YOUR WORD IS A LAMP TO MY FEET AND A LIGHT FOR MY PATH. PS 119:105

PRESENTED

TO

BY

ON

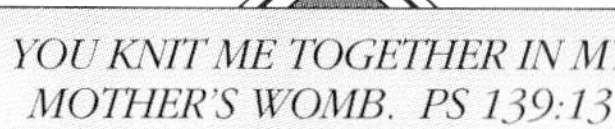

BIRTHS

NAME

BORN TO DATE

NAME

BORN TO DATE

NAME

BORN TO DATE

NAME

BORN TO DATE

NAME

BORN TO DATE

NAME

BORN TO DATE

NAME

BORN TO DATE

THE LORD REIGNS,
LET THE EARTH BE GLAD. PS 97:1

SPECIAL EVENTS

EVENT

PLACE DATE

EVENT

PLACE DATE

EVENT

PLACE DATE

EVENT

PLACE DATE

EVENT

PLACE DATE

EVENT

PLACE DATE

A MAN WILL... BE UNITED TO HIS WIFE, AND THEY WILL BECOME ONE FLESH. GE 2:24

THIS CERTIFIES THAT

---

and

---

were united in

HOLY MATRIMONY

on *the*

day of *A.D.*

at

in accordance with the laws of

Officiating

Witness

Witness

LOVE IS PATIENT, LOVE IS KIND…
LOVE NEVER FAILS. 1 CO 13:4,8

MARRIAGES

HUSBAND

WIFE

PLACE DATE

HUSBAND

WIFE

PLACE DATE

HUSBAND

WIFE

PLACE DATE

HUSBAND

WIFE

PLACE DATE

HUSBAND

WIFE

PLACE DATE

HUSBAND

WIFE

PLACE DATE

BLESSED IS THE MAN
WHO FEARS THE LORD. PS 112:1

HUSBAND'S FAMILY TREE

NAME

BIRTHPLACE DATE

BROTHERS AND SISTERS

PARENTS

FATHER

NAME

BIRTHPLACE DATE

MOTHER

NAME

BIRTHPLACE DATE

GRANDPARENTS

PATERNAL

GRANDFATHER

BIRTHPLACE DATE

GRANDMOTHER

BIRTHPLACE DATE

MATERNAL

GRANDFATHER

BIRTHPLACE DATE

GRANDMOTHER

BIRTHPLACE DATE

GREAT-GRANDPARENTS

PATERNAL

GRANDFATHER'S FATHER

BIRTHPLACE DATE

GRANDFATHER'S MOTHER

BIRTHPLACE DATE

GRANDMOTHER'S FATHER

BIRTHPLACE DATE

GRANDMOTHER'S MOTHER

BIRTHPLACE DATE

MATERNAL

GRANDFATHER'S FATHER

BIRTHPLACE DATE

GRANDFATHER'S MOTHER

BIRTHPLACE DATE

GRANDMOTHER'S FATHER

BIRTHPLACE DATE

GRANDMOTHER'S MOTHER

BIRTHPLACE DATE

A WOMAN WHO FEARS THE LORD IS TO BE PRAISED. PR 31:30

WIFE'S FAMILY TREE

NAME

BIRTHPLACE DATE

BROTHERS AND SISTERS

PARENTS

FATHER

NAME

BIRTHPLACE DATE

MOTHER

NAME

BIRTHPLACE DATE

GRANDPARENTS

PATERNAL

GRANDFATHER

BIRTHPLACE DATE

GRANDMOTHER

BIRTHPLACE DATE

MATERNAL

GRANDFATHER

BIRTHPLACE DATE

GRANDMOTHER

BIRTHPLACE DATE

GREAT-GRANDPARENTS

PATERNAL

GRANDFATHER'S FATHER

BIRTHPLACE DATE

GRANDFATHER'S MOTHER

BIRTHPLACE DATE

GRANDMOTHER'S FATHER

BIRTHPLACE DATE

GRANDMOTHER'S MOTHER

BIRTHPLACE DATE

MATERNAL

GRANDFATHER'S FATHER

BIRTHPLACE DATE

GRANDFATHER'S MOTHER

BIRTHPLACE DATE

GRANDMOTHER'S FATHER

BIRTHPLACE DATE

GRANDMOTHER'S MOTHER

BIRTHPLACE DATE

FOR TO ME, TO LIVE IS CHRIST
AND TO DIE IS GAIN. PHP 1:21

DEATHS

NAME

DATE

NAME

DATE

NAME

DATE

NAME

DATE

NAME

DATE

NAME

DATE

NAME

DATE

NEW AMERICAN STANDARD BIBLE

ZondervanPublishingHouse
Grand Rapids, Michigan 49530, USA

Library of Congress Card Number 00-130208

Published by Zondervan Publishing House
Grand Rapids, Michigan 49530, U.S.A.
http:\\www.zondervan.com

Printed in the United States of America

00 01 02 03 04 05/ 9 8 7 6 5 4 3 2 1
RRD-C

CONTENTS

LIST OF THE BOOKS OF THE BIBLE

EXPLANATION OF GENERAL FORMAT

CROSS REFERENCES are placed in a column adjoining the text on the page and listed under verse numbers to which they refer. In the event that cross references are included for more than one portion of a Scripture verse, the references may appear to start over (e.g., a Genesis reference might follow a reference from a later book of the Bible.)

PARAGRAPHS are designated by bold face verse numbers or letters.

QUOTATION MARKS are used in the text in accordance with modern English usage.

"THOU," "THEE" AND "THY" are not used in this edition and have been rendered as "YOU" and "YOUR."

PERSONAL PRONOUNS in the Scripture text (not the study notes) are capitalized when pertaining to Deity.

ITALICS are used in the text to indicate words that are not found in the original Hebrew, Aramaic, or Greek but implied by it. Italics are not used when the verse or verse portion is quoted in the study notes. Italics are used in the textual footnotes to signify alternate readings for the text. Roman text in the alternate readings is the same as italics in the Bible text.

SMALL CAPS in the New Testament are used in the text to indicate Old Testament quotations or obvious references to Old Testament texts. Variations of Old Testament wording are found in New Testament citations depending on whether the New Testament writer translated from a Hebrew text, used existing Greek or Aramaic translations, or paraphrased the material. It should be noted that modern rules for the indication of direct quotation were not used in biblical times; thus, the ancient writer would use exact quotations or references to quotations without specific indication of such.

STARS are used to mark verbs that are historical presents in the Greek but which have been translated with an English past tense in order to conform to modern usage. The translators recognized that in some contexts the present tense seems more unexpected and unjustified to the English reader than a past tense would have been. But Greek authors frequently used the present tense for the sake of heightened vividness, thereby transporting their readers in imagination to the actual scene at the time of occurrence. However, the translators felt that it would be wise to change these historical presents to English past tenses.

ABBREVIATIONS AND SPECIAL MARKINGS:

Aram = Aramaic
DSS = Dead Sea Scrolls
Gr = Greek translation of O.T. (Septuagint or LXX) or Greek text of N.T.
Heb = Hebrew text, usually Masoretic
Lat = Latin
M.T. = Masoretic text
Syr = Syriac
Lit = A literal translation
Or = An alternate translation justified by the Hebrew, Aramaic, or Greek
[ ] = In text, brackets indicate words probably not in the original writings
[ ] = In footnotes, brackets indicate references to a name, place or thing similar to, but not identical with that in the text
cf = compare
f, ff = following verse or verses
mg = Refers to a marginal reading on another verse
ms, mss = manuscript, manuscripts
v, vv = verse, verses

A NOTE TO THE READERS

SCRIPTURAL PROMISE

"The grass withers, the flower fades,
but the word of our God stands forever."
ISAIAH 40:8

The New American Standard Bible has been produced with the conviction that the words of Scripture as originally penned in the Hebrew, Aramaic, and Greek were inspired by God. Since they are the eternal Word of God, the Holy Scriptures speak with fresh power to each generation, to give wisdom that leads to salvation, that men may serve Christ to the glory of God.

The purpose of the Editorial Board in making this translation was to adhere as closely as possible to the original languages of the Holy Scriptures, and to make the translation in a fluent and readable style according to current English usage.

THE FOURFOLD AIM OF THE LOCKMAN FOUNDATION

1. These publications shall be true to the original Hebrew, Aramaic, and Greek.
2. They shall be grammatically correct.
3. They shall be understandable.
4. They shall give the Lord Jesus Christ His proper place, the place which the Word gives Him; therefore, no work will ever be personalized.

PREFACE TO THE NEW AMERICAN STANDARD BIBLE

In the history of English Bible translations, the King James Version is the most prestigious. This time-honored version of 1611, itself a revision of the Bishops' Bible of 1568, became the basis for the English Revised Version appearing in 1881 (New Testament) and 1885 (Old Testament). The American counterpart of this last work was published in 1901 as the American Standard Version. The ASV, a product of both British and American scholarship, has been highly regarded for its scholarship and accuracy. Recognizing the values of the American Standard Version, The Lockman Foundation felt an urgency to preserve these and other lasting values of the ASV by incorporating recent discoveries of Hebrew and Greek textual sources and by rendering them into more current English. Therefore, in 1959 a new translation project was launched, based on the time-honored principles of translation of the ASV and KJV. The result is the New American Standard Bible.

Translation work for the NASB was begun in 1959. In the preparation of this work numerous other translations have been consulted along with the linguistic tools and literature of biblical scholarship. Decisions about English renderings were made by consensus of a team composed of educators and pastors. Subsequently, review and evaluation by other Hebrew and Greek scholars outside the Editorial Board were sought and carefully considered.

The Editorial Board has continued to function since publication of the complete Bible in 1971. This edition of the NASB represents revisions and refinements recommended over the last several years as well as thorough research based on modern English usage.

PRINCIPLES OF TRANSLATION

MODERN ENGLISH USAGE: The attempt has been made to render the grammar and terminology in contemporary English. When it was felt that the word-for-word literalness was unacceptable to the modern reader, a change was made in the direction of a more current English idiom. In the instances where this has been done, the more literal rendering has been indicated in the notes. There are a few exceptions to this procedure. In particular, frequently "And" is not translated at the beginning of sentences because of differences in style between ancient and modern writing. Punctuation is a relatively modern invention, and ancient writers often linked most of their sentences with "and" or other connectives. Also, the Hebrew idiom "answered and said" is sometimes reduced to "answered" or "said" as demanded by the context. For current English the idiom "it came about that" has not been translated in the New Testament except when a major transition is needed.

ALTERNATIVE READINGS: In addition to the more literal renderings, notations have been made to include alternate translations, reading of variant manuscripts and explanatory equivalents of the text. Only such notations have been used as have been felt justified in assisting the reader's comprehension of the terms used by the original author.

HEBREW TEXT: In the present translation the latest edition of Rudolf Kittel's BIBLIA HEBRAICA has been employed together with the most recent light from lexicography, cognate languages, and the Dead Sea Scrolls.

HEBREW TENSES: Consecution of tenses in Hebrew remains a puzzling factor in translation. The translators have been guided by the requirements of a literal translation, the sequence of tenses, and the immediate and broad contexts.

THE PROPER NAME OF GOD IN THE OLD TESTAMENT: In the Scriptures, the name of God is most significant, and understandably so. It is inconceivable to think of spiritual matters without a proper designation for the Supreme Deity. Thus the most common name for the Deity is God, a translation of the original *Elohim*. One of the titles for God is Lord, a translation of *Adonai*. There is yet another name which is particularly assigned to God as His special or proper name, that is, the four letters YHWH (Exodus 3:14 and Isaiah 42:8). This name has not been pronounced by the Jews because of reverence for the great sacredness of the divine name. Therefore, it has been consistently translated LORD. The only exception to this translation of YHWH is when it occurs in immediate proximity to the word Lord, that is, *Adonai*. In that case it is regularly translated GOD in order to avoid confusion.

It is known that for many years YHWH has been transliterated as Yahweh; however no complete certainty attaches to this pronunciation.

GREEK TEXT: Consideration was given to the latest available manuscripts with a view to determining the best Greek text. In most instances the 26th edition of Eberhard Nestle's NOVUM TESTAMENTUM GRAECE was followed.

GREEK TENSES: A careful distinction has been made in the treatment of the Greek aorist tense (usually translated as the English past, "He did") and the Greek imperfect tense (normally rendered either as English past progressive, "He was doing"; or, if inceptive, as "He began to do" or "He started to do"; or else if customary past, as "He used to do"). "Began" is italicized if it renders an imperfect tense, in order to distinguish it from the Greek verb for "begin." In some contexts the difference between the Greek imperfect and the English past is conveyed better by the choice of vocabulary or by other words in the context, and in such cases the Greek imperfect may be rendered as a simple past tense (e.g. "had an illness for many years" would be preferable to "was having an illness for many years" and would be understood in the same way).

On the other hand, not all aorists have been rendered as English pasts ("He did"), for some of them are clearly to be rendered as English perfects ("He has done"), or even as past perfects ("He had done"), judging from the context in which they occur. Such aorists have been rendered as perfects or past perfects in this translation.

As for the distinction between aorist and present imperatives, the translators have usually rendered these imperatives in the customary manner, rather than attempting any such fine distinction as "Begin to do!" (for the aorist imperative), or, "Continually do!" (for the present imperative).

As for sequence of tenses, the translators took care to follow English rules rather than Greek in translating Greek presents, imperfects and aorists. Thus, where English says, "We knew that he was doing," Greek puts it, "We knew that he does"; similarly, "We knew that he had done" is the Greek, "We knew that he did." Likewise, the English, "When he had come, they met him," is represented in Greek by, "When he came, they met him." In all cases a consistent transfer has been made from the Greek tense in the subordinate clause to the appropriate tense in English.

In the rendering of negative questions introduced by the particle *me*—(which always expects the answer "No") the wording has been altered from a mere, "Will he not do this?" to a more accurate, "He will not do this, will he?"

THE LOCKMAN FOUNDATION

CONTRIBUTORS

Senior Editorial Team
Dr. Bruce B. Barton
Ronald A. Beers
Dr. James C. Galvin
LaVonne Neff
Linda Chaffee Taylor
David R. Veerman

General Editor
Ronald A. Beers

Tyndale House Bible Editors
Dr. Philip W. Comfort
Mark Norton

Zondervan Bible Editors
Dirk Buursma
Donna Huisjen
June Gunden

Book Introductions
David R. Veerman

Book Outlines, Blueprints, Harmony
Dr. James C. Galvin

Megathemes
Dr. Bruce B. Barton

Map Development & Computer Operation
Linda Chaffee Taylor

Color Map Consultant
Dr. Barry Beitzel

Charts & Diagrams
Neil S. Wilson
Ronald A. Beers
David R. Veerman
Pamela York

Personality Profiles
Neil S. Wilson

Design & Development Team
Dr. Bruce B. Barton
Ronald A. Beers
Dr. James C. Galvin
David R. Veerman

Production
Christopher D. Hudson
Katie Gieser
Thomas Ristow
Kathleen Ristow
Joan Major
Lois Rusch
Gwen Elliott
Joan Woodhead
Betsy Schmitt
Ashley Jones

Tyndale House Graphic Design
Timothy R. Botts

A Chronology of Bible Events and World Events
Dr. David Maas

Theological Reviewers
Dr. Kenneth S. Kantzer

General Theological Reviewer
Dean Emeritus and
Distinguished Professor of Bible
and Systematic Theology
Trinity Evangelical Divinity School

Dr. V. Gilbert Beers

Dr. Barry Beitzel
Associate Academic Dean
and Professor of Old Testament
and Semitic Languages
Trinity Evangelical Divinity School

Dr. Edwin A. Blum
Associate Professor of
Historical Theology
Dallas Theological Seminary

Dr. Geoffrey W. Bromiley
Professor
Fuller Theological Seminary

Dr. George K. Brushaber
President
Bethel College & Seminary

Dr. L. Russ Bush
Associate Professor
Philosophy & Religion
Southwestern Baptist
Theological Seminary

C. Donald Cole
Pastor, Moody Radio Network

Mrs. Naomi E. Cole
Speaker & Seminar Leader

Dr. Walter A. Elwell
Dean
Wheaton College Graduate School

Dr. Gerald F. Hawthorne
Professor Emeritus
Wheaton College

Dr. Howard G. Hendricks
Professor-at-Large
Chairman
Center for Christian Leadership
Dallas Theological Seminary

Dr. Grant R. Osborne
Professor of New Testament
Trinity Evangelical Divinity School

A special thanks to the nationwide staff of Youth for Christ/USA for their suggestions and field testing, and to the following additional contributing writers: V. Gilbert Beers, Neil Wilson, John Crosby, Joan Young, Jack Crabtree, Philip Craven, Bob Black, Bur Shilling, Arthur Deyo, Annie Lafrentz, Danny Sartin, William Hanawalt, William Bonikowsky, Brian Rathbun, Pamela Barden, Thomas Stobie, Robert Arnold, Greg Monaco, Larry Dunn, Lynn Ziegenfuss, Mitzie Barton, Marijean Hamilton, Larry Kreider, Gary Dausey, William Roland, Kathy Howell, Philip Steffeck, James Coleman, Marty Grasley, O'Ann Steere, Julia Amstutz.

A special thanks also to the following people whose personal counsel, encouragement, and determination helped make this product a reality:

Dr. Kenneth N. Taylor
Translator of *The Living Bible*
Chairman of the Board
Tyndale House Publishers, Inc.

Mark D. Taylor
President
Tyndale House Publishers, Inc.

Dr. Wendell C. Hawley
Senior Vice President
Editorial
Tyndale House Publishers, Inc.

Virginia Muir
Retired Assistant Editor-in-Chief
Tyndale House Publishers, Inc.

Dr. Jay L. Kesler
President, Taylor University

A CHRONOLOGY OF BIBLE EVENTS AND WORLD EVENTS

Creation
undated

Noah builds the ark
undated

Abraham born
2166

Abrahan enters Canaan
2091

2500 BC.
Egyptians discover papyrus and ink for writing and build the first libraries; iron objects manufactured in the ancient Near East

2400
Egyptians import gold from other parts of Africa

2331
Semitic chieftain, Sargon, conquers Sumer to become first "world conqueror"

2300
Horses domesticated in Egypt; chickens domesticated in Babylon; bows & arrows used in wars

2100
Glass made by the Mesopotamia ziggurats (like the towe of Babel) built in Mesopotamia earliest discovered dr ethyl alcohol, used to alleviate pain

WHY THE
LIFE APPLICATION STUDY BIBLE
IS UNIQUE

Have you ever opened your Bible and asked the following:

- What does this passage really mean?
- How does it apply to my life?
- Why does some of the Bible seem irrelevant?
- What do these ancient cultures have to do with today?
- I love God; why can't I understand what he is saying to me through his Word?
- What's going on in the lives of these Bible people?

Many Christians do not read the Bible regularly. Why? Because in the pressures of daily living, they cannot find a connection between the timeless principles of Scripture and the ever-present problems of day-by-day living.

God urges us to apply his Word (Isaiah 42:23; 1 Corinthians 10:11; 2 Thessalonians 3:4), but too often we stop at accumulating Bible knowledge. This is why the *Life Application Study Bible* was developed—to show how to put into practice what we have learned.

Applying God's Word is a vital part of one's relationship with God; it is the evidence that we are obeying him. The difficulty in applying the Bible is not with the

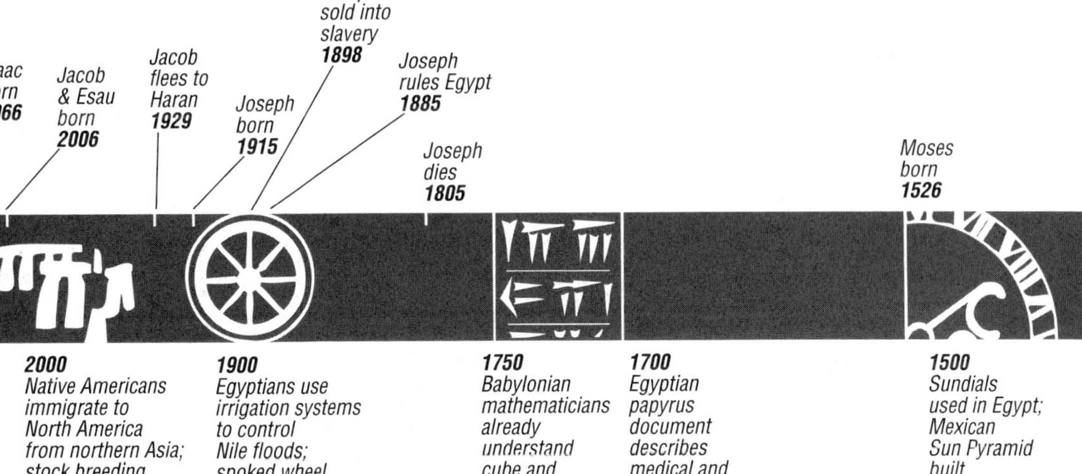

Jacob & Esau born 2006
Jacob flees to Haran 1929
Joseph born 1915
Joseph sold into slavery 1898
Joseph rules Egypt 1885
Joseph dies 1805
Moses born 1526
2000 Native Americans immigrate to North America from northern Asia; stock breeding and irrigation used in China; Stonehenge, England, a center for religious worship is erected; bellows used in India, allowing for higher furnace temperatures
1900 Egyptians use irrigation systems to control Nile floods; spoked wheel invented in the ancient Near East; horses used to pull vehicles
1750 Babylonian mathematicians already understand cube and square root; Hammurapi of Babylon provides first of all legal codes
1700 Egyptian papyrus document describes medical and surgical procedures
1500 Sundials used in Egypt; Mexican Sun Pyramid built

Bible itself, but with the reader's inability to bridge the gap between the past and present, the conceptual and practical. When we don't or can't do this, spiritual dryness, shallowness, and indifference are the results.

The words of Scripture itself cry out to us, "And remember, it is a message to obey, not just to listen to. If you don't obey, you are only fooling yourself" (James 1:22). The *Life Application Study Bible* does just that. Developed by an interdenominational team of pastors, scholars, family counselors, and a national organization dedicated to promoting God's Word and spreading the gospel, the *Life Application Study Bible* took many years to complete, and all the work was reviewed by several renowned theologians under the directorship of Dr. Kenneth Kantzer.

The *Life Application Study Bible* does what a good resource Bible should—it helps you understand the context of a passage, gives important background and historical information, explains difficult words and phrases, and helps you see the interrelationships within Scripture. But it does much more. The *Life Application Study Bible* goes deeper into God's Word, helping you discover the timeless truth being communicated, see the relevance for your life, and make a personal application. While some study Bibles attempt application, over 75% of this Bible is application-oriented. The notes answer the questions, "So what?" and "What does this passage mean to me, my family, my friends, my job, my neighborhood, my church, my country?"

Imagine reading a familiar passage of Scripture and gaining fresh insight, as if it were the first time you had ever read it. How much richer your life would be if you left each Bible reading with a new perspective and a small change for the better. A small change every day adds up to a changed life—and that is the very purpose of Scripture.

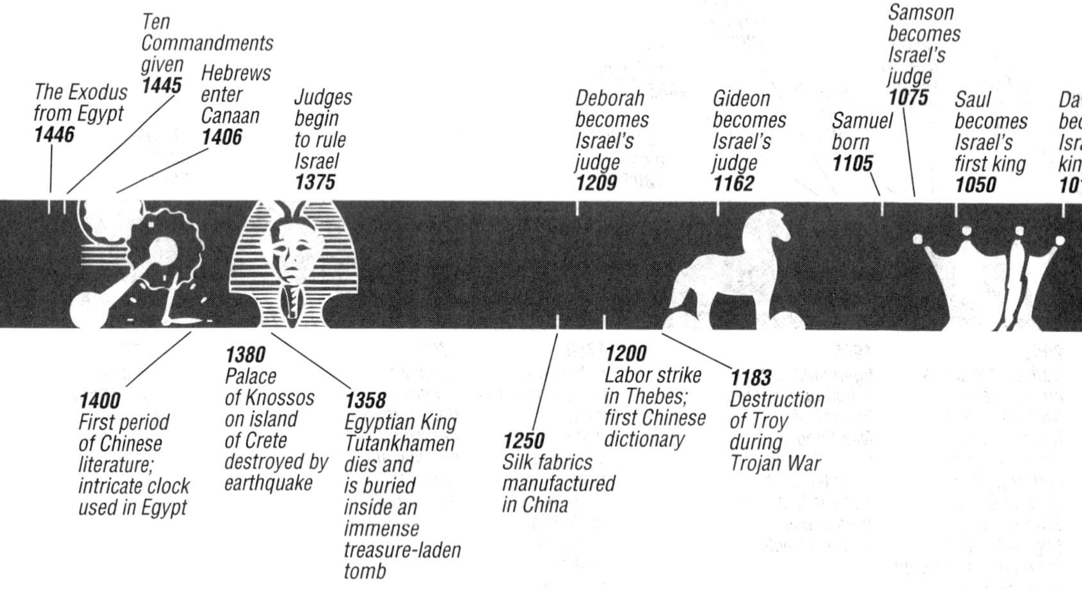

The best way to define application is to first determine what it is *not.* Application is *not* just accumulating knowledge. This helps us discover and understand facts and concepts, but it stops there. History is filled with philosophers who knew what the Bible said but failed to apply it to their lives, keeping them from believing and changing. Many think that understanding is the end goal of Bible study, but it is really only the beginning.

Application is *not* just illustration. Illustration only tells us how someone else handled a similar situation. While we may empathize with that person, we still have little direction for our personal situation.

Application is *not* just making a passage "relevant." Making the Bible relevant only helps us to see that the same lessons that were true in Bible times are true today; it does not show us how to apply them to the problems and pressures of our individual lives.

What, then, is application? Application begins by knowing and understanding God's Word and its timeless truths. *But you cannot stop there.* If you do, God's Word may not change your life, and it may become dull, difficult, tedious, and tiring. A good application focuses the truth of God's Word, shows the reader what to do about what is being read, and motivates the reader to respond to what God is teaching. All three are essential to application.

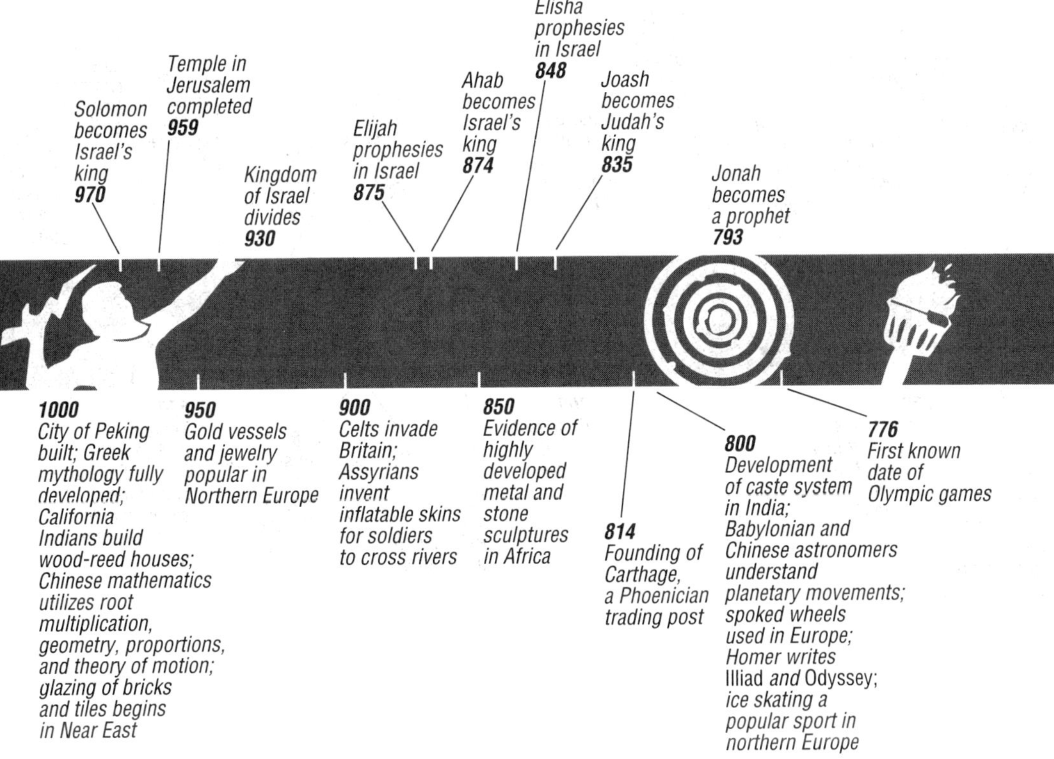
Solomon becomes Israel's king 970
Temple in Jerusalem completed 959
Kingdom of Israel divides 930
Elijah prophesies in Israel 875
Ahab becomes Israel's king 874
Elisha prophesies in Israel 848
Joash becomes Judah's king 835
Jonah becomes a prophet 793
1000 City of Peking built; Greek mythology fully developed; California Indians build wood-reed houses; Chinese mathematics utilizes root multiplication, geometry, proportions, and theory of motion; glazing of bricks and tiles begins in Near East
950 Gold vessels and jewelry popular in Northern Europe
900 Celts invade Britain; Assyrians invent inflatable skins for soldiers to cross rivers
850 Evidence of highly developed metal and stone sculptures in Africa
814 Founding of Carthage, a Phoenician trading post
800 Development of caste system in India; Babylonian and Chinese astronomers understand planetary movements; spoked wheels used in Europe; Homer writes Illiad and Odyssey; ice skating a popular sport in northern Europe
776 First known date of Olympic games

Application is putting into practice what we already know (see Mark 4:24 and Hebrews 5:14) and answering the question, "So what? " by confronting us with the right questions and motivating us to take action (see 1 John 2:5–6 and James 2:17). Application is deeply personal—unique for each individual. It is making a relevant truth a personal truth, and it involves developing a strategy and action plan to live your life in harmony with the Bible. It is the Biblical "how to " of life.

You may ask, "How can your application notes be relevant to my life? " Each application note has three parts: (1) an *explanation* that ties the note directly to the Scripture passage and sets up the truth that is being taught, (2) the *bridge* that explains the timeless truth and makes it relevant for today, (3) the *application* that shows you how to take the timeless truth and apply it to your personal situation. No note, by itself, can apply Scripture directly to your life. It can only teach, direct, lead, guide, inspire, recommend, and urge. It can give you the resources and direction you need to apply the Bible, but only *you* can take these resources and put them into practice.

A good note, therefore, should not only give you knowledge and understanding, but point you to application. Before you buy any kind of resource Bible, you should evaluate the notes and ask the following questions: (1) Does the note contain enough information to help me understand the point of the Scripture passage? (2) Does the note assume I know too much? (3) Does the note avoid denominational bias? (4) Do the notes touch most of life's experiences? (5) Does the note help me *apply* God's Word?

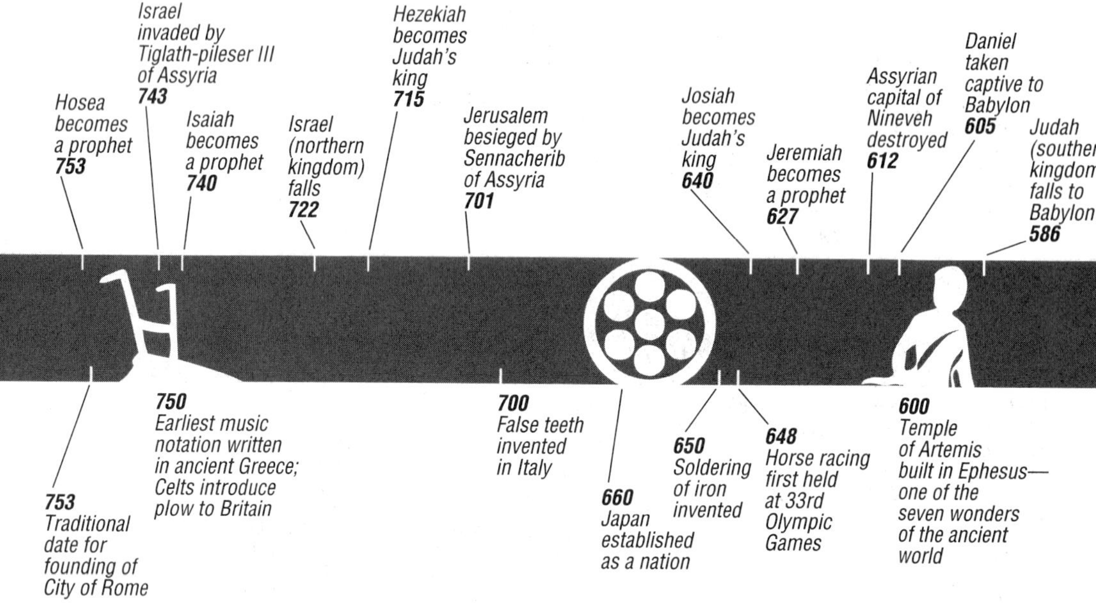

FEATURES OF THE
LIFE APPLICATION STUDY BIBLE

NOTES
In addition to providing the reader with many application notes, the *Life Application Study Bible* offers several explanatory notes, which are notes that help the reader understand culture, history, context, difficult-to-understand passages, background, places, theological concepts, and the relationship of various passages in Scripture to other passages. Maps, charts, and diagrams are also found on the same page as the passages to which they relate. For an example of an application note, see Mark 15:47. For an example of an explanatory note, see Mark 11:1–2.

BOOK INTRODUCTIONS
The Book Introductions are divided into several easy-to-find parts:

Timeline. This puts the Bible book into its historical setting. It lists the key events of each book and the dates when they occurred. The alternative dates in parenthesis are based on a later dating of the Exodus.

Vital Statistics. This is a list of straight facts about the book—those pieces of information you need to know at a glance.

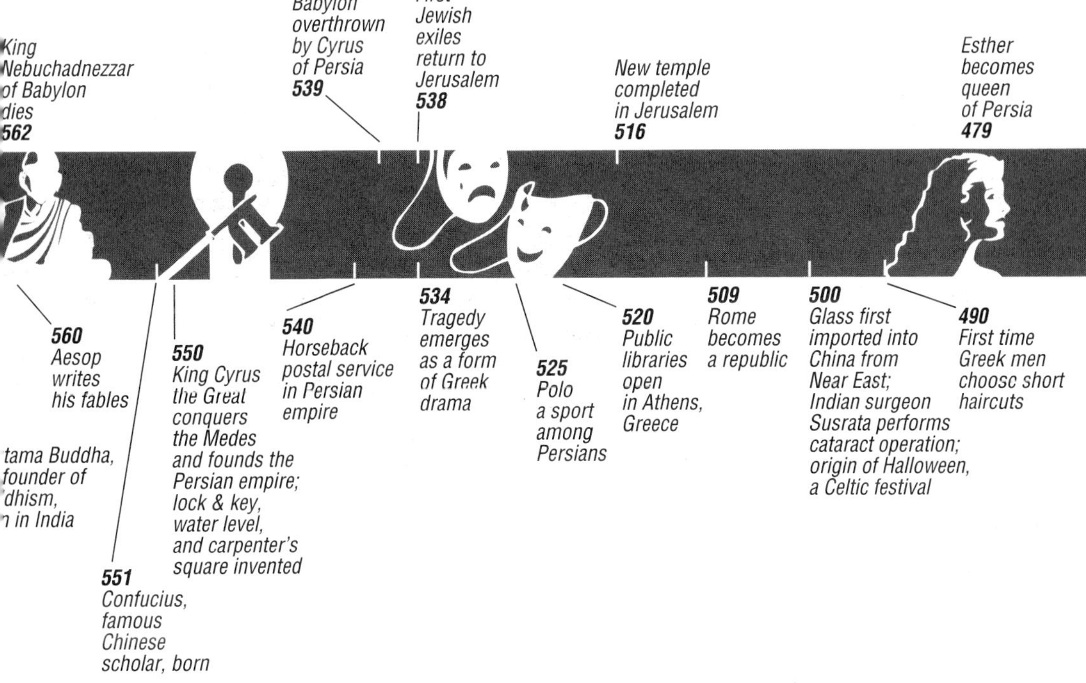
King Nebuchadnezzar of Babylon dies 562
Babylon overthrown by Cyrus of Persia 539
First Jewish exiles return to Jerusalem 538
New temple completed in Jerusalem 516
Esther becomes queen of Persia 479
560 Aesop writes his fables
tama Buddha, founder of dhism, in India
551 Confucius, famous Chinese scholar, born
550 King Cyrus the Great conquers the Medes and founds the Persian empire; lock & key, water level, and carpenter's square invented
540 Horseback postal service in Persian empire
534 Tragedy emerges as a form of Greek drama
525 Polo a sport among Persians
520 Public libraries open in Athens, Greece
509 Rome becomes a republic
500 Glass first imported into China from Near East; Indian surgeon Susrata performs cataract operation; origin of Halloween, a Celtic festival
490 First time Greek men choose short haircuts

Overview. This is a summary of the book with general lessons and application that can be learned from the book as a whole.

Blueprint. This is the outline of the book. It is printed in easy-to-understand language and is designed for easy memorization. To the right of each main heading is a key lesson that is taught in that particular section.

Megathemes. This section gives the main themes of the Bible book, explains their significance, and then tells why they are still important for us today.

Map. This shows the key places found in that book and retells the story of the book from a geographical point of view.

OUTLINE

The *Life Application Study Bible* has a custom made outline that was designed specifically from an application point of view. Several unique features should be noted:

1. To avoid confusion and to aid memory work, each book outline has only three levels for headings. Main outline heads are marked with a capital letter. Subheads are marked by a number. Minor explanatory heads have no letter or number.

2. Each main outline head marked by a letter also has a brief paragraph below it summarizing the Bible text and offering a general application.

3. Parallel passages are listed where they apply in the Gospels.

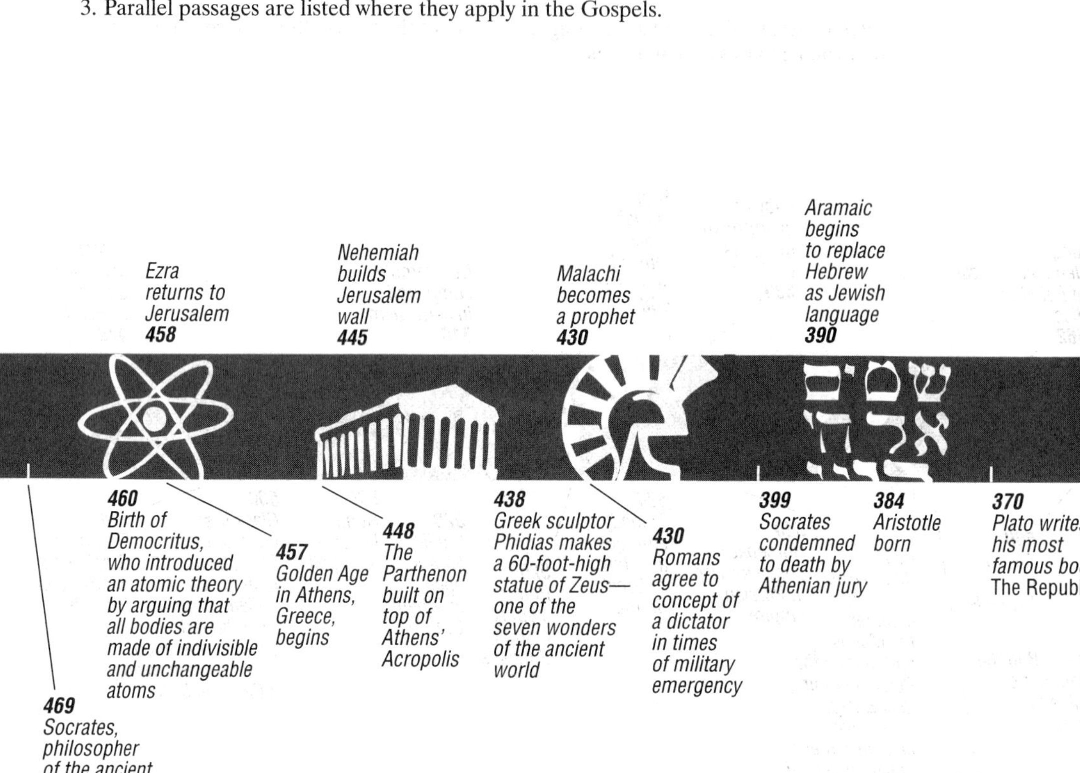
Ezra returns to Jerusalem 458
Nehemiah builds Jerusalem wall 445
Malachi becomes a prophet 430
Aramaic begins to replace Hebrew as Jewish language 390
469 Socrates, philosopher of the ancient world, born
460 Birth of Democritus, who introduced an atomic theory by arguing that all bodies are made of indivisible and unchangeable atoms
457 Golden Age in Athens, Greece, begins
448 The Parthenon built on top of Athens' Acropolis
438 Greek sculptor Phidias makes a 60-foot-high statue of Zeus—one of the seven wonders of the ancient world
430 Romans agree to concept of a dictator in times of military emergency
399 Socrates condemned to death by Athenian jury
384 Aristotle born
370 Plato writes his most famous boo The Republi

HARMONY OF THE GOSPELS

A harmony of the Gospels was developed specifically for this Bible. It is the first harmony that has ever been incorporated into the Bible text. Through a unique and simple numbering system (found both in the harmony feature and parenthesized in the subheads throughout the Gospels), you can read any Gospel account and see just where you are in relation to other events in the life of Christ. The harmony feature is located after the Gospel of John and explained in detail there.

PROFILE NOTES

Another unique feature of this Bible is the profiles of many Bible people, including their strengths and weaknesses, greatest accomplishments and mistakes, and key lessons from their lives. The profiles of these people are found in the Bible books where their stories occur.

MAPS

The *Life Application Study Bible* has more maps than any other Bible. A thorough and comprehensive Bible atlas is built right into each Bible book. There are two kinds of maps: (1) a book introduction map, telling the story of that Bible book; (2) thumbnail maps in the notes, plotting most geographic movements in the Bible. In addition to these numerous black-and-white maps, there is an entirely new and comprehensive set of color maps and diagrams at the back of this Bible.

CHARTS AND DIAGRAMS

Hundreds of charts and diagrams are included to help the reader better visualize difficult concepts or relationships. Most charts not only present the needed information but show the significance of the information as well.

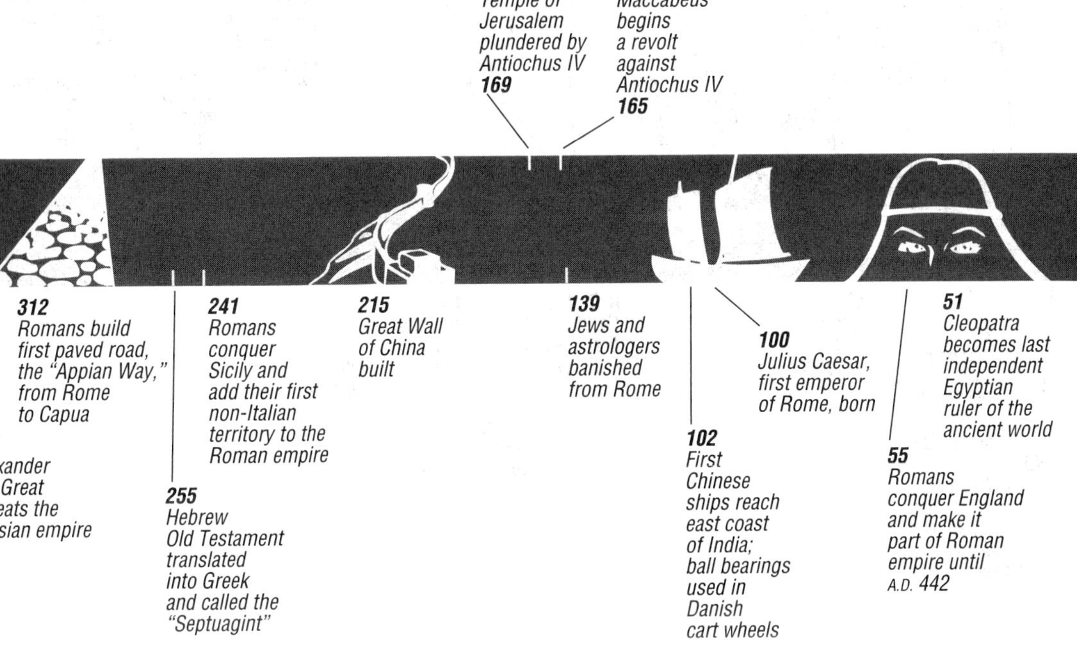
Temple of Jerusalem plundered by Antiochus IV 169
Judas Maccabeus begins a revolt against Antiochus IV 165
1 exander e Great feats the rsian empire
312 Romans build first paved road, the "Appian Way," from Rome to Capua
255 Hebrew Old Testament translated into Greek and called the "Septuagint"
241 Romans conquer Sicily and add their first non-Italian territory to the Roman empire
215 Great Wall of China built
139 Jews and astrologers banished from Rome
102 First Chinese ships reach east coast of India; ball bearings used in Danish cart wheels
100 Julius Caesar, first emperor of Rome, born
55 Romans conquer England and make it part of Roman empire until A.D. 442
51 Cleopatra becomes last independent Egyptian ruler of the ancient world

CROSS-REFERENCES

A carefully organized cross-reference system in the margins of the Bible text helps the reader find related passages quickly. In the event that cross references are included for more than one portion of a Scripture verse, the references may appear to start over (e.g., a Genesis reference might follow a reference from a later book of the Bible.)

TEXTUAL NOTES AND SECTIONAL HEADINGS

Directly related to the New American Standard Bible text, the textual notes examine such issues as alternate translations, meanings of Hebrew and Greek terms, Old Testament quotations, and variant readings in ancient biblical manuscripts. The New American Standard Bible text also contains sectional headings in order to help you more easily understand the subject and content of each section. Note that the sectional headings used in the four Gospels follow the Harmony of the Gospels which appears after the Book of John rather than the usual NASB headings.

INDEX

This book contains a complete index to all the notes, charts, maps, and personality profiles. With its emphasis on application, it is helpful for group Bible study, sermon preparation, teaching, or personal Bible study.

DICTIONARY-CONCORDANCE-THESAURUS

For a complete description of the features of this unique Dictionary-Concordance-Thesaurus see page 2389 near the back of this Bible.

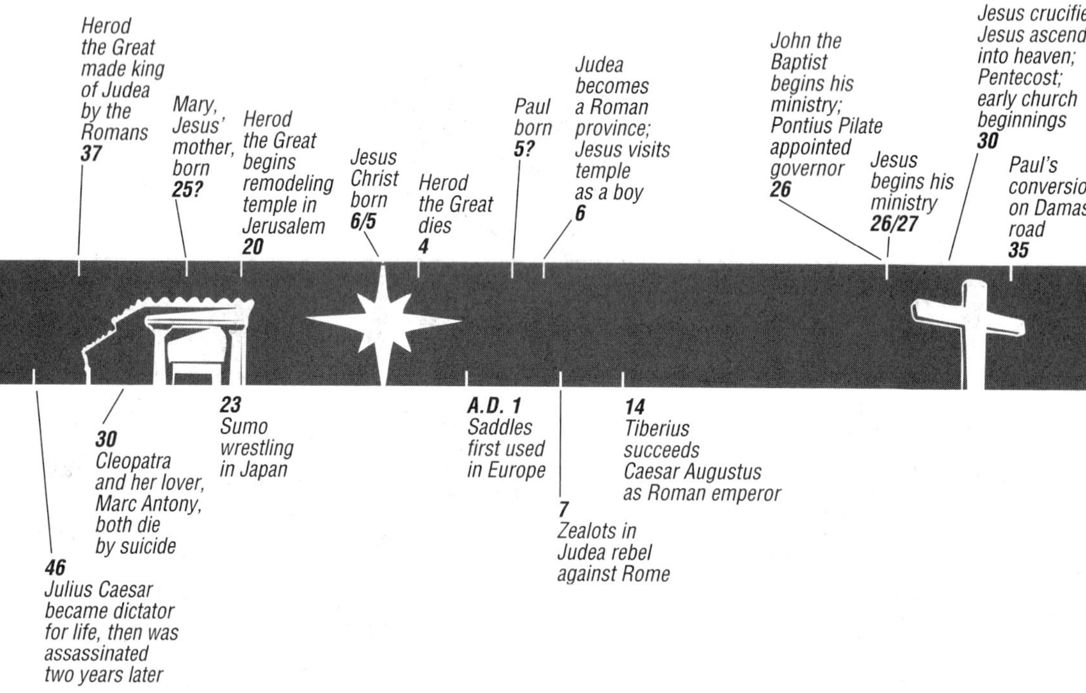

Herod the Great made king of Judea by the Romans 37
Mary, Jesus' mother, born 25?
Herod the Great begins remodeling temple in Jerusalem 20
Jesus Christ born 6/5
Herod the Great dies 4
Paul born 5?
Judea becomes a Roman province; Jesus visits temple as a boy 6
John the Baptist begins his ministry; Pontius Pilate appointed governor 26
Jesus begins his ministry 26/27
Jesus crucified; Jesus ascends into heaven; Pentecost; early church beginnings 30
Paul's conversion on Damasc road 35
46 Julius Caesar became dictator for life, then was assassinated two years later
30 Cleopatra and her lover, Marc Antony, both die by suicide
23 Sumo wrestling in Japan
A.D. 1 Saddles first used in Europe
7 Zealots in Judea rebel against Rome
14 Tiberius succeeds Caesar Augustus as Roman emperor

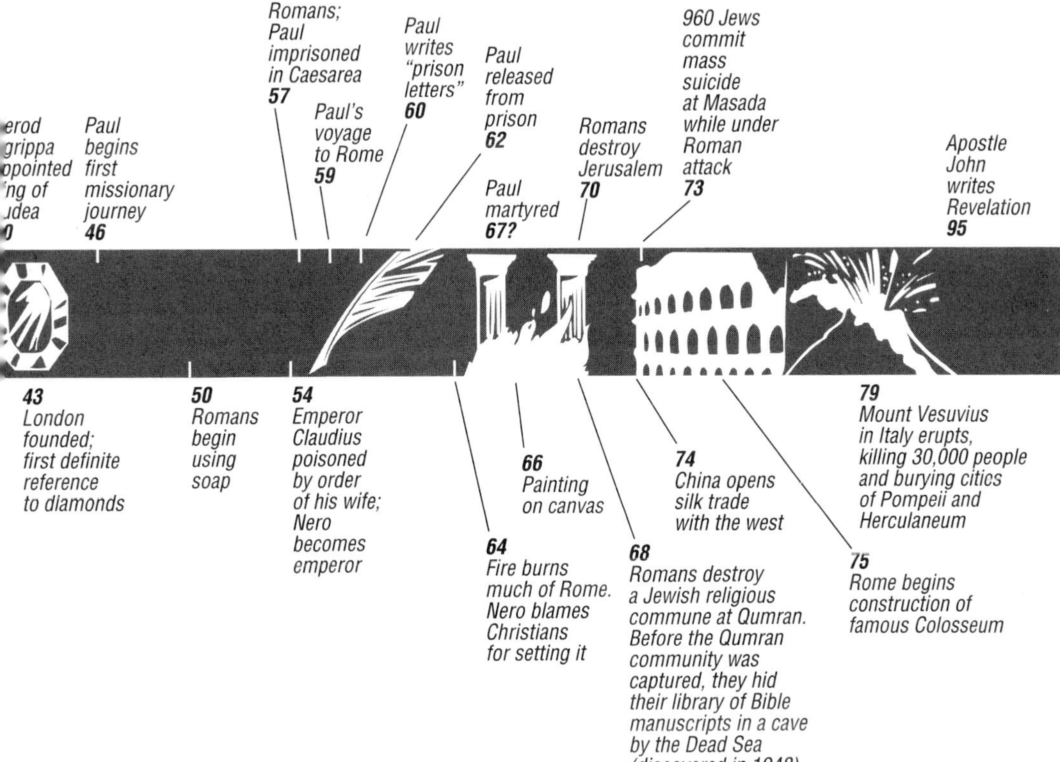
Paul writes Romans; Paul imprisoned in Caesarea 57
Paul writes "prison letters" 60
Paul released from prison 62
960 Jews commit mass suicide at Masada while under Roman attack 73
erod grippa opointed ng of ıdea 0
Paul begins first missionary journey 46
Paul's voyage to Rome 59
Romans destroy Jerusalem 70
Apostle John writes Revelation 95
Paul martyred 67?
43 London founded; first definite reference to diamonds
50 Romans begin using soap
54 Emperor Claudius poisoned by order of his wife; Nero becomes emperor
66 Painting on canvas
74 China opens silk trade with the west
79 Mount Vesuvius in Italy erupts, killing 30,000 people and burying cities of Pompeii and Herculaneum
64 Fire burns much of Rome. Nero blames Christians for setting it
68 Romans destroy a Jewish religious commune at Qumran. Before the Qumran community was captured, they hid their library of Bible manuscripts in a cave by the Dead Sea (discovered in 1948).
75 Rome begins construction of famous Colosseum

THE OLD TESTAMENT

GENESIS

Creation	Noah undated	Abram born 2166 B.C. (2000 B.C.)	Abram enters Canaan 2091 (1925)	Isaac born 2066 (1900)

VITAL STATISTICS

PURPOSE:
To record God's creation of the world and his desire to have a people set apart to worship him

AUTHOR:
Moses

TO WHOM WRITTEN:
The people of Israel

DATE WRITTEN:
1450–1410 B.C.

SETTING:
The region presently known as the Middle East

KEY VERSES:
"God created man in His own image, in the image of God He created him; male and female He created them" (1:27). " 'And I will make you a great nation, and I will bless you, and make your name great; and so you shall be a blessing; and I will bless those who bless you, and the one who curses you I will curse. And in you all the families of the earth will be blessed' " (12:2–3).

KEY PEOPLE:
Adam, Eve, Noah, Abraham, Sarah, Isaac, Rebekah, Jacob, Joseph

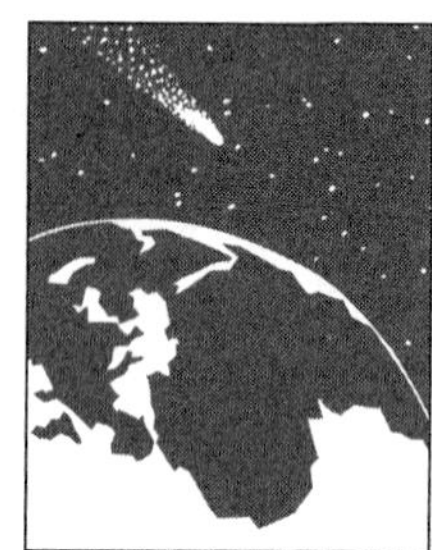

BEGIN . . . start . . . commence . . . open. . . . There's something refreshing and optimistic about these words, whether they refer to the dawn of a new day, the birth of a child, the prelude of a symphony, or the first miles of a family vacation. Free of problems and full of promise, beginnings stir hope and imaginative visions of the future. *Genesis* means "beginnings" or "origin," and it unfolds the record of the beginning of the world, of human history, of family, of civilization, of salvation. It is the story of God's purpose and plan for his creation. As the book of beginnings, Genesis sets the stage for the entire Bible. It reveals the person and nature of God (Creator, Sustainer, Judge, Redeemer); the value and dignity of human beings (made in God's image, saved by grace, used by God in the world); the tragedy and consequences of sin (the Fall, separation from God, judgment); and the promise and assurance of salvation (covenant, forgiveness, promised Messiah).

God. That's where Genesis begins. All at once we see him creating the world in a majestic display of power and purpose, culminating with a man and woman made like himself (1:26–27). But before long, sin entered the world, and Satan was unmasked. Bathed in innocence, creation was shattered by the fall (the willful disobedience of Adam and Eve). Fellowship with God was broken, and evil began weaving its destructive web. In rapid succession, we read how Adam and Eve were expelled from the beautiful garden, their first son turned murderer, and evil bred evil until God finally destroyed everyone on earth except a small family led by Noah, the only godly person left.

As we come to Abraham on the plains of Canaan, we discover the beginning of God's covenant people and the broad strokes of his salvation plan: Salvation comes by faith, Abraham's descendants will be God's people, and the Savior of the world will come through this chosen nation. The stories of Isaac, Jacob, and Joseph that follow are more than interesting biographies. They emphasize the promises of God and the proof that he is faithful. The people we meet in Genesis are simple, ordinary people, yet through them, God did great things. These are vivid pictures of how God can and does use all kinds of people to accomplish his good purposes—even people like you and me.

Read Genesis and be encouraged. There is hope! No matter how dark the world situation seems, God has a plan. No matter how insignificant or useless you feel, God loves you and wants to use you in his plan. No matter how sinful and separated from God you are, his salvation is available. Read Genesis . . . and hope!

Jacob & Esau born 2006 (1840)	Jacob flees to Haran 1929 (1764)	Joseph born 1915 (1750)	Joseph sold into slavery 1898 (1733)	Joseph rules Egypt 1885 (1720)	Joseph dies 1805 (1640)

THE BLUEPRINT

A. THE STORY OF CREATION (1:1—2:3)	God created the sky, seas, and land. He created the plants, animals, fish, and birds. But he created human beings in his own image. At times, others may treat us disrespectfully. But we can be certain of our dignity and worth because we have been created in the image of God.
B. THE STORY OF ADAM (2:4—5:32) 1. Adam and Eve 2. Cain and Abel 3. Adam's descendants	When Adam and Eve were created by God, they were without sin. But they became sinful when they disobeyed God and ate some fruit from the tree. Through Adam and Eve we learn about the destructive power of sin and its bitter consequences.
C. THE STORY OF NOAH (6:1—11:32) 1. The flood 2. Repopulating the earth 3. The tower of Babel	Noah was spared from the destruction of the flood because he obeyed God and built the boat. Just as God protected Noah and his family, he still protects those who are faithful to him today.
D. THE STORY OF ABRAHAM (12:1—25:18) 1. God promises a nation to Abram 2. Abram and Lot 3. God promises a son to Abram 4. Sodom and Gomorrah 5. Birth and near sacrifice of Isaac 6. Isaac and Rebekah 7. Abraham dies	Abraham was asked to leave his country, wander in Canaan, wait years for a son, and then sacrifice him as a burnt offering. Through these periods of sharp testing, Abraham remained faithful to God. His example teaches us what it means to live a life of faith.
E. THE STORY OF ISAAC (25:19—28:9) 1. Jacob and Esau 2. Isaac and Abimelech 3. Jacob gets Isaac's blessing	Isaac did not demand his own way. He did not resist when he was about to be sacrificed, and he gladly accepted a wife chosen for him by others. Like Isaac, we must learn to put God's will ahead of our own.
F. THE STORY OF JACOB (28:10—36:43) 1. Jacob starts a family 2. Jacob returns home	Jacob did not give up easily. He faithfully served Laban for over 14 years. Later, he wrestled with God. Although Jacob made many mistakes, his hard work teaches us about living a life of service for our Lord.
G. THE STORY OF JOSEPH (37:1—50:26) 1. Joseph is sold into slavery 2. Judah and Tamar 3. Joseph is thrown into prison 4. Joseph is placed in charge of Egypt 5. Joseph and his brothers meet in Egypt 6. Jacob's family moves to Egypt 7. Jacob and Joseph die in Egypt	Joseph was sold into slavery by his brothers and unjustly thrown into prison by his master. Through the life of Joseph, we learn that suffering, no matter how unfair, can develop strong character in us.

MEGATHEMES

THEME	EXPLANATION	IMPORTANCE
Beginnings	Genesis explains the beginning of many important realities: the universe, the earth, people, sin, and God's plan of salvation.	Genesis teaches us that the earth is well made and good. People are special to God and unique. God creates and sustains all life.
Disobedience	People are always facing great choices. Disobedience occurs when people choose not to follow God's plan of living.	Genesis explains why people are evil: They choose to do wrong. Even great Bible heroes failed God and disobeyed.
Sin	Sin ruins people's lives. It happens when we disobey God.	Living God's way makes life productive and fulfilling.
Promises	God makes promises to help and protect people. This kind of promise is called a "covenant."	God kept his promises then, and he keeps them now. He promises to love us, accept us, forgive us.

Obedience	The opposite of sin is obedience. Obeying God restores our relationship to him.	The only way to enjoy the benefits of God's promises is to obey him.
Prosperity	Prosperity is deeper than mere material wealth. True prosperity and fulfillment come as a result of obeying God.	When people obey God, they find peace with him, with others, and with themselves.
Israel	God started the nation of Israel in order to have a dedicated people who would (1) keep his ways alive in the world, (2) proclaim to the world what he is really like, and (3) prepare the world for the birth of Christ.	God is looking for people today to follow him. We are to proclaim God's truth and love to all nations, not just our own. We must be faithful to carry out the mission God has given us.

KEY PLACES IN GENESIS

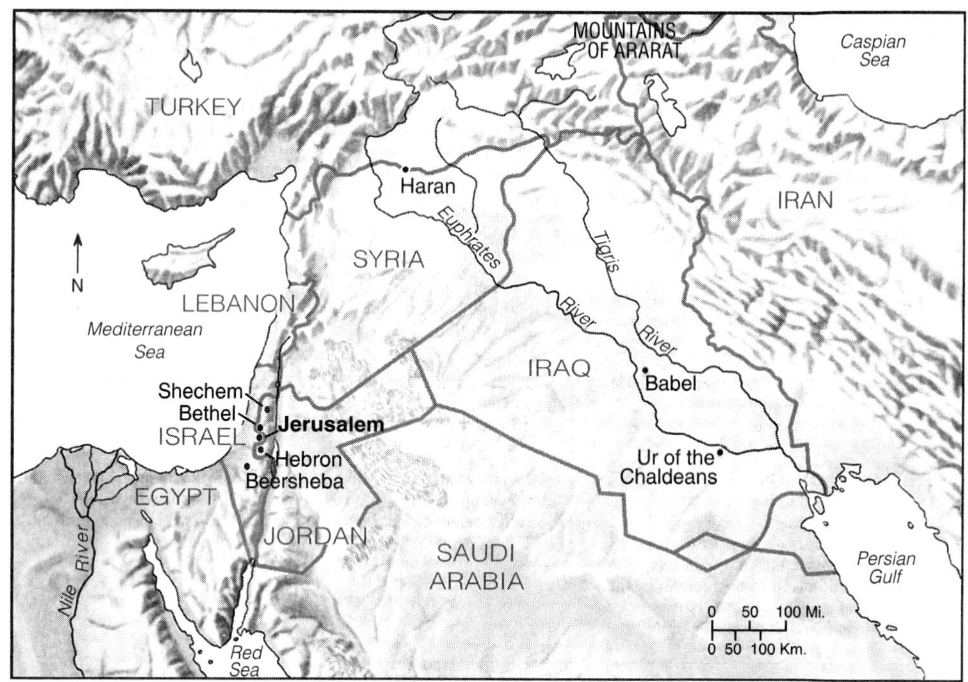

Modern names and boundaries are shown in gray.

God created the universe and the earth. Then he made man and woman, giving them a home in a beautiful garden. Unfortunately, Adam and Eve disobeyed God and were banished from the garden (3:24).

1 **Mountains of Ararat** Adam and Eve's sin brought sin into the human race. Years later, sin had run rampant and God decided to destroy the earth with a great flood. But Noah, his family, and two of each animal were safe in the boat. When the floods receded, the boat rested on the mountains of Ararat (8:4).

2 **Babel** People never learn. Again sin abounded, and the pride of the people led them to build a huge tower as a monument to their own greatness—obviously they had no thought of God. As punishment, God scattered the people by giving them different languages (11:8–9).

3 **Ur of the Chaldeans** Abram, a descendant of Shem and father of the Hebrew nation, was born in this great city (11:28).

4 **Haran** Terah, Abram, Lot, and Sarai left Ur and, following the fertile crescent of the Euphrates River, headed toward the land of Canaan. Along the way, they settled in the city of Haran for a while (11:31).

5 **Shechem** God urged Abram to leave Haran and go to a place where he would become the father of a great nation (12:1–2). So Abram, Lot, and Sarai traveled to the land of Canaan and settled near a city called Shechem (12:6).

6 **Hebron** Abraham moved on to Hebron where he put down his deepest roots (13:18). Abraham, Isaac, and Jacob all lived and were buried here.

7 **Beersheba** The well at Beersheba was a source of conflict between Abraham and King Abimelech and later became a sign of the oath that they swore there (21:31). Years later, as Isaac was moving from place to place, God appeared to him here and passed on to him the covenant he had made with his father, Abraham (26:23–25).

8 **Bethel** After deceiving his brother, Jacob left Beersheba and

fled to Haran. Along the way, God revealed himself to Jacob in a dream and passed on the covenant he had made with Abraham and Isaac (28:10–22). Jacob lived in Haran, worked for Laban, and married Leah and Rachel (29:15–28). After a tense meeting with his brother, Esau, Jacob returned to Bethel (35:1).

9 Egypt Jacob had 12 sons, including Joseph, Jacob's favorite. Joseph's 10 older brothers grew jealous, until one day the brothers sold him to Midianite traders going to Egypt. Eventually, Joseph rose from Egyptian slave to Pharaoh's "right-hand man," saving Egypt from famine. His entire family moved from Canaan to Egypt and settled there (46:3–7).

A. THE STORY OF CREATION (1:1—2:3)

We sometimes wonder how our world came to be. But here we find the answer. God created the earth and everything in it, and made man like himself. Although we may not understand the complexity of just how he did it, it is clear that God did create all life. This shows not only God's authority over humanity, but his deep love for all people.

1:1 John 1:1, 2; Heb 1:10; Ps 89:11; 90:2; Acts 17:24; Rom 1:20
1:2 Ps 104:30; Is 40:13
1:3 Ps 33:6, 9; 2 Cor 4:6
1:4 Ps 145:9, 10; Is 45:7
1:5 Ps 74:16; Ps 65:8
1:6 Is 40:22; Jer 10:12
1:7 Job 38:8-11
1:9 Ps 104:6-9; Jer 5:22
1:10 Ps 33:7; 95:5; 146:6

The Creation

1 In the beginning God created the heavens and the earth.
2 The earth was [1]formless and void, and darkness was over the surface of the deep,
and the Spirit of God was [2]moving over the surface of the waters.
3 Then God said, "Let there be light"; and there was light.
4 God saw that the light was good; and God separated the light from the darkness.
5 God called the light day, and the darkness He called night. And there was evening
and there was morning, one day.
6 Then God said, "Let there be an expanse in the midst of the waters, and let it separate the waters from the waters."
7 God made the [3]expanse, and separated the waters which were below the expanse
from the waters which were above the expanse; and it was so.
8 God called the expanse heaven. And there was evening and there was morning, a
second day.
9 Then God said, "Let the waters below the heavens be gathered into one place, and
let the dry land appear"; and it was so.
10 God called the dry land earth, and the gathering of the waters He called seas; and
God saw that it was good.

1 Or *a waste and emptiness* **2** Or *hovering* **3** Or *firmament*

1:1 The simple statement that God created the heavens and the earth is one of the most challenging concepts confronting the modern mind. The vast galaxy we live in is spinning at the incredible speed of 490,000 miles an hour. But even at this breakneck speed, our galaxy still needs 200 million years to make one rotation. And there are over one billion other galaxies just like ours in the universe.

Some scientists say that the number of stars in creation is equal to all the grains of all the sands on all the beaches of the world. Yet this complex sea of spinning stars functions with remarkable order and efficiency. To say that the universe "just happened" or "evolved" requires more faith than to believe that God is behind these amazing statistics. God truly did create a wonderful universe.

God did not *need* to create the universe; he *chose* to create it. Why? God is love, and love is best expressed toward something or someone else—so God created the world and people as an expression of his love. We should avoid reducing God's creation to merely scientific terms. Remember that God created the universe because he loves each of us.

1:1ff The creation story teaches us much about God and ourselves. First, we learn about God: (1) He is creative; (2) as the Creator he is distinct from his creation; (3) he is eternal and in control of the world. We also learn about ourselves: (1) since God chose to create us, we are valuable in his eyes; (2) we are more important than the animals. (See 1:28 for more on our role in the created order.)

1:1ff Just how did God create the earth? This is still a subject of great debate. Some say that there was a sudden explosion, and the universe appeared. Others say God started the process, and the universe evolved over billions of years. Almost every ancient religion has its own story to explain how the earth came to be. And almost every scientist has an opinion on the origin of the universe. But only the Bible shows one supreme God creating the earth out of his great love and giving all people a special place in it. We will never know all the answers to how God created the earth, but the Bible tells us that God did create it. That fact alone gives worth and dignity to all people.

1:2 The statement "the earth was formless and void" provides the setting for the creation narrative that follows. During the second and third days of creation, God gave *form* to the universe; during the next three days, God *filled* the earth with living beings. The "darkness . . . over the surface of the deep" was dispelled on the first day, when God created light.

1:2 The image of the Spirit of God moving over the waters is similar to a mother bird caring for and protecting her young (see Deuteronomy 32:11–12; Isaiah 31:5). God's Spirit was actively involved in the creation of the world (see Job 33:4; Psalm 104:30). God's care and protection are still active.

1:3—2:7 How long did it take God to create the world? There are two basic views about the days of creation: (1) Each day was a literal 24-hour period; (2) each day represents an indefinite period of time (even millions of years).

The Bible does not say how long these time periods were. The real question, however, is not how long God took, but how he did it. God created the earth in an orderly fashion (he did not make plants before light), and he created men and women as unique beings capable of communication with him. No other part of creation can claim that remarkable privilege. It is not important how long it took God to create the world, whether a few days or a few billion years, but that he created it just the way he wanted it.

1:6 The "expanse in the midst of the waters" was a separation between the sea and the mists of the skies.

11 Then God said, "Let the earth sprout vegetation: plants yielding seed, *and* fruit trees
on the earth bearing fruit after their kind with seed in them"; and it was so.
12 The earth brought forth vegetation, plants yielding seed after their kind, and trees
bearing fruit with seed in them, after their kind; and God saw that it was good.
13 There was evening and there was morning, a third day.
14 Then God said, "Let there be lights in the expanse of the heavens to separate the
day from the night, and let them be for signs and for seasons and for days and years;
15 and let them be for lights in the expanse of the heavens to give light on the earth";
and it was so.
16 God made the two great lights, the greater light to govern the day, and the lesser
light to govern the night; *He made* the stars also.
17 God placed them in the expanse of the heavens to give light on the earth,
18 and to govern the day and the night, and to separate the light from the darkness;
and God saw that it was good.
19 There was evening and there was morning, a fourth day.
20 Then God said, "Let the waters teem with swarms of living creatures, and let birds
fly above the earth in the open expanse of the heavens."
21 God created the great sea monsters and every living creature that moves, with which
the waters swarmed after their kind, and every winged bird after its kind; and God saw
that it was good.
22 God blessed them, saying, "Be fruitful and multiply, and fill the waters in the seas,
and let birds multiply on the earth."
23 There was evening and there was morning, a fifth day.
24 Then God said, "Let the earth bring forth living creatures after their kind: cattle
and creeping things and beasts of the earth after their kind"; and it was so.
25 God made the beasts of the earth after their kind, and the cattle after their kind,
and everything that creeps on the ground after its kind; and God saw that it was good.
26 Then God said, "Let Us make man in Our image, according to Our likeness; and let
them rule over the fish of the sea and over the birds of the sky and over the cattle and
over all the earth, and over every creeping thing that creeps on the earth."

1:11 Ps 65:9-13; 104:14; Heb 6:7
1:14 Ps 74:16; 136:7; Ps 19:1; 150:1; Jer 10:2; Ps 104:19
1:16 Ps 136:8, 9; Job 38:7; Ps 8:3; Is 40:26
1:17 Jer 33:20, 25
1:18 Jer 31:35
1:21 Ps 104:25-28
1:24 Gen 2:19; 6:20; 7:14; 8:19
1:25 Gen 7:21, 22; Jer 27:5
1:26 Gen 3:22; 11:7; Gen 5:1; 9:6; 1 Cor 11:7; Eph 4:24; James 3:9; Ps 8:6-8

BEGINNINGS

The Bible does not discuss the subject of evolution. Rather, its worldview assumes God created the world. The Biblical view of creation is not in conflict with science; rather, it is in conflict with any worldview that starts without a creator.

Equally committed and sincere Christians have struggled with the subject of beginnings and come to differing conclusions. This, of course, is to be expected because the evidence is very old and, due to the ravages of the ages, quite fragmented. Students of the Bible and of science should avoid polarizations and black/white thinking. Students of the Bible must be careful not to make the Bible say what it doesn't say, and students of science must not make science say what it doesn't say.

The most important aspect of the continuing discussion is not the process of creation, but the origin of creation. The world is not a product of blind chance and probability; God created it.

The Bible not only tells us that the world was created by God; more important, it tells us who this God is. It reveals God's personality, his character, and his plan for his creation. It also reveals God's deepest desire: to relate to and fellowship with the people he created. God took the ultimate step toward fellowship with us through his historic visit to this planet in the person of his Son, Jesus Christ. We can know this God who created the universe in a very personal way.

The heavens and the earth are here. We are here. God created all that we see and experience. The book of Genesis begins, "God created the heavens and the earth."

Here we begin the most exciting and fulfilling journey imaginable.

1:25 God saw that his work was good. People sometimes feel guilty for having a good time or for feeling good about an accomplishment. This need not be so. Just as God felt good about his work, we can be pleased with ours. However, we should not feel good about our work if God would not be pleased with it. What are you doing that pleases both you and God?

1:26 Why does God use the plural form, "Let *Us* make man in *Our* image"? One view says this is a reference to the Trinity—God the Father, Jesus Christ his Son, and the Holy Spirit—all of whom are God. Another view is that the plural wording is used to denote majesty. Kings traditionally use the plural form in speaking of themselves. From Job 33:4 and Psalm 104:30, we do know that God's Spirit was present in the creation. From Colossians 1:16 we know that Christ, God's Son, was at work in the creation.

1:26 In what ways are we made in God's image? God obviously did not create us exactly like himself because God has no physical body. Instead, we are reflections of God's glory. Some feel that our reason, creativity, speech, or self-determination is the image of God. More likely, it is our entire self that reflects the image of God. We will never be totally like God because he is our supreme Creator. But we do have the ability to reflect his character in our love, patience, forgiveness, kindness, and faithfulness.

Knowing that we are made in God's image and thus share many of his characteristics provides a solid basis for self-worth. Human

1:27 Gen 5:1f; 1 Cor 11:7; Eph 4:24; Col 3:10; Matt 19:4; Mark 10:6
1:28 Gen 9:1, 7; Lev 26:9; Ps 127:3, 5
1:29 Ps 104:14; 136:25
1:30 Ps 145:15, 16; 147:9
1:31 Ps 104:24, 28; 119:68; 1 Tim 4:4

27 God created man in His own image, in the image of God He created him; male and
female He created them.
28 God blessed them; and God said to them, "Be fruitful and multiply, and fill the earth,
and subdue it; and rule over the fish of the sea and over the birds of the sky and over
every living thing that moves on the earth."
29 Then God said, "Behold, I have given you every plant yielding seed that is on
the surface of all the earth, and every tree which has fruit yielding seed; it shall be food
for you;
30 and to every beast of the earth and to every bird of the sky and to every thing that
moves on the earth which has life, *I have given* every green plant for food"; and it was so.
31 God saw all that He had made, and behold, it was very good. And there was evening and there was morning, the sixth day.

The Creation of Man and Woman

2:1 Deut 4:19; 17:3
2:2 Ex 20:8-11; 31:17; Heb 4:4, 10

2 Thus the heavens and the earth were completed, and all their hosts.
2 By the seventh day God completed His work which He had done, and He rested
on the seventh day from all His work which He had done.
3 Then God blessed the seventh day and sanctified it, because in it He rested from all
His work which God had created and made.

B. THE STORY OF ADAM (2:4—5:32)

Learning about our ancestors often helps us understand ourselves. Adam and Eve, our first ancestors, were the highlight of God's creation-the very reason God made the world. But they didn't always live the way God intended. Through their mistakes, we can learn important lessons on how to live rightly. Adam and Eve teach us much about the nature of sin and its consequences.

1. Adam and Eve

2:4 Job 38:4-11; Gen 1:3-31
2:5 Gen 1:11; Ps 65:9, 10; Jer 10:12, 13

4 This is the account of the heavens and the earth when they were created, in the day
that the LORD God made earth and heaven.
5 Now no shrub of the field was yet in the earth, and no plant of the field had yet
sprouted, for the LORD God had not sent rain upon the earth, and there was no man to
cultivate the ground.

DAYS OF CREATION

First Day	Light (so there was light and darkness)
Second Day	Sky and water (waters separated)
Third Day	Land and seas (waters gathered); vegetation
Fourth Day	Sun, moon, and stars (to govern the day and the night and to mark seasons, days, and years)
Fifth Day	Fish and birds (to fill the waters and the sky)
Sixth Day	Animals (to fill the earth)
	Man and woman (to care for the earth and to commune with God)
Seventh Day	God rested and declared all he had made to be very good

worth is not based on possessions, achievements, physical attractiveness, or public acclaim. Instead it is based on being made in God's image. Because we bear God's image, we can feel positive about ourselves. Criticizing or downgrading ourselves is criticizing what God has made and the abilities he has given us. Knowing that you are a person of worth helps you love God, know him personally, and make a valuable contribution to those around you.

1:27 God made both man and woman in his image. Neither man nor woman is made more in the image of God than the other. From the beginning the Bible places both man and woman at the pinnacle of God's creation. Neither sex is exalted, and neither is depreciated.

1:28 To "rule over" something is to have absolute authority and control over it. God has ultimate rule over the earth, and he exercises his authority with loving care. When God delegated some of his authority to the human race, he expected us to take responsibility for the environment and the other creatures that share our planet. We must not be careless and wasteful as we fulfill this charge. God was careful how he made this earth. We must not be careless about how we take care of it.

1:31 God saw that all he had created was very good. You are part of God's creation, and he is pleased with how he made you. If at times you feel worthless or of little value, remember that God made you for a good reason. You are valuable to him.

2:2-3 We live in an action-oriented world! There always seems to be something to do and no time to rest. Yet God demonstrated that rest is appropriate and right. If God himself rested from his work, then it should not amaze us that we also need rest. Jesus demonstrated this principle when he and his disciples left in a boat to get away from the crowds (see Mark 6:31–32). Our times of rest refresh us for times of service.

2:3 That God *blessed* the seventh day means that he set it apart for holy use. This act is picked up in the Ten Commandments (Exodus 20:1-17) where God commanded the observance of the Sabbath.

6 But a mist used to rise from the earth and water the whole surface of the ground.
7 Then the LORD God formed man of dust from the ground, and breathed into his
nostrils the breath of life; and man became a living being.
8 The LORD God planted a garden toward the east, in Eden; and there He placed the
man whom He had formed.
9 Out of the ground the LORD God caused to grow every tree that is pleasing to the
sight and good for food; the tree of life also in the midst of the garden, and the tree of
the knowledge of good and evil.
10 Now a river flowed out of Eden to water the garden; and from there it divided and
became four rivers.
11 The name of the first is Pishon; it flows around the whole land of Havilah, where
there is gold.
12 The gold of that land is good; the bdellium and the onyx stone are there.
13 The name of the second river is Gihon; it flows around the whole land of Cush.
14 The name of the third river is Tigris; it flows east of Assyria. And the fourth river is
the Euphrates.
15 Then the LORD God took the man and put him into the garden of Eden to cultivate
it and keep it.
16 The LORD God commanded the man, saying, "From any tree of the garden you may
eat freely;
17 but from the tree of the knowledge of good and evil you shall not eat, for in the day
that you eat from it you will surely die."
18 Then the LORD God said, "It is not good for the man to be alone; I will make him
a helper [4]suitable for him."

2:7 Gen 3:19; 1 Cor 15:45
2:8 Gen 13:10; Is 51:3; Ezek 28:13
2:9 Ezek 47:12; Gen 3:22; Rev 2:7; 22:2, 14
2:10 Ps 46:4
2:11 Gen 25:18
2:14 Dan 10:4; Gen 15:18
2:16 Gen 3:2, 3
2:17 Deut 30:15, 19, 20; Rom 6:23; 1 Tim 5:6; James 1:15
2:18 1 Cor 11:9

4 Lit *corresponding to*

WHAT THE BIBLE SAYS ABOUT MARRIAGE

Genesis 2:18-24	Marriage is God's idea
Genesis 24:58-60	Commitment is essential to a successful marriage
Song 4:9–10	Romance is important
Jeremiah 33:10–11	Marriage holds times of great joy
Malachi 2:14–15	Marriage creates the best environment for raising children
Matthew 5:32	Unfaithfulness breaks the bond of trust, the foundation of all relationships
Matthew 19:6	Marriage is permanent
Romans 7:2-3	Ideally, only death should dissolve marriage
Ephesians 5:21-33	Marriage is based on the principled practice of love, not on feelings
Ephesians 5:23, 32	Marriage is a living symbol of Christ and the church
Hebrews 13:4	Marriage is good and honorable

2:7 "Dust from the ground" implies that there is nothing fancy about the chemical elements making up our bodies. The body is a lifeless shell until God brings it alive with his "breath of life." When God removes his life-giving breath, our bodies once again return to dust. Therefore our life and worth come from God's Spirit. Many boast of their achievements and abilities as though they were the originator of their own strengths. Others feel worthless because their abilities do not stand out. In reality, our worth comes not from our achievements but from the God of the universe, who chooses to give us the mysterious and miraculous gift of life. Value life, as he does.

2:9 The name of the tree of the knowledge of good and evil implies that evil had already occurred, if not in the garden, then at the time of Satan's fall.

2:9, 16–17 Were the tree of life and the tree of the knowledge of good and evil real trees? Two views are often expressed: (1) *The trees were real, but symbolic.* Eternal life with God was pictured as eating from the tree of life. (2) *The trees were real, possessing special properties.* By eating the fruit from the tree of life, Adam and Eve could have had eternal life, enjoying a permanent relationship as God's children.

In either case, Adam and Eve's sin separated them from the tree of life and thus kept them from obtaining eternal life. Interestingly, the tree of life again appears in a description in Revelation 22 of people enjoying eternal life with God.

2:15–17 God gave Adam responsibility for the garden and told him not to eat from the tree of the knowledge of good and evil. Rather than physically preventing him from eating, God gave Adam a choice, and thus the possibility of choosing wrongly. God still gives us choices, and we, too, often choose wrongly. These wrong choices may cause us pain, but they can help us learn and grow and make better choices in the future. Living with the consequences of our choices teaches us to think and choose more carefully.

2:16–17 Why would God place a tree in the garden and then forbid Adam to eat from it? God wanted Adam to obey, but God gave Adam the freedom to choose. Without choice, Adam would have been like a prisoner, and his obedience would have been hollow. The two trees provided an exercise in choice, with rewards for choosing to obey and sad consequences for choosing to disobey. When you are faced with the choice, always choose to obey God.

2:19 Gen 1:24; Gen 1:26

19 Out of the ground the LORD God formed every beast of the field and every bird of
the sky, and brought *them* to the man to see what he would call them; and whatever the
man called a living creature, that was its name.

2:20 Gen 2:18

20 The man gave names to all the cattle, and to the birds of the sky, and to every beast
of the field, but for [5]Adam there was not found a helper suitable for him.

2:21 Gen 15:12

21 So the LORD God caused a deep sleep to fall upon the man, and he slept; then He
took one of his ribs and closed up the flesh at that place.

2:22 1 Cor 11:8, 9

22 The LORD God [6]fashioned into a woman the rib which He had taken from the man,
and brought her to the man.

2:23 Gen 29:14; Eph 5:28, 29

23 The man said,
"This is now bone of my bones,
And flesh of my flesh;
She shall be called Woman,
Because she was taken out of Man."

2:24 Matt 19:5; Mark 10:7, 8; 1 Cor 6:16; Eph 5:31

24 For this reason a man shall leave his father and his mother, and be joined to his
wife; and they shall become one flesh.

2:25 Gen 3:7, 10, 11

25 And the man and his wife were both naked and were not ashamed.

The Fall of Man

3:1 2 Cor 11:3; Rev 12:9; 20:2

3 Now the serpent was more crafty than any beast of the field which the LORD God
had made. And he said to the woman, "Indeed, has God said, 'You shall not eat
from any tree of the garden'?"

3:2 Gen 2:16, 17

2 The woman said to the serpent, "From the fruit of the trees of the garden we may eat;
3 but from the fruit of the tree which is in the middle of the garden, God has said,
'You shall not eat from it or touch it, or you will die.' "

3:4 John 8:44; 2 Cor 11:3

4 The serpent said to the woman, "You surely will not die!

5 Or *man* **6** Lit *built*

2:18–24 God's creative work was not complete until he made woman. He could have made her from the dust of the ground, as he made man. God chose, however, to make her from the man's flesh and bone. In so doing, he illustrated for us that in marriage man and woman symbolically become one flesh. This is a mystical union of the couple's hearts and lives. Throughout the Bible, God treats this special partnership seriously. If you are married or planning to be married, are you willing to keep the commitment that makes the two of you one? The goal in marriage should be more than friendship; it should be oneness.

2:21–23 God forms and equips men and women for various tasks, but all these tasks lead to the same goal—honoring God. Man gives life to woman; woman gives life to the world. Each role carries exclusive privileges; there is no room for thinking that one sex is superior to the other.

2:24 God gave marriage as a gift to Adam and Eve. They were created perfect for each other. Marriage was not just for convenience, nor was it brought about by any culture. It was instituted by God and has three basic aspects: (1) The man leaves his parents and, in a public act, promises himself to his wife; (2) the man and woman are joined together by taking responsibility for each other's welfare and by loving the mate above all others; (3) the two become one flesh in the intimacy and commitment of sexual union that is reserved for marriage. Strong marriages include all three of these aspects.

2:25 Have you ever noticed how a little child can run naked through a room full of strangers without embarrassment? He is not aware of his nakedness, just as Adam and Eve were not embarrassed in their innocence. But after Adam and Eve sinned, shame and awkwardness followed, creating barriers between themselves and God. We often experience these same barriers in marriage. Ideally a husband and wife have no barriers, feeling no embarrassment in exposing themselves to each other or to God. But, like Adam and Eve (3:7), we put on fig leaves (barriers) because we have areas we don't want our spouse, or God, to know about. Then we hide, just as Adam and Eve hid from God. In marriage, lack of spiritual, emotional, and intellectual intimacy usually precedes a breakdown of physical intimacy. In the same way, when we fail to expose our secret thoughts to God, we break our lines of communication with him.

3:1 Disguised as a crafty serpent, Satan came to tempt Eve. Satan at one time was an angel who rebelled against God and was thrown out of heaven. As a created being, Satan has definite limitations. Although he is trying to tempt everyone away from God, he will not be the final victor. In 3:14–15, God promises that Satan will be crushed by one of the woman's offspring, the Messiah.

3:1–6 Why does Satan tempt us? Temptation is Satan's invitation to give in to his kind of life and give up on God's kind of life. Satan tempted Eve and succeeded in getting her to sin. Ever since then, he's been busy getting people to sin. He even tempted Jesus (Matthew 4:11). But Jesus did not sin!

How could Eve have resisted temptation? By following the same guidelines we can follow. First, we must realize that *being tempted* is not a sin. We have not sinned until we *give in* to the temptation. Then, to resist temptation, we must (1) pray for strength to resist, (2) run, sometimes literally, and (3) say no when confronted with what we know is wrong. James 1:12 tells of the blessings and rewards for those who don't give in when tempted.

3:1–6 The serpent, Satan, tempted Eve by getting her to doubt God's goodness. He implied that God was strict, stingy, and selfish for not wanting Eve to share his knowledge of good and evil. Satan made Eve forget all that God had given her and, instead, focus on the one thing she couldn't have. We fall into trouble, too, when we dwell on the few things we don't have rather than on the countless things God has given us. The next time you are feeling sorry for yourself and what you don't have, consider all you *do* have and thank God. Then your doubts won't lead you into sin.

5 "For God knows that in the day you eat from it your eyes will be opened, and you will
be like God, knowing good and evil."
6 When the woman saw that the tree was good for food, and that it was a delight to
the eyes, and that the tree was desirable to make *one* wise, she took from its fruit and
ate; and she gave also to her husband with her, and he ate.
7 Then the eyes of both of them were opened, and they knew that they were naked;
and they sewed fig leaves together and made themselves loin coverings.
8 They heard the sound of the LORD God walking in the garden in the cool of the
day, and the man and his wife hid themselves from the presence of the LORD God among
the trees of the garden.
9 Then the LORD God called to the man, and said to him, "Where are you?"
10 He said, "I heard the sound of You in the garden, and I was afraid because I was
naked; so I hid myself."
11 And He said, "Who told you that you were naked? Have you eaten from the tree of
which I commanded you not to eat?"
12 The man said, "The woman whom You gave *to be* with me, she gave me from the
tree, and I ate."

3:5
Is 14:14; Ezek 28:2, 12-17

3:6
Rom 5:12-19; 1 Tim 2:14; James 1:14, 15; 1 John 2:16

3:7
Is 47:3; Lam 1:8

3:8
Gen 18:33; Lev 26:12; Deut 23:14; Job 31:33; Ps 139:1-12; Hos 10:8; Amos 9:3; Rev 6:15-17

3:9
Gen 4:9; 18:9

3:10
Ex 20:18, 19; Deut 5:25

3:12
Job 31:33; Prov 28:13

3:5 Adam and Eve got what they wanted: an intimate knowledge of both good and evil. But they got it by doing evil, and the results were disastrous. Sometimes we have the illusion that freedom is doing anything we want. But God says that true freedom comes from obedience and knowing what *not* to do. The restrictions he gives us are for our good, helping us avoid evil. We have the freedom to walk in front of a speeding car, but we don't need to be hit to realize it would be foolish to do so. Don't listen to Satan's temptations. You don't have to do evil to gain more experience and learn more about life.

3:5 Satan used a sincere motive to tempt Eve—"you will be like God." It wasn't wrong of Eve to want to be like God. To become more like God is humanity's highest goal. It is what we are supposed to do. But Satan misled Eve concerning the right way to accomplish this goal. He told her that she could become more like God by defying God's authority, by taking God's place and deciding for herself what was best for her life. In effect, he told her to become her own god.

But to become like God is not the same as trying to become God. Rather, it is to reflect his characteristics and to recognize his authority over your life. Like Eve, we often have a worthy goal but try to achieve it in the wrong way. We act like a political candidate who pays off an election judge to be "voted" into office. When he does this, serving the people is no longer his highest goal.

Self-exaltation leads to rebellion against God. As soon as we begin to leave God out of our plans, we are placing ourselves above him. This is exactly what Satan wants us to do.

3:6 Satan tried to make Eve think that sin is good, pleasant, and desirable. A knowledge of both good and evil seemed harmless to her. People usually choose wrong things because they have become convinced that those things are good, at least for themselves. Our sins do not always appear ugly to us, and the pleasant sins are the hardest to avoid. So prepare yourself for the attractive temptations that may come your way. We cannot always prevent temptation, but there is always a way of escape (1 Corinthians 10:13). Use God's Word and God's people to help you stand against it.

3:6–7 Notice what Eve did: She looked, she took, she ate, and she gave. The battle is often lost at the first look. Temptation often begins by simply seeing something you want. Are you struggling with temptation because you have not learned that looking is the first step toward sin? You would win over temptation more often if you followed Paul's advice to run from those things that produce evil thoughts (2 Timothy 2:22).

3:6–7 One of the realities of sin is that its effects spread. After Eve sinned, she involved Adam in her wrongdoing. When we do something wrong, often we try to relieve our guilt by involving someone else. Like toxic waste spilled in a river, sin swiftly spreads. Recognize and confess your sin to God before you are tempted to pollute those around you.

3:7–8 After sinning, Adam and Eve felt guilt and embarrassment over their nakedness. Their guilty feelings made them try to hide from God. A guilty conscience is a warning signal God placed inside you that goes off when you've done wrong. The worst step you could take is to eliminate the guilty feelings without eliminating the cause. That would be like using a pain killer but not treating the disease. Be glad those guilty feelings are there. They make you aware of your sin so you can ask God's forgiveness and then correct your wrongdoing.

3:8 The thought of two humans covered with fig leaves trying to hide from the all-seeing, all-knowing God is humorous. How could they be so silly as to think they could actually hide? Yet we do the same, acting as though God doesn't know what we're doing. Have the courage to share all you do and think with him. And don't try to hide—it can't be done. Honesty will strengthen your relationship with God.

3:8–9 These verses show God's desire to have fellowship with us. They also show why we are afraid to have fellowship with him. Adam and Eve hid from God when they heard him approaching. God wanted to be with them, but because of their sin they were afraid to show themselves. Sin had broken their close relationship with God, just as it has broken ours. But Jesus Christ, God's Son, opens the way for us to renew our fellowship with him. God longs to be with us. He actively offers us his unconditional love. Our natural response is fear because we feel we can't live up to his standards. But understanding that he loves us, regardless of our faults, can help remove that dread.

3:11–13 Adam and Eve failed to heed God's warning recorded in 2:16–17. They did not understand the reasons for his command, so they chose to act in another way that looked better to them. All of God's commands are for our own good, but we may not always understand the reasons behind them. People who trust God will obey because God asks them to, whether or not they understand why God commands it.

3:11–13 When God asked Adam about his sin, Adam blamed Eve. Then Eve blamed the serpent. How easy it is to excuse our sins by blaming someone else or circumstances. But God knows the truth, and he holds each of us responsible for what we do (see 3:14–19). Admit your wrong attitudes and actions and apologize to God. Don't try to get away with sin by blaming someone else.

3:13 2 Cor 11:3; 1 Tim 2:14

3:14 Deut 28:15-20; Is 65:25; Mic 7:17

13 Then the LORD God said to the woman, "What is this you have done?" And the
woman said, "The serpent deceived me, and I ate."
14 The LORD God said to the serpent,
"Because you have done this,
Cursed are you more than all cattle,
And more than every beast of the field;

We can hardly imagine what it must have been like to be the first and only person on earth. It's one thing for us to be lonely; it was another for Adam, who had never known another human being. He missed much that makes us who we are—he had no childhood, no parents, no family or friends. He had to learn to be human on his own. Fortunately, God didn't let him struggle too long before presenting him with an ideal companion and mate, Eve. Theirs was a complete, innocent, and open oneness, without a hint of shame.

One of Adam's first conversations with his delightful new companion must have been about the rules of the garden. Before God made Eve he had already given Adam complete freedom in the garden, with the responsibility to tend and care for it. But one tree was off limits, the tree of the knowledge of good and evil. Adam would have told Eve all about this. She knew, when Satan approached her, that the tree's fruit was not to be eaten. However, she decided to eat the forbidden fruit. Then she offered some to Adam. At that moment, the fate of creation was on the line. Sadly, Adam didn't pause to consider the consequences. He went ahead and ate.

In that moment of small rebellion something large, beautiful, and free was shattered . . . God's perfect creation. Man was separated from God by his desire to act on his own. The effect on a plate glass window is the same whether a pebble or a boulder is hurled at it—the thousands of fragments can never be regathered.

In the case of man's sin, however, God already had a plan in motion to overcome the effects of the rebellion. The entire Bible is the story of how that plan unfolds, ultimately leading to God's own visit to earth through his Son, Jesus. His sinless life and death made it possible for God to offer forgiveness to all who want it. Our small and large acts of rebellion prove that we are descendants of Adam. Only by asking forgiveness of Jesus Christ can we become children of God.

Strengths and accomplishments:
- The first zoologist—namer of animals
- The first landscape architect, placed in the garden to care for it
- Father of the human race
- The first person made in the image of God, and the first human to share an intimate personal relationship with God

Weaknesses and mistakes:
- Avoided responsibility and blamed others; chose to hide rather than to confront; made excuses rather than admitting the truth
- Greatest mistake: teamed up with Eve to bring sin into the world

Lessons from his life:
- As Adam's descendants, we all reflect to some degree the image of God
- God wants people who, though free to do wrong, choose instead to love him
- We should not blame others for our faults
- We cannot hide from God

Vital statistics:
- Where: Garden of Eden
- Occupation: Caretaker, gardener, farmer
- Relatives: Wife: Eve. Sons: Cain, Abel, Seth. Numerous other children. The only man who never had an earthly mother or father

Key verses:
"The man said, 'The woman whom You gave to be with me, she gave me from the tree, and I ate' " (Genesis 3:12).
"For as in Adam all die, so also in Christ all will be made alive" (1 Corinthians 15:22).

Adam's story is told in Genesis 1:26—5:5. He is also mentioned in 1 Chronicles 1:1; Job 31:33; Luke 3:38; Romans 5:14; 1 Corinthians 15:22, 45; 1 Timothy 2:13–14.

3:14ff Adam and Eve chose their course of action (disobedience), and then God chose his. As a holy God, he could respond only in a way consistent with his perfect moral nature. He could not allow sin to go unchecked; he had to punish it. If the consequences of Adam and Eve's sin seem extreme, remember that their sin set in motion the world's tendency toward disobeying God. That is why we sin today: Every human being ever born, with the exception of Jesus, has inherited the sinful nature of Adam and Eve (Romans 5:12–21). Adam and Eve's punishment reflects how seriously God views sin of any kind.

On your belly you will go,
And dust you will eat
All the days of your life;
15 And I will put enmity
Between you and the woman,
And between your seed and her seed;
He shall bruise you on the head,
And you shall bruise him on the heel."
16 To the woman He said,
"I will greatly multiply
Your pain in childbirth,
In pain you will bring forth children;
Yet your desire will be for your husband,
And he will rule over you."
17 Then to Adam He said, "Because you have listened to the voice of your wife,
and have eaten from the tree about which I commanded you, saying, 'You shall not eat
from it';
Cursed is the ground because of you;
In toil you will eat of it
All the days of your life.
18 "Both thorns and thistles it shall grow for you;
And you will eat the plants of the field;
19 By the sweat of your face
You will eat bread,
Till you return to the ground,
Because from it you were taken;
For you are dust,
And to dust you shall return."
20 Now the man called his wife's name [7]Eve, because she was the mother of all *the* living.
21 The LORD God made garments of skin for Adam and his wife, and clothed them.
22 Then the LORD God said, "Behold, the man has become like one of Us, knowing
good and evil; and now, he might stretch out his hand, and take also from the tree of life,
and eat, and live forever"—
23 therefore the LORD God sent him out from the garden of Eden, to cultivate the
ground from which he was taken.

3:15 Rev 12:17; Rom 16:20

3:16 John 16:21; 1 Tim 2:15; 1 Cor 14:34

3:17 Gen 5:29; Rom 8:20-22; Heb 6:8; Job 5:7; 14:1; Eccl 2:23

3:19 Ps 90:3; 104:29; Eccl 12:7; Gen 2:7

3:20 2 Cor 11:3; 1 Tim 2:13

3:22 Gen 1:26; Gen 2:9; Rev 22:14

7 I.e. living; or life

SATAN'S PLAN

Doubt	Makes you question God's Word and his goodness
Discouragement	Makes you look at your problems rather than at God
Diversion	Makes the wrong things seem attractive so that you will want them more than the right things
Defeat	Makes you feel like a failure so that you don't even try
Delay	Makes you put off doing something so that it never gets done

3:14–19 Adam and Eve learned by painful experience that because God is holy and hates sin, he must punish sinners. The rest of the book of Genesis recounts painful stories of lives ruined as a result of the fall. Disobedience is sin, and it breaks our fellowship with God. But, fortunately, when we disobey, God is willing to forgive us and to restore our relationship with him.

3:15 Satan is our enemy. He will do anything he can to get us to follow his evil, deadly path. The phrase "you shall bruise him on the heel" refers to Satan's repeated attempts to defeat Christ during his life on earth. "He shall bruise you on the head" foreshadows Satan's defeat when Christ rose from the dead. A bruise on the heel is not deadly; but a crushing blow to the head is. Already God was revealing his plan to defeat Satan and offer salvation to the world through his Son, Jesus Christ.

3:17–19 Adam and Eve's disobedience and fall from God's gracious presence affected all creation, including the environment. Years ago people thought nothing of polluting streams with chemical wastes and garbage. This seemed so insignificant, so small. Now we know that just two or three parts per million of certain chemicals can damage human health. Sin in our lives is similar to pollution in streams. A small amount is deadly.

3:22–24 Life in the Garden of Eden was like living in heaven. Everything was perfect, and if Adam and Eve had obeyed God, they could have lived there forever. But after disobeying, Adam and Eve no longer deserved paradise, and God told them to leave. If they had continued to live in the garden and eat from the tree of life, they would have lived forever. But eternal life in a state of sin would mean forever trying to hide from God. Like Adam and Eve, all of us have sinned and are separated from fellowship with God. We do not have to stay separated, however. God is preparing a new earth as an eternal paradise for his people (see Revelation 22).

3:24 Ezek 31:11; Gen 2:8; Ex 25:18-22; Ps 104:4; Ezek 10:1-20; Heb 1:7; Gen 2:9

24 So He drove the man out; and at the east of the garden of Eden He stationed the cherubim and the flaming sword which turned every direction to guard the way to the tree of life.

2. Cain and Abel

4 Now the man had relations with his wife Eve, and she conceived and gave birth to Cain, and she said, "I have gotten a manchild with *the help of* the LORD."

4:2 Luke 11:50, 51; Gen 46:32; 47:3

2 Again, she gave birth to his brother Abel. And Abel was a keeper of flocks, but Cain was a tiller of the ground.

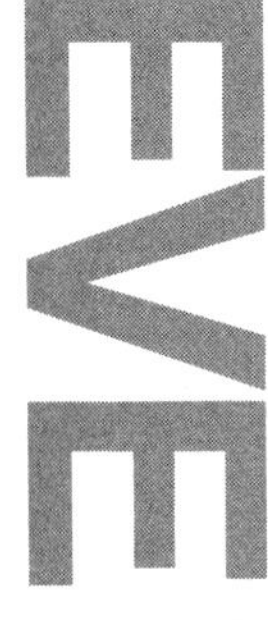

We know very little about Eve, the first woman in the world, yet she is the mother of us all. She was the final piece in the intricate and amazing puzzle of God's creation. Adam now had another human being with whom to fellowship—someone with an equal share in God's image. Here was someone alike enough for companionship, yet different enough for relationship. Together they were greater than either could have been alone.

Eve was approached by Satan in the Garden of Eden, where she and Adam lived. He questioned her contentment. How could she be happy when she was not allowed to eat from one of the fruit trees? Satan helped Eve shift her focus from all that God had done and given to the one thing he had withheld. And Eve was willing to accept Satan's viewpoint without checking with God.

Sound familiar? How often is our attention drawn from the much which is ours to the little that isn't? We get that "I've got to have it" feeling. Eve was typical of us all, and we consistently show we are her descendants by repeating her mistakes. Our desires, like Eve's, can be quite easily manipulated. They are not the best basis for actions. We need to keep God in our decision-making process always. His Word, the Bible, is our guidebook in decision making.

Strengths and accomplishments:
- First wife and mother
- First female. As such she shared a special relationship with God, had co-responsibility with Adam over creation, and displayed certain characteristics of God

Weaknesses and mistakes:
- Allowed her contentment to be undermined by Satan
- Acted impulsively without talking either to God or to her mate
- Not only sinned, but shared her sin with Adam
- When confronted, blamed others

Lessons from her life:
- The female shares in the image of God
- The necessary ingredients for a strong marriage are commitment to each other, companionship with each other, complete oneness, absence of shame (2:24–25)
- The basic human tendency to sin goes back to the beginning of the human race

Vital statistics:
- Where: Garden of Eden
- Occupation: Wife, helper, companion, co-manager of Eden
- Relatives: Husband: Adam. Sons: Cain, Abel, Seth. Numerous other children

Key verse:
"The LORD God said, 'It is not good for the man to be alone; I will make him a helper suitable for him' " (Genesis 2:18).

Eve's story is told in Genesis 2:19—4:26. Her death is not mentioned in Scripture.

3:24 The cherubim were mighty angels of the Lord.

3:24 This is how Adam and Eve broke their relationship with God: (1) they became convinced that their way was better than God's; (2) they became self-conscious and hid; (3) they tried to excuse and defend themselves. To build a relationship with God we must reverse those steps: (1) we must drop our excuses and self-defenses; (2) we must stop trying to hide from God; (3) we must become convinced that God's way is better than our way.

4:1 The phrase *had relations with* is literally *knew* and means he "had sexual intercourse with." Sexual union means oneness and total knowledge of the other person. Sexual intercourse is the most intimate of acts, sealing a social, physical, and spiritual relationship. That is why God has reserved it for marriage alone.

4:2 No longer was everything provided for Adam and Eve as it had been in the Garden of Eden where their daily tasks were refreshing and delightful. Now they had to struggle against the elements in order to provide food, clothing, and shelter for themselves and their family. Cain became a farmer, while Abel was a shepherd. In parts of the Middle East today, these ancient occupations are still practiced much as they were in Cain and Abel's time.

3 So it came about in the course of time that Cain brought an offering to the LORD of
the fruit of the ground.
4 Abel, on his part also brought of the firstlings of his flock and of their fat portions.
And the LORD had regard for Abel and for his offering;
5 but for Cain and for his offering He had no regard. So Cain became very angry and
his countenance fell.
6 Then the LORD said to Cain, "Why are you angry? And why has your countenance
fallen?
7 "If you do well, will not *your countenance* be lifted up? And if you do not do well, sin
is crouching at the door; and its desire is for you, but you must master it."
8 Cain told Abel his brother. And it came about when they were in the field, that Cain
rose up against Abel his brother and killed him.
9 Then the LORD said to Cain, "Where is Abel your brother?" And he said, "I do not
know. Am I my brother's keeper?"
10 He said, "What have you done? The voice of your brother's blood is crying to Me
from the ground.
11 "Now you are cursed from the ground, which has opened its mouth to receive your
brother's blood from your hand.
12 "When you cultivate the ground, it will no longer yield its strength to you; you will be
a vagrant and a wanderer on the earth."
13 Cain said to the LORD, "My punishment is too great to bear!
14 "Behold, You have driven me this day from the face of the ground; and from Your
face I will be hidden, and I will be a vagrant and a wanderer on the earth, and whoever
finds me will kill me."
15 So the LORD said to him, "Therefore whoever kills Cain, vengeance will be taken
on him sevenfold." And the LORD appointed a sign for Cain, so that no one finding him
would slay him.
16 Then Cain went out from the presence of the LORD, and settled in the land of Nod,
east of Eden.
17 Cain had relations with his wife and she conceived, and gave birth to Enoch; and he
built a city, and called the name of the city Enoch, after the name of his son.

4:4 Heb 11:4; 1 Sam 15:22
4:5 1 Sam 16:7; Is 3:9; Jude 11
4:6 Jon 4:4
4:7 Jer 3:12; Mic 7:18; Num 32:23; Job 11:14, 15; Rom 6:12, 16
4:8 Matt 23:35; Luke 11:51; 1 John 3:12-15; Jude 11
4:9 Gen 3:9
4:10 Num 35:33; Deut 21:1-9; Heb 12:24; Rev 6:9, 10
4:11 Gen 3:14; Deut 28:15-20; Gal 3:10
4:12 Deut 28:15-24; Joel 1:10-20; Lev 26:17, 36
4:14 Gen 3:24; Jer 52:3; Deut 28:64-67; Num 35:19
4:15 Gen 4:24; Ezek 9:4, 6
4:16 2 Kin 24:20; Jer 23:39; 52:3

4:3–5 The Bible does not say why God rejected Cain's sacrifice. Perhaps Cain's attitude was improper, or perhaps his offering was not up to God's standards. Proverbs 21:27 says, "The sacrifice of the wicked is an abomination, how much more when he brings it with evil intent!" God evaluates both our motives and the quality of what we offer him. When we give to God and others, we should have a joyful heart because of what we are able to give. We should not worry about how much we are giving up, for all things are God's in the first place. Instead, we should joyfully give to God our best in time, money, possessions, and talents.

4:6–7 How do you react when someone suggests you have done something wrong? Do you move to correct the mistake or deny that you need to correct it? After Cain's sacrifice was rejected, God gave him the chance to right his wrong and try again. God even encouraged him to do this! But Cain refused, and the rest of his life is a startling example of what happens to those who refuse to admit their mistakes. The next time someone suggests you are wrong, take an honest look at yourself and choose God's way instead of Cain's.

4:7 For Cain to master the sin crouching at the entrance to his desires, he would have to give up his jealous anger so that sin would not find a foothold in his life. Sin is still crouching at our doors today. Like Cain, we will be victims of sin if we do not master it. But we cannot master sin in our own strength. Instead, we must turn to God to receive faith for ourselves and faith and strength from other believers. The Holy Spirit will help us master sin. This will be a lifelong battle that will not be over until we are face to face with Christ.

4:8–10 This is the first murder—taking a life by shedding human blood. Blood represents life (Leviticus 17:10–14). If blood is removed from a living creature, it will die. Because God created life, only God should take life away.

4:8–10 Adam and Eve's disobedience brought sin into the human race. They may have thought their sin—eating a piece of fruit—wasn't very bad, but notice how quickly their sinful nature developed in their children. Simple disobedience quickly degenerated into outright murder. Adam and Eve acted only against God, but Cain acted against both God and man. A small sin has a way of growing out of control. Let God help you with your "little" sins before they turn into tragedies.

4:11–15 Cain was severely punished for this murder. God judges all sins and punishes appropriately, but not simply out of anger or vengeance. Rather, God's punishment is meant to correct us and restore our fellowship with him. When you're corrected, don't resent it. Instead, renew your fellowship with God.

4:14 We have heard about only four people so far—Adam, Eve, Cain, and Abel. Two questions arise: Why was Cain worried about being killed by others, and where did he get his wife (see 4:17)?

Adam and Eve had numerous children; they had been told to "fill the earth" (1:28). Cain's guilt and fear over killing his brother were heavy, and he probably feared repercussions from his family. If he was capable of killing, so were they. The wife Cain chose may have been one of his sisters or a niece. The human race was still genetically pure, and there was no fear of side effects from marrying relatives.

4:15 The expression, "vengeance will be taken on him sevenfold" means that the person's punishment would be complete, thorough, and much worse than that received by Cain for his sin.

18 Now to Enoch was born Irad, and Irad became the father of Mehujael, and Mehujael became the father of Methushael, and Methushael became the father of Lamech.

4:19 Gen 2:24

19 Lamech took to himself two wives; the name of the one was Adah, and the name of
the other, Zillah.
20 Adah gave birth to Jabal; he was the father of those who dwell in tents and *have*
livestock.
21 His brother's name was Jubal; he was the father of all those who play the lyre and
pipe.
22 As for Zillah, she also gave birth to Tubal-cain, the forger of all implements of bronze
and iron; and the sister of Tubal-cain was Naamah.

4:23 Ex 20:13; Lev 19:18; Deut 32:35; Ps 94:1

23 Lamech said to his wives,
"Adah and Zillah,
Listen to my voice,
You wives of Lamech,
Give heed to my speech,
For I have killed a man for wounding me;
And a boy for striking me;

4:24 Gen 4:15

24 If Cain is avenged sevenfold,
Then Lamech seventy-sevenfold."

4:25 Gen 5:3; Gen 4:8

25 Adam had relations with his wife again; and she gave birth to a son, and named him
Seth, for, *she said,* " God has appointed me another offspring in place of Abel, for Cain
killed him."

4:26 Luke 3:38; Gen 12:8; 26:25; 1 Kin 18:24; Ps 116:17; Joel 2:32; Zeph 3:9; 1 Cor 1:2

26 To Seth, to him also a son was born; and he called his name Enosh. Then *men* began to call upon the name of the LORD.

3. Adam's descendants

Descendants of Adam

5:1 Gen 1:26, 27; Eph 4:24; Col 3:10

5:2 Matt 19:4; Mark 10:6; Gen 1:28

5 This is the book of the generations of Adam. In the day when God created man, He
made him in the likeness of God.
2 He created them male and female, and He blessed them and named them [8]Man in
the day when they were created.
3 When Adam had lived one hundred and thirty years, he [9]became the father of *a son*
in his own likeness, according to his image, and named him Seth.
4 Then the days of Adam after he became the father of Seth were eight hundred years,
and he had *other* sons and daughters.
5 So all the days that Adam lived were nine hundred and thirty years, and he died.
6 Seth lived one hundred and five years, and became the father of Enosh.
7 Then Seth lived eight hundred and seven years after he became the father of Enosh,
and he had *other* sons and daughters.
8 So all the days of Seth were nine hundred and twelve years, and he died.
9 Enosh lived ninety years, and became the father of Kenan.

8 Lit *Adam* **9** Lit *begot,* and so throughout the ch

4:19–26 Unfortunately, when left to themselves, people tend to get worse instead of better. This short summary of Lamech's family shows us the variety of talent and ability God gives humans. It also presents the continuous development of sin as time passes. Another killing occurred, presumably in self-defense. Violence is on the rise. Two distinct groups are appearing: (1) those who show indifference to sin and evil, and (2) those who call on the name of the Lord (the descendants of Seth, 4:26). Seth would take Abel's place as leader of a line of God's faithful people.

5:1ff The Bible contains several lists of ancestors, called *genealogies.* There are two basic views concerning these lists: (1) they are complete, recording the entire history of a family, tribe, or nation; or (2) they are not intended to be exhaustive and may include only famous people or the heads of families. "Became the father of" could also mean "was the ancestor of."

Why are genealogies included in the Bible? The Hebrews passed on their beliefs through oral tradition. For many years in many places, writing was primitive or nonexistent. Stories were told to children who passed them on to their children. Genealogies gave a skeletal outline that helped people remember the stories. For centuries these genealogies were added to and passed down from family to family. Even more important than preserving family tradition, genealogies were included to confirm the Bible's promise that the coming Messiah, Jesus Christ, would be born into the line of Abraham.

Genealogies point out an interesting characteristic of God. People are important to him as individuals, not just as races or nations. Therefore God refers to people by name, mentioning their life span and descendants. The next time you feel overwhelmed in a vast crowd, remember that the focus of God's attention and love is on the individual—and on you!

5:3–5 All human beings are related, going back to Adam and Eve. Mankind is a family that shares one flesh and blood. Remember this when prejudice enters your mind or hatred invades your feelings. Each person is a valuable and unique creation of God.

10 Then Enosh lived eight hundred and fifteen years after he became the father of Kenan, and he had *other* sons and daughters.
11 So all the days of Enosh were nine hundred and five years, and he died.
12 Kenan lived seventy years, and became the father of Mahalalel.
13 Then Kenan lived eight hundred and forty years after he became the father of Mahalalel, and he had *other* sons and daughters.
14 So all the days of Kenan were nine hundred and ten years, and he died.
15 Mahalalel lived sixty-five years, and became the father of Jared.
16 Then Mahalalel lived eight hundred and thirty years after he became the father of
Jared, and he had *other* sons and daughters.
17 So all the days of Mahalalel were eight hundred and ninety-five years, and he died.
18 Jared lived one hundred and sixty-two years, and became the father of Enoch.
19 Then Jared lived eight hundred years after he became the father of Enoch, and he
had *other* sons and daughters.
20 So all the days of Jared were nine hundred and sixty-two years, and he died.
21 Enoch lived sixty-five years, and became the father of Methuselah.
22 Then Enoch walked with God three hundred years after he became the father of
Methuselah, and he had *other* sons and daughters.
23 So all the days of Enoch were three hundred and sixty-five years.
24 Enoch walked with God; and he was not, for God took him.

5:22 Gen 6:9; 17:1; 24:40; 48:15; Mic 6:8; Mal 2:6; 1 Thess 2:12

25 Methuselah lived one hundred and eighty-seven years, and became the father of
Lamech.
26 Then Methuselah lived seven hundred and eighty-two years after he became the
father of Lamech, and he had *other* sons and daughters.

5:24 2 Kin 2:11; Jude 14; 2 Kin 2:10; Ps 49:15; 73:24; Heb 11:5

27 So all the days of Methuselah were nine hundred and sixty-nine years, and he died.
28 Lamech lived one hundred and eighty-two years, and became the father of a son.
29 Now he called his name Noah, saying, "This one will give us rest from our work and
from the toil of our hands *arising* from the ground which the Lord has cursed."

5:29 Gen 3:17-19; 4:11

30 Then Lamech lived five hundred and ninety-five years after he became the father
of Noah, and he had *other* sons and daughters.
31 So all the days of Lamech were seven hundred and seventy-seven years, and he died.
32 Noah was five hundred years old, and Noah became the father of Shem, Ham, and
Japheth.

5:32 Gen 7:6

C. THE STORY OF NOAH (6:1—11:32)

Earth was no longer the perfect paradise that God had intended. It is frightening to see how quickly all of humanity forgot about God. Incredibly, in all the world, only one man and his family still worshiped God. That man was Noah. Because of his faithfulness and obedience, God saved him and his family from a vast flood that destroyed every other human being on earth. This section shows us how God hates sin and judges those who enjoy it.

1. The flood

The Corruption of Mankind

6 Now it came about, when men began to multiply on the face of the land, and daughters were born to them,
2 that the sons of God saw that the daughters of men were beautiful; and they took
wives for themselves, whomever they chose.
3 Then the LORD said, "My Spirit shall not strive with man forever, because he also
is flesh; nevertheless his days shall be one hundred and twenty years."

6:3 Gal 5:16, 17; 1 Pet 3:20; Ps 78:39

5:25–27 How did these people live so long? Some believe that the ages listed here were lengths of family dynasties rather than ages of individual men. Those who think these were actual ages offer three explanations: (1) the human race was more genetically pure in this early time period, so there was less disease to shorten life spans; (2) no rain had yet fallen on the earth, and the expanse of water "above" (1:7) kept out harmful cosmic rays and shielded people from environmental factors that hasten aging; (3) God gave people longer lives so they would have time to "fill the earth" (1:28).

6:1–4 Some people have thought that the "sons of God" were fallen angels. But the "sons of God" were probably not angels, because angels do not marry or reproduce (Matthew 22:30; Mark 12:25). Some scholars believe this phrase refers to the descendants of Seth who intermarried with Cain's evil descendants ("the daughters of men"). This would have weakened the good influence of the faithful and increased moral depravity in the world, resulting in an explosion of evil. *Nephilim* refers to a powerful race of giants.

6:3 "His days shall be one hundred and twenty years" means that God was allowing the people of Noah's day 120 years to change their sinful ways. God shows his great patience with us as well. He is giving us time to quit living our way and begin living his way, the

6:5 Gen 8:21; Ps 14:1-3; Prov 6:18; Matt 15:19; Rom 1:28-32
6:6 Gen 6:7; Jer 18:7-10; Is 63:10
6:7 Deut 28:63; 29:20
6:8 Matt 24:37; Luke 17:26; 1 Pet 3:20; Gen 19:19; Ex 33:17; Luke 1:30
6:9 Ps 37:39; 2 Pet 2:5; Gen 17:1
6:11 Ezek 8:17
6:12 Ps 14:1-3
6:13 Is 34:1-4; Ezek 7:2

4 The Nephilim were on the earth in those days, and also afterward, when the sons of
God came in to the daughters of men, and they bore *children* to them. Those were the
mighty men who *were* of old, men of renown.
5 Then the LORD saw that the wickedness of man was great on the earth, and that
every intent of the thoughts of his heart was only evil continually.
6 The LORD was sorry that He had made man on the earth, and He was grieved in
His heart.
7 The LORD said, "I will blot out man whom I have created from the face of the land,
from man to animals to creeping things and to birds of the sky; for I am sorry that I have
made them."
8 But Noah found favor in the eyes of the LORD.
9 These are *the records of* the generations of Noah. Noah was a righteous man, blameless in his time; Noah walked with God.
10 Noah became the father of three sons: Shem, Ham, and Japheth.
11 Now the earth was corrupt in the sight of God, and the earth was filled with violence.
12 God looked on the earth, and behold, it was corrupt; for all flesh had corrupted their
way upon the earth.
13 Then God said to Noah, "The end of all flesh has come before Me; for the earth is

---

Abel was the second child born into the world, but the first one to obey God. All we know about this man is that his parents were Adam and Eve, he was a shepherd, he presented pleasing sacrifices to God, and his short life was ended at the hands of his jealous older brother, Cain.

The Bible doesn't tell us why God liked Abel's gift and disliked Cain's, but both Cain and Abel knew what God expected. Only Abel obeyed. Throughout history, Abel is remembered for his obedience and faith (Hebrews 11:4), and he is called "righteous" (Matthew 23:35).

The Bible is filled with God's general guidelines and expectations for our lives. It is also filled with more specific directions. Like Abel, we must obey regardless of the cost and trust God to make things right.

Strengths and accomplishments:
- First member of the Hall of Faith in Hebrews 11
- First shepherd
- First martyr for truth (Matthew 23:35)

Lessons from his life:
- God hears those who come to him
- God recognizes the innocent person and sooner or later punishes the guilty

Vital statistics:
- Where: Just outside of Eden
- Occupation: Shepherd
- Relatives: Parents: Adam and Eve. Brother: Cain

Key verse:
"By faith Abel offered to God a better sacrifice than Cain, through which he obtained the testimony that he was righteous, God testifying about his gifts, and through faith, though he is dead, he still speaks" (Hebrews 11:4).

Abel's story is told in Genesis 4:1–8. He is also mentioned in Matthew 23:35; Luke 11:51; Hebrews 11:4 and 12:24.

---

way he shows us in his Word. While 120 years seems like a long time, eventually the time ran out and the floodwaters swept across the earth. Your time also may be running out. Turn to God to forgive your sins. You can't see the stopwatch of God's patience, and there is no bargaining for additional time.

6:4 The Nephilim were giants, people probably nine or ten feet tall. These may have been the same people mentioned in Numbers 13:33. Goliath, who was nine feet tall, appears in 1 Samuel 17. The Nephilim used their physical advantage to oppress the people around them.

6:6–7 Does this mean that God regretted creating humanity? Was he admitting that he made a mistake? No, God does not change his mind (1 Samuel 15:29). Instead, he was expressing sorrow for what the people had done to themselves, as a parent might express sorrow over a rebellious child. God was sorry that the people chose sin and death instead of a relationship with him.

6:6–8 The people's sin grieved God. Our sins break God's heart as much as sin did in Noah's day. Noah, however, pleased God, although he was far from perfect. We can follow Noah's example and find "favor in the eyes of the LORD" in spite of the sin that surrounds us.

6:9 To say that Noah was *righteous* and *blameless* does not mean that he never sinned (the Bible records one of his sins in 9:20ff). Rather it means that he wholeheartedly loved and obeyed God. For a lifetime he walked step by step in faith as a living example to his generation. Like Noah, we live in a world filled with evil. Are we influencing others or being influenced by them?

filled with violence because of them; and behold, I am about to destroy them with the
earth.
14 "Make for yourself an ark of gopher wood; you shall make the ark with rooms, and
shall cover it inside and out with pitch.
15 "This is how you shall make it: the length of the ark three hundred [10]cubits, its breadth
fifty cubits, and its height thirty cubits.
16 "You shall make a window for the ark, and finish it to a cubit from the top; and set
the door of the ark in the side of it; you shall make it with lower, second, and third decks.
17 "Behold, I, even I am bringing the flood of water upon the earth, to destroy all flesh
in which is the breath of life, from under heaven; everything that is on the earth shall
perish.
18 "But I will establish My covenant with you; and you shall enter the ark—you and your
sons and your wife, and your sons' wives with you.
19 "And of every living thing of all flesh, you shall bring two of every *kind* into the ark,
to keep *them* alive with you; they shall be male and female.
20 "Of the birds after their kind, and of the animals after their kind, of every creeping
thing of the ground after its kind, two of every *kind* will come to you to keep *them* alive.
21 "As for you, take for yourself some of all food which is edible, and gather *it* to yourself; and it shall be for food for you and for them."
22 Thus Noah did; according to all that God had commanded him, so he did.

The Flood

7 Then the LORD said to Noah, "Enter the ark, you and all your household, for you
alone I have seen *to be* righteous before Me in this time.
2 "You shall take with you of every clean animal by sevens, a male and his female; and
of the animals that are not clean two, a male and his female;
3 also of the birds of the sky, by sevens, male and female, to keep offspring alive on
the face of all the earth.
4 "For after seven more days, I will send rain on the earth forty days and forty nights;
and I will blot out from the face of the land every living thing that I have made."
5 Noah did according to all that the LORD had commanded him.
6 Now Noah was six hundred years old when the flood of water came upon the earth.
7 Then Noah and his sons and his wife and his sons' wives with him entered the ark
because of the water of the flood.
8 Of clean animals and animals that are not clean and birds and everything that creeps
on the ground,
9 there went into the ark to Noah by twos, male and female, as God had commanded
Noah.
10 It came about after the seven days, that the water of the flood came upon the earth.
11 In the six hundredth year of Noah's life, in the second month, on the seventeenth
day of the month, on the same day all the fountains of the great deep burst open, and
the floodgates of the sky were opened.
12 The rain fell upon the earth for forty days and forty nights.
13 On the very same day Noah and Shem and Ham and Japheth, the sons of Noah,
and Noah's wife and the three wives of his sons with them, entered the ark,

6:17 2 Pet 2:5
6:18 Gen 9:9-16; 17:7; Gen 7:7
6:19 Gen 7:2, 14, 15
6:20 Gen 7:3
6:21 Gen 1:29, 30
6:22 Gen 7:5; Heb 11:7
7:1 Gen 6:9
7:2 Lev 11:1-31; Deut 14:3-20
7:4 Gen 7:10; Gen 7:12, 17; Gen 6:7, 13
7:5 Gen 6:22
7:6 Gen 5:32
7:7 Gen 6:18; 7:13; Matt 24:38f; Luke 17:27
7:8 Gen 6:19, 20; 7:2, 3
7:10 Gen 7:4
7:11 Gen 7:6; Gen 8:2
7:12 Gen 7:4, 17
7:13 Gen 6:18; 7:7

10 I.e. One cubit equals approx 18 in.

6:14 *Pitch* was a tarlike substance used to make the ark watertight.

6:15 The boat Noah built was no canoe! Picture yourself building a boat the length of one and a half football fields and as high as a four-story building. The ark was exactly six times longer than it was wide—the same ratio used by modern shipbuilders. This huge boat was probably built miles from any body of water by only a few faithful men who believed God's promises and obeyed his commands.

6:18 A *covenant* is a promise. This is a familiar theme in Scripture—God making covenants with his people. How reassuring it is to know God's covenant is established with us. He is still our salvation and we are kept safe through our relationship with him. For more on the covenant see 9:8–17; 12:1–3; and 15:17.

6:22 Noah got right to work when God told him to build the ark. Other people must have been warned about the coming disaster (1 Peter 3:20), but apparently they did not expect it to happen. Today things haven't changed much. Each day thousands of people are warned of God's inevitable judgment, yet most of them don't really believe it will happen. Don't expect people to welcome or accept your message of God's coming judgment on sin. Those who don't believe in God will deny his judgment and try to get you to deny God as well. But remember God's promise to Noah to keep him safe. This can inspire you to trust God for deliverance in the judgment that is sure to come.

7:1ff Pairs of every animal joined Noah in the ark; seven pairs were taken of those animals used for sacrifice—the "clean" animals. Scholars have estimated that almost 45,000 animals could have fit into the ark.

14 they and every beast after its kind, and all the cattle after their kind, and every creeping thing that creeps on the earth after its kind, and every bird after its kind, all sorts of
birds.
7:15 Gen 6:19; 7:9 15 So they went into the ark to Noah, by twos of all flesh in which was the breath of
life.
16 Those that entered, male and female of all flesh, entered as God had commanded
him; and the LORD closed *it* behind him.
7:17 Gen 7:4 **17** Then the flood came upon the earth for forty days, and the water increased and lifted up the ark, so that it rose above the earth.
18 The water prevailed and increased greatly upon the earth, and the ark floated on
the surface of the water.
19 The water prevailed more and more upon the earth, so that all the high mountains
everywhere under the heavens were covered.

CAIN

In spite of parents' efforts and worries, conflicts between children in a family seem inevitable. Sibling relationships allow both competition and cooperation. In most cases, the mixture of loving and fighting eventually creates a strong bond between brothers and sisters. It isn't unusual, though, to hear parents say, "They fight so much I hope they don't kill each other before they grow up." In Cain's case, the troubling potential became a tragedy. And while we don't know many details of this first child's life, his story can still teach us.

Cain got angry. Furious. Both he and his brother Abel had made sacrifices to God, and his had been rejected. Cain's reaction gives us a clue that his attitude was probably wrong from the start. Cain had a choice to make. He could correct his attitude about his sacrifice to God, or he could take out his anger on his brother. His decision is a clear reminder of how often we are aware of opposite choices, yet choose the wrong just as Cain did. We may not be choosing to murder, but we are still intentionally choosing what we shouldn't.

The feelings motivating our behavior can't always be changed by simple thought-power. But here we can begin to experience God's willingness to help. Asking for his help to do what is right can prevent us from setting into motion actions that we will later regret.

Strengths and accomplishments:
- First human child
- First to follow in father's profession, farming

Weaknesses and mistakes:
- When disappointed, reacted in anger
- Took the negative option even when a positive possibility was offered
- Was the first murderer

Lessons from his life:
- Anger is not necessarily a sin, but actions motivated by anger can be sinful. Anger should be the energy behind good action, not evil action
- What we offer to God must be from the heart—the best we are and have
- The consequences of sin may last a lifetime

Vital statistics:
- Where: Near Eden, which was probably located in present-day Iraq or Iran
- Occupation: Farmer, then wanderer
- Relatives: Parents: Adam and Eve. Brothers: Abel, Seth, and others not mentioned by name

Key verse:
"If you do well, will not your countenance be lifted up? And if you do not do well, sin is crouching at the door; and its desire is for you, but you must master it" (Genesis 4:7).

Cain's story is told in Genesis 4:1–17. He is also mentioned in Hebrews 11:4; 1 John 3:12; Jude 11.

7:16 Many have wondered how this animal kingdom roundup happened. Did Noah and his sons spend years collecting all the animals? In reality the creation, along with Noah, was doing just as God had commanded. There seemed to be no problem gathering the animals—God took care of the details of that job while Noah was doing his part by building the ark. Often we do just the opposite of Noah. We worry about details over which we have no control, while neglecting specific areas (such as attitudes, relationships, responsibilities) that *are* under our control. Like Noah, concentrate on what God has given you to do, and leave the rest to God.

7:17–24 Was the flood a local event, or did it cover the entire earth? A universal flood was certainly possible. There is enough water on the earth to cover all dry land (the earth began that way; see 1:9–10). Afterward, God promised never again to destroy the earth with a flood. Thus this flood must have either covered the entire earth or destroyed all the inhabitants of the earth. Remember, God's reason for sending the flood was to destroy all the earth's wickedness. It would have taken a major flood to accomplish this.

20 The water prevailed fifteen cubits higher, and the mountains were covered.
21 All flesh that moved on the earth perished, birds and cattle and beasts and every
swarming thing that swarms upon the earth, and all mankind;
22 of all that was on the dry land, all in whose nostrils was the breath of the spirit of
life, died.
23 Thus He blotted out every living thing that was upon the face of the land, from man
to animals to creeping things and to birds of the sky, and they were blotted out from the
earth; and only Noah was left, together with those that were with him in the ark.
24 The water prevailed upon the earth one hundred and fifty days.

The Flood Subsides

8 But God remembered Noah and all the beasts and all the cattle that were with him
in the ark; and God caused a wind to pass over the earth, and the water subsided.
2 Also the fountains of the deep and the floodgates of the sky were closed, and the
rain from the sky was restrained;
3 and the water receded steadily from the earth, and at the end of one hundred and
fifty days the water decreased.
4 In the seventh month, on the seventeenth day of the month, the ark rested upon the
mountains of Ararat.
5 The water decreased steadily until the tenth month; in the tenth month, on the first
day of the month, the tops of the mountains became visible.
6 Then it came about at the end of forty days, that Noah opened the window of the
ark which he had made;
7 and he sent out a raven, and it flew here and there until the water was dried up from
the earth.
8 Then he sent out a dove from him, to see if the water was abated from the face of
the land;
9 but the dove found no resting place for the sole of her foot, so she returned to him
into the ark, for the water was on the surface of all the earth. Then he put out his hand
and took her, and brought her into the ark to himself.
10 So he waited yet another seven days; and again he sent out the dove from the ark.
11 The dove came to him toward evening, and behold, in her beak was a freshly picked
olive leaf. So Noah knew that the water was abated from the earth.
12 Then he waited yet another seven days, and sent out the dove; but she did not return to him again.
13 Now it came about in the six hundred and first year, in the first *month,* on the first
of the month, the water was dried up from the earth. Then Noah removed the covering
of the ark, and looked, and behold, the surface of the ground was dried up.
14 In the second month, on the twenty-seventh day of the month, the earth was dry.

7:20 Gen 8:4
7:21 Gen 6:7, 13, 17; 7:4
7:22 Gen 2:7
7:23 Matt 24:38, 39; Luke 17:26, 27; Heb 11:7; 1 Pet 3:20; 2 Pet 2:5
7:24 Gen 8:3
8:1 Gen 19:29; Ex 2:24; 1 Sam 1:19; Ps 105:42; Ex 14:21; 15:10; Job 12:15; Ps 29:10; Is 44:27; Nah 1:4
8:2 Gen 7:11; Gen 7:4, 12
8:3 Gen 7:24
8:4 Gen 7:20
8:6 Gen 6:16
8:12 Jer 48:28
8:13 Gen 7:6

8:6–16 Occasionally Noah would send a bird out to test the earth and see if it was dry. But Noah didn't get out of the ark until God told him to. He was waiting for God's timing. God knew that even though the water was gone, the earth was not dry enough for Noah and his family to venture out. What patience Noah showed, especially after spending an entire year inside his boat! We, like Noah, must trust God to give us patience during those difficult times when we must wait.

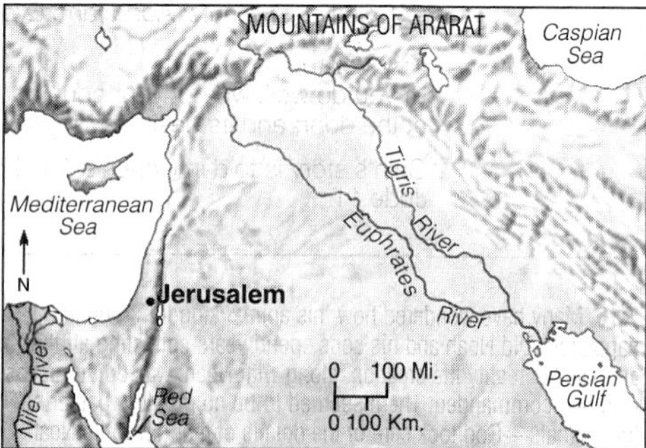

MOUNTAINS OF ARARAT The boat touched land in the mountains of Ararat, located in present-day Turkey. There it rested for almost eight months before Noah, his family, and the animals stepped onto dry land.

15 Then God spoke to Noah, saying,
16 "Go out of the ark, you and your wife and your sons and your sons' wives with you.
17 "Bring out with you every living thing of all flesh that is with you, birds and animals
and every creeping thing that creeps on the earth, that they may breed abundantly on
the earth, and be fruitful and multiply on the earth."
18 So Noah went out, and his sons and his wife and his sons' wives with him.
19 Every beast, every creeping thing, and every bird, everything that moves on the earth,
went out by their families from the ark.
20 Then Noah built an altar to the LORD, and took of every clean animal and of every
clean bird and offered burnt offerings on the altar.
21 The LORD smelled the soothing aroma; and the LORD said to Himself, "I will never
again curse the ground on account of man, for the intent of man's heart is evil from his
youth; and I will never again destroy every living thing, as I have done.
22 "While the earth remains,
Seedtime and harvest,
And cold and heat,
And summer and winter,
And day and night
Shall not cease."

8:17 Gen 1:22, 28

8:20 Gen 12:7, 8; 13:18; 22:9; Gen 7:2; Lev 11:1-47; Gen 22:2; Ex 10:25

8:21 Ex 29:18, 25; Gen 3:17; 6:7, 13, 17; Is 54:9; Gen 6:5; Ps 51:5; Jer 17:9; Rom 1:21; 3:23; Eph 2:1-3; Gen 9:11, 15

8:22 Ps 74:17; Jer 33:20, 25

NOAH

The story of Noah's life involves not one, but two great and tragic floods. The world in Noah's day was flooded with evil. The number of those who remembered the God of creation, perfection, and love had dwindled to one. Of God's people, only Noah was left. God's response to the severe situation was a 120-year-long last chance, during which he had Noah build a graphic illustration of the message of his life. Nothing like a huge boat on dry land to make a point! For Noah, obedience meant a long-term commitment to a project.

Many of us have trouble sticking to any project, whether or not it is directed by God. It is interesting that the length of Noah's obedience was greater than the lifespan of people today. The only comparable long-term project is our very lives. But perhaps this is one great challenge Noah's life gives us—to live, in acceptance of God's grace, an entire lifetime of obedience and gratitude.

Strengths and accomplishments:
- Only follower of God left in his generation
- Second father of the human race
- Man of patience, consistency, and obedience
- First major shipbuilder

Weakness and mistake:
- Got drunk and embarrassed himself in front of his sons

Lessons from his life:
- God is faithful to those who obey him
- God does not always protect us from trouble, but cares for us in spite of trouble
- Obedience is a long-term commitment
- A man may be faithful, but his sinful nature always travels with him

Vital statistics:
- Where: We're not told how far from the Garden of Eden people had settled
- Occupation: Farmer, shipbuilder, preacher
- Relatives: Grandfather: Methuselah. Father: Lamech. Sons: Ham, Shem, and Japheth

Key verse:
"Thus Noah did; according to all that God had commanded him, so he did" (Genesis 6:22).

Noah's story is told in Genesis 5:29—10:32. He is also mentioned in 1 Chronicles 1:3–4; Isaiah 54:9; Ezekiel 14:14, 20; Matthew 24:37–38; Luke 3:36; 17:26–27; Hebrews 11:7; 1 Peter 3:20; 2 Peter 2:5.

8:21–22 Countless times throughout the Bible we see God showing his love and patience toward men and women in order to save them. Although he realizes that their hearts are evil, he continues to try to reach them. When we sin or fall away from God, we surely deserve to be destroyed by his judgment. But God has promised never again to destroy everything on earth until the judgment day when Christ returns to destroy evil forever. Now every change of season is a reminder of his promise.

2. Repopulating the earth

Covenant of the Rainbow

9 And God blessed Noah and his sons and said to them, "Be fruitful and multiply, and
fill the earth.
2 "The fear of you and the terror of you will be on every beast of the earth and on every
bird of the sky; with everything that creeps on the ground, and all the fish of the sea, into
your hand they are given.
3 "Every moving thing that is alive shall be food for you; I give all to you, as *I gave* the
green plant.
4 "Only you shall not eat flesh with its life, *that is,* its blood.
5 "Surely I will require your lifeblood; from every beast I will require it. And from *every*
man, from every man's brother I will require the life of man.
6 "Whoever sheds man's blood,
By man his blood shall be shed,
For in the image of God
He made man.
7 "As for you, be fruitful and multiply;
Populate the earth abundantly and multiply in it."
8 Then God spoke to Noah and to his sons with him, saying,
9 "Now behold, I Myself do establish My covenant with you, and with your descendants after you;
10 and with every living creature that is with you, the birds, the cattle, and every beast
of the earth with you; of all that comes out of the ark, even every beast of the earth.
11 "I establish My covenant with you; and all flesh shall never again be cut off by the
water of the flood, neither shall there again be a flood to destroy the earth."
12 God said, "This is the sign of the covenant which I am making between Me and you
and every living creature that is with you, for all successive generations;
13 I set My bow in the cloud, and it shall be for a sign of a covenant between Me and
the earth.
14 "It shall come about, when I bring a cloud over the earth, that the bow will be seen in
the cloud,
15 and I will remember My covenant, which is between Me and you and every living
creature of all flesh; and never again shall the water become a flood to destroy all flesh.
16 "When the bow is in the cloud, then I will look upon it, to remember the everlasting
covenant between God and every living creature of all flesh that is on the earth."
17 And God said to Noah, "This is the sign of the covenant which I have established
between Me and all flesh that is on the earth."
18 Now the sons of Noah who came out of the ark were Shem and Ham and Japheth;
and Ham was the father of Canaan.
19 These three *were* the sons of Noah, and from these the whole earth was populated.
20 Then Noah began farming and planted a vineyard.
21 He drank of the wine and became drunk, and uncovered himself inside his tent.
22 Ham, the father of Canaan, saw the nakedness of his father, and told his two brothers outside.
23 But Shem and Japheth took a garment and laid it upon both their shoulders and
walked backward and covered the nakedness of their father; and their faces were turned
away, so that they did not see their father's nakedness.

9:1 Gen 1:28; 9:7
9:3 Gen 1:29
9:4 Lev 7:26f; 17:10-16; 19:26; Deut 12:16, 23; 15:23; 1 Sam 14:34; Acts 15:20, 29
9:5 Ex 20:13; 21:12; Ex 21:28, 29
9:6 Ex 21:12-14; Lev 24:17; Num 35:33; Matt 26:52; Gen 1:26, 27
9:7 Gen 9:1
9:9 Gen 6:18
9:11 Gen 8:21; Is 54:9
9:12 Gen 9:13, 17; 17:11
9:13 Ezek 1:28
9:15 Lev 26:42, 45; Deut 7:9; Ezek 16:60; Gen 9:11
9:16 Gen 17:13, 19; 2 Sam 23:5
9: 18 Gen 9:25-27; 10:6
9:19 Gen 9:1, 7; 10:32; 1 Chr 1:4
9:21 Prov 20:1
9:22 Hab 2:15

9:5 "And from every man, from every man's brother I will require the life of man" means that God will require each person to account for his or her actions. We cannot harm or kill another human being without answering to God. A penalty must be paid. Justice will be served.

9:5–6 Here God explains why murder is so wrong: To kill a person is to kill one made in God's image. Because all human beings are made in God's image, all people possess the qualities that distinguish them from animals: morality, reason, creativity, and self-worth. When we interact with others, we are interacting with beings made by God, beings to whom God offers eternal life. God wants us to recognize his image in all people.

9:8–17 Noah stepped out of the ark onto an earth devoid of human life. But God gave him a reassuring promise. This covenant had three parts: (1) never again will a flood do such destruction; (2) as long as the earth remains, the seasons will always come as expected; (3) a rainbow will be visible when it rains as a sign to all that God will keep his promises. The earth's order and seasons are still preserved, and rainbows still remind us of God's faithfulness to his Word.

9:20–27 Noah, the great hero of faith, got drunk—a poor example of godliness to his sons. Perhaps this story is included to show us that even godly people can sin and that their bad influence affects their families. Although the wicked people had all been killed, the possibility of evil still existed in the hearts of Noah and his family. Ham's mocking attitude revealed a severe lack of respect for his father and for God.

24 When Noah awoke from his wine, he knew what his youngest son had done to him.
25 So he said,
"Cursed be Canaan;
[11]A servant of servants
He shall be to his brothers."
26 He also said,
"Blessed be the LORD,
The God of Shem;
And let Canaan be his servant.
27 "May God enlarge Japheth,
And let him dwell in the tents of Shem;
And let Canaan be his servant."
28 Noah lived three hundred and fifty years after the flood.
29 So all the days of Noah were nine hundred and fifty years, and he died.

9:25 Deut 27:16; Josh 9:23
9:26 Gen 14:20; 24:27
9:27 Gen 10:2-5; Is 66:19

Descendants of Noah

10 Now these are *the records of* the generations of Shem, Ham, and Japheth, the sons
of Noah; and sons were born to them after the flood.
2 The sons of Japheth *were* Gomer and Magog and Madai and Javan and Tubal and
Meshech and Tiras.
3 The sons of Gomer *were* Ashkenaz and Riphath and Togarmah.
4 The sons of Javan *were* Elishah and Tarshish, Kittim and Dodanim.
5 From these the coastlands of the nations were separated into their lands, every one
according to his language, according to their families, into their nations.
6 The sons of Ham *were* Cush and Mizraim and Put and Canaan.
7 The sons of Cush *were* Seba and Havilah and Sabtah and Raamah and Sabteca; and
the sons of Raamah *were* Sheba and Dedan.
8 Now Cush became the father of Nimrod; he became a mighty one on the earth.
9 He was a mighty hunter before the LORD; therefore it is said, "Like Nimrod a mighty
hunter before the LORD."
10 The beginning of his kingdom was [12]Babel and Erech and Accad and Calneh, in the
land of Shinar.
11 From that land he went forth into Assyria, and built Nineveh and Rehoboth-Ir and
Calah,
12 and Resen between Nineveh and Calah; that is the great city.
13 Mizraim became the father of Ludim and Anamim and Lehabim and Naphtuhim
14 and Pathrusim and Casluhim (from which came the Philistines) and Caphtorim.
15 Canaan became the father of Sidon, his firstborn, and Heth
16 and the Jebusite and the Amorite and the Girgashite
17 and the Hivite and the Arkite and the Sinite
18 and the Arvadite and the Zemarite and the Hamathite; and afterward the families
of the Canaanite were spread abroad.
19 The territory of the Canaanite extended from Sidon as you go toward Gerar, as far

10:2 1 Chr 1:5-7; Ezek 38:2, 6; 2 Kin 17:6; Is 66:19; Ezek 38:2
10:3 Jer 51:27; Ezek 27:14
10:4 Ezek 27:12, 25
10:6 1 Chr 1:8-10
10:7 Is 43:3; Ezek 27:22; Ezek 27:15, 20
10:10 Gen 11:9; Gen 11:2; 14:1
10:11 Mic 5:6
10:13 Jer 46:9
10:14 1 Chr 1:12
10:15 1 Chr 1:13; Jer 47:4; Gen 23:3
10:16 Gen 15:19-21
10:19 Num 34:2-12; Gen 14:2, 3

11 I.e. The lowest of servants **12** Or *Babylon*

BIBLE NATIONS DESCENDED FROM NOAH'S SONS

Shem	*Ham*	*Japheth*
Hebrews	Canaanites	Greeks
Chaldeans	Egyptians	Thracians
Assyrians	Philistines	Scythians
Persians	Hittites	
Syrians	Amorites	

Shem's descendants were called Semites. Abraham, David, and Jesus descended from Shem. Ham's descendants settled in Canaan, Egypt, and the rest of Africa. Japheth's descendants settled for the most part in Europe and Asia Minor.

9:25 This verse has been wrongfully used to support racial prejudice and even slavery. Noah's curse, however, wasn't directed toward any particular race, but rather at the Canaanite nation—a nation God knew would become wicked. The curse was fulfilled when the Israelites entered the promised land and drove the Canaanites out (see the book of Joshua).

10:8–9 Who was Nimrod? Not much is known about him except that he was a mighty hunter. But people with great gifts can become proud, and that is probably what happened to Nimrod. Some consider him the founder of the great, godless Babylonian empire.

as Gaza; as you go toward Sodom and Gomorrah and Admah and Zeboiim, as far as
Lasha.
20 These are the sons of Ham, according to their families, according to their languages,
by their lands, by their nations.
21 Also to Shem, the father of all the children of Eber, *and* the older brother of Japheth, children were born.
22 The sons of Shem *were* Elam and Asshur and Arpachshad and Lud and Aram.
23 The sons of Aram *were* Uz and Hul and Gether and Mash.
24 Arpachshad became the father of Shelah; and Shelah became the father of Eber.
25 Two sons were born to Eber; the name of the one *was* Peleg, for in his days the earth
was divided; and his brother's name *was* Joktan.
26 Joktan became the father of Almodad and Sheleph and Hazarmaveth and Jerah
27 and Hadoram and Uzal and Diklah
28 and Obal and Abimael and Sheba
29 and Ophir and Havilah and Jobab; all these were the sons of Joktan.
30 Now their settlement extended from Mesha as you go toward Sephar, the hill country of the east.
31 These are the sons of Shem, according to their families, according to their languages,
by their lands, according to their nations.
32 These are the families of the sons of Noah, according to their genealogies, by their
nations; and out of these the nations were separated on the earth after the flood.

10:22 1 Chr 1:17; Gen 14:1, 9; Gen 11:10; Is 66:19
10:23 Job 1:1; Jer 25:20
10:24 Gen 11:12; Luke 3:35
10:25 1 Chr 1:19
10:32 Gen 9:19

3. The tower of Babel

Universal Language, Babel, Confusion

11 Now the whole earth used the same language and the same words.
2 It came about as they journeyed east, that they found a plain in the land of Shinar and settled there.
3 They said to one another, "Come, let us make bricks and burn *them* thoroughly."
And they used brick for stone, and they used tar for mortar.
4 They said, "Come, let us build for ourselves a city, and a tower whose top *will reach*
into heaven, and let us make for ourselves a name, otherwise we will be scattered abroad
over the face of the whole earth."
5 The LORD came down to see the city and the tower which the sons of men had built.
6 The LORD said, "Behold, they are one people, and they all have the same language.
And this is what they began to do, and now nothing which they purpose to do will be
impossible for them.
7 "Come, let Us go down and there confuse their language, so that they will not understand one another's speech."
8 So the LORD scattered them abroad from there over the face of the whole earth;
and they stopped building the city.
9 Therefore its name was called [13]Babel, because there the LORD confused the language of the whole earth; and from there the LORD scattered them abroad over the face
of the whole earth.

Descendants of Shem

10 These are *the records of* the generations of Shem. Shem was one hundred years old,
and became the father of Arpachshad two years after the flood;

13 Or *Babylon;* cf Heb *balal,* confuse

11:2 Gen 10:10; 14:1; Dan 1:2
11:3 Gen 14:10
11:4 Deut 1:28; 9:1; Ps 107:26; Gen 6:4; 2 Sam 8:13; Deut 4:27
11:5 Gen 18:21; Ex 3:8; 19:11, 18, 20
11:6 Gen 11:1
11:7 Gen 1:26; Gen 42:23; Ex 4:11; Deut 28:49; Is 33:19; Jer 5:15
11:8 Gen 11:4; Ps 92:9; Luke 1:51
11:9 Gen 10:10
11:10 Gen 10:22-25

11:3 The brick used to build this tower was man-made and not as hard as stone.

11:3–4 The tower of Babel was most likely a ziggurat, a common structure in Babylonia at this time. Most often built as temples, ziggurats looked like pyramids with steps or ramps leading up the sides. Ziggurats stood as high as 300 feet and were often just as wide; thus they were the focal point of the city. The people in this story built their tower as a monument to their own greatness, something for the whole world to see.

11:4 The tower of Babel was a great human achievement, a wonder of the world. But it was a monument to the people themselves rather than to God. We may build monuments to ourselves (expensive clothes, big house, fancy car, important job) to call attention to our achievements. These may not be wrong in themselves, but when we use them to give us identity and self-worth, they take God's place in our lives. We are free to develop in many areas, but we are not free to think we have replaced God. What "towers" have you built in your life?

11:10–27 In 9:24–27 we read Noah's curse on Canaan, Ham's son (10:6), ancestor of the evil Canaanites. Here and in 10:22–31 we have a list of Shem's descendants, who were blessed (9:26). From Shem's line came Abram and the entire Jewish nation, which would eventually conquer the land of Canaan in the days of Joshua.

11 and Shem lived five hundred years after he became the father of Arpachshad, and
he had *other* sons and daughters.
12 Arpachshad lived thirty-five years, and became the father of Shelah;
13 and Arpachshad lived four hundred and three years after he became the father of
Shelah, and he had *other* sons and daughters.
14 Shelah lived thirty years, and became the father of Eber;
15 and Shelah lived four hundred and three years after he became the father of Eber,
and he had *other* sons and daughters.
16 Eber lived thirty-four years, and became the father of Peleg;
17 and Eber lived four hundred and thirty years after he became the father of Peleg,
and he had *other* sons and daughters.
18 Peleg lived thirty years, and became the father of Reu;
19 and Peleg lived two hundred and nine years after he became the father of Reu, and
he had *other* sons and daughters.
20 Reu lived thirty-two years, and became the father of Serug;
21 and Reu lived two hundred and seven years after he became the father of Serug,
and he had *other* sons and daughters.
22 Serug lived thirty years, and became the father of Nahor;
23 and Serug lived two hundred years after he became the father of Nahor, and he had
other sons and daughters.

11:24 Josh 24:2

24 Nahor lived twenty-nine years, and became the father of Terah;
25 and Nahor lived one hundred and nineteen years after he became the father of Terah, and he had *other* sons and daughters.

11:26 Josh 24:2

26 Terah lived seventy years, and became the father of Abram, Nahor and Haran.

11:27 Gen 11:31; 12:4; Gen 13:10; 14:12; 19:1, 29

27 Now these are *the records of* the generations of Terah. Terah became the father of
Abram, Nahor and Haran; and Haran became the father of Lot.

11:28 Gen 11:31

28 Haran died in the presence of his father Terah in the land of his birth, in Ur of the
Chaldeans.

11:29 Gen 24:10; Gen 17:15; 20:12; Gen 22:20, 23; 24:15

29 Abram and Nahor took wives for themselves. The name of Abram's wife was Sarai;
and the name of Nahor's wife was Milcah, the daughter of Haran, the father of Milcah
and Iscah.

11:30 Gen 16:1

30 Sarai was barren; she had no child.

11:31 Gen 15:7; Neh 9:7; Acts 7:4

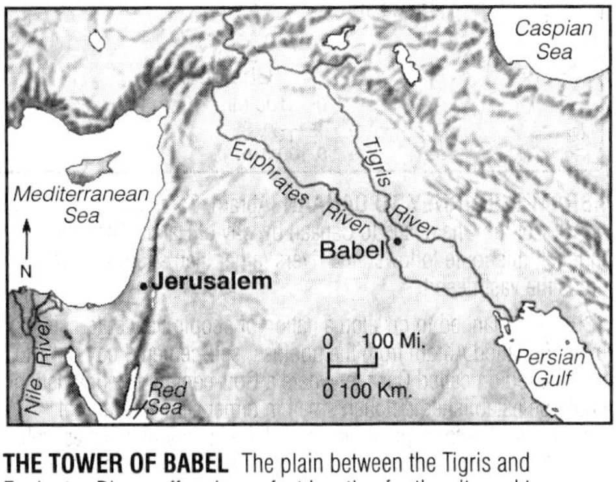

31 Terah took Abram his son, and Lot the son of Haran, his grandson, and Sarai his
daughter-in-law, his son Abram's wife; and they went out together from Ur of the Chaldeans in order to enter the land of Canaan; and they went as far as Haran, and settled
there.
32 The days of Terah were two hundred and five years; and Terah died in Haran.

THE TOWER OF BABEL The plain between the Tigris and Euphrates Rivers offered a perfect location for the city and tower "whose top will reach into heaven."

11:26–28 Abram grew up in Ur of the Chaldeans, an important city in the ancient world. Archaeologists have discovered evidence of a flourishing civilization there in Abram's day. The city carried on an extensive trade with its neighbors and had a vast library. Growing up in Ur, Abram was probably well educated.

11:31 Terah left Ur to go to Canaan but settled in Haran instead. Why did he stop halfway? It may have been his health, the climate, or even fear. But this did not change Abram's calling ("the LORD said to Abram," 12:1). He had respect for his father's leadership, but when Terah died Abram moved on to Canaan. God's will may come in stages. Just as the time in Haran was a transition period for Abram, so God may give us transition periods and times of waiting to help us depend on him and trust his timing. If we patiently do his will during the transition times, we will be better prepared to serve him as we should when he calls us.

D. THE STORY OF ABRAHAM (12:1—25:18)

Despite God's swift judgment of sin, most people ignored him and continued to sin. But a handful of people really tried to follow him. One of these was Abraham. God appeared to Abraham one day and promised to make his descendants into a great nation. Abraham's part of the agreement was to obey God. Through sharp testing and an incident that almost destroyed his family, Abraham remained faithful to God. Throughout this section we discover how to live a life of faith.

1. God promises a nation to Abram

Abram Journeys to Egypt

12 Now the LORD said to Abram,
"Go forth from your country,
And from your relatives
And from your father's house,
To the land which I will show you;
2 And I will make you a great nation,
And I will bless you,
And make your name great;
And so you shall be a blessing;
3 And I will bless those who bless you,
And the one who curses you I will curse.
And in you all the families of the earth will be blessed."
4 So Abram went forth as the LORD had spoken to him; and Lot went with him. Now
Abram was seventy-five years old when he departed from Haran.
5 Abram took Sarai his wife and Lot his nephew, and all their possessions which they
had accumulated, and the persons which they had acquired in Haran, and they set out
for the land of Canaan; thus they came to the land of Canaan.
6 Abram passed through the land as far as the site of Shechem, to the oak of Moreh.
Now the Canaanite *was* then in the land.
7 The LORD appeared to Abram and said, "To your descendants I will give this land."
So he built an altar there to the LORD who had appeared to him.

12:1 Gen 15:7; Acts 7:3; Heb 11:8

12:2 Gen 17:4-6; 18:18; 46:3; Deut 26:5; Gen 22:17; Zech 8:13

12:3 Gen 24:35; 27:29; Num 24:9; Gen 22:18; 26:4; 28:14; Acts 3:25; Gal 3:8

12:4 Gen 11:27, 31

12:5 Gen 13:6; Gen 14:14; Lev 22:11; Gen 11:31; Heb 11:8

12:6 Gen 35:4; Deut 11:30

12:7 Gen 17:1; 18:1; Gen 13:15; 15:18; Deut 34:4; Ps 105: 9-12; Acts 7:5; Gal 3:16; Gen 13:4, 18; 22:9

12:1–3 When God called him, Abram moved out in faith from Ur to Haran and finally to Canaan. God then established a covenant with Abram, telling him that he would found a great nation. Not only would this nation be blessed, God said, but the other nations of the earth would be blessed through Abram's descendants. Israel, the nation that would come from Abram, was to follow God and influence those with whom it came in contact. Through Abram's family tree, Jesus Christ was born to save humanity. Through Christ, people can have a personal relationship with God and be blessed beyond measure.

12:2 God promised to bless Abram and make him great, but there was one condition. Abram had to do what God wanted him to do. This meant leaving his home and friends and traveling to a new land where God promised to build a great nation from Abram's family. Abram obeyed, walking away from his home for God's promise of even greater blessings in the future. God may be trying to lead you to a place of greater service and usefulness for him. Don't let the comfort and security of your present position make you miss God's plan for you.

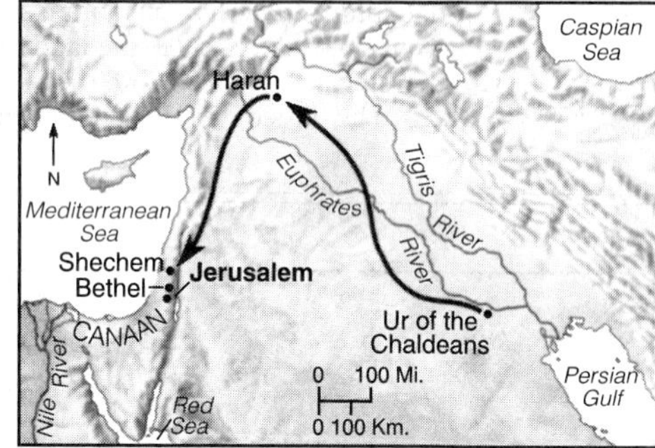

ABRAM'S JOURNEY TO CANAAN Abram, Sarai, and Lot traveled from Ur of the Chaldeans to Canaan by way of Haran. Though indirect, this route followed the rivers rather than attempting to cross the vast desert.

12:5 God planned to develop a nation of people he would call his own. He called Abram from the godless, self-centered city of Ur to a fertile region called Canaan, where a God-centered, moral nation could be established. Though small in dimension, the land of Canaan was the focal point for most of the history of Israel as well as for the rise of Christianity. This small land given to one man, Abram, has had a tremendous impact on world history.

12:7 Abram built an altar to the Lord. Altars were used in many religions, but for God's people, altars were more than places of sacrifice. For them, altars symbolized communion with God and commemorated notable encounters with him. Built of rough stones and earth, altars often remained in place for years as continual reminders of God's protection and promises.

12:8 Josh 8:9, 12; Gen 4:26; 21:33
12:9 Gen 13:1, 3; 20:1; 24:62
12:10 Gen 26:1; Gen 43:1
12:11 Gen 26:7; 29:17
12:12 Gen 20:11
12:13 Gen 20:2, 5, 12; 26:7; Jer 38:17, 20
12:15 Gen 20:2
12:16 Gen 20:14; Gen 13:2
12:17 Gen 20:18; 1 Chr 16:21; Ps 105:14
12:18 Gen 20:9, 10; 26:10

8 Then he proceeded from there to the mountain on the east of Bethel, and pitched
his tent, with Bethel on the west and Ai on the east; and there he built an altar to the
LORD and called upon the name of the LORD.
9 Abram journeyed on, continuing toward the [14]Negev.
10 Now there was a famine in the land; so Abram went down to Egypt to sojourn there,
for the famine was severe in the land.
11 It came about when he came near to Egypt, that he said to Sarai his wife, "See now,
I know that you are a beautiful woman;
12 and when the Egyptians see you, they will say, 'This is his wife'; and they will kill
me, but they will let you live.
13 "Please say that you are my sister so that it may go well with me because of you, and
that I may live on account of you."
14 It came about when Abram came into Egypt, the Egyptians saw that the woman
was very beautiful.
15 Pharaoh's officials saw her and praised her to Pharaoh; and the woman was taken
into Pharaoh's house.
16 Therefore he treated Abram well for her sake; and gave him sheep and oxen and
donkeys and male and female servants and female donkeys and camels.
17 But the LORD struck Pharaoh and his house with great plagues because of Sarai,
Abram's wife.
18 Then Pharaoh called Abram and said, "What is this you have done to me? Why did
you not tell me that she was your wife?
19 "Why did you say, 'She is my sister,' so that I took her for my wife? Now then, here
is your wife, take her and go."
20 Pharaoh commanded *his* men concerning him; and they escorted him away, with
his wife and all that belonged to him.

2. Abram and Lot

13:1 Gen 12:9
13:2 Gen 24:35

13 So Abram went up from Egypt to the [14]Negev, he and his wife and all that belonged to him, and Lot with him.
2 Now Abram was very rich in livestock, in silver and in gold.

14 I.e. South country

Abram regularly built altars to God for two reasons: (1) for prayer and worship, and (2) as reminders of God's promise to bless him. Abram couldn't survive spiritually without regularly renewing his love and loyalty to God. Building altars helped Abram remember that God was at the center of his life. Regular worship helps us remember what God desires and motivates us to obey him.

12:10 When famine struck, Abram went to Egypt where there was food. Why would there be a famine in the land where God had just called Abram? This was a test of Abram's faith, and Abram passed. He didn't question God's leading when facing this difficulty. Many believers find that when they determine to follow God, they immediately encounter great obstacles. The next time you face such a test, don't try to second-guess what God is doing. Use the intelligence God gave you, as Abram did when he temporarily moved to Egypt, and wait for new opportunities.

12:11–13 Abram, acting out of fear, asked Sarai to tell a half-truth by saying she was his sister. She *was* his half sister, but she was also his wife (see 20:12).

Abram's intent was to deceive the Egyptians. He feared that if they knew the truth, they would kill him to get Sarai. She would have been a desirable addition to Pharaoh's harem because of her wealth, beauty, and potential for political alliance. As Sarai's brother, Abram would have been given a place of honor. As her husband, however, his life would be in danger because Sarai could not enter Pharaoh's harem unless Abram was dead. So Abram lost faith in God's protection, even after all God had promised him, and told a half-truth. This shows how lying compounds the effects of sin. When he lied, Abram's problems multiplied.

13:1–2 In Abram's day, sheep and cattle owners could acquire great wealth. Abram's wealth not only included silver and gold, but also livestock. These animals were a valuable commodity used for food, clothing, tent material, and sacrifices. They were often traded for other goods and services. Abram was able to watch his wealth grow and multiply daily.

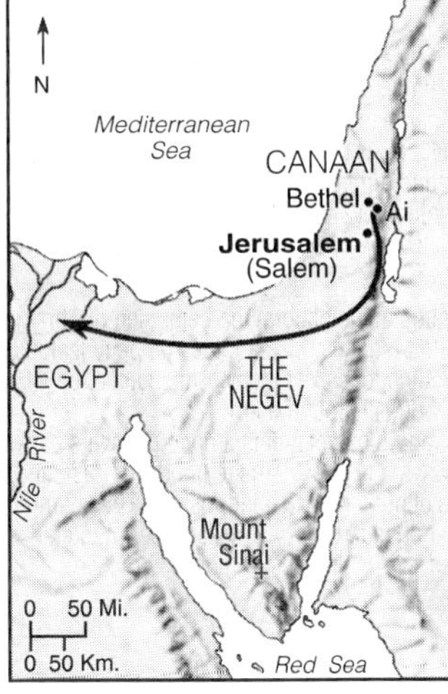

ABRAM'S JOURNEY TO EGYPT
A famine could cause the loss of a shepherd's wealth. So Abram traveled through the Negev to Egypt, where there was plenty of food and good land for his flocks.

3 He went on his journeys from the [15]Negev as far as Bethel, to the place where his
tent had been at the beginning, between Bethel and Ai,
4 to the place of the altar which he had made there formerly; and there Abram called
on the name of the LORD.
5 Now Lot, who went with Abram, also had flocks and herds and tents.
6 And the land could not sustain them while dwelling together, for their possessions
were so great that they were not able to remain together.
7 And there was strife between the herdsmen of Abram's livestock and the herdsmen
of Lot's livestock. Now the Canaanite and the Perizzite were dwelling then in the land.
8 So Abram said to Lot, "Please let there be no strife between you and me, nor between my herdsmen and your herdsmen, for we are brothers.
9 "Is not the whole land before you? Please separate from me; if *to* the left, then I will
go to the right; or if *to* the right, then I will go to the left."
10 Lot lifted up his eyes and saw all the valley of the Jordan, that it was well watered
everywhere—*this was* before the LORD destroyed Sodom and Gomorrah—like the garden of the LORD, like the land of Egypt as you go to Zoar.
11 So Lot chose for himself all the valley of the Jordan, and Lot journeyed eastward.
Thus they separated from each other.
12 Abram settled in the land of Canaan, while Lot settled in the cities of the valley,
and moved his tents as far as Sodom.
13 Now the men of Sodom were wicked exceedingly and sinners against the LORD.
14 The LORD said to Abram, after Lot had separated from him, "Now lift up your eyes
and look from the place where you are, northward and southward and eastward and
westward;
15 for all the land which you see, I will give it to you and to your descendants forever.
16 "I will make your descendants as the dust of the earth, so that if anyone can number
the dust of the earth, then your descendants can also be numbered.
17 "Arise, walk about the land through its length and breadth; for I will give it to you."
18 Then Abram moved his tent and came and dwelt by the oaks of Mamre, which are
in Hebron, and there he built an altar to the LORD.

War of the Kings

14 And it came about in the days of Amraphel king of Shinar, Arioch king of Ellasar,
Chedorlaomer king of Elam, and Tidal king of Goiim,
2 *that* they made war with Bera king of Sodom, and with Birsha king of Gomorrah,
Shinab king of Admah, and Shemeber king of Zeboiim, and the king of Bela (that is,
Zoar).
3 All these came as allies to the valley of Siddim (that is, the Salt Sea).

15 I.e. South country

13:3 Gen 12:8
13:5 Gen 12:5
13:6 Gen 36:7; Gen 12:5, 16; 13:2
13:7 Gen 26:20; Gen 12:6; 15:20, 21
13:8 Prov 15:18; 20:3
13:10 Gen 19:17-29; Deut 34:3; Gen 19:24; Gen 2:8, 10; Gen 47:6; Gen 14:2, 8; 19:22; Deut 34:3
13:12 Gen 14:2; 19:24, 25
13:13 Gen 18:20; Ezek 16:49; Gen 39:9; Num 32:23; 2 Pet 2:7, 8
13:14 Deut 3:27; 34:1-4; Is 49:18; Gen 28:14
13:15 Gen 12:7; Gen 13:17; 15:7; 17:8; 2 Chr 20:7; Acts 7:5
13:16 Gen 16:10; 28:14
13:17 Num 13:17-24
13:18 Gen 14:13; Gen 8:20; 12:7, 8
14:1 Gen 10:22; Is 11:11; Dan 8:2
14:2 Gen 10:19; Deut 29:23
14:3 Num 34:12; Deut 3:17; Josh 3:16

13:5–9 Facing a potential conflict with his nephew Lot, Abram took the initiative in settling the dispute. He gave Lot first choice, even though Abram, being older, had the right to choose first. Abram also showed a willingness to risk being cheated. Abram's example shows us how to respond to difficult family situations: (1) take the initiative in resolving conflicts; (2) let others have first choice, even if that means not getting what we want; (3) put family peace above personal desires.

13:7–8 Surrounded by hostile neighbors, the herdsmen of Abram and Lot should have pulled together. Instead, they let petty jealousy tear them apart. Similar situations exist today. Christians often bicker while Satan is at work all around them.

Rivalries, arguments, and disagreements among believers can be destructive in three ways. (1) They damage goodwill, trust, and peace—the foundations of good human relations. (2) They hamper progress toward important goals. (3) They make us self-centered rather than love-centered. Jesus understood how destructive arguments among brothers could be. In his final prayer before being betrayed and arrested, Jesus asked God that his followers be "one" (John 17:21).

13:10–11 Lot's character is revealed by his choices. He took the best share of the land even though it meant living near Sodom, a city known for its sin. He was greedy, wanting the best for himself, without thinking about his uncle Abram's needs or what was fair.

Life is a series of choices. We too can choose the best while ignoring the needs and feelings of others. But this kind of choice, as Lot's life shows, leads to problems. When we stop making choices in God's direction, all that is left is to make choices in the wrong direction.

13:12 Good pasture and available water seemed like a wise choice to Lot at first. But he failed to recognize that wicked Sodom could provide temptations strong enough to destroy his family. Have you chosen to live or work in a "Sodom"? Even though you may be strong enough to resist the temptations, other members of your family may not. While God commands us to reach people in the "Sodom" near us, we must be careful not to become like the very people we are trying to reach.

4 Twelve years they had served Chedorlaomer, but the thirteenth year they rebelled.
5 In the fourteenth year Chedorlaomer and the kings that were with him, came and
defeated the Rephaim in Ashteroth-karnaim and the Zuzim in Ham and the Emim in
Shaveh-kiriathaim,
6 and the Horites in their Mount Seir, as far as El-paran, which is by the wilderness.
7 Then they turned back and came to En-mishpat (that is, Kadesh), and conquered
all the country of the Amalekites, and also the Amorites, who lived in Hazazon-tamar.
8 And the king of Sodom and the king of Gomorrah and the king of Admah and the
king of Zeboiim and the king of Bela (that is, Zoar) came out; and they arrayed for battle against them in the valley of Siddim,
9 against Chedorlaomer king of Elam and Tidal king of Goiim and Amraphel king of
Shinar and Arioch king of Ellasar—four kings against five.
10 Now the valley of Siddim was full of tar pits; and the kings of Sodom and Gomorrah
fled, and they fell into them. But those who survived fled to the hill country.

14:5 Deut 3:11, 13; Deut 1:4; Josh 9:10; Num 32:37

14:6 Gen 36:20; Deut 2:12, 22; Gen 21:21; Num 10:12

14:7 Num 13:26; 2 Chr 20:2

14:8 Gen 14:3

14:10 Gen 14:17, 21, 22; Gen 19:17

LOT

Some people simply drift through life. Their choices, when they can muster the will to choose, tend to follow the course of least resistance. Lot, Abram's nephew, was such a person.

While still young, Lot lost his father. Although this must have been hard on him, he was not left without strong role models in his grandfather Terah and his uncle Abram, who raised him. Still, Lot did not develop their sense of purpose. Throughout his life he was so caught up in the present moment that he seemed incapable of seeing the consequences of his actions. It is hard to imagine what his life would have been like without Abram's careful attention and God's intervention.

By the time Lot drifted out of the picture, his life had taken an ugly turn. He had so blended into the sinful culture of his day that he did not want to leave it. Then his daughters committed incest with him. His drifting finally took him in a very specific direction—destruction.

Lot, however, is called "righteous" in the New Testament (2 Peter 2:7–8). Ruth, a descendant of Moab, was an ancestor of Jesus, even though Moab was born as a result of Lot's incestuous relationship with one of his daughters. Lot's story gives hope to us that God forgives and often brings about positive circumstances from evil.

What is the direction of your life? Are you headed toward God or away from him? If you're a drifter, the choice for God may seem difficult, but it is the one choice that puts all other choices in a different light.

Strengths and accomplishments:
- He was a successful businessman
- Peter calls him a righteous man (2 Peter 2:7–8)

Weaknesses and mistakes:
- When faced with decisions, he tended to put off deciding, then chose the easiest course of action
- When given a choice, his first reaction was to think of himself

Lesson from his life:
- God wants us to do more than drift through life; he wants us to be an influence for him

Vital statistics:
- Where: Lived first in Ur of the Chaldeans, then moved to Canaan with Abram. Eventually he moved to the wicked city of Sodom
- Occupation: Wealthy sheep and cattle rancher; also a city official
- Relatives: Father: Haran. Adopted by Abram when his father died. The name of his wife, who turned into a pillar of salt, is not mentioned

Key verse:
"But he hesitated. So the men seized his hand and the hand of his wife and the hands of his two daughters, for the compassion of the LORD was upon him; and they brought him out, and put him outside the city" (Genesis 19:16).

Lot's story is told in Genesis 11—14; 19. He is also mentioned in Deuteronomy 2:9; Luke 17:28–32; 2 Peter 2:7–8.

14:4–16 Who was Chedorlaomer, and why was he important? In Abram's time, most cities had their own kings. Wars and rivalries among kings were common. A conquered city paid tribute to the victorious king. Nothing is known about Chedorlaomer except what we read in the Bible, but apparently he was quite powerful. Five cities including Sodom had paid tribute to him for 12 years. The five cities formed an alliance and rebelled by withholding tribute. Chedorlaomer reacted swiftly and reconquered them all. When he defeated Sodom, he captured Lot, his family, and his possessions. Abram, with only 318 men, chased Chedorlaomer's army and attacked him near Damascus. With God's help, he defeated them and recovered Lot, his family, and their possessions.

11 Then they took all the goods of Sodom and Gomorrah and all their food supply,
and departed.
12 They also took Lot, Abram's nephew, and his possessions and departed, for he was
living in Sodom.
13 Then a fugitive came and told Abram the Hebrew. Now he was living by the oaks of
Mamre the Amorite, brother of Eshcol and brother of Aner, and these were allies with
Abram.
14 When Abram heard that his relative had been taken captive, he led out his trained
men, born in his house, three hundred and eighteen, and went in pursuit as far as Dan.
15 He divided his forces against them by night, he and his servants, and defeated them,
and pursued them as far as Hobah, which is north of Damascus.
16 He brought back all the goods, and also brought back his relative Lot with his possessions, and also the women, and the people.

God's Promise to Abram

17 Then after his return from the defeat of Chedorlaomer and the kings who were with
him, the king of Sodom went out to meet him at the valley of Shaveh (that is, the King's
Valley).
18 And Melchizedek king of Salem brought out bread and wine; now he was a priest of
God Most High.
19 He blessed him and said,
"Blessed be Abram of God Most High,
Possessor of heaven and earth;
20 And blessed be God Most High,
Who has delivered your enemies into your hand."
He gave him a tenth of all.
21 The king of Sodom said to Abram, "Give the people to me and take the goods for
yourself."

14:12 Gen 11:27; Gen 13:12

14:13 Gen 40:15; Ex 3:18; Gen 13:18; 14:24; Gen 21:27, 32

14:14 Gen 14:12; Gen 12:5; 15:3; 17:27; Eccl 2:7; Deut 34:1; Judg 18:29; 1 Kin 15:20

14:15 Judg 7:16; Gen 15:2

14:16 1 Sam 30:8, 18, 19; Gen 14:12, 14

14:17 Gen 14:10; 2 Sam 18:18

14:18 Heb 7:1-10; Ps 104:15; Ps 110:4; Heb 5:6, 10

14:19 Gen 14:22

14:20 Heb 7:4

14:12 Lot's greedy desire for the best of everything led him into sinful surroundings. His burning desire for possessions and success cost him his freedom and enjoyment. As a captive to Chedorlaomer, he faced torture, slavery, or death. In much the same way, we can be enticed into doing things or going places we shouldn't. The prosperity we long for is captivating; it can both entice us and enslave us if our motives are not in line with God's desires.

LOT'S RESCUE
Having conquered Sodom, Chedorlaomer left for his home country, taking many captives with him. Abram learned what had happened and chased Chedorlaomer past Dan and beyond Damascus. There he defeated the king and rescued the captives, among them Lot.

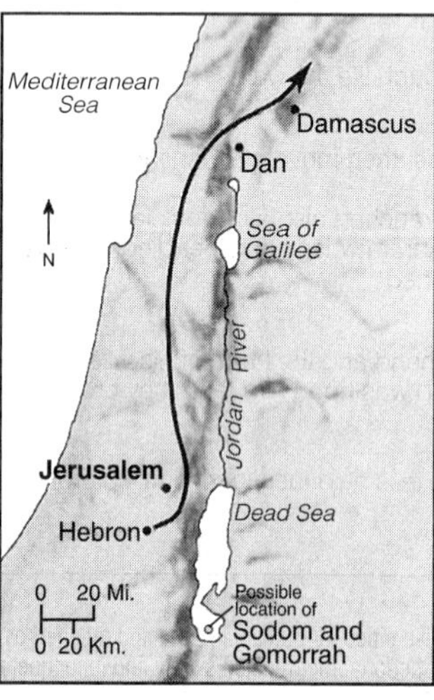

14:14–16 These incidents portray two of Abram's characteristics: (1) He had courage that came from God. Facing a powerful foe, he attacked. (2) He was prepared. He had taken time to train his men for a potential conflict. We never know when we will be called upon to complete difficult tasks. Like Abram, we should prepare for those times and take courage from God when they come.

14:14–16 When Abram learned that Lot was a prisoner, he immediately tried to rescue his nephew. It is easier and safer not to become involved. But with Lot in serious trouble, Abram acted at once. Sometimes we must get involved in a messy or painful situation in order to help others. We should be willing to act immediately when others need our help.

14:18 Who was Melchizedek? He was obviously a God-fearing man, for his name means "king of righteousness," and king of Salem means "king of peace." He was a "priest of the Most High God" (Hebrews 7:1–2). He recognized God as Creator of heaven and earth. What else is known about him? Four main theories have been suggested. (1) Melchizedek was a respected king of that region. Abram was simply showing him the respect he deserved. (2) The name Melchizedek may have been a standing title for all the kings of Salem. (3) Melchizedek was a type of Christ (Hebrews 7:3). A type is an Old Testament event or teaching that is so closely related to what Christ did that it illustrates a lesson about Christ. (4) Melchizedek was the appearance on earth of the preincarnate Christ in a temporary bodily form.

14:20 Abram gave a tenth of the booty to Melchizedek. Even in some pagan religions, it was traditional to give a tenth of one's earnings to the gods. Abram followed accepted tradition; however, he refused to take any booty from the king of Sodom. Even though this huge amount would significantly increase what he could have given to God, he chose to reject it for more important reasons—he didn't want the ungodly king of Sodom to say, "I have made Abram rich." Instead, Abram wanted him to say, "God has made Abram rich." In this case, accepting the gifts would have focused everyone's attention on Abram or the king of Sodom rather than on God, the giver of victory. When people look at us, they need to see what God has accomplished in our lives.

22 Abram said to the king of Sodom, "I have sworn to the LORD God Most High, possessor of heaven and earth,
23 that I will not take a thread or a sandal thong or anything that is yours, for fear you
would say, 'I have made Abram rich.'
24 "I will take nothing except what the young men have eaten, and the share of the men
who went with me, Aner, Eshcol, and Mamre; let them take their share."

3. God promises a son to Abram

Abram Promised a Son

15 After these things the word of the LORD came to Abram in a vision, saying,
"Do not fear, Abram,
I am a shield to you;
Your reward shall be very great."
2 Abram said, "O Lord GOD, what will You give me, since I am childless, and the heir
of my house is Eliezer of Damascus?"
3 And Abram said, "Since You have given no offspring to me, one born in my house
is my heir."
4 Then behold, the word of the LORD came to him, saying, "This man will not be your
heir; but one who will come forth from your own body, he shall be your heir."
5 And He took him outside and said, "Now look toward the heavens, and count the
stars, if you are able to count them." And He said to him, "So shall your descendants be."
6 Then he believed in the LORD; and He reckoned it to him as righteousness.
7 And He said to him, "I am the LORD who brought you out of Ur of the Chaldeans,
to give you this land to possess it."
8 He said, "O Lord GOD, how may I know that I will possess it?"
9 So He said to him, "Bring Me a three year old heifer, and a three year old female
goat, and a three year old ram, and a turtledove, and a young pigeon."
10 Then he brought all these to Him and cut them in two, and laid each half opposite
the other; but he did not cut the birds.
11 The birds of prey came down upon the carcasses, and Abram drove them away.
12 Now when the sun was going down, a deep sleep fell upon Abram; and behold, terror *and* great darkness fell upon him.
13 *God* said to Abram, "Know for certain that your descendants will be strangers in a
land that is not theirs, where they will be enslaved and oppressed four hundred years.
14 "But I will also judge the nation whom they will serve, and afterward they will come
out with many possessions.
15 "As for you, you shall go to your fathers in peace; you will be buried at a good old
age.

14:22 Gen 14:19; Ps 24:1
14:23 2 Kin 5:16
14:24 Gen 14:13
15:1 Gen 15:4; 46:2; 1 Sam 15:10; Gen 21:17; 26:24; Is 41:10; Deut 33:29; Num 18:20; Ps 58:11
15:3 Gen 14:14
15:4 Gal 4:28
15:5 Gen 22:17; 26:4; Deut 1:10; Ex 32:13; Rom 4:18; Heb 11:12
15:6 Rom 4:3, 20-22; Gal 3:6; James 2:23
15:7 Gen 11:31; Gen 13:15, 17
15:8 Judg 6:36-40; Luke 1:18
15:10 Gen 15:17; Lev 1:17
15:12 Gen 2:21; 28:11; Job 33:15
15:13 Acts 7:6, 17; Ex 1:11; Deut 5:15; Ex 12:40; Gal 3:17
15:14 Ex 12:32-38
15:15 Gen 25:8; 47:30

15:1 Why would Abram be afraid? Perhaps he feared revenge from the kings he had just defeated (14:15). God gave him two good reasons for courage: (1) he promised to defend Abram ("I am a shield to you"), and (2) he promised to be Abram's "reward." When you fear what lies ahead, remember that God will stay with you through difficult times and that he has promised you great blessings.

15:2–3 Eliezer was Abram's most trusted servant, acting as household administrator (a chief servant, see Genesis 24). According to custom, if Abram were to die without a son, his eldest servant would become his heir. Although Abram loved his servant, he wanted a son to carry on the family line.

15:5 Abram wasn't promised wealth or fame; he already had that. Instead God promised descendants like the stars in the sky or the grains of sand on the seashore (22:17), too numerous to count. To appreciate the vast number of stars scattered through the sky, you need to be, like Abram, away from any distractions. Or pick up a handful of sand and try to count the grains—it can't be done! Just when Abram was despairing of ever having an heir, God promised descendants too numerous to imagine. God's blessings are beyond our imaginations!

15:6 Although Abram had been demonstrating his faith through his actions, it was his belief in the Lord, not his actions, that made Abram right with God (Romans 4:1–5). We too can have a right relationship with God by trusting him. Our outward actions—church attendance, prayer, good deeds—will not by themselves make us right with God. A right relationship is based on faith—the heartfelt inner confidence that God is who he says he is and does what he says he will do. Right actions will follow naturally as by-products.

15:8 Abram was looking for confirmation and assurance that he was doing God's will. We also want assurance when we ask for guidance. But we can know for sure that what we are doing is right if we do what the Bible says. Abram didn't have the Bible—we do.

15:13–14 The book of Exodus tells the story of the enslavement and miraculous deliverance of Abram's descendants.

16 "Then in the fourth generation they will return here, for the iniquity of the Amorite
is not yet complete."
17 It came about when the sun had set, that it was very dark, and behold, *there appeared*
a smoking oven and a flaming torch which passed between these pieces.
18 On that day the LORD made a covenant with Abram, saying,
"To your descendants I have given this land,
From the river of Egypt as far as the great river, the river Euphrates:
19 the Kenite and the Kenizzite and the Kadmonite
20 and the Hittite and the Perizzite and the Rephaim
21 and the Amorite and the Canaanite and the Girgashite and the Jebusite."

Sarai and Hagar

16 Now Sarai, Abram's wife had borne him no *children,* and she had an Egyptian maid
whose name was Hagar.
2 So Sarai said to Abram, "Now behold, the LORD has prevented me from bearing
children. Please go in to my maid; perhaps I will obtain children through her." And Abram
listened to the voice of Sarai.
3 After Abram had lived ten years in the land of Canaan, Abram's wife Sarai took
Hagar the Egyptian, her maid, and gave her to her husband Abram as his wife.
4 He went in to Hagar, and she conceived; and when she saw that she had conceived,
her mistress was despised in her sight.
5 And Sarai said to Abram, "May the wrong done me be upon you. I gave my maid
into your arms, but when she saw that she had conceived, I was despised in her sight.
May the LORD judge between you and me."
6 But Abram said to Sarai, "Behold, your maid is in your power; do to her what is
good in your sight." So Sarai treated her harshly, and she fled from her presence.
7 Now the angel of the LORD found her by a spring of water in the wilderness, by the
spring on the way to Shur.
8 He said, "Hagar, Sarai's maid, where have you come from and where are you going?" And she said, "I am fleeing from the presence of my mistress Sarai."
9 Then the angel of the LORD said to her, "Return to your mistress, and submit yourself to her authority."
10 Moreover, the angel of the LORD said to her, "I will greatly multiply your descendants
so that they will be too many to count."

15:16 Gen 15:13; Lev 18:24-28

15:17 Jer 34:18, 19

15:18 Gen 17:8; Josh 21:43; Acts 7:5; Ex 23:31; Num 34:1-15; Deut 1:7, 8

15:19 Ex 3:17; 23:28; Josh 24:11; Neh 9:8

16:1 Gen 11:30; Gen 12:16

16:2 Gen 30:3, 4, 9, 10

16:3 Gen 12:4

16:5 Jer 51:35; Gen 31:53; Ex 5:21

16:6 Gen 16:9

16:7 Gen 21:17, 18; 22:11, 15; 31:11; Gen 20:1; 25:18

16:8 Gen 3:9; 1 Kin 19:9, 13

16:10 Gen 22:15-18; Gen 17:20

15:16 The Amorites were one of the nations living in Canaan, the land God promised Abram. God knew the people would grow more wicked and would someday need to be punished. Part of that punishment would involve taking away their land and giving it to Abram's descendants. God in his mercy was giving the Amorites plenty of time to repent, but he already knew they would not. At the right time, they would have to be punished. Everything God does is true to his character. He is merciful, knows all, and acts justly—and his timing is perfect.

15:17 Why did God send this strange vision to Abram? God's covenant with Abram was serious business. It represented an incredible promise from God and a huge responsibility for Abram. To confirm his promise, God gave Abram a sign—a smoking oven and a flaming torch. The fire and smoke suggest God's holiness, his zeal for righteousness, and his judgment on all the nations. God took the initiative, gave the confirmation, and followed through on his promises. God's passing between the pieces was a visible assurance to Abram that the covenant God had made was real.

16:1–3 Sarai gave Hagar to Abram as a substitute wife, a common practice of that time. A married woman who could not have children was shamed by her peers and was often required to give a female servant to her husband in order to produce heirs. The children born to the servant woman were considered the children of the wife. Abram was acting in line with the custom of the day, but his action showed a lack of faith that God would fulfill his promise.

16:3 Sarai took matters into her own hands by giving Hagar to Abram. Like Abram she had trouble believing God's promise that was apparently directed specifically toward Abram and Sarai. Out of this lack of faith came a series of problems. This invariably happens when we take over for God, trying to make his promise come true through efforts that are not in line with his specific directions. In this case, time was the greatest test of Abram and Sarai's willingness to let God work in their lives. Sometimes we too must simply wait. When we ask God for something and have to wait, it is a temptation to take matters into our own hands and interfere with God's plans.

16:5 Although Sarai arranged for Hagar to have a child by Abram, she later blamed Abram for the results. It is often easier to strike out in frustration and accuse someone else than to admit an error and ask forgiveness. (Adam and Eve did the same thing in 3:12–13.)

16:6 Sarai took out her anger against Abram and herself on Hagar, and her treatment was harsh enough to cause Hagar to run away. Anger, especially when it arises from our own shortcomings, can be dangerous.

16:8 Hagar was running away from her mistress and her problem. The angel of the Lord gave her this advice: (1) to return and face Sarai, the cause of her problem, and (2) to submit to her. Hagar needed to work on her attitude toward Sarai, no matter how justified it may have been. Running away from our problems rarely solves them. It is wise to return to our problems, face them squarely, accept God's promise of help, correct our attitudes, and act as we should.

16:11 Ex 2:23, 24; 3:7, 9

16:12 Job 24:5; 39:5-8; Gen 25:18

11 The angel of the LORD said to her further,
"Behold, you are with child,
And you will bear a son;
And you shall call his name [16]Ishmael,
Because the LORD has given heed to your affliction.
12 "He will be a wild donkey of a man,
His hand *will be* against everyone,
And everyone's hand *will be* against him;
And he will live to the east of all his brothers."

16 I.e. God hears

MELCHIZEDEK

Do you like a good mystery? History is full of them! They usually involve people. One of the most mysterious people in the Bible is the King of Peace, Melchizedek. He appeared one day in the life of Abraham (then Abram) and was never heard from again. What happened that day, however, was to be remembered throughout history and eventually became a subject of a New Testament letter (Hebrews).

This meeting between Abram and Melchizedek was most unusual. Although the two men were strangers and foreigners to each other, they shared a most important characteristic: both worshiped and served the one God who made heaven and earth. This was a great moment of triumph for Abram. He had just defeated an army and regained the freedom of a large group of captives. If there was any doubt in his mind about whose victory it was, Melchizedek set the record straight by reminding Abram, "Blessed be God Most High, Who has delivered your enemies into your hand" (Genesis 14:20). Abram recognized that this man worshiped the same God he did.

Melchizedek was one of a small group of God-honoring people throughout the Old Testament who came in contact with the Jews (Israelites) but were not Jews themselves. This indicates that the requirement to be a follower of God is not genetic, but is based on faithfully obeying his teachings and recognizing his greatness.

Do you let God speak to you through other people? In evaluating others, do you consider God's impact on their lives? Are you aware of the similarities between yourself and others who worship God, even if their form of worship is quite different from yours? Do you know the God of the Bible well enough to know if you truly worship him? Allow Melchizedek, Abraham, David, and Jesus, along with many other persons in the Bible, to show you this great God, Creator of heaven and earth. He wants you to know how much he loves you; he wants you to know him personally.

Strengths and accomplishments:
- The first priest/king of Scripture—a leader with a heart tuned to God
- Good at encouraging others to serve God wholeheartedly
- A man whose character reflected his love for God
- A person in the Old Testament who reminds us of Jesus and who some believe really was Jesus

Lesson from his life:
- Live for God and you're likely to be at the right place at the right time. Examine your heart: to whom or what is your greatest loyalty? If you can honestly answer [God,] you are living for him

Vital statistics:
- Where: Ruled in Salem, site of the future Jerusalem
- Occupation: King of Salem and priest of God Most High

Key verses:
"This Melchizedek, king of Salem, priest of the Most High God . . . met Abraham as he was returning from the slaughter of the kings and blessed him . . . Now observe how great this man was to whom Abraham, the patriarch, gave a tenth of the choicest spoils" (Hebrews 7:1, 4).

Melchizedek's story is told in Genesis 14:17–20. He is also mentioned in Psalm 110:4; Hebrews 5—7.

13 Then she called the name of the LORD who spoke to her, "You are a God who sees";
for she said, "Have I even remained alive here after seeing Him?"
14 Therefore the well was called [17]Beer-lahai-roi; behold, it is between Kadesh and
Bered.
15 So Hagar bore Abram a son; and Abram called the name of his son, whom Hagar
bore, Ishmael.
16 Abram was eighty-six years old when Hagar bore Ishmael to him.

Abraham and the Covenant of Circumcision

17 Now when Abram was ninety-nine years old, the LORD appeared to Abram and
said to him,
"I am God Almighty;
Walk before Me, and be blameless.
2 "I will establish My covenant between Me and you,
And I will multiply you exceedingly."
3 Abram fell on his face, and God talked with him, saying,
4 "As for Me, behold, My covenant is with you,
And you will be the father of a multitude of nations.
5 "No longer shall your name be called [18]Abram,
But your name shall be [19]Abraham;
For I will make you the father of a multitude of nations.
6 "I will make you exceedingly fruitful, and I will make nations of you, and kings will
come forth from you.
7 "I will establish My covenant between Me and you and your descendants after you
throughout their generations for an everlasting covenant, to be God to you and to your
descendants after you.
8 "I will give to you and to your descendants after you, the land of your sojournings, all
the land of Canaan, for an everlasting possession; and I will be their God."
9 God said further to Abraham, "Now as for you, you shall keep My covenant, you
and your descendants after you throughout their generations.
10 "This is My covenant, which you shall keep, between Me and you and your descendants after you: every male among you shall be circumcised.
11 "And you shall be circumcised in the flesh of your foreskin, and it shall be the sign of
the covenant between Me and you.
12 "And every male among you who is eight days old shall be circumcised throughout
your generations, a *servant* who is born in the house or who is bought with money from
any foreigner, who is not of your descendants.

17 I.e. the well of the living one who sees me **18** I.e. exalted father **19** I.e. father of a multitude

16:13 Gen 32:30; Ps 139:1-12
16:14 Gen 14:7
16:16 Gen 12:4; 16:3
17:1 Gen 12:7; 18:1; Gen 28:3; 35:11; Gen 6:9; Deut 18:13
17:2 Gen 15:18; Gen 13:16; 15:5
17:3 Gen 17:17; 18:2
17:4 Gen 35:11; 48:19
17:5 Neh 9:7; Rom 4:17
17:6 Gen 17:16; 35:11
17:7 Gen 17:13, 19; Ps 105:9, 10; Luke 1:55; Gen 26:24; Lev 11:45; 26:12, 45; Heb 11:16; Gen 28:13; Gal 3:16
17:8 Gen 12:7; 13:15, 17; Acts 7:5; Ex 6:7; 29:45; Lev 26:12; Deut 29:13; Rev 21:7
17:9 Ex 19:5
17:10 John 7:22; Acts 7:8; Rom 4:11
17:11 Ex 12:48; Deut 10:16; Acts 7:8; Rom 4:11
17:12 Lev 12:3

16:13 We have watched three people make serious mistakes: (1) Sarai, who took matters into her own hands and gave her maid to Abram; (2) Abram, who went along with the plan but, when circumstances began to go wrong, refused to help solve the problem; and (3) Hagar, who ran away from the problem. In spite of this messy situation, God demonstrated his ability to work in all things for good (Romans 8:28). Sarai and Abram still received the son they so desperately wanted, and God solved Hagar's problem despite Abram's refusal to get involved. No problem is too complicated for God if you are willing to let him help you.

17:1 The Lord told Abram, "I am God Almighty; walk before Me, and be blameless." God has the same message for us today. We are to obey the Lord in every respect because he is God—that is reason enough. If you don't think the benefits of obedience are worth it, consider who God is—the only one with the power and ability to meet your every need.

17:2–8 Why did God repeat his covenant to Abram? Twice before, he had mentioned this agreement (Genesis 12 and 15). Here, however, God was bringing it into focus and preparing to carry it out. He revealed to Abram several specific parts of his covenant: (1) God would give Abram many descendants; (2) many nations would descend from him; (3) God would maintain his covenant with Abram's descendants; (4) God would give Abram's descendants the land of Canaan.

17:5 God changed Abram's name to Abraham ("father of a multitude") shortly before the promised son was conceived. From this point on, the Bible calls him Abraham.

17:5–14 God was making a covenant, or contract, between himself and Abraham. The terms were simple: Abraham would obey God and circumcise all the males in his household; God's part was to give Abraham heirs, property, power, and wealth. Most contracts are even trades: We give something and in turn receive something of equal value. But when we become part of God's covenant family, the blessings we receive far outweigh what we must give up.

17:9–10 Why did God require circumcision? (1) As a sign of obedience to him in all matters. (2) As a sign of belonging to his covenant people. Once circumcised, there was no turning back. The man would be identified as a Jew forever. (3) As a symbol of "cutting off" the old life of sin, purifying one's heart, and dedicating oneself to God. (4) Possibly as a health measure.

Circumcision more than any other practice separated God's people from their pagan neighbors. In Abraham's day, this was essential to develop the pure worship of the one true God.

17:13 Ex 12:44
17:14 Ex 4:24-26
17:16 Gen 18:10; Gen 17:6; 36:31
17:17 Gen 17:3; 18:12; 21:6; Gen 21:7

13 "A *servant* who is born in your house or who is bought with your money shall surely
be circumcised; thus shall My covenant be in your flesh for an everlasting covenant.
14 "But an uncircumcised male who is not circumcised in the flesh of his foreskin, that
person shall be cut off from his people; he has broken My covenant."
15 Then God said to Abraham, "As for Sarai your wife, you shall not call her name
Sarai, but [20]Sarah *shall be* her name.
16 "I will bless her, and indeed I will give you a son by her. Then I will bless her, and she
shall be *a mother of* nations; kings of peoples will come from her."
17 Then Abraham fell on his face and laughed, and said in his heart, "Will a child be
born to a man one hundred years old? And will Sarah, who is ninety years old, bear *a
child?*"

20 I.e. princess

ISHMAEL

Have you ever wondered if you were born into the wrong family? We don't know much about how Ishmael viewed life, but that question must have haunted him at times. His life, his name, and his position were bound up in a conflict between two jealous women. Sarah (Sarai), impatient with God's timetable, had taken matters into her own hands, deciding to have a child through another woman. Hagar, servant that she was, submitted to being used this way. But her pregnancy gave birth to strong feelings of superiority toward Sarah. Into this tense atmosphere, Ishmael was born.

For 13 years Abraham thought Ishmael's birth had fulfilled God's promise. He was surprised to hear God say that the promised child would be Abraham and Sarah's very own. Sarah's pregnancy and Isaac's birth must have had a devastating impact on Ishmael. Until then he had been treated as a son and heir, but this late arrival made his future uncertain. During Isaac's weaning celebration, Sarah caught Ishmael teasing his half brother. As a result, Hagar and Ishmael were permanently expelled from Abraham's family.

Much of what happened throughout his life cannot be blamed on Ishmael. He was caught in a process much bigger than himself. However, his own actions showed that he had chosen to become part of the problem and not part of the solution. He chose to live under his circumstances rather than above them.

The choice he made is one we must all make. There are circumstances over which we have no control (heredity, for instance), but there are others that we can control (decisions we make). At the heart of the matter is the sin-oriented nature we have all inherited. It can be partly controlled, although not overcome, by human effort. In the context of history, Ishmael's life represents the mess we make when we don't try to change the things we could change. The God of the Bible has offered a solution. His answer is not control, but a changed life. To have a changed life, turn to God, trust him to forgive your sinful past, and begin to change your attitude toward him and others.

Strengths and accomplishments:
- One of the first to experience the physical sign of God's covenant, circumcision
- Known for his ability as an archer and hunter
- Fathered 12 sons who became leaders of warrior tribes

Weakness and mistake:
- Failed to recognize the place of his half brother, Isaac, and mocked him

Lesson from his life:
- God's plans incorporate people's mistakes

Vital statistics:
- Where: Canaan and Egypt
- Occupation: Hunter, archer, warrior
- Relatives: Parents: Hagar and Abraham. Half brother: Isaac

Key verses:
"God heard the lad crying; and the angel of God called to Hagar from heaven and said to her, 'What is the matter with you, Hagar? Do not fear, for God has heard the voice of the lad where he is. Arise, lift up the lad, and hold him by the hand, for I will make a great nation of him' " (Genesis 21:17–18).

Ishmael's story is told in Genesis 16—17; 25:12–18; 28:8–9; 36:1–3. He is also mentioned in 1 Chronicles 1:28–31; Romans 9:7–9; Galatians 4:21–31.

17:17–27 How could Abraham doubt God? It seemed incredible that he and Sarah in their advanced years could have a child. Abraham, the man God considered righteous because of his faith, had trouble believing God's promise to him. Despite his doubts, however, he followed God's commands (17:22–27). Even people of great faith may have doubts. When God seems to want the impossible and you begin to doubt his leading, be like Abraham. Focus on God's commitment to fulfill his promises to you, and then continue to obey.

18 And Abraham said to God, "Oh that Ishmael might live before You!"

19 But God said, "No, but Sarah your wife will bear you a son, and you shall call his name [21]Isaac; and I will establish My covenant with him for an everlasting covenant for his descendants after him.

17:19 Gen 17:16; 18:10; 21:2; Gen 26:2-5

20 "As for Ishmael, I have heard you; behold, I will bless him, and will make him fruitful and will multiply him exceedingly. He shall become the father of twelve princes, and I will make him a great nation.

17:20 Gen 16:10; Gen 25:12-16; Gen 21:18

21 "But My covenant I will establish with Isaac, whom Sarah will bear to you at this season next year."

17:21 Gen 17:19; 18:10, 14; Gen 21:2

22 When He finished talking with him, God went up from Abraham.

17:22 Gen 18:33; 35:13

23 Then Abraham took Ishmael his son, and all *the servants* who were born in his house and all who were bought with his money, every male among the men of Abraham's household, and circumcised the flesh of their foreskin in the very same day, as God had said to him.

17:23 Gen 14:14; Gen 17:9-11

24 Now Abraham was ninety-nine years old when he was circumcised in the flesh of his foreskin.

17:24 Rom 4:11

25 And Ishmael his son was thirteen years old when he was circumcised in the flesh of his foreskin.

17:25 Gen 16:16

26 In the very same day Abraham was circumcised, and Ishmael his son.

27 All the men of his household, who were born in the house or bought with money from a foreigner, were circumcised with him.

17:27 Gen 14:14

4. Sodom and Gomorrah

Birth of Isaac Promised

18 Now the LORD appeared to him by the oaks of Mamre, while he was sitting at the tent door in the heat of the day.

18:1 Gen 12:7; 17:1; Gen 13:18; 14:13

2 When he lifted up his eyes and looked, behold, three men were standing opposite him; and when he saw *them,* he ran from the tent door to meet them and bowed himself to the earth,

3 and said, "My lord, if now I have found favor in your sight, please do not pass your servant by.

18:2 Gen 18:16, 22; 32:24; Josh 5:13; Judg 13:6-11; Heb 13:2

4 "Please let a little water be brought and wash your feet, and rest yourselves under the tree;

18:4 Gen 19:2; 24:32; 43:24

5 and I will bring a piece of bread, that you may refresh yourselves; after that you may go on, since you have visited your servant." And they said, "So do, as you have said."

18:5 Judg 6:18, 19; 13:15, 16

6 So Abraham hurried into the tent to Sarah, and said, "Quickly, prepare three measures of fine flour, knead *it* and make bread cakes."

7 Abraham also ran to the herd, and took a tender and choice calf and gave *it* to the servant, and he hurried to prepare it.

8 He took curds and milk and the calf which he had prepared, and placed *it* before them; and he was standing by them under the tree as they ate.

9 Then they said to him, "Where is Sarah your wife?" And he said, "There, in the tent."

10 He said, "I will surely return to you at this time next year; and behold, Sarah your wife will have a son." And Sarah was listening at the tent door, which was behind him.

18:10 Gen 21:2; Rom 9:9

11 Now Abraham and Sarah were old, advanced in age; Sarah was past childbearing.

18:11 Gen 17:17; Rom 4:19; Heb 11:11

12 Sarah laughed to herself, saying, "After I have become old, shall I have pleasure, my lord being old also?"

13 And the LORD said to Abraham, "Why did Sarah laugh, saying, 'Shall I indeed bear *a child,* when I am *so* old?'

18:12 Gen 17:17; Luke 1:18; 1 Pet 3:6

21 I.e. he laughs

17:20 God did not forget Ishmael. Although he was not to be Abraham's heir, he would also be the father of a great nation. Regardless of your circumstances, God has not forgotten you. Obey him and trust in his plan.

18:2–5 Abraham was eager to show hospitality to these three visitors, as was Lot (19:2). In Abraham's day, a person's reputation was largely connected to his hospitality—the sharing of home and food. Even strangers were to be treated as highly honored guests. Meeting another's need for food or shelter was and still is one of the most immediate and practical ways to obey God. It is also a time-honored relationship builder. Hebrews 13:2 suggests that we, like Abraham, might actually entertain angels. This thought should be on our minds the next time we have the opportunity to meet a stranger's needs.

18:14 Jer 32:17, 27; Zech 8:6; Matt 19:26; Luke 1:37; Rom 4:21; Gen 17:21

18:17 Gen 18:22, 26, 33; Amos 3:7; Gen 18:21; 19:24

18:18 Gen 12:3; 22:18; Acts 3:25; Gal 3:8

18:19 Neh 9:7; Amos 3:2; Deut 6:6, 7

14 "Is anything too difficult for the LORD? At the appointed time I will return to you, at
this time next year, and Sarah will have a son."
15 Sarah denied *it* however, saying, "I did not laugh"; for she was afraid. And He said,
"No, but you did laugh."
16 Then the men rose up from there, and looked down toward Sodom; and Abraham
was walking with them to send them off.
17 The LORD said, "Shall I hide from Abraham what I am about to do,
18 since Abraham will surely become a great and mighty nation, and in him all the
nations of the earth will be blessed?
19 "For I have chosen him, so that he may command his children and his household after
him to keep the way of the LORD by doing righteousness and justice, so that the LORD
may bring upon Abraham what He has spoken about him."

ABRAHAM

We all know that there are consequences to any action we take. What we do can set into motion a series of events that may continue long after we're gone. Unfortunately, when we are making a decision most of us think only of the immediate consequences. These are often misleading because they are short-lived.

Abraham had a choice to make. His decision was between setting out with his family and belongings for parts unknown or staying right where he was. He had to decide between the security of what he already had and the uncertainty of traveling under God's direction. All he had to go on was God's promise to guide and bless him. Abraham could hardly have been expected to visualize how much of the future was resting on his decision of whether to go or stay, but his obedience affected the history of the world. His decision to follow God set into motion the development of the nation that God would eventually use as his own when he visited earth himself. When Jesus Christ came to earth, God's promise was fulfilled; through Abraham the entire world was blessed.

You probably don't know the long-term effects of most decisions you make. But shouldn't the fact that there will be long-term results cause you to think carefully and seek God's guidance as you make choices and take action today?

Strengths and accomplishments:
- His faith pleased God
- Became the founder of the Jewish nation
- Was respected by others and was courageous in defending his family at any cost
- Was not only a caring father to his own family, but practiced hospitality to others
- Was a successful and wealthy rancher
- Usually avoided conflicts, but when they were unavoidable, he allowed his opponent to set the rules for settling the dispute

Weakness and mistake:
- Under direct pressure, he distorted the truth

Lessons from his life:
- God desires dependence, trust, and faith in him—not faith in our ability to please him
- God's plan from the beginning has been to make himself known to all people

Vital statistics:
- Where: Born in Ur of the Chaldeans; spent most of his life in the land of Canaan
- Occupation: Wealthy livestock owner
- Relatives: Brothers: Nahor and Haran. Father: Terah. Wife: Sarah. Nephew: Lot. Sons: Ishmael and Isaac
- Contemporaries: Abimelech, Melchizedek

Key verse:
"Then he believed in the LORD; and He reckoned it to him as righteousness" (Genesis 15:6).

Abraham's story is told in Genesis 11—25. He is also mentioned in Exodus 2:24; Acts 7:2–8; Romans 4; Galatians 3; Hebrews 2, 6–7, 11.

18:14 "Is anything too difficult for the LORD?" The obvious answer is, "Of course not!" This question reveals much about God. Make it a habit to insert your specific needs into the question. "Is this day in my life too hard for the Lord?" "Is this habit I'm trying to break too hard for him?" "Is the communication problem I'm having too hard for him?" Asking the question this way reminds you that God is personally involved in your life and nudges you to ask for his power to help you.

18:15 Sarah lied because she was afraid of being discovered. Fear is the most common motive for lying. We are afraid that our inner thoughts and emotions will be exposed or our wrongdoings discovered. But lying causes greater complications than telling the truth and brings even more problems. If God can't be trusted with our innermost thoughts and fears, we are in greater trouble than we first imagined.

20 And the LORD said, "The outcry of Sodom and Gomorrah is indeed great, and their
sin is exceedingly grave.
21 "I will go down now, and see if they have done entirely according to its outcry, which
has come to Me; and if not, I will know."
22 Then the men turned away from there and went toward Sodom, while Abraham was
still standing before the LORD.
23 Abraham came near and said, "Will You indeed sweep away the righteous with the
wicked?
24 "Suppose there are fifty righteous within the city; will You indeed sweep *it* away and
not spare the place for the sake of the fifty righteous who are in it?
25 "Far be it from You to do such a thing, to slay the righteous with the wicked, so that
the righteous and the wicked are *treated* alike. Far be it from You! Shall not the Judge of
all the earth deal justly?"
26 So the LORD said, "If I find in Sodom fifty righteous within the city, then I will spare
the whole place on their account."
27 And Abraham replied, "Now behold, I have ventured to speak to the Lord, although
I am *but* dust and ashes.
28 "Suppose the fifty righteous are lacking five, will You destroy the whole city because
of five?" And He said, "I will not destroy *it* if I find forty-five there."
29 He spoke to Him yet again and said, "Suppose forty are found there?" And He said,
"I will not do *it* on account of the forty."
30 Then he said, "Oh may the Lord not be angry, and I shall speak; suppose thirty are
found there?" And He said, "I will not do *it* if I find thirty there."
31 And he said, "Now behold, I have ventured to speak to the Lord; suppose twenty
are found there?" And He said, "I will not destroy *it* on account of the twenty."
32 Then he said, "Oh may the Lord not be angry, and I shall speak only this once; suppose ten are found there?" And He said, "I will not destroy *it* on account of the ten."
33 As soon as He had finished speaking to Abraham the LORD departed, and Abraham returned to his place.

18:20 Gen 19:13; Ezek 16:49, 50
18:21 Gen 11:5; Ex 3:8; Ps 14:2
18:22 Gen 18:16; 19:1; Gen 18:1, 17
18:23 Ex 23:7; Num 16:22; 2 Sam 24:17; Ps 11:4-7
18:25 Deut 1:16, 17; 32:4; Job 8:3, 20; Ps 58:11; 94:2; Is 3:10, 11; Rom 3:5, 6
18:26 Jer 5:1
18:27 Gen 3:19; Job 30:19; 42:6
18:32 Judg 6:39
18:33 Gen 17:22; 35:13

The Doom of Sodom

19 Now the two angels came to Sodom in the evening as Lot was sitting in the gate of
Sodom. When Lot saw *them,* he rose to meet them and bowed down *with his* face
to the ground.
2 And he said, "Now behold, my lords, please turn aside into your servant's house,
and spend the night, and wash your feet; then you may rise early and go on your way."
They said however, "No, but we shall spend the night in the square."

19:1 Gen 18:2, 22; Gen 18:2-5

18:20-33 Did Abraham change God's mind? Of course not. The more likely answer is that God changed Abraham's mind. Abraham knew that God is just and that he punishes sin, but he may have wondered about God's mercy. Abraham seemed to be probing God's mind to see how merciful he really was. He left his conversation with God convinced that God was both kind and fair. Our prayers won't change God's mind, but they may change ours just as Abraham's prayer changed his. Prayer helps us better understand the mind of God.

18:20-33 Why did God let Abraham question his justice and intercede for a wicked city? Abraham knew that God must punish sin, but he also knew from experience that God is merciful to sinners. God knew there were not ten righteous people in the city, but he was merciful enough to allow Abraham to intercede. He was also merciful enough to help Lot, Abraham's nephew, get out of Sodom before it was destroyed. God does not take pleasure in destroying the wicked, but he must punish sin. He is both just and merciful. We should be thankful that God's mercy extends to us.

18:21 God gave the men of Sodom a fair test. He was not ignorant of the city's wicked practices, but in his fairness and patience he gave the people of Sodom one last chance to repent. God is still waiting, giving people the opportunity to turn to him (2 Peter 3:9). Those who are wise will turn to him before his patience wears out.

18:25 Was God being unfair to the people of Sodom? Did he really plan to destroy the righteous with the wicked? On the contrary, God's fairness stood out. (1) He agreed to spare the entire city if only ten righteous people lived there. (2) He showed great mercy toward Lot, apparently the only man in the city who had any kind of relationship with him (and even that was questionable). (3) He showed great patience toward Lot, almost forcing him to leave Sodom before it was destroyed. Remember God's patience when you are tempted to think he is unfair. Even the most godly people deserve his justice. We should be glad God doesn't direct his justice toward us as he did toward Sodom.

18:33 God showed Abraham that asking for anything is allowed, with the understanding that God's answers come from God's perspective. They are not always in harmony with our expectations, for only he knows the whole story. Are you missing God's answer to a prayer because you haven't considered any possible answer other than the one you want?

19:1 The gateway of the city was the meeting place for city officials and other men to discuss current events and transact business. It was a place of authority and status where a person could see and be seen. Evidently Lot held an important position in the government or associated with those who did because the angels found him at the city gate. Perhaps Lot's status in Sodom was one reason he was so reluctant to leave (19:16, 18-22).

19:3 Gen 18:6-8
19:4 Gen 13:13, 18:20
19:5 Lev 18:22; Judg 19:22
19:8 Judg 19:24
19:9 Ex 2:14

3 Yet he urged them strongly, so they turned aside to him and entered his house; and
he prepared a feast for them, and baked unleavened bread, and they ate.
4 Before they lay down, the men of the city, the men of Sodom, surrounded the house,
both young and old, all the people from every quarter;
5 and they called to Lot and said to him, "Where are the men who came to you tonight? Bring them out to us that we may have relations with them."
6 But Lot went out to them at the doorway, and shut the door behind him,
7 and said, "Please, my brothers, do not act wickedly.
8 "Now behold, I have two daughters who have not had relations with man; please let
me bring them out to you, and do to them whatever you like; only do nothing to these
men, inasmuch as they have come under the shelter of my roof."
9 But they said, "Stand aside." Furthermore, they said, "This one came in as an alien,

---

SARAH

There probably isn't anything harder to do than wait, whether we are expecting something good, something bad, or an unknown.

One way we often cope with a long wait (or even a short one) is to begin helping God get his plan into action. Sarah tried this approach. She was too old to expect to have a child of her own, so she thought God must have something else in mind. From Sarah's limited point of view this could only be to give Abraham a son through another woman—a common practice in her day. The plan seemed harmless enough. Abraham would sleep with Sarah's maidservant, who would then give birth to a child. Sarah would take the child as her own. The plan worked beautifully—at first. But as you read about the events that followed, you will be struck by how often Sarah must have regretted the day she decided to push God's timetable ahead.

Another way we cope with a long wait is to gradually conclude that what we're waiting for is never going to happen. Sarah waited 90 years for a baby! When God told her she would finally have one of her own, she laughed, not so much from a lack of faith in what God could do, but from doubt about what he could do [through her.] When confronted about her laughter, she lied—as she had seen her husband do from time to time. She probably didn't want her true feelings to be known.

What parts of your life seem to be on hold right now? Do you understand that this may be part of God's plan for you? The Bible has more than enough clear direction to keep us busy while we're waiting for some particular part of life to move ahead.

Strengths and accomplishments:
- Was intensely loyal to her own child
- Became the mother of a nation and an ancestor of Jesus
- Was a woman of faith, the first woman listed in the Hall of Faith in Hebrews 11

Weaknesses and mistakes:
- Had trouble believing God's promises to her
- Attempted to work problems out on her own, without consulting God
- Tried to cover her faults by blaming others

Lessons from her life:
- God responds to faith even in the midst of failure
- God is not bound by what usually happens; he can stretch the limits and cause unheard-of events to occur

Vital statistics:
- Where: Married Abram in Ur of the Chaldeans, then moved with him to Canaan
- Occupation: Wife, mother, household manager
- Relatives: Father: Terah. Husband: Abraham. Half brothers: Nahor and Haran. Nephew: Lot. Son: Isaac

Key verse:
"By faith even Sarah herself received ability to conceive, even beyond the proper time of life, since she considered Him faithful who had promised" (Hebrews 11:11).

Sarah's story is told in Genesis 11—25. She is also mentioned in Isaiah 51:2; Romans 4:19; 9:9; Hebrews 11:11; 1 Peter 3:6.

19:8 How could any father give his daughters to be ravished by a mob of perverts, just to protect two strangers? Possibly Lot was scheming to save both the girls and the visitors, hoping the girls' fiancés would rescue them or that the homosexual men would be disinterested in the girls and simply go away. Although it was the custom of the day to protect guests at any cost, this terrible suggestion reveals how deeply sin had been absorbed into Lot's life. He had become hardened to evil acts in an evil city. Whatever Lot's motives were, we see here an illustration of Sodom's terrible wickedness—a wickedness so great that God had to destroy the entire city.

and already he is acting like a judge; now we will treat you worse than them." So they
pressed hard against Lot and came near to break the door.
10 But the men reached out their hands and brought Lot into the house with them,
and shut the door.
11 They struck the men who were at the doorway of the house with blindness, both
small and great, so that they wearied *themselves trying* to find the doorway.
12 Then the *two* men said to Lot, "Whom else have you here? A son-in-law, and your
sons, and your daughters, and whomever you have in the city, bring *them* out of the place;
13 for we are about to destroy this place, because their outcry has become so great before the LORD that the LORD has sent us to destroy it."
14 Lot went out and spoke to his sons-in-law, who were to marry his daughters, and
said, "Up, get out of this place, for the LORD will destroy the city." But he appeared to
his sons-in-law to be jesting.
15 When morning dawned, the angels urged Lot, saying, "Up, take your wife and your
two daughters who are here, or you will be swept away in the punishment of the city."
16 But he hesitated. So the men seized his hand and the hand of his wife and the hands
of his two daughters, for the compassion of the LORD *was* upon him; and they brought
him out, and put him outside the city.
17 When they had brought them outside, one said, "Escape for your life! Do not look
behind you, and do not stay anywhere in the valley; escape to the mountains, or you will
be swept away."
18 But Lot said to them, "Oh no, my lords!
19 "Now behold, your servant has found favor in your sight, and you have magnified
your lovingkindness, which you have shown me by saving my life; but I cannot escape to
the mountains, for the disaster will overtake me and I will die;
20 now behold, this town is near *enough* to flee to, and it is small. Please, let me escape
there (is it not small?) that my life may be saved."
21 He said to him, "Behold, I grant you this request also, not to overthrow the town of
which you have spoken.
22 "Hurry, escape there, for I cannot do anything until you arrive there." Therefore the
name of the town was called [22]Zoar.
23 The sun had risen over the earth when Lot came to Zoar.
24 Then the LORD rained on Sodom and Gomorrah brimstone and fire from the LORD
out of heaven,
25 and He overthrew those cities, and all the valley, and all the inhabitants of the cities, and what grew on the ground.
26 But his wife, from behind him, looked *back,* and she became a pillar of salt.
27 Now Abraham arose early in the morning *and went* to the place where he had stood
before the LORD;

19:10 Gen 19:1
19:11 Deut 28:28, 29; 2 Kin 6:18; Acts 13:11
19:13 Gen 18:20; Lev 26:30-33; Deut 4:26; 28:45; 1 Chr 21:15
19:14 Num 16:21, 45; Rev 18:4; Jer 43:1, 2
19:16 Deut 5:15; 6:21; 7:8; 2 Pet 2:7; Ex 34:7; Ps 32:10; 33:18, 19
19:17 Jer 48:6; Gen 19:26; Gen 13:10; Gen 14:10
19:22 Gen 13:10; 14:2
19:24 Deut 29:23; Ps 11:6; Is 13:19; Ezek 16:49, 50; Luke 17:29; Jude 7
19:25 Deut 29:23; Ps 107:34; Is 13:19; Lam 4:6; 2 Pet 2:6
19:26 Gen 19:17; Luke 17:32
19:27 Gen 18:22

22 I.e. small

19:13 God promised to spare Sodom if only ten righteous people lived there (18:32). Obviously not even ten could be found, because the angels arrived to destroy the city. Archaeological evidence points to an advanced civilization in this area during Abraham's day. Most researchers also confirm some kind of sudden and devastating destruction. It is now widely thought that the buried city lies beneath the waters of the southern end of the Dead Sea. The story of Sodom reveals that the people of Lot's day had to deal with the same kinds of repulsive sins the world faces today. We should follow Abraham's example of trusting God. His selfless faith contrasts with the self-gratifying people of Sodom.

19:14 Lot had lived so long and so contented among ungodly people that he was no longer a believable witness for God. He had allowed his environment to shape him, rather than he shaping his environment. Do those who know you see you as a witness for God, or are you just one of the crowd, blending in unnoticed? Lot had compromised to the point that he was almost useless to God. When he finally made a stand, nobody listened. Have you too become useless to God because you are too much like your environment? To make a difference, you must first decide to be different in your faith and your conduct.

19:16 Lot hesitated, so the angel seized his hand and rushed him to safety. Lot did not want to abandon the wealth, position, and comfort he enjoyed in Sodom. It is easy to criticize Lot for being hypnotized by Sodom when the choice seems so clear to us. To be wiser than Lot, we must see that our hesitation to obey stems from the false attractions of our culture's pleasures.

19:16–29 Notice how God's mercy toward Abraham extended to Lot and his family. Because Abraham pleaded for Lot, God was merciful and saved Lot from the fiery destruction of Sodom. A righteous person can often affect others for good. James says that the prayers of a righteous person are powerful (see James 5:16). All Christians should follow Abraham's example and pray for others to be saved.

19:24 In the story of Sodom and Gomorrah, we see two facets of God's character: his great patience (agreeing to spare a wicked city for ten good people) and his fierce anger (destroying both cities). As we grow spiritually, we should find ourselves developing a deeper respect for God because of his anger toward sin, and also a deeper love for God because of his patience when we sin.

19:26 Lot's wife turned back to look at the smoldering city of Sodom. Clinging to the past, she was unwilling to turn completely away. Are you looking back longingly at sin while trying to move forward with God? You can't make progress with God as long as you

19:28 Rev 9:2; 18:9
19:29 Deut 7:8; 9:5, 27; 2 Pet 2:7
19:30 Gen 19:17, 19
19:31 Gen 16:2, 4; 38:8; Deut 25:5
19:32 Luke 21:34
19:37 Deut 2:9
19:38 Deut 2:19
20:1 Gen 18:1; Gen 12:9; Gen 26:1, 6
20:2 Gen 12:11-13; 20:12; 26:7; Gen 12:15
20:3 Gen 12:17, 18; Gen 20:7
20:4 Gen 18:23-25
20:5 Gen 20:13; 1 Kin 9:4; Ps 7:8; 26:6
20:6 1 Sam 25:26, 34

28 and he looked down toward Sodom and Gomorrah, and toward all the land of
the valley, and he saw, and behold, the smoke of the land ascended like the smoke of a
furnace.
29 Thus it came about, when God destroyed the cities of the valley, that God remembered Abraham, and sent Lot out of the midst of the overthrow, when He overthrew the
cities in which Lot lived.

Lot Is Debased

30 Lot went up from Zoar, and stayed in the mountains, and his two daughters with
him; for he was afraid to stay in Zoar; and he stayed in a cave, he and his two daughters.
31 Then the firstborn said to the younger, "Our father is old, and there is not a man on
earth to come in to us after the manner of the earth.
32 "Come, let us make our father drink wine, and let us lie with him that we may preserve our family through our father."
33 So they made their father drink wine that night, and the firstborn went in and lay
with her father; and he did not know when she lay down or when she arose.
34 On the following day, the firstborn said to the younger, "Behold, I lay last night with
my father; let us make him drink wine tonight also; then you go in and lie with him, that
we may preserve our family through our father."
35 So they made their father drink wine that night also, and the younger arose and lay
with him; and he did not know when she lay down or when she arose.
36 Thus both the daughters of Lot were with child by their father.
37 The firstborn bore a son, and called his name Moab; he is the father of the Moabites to this day.
38 As for the younger, she also bore a son, and called his name Ben-ammi; he is the
father of the sons of Ammon to this day.

Abraham's Treachery

20 Now Abraham journeyed from there toward the land of the [23]Negev, and settled
between Kadesh and Shur; then he sojourned in Gerar.
2 Abraham said of Sarah his wife, "She is my sister." So Abimelech king of Gerar sent
and took Sarah.
3 But God came to Abimelech in a dream of the night, and said to him, "Behold, you
are a dead man because of the woman whom you have taken, for she is married."
4 Now Abimelech had not come near her; and he said, "Lord, will You slay a nation,
even *though* blameless?
5 "Did he not himself say to me, 'She is my sister'? And she herself said, 'He is my
brother.' In the integrity of my heart and the innocence of my hands I have done this."
6 Then God said to him in the dream, "Yes, I know that in the integrity of your heart

23 I.e. South country

---

are holding on to pieces of your old life. Jesus said it this way in Matthew 6:24: "No one can serve two masters."

19:30–38 In this pitiful sequel to the story of the destruction of Sodom, we see two women compelled to preserve their family line. They were driven not by lust, but by desperation—they feared they would never marry. Lot's tendency to compromise and refusal to act reached its peak. He should have found right partners for his daughters long before this; Abraham's family wasn't far away. Now the two daughters stooped to incest, showing their acceptance of the morals of Sodom. We are most likely to sin when we are desperate for what we feel we must have.

19:30–38 Why doesn't the Bible openly condemn these sisters for what they did? In many cases, the Bible does not judge people for their actions. It simply reports the events. However, incest is clearly condemned in other parts of Scripture (Leviticus 18:6–18; 20:11–12, 17, 19–21; Deuteronomy 22:30; 27:20–23; Ezekiel 22:11; 1 Corinthians 5:1). Perhaps the consequence of their action—Moab and Ammon became enemies of Israel—was God's way of judging their sin.

19:37–38 Moab and Ben-ammi were the products of incest. They became the fathers of two of Israel's greatest enemies, the Moabites and the Ammonites. These nations settled east of the Jordan River, and Israel never conquered them. Because of the family connection, Moses was forbidden to attack them (Deuteronomy 2:9). Ruth, great-grandmother of David and an ancestor of Jesus, was from Moab.

20:2 Abraham had used this same trick before to protect himself (12:11–13). Although Abraham is one of our heroes of faith, he did not learn his lesson well enough the first time. In fact, by giving in to the temptation again, he risked turning a sinful act into a sinful pattern of lying whenever he suspected his life was in danger.

No matter how much we love God, certain temptations are especially difficult to resist. These are the vulnerable spots in our spiritual armor. As we struggle with these weaknesses, we can be encouraged to know that God is watching out for us just as he did for Abraham.

20:6 Abimelech had unknowingly taken a married woman to be his wife and was about to commit adultery. But God somehow prevented him from touching Sarah and held him back from sinning. What mercy on God's part! How many times has God done the same for us, holding us back from sin in ways we can't even detect? We have no way of knowing—we just know from this story that he can. God works just as often in ways we can't see as in ways we can.

you have done this, and I also kept you from sinning against Me; therefore I did not let
you touch her.
7 "Now therefore, restore the man's wife, for he is a prophet, and he will pray for you
and you will live. But if you do not restore *her,* know that you shall surely die, you and all
who are yours."
8 So Abimelech arose early in the morning and called all his servants and told all these
things in their hearing; and the men were greatly frightened.
9 Then Abimelech called Abraham and said to him, "What have you done to us? And
how have I sinned against you, that you have brought on me and on my kingdom a great
sin? You have done to me things that ought not to be done."
10 And Abimelech said to Abraham, "What have you encountered, that you have done
this thing?"
11 Abraham said, "Because I thought, surely there is no fear of God in this place, and
they will kill me because of my wife.
12 "Besides, she actually is my sister, the daughter of my father, but not the daughter of
my mother, and she became my wife;
13 and it came about, when God caused me to wander from my father's house, that I
said to her, 'This is the kindness which you will show to me: everywhere we go, say of
me, "He is my brother." ' "
14 Abimelech then took sheep and oxen and male and female servants, and gave them
to Abraham, and restored his wife Sarah to him.
15 Abimelech said, "Behold, my land is before you; settle wherever you please."
16 To Sarah he said, "Behold, I have given your brother a thousand pieces of silver;
behold, it is your vindication before all who are with you, and before all men you are
cleared."
17 Abraham prayed to God, and God healed Abimelech and his wife and his maids, so
that they bore *children.*
18 For the LORD had closed fast all the wombs of the household of Abimelech because
of Sarah, Abraham's wife.

5. Birth and near sacrifice of Isaac

Isaac Is Born

21 Then the LORD took note of Sarah as He had said, and the LORD did for Sarah as
He had promised.
2 So Sarah conceived and bore a son to Abraham in his old age, at the appointed time
of which God had spoken to him.
3 Abraham called the name of his son who was born to him, whom Sarah bore to him,
Isaac.
4 Then Abraham circumcised his son Isaac when he was eight days old, as God had
commanded him.
5 Now Abraham was one hundred years old when his son Isaac was born to him.
6 Sarah said, "God has made laughter for me; everyone who hears will laugh with me."
7 And she said, "Who would have said to Abraham that Sarah would nurse children?
Yet I have borne him a son in his old age."

20:7 1 Sam 7:5; 2 Kin 5:11; Job 42:8
20:9 Gen 12:18; Gen 39:9
20:11 Neh 5:15; Prov 16:6; Gen 12:12; 26:7
20:13 Gen 12:1-9; Gen 12:13; 20:5
20:14 Gen 12:16
20:15 Gen 13:9; 34:10; 47:6
20:16 Gen 20:5
20:17 Num 12:13; 21:7; James 5:16
20:18 Gen 12:17
21:1 Gen 17:16, 21; 18:10, 14; Gal 4:23
21:2 Acts 7:8; Gal 4:22; Heb 11:11; Gen 17:21; 18:10, 14
21:3 Gen 17:19, 21
21:4 Gen 17:12; Acts 7:8
21:5 Gen 17:17
21:6 Gen 18:13; Ps 126:2; Is 54:1
21:7 Gen 18:11, 13

20:11–13 Because Abraham mistakenly assumed that Abimelech was a wicked man, he made a quick decision to tell a half-truth. Abraham thought it would be more effective to deceive Abimelech than to trust God to work in the king's life. Don't assume that God will not work in a situation that has potential problems. You may not completely understand the situation, and God may intervene when you least expect it.

20:17–18 Why did God punish Abimelech when he had no idea Sarah was married? (1) Even though Abimelech's intentions were good, as long as Sarah was living in his harem he was in danger of sinning. A person who eats a poisonous toadstool, thinking it's a harmless mushroom, no doubt has perfectly good intentions—but will still suffer. Sin is a poison that damages us and those around us, whatever our intentions. (2) The punishment, closing up "all the wombs of the household of Abimelech," lasted only as long as Abimelech was in danger of sleeping with Sarah. It was meant to change the situation, not to harm Abimelech. (3) The punishment clearly showed that Abraham was in league with almighty God. This incident may have made Abimelech respect and fear Abraham's God.

21:1–7 Who could believe that Abraham would have a son at 100 years of age—and live to raise him to adulthood? But doing the impossible is everyday business for God. Our big problems won't seem so impossible if we let God handle them.

21:7 After repeated promises, a visit by two angels, and the appearance of the Lord himself, Sarah finally cried out with surprise and joy at the birth of her son. Because of her doubt, worry, and fear, she had forfeited the peace she could have felt in God's wonderful promise to her. The way to bring peace to a troubled heart is to focus on God's promises. Trust him to do what he says.

8 The child grew and was weaned, and Abraham made a great feast on the day that Isaac was weaned.

Sarah Turns against Hagar

21:9 Gen 16:1, 4, 15; Gal 4:29

9 Now Sarah saw the son of Hagar the Egyptian, whom she had borne to Abraham, mocking.

21:10 Gal 4:30

10 Therefore she said to Abraham, "Drive out this maid and her son, for the son of this maid shall not be an heir with my son Isaac."

21:11 Gen 17:18

11 The matter distressed Abraham greatly because of his son.

21:12 Rom 9:7; Heb 11:18

12 But God said to Abraham, "Do not be distressed because of the lad and your maid; whatever Sarah tells you, listen to her, for through Isaac your descendants shall be named.

21:13 Gen 16:10; 21:18; 25:12-18

13 "And of the son of the maid I will make a nation also, because he is your descendant."

14 So Abraham rose early in the morning and took bread and a skin of water and gave *them* to Hagar, putting *them* on her shoulder, and *gave her* the boy, and sent her away. And she departed and wandered about in the wilderness of Beersheba.

15 When the water in the skin was used up, she left the boy under one of the bushes.

21:16 Jer 6:26; Amos 8:10

16 Then she went and sat down opposite him, about a bowshot away, for she said, "Do not let me see the boy die." And she sat opposite him, and lifted up her voice and wept.

21:17 Ex 3:7; Deut 26:7; Ps 6:8; Gen 26:24

17 God heard the lad crying; and the angel of God called to Hagar from heaven and said to her, "What is the matter with you, Hagar? Do not fear, for God has heard the voice of the lad where he is.

21:18 Gen 16:10; 21:13; 25:12-16

18 "Arise, lift up the lad, and hold him by the hand, for I will make a great nation of him."

21:19 Num 22:31; 2 Kin 6:17; Gen 16:7, 14

19 Then God opened her eyes and she saw a well of water; and she went and filled the skin with water and gave the lad a drink.

21:20 Gen 28:15; 39:2, 3, 21

20 God was with the lad, and he grew; and he lived in the wilderness and became an archer.

21:21 Gen 25:18

21 He lived in the wilderness of Paran, and his mother took a wife for him from the land of Egypt.

Covenant with Abimelech

21:22 Gen 20:2, 14; 26:26; Gen 26:28; Is 8:10

22 Now it came about at that time that Abimelech and Phicol, the commander of his army, spoke to Abraham, saying, "God is with you in all that you do;

21:23 Josh 2:12; 1 Sam 24:21

23 now therefore, swear to me here by God that you will not deal falsely with me or with my offspring or with my posterity, but according to the kindness that I have shown to you, you shall show to me and to the land in which you have sojourned."

24 Abraham said, "I swear it."

21:18 What happened to Ishmael, and who are his descendants? Ishmael became ruler of a large tribe or nation. The Ishmaelites were nomads living in the desert of Sinai and Paran, south of Israel. One of Ishmael's daughters married Esau, Ishmael's nephew (28:9). The Bible pictures the Ishmaelites as hostile to Israel and to God (Psalm 83:6).

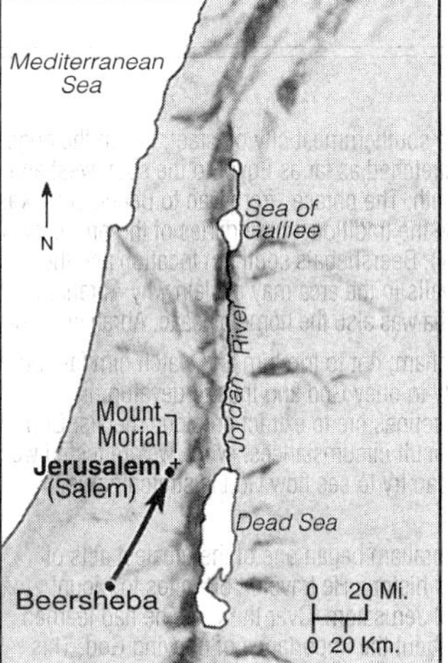

ABRAHAM'S TRIP TO MOUNT MORIAH
Abraham and Isaac traveled the 50 or 60 miles from Beersheba to Mount Moriah in about three days. This was a very difficult time for Abraham, who was on his way to sacrifice his beloved son, Isaac.

25 But Abraham complained to Abimelech because of the well of water which the servants of Abimelech had seized.
26 And Abimelech said, "I do not know who has done this thing; you did not tell me,
nor did I hear of it until today."
27 Abraham took sheep and oxen and gave them to Abimelech, and the two of them
made a covenant.
28 Then Abraham set seven ewe lambs of the flock by themselves.
29 Abimelech said to Abraham, "What do these seven ewe lambs mean, which you have
set by themselves?"
30 He said, "You shall take these seven ewe lambs from my hand so that it may be a
witness to me, that I dug this well."
31 Therefore he called that place Beersheba, because there the two of them took an
oath.
32 So they made a covenant at Beersheba; and Abimelech and Phicol, the commander
of his army, arose and returned to the land of the Philistines.
33 *Abraham* planted a tamarisk tree at Beersheba, and there he called on the name of
the LORD, the Everlasting God.
34 And Abraham sojourned in the land of the Philistines for many days.

The Offering of Isaac

22 Now it came about after these things, that God tested Abraham, and said to him,
"Abraham!" And he said, "Here I am."
2 He said, "Take now your son, your only son, whom you love, Isaac, and go to the
land of Moriah, and offer him there as a burnt offering on one of the mountains of which
I will tell you."
3 So Abraham rose early in the morning and saddled his donkey, and took two of his
young men with him and Isaac his son; and he split wood for the burnt offering, and arose
and went to the place of which God had told him.
4 On the third day Abraham raised his eyes and saw the place from a distance.
5 Abraham said to his young men, "Stay here with the donkey, and I and the lad will
go over there; and we will worship and return to you."
6 Abraham took the wood of the burnt offering and laid it on Isaac his son, and he
took in his hand the fire and the knife. So the two of them walked on together.
7 Isaac spoke to Abraham his father and said, "My father!" And he said, "Here I am,
my son." And he said, "Behold, the fire and the wood, but where is the lamb for the burnt
offering?"
8 Abraham said, "God will provide for Himself the lamb for the burnt offering, my
son." So the two of them walked on together.
9 Then they came to the place of which God had told him; and Abraham built the
altar there and arranged the wood, and bound his son Isaac and laid him on the altar, on
top of the wood.
10 Abraham stretched out his hand and took the knife to slay his son.

21:25 Gen 26:15, 18, 20-22

21:27 Gen 26:31

21:30 Gen 31:48

21:31 Gen 21:14; 26:33

21:33 Gen 12:8; Ex 15:18; Deut 32:40; Ps 90:2; 93:2; Is 40:28; Jer 10:10; Hab 1:12; Heb 13:8

21:34 Gen 22:19

22:1 Deut 8:2, 16; Heb 11:17; James 1:12-14; Gen 22:11

22:2 Gen 22:12, 16; John 3:16; 1 John 4:9; 2 Chr 3:1; Gen 8:20

22:6 John 19:17

22:7 Ex 29:38-42; John 1:29, 36; Rev 13:8

22:9 Gen 22:2; Gen 12:7, 8; 13:18; Heb 11:17-19; James 2:21

21:31 Beersheba, the southernmost city of Israel, lay on the edge of a vast desert that stretched as far as Egypt to the southwest and Mount Sinai to the south. The phrase "from Dan to Beersheba" was often used to describe the traditional boundaries of the promised land (2 Samuel 17:11). Beersheba's southern location and the presence of several wells in the area may explain why Abraham settled there. Beersheba was also the home of Isaac, Abraham's son.

22:1 God tested Abraham, not to trip him and watch him fall, but to deepen his capacity to obey God and thus to develop his character. Just as fire refines ore to extract precious metals, God refines us through difficult circumstances. When we are tested we can complain, or we can try to see how God is stretching us to develop our character.

22:3 That morning Abraham began one of the greatest acts of obedience in recorded history. He traveled 50 miles to Mount Moriah near the site of Jerusalem. Over the years he had learned many tough lessons about the importance of obeying God. This time his obedience was prompt and complete. Obeying God is often a struggle because it may mean giving up something we truly want. We should not expect our obedience to God to be easy or to come naturally.

22:6 We don't know how Abraham "took in his hand the fire," that is, how he carried the fire. Perhaps he carried a live coal or a flint to start a fire.

22:7–8 Why did God ask Abraham to perform human sacrifice? Pagan nations practiced human sacrifice, but God condemned this as a terrible sin (Leviticus 20:1–5). God did not want Isaac to die, but he wanted Abraham to sacrifice Isaac in his heart so it would be clear that Abraham loved God more than he loved his promised and long-awaited son. God was testing Abraham. The purpose of testing is to strengthen our character and deepen our commitment to God and his perfect timing. Through this difficult experience, Abraham strengthened his commitment to obey God. He also learned about God's ability to provide.

22:11 Gen 16:7-11; 21:17, 18

22:12 James 2:21, 22; Gen 22:2, 16

11 But the angel of the LORD called to him from heaven and said, "Abraham, Abraham!" And he said, "Here I am."
12 He said, "Do not stretch out your hand against the lad, and do nothing to him;
for now I know that you fear God, since you have not withheld your son, your only son,
from Me."
13 Then Abraham raised his eyes and looked, and behold, behind *him* a ram caught in

---

ISAAC

A name carries great authority. It sets you apart. It triggers memories. The sound of it calls you to attention anywhere.

Many Bible names accomplished even more. They were often descriptions of important facts about one's past and hopes for the future. The choice of the name *Isaac,* "he laughs," for Abraham and Sarah's son must have created a variety of feelings in them each time it was spoken. At times it must have recalled their shocked laughter at God's announcement that they would be parents in their old age. At other times, it must have brought back the joyful feelings of receiving their long-awaited answer to prayer for a child. Most important, it was a testimony to God's power in making his promise a reality.

In a family of forceful initiators, Isaac was the quiet, "mind-my-own-business" type unless he was specifically called on to take action. He was the protected only child from the time Sarah got rid of Ishmael until Abraham arranged his marriage to Rebekah.

In his own family, Isaac had the patriarchal position, but Rebekah had the power. Rather than stand his ground, Isaac found it easier to compromise or lie to avoid confrontations.

In spite of these shortcomings, Isaac was part of God's plan. The model his father gave him included a great gift of faith in the one true God. God's promise to create a great nation through which he would bless the world was passed on by Isaac to his twin sons.

It is usually not hard to identify with Isaac in his weaknesses. But consider for a moment that God works through people in spite of their shortcomings and, often, through them. As you pray, put into words your desire to be available to God. You will discover that his willingness to use you is even greater than your desire to be used.

Strengths and accomplishments:
- He was the miracle child born to Sarah and Abraham when she was 90 years old and he was 100
- He was the first descendant in fulfillment of God's promise to Abraham
- He seems to have been a caring and consistent husband, at least until his sons were born
- He demonstrated great patience

Weaknesses and mistakes:
- Under pressure he tended to lie
- In conflict he sought to avoid confrontation
- He played favorites between his sons and alienated his wife

Lessons from his life:
- Patience often brings rewards
- Both God's plans and his promises are larger than people
- God keeps his promises! He remains faithful though we are often faithless
- Playing favorites is sure to bring family conflict

Vital statistics:
- Where: The area called the Negev, in the southern part of Palestine, between Kadesh and Shur (Genesis 20:1)
- Occupation: Wealthy livestock owner
- Relatives: Parents: Abraham and Sarah. Half brother: Ishmael. Wife: Rebekah. Sons: Jacob and Esau

Key verse:
"But God said, 'No, but Sarah your wife will bear you a son, and you shall call his name Isaac; and I will establish My covenant with him for an everlasting covenant for his descendants after him' " (Genesis 17:19).

Isaac's story is told in Genesis 17:15—35:29. He is also mentioned in Romans 9:7–8; Hebrews 11:17–20; James 2:21–24.

22:12 It is difficult to let go of what we deeply love. What could be more proper than to love your only child? Yet when we do give to God what he asks, he returns to us far more than we could dream. The spiritual benefits of his blessings far outweigh our sacrifices. Have you withheld your love, your children, or your time from him? Trust him to provide (22:8).

22:13 Notice the parallel between the ram offered on the altar as a substitute for Isaac and Christ offered on the cross as a substitute for us. Whereas God stopped Abraham from sacrificing his son, God did not spare his own Son, Jesus, from dying on the cross. If Jesus had lived, the rest of humankind would have died. God sent his only Son to die for us so that we can be spared from the eternal death we deserve and instead receive eternal life (John 3:16).

the thicket by his horns; and Abraham went and took the ram and offered him up for a
burnt offering in the place of his son.
14 Abraham called the name of that place The LORD Will Provide, as it is said to this
day, "In the mount of the LORD it will be provided."
15 Then the angel of the LORD called to Abraham a second time from heaven,
16 and said, "By Myself I have sworn, declares the LORD, because you have done this
thing and have not withheld your son, your only son,
17 indeed I will greatly bless you, and I will greatly multiply your seed as the stars of
the heavens and as the sand which is on the seashore; and your seed shall possess the
gate of their enemies.
18 "In your seed all the nations of the earth shall be blessed, because you have obeyed
My voice."
19 So Abraham returned to his young men, and they arose and went together to Beersheba; and Abraham lived at Beersheba.
20 Now it came about after these things, that it was told Abraham, saying, "Behold,
Milcah also has borne children to your brother Nahor:
21 Uz his firstborn and Buz his brother and Kemuel the father of Aram
22 and Chesed and Hazo and Pildash and Jidlaph and Bethuel."
23 Bethuel became the father of Rebekah; these eight Milcah bore to Nahor, Abraham's
brother.
24 His concubine, whose name was Reumah, also bore Tebah and Gaham and Tahash
and Maacah.

22:14 Gen 22:8
22:16 Ps 105:9; Luke 1:73; Heb 6:13, 14
22:17 Gen 15:5; 26:4; Jer 33:22; Heb 11:12; Gen 32:12; Gen 24:60
22:18 Gen 12:3; 18:18; Acts 3:25; Gal 3:8, 16; Gen 18:19; 22:3, 10; 26:5
22:19 Gen 22:5
22:20 Gen 11:29
22:23 Gen 24:15

Death and Burial of Sarah

23 Now Sarah lived one hundred and twenty-seven years; *these were* the years of the
life of Sarah.
2 Sarah died in Kiriath-arba (that is, Hebron) in the land of Canaan; and Abraham
went in to mourn for Sarah and to weep for her.
3 Then Abraham rose from before his dead, and spoke to the sons of Heth, saying,
4 "I am a stranger and a sojourner among you; give me a burial site among you that I
may bury my dead out of my sight."
5 The sons of Heth answered Abraham, saying to him,
6 "Hear us, my lord, you are a mighty prince among us; bury your dead in the choicest
of our graves; none of us will refuse you his grave for burying your dead."
7 So Abraham rose and bowed to the people of the land, the sons of Heth.

23:2 Josh 14:15; 15:13; 21:11
23:3 Gen 10:15; 15:20
23:4 Gen 17:8; Lev 25:23; 1 Chr 29:15; Ps 39:12; 105:12; 119:19; Heb 11:9, 13; Acts 7:16; Gen 49:30
23:6 Gen 14:14; 20:7

22:15-18 Abraham received abundant blessings because he did not hold back, but obeyed God. First, God gave Abraham's descendants the ability to conquer their enemies. Second, God promised Abraham children and grandchildren who would in turn bless the whole earth. People's lives would be changed as a result of knowing of the faith of Abraham and his descendants. Most often we think of blessings as gifts to be enjoyed. But when God blesses us, his blessings are intended to overflow to others.

23:1-4 In Abraham's day, death and burial were steeped in ritual and traditions. Failing to honor a dead person demonstrated the greatest possible lack of respect. An improper burial was the equivalent of a curse. Mourning was an essential part of the death ritual. Friends and relatives let out loud cries for the whole neighborhood to hear. Because there were no funeral homes or undertakers, these same friends and relatives helped prepare the body for burial, which usually took place on the same day because of the warm climate.

23:4-6 Abraham was in a foreign land looking for a place to bury his wife. Strangers offered to help him because he was "a mighty prince," and they respected him. Although Abraham had not established roots in the area, his reputation was above reproach. Those who invest their time and money in serving God often earn a pleasant return on their investment—a good reputation and the respect of others.

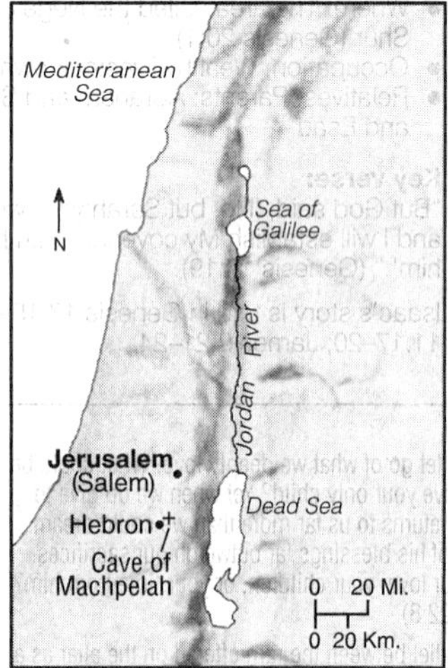

CAVE OF MACHPELAH
Sarah died in Hebron. Abraham bought the cave of Machpelah, near Hebron, as her burial place. Abraham was also buried there, as were his son and grandson, Isaac and Jacob.

23:8 Gen 25:9

8 And he spoke with them, saying, "If it is your wish *for me* to bury my dead out of my
sight, hear me, and approach Ephron the son of Zohar for me,
9 that he may give me the cave of Machpelah which he owns, which is at the end of his
field; for the full price let him give it to me in your presence for a burial site."

23:10 Gen 23:18; 34:20, 24; Ruth 4:1, 11

10 Now Ephron was sitting among the sons of Heth; and Ephron the Hittite answered
Abraham in the hearing of the sons of Heth; *even* of all who went in at the gate of his
city, saying,

23:11 2 Sam 24:21-24

11 "No, my lord, hear me; I give you the field, and I give you the cave that is in it. In the
presence of the sons of my people I give it to you; bury your dead."
12 And Abraham bowed before the people of the land.
13 He spoke to Ephron in the hearing of the people of the land, saying, "If you will
only please listen to me; I will give the price of the field, accept *it* from me that I may
bury my dead there."
14 Then Ephron answered Abraham, saying to him,

23:15 Ex 30:13; Ezek 45:12

15 "My lord, listen to me; a piece of land worth four hundred shekels of silver, what is
that between me and you? So bury your dead."

HAGAR

Escape of some kind is usually the most tempting solution to our problems. In fact, it can become a habit. Hagar was a person who used that approach. When the going got tough, she usually got going—in the other direction.

However, it is worthwhile to note that the biggest challenges Hagar faced were brought on by [other] people's choices. Sarah chose her to bear Abraham's child, and Hagar probably had little to say in the matter.

It isn't hard to understand how Hagar's pregnancy caused her to look down on Sarah. But that brought on hard feelings, and Sarah consequently punished Hagar. This motivated her first escape. When she returned to the family and gave birth to Ishmael, Sarah's continued barrenness must have contributed to bitterness on both sides.

When Isaac was finally born, Sarah looked for any excuse to have Hagar and Ishmael sent away. She found it when she caught Ishmael teasing Isaac. In the desert, out of water and facing the death of her son, Hagar once again tried to escape. She walked away so she wouldn't have to watch her son die. Once again, God graciously intervened.

Have you noticed how patiently God operates to make our escape attempts fail? Have you begun to learn that escape is only a temporary solution? God's continual desire is for us to face our problems with his help. We experience his help most clearly in and through conflicts and difficulties, not away from them. Are there problems in your life for which you've been using the "Hagar solution"? Choose one of those problems, ask for God's help, and begin to face it today.

Strength and accomplishment:
- Mother of Abraham's first child, Ishmael, who became founder of the Arab nations

Weaknesses and mistakes:
- When faced with problems, she tended to run away
- Her pregnancy brought out strong feelings of pride and arrogance

Lessons from her life:
- God is faithful to his plan and promises, even when humans complicate the process
- God shows himself as one who knows us and wants to be known by us
- The New Testament uses Hagar as a symbol of those who would pursue favor with God by their own efforts, rather than by trusting in his mercy and forgiveness

Vital statistics:
- Where: Canaan and Egypt
- Occupation: Servant, mother
- Relatives: Son: Ishmael

Key verse:
"Then the angel of the LORD said to her, 'Return to your mistress, and submit yourself to her authority' " (Genesis 16:9).

Hagar's story is told in Genesis 16—21. She is also mentioned in Galatians 4:24-25.

23:10-15 The polite interchange between Abraham and Ephron was typical of bargaining at that time. Ephron graciously offered to give his land to Abraham at no charge; Abraham insisted on paying for it; Ephron politely mentioned the price but said, in effect, that it wasn't important; Abraham paid the 400 shekels of silver. Both men knew what was going on as they went through the bargaining process. If Abraham had accepted the land as a gift when it was offered, he would have insulted Ephron, who then would have rescinded his offer. Many Middle Eastern shopkeepers still follow this ritual with their customers.

16 Abraham listened to Ephron; and Abraham weighed out for Ephron the silver which
he had named in the hearing of the sons of Heth, four hundred shekels of silver, commercial standard.
17 So Ephron's field, which was in Machpelah, which faced Mamre, the field and cave
which was in it, and all the trees which were in the field, that were within all the confines
of its border, were deeded over
18 to Abraham for a possession in the presence of the sons of Heth, before all who
went in at the gate of his city.
19 After this, Abraham buried Sarah his wife in the cave of the field at Machpelah facing
Mamre (that is, Hebron) in the land of Canaan.
20 So the field and the cave that is in it, were deeded over to Abraham for a burial site
by the sons of Heth.

6. Isaac and Rebekah

A Bride for Isaac

24 Now Abraham was old, advanced in age; and the LORD had blessed Abraham in
every way.
2 Abraham said to his servant, the oldest of his household, who had charge of all that
he owned, "Please place your hand under my thigh,
3 and I will make you swear by the LORD, the God of heaven and the God of earth,
that you shall not take a wife for my son from the daughters of the Canaanites, among
whom I live,
4 but you will go to my country and to my relatives, and take a wife for my son Isaac."
5 The servant said to him, "Suppose the woman is not willing to follow me to this land;
should I take your son back to the land from where you came?"
6 Then Abraham said to him, "Beware that you do not take my son back there!
7 "The LORD, the God of heaven, who took me from my father's house and from the
land of my birth, and who spoke to me and who swore to me, saying, 'To your descendants I will give this land,' He will send His angel before you, and you will take a wife for
my son from there.
8 "But if the woman is not willing to follow you, then you will be free from this my
oath; only do not take my son back there."
9 So the servant placed his hand under the thigh of Abraham his master, and swore
to him concerning this matter.
10 Then the servant took ten camels from the camels of his master, and set out with a
variety of good things of his master's in his hand; and he arose and went to Mesopotamia, to the city of Nahor.
11 He made the camels kneel down outside the city by the well of water at evening time,
the time when women go out to draw water.
12 He said, "O LORD, the God of my master Abraham, please grant me success today,
and show lovingkindness to my master Abraham.

23:16 2 Sam 14:26; Jer 32:9, 10; Zech 11:12
23:17 Gen 25:9; 49:29, 30; 50:13
23:18 Gen 23:10
23:20 Jer 32:10-14
24:1 Gen 18:11; Gen 12:2; 13:2; 24:35; Gal 3:9
24:2 Gen 39:4-6; Gen 24:9; 47:29
24:3 Gen 14:19, 22; Deut 7:3; 2 Cor 6:14-17; Gen 10:15-19; 26:34, 35; 28:1, 8
24:4 Gen 12:1; Heb 11:15
24:6 Gen 24:8
24:7 Gen 24:3; Gen 12:7; 13:15; 15:18; Ex 32:13; Gen 16:7; 21:17; 22:11; Ex 23:20, 23
24:8 Josh 2:17-20; Gen 24:6
24:9 Gen 24:2
24:10 Gen 24:22, 53; Gen 11:31, 32
24:11 Gen 24:42; Ex 2:16; 1 Sam 9:11
24:12 Gen 24:27, 42, 48; 26:24; Ex 3:6, 15; Gen 27:20

23:16 Four hundred shekels of silver was a high price for the piece of property Abraham bought. The Hittites weren't thrilled about foreigners buying their property, so Abraham had little bargaining leverage.

Ephron asked an outrageous price. The custom of the day was to ask double the fair market value of the land, fully expecting the buyer to offer half the stated price. Abraham, however, did not bargain. He simply paid the initial price. He was not trying to take anything he didn't deserve. Even though God had promised the land to Abraham, he did not just take it away from Ephron.

24:2, 9 In Abraham's culture, putting a hand under the thigh was how an agreement was sealed or a covenant ratified. To accomplish the same purpose, we shake hands, swear oaths, or sign documents in the presence of a notary public.

24:4 Abraham wanted Isaac to marry within the family. This was a common and acceptable practice at this time that had the added advantage of avoiding intermarriage with pagan neighbors. A son's wife was usually chosen by the parents. It was common for a woman to be married in her early teens although Rebekah was probably older.

24:6 Abraham wanted Isaac to stay in Canaan, but he didn't want him to marry one of the local girls. This contrasts to the way Hagar selected a wife for Ishmael in 21:21. To have Isaac stay and marry, or send him back to marry a relative would have been easier. But Abraham wanted to obey God in the *who* as well as in the *where.* Make your obedience full and complete.

24:11 The well, the chief source of water for an entire village, was usually located outside town along the main road. Many people had to walk a mile or more for their water. They could use only what they could carry home. Farmers and shepherds would come from nearby fields to draw water for their animals. The well was a good place to meet new friends or to chat with old ones. Rebekah would have visited the well twice daily to draw water for her family.

24:12 Abraham's servant asked God for guidance in this very important task. Obviously Eliezer had learned much about faith and about God from his master (15:2). What are your family members, friends, and associates learning about God from watching you? Be like Abraham, setting an example of dependent faith. And be like Eliezer, asking God for guidance before any venture.

24:13 Gen 24:43

13 "Behold, I am standing by the spring, and the daughters of the men of the city are coming out to draw water;
14 now may it be that the girl to whom I say, 'Please let down your jar so that I may drink,' and who answers, 'Drink, and I will water your camels also'—*may* she *be the one* whom You have appointed for Your servant Isaac; and by this I will know that You have shown lovingkindness to my master."

24:15 Gen 24:45; Gen 22:20, 23; Gen 11:29

Rebekah Is Chosen

15 Before he had finished speaking, behold, Rebekah who was born to Bethuel the son of Milcah, the wife of Abraham's brother Nahor, came out with her jar on her shoulder.

REBEKAH

Some people are initiators. They help get the ball rolling. Rebekah would easily stand out in this group. Her life was characterized by initiative. When she saw a need she took action, even though the action was not always right.

It was Rebekah's initiative that first caught the attention of Eliezer, the servant Abraham sent to find a wife for Isaac. It was common courtesy to give a drink to a stranger, but it took added character to also fetch water for ten thirsty camels. Later, after hearing the details of Eliezer's mission, Rebekah was immediately willing to be Isaac's bride.

Several later events help us see how initiative can be misdirected. Rebekah was aware that God's plan would be channeled through Jacob, not Esau (Genesis 25:23). So not only did Jacob become her favorite; she actually planned ways to ensure that he would overshadow his older twin. Meanwhile, Isaac preferred Esau. This created a conflict between the couple. She felt justified in deceiving her husband when the time came to bless the sons, and her ingenious plan was carried out to perfection.

Most of the time we try to justify the things we choose to do. Often we attempt to add God's approval to our actions. While it is true that our actions will not spoil God's plan, it is also true that we are responsible for what we do and must always be cautious about our motives. When thinking about a course of action, are you simply seeking God's stamp of approval on something you've already decided to do? Or are you willing to set the plan aside if the principles and commands of God's Word are against the action? Initiative and action are admirable and right when they are controlled by God's wisdom.

Strengths and accomplishments:
- When confronted with a need, she took immediate action
- She was accomplishment oriented

Weaknesses and mistakes:
- Her initiative was not always balanced by wisdom
- She favored one of her sons
- She deceived her husband

Lessons from her life:
- Our actions must be guided by God's Word
- God makes use even of our mistakes in his plan
- Parental favoritism hurts a family

Vital statistics:
- Where: Haran, Canaan
- Occupation: Wife, mother, household manager
- Relatives: Grandparents: Nahor and Milcah. Father: Bethuel. Husband: Isaac. Brother: Laban. Twin sons: Esau and Jacob

Key verses:
"Then Isaac brought her into his mother Sarah's tent, and he took Rebekah, and she became his wife, and he loved her; thus Isaac was comforted after his mother's death" (Genesis 24:67). "Now Isaac loved Esau, because he had a taste for game, but Rebekah loved Jacob" (Genesis 25:28).

Rebekah's story is told in Genesis 24—49. She is also mentioned in Romans 9:10.

24:14 Was it right for Abraham's servant to ask God for such a specific sign? The sign he requested was only slightly out of the ordinary. The hospitality of the day required women at the well to offer water to weary travelers, but not to their animals. Eliezer was simply asking God to show him a woman with an attitude of service—someone who would go beyond the expected. An offer to water his camels would indicate that kind of attitude. Eliezer did not ask for a woman with looks or wealth. He knew the importance of having the right heart, and he asked God to help him with his task.

24:15–16 Rebekah had physical beauty, but the servant was looking for a sign of inner beauty. Appearance is important to us, and we spend time and money improving it. But how much effort do we put into developing our inner beauty? Patience, kindness, and joy are the beauty treatments that help us become truly lovely—on the inside.

16 The girl was very beautiful, a virgin, and no man had had relations with her; and she
went down to the spring and filled her jar and came up.
17 Then the servant ran to meet her, and said, "Please let me drink a little water from
your jar."
18 She said, "Drink, my lord"; and she quickly lowered her jar to her hand, and gave
him a drink.
19 Now when she had finished giving him a drink, she said, "I will draw also for your
camels until they have finished drinking."
20 So she quickly emptied her jar into the trough, and ran back to the well to draw, and
she drew for all his camels.
21 Meanwhile, the man was gazing at her in silence, to know whether the LORD had
made his journey successful or not.
22 When the camels had finished drinking, the man took a gold ring weighing a half-
shekel and two bracelets for her wrists weighing ten shekels in gold,
23 and said, "Whose daughter are you? Please tell me, is there room for us to lodge in
your father's house?"
24 She said to him, "I am the daughter of Bethuel, the son of Milcah, whom she bore
to Nahor."
25 Again she said to him, "We have plenty of both straw and feed, and room to lodge in."
26 Then the man bowed low and worshiped the LORD.
27 He said, "Blessed be the LORD, the God of my master Abraham, who has not forsaken His lovingkindness and His truth toward my master; as for me, the LORD has guided
me in the way to the house of my master's brothers."
28 Then the girl ran and told her mother's household about these things.
29 Now Rebekah had a brother whose name was Laban; and Laban ran outside to the
man at the spring.
30 When he saw the ring and the bracelets on his sister's wrists, and when he heard the
words of Rebekah his sister, saying, "This is what the man said to me," he went to the
man; and behold, he was standing by the camels at the spring.
31 And he said, "Come in, blessed of the LORD! Why do you stand outside since I have
prepared the house, and a place for the camels?"
32 So the man entered the house. Then Laban unloaded the camels, and he gave straw
and feed to the camels, and water to wash his feet and the feet of the men who were
with him.
33 But when *food* was set before him to eat, he said, "I will not eat until I have told my
business." And he said, "Speak on."
34 So he said, "I am Abraham's servant.

24:16 Gen 12:11; 26:7; 29:17
24:17 John 4:7
24:18 Gen 24:14, 46
24:19 Gen 24:14
24:21 Gen 24:12-14, 27, 52
24:22 Gen 24:47; Ex 32:2, 3
24:24 Gen 24:15
24:26 Gen 24:48, 52; Ex 4:31
24:27 Gen 24:12, 42, 48; Ex 18:10; Ruth 4:14; 1 Sam 25:32; 2 Sam 18:28; Luke 1:68; Gen 32:10; Ps 98:3; Gen 24:21, 48
24:28 Gen 29:12
24:29 Gen 29:5, 13
24:31 Gen 29:13; Gen 26:29; Ruth 3:10; Ps 115:15; Gen 18:3-5; 19:2, 3
24:32 Gen 43:24; Judg 19:21
24:34 Gen 24:2

ELIEZER: PROFILE OF A TRUE SERVANT

Have you ever approached a responsibility with this kind of single-mindedness and careful planning, while ultimately depending on God?

24:3, 9	Accepted the challenge
24:5	Examined alternatives
24:9	Promised to follow instructions
24:12–14	Made a plan
24:12–14	Submitted the plan to God
24:12–14	Prayed for guidance
24:12–14	Devised a strategy with room for God to operate
24:21	Waited
24:21	Watched closely
24:26	Accepted the answer thankfully
24:34–49	Explained the situation to concerned parties
24:56	Refused unnecessary delay
24:66	Followed through with entire plan

24:18–21 Rebekah's servant spirit was clearly demonstrated as she willingly and quickly drew water for Eliezer and his camels. The pots used for carrying water were large and heavy. It took a lot of water to satisfy a thirsty camel—up to 25 gallons per camel after a week's travel. Seeing Rebekah go to work, Eliezer knew this was a woman with a heart for doing far more than the bare minimum. Do you have a servant spirit? When asked to help or when you see a need, go beyond the minimum.

24:26–27 As soon as Abraham's servant knew that God had answered his prayer, he prayed and thanked God for his goodness and guidance. God will also use and lead us if we are available like Eliezer. And our first response should be praise and thanksgiving that God would choose to work in and through us.

35 "The LORD has greatly blessed my master, so that he has become rich; and He has
given him flocks and herds, and silver and gold, and servants and maids, and camels and
donkeys.
36 "Now Sarah my master's wife bore a son to my master in her old age, and he has
given him all that he has.
37 "My master made me swear, saying, 'You shall not take a wife for my son from the
daughters of the Canaanites, in whose land I live;
38 but you shall go to my father's house and to my relatives, and take a wife for my son.'
39 "I said to my master, 'Suppose the woman does not follow me.'
40 "He said to me, 'The LORD, before whom I have walked, will send His angel with
you to make your journey successful, and you will take a wife for my son from my relatives and from my father's house;
41 then you will be free from my oath, when you come to my relatives; and if they do
not give her to you, you will be free from my oath.'
42 "So I came today to the spring, and said, 'O LORD, the God of my master Abraham,
if now You will make my journey on which I go successful;
43 behold, I am standing by the spring, and may it be that the maiden who comes out
to draw, and to whom I say, "Please let me drink a little water from your jar";
44 and she will say to me, "You drink, and I will draw for your camels also"; let her be
the woman whom the LORD has appointed for my master's son.'
45 "Before I had finished speaking in my heart, behold, Rebekah came out with her jar
on her shoulder, and went down to the spring and drew, and I said to her, 'Please let me
drink.'
46 "She quickly lowered her jar from her *shoulder,* and said, 'Drink, and I will water your
camels also'; so I drank, and she watered the camels also.
47 "Then I asked her, and said, 'Whose daughter are you?' And she said, 'The daughter
of Bethuel, Nahor's son, whom Milcah bore to him'; and I put the ring on her nose, and
the bracelets on her wrists.
48 "And I bowed low and worshiped the LORD, and blessed the LORD, the God of my
master Abraham, who had guided me in the right way to take the daughter of my master's
kinsman for his son.
49 "So now if you are going to [24]deal kindly and truly with my master, tell me; and if not,
let me know, that I may turn to the right hand or the left."
50 Then Laban and Bethuel replied, "The matter comes from the LORD; *so* we cannot
speak to you bad or good.
51 "Here is Rebekah before you, take *her* and go, and let her be the wife of your master's
son, as the LORD has spoken."
52 When Abraham's servant heard their words, he bowed himself to the ground before the LORD.
53 The servant brought out articles of silver and articles of gold, and garments, and
gave them to Rebekah; he also gave precious things to her brother and to her mother.
54 Then he and the men who were with him ate and drank and spent the night. When
they arose in the morning, he said, "Send me away to my master."
55 But her brother and her mother said, "Let the girl stay with us *a few* days, say ten;
afterward she may go."
56 He said to them, "Do not delay me, since the LORD has prospered my way. Send
me away that I may go to my master."
57 And they said, "We will call the girl and consult her wishes."
58 Then they called Rebekah and said to her, "Will you go with this man?" And she
said, "I will go."
59 Thus they sent away their sister Rebekah and her nurse with Abraham's servant and
his men.
60 They blessed Rebekah and said to her,
"May you, our sister,

24 Lit *show lovingkindness and truth*

24:35 Gen 24:1; Gen 13:2
24:36 Gen 21:1-7; Gen 25:5
24:37 Gen 24:2-4
24:39 Gen 24:5
24:40 Gen 24:7; Gen 5:22, 24; 17:1; Ex 23:20
24:41 Gen 24:8
24:42 Gen 24:11, 12; Neh 1:11
24:43 Gen 24:13; Gen 24:14
24:45 1 Sam 1:13; Gen 24:15; Gen 24:17
24:46 Gen 24:18, 19
24:47 Gen 24:23, 24; Ezek 16:11, 12
24:48 Gen 24:26, 52; Gen 24:27; Ps 32:8; 48:14; Is 48:17
24:49 Gen 47:29; Josh 2:14
24:50 Ps 118:23; Mark 12:11; Gen 31:24, 29
24:52 Gen 24:26, 48
24:53 Gen 24:10, 22; Ex 3:22; 11:2; 12:35
24:54 Gen 24:56, 59; 30:25
24:55 Judg 19:4
24:56 Gen 24:40
24:59 Gen 35:8
24:60 Gen 17:16; Gen 22:17

24:42, 48 When Eliezer told his story to Laban, he spoke openly of God and his goodness. Often we do the opposite, afraid that we will be misunderstood or rejected or seen as too religious. Instead, we should share openly what God is doing for us.

24:60 "May your descendants possess the gate of those who hate them" means "May you overcome all your enemies."

Become thousands of ten thousands,
And may your descendants possess
The gate of those who hate them."
61 Then Rebekah arose with her maids, and they mounted the camels and followed
the man. So the servant took Rebekah and departed.

Isaac Marries Rebekah

62 Now Isaac had come from going to Beer-lahai-roi; for he was living in the Negev.
63 Isaac went out to meditate in the field toward evening; and he lifted up his eyes and
looked, and behold, camels were coming.
64 Rebekah lifted up her eyes, and when she saw Isaac she dismounted from the camel.
65 She said to the servant, "Who is that man walking in the field to meet us?" And the
servant said, "He is my master." Then she took her veil and covered herself.
66 The servant told Isaac all the things that he had done.
67 Then Isaac brought her into his mother Sarah's tent, and he took Rebekah, and she
became his wife, and he loved her; thus Isaac was comforted after his mother's death.

24:62 Gen 16:14; 25:11; Gen 20:1
24:63 Josh 1:8; Ps 1:2; 77:12; 119:15, 27, 48; 143:5; 145:5; Gen 18:2
24:67 Gen 25:20; Gen 29:18; Gen 23:1, 2

7. Abraham dies

25 Now Abraham took another wife, whose name was Keturah.
2 She bore to him Zimran and Jokshan and Medan and Midian and Ishbak
and Shuah.
3 Jokshan became the father of Sheba and Dedan. And the sons of Dedan were
Asshurim and Letushim and Leummim.
4 The sons of Midian *were* Ephah and Epher and Hanoch and Abida and Eldaah. All
these *were* the sons of Keturah.
5 Now Abraham gave all that he had to Isaac;
6 but to the sons of his concubines, Abraham gave gifts while he was still living, and
sent them away from his son Isaac eastward, to the land of the east.
7 These are all the years of Abraham's life that he lived, one hundred and seventy-
five years.
8 Abraham breathed his last and died in a ripe old age, an old man and satisfied *with
life;* and he was gathered to his people.
9 Then his sons Isaac and Ishmael buried him in the cave of Machpelah, in the field
of Ephron the son of Zohar the Hittite, facing Mamre,
10 the field which Abraham purchased from the sons of Heth; there Abraham was
buried with Sarah his wife.
11 It came about after the death of Abraham, that God blessed his son Isaac; and Isaac
lived by Beer-lahai-roi.

Descendants of Ishmael

12 Now these are *the records of* the generations of Ishmael, Abraham's son, whom Hagar
the Egyptian, Sarah's maid, bore to Abraham;
13 and these are the names of the sons of Ishmael, by their names, in the order of their
birth: Nebaioth, the firstborn of Ishmael, and Kedar and Adbeel and Mibsam
14 and Mishma and Dumah and Massa,
15 Hadad and Tema, Jetur, Naphish and Kedemah.
16 These are the sons of Ishmael and these are their names, by their villages, and by
their camps; twelve princes according to their tribes.
17 These are the years of the life of Ishmael, one hundred and thirty-seven years; and
he breathed his last and died, and was gathered to his people.
18 They settled from Havilah to Shur which is east of Egypt as one goes toward Assyria;
he settled in defiance of all his relatives.

25:2 1 Chr 1:32, 33
25:5 Gen 24:35, 36
25:6 Gen 21:14
25:7 Gen 12:4
25:8 Gen 15:15; 47:8, 9; Gen 25:17; 35:29; 49:29, 33
25:9 Gen 23:17, 18; 49:29, 30; 50:13
25:10 Gen 23:3-16
25:11 Gen 12:2, 3; 22:17; 26:3; Gen 16:14; 24:62
25:12 Gen 16:15
25:13 1 Chr 1:29-31
25:16 Gen 17:20
25:17 Gen 16:16; Gen 25:8; 49:33
25:18 1 Sam 15:7; Gen 20:1; Gen 16:12

24:64–65 When Rebekah learned that the man coming to greet them was Isaac, her husband-to-be, she followed two oriental customs. She dismounted from her camel to show respect, and she placed a veil over her face as a bride.

25:1–6 Abraham took another wife, Keturah, after Sarah died. Although the sons and grandson of Abraham and Keturah received many gifts from Abraham, all his property and authority went to Isaac, his principle heir.

E. THE STORY OF ISAAC (25:19—28:9)

Isaac inherited everything from his father, including God's promise to make his descendants into a great nation. As a boy, Isaac did not resist as his father prepared to sacrifice him, and as a man, he gladly accepted the wife that others chose for him. Through Isaac, we learn how to let God guide our life and place his will ahead of our own.

25:19 Matt 1:2

25:20 Gen 24:15, 29, 67; Gen 22:23; Gen 24:29

25:21 1 Sam 1:17; 1 Chr 5:20; 2 Chr 33:13; Ezra 8:23; Ps 127:3; Rom 9:10

1. Jacob and Essau

Isaac's Sons

19 Now these are *the records of* the generations of Isaac, Abraham's son: Abraham became the father of Isaac;
20 and Isaac was forty years old when he took Rebekah, the daughter of Bethuel the Aramean of Paddan-aram, the sister of Laban the Aramean, to be his wife.
21 Isaac prayed to the LORD on behalf of his wife, because she was barren; and the LORD answered him and Rebekah his wife conceived.

Common sense isn't all that common. In fact, the common thread in many decisions is that they don't make sense. Esau's life was filled with choices he must have regretted bitterly. He appears to have been a person who found it hard to consider consequences, reacting to the need of the moment without realizing what he was giving up to meet that need. Trading his birthright for a bowl of stew was the clearest example of this weakness. He also chose wives in direct opposition to his parents' wishes. He learned the hard way.

What are you willing to trade for the things you want? Do you find yourself, at times, willing to negotiate [anything] for what you feel you need *now*? Do your family, spouse, integrity, body, or soul get included in these deals? Do you sometimes feel that the important parts of life escaped while you were grabbing for something else?

If so, your initial response, like Esau's, may be deep anger. In itself that isn't wrong, as long as you direct the energy of that anger toward a solution and not toward yourself or others as the cause of the problem. Your greatest need is to find a focal point other than "what I need now." The only worthy focal point is God. A relationship with him will not only give an ultimate purpose to your life; it will also be a daily guideline for living. Meet him in the pages of the Bible.

Strengths and accomplishments:
- Ancestor of the Edomites
- Known for his archery skill
- Able to forgive after explosive anger

Weaknesses and mistakes:
- When faced with important decisions, tended to choose according to the immediate need rather than the long-range effect
- Angered his parents by poor marriage choices

Lessons from his life:
- God allows certain events in our lives to accomplish his overall purposes, but we are still responsible for our actions
- Consequences are important to consider
- It is possible to have great anger and yet not sin

Vital statistics:
- Where: Canaan
- Occupation: Skillful hunter
- Relatives: Parents: Isaac and Rebekah. Brother: Jacob. Wives: Judith, Basemath, and Mahalath

Key verses:
"Pursue peace with all men, and the sanctification without which no one will see the Lord. See to it that no one comes short of the grace of God; that no root of bitterness springing up causes trouble, and by it many be defiled; that there be no immoral or godless person like Esau, who sold his own birthright for a single meal. For you know that even afterwards, when he desired to inherit the blessing, he was rejected, for he found no place for repentance, though he sought for it with tears" (Hebrews 12:14–17).

Esau's story is told in Genesis 25—36. He is also mentioned in Malachi 1:2–3; Romans 9:13; Hebrews 12:16–17.

25:21 As Isaac pleaded with God for children, so the Bible encourages us to ask and even plead for our most personal and important requests. God wants to grant our requests, but he wants us to ask him. Even then, as Isaac learned, God may decide to withhold his answer for a while in order to (1) deepen our insight into what we really need, (2) broaden our appreciation for his answers, or (3) allow us to mature so we can use his gifts more wisely.

22 But the children struggled together within her; and she said, "If it is so, why then
am I *this way?*" So she went to inquire of the LORD.
23 The LORD said to her,
"Two nations are in your womb;
And two peoples will be separated from your body;
And one people shall be stronger than the other;
And the older shall serve the younger."
24 When her days to be delivered were fulfilled, behold, there were twins in her womb.
25 Now the first came forth red, all over like a hairy garment; and they named him
Esau.
26 Afterward his brother came forth with his hand holding on to Esau's heel, so his
name was called [25]Jacob; and Isaac was sixty years old when she gave birth to them.
27 When the boys grew up, Esau became a skillful hunter, a man of the field, but Jacob
was a peaceful man, living in tents.
28 Now Isaac loved Esau, because he had a taste for game, but Rebekah loved Jacob.
29 When Jacob had cooked stew, Esau came in from the field and he was famished;
30 and Esau said to Jacob, "Please let me have a swallow of that red stuff there, for I
am famished." Therefore his name was called [26]Edom.
31 But Jacob said, "First sell me your birthright."
32 Esau said, "Behold, I am about to die; so of what *use* then is the birthright to me?"
33 And Jacob said, "First swear to me"; so he swore to him, and sold his birthright to
Jacob.
34 Then Jacob gave Esau bread and lentil stew; and he ate and drank, and rose and
went on his way. Thus Esau despised his birthright.

2. Isaac and Abimelech

Isaac Settles in Gerar

26 Now there was a famine in the land, besides the previous famine that had occurred
in the days of Abraham. So Isaac went to Gerar, to Abimelech king of the Philistines.
2 The LORD appeared to him and said, "Do not go down to Egypt; stay in the land of
which I shall tell you.
3 "Sojourn in this land and I will be with you and bless you, for to you and to your descendants I will give all these lands, and I will establish the oath which I swore to your
father Abraham.
4 "I will multiply your descendants as the stars of heaven, and will give your descendants all these lands; and by your descendants all the nations of the earth shall be blessed;
5 because Abraham obeyed Me and kept My charge, My commandments, My statutes and My laws."
6 So Isaac lived in Gerar.

25:22 1 Sam 9:9; 10:22
25:23 Gen 17:4-6, 16; Num 20:14; Deut 2:4, 8; Gen 27:29; Gen 27:40; Mal 1:2, 3; Rom 9:12
25:25 Gen 27:11
25:26 Hos 12:3; Gen 27:36; Gen 25:20
25:27 Heb 11:9
25:28 Gen 27:19; Gen 27:6-10
25:29 2 Kin 4:38
25:31 Deut 21:16, 17; 1 Chr 5:1, 2
25:33 Heb 12:16
26:1 Gen 12:10; Gen 20:1, 2
26:2 Gen 12:7; 17:1; 18:1; Gen 12:1
26:3 Gen 26:24; 28:15; 31:3; Gen 12:2; Gen 12:7; 13:15; 15:18; Gen 22:16-18; Ps 105:9
26:4 Gen 15:5; 22:17; Ex 32:13; Gen 22:18; Gal 3:8
26:5 Gen 22:16

25 I.e. one who takes by the heel or supplants **26** I.e. red

---

25:31 A birthright was a special honor given to the firstborn son. It included a double portion of the family inheritance along with the honor of one day becoming the family's leader. The oldest son could sell his birthright or give it away if he chose, but in so doing, he would lose both material goods and his leadership position. By trading his birthright, Esau showed complete disregard for the spiritual blessings that would have come his way if he had kept it. In effect, Esau "despised" his birthright (25:34).

25:32–33 Esau traded the lasting benefits of his birthright for the immediate pleasure of food. He acted on impulse, satisfying his immediate desires without pausing to consider the long-range consequences of what he was about to do. We can fall into the same trap. When we see something we want, our first impulse is to get it. At first we feel intensely satisfied and sometimes even powerful because we have obtained what we set out to get. But immediate pleasure often loses sight of the future. We can avoid making Esau's mistake by comparing the short-term satisfaction with its long-range consequences before we act.

Esau exaggerated his hunger. "I am about to die," he said. This thought made his choice much easier because if he was starving, what good was an inheritance anyway? The pressure of the moment distorted his perspective and made his decision seem urgent. We often experience similar pressures. For example, when we feel sexual pressure, a marriage vow may seem unimportant. We might feel such great pressure in one area that nothing else seems to matter and we lose our perspective. Getting through that short, pressure-filled moment is often the most difficult part of overcoming a temptation.

26:1 The Philistine tribe would become one of Israel's fiercest enemies. The Philistines were one group of a number of migrating sea peoples from the Aegean Sea who settled in Palestine. They arrived by way of Crete and Cyprus and were used as mercenaries by Canaanite rulers. These people, living along the southwest coast, were few but ferocious in battle. Although friendly to Isaac, this small group was the forerunner of the nation that would plague Israel during the time of Joshua, the judges, and David. This King Abimelech was not the same Abimelech that Abraham encountered (chapter 22). *Abimelech* may have been a dynastic name of the Philistine rulers.

26:7 Gen 12:13; 20:2, 12; Prov 29:25; Gen 12:11; 24:16; 29:17

7 When the men of the place asked about his wife, he said, "She is my sister," for he
was afraid to say, "my wife," *thinking,* "the men of the place might kill me on account of
Rebekah, for she is beautiful."
8 It came about, when he had been there a long time, that Abimelech king of the Philistines looked out through a window, and saw, and behold, Isaac was caressing his wife
Rebekah.
9 Then Abimelech called Isaac and said, "Behold, certainly she is your wife! How then
did you say, 'She is my sister'?" And Isaac said to him, "Because I said, 'I might die on
account of her.' "

26:10 Gen 20:9

10 Abimelech said, "What is this you have done to us? One of the people might easily
have lain with your wife, and you would have brought guilt upon us."

26:11 Ps 105:15

11 So Abimelech charged all the people, saying, "He who touches this man or his wife
shall surely be put to death."

26:12 Gen 24:1; 26:3; Job 42:12; Prov 10:22

12 Now Isaac sowed in that land and reaped in the same year a hundredfold. And the
LORD blessed him,

26:13 Prov 10:22

13 and the man became rich, and continued to grow richer until he became very wealthy;

26:14 Gen 24:35; 25:5

14 for he had possessions of flocks and herds and a great household, so that the Philistines envied him.

26:15 Gen 21:25, 30

15 Now all the wells which his father's servants had dug in the days of Abraham his
father, the Philistines stopped up by filling them with earth.

26:16 Ex 1:9

16 Then Abimelech said to Isaac, "Go away from us, for you are too powerful for us."
17 And Isaac departed from there and camped in the valley of Gerar, and settled there.

Quarrel over the Wells

18 Then Isaac dug again the wells of water which had been dug in the days of his father
Abraham, for the Philistines had stopped them up after the death of Abraham; and he
gave them the same names which his father had given them.
19 But when Isaac's servants dug in the valley and found there a well of flowing water,

26:20 Gen 21:25

20 the herdsmen of Gerar quarreled with the herdsmen of Isaac, saying, "The water is
ours!" So he named the well Esek, because they contended with him.

26:22 Ps 4:1; Is 54:2, 3; Gen 17:6; Ex 1:7

21 Then they dug another well, and they quarreled over it too, so he named it Sitnah.
22 He moved away from there and dug another well, and they did not quarrel over it;

ISAAC'S MOVE TO GERAR
Isaac had settled near Beer-lahai-roi ("the well of the Living One who sees me"), where his sons, Jacob and Esau, were born. A famine drove him to Gerar. But when he became wealthy, his jealous neighbors asked him to leave. From Gerar he moved to Beersheba.

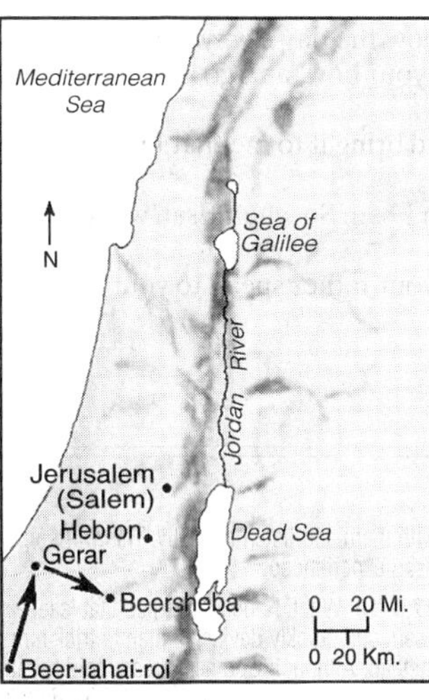

26:7–11 Isaac was afraid that the men in Gerar would kill him to get his beautiful wife, Rebekah. So he lied, claiming that Rebekah was his sister. Where did he learn that trick? He may have known about the actions of his father, Abraham (see 12:10–14 and 20:1–4). Parents help shape the world's future by the way they shape their children's values. The first step toward helping children live rightly is for the parents to live rightly. Your actions are often copied by those closest to you. What kind of example are you setting for your children?

26:12–16 God kept his promise to bless Isaac. The neighboring Philistines grew jealous because everything Isaac did seemed to go right. So they stopped up his wells and tried to get rid of him. Jealousy is a dividing force strong enough to tear apart the mightiest of nations or the closest of friends. It forces you to separate yourself from what you were longing for in the first place. When you find yourself becoming jealous of others, try thanking God for their good fortune. Before striking out in anger, consider what you could lose—a friend, a job, a spouse?

26:17–18 The desolate Gerar area was located on the edge of a desert. Water was as precious as gold. If someone dug a well, he was staking a claim to the land. Some wells had locks to keep thieves from stealing the water. To "stop" or plug up someone's well was an act of war; it was one of the most serious crimes in the land. Isaac had every right to fight back when the Philistines ruined his wells, and yet he chose to keep the peace. In the end, the Philistines respected him for his patience.

26:17–22 Three times Isaac and his men dug new wells. When the first two disputes arose, Isaac moved on. Finally there was enough room for everyone. Rather than start a huge conflict, Isaac compromised for the sake of peace. Would you be willing to forsake an important position or valuable possession to keep peace? Ask God for the wisdom to know when to withdraw and when to stand and fight.

so he named it Rehoboth, for he said, "At last the LORD has made room for us, and we
will be fruitful in the land."
23 Then he went up from there to Beersheba.
24 The LORD appeared to him the same night and said,
"I am the God of your father Abraham;
Do not fear, for I am with you.
I will bless you, and multiply your descendants,
For the sake of My servant Abraham."
25 So he built an altar there and called upon the name of the LORD, and pitched his
tent there; and there Isaac's servants dug a well.

Covenant with Abimelech

26 Then Abimelech came to him from Gerar with his adviser Ahuzzath and Phicol the
commander of his army.
27 Isaac said to them, "Why have you come to me, since you hate me and have sent me
away from you?"
28 They said, "We see plainly that the LORD has been with you; so we said, 'Let there
now be an oath between us, *even* between you and us, and let us make a covenant with you,
29 that you will do us no harm, just as we have not touched you and have done to you
nothing but good and have sent you away in peace. You are now the blessed of the
LORD.'"
30 Then he made them a feast, and they ate and drank.
31 In the morning they arose early and exchanged oaths; then Isaac sent them away
and they departed from him in peace.
32 Now it came about on the same day, that Isaac's servants came in and told him about
the well which they had dug, and said to him, "We have found water."
33 So he called it Shibah; therefore the name of the city is Beersheba to this day.
34 When Esau was forty years old he married Judith the daughter of Beeri the Hittite,
and Basemath the daughter of Elon the Hittite;
35 and they [27]brought grief to Isaac and Rebekah.

3. Jacob gets Isaac's blessing

Jacob's Deception

27 Now it came about, when Isaac was old and his eyes were too dim to see, that
he called his older son Esau and said to him, "My son." And he said to him, "Here
I am."
2 Isaac said, "Behold now, I am old *and* I do not know the day of my death.
3 "Now then, please take your gear, your quiver and your bow, and go out to the field
and hunt game for me;
4 and prepare a savory dish for me such as I love, and bring it to me that I may eat, so
that my soul may bless you before I die."
5 Rebekah was listening while Isaac spoke to his son Esau. So when Esau went to the
field to hunt for game to bring *home*,
6 Rebekah said to her son Jacob, "Behold, I heard your father speak to your brother
Esau, saying,

26:23 Gen 22:19
26:24 Gen 26:2; Gen 17:7, 8; 24:12; Ex 3:6; Acts 7:32; Gen 15:1; Gen 22:17; 26:3, 4
26:25 Gen 12:7, 8; 13:4, 18; Ps 116:17
26:26 Gen 21:22
26:27 Judg 11:7
26:28 Gen 21:22, 23
26:29 Gen 24:31; Ps 115:15
26:30 Gen 19:3
26:31 Gen 21:31
26:33 Gen 21:31
26:34 Gen 28:8; 36:2
26:35 Gen 27:46
27:1 Gen 48:10; 1 Sam 3:2; Gen 25:25, 33, 34
27:2 Gen 47:29
27:3 Gen 25:28
27:4 Gen 27:19, 25, 31; 48:9, 15, 16; Deut 33:1; Heb 11:20
27:6 Gen 25:28

27 Lit *were a bitterness of spirit to*

26:26–31 With his enemies wanting to make a peace treaty, Isaac was quick to respond, turning the occasion into a celebration. We should be just as receptive to those who want to make peace with us. When God's influence in our lives attracts people—even enemies—we must take the opportunity to reach out to them with God's love.

26:34–35 Esau married pagan women, and this upset his parents greatly. Most parents can be a storehouse of good advice, because they have a lifetime of insight into their children's character. You may not agree with everything your parents say, but at least talk with them and listen carefully. This will help avoid the hard feelings Esau experienced.

27:5–10 When Rebekah learned that Isaac was preparing to bless Esau, she quickly devised a plan to trick him into blessing Jacob instead. Although God had already told her that Jacob would become the family leader (25:23–26), Rebekah took matters into her own hands. She resorted to doing something wrong to try to bring about what God had already said would happen. For Rebekah, the end justified the means. No matter how good we think our goals are, we should not attempt to achieve them by doing what is wrong. Would God approve of the methods you are using to accomplish your goals?

7 'Bring me *some* game and prepare a savory dish for me, that I may eat, and bless you
in the presence of the LORD before my death.'
8 "Now therefore, my son, listen to me as I command you.
9 "Go now to the flock and bring me two choice young goats from there, that I may
prepare them *as* a savory dish for your father, such as he loves.
10 "Then you shall bring *it* to your father, that he may eat, so that he may bless you before his death."

27:8 Gen 27:13, 43

JACOB

Abraham, Isaac, and Jacob are among the most significant people in the Old Testament. It is important to realize that this significance is not based upon their personal characters, but upon the character of God. They were all men who earned the grudging respect and even fear of their peers; they were wealthy and powerful, and yet each was capable of lying, deceit, and selfishness. They were not the perfect heroes we might have expected; instead, they were just like us, trying to please God, but often falling short.

Jacob was the third link in God's plan to start a nation from Abraham. The success of that plan was more often in spite of than because of Jacob's life. Before Jacob was born, God promised that his plan would be worked out through Jacob and not his twin brother, Esau. Although Jacob's methods were not always respectable, his skill, determination, and patience have to be admired. As we follow him from birth to death, we are able to see God's work.

Jacob's life had four stages, each marked by a personal encounter with God. In the first stage, Jacob lived up to his name, which means "he grasps the heel" (figuratively, "he deceives"). He grabbed Esau's heel at birth, and by the time he fled from home, he had also grabbed his brother's birthright and blessing. During his flight, God first appeared to him. Not only did God confirm to Jacob his blessing, but he awakened in Jacob a personal knowledge of himself. In the second stage, Jacob experienced life from the other side, being manipulated and deceived by Laban. But there is a curious change: the Jacob of stage one would simply have left Laban, whereas the Jacob of stage two, after deciding to leave, waited six years for God's permission. In the third stage, Jacob was in a new role as grabber. This time, by the Jordan River, he grabbed on to God and wouldn't let go. He realized his dependence on the God who had continued to bless him. His relationship to God became essential to his life, and his name was changed to Israel, "he struggles with God." Jacob's last stage of life was to *be* grabbed—God achieved a firm hold on him. In responding to Joseph's invitation to come to Egypt, Jacob was clearly unwilling to make a move without God's approval.

Can you think of times when God has made himself known to you? Do you allow yourself to meet him as you study his Word? What difference have these experiences made in your life? Are you more like the young Jacob, forcing God to track you down in the desert of your own plans and mistakes? Or are you more like the Jacob who placed his desires and plans before God for his approval before taking any action?

Strengths and accomplishments:
- Father of the 12 tribes of Israel
- Third in the Abrahamic line of God's plan
- Determined, willing to work long and hard for what he wanted
- Good businessman

Weaknesses and mistakes:
- When faced with conflict, relied on his own resources rather than going to God for help
- Tended to accumulate wealth for its own sake

Lessons from his life:
- Security does not lie in the accumulation of goods
- All human intentions and actions—for good or evil—are woven by God into his ongoing plan

Vital statistics:
- Where: Canaan
- Occupation: Shepherd, livestock owner
- Relatives: Parents: Isaac and Rebekah. Brother: Esau. Father-in-law: Laban. Wives: Rachel and Leah. Twelve sons and one daughter are mentioned in the Bible

Key verse:
"Behold, I am with you and will keep you wherever you go, and will bring you back to this land; for I will not leave you until I have done what I have promised you" (Genesis 28:15).

Jacob's story is told in Genesis 25—50. He is also mentioned in Hosea 12:2-5; Matthew 1:2; 22:32; Acts 3:13; 7:46; Romans 9:11–13; 11:26; Hebrews 11:9, 20–21.

11 Jacob answered his mother Rebekah, "Behold, Esau my brother is a hairy man and
I am a smooth man.
12 "Perhaps my father will feel me, then I will be as a deceiver in his sight, and I will
bring upon myself a curse and not a blessing."
13 But his mother said to him, "Your curse be on me, my son; only obey my voice, and
go, get *them* for me."
14 So he went and got *them,* and brought *them* to his mother; and his mother made
savory food such as his father loved.
15 Then Rebekah took the best garments of Esau her elder son, which were with her
in the house, and put them on Jacob her younger son.
16 And she put the skins of the young goats on his hands and on the smooth part of his
neck.
17 She also gave the savory food and the bread, which she had made, to her son Jacob.
18 Then he came to his father and said, "My father." And he said, "Here I am. Who
are you, my son?"
19 Jacob said to his father, "I am Esau your firstborn; I have done as you told me. Get
up, please, sit and eat of my game, that you may bless me."
20 Isaac said to his son, "How is it that you have *it* so quickly, my son?" And he said,
"Because the LORD your God caused *it* to happen to me."
21 Then Isaac said to Jacob, "Please come close, that I may feel you, my son, whether
you are really my son Esau or not."
22 So Jacob came close to Isaac his father, and he felt him and said, "The voice is the
voice of Jacob, but the hands are the hands of Esau."
23 He did not recognize him, because his hands were hairy like his brother Esau's hands;
so he blessed him.
24 And he said, "Are you really my son Esau?" And he said, "I am."
25 So he said, "Bring *it* to me, and I will eat of my son's game, that I may bless you."
And he brought *it* to him, and he ate; he also brought him wine and he drank.
26 Then his father Isaac said to him, "Please come close and kiss me, my son."
27 So he came close and kissed him; and when he smelled the smell of his garments, he
blessed him and said,

"See, the smell of my son
Is like the smell of a field which the LORD has blessed;
28 Now may God give you of the dew of heaven,
And of the fatness of the earth,
And an abundance of grain and new wine;
29 May peoples serve you,
And nations bow down to you;
Be master of your brothers,
And may your mother's sons bow down to you.
Cursed be those who curse you,
And blessed be those who bless you."

27:11 Gen 25:25
27:12 Gen 27:21, 22
27:13 Gen 27:8
27:15 Gen 27:27
27:19 Gen 27:31; Gen 27:4
27:20 Gen 24:12
27:21 Gen 27:12
27:23 Gen 27:16
27:25 Gen 27:4
27:27 Heb 11:20; Song 4:11; Ps 65:10
27:28 Gen 27:39; Deut 33:13, 28; Prov 3:20; Zech 8:12; Num 18:12
27:29 Gen 25:23; Is 45:14; 49:7, 23; 60:12, 14; Gen 9:26, 27; 27:37; Gen 37:7, 10; Gen 12:3; Num 24:9

The Stolen Blessing

30 Now it came about, as soon as Isaac had finished blessing Jacob, and Jacob had hardly
gone out from the presence of Isaac his father, that Esau his brother came in from his
hunting.

27:11–12 How we react to a moral dilemma often exposes our real motives. Frequently we are more worried about getting caught than about doing what is right. Jacob did not seem concerned about the deceitfulness of his mother's plan; instead he was afraid of getting in trouble while carrying it out. If you are worried about getting caught, you are probably in a position that is less than honest. Let your fear of getting caught be a warning to do right. Jacob paid a huge price for carrying out this dishonest plan.

27:11–13 Jacob hesitated when he heard Rebekah's deceitful plan. Although he questioned it for the wrong reason (fear of getting caught), he protested and thus gave her one last chance to reconsider. But Rebekah had become so wrapped up in her plan that she no longer saw clearly what she was doing. Sin had trapped her and was degrading her character. Correcting yourself in the middle of doing wrong may bring hurt and disappointment, but it also will bring freedom from sin's control.

27:24 Although Jacob got the blessing he wanted, deceiving his father cost him dearly. These are some of the consequences of that deceit: (1) he never saw his mother again; (2) his brother wanted to kill him; (3) he was deceived by his uncle, Laban; (4) his family became torn by strife; (5) Esau became the founder of an enemy nation; (6) he was exiled from his family for years. Ironically, Jacob would have received the birthright and blessing anyway (25:23). Imagine how different his life would have been had he and his mother waited for God to work his way, in his time!

27:31 Gen 27:19; Gen 27:4
27:32 Gen 27:18; Gen 25:33, 34
27:33 Gen 27:35; Gen 25:23; 28:3, 4; Num 23:20
27:34 Heb 12:17
27:35 Gen 27:19
27:36 Gen 25:26, 32-34
27:37 Gen 27:28, 29
27:38 Heb 12:17
27:39 Heb 11:20; Gen 27:28; Deut 33:13, 28
27:40 Gen 25:23; 27:29; 2 Kin 8:20-22
27:41 Gen 32:3-11; 37:4, 8; Gen 50:2-4, 10
27:43 Gen 27:8, 13; Gen 11:31; Gen 24:29
27:44 Gen 31:41
27:45 Gen 27:12, 19, 35
27:46 Gen 26:34, 35; 28:8; Gen 24:3
28:1 Gen 27:33; Gen 24:3, 4
28:2 Gen 25:20

31 Then he also made savory food, and brought it to his father; and he said to his father, "Let my father arise and eat of his son's game, that you may bless me."
32 Isaac his father said to him, "Who are you?" And he said, "I am your son, your firstborn, Esau."
33 Then Isaac trembled violently, and said, "Who was he then that hunted game and
brought *it* to me, so that I ate of all *of it* before you came, and blessed him? Yes, and he
shall be blessed."
34 When Esau heard the words of his father, he cried out with an exceedingly great
and bitter cry, and said to his father, "Bless me, *even* me also, O my father!"
35 And he said, "Your brother came deceitfully and has taken away your blessing."
36 Then he said, "Is he not rightly named Jacob, for he has supplanted me these two
times? He took away my birthright, and behold, now he has taken away my blessing."
And he said, "Have you not reserved a blessing for me?"
37 But Isaac replied to Esau, "Behold, I have made him your master, and all his relatives I have given to him as servants; and with grain and new wine I have sustained him.
Now as for you then, what can I do, my son?"
38 Esau said to his father, "Do you have only one blessing, my father? Bless me, *even*
me also, O my father." So Esau lifted his voice and wept.
39 Then Isaac his father answered and said to him,
"Behold, away from the fertility of the earth shall be your dwelling,
And away from the dew of heaven from above.
40 "By your sword you shall live,
And your brother you shall serve;
But it shall come about when you become restless,
That you will break his yoke from your neck."
41 So Esau bore a grudge against Jacob because of the blessing with which his father
had blessed him; and Esau said to himself, "The days of mourning for my father are near;
then I will kill my brother Jacob."
42 Now when the words of her elder son Esau were reported to Rebekah, she sent and
called her younger son Jacob, and said to him, "Behold your brother Esau is consoling
himself concerning you *by planning* to kill you.
43 "Now therefore, my son, obey my voice, and arise, flee to Haran, to my brother
Laban!
44 "Stay with him a few days, until your brother's fury subsides,
45 until your brother's anger against you subsides and he forgets what you did to him.
Then I will send and get you from there. Why should I be bereaved of you both in one
day?"
46 Rebekah said to Isaac, "I am tired of living because of the daughters of Heth; if
Jacob takes a wife from the daughters of Heth, like these, from the daughters of the land,
what good will my life be to me?"

Jacob Is Sent Away

28 So Isaac called Jacob and blessed him and charged him, and said to him, "You
shall not take a wife from the daughters of Canaan.
2 "Arise, go to Paddan-aram, to the house of Bethuel your mother's father; and from
there take to yourself a wife from the daughters of Laban your mother's brother.

27:33 In ancient times, a person's word was binding (much like a written contract today), especially when it was a formal oath. This is why Isaac's blessing was irrevocable.

27:33–37 Before the father died, he performed a ceremony of blessing, in which he officially handed over the birthright to the rightful heir. Although the firstborn son was entitled to the birthright, it was not actually his until the blessing was pronounced. Before the blessing was given, the father could take the birthright away from the oldest son and give it to a more deserving son. But after the blessing was given, the birthright could no longer be taken away. This is why fathers usually waited until late in life to pronounce the blessing. Although Jacob had been given the birthright by his older brother years before, he still needed his father's blessing to make it binding.

27:41 Esau was so angry at Jacob that he failed to see his own wrong in giving away the birthright in the first place. Jealous anger blinds us from seeing the benefits we have and makes us dwell on what we don't have.

27:41 When Esau lost the valuable family blessing, his future suddenly changed. Reacting in anger, he decided to kill Jacob. When you lose something of great value, or if others conspire against you and succeed, anger is the first and most natural reaction. But you can control your feelings by (1) recognizing your reaction for what it is, (2) praying for strength, and (3) asking God for help to see the opportunities that even your bad situation may provide.

3 "May God Almighty bless you and make you fruitful and multiply you, that you may
become a company of peoples.
4 "May He also give you the blessing of Abraham, to you and to your descendants with
you, that you may possess the land of your sojournings, which God gave to Abraham."
5 Then Isaac sent Jacob away, and he went to Paddan-aram to Laban, son of Bethuel
the Aramean, the brother of Rebekah, the mother of Jacob and Esau.
6 Now Esau saw that Isaac had blessed Jacob and sent him away to Paddan-aram to
take to himself a wife from there, *and that* when he blessed him he charged him, saying,
"You shall not take a wife from the daughters of Canaan,"
7 and that Jacob had obeyed his father and his mother and had gone to Paddan-aram.
8 So Esau saw that the daughters of Canaan displeased his father Isaac;
9 and Esau went to Ishmael, and married, besides the wives that he had, Mahalath
the daughter of Ishmael, Abraham's son, the sister of Nebaioth.

F. THE STORY OF JACOB (28:10—36:43)

Jacob did everything, both right and wrong, with great zeal. He deceived his own brother Esau and his father Isaac. He wrestled with an angel and worked fourteen years to marry the woman he loved. Through Jacob we learn how a strong leader can also be a servant. We also see how wrong actions will always come back to haunt us.

1. Jacob starts a family

Jacob's Dream

10 Then Jacob departed from Beersheba and went toward Haran.
11 He came to a certain place and spent the night there, because the sun had set; and
he took one of the stones of the place and put it under his head, and lay down in that
place.
12 He had a dream, and behold, a ladder was set on the earth with its top reaching to
heaven; and behold, the angels of God were ascending and descending on it.
13 And behold, the LORD stood above it and said, "I am the LORD, the God of your
father Abraham and the God of Isaac; the land on which you lie, I will give it to you and
to your descendants.
14 "Your descendants will also be like the dust of the earth, and you will spread out to
the west and to the east and to the north and to the south; and in you and in your descendants shall all the families of the earth be blessed.
15 "Behold, I am with you and will keep you wherever you go, and will bring you back to
this land; for I will not leave you until I have done what I have promised you."
16 Then Jacob awoke from his sleep and said, "Surely the LORD is in this place, and I
did not know it."
17 He was afraid and said, "How awesome is this place! This is none other than the
house of God, and this is the gate of heaven."

28:3 Gen 17:1; 35:11; 48:3; Gen 22:17; Gen 17:6, 20; Gen 17:2; 26:4, 24; Gen 35:11; 48:4
28:4 Gen 12:2; 22:17; Gen 15:7, 8; 17:8; 1 Chr 29:15; Ps 39:12
28:5 Gen 27:43
28:6 Gen 28:1
28:8 Gen 24:3; 26:34, 35; 27:46
28:9 Gen 26:34; 36:2
28:10 Gen 26:23; Gen 12:4, 5; 27:43
28:11 Gen 28:19
28:12 Gen 41:1; Num 12:6; John 1:51
28:13 Gen 35:1; Amos 7:7; Gen 26:3, 24; Gen 13:15, 17; 26:3; Gen 12:7; 15:18
28:14 Gen 13:16; 22:17; Gen 13:14, 15; Gen 12:3; 18:18; 22:18; 26:4
28:15 Gen 26:3, 24; 31:3; Num 6:24; Ps 121:5, 7, 8; Gen 48:21; Deut 30:3; Num 23:19; Deut 7:9; 31:6, 8
28:16 1 Kin 3:15; Jer 31:26; Ex 3:4-6; Josh 5:13-15; Ps 139:7-12
28:17 Ps 68:35

28:9 Ishmael was Isaac's half brother, the son of Abraham and Hagar, Sarah's maidservant (16:1–4, 15). After marrying two foreign girls (26:34), Esau hoped his marriage into Ishmael's family would please his parents, Isaac and Rebekah.

28:10–15 God's covenant promise to Abraham and Isaac was offered to Jacob as well. But it was not enough to be Abraham's grandson; Jacob had to establish his own personal relationship with God. God has no grandchildren; each of us must have a personal relationship with him. It is not enough to hear wonderful stories about Christians in your family. You need to become part of the story yourself (see Galatians 3:6–7).

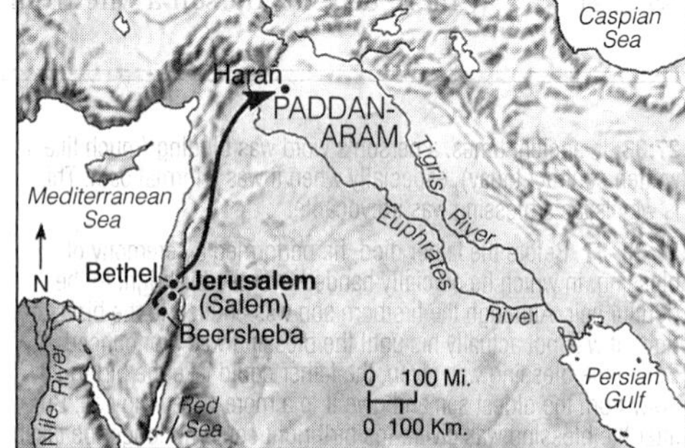

JACOB'S TRIP TO HARAN After deceiving Esau, Jacob ran for his life, traveling more than 400 miles to Haran, where an uncle, Laban, lived. In Haran, Jacob married and started a family.

28:18 Gen 28:11; 35:14
28:19 Judg 1:23; Gen 35:6; 48:3
28:20 Gen 31:13; Judg 11:30; 2 Sam 15:8; Gen 28:15; 1 Tim 6:8
28:21 Judg 11:31; Deut 26:17
28:22 Gen 35:7; Lev 27:30; Deut 14:22
29:1 Judg 6:3, 33
29:2 Gen 24:10, 11; Ex 2:15, 16
29:4 Gen 28:10
29:5 Gen 24:24, 29
29:6 Ex 2:16
29:11 Gen 33:4
29:12 Gen 28:5; Gen 24:28
29:13 Gen 24:29-31; Gen 33:4
29:14 Gen 2:23; Judg 9:2; 2 Sam 5:1; 19:12, 13
29:15 Gen 31:41
29:17 Gen 12:11, 14; 26:7
29:18 Gen 24:67; Hos 12:12

18 So Jacob rose early in the morning, and took the stone that he had put under his head and set it up as a pillar and poured oil on its top.

19 He called the name of that place [28]Bethel; however, previously the name of the city had been Luz.

20 Then Jacob made a vow, saying, "If God will be with me and will keep me on this journey that I take, and will give me food to eat and garments to wear,

21 and I return to my father's house in safety, then the LORD will be my God.

22 "This stone, which I have set up as a pillar, will be God's house, and of all that You give me I will surely give a tenth to You."

Jacob Meets Rachel

29 Then Jacob [29]went on his journey, and came to the land of the sons of the east.
2 He looked, and saw a well in the field, and behold, three flocks of sheep were lying there beside it, for from that well they watered the flocks. Now the stone on the mouth of the well was large.

3 When all the flocks were gathered there, they would then roll the stone from the mouth of the well and water the sheep, and put the stone back in its place on the mouth of the well.

4 Jacob said to them, "My brothers, where are you from?" And they said, "We are from Haran."

5 He said to them, "Do you know Laban the son of Nahor?" And they said, "We know *him.*"

6 And he said to them, "Is it well with him?" And they said, "It is well, and here is Rachel his daughter coming with the sheep."

7 He said, "Behold, it is still high day; it is not time for the livestock to be gathered. Water the sheep, and go, pasture them."

8 But they said, "We cannot, until all the flocks are gathered, and they roll the stone from the mouth of the well; then we water the sheep."

9 While he was still speaking with them, Rachel came with her father's sheep, for she was a shepherdess.

10 When Jacob saw Rachel the daughter of Laban his mother's brother, and the sheep of Laban his mother's brother, Jacob went up and rolled the stone from the mouth of the well and watered the flock of Laban his mother's brother.

11 Then Jacob kissed Rachel, and lifted his voice and wept.

12 Jacob told Rachel that he was a relative of her father and that he was Rebekah's son, and she ran and told her father.

13 So when Laban heard the news of Jacob his sister's son, he ran to meet him, and embraced him and kissed him and brought him to his house. Then he related to Laban all these things.

14 Laban said to him, "Surely you are my bone and my flesh." And he stayed with him a month.

15 Then Laban said to Jacob, "Because you are my relative, should you therefore serve me for nothing? Tell me, what shall your wages be?"

16 Now Laban had two daughters; the name of the older was Leah, and the name of the younger was Rachel.

17 And Leah's eyes were weak, but Rachel was beautiful of form and face.

18 Now Jacob loved Rachel, so he said, "I will serve you seven years for your younger daughter Rachel."

28 I.e. the house of God **29** Lit *lifted up his feet*

28:19 Bethel was about ten miles north of Jerusalem and 60 miles north of Beersheba, where Jacob left his family. This was where Abraham made one of his first sacrifices to God when he entered the land. At first, Bethel became an important center for worship; later, it was a center of idol worship. The prophet Hosea condemned its evil practices.

28:20–22 Was Jacob trying to bargain with God? It is possible that he, in his ignorance of how to worship and serve God, treated God like a servant who would perform a service for a tip. More likely, Jacob was not bargaining, but pledging his future to God. He may have been saying, in effect, "Because you have blessed me, I will follow you." Whether Jacob was bargaining or pledging, God blessed him. But God also had some difficult lessons for Jacob to learn.

29:18–27 It was the custom of the day for a man to present a dowry, or substantial gift, to the family of his future wife. This was to compensate the family for the loss of the girl. Jacob's dowry was not a material possession, for he had none to offer. Instead he agreed to work seven years for Laban. But there was another custom of the land that Laban did not tell Jacob. The older daughter had to be married first. By giving Jacob Leah and not Rachel, Laban tricked him into promising another seven years of hard work.

19 Laban said, "It is better that I give her to you than to give her to another man; stay
with me."
20 So Jacob served seven years for Rachel and they seemed to him but a few days be- **29:20** Song 8:7
cause of his love for her.

Laban's Treachery

21 Then Jacob said to Laban, "Give *me* my wife, for my time is completed, that I may **29:21** Judg 15:1
go in to her."
22 Laban gathered all the men of the place and made a feast.
23 Now in the evening he took his daughter Leah, and brought her to him; and *Jacob*
went in to her.
24 Laban also gave his maid Zilpah to his daughter Leah as a maid.
25 So it came about in the morning that, behold, it was Leah! And he said to Laban, **29:25** Gen 12:18; 20:9; 26:10; 1 Sam 28:12
"What is this you have done to me? Was it not for Rachel that I served with you? Why
then have you deceived me?"
26 But Laban said, "It is not the practice in our place to marry off the younger before
the firstborn.
27 "Complete the week of this one, and we will give you the other also for the service **29:27** Gen 31:41
which you shall serve with me for another seven years."
28 Jacob did so and completed her week, and he gave him his daughter Rachel as his
wife.
29 Laban also gave his maid Bilhah to his daughter Rachel as her maid.
30 So *Jacob* went in to Rachel also, and indeed he loved Rachel more than Leah, and **29:30** Gen 29:17, 18; Gen 31:41
he served with Laban for another seven years.
31 Now the LORD saw that Leah was unloved, and He opened her womb, but Rachel
was barren.
32 Leah conceived and bore a son and named him Reuben, for she said, "Because the **29:32** Gen 16:11; 31:42; Ex 3:7; 4:31; Deut 26:7; Ps 25:18
LORD has seen my affliction; surely now my husband will love me."
33 Then she conceived again and bore a son and said, "Because the LORD has heard
that I am unloved, He has therefore given me this *son* also." So she named him **29:33** Deut 21:15
Simeon.
34 She conceived again and bore a son and said, "Now this time my husband will be- **29:34** Gen 49:5
come attached to me, because I have borne him three sons." Therefore he was named
Levi. **29:35** Gen 49:8; Matt 1:2
35 And she conceived again and bore a son and said, "This time I will praise the LORD."
Therefore she named him Judah. Then she stopped bearing.

The Sons of Jacob

30 Now when Rachel saw that she bore Jacob no children, she became jealous of **30:1** Gen 29:31; 1 Sam 1:5, 6
her sister; and she said to Jacob, "Give me children, or else I die."
2 Then Jacob's anger burned against Rachel, and he said, "Am I in the place of God, **30:2** Gen 20:18; 29:31
who has withheld from you the fruit of the womb?"

29:20–28 People often wonder if working a long time for something they desire is worth it. Jacob worked seven years to marry Rachel. After being tricked, he agreed to work seven more years for her (although he did get to marry Rachel shortly after he married Leah)! The most important goals and desires are worth working and waiting for. Movies and television have created the illusion that people have to wait only about an hour to solve their problems or get what they want. Don't be trapped into thinking the same is true in real life. Patience is hardest when we need it the most, but it is the key to achieving our goals.

29:23–25 Jacob was enraged when he learned that Laban had tricked him. The deceiver of Esau was now deceived himself. How natural it is for us to become upset at an injustice done to us while closing our eyes to the injustices we do to others. Sin has a way of coming back to haunt us.

29:28–30 Although Jacob was tricked by Laban, he kept his part of the bargain. There was more at stake than just Jacob's hurt. There was Rachel to think about, as well as God's plan for his life. When we are tricked by others, keeping our part of the bargain may still be wise. Nursing our wounds or plotting revenge makes us unable to see from God's perspective.

29:32 Today parents usually give their children names that sound good or have sentimental appeal. But the Old Testament portrays a more dynamic use of names. Parents often chose names that reflected the situation at the time of the birth. They sometimes hoped their children would fulfill the meaning of the names given them. Later the parents could look back and see if their grown children had lived up to their names. Sometimes a person's name was changed because his or her character and name did not match. This happened to Jacob ("he grasps the heel," figuratively, "he deceives," 25:26), whose name was changed to Israel ("[he has] striven with God," 32:28). Jacob's character had changed to the point that he was no longer seen as a deceiver, but as a God-honoring man.

30:3 Gen 16:2; Gen 50:23; Job 3:12

30:4 Gen 16:3, 4

30:6 Ps 35:24; 43:1; Lam 3:59

3 She said, "Here is my maid Bilhah, go in to her that she may bear on my knees, that
through her I too may have children."
4 So she gave him her maid Bilhah as a wife, and Jacob went in to her.
5 Bilhah conceived and bore Jacob a son.
6 Then Rachel said, "God has vindicated me, and has indeed heard my voice and has
given me a son." Therefore she named him Dan.
7 Rachel's maid Bilhah conceived again and bore Jacob a second son.

History seems to repeat itself here. Twice a town well at Haran was the site of significant events in one family's story. It was here that Rebekah met Eliezer, Abraham's servant, who had come to find a wife for Isaac. Some 40 years later, Rebekah's son Jacob returned the favor by serving his cousin Rachel and her sheep from the same well. The relationship that developed between them not only reminds us that romance is not a modern invention, but also teaches us a few lessons about patience and love.

Jacob's love for Rachel was both patient and practical. Jacob had the patience to wait seven years for her, but he kept busy in the meantime. His commitment to Rachel kindled a strong loyalty within her. In fact, her loyalty to Jacob got out of hand and became self-destructive. She was frustrated by her barrenness and desperate to compete with her sister for Jacob's affection. She was trying to gain from Jacob what he had already given: devoted love.

Rachel's attempts to earn the unearnable are a picture of a much greater error we can make. Like her, we find ourselves trying somehow to earn love—God's love. But apart from his Word, we end up with one of two false ideas. Either we think we've been good enough to deserve his love or we recognize we aren't able to earn his love and assume that it cannot be ours. If the Bible makes no other point, it shouts this one: God loves us! His love had no beginning and is incredibly patient. All we need to do is respond, not try to earn what is freely offered. God has said in many ways, "I love you. I have demonstrated that love to you by all I've done for you. I have even sacrificed my Son, Jesus, to pay the price for what is unacceptable about you—your sin. Now, live because of my love. Respond to me; love me with your whole being; give yourself to me in thanksgiving, not as payment." Live life fully, in the freedom of knowing you are loved.

Strengths and accomplishments:
- She showed great loyalty to her family
- She mothered Joseph and Benjamin after being barren for many years

Weaknesses and mistakes:
- Her envy and competitiveness marred her relationship with her sister, Leah
- She was capable of dishonesty when she took her loyalty too far
- She failed to recognize that Jacob's devotion was not dependent on her ability to have children

Lessons from her life:
- Loyalty must be controlled by what is true and right
- Love is accepted, not earned

Vital statistics:
- Where: Haran
- Occupation: Shepherdess, housewife
- Relatives: Father: Laban. Aunt: Rebekah. Sister: Leah. Husband: Jacob. Sons: Joseph and Benjamin

Key verse:
"So Jacob served seven years for Rachel and they seemed to him but a few days because of his love for her" (Genesis 29:20).

Rachel's story is told in Genesis 29—35:20. She is also mentioned in Ruth 4:11.

30:3 Each of the three great patriarchs (Abraham, Isaac, and Jacob) had wives who had difficulty conceiving children. It is interesting to note how each man reacted to his wife's predicament. Abraham had relations with Sarah's maid in order to have his own child, thus introducing bitterness and jealousy into his family. Isaac, by contrast, prayed to God when his wife was barren. God eventually answered his prayers, and Rebekah had twin sons. Jacob, however, followed his grandfather's example and had children by his wives' maidservants, leading to sad and sometimes bitter consequences.

30:4–13 Rachel and Leah were locked in a cruel contest. In their race to have more children, they both gave their maids to Jacob as concubines. Jacob would have been wise to refuse, even though this was an accepted custom of the day. The fact that a custom is socially acceptable does not mean it is wise or right. You will be spared much heartbreak if you look at the potential consequences, to you or others, of your actions. Are you doing anything now that might cause future problems?

8 So Rachel said, "With mighty wrestlings I have wrestled with my sister, *and* I have
indeed prevailed." And she named him Naphtali.
9 When Leah saw that she had stopped bearing, she took her maid Zilpah and gave
her to Jacob as a wife.
10 Leah's maid Zilpah bore Jacob a son.
11 Then Leah said, "How fortunate!" So she named him Gad.
12 Leah's maid Zilpah bore Jacob a second son.
13 Then Leah said, "Happy am I! For women will call me happy." So she named him
Asher.
14 Now in the days of wheat harvest Reuben went and found mandrakes in the field,
and brought them to his mother Leah. Then Rachel said to Leah, "Please give me some
of your son's mandrakes."
15 But she said to her, "Is it a small matter for you to take my husband? And would
you take my son's mandrakes also?" So Rachel said, "Therefore he may lie with you tonight in return for your son's mandrakes."
16 When Jacob came in from the field in the evening, then Leah went out to meet him
and said, "You must come in to me, for I have surely hired you with my son's mandrakes."
So he lay with her that night.
17 God gave heed to Leah, and she conceived and bore Jacob a fifth son.
18 Then Leah said, "God has given me my wages because I gave my maid to my husband." So she named him Issachar.
19 Leah conceived again and bore a sixth son to Jacob.
20 Then Leah said, "God has endowed me with a good gift; now my husband will dwell
with me, because I have borne him six sons." So she named him Zebulun.
21 Afterward she bore a daughter and named her Dinah.
22 Then God remembered Rachel, and God gave heed to her and opened her womb.
23 So she conceived and bore a son and said, "God has taken away my reproach."
24 She named him Joseph, saying, "May the LORD give me another son."

Jacob Prospers

25 Now it came about when Rachel had borne Joseph, that Jacob said to Laban, "Send
me away, that I may go to my own place and to my own country.

30:13 Luke 1:48
30:14 Song 7:13
30:22 1 Sam 1:19, 20; Gen 29:31
30:23 Is 4:1; Luke 1:25
30:24 Gen 35:17
30:25 Gen 24:54, 56

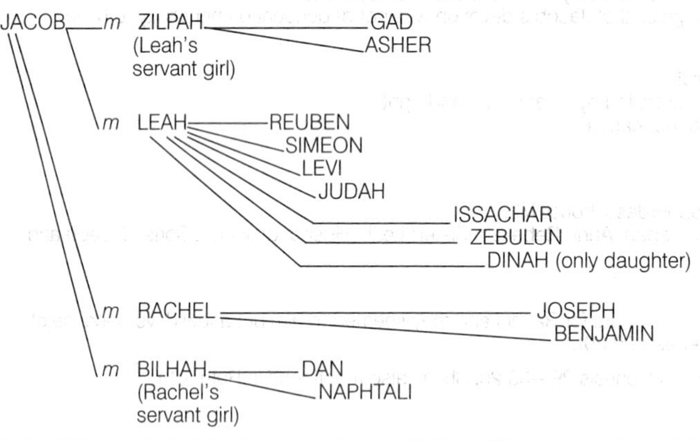

JACOB'S CHILDREN This chart shows from left to right Jacob's children in the order in which they were born.

Jacob's many wives (two wives and two "substitute" wives) led to sad and bitter consequences among the children. Anger, resentment, and jealousy were common among Jacob's sons. It is interesting to note that the worst fighting and rivalry occurred between Leah's children and Rachel's children, and among the tribes that descended from them.

30:22–24 Eventually God answered Rachel's prayers and gave her a child of her own. In the meantime, however, she had given her maid to Jacob. Trusting God when nothing seems to happen is difficult. But it is harder still to live with the consequences of taking matters into our own hands. Resist the temptation to think God has forgotten you. Have patience and courage to wait for God to act.

30:26 Gen 29:18, 20, 27; Hos 12:12

26 "Give *me* my wives and my children for whom I have served you, and let me depart;
for you yourself know my service which I have rendered you."

30:27 Gen 26:24; 39:3, 5; Is 61:9

27 But Laban said to him, "If now [30]it pleases you, *stay with me;* I have divined that the
LORD has blessed me on your account."
28 He continued, "Name me your wages, and I will give it."

30:28 Gen 29:15; 31:7, 41

29 But he said to him, "You yourself know how I have served you and how your cattle
have fared with me.

30:29 Gen 31:6

30 "For you had little before I came and it has increased to a multitude, and the LORD
has blessed you wherever I turned. But now, when shall I provide for my own household
also?"
31 So he said, "What shall I give you?" And Jacob said, "You shall not give me anything. If you will do this *one* thing for me, I will again pasture *and* keep your flock:

30:32 Gen 31:8

32 let me pass through your entire flock today, removing from there every speckled
and spotted sheep and every black one among the lambs and the spotted and speckled
among the goats; and *such* shall be my wages.
33 "So my honesty will answer for me later, when you come concerning my wages. Every
one that is not speckled and spotted among the goats and black among the lambs, *if found*
with me, will be considered stolen."
34 Laban said, "Good, let it be according to your word."
35 So he removed on that day the striped and spotted male goats and all the speckled
and spotted female goats, every one with white in it, and all the black ones among the
sheep, and gave them into the care of his sons.
36 And he put *a distance of* three days' journey between himself and Jacob, and Jacob
fed the rest of Laban's flocks.
37 Then Jacob took fresh rods of poplar and almond and plane trees, and peeled white
stripes in them, exposing the white which *was* in the rods.
38 He set the rods which he had peeled in front of the flocks in the gutters, *even* in the
watering troughs, where the flocks came to drink; and they mated when they came to
drink.
39 So the flocks mated by the rods, and the flocks brought forth striped, speckled, and
spotted.
40 Jacob separated the lambs, and made the flocks face toward the striped and all the
black in the flock of Laban; and he put his own herds apart, and did not put them with
Laban's flock.
41 Moreover, whenever the stronger of the flock were mating, Jacob would place the
rods in the sight of the flock in the gutters, so that they might mate by the rods;
42 but when the flock was feeble, he did not put *them* in; so the feebler were Laban's
and the stronger Jacob's.

30:43 Gen 12:16; 13:2; 24:35; 26:13, 14; 30:30

43 So the man became exceedingly prosperous, and had large flocks and female and
male servants and camels and donkeys.

2. Jacob returns home

Jacob Leaves Secretly for Canaan

31 Now Jacob heard the words of Laban's sons, saying, "Jacob has taken away all that
was our father's, and from what belonged to our father he has made all this wealth."
2 Jacob saw the [31]attitude of Laban, and behold, it was not *friendly* toward him as
formerly.

30 Lit *I have found favor in your eyes* **31** Lit *face*

30:27 Laban claimed to have learned by divination that God had blessed him because of Jacob. In other words, he thought his idols had given him this insight.

30:37–43 It is unclear what this method was or how it worked. Some say that there was a belief among herdsmen that vivid impressions at mating time influenced the offspring. Most likely, the selective breeding and God's promise of provision were the main reasons that Jacob's flocks increased.

31:1–2 Jacob's wealth made Laban's sons jealous. It is sometimes difficult to be happy when others are doing better than we are. To compare our success with that of others is a dangerous way to judge the quality of our lives. By comparing ourselves to others, we may be giving jealousy a foothold. We can avoid jealousy by rejoicing in others' successes (see Romans 12:15).

3 Then the LORD said to Jacob, "Return to the land of your fathers and to your relatives, and I will be with you."
4 So Jacob sent and called Rachel and Leah to his flock in the field,
5 and said to them, "I see your father's attitude, that it is not *friendly* toward me as formerly, but the God of my father has been with me.
6 "You know that I have served your father with all my strength.
7 "Yet your father has cheated me and changed my wages ten times; however, God did not allow him to hurt me.
8 "If he spoke thus, 'The speckled shall be your wages,' then all the flock brought forth speckled; and if he spoke thus, 'The striped shall be your wages,' then all the flock brought forth striped.
9 "Thus God has taken away your father's livestock and given *them* to me.
10 "And it came about at the time when the flock were mating that I lifted up my eyes and saw in a dream, and behold, the male goats which were mating *were* striped, speckled, and mottled.
11 "Then the angel of God said to me in the dream, 'Jacob,' and I said, 'Here I am.'
12 "He said, 'Lift up now your eyes and see *that* all the male goats which are mating are striped, speckled, and mottled; for I have seen all that Laban has been doing to you.
13 'I am the God *of* Bethel, where you anointed a pillar, where you made a vow to Me; now arise, leave this land, and return to the land of your birth.' "
14 Rachel and Leah said to him, "Do we still have any portion or inheritance in our father's house?
15 "Are we not reckoned by him as foreigners? For he has sold us, and has also entirely consumed our purchase price.
16 "Surely all the wealth which God has taken away from our father belongs to us and our children; now then, do whatever God has said to you."
17 Then Jacob arose and put his children and his wives upon camels;
18 and he drove away all his livestock and all his property which he had gathered, his acquired livestock which he had gathered in Paddan-aram, to go to the land of Canaan to his father Isaac.
19 When Laban had gone to shear his flock, then Rachel stole the household idols that were her father's.
20 And Jacob deceived Laban the Aramean by not telling him that he was fleeing.
21 So he fled with all that he had; and he arose and crossed the *Euphrates* River, and set his face toward the hill country of Gilead.

31:3 Gen 32:9; Gen 28:15
31:5 Gen 31:2; Gen 21:22; 28:13, 15; 31:29, 42, 53; Is 41:10; Heb 13:5
31:6 Gen 30:29
31:7 Gen 29:25; Gen 31:41; Gen 15:1; 31:29
31:8 Gen 30:32
31:9 Gen 31:1, 16
31:11 Gen 16:7-11; 22:11, 15; 31:13; 48:16
31:12 Ex 3:7
31:13 Gen 28:13, 19; Gen 28:18, 20; Gen 28:15; 32:9
31:15 Gen 29:20, 23, 27
31:18 Gen 35:27
31:19 Gen 31:30, 34; 35:2; Judg 17:5; 1 Sam 19:13; Hos 3:4
31:21 Gen 37:25

Laban Pursues Jacob

22 When it was told Laban on the third day that Jacob had fled,
23 then he took his kinsmen with him and pursued him *a distance of* seven days' journey, and he overtook him in the hill country of Gilead.

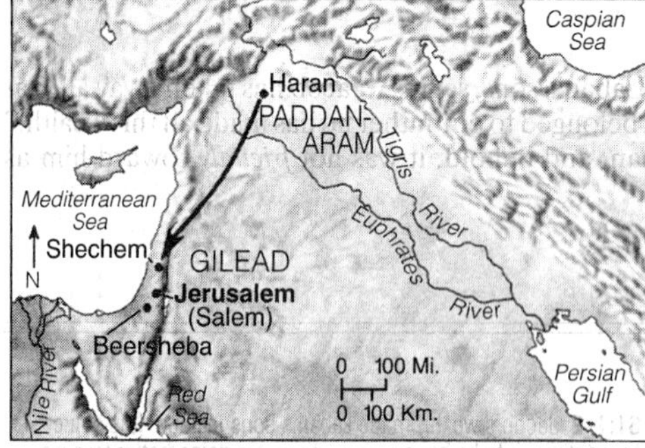

JACOB'S RETURN TO CANAAN God told Jacob to leave Haran and return to his homeland. Jacob took his family, crossed the Euphrates River, and headed first for the hill country of Gilead. Laban caught up with him there.

31:4–13 Although Laban treated Jacob unfairly, God still increased Jacob's prosperity. God's power is not limited by lack of fair play. He has the ability to meet our needs and make us thrive even though others mistreat us. To give in and respond unfairly is to be no different from your enemies.

31:14–15 Leaving home was not difficult for Rachel and Leah because their father had treated them as poorly as he had Jacob. According to custom, they were supposed to receive the benefits of the dowry Jacob paid for them, which was 14 years of hard work. When Laban did not give them what was rightfully theirs, they knew they would never inherit anything from their father. Thus they wholeheartedly approved of Jacob's plan to take the wealth he had gained and leave.

31:19 Many people kept small wooden or metal idols ("gods") in their homes. These idols were called *teraphim,* and they were thought to protect the home and offer advice in times of need. They had legal significance as well, for when they were passed on to an heir, the person who received them could rightfully claim the greatest part of the family inheritance. No wonder Laban was concerned when he realized his idols were missing (31:30). Most likely Rachel stole her father's idols because she was afraid Laban would consult them and learn where she and Jacob had gone, or perhaps she wanted to claim the family inheritance.

31:24 Gen 20:3; 31:29; Gen 20:3, 6; 31:11; Gen 24:50; 31:7, 29

24 God came to Laban the Aramean in a dream of the night and said to him, "Be careful that you do not speak to Jacob either good or bad."
25 Laban caught up with Jacob. Now Jacob had pitched his tent in the hill country, and
Laban with his kinsmen camped in the hill country of Gilead.
26 Then Laban said to Jacob, "What have you done by deceiving me and carrying away
my daughters like captives of the sword?

31:27 Ex 15:20; Gen 4:21

27 "Why did you flee secretly and deceive me, and did not tell me so that I might have
sent you away with joy and with songs, with timbrel and with lyre;

31:28 Gen 31:55

28 and did not allow me to kiss my sons and my daughters? Now you have done foolishly.

31:29 Gen 31:5, 24, 42, 53; Gen 31:24

29 "It is in my power to do you harm, but the God of your father spoke to me last night,
saying, 'Be careful not to speak either good or bad to Jacob.'

31:30 Gen 31:19; Josh 24:2; Judg 18:24

30 "Now you have indeed gone away because you longed greatly for your father's house;
but why did you steal my gods?"
31 Then Jacob replied to Laban, "Because I was afraid, for I thought that you would
take your daughters from me by force.

31:32 Gen 44:9

32 "The one with whom you find your gods shall not live; in the presence of our kinsmen point out what is yours among my belongings and take *it* for yourself." For Jacob
did not know that Rachel had stolen them.

We're all selfish, but some of us have a real corner on the weakness. Laban's whole life was stamped by self-centeredness. His chief goal was to look out for himself. The way he treated others was controlled by that goal. He made profitable arrangements for his sister Rebekah's marriage to Isaac and used his daughters' lives as bargaining chips. Jacob eventually outmaneuvered Laban, but the older man was unwilling to admit defeat. His hold on Jacob was broken, but he still tried to maintain some kind of control by getting Jacob to promise to be gone for good. He realized that Jacob and Jacob's God were more than he could handle.

On the surface, we may find it difficult to identify with Laban. But his selfishness is one point we have in common. Like him, we often have a strong tendency to control people and events to our benefit. Our "good" reasons for treating others the way we do may simply be a thin cover on our self-centered motives. We may not even recognize our own selfishness. One way to discover it is to examine our willingness to admit we're wrong. Laban could not bring himself to do this. If you ever amaze yourself by what you say and do to avoid facing up to wrong actions, you are getting a glimpse of your selfishness in action. Recognizing selfishness is painful, but it is the first step on the road back to God.

Strengths and accomplishments:
- Controlled two generations of marriages in the Abrahamic family (Rebekah, Rachel, Leah)
- Quick-witted

Weaknesses and mistakes:
- Manipulated others for his own benefit
- Unwilling to admit wrongdoing
- Benefited financially by using Jacob, but never fully benefited spiritually by knowing and worshiping Jacob's God

Lessons from his life:
- Those who set out to use people will eventually find themselves used
- God's plan cannot be blocked

Vital statistics:
- Where: Haran
- Occupation: Wealthy sheep breeder
- Relatives: Father: Bethuel. Sister: Rebekah. Brother-in-law: Isaac. Daughters: Rachel and Leah. Son-in-law: Jacob

Key verse:
"If the God of my father, the God of Abraham, and the fear of Isaac, had not been for me, surely now you would have sent me away empty-handed. God has seen my affliction and the toil of my hands, so He rendered judgment last night" (Genesis 31:42).

Laban's story is told in Genesis 24:1—31:55.

31:32 Do you remember feeling absolutely sure about something? Jacob was so sure that no one had stolen Laban's idols that he vowed to kill the offender. Because Rachel took them, this statement put her safety in serious jeopardy. Even when you are absolutely sure about a matter, it is safer to avoid rash statements. Someone may hold you to them.

33 So Laban went into Jacob's tent and into Leah's tent and into the tent of the two
maids, but he did not find *them.* Then he went out of Leah's tent and entered Rachel's
tent.
34 Now Rachel had taken the household idols and put them in the camel's saddle, and
she sat on them. And Laban felt through all the tent but did not find *them.*
35 She said to her father, "Let not my lord be angry that I cannot rise before you, for
the manner of women is upon me." So he searched but did not find the household idols.
36 Then Jacob became angry and contended with Laban; and Jacob said to Laban,
"What is my transgression? What is my sin that you have hotly pursued me?
37 "Though you have felt through all my goods, what have you found of all your household goods? Set *it* here before my kinsmen and your kinsmen, that they may decide between us two.
38 "These twenty years I *have been* with you; your ewes and your female goats have not
miscarried, nor have I eaten the rams of your flocks.
39 "That which was torn *of beasts* I did not bring to you; I bore the loss of it myself. You
required it of my hand *whether* stolen by day or stolen by night.
40 "*Thus* I was: by day the heat consumed me and the frost by night, and my sleep fled
from my eyes.
41 "These twenty years I have been in your house; I served you fourteen years for your
two daughters and six years for your flock, and you changed my wages ten times.
42 "If the God of my father, the God of Abraham, and the fear of Isaac, had not been
for me, surely now you would have sent me away empty-handed. God has seen my affliction and the toil of my hands, so He rendered judgment last night."

The Covenant of Mizpah

43 Then Laban replied to Jacob, "The daughters are my daughters, and the children
are my children, and the flocks are my flocks, and all that you see is mine. But what can
I do this day to these my daughters or to their children whom they have borne?
44 "So now come, let us make a covenant, you and I, and let it be a witness between you
and me."
45 Then Jacob took a stone and set it up *as* a pillar.
46 Jacob said to his kinsmen, "Gather stones." So they took stones and made a heap,
and they ate there by the heap.
47 Now Laban called it [32]Jegar-sahadutha, but Jacob called it [33]Galeed.
48 Laban said, "This heap is a witness between you and me this day." Therefore it was
named Galeed,
49 and [34]Mizpah, for he said, "May the LORD watch between you and me when we are
absent one from the other.
50 "If you mistreat my daughters, or if you take wives besides my daughters, *although*
no man is with us, see, God is witness between you and me."
51 Laban said to Jacob, "Behold this heap and behold the pillar which I have set between you and me.
52 "This heap is a witness, and the pillar is a witness, that I will not pass by this heap to
you for harm, and you will not pass by this heap and this pillar to me, for harm.
53 "The God of Abraham and the God of Nahor, the God of their father, judge between
us." So Jacob swore by the fear of his father Isaac.
54 Then Jacob offered a sacrifice on the mountain, and called his kinsmen to the meal;
and they ate the meal and spent the night on the mountain.
55 Early in the morning Laban arose, and kissed his sons and his daughters and blessed
them. Then Laban departed and returned to his place.

32 I.e. the heap of witness, in Aram **33** I.e. the heap of witness, in Heb **34** Lit *the Mizpah;* i.e. the watchtower

31:35 Lev 19:32; Gen 31:19
31:41 Gen 29:27, 30; Gen 31:7
31:42 Gen 31:5, 29, 53; Gen 29:32; Ex 3:7; Gen 31:24, 29
31:43 Gen 31:1
31:44 Gen 21:27, 32; 26:28; Josh 24:27
31:45 Gen 28:18; Josh 24:26, 27
31:47 Josh 22:34
31:48 Josh 24:27
31:49 Judg 11:29; 1 Sam 7:5, 6
31:50 Jer 29:23; 42:5
31:53 Gen 28:13; Gen 16:5; Gen 31:42
31:54 Ex 18:12
31:55 Gen 31:28, 43

31:38–42 Jacob made it a habit to do more than was expected of him. When his flocks were attacked, he took the losses rather than splitting them with Laban. He worked hard even after several pay cuts. His diligence eventually paid off; his flocks began to multiply. Making a habit of doing more than expected can pay off. It (1) pleases God, (2) earns recognition and advancement, (3) enhances your reputation, (4) builds others' confidence in you, (5) gives you more experience and knowledge, and (6) develops your spiritual maturity.

31:49 To be binding, an agreement had to be witnessed by a third party. In this case, Jacob and Laban used God as their witness that they would keep their word.

Jacob's Fear of Esau

32 Now as Jacob went on his way, the angels of God met him.
2 Jacob said when he saw them, "This is God's [35]camp." So he named that place
[36]Mahanaim
3 Then Jacob sent messengers before him to his brother Esau in the land of Seir, the
country of Edom.
4 He also commanded them saying, "Thus you shall say to my lord Esau: 'Thus says
your servant Jacob, "I have sojourned with Laban, and stayed until now;
5 I have oxen and donkeys *and* flocks and male and female servants; and I have sent
to tell my lord, that I may find favor in your sight." ' "
6 The messengers returned to Jacob, saying, "We came to your brother Esau, and furthermore he is coming to meet you, and four hundred men are with him."
7 Then Jacob was greatly afraid and distressed; and he divided the people who were
with him, and the flocks and the herds and the camels, into two companies;
8 for he said, "If Esau comes to the one company and attacks it, then the company
which is left will escape."
9 Jacob said, "O God of my father Abraham and God of my father Isaac, O LORD,
who said to me, 'Return to your country and to your relatives, and I will prosper you,'
10 I am unworthy of all the lovingkindness and of all the faithfulness which You have
shown to Your servant; for with my staff *only* I crossed this Jordan, and now I have become two companies.
11 "Deliver me, I pray, from the hand of my brother, from the hand of Esau; for I fear
him, that he will come and attack me *and* the mothers with the children.
12 "For You said, 'I will surely prosper you and make your descendants as the sand of
the sea, which is too great to be numbered.' "
13 So he spent the night there. Then he selected from what he had with him a present
for his brother Esau:
14 two hundred female goats and twenty male goats, two hundred ewes and twenty rams,
15 thirty milking camels and their colts, forty cows and ten bulls, twenty female donkeys and ten male donkeys.
16 He delivered *them* into the hand of his servants, every drove by itself, and said to his
servants, "Pass on before me, and put a space between droves."
17 He commanded the one in front, saying, "When my brother Esau meets you and
asks you, saying, 'To whom do you belong, and where are you going, and to whom do
these *animals* in front of you belong?'
18 then you shall say, '*These* belong to your servant Jacob; it is a present sent to my
lord Esau. And behold, he also is behind us.' "
19 Then he commanded also the second and the third, and all those who followed the
droves, saying, "After this manner you shall speak to Esau when you find him;
20 and you shall say, 'Behold, your servant Jacob also is behind us.' " For he said, "I
will appease him with the present that goes before me. Then afterward I will see his face;
perhaps he will accept me."
21 So the present passed on before him, while he himself spent that night in the camp.
22 Now he arose that same night and took his two wives and his two maids and his eleven
children, and crossed the ford of the Jabbok.
23 He took them and sent them across the stream. And he sent across whatever he
had.

32:1 2 Kin 6:16, 17; Ps 34:7
32:2 Josh 21:38; 2 Sam 2:8
32:3 Gen 27:41, 42; 32:7, 11; Gen 14:6; 33:14; Gen 25:30; 36:8, 9
32:4 Gen 31:41
32:5 Gen 30:43; Gen 33:8
32:6 Gen 33:1
32:7 Gen 32:11
32:9 Gen 28:13; 31:42; Gen 28:15; 31:3, 13
32:10 Gen 24:27
32:11 Ps 59:1, 2; Gen 27:41, 42; 33:4; Hos 10:14
32:12 Gen 28:14; Gen 22:17
32:13 Gen 43:11
32:22 Deut 3:16; Josh 12:2

35 Or *company* **36** I.e. Two Camps, or Two Companies

32:1 Why did angels of God meet Jacob? In the Bible, angels often intervened in human situations. Although angels often came in human form, these angels must have looked different, for Jacob recognized them at once. The reason these angels met Jacob is unclear; but because of their visit, Jacob knew God was with him.

32:3 The last time Jacob had seen Esau, his brother was ready to kill him for stealing the family blessing (25:29—27:42). Esau was so angry he had vowed to kill Jacob as soon as their father, Isaac, died (27:41). Fearing their reunion, Jacob sent messengers ahead with gifts. He hoped to buy Esau's favor.

32:9–12 How would you feel knowing you were about to meet the person you had cheated out of his most precious possession? Jacob had taken Esau's birthright (25:33) and his blessing (27:27–40). Now he was about to meet this brother for the first time in 20 years, and he was frantic with fear. He collected his thoughts, however, and decided to pray. When we face a difficult conflict, we can run about frantically or we can pause to pray. Which approach will be more effective?

Jacob Wrestles

24 Then Jacob was left alone, and a man wrestled with him until daybreak.
25 When he saw that he had not prevailed against him, he touched the socket of his
thigh; so the socket of Jacob's thigh was dislocated while he wrestled with him.
26 Then he said, "Let me go, for the dawn is breaking." But he said, "I will not let you
go unless you bless me."
27 So he said to him, "What is your name?" And he said, "Jacob."
28 He said, "Your name shall no longer be Jacob, but [37]Israel; for you have striven with
God and with men and have prevailed."
29 Then Jacob asked him and said, "Please tell me your name." But he said, "Why is it
that you ask my name?" And he blessed him there.
30 So Jacob named the place [38]Peniel, for *he said,* "I have seen God face to face, yet
my life has been preserved."
31 Now the sun rose upon him just as he crossed over Penuel, and he was limping on
his thigh.
32 Therefore, to this day the sons of Israel do not eat the sinew of the hip which is on
the socket of the thigh, because he touched the socket of Jacob's thigh in the sinew of
the hip.

32:24 Hos 12:3, 4
32:26 Hos 12:4
32:28 Gen 35:10; 1 Kin 18:31
32:29 Judg 13:17, 18
32:30 Gen 16:13; Ex 24:10, 11; 33:20; Num 12:8; Judg 6:22; 13:22
32:31 Judg 8:8

Jacob Meets Esau

33 Then Jacob lifted his eyes and looked, and behold, Esau was coming, and four
hundred men with him. So he divided the children among Leah and Rachel and
the two maids.
2 He put the maids and their children in front, and Leah and her children next, and
Rachel and Joseph last.
3 But he himself passed on ahead of them and bowed down to the ground seven times,
until he came near to his brother.
4 Then Esau ran to meet him and embraced him, and fell on his neck and kissed him,
and they wept.
5 He lifted his eyes and saw the women and the children, and said, "Who are these
with you?" So he said, "The children whom God has graciously given your servant."
6 Then the maids came near with their children, and they bowed down.
7 Leah likewise came near with her children, and they bowed down; and afterward
Joseph came near with Rachel, and they bowed down.
8 And he said, "What do you mean by all this company which I have met?" And he
said, "To find favor in the sight of my lord."
9 But Esau said, "I have plenty, my brother; let what you have be your own."
10 Jacob said, "No, please, if now I have found favor in your sight, then take my present
from my hand, for I see your face as one sees the face of God, and you have received me
favorably.

33:1 Gen 32:6
33:3 Gen 42:6; 43:26
33:4 Gen 45:14, 15
33:5 Gen 48:9; Ps 127:3; Is 8:18
33:8 Gen 32:13-16; Gen 32:5
33:9 Gen 27:39, 40

37 I.e. he who strives with God; or God strives **38** I.e. the face of God

---

32:26 Jacob continued this wrestling match all night just to be blessed. He was persistent. God encourages persistence in all areas of our lives, including the spiritual. Where in your spiritual life do you need more persistence? Strong character develops as you struggle through tough conditions.

32:27–29 God gave many Bible people new names (Abraham, Sarah, Peter). Their new names were symbols of how God had changed their lives. Here we see how Jacob's character had changed. Jacob, the ambitious deceiver, had now become Israel, the one who struggles with God and prevails.

33:1–11 It is refreshing to see Esau's change of heart when the two brothers meet again. The bitterness over losing his birthright and blessing (25:29–34) seems gone. Instead Esau was content with what he had. Jacob even exclaimed how great it was to see his brother obviously pleased with him (33:10).

Life can bring us some bad situations. We can feel cheated, as Esau did, but we don't have to remain bitter. We can remove bitterness from our lives by honestly expressing our feelings to God, forgiving those who have wronged us, and being content with what we have.

33:3 Bowing to the ground seven times was the sign of respect given to a king. Jacob was taking every precaution as he met Esau, hoping to dispel any thoughts of revenge.

33:4 Esau greeted his brother, Jacob, with a great hug. Imagine how difficult this must have been for a man who once had actually plotted his brother's death (27:41). But time away from each other allowed the bitter wounds to heal. With the passing of time, each brother was able to see that their relationship was more important than their real estate.

33:11 1 Sam 25:27; Gen 30:43

11 "Please take my gift which has been brought to you, because God has dealt graciously with me and because I have plenty." Thus he urged him and he took *it.*
12 Then Esau said, "Let us take our journey and go, and I will go before you."
13 But he said to him, "My lord knows that the children are frail and that the flocks
and herds which are nursing are a care to me. And if they are driven hard one day, all
the flocks will die.

33:14 Gen 32:3

14 "Please let my lord pass on before his servant, and I will proceed at my leisure, according to the pace of the cattle that are before me and according to the pace of the
children, until I come to my lord at Seir."

33:15 Ruth 2:13

15 Esau said, "Please let me leave with you some of the people who are with me." But
he said, "[39]What need is there? Let me find favor in the sight of my lord."
16 So Esau returned that day on his way to Seir.

33:17 Josh 13:27; Judg 8:5, 14; Ps 60:6

17 Jacob journeyed to [40]Succoth, and built for himself a house and made booths for his
livestock; therefore the place is named Succoth.

Jacob Settles in Shechem

33:18 Gen 12:6; Josh 24:1; Judg 9:1; Gen 25:20; 28:2

33:19 Josh 24:32; John 4:5

18 Now Jacob came safely to the city of Shechem, which is in the land of Canaan, when
he came from Paddan-aram, and camped before the city.
19 He bought the piece of land where he had pitched his tent from the hand of the
sons of Hamor, Shechem's father, for one hundred pieces of money.
20 Then he erected there an altar and called it [41]El-Elohe-Israel.

The Treachery of Jacob's Sons

34:1 Gen 30:21

34:2 Gen 34:30

34 Now Dinah the daughter of Leah, whom she had borne to Jacob, went out to visit
the daughters of the land.
2 When Shechem the son of Hamor the Hivite, the prince of the land, saw her, he
took her and lay with her by force.
3 He was deeply attracted to Dinah the daughter of Jacob, and he loved the girl and
spoke tenderly to her.

34:4 Judg 14:2

4 So Shechem spoke to his father Hamor, saying, "Get me this young girl for a wife."
5 Now Jacob heard that he had defiled Dinah his daughter; but his sons were with his
livestock in the field, so Jacob kept silent until they came in.
6 Then Hamor the father of Shechem went out to Jacob to speak with him.

34:7 Deut 22:20-30; Judg 20:6; 2 Sam 13:12

7 Now the sons of Jacob came in from the field when they heard *it;* and the men were
grieved, and they were very angry because he had done a disgraceful thing in Israel by
lying with Jacob's daughter, for such a thing ought not to be done.

39 Lit *Why this?* **40** I.e. booths **41** I.e. God, the God of Israel

---

33:11 Why did Jacob send gifts ahead for Esau? In Bible times, gifts were given for several reasons. (1) This may have been a bribe. Gifts are still given to win someone over or buy his or her support. Esau may first have refused Jacob's gifts (33:9) because he didn't want or need a bribe. He had already forgiven Jacob, and he had ample wealth of his own. (2) This may have been an expression of affection. (3) It may have been the customary way of greeting someone before an important meeting. Such gifts were often related to a person's occupation. This explains why Jacob sent Esau—who was a herdsman— sheep, goats, and cattle.

33:14–17 Why did Jacob imply that he was going to Seir but then stop at Succoth? We don't know the answer, but perhaps Jacob decided to stop there as they journeyed because Succoth is a beautiful site on the eastern side of the Jordan River. Whatever the reason, Jacob and Esau parted in peace. But they still lived fairly close to each other until after their father's death (36:6-8).

34:1–4 Shechem may have been a victim of "love at first sight," but his actions were impulsive and evil. Not only did he sin against Dinah; he sinned against the entire family (34:6–7). The consequences of his deed were severe both for his family and for Jacob's (34:25–31). Even Shechem's declared love for Dinah could not excuse the evil he did by raping her. Don't allow sexual passion to boil over into evil actions. Passion must be controlled.

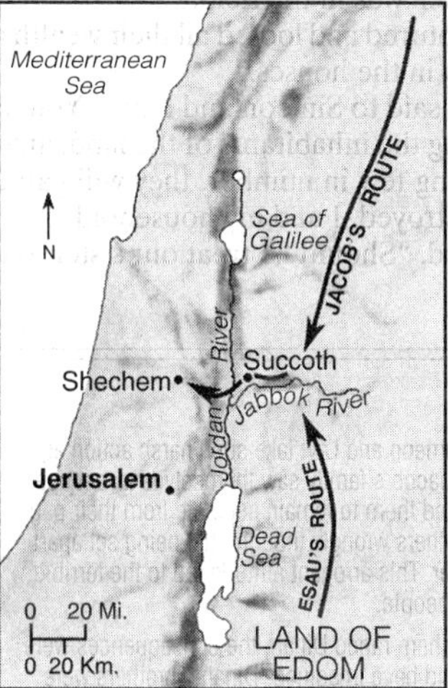

JACOB'S JOURNEY TO SHECHEM
After a joyful reunion with his brother, Esau (who journeyed from Edom), Jacob set up camp in Succoth. Later he moved on to Shechem where his daughter, Dinah, was raped and two of his sons took revenge on the city.

8 But Hamor spoke with them, saying, "The soul of my son Shechem longs for your
daughter; please give her to him in marriage.
9 "Intermarry with us; give your daughters to us and take our daughters for yourselves.
10 "Thus you shall live with us, and the land shall be *open* before you; live and trade in **34:10**
it and acquire property in it." Gen 13:9; 20:15; Gen 42:34; Gen
11 Shechem also said to her father and to her brothers, "If I find favor in your sight, 47:27
then I will give whatever you say to me.
12 "Ask me ever so much bridal payment and gift, and I will give according as you say to
me; but give me the girl in marriage."
13 But Jacob's sons answered Shechem and his father Hamor with deceit, because he
had defiled Dinah their sister.
14 They said to them, "We cannot do this thing, to give our sister to one who is uncir- **34:14**
cumcised, for that would be a disgrace to us." Gen 17:14
15 "Only on this *condition* will we consent to you: if you will become like us, in that every
male of you be circumcised,
16 then we will give our daughters to you, and we will take your daughters for ourselves,
and we will live with you and become one people.
17 "But if you will not listen to us to be circumcised, then we will take our daughter
and go."
18 Now their words seemed reasonable to Hamor and Shechem, Hamor's son.
19 The young man did not delay to do the thing, because he was delighted with Jacob's
daughter. Now he was more respected than all the household of his father.
20 So Hamor and his son Shechem came to the gate of their city and spoke to the men **34:20**
of their city, saying, Ruth 4:1; 2 Sam 15:2
21 "These men are friendly with us; therefore let them live in the land and trade in it,
for behold, the land is large enough for them. Let us take their daughters in marriage,
and give our daughters to them.
22 "Only on this *condition* will the men consent to us to live with us, to become one
people: that every male among us be circumcised as they are circumcised.
23 "Will not their livestock and their property and all their animals be ours? Only let us
consent to them, and they will live with us."
24 All who went out of the gate of his city listened to Hamor and to his son Shechem, **34:24**
and every male was circumcised, all who went out of the gate of his city. Gen 23:10
25 Now it came about on the third day, when they were in pain, that two of Jacob's **34:25**
sons, Simeon and Levi, Dinah's brothers, each took his sword and came upon the city Gen 49:5-7
unawares, and killed every male.
26 They killed Hamor and his son Shechem with the edge of the sword, and took Dinah from Shechem's house, and went forth.
27 Jacob's sons came upon the slain and looted the city, because they had defiled their
sister.
28 They took their flocks and their herds and their donkeys, and that which was in the
city and that which was in the field;
29 and they captured and looted all their wealth and all their little ones and their wives,
even all that *was* in the houses.
30 Then Jacob said to Simeon and Levi, "You have brought trouble on me by making **34:30**
me odious among the inhabitants of the land, among the Canaanites and the Perizzites; Josh 7:25; Ex 5:21; 1 Sam 13:4; 2 Sam
and my men being few in number, they will gather together against me and attack me 10:6; Gen 13:7;
and I will be destroyed, I and my household." 34:2; Gen 46:26, 27; Deut 4:27; 1 Chr
31 But they said, "Should he treat our sister as a harlot?" 16:19; Ps 105:12

34:25–31 Why did Simeon and Levi take such harsh action against the city of Shechem? Jacob's family saw themselves as set apart from others. God wanted them to remain separate from their pagan neighbors. But the brothers wrongly thought that being set apart also meant being better. This arrogant attitude led to the terrible slaughter of innocent people.

34:27–29 When Shechem raped Dinah, the consequences were far greater than he could have imagined. Dinah's brothers were outraged and took revenge. Pain, deceit, and murder followed. Sexual sin is devastating because its consequences are so far reaching.

34:30–31 In seeking revenge against Shechem, Simeon and Levi lied, stole, and murdered. Their desire for justice was right, but their ways of achieving it were wrong. Because of their sin, their father cursed them with his dying breath (49:5–7). Generations later, their descendants lost the part of the promised land allotted to them. When tempted to return evil for evil, leave revenge to God and spare yourself the dreadful consequences of sin.

Jacob Moves to Bethel

35 Then God said to Jacob, "Arise, go up to Bethel and live there, and make an altar
there to God, who appeared to you when you fled from your brother Esau."
2 So Jacob said to his household and to all who were with him, "Put away the foreign
gods which are among you, and purify yourselves and change your garments;
3 and let us arise and go up to Bethel, and I will make an altar there to God, who
answered me in the day of my distress and has been with me wherever I have gone."
4 So they gave to Jacob all the foreign gods which they had and the rings which were
in their ears, and Jacob hid them under the oak which was near Shechem.
5 As they journeyed, there was a great terror upon the cities which were around them,
and they did not pursue the sons of Jacob.
6 So Jacob came to Luz (that is, Bethel), which is in the land of Canaan, he and all the
people who were with him.
7 He built an altar there, and called the place El-bethel, because there God had revealed Himself to him when he fled from his brother.
8 Now Deborah, Rebekah's nurse, died, and she was buried below Bethel under the
oak; it was named [42]Allon-bacuth.

Jacob Is Named Israel

9 Then God appeared to Jacob again when he came from Paddan-aram, and He
blessed him.
10 God said to him,
"Your name is Jacob;
You shall no longer be called Jacob,
But Israel shall be your name."
Thus He called him Israel.
11 God also said to him,
"I am God Almighty;
Be fruitful and multiply;
A nation and a company of nations shall come from you,
And kings shall come forth from you.
12 "The land which I gave to Abraham and Isaac,
I will give it to you,
And I will give the land to your descendants after you."

35:1 Gen 28:19; Gen 28:13; Gen 27:43
35:2 Gen 10.19, Josh 24:15; Gen 31:19, 30, 34; Ex 19:10, 14
35:3 Gen 28:20-22; Ps 107:6; Gen 28:15; 31:3, 42
35:5 Ex 15:16; 23:27; Deut 2:25
35:6 Gen 28:19; 48:3
35:7 Gen 35:3
35:8 Gen 24:59
35:9 Gen 32:29
35:10 Gen 17:5; 32:28
35:11 Gen 17:1; 28:3; Ex 6:3; Gen 9:1, 7; Gen 48:4; Gen 17:6, 16; 36:31
35:12 Gen 12:7; 13:15; 26:3, 4; 28:13; Ex 32:13

42 I.e. oak of weeping

35:2 Why did the people have these idols ("foreign gods")? Idols were sometimes seen more as good luck charms than as gods. Some Israelites, even though they worshiped God, had idols in their homes, just as some Christians today own good luck trinkets. Jacob believed that idols should have no place in his household. He wanted nothing to divert his family's spiritual focus.

Jacob ordered his household to get rid of their gods. Unless we remove idols from our lives, they can ruin our faith. What idols do we have? An idol is anything we put before God. Idols don't have to be physical objects; they can be thoughts or desires. Like Jacob, we should get rid of anything that could stand between us and God.

35:4 Why did the people give Jacob their earrings? Jewelry in itself was not evil, but in Jacob's day earrings were often worn as good luck charms to ward off evil. The people in his family had to cleanse themselves of all pagan influences, including reminders of foreign gods.

35:10 God reminded Jacob of his new name, Israel, which meant "he struggles with God." Although Jacob's life was littered with difficulties and trials, his new name was a tribute to his desire to stay close to God despite life's disappointments.

Many people believe that Christianity should offer a problem-free life. Consequently, as life gets tough, they draw back disappointed. Instead, they should determine to prevail with God through life's storm. Problems and difficulties are painful but inevitable; you might as well see them as opportunities for growth. You can't prevail with God unless you have troubles to prevail over.

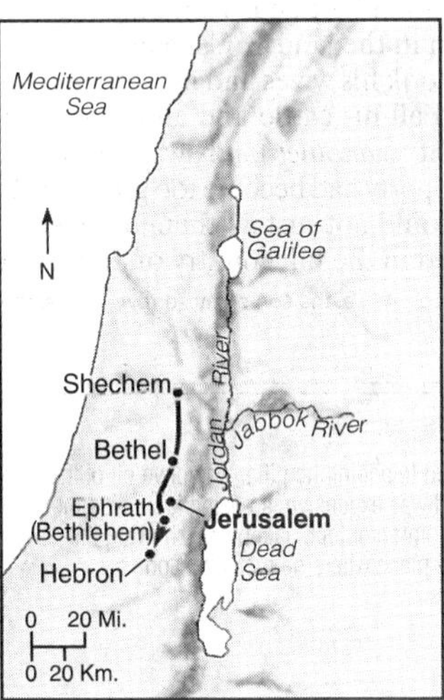

JACOB'S JOURNEY BACK TO HEBRON
After Jacob's sons Simeon and Levi destroyed Shechem, God told Jacob to move to Bethel, where God reminded him that his name had been changed to Israel. He then traveled to Hebron, but along the way, his dear wife Rachel died near Ephrath (Bethlehem).

13 Then God went up from him in the place where He had spoken with him.
14 Jacob set up a pillar in the place where He had spoken with him, a pillar of stone,
and he poured out a drink offering on it; he also poured oil on it.
15 So Jacob named the place where God had spoken with him,[43]Bethel.
16 Then they journeyed from Bethel; and when there was still some distance to go to
Ephrath, Rachel began to give birth and she suffered severe labor.
17 When she was in severe labor the midwife said to her, "Do not fear, for now you
have another son."
18 It came about as her soul was departing (for she died), that she named him [44]Ben-
oni; but his father called him [45]Benjamin.
19 So Rachel died and was buried on the way to Ephrath (that is, Bethlehem).
20 Jacob set up a pillar over her grave; that is the pillar of Rachel's grave to this day.
21 Then Israel journeyed on and pitched his tent beyond the tower of Eder.
22 It came about while Israel was dwelling in that land, that Reuben went and lay with
Bilhah his father's concubine, and Israel heard *of it.*

The Sons of Israel

Now there were twelve sons of Jacob—
23 the sons of Leah: Reuben, Jacob's firstborn, then Simeon and Levi and Judah and
Issachar and Zebulun;
24 the sons of Rachel: Joseph and Benjamin;
25 and the sons of Bilhah, Rachel's maid: Dan and Naphtali;
26 and the sons of Zilpah, Leah's maid: Gad and Asher. These are the sons of Jacob
who were born to him in Paddan-aram.
27 Jacob came to his father Isaac at Mamre of Kiriath-arba (that is, Hebron), where
Abraham and Isaac had sojourned.
28 Now the days of Isaac were one hundred and eighty years.
29 Isaac breathed his last and died and was gathered to his people, an old man of ripe
age; and his sons Esau and Jacob buried him.

Esau Moves

36 Now these are *the records of* the generations of Esau (that is, Edom).
2 Esau took his wives from the daughters of Canaan: Adah the daughter of Elon
the Hittite, and Oholibamah the daughter of Anah and the granddaughter of Zibeon
the Hivite;
3 also Basemath, Ishmael's daughter, the sister of Nebaioth.
4 Adah bore Eliphaz to Esau, and Basemath bore Reuel,
5 and Oholibamah bore Jeush and Jalam and Korah. These are the sons of Esau who
were born to him in the land of Canaan.
6 Then Esau took his wives and his sons and his daughters and all his household, and
his livestock and all his cattle and all his goods which he had acquired in the land of
Canaan, and went to *another* land away from his brother Jacob.
7 For their property had become too great for them to live together, and the land where
they sojourned could not sustain them because of their livestock.
8 So Esau lived in the hill country of Seir; Esau is Edom.

43 I.e. the house of God **44** I.e. the son of my sorrow **45** I.e. the son of the right hand

35:13 Gen 17:22; 18:33
35:14 Gen 28:18, 19; 31:45
35:15 Gen 28:19
35:16 Gen 35:19; 48:7; Ruth 4:11; Mic 5:2
35:17 Gen 30:24
35:19 Gen 48:7; Ruth 1:2; 4:11; Mic 5:2
35:20 1 Sam 10:2
35:21 Mic 4:8
35:22 Gen 49:4; 1 Chr 5:1
35:23 Gen 29:31-35; 30:18-20; 46:8; Ex 1:1-4
35:24 Gen 30:22-24; 35:18
35:25 Gen 30:5-8
35:26 Gen 30:10-13
35:27 Gen 13:18; 18:1; 23:19; Josh 14:15
35:28 Gen 25:26
35:29 Gen 25:8; 49:33; Gen 15:15; Gen 25:9
36:1 Gen 25:30
36:2 Gen 28:9; Gen 36:25; Gen 36:24
36:4 1 Chr 1:35
36:6 Gen 12:5
36:7 Gen 13:6; Gen 17:8; Heb 11:9; 1 Chr 29:15; Ps 39:12
36:8 Gen 32:3; Gen 36:1, 19

35:13–14 This oil used to anoint the pillar was olive oil of the finest grade of purity. It was expensive, so using it showed the high value placed on the anointed object. Jacob was showing the greatest respect for the place where he met with God.

35:22 Reuben's sin was costly, although not right away. As the oldest son, he stood to receive a double portion of the family inheritance and a place of leadership among his people. Reuben may have thought he got away with his sin. No more is mentioned of it until Jacob, on his deathbed, assembled his family for the final blessing. Suddenly Jacob took away Reuben's double portion and gave it to someone else. The reason? "You went up to your father's bed; then you defiled it" (49:4).

Sin's consequences can plague us long after the sin is committed. When we do something wrong, we may think we can escape unnoticed, only to discover later that the sin has been quietly breeding serious consequences.

Descendants of Esau

9 These then are *the records of* the generations of Esau the father of the Edomites in
the hill country of Seir.
10 These are the names of Esau's sons: Eliphaz the son of Esau's wife Adah, Reuel the
son of Esau's wife Basemath.
11 The sons of Eliphaz were Teman, Omar, Zepho and Gatam and Kenaz.
36:12 Ex 17:8-16; Num 24:20; Deut 25:17-19; 1 Sam 15:2, 3
12 Timna was a concubine of Esau's son Eliphaz and she bore Amalek to Eliphaz. These
are the sons of Esau's wife Adah.
13 These are the sons of Reuel: Nahath and Zerah, Shammah and Mizzah. These were
the sons of Esau's wife Basemath.
14 These were the sons of Esau's wife Oholibamah, the daughter of Anah and the granddaughter of Zibeon: she bore to Esau, Jeush and Jalam and Korah.
15 These are the chiefs of the sons of Esau. The sons of Eliphaz, the firstborn of Esau,
are chief Teman, chief Omar, chief Zepho, chief Kenaz,
16 chief Korah, chief Gatam, chief Amalek. These are the chiefs descended from Eliphaz in the land of Edom; these are the sons of Adah.
17 These are the sons of Reuel, Esau's son: chief Nahath, chief Zerah, chief Shammah, chief Mizzah. These are the chiefs descended from Reuel in the land of Edom;
these are the sons of Esau's wife Basemath.
18 These are the sons of Esau's wife Oholibamah: chief Jeush, chief Jalam, chief Korah. These are the chiefs descended from Esau's wife Oholibamah, the daughter of Anah.
19 These are the sons of Esau (that is, Edom), and these are their chiefs.
36:20 Gen 14:6; Deut 2:12, 22; 1 Chr 1:38-42
20 These are the sons of Seir the Horite, the inhabitants of the land: Lotan and Shobal
and Zibeon and Anah,
21 and Dishon and Ezer and Dishan. These are the chiefs descended from the Horites,
the sons of Seir in the land of Edom.
22 The sons of Lotan were Hori and Hemam; and Lotan's sister was Timna.
23 These are the sons of Shobal: Alvan and Manahath and Ebal, Shepho and Onam.
24 These are the sons of Zibeon: Aiah and Anah—he is the Anah who found the hot
springs in the wilderness when he was pasturing the donkeys of his father Zibeon.
25 These are the children of Anah: Dishon, and Oholibamah, the daughter of Anah.
36:26 1 Chr 1:41
26 These are the sons of Dishon: Hemdan and Eshban and Ithran and Cheran.
27 These are the sons of Ezer: Bilhan and Zaavan and Akan.
28 These are the sons of Dishan: Uz and Aran.
29 These are the chiefs descended from the Horites: chief Lotan, chief Shobal, chief
Zibeon, chief Anah,
30 chief Dishon, chief Ezer, chief Dishan. These are the chiefs descended from the
Horites, according to their *various* chiefs in the land of Seir.
36:31 Gen 17:6, 16; 35:11; 1 Chr 1:43
31 Now these are the kings who reigned in the land of Edom before any king reigned
over the sons of Israel.
36:32 1 Chr 1:43
32 Bela the son of Beor reigned in Edom, and the name of his city was Dinhabah.
33 Then Bela died, and Jobab the son of Zerah of Bozrah became king in his place.
34 Then Jobab died, and Husham of the land of the Temanites became king in his place.
35 Then Husham died, and Hadad the son of Bedad, who defeated Midian in the field
of Moab, became king in his place; and the name of his city was Avith.
36 Then Hadad died, and Samlah of Masrekah became king in his place.
37 Then Samlah died, and Shaul of Rehoboth on the *Euphrates* River became king in
his place.
38 Then Shaul died, and Baal-hanan the son of Achbor became king in his place.
39 Then Baal-hanan the son of Achbor died, and Hadar became king in his place; and
the name of his city was Pau; and his wife's name was Mehetabel, the daughter of Matred, daughter of Mezahab.

36:9 The Edomites were descendants of Esau who lived south and east of the Dead Sea. The country featured rugged mountains and desolate desert. Several major roads led through Edom because it was rich in natural resources. During the exodus, God told Israel to leave the Edomites alone (Deuteronomy 2:4–5) because they were "brothers." But Edom refused to let them enter the land, and later they became bitter enemies of King David. The nations of Edom and Israel shared the same ancestor, Isaac, and the same border. Israel looked down on the Edomites because they intermarried with the Canaanites.

36:15ff The title "chief" is equivalent to "head of the clan."

40 Now these are the names of the chiefs descended from Esau, according to their
families *and* their localities, by their names: chief Timna, chief Alvah, chief Jetheth,
41 chief Oholibamah, chief Elah, chief Pinon,
42 chief Kenaz, chief Teman, chief Mibzar,
43 chief Magdiel, chief Iram. These are the chiefs of Edom (that is, Esau, the father of
the Edomites), according to their habitations in the land of their possession.

G. THE STORY OF JOSEPH (37:1—50:26)

Joseph, one of Jacob's 12 sons, was obviously the favorite. Hated by his brothers for this, Joseph was sold to slave traders only to emerge as ruler of all Egypt. Through Joseph, we learn how suffering, no matter how unfair, develops strong character and deep wisdom.

1. Joseph is sold into slavery

Joseph's Dream

37 Now Jacob lived in the land where his father had sojourned, in the land of
Canaan.
2 These are *the records of* the generations of Jacob.
Joseph, when seventeen years of age, was pasturing the flock with his brothers while
he was *still* a youth, along with the sons of Bilhah and the sons of Zilpah, his father's
wives. And Joseph brought back a bad report about them to their father.
3 Now Israel loved Joseph more than all his sons, because he was the son of his old
age; and he made him a [46]varicolored tunic.
4 His brothers saw that their father loved him more than all his brothers; and *so* they
hated him and could not speak to him [47]on friendly terms.
5 Then Joseph had a dream, and when he told it to his brothers, they hated him even
more.
6 He said to them, "Please listen to this dream which I have had;
7 for behold, we were binding sheaves in the field, and lo, my sheaf rose up and also
stood erect; and behold, your sheaves gathered around and bowed down to my sheaf."
8 Then his brothers said to him, "Are you actually going to reign over us? Or are you
really going to rule over us?" So they hated him even more for his dreams and for his
words.
9 Now he had still another dream, and related it to his brothers, and said, "Lo, I have
had still another dream; and behold, the sun and the moon and eleven stars were bowing down to me."
10 He related *it* to his father and to his brothers; and his father rebuked him and said
to him, "What is this dream that you have had? Shall I and your mother and your brothers actually come to bow ourselves down before you to the ground?"
11 His brothers were jealous of him, but his father kept the saying *in mind.*

37:1 Gen 17:8; 28:4
37:2 Gen 41:46; Gen 35:25, 26; 1 Sam 2:22-24
37:3 Gen 44:20; Gen 37:23, 32
37:4 Gen 27:41; 1 Sam 17:28
37:5 Gen 28:12; 31:10, 11, 24
37:7 Gen 42:6, 9; 43:26; 44:14
37:8 Gen 49:26; Deut 33:16
37:10 Gen 27:29
37:11 Acts 7:9; Dan 7:28; Luke 2:19, 51

46 Or *full-length robe* **47** Lit *in peace*

37:3 In Joseph's day, everyone had a tunic or cloak. Tunics were used to warm oneself, to bundle up belongings for a trip, to wrap babies, to sit on, or even to serve as security for a loan. Most tunics were knee length, short sleeved, and plain. In contrast, Joseph's tunic was probably of the kind worn by royalty—long sleeved, ankle length, and colorful. The tunic became a symbol of Jacob's favoritism toward Joseph, and it aggravated the already strained relations between Joseph and his brothers. Favoritism in families may be unavoidable, but its divisive effects should be minimized. Parents may not be able to change their feelings toward a favorite child, but they can change their actions toward the others.

37:6–11 Joseph's brothers were already angry over the possibility of being ruled by their little brother. Joseph then fueled the fire with his immature attitude and boastful manner. No one enjoys a braggart. Joseph learned his lesson the hard way. His angry brothers sold him into slavery to get rid of him. After several years of hardship, Joseph learned an important lesson: Because our talents and knowledge come from God, it is more appropriate to thank him for them than to brag about them. Later, Joseph gives God the credit (41:16).

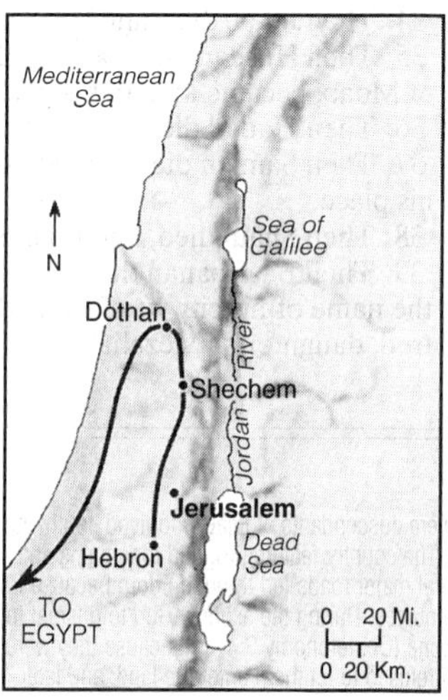

JOSEPH GOES TO MEET HIS BROTHERS
Jacob asked Joseph to go find his brothers, who were grazing their flocks near Shechem. When Joseph arrived, he learned that his brothers had gone on to Dothan, which lay along a major trade route to Egypt. There the jealous brothers sold Joseph as a slave to a group of Midianite traders on their way to Egypt.

12 Then his brothers went to pasture their father's flock in Shechem.

37:13 Gen 33:18-20

13 Israel said to Joseph, "Are not your brothers pasturing *the flock* in Shechem? Come,
and I will send you to them." And he said to him, "I will go."

37:14 Gen 13:18; 23:2, 19; 35:27; Josh 14:14, 15; Judg 1:10

14 Then he said to him, "Go now and see about the welfare of your brothers and the
welfare of the flock, and bring word back to me." So he sent him from the valley of Hebron,
and he came to Shechem.
15 A man found him, and behold, he was wandering in the field; and the man asked
him, "What are you looking for?"
16 He said, "I am looking for my brothers; please tell me where they are pasturing *the
flock.*"

37:17 2 Kin 6:13

17 Then the man said, "They have moved from here; for I heard *them* say, 'Let us go to
Dothan.' " So Joseph went after his brothers and found them at Dothan.

The Plot against Joseph

37:18 Ps 31:13; 37:12, 32; Mark 14:1; John 11:53; Acts 23:12

18 When they saw him from a distance and before he came close to them, they plotted
against him to put him to death.
19 They said to one another, "Here comes this dreamer!

JOSEPH

As a youngster, Joseph was overconfident. His natural self-assurance, increased by being Jacob's favorite son and by knowing of God's designs on his life, was unbearable to his ten older brothers, who eventually conspired against him. But this self-assurance, molded by pain and combined with a personal knowledge of God, allowed him to survive and prosper where most would have failed. He added quiet wisdom to his confidence and won the hearts of everyone he met—Potiphar, the warden, other prisoners, the king, and after many years, even those ten brothers.

Perhaps you can identify with one or more of these hardships Joseph experienced: he was betrayed and deserted by his family, exposed to sexual temptation, and punished for doing the right thing; he endured a long imprisonment and was forgotten by those he helped. As you read his story, note what Joseph did in each case. His positive response transformed each setback into a step forward. He didn't spend much time asking "Why?" His approach was "What shall I do now?" Those who met Joseph were aware that wherever he went and whatever he did, God was with him. When you're facing a setback, the beginning of a Joseph-like attitude is to acknowledge that God is with you. There is nothing like his presence to shed new light on a dark situation.

Strengths and accomplishments:
- Rose in power from slave to ruler of Egypt
- Was known for his personal integrity
- Was a man of spiritual sensitivity
- Prepared a nation to survive a famine

Weakness and mistake:
- His youthful pride caused friction with his brothers

Lessons from his life:
- What matters is not so much the events or circumstances of life, but your response to them
- With God's help, any situation can be used for good, even when others intend it for evil

Vital statistics:
- Where: Canaan, Egypt
- Occupation: Shepherd, slave, convict, ruler
- Relatives: Parents: Jacob and Rachel. Eleven brothers and one sister named in the Bible. Wife: Asenath. Sons: Manasseh and Ephraim

Key verse:
"Then Pharaoh said to his servants, 'Can we find a man like this, in whom is a divine spirit?' " (Genesis 41:38).

Joseph's story is told in Genesis 30—50. He is also mentioned in Hebrews 11:22.

37:19–20 Could jealousy ever make you feel like killing someone? Before saying, "Of course not," look at what happened in this story. Ten men were willing to kill their younger brother over a tunic and a few reported dreams. Their deep jealousy had grown into ugly rage, completely blinding them to what was right. Jealousy can be difficult to recognize because our reasons for it seem to make sense. But left unchecked, jealousy grows quickly and leads to serious sins. The longer you cultivate jealous feelings, the harder it is to uproot them. The time to deal with jealousy is when you notice yourself keeping score of what others have.

20 "Now then, come and let us kill him and throw him into one of the pits; and we will
say, 'A wild beast devoured him.' Then let us see what will become of his dreams!"
21 But Reuben heard *this* and rescued him out of their hands and said, "Let us not
take his life."
22 Reuben further said to them, "Shed no blood. Throw him into this pit that is in the
wilderness, but do not lay hands on him"—that he might rescue him out of their hands,
to restore him to his father.
23 So it came about, when Joseph reached his brothers, that they stripped Joseph of
his tunic, the varicolored tunic that was on him;
24 and they took him and threw him into the pit. Now the pit was empty, without any
water in it.
25 Then they sat down to eat a meal. And as they raised their eyes and looked, behold,
a caravan of Ishmaelites was coming from Gilead, with their camels bearing aromatic
gum and balm and myrrh, on their way to bring *them* down to Egypt.
26 Judah said to his brothers, "What profit is it for us to kill our brother and cover up
his blood?
27 "Come and let us sell him to the Ishmaelites and not lay our hands on him, for he is
our brother, our *own* flesh." And his brothers listened *to him.*
28 Then some Midianite traders passed by, so they pulled *him* up and lifted Joseph out
of the pit, and sold him to the Ishmaelites for twenty *shekels* of silver. Thus they brought
Joseph into Egypt.
29 Now Reuben returned to the pit, and behold, Joseph was not in the pit; so he tore
his garments.
30 He returned to his brothers and said, "The boy is not *there;* as for me, where am I
to go?"
31 So they took Joseph's tunic, and slaughtered a male goat and dipped the tunic in
the blood;
32 and they sent the varicolored tunic and brought it to their father and said, "We found
this; please examine *it* to *see* whether it is your son's tunic or not."
33 Then he examined it and said, "It is my son's tunic. A wild beast has devoured him;
Joseph has surely been torn to pieces!"
34 So Jacob tore his clothes, and put sackcloth on his loins and mourned for his son
many days.
35 Then all his sons and all his daughters arose to comfort him, but he refused to be
comforted. And he said, "Surely I will go down to Sheol in mourning for my son." So his
father wept for him.
36 Meanwhile, the Midianites sold him in Egypt to Potiphar, Pharaoh's officer, the captain of the bodyguard.

37:20 Gen 37:32, 33
37:21 Gen 42:22
37:25 Gen 16:11, 12; 37:28; 39:1; Gen 43:11; Jer 8:22; 46:11
37:26 Gen 37:20
37:27 Gen 42:21
37:28 Gen 37:25; Judg 6:1-3; 8:22, 24; Gen 45:4, 5; Ps 105:17; Acts 7:9; Gen 39:1
37:29 Gen 37:34; 44:13
37:30 Gen 42:13, 36
37:31 Gen 37:3, 23
37:33 Gen 37:20; Gen 44:28
37:34 Gen 37:29
37:35 Gen 25:8; 35:29; 42:38; 44:29, 31
37:36 Gen 39:1

37:26–27 The brothers were worried about bearing the guilt of Joseph's death. Judah suggested an option that was not right but would leave them guiltless of murder. Sometimes we jump at a solution because it is the lesser of two evils, but it still is not the right action to take. When someone proposes a seemingly workable solution, first ask, "Is it right?"

37:28 Although Joseph's brothers didn't kill him outright, they wouldn't expect him to survive for long as a slave. They were quite willing to let cruel slave traders do their dirty work for them. Joseph faced a 30-day journey through the desert, probably chained and on foot. He would be treated like baggage, and once in Egypt, would be sold as a piece of merchandise. His brothers thought they would never see him again. But God was in control of Joseph's life.

37:29–30 Reuben returned to the pit to find Joseph, but his little brother was gone. His first response, in effect, was "What is going to happen to me?" rather than "What is going to happen to Joseph?" In a tough situation, are you usually concerned first about yourself? Consider the person most affected by the problem, and you will be more likely to find a solution for it.

37:31–35 To cover their evil action, Jacob's sons deceived their father into thinking Joseph was dead. Jacob himself had deceived others many times (including his own father; 27:35). Now, though blessed by God, he still had to face the consequences of his sins. God may not have punished Jacob immediately for his deceit, but the consequences came nevertheless and stayed with him for the rest of his life.

37:34 Tearing one's clothes and wearing sackcloth were signs of mourning, much like wearing black today.

37:36 Imagine the culture shock Joseph experienced upon arriving in Egypt. Joseph had lived as a nomad, traveling the countryside with his family, caring for sheep. Suddenly he was thrust into the world's most advanced civilization with great pyramids, beautiful homes, sophisticated people, and a new language. While Joseph saw Egypt's skill and intelligence at their best, he also saw the Egyptians' spiritual blindness. They worshiped countless gods related to every aspect of life.

38:1 Josh 15:35; 1 Sam 22:1
38:2 1 Chr 2:3
38:3 Gen 46:12; Num 26:19
38:4 Gen 46:12
38:5 Num 26:20
38:7 Gen 46:12; Num 26:19; 1 Chr 2:3
38:8 Deut 25:5, 6; Matt 22:24
38:9 Deut 25:6

2. Judah and Tamar

38 And it came about at that time, that Judah departed from his brothers and visited a certain Adullamite, whose name was Hirah.
2 Judah saw there a daughter of a certain Canaanite whose name was Shua; and he
took her and went in to her.
3 So she conceived and bore a son and he named him Er.
4 Then she conceived again and bore a son and named him Onan.
5 She bore still another son and named him Shelah; and it was at Chezib that she
bore him.
6 Now Judah took a wife for Er his firstborn, and her name *was* Tamar.
7 But Er, Judah's firstborn, was evil in the sight of the LORD, so the LORD took
his life.
8 Then Judah said to Onan, "Go in to your brother's wife, and perform your duty as
a brother-in-law to her, and raise up offspring for your brother."
9 Onan knew that the offspring would not be his; so when he went in to his brother's
wife, he wasted his seed on the ground in order not to give offspring to his brother.

REUBEN

Parents are usually the best judges of their children's character. Jacob summarized the personality of his son Reuben by comparing him to water. Except when frozen, water has no stable shape of its own. It always shapes itself to its container or environment. Reuben usually had good intentions, but he seemed unable to stand against a crowd. His instability made him hard to trust. He had both private and public values, but these contradicted each other. He went along with his brothers in their action against Joseph while hoping to counteract the evil in private. The plan failed. Compromise has a way of destroying convictions. Without convictions, lack of direction will destroy life. Reuben's sleeping with his father's concubine showed how little he had left of the integrity he had displayed earlier in life.

How consistent are your public and private lives? We may want to think they are separate, but we can't deny that they affect each other. What convictions are present in your life at all times? How closely does Jacob's description of his son—"uncontrolled as water"—describe your life?

Strengths and accomplishments:
- Saved Joseph's life by talking the other brothers out of murder
- Showed intense love for his father by offering his own sons as a guarantee that Benjamin's life would be safe

Weaknesses and mistakes:
- Gave in quickly to group pressure
- Did not directly protect Joseph from his brothers, although as oldest son he had the authority to do so
- Slept with his father's concubine

Lessons from his life:
- Public and private integrity must be the same, or one will destroy the other
- Punishment for sin may not be immediate, but it is certain

Vital statistics:
- Where: Canaan, Egypt
- Occupation: Shepherd
- Relatives: Parents: Jacob and Leah. Eleven brothers, one sister

Key verses:
"Reuben, you are my firstborn; my might and the beginning of my strength, preeminent in dignity and preeminent in power. Uncontrolled as water, you shall not have preeminence, because you went up to your father's bed; then you defiled it—he went up to my couch" (Genesis 49:3–4).

Reuben's story is told in Genesis 29—50.

38:1ff This chapter vividly contrasts the immoral character of Judah with the moral character of Joseph. Judah's lack of integrity resulted in family strife and deception. In chapter 39, we see how Joseph's integrity and wise choices reflect his godly character. His faithfulness was rewarded with blessings greater than he could imagine, both for himself and for his family.

38:8-10 This law about marrying a widow in the family is explained in Deuteronomy 25:5–10. Its purpose was to ensure that a childless widow would have a son who would receive her late husband's inheritance and who, in turn, would care for her. Because Judah's son (Tamar's husband) had no children, there was no family line through which the inheritance and the blessing of the covenant could continue. God killed Onan because he refused to fulfill his obligation to his brother and to Tamar.

10 But what he did was displeasing in the sight of the LORD; so He took his life also.
11 Then Judah said to his daughter-in-law Tamar, "Remain a widow in your father's
house until my son Shelah grows up"; for he thought, "*I am afraid* that he too may die
like his brothers." So Tamar went and lived in her father's house.
12 Now after a considerable time Shua's daughter, the wife of Judah, died; and when
the time of mourning was ended, Judah went up to his sheepshearers at Timnah, he and
his friend Hirah the Adullamite.
13 It was told to Tamar, "Behold, your father-in-law is going up to Timnah to shear his
sheep."
14 So she removed her widow's garments and covered *herself* with a [48]veil, and wrapped
herself, and sat in the gateway of Enaim, which is on the road to Timnah; for she saw
that Shelah had grown up, and she had not been given to him as a wife.
15 When Judah saw her, he thought she *was* a harlot, for she had covered her face.
16 So he turned aside to her by the road, and said, "Here now, let me come in to you";
for he did not know that she was his daughter-in-law. And she said, "What will you give
me, that you may come in to me?"
17 He said, therefore, "I will send you a young goat from the flock." She said, moreover, "Will you give a pledge until you send *it?*"
18 He said, "What pledge shall I give you?" And she said, "Your seal and your cord,
and your staff that is in your hand." So he gave *them* to her and went in to her, and she
conceived by him.
19 Then she arose and departed, and removed her veil and put on her widow's garments.
20 When Judah sent the young goat by his friend the Adullamite, to receive the pledge
from the woman's hand, he did not find her.
21 He asked the men of her place, saying, "Where is the temple prostitute who was by
the road at Enaim?" But they said, "There has been no temple prostitute here."
22 So he returned to Judah, and said, "I did not find her; and furthermore, the men of
the place said, 'There has been no temple prostitute here.' "
23 Then Judah said, "Let her keep them, otherwise we will become a laughingstock.
After all, I sent this young goat, but you did not find her."

38:10 Gen 46:12; Num 26:19
38:11 Ruth 1:12, 13
38:12 Josh 15:10, 57
38:13 Josh 15:10, 57; Judg 14:1
38:14 Gen 24:65; Gen 38:11, 26
38:18 Gen 38:25; 41:42

48 Or *shawl*

WOMEN IN JESUS' FAMILY TREE

Tamar	Canaanite	Genesis 38:1–30
Rahab	Canaanite	Joshua 6:22–25
Ruth	Moabite	Ruth 4:13–22
Bathsheba	Israelite	2 Samuel 12:24–25

38:15–23 Why does this story seem to take a light view of prostitution? Prostitutes (harlots) were common in pagan cultures such as Canaan. Public prostitutes served Canaanite goddesses and were common elements of the religious cults. Fornication was encouraged to improve fertility in crops and flocks. They were more highly respected than private prostitutes who were sometimes punished when caught. Tamar was driven to seduce Judah because of her intense desire to have children and be the matriarch of Judah's oldest line; Judah was driven by his lust. Neither case was justified.

38:15–24 Why was Judah so open about his relations with a prostitute, yet ready to execute his daughter-in-law for being one? To understand this apparent contradiction, we must understand the place of women in Canaan. A woman's most important function was bearing children who would perpetuate the family line. To ensure that children belonged to the husband, the bride was expected to be a virgin and the wife was expected to have relations only with him. If a wife committed adultery, she could be executed. Some women, however, did not belong to families. They might be shrine prostitutes supported by offerings or common prostitutes supported by the men who used their services. Their children were nobody's heirs, and men who hired them adulterated nobody's bloodlines.

Judah saw no harm in hiring a prostitute for a night; after all, he was more than willing to pay. He was ready to execute Tamar, however, because if she was pregnant as a result of prostitution, his grandchild would not be part of his family line. Apparently the question of sexual morality never entered Judah's mind; his concern was for keeping his inheritance in the family. Ironically, it was Tamar, not Judah, who acted to provide him with legal heirs. By seducing him, she acted more in the spirit of the law than he did when he refused to send his third son to her.

This story in no way implies that God winks at prostitution. Throughout Scripture, prostitution is condemned as a serious sin. If the story has a moral, it is that faithfulness to family obligations is important. Incidentally, Judah and Tamar are direct ancestors of Jesus Christ (see Matthew 1:1–6).

38:18 A seal was a form of identification used to authenticate legal documents. Usually a unique design carved in stone and worn on a ring or necklace inseparable from its owner, the seal was used by the wealthy and powerful to mark clay or wax. Because Tamar had Judah's seal, she could prove beyond a doubt that he had been with her.

24 Now it was about three months later that Judah was informed, "Your daughter-in-
law Tamar has played the harlot, and behold, she is also with child by harlotry." Then
Judah said, "Bring her out and let her be burned!"
25 It was while she was being brought out that she sent to her father-in-law, saying, "I
am with child by the man to whom these things belong." And she said, "Please examine
and see, whose signet ring and cords and staff are these?"
26 Judah recognized *them,* and said, "She is more righteous than I, inasmuch as I did
not give her to my son Shelah." And he did not have relations with her again.
27 It came about at the time she was giving birth, that behold, there were twins in her
womb.
28 Moreover, it took place while she was giving birth, one put out a hand, and the midwife took and tied a scarlet *thread* on his hand, saying, "This one came out first."
29 But it came about as he drew back his hand, that behold, his brother came out. Then
she said, "What a breach you have made for yourself!" So he was named [49]Perez.
30 Afterward his brother came out who had the scarlet *thread* on his hand; and he was
named [50]Zerah.

3. Joseph is thrown into prison

Joseph's Success in Egypt

39 Now Joseph had been taken down to Egypt; and Potiphar, an Egyptian officer of
Pharaoh, the captain of the bodyguard, bought him from the Ishmaelites, who
had taken him down there.
2 The LORD was with Joseph, so he became a successful man. And he was in the house
of his master, the Egyptian.
3 Now his master saw that the LORD was with him and *how* the LORD caused all that
he did to prosper in his hand.
4 So Joseph found favor in his sight and became his personal servant; and he made
him overseer over his house, and all that he owned he put in his charge.
5 It came about that from the time he made him overseer in his house and over all
that he owned, the LORD blessed the Egyptian's house on account of Joseph; thus the
LORD's blessing was upon all that he owned, in the house and in the field.
6 So he left everything he owned in Joseph's charge; and with him *there* he did not
concern himself with anything except the food which he ate.
Now Joseph was handsome in form and appearance.
7 It came about after these events that his master's wife looked with desire at Joseph,
and she said, "Lie with me."
8 But he refused and said to his master's wife, "Behold, with me *here,* my master does
not concern himself with anything in the house, and he has put all that he owns in my charge.
9 "There is no one greater in this house than I, and he has withheld nothing from
me except you, because you are his wife. How then could I do this great evil and sin
against God?"

38:24 Lev 21:9
38:25 Gen 37:32
38:26 1 Sam 24:17; Gen 38:14
38:27 Gen 25:24-26
38:29 Gen 46:12; Ruth 4:12
38:30 1 Chr 2:4
39:1 Gen 37:25, 28, 36; Ps 105:17
39:2 Gen 39:3, 21, 23; Acts 7:9
39:3 Gen 21:22; 26:28; Ps 1:3
39:4 Gen 18:3; 19:19; Gen 24:2; 39:8, 22
39:5 Gen 30:27; Deut 28:3, 4, 11
39:6 Gen 29:17; 1 Sam 16:12
39:7 Prov 7:15-20; 2 Sam 13:11
39:8 Prov 6:23, 24
39:9 Gen 41:40; Gen 20:6; 42:18; 2 Sam 12:13; Ps 51:4

49 I.e. a breach **50** I.e. a dawning or brightness

38:24–26 When Tamar revealed she was pregnant, Judah, who unknowingly had gotten her pregnant, moved to have her killed. Judah had concealed his own sin, yet he came down harshly on Tamar. Often the sins we try to cover up are the ones that anger us most when we see them in others. If you become indignant at the sins of others, you may have a similar tendency to sin that you don't wish to face. When we admit our sins and ask God to forgive us, forgiving others becomes easier.

39:1 The date of Joseph's arrival in Egypt is debatable. Many believe he arrived during the period of the Hyksos rulers, foreigners who came from the region of Canaan. They invaded Egypt and controlled the land for almost 150 years. If Joseph arrived during their rule, it is easy to see why he was rapidly promoted up the royal ladder. Because the Hyksos were foreigners themselves, they would not hold this brilliant young foreigner's ancestry against him.

39:1 *Pharaoh* was the general name for all the kings of Egypt. It was a title like "King" or "President" used to address the country's leader. The Pharaohs in Genesis and Exodus were different men.

39:1 Ancient Egypt was a land of great contrasts. People were either rich beyond measure or poverty stricken. There wasn't much middle ground. Joseph found himself serving Potiphar, an extremely rich officer in Pharaoh's service. Rich families like Potiphar's had elaborate homes two or three stories tall with beautiful gardens and balconies. They enjoyed live entertainment at home as they chose delicious fruit from expensive bowls. They surrounded themselves with alabaster vases, paintings, beautiful rugs, and hand-carved chairs. Dinner was served on golden tableware, and the rooms were lighted with gold lampstands. Servants, like Joseph, worked on the first floor, while the family occupied the upper stories.

39:9 Potiphar's wife failed to seduce Joseph, who resisted this temptation by saying it would be a sin against God. Joseph didn't say, "I'd be hurting you," or "I'd be sinning against Potiphar," or "I'd be sinning against myself." Under pressure, such excuses are easily rationalized away. Remember that sexual sin is not just between two consenting adults. It is an act of disobedience against God.

10 As she spoke to Joseph day after day, he did not listen to her to lie beside her *or* be
with her.
11 Now it happened one day that he went into the house to do his work, and none of
the men of the household was there inside.
12 She caught him by his garment, saying, "Lie with me!" And he left his garment in
her hand and fled, and went outside.
13 When she saw that he had left his garment in her hand and had fled outside,
14 she called to the men of her household and said to them, "See, he has brought in a
Hebrew to us to make sport of us; he came in to me to lie with me, and I screamed.
15 "When he heard that I raised my voice and [51]screamed, he left his garment beside
me and fled and went outside."
16 So she left his garment beside her until his master came home.
17 Then she spoke to him with these words, "The Hebrew slave, whom you brought to
us, came in to me to make sport of me;
18 and as I raised my voice and screamed, he left his garment beside me and fled outside."

39:17 Ex 23:1; Prov 26:28

Joseph Imprisoned

19 Now when his master heard the words of his wife, which she spoke to him, saying,
"This is what your slave did to me," his anger burned.
20 So Joseph's master took him and put him into the jail, the place where the king's
prisoners were confined; and he was there in the jail.
21 But the LORD was with Joseph and extended kindness to him, and gave him favor
in the sight of the chief jailer.
22 The chief jailer committed to Joseph's charge all the prisoners who were in the jail;
so that whatever was done there, he was responsible *for it.*
23 The chief jailer did not supervise anything under Joseph's charge because the LORD
was with him; and whatever he did, the LORD made to prosper.

39:19 Prov 6:34
39:20 Gen 40:3; Ps 105:18
39:21 Gen 39:2; Ps 105:19; Acts 7:9; Ex 3:21; 11:3; 12:36
39:22 Gen 39:4; 40:3, 4
39:23 Gen 39:3, 8; Gen 39:2, 3; Gen 39:3

Joseph Interprets a Dream

40 Then it came about after these things, the cupbearer and the baker for the king
of Egypt offended their lord, the king of Egypt.
2 Pharaoh was furious with his two officials, the chief cupbearer and the chief baker.
3 So he put them in confinement in the house of the captain of the bodyguard, in the
jail, the *same* place where Joseph was imprisoned.
4 The captain of the bodyguard put Joseph in charge of them, and he took care of
them; and they were in confinement for some time.
5 Then the cupbearer and the baker for the king of Egypt, who were confined in jail,
both had a dream the same night, each man with his *own* dream *and* each dream with its
own interpretation.
6 When Joseph came to them in the morning and observed them, behold, they were
dejected.
7 He asked Pharaoh's officials who were with him in confinement in his master's house,
"Why are your faces so sad today?"

40:1 Gen 40:11, 13; Neh 1:11
40:2 Prov 16:14
40:3 Gen 39:1, 20
40:7 Neh 2:2

51 Lit *called out*

39:10–15 Joseph avoided Potiphar's wife as much as possible. He refused her advances and finally *fled* from her. Sometimes merely trying to avoid temptation is not enough. We must turn and run, especially when the temptations seem very strong, as is often the case in sexual temptations.

39:20 Jails were grim places with vile conditions. They were used to house forced laborers or, like Joseph, the accused who were awaiting trial. Prisoners were guilty until proven innocent, and there was no right to a speedy trial. Many prisoners never made it to court, because trials were held at the whim of the ruler. Joseph was in jail two years until he appeared before Pharaoh, and then he was called out to interpret a dream, not to stand trial.

39:21–23 As a prisoner and slave, Joseph could have seen his situation as hopeless. Instead, he did his best with each small task given him. His diligence and positive attitude were soon noticed by the chief jailer, who promoted him to prison administrator. Are you facing a seemingly hopeless predicament? At work, at home, or at school, follow Joseph's example by taking each small task and doing your best. Remember how God turned Joseph's situation around. He will see your efforts and can reverse even overwhelming odds.

40:1–3 The cupbearer and the baker were two of the most trusted men in Pharaoh's kingdom. The baker was in charge of making the Pharaoh's food, and the cupbearer tasted all of his food and drink before giving it to him, in case any of it was contaminated or poisoned. These trusted men must have been suspected of a serious wrong, perhaps of conspiring against Pharaoh. Later the cupbearer was released and the baker executed.

40:8 Gen 41:15; Gen 41:16; Dan 2:27, 28

8 Then they said to him, "We have had a dream and there is no one to interpret it." Then Joseph said to them, "Do not interpretations belong to God? Tell *it* to me, please."
9 So the chief cupbearer told his dream to Joseph, and said to him, "In my dream, behold, *there was* a vine in front of me;
10 and on the vine *were* three branches. And as it was budding, its blossoms came out, *and* its clusters produced ripe grapes.
11 "Now Pharaoh's cup was in my hand; so I took the grapes and squeezed them into Pharaoh's cup, and I put the cup into Pharaoh's hand."

40:12 Dan 2:36; 4:18, 19

12 Then Joseph said to him, "This is the interpretation of it: the three branches are three days;
13 within three more days Pharaoh will [52]lift up your head and restore you to your office; and you will put Pharaoh's cup into his hand according to your former custom when you were his cupbearer.

40:14 Josh 2:12; 1 Sam 20:14; 1 Kin 2:7

14 "Only keep me in mind when it goes well with you, and please do me a kindness by mentioning me to Pharaoh and get me out of this house.

40:15 Gen 37:26-28

15 "For I was in fact kidnapped from the land of the Hebrews, and even here I have done nothing that they should have put me into the dungeon."
16 When the chief baker saw that he had interpreted favorably, he said to Joseph, "I also *saw* in my dream, and behold, *there were* three baskets of white bread on my head;
17 and in the top basket *there were* some of all sorts of baked food for Pharaoh, and the birds were eating them out of the basket on my head."
18 Then Joseph answered and said, "This is its interpretation: the three baskets are three days;
19 within three more days Pharaoh will lift up your head from you and will hang you on a tree, and the birds will eat your flesh off you."

40:20 Matt 14:6; 2 Kin 25:27; Jer 52:31

20 Thus it came about on the third day, *which was* Pharaoh's birthday, that he made a feast for all his servants; and he lifted up the head of the chief cupbearer and the head of the chief baker among his servants.

40:21 Gen 40:13

21 He restored the chief cupbearer to his office, and he put the cup into Pharaoh's hand;

40:22 Gen 40:19; Esth 7:10

22 but he hanged the chief baker, just as Joseph had interpreted to them.
23 Yet the chief cupbearer did not remember Joseph, but forgot him.

40:23 Job 19:14; Ps 31:12; Eccl 9:15

4. Joseph is placed in charge of Egypt

Pharaoh's Dream

41 Now it happened at the end of two full years that Pharaoh had a dream, and behold, he was standing by the Nile.

41:2 Job 8:11; Is 19:6, 7

2 And lo, from the Nile there came up seven cows, sleek and fat; and they grazed in the marsh grass.
3 Then behold, seven other cows came up after them from the Nile, ugly and gaunt, and they stood by the *other* cows on the bank of the Nile.
4 The ugly and gaunt cows ate up the seven sleek and fat cows. Then Pharaoh awoke.
5 He fell asleep and dreamed a second time; and behold, seven ears of grain came up on a single stalk, plump and good.
6 Then behold, seven ears, thin and scorched by the east wind, sprouted up after them.

41:8 Dan 2:1, 3; Ex 7:11, 22; Dan 1:20; 2:2; Matt 2:1; Dan 2:27; 4:7

7 The thin ears swallowed up the seven plump and full ears. Then Pharaoh awoke, and behold, *it was* a dream.
8 Now in the morning his spirit was troubled, so he sent and called for all the magicians

52 Or possibly *forgive you*

40:8 When the subject of dreams came up, Joseph focused everyone's attention on God. Rather than using the situation to make himself look good, he turned it into a powerful witness for the Lord. One secret of effective witnessing is to recognize opportunities to relate God to the other person's experience. When the opportunity arises, we must have the courage to speak, as Joseph did.

40:23 When Pharaoh's cupbearer was freed from jail, he forgot about Joseph, even though he had Joseph to thank for letting him know of his coming freedom. It was two full years before Joseph had another opportunity to be freed (41:1). Yet Joseph's faith was deep, and he would be ready when the next chance came. When we feel passed by, overlooked, or forgotten, we shouldn't be surprised that people are often ungrateful. In similar situations, trust God as Joseph did. More opportunities may be waiting.

41:8 Magicians and wise men were common in the palaces of ancient rulers. Their job description included studying sacred arts and sciences, reading the stars, interpreting dreams, predicting the future, and performing magic. These men had power (see Exodus 7:11–12), but their power was satanic. They were unable to interpret Pharaoh's dream, but God had revealed it to Joseph in prison.

of Egypt, and all its wise men. And Pharaoh told them his dreams, but there was no one
who could interpret them to Pharaoh.
9 Then the chief cupbearer spoke to Pharaoh, saying, "I would make mention today **41:9**
of my *own* offenses. Gen 40:14, 23
10 "Pharaoh was furious with his servants, and he put me in confinement in the house **41:10**
of the captain of the bodyguard, *both* me and the chief baker. Gen 40:2, 3; Gen 39:20
11 "We had a dream on the same night, he and I; each of us dreamed according to the **41:11**
interpretation of his *own* dream. Gen 40:5
12 "Now a Hebrew youth *was* with us there, a servant of the captain of the bodyguard, **41:12**
and we related *them* to him, and he interpreted our dreams for us. To each one he inter- Gen 37:36; Gen
preted according to his *own* dream. 40:12
13 "And just as he interpreted for us, so it happened; he restored me in my office, but **41:13**
he hanged him." Gen 40:21, 22

Joseph Interprets

14 Then Pharaoh sent and called for Joseph, and they hurriedly brought him out **41:14**
of the dungeon; and when he had shaved himself and changed his clothes, he came to Ps 105:20; Dan 2:25
Pharaoh.
15 Pharaoh said to Joseph, "I have had a dream, but no one can interpret it; and I have **41:15**
heard it said about you, that when you hear a dream you can interpret it." Gen 41:8; Dan 5:16
16 Joseph then answered Pharaoh, saying, "It is not in me; God will give Pharaoh a **41:16**
favorable answer." Dan 2:30; Zech 4:6; Acts 3:12; 2 Cor 3:5;
17 So Pharaoh spoke to Joseph, "In my dream, behold, I was standing on the bank of Gen 40:8; 41:25, 28,
the Nile; 32; Deut 29:29; Dan 2:22, 28, 47
18 and behold, seven cows, fat and sleek came up out of the Nile, and they grazed in
the marsh grass.
19 "Lo, seven other cows came up after them, poor and very ugly and gaunt, such as I
had never seen for ugliness in all the land of Egypt;
20 and the lean and ugly cows ate up the first seven fat cows.
21 "Yet when they had devoured them, it could not be detected that they had devoured
them, for they were just as ugly as before. Then I awoke.
22 "I saw also in my dream, and behold, seven ears, full and good, came up on a single
stalk;
23 and lo, seven ears, withered, thin, *and* scorched by the east wind, sprouted up after
them;
24 and the thin ears swallowed the seven good ears. Then I told it to the magicians, but **41:24**
there was no one who could explain it to me." Is 8:19; Dan 4:7
25 Now Joseph said to Pharaoh, "Pharaoh's dreams are one *and the same;* God has **41:25**
told to Pharaoh what He is about to do. Gen 41:28, 32; Dan 2:28, 29, 45
26 "The seven good cows are seven years; and the seven good ears are seven years; the
dreams are one *and the same.*
27 "The seven lean and ugly cows that came up after them are seven years, and the seven **41:27**
thin ears scorched by the east wind will be seven years of famine. 2 Kin 8:1
28 "It is as I have spoken to Pharaoh: God has shown to Pharaoh what He is about to do. **41:28**
29 "Behold, seven years of great abundance are coming in all the land of Egypt; Gen 41:25, 32
30 and after them seven years of famine will come, and all the abundance will be for- **41:29**
gotten in the land of Egypt, and the famine will ravage the land. Gen 41:47
31 "So the abundance will be unknown in the land because of that subsequent famine; **41:30**
for it *will be* very severe. Gen 41:54, 56; 47:13; Ps 105:16

41:14 Our most important opportunities may come when we least expect them. Joseph was brought hastily from the dungeon and pushed before Pharaoh. Did he have time to prepare? Yes and no. He had no warning that he would be suddenly pulled from jail and questioned by the king. Yet Joseph was ready for almost anything because of his right relationship with God. It was not Joseph's knowledge of dreams that helped him interpret their meaning. It was his knowledge of God. Be ready for opportunities by getting to know more about God. Then you will be ready to call on him when opportunities come your way.

41:16 Joseph made sure that he gave the credit to God. We should be careful to do the same. To take the honor for ourselves is a form of stealing God's honor. Don't be silent when you know you should be giving glory and credit to God.

41:28–36 After interpreting Pharaoh's dream, Joseph gave the king a survival plan for the next 14 years. The only way to prevent starvation was through careful planning; without a famine plan Egypt would have turned from prosperity to ruin. Many find detailed planning boring and unnecessary. But planning is a responsibility, not an option. Joseph was able to save a nation by translating God's plan for Egypt into practical actions (implementation). We must take time to translate God's plan for us into practical actions too.

41:32 Gen 41:25, 28

32 "Now as for the repeating of the dream to Pharaoh twice, *it means* that the matter is determined by God, and God will quickly bring it about.

41:33 Gen 41:39

33 "Now let Pharaoh look for a man discerning and wise, and set him over the land of Egypt.

34 "Let Pharaoh take action to appoint overseers in charge of the land, and let him exact a fifth *of the produce* of the land of Egypt in the seven years of abundance.

41:35 Gen 41:48

35 "Then let them gather all the food of these good years that are coming, and store up the grain for food in the cities under Pharaoh's authority, and let them guard *it*.

36 "Let the food become as a reserve for the land for the seven years of famine which will occur in the land of Egypt, so that the land will not perish during the famine."

37 Now the proposal seemed good to Pharaoh and to all his servants.

Joseph Is Made a Ruler of Egypt

41:38 Job 32:8; Dan 4:8, 9, 18; 5:11, 14

38 Then Pharaoh said to his servants, "Can we find a man like this, in whom is a divine spirit?"

41:39 Gen 41:33

39 So Pharaoh said to Joseph, "Since God has informed you of all this, there is no one so discerning and wise as you are.

41:40 Ps 105:21; Acts 7:10

40 "You shall be over my house, and according to your command all my people shall do homage; only in the throne I will be greater than you."

41:41 Gen 42:6; Ps 105:21; Dan 6:3; Acts 7:10

41 Pharaoh said to Joseph, "See, I have set you over all the land of Egypt."

42 Then Pharaoh took off his signet ring from his hand and put it on Joseph's hand, and clothed him in garments of fine linen and put the gold necklace around his neck.

41:42 Esth 3:10; 8:2; Dan 5:7, 16, 29

43 He had him ride in his second chariot; and they proclaimed before him, "Bow the knee!" And he set him over all the land of Egypt.

41:44 Ps 105:22

44 Moreover, Pharaoh said to Joseph, "*Though* I am Pharaoh, yet without your permission no one shall raise his hand or foot in all the land of Egypt."

41:45 Jer 43:13; Ezek 30:17

45 Then Pharaoh named Joseph [53]Zaphenath-paneah; and he gave him Asenath, the daughter of Potiphera priest of On, as his wife. And Joseph went forth over the land of Egypt.

41:46 Gen 37:2

46 Now Joseph was thirty years old when he [54]stood before Pharaoh, king of Egypt. And Joseph went out from the presence of Pharaoh and went through all the land of Egypt.

47 During the seven years of plenty the land brought forth abundantly.

48 So he gathered all the food of *these* seven years which occurred in the land of Egypt and placed the food in the cities; he placed in every city the food from its own surrounding fields.

49 Thus Joseph stored up grain in great abundance like the sand of the sea, until he stopped measuring *it*, for it was beyond measure.

The Sons of Joseph

41:50 Gen 48:5

50 Now before the year of famine came, two sons were born to Joseph, whom Asenath, the daughter of Potiphera priest of [55]On, bore to him.

51 Joseph named the firstborn [56]Manasseh, "For," *he said,* "God has made me forget all my trouble and all my father's household."

41:52 Gen 17:6; 28:3; 49:22

52 He named the second [57]Ephraim, "For," *he said,* "God has made me fruitful in the land of my affliction."

53 When the seven years of plenty which had been in the land of Egypt came to an end,

53 Probably Egyptian for "God speaks; he lives" **54** Or *entered the service of* **55** Or *Heliopolis* **56** I.e. making to forget **57** I.e. fruitfulness

---

41:38 Pharaoh recognized that Joseph was a man "in whom is a divine spirit." You probably won't get to interpret dreams for a king, but those who know you should be able to see God in you, through your kind words, merciful acts, and wise advice. Do your relatives, neighbors, and coworkers see you as a person in whom the Spirit of God lives?

41:39–40 Joseph rose quickly to the top, from dungeon walls to Pharaoh's palace. His training for this important position involved being first a slave and then a prisoner. In each situation he learned the importance of serving God and others. Whatever your situation, no matter how undesirable, consider it part of your training program for serving God.

41:45 Pharaoh may have been trying to make Joseph more acceptable by giving him an Egyptian name and wife. He probably wanted to (1) play down the fact that Joseph was a nomadic shepherd, an occupation disliked by the Egyptians, (2) make Joseph's name easier for Egyptians to pronounce and remember, and (3) show how highly he was honored by giving him the daughter of a prominent Egyptian official.

41:46 Joseph was 30 years old when he became governor of Egypt. He was 17 when he was sold into slavery by his brothers. Thus he must have spent 11 years as an Egyptian slave and two years in prison.

54 and the seven years of famine began to come, just as Joseph had said, then there
was famine in all the lands, but in all the land of Egypt there was bread.

41:54 Gen 41:30; Ps 105:16; Acts 7:11

55 So when all the land of Egypt was famished, the people cried out to Pharaoh for
bread; and Pharaoh said to all the Egyptians, "Go to Joseph; whatever he says to you,
you shall do."

41:55 John 2:5

56 When the famine was *spread* over all the face of the earth, then Joseph opened all
the storehouses, and sold to the Egyptians; and the famine was severe in the land of Egypt.
57 *The people of* all the earth came to Egypt to buy grain from Joseph, because the famine was severe in all the earth.

41:57 Gen 12:10

5. Joseph and his brothers meet in Egypt

Joseph's Brothers Sent to Egypt

42 Now Jacob saw that there was grain in Egypt, and Jacob said to his sons, "Why
are you staring at one another?"

42:1 Acts 7:12

2 He said, "Behold, I have heard that there is grain in Egypt; go down there and buy
some for us from that place, so that we may live and not die."

42:2 Acts 7:12; Gen 43:8; Ps 33:18, 19

3 Then ten brothers of Joseph went down to buy grain from Egypt.
4 But Jacob did not send Joseph's brother Benjamin with his brothers, for he said, "I
am afraid that harm may befall him."

42:4 Gen 35:24; Gen 42:38

5 So the sons of Israel came to buy grain among those who were coming, for the famine was in the land of Canaan *also.*

42:5 Gen 12:10; 26:1; 41:57; Acts 7:11

6 Now Joseph was the ruler over the land; he was the one who sold to all the people
of the land. And Joseph's brothers came and bowed down to him with *their* faces to the
ground.

42:6 Gen 41:41, 55; Gen 37:7-10; 41:43; Is 60:14

7 When Joseph saw his brothers he recognized them, but he disguised himself to them
and spoke to them harshly. And he said to them, "Where have you come from?" And
they said, "From the land of Canaan, to buy food."

42:7 Gen 42:30

8 But Joseph had recognized his brothers, although they did not recognize him.

42:8 Gen 37:2; 41:46

9 Joseph remembered the dreams which he had about them, and said to them, "You
are spies; you have come to look at the undefended parts of our land."

42:9 Gen 37:6-9

10 Then they said to him, "No, my lord, but your servants have come to buy food.

42:10 Gen 37:8

11 "We are all sons of one man; we are honest men, your servants are not spies."

42:11 Gen 42:16, 19, 31, 34

12 Yet he said to them, "No, but you have come to look at the undefended parts of our
land!"
13 But they said, "Your servants are twelve brothers *in all,* the sons of one man in the
land of Canaan; and behold, the youngest is with our father today, and one is no longer
alive."

42:13 Gen 43:7; Gen 37:30; 42:32; 44:20

14 Joseph said to them, "It is as I said to you, you are spies;
15 by this you will be tested: by the life of Pharaoh, you shall not go from this place
unless your youngest brother comes here!

42:15 1 Sam 17:55

16 "Send one of you that he may get your brother, while you remain confined, that your
words may be tested, whether there is truth in you. But if not, by the life of Pharaoh,
surely you are spies."

42:16 Gen 42:11

41:54 Famine was a catastrophe in ancient times, just as it still is in many parts of the world today. Almost perfect conditions were needed to produce good crops because there were no chemical fertilizers or pesticides. Any variances in rainfall or insect activity could cause crop failure and great hunger because the people relied almost exclusively on their own crops for food. Lack of storage, refrigeration, or transportation turned a moderate famine into a desperate situation. The famine Joseph prepared for was severe. Without God's intervention, the Egyptian nation would have crumbled.

42:1–2 Why was grain so valuable in those days? As a food source it was universal and used in nearly everything eaten. It could be dried and stored much longer than any vegetables, milk products, or meat. It was so important that it was even used as money.

42:4 Jacob was especially fond of Benjamin because he was Joseph's only full brother and—as far as Jacob knew—the only surviving son of his beloved wife, Rachel. Benjamin was Jacob's youngest son and a child of his old age.

42:7 Joseph could have revealed his identity to his brothers at once. But Joseph's last memory of them was of staring in horror at their faces as slave traders carried him away. Were his brothers still evil and treacherous, or had they changed over the years? Joseph decided to put them through a few tests to find out.

42:8–9 Joseph remembered his dreams about his brothers bowing down to him (37:6–9). Those dreams were coming true! As a young boy, Joseph was boastful about his dreams. As a man, he no longer flaunted his superior status. He did not feel the need to say "I told you so." It was not yet time to reveal his identity, so he kept quiet. Sometimes it is best for us to remain quiet, even when we would like to have the last word.

42:15 Joseph was testing his brothers to make sure they had not been as cruel to Benjamin as they had been to him. Benjamin was his only full brother, and he wanted to see him face to face.

17 So he put them all together in prison for three days.
18 Now Joseph said to them on the third day, "Do this and live, for I fear God:
19 if you are honest men, let one of your brothers be confined in your prison; but as for
the rest of you, go, carry grain for the famine of your households,
20 and bring your youngest brother to me, so your words may be verified, and you will
not die." And they did so.
21 Then they said to one another, "Truly we are guilty concerning our brother, because
we saw the distress of his soul when he pleaded with us, yet we would not listen; therefore this distress has come upon us."
22 Reuben answered them, saying, "Did I not tell you, 'Do not sin against the boy';
and you would not listen? Now comes the reckoning for his blood."
23 They did not know, however, that Joseph understood, for there was an interpreter
between them.
24 He turned away from them and wept. But when he returned to them and spoke to
them, he took Simeon from them and bound him before their eyes.
25 Then Joseph gave orders to fill their bags with grain and to restore every man's money
in his sack, and to give them provisions for the journey. And thus it was done for them.
26 So they loaded their donkeys with their grain and departed from there.
27 As one *of them* opened his sack to give his donkey fodder at the lodging place, he
saw his money; and behold, it was in the mouth of his sack.
28 Then he said to his brothers, "My money has been returned, and behold, it is even
in my sack." And their hearts sank, and they *turned* trembling to one another, saying,
"What is this that God has done to us?"

Simeon Is Held Hostage

29 When they came to their father Jacob in the land of Canaan, they told him all that
had happened to them, saying,
30 "The man, the lord of the land, spoke harshly with us, and took us for spies of the
country.
31 "But we said to him, 'We are honest men; we are not spies.
32 'We are twelve brothers, sons of our father; one is no longer alive, and the youngest
is with our father today in the land of Canaan.'
33 "The man, the lord of the land, said to us, 'By this I will know that you are honest
men: leave one of your brothers with me and take *grain for* the famine of your households, and go.
34 'But bring your youngest brother to me that I may know that you are not spies, but
honest men. I will give your brother to you, and you may trade in the land.' "
35 Now it came about as they were emptying their sacks, that behold, every man's bundle of money *was* in his sack; and when they and their father saw their bundles of money,
they were dismayed.
36 Their father Jacob said to them, "You have bereaved me of my children: Joseph is
no more, and Simeon is no more, and you would take Benjamin; all these things are
against me."
37 Then Reuben spoke to his father, saying, "You may put my two sons to death if I do
not bring him *back* to you; put him in my care, and I will return him to you."
38 But Jacob said, "My son shall not go down with you; for his brother is dead, and he
alone is left. If harm should befall him on the journey you are taking, then you will bring
my gray hair down to Sheol in sorrow."

The Return to Egypt

43 Now the famine was severe in the land.
2 So it came about when they had finished eating the grain which they had
brought from Egypt, that their father said to them, "Go back, buy us a little food."

42:17 Gen 40:4, 7
42:18 Gen 39:9; Lev 25:43; Neh 5:15
42:20 Gen 42:34; 43:5; 44:23
42:21 Gen 37:26-28; 45:3; Hos 5:15
42:22 Gen 37:21, 22; Gen 9:5, 6; 1 Kin 2:32; 2 Chr 24:22; Ps 9:12
42:24 Gen 43:30; 45:14, 15; Gen 43:14, 23
42:25 Gen 44:1; Rom 12:17, 20, 21; 1 Pet 3:9
42:27 Gen 43:21, 22
42:28 Gen 43:23
42:30 Gen 42:7
42:31 Gen 42:11
42:33 Gen 42:19, 20
42:34 Gen 34:10
42:35 Gen 43:12, 15, 21
42:36 Gen 43:14
42:38 Gen 37:33, 34; 42:13; 44:27, 28; Gen 42:4; Gen 37:35; 44:29, 31
43:1 Gen 12:10; 26:1; 41:56, 57

42:22 Reuben couldn't resist saying "I told you so." "The reckoning for his blood" means that they thought they were being punished by God for what they had done to Joseph.

43:1 Jacob and his sons had no relief from the famine. They could not see God's overall plan of sending them to Egypt to be reunited with Joseph and fed from Egypt's storehouses. If you are praying for relief from suffering or pressure and God is not bringing it as quickly as you would like, remember that God may be leading you to special treasures.

3 Judah spoke to him, however, saying, "The man solemnly warned us, 'You shall not see my face unless your brother is with you.'

43:3 Gen 43:5; 44:23

4 "If you send our brother with us, we will go down and buy you food.

5 "But if you do not send *him,* we will not go down; for the man said to us, 'You will not see my face unless your brother is with you.' "

6 Then Israel said, "Why did you treat me so badly by telling the man whether you still had *another* brother?"

7 But they said, "The man questioned particularly about us and our relatives, saying, 'Is your father still alive? Have you *another* brother?' So we answered his questions. Could we possibly know that he would say, 'Bring your brother down'?"

43:7 Gen 42:13; 43:27

8 Judah said to his father Israel, "Send the lad with me and we will arise and go, that we may live and not die, we as well as you and our little ones.

43:8 Gen 42:2

9 "I myself will be surety for him; you may hold me responsible for him. If I do not bring him *back* to you and set him before you, then let me bear the blame before you forever.

43:9 Gen 42:37; 44:32; Philem 18, 19

10 "For if we had not delayed, surely by now we could have returned twice."

11 Then their father Israel said to them, "If *it must be* so, then do this: take some of the best products of the land in your bags, and carry down to the man as a present, a little balm and a little honey, aromatic gum and myrrh, pistachio nuts and almonds.

43:11 Gen 32:20; 43:25, 26; Gen 37:25; Jer 8:22; Ezek 27:17

12 "Take double *the* money in your hand, and take back in your hand the money that was returned in the mouth of your sacks; perhaps it was a mistake.

43:12 Gen 42:25, 35; 43:21, 22

13 "Take your brother also, and arise, return to the man;

14 and may God Almighty grant you compassion in the sight of the man, so that he will release to you your other brother and Benjamin. And as for me, if I am bereaved of my children, I am bereaved."

43:14 Gen 17:1; 28:3; 35:11; Ps 106:46; Gen 42:24; Gen 42:36

15 So the men took this present, and they took double *the* money in their hand, and Benjamin; then they arose and went down to Egypt and stood before Joseph.

43:15 Gen 43:11

Joseph Sees Benjamin

16 When Joseph saw Benjamin with them, he said to his house steward, "Bring the men into the house, and slay an animal and make ready; for the men are to dine with me at noon."

43:16 Gen 44:1

17 So the man did as Joseph said, and brought the men to Joseph's house.

18 Now the men were afraid, because they were brought to Joseph's house; and they said, "*It is* because of the money that was returned in our sacks the first time that we are being brought in, that he may seek occasion against us and fall upon us, and take us for slaves with our donkeys."

19 So they came near to Joseph's house steward, and spoke to him at the entrance of the house,

20 and said, "Oh, my lord, we indeed came down the first time to buy food,

21 and it came about when we came to the lodging place, that we opened our sacks, and behold, each man's money was in the mouth of his sack, our money in full. So we have brought it back in our hand.

43:21 Gen 42:27, 35; Gen 43:12, 15

22 "We have also brought down other money in our hand to buy food; we do not know who put our money in our sacks."

23 He said, "[58]Be at ease, do not be afraid. Your God and the God of your father has given you treasure in your sacks; I had your money." Then he brought Simeon out to them.

43:23 Gen 42:28; Gen 42:24

58 Lit *Peace be to you*

43:9 Judah accepted full responsibility for Benjamin's safety. He did not know what that might mean for him, but he was determined to do his duty. In the end it was Judah's stirring words that caused Joseph to break down with emotion and reveal himself to his brothers (44:18–34). Accepting responsibilities is difficult, but it builds character and confidence, earns others' respect, and motivates us to complete our work. When you have been given an assignment to complete or a responsibility to fulfill, commit yourself to seeing it through.

43:11 These gifts of balm, honey, aromatic gum, myrrh, pistachio nuts, and almonds were highly valuable specialty items not common in Egypt. Because of the famine, they were even more rare.

43:12 Joseph's brothers arrived home from Egypt only to find in their grain sacks the money they had used to pay for the grain (42:35). Some months later, when it was time to return to Egypt for more food, Jacob instructed them to take extra money so they could pay for the previous purchase as well as for additional grain. Jacob did not try to get away with anything. He was a man of integrity who paid for what he bought, whether he had to or not. We should follow his example and guard our integrity. A reputation for honesty is worth far more than the money we might save by compromising it.

43:23 How did the money get into the sacks? Most likely, Joseph instructed his steward to replace the money and then explain it with

43:24 Gen 18:4; 19:2; 24:32; Luke 7:44; John 13:5; 1 Tim 5:10

24 Then the man brought the men into Joseph's house and gave them water, and they washed their feet; and he gave their donkeys fodder.

25 So they prepared the present for Joseph's coming at noon; for they had heard that they were to eat a meal there.

43:25 Gen 43:11, 15

26 When Joseph came home, they brought into the house to him the present which was in their hand and bowed to the ground before him.

43:26 Gen 37:7, 10

27 Then he asked them about their welfare, and said, "Is your old father well, of whom you spoke? Is he still alive?"

43:27 Gen 43:7; 45:3

28 They said, "Your servant our father is well; he is still alive." They bowed down in homage.

43:28 Gen 37:7, 10

29 As he lifted his eyes and saw his brother Benjamin, his mother's son, he said, "Is this your youngest brother, of whom you spoke to me?" And he said, "May God be gracious to you, my son."

43:29 Gen 42:13; Num 6:25; Ps 67:1

30 Joseph hurried *out* for he was deeply stirred over his brother, and he sought *a place* to weep; and he entered his chamber and wept there.

43:30 1 Kin 3:26; Gen 42:24; 45:2, 14, 15; 46:29

31 Then he washed his face and came out; and he controlled himself and said, "Serve the meal."

43:31 Gen 45:1

32 So they served him by himself, and them by themselves, and the Egyptians who ate with him by themselves, because the Egyptians could not eat bread with the Hebrews, for that is loathsome to the Egyptians.

43:32 Gen 46:34; Ex 8:26

33 Now they were seated before him, the firstborn according to his birthright and the youngest according to his youth, and the men looked at one another in astonishment.

43:33 Gen 42:7

34 He took portions to them from his own table, but Benjamin's portion was five times as much as any of theirs. So they feasted and drank freely with him.

43:34 Gen 35:24; 45:22

The Brothers Are Brought Back

44:1 Gen 42:25

44 Then he commanded his house steward, saying, "Fill the men's sacks with food, as much as they can carry, and put each man's money in the mouth of his sack.

2 "Put my cup, the silver cup, in the mouth of the sack of the youngest, and his money for the grain." And he did as Joseph had told *him.*

3 As soon as it was light, the men were sent away, they with their donkeys.

44:4 Gen 44:13

4 They had *just* gone out of the city, *and* were not far off, when Joseph said to his house steward, "Up, follow the men; and when you overtake them, say to them, 'Why have you repaid evil for good?

44:5 Gen 30:27; 44:15; Lev 19:26; Deut 18:10-14

5 'Is not this the one from which my lord drinks and which he indeed uses for divination? You have done wrong in doing this.' "

6 So he overtook them and spoke these words to them.

7 They said to him, "Why does my lord speak such words as these? Far be it from your servants to do such a thing.

44:8 Gen 43:21

8 "Behold, the money which we found in the mouth of our sacks we have brought back to you from the land of Canaan. How then could we steal silver or gold from your lord's house?

44:9 Gen 31:32; Gen 44:16

9 "With whomever of your servants it is found, let him die, and we also will be my lord's slaves."

10 So he said, "Now let it also be according to your words; he with whom it is found shall be my slave, and *the rest of* you shall be innocent."

11 Then they hurried, each man lowered his sack to the ground, and each man opened his sack.

44:12 Gen 44:2

12 He searched, beginning with the oldest and ending with the youngest, and the cup was found in Benjamin's sack.

---

this response. Note that the steward credited their God, not some Egyptian deity.

43:32 Why did Joseph eat by himself? He was following the laws of the Egyptians' caste system. Egyptians considered themselves highly intelligent and sophisticated. They looked upon shepherds and nomads as uncultured and even vulgar. As a Hebrew, Joseph could not eat with Egyptians even though he outranked them. As foreigners and shepherds, his brothers were lower in rank than any Egyptian citizens, so they had to eat separately too.

44:2 Joseph's silver cup was a symbol of his authority. It was thought to have supernatural powers, and to steal it was a serious crime. Such goblets were used for predicting the future. A person poured water into the cup and interpreted the reflections, ripples, and bubbles. Joseph wouldn't have needed his cup, since God told him everything he needed to know about the future.

13 Then they tore their clothes, and when each man loaded his donkey, they returned
to the city.
14 When Judah and his brothers came to Joseph's house, he was still there, and they
fell to the ground before him.
15 Joseph said to them, "What is this deed that you have done? Do you not know that
such a man as I can indeed practice divination?"
16 So Judah said, "What can we say to my lord? What can we speak? And how can we
justify ourselves? God has found out the iniquity of your servants; behold, we are my
lord's slaves, both we and the one in whose possession the cup has been found."
17 But he said, "Far be it from me to do this. The man in whose possession the cup has
been found, he shall be my slave; but as for you, go up in peace to your father."
18 Then Judah approached him, and said, "Oh my lord, may your servant please speak
a word in my lord's ears, and do not be angry with your servant; for you are equal to
Pharaoh.
19 "My lord asked his servants, saying, 'Have you a father or a brother?'
20 "We said to my lord, 'We have an old father and a little child of *his* old age. Now his
brother is dead, so he alone is left of his mother, and his father loves him.'
21 "Then you said to your servants, 'Bring him down to me that I may set my eyes on
him.'
22 "But we said to my lord, 'The lad cannot leave his father, for if he should leave his
father, his father would die.'
23 "You said to your servants, however, 'Unless your youngest brother comes down with
you, you will not see my face again.'
24 "Thus it came about when we went up to your servant my father, we told him the
words of my lord.
25 "Our father said, 'Go back, buy us a little food.'
26 "But we said, 'We cannot go down. If our youngest brother is with us, then we will go
down; for we cannot see the man's face unless our youngest brother is with us.'
27 "Your servant my father said to us, 'You know that my wife bore me two sons;
28 and the one went out from me, and I said, "Surely he is torn in pieces," and I have
not seen him since.
29 'If you take this one also from me, and harm befalls him, you will bring my gray hair
down to Sheol in sorrow.'
30 "Now, therefore, when I come to your servant my father, and the lad is not with us,
since his life is bound up in the lad's life,
31 when he sees that the lad is not *with us,* he will die. Thus your servants will bring the
gray hair of your servant our father down to Sheol in sorrow.
32 "For your servant became surety for the lad to my father, saying, 'If I do not bring
him *back* to you, then let me bear the blame before my father forever.'
33 "Now, therefore, please let your servant remain instead of the lad a slave to my lord,
and let the lad go up with his brothers.

44:13 Gen 37:29, 34; Num 14:6; 2 Sam 1:11; Gen 44:4
44:14 Gen 37:7, 10
44:15 Gen 44:5
44:16 Gen 44:9
44:18 Gen 18:30, 32; Ex 32:22; Gen 37:7, 8; 41:40-44
44:19 Gen 43:7
44:20 Gen 37:3; 43:8; 44:30; Gen 37:33; 42:13, 38
44:21 Gen 42:15, 20
44:23 Gen 43:3, 5
44:25 Gen 43:2
44:27 Gen 46:19
44:28 Gen 37:31-35
44:29 Gen 42:38; 44:31
44:30 1 Sam 18:1
44:31 Gen 44:29
44:32 Gen 43:9

44:13 Tearing clothes was an expression of deep sorrow, a customary manner of showing grief. The brothers were terrified that Benjamin might be harmed.

44:15 Did Joseph really practice divination? Probably not—he would have no desire or need to because of his relationship with God. This statement was probably part of the test to emphasize how important the cup was.

44:16–34 When Judah was younger, he showed no regard for his brother Joseph or his father, Jacob. First he convinced his brothers to sell Joseph as a slave (37:27); then he joined his brothers in lying to his father about Joseph's fate (37:32). But what a change had taken place in Judah! The man who sold one favored little brother into slavery now offered to become a slave himself to save another favored little brother. He was so concerned for his father and younger brother that he was willing to die for them. When you are ready to give up hope on yourself or others, remember that God can work a complete change in even the most selfish personality.

44:18–34 Judah finally could take no more and stepped forward to plead their case. This was risky because Joseph could have had him killed. But Judah courageously defended himself and his brothers and pled for mercy. And he offered to put himself in Benjamin's place. There are times when we should be silent, but there are also times when we should speak up, even if there could be serious repercussions. When faced with a situation that needs a strong voice and courageous action, remember Judah, and speak up.

44:32–33 Judah had promised Jacob that he would guarantee young Benjamin's safety (43:9). Now Judah had a chance to keep that promise. Becoming a slave was a terrible fate, but Judah was determined to keep his word to his father. He showed great courage in carrying out his promise. Accepting a responsibility means carrying it out with determination and courage, regardless of the personal sacrifice.

44:33 Joseph wanted to see if his brothers' attitudes had changed for the better, so he tested the way they treated each other. Judah, the brother who had stepped forward with the plan to sell Joseph (37:27), now stepped forward to take Benjamin's punishment so that Benjamin could return to their father. This courageous act convinced Joseph that his brothers had dramatically changed for the better.

34 "For how shall I go up to my father if the lad is not with me—for fear that I see the
evil that would overtake my father?"

Joseph Deals Kindly with His Brothers

45:1 Acts 7:13

45:2 Gen 45:14, 15; 46:29

45:3 Acts 7:13; Gen 43:27; Gen 37:20-28; 42:21, 22

45:4 Gen 37:28

45 Then Joseph could not control himself before all those who stood by him, and he
cried, "Have everyone go out from me." So there was no man with him when
Joseph made himself known to his brothers.
2 He wept so loudly that the Egyptians heard *it,* and the household of Pharaoh heard
of it.
3 Then Joseph said to his brothers, "I am Joseph! Is my father still alive?" But his
brothers could not answer him, for they were dismayed at his presence.
4 Then Joseph said to his brothers, "Please come closer to me." And they came closer. And he said, "I am your brother Joseph, whom you sold into Egypt.

JUDAH

People who are leaders stand out. They don't necessarily look or act a certain way until the need for their action is apparent. Among their skills are outspokenness, decisiveness, action, and control. These skills can be used for great good or great evil. Jacob's fourth son, Judah, was a natural leader. The events of his life provided many opportunities to exercise those skills. Unfortunately Judah's decisions were often shaped more by the pressures of the moment than by a conscious desire to cooperate with God's plan. But when he did recognize his mistakes, he was willing to admit them. His experience with Tamar and the final confrontation with Joseph are both examples of Judah's willingness to bear the blame when confronted. It was one of the qualities he passed on to his descendant David.

Whether or not we have Judah's natural leadership qualities, we share with him a tendency to be blind toward our own sin. Too often, however, we don't share his willingness to admit mistakes. From Judah we can learn that it is not wise to wait until our errors force us to admit to wrongdoing. It is far better to admit our mistakes openly, to shoulder the blame, and to seek forgiveness.

Strengths and accomplishments:
- Was a natural leader—outspoken and decisive
- Thought clearly and took action in high-pressure situations
- Was willing to stand by his word and put himself on the line when necessary
- Was the fourth son of 12, through whom God would eventually bring David and Jesus, the Messiah

Weaknesses and mistakes:
- Suggested to his brothers they sell Joseph into slavery
- Failed to keep his promise to his daughter-in-law, Tamar

Lessons from his life:
- God is in control, far beyond the immediate situation
- Procrastination often makes matters worse
- Judah's offer to substitute his life for Benjamin's is a picture of what his descendant Jesus would do for all people

Vital statistics:
- Where: Canaan and Egypt
- Occupation: Shepherd
- Relatives: Parents: Jacob and Leah. Wife: Bath-shua (1 Chronicles 2.3). Daughter-in-law: Tamar. Eleven brothers, at least one sister, and at least five sons

Key verses:
"Judah, your brothers shall praise you; your hand shall be on the neck of your enemies; your father's sons shall bow down to you. Judah is a lion's whelp; from the prey, my son, you have gone up. He couches, he lies down as a lion, and as a lion, who dares rouse him up? The scepter shall not depart from Judah, nor the ruler's staff from between his feet, until Shiloh comes, and to him shall be the obedience of the peoples" (Genesis 49:8–10).

Judah's story is told in Genesis 29:35—50:26. He is also mentioned in 1 Chronicles 2—4.

45:4–8 Although Joseph's brothers had wanted to get rid of him, God used even their evil actions to fulfill his ultimate plan. He sent Joseph ahead to preserve their lives, save Egypt, and prepare the way for the beginning of the nation of Israel. God is sovereign. His plans are not dictated by human actions. When others intend evil toward you, remember that they are only God's tools. As Joseph said to his brothers, "You meant evil against me, but God meant it for good in order to bring about this present result, to preserve many people alive" (50:20).

5 "Now do not be grieved or angry with yourselves, because you sold me here, for God
sent me before you to preserve life.
6 "For the famine *has been* in the land these two years, and there are still five years in
which there will be neither plowing nor harvesting.
7 "God sent me before you to preserve for you a remnant in the earth, and to keep you
alive by a great deliverance.
8 "Now, therefore, it was not you who sent me here, but God; and He has made me a
father to Pharaoh and lord of all his household and ruler over all the land of Egypt.
9 "Hurry and go up to my father, and say to him, 'Thus says your son Joseph, "God has
made me lord of all Egypt; come down to me, do not delay.
10 "You shall live in the land of Goshen, and you shall be near me, you and your children and your children's children and your flocks and your herds and all that you have.
11 "There I will also provide for you, for there are still five years of famine *to come,* and
you and your household and all that you have would be impoverished." '
12 "Behold, your eyes see, and the eyes of my brother Benjamin *see,* that it is my mouth
which is speaking to you.
13 "Now you must tell my father of all my splendor in Egypt, and all that you have seen;
and you must hurry and bring my father down here."
14 Then he fell on his brother Benjamin's neck and wept, and Benjamin wept on his
neck.
15 He kissed all his brothers and wept on them, and afterward his brothers talked
with him.
16 Now when the news was heard in Pharaoh's house that Joseph's brothers had come,
it pleased Pharaoh and his servants.
17 Then Pharaoh said to Joseph, "Say to your brothers, 'Do this: load your beasts and
go to the land of Canaan,
18 and take your father and your households and come to me, and I will give you the
best of the land of Egypt and you will eat the fat of the land.'
19 "Now you are ordered, 'Do this: take wagons from the land of Egypt for your little
ones and for your wives, and bring your father and come.
20 'Do not concern yourselves with your goods, for the best of all the land of Egypt is
yours.' "
21 Then the sons of Israel did so; and Joseph gave them wagons according to the command of Pharaoh, and gave them provisions for the journey.
22 To each of them he gave changes of garments, but to Benjamin he gave three hundred *pieces of* silver and five changes of garments.
23 To his father he sent as follows: ten donkeys loaded with the best things of Egypt,
and ten female donkeys loaded with grain and bread and sustenance for his father on
the journey.
24 So he sent his brothers away, and as they departed, he said to them, "Do not quarrel on the journey."
25 Then they went up from Egypt, and came to the land of Canaan to their father Jacob.
26 They told him, saying, "Joseph is still alive, and indeed he is ruler over all the land
of Egypt." But he was stunned, for he did not believe them.
27 When they told him all the words of Joseph that he had spoken to them, and when
he saw the wagons that Joseph had sent to carry him, the spirit of their father Jacob revived.
28 Then Israel said, "It is enough; my son Joseph is still alive. I will go and see him
before I die."

45:5 Gen 37:28; Gen 45:7, 8; 50:20; Ps 105:17
45:6 Gen 37:2; 41:46, 53
45:7 Gen 45:5
45:8 Judg 17:10
45:9 Acts 7:14
45:10 Gen 46:28, 34; 47:1
45:11 Gen 47:12
45:13 Acts 7:14
45:14 Gen 45:2
45:16 Acts 7:13
45:18 Gen 27:28
45:19 Gen 45:21, 27; 46:5; Num 7:3-8
45:21 Gen 45:19
45:22 2 Kin 5:5; Gen 43:34
45:26 Gen 37:31-35
45:27 Gen 45:19

45:17–20 Joseph was rejected, kidnapped, enslaved, and imprisoned. Although his brothers had been unfaithful to him, he graciously forgave them and shared his prosperity. Joseph demonstrated how God forgives us and showers us with goodness even though we have sinned against him. The same forgiveness and blessings are ours if we ask for them.

45:26–27 Jacob needed some evidence before he could believe the incredible news that Joseph was alive. Similarly, Thomas refused to believe that Jesus had risen from the dead until he could see and touch him (John 20:25). It is hard to change what you believe without all the facts—or sometimes even with the facts. Good news can be hard to believe. Don't ever give up hope that God has a wonderful future in store for you.

6. Jacob's family moves to Egypt

46 So Israel set out with all that he had, and came to Beersheba, and offered sacrifices to the God of his father Isaac.
2 God spoke to Israel in visions of the night and said, "Jacob, Jacob." And he said,
"Here I am."
3 He said, "I am God, the God of your father; do not be afraid to go down to Egypt,
for I will make you a great nation there.
4 "I will go down with you to Egypt, and I will also surely bring you up again; and Joseph will close your eyes."
5 Then Jacob arose from Beersheba; and the sons of Israel carried their father Jacob
and their little ones and their wives in the wagons which Pharaoh had sent to carry him.
6 They took their livestock and their property, which they had acquired in the land of
Canaan, and came to Egypt, Jacob and all his descendants with him:
7 his sons and his grandsons with him, his daughters and his granddaughters, and all
his descendants he brought with him to Egypt.

Those Who Came to Egypt

8 Now these are the names of the sons of Israel, Jacob and his sons, who went to Egypt:
Reuben, Jacob's firstborn.
9 The sons of Reuben: Hanoch and Pallu and Hezron and Carmi.
10 The sons of Simeon: Jemuel and Jamin and Ohad and Jachin and Zohar and Shaul
the son of a Canaanite woman.
11 The sons of Levi: Gershon, Kohath, and Merari.
12 The sons of Judah: Er and Onan and Shelah and Perez and Zerah (but Er and Onan
died in the land of Canaan). And the sons of Perez were Hezron and Hamul.
13 The sons of Issachar: Tola and Puvvah and Iob and Shimron.
14 The sons of Zebulun: Sered and Elon and Jahleel.
15 These are the sons of Leah, whom she bore to Jacob in Paddan-aram, with his daughter Dinah; all his sons and his daughters *numbered* thirty-three.
16 The sons of Gad: Ziphion and Haggi, Shuni and Ezbon, Eri and Arodi and Areli.
17 The sons of Asher: Imnah and Ishvah and Ishvi and Beriah and their sister Serah.
And the sons of Beriah: Heber and Malchiel.
18 These are the sons of Zilpah, whom Laban gave to his daughter Leah; and she bore
to Jacob these sixteen persons.
19 The sons of Jacob's wife Rachel: Joseph and Benjamin.
20 Now to Joseph in the land of Egypt were born Manasseh and Ephraim, whom Asenath, the daughter of Potiphera, priest of On, bore to him.

46:1 Gen 21:31; 28:10; Gen 26:24; 28:13; 31:42
46:2 Gen 15:1; Num 12:6; Job 33:14, 15; Gen 22:11; 31:11
46:3 Gen 17:1; 28:13; Gen 12:2; Ex 1:9; Deut 26:5
46:4 Gen 28:15; 48:21; Gen 50:24; Ex 3:8; Gen 50:1
46:5 Gen 45:21
46:6 Deut 26:5; Josh 24:4; Ps 105:23; Is 52:4; Acts 7:15
46:8 Ex 1:1-4; Num 26:4, 5; 1 Chr 2:1ff
46:10 Ex 6:15
46:12 1 Chr 2:5
46:16 Num 26:15-18
46:17 1 Chr 7:30; 1 Chr 7:31
46:20 Gen 41:50-52

JACOB MOVES TO EGYPT
After hearing the joyful news that Joseph was alive, Jacob packed up and moved his family to Egypt. Stopping first in Beersheba, Jacob offered sacrifices and received assurance from God that Egypt was where he should go. Jacob and his family settled in the region of Goshen, in the northeastern part of Egypt.

46:3–4 The Israelites did become a great nation, and Jacob's descendants eventually returned to Canaan. The book of Exodus recounts the story of Israel's slavery in Egypt for 400 years (fulfilling God's words to Abraham in 15:13–16), and the book of Joshua gives an exciting account of the Israelites entering and conquering Canaan, the promised land.

46:3–4 God told Jacob to leave his home and travel to a strange and faraway land. But God reassured him by promising to go with him and take care of him. When new situations or surroundings frighten you, recognize that experiencing fear is normal. To be paralyzed by fear, however, is an indication that you question God's ability to take care of you.

46:4 Jacob never returned to Canaan. This was a promise to his descendants that they would return. "Joseph will close your eyes" refers to Joseph attending to Jacob as he faced death. It was God's promise to Jacob that he would never know the bitterness of being lonely again.

21 The sons of Benjamin: Bela and Becher and Ashbel, Gera and Naaman, Ehi and
Rosh, Muppim and Huppim and Ard.
22 These are the sons of Rachel, who were born to Jacob; *there were* fourteen persons
in all.
23 The sons of Dan: Hushim.
24 The sons of Naphtali: Jahzeel and Guni and Jezer and Shillem.
25 These are the sons of Bilhah, whom Laban gave to his daughter Rachel, and she
bore these to Jacob; *there were* seven persons in all.
26 All the persons belonging to Jacob, who came to Egypt, his direct descendants, not
including the wives of Jacob's sons, *were* sixty-six persons in all,
27 and the sons of Joseph, who were born to him in Egypt were two; all the persons of
the house of Jacob, who came to Egypt, *were* seventy.
28 Now he sent Judah before him to Joseph, to point out *the way* before him to Goshen; and they came into the land of Goshen.
29 Joseph prepared his chariot and went up to Goshen to meet his father Israel; as
soon as he appeared before him, he fell on his neck and wept on his neck a long time.
30 Then Israel said to Joseph, "Now let me die, since I have seen your face, that you
are still alive."
31 Joseph said to his brothers and to his father's household, "I will go up and tell Pharaoh, and will say to him, 'My brothers and my father's household, who *were* in the land
of Canaan, have come to me;
32 and the men are shepherds, for they have been keepers of livestock; and they have
brought their flocks and their herds and all that they have.'
33 "When Pharaoh calls you and says, 'What is your occupation?'
34 you shall say, 'Your servants have been keepers of livestock from our youth even
until now, both we and our fathers,' that you may live in the land of Goshen; for every
shepherd is loathsome to the Egyptians."

46:21 1 Chr 7:6
46:25 Gen 30:5, 7; Gen 29:29
46:26 Ex 1:5
46:27 Ex 1:5; Deut 10:22; Acts 7:14
46:28 Gen 45:10
46:29 Gen 45:14, 15
46:31 Gen 47:1
46:33 Gen 47:2, 3
46:34 Gen 13:7, 8; 26:20; 37:2; Gen 45:10, 18; 47:6, 11; Gen 43:32; Ex 8:26

Jacob's Family Settles in Goshen

47 Then Joseph went in and told Pharaoh, and said, "My father and my brothers
and their flocks and their herds and all that they have, have come out of the land
of Canaan; and behold, they are in the land of Goshen."
2 He took five men from among his brothers and presented them to Pharaoh.
3 Then Pharaoh said to his brothers, "What is your occupation?" So they said to Pharaoh, "Your servants are shepherds, both we and our fathers."
4 They said to Pharaoh, "We have come to sojourn in the land, for there is no pasture
for your servants' flocks, for the famine is severe in the land of Canaan. Now, therefore,
please let your servants live in the land of Goshen."
5 Then Pharaoh said to Joseph, "Your father and your brothers have come to you.
6 "The land of Egypt is [59]at your disposal; settle your father and your brothers in the
best of the land, let them live in the land of Goshen; and if you know any capable men
among them, then put them in charge of my livestock."
7 Then Joseph brought his father Jacob and presented him to Pharaoh; and Jacob
blessed Pharaoh.
8 Pharaoh said to Jacob, "How many years have you lived?"
9 So Jacob said to Pharaoh, "The years of my sojourning are one hundred and thirty;
few and unpleasant have been the years of my life, nor have they attained the years that
my fathers lived during the days of their sojourning."
10 And Jacob blessed Pharaoh, and went out from his presence.

59 Lit *before you*

47:1 Gen 46:31; Gen 45:10; 46:28
47:2 Acts 7:13
47:3 Gen 46:33; Gen 46:34
47:4 Gen 15:13; Deut 26:5; Ps 105:23; Gen 43:1; Acts 7:11; Gen 46:34
47:6 Gen 45:10, 18; 47:11; Ex 18:21, 25; 1 Kin 11:28; Prov 22:29
47:7 Gen 47:10; 2 Sam 14:22; 1 Kin 8:66
47:9 Heb 11:9, 13; Gen 25:7; 35:28
47:10 Gen 47:7

46:31–34 Jacob moved his whole family to Egypt, but they wanted to live apart from the Egyptians. To ensure this, Joseph told them to let Pharaoh know they were shepherds. Although Pharaoh may have been sympathetic to shepherds (for he was probably descended from the nomadic Hyksos line), the Egyptian culture would not willingly accept shepherds among them. The strategy worked, and Jacob's family was able to benefit from Pharaoh's generosity as well as from the Egyptians' prejudice.

47:1–6 The faithfulness of Joseph affected his entire family. When he was in the pit and in prison, Joseph must have wondered about his future. Instead of despairing, he faithfully obeyed God and did what was right. Here we see one of the exciting results. We may not always see the effects of our faith, but we can be sure that God will honor faithfulness.

11 So Joseph settled his father and his brothers and gave them a possession in the land
of Egypt, in the best of the land, in the land of Rameses, as Pharaoh had ordered.
12 Joseph provided his father and his brothers and all his father's household with food,
according to their little ones.
13 Now there was no food in all the land, because the famine was very severe, so that
the land of Egypt and the land of Canaan languished because of the famine.
14 Joseph gathered all the money that was found in the land of Egypt and in the land
of Canaan for the grain which they bought, and Joseph brought the money into Pharaoh's
house.
15 When the money was all spent in the land of Egypt and in the land of Canaan, all
the Egyptians came to Joseph and said, "Give us food, for why should we die in your
presence? For *our* money is gone."
16 Then Joseph said, "Give up your livestock, and I will give you *food* for your livestock, since *your* money is gone."
17 So they brought their livestock to Joseph, and Joseph gave them food in exchange
for the horses and the flocks and the herds and the donkeys; and he fed them with food
in exchange for all their livestock that year.
18 When that year was ended, they came to him the next year and said to him, "We
will not hide from my lord that our money is all spent, and the cattle are my lord's. There
is nothing left for my lord except our bodies and our lands.
19 "Why should we die before your eyes, both we and our land? Buy us and our land for
food, and we and our land will be slaves to Pharaoh. So give us seed, that we may live
and not die, and that the land may not be desolate."

Result of the Famine

20 So Joseph bought all the land of Egypt for Pharaoh, for every Egyptian sold his field,
because the famine was severe upon them. Thus the land became Pharaoh's.
21 As for the people, he removed them to the cities from one end of Egypt's border to
the other.
22 Only the land of the priests he did not buy, for the priests had an allotment from
Pharaoh, and they lived off the allotment which Pharaoh gave them. Therefore, they did
not sell their land.
23 Then Joseph said to the people, "Behold, I have today bought you and your land
for Pharaoh; now, *here* is seed for you, and you may sow the land.
24 "At the harvest you shall give a fifth to Pharaoh, and four-fifths shall be your own for
seed of the field and for your food and for those of your households and as food for your
little ones."
25 So they said, "You have saved our lives! Let us find favor in the sight of my lord,
and we will be Pharaoh's slaves."
26 Joseph made it a statute concerning the land of Egypt *valid* to this day, that Pharaoh should have the fifth; only the land of the priests did not become Pharaoh's.
27 Now Israel lived in the land of Egypt, in Goshen, and they acquired property in it
and were fruitful and became very numerous.

7. Jacob and Joseph die in Egypt

28 Jacob lived in the land of Egypt seventeen years; so the length of Jacob's life was
one hundred and forty-seven years.
29 When the time for Israel to die drew near, he called his son Joseph and said to him,
"Please, if I have found favor in your sight, place now your hand under my thigh and
deal with me in kindness and [60]faithfulness. Please do not bury me in Egypt,
30 but when I lie down with my fathers, you shall carry me out of Egypt and bury me in
their burial place." And he said, "I will do as you have said."

60 Lit *truth*

47:11 Gen 47:6, 27; Ex 1:11; 12:37
47:12 Gen 45:11
47:13 Gen 41:30; Acts 7:11
47:14 Gen 41:56
47:15 Gen 47:19
47:24 Gen 41:34
47:26 Gen 47:22
47:27 Gen 47:11; Gen 17:6; 26:4; 35:11; Ex 1:7; Deut 26:5; Acts 7:17
47:28 Gen 47:9
47:29 Deut 31:14; 1 Kin 2:1; Gen 24:2; Gen 24:49
47:30 Gen 15:15; Deut 31:16; Gen 23:17-20; 25:9, 10; 35:29; 49:29-32; 50:5, 13; Acts 7:15, 16

47:29–31 Putting a hand under the thigh was a sign of making a promise, much like shaking hands today. Jacob had Joseph promise to bury him in his homeland. Few things were written in this culture, so a person's word then carried as much force as a written contract today. People today seem to find it easy to say, "I didn't mean that." God's people, however, are to speak the truth and live the truth. Let your words be as binding as a written contract.

31 He said, "Swear to me." So he swore to him. Then Israel bowed *in worship* at the
head of the bed.

Israel's Last Days

48 Now it came about after these things that Joseph was told, "Behold, your father
is sick." So he took his two sons Manasseh and Ephraim with him.
2 When it was told to Jacob, "Behold, your son Joseph has come to you," Israel collected his strength and sat up in the bed.
3 Then Jacob said to Joseph, "God Almighty appeared to me at Luz in the land of
Canaan and blessed me,
4 and He said to me, 'Behold, I will make you fruitful and numerous, and I will make
you a company of peoples, and will give this land to your descendants after you for an
everlasting possession.'
5 "Now your two sons, who were born to you in the land of Egypt before I came to you
in Egypt, are mine; Ephraim and Manasseh shall be mine, as Reuben and Simeon are.
6 "But your offspring that have been born after them shall be yours; they shall be called
by the names of their brothers in their inheritance.
7 "Now as for me, when I came from Paddan, Rachel died, to my sorrow, in the land of
Canaan on the journey, when there was still some distance to go to Ephrath; and I buried her there on the way to Ephrath (that is, Bethlehem)."
8 When Israel saw Joseph's sons, he said, "Who are these?"
9 Joseph said to his father, "They are my sons, whom God has given me here." So he
said, "Bring them to me, please, that I may bless them."
10 Now the eyes of Israel were *so* dim from age *that* he could not see. Then Joseph
brought them close to him, and he kissed them and embraced them.
11 Israel said to Joseph, "I never expected to see your face, and behold, God has let
me see your children as well."
12 Then Joseph took them from his knees, and bowed with his face to the ground.
13 Joseph took them both, Ephraim with his right hand toward Israel's left, and Manasseh with his left hand toward Israel's right, and brought them close to him.
14 But Israel stretched out his right hand and laid it on the head of Ephraim, who was
the younger, and his left hand on Manasseh's head, crossing his hands, although Manasseh was the firstborn.
15 He blessed Joseph, and said,
"The God before whom my fathers Abraham and Isaac walked,
The God who has been my shepherd all my life to this day,
16 The angel who has redeemed me from all evil,
Bless the lads;
And may my name live on in them,
And the names of my fathers Abraham and Isaac;
And may they grow into a multitude in the midst of the earth."
17 When Joseph saw that his father laid his right hand on Ephraim's head, it displeased
him; and he grasped his father's hand to remove it from Ephraim's head to Manasseh's
head.
18 Joseph said to his father, "Not so, my father, for this one is the firstborn. Place your
right hand on his head."
19 But his father refused and said, "I know, my son, I know; he also will become a peo-

47:31 Gen 21:23, 24; 24:3; 31:53; 50:25; 1 Kin 1:47
48:1 Gen 41:51, 52; Josh 14:4
48:3 Gen 28:13f; 35:9-12; Gen 28:19; 35:6
48:4 Gen 17:8
48:5 Gen 41:50-52; 46:20; 48:1; Josh 14:4; 1 Chr 5:1, 2
48:7 Gen 33:18; Gen 35:19, 20
48:8 Gen 48:10
48:9 Gen 33:5; Gen 27:4
48:10 Gen 27:1; Gen 27:27
48:12 Gen 42:6
48:14 Gen 41:51, 52
48:15 Gen 17:1; Gen 49:24
48:16 Gen 22:11, 15-18; 28:13-15; 31:11; Heb 11:21; Gen 28:14; 46:3
48:17 Gen 48:14
48:19 Gen 28:14; 46:3

48:8–20 Jacob gave Ephraim, instead of his older brother Manasseh, the greater blessing. When Joseph objected, Jacob refused to listen because God had told him that Ephraim would become greater. God often works in unexpected ways. When he chooses people to fulfill his plans, he always goes deeper than appearance, tradition, or position. He sometimes surprises us by choosing the less obvious person, at least by human reasoning. God can use you to carry out his plans, even if you don't think you have all the qualifications.

48:11 When Joseph became a slave, Jacob thought he was dead and wept in despair (37:30). But eventually God's plan allowed Jacob to regain not only his son, but his grandchildren as well. Circumstances are never so bad that they are beyond God's help. Jacob regained his son. Job got a new family (Job 42:10–17). Mary regained her brother Lazarus (John 11:1–44). We need never despair because we belong to a loving God. We never know what good he will bring out of a seemingly hopeless situation.

48:15 Jacob spoke of God as his shepherd throughout his life. In his old age, he could clearly see his dependence upon God. This marks a total attitude change from that of his scheming and dishonest youth. To develop an attitude like Jacob's, let God shepherd you as you trust in his provision and care. When you realize that every good thing comes from God, you can quit trying to grab them for yourself.

ple and he also will be great. However, his younger brother shall be greater than he, and
his descendants shall become a multitude of nations."

48:20 Heb 11:21

20 He blessed them that day, saying,
"By you Israel will pronounce blessing, saying,
'May God make you like Ephraim and Manasseh!' "
Thus he put Ephraim before Manasseh.

48:21 Gen 26:3; Gen 28:15; 46:4; 50:24

21 Then Israel said to Joseph, "Behold, I am about to die, but God will be with you,
and bring you back to the land of your fathers.

48:22 Josh 24:32; John 4:5

22 "I give you one portion more than your brothers, which I took from the hand of the
Amorite with my sword and my bow."

Israel's Prophecy concerning His Sons

49:1 Num 24:14

49 Then Jacob summoned his sons and said, "Assemble yourselves that I may tell
you what will befall you in the days to come.

49:2 Ps 34:11

2 "Gather together and hear, O sons of Jacob;
And listen to Israel your father.

49:3 Deut 21:17; Ps 78:51; 105:36

3 "Reuben, you are my firstborn;
My might and the beginning of my strength,
Preeminent in dignity and preeminent in power.

49:4 Gen 35:22; Deut 27:20; 1 Chr 5:1

4 "Uncontrolled as water, you shall not have preeminence,
Because you went up to your father's bed;
Then you defiled *it*—he went up to my couch.

49:5 Gen 34:25-30

5 "Simeon and Levi are brothers;
Their swords are implements of violence.

49:6 Ps 64:2

6 "Let my soul not enter into their council;
Let not my glory be united with their assembly;
Because in their anger they slew men,
And in their self-will they lamed oxen.

49:7 Josh 19:1, 9; 21:1-42

7 "Cursed be their anger, for it is fierce;
And their wrath, for it is cruel.
I will disperse them in Jacob,
And scatter them in Israel.

49:8 Gen 27:29; 1 Chr 5:2

8 "Judah, your brothers shall praise you;
Your hand shall be on the neck of your enemies;
Your father's sons shall bow down to you.

49:9 Ezek 19:5-7; Mic 5:8; Num 24:9

9 " Judah is a lion's whelp;
From the prey, my son, you have gone up.
He couches, he lies down as a lion,
And as a lion, who dares rouse him up?

49:10 Num 24:17; Ps 60:7; 108:8; Ps 2:6-9; 72:8-11; Is 42:1, 4; 49:6

10 "The scepter shall not depart from Judah,
Nor the ruler's staff from between his feet,
[61]Until Shiloh comes,

61 Or *Until he comes to Shiloh;* or *Until he comes to whom it belongs*

48:20–22 Jacob was giving these young boys land occupied by the Philistines and Canaanites. His gift became reality when the tribes of Ephraim and Manasseh occupied the east and west sides of the Jordan River (Joshua 16).

49:3–28 Jacob blessed each of his sons and then made a prediction about each one's future. The way the men had lived played an important part in Jacob's blessing and prophecy. Our past also affects our present and future. By sunrise tomorrow, our actions of today will have become part of the past. Yet they will already have begun to shape the future. What actions can you choose or avoid that will positively shape your future?

49:4 The oldest son was supposed to receive a double inheritance, but Reuben lost his special honor. Unstable and untrustworthy, especially in his younger days, he had gone so far as to sleep with one of his father's concubines. Jacob could not give the birthright blessing to such a dishonorable son.

49:8–12 Why was Judah—known for selling Joseph into slavery and trying to defraud his daughter-in-law—so greatly blessed? God had chosen Judah to be the ancestor of Israel's line of kings (that is the meaning of "the scepter shall not depart from Judah"). This may have been due to Judah's dramatic change of character (44:33–34). Judah's line would produce the promised Messiah, Jesus.

49:10 What is *Shiloh?* The meaning of this difficult passage is disputed. Shiloh may be another name for the Messiah, because its literal meaning is "sent." Shiloh might also refer to the Tent of Meeting set up at the city of Shiloh (Joshua 18:1).

And to him *shall be* the obedience of the peoples.
11 "He ties *his* foal to the vine,
And his donkey's colt to the choice vine;
He washes his garments in wine,
And his robes in the blood of grapes.
12 "His eyes are [62]dull from wine,
And his teeth [63]white from milk.

49:11 Deut 8:7, 8; 2 Kin 18:32; Is 63:2

13 "Zebulun will dwell at the seashore;
And he *shall be* a haven for ships,
And his flank *shall be* toward Sidon.

49:13 Deut 33:18, 19

14 "Issachar is a strong donkey,
Lying down between the sheepfolds.
15 "When he saw that a resting place was good
And that the land was pleasant,
He bowed his shoulder to bear *burdens,*
And became a slave at forced labor.

49:14 Judg 5:16; Ps 68:13

16 "Dan shall judge his people,
As one of the tribes of Israel.
17 "Dan shall be a serpent in the way,
A horned snake in the path,
That bites the horse's heels,
So that his rider falls backward.
18 "For Your salvation I wait, O LORD.

49:16 Deut 33:22; Judg 18:26, 27; Gen 30:6

49:18 Ex 15:2; Ps 25:5; 40:1-3; 119:166, 174; Is 25:9; Mic 7:7

19 "As for Gad, raiders shall raid him,
But he will raid *at* their heels.

49:19 Deut 33:20

20 "As for Asher, his food shall be rich,
And he will yield royal dainties.

49:20 Deut 33:24, 25; Gen 30:13

21 "Naphtali is a doe let loose,
He gives beautiful words.

49:21 Deut 33:23

62 Or *darker than* **63** Or *whiter than*

PARALLELS BETWEEN JOSEPH AND JESUS
Genesis 37—50

Joseph	*Parallels*	*Jesus*
37:3	Their fathers loved them dearly	Matthew 3:17
37:2	Shepherds of their fathers' sheep	John 10:11, 27
37:13–14	Sent by father to brothers	Hebrews 2:11
37:4	Hated by brothers	John 7:5
37:20	Others plotted to harm them	John 11:53
39:7	Tempted	Matthew 4:1
37:25	Taken to Egypt	Matthew 2:14–15
37:23	Robes taken from them	John 19:23
37:28	Sold for the price	Matthew 26:15
39:20	Bound in chains	Matthew 27:2
39:16–18	Falsely accused	Matthew 26:59–60
40:2–3	Placed with two other prisoners, one who was saved and the other lost	Luke 23:32
41:46	Both 30 years old at the beginning of public recognition	Luke 3:23
41:41	Exalted after suffering	Philippians 2:9–11
45:1–15	Forgave those who wronged them	Luke 23:34
45:7	Saved their nation	Matthew 1:21
50:20	What people did to hurt them God turned to good	1 Corinthians 2:7–8

49:18 In the middle of his prophecy to Dan, Jacob exclaimed, "For Your salvation I wait, O LORD." He was emphasizing to Dan that he would be a strong leader only if his trust was in God, not in his natural strength or ability. Those who are strong, attractive, or talented often find it easier to trust in themselves than in God who gave them their gifts. Remember to thank God for what you are and have so your trust does not become misplaced.

49:22 Deut 33:13-17

22 "Joseph is a fruitful [64]bough,
A fruitful bough by a spring;
Its [65]branches run over a wall.
23 "The archers bitterly attacked him,
And shot *at him* and harassed him;

49:24 Job 29:20; Ps 18:34; 73:23; Is 41:10; Ps 132:2, 5; Is 1:24; 49:26; Ps 23:1; 80:1; Ps 118:22; Is 28:16; 1 Pet 2:6-8

24 But his bow remained firm,
And his arms were agile,
From the hands of the Mighty One of Jacob
(From there is the Shepherd, the Stone of Israel),
25 From the God of your father who helps you,

49:25 Gen 28:13; 32:9; Gen 28:3; 48:3; Gen 27:28

And by the Almighty who blesses you
With blessings of heaven above,
Blessings of the deep that lies beneath,
Blessings of the breasts and of the womb.

49:26 Deut 33:15, 16

26 "The blessings of your father
Have surpassed the blessings of my ancestors
Up to the utmost bound of the everlasting hills;
May they be on the head of Joseph,
And on the crown of the head of the one distinguished among his brothers.

27 "Benjamin is a ravenous wolf;
In the morning he devours the prey,
And in the evening he divides the spoil."

28 All these are the twelve tribes of Israel, and this is what their father said to them
when he blessed them. He blessed them, every one with the blessing appropriate to him.

49:29 Gen 25:8; Gen 47:30; Gen 23:16-20; 50:13

29 Then he charged them and said to them, 'I am about to be gathered to my people;
bury me with my fathers in the cave that is in the field of Ephron the Hittite,

49:30 Gen 23:3-20

30 in the cave that is in the field of Machpelah, which is before Mamre, in the land of
Canaan, which Abraham bought along with the field from Ephron the Hittite for a burial
site.

49:31 Gen 25:9; Gen 23:19; Gen 35:29

31 "There they buried Abraham and his wife Sarah, there they buried Isaac and his wife
Rebekah, and there I buried Leah—
32 the field and the cave that is in it, purchased from the sons of Heth."

49:33 Gen 25:8; Acts 7:15; Gen 49:29

33 When Jacob finished charging his sons, he drew his feet into the bed and breathed
his last, and was gathered to his people.

The Death of Israel

50 Then Joseph fell on his father's face, and wept over him and kissed him.

50:2 Gen 50:26; 2 Chr 16:14; Matt 26:12; Mark 16:1; John 19:39, 40

2 Joseph commanded his servants the physicians to embalm his father. So the
physicians embalmed Israel.

50:3 Gen 50:10; Num 20:29; Deut 34:8

3 Now forty days were required for it, for such is the period required for embalming.
And the Egyptians wept for him seventy days.
4 When the days of mourning for him were past, Joseph spoke to the household of
Pharaoh, saying, 'If now I have found favor in your sight, please speak to Pharaoh, saying,

64 Lit *son* **65** Lit *daughters*

49:22 Joseph was indeed fruitful, with some heroic descendants. Among them were Joshua, who would lead the Israelites into the promised land (Joshua 1:10–11); Deborah, Gideon, and Jephthah, judges of Israel (Judges 4:4; 6:11–12; 11:11); and Samuel, a great prophet (1 Samuel 3:19).

49:23–24 These verses celebrate the times God rescued Joseph when his enemies attacked him. So often we struggle by ourselves, forgetting that God is able to help us fight our battles, whether they are against men with weapons or against spiritual forces. Joseph was able to draw closer to God as adversity mounted. To trust God to rescue you shows great faith. Can you trust him when injury or persecution is directed at you? Such spiritual battles require teamwork between courageous, faithful people and a mighty God.

50:1–11 When Jacob died at the age of 147, Joseph wept and mourned for months. When someone close to us dies, we need a long period of time to work through our grief. Crying and sharing our feelings with others helps us recover and go on with life. Allow yourself and others the freedom to grieve over the loss of a loved one, and give yourself time enough to complete your grieving process.

50:2–3 Embalming was typical for Egyptians but unusual for nomadic shepherds. Believing that the dead went to the next world in their physical bodies, the Egyptians embalmed bodies to preserve them so they could function in the world to come. Jacob's family allowed him to be embalmed as a sign of courtesy and respect to the Egyptians.

5 'My father made me swear, saying, "Behold, I am about to die; in my grave which I **50:5**
dug for myself in the land of Canaan, there you shall bury me." Now therefore, please Gen 47:29-31; 2 Chr 16:14; Is 22:16; Matt
let me go up and bury my father; then I will return.' " 27:60
6 Pharaoh said, "Go up and bury your father, as he made you swear."
7 So Joseph went up to bury his father, and with him went up all the servants of Pharaoh, the elders of his household and all the elders of the land of Egypt,
8 and all the household of Joseph and his brothers and his father's household; they
left only their little ones and their flocks and their herds in the land of Goshen.
9 There also went up with him both chariots and horsemen; and it was a very great
company.
10 When they came to the threshing floor of Atad, which is beyond the Jordan, they **50:10**
lamented there with a very great and sorrowful lamentation; and he observed seven days Acts 8:2
mourning for his father.
11 Now when the inhabitants of the land, the Canaanites, saw the mourning at the
threshing floor of Atad, they said, "This is a grievous mourning for the Egyptians." Therefore it was named Abel-mizraim, which is beyond the Jordan.

Burial at Machpelah

12 Thus his sons did for him as he had charged them;
13 for his sons carried him to the land of Canaan and buried him in the cave of the **50:13**
field of Machpelah before Mamre, which Abraham had bought along with the field for Gen 23:16-20; Acts
a burial site from Ephron the Hittite. 7:16
14 After he had buried his father, Joseph returned to Egypt, he and his brothers, and
all who had gone up with him to bury his father.
15 When Joseph's brothers saw that their father was dead, they said, "What if Joseph **50:15**
bears a grudge against us and pays us back in full for all the wrong which we did to him!" Gen 37:28; 42:21,
16 So they sent *a message* to Joseph, saying, "Your father charged before he died, saying, 22
17 'Thus you shall say to Joseph, "Please forgive, I beg you, the transgression of your
brothers and their sin, for they did you wrong." ' And now, please forgive the transgression of the servants of the God of your father." And Joseph wept when they spoke to him.
18 Then his brothers also came and fell down before him and said, "Behold, we are **50:18**
your servants." Gen 37:8-10; 41:43
19 But Joseph said to them, "Do not be afraid, for am I in God's place?

JACOB'S SONS AND THEIR NOTABLE DESCENDANTS
Jacob's 12 sons were the ancestors of the 12 tribes of Israel. The entire nation of Israel came from these men.

REUBEN	none
SIMEON	none
LEVI	Aaron, Moses, Eli, John the Baptist
JUDAH	David, Jesus
DAN	Samson
NAPHTALI	Barak, Elijah (?)
GAD	Jephthah (?)
ASHER	none
ISSACHAR	none
ZEBULUN	none
JOSEPH	Joshua, Gideon, Samuel
BENJAMIN	Saul, Esther, Paul

50:5 Joseph had proven himself trustworthy as Pharaoh's adviser. Because of his good record, Pharaoh had little doubt that he would return to Egypt as promised after burying his father in Canaan. Privileges and freedom often result when we have demonstrated our trustworthiness. Since trust must be built gradually over time, take every opportunity to prove your reliability even in minor matters.

50:12–13 Abraham had purchased the cave in the field of Machpelah as a burial place for his wife, Sarah (23:1–9). It was to be a burial place for his entire family. Jacob was Abraham's grandson, and Jacob's sons returned to Canaan to bury him in this cave along with Abraham and Isaac. Their desire to be buried in this cave expressed their faith in God's promise to give their descendants the land of Canaan.

50:15–21 Now that Jacob (or Israel) was dead, the brothers feared revenge from Joseph. Could he really have forgiven them for selling him into slavery? But to their surprise, Joseph not only forgave them but reassured them, offering to care for them and their families. Joseph's forgiveness was complete. He demonstrated how God graciously accepts us even though we don't deserve it. Because God forgives us even when we have ignored or rejected him, we should graciously forgive others.

50:20 Gen 37:26, 27; 45:5, 7

50:21 Gen 45:11; 47:12

50:23 Gen 30:3

50:24 Gen 48:21; Ex 3:16, 17; Heb 11:22; Gen 13:15, 17; 15:7, 8, 18; Gen 26:3; Gen 28:13; 35:12

50:25 Gen 47:29, 30; Ex 13:19; Josh 24:32; Heb 11:22

50:26 Gen 50:2

20 "As for you, you meant evil against me, *but* God meant it for good in order to bring
about this present result, to preserve many people alive.
21 "So therefore, do not be afraid; I will provide for you and your little ones." So he
comforted them and spoke kindly to them.

Death of Joseph

22 Now Joseph stayed in Egypt, he and his father's household, and Joseph lived one
hundred and ten years.
23 Joseph saw the third generation of Ephraim's sons; also the sons of Machir, the son
of Manasseh, were born on Joseph's knees.
24 Joseph said to his brothers, "I am about to die, but God will surely take care of you
and bring you up from this land to the land which He promised on oath to Abraham, to
Isaac and to Jacob."
25 Then Joseph made the sons of Israel swear, saying, "God will surely take care of
you, and you shall carry my bones up from here."
26 So Joseph died at the age of one hundred and ten years; and he was embalmed and
placed in a coffin in Egypt.

50:20 God brought good from the brothers' evil deed, Potiphar's wife's false accusation, the cupbearer's neglect, and seven years of famine. The experiences in Joseph's life taught him that God brings good from evil for those who trust him. Do you trust God enough to wait patiently for him to bring good out of bad situations? You can trust him because, as Joseph learned, God can overrule people's evil intentions to bring about his intended results.

50:24 Joseph was ready to die. He had no doubts that God would keep his promise and one day bring the Israelites back to their homeland. What a tremendous example! The secret of that kind of faith is a lifetime of trusting God. Your faith is like a muscle—it grows with exercise, gaining strength over time. After a lifetime of exercising trust, your faith can be as strong as Joseph's. Then at your death, you can be confident that God will fulfill all his promises to you and to all those faithful to him who may live after you.

50:24 This verse sets the stage for what would begin to happen in Exodus and come to completion in Joshua. God was going to make Jacob's family into a great nation, lead them out of Egypt, and bring them into the land he had promised them. The nation would rely heavily on this promise, and Joseph emphasized his belief that God would do what he had promised.

50:26 The book of Genesis gives us rich descriptions of the lives of many great men and women who walked with God. They sometimes succeeded and often failed. Yet we learn much by reading the biographies of these people. Where did they get their motivation and courage? They got it by realizing God was with them despite their inadequacies. Knowing this should encourage us to be faithful to God, to rely on him for guidance, and to utilize the potential he has given us.

E X O D U S

Joseph dies 1805 B.C. (1640 B.C.)   S L A V E R Y   I N   E G Y P T

VITAL STATISTICS

PURPOSE:
To record the events of Israel's deliverance from Egypt and development as a nation

AUTHOR:
Moses

DATE WRITTEN:
1450–1410 B.C., approximately the same as Genesis

WHERE WRITTEN:
In the wilderness during Israel's wanderings, somewhere in the Sinai peninsula

SETTING:
Egypt. God's people, once highly favored in the land, are now slaves. God is about to set them free.

KEY VERSES:
"Then the LORD said, 'I have surely seen the affliction of My people who are in Egypt, and have given heed to their cry because of their taskmasters, for I am aware of their sufferings. . . . Come now, and I will send you to Pharaoh, so that you may bring My people, the sons of Israel, out of Egypt' " (3:7, 10).

KEY PEOPLE:
Moses, Miriam, Pharaoh, Pharaoh's daughter, Jethro, Aaron, Joshua, Bezalel

KEY PLACES:
Egypt, Goshen, Nile River, Midian, Red Sea, Sinai peninsula, Mount Sinai

SPECIAL FEATURES:
Exodus relates more miracles than any other Old Testament book and is noted for containing the Ten Commandments

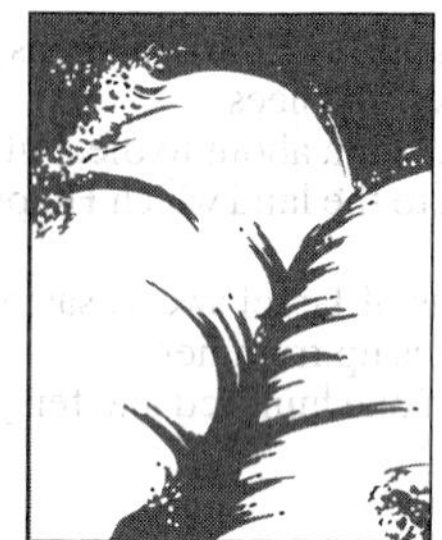

GET UP . . . leave . . . take off—these words are good ones for those trapped or enslaved. Some resist their marching orders, however, preferring present surroundings to a new, unknown environment. It's not easy to trade the comfortable security of the known for an uncertain future. But what if God gives the order to move? Will we follow his lead? Exodus describes a series of God's calls and the responses of his people.

Four hundred years had passed since Joseph moved his family to Egypt. These descendants of Abraham had now grown to over two million strong. To Egypt's new pharaoh, these Hebrews were foreigners, and their numbers were frightening. Pharaoh decided to make them slaves so they wouldn't upset his balance of power. As it turned out, that was his biggest mistake, for God then came to the rescue of his people.

Through a series of strange events, a Hebrew boy named Moses became a prince in Pharaoh's palace and then an outcast in a wilderness land. God visited Moses in the mysterious flames of a burning bush, and after some discussion, Moses agreed to return to Egypt to lead God's people out of slavery. Pharaoh was confronted, and through a cycle of plagues and promises made and broken, Israel was torn from his grasp.

It was no easy task to mobilize this mass of humanity, but they marched out of Egypt, through the Red Sea, and into the wilderness behind Moses and the pillars of cloud and fire. Despite continual evidence of God's love and power, the people complained and began to yearn for their days in Egypt. God provided for their physical and spiritual needs with food and a place to worship, but he also judged their disobedience and unbelief. Then in the dramatic Sinai meeting with Moses, God gave his laws for right living.

God led Moses and the nation of Israel, and he wants to lead us as well. Is he preparing you, like Moses, for a specific task? He will be with you; obey and follow. Is he delivering you from an enemy or a temptation? Trust him, and do what he says. Have you heard his clear moral directions? Read, study, and obey his Word. Is he calling you to true worship? Discover God's presence in your life, in your home, and in the body of assembled believers. Exodus is the exciting story of God's guidance. Read with the determination to follow God wherever he leads.

Moses born 1526 (1350)	Exodus from Egypt 1446 (1280)	Ten Commandments given 1445 (1279)	Israel enters Canaan 1406 (1240)	Judges begin to rule 1375 (1220)

THE BLUEPRINT

A. ISRAEL IN EGYPT (1:1—12:30)
1. Slavery in Egypt
2. God chooses Moses
3. God sends Moses to Pharaoh
4. Plagues strike Egypt
5. The Passover

When the Israelites were enslaved in Egypt, God heard their cries and rescued them. We can be confident that God still hears the cries of his people. Just as he delivered the Israelites from their captors, he delivers us from sin, death, and evil.

B. ISRAEL IN THE WILDERNESS (12:31—18:27)
1. The exodus
2. Crossing the sea
3. Complaining in the wilderness

After crossing the Red Sea, the Israelites became quarrelsome and discontent. Like the Israelites, we find it easy to complain and be dissatisfied. Christians still have struggles, but we should never allow difficulties and unpleasant circumstances to turn us away from trusting God.

C. ISRAEL AT SINAI (19:1—40:38)
1. Giving the law
2. Tabernacle instructions
3. Breaking the law
4. Tabernacle construction

God revealed his law to the Israelites at Sinai. Through the law, they learned more about what God is like and how he expected his people to live. The law is still instructional for us, for it exposes our sin and shows us God's standard for living.

MEGATHEMES

THEME	EXPLANATION	IMPORTANCE
Slavery	During the Israelites' 400-year stay in the land of Egypt, they became enslaved to the Egyptians. Pharaoh, the king of Egypt, oppressed them cruelly. They prayed to God for deliverance from this situation.	Like the Israelites, we need both human and divine leadership to escape from the slavery of sin. After their escape, the memory of slavery helped the Israelites learn to treat others generously. We need to stand against those who oppress others.
Rescue/ Redemption	God rescued Israel through the leader Moses and through mighty miracles. The Passover celebration was an annual reminder of their escape from slavery.	God delivers us from the slavery of sin. Jesus Christ celebrated the Passover with his disciples at the Last Supper and then went on to rescue us from sin by dying in our place.
Guidance	God guided Israel out of Egypt by using the plagues, Moses' heroic courage, the miracle of the Red Sea, and the Ten Commandments. God is a trustworthy guide.	Although God is all-powerful and can do miracles, he normally leads us by wise leadership and team effort. His Word gives us the wisdom to make daily decisions and govern our lives.
Ten Commandments	God's law system had three parts. The Ten Commandments were the first part, containing the absolutes of spiritual and moral life. The civil law was the second part, giving the people rules to manage their lives. The ceremonial law was the third part, showing them patterns for building the tabernacle and for regular worship.	God was teaching Israel the importance of choice and responsibility. When they obeyed the conditions of the law, he blessed them; if they forgot or disobeyed, he punished them or allowed calamities to come. Many great countries of the world base their laws on the moral system set up in the book of Exodus. God's moral law is valid today.
The Nation	God founded the nation of Israel to be the source of truth and salvation to all the world. His relationship to his people was loving yet firm. The Israelites had no army, schools, governors, mayors, or police when they left Egypt. God had to instruct them in their constitutional laws and daily practices. He showed them how to worship and how to have national holidays.	Israel's newly formed nation had all the behavioral characteristics of Christians today. We are often disorganized, sometimes rebellious, and sometimes victorious. God's Person and Word are still our only guides. If our churches reflect his leadership, they will be effective in serving him.

KEY PLACES IN EXODUS

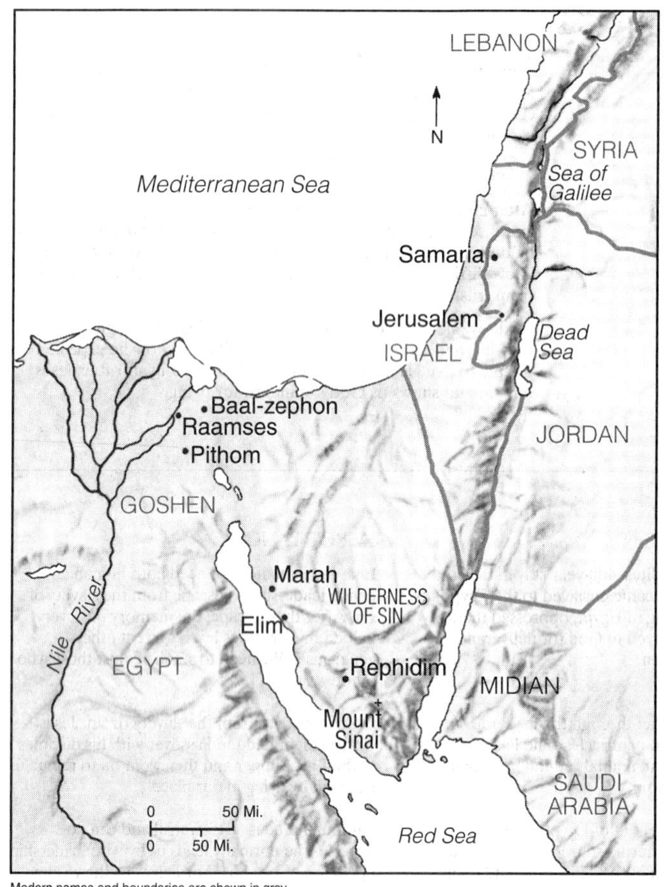

Modern names and boundaries are shown in gray.

1 Goshen This area was given to Jacob and his family when they moved to Egypt (Genesis 47:5–6). It became the Hebrews' homeland for 400 years and remained separate from the main Egyptian centers, for Egyptian culture looked down upon shepherds and nomads. As the years passed, Jacob's family grew into a large nation (1:7).

2–3 Pithom and Raamses During the Israelites' stay in the land of Egypt, a pharaoh came to the throne who had no respect for these descendants of Joseph and feared their large numbers. He forced them into slavery in order to oppress and subdue them. Out of their slave labor, the supply cities of Pithom and Raamses were built (1:11).

4 Midian Moses, an Egyptian prince who was born a Hebrew, killed an Egyptian and fled for his life to Midian. Here he became a shepherd and married a woman named Zipporah. It was while he was here that God commissioned him for the job of leading the Hebrew people out of Egypt (2:15—4:31).

5 Baal-zephon Slavery was not to last because God planned to deliver his people. After choosing Moses and Aaron to be his spokesmen to Pharaoh, God worked a series of dramatic miracles in the land of Egypt to convince Pharaoh to let the Hebrews go (5:1—12:33). When finally freed, the entire nation set out with the riches of Egypt (12:34–36). One of their first stops was at Baal-zephon (14:2), where Pharaoh, who had changed his mind, chased the Hebrews and trapped them against the sea. But God parted the waters and led the people through the sea on dry land. When Pharaoh's army tried to pursue, the waters collapsed around them, and they were drowned (14:5–31).

6 Marah Moses now led the people southward. The long trek across the wilderness brought hot tempers and parched throats for this mass of people. At Marah, the water they found was bitter, but God sweetened it (15:22–25).

7 Elim As they continued their journey, the Hebrews (now called Israelites) came to Elim, an oasis with 12 springs (15:27).

8 Wilderness of Sin Leaving Elim, the people headed into the wilderness of Sin. Here the people became hungry, so God provided them with manna that came from heaven and covered the ground each morning (16:1, 13–15). The people ate this manna until they entered the promised land.

9 Rephidim Moses led the people to Rephidim where they found no water. But God miraculously provided water from a rock (17:1, 5–6). Here the Israelites encountered their first test in battle: the Amalekites attacked and were defeated (17:9–13). Moses' father-in-law, Jethro, then arrived on the scene with some sound advice on delegating responsibilities (18).

10 Mount Sinai God had previously appeared to Moses on this mountain and commissioned him to lead Israel (3:1–10). Now Moses returned with the people God had asked him to lead. For almost a year the people camped at the foot of Mount Sinai. During this time God gave them his Ten Commandments as well as other laws for right living. He also provided the blueprint for building the tabernacle (19—40).

God was forging a holy nation, prepared to live for and serve him alone.

A. ISRAEL IN EGYPT (1:1—12:30)

Joseph brought his family to Egypt and protected them there. But after Joseph's death, as they multiplied into a nation, they were forced into slavery. God then prepared Moses to free his people from slavery and lead them out of Egypt. To help Moses, God unleashed ten plagues upon the land. After the tenth plague, Pharaoh let the people go. On the night before the great exodus, God's new nation celebrated the Passover. Just as God delivered Israel from Egypt, he delivers us from sin, death, and evil.

1. Slavery in Egypt

Israel Multiplies in Egypt

1 Now these are the names of the sons of Israel who came to Egypt with Jacob; they
came each one with his household:
2 Reuben, Simeon, Levi and Judah;
3 Issachar, Zebulun and Benjamin;
4 Dan and Naphtali, Gad and Asher.
5 All the persons who came from the loins of Jacob were seventy in number, but Joseph was *already* in Egypt.
6 Joseph died, and all his brothers and all that generation.
7 But the sons of Israel were fruitful and increased greatly, and multiplied, and became exceedingly mighty, so that the land was filled with them.
8 Now a new king arose over Egypt, who did not know Joseph.
9 He said to his people, "Behold, the people of the sons of Israel are more and mightier than we.
10 "Come, let us deal wisely with them, or else they will multiply and in the event of
war, they will also join themselves to those who hate us, and fight against us and depart
from the land."
11 So they appointed taskmasters over them to afflict them with hard labor. And they
built for Pharaoh storage cities, Pithom and Raamses.
12 But the more they afflicted them, the more they multiplied and the more they spread
out, so that they were in dread of the sons of Israel.
13 The Egyptians compelled the sons of Israel to labor rigorously;
14 and they made their lives bitter with hard labor in mortar and bricks and at all *kinds*
of labor in the field, all their labors which they rigorously imposed on them.
15 Then the king of Egypt spoke to the Hebrew midwives, one of whom was named
Shiphrah and the other was named Puah;

1:1 Gen 46:8-27
1:5 Gen 46:26, 27; Deut 10:22
1:6 Gen 50:26
1:7 Gen 12:2; 28:3; 35:11; 46:3; 47:27; 48:4; Deut 26:5; Ps 105:24; Acts 7:17
1:8 Acts 7:18, 19
1:9 Ps 105:24, 25
1:10 Acts 7:19
1:11 Gen 15:13; Ex 3:7; 5:6; Ex 1:14; 2:11; 5:4-9; 6:6f; 1 Kin 9:19; 2 Chr 8:4; Gen 47:11
1:12 Ex 1:7
1:13 Gen 15:13; Deut 4:20
1:14 Ex 2:23; 6:9; Num 20:15; Acts 7:19

1:1 The children of Israel, or Israelites, were the descendants of Jacob, whose name was changed to Israel after he wrestled with the angel (see Genesis 32:24–30). Jacob's family had moved to Egypt at the invitation of Joseph, one of Jacob's sons who had become a great ruler under Pharaoh. Jacob's family grew into a large nation. But, as foreigners and newcomers, their lives were quite different from the Egyptians. The Hebrews worshiped one God; the Egyptians worshiped many gods. The Hebrews were wanderers; the Egyptians had a deeply rooted culture. The Hebrews were shepherds; the Egyptians were builders. The Hebrews were also physically separated from the rest of the Egyptians: They lived in Goshen, north of the great Egyptian cultural centers.

1:9–10 Pharaoh was afraid the Israelites were becoming so numerous that they would organize and threaten his kingdom, so he made them slaves and oppressed them to kill their spirit and stop their growth. Slavery was an ancient practice used by almost all nations to employ conquered people and other captives. Most likely, the great pyramids of Egypt were built with slave labor. Although Israel was not a conquered nation, the people were foreigners and thus lacked the rights of native Egyptians.

1:11 There were levels of slavery in Egypt. Some slaves worked long hours in mud pits while others were skilled carpenters, jewelers, and craftsmen. Regardless of their skill or level, all slaves were watched closely by ruthless slave masters, supervisors whose assignment was to keep the slaves working as fast as possible. They were specialists at making a slave's life miserable.

1:11 Ancient records indicate that these cities were built in 1290 B.C., which is why some scholars believe the exodus occurred early in the 13th century. Looking at other evidence, however, other scholars believe the Hebrews left Egypt in 1446 B.C. How could they build two cities 150 years after they left? These scholars suggest that Raamses II, the pharaoh in 1290 B.C., did not build the cities of Pithom and Raamses. Instead, he renamed two cities that actually had been built 150 years previously. It was a common practice for an Egyptian ruler to make improvements on a city and then take credit for building it, thus wiping out all records of previous founders. Also see the second note on 13:17–18.

1:12 The Egyptians tried to wear down the Hebrew people by forcing them into slavery and mistreating them. Instead, the Hebrews multiplied and grew stronger. When we are burdened or mistreated, we may feel defeated. But our burdens can make us stronger and develop qualities in us that will prepare us for the future. We cannot be overcomers without troubles to overcome. Be true to God in the hard times because even the worst situations can make us better people.

1:15–17 Shiphrah and Puah may have been supervisors over the midwives, or else these two were given special mention. Hebrew midwives helped women give birth and cared for the baby until the mother was stronger. When Pharaoh ordered the midwives to kill the Hebrew baby boys, he was asking the wrong group of people. Midwives were committed to helping babies be born, not to killing them. These women showed great courage and love for God by risking their lives to disobey Pharaoh's command. Note: A birthstool was the stool upon which a woman crouched when delivering her baby.

16 and he said, "When you are helping the Hebrew women to give birth and see *them*
upon the birthstool, if it is a son, then you shall put him to death; but if it is a daughter,
then she shall live."
17 But the midwives feared God, and did not do as the king of Egypt had commanded
them, but let the boys live.
18 So the king of Egypt called for the midwives and said to them, "Why have you done
this thing, and let the boys live?"
19 The midwives said to Pharaoh, "Because the Hebrew women are not as the Egyptian women; for they are vigorous and give birth before the midwife can get to them."
20 So God was good to the midwives, and the people multiplied, and became very
mighty.
21 Because the midwives feared God, He established households for them.
22 Then Pharaoh commanded all his people, saying, "Every son who is born [1]you are
to cast into the Nile, and every daughter you are to keep alive."

1:16 Acts 7:19
1:17 Ex 1:21; Prov 16:6; Acts 4:18-20; 5:29
1:20 Prov 11:18; Eccl 8:12; Heb 6:10; Ex 1:12; Is 3:10
1:21 Ex 1:17
1 Sam 2:35; 2 Sam 7:11, 27; 1 Kin 2:24; 11:38
1:22 Acts 7:19; Gen 41:1

2. God chooses Moses

The Birth of Moses

2 Now a man from the house of Levi went and married a daughter of Levi.
2 The woman conceived and bore a son; and when she saw that he was beautiful,
she hid him for three months.
3 But when she could hide him no longer, she got him a [2]wicker basket and covered it
over with tar and pitch. Then she put the child into it and set *it* among the reeds by the
bank of the Nile.
4 His sister stood at a distance to find out what would happen to him.
5 The daughter of Pharaoh came down to bathe at the Nile, with her maidens walking alongside the Nile; and she saw the basket among the reeds and sent her maid, and
she brought it *to her.*
6 When she opened *it,* she saw the child, and behold, *the* boy was crying. And she had
pity on him and said, "This is one of the Hebrews' children."
7 Then his sister said to Pharaoh's daughter, "Shall I go and call a nurse for you from
the Hebrew women that she may nurse the child for you?"
8 Pharaoh's daughter said to her, "Go *ahead.*" So the girl went and called the child's
mother.

2:1 Ex 6:16, 18, 20
2:2 Acts 7:20; Heb 11:23
2:3 Is 18:2; Is 19:6
2:4 Ex 15:20; Num 26:59
2:5 Ex 7:15; 8:20

1 Some versions insert *to the Hebrews* **2** I.e. papyrus reeds

---

1:17–21 Against Pharaoh's orders, the midwives spared the Hebrew babies. Their faith in God gave them the courage to take a stand for what they knew was right. In this situation, disobeying the authority was proper. God does not expect us to obey those in authority when they ask us to disobey him or his Word. The Bible is filled with examples of those who were willing to sacrifice their very lives in order to obey God or save others. Esther and Mordecai (Esther 3:2; 4:13–16) and Shadrach, Meshach, and Abed-nego (Daniel 3:16–18) are some of the people who took a bold stand for what was right. Whole nations can be caught up in immorality (racial hatred, slavery, prison cruelty); thus following the majority or the authority is not always right. Whenever we are ordered to disobey God's Word, we must "obey God rather than men" (Acts 5:29).

1:19–21 Did God bless the Hebrew midwives for lying to Pharaoh? God blessed them not because they lied, but because they saved the lives of innocent children. This doesn't mean that a lie was necessarily the best way to answer Pharaoh. The midwives were blessed, however, for not violating the higher law of God that forbids the senseless slaughter of innocent lives.

2:1–2 Although a name is not mentioned yet, the baby in this story was Moses. Moses' mother and father were named Jochebed and Amram. His brother was Aaron and his sister, Miriam.

2:3 This tiny wicker boat, made of papyrus reeds, was fashioned by a woman who knew what she was doing. Egyptian river boats were made with these same reeds and waterproofed with tar. The reeds, which grew as tall as sixteen feet, could be gathered in swampy areas along the Nile. Thus a small basket hidden among the reeds would be well insulated from the weather and difficult to see.

2:3ff Moses' mother knew how wrong it would be to destroy her child. But there was little she could do to change Pharaoh's new law. Her only alternative was to hide the child and later place him in a tiny wicker basket on the river. God used her courageous act to place her son, the Hebrew of his choice, in the house of Pharaoh. Do you sometimes feel surrounded by evil and frustrated by how little you can do about it? When faced with evil, look for ways to act against it. Then trust God to use your effort, however small it seems, in his war against evil.

2:5 Who was Pharaoh's daughter? There are two popular explanations. (1) Some think that Hatshepsut was the woman who pulled Moses from the river. Her husband was Pharaoh Thutmose II. (This would match the earlier exodus date.) Apparently Hatshepsut could not have children, so Thutmose had a son by another woman, and this son became heir to the throne. Hatshepsut would have considered Moses a gift from the gods because now she had her own son who would be the legal heir to the throne. (2) Some think the princess who rescued baby Moses was the daughter of Raamses II, an especially cruel Pharaoh who would have made life miserable for the Hebrew slaves. (This would match the later exodus date.)

2:7–8 Miriam, the baby's sister, saw that Pharaoh's daughter had discovered Moses. Quickly she took the initiative to suggest a nurse (her mother) who might care for the baby. The Bible doesn't say if Miriam was afraid to approach the Egyptian princess, or if the princess was suspicious of the Hebrew girl. But Miriam did approach her, and the princess bought the services of Miriam and her mother. Their family was reunited. Special opportunities may come our way unexpectedly. Don't let the fear of what might happen cause you to miss an opportunity. Be alert for the opportunities God gives you, and take full advantage of them.

9 Then Pharaoh's daughter said to her, "Take this child away and nurse him for me and I will give *you* your wages." So the woman took the child and nursed him.
10 The child grew, and she brought him to Pharaoh's daughter and he became her son. And she named him Moses, and said, "Because I drew him out of the water."
11 Now it came about in those days, when Moses had grown up, that he went out to his brethren and looked on their hard labors; and he saw an Egyptian beating a Hebrew, one of his brethren.
12 So he looked this way and that, and when he saw there was no one *around,* he struck down the Egyptian and hid him in the sand.
13 He went out the next day, and behold, two Hebrews were fighting with each other; and he said to the offender, "Why are you striking your companion?"
14 But he said, "Who made you a prince or a judge over us? Are you intending to kill me as you killed the Egyptian?" Then Moses was afraid and said, "Surely the matter has become known."

2:10 Acts 7:21
2:11 Acts 7:23; Heb 11:24-26; Ex 1:11; 5:4, 5; 6:6, 7; Acts 7:24
2:12 Acts 7:24, 25
2:13 Acts 7:26-28
2:14 Gen 19:9; Acts 7:27, 28
2:15 Acts 7:29; Heb 11:27; Gen 24:11; 29:2
2:16 Ex 3:1; 18:12; Gen 24:11, 13, 19; 29:9, 10; 1 Sam 9:11
2:17 Gen 29:3, 10
2:18 Ex 3:1; Num 10:29
2:21 Acts 7:29; Ex 4:25; 18:2
2:22 Ex 4:20; 18:3, 4; Gen 23:4; Lev 25:23; Acts 7:29; Heb 11:13, 14
2:23 Ex 6:5, 9; Ex 3:7, 9; Deut 26:7; James 5:4

Moses Escapes to Midian

15 When Pharaoh heard of this matter, he tried to kill Moses. But Moses fled from the presence of Pharaoh and settled in the land of Midian, and he sat down by a well.
16 Now the priest of Midian had seven daughters; and they came to draw water and filled the troughs to water their father's flock.
17 Then the shepherds came and drove them away, but Moses stood up and helped them and watered their flock.
18 When they came to Reuel their father, he said, "Why have you come *back* so soon today?"
19 So they said, "An Egyptian delivered us from the hand of the shepherds, and what is more, he even drew the water for us and watered the flock."
20 He said to his daughters, "Where is he then? Why is it that you have left the man behind? Invite him to have something to eat."
21 Moses was willing to dwell with the man, and he gave his daughter Zipporah to Moses.
22 Then she gave birth to a son, and he named him Gershom, for he said, "I have been a sojourner in a foreign land."
23 Now it came about in *the course of* those many days that the king of Egypt died.

2:9 Moses' mother was reunited with her baby! God used her courageous act of saving and hiding her baby to begin his plan to rescue his people from Egypt. God doesn't need much from us to accomplish his plan for our lives. Focusing on our human predicament may paralyze us because the situation may appear humanly impossible. But concentrating on God and his power will help us see the way out. Right now you may feel unable to see through your troubles. Focus instead on God, and trust him for the way out. That is all he needs to begin his work in you.

2:12–14 Moses tried to make sure no one was watching before he killed the Egyptian. But as it turned out, someone did see, and Moses had to flee the country. Sometimes we mistakenly think we can get away with doing wrong if no one sees or catches us. Sooner or later, however, doing wrong will catch up with us as it did with Moses. Even if we are not caught in this life, we will still have to face God and his evaluation of our actions.

2:15 To escape punishment for killing the Egyptian, Moses ran away to Midian. He became a stranger in a strange land, separated from his home and family. It took many years after this incident for Moses to be ready to serve God. But he trusted God instead of fearing the king (Hebrews 11:27). We may feel abandoned or isolated because of something we have done. But though we feel afraid and separated, we should not give up. Moses didn't. He trusted God to deliver him, no matter how dark his past or bleak his future.

2:17 How did Moses handle these shepherds so easily? As an Egyptian prince, Moses would have been well trained in the Egyptian military, the most advanced army in the world. Even a large group of shepherds would have been no match for the sophisticated fighting techniques of this trained warrior.

2:18 Reuel is also called Jethro in 3:1.

2:23–25 God's rescue doesn't always come the moment we want it. God had promised to bring the Hebrew slaves out of Egypt (Genesis 15:16; 46:3–4). The people had waited a long time for that promise to be kept, but God rescued them when he knew the right time had come. God knows the best time to act. When you feel that God has forgotten you in your troubles, remember that God has a time schedule we can't see.

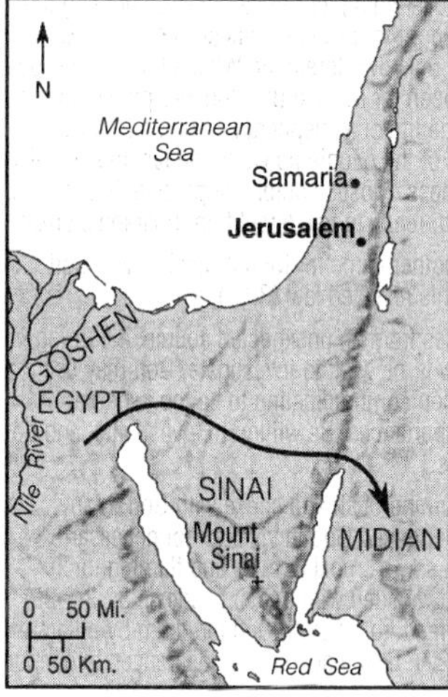

MOSES FLEES TO MIDIAN
After murdering an Egyptian, Moses escaped into Midian. There he married Zipporah and became a shepherd.

And the sons of Israel sighed because of the bondage, and they cried out; and their cry
for help because of *their* bondage rose up to God.
24 So God heard their groaning; and God remembered His covenant with Abraham,
Isaac, and Jacob.
25 God saw the sons of Israel, and God took notice *of them.*

The Burning Bush

3 Now Moses was pasturing the flock of Jethro his father-in-law, the priest of Midian;
and he led the flock to the west side of the wilderness and came to Horeb, the mountain of God.
2 The angel of the LORD appeared to him in a blazing fire from the midst of a bush; and
he looked, and behold, the bush was burning with fire, yet the bush was not consumed.
3 So Moses said, "I must turn aside now and see this marvelous sight, why the bush is
not burned up."
4 When the LORD saw that he turned aside to look, God called to him from the midst
of the bush and said, "Moses, Moses!" And he said, "Here I am."
5 Then He said, "Do not come near here; remove your sandals from your feet, for the
place on which you are standing is holy ground."
6 He said also, "I am the God of your father, the God of Abraham, the God of Isaac,
and the God of Jacob." Then Moses hid his face, for he was afraid to look at God.
7 The LORD said, "I have surely seen the affliction of My people who are in Egypt, and
have given heed to their cry because of their taskmasters, for I am aware of their sufferings.
8 "So I have come down to deliver them from the power of the Egyptians, and to bring
them up from that land to a good and spacious land, to a land flowing with milk and
honey, to the place of the Canaanite and the Hittite and the Amorite and the Perizzite
and the Hivite and the Jebusite.
9 "Now, behold, the cry of the sons of Israel has come to Me; furthermore, I have seen
the oppression with which the Egyptians are oppressing them.

The Mission of Moses

10 "Therefore, come now, and I will send you to Pharaoh, so that you may bring My
people, the sons of Israel, out of Egypt."
11 But Moses said to God, "Who am I, that I should go to Pharaoh, and that I should
bring the sons of Israel out of Egypt?"
12 And He said, "Certainly I will be with you, and this shall be the sign to you that it is
I who have sent you: when you have brought the people out of Egypt, you shall worship
God at this mountain."
13 Then Moses said to God, "Behold, I am going to the sons of Israel, and I will say to

2:24 Ex 6:5; Acts 7:34; Gen 15:13f; 22:16-18; 26:2-5

2:25 Ex 3:7; 4:31; Acts 7:34

3:2 Gen 16:7-11; 21:17; 22:11, 15; Judg 13:13-21; Acts 7:30; Deut 33:16; Mark 12:26; Luke 20:37; Acts 7:30

3:3 Acts 7:31

3:4 Ex 4:5

3:5 Josh 5:15; Acts 7:33

3:6 Gen 28:13; Ex 3:16; 4:5; Matt 22:32; Mark 12:26; Luke 20:37; Acts 7:32; Judg 13:22

3:7 Ex 2:25; Neh 9:9; Ps 106:44; Is 63:9; Acts 7:34

3:8 Gen 15:13-16; 46:4; 50:24, 25; Jer 11:5; Ezek 20:6; Gen 15:19-21; Josh 24:11

3:10 Gen 15:13, 14; Ex 12:40, 41; Mic 6:4; Acts 7:6, 7

3:11 Ex 4:10; 6:12; 1 Sam 18:18

3:12 Gen 31:3; Ex 4:12, 15; 33:14-16; Deut 31:23; Josh 1:5; Is 43:2; Ex 19:1; Ex 19:2, 3; Acts 7:7

3:1 What a contrast between Moses' life as an Egyptian prince and his life as a Midianite shepherd! As a prince he had everything done for him; he was the famous son of an Egyptian princess. As a shepherd he had to do everything for himself; he was holding the very job he had been taught to despise (Genesis 43:32; 46:32–34), and he lived as an unknown foreigner. What a humbling experience this must have been for Moses! But God was preparing him for leadership. Living the life of a shepherd and nomad, Moses learned about the ways of the people he would be leading and also about life in the wilderness. Moses couldn't appreciate this lesson, but God was getting him ready to free Israel from Pharaoh's grasp.

3:1 Mount Horeb is another name for Mount Sinai, where God would give the people his revealed law (3:12).

3:2 God spoke to Moses from an unexpected source: a burning bush. When Moses saw it, he went to investigate. God may use unexpected sources when communicating to us too, whether people, thoughts, or experiences. Be willing to investigate, and be open to God's surprises.

3:2–4 Moses saw a burning bush and spoke with God. Many people in the Bible experienced God in visible (not necessarily human) form. Abraham saw a smoking oven and flaming torch (Genesis 15:17); Jacob wrestled with a man (Genesis 32:24–29). When the slaves were freed from Egypt, God led them by pillars of cloud and fire (13:17–22). God made such appearances to encourage his new nation, to guide them, and to prove the reliability of his verbal message.

3:5–6 At God's command, Moses removed his sandals and covered his face. Taking off his shoes was an act of reverence, conveying his own unworthiness before God. God is our friend, but he is also our sovereign Lord. To approach him frivolously shows a lack of respect and sincerity. When you come to God in worship, do you approach him casually, or do you come as though you were an invited guest before a king? If necessary, adjust your attitude so it is suitable for approaching a holy God.

3:8 "The place of the Canaanite" is the land of Israel and Jordan today. *Canaanites* was a term for all the various tribes living in that land.

3:10ff Moses made excuses because he felt inadequate for the job God asked him to do. It was natural for him to feel that way. He *was* inadequate all by himself. But God wasn't asking Moses to work alone. He offered other resources to help (God himself, Aaron, and the ability to do miracles). God often calls us to tasks that seem too difficult, but he doesn't ask us to do them alone. God offers us his resources, just as he did to Moses. We should not hide behind our inadequacies, as Moses did, but look beyond ourselves to the great resources available. Then we can allow God to use our unique contributions.

3:13–15 The Egyptians had many gods by many different names. Moses wanted to know God's name so the Hebrew people would

them, 'The God of your fathers has sent me to you.' Now they may say to me, 'What is
His name?' What shall I say to them?"
14 God said to Moses, "[3]I AM WHO [3]I AM"; and He said, "Thus you shall say to the
sons of Israel, '[3]I AM has sent me to you.' "
15 God, furthermore, said to Moses, "Thus you shall say to the sons of Israel, 'The
LORD, the God of your fathers, the God of Abraham, the God of Isaac, and the God of
Jacob, has sent me to you.' This is My name forever, and this is My memorial-name to
all generations.
16 "Go and gather the elders of Israel together and say to them, 'The LORD, the God of
your fathers, the God of Abraham, Isaac and Jacob, has appeared to me, saying, "I am
indeed concerned about you and what has been done to you in Egypt.
17 "So I said, I will bring you up out of the affliction of Egypt to the land of the Canaanite and the Hittite and the Amorite and the Perizzite and the Hivite and the Jebusite, to
a land flowing with milk and honey." '
18 "They will pay heed to what you say; and you with the elders of Israel will come to
the king of Egypt and you will say to him, 'The LORD, the God of the Hebrews, has met
with us. So now, please, let us go a three days' journey into the wilderness, that we may
sacrifice to the LORD our God.'
19 "But I know that the king of Egypt will not permit you to go, except under compulsion.
20 "So I will stretch out My hand and strike Egypt with all My miracles which I shall do
in the midst of it; and after that he will let you go.
21 "I will grant this people favor in the sight of the Egyptians; and it shall be that when
you go, you will not go empty-handed.
22 "But every woman shall ask of her neighbor and the woman who lives in her house,
articles of silver and articles of gold, and clothing; and you will put them on your sons
and daughters. Thus you will plunder the Egyptians."

Moses Given Powers

4 Then Moses said, "What if they will not believe me or listen to what I say? For they
may say, 'The LORD has not appeared to you.' "
2 The LORD said to him, "What is that in your hand?"
And he said, "A staff."
3 Then He said, "Throw it on the ground." So he threw it on the ground, and it became a serpent; and Moses fled from it.

3 Related to the name of God, *YHWH*, rendered *LORD*, which is derived from the verb *HAYAH, to be*

3:14 Ex 6:3; John 8:24, 28, 58; Heb 13:8; Rev 1:8; 4:8

3:15 Ex 3:6, 13; Ps 30:4; 97:12; 102:12; 135:13; Hos 12:5

3:16 Ex 4:29; Gen 28:13; 48:15; Ex 3:2, 6; 4:5; Ex 4:31; Ps 33:18f

3:17 Gen 15:13-21; 46:4; 50:24, 25; Josh 24:11; Ex 3:8

3:18 Ex 4:31; Ex 5:1; Ex 5:3; 8:27

3:19 Ex 5:2; Ex 6:1

3:20 Ex 6:1; 7:4, 5; 9:15; 13:3, 9, 14; Ex 7:3; 15:11; Deut 6:22; Neh 9:10; Ps 105:27; 135:9; Jer 32:20; Acts 7:36; Ex 11:1; 12:31-33

3:21 Ex 11:3; 12:36; 1 Kin 8:50; Ps 105:37f; 106:46; Prov 16:7

3:22 Gen 15:14; Ex 11:2; 12:35; Ezek 39:10

4:1 Ex 3:18; 6:30; Ex 3:15, 16

4:2 Ex 4:17, 20

4:3 Ex 7:10-12

know exactly who had sent him to them. God called himself, *I AM*, a name describing his eternal power and unchangeable character. In a world where values, morals, and laws change constantly, we can find stability and security in our unchanging God. The God who appeared to Moses is the same God who can live in us today. Hebrews 13:8 says God is the same "yesterday and today and forever." Because God's nature is stable and trustworthy, we are free to follow and enjoy him rather than spend our time trying to figure him out.

3:14–15 *Yahweh* is derived from the Hebrew word for "I AM." God reminded Moses of his covenant promises to Abraham (Genesis 12:1–3; 15; 17), Isaac (Genesis 26:2–5), and Jacob (Genesis 28:13–15), and used the name *I AM* to show his unchanging nature. What God promised to the great patriarchs hundreds of years earlier he would fulfill through Moses.

3:16–17 God told Moses to tell the people what he saw and heard at the burning bush. Our God is a God who acts and speaks. One of the most convincing ways to tell others about him is to describe what he has done and how he has spoken to his people. If you are trying to explain God to others, talk about what he has done for you, for people you know, or for people whose stories are told in the Bible.

3:17 "A land flowing with milk and honey" is a poetic word picture expressing the beauty and productivity of the promised land.

3:18–20 The leaders of Israel would accept God's message, and the leaders of Egypt would reject it. God knew what both reactions would be before they happened. This is more than good psychology—God knows the future. Any believer can trust his or her future to God because God already knows what is going to happen.

3:22 The jewels and clothing were not merely borrowed—they were asked for and easily received. The Egyptians would be so glad to see the Israelites go that they would send them out with gifts (12:35–36). These items were used later in building the tabernacle (35:5, 22). The promise of being able to plunder the Egyptians seemed impossible to Moses at this time.

4:1 Moses' reluctance and fear were caused by overanticipation. He was worried about how the people might respond to him. We often build up events in our minds and then panic over what might go wrong. God does not ask us to go where he has not provided the means to help. Go where he leads, trusting him to supply courage, confidence, and resources at the right moment.

4:2–4 A shepherd's staff was commonly a three- to six-foot wooden rod with a curved hook at the top. The shepherd used it for walking, guiding his sheep, killing snakes, and many other tasks. Still, it was just a stick. But God used the simple shepherd's staff Moses carried as a sign to teach him an important lesson. God sometimes takes joy in using ordinary things for extraordinary purposes. What are the ordinary things in your life—your voice, a pen, a hammer, a broom, a musical instrument? While it is easy to assume God can use only special skills, you must not hinder his use of the everyday contributions you can make. Little did Moses imagine the power his simple staff would wield when it became the staff of God.

4 But the LORD said to Moses, "Stretch out your hand and grasp *it* by its tail"—so he
stretched out his hand and caught it, and it became a staff in his hand—
5 "that they may believe that the LORD, the God of their fathers, the God of Abraham, the God of Isaac, and the God of Jacob, has appeared to you."
6 The LORD furthermore said to him, "Now put your hand into your bosom." So he put his hand into his bosom, and when he took it out, behold, his hand was leprous like snow.
7 Then He said, "Put your hand into your bosom again." So he put his hand into his bosom again, and when he took it out of his bosom, behold, it was restored like *the rest of* his flesh.
8 "If they will not believe you or heed the witness of the first sign, they may believe the witness of the last sign.
9 "But if they will not believe even these two signs or heed what you say, then you shall take some water from the Nile and pour it on the dry ground; and the water which you take from the Nile will become blood on the dry ground."
10 Then Moses said to the LORD, "Please, Lord, I have never been eloquent, neither recently nor in time past, nor since You have spoken to Your servant; for I am slow of speech and slow of tongue."
11 The LORD said to him, "Who has made man's mouth? Or who makes *him* mute or deaf, or seeing or blind? Is it not I, the LORD?
12 "Now then go, and I, even I, will be with your mouth, and teach you what you are to say."
13 But he said, "Please, Lord, now send *the message* by whomever You will."

Aaron to Be Moses' Mouthpiece

14 Then the anger of the LORD burned against Moses, and He said, "Is there not your brother Aaron the Levite? I know that he speaks fluently. And moreover, behold, he is coming out to meet you; when he sees you, he will be glad in his heart.
15 "You are to speak to him and put the words in his mouth; and I, even I, will be with your mouth and his mouth, and I will teach you what you are to do.
16 "Moreover, he shall speak for you to the people; and he will be as a mouth for you and you will be as God to him.
17 "You shall take in your hand this staff, with which you shall perform the signs."
18 Then Moses departed and returned to Jethro his father-in-law and said to him, "Please, let me go, that I may return to my brethren who are in Egypt, and see if they are still alive." And Jethro said to Moses, "Go in peace."
19 Now the LORD said to Moses in Midian, "Go back to Egypt, for all the men who were seeking your life are dead."
20 So Moses took his wife and his sons and mounted them on a donkey, and returned to the land of Egypt. Moses also took the staff of God in his hand.
21 The LORD said to Moses, "When you go back to Egypt see that you perform before Pharaoh all the wonders which I have put in your power; but I will harden his heart so that he will not let the people go.
22 "Then you shall say to Pharaoh, 'Thus says the LORD, "Israel is My son, My firstborn.
23 "So I said to you, 'Let My son go that he may serve Me'; but you have refused to let him go. Behold, I will kill your son, your firstborn." ' "

4:5 Ex 4:31; 19:9; Gen 28:13; 48:15
4:6 Num 12:10
4:7 Num 12:13-15; Matt 8:3; Luke 17:12-14
4:9 Ex 7:19, 20
4:10 Ex 3:11; 4:1; 6:12
4:11 Ps 94:9; 146:8; Matt 11:5; Luke 1:20, 64
4:12 Ex 4:15, 16; Jer 1:9; Matt 10:19, 20; Mark 13:11; Luke 12:11, 12; 21:14, 15
4:14 Ex 4:27
4:15 Ex 4:12, 30; 7:1f; Num 23:5, 12, 16
4:16 Ex 7:1, 2
4:17 Ex 4:2, 20; 17:9; Ex 7:9-20; 14:16
4:18 Ex 2:21; 3:1
4:19 Ex 2:15, 23
4:20 Ex 18:3, 4; Acts 7:29; Ex 4:17; 17:9; Num 20:8, 9, 11
4:21 Ex 3:20; 11:9, 10; Ex 7:3, 13; 9:12, 35; 10:1, 20, 27; 14:4, 8; Deut 2:30; Josh 11:20; 1 Sam 6:6; Is 63:17; John 12:40; Rom 9:18
4:22 Jer 31:9; Rom 9:4
4:23 Ex 5:1; 6:11; 7:16; Ps 105:36; 135:8; 136:10

4:6–7 Leprosy was one of the most feared diseases of this time. There was no cure, and a great deal of suffering preceded eventual death. Through this experience, Moses learned that God could cause or cure any kind of problem. He saw that God indeed had all power and was commissioning him to exercise that power to lead the Hebrews out of Egypt.

4:10–13 Moses pleaded with God to let him out of his mission. After all, he was not a good speaker and would probably embarrass both himself and God. But God looked at Moses' problem quite differently. All Moses needed was some help, and who better than God could help him say and do the right things. God made his mouth and would give him the words to say. It is easy for us to focus on our weaknesses, but if God asks us to do something, then he will help us get the job done. If the job involves some of our weak areas, then we can trust that he will provide words, strength, courage, and ability where needed.

4:14 God finally agreed to let Aaron speak for Moses. Moses' feelings of inadequacy were so strong that he could not trust even God's ability to help him. Moses had to deal with his deep sense of inadequacy many times. When we face difficult or frightening situations, we must be willing to let God help us.

4:16 The phrase, "you will be as God to him," means that Moses would tell Aaron what to say as God was telling him.

4:17–20 Moses clung tightly to the shepherd's staff as he left for Egypt to face the greatest challenge of his life. The staff was his assurance of God's presence and power. When feeling uncertain, some people need something to stabilize and reassure them. For assurance when facing great trials, God has given promises from his Word and examples from great heroes of faith. Any Christian may cling tightly to these.

4:24 Num 22:22

4:25 Gen 17:14; Josh 5:2, 3

4:27 Ex 4:14; Ex 3:1; 18:5; 24:13

4:28 Ex 4:15f; Ex 4:8f

4:29 Ex 3:16

4:30 Ex 4:15, 16; Ex 4:1-9

4:31 Ex 3:18; 4:8f; 19:9; Gen 50:24; Ex 3:16; Gen 24:26; Ex 12:27; 1 Chr 29:20

24 Now it came about at the lodging place on the way that the LORD met him and sought
to put him to death.
25 Then Zipporah took a flint and cut off her son's foreskin and threw it at Moses'
feet, and she said, "You are indeed a bridegroom of blood to me."
26 So He let him alone. At that time she said, "*You are* a bridegroom of blood"—because of the circumcision.
27 Now the LORD said to Aaron, "Go to meet Moses in the wilderness." So he went
and met him at the mountain of God and kissed him.
28 Moses told Aaron all the words of the LORD with which He had sent him, and all
the signs that He had commanded him *to do.*
29 Then Moses and Aaron went and assembled all the elders of the sons of Israel;
30 and Aaron spoke all the words which the LORD had spoken to Moses. He then performed the signs in the sight of the people.
31 So the people believed; and when they heard that the LORD was concerned about
the sons of Israel and that He had seen their affliction, then they bowed low and worshiped.

3. God sends Moses to Pharaoh

Israel's Labor Increased

5:1 Ex 3:18; Ex 4:23; 6:11; 7:16

5:2 2 Kin 18:35; 2 Chr 32:14; Job 21:15; Ex 3:19

5:4 Ex 1:11; 2:11; 6:5-7

5:5 Ex 1:7, 9

5 And afterward Moses and Aaron came and said to Pharaoh, "Thus says the LORD,
the God of Israel, 'Let My people go that they may celebrate a feast to Me in the
wilderness.' "
2 But Pharaoh said, "Who is the LORD that I should obey His voice to let Israel go?
I do not know the LORD, and besides, I will not let Israel go."
3 Then they said, "The God of the Hebrews has met with us. Please, let us go a three
days' journey into the wilderness that we may sacrifice to the LORD our God, otherwise
He will fall upon us with pestilence or with the sword."
4 But the king of Egypt said to them, "Moses and Aaron, why do you draw the people
away from their work? Get *back* to your labors!"
5 Again Pharaoh said, "Look, the people of the land are now many, and you would
have them cease from their labors!"

4:24–26 God was about to kill Moses because Moses had not circumcised his son. Why hadn't Moses done this? Remember that Moses had spent half his life in Pharaoh's palace and half his life in the Midianite wilderness. He might not have been too familiar with God's laws, especially since all the requirements of God's covenant with Israel (Genesis 17) had not been actively carried out for over 400 years. In addition, Moses' wife, due to her Midianite background, may have opposed circumcision. But Moses could not effectively serve as deliverer of God's people until he had fulfilled the conditions of God's covenant, and one of those conditions was circumcision. Before they could go any farther, Moses and his family had to follow God's commands completely. Under Old Testament law, failing to circumcise your son was to remove yourself and your family from God's blessings. Moses learned that disobeying God was even more dangerous than tangling with an Egyptian pharaoh.

4:25–26 Why did Zipporah perform the circumcision? It may have been Zipporah who, as a Midianite unfamiliar with the circumcision requirement, had persuaded Moses not to circumcise their son. If she prevented the action, now she would have to perform it. It is also possible that Moses became ill as a result of permitting disobedience, and so Zipporah had to perform the circumcision herself to save both her husband and son. This would not have made her happy—hence, her unflattering comment to Moses.

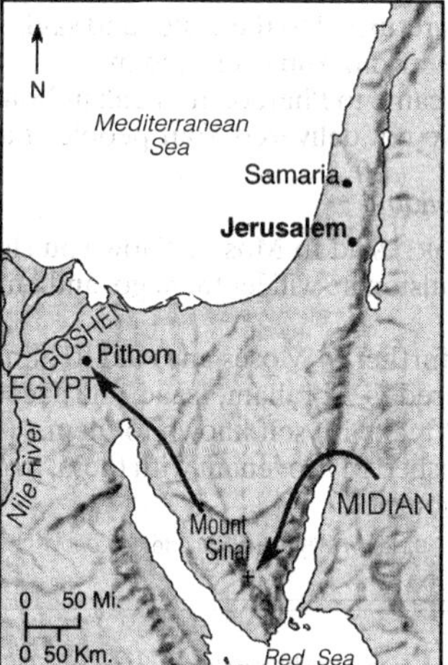

MOSES RETURNS TO EGYPT
God appeared to Moses in a mysterious burning bush on Mount Sinai. Later Aaron met Moses at the mountain, and together they returned to Egypt, a 200-mile trip.

5:1–2 Pharaoh was familiar with many gods (Egypt was filled with them), but he had never heard of the God of Israel. Pharaoh assumed that the God of the Hebrew slaves couldn't be very powerful. At first, Pharaoh was not at all worried about Moses' message, for he had not yet seen any evidence of the Lord's power.

5:3 Pharaoh would not listen to Moses and Aaron because he did not know or respect God. People who do not know God may not listen to his word or his messengers. Like Moses and Aaron, we need to persist. When others reject you or your faith, don't be surprised or discouraged. Continue to tell them about God, trusting him to open minds and soften stubborn hearts.

5:4–9 Moses and Aaron took their message to Pharaoh just as God directed. The unhappy result was harder work and more oppression for the Hebrews. Sometimes hardship comes as a result of obeying God. Are you following God but still suffering—or suffering even worse than before? If your life is miserable, don't assume you have fallen out of God's favor. You may be suffering for doing good in an evil world.

6 So the same day Pharaoh commanded the taskmasters over the people and their **5:6** Ex 1:11; 3:7; 5:10,
foremen, saying, 13, 14; Ex 5:10, 14,
7 "You are no longer to give the people straw to make brick as previously; let them go 15, 19
and gather straw for themselves.
8 "But the quota of bricks which they were making previously, you shall impose on them; **5:8**
you are not to reduce any of it. Because they are lazy, therefore they cry out, 'Let us go Ex 5:17
and sacrifice to our God.'
9 "Let the labor be heavier on the men, and let them work at it so that they will pay no
attention to false words."
10 So the taskmasters of the people and their foremen went out and spoke to the peo- **5:10**
ple, saying, "Thus says Pharaoh, 'I am not going to give you *any* straw. Ex 1:11; 3:7; 5:6
11 'You go *and* get straw for yourselves wherever you can find *it,* but none of your labor
will be reduced.' "
12 So the people scattered through all the land of Egypt to gather stubble for straw.
13 The taskmasters pressed them, saying, "Complete your work quota, *your* daily
amount, just as when you had straw."
14 Moreover, the foremen of the sons of Israel, whom Pharaoh's taskmasters had set **5:14**
over them, were beaten and were asked, "Why have you not completed your required Ex 5:6; Is 10:24
amount either yesterday or today in making brick as previously?"
15 Then the foremen of the sons of Israel came and cried out to Pharaoh, saying, "Why
do you deal this way with your servants?
16 "There is no straw given to your servants, yet they keep saying to us, 'Make bricks!'
And behold, your servants are being beaten; but it is the fault of your *own* people."
17 But he said, "You are lazy, *very* lazy; therefore you say, 'Let us go *and* sacrifice to **5:17**
the LORD.' Ex 5:8
18 "So go now *and* work; for you will be given no straw, yet you must deliver the quota
of bricks."
19 The foremen of the sons of Israel saw that they were in trouble because they were
told, "You must not reduce *your* daily amount of bricks." **5:21**
20 When they left Pharaoh's presence, they met Moses and Aaron as they were wait- Ex 14:11; 15:24;
ing for them. 16:2; Gen 16:5; 31:53; Gen 34:30;
21 They said to them, "May the LORD look upon you and judge *you,* for you have made 1 Sam 13:4; 27:12;
[4]us odious in Pharaoh's sight and in the sight of his servants, to put a sword in their hand 2 Sam 10:6; 1 Chr
to kill us." 19:6
22 Then Moses returned to the LORD and said, "O Lord, why have You brought harm **5:22** Num 11:11; Jer 4:10
to this people? Why did You ever send me?
23 "Ever since I came to Pharaoh to speak in Your name, he has done harm to this peo- **5:23** Ex 3:8
ple, and You have not delivered Your people at all."

God Promises Action

6 Then the LORD said to Moses, "Now you shall see what I will do to Pharaoh; for **6:1** Ex 3:19, 20; 7:4, 5; 11:1; 12:31, 33, 39; 13:3
under compulsion he will let them go, and under compulsion he will drive them out **6:2** Ex 3:14, 15
of his land."
2 God spoke further to Moses and said to him, "I am the LORD; **6:3** Gen 17:1; 35:11; 48:3; Ps 68:4; 83:18;
3 and I appeared to Abraham, Isaac, and Jacob, as God Almighty, but *by* My name, Is 52:6; Jer 16:21;
[5]LORD, I did not make Myself known to them. Ezek 37:6, 13
4 "I also established My covenant with them, to give them the land of Canaan, the land **6:4**
in which they sojourned. Gen 12:7; 15:18; 17:4, 7; 26:3, 4; 28:4, 13

4 Lit *our savor to stink* **5** Heb *YHWH,* usually rendered *LORD*

5:7–8 Mixing straw with mud made bricks stronger and more durable. Pharaoh had supplied the slaves with straw, but now he made them find their own straw and keep up their production quota as well.

5:15–21 The foremen were caught in the middle. First they tried to get the people to produce the same amount, then they complained to Pharaoh, finally they turned on Moses. Perhaps you have felt caught in the middle at work, or in relationships in your family or church. Complaining or turning on the leadership does not solve the problem. In the case of these supervisors, God had a larger purpose in mind, just as he might in your situation. So rather than turning on the leadership when you feel pressured by both sides, turn to God to see what else he might be doing in this situation.

5:22–23 Pharaoh had just increased the Hebrews' workload, and Moses protested that God had not rescued his people. Moses expected faster results and fewer problems. When God is at work, suffering, setbacks, and hardship may still occur. In James 1:2–4, we are encouraged to be happy when difficulties come our way. Problems develop our patience and character by teaching us to (1) trust God to do what is best for us, (2) look for ways to honor God in our present situation, (3) remember that God will not abandon us, and (4) watch for God's plan for us.

6:6
Deut 6:12; Ex 3:17; 7:4; 12:51; 16:6; 18:1; Deut 26:8; Ps 136:11; Ex 15:13; Deut 7:8; 1 Chr 17:21; Neh 1:10; Deut 4:34; 5:15; 26:8; Ps 136:11f

6:7
Ex 19:5; Deut 4:20; 7:6; 2 Sam 7:24; Gen 17:7

6:8
Gen 15:18; 26:3; Num 14:30; Neh 9:15; Ezek 20:5, 6; Josh 24:13; Ps 136:21, 22; Ex 6:6

6:12
Ex 4:1, 10; 6:30; Jer 1:6

6:14
Gen 46:9; Num 26:5-11; 1 Chr 5:3

6:15
Gen 46:10; 1 Chr 4:24

6:16
Num 3:17; 26:57f; 1 Chr 6:1, 16-19

6:17
Num 3:18-20

6:18
Num 3:19

6:19
Num 3:20

6:20
Num 26:59

6:21
Num 16:1

6:22
Lev 10:4; Num 3:30

6:23
Ruth 4:19, 20; 1 Chr 2:10; Num 1:7; 2:3

6:24
Num 26:11; 1 Chr 6:22, 23, 37

6:25
Josh 24:33; Num 25:7-13; Josh 24:33; Ps 106:30

5 "Furthermore I have heard the groaning of the sons of Israel, because the Egyptians
are holding them in bondage, and I have remembered My covenant.
6 "Say, therefore, to the sons of Israel, 'I am the LORD, and I will bring you out from
under the burdens of the Egyptians, and I will deliver you from their bondage. I will also
redeem you with an outstretched arm and with great judgments.
7 'Then I will take you for My people, and I will be your God; and you shall know that
I am the LORD your God, who brought you out from under the burdens of the Egyptians.
8 'I will bring you to the land which I swore to give to Abraham, Isaac, and Jacob, and
I will give it to you *for* a possession; I am the LORD.' "
9 So Moses spoke thus to the sons of Israel, but they did not listen to Moses on account of *their* despondency and cruel bondage.
10 Now the LORD spoke to Moses, saying,
11 "Go, tell Pharaoh king of Egypt to let the sons of Israel go out of his land."
12 But Moses spoke before the LORD, saying, "Behold, the sons of Israel have not listened to me; how then will Pharaoh listen to me, for I am unskilled in speech?"
13 Then the LORD spoke to Moses and to Aaron, and gave them a charge to the sons
of Israel and to Pharaoh king of Egypt, to bring the sons of Israel out of the land of Egypt.

The Heads of Israel

14 These are the heads of their fathers' households. The sons of Reuben, Israel's firstborn: Hanoch and Pallu, Hezron and Carmi; these are the families of Reuben.
15 The sons of Simeon: Jemuel and Jamin and Ohad and Jachin and Zohar and Shaul
the son of a Canaanite woman; these are the families of Simeon.
16 These are the names of the sons of Levi according to their generations: Gershon
and Kohath and Merari; and the length of Levi's life was one hundred and thirty-seven
years.
17 The sons of Gershon: Libni and Shimei, according to their families.
18 The sons of Kohath: Amram and Izhar and Hebron and Uzziel; and the length of
Kohath's life was one hundred and thirty-three years.
19 The sons of Merari: Mahli and Mushi. These are the families of the Levites according to their generations.
20 Amram married his father's sister Jochebed, and she bore him Aaron and Moses;
and the length of Amram's life was one hundred and thirty-seven years.
21 The sons of Izhar: Korah and Nepheg and Zichri.
22 The sons of Uzziel: Mishael and Elzaphan and Sithri.
23 Aaron married Elisheba, the daughter of Amminadab, the sister of Nahshon, and
she bore him Nadab and Abihu, Eleazar and Ithamar.
24 The sons of Korah: Assir and Elkanah and Abiasaph; these are the families of the
Korahites.
25 Aaron's son Eleazar married one of the daughters of Putiel, and she bore him Phinehas. These are the heads of the fathers' *households* of the Levites according to their
families.

6:6 Small problems need only small answers. But when we face great problems, God has an opportunity to exercise his great power. As the Hebrews' troubles grew steadily worse, God planned to intervene with his mighty power and perform great miracles to deliver them. How big are your problems? Big problems put you in a perfect position to watch God give big answers.

6:6–8 God's promises in these verses were fulfilled to the letter when the Hebrews left Egypt. He freed them from slavery, became their God, and accepted them as his people. Then he led them toward the land he had promised. When the Hebrews were rescued from slavery, they portrayed the drama of salvation for all of us. When God redeems us from sin he delivers us, accepts us, and becomes our God. Then he leads us to a new life as we follow him.

6:9–12 When Moses gave God's message to the people, they were too discouraged to listen. The Hebrews didn't want to hear any more about God and his promises because the last time they listened to Moses, all they got was more work and greater suffering. Sometimes a clear message from God is followed by a period when no change in the situation is apparent. During that time, seeming setbacks may turn people away from wanting to hear more about God. If you are a leader, don't give up. Keep bringing people God's message as Moses did. By focusing on God who must be obeyed rather than on the results to be achieved, good leaders see beyond temporary setbacks and reversals.

6:10–12 Think how hard it must have been for Moses to bring God's message to Pharaoh when his own people had trouble believing it. Eventually the Hebrews believed that God had sent Moses, but for a time he must have felt very alone. Moses obeyed God, however, and what a difference it made! When the chances for success appear slim, remember that anyone can obey God when the task is easy and everyone is behind it. Only those with persistent faith can obey when the task seems impossible.

6:14–25 This genealogy or family tree was placed here to identify more firmly Moses and Aaron. Genealogies were used to establish credentials and authority as well as outlining the history of a family.

26 It was *the same* Aaron and Moses to whom the LORD said, "Bring out the sons of
Israel from the land of Egypt according to their hosts."
27 They were the ones who spoke to Pharaoh king of Egypt about bringing out the sons
of Israel from Egypt; it was *the same* Moses and Aaron.
28 Now it came about on the day when the LORD spoke to Moses in the land of Egypt,
29 that the LORD spoke to Moses, saying, "I am the LORD; speak to Pharaoh king of
Egypt all that I speak to you."
30 But Moses said before the LORD, "Behold, I am unskilled in speech; how then will
Pharaoh listen to me?"

"I Will Stretch Out My Hand"

7 Then the LORD said to Moses, "See, I make you *as* God to Pharaoh, and your brother
Aaron shall be your prophet.
2 "You shall speak all that I command you, and your brother Aaron shall speak to
Pharaoh that he let the sons of Israel go out of his land.
3 "But I will harden Pharaoh's heart that I may multiply My signs and My wonders in
the land of Egypt.
4 "When Pharaoh does not listen to you, then I will lay My hand on Egypt and bring
out My hosts, My people the sons of Israel, from the land of Egypt by great judgments.
5 "The Egyptians shall know that I am the LORD, when I stretch out My hand on Egypt
and bring out the sons of Israel from their midst."
6 So Moses and Aaron did *it;* as the LORD commanded them, thus they did.
7 Moses was eighty years old and Aaron eighty-three, when they spoke to Pharaoh.

4. Plagues strike Egypt

Aaron's Rod Becomes a Serpent

8 Now the LORD spoke to Moses and Aaron, saying,
9 "When Pharaoh speaks to you, saying, 'Work a miracle,' then you shall say to Aaron,
'Take your staff and throw *it* down before Pharaoh, *that* it may become a serpent.' "
10 So Moses and Aaron came to Pharaoh, and thus they did just as the LORD had commanded; and Aaron threw his staff down before Pharaoh and his servants, and it became a serpent.
11 Then Pharaoh also called for *the* wise men and *the* sorcerers, and they also, the
magicians of Egypt, did the same with their secret arts.
12 For each one threw down his staff and they turned into serpents. But Aaron's staff
swallowed up their staffs.
13 Yet Pharaoh's heart was hardened, and he did not listen to them, as the LORD had
said.

Water Is Turned to Blood

14 Then the LORD said to Moses, "Pharaoh's heart is stubborn; he refuses to let the
people go.
15 "Go to Pharaoh in the morning as he is going out to the water, and station yourself
to meet him on the bank of the Nile; and you shall take in your hand the staff that was
turned into a serpent.
16 "You shall say to him, 'The LORD, the God of the Hebrews, sent me to you, saying,
"Let My people go, that they may serve Me in the wilderness. But behold, you have not
listened until now."

6:26 Ex 3:10; 6:13; Ex 7:4; 12:17, 51
6:27 Ex 5:1
6:29 Ex 6:2, 6, 8; Ex 6:11; 7:2
6:30 Ex 4:10; 6:12; Jer 1:6
7:1 Ex 4:16
7:2 Ex 4:15
7:3 Ex 4:21; Ex 11:9; Acts 7:36
7:4 Ex 3:19, 20; 7:13, 16, 22; 8:15, 19; 9:12; 11:9; Ex 12:51; 13:3, 9; Ex 6:6
7:5 Ex 7:17; 8:19, 22; 10:7; 14:4, 18, 25; Ex 3:20
7:6 Gen 6:22; 7:5; Ex 7:2
7:7 Deut 29:5; 31:2; 34:7; Acts 7:23, 30
7:9 Is 7:11; John 2:18; 6:30; Ex 4:2, 17
7:10 Ex 4:3; 7:9
7:11 Dan 2:2; 4:6; 5:7; Gen 41:8; Ex 7:22; Dan 2:2; 2 Tim 3:8; Ex 7:22; 8:7, 18; 2 Tim 3:9; Rev 13:13, 14
7:13 Ex 4:21; 7:3, 22; 8:15, 19, 32; 9:7, 12, 34, 35; 10:1, 20, 27
7:15 Ex 2:5; 8:20; Ex 4:2, 3; 7:10
7:16 Ex 3:13, 18; 4:22; 5:1; Ex 4:23; 5:1, 3

6:26 To bring the Israelites out of Egypt according to their hosts means that they would be brought out in tribes, clans, or family groups.

7:1 God made Moses "as God to Pharaoh"—in other words, a powerful person who deserved to be listened to. Pharaoh himself was considered a god, so he recognized Moses as one of his peers. His refusal to give in to Moses shows, however, that he did not feel inferior to Moses.

7:11 How were these sorcerers and magicians able to duplicate Moses' miracles? Some of their feats involved trickery or illusion, and some may have used satanic power since worshiping gods of the underworld was part of their religion. Ironically, whenever the sorcerers duplicated one of Moses' plagues, it only made matters worse. If the magicians had been as powerful as God, they would have reversed the plagues, not added to them.

7:12 God performed a miracle by turning Aaron's staff into a serpent, and Pharaoh's magicians did the same through trickery or sorcery. Although miracles can help us believe, it is dangerous to rely on them alone. Satan can imitate some parts of God's work and lead people astray. Pharaoh focused on the miracle rather than the message. We can avoid this error by letting the Word of God be the basis of our faith. No miracle from God would endorse any message that is contrary to the teachings of his Word.

7:17 Ex 5:2; 7:5; 10:2; Ps 9:16; Ezek 25:17; Ex 4:9; 7:20; Rev 11:6; 16:4, 6

17 'Thus says the LORD, "By this you shall know that I am the LORD: behold, I will strike
the water that is in the Nile with the staff that is in my hand, and it will be turned to
blood.

7:18 Ex 7:21; Ex 7:24

18 "The fish that are in the Nile will die, and the Nile will become foul, and the Egyptians will find difficulty in drinking water from the Nile." ' "

7:19 Ex 8:5, 6, 16; 9:22; 10:12, 21; 14:21, 26

19 Then the LORD said to Moses, "Say to Aaron, 'Take your staff and stretch out your
hand over the waters of Egypt, over their rivers, over their streams, and over their pools,
and over all their reservoirs of water, that they may become blood; and there will be blood
throughout all the land of Egypt, both in *vessels of* wood and in *vessels of* stone.' "

7:20 Ex 17:5; Ps 78:44; 105:29

20 So Moses and Aaron did even as the LORD had commanded. And he lifted up the
staff and struck the water that *was* in the Nile, in the sight of Pharaoh and in the sight of
his servants, and all the water that *was* in the Nile was turned to blood.
21 The fish that *were* in the Nile died, and the Nile became foul, so that the Egyptians
could not drink water from the Nile. And the blood was through all the land of Egypt.

7:22 Ex 7:11; 8:7

22 But the magicians of Egypt did the same with their secret arts; and Pharaoh's heart
was hardened, and he did not listen to them, as the LORD had said.
23 Then Pharaoh turned and went into his house with no concern even for this.
24 So all the Egyptians dug around the Nile for water to drink, for they could not drink
of the water of the Nile.
25 Seven days passed after the LORD had struck the Nile.

Frogs over the Land

8:1 Ex 3:18; 4:23; 5:1, 3

8 Then the LORD said to Moses, "Go to Pharaoh and say to him, 'Thus says the LORD,
"Let My people go, that they may serve Me.
2 "But if you refuse to let *them* go, behold, I will smite your whole territory with frogs.

8:3 Ps 105:30

3 "The Nile will swarm with frogs, which will come up and go into your house and into
your bedroom and on your bed, and into the houses of your servants and on your people, and into your ovens and into your kneading bowls.
4 "So the frogs will come up on you and your people and all your servants." ' "

8:5 Ex 7:19

5 Then the LORD said to Moses, "Say to Aaron,
'Stretch out your hand with your staff over the rivers, over the streams and over the pools,
and make frogs come up on the land of Egypt.' "

8:6 Ps 78:45; 105:30

6 So Aaron stretched out his hand over the waters of Egypt, and the frogs came up
and covered the land of Egypt.

8:7 Ex 7:11, 22

7 The magicians did the same with their secret arts, making frogs come up on the land
of Egypt.

8:8 Ex 8:25; 9:27; 10:16; Ex 8:28; 9:28; 10:17; Num 21:7; 1 Kin 13:6; Ex 8:15, 29, 32

8 Then Pharaoh called for Moses and Aaron and said, "Entreat the LORD that He
remove the frogs from me and from my people; and I will let the people go, that they
may sacrifice to the LORD."
9 Moses said to Pharaoh, "The honor is yours to tell me: when shall I entreat for you

8:10 Ex 9:14; Deut 4:35, 39; 33:26; 2 Sam 7:22; 1 Chr 17:20; Ps 86:8; Is 46:9; Jer 10:6, 7

and your servants and your people, that the frogs be destroyed from you and your houses,
that they may be left only in the Nile?"
10 Then he said, "Tomorrow." So he said, "*May it be* according to your word, that you
may know that there is no one like the LORD our God.

8:11 Ex 8:13

11 "The frogs will depart from you and your houses and your servants and your people;
they will be left only in the Nile."

8:12 Ex 8:30; 9:33, 10:18

12 Then Moses and Aaron went out from Pharaoh, and Moses cried to the LORD concerning the frogs which He had inflicted upon Pharaoh.

7:17 God dramatically turned the waters of the Nile into blood to show Pharaoh who he was. Do you sometimes wish for miraculous signs so you can be sure about God? God has given you the miracle of eternal life through your faith in him, something Pharaoh never obtained. This is a quiet miracle and, though less evident right now, just as extraordinary as water turned to blood. The desire for spectacular signs may cause us to ignore the more subtle miracles God is working every day.

7:20 Egypt was a large country, but most of the population lived along the banks of the Nile River. This 3,000-mile waterway was truly a river of life for the Egyptians. It made life possible in a land that was mostly desert by providing water for drinking, farming, bathing, and fishing. Egyptian society was a ribbon of civilization lining the banks of this life source, rarely reaching very far into the surrounding desert. Without the Nile's water, Egypt could not have existed. Imagine Pharaoh's dismay when Moses turned this sacred river to blood!

8:3ff Moses predicted that every house in Egypt would be infested with frogs. The poor of Egypt lived in small, mud-brick houses of one or two rooms with palm-trunk roofs. The homes of the rich, however, were often two or three stories high, surrounded by landscaped gardens and enclosed by a high wall. Servants lived and worked on the first floor while the family occupied the upper floors. Thus if the frogs got into the royal bedrooms, they had infiltrated even the upper floors. No place in Egypt would be safe from them.

13 The LORD did according to the word of Moses, and the frogs died out of the houses,
the courts, and the fields.
14 So they piled them in heaps, and the land became foul.
15 But when Pharaoh saw that there was relief, he hardened his heart and did not listen to them, as the LORD had said.

8:15 Ex 7:4

The Plague of Insects

16 Then the LORD said to Moses, "Say to Aaron, 'Stretch out your staff and strike the
dust of the earth, that it may become [6]gnats through all the land of Egypt.' "
17 They did so; and Aaron stretched out his hand with his staff, and struck the dust of
the earth, and there were gnats on man and beast. All the dust of the earth became gnats
through all the land of Egypt.
18 The magicians tried with their secret arts to bring forth gnats, but they could not; so
there were gnats on man and beast.
19 Then the magicians said to Pharaoh, "This is the finger of God." But Pharaoh's heart
was hardened, and he did not listen to them, as the LORD had said.
20 Now the LORD said to Moses, "Rise early in the morning and present yourself before Pharaoh, as he comes out to the water, and say to him, 'Thus says the LORD, "Let
My people go, that they may serve Me.
21 "For if you do not let My people go, behold, I will send swarms of insects on you and
on your servants and on your people and into your houses; and the houses of the Egyptians will be full of swarms of insects, and also the ground on which they *dwell.*
22 "But on that day I will set apart the land of Goshen, where My people are living, so
that no swarms of insects will be there, in order that you may know that I, the LORD, am
in the midst of the land.
23 "I will [7]put a division between My people and your people. Tomorrow this sign will
occur." ' "

8:17 Ps 105:31
8:18 Ex 7:11, 12; 8:7; 9:11
8:19 Ex 7:5; 10:7; Ps 8:3; Luke 11:20
8:20 Ex 7:15; 9:13; Ex 2:5; 7:15; Ex 3:18; 4:23; 5:1, 3; 8:1
8:22 Ex 9:4, 6, 24; 10:23; 11:7; Ex 9:29; 19:5; 20:11

24 Then the LORD did so. And there came great swarms of insects into the house of
Pharaoh and the houses of his servants and the land was laid waste because of the swarms
of insects in all the land of Egypt.
25 Pharaoh called for Moses and Aaron and said, "Go, sacrifice to your God within
the land."
26 But Moses said, "It is not right to do so, for we will sacrifice to the LORD our God
what is an abomination to the Egyptians. If we sacrifice what is an abomination to the
Egyptians before their eyes, will they not then stone us?
27 "We must go a three days' journey into the wilderness and sacrifice to the LORD our
God as He commands us."
28 Pharaoh said, "I will let you go, that you may sacrifice to the LORD your God in the
wilderness; only you shall not go very far away. Make supplication for me."
29 Then Moses said, "Behold, I am going out from you, and I shall make supplication
to the LORD that the swarms of insects may depart from Pharaoh, from his servants, and
from his people tomorrow; only do not let Pharaoh deal deceitfully again in not letting
the people go to sacrifice to the LORD."
30 So Moses went out from Pharaoh and made supplication to the LORD.
31 The LORD did as Moses asked, and removed the swarms of insects from Pharaoh,
from his servants and from his people; not one remained.
32 But Pharaoh hardened his heart this time also, and he did not let the people go.

8:24 Ps 78:45; 105:31
8:25 Ex 8:8; 9:27; 10:16; Ex 9:28; 10:8, 24; 12:31
8:26 Gen 43:32; 46:34; Deut 7:25f
8:27 Ex 3:18; 5:3
8:28 Ex 8:8, 15, 29, 32; Ex 8:8; 9:28; 1 Kin 13:6
8:29 Ex 8:8, 15
8:30 Ex 8:12
8:32 Ex 4:21; 8:8, 15

6 Or *lice* **7** Lit *set a ransom*

8:15 After repeated warnings, Pharaoh still refused to obey God. He hardened his heart every time there was a break in the plagues. His stubborn disobedience brought suffering upon himself and his entire country. While persistence is good, stubbornness is usually self-centered. Stubbornness toward God is always disobedience. Avoid disobedience because the consequences may spill onto others.

8:19 Some people think, "If only I could see a miracle, I could believe in God." God gave Pharaoh just such an opportunity. When gnats infested Egypt, even the magicians agreed that this was God's work ("the finger of God")—but still Pharaoh refused to believe. He was stubborn, and stubbornness can blind a person to the truth. When you rid yourself of stubbornness, you may be surprised by abundant evidence of God's work in your life.

8:25–29 Pharaoh wanted a compromise. He would allow the Hebrews to sacrifice, but only if they would do it nearby. God's requirement, however, was firm: The Hebrews had to leave Egypt. Sometimes people urge believers to compromise and give only partial obedience to God's commands. But commitment and obedience to God cannot be negotiated. When it comes to obeying God, half measures won't do.

8:26 The Israelites would be sacrificing animals that the Egyptians regarded as sacred, and this would be offensive to them. Moses was concerned about a violent reaction to sacrificing these animals near the Egyptians.

Egyptian Cattle Die

9 Then the LORD said to Moses, "Go to Pharaoh and speak to him, 'Thus says the
LORD, the God of the Hebrews, "Let My people go, that they may serve Me.
2 "For if you refuse to let *them* go and continue to hold them,
3 behold, the hand of the LORD will come *with* a very severe pestilence on your livestock which are in the field, on the horses, on the donkeys, on the camels, on the herds,
and on the flocks.
4 "But the LORD will make a distinction between the livestock of Israel and the livestock of Egypt, so that nothing will die of all that belongs to the sons of Israel." ' "
5 The LORD set a definite time, saying, "Tomorrow the LORD will do this thing in the
land."
6 So the LORD did this thing on the next day, and all the livestock of Egypt died; but
of the livestock of the sons of Israel, not one died.
7 Pharaoh sent, and behold, there was not even one of the livestock of Israel dead.
But the heart of Pharaoh was hardened, and he did not let the people go.

9:1 Ex 4:23; 8:1
9:2 Ex 8:2
9:3 Ex 7:4; 1 Sam 5:6; Ps 39:10; Acts 13:11
9:4 Ex 8:22; Ex 9:6
9:6 Ex 9:19, 20, 25; Ps 78:48; Ex 9:4
9:7 Ex 7:14; 8:32

THE PLAGUES

Reference	*Plague*	*What Happened*	*Result*
7:14–24	Blood	Fish die, the river smells, the people are without water	Pharaoh's magicians duplicate the miracle by "secret arts" and Pharaoh is unmoved
8:1–15	Frogs	Frogs come up from the water and completely cover the land	Again Pharaoh's magicians duplicate the miracle by sorcery and Pharaoh is unmoved
8:16–19	Gnats	All the dust of Egypt becomes a massive swarm of gnats	Magicians are unable to duplicate this; they say it is the "finger of God," but Pharaoh's heart remains hard
8:20–32	Flies	Swarms of flies cover the land	Pharaoh promises to let the Hebrews go, but then hardens his heart and refuses
9:1–7	Livestock	All the Egyptian livestock dies— but none of Israel's is even sick	Pharaoh still refuses to let the people go
9:8–12	Boils	Horrible boils break out on everyone in Egypt	Magicians cannot respond because they are struck down with boils as well—Pharaoh refuses to listen
9:13–35	Hail	Hailstorms kill all the slaves and animals left out or unprotected and strip or destroy almost every plant	Pharaoh admits his sin, but then changes his mind and refuses to let Israel go
10:1–20	Locusts	Locusts cover Egypt and eat everything left after the hail	Everyone advises Pharaoh to let the Hebrews go, but God hardens Pharaoh's heart and he refuses
10:21–29	Darkness	Total darkness covers Egypt for three days so no one can even move—except the Hebrews, who have light as usual	Pharaoh again promises to let Israel go, but again changes his mind
11:1—12:33	Death of Firstborn	The firstborn of all the people and cattle of Egypt die—but Israel is spared	Pharaoh and the Egyptians urge Israel to leave quickly; after they are gone, Pharaoh again changes his mind and chases after them

9:1 This was the fifth time God sent Moses back to Pharaoh with the demand, "Let My people go"! By this time, Moses may have been tired and discouraged, but he continued to obey. Is there a difficult conflict you must face again and again? Don't give up when you know what is right to do. As Moses discovered, persistence is rewarded.

The Plague of Boils

8 Then the LORD said to Moses and Aaron, "Take for yourselves handfuls of soot
from a kiln, and let Moses throw it toward the sky in the sight of Pharaoh.
9 "It will become fine dust over all the land of Egypt, and will become boils breaking
out with sores on man and beast through all the land of Egypt."
10 So they took soot from a kiln, and stood before Pharaoh; and Moses threw it toward the sky, and it became boils breaking out with sores on man and beast.
11 The magicians could not stand before Moses because of the boils, for the boils were
on the magicians as well as on all the Egyptians.
12 And the LORD hardened Pharaoh's heart, and he did not listen to them, just as the
LORD had spoken to Moses.
13 Then the LORD said to Moses, "Rise up early in the morning and stand before Pharaoh and say to him, 'Thus says the LORD, the God of the Hebrews, "Let My people go,
that they may serve Me.
14 "For this time I will send all My plagues on you and your servants and your people,
so that you may know that there is no one like Me in all the earth.
15 "For *if by* now I had put forth My hand and struck you and your people with pestilence, you would then have been cut off from the earth.
16 "But, indeed, for this reason I have allowed you to remain, in order to show you My
power and in order to proclaim My name through all the earth.
17 "Still you exalt yourself against My people by not letting them go.

The Plague of Hail

18 "Behold, about this time tomorrow, I will send a very heavy hail, such as has not been
seen in Egypt from the day it was founded until now.
19 "Now therefore send, bring your livestock and whatever you have in the field to safety. Every man and beast that is found in the field and is not brought home, when the hail
comes down on them, will die."' "
20 The one among the servants of Pharaoh who feared the word of the LORD made his
servants and his livestock flee into the houses;
21 but he who paid no regard to the word of the LORD left his servants and his livestock in the field.
22 Now the LORD said to Moses, "Stretch out your hand toward the sky, that hail may
fall on all the land of Egypt, on man and on beast and on every plant of the field, throughout the land of Egypt."
23 Moses stretched out his staff toward the sky, and the LORD sent thunder and hail,
and fire ran down to the earth. And the LORD rained hail on the land of Egypt.
24 So there was hail, and fire flashing continually in the midst of the hail, very severe,
such as had not been in all the land of Egypt since it became a nation.
25 The hail struck all that was in the field through all the land of Egypt, both man and
beast; the hail also struck every plant of the field and shattered every tree of the field.
26 Only in the land of Goshen, where the sons of Israel *were,* there was no hail.
27 Then Pharaoh sent for Moses and Aaron, and said to them, "I have sinned this time;
the LORD is the righteous one, and I and my people are the wicked ones.
28 "Make supplication to the LORD, for there has been enough of God's thunder and
hail; and I will let you go, and you shall stay no longer."
29 Moses said to him, "As soon as I go out of the city, I will spread out my hands to the
LORD; the thunder will cease and there will be hail no longer, that you may know that
the earth is the LORD'S.
30 "But as for you and your servants, I know that you do not yet fear the LORD God."
31 (Now the flax and the barley were ruined, for the barley was in the ear and the flax
was in bud.

9:9 Deut 28:27; Rev 16:2
9:11 Ex 8:18
9:12 Ex 4:21; 10:1, 20; 14:8; Josh 11:20; John 12:40
9:13 Ex 8:20; Ex 4:23
9:14 Ex 8:10; Deut 3:24; 2 Sam 7:22; 1 Chr 17:20; Ps 86:8; Is 45:5-8; 46:9; Jer 10:6, 7
9:16 Prov 16:4; Rom 9:17
9:18 Ex 9:23, 24
9:19 Ex 9:6; Ex 9:25
9:20 Prov 13:13
9:22 Rev 16:21
9:23 Gen 19:24; Josh 10:11; Ps 18:13; 78:47; 105:32; Is 30:30; Ezek 38:22; Rev 8:7
9:25 Ex 9:19; Ps 78:47, 48; 105:32, 33
9:26 Ex 8:22; 9:4, 6; 11:7
9:27 Ex 8:8; Ex 10:16, 17; 2 Chr 12:6; Ps 129:4; 145:17; Lam 1:18
9:28 Ex 8:8, 28; 10:17; Ex 8:25; 10:8, 24
9:29 1 Kin 8:22, 38; Ps 143:6; Is 1:15; Ex 8:22; 19:5; 20:11; Ps 24:1; 1 Cor 10:26
9:30 Ex 8:29; Is 26:10
9:31 Ruth 1:22; 2:23

9:12 God gave Pharaoh many opportunities to heed Moses' warnings. But finally God seemed to say, "All right, Pharaoh, have it your way," and Pharaoh's heart became permanently hardened. Did God intentionally harden Pharaoh's heart and overrule his free will? No, he simply confirmed that Pharaoh freely chose a life of resisting God. Similarly, after a lifetime of resisting God, you may find it impossible to turn to him. Don't wait until just the *right* time before turning to God. Do it now while you still have the chance. If you continually ignore God's voice, eventually you will be unable to hear it at all.

9:20–21 If all the Egyptian livestock were killed in the earlier plague (9:6), how could the slaves of Pharaoh put their livestock inside? The answer is probably that the earlier plague killed all the animals in the fields (9:3), but not those in the shelters.

9:27–34 After promising to let the Hebrews go, Pharaoh immediately broke his promise and brought even more trouble upon the land. His actions reveal that his repentance was not real. We do damage to ourselves and to others if we pretend to change but don't mean it.

32 But the wheat and the spelt were not ruined, for they *ripen* late.)

33 So Moses went out of the city from Pharaoh, and spread out his hands to the LORD; and the thunder and the hail ceased, and rain no longer poured on the earth.

34 But when Pharaoh saw that the rain and the hail and the thunder had ceased, he sinned again and hardened his heart, he and his servants.

35 Pharaoh's heart was hardened, and he did not let the sons of Israel go, just as the LORD had spoken through Moses.

The Plague of Locusts

10 Then the LORD said to Moses, "Go to Pharaoh, for I have [8]hardened his heart and the heart of his servants, that I may perform these signs of Mine among them,

2 and that you may tell in the hearing of your son, and of your grandson, how I made a mockery of the Egyptians and how I performed My signs among them, that you may know that I am the LORD."

3 Moses and Aaron went to Pharaoh and said to him, "Thus says the LORD, the God of the Hebrews, 'How long will you refuse to humble yourself before Me? Let My people go, that they may serve Me.

4 'For if you refuse to let My people go, behold, tomorrow I will bring locusts into your territory.

5 'They shall cover the surface of the land, so that no one will be able to see the land. They will also eat the rest of what has escaped—what is left to you from the hail—and they will eat every tree which sprouts for you out of the field.

6 'Then your houses shall be filled and the houses of all your servants and the houses of all the Egyptians, *something* which neither your fathers nor your grandfathers have seen, from the day that they came upon the earth until this day.' " And he turned and went out from Pharaoh.

7 Pharaoh's servants said to him, "How long will this man be a snare to us? Let the men go, that they may serve the LORD their God. Do you not realize that Egypt is destroyed?"

8 So Moses and Aaron were brought back to Pharaoh, and he said to them, "Go, serve the LORD your God! Who are the ones that are going?"

9 Moses said, "We shall go with our young and our old; with our sons and our daughters, with our flocks and our herds we shall go, for we must hold a feast to the LORD."

10 Then he said to them, "Thus may the LORD be with you, if ever I let you and your little ones go! Take heed, for evil is in your mind.

11 "Not so! Go now, the men *among you,* and serve the LORD, for that is what you desire." So they were driven out from Pharaoh's presence.

12 Then the LORD said to Moses, "Stretch out your hand over the land of Egypt for the locusts, that they may come up on the land of Egypt and eat every plant of the land, *even* all that the hail has left."

13 So Moses stretched out his staff over the land of Egypt, and the LORD directed an east wind on the land all that day and all that night; and when it was morning, the east wind brought the locusts.

14 The locusts came up over all the land of Egypt and settled in all the territory of Egypt; *they were* very numerous. There had never been so *many* locusts, nor would there be so *many* again.

15 For they covered the surface of the whole land, so that the land was darkened; and they ate every plant of the land and all the fruit of the trees that the hail had left. Thus nothing green was left on tree or plant of the field through all the land of Egypt.

16 Then Pharaoh hurriedly called for Moses and Aaron, and he said, "I have sinned against the LORD your God and against you.

17 "Now therefore, please forgive my sin only this once, and make supplication to the LORD your God, that He would only remove this death from me."

18 He went out from Pharaoh and made supplication to the LORD.

19 So the LORD shifted *the wind* to a very strong west wind which took up the locusts

9:33 Ex 8:12; 9:29
9:35 Ex 4:21
10:1 Ex 4:21; 7:13; Josh 11:20; John 12:40; Rom 9:18
10:2 Ex 12:26, 27; 13:8, 14, 15; Deut 4:9; Ps 44:1; 78:5; Joel 1:3; Ex 7:5, 17
10:3 1 Kin 21:29; 2 Chr 34:27; James 4:10; 1 Pet 5:6; Ex 4:23
10:5 Joel 1:4; 2:25
10:6 Ex 8:3, 21
10:7 Ex 7:5; 8:19; 12:33; Ex 23:33; Josh 23:13; 1 Sam 18:21; Eccl 7:26
10:8 Ex 8:8; Ex 8:25
10:9 Ex 12:37, 38; Ex 10:26
10:11 Ex 10:28
10:12 Ex 7:19; Ex 10:5, 15
10:13 Ps 78:46; 105:34
10:14 Deut 28:38; Ps 78:46; 105:34; Joel 1:4, 7; 2:1-11; Rev 9:3
10:15 Ex 10:5; Ps 105:34f
10:16 Ex 8:8; Ex 9:27
10:17 Ex 8:8, 28; 9:28; 1 Kin 13:6
10:18 Ex 8:30

8 Lit *made heavy*

10:2 God told Moses that his miraculous experiences with Pharaoh should be retold to his descendants. What stories Moses had to tell! Living out one of the greatest dramas in Biblical history, he witnessed events few people would ever see. It is important to tell our children about God's work in our past and to help them see what he is doing right now. What are the turning points in your life where God intervened? What is God doing for you now? Your stories will form the foundations of your children's belief in God.

and drove them into the [9]Red Sea; not one locust was left in all the territory of Egypt.
20 But the LORD hardened Pharaoh's heart, and he did not let the sons of Israel go.

Darkness over the Land

21 Then the LORD said to Moses, "Stretch out your hand toward the sky, that there
may be darkness over the land of Egypt, even a darkness which may be felt."
22 So Moses stretched out his hand toward the sky, and there was thick darkness in all
the land of Egypt for three days.
23 They did not see one another, nor did anyone rise from his place for three days, but
all the sons of Israel had light in their dwellings.
24 Then Pharaoh called to Moses, and said, "Go, serve the LORD; only let your flocks
and your herds be detained. Even your little ones may go with you."
25 But Moses said, "You must also let us have sacrifices and burnt offerings, that we
may sacrifice *them* to the LORD our God.
26 "Therefore, our livestock too shall go with us; not a hoof shall be left behind, for we
shall take some of them to serve the LORD our God. And until we arrive there, we ourselves do not know with what we shall serve the LORD."
27 But the LORD hardened Pharaoh's heart, and he was not willing to let them go.
28 Then Pharaoh said to him, "Get away from me!
Beware, do not see my face again, for in the day you see my face you shall die!"
29 Moses said, "You are right; I shall never see your face again!"

The Last Plague

11 Now the LORD said to Moses, "One more plague I will bring on Pharaoh and on
Egypt; after that he will let you go from here. When he lets you go, he will surely
drive you out from here completely.
2 "Speak now in the hearing of the people that each man ask from his neighbor and
each woman from her neighbor for articles of silver and articles of gold."
3 The LORD gave the people favor in the sight of the Egyptians. Furthermore, the
man Moses *himself* was greatly esteemed in the land of Egypt, *both* in the sight of
Pharaoh's servants and in the sight of the people.
4 Moses said, "Thus says the LORD, 'About midnight I am going out into the midst of
Egypt,
5 and all the firstborn in the land of Egypt shall die, from the firstborn of the Pharaoh
who sits on his throne, even to the firstborn of the slave girl who is behind the millstones;
all the firstborn of the cattle as well.
6 'Moreover, there shall be a great cry in all the land of Egypt, such as there has not
been *before* and such as shall never be again.
7 'But against any of the sons of Israel a dog will not *even* bark, whether against man
or beast, that you may understand how the LORD makes a distinction between Egypt
and Israel.'
8 "All these your servants will come down to me and bow themselves before me, saying, 'Go out, you and all the people who follow you,' and after that I will go out." And he
went out from Pharaoh in hot anger.
9 Then the LORD said to Moses, "Pharaoh will not listen to you, so that My wonders
will be multiplied in the land of Egypt."

10:20 Ex 4:21; 11:10
10:21 Ex 9:22; Deut 28:29
10:22 Ps 105:28; Rev 16:10
10:23 Ex 8:22
10:24 Ex 8:8, 25; Ex 10:10
10:26 Ex 10:9
10:27 Ex 4:21; 10:20; 14:4, 8
10:28 Ex 10:11
10:29 Ex 11:8; Heb 11:27
11:1 Ex 12:31, 33, 39
11:2 Ex 3:22; 12:35, 36
11:3 Ex 3:21; 12:36; Ps 106:46; Deut 34:10-12
11:4 Ex 12:29
11:5 Ex 12:12, 29; Ps 78:51; 105:36; 135:8; 136:10
11:6 Ex 12:30
11:7 Ex 8:22; Josh 10:21
11:8 Ex 12:31-33; Heb 11:27
11:9 Ex 7:4; Ex 7:3

9 Lit *Sea of Reeds*

10:22 As each gloomy plague descended upon the land, the Egyptian people realized how powerless their own gods were to stop it. Hapi, the god of the Nile River, could not prevent the waters from turning to blood (7:20). Hathor, the crafty cow-goddess, was helpless as Egyptian livestock died in droves (9:6). Amon-Re, the sun-god and chief of the Egyptian gods, could not stop an eerie darkness from covering the land for three full days (10:21, 22). The Egyptian gods were (1) nonpersonal, centering around images like the sun or the river; (2) numerous; (3) nonexclusive. By contrast, the God of the Hebrews was (1) a living personal Being, (2) the only true God, and (3) the only God who should be worshiped. God was proving to both the Hebrews and the Egyptians that he alone is the living and all-powerful God.

10:27, 28 Why was Pharaoh so reluctant to let the people go? The Hebrews were Egypt's free labor—the builders of their great cities. As Egypt's leader, Pharaoh would not easily let such a great resource go.

11:7 Moses told Pharaoh that God made a distinction between Egypt and Israel. At this time the distinction was very clear in God's mind: He knew the Hebrews would become his chosen people. The distinction was taking shape in Moses' mind also. But the Hebrews still saw the distinction only in terms of slave and free. Later, when they were in the wilderness, God would teach them the laws, principles, and values that would make them distinct as his people. Remember that God sees us in terms of what we will become and not just what we are right now.

11:9, 10 You may wonder how Pharaoh could be so foolish as to see God's miraculous power and still not listen to Moses. But

11:10
Ex 4:21; Ex 7:3; 9:12; 10:20, 27; Josh 11:20; Is 63:17; John 12:40

10 Moses and Aaron performed all these wonders before Pharaoh; yet the LORD hardened Pharaoh's heart, and he did not let the sons of Israel go out of his land.

5. The Passover

The Passover Lamb

12:2
Ex 13:4; 23:15; 34:18; Deut 16:1

12 Now the LORD said to Moses and Aaron in the land of Egypt,
2 "This month shall be the beginning of months for you; it is to be the first month
of the year to you.
3 "Speak to all the congregation of Israel, saying, 'On the tenth of this month they are
each one to take a lamb for themselves, according to their fathers' households, a lamb
for each household.

THE HEBREW CALENDAR
A Hebrew month began in the middle of a month on our calendar today. Crops are planted in November and December and harvested in March and April.

	Month	*Today's Calendar*	*Bible Reference*	*Israel's Holidays*
1	Nisan (Abib)	March–April	Exodus 13:4; Exodus 23:15; Exodus 34:18; Deuteronomy 16:1	Passover (Leviticus 23:5) Unleavened Bread (Leviticus 23:6) Firstfruits (Leviticus 23:10)
2	Iyyar (Ziv)	April–May	1 Kings 6:1, 37	Second Passover (Numbers 9:10, 11)
3	Sivan	May–June	Esther 8:9	Pentecost (Weeks) (Leviticus 23:16)
4	Tammuz	June–July		
5	Ab	July–Aug.		
6	Elul	Aug.–Sept.	Nehemiah 6:15	
7	Tishri (Ethanim)	Sept.–Oct.	1 Kings 8:2	Trumpets (Numbers 29:1; Leviticus 23:24) Day of Atonement (Leviticus 23:27) Tabernacles (Booths) (Leviticus 23:34)
8	Marcheshvan (Bul)	Oct.–Nov.	1 Kings 6:38	
9	Kislev	Nov.–Dec.	Nehemiah 1:1	Dedication (John 10:22)
10	Tebeth	Dec.–Jan.	Esther 2:16	
11	Shebat	Jan.–Feb.	Zechariah 1:7	
12	Adar	Feb.–March	Esther 3:7	Purim (Esther 9:24–32)

Pharaoh had his mind made up long before the plagues began. He couldn't believe that someone was greater than he. This stubborn unbelief led to a heart so hard that even a major catastrophe couldn't soften him. Finally, it took the greatest of all calamities, the loss of his son, to force him to recognize God's authority. But even then he wanted God to leave, not to rule his country. We must not wait for great calamities to drive us to God, but must open our hearts and minds to his direction now.

11:10 Did God really harden Pharaoh's heart and force him to do wrong? Before the ten plagues began, Moses and Aaron announced what God would do if Pharaoh didn't let the people go. But their message only made Pharaoh stubborn—he was hardening his own heart. In so doing, he defied both God and his messengers. Through the first six plagues, Pharaoh's heart grew even more stubborn. After the sixth plague, God passed judgment. Sooner or later, evil people will be punished for their sins. When it became evident that Pharaoh wouldn't change, God confirmed Pharaoh's prideful decision and set the painful consequences of his actions in motion. God didn't force Pharaoh to reject him; rather, he gave him every opportunity to change his mind. In Ezekiel 33:11, God says, "I take no pleasure in the death of the wicked."

12:1–3 Certain holidays were instituted by God himself. Passover was a holiday designed to celebrate Israel's deliverance from Egypt and to remind the people of what God had done. Holidays can be important today, too, as annual reminders of what God has done for us. Develop traditions in your family to highlight the religious significance of certain holidays. These serve as reminders to the older people and learning experiences for the younger ones.

12:3ff For the Israelites to be spared from the plague of death, an unblemished male lamb had to be killed and its blood placed on the doorposts of each home. What was the significance of the lamb? In killing the lamb, the Israelites shed innocent blood. The lamb was a sacrifice, a substitute for the person who would have died in the plague. From this point on, the Hebrew people would clearly understand that for them to be spared from death, an innocent life had to be sacrificed in their place.

4 'Now if the household is too small for a lamb, then he and his neighbor nearest to his house are to take one according to the number of persons *in them;* according to what each man should eat, you are to divide the lamb.

5 'Your lamb shall be an unblemished male a year old; you may take it from the sheep or from the goats.

6 'You shall keep it until the fourteenth day of the same month, then the whole assembly of the congregation of Israel is to kill it at twilight.

7 'Moreover, they shall take some of the blood and put it on the two doorposts and on the lintel of the houses in which they eat it.

8 'They shall eat the flesh that *same* night, roasted with fire, and they shall eat it with unleavened bread and bitter herbs.

9 'Do not eat any of it raw or boiled at all with water, but rather roasted with fire, *both* its head and its legs along with its entrails.

10 'And you shall not leave any of it over until morning, but whatever is left of it until morning, you shall burn with fire.

11 'Now you shall eat it in this manner: *with* your loins girded, your sandals on your feet, and your staff in your hand; and you shall eat it in haste—it is the LORD'S Passover.

12 'For I will go through the land of Egypt on that night, and will strike down all the firstborn in the land of Egypt, both man and beast; and against all the gods of Egypt I will execute judgments—I am the LORD.

13 'The blood shall be a sign for you on the houses where you live; and when I see the blood I will pass over you, and no plague will befall you to destroy *you* when I strike the land of Egypt.

Feast of Unleavened Bread

14 'Now this day will be a memorial to you, and you shall celebrate it *as* a feast to the LORD; throughout your generations you are to celebrate it *as* a permanent ordinance.

15 'Seven days you shall eat unleavened bread, but on the first day you shall remove leaven from your houses; for whoever eats anything leavened from the first day until the seventh day, that person shall be cut off from Israel.

16 'On the first day you shall have a holy assembly, and *another* holy assembly on the seventh day; no work at all shall be done on them, except what must be eaten by every person, that alone may be prepared by you.

17 'You shall also observe the *Feast of* Unleavened Bread, for on this very day I brought your hosts out of the land of Egypt; therefore you shall observe this day throughout your generations as a permanent ordinance.

18 'In the first *month,* on the fourteenth day of the month at evening, you shall eat unleavened bread, until the twenty-first day of the month at evening.

19 'Seven days there shall be no leaven found in your houses; for whoever eats what is leavened, that person shall be cut off from the congregation of Israel, whether *he is* an alien or a native of the land.

20 'You shall not eat anything leavened; in all your dwellings you shall eat unleavened bread.' "

21 Then Moses called for all the elders of Israel and said to them, "Go and take for yourselves lambs according to your families, and slay the Passover *lamb.*

22 "You shall take a bunch of hyssop and dip it in the blood which is in the basin, and

12:5 Lev 22:18-21; 23:12; Heb 9:14; 1 Pet 1:19

12:6 Ex 12:14, 17; Lev 23:5; Num 9:1-3, 11; 28:16; Ex 16:12; Deut 16:4, 6

12:7 Ex 12:22

12:8 Ex 34:25; Num 9:12; Deut 16:7; Deut 16:3, 4; 1 Cor 5:8; Num 9:11

12:9 Ex 12:8; Ex 29:13, 17, 22

12:10 Ex 16:19; 23:18; 34:25

12:11 Ex 12:13, 21, 27, 43

12:12 Ex 11:4, 5; Num 33:4; Ps 82:1; Ex 6:2

12:13 Heb 11:28

12:14 Ex 12:6; Lev 23:4, 5; 2 Kin 23:21; Ex 13:9; Ex 12:17, 24; 13:10

12:15 Ex 13:6, 7; 23:15; 34:18; Lev 23:6; Num 28:17; Deut 16:3, 8; Gen 17:14; Ex 12:19; Num 9:13

12:16 Lev 23:7, 8; Num 28:18, 25

12:17 Deut 16:3-8; Ex 12:41; Ex 12:14; 13:3, 10

12:18 Ex 12:2; Lev 23:5-8; Num 28:16-25

12:19 Ex 12:15; 23:15; 34:18; Num 9:13

12:21 Num 9:4; Heb 11:28; Ex 12:3; Ex 12:11

12:22 Ex 12:7

12:6–11 The Feast of the Passover was to be an annual holiday in honor of the night when the Lord "passed over" the homes of the Israelites. The Hebrews followed God's instructions by placing the blood of a lamb on the doorposts of their homes. That night the firstborn son of every family who did not have blood on the doorposts was killed. The lamb had to be killed in order to get the blood that would protect them. (This foreshadowed the blood of Christ, the Lamb of God, who gave his blood for the sins of all people.) Inside their homes, the Israelites ate a meal of roast lamb, bitter herbs, and bread made without leaven (yeast). Unleavened bread could be made quickly because the dough did not have to rise. Thus they could leave at any time. Bitter herbs signified the bitterness of slavery.

12:11 Eating the Passover feast while dressed for travel was a sign of the Hebrews' faith. Although they were not yet free, they were to prepare themselves, for God had said he would lead them out of Egypt. Their preparation was an act of faith. Preparing ourselves for the fulfillment of God's promises, however unlikely they may seem, demonstrates our faith.

12:17, 23 Passover became an annual remembrance of how God delivered the Hebrews from Egypt. Each year the people would pause to remember the day when the destroyer (God's angel of death) passed over their homes. They gave thanks to God for saving them from death and bringing them out of a land of slavery and sin. Believers today have experienced a day of deliverance as well—the day we were delivered from spiritual death and slavery to sin. The Lord's Supper is our Passover remembrance of our new life and freedom from sin. The next time struggles and trials come, remember how God has delivered you in the past and focus on his promise of new life with him.

apply some of the blood that is in the basin to the lintel and the two doorposts; and none
of you shall go outside the door of his house until morning.

A Memorial of Redemption

23 "For the LORD will pass through to smite the Egyptians; and when He sees the blood
on the lintel and on the two doorposts, the LORD will pass over the door and will not
allow the destroyer to come in to your houses to smite *you.*
24 "And you shall observe this event as an ordinance for you and your children forever.
25 "When you enter the land which the LORD will give you, as He has promised, you
shall observe this rite.
26 "And when your children say to you, 'What does this rite mean to you?'
27 you shall say, 'It is a Passover sacrifice to the LORD who passed over the houses of
the sons of Israel in Egypt when He smote the Egyptians, but spared our homes.' "
And the people bowed low and worshiped.
28 Then the sons of Israel went and did *so;* just as the LORD had commanded Moses
and Aaron, so they did.
29 Now it came about at midnight that the LORD struck all the firstborn in the land of
Egypt, from the firstborn of Pharaoh who sat on his throne to the firstborn of the captive who was in the dungeon, and all the firstborn of cattle.
30 Pharaoh arose in the night, he and all his servants and all the Egyptians, and there
was a great cry in Egypt, for there was no home where there was not someone dead.

B. ISRAEL IN THE DESERT (12:31—18:27)

As Egypt buried its dead, the Hebrew slaves left the country, a free people at last. Pharaoh made one last attempt to bring them back, but the people escaped when God miraculously parted the waters of the Red Sea. But on the other side, the people soon became dissatisfied and complained bitterly to Moses and Aaron about their trek through the desert. Through these experiences of the Hebrews, we learn that the Christian life is not always trouble-free. We still have struggles and often complain bitterly to God about conditions in our lives.

1. The Exodus

31 Then he called for Moses and Aaron at night and said, "Rise up, get out from among
my people, both you and the sons of Israel; and go, worship the LORD, as you have said.
32 "Take both your flocks and your herds, as you have said, and go, and bless me also."

Exodus of Israel

33 The Egyptians urged the people, to send them out of the land in haste, for they said,
"We will all be dead."
34 So the people took their dough before it was leavened, *with* their kneading bowls
bound up in the clothes on their shoulders.
35 Now the sons of Israel had done according to the word of Moses, for they had requested from the Egyptians articles of silver and articles of gold, and clothing;
36 and the LORD had given the people favor in the sight of the Egyptians, so that they
let them have their request. Thus they plundered the Egyptians.
37 Now the sons of Israel journeyed from Rameses to Succoth, about six hundred thousand men on foot, aside from children.
38 A mixed multitude also went up with them, along with flocks and herds, a very large
number of livestock.

12:23 Ex 11:4; 12:12, 13; Rev 7:3; 9:4 1 Cor 10:10; Heb 11:28

12:24 Ex 12:14, 17; 13:5, 10

12:26 Ex 10:2; 13:8, 14, 15; Deut 32:7; Josh 4:6; Ps 78:6

12:27 Ex 12:11; Ex 4:31

12:29 Ex 11:4, 5; Num 8:17; 33:4; Ps 135:8; 136:10; Ex 4:23; Ps 78:51; 105:36; Ex 9:6

12:30 Ex 11:6

12:31 Ex 8:8; Ex 8:25

12:32 Ex 10:9, 26

12:33 Ex 10:7; 11:1; 12:39; Ps 105:38

12:34 Ex 12:39

12:35 Ex 3:21, 22; 11:2, 3; Ps 105:37

12:36 Ex 3:22

12:37 Num 33:3, 5; Gen 47:11; Ex 38:26; Num 1:46; 2:32; 11:21; 26:51

12:38 Num 11:4; Ex 17:3; Num 20:19; 32:1; Deut 3:19

12:29–30 Every firstborn child of the Egyptians died, but the Israelite children were spared because the blood of a lamb had been placed on their doorposts. So begins the story of redemption, the central theme of the Bible.

Redemption means "to buy back" or "to save from captivity by paying a ransom." One way to buy back a slave was to offer an equivalent or superior slave in exchange. That is the way God chose to buy us back—he offered his Son in exchange for us.

In Old Testament times, God accepted symbolic offerings. Jesus had not yet been sacrificed, so God accepted the life of an animal in place of the life of the sinner. When Jesus came, he substituted his perfect life for our sinful lives, taking the penalty for sin that we deserve. Thus he redeemed us from the power of sin and restored us to God. Jesus' sacrifice made animal sacrifice no longer necessary.

We must recognize that if we want to be freed from the deadly consequences of our sins, a tremendous price must be paid. But we don't have to pay it. Jesus Christ, our substitute, has already redeemed us by his death on the cross. Our part is to trust him and accept his gift of eternal life. Our sins have been paid for, and the way has been cleared for us to begin a relationship with God (Titus 2:14; Hebrews 9:13–15, 23–26).

12:34 A kneading bowl was a large bowl made of wood, bronze, or pottery and used for kneading dough. Bread was made by mixing water and flour in the bowl with a small piece of leavened dough saved from the previous day's batch. Bread was the primary food in the Hebrews' diet, and thus it was vital to bring the kneading bowl along. It could be easily carried on the shoulder.

12:37–38 The total number of people leaving Egypt is estimated to have been about two million. The "mixed multitude" may have been Egyptians and others who were drawn to the Hebrews by God's mighty works and who decided to leave Egypt with them.

39 They baked the dough which they had brought out of Egypt into cakes of unleavened bread. For it had not become leavened, since they were driven out of Egypt and
could not delay, nor had they prepared any provisions for themselves.
40 Now the time that the sons of Israel lived in Egypt was four hundred and thirty years.
41 And at the end of four hundred and thirty years, to the very day, all the hosts of the
LORD went out from the land of Egypt.

Ordinance of the Passover

42 It is a night to be observed for the LORD for having brought them out from the land
of Egypt; this night is for the LORD, to be observed by all the sons of Israel throughout
their generations.
43 The LORD said to Moses and Aaron, "This is the ordinance of the Passover: no [10]for-
eigner is to eat of it;
44 but every man's slave purchased with money, after you have circumcised him, then
he may eat of it.
45 "A sojourner or a hired servant shall not eat of it.
46 "It is to be eaten in a single house; you are not to bring forth any of the flesh outside
of the house, nor are you to break any bone of it.
47 "All the congregation of Israel are to celebrate this.
48 "But if a stranger sojourns with you, and celebrates the Passover to the LORD, let all
his males be circumcised, and then let him come near to celebrate it; and he shall be like
a native of the land. But no uncircumcised person may eat of it.
49 "The same law shall apply to the native as to the stranger who sojourns among you."
50 Then all the sons of Israel did *so;* they did just as the LORD had commanded Moses
and Aaron.
51 And on that same day the LORD brought the sons of Israel out of the land of Egypt
by their hosts.

Consecration of the Firstborn

13 Then the LORD spoke to Moses, saying,
2 "Sanctify to Me every firstborn, the first offspring of every womb among the
sons of Israel, both of man and beast; it belongs to Me."
3 Moses said to the people, "Remember this day in which you went out from Egypt,
from the house of slavery; for by a powerful hand the LORD brought you out from this
place. And nothing leavened shall be eaten.
4 "On this day in the month of Abib, you are about to go forth.
5 "It shall be when the LORD brings you to the land of the Canaanite, the Hittite, the
Amorite, the Hivite and the Jebusite, which He swore to your fathers to give you, a land
flowing with milk and honey, that you shall observe this rite in this month.
6 "For seven days you shall eat unleavened bread, and on the seventh day there shall
be a feast to the LORD.
7 "Unleavened bread shall be eaten throughout the seven days; and nothing leavened
shall be seen among you, nor shall any leaven be seen among you in all your borders.
8 "You shall tell your son on that day, saying, 'It is because of what the LORD did for
me when I came out of Egypt.'
9 "And it shall serve as a sign to you on your hand, and as a reminder on your forehead, that the law of the LORD may be in your mouth; for with a powerful hand the LORD
brought you out of Egypt.
10 "Therefore, you shall keep this ordinance at its appointed time from year to year.
11 "Now when the LORD brings you to the land of the Canaanite, as He swore to you
and to your fathers, and gives it to you,
12 you shall devote to the LORD the first offspring of every womb, and the first offspring of every beast that you own; the males belong to the LORD.

10 Lit *son of a stranger*

12:39 Ex 6:1; 11:1; 12:31-33
12:40 Gen 15:13, 16; Acts 7:6; Gal 3:17
12:41 Ex 12:17; Ex 3:8, 10
12:42 Ex 13:10; 34:18; Deut 16:1
12:43 Ex 12:11; Num 9:14; Ex 12:48
12:44 Gen 17:12, 13; Lev 22:11
12:45 Lev 22:10
12:46 Num 9:12; Ps 34:20; John 19:33, 36
12:47 Ex 12:6; Num 9:13
12:48 Num 9:14
13:2 Ex 13:12, 13, 15; 22:29; Lev 27:26; Num 3:13; 8:16f; 18:15; Deut 15:19; Luke 2:23
13:3 Ex 12:42; Deut 16:3; Ex 3:20; 6:1; Ex 12:19
13:5 Ex 3:8, 17; Josh 24:11; Ex 6:8
13:6 Ex 12:15-20
13:7 Ex 12:19
13:8 Ex 10:2; 12:26f; 13:14; Ps 44:1
13:9 Ex 12:14; 13:16; Num 15:39; Deut 6:8; 11:18; Ex 13:3
13:10 Ex 12:24, 25; 13:5
13:11 Ex 13:5; Gen 15:18; 17:8; 28:15; Ps 105:42-45
13:12 Ex 13:1, 2; 22:29; 34:19; Lev 27:26; Num 18:15; Ezek 44:30; Luke 2:23

13:2 *Sanctify* means to sacrifice or to consider something as belonging to God. This dedication practice described in 13:11–16 was to remind the people of their deliverance through God.

13:4 "In the month of Abib" corresponds to late March and early April on our calendar.

13:6–9 The Feast of Unleavened Bread marked the Hebrews as a unique people—as though they were branded on their hands and foreheads. What do you do that marks you as a follower of God? The way you raise your children, demonstrate love for others, show concern for the poor, and live in devotion to God—these actions will leave visible marks for all to see. While national groups are marked by customs and traditions, Christians are marked by loving one another (John 13:34–35).

13:12–14 What did it mean to "devote to the LORD the first offspring of every womb"? During the night the Israelites escaped

13:13 Ex 34:20; Num 18:15; Num 3:46
13:14 Ex 10:2; 12:26, 27; 13:8; Deut 6:20; Josh 4:6, 21; Ex 13:3, 9
13:15 Ex 12:29
13:16 Ex 13:9; Deut 6:8

13 "But every first offspring of a donkey you shall redeem with a lamb, but if you do not
redeem *it,* then you shall break its neck; and every firstborn of man among your sons you
shall redeem.
14 "And it shall be when your son asks you in time to come, saying, 'What is this?' then
you shall say to him, 'With a powerful hand the LORD brought us out of Egypt, from the
house of slavery.
15 'It came about, when Pharaoh was stubborn about letting us go, that the LORD killed
every firstborn in the land of Egypt, both the firstborn of man and the firstborn of beast.
Therefore, I sacrifice to the LORD the males, the first offspring of every womb, but every
firstborn of my sons I redeem.'
16 "So it shall serve as a sign on your hand and as phylacteries on your forehead, for
with a powerful hand the LORD brought us out of Egypt."

2. Crossing the sea

God Leads the People

13:17 Ex 14:11, 12; Num 14:1-4; Deut 17:16
13:18 Josh 1:14; 4:12, 13
13:19 Gen 50:24, 25; Josh 24:32; Acts 7:15, 16
13:20 Ex 12:37; Num 33:6
13:21 Ex 14:19, 24; 33:9, 10; Num 9:15; 14:14; Deut 1:33; Neh 9:12; Ps 78:14; 99:7; 105:39; Is 4:5; 1 Cor 10:1
13:22 Neh 9:19

17 Now when Pharaoh had let the people go, God did not lead them by the way of the
land of the Philistines, even though it was near; for God said, "The people might change
their minds when they see war, and return to Egypt."
18 Hence God led the people around by the way of the wilderness to the Red Sea; and
the sons of Israel went up in martial array from the land of Egypt.
19 Moses took the bones of Joseph with him, for he had made the sons of Israel solemnly swear, saying, "God will surely take care of you, and you shall carry my bones from
here with you."
20 Then they set out from Succoth and camped in Etham on the edge of the wilderness.
21 The LORD was going before them in a pillar of cloud by day to lead them on the
way, and in a pillar of fire by night to give them light, that they might travel by day and
by night.
22 He did not take away the pillar of cloud by day, nor the pillar of fire by night, from
before the people.

---

from Egypt, God spared the oldest son of every house marked with blood on the doorposts. Because God saved the lives of the firstborn, he had a rightful claim to them. But God commanded the Israelites to buy their sons back from him. This ritual served three main purposes: (1) it was a reminder to the people of how God had spared their sons from death and freed them all from slavery; (2) it showed God's high respect for human life in contrast to the pagan gods who, their worshipers believed, demanded human sacrifice; (3) it looked forward to the day when Jesus Christ would buy us back by paying the price for our sin once and for all.

13:17–18 God doesn't always work in the way that seems best to us. Instead of guiding the Israelites along the direct route from Egypt to the promised land, he took them by a longer route to avoid fighting with the Philistines. If God does not lead you along the shortest path to your goal, don't complain or resist. Follow him willingly and trust him to lead you safely around unseen obstacles. He can see the end of your journey from the beginning, and he knows the safest and best route.

THE EXODUS The Israelites left Succoth and camped first at Etham before going toward Baal-zephon to camp by the sea (14:2). God miraculously brought them across the sea, into the wilderness of Shur (15:22). After stopping at the oasis of Elim, the people moved into the wilderness of Sin (16:1).

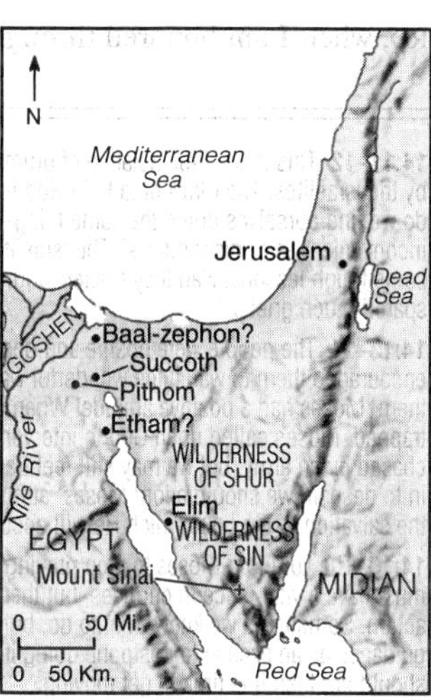

13:17–18 When did the Hebrews leave Egypt? There are two theories. The *early* theory says the exodus occurred around 1446–1445 B.C. The *late* theory suggests the exodus happened between 1300 and 1200 B.C. Those who hold to the earlier date point to 1 Kings 6:1, where the Bible clearly states that Solomon began building the temple 480 years after the Hebrews left Egypt. Since almost all scholars agree that Solomon began building the temple in 966, this puts the exodus in the year 1446. But those who hold to the later date suggest that the 480 years cannot be taken literally. They point to Exodus 1:11, which says that the Hebrews built the store cities of Pithom and Raamses, named after Pharaoh Raamses II, who reigned around 1290 B.C. Regardless of which date is correct, the fact is that God led the Hebrews out of Egypt, just as he had promised. This showed his great power and his great love for his people.

13:21–22 God gave the Hebrews a pillar of cloud and a pillar of fire so they would know day and night that God was with them on their journey to the promised land. What has God given us so that we can have the same assurance? The Bible—something the Israelites did not have. Look to God's Word for reassurance of his presence. As the Hebrews looked to the pillars of cloud and fire, we can look to God's Word day and night to know he is with us, helping us on our journey.

13:21–22 The pillars of fire and cloud were examples of *theophany*—God appearing in a physical form. In this form, God lighted Israel's path, protected them from their enemies, provided reassurance, controlled their movements, and inspired the burning zeal that Israel should have for their God.

Pharaoh in Pursuit

14 Now the LORD spoke to Moses, saying,
2 "Tell the sons of Israel to turn back and camp before Pi-hahiroth, between
Migdol and the sea; you shall camp in front of Baal-zephon, opposite it, by the sea.
3 "For Pharaoh will say of the sons of Israel, 'They are wandering aimlessly in the land;
the wilderness has shut them in.'
4 "Thus I will harden Pharaoh's heart, and he will chase after them; and I will be honored through Pharaoh and all his army, and the Egyptians will know that I am the LORD."
And they did so.
5 When the king of Egypt was told that the people had fled, Pharaoh and his servants
had a change of heart toward the people, and they said, "What is this we have done, that
we have let Israel go from serving us?"
6 So he made his chariot ready and took his people with him;
7 and he took six hundred select chariots, and all the *other* chariots of Egypt with officers over all of them.
8 The LORD hardened the heart of Pharaoh, king of Egypt, and he chased after the
sons of Israel as the sons of Israel were going out boldly.
9 Then the Egyptians chased after them *with* all the horses *and* chariots of Pharaoh,
his horsemen and his army, and they overtook them camping by the sea, beside Pi-hahiroth, in front of Baal-zephon.
10 As Pharaoh drew near, the sons of Israel looked, and behold, the Egyptians were
marching after them, and they became very frightened; so the sons of Israel cried out to
the LORD.
11 Then they said to Moses, "Is it because there were no graves in Egypt that you have
taken us away to die in the wilderness? Why have you dealt with us in this way, bringing
us out of Egypt?
12 "Is this not the word that we spoke to you in Egypt, saying, 'Leave us alone that we
may serve the Egyptians'? For it would have been better for us to serve the Egyptians
than to die in the wilderness."

The Sea Is Divided

13 But Moses said to the people, "Do not fear! Stand by and see the salvation of the
LORD which He will accomplish for you today; for the Egyptians whom you have seen
today, you will never see them again forever.
14 "The LORD will fight for you while you keep silent."
15 Then the LORD said to Moses, "Why are you crying out to Me? Tell the sons of
Israel to go forward.
16 "As for you, lift up your staff and stretch out your hand over the sea and divide it,
and the sons of Israel shall go through the midst of the sea on dry land.
17 "As for Me, behold, I will harden the hearts of the Egyptians so that they will go in
after them; and I will be honored through Pharaoh and all his army, through his chariots
and his horsemen.
18 "Then the Egyptians will know that I am the LORD, when I am honored through
Pharaoh, through his chariots and his horsemen."

14:2 Num 33:7; Jer 44:1
14:4 Ex 4:21; 7:3; 14:17; Ex 14:23; Ex 7:5; 14:25
14:8 Ex 14:4; Num 33:3; Acts 13:17
14:9 Ex 15:9; Josh 24:6; Ex 14:2
14:10 Josh 24:7; Neh 9:9; Ps 34:17; 107:6
14:11 Ex 5:21; 15:24; 16:2; Ps 106:7, 8
14:12 Ex 6:9
14:13 Gen 15:1; 46:3; Ex 20:20; 2 Chr 20:15, 17; Is 41:10, 13, 14; Ex 14:30; 15:2
14:14 Ex 14:25; 15:3; Deut 1:30; 3:22; Josh 23:3; 2 Chr 20:29; Neh 4:20; Is 30:15
14:16 Ex 4:17, 20; 7:19; 14:21, 26; 17:5, 6, 9; Num 20:8, 9, 11; Is 10:26
14:17 Ex 14:4, 8
14:18 Ex 14:25

14:6–9 Six hundred Egyptian war chariots were bearing down on the helpless Israelites, who were trapped between the mountains and the sea. The war chariots each carried two people—one to drive and one to fight. These chariots were made of a wood or leather cab placed over two wheels, and they were pulled by horses. These were the armored tanks of Bible times. But even their power was no match for God, who destroyed both the chariots and their soldiers.

14:10–11 Trapped against the sea, the Israelites faced the Egyptian army sweeping in for the kill. The Israelites thought they were doomed. After watching God's powerful hand deliver them from Egypt, their only response was fear, whining, and despair. Where was their trust in God? Israel had to learn from repeated experience that God was able to provide for them. God has preserved these examples in the Bible so that we can learn to trust him the first time. By focusing on God's faithfulness in the past we can face crises with confidence rather than with fear and complaining.

14:11–12 This is the first instance of grumbling and complaining by the Israelites. Their lack of faith in God is startling. Yet how often do we find ourselves doing the same thing—complaining over inconveniences or discomforts? The Israelites were about to learn some tough lessons. Had they trusted God, they would have been spared much grief.

14:13–14 The people were hostile and despairing, but Moses encouraged them to watch the wonderful way God would rescue them. Moses had a positive attitude! When it looked as if they were trapped, Moses called upon God to intervene. We may not be chased by an army, but we may still feel trapped. Instead of giving in to despair, we should adopt Moses' attitude to "stand by and see the salvation of the LORD which He will accomplish for you today."

14:15 The Lord told Moses to stop praying and get moving! Prayer must have a vital place in our lives, but there is also a place for action. Sometimes we know what to do, but we pray for more guidance as an excuse to postpone doing it. If we know what we should do, then it is time to get moving.

14:19 Ex 13:21, 22

14:21 Ex 7:19; 14:16; Ps 66:6; 106:9; 136:13, 14; Ex 15:8; Josh 3:16; 4:23; Neh 9:11; Ps 74:13; 78:13; 114:3, 5; Is 63:12, 13

19 The angel of God, who had been going before the camp of Israel, moved and went
behind them; and the pillar of cloud moved from before them and stood behind them.
20 So it came between the camp of Egypt and the camp of Israel; and there was the
cloud along with the darkness, yet it gave light at night. Thus the one did not come near
the other all night.
21 Then Moses stretched out his hand over the sea; and the LORD swept the sea *back*
by a strong east wind all night and turned the sea into dry land, so the waters were divided.

MOSES

Some people can't stay out of trouble. When conflict breaks out, they always manage to be nearby. Reaction is their favorite action. This was Moses. He seemed drawn to what needed to be righted. Throughout his life, he was at his finest and his worst responding to the conflicts around him. Even the burning bush experience was an illustration of his character. Having spotted the fire and seen that the bush did not burn, he had to investigate. Whether jumping into a fight to defend a Hebrew slave or trying to referee a struggle between two kinsmen, when Moses saw conflict, he reacted.

Over the years, however, an amazing thing happened to Moses' character. He didn't stop reacting, but rather learned to react correctly. The kaleidoscopic action of each day of leading two million people in the wilderness was more than enough challenge for Moses' reacting ability. Much of the time he served as a buffer between God and the people. At one moment he had to respond to God's anger at the people's stubbornness and forgetfulness. At another moment he had to react to the people's bickering and complaining. At still another moment he had to react to their unjustified attacks on his character.

Leadership often involves reaction. If we want to react with instincts consistent with God's will, we must develop habits of obedience to God. Consistent obedience to God is best developed in times of less stress. Then when stress comes, our natural reaction will be to obey God.

In our age of lowering moral standards, we find it almost impossible to believe that God would punish Moses for the one time he disobeyed outright. What we fail to see, however, is that God did not reject Moses; Moses simply disqualified himself to enter the promised land. Personal greatness does not make a person immune to error or its consequences.

In Moses we see an outstanding personality shaped by God. But we must not misunderstand what God did. He did not change who or what Moses was; he did not give Moses new abilities and strengths. Instead, he took Moses' characteristics and molded them until they were suited to his purposes. Does knowing this make a difference in your understanding of God's purpose in your life? He is trying to take what he created in the first place and use it for its intended purposes. The next time you talk with God, don't ask, "What should I change into?" but "How should I use my own abilities and strengths to do your will?"

Strengths and accomplishments:
- Egyptian education; desert training
- Greatest Jewish leader; set the exodus in motion
- Prophet and lawgiver; recorder of the Ten Commandments
- Author of the Pentateuch

Weaknesses and mistakes:
- Failed to enter the promised land because of disobedience to God
- Did not always recognize and use the talents of others

Lessons from his life:
- God prepares, then uses. His timetable is life-sized
- God does his greatest work through frail people

Vital statistics:
- Where: Egypt, Midian, wilderness of Sinai
- Occupations: Prince, shepherd, leader of the Israelites
- Relatives: Sister: Miriam. Brother: Aaron. Wife: Zipporah. Sons: Gershom and Eliezer

Key verses:
"By faith Moses, when he had grown up, refused to be called the son of Pharaoh's daughter, choosing rather to endure ill-treatment with the people of God than to enjoy the passing pleasures of sin" (Hebrews 11:24–25).

Moses' story is told in the books of Exodus through Deuteronomy. He is also mentioned in Acts 7:20–44; Hebrews 11:23–29.

14:21 There was no apparent way of escape, but the Lord opened up a dry path through the sea. Sometimes we find ourselves caught in a problem and see no way out. Don't panic; God can open up a way.

14:21–22 Some scholars believe the Israelites did not cross the main body of the Red Sea but one of the shallow lakes or marshes north of it that dry up at certain times of the year, or perhaps a smaller branch of the Red Sea where the water would have been shallow enough to wade across. But the Bible clearly states that the Lord "swept the sea back by a strong east wind all night and turned the sea into dry land" (14:21; see also Joshua 3:15–16 and 2 Kings 2:13–14). Also, the water was deep enough to cover the chariots (14:28). The God who created the earth and water performed a mighty miracle at exactly the right time to demonstrate his great power and love for his people.

22 The sons of Israel went through the midst of the sea on the dry land, and the waters
were like a wall to them on their right hand and on their left.
23 Then the Egyptians took up the pursuit, and all Pharaoh's horses, his chariots and
his horsemen went in after them into the midst of the sea.
24 At the morning watch, the LORD looked down on the army of the Egyptians through
the pillar of fire and cloud and brought the army of the Egyptians into confusion.
25 He caused their chariot wheels to swerve, and He made them drive with difficulty;
so the Egyptians said, "Let us flee from Israel, for the LORD is fighting for them against
the Egyptians."
26 Then the LORD said to Moses, "Stretch out your hand over the sea so that the waters may come back over the Egyptians, over their chariots and their horsemen."
27 So Moses stretched out his hand over the sea, and the sea returned to its normal
state at daybreak, while the Egyptians were fleeing right into it; then the LORD overthrew the Egyptians in the midst of the sea.
28 The waters returned and covered the chariots and the horsemen, even Pharaoh's
entire army that had gone into the sea after them; not even one of them remained.
29 But the sons of Israel walked on dry land through the midst of the sea, and the waters
were like a wall to them on their right hand and on their left.
30 Thus the LORD saved Israel that day from the hand of the Egyptians, and Israel saw
the Egyptians dead on the seashore.
31 When Israel saw the great power which the LORD had used against the Egyptians,
the people feared the LORD, and they believed in the LORD and in His servant Moses.

The Song of Moses and Israel

15 Then Moses and the sons of Israel sang this song to the LORD, and said,
"I will sing to the LORD, for He is highly exalted;
The horse and its rider He has hurled into the sea.
2 "The LORD is my strength and song,
And He has become my salvation;
This is my God, and I will praise Him;
My father's God, and I will extol Him.
3 "The LORD is a warrior;
The LORD is His name.
4 "Pharaoh's chariots and his army He has cast into the sea;
And the choicest of his officers are drowned in the [11]Red Sea.
5 "The deeps cover them;
They went down into the depths like a stone.
6 "Your right hand, O LORD, is majestic in power,
Your right hand, O LORD, shatters the enemy.
7 "And in the greatness of Your excellence You overthrow those who rise up against
You;
You send forth Your burning anger, *and* it consumes them as chaff.
8 "At the blast of Your nostrils the waters were piled up,
The flowing waters stood up like a heap;
The deeps were congealed in the heart of the sea.
9 "The enemy said, 'I will pursue, I will overtake, I will divide the spoil;
My desire shall be gratified against them;
I will draw out my sword, my hand will destroy them.'
10 "You blew with Your wind, the sea covered them;

14:22 Ex 15:19; Josh 3:17; 4:22; Neh 9:11; Ps 66:6; 78:13; Heb 11:29
14:24 Ex 13:21
14:25 Ex 14:4, 14, 18
14:26 Ex 14:16
14:27 Josh 4:18; Ex 15:1, 7; Deut 11:4; Ps 78:53; Heb 11:29
14:28 Ps 78:53; 106:11
14:29 Ex 14:22; Ps 66:6
14:30 Ex 14:13; Ps 106:8, 10; Is 63:8, 11; Ps 58:10; 59:10
14:31 Ex 4:31; 19:9; Ps 106:12; John 2:11
15:1 Ps 106:12; Rev 15:3
15:2 Ps 18:1, 2; Is 12:2; Hab 3:18f; Ps 48:14; Ex 3:6, 15, 16; 2 Sam 22:47; Ps 99:5
15:3 Ex 14:14; Rev 19:11; Ex 3:15; 6:2, 3, 7, 8; Ps 24:8; 83:18
15:4 Ex 14:6, 7, 17, 28
15:5 Ex 15:10; Neh 9:11
15:6 Ex 3:20; 6:1; Ps 118:15, 16
15:7 Ex 14:27; Ps 78:49, 50; Deut 4:24; Is 5:24; Heb 12:29
15:8 Ex 14:22, 29; Job 4:9; Ps 78:13
15:9 Ex 14:5, 8, 9; Judg 5:30; Is 53:12; Luke 11:22
15:10 Ex 14:27, 28; Ex 15:5

11 Lit *Sea of Reeds*

14:27–28 No evidence of this great exodus has been discovered in Egyptian historical records. This was because it was a common practice for Egyptian pharaohs not to record their defeats. They even went so far as to take existing records and delete the names of traitors and political adversaries. Pharaoh would have been especially anxious not to record that his great army was destroyed chasing a band of runaway slaves. Since either the Egyptians failed to record the exodus or the record has not yet been found, it is impossible to place a precise date on the event.

15:1ff Music played an important part in Israel's worship and celebration. Singing was an expression of love and thanks, and it was a creative way to pass down oral traditions. Some say this song of Moses is the oldest recorded song in the world. It was a festive epic poem celebrating God's victory, lifting the hearts and voices of the people outward and upward. After having been delivered from great danger, they sang with joy! Psalms and hymns can be great ways to express relief, praise, and thanks when you have been through trouble.

15:8 The phrase, "the deeps were congealed in the heart of the sea" means that the waters became like hard walls for them to walk between.

They sank like lead in the mighty waters.
11 "Who is like You among the gods, O LORD?
Who is like You, majestic in holiness,
Awesome in praises, working wonders?
12 "You stretched out Your right hand,
The earth swallowed them.
13 "In Your lovingkindness You have led the people whom You have redeemed;
In Your strength You have guided *them* to Your holy habitation.
14 "The peoples have heard, they tremble;
Anguish has gripped the inhabitants of Philistia.
15 "Then the chiefs of Edom were dismayed;
The leaders of Moab, trembling grips them;
All the inhabitants of Canaan have melted away.
16 "Terror and dread fall upon them;
By the greatness of Your arm they are motionless as stone;
Until Your people pass over, O LORD,
Until the people pass over whom You have purchased.
17 "You will bring them and plant them in the mountain of Your inheritance,
The place, O LORD, which You have made for Your dwelling,
The sanctuary, O Lord, which Your hands have established.
18 "The LORD shall reign forever and ever."
19 For the horses of Pharaoh with his chariots and his horsemen went into the sea, and
the LORD brought back the waters of the sea on them, but the sons of Israel walked on
dry land through the midst of the sea.
20 Miriam the prophetess, Aaron's sister, took the timbrel in her hand, and all the
women went out after her with timbrels and with dancing.
21 Miriam answered them,
"Sing to the LORD, for He is highly exalted;
The horse and his rider He has hurled into the sea."

15:11 Ex 8:10; 9:14; Deut 3:24; 2 Sam 7:22; 1 Kin 8:23; Ps 71:19; 86:8; Mic 7:18; Is 6:3; Rev 4:8; Ps 22:23; Ps 72:18; 136:4

15:13 Neh 9:12; Ps 77:20; Ex 15:16; Ps 77:15

15:15 Gen 36:15, 40; Num 22:3, 4; Josh 2:9

15:16 Ex 23:27; Deut 2:25; Josh 2:9; Ex 15:5, 6; Ex 15:13; Ps 74:2; Is 43:1; Jer 31:11; Titus 2:14; 2 Pet 2:1

15:17 Ex 23:20; 32:34; Ps 44:2; 80:8, 15; Ps 2:6; 78:54, 68; Ps 68:16; 76:2

15:18 Ps 10:16; 29:10; Is 57:15

15:20 Ex 2:4; Num 26:59; 1 Chr 6:3; Mic 6:4; Judg 11:34; 1 Sam 18:6; 1 Chr 15:16; Ps 68:25; 81:2; 149:3; Jer 31:4; Judg 11:34; 21:21; 1 Sam 18:6; Ps 30:11; 150:4

FAMOUS SONGS IN THE BIBLE

Where	*Purpose of Song*
Exodus 15:1–21	Moses' song of victory and praise after God led Israel out of Egypt and saved them by parting the Red Sea; Miriam joined in the singing too
Numbers 21:17	Israel's song of praise to God for giving them water in the wilderness
Deuteronomy 32:1–43	Moses' song of Israel's history with thanksgiving and praise as the Hebrews were about to enter the promised land
Judges 5:2–31	Deborah and Barak's song of praise thanking God for Israel's victory over King Jabin's army at Mount Tabor
2 Samuel 22:2–51	David's song of thanks and praise to God for rescuing him from Saul and his other enemies
Song of Solomon 1–8	Solomon's song of love celebrating the union of husband and wife
Isaiah 26:1	Isaiah's prophetic song about how the redeemed will sing in the new Jerusalem
Ezra 3:11	Israel's song of praise at the completion of the temple's foundation
Luke 1:46–55	Mary's song of praise to God for the conception of Jesus
Luke 1:68–79	Zacharias's song of praise for the promise of a son
Acts 16:25	Paul and Silas sang hymns in prison
Revelation 5:9–10	The "new song" of the 24 elders acclaiming Christ as worthy to break the seven seals of God's scroll
Revelation 14:3	The song of the 144,000 redeemed from the earth
Revelation 15:3–4	The song of all the redeemed in praise of the Lamb who redeemed them

15:20 Miriam was called a prophetess not only because she received revelations from God (Numbers 12:1–2; Micah 6:4) but also for her musical skill. Prophecy and music were often closely related in the Bible (1 Samuel 10:5; 1 Chronicles 25:1).

3. Complaining in the desert

The LORD Provides Water

22 Then Moses led Israel from the Red Sea, and they went out into the wilderness of
Shur; and they went three days in the wilderness and found no water.
23 When they came to Marah, they could not drink the waters of Marah, for they were
bitter; therefore it was named [12]Marah.
24 So the people grumbled at Moses, saying, "What shall we drink?"
25 Then he cried out to the LORD, and the LORD showed him a tree; and he threw *it*
into the waters, and the waters became sweet.
There He made for them a statute and regulation, and there He tested them.
26 And He said, "If you will give earnest heed to the voice of the LORD your God, and
do what is right in His sight, and give ear to His commandments, and keep all His statutes, I will put none of the diseases on you which I have put on the Egyptians; for I, the
LORD, am your healer."
27 Then they came to Elim where there *were* twelve springs of water and seventy date
palms, and they camped there beside the waters.

The LORD Provides Manna

16 Then they set out from Elim, and all the congregation of the sons of Israel came
to the wilderness of Sin, which is between Elim and Sinai, on the fifteenth day of
the second month after their departure from the land of Egypt.
2 The whole congregation of the sons of Israel grumbled against Moses and Aaron in
the wilderness.
3 The sons of Israel said to them, "Would that we had died by the LORD'S hand in the
land of Egypt, when we sat by the pots of meat, when we ate bread to the full; for you
have brought us out into this wilderness to kill this whole assembly with hunger."
4 Then the LORD said to Moses, "Behold, I will rain bread from heaven for you; and
the people shall go out and gather a day's portion every day, that I may test them, whether
or not they will walk in My [13]instruction.
5 "On the sixth day, when they prepare what they bring in, it will be twice as much as
they gather daily."
6 So Moses and Aaron said to all the sons of Israel, "At evening you will know that
the LORD has brought you out of the land of Egypt;
7 and in the morning you will see the glory of the LORD, for He hears your grumblings
against the LORD; and what are we, that you grumble against us?"

The LORD Provides Meat

8 Moses said, "*This will happen* when the LORD gives you meat to eat in the evening,
and bread to the full in the morning; for the LORD hears your grumblings which you
grumble against Him. And what are we? Your grumblings are not against us but against
the LORD."

12 I.e. bitterness 13 Or *law*

15:22 Ps 77:20; 78:52, 53; Num 33:8; Gen 16:7; 20:1; 25:18
15:23 Num 33:8; Ruth 1:20
15:24 Ex 14:11; 16:2; Ps 106:13
15:25 Ex 14:10; Ezek 47:7, 8; Josh 24:25; Ex 16:4; Deut 8:2, 16; Judg 2:22; 3:1, 4; Ps 66:10
15:26 Ex 19:5, 6; Deut 7:12; Ex 20:2-17; Deut 7:15; 28:58, 60; Ex 23:25; Deut 32:39; Ps 41:3, 4; 103:3; 147:3
15:27 Num 33:9
16:1 Num 33:10, 11; Ezek 30:15; Ex 12:6, 51; 19:1
16:2 Ex 14:11; 15:24; Ps 106:25; 1 Cor 10:10
16:3 Ex 17:3; Num 14:2, 3; 20:3; Lam 4:9; Num 11:4, 5
16:4 Neh 9:15; Ps 78:23-25; 105:40; John 6:31; 1 Cor 10:3; Ex 15:25; Deut 8:2, 16
16:5 Ex 16:22
16:6 Ex 6:7
16:7 Ex 16:10, 12; Is 35:2; 40:5; John 11:4, 40; Num 14:27; 17:5; Num 16:11
16:8 1 Sam 8:7; Luke 10:16; Rom 13:2; 1 Thess 4:8

15:23, 27 The waters of Marah are contrasted with the springs of Elim. Marah stood for the unbelieving, grumbling attitude of the people who would not trust God. Elim stands for God's bountiful provision. How easy it is to grumble and complain too quickly, only to be embarrassed by God's help!

15:26 God promised that if the people obeyed him they would be free from the diseases that plagued the Egyptians. Little did they know that many of the moral laws he later gave them were designed to keep them free from sickness. For example, following God's law against prostitution would keep them free of venereal disease. God's laws for us are often designed to keep us from harm. Men and women are complex beings. Our physical, emotional, and spiritual lives are intertwined. Modern medicine is now acknowledging what these laws assumed. If we want God to care for us, we need to submit to his directions for living.

16:1 The wilderness of Sin was a vast and hostile environment of sand and stone. Its barren surroundings provided the perfect place for God to test and shape the character of his people.

16:2 It happened again. As the Israelites encountered danger, shortages, and inconvenience, they complained bitterly and longed to be back in Egypt. But as always, God provided for their needs. Difficult circumstances often lead to stress, and complaining is a natural response. The Israelites didn't really want to be back in Egypt; they just wanted life to get a little easier. In the pressure of the moment, they could not focus on the cause of their stress (in this case, lack of trust in God); they could only think about the quickest way of escape. When pressure comes your way, resist the temptation to make a quick escape. Instead, focus on God's power and wisdom to help you deal with the cause of your stress.

16:4–5 God promised to meet the Hebrews' need for food in the wilderness, but he decided to test their obedience. God wanted to see if they would obey his detailed instructions. We can learn to trust him as our Lord only by following. We can learn to obey by taking small steps of obedience.

9 Then Moses said to Aaron, "Say to all the congregation of the sons of Israel, 'Come
near before the LORD, for He has heard your grumblings.' "
10 It came about as Aaron spoke to the whole congregation of the sons of Israel, that
they looked toward the wilderness, and behold, the glory of the LORD appeared in the
cloud.
11 And the LORD spoke to Moses, saying,
12 "I have heard the grumblings of the sons of Israel; speak to them, saying, 'At twilight
you shall eat meat, and in the morning you shall be filled with bread; and you shall know
that I am the LORD your God.' "
13 So it came about at evening that the quails came up and covered the camp, and in
the morning there was a layer of dew around the camp.
14 When the layer of dew evaporated, behold, on the surface of the wilderness there
was a fine flake-like thing, fine as the frost on the ground.
15 When the sons of Israel saw *it,* they said to one another, "What is it?" For they did
not know what it was. And Moses said to them, "It is the bread which the LORD has given
you to eat.
16 "This is what the LORD has commanded, 'Gather of it every man as much as he should
eat; you shall take an omer apiece according to the number of persons each of you has in
his tent.' "
17 The sons of Israel did so, and *some* gathered much and *some* little.
18 When they measured it with an omer, he who had gathered much had no excess,
and he who had gathered little had no lack; every man gathered as much as he should
eat.
19 Moses said to them, "Let no man leave any of it until morning."
20 But they did not listen to Moses, and some left part of it until morning, and it bred
worms and became foul; and Moses was angry with them.
21 They gathered it morning by morning, every man as much as he should eat; but when
the sun grew hot, it would melt.

The Sabbath Observed

22 Now on the sixth day they gathered twice as much bread, two omers for each one.
When all the leaders of the congregation came and told Moses,
23 then he said to them, "This is what the LORD meant: Tomorrow is a sabbath observance, a holy sabbath to the LORD. Bake what you will bake and boil what you will boil,
and all that is left over put aside to be kept until morning."
24 So they put it aside until morning, as Moses had ordered, and it did not become
foul nor was there any worm in it.
25 Moses said, "Eat it today, for today is a sabbath to the LORD; today you will not
find it in the field.
26 "Six days you shall gather it, but on the seventh day, *the* sabbath, there will be none."
27 It came about on the seventh day that some of the people went out to gather, but
they found none.
28 Then the LORD said to Moses, "How long do you refuse to keep My commandments
and My [14]instructions?
29 "See, the LORD has given you the sabbath; therefore He gives you bread for two days
on the sixth day. Remain every man in his place; let no man go out of his place on the
seventh day."
30 So the people rested on the seventh day.
31 The house of Israel named it manna, and it was like coriander seed, white, and its
taste was like wafers with honey.

16:9 Num 16:16
16:10 Ex 13:21; 16:7; Num 16:19; 1 Kin 8:10f
16:12 Ex 16:8; Num 14:27; Ex 6:7; 16:7; 1 Kin 20:28; Joel 3:17
16:13 Num 11:31; Ps 78:27-29; 105:40; Num 11:9
16:14 Num 11:7-9; Ex 16:31; Neh 9:15; Ps 78:24; 105:40
16:15 Ex 16:4; Neh 9:15; Ps 78:24; John 6:31; 1 Cor 10:3
16:16 Ex 16:32, 36
16:18 2 Cor 8:15
16:19 Ex 12:10; 16:23; 23:18
16:22 Ex 16:5; Ex 34:31
16:23 Gen 2:3; Ex 20:8-11; 23:12; 31:15; 35:2; Lev 23:3; Neh 9:13, 14; Ex 16:19
16:24 Ex 16:20
16:26 Ex 20:9, 10
16:28 2 Kin 17:14; Ps 78:10; 106:13
16:31 Num 11:7-9; Deut 8:3, 16; Ex 16:14

14 Or *laws*

16:14–16 Manna (16:31) appeared on the ground each day as thin flakes like frost. The people gathered it, ground it like grain, and made it into honey-tasting pancakes. For the Israelites the manna was a gift—it came every day and was just what they needed. It satisfied their temporary physical need. In John 6:48–51 Jesus compares himself to manna. Christ is our daily bread who satisfies our eternal, spiritual need.

16:23 The Israelites were not to work on the Sabbath—not even to cook food. Why? God knew that the busy routine of daily living could distract people from worshiping him. It is so easy to let work, family responsibilities, and recreation crowd our schedules so tightly that we don't take time to worship. Carefully guard your time with God.

32 Then Moses said, "This is what the LORD has commanded, 'Let an omerful of it be
kept throughout your generations, that they may see the bread that I fed you in the wilderness, when I brought you out of the land of Egypt.' "
33 Moses said to Aaron, "Take a jar and put an omerful of manna in it, and place it
before the LORD to be kept throughout your generations."
34 As the LORD commanded Moses, so Aaron placed it before the Testimony, to be
kept.
35 The sons of Israel ate the manna forty years, until they came to an inhabited land;
they ate the manna until they came to the border of the land of Canaan.
36 (Now an omer is a tenth of an ephah.)

Water in the Rock

17 Then all the congregation of the sons of Israel journeyed by stages from the wilderness of Sin, according to the command of the LORD, and camped at Rephidim,
and there was no water for the people to drink.
2 Therefore the people quarreled with Moses and said, "Give us water that we may
drink." And Moses said to them, "Why do you quarrel with me? Why do you test the
LORD?"
3 But the people thirsted there for water; and they grumbled against Moses and said,
"Why, now, have you brought us up from Egypt, to kill us and our children and our livestock with thirst?"
4 So Moses cried out to the LORD, saying, "What shall I do to this people? A little
more and they will stone me."
5 Then the LORD said to Moses, "Pass before the people and take with you some
of the elders of Israel; and take in your hand your staff with which you struck the Nile,
and go.
6 "Behold, I will stand before you there on the rock at Horeb; and you shall strike the
rock, and water will come out of it, that the people may drink." And Moses did so in the
sight of the elders of Israel.
7 He named the place [15]Massah and [16]Meribah because of the quarrel of the sons of
Israel, and because they tested the LORD, saying, "Is the LORD among us, or not?"

Amalek Fought

8 Then Amalek came and fought against Israel at Rephidim.
9 So Moses said to Joshua, "Choose men for us and go out, fight against Amalek.
Tomorrow I will station myself on the top of the hill with the staff of God in my hand."
10 Joshua did as Moses told him, and fought against Amalek; and Moses, Aaron, and
Hur went up to the top of the hill.
11 So it came about when Moses held his hand up, that Israel prevailed, and when he
let his hand down, Amalek prevailed.
12 But Moses' hands were heavy. Then they took a stone and put it under him, and he

15 I.e. test **16** I.e. quarrel

16:33 Heb 9:4; Rev 2:17
16:34 Ex 25:16, 21; 27:21; 40:20; Num 17:10
16:35 Deut 8:2f; Josh 5:12; Neh 9:20, 21
16:36 Ex 16:16
17:1 Ex 16:1; Num 33:12; Ex 19:2; Num 33:14
17:2 Ex 14:11; Num 20:2, 3, 13; Ex 16:8; Deut 6:16; Ps 78:18, 41; Matt 4:7; 1 Cor 10:9
17:3 Ex 16:2, 3; Ex 12:38
17:4 Num 14:10; 1 Sam 30:6
17:5 Ex 3:16, 18; Ex 7:20
17:6 Ex 3:1; Num 20:10, 11; Deut 8:15; Neh 9:15; Ps 78:15; 105:41; 114:8; 1 Cor 10:4
17:7 Deut 6:16; 9:22; Ps 95:8; Num 20:13, 24; 27:14; Ps 81:7; Num 14:22; Deut 33:8
17:8 Gen 36:12; Num 24:20; Deut 25:17-19; 1 Sam 15:2; Ex 17:1
17:9 Ex 24:13; Ex 4:20
17:10 Ex 24:14; 31:2
17:12 Is 35:3

16:32–33 The Hebrews put some manna in a special jar as a reminder of the way God provided for them in the wilderness. Symbols have always been an important part of Christian worship also. We use special objects as symbols to remind us of God's work. Such symbols can be valuable aids to our worship as long as we are careful to keep them from becoming objects of worship.

16:36 "An omer is a tenth of an ephah"—this is about two quarts or one tenth of a bushel.

17:2 Again the people complained about their problem instead of praying. Some problems can be solved by careful thought or by rearranging our priorities. Some can be solved by discussion and good counsel. But some problems can be solved only by prayer. We should make a determined effort to pray when we feel like complaining, because complaining only raises our level of stress. Prayer quiets our thoughts and emotions and prepares us to listen.

17:8 The Amalekites were descendants of Amalek, a grandson of Esau. They were a fierce nomadic tribe that lived in the desert region of the Dead Sea. They made part of their livelihood by conducting frequent raids on other settlements and carrying off booty. They killed for pleasure. One of the greatest insults in Israelite culture was to call someone "a friend of Amalek." When the Israelites entered the region, the Amalekites saw this as a perfect opportunity for both pleasure and profit. But this hostile tribe was moving in on the wrong group—a people led by God. For the Israelite slaves to defeat such a warlike nation was more than enough proof that God was with them as he had promised to be.

17:9 Here we meet Joshua for the first time. Later he would become the great leader who brought God's people into the promised land. As a general of the Israelite army, he was gaining valuable experience for the greater battles to come.

sat on it; and Aaron and Hur supported his hands, one on one side and one on the other.
Thus his hands were steady until the sun set.
13 So Joshua overwhelmed Amalek and his people with the edge of the sword.
14 Then the LORD said to Moses, "Write this in a book as a memorial and recite it to
Joshua, that I will utterly blot out the memory of Amalek from under heaven."
15 Moses built an altar and named it The LORD is My Banner;
16 and he said, "The LORD has sworn; the LORD will have war against Amalek from
generation to generation."

Jethro, Moses' Father-in-law

18 Now Jethro, the priest of Midian, Moses' father-in-law, heard of all that God had
done for Moses and for Israel His people, how the LORD had brought Israel out
of Egypt.
2 Jethro, Moses' father-in-law, took Moses' wife Zipporah, after he had sent her away,
3 and her two sons, of whom one was named Gershom, for Moses said, "I have been
a sojourner in a foreign land."
4 The other was named Eliezer, for *he said,* "The God of my father was my help, and
delivered me from the sword of Pharaoh."
5 Then Jethro, Moses' father-in-law, came with his sons and his wife to Moses in the
wilderness where he was camped, at the mount of God.
6 He sent word to Moses, "I, your father-in-law Jethro, am coming to you with your
wife and her two sons with her."
7 Then Moses went out to meet his father-in-law, and he bowed down and kissed him;
and they asked each other of their welfare and went into the tent.
8 Moses told his father-in-law all that the LORD had done to Pharaoh and to the
Egyptians for Israel's sake, all the hardship that had befallen them on the journey, and
how the LORD had delivered them.
9 Jethro rejoiced over all the goodness which the LORD had done to Israel, in delivering them from the hand of the Egyptians.
10 So Jethro said, "Blessed be the LORD who delivered you from the hand of the Egyptians and from the hand of Pharaoh, *and* who delivered the people from under the hand
of the Egyptians.
11 "Now I know that the LORD is greater than all the gods; indeed, it was proven when
they dealt proudly against the people."
12 Then Jethro, Moses' father-in-law, took a burnt offering and sacrifices for God,
and Aaron came with all the elders of Israel to eat a meal with Moses' father-in-law
before God.

17:14 Ex 24:4; 34:27; Num 33:2; Deut 25:19; 1 Sam 15:3
17:15 Ex 24:4; Gen 22:14; Judg 6:24
17:16 Gen 22:16
18:1 Ex 2:16, 18; 3:1
18:2 Ex 2:21; 4:25
18:3 Ex 2:22; 4:20; Acts 7:29; Ex 2:22
18:4 1 Chr 23:15, 17; Gen 49:25
18:5 Ex 3:1, 12; 4:27; 24:13
18:7 Gen 43:26, 28; Gen 29:13; Ex 4:27; Gen 43:27; 2 Sam 11:7
18:8 Ex 4:23; 7:4, 5; Num 20:14; Neh 9:32; Ex 15:6, 16
18:9 Is 63:7-14
18:10 Gen 14:20; 2 Sam 18:28; 1 Kin 8:56; Ps 68:19, 20
18:11 Ex 12:12; 15:11; 2 Chr 2:5; Ps 95:3; 97:9; 135:5; Luke 1:51
18:12 Gen 31:54; Ex 24:5

17:10–13 Aaron and Hur stood by Moses' side and held up his arms to ensure victory against Amalek. We need to "lift up the hands" of our spiritual leaders as well. Shouldering some responsibility, lending a word of encouragement, or offering a prayer are ways of refreshing spiritual leaders in their work.

18:7 Jethro entered Moses' tent where the two talked. Tents were the homes of shepherds. In shape and design, they resembled the tents of today, but they were very large and made of a thick cloth woven from goat or camel hair. This fabric breathed in warm weather and contracted in stormy weather to offer protection from the winter winds and rains. The floor was often covered with animal-skin rugs, while curtains divided the inside space into rooms.

18:8–11 Moses told his father-in-law all that God had done, convincing him that the Lord was greater than any other god. Our relatives are often the hardest people to tell about God. Yet we should look for opportunities to tell them what God is doing in our lives because we can have an important influence on them.

18:12 This reunion turned into a large celebration. The Israelites frequently shared a sacrificial meal among themselves. A burnt offering was sacrificed to God, and then the meal taken from the sacrifice was dedicated to God and eaten ceremonially as a fellowship dinner.

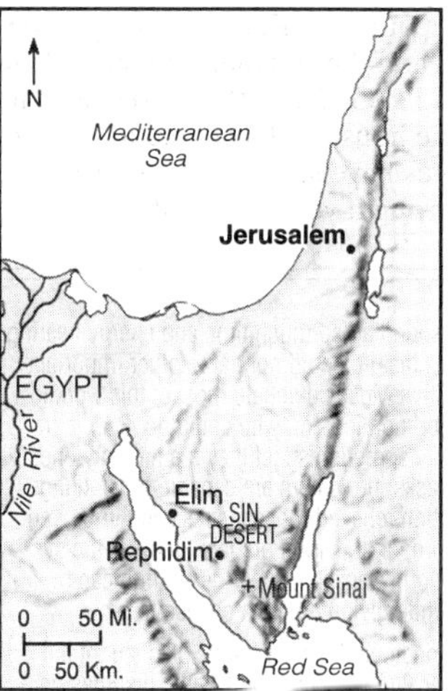

JOURNEY TO MOUNT SINAI
God miraculously supplied food and water in the wilderness for the Israelites. In the wildnerness of Sin, he provided manna (16). At Rephidim, he provided water from a rock (17:1–7). Finally God brought them to the foot of Mount Sinai, where he gave them his holy laws.

13 It came about the next day that Moses sat to judge the people, and the people stood
about Moses from the morning until the evening.
14 Now when Moses' father-in-law saw all that he was doing for the people, he said,
"What is this thing that you are doing for the people? Why do you alone sit *as judge* and
all the people stand about you from morning until evening?"
15 Moses said to his father-in-law, "Because the people come to me to inquire of God.
16 "When they have a dispute, it comes to me, and I judge between a man and his neighbor and make known the statutes of God and His laws."

Jethro Counsels Moses

17 Moses' father-in-law said to him, "The thing that you are doing is not good.
18 "You will surely wear out, both yourself and these people who are with you, for the
task is too heavy for you; you cannot do it alone.
19 "Now listen to me: I will give you counsel, and God be with you. You be the people's
representative before God, and you bring the disputes to God,
20 then teach them the statutes and the laws, and make known to them the way in which
they are to walk and the work they are to do.
21 "Furthermore, you shall select out of all the people able men who fear God, men of
truth, those who hate dishonest gain; and you shall place *these* over them *as* leaders of
thousands, of hundreds, of fifties and of tens.
22 "Let them judge the people at all times; and let it be that every major dispute they
will bring to you, but every minor dispute they themselves will judge. So it will be easier
for you, and they will bear *the burden* with you.
23 "If you do this thing and God *so* commands you, then you will be able to endure, and
all these people also will go to their place in peace."
24 So Moses listened to his father-in-law and did all that he had said.
25 Moses chose able men out of all Israel and made them heads over the people, leaders of thousands, of hundreds, of fifties and of tens.
26 They judged the people at all times; the difficult dispute they would bring to Moses,
but every minor dispute they themselves would judge.
27 Then Moses bade his father-in-law farewell, and he went his way into his own land.

18:15 Num 9:6, 8; 27:5; Deut 17:8-13
18:16 Ex 24:14
18:18 Num 11:14, 17; Deut 1:12; Deut 1:9
18:19 Num 27:5
18:20 Deut 1:18; 4:1, 5; 5:1; Ps 143:8
18:21 Ex 18:25; Deut 1:13, 15; 2 Chr 19:5-10; Ps 15:1-5; Acts 6:3; Gen 42:18; 2 Sam 23:3; Deut 16:19
18:22 Deut 1:17, 18; Num 11:17
18:25 Ex 18:21; Deut 1:15
18:26 Ex 18:22
18:27 Num 10:29, 30

C. ISRAEL AT SINAI (19:1—40:38)

After escaping through the Red Sea, the Hebrews traveled through the desert and arrived at Sinai, God's holy mountain. There they received the Ten Commandments, as well as instructions for building a tabernacle as a center of worship. Through Israel's experiences at Mount Sinai, we learn about the importance of obedience in our relationship with God. His laws help expose sin, and they give standards for righteous living.

1. Giving the law

Moses on Sinai

19 In the third month after the sons of Israel had gone out of the land of Egypt, on
that very day they came into the wilderness of Sinai.
2 When they set out from Rephidim, they came to the wilderness of Sinai and camped
in the wilderness; and there Israel camped in front of the mountain.
3 Moses went up to God, and the LORD called to him from the mountain, saying, "Thus
you shall say to the house of Jacob and tell the sons of Israel:
4 'You yourselves have seen what I did to the Egyptians, and *how* I bore you on eagles' wings, and brought you to Myself.

19:1 Ex 12:6, 51; 16:1; Deut 1:6; 4:10, 15; 5:2
19:2 Ex 17:1; Num 33:15; Ex 3:1, 12; 18:5
19:3 Ex 3:4
19:4 Deut 29:2; Deut 32:11; Rev 12:14

18:13–26 Moses was spending so much time and energy hearing the Hebrews' complaints that he could not get to other important work. Jethro suggested that Moses delegate most of this work to others and focus his efforts on jobs only he could do. People in positions of responsibility sometimes feel they are the only ones who can do necessary tasks; but others are capable of handling part of the load. Delegation relieved Moses' stress and improved the quality of the government. It helped prepare them for the system of government set up in Canaan. Proper delegation can multiply your effectiveness while giving others a chance to grow.

18:16 Moses not only decided these cases, he also taught the people God's laws. Whenever we help others settle disputes or resolve conflicts, we should also look for opportunities to teach about God.

19:2–3 Mount Sinai (also called Mount Horeb) is one of the most sacred locations in Israel's history. Located in the south-central Sinai peninsula, this mountain is where Moses met God in a burning bush, God made his covenant with Israel, and Elijah heard God. Here God gave his people the laws and guidelines for right living. They learned the potential blessings of obedience (34:4–28) and the tragic consequences of disobedience (34:32).

19:4–6 God had a reason for rescuing the Israelites from slavery. Now he was ready to tell them what it was: Israel was to become a kingdom of priests and a holy nation where anyone could approach

19:5 Ex 15:26; Deut 5:2f; Ps 78:10; Ps 135:4; Titus 2:14; 1 Pet 2:9; Deut 10:14; Job 41:11; Ps 50:12; 1 Cor 10:26

19:6 1 Pet 2:5, 9; Rev 1:6; 5:10; Is 62:12

19:9 Deut 4:11; Ps 99:7

5 'Now then, if you will indeed obey My voice and keep My covenant, then you shall
be My [17]own possession among all the peoples, for all the earth is Mine;
6 and you shall be to Me a kingdom of priests and a holy nation.' These are the words
that you shall speak to the sons of Israel."
7 So Moses came and called the elders of the people, and set before them all these
words which the LORD had commanded him.
8 All the people answered together and said, "All that the LORD has spoken we will
do!" And Moses brought back the words of the people to the LORD.
9 The LORD said to Moses, "Behold, I will come to you in a thick cloud, so that the

17 Or *special treasure*

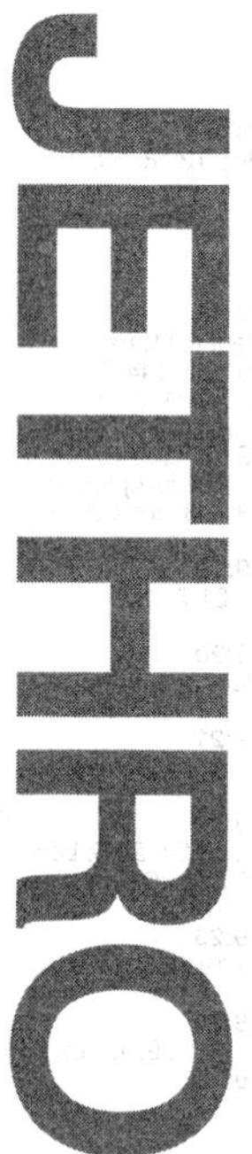

People such as Jethro and Melchizedek—not Israelites, but nevertheless worshipers of the true God—play an important role in the Old Testament. They remind us of God's commitment to the world. God chose one nation through which to work, but his love and concern are for all nations!

Jethro's religious background prepared him for, rather than prevented him from, responding in faith to God. When he saw and heard what God had done for the Israelites, he worshiped God wholeheartedly. We can guess that for 40 years as Moses' father-in-law, Jethro had been watching God at work, molding a leader. Moses and Jethro's relationship must have been close, for Moses readily accepted his father-in-law's advice. Each benefited from knowing the other. Jethro met God through Moses, and Moses received hospitality, his wife, and wisdom from Jethro.

The greatest gift one person can give another is an introduction to God. But that gift is hindered if the believer's attitude is, "I have the greatest gift to pass on to you, while you have nothing to give me in return." Real friends give to and receive from each other. The importance of introducing a friend to God does not make the friend's gifts to us insignificant. Rather, the believer is doubly blessed—first by receiving the gifts the friend wishes to give; then by growing in knowledge of the Lord. For we discover that in introducing another person to God, we increase our own awareness of God. As we give God away, he gives himself even more to us.

Is all you know about God a miscellaneous collection of trivia, or do you have a living relationship with him? Only with a vital relationship can you pass on to others the excitement of allowing God to guide your life. Have you reached the point of saying, with Jethro, "Now I know that the LORD is greater than all the gods" (Exodus 18:11)?

Strengths and accomplishments:
- As father-in-law to Moses, he came to recognize the one true God
- He was a practical troubleshooter and organizer

Lessons from his life:
- Supervision and administration are team efforts
- God's plan includes all nations

Vital statistics:
- Where: The land of Midian and the wilderness of Sinai
- Occupations: Shepherd, priest
- Relatives: Daughter: Zipporah. Son-in-law: Moses. Son: Hobab

Key verse:
"Jethro rejoiced over all the goodness which the LORD had done to Israel, in delivering them from the hand of the Egyptians" (Exodus 18:9).

Jethro's story is told in Exodus 2:15—3:1; 18:1–27. He is also mentioned in Judges 1:16.

God freely. It didn't take long, however, for the people to corrupt God's plan. God then established Aaron's descendants from the tribe of Levi as priests, representing what the entire nation should have been (Leviticus 8–9). But with the coming of Jesus Christ, God has once again extended his plan to all believers. We are to become holy, a "royal PRIESTHOOD" (1 Peter 2:9). The death and resurrection of Christ has allowed each of us to approach God freely.

19:5 Why did God choose Israel as his nation? God knew that no nation on earth was good enough to deserve to be called his people. He chose Israel, not because of anything they had done, but in his love and mercy in spite of the wrong the nation had done and would do. Why did he want to have a special nation on earth? To represent his way of life, to teach his Word, and to be an agent of salvation to the world. "All the nations of the earth" would be blessed through Abraham's descendants (Genesis 18:18). Gentiles and kings would come to the Lord through Israel, predicted Isaiah (Isaiah 60:3). Through the nation of Israel, the Messiah, God's chosen Son, would be born. God chose one nation and put it through a rigorous training program, so that one day it could be a channel for his blessings to the whole world.

19:5–8 In Genesis 15 and 17, God made a covenant with Abraham, promising to make his descendants into a great nation. Now that promise was being realized as God restated his agreement with the Israelite nation, the descendants of Abraham. God promised to bless and care for them. The people promised to obey him. The covenant was thus sealed. But the good intentions of the people quickly wore off. Have you made a commitment to God? How are you holding up your end of the bargain?

people may hear when I speak with you and may also believe in you forever." Then Moses
told the words of the people to the LORD.
10 The LORD also said to Moses, "Go to the people and consecrate them today and
tomorrow, and let them wash their garments;
11 and let them be ready for the third day, for on the third day the LORD will come
down on Mount Sinai in the sight of all the people.
12 "You shall set bounds for the people all around, saying, 'Beware that you do not go
up on the mountain or touch the border of it; whoever touches the mountain shall surely
be put to death.
13 'No hand shall touch him, but he shall surely be stoned or [18]shot through; whether
beast or man, he shall not live.' When the ram's horn sounds a long blast, they shall come
up to the mountain."
14 So Moses went down from the mountain to the people and consecrated the people,
and they washed their garments.
15 He said to the people, "Be ready for the third day; do not go near a woman."
16 So it came about on the third day, when it was morning, that there were thunder
and lightning flashes and a thick cloud upon the mountain and a very loud trumpet sound,
so that all the people who *were* in the camp trembled.
17 And Moses brought the people out of the camp to meet God, and they stood at the
foot of the mountain.

The LORD Visits Sinai

18 Now Mount Sinai *was* all in smoke because the LORD descended upon it in fire;
and its smoke ascended like the smoke of a furnace, and the whole mountain quaked
violently.
19 When the sound of the trumpet grew louder and louder, Moses spoke and God
answered him with thunder.
20 The LORD came down on Mount Sinai, to the top of the mountain; and the LORD
called Moses to the top of the mountain, and Moses went up.
21 Then the LORD spoke to Moses, "Go down, warn the people, so that they do not
break through to the LORD to gaze, and many of them perish.
22 "Also let the priests who come near to the LORD consecrate themselves, or else the
LORD will break out against them."
23 Moses said to the LORD, "The people cannot come up to Mount Sinai, for You
warned us, saying, 'Set bounds about the mountain and consecrate it.' "
24 Then the LORD said to him, "Go down and come up *again,* you and Aaron with you;
but do not let the priests and the people break through to come up to the LORD, or He
will break forth upon them."
25 So Moses went down to the people and told them.

The Ten Commandments

20 Then God spoke all these words, saying,
2 "I am the LORD your God, who brought you out of the land of Egypt, out of
the house of slavery.
3 "You shall have no other gods [19]before Me.

18 I.e. with arrows **19** Or *besides Me*

19:10 Lev 11:44, 45; Gen 35:2; Lev 15:5; Num 8:7, 21; 19:19; Rev 22:14
19:11 Ex 19:16
19:12 Heb 12:20
19:13 Heb 12:20; Ex 19:17
19:16 Heb 12:18, 19, 21
19:18 Deut 4:11; Ps 104:32; 144:5; Ex 3:2; 24:17; Deut 5:4; 2 Chr 7:1-3; Heb 12:18; Gen 15:17; 19:28; Judg 5:5; Ps 68:7, 8; Jer 4:24
19:19 Ps 81:7
19:20 Neh 9:13
19:21 Ex 3:5; 1 Sam 6:19
19:22 Ex 19:24; 24:5; Lev 10:3; 21:6-8
19:23 Ex 19:12
19:24 Ex 24:1, 9, 12; Ex 19:22
20:2 Lev 26:1; Deut 5:6; Ps 81:10; Ex 13:3; 15:13, 16; Deut 7:8
20:3 Deut 6:14; 2 Kin 17:35; Jer 25:6; 35:15; Ex 15:11; 20:23

19:9–11 Moses was told to consecrate the people. This meant getting them physically and spiritually ready to meet God. The people were to set themselves apart from sin and even ordinary daily routine in order to dedicate themselves to God. The act of washing and preparing served to get their minds and hearts ready. When we meet God for worship, we should set aside the cares and preoccupations of everyday life. Use your time of physical preparation to get your mind ready to meet God.

19:22 By stating that he "will break out against them," the Lord was saying that he would destroy anyone who was not fully consecrated and ready to meet him.

20:1ff Why were the Ten Commandments necessary for God's new nation? At the foot of Mount Sinai, God showed his people the true function and beauty of his laws. The commandments were designed to lead Israel to a life of practical holiness. In them, people could see the nature of God and his plan for how they should live. The commands and guidelines were intended to direct the community to meet the needs of each individual in a loving and responsible manner. By Jesus' time, however, most people looked at the law the wrong way. They saw it as a means to prosperity in both this world and the next. And they thought that to obey every law was the way to earn God's protection from foreign invasion and natural disaster. Lawkeeping became an end in itself, not the means to fulfill God's ultimate law of love.

20:1–6 The Israelites had just come from Egypt, a land of many idols and many gods. Because each god represented a different aspect of life, it was common to worship many gods in order to get the maximum number of blessings. When God told his people to worship and believe in him, that wasn't so hard for them—he was

4 "You shall not make for yourself [20]an idol, or any likeness of what is in heaven above
or on the earth beneath or in the water under the earth.
5 "You shall not worship them or serve them; for I, the LORD your God, am a jealous
God, visiting the iniquity of the fathers on the children, on the third and the fourth generations of those who hate Me,
6 but showing lovingkindness to thousands, to those who love Me and keep My commandments.
7 "You shall not take the name of the LORD your God in vain, for the LORD will not
leave him unpunished who takes His name in vain.
8 "Remember the sabbath day, to keep it holy.
9 "Six days you shall labor and do all your work,
10 but the seventh day is a sabbath of the LORD your God; *in it* you shall not do any
work, you or your son or your daughter, your male or your female servant or your cattle
or your sojourner who stays with you.

20 Or *a graven image*

20:4 Deut 4:15-19; 27:15
20:5 Ex 23:24; Josh 23:7; 2 Kin 17:35; Ex 34:14; Josh 24:19; Nah 1:2; Ex 34:6, 7; Num 14:18, 33; Deut 5:9, 10; 1 Kin 21:29; Jer 32:18
20:6 Deut 7:9
20:9 Ex 34:21; 35:2, 3; Deut 5:13; Luke 13:14
20:10 Neh 13:16-19

JESUS AND THE TEN COMMANDMENTS

The Ten Commandments said. . .	*Jesus said. . .*
Exodus 20:3 "You shall have no other gods before Me"	Matthew 4:10 "WORSHIP THE LORD YOUR GOD, AND SERVE HIM ONLY"
Exodus 20:4 "You shall not make for yourself an idol"	Luke 16:13 "No servant can serve two masters"
Exodus 20:7 "You shall not take the name of the LORD your God in vain"	Matthew 5:34 "Make no oath at all, either by heaven, for it is the throne of God . . ."
Exodus 20:8 "Remember the sabbath day, to keep it holy"	Mark 2:27–28 "The Sabbath was made for man, and not man for the Sabbath. So the Son of Man is Lord even of the Sabbath"
Exodus 20:12 "Honor your father and your mother"	Matthew 10:37 "He who loves father or mother more than Me is not worthy of Me"
Exodus 20:13 "You shall not murder"	Matthew 5:22 "Everyone who is angry with his brother shall be guilty before the court"
Exodus 20:14 "You shall not commit adultery"	Matthew 5:28 "Everyone who looks at a woman with lust for her has already committed adultery with her in his heart"
Exodus 20:15 "You shall not steal"	Matthew 5:40 "If anyone wants to sue you and take your shirt, let him have your coat also"
Exodus 20:16 "You shall not bear false witness"	Matthew 12:36 "Every careless word that people speak, they shall give an accounting for it in the day of judgment"
Exodus 20:17 "You shall not covet"	Luke 12:15 "Be on your guard against every form of greed"

just one more god to add to the list. But when he said, "You shall have no other gods before Me," that was difficult for the people to accept. But if they didn't learn that the God who led them out of Egypt was the only true God, they could not be his people—no matter how faithfully they kept the other nine commandments. Thus, God made this his first commandment and emphasized it more than the others. Today we can allow many things to become gods to us. Money, fame, work, or pleasure can become gods when we concentrate too much on them for personal identity, meaning, and security. No one sets out with the intention of worshiping these things. But by the amount of time we devote to them, they can grow into gods that ultimately control our thoughts and energies. Letting God hold the central place in our lives keeps these things from turning into gods.

20:7 God's name is special because it carries his personal identity. Using it frivolously or in a curse is so common today that we may fail to realize how serious it is. The way we use God's name conveys how we really feel about him. We should respect his name and use it appropriately, speaking it in praise or worship rather than in curse or jest. We should not take lightly the abuse or dishonor of his name.

20:8–11 The Sabbath was a day set aside for rest and worship. God commanded a Sabbath because human beings need to spend unhurried time in worship and rest each week. A God who is concerned enough to provide a day each week for us to rest is indeed wonderful. To observe a regular time of rest and worship in our fast-paced world demonstrates how important God is to us, and it gives us the extra benefit of refreshing our spirits. Don't neglect God's provision.

11 "For in six days the LORD made the heavens and the earth, the sea and all that is in
them, and rested on the seventh day; therefore the LORD blessed the sabbath day and
made it holy.
12 "Honor your father and your mother, that your days may be prolonged in the land
which the LORD your God gives you.
13 "You shall not murder.
14 "You shall not commit adultery.
15 "You shall not steal.
16 "You shall not bear false witness against your neighbor.
17 "You shall not covet your neighbor's house; you shall not covet your neighbor's wife
or his male servant or his female servant or his ox or his donkey or anything that belongs
to your neighbor."
18 All the people perceived the thunder and the lightning flashes and the sound of the
trumpet and the mountain smoking; and when the people saw *it,* they trembled and stood
at a distance.
19 Then they said to Moses, "Speak to us yourself and we will listen; but let not God
speak to us, or we will die."
20 Moses said to the people, "Do not be afraid; for God has come in order to test you,
and in order that the fear of Him may remain with you, so that you may not sin."
21 So the people stood at a distance, while Moses approached the thick cloud where
God *was.*
22 Then the LORD said to Moses, "Thus you shall say to the sons of Israel, 'You yourselves have seen that I have spoken to you from heaven.
23 'You shall not make *other gods* besides Me; gods of silver or gods of gold, you shall
not make for yourselves.
24 'You shall make an altar of earth for Me, and you shall sacrifice on it your burnt
offerings and your peace offerings, your sheep and your oxen; in every place where I
cause My name to be remembered, I will come to you and bless you.
25 'If you make an altar of stone for Me, you shall not build it of cut stones, for if you
wield your tool on it, you will profane it.
26 'And you shall not go up by steps to My altar, so that your nakedness will not be
exposed on it.'

20:11 Gen 2:2, 3; Ex 31:17

20:12 Deut 27:16; Matt 15:4; 19:19; Mark 7:10; 10:19; Luke 18:20; Eph 6:2

20:13 Gen 9:6; Ex 21:12; Lev 24:17; Matt 5:21; 19:18; Mark 10:19; Luke 18:20; Rom 13:9; James 2:11

20:14 Deut 5:18; Matt 5:27; 19:18; Rom 13:9

20:15 Ex 21:16; Matt 19:18; Rom 13:9

20:16 Ex 23:1, 7; Deut 5:20; Matt 19:18

20:17 Deut 5:21; Rom 7:7; 13:9; Eph 5:3, 5; Prov 6:29; Matt 5:28

20:18 Ex 19:16, 18; Heb 12:18, 19

20:19 Deut 5:5, 23-27; Gal 3:19; Heb 12:19

20:20 Ex 14:13; Is 41:10, 13; Prov 3:7; 16:6; Is 8:13

20:22 Neh 9:13

20:12 This is the first commandment with a promise attached. To live in peace for generations in the promised land, the Israelites would need to respect authority and build strong families. But what does it mean to "honor" parents? Partly, it means speaking well of them and politely to them. It also means acting in a way that shows them courtesy and respect (but not to obey them if this means disobedience to God). It means following their teaching and example of putting God first. Parents have a special place in God's sight. Even those who find it difficult to get along with their parents are still commanded to honor them.

20:16 Bearing false testimony means lying in court. God knew that Israel could not survive unless its system of justice was incorruptible. We should be honest in our private dealings as well as in our public statements. In either situation, we "bear false testimony" by leaving something out of a story, telling a half-truth, twisting the facts, or inventing a falsehood. God warns us against deception. Even though deception is a way of life for many people, God's people must not give in to it!

20:17 To covet is to wish to have the possessions of others. It goes beyond simply admiring someone else's possessions or thinking, "I'd like to have one of those." Coveting includes envy—resenting the fact that others have what you don't. God knows, however, that possessions never make anyone happy for long. Since only God can supply all our needs, true contentment is found only in him. When you begin to covet, try to determine if a more basic need is leading you to envy. For example, you may covet someone's success, not because you want to take it away from him, but because you would like to feel as appreciated by others as he is. If this is the case, pray that God will help you deal with your resentment and meet your basic needs.

20:18 Sometimes God speaks to his people with a majestic display of power; at other times he speaks quietly. Why the difference? God speaks in the way that best accomplishes his purposes. At Sinai, the awesome display of light and sound was necessary to show Israel God's great power and authority. Only then would they listen to Moses and Aaron.

20:20 Throughout the Bible we find this phrase, "Do not be afraid." God wasn't trying to scare the people. He was showing his mighty power so the Israelites would know he was the true God and would therefore obey him. If they would do this, he would make his power available to them. God wants us to follow him out of love rather than fear. To overcome fear, we must think more about his love. First John 4:18 says, "Perfect love casts out fear."

20:24–26 Why were specific directions given for building altars? God's people had no Bible and few religious traditions to learn from. God had to start from scratch and teach them how to worship him. God gave specific instructions about building altars because he wanted to control the way sacrifices were offered. To prevent idolatry from creeping into worship, God did not allow the altar stones to be cut or shaped into any form. Nor did God let the people build an altar just anywhere. This was designed to prevent them from starting their own religions or making changes in the way God wanted things done. God is not against creativity, but he is against us creating our own religion.

Ordinances for the People

21 "Now these are the ordinances which you are to set before them:
2 "If you buy a Hebrew slave, he shall serve for six years; but on the seventh he
shall go out as a free man without payment.
3 "If he comes alone, he shall go out alone; if he is the husband of a wife, then his wife
shall go out with him.
4 "If his master gives him a wife, and she bears him sons or daughters, the wife and her
children shall belong to her master, and he shall go out alone.
5 "But if the slave plainly says, 'I love my master, my wife and my children; I will not go
out as a free man,'
6 then his master shall bring him to [21]God, then he shall bring him to the door or the
doorpost. And his master shall pierce his ear with an awl; and he shall serve him permanently.
7 "If a man sells his daughter as a female slave, she is not to go free as the male
slaves do.
8 "If she is displeasing in the eyes of her master who designated her for himself, then
he shall let her be redeemed. He does not have authority to sell her to a foreign people
because of his unfairness to her.
9 "If he designates her for his son, he shall deal with her according to the custom of
daughters.
10 "If he takes to himself another woman, he may not reduce her food, her clothing, or
her conjugal rights.
11 "If he will not do these three *things* for her, then she shall go out for nothing, without
payment of money.

Personal Injuries

12 "He who strikes a man so that he dies shall surely be put to death.
13 "But if he did not lie in wait *for him,* but God let *him* fall into his hand, then I will
appoint you a place to which he may flee.
14 "If, however, a man acts presumptuously toward his neighbor, so as to kill him craftily, you are to take him *even* from My altar, that he may die.
15 "He who strikes his father or his mother shall surely be put to death.
16 "He who kidnaps a man, whether he sells him or he is found in his possession, shall
surely be put to death.
17 "He who curses his father or his mother shall surely be put to death.
18 "If men have a quarrel and one strikes the other with a stone or with *his* fist, and he
does not die but remains in bed,
19 if he gets up and walks around outside on his staff, then he who struck him shall go
unpunished; he shall only pay for his loss of time, and shall take care of him until he is
completely healed.
20 "If a man strikes his male or female slave with a rod and he dies at his hand, he shall
be punished.
21 "If, however, he survives a day or two, no vengeance shall be taken; for he is his property.
22 "If men struggle with each other and strike a woman with child so that she gives birth
prematurely, yet there is no injury, he shall surely be fined as the woman's husband may
demand of him, and he shall pay as the judges *decide.*
23 "But if there is *any further* injury, then you shall appoint *as a penalty* life for life,
24 eye for eye, tooth for tooth, hand for hand, foot for foot,

21:1 Ex 24:3, 4; Deut 4:14; 6:1
21:2 Lev 25:39-43; Deut 15:12-18; Jer 34:14
21:5 Deut 15:16, 17
21:7 Neh 5:5; Ex 21:2, 3
21:10 1 Cor 7:3, 5
21:12 Gen 9:6; Lev 24:17; Num 35:30; Matt 26:52
21:13 Num 35:10-34; Deut 19:1-13; Josh 20:1-9 1 Sam 24:4, 10, 18
21:14 Deut 19:11, 12; 1 Kin 2:28-34
21:16 Deut 24:7
21:17 Lev 20:9; Prov 20:20; Matt 15:4; Mark 7:10
21:21 Lev 25:44-46
21:22 Ex 21:30; Deut 22:18, 19
21:23 Lev 24:19; Deut 19:21
21:24 Lev 24:20; Deut 19:21; Matt 5:38

21 Or *the judges who acted in God's name*

21:1ff These laws were given because everything we do has consequences. It is vital to think before acting, to consider the effects of our choices. Think of your plans for today and consider what their long-range results will be. As we deal with others, we should keep the principles of these laws in mind. We should act responsibly and justly with all people—friends and enemies alike.

21:2 The Hebrews, though freed from slavery, had slaves (or servants) themselves. A person could become a slave because of poverty, debt, or even crime. But Hebrew slaves were treated as humans, not property, and were allowed to work their way to freedom. The Bible acknowledges the existence of slavery but never encourages it.

21:24–25 The "eye for eye" rule was instituted as a guide for judges, not as a rule for personal relationships or to justify revenge. This rule made the punishment fit the crime, thereby preventing the cruel and barbaric punishments that characterized many ancient countries. Jesus used this principle to teach us not to retaliate (Matthew 5:38–48). Judges, parents, teachers, and others who work with people must make wise decisions in order for discipline to be effective. A punishment too harsh is unfair, and one too lenient is powerless to teach. Ask God for wisdom before you judge.

25 burn for burn, wound for wound, bruise for bruise.
26 "If a man strikes the eye of his male or female slave, and destroys it, he shall let him
go free on account of his eye.
27 "And if he knocks out a tooth of his male or female slave, he shall let him go free on
account of his tooth.
28 "If an ox gores a man or a woman to death, the ox shall surely be stoned and its flesh **21:28**
shall not be eaten; but the owner of the ox shall go unpunished. Gen 9:5; Ex 21:32
29 "If, however, an ox was previously in the habit of goring and its owner has been warned,
yet he does not confine it and it kills a man or a woman, the ox shall be stoned and its
owner also shall be put to death.
30 "If a ransom is demanded of him, then he shall give for the redemption of his life
whatever is demanded of him.
31 "Whether it gores a son or a daughter, it shall be done to him according to the same
rule.
32 "If the ox gores a male or female slave, the owner shall give his *or her* master thirty **21:32**
shekels of silver, and the ox shall be stoned. Zech 11:12; Matt 26:15; 27:3, 9
33 "If a man opens a pit, or digs a pit and does not cover it over, and an ox or a donkey
falls into it,
34 the owner of the pit shall make restitution; he shall give money to its owner, and the
dead *animal* shall become his.
35 "If one man's ox hurts another's so that it dies, then they shall sell the live ox and
divide its price equally; and also they shall divide the dead *ox.*
36 "Or *if* it is known that the ox was previously in the habit of goring, yet its owner has
not confined it, he shall surely pay ox for ox, and the dead *animal* shall become his.

Property Rights

22 "If a man steals an ox or a sheep and slaughters it or sells it, he shall pay five oxen **22:1**
for the ox and four sheep for the sheep. 2 Sam 12:6; Luke 19:8
2 "If the thief is caught while breaking in and is struck so that he dies, there will be no
bloodguiltiness on his account. **22:2** Matt 6:19; 24:43;
3 "*But* if the sun has risen on him, there will be bloodguiltiness on his account. He shall 1 Pet 4:15
surely make restitution; if he owns nothing, then he shall be sold for his theft. **22:3**
4 "If what he stole is actually found alive in his possession, whether an ox or a donkey Matt 18:25
or a sheep, he shall pay double. **22:4**
5 "If a man lets a field or vineyard be grazed *bare* and lets his animal loose so that it Ex 22:7
grazes in another man's field, he shall make restitution from the best of his own field
and the best of his own vineyard.
6 "If a fire breaks out and spreads to thorn bushes, so that stacked grain or the standing grain or the field *itself* is consumed, he who started the fire shall surely make restitution.
7 "If a man gives his neighbor money or goods to keep *for him* and it is stolen from the **22:7**
man's house, if the thief is caught, he shall pay double. Lev 6:1-7
8 "If the thief is not caught, then the owner of the house shall appear before the judges, **22:8**
to determine whether he laid his hands on his neighbor's property. Ex 22:9; Deut 17:8, 9; 19:17
9 "For every breach of trust, *whether it is* for ox, for donkey, for sheep, for clothing, *or*
for any lost thing about which one says, 'This is it,' the case of both parties shall come **22:9**
before the judges; he whom the judges condemn shall pay double to his neighbor. Ex 22:8, 28; Deut 25:1
10 "If a man gives his neighbor a donkey, an ox, a sheep, or any animal to keep *for him,*
and it dies or is hurt or is driven away while no one is looking,
11 an oath before the LORD shall be made by the two of them that he has not laid hands **22:11**
on his neighbor's property; and its owner shall accept *it,* and he shall not make restitution. Heb 6:16

22:1ff These are not a collection of picky laws but are case studies of God's principles in action. God was taking potential situations and showing how his laws would work in the Israelites' everyday lives. These case studies had several objectives: (1) to protect the nation, (2) to organize the nation, and (3) to focus the nation's attention on God. The laws listed here do not cover every possible situation but give practical examples that make it easier to decide what God wants.

22:3ff Throughout chapter 22 we find examples of the principle of restitution—making wrongs right. For example, if a man stole an animal, he had to repay double the beast's market value. If you have done someone wrong, perhaps you should go beyond what is expected to make things right. This will (1) help ease any pain you've caused, (2) help the other person be more forgiving, and (3) make you more likely to think before you do it again.

12"But if it is actually stolen from him, he shall make restitution to its owner.
13"If it is all torn to pieces, let him bring it as evidence; he shall not make restitution
for what has been torn to pieces.
14"If a man borrows *anything* from his neighbor, and it is injured or dies while its owner is not with it, he shall make full restitution.
15"If its owner is with it, he shall not make restitution; if it is hired, it came for its hire.

Sundry Laws

16"If a man seduces a virgin who is not engaged, and lies with her, he must pay a dowry
for her *to be* his wife.
17"If her father absolutely refuses to give her to him, he shall pay money equal to the
dowry for virgins.
18"You shall not allow a sorceress to live.
19"Whoever lies with an animal shall surely be put to death.
20"He who sacrifices to any god, other than to the LORD alone, shall be utterly destroyed.
21"You shall not wrong a stranger or oppress him, for you were strangers in the land of
Egypt.
22"You shall not afflict any widow or orphan.
23"If you afflict him at all, *and* if he does cry out to Me, I will surely hear his cry;
24 and My anger will be kindled, and I will kill you with the sword, and your wives shall
become widows and your children fatherless.
25"If you lend money to My people, to the poor among you, you are not to act as a
creditor to him; you shall not charge him interest.
26"If you ever take your neighbor's cloak as a pledge, you are to return it to him before
the sun sets,
27 for that is his only covering; it is his cloak for his body. What else shall he sleep in?
And it shall come about that when he cries out to Me, I will hear *him,* for I am gracious.
28"You shall not curse God, nor curse a ruler of your people.
29"You shall not delay *the offering from* your harvest and your vintage. The firstborn of
your sons you shall give to Me.
30"You shall do the same with your oxen *and* with your sheep. It shall be with its mother seven days; on the eighth day you shall give it to Me.
31"You shall be holy men to Me, therefore you shall not eat *any* flesh torn to pieces in
the field; you shall throw it to the dogs.

Sundry Laws

23 "You shall not bear a false report; do not join your hand with a wicked man to be
a malicious witness.

22:16 Deut 22:28, 29

22:17 Gen 34:12; 1 Sam 18:25

22:18 Lev 19:31; 20:6, 27; Deut 18:10, 11; 1 Sam 28:3; Jer 27:9, 10

22:19 Lev 18:23; 20:15, 16; Deut 27:21

22:20 Ex 32:8; 34:15; Lev 17:7; Num 25:2; Deut 17:2, 3, 5; 1 Kin 18:40; 2 Kin 10:25

22:21 Ex 23:9; Lev 19:33, 34; 25:35; Deut 1:16; 10:19; 27:19; Zech 7:10

22:22 Deut 24:17, 18; Prov 23:10, 11; Jer 7:6, 7

22:23 Deut 15:9; Job 35:9; Luke 18:7; Deut 10:18; Job 34:28; Ps 10:14, 17, 18; 18:6; 68:5; James 5:4

22:24 Ps 109:2, 9

22:25 Neh 5:7; Ps 15:5; Ezek 18:8

22:26 Job 24:3; Prov 20:16; Amos 2:8

22:28 Eccl 10:20; Acts 23:5

23:1 Ps 101:5; Prov 10:18; Deut 19:16-21; Ps 35:11; Prov 19:5; Acts 6:11

22:18 Why did God's laws speak so strongly against sorcery (Leviticus 19:31; 20:6, 27; Deuteronomy 18:10–12)? Sorcery was punishable by death because it was a crime against God himself. To invoke evil powers violated the first commandment to "have no other gods." Sorcery was rebellion against God and his authority. In essence, it was teaming up with Satan instead of with God.

22:21 God warned the Israelites not to treat strangers unfairly because they themselves were once strangers in Egypt. It is not easy coming into a new environment where you feel alone and out of place. Are there strangers in your corner of the world? Refugees? New arrivals at school? Immigrants from another country? Be sensitive to their struggles, and express God's love by your kindness and generosity.

22:22–27 The Hebrew law code is noted for its fairness and social responsibility toward the poor. God insisted that the poor and powerless be well treated and given the chance to restore their fortunes. We should reflect God's concern for the poor by helping those less fortunate than ourselves.

22:26 Why did the law insist on returning a person's cloak by evening? The cloak was one of an Israelite's most valuable possessions. Making clothing was difficult and time-consuming. As a result, cloaks were expensive, and most people owned only one. The cloak was used as a blanket, a sack to carry things in, a place to sit, a pledge for a debt, and, of course, clothing.

22:29 The Israelites were to be prompt in giving God their offerings. The first of the harvest was to be dedicated to him. Since God doesn't send payment overdue notices, it is easy to take care of other financial responsibilities while letting our gifts to him slide. Giving to God first out of what he has allowed you to have demonstrates that he has first priority in your life.

23:1 Making up or spreading false reports was strictly forbidden by God. Gossip, slander, and false witnessing undermined families, strained neighborhood cooperation, and made chaos of the justice system. Destructive gossip still causes problems. Even if you do not initiate a lie, you become responsible if you pass it along. Don't circulate rumors; squelch them.

2 "You shall not follow the masses in doing evil, nor shall you testify in a dispute so as
to turn aside after a multitude in order to pervert *justice;*
3 nor shall you be partial to a poor man in his dispute.
4 "If you meet your enemy's ox or his donkey wandering away, you shall surely return
it to him.
5 "If you see the donkey of one who hates you lying *helpless* under its load, you shall
refrain from leaving it to him, you shall surely release *it* with him.
6 "You shall not pervert the justice *due* to your needy *brother* in his dispute.
7 "Keep far from a false charge, and do not kill the innocent or the righteous, for I will
not acquit the guilty.
8 "You shall not take a bribe, for a bribe blinds the clear-sighted and subverts the cause
of the just.
9 "You shall not oppress a stranger, since you yourselves know the feelings of a stranger, for you *also* were strangers in the land of Egypt.

The Sabbath and Land

10 "You shall sow your land for six years and gather in its yield,
11 but *on* the seventh year you shall let it rest and lie fallow, so that the needy of your
people may eat; and whatever they leave the beast of the field may eat. You are to do
the same with your vineyard *and* your olive grove.
12 "Six days you are to do your work, but on the seventh day you shall cease *from labor*
so that your ox and your donkey may rest, and the son of your female slave, as well as
your stranger, may refresh themselves.
13 "Now concerning everything which I have said to you, be on your guard; and do not
mention the name of other gods, nor let *them* be heard from your mouth.

Three National Feasts

14 "Three times a year you shall celebrate a feast to Me.
15 "You shall observe the Feast of Unleavened Bread; for seven days you are to eat
unleavened bread, as I commanded you, at the appointed time in the month Abib, for in
it you came out of Egypt. And none shall appear before Me empty-handed.
16 "Also *you shall observe* the Feast of the Harvest *of* the first fruits of your labors *from*
what you sow in the field; also the Feast of the Ingathering at the end of the year when
you gather in *the fruit of* your labors from the field.
17 "Three times a year all your males shall appear before the Lord GOD.
18 "You shall not offer the blood of My sacrifice with leavened bread; nor is the fat of
My feast to remain overnight until morning.
19 "You shall bring the choice first fruits of your soil into the house of the LORD
your God.
"You are not to boil a young goat in the milk of its mother.

Conquest of the Land

20 "Behold, I am going to send an angel before you to guard you along the way and to
bring you into the place which I have prepared.
21 "Be on your guard before him and obey his voice; do not be rebellious toward him,
for he will not pardon your transgression, since My name is in him.
22 "But if you truly obey his voice and do all that I say, then I will be an enemy to your
enemies and an adversary to your adversaries.

23:2 Deut 16:19; 24:17
23:3 Ex 23:6; Lev 19:15; Deut 1:17; 16:19
23:4 Deut 22:1-4
23:5 Deut 22:4
23:6 Ex 23:2, 3; Lev 19:15
23:7 Ex 20:16; Ps 119:29; Eph 4:25; Ex 20:13; Deut 27:25; Ex 34:7; Deut 25:1; Rom 1:18
23:8 Deut 10:17; 16:19; Prov 15:27; 17:8, 23; Is 5:22, 23
23:9 Ex 22:21; Lev 19:33f; Deut 24:17f; 27:19
23:10 Lev 25:1-7
23:12 Ex 20:8-11; 31:15; 34:21; 35:2, 3; Lev 23:3; Deut 5:13f
23:13 Deut 4:9, 23; 1 Tim 4:16; Josh 23:7; Ps 16:4; Hos 2:17
23:16 Num 28:26; Lev 23:39
23:17 Ex 23:14; 34:23; Deut 16:16
23:19 Ex 22:29; 34:26; Deut 26:2, 10; Neh 10:35; Prov 3:9; Deut 14:21
23:21 Deut 9:7; Ps 78:40, 56; Ex 3:14; 6:3; 34:5-7
23:22 Gen 12:3; Num 24:9; Deut 30:7

23:2–3 Justice is often perverted in favor of the rich. Here the people are warned against twisting justice in favor of the poor. Justice should be impartial, treating rich and poor alike. Giving special privileges to either rich or poor only makes justice for everyone more unlikely. Withstand the pressure of the crowd to sway your decision about a person. Let the fairness God shows to each of us guide your judgment.

23:4–5 The thought of being kind to enemies was new and startling in a world where revenge was the common form of justice. God not only introduced this idea to the Israelites, he made it law! If a man found a lost animal owned by his enemy, he was to return it at once, even if his enemy might use it to harm him. Jesus clearly taught in Luke 10:30–37 to reach out to all people in need, even our enemies. Following the laws of right living is hard enough with friends. When we apply God's laws of fairness and kindness to our enemies, we show how different we are from the world.

23:20–21 Who was this angel that went with the Israelites? Most likely the angel was a manifestation of God. God was in the angel in the same way he was present in the pillars of cloud and fire (13:21–22). "My name is in him" means the essential nature and power of God were made known in this angel.

23 "For My angel will go before you and bring you in to *the land of* the Amorites, the
Hittites, the Perizzites, the Canaanites, the Hivites and the Jebusites; and I will completely destroy them.
24 "You shall not worship their gods, nor serve them, nor do according to their deeds;
but you shall utterly overthrow them and break their *sacred* pillars in pieces.
25 "But you shall serve the LORD your God, and He will bless your bread and your water;
and I will remove sickness from your midst.
26 "There shall be no one miscarrying or barren in your land; I will fulfill the number of
your days.
27 "I will send My terror ahead of you, and throw into confusion all the people among
whom you come, and I will make all your enemies turn *their* backs to you.
28 "I will send hornets ahead of you so that they will drive out the Hivites, the Canaanites, and the Hittites before you.
29 "I will not drive them out before you in a single year, that the land may not become
desolate and the beasts of the field become too numerous for you.
30 "I will drive them out before you little by little, until you become fruitful and take
possession of the land.
31 "I will fix your boundary from the Red Sea to the sea of the Philistines, and from the
wilderness to the River *Euphrates;* for I will deliver the inhabitants of the land into your
hand, and you will drive them out before you.
32 "You shall make no covenant with them or with their gods.
33 "They shall not live in your land, because they will make you sin against Me; for *if*
you serve their gods, it will surely be a snare to you."

People Affirm Their Covenant with God

24 Then He said to Moses, "Come up to the LORD, you and Aaron, Nadab and Abihu
and seventy of the elders of Israel, and you shall worship at a distance.
2 "Moses alone, however, shall come near to the LORD, but they shall not come near,
nor shall the people come up with him."
3 Then Moses came and recounted to the people all the words of the LORD and all
the ordinances; and all the people answered with one voice and said, "All the words which
the LORD has spoken we will do!"
4 Moses wrote down all the words of the LORD. Then he arose early in the morning,
and built an altar at the foot of the mountain with twelve pillars for the twelve tribes of
Israel.
5 He sent young men of the sons of Israel, and they offered burnt offerings and sacrificed young bulls as peace offerings to the LORD.
6 Moses took half of the blood and put *it* in basins, and the *other* half of the blood he
sprinkled on the altar.

23:23 Ex 23:20; Josh 24:8, 11

23:24 Ex 20:5; 23:13, 33; Deut 12:30f; Num 33:52; Deut 7:5; 12:3; 2 Kin 18:4; Ex 34:13; Lev 26:1; 2 Kin 3:2

23:25 Lev 26:3-13; Deut 6:13; 10:12; 28:1-14; Josh 22:5; 1 Sam 12:20; Matt 4:10; Ex 15:26; Deut 7:15

23:26 Deut 7:14; Deut 4:40; Job 5:26

23:27 Gen 35:5; Ex 15:16; Deut 2:25; Josh 2:9; Deut 7:23; Ps 18:40; 21:12

23:28 Deut 7:20; Josh 24:12; Ex 33:2; 34:11

23:29 Deut 7:22

23:30 Deut 7:22

23:31 Gen 15:18; Deut 1:7, 8; 11:24; Deut 2:36; Josh 21:44; Josh 24:12, 18

23:33 Deut 7:1-5, 16; Ex 34:12; Deut 12:30; Josh 23:13; Judg 2:3; Ps 106:36

24:1 Ex 19:24; Ex 6:23; 28:1; Lev 10:1, 2; Num 11:16

24:6 Heb 9:18

23:24–25 If you're in the furnace, it's easy to catch on fire. God warned the Israelites about their neighbors whose beliefs and actions could turn them away from him. We also live with neighbors whose values may be completely different from ours. We are called to maintain a life-style that shows our faith. This can be a struggle, especially if our Christian life-style differs from the norm. Our lives should show that we put obeying God before doing what is praised and accepted by society.

23:29 Not all of God's solutions are instantaneous. Nor does delay justify inaction. In this case, God's cause would require constant cooperation, persistence, and effort by the Israelites. Success would come step-by-step.

23:32–33 God continually warned the people to avoid false religions and false gods. In Egypt they had been surrounded by idols and sorcerers, but leaving that land did not mean they were free from pagan religious influences. The land of Canaan was just as infested with idol worship. God knew his people needed extra strength, so he continually emphasized guarding against the influence of pagan religions.

24:6–8 To understand this unusual covenant ratification ceremony, we need to understand the Bible's view of sin and forgiveness. God is the sovereign judge of the universe. He is also absolutely holy. As the holy judge of all, he condemns sin and judges it worthy of death. In the Old Testament God accepted the death of an animal as a substitute for the sinner. The animal's shed blood was proof that one life had been given for another. So on the one hand, blood symbolized the death of the animal, but it also symbolized the life that was spared as a result. Of course the death of the animal that brought forgiveness in the Old Testament was only a temporary provision, looking forward to the death of Jesus Christ (Hebrews 9:9—10:24).

In this ceremony described here, Moses sprinkled half the blood from the sacrificed animals on the altar to show that the sinner could once again approach God because something had died in his place. He sprinkled the other half of the blood on the people to show that the penalty for their sin had been paid and they could be reunited with God. Through this symbolic act God's promises to Israel were reaffirmed and lessons are taught to us about the future sacrificial death (or atonement) of Jesus Christ.

7 Then he took the book of the covenant and read *it* in the hearing of the people; and
they said, "All that the LORD has spoken we will do, and we will be obedient!"
8 So Moses took the blood and sprinkled *it* on the people, and said, "Behold the blood
of the covenant, which the LORD has made with you in accordance with all these words."
9 Then Moses went up with Aaron, Nadab and Abihu, and seventy of the elders of
Israel,
10 and they saw the God of Israel; and under His feet there appeared to be a pavement of sapphire, as clear as the sky itself.
11 Yet He did not stretch out His hand against the nobles of the sons of Israel; and
they saw God, and they ate and drank.
12 Now the LORD said to Moses, "Come up to Me on the mountain and remain there,
and I will give you the stone tablets with the law and the commandment which I have
written for their instruction."
13 So Moses arose with Joshua his servant, and Moses went up to the mountain of God.
14 But to the elders he said, "Wait here for us until we return to you. And behold, Aaron
and Hur are with you; whoever has a legal matter, let him approach them."
15 Then Moses went up to the mountain, and the cloud covered the mountain.
16 The glory of the LORD rested on Mount Sinai, and the cloud covered it for six days;
and on the seventh day He called to Moses from the midst of the cloud.
17 And to the eyes of the sons of Israel the appearance of the glory of the LORD was
like a consuming fire on the mountain top.
18 Moses entered the midst of the cloud as he went up to the mountain; and Moses
was on the mountain forty days and forty nights.

2. Tabernacle instructions

Offerings for the Sanctuary

25 Then the LORD spoke to Moses, saying,
2 "Tell the sons of Israel to raise a contribution for Me; from every man whose
heart moves him you shall raise My contribution.
3 "This is the contribution which you are to raise from them: gold, silver and bronze,
4 blue, purple and scarlet *material,* fine linen, goat *hair,*
5 rams' skins dyed red, porpoise skins, acacia wood,
6 oil for lighting, spices for the anointing oil and for the fragrant incense,
7 onyx stones and setting stones for the ephod and for the breastpiece.
8 "Let them construct a sanctuary for Me, that I may dwell among them.
9 "According to all that I am going to show you, *as* the pattern of the tabernacle and
the pattern of all its furniture, just so you shall construct *it.*

Ark of the Covenant

10 "They shall construct an ark of acacia wood two and a half cubits long, and one and
a half cubits wide, and one and a half cubits high.
11 "You shall overlay it with pure gold, inside and out you shall overlay it, and you shall
make a gold molding around it.
12 "You shall cast four gold rings for it and fasten them on its four feet, and two rings
shall be on one side of it and two rings on the other side of it.
13 "You shall make poles of acacia wood and overlay them with gold.
14 "You shall put the poles into the rings on the sides of the ark, to carry the ark with
them.
15 "The poles shall remain in the rings of the ark; they shall not be removed from it.

24:7 Ex 24:4; Heb 9:19; Ex 24:3

24:8 Heb 9:19, 20; Zech 9:11; Matt 26:28; Mark 14:24; Luke 22:20; 1 Cor 11:25; Heb 13:20

24:9 Ex 24:1

24:10 Ex 24:11; Num 12:8; Is 6:5; John 1:18; 6:46; Ezek 1:26; 10:1; Rev 4:3

24:11 Gen 16:13; 32:30; Ex 24:10

24:12 Ex 31:18; 32:15; Deut 5:22

24:13 Ex 17:9-14; 33:11; Ex 3:1

24:14 Gen 22:5; Ex 17:10, 12

24:15 Ex 19:9

24:16 Ex 16:10; Num 14:10; Ps 99:7

24:17 Ex 3:2; Ezek 1:28; Deut 4:24; 9:3; Heb 12:29

24:18 Ex 34:28; Deut 9:9; 10:10

25:2 Ex 35:4-9; Ex 35:21; 1 Chr 29:3, 5, 9; Ezra 2:68; 2 Cor 8:11, 12; 9:7

25:8 Ex 36:1-5; Ex 29:45, 46; Num 5:3; Deut 12:11; 1 Kin 6:13; 2 Cor 6:16; Rev 21:3

25:9 Ex 25:40; 26:30; Acts 7:44; Heb 8:2, 5

25:10 Ex 37:1-9; Deut 10:3; Heb 9:4

25:11 Heb 9:4

25:15 1 Kin 8:8

25:1ff Chapters 25 through 31 record God's directions for building the tabernacle. Chapters 35 through 39 tell how these instructions were carried out. But what can all these ancient, complicated construction details show us today? First, the high quality of the precious materials making up the tabernacle shows God's greatness and transcendence. Second, the curtain surrounding the holy of holies shows God's moral perfection as symbolized by his separation from the common and unclean. Third, the portable nature of the tabernacle shows God's desire to be with his people as they traveled.

25:10 Much of the tabernacle and its furniture was made of acacia wood. Acacia trees flourished in barren regions and were fairly common in Old Testament times. The wood was brownish-orange and very hard, making it an excellent material for furniture. Acacia wood is still used in furniture-making today. A cubit is about 1 1/2 feet or .43 meter.

25:16 Ex 40:20; Deut 10:2; 31:26; 1 Kin 8:9; Heb 9:4

16 "You shall put into the ark the testimony which I shall give you.
17 "You shall make a [22]mercy seat of pure gold, two and a half cubits long and one and
a half cubits wide.

25:17 Ex 37:6

18 "You shall make two cherubim of gold, make them of hammered work at the two
ends of the mercy seat.
19 "Make one cherub at one end and one cherub at the other end; you shall make the
cherubim *of one piece* with the mercy seat at its two ends.

25:20 1 Kin 8:7; 1 Chr 28:18; Heb 9:5

20 "The cherubim shall have *their* wings spread upward, covering the mercy seat with
their wings and facing one another; the faces of the cherubim are to be *turned* toward
the mercy seat.

25:21 Ex 26:34; 40:20; Ex 25:16

21 "You shall put the mercy seat on top of the ark, and in the ark you shall put the testimony which I will give to you.

25:22 Ex 29:42, 43; 30:6, 36; Lev 16:2; Num 17:4; Num 7:89; 1 Sam 4:4; 2 Sam 6:2; 2 Kin 19:15; Ps 80:1; Is 37:16

22 "There I will meet with you; and from above the mercy seat, from between the two
cherubim which are upon the ark of the testimony, I will speak to you about all that I will
give you in commandment for the sons of Israel.

The Table of Showbread

25:23 Ex 37:10-16

23 "You shall make a table of acacia wood, two cubits long and one cubit wide and one
and a half cubits high.

25:24 Ex 25:11

24 "You shall overlay it with pure gold and make a gold border around it.
25 "You shall make for it a rim of a handbreadth around *it;* and you shall make a gold
border for the rim around it.
26 "You shall make four gold rings for it and put rings on the four corners which are on
its four feet.
27 "The rings shall be close to the rim as holders for the poles to carry the table.
28 "You shall make the poles of acacia wood and overlay them with gold, so that with
them the table may be carried.

25:29 Ex 37:16; Num 4:7

29 "You shall make its dishes and its pans and its jars and its bowls with which to pour
drink offerings; you shall make them of pure gold.

25:30 Ex 39:36; 40:23; Lev 24:5-9

30 "You shall set the bread of the Presence on the table before Me at all times.

The Golden Lampstand

25:31 Ex 37:17-24; 1 Kin 7:49; Zech 4:2

31 "Then you shall make a lampstand of pure gold. The lampstand *and* its base and its
shaft are to be made of hammered work; its cups, its bulbs and its flowers shall be *of one
piece* with it.

25:32 Ex 37:18

32 "Six branches shall go out from its sides; three branches of the lampstand from its
one side and three branches of the lampstand from its other side.

25:33 Ex 37:19

33 "Three cups *shall be* shaped like almond *blossoms* in the one branch, a [23]bulb and a
flower, and three cups shaped like almond *blossoms* in the other branch, a bulb and a
flower—so for six branches going out from the lampstand;

22 Lit *propitiatory,* and so through v 22 23 Or *calyx*

THEOPHANIES IN THE SCRIPTURE

At the foot of Mount Sinai, God appeared to the people of Israel in a physical form. This is called a *theophany.* Here are some of the other times God appeared to Bible people.

Verse	*Theophany*
Genesis 16:7	The angel of the Lord appeared to Sarah's maid, Hagar, announcing the birth of Abraham's son, Ishmael
Genesis 18:1–11	The Lord appeared to Abraham, foretelling Isaac's birth
Genesis 22:11–12	The angel of the Lord stopped Abraham from sacrificing Isaac
Exodus 3:2	The angel of the Lord appeared to Moses in flames in a bush
Exodus 14:19	God appeared to Israel in pillars of cloud and fire to guide them through the wilderness
Exodus 33:11	The Lord spoke to Moses face to face
Daniel 3:25	One "like a son of the gods" appeared as the fourth man with Shadrach, Meshach, and Abed-nego in the fiery furnace

("Angel of the LORD" is a reverential way to refer to God in these passages.)

25:17 The cover of the ark of the testimony was called the mercy seat. This is where, between the two golden cherubim (mighty angels), the presence of God would dwell in a cloud above their outstretched wings. The mercy seat was where the highest and most perfect act of atonement would be made when the high priest would enter the holy of holies on the day of atonement to atone for the sins of all the people (30:10).

34 and in the lampstand four cups shaped like almond *blossoms,* its bulbs and its flowers. **25:34**
35 "A bulb shall be under the *first* pair of branches *coming* out of it, and a bulb under Ex 37:20
the *second* pair of branches *coming* out of it, and a bulb under the *third* pair of branches **25:35**
coming out of it, for the six branches coming out of the lampstand. Ex 37:21
36 "Their bulbs and their branches *shall be of one piece* with it; all of it shall be one piece **25:36**
of hammered work of pure gold. Ex 37:22
37 "Then you shall make its lamps seven *in number;* and they shall mount its lamps so as **25:37**
to shed light on the space in front of it. Num 8:2
38 "Its snuffers and their trays *shall be* of pure gold.
39 "It shall be made from a talent of pure gold, with all these utensils.
40 "See that you make *them* after the pattern for them, which was shown to you on the **25:40**
mountain. Heb 8:5; Ex 25:9; 26:30; Num 8:4; Acts 7:44

Curtains of Linen

26 "Moreover you shall make the tabernacle with ten curtains of fine twisted linen **26:1**
and [24]blue and purple and scarlet *material;* you shall make them with cherubim, Ex 36:8-19
the work of a skillful workman.
2 "The length of each curtain shall be twenty-eight cubits, and the width of each curtain four cubits; all the curtains shall have the same measurements.
3 "Five curtains shall be joined to one another, and *the other* five curtains *shall be* joined to one another.
4 "You shall make loops of blue on the edge of the outermost curtain in the *first* set, and likewise you shall make *them* on the edge of the curtain that is outermost in the second set.
5 "You shall make fifty loops in the one curtain, and you shall make fifty loops on the edge of the curtain that is in the second set; the loops shall be opposite each other.
6 "You shall make fifty clasps of gold, and join the curtains to one another with the clasps so that the [25]tabernacle will be a unit.

Curtains of Goats' Hair

7 "Then you shall make curtains of goats' *hair* for a tent over the tabernacle; you shall **26:7**
make eleven curtains in all. Ex 36:14
8 "The length of each curtain *shall be* thirty cubits, and the width of each curtain four cubits; the eleven curtains shall have the same measurements.
9 "You shall join five curtains by themselves and the *other* six curtains by themselves, and you shall double over the sixth curtain at the front of the tent.
10 "You shall make fifty loops on the edge of the curtain that is outermost in the *first* set, and fifty loops on the edge of the curtain *that is outermost in* the second set.
11 "You shall make fifty clasps of [26]bronze, and you shall put the clasps into the loops and join the tent together so that it will be a unit.
12 "The overlapping part that is left over in the curtains of the tent, the half curtain that is left over, shall lap over the back of the tabernacle.
13 "The cubit on one side and the cubit on the other, of what is left over in the length of the curtains of the tent, shall lap over the sides of the tabernacle on one side and on the other, to cover it.
14 "You shall make a covering for the tent of rams' skins dyed red and a covering of **26:14**
porpoise skins above. Ex 36:19

Boards and Sockets

15 "Then you shall make the boards for the tabernacle of acacia wood, standing upright. **26:15**
16 "Ten cubits *shall be* the length of each board and one and a half cubits the width of Ex 36:20-34
each board.
17 "*There shall be* two tenons for each board, fitted to one another; thus you shall do for all the boards of the tabernacle.
18 "You shall make the boards for the tabernacle: twenty boards for the south side.
19 "You shall make forty [27]sockets of silver under the twenty boards, two sockets **26:19**
under one board for its two tenons and two sockets under another board for its two Ex 38:27
tenons;
20 and for the second side of the tabernacle, on the north side, twenty boards,

24 Or *violet* **25** Or *dwelling place,* and so throughout the ch **26** Or *copper* **27** Or *bases*

21 and their forty sockets of silver; two sockets under one board and two sockets under another board.

22 "For the rear of the tabernacle, to the west, you shall make six boards.

23 "You shall make two boards for the corners of the tabernacle at the rear.

24 "They shall be double beneath, and together they shall be complete to its top to the first ring; thus it shall be with both of them: they shall form the two corners.

25 "There shall be eight boards with their sockets of silver, sixteen sockets; two sockets under one board and two sockets under another board.

26:26 Ex 36:31

26 "Then you shall make bars of acacia wood, five for the boards of one side of the tabernacle,

27 and five bars for the boards of the other side of the tabernacle, and five bars for the boards of the side of the tabernacle for the rear *side* to the west.

28 "The middle bar in the center of the boards shall pass through from end to end.

29 "You shall overlay the boards with gold and make their rings of gold *as* holders for the bars; and you shall overlay the bars with gold.

26:30 Ex 25:9, 40; Acts 7:44; Heb 8:5

30 "Then you shall erect the tabernacle according to its plan which you have been shown in the mountain.

The Veil and Screen

26:31 Ex 36:35, 36; 2 Chr 3:14; Matt 27:51; Heb 9:3

31 "You shall make a veil of blue and purple and scarlet *material* and fine twisted linen; it shall be made with cherubim, the work of a skillful workman.

32 "You shall hang it on four pillars of acacia overlaid with gold, their hooks *also being of* gold, on four sockets of silver.

26:33 Ex 25:16; 40:21; Heb 9:2f

33 "You shall hang up the veil under the clasps, and shall bring in the ark of the testimony there within the veil; and the veil shall serve for you as a partition between the holy place and the holy of holies.

26:34 Ex 25:21; 40:20; Lev 16:2

34 "You shall put the mercy seat on the ark of the testimony in the holy of holies.

35 "You shall set the table outside the veil, and the lampstand opposite the table on the side of the tabernacle toward the south; and you shall put the table on the north side.

26:35 Ex 40:22; Ex 40:24

36 "You shall make a screen for the doorway of the tent of blue and purple and scarlet *material* and fine twisted linen, the work of a weaver.

26:36 Ex 36:37

37 "You shall make five pillars of acacia for the screen and overlay them with gold, their hooks *also being of* gold; and you shall cast five sockets of bronze for them.

26:37 Ex 36:38

The Bronze Altar

27:1 Ex 38:1-7

27 "And you shall make the altar of acacia wood, five cubits long and five cubits wide; the altar shall be square, and its height shall be three cubits.

27:2 Ps 118:27

2 "You shall make its horns on its four corners; its horns shall be of one piece with it, and you shall overlay it with bronze.

3 "You shall make its pails for removing its ashes, and its shovels and its basins and its forks and its firepans; you shall make all its utensils of bronze.

4 "You shall make for it a grating of network of bronze, and on the net you shall make four bronze rings at its four corners.

5 "You shall put it beneath, under the ledge of the altar, so that the net will reach halfway up the altar.

6 "You shall make poles for the altar, poles of acacia wood, and overlay them with bronze.

27:7 Num 4:15

7 "Its poles shall be inserted into the rings, so that the poles shall be on the two sides of the altar when it is carried.

27:8 Ex 25:40; 26:30; Acts 7:44; Heb 8:5

8 "You shall make it hollow with planks; as it was shown to you in the mountain, so they shall make *it.*

26:31–33 This veil separated the two sacred rooms in the tabernacle—the holy place and the holy of holies. The priest entered the holy place each day to commune with God and to tend to the altar of incense, the lampstand, and the table with the bread of the Presence. The holy of holies was where God himself dwelt, his presence resting on the mercy seat, which covered the ark of the testimony. Only the high priest could enter the holy of holies. Even he could do so only once a year (on the day of atonement) to make atonement for the sins of the nation as a whole. When Jesus Christ died on the cross, the veil in the temple (which had replaced the tabernacle) tore from top to bottom (Mark 15:38), symbolizing our free access to God because of Jesus' death. No longer did people have to approach God through priests and sacrifices.

27:1 The altar of burnt offering was the first thing the Israelites saw as they entered the tabernacle courtyard. Here sacrifices were constantly made. Its vivid presence constantly reminded the people that they could only come to God by means of the sacrifice. It was the only way their sins could be forgiven and taken away. In Hebrews 10:1–18, Jesus Christ is portrayed as the ultimate sacrifice.

Court of the Tabernacle

9 "You shall make the court of the tabernacle. On the south side *there shall be* hangings for the court of fine twisted linen one hundred cubits long for one side;
10 and its pillars *shall be* twenty, with their twenty sockets of bronze; the hooks of the
pillars and their bands *shall be* of silver.
11 "Likewise for the north side in length *there shall be* hangings one hundred *cubits* long,
and its twenty pillars with their twenty sockets of bronze; the hooks of the pillars and
their bands *shall be* of silver.
12 "*For* the width of the court on the west side *shall be* hangings of fifty cubits *with* their
ten pillars and their ten sockets.
13 "The width of the court on the east side *shall be* fifty cubits.
14 "The hangings for the *one* side *of the gate shall be* fifteen cubits *with* their three pillars and their three sockets.
15 "And for the other side *shall be* hangings of fifteen cubits *with* their three pillars and
their three sockets.
16 "For the gate of the court *there shall be* a screen of twenty cubits, of blue and purple
and scarlet *material* and fine twisted linen, the work of a weaver, *with* their four pillars
and their four sockets.
17 "All the pillars around the court shall be furnished with silver bands *with* their hooks
of silver and their sockets of bronze.
18 "The length of the court *shall be* one hundred cubits, and the width fifty throughout,
and the height five cubits of fine twisted linen, and their sockets of bronze.
19 "All the utensils of the tabernacle *used* in all its service, and all its pegs, and all the
pegs of the court, *shall be* of bronze.
20 "You shall charge the sons of Israel, that they bring you clear oil of beaten olives for
the light, to make a lamp burn continually.
21 "In the tent of meeting, outside the veil which is before the testimony, Aaron and his
sons shall keep it in order from evening to morning before the LORD; *it shall be* a perpetual statute throughout their generations for the sons of Israel.

27:9 Ex 38:9-20

27:20 Ex 35:8, 28; Lev 24:1-4

27:21 Ex 25:22; 29:42; 30:36; Ex 26:31, 33; Ex 30:8; 1 Sam 3:3; 2 Chr 13:11; Ex 28:43; 29:9; Lev 3:17; 16:34; Num 18:23; 19:21; 1 Sam 30:25

Garments of the Priests

28 "Then bring near to yourself Aaron your brother, and his sons with him, from
among the sons of Israel, to minister as priest to Me—Aaron, Nadab and Abihu,
Eleazar and Ithamar, Aaron's sons.
2 "You shall make holy garments for Aaron your brother, for glory and for beauty.
3 "You shall speak to all the skillful persons whom I have endowed with the spirit of
wisdom, that they make Aaron's garments to consecrate him, that he may minister as
priest to Me.
4 "These are the garments which they shall make: a [28]breastpiece and an ephod and a
robe and a tunic of checkered work, a turban and a sash, and they shall make holy garments for Aaron your brother and his sons, that he may minister as priest to Me.
5 "They shall take the gold and the blue and the purple and the scarlet *material* and
the fine linen.
6 "They shall also make the ephod of gold, of blue and purple *and* scarlet *material* and
fine twisted linen, the work of the skillful workman.

28:1 Num 18:7; Ps 99:6; Heb 5:1, 4; Ex 24:1, 9

28:2 Ex 29:5, 29; 31:10; 39:1-31; Lev 8:7-9, 30

28:3 Ex 31:6; 35:25, 31-35; 36:1; Ex 31:3; Is 11:2; 1 Cor 12:7-11; Eph 1:17

28:4 Ex 28:15-43

28:5 Ex 25:3

28:6 Ex 39:2-7; Lev 8:7

28 Or *pouch*

28:1ff God was teaching his people how to worship him. To do so, he needed ministers to oversee the operations of the tabernacle and to help the people maintain their relationship with God. These men were called priests and Levites, and they could only be members of the tribe of Levi. Chapters 28 and 29 give some details about priests. Not only was a priest from the tribe of Levi, but he also was a descendant of Aaron, Israel's first high priest. Priests had more responsibilities than Levites. As high priest, Aaron was in charge of all the priests and Levites. The priests performed the daily sacrifices, maintained the tabernacle, and counseled the people on how to follow God. They were the people's representatives before God and thus were required to live worthy of their office. Jesus is now our high priest (Hebrews 8). Daily sacrifices are no longer required because he sacrificed himself on the cross for our sins. Today ministers no longer sacrifice animals. Instead they lead us in prayer and teach us about both the benefits and the commandments that characterize our new life as Christians.

28:3 The tailors who made Aaron's garments were given wisdom by God in order to do their task. All of us have special skills. God wants to fill us with his Spirit so we will use them for his glory. Think about your special talents and abilities and the ways you could use them for God's work in the world. A talent must be used or it will diminish.

28:6–13 The ephod was a kind of apron elaborately embroidered with two pieces, back and front, joined at the shoulder with a band

7 "It shall have two shoulder pieces joined to its two ends, that it may be joined.
8 "The skillfully woven band, which is on it, shall be like its workmanship, of the same
material: of gold, of blue and purple and scarlet *material* and fine twisted linen.
9 "You shall take two onyx stones and engrave on them the names of the sons of Israel,
10 six of their names on the one stone and the names of the remaining six on the other
stone, according to their birth.
11 "As a jeweler engraves a signet, you shall engrave the two stones according to the
names of the sons of Israel; you shall set them in filigree *settings* of gold.

28:12 Ex 28:29; 39:6f; Ex 39:7; Lev 24:7; Num 31:54; Josh 4:7; 1 Cor 11:24f

12 "You shall put the two stones on the shoulder pieces of the ephod, *as* stones of memorial for the sons of Israel, and Aaron shall bear their names before the LORD on his
two shoulders for a memorial.

28:13 Ex 39:16-18

13 "You shall make filigree *settings* of gold,
14 and two chains of pure gold; you shall make them of twisted cordage work, and you
shall put the corded chains on the filigree *settings*.

28:15 Ex 39:8-21

15 "You shall make a breastpiece of judgment, the work of a skillful workman; like the
work of the ephod you shall make it: of gold, of blue and purple and scarlet *material* and
fine twisted linen you shall make it.
16 "It shall be square *and* folded double, a span in length and a span in width.
17 "You shall mount on it four rows of stones; the first row *shall be* a row of ruby, topaz
and emerald;
18 and the second row a turquoise, a sapphire and a diamond;
19 and the third row a jacinth, an agate and an amethyst;
20 and the fourth row a beryl and an onyx and a jasper; they shall be set in gold filigree.

28:21 Rev 7:4-8; 21:12

21 "The stones shall be according to the names of the sons of Israel: twelve, according
to their names; they shall be *like* the engravings of a seal, each according to his name for
the twelve tribes.
22 "You shall make on the breastpiece chains of twisted cordage work in pure gold.
23 "You shall make on the breastpiece two rings of gold, and shall put the two rings on
the two ends of the breastpiece.
24 "You shall put the two cords of gold on the two rings at the ends of the breastpiece.
25 "You shall put the *other* two ends of the two cords on the two filigree *settings*, and put
them on the shoulder pieces of the ephod, at the front of it.
26 "You shall make two rings of gold and shall place them on the two ends of the breastpiece, on the edge of it, which is toward the inner side of the ephod.
27 "You shall make two rings of gold and put them on the bottom of the two shoulder
pieces of the ephod, on the front of it close to the place where it is joined, above the
skillfully woven band of the ephod.
28 "They shall bind the breastpiece by its rings to the rings of the ephod with a blue
cord, so that it will be on the skillfully woven band of the ephod, and that the breastpiece
will not come loose from the ephod.
29 "Aaron shall carry the names of the sons of Israel in the breastpiece of judgment over
his heart when he enters the holy place, for a memorial before the LORD continually.

28:30 Lev 8:8; Num 27:21; Deut 33:8; Ezra 2:63; Neh 7:65

30 "You shall put in the breastpiece of judgment the [29]Urim and the Thummim,
and they shall be over Aaron's heart when he goes in before the LORD; and Aaron shall
carry the judgment of the sons of Israel over his heart before the LORD continually.

28:31 Ex 39:22-26

31 "You shall make the robe of the ephod all of blue.
32 "There shall be an opening at its top in the middle of it; around its opening there
shall be a binding of woven work, as like the opening of a coat of mail, so that it will not
be torn.
33 "You shall make on its hem pomegranates of blue and purple and scarlet *material*,
all around on its hem, and bells of gold between them all around:
34 a golden bell and a pomegranate, a golden bell and a pomegranate, all around on
the hem of the robe.

29 I.e. lights and perfections

---

at the waist. On each shoulder strap was a stone with six of the 12 tribes of Israel engraved on it. The priest symbolically carried the burden of the whole nation on his shoulders as he represented them before God.

28:30 The Urim and the Thummim were used by the priest to make decisions. These names mean "Curses" and "Perfections" and refer to the nature of God whose will they revealed. They were kept in a pouch and taken out or shaken out to get either a yes or no decision.

35 "It shall be on Aaron when he ministers; and its tinkling shall be heard when he enters and leaves the holy place before the LORD, so that he will not die.

36 "You shall also make a plate of pure gold and shall engrave on it, like the engravings of a seal, 'Holy to the LORD.'

37 "You shall fasten it on a blue cord, and it shall be on the turban; it shall be at the front of the turban.

38 "It shall be on Aaron's forehead, and Aaron shall take away the iniquity of the holy things which the sons of Israel consecrate, with regard to all their holy gifts; and it shall always be on his forehead, that they may be accepted before the LORD.

39 "You shall weave the tunic of checkered work of fine linen, and shall make a turban of fine linen, and you shall make a sash, the work of a weaver.

40 "For Aaron's sons you shall make tunics; you shall also make sashes for them, and you shall make caps for them, for glory and for beauty.

41 "You shall put them on Aaron your brother and on his sons with him; and you shall anoint them and ordain them and consecrate them, that they may serve Me as priests.

42 "You shall make for them linen breeches to cover *their* bare flesh; they shall reach from the loins even to the thighs.

43 "They shall be on Aaron and on his sons when they enter the tent of meeting, or when they approach the altar to minister in the holy place, so that they do not incur guilt and die. It *shall be* a statute forever to him and to his descendants after him.

Consecration of the Priests

29 "Now this is what you shall do to them to consecrate them to minister as priests to Me: take one young bull and two rams without blemish,

2 and unleavened bread and unleavened cakes mixed with oil, and unleavened wafers spread with oil; you shall make them of fine wheat flour.

3 "You shall put them in one basket, and present them in the basket along with the bull and the two rams.

4 "Then you shall bring Aaron and his sons to the doorway of the tent of meeting and wash them with water.

5 "You shall take the garments, and put on Aaron the tunic and the robe of the ephod and the ephod and the breastpiece, and gird him with the skillfully woven band of the ephod;

6 and you shall set the turban on his head and put the holy crown on the turban.

7 "Then you shall take the anointing oil and pour it on his head and anoint him.

8 "You shall bring his sons and put tunics on them.

9 "You shall gird them with sashes, Aaron and his sons, and bind caps on them, and they shall have the priesthood by a perpetual statute. So you shall ordain Aaron and his sons.

The Sacrifices

10 "Then you shall bring the bull before the tent of meeting, and Aaron and his sons shall lay their hands on the head of the bull.

11 "You shall slaughter the bull before the LORD at the doorway of the tent of meeting.

12 "You shall take some of the blood of the bull and put *it* on the horns of the altar with your finger; and you shall pour out all the blood at the base of the altar.

13 "You shall take all the fat that covers the entrails and the lobe of the liver, and the two kidneys and the fat that is on them, and offer them up in smoke on the altar.

28:36 Ex 39:30, 31; Lev 8:9; Zech 14:20
28:38 Lev 10:17; 22:16; Num 18:1; Lev 1:4; 22:27; 23:11; Is 56:7
28:39 Ex 39:27-29
28:40 Ex 28:4; 39:27, 41; Ex 29:9; 39:28; Lev 8:13; Ezek 44:18
28:41 Ex 29:7, 9; 30:30; 40:15; Lev 8:1-36; 10:7
28:42 Ex 39:28; Lev 6:10; 16:4; Ezek 44:18
28:43 Ex 20:26; Ex 27:21
29:1 Lev 8:1-34
29:2 Lev 2:4; 6:19-23
29:4 Ex 40:12; Lev 8:6
29:5 Ex 28:39; Lev 8:7; Ex 28:31; Ex 28:6; Ex 28:15; Ex 28:8
29:6 Ex 28:4, 39; Ex 28:36, 37; Lev 8:9
29:7 Ex 30:25; Lev 8:12; 21:10; Num 35:25; Ps 133:2
29:8 Ex 28:39, 40; Lev 8:13
29:9 Ex 28:40; Ex 40:15; Num 3:10; 18:7; 25:13; Deut 18:5; Ex 28:41; Lev 8:1-36
29:10 Lev 1:4; 8:14
29:12 Lev 8:15; Ex 27:2; 30:2
29:13 Lev 3:3, 4

29:1ff Why did God set up the priesthood? God had originally intended that his chosen people be a "kingdom of priests" with both the nation as a whole and each individual dealing directly with God. But the people's sin prevented this from happening because a sinful person is not worthy to approach a perfect God. God then appointed priests from the tribe of Levi and set up the system of sacrifices to help the people approach him. He promised to forgive the people's sins if they would offer certain sacrifices administered by the priests on behalf of the people. Through these priests and their work, God wished to prepare all people for the coming of Jesus Christ, who would once again offer a direct relationship with God for anyone who would come to him. But until Christ came, the priests were the people's representatives before God. Through this Old Testament system, we can better understand the significance of what Christ did for us (see Hebrews 10:1–14).

29:10–41 Why were there such detailed rituals in connection with these sacrifices? Partly, it was for quality control. A centralized, standardized form of worship prevented problems of belief which could arise from individuals creating their own worship. Also, it differentiated the Hebrews from the pagan Canaanites they would meet in the promised land. By closely following God's instructions, the Hebrews could not possibly join the Canaanites in their immoral religious practices. Finally, it showed Israel that God was serious about his relationship with them.

14"But the flesh of the bull and its hide and its refuse, you shall burn with fire outside
the camp; it is a sin offering.

29:14 Lev 4:11, 12, 21; Heb 13:11

15"You shall also take the one ram, and Aaron and his sons shall lay their hands on the
head of the ram;

29:15 Lev 8:18

16 and you shall slaughter the ram and shall take its blood and sprinkle it around on
the altar.
17"Then you shall cut the ram into its pieces, and wash its entrails and its legs, and put
them with its pieces and its head.
18"You shall offer up in smoke the whole ram on the altar; it is a burnt offering to the
LORD: it is a soothing aroma, an offering by fire to the LORD.

29:18 Gen 8:21; Ex 29:25

19"Then you shall take the other ram, and Aaron and his sons shall lay their hands on
the head of the ram.

29:19 Lev 8:22f

20"You shall slaughter the ram, and take some of its blood and put *it* on the lobe of
Aaron's right ear and on the lobes of his sons' right ears and on the thumbs of their right
hands and on the big toes of their right feet, and sprinkle the *rest of the* blood around on
the altar.
21"Then you shall take some of the blood that is on the altar and some of the anointing
oil, and sprinkle *it* on Aaron and on his garments and on his sons and on his sons' garments with him; so he and his garments shall be consecrated, as well as his sons and his
sons' garments with him.

29:21 Ex 30:25, 31; Lev 8:30

22"You shall also take the fat from the ram and the fat tail, and the fat that covers the
entrails and the lobe of the liver, and the two kidneys and the fat that is on them and the
right thigh (for it is a ram of ordination),
23 and one cake of bread and one cake of bread *mixed with* oil and one wafer from the
basket of unleavened bread which is *set* before the LORD;

29:23 Lev 8:26

24 and you shall put all these in the hands of Aaron and in the hands of his sons, and
shall wave them as a wave offering before the LORD.
25"You shall take them from their hands, and offer them up in smoke on the altar on the
burnt offering for a soothing aroma before the LORD; it is an offering by fire to the LORD.

29:25 Lev 8:28

26"Then you shall take the breast of Aaron's ram of ordination, and wave it as a wave
offering before the LORD; and it shall be your portion.

29:26 Lev 7:31, 34; 8:29

27"You shall consecrate the breast of the wave offering and the thigh of the heave offering which was waved and which was offered from the ram of ordination, from the one
which was for Aaron and from the one which was for his sons.
28"It shall be for Aaron and his sons as *their* portion forever from the sons of Israel, for
it is a heave offering; and it shall be a heave offering from the sons of Israel from the
sacrifices of their peace offerings, *even* their heave offering to the LORD.
29"The holy garments of Aaron shall be for his sons after him, that in them they may
be anointed and ordained.

29:29 Num 20:26, 28

30"For seven days the one of his sons who is priest in his stead shall put them on when
he enters the tent of meeting to minister in the holy place.

Food of the Priests

31"You shall take the ram of ordination and boil its flesh in a holy place.

29:31 Lev 8:31

32"Aaron and his sons shall eat the flesh of the ram and the bread that is in the basket,
at the doorway of the tent of meeting.
33"Thus they shall eat those things by which atonement was made at their ordination
and consecration; but a layman shall not eat *them,* because they are holy.

29:33 Lev 10:14; Lev 22:10, 13

34"If any of the flesh of ordination or any of the bread remains until morning, then you
shall burn the remainder with fire; it shall not be eaten, because it is holy.

29:34 Ex 12:10; 23:18; 34:25; Lev 8:32

35"Thus you shall do to Aaron and to his sons, according to all that I have commanded
you; you shall ordain them through seven days.

29:35 Lev 8:33

36"Each day you shall offer a bull as a sin offering for atonement, and you shall purify
the altar when you make atonement for it, and you shall anoint it to consecrate it.

29:36 Heb 10:11; Ex 40:10

37"For seven days you shall make atonement for the altar and consecrate it; then the
altar shall be most holy, *and* whatever touches the altar shall be holy.

29:37 Ex 30:28f

29:37 Notice the overwhelming emphasis on the holiness of God. The priests, the clothes, the tabernacle, and the sacrifice had to be clean and consecrated, prepared to meet God. In contrast, today we tend to take God for granted, rushing into worship and treating him with almost casual disregard. But we worship the almighty Creator and Sustainer of the universe. Remember that profound truth when you pray or worship, and come before him with reverence and repentance.

38 "Now this is what you shall offer on the altar: two one year old lambs each day, con- 29:38
tinuously. Num 28:3-31; 29:6-38
39 "The one lamb you shall offer in the morning and the other lamb you shall offer at
twilight; 29:39
40 and there *shall be* one-tenth *of an ephah* of fine flour mixed with one-fourth of a hin Ezek 46:13-15
of beaten oil, and one-fourth of a hin of wine for a drink offering with one lamb.
41 "The other lamb you shall offer at twilight, and shall offer with it the same grain offering and the same drink offering as in the morning, for a soothing aroma, an offering
by fire to the LORD.
42 "It shall be a continual burnt offering throughout your generations at the doorway 29:42
of the tent of meeting before the LORD, where I will meet with you, to speak to you there. Ex 25:22; Num 17:4
43 "I will meet there with the sons of Israel, and it shall be consecrated by My glory. 29:45
44 "I will consecrate the tent of meeting and the altar; I will also consecrate Aaron and Ex 25:8; Lev 26:12; Num 5:3; Deut
his sons to minister as priests to Me. 12:11; Zech 2:10;
45 "I will dwell among the sons of Israel and will be their God. 2 Cor 6:16; Rev 21:3
46 "They shall know that I am the LORD their God who brought them out of the land of 29:46
Egypt, that I might dwell among them; I am the LORD their God. Ex 20:2

The Altar of Incense

30 "Moreover, you shall make an altar as a place for burning incense; you shall make 30:1
it of acacia wood. Ex 37:25-29
2 "Its length *shall be* a cubit, and its width a cubit, it shall be square, and its height *shall*
be two cubits; its horns *shall be* of one piece with it.
3 "You shall overlay it with pure gold, its top and its sides all around, and its horns;
and you shall make a gold molding all around for it.
4 "You shall make two gold rings for it under its molding; you shall make *them* on
its two side walls—on opposite sides—and they shall be holders for poles with which to
carry it.
5 "You shall make the poles of acacia wood and overlay them with gold.
6 "You shall put this altar in front of the veil that is near the ark of the testimony, in 30:6
front of the mercy seat that is over *the ark of* the testimony, where I will meet with you. Ex 25:21f
7 "Aaron shall burn fragrant incense on it; he shall burn it every morning when he trims
the lamps.
8 "When Aaron trims the lamps at twilight, he shall burn incense. *There shall be* perpetual incense before the LORD throughout your generations.
9 "You shall not offer any strange incense on this altar, or burnt offering or meal offering; and you shall not pour out a drink offering on it.
10 "Aaron shall make atonement on its horns once a year; he shall make atonement on 30:10
it with the blood of the sin offering of atonement once a year throughout your genera- Lev 16:18
tions. It is most holy to the LORD."
11 The LORD also spoke to Moses, saying,
12 "When you take a census of the sons of Israel to number them, then each one of them 30:12
shall give a ransom for himself to the LORD, when you number them, so that there will Ex 38:25, 26; Num 1:2; 26:2; Num
be no plague among them when you number them. 31:50
13 "This is what everyone who is numbered shall give: half a shekel according to the 30:13
shekel of the sanctuary (the shekel is twenty gerahs), half a shekel as a contribution to Lev 27:25; Num
the LORD. 3:47; Ezek 45:12
14 "Everyone who is numbered, from twenty years old and over, shall give the contribution to the LORD.
15 "The rich shall not pay more and the poor shall not pay less than the half shekel,
when you give the contribution to the LORD to make atonement for yourselves.

29:45–46 God's action in bringing the Israelites out of Egypt showed his great desire to be with them and protect them. Throughout the Bible, God shows that he is not an absentee landlord. He wants to live among us, even in our hearts. Don't exclude God from your life. Allow him to be your God as you obey his Word and communicate with him in prayer. Let him be your resident landlord.

30:10 This once-a-year ceremony was called the day of atonement. On this day a sacrifice was made for the sins of the entire Israelite nation. This was the only day the high priest could enter the holy of holies, the innermost room of the tabernacle. Here he asked God to forgive the people. The day of atonement served as a reminder that the daily, weekly, and monthly sacrifices could cover sins only temporarily. It pointed toward Jesus Christ, the perfect atonement, who could remove sins forever.

30:11–16 The ransom was like a census tax. It continued the principle that all the people belonged to God and therefore needed to be redeemed by a sacrifice. Whenever a census took place,

16 "You shall take the atonement money from the sons of Israel and shall give it for the service of the tent of meeting, that it may be a memorial for the sons of Israel before the LORD, to make atonement for yourselves."
17 The LORD spoke to Moses, saying,
30:18 Ex 38:8; Ex 40:30
18 "You shall also make a laver of bronze, with its base of bronze, for washing; and you shall put it between the tent of meeting and the altar, and you shall put water in it.
30:19 Ex 40:31f; Is 52:11
19 "Aaron and his sons shall wash their hands and their feet from it;
20 when they enter the tent of meeting, they shall wash with water, so that they will not die; or when they approach the altar to minister, by offering up in smoke a fire *sacrifice* to the LORD.
30:21 Ex 28:43
21 "So they shall wash their hands and their feet, so that they will not die; and it shall be a perpetual statute for them, for Aaron and his descendants throughout their generations."

The Anointing Oil

22 Moreover, the LORD spoke to Moses, saying,
23 "Take also for yourself the finest of spices: of flowing myrrh five hundred *shekels,* and of fragrant cinnamon half as much, two hundred and fifty, and of fragrant cane two hundred and fifty,
24 and of cassia five hundred, according to the shekel of the sanctuary, and of olive oil a hin.
30:25 Ex 37:29; 40:9; Lev 8:10
25 "You shall make of these a holy anointing oil, a perfume mixture, the work of a perfumer; it shall be a holy anointing oil.
30:26 Ex 40:9; Lev 8:10; Num 7:1
26 "With it you shall anoint the tent of meeting and the ark of the testimony,
27 and the table and all its utensils, and the lampstand and its utensils, and the altar of incense,
28 and the altar of burnt offering and all its utensils, and the laver and its stand.
29 "You shall also consecrate them, that they may be most holy; whatever touches them shall be holy.
30:30 Ex 29:7; Lev 8:12
30 "You shall anoint Aaron and his sons, and consecrate them, that they may minister as priests to Me.
31 "You shall speak to the sons of Israel, saying, 'This shall be a holy anointing oil to Me throughout your generations.
30:32 Ex 30:25, 37
32 'It shall not be poured on anyone's body, nor shall you make *any* like it in the same proportions; it is holy, *and* it shall be holy to you.
30:33 Ex 30:38; Gen 17:14; Ex 12:15; Lev 7:20f
33 'Whoever shall mix *any* like it or whoever puts any of it on a layman shall be cut off from his people.' "

The Incense

34 Then the LORD said to Moses, "Take for yourself spices, stacte and onycha and galbanum, spices with pure frankincense; there shall be an equal part of each.
35 "With it you shall make incense, a perfume, the work of a perfumer, salted, pure, *and* holy.
30:36 Ex 29:42
36 "You shall beat some of it very fine, and put part of it before the testimony in the tent of meeting where I will meet with you; it shall be most holy to you.
30:37 Ex 30:32
37 "The incense which you shall make, you shall not make in the same proportions for yourselves; it shall be holy to you for the LORD.
30:38 Ex 30:33
38 "Whoever shall make *any* like it, to use as perfume, shall be cut off from his people."

---

everyone, both rich and poor, was required to pay a ransom. God does not discriminate between people (see Acts 10:34; Galatians 3:28). All of us need mercy and forgiveness because of our sinful thoughts and actions. There is no way the rich person can buy off God, and no way the poor can avoid paying. God's demand is that all of us come humbly before him to be forgiven and brought into his family.

30:34–38 The Israelites often burned incense, but this holy incense could be burned only in the tabernacle. Here God gave the recipe for this special incense. The sweet-smelling incense was burned in shallow dishes called censers (or firepans) and was used to show honor and reverence to God. It was like prayer lifting up to God. It was also a vital part of the sacred ceremony on the day of atonement, when the high priest carried his smoking censer into the holy of holies. This incense, like the sacred anointing oil, was so holy that the people were strictly forbidden to copy it for personal use.

The Skilled Craftsmen

31 Now the LORD spoke to Moses, saying,
2 "See, I have called by name Bezalel, the son of Uri, the son of Hur, of the tribe
of Judah.
3 "I have filled him with the Spirit of God in wisdom, in understanding, in knowledge,
and in all *kinds of* craftsmanship,
4 to make artistic designs for work in gold, in silver, and in bronze,
5 and in the cutting of stones for settings, and in the carving of wood, that he may
work in all *kinds of* craftsmanship.
6 "And behold, I Myself have appointed with him Oholiab, the son of Ahisamach, of
the tribe of Dan; and in the hearts of all who are skillful I have put skill, that they may
make all that I have commanded you:
7 the tent of meeting, and the ark of testimony, and the mercy seat upon it, and all
the furniture of the tent,
8 the table also and its utensils, and the pure *gold* lampstand with all its utensils, and
the altar of incense,
9 the altar of burnt offering also with all its utensils, and the laver and its stand,
10 the woven garments as well, and the holy garments for Aaron the priest, and the
garments of his sons, *with which* to carry on their priesthood;
11 the anointing oil also, and the fragrant incense for the holy place, they are to make
them according to all that I have commanded you."

31:1 Ex 35:30-36:1
31:2 1 Chr 2:20
31:3 Ex 35:31; 1 Kin 7:14; 1 Cor 12:4-8
31:6 Ex 35:34
31:7 Ex 36:8-38; Ex 37:1-5; Ex 37:6-9
31:8 Ex 37:10-16; Ex 37:17-24; Lev 24:4; Ex 37:25-29
31:9 Ex 38:1-7; Ex 38:8
31:10 Ex 39:1
31:11 Ex 30:23-32; Ex 30:34-38

The Sign of the Sabbath

12 The LORD spoke to Moses, saying,
13 "But as for you, speak to the sons of Israel, saying, 'You shall surely observe My sabbaths; for *this* is a sign between Me and you throughout your generations, that you may
know that I am the LORD who sanctifies you.
14 'Therefore you are to observe the sabbath, for it is holy to you. Everyone who profanes it shall surely be put to death; for whoever does any work on it, that person shall
be cut off from among his people.
15 'For six days work may be done, but on the seventh day there is a sabbath of complete rest, holy to the LORD; whoever does any work on the sabbath day shall surely be
put to death.
16 'So the sons of Israel shall observe the sabbath, to celebrate the sabbath throughout
their generations as a perpetual covenant.'
17 "It is a sign between Me and the sons of Israel forever; for in six days the LORD made
heaven and earth, but on the seventh day He ceased *from labor,* and was refreshed."
18 When He had finished speaking with him upon Mount Sinai, He gave Moses the
two tablets of the testimony, tablets of stone, written by the finger of God.

31:13 Ex 20:8; Ex 31:17; Ezek 20:12, 20
31:14 Ex 31:15; 35:2; Num 15:32, 35; John 7:23
31:15 Ex 20:9-11; 23:12; 34:21; 35:2; Lev 23:3; Deut 5:12-14; Gen 2:2f; Ex 16:23; 20:8; 35:2, 3; Ex 31:14
31:17 Ex 31:13; Ezek 20:12; Gen 1:31; 2:2, 3; Ex 20:11
31:18 Ex 24:12; 34:29; Deut 4:13; 5:22; 9:10f; Ex 32:15, 16; 34:1, 28; Deut 9:10

3. Breaking the law

The Golden Calf

32 Now when the people saw that Moses delayed to come down from the mountain,
the people assembled about Aaron and said to him, "Come, make us a god who
will go before us; as for this Moses, the man who brought us up from the land of Egypt,
we do not know what has become of him."

32:1 Ex 24:18; Deut 9:11, 12; Acts 7:40; Ex 14:11

31:1–11 God regards all the skills of his people, not merely those with theological or ministerial abilities. Our tendency is to regard only those who are up front and in leadership roles. God gave Bezalel and Oholiab Spirit-filled abilities in artistic craftsmanship. Take notice of all the abilities God gives his people. Don't diminish your skills if they are not like Moses' and Aaron's.

31:12–17 The Sabbath had two purposes: It was a time *to rest* and a time *to remember* what God had done. We need rest. Without time out from the bustle, life loses its meaning. In our day, as in Moses' day, taking time out is not easy. But God reminds us that without Sabbaths we will forget the purpose for all of our activity and lose the balance crucial to a faithful life. Make sure your Sabbath provides a time of both refreshment and remembrance of God.

31:18 The two tablets of the testimony contained the Ten Commandments. These were not the only code of laws in the ancient world. Other law codes had come into existence when cities or nations decided that there must be standards of judgment, ways to correct specific wrongs. But God's laws for Israel were unique in that: (1) they alleviated the harsh judgments typical of the day; (2) they were egalitarian—the poor and the powerful received the same punishment; (3) they did not separate religious and social law. All law rested on God's authority.

32:1–10 Idols again! Even though Israel had seen the invisible God in action, they still wanted the familiar gods they could see and shape into whatever image they desired. How much like them we are! Our great temptation is still to shape God to our liking, to make him convenient to obey or ignore. God responds in great

32:2 Ex 35:22

2 Aaron said to them, "Tear off the gold rings which are in the ears of your wives,
your sons, and your daughters, and bring *them* to me."
3 Then all the people tore off the gold rings which were in their ears and brought *them*
to Aaron.

32:4 Deut 9:16; Neh 9:18; Ps 106:19; Acts 7:41

4 He took *this* from their hand, and fashioned it with a graving tool and made it into
a molten calf; and they said, "This is your god, O Israel, who brought you up from the
land of Egypt."

32:6 Acts 7:41 1 Cor 10:7; Ex 32:17-19; Num 25:2

5 Now when Aaron saw *this,* he built an altar before it; and Aaron made a proclamation and said, "Tomorrow *shall be* a feast to the LORD."
6 So the next day they rose early and offered burnt offerings, and brought peace offerings; and the people sat down to eat and to drink, and rose up to play.

32:7 Ex 32:4, 11; Deut 9:12; Gen 6:11f

7 Then the LORD spoke to Moses, "Go down at once, for your people, whom you
brought up from the land of Egypt, have corrupted *themselves.*

32:8 Ex 20:3, 4, 23; Ex 22:20; 34:15; Deut 32:17; 1 Kin 12:28

8 "They have quickly turned aside from the way which I commanded them. They have
made for themselves a molten calf, and have worshiped it and have sacrificed to it and
said, 'This is your god, O Israel, who brought you up from the land of Egypt!' "

32:9 Num 14:11-20; Ex 33:3, 5; 34:9; Is 48:4; Acts 7:51

9 The LORD said to Moses, "I have seen this people, and behold, they are an obstinate people.

32:10 Deut 9:14; Num 14:12

10 "Now then let Me alone, that My anger may burn against them and that I may destroy them; and I will make of you a great nation."

Moses' Entreaty

32:11 Deut 9:18, 26

11 Then Moses entreated the LORD his God, and said, "O LORD, why does Your anger burn against Your people whom You have brought out from the land of Egypt with
great power and with a mighty hand?

32:12 Num 14:13-19; Deut 9:28; Josh 7:9

12 "Why should the Egyptians speak, saying, 'With evil *intent* He brought them out to
kill them in the mountains and to destroy them from the face of the earth'? Turn from
Your burning anger and change Your mind about *doing* harm to Your people.

32:13 Gen 22:16-18; Heb 6:13; Gen 15:5; 26:4; Gen 12:7; 13:15; 15:18; 17:8; 35:12; Ex 13:5, 11; 33:1

13 "Remember Abraham, Isaac, and Israel, Your servants to whom You swore by Yourself, and said to them, 'I will multiply your descendants as the stars of the heavens, and
all this land of which I have spoken I will give to your descendants, and they shall inherit
it forever.' "

32:14 Ps 106:45

14 So the LORD changed His mind about the harm which He said He would do to His
people.

32:15 Deut 9:15; Ex 31:18

15 Then Moses turned and went down from the mountain with the two tablets of the
testimony in his hand, tablets which were written on both sides; they were written on
one *side* and the other.
16 The tablets were God's work, and the writing was God's writing engraved on the
tablets.
17 Now when Joshua heard the sound of the people as they shouted, he said to Moses,
"There is a sound of war in the camp."

---

anger when his mercy is trampled on. The gods we create blind us to the love our loving God wants to shower on us. God cannot work in us when we elevate anyone or anything above him. What false gods in your life are preventing the true God from living in you?

32:4–5 Two popular Egyptian gods, Hapi (Apis) and Hathor, were thought of as a bull and a heifer. The Canaanites around them worshiped Baal, thought of as a bull. Baal was their sacred symbol of power and fertility and was closely connected to immoral sexual practices. No doubt the Israelites, fresh from Egypt, found it quite natural to make a golden calf to represent the God that had just delivered them from their oppressors. They were weary of a god without a face. But in doing so, they were ignoring the command he had just given them: "You shall not make for yourself an idol, or any likeness of what is in heaven above or on the earth beneath or in the water under the earth" (20:4). They may even have thought they were worshiping God. Their apparent sincerity was no substitute for obedience or excuse for disobedience.

Even if we do not make idols, we are often guilty of trying to make God in our image, molding him to fit our expectations, desires, and circumstances. When we do this, we end up worshiping ourselves rather than the God who created us—and self-worship, today as in the Israelites' time, leads to all kinds of immorality. What is your favorite image of God? Is it Biblical? Is it adequate? Do you need to destroy it in order to worship the immeasurably powerful God who delivered you from bondage to sin?

32:9–14 God was ready to destroy the whole nation because of their sin. But Moses pleaded for mercy, and God spared them. This is one of the countless examples in the Bible of God's mercy. Although we deserve his anger, he is willing to forgive and restore us to himself. We can receive God's forgiveness from sin by asking him. Like Moses, we can pray that he will forgive others and use us to bring them the message of his mercy.

32:14 How could God relent? God did not change his mind in the same way that a parent decides not to discipline a child. Instead, God changed his behavior to remain consistent with his nature. When God first wanted to destroy the people, he was acting consistently with his justice. When Moses interceded for the people, God relented in order to act consistently with his mercy. God had often told the people that if they changed their ways, he would not condemn them. They changed, and God did as he promised.

18 But he said,
"It is not the sound of the cry of triumph,
Nor is it the sound of the cry of defeat;
But the sound of singing I hear."

Moses' Anger

19 It came about, as soon as Moses came near the camp, that he saw the calf and *the* dancing; and Moses' anger burned, and he threw the tablets from his hands and shattered them at the foot of the mountain.

20 He took the calf which they had made and burned *it* with fire, and ground it to powder, and scattered it over the surface of the water and made the sons of Israel drink *it.*

21 Then Moses said to Aaron, "What did this people do to you, that you have brought *such* great sin upon them?"

22 Aaron said, "Do not let the anger of my lord burn; you know the people yourself, that they are prone to evil.

23 "For they said to me, 'Make a god for us who will go before us; for this Moses, the man who brought us up from the land of Egypt, we do not know what has become of him.'

24 "I said to them, 'Whoever has any gold, let them tear it off.' So they gave *it* to me, and I threw it into the fire, and out came this calf."

25 Now when Moses saw that the people were out of control—for Aaron had let them get out of control to be a derision among their enemies—

26 then Moses stood in the gate of the camp, and said, "Whoever is for the LORD, *come* to me!" And all the sons of Levi gathered together to him.

27 He said to them, "Thus says the LORD, the God of Israel, 'Every man *of you* put his sword upon his thigh, and go back and forth from gate to gate in the camp, and kill every man his brother, and every man his friend, and every man his neighbor.' "

28 So the sons of Levi did as Moses instructed, and about three thousand men of the people fell that day.

29 Then Moses said, "Dedicate yourselves today to the LORD—for every man has been against his son and against his brother—in order that He may bestow a blessing upon you today."

30 On the next day Moses said to the people, "You yourselves have committed a great sin; and now I am going up to the LORD, perhaps I can make atonement for your sin."

31 Then Moses returned to the LORD, and said, "Alas, this people has committed a great sin, and they have made a god of gold for themselves.

32 "But now, if You will, forgive their sin—and if not, please blot me out from Your book which You have written!"

33 The LORD said to Moses, "Whoever has sinned against Me, I will blot him out of My book.

34 "But go now, lead the people where I told you. Behold, My angel shall go before you; nevertheless in the day when I punish, I will punish them for their sin."

35 Then the LORD smote the people, because of what they did with the calf which Aaron had made.

The Journey Resumed

33 Then the LORD spoke to Moses, "Depart, go up from here, you and the people whom you have brought up from the land of Egypt, to the land of which I swore to Abraham, Isaac, and Jacob, saying, 'To your descendants I will give it.'

2 "I will send an angel before you and I will drive out the Canaanite, the Amorite, the Hittite, the Perizzite, the Hivite and the Jebusite.

32:19 Ex 32:6; Deut 9:16; Deut 9:17
32:20 Deut 9:21
32:22 Deut 9:24
32:23 Ex 32:1-4
32:24 Ex 32:4
32:25 1 Kin 12:28-30; 14:16
32:28 Num 25:7-13; Deut 33:9
32:30 1 Sam 12:20, 23; Num 25:13
32:31 Ex 20:23
32:32 Ps 69:28; Is 4:3; Dan 12:1; Mal 3:16, 17; Phil 4:3; Rev 3:5; 21:27
32:33 Ex 17:14; Deut 29:20; Ps 9:5; Rev 3:5
32:34 Ex 3:17; Ex 23:20; Deut 32:35; Rom 2:5, 6; Ps 99:8
32:35 Ex 32:28; Ex 32:4, 24
33:1 Ex 32:13; Gen 26:1-3; Gen 28:10; Gen 12:7
33:2 Ex 32:34; Ex 23:27-31; Josh 24:11

32:19–20 Overwhelmed by the actual sight of the blatant idolatry and revelry, Moses broke the tablets containing the commandments which had already been broken in the hearts and actions of the people. There is a place for righteous anger. However angry Moses might have been, God was angrier still—he wanted to kill all the people. Anger at sin is a sign of spiritual vitality. Don't squelch this kind of anger. But when you are justifiably angry at sin, be careful not to do anything that you will regret later.

32:21–24 Aaron's decision nearly cost him his life. His absurd excuse shows the spiritual decline in his leadership and in the people. Those who function as spokespersons and assistants need to be doubly sure their theology and morality are in tune with God so they will not be influenced by pressure from people. For more information on Aaron, see his Profile in chapter 33.

33:3 Ex 3:8, 17; Ex 32:9; 33:5; Ex 32:10
3 "*Go up* to a land flowing with milk and honey; for I will not go up in your midst,
because you are an obstinate people, and I might destroy you on the way."
33:4 Num 14:1, 39
4 When the people heard this sad word, they went into mourning, and none of them
put on his ornaments.
33:5 Ex 33:3
5 For the LORD had said to Moses, "Say to the sons of Israel, 'You are an obstinate
people; should I go up in your midst for one moment, I would destroy you. Now therefore, put off your ornaments from you, that I may know what I shall do with you.' "
6 So the sons of Israel stripped themselves of their ornaments, from Mount Horeb
onward.
33:7 Ex 18:7, 12-16; Ex 29:42f
7 Now Moses used to take the tent and pitch it outside the camp, a good distance
from the camp, and he called it the tent of meeting. And everyone who sought the LORD
would go out to the tent of meeting which was outside the camp.
8 And it came about, whenever Moses went out to the tent, that all the people would
arise and stand, each at the entrance of his tent, and gaze after Moses until he entered
the tent.
33:9 Ex 13:21; Ps 99:7
9 Whenever Moses entered the tent, the pillar of cloud would descend and stand at
the entrance of the tent; and the LORD would speak with Moses.
33:11 Num 12:8; Deut 34:10; Ex 24:13
10 When all the people saw the pillar of cloud standing at the entrance of the tent, all
the people would arise and worship, each at the entrance of his tent.
11 Thus the LORD used to speak to Moses face to face, just as a man speaks to his friend.

AARON

Effective teamwork happens when each team member uses his or her special skills. Ideally, each member's strengths will contribute something important to the team effort. In this way, members make up for one another's weaknesses. Aaron made a good team with Moses. He provided Moses with one skill Moses lacked—effective public speaking. But while Aaron was necessary to Moses, he needed Moses as well. Without a guide, Aaron had little direction of his own. There was never any doubt as to who God's chosen and trained leader was. The pliability that made Aaron a good follower made him a weak leader. His major failures were caused by his inability to stand alone. His yielding to public pressure and making an idol was a good example of this weakness.

Most of us have more of the follower than the leader in us. We may even be good followers, following a good leader. But no leader is perfect, and no human deserves our complete allegiance. Only God deserves our complete loyalty and obedience. We need to be effective team members in using the skills and abilities God has given us. But if the team or the leader goes against God's Word, we must be willing to stand alone.

Strengths and accomplishments:
- First high priest of God in Israel
- Effective communicator; Moses' mouthpiece

Weaknesses and mistakes:
- Pliable personality; gave in to people's demands for a golden calf
- Joined with Moses in disobeying God's orders about the water-giving rock
- Joined sister Miriam in complaining against Moses

Lessons from his life:
- God gives individuals special abilities, which he weaves together for his use
- The very skills that make a good team player sometimes also make a poor leader

Vital statistics:
- Where: Egypt, wilderness of Sinai
- Occupations: Priest; Moses' second in command
- Relatives: Brother: Moses. Sister: Miriam. Sons: Nadab, Abihu, Eleazar, and Ithamar

Key verses:
"Then the anger of the LORD burned against Moses, and He said, 'Is there not your brother Aaron the Levite? I know that he speaks fluently. And moreover, behold, he is coming out to meet you; when he sees you, he will be glad in his heart . . . He shall speak for you to the people; and he will be as a mouth for you and you will be as God to him' " (Exodus 4:14, 16).

Aaron's story is told in Exodus—Deuteronomy 10:6. He is also mentioned in Hebrews 7:11.

33:5–6 This ban on ornaments was not a permanent ban on all jewelry. It was a temporary sign of repentance and mourning. In 35:22 we read that the people had jewelry.

33:11 God and Moses talked face-to-face in the tent of meeting, just as friends do. Why did Moses find such favor with God? It certainly was not because he was perfect, gifted, or powerful. Rather, it was because God chose Moses, and Moses in turn relied wholeheartedly on God's wisdom and direction. Friendship with God was a true privilege for Moses, out of reach for the other Hebrews. But it is not out of reach for us today. Jesus called his disciples—and, by extension, all of his followers—his friends (John 15:15). He has called you to be his friend. Will you trust him as Moses did?

When Moses returned to the camp, his servant Joshua, the son of Nun, a young man,
would not depart from the tent.

Moses Intercedes

12 Then Moses said to the LORD, "See, You say to me, 'Bring up this people!' But You
Yourself have not let me know whom You will send with me. Moreover, You have said,
'I have known you by name, and you have also found favor in My sight.'
13 "Now therefore, I pray You, if I have found favor in Your sight, let me know Your
ways that I may know You, so that I may find favor in Your sight. Consider too, that this
nation is Your people."
14 And He said, "My presence shall go *with you,* and I will give you rest."
15 Then he said to Him, "If Your presence does not go *with us,* do not lead us up from
here.
16 "For how then can it be known that I have found favor in Your sight, I and Your
people? Is it not by Your going with us, so that we, I and Your people, may be distinguished from all the *other* people who are upon the face of the earth?"
17 The LORD said to Moses, "I will also do this thing of which you have spoken; for
you have found favor in My sight and I have known you by name."
18 Then Moses said, "I pray You, show me Your glory!"
19 And He said, "I Myself will make all My goodness pass before you, and will proclaim the name of the LORD before you; and I will be gracious to whom I will be gracious, and will show compassion on whom I will show compassion."
20 But He said, "You cannot see My face, for no man can see Me and live!"
21 Then the LORD said, "Behold, there is a place by Me, and you shall stand *there* on
the rock;
22 and it will come about, while My glory is passing by, that I will put you in the cleft of
the rock and cover you with My hand until I have passed by.
23 "Then I will take My hand away and you shall see My back, but My face shall not be
seen."

The Two Tablets Replaced

34 Now the LORD said to Moses, "Cut out for yourself two stone tablets like the former ones, and I will write on the tablets the words that were on the former tablets
which you shattered.
2 "So be ready by morning, and come up in the morning to Mount Sinai, and present
yourself there to Me on the top of the mountain.
3 "No man is to come up with you, nor let any man be seen anywhere on the mountain;
even the flocks and the herds may not graze in front of that mountain."
4 So he cut out two stone tablets like the former ones, and Moses rose up early in the
morning and went up to Mount Sinai, as the LORD had commanded him, and he took
two stone tablets in his hand.
5 The LORD descended in the cloud and stood there with him as he called upon the
name of the LORD.
6 Then the LORD passed by in front of him and proclaimed, "The LORD, the LORD
God, compassionate and gracious, slow to anger, and abounding in lovingkindness and
truth;
7 who keeps lovingkindness for thousands, who forgives iniquity, transgression and

33:12 Ex 3:10; 32:34; Ex 33:2; Ex 33:17

33:13 Ps 25:4; 27:11; 51:13; 86:11; 119:33; Ex 3:7, 10; 5:1; 32:12, 14; Deut 9:26, 29

33:14 Deut 4:37; Is 63:9; Deut 12:10; 25:19; Josh 21:44; 22:4

33:15 Ps 80:3, 7, 19

33:16 Lev 20:24, 26

33:17 Ex 33:12

33:18 Ex 33:20-23

33:19 Ex 34:6, 7; Rom 9:15

33:20 Is 6:5; 1 Tim 6:16

33:21 Ps 18:2, 46; 27:5; 61:2; 62:7

33:22 Ps 91:1, 4; Is 49:2; 51:16

33:23 Ex 33:20; John 1:18

34:1 Ex 24:12; 31:18; 32:16, 19; Deut 10:2, 4

34:2 Ex 19:11, 18, 20

34:3 Ex 19:12, 13

34:4 Ex 34:1

34:5 Ex 19:9; 33:9

34:6 Num 14:18; Deut 4:31; Neh 9:17; Ps 86:15; 103:8; 108:4; 145:8; Joel 2:13; Rom 2:4

34:7 Ex 20:5, 6; Deut 5:10; 7:9; Ps 103:3; 130:3, 4; 1 John 1:9; Ex 23:7; Deut 7:10; Job 10:14; Nah 1:3

33:11 Joshua, Moses' aide, would not leave the tent, probably because he was guarding it. No doubt there were curious people who would have dared to go inside.

33:18–23 Moses' prayer was to see the manifest glory of God. He wanted assurance of God's presence with him, Aaron, and Joshua, and also he desired to know that presence experientially. Because we are finite and morally imperfect, we cannot exist and see God as he is. To see God's back means we can only see where God has passed by. We can only know him by what he does and how he acts. We cannot comprehend God as he really is apart from Jesus Christ (John 14:9). Jesus promised to show himself to those who believe (John 14:21).

34:6–7 Moses had asked to see God's glory (33:18), and this was God's response. What is God's glory? It is his character, his nature, his way of relating to his creatures. Notice that God did not give Moses a vision of his power and majesty, but rather of his love. God's glory is revealed in his mercy, grace, compassion, faithfulness, forgiveness, and justice. God's love and mercy are truly wonderful, and we benefit from them. We can respond and give glory to God when our characters resemble his.

34:7 Why would sins affect children and grandchildren? This is no arbitrary punishment. Children still suffer for the sins of their parents. Consider child abuse or alcoholism, for example. While these sins are obvious, sins like selfishness and greed can be passed along as well. The dire consequences of sin are not limited to the

34:8 Ex 4:31
34:9 Ex 33:13; Ex 32:9; Ex 34:7; Deut 4:20; 9:26, 29; 32:9; Ps 33:12
34:10 Ex 34:27, 28; Deut 5:2; Deut 4:32; Ps 72:18; 136:4
34:11 Ex 33:2
34:12 Ex 23:32, 33
34:13 Ex 23:24; Deut 12:3; Deut 16:21; Judg 6:25, 26; 2 Kin 18:4; 2 Chr 34:3f
34:14 Ex 20:3, 5; Deut 4:24
34:15 Ex 22:20; 32:8; Num 25:1, 2; Deut 32:37, 38
34:16 Deut 7:3; Josh 23:12, 13; 1 Kin 11:1-4
34:17 Ex 20:4, 23; Lev 19:4; Deut 5:8
34:18 Ex 12:17; Lev 23:6; Num 28:16f; Ex 12:15, 16; Ex 12:2; 13:4
34:19 Ex 13:2; 22:29f
34:20 Ex 13:13; Ex 13:15; Num 3:45; Ex 22:29; 23:15; Deut 16:16
34:21 Ex 20:9f; 23:12; 31:15; 35:2; Lev 23:3; Deut 5:13f
34:22 Ex 23:16; Num 28:26
34:23 Ex 23:14-17
34:24 Ex 33:2; Ps 78:55
34:25 Ex 23:18; Ex 12:10
34:26 Ex 23:19; Deut 26:2

sin; yet He will by no means leave *the guilty* unpunished, visiting the iniquity of fathers
on the children and on the grandchildren to the third and fourth generations."
8 Moses made haste to bow low toward the earth and worship.
9 He said, "If now I have found favor in Your sight, O Lord, I pray, let the Lord go
along in our midst, even though the people are so obstinate, and pardon our iniquity
and our sin, and take us as Your own possession."

The Covenant Renewed

10 Then God said, "Behold, I am going to make a covenant. Before all your people I
will perform miracles which have not been produced in all the earth nor among any of
the nations; and all the people among whom you live will see the working of the LORD,
for it is a fearful thing that I am going to perform with you.
11 "Be sure to observe what I am commanding you this day: behold, I am going to drive
out the Amorite before you, and the Canaanite, the Hittite, the Perizzite, the Hivite and
the Jebusite.
12 "Watch yourself that you make no covenant with the inhabitants of the land into which
you are going, or it will become a snare in your midst.
13 "But *rather,* you are to tear down their altars and smash their *sacred* pillars and cut
down their [30]Asherim
14 —for you shall not worship any other god, for the LORD, whose name is Jealous, is
a jealous God—
15 otherwise you might make a covenant with the inhabitants of the land and they would
play the harlot with their gods and sacrifice to their gods, and someone might invite you
to eat of his sacrifice,
16 and you might take some of his daughters for your sons, and his daughters might
play the harlot with their gods and cause your sons *also* to play the harlot with their gods.
17 "You shall make for yourself no molten gods.
18 "You shall observe the Feast of Unleavened Bread. For seven days you are to eat
unleavened bread, as I commanded you, at the appointed time in the month of Abib, for
in the month of Abib you came out of Egypt.
19 "The first offspring from every womb belongs to Me, and all your male livestock, the
first offspring from cattle and sheep.
20 "You shall redeem with a lamb the first offspring from a donkey; and if you do not
redeem *it,* then you shall break its neck. You shall redeem all the firstborn of your sons.
None shall appear before Me empty-handed.
21 "You shall work six days, but on the seventh day you shall rest; *even* during plowing
time and harvest you shall rest.
22 "You shall celebrate the Feast of Weeks, *that is,* the first fruits of the wheat harvest,
and the Feast of Ingathering at the turn of the year.
23 "Three times a year all your males are to appear before the Lord GOD, the God of
Israel.
24 "For I will drive out nations before you and enlarge your borders, and no man shall
covet your land when you go up three times a year to appear before the LORD your God.
25 "You shall not offer the blood of My sacrifice with leavened bread, nor is the sacrifice of the Feast of the Passover to be left over until morning.
26 "You shall bring the very first of the first fruits of your soil into the house of the LORD
your God.
"You shall not boil a young goat in its mother's milk."
27 Then the LORD said to Moses, "Write down these words, for in accordance with
these words I have made a covenant with you and with Israel."

30 I.e. wooden symbols of a female deity

---

individual family member. Be careful not to treat sin casually, but repent and turn from it. The sin may cause you little pain now, but it could sting in a most tender area of your life later—your children and grandchildren.

34:12–14 God told the Israelites not to join in religious rites with the sinful people around them, but to give their absolute loyalty and exclusive devotion to him. Pagan worship simply cannot be mixed with the worship of the holy God. As Jesus pointed out, "No servant can serve two masters. . . . You cannot serve God and wealth" (Luke 16:13). Love of money is the god of this age, and many Christians attempt to make a treaty with this enslaving god. Are you trying to worship two gods at once? Where is your first allegiance?

34:13 Asherim were wooden poles that stood by Baal's altar (see Judges 6:25). Asherah was the goddess who was the consort (wife) of Baal. She represented good luck in agriculture and fertility.

34:18 The month of Abib corresponds to the end of March and the beginning of April.

28 So he was there with the LORD forty days and forty nights; he did not eat bread or
drink water. And he wrote on the tablets the words of the covenant, the Ten Commandments.

Moses' Face Shines

29 It came about when Moses was coming down from Mount Sinai (and the two tablets of the testimony *were* in Moses' hand as he was coming down from the mountain),
that Moses did not know that the skin of his face shone because of his speaking with
Him.
30 So when Aaron and all the sons of Israel saw Moses, behold, the skin of his face
shone, and they were afraid to come near him.
31 Then Moses called to them, and Aaron and all the rulers in the congregation returned to him; and Moses spoke to them.
32 Afterward all the sons of Israel came near, and he commanded them *to do* everything that the LORD had spoken to him on Mount Sinai.
33 When Moses had finished speaking with them, he put a veil over his face.
34 But whenever Moses went in before the LORD to speak with Him, he would take
off the veil until he came out; and whenever he came out and spoke to the sons of Israel
what he had been commanded,
35 the sons of Israel would see the face of Moses, that the skin of Moses' face shone.
So Moses would replace the veil over his face until he went in to speak with Him.

4. Tabernacle construction

The Sabbath Emphasized

35 Then Moses assembled all the congregation of the sons of Israel, and said to them,
"These are the things that the LORD has commanded *you* to do:
2 "For six days work may be done, but on the seventh day you shall have a holy *day*, a
sabbath of complete rest to the LORD; whoever does any work on it shall be put to death.
3 "You shall not kindle a fire in any of your dwellings on the sabbath day."
4 Moses spoke to all the congregation of the sons of Israel, saying, "This is the thing
which the LORD has commanded, saying,
5 'Take from among you a contribution to the LORD; whoever is of a willing heart, let
him bring it as the LORD'S contribution: gold, silver, and bronze,
6 and blue, purple and scarlet *material,* fine linen, goats' *hair,*
7 and rams' skins dyed red, and porpoise skins, and acacia wood,
8 and oil for lighting, and spices for the anointing oil, and for the fragrant incense,
9 and onyx stones and setting stones for the ephod and for the breastpiece.

Tabernacle Workmen

10 'Let every skillful man among you come, and make all that the LORD has commanded:
11 the tabernacle, its tent and its covering, its hooks and its boards, its bars, its pillars,
and its sockets;
12 the ark and its poles, the mercy seat, and the curtain of the screen;
13 the table and its poles, and all its utensils, and the bread of the [31]Presence;
14 the lampstand also for the light and its utensils and its lamps and the oil for the light;
15 and the altar of incense and its poles, and the anointing oil and the fragrant incense,
and the screen for the doorway at the entrance of the tabernacle;
16 the altar of burnt offering with its bronze grating, its poles, and all its utensils, the
basin and its stand;

34:28 Ex 24:18; Ex 31:18; 34:1; Deut 4:13; 10:4
34:29 Ex 32:15; Matt 17:2; 2 Cor 3:7
34:30 2 Cor 3:7
34:33 2 Cor 3:13
34:34 2 Cor 3:16
34:35 2 Cor 3:13
35:1 Ex 34:32
35:2 Ex 20:9, 10; 23:12; 31:15; 34:21; Lev 23:3; Deut 5:13f; Ex 16:23; Num 15:32-36
35:3 Ex 12:16; 16:23
35:5 Ex 25:1-9
35:10 Ex 31:6
35:11 Ex 26:1-30
35:12 Ex 25:10-22
35:13 Ex 25:23-30
35:14 Ex 25:31ff
35:15 Ex 30:1-6; Ex 30:25; Ex 30:34-38
35:16 Ex 27:1-8

31 Lit *Face*

34:28–35 Moses' face was radiant after he spent time with God. The people could clearly see God's presence in him. How often do you spend time alone with God? Although your face may not light up a room, time spent in prayer, reading the Bible, and meditating should have such an effect on your life that people will know you have been with God.

35:5–21 God did not require these special offerings, but he appealed to people with generous hearts. Only those who were willing to give were invited to participate. God loves cheerful givers (2 Corinthians 9:7). Our giving should be from love and generosity, not from a guilty conscience.

35:10–19 Moses asked people with various abilities to help with the tabernacle. Every one of God's people has been given special abilities. We are responsible to develop these abilities—even the ones not considered religious—and to use them for God's glory. We can become skilled through study, by watching others, and through practice. Work on your skills or abilities that could help your church or community.

35:17 Ex 27:9-18

17 the hangings of the court, its pillars and its sockets, and the screen for the gate of
the court;
18 the pegs of the tabernacle and the pegs of the court and their cords;

35:19 Ex 31:10; 39:1

19 the woven garments for ministering in the holy place, the holy garments for Aaron
the priest and the garments of his sons, to minister as priests.' "

Gifts Received

20 Then all the congregation of the sons of Israel departed from Moses' presence.

35:21 Ex 25:2; 35:5, 22, 26, 29; 36:2

21 Everyone whose heart stirred him and everyone whose spirit moved him came *and*
brought the LORD'S contribution for the work of the tent of meeting and for all its service and for the holy garments.
22 Then all whose hearts moved them, both men and women, came *and* brought
brooches and earrings and signet rings and bracelets, all articles of gold; so *did* every
man who presented an offering of gold to the LORD.
23 Every man, who had in his possession blue and purple and scarlet *material* and fine
linen and goats' *hair* and rams' skins dyed red and porpoise skins, brought them.
24 Everyone who could make a contribution of silver and bronze brought the LORD'S
contribution; and every man who had in his possession acacia wood for any work of the
service brought it.
25 All the skilled women spun with their hands, and brought what they had spun, *in*
blue and purple *and* scarlet *material* and *in* fine linen.
26 All the women whose heart stirred with a skill spun the goats' *hair.*
27 The rulers brought the onyx stones and the stones for setting for the ephod and for
the breastpiece;

35:28 Ex 30:23ff

28 and the spice and the oil for the light and for the anointing oil and for the fragrant
incense.

35:29 Ex 35:21; 1 Chr 29:9

29 The Israelites, all the men and women, whose heart moved them to bring *material*
for all the work, which the LORD had commanded through Moses to be done, brought a
freewill offering to the LORD.

35:30 Ex 31:1-6

30 Then Moses said to the sons of Israel, "See, the LORD has called by name Bezalel
the son of Uri, the son of Hur, of the tribe of Judah.
31 "And He has filled him with the Spirit of God, in wisdom, in understanding and in
knowledge and in all craftsmanship;
32 to make designs for working in gold and in silver and in bronze,
33 and in the cutting of stones for settings and in the carving of wood, so as to perform
in every inventive work.

35:34 Ex 31:6

34 "He also has put in his heart to teach, both he and Oholiab, the son of Ahisamach, of
the tribe of Dan.

35:35 Ex 31:3, 6; 35:31; 1 Kin 7:14

35 "He has filled them with skill to perform every work of an engraver and of a designer
and of an embroiderer, in blue and in purple *and* in scarlet *material,* and in fine linen,
and of a weaver, as performers of every work and makers of designs.

The Tabernacle Underwritten

36 "Now Bezalel and Oholiab, and every skillful person in whom the LORD has put
skill and understanding to know how to perform all the work in the construction
of the sanctuary, shall perform in accordance with all that the LORD has commanded."

36:2 Ex 35:21, 26

2 Then Moses called Bezalel and Oholiab and every skillful person in whom the LORD
had put skill, everyone whose heart stirred him, to come to the work to perform it.

35:20–24 Where did the Israelites, who were once Egyptian slaves, get all this gold and jewelry? When the Hebrews left Egypt, they took with them the spoils from the land—all the booty they could carry (12:35–36). This included gold, silver, jewels, linen, skins, and other valuables.

35:21 Those whose hearts were stirred gave cheerfully to the tent of meeting (also called the tabernacle). With great enthusiasm they gave because they knew how important their giving was to the completion of God's house. Airline pilots and computer operators can push test buttons to see if their equipment is functioning properly. God has a quick test button he can push to see the level of our commitment—our pocketbooks. Generous people aren't necessarily faithful to God. But faithful people are always generous.

35:26 Those who spun cloth made a beautiful contribution to the tabernacle. Good workers take pride in the quality and beauty of their work. God is concerned with the quality and beauty of what you do. Whether you are a corporate executive or a drugstore cashier, your work should reflect the creative abilities God has given you.

3 They received from Moses all the contributions which the sons of Israel had brought
to perform the work in the construction of the sanctuary. And they still *continued* bringing to him freewill offerings every morning.
4 And all the skillful men who were performing all the work of the sanctuary came,
each from the work which he was performing,
5 and they said to Moses, "The people are bringing much more than enough for the 36:5
construction work which the LORD commanded *us* to perform." 2 Chr 24:14; 31:6-10
6 So Moses issued a command, and a proclamation was circulated throughout the
camp, saying, "Let no man or woman any longer perform work for the contributions of
the sanctuary." Thus the people were restrained from bringing *any more.*
7 For the material they had was sufficient and more than enough for all the work, to 36:7
perform it. 1 Kin 8:64

Construction Proceeds

8 All the skillful men among those who were performing the work made the taber- 36:8
nacle with ten curtains; of fine twisted linen and blue and purple and scarlet *material,* Ex 26:1-14
with cherubim, the work of a skillful workman, Bezalel made them.
9 The length of each curtain was twenty-eight cubits and the width of each curtain
four cubits; all the curtains had the same measurements.
10 He joined five curtains to one another and *the other* five curtains he joined to one
another.
11 He made loops of blue on the edge of the outermost curtain in the first set; he did
likewise on the edge of the curtain that was outermost in the second set.
12 He made fifty loops in the one curtain and he made fifty loops on the edge of the 36:12
curtain that was in the second set; the loops were opposite each other. Ex 26:5
13 He made fifty clasps of gold and joined the curtains to one another with the clasps, 36:13
so the tabernacle was a unit. Ex 26:6
14 Then he made curtains of goats' *hair* for a tent over the tabernacle; he made eleven 36:14
curtains in all. Ex 26:7-14
15 The length of each curtain *was* thirty cubits and four cubits the width of each curtain; the eleven curtains had the same measurements.
16 He joined five curtains by themselves and *the other* six curtains by themselves.
17 Moreover, he made fifty loops on the edge of the curtain that was outermost in the
first set, and he made fifty loops on the edge of the curtain *that was outermost in* the second set.
18 He made fifty clasps of bronze to join the tent together so that it would be a unit.
19 He made a covering for the tent of rams' skins dyed red, and a covering of porpoise
skins above.
20 Then he made the boards for the tabernacle of acacia wood, standing upright. 36:20
21 Ten cubits *was* the length of each board and one and a half cubits the width of each Ex 26:15-29
board.
22 *There were* two tenons for each board, fitted to one another; thus he did for all the
boards of the tabernacle.
23 He made the boards for the tabernacle: twenty boards for the south side;
24 and he made forty sockets of silver under the twenty boards; two sockets under one
board for its two tenons and two sockets under another board for its two tenons.
25 Then for the second side of the tabernacle, on the north side, he made twenty boards,
26 and their forty sockets of silver; two sockets under one board and two sockets under another board.
27 For the rear of the tabernacle, to the west, he made six boards.
28 He made two boards for the corners of the tabernacle at the rear.
29 They were double beneath, and together they were complete to its top to the first
ring; thus he did with both of them for the two corners.

36:8–9 Making cloth (spinning and weaving) took a great deal of time in Moses' day. To own more than two or three changes of clothes was a sign of wealth. The effort involved in making enough cloth for the tabernacle was staggering. The tabernacle would never have been built without tremendous community involvement. Today, churches and neighborhoods often require this same kind of pulling together. Without it, many essential services wouldn't get done.

30 There were eight boards with their sockets of silver, sixteen sockets, two under every
board.
36:31 Ex 26:26-29 **31** Then he made bars of acacia wood, five for the boards of one side of the tabernacle,
32 and five bars for the boards of the other side of the tabernacle, and five bars for the
boards of the tabernacle for the rear *side* to the west.
33 He made the middle bar to pass through in the center of the boards from end
to end.
34 He overlaid the boards with gold and made their rings of gold *as* holders for the
bars, and overlaid the bars with gold.
36:35 Ex 26:31-37 **35** Moreover, he made the veil of blue and purple and scarlet *material,* and fine twisted linen; he made it with cherubim, the work of a skillful workman.
36 He made four pillars of acacia for it, and overlaid them with gold, with their hooks
of gold; and he cast four sockets of silver for them.
36:37 Ex 26:36 37 He made a screen for the doorway of the tent, of blue and purple and scarlet *material,* and fine twisted linen, the work of a weaver;
36:38 Ex 26:37 38 and *he made* its five pillars with their hooks, and he overlaid their tops and their
bands with gold; but their five sockets were of bronze.

KEY TABERNACLE PIECES

Name	*Function and Significance*
Ark of the Testimony	• A golden rectangular box that contained the Ten Commandments • Symbolized God's covenant with Israel's people • Located in the holy of holies
Mercy Seat	• The lid to the ark of the testimony • Symbolized the presence of God among his people
Veil	• The curtain that divided the two sacred rooms of the tabernacle—the holy place and the holy of holies • Symbolized how the people were separated from God because of sin
Table	• A wooden table located in the holy place of the tabernacle. The bread of the Presence and various utensils were kept on this table
Bread of the Presence	• Twelve loaves of baked bread, one for each tribe of Israel • Symbolized the spiritual nourishment God offers his people
Lampstands and Lamps	• A golden lampstand located in the holy place, which held seven burning oil lamps • The lampstand lighted the holy place for the priests
Altar of Incense	• An altar in the holy place in front of the veil • Used for burning God's special incense and symbolic of acceptable prayer
Anointing Oil	• A special oil used to anoint the priests and all the pieces in the tabernacle • A sign of being set apart for God
Altar of Burnt Offering	• The bronze altar outside the tabernacle used for the sacrifices • Symbolized how sacrifice restored one's relationship with God
Basin	• A large wash basin outside the tabernacle used by the priests to cleanse themselves before performing their duties • Symbolized the need for spiritual cleansing

36:35 Cherubim are mighty angels.

Construction Continues

37 Now Bezalel made the ark of acacia wood; its length was two and a half cubits, and its width one and a half cubits, and its height one and a half cubits; **37:1** Ex 25:10-20
2 and he overlaid it with pure gold inside and out, and made a gold molding for it all around.
3 He cast four rings of gold for it on its four feet; even two rings on one side of it, and two rings on the other side of it.
4 He made poles of acacia wood and overlaid them with gold.
5 He put the poles into the rings on the sides of the ark, to carry it.
6 He made a mercy seat of pure gold, two and a half cubits long and one and a half cubits wide.
7 He made two cherubim of gold; he made them of hammered work at the two ends of the mercy seat;
8 one cherub at the one end and one cherub at the other end; he made the cherubim *of one piece* with the mercy seat at the two ends.
9 The cherubim had *their* wings spread upward, covering the mercy seat with their wings, with their faces toward each other; the faces of the cherubim were toward the mercy seat.
10 Then he made the table of acacia wood, two cubits long and a cubit wide and one and a half cubits high. **37:10** Ex 25:23-29
11 He overlaid it with pure gold, and made a gold molding for it all around.
12 He made a rim for it of a handbreadth all around, and made a gold molding for its rim all around.
13 He cast four gold rings for it and put the rings on the four corners that were on its four feet.
14 Close by the rim were the rings, the holders for the poles to carry the table.
15 He made the poles of acacia wood and overlaid them with gold, to carry the table.
16 He made the utensils which were on the table, its dishes and its pans and its bowls and its jars, with which to pour out drink offerings, of pure gold.
17 Then he made the lampstand of pure gold. He made the lampstand of hammered work, its base and its shaft; its cups, its bulbs and its flowers were *of one piece* with it. **37:17** Ex 25:31-39
18 There were six branches going out of its sides; three branches of the lampstand from the one side of it and three branches of the lampstand from the other side of it;
19 three cups shaped like almond *blossoms,* a bulb and a flower in one branch, and three cups shaped like almond *blossoms,* a bulb and a flower in the other branch—so for the six branches going out of the lampstand.
20 In the lampstand *there were* four cups shaped like almond *blossoms,* its bulbs and its flowers;
21 and a bulb was under the *first* pair of branches *coming* out of it, and a bulb under the *second* pair of branches *coming* out of it, and a bulb under the *third* pair of branches *coming* out of it, for the six branches coming out of the lampstand.
22 Their bulbs and their branches were *of one piece* with it; the whole of it *was* a single hammered work of pure gold.
23 He made its seven lamps with its snuffers and its trays of pure gold.
24 He made it and all its utensils from a talent of pure gold.
25 Then he made the altar of incense of acacia wood: a cubit long and a cubit wide, square, and two cubits high; its horns were *of one piece* with it. **37:25** Ex 30:1-5
26 He overlaid it with pure gold, its top and its sides all around, and its horns; and he made a gold molding for it all around.
27 He made two golden rings for it under its molding, on its two sides—on opposite sides—as holders for poles with which to carry it.
28 He made the poles of acacia wood and overlaid them with gold.
29 And he made the holy anointing oil and the pure, fragrant incense of spices, the work of a perfumer. **37:29** Ex 30:23-25, 34, 35

37:1 The ark (also called the ark of the testimony or ark of the covenant) was built to hold the Ten Commandments. It symbolized God's covenant with his people. Two gold angels called cherubim were placed on its top. The ark was Israel's most sacred object and was kept in the holy of holies in the tabernacle. Only once each year, the high priest entered the holy of holies to sprinkle blood on the top of the ark (called the mercy seat) to atone for the sins of the entire nation.

The Tabernacle Completed

38:1 Ex 27:1-8 **38** Then he made the altar of burnt offering of acacia wood, five cubits long, and five cubits wide, square, and three cubits high.

2 He made its horns on its four corners, its horns being *of one piece* with it, and he overlaid it with bronze.

3 He made all the utensils of the altar, the pails and the shovels and the basins, the flesh hooks and the firepans; he made all its utensils of bronze.

4 He made for the altar a grating of bronze network beneath, under its ledge, reaching halfway up.

5 He cast four rings on the four ends of the bronze grating *as* holders for the poles.

6 He made the poles of acacia wood and overlaid them with bronze.

7 He inserted the poles into the rings on the sides of the altar, with which to carry it. He made it hollow with planks.

38:8 Ex 30:18 **8** Moreover, he made the laver of bronze with its base of bronze, from the mirrors of the serving women who served at the doorway of the tent of meeting.

38:9 Ex 27:9-19 **9** Then he made the court: for the south side the hangings of the court were of fine twisted linen, one hundred cubits;

10 their twenty pillars, and their twenty sockets, *made* of bronze; the hooks of the pillars and their bands *were* of silver.

11 For the north side *there were* one hundred cubits; their twenty pillars and their twenty sockets *were* of bronze, the hooks of the pillars and their bands *were* of silver.

12 For the west side *there were* hangings of fifty cubits *with* their ten pillars and their ten sockets; the hooks of the pillars and their bands *were* of silver.

13 For the east side fifty cubits.

14 The hangings for the *one* side *of the gate were* fifteen cubits, *with* their three pillars and their three sockets,

15 and so for the other side. On both sides of the gate of the court *were* hangings of fifteen cubits, *with* their three pillars and their three sockets.

16 All the hangings of the court all around *were* of fine twisted linen.

17 The sockets for the pillars *were* of bronze, the hooks of the pillars and their bands, of silver; and the overlaying of their tops, of silver, and all the pillars of the court were furnished with silver bands.

18 The screen of the gate of the court was the work of the weaver, of blue and purple and scarlet *material* and fine twisted linen. And the length *was* twenty cubits and the height *was* five cubits, corresponding to the hangings of the court.

19 Their four pillars and their four sockets *were* of bronze; their hooks *were* of silver, and the overlaying of their tops and their bands *were* of silver.

20 All the pegs of the tabernacle and of the court all around *were* of bronze.

The Cost of the Tabernacle

21 This is the number of the things for the tabernacle, the tabernacle of the testimony, as they were numbered according to the command of Moses, for the service of the Levites, by the hand of Ithamar the son of Aaron the priest.

38:22 Ex 31:2 22 Now Bezalel the son of Uri, the son of Hur, of the tribe of Judah, made all that the LORD had commanded Moses.

38:23 Ex 31:6 23 With him *was* Oholiab the son of Ahisamach, of the tribe of Dan, an engraver and a skillful workman and a weaver in blue and in purple and in scarlet *material,* and fine linen.

38:24 Ex 30:13; Lev 27:25; Num 3:47; 18:16 **24** All the gold that was used for the work, in all the work of the sanctuary, even the gold of the wave offering, was 29 talents and 730 shekels, according to the shekel of the sanctuary.

38:25 Ex 30:11-16 25 The silver of those of the congregation who were numbered was 100 talents and 1,775 shekels, according to the shekel of the sanctuary;

38:26 Ex 30:13, 15; Ex 12:37; Num 1:46; 26:51 26 a beka a head (*that is,* half a shekel according to the shekel of the sanctuary), for each one who passed over to those who were numbered, from twenty years old and upward, for 603,550 men.

38:21 In building the tabernacle, Moses laid out the steps, but Ithamar supervised the project. We all have different talents and abilities. God didn't ask Moses to build the tabernacle but to motivate the experts to do it. Look for the areas where God has gifted you and then seek opportunities to allow God to use your gifts.

27 The hundred talents of silver were for casting the sockets of the sanctuary and the
sockets of the veil; one hundred sockets for the hundred talents, a talent for a socket.
28 Of the 1,775 *shekels,* he made hooks for the pillars and overlaid their tops and made
bands for them.
29 The bronze of the wave offering was 70 talents and 2,400 shekels.
30 With it he made the sockets to the doorway of the tent of meeting, and the bronze
altar and its bronze grating, and all the utensils of the altar,
31 and the sockets of the court all around and the sockets of the gate of the court, and
all the pegs of the tabernacle and all the pegs of the court all around.

The Priestly Garments

39 Moreover, from the blue and purple and scarlet *material,* they made finely woven
garments for ministering in the holy place as well as the holy garments which were
for Aaron, just as the LORD had commanded Moses.
2 He made the ephod of gold, *and* of blue and purple and scarlet *material,* and fine
twisted linen.
3 Then they hammered out gold sheets and cut *them* into threads to be woven in *with*
the blue and the purple and the scarlet *material,* and the fine linen, the work of a skillful
workman.
4 They made attaching shoulder pieces for the ephod; it was attached at its two *upper*
ends.
5 The skillfully woven band which was on it was like its workmanship, of the same
material: of gold *and* of blue and purple and scarlet *material,* and fine twisted linen, just
as the LORD had commanded Moses.
6 They made the onyx stones, set in gold filigree *settings;* they were engraved *like* the
engravings of a signet, according to the names of the sons of Israel.
7 And he placed them on the shoulder pieces of the ephod, *as* memorial stones for
the sons of Israel, just as the LORD had commanded Moses.
8 He made the breastpiece, the work of a skillful workman, like the workmanship of
the ephod: of gold *and* of blue and purple and scarlet *material* and fine twisted linen.
9 It was square; they made the breastpiece folded double, a span long and a span wide
when folded double.
10 And they mounted four rows of stones on it. The first row *was* a row of ruby, topaz,
and emerald;
11 and the second row, a turquoise, a sapphire and a diamond;
12 and the third row, a jacinth, an agate, and an amethyst;
13 and the fourth row, a beryl, an onyx, and a jasper. They were set in gold filigree *settings* when they were mounted.
14 The stones were corresponding to the names of the sons of Israel; they were twelve,
corresponding to their names, *engraved with* the engravings of a signet, each with its name
for the twelve tribes.
15 They made on the breastpiece chains like cords, of twisted cordage work in pure
gold.
16 They made two gold filigree *settings* and two gold rings, and put the two rings on the
two ends of the breastpiece.
17 Then they put the two gold cords in the two rings at the ends of the breastpiece.
18 They put the *other* two ends of the two cords on the two filigree *settings,* and put
them on the shoulder pieces of the ephod at the front of it.
19 They made two gold rings and placed *them* on the two ends of the breastpiece, on
its inner edge which was next to the ephod.
20 Furthermore, they made two gold rings and placed them on the bottom of the two
shoulder pieces of the ephod, on the front of it, close to the place where it joined, above
the woven band of the ephod.

39:1 Ex 35:23; Ex 31:10; 35:19
39:2 Ex 28:6-12
39:6 Ex 28:9-11
39:7 Ex 28:12
39:8 Ex 28:15-28

39:1–21 The priests wore a uniform to the tabernacle each day. Some of the pieces of their uniform were not only beautiful but also significant. Two parts of the high priest's uniform were the ephod and breastpiece. The ephod looked like a vest and was worn over the outer clothing. The breastpiece was fitted to the ephod (and sometimes was called the ephod). The breastpiece was made of colored linens about nine inches square. On its front were attached 12 precious stones, each inscribed with the name of a tribe of Israel. This symbolized how the high priest represented all the people before God. The breastpiece also contained pockets that held two stones or plates called the Urim and Thummim. The high priest could determine God's will for the nation by consulting the Urim and Thummim. (See the note on 28:30.)

21 They bound the breastpiece by its rings to the rings of the ephod with a blue cord,
so that it would be on the woven band of the ephod, and that the breastpiece would not
come loose from the ephod, just as the LORD had commanded Moses.
39:22 Ex 28:31, 34 **22** Then he made the robe of the ephod of woven work, all of blue;
23 and the opening of the robe was *at the top* in the center, as the opening of a coat of
39:23 Ex 28:32 mail, with a binding all around its opening, so that it would not be torn.
24 They made pomegranates of blue and purple and scarlet *material and* twisted *linen*
on the hem of the robe.
25 They also made bells of pure gold, and put the bells between the pomegranates all
around on the hem of the robe,
26 alternating a bell and a pomegranate all around on the hem of the robe for the service, just as the LORD had commanded Moses.
39:27 Ex 28:39, 40, 42 **27** They made the tunics of finely woven linen for Aaron and his sons,
28 and the turban of fine linen, and the decorated caps of fine linen, and the linen
breeches of fine twisted linen,
29 and the sash of fine twisted linen, and blue and purple and scarlet *material,* the work
of the weaver, just as the LORD had commanded Moses.
39:30 Ex 28:36, 37 **30** They made the plate of the holy crown of pure gold, and inscribed it like the engravings of a signet, "Holy to the LORD."
31 They fastened a blue cord to it, to fasten it on the turban above, just as the LORD
had commanded Moses.
32 Thus all the work of the tabernacle of the tent of meeting was completed; and the
sons of Israel did according to all that the LORD had commanded Moses; so they did.
33 They brought the tabernacle to Moses, the tent and all its [32]furnishings: its clasps,
its boards, its bars, and its pillars and its sockets;
34 and the covering of rams' skins dyed red, and the covering of porpoise skins, and
the screening veil;
35 the ark of the testimony and its poles and the mercy seat;
36 the table, all its utensils, and the bread of the Presence;
37 the pure *gold* lampstand, with its arrangement of lamps and all its utensils, and the
oil for the light;
38 and the gold altar, and the anointing oil and the fragrant incense, and the veil for
the doorway of the tent;
39 the bronze altar and its bronze grating, its poles and all its utensils, the laver and its
stand;
40 the hangings for the court, its pillars and its sockets, and the screen for the gate of
the court, its cords and its pegs and all the equipment for the service of the tabernacle,
for the tent of meeting;
41 the woven garments for ministering in the holy place and the holy garments for Aaron
the priest and the garments of his sons, to minister as priests.
42 So the sons of Israel did all the work according to all that the LORD had commanded Moses.
39:43 Lev 9:22, 23; Num 6:23-26 43 And Moses examined all the work and behold, they had done it; just as the LORD
had commanded, this they had done. So Moses blessed them.

The Tabernacle Erected

40 Then the LORD spoke to Moses, saying,
40:2 Ex 19:1; 40:17; Num 1:1 2 "On the first day of the first month you shall set up the tabernacle of the tent
of meeting.

32 Or *utensils*

39:32 The tabernacle was finally complete to the last detail. God was keenly interested in every minute part. The Creator of the universe was concerned about even the little things. Matthew 10:30 says that God knows the number of hairs on our heads. This shows that God is greatly interested in you. Don't be afraid to talk with him about any of your concerns—no matter how small or unimportant they might seem.

39:42 Moses had learned his management lesson well. He gave important responsibilities to others and then trusted them to do the job. Great leaders, like Moses, give plans and direction while letting others participate on the team. If you are a leader, trust your assistants with key responsibilities.

39:43 Moses inspected the finished work, saw that it was done the way God wanted, and then blessed the people. A good leader follows up on assigned tasks and gives rewards for good work. In whatever responsible position you find yourself, follow up to make sure that tasks are completed as intended, and show your appreciation to the people who have helped.

3 "You shall place the ark of the testimony there, and you shall screen the ark with the veil.
4 "You shall bring in the table and arrange what belongs on it; and you shall bring in the lampstand and mount its lamps.
5 "Moreover, you shall set the gold altar of incense before the ark of the testimony, and set up the veil for the doorway to the tabernacle.
6 "You shall set the altar of burnt offering in front of the doorway of the tabernacle of the tent of meeting.
7 "You shall set the laver between the tent of meeting and the altar and put water in it.
8 "You shall set up the court all around and hang up the veil for the gateway of the court.
9 "Then you shall take the anointing oil and anoint the tabernacle and all that is in it, and shall consecrate it and all its furnishings; and it shall be holy.
10 "You shall anoint the altar of burnt offering and all its utensils, and consecrate the altar, and the altar shall be most holy.
11 "You shall anoint the laver and its stand, and consecrate it.
12 "Then you shall bring Aaron and his sons to the doorway of the tent of meeting and wash them with water.
13 "You shall put the holy garments on Aaron and anoint him and consecrate him, that he may minister as a priest to Me.
14 "You shall bring his sons and put tunics on them;
15 and you shall anoint them even as you have anointed their father, that they may minister as priests to Me; and their anointing will qualify them for a perpetual priesthood throughout their generations."
16 Thus Moses did; according to all that the LORD had commanded him, so he did.
17 Now in the first month of the second year, on the first *day* of the month, the tabernacle was erected.
18 Moses erected the tabernacle and laid its sockets, and set up its boards, and inserted its bars and erected its pillars.
19 He spread the tent over the tabernacle and put the covering of the tent on top of it, just as the LORD had commanded Moses.
20 Then he took the testimony and put *it* into the ark, and attached the poles to the ark, and put the mercy seat on top of the ark.
21 He brought the ark into the tabernacle, and set up a veil for the screen, and screened off the ark of the testimony, just as the LORD had commanded Moses.
22 Then he put the table in the tent of meeting on the north side of the tabernacle, outside the veil.
23 He set the arrangement of bread in order on it before the LORD, just as the LORD had commanded Moses.
24 Then he placed the lampstand in the tent of meeting, opposite the table, on the south side of the tabernacle.
25 He lighted the lamps before the LORD, just as the LORD had commanded Moses.
26 Then he placed the gold altar in the tent of meeting in front of the veil;
27 and he burned fragrant incense on it, just as the LORD had commanded Moses.
28 Then he set up the veil for the doorway of the tabernacle.
29 He set the altar of burnt offering *before* the doorway of the tabernacle of the tent of meeting, and offered on it the burnt offering and the meal offering, just as the LORD had commanded Moses.
30 He placed the laver between the tent of meeting and the altar and put water in it for washing.

40:3 Ex 26:33; 40:21; Num 4:5
40:4 Ex 26:35; 40:22; Ex 25:30; 40:23; Ex 40:24f
40:5 Ex 40:26
40:7 Ex 30:18; 40:30
40:9 Ex 30:26; Lev 8:10
40:10 Ex 29:37
40:12 Lev 8:1-6
40:13 Ex 28:41; Lev 8:13
40:15 Ex 29:9; Num 25:13
40:17 Ex 40:2
40:20 Ex 25:16; Deut 10:5; 1 Kin 8:9; 2 Chr 5:10; Heb 9:4
40:21 Ex 26:33
40:22 Ex 26:35
40:23 Ex 25:30; Lev 24:5, 6
40:25 Ex 25:37; 40:4
40:26 Ex 30:6; 40:5
40:27 Ex 30:7
40:29 Ex 40:6; Ex 29:38-42

40:1ff Moses was careful to obey God's instructions in the smallest detail. Notice that he didn't make a reasonable facsimile of God's description, but an exact copy. We should follow Moses' example and be fastidious about our obedience. If God has told you to do something, do it, do it right, and do it completely.

40:16 God told Moses how to build the tabernacle, and Moses delegated jobs in order to do it. God allows people to participate with him in carrying out his will. Your task is not just to sit and watch God work, but to give your best effort when work needs to be done.

40:17–33 The physical care of the tabernacle required a long list of tasks, and each was important to the work of God's house. This principle is important to remember today when God's house is the church. There are many seemingly unimportant tasks that must be done to keep your church building maintained. Washing dishes, painting walls, or shoveling snow may not seem very spiritual. But they are vital to the ministry of the church and have an important role in our worship of God.

40:31
Ex 30:19, 20

31 From it Moses and Aaron and his sons washed their hands and their feet.
32 When they entered the tent of meeting, and when they approached the altar, they
washed, just as the LORD had commanded Moses.

40:33
Ex 27:9-18; 40:8

33 He erected the court all around the tabernacle and the altar, and hung up the veil
for the gateway of the court. Thus Moses finished the work.

40:34
Num 9:15-23
1 Kin 8:11; Ezek 43:4f; Rev 15:8

The Glory of the LORD

34 Then the cloud covered the tent of meeting, and the glory of the LORD filled the
tabernacle.

40:35
1 Kin 8:11; 2 Chr 5:13, 14

35 Moses was not able to enter the tent of meeting because the cloud had settled on it,
and the glory of the LORD filled the tabernacle.

40:36
Num 9:17; Neh 9:19

36 Throughout all their journeys whenever the cloud was taken up from over the tabernacle, the sons of Israel would set out;

40:37
Num 9:19-22

37 but if the cloud was not taken up, then they did not set out until the day when it was
taken up.

40:38
Ex 13:21; Num 9:12, 15; Ps 78:14; Is 4:5

38 For throughout all their journeys, the cloud of the LORD was on the tabernacle by
day, and there was fire in it by night, in the sight of all the house of Israel.

40:34 The tabernacle was God's home on earth. He filled it with his glory—the overpowering sense of his presence. Almost 500 years later, Solomon built the temple, which replaced the tabernacle as the central place of worship. God also filled the temple with his glory (2 Chronicles 5:13–14). But when Israel turned from God, his glory and presence departed from the temple and it was destroyed by invading armies (2 Kings 25). The temple was rebuilt in 516 B.C. God's glory returned in even greater splendor nearly five centuries later when Jesus Christ, God's Son, entered it and taught. When Jesus was crucified, God's glory again left the temple. However, God no longer needed a physical building after Jesus rose from the dead. God's temple now is his church, the body of believers.

40:38 The Israelites were once Egyptian slaves making bricks without straw. Here they were following the pillar of cloud and the pillar of fire, carrying the tabernacle they had built for God. Exodus begins in gloom and ends in glory. This parallels our progress through the Christian life. We begin as slaves to sin, are redeemed by God, and end our pilgrimage living with God forever. The lessons the Israelites learned along the way are lessons that we also need to learn.

LEVITICUS

Joseph dies 1805 B.C. (1640 B.C.)

S L A V E R Y I N E G Y P T

VITAL STATISTICS

PURPOSE:
A handbook for the priests and Levites outlining their duties in worship, and a guidebook of holy living for the Hebrews

AUTHOR:
Moses

DATE OF EVENTS:
1445–1444 B.C.

SETTING:
At the foot of Mount Sinai. God is teaching the Israelites how to live as holy people.

KEY VERSE:
"You shall be holy, for I the LORD your God am holy" (19:2).

KEY PEOPLE:
Moses, Aaron, Nadab, Abihu, Eleazar, Ithamar

KEY PLACE:
Mount Sinai

SPECIAL FEATURE:
Holiness is mentioned more times (152) than in any other book of the Bible.

"GOD seems so far away . . . if only I could see or hear him." Have you ever felt this way—struggling with loneliness, burdened by despair, riddled with sin, overwhelmed by problems? Made in God's image, we were created to have a close relationship with him; and when fellowship is broken, we are incomplete and need restoration. Communion with the living God is the essence of worship. It is vital, touching the very core of our lives. Perhaps this is why a whole book of the Bible is dedicated to worship. After Israel's dramatic exit from Egypt, the nation was camped at the foot of Mount Sinai for two years to listen to God (Exodus 19 to Numbers 10). It was a time of resting, teaching, building, and meeting with him face to face. Redemption in Exodus is the foundation for cleansing, worship, and service in Leviticus.

The overwhelming message of Leviticus is the holiness of God—"You shall be holy, for I the LORD your God am holy" (19:2). But how can unholy people approach a holy God? The answer—first sin must be dealt with. Thus the opening chapters of Leviticus give detailed instructions for offering sacrifices, which were the active symbols of repentance and obedience. Whether bulls, grain, goats, or sheep, the sacrificial offerings had to be perfect, with no defects or bruises—pictures of the ultimate sacrifice to come, Jesus, the Lamb of God. Jesus has come and opened the way to God by giving up his life as the final sacrifice in our place. True worship and oneness with God begin as we confess our sin and accept Christ as the only one who can redeem us from sin and help us approach God.

In Leviticus, sacrifices, priests, and the sacred day of atonement opened the way for the Israelites to come to God. God's people were also to worship him with their lives. Thus we read of purity laws (chapters 11—15) and rules for daily living concerning family responsibilities, sexual conduct, relationships, worldliness (chapters 18—20), and vows (chapter 27). These instructions involve one's holy walk with God, and the patterns of spiritual living still apply today. Worship, therefore, has a horizontal aspect—that is, God is honored by our lives as we relate to others.

The final emphasis in Leviticus is celebration. The book gives instructions for the feasts. These were special, regular, and corporate occasions for remembering what God had done, giving thanks to him, and rededicating lives to his service (chapter 23). Our Christian traditions and holidays are different, but they are necessary ingredients of worship. We, too, need special days of worship and celebration with our brothers and sisters to remember God's goodness in our lives.

As you read Leviticus, rededicate yourself to holiness, worshiping God in private confession, public service, and group celebration.

Exodus from Egypt 1446 (1280)	Ten Command-ments given 1445 (1279)	Israel camps at Mount Sinai 1444 (1278)	Moses dies, Canaan entered 1406 (1240)	Judges begin to rule 1375 (1220)	United kingdom under Saul 1050 (1045)

THE BLUEPRINT

A. WORSHIPING A HOLY GOD (1:1—17:16)
1. Instructions for the offerings
2. Instructions for the priests
3. Instructions for the people
4. Instructions for the altar

God provided specific directions for the kind of worship that would be pleasing to him. These instructions teach us about the nature of God and can help us develop a right attitude toward worship. Through the offerings we learn of the seriousness of sin and the importance of bringing our sins to God for forgiveness.

B. LIVING A HOLY LIFE (18:1—27:34)
1. Standards for the people
2. Rules for priests
3. Seasons and feasts
4. Receiving God's blessing

God gave clear standards to the Israelites for living a holy life. They were to be separate and distinct from the pagan nations around them. In the same way, all believers should be separated from sin and dedicated to God. God still wants to remove sin from the lives of his people.

MEGATHEMES

THEME	EXPLANATION	IMPORTANCE
Sacrifice/Offering	There are five kinds of offerings that fulfill two main purposes: one to show praise, thankfulness, and devotion; the other for atonement, the covering and removal of guilt and sin. Animal offerings demonstrated that the person was giving his or her life to God by means of the life of the animal.	The sacrifices (offerings) were for worship and forgiveness of sin. Through them we learn about the cost of sin, for we see that we cannot forgive ourselves. God's system says that a life must be given for a life. In the Old Testament, an animal's life was given to save the life of a person. But this was only a temporary measure until Jesus' death paid the penalty of sin for all people forever.
Worship	Seven feasts were designated as religious and national holidays. They were often celebrated in family settings. These events teach us much about worshiping God in both celebration and quiet dedication.	God's rules about worship set up an orderly, regular pattern of fellowship with him. They allowed times for celebration and thanksgiving as well as for reverence and rededication. Our worship should demonstrate our deep devotion.
Health	Civil rules for handling food, disease, and sex were taught. In these physical principles, many spiritual principles were suggested. Israel was to be different from the surrounding nations. God was preserving Israel from disease and community health problems.	We are to be different morally and spiritually from the unbelievers around us. Principles for healthy living are as important today as in Moses' time. A healthy environment and a healthy body make our service to God more effective.
Holiness	*Holy* means "separated" or "devoted." God removed his people from Egypt; now he was removing Egypt from the people. He was showing them how to exchange Egyptian ways of living and thinking for his ways.	We must devote every area of life to God. God desires absolute obedience in motives as well as practices. Though we do not observe all the worship practices of Israel, we are to have the same spirit of preparation and devotion.
Levites	The Levites and priests instructed the people in their worship. They were the ministers of their day. They also regulated the moral, civil, and ceremonial laws and supervised the health, justice, and welfare of the nation.	The Levites were servants who showed Israel the way to God. They provide the historical backdrop for Christ, who is our high priest and yet our servant. God's true servants care for all the needs of their people.

A. WORSHIPING A HOLY GOD (1:1—17:16)

The Israelites have arrived safely at the foot of Mount Sinai, and the tabernacle has been completed. The people will spend a great deal of time here as God shows them a new way of life with clear instructions on how sinful people can relate to a holy God. These instructions help us avoid taking our relationship with the same holy God too lightly. We learn about the holiness and majesty of the God with whom we are allowed to have a personal relationship.

1. Instructions for the offerings

The Law of Burnt Offerings

1 Then the LORD called to Moses and spoke to him from the tent of meeting, saying,
2 "Speak to the sons of Israel and say to them, 'When any man of you brings an
offering to the LORD, you shall bring your offering of animals from the herd or the flock.
3 'If his offering is a burnt offering from the herd, he shall offer it, a male without defect;
he shall offer it at the doorway of the tent of meeting, that he may be accepted before
the LORD.

1:1 The book of Leviticus begins where the book of Exodus ends—at the foot of Mount Sinai. The tabernacle was just completed (Exodus 35—40), and God was ready to teach the people how to worship there.

THE ISRAELITES AT MOUNT SINAI
Throughout the book of Leviticus, the Israelites were camped at the foot of Mount Sinai. It was time to regroup as a nation and learn the importance of following God as they prepared to march toward the promised land.

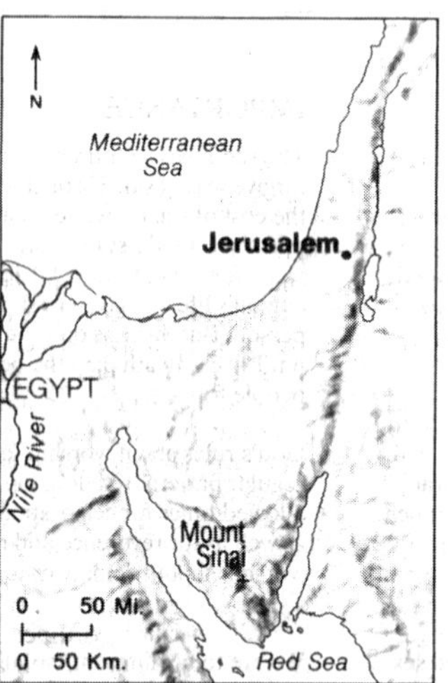

1:1 The tent of meeting was the smaller structure inside the larger tabernacle. The tent of meeting contained the sanctuary in one part and the holy of holies with the ark in another part. These two sections were separated by a veil. God revealed himself to Moses in the holy of holies. Exodus 33:7 mentions a "tent of meeting" where Moses met God before the tabernacle was constructed. Many believe it served the same function as the one described here.

1:1ff We may be tempted to dismiss Leviticus as a record of bizarre rituals of a different age. But its practices made sense to the people of the day and offer important insights for us into God's nature and character. Animal sacrifice seems obsolete and repulsive to many people today, but animal sacrifices were practiced in many cultures in the Middle East. God used the form of sacrifice to teach his people about faith. Sin needed to be taken seriously. When people saw the sacrificial animals being killed, they were sensitized to the importance of their sin and guilt. Our culture's casual attitude toward sin ignores the cost of sin and need for repentance and restoration. Although many of the rituals of Leviticus were designed for the culture of the day, their purpose was to reveal a high and holy God who should be loved, obeyed, and worshiped. God's laws and sacrifices were intended to bring out true devotion of the heart. The ceremonies and rituals were the best way for the Israelites to focus their lives on God.

1:2 Was there any difference between a sacrifice and an offering? In Leviticus the words are interchanged. Usually a specific sacrifice is called an offering (burnt offering, grain offering, peace offering). Offerings in general are called sacrifices. The point is that each person *offered* a gift to God by *sacrificing* it on the altar. In the Old Testament, the sacrifice was the only way to approach God and restore a relationship with him. There was more than one kind of offering or sacrifice. The variety of sacrifices made them more meaningful because each one related to a specific life situation. Sacrifices were given in praise, worship, and thanksgiving, as well as for forgiveness and fellowship. The first seven chapters of Leviticus describe the variety of offerings and how they were to be used.

1:2 When God taught his people to worship him, he placed great emphasis on sacrifices. Why? Sacrifices were God's Old Testament way for people to ask forgiveness for their sins. Since creation, God has made it clear that sin separates people from him, and that those who sin deserve to die. Because "all have sinned" (Romans 3:23), God designed sacrifice as a way to seek forgiveness and restore a relationship with him. Because he is a God of love and mercy, God decided from the very first that he would come into our world and die to pay the penalty for all humans. This he did in his Son who, while still God, became a human being. In the meantime, before God made this ultimate sacrifice of his Son, he instructed people to kill animals as sacrifices for sin.

Animal sacrifice accomplished two purposes: (1) the animal symbolically took the sinner's place and paid the penalty for sin, and (2) the animal's death represented one life given so that another life could be saved. This method of sacrifice continued throughout Old Testament times. It was effective in teaching and guiding the people and bringing them back to God. But in New Testament times, Christ's death became the last sacrifice needed. He took our punishment once and for all. Animal sacrifice is no longer required. Now, all people can be freed from the penalty of sin by simply believing in Jesus and accepting the forgiveness he offers.

1:3–4 The first offering God describes is the burnt offering. A person who had sinned brought an animal with no defects to a priest. The unblemished animal symbolized the moral perfection demanded by a holy God and the perfect nature of the real sacrifice to come—Jesus Christ. The person then laid his hand on the head of the animal to symbolize the person's complete identification with the animal as his substitute. Then he killed the animal and the priest sprinkled the blood. He symbolically transferred his sins to the animal, and thus his sins were taken away (atonement). Finally the animal (except for the blood and skin) was burned on the altar, signifying the person's complete dedication to God. God required more than a sacrifice, of course. He also asked the sinner to have an attitude of repentance. The outward symbol (the sacrifice) and the inner change (repentance) were to work together. But it is important to remember that neither sacrifice nor repentance actually caused the sin to be taken away. God alone forgives sin. Fortunately for us, forgiveness is part of God's loving nature. Have you come to him to receive forgiveness?

4 'He shall lay his hand on the head of the burnt offering, that it may be accepted for
him to make atonement on his behalf.
5 'He shall slay the young bull before the LORD; and Aaron's sons the priests shall
offer up the blood and sprinkle the blood around on the altar that is at the doorway of
the tent of meeting.
6 'He shall then skin the burnt offering and cut it into its pieces.
7 'The sons of Aaron the priest shall put fire on the altar and arrange wood on the
fire.
8 'Then Aaron's sons the priests shall arrange the pieces, the head and the suet over
the wood which is on the fire that is on the altar.
9 'Its entrails, however, and its legs he shall wash with water. And the priest shall offer
up in smoke all of it on the altar for a burnt offering, an offering by fire of a soothing
aroma to the LORD.
10 'But if his offering is from the flock, of the sheep or of the goats, for a burnt offering,
he shall offer it a male without defect.
11 'He shall slay it on the side of the altar northward before the LORD, and Aaron's
sons the priests shall sprinkle its blood around on the altar.
12 'He shall then cut it into its pieces with its head and its suet, and the priest shall arrange them on the wood which is on the fire that is on the altar.
13 'The entrails, however, and the legs he shall wash with water. And the priest shall
offer all of it, and offer it up in smoke on the altar; it is a burnt offering, an offering by
fire of a soothing aroma to the LORD.
14 'But if his offering to the LORD is a burnt offering of birds, then he shall bring his
offering from the turtledoves or from young pigeons.

THE OFFERINGS Listed here are the five key offerings the Israelites made to God. The Jews made these offerings in order to have their sins forgiven and to restore their fellowship with God. The death of Jesus Christ made these sacrifices unnecessary. Because of his death our sins were completely forgiven and fellowship with God has been restored.

Offering	*Purpose*	*Significance*	*Christ, the Perfect Offering*
Burnt Offering (Lev. 1— voluntary)	To make payment for sins in general	Showed a person's devotion to God	Christ's death was the perfect offering
Grain Offering (Lev. 2— voluntary)	To show honor and respect to God in worship	Acknowledged that all we have belongs to God	Christ was the perfect man, who gave all of himself to God and others
Peace Offering (Lev. 3— voluntary)	To express gratitude to God	Symbolized peace and fellowship with God	Christ is the only way to peace with God
Sin Offering (Lev. 4— required)	To make payment for unintentional neglect, sins of uncleanness, or thoughtlessness	Restored the sinner to fellowship with God; showed seriousness of sin	Christ's death restores our fellowship with God
Guilt Offering (Lev. 5— required)	To make payment for sins against God and others. A sacrifice was made to God and the injured person was repaid or compensated	Provided compensation for injured parties	Christ's death takes away the deadly consequences of sin

1:3ff What did sacrifices teach the people? (1) By requiring perfect animals and holy priests, they taught reverence for a holy God. (2) By demanding exact obedience, they taught total submission to God's laws. (3) By requiring an animal of great value, they showed the high cost of sin and demonstrated the sincerity of their commitment to God.

1:3–13 Why are there such detailed regulations for each offering? God had a purpose in giving these commands. Starting from scratch, he was teaching his people a whole new way of life, cleansing them from the many pagan practices they had learned in Egypt, and restoring true worship of himself. The strict details kept Israel from slipping back into their old life-style. In addition, each law paints a graphic picture of the seriousness of sin and of God's great mercy in forgiving sinners.

1:4ff Israel was not the only nation to sacrifice animals. Many other religions did it as well to try to please their gods. Some cultures even included human sacrifice, which was strictly forbidden by God. However, the meaning of Israel's animal sacrifices was clearly different from that of their pagan neighbors. Israelites sacrificed animals, not just to appease God's wrath, but as a substitute for the punishment they deserved for their sins. A sacrifice showed faith in God and commitment to his laws. Most important, this system foreshadowed the day when the Lamb of God (Jesus Christ) would die and conquer sin once and for all.

1:13 The "soothing aroma to the LORD" is a way of saying that God accepted the sacrifice because of the people's attitude.

15 'The priest shall bring it to the altar, and wring off its head and offer it up in smoke
on the altar; and its blood is to be drained out on the side of the altar.
16 'He shall also take away its crop with its feathers and cast it beside the altar eastward, to the place of the ashes.
17 'Then he shall tear it by its wings, *but* shall not sever *it.* And the priest shall offer it
up in smoke on the altar on the wood which is on the fire; it is a burnt offering, an offering by fire of a soothing aroma to the LORD.

The Law of Grain Offerings

2 'Now when anyone presents a grain offering as an offering to the LORD, his offering
shall be of fine flour, and he shall pour oil on it and put frankincense on it.
2 'He shall then bring it to Aaron's sons the priests; and shall take from it his handful
of its fine flour and of its oil with all of its frankincense. And the priest shall offer *it* up in
smoke *as* its memorial portion on the altar, an offering by fire of a soothing aroma to
the LORD.
3 'The remainder of the grain offering belongs to Aaron and his sons: a thing most
holy, of the offerings to the LORD by fire.
4 'Now when you bring an offering of a grain offering baked in an oven, *it shall be* unleavened cakes of fine flour mixed with oil, or unleavened wafers spread with oil.
5 'If your offering is a grain offering *made* on the griddle, *it shall be* of fine flour, unleavened, mixed with oil;
6 you shall break it into bits and pour oil on it; it is a grain offering.
7 'Now if your offering is a grain offering *made* in a pan, it shall be made of fine flour
with oil.
8 'When you bring in the grain offering which is made of these things to the LORD, it
shall be presented to the priest and he shall bring it to the altar.
9 'The priest then shall take up from the grain offering its memorial portion, and shall
offer *it* up in smoke on the altar *as* an offering by fire of a soothing aroma to the LORD.
10 'The remainder of the grain offering belongs to Aaron and his sons: a thing most
holy of the offerings to the LORD by fire.
11 'No grain offering, which you bring to the LORD, shall be made with leaven, for you
shall not offer up in smoke any leaven or any honey as an offering by fire to the LORD.
12 'As an offering of first fruits you shall bring them to the LORD, but they shall not
ascend for a soothing aroma on the altar.
13 'Every grain offering of yours, moreover, you shall season with salt, so that the salt
of the covenant of your God shall not be lacking from your grain offering; with all your
offerings you shall offer salt.
14 'Also if you bring a grain offering of early ripened things to the LORD, you shall bring
fresh heads of grain roasted in the fire, grits of new growth, for the grain offering of your
early ripened things.
15 'You shall then put oil on it and lay incense on it; it is a grain offering.
16 'The priest shall offer up in smoke its memorial portion, part of its grits and its oil
with all its incense as an offering by fire to the LORD.

2:1 Lev 6:14-18; Num 15:4
2:2 Lev 5:12; 6:15; Lev 2:9, 16; 5:12; 24:7; Acts 10:4
2:3 Lev 2:10; 6:16; Lev 10:12, 13
2:4 Ex 29:2
2:5 Lev 6:21; 7:9
2:7 Lev 7:9
2:9 Lev 2:2, 16; 5:12
2:10 Lev 2:3; 6:16
2:11 Ex 23:18; 34:25; Lev 6:16, 17; Ex 29:25; Lev 1:13
2:12 Ex 34:22; Lev 7:13; 23:10, 17, 18
2:13 Num 18:19; 2 Chr 13:5; Ezek 43:24
2:14 Lev 23:14
2:16 Lev 2:2

2:1ff The grain offering accompanied all burnt offerings and was a gift of thanks to God. It reminded the people that their food came from God and that therefore they owed their lives to him. Three kinds of grain offerings are listed: (1) fine flour with oil and frankincense, (2) unleavened cakes or wafers of fine flour and oil, and (3) roasted kernels of grain (corn) with oil and incense. The absence of leaven (yeast) symbolized the absence of sin, and the oil symbolized God's presence. Part of the grain offering was burned on the altar as a gift to God, and the rest was eaten by the priests. The offerings helped support them in their work.

2:11 Why was no leaven (yeast) allowed in the grain offerings? Yeast is a bacterial fungus or mold and is, therefore, an appropriate symbol for sin. It grows in bread dough just as sin grows in a life. A little yeast will affect the whole loaf, just as a little sin can ruin a whole life. Jesus continued this analogy by warning about the "leaven of the Pharisees and Sadducees" (Matthew 16:6; Mark 8:15).

2:13 The offerings were seasoned with salt as a reminder of the people's covenant (contract) with God. Salt is a good symbol of God's activity in a person's life, because it penetrates, preserves, and aids in healing. God wants to be active in your life. Let him become part of you, penetrating every aspect of your life, preserving you from the evil all around, and healing you of your sins and shortcomings.

2:13 In Arab countries, an agreement was sealed with a gift of salt to show the strength and permanence of the contract. In Matthew 5:13 believers are called "the salt of the earth." Let the salt you use each day remind you that you are now one of God's covenant people who actively help preserve and purify the world.

2:14–15 Crushed heads of new grain mixed with oil and baked was typical food for the average person. This offering was a token presentation of a person's daily food. In this way, people acknowledged God as provider of their food. Even a poor person could fulfill this offering. God was pleased by the motivation and the dedication of the persons making it.

The Law of Peace Offerings

3 'Now if his offering is a sacrifice of peace offerings, if he is going to offer out of the
herd, whether male or female, he shall offer it without defect before the LORD.
2 'He shall lay his hand on the head of his offering and slay it at the doorway of
the tent of meeting, and Aaron's sons the priests shall sprinkle the blood around on the
altar.
3 'From the sacrifice of the peace offerings he shall present an offering by fire to the
LORD, the fat that covers the entrails and all the fat that is on the entrails,
4 and the two kidneys with the fat that is on them, which is on the loins, and the lobe
of the liver, which he shall remove with the kidneys.
5 'Then Aaron's sons shall offer *it* up in smoke on the altar on the burnt offering, which
is on the wood that is on the fire; it is an offering by fire of a soothing aroma to the LORD.
6 'But if his offering for a sacrifice of peace offerings to the LORD is from the flock, he
shall offer it, male or female, without defect.
7 'If he is going to offer a lamb for his offering, then he shall offer it before the LORD,
8 and he shall lay his hand on the head of his offering and slay it before the tent of
meeting, and Aaron's sons shall sprinkle its blood around on the altar.
9 'From the sacrifice of peace offerings he shall bring as an offering by fire to the LORD,
its fat, the entire fat tail which he shall remove close to the backbone, and the fat that
covers the entrails and all the fat that is on the entrails,
10 and the two kidneys with the fat that is on them, which is on the loins, and the lobe
of the liver, which he shall remove with the kidneys.
11 'Then the priest shall offer *it* up in smoke on the altar *as* food, an offering by fire to
the LORD.
12 'Moreover, if his offering is a goat, then he shall offer it before the LORD,
13 and he shall lay his hand on its head and slay it before the tent of meeting, and the
sons of Aaron shall sprinkle its blood around on the altar.
14 'From it he shall present his offering as an offering by fire to the LORD, the fat that
covers the entrails and all the fat that is on the entrails,
15 and the two kidneys with the fat that is on them, which is on the loins, and the lobe
of the liver, which he shall remove with the kidneys.
16 'The priest shall offer them up in smoke on the altar *as* food, an offering by fire for
a soothing aroma; all fat is the LORD'S.
17 'It is a perpetual statute throughout your generations in all your dwellings: you shall
not eat any fat or any blood.' "

The Law of Sin Offerings

4 Then the LORD spoke to Moses, saying,
2 "Speak to the sons of Israel, saying, 'If a person sins unintentionally in any of the
things which the LORD has commanded not to be done, and commits any of them,
3 if the anointed priest sins so as to bring guilt on the people, then let him offer to the
LORD a bull without defect as a sin offering for the sin he has committed.
4 'He shall bring the bull to the doorway of the tent of meeting before the LORD, and
he shall lay his hand on the head of the bull and slay the bull before the LORD.
5 'Then the anointed priest is to take some of the blood of the bull and bring it to the
tent of meeting,
6 and the priest shall dip his finger in the blood and sprinkle some of the blood seven
times before the LORD, in front of the veil of the sanctuary.
7 'The priest shall also put some of the blood on the horns of the altar of fragrant

3:1 Lev 7:11-34; 17:5; Lev 1:3; 22:20 21
3:2 Lev 1:4; Ex 29:11, 16, 20
3:5 Lev 7:28-34; Ex 29:38-42; Num 28:3-10; Num 15:8-10; 28:12-14
3:6 Lev 3:1; 22:20-24
3:7 Num 15:4, 5; 28:4-8; Lev 17:8, 9; 1 Kin 8:62
3:8 Lev 1:4; Lev 3:2; Lev 1:5
3:9 Lev 17:5; Num 7:88; 1 Sam 10:8; 2 Sam 6:17; 1 Kin 3:15; 8:63, 64; 1 Chr 16:1
3:10 Lev 3:4, 15
3:11 Lev 3:5; Lev 3:16; 21:6, 8, 17, 22
3:12 Num 15:6-11
3:15 Lev 3:4; 7:4
3:16 Lev 7:23-25
3:17 Lev 6:18, 22; 7:34, 36; 10:9, 15; 16:29; 17:7; 23:14, 21; 24:3; Lev 7:26; 17:10-16
4:2 Lev 4:22, 27; 5:15-18; 22:14; Lev 4:13
4:3 Lev 4:14, 23, 28
4:4 Lev 1:4; 4:15; Num 8:12
4:5 Lev 4:3, 17
4:6 Ex 40:21, 26
4:7 Lev 4:18, 25, 30, 34; 8:15; 9:9; 16:18

3:1ff A person gave a peace (or fellowship) offering as an expression of gratitude and a means of establishing peace between himself and God. Because it symbolized peace with God, part of the offering could be eaten by the person presenting it.

3:2 The altar was inside the walls of the tabernacle gate but outside the tent of meeting.

4:1ff Have you ever done something wrong without realizing it until later? Although your sin was unintentional, it was still sin. One of the purposes of God's commands was to make the Israelites aware of their unintentional sins so they would not repeat them and so they could be forgiven for them. Leviticus 4 and 5 mention some of these unintentional sins and the way the Israelites could be forgiven for them. As you read more of God's laws, keep in mind that they were meant to teach and guide the people. Let them help you become more aware of sin in your life.

4:3 The sin offering was for those who (1) committed a sin without realizing it or (2) committed a sin out of weakness or negligence as opposed to outright rebellion against God. Different animals were sacrificed for the different kinds of sin. The death of Jesus Christ was the final sin offering in the Bible (Hebrews 9:25–28 tells why).

incense which is before the LORD in the tent of meeting; and all the blood of the bull he
shall pour out at the base of the altar of burnt offering which is at the doorway of the
tent of meeting.
8 'He shall remove from it all the fat of the bull of the sin offering: the fat that covers
the entrails, and all the fat which is on the entrails,
9 and the two kidneys with the fat that is on them, which is on the loins, and the lobe
of the liver, which he shall remove with the kidneys
10 (just as it is removed from the ox of the sacrifice of peace offerings), and the priest
is to offer them up in smoke on the altar of burnt offering.
11 'But the hide of the bull and all its flesh with its head and its legs and its entrails and
its refuse,
12 that is, all *the rest of* the bull, he is to bring out to a clean place outside the camp
where the ashes are poured out, and burn it on wood with fire; where the ashes are poured
out it shall be burned.
13 'Now if the whole congregation of Israel commits error and the matter escapes the
notice of the assembly, and they commit any of the things which the LORD has commanded
not to be done, and they become guilty;
14 when the sin which they have committed becomes known, then the assembly shall
offer a bull of the herd for a sin offering and bring it before the tent of meeting.
15 'Then the elders of the congregation shall lay their hands on the head of the bull
before the LORD, and the bull shall be slain before the LORD.
16 'Then the anointed priest is to bring some of the blood of the bull to the tent of
meeting;
17 and the priest shall dip his finger in the blood and sprinkle *it* seven times before the
LORD, in front of the veil.
18 'He shall put some of the blood on the horns of the altar which is before the LORD
in the tent of meeting; and all the blood he shall pour out at the base of the altar of burnt
offering which is at the doorway of the tent of meeting.
19 'He shall remove all its fat from it and offer it up in smoke on the altar.
20 'He shall also do with the bull just as he did with the bull of the sin offering; thus he
shall do with it. So the priest shall make atonement for them, and they will be forgiven.
21 'Then he is to bring out the bull to *a place* outside the camp and burn it as he burned
the first bull; it is the sin offering for the assembly.
22 'When a leader sins and unintentionally does any one of all the things which the LORD
his God has commanded not to be done, and he becomes guilty,
23 if his sin which he has committed is made known to him, he shall bring for his offering a goat, a male without defect.
24 'He shall lay his hand on the head of the male goat and slay it in the place where
they slay the burnt offering before the LORD; it is a sin offering.
25 'Then the priest is to take some of the blood of the sin offering with his finger and
put it on the horns of the altar of burnt offering; and *the rest of* its blood he shall pour
out at the base of the altar of burnt offering.
26 'All its fat he shall offer up in smoke on the altar as *in the case of* the fat of the sacrifice of peace offerings. Thus the priest shall make atonement for him in regard to his
sin, and he will be forgiven.
27 'Now if anyone of the common people sins unintentionally in doing any of the things
which the LORD has commanded not to be done, and becomes guilty,
28 if his sin which he has committed is made known to him, then he shall bring for his
offering a goat, a female without defect, for his sin which he has committed.
29 'He shall lay his hand on the head of the sin offering and slay the sin offering at the
place of the burnt offering.
30 'The priest shall take some of its blood with his finger and put it on the horns of the
altar of burnt offering; and all *the rest of* its blood he shall pour out at the base of the
altar.
31 'Then he shall remove all its fat, just as the fat was removed from the sacrifice of
peace offerings; and the priest shall offer it up in smoke on the altar for a soothing aroma to the LORD. Thus the priest shall make atonement for him, and he will be forgiven.
32 'But if he brings a lamb as his offering for a sin offering, he shall bring it, a female
without defect.
33 'He shall lay his hand on the head of the sin offering and slay it for a sin offering in
the place where they slay the burnt offering.

4:8 Lev 3:3, 4
4:9 Lev 3:4
4:11 Lev 9:11; Num 19:5
4:12 Lev 4:21; 6:10, 11; 16:27
4:13 Num 15:24-26
4:14 Lev 4:3; Lev 4:3, 23, 28
4:15 Lev 8:14, 18, 22; Num 8:10, 12; Lev 1:3
4:17 Lev 4:6
4:18 Lev 4:7, 25, 30, 34
4:19 Lev 4:8
4:20 Lev 4:8, 21; Num 15:25, 28
4:21 Lev 4:13f; 16:15-17; Num 15:24-26
4:22 Num 31:13; 32:2; Lev 4:2, 27
4:23 Lev 4:3; Lev 4:3, 14, 28; Lev 4:28
4:25 Lev 4:7, 18, 30, 34
4:26 Lev 4:19; Lev 4:20, 31; 5:10, 13, 16, 18; 6:7
4:27 Lev 4:2; Num 15:27
4:28 Lev 4:3; Lev 4:3, 14, 23, 32; Lev 4:23
4:29 Lev 1:4; 4:4, 24; Lev 1:5, 11
4:30 Lev 4:7, 18, 25, 34; Lev 4:7
4:31 Lev 4:8; Gen 8:21; Ex 29:18; Lev 1:9, 13; 2:2, 9, 12
4:32 Lev 4:28
4:33 Lev 1:4, 5; Lev 4:29

4:34 Lev 4:7, 18, 25, 30; Lev 4:7

34 'The priest is to take some of the blood of the sin offering with his finger and put it
on the horns of the altar of burnt offering, and all *the rest of* its blood he shall pour out
at the base of the altar.

4:35 Lev 4:26, 31; Lev 4:20

35 'Then he shall remove all its fat, just as the fat of the lamb is removed from the sacrifice of the peace offerings, and the priest shall offer them up in smoke on the altar, on
the offerings by fire to the LORD. Thus the priest shall make atonement for him in regard to his sin which he has committed, and he will be forgiven.

The Law of Guilt Offerings

5:1 Prov 29:24; Jer 23:10

5 'Now if a person sins after he hears a public adjuration *to testify* when he is a witness,
whether he has seen or *otherwise* known, if he does not tell *it,* then he will bear his
guilt.

5:2 Lev 11:8, 11, 24-40; Num 19:11-16; Deut 14:8

2 'Or if a person touches any unclean thing, whether a carcass of an unclean beast or
the carcass of unclean cattle or a carcass of unclean swarming things, though it is hidden
from him and he is unclean, then he will be guilty.
3 'Or if he touches human uncleanness, of whatever *sort* his uncleanness *may* be with
which he becomes unclean, and it is hidden from him, and then he comes to know *it,* he
will be guilty.

5:4 Num 30:6, 8; Ps 106:33

4 'Or if a person swears thoughtlessly with his lips to do evil or to do good, in whatever
matter a man may speak thoughtlessly with an oath, and it is hidden from him, and then
he comes to know *it,* he will be guilty in one of these.

5:5 Lev 16:21; 26:40; Num 5:7; Prov 28:13

5 'So it shall be when he becomes guilty in one of these, that he shall confess that in
which he has sinned.

5:6 Lev 4:28, 32

6 'He shall also bring his guilt offering to the LORD for his sin which he has committed, a female from the flock, a lamb or a goat as a sin offering. So the priest shall make
atonement on his behalf for his sin.

5:7 Lev 12:6, 8; 14:22, 30, 31

7 'But if he cannot afford a lamb, then he shall bring to the LORD his guilt offering for
that in which he has sinned, two turtledoves or two young pigeons, one for a sin offering
and the other for a burnt offering.

5:8 Lev 1:17

8 'He shall bring them to the priest, who shall offer first that which is for the sin offering and shall nip its head at the front of its neck, but he shall not sever *it.*

5:9 Lev 1:15; Lev 4:7, 18

9 'He shall also sprinkle some of the blood of the sin offering on the side of the altar,
while the rest of the blood shall be drained out at the base of the altar: it is a sin offering.

5:10 Lev 1:14-17; Lev 4:20, 26; 5:13, 16

10 'The second he shall then prepare as a burnt offering according to the ordinance. So
the priest shall make atonement on his behalf for his sin which he has committed, and it
will be forgiven him.

5:11 Lev 14:21-32; 27:8; Lev 2:1, 2

11 'But if his means are insufficient for two turtledoves or two young pigeons, then for
his offering for that which he has sinned, he shall bring the tenth of an [1]ephah of fine
flour for a sin offering; he shall not put oil on it or place incense on it, for it is a sin offering.
12 'He shall bring it to the priest, and the priest shall take his handful of it as its memorial portion and offer *it* up in smoke on the altar, with the offerings of the LORD by fire:
it is a sin offering.

5:13 Lev 5:4, 5; Lev 2:3

13 'So the priest shall make atonement for him concerning his sin which he has committed from one of these, and it will be forgiven him; then *the rest* shall become the priest's,
like the grain offering.' "
14 Then the LORD spoke to Moses, saying,

1 I.e. Approx one bu

5:4 Have you ever sworn to do or not do something and then realized how foolish your promise was? God's people are called to keep their word, even if they make promises that are tough to keep. Jesus was warning against swearing (in the sense of making vows or oaths) when he said, "Let your statement be, 'Yes, yes' or 'No, no'; anything beyond these is of evil" (Matthew 5:37). Our word should be enough. If we feel we have to strengthen it with an oath, something is wrong with our sincerity. The only promises we ought not to keep are promises that lead to sin. A wise and self-controlled person avoids making rash promises.

5:5 The entire system of sacrifices could not help a sinner unless he brought his offering with an attitude of repentance and a willingness to confess sin. Today, because of Christ's death on the cross, we do not have to sacrifice animals. But it is still vital to confess sin, because confession shows realization of sin, awareness of God's holiness, humility before God, and willingness to turn from this sin (Psalm 51:16–17). Even Jesus' death will be of little value to us if we do not repent and follow him. It is like a vaccine for a dangerous disease—it won't help unless it enters the bloodstream.

5:14–19 The guilt offering was a way of taking care of sin committed unintentionally. It was for those who sinned in some way against "holy things"—the tabernacle or the priesthood—as well as for those who unintentionally sinned against someone. In either case, a ram with no defects had to be sacrificed, plus those harmed by the sin had to be compensated for their loss, plus a 20 percent penalty. Even though Christ's death has made guilt offerings unnecessary for us today, we still need to make things right with those we hurt.

15"If a person acts unfaithfully and sins unintentionally against the LORD'S holy things, **5:15**
then he shall bring his guilt offering to the LORD: a ram without defect from the flock, Num 5:5-8; Lev 4:2;
according to your valuation in silver by shekels, in *terms of* the shekel of the sanctuary, 22:14; Lev 7:1-10; Lev 6:6; Ex 30:13
for a guilt offering.
16"He shall make restitution for that which he has sinned against the holy thing, and **5:16**
shall add to it a fifth part of it and give it to the priest. The priest shall then make atone- Lev 6:5; 22:14; Num 5:7, 8; Lev 7:2-7
ment for him with the ram of the guilt offering, and it will be forgiven him.
17"Now if a person sins and does any of the things which the LORD has commanded **5:17**
not to be done, though he was unaware, still he is guilty and shall bear his punishment. Lev 4:2; 5:19
18"He is then to bring to the priest a ram without defect from the flock, according to **5:18**
your valuation, for a guilt offering. So the priest shall make atonement for him concern- Lev 5:15; Lev 5:17
ing his error in which he sinned unintentionally and did not know *it,* and it will be forgiven him.
19"It is a guilt offering; he was certainly guilty before the LORD."

Guilt Offering

6 Then the LORD spoke to Moses, saying,
2 "When a person sins and acts unfaithfully against the LORD, and deceives his **6:2**
companion in regard to a deposit or a security entrusted *to him,* or through robbery, or Ex 22:7-15
if he has extorted from his companion,
3 or has found what was lost and lied about it and sworn falsely, so that he sins in **6:3**
regard to any one of the things a man may do; Ex 23:4; Deut 22:1-4
4 then it shall be, when he sins and becomes guilty, that he shall restore what he took **6:4**
by robbery or what he got by extortion, or the deposit which was entrusted to him or the Lev 24:18, 21
lost thing which he found,
5 or anything about which he swore falsely; he shall make restitution for it in full and **6:5**
add to it one-fifth more. He shall give it to the one to whom it belongs on the day *he* Lev 5:16; Num 5:8
presents his guilt offering.
6"Then he shall bring to the priest his guilt offering to the LORD, a ram without de- **6:6**
fect from the flock, according to your valuation, for a guilt offering, Lev 5:15
7 and the priest shall make atonement for him before the LORD, and he will be for- **6:7**
given for any one of the things which he may have done to incur guilt." Lev 7:2-5

The Priest's Part in the Offerings

8 Then the LORD spoke to Moses, saying,
9"Command Aaron and his sons, saying, 'This is the law for the burnt offering: the **6:9**
burnt offering itself *shall remain* on the hearth on the altar all night until the morning, Ex 29:38-42; Num 28:3-10; Lev 6:12,
and the fire on the altar is to be kept burning on it. 13
10 'The priest is to put on his linen robe, and he shall put on undergarments next to his **6:10**
flesh; and he shall take up the ashes *to* which the fire reduces the burnt offering on the Ex 28:39, 42; 39:27,
altar and place them beside the altar. 28
11 'Then he shall take off his garments and put on other garments, and carry the ashes
outside the camp to a clean place.
12 'The fire on the altar shall be kept burning on it. It shall not go out, but the priest **6:12**
shall burn wood on it every morning; and he shall lay out the burnt offering on it, and Lev 3:5
offer up in smoke the fat portions of the peace offerings on it.
13 'Fire shall be kept burning continually on the altar; it is not to go out.
14 'Now this is the law of the grain offering: the sons of Aaron shall present it before
the LORD in front of the altar.
15 'Then one *of them* shall lift up from it a handful of the fine flour of the grain offer- **6:15** Lev 2:2, 9

6:1–7 Here we discover that stealing involves more than just taking from someone. Finding something and not returning it or refusing to return something borrowed are other forms of stealing. These are sins against God and not just your neighbor, a stranger, or a large business. If you have gotten something deceitfully, then confess your sin to God, apologize to the owner, and return the stolen items—with interest.

6:12–13 While the previous offerings and sacrifices were ones that the people did, the section from 6:8—7:38 deals with priestly procedure. The burnt offering was presented in the morning and evening for the whole nation (see Exodus 29:38–43). The holy fire on the altar had to keep burning because God had started it. This represented God's eternal presence in the sacrificial system. It showed the people that only by God's gracious favor could their sacrifices be acceptable. God's fire is present in each believer's life today. He lights the fire when the Holy Spirit comes to live in us, and he tends it so that we will grow in grace as we walk with him. When we are aware that God lives in us, we have confidence to come to him for forgiveness and restoration. We can carry out our work with strength and enthusiasm.

ing, with its oil and all the incense that is on the grain offering, and he shall offer *it* up in
smoke on the altar, a soothing aroma, as its memorial offering to the LORD.
16 'What is left of it Aaron and his sons are to eat. It shall be eaten as unleavened cakes
in a holy place; they are to eat it in the court of the tent of meeting.
17 'It shall not be baked with leaven. I have given it as their share from My offerings by
fire; it is most holy, like the sin offering and the guilt offering.
18 'Every male among the sons of Aaron may eat it; it is a permanent ordinance throughout your generations, from the offerings by fire to the LORD. Whoever touches them
will become consecrated.' "
19 Then the LORD spoke to Moses, saying,
20 "This is the offering which Aaron and his sons are to present to the LORD on the day
when he is anointed; the tenth of an ephah of fine flour as a regular grain offering, half
of it in the morning and half of it in the evening.
21 "It shall be prepared with oil on a griddle. When it is *well* stirred, you shall bring it.
You shall present the grain offering in baked pieces as a soothing aroma to the LORD.
22 "The anointed priest who will be in his place among his sons shall offer it. By a permanent ordinance it shall be entirely offered up in smoke to the LORD.
23 "So every grain offering of the priest shall be burned entirely. It shall not be eaten."
24 Then the LORD spoke to Moses, saying,
25 "Speak to Aaron and to his sons, saying, 'This is the law of the sin offering: in the
place where the burnt offering is slain the sin offering shall be slain before the LORD; it
is most holy.
26 'The priest who offers it for sin shall eat it. It shall be eaten in a holy place, in the
court of the tent of meeting.
27 'Anyone who touches its flesh will become consecrated; and when any of its blood
splashes on a garment, in a holy place you shall wash what was splashed on.
28 'Also the earthenware vessel in which it was boiled shall be broken; and if it was boiled
in a bronze vessel, then it shall be scoured and rinsed in water.
29 'Every male among the priests may eat of it; it is most holy.
30 'But no sin offering of which any of the blood is brought into the tent of meeting to
make atonement in the holy place shall be eaten; it shall be burned with fire.

The Priest's Part in the Offerings

7 'Now this is the law of the guilt offering; it is most holy.
2 'In the place where they slay the burnt offering they are to slay the guilt offering,
and he shall sprinkle its blood around on the altar.
3 'Then he shall offer from it all its fat: the fat tail and the fat that covers the entrails,
4 and the two kidneys with the fat that is on them, which is on the loins, and the lobe
on the liver he shall remove with the kidneys.
5 'The priest shall offer them up in smoke on the altar as an offering by fire to the
LORD; it is a guilt offering.
6 'Every male among the priests may eat of it. It shall be eaten in a holy place; it is
most holy.
7 'The guilt offering is like the sin offering, there is one law for them; the priest who
makes atonement with it shall have it.
8 'Also the priest who presents any man's burnt offering, that priest shall have for himself the skin of the burnt offering which he has presented.
9 'Likewise, every grain offering that is baked in the oven and everything prepared in
a pan or on a griddle shall belong to the priest who presents it.
10 'Every grain offering, mixed with oil or dry, shall belong to all the sons of Aaron, to
all alike.
11 'Now this is the law of the sacrifice of peace offerings which shall be presented to
the LORD.
12 'If he offers it by way of thanksgiving, then along with the sacrifice of thanksgiving
he shall offer unleavened cakes mixed with oil, and unleavened wafers spread with oil,
and cakes *of well* stirred fine flour mixed with oil.

6:16 Lev 2:3; 10:12-14; Ezek 44:29
6:17 Lev 2:11; Ex 40:10; Lev 6:25, 26, 29, 30; Num 18:9; Lev 7:7; 10:16-18
6:18 Lev 6:29; 7:6; Num 18:10; 1 Cor 9:13; Lev 6:27
6:20 Lev 5:11; Num 4:16
6:21 Lev 2:5
6:25 Lev 1:11
6:26 Lev 6:29
6:27 Lev 7:19
6:28 Lev 11:33; 15:12
6:29 Lev 6:18; Lev 6:17, 25
6:30 Lev 4:1-21; Lev 4:7, 18; Lev 4:11, 12, 21
7:1 Lev 5:14-6:7
7:2 Lev 1:11
7:3 Lev 3:9
7:4 Lev 3:4
7:6 Lev 6:18, 29; Num 18:9
7:7 Lev 6:25, 26, 30 1 Cor 9:13; 10:18
7:9 Lev 2:5
7:11 Lev 3:1
7:12 Lev 7:15; Lev 2:4; Num 6:15

7:11–18 The peace offering was divided into three kinds according to purpose: thanksgiving offering, votive (vow) offering, and freewill offering. A thanksgiving offering was appropriate whenever one wished to show thanks to God, as when recovering from a serious illness, or surviving a dangerous calamity (Psalm 107). A votive offering was given in fulfillment of a vow (2 Samuel 15:7–8). The freewill offering, however, needed no special occasion or reason.

13 'With the sacrifice of his peace offerings for thanksgiving, he shall present his offering with cakes of leavened bread.
14 'Of this he shall present one of every offering as a contribution to the LORD; it shall
belong to the priest who sprinkles the blood of the peace offerings.
15 'Now *as for* the flesh of the sacrifice of his thanksgiving peace offerings, it shall be
eaten on the day of his offering; he shall not leave any of it over until morning.
16 'But if the sacrifice of his offering is a votive or a freewill offering, it shall be eaten
on the day that he offers his sacrifice, and on the next day what is left of it may be eaten;
17 but what is left over from the flesh of the sacrifice on the third day shall be burned
with fire.
18 'So if any of the flesh of the sacrifice of his peace offerings should *ever* be eaten on
the third day, he who offers it will not be accepted, *and* it will not be reckoned to his
benefit. It shall be an offensive thing, and the person who eats of it will bear his *own* iniquity.
19 'Also the flesh that touches anything unclean shall not be eaten; it shall be burned
with fire. As for *other* flesh, anyone who is clean may eat *such* flesh.
20 'But the person who eats the flesh of the sacrifice of peace offerings which belong to
the LORD, in his uncleanness, that person shall be cut off from his people.
21 'When anyone touches anything unclean, whether human uncleanness, or an unclean
animal, or any unclean [2]detestable thing, and eats of the flesh of the sacrifice of peace
offerings which belong to the LORD, that person shall be cut off from his people.' "
22 Then the LORD spoke to Moses, saying,
23 "Speak to the sons of Israel, saying, 'You shall not eat any fat *from* an ox, a sheep or
a goat.
24 'Also the fat of *an animal* which dies and the fat of an animal torn *by beasts* may be
put to any other use, but you must certainly not eat it.
25 'For whoever eats the fat of the animal from which an offering by fire is offered to
the LORD, even the person who eats shall be cut off from his people.
26 'You are not to eat any blood, either of bird or animal, in any of your dwellings.
27 'Any person who eats any blood, even that person shall be cut off from his people.' "
28 Then the LORD spoke to Moses, saying,
29 "Speak to the sons of Israel, saying, 'He who offers the sacrifice of his peace offerings to the LORD shall bring his offering to the LORD from the sacrifice of his peace
offerings.
30 'His own hands are to bring offerings by fire to the LORD. He shall bring the fat with
the breast, that the breast may be presented as a wave offering before the LORD.
31 'The priest shall offer up the fat in smoke on the altar, but the breast shall belong to
Aaron and his sons.
32 'You shall give the right thigh to the priest as a contribution from the sacrifices of
your peace offerings.
33 'The one among the sons of Aaron who offers the blood of the peace offerings and
the fat, the right thigh shall be his as *his* portion.
34 'For I have taken the breast of the wave offering and the thigh of the contribution
from the sons of Israel from the sacrifices of their peace offerings, and have given them
to Aaron the priest and to his sons as *their* due forever from the sons of Israel.
35 'This is that which is consecrated to Aaron and that which is consecrated to his sons
from the offerings by fire to the LORD, in that day when he presented them to serve as
priests to the LORD.

2 Some mss read *swarming thing*

7:13 Lev 2:12; 23:17, 18; Amos 4:5
7:14 Num 18:8, 11, 19
7:15 Lev 22:29, 30
7:16 Lev 19:5-8
7:17 Ex 12:10
7:18 Lev 19:7; Prov 15:8
7:20 Lev 22:3-7; Num 19:13; Lev 7:25
7:21 Lev 5:2, 3
7:23 Lev 3:17
7:24 Ex 22:31; Lev 17:15; 22:8
7:26 Gen 9:4; Lev 17:10-16; 19:26; Deut 12:23; 1 Sam 14:33; Acts 15:20
7:29 Lev 3:1
7:30 Ex 29:26, 27; Lev 8:29; Num 6:20
7:31 Num 18:11; Deut 18:3
7:32 Ex 29:27; Lev 7:34; 9:21; Num 6:20
7:34 Ex 29:27; Lev 10:14, 15; Num 18:18
7:35 Num 18:8

7:22–27 The fat portions were regarded as the best portions; therefore, it was appropriate to dedicate them only to God. Because blood was the river of life, and life was God's gift and his alone, blood had to be returned to God and not used by people.

7:28–30 God told the people of Israel to bring their peace offerings personally, with their own hands. They were to take time and effort to express thanks to God. You are the only person who can express your thankfulness to God and to others. Do you leave it to others to express thanks for what people have done? Do you rely on the one leading the prayer to thank God for you? Take time yourself to express thanks both to God and to others who have helped and blessed you.

7:31–36 The offering that was waved before the altar was called the wave offering. The part of the offering the priests waved was theirs to keep. The waving motion toward and away from the altar symbolized the offering of the sacrifice to God and his returning it to the priests. These offerings helped to care for the priests, who cared for God's house. The New Testament teaches that ministers should be paid by the people they serve (1 Corinthians 9:10). We should give generously to those who minister to us.

7:36 Ex 40:13-15; Lev 8:12, 30
7:37 Ex 29:22-34; Lev 8:22, 23
7:38 Lev 1:1; 26:46; 27:34; Deut 4:5
8:2 Ex 28:1; Lev 6:10; Ex 30:25
8:6 Ex 29:4-6; Ex 30:19, 20; Ps 26:6; 1 Cor 6:11; Eph 5:26
8:7 Ex 28:4
8:8 Ex 28:30; Num 27:21; Deut 33:8; 1 Sam 28:6; Ezra 2:63; Neh 7:65
8:9 Ex 28:36
8:10 Ex 30:26-29; Lev 8:2
8:11 Ex 29:36, 37; 30:29
8:12 Ex 29:7; 30:30; Lev 21:10, 12; Ps 133:2

36 'These the LORD had commanded to be given them from the sons of Israel in the
day that He anointed them. It is *their* due forever throughout their generations.' "
37 This is the law of the burnt offering, the grain offering and the sin offering and the
guilt offering and the ordination offering and the sacrifice of peace offerings,
38 which the LORD commanded Moses at Mount Sinai in the day that He commanded
the sons of Israel to present their offerings to the LORD in the wilderness of Sinai.

2. Instructions for the priests

The Consecration of Aaron and His Sons

8 Then the LORD spoke to Moses, saying,
2 "Take Aaron and his sons with him, and the garments and the anointing oil and
the bull of the sin offering, and the two rams and the basket of unleavened bread,
3 and assemble all the congregation at the doorway of the tent of meeting."
4 So Moses did just as the LORD commanded him. When the congregation was assembled at the doorway of the tent of meeting,
5 Moses said to the congregation, "This is the thing which the LORD has commanded
to do."
6 Then Moses had Aaron and his sons come near and washed them with water.
7 He put the tunic on him and girded him with the sash, and clothed him with the
robe and put the ephod on him; and he girded him with the artistic band of the ephod,
with which he tied *it* to him.
8 He then placed the breastpiece on him, and in the breastpiece he put [3]the Urim and
the Thummim.
9 He also placed the turban on his head, and on the turban, at its front, he placed the
golden plate, the holy crown, just as the LORD had commanded Moses.
10 Moses then took the anointing oil and anointed the tabernacle and all that was in it,
and consecrated them.
11 He sprinkled some of it on the altar seven times and anointed the altar and all its
utensils, and the basin and its stand, to consecrate them.
12 Then he poured some of the anointing oil on Aaron's head and anointed him, to
consecrate him.

3 I.e. the lights and perfections

7:37 The ordination offering refers to the offering given at the ceremony when priests were inducted into office (8:22).

7:38 God gave his people many rituals and instructions to follow. All the rituals in Leviticus were meant to teach the people valuable lessons. But over time, the people became indifferent to the meanings of these rituals and they began to lose touch with God. When your church appears to be conducting dry, meaningless rituals, try rediscovering the original meaning and purpose behind each. Your worship will be revitalized.

8:1ff Why did Aaron and his sons need to be cleansed and set apart? Although all the men from the tribe of Levi were dedicated for service to God, only Aaron's descendants could be priests. They alone had the honor and responsibility of performing the sacrifices. These priests had to cleanse and dedicate themselves before they could help the people do the same.

The ceremony described in Leviticus 8 and 9 was their ordination ceremony. Aaron and his sons were washed with water (8:6), clothed with special garments (8:7–9), and anointed with oil (8:12). They placed their hands on a young bull as it was killed (8:14), and on two rams as they were killed (8:18–19, 22). This showed that holiness came from God alone, not from the priestly role. Similarly, we are not spiritually cleansed because we have a religious position. Spiritual cleansing comes only from God. No matter how high our position or how long we have held it, we must depend on God for spiritual vitality.

8:2–3 Why were priests needed in Israel? In Exodus 19:6, the Israelites were instructed to be a kingdom of priests; ideally they would all be holy and relate to God. But from the time of Adam's fall, sin has separated man and God, and people have needed mediators to help them find forgiveness. At first, the patriarchs—heads of households like Abraham and Job—were priests of the house or clan and made sacrifices for the family. When the Israelites left Egypt, the descendants of Aaron were chosen to serve as priests for the nation. The priests stood in the gap between God and man. They were the full-time spiritual leaders and overseers of offerings. The priestly system was a concession to people's inability, because of sin, to confront and relate to God individually and corporately. In Christ, this imperfect system was transformed. Jesus Christ himself is our high priest. Now all believers can approach God through him.

8:8 What were the Urim and Thummim? Little is known about them, but they were probably precious stones or flat objects that God used to give guidance to his people. The high priest kept them in a pouch attached to his breastpiece. Some scholars think the Urim may have been the *no* answer and the Thummim the *yes* answer. After a time of prayer for guidance, the priest would shake one of the stones out of the pouch, and God would cause the proper one to fall out. Another view is that the Urim and Thummim were small flat objects, each with a *yes* side and a *no* side. The priest spilled both from his pouch. If both landed on their *yes* sides, God's answer was positive. Two *no* sides were negative. A *yes* and a *no* meant no reply. God had a specific purpose for using this method of guidance—he was teaching a nation the principles of following him. Our situation is not the same, however, so we must not invent ways like this for God to guide us.

8:12 What was the significance of anointing Aaron as high priest? The high priest had special duties that no other priest had. He alone could enter the holy of holies in the tabernacle on the yearly day of atonement to atone for the sins of the nation. Therefore he was in charge of all the other priests. The high priest was a picture of Jesus Christ, who is our high priest (Hebrews 7:26–28).

13 Next Moses had Aaron's sons come near and clothed them with tunics, and girded
them with sashes and bound caps on them, just as the LORD had commanded Moses.
14 Then he brought the bull of the sin offering, and Aaron and his sons laid their hands
on the head of the bull of the sin offering.
15 Next Moses slaughtered *it* and took the blood and with his finger put *some of it* around
on the horns of the altar, and purified the altar. Then he poured out *the rest of* the blood
at the base of the altar and consecrated it, to make atonement for it.
16 He also took all the fat that was on the entrails and the lobe of the liver, and the two
kidneys and their fat; and Moses offered it up in smoke on the altar.
17 But the bull and its hide and its flesh and its refuse he burned in the fire outside the
camp, just as the LORD had commanded Moses.
18 Then he presented the ram of the burnt offering, and Aaron and his sons laid their
hands on the head of the ram.
19 Moses slaughtered *it* and sprinkled the blood around on the altar.
20 When he had cut the ram into its pieces, Moses offered up the head and the pieces
and the suet in smoke.
21 After he had washed the entrails and the legs with water, Moses offered up the whole
ram in smoke on the altar. It was a burnt offering for a soothing aroma; it was an offering by fire to the LORD, just as the LORD had commanded Moses.
22 Then he presented the second ram, the ram of [4]ordination, and Aaron and his sons
laid their hands on the head of the ram.
23 Moses slaughtered *it* and took some of its blood and put it on the lobe of Aaron's
right ear, and on the thumb of his right hand and on the big toe of his right foot.
24 He also had Aaron's sons come near; and Moses put some of the blood on the lobe
of their right ear, and on the thumb of their right hand and on the big toe of their right
foot. Moses then sprinkled *the rest of* the blood around on the altar.
25 He took the fat, and the fat tail, and all the fat that was on the entrails, and the lobe
of the liver and the two kidneys and their fat and the right thigh.
26 From the basket of unleavened bread that was before the LORD, he took one unleavened cake and one cake of bread *mixed with* oil and one wafer, and placed *them* on
the portions of fat and on the right thigh.
27 He then put all *these* on the hands of Aaron and on the hands of his sons and presented them as a wave offering before the LORD.
28 Then Moses took them from their hands and offered them up in smoke on the altar
with the burnt offering. They were an ordination offering for a soothing aroma; it was
an offering by fire to the LORD.
29 Moses also took the breast and presented it for a wave offering before the LORD; it
was Moses' portion of the ram of ordination, just as the LORD had commanded Moses.
30 So Moses took some of the anointing oil and some of the blood which was on the
altar and sprinkled it on Aaron, on his garments, on his sons, and on the garments of his
sons with him; and he consecrated Aaron, his garments, and his sons, and the garments
of his sons with him.
31 Then Moses said to Aaron and to his sons, "Boil the flesh at the doorway of the tent
of meeting, and eat it there together with the bread which is in the basket of the ordination offering, just as I commanded, saying, 'Aaron and his sons shall eat it.'
32 "The remainder of the flesh and of the bread you shall burn in the fire.
33 "You shall not go outside the doorway of the tent of meeting for seven days, until the
day that the period of your ordination is fulfilled; for he will ordain you through seven days.
34 "The LORD has commanded to do as has been done this day, to make atonement on
your behalf.
35 "At the doorway of the tent of meeting, moreover, you shall remain day and night
for seven days and keep the charge of the LORD, so that you will not die, for so I have
been commanded."
36 Thus Aaron and his sons did all the things which the LORD had commanded through
Moses.

8:13 Ex 29:8, 9
8:14 Ex 29:10; Lev 4:4; Ps 66:15; Ezek 43:19
8:15 Ex 29:12; Lev 4:7; Ezek 43:20
8:16 Ex 29:13
8:17 Ex 29:14; Lev 4:11, 12
8:18 Ex 29:15; Lev 8:2
8:20 Lev 1:8
8:21 Ex 29:18
8:22 Ex 29:31; Lev 8:2
8:23 Ex 29:20, 21
8:24 Heb 9:18-22
8:26 Ex 29:23
8:27 Ex 29:24
8:28 Ex 29:25; Gen 8:21
8:29 Lev 7:31-34; Ex 29:26; Ps 99:6
8:30 Ex 29:21
8:31 Ex 29:31; Ex 29:32
8:32 Ex 29:34
8:33 Ex 29:35
8:35 Num 3:7; 9:19; Deut 11:1; 1 Kin 2:3; Ezek 48:11

4 Lit *filling*, and so throughout the ch

8:36 Aaron and his sons did "all the things which the LORD had commanded." Considering the many detailed lists of Leviticus, that was a remarkable feat. They knew what God wanted, how he wanted it done, and with what attitude it was to be carried out. This can serve as a model for how carefully we ought to obey God. God wants us to be thoroughly holy people, not a rough approximation of the way his followers should be.

Aaron Offers Sacrifices

9:1 Ezek 43:27
9 Now it came about on the eighth day that Moses called Aaron and his sons and the
elders of Israel;
9:2 Ezek 29:1; Lev 4:3
2 and he said to Aaron, "Take for yourself a calf, a bull, for a sin offering and a ram
for a burnt offering, *both* without defect, and offer *them* before the LORD.
3 "Then to the sons of Israel you shall speak, saying, 'Take a male goat for a sin offering, and a calf and a lamb, both one year old, without defect, for a burnt offering,
9:4 Ex 29:43
4 and an ox and a ram for peace offerings, to sacrifice before the LORD, and a grain
offering mixed with oil; for today the LORD will appear to you.' "
5 So they took what Moses had commanded to the front of the tent of meeting, and
the whole congregation came near and stood before the LORD.
9:6 Ex 24:16; Lev 9:23
6 Moses said, "This is the thing which the LORD has commanded you to do, that the
glory of the LORD may appear to you."
9:7 Heb 5:3; 7:27
7 Moses then said to Aaron, "Come near to the altar and offer your sin offering and
your burnt offering, that you may make atonement for yourself and for the people; then
make the offering for the people, that you may make atonement for them, just as the
LORD has commanded."
9:8 Lev 4:1-12
8 So Aaron came near to the altar and slaughtered the calf of the sin offering which
was for himself.
9:9 Lev 9:12, 18; Lev 4:7
9 Aaron's sons presented the blood to him; and he dipped his finger in the blood and
put *some* on the horns of the altar, and poured out *the rest of* the blood at the base of the
altar.
10 The fat and the kidneys and the lobe of the liver of the sin offering, he then offered
up in smoke on the altar just as the LORD had commanded Moses.
9:11 Lev 4:11, 12; 8:17
11 The flesh and the skin, however, he burned with fire outside the camp.
12 Then he slaughtered the burnt offering; and Aaron's sons handed the blood to him
and he sprinkled it around on the altar.
13 They handed the burnt offering to him in pieces, with the head, and he offered *them*
up in smoke on the altar.
14 He also washed the entrails and the legs, and offered *them* up in smoke with the
burnt offering on the altar.
9:15 Lev 4:27-31
15 Then he presented the people's offering, and took the goat of the sin offering which
was for the people, and slaughtered it and offered it for sin, like the first.
9:16 Lev 1:1-13
16 He also presented the burnt offering, and offered it according to the ordinance.
9:17 Lev 2:1-3; Lev 3:5
17 Next he presented the grain offering, and filled his hand with some of it and offered
it up in smoke on the altar, besides the burnt offering of the morning.
9:18 Lev 3:1-11
18 Then he slaughtered the ox and the ram, the sacrifice of peace offerings which was
for the people; and Aaron's sons handed the blood to him and he sprinkled it around on
the altar.
9:19 Lev 3:9
19 As for the portions of fat from the ox and from the ram, the fat tail, and the *fat* covering, and the kidneys and the lobe of the liver,
20 they now placed the portions of fat on the breasts; and he offered them up in smoke
on the altar.
9:21 Ex 29:26, 27; Lev 7:30-34
21 But the breasts and the right thigh Aaron presented as a wave offering before the
LORD, just as Moses had commanded.
9:22 Num 6:22-26; Deut 21:5; Luke 24:50
22 Then Aaron lifted up his hands toward the people and blessed them, and he stepped
down after making the sin offering and the burnt offering and the peace offerings.
9:23 Lev 9:6; Num 16:19
23 Moses and Aaron went into the tent of meeting. When they came out and blessed
the people, the glory of the LORD appeared to all the people.
9:24 1 Kin 18:38, 39; 2 Chr 7:1
24 Then fire came out from before the LORD and consumed the burnt offering and
the portions of fat on the altar; and when all the people saw *it,* they shouted and fell on
their faces.

9:22–23 In 9:6 Moses said to the people, "This is the thing which the LORD has commanded you to do, that the glory of the LORD may appear to you." Moses, Aaron, and the people then got to work and followed God's instructions. Soon after, the glory of the Lord appeared. Often we look for God's glorious acts without concern for following his instructions. Do you serve God in the daily routines of life, or do you wait for him to do a mighty act? If you depend on his glorious acts, you may find yourself sidestepping your everyday duty to obey.

9:24 As a display of his mighty power, God sent fire from the sky to consume Aaron's offering. The people fell to the ground in awe. Some people wonder if God really exists because they don't see his activity in the world. But God is at work in today's world just as he was in Moses' world. Where a large body of believers is active for him, God tends not to display his power in the form of mighty physical acts. Instead he works to change the world through the work of these believers. When you realize that, you will begin to see acts of love and faith that are just as supernatural.

The Sin of Nadab and Abihu

10 Now Nadab and Abihu, the sons of Aaron, took their respective firepans, and
after putting fire in them, placed incense on it and offered strange fire before the
LORD, which He had not commanded them.
2 And fire came out from the presence of the LORD and consumed them, and they
died before the LORD.
3 Then Moses said to Aaron, "It is what the LORD spoke, saying,
'By those who come near Me I will be treated as holy,
And before all the people I will be honored.' "
So Aaron, therefore, kept silent.
4 Moses called also to Mishael and Elzaphan, the sons of Aaron's uncle Uzziel, and
said to them, "Come forward, carry your relatives away from the front of the sanctuary
to the outside of the camp."
5 So they came forward and carried them still in their tunics to the outside of the camp,
as Moses had said.
6 Then Moses said to Aaron and to his sons Eleazar and Ithamar, "Do not [5]uncover
your heads nor tear your clothes, so that you will not die and that He will not become
wrathful against all the congregation. But your kinsmen, the whole house of Israel, shall
bewail the burning which the LORD has brought about.
7 "You shall not even go out from the doorway of the tent of meeting, or you will die;
for the LORD'S anointing oil is upon you." So they did according to the word of Moses.
8 The LORD then spoke to Aaron, saying,
9 "Do not drink wine or strong drink, neither you nor your sons with you, when you
come into the tent of meeting, so that you will not die—it is a perpetual statute throughout your generations—
10 and so as to make a distinction between the holy and the profane, and between the
unclean and the clean,
11 and so as to teach the sons of Israel all the statutes which the LORD has spoken to
them through Moses."
12 Then Moses spoke to Aaron, and to his surviving sons, Eleazar and Ithamar, "Take
the grain offering that is left over from the LORD'S offerings by fire and eat it unleavened beside the altar, for it is most holy.
13 "You shall eat it, moreover, in a holy place, because it is your due and your sons' due
out of the LORD'S offerings by fire; for thus I have been commanded.
14 "The breast of the wave offering, however, and the thigh of the offering you may eat
in a clean place, you and your sons and your daughters with you; for they have been given
as your due and your sons' due out of the sacrifices of the peace offerings of the sons of
Israel.
15 "The thigh offered by lifting up and the breast offered by waving they shall bring along
with the offerings by fire of the portions of fat, to present as a wave offering before the
LORD; so it shall be a thing perpetually due you and your sons with you, just as the LORD
has commanded."

10:1 Ex 24:1, 9; Num 3:2; 26:61; Lev 16:12
10:2 Num 3:4; 16:35; 26:61
10:3 Ex 19:22; Lev 21:6; Ex 30:30; Ezek 38:16; Ex 14:4, 17; Is 49:3; Ezek 28:22
10:4 Ex 6:22
10:5 Ex 29:5; Lev 8:13
10:6 Lev 21:1-5, 10-12; Num 1:53; 16:22, 46; 18:5; Josh 7:1; 22:18, 20; 2 Sam 24:1
10:7 Ex 28:41; Lev 21:12
10:9 Prov 20:1; 31:5; Is 28:7; Ezek 44:21; Hos 4:11; Luke 1:15; Eph 5:18; 1 Tim 3:3; Titus 1:7
10:10 Lev 11:47; 20:25; Ezek 22:26
10:11 Deut 17:10, 11; 33:10
10:12 Ex 6:23; Num 3:2; Lev 6:14-18
10:14 Lev 7:30-34; Num 18:11
10:15 Lev 7:34

5 Lit *unbind*

10:1 What was the strange fire that Nadab and Abihu offered before the Lord? The fire on the altar of burnt offering was never to go out (6:12–13), implying that it was holy. It is possible that Nadab and Abihu brought coals of fire to the altar from another source, making the sacrifice unholy. It has also been suggested that the two priests gave an offering at an unprescribed time. Whatever explanation is correct, the point is that Nadab and Abihu abused their office as priests in a flagrant act of disrespect to God, who had just reviewed with them precisely how they were to conduct worship. As leaders, they had special responsibility to obey God. In their position, they could easily lead many people astray. If God has commissioned you to lead or teach others, be sure to stay close to him and follow his advice.

10:2 Aaron's sons were careless about following the laws for sacrifices. In response, God destroyed them with a blast of fire. Performing the sacrifices was an act of obedience. Doing them correctly showed respect for God. It is easy for us to grow careless about obeying God, to live our way instead of God's. But if one way were just as good as another, God would not have commanded us to live his way. He always has good reasons for his commands, and we always place ourselves in danger when we consciously or carelessly disobey them.

10:8–11 The priests were not to drink wine or other alcoholic beverages before going into the tabernacle. If their senses were dulled by alcohol, they might repeat Nadab and Abihu's sin and bring something unholy into the worship ceremony. In addition, drinking would disqualify them to teach the people God's requirements of self-discipline. Drunkenness was associated with pagan practices, and the Jewish priests were supposed to be distinctively different.

10:10–11 This passage (along with 19:1–2) shows the focus of Leviticus. The Ten Commandments recorded in Exodus 20 were God's fundamental laws. Leviticus explained and supplemented those laws with many other guidelines and principles that helped the Israelites put them into practice. The purpose of God's laws was to teach people how to distinguish right from wrong, the holy from the common. The nation who lived by God's laws would obviously be set apart, dedicated to his service.

10:16 Lev 9:3, 15

10:17 Lev 6:24-30; Ex 28:38; Lev 22:16; Num 18:1

10:18 Lev 6:30; Lev 6:26

10:19 Lev 9:8, 12

16 But Moses searched carefully for the goat of the sin offering, and behold, it had been burned up! So he was angry with Aaron's surviving sons Eleazar and Ithamar, saying,
17 "Why did you not eat the sin offering at the holy place? For it is most holy, and He gave it to you to bear away the guilt of the congregation, to make atonement for them before the LORD.
18 "Behold, since its blood had not been brought inside, into the sanctuary, you should certainly have eaten it in the sanctuary, just as I commanded."
19 But Aaron spoke to Moses, "Behold, this very day they presented their sin offering and their burnt offering before the LORD. When things like these happened to me, if I had eaten a sin offering today, would it have been good in the sight of the LORD?"
20 When Moses heard *that,* it seemed good in his sight.

3. Instructions for the people

Laws about Animals for Food

11:2 Deut 14:3-21

11 The LORD spoke again to Moses and to Aaron, saying to them,
2 "Speak to the sons of Israel, saying, 'These are the creatures which you may eat from all the animals that are on the earth.
3 'Whatever divides a hoof, thus making split hoofs, *and* chews the cud, among the animals, that you may eat.

NADAB/ABIHU

Some brothers, like Cain and Abel or Jacob and Esau, get each other in trouble. Nadab and Abihu got in trouble together.

Although little is known of their early years, the Bible gives us an abundance of information about the environment in which they grew up. Born in Egypt, they were eyewitnesses of God's mighty acts of the exodus. They saw their father, Aaron, their uncle, Moses, and their aunt, Miriam, in action many times. They had firsthand knowledge of God's holiness as few men have ever had, and for a while at least, they followed God wholeheartedly (Leviticus 8:36). But at a crucial moment they chose to treat with indifference the clear instructions from God. The consequence of their sin was fiery, instant, and shocking to all.

We are in danger of making the same mistake as these brothers when we treat lightly the justice and holiness of God. We must draw near to God while realizing that there is a proper fear of God. Don't forget that the opportunity to know God personally is based on his gracious invitation to an always unworthy people, not a gift to be taken for granted. Do your thoughts about God include a humble recognition of his great holiness?

Strengths and accomplishments:
- Oldest sons of Aaron
- Primary candidates to become high priest after their father
- Involved with the original consecration of the tabernacle
- Commended for doing "all the things which the LORD had commanded" (Leviticus 8:36)

Weakness and mistake:
- Treated lightly God's direct commands

Lesson from their lives:
- Sin has deadly consequences

Vital statistics:
- Where: The Sinai peninsula
- Occupation: Priests-in-training
- Relatives: Father: Aaron. Uncle and Aunt: Moses and Miriam. Brothers: Eleazar and Ithamar

Key verses:
"Now Nadab and Abihu, the sons of Aaron, took their respective firepans, and after putting fire in them, placed incense on it and offered strange fire before the LORD, which He had not commanded them. And fire came out from the presence of the LORD and consumed them, and they died before the LORD" (Leviticus 10:1–2).

The story of Nadab and Abihu is told in Leviticus 8—10. They are also mentioned in Exodus 24:1, 9; 28:1; Numbers 3:2-4; 26:60–61.

10:16–20 The priest who offered the sin offering was supposed to eat a portion of the animal and then burn the rest (6:24–30). Moses was angry because Eleazar and Ithamar burned the sin offering, but did not eat any of it. Aaron explained to Moses that his two sons did not feel it appropriate to eat the sacrifice after their two brothers, Nadab and Abihu, had just been killed for sacrificing wrongly. Moses then understood that Eleazar and Ithamar were not trying to disobey God. They were simply afraid and upset over what had just happened to their brothers.

4 'Nevertheless, you are not to eat of these, among those which chew the cud, or among **11:4**
those which divide the hoof: the camel, for though it chews cud, it does not divide the Acts 10:14
hoof, it is unclean to you.
5 'Likewise, the shaphan, for though it chews cud, it does not divide the hoof, it is
unclean to you;
6 the rabbit also, for though it chews cud, it does not divide the hoof, it is unclean
to you;
7 and the pig, for though it divides the hoof, thus making a split hoof, it does not chew
cud, it is unclean to you.
8 'You shall not eat of their flesh nor touch their carcasses; they are unclean to you.
9 'These you may eat, whatever is in the water: all that have fins and scales, those in **11:9**
the water, in the seas or in the rivers, you may eat. Deut 14:9
10 'But whatever is in the seas and in the rivers that does not have fins and scales among **11:10**
all the teeming life of the water, and among all the living creatures that are in the water, Deut 14:10
they are detestable things to you,
11 and they shall be [6]abhorrent to you; you may not eat of their flesh, and their carcasses you shall detest.
12 'Whatever in the water does not have fins and scales is abhorrent to you.

Avoid the Unclean

13 'These, moreover, you shall detest among the birds; they are abhorrent, not to be **11:13**
eaten: the eagle and the vulture and the buzzard, Deut 14:12-19
14 and the kite and the falcon in its kind,
15 every raven in its kind,
16 and the ostrich and the owl and the sea gull and the hawk in its kind,
17 and the little owl and the cormorant and the great owl,
18 and the white owl and the pelican and the carrion vulture,
19 and the stork, the heron in its kinds, and the hoopoe, and the bat.
20 'All the winged insects that walk on *all* fours are detestable to you.
21 'Yet these you may eat among all the winged insects which walk on *all* fours: those
which have above their feet jointed legs with which to jump on the earth.
22 'These of them you may eat: the locust in its kinds, and the devastating locust in its
kinds, and the cricket in its kinds, and the grasshopper in its kinds.
23 'But all other winged insects which are four-footed are detestable to you.
24 'By these, moreover, you will be made unclean: whoever touches their carcasses becomes unclean until evening,
25 and whoever picks up any of their carcasses shall wash his clothes and be unclean **11:25**
until evening. Lev 11:40
26 'Concerning all the animals which divide the hoof but do not make a split *hoof,* or
which do not chew cud, they are unclean to you: whoever touches them becomes unclean.
27 'Also whatever walks on its paws, among all the creatures that walk on *all* fours, are
unclean to you; whoever touches their carcasses becomes unclean until evening,
28 and the one who picks up their carcasses shall wash his clothes and be unclean until
evening; they are unclean to you.
29 'Now these are to you the unclean among the swarming things which swarm on the
earth: the mole, and the mouse, and the great lizard in its kinds,
30 and the gecko, and the crocodile, and the lizard, and the sand reptile, and the
chameleon.

6 Lit *detestable things*

11:8 God had strictly forbidden eating the meat of certain "unclean" animals; to make sure, he forbade even touching them. He wanted the people to be totally separated from those things he had forbidden. So often we flirt with temptation, rationalizing that at least we are technically keeping the commandment not to commit the sin. But God wants us to separate ourselves completely from all sin and tempting situations.

11:25 In order to worship, people need to be prepared. There were some acts of disobedience, some natural acts (such as childbirth, menstruation, or sex), or some accidents (such as touching a dead or diseased body) that would make a person ceremonially unclean and thus forbidden to participate in worship. This did not imply that they had sinned or were rejected by God, but it ensured that all worship was done decently and in order. This chapter describes many of the intentional or accidental occurrences that would disqualify a person from worship until they were "cleansed" or straightened out. A person had to be *prepared* for worship. Similarly, we cannot live any way we want during the week and then rush into God's presence on Sunday. We should prepare ourselves through repentance and cleansing.

31 'These are to you the unclean among all the swarming things; whoever touches them
when they are dead becomes unclean until evening.

11:32 Lev 15:12

32 'Also anything on which one of them may fall when they are dead becomes unclean,
including any wooden article, or clothing, or a skin, or a sack—any article of which use
is made—it shall be put in the water and be unclean until evening, then it becomes clean.

11:33 Lev 6:28; 15:12

33 'As for any earthenware vessel into which one of them may fall, whatever is in it
becomes unclean and you shall break the vessel.
34 'Any of the food which may be eaten, on which water comes, shall become unclean,
and any liquid which may be drunk in every vessel shall become unclean.
35 'Everything, moreover, on which part of their carcass may fall becomes unclean; an
oven or a [7]stove shall be smashed; they are unclean and shall continue as unclean to you.
36 'Nevertheless a spring or a cistern collecting water shall be clean, though the one
who touches their carcass shall be unclean.
37 'If a part of their carcass falls on any seed for sowing which is to be sown, it is clean.
38 'Though if water is put on the seed and a part of their carcass falls on it, it is unclean
to you.
39 'Also if one of the animals dies which you have for food, the one who touches its
carcass becomes unclean until evening.

11:40 Lev 17:15; 22:8; Deut 14:21; Ezek 44:31

40 'He too, who eats some of its carcass shall wash his clothes and be unclean until evening, and the one who picks up its carcass shall wash his clothes and be unclean until
evening.

11:41 Lev 11:29

41 'Now every swarming thing that swarms on the earth is detestable, not to be eaten.
42 'Whatever crawls on its belly, and whatever walks on *all* fours, whatever has many
feet, in respect to every swarming thing that swarms on the earth, you shall not eat them,
for they are detestable.

11:43 Lev 20:25

43 'Do not render yourselves detestable through any of the swarming things that swarm;
and you shall not make yourselves unclean with them so that you become unclean.

11:44 Ex 6:7; 16:12; 23:25; Is 43:3; 51:15; Lev 19:2; 1 Pet 1:16

44 'For I am the LORD your God. Consecrate yourselves therefore, and be holy, for I
am holy. And you shall not make yourselves unclean with any of the swarming things
that swarm on the earth.

11:45 Ex 6:7; 20:2; Lev 22:33; 25:38; 26:45; Lev 19:2; 1 Pet 1:16

45 'For I am the LORD who brought you up from the land of Egypt to be your God;
thus you shall be holy, for I am holy.' "
46 This is the law regarding the animal and the bird, and every living thing that moves
in the waters and everything that swarms on the earth,

11:47 Lev 10:10; Ezek 22:26; 44:23

47 to make a distinction between the unclean and the clean, and between the edible
creature and the creature which is not to be eaten.

Laws of Motherhood

12:2 Lev 15:19; 18:19

12 Then the LORD spoke to Moses, saying,
2 "Speak to the sons of Israel, saying:

7 Lit *hearth for supporting (two) pots*

11:44–45 There is more to this chapter than eating right. These verses provide a key to understanding all the laws and regulations in Leviticus. God wanted his people to be *holy* (set apart, different, unique), just as he is holy. He knew they had only two options: to be separate and holy, or to compromise with their pagan neighbors and become corrupt. That is why he called them out of idolatrous Egypt and set them apart as a unique nation, dedicated to worshiping him alone and leading moral lives. That is also why he designed laws and restrictions to help them remain separate—both socially and spiritually—from the wicked pagan nations they would encounter in Canaan. Christians also are called to be holy (1 Peter 1:15). Like the Israelites, we should remain spiritually separate from the world's wickedness, even though unlike them, we rub shoulders with unbelievers every day. It is no easy task to be holy in an unholy world, but God doesn't ask you to accomplish this on your own. Through the death of his Son, he will "present you before Him holy and blameless and beyond reproach" (Colossians 1:22).

11:47 The designations *clean* and *unclean* were used to define the kind of animals the Israelites could and could not eat. There were several reasons for this restricted diet: (1) To ensure the health of the nation. The forbidden foods were usually scavenging animals that fed on dead animals; thus disease could be transmitted through them. (2) To visibly distinguish Israel from other nations. The pig, for example, was a common sacrifice of pagan religions. (3) To avoid objectionable associations. The creatures that move about on the ground, for example, were reminiscent of serpents, which often symbolized sin.

12:1–4 Why was a woman considered "unclean" after the wonderful miracle of birth? It was due to the bodily emissions and secretions occurring during and after childbirth. These were considered unclean and made the woman unprepared to enter the pure surroundings of the tabernacle.

12:1–4 *Unclean* did not mean sinful or dirty. God created us male and female, and he ordered us to be fruitful and multiply (Genesis 1:27–28). He did not change his mind and say that sex and procreation were now somehow unclean. Instead, he made a distinction between his worship and the popular worship of fertility gods and goddesses. Canaanite religions incorporated prostitution and immoral rites as the people begged their gods to make their crops, herds, and families increase. By contrast, Israel's religion avoided all sexual connotations. By keeping worship and sex entirely separate, God helped the Israelites avoid confusion with pagan rites. The Israelites worshiped God as their loving Creator and Provider, and they thanked him for bountiful crops and safe childbirth.

"When a woman gives birth and bears a male *child,* then she shall be unclean for seven
days, as in the days of her menstruation she shall be unclean.
3 'On the eighth day the flesh of his foreskin shall be circumcised. **12:3**
4 'Then she shall remain in the blood of *her* purification for thirty-three days; she shall Gen 17:12; Luke
not touch any consecrated thing, nor enter the sanctuary until the days of her purifica- 1:59; 2:21
tion are completed.
5 'But if she bears a female *child,* then she shall be unclean for two weeks, as in her
menstruation; and she shall remain in the blood of *her* purification for sixty-six days.
6 'When the days of her purification are completed, for a son or for a daughter, she **12:6**
shall bring to the priest at the doorway of the tent of meeting a one year old lamb for a Luke 2:22; Lev 5:7
burnt offering and a young pigeon or a turtledove for a sin offering.
7 'Then he shall offer it before the LORD and make atonement for her, and she shall
be cleansed from the flow of her blood. This is the law for her who bears *a child, whether*
a male or a female.
8 'But if she cannot afford a lamb, then she shall take two turtledoves or two young **12:8**
pigeons, the one for a burnt offering and the other for a sin offering; and the priest shall Luke 2:22-24; Lev
make atonement for her, and she will be clean.' " 5:7; Lev 4:26

The Test for Leprosy

13 Then the LORD spoke to Moses and to Aaron, saying,
2 "When a man has on the skin of his body a swelling or a scab or a bright spot, **13:2**
and it becomes [8]an infection of leprosy on the skin of his body, then he shall be brought Deut 24:8
to Aaron the priest or to one of his sons the priests.
3 "The priest shall look at the mark on the skin of the body, and if the hair in the infection has turned white and the infection appears to be deeper than the skin of his body, it
is an infection of leprosy; when the priest has looked at him, he shall pronounce him
unclean.
4 "But if the bright spot is white on the skin of his body, and it does not appear to be
deeper than the skin, and the hair on it has not turned white, then the priest shall isolate
him who has the infection for seven days.
5 "The priest shall look at him on the seventh day, and if in his eyes the infection has
not changed *and* the infection has not spread on the skin, then the priest shall isolate
him for seven more days.
6 "The priest shall look at him again on the seventh day, and if the infection has faded **13:6**
and the mark has not spread on the skin, then the priest shall pronounce him clean; it is Lev 11:25; 14:8
only a scab. And he shall wash his clothes and be clean.
7 "But if the scab spreads farther on the skin after he has shown himself to the priest
for his cleansing, he shall appear again to the priest.
8 "The priest shall look, and if the scab has spread on the skin, then the priest shall
pronounce him unclean; it is leprosy.
9 "When the infection of leprosy is on a man, then he shall be brought to the priest.
10 "The priest shall then look, and if there is a white swelling in the skin, and it has turned **13:10**
the hair white, and there is quick raw flesh in the swelling, Num 12:10; 2 Kin
11 it is a chronic leprosy on the skin of his body, and the priest shall pronounce him 5:27; 2 Chr 26:19,
unclean; he shall not isolate him, for he is unclean. 20
12 "If the leprosy breaks out farther on the skin, and the leprosy covers all the skin of
him who has the infection from his head even to his feet, as far as the priest can see,
13 then the priest shall look, and behold, *if* the leprosy has covered all his body, he shall
pronounce clean *him who has* the infection; it has all turned white *and* he is clean.
14 "But whenever raw flesh appears on him, he shall be unclean.
15 "The priest shall look at the raw flesh, and he shall pronounce him unclean; the raw
flesh is unclean, it is leprosy.
16 "Or if the raw flesh turns again and is changed to white, then he shall come to the **13:16**
priest, Luke 5:12-14

8 Lit *a mark, stroke,* and so throughout the ch

13:1ff Leprosy is a name applied to several different diseases, and it was greatly feared in Bible times. Some of these diseases, unlike the disease we call leprosy or Hansen's disease today, were highly contagious. The worst of them slowly ruined the body and, in most cases, were fatal. Lepers were separated from family and friends and confined outside the camp. Since priests were responsible for the health of the camp, it was their duty to expel and readmit lepers. If someone's leprosy appeared to go away, only the priest could decide if that person was truly cured. Leprosy is often used in the Bible as an illustration of sin because sin is contagious and destructive and leads to separation.

17 and the priest shall look at him, and behold, *if* the infection has turned to white,
then the priest shall pronounce clean *him who has* the infection; he is clean.
18"When the body has a boil on its skin and it is healed,
19 and in the place of the boil there is a white swelling or a reddish-white, bright spot,
then it shall be shown to the priest;
20 and the priest shall look, and behold, *if* it appears to be lower than the skin, and the
hair on it has turned white, then the priest shall pronounce him unclean; it is the infection of leprosy, it has broken out in the boil.
21"But if the priest looks at it, and behold, there are no white hairs in it and it is not
lower than the skin and is faded, then the priest shall isolate him for seven days;
22 and if it spreads farther on the skin, then the priest shall pronounce him unclean; it
is an infection.
23"But if the bright spot remains in its place and does not spread, it is *only* the scar of
the boil; and the priest shall pronounce him clean.
24"Or if the body sustains in its skin a burn by fire, and the raw *flesh* of the burn becomes a bright spot, reddish-white, or white,

13:25
Ex 4:6; Num 12:10;
2 Kin 5:27

25 then the priest shall look at it. And if the hair in the bright spot has turned white
and it appears to be deeper than the skin, it is leprosy; it has broken out in the burn.
Therefore, the priest shall pronounce him unclean; it is an infection of leprosy.
26"But if the priest looks at it, and indeed, there is no white hair in the bright spot and
it is no deeper than the skin, but is dim, then the priest shall isolate him for seven days;
27 and the priest shall look at him on the seventh day. If it spreads farther in the skin,
then the priest shall pronounce him unclean; it is an infection of leprosy.
28"But if the bright spot remains in its place and has not spread in the skin, but is dim,
it is the swelling from the burn; and the priest shall pronounce him clean, for it is *only*
the scar of the burn.
29"Now if a man or woman has an infection on the head or on the beard,
30 then the priest shall look at the infection, and if it appears to be deeper than the
skin and there is thin yellowish hair in it, then the priest shall pronounce him unclean; it
is a scale, it is leprosy of the head or of the beard.
31"But if the priest looks at the infection of the scale, and indeed, it appears to be no
deeper than the skin and there is no black hair in it, then the priest shall isolate *the person* with the scaly infection for seven days.
32"On the seventh day the priest shall look at the infection, and if the scale has not
spread and no yellowish hair has grown in it, and the appearance of the scale is no deeper than the skin,
33 then he shall shave himself, but he shall not shave the scale; and the priest shall isolate *the person* with the scale seven more days.
34"Then on the seventh day the priest shall look at the scale, and if the scale has not
spread in the skin and it appears to be no deeper than the skin, the priest shall pronounce
him clean; and he shall wash his clothes and be clean.
35"But if the scale spreads farther in the skin after his cleansing,
36 then the priest shall look at him, and if the scale has spread in the skin, the priest
need not seek for the yellowish hair; he is unclean.
37"If in his sight the scale has remained, however, and black hair has grown in it, the
scale has healed, he is clean; and the priest shall pronounce him clean.
38"When a man or a woman has bright spots on the skin of the body, *even* white bright
spots,
39 then the priest shall look, and if the bright spots on the skin of their bodies are a
faint white, it is eczema that has broken out on the skin; he is clean.

13:40
2 Kin 2:23; Is 15:2;
Amos 8:10

40"Now if a man loses the hair of his head, he is bald; he is clean.
41"If his head becomes bald at the front and sides, he is bald on the forehead; he is clean.
42"But if on the bald head or the bald forehead, there occurs a reddish-white infection,
it is leprosy breaking out on his bald head or on his bald forehead.

13:43
Lev 10:10; Ezek
22:26

43"Then the priest shall look at him; and if the swelling of the infection is reddish-white
on his bald head or on his bald forehead, like the appearance of leprosy in the skin of
the body,
44 he is a leprous man, he is unclean. The priest shall surely pronounce him unclean;
his infection is on his head.

13:45
Lev 10:6; Ezek
24:17, 22; Mic 3:7;
Lam 4:15

45"As for the leper who has the infection, his clothes shall be torn, and the hair of his
head shall be uncovered, and he shall cover his mustache and cry, 'Unclean! Unclean!'

46 "He shall remain unclean all the days during which he has the infection; he is un- 13:46
clean. He shall live alone; his dwelling shall be outside the camp. Num 5:1-4; 12:14
47 "When a garment has a mark of leprosy in it, whether it is a wool garment or a linen
garment,
48 whether in warp or woof, of linen or of wool, whether in leather or in any article
made of leather,
49 if the mark is greenish or reddish in the garment or in the leather, or in the warp or
in the woof, or in any article of leather, it is a leprous mark and shall be shown to the priest.
50 "Then the priest shall look at the mark and shall quarantine the article with the mark 13:50
for seven days. Ezek 44:23
51 "He shall then look at the mark on the seventh day; if the mark has spread in the
garment, whether in the warp or in the woof, or in the leather, whatever the purpose for
which the leather is used, the mark is a leprous malignancy, it is unclean.
52 "So he shall burn the garment, whether the warp or the woof, in wool or in linen, or
any article of leather in which the mark occurs, for it is a leprous malignancy; it shall be
burned in the fire.
53 "But if the priest shall look, and indeed the mark has not spread in the garment, either in the warp or in the woof, or in any article of leather,
54 then the priest shall order them to wash the thing in which the mark occurs and he
shall quarantine it for seven more days.
55 "After the article with the mark has been washed, the priest shall again look, and if
the mark has not changed its appearance, even though the mark has not spread, it is
unclean; you shall burn it in the fire, whether an eating away has produced bareness on
the top or on the front of it.
56 "Then if the priest looks, and if the mark has faded after it has been washed, then he
shall tear it out of the garment or out of the leather, whether from the warp or from the
woof;
57 and if it appears again in the garment, whether in the warp or in the woof, or in any
article of leather, it is an outbreak; the article with the mark shall be burned in the fire.
58 "The garment, whether the warp or the woof, or any article of leather from which
the mark has departed when you washed it, it shall then be washed a second time and
will be clean."
59 This is the law for the mark of leprosy in a garment of wool or linen, whether in the
warp or in the woof, or in any article of leather, for pronouncing it clean or unclean.

Law of Cleansing a Leper

14 Then the LORD spoke to Moses, saying,
2 "This shall be the law of the leper in the day of his cleansing. Now he shall be 14:2
brought to the priest, Matt 8:4; Mark 1:44; Luke 5:14; 17:14
3 and the priest shall go out to the outside of the camp. Thus the priest shall look,
and if the infection of leprosy has been healed in the leper, 14:3 Lev 13:46
4 then the priest shall give orders to take two live clean birds and cedar wood and a
scarlet string and hyssop for the one who is to be cleansed. 14:4 Lev 14:6, 49, 51, 52; Num 19:6
5 "The priest shall also give orders to slay the one bird in an earthenware vessel over
running water.
6 "*As for* the live bird, he shall take it together with the cedar wood and the scarlet 14:6 Lev 14:4; Ps 51:7
string and the hyssop, and shall dip them and the live bird in the blood of the bird that
was slain over the running water. 14:7 Ezek 36:25
7 "He shall then sprinkle seven times the one who is to be cleansed from the leprosy
and shall pronounce him clean, and shall let the live bird go free over the open field. 14:8 Lev 11:25; 13:6;
8 "The one to be cleansed shall then wash his clothes and shave off all his hair and Num 8:7; Lev 14:9,
bathe in water and be clean. Now afterward, he may enter the camp, but he shall stay 20; Num 5:2, 3; 12:14, 15; 2 Chr
outside his tent for seven days. 26:21
9 "It will be on the seventh day that he shall shave off all his hair: he shall shave his 14:9
head and his beard and his eyebrows, even all his hair. He shall then wash his clothes Lev 14:8, 20
and bathe his body in water and be clean. 14:10
10 "Now on the eighth day he is to take two male lambs without defect, and a yearling Lev 14:12, 15, 21, 24

13:45–46 A person with leprosy (a leper) had to perform this strange ritual to protect others from coming too near. Because the disease described in Leviticus was often contagious, it was important that people stay away from those who had it.

ewe lamb without defect, and three-tenths *of an ephah* of fine flour mixed with oil for a
grain offering, and one [9]log of oil;
11 and the priest who pronounces him clean shall present the man to be cleansed and
the aforesaid before the LORD at the doorway of the tent of meeting.

14:12 Lev 5:6, 18; 6:6; 14:19; Lev 14:10; Ex 29:22-24, 26

12 "Then the priest shall take the one male lamb and bring it for a guilt offering, with
the log of oil, and present them as a wave offering before the LORD.
13 "Next he shall slaughter the male lamb in the place where they slaughter the sin offering and the burnt offering, at the place of the sanctuary—for the guilt offering, like
the sin offering, belongs to the priest; it is most holy.

14:13 Ex 29:11; Lev 1:11; 4:24; Lev 6:24-30; 7:7

14 "The priest shall then take some of the blood of the guilt offering, and the priest shall
put *it* on the lobe of the right ear of the one to be cleansed, and on the thumb of his right
hand and on the big toe of his right foot.

14:14 Lev 14:19; Ex 29:20; Lev 8:23, 24

15 "The priest shall also take some of the log of oil, and pour *it* into his left palm;

14:15 Lev 14:10

16 the priest shall then dip his right-hand finger into the oil that is in his left palm, and
with his finger sprinkle some of the oil seven times before the LORD.
17 "Of the remaining oil which is in his palm, the priest shall put some on the right ear
lobe of the one to be cleansed, and on the thumb of his right hand, and on the big toe of
his right foot, on the blood of the guilt offering;

14:18 Lev 4:26; Num 15:28; Heb 2:17

18 while the rest of the oil that is in the priest's palm, he shall put on the head of the
one to be cleansed. So the priest shall make atonement on his behalf before the LORD.

14:19 Lev 14:12

19 "The priest shall next offer the sin offering and make atonement for the one to be
cleansed from his uncleanness. Then afterward, he shall slaughter the burnt offering.

14:20 Lev 14:8, 9

20 "The priest shall offer up the burnt offering and the grain offering on the altar. Thus
the priest shall make atonement for him, and he will be clean.

14:21 Lev 5:11; 12:8; 27:8; Lev 14:22; Lev 14:10

21 "But if he is poor and his means are insufficient, then he is to take one male lamb for
a guilt offering as a wave offering to make atonement for him, and one-tenth *of an ephah*
of fine flour mixed with oil for a grain offering, and a log of oil,

14:22 Lev 5:7; Lev 14:21, 24, 25

22 and two turtledoves or two young pigeons which are within his means, the one shall
be a sin offering and the other a burnt offering.

14:23 Lev 14:10, 11

23 "Then the eighth day he shall bring them for his cleansing to the priest, at the doorway of the tent of meeting, before the LORD.

14:24 Lev 14:10

24 "The priest shall take the lamb of the guilt offering and the log of oil, and the priest
shall offer them for a wave offering before the LORD.

14:25 Lev 14:14

25 "Next he shall slaughter the lamb of the guilt offering; and the priest is to take some
of the blood of the guilt offering and put *it* on the lobe of the right ear of the one to be
cleansed and on the thumb of his right hand and on the big toe of his right foot.
26 "The priest shall also pour some of the oil into his left palm;
27 and with his right-hand finger the priest shall sprinkle some of the oil that is in his
left palm seven times before the LORD.
28 "The priest shall then put some of the oil that is in his palm on the lobe of the right
ear of the one to be cleansed, and on the thumb of his right hand and on the big toe of
his right foot, on the place of the blood of the guilt offering.
29 "Moreover, the rest of the oil that is in the priest's palm he shall put on the head of
the one to be cleansed, to make atonement on his behalf before the LORD.
30 "He shall then offer one of the turtledoves or young pigeons, which are within his means.

14:31 Lev 5:7

31 "*He shall offer* what he can afford, the one for a sin offering and the other for a burnt
offering, together with the grain offering. So the priest shall make atonement before the
LORD on behalf of the one to be cleansed.
32 "This is the law *for him* in whom there is an infection of leprosy, whose means are
limited for his cleansing."

Cleansing a Leprous House

14:34 Gen 17:8; Num 32:22; Deut 7:1; 32:49

33 The LORD further spoke to Moses and to Aaron, saying:
34 "When you enter the land of Canaan, which I give you for a possession, and I put a
mark of leprosy on a house in the land of your possession,

9 I.e. Approx one pt

14:34–35 This leprosy on a house was dry rot or mineral crystals affecting stone walls. There were specific cleansing procedures designated for mildewed clothing and buildings. These were fully required by the law (vv. 44–57). Why was mildew so dangerous? This fungus could spread rapidly and promote disease. It was therefore important to check its spread as soon as possible. In extreme cases, if the fungus had done enough damage, the clothing was burned or the house destroyed.

35 then the one who owns the house shall come and tell the priest, saying, '*Something* **14:35**
like a mark *of leprosy* has become visible to me in the house.' Ps 91:10
36 "The priest shall then command that they empty the house before the priest goes in
to look at the mark, so that everything in the house need not become unclean; and afterward the priest shall go in to look at the house.
37 "So he shall look at the mark, and if the mark on the walls of the house has greenish
or reddish depressions and appears deeper than the surface,
38 then the priest shall come out of the house, to the doorway, and quarantine the house
for seven days.
39 "The priest shall return on the seventh day and make an inspection. If the mark has
indeed spread in the walls of the house,
40 then the priest shall order them to tear out the stones with the mark in them and
throw them away at an unclean place outside the city.
41 "He shall have the house scraped all around inside, and they shall dump the plaster
that they scrape off at an unclean place outside the city.
42 "Then they shall take other stones and replace *those* stones, and he shall take other
plaster and replaster the house.
43 "If, however, the mark breaks out again in the house after he has torn out the stones
and scraped the house, and after it has been replastered,
44 then the priest shall come in and make an inspection. If he sees that the mark has **14:44**
indeed spread in the house, it is a malignant mark in the house; it is unclean. Lev 13:51
45 "He shall therefore tear down the house, its stones, and its timbers, and all the plas- **14:45**
ter of the house, and he shall take *them* outside the city to an unclean place. Lev 14:41
46 "Moreover, whoever goes into the house during the time that he has quarantined it, **14:46**
becomes unclean until evening. Num 19:7, 10, 21, 22
47 "Likewise, whoever lies down in the house shall wash his clothes, and whoever eats
in the house shall wash his clothes.
48 "If, on the other hand, the priest comes in and makes an inspection and the mark has
not indeed spread in the house after the house has been replastered, then the priest shall
pronounce the house clean because the mark has not reappeared.
49 "To cleanse the house then, he shall take two birds and cedar wood and a scarlet string **14:49**
and hyssop, Lev 14:4
50 and he shall slaughter the one bird in an earthenware vessel over running water.
51 "Then he shall take the cedar wood and the hyssop and the scarlet string, with the **14:51**
live bird, and dip them in the blood of the slain bird as well as in the running water, and 1 Kin 4:33; Ps 51:7
sprinkle the house seven times.
52 "He shall thus cleanse the house with the blood of the bird and with the running water,
along with the live bird and with the cedar wood and with the hyssop and with the scarlet
string.
53 "However, he shall let the live bird go free outside the city into the open field. So he **14:54**
shall make atonement for the house, and it will be clean." Lev 13:30
54 This is the law for any mark of leprosy—even for a scale, **14:55**
55 and for the leprous garment or house, Lev 13:47-52
56 and for a swelling, and for a scab, and for a bright spot— **14:56**
57 to teach when they are unclean and when they are clean. This is the law of leprosy. Lev 13:2

14:54–57 God told the Israelites how to diagnose leprosy and mildew so they could avoid them or treat them. These laws were given for the people's health and protection. They helped the Israelites avoid diseases that were serious threats in that time and place. Although they wouldn't have understood the medical reasons for some of these laws, their obedience to them made them healthier. Many of God's laws must have seemed strange to the Israelites. His laws, however, helped them avoid not only physical contamination, but also moral and spiritual infection.

The Word of God still provides a pattern for physically, spiritually, and morally healthy living. We may not always understand the wisdom of God's laws, but if we obey them, we will thrive. Does this mean we are to follow the Old Testament health and dietary restrictions? In general, the basic principles of health and cleanliness are still healthful practices, but it would be legalistic, if not wrong, to adhere to each specific restriction today. Some of these regulations were intended to mark the Israelites as different from the wicked people around them. Others were given to prevent God's people from becoming involved in pagan religious practices, one of the most serious problems of the day. Still others related to quarantines in a culture where exact medical diagnosis was impossible. Today, for example, physicians can diagnose the different forms of leprosy, and they know which ones are contagious. Treatment methods have greatly improved, and quarantine for leprosy is rarely necessary.

Cleansing Unhealthiness

15 The LORD also spoke to Moses and to Aaron, saying,
2 "Speak to the sons of Israel, and say to them, 'When any man has a discharge
from his body, his discharge is unclean.

15:2 Lev 22:4; Num 5:2; 2 Sam 3:29

3 'This, moreover, shall be his uncleanness in his discharge: it is his uncleanness whether
his body allows its discharge to flow or whether his body obstructs its discharge.
4 'Every bed on which the person with the discharge lies becomes unclean, and everything on which he sits becomes unclean.
5 'Anyone, moreover, who touches his bed shall wash his clothes and bathe in water
and be unclean until evening;
6 and whoever sits on the thing on which the man with the discharge has been sitting,
shall wash his clothes and bathe in water and be unclean until evening.
7 'Also whoever touches the person with the discharge shall wash his clothes and bathe
in water and be unclean until evening.
8 'Or if the man with the discharge spits on one who is clean, he too shall wash his
clothes and bathe in water and be unclean until evening.
9 'Every saddle on which the person with the discharge rides becomes unclean.
10 'Whoever then touches any of the things which were under him shall be unclean until
evening, and he who carries them shall wash his clothes and bathe in water and be unclean until evening.
11 'Likewise, whomever the one with the discharge touches without having rinsed his
hands in water shall wash his clothes and bathe in water and be unclean until evening.
12 'However, an earthenware vessel which the person with the discharge touches shall
be broken, and every wooden vessel shall be rinsed in water.

15:12 Lev 6:28; 11:33

13 'Now when the man with the discharge becomes cleansed from his discharge, then
he shall count off for himself seven days for his cleansing; he shall then wash his clothes
and bathe his body in running water and will become clean.

15:13 Lev 8:33; 14:8

14 'Then on the eighth day he shall take for himself two turtledoves or two young pigeons, and come before the LORD to the doorway of the tent of meeting and give them
to the priest;

15:14 Lev 14:22, 23

15 and the priest shall offer them, one for a sin offering and the other for a burnt offering. So the priest shall make atonement on his behalf before the LORD because of his
discharge.

15:15 Lev 5:7; 14:31; Lev 14:19, 31

16 'Now if a man has a seminal emission, he shall bathe all his body in water and be
unclean until evening.

15:16 Lev 22:4; Deut 23:10, 11

17 'As for any garment or any leather on which there is seminal emission, it shall be
washed with water and be unclean until evening.
18 'If a man lies with a woman *so that* there is a seminal emission, they shall both bathe
in water and be unclean until evening.

15:18 1 Sam 21:4

19 'When a woman has a discharge, *if* her discharge in her body is blood, she shall continue in her menstrual impurity for seven days; and whoever touches her shall be unclean until evening.

15:19 Lev 12:2

20 'Everything also on which she lies during her menstrual impurity shall be unclean,
and everything on which she sits shall be unclean.
21 'Anyone who touches her bed shall wash his clothes and bathe in water and be unclean until evening.
22 'Whoever touches any thing on which she sits shall wash his clothes and bathe in
water and be unclean until evening.
23 'Whether it be on the bed or on the thing on which she is sitting, when he touches it,
he shall be unclean until evening.
24 'If a man actually lies with her so that her menstrual impurity is on him, he shall be
unclean seven days, and every bed on which he lies shall be unclean.

15:24 Lev 18:19; 20:18

25 'Now if a woman has a discharge of her blood many days, not at the period of her
menstrual impurity, or if she has a discharge beyond that period, all the days of her impure discharge she shall continue as though in her menstrual impurity; she is unclean.

15:25 Matt 9:20; Mark 5:25; Luke 8:43

15:18 This verse is not implying that sex is dirty or disgusting. God created sex for the enjoyment of married couples as well as for continuing the race and continuing the covenant. Everything must be seen and done with a view toward God's love and control. Sex is not separate from spirituality and God's care. God is concerned about our sexual habits. We tend to separate our physical and spiritual lives, but there is an inseparable intertwining. God must be Lord over our whole selves—including our private lives.

26 'Any bed on which she lies all the days of her discharge shall be to her like her bed
at menstruation; and every thing on which she sits shall be unclean, like her uncleanness
at that time.
27 'Likewise, whoever touches them shall be unclean and shall wash his clothes and bathe
in water and be unclean until evening.
28 'When she becomes clean from her discharge, she shall count off for herself seven
days; and afterward she will be clean.
29 'Then on the eighth day she shall take for herself two turtledoves or two young pigeons and bring them in to the priest, to the doorway of the tent of meeting.
30 'The priest shall offer the one for a sin offering and the other for a burnt offering. So **15:30**
the priest shall make atonement on her behalf before the LORD because of her impure Lev 5:7
discharge.'
31 "Thus you shall keep the sons of Israel separated from their uncleanness, so that they **15:31**
will not die in their uncleanness by their defiling My tabernacle that is among them." Lev 20:3; Num 19:13, 20; Ezek
32 This is the law for the one with a discharge, and for the man who has a seminal 5:11; 36:17
emission so that he is unclean by it,
33 and for the woman who is ill because of menstrual impurity, and for the one who
has a discharge, whether a male or a female, or a man who lies with an unclean woman.

2. Instructions for the altar

Law of Atonement

16 Now the LORD spoke to Moses after the death of the two sons of Aaron, when **16:1**
they had approached the presence of the LORD and died. Lev 10:1, 2
2 The LORD said to Moses: **16:2**
"Tell your brother Aaron that he shall not enter at any time into the holy place inside Ex 30:10; Heb 6:19; 9:7, 25; Ex 25:21,
the veil, before the [10]mercy seat which is on the ark, or he will die; for I will appear in the 22; 40:34; 1 Kin
cloud over the mercy seat. 8:10-12
3 "Aaron shall enter the holy place with this: with a bull for a sin offering and a ram for **16:3**
a burnt offering. Lev 4:1-12; 16:6; Heb 9:7
4 "He shall put on the holy linen tunic, and the linen undergarments shall be next to **16:4**
his body, and he shall be girded with the linen sash and attired with the linen turban Ex 28:39, 42; Ex
(these are holy garments). Then he shall bathe his body in water and put them on. 30:20; Lev 16:24; Heb 10:22
5 "He shall take from the congregation of the sons of Israel two male goats for a sin **16:5**
offering and one ram for a burnt offering. Lev 4:13-21; 2 Chr
6 "Then Aaron shall offer the bull for the sin offering which is for himself, that he may 29:21; Ezek 45:22
make atonement for himself and for his household. **16:6**
7 "He shall take the two goats and present them before the LORD at the doorway of Heb 5:3
the tent of meeting.
8 "Aaron shall cast lots for the two goats, one lot for the LORD and the other lot for
the [11]scapegoat.
9 "Then Aaron shall offer the goat on which the lot for the LORD fell, and make it a
sin offering.

10 Lit *propitiatory* **11** Lit *goat of removal,* or else a name: *Azazel*

15:32–33 God is concerned about health, the dignity of the person, the dignity of the body, and the dignity of the sexual experience. His commands call the people to avoid unhealthy practices and promote healthy ones. To wash was the physical health response; to be purified or cleansed was the spiritual dignity response. This shows God's high regard for sex and sexuality. In our day, sex has been degraded by publicity; it has become public domain, not private celebration. We are called to have a high regard for sex, both in good health and purity.

16:1ff The day of atonement was the greatest day of the year for Israel. The Hebrew word for *atone* means "to cover." Old Testament sacrifices could not actually remove sins, only cover them. On this day, the people confessed their sins as a nation, and the high priest went into the holy of holies to make atonement for them. Sacrifices were made and blood was shed so that the people's sins could be "covered" until Christ's sacrifice on the cross would give people the opportunity to have their sin removed forever.

16:1–25 Aaron had to spend hours preparing himself to meet God. But we can approach God anytime (Hebrews 4:16). What a privilege! We are offered easier access to God than the high priests of Old Testament times! Still, we must never forget that God is holy nor let this privilege cause us to approach God carelessly. The way to God has been opened to us by Christ. But easy access to God does not eliminate our need to prepare our hearts as we draw near in prayer.

16:5–28 This event with the two goats occurred on the day of atonement. The two goats represented the two ways God was dealing with the Israelites' sin: (1) he was forgiving their sin through the first goat, which was sacrificed, and (2) he was removing their guilt through the second goat, the scapegoat that was sent into the wilderness. The same ritual had to be repeated every year. Jesus Christ's death replaced this system once and for all. We can have our sins forgiven and guilt removed by placing our trust in Christ (Hebrews 10:1–18).

16:10 Is 53:4-10; Rom 3:25; 1 John 2:2

10 "But the goat on which the lot for the scapegoat fell shall be presented alive before
the LORD, to make atonement upon it, to send it into the wilderness as the scapegoat.

16:11 Heb 7:27; 9:7; Lev 16:33

11 "Then Aaron shall offer the bull of the sin offering which is for himself and make
atonement for himself and for his household, and he shall slaughter the bull of the sin
offering which is for himself.

16:12 Lev 10:1; Num 16:18; Ex 30:34-38

12 "He shall take a firepan full of coals of fire from upon the altar before the LORD and
two handfuls of finely ground sweet incense, and bring *it* inside the veil.

16:13 Ex 25:21; Ex 28:43; Lev 22:9; Num 4:15, 20

13 "He shall put the incense on the fire before the LORD, that the cloud of incense may
cover the mercy seat that is on *the ark of* the testimony, otherwise he will die.

16:14 Heb 9:25; Lev 4:6, 17

14 "Moreover, he shall take some of the blood of the bull and sprinkle *it* with his finger
on the mercy seat on the east *side;* also in front of the mercy seat he shall sprinkle some
of the blood with his finger seven times.

16:15 Heb 7:27; 9:7, 12

15 "Then he shall slaughter the goat of the sin offering which is for the people, and bring
its blood inside the veil and do with its blood as he did with the blood of the bull, and
sprinkle it on the mercy seat and in front of the mercy seat.

16:16 Ex 29:36, 37; 30:10; Heb 2:17

16 "He shall make atonement for the holy place, because of the impurities of the sons
of Israel and because of their transgressions in regard to all their sins; and thus he shall
do for the tent of meeting which abides with them in the midst of their impurities.
17 "When he goes in to make atonement in the holy place, no one shall be in the tent of
meeting until he comes out, that he may make atonement for himself and for his household and for all the assembly of Israel.

16:18 Lev 4:25; Ezek 43:20, 22

18 "Then he shall go out to the altar that is before the LORD and make atonement for
it, and shall take some of the blood of the bull and of the blood of the goat and put it on
the horns of the altar on all sides.

16:19 Lev 16:14; Ezek 43:20

19 "With his finger he shall sprinkle some of the blood on it seven times and cleanse it,
and from the impurities of the sons of Israel consecrate it.
20 "When he finishes atoning for the holy place and the tent of meeting and the altar,
he shall offer the live goat.

16:21 Lev 5:5

21 "Then Aaron shall lay both of his hands on the head of the live goat, and confess
over it all the iniquities of the sons of Israel and all their transgressions in regard to all
their sins; and he shall lay them on the head of the goat and send *it* away into the wilderness by the hand of a man who *stands* in readiness.
22 "The goat shall bear on itself all their iniquities to a solitary land; and he shall release the goat in the wilderness.

16:23 Lev 16:4; Ezek 42:14; 44:19

23 "Then Aaron shall come into the tent of meeting and take off the linen garments
which he put on when he went into the holy place, and shall leave them there.

16:24 Lev 16:4; Ex 28:40, 41

24 "He shall bathe his body with water in a holy place and put on his clothes, and come
forth and offer his burnt offering and the burnt offering of the people and make atonement for himself and for the people.
25 "Then he shall offer up in smoke the fat of the sin offering on the altar.

16:26 Lev 11:25, 40

26 "The one who released the goat as the scapegoat shall wash his clothes and bathe his
body with water; then afterward he shall come into the camp.

16:27 Lev 6:30; Heb 13:11

27 "But the bull of the sin offering and the goat of the sin offering, whose blood was
brought in to make atonement in the holy place, shall be taken outside the camp, and
they shall burn their hides, their flesh, and their refuse in the fire.

16:28 Num 19:8

28 "Then the one who burns them shall wash his clothes and bathe his body with water,
then afterward he shall come into the camp.

An Annual Atonement

16:29 Lev 23:27; Num 29:7; Ex 31:14, 15

29 "*This* shall be a permanent statute for you: in the seventh month, on the tenth day of
the month, you shall humble your souls and not do any work, whether the native, or the
alien who sojourns among you;

16:30 Ps 51:2; Jer 33:8; Eph 5:26

30 for it is on this day that atonement shall be made for you to cleanse you; you will be
clean from all your sins before the LORD.

16:12 A firepan (or censer) was a dish or shallow bowl that hung by a chain or was carried with tongs. Inside the censer were placed incense (a combination of sweet-smelling spices) and burning coals from the altar. On the day of atonement, the high priest entered the holy of holies carrying a smoking firepan. The smoke shielded him from the ark of the testimony and the presence of God—otherwise he would die. Incense may also have had a very practical purpose. The sweet smell drew the people's attention to the morning and evening sacrifices and helped cover the sometimes foul smell.

31 "It is to be a sabbath of solemn rest for you, that you may humble your souls; it is a
permanent statute.
32 "So the priest who is anointed and ordained to serve as priest in his father's place
shall make atonement: he shall thus put on the linen garments, the holy garments,
33 and make atonement for the holy sanctuary, and he shall make atonement for the
tent of meeting and for the altar. He shall also make atonement for the priests and for
all the people of the assembly.
34 "Now you shall have this as a permanent statute, to make atonement for the sons of
Israel for all their sins once every year." And just as the LORD had commanded Moses,
so he did.

16:31 Lev 23:32; Ezra 8:21; Is 58:3, 5; Dan 10:12
16:32 Lev 16:4
16:33 Lev 16:11
16:34 Lev 23:31; Heb 9:7

Blood for Atonement

17 Then the LORD spoke to Moses, saying,
2 "Speak to Aaron and to his sons and to all the sons of Israel and say to them,
'This is what the LORD has commanded, saying,
3 "Any man from the house of Israel who slaughters an ox or a lamb or a goat in the
camp, or who slaughters it outside the camp,
4 and has not brought it to the doorway of the tent of meeting to present *it* as an offering to the LORD before the tabernacle of the LORD, bloodguiltiness is to be reckoned
to that man. He has shed blood and that man shall be cut off from among his people.
5 "The reason is so that the sons of Israel may bring their sacrifices which they were
sacrificing in the open field, that they may bring them in to the LORD, at the doorway of
the tent of meeting to the priest, and sacrifice them as sacrifices of peace offerings to
the LORD.
6 "The priest shall sprinkle the blood on the altar of the LORD at the doorway of the
tent of meeting, and offer up the fat in smoke as a soothing aroma to the LORD.
7 "They shall no longer sacrifice their sacrifices to the goat demons with which they
play the harlot. This shall be a permanent statute to them throughout their generations." '
8 "Then you shall say to them, 'Any man from the house of Israel, or from the aliens
who sojourn among them, who offers a burnt offering or sacrifice,
9 and does not bring it to the doorway of the tent of meeting to offer it to the LORD,
that man also shall be cut off from his people.
10 'And any man from the house of Israel, or from the aliens who sojourn among them,
who eats any blood, I will set My face against that person who eats blood and will cut
him off from among his people.
11 'For the life of the flesh is in the blood, and I have given it to you on the altar to
make atonement for your souls; for it is the blood by reason of the life that makes atonement.'
12 "Therefore I said to the sons of Israel, 'No person among you may eat blood, nor
may any alien who sojourns among you eat blood.'
13 "So when any man from the sons of Israel, or from the aliens who sojourn among
them, in hunting catches a beast or a bird which may be eaten, he shall pour out its blood
and cover it with earth.
14 "For *as for the* life of all flesh, its blood is *identified* with its life. Therefore I said to

17:4 Deut 12:5-21
17:6 Num 18:17
17:7 Ex 22:20; 32:8; 34:15; Deut 32:17; 2 Chr 11:15; Ps 106:37f; 1 Cor 10:20
17:9 Ex 20:24; Lev 17:4
17:10 Gen 9:4; Lev 3:17; 7:26, 27; Deut 12:16, 23-25; 1 Sam 14:33; Lev 20:3, 6; Jer 44:11
17:11 Gen 9:4; Lev 17:14; Heb 9:22
17:13 Deut 12:16
17:14 Gen 9:4; Lev 17:11

17:1ff Chapters 17—26 are sometimes called the "holiness code" because they focus on what it means to live a holy life. The central verse is 19:2, "You shall be holy, for I the LORD your God am holy."

17:3–9 Why were the Israelites prohibited from sacrificing outside the tabernacle area? God had established specific times and places for sacrifices, and each occasion was permeated with symbolism. If people sacrificed on their own, they might easily add to or subtract from God's laws to fit their own life-styles. Many pagan religions allowed every individual priest to set his own rules; God's command helped the Israelites resist the temptation to follow the pagan pattern. When the Israelites slipped into idolatry, it was because "every man did what was right in his own eyes" (Judges 17:6).

17:7 The goat demons were objects of worship and sacrifice in ancient times, particularly in Egypt from which they had recently escaped. God did not want the people to make this kind of sacrifice in the wilderness or in the promised land where they were heading.

17:11–14 How does blood make atonement for sin? When offered with the right attitude, the sacrifice and the blood shed from it made forgiveness of sin possible. On the one hand, blood represented the sinner's life, infected by his sin and headed for death. On the other hand, the blood represented the innocent life of the animal that was sacrificed in place of the guilty person making the offering. The death of the animal (of which the blood was proof) fulfilled the penalty of death. God therefore granted forgiveness to the sinner. It is God who forgives based on the faith of the person doing the sacrificing.

17:14 Why was eating or drinking blood prohibited? The prohibition against eating blood can be traced all the way back to Noah (Genesis 9:4). God prohibited eating or drinking blood for several reasons. (1) To discourage pagan practices. Israel was to be separate and distinct from the foreign nations around them. Eating blood was a common pagan practice. It was often done in hopes of gain-

the sons of Israel, 'You are not to eat the blood of any flesh, for the life of all flesh is its
blood; whoever eats it shall be cut off.'

17:15 Ex 22:31; Lev 7:24; 22:8; Deut 14:21

15 "When any person eats *an animal* which dies or is torn *by beasts,* whether he is a native
or an alien, he shall wash his clothes and bathe in water, and remain unclean until evening; then he will become clean.

17:16 Num 19:20

16 "But if he does not wash *them* or bathe his body, then he shall bear his guilt."

B. LIVING A HOLY LIFE (18:1—27:34)

After the sacrificial system for forgiving sins was in place, the people were instructed on how to live as forgiven people. Applying these standards to our lives helps us grow in obedience and live a life pleasing to God.

1. Standards for the people

Laws on Immoral Relations

18:2 Ex 6:7; Lev 11:44; Ezek 20:5

18:3 Ezek 20:7, 8; Lev 18:24-30; 20:23

18:4 Lev 18:2

18:5 Neh 9:29; Ezek 18:9; 20:11; Luke 10:28; Rom 10:5; Gal 3:12

18 Then the LORD spoke to Moses, saying,
2 "Speak to the sons of Israel and say to them, 'I am the LORD your God.
3 'You shall not do what is done in the land of Egypt where you lived, nor are you to
do what is done in the land of Canaan where I am bringing you; you shall not walk in
their statutes.
4 'You are to perform My judgments and keep My statutes, to live in accord with them;
I am the LORD your God.
5 'So you shall keep My statutes and My judgments, by which a man may live if he
does them; I am the LORD.
6 'None of you shall approach any blood relative of his to uncover nakedness; I am
the LORD.

OLD/NEW SYSTEMS OF SACRIFICE

Old System of Sacrifice	*New System of Sacrifice*
Was temporary (Hebrews 8:13)	Is permanent (Hebrews 7:21)
Aaron first high priest (Leviticus 16:32)	Jesus only high priest (Hebrews 4:14)
From tribe of Levi (Hebrews 7:5)	From tribe of Judah (Hebrews 7:14)
Ministered on earth (Hebrews 8:4)	Ministers in heaven (Hebrews 8:1–2)
Used blood of animals (Leviticus 16:15)	Uses blood of Christ (Hebrews 10:5)
Required many sacrifices (Leviticus 22:19)	Requires one sacrifice (Hebrews 9:28)
Needed perfect animals (Leviticus 22:19)	Needs a perfect life (Hebrews 5:9)
Required careful approach to tabernacle (Leviticus 16:2)	Encourages confident approach to throne (Hebrews 4:16)
Looked forward to new system (Hebrews 10:1)	Sets aside old system (Hebrews 10:9)

ing the characteristics of the slain animal (strength, speed, etc.). God's people were to rely on him, not on ingested blood, for their strength. (2) To preserve the symbolism of the sacrifice. Blood symbolized the life of the animal that was sacrificed in the sinner's place. To drink it would change the symbolism of the sacrificial penalty and destroy the evidence of the sacrifice. (3) To protect the people from infection because many deadly diseases are transmitted through the blood. The Jews took this prohibition seriously, and that is why Jesus' hearers were so upset when Jesus told them to drink his blood (John 6:53–56). However, Jesus, as God himself and the last sacrifice ever needed for sins, was asking believers to identify with him completely. He wants us to take his life into us, and he wants to participate in our lives as well.

18:3 The Israelites moved from one idol-infested country to another. As God helped them form a new culture, he warned them to leave all aspects of their pagan background behind. He also warned them how easy it would be to slip into the pagan culture of Canaan, where they were going. Canaan's society and religions appealed to worldly desires, especially sexual immorality and drunkenness. The Israelites were to keep themselves pure and set apart for God. God did not want his people absorbed into the surrounding culture and environment. Society may pressure us to conform to its way of life and thought, but yielding to that pressure will (1) create confusion as to which side we should be on and (2) eliminate our effectiveness in serving God. Follow God, and don't let the culture around you mold your thoughts and actions.

18:6–18 This section is referring to marriage between close relatives. Marrying relatives was prohibited by God for physical, social, and moral reasons. Children born to near relatives may experience serious health problems. Without these specific laws, sexual promiscuity would have been more likely, first in families, then outside. Improper sexual relations destroy family life.

7 'You shall not uncover the nakedness of your father, that is, the nakedness of your
mother. She is your mother; you are not to uncover her nakedness.
8 'You shall not uncover the nakedness of your father's wife; it is your father's nakedness.
9 'The nakedness of your sister, *either* your father's daughter or your mother's daughter, whether born at home or born outside, their nakedness you shall not uncover.
10 'The nakedness of your son's daughter or your daughter's daughter, their nakedness
you shall not uncover; for their nakedness is yours.
11 'The nakedness of your father's wife's daughter, born to your father, she is your sister, you shall not uncover her nakedness.
12 'You shall not uncover the nakedness of your father's sister; she is your father's blood
relative.
13 'You shall not uncover the nakedness of your mother's sister, for she is your mother's
blood relative.
14 'You shall not uncover the nakedness of your father's brother; you shall not approach
his wife, she is your aunt.
15 'You shall not uncover the nakedness of your daughter-in-law; she is your son's wife,
you shall not uncover her nakedness.
16 'You shall not uncover the nakedness of your brother's wife; it is your brother's nakedness.
17 'You shall not uncover the nakedness of a woman and of her daughter, nor shall you
take her son's daughter or her daughter's daughter, to uncover her nakedness; they are
blood relatives. It is lewdness.
18 'You shall not marry a woman in addition to her sister as a rival while she is alive, to
uncover her nakedness.
19 'Also you shall not approach a woman to uncover her nakedness during her menstrual impurity.
20 'You shall not have intercourse with your neighbor's wife, to be defiled with her.
21 'You shall not give any of your offspring to offer them to Molech, nor shall you profane the name of your God; I am the LORD.
22 'You shall not lie with a male as one lies with a female; it is an abomination.
23 'Also you shall not have intercourse with any animal to be defiled with it, nor shall
any woman stand before an animal to mate with it; it is a perversion.
24 'Do not defile yourselves by any of these things; for by all these the nations which I
am casting out before you have become defiled.
25 'For the land has become defiled, therefore I have brought its punishment upon it,
so the land has spewed out its inhabitants.
26 'But as for you, you are to keep My statutes and My judgments and shall not do any
of these abominations, *neither* the native, nor the alien who sojourns among you
27 (for the men of the land who have been before you have done all these abominations, and the land has become defiled);
28 so that the land will not spew you out, should you defile it, as it has spewed out the
nation which has been before you.
29 'For whoever does any of these abominations, those persons who do *so* shall be cut
off from among their people.
30 'Thus you are to keep My charge, that you do not practice any of the abominable
customs which have been practiced before you, so as not to defile yourselves with them;
I am the LORD your God.' "

18:7 Lev 20:11; Deut 27:20; Ezek 22:10
18:8 Lev 20:11; Deut 22:30; 27:20; 1 Cor 5:1
18:9 Lev 18:11; 20:17; Deut 27:22
18:12 Lev 20:19
18:14 Lev 20:20
18:15 Lev 20:12
18:16 Lev 20:21
18:17 Lev 20:14
18:19 Lev 15:24; 20:18; Lev 12:2
18:20 Lev 20:10; Prov 6:29; Matt 5:27, 28; 1 Cor 6:9; Heb 13:4
18:21 Lev 20:2-5; Deut 12:31; Lev 19:12; 20:3; 21:6; Ezek 36:20; Mal 1:12
18:22 Lev 20:13; Deut 23:18; Rom 1:27
18:23 Ex 22:19; Lev 20:15, 16; Deut 27:21
18:24 Lev 18:3; Deut 18:12
18:25 Lev 20:23; Deut 9:5; 18:12; Lev 18:28; 20:22
18:30 Lev 22:9; Deut 11:1; Lev 18:2

Idolatry Forbidden

19 Then the LORD spoke to Moses, saying:
2 "Speak to all the congregation of the sons of Israel and say to them, 'You shall
be holy, for I the LORD your God am holy.

19:2 Ex 19:6; Lev 11:44; 20:7, 26; Eph 1:4; 1 Pet 1:16

18:6–27 Several abominations, or wicked actions, are listed here: (1) having sexual relations with close relatives, (2) committing adultery, (3) offering children as sacrifices, (4) having homosexual relations, and (5) having sexual relations with animals. These practices were common in pagan religions and cultures, and it is easy to see why God dealt harshly with those who began to follow them. Such practices lead to disease, deformity, and death. They disrupt family life and society and reveal a low regard for the value of oneself and of others. Society today takes some of these practices lightly, even trying to make them acceptable. But they are still sins in God's eyes. If you consider them acceptable, you are not judging by God's standards.

3 'Every one of you shall reverence his mother and his father, and you shall keep My
sabbaths; I am the LORD your God.
4 'Do not turn to idols or make for yourselves molten gods; I am the LORD your God.
5 'Now when you offer a sacrifice of peace offerings to the LORD, you shall offer it so
that you may be accepted.
6 'It shall be eaten the same day you offer *it,* and the next day; but what remains until
the third day shall be burned with fire.
7 'So if it is eaten at all on the third day, it is an offense; it will not be accepted.
8 'Everyone who eats it will bear his iniquity, for he has profaned the holy thing of the
LORD; and that person shall be cut off from his people.

Sundry Laws

9 'Now when you reap the harvest of your land, you shall not reap to the very corners
of your field, nor shall you gather the gleanings of your harvest.
10 'Nor shall you glean your vineyard, nor shall you gather the fallen fruit of your vineyard; you shall leave them for the needy and for the stranger. I am the LORD your God.
11 'You shall not steal, nor deal falsely, nor lie to one another.
12 'You shall not swear falsely by My name, so as to profane the name of your God; I
am the LORD.
13 'You shall not oppress your neighbor, nor rob *him.* The wages of a hired man are
not to remain with you all night until morning.
14 'You shall not curse a deaf man, nor place a stumbling block before the blind, but
you shall revere your God; I am the LORD.
15 'You shall do no injustice in judgment; you shall not be partial to the poor nor defer
to the great, but you are to judge your neighbor fairly.
16 'You shall not go about as a slanderer among your people, and you are not to act
against the life of your neighbor; I am the LORD.
17 'You shall not hate your fellow countryman in your heart; you may surely reprove
your neighbor, but shall not incur sin because of him.
18 'You shall not take vengeance, nor bear any grudge against the sons of your people,
but you shall love your neighbor as yourself; I am the LORD.
19 'You are to keep My statutes. You shall not breed together two kinds of your cattle;
you shall not sow your field with two kinds of seed, nor wear a garment upon you of two
kinds of material mixed together.
20 'Now if a man lies carnally with a woman who is a slave acquired for *another* man,
but who has in no way been redeemed nor given her freedom, there shall be punishment;
they shall not, *however,* be put to death, because she was not free.
21 'He shall bring his guilt offering to the LORD to the doorway of the tent of meeting,
a ram for a guilt offering.
22 'The priest shall also make atonement for him with the ram of the guilt offering before
the LORD for his sin which he has committed, and the sin which he has committed will
be forgiven him.
23 'When you enter the land and plant all kinds of trees for food, then you shall count
their fruit as forbidden. Three years it shall be forbidden to you; *it* shall not be eaten.
24 'But in the fourth year all its fruit shall be holy, an offering of praise to the LORD.
25 'In the fifth year you are to eat of its fruit, that its yield may increase for you; I am
the LORD your God.
26 'You shall not eat *anything* with the blood, nor practice divination or soothsaying.
27 'You shall not round off the side-growth of your heads nor harm the edges of your
beard.

19:3 Ex 20:12; 31:13; Deut 5:16; Ex 20:8; Lev 11:44

19:4 Lev 26:1; Ps 96:5; 115:4-7; Ex 20:23; 34:17

19:9 Lev 23:22; Deut 24:20-22

19:11 Ex 20:15, 16; Jer 9:3-5; Eph 4:25

19:12 Ex 20:7; Deut 5:11; Matt 5:33; Lev 18:21

19:13 Ex 22:7-15, 21-27; Deut 24:15; James 5:4

19:14 Deut 27:18

19:15 Ex 23:3, 6; Deut 1:17; 10:17; 16:19

19:16 Ps 15:3; Jer 6:28; 9:4; Ezek 22:9; Ex 23:7; Deut 27:25

19:17 1 John 2:9, 11; 3:15; Matt 18:15; Luke 17:3

19:18 Deut 32:35; Rom 12:19; Heb 10:30; Ps 103:9; Matt 19:19; Mark 12:31; Luke 10:27; Rom 13:9; Gal 5:14; James 2:8

19:19 Deut 22:9, 11

19:20 Deut 22:23-27

19:21 Lev 6:1-7

19:26 Gen 9:4; Lev 7:26f; 17:10; Deut 12:16, 23; Deut 18:10; 2 Kin 17:17

19:27 Lev 21:5; Deut 14:1

19:9–10 This law was a protection for the poor and the stranger (foreigner) and a reminder that God owned the land; the people were only caretakers. Laws such as this showed God's generosity and liberality. As people of God, the Israelites were to reflect his nature and characteristics in their attitudes and actions. Ruth and Naomi were two people who benefited from this merciful law (Ruth 2:2).

19:9–10 God instructed the Hebrews to provide for those in need. He required that the people leave the edges of their fields unharvested, providing food for travelers and the poor. It is easy to ignore the poor or forget about those who have less than we do. But God desires generosity. In what ways can you leave the "corners of your field" for those in need?

19:10–35 "You shall not . . ." Some people think the Bible is nothing but a book of don'ts. But Jesus neatly summarized all these rules when he said to love God with all your heart, and your neighbor as yourself. He called these the greatest commandments (or rules) of all (Matthew 22:34–40). By carrying out Jesus' simple commands, we find ourselves following all of God's other laws as well.

28 'You shall not make any cuts in your body for the dead nor make any tattoo marks
on yourselves: I am the LORD.
29 'Do not profane your daughter by making her a harlot, so that the land will not fall
to harlotry and the land become full of lewdness.
30 'You shall keep My sabbaths and revere My sanctuary; I am the LORD.
31 'Do not turn to mediums or spiritists; do not seek them out to be defiled by them. I
am the LORD your God.
32 'You shall rise up before the grayheaded and honor the aged, and you shall revere
your God; I am the LORD.
33 'When a stranger resides with you in your land, you shall not do him wrong.
34 'The stranger who resides with you shall be to you as the native among you, and
you shall love him as yourself, for you were aliens in the land of Egypt; I am the LORD
your God.
35 'You shall do no wrong in judgment, in measurement of weight, or capacity.
36 'You shall have just balances, just weights, a just [12]ephah, and a just [13]hin; I am the
LORD your God, who brought you out from the land of Egypt.
37 'You shall thus observe all My statutes and all My ordinances and do them; I am the
LORD.' "

On Human Sacrifice and Immoralities

20 Then the LORD spoke to Moses, saying,
2 "You shall also say to the sons of Israel:
'Any man from the sons of Israel or from the aliens sojourning in Israel who gives any
of his offspring to Molech, shall surely be put to death; the people of the land shall stone
him with stones.
3 'I will also set My face against that man and will cut him off from among his people,
because he has given some of his offspring to Molech, so as to defile My sanctuary and
to profane My holy name.
4 'If the people of the land, however, should ever disregard that man when he gives
any of his offspring to Molech, so as not to put him to death,
5 then I Myself will set My face against that man and against his family, and I will cut
off from among their people both him and all those who play the harlot after him, by
playing the harlot after Molech.
6 'As for the person who turns to mediums and to spiritists, to play the harlot after
them, I will also set My face against that person and will cut him off from among his
people.
7 'You shall consecrate yourselves therefore and be holy, for I am the LORD your God.
8 'You shall keep My statutes and practice them; I am the LORD who sanctifies you.
9 'If *there is* anyone who curses his father or his mother, he shall surely be put to death;
he has cursed his father or his mother, his bloodguiltiness is upon him.

12 I.e. Approx one bu **13** I.e. Approx one gal.

19:29 Lev 21:9; Deut 22:21; 23:17, 18

19:30 Lev 19:3; Lev 26:2

19:31 Lev 20:6, 27; Deut 18:11; 1 Sam 28:3; Is 8:19

19:32 Prov 23:22; Lam 5:12; 1 Tim 5:1

19:33 Ex 22:21; Deut 24:17, 18

19:34 Lev 19:18

19:35 Deut 25:13-16; Ezek 45:10

19:36 Deut 25:13-15; Prov 20:10

20:2 Lev 18:21; Lev 20:27; 24:14-23; Num 15:35, 36; Deut 21:21

20:3 Lev 15:31; Lev 18:21

20:6 Lev 19:31

20:7 Eph 1:4; 1 Pet 1:16

20:8 Ex 31:13

20:9 Ex 21:17; Deut 27:16

19:32 People often find it easy to dismiss the opinions of the elderly and avoid taking time to visit with them. But the fact that God commanded the Israelites to honor the elderly shows how seriously we should take the responsibility of respecting those older than we. Their wisdom gained from experience can save us from many pitfalls.

19:33–34 How do you feel when you encounter foreigners (strangers), especially those who don't speak your language? Are you impatient? Do you think or act as if they should go back where they came from? Are you tempted to take advantage of them? God says to treat foreigners as you'd treat fellow countrymen, to love them as you love yourself. In reality, we are all foreigners in this world, because it is only our temporary home. View strangers, newcomers, and foreigners as opportunities to demonstrate God's love.

20:1–3 Sacrificing children to the gods was a common practice in ancient religions. The Ammonites, Israel's neighbors, made child sacrifice to Molech (their national god) a vital part of their religion. They saw this as the greatest gift they could offer to ward off evil or appease angry gods. God made it clear that this practice was detestable and strictly forbidden. In Old Testament times as well as New, his character made human sacrifice unthinkable. (1) Unlike the pagan gods, he is a God of love, who does not need to be appeased (Exodus 34:6). (2) He is a God of life, who prohibits murder and encourages practices that lead to health and happiness (Deuteronomy 30:15–16). (3) He is God of the helpless, who shows special concern for children (Psalm 72:4). (4) He is a God of unselfishness, who instead of demanding blood gives his life for others (Isaiah 53:4–5).

20:6 Everyone is interested in what the future holds, and we often look to others for guidance. But God warned about looking to the occult for advice. Mediums and spiritists were outlawed because God was not the source of their information. At best, occult practitioners are fakes whose predictions cannot be trusted. At worst, they are in contact with evil spirits and are thus extremely dangerous. We don't need to look to the occult for information about the future. God has given us the Bible so that we may obtain all the information we need—and the Bible's teaching is trustworthy.

20:10 Ex 20:14; Lev 18:20; Deut 5:18
20:11 Lev 18:7, 8; Deut 27:20
20:12 Lev 18:15
20:13 Lev 18:22
20:14 Lev 18:17; Deut 27:23
20:15 Lev 18:23; Deut 27:21
20:17 Lev 18:9; Deut 27:22
20:18 Lev 15:24; 18:19
20:19 Lev 18:12, 13
20:20 Lev 18:14
20:21 Lev 18:16
20:22 Lev 18:28
20:23 Lev 18:3; Lev 18:25
20:24 Ex 13:5; 33:1-3; Ex 33:16; Lev 20:26
20:25 Lev 10:10; 11:1-47; Deut 14:3-21
20:26 Lev 20:24
20:27 Lev 19:31

10 'If *there is* a man who commits adultery with another man's wife, one who commits
adultery with his friend's wife, the adulterer and the adulteress shall surely be put to death.
11 'If *there is* a man who lies with his father's wife, he has uncovered his father's nakedness; both of them shall surely be put to death, their bloodguiltiness is upon them.
12 'If *there is* a man who lies with his daughter-in-law, both of them shall surely be put
to death; they have committed incest, their bloodguiltiness is upon them.
13 'If *there is* a man who lies with a male as those who lie with a woman, both of them
have committed a detestable act; they shall surely be put to death. Their bloodguiltiness
is upon them.
14 'If *there is* a man who marries a woman and her mother, it is immorality; both he and
they shall be burned with fire, so that there will be no immorality in your midst.
15 'If *there is* a man who lies with an animal, he shall surely be put to death; you shall
also kill the animal.
16 'If *there is* a woman who approaches any animal to mate with it, you shall kill the
woman and the animal; they shall surely be put to death. Their bloodguiltiness is upon
them.
17 'If *there is* a man who takes his sister, his father's daughter or his mother's daughter,
so that he sees her nakedness and she sees his nakedness, it is a disgrace; and they shall
be cut off in the sight of the sons of their people. He has uncovered his sister's nakedness; he bears his guilt.
18 'If *there is* a man who lies with a menstruous woman and uncovers her nakedness, he
has laid bare her flow, and she has exposed the flow of her blood; thus both of them shall
be cut off from among their people.
19 'You shall also not uncover the nakedness of your mother's sister or of your father's
sister, for such a one has made naked his blood relative; they will bear their guilt.
20 'If *there is* a man who lies with his uncle's wife he has uncovered his uncle's nakedness; they will bear their sin. They will die childless.
21 'If *there is* a man who takes his brother's wife, it is abhorrent; he has uncovered his
brother's nakedness. They will be childless.
22 'You are therefore to keep all My statutes and all My ordinances and do them, so
that the land to which I am bringing you to live will not spew you out.
23 'Moreover, you shall not follow the customs of the nation which I will drive out before you, for they did all these things, and therefore I have abhorred them.
24 'Hence I have said to you, "You are to possess their land, and I Myself will give it to
you to possess it, a land flowing with milk and honey." I am the LORD your God, who
has separated you from the peoples.
25 'You are therefore to make a distinction between the clean animal and the unclean,
and between the unclean bird and the clean; and you shall not make yourselves detestable by animal or by bird or by anything that creeps on the ground, which I have separated for you as unclean.
26 'Thus you are to be holy to Me, for I the LORD am holy; and I have set you apart
from the peoples to be Mine.
27 'Now a man or a woman who is a medium or a spiritist shall surely be put to death.
They shall be stoned with stones, their bloodguiltiness is upon them.' "

20:10–21 This list of commands against sexual sins includes extremely harsh punishments. Why? God had no tolerance for such acts for the following reasons: (1) they shatter the mutual commitment of married partners; (2) they destroy the sanctity of the family; (3) they twist people's mental well-being; and (4) they spread disease. Sexual sin has always been widely available, but the glorification of sex between people who are not married to each other often hides deep tragedy and hurt behind the scenes. When society portrays sexual sins as attractive, it is easy to forget the dark side. God had good reasons for prohibiting sexual sins: He loves us and wants the very best for us.

20:10–21 The detestable acts listed here were very common in the pagan nations of Canaan; their religions were rampant with sex goddesses, temple prostitution, and other gross sins. The Canaanites' immoral religious practices reflected a decadent culture that tended to corrupt whoever came in contact with it. By contrast, God was building a nation to make a positive influence on the world. He did not want the Israelites to adopt the Canaanites' practices and slide into debauchery. So he prepared the people for what they would face in the promised land by commanding them to steer clear of sexual sins.

20:22–23 God gave many rules to his people—but not without reason. He did not withhold good from them; he only prohibited those acts that would bring them to ruin. All of us understand God's physical laws of nature. For example, jumping off a ten-story building means death because of the law of gravity. But some of us don't understand how God's spiritual laws work. God forbids us to do certain things because he wants to keep us from self-destruction. Next time you are drawn to a forbidden physical or emotional pleasure, remind yourself that its consequences might be suffering and separation from the God who is trying to help you.

2. Rules for priests

Regulations concerning Priests

21 Then the LORD said to Moses, "Speak to the priests, the sons of Aaron, and say
to them:
'No one shall defile himself for a *dead* person among his people,
2 except for his relatives who are nearest to him, his mother and his father and his
son and his daughter and his brother,
3 also for his virgin sister, who is near to him because she has had no husband; for her
he may defile himself.
4 'He shall not defile himself as a relative by marriage among his people, and so profane himself.
5 'They shall not make any baldness on their heads, nor shave off the edges of their
beards, nor make any cuts in their flesh.
6 'They shall be holy to their God and not profane the name of their God, for they
present the offerings by fire to the LORD, the food of their God; so they shall be holy.
7 'They shall not take a woman who is profaned by harlotry, nor shall they take a woman
divorced from her husband; for he is holy to his God.
8 'You shall consecrate him, therefore, for he offers the food of your God; he shall be
holy to you; for I the LORD, who sanctifies you, am holy.
9 'Also the daughter of any priest, if she profanes herself by harlotry, she profanes her
father; she shall be burned with fire.
10 'The priest who is the highest among his brothers, on whose head the anointing oil
has been poured and who has been consecrated to wear the garments, shall not uncover
his head nor tear his clothes;
11 nor shall he approach any dead person, nor defile himself *even* for his father or his
mother;
12 nor shall he go out of the sanctuary nor profane the sanctuary of his God, for the
consecration of the anointing oil of his God is on him; I am the LORD.
13 'He shall take a wife in her virginity.
14 'A widow, or a divorced woman, or one who is profaned by harlotry, these he may
not take; but rather he is to marry a virgin of his own people,
15 so that he will not profane his offspring among his people; for I am the LORD who
sanctifies him.'"
16 Then the LORD spoke to Moses, saying,
17 "Speak to Aaron, saying, 'No man of your offspring throughout their generations who
has a defect shall approach to offer the food of his God.
18 'For no one who has a defect shall approach: a blind man, or a lame man, or he who
has a disfigured *face,* or any deformed *limb,*
19 or a man who has a broken foot or broken hand,
20 or a hunchback or a dwarf, or *one who has* a defect in his eye or eczema or scabs or
crushed testicles.
21 'No man among the descendants of Aaron the priest who has a defect is to come
near to offer the LORD'S offerings by fire; *since* he has a defect, he shall not come near
to offer the food of his God.

21:1 Lev 19:28; Ezek 44:25
21:2 Lev 21:11
21:5 Deut 14:1; Ezek 44:20; Lev 19:27; Deut 14:1
21:6 Lev 18:21; Lev 3:11
21:7 Lev 21:13, 14
21:8 Lev 21:6
21:9 Gen 38:24; Lev 19:29
21:10 Lev 10:6
21:11 Lev 19:28; Num 19:14
21:12 Lev 10:7; Ex 29:6, 7
21:14 Lev 21:7; Ezek 44:22
21:17 Lev 21:6
21:18 Lev 22:19-25
21:20 Deut 23:1; Is 56:3-5
21:21 Lev 21:6

21:1–2 To become ceremonially unclean (defiled) "for a dead person among his people" means touching a dead body.

21:16–23 Was God unfairly discriminating against handicapped people when he said they were unqualified to offer sacrifices? Just as God demanded that no imperfect animals be used for sacrifice, he required that no handicapped priests offer sacrifices. This was not meant as an insult; rather, it had to do with the fact that the priest must match as closely as possible the perfect God he served. Of course, such perfection was not fully realized until Jesus Christ came. As Levites, the handicapped priests were protected and supported with food from the sacrifices. They were not abandoned because they still performed many essential services within the tabernacle.

22:1–9 Why were there so many specific guidelines for the priests? The Israelites would have been quite familiar with priests from Egypt. Egyptian priests were mainly interested in politics. They viewed religion as a way to gain power. Thus the Israelites would have been suspicious of the establishment of a new priestly order. But God wanted his priests to serve him and the people. Their duties were religious—to help people draw near to God and worship him. They could not use their position to gain power because they were not allowed to own land or take money from anyone. All these guidelines reassured the people and helped the priests accomplish their purpose.

22:19–25 Animals with defects were not acceptable as sacrifices because they did not represent God's holy nature. Furthermore, the animal had to be without blemish in order to foreshadow the perfect, sinless life of Jesus Christ. When we give our best time, talent, and treasure to God rather than what is tarnished or common, we show the true meaning of worship and testify to God's supreme worth.

21:22 1 Cor 9:13

22 'He may eat the food of his God, *both* of the most holy and of the holy,

23 only he shall not go in to the veil or come near the altar because he has a defect, so that he will not profane My sanctuaries. For I am the LORD who sanctifies them.' "

24 So Moses spoke to Aaron and to his sons and to all the sons of Israel.

Sundry Rules for Priests

22 Then the LORD spoke to Moses, saying,

2 "Tell Aaron and his sons to be careful with the holy *gifts* of the sons of Israel, which they dedicate to Me, so as not to profane My holy name; I am the LORD.

22:3 Lev 7:20, 21; Num 19:13

3 "Say to them, 'If any man among all your descendants throughout your generations approaches the holy *gifts* which the sons of Israel dedicate to the LORD, while he has an uncleanness, that person shall be cut off from before Me; I am the LORD.

22:4 Lev 14:1-32; Lev 11:24-28, 39, 40; Lev 15:16, 17

4 'No man of the descendants of Aaron, who is a leper or who has a discharge, may eat of the holy *gifts* until he is clean. And if one touches anything made unclean by a corpse or if a man has a seminal emission,

22:5 Lev 11:23-28

5 or if a man touches any teeming things by which he is made unclean, or any man by whom he is made unclean, whatever his uncleanness;

6 a person who touches any such shall be unclean until evening, and shall not eat of the holy *gifts* unless he has bathed his body in water.

22:7 Num 18:11

7 'But when the sun sets, he will be clean, and afterward he shall eat of the holy *gifts,* for it is his food.

22:8 Lev 7:24; 11:39, 40; 17:15

8 'He shall not eat *an animal* which dies or is torn *by beasts,* becoming unclean by it; I am the LORD.

22:9 Lev 18:30; Ex 28:43; Lev 22:16; Num 18:22

9 'They shall therefore keep My charge, so that they will not bear sin because of it and die thereby because they profane it; I am the LORD who sanctifies them.

22:10 Ex 29:33; Lev 22:13; Num 3:10

10 'No [14]layman, however, is to eat the holy *gift;* a sojourner with the priest or a hired man shall not eat of the holy *gift.*

22:11 Gen 17:13; Ex 12:44

11 'But if a priest buys a slave as *his* property with his money, that one may eat of it, and those who are born in his house may eat of his food.

12 'If a priest's daughter is married to a layman, she shall not eat of the offering of the *gifts.*

22:13 Lev 22:10

13 'But if a priest's daughter becomes a widow or divorced, and has no child and returns to her father's house as in her youth, she shall eat of her father's food; but no layman shall eat of it.

22:14 Lev 5:15, 16

14 'But if a man eats a holy *gift* unintentionally, then he shall add to it a fifth of it and shall give the holy *gift* to the priest.

22:15 Num 18:32

15 'They shall not profane the holy *gifts* of the sons of Israel which they offer to the LORD,

22:16 Lev 10:17; 22:9

16 and *so* cause them to bear punishment for guilt by eating their holy *gifts;* for I am the LORD who sanctifies them.' "

Flawless Animals for Sacrifice

17 Then the LORD spoke to Moses, saying,

22:18 Num 15:14

18 "Speak to Aaron and to his sons and to all the sons of Israel and say to them, 'Any man of the house of Israel or of the aliens in Israel who presents his offering, whether it is any of their votive or any of their freewill offerings, which they present to the LORD for a burnt offering—

22:19 Lev 21:18-21; Deut 15:21

19 for you to be accepted—*it must be* a male without defect from the cattle, the sheep, or the goats.

20 'Whatever has a defect, you shall not offer, for it will not be accepted for you.

22:20 Deut 15:21; 17:1; Mal 1:8, 14; Heb 9:14; 1 Pet 1:19

21 'When a man offers a sacrifice of peace offerings to the LORD to fulfill a special vow or for a freewill offering, of the herd or of the flock, it must be perfect to be accepted; there shall be no defect in it.

22:21 Num 15:3, 8

22 'Those *that are* blind or fractured or maimed or having a running sore or eczema or scabs, you shall not offer to the LORD, nor make of them an offering by fire on the altar to the LORD.

23 'In respect to an ox or a lamb which has an overgrown or stunted *member,* you may present it for a freewill offering, but for a vow it will not be accepted.

22:24 Lev 21:20

24 'Also anything *with its testicles* bruised or crushed or torn or cut, you shall not offer to the LORD, or sacrifice in your land,

22:25 Lev 21:22

25 nor shall you accept any such from the hand of a foreigner for offering as the food

14 Lit *stranger*

of your God; for their corruption is in them, they have a defect, they shall not be accepted for you.' "
26 Then the LORD spoke to Moses, saying,
27 "When an ox or a sheep or a goat is born, it shall remain seven days with its mother,
and from the eighth day on it shall be accepted as a sacrifice of an offering by fire to the
LORD.
28 "But, *whether* it is an ox or a sheep, you shall not kill *both* it and its young in one day.
29 "When you sacrifice a sacrifice of thanksgiving to the LORD, you shall sacrifice it so
that you may be accepted.
30 "It shall be eaten on the same day, you shall leave none of it until morning; I am the
LORD.
31 "So you shall keep My commandments, and do them; I am the LORD.
32 "You shall not profane My holy name, but I will be sanctified among the sons of Israel;
I am the LORD who sanctifies you,
33 who brought you out from the land of Egypt, to be your God; I am the LORD."

22:27 Ex 22:30
22:28 Deut 22:6, 7
22:29 Lev 7:12
22:31 Lev 19:37; Num 15:40; Deut 4:40
22:33 Lev 11:45

3. Seasons and festivals

Laws of Religious Festivals

23 The LORD spoke again to Moses, saying,
2 "Speak to the sons of Israel and say to them, 'The LORD'S appointed times
which you shall proclaim as holy convocations—My appointed times are these:
3 'For six days work may be done, but on the seventh day there is a sabbath of complete rest, a holy convocation. You shall not do any work; it is a sabbath to the LORD in
all your dwellings.
4 'These are the appointed times of the LORD, holy convocations which you shall proclaim at the times appointed for them.
5 'In the first month, on the fourteenth day of the month at twilight is the LORD'S
Passover.
6 'Then on the fifteenth day of the same month there is the Feast of Unleavened Bread
to the LORD; for seven days you shall eat unleavened bread.
7 'On the first day you shall have a holy convocation; you shall not do any laborious
work.
8 'But for seven days you shall present an offering by fire to the LORD. On the seventh
day is a holy convocation; you shall not do any laborious work.' "
9 Then the LORD spoke to Moses, saying,
10 "Speak to the sons of Israel and say to them, 'When you enter the land which I am
going to give to you and reap its harvest, then you shall bring in the sheaf of the first
fruits of your harvest to the priest.
11 'He shall wave the sheaf before the LORD for you to be accepted; on the day after
the sabbath the priest shall wave it.
12 'Now on the day when you wave the sheaf, you shall offer a male lamb one year old
without defect for a burnt offering to the LORD.
13 'Its grain offering shall then be two-tenths *of an ephah* of fine flour mixed with oil,
an offering by fire to the LORD *for* a soothing aroma, with its drink offering, a fourth of
a [15]hin of wine.

23:2 Lev 23:4, 37, 44; Num 29:39; Lev 23:21
23:3 Ex 20:9, 10; 23:12; 31:13-17; 35:2, 3; Lev 19:3; Deut 5:13, 14
23:4 Ex 23:14; Lev 23:2
23:5 Ex 12:18, 19; Num 28:16-25; Deut 16:1; Josh 5:10
23:6 Ex 12:14-20; 23:15; 34:18; Deut 16:3-8
23:7 Lev 23:8, 21, 25, 35, 36
23:10 Ex 23:19; 34:26
23:13 Lev 6:20

15 I.e. Approx one gal.

23:Iff Convocations (appointed feasts) played a major role in Israel's culture. Israel's feasts were different from those of any other nation because, being ordained by God, they were times of celebrating with him, not times of moral depravity. God wanted to set aside special days for the people to come together for rest, refreshment, and remembering with thanksgiving all he had done for them.

23:1–4 God established several national holidays each year for celebration, fellowship, and worship. Much can be learned about people by observing the holidays they celebrate and the way they celebrate them. Take note of your holiday traditions. What do they say about your values?

23:6 The Feast of Unleavened Bread reminded Israel of their escape from Egypt. For seven days they ate unleavened bread, just as they had eaten it back then (Exodus 12:14–15). The symbolism of this bread made without yeast was important to the Israelites. First, because the bread was unique, it illustrated Israel's uniqueness as a nation. Second, because yeast was a symbol of sin, the bread represented Israel's moral purity. Third, the bread reminded them to obey quickly. Their ancestors left the yeast out of their dough so they could leave Egypt quickly without waiting for the dough to rise.

23:9–14 The Feast of Firstfruits required that the first crops harvested be offered to God. The Israelites could not eat the food from their harvest until they had made this offering. Today God still expects us to set aside his portion first, not last. Giving leftovers to God is no way to express thanks.

23:14 Ex 34:26; Num 15:20, 21

14 'Until this same day, until you have brought in the offering of your God, you shall
eat neither bread nor roasted grain nor new growth. It is to be a perpetual statute throughout your generations in all your dwelling places.

23:15 Num 28:26-31; Deut 16:9-12

15 'You shall also count for yourselves from the day after the sabbath, from the day
when you brought in the sheaf of the wave offering; there shall be seven complete sabbaths.

23:16 Num 28:26

16 'You shall count fifty days to the day after the seventh sabbath; then you shall present a new grain offering to the LORD.

23:17 Lev 2:12; 7:13

17 'You shall bring in from your dwelling places two *loaves* of bread for a wave offering, made of two-tenths *of an ephah;* they shall be of a fine flour, baked with leaven as
first fruits to the LORD.
18 'Along with the bread you shall present seven one year old male lambs without defect, and a bull of the herd and two rams; they are to be a burnt offering to the LORD,
with their grain offering and their drink offerings, an offering by fire of a soothing aroma to the LORD.

23:19 Lev 4:23; Num 28:30

19 'You shall also offer one male goat for a sin offering and two male lambs one year
old for a sacrifice of peace offerings.
20 'The priest shall then wave them with the bread of the first fruits for a wave offering
with two lambs before the LORD; they are to be holy to the LORD for the priest.

23:21 Lev 23:2, 4; Lev 23:7

21 'On this same day you shall make a proclamation as well; you are to have a holy
convocation. You shall do no laborious work. It is to be a perpetual statute in all your
dwelling places throughout your generations.

23:22 Lev 19:9, 10; Deut 24:19; Ruth 2:15f

22 'When you reap the harvest of your land, moreover, you shall not reap to the very
corners of your field nor gather the gleaning of your harvest; you are to leave them for
the needy and the alien. I am the LORD your God.' "
23 Again the LORD spoke to Moses, saying,

23:24 Num 29:1; Num 10:9, 10

24 "Speak to the sons of Israel, saying, 'In the seventh month on the first of the month
you shall have a rest, a reminder by blowing *of trumpets,* a holy convocation.

23:25 Lev 23:21

25 'You shall not do any laborious work, but you shall present an offering by fire to the
LORD.' "

THE FEASTS
Besides enjoying one Sabbath day of rest each week, the Israelites also enjoyed 19 days when national holidays were celebrated.

Feast	*What It Celebrated*	*Its Importance*
Passover One day (Leviticus 23:5)	When God spared the lives of Israel's firstborn children in Egypt and freed the Hebrews from slavery	Reminded the people of God's deliverance
Unleavened Bread Seven days (Leviticus 23:6–8)	The exodus from Egypt	Reminded the people they were leaving the old life behind and entering a new way of living
Firstfruits One day (Leviticus 23:9–14)	The first crops of the barley harvest	Reminded the people how God provided for them
Pentecost (Weeks) One day (Leviticus 23:15–22)	The end of the barley harvest and beginning of the wheat harvest	Showed joy and thanksgiving over the bountiful harvest
Trumpets One day (Leviticus 23:23–25)	The beginning of the seventh month (civil new year)	Expressed joy and thanksgiving to God
Day of Atonement One day (Leviticus 23:26–32)	The removal of sin from the people and the nation	Restored fellowship with God
Booths (Tabernacles) Seven days (Leviticus 23:33–43)	God's protection and guidance in the wilderness	Renewed Israel's commitment to God and trust in his guidance and protection

---

23:15–22 The Feast of Weeks (Pentecost) was a festival praising God for a bountiful harvest.

23:23–24 Most of the trumpets used were rams' horns, although some of the more special trumpets were made of beaten silver. Trumpets were blown to announce the beginning of each month as well as the start of festivals.

The Day of Atonement

26 The LORD spoke to Moses, saying,
27 "On exactly the tenth day of this seventh month is the day of atonement; it shall be a
holy convocation for you, and you shall humble your souls and present an offering by
fire to the LORD.
28 "You shall not do any work on this same day, for it is a day of atonement, to make
atonement on your behalf before the LORD your God.
29 "If there is any person who will not humble himself on this same day, he shall be cut
off from his people.
30 "As for any person who does any work on this same day, that person I will destroy
from among his people.
31 "You shall do no work at all. It is to be a perpetual statute throughout your generations in all your dwelling places.
32 "It is to be a sabbath of complete rest to you, and you shall humble your souls; on the
ninth of the month at evening, from evening until evening you shall keep your sabbath."
33 Again the LORD spoke to Moses, saying,
34 "Speak to the sons of Israel, saying, 'On the fifteenth of this seventh month is the
Feast of Booths for seven days to the LORD.
35 'On the first day is a holy convocation; you shall do no laborious work of any kind.
36 'For seven days you shall present an offering by fire to the LORD. On the eighth day
you shall have a holy convocation and present an offering by fire to the LORD; it is an
assembly. You shall do no laborious work.
37 'These are the appointed times of the LORD which you shall proclaim as holy convocations, to present offerings by fire to the LORD—burnt offerings and grain offerings,
sacrifices and drink offerings, *each* day's matter on its own day—
38 besides *those of* the sabbaths of the LORD, and besides your gifts and besides all
your votive and freewill offerings, which you give to the LORD.
39 'On exactly the fifteenth day of the seventh month, when you have gathered in the
crops of the land, you shall celebrate the feast of the LORD for seven days, with a rest on
the first day and a rest on the eighth day.
40 'Now on the first day you shall take for yourselves the foliage of beautiful trees, palm
branches and boughs of leafy trees and willows of the brook, and you shall rejoice before the LORD your God for seven days.
41 'You shall thus celebrate it *as* a feast to the LORD for seven days in the year. It *shall
be* a perpetual statute throughout your generations; you shall celebrate it in the seventh
month.
42 'You shall live in booths for seven days; all the native-born in Israel shall live in booths,
43 so that your generations may know that I had the sons of Israel live in booths when
I brought them out from the land of Egypt. I am the LORD your God.' "
44 So Moses declared to the sons of Israel the appointed times of the LORD.

23:27 Lev 16:29; 25:9; Num 29:7; Ex 30:10; Lev 16:30; 23:28; Num 29:7-11
23:28 Lev 23:27; Lev 16:34
23:29 Gen 17:14; Lev 13:46; Num 5:2
23:34 Num 29:12; Lev 23:42, 43; Deut 16:13, 16; Ezra 3:4; Neh 8:14; Zech 14:16; John 7:2
23:35 Lev 23:25
23:36 Num 29:12-34; Num 29:35-38
23:37 Lev 23:2; Num 28:1-29:38
23:39 Ex 23:16
23:42 Lev 23:34
23:43 Deut 31:13; Ps 78:5f
23:44 Lev 23:37

The Lamp and the Bread of the Sanctuary

24 Then the LORD spoke to Moses, saying,
2 "Command the sons of Israel that they bring to you clear oil from beaten olives
for the light, to make a lamp burn continually.
3 "Outside the veil of testimony in the tent of meeting, Aaron shall keep it in order
from evening to morning before the LORD continually; *it shall be* a perpetual statute
throughout your generations.
4 "He shall keep the lamps in order on the pure *gold* lampstand before the LORD continually.

24:2 Ex 27:20, 21
24:4 Ex 25:31; 31:8; 37:17

23:33-43 The Feast of Booths, also called the Feast of Ingathering or Tabernacles, was a special celebration involving the whole family (see 23:34; Exodus 23:16; Deuteronomy 16:13). Like Passover, this feast taught family members of all ages about God's nature and what he had done for them and was a time of renewed commitment to God. Our families also need rituals of celebration to renew our faith and to pass it on to our children. In addition to Christmas and Easter, we should select other special days to commemorate God's goodness.

23:44 Worship involves both celebration and confession. But in Israel's national holidays, the balance seems heavily tipped in favor of celebration—five joyous occasions to two solemn ones. The God of the Bible encourages joy! God does not intend for religion to be only meditation and introspection. He also wants us to celebrate. Serious reflection and immediate confession of sin is essential, of course. But this should be balanced by celebrating who God is and what he has done for his people.

24:5 Ex 25:30; 39:36; 40:23
5 "Then you shall take fine flour and bake twelve cakes with it; two-tenths *of an ephah*
shall be *in* each cake.
24:6 Ex 25:24; 1 Kin 7:48
6 "You shall set them *in* two rows, six *to* a row, on the pure *gold* table before the LORD.
24:7 Lev 2:2, 9, 16
7 "You shall put pure frankincense on each row that it may be a memorial portion for
the bread, *even* an offering by fire to the LORD.
24:8 Matt 12:5; Ex 25:30; Num 4:7; 2 Chr 2:4
8 "Every sabbath day he shall set it in order before the LORD continually; it is an everlasting covenant for the sons of Israel.
24:9 Matt 12:4; Mark 2:26; Luke 6:4
9 "It shall be for Aaron and his sons, and they shall eat it in a holy place; for it is most
holy to him from the LORD'S offerings by fire, *his* portion forever."
10 Now the son of an Israelite woman, whose father was an Egyptian, went out among
the sons of Israel; and the Israelite woman's son and a man of Israel struggled with each
other in the camp.
24:11 Ex 3:15; 22:28; Job 2:5, 9; Is 8:21
11 The son of the Israelite woman blasphemed the Name and cursed. So they brought
him to Moses. (Now his mother's name was Shelomith, the daughter of Dibri, of the tribe
of Dan.)
24:12 Ex 18:15; Num 15:34
12 They put him in custody so that the command of the LORD might be made clear to
them.
13 Then the LORD spoke to Moses, saying,
24:14 Deut 13:9; 17:7; Lev 20:2, 27; Deut 21:21
14 "Bring the one who has cursed outside the camp, and let all who heard him lay their
hands on his head; then let all the congregation stone him.
24:15 Ex 22:28
15 "You shall speak to the sons of Israel, saying, 'If anyone curses his God, then he will
bear his sin.
24:16 1 Kin 21:10; Matt 12:31; Mark 3:28f
16 'Moreover, the one who blasphemes the name of the LORD shall surely be put to
death; all the congregation shall certainly stone him. The alien as well as the native, when
he blasphemes the Name, shall be put to death.

"An Eye for an Eye"

24:17 Gen 9:6; Ex 21:12; Num 35:30, 31; Deut 27:24
17 'If a man takes the life of any human being, he shall surely be put to death.
24:18 Lev 24:21
18 'The one who takes the life of an animal shall make it good, life for life.
19 'If a man injures his neighbor, just as he has done, so it shall be done to him:
24:20 Ex 21:23; Deut 19:21; Matt 5:38
20 fracture for fracture, eye for eye, tooth for tooth; just as he has injured a man, so it
shall be inflicted on him.
24:21 Lev 24:17
21 'Thus the one who kills an animal shall make it good, but the one who kills a man
shall be put to death.
24:22 Ex 12:49; Num 9:14; 15:15, 16, 29
22 'There shall be one standard for you; it shall be for the stranger as well as the native,
for I am the LORD your God.' "
23 Then Moses spoke to the sons of Israel, and they brought the one who had cursed
outside the camp and stoned him with stones. Thus the sons of Israel did, just as the
LORD had commanded Moses.

The Sabbatic Year and Year of Jubilee

25 The LORD then spoke to Moses at Mount Sinai, saying,
2 "Speak to the sons of Israel and say to them, 'When you come into the land
which I shall give you, then the land shall have a sabbath to the LORD.
25:3 Ex 23:10, 11
3 'Six years you shall sow your field, and six years you shall prune your vineyard and
gather in its crop,
25:4 Lev 25:20
4 but during the seventh year the land shall have a sabbath rest, a sabbath to the LORD;
you shall not sow your field nor prune your vineyard.
5 'Your harvest's [16]aftergrowth you shall not reap, and your grapes of untrimmed vines
you shall not gather; the land shall have a sabbatical year.
25:6 Lev 25:20, 21
6 'All of you shall have the sabbath *products* of the land for food; yourself, and your

16 Lit *growth from spilled kernels*

24:13 This punishment for blasphemy (cursing God) seems extreme by modern standards. But it shows how seriously God expects us to take our relationship with him. Often we use his name in swearing, or we act as though he doesn't exist. We should be careful how we speak and act, treating God with reverence. Eventually, he will have the last word.

24:17–22 This was a code for judges, not an endorsement of personal vengeance. In effect, it was saying that the punishment should fit the crime, but it should not go beyond.

25:1–7 The sabbatical (or sabbath) year provided one year in seven for the fields to lay fallow (unplowed). This was good management of natural resources and reminded the people of God's control and provision for them.

male and female slaves, and your hired man and your foreign resident, those who live as
aliens with you.
7 'Even your cattle and the animals that are in your land shall have all its crops to eat.
8 'You are also to count off seven sabbaths of years for yourself, seven times seven
years, so that you have the time of the seven sabbaths of years, *namely,* forty-nine years.
9 'You shall then sound a ram's horn abroad on the tenth day of the seventh month;
on the day of atonement you shall sound a horn all through your land.
10 'You shall thus consecrate the fiftieth year and proclaim [17]a release through the land
to all its inhabitants. It shall be a jubilee for you, and each of you shall return to his own
property, and each of you shall return to his family.
11 'You shall have the fiftieth year as a jubilee; you shall not sow, nor reap its aftergrowth,
nor gather in *from* its untrimmed vines.
12 'For it is a jubilee; it shall be holy to you. You shall eat its crops out of the field.
13 'On this year of jubilee each of you shall return to his own property.
14 'If you make a sale, moreover, to your friend or buy from your friend's hand, you
shall not wrong one another.
15 'Corresponding to the number of years after the jubilee, you shall buy from your
friend; he is to sell to you according to the number of years of crops.
16 'In proportion to the extent of the years you shall increase its price, and in proportion to the fewness of the years you shall diminish its price, for *it is* a number of crops he
is selling to you.
17 'So you shall not wrong one another, but you shall fear your God; for I am the LORD
your God.
18 'You shall thus observe My statutes and keep My judgments, so as to carry them
out, that you may live securely on the land.
19 'Then the land will yield its produce, so that you can eat your fill and live securely on it.
20 'But if you say, "What are we going to eat on the seventh year if we do not sow or
gather in our crops?"
21 then I will so order My blessing for you in the sixth year that it will bring forth the
crop for three years.
22 'When you are sowing the eighth year, you can still eat old things from the crop, eating
the old until the ninth year when its crop comes in.

The Law of Redemption

23 'The land, moreover, shall not be sold permanently, for the land is Mine; for you are
but aliens and sojourners with Me.
24 'Thus for every piece of your property, you are to provide for the redemption of the
land.
25 'If a fellow countryman of yours becomes so poor he has to sell part of his property,
then his nearest kinsman is to come and buy back what his relative has sold.
26 'Or in case a man has no kinsman, but so recovers his means as to find sufficient for
its redemption,
27 then he shall calculate the years since its sale and refund the balance to the man to
whom he sold it, and so return to his property.
28 'But if he has not found sufficient means to get it back for himself, then what he has
sold shall remain in the hands of its purchaser until the year of jubilee; but at the jubilee
it shall revert, that he may return to his property.
29 'Likewise, if a man sells a dwelling house in a walled city, then his redemption right
remains valid until a full year from its sale; his right of redemption lasts a full year.
30 'But if it is not bought back for him within the space of a full year, then the house

25:9 Lev 23:27
25:10 Jer 34:8, 15, 17; Lev 25:13, 28, 54
25:13 Lev 25:10; 27:24
25:14 Lev 25:17
25:16 Lev 25:27, 51, 52
25:17 Lev 25:14; Prov 14:31; 22:22; Jer 7:5, 6; 1 Thess 4:6
25:18 Lev 26:5; Deut 12:10; Jer 23:6
25:20 Lev 25:4
25:21 Deut 28:8
25:22 Lev 26:10
25:23 Ex 19:5; Gen 23:4; 1 Chr 29:15; Ps 39:12; Heb 11:13; 1 Pet 2:11
25:25 Ruth 2:20; 4:4, 6
25:27 Lev 25:16
25:28 Lev 25:10, 13

17 Or *liberty*

25:8–17 The Year of Jubilee was meant to be celebrated every 50 years. It included canceling all debts, freeing all slaves, and returning to its original owners all land that had been sold. There is no indication in the Bible that the Year of Jubilee was ever carried out. If Israel had followed this practice faithfully, they would have been a society without permanent poverty.

25:23 The people would one day possess land in Canaan, but in God's plan, only God's ownership was absolute. He wanted his people to avoid greed and materialism. If you have the attitude that you are taking care of the Lord's property, you will make what you have more available to others. This is difficult to do if you have an attitude of ownership. Think of yourself as a manager of all that is under your care, not as an owner.

that is in the walled city passes permanently to its purchaser throughout his generations; it does not revert in the jubilee.

31 'The houses of the villages, however, which have no surrounding wall shall be considered as open fields; they have redemption rights and revert in the jubilee.

25:32 Num 35:1-8; Josh 21:2

32 'As for cities of the Levites, the Levites have a permanent right of redemption for the houses of the cities which are their possession.

33 'What, therefore, belongs to the Levites may be redeemed and a house sale in the city of this possession reverts in the jubilee, for the houses of the cities of the Levites are their possession among the sons of Israel.

25:34 Num 35:2-5

34 'But pasture fields of their cities shall not be sold, for that is their perpetual possession.

Of Poor Countrymen

25:35 Deut 15:7-11; 24:14, 15

35 'Now in case a countryman of yours becomes poor and his means with regard to you falter, then you are to sustain him, like a stranger or a sojourner, that he may live with you.

25:36 Ex 22:25; Deut 23:19, 20

36 'Do not take usurious interest from him, but revere your God, that your countryman may live with you.

37 'You shall not give him your silver at interest, nor your food for gain.

25:38 Lev 11:45; Gen 17:7

38 'I am the LORD your God, who brought you out of the land of Egypt to give you the land of Canaan *and* to be your God.

25:39 Ex 21:2-6; Deut 15:12-18; 1 Kin 9:22

39 'If a countryman of yours becomes so poor with regard to you that he sells himself to you, you shall not subject him to a slave's service.

25:40 Ex 21:2

40 'He shall be with you as a hired man, as if he were a sojourner; he shall serve with you until the year of jubilee.

41 'He shall then go out from you, he and his sons with him, and shall go back to his family, that he may return to the property of his forefathers.

42 'For they are My servants whom I brought out from the land of Egypt; they are not to be sold *in* a slave sale.

25:43 Ex 1:13, 14; Lev 25:46, 53; Ezek 34:4; Col 4:1

43 'You shall not rule over him with severity, but are to revere your God.

44 'As for your male and female slaves whom you may have—you may acquire male and female slaves from the pagan nations that are around you.

45 'Then, too, *it is* out of the sons of the sojourners who live as aliens among you that you may gain acquisition, and out of their families who are with you, whom they will have produced in your land; they also may become your possession.

25:46 Lev 25:43

46 'You may even bequeath them to your sons after you, to receive as a possession; you can use them as permanent slaves. But in respect to your countrymen, the sons of Israel, you shall not rule with severity over one another.

Of Redeeming a Poor Man

47 'Now if the means of a stranger or of a sojourner with you becomes sufficient, and a countryman of yours becomes so poor with regard to him as to sell himself to a stranger who is sojourning with you, or to the descendants of a stranger's family,

48 then he shall have redemption right after he has been sold. One of his brothers may redeem him,

25:49 Lev 25:26, 27

49 or his uncle, or his uncle's son, may redeem him, or one of his blood relatives from his family may redeem him; or if he prospers, he may redeem himself.

25:35ff The Bible places great emphasis on assisting the poor and helpless, especially orphans, widows, and the handicapped. In Israelite society, no paid work was available to women; thus, a widow and her children had no livelihood. Neither was there work available for the seriously handicapped in this nation of farmers and shepherds. The poor were to be helped without charging any interest. Individual and family responsibility for the poor was crucial since there was no government aid.

25:35–37 God said that neglecting the poor was a sin. Permanent poverty was not allowed in Israel. Financially secure families were responsible to help and house those in need. Many times we do nothing, not because we lack compassion, but because we are overwhelmed by the size of the problem and don't know where to begin. God doesn't expect you to eliminate poverty, nor does he expect you to neglect your family while providing for others. He does, however, expect that when you see an individual in need, you will reach out with whatever help you can offer, including hospitality.

25:44 Why did God allow the Israelites to purchase slaves? Under Hebrew laws, slaves were treated differently from slaves in other nations. They were seen as human beings with dignity, and not as animals. Hebrew slaves, for example, took part in the religious festivals and rested on the Sabbath. Nowhere does the Bible condone slavery, but it recognizes its existence. God's laws offered many guidelines for treating slaves properly.

50 'He then with his purchaser shall calculate from the year when he sold himself to
him up to the year of jubilee; and the price of his sale shall correspond to the number of
years. *It is* like the days of a hired man *that* he shall be with him.
51 'If there are still many years, he shall refund part of his purchase price in proportion
to them for his own redemption;
52 and if few years remain until the year of jubilee, he shall so calculate with him. In
proportion to his years he is to refund *the amount for* his redemption.
53 'Like a man hired year by year he shall be with him; he shall not rule over him with
severity in your sight.
54 'Even if he is not redeemed by these *means,* he shall still go out in the year of jubilee,
he and his sons with him.
55 'For the sons of Israel are My servants; they are My servants whom I brought out
from the land of Egypt. I am the LORD your God.

4. Receiving God's blessing

Blessings of Obedience

26 'You shall not make for yourselves idols, nor shall you set up for yourselves an
image or a *sacred* pillar, nor shall you place a figured stone in your land to bow
down to it; for I am the LORD your God.
2 'You shall keep My sabbaths and reverence My sanctuary; I am the LORD.
3 'If you walk in My statutes and keep My commandments so as to carry them out,
4 then I shall give you rains in their season, so that the land will yield its produce and
the trees of the field will bear their fruit.
5 'Indeed, your threshing will last for you until grape gathering, and grape gathering
will last until sowing time. You will thus eat your food to the full and live securely in your
land.
6 'I shall also grant peace in the land, so that you may lie down with no one making
you tremble. I shall also eliminate harmful beasts from the land, and no sword will pass
through your land.
7 'But you will chase your enemies and they will fall before you by the sword;
8 five of you will chase a hundred, and a hundred of you will chase ten thousand, and
your enemies will fall before you by the sword.
9 'So I will turn toward you and make you fruitful and multiply you, and I will confirm
My covenant with you.
10 'You will eat the old supply and clear out the old because of the new.
11 'Moreover, I will make My dwelling among you, and My soul will not reject you.
12 'I will also walk among you and be your God, and you shall be My people.
13 'I am the LORD your God, who brought you out of the land of Egypt so that *you*
would not be their slaves, and I broke the bars of your yoke and made you walk erect.

Penalties of Disobedience

14 'But if you do not obey Me and do not carry out all these commandments,
15 if, instead, you reject My statutes, and if your soul abhors My ordinances so as not
to carry out all My commandments, *and* so break My covenant,
16 I, in turn, will do this to you: I will appoint over you a sudden terror, consumption
and fever that will waste away the eyes and cause the soul to pine away; also, you will
sow your seed uselessly, for your enemies will eat it up.
17 'I will set My face against you so that you will be struck down before your enemies;
and those who hate you will rule over you, and you will flee when no one is pursuing you.

25:51 Lev 25:16
25:53 Lev 25:43
25:54 Lev 25:10, 13, 28
26:1 Lev 19:4; Deut 5:8; Ex 20:4; Deut 16:21f; Ex 23:24; Num 33:52
26:2 Lev 19:30
26:3 Deut 7:12-26; 11:13; 28:1-14
26:4 Deut 11:14
26:5 Deut 11:15; Joel 2:19, 26; Amos 9:13; Lev 25:18, 19; Ezek 34:25
26:6 Ps 29:11; 85:8; 147:14; Zeph 3:13; Lev 26:22; Lev 26:25
26:8 Deut 32:30
26:9 Gen 17:6; 22:17; 48:4; Gen 17:7
26:10 Lev 25:22
26:11 Ex 25:8; 29:45, 46; Ezek 37:26
26:12 Gen 3:8; Deut 23:14; 2 Cor 6:16
26:13 Ex 20:2; Ezek 34:27
26:14 Deut 28:15-68; Josh 23:15
26:15 Lev 26:11; 2 Kin 17:15; Lev 26:9
26:16 Deut 28:22; Ps 78:33; 1 Sam 2:33; Ezek 24:23; 33:10; Judg 6:3-6; Job 31:8
26:17 Ps 106:41; Lev 26:36, 37; Ps 53:5; Prov 28:1

26:1ff This chapter presents the two paths of obedience and disobedience that God set before the people (see also Deuteronomy 28). The people of the Old Testament were warned over and over against worshiping idols. We wonder how they could deceive themselves with these objects of wood and stone. Yet God could well give us the same warning, for we are prone to put idols before him. Idolatry is making anything more important than God, and our lives are full of that temptation. Money, looks, success, reputation, security—these are today's idols. As you look at these false gods that promise everything you want but nothing you need, does idolatry seem so far removed from your experience?

26:13 Imagine the joy of a slave set free. God took the children of Israel out of bitter slavery and gave them freedom and dignity. We too are set free when we accept Christ's payment that redeems us from sin's slavery. We no longer need to be bogged down in shame over our past sins; we can walk with dignity because God has forgiven us and forgotten them. But just as the Israelites were still in danger of returning to a slave mentality, we need to beware of the temptation to return to our former sinful patterns.

18 'If also after these things you do not obey Me, then I will punish you seven times
more for your sins.
19 'I will also break down your pride of power; I will also make your sky like iron and
your earth like bronze.
20 'Your strength will be spent uselessly, for your land will not yield its produce and the
trees of the land will not yield their fruit.
21 'If then, you act with hostility against Me and are unwilling to obey Me, I will increase the plague on you seven times according to your sins.
22 'I will let loose among you the beasts of the field, which will bereave you of your
children and destroy your cattle and reduce your number so that your roads lie deserted.
23 'And if by these things you are not turned to Me, but act with hostility against Me,
24 then I will act with hostility against you; and I, even I, will strike you seven times for
your sins.
25 'I will also bring upon you a sword which will execute vengeance for the covenant;
and when you gather together into your cities, I will send pestilence among you, so that
you shall be delivered into enemy hands.
26 'When I break your staff of bread, ten women will bake your bread in one oven, and
they will bring back your bread [18]in rationed amounts, so that you will eat and not be
satisfied.
27 'Yet if in spite of this you do not obey Me, but act with hostility against Me,
28 then I will act with wrathful hostility against you, and I, even I, will punish you seven
times for your sins.
29 'Further, you will eat the flesh of your sons and the flesh of your daughters you
will eat.
30 'I then will destroy your high places, and cut down your incense altars, and heap your
remains on the remains of your idols, for My soul shall abhor you.
31 'I will lay waste your cities as well and will make your sanctuaries desolate, and I will
not smell your soothing aromas.
32 'I will make the land desolate so that your enemies who settle in it will be appalled
over it.
33 'You, however, I will scatter among the nations and will draw out a sword after you,
as your land becomes desolate and your cities become waste.
34 'Then the land will enjoy its sabbaths all the days of the desolation, while you are in
your enemies' land; then the land will rest and enjoy its sabbaths.
35 'All the days of *its* desolation it will observe the rest which it did not observe on your
sabbaths, while you were living on it.
36 'As for those of you who may be left, I will also bring weakness into their hearts in
the lands of their enemies. And the sound of a driven leaf will chase them, and even when
no one is pursuing they will flee as though from the sword, and they will fall.
37 'They will therefore stumble over each other as if *running* from the sword, although
no one is pursuing; and you will have *no strength* to stand up before your enemies.
38 'But you will perish among the nations, and your enemies' land will consume you.
39 'So those of you who may be left will rot away because of their iniquity in the lands
of your enemies; and also because of the iniquities of their forefathers they will rot away
with them.

18 Lit *by weight*

26:18 Lev 26:21, 24, 28
26:19 Is 25:11; Ezek 24:21
26:20 Ps 127:1; Is 17:10, 11; 49:4; Jer 12:13
26:21 Lev 26:23, 27, 40; Lev 26:18
26:22 2 Kin 17:25; Judg 5:6
26:23 Lev 26:21; Jer 5:3
26:24 Lev 26:28, 41; Lev 26:21
26:25 Jer 50:28; 51:11; Num 14:12
26:26 Is 3:1; Ezek 4:16, 17; 5:16; Mic 6:14
26:28 Lev 26:24, 41; Is 59:18
26:29 2 Kin 6:29
26:30 2 Kin 23:20; Ezek 6:3, 6; Amos 7:9; 2 Chr 34:4, 7; Is 27:9
26:31 Neh 2:3; Jer 44:2, 6, 22; Is 63:18; Lam 2:7; Amos 5:21
26:32 Jer 9:11; 12:11; 25:11; 33:10; Jer 18:16; 19:8
26:33 Deut 4:27; 28:64; Ps 44:11; 106:27; Jer 31:10; Ezek 12:15; 20:23; Zech 7:14
26:34 Lev 26:43; 2 Chr 36:21
26:36 Is 30:17; Lam 1:3, 6; 4:19; Ezek 21:7
26:37 Jer 6:21; Nah 3:3
26:38 Deut 4:26

26:18 If the Israelites obeyed, there would be peace in the land. If they disobeyed, disaster would follow. God used sin's consequences to draw them to repentance, not to get back at them. Today, sin's consequences are not always so apparent. When calamity strikes us we may not know the reason. It may be (1) the result of our own disobedience, (2) the result of someone else's sin, (3) the result of natural disaster. Because we don't know, we should search our hearts and be sure we are at peace with God. His Spirit, like a great searchlight, will reveal those areas we need to deal with. Because calamity is not always the result of wrongdoing, we must guard against assigning or accepting blame for every tragedy we encounter. Misplaced guilt is one of Satan's favorite weapons against believers.

26:33–35 In 2 Kings 17 and 25 the warning pronounced in these verses came true. The people persistently disobeyed, and eventually they were conquered and carried off to the lands of Assyria and Babylonia. The nation was held in captivity for 70 years, making up for all of the years that the Israelites did not observe the law of the sabbath year (2 Chronicles 36:21).

40 'If they confess their iniquity and the iniquity of their forefathers, in their unfaithfulness which they committed against Me, and also in their acting with hostility
against Me—
41 I also was acting with hostility against them, to bring them into the land of their
enemies—or if their uncircumcised heart becomes humbled so that they then make
amends for their iniquity,
42 then I will remember My covenant with Jacob, and I will remember also My covenant with Isaac, and My covenant with Abraham as well, and I will remember the land.
43 'For the land will be abandoned by them, and will make up for its sabbaths while it
is made desolate without them. They, meanwhile, will be making amends for their iniquity, because they rejected My ordinances and their soul abhorred My statutes.
44 'Yet in spite of this, when they are in the land of their enemies, I will not reject them,
nor will I so abhor them as to destroy them, breaking My covenant with them; for I am
the LORD their God.
45 'But I will remember for them the covenant with their ancestors, whom I brought
out of the land of Egypt in the sight of the nations, that I might be their God. I am the
LORD.' "
46 These are the statutes and ordinances and laws which the LORD established between
Himself and the sons of Israel through Moses at Mount Sinai.

26:40 Jer 3:12-15; 14:20; Hos 5:15
26:41 Jer 4:4; 9:25, 26; Ezek 44:7, 9; Acts 7:51; Ezek 20:43
26:42 Gen 28:13-15; 35:11, 12; Gen 26:2-5; Gen 22:15-18
26:43 Lev 26:34; Lev 26:11
26:44 Lev 26:11; Deut 4:31; Jer 30:11; Jer 33:20-26
26:45 Ex 6:6-8; Gen 17:7
26:46 Lev 7:38; 27:34; Deut 4:5; 29:1

Rules concerning Valuations

27 Again, the LORD spoke to Moses, saying,
2 "Speak to the sons of Israel and say to them, 'When a man makes a difficult
vow, he *shall be valued* according to your valuation of persons belonging to the LORD.
3 'If your valuation is of the male from twenty years even to sixty years old, then your
valuation shall be fifty shekels of silver, after the shekel of the sanctuary.
4 'Or if it is a female, then your valuation shall be thirty shekels.
5 'If it be from five years even to twenty years old then your valuation for the male
shall be twenty shekels and for the female ten shekels.
6 'But if *they are* from a month even up to five years old, then your valuation shall be
five shekels of silver for the male, and for the female your valuation shall be three shekels of silver.
7 'If *they are* from sixty years old and upward, if it is a male, then your valuation shall
be fifteen shekels, and for the female ten shekels.
8 'But if he is poorer than your valuation, then he shall be placed before the priest and
the priest shall value him; according to the means of the one who vowed, the priest shall
value him.
9 'Now if it is an animal of the kind which men can present as an offering to the LORD,
any such that one gives to the LORD shall be holy.
10 'He shall not replace it or exchange it, a good for a bad, or a bad for a good; or if he
does exchange animal for animal, then both it and its substitute shall become holy.
11 'If, however, it is any unclean animal of the kind which men do not present as an
offering to the LORD, then he shall place the animal before the priest.
12 'The priest shall value it as either good or bad; as you, the priest, value it, so it
shall be.

27:2 Num 6:2; Deut 23:21-23
27:3 Ex 30:13; Lev 27:25; Num 3:47; 18:16
27:6 Num 18:16
27:8 Lev 5:11; 14:21-24
27:10 Lev 27:33

26:40–45 These verses show what God meant when he said he is slow to anger (Exodus 34:6). Even if the Israelites chose to disobey and were scattered among their enemies, God would still give them the opportunity to repent and return to him. His purpose was not to destroy them, but to help them grow. Our day-to-day experiences and hardships are sometimes overwhelming; unless we can see that God's purpose is to bring about continual growth in us, we may despair. The hope we need is well expressed in Jeremiah 29:11–12: " 'For I know the plans that I have for you,' declares the LORD, 'plans for welfare and not for calamity to give you a future and a hope. Then you will call upon Me and come and pray to Me, and I will listen to you.' " To retain hope while we suffer shows we understand God's merciful ways of relating to his people.

27:1ff The Israelites were required to give or dedicate certain things to the Lord and to his service: the firstfruits of their harvests, firstborn animals, their firstborn sons, a tithe of their increase. Many wished to go beyond this and dedicate themselves or another family member, additional animals, a house, or a field to God. In these cases, it was possible to donate money instead of the actual person, animal, or property. Some people made rash or unrealistic vows. To urge them to think about it first, a 20 percent penalty was put on those items purchased back by money. This chapter explains how valuations were to be made and what to do if a donor later wished to buy back what had been donated to God.

27:9–10 God taught the Israelites that when they made a vow to him, they must not go back on their promise even if it turned out to cost more than expected. (This applied to animals; humans could be redeemed or purchased back.) God takes our promises seriously. If you vow to give 10 percent of your income and suddenly some unexpected bills come along, your faithful stewardship will be costly. God, however, expects you to fulfill your vow even if it is difficult to do so.

13 'But if he should ever *wish to* redeem it, then he shall add one-fifth of it to your valuation.
14 'Now if a man consecrates his house as holy to the LORD, then the priest shall value
it as either good or bad; as the priest values it, so it shall stand.
15 'Yet if the one who consecrates it should *wish to* redeem his house, then he shall add
one-fifth of your valuation price to it, so that it may be his.
16 'Again, if a man consecrates to the LORD part of the fields of his own property, then
your valuation shall be proportionate to the seed needed for it: a homer of barley seed
at fifty shekels of silver.
17 'If he consecrates his field as of the year of jubilee, according to your valuation it
shall stand.
18 'If he consecrates his field after the jubilee, however, then the priest shall calculate
the price for him proportionate to the years that are left until the year of jubilee; and it
shall be deducted from your valuation.
19 'If the one who consecrates it should ever wish to redeem the field, then he shall add
one-fifth of your valuation price to it, so that it may pass to him.
20 'Yet if he will not redeem the field, but has sold the field to another man, it may no
longer be redeemed;

27:21 Num 18:14; Ezek 44:29

21 and when it reverts in the jubilee, the field shall be holy to the LORD, like a field set
apart; it shall be for the priest as his property.
22 'Or if he consecrates to the LORD a field which he has bought, which is not a part of
the field of his own property,
23 then the priest shall calculate for him the amount of your valuation up to the year
of jubilee; and he shall on that day give your valuation as holy to the LORD.
24 'In the year of jubilee the field shall return to the one from whom he bought it, to
whom the possession of the land belongs.

27:25 Ex 30:13; Lev 27:3; Num 3:47; 18:16

25 'Every valuation of yours, moreover, shall be after the shekel of the sanctuary. The
shekel shall be twenty gerahs.

27:26 Ex 13:2

26 'However, a firstborn among animals, which as a firstborn belongs to the LORD, no
man may consecrate it; whether ox or sheep, it is the LORD'S.
27 'But if *it is* among the unclean animals, then he shall redeem it according to your
valuation and add to it one-fifth of it; and if it is not redeemed, then it shall be sold according to your valuation.

27:28 Num 18:14; Josh 6:17-19

28 'Nevertheless, anything which a man [19]sets apart to the LORD out of all that he has,
of man or animal or of the fields of his own property, shall not be sold or redeemed.
Anything devoted to destruction is most holy to the LORD.
29 'No one who may have been set apart among men shall be ransomed; he shall surely
be put to death.

27:30 Gen 28:22; 2 Chr 31:5; Neh 13:12

30 'Thus all the tithe of the land, of the seed of the land or of the fruit of the tree, is the
LORD'S; it is holy to the LORD.
31 'If, therefore, a man wishes to redeem part of his tithe, he shall add to it one-fifth of it.

27:32 Jer 33:13; Ezek 20:37

32 'For every tenth part of herd or flock, whatever passes under the rod, the tenth one
shall be holy to the LORD.

27:33 Lev 27:10

33 'He is not to be concerned whether *it is* good or bad, nor shall he exchange it; or if he
does exchange it, then both it and its substitute shall become holy. It shall not be redeemed.' "

27:34 Lev 26:46; Deut 4:5

34 These are the commandments which the LORD commanded Moses for the sons of
Israel at Mount Sinai.

19 Lit *anything devoted;* or *banned*

27:14–25 Real estate could be given as a voluntary offering in much the same way that today people give property through a will or donate the proceeds from the sale of property to the church or Christian organizations.

27:29 Things set apart (or devoted to destruction) applies to personal property or persons placed under God's ban, such as captured booty from idol-worshipers or idols themselves. These were to be destroyed and could not be redeemed.

27:33 Many of the principles regarding sacrifices and tithes were intended to encourage inward attitudes as well as outward actions. If a person gives grudgingly, he shows that he has a stingy heart. God wants us to be cheerful givers (2 Corinthians 9:7) who give with gratitude to him.

27:34 The book of Leviticus is filled with the commands God gave his people at the foot of Mount Sinai. From these commands we can learn much about God's nature and character. At first glance, Leviticus seems irrelevant to our high-tech world. But digging a little deeper, we realize that the book still speaks to us today—God has not changed, and his principles are for all times. As people and society change, we need constantly to search for ways to apply the principles of God's law to our present circumstances. God was the same in Leviticus as he is today and will be forever (Hebrews 13:8).

NUMBERS

Joseph dies 1805 B.C. (1640 B.C.)	SLAVERY IN EGYPT	Exodus from Egypt 1446 (1280)	Ten Commandments given 1445 (1279)	First census 1444 (1278)	First spy mission 1443 (1277)

VITAL STATISTICS

PURPOSE:
To tell the story of how Israel prepared to enter the promised land, how they sinned and were punished, and how they prepared to try again

AUTHOR:
Moses

TO WHOM WRITTEN:
The people of Israel

DATE WRITTEN:
1450–1410 B.C.

SETTING:
The vast wilderness of the Sinai region, as well as lands just south and east of Canaan

KEY VERSES:
"Surely all the men who have seen My glory and My signs which I performed in Egypt and in the wilderness, yet have put Me to the test these ten times and have not listened to My voice, shall by no means see the land which I swore to their fathers, nor shall any of those who spurned Me see it" (14:22–23).

KEY PEOPLE:
Moses, Aaron, Miriam, Joshua, Caleb, Eleazar, Korah, Balaam

KEY PLACES:
Mount Sinai, promised land (Canaan), Kadesh, Mount Hor, plains of Moab

EVERY parent knows the shrill whine of a young child—a slow, high-pitched complaint that grates on the eardrums and aggravates the soul. The tone of voice is difficult to bear, but the real irritation is the underlying cause—discontentment and disobedience. As the "children" of Israel journeyed from the foot of Mount Sinai to the land of Canaan, they grumbled, whined, and complained at every turn. They focused on their present discomforts. Faith had fled, and they added an extra 40 years to their trip.

Numbers, which records the tragic story of Israel's unbelief, should serve as a dramatic lesson for all of God's people. God loves us and wants the very best for us. He can and should be trusted. Numbers also gives a clear portrayal of God's patience. Again and again he withholds judgment and preserves the nation. But his patience must not be taken for granted. His judgment will come. We must obey.

As Numbers begins, the nation of Israel was camped at the foot of Mount Sinai. The people had received God's laws and were preparing to move. A census was taken to determine the number of men fit for military service. Next, the people were set apart for God. God was making the people, both spiritually and physically, ready to receive their inheritance.

But then the complaining began. First, the people complained about the food. Next, it was over Moses' authority. God punished some people but spared the nation because of Moses' prayers. The nation then arrived at Kadesh, and spies were sent into Canaan to assess its strength. Ten returned with fearful stories of giants. Only Caleb and Joshua encouraged them to "go up and take possession" of the land (13:30). The minority report fell on deaf ears full of the ominous message of the majority. Because of their unbelief, God declared that the present generation would not live to see the promised land. Thus the "wanderings" began. During these wilderness wanderings there was a continuous pattern of grumbling, defiance, discipline, and death. How much better it would have been to have trusted God and entered his land! Then the terrible waiting began—waiting for the old generation to die off and waiting to see if the new generation could faithfully obey God.

Numbers ends as it begins, with preparation. This new generation of Israelites was numbered and sanctified. After defeating numerous armies, they settle the east side of the Jordan River. Then they faced their greatest test: to cross the river and possess the beautiful land God promised them.

The lesson is clear. God's people must trust him, moving ahead by *faith* if they are to claim his promised land.

WILDERNESS WANDERINGS	Second census, Balaam prophesies 1407 (1241)	Joshua appointed, Canaan entered 1406 (1240)	Judges begin to rule 1375 (1220)	United kingdom under Saul 1050 (1045)

THE BLUEPRINT

A. PREPARING FOR THE JOURNEY (1:1—10:10)
1. The first census of the nation
2. The role of the Levites
3. The purity of the camp
4. Receiving guidance for the journey

As part of their preparations, the Lord gave strict guidelines to the Israelites regarding purity in the camp. He wanted them to have a life-style distinct from the nations around them. He wanted them to be a holy people. Similarly, we should concern ourselves with purity in the church.

B. FIRST APPROACH TO THE PROMISED LAND (10:11—14:45)
1. The people complain
2. Miriam and Aaron oppose Moses
3. The spies incite rebellion

The Israelites were prevented from entering the promised land because of their unbelief. Throughout history, God's people have continued to struggle with lack of faith. We must prevent unbelief from gaining a foothold in our lives, for it will keep us from enjoying the blessings that God has promised.

C. WANDERING IN THE WILDERNESS (15:1—21:35)
1. Additional regulations
2. Many leaders rebel against Moses
3. Duties of priests and Levites
4. The new generation

When the people complained against God and criticized Moses, they were severely punished. Over 14,000 people died as a result of rebellion against Moses. As a result of Korah's rebellion, Korah, Dathan, and Abiram and their households died, along with 250 false priests. Dissatisfaction and discontent, if allowed to remain in our lives, can easily lead to disaster. We should refrain from complaining and criticizing our leaders.

D. SECOND APPROACH TO THE PROMISED LAND (22:1—36:13)
1. The story of Balaam
2. The second census of the nation
3. Instructions concerning offerings
4. Vengeance on the Midianites
5. The Transjordan tribes
6. Camped on the plains of Moab

The Moabites and Midianites could not get Balaam to curse Israel, but they did get him to give advice on how to draw the Israelites to idol worship. Balaam knew what was right, but he gave in to the temptation of material rewards and sinned. Knowing what is right alone is never enough. We must also do what is right.

MEGATHEMES

THEME	EXPLANATION	IMPORTANCE
Census	Moses counted the Israelites twice. The first census organized the people into marching units to better defend themselves. The second prepared them to conquer the country east of the Jordan River.	People have to be organized, trained, and led to be effective in great movements. It is always wise to count the cost before setting out on some great undertaking. When we are aware of the obstacles before us, we can more easily avoid them. In God's work, we must remove barriers in our relationships with others so that our effectiveness is not diminished.
Rebellion	At Kadesh, 12 spies were sent out into the land of Canaan to report on the fortifications of the enemies. When the spies returned, 10 said that they should give up and go back to Egypt. As a result, the people refused to enter the land. Faced with a choice, Israel rebelled against God. Rebellion did not start with an uprising, but with griping and murmuring against Moses and God.	Rebellion against God is always a serious matter. It is not something to take lightly, for God's punishment for sin is often very severe. Our rebellion does not usually begin with all-out warfare, but in subtle ways—with griping and criticizing. Make sure your negative comments are not the product of a rebellious spirit.

Wandering	Because they rebelled, the Israelites wandered 40 years in the wilderness. This shows how severely God can punish sin. Forty years was enough time for all those who held on to Egypt's customs and values to die off. It gave time to train up a new generation in the ways of God.	God judges sin harshly because he is holy. The wanderings in the wilderness demonstrate how serious God considers flagrant disobedience of his commands. Purging our lives of sin is vital to God's purpose.
Canaan	Canaan is the promised land. It was the land God had promised to Abraham, Isaac, and Jacob—the land of the covenant. Canaan was to be the dwelling place of God's people, those set apart for true spiritual worship.	Although God's punishment for sin is often severe, he offers reconciliation and hope— his love is truly amazing. Just as God's love and law led Israel to the promised land, God desires to give purpose and destiny to our lives.

KEY PLACES IN NUMBERS

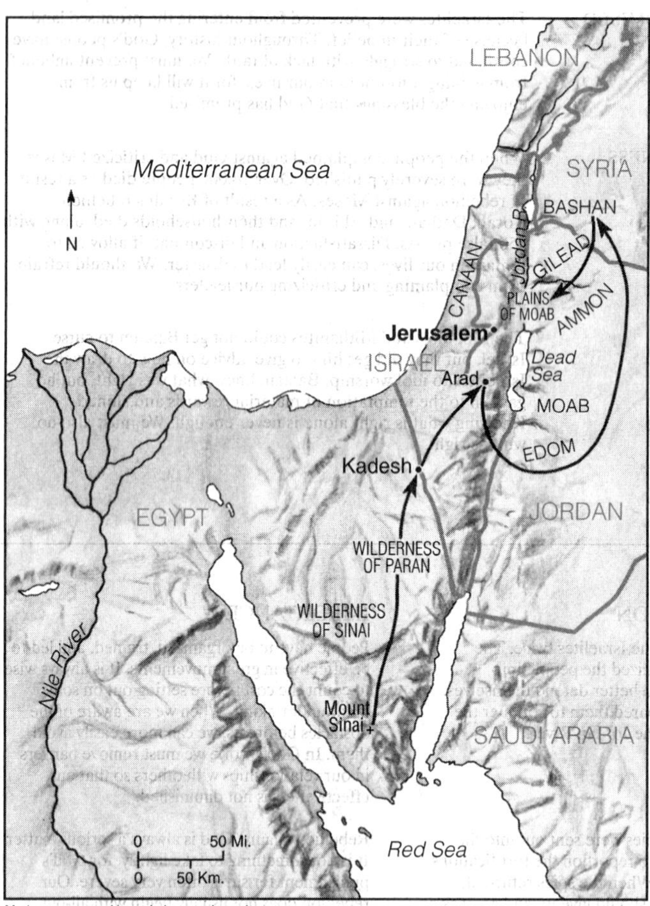

Modern names and boundaries are shown in gray.

1 Mount Sinai Numbers begins at Mount Sinai in the wilderness of Sinai with Moses taking a census of the men eligible for battle. As the battle preparations began, the people also prepared for the spiritual warfare they would face. The promised land was full of wicked people who would try to entice the Israelites to sin. God, therefore, taught Moses and the Israelites how to live right (1:1—12:15).

2 Wilderness of Paran After a full year at Mount Sinai, the Israelites broke camp and began their march toward the promised land by moving into the wilderness of Paran. From there, one leader from each tribe was sent to spy out the new land. After 40 days they returned, and all but Joshua and Caleb were too afraid to enter. Because of their lack of faith, the Israelites were made to wander in the wilderness for 40 years (12:16—19:22).

3 Kadesh With the years of wandering nearing an end, the Israelites set their sights once again on the promised land. Kadesh was the oasis where they spent most of their wilderness years. Miriam died here. And it was here that Moses angrily struck the rock, which kept him from entering the promised land (20).

4 Arad When the king there heard that Israel was on the move, he attacked, but he was soundly defeated. Moses then led the people southward and eastward around the Dead Sea (21:1–3).

5 Edom The Israelites wanted to travel through Edom, but the king of Edom refused them passage (20:14–22). So they traveled around Edom and became very discouraged. The people complained, and God sent poisonous serpents to punish them. Only by looking at a bronze serpent on a pole could those bitten be healed (21:4–9).

6 Ammon Next, King Sihon of the Amorites refused Israel passage. When he attacked, Israel defeated his army and conquered the territory as far as the border of Ammon (21:21–32).

7 Bashan Moses sent spies to Bashan. King Og attacked, but he was also defeated (21:33–35).

8 Plains of Moab The people camped on the plains of Moab, east of the Jordan River across from Jericho. They were on the verge of entering the promised land (22:1).

9 Moab King Balak of Moab, terrified of the Israelites, called upon Balaam, a famous sorcerer, to curse Israel from the mountains above where the Israelites camped. But the Lord caused Balaam to bless them instead (22:2—24:25).

10 Gilead The tribes of Reuben and Gad decided to settle in the fertile country of Gilead east of the Jordan River because it was a good land for their sheep. But first they promised to help the other tribes conquer the land west of the Jordan River (32).

A. PREPARING FOR THE JOURNEY (1:1—10:10)

At Mount Sinai, the Israelites received specific directions for their life-style in the new land God would give to them. A census was taken and the second Passover was celebrated, marking one year of freedom from slavery in Egypt. The people were now prepared to continue their journey to the promised land. Just as the Lord prepared the Israelites, he prepares us for our journey through life.

1. The first census of the nation

The Census of Israel's Warriors

1:1 Ex 40:2, 17
1 Then the LORD spoke to Moses in the wilderness of Sinai, in the tent of meeting, on
the first of the second month, in the second year after they had come out of the land
of Egypt, saying,
1:2 Ex 12:37; 38:25, 26; Num 26:2
2 "Take a [1]census of all the congregation of the sons of Israel, by their families, by their
fathers' households, according to the number of names, every male, head by head
1:3 Ex 30:14; 38:26
3 from twenty years old and upward, whoever *is able to* go out to war in Israel, you
and Aaron shall [2]number them by their armies.
1:4 Ex 18:21, 25; Num 1:16; Deut 1:15
4 "With you, moreover, there shall be a man of each tribe, each one head of his father's
household.
1:5 Gen 29:32; Ex 1:2; Deut 33:6; Rev 7:5
5 "These then are the names of the men who shall stand with you: of Reuben, Elizur
the son of Shedeur;
6 of Simeon, Shelumiel the son of Zurishaddai;
1:7 Ruth 4:20; 1 Chr 2:10; Luke 3:32
7 of Judah, Nahshon the son of Amminadab;
8 of Issachar, Nethanel the son of Zuar;
9 of Zebulun, Eliab the son of Helon;
10 of the sons of Joseph: of Ephraim, Elishama the son of Ammihud; of Manasseh,
Gamaliel the son of Pedahzur;
11 of Benjamin, Abidan the son of Gideoni;
12 of Dan, Ahiezer the son of Ammishaddai;
13 of Asher, Pagiel the son of Ochran;
1:14 Num 2:14
14 of Gad, Eliasaph the son of Deuel;
15 of Naphtali, Ahira the son of Enan.
1:16 Ex 18:21; Num 7:2; 16:2; 26:9; Ex 18:25
16 "These are they who were called of the congregation, the leaders of their fathers'
tribes; they were the heads of [3]divisions of Israel."
17 So Moses and Aaron took these men who had been designated by name,
1:18 Num 1:1; Ezra 2:59; Heb 7:3
18 and they assembled all the congregation together on the first of the second month.
Then they registered by ancestry in their families, by their fathers' households, according to the number of names, from twenty years old and upward, head by head,
1:19 2 Sam 24:1
19 just as the LORD had commanded Moses. So he numbered them in the wilderness
of Sinai.
1:20 Num 26:5-7
20 Now the sons of Reuben, Israel's firstborn, their genealogical registration by their

1 Lit *sum* **2** Lit *muster,* and so throughout the ch **3** Lit *thousands;* or *clans*

1:1 As the book of Numbers opens, the Israelites had been camped near Mount Sinai for more than a year. There they had received all the laws and regulations recorded in the book of Leviticus. They had been transformed into a new nation and equipped for their task. At this time, they were ready to move out and receive their land. In preparation, Moses and Aaron were told to number all the men who were able to serve in the army. This book is named for this census, or numbering, of the people.

1:1 The tent of meeting was the smaller structure inside the larger tabernacle. The tent of meeting contained the sanctuary (or holy place) in one part, and the holy of holies with the ark in another part. These two parts were separated by a veil, or curtain. God revealed himself to Moses in the holy of holies. Sometimes the tent of meeting refers to the whole tabernacle (see 2:2).

Exodus 33:7 mentions the "tent of meeting" as the place where Moses met with God before the tabernacle was constructed. Many believe that the tent of meeting in Exodus served the same function as the one described here.

1:2–15 Taking a census was long and tedious, but it was an important task. The fighting men had to be counted to determine Israel's military strength before entering the promised land. In addition, the tribes had to be organized to determine the amount of land each would need, as well as to provide genealogical records. Without such a census, the task of conquering and organizing the promised land would have been more difficult. Whenever we are at a crossroads, it is important to take inventory of our resources. We will serve more effectively if, before plunging in, we set aside time to take a "census" of all we have—possessions, relationships, spiritual condition, time, goals.

1:20–46 If there were 603,550 men, not counting the Levites or women and children, the total population must have numbered more than two million Israelites. How could such a large population have grown from Jacob's family of 70 who moved down to Egypt? The book of Exodus tells us that the Israelites who descended from Jacob's family "increased greatly, and multiplied" (Exodus 1:7). Because they remained in Egypt more than 400 years, they had plenty of time to grow into a large group of people. After leaving Egypt, they were able to survive in the wilderness because God miraculously provided the food and water they needed. The leaders of Moab were terrified because of the large number of Israelites (22:3).

families, by their fathers' households, according to the number of names, head by head,
every male from twenty years old and upward, whoever *was able to* go out to war,
21 their numbered men of the tribe of Reuben *were* 46,500.
22 Of the sons of Simeon, their genealogical registration by their families, by their fathers' households, their numbered men, according to the number of names, head by head,
every male from twenty years old and upward, whoever *was able to* go out to war,
23 their numbered men of the tribe of Simeon *were* 59,300.

1:22 Num 26:12-14; Ps 144:1

24 Of the sons of Gad, their genealogical registration by their families, by their fathers'
households, according to the number of names, from twenty years old and upward, whoever *was able to* go out to war,
25 their numbered men of the tribe of Gad *were* 45,650.

1:24 Gen 30:11; Num 26:15-18; Josh 4:12; Jer 49:1

26 Of the sons of Judah, their genealogical registration by their families, by their fathers' households, according to the number of names, from twenty years old and upward,
whoever *was able to* go out to war,
27 their numbered men of the tribe of Judah *were* 74,600.

1:26 Gen 29:35; Num 26:19-22; 2 Sam 24:9; Ps 78:68; Matt 1:2

28 Of the sons of Issachar, their genealogical registration by their families, by their
fathers' households, according to the number of names, from twenty years old and upward, whoever *was able to* go out to war,
29 their numbered men of the tribe of Issachar *were* 54,400.

1:28 Num 26:23-25

30 Of the sons of Zebulun, their genealogical registration by their families, by their
fathers' households, according to the number of names, from twenty years old and upward, whoever *was able to* go out to war,
31 their numbered men of the tribe of Zebulun *were* 57,400.

1:30 Num 26:26, 27

32 Of the sons of Joseph, *namely,* of the sons of Ephraim, their genealogical registration by their families, by their fathers' households, according to the number of names,
from twenty years old and upward, whoever *was able to* go out to war,
33 their numbered men of the tribe of Ephraim *were* 40,500.

1:32 Num 26:35-37; Deut 33:13-17; Jer 7:15; Obad 19

34 Of the sons of Manasseh, their genealogical registration by their families, by their
fathers' households, according to the number of names, from twenty years old and upward, whoever *was able to* go out to war,
35 their numbered men of the tribe of Manasseh *were* 32,200.

1:34 Num 26:28-34

36 Of the sons of Benjamin, their genealogical registration by their families, by their
fathers' households, according to the number of names, from twenty years old and upward, whoever *was able to* go out to war,
37 their numbered men of the tribe of Benjamin *were* 35,400.

1:36 Gen 49:27; Num 26:38-41; 2 Chr 17:17; Rev 7:8

38 Of the sons of Dan, their genealogical registration by their families, by their fathers'
households, according to the number of names, from twenty years old and upward, whoever *was able to* go out to war,
39 their numbered men of the tribe of Dan *were* 62,700.

1:38 Gen 30:6; 46:23; Num 2:25; 26:42, 43

40 Of the sons of Asher, their genealogical registration by their families, by their fathers' households, according to the number of names, from twenty years old and upward,
whoever *was able to* go out to war,
41 their numbered men of the tribe of Asher *were* 41,500.

1:40 Num 26:44-47

42 Of the sons of Naphtali, their genealogical registration by their families, by their
fathers' households, according to the number of names, from twenty years old and upward, whoever *was able to* go out to war,
43 their numbered men of the tribe of Naphtali *were* 53,400.

1:42 Num 26:48-50

44 These are the ones who were numbered, whom Moses and Aaron numbered, with
the leaders of Israel, twelve men, each of whom was of his father's household.
45 So all the numbered men of the sons of Israel by their fathers' households, from
twenty years old and upward, whoever *was able to* go out to war in Israel,
46 even all the numbered men were 603,550.

1:46 Ex 12:37; 38:26; Num 2:32; 26:51

Levites Exempted

47 The Levites, however, were not numbered among them by their fathers' tribe.
48 For the LORD had spoken to Moses, saying,
49 "Only the tribe of Levi you shall not number, nor shall you take their census among
the sons of Israel.
50 "But you shall appoint the Levites over the [4]tabernacle of the testimony, and over all
its furnishings and over all that belongs to it. They shall carry the tabernacle and all its
furnishings, and they shall take care of it; they shall also camp around the tabernacle.

1:47 Num 2:33; 3:14-39; 4:49; 26:57-64

1:49 Num 26:62

1:50 Ex 38:21; Num 3:6-8, 25-37; 4:15, 25-27, 31, 32

4 Lit *dwelling place,* and so throughout the ch

1:51 Num 4:1-33; Num 3:10, 38; 4:15, 19, 20
51 "So when the tabernacle is to set out, the Levites shall take it down; and when the
tabernacle encamps, the Levites shall set it up. But the [5]layman who comes near shall be
put to death.
1:52 Num 2:2, 34
52 "The sons of Israel shall camp, each man by his own camp, and each man by his own
standard, according to their armies.
1:53 Num 3:23, 29, 35, 38; Lev 10:6; Num 16:46; 18:5; Num 8:24; 18:2-4; 1 Chr 23:32
53 "But the Levites shall camp around the tabernacle of the testimony, so that there
will be no wrath on the congregation of the sons of Israel. So the Levites shall keep charge
of the tabernacle of the testimony."
54 Thus the sons of Israel did; according to all which the LORD had commanded Moses, so they did.

Arrangement of the Camps

2 Now the LORD spoke to Moses and to Aaron, saying,
2:2 Num 1:52; 24:2
2 "The sons of Israel shall camp, each by his own standard, with the banners of their
fathers' households; they shall camp around the tent of meeting at a distance.
2:3 Num 1:7; 10:14; Ruth 4:20; 1 Chr 2:10; Luke 3:32, 33
3 "Now those who camp on the east side toward the sunrise *shall be* of the standard of
the camp of Judah, by their armies, and the leader of the sons of Judah: Nahshon the
son of Amminadab,
4 and his army, even their numbered men, 74,600.
2:5 Num 1:8; 7:18, 23
5 "Those who camp next to him *shall be* the tribe of Issachar, and the leader of the
sons of Issachar: Nethanel the son of Zuar,
6 and his army, even their numbered men, 54,400.
2:7 Num 1:9
7 "*Then comes* the tribe of Zebulun, and the leader of the sons of Zebulun: Eliab the
son of Helon,
8 and his army, even his numbered men, 57,400.
2:9 Num 10:14
9 "The total of the numbered men of the camp of Judah: 186,400, by their armies. They
shall set out first.
2:10 Num 1:5
10 "On the south side *shall be* the standard of the camp of Reuben by their armies, and
the leader of the sons of Reuben: Elizur the son of Shedeur,
11 and his army, even their numbered men, 46,500.
2:12 Num 1:6
12 "Those who camp next to him *shall be* the tribe of Simeon, and the leader of the sons
of Simeon: Shelumiel the son of Zurishaddai,
13 and his army, even their numbered men, 59,300.
2:14 Num 1:14; 7:42
14 "Then *comes* the tribe of Gad, and the leader of the sons of Gad: Eliasaph the son of
Deuel,
15 and his army, even their numbered men, 45,650.
2:16 Num 10:18
16 "The total of the numbered men of the camp of Reuben: 151,450 by their armies.
And they shall set out second.
2:17 Num 1:53
17 "Then the tent of meeting shall set out *with* the camp of the Levites in the midst of

5 Lit *stranger*

ARRANGEMENT OF TRIBES AROUND THE TABERNACLE WHILE IN THE WILDERNESS

	ASHER	DAN	NAPHTALI	
BENJAMIN		Merari (Son of Levi)		ISSACHAR
EPHRAIM	Gershon (Son of Levi)	TABERNACLE	Moses, Aaron, Sons of Aaron	JUDAH
MANASSEH		Kohath (Son of Levi)		ZEBULUN
	GAD	REUBEN	SIMEON	

2:2 The nation of Israel was organized according to tribes for several reasons. (1) It was an effective way to manage and govern a large group. (2) It made dividing the promised land easier. (3) It was part of their culture and heritage (people were not known by a last name, but by their family, clan, and tribe). (4) It made it easier to keep detailed genealogies, and genealogies were the only way to prove membership in God's chosen nation. (5) It made travel much more efficient. The people followed the tribe's standard (a kind of flag) and thus stayed together and kept from getting lost.

the camps; just as they camp, so they shall set out, every man in his place by their standards.
18 "On the west side *shall be* the standard of the camp of Ephraim by their armies, and
the leader of the sons of Ephraim *shall be* Elishama the son of Ammihud,
19 and his army, even their numbered men, 40,500.
20 "Next to him *shall be* the tribe of Manasseh, and the leader of the sons of Manasseh:
Gamaliel the son of Pedahzur,
21 and his army, even their numbered men, 32,200.
22 "Then *comes* the tribe of Benjamin, and the leader of the sons of Benjamin: Abidan
the son of Gideoni,
23 and his army, even their numbered men, 35,400.
24 "The total of the numbered men of the camp of Ephraim: 108,100, by their armies.
And they shall set out third.
25 "On the north side *shall be* the standard of the camp of Dan by their armies, and the
leader of the sons of Dan: Ahiezer the son of Ammishaddai,
26 and his army, even their numbered men, 62,700.
27 "Those who camp next to him *shall be* the tribe of Asher, and the leader of the sons
of Asher: Pagiel the son of Ochran,
28 and his army, even their numbered men, 41,500.
29 "Then *comes* the tribe of Naphtali, and the leader of the sons of Naphtali: Ahira the
son of Enan,
30 and his army, even their numbered men, 53,400.
31 "The total of the numbered men of the camp of Dan *was* 157,600. They shall set out
last by their standards."
32 These are the numbered men of the sons of Israel by their fathers' households; the
total of the numbered men of the camps by their armies, 603,550.
33 The Levites, however, were not numbered among the sons of Israel, just as the LORD
had commanded Moses.
34 Thus the sons of Israel did; according to all that the LORD commanded Moses, so
they camped by their standards, and so they set out, every one by his family according to
his father's household.

2:18 Gen 48:14-20; Jer 31:9, 18-20; Num 1:10
2:20 Num 1:10
2:22 Ps 68:27; Num 1:11
2:24 Num 10:22
2:25 Num 1:12
2:27 Num 1:13
2:29 Gen 30:8; Num 1:15
2:31 Num 10:25
2:32 Ex 38:26; Num 1:46
2:33 Num 1:47; 26:57-62

2. The role of the Levites

Levites to Be Priesthood

3 Now these are *the records of* the generations of Aaron and Moses at the time when
the LORD spoke with Moses on Mount Sinai.
2 These then are the names of the sons of Aaron: Nadab the firstborn, and Abihu,
Eleazar and Ithamar.
3 These are the names of the sons of Aaron, the anointed priests, whom he ordained
to serve as priests.
4 But Nadab and Abihu died before the LORD when they offered strange fire before
the LORD in the wilderness of Sinai; and they had no children. So Eleazar and Ithamar
served as priests in the lifetime of their father Aaron.
5 Then the LORD spoke to Moses, saying,
6 "Bring the tribe of Levi near and set them before Aaron the priest, that they may
serve him.
7 "They shall perform the duties for him and for the whole congregation before the
tent of meeting, to do the service of the tabernacle.

3:1 Ex 6:20-27
3:2 Ex 6:23; Num 26:60
3:3 Ex 28:41
3:4 Lev 10:1, 2; Num 26:61
3:6 Num 8:6-22; 18:1-7; Deut 10:8
3:7 Num 1:50

2:34 This must have been one of the biggest campsites the world has ever seen! It would have taken about 12 square miles to set up tents for just the 600,000 fighting men—not to mention the women and children. Moses must have had a difficult time managing such a group. In the early stages of the journey and at Mount Sinai, the people were generally obedient to both God and Moses. But when the people left Mount Sinai and traveled across the rugged wilderness, they began to complain, grumble, and disobey. Soon problems erupted, and Moses could no longer effectively manage the Israelites. The books of Exodus, Leviticus, and Numbers present a striking contrast between how much we can accomplish when we obey God and how little we can accomplish when we don't.

3:4 See Leviticus 10:1–2 for the story of Nadab and Abihu.

3:5–13 At the time of the first Passover (Exodus 13:2), God instructed every Israelite family to dedicate its firstborn son to him (see 3:40–51 and 8:16). They were set apart to assist Moses and Aaron in ministering to the people. This was only a temporary measure, however. Here God chose all the men from the tribe of Levi to replace the firstborn sons from every Israelite tribe. These men, called Levites, were set apart to care for the tabernacle and minister to the people. All the priests had to belong to the tribe of Levi, but not all Levites were priests. The Levites were to be 25 years old before entering service. They probably received five years of on-the-job training before being admitted to full service at age 30.

8 "They shall also keep all the furnishings of the tent of meeting, along with the duties
of the sons of Israel, to do the service of the tabernacle.

3:9 Num 18:6

9 "You shall thus give the Levites to Aaron and to his sons; they are wholly given to
him from among the sons of Israel.

3:10 Ex 29:9; Num 1:51

10 "So you shall appoint Aaron and his sons that they may keep their priesthood, but
the layman who comes near shall be put to death."
11 Again the LORD spoke to Moses, saying,

3:12 Num 3:45; 8:14; Ex 13:2

12 "Now, behold, I have taken the Levites from among the sons of Israel instead of every
firstborn, the first issue of the womb among the sons of Israel. So the Levites shall be
Mine.

3:13 Ex 13:2; Lev 27:26; Neh 10:36

13 "For all the firstborn are Mine; on the day that I struck down all the firstborn in the
land of Egypt, I sanctified to Myself all the firstborn in Israel, from man to beast. They
shall be Mine; I am the LORD."

3:14 Ex 19:1

14 Then the LORD spoke to Moses in the wilderness of Sinai, saying,

3:15 Num 1:47

15 "Number the sons of Levi by their fathers' households, by their families; every male
from a month old and upward you shall number."
16 So Moses numbered them according to the word of the LORD, just as he had been
commanded.

3:17 Ex 6:16-22

17 These then are the sons of Levi by their names: Gershon and Kohath and Merari.
18 These are the names of the sons of Gershon by their families: Libni and Shimei;

3:18 Ex 6:17

19 and the sons of Kohath by their families: Amram and Izhar, Hebron and Uzziel;
20 and the sons of Merari by their families: Mahli and Mushi. These are the families of
the Levites according to their fathers' households.
21 Of Gershon *was* the family of the Libnites and the family of the Shimeites; these
were the families of the Gershonites.
22 Their numbered men, in the numbering of every male from a month old and upward, *even* their numbered men *were* 7,500.
23 The families of the Gershonites were to camp behind the tabernacle westward,
24 and the leader of the fathers' households of the Gershonites *was* Eliasaph the son
of Lael.

Duties of the Priests

3:25 Num 4:24-26; Ex 26:1, 7, 14; Ex 26:36

25 Now the duties of the sons of Gershon in the tent of meeting *involved* the tabernacle and the tent, its covering, and the screen for the doorway of the tent of meeting,

3:26 Ex 27:9, 12, 14, 15; Ex 27:16

26 and the hangings of the court, and the screen for the doorway of the court which is
around the tabernacle and the altar, and its cords, according to all the service concerning them.
27 Of Kohath *was* the family of the Amramites and the family of the Izharites and the
family of the Hebronites and the family of the Uzzielites; these were the families of the
Kohathites.
28 In the numbering of every male from a month old and upward, *there were* 8,600,
performing the duties of the sanctuary.
29 The families of the sons of Kohath were to camp on the southward side of the tabernacle,
30 and the leader of the fathers' households of the Kohathite families was Elizaphan
the son of Uzziel.

3:31 Num 4:15; Ex 25:10-22; Ex 25:23-28; Ex 25:31-40; Ex 27:1, 2; 30:1-5

31 Now their duties *involved* the ark, the table, the lampstand, the altars, and the utensils of the sanctuary with which they minister, and the screen, and all the service concerning them;
32 and Eleazar the son of Aaron the priest *was* the chief of the leaders of Levi, *and
had* the oversight of those who perform the duties of the sanctuary.
33 Of Merari *was* the family of the Mahlites and the family of the Mushites; these *were*
the families of Merari.

3:10 Aaron and his descendants were appointed to the priesthood. There is a tremendous contrast between the priesthood of Aaron in the Old Testament and the priesthood of Christ in the New Testament. Aaron and his descendants were the only ones who could carry out the duties of the priests and approach God's dwelling place. Now that Christ is our high priest—our intermediary with God—anyone who follows him is also called a priest (1 Peter 2:5, 9). Now all Christians may come into God's presence without fear because God's own Son encourages his followers to do so. We can put guilt behind us when we have a special relationship with God based on what Christ has done for us.

34 Their numbered men in the numbering of every male from a month old and upward, *were* 6,200.

35 The leader of the fathers' households of the families of Merari *was* Zuriel the son of Abihail. They *were* to camp on the northward side of the tabernacle.

3:35 Num 1:53; 2:25

36 Now the appointed duties of the sons of Merari *involved* the frames of the tabernacle, its bars, its pillars, its sockets, all its equipment, and the service concerning them,

37 and the pillars around the court with their sockets and their pegs and their cords.

38 Now those who were to camp before the tabernacle eastward, before the tent of meeting toward the sunrise, are Moses and Aaron and his sons, performing the duties of the sanctuary for the obligation of the sons of Israel; but the layman coming near was to be put to death.

3:38 Num 1:53; 2:3; Num 1:51

39 All the numbered men of the Levites, whom Moses and Aaron numbered at the command of the LORD by their families, every male from a month old and upward, *were* 22,000.

3:39 Num 3:43; 4:48; 26:62

Firstborn Redeemed

40 Then the LORD said to Moses, "Number every firstborn male of the sons of Israel from a month old and upward, and make a list of their names.

3:40 Num 3:15

41 "You shall take the Levites for Me, I am the LORD, instead of all the firstborn among the sons of Israel, and the cattle of the Levites instead of all the firstborn among the cattle of the sons of Israel."

3:41 Num 3:12, 45

42 So Moses numbered all the firstborn among the sons of Israel, just as the LORD had commanded him;

43 and all the firstborn males by the number of names from a month old and upward, for their numbered men were 22,273.

3:43 Num 3:39

44 Then the LORD spoke to Moses, saying,

45 "Take the Levites instead of all the firstborn among the sons of Israel and the cattle of the Levites. And the Levites shall be Mine; I am the LORD.

3:45 Num 3:12

46 "For the ransom of the 273 of the firstborn of the sons of Israel who are in excess beyond the Levites,

3:46 Ex 13:13, 15; Num 18:15, 16

47 you shall take five shekels apiece, per head; you shall take *them* in terms of the shekel of the sanctuary (the shekel is twenty [6]gerahs),

3:47 Lev 27:6; Num 18:16; Ex 30:13; Lev 27:25; Ezek 45:12

48 and give the money, the ransom of those who are in excess among them, to Aaron and to his sons."

49 So Moses took the ransom money from those who were in excess, beyond those ransomed by the Levites;

50 from the firstborn of the sons of Israel he took the money in terms of the shekel of the sanctuary, 1,365.

51 Then Moses gave the ransom money to Aaron and to his sons, at the command of the LORD, just as the LORD had commanded Moses.

Duties of the Kohathites

4 Then the LORD spoke to Moses and to Aaron, saying,

2 "Take a census of the descendants of Kohath from among the sons of Levi, by their families, by their fathers' households,

3 from thirty years and upward, even to fifty years old, all who enter the service to do the work in the tent of meeting.

4:3 Num 4:23, 30, 35; 8:24; 1 Chr 23:3, 24, 27; Ezra 3:8

4 "This is the work of the descendants of Kohath in the tent of meeting, *concerning* the most holy things.

5 "When the camp sets out, Aaron and his sons shall go in and they shall take down the veil of the screen and cover the ark of the testimony with it;

4:5 Ex 40:5; Lev 16:2; 2 Chr 3:14; Matt 27:51; Heb 9:3; Ex 25:10-16

6 and they shall lay a covering of porpoise skin on it, and shall spread over *it* a cloth of pure blue, and shall insert its poles.

4:6 Num 4:25

7 "Over the table of the bread of the Presence they shall also spread a cloth of blue

4:7 Ex 25:30; Lev 24:5-9

6 I.e. A gerah equals approx one-fortieth oz

4:2ff The descendants of Kohath, Gershon (4:21), and Merari (4:29) were families of Levites who were assigned special tasks in Israel's worship. For the jobs described in this chapter, a Levite had to be between 30 and 50 years old. They were expected to carry out their duties as described here in every detail. In fact, failure to do so would mean death (4:20). Worshiping our holy God must not be taken lightly.

and put on it the dishes and the pans and the sacrificial bowls and the jars for the drink
offering, and the continual bread shall be on it.
8 "They shall spread over them a cloth of scarlet *material,* and cover the same with a
covering of porpoise skin, and they shall insert its poles.

4:9 Ex 25:31; Ex 25:37, 38

9 "Then they shall take a blue cloth and cover the lampstand for the light, along with
its lamps and its snuffers, and its trays and all its oil vessels, by which they serve it;
10 and they shall put it and all its utensils in a covering of porpoise skin, and shall put
it on the carrying bars.
11 "Over the golden altar they shall spread a blue cloth and cover it with a covering of
porpoise skin, and shall insert its poles;
12 and they shall take all the utensils of service, with which they serve in the sanctuary,
and put them in a blue cloth and cover them with a covering of porpoise skin, and put
them on the carrying bars.

4:13 Ex 27:1-8

13 "Then they shall take away the ashes from the altar, and spread a purple cloth over it.
14 "They shall also put on it all its utensils by which they serve in connection with it: the
firepans, the forks and shovels and the basins, all the utensils of the altar; and they shall
spread a cover of porpoise skin over it and insert its poles.

4:15 Num 1:51; 4:19, 20; 2 Sam 6:6, 7

15 "When Aaron and his sons have finished covering the holy *objects* and all the furnishings of the sanctuary, when the camp is to set out, after that the sons of Kohath shall
come to carry *them,* so that they will not touch the holy *objects* and die. These are the
things in the tent of meeting which the sons of Kohath are to carry.

4:16 Lev 24:1-3; Ex 30:34-38; Lev 6:20; Ex 30:22-33

16 "The responsibility of Eleazar the son of Aaron the priest is the oil for the light and
the fragrant incense and the continual grain offering and the anointing oil—the responsibility of all the tabernacle and of all that is in it, with the sanctuary and its furnishings."
17 Then the LORD spoke to Moses and to Aaron, saying,
18 "Do not let the tribe of the families of the Kohathites be cut off from among the
Levites.

4:19 Num 4:15

19 "But do this to them that they may live and not die when they approach the most
holy *objects:* Aaron and his sons shall go in and assign each of them to his work and to
his load;

4:20 Ex 19:21; 1 Sam 6:19

20 but they shall not go in to see the holy *objects* even for a moment, or they will die."

Duties of the Gershonites

21 Then the LORD spoke to Moses, saying,
22 "Take a census of the sons of Gershon also, by their fathers' households, by their
families;

4:23 Num 4:3; 1 Chr 23:3, 24, 27

23 from thirty years and upward to fifty years old, you shall number them; all who enter to perform the service to do the work in the tent of meeting.
24 "This is the service of the families of the Gershonites, in serving and in carrying:

4:25 Ex 40:19; Ex 26:14; Num 4:6

25 they shall carry the curtains of the tabernacle and the tent of meeting *with* its covering and the covering of porpoise skin that is on top of it, and the screen for the doorway
of the tent of meeting,

4:26 Ex 38:9

26 and the hangings of the court, and the screen for the doorway of the gate of the
court which is around the tabernacle and the altar, and their cords and all the equipment for their service; and all that is to be done, they shall perform.
27 "All the service of the sons of the Gershonites, in all their loads and in all their work,
shall be *performed* at the command of Aaron and his sons; and you shall assign to them
as a duty all their loads.
28 "This is the service of the families of the sons of the Gershonites in the tent of meeting, and their duties *shall be* under the direction of Ithamar the son of Aaron the priest.

Duties of the Merarites

29 "*As for* the sons of Merari, you shall number them by their families, by their fathers'
households;

4:30 Num 4:3; 8:24-26

30 from thirty years and upward even to fifty years old, you shall number them, everyone who enters the service to do the work of the tent of meeting.

4:27–28 The Gershonites could receive directions from any of Aaron's sons, but they were directly responsible to Ithamar only. The lines of authority and accountability were clearly communicated to all. As you function with others in service to God, make sure the lines of authority between you and those you work with are clearly understood. Good communication builds good relationships.

31 "Now this is the duty of their loads, for all their service in the tent of meeting: the
boards of the tabernacle and its bars and its pillars and its sockets,
32 and the pillars around the court and their sockets and their pegs and their cords,
with all their equipment and with all their service; and you shall assign *each man* by name
the items he is to carry.
33 "This is the service of the families of the sons of Merari, according to all their service
in the tent of meeting, under the direction of Ithamar the son of Aaron the priest."
34 So Moses and Aaron and the leaders of the congregation numbered the sons of the
Kohathites by their families and by their fathers' households,
35 from thirty years and upward even to fifty years old, everyone who entered the ser- **4:35**
vice for work in the tent of meeting. 1 Chr 23:24
36 Their numbered men by their families were 2,750.
37 These are the numbered men of the Kohathite families, everyone who was serving
in the tent of meeting, whom Moses and Aaron numbered according to the commandment of the LORD through Moses.
38 The numbered men of the sons of Gershon by their families and by their fathers'
households,
39 from thirty years and upward even to fifty years old, everyone who entered the service for work in the tent of meeting.
40 Their numbered men by their families, by their fathers' households, were 2,630.
41 These are the numbered men of the families of the sons of Gershon, everyone who
was serving in the tent of meeting, whom Moses and Aaron numbered according to the
commandment of the LORD.
42 The numbered men of the families of the sons of Merari by their families, by their
fathers' households,
43 from thirty years and upward even to fifty years old, everyone who entered the ser- **4:43**
vice for work in the tent of meeting. Num 8:24-26
44 Their numbered men by their families were 3,200.
45 These are the numbered men of the families of the sons of Merari, whom Moses
and Aaron numbered according to the commandment of the LORD through Moses.
46 All the numbered men of the Levites, whom Moses and Aaron and the leaders of
Israel numbered, by their families and by their fathers' households,
47 from thirty years and upward even to fifty years old, everyone who could enter to
do the work of service and the work of carrying in the tent of meeting.
48 Their numbered men were 8,580. **4:48**
49 According to the commandment of the LORD through Moses, they were numbered, Num 3:39
everyone by his serving or carrying; thus *these were* his numbered men, just as the LORD **4:49**
had commanded Moses. Num 1:47

3. The purity of the camp

On Defilement

5 Then the LORD spoke to Moses, saying,
2 "Command the sons of Israel that they send away from the camp every leper and **5:2**
everyone having a discharge and everyone who is unclean because of a *dead* person. Lev 13:8, 46; Num 12:10, 14, 15; Lev
3 "You shall send away both male and female; you shall send them outside the camp 15:2; Lev 21:1; Num
so that they will not defile their camp where I dwell in their midst." 9:6-10; 19:11
4 The sons of Israel did so and sent them outside the camp; just as the LORD had **5:3**
spoken to Moses, thus the sons of Israel did. Lev 26:12; Num 35:34
5 Then the LORD spoke to Moses, saying, **5:6**
6 "Speak to the sons of Israel, 'When a man or woman commits any of the sins of man- Lev 5:14-6:7
kind, acting unfaithfully against the LORD, and that person is guilty,
7 then he shall confess his sins which he has committed, and he shall make restitution **5:7** Lev 5:5; 26:40, 41;
in full for his wrong and add to it one-fifth of it, and give *it* to him whom he has wronged. Josh 7:19; Lev 6:4, 5

5:5–8 God included restitution, a unique concept for that day, as part of his law for Israel. When someone was robbed, the guilty person was required to restore the loss to the victim and pay an additional interest penalty. When we have wronged others, we ought to do more than apologize. We should look for ways to set matters right and, if possible, leave the victim even better off than when we harmed him or her. When we have been wronged, we should still seek restoration rather than striking out in revenge.

8 'But if the man has no [7]relative to whom restitution may be made for the wrong, the
restitution which is made for the wrong *must go* to the LORD for the priest, besides the
ram of atonement, by which atonement is made for him.

5:9 Lev 7:32, 34; 10:14, 15

9 'Also every contribution pertaining to all the holy *gifts* of the sons of Israel, which
they offer to the priest, shall be his.

5:10 Lev 10:13

10 'So every man's holy *gifts* shall be his; whatever any man gives to the priest, it becomes his.' "

The Adultery Test

11 Then the LORD spoke to Moses, saying,

5:12 Num 5:19-21, 29

12 "Speak to the sons of Israel and say to them, 'If any man's wife goes astray and is
unfaithful to him,

5:13 Lev 18:20; 20:10

13 and a man has intercourse with her and it is hidden from the eyes of her husband
and she is undetected, although she has defiled herself, and there is no witness against
her and she has not been caught in the act,

5:14 Prov 6:34; Song 8:6

14 if a spirit of jealousy comes over him and he is jealous of his wife when she has defiled herself, or if a spirit of jealousy comes over him and he is jealous of his wife when
she has not defiled herself,

5:15 1 Kin 17:18; Ezek 29:16

15 the man shall then bring his wife to the priest, and shall bring *as* an offering for her
one-tenth of an ephah of barley meal; he shall not pour oil on it nor put frankincense
on it, for it is a grain offering of jealousy, a grain offering of memorial, a reminder of
iniquity.
16 'Then the priest shall bring her near and have her stand before the LORD,
17 and the priest shall take holy water in an earthenware vessel; and he shall take some
of the dust that is on the floor of the tabernacle and put *it* into the water.
18 'The priest shall then have the woman stand before the LORD and let *the hair of* the
woman's head go loose, and place the grain offering of memorial in her hands, which is
the grain offering of jealousy, and in the hand of the priest is to be the water of bitterness that brings a curse.

5:19 Num 5:12

19 'The priest shall have her take an oath and shall say to the woman, "If no man has
lain with you and if you have not gone astray into uncleanness, *being* under *the authority
of* your husband, be immune to this water of bitterness that brings a curse;

5:20 Num 5:12

20 if you, however, have gone astray, *being* under *the authority of* your husband, and
if you have defiled yourself and a man other than your husband has had intercourse
with you"

5:21 Josh 6:26; 1 Sam 14:24; Neh 10:29

21 (then the priest shall have the woman swear with the oath of the curse, and the priest
shall say to the woman), "the LORD make you a curse and an oath among your people by
the LORD'S making your thigh waste away and your abdomen swell;

5:22 Deut 27:15

22 and this water that brings a curse shall go into your stomach, and make your abdomen swell and your thigh waste away." And the woman shall say, "Amen. Amen."
23 'The priest shall then write these curses on a scroll, and he shall wash them off into
the water of bitterness.
24 'Then he shall make the woman drink the water of bitterness that brings a curse, so
that the water which brings a curse will go into her and *cause* bitterness.
25 'The priest shall take the grain offering of jealousy from the woman's hand, and he
shall wave the grain offering before the LORD and bring it to the altar;

5:26 Lev 2:2, 9

26 and the priest shall take a handful of the grain offering as its memorial offering and
offer *it* up in smoke on the altar, and afterward he shall make the woman drink the
water.

5:27 Jer 29:18; 42:18; 44:12

27 'When he has made her drink the water, then it shall come about, if she has defiled
herself and has been unfaithful to her husband, that the water which brings a curse will
go into her and *cause* bitterness, and her abdomen will swell and her thigh will waste
away, and the woman will become a curse among her people.

7 Lit *redeemer*

5:11–31 This test for adultery served to remove a jealous husband's suspicion. Trust between husband and wife had to be completely eroded for a man to bring his wife to the priest for this type of test. Today priests and pastors help restore marriages by counseling couples who have lost faith in each other. Whether justified or not, suspicion must be removed for a marriage to survive and trust to be restored.

28 'But if the woman has not defiled herself and is clean, she will then be free and conceive children.
29 'This is the law of jealousy: when a wife, *being* under *the authority of* her husband, **5:29** Num 5:12
goes astray and defiles herself,
30 or when a spirit of jealousy comes over a man and he is jealous of his wife, he
shall then make the woman stand before the LORD, and the priest shall apply all this law
to her.
31 'Moreover, the man will be free from guilt, but that woman shall bear her guilt.' " **5:31** Lev 20:17

Law of the Nazirites

6 Again the LORD spoke to Moses, saying,
2 "Speak to the sons of Israel and say to them, 'When a man or woman makes a **6:2** Judg 13:5; 16:17; Amos 2:11, 12
special vow, the vow of a [8]Nazirite, to dedicate himself to the LORD,
3 he shall abstain from wine and strong drink; he shall drink no vinegar, whether made **6:3** Luke 1:15
from wine or strong drink, nor shall he drink any grape juice nor eat fresh or dried grapes.
4 'All the days of his [9]separation he shall not eat anything that is produced by the grape
vine, from *the* seeds even to *the* skin.
5 'All the days of his vow of separation no razor shall pass over his head. He shall be **6:5** 1 Sam 1:11
holy until the days are fulfilled for which he separated himself to the LORD; he shall let
the locks of hair on his head grow long.
6 'All the days of his separation to the LORD he shall not go near to a dead person. **6:6** Lev 21:1-3; Num 19:11-22
7 'He shall not make himself unclean for his father or for his mother, for his brother
or for his sister, when they die, because his separation to God is on his head.
8 'All the days of his separation he is holy to the LORD. **6:7** Num 9:6
9 'But if a man dies very suddenly beside him and he defiles his dedicated head *of hair,*
then he shall shave his head on the day when he becomes clean; he shall shave it on the **6:9** Lev 14:8, 9; Num 6:18
seventh day.
10 'Then on the eighth day he shall bring two turtledoves or two young pigeons to the **6:10** Lev 5:7; 14:22
priest, to the doorway of the tent of meeting.
11 'The priest shall offer one for a sin offering and *the* other for a burnt offering, and **6:11** Lev 5:7
make atonement for him concerning his sin because of the *dead* person. And that same
day he shall consecrate his head,
12 and shall dedicate to the LORD his days as a Nazirite, and shall bring a male lamb a
year old for a guilt offering; but the former days will be void because his separation was
defiled.
13 'Now this is the law of the Nazirite when the days of his separation are fulfilled, he **6:13** Acts 21:26
shall bring the offering to the doorway of the tent of meeting.
14 'He shall present his offering to the LORD: one male lamb a year old without defect **6:14** Lev 14:10; Num 15:27
for a burnt offering and one ewe-lamb a year old without defect for a sin offering and
one ram without defect for a peace offering,
15 and a basket of unleavened cakes of fine flour mixed with oil and unleavened wa- **6:15** Ex 29:2; Lev 2:4; Num 15:1-7
fers spread with oil, along with their grain offering and their drink offering.
16 'Then the priest shall present *them* before the LORD and shall offer his sin offering
and his burnt offering.
17 'He shall also offer the ram for a sacrifice of peace offerings to the LORD, together
with the basket of unleavened cakes; the priest shall likewise offer its grain offering and
its drink offering.
18 'The Nazirite shall then shave his dedicated head *of hair* at the doorway of the tent **6:18** Num 6:9; Acts 21:23, 24
of meeting, and take the dedicated hair of his head and put *it* on the fire which is under
the sacrifice of peace offerings.
19 'The priest shall take the ram's shoulder *when it has been* boiled, and one unleav- **6:19** Lev 7:28-34

8 I.e. one separated 9 Or *living as a Nazirite,* and so through v 21

6:1–2 In Moses' day, a personal vow was as binding as a written contract. It was one thing to say you would do something, but it was considered much more serious when you made a solemn vow to do it. God instituted the Nazirite vow for people who wanted to devote some time exclusively to serving him. This vow could be taken for as little as 30 days or as long as a lifetime. It was voluntary, with one exception—parents could take the vow for their young children, making them Nazirites for life. The vow included three distinct restrictions: (1) he must abstain from wine and fermented drink; (2) the hair could not be cut, and the beard could not be shaved; (3) touching a dead body was prohibited. The purpose of the Nazirite vow was to raise up a group of leaders devoted completely to God. Samson, Samuel, and John the Baptist were probably Nazirites for life.

ened cake out of the basket and one unleavened wafer, and shall put *them* on the hands
of the Nazirite after he has shaved his dedicated *hair.*
20 'Then the priest shall wave them for a wave offering before the LORD. It is holy for
the priest, together with the breast offered by waving and the thigh offered by lifting up;
and afterward the Nazirite may drink wine.'
21 "This is the law of the Nazirite who vows his offering to the LORD according to his
separation, in addition to what *else* he can afford; according to his vow which he takes,
so he shall do according to the law of his separation."

Aaron's Benediction

22 Then the LORD spoke to Moses, saying,
23 "Speak to Aaron and to his sons, saying, 'Thus you shall bless the sons of Israel. You
shall say to them:
24 The LORD bless you, and keep you;
25 The LORD make His face shine on you,
And be gracious to you;
26 The LORD lift up His countenance on you,
And give you peace.'
27 "So they shall invoke My name on the sons of Israel, and I *then* will bless them."

Offerings of the Leaders

7 Now on the day that Moses had finished setting up the tabernacle, he anointed it
and consecrated it with all its furnishings and the altar and all its utensils; he anointed them and consecrated them also.
2 Then the leaders of Israel, the heads of their fathers' households, made an offering
(they were the leaders of the tribes; they were the ones who were over the numbered
men).
3 When they brought their offering before the LORD, six covered carts and twelve oxen,
a cart for *every* two of the leaders and an ox for each one, then they presented them before the tabernacle.
4 Then the LORD spoke to Moses, saying,
5 "Accept *these things* from them, that they may be used in the service of the tent of
meeting, and you shall give them to the Levites, *to* each man according to his service."
6 So Moses took the carts and the oxen and gave them to the Levites.
7 Two carts and four oxen he gave to the sons of Gershon, according to their service,
8 and four carts and eight oxen he gave to the sons of Merari, according to their service, under the direction of Ithamar the son of Aaron the priest.
9 But he did not give *any* to the sons of Kohath because theirs *was* the service of the
holy *objects, which* they carried on the shoulder.
10 The leaders offered the dedication *offering* for the altar when it was anointed, so
the leaders offered their offering before the altar.
11 Then the LORD said to Moses, "Let them present their offering, one leader each
day, for the dedication of the altar."
12 Now the one who presented his offering on the first day was Nahshon the son of
Amminadab, of the tribe of Judah;
13 and his offering *was* one silver [10]dish whose weight *was* one hundred and thirty *shekels,* one silver bowl of seventy shekels, according to [11]the shekel of the sanctuary, both of
them full of fine flour mixed with oil for a grain offering;
14 one gold pan of ten *shekels,* full of incense;
15 one bull, one ram, one male lamb one year old, for a burnt offering;
16 one male goat for a sin offering;

10 Or *platter,* and so through v 85 **11** I.e. Approx one-half oz, and so through v 86

6:20 Eccl 9:7
6:23 1 Chr 23:13
6:24 Deut 28:3-6; Ps 28:9 1 Sam 2:9; Ps 17:8
6:25 Ps 80:3, 7, 19; Ps 86:16
6:26 Ps 4:6; 44:3; Ps 29:11; 37:37
6:27 2 Sam 7:23; 2 Chr 7:14
7:1 Ex 40:17; Ex 40:9-11; Num 7:10, 84, 88
7:2 Num 1:5-16; 2 Chr 35:8
7:3 Is 66:20
7:7 Num 4:24-26
7:8 Num 4:31, 32
7:9 Num 4:5-15
7:10 Num 7:1; 2 Chr 7:9
7:13 Ex 25:29; 37:16; Num 3:47
7:16 Lev 4:23

6:24–26 A blessing was one way of asking for God's divine favor to rest upon others. The ancient blessing in these verses helps us understand what a blessing was supposed to do. Its five parts conveyed hope that God would (1) bless and keep them (favor and protect); (2) make his face shine upon them (be pleased); (3) be gracious (merciful and compassionate); (4) turn his face (countenance) toward them (give his approval); (5) give peace. When you ask God to bless others or yourself, you are asking him to do these five things. The blessing you offer will not only help the one receiving it, but it will also demonstrate love, encourage others, and provide a model of caring to others.

7:1ff After the tabernacle was set up, anointed, and consecrated, the leaders of the 12 tribes brought gifts and offerings for its use and maintenance. All of the people participated—it was everyone's tabernacle.

17 and for the sacrifice of peace offerings, two oxen, five rams, five male goats, five
male lambs one year old. This *was* the offering of Nahshon the son of Amminadab.
18 On the second day Nethanel the son of Zuar, leader of Issachar, presented *an offering;*
19 he presented as his offering one silver dish whose weight *was* one hundred and thirty
shekels, one silver bowl of seventy shekels, according to the shekel of the sanctuary, both
of them full of fine flour mixed with oil for a grain offering;
20 one gold pan of ten *shekels,* full of incense;
21 one bull, one ram, one male lamb one year old, for a burnt offering;
22 one male goat for a sin offering;
23 and for the sacrifice of peace offerings, two oxen, five rams, five male goats, five
male lambs one year old. This *was* the offering of Nethanel the son of Zuar.
24 On the third day *it was* Eliab the son of Helon, leader of the sons of Zebulun;
25 his offering *was* one silver dish whose weight *was* one hundred and thirty *shekels,*
one silver bowl of seventy shekels, according to the shekel of the sanctuary, both of them
full of fine flour mixed with oil for a grain offering;
26 one gold pan of ten *shekels,* full of incense;
27 one young bull, one ram, one male lamb one year old, for a burnt offering;
28 one male goat for a sin offering;
29 and for the sacrifice of peace offerings, two oxen, five rams, five male goats, five
male lambs one year old. This *was* the offering of Eliab the son of Helon.
30 On the fourth day *it was* Elizur the son of Shedeur, leader of the sons of Reuben;
31 his offering *was* one silver dish whose weight *was* one hundred and thirty *shekels,*
one silver bowl of seventy shekels, according to the shekel of the sanctuary, both of them
full of fine flour mixed with oil for a grain offering;
32 one gold pan of ten *shekels,* full of incense;
33 one bull, one ram, one male lamb one year old, for a burnt offering;
34 one male goat for a sin offering;
35 and for the sacrifice of peace offerings, two oxen, five rams, five male goats, five
male lambs one year old. This *was* the offering of Elizur the son of Shedeur.
36 On the fifth day *it was* Shelumiel the son of Zurishaddai, leader of the children of
Simeon;
37 his offering *was* one silver dish whose weight *was* one hundred and thirty *shekels,*
one silver bowl of seventy shekels, according to the shekel of the sanctuary, both of them
full of fine flour mixed with oil for a grain offering;
38 one gold pan of ten *shekels,* full of incense;
39 one bull, one ram, one male lamb one year old, for a burnt offering;
40 one male goat for a sin offering;
41 and for the sacrifice of peace offerings, two oxen, five rams, five male goats, five
male lambs one year old. This *was* the offering of Shelumiel the son of Zurishaddai.
42 On the sixth day *it was* Eliasaph the son of Deuel, leader of the sons of Gad;
43 his offering *was* one silver dish whose weight *was* one hundred and thirty *shekels,*
one silver bowl of seventy shekels, according to the shekel of the sanctuary, both of them
full of fine flour mixed with oil for a grain offering;
44 one gold pan of ten *shekels,* full of incense;
45 one bull, one ram, one male lamb one year old, for a burnt offering;
46 one male goat for a sin offering;
47 and for the sacrifice of peace offerings, two oxen, five rams, five male goats, five
male lambs one year old. This *was* the offering of Eliasaph the son of Deuel.
48 On the seventh day *it was* Elishama the son of Ammihud, leader of the sons of
Ephraim;
49 his offering *was* one silver dish whose weight *was* one hundred and thirty *shekels,*
one silver bowl of seventy shekels, according to the shekel of the sanctuary, both of them
full of fine flour mixed with oil for a grain offering;
50 one gold pan of ten *shekels,* full of incense;
51 one bull, one ram, one male lamb one year old, for a burnt offering;
52 one male goat for a sin offering;
53 and for the sacrifice of peace offerings, two oxen, five rams, five male goats, five
male lambs one year old. This *was* the offering of Elishama the son of Ammihud.
54 On the eighth day *it was* Gamaliel the son of Pedahzur, leader of the sons of Manasseh;
55 his offering *was* one silver dish whose weight *was* one hundred and thirty *shekels,*

7:17 Luke 3:32, 33
7:23 Lev 7:11-13
7:27 Is 53:7; John 1:29; 1 Pet 1:19
7:33 Heb 9:28
7:42 Num 1:14; 10:20
7:43 Lev 2:5; 14:10
7:45 Ps 50:8-14; Is 1:11
7:48 Num 1:10; 2:18; 1 Chr 7:26
7:50 Deut 33:10; Ezek 8:11; Luke 1:10
7:51 Mic 6:6-8
7:54 Num 2:20

one silver bowl of seventy shekels, according to the shekel of the sanctuary, both of them
full of fine flour mixed with oil for a grain offering;
56 one gold pan of ten *shekels,* full of incense;
57 one bull, one ram, one male lamb one year old, for a burnt offering;
58 one male goat for a sin offering;
59 and for the sacrifice of peace offerings, two oxen, five rams, five male goats, five
male lambs one year old. This *was* the offering of Gamaliel the son of Pedahzur.
60 On the ninth day *it was* Abidan the son of Gideoni, leader of the sons of Benjamin;
61 his offering *was* one silver dish whose weight *was* one hundred and thirty *shekels,*
one silver bowl of seventy shekels, according to the shekel of the sanctuary, both of them
full of fine flour mixed with oil for a grain offering;
62 one gold pan of ten *shekels,* full of incense;
63 one bull, one ram, one male lamb one year old, for a burnt offering;
64 one male goat for a sin offering;
65 and for the sacrifice of peace offerings, two oxen, five rams, five male goats, five
male lambs one year old. This *was* the offering of Abidan the son of Gideoni.
66 On the tenth day *it was* Ahiezer the son of Ammishaddai, leader of the sons of Dan;
67 his offering *was* one silver dish whose weight *was* one hundred and thirty *shekels,*
one silver bowl of seventy shekels, according to the shekel of the sanctuary, both of them
full of fine flour mixed with oil for a grain offering;
68 one gold pan of ten *shekels,* full of incense;
69 one bull, one ram, one male lamb one year old, for a burnt offering;
70 one male goat for a sin offering;
71 and for the sacrifice of peace offerings, two oxen, five rams, five male goats, five
male lambs one year old. This *was* the offering of Ahiezer the son of Ammishaddai.
72 On the eleventh day *it was* Pagiel the son of Ochran, leader of the sons of Asher;
73 his offering *was* one silver dish whose weight *was* one hundred and thirty *shekels,*
one silver bowl of seventy shekels, according to the shekel of the sanctuary, both of them
full of fine flour mixed with oil for a grain offering;
74 one gold pan of ten *shekels,* full of incense;
75 one bull, one ram, one male lamb one year old, for a burnt offering;
76 one male goat for a sin offering;
77 and for the sacrifice of peace offerings, two oxen, five rams, five male goats, five
male lambs one year old. This *was* the offering of Pagiel the son of Ochran.
78 On the twelfth day *it was* Ahira the son of Enan, leader of the sons of Naphtali;
79 his offering *was* one silver dish whose weight *was* one hundred and thirty *shekels,*
one silver bowl of seventy shekels, according to the shekel of the sanctuary, both of them
full of fine flour mixed with oil for a grain offering;
80 one gold pan of ten *shekels,* full of incense;
81 one bull, one ram, one male lamb one year old, for a burnt offering;
82 one male goat for a sin offering;
83 and for the sacrifice of peace offerings, two oxen, five rams, five male goats, five
male lambs one year old. This *was* the offering of Ahira the son of Enan.
84 This *was* the dedication *offering* for the altar from the leaders of Israel when it was
anointed: twelve silver dishes, twelve silver bowls, twelve gold pans,
85 each silver dish *weighing* one hundred and thirty *shekels* and each bowl seventy; all
the silver of the utensils *was* 2,400 *shekels,* according to the shekel of the sanctuary;
86 the twelve gold pans, full of incense, *weighing* ten *shekels* apiece, according to the
shekel of the sanctuary, all the gold of the pans 120 *shekels;*
87 all the oxen for the burnt offering twelve bulls, *all* the rams twelve, the male lambs
one year old with their grain offering twelve, and the male goats for a sin offering twelve;
88 and all the oxen for the sacrifice of peace offerings 24 bulls, *all* the rams 60, the male
goats 60, the male lambs one year old 60. This *was* the dedication *offering* for the altar
after it was anointed.
89 Now when Moses went into the tent of meeting to speak with Him, he heard the

7:56 Ex 30:7
7:57 Ex 12:5; Acts 8:32; Rev 5:6
7:59 Lev 3:1-17
7:60 Num 1:11; 2:22
7:62 Rev 5:8; 8:3, 4
7:64 2 Cor 5:21
7:65 Col 1:20
7:66 Num 1:12; 2:25
7:67 Ex 30:13; Lev 27:25
7:68 Ps 141:2
7:72 Num 1:13; 2:27
7:74 Mal 1:11
7:78 Num 1:15; 2:29
7:79 Ezra 1:9, 10; Dan 5:2
7:84 Num 7:10; Num 7:1
7:86 Ex 30:13
7:88 Num 7:1, 10
7:89 Ex 40:34, 35; Ex 25:21, 22; Ps 80:1; 99:1

7:89 Imagine hearing the very voice of God! Moses must have trembled at the sound. Yet we have God's words recorded for us in the Bible, and we should have no less reverence and awe for them. God sometimes spoke directly to his people to tell them the proper way to live. The Bible records these conversations to give us insights into God's character. How tragic when we take these very words of God lightly. Like Moses, we have the privilege of talking to God, but God answers us differently—through his written Word and the guidance of his Holy Spirit. To receive this guidance, we need to seek to know God as Moses did.

voice speaking to him from above the mercy seat that was on the ark of the testimony,
from between the two cherubim, so He spoke to him.

The Seven Lamps

8 Then the LORD spoke to Moses, saying,
2 "Speak to Aaron and say to him, 'When you mount the lamps, the seven lamps
will give light in the front of the lampstand.' "
3 Aaron therefore did so; he mounted its lamps at the front of the lampstand, just as
the LORD had commanded Moses.
4 Now this was the workmanship of the lampstand, hammered work of gold; from its
base to its flowers it was hammered work; according to the pattern which the LORD had
showed Moses, so he made the lampstand.

Cleansing the Levites

5 Again the LORD spoke to Moses, saying,
6 "Take the Levites from among the sons of Israel and cleanse them.
7 "Thus you shall do to them, for their cleansing: *sprinkle* purifying water on them, and
let them use a razor over their whole body and wash their clothes, and they will be clean.
8 "Then let them take a bull with its grain offering, fine flour mixed with oil; and a
second bull you shall take for a sin offering.
9 "So you shall present the Levites before the tent of meeting. You shall also assemble
the whole congregation of the sons of Israel,
10 and present the Levites before the LORD; and the sons of Israel shall lay their hands
on the Levites.
11 "Aaron then shall present the Levites before the LORD as a wave offering from the
sons of Israel, that they may qualify to perform the service of the LORD.
12 "Now the Levites shall lay their hands on the heads of the bulls; then offer the one
for a sin offering and the other for a burnt offering to the LORD, to make atonement for
the Levites.
13 "You shall have the Levites stand before Aaron and before his sons so as to present
them as a wave offering to the LORD.
14 "Thus you shall separate the Levites from among the sons of Israel, and the Levites
shall be Mine.
15 "Then after that the Levites may go in to serve the tent of meeting. But you shall
cleanse them and present them as a wave offering;
16 for they are wholly given to Me from among the sons of Israel. I have taken them
for Myself instead of every first issue of the womb, the firstborn of all the sons of Israel.
17 "For every firstborn among the sons of Israel is Mine, among the men and among
the animals; on the day that I struck down all the firstborn in the land of Egypt I sanctified them for Myself.
18 "But I have taken the Levites instead of every firstborn among the sons of Israel.
19 "I have given the Levites as a gift to Aaron and to his sons from among the sons of
Israel, to perform the service of the sons of Israel at the tent of meeting and to make
atonement on behalf of the sons of Israel, so that there will be no plague among the sons
of Israel by their coming near to the sanctuary."
20 Thus did Moses and Aaron and all the congregation of the sons of Israel to the
Levites; according to all that the LORD had commanded Moses concerning the Levites,
so the sons of Israel did to them.
21 The Levites, too, purified themselves from sin and washed their clothes; and Aaron
presented them as a wave offering before the LORD. Aaron also made atonement for
them to cleanse them.
22 Then after that the Levites went in to perform their service in the tent of meeting
before Aaron and before his sons; just as the LORD had commanded Moses concerning
the Levites, so they did to them.

8:2 Ex 25:37; Lev 24:2, 4
8:4 Ex 25:31-40; Ex 25:9, 31-40; 26:30; 37:17-24
8:6 Is 52:11
8:7 Num 19:9, 13, 20; Lev 14:8, 9; Num 8:21
8:8 Lev 2:1; Num 15:8-10
8:9 Ex 29:4; 40:12; Lev 8:3
8:10 Lev 1:4
8:11 Lev 7:30, 34
8:12 Ex 29:10
8:14 Num 3:12; 16:9
8:15 Ex 29:24
8:16 Num 3:9; Ex 13:2; Num 3:12, 45
8:17 Ex 13:2, 12, 13, 15; Luke 2:23
8:19 Num 3:9; Num 1:53; 16:46
8:21 Num 8:7

8:1–4 The lamps provided light for the priests as they carried out their duties. The light was also an expression of God's presence. Jesus said, "I am the Light of the world" (John 8:12). The golden lampstand is still one of the major symbols of the Jewish faith.

Retirement

23 Now the LORD spoke to Moses, saying,

8:24 Num 4:3; 1 Chr 23:3, 24, 27

24 "This is what *applies* to the Levites: from twenty-five years old and upward they shall
enter to perform service in the work of the tent of meeting.
25 "But at the age of fifty years they shall retire from service in the work and not work
any more.

8:26 Num 1:53

26 "They may, however, assist their brothers in the tent of meeting, to keep an obligation, but they *themselves* shall do no work. Thus you shall deal with the Levites concerning their obligations."

The Passover

9:1 Ex 40:2, 17; Num 1:1

9 Thus the LORD spoke to Moses in the wilderness of Sinai, in the first month of the
second year after they had come out of the land of Egypt, saying,

9:2 Ex 12:6; Lev 23:5; Deut 16:1, 2

2 "Now, let the sons of Israel observe the Passover at its appointed time.
3 "On the fourteenth day of this month, at twilight, you shall observe it at its appointed
time; you shall observe it according to all its statutes and according to all its ordinances."
4 So Moses told the sons of Israel to observe the Passover.

9:5 Josh 5:10; Ex 12:1-13

5 They observed the Passover in the first *month,* on the fourteenth day of the month,
at twilight, in the wilderness of Sinai; according to all that the LORD had commanded
Moses, so the sons of Israel did.

9:6 Num 5:2; 19:11-22; Ex 18:15; Num 27:2

6 But there were *some* men who were unclean because of *the* dead person, so that
they could not observe Passover on that day; so they came before Moses and Aaron on
that day.
7 Those men said to him, "*Though* we are unclean because of *the* dead person, why
are we restrained from presenting the offering of the LORD at its appointed time among
the sons of Israel?"

9:8 Ex 18:15; Ps 85:8

8 Moses therefore said to them, "Wait, and I will listen to what the LORD will command concerning you."
9 Then the LORD spoke to Moses, saying,
10 "Speak to the sons of Israel, saying, 'If any one of you or of your generations becomes
unclean because of a *dead* person, or is on a distant journey, he may, however, observe
the Passover to the LORD.

9:11 2 Chr 30:2, 15; Ex 12:8

11 'In the second month on the fourteenth day at twilight, they shall observe it; they
shall eat it with unleavened bread and bitter herbs.

9:12 Ex 12:10; Ex 12:46; John 19:36

12 'They shall leave none of it until morning, nor break a bone of it; according to all the
statute of the Passover they shall observe it.

9:13 Gen 17:14; Ex 12:15, 47; Num 5:31

13 'But the man who is clean and is not on a journey, and yet neglects to observe the
Passover, that person shall then be cut off from his people, for he did not present the
offering of the LORD at its appointed time. That man will bear his sin.

9:14 Ex 12:48; Ex 12:49; Lev 24:22; Num 15:15, 16, 29

14 'If an alien sojourns among you and observes the Passover to the LORD, according
to the statute of the Passover and according to its ordinance, so he shall do; you shall
have one statute, both for the alien and for the native of the land.' "

8:25–26 Why were the Levites supposed to retire at age 50? The reasons were probably more practical than theological. (1) Moving the tabernacle and its furniture through the wilderness required strength. The younger men were more suited for the work of lifting the heavy articles. (2) The Levites over 50 did not stop working altogether. They were allowed to assist with various light duties in the tabernacle. This helped the younger men assume more responsibilities, and it allowed the older men to be in a position to advise and counsel them.

9:2 This is the second Passover. The first was instituted in Egypt and recorded in Exodus 12. Passover and the Feast of Unleavened Bread were an eight-day religious observance (Leviticus 23:5–6) commemorating the Israelites' escape from slavery in Egypt by God's power.

9:6–12 Several men came to Moses because of the predicament they faced: They were "unclean" because of contact with a dead body (or entering the home of a person who had died), and this prevented them from participating in the Passover meal. Notice that God did not adjust the requirements of the Passover. The standards of holiness were maintained, and the men were not allowed to participate. But God did make an exception and allowed the men to celebrate the Passover at a later date. This upheld the sacred requirements while allowing the men to participate in the feast—a duty for all Israelite men. Sometimes we face predicaments where the most obvious solution might cause us to compromise God's standards. Like Moses, we should use wisdom and prayer to reach a workable solution.

9:14 Sometimes we are tempted to excuse non-Christians from following God's guidelines for living. Christmas and Easter, for example, often have other meanings for them. We would not expect them to understand Lent. Yet aliens (foreigners) at this time were expected to follow the same laws and ordinances as the Israelites. God did not have a separate set of standards for unbelievers, and he still does not today. The phrase "You shall have one statute" emphasizes that non-Israelites were also subject to God's commands and promises. God singled out Israel for a special purpose—to be an example of how one nation could, and should, follow him. His aim, however, was to have all people obey and worship him.

4. Receiving guidance for the journey

The Cloud on the Tabernacle

15 Now on the day that the tabernacle was erected the cloud covered the tabernacle,
the tent of the testimony, and in the evening it was like the appearance of fire over the
tabernacle, until morning.
16 So it was continuously; the cloud would cover it *by day,* and the appearance of fire
by night.
17 Whenever the cloud was lifted from over the tent, afterward the sons of Israel would
then set out; and in the place where the cloud settled down, there the sons of Israel would
camp.
18 At the command of the LORD the sons of Israel would set out, and at the command
of the LORD they would camp; as long as the cloud settled over the tabernacle, they remained camped.
19 Even when the cloud lingered over the tabernacle for many days, the sons of Israel
would keep the LORD'S charge and not set out.
20 If sometimes the cloud remained a few days over the tabernacle, according to the
command of the LORD they remained camped. Then according to the command of the
LORD they set out.
21 If sometimes the cloud remained from evening until morning, when the cloud was
lifted in the morning, they would move out; or *if it remained* in the daytime and at night,
whenever the cloud was lifted, they would set out.
22 Whether it was two days or a month or a year that the cloud lingered over the tabernacle, staying above it, the sons of Israel remained camped and did not set out; but
when it was lifted, they did set out.
23 At the command of the LORD they camped, and at the command of the LORD they
set out; they kept the LORD'S charge, according to the command of the LORD through
Moses.

9:15 Ex 40:2, 17; Ex 40:34; Num 17:7; Ex 13:21, 22
9:16 Ex 40:34; Neh 9:12
9:17 Ex 40:36-38; Num 10:11, 12
9:18 1 Cor 10:1
9:20 Ps 48:14; Prov 3:5, 6
9:22 Ex 40:36, 37
9:23 Ps 73:24; 107:7; Is 63:14

The Silver Trumpets

10 The LORD spoke further to Moses, saying,
2 "Make yourself two trumpets of silver, of hammered work you shall make them;
and you shall use them for summoning the congregation and for having the camps
set out.
3 "When both are blown, all the congregation shall gather themselves to you at the
doorway of the tent of meeting.
4 "Yet if *only* one is blown, then the leaders, the heads of the divisions of Israel, shall
assemble before you.
5 "But when you blow an alarm, the camps that are pitched on the east side shall
set out.
6 "When you blow an alarm the second time, the camps that are pitched on the south
side shall set out; an alarm is to be blown for them to set out.
7 "When convening the assembly, however, you shall blow without sounding an alarm.
8 "The priestly sons of Aaron, moreover, shall blow the trumpets; and this shall be for
you a perpetual statute throughout your generations.
9 "When you go to war in your land against the adversary who attacks you, then you
shall sound an alarm with the trumpets, that you may be remembered before the LORD
your God, and be saved from your enemies.

10:2 Is 1:13
10:3 Jer 4:5; Joel 2:15
10:4 Ex 18:21; Num 1:16; 7:2
10:5 Num 10:14
10:6 Num 10:18
10:7 Joel 2:1
10:8 Num 31:6; Josh 6:4; 2 Chr 13:12
10:9 Judg 2:18; 1 Sam 10:18; Ps 106:42; Gen 8:1; Ps 106:4

9:15–22 A pillar of cloud by day and a pillar of fire by night guided and protected the Israelites as they traveled across the wilderness. Some have said this pillar may have been a burning bowl of pitch whose smoke was visible during the day and whose fire could be seen at night. However, a bowl of pitch would not have lifted itself up and moved ahead of the people, and the Bible is clear that the cloud and fire moved in accordance with the will of God. The cloud and the fire were not merely natural phenomena; they were the vehicle of God's presence and the visible evidence of his moving and directing his people.

9:23 The Israelites traveled and camped as God guided. When you follow God's guidance, you know you are where God wants you, whether you're moving or staying in one place. You are physically somewhere right now. Instead of praying, "God, what do you want me to do next?" ask, "God, what do you want me to do while I'm right here?" Direction from God is not just for your next big move. He has a purpose in placing you where you are right now. Begin to understand God's purpose for your life by discovering what he wants you to do now!

10:1–10 The two silver trumpets were used to coordinate the tribes as they moved through the wilderness. To keep so many people in tight formations required clear communication and control. Trumpet blasts also reminded Israel of God's protection over them.

10:10 Ps 81:3-5

10 "Also in the day of your gladness and in your appointed feasts, and on the first *days*
of your months, you shall blow the trumpets over your burnt offerings, and over the sacrifices of your peace offerings; and they shall be as a reminder of you before your God.
I am the LORD your God."

B. FIRST APPROACH TO THE PROMISED LAND (10:11—14:45)

As the Israelites approached the promised land, Moses sent leaders to spy out the land and its people. But the spies returned with a discouraging report. Although Joshua and Caleb disagreed, the Israelites had already made up their minds and began to complain. As punishment for their lack of faith, God condemned them to wander in the desert for 40 years. Our obedience must be complete and timely.

1. The people complain

The Tribes Leave Sinai

10:11 Ex 40:17
10:12 Ex 40:36; Gen 21:21; Num 12:16
10:13 Deut 1:6
10:14 Num 2:3-9

11 Now in the second year, in the second month, on the twentieth of the month, the
cloud was lifted from over the tabernacle of the testimony;
12 and the sons of Israel set out on their journeys from the wilderness of Sinai. Then
the cloud settled down in the wilderness of Paran.
13 So they moved out for the first time according to the commandment of the LORD
through Moses.
14 The standard of the camp of the sons of Judah, according to their armies, set out
first, with Nahshon the son of Amminadab, over its army,
15 and Nethanel the son of Zuar, over the tribal army of the sons of Issachar;
16 and Eliab the son of Helon over the tribal army of the sons of Zebulun.

10:17 Num 4:21-32
10:18 Num 2:10-16

17 Then the tabernacle was taken down; and the sons of Gershon and the sons of Merari,
who were carrying the tabernacle, set out.
18 Next the standard of the camp of Reuben, according to their armies, set out with
Elizur the son of Shedeur, over its army,
19 and Shelumiel the son of Zurishaddai over the tribal army of the sons of Simeon,
20 and Eliasaph the son of Deuel was over the tribal army of the sons of Gad.

10:21 Num 4:4-20; Num 10:17
10:22 Num 2:18-24

21 Then the Kohathites set out, carrying the holy *objects;* and the tabernacle was set
up before their arrival.
22 Next the standard of the camp of the sons of Ephraim, according to their armies,
was set out, with Elishama the son of Ammihud over its army,
23 and Gamaliel the son of Pedahzur over the tribal army of the sons of Manasseh;
24 and Abidan the son of Gideoni over the tribal army of the sons of Benjamin.

10:25 Num 2:25-31; Josh 6:9, 13

25 Then the standard of the camp of the sons of Dan, according to their armies, *which*
formed the rear guard for all the camps, set out, with Ahiezer the son of Ammishaddai
over its army,
26 and Pagiel the son of Ochran over the tribal army of the sons of Asher;
27 and Ahira the son of Enan over the tribal army of the sons of Naphtali.

10:21 Those who travel, move, or face new challenges know what it is to be uprooted. Life is full of changes, and few things remain stable. The Israelites were constantly moving through the wilderness. They were able to handle change only because God's presence in the tabernacle was always with them. The portable tabernacle signified God and his people moving together. For us, stability does not mean lack of change, but moving with God in every circumstance.

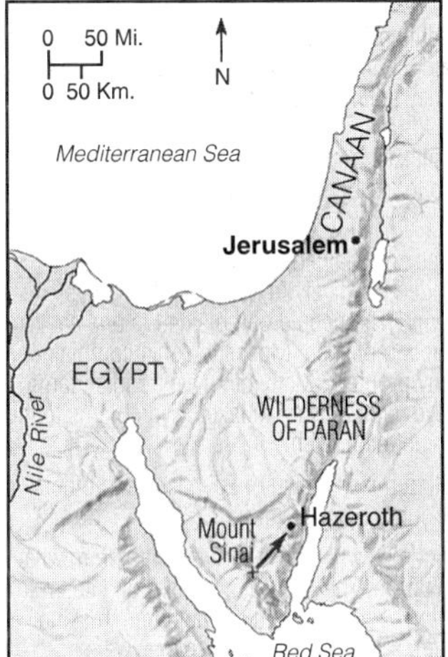

ISRAEL'S DEPARTURE FROM SINAI
It has been two years since Israel left Egypt. Having received God's travel instructions through Moses, Israel set out from Mount Sinai into the wilderness of Paran on their way toward the promised land.

28 This was the order of march of the sons of Israel by their armies as they set out.
29 Then Moses said to Hobab the son of Reuel the Midianite, Moses' father-in-law,
"We are setting out to the place of which the LORD said, 'I will give it to you'; come with
us and we will do you good, for the LORD has promised good concerning Israel."
30 But he said to him, "I will not come, but rather will go to my *own* land and relatives."
31 Then he said, "Please do not leave us, inasmuch as you know where we should camp
in the wilderness, and you will be as eyes for us.
32 "So it will be, if you go with us, that whatever good the LORD does for us, we will do
for you."
33 Thus they set out from the mount of the LORD three days' journey, with the ark of
the covenant of the LORD journeying in front of them for the three days, to seek out a
resting place for them.
34 The cloud of the LORD was over them by day when they set out from the camp.
35 Then it came about when the ark set out that Moses said,
"Rise up, O LORD!
And let Your enemies be scattered,
And let those who hate You flee [12]before You."
36 When it came to rest, he said,
"Return, O LORD,
To the myriad thousands of Israel."

The People Complain

11 Now the people became like those who complain of adversity in the hearing of the
LORD; and when the LORD heard *it,* His anger was kindled, and the fire of the
LORD burned among them and consumed *some* of the outskirts of the camp.
2 The people therefore cried out to Moses, and Moses prayed to the LORD and the
fire died out.
3 So the name of that place was called [13]Taberah, because the fire of the LORD burned
among them.
4 The rabble who were among them had greedy desires; and also the sons of Israel
wept again and said, "Who will give us meat to eat?
5 "We remember the fish which we used to eat free in Egypt, the cucumbers and the
melons and the leeks and the onions and the garlic,
6 but now our [14]appetite is gone. There is nothing at all to look at except this manna."
7 Now the manna was like coriander seed, and its appearance like that of bdellium.
8 The people would go about and gather *it* and grind *it* between two millstones or beat
it in the mortar, and boil *it* in the pot and make cakes with it; and its taste was as the taste
of cakes baked with oil.
9 When the dew fell on the camp at night, the manna would fall with it.

10:29 Judg 4:11; Ex 2:18; 3:1; 18:12; Gen 12:7; Ex 6:4-8; Ps 95:1-7; 100:1-5; Deut 4:40; 30:5
10:30 Judg 1:16; Matt 21:28, 29
10:31 Job 29:15
10:32 Ps 22:27-31; 67:5-7; Lev 19:34; Deut 10:18
10:33 Num 10:12; Deut 1:33; Is 11:10
10:34 Num 9:15-23
10:35 Ps 68:1, 2; Is 17:12-14; Deut 7:10; 32:41
10:36 Is 63:17; Deut 1:10
11:1 Num 14:2; 16:11; 17:5; Num 11:18; 14:28
11:2 Num 12:11, 13; 21:7
11:3 Deut 9:22
11:4 Ex 12:38; 1 Cor 10:6; Ps 78:20
11:5 Ex 16:3
11:6 Num 21:5
11:7 Ex 16:31; Gen 2:12
11:9 Ex 16:13, 14

12 Or *from Your presence* **13** I.e. burning **14** Lit *soul is dried up*

10:29–32 By complimenting Hobab's wilderness skills, Moses let him know he was needed. People cannot know you appreciate them if you do not tell them they are important to you. Complimenting those who deserve it builds lasting relationships and helps people know they are valued. Think about those who have helped you this month. What can you do to let them know how much you need and appreciate them?

11:1, 6–15 The Israelites complained, and then Moses complained. But God responded positively to Moses and negatively to the rest of the people. Why? The people complained *to one another,* and nothing was accomplished. Moses took his complaint *to God,* who could solve any problem. Many of us are good at complaining to each other. We need to learn to take our problems to the One who can do something about them.

11:4 The *rabble* refers to a mixed crowd of Egyptians and others who had followed Israel out of Egypt (Exodus 12:38).

11:4–6 Dissatisfaction comes when our attention shifts from what we have to what we don't have. The people of Israel didn't seem to notice what God was doing for them—setting them free, making them a nation, giving them a new land—because they were so wrapped up in what God wasn't doing for them. They could think of nothing but the delicious Egyptian food they had left behind. Somehow they forgot that the brutal whip of Egyptian slavery was the cost of eating that food. Before we judge the Israelites too harshly, it's helpful to think about what occupies our attention most of the time. Are we grateful for what God has given us, or are we always thinking about what we would like to have? We should not allow our unfulfilled desires to cause us to forget God's gifts of life, food, health, work, and friends.

11:4–9 Every morning the Israelites drew back their tent doors and witnessed a miracle. Covering the ground was white, fluffy manna—food from heaven. But soon that wasn't enough. Feeling it was their right to have more, they forgot what they already had. They didn't ask God to fill their need; instead they demanded meat, and they stopped trusting God to care for them. "Who will give us meat to eat?" they complained to Moses as they reminisced about the good food they had in Egypt. God gave them what they asked for, but they paid dearly for it when a plague struck the camp (see 11:18–20, 31–34). When you ask God for something, he may grant your request. But if you approach him with a sinful attitude, getting what you want may prove costly.

The Complaint of Moses

10 Now Moses heard the people weeping throughout their families, each man at the
doorway of his tent; and the anger of the LORD was kindled greatly, and Moses was displeased.

11:11 Ex 5:22; Deut 1:12

11 So Moses said to the LORD, "Why have You [15]been so hard on Your servant? And
why have I not found favor in Your sight, that You have laid the burden of all this people on me?

11:12 2 Kin 10:1, 5; Is 49:23; Gen 24:7; Ex 13:5, 11; 33:1

12 "Was it I who conceived all this people? Was it I who brought them forth, that You
should say to me, 'Carry them in your bosom as a nurse carries a nursing infant, to the
land which You swore to their fathers'?

11:13 Num 11:21, 22; John 6:5-9

13 "Where am I to get meat to give to all this people? For they weep before me, saying,
'Give us meat that we may eat!'

11:14 Ex 18:18; Deut 1:12

14 "I alone am not able to carry all this people, because it is too burdensome for me.

11:15 Ex 32:32

15 "So if You are going to deal thus with me, please kill me at once, if I have found
favor in Your sight, and do not let me see my wretchedness."

Seventy Elders to Assist

11:16 Ex 24:1, 9; Ex 18:25

16 The LORD therefore said to Moses, "Gather for Me seventy men from the elders of
Israel, whom you know to be the elders of the people and their officers and bring them
to the tent of meeting, and let them take their stand there with you.

11:17 Num 11:25 1 Sam 10:6; Joel 2:28

17 "Then I will come down and speak with you there, and I will take of the Spirit who is
upon you, and will put *Him* upon them; and they shall bear the burden of the people
with you, so that you will not bear *it* all alone.

11:18 Ex 19:10, 22; Num 11:1

18 "Say to the people, 'Consecrate yourselves for tomorrow, and you shall eat meat; for
you have wept in the ears of the LORD, saying, "Oh that someone would give us meat to
eat! For we were well-off in Egypt." Therefore the LORD will give you meat and you
shall eat.

19 'You shall eat, not one day, nor two days, nor five days, nor ten days, nor twenty days,

15 Lit *dealt ill with*

ISRAEL'S COMPLAINING

Reference	*Complaint*	*Sin*	*Result*
11:1	About their hardships	Complained about their problems instead of praying to God about them	Thousands of people were destroyed when God sent a plague of fire to punish them
11:4	About the lack of meat	Lusted after things they didn't have	God sent quail; but as the people began to eat, God struck them with a plague that killed many
14:1–4	About being stuck in the wilderness, facing the giants of the promised land, and wishing to return to Egypt	Openly rebelled against God's leaders and failed to trust in his promises	All who complained were not allowed to enter the promised land, being doomed to wander in the wilderness until they died
16:3	About Moses' and Aaron's authority and leadership	Were greedy for more power and authority	The families, friends, and possessions of Korah, Dathan, and Abiram were swallowed up by the earth. Fire then burned up the 250 other men who rebelled
16:41	That Moses and Aaron caused the deaths of Korah and his conspirators	Blamed others for their own troubles	God began to destroy Israel with a plague. Moses and Aaron made atonement for the people, but 14,700 of them were killed
20:2–3	About the lack of water	Refused to believe that God would provide as he had promised	Moses sinned along with the people. For this he was barred from entering the promised land
21:5	That God and Moses brought them into the wilderness	Failed to recognize that their problems were brought on by their own disobedience	God sent fiery serpents that killed many people and seriously injured many others

20 but a whole month, until it comes out of your nostrils and becomes loathsome to
you; because you have rejected the LORD who is among you and have wept before Him,
saying, "Why did we ever leave Egypt?" ' "
21 But Moses said, "The people, among whom I am, are 600,000 on foot; yet You have
said, 'I will give them meat, so that they may eat for a whole month.'
22 "Should flocks and herds be slaughtered for them, to be sufficient for them? Or should
all the fish of the sea be gathered together for them, to be sufficient for them?"
23 The LORD said to Moses, "Is the LORD'S power limited? Now you shall see whether
My word will come true for you or not."
24 So Moses went out and told the people the words of the LORD. Also, he gathered
seventy men of the elders of the people, and stationed them around the tent.
25 Then the LORD came down in the cloud and spoke to him; and He took of the Spirit
who was upon him and placed *Him* upon the seventy elders. And when the Spirit rested
upon them, they prophesied. But they did not do *it* again.
26 But two men had remained in the camp; the name of one was Eldad and the name
of the other Medad. And the Spirit rested upon them (now they were among those who
had been registered, but had not gone out to the tent), and they prophesied in the camp.
27 So a young man ran and told Moses and said, "Eldad and Medad are prophesying
in the camp."
28 Then Joshua the son of Nun, the attendant of Moses from his youth, said, "Moses,
my lord, restrain them."
29 But Moses said to him, "Are you jealous for my sake? Would that all the LORD'S
people were prophets, that the LORD would put His Spirit upon them!"
30 Then Moses returned to the camp, *both* he and the elders of Israel.

11:20 Josh 24:27; 1 Sam 10:19
11:23 Is 50:2; 59:1; Ezek 12:25; 24:14
11:24 Num 11:16
11:25 Num 11:17; 12:5
11:26 Num 24:2; 1 Sam 10:6; 2 Chr 15:1; Neh 9:30
11:28 Ex 33:11; Josh 1:1; Mark 9:38-40
11:29 1 Cor 14:5

The Quail and the Plague

31 Now there went forth a wind from the LORD and it brought quail from the sea, and
let *them* fall beside the camp, about a day's journey on this side and a day's journey on
the other side, all around the camp and about two cubits *deep* on the surface of the ground.
32 The people spent all day and all night and all the next day, and gathered the quail
(he who gathered least gathered ten homers) and they spread *them* out for themselves
all around the camp.
33 While the meat was still between their teeth, before it was chewed, the anger of the
LORD was kindled against the people, and the LORD struck the people with a very severe plague.
34 So the name of that place was called [16]Kibroth-hattaavah, because there they buried the people who had been greedy.
35 From Kibroth-hattaavah the people set out for Hazeroth, and they remained at
Hazeroth.

11:31 Ex 16:13; Ps 78:26-28; 105:40
11:32 Ezek 45:11
11:33 Ps 78:29-31; 106:15
11:34 Deut 9:22
11:35 Num 33:17

2. Miriam and Aaron oppose Moses

The Murmuring of Miriam and Aaron

12 Then Miriam and Aaron spoke against Moses because of the Cushite woman whom
he had married (for he had married a Cushite woman);

12:1 Ex 2:21

16 I.e. the graves of greediness

11:21–22 Moses had witnessed God's power in spectacular miracles, yet at this time he questioned God's ability to feed the wandering Israelites. If Moses doubted God's power, how much easier it is for us to do the same. But completely depending upon God is essential, regardless of our level of spiritual maturity. When we begin to rely on our own understanding, we are in danger of ignoring God's assessment of the situation. By remembering his past works and his present power, we can be sure that we are not cutting off his potential help.

11:23 How strong is God? It is easy to trust God when we see his mighty acts (the Israelites saw many), but after a while, in the routine of daily life, his strength may appear to diminish. God doesn't change, but our view of him often does. The monotony of day-by-day living lulls us into forgetting how powerful God can be. As Moses learned, God's strength is always available.

11:26–29 This incident is similar to a story told in Mark 9:38–41. The disciples wanted Jesus to forbid others to drive out demons because they were not part of the disciples' group. But this type of narrow attitude was condemned by both Moses and Jesus. Beware of putting limits on God—he can work through whomever he chooses.

11:34 Craving or lusting is more than inappropriate sexual desire. It can be an unnatural or greedy desire for anything (sports, knowledge, possessions, influence over others). In this circumstance, God punished the Israelites for craving good food! Their desire was not wrong; the sin was in allowing that desire to turn into greed. They felt it was their right to have fine food, and they could think of nothing else. When you become preoccupied with something until it affects your perspective on everything else, you have moved from desire to lust.

2 and they said, "Has the LORD indeed spoken only through Moses? Has He not spoken through us as well?" And the LORD heard it.
3 (Now the man Moses was very humble, more than any man who was on the face of
the earth.)
4 Suddenly the LORD said to Moses and Aaron and to Miriam, "You three come out
to the tent of meeting." So the three of them came out.
5 Then the LORD came down in a pillar of cloud and stood at the doorway of the tent,
and He called Aaron and Miriam. When they had both come forward,
6 He said,
"Hear now My words:
If there is a prophet among you,
I, the LORD, shall make Myself known to him in a vision.
I shall speak with him in a dream.
7 "Not so, with My servant Moses,
He is faithful in all My household;
8 With him I speak mouth to mouth,
Even openly, and not in dark sayings,
And he beholds the form of the LORD.
Why then were you not afraid
To speak against My servant, against Moses?"
9 So the anger of the LORD burned against them and He departed.
10 But when the cloud had withdrawn from over the tent, behold, Miriam *was* leprous,
as *white as* snow. As Aaron turned toward Miriam, behold, she *was* leprous.
11 Then Aaron said to Moses, "Oh, my lord, I beg you, do not account *this* sin to us, in
which we have acted foolishly and in which we have sinned.
12 "Oh, do not let her be like one dead, whose flesh is half eaten away when he comes
from his mother's womb!"
13 Moses cried out to the LORD, saying, "O God, heal her, I pray!"
14 But the LORD said to Moses, "If her father had but spit in her face, would she not
bear her shame for seven days? Let her be shut up for seven days outside the camp, and
afterward she may be received again."
15 So Miriam was shut up outside the camp for seven days, and the people did not move
on until Miriam was received again.
16 Afterward, however, the people moved out from Hazeroth and camped in the wilderness of Paran.

3. The spies incite rebellion

Spies View the Land

13 Then the LORD spoke to Moses saying,
2 "Send out for yourself men so that they may spy out the land of Canaan, which
I am going to give to the sons of Israel; you shall send a man from each of their fathers'
tribes, every one a leader among them."

12:2 Num 16:3
12:3 Matt 11:29
12:5 Ex 19:9; 34:5
12:6 Gen 46:2; 1 Sam 3:15; Gen 31:11; 1 Kin 3:5, 15
12:7 Josh 1:1; Heb 3:2, 5
12:8 Deut 34:10; Hos 12:13; Ex 20:4; 24:10, 11; Deut 5:8; Ps 17:15
12:9 Gen 17:22; 18:33
12:10 Deut 24:9; Ex 4:6; 2 Kin 5:27
12:11 2 Sam 19:19; 24:10
12:13 Ps 30:2; 41:4; Is 30:26; Jer 17:14
12:14 Deut 25:9; Job 17:6; 30:10; Is 50:6; Num 5:1-4
12:15 Deut 24:9
13:1 Deut 1:22, 23
13:2 Deut 1:22; 9:23

12:1 Moses didn't have a Jewish wife because he lived with the Egyptians the first 40 years of his life, and he was in the wilderness the next 40 years. The woman is probably not Zipporah, his first wife, who was a Midianite (see Exodus 2:21). A Cushite was an Ethiopian. There is no explanation given for why Miriam objected to this woman.

12:1 People often argue over minor disagreements, leaving the real issue untouched. Such was the case when Miriam and Aaron came to Moses with a complaint. They represented the priests and the prophets, the two most powerful groups next to Moses. The real issue was their growing jealousy of Moses' position and influence. Since they could not find fault with the way Moses was leading the people, they chose to criticize his wife. Rather than face the problem squarely by dealing with their envy and pride, they chose to create a diversion from the real issue. When you are in a disagreement, stop and ask yourself if you are arguing over the real issue or if you have introduced a smoke screen by attacking someone's character. If you are unjustly criticized, remember that your critics may be afraid to face the real problem. Don't take this type of criticism personally. Ask God to help you identify the real issue and deal with it.

12:11 Aaron asked that the sin he and Miriam committed not be held against them. It is easy to look back at our mistakes and recognize their foolishness. It is much harder to recognize foolish plans while we are carrying them out because somehow then they seem appropriate. To get rid of foolish ideas before they turn into foolish actions requires eliminating our wrong thoughts and motives. Failing to do this caused Miriam and Aaron much grief.

12:14 Spitting in someone's face was considered the ultimate insult and a sign of shame imposed on wrongdoers. The religious leaders spat in Jesus' face to insult him (Matthew 26:67). God punished Miriam for her smug attitude toward not only Moses' authority, but also God's. He struck her with leprosy, then ordered her out of the camp for a week. This punishment was actually quite lenient. A week was the length of time she would have been excluded if her father had spat in her face. How much more she deserved for wronging God! Once again, God was merciful while retaining an effective discipline.

3 So Moses sent them from the wilderness of Paran at the command of the LORD, all
of them men who were heads of the sons of Israel.
4 These then *were* their names: from the tribe of Reuben, Shammua the son of
Zaccur;
5 from the tribe of Simeon, Shaphat the son of Hori;
6 from the tribe of Judah, Caleb the son of Jephunneh;
7 from the tribe of Issachar, Igal the son of Joseph;
8 from the tribe of Ephraim, Hoshea the son of Nun;
9 from the tribe of Benjamin, Palti the son of Raphu;
10 from the tribe of Zebulun, Gaddiel the son of Sodi;
11 from the tribe of Joseph, from the tribe of Manasseh, Gaddi the son of Susi;
12 from the tribe of Dan, Ammiel the son of Gemalli;
13 from the tribe of Asher, Sethur the son of Michael;
14 from the tribe of Naphtali, Nahbi the son of Vophsi;
15 from the tribe of Gad, Geuel the son of Machi.
16 These are the names of the men whom Moses sent to spy out the land; but Moses
called Hoshea the son of Nun, Joshua.
17 When Moses sent them to spy out the land of Canaan, he said to them, "Go up there
into the [17]Negev; then go up into the hill country.
18 "See what the land is like, and whether the people who live in it are strong *or* weak,
whether they are few or many.
19 "How is the land in which they live, is it good or bad? And how are the cities in which
they live, are *they* like *open* camps or with fortifications?
20 "How is the land, is it fat or lean? Are there trees in it or not? Make an effort then to
get some of the fruit of the land." Now the time was the time of the first ripe grapes.
21 So they went up and spied out the land from the wilderness of Zin as far as Rehob,
at Lebo-hamath.
22 When they had gone up into the Negev, they came to Hebron where Ahiman, Sheshai and Talmai, the descendants of Anak were. (Now Hebron was built seven years before
Zoan in Egypt.)
23 Then they came to the valley of [18]Eshcol and from there cut down a branch with a
single cluster of grapes; and they carried it on a pole between two *men,* with some of the
pomegranates and the figs.
24 That place was called the valley of Eshcol, because of the cluster which the sons of
Israel cut down from there.

The Spies' Reports

25 When they returned from spying out the land, at the end of forty days,
26 they proceeded to come to Moses and Aaron and to all the congregation of the sons
of Israel in the wilderness of Paran, at Kadesh; and they brought back word to them and
to all the congregation and showed them the fruit of the land.
27 Thus they told him, and said, "We went in to the land where you sent us; and it certainly does flow with milk and honey, and this is its fruit.

13:6 Num 14:6, 30; Josh 14:6
13:8 Num 13:16; Deut 32:44
13:16 Num 13:8; Deut 32:44
13:17 Gen 12:9; 13:1, 3
13:20 Deut 1:24, 25; Deut 31:6, 23
13:21 Num 20:1; 27:14; 33:36; Josh 13:5
13:22 Num 13:17; Josh 15:14; Num 13:28, 33; Ps 78:12, 43
13:23 Gen 14:13; Num 13:24; 32:9; Deut 1:24
13:26 Num 20:1, 14; 32:8
13:27 Ex 3:8, 17; 13:5; Deut 1:25

17 I.e. South country, and so throughout the ch **18** I.e. cluster

13:17–20 Moses decided what information was needed before the people could enter the promised land, and he took careful steps to get that information. When you are making decisions or assuming new responsibilities, remember these two important steps. Ask yourself what you need to know about the opportunity, and then obtain that knowledge. Common sense is a valuable aid in accomplishing God's purposes.

13:25–29 God told the Israelites that the promised land was rich and fertile. Not only that, he promised that this bountiful land would be theirs. When the spies reported back to Moses, they gave plenty of good reasons for entering the land, but they couldn't stop focusing on their fear. Talk of giants (descendants of Anak) and fortified cities made it easy to forget about God's promise to help. When facing a tough decision, don't let the negatives cause you to lose sight of the positives. Weigh both sides carefully. Don't let potential difficulties blind you to God's power to help and his promise to guide.

13:26 Although Kadesh was only a wilderness oasis, it was a crossroads in Israel's history. When the spies returned to Kadesh from scouting the new land, the people had to decide either to enter the land or to retreat. They chose to retreat and were condemned to wander 40 years in the wilderness. It was also at Kadesh that Moses disobeyed God (20:7–12). For this, he too was denied entrance into the promised land. Aaron and Miriam died there, for they could not enter the new land either. Kadesh was near Canaan's southern borders, but because of the Israelites' lack of faith, they needed more than a lifetime to go from Kadesh to the promised land.

13:27 The promised land, also called the land of Canaan, was indeed magnificent, as the 12 spies discovered. The Bible often calls it the land flowing with milk and honey. Although the land was relatively small—150 miles long and 60 miles wide—its lush hillsides were covered with fig, date, and nut trees. It was the land God had promised to Abraham, Isaac, and Jacob.

13:28 Deut 1:28; 9:1, 2; Num 13:33

13:29 Num 13:17; 14:25, 45; Josh 10:6; Num 14:43, 45

13:31 Deut 1:28; 9:1-3

13:32 Num 14:36, 37; Ps 106:24; Ezek 36:13, 14; Amos 2:9

28 "Nevertheless, the people who live in the land are strong, and the cities are fortified
and very large; and moreover, we saw the descendants of Anak there.
29 "Amalek is living in the land of the Negev and the Hittites and the Jebusites and the
Amorites are living in the hill country, and the Canaanites are living by the sea and by
the side of the Jordan."
30 Then Caleb quieted the people before Moses and said, "We should by all means go
up and take possession of it, for we will surely overcome it."
31 But the men who had gone up with him said, "We are not able to go up against the
people, for they are too strong for us."
32 So they gave out to the sons of Israel a bad report of the land which they had spied
out, saying, "The land through which we have gone, in spying it out, is a land that devours its inhabitants; and all the people whom we saw in it are men of *great* size.

MIRIAM

Ask older brothers or sisters what their greatest trial in life is and they will often answer, "My younger brother (or sister)!" This is especially true when the younger sibling is more successful than the older. The bonds of family loyalty can be strained to the breaking point.

When we first meet Miriam she is involved in one of history's most unusual baby-sitting jobs. She is watching her infant brother float on the Nile River in a waterproof cradle. Miriam's quick thinking allowed Moses to be raised by his own mother. Her protective superiority, reinforced by that event, must have been hard to give up as she watched her little brother rise to greatness.

Eventually Moses' choice of a wife gave Miriam an opportunity to criticize. It was natural for her insecurity to break out over this issue. With Moses married, Miriam was clearly no longer the most important woman in his life. The real issue, however, was not the kind of woman Moses had married. It was the fact that he was now the most important man in Israel. "Has the LORD indeed spoken only through Moses? . . . Has He not spoken through us as well?" No mention is made of Moses' response, but God had a quick answer for Miriam and Aaron. Without denying their role in his plan, God clearly pointed out his special relationship with Moses. Miriam was stricken with leprosy, a deadly disease, as punishment for her insubordination. But Moses, true to his character, intervened for his sister so that God healed Miriam of her leprosy.

Before criticizing someone else, we need to pause long enough to discover our own motives. Failing to do this can bring disastrous results. What is often labeled "constructive criticism" may actually be destructive jealousy, since the easiest way to raise our own status is to bring someone else down. Are you willing to question your motives before you offer criticism? Does the critical finger you point need to be pointed first toward yourself?

Strengths and accomplishments:
- Quick thinker under pressure
- Able leader
- Songwriter
- Prophetess

Weaknesses and mistakes:
- Was jealous of Moses' authority
- Openly criticized Moses' leadership

Lesson from her life:
- The motives behind criticism are often more important to deal with than the criticism itself

Vital statistics:
- Where: Egypt, Sinai peninsula
- Relatives: Brothers: Aaron and Moses

Key verses:
"Miriam the prophetess, Aaron's sister, took the timbrel in her hand, and all the women went out after her with timbrels and with dancing. Miriam answered them, 'Sing to the LORD, for He is highly exalted; the horse and his rider He has hurled into the sea' " (Exodus 15:20–21).

Miriam's story is told in Exodus 2; 15; and Numbers 12; 20. She is also mentioned in Deuteronomy 24:9; 1 Chronicles 6:3; Micah 6:4.

13:28 The "descendants of Anak" were a race of abnormally large people. The family of Goliath may have been descended from these people (see 2 Samuel 21:16–22).

13:28–29 The fortified cities the spies talked about were surrounded by high walls as much as 20 feet thick and 25 feet tall. Guards were often stationed on top, where there was a commanding view of the countryside. Some of the inhabitants, said the spies, were formidable men—from seven to nine feet tall—so that the Israelites felt like grasshoppers next to them (13:33). The fortified cities and the giants struck fear into the hearts of most of the spies.

13:30–32 Imagine standing before a crowd and loudly voicing an unpopular opinion! Caleb was willing to take the unpopular stand to do as God had commanded. To be effective when you go against the crowd, you must: (1) have the facts (Caleb had seen the land himself); (2) have the right attitude (Caleb trusted God's promise to give Israel the land); (3) state clearly what you believe (Caleb said, "We will surely overcome it").

33 "There also we saw the Nephilim (the sons of Anak are part of the Nephilim); and
we became like grasshoppers in our own sight, and so we were in their sight."

The People Rebel

14 Then all the congregation lifted up their voices and cried, and the people wept
that night.
2 All the sons of Israel grumbled against Moses and Aaron; and the whole congregation said to them, "Would that we had died in the land of Egypt! Or would that we had
died in this wilderness!
3 "Why is the LORD bringing us into this land, to fall by the sword? Our wives and our
little ones will become plunder; would it not be better for us to return to Egypt?"
4 So they said to one another, "Let us appoint a leader and return to Egypt."
5 Then Moses and Aaron fell on their faces in the presence of all the assembly of the
congregation of the sons of Israel.
6 Joshua the son of Nun and Caleb the son of Jephunneh, of those who had spied out
the land, tore their clothes;
7 and they spoke to all the congregation of the sons of Israel, saying, "The land which
we passed through to spy out is an exceedingly good land.
8 "If the LORD is pleased with us, then He will bring us into this land and give it to
us—a land which flows with milk and honey.
9 "Only do not rebel against the LORD; and do not fear the people of the land, for they
will be our prey. Their protection has been removed from them, and the LORD is with
us; do not fear them."
10 But all the congregation said to stone them with stones. Then the glory of the LORD
appeared in the tent of meeting to all the sons of Israel.

13:33 Gen 6:4; Deut 1:28; 9:2; Josh 11:21
14:2 Num 11:1; Num 11:5; 16:13; 20:3, 4; 21:5
14:3 Ex 5:21; 16:3; Num 14:31; Deut 1:39
14:4 Neh 9:17
14:5 Num 16:4
14:7 Num 13:27; Deut 1:25
14:8 Deut 10:15; Ex 3:8; Num 13:27
14:9 Deut 1:26; 9:23, 24; Deut 1:21, 29
14:10 Ex 17:4; Ex 16:10; Lev 9:23

13:33 The Nephilim were giants who lived on the earth before the flood (Genesis 6:4).

13:33—14:4 The negative opinion of ten men caused a great rebellion among the people. Because it is human nature to accept opinion as fact, we must be especially careful when voicing our negative opinions. What we say may heavily influence the actions of those who trust us to give sound advice.

14:1–4 When the chorus of despair went up, everyone joined in. Their greatest fears were being realized. Losing their perspective, the people were caught up in the emotion of the moment, forgetting what they knew about God's character. What if the people had spent as much energy moving forward as they did moving back? They could have enjoyed their land—instead they never even entered it. When a cry of despair goes up around you, consider the larger perspective before you join in. You have better ways to use your energy than to complain.

14:5–9 With great miracles, God had led the Israelites out of slavery, through the desolate wilderness, and up to the very edge of the promised land. He had protected them, fed them, and fulfilled every promise. Yet when encouraged to take that last step of faith and enter the land, the people refused. After witnessing so many miracles, why did they stop trusting God? Why did they refuse to enter the promised land when that had been their goal since leaving Egypt? They were afraid. Often we do the same thing. We trust God to handle the smaller issues but doubt his ability to take care of the big problems, the tough decisions, the frightening situations. Don't stop trusting God just as you are ready to reach your goal. He brought you this far and won't let you down now. We can continue trusting God by remembering all he has done for us.

14:6 Tearing clothing was a customary way of showing deep sorrow, mourning, or despair. Joshua and Caleb were greatly distressed by the people's refusal to enter the land.

14:6–10 Two wise men, Joshua and Caleb, encouraged the people to act on God's promise and move ahead into the land. The people rejected their advice and even talked of killing them. Don't be too quick to reject advice you don't like. Evaluate it carefully, comparing it to the teaching in God's Word. The advice may be God's message.

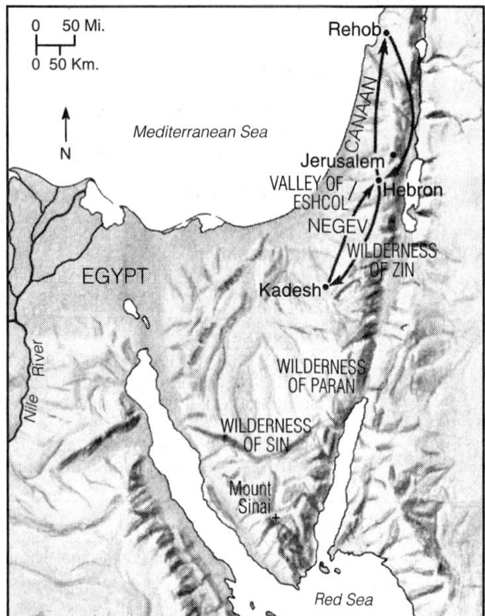

ROUTE OF THE SCOUTS
The scouts traveled from Kadesh at the southernmost edge of the wilderness of Zin to Rehob at the northernmost edge and back, a round trip of about 500 miles.

Moses Pleads for the People

11 The LORD said to Moses, "How long will this people spurn Me? And how long will
they not believe in Me, despite all the signs which I have performed in their midst?
12 "I will smite them with pestilence and dispossess them, and I will make you into a
nation greater and mightier than they."
13 But Moses said to the LORD, "Then the Egyptians will hear of it, for by Your strength
You brought up this people from their midst,
14 and they will tell *it* to the inhabitants of this land. They have heard that You, O LORD,
are in the midst of this people, for You, O LORD, are seen eye to eye, while Your cloud
stands over them; and You go before them in a pillar of cloud by day and in a pillar of
fire by night.
15 "Now if You slay this people as one man, then the nations who have heard of Your
fame will say,
16 'Because the LORD could not bring this people into the land which He promised them
by oath, therefore He slaughtered them in the wilderness.'
17 "But now, I pray, let the power of the Lord be great, just as You have declared,
18 'The LORD is slow to anger and abundant in lovingkindness, forgiving iniquity and
transgression; but He will by no means clear *the guilty,* visiting the iniquity of the fathers
on the children to the third and the fourth *generations.*'
19 "Pardon, I pray, the iniquity of this people according to the greatness of Your
lovingkindness, just as You also have forgiven this people, from Egypt even until now."

The LORD Pardons and Rebukes

20 So the LORD said, "I have pardoned *them* according to your word;
21 but indeed, as I live, all the earth will be filled with the glory of the LORD.
22 "Surely all the men who have seen My glory and My signs which I performed in Egypt
and in the wilderness, yet have put Me to the test these ten times and have not listened
to My voice,
23 shall by no means see the land which I swore to their fathers, nor shall any of those
who spurned Me see it.
24 "But My servant Caleb, because he has had a different spirit and has followed Me
fully, I will bring into the land which he entered, and his descendants shall take possession of it.
25 "Now the Amalekites and the Canaanites live in the valleys; turn tomorrow and set
out to the wilderness by the way of the Red Sea."
26 The LORD spoke to Moses and Aaron, saying,
27 "How long *shall I bear* with this evil congregation who are grumbling against Me? I
have heard the complaints of the sons of Israel, which they are making against Me.
28 "Say to them, 'As I live,' says the LORD, 'just as you have spoken in My hearing,
so I will surely do to you;
29 your corpses will fall in this wilderness, even all your numbered men, according to
your complete number from twenty years old and upward, who have grumbled
against Me.
30 'Surely you shall not come into the land in which I swore to settle you, except Caleb
the son of Jephunneh and Joshua the son of Nun.

14:11 Ex 32:9 13; Ps 106:24
14:12 Lev 26:25; Deut 28:21; Ex 32:10
14:13 Ex 32:11-14; Ps 106:23
14:14 Ex 13:21; Deut 5:4
14:15 Ex 32:12
14:16 Josh 7:7
14:18 Ex 20:6; 34:6, 7; Deut 5:10; 7:9; Ps 103:8; 145:8; Jon 4:2; Ex 20:5; Deut 5:9; 7:10; Ex 34:7
14:19 Ex 32:32; 34:9
14:20 Mic 7:18-20
14:21 Num 14:28; Deut 32:40; Is 49:18; Is 6:3; Hab 2:14
14:22 1 Cor 10:5; Ex 5:21; 14:11; 15:24; 16:2; 17:2, 3; 32:1; Num 11:1, 4; 12:1; 14:2
14:23 Num 26:65; 32:11; Heb 3:18
14:24 Num 14:6-9; Num 26:65; 32:12; Deut 1:36; Josh 14:6-15
14:25 Num 13:29
14:27 Num 11:1
14:28 Num 14:21; Num 14:2; Deut 2:14, 15; Heb 3:17
14:29 Heb 3:17; Num 1:45, 46

14:17–20 Moses pleaded with God, asking him to forgive his people. His plea reveals several characteristics of God: (1) God is immensely patient; (2) God's love is one promise we can always count on; (3) God forgives again and again; and (4) God is merciful, listening to and answering our requests. God has not changed since Moses' day. Like Moses, we can rely on God's love, patience, forgiveness, and mercy.

14:20–23 The people of Israel had a clearer view of God than any people before them, for they had both his laws and his physical presence. Their refusal to follow God after witnessing his miraculous deeds and listening to his words made the judgment against them more severe. Increased opportunity brings increased responsibility. As Jesus said: "From everyone who has been given much, much will be required" (Luke 12:48). How much greater is our responsibility to obey and serve God—we have the whole Bible, and we know God's Son, Jesus Christ.

14:22 God wasn't exaggerating when he said that the Israelites had already failed ten times to trust and obey him. Here is a list of their ten failures: (1) lacking trust at the crossing of the Red Sea (Exodus 14:11–12); (2) complaining over bitter water at Marah (Exodus 15:24); (3) complaining in the wilderness of Sin (Exodus 16:3); (4) collecting more than the daily quota of manna (Exodus 16:20); (5) collecting manna on the Sabbath (Exodus 16:27–29); (6) complaining over lack of water at Rephidim (Exodus 17:2–3); (7) engaging in idolatry with a golden calf (Exodus 32:7–10); (8) complaining at Taberah (Numbers 11:1–2); (9) more complaining over the lack of delicious food (Numbers 11:4); (10) failing to trust God and enter the promised land (Numbers 14:1–4).

14:24 The fulfillment of this verse is recorded in Joshua 14:6–15 when Caleb received his inheritance in the promised land. Caleb followed God with all his heart and was rewarded for his obedience. Are you wholehearted in your commitment to obey God?

31 'Your children, however, whom you said would become a prey—I will bring them in, and they will know the land which you have rejected.

32 'But as for you, your corpses will fall in this wilderness.

33 'Your sons shall be shepherds for forty years in the wilderness, and they will suffer *for* your unfaithfulness, until your corpses lie in the wilderness.

34 'According to the number of days which you spied out the land, forty days, for every day you shall bear your guilt a year, *even* forty years, and you will know My opposition.

35 'I, the LORD, have spoken, surely this I will do to all this evil congregation who are gathered together against Me. In this wilderness they shall be destroyed, and there they will die.' "

36 As for the men whom Moses sent to spy out the land and who returned and made all the congregation grumble against him by bringing out a bad report concerning the land,

37 even those men who brought out the very bad report of the land died by a plague before the LORD.

38 But Joshua the son of Nun and Caleb the son of Jephunneh remained alive out of those men who went to spy out the land.

14:31 Num 14:3
14:32 Num 26:64, 65; 32:13; 1 Cor 10:5
14:33 Deut 2:7; 8:2, 4; 29:5
14:34 Num 13:25
14:35 Num 23:19
14:36 Num 13:4-16, 32
14:37 1 Cor 10:10; Heb 3:17, 18; Num 16:49

Israel Repulsed

39 When Moses spoke these words to all the sons of Israel, the people mourned greatly.

40 In the morning, however, they rose up early and went up to the ridge of the hill country, saying, "Here we are; we have indeed sinned, but we will go up to the place which the LORD has promised."

41 But Moses said, "Why then are you transgressing the commandment of the LORD, when it will not succeed?

42 "Do not go up, or you will be struck down before your enemies, for the LORD is not among you.

43 "For the Amalekites and the Canaanites will be there in front of you, and you will fall by the sword, inasmuch as you have turned back from following the LORD. And the LORD will not be with you."

44 But they went up heedlessly to the ridge of the hill country; neither the ark of the covenant of the LORD nor Moses left the camp.

45 Then the Amalekites and the Canaanites who lived in that hill country came down, and struck them and beat them down as far as Hormah.

14:39 Num 14:28-35; Ex 33:4
14:40 Deut 1:41-44
14:41 2 Chr 24:20
14:42 Deut 1:42
14:44 Num 31:6
14:45 Num 21:3

C. WANDERING IN THE WILDERNESS (15:1—21:35)

After their disobedience and unsuccessful attempt to enter the promised land, the Israelites were condemned to wander 40 years in the wilderness. Even in the midst of this punishment, the people continued to rebel and thus God continued to punish them. But the hearts of the people remained hard and rebellious. Hard hearts toward God may bring similar calamity to us.

1. Additional regulations

Laws for Canaan

15 Now the LORD spoke to Moses, saying,

2 "Speak to the sons of Israel and say to them, 'When you enter the land where you are to live, which I am giving you,

3 then make an offering by fire to the LORD, a burnt offering or a sacrifice to fulfill a

15:2 Lev 23:10
15:3 Lev 1:2, 3; Lev 22:21; Lev 23:1-44; Gen 8:21; 2 Cor 2:15, 16; Phil 4:18

14:34 God's judgment came in the form the people feared most. The people were afraid of dying in the wilderness, so God punished them by making them wander in the wilderness until they died. Now they wished they had the problem of facing the giants and the fortified cities of the promised land. Failing to trust God often brings even greater problems than those we originally faced. When we run from God, we inevitably run into problems.

14:35 Was this judgment—wandering 40 years in the wilderness—too harsh? Not compared to the instant death that God first threatened (14:12). Instead, God allowed the people to live. God had brought his people to the edge of the promised land, just as he said he would. He was ready to give them the rich land, but the people didn't want it (14:1–2). By this time, God had put up with a lot. At least ten times the people had refused to trust and obey him (14:22). The whole nation (except for Joshua, Caleb, Moses, and Aaron) showed contempt for and distrust of God. But God's punishment was not permanent. In 40 years, a new generation would have a chance to enter Canaan (Joshua 1—3).

14:40–44 When the Israelites realized their foolish mistake, they were suddenly ready to return to God. But God didn't confuse their admission of guilt with true repentance because he knew their hearts. Sure enough, they soon went their own way again. Sometimes right actions or good intentions come too late. We must not only do what is right, but also do it at the right time. God wants complete and instant obedience.

special vow, or as a freewill offering or in your appointed times, to make a soothing aroma
to the LORD, from the herd or from the flock.

15:4 Num 28:1-29:40

4 'The one who presents his offering shall present to the LORD a grain offering of one-
tenth *of an ephah* of fine flour mixed with one-fourth of a [19]hin of oil,

15:5 Lev 1:10; 3:6; Num 15:11

5 and you shall prepare wine for the drink offering, one-fourth of a hin, with the burnt
offering or for the sacrifice, for each lamb.
6 'Or for a ram you shall prepare as a grain offering two-tenths *of an ephah* of fine
flour mixed with one-third of a hin of oil;
7 and for the drink offering you shall offer one-third of a hin of wine as a soothing
aroma to the LORD.

15:8 Lev 1:3; 3:1

8 'When you prepare a bull as a burnt offering or a sacrifice, to fulfill a special vow, or
for peace offerings to the LORD,
9 then you shall offer with the bull a grain offering of three-tenths *of an ephah* of fine
flour mixed with one-half a hin of oil;
10 and you shall offer as the drink offering one-half a hin of wine as an offering by fire,
as a soothing aroma to the LORD.
11 'Thus it shall be done for each ox, or for each ram, or for each of the male lambs, or
of the goats.
12 'According to the number that you prepare, so you shall do for everyone according
to their number.
13 'All who are native shall do these things in this manner, in presenting an offering by
fire, as a soothing aroma to the LORD.

19 I.e. Approx one gal., and so through v 10

The voice of the minority is not often given a hearing. Nevertheless, truth cannot be measured by numbers. On the contrary, it often stands against majority opinion. Truth remains unchanged because it is guaranteed by the character of God. God is truth; what he says is the last word. At times, a person must even stand alone on the side of truth.

Caleb was not so much a man of great faith as a man of faith in a great God! His boldness rested on his understanding of God, not on his confidence in Israel's abilities to conquer the land. He could not agree with the majority, for that would be to disagree with God.

We, on the other hand, often base our decisions on what everyone else is doing. Few of us are first-order cowards like the ten spies. We are more like the people of Israel, getting our cowardice secondhand. Our search for right and wrong usually starts with questions such as "What do the experts say?" or "What do my friends say?" The question we most often avoid is "What does God say?" The principles we learn as we study the Bible provide a dependable road map for life. They draw us into a personal relationship with the God whose Word is the Bible. The God who gave Caleb his boldness is the same God who offers us the gift of eternal life through his Son, Jesus. That's truth worth believing!

Strengths and accomplishments:
- One of the spies sent by Moses to survey the land of Canaan
- One of the only two adults who left Egypt and entered the promised land
- Voiced the minority opinion in favor of conquering the land
- Expressed faith in God's promises, in spite of apparent obstacles

Lessons from his life:
- Majority opinion is not an accurate measurement of right and wrong
- Boldness based on God's faithfulness is appropriate
- For courage and faith to be effective, they must combine words and actions

Vital statistics:
- Where: From Egypt to the Sinai peninsula to the promised land, specifically Hebron
- Occupations: Spy, soldier, shepherd

Key verse:
"But My servant Caleb, because he has had a different spirit and has followed Me fully, I will bring into the land which he entered, and his descendants shall take possession of it" (Numbers 14:24).

Caleb's story is told in Numbers 13; 14 and Joshua 14; 15. He is also mentioned in Judges 1 and 1 Chronicles 4:15.

15:3 "A soothing aroma to the LORD" means that God would be pleased with their sacrifices.

Law of the Sojourner

14 'If an alien sojourns with you, or one who may be among you throughout your generations, and he *wishes to* make an offering by fire, as a soothing aroma to the LORD,
just as you do so he shall do.
15 '*As for* the assembly, there shall be one statute for you and for the alien who sojourns **15:15**
with you, a perpetual statute throughout your generations; as you are, so shall the alien Num 9:14; 15:29
be before the LORD.
16 'There is to be one law and one ordinance for you and for the alien who sojourns **15:16**
with you.' " Lev 24:22
17 Then the LORD spoke to Moses, saying,
18 "Speak to the sons of Israel and say to them, 'When you enter the land where I
bring you,
19 then it shall be, that when you eat of the food of the land, you shall lift up an offer- **15:19**
ing to the LORD. Josh 5:11, 12
20 'Of the first of your [20]dough you shall lift up a cake as an offering; as the offering of **15:20**
the threshing floor, so you shall lift it up. Ex 34:26; Lev 23:14; Deut 14:22, 23;
21 'From the first of your [20]dough you shall give to the LORD an offering throughout 16:13
your generations.
22 'But when you unwittingly fail and do not observe all these commandments, which **15:22**
the LORD has spoken to Moses, Lev 4:2
23 *even* all that the LORD has commanded you through Moses, from the day when the
LORD gave commandment and onward throughout your generations,
24 then it shall be, if it is done unintentionally, without the knowledge of the congre- **15:24**
gation, that all the congregation shall offer one bull for a burnt offering, as a soothing Lev 4:2, 22, 27;
aroma to the LORD, with its grain offering and its drink offering, according to the ordi- 5:15, 18; Num 15:8-10
nance, and one male goat for a sin offering.
25 'Then the priest shall make atonement for all the congregation of the sons of Israel, **15:25**
and they will be forgiven; for it was an error, and they have brought their offering, an Lev 4:20; Heb 2:17
offering by fire to the LORD, and their sin offering before the LORD, for their error.
26 'So all the congregation of the sons of Israel will be forgiven, with the alien who **15:26**
sojourns among them, for *it happened* to all the people through error. Num 15:24
27 'Also if one person sins unintentionally, then he shall offer a one year old female **15:27**
goat for a sin offering. Lev 4:27-31; Luke 12:48
28 'The priest shall make atonement before the LORD for the person who goes astray
when he sins unintentionally, making atonement for him that he may be forgiven. **15:28** Lev 4:35
29 'You shall have one law for him who does *anything* unintentionally, for him who is
native among the sons of Israel and for the alien who sojourns among them.
30 'But the person who does *anything* defiantly, whether he is native or an alien, that **15:30**
one is blaspheming the LORD; and that person shall be cut off from among his people. Num 14:40-44; Deut 1:43; 17:12, 13
31 'Because he has despised the word of the LORD and has broken His commandment,
that person shall be completely cut off; his guilt *will be* on him.' " **15:31** 2 Sam 12:9; Prov 13:13; Ezek 18:20

Sabbath-breaking Punished

32 Now while the sons of Israel were in the wilderness, they found a man gathering **15:32**
wood on the sabbath day. Ex 31:14, 15; 35:2, 3
33 Those who found him gathering wood brought him to Moses and Aaron and to all
the congregation;
34 and they put him in custody because it had not been declared what should be done **15:34**
to him. Num 9:8
35 Then the LORD said to Moses, "The man shall surely be put to death; all the con- **15:35**
gregation shall stone him with stones outside the camp." Lev 20:2, 27; 24:14-23; Deut 21:21
36 So all the congregation brought him outside the camp and stoned him to death with
stones, just as the LORD had commanded Moses.

20 Or *coarse meal*

15:30–31 God was willing to forgive those who made unintentional errors if they realized their mistakes quickly and corrected them. However, those who defiantly and deliberately sinned received a harsher judgment. Intentional sin grows out of an improper attitude toward God. A child who knowingly disobeys his parents challenges their authority and dares them to respond. Both the act and the attitude have to be dealt with.

15:32–36 Stoning a man for gathering wood on the Sabbath seems like a severe punishment, and it was. This act was a deliberate sin, defying God's law against working on the Sabbath. Perhaps the man was trying to get ahead of everyone else, in addition to breaking the Sabbath.

37 The LORD also spoke to Moses, saying,
15:38 Deut 22:12; Matt 23:5
38 "Speak to the sons of Israel, and tell them that they shall make for themselves tassels on the corners of their garments throughout their generations, and that they shall put on the tassel of each corner a cord of blue.
15:39 Deut 4:23; 6:12; 8:11, 14, 19
39 "It shall be a tassel for you to look at and remember all the commandments of the LORD, so as to do them and not follow after your own heart and your own eyes, after which you played the harlot,
15:40 Lev 11:44, 45
40 so that you may remember to do all My commandments and be holy to your God.
41 "I am the LORD your God who brought you out from the land of Egypt to be your God; I am the LORD your God."

2. Many leaders rebel against Moses

Korah's Rebellion

16:1 Ex 6:21; Jude 11; Num 26:9; Deut 11:6
16 Now Korah the son of Izhar, the son of Kohath, the son of Levi, with Dathan and Abiram, the sons of Eliab, and On the son of Peleth, sons of Reuben, took *action,*
16:2 Num 1:16; 26:9
2 and they rose up before Moses, together with some of the sons of Israel, two hundred and fifty leaders of the congregation, chosen in the assembly, men of renown.
16:3 Num 12:2; Ps 106:16; Num 16:7; Num 5:3
3 They assembled together against Moses and Aaron, and said to them, "You have gone far enough, for all the congregation are holy, every one of them, and the LORD is in their midst; so why do you exalt yourselves above the assembly of the LORD?"
16:4 Num 14:5
4 When Moses heard *this,* he fell on his face;
16:5 Lev 10:3; Ps 65:4; Num 17:5, 8
5 and he spoke to Korah and all his company, saying, "Tomorrow morning the LORD will show who is His, and who is holy, and will bring *him* near to Himself; even the one whom He will choose, He will bring near to Himself.
6 "Do this: take censers for yourselves, Korah and all your company,
16:7 Num 16:3
7 and put fire in them, and lay incense upon them in the presence of the LORD tomorrow; and the man whom the LORD chooses *shall be* the one who is holy. You have gone far enough, you sons of Levi!"
8 Then Moses said to Korah, "Hear now, you sons of Levi,
16:9 Is 7:13; Num 3:6, 9; Deut 10:8
9 is it not enough for you that the God of Israel has separated you from the *rest of* the congregation of Israel, to bring you near to Himself, to do the service of the tabernacle of the LORD, and to stand before the congregation to minister to them;
16:10 Num 3:10; 18:1-7
10 and that He has brought you near, *Korah,* and all your brothers, sons of Levi, with you? And are you seeking for the priesthood also?
16:11 Ex 16:7 1 Cor 10:10
11 "Therefore you and all your company are gathered together against the LORD; but as for Aaron, who is he that you grumble against him?"
12 Then Moses sent a summons to Dathan and Abiram, the sons of Eliab; but they said, "We will not come up.
16:13 Ex 16:3; Num 11:4-6; Num 14:2, 3
13 "Is it not enough that you have brought us up out of a land flowing with milk and honey to have us die in the wilderness, but you would also lord it over us?
16:14 Num 13:27; 14:8; Ex 22:5; 23:10, 11; Num 20:5; Judg 16:21; 1 Sam 11:2
14 "Indeed, you have not brought us into a land flowing with milk and honey, nor have you given us an inheritance of fields and vineyards. Would you put out the eyes of these men? We will not come up!"

15:39 The tassels were to remind people not to seek after their own lustful desires, but to seek the Lord. Idol worship is self-centered, focusing on what a person can get from serving an idol. Good luck, prosperity, long life, and success in battle were expected from the gods. So were power and prestige. The worship of God is the opposite. Believers are to be selfless rather than self-centered. Instead of expecting God to serve us, we are to serve him, expecting nothing in return. We serve God for who he is, not for what we get from him.

16:1–3 Korah and his associates had seen the advantages of the priesthood in Egypt. Egyptian priests had great wealth and political influence, something Korah wanted for himself. Korah may have assumed that Moses, Aaron, and his sons were trying to make the Israelite priesthood the same kind of political machine, and he wanted to be a part of it. He did not understand that Moses' main ambition was to serve God rather than to control others.

16:8–10 Moses saw through their charge to their true motivation—some of the Levites wanted the power of the priesthood. Like Korah, we often desire the special qualities God has given others. Korah had significant, worthwhile abilities and responsibilities of his own. In the end, however, his ambition for more caused him to lose everything. Inappropriate ambition is greed in disguise. Concentrate on finding the special purpose God has for you.

16:13–14 One of the easiest ways to fall away from following God is to look at our present problems and exaggerate them. Dathan and Abiram did just that when they began to long for better food and more pleasant surroundings. Egypt, the place they had longed to leave, was now looking better and better—not because of slavery and taskmasters, of course, but because of its mouth-watering food! These two men and their followers had completely lost their perspective. When we take our eyes off God and start looking at ourselves and our problems, we begin to lose our perspective as well. Overrating problems can hinder our relationship with God. Don't let difficulties make you lose sight of God's direction for your life.

15 Then Moses became very angry and said to the LORD, "Do not regard their offering! I have not taken a single donkey from them, nor have I done harm to any of them."
16 Moses said to Korah, "You and all your company be present before the LORD tomorrow, both you and they along with Aaron.
17 "Each of you take his firepan and put incense on it, and each of you bring his censer
before the LORD, two hundred and fifty firepans; also you and Aaron *shall* each *bring*
his firepan."
18 So they each took his *own* censer and put fire on it, and laid incense on it; and they
stood at the doorway of the tent of meeting, with Moses and Aaron.
19 Thus Korah assembled all the congregation against them at the doorway of the tent
of meeting. And the glory of the LORD appeared to all the congregation.
20 Then the LORD spoke to Moses and Aaron, saying,
21 "Separate yourselves from among this congregation, that I may consume them instantly."
22 But they fell on their faces and said, "O God, God of the spirits of all flesh, when
one man sins, will You be angry with the entire congregation?"
23 Then the LORD spoke to Moses, saying,
24 "Speak to the congregation, saying, 'Get back from around the dwellings of Korah,
Dathan and Abiram.' "
25 Then Moses arose and went to Dathan and Abiram, with the elders of Israel following him,
26 and he spoke to the congregation, saying, "Depart now from the tents of these wicked
men, and touch nothing that belongs to them, or you will be swept away in all their sin."
27 So they got back from around the dwellings of Korah, Dathan and Abiram; and
Dathan and Abiram came out *and* stood at the doorway of their tents, along with their
wives and their sons and their little ones.
28 Moses said, "By this you shall know that the LORD has sent me to do all these deeds;
for this is not my doing.
29 "If these men die the death of all men or if they suffer the fate of all men, *then* the
LORD has not sent me.
30 "But if the LORD brings about an entirely new thing and the ground opens its mouth
and swallows them up with all that is theirs, and they descend alive into Sheol, then you
will understand that these men have spurned the LORD."
31 As he finished speaking all these words, the ground that was under them split open;
32 and the earth opened its mouth and swallowed them up, and their households, and
all the men who belonged to Korah with *their* possessions.
33 So they and all that belonged to them went down alive to Sheol; and the earth closed
over them, and they perished from the midst of the assembly.
34 All Israel who *were* around them fled at their outcry, for they said, "The earth may
swallow us up!"
35 Fire also came forth from the LORD and consumed the two hundred and fifty men
who were offering the incense.
36 Then the LORD spoke to Moses, saying,
37 "Say to Eleazar, the son of Aaron the priest, that he shall take up the censers out of
the midst of the blaze, for they are holy; and you scatter the burning coals abroad.
38 "As for the censers of these men who have sinned at the cost of their lives, let them
be made into hammered sheets for a plating of the altar, since they did present them
before the LORD and they are holy; and they shall be for a sign to the sons of Israel."
39 So Eleazar the priest took the bronze censers which the men who were burned had
offered, and they hammered them out as a plating for the altar,
40 as a reminder to the sons of Israel that no layman who is not of the descendants of
Aaron should come near to burn incense before the LORD; so that he will not become
like Korah and his company—just as the LORD had spoken to him through Moses.

16:15 Gen 4:4, 5; 1 Sam 12:3
16:19 Num 14:10; 16:42; 20:6
16:21 Num 16:45; Ex 32:10, 12
16:22 Num 27:16; Gen 18:23-32; Lev 4:3
16:24 Num 16:45
16:26 Is 52:11; Gen 19:15, 17
16:27 Num 26:11
16:28 Ex 3:12-15; 4:12, 15
16:29 Eccl 3:19
16:30 Job 31:2, 3; Ps 55:15
16:32 Num 26:10; Deut 11:6; Ps 106:17; Num 26:11
16:35 Num 11:1-3; 26:10; Num 16:2
16:38 Ezek 14:8; 2 Pet 2:6
16:40 Num 1:51; Ex 30:7-10

16:26 The Israelites were told not even to touch the belongings of the wicked rebels. In this case, doing so would have shown sympathy to their cause and agreement with their principles. Korah, Dathan, and Abiram were directly challenging Moses and God. Moses clearly stated what God intended to do to the rebels (16:28–30). He did this so that everyone would have to choose between following Korah or following Moses, God's chosen leader. When God asks us to make a fundamental choice between siding with wicked people or siding with him, we should not hesitate but commit ourselves to be 100 percent on the Lord's side.

16:27–35 Although the families of Dathan and Abiram were swallowed up, the sons of Korah were not wiped out (see 26:11).

Murmuring and Plague

16:41 Num 16:3
16:42 Num 16:19
16:45 Num 16:21, 24
16:46 Num 25:13; Is 6:6, 7; Num 18:5; Deut 9:22

41 But on the next day all the congregation of the sons of Israel grumbled against Moses
and Aaron, saying, "You are the ones who have caused the death of the LORD'S people."
42 It came about, however, when the congregation had assembled against Moses and
Aaron, that they turned toward the tent of meeting, and behold, the cloud covered it
and the glory of the LORD appeared.
43 Then Moses and Aaron came to the front of the tent of meeting,
44 and the LORD spoke to Moses, saying,
45 "Get away from among this congregation, that I may consume them instantly." Then
they fell on their faces.
46 Moses said to Aaron, "Take your censer and put in it fire from the altar, and lay

Some notorious historical figures might have remained anonymous if they hadn't tried to grab on to more than they could hold. But by refusing to be content with what they had, and by trying to get more than they deserved, they ended up with nothing. Korah, one of the Israelite leaders, was such a person.

Korah was a Levite who assisted in the daily functions of the tabernacle. Shortly after Israel's great rebellion against God (Numbers 13; 14), Korah instigated his own mini-rebellion. He recruited a grievance committee and confronted Moses and Aaron. Their list of complaints boils down to three statements: (1) you are no better than anyone else; (2) everyone in Israel has been chosen of the Lord; (3) we don't need to obey you. It is amazing to see how Korah twisted the first two statements—both true—to reach the wrong conclusion.

Moses would have agreed that he was no better than anyone else. He would also have agreed that all Israelites were God's chosen people. But Korah's application of these truths was wrong. Not all Israelites were chosen to lead. Korah's hidden claim was this: "I have as much right to lead as Moses does." His error cost him not only his job—a position of service that he enjoyed—but also his life.

Korah's story gives us numerous warnings: (1) Don't let desire for what someone else has make you discontented with what you already have. (2) Don't try to raise your own self-esteem by attacking someone else's. (3) Don't use part of God's Word to support what you want, rather than allowing its entirety to shape your wants. (4) Don't expect to find satisfaction in power and position; God may want to work through you in the position you are now in.

Strengths and accomplishments:
- Popular leader; influential figure during the exodus
- Mentioned among the chief men of Israel (Exodus 6)
- One of the first Levites appointed for special service in the tabernacle

Weaknesses and mistakes:
- Failed to recognize the significant position God had placed him in
- Forgot that his fight was against someone greater than Moses
- Allowed greed to blind his common sense

Lessons from his life:
- There is sometimes a fine line between goals and greed
- If we are discontented with what we have, we may lose it without gaining anything better

Vital statistics:
- Where: Egypt, Sinai peninsula
- Occupation: Levite (tabernacle assistant)

Key verses:
"Then Moses said to Korah, 'Hear now, you sons of Levi, is it not enough for you that the God of Israel has separated you from the rest of the congregation of Israel, to bring you near to Himself, to do the service of the tabernacle of the LORD, and to stand before the congregation to minister to them; and that He has brought you near, Korah, and all your brothers, sons of Levi, with you? And are you seeking for the priesthood also?' " (Numbers 16:8–10).

Korah's story is told in Numbers 16:1–40. He is also mentioned in Numbers 26:9; Jude 11.

16:41 Just one day after Korah and his followers were executed for grumbling and complaining against God, the Israelites started all over with more muttering and complaining. Their negative attitude only caused them to rebel even more and to bring about even greater trouble. It eroded their faith in God and encouraged thoughts of giving up and turning back. The path to open rebellion against God begins with dissatisfaction and skepticism, then moves to grumbling about both God and present circumstances. Next comes bitterness and resentment, followed finally by rebellion and open hostility. If you are often dissatisfied, skeptical, complaining, or bitter—beware! These attitudes lead to rebellion and separation from God. Any choice to side against God is a step in the direction of letting go of him completely and making your own way through life.

incense *on it;* then bring it quickly to the congregation and make atonement for them,
for wrath has gone forth from the LORD, the plague has begun!"
47 Then Aaron took *it* as Moses had spoken, and ran into the midst of the assembly, **16:47** Num 25:6-8, 13
for behold, the plague had begun among the people. So he put *on* the incense and made
atonement for the people.
48 He took his stand between the dead and the living, so that the plague was checked.
49 But those who died by the plague were 14,700, besides those who died on account **16:49** Num 25:9; Num 16:32, 35
of Korah.
50 Then Aaron returned to Moses at the doorway of the tent of meeting, for the plague
had been checked.

Aaron's Rod Buds

17 Then the LORD spoke to Moses, saying,
2 "Speak to the sons of Israel, and get from them a rod for each father's household: twelve rods, from all their leaders according to their fathers' households. You shall
write each name on his rod,
3 and write Aaron's name on the rod of Levi; for there is one rod for the head *of each*
of their fathers' households.
4 "You shall then deposit them in the tent of meeting in front of the testimony, where **17:4** Ex 25:16, 21, 22; Num 17:7
I meet with you.
5 "It will come about that the rod of the man whom I choose will sprout. Thus I will
lessen from upon Myself the grumblings of the sons of Israel, who are grumbling against **17:5** Num 16:5
you."
6 Moses therefore spoke to the sons of Israel, and all their leaders gave him a rod
apiece, for each leader according to their fathers' households, twelve rods, with the rod
of Aaron among their rods.
7 So Moses deposited the rods before the LORD in the tent of the testimony. **17:7** Num 1:50, 53; 9:15
8 Now on the next day Moses went into the tent of the testimony; and behold, the rod
of Aaron for the house of Levi had sprouted and put forth buds and produced blossoms, **17:8** Ezek 17:24; Heb 9:4
and it bore ripe almonds.
9 Moses then brought out all the rods from the presence of the LORD to all the sons
of Israel; and they looked, and each man took his rod.
10 But the LORD said to Moses, "Put back the rod of Aaron before the testimony to be **17:10** Num 17:4; Deut 9:7, 24
kept as a sign against the rebels, that you may put an end to their grumblings against
Me, so that they will not die."
11 Thus Moses did; just as the LORD had commanded him, so he did.
12 Then the sons of Israel spoke to Moses, saying, "Behold, we perish, we are dying, **17:12** Is 6:5
we are all dying!
13 "Everyone who comes near, who comes near to the tabernacle of the LORD, must **17:13** Num 1:51
die. Are we to perish completely?"

3. Duties of priests and Levites

Duties of Levites

18 So the LORD said to Aaron, "You and your sons and your father's household with **18:1** Ex 28:38; Lev 10:17; 22:16
you shall bear the guilt in connection with the sanctuary, and you and your sons
with you shall bear the guilt in connection with your priesthood.
2 "But bring with you also your brothers, the tribe of Levi, the tribe of your father, that **18:2** Num 3:5-10
they may be joined with you and serve you, while you and your sons with you are before
the tent of the testimony. **18:3** Num 4:15-20; Num 1:51; 18:7
3 "And they shall thus attend to your obligation and the obligation of all the tent, but
they shall not come near to the furnishings of the sanctuary and the altar, or both they
and you will die.

17:5, 10 After witnessing spectacular miracles, seeing the Egyptians punished by the plagues, and experiencing the actual presence of God, the Israelites still complained and rebelled. We wonder how they could be so blind and ignorant, and yet we often repeat this same pattern. We have centuries of evidence, the Bible in many translations, and the convincing results of archaeological and historical studies. But people today continue to disobey God and go their own way. Like the Israelites, we are more concerned about our physical condition than our spiritual condition. We can escape this pattern only by paying attention to all the signs of God's presence that we have been given. Has God guided and protected you? Has he answered your prayers? Do you know people who have experienced remarkable blessings and healings? Do you know Bible stories about the way God has led his people? Focus your thoughts on what God has done, and rebellion will become unthinkable.

4 "They shall be joined with you and attend to the obligations of the tent of meeting, for all the service of the tent; but an outsider may not come near you.

5 "So you shall attend to the obligations of the sanctuary and the obligations of the altar, so that there will no longer be wrath on the sons of Israel.

6 "Behold, I Myself have taken your fellow Levites from among the sons of Israel; they are a gift to you, dedicated to the LORD, to perform the service for the tent of meeting.

7 "But you and your sons with you shall attend to your priesthood for everything concerning the altar and inside the veil, and you are to perform service. I am giving you the priesthood as a bestowed service, but the outsider who comes near shall be put to death."

The Priests' Portion

8 Then the LORD spoke to Aaron, "Now behold, I Myself have given you charge of My offerings, even all the holy gifts of the sons of Israel I have given them to you as a portion and to your sons as a perpetual allotment.

9 "This shall be yours from the most holy *gifts reserved* from the fire; every offering of theirs, even every grain offering and every sin offering and every guilt offering, which they shall render to Me, shall be most holy for you and for your sons.

10 "As the most holy *gifts* you shall eat it; every male shall eat it. It shall be holy to you.

11 "This also is yours, the offering of their gift, even all the wave offerings of the sons of Israel; I have given them to you and to your sons and daughters with you as a perpetual allotment. Everyone of your household who is clean may eat it.

12 "All the best of the fresh oil and all the best of the fresh wine and of the grain, the first fruits of those which they give to the LORD, I give them to you.

13 "The first ripe fruits of all that is in their land, which they bring to the LORD, shall be yours; everyone of your household who is clean may eat it.

14 "Every devoted thing in Israel shall be yours.

15 "Every first issue of the womb of all flesh, whether man or animal, which they offer to the LORD, shall be yours; nevertheless the firstborn of man you shall surely redeem, and the firstborn of unclean animals you shall redeem.

16 "As to their redemption price, from a month old you shall redeem them, by your valuation, five [21]shekels in silver, according to the shekel of the sanctuary, which is twenty gerahs.

17 "But the firstborn of an ox or the firstborn of a sheep or the firstborn of a goat, you shall not redeem; they are holy. You shall sprinkle their blood on the altar and shall offer up their fat in smoke *as* an offering by fire, for a soothing aroma to the LORD.

18 "Their meat shall be yours; it shall be yours like the breast of a wave offering and like the right thigh.

19 "All the offerings of the holy *gifts,* which the sons of Israel offer to the LORD, I have given to you and your sons and your daughters with you, as a perpetual allotment. It is an everlasting covenant of salt before the LORD to you and your descendants with you."

20 Then the LORD said to Aaron, "You shall have no inheritance in their land nor own any portion among them; I am your portion and your inheritance among the sons of Israel.

21 "To the sons of Levi, behold, I have given all the tithe in Israel for an inheritance, in return for their service which they perform, the service of the tent of meeting.

22 "The sons of Israel shall not come near the tent of meeting again, or they will bear sin and die.

23 "Only the Levites shall perform the service of the tent of meeting, and they shall bear their iniquity; it shall be a perpetual statute throughout your generations, and among the sons of Israel they shall have no inheritance.

24 "For the tithe of the sons of Israel, which they offer as an offering to the LORD, I have given to the Levites for an inheritance; therefore I have said concerning them, 'They shall have no inheritance among the sons of Israel.' "

25 Then the LORD spoke to Moses, saying,

18:5 Ex 27:21; Lev 24:3; Num 16:46

18:6 Num 3:12, 45; Num 3:9

18:7 Ex 29:9; Num 18:20; Deut 18:2; Matt 10:8; 1 Pet 5:2, 3; Num 1:51

18:8 Lev 6:16, 18; 7:28-34

18:9 Lev 2:1-16; Lev 6:30

18:11 Num 18:1; Deut 18:3; Lev 22:1-16

18:12 Deut 18:4; 32:14; Ps 81:16; 147:14

18:13 Ex 22:29; 23:19; 34:26

18:14 Lev 27:1-33

18:15 Ex 13:13, 15; Num 3:46

18:17 Deut 15:19; Lev 3:2

18:18 Lev 7:31

18:19 Num 18:11; 2 Chr 13:5

18:20 Deut 10:9; 12:12; 14:27, 29; Deut 18:2; Josh 13:33; Ezek 44:28

18:21 Lev 27:30-33; Deut 14:22-29

18:22 Num 1:51

18:23 Num 18:1; Num 18:20

18:24 Deut 10:9

21 I.e. A shekel equals approx one-half oz

18:25–26 Even the Levites, who were ministers, had to tithe to support the Lord's work. No one was exempt from returning to God a portion of what was received. Though the Levites owned no land and operated no great enterprises, they were to treat their income the same as everyone else did by giving a portion to care for the needs of the other Levites and of the tabernacle. The tithing principle is still relevant. God expects all his followers to supply the material needs of those who devote themselves to meeting the spiritual needs of the community of faith.

26 "Moreover, you shall speak to the Levites and say to them, 'When you take from the
sons of Israel the tithe which I have given you from them for your inheritance, then you
shall present an offering from it to the LORD, a tithe of the tithe.
27 'Your offering shall be reckoned to you as the grain from the threshing floor or the
full produce from the wine vat.
28 'So you shall also present an offering to the LORD from your tithes, which you receive from the sons of Israel; and from it you shall give the LORD'S offering to Aaron the
priest.
29 'Out of all your gifts you shall present every offering due to the LORD, from all the
best of them, the sacred part from them.'
30 "You shall say to them, 'When you have offered from it the best of it, then *the rest*
shall be reckoned to the Levites as the product of the threshing floor, and as the product
of the wine vat.
31 'You may eat it anywhere, you and your households, for it is your compensation in
return for your service in the tent of meeting.
32 'You will bear no sin by reason of it when you have offered the best of it. But you
shall not profane the sacred gifts of the sons of Israel, or you will die.' "

18:26 Num 18:21; Neh 10:38
18:32 Lev 22:15, 16

Ordinance of the Red Heifer

19 Then the LORD spoke to Moses and Aaron, saying,
2 "This is the statute of the law which the LORD has commanded, saying, 'Speak
to the sons of Israel that they bring you an unblemished red heifer in which is no defect
and on which a yoke has never been placed.
3 'You shall give it to Eleazar the priest, and it shall be brought outside the camp and
be slaughtered in his presence.
4 'Next Eleazar the priest shall take some of its blood with his finger and sprinkle some
of its blood toward the front of the tent of meeting seven times.
5 'Then the heifer shall be burned in his sight; its hide and its flesh and its blood, with
its refuse, shall be burned.
6 'The priest shall take cedar wood and hyssop and scarlet *material* and cast it into the
midst of the burning heifer.
7 'The priest shall then wash his clothes and bathe his body in water, and afterward
come into the camp, but the priest shall be unclean until evening.
8 'The one who burns it shall also wash his clothes in water and bathe his body in water,
and shall be unclean until evening.
9 'Now a man who is clean shall gather up the ashes of the heifer and deposit them
outside the camp in a clean place, and the congregation of the sons of Israel shall keep
it as water to remove impurity; it is purification from sin.
10 'The one who gathers the ashes of the heifer shall wash his clothes and be unclean
until evening; and it shall be a perpetual statute to the sons of Israel and to the alien who
sojourns among them.
11 'The one who touches the corpse of any person shall be unclean for seven days.
12 'That one shall purify himself from uncleanness with the water on the third day and
on the seventh day, *and then* he will be clean; but if he does not purify himself on the
third day and on the seventh day, he will not be clean.
13 'Anyone who touches a corpse, the body of a man who has died, and does not purify
himself, defiles the tabernacle of the LORD; and that person shall be cut off from Israel.
Because the water for impurity was not sprinkled on him, he shall be unclean; his uncleanness is still on him.
14 'This is the law when a man dies in a tent: everyone who comes into the tent and
everyone who is in the tent shall be unclean for seven days.
15 'Every open vessel, which has no covering tied down on it, shall be unclean.

19:2 Lev 22:20-25; Deut 21:3
19:3 Num 3:4; Lev 4:11, 12, 21; Num 19:9
19:4 Lev 4:6, 17; 16:14
19:5 Ex 29:14; Lev 4:11, 12
19:6 Lev 14:4
19:7 Lev 16:26, 28; 22:6
19:9 Num 8:7; 31:23
19:10 Num 19:7
19:11 Lev 21:1, 11; Num 5:2; 6:6; Acts 21:26, 27
19:12 Num 19:19; 31:19
19:13 Lev 7:21; 22:3-7; Lev 15:31; 20:3; Num 19:20; Num 19:19

19:9–10 What is the significance of the red heifer's ashes? When a person touched a dead body, he was considered unclean (i.e., unable to approach God in worship). This ritual purified the unclean person so that once again he could offer sacrifices and worship God. Death was the strongest of defilements because it was the final result of sin. Thus a special sacrifice—a red heifer—was required. It had to be offered by someone who was not unclean. When it had been burned on the altar, its ashes were used to purify water for ceremonial cleansing—not so much literally as symbolically. The unclean person then washed himself, and often his clothes and belongings, with this purified water as an act of becoming clean again.

19:16 Num 31:19
16 'Also, anyone who in the open field touches one who has been slain with a sword or
who has died *naturally,* or a human bone or a grave, shall be unclean for seven days.
19:17 Num 19:9
17 'Then for the unclean *person* they shall take some of the ashes of the burnt purification from sin and flowing water shall be added to them in a vessel.
18 'A clean person shall take hyssop and dip *it* in the water, and sprinkle *it* on the tent
and on all the furnishings and on the persons who were there, and on the one who touched
the bone or the one slain or the one dying *naturally* or the grave.
19:19 Ezek 36:25; Heb 10:22
19 'Then the clean *person* shall sprinkle on the unclean on the third day and on the seventh day; and on the seventh day he shall purify him from uncleanness, and he shall wash
his clothes and bathe *himself* in water and shall be clean by evening.
19:20 Num 19:13
20 'But the man who is unclean and does not purify himself from uncleanness, that person shall be cut off from the midst of the assembly, because he has defiled the sanctuary
of the LORD; the water for impurity has not been sprinkled on him, he is unclean.
19:21 Num 19:7
21 'So it shall be a perpetual statute for them. And he who sprinkles the water for impurity shall wash his clothes, and he who touches the water for impurity shall be unclean
until evening.
19:22 Lev 5:2, 3; 7:21; 22:5, 6
22 'Furthermore, anything that the unclean *person* touches shall be unclean; and the
person who touches *it* shall be unclean until evening.' "

4. The new generation

Death of Miriam

20:1 Num 13:21; 27:14; 33:36
20 Then the sons of Israel, the whole congregation, came to the wilderness of Zin in
the first month; and the people stayed at Kadesh. Now Miriam died there and
was buried there.
20:2 Ex 17:1; Num 16:19, 42
2 There was no water for the congregation, and they assembled themselves against
Moses and Aaron.
20:3 Ex 17:2; Num 14:2, 3; Num 16:31-35
3 The people thus contended with Moses and spoke, saying, "If only we had perished
when our brothers perished before the LORD!
20:4 Ex 17:3
4 "Why then have you brought the LORD'S assembly into this wilderness, for us and
our beasts to die here?
20:5 Num 16:14
5 "Why have you made us come up from Egypt, to bring us in to this wretched place?
It is not a place of grain or figs or vines or pomegranates, nor is there water to drink."
20:6 Num 14:5
6 Then Moses and Aaron came in from the presence of the assembly to the doorway of
the tent of meeting and fell on their faces. Then the glory of the LORD appeared to them;
7 and the LORD spoke to Moses, saying,

The Water of Meribah

20:8 Ex 4:17, 20; 17:5, 6
8 "Take the rod; and you and your brother Aaron assemble the congregation and speak
to the rock before their eyes, that it may yield its water. You shall thus bring forth water
for them out of the rock and let the congregation and their beasts drink."

EVENTS AT KADESH
After wandering in the wilderness for 40 years, Israel arrived at Kadesh, where Miriam died. There was not enough water, and the people complained bitterly. Moses struck a rock, and it gave enough water for everyone. The king of Edom refused Israel passage through his land, forcing them to travel around his country.

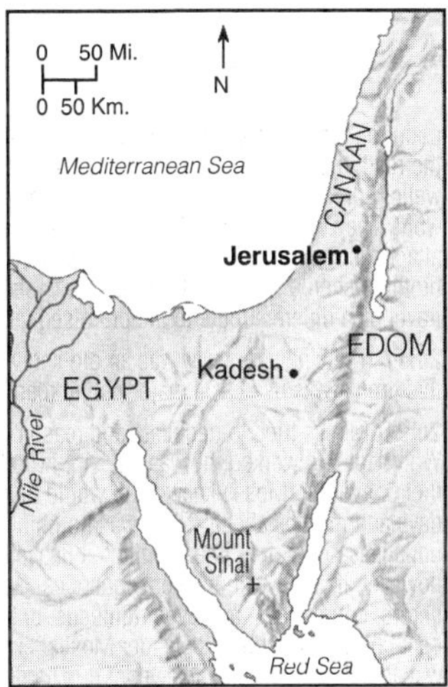

20:1 It had been 37 years since Israel's first spy mission into the promised land (Numbers 13–14) and 40 years since the exodus from Egypt. The Bible is virtually silent about those 37 years of aimless wandering. The generation of those who had lived in Egypt had almost died off, and the new generation would soon be ready to enter the land. Moses, Aaron, Joshua, and Caleb were among the few who remained from those who had left Egypt. Once again they camped at Kadesh, the site of the first spy mission that had ended in disaster. Moses hoped the people were ready for a fresh start.

20:3–5 After 37 years in the wilderness, the Israelites forgot that their wanderings were a result of their parents' and their own sin. They could not accept the fact that they had brought their problems upon themselves, so they blamed Moses for their condition. Often our troubles result from our own disobedience or lack of faith. We cannot blame God for our sins. Until we face this reality, we will have little peace and no spiritual growth.

9 So Moses took the rod from before the LORD, just as He had commanded him;
10 and Moses and Aaron gathered the assembly before the rock. And he said to them,
"Listen now, you rebels; shall we bring forth water for you out of this rock?"
11 Then Moses lifted up his hand and struck the rock twice with his rod; and water
came forth abundantly, and the congregation and their beasts drank.
12 But the LORD said to Moses and Aaron, "Because you have not believed Me, to
treat Me as holy in the sight of the sons of Israel, therefore you shall not bring this assembly into the land which I have given them."
13 Those *were* the waters of [22]Meribah, because the sons of Israel contended with the
LORD, and He proved Himself holy among them.
14 From Kadesh Moses then sent messengers to the king of Edom: "Thus your brother Israel has said, 'You know all the hardship that has befallen us;
15 that our fathers went down to Egypt, and we stayed in Egypt a long time, and the
Egyptians treated us and our fathers badly.
16 'But when we cried out to the LORD, He heard our voice and sent an angel and
brought us out from Egypt; now behold, we are at Kadesh, a town on the edge of your
territory.
17 'Please let us pass through your land. We will not pass through field or through vineyard; we will not even drink water from a well. We will go along the king's highway, not
turning to the right or left, until we pass through your territory.' "
18 Edom, however, said to him, "You shall not pass through us, or I will come out with
the sword against you."
19 Again, the sons of Israel said to him, "We will go up by the highway, and if I and my
livestock do drink any of your water, then I will pay its price. Let me only pass through
on my feet, nothing *else.*"
20 But he said, "You shall not pass through." And Edom came out against him with a
heavy force and with a strong hand.
21 Thus Edom refused to allow Israel to pass through his territory; so Israel turned
away from him.
22 Now when they set out from Kadesh, the sons of Israel, the whole congregation,
came to Mount Hor.

Death of Aaron

23 Then the LORD spoke to Moses and Aaron at Mount Hor by the border of the land
of Edom, saying,
24 "Aaron will be gathered to his people; for he shall not enter the land which I have
given to the sons of Israel, because you rebelled against My command at the waters of
Meribah.
25 "Take Aaron and his son Eleazar and bring them up to Mount Hor;
26 and strip Aaron of his garments and put them on his son Eleazar. So Aaron will be
gathered *to his people,* and will die there."

22 I.e. contention

20:9 Num 17:10
20:10 Ps 106:33
20:11 Ps 78:16; Is 48:21; 1 Cor 10:4
20:12 Num 20:24; 27:14; Deut 1:37; 3:26, 27
20:13 Ex 17:7; Ps 95:8
20:14 Gen 36:31-39; Deut 2:4; Josh 2:9, 10; 9:9, 10, 24
20:16 Ex 2:23; 3:7; Ex 14:19
20:17 Num 21:22
20:18 Num 24:18
20:19 Ex 12:38; Deut 2:6, 28
20:20 Judg 11:17
20:21 Judg 11:17; Deut 2:8
20:22 Num 20:1, 14
20:23 Num 33:37
20:24 Gen 25:8; Num 20:5, 10
20:25 Num 3:4
20:26 Num 20:24

20:12 The Lord had told Moses to speak to the rock; however, Moses struck it, not once, but twice. God did the miracle; yet Moses was taking credit for it when he asked, "Shall we bring forth water for you out of this rock?" For this he was forbidden to enter the promised land. Was God's punishment of Moses too harsh? After all, the people had nagged him, slandered him, and rebelled against both him and God. Now they were at it again (20:5). But Moses was the leader and model for the entire nation. Because of this great responsibility to the people, he could not be let off lightly. By striking the rock, Moses disobeyed God's direct command and dishonored God in the presence of his people.

20:14 Two brothers became the ancestors of two nations. The Edomites descended from Esau; the Israelites from Jacob. Thus the Edomites were "brothers" to the Israelites. Israel sent a brotherly message to Edom requesting passage through their land on the main road, a well-traveled trade route. Israel promised to stay on the road, thus harmlessly bypassing Edom's fields, vineyards, and wells. Edom refused, however, because they did not trust Israel's word. They were afraid that this great horde of people would either attack them or devour their crops (Deuteronomy 2:4–5). Because brothers should not fight, God told the Israelites to turn back and travel by a different route to the promised land.

20:17 The king's highway was an old caravan route. Long before this time it was used as a major public road.

20:21 Moses tried to negotiate and reason with the Edomite king. When nothing worked, he was left with two choices—force a conflict or avoid it. Moses knew there would be enough barriers in the days and months ahead. There was no point in adding another one unnecessarily. Sometimes conflict is unavoidable. Sometimes, however, it isn't worth the consequences. Open warfare may seem heroic, courageous, and even righteous, but it is not always the best choice. We should consider Moses' example and find another way to solve our problems, even if it is harder for us to do.

27 So Moses did just as the LORD had commanded, and they went up to Mount Hor in
the sight of all the congregation.
20:28 Ex 29:29; Num 33:38; Deut 10:6; 32:50
28 After Moses had stripped Aaron of his garments and put them on his son Eleazar,
Aaron died there on the mountain top. Then Moses and Eleazar came down from the
mountain.
20:29 Gen 1:5; 50:3, 10; Deut 34:8
29 When all the congregation saw that Aaron had died, all the house of Israel wept for
Aaron thirty days.

Arad Conquered

21:1 Num 33:40; Josh 12:14; Judg 1:16
21 When the Canaanite, the king of Arad, who lived in the [23]Negev, heard that
Israel was coming by the way of [24]Atharim, then he fought against Israel and took
some of them captive.
21:2 Gen 28:20; Judg 11:30
2 So Israel made a vow to the LORD and said, "If You will indeed deliver this people
into my hand, then I will utterly destroy their cities."
21:3 Num 14:45
3 The LORD heard the voice of Israel and delivered up the Canaanites; then they utterly
destroyed them and their cities. Thus the name of the place was called [25]Hormah.
21:4 Deut 2:8
4 Then they set out from Mount Hor by the way of the Red Sea, to go around the
land of Edom; and the people became impatient because of the journey.
21:5 Num 14:2, 3; Num 11:6
5 The people spoke against God and Moses, "Why have you brought us up out of Egypt
to die in the wilderness? For there is no food and no water, and we loathe this miserable
food."

23 I.e. South country **24** Or *the spies* **25** I.e. a devoted thing; or Destruction

An understudy must know the lead role completely and be willing to step into it at a moment's notice. Eleazar was an excellent understudy, well trained for his eventual leading role. However, his moments in the spotlight were painful. On one occasion, he watched his two older brothers burn to death for failing to take God's holiness seriously. Later, as his father was dying, he was made high priest, surely one of the most responsible—and therefore potentially most stressful—positions in Israel.

An understudy benefits from having both the script and a human model of the role. Ever since childhood, Eleazar had been able to observe Moses and Aaron. Now he could learn from watching Joshua. In addition, he had God's laws to guide him as he worked as priest and adviser to Joshua.

Strengths and accomplishments:
- Succeeded his father, Aaron, as high priest
- Completed his father's work by helping lead the people into the promised land
- Teamed up with Joshua
- Acted as God's spokesman to the people

Lessons from his life:
- Concentrating on our present challenges and responsibilities is the best way to prepare for what God has planned for our future
- God's desire is consistent obedience throughout our lives

Vital statistics:
- Where: Wilderness of Sinai, promised land
- Occupations: Priest and high priest
- Relatives: Father: Aaron. Brothers: Nadab and Abihu. Aunt and uncle: Miriam and Moses
- Contemporaries: Joshua, Caleb

Key verses:
"Then the LORD spoke to Moses and Aaron at Mount Hor by the border of the land of Edom, saying, 'Aaron will be gathered to his people . . . Take Aaron and his son Eleazar and bring them up to Mount Hor; and strip Aaron of his garments and put them on his son Eleazar'" (Numbers 20:23–26).

Eleazar is mentioned in Exodus 6:23; Leviticus 10:16–20; Numbers 3:1–4; 4:16; 16:36–40; 20:25–29; 26:1–3, 63; 27:2, 15–23; 32:2; 34:17; Deuteronomy 10:6; Joshua 14:1; 17:4; 24:33.

20:28 Aaron died just before entering the promised land, probably as punishment for his sin of rebellion (Exodus 32; Numbers 12:1–9). This was the first time that a new high priest was appointed. The priestly clothing was removed from Aaron and placed on his son Eleazar, following the commands recorded in the book of Leviticus.

21:5 In Psalm 78, we learn the sources of Israel's complaining: (1) their spirits were not faithful to God (78:8); (2) they refused to obey God's law (78:10); (3) they forgot the miracles God had done for them (78:11). Our complaining often has its roots in one of these thoughtless actions and attitudes. If we can deal with the cause of our complaining, it will not take hold and grow in our lives.

The Bronze Serpent

6 The LORD sent fiery serpents among the people and they bit the people, so that
many people of Israel died.
7 So the people came to Moses and said, "We have sinned, because we have spoken
against the LORD and you; intercede with the LORD, that He may remove the serpents
from us." And Moses interceded for the people.
8 Then the LORD said to Moses, "Make a fiery *serpent,* and set it on a standard; and
it shall come about, that everyone who is bitten, when he looks at it, he will live."
9 And Moses made a bronze serpent and set it on the standard; and it came about,
that if a serpent bit any man, when he looked to the bronze serpent, he lived.
10 Now the sons of Israel moved out and camped in Oboth.
11 They journeyed from Oboth and camped at Iyeabarim, in the wilderness which is
opposite Moab, to the east.
12 From there they set out and camped in [26]Wadi Zered.
13 From there they journeyed and camped on the other side of the Arnon, which is in
the wilderness that comes out of the border of the Amorites, for the Arnon is the border
of Moab, between Moab and the Amorites.
14 Therefore it is said in the Book of the Wars of the LORD,
"Waheb in Suphah,
And the wadis of the Arnon,
15 And the slope of the wadis
That extends to the site of Ar,
And leans to the border of Moab."
16 From there *they continued* to Beer, that is the well where the LORD said to Moses,
"Assemble the people, that I may give them water."
17 Then Israel sang this song:
"Spring up, O well! Sing to it!
18 "The well, which the leaders sank,

21:6 Deut 8:15; Jer 8:17; 1 Cor 10:9
21:7 Num 11:2; Ps 78:34; Is 26:16; Hos 5:15; Ex 8:8; 1 Sam 12:19; Acts 8:24
21:8 Is 14:29; 30:6; John 3:14
21:9 2 Kin 18:4; John 3:14, 15
21:10 Num 33:43, 44
21:12 Num 33:45
21:13 Num 22:36; Judg 11:18
21:15 Num 21:28; Deut 2:9, 18, 29
21:16 Num 33:46-49
21:17 Ex 15:1; Ps 105:2

26 I.e. a dry ravine except during rainy season

21:6 God used fiery (poisonous) serpents to punish the people for their unbelief and complaining. The wilderness of Sinai has a variety of snakes. Some hide in the sand and attack without warning. Both the Israelites and the Egyptians had a great fear of snakes. A bite by a poisonous snake often meant a slow death with intense suffering.

21:8–9 When the bronze serpent was hung on the standard (pole), the Israelites didn't know the fuller meaning Jesus Christ would bring to this event (see John 3:14–15). Jesus explained that just as the Israelites were healed of their sickness by looking at the serpent on the pole, all believers today can be saved from the sickness of sin by looking to Jesus' death on the cross. It was not the snake that healed the people, but their belief that God could heal them. This belief was demonstrated by their obedience to God's instructions. In the same way, we should continue to look to Christ (see Hebrews 12:2).

21:14 There is no existing record of the Book of the Wars of the LORD. Most likely, it was a collection of victory songs or poems.

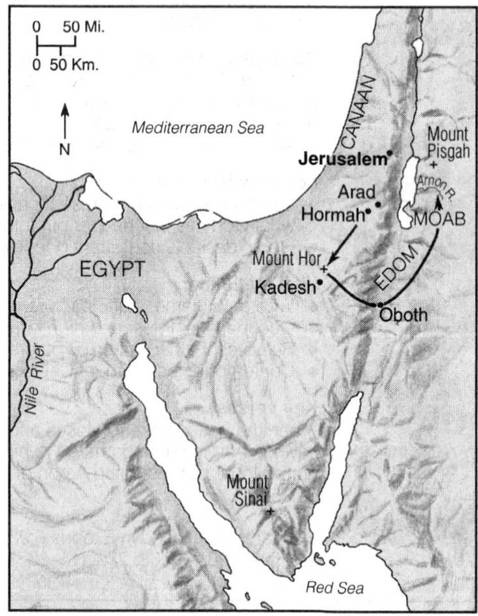

EVENTS IN THE WILDERNESS
Israel next met resistance from the king of Arad but soundly defeated him. The next stop was Mount Hor (where Aaron had died); then they traveled south and east around Edom. After camping at Oboth, they moved toward the Arnon River and onto the plains of Moab near Mount Pisgah.

Which the nobles of the people dug,
With the scepter *and* with their staffs."
And from the wilderness *they continued* to Mattanah,
19 and from Mattanah to Nahaliel, and from Nahaliel to Bamoth,
20 and from Bamoth to the valley that is in the land of Moab, at the top of Pisgah which
overlooks the wasteland.

Two Victories

21:21 Deut 2:26-37; Judg 11:19
21:22 Num 20:16, 17
21:23 Num 20:21; Deut 2:32
21:24 Amos 2:9; Deut 2:37

21 Then Israel sent messengers to Sihon, king of the Amorites, saying,
22 "Let me pass through your land. We will not turn off into field or vineyard; we will
not drink water from wells. We will go by the king's highway until we have passed through
your border."
23 But Sihon would not permit Israel to pass through his border. So Sihon gathered all
his people and went out against Israel in the wilderness, and came to Jahaz and fought
against Israel.
24 Then Israel struck him with the edge of the sword, and took possession of his land
from the Arnon to the Jabbok, as far as the sons of Ammon; for the border of the sons
of Ammon *was* Jazer.

21:25 Amos 2:10

25 Israel took all these cities and Israel lived in all the cities of the Amorites, in Heshbon, and in all her villages.
26 For Heshbon was the city of Sihon, king of the Amorites, who had fought against
the former king of Moab and had taken all his land out of his hand, as far as the Arnon.
27 Therefore those who use proverbs say,
"Come to Heshbon! Let it be built!
So let the city of Sihon be established.

21:28 Jer 48:45; Num 21:15; Num 22:41; Is 15:2; 16:12

28 "For a fire went forth from Heshbon,
A flame from the town of Sihon;
It devoured Ar of Moab,
The dominant heights of the Arnon.

21:29 Jer 48:46; Judg 11:24; 1 Kin 11:33; 2 Kin 23:13; Is 15:5; Is 16:2

29 "Woe to you, O Moab!
You are ruined, O people of Chemosh!
He has given his sons as fugitives,
And his daughters into captivity,
To an Amorite king, Sihon.

21:30 Num 32:3, 34; Jer 48:18, 22

30 "But we have cast them down,
Heshbon is ruined as far as Dibon,
Then we have laid waste even to Nophah,
Which *reaches* to Medeba."

21:32 Num 32:1, 3, 35; Jer 48:32
21:33 Deut 3:1-7; Josh 13:12
21:34 Deut 3:2

31 Thus Israel lived in the land of the Amorites.
32 Moses sent to spy out Jazer, and they captured its villages and dispossessed the
Amorites who *were* there.
33 Then they turned and went up by the way of Bashan, and Og the king of Bashan
went out with all his people, for battle at Edrei.
34 But the LORD said to Moses, "Do not fear him, for I have given him into your hand,

---

THE SERPENT IN THE WILDERNESS
Compare the texts for yourself: Numbers 21:7–9 and John 3:14–15.

Israelites	*Christians*
Bitten by serpents	Bitten by sin
Little initial pain, then intense suffering	Little initial pain, then intense suffering
Physical death from serpents' poison	Spiritual death from sin's poison
Bronze serpent lifted up in the wilderness	Christ lifted up on the cross
Looking to the serpent spared one's life	Looking to Christ saves from eternal death

---

21:27–30 Chemosh, the national god of Moab, was worshiped as a god of war. This false god, however, was no help to this nation when it fought against Israel. Israel's God was stronger than any of Canaan's war gods.

21:34 God assured Moses that Israel's enemy was conquered even before the battle began! God wants to give us victory over our enemies (which are usually problems related to sin rather than armed soldiers). But first we must believe that he can help us. Second, we must trust him to help us. Third, we must take the steps he shows us.

and all his people and his land; and you shall do to him as you did to Sihon, king of the Amorites, who lived at Heshbon."

35 So they killed him and his sons and all his people, until there was no remnant left
him; and they possessed his land.

21:35 Deut 3:3, 4

D. SECOND APPROACH TO THE PROMISED LAND (22:1—36:13)

Now the old generation has died and a new generation stands poised at the border, ready to enter the promised land. Neighboring nations, however, cause Israel to begin worshiping other gods. Without Moses' quick action, the nation may never have entered Canaan. We must never let down our guard in resisting sin.

1. The story of Balaam

Balak Sends for Balaam

22 Then the sons of Israel journeyed, and camped in the plains of Moab beyond the
Jordan *opposite* Jericho.
2 Now Balak the son of Zippor saw all that Israel had done to the Amorites.
3 So Moab was in great fear because of the people, for they were numerous; and Moab
was in dread of the sons of Israel.
4 Moab said to the elders of Midian, "Now this horde will lick up all that is around us,
as the ox licks up the grass of the field." And Balak the son of Zippor was king of Moab
at that time.
5 So he sent messengers to Balaam the son of Beor, at Pethor, which is near the [27]River,
in the land of the sons of his people, to call him, saying, "Behold, a people came out of
Egypt; behold, they cover the surface of the land, and they are living opposite me.
6 "Now, therefore, please come, curse this people for me since they are too mighty for
me; perhaps I may be able to defeat them and drive them out of the land. For I know
that he whom you bless is blessed, and he whom you curse is cursed."
7 So the elders of Moab and the elders of Midian departed with the *fees for* divination
in their hand; and they came to Balaam and repeated Balak's words to him.
8 He said to them, "Spend the night here, and I will bring word back to you as the
LORD may speak to me." And the leaders of Moab stayed with Balaam.
9 Then God came to Balaam and said, "Who are these men with you?"
10 Balaam said to God, "Balak the son of Zippor, king of Moab, has sent *word* to me,
11 'Behold, there is a people who came out of Egypt and they cover the surface of the
land; now come, curse them for me; perhaps I may be able to fight against them and
drive them out.' "
12 God said to Balaam, "Do not go with them; you shall not curse the people, for they
are blessed."
13 So Balaam arose in the morning and said to Balak's leaders, "Go back to your land,
for the LORD has refused to let me go with you."

22:1 Num 33:48, 49
22:2 Judg 11:25
22:3 Ex 15:15
22:4 Num 25:15-18; 31:1-3
22:5 Josh 24:9; 2 Pet 2:15f; Jude 11; Deut 23:4
22:6 Num 22:17; 23:7, 8; Num 22:12; 24:9
22:7 Num 23:23; 24:1; Josh 13:22
22:9 Gen 20:3
22:12 Num 23:8; 24:9; Gen 12:2; 22:17

27 I.e. Euphrates

22:4–6 Balaam was a sorcerer, one called upon to place curses on others. Belief in curses and blessings was common in Old Testament times. Sorcerers were thought to have power with the gods. Thus the king of Moab wanted Balaam to use his powers with the God of Israel to place a curse on Israel—hoping that, by magic, God would turn against his people. Neither Balaam nor Balak had any idea whom they were dealing with!

22:9 Why would God speak through a sorcerer like Balaam? God wanted to give a message to the Moabites, and they had already chosen to employ Balaam. So Balaam was available for God to use, much as he used the wicked pharaoh to accomplish his will in Egypt (Exodus 10:1). Balaam entered into his prophetic role seriously, but his heart was mixed. He had some knowledge of God, but not enough to forsake his magic and turn wholeheartedly to God. Although this story leads us to believe he turned completely to God, later passages in the Bible show that Balaam couldn't resist the tempting pull of money and idolatry (31:16; 2 Peter 2:15; Jude 1:11).

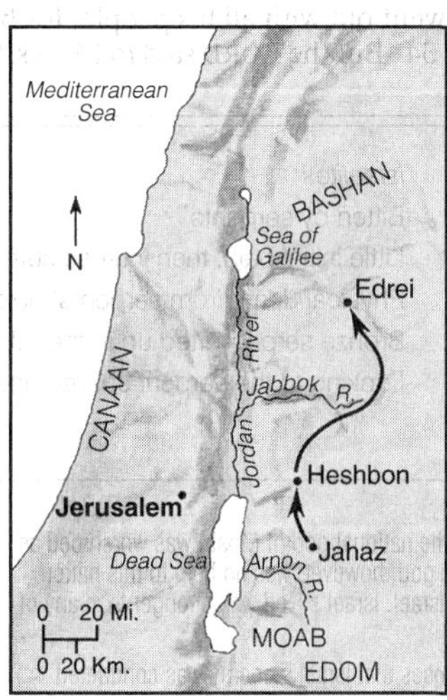

BATTLES WITH SIHON AND OG
King Sihon refused passage to the Israelites through his land, and he attacked Israel at Jahaz. Israel defeated him, occupying the land between the Arnon and Jabbok Rivers, including the capital city, Heshbon. As they moved north, they defeated King Og of Bashan at Edrei.

14 The leaders of Moab arose and went to Balak and said, "Balaam refused to come
with us."
15 Then Balak again sent leaders, more numerous and more distinguished than the
former.
16 They came to Balaam and said to him, "Thus says Balak the son of Zippor, 'Let
nothing, I beg you, hinder you from coming to me;
22:17 Num 22:6 17 for I will indeed honor you richly, and I will do whatever you say to me. Please come
then, curse this people for me.' "
22:18 Num 22:38; 24:13; 1 Kin 22:14; 2 Chr 18:13 18 Balaam replied to the servants of Balak, "Though Balak were to give me his house
full of silver and gold, I could not do anything, either small or great, contrary to the com-
mand of the LORD my God.
19 "Now please, you also stay here tonight, and I will find out what else the LORD will
speak to me."
22:20 Num 22:35; 23:5, 12, 16, 26; 24:13 20 God came to Balaam at night and said to him, "If the men have come to call you,
rise up *and* go with them; but only the word which I speak to you shall you do."
22:21 2 Pet 2:15 **21** So Balaam arose in the morning, and saddled his donkey and went with the leaders
of Moab.

BALAAM

Balaam was one of those noteworthy Old Testament characters who, though not one of God's chosen people, was willing to acknowledge that Yahweh (the LORD) was indeed a powerful God. But he did not believe in the Lord as the only true God. His story exposes the deception of maintaining an outward facade of spirituality over a corrupt inward life. Balaam was a man ready to obey God's command as long as he could profit from doing so. This mixture of motives—obedience and profit—eventually led to Balaam's death. Although he realized the awesome power of Israel's God, his heart was occupied with the wealth he could gain in Moab. There he returned to die when the armies of Israel invaded.

Eventually, each of us lives through the same process. Who and what we are will somehow come to the surface, destroying any masks we may have put on to cover up our real selves. Efforts spent on keeping up appearances would be much better spent on finding the answer to sin in our lives. We can avoid Balaam's mistake by facing ourselves and realizing that God is willing to accept us, forgive us, and literally make us over from within. Don't miss this great discovery that eluded Balaam.

Strengths and accomplishments:
- Widely known for his effective curses and blessings
- Obeyed God and blessed Israel, in spite of Balak's bribe

Weaknesses and mistakes:
- Encouraged the Israelites to worship idols (Numbers 31:16)
- Returned to Moab and was killed in war

Lessons from his life:
- Motives are just as important as actions
- Your treasure is where your heart is

Vital statistics:
- Where: Lived near the Euphrates River, traveled to Moab
- Occupations: Sorcerer, prophet
- Relative: Father: Beor
- Contemporaries: Balak (king of Moab), Moses, Aaron

Key verses:
"Forsaking the right way, they have gone astray, having followed the way of Balaam, the son of Beor, who loved the wages of unrighteousness; but he received a rebuke for his own transgression, for a mute donkey, speaking with a voice of a man, restrained the madness of the prophet" (2 Peter 2:15–16).

Balaam's story is told in Numbers 22:1—24:25. He is also mentioned in Numbers 31:7–8, 16; Deuteronomy 23:4–5; Joshua 24:9–10; Nehemiah 13:2; Micah 6:5; 2 Peter 2:15–16; Jude 1:11; Revelation 2:14.

22:20–23 God let Balaam go with Balak's messengers, but he was angry about Balaam's greedy attitude. Balaam claimed that he would not go against God just for money, but his resolve was beginning to slip. His greed for the wealth offered by the king blinded him so that he could not see how God was trying to stop him. Though we may know what God wants us to do, we can become blinded by the desire for money, possessions, or prestige. We can avoid Balaam's mistake by looking past the allure of fame or fortune to the long-range benefits of following God.

The Angel and Balaam

22 But God was angry because he was going, and the angel of the LORD took his stand in the way as an adversary against him. Now he was riding on his donkey and his two servants were with him.
23 When the donkey saw the angel of the LORD standing in the way with his drawn sword in his hand, the donkey turned off from the way and went into the field; but Balaam struck the donkey to turn her back into the way.
24 Then the angel of the LORD stood in a narrow path of the vineyards, *with* a wall on this side and a wall on that side.
25 When the donkey saw the angel of the LORD, she pressed herself to the wall and pressed Balaam's foot against the wall, so he struck her again.
26 The angel of the LORD went further, and stood in a narrow place where there was no way to turn to the right hand or the left.
27 When the donkey saw the angel of the LORD, she lay down under Balaam; so Balaam was angry and struck the donkey with his stick.
28 And the LORD opened the mouth of the donkey, and she said to Balaam, "What have I done to you, that you have struck me these three times?"
29 Then Balaam said to the donkey, "Because you have made a mockery of me! If there had been a sword in my hand, I would have killed you by now."
30 The donkey said to Balaam, "Am I not your donkey on which you have ridden all your life to this day? Have I ever been accustomed to do so to you?" And he said, "No."
31 Then the LORD opened the eyes of Balaam, and he saw the angel of the LORD standing in the way with his drawn sword in his hand; and he bowed all the way to the ground.
32 The angel of the LORD said to him, "Why have you struck your donkey these three times? Behold, I have come out as an adversary, because your way was contrary to me.
33 "But the donkey saw me and turned aside from me these three times. If she had not turned aside from me, I would surely have killed you just now, and let her live."
34 Balaam said to the angel of the LORD, "I have sinned, for I did not know that you were standing in the way against me. Now then, if it is displeasing to you, I will turn back."
35 But the angel of the LORD said to Balaam, "Go with the men, but you shall speak only the word which I tell you." So Balaam went along with the leaders of Balak.
36 When Balak heard that Balaam was coming, he went out to meet him at the city of Moab, which is on the Arnon border, at the extreme end of the border.
37 Then Balak said to Balaam, "Did I not urgently send to you to call you? Why did you not come to me? Am I really unable to honor you?"
38 So Balaam said to Balak, "Behold, I have come now to you! Am I able to speak anything at all? The word that God puts in my mouth, that I shall speak."
39 And Balaam went with Balak, and they came to Kiriath-huzoth.
40 Balak sacrificed oxen and sheep, and sent *some* to Balaam and the leaders who were with him.

22:22 Ex 23:20
22:27 James 1:19
22:28 2 Pet 2:16
22:29 Prov 12:10; Matt 15:19
22:31 Josh 5:13-15
22:32 2 Pet 2:15
22:34 Num 14:40
22:35 Num 22:20
22:38 Num 22:18

THE STORY OF BALAAM
At King Balak's request, Balaam traveled nearly 400 miles to curse Israel. Balak took Balaam to the high places of Baal, then to the top of Pisgah, and finally to Mount Peor. Each place looked over the plains of Moab, where the Israelites were camped. But to the king's dismay, Balaam blessed, not cursed, Israel.

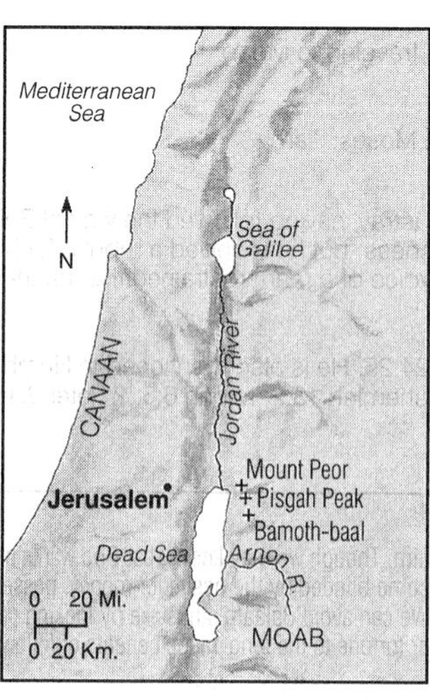

22:27 Donkeys were all-purpose vehicles used for transportation, carrying loads, grinding grain, and plowing fields. They were usually highly dependable, which explains why Balaam became so angry when his donkey refused to move.

22:29 The donkey saved Balaam's life but made him look foolish in the process, so Balaam lashed out at the donkey. We sometimes strike out at blameless people who get in our way because we are embarrassed or our pride is hurt. Lashing out at others can be a sign that something is wrong with us. Don't allow your own hurt pride to lead you to hurt others.

22:41 Num 21:28; Num 23:13

41 Then it came about in the morning that Balak took Balaam and brought him up to
the high places of Baal, and he saw from there a portion of the people.

The Prophecies of Balaam

23 Then Balaam said to Balak, "Build seven altars for me here, and prepare seven
bulls and seven rams for me here."
2 Balak did just as Balaam had spoken, and Balak and Balaam offered up a bull and
a ram on each altar.
3 Then Balaam said to Balak, "Stand beside your burnt offering, and I will go; perhaps the LORD will come to meet me, and whatever He shows me I will tell you." So he
went to a bare hill.
4 Now God met Balaam, and he said to Him, "I have set up the seven altars, and I
have offered up a bull and a ram on each altar."

23:5 Num 22:20; Deut 18:18; Jer 1:9

5 Then the LORD put a word in Balaam's mouth and said, "Return to Balak, and you
shall speak thus."
6 So he returned to him, and behold, he was standing beside his burnt offering, he
and all the leaders of Moab.

23:7 Num 22:5; Deut 23:4; Num 22:6

7 He took up his [28]discourse and said,
"From Aram Balak has brought me,
Moab's king from the mountains of the East,
'Come curse Jacob for me,
And come, denounce Israel!'

23:8 Num 22:12

8 "How shall I curse whom God has not cursed?
And how can I denounce whom the LORD has not denounced?

23:9 Deut 32:8; 33:28

9 "As I see him from the top of the rocks,
And I look at him from the hills;
Behold, a people *who* dwells apart,
And will not be reckoned among the nations.

23:10 Gen 13:16; 28:14; Is 57:1; Ps 37:37

10 "Who can count the dust of Jacob,
Or number the fourth part of Israel?
Let me die the death of the upright,
And let my end be like his!"

23:11 Neh 13:2

11 Then Balak said to Balaam, "What have you done to me? I took you to curse my
enemies, but behold, you have actually blessed them!"

23:12 Num 22:20

12 He replied, "Must I not be careful to speak what the LORD puts in my mouth?"
13 Then Balak said to him, "Please come with me to another place from where you
may see them, although you will only see the extreme end of them and will not see all of
them; and curse them for me from there."
14 So he took him to the field of Zophim, to the top of Pisgah, and built seven altars
and offered a bull and a ram on *each* altar.
15 And he said to Balak, "Stand here beside your burnt offering while I myself meet
the LORD over there."

23:16 Num 22:20

16 Then the LORD met Balaam and put a word in his mouth and said, "Return to Balak, and thus you shall speak."
17 He came to him, and behold, he was standing beside his burnt offering, and the leaders of Moab with him. And Balak said to him, "What has the LORD spoken?"
18 Then he took up his [28]discourse and said,
"Arise, O Balak, and hear;
Give ear to me, O son of Zippor!

23:19 1 Sam 15:29; Is 40:8; 55:11

19 "God is not a man, that He should lie,
Nor a son of man, that He should repent;
Has He said, and will He not do it?
Or has He spoken, and will He not make it good?

28 Lit *parable*

22:41 The high places of Baal were located near Heshbon and Dibon. It was the first stopping point on the way to the high plains of Moab. From this vantage point, they could see the entire Israelite camp.

23:1–3 The number seven was sacred among many of the nations and religions at this time. A "bare hill" means a place at a higher elevation on the mountain, without foliage.

20 "Behold, I have received *a command* to bless;
When He has blessed, then I cannot revoke it.
21 "He has not observed misfortune in Jacob;
Nor has He seen trouble in Israel;
The LORD his God is with him,
And the shout of a king is among them.
22 "God brings them out of Egypt,
He is for them like the horns of the wild ox.
23 "For there is no omen against Jacob,
Nor is there any divination against Israel;
At the proper time it shall be said to Jacob
And to Israel, what God has done!
24 "Behold, a people rises like a lioness,
And as a lion it lifts itself;
It will not lie down until it devours the prey,
And drinks the blood of the slain."
25 Then Balak said to Balaam, "Do not curse them at all nor bless them at all!"
26 But Balaam replied to Balak, "Did I not tell you, 'Whatever the LORD speaks, that
I must do'?"
27 Then Balak said to Balaam, "Please come, I will take you to another place; perhaps
it will be agreeable with God that you curse them for me from there."
28 So Balak took Balaam to the top of Peor which overlooks the wasteland.
29 Balaam said to Balak, "Build seven altars for me here and prepare seven bulls and
seven rams for me here."
30 Balak did just as Balaam had said, and offered up a bull and a ram on *each* altar.

23:20 Gen 12:2; 22:17; Num 22:12; Is 43:13

23:21 Num 14:18, 19, 34; Ps 32:2, 5; Deut 9:24; 32:5; Jer 50:20; Ex 3:12; Deut 31:23; Deut 33:5; Ps 89:15-18

23:22 Num 24:8; Deut 33:17

23:23 Num 22:7; 24:1; Josh 13:22

23:24 Gen 49:9; Nah 2:11, 12

23:26 Num 22:18

The Prophecy from Peor

24 When Balaam saw that it pleased the LORD to bless Israel, he did not go as at
other times to seek omens but he set his face toward the wilderness.
2 And Balaam lifted up his eyes and saw Israel camping tribe by tribe; and the Spirit
of God came upon him.
3 He took up his discourse and said,
"The oracle of Balaam the son of Beor,
And the oracle of the man whose eye is opened;
4 The oracle of him who hears the words of God,
Who sees the vision of the Almighty,
Falling down, yet having his eyes uncovered,
5 How fair are your tents, O Jacob,
Your dwellings, O Israel!
6 "Like valleys that stretch out,
Like gardens beside the river,
Like aloes planted by the LORD,
Like cedars beside the waters.
7 "Water will flow from his buckets,
And his seed *will be* by many waters,
And his king shall be higher than Agag,
And his kingdom shall be exalted.
8 "God brings him out of Egypt,
He is for him like the horns of the wild ox.
He will devour the nations *who are* his adversaries,
And will crush their bones in pieces,

24:1 Num 22:7; 23:23; Num 23:28

24:2 Num 11:26; 1 Sam 19:20; Rev 1:10

24:3 Num 24:15, 16

24:4 Num 22:20; Gen 15:1; Num 12:6

24:6 Ps 45:8; Ps 1:3

24:7 Num 24:20; 1 Sam 15:8; Ps 145:11-13

24:8 Num 23:22; Num 23:24; Ps 2:9; Ps 45:5

23:27 Balak took Balaam to several places to try to entice him to curse the Israelites. He thought a change of scenery might help change Balaam's mind. But changing locations won't change God's will. We must learn to face the source of our problems. Moving to escape problems only makes solving them more difficult. Problems rooted in us are not solved by a change of scenery. A change in location or job may only distract us from the need for us to change our heart.

24:1 Because Balaam was a sorcerer, he would look for omens or signs to help him tell the future. In this situation, however, it was clear that God himself was speaking, and so Balaam needed no other signs, real or imagined.

24:7 Who was Agag? *Agag* was the title for the king of the Amalekites, just as *Pharaoh* was the ruler of Egypt. Saul, the first king of Israel, defeated Agag (1 Samuel 15:8). Balaam has prophesied correctly the ruin of Israel's oldest enemy (Exodus 17:14–16).

And shatter *them* with his arrows.
9 "He couches, he lies down as a lion,
And as a lion, who dares rouse him?
Blessed is everyone who blesses you,
And cursed is everyone who curses you."
10 Then Balak's anger burned against Balaam, and he struck his hands together; and
Balak said to Balaam, "I called you to curse my enemies, but behold, you have persisted
in blessing them these three times!
11 "Therefore, flee to your place now. I said I would honor you greatly, but behold, the
LORD has held you back from honor."
12 Balaam said to Balak, "Did I not tell your messengers whom you had sent to me,
saying,
13 'Though Balak were to give me his house full of silver and gold, I could not do anything contrary to the command of the LORD, either good or bad, of my own accord. What
the LORD speaks, that I will speak'?
14 "And now, behold, I am going to my people; come, *and* I will advise you what this
people will do to your people in the days to come."
15 He took up his discourse and said,
"The oracle of Balaam the son of Beor,
And the oracle of the man whose eye is opened,
16 The oracle of him who hears the words of God,
And knows the knowledge of the Most High,
Who sees the vision of the Almighty,
Falling down, yet having his eyes uncovered.
17 "I see him, but not now;
I behold him, but not near;
A star shall come forth from Jacob,
A scepter shall rise from Israel,
And shall crush through the forehead of Moab,
And tear down all the sons of [29]Sheth.
18 "Edom shall be a possession,
Seir, its enemies, also will be a possession,
While Israel performs valiantly.
19 "One from Jacob shall have dominion,
And will destroy the remnant from the city."
20 And he looked at Amalek and took up his discourse and said,
"Amalek was the first of the nations,
But his end *shall be* destruction."
21 And he looked at the Kenite, and took up his discourse and said,
"Your dwelling place is enduring,
And your nest is set in the cliff.
22 "Nevertheless Kain will be consumed;
How long will Asshur keep you captive?"
23 Then he took up his discourse and said,
"Alas, who can live except God has ordained it?
24 "But ships *shall come* from the coast of Kittim,
And they shall afflict Asshur and will afflict Eber;
So they also *will come* to destruction."
25 Then Balaam arose and departed and returned to his place, and Balak also went
his way.

29 I.e. tumult

24:9 Gen 49:9; Num 23:24; Gen 12:3; 27:29
24:12 Num 22:18
24:13 Num 16:28; Num 22:20
24:14 Num 31:8, 16; Josh 13:22
24:15 Num 24:3, 4
24:17 Gen 49:10; Num 21:29; Is 15:1-16:14
24:18 Gen 27:29; Amos 9:11, 12; Gen 32:3
24:20 Num 24:24
24:21 Gen 15:19
24:22 Gen 10:21, 22
24:24 Gen 10:4; Ezek 27:6; Gen 10:21; Num 24:20
24:25 Num 24:14

24:11 Although Balaam's motives were not correct, in blessing Israel he acted with integrity. God's message had so filled him that Balaam spoke the truth. In so doing, he forfeited the reward that had lured him to speak in the first place. Staying true to God's Word may cost us promotions and advantages in the short run, but those who choose God over money will one day acquire heavenly wealth beyond measure (Matthew 6:19–21).

24:15–19 The star out of Jacob is often thought to refer to the coming Messiah. It was probably this prophecy that convinced the magi to travel to Israel to search for the baby Jesus (see Matthew 2:1, 2). It seems strange that God would use a sorcerer like Balaam to foretell the coming of the Messiah. But this teaches us that God can use anything or anyone to accomplish his plans. By using a sorcerer, God did not make sorcery acceptable; in fact, the Bible condemns it in several places (Exodus 22:18; 2 Chronicles 33:6; Revelation 18:23). Rather, God showed his ultimate sovereignty over good and evil.

The Sin of Peor

25 While Israel remained at Shittim, the people began to play the harlot with the
daughters of Moab.
2 For they invited the people to the sacrifices of their gods, and the people ate and
bowed down to their gods.
3 So Israel joined themselves to Baal of Peor, and the LORD was angry against Israel.
4 The LORD said to Moses, "Take all the leaders of the people and execute them in
broad daylight before the LORD, so that the fierce anger of the LORD may turn away
from Israel."
5 So Moses said to the judges of Israel, "Each of you slay his men who have joined
themselves to Baal of Peor."
6 Then behold, one of the sons of Israel came and brought to his relatives a Midianite woman, in the sight of Moses and in the sight of all the congregation of the sons of
Israel, while they were weeping at the doorway of the tent of meeting.
7 When Phinehas the son of Eleazar, the son of Aaron the priest, saw it, he arose from
the midst of the congregation and took a spear in his hand,
8 and he went after the man of Israel into the tent and pierced both of them through,
the man of Israel and the woman, through the body. So the plague on the sons of Israel
was checked.
9 Those who died by the plague were 24,000.

The Zeal of Phinehas

10 Then the LORD spoke to Moses, saying,
11 "Phinehas the son of Eleazar, the son of Aaron the priest, has turned away My wrath
from the sons of Israel in that he was jealous with My jealousy among them, so that I did
not destroy the sons of Israel in My jealousy.
12 "Therefore say, 'Behold, I give him My covenant of peace;
13 and it shall be for him and his descendants after him, a covenant of a perpetual priesthood, because he was jealous for his God and made atonement for the sons of Israel.' "
14 Now the name of the slain man of Israel who was slain with the Midianite woman,
was Zimri the son of Salu, a leader of a father's household among the Simeonites.
15 The name of the Midianite woman who was slain was Cozbi the daughter of Zur,
who was head of the people of a father's household in Midian.
16 Then the LORD spoke to Moses, saying,
17 "Be hostile to the Midianites and strike them;
18 for they have been hostile to you with their tricks, with which they have deceived

25:1 Num 33:49; Josh 2:1; Num 31:16; 1 Cor 10:8; Rev 2:14
25:2 Ex 34:15; Deut 32:38
25:3 Ps 106:28, 29; Hos 9:10
25:4 Deut 13:17
25:5 Ex 32:27
25:6 Num 22:4; Joel 2:17
25:7 Ps 106:30
25:8 Num 16:46-48
25:9 Num 14:37; 16:48-50; 31:16
25:11 Ps 106:30; Ex 20:5
25:12 Ps 106:30, 31; Is 54:10; Ezek 34:25; 37:26
25:13 Ex 29:9; Num 16:46
25:15 Num 25:18; Num 31:8
25:17 Num 25:1; 22:4; 31:1-3

25:1 This verse shows the great challenge Israel had to face. The most dangerous problem for Moses and Joshua was not Jericho's hostile army, but the ever-present temptation to compromise with the pagan Canaanite religions and cultures.

25:1–2 The Bible doesn't say how the Israelite men got involved in sexual immorality. We do know that sacred prostitution was a common practice among Canaanite religions. At first, they didn't think about worshiping idols; they were just interested in sex. Before long they started attending local feasts and family celebrations that involved idol worship. Soon they were in over their heads, absorbed into the practices of the pagan culture. Their desire for fun and pleasure caused them to loosen their spiritual commitment. Have you relaxed your standards in order to justify your desires?

25:1–3 This combination of sexual sin and idolatry, it turns out, was Balaam's idea (see 31:16; Revelation 2:14), the same Balaam who had just blessed Israel and who appeared to be on their side. It is easy to see how the Israelites were misled, for Balaam seemed to say and do all the right things—at least for a while (22—24). Not until Balaam had inflicted great damage on them did the Israelites realize that he was greedy, used sorcery, and was deeply involved in pagan religious practices. We must be careful to weigh both the words and the deeds of those who claim to offer spiritual help.

25:3 Baal was the most popular god in Canaan, the land Israel was about to enter. Represented by a bull, symbol of strength and fertility, he was the god of the rains and harvest. The Israelites were continually attracted to Baal worship, in which prostitution played a large part, throughout their years in Canaan. Because Baal was so popular, his name was often used as a generic title for all the local gods.

25:6 The phrase "brought to his relatives" referred to the person's inner room of his tent. Clearly the woman was brought into his tent for sex. Zimri (25:14) so disregarded the law of God that he brought that woman right into the camp.

25:10–11 It is clear from Phinehas's story that some anger is proper and justified. Phinehas was angry because of his zeal for the Lord. But how can we know when our anger is appropriate and when it should be restrained? Ask these questions when you become angry: (1) Why am I angry? (2) Whose rights are being violated (mine or another's)? (3) Is the truth (a principle of God) being violated? If only your rights are at stake, it may be wiser to keep angry feelings under control. But if the truth is at stake, anger is often justified, although violence and retaliation are usually the wrong way to express it (Phinehas's case was unique). If we are becoming more and more like God, we should be angered by sin.

25:12–13 Phinehas's act made atonement for the nation of Israel; in effect, what he did averted God's judgment. Because of this, his descendants would become the high priests of Israel. They continued so throughout the history of the tabernacle and the temple.

you in the affair of Peor and in the affair of Cozbi, the daughter of the leader of Midian,
their sister who was slain on the day of the plague because of Peor."

2. The second census of the nation

Census of a New Generation

26:1 Num 25:9
26 Then it came about after the plague, that the LORD spoke to Moses and to Eleazar the son of Aaron the priest, saying,
26:2 Ex 30:11-16; 38:25, 26; Num 1:2
2 "Take a census of all the congregation of the sons of Israel from twenty years old and
upward, by their fathers' households, whoever is able to go out to war in Israel."
26:3 Num 22:1; 33:48; 35:1
3 So Moses and Eleazar the priest spoke with them in the plains of Moab by the Jordan at Jericho, saying,
4 "*Take a census of the people* from twenty years old and upward, as the LORD has commanded Moses."
Now the sons of Israel who came out of the land of Egypt *were:*
5 Reuben, Israel's firstborn, the sons of Reuben: *of* Hanoch, the family of the
Hanochites; of Pallu, the family of the Palluites;
6 of Hezron, the family of the Hezronites; of Carmi, the family of the Carmites.
26:7 Num 1:21
7 These are the families of the Reubenites, and those who were numbered of them
were 43,730.
8 The son of Pallu: Eliab.
26:9 Num 1:16; 16:2
9 The sons of Eliab: Nemuel and Dathan and Abiram. These are the Dathan and
Abiram who were called by the congregation, who contended against Moses and against
Aaron in the company of Korah, when they contended against the LORD,
26:10 Num 16:32; Num 16:35, 38
10 and the earth opened its mouth and swallowed them up along with Korah, when
that company died, when the fire devoured 250 men, so that they became a warning.
26:11 Num 16:27, 33; Deut 24:16
11 The sons of Korah, however, did not die.
12 The sons of Simeon according to their families: of Nemuel, the family of the
Nemuelites; of Jamin, the family of the Jaminites; of Jachin, the family of the Jachinites;
13 of Zerah, the family of the Zerahites; of Shaul, the family of the Shaulites.
26:14 Num 1:23
14 These are the families of the Simeonites, 22,200.
15 The sons of Gad according to their families: of Zephon, the family of the Zephonites;
of Haggi, the family of the Haggites; of Shuni, the family of the Shunites;
16 of Ozni, the family of the Oznites; of Eri, the family of the Erites;
17 of Arod, the family of the Arodites; of Areli, the family of the Arelites.
26:18 Num 1:25
18 These are the families of the sons of Gad according to those who were numbered of
them, 40,500.
26:19 Gen 38:2; 46:12
19 The sons of Judah *were* Er and Onan, but Er and Onan died in the land of Canaan.
26:20 Gen 49:8; 1 Chr 2:3; Rev 7:5
20 The sons of Judah according to their families were: of Shelah, the family of the
Shelanites; of Perez, the family of the Perezites; of Zerah, the family of the Zerahites.
21 The sons of Perez were: of Hezron, the family of the Hezronites; of Hamul, the family
of the Hamulites.
26:22 Num 1:27
22 These are the families of Judah according to those who were numbered of them,
76,500.
26:23 Gen 46:13; 1 Chr 7:1
23 The sons of Issachar according to their families: *of* Tola, the family of the Tolaites;
of Puvah, the family of the Punites;
24 of Jashub, the family of the Jashubites; of Shimron, the family of the Shimronites.
26:25 Num 1:29
25 These are the families of Issachar according to those who were numbered of them,
64,300.
26:26 Gen 46:14
26 The sons of Zebulun according to their families: of Sered, the family of the Seredites;
of Elon, the family of the Elonites; of Jahleel, the family of the Jahleelites.
26:27 Num 1:31
27 These are the families of the Zebulunites according to those who were numbered
of them, 60,500.
26:28 Gen 46:20; Deut 33:16f
28 The sons of Joseph according to their families: Manasseh and Ephraim.
29 The sons of Manasseh: of Machir, the family of the Machirites; and Machir became
the father of Gilead: of Gilead, the family of the Gileadites.
26:29 Josh 17:1; 1 Chr 7:14f
30 These are the sons of Gilead: *of* Iezer, the family of the Iezerites; of Helek, the family of the Helekites;
26:30 Judg 6:11, 24, 34
31 and *of* Asriel, the family of the Asrielites; and *of* Shechem, the family of the She-
chemites;
32 and *of* Shemida, the family of the Shemidaites; and *of* Hepher, the family of the
Hepherites.

33 Now Zelophehad the son of Hepher had no sons, but only daughters; and the **26:33** Num 27:1
names of the daughters of Zelophehad were Mahlah, Noah, Hoglah, Milcah and
Tirzah.
34 These are the families of Manasseh; and those who were numbered of them were **26:34** Num 1:35
52,700.
35 These are the sons of Ephraim according to their families: of Shuthelah, the family
of the Shuthelahites; of Becher, the family of the Becherites; of Tahan, the family of the
Tahanites.
36 These are the sons of Shuthelah: of Eran, the family of the Eranites.
37 These are the families of the sons of Ephraim according to those who were num- **26:37** Num 1:33
bered of them, 32,500. These are the sons of Joseph according to their families.
38 The sons of Benjamin according to their families: of Bela, the family of the Belaites;
of Ashbel, the family of the Ashbelites; of Ahiram, the family of the Ahiramites;
39 of Shephupham, the family of the Shuphamites; of Hupham, the family of the
Huphamites.
40 The sons of Bela were Ard and Naaman: *of Ard,* the family of the Ardites; of Naaman, the family of the Naamites.
41 These are the sons of Benjamin according to their families; and those who were **26:41** Num 1:37
numbered of them were 45,600.
42 These are the sons of Dan according to their families: of Shuham, the family of the
Shuhamites. These are the families of Dan according to their families.
43 All the families of the Shuhamites, according to those who were numbered of them, **26:43** Num 1:39
were 64,400.
44 The sons of Asher according to their families: of Imnah, the family of the Imnites; **26:44** Gen 46:17; 1 Chr 7:30
of Ishvi, the family of the Ishvites; of Beriah, the family of the Beriites.
45 Of the sons of Beriah: of Heber, the family of the Heberites; of Malchiel, the family
of the Malchielites.
46 The name of the daughter of Asher *was* Serah.
47 These are the families of the sons of Asher according to those who were numbered **26:47** Num 1:41
of them, 53,400.
48 The sons of Naphtali according to their families: of Jahzeel, the family of the **26:48** Gen 46:24; 1 Chr 7:13
Jahzeelites; of Guni, the family of the Gunites;
49 of Jezer, the family of the Jezerites; of Shillem, the family of the Shillemites. **26:49** 1 Chr 7:13
50 These are the families of Naphtali according to their families; and those who were
numbered of them were 45,400. **26:50** Num 1:43
51 These are those who were numbered of the sons of Israel, 601,730.
52 Then the LORD spoke to Moses, saying, **26:51** Ex 12:37; 38:26; Num 1:46; 11:21
53 "Among these the land shall be divided for an inheritance according to the number
of names.
54 "To the larger *group* you shall increase their inheritance, and to the smaller *group* **26:54** Num 33:54
you shall diminish their inheritance; each shall be given their inheritance according to
those who were numbered of them.
55 "But the land shall be divided by lot. They shall receive their inheritance according **26:55** Num 33:54; 34:13
to the names of the tribes of their fathers.
56 "According to the selection by lot, their inheritance shall be divided between the larger
and the smaller *groups.*"
57 These are those who were numbered of the Levites according to their families: of **26:57** Gen 46:11; Ex 6:16; 1 Chr 6:1, 16
Gershon, the family of the Gershonites; of Kohath, the family of the Kohathites; of
Merari, the family of the Merarites.
58 These are the families of Levi: the family of the Libnites, the family of the Hebron- **26:58** Ex 6:20
ites, the family of the Mahlites, the family of the Mushites, the family of the Korahites.
Kohath became the father of Amram.
59 The name of Amram's wife was Jochebed, the daughter of Levi, who was born to **26:59** Ex 2:1, 2; 6:20
Levi in Egypt; and she bore to Amram: Aaron and Moses and their sister Miriam.
60 To Aaron were born Nadab and Abihu, Eleazar and Ithamar. **26:60** Num 3:2
61 But Nadab and Abihu died when they offered strange fire before the LORD.
62 Those who were numbered of them were 23,000, every male from a month old and **26:61** Lev 10:1, 2; Num 3:4
upward, for they were not numbered among the sons of Israel since no inheritance was
given to them among the sons of Israel. **26:62** Num 3:39; Num 1:47; Num 18:23, 24
63 These are those who were numbered by Moses and Eleazar the priest, who numbered the sons of Israel in the plains of Moab by the Jordan at Jericho.

26:64 Num 14:29-35; Deut 2:14 16; Heb 3:17

64 But among these there was not a man of those who were numbered by Moses and Aaron the priest, who numbered the sons of Israel in the wilderness of Sinai.

26:65 Num 14:26-35; Ps 90:3-10; 1 Cor 10:5; Deut 1:36; Josh 14:6-10

65 For the LORD had said of them, "They shall surely die in the wilderness." And not a man was left of them, except Caleb the son of Jephunneh and Joshua the son of Nun.

A Law of Inheritance

27:1 Num 26:33; 36:1; Num 26:33

27 Then the daughters of Zelophehad, the son of Hepher, the son of Gilead, the son of Machir, the son of Manasseh, of the families of Manasseh the son of Joseph, came near; and these are the names of his daughters: Mahlah, Noah and Hoglah and Milcah and Tirzah.

27:3 Num 26:64, 65; Num 26:33

2 They stood before Moses and before Eleazar the priest and before the leaders and all the congregation, at the doorway of the tent of meeting, saying,

3 "Our father died in the wilderness, yet he was not among the company of those who gathered themselves together against the LORD in the company of Korah; but he died in his own sin, and he had no sons.

4 "Why should the name of our father be withdrawn from among his family because he had no son? Give us a possession among our father's brothers."

27:5 Num 9:8; 27:21

5 So Moses brought their case before the LORD.

6 Then the LORD spoke to Moses, saying,

27:7 Num 36:2; Josh 17:4

7 "The daughters of Zelophehad are right in *their* statements. You shall surely give them a hereditary possession among their father's brothers, and you shall transfer the inheritance of their father to them.

8 "Further, you shall speak to the sons of Israel, saying, 'If a man dies and has no son, then you shall transfer his inheritance to his daughter.

9 'If he has no daughter, then you shall give his inheritance to his brothers.

10 'If he has no brothers, then you shall give his inheritance to his father's brothers.

27:11 Num 35:29

11 'If his father has no brothers, then you shall give his inheritance to his nearest relative in his own family, and he shall possess it; and it shall be a statutory ordinance to the sons of Israel, just as the LORD commanded Moses.' "

27:12 Deut 3:23-27; 32:48-52; Num 33:47, 48

12 Then the LORD said to Moses, "Go up to this mountain of Abarim, and see the land which I have given to the sons of Israel.

27:13 Num 31:2; Num 20:24, 28; Deut 10:6

13 "When you have seen it, you too will be gathered to your people, as Aaron your brother was;

27:14 Num 20:12; Deut 32:51; Ps 106:32

14 for in the wilderness of Zin, during the strife of the congregation, you rebelled against My command to treat Me as holy before their eyes at the water." (These are the waters of Meribah of Kadesh in the wilderness of Zin.)

Joshua to Succeed Moses

15 Then Moses spoke to the LORD, saying,

27:16 Num 16:22

16 "May the LORD, the God of the spirits of all flesh, appoint a man over the congregation,

---

26:64 A new census for a new generation. Thirty-eight years had elapsed since the first great census recorded in Numbers (see 1:1—2:33). During that time, every Israelite man and woman over 20 years of age—except Caleb, Joshua, and Moses—had died, and yet God's laws and the spiritual character of the nation were still intact. Numbers records some dramatic miracles. This is a quiet but powerful miracle often overlooked: A whole nation moved from one land to another, lost its entire adult population, yet managed to maintain its spiritual direction. Sometimes it may feel like God isn't working dramatic miracles in our lives. But God often works in quiet ways to bring about his long-range purposes.

27:3 "Died in his own sin" means that he died a natural death. His death fell under the judgment of the entire nation for believing the faithless spies.

27:3–4 Up to this point, the Hebrew law gave sons alone the right to inherit. The daughters of Zelophehad, having no brothers, came to Moses to ask for their father's possessions. God told Moses that if a man died without sons, his inheritance would go to his daughters (27:8). But the daughters could keep it only if they married within their own tribe, probably so the territorial lines would remain intact (36:5–12).

27:15–17 Moses asked God to appoint a leader who was capable of directing both external and internal affairs—one who could lead them in battle, but who would also care for their needs. The Lord responded by appointing Joshua. Many people want to be known as leaders. Some are very capable of reaching their goals, while others care deeply for the people in their charge. The best leaders are both goal-oriented and people-oriented.

27:15–21 Moses did not want to leave his work without making sure a new leader was ready to replace him. First he asked God to help him find a replacement. Then, when Joshua was selected, Moses gave him a variety of tasks to ease the transition into his new position. Moses also clearly told the people that Joshua had the authority and the ability to lead the nation. His display of confidence in Joshua was good for both Joshua and the people. To minimize leadership gaps, anyone in a leadership position should train others to carry on the duties should he or she suddenly or eventually have to leave. While you have the opportunity, follow Moses' pattern: pray, select, develop, and commission.

17 who will go out and come in before them, and who will lead them out and bring
them in, so that the congregation of the LORD will not be like sheep which have no shepherd."

27:17 Deut 31:2; 2 Chr 1:10; 1 Kin 22:17; Ezek 34:5; Matt 9:36; Mark 6:34

18 So the LORD said to Moses, "Take Joshua the son of Nun, a man in whom is the
Spirit, and lay your hand on him;

27:18 Num 11:25-29; Deut 34:9; Num 27:23

19 and have him stand before Eleazar the priest and before all the congregation, and
commission him in their sight.
20 "You shall put some of your authority on him, in order that all the congregation of
the sons of Israel may obey *him.*

27:19 Deut 3:28; 31:3, 7, 8, 23

21 "Moreover, he shall stand before Eleazar the priest, who shall inquire for him by the
judgment of the Urim before the LORD. At his command they shall go out and at his
command they shall come in, *both* he and the sons of Israel with him, even all the congregation."

27:21 Ex 28:30; 1 Sam 28:6

22 Moses did just as the LORD commanded him; and he took Joshua and set him before Eleazar the priest and before all the congregation.
23 Then he laid his hands on him and commissioned him, just as the LORD had spoken
through Moses.

27:23 Deut 31:23

3. Instructions concerning offerings

Laws for Offerings

28 Then the LORD spoke to Moses, saying,
2 "Command the sons of Israel and say to them, 'You shall be careful to present
My offering, My food for My offerings by fire, of a soothing aroma to Me, at their appointed time.'

28:2 Lev 3:11

3 "You shall say to them, 'This is the offering by fire which you shall offer to the
LORD: two male lambs one year old without defect *as* a continual burnt offering
every day.

28:3 Ex 29:38-42

4 'You shall offer the one lamb in the morning and the other lamb you shall offer at
twilight;
5 also a tenth of an ephah of fine flour for a grain offering, mixed with a fourth of a
hin of beaten oil.

28:5 Ex 16:36; Num 15:4; Lev 2:1

6 'It is a continual burnt offering which was ordained in Mount Sinai as a soothing
aroma, an offering by fire to the LORD.
7 'Then the drink offering with it *shall be* a fourth of a hin for each lamb, in the holy
place you shall pour out a drink offering of strong drink to the LORD.

28:7 Ex 29:42

8 'The other lamb you shall offer at twilight; as the grain offering of the morning
and as its drink offering, you shall offer it, an offering by fire, a soothing aroma to the
LORD.
9 'Then on the sabbath day two male lambs one year old without defect, and two-tenths
of an ephah of fine flour mixed with oil as a grain offering, and its drink offering:
10 '*This is* the burnt offering of every sabbath in addition to the continual burnt offering and its drink offering.

28:10 Num 28:3

11 'Then at the beginning of each of your months you shall present a burnt offering to
the LORD: two bulls and one ram, seven male lambs one year old without defect;

28:11 Num 10:10; Ezek 46:6, 7

12 and three-tenths *of an ephah* of fine flour mixed with oil for a grain offering,
for each bull; and two-tenths of fine flour mixed with oil for a grain offering, for the
one ram;

28:12 Num 15:4-12

13 and a tenth *of an ephah* of fine flour mixed with oil for a grain offering for each
lamb, for a burnt offering of a soothing aroma, an offering by fire to the LORD.
14 'Their drink offerings shall be half a hin of wine for a bull and a third of a hin for the
ram and a fourth of a hin for a lamb; this is the burnt offering of each month throughout
the months of the year.

28:1–2 Offerings had to be brought regularly and presented according to prescribed rituals under the priests' supervision. Following these rituals took time, and this gave the people the opportunity to prepare their hearts for worship. Unless our hearts are ready, worship is meaningless. By contrast, God is delighted, and we get more from it, when our hearts are prepared to come before him in a spirit of thankfulness.

28:9–10 Why were extra offerings made on the Sabbath day? The Sabbath was a special day of rest and worship commemorating both creation (Exodus 20:8–11) and the deliverance from Egypt (Deuteronomy 5:12–15). Because of the significance of this special day, it was only natural to offer extra sacrifices on it.

15 'And one male goat for a sin offering to the LORD; it shall be offered with its drink
offering in addition to the continual burnt offering.
16 'Then on the fourteenth day of the first month shall be the LORD'S Passover.
17 'On the fifteenth day of this month *shall be* a feast, unleavened bread *shall be* eaten
for seven days.
18 'On the first day *shall be* a holy convocation; you shall do no laborious work.
19 'You shall present an offering by fire, a burnt offering to the LORD: two bulls and
one ram and seven male lambs one year old, having them without defect.
20 'For their grain offering, you shall offer fine flour mixed with oil: three-tenths *of an*
ephah for a bull and two-tenths for the ram.
21 'A tenth *of an ephah* you shall offer for each of the seven lambs;
22 and one male goat for a sin offering to make atonement for you.
23 'You shall present these besides the burnt offering of the morning, which is for a
continual burnt offering.
24 'After this manner you shall present daily, for seven days, the food of the offering by
fire, of a soothing aroma to the LORD; it shall be presented with its drink offering in
addition to the continual burnt offering.
25 'On the seventh day you shall have a holy convocation; you shall do no laborious
work.
26 'Also on the day of the first fruits, when you present a new grain offering to the LORD
in your *Feast of* Weeks, you shall have a holy convocation; you shall do no laborious work.
27 'You shall offer a burnt offering for a soothing aroma to the LORD: two young bulls,
one ram, seven male lambs one year old;
28 and their grain offering, fine flour mixed with oil: three-tenths *of an ephah* for each
bull, two-tenths for the one ram,
29 a tenth for each of the seven lambs;
30 *also* one male goat to make atonement for you.
31 'Besides the continual burnt offering and its grain offering, you shall present *them*
with their drink offerings. They shall be without defect.

28:15 Num 28:3
28:16 Ex 12:1-20; Lev 23:5-8; Deut 16:1-8
28:17 Lev 23:6; Ex 23:15; 34:18; Deut 16:3-8
28:18 Lev 23:7
28:19 Deut 15:21
28:22 Lev 16:18; Rom 8:3; Gal 4:4f
28:23 Num 28:3
28:24 Lev 3:11; Num 28:3
28:25 Num 28:18
28:26 Ex 23:16; 34:22; Lev 23:15-21; Deut 16:9-12; Num 28:18
28:31 Num 28:3

Offerings of the Seventh Month

29 'Now in the seventh month, on the first day of the month, you shall also have a
holy convocation; you shall do no laborious work. It will be to you a day for blowing trumpets.
2 'You shall offer a burnt offering as a soothing aroma to the LORD: one bull, one ram,
and seven male lambs one year old without defect;
3 also their grain offering, fine flour mixed with oil: three-tenths *of an ephah* for the
bull, two-tenths for the ram,
4 and one-tenth for each of the seven lambs.
5 '*Offer* one male goat for a sin offering, to make atonement for you,
6 besides the burnt offering of the new moon and its grain offering, and the continual
burnt offering and its grain offering, and their drink offerings, according to their ordinance, for a soothing aroma, an offering by fire to the LORD.
7 'Then on the tenth day of this seventh month you shall have a holy convocation, and
you shall humble yourselves; you shall not do any work.
8 'You shall present a burnt offering to the LORD *as* a soothing aroma: one bull, one
ram, seven male lambs one year old, having them without defect;
9 and their grain offering, fine flour mixed with oil: three-tenths *of an ephah* for the
bull, two-tenths for the one ram,

29:1 Ex 23:16; 34:22; Lev 23:23-25; Num 28:26
29:6 Num 28:27; Num 28:3
29:7 Lev 16:29-34; 23:26-32
29:8 Lev 22:20; Deut 15:21; 17:1

29:1ff God placed many holidays on Israel's calendar. The Feast of Trumpets was one of three great holidays celebrated in the seventh month (the Feast of Booths and day of atonement were the other two). These holidays provided a time to refresh the mind and body and to renew one's commitment to God. If you feel tired or far from God, try taking a "spiritual holiday." Separate yourself from your daily routine and concentrate on renewing your commitment to God.

29:1–2 The Feast of Trumpets demonstrated three important principles that we should follow in our worship today: (1) The people gathered together to celebrate and worship. There is an extra benefit to be gained from worshiping with other believers. (2) The normal daily routine was suspended, and no hard work was done. It takes time to worship, and setting aside the time allows us to adjust our attitudes before and reflect afterwards. (3) The people sacrificed animals as burnt offerings to God. We show our commitment to God when we give something of value to him. The best gift, of course, is ourselves.

10 a tenth for each of the seven lambs;
11 one male goat for a sin offering, besides the sin offering of atonement and the con- 29:11
tinual burnt offering and its grain offering, and their drink offerings. Lev 16:3, 5; Num 28:3
12 'Then on the fifteenth day of the seventh month you shall have a holy convocation;
you shall do no laborious work, and you shall observe a feast to the LORD for seven days. 29:12 Lev 23:33-35; Deut 16:13-15; Num 29:1
13 'You shall present a burnt offering, an offering by fire as a soothing aroma to the
LORD: thirteen bulls, two rams, fourteen male lambs one year old, which are without
defect;
14 and their grain offering, fine flour mixed with oil: three-tenths *of an ephah* for each
of the thirteen bulls, two-tenths for each of the two rams,
15 and a tenth for each of the fourteen lambs;
16 and one male goat for a sin offering, besides the continual burnt offering, its grain 29:16
offering and its drink offering. Num 28:3
17 'Then on the second day: twelve bulls, two rams, fourteen male lambs one year old 29:17
without defect; Lev 23:36
18 and their grain offering and their drink offerings for the bulls, for the rams and for 29:18
the lambs, by their number according to the ordinance; Lev 2:1-16
19 and one male goat for a sin offering, besides the continual burnt offering and its 29:19 Num 28:8
grain offering, and their drink offerings.
20 'Then on the third day: eleven bulls, two rams, fourteen male lambs one year old
without defect;
21 and their grain offering and their drink offerings for the bulls, for the rams and for
the lambs, by their number according to the ordinance;
22 and one male goat for a sin offering, besides the continual burnt offering and its
grain offering and its drink offering.
23 'Then on the fourth day: ten bulls, two rams, fourteen male lambs one year old without defect;
24 their grain offering and their drink offerings for the bulls, for the rams and for the
lambs, by their number according to the ordinance;
25 and one male goat for a sin offering, besides the continual burnt offering, its grain
offering and its drink offering.
26 'Then on the fifth day: nine bulls, two rams, fourteen male lambs one year old with- 29:26
out defect; Heb 7:26
27 and their grain offering and their drink offerings for the bulls, for the rams and for
the lambs, by their number according to the ordinance;
28 and one male goat for a sin offering, besides the continual burnt offering and its
grain offering and its drink offering.
29 'Then on the sixth day: eight bulls, two rams, fourteen male lambs one year old without defect;
30 and their grain offering and their drink offerings for the bulls, for the rams and for
the lambs, by their number according to the ordinance;
31 and one male goat for a sin offering, besides the continual burnt offering, its grain
offering and its drink offerings.
32 'Then on the seventh day: seven bulls, two rams, fourteen male lambs one year old
without defect;
33 and their grain offering and their drink offerings for the bulls, for the rams and for
the lambs, by their number according to the ordinance;
34 and one male goat for a sin offering, besides the continual burnt offering, its grain
offering and its drink offering.
35 'On the eighth day you shall have a solemn assembly; you shall do no laborious work. 29:35
36 'But you shall present a burnt offering, an offering by fire, as a soothing aroma to Lev 23:36
the LORD: one bull, one ram, seven male lambs one year old without defect;
37 their grain offering and their drink offerings for the bull, for the ram and for the
lambs, by their number according to the ordinance;
38 and one male goat for a sin offering, besides the continual burnt offering and its
grain offering and its drink offering.
39 'You shall present these to the LORD at your appointed times, besides your votive 29:39
offerings and your freewill offerings, for your burnt offerings and for your grain offer- Lev 23:2
ings and for your drink offerings and for your peace offerings.' "
40 Moses spoke to the sons of Israel in accordance with all that the LORD had commanded Moses.

The Law of Vows

30:1 Num 1:4, 16; 7:2

30 Then Moses spoke to the heads of the tribes of the sons of Israel, saying, "This is
the word which the LORD has commanded.

30:2 Deut 23:21-23; Matt 5:33

2 "If a man makes a vow to the LORD, or takes an oath to bind himself with a binding
obligation, he shall not violate his word; he shall do according to all that proceeds out of
his mouth.
3 "Also if a woman makes a vow to the LORD, and binds herself by an obligation in her
father's house in her youth,
4 and her father hears her vow and her obligation by which she has bound herself,
and her father says nothing to her, then all her vows shall stand and every obligation by
which she has bound herself shall stand.
5 "But if her father should forbid her on the day he hears *of it,* none of her vows or her
obligations by which she has bound herself shall stand; and the LORD will forgive her
because her father had forbidden her.
6 "However, if she should marry while under her vows or the rash statement of her lips
by which she has bound herself,
7 and her husband hears of it and says nothing to her on the day he hears *it,* then her
vows shall stand and her obligations by which she has bound herself shall stand.
8 "But if on the day her husband hears *of it,* he forbids her, then he shall annul her vow
which she is under and the rash statement of her lips by which she has bound herself;
and the LORD will forgive her.
9 "But the vow of a widow or of a divorced woman, everything by which she has bound
herself, shall stand against her.
10 "However, if she vowed in her husband's house, or bound herself by an obligation
with an oath,
11 and her husband heard *it,* but said nothing to her *and* did not forbid her, then all
her vows shall stand and every obligation by which she bound herself shall stand.
12 "But if her husband indeed annuls them on the day he hears *them,* then whatever
proceeds out of her lips concerning her vows or concerning the obligation of herself shall
not stand; her husband has annulled them, and the LORD will forgive her.
13 "Every vow and every binding oath to humble herself, her husband may confirm it or
her husband may annul it.
14 "But if her husband indeed says nothing to her from day to day, then he confirms all
her vows or all her obligations which are on her; he has confirmed them, because he said
nothing to her on the day he heard them.
15 "But if he indeed annuls them after he has heard them, then he shall bear her guilt."
16 These are the statutes which the LORD commanded Moses, *as* between a man and
his wife, *and as* between a father and his daughter, *while she is* in her youth in her father's
house.

4. Vengeance on the Midianites

The Slaughter of Midian

31:2 Num 25:1, 16, 17; Num 20:24, 26; 27:13

31 Then the LORD spoke to Moses, saying,
2 "Take full vengeance for the sons of Israel on the Midianites; afterward you
will be gathered to your people."

30:1–2 Moses reminded the people that their promises to God and others must be kept. In ancient times, people did not sign written contracts. A person's word was as binding as a signature. To make a vow even more binding, an offering was given along with it. No one was forced by law to make a vow; but once made, vows had to be fulfilled. Breaking a vow meant a broken trust and a broken relationship. Trust is still the basis of our relationships with God and others. A broken promise today is just as harmful as it was in Moses' day.

30:3–8 Under Israelite law, parents could overrule their children's vows. This helped young people avoid the consequences of making foolish promises or costly commitments. From this law comes an important principle for both parents and children. Young people still living at home should seek their parents' help when they make decisions. A parent's experience could save a child from a serious mistake. Parents, however, should exercise their authority with caution and grace. They should let children learn from their mistakes while protecting them from disaster.

31:1ff The Midianites were a nomadic people who descended from Abraham and his second wife, Keturah. The land of Midian lay far to the south of Canaan, but large bands of Midianites roamed many miles from their homeland, searching for grazing areas for their flocks. Such a group was near the promised land when the Israelites arrived. When Moses fled from Egypt (Exodus 2), he took refuge in the land of Midian. His wife and father-in-law were Midianites. Despite this alliance, the Israelites and Midianites were always bitter enemies.

3 Moses spoke to the people, saying, "Arm men from among you for the war, that **31:3**
they may go against Midian to execute the LORD'S vengeance on Midian. Lev 26:25
4 "A thousand from each tribe of all the tribes of Israel you shall send to the war."
5 So there were furnished from the thousands of Israel, a thousand from each tribe,
twelve thousand armed for war.
6 Moses sent them, a thousand from each tribe, to the war, and Phinehas the son of **31:6**
Eleazar the priest, to the war with them, and the holy vessels and the trumpets for the Num 14:44; Num 10:8, 9
alarm in his hand.
7 So they made war against Midian, just as the LORD had commanded Moses, and **31:7**
they killed every male. Deut 20:13; Judg 21:11; 1 Kin 11:15, 16
8 They killed the kings of Midian along with the *rest of* their slain: Evi and Rekem
and Zur and Hur and Reba, the five kings of Midian; they also killed Balaam the son of **31:8**
Beor with the sword. Josh 13:21; Num 25:15; Num 31:16; Josh 13:22
9 The sons of Israel captured the women of Midian and their little ones; and all their
cattle and all their flocks and all their goods they plundered.
10 Then they burned all their cities where they lived and all their camps with fire.
11 They took all the spoil and all the prey, both of man and of beast. **31:11**
12 They brought the captives and the prey and the spoil to Moses, and to Eleazar the Deut 20:14
priest and to the congregation of the sons of Israel, to the camp at the plains of Moab,
which are by the Jordan *opposite* Jericho.
13 Moses and Eleazar the priest and all the leaders of the congregation went out to
meet them outside the camp.
14 Moses was angry with the officers of the army, the captains of thousands and the
captains of hundreds, who had come from service in the war.
15 And Moses said to them, "Have you spared all the women? **31:15**
16 "Behold, these caused the sons of Israel, through the counsel of Balaam, to trespass Deut 20:14
against the LORD in the matter of Peor, so the plague was among the congregation of **31:16**
the LORD. Num 25:1-9; Num 31:8
17 "Now therefore, kill every male among the little ones, and kill every woman who has **31:17**
known man intimately. Deut 7:2; 20:16-18
18 "But all the girls who have not known man intimately, spare for yourselves.
19 "And you, camp outside the camp seven days; whoever has killed any person and **31:19**
whoever has touched any slain, purify yourselves, you and your captives, on the third Num 19:11-22
day and on the seventh day.
20 "You shall purify for yourselves every garment and every article of leather and all
the work of goats' *hair,* and all articles of wood."
21 Then Eleazar the priest said to the men of war who had gone to battle, "This is the
statute of the law which the LORD has commanded Moses:
22 only the gold and the silver, the bronze, the iron, the tin and the lead,
23 everything that can stand the fire, you shall pass through the fire, and it shall be **31:23**
clean, but it shall be purified with water for impurity. But whatever cannot stand the fire Num 19:9, 17
you shall pass through the water.
24 "And you shall wash your clothes on the seventh day and be clean, and afterward
you may enter the camp."

Division of the Booty

25 Then the LORD spoke to Moses, saying,
26 "You and Eleazar the priest and the heads of the fathers' *households* of the congregation take a count of the booty that was captured, both of man and of animal;

31:14–16 Because Midianites were responsible for enticing Israel into Baal worship, God commanded Israel to destroy them (25:16–18). But Israel took the women as captives, rather than killing them, probably because of the tempting enticements of the Midianites' sinful life-style. When we discover sin in our lives, we must deal with it completely. When the Israelites later entered the promised land, it was their indifferent attitude to sin that eventually ruined them. Moses dealt with the sin promptly and completely. When God points out sin, move quickly to remove it from your life.

31:16 Balaam's story (22:1—24:25), taken alone, would lead us to believe that Balaam was an honest and God-fearing man. But here is the first of much Biblical evidence that Balaam was not the good man he might appear to be. For more on Balaam, see the notes on 22:9 and 25:1–3, and Balaam's Profile in chapter 22.

31:25–30 Moses told the Israelites to give a portion of the war booty to God. Another portion was to go to the people who remained behind. Similarly, the money we earn is not ours alone. Everything we possess comes directly or indirectly from God and ultimately belongs to him. We should return a portion to him and also share a portion with those in need.

31:27 Josh 22:8

27 and divide the booty between the warriors who went out to battle and all the congregation.

31:28 Num 18:21-30

28 "Levy a tax for the LORD from the men of war who went out to battle, one in five hundred of the persons and of the cattle and of the donkeys and of the sheep;
29 take it from their half and give it to Eleazar the priest, as an offering to the LORD.

31:30 Num 3:7, 8, 25, 26, 31, 36, 37; 18:3, 4

30 "From the sons of Israel's half, you shall take one drawn out of every fifty of the persons, of the cattle, of the donkeys and of the sheep, from all the animals, and give them to the Levites who keep charge of the tabernacle of the LORD."
31 Moses and Eleazar the priest did just as the LORD had commanded Moses.
32 Now the booty that remained from the spoil which the men of war had plundered was 675,000 sheep,
33 and 72,000 cattle,
34 and 61,000 donkeys,
35 and of human beings, of the women who had not known man intimately, all the persons were 32,000.
36 The half, the portion of those who went out to war, was *as follows:* the number of sheep was 337,500,
37 and the LORD'S levy of the sheep was 675;
38 and the cattle were 36,000, from which the LORD'S levy was 72;
39 and the donkeys were 30,500, from which the LORD'S levy was 61;
40 and the human beings were 16,000, from whom the LORD'S levy was 32 persons.

31:41 Num 5:9, 10; 18:19

41 Moses gave the levy *which was* the LORD'S offering to Eleazar the priest, just as the LORD had commanded Moses.
42 As for the sons of Israel's half, which Moses separated from the men who had gone to war—
43 now the congregation's half was 337,500 sheep,
44 and 36,000 cattle,
45 and 30,500 donkeys,
46 and the human beings were 16,000—
47 and from the sons of Israel's half, Moses took one drawn out of every fifty, both of man and of animals, and gave them to the Levites, who kept charge of the tabernacle of the LORD, just as the LORD had commanded Moses.
48 Then the officers who were over the thousands of the army, the captains of thousands and the captains of hundreds, approached Moses,
49 and they said to Moses, "Your servants have taken a census of men of war who are in our charge, and no man of us is missing.

31:50 Ex 30:12-16

50 "So we have brought as an offering to the LORD what each man found, articles of gold, armlets and bracelets, signet rings, earrings and necklaces, to make atonement for ourselves before the LORD."
51 Moses and Eleazar the priest took the gold from them, all kinds of wrought articles.
52 All the gold of the offering which they offered up to the LORD, from the captains of thousands and the captains of hundreds, was 16,750 shekels.

31:53 Num 31:32; Deut 20:14

53 The men of war had taken booty, every man for himself.

31:54 Ex 30:16

54 So Moses and Eleazar the priest took the gold from the captains of thousands and of hundreds, and brought it to the tent of meeting as a memorial for the sons of Israel before the LORD.

5. The Transjordan tribes

Reuben and Gad Settle in Gilead

32:1 Ex 12:38; Num 21:32

32 Now the sons of Reuben and the sons of Gad had an exceedingly large number of livestock. So when they saw the land of Jazer and the land of Gilead, that it was indeed a place suitable for livestock,

---

31:48–50 After carefully accounting for all their men, the officers discovered that not one soldier had been lost in battle. At once they thanked God. After going through tough times, we should be quick to thank God for delivering us and protecting us from severe loss.

32:1ff Three tribes (Reuben, Gad, and the half-tribe of Manasseh) wanted to live east of the Jordan River on land they had already conquered. Moses immediately assumed they had selfish motives and were trying to avoid helping the others fight for the land across the river. But Moses jumped to the wrong conclusion. In dealing with people, we must find out all the facts before making up our minds. We shouldn't automatically assume that their motives are wrong, even if their plans sound suspicious.

2 the sons of Gad and the sons of Reuben came and spoke to Moses and to Eleazar
the priest and to the leaders of the congregation, saying,
3 "Ataroth, Dibon, Jazer, Nimrah, Heshbon, Elealeh, Sebam, Nebo and Beon,
4 the land which the LORD conquered before the congregation of Israel, is a land for
livestock, and your servants have livestock."
5 They said, "If we have found favor in your sight, let this land be given to your servants as a possession; do not take us across the Jordan."
6 But Moses said to the sons of Gad and to the sons of Reuben, "Shall your brothers
go to war while you yourselves sit here?
7 "Now why are you discouraging the sons of Israel from crossing over into the land
which the LORD has given them?
8 "This is what your fathers did when I sent them from Kadesh-barnea to see the land.
9 "For when they went up to the valley of Eshcol and saw the land, they discouraged
the sons of Israel so that they did not go into the land which the LORD had given them.
10 "So the LORD'S anger burned in that day, and He swore, saying,
11 'None of the men who came up from Egypt, from twenty years old and upward, shall
see the land which I swore to Abraham, to Isaac and to Jacob; for they did not follow Me
fully,
12 except Caleb the son of Jephunneh the Kenizzite and Joshua the son of Nun, for
they have followed the LORD fully.'
13 "So the LORD'S anger burned against Israel, and He made them wander in the wilderness forty years, until the entire generation of those who had done evil in the sight of
the LORD was destroyed.
14 "Now behold, you have risen up in your fathers' place, a brood of sinful men, to add
still more to the burning anger of the LORD against Israel.
15 "For if you turn away from following Him, He will once more abandon them in the
wilderness, and you will destroy all these people."
16 Then they came near to him and said, "We will build here sheepfolds for our livestock and cities for our little ones;
17 but we ourselves will be armed ready *to go* before the sons of Israel, until we have
brought them to their place, while our little ones live in the fortified cities because of the
inhabitants of the land.
18 "We will not return to our homes until every one of the sons of Israel has possessed
his inheritance.
19 "For we will not have an inheritance with them on the other side of the Jordan and
beyond, because our inheritance has fallen to us on this side of the Jordan toward the east."
20 So Moses said to them, "If you will do this, if you will arm yourselves before the
LORD for the war,
21 and all of you armed men cross over the Jordan before the LORD until He has driven
His enemies out from before Him,

32:3 Num 32:34-38
32:4 Num 21:34
32:7 Num 13:27-14:4
32:8 Num 13:3, 26; Deut 1:19-25
32:9 Num 13:24; Deut 1:24
32:10 Num 14:11f; Deut 1:34
32:11 Num 14:28-30
32:12 Deut 1:36; Josh 14:8f
32:13 Num 14:33-35
32:14 Deut 1:34f
32:15 Deut 30:17, 18; 2 Chr 7:19, 20
32:17 Josh 4:12, 13
32:18 Josh 22:1-4
32:19 Josh 12:1; 13:8
32:20 Deut 3:18

32:16 A simple sheepfold for livestock had four roughly built stone walls, high enough to keep wild animals out. Sometimes the top of the wall was lined with thorns to further discourage predators and thieves. The sheepfold's single entrance made it easier for a shepherd to guard his flock. Often several shepherds used a single fold and took turns guarding the entrance. Mingling the animals was no problem since each flock responded readily to its own shepherd's voice. The three tribes who chose to remain east of the Jordan River wanted to build sheepfolds to protect their flocks and cities to protect their families before the men crossed the river to help the rest of the tribes conquer the promised land.

32:16–19 The land on the east side of the Jordan had been conquered. The hard work was done by all of the tribes together. But the tribes of Reuben and Gad and the half-tribe of Manasseh did not stop after their land was cleared. They promised to keep working with the others until everyone's land was conquered. After others have helped you, do you make excuses to escape helping them? Finish the whole job, even those parts that may not benefit you directly.

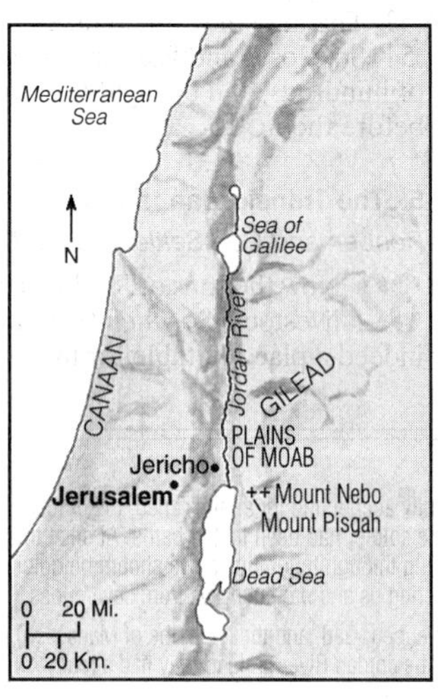

PREPARING TO ENTER THE PROMISED LAND
The Israelites had been camped in the plains of Moab, across from Jericho. From this position, they were ready to enter the promised land.

32:22 Deut 3:20

22 and the land is subdued before the LORD, then afterward you shall return and be
free of obligation toward the LORD and toward Israel, and this land shall be yours for a
possession before the LORD.

32:23 Gen 4:7; 44:16; Is 59:12

23 "But if you will not do so, behold, you have sinned against the LORD, and be sure
your sin will find you out.

32:24 Num 30:2

24 "Build yourselves cities for your little ones, and sheepfolds for your sheep, and do
what you have promised."

25 The sons of Gad and the sons of Reuben spoke to Moses, saying, "Your servants
will do just as my lord commands.

32:26 Josh 1:14

26 "Our little ones, our wives, our livestock and all our cattle shall remain there in the
cities of Gilead;

32:27 Josh 4:12

27 while your servants, everyone who is armed for war, will cross over in the presence
of the LORD to battle, just as my lord says."

28 So Moses gave command concerning them to Eleazar the priest, and to Joshua
the son of Nun, and to the heads of the fathers' *households* of the tribes of the sons of
Israel.

29 Moses said to them, "If the sons of Gad and the sons of Reuben, everyone who is
armed for battle, will cross with you over the Jordan in the presence of the LORD, and
the land is subdued before you, then you shall give them the land of Gilead for a possession;

30 but if they will not cross over with you armed, they shall have possessions among
you in the land of Canaan."

31 The sons of Gad and the sons of Reuben answered, saying, "As the LORD has said
to your servants, so we will do.

32 "We ourselves will cross over armed in the presence of the LORD into the land
of Canaan, and the possession of our inheritance *shall remain* with us across the
Jordan."

32:33 Deut 3:8-17; Josh 12:1-6

33 So Moses gave to them, to the sons of Gad and to the sons of Reuben and to the
half-tribe of Joseph's son Manasseh, the kingdom of Sihon, king of the Amorites and
the kingdom of Og, the king of Bashan, the land with its cities with *their* territories, the
cities of the surrounding land.

32:34 Deut 2:36

34 The sons of Gad built Dibon and Ataroth and Aroer,

35 and Atroth-shophan and Jazer and Jogbehah,

32:36 Num 32:3

36 and Beth-nimrah and Beth-haran as fortified cities, and sheepfolds for sheep.

37 The sons of Reuben built Heshbon and Elealeh and Kiriathaim,

32:38 Is 46:1

38 and Nebo and Baal-meon—*their* names being changed—and Sibmah, and they gave
other names to the cities which they built.

32:39 Gen 50:23

39 The sons of Machir the son of Manasseh went to Gilead and took it, and dispossessed the Amorites who were in it.

32:40 Deut 3:12, 13, 15; Josh 17:1

40 So Moses gave Gilead to Machir the son of Manasseh, and he lived in it.

32:41 Deut 3:14; Judg 10:4

41 Jair the son of Manasseh went and took its towns, and called them Havvoth-jair.

32:42 2 Sam 18:18; Ps 49:11

42 Nobah went and took Kenath and its villages, and called it Nobah after his own name.

6. Camped on the plains of Moab

Review of the Journey from Egypt to Jordan

33:1 Ps 77:20; 105:26; Mic 6:4

33 These are the journeys of the sons of Israel, by which they came out from the land
of Egypt by their armies, under the leadership of Moses and Aaron.

2 Moses recorded their starting places according to their journeys by the command
of the LORD, and these are their journeys according to their starting places.

33:3 Ex 12:37; Ex 14:8

3 They journeyed from Rameses in the first month, on the fifteenth day of the first
month; on the next day after the Passover the sons of Israel started out boldly in the
sight of all the Egyptians,

33:1ff Look at the map in the introduction to the book of Numbers to see the travels of the Israelites.

33:2 Moses recorded the Israelites' journeys as God instructed him, providing a record of their spiritual as well as geographic progress. Have you made spiritual progress lately? Recording your thoughts about God and lessons you have learned over a period of time can be a valuable aid to spiritual growth. A record of your spiritual pilgrimage will let you check up on your progress and avoid repeating past mistakes.

4 while the Egyptians were burying all their firstborn whom the LORD had struck down
among them. The LORD had also executed judgments on their gods.
5 Then the sons of Israel journeyed from Rameses and camped in Succoth.
6 They journeyed from Succoth and camped in Etham, which is on the edge of the
wilderness.
7 They journeyed from Etham and turned back to Pi-hahiroth, which faces Baal-
zephon, and they camped before Migdol.
8 They journeyed from before Hahiroth and passed through the midst of the sea into
the wilderness; and they went three days' journey in the wilderness of Etham and camped
at Marah.
9 They journeyed from Marah and came to Elim; and in Elim there were twelve springs
of water and seventy palm trees, and they camped there.
10 They journeyed from Elim and camped by the Red Sea.
11 They journeyed from the Red Sea and camped in the wilderness of Sin.
12 They journeyed from the wilderness of Sin and camped at Dophkah.
13 They journeyed from Dophkah and camped at Alush.
14 They journeyed from Alush and camped at Rephidim; now it was there that the
people had no water to drink.
15 They journeyed from Rephidim and camped in the wilderness of Sinai.
16 They journeyed from the wilderness of Sinai and camped at Kibroth-hattaavah.
17 They journeyed from Kibroth-hattaavah and camped at Hazeroth.
18 They journeyed from Hazeroth and camped at Rithmah.
19 They journeyed from Rithmah and camped at Rimmon-perez.
20 They journeyed from Rimmon-perez and camped at Libnah.
21 They journeyed from Libnah and camped at Rissah.
22 They journeyed from Rissah and camped in Kehelathah.
23 They journeyed from Kehelathah and camped at Mount Shepher.
24 They journeyed from Mount Shepher and camped at Haradah.
25 They journeyed from Haradah and camped at Makheloth.
26 They journeyed from Makheloth and camped at Tahath.
27 They journeyed from Tahath and camped at Terah.
28 They journeyed from Terah and camped at Mithkah.
29 They journeyed from Mithkah and camped at Hashmonah.
30 They journeyed from Hashmonah and camped at Moseroth.
31 They journeyed from Moseroth and camped at Bene-jaakan.
32 They journeyed from Bene-jaakan and camped at Hor-haggidgad.
33 They journeyed from Hor-haggidgad and camped at Jotbathah.
34 They journeyed from Jotbathah and camped at Abronah.
35 They journeyed from Abronah and camped at Ezion-geber.
36 They journeyed from Ezion-geber and camped in the wilderness of Zin, that is,
Kadesh.
37 They journeyed from Kadesh and camped at Mount Hor, at the edge of the land of
Edom.
38 Then Aaron the priest went up to Mount Hor at the command of the LORD, and
died there in the fortieth year after the sons of Israel had come from the land of Egypt,
on the first *day* in the fifth month.
39 Aaron was one hundred twenty-three years old when he died on Mount Hor.
40 Now the Canaanite, the king of Arad who lived in the Negev in the land of Canaan,
heard of the coming of the sons of Israel.
41 Then they journeyed from Mount Hor and camped at Zalmonah.
42 They journeyed from Zalmonah and camped at Punon.
43 They journeyed from Punon and camped at Oboth.
44 They journeyed from Oboth and camped at Iye-abarim, at the border of Moab.
45 They journeyed from Iyim and camped at Dibon-gad.
46 They journeyed from Dibon-gad and camped at Almon-diblathaim.
47 They journeyed from Almon-diblathaim and camped in the mountains of Abarim,
before Nebo.

33:4 Ex 12:12
33:5 Ex 12:37
33:6 Ex 13:20
33:7 Ex 14:1, 2
33:8 Ex 14:22; Ex 15:22, 23
33:9 Ex 15:27
33:11 Ex 16:1
33:14 Ex 17:1
33:15 Ex 19:1
33:16 Num 11:34
33:17 Num 11:35
33:20 Deut 1:1
33:30 Deut 10:6
33:32 Gen 36:27; Deut 10:6; 1 Chr 1:42
33:33 Deut 10:7
33:35 Deut 2:8
33:36 Num 20:1
33:37 Num 20:22; Num 20:16
33:38 Num 20:28; Deut 10:6
33:40 Num 21:1
33:43 Num 21:10, 11
33:47 Num 27:12

33:4 God "executed judgments on their gods" by sending the plagues. See the note on Exodus 10:22 for a further explanation.

33:48 Num 22:1 48 They journeyed from the mountains of Abarim and camped in the plains of Moab
by the Jordan *opposite* Jericho.
33:49 Num 25:1 49 They camped by the Jordan, from Beth-jeshimoth as far as Abel-shittim in the plains
of Moab.

Law of Possessing the Land

50 Then the LORD spoke to Moses in the plains of Moab by the Jordan *opposite* Jericho, saying,
33:51 Josh 3:17 51 "Speak to the sons of Israel and say to them, 'When you cross over the Jordan into
the land of Canaan,
33:52 Ex 23:24; Lev 26:1; Deut 7:5; 12:3, 30; Ps 106:34-36 52 then you shall drive out all the inhabitants of the land from before you, and destroy
all their figured stones, and destroy all their molten images and demolish all their high
places;
33:53 Deut 11:31; 17:14; Josh 21:43 53 and you shall take possession of the land and live in it, for I have given the land to
you to possess it.
33:54 Num 26:53-56 54 'You shall inherit the land by lot according to your families; to the larger you shall
give more inheritance, and to the smaller you shall give less inheritance. Wherever the
lot falls to anyone, that shall be his. You shall inherit according to the tribes of your fathers.
33:55 Josh 23:13 55 'But if you do not drive out the inhabitants of the land from before you, then it shall
come about that those whom you let remain of them *will become* as pricks in your eyes
and as thorns in your sides, and they will trouble you in the land in which you live.
56 'And as I plan to do to them, so I will do to you.' "

Instruction for Apportioning Canaan

34 Then the LORD spoke to Moses, saying,
34:2 Gen 17:8; Ps 78:54, 55; 105:11 2 "Command the sons of Israel and say to them, 'When you enter the land of
Canaan, this is the land that shall fall to you as an inheritance, *even the* land of Canaan
according to its borders.

33:50–53 God told Moses that before the Israelites settled in the promised land they should drive out the wicked inhabitants and destroy their idols. In Colossians 3, Paul encourages us to live as Christians in the same manner: throwing away our old way of living and moving ahead into our new life of obedience to God and faith in Jesus Christ. Like the Israelites moving into the promised land, we can destroy the wickedness in our lives or we can settle down and live with it. To move in and possess the new life, we must drive out the sinful thoughts and practices to make room for the new.

33:50–56 Why were the Israelites told to destroy the people living in Canaan? God had several compelling reasons for giving this command: (1) God was stamping out the wickedness of an extremely sinful nation. The Canaanites brought on their own punishment. Idol worship expressed their deepest evil desires. It ultimately led to the worship of Satan and the total rejection of God. (2) God was using Moses and Israel to judge Canaan for its sins in fulfillment of the prophecy in Genesis 9:25. (3) God wanted to remove all trace of pagan beliefs and practices from the land. He did not want his people to mix or compromise with idolatry in any way. The Israelites did not fully understand God's reasons, and they did not carry out his command. This eventually led them to compromise and corruption. In all areas of life, we should obey God's Word without question because we know he is just, even if we cannot fully understand his overall purposes.

33:55 If you don't do the job right the first time, it often becomes much more difficult to accomplish. God warned that if the Israelites did not drive the wicked inhabitants out of the promised land, later these people would become a source of great irritation. That is exactly what happened. Just as the Israelites were hesitant to clear out all the wicked people, we are sometimes hesitant to clear out all the sin in our lives, either because we are afraid of it (as the Israelites feared the giants), or because it seems harmless and attractive (as sexual sin seemed). But Hebrews 12:1–2 tells us to throw off "the sin which so easily entangles" us. We all have "idols" we don't want to let go of (a bad habit, an unhealthy relationship, a certain life-style). If we allow these idols to dominate us, they will cause serious problems later.

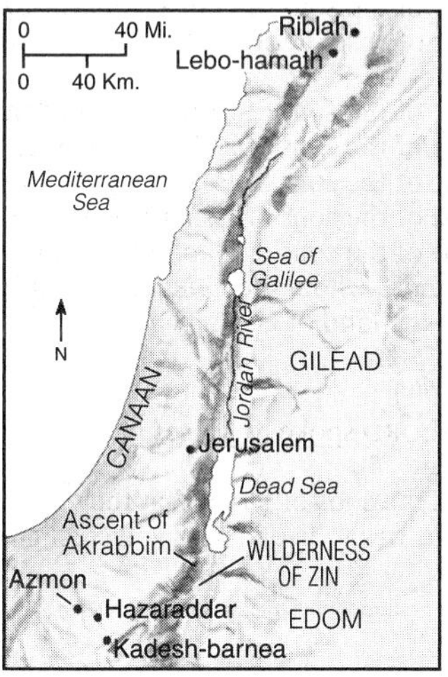

THE BORDERS OF THE PROMISED LAND The borders of the promised land stretched from the wilderness of Zin and Kadesh in the south to Lebo-hamath and Riblah in the north, and from the Mediterranean seacoast on the west to the Jordan River on the east. The land of Gilead was also included.

34:1ff The land was given by God as an inheritance; no tribe was to claim its own land. The boundaries declared by God are larger than the area actually occupied by the Hebrews. The boundaries correspond more to the land conquered by David and to the ideal territory portrayed by Ezekiel (Ezekiel 47–48). The size of the land portrays God's generosity. He always gives us more than we could ask or think.

3 'Your southern sector shall extend from the wilderness of Zin along the side of Edom,
and your southern border shall extend from the end of the Salt Sea eastward.
4 'Then your border shall turn *direction* from the south to the ascent of Akrabbim and
continue to Zin, and its [30]termination shall be to the south of Kadesh-barnea; and it shall
reach Hazaraddar and continue to Azmon.
5 'The border shall turn *direction* from Azmon to the brook of Egypt, and its termination shall be at the sea.
6 'As for the western border, you shall have the Great Sea, that is, *its* coastline; this
shall be your west border.
7 'And this shall be your north border: you shall draw your *border* line from the Great
Sea to Mount Hor.
8 'You shall draw a line from Mount Hor to the Lebo-hamath, and the termination of
the border shall be at Zedad;
9 and the border shall proceed to Ziphron, and its termination shall be at Hazar-enan.
This shall be your north border.
10 'For your eastern border you shall also draw a line from Hazar-enan to Shepham,
11 and the border shall go down from Shepham to Riblah on the east side of Ain; and
the border shall go down and reach to the [31]slope on the east side of the Sea of Chinnereth.
12 'And the border shall go down to the Jordan and its termination shall be at the Salt
Sea. This shall be your land according to its borders all around.' "
13 So Moses commanded the sons of Israel, saying, "This is the land that you are to
apportion by lot among you as a possession, which the LORD has commanded to give to
the nine and a half tribes.
14 "For the tribe of the sons of Reuben have received *theirs* according to their fathers'
households, and the tribe of the sons of Gad according to their fathers' households, and
the half-tribe of Manasseh have received their possession.
15 "The two and a half tribes have received their possession across the Jordan opposite
Jericho, eastward toward the sunrising."
16 Then the LORD spoke to Moses, saying,
17 "These are the names of the men who shall apportion the land to you for inheritance:
Eleazar the priest and Joshua the son of Nun.
18 "You shall take one leader of every tribe to apportion the land for inheritance.
19 "These are the names of the men: of the tribe of Judah, Caleb the son of Jephunneh.
20 "Of the tribe of the sons of Simeon, Samuel the son of Ammihud.
21 "Of the tribe of Benjamin, Elidad the son of Chislon.
22 "Of the tribe of the sons of Dan a leader, Bukki the son of Jogli.
23 "Of the sons of Joseph: of the tribe of the sons of Manasseh a leader, Hanniel the
son of Ephod.
24 "Of the tribe of the sons of Ephraim a leader, Kemuel the son of Shiphtan.
25 "Of the tribe of the sons of Zebulun a leader, Elizaphan the son of Parnach.
26 "Of the tribe of the sons of Issachar a leader, Paltiel the son of Azzan.
27 "Of the tribe of the sons of Asher a leader, Ahihud the son of Shelomi.
28 "Of the tribe of the sons of Naphtali a leader, Pedahel the son of Ammihud."
29 These are those whom the LORD commanded to apportion the inheritance to the
sons of Israel in the land of Canaan.

Cities for the Levites

35 Now the LORD spoke to Moses in the plains of Moab by the Jordan *opposite* Jericho, saying,
2 "Command the sons of Israel that they give to the Levites from the inheritance of
their possession cities to live in; and you shall give to the Levites pasture lands around
the cities.

30 Lit *goings out,* and so throughout the ch **31** Lit *shoulder*

34:3 Josh 15:1-3; Josh 15:5
34:4 Num 32:8
34:5 Josh 15:4
34:7 Ezek 47:15-17
34:8 Josh 13:5
34:11 2 Kin 23:33; Deut 3:17; Josh 13:27
34:13 Gen 15:18; Num 26:52-56; Deut 11:24; Josh 14:1-5
34:14 Num 32:33
34:17 Josh 14:1, 2
34:19 Gen 29:35; Deut 33:7; Ps 60:7; Num 13:6, 30; 26:65; Deut 1:36
34:20 Gen 29:33; 49:5; Ezek 48:24
34:21 Gen 49:27; Deut 33:12; Ps 68:27
35:1 Lev 25:32-34

34:16–29 In God's plan for settling the land, he (1) explained what to do, (2) communicated this clearly to Moses, and (3) assigned specific people to oversee the apportionment of the land. No plan is complete until each job is assigned and everyone understands his or her responsibilities. When you have a job to do, determine what must be done, give clear instructions, and put people in charge of each part.

35:2–3 The Levites were ministers. They were supported by the tithes of the people who gave them homes, flocks, and pasturelands. Likewise, we are responsible to provide for the needs of our ministers and missionaries so they can be free to do their God-ordained work.

3 "The cities shall be theirs to live in; and their pasture lands shall be for their cattle
and for their herds and for all their beasts.
4 "The pasture lands of the cities which you shall give to the Levites *shall extend* from
the wall of the city outward a thousand cubits around.
5 "You shall also measure outside the city on the east side two thousand cubits, and on
the south side two thousand cubits, and on the west side two thousand cubits, and on the
north side two thousand cubits, with the city in the center. This shall become theirs as
pasture lands for the cities.

Cities of Refuge

35:6 Josh 20:7-9

6 "The cities which you shall give to the Levites *shall be* the six cities of refuge, which
you shall give for the manslayer to flee to; and in addition to them you shall give forty-
two cities.

35:7 Josh 21:41

7 "All the cities which you shall give to the Levites *shall be* forty-eight cities, together
with their pasture lands.

35:8 Lev 25:32-34; Num 26:54; 33:54; Josh 21:1-42

8 "As for the cities which you shall give from the possession of the sons of Israel, you
shall take more from the larger and you shall take less from the smaller; each shall give
some of his cities to the Levites in proportion to his possession which he inherits."
9 Then the LORD spoke to Moses, saying,

35:10 Josh 20:1-9

10 "Speak to the sons of Israel and say to them, 'When you cross the Jordan into the
land of Canaan,

35:11 Deut 19:1-13; Josh 20:2f; Ex 21:13; Lev 4:2f, 22f; Num 35:22-25

11 then you shall select for yourselves cities to be your cities of refuge, that the manslayer
who has killed any person unintentionally may flee there.
12 'The cities shall be to you as a refuge from the avenger, so that the manslayer will
not die until he stands before the congregation for trial.

35:12 Deut 19:4-6; Josh 20:2, 3

13 'The cities which you are to give shall be your six cities of refuge.
14 'You shall give three cities across the Jordan and three cities in the land of Canaan;
they are to be cities of refuge.

35:14 Deut 4:41

15 'These six cities shall be for refuge for the sons of Israel, and for the alien and for
the sojourner among them; that anyone who kills a person unintentionally may flee there.

35:15 Num 35:11

16 'But if he struck him down with an iron object, so that he died, he is a murderer; the
murderer shall surely be put to death.

35:16 Ex 21:12, 14; Lev 24:17

17 'If he struck him down with a stone in the hand, by which he will die, and *as a result*
he died, he is a murderer; the murderer shall surely be put to death.

35:17 Num 35:31

18 'Or if he struck him with a wooden object in the hand, by which he might die, and *as
a result* he died, he is a murderer; the murderer shall surely be put to death.

CITIES OF REFUGE
Six of the Levites' cities were designated as cities of refuge. They were spaced throughout the land and protected those who had accidentally committed a crime or who were awaiting trial.

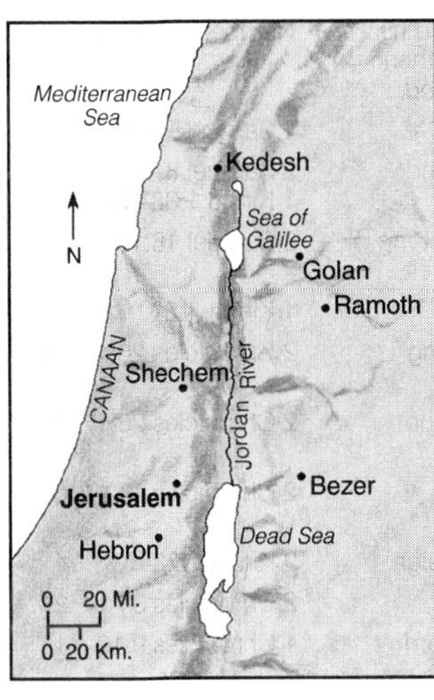

35:6 Of the 48 cities given to the Levites, six were cities of refuge. These six cities were probably put under the Levites' supervision because they would be the most impartial judges. Such cities were needed because the ancient customs of justice called for revenge in the event of the death of a relative or loved one (2 Samuel 14:7). The Levites would hold a preliminary hearing outside the gates while the accused person was kept in the city until the time of his trial. If the killing was judged accidental, the person would stay in the city until the death of the high priest. At that time, he would be allowed to go free, and he could start a new life without worrying about avengers. If it was not accidental, the person would be delivered to the slain person's avengers. This system of justice shows how God's law and his mercy go hand in hand.

35:11–28 If anyone died because of violence, murder was assumed, but the murder suspect was not automatically assumed guilty. The cities of refuge assured the accused that justice would be served. But if he or she left the city, then he or she would be assumed guilty and able to be killed by the avenging party. The people were to be intolerant of the sin, yet impartial to the accused so that he or she could have a fair trial. The cities of refuge represented God's concern for justice in a culture that did not always protect the innocent. It is unjust both to overlook wrongdoing and to jump to conclusions about guilt. When someone is accused of wrongdoing, stand up for justice, protect those not yet proven guilty, and listen carefully to all sides of the story.

19 'The blood avenger himself shall put the murderer to death; he shall put him to death
when he meets him.
20 'If he pushed him of hatred, or threw something at him lying in wait and *as a result*
he died,
21 or if he struck him down with his hand in enmity, and *as a result* he died, the one
who struck him shall surely be put to death, he is a murderer; the blood avenger shall
put the murderer to death when he meets him.
22 'But if he pushed him suddenly without enmity, or threw something at him without
lying in wait,
23 or with any deadly object of stone, and without seeing it dropped on him so that he
died, while he was not his enemy nor seeking his injury,
24 then the congregation shall judge between the slayer and the blood avenger according to these ordinances.
25 'The congregation shall deliver the manslayer from the hand of the blood avenger,
and the congregation shall restore him to his city of refuge to which he fled; and he shall
live in it until the death of the high priest who was anointed with the holy oil.
26 'But if the manslayer at any time goes beyond the border of his city of refuge to which
he may flee,
27 and the blood avenger finds him outside the border of his city of refuge, and the
blood avenger kills the manslayer, he will not be guilty of blood
28 because he should have remained in his city of refuge until the death of the high
priest. But after the death of the high priest the manslayer shall return to the land of his
possession.
29 'These things shall be for a statutory ordinance to you throughout your generations
in all your dwellings.
30 'If anyone kills a person, the murderer shall be put to death at the evidence of witnesses, but no person shall be put to death on the testimony of one witness.
31 'Moreover, you shall not take ransom for the life of a murderer who is guilty of death,
but he shall surely be put to death.
32 'You shall not take ransom for him who has fled to his city of refuge, that he may
return to live in the land before the death of the priest.
33 'So you shall not pollute the land in which you are; for blood pollutes the land and

35:20 Gen 4:8; 2 Sam 3:27; 20:10; Ex 21:14; Deut 19:11

35:22 Num 35:11

35:24 Josh 20:6

35:29 Num 27:11

35:30 Num 35:16; Deut 17:6; 19:15; Matt 18:16; John 7:51; 8:17, 18

35:33 Deut 21:7, 8; Ps 106:38; Gen 9:6

PRIESTS IN ISRAEL'S HISTORY

Numbers 35:25–28 mentions the death of a high priest. Each new high priest had to come from the lineage of Aaron. Listed here are the ones whose stories are told elsewhere in the Bible.

Priest	*Importance*	*Reference*
Aaron	Moses' brother and first priest	Exodus 28:1–3
Eleazar	Watched two of his brothers die in a fire from God because they did not follow God's instructions. He obeyed God and became chief leader of the tabernacle.	Leviticus 10 Numbers 3:32
Phinehas	Executed a young Israelite idol worshiper and his Midianite mistress to end a plague. He was then promised that his priestly line would never end.	Numbers 25:1–15
Ahitub	A priest during King Saul's reign	1 Samuel 14:3
Zadok	A faithful high priest under King David. He and Nathan anointed Solomon as the next king.	2 Samuel 8:17 1 Kings 1:38–39
Ahimaaz	Carried the message of Absalom's death to King David, but was apparently afraid to tell about it.	2 Samuel 18:19–29
Azariah	High priest under King Solomon	1 Kings 4:2
Azariah	High priest under Uzziah. He rebuked the king for burning incense himself.	2 Chronicles 26:17–21
	When Hezekiah became king he reopened the temple. Azariah again served as high priest.	2 Chronicles 26:17–21
Amariah	King Jehoshaphat appointed him to judge religious disputes.	2 Chronicles 19:11
Hilkiah	Found the book of the law during Josiah's reign	2 Kings 22:3–13 2 Chronicles 34:14–21
Azariah	Probably one of the first to return to Israel from Babylon	1 Chronicles 9:10–11
Seraiah	The father of Ezra	Ezra 7:1–5

no expiation can be made for the land for the blood that is shed on it, except by the blood
of him who shed it.

35:34 Lev 18:24, 25; Num 5:3

34 'You shall not defile the land in which you live, in the midst of which I dwell; for I
the LORD am dwelling in the midst of the sons of Israel.' "

Inheritance by Marriage

36:1 Num 27:1

36 And the heads of the fathers' *households* of the family of the sons of Gilead, the
son of Machir, the son of Manasseh, of the families of the sons of Joseph, came
near and spoke before Moses and before the leaders, the heads of the fathers' *households* of the sons of Israel,

36:2 Num 27:5-7

2 and they said, "The LORD commanded my lord to give the land by lot to the sons of
Israel as an inheritance, and my lord was commanded by the LORD to give the inheritance of Zelophehad our brother to his daughters.
3 "But if they marry one of the sons of the *other* tribes of the sons of Israel, their inheritance will be withdrawn from the inheritance of our fathers and will be added to the
inheritance of the tribe to which they belong; thus it will be withdrawn from our allotted
inheritance.

36:4 Lev 25:10

4 "When the jubilee of the sons of Israel comes, then their inheritance will be added to
the inheritance of the tribe to which they belong; so their inheritance will be withdrawn
from the inheritance of the tribe of our fathers."
5 Then Moses commanded the sons of Israel according to the word of the LORD,
saying, "The tribe of the sons of Joseph are right in *their* statements.

36:6 Num 27:7

6 "This is what the LORD has commanded concerning the daughters of Zelophehad,
saying, 'Let them marry whom they wish; only they must marry within the family of the
tribe of their father.'

36:7 1 Kin 21:3

7 "Thus no inheritance of the sons of Israel shall be transferred from tribe to tribe, for
the sons of Israel shall each hold to the inheritance of the tribe of his fathers.

36:8 1 Chr 23:22

8 "Every daughter who comes into possession of an inheritance of any tribe of the sons
of Israel shall be wife to one of the family of the tribe of her father, so that the sons of
Israel each may possess the inheritance of his fathers.
9 "Thus no inheritance shall be transferred from one tribe to another tribe, for the tribes
of the sons of Israel shall each hold to his own inheritance."
10 Just as the LORD had commanded Moses, so the daughters of Zelophehad did:

36:11 Num 26:33

11 Mahlah, Tirzah, Hoglah, Milcah and Noah, the daughters of Zelophehad married
their uncles' sons.

36:13 Lev 26:46; 27:34; Num 22:1

12 They married *those* from the families of the sons of Manasseh the son of Joseph,
and their inheritance remained with the tribe of the family of their father.
13 These are the commandments and the ordinances which the LORD commanded to
the sons of Israel through Moses in the plains of Moab by the Jordan *opposite* Jericho.

36:1–9 Zelophehad had five daughters but no sons. After he died, his daughters appealed to Moses. Because the inheritance normally passed only through the male line, the family line of Zelophehad would have disappeared. God told Moses that if a man died without sons, then the inheritance would go to his daughters (27:8). But the question of marriage arose. If the daughters were to marry outside of their tribe, the land would belong to another tribe at the Year of Jubilee. So Moses commanded that in such cases the women should marry men in their own clan and tribe so that each tribe would retain its original inheritance. Later, when the tribes received their land under Joshua, the daughters of Zelophehad received their inheritance as God had instructed (Joshua 17:3–6).

We don't have to look far to find those who want to be considered "special cases" and "exceptions to the rule," but wise leaders will sort out those who have legitimate concerns and make sure that justice is done in these special situations.

36:13 The book of Numbers covers 39 years and closes with the Israelites poised near the banks of the Jordan River with the promised land in sight. The wanderings in the wilderness have come to an end, and the people are preparing for their next big move—the conquest of the land. The apostle Paul says that the events described in Numbers are examples that warn us and help us avoid the Israelites' mistakes (1 Corinthians 10:1–12). From their experiences we learn that unbelief is disastrous. We also learn not to long for the sinful pleasures of the past, to avoid complaining, and to stay away from all forms of compromise. If we choose to let God lead our lives, we should not ignore his message in the book of Numbers.

DEUTERONOMY

Joseph dies 1805 B.C. (1640 B.C.)	*SLAVERY IN EGYPT*	*Exodus from Egypt 1446 (1280)*	*Ten Commandments given 1445 (1279)*
		WILDERNESS WANDERINGS	

VITAL STATISTICS

PURPOSE:
To remind the people of what God had done and encourage them to rededicate their lives to him

AUTHOR:
Moses (except for the final summary, which was probably written by Joshua after Moses' death)

TO WHOM WRITTEN:
Israel (the new generation entering the promised land)

DATE WRITTEN:
About 1407/6 B.C.

SETTING:
The east side of the Jordan River, in view of Canaan

KEY VERSE:
"Know therefore that the LORD your God, He is God, the faithful God, who keeps His covenant and His lovingkindness to a thousandth generation with those who love Him and keep His commandments" (7:9).

KEY PEOPLE:
Moses, Joshua

KEY PLACE:
The Arabah in Moab

CLASS reunions, scrapbooks and photo albums, familiar songs, and old neighborhoods—like long-time friends they awaken our memories and stir our emotions. The past is a kaleidoscope of promises, failures, victories, and embarrassments. Sometimes we want to forget memories that are too painful. However, as the years pass, remembrances of unpleasant events usually fade into our subconscious. But there is a time to remember: Mistakes should not be repeated; commitments made must be fulfilled; and the memory of special events can encourage us and move us to action.

The book of Deuteronomy is written in the form of a treaty between a king and his vassal state typical of the second millenium B.C. It calls Israel to remember who God is and what he has done. Lacking faith, the old generation had wandered for 40 years and died in the wilderness. They left Egypt behind, but never knew the promised land. Then on the east bank of the Jordan River, Moses prepared the sons and daughters of that faithless generation to possess the land. After a brief history lesson emphasizing God's great acts on behalf of his people, Moses reviewed the law. Then he restated the covenant—God's contract with his people.

The lessons are clear. Because of what God has done, Israel should have hope and follow him; because of what he expects, they should listen and obey; because of who he is, they should love him completely. Learning these lessons will prepare them to possess the promised land.

As you hear the message of Deuteronomy, remember how God has expressed his kindness in your life, and then commit yourself anew to trust, love, and obey him.

THE BLUEPRINT

A. WHAT GOD HAS DONE FOR US: MOSES' FIRST ADDRESS (1:1—4:43)

Moses reviewed the mighty acts of God for the nation of Israel. Remembering God's special involvement in our lives gives us hope and encouragement for the future.

B. PRINCIPLES FOR GODLY LIVING: MOSES' SECOND ADDRESS (4:44—29:1)

1. The Ten Commandments
2. Love the Lord your God
3. Laws for proper worship
4. Laws for ruling the nation
5. Laws for human relationships
6. Consequences of obedience and disobedience

Obeying God's laws brought blessings to the Israelites and disobeying brought misfortune. This was part of the written agreement God made with his people. Although we are not part of this covenant, the principle holds true: Obedience and disobedience carry inevitable consequences in this life and the next.

Moses' death; Israelites enter Canaan 1406 (1240)	Judges begin to rule 1375 (1220)	United kingdom under Saul 1050 (1045)

C. A CALL FOR COMMITMENT TO GOD: MOSES' THIRD ADDRESS (29:2—30:20)

Moses called the people to commitment. God still calls us to be committed to love him with all our heart, soul, mind, and strength.

D. THE CHANGE IN LEADERSHIP: MOSES' LAST DAYS (31:1—34:12)

Although Moses made some serious mistakes, he had lived uprightly and carried out God's commands. Moses died with integrity. We too may make some serious mistakes, but that should not stop us from living with integrity and godly commitment.

MEGATHEMES

THEME	EXPLANATION	IMPORTANCE
History	Moses reviewed the mighty acts of God whereby he liberated Israel from slavery in Egypt. He recounted how God had helped them and how the people had disobeyed.	By reviewing God's promises and mighty acts in history, we can learn about his character. We come to know God more intimately through understanding how he has acted in the past. We can also avoid mistakes in our own lives through learning from Israel's past failures.
Laws	God reviewed his laws for the people. The legal contract between God and his people had to be renewed by the new generation about to enter the promised land.	Commitment to God and his truth cannot be taken for granted. Each generation and each person must respond afresh to God's call for obedience.
Love	God's faithful and patient love is portrayed more often than his punishment. God shows his love by being faithful to his people and his promises. In response, God desires love from the heart, not merely a legalistic keeping of his law.	God's love forms the foundation for our trust in him. We trust him because he loves us. Because God loves us, we should maintain justice and respect.
Choices	God reminded his people that in order to ratify his agreement, they must choose the path of obedience. A personal decision to obey would bring benefits to their lives; rebellion would bring severe calamity.	Our choices make a difference. Choosing to follow God benefits us and improves our relationships with others. Choosing to abandon God's ways brings harm to ourselves and others.
Teaching	God commanded the Israelites to teach their children his ways. They were to use ritual, instruction, and memorization to make sure their children understood God's principles and passed them on to the next generation.	Quality teaching for our children must be a priority. It is important to pass on God's truth to future generations in our traditions. But God desires that his truth be in our hearts and minds and not merely in our traditions.

A. WHAT GOD HAS DONE FOR US: MOSES' FIRST ADDRESS (1:1—4:43)

God has led his people out of Egypt and across the great desert. Now they stand ready to enter the promised land. But before the Israelites go into the land, Moses has some important advice to give them. He delivers his advice in three parts. In the first part, Moses reviews the history of God's previous care for the people of Israel. Through God's actions in the past, we can learn about the God we serve today.

Israel's History after the Exodus

1 These are the words which Moses spoke to all Israel across the Jordan in the wilderness, in the Arabah opposite Suph, between Paran and Tophel and Laban and
Hazeroth and Dizahab.
2 It is eleven days' *journey* from Horeb by the way of Mount Seir to Kadesh-barnea.
3 In the fortieth year, on the first *day* of the eleventh month, Moses spoke to the children of Israel, according to all that the LORD had commanded him *to give* to them,
4 after he had defeated Sihon the king of the Amorites, who lived in Heshbon, and
Og the king of Bashan, who lived in Ashtaroth and Edrei.
5 Across the Jordan in the land of Moab, Moses undertook to expound this law,
saying,
6 "The LORD our God spoke to us at Horeb, saying, 'You have stayed long enough at
this mountain.
7 'Turn and set your journey, and go to the hill country of the Amorites, and to all their
neighbors in the Arabah, in the hill country and in the lowland and in the [1]Negev and by
the seacoast, the land of the Canaanites, and Lebanon, as far as the great river, the river
Euphrates.
8 'See, I have placed the land before you; go in and possess the land which the LORD
swore to give to your fathers, to Abraham, to Isaac, and to Jacob, to them and their
descendants after them.'
9 "I spoke to you at that time, saying, 'I am not able to bear *the burden* of you alone.
10 'The LORD your God has multiplied you, and behold, you are this day like the stars
of heaven in number.

1:1 Deut 4:46; Deut 2:8
1:2 Ex 3:1; 17:6; Gen 32:3; Num 13:26; 32:8; Deut 9:23
1:3 Num 33:38; Deut 4:1, 2
1:4 Num 21:21-26; Deut 2:26-35; Josh 13:10; Neh 9:22; Num 21:33-35; Josh 13:12; Josh 12:4
1:6 Num 10:11-13
1:7 Gen 15:18; Deut 11:24; Josh 10:40; Gen 12:9
1:8 Gen 12:7; 26:3; 28:13; Ex 33:1; Num 14:23; 32:11; Heb 6:13, 14
1:9 Ex 18:18, 24; Num 11:14
1:10 Gen 15:5; 22:17; Ex 32:13; Deut 7:7; 10:22; 26:5; 28:62

1 I.e. South country

1:1–2 The Israelites spent 40 years on a journey that should have lasted 11 days. It wasn't distance that stood between them and the promised land. It was the condition of their hearts. God's purpose went deeper than simply transporting a huge group of people to a new land. He was preparing them to live in obedience to him once they arrived. What good was the promised land if the Israelites were just as wicked as the nations already living there? The journey was a painful but necessary part of their preparation. Through it God taught the Israelites who he was: the living God, the Leader of their nation. He also taught them who they were: people who were fallen, sinful, prone to rebellion and doubt. He gave his rebellious people the law to help them understand how to relate to God and to other people. Your spiritual pilgrimage may be lengthy, and you may face pain, discouragement, and difficulties. But remember that God isn't just trying to keep you alive. He wants to prepare you to live in service and devotion to him.

1:1–5 The 40 years of wilderness wandering come to an end in this book. The events of Deuteronomy cover only a week or two of the 11th month of the 40th year (1:3). The 12th and last month was spent in mourning for Moses (34:8). Then the Israelites entered the promised land the first month of the 41st year after the exodus (Joshua 4:19).

1:6–7 Notice that Moses' summary of Israel's 40-year journey begins at Mount Horeb (Sinai), not in Egypt. Why did Moses leave out the first part of the exodus? Moses was not giving an itinerary—he was summarizing the nation's development. In Moses' mind the nation of Israel began at the base of Mount Sinai, not in Egypt, for it was at Mount Sinai that God gave his covenant to the people (Exodus 19–20). Along with this covenant came knowledge and responsibility. After the people chose to follow God (and it was their choice), they had to know *how* to follow him. Therefore, God gave them a comprehensive set of laws and guidelines that stated how he wanted them to live (these are found in the books of Exodus, Leviticus, and Numbers). The people could no longer say they didn't know the difference between right and wrong. Now that the people had promised to follow God and knew how to follow him, they had a responsibility to do it. When God tells you to break camp and move out to face a challenge he gives you, will you be ready to obey?

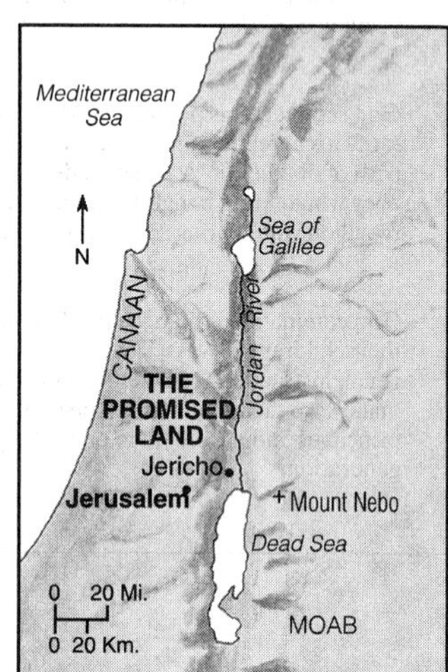

EVENTS IN DEUTERONOMY
The book of Deuteronomy opens with Israel camped east of the Jordan River in the land of Moab. Just before the people crossed the river into the promised land, Moses delivered an inspirational speech indicating how they were to live.

1:9–13 It was a tremendous burden for Moses to lead the nation by himself. He could not accomplish the task single-handedly. Like nations, as organizations and churches grow, they become increasingly complex. Conflicting needs and quarrels arise. No longer can one leader make all the decisions. Like Moses, you may have a

1:11 Deut 1:8, 10
1:13 Ex 18:21
1:16 Deut 16:18; John 7:24
1:17 Deut 10:17; 16:19; 24:17; 2 Chr 19:5, 6; Prov 24:23-26; Acts 10:34; James 2:1, 9; Prov 29:25; Ex 18:22, 26
1:18 Ex 18:20
1:19 Deut 1:2; Deut 2:7; 8:15; 32:10; Jer 2:6; Deut 1:7
1:21 Josh 1:6, 9
1:22 Num 13:1-3
1:24 Num 13:21-25
1:26 Num 14:1-4; Deut 9:23
1:27 Deut 9:28; Ps 106:25
1:28 Num 13:28, 33; Deut 9:2
1:30 Ex 14:14; Deut 3:22; 20:4; Neh 4:20

11 'May the LORD, the God of your fathers, increase you a thousand-fold more than
you are and bless you, just as He has promised you!
12 'How can I alone bear the load and burden of you and your strife?
13 'Choose wise and discerning and experienced men from your tribes, and I will appoint them as your heads.'
14 "You answered me and said, 'The thing which you have said to do is good.'
15 "So I took the heads of your tribes, wise and experienced men, and appointed them
heads over you, leaders of thousands and of hundreds, of fifties and of tens, and officers
for your tribes.
16 "Then I charged your judges at that time, saying, 'Hear *the cases* between your fellow countrymen, and judge righteously between a man and his fellow countryman, or
the alien who is with him.
17 'You shall not show partiality in judgment; you shall hear the small and the great
alike. You shall not fear man, for the judgment is God's. The case that is too hard for
you, you shall bring to me, and I will hear it.'
18 "I commanded you at that time all the things that you should do.
19 "Then we set out from Horeb, and went through all that great and terrible wilderness which you saw on the way to the hill country of the Amorites, just as the LORD our
God had commanded us; and we came to Kadesh-barnea.
20 "I said to you, 'You have come to the hill country of the Amorites which the LORD
our God is about to give us.
21 'See, the LORD your God has placed the land before you; go up, take possession, as
the LORD, the God of your fathers, has spoken to you. Do not fear or be dismayed.'
22 "Then all of you approached me and said, 'Let us send men before us, that they may
search out the land for us, and bring back to us word of the way by which we should go
up and the cities which we shall enter.'
23 "The thing pleased me and I took twelve of your men, one man for each tribe.
24 "They turned and went up into the hill country, and came to the valley of Eshcol and
spied it out.
25 "Then they took *some* of the fruit of the land in their hands and brought it down to
us; and they brought us back a report and said, 'It is a good land which the LORD our
God is about to give us.'
26 "Yet you were not willing to go up, but rebelled against the command of the LORD
your God;
27 and you grumbled in your tents and said, 'Because the LORD hates us, He has brought
us out of the land of Egypt to deliver us into the hand of the Amorites to destroy us.
28 'Where can we go up? Our brethren have made our hearts melt, saying, "The people are bigger and taller than we; the cities are large and fortified to heaven. And besides, we saw the sons of the Anakim there." '
29 "Then I said to you, 'Do not be shocked, nor fear them.
30 'The LORD your God who goes before you will Himself fight on your behalf, just as
He did for you in Egypt before your eyes,

---

natural tendency to try to do all the work alone. You may be afraid or embarrassed to ask for help. Moses made a wise decision to share the leadership with others. Rather than trying to handle larger responsibilities alone, look for ways of sharing the load so that others may exercise their God-given gifts and abilities.

1:13–18 Moses identified some of the inner qualities of good leaders: (1) wisdom, (2) understanding, and (3) respect. These characteristics differ markedly from the ones that often help elect leaders today: good looks, wealth, popularity, willingness to do anything to get to the top. The qualities Moses identified should be evident in us as we lead, and we should look for them in those we elect to positions of leadership.

1:22 The spies were sent into the land to determine not *whether* they should enter, but *where* they should enter. Upon returning, however, most of the spies concluded that the land was not worth the obstacles. God would give the Israelites the power to conquer the land, but they were afraid of the risk and decided not to enter. God gives us the power to overcome our obstacles, but like the Israelites filled with fear and skepticism, we often let difficulties control our lives. Following God regardless of the difficulties is the way to have courageous, overcoming faith.

1:23–40 Moses retold the story of the spy mission into the promised land (Numbers 13—14). When the spies returned with reports of giants (Anakim) and walled cities, the people were afraid to move ahead and began to complain about their predicament. But the minority report of Joshua and Caleb pointed out that the land was fertile, the enemy was vulnerable, and God was on their side. We become fearful and immobile when we focus on the negative aspects of a situation. How much better it is to focus on the positive—God's direction and promises. When confronted with an important decision and you know what you should do, move out in faith. Focus on the positives while trusting God to overcome the negatives. Problems don't have to rob you of the victory.

1:28 Canaan was a land with giants and imposing fortresses. The "Anakim" may have been seven to nine feet tall. Many of the land's fortified cities had walls as high as 30 feet. The Israelites' fear was understandable, but not justified, for the all-powerful God had already promised them victory.

31 and in the wilderness where you saw how the LORD your God carried you, just as a
man carries his son, in all the way which you have walked until you came to this place.'
32 "But for all this, you did not trust the LORD your God,
33 who goes before you on *your* way, to seek out a place for you to encamp, in fire by
night and cloud by day, to show you the way in which you should go.
34 "Then the LORD heard the sound of your words, and He was angry and took an oath,
saying,
35 'Not one of these men, this evil generation, shall see the good land which I swore to
give your fathers,
36 except Caleb the son of Jephunneh; he shall see it, and to him and to his sons I will
give the land on which he has set foot, because he has followed the LORD fully.'
37 "The LORD was angry with me also on your account, saying, 'Not even you shall enter there.
38 'Joshua the son of Nun, who stands before you, he shall enter there; encourage him,
for he will cause Israel to inherit it.
39 'Moreover, your little ones who you said would become a prey, and your sons, who
this day have no knowledge of good or evil, shall enter there, and I will give it to them
and they shall possess it.
40 'But as for you, turn around and set out for the wilderness by the way to the Red
Sea.'
41 "Then you said to me, 'We have sinned against the LORD; we will indeed go up and
fight, just as the LORD our God commanded us.' And every man of you girded on his
weapons of war, and regarded it as easy to go up into the hill country.
42 "And the LORD said to me, 'Say to them, "Do not go up nor fight, for I am not among
you; otherwise you will be defeated before your enemies." '
43 "So I spoke to you, but you would not listen. Instead you rebelled against the command of the LORD, and acted presumptuously and went up into the hill country.
44 "The Amorites who lived in that hill country came out against you and chased you as
bees do, and crushed you from Seir to Hormah.
45 "Then you returned and wept before the LORD; but the LORD did not listen to your
voice nor give ear to you.
46 "So you remained in Kadesh many days, the days that you spent *there.*

Wanderings in the Wilderness

2 "Then we turned and set out for the wilderness by the way to the Red Sea, as the
LORD spoke to me, and circled Mount Seir for many days.
2 "And the LORD spoke to me, saying,
3 'You have circled this mountain long enough. *Now* turn north,
4 and command the people, saying, "You will pass through the territory of your brothers the sons of Esau who live in Seir; and they will be afraid of you. So be very careful;
5 do not provoke them, for I will not give you any of their land, even *as little as* a foot-
step because I have given Mount Seir to Esau as a possession.
6 "You shall buy food from them with money so that you may eat, and you shall also
purchase water from them with money so that you may drink.
7 "For the LORD your God has blessed you in all that you have done; He has known
your wanderings through this great wilderness. These forty years the LORD your God
has been with you; you have not lacked a thing." '
8 "So we passed beyond our brothers the sons of Esau, who live in Seir, away from the
Arabah road, away from Elath and from Ezion-geber. And we turned and passed through
by the way of the wilderness of Moab.
9 "Then the LORD said to me, 'Do not harass Moab, nor provoke them to war, for I
will not give you any of their land as a possession, because I have given Ar to the sons of
Lot as a possession.

1:31 Deut 32:10-12; Is 46:3, 4; 63:9; Hos 11:3; Acts 13:18

1:32 Num 14:11; Ps 106:24; Heb 3:19; 4:2; Jude 5

1:33 Ex 13:21; Num 9:15-23; Neh 9:12; Ps 78:14; Num 10:33

1:34 Num 14:28-30; Heb 3:18

1:35 Ps 95:11; 106:26; Ezek 20:15; 1 Cor 10:5; Heb 3:14-19

1:36 Num 14:24; Josh 14:9

1:37 Num 20:12; Deut 3:26; 4:21; Num 27:13, 18

1:38 Num 14:30; Num 34:17; Deut 3:28; 31:7; Josh 11:23

1:39 Num 14:3, 31; Is 7:15, 16

1:40 Num 14:25

1:42 Num 14:41-43

1:43 Num 14:40

1:44 Num 14:45; Ps 118:12

1:45 Job 27:8, 9; Ps 66:18; John 9:31

1:46 Num 20:1, 22; Deut 2:7, 14; Judg 11:17

2:4 Num 20:14-21; Gen 36:8; Ex 15:15, 16

2:5 Gen 36:8; Josh 24:4

2:7 Deut 1:19; Num 14:33, 34; 32:13; Deut 2:14

2:8 Deut 1:1; Num 33:35; 1 Kin 9:26

2:9 Num 21:15, 28; Deut 2:18, 29; Gen 19:36, 37

2:4–6 When the Israelites passed through Seir, God advised them to be careful. The Israelites were known as warriors, and the children of Esau—the Edomites—would be understandably nervous as the great crowd passed through their land. God warned the Israelites not to start a fight, to respect the Edomites' territory, and to pay for whatever they used. God wanted the Israelites to deal justly with these neighbors. We must also act justly in dealing with others. Recognize the rights of others, even your opponents. By behaving wisely and justly you may be able to establish or restore a relationship.

2:10 Gen 14:5
2:11 Gen 14:5; Deut 2:20
2:12 Gen 36:20; Deut 2:22; Num 21:25, 35
2:14 Deut 2:7; Num 14:29-35; 26:64, 65; Ps 106:26; 1 Cor 10:5; Deut 1:34, 35
2:15 Jude 5
2:16 Deut 2:14
2:18 Deut 2:9
2:19 Gen 19:38; Deut 2:9
2:20 Deut 2:11
2:22 Gen 36:8; Deut 2:5; Deut 2:12
2:23 Josh 13:3; Gen 10:14; 1 Chr 1:12; Jer 47:4; Amos 9:7
2:24 Num 21:13, 14; Judg 11:18
2:25 Ex 23:27; Deut 11:25; Josh 2:9; Ex 15:14-16
2:26 Num 21:21-32; Deut 1:4; Judg 11:19-21
2:28 Num 20:19
2:29 Deut 2:9
2:30 Num 21:23; Ex 4:21; Josh 11:20

10 (The Emim lived there formerly, a people as great, numerous, and tall as the Anakim.
11 Like the Anakim, they are also regarded as Rephaim, but the Moabites call them
Emim.
12 The Horites formerly lived in Seir, but the sons of Esau dispossessed them and
destroyed them from before them and settled in their place, just as Israel did to the land
of their possession which the LORD gave to them.)
13 'Now arise and cross over the brook Zered yourselves.' So we crossed over the brook
Zered.
14 "Now the time that it took for us to come from Kadesh-barnea until we crossed over
the brook Zered was thirty-eight years, until all the generation of the men of war perished from within the camp, as the LORD had sworn to them.
15 "Moreover the hand of the LORD was against them, to destroy them from within the
camp until they all perished.
16 "So it came about when all the men of war had finally perished from among the
people,
17 that the LORD spoke to me, saying,
18 'Today you shall cross over Ar, the border of Moab.
19 'When you come opposite the sons of Ammon, do not harass them nor provoke them,
for I will not give you any of the land of the sons of Ammon as a possession, because I
have given it to the sons of Lot as a possession.'
20 (It is also regarded as the land of the Rephaim, *for* Rephaim formerly lived in it, but
the Ammonites call them Zamzummin,
21 a people as great, numerous, and tall as the Anakim, but the LORD destroyed them
before them. And they dispossessed them and settled in their place,
22 just as He did for the sons of Esau, who live in Seir, when He destroyed the Horites
from before them; they dispossessed them and settled in their place even to this day.
23 And the Avvim, who lived in villages as far as Gaza, the [2]Caphtorim who came from
[3]Caphtor, destroyed them and lived in their place.)
24 'Arise, set out, and pass through the valley of Arnon. Look! I have given Sihon the
Amorite, king of Heshbon, and his land into your hand; begin to take possession and
contend with him in battle.
25 'This day I will begin to put the dread and fear of you upon the peoples everywhere
under the heavens, who, when they hear the report of you, will tremble and be in anguish because of you.'
26 "So I sent messengers from the wilderness of Kedemoth to Sihon king of Heshbon
with words of peace, saying,
27 'Let me pass through your land, I will travel only on the highway; I will not turn aside
to the right or to the left.
28 'You will sell me food for money so that I may eat, and give me water for money so
that I may drink, only let me pass through on foot,
29 just as the sons of Esau who live in Seir and the Moabites who live in Ar did for me,
until I cross over the Jordan into the land which the LORD our God is giving to us.'
30 "But Sihon king of Heshbon was not willing for us to pass through his land; for the
LORD your God hardened his spirit and made his heart obstinate, in order to deliver
him into your hand, as *he is* today.
31 "The LORD said to me, 'See, I have begun to deliver Sihon and his land over to you.
Begin to occupy, that you may possess his land.'
32 "Then Sihon with all his people came out to meet us in battle at Jahaz.

2 I.e. Philistines **3** I.e. Crete

2:11 Both Moab and Ammon had removed a tall Anakim-like people usually known as the Rephaim, but called Emim by the Moabites and Zamzummin by the Ammonites (2:20). If our enemies seem overwhelming, we must remember that God can deliver us as he did the Israelites.

2:14–15 Israel did not have to spend 40 years on the way to the promised land. God sentenced them to wilderness wanderings because they rejected his love, rebelled against his authority, ignored his commands for right living, and willfully broke their end of the agreement made in Exodus 19:8 and 24:3–8. In short, they disobeyed God. We often make life's journey more difficult than necessary by disobedience. Accept God's love, read and follow his commands in the Bible, and make a promise to stick with God whatever your situation. You will find that your life will be less complicated and more rewarding.

2:25 God told Moses he would make the enemy nations afraid of Israel. By worldly standards, Israel's army was not intimidating, but Israel had God on its side. Moses no longer had to worry about his enemies because his enemies were worried about him. God often goes before us in our daily battles, preparing the way and overcoming barriers. We need to follow him wholeheartedly and be alert to his leading.

33 "The LORD our God delivered him over to us, and we defeated him with his sons and all his people.

34 "So we captured all his cities at that time and utterly destroyed the men, women and children of every city. We left no survivor.

35 "We took only the animals as our booty and the spoil of the cities which we had captured.

36 "From Aroer which is on the edge of the valley of Arnon and *from* the city which is in the valley, even to Gilead, there was no city that was too high for us; the LORD our God delivered all over to us.

37 "Only you did not go near to the land of the sons of Ammon, all along the river Jabbok and the cities of the hill country, and wherever the LORD our God had commanded us.

2:33 Ex 23:31; Deut 7:2; Deut 29:7
2:34 Deut 3:6; 7:2
2:35 Deut 3:7
2:36 Deut 3:12; 4:48; Josh 12:2; 13:9
2:37 Deut 2:19; Gen 32:22; Num 21:24; Deut 3:16

Conquests Recounted

3 "Then we turned and went up the road to Bashan, and Og, king of Bashan, with all his people came out to meet us in battle at Edrei.

2 "But the LORD said to me, 'Do not fear him, for I have delivered him and all his people and his land into your hand; and you shall do to him just as you did to Sihon king of the Amorites, who lived at Heshbon.'

3 "So the LORD our God delivered Og also, king of Bashan, with all his people into our hand, and we smote them until no survivor was left.

4 "We captured all his cities at that time; there was not a city which we did not take from them: sixty cities, all the region of Argob, the kingdom of Og in Bashan.

5 "All these were cities fortified with high walls, gates and bars, besides a great many unwalled towns.

6 "We utterly destroyed them, as we did to Sihon king of Heshbon, utterly destroying the men, women and children of every city.

7 "But all the animals and the spoil of the cities we took as our booty.

8 "Thus we took the land at that time from the hand of the two kings of the Amorites who were beyond the Jordan, from the valley of Arnon to Mount Hermon

9 (Sidonians call Hermon Sirion, and the Amorites call it Senir):

10 all the cities of the plateau and all Gilead and all Bashan, as far as Salecah and Edrei, cities of the kingdom of Og in Bashan.

11 (For only Og king of Bashan was left of the remnant of the Rephaim. Behold, his bedstead was an iron bedstead; it is in Rabbah of the sons of Ammon. Its length was nine cubits and its width four cubits by ordinary cubit.)

12 "So we took possession of this land at that time. From Aroer, which is by the valley of Arnon, and half the hill country of Gilead and its cities I gave to the Reubenites and to the Gadites.

13 "The rest of Gilead and all Bashan, the kingdom of Og, I gave to the half-tribe of Manasseh, all the region of Argob (concerning all Bashan, it is called the land of Rephaim.

14 Jair the son of Manasseh took all the region of Argob as far as the border of the Geshurites and the Maacathites, and called it, *that is,* Bashan, after his own name, Havvoth-jair, *as it is* to this day.)

15 "To Machir I gave Gilead.

16 "To the Reubenites and to the Gadites I gave from Gilead even as far as the valley of Arnon, the middle of the valley as a border and as far as the river Jabbok, the border of the sons of Ammon;

17 the Arabah also, with the Jordan as *a* border, from [4]Chinnereth even as far as the sea of the Arabah, the Salt Sea, at the foot of the slopes of Pisgah on the east.

18 "Then I commanded you at that time, saying, 'The LORD your God has given you this land to possess it; all you valiant men shall cross over armed before your brothers, the sons of Israel.

3:1 Num 21:33-35
3:4 Deut 3:13, 14; 1 Kin 4:13
3:6 Deut 1:4; Deut 2:34
3:7 Deut 2:35
3:8 Num 32:33; Josh 12:1-7; 13:8-12
3:9 Deut 4:48; Josh 11:17; Ps 42:6; 133:3; Ps 29:6 1 Chr 5:23
3:10 Josh 13:11
3:11 Gen 14:5; Deut 2:11, 20; 2 Sam 11:1; 12:26; Jer 49:2
3:12 Deut 2:36; Num 32:32-38; Josh 13:8-13
3:14 Num 32:41; 1 Chr 2:22
3:15 Num 32:39, 40
3:16 Num 21:24; Deut 2:37
3:17 Num 34:11; Josh 13:27; Josh 12:3; Gen 14:3; Josh 3:16
3:18 Josh 1:13; Num 32:20; Josh 4:12, 13

4 I.e. the Sea of Galilee

3:1–3 The Israelites faced a big problem—the well-trained army of Og, king of Bashan. The Israelites hardly stood a chance. But they won because God fought for them. God can help his people regardless of the problems they face. No matter how insurmountable the obstacles may seem, remember that God is sovereign, and he will keep his promises.

19 'But your wives and your little ones and your livestock (I know that you have much
livestock) shall remain in your cities which I have given you,
20 until the LORD gives rest to your fellow countrymen as to you, and they also possess
the land which the LORD your God will give them beyond the Jordan. Then you may
return every man to his possession which I have given you.'
21 "I commanded Joshua at that time, saying, 'Your eyes have seen all that the LORD
your God has done to these two kings; so the LORD shall do to all the kingdoms into
which you are about to cross.
22 'Do not fear them, for the LORD your God is the one fighting for you.'
23 "I also pleaded with the LORD at that time, saying,
24 'O Lord GOD, You have begun to show Your servant Your greatness and Your strong
hand; for what god is there in heaven or on earth who can do such works and mighty acts
as Yours?
25 'Let me, I pray, cross over and see the fair land that is beyond the Jordan, that good
hill country and Lebanon.'
26 "But the LORD was angry with me on your account, and would not listen to me; and
the LORD said to me, 'Enough! Speak to Me no more of this matter.
27 'Go up to the top of Pisgah and lift up your eyes to the west and north and south and
east, and see *it* with your eyes, for you shall not cross over this Jordan.
28 'But charge Joshua and encourage him and strengthen him, for he shall go across
at the head of this people, and he will give them as an inheritance the land which you
will see.'
29 "So we remained in the valley opposite Beth-peor.

Israel Urged to Obey God's Law

4 "Now, O Israel, listen to the statutes and the judgments which I am teaching you to
perform, so that you may live and go in and take possession of the land which the
LORD, the God of your fathers, is giving you.
2 "You shall not add to the word which I am commanding you, nor take away from it,
that you may keep the commandments of the LORD your God which I command you.
3 "Your eyes have seen what the LORD has done in the case of Baal-peor, for all the
men who followed Baal-peor, the LORD your God has destroyed them from among you.
4 "But you who held fast to the LORD your God are alive today, every one of you.
5 "See, I have taught you statutes and judgments just as the LORD my God commanded me, that you should do thus in the land where you are entering to possess it.
6 "So keep and do *them,* for that is your wisdom and your understanding in the sight of
the peoples who will hear all these statutes and say, 'Surely this great nation is a wise
and understanding people.'
7 "For what great nation is there that has a god so near to it as is the LORD our God
whenever we call on Him?

3:19 Josh 1:14; Ex 12:38
3:20 Josh 1:15; Josh 22:4
3:22 Ex 14:14; Deut 1:30; 20:4; Neh 4:20
3:24 Deut 11:2; Ex 8:10; 15:11; 2 Sam 7:22; Ps 71:19; 86:8
3:25 Deut 4:22
3:26 Deut 1:37
3:27 Num 23:14; 27:12; Deut 1:37
3:28 Num 27:18; Deut 31:3, 7, 8, 23; Deut 1:38
3:29 Num 25:1-3; Deut 4:46; 34:6
4:1 Deut 1:3; Lev 18:5; Deut 5:33; 8:1; 16:20; 30:16, 19; Ezek 20:11; Rom 10:5
4:2 Deut 12:32; Prov 30:6; Rev 22:18; Deut 4:5, 14, 40
4:3 Num 25:1-9
4:5 Lev 26:46; 27:34
4:6 Deut 30:19, 20; 32:46, 47; Job 28:28; Ps 19:7; 111:10; Prov 1:7; 2 Tim 3:15
4:7 Deut 4:32-34; 2 Sam 7:23; Ps 34:17, 18; 145:18; 148:14; Is 55:6; Ps 34:18; 85:9

3:21–22 What encouraging news for Joshua, who was to lead his men against the persistent forces of evil in the promised land! Since God promised to help him win every battle, he had nothing to fear. Our battles may not be against godless armies, but they are just as real as Joshua's. Whether we are resisting temptation or battling fear, God has promised to fight with and for us as we obey him.

3:26–28 God had made it clear that Moses would not enter the promised land (Numbers 20:12). So God told Moses to commission Joshua as the new leader and encourage him in this new role. This is a good example to churches and organizations who must eventually replace their leaders. Good leaders prepare their people to function without them by discovering those with leadership potential, providing the training they need, and looking for ways to encourage them.

4:2 What is meant by adding to or taking away from God's commands? These laws were the word of God, and they were complete. How could any human being, with limited wisdom and knowledge, edit God's perfect laws? To add to the laws would make them a burden; to subtract from the laws would make them incomplete. Thus the laws were to remain unchanged. To presume to make changes in God's law is to assume a position of authority over God who gave the laws (Matthew 5:17–19; 15:3–9; Revelation 22:18, 19). The religious leaders at the time of Christ did exactly this; they elevated their own laws to the same level as God's. Jesus rebuked them for this (Matthew 23:1–4).

8 "Or what great nation is there that has statutes and judgments as righteous as this
whole law which I am setting before you today?
9 "Only give heed to yourself and keep your soul diligently, so that you do not forget
the things which your eyes have seen and they do not depart from your heart all the days
of your life; but make them known to your sons and your grandsons.
10 "*Remember* the day you stood before the LORD your God at Horeb, when the LORD
said to me, 'Assemble the people to Me, that I may let them hear My words so they may
learn to [5]fear Me all the days they live on the earth, and that they may teach their children.'
11 "You came near and stood at the foot of the mountain, and the mountain burned
with fire to the *very* heart of the heavens: darkness, cloud and thick gloom.
12 "Then the LORD spoke to you from the midst of the fire; you heard the sound of
words, but you saw no form—only a voice.
13 "So He declared to you His covenant which He commanded you to perform, *that is,*
the Ten Commandments; and He wrote them on two tablets of stone.
14 "The LORD commanded me at that time to teach you statutes and judgments, that
you might perform them in the land where you are going over to possess it.
15 "So watch yourselves carefully, since you did not see any form on the day the LORD
spoke to you at Horeb from the midst of the fire,
16 so that you do not act corruptly and make a graven image for yourselves in the form
of any figure, the likeness of male or female,
17 the likeness of any animal that is on the earth, the likeness of any winged bird that
flies in the sky,
18 the likeness of anything that creeps on the ground, the likeness of any fish that is in
the water below the earth.
19 "And *beware* not to lift up your eyes to heaven and see the sun and the moon and the
stars, all the host of heaven, and be drawn away and worship them and serve them, those
which the LORD your God has allotted to all the peoples under the whole heaven.
20 "But the LORD has taken you and brought you out of the iron furnace, from Egypt,
to be a people for His own possession, as today.
21 "Now the LORD was angry with me on your account, and swore that I would not cross
the Jordan, and that I would not enter the good land which the LORD your God is giving
you as an inheritance.
22 "For I will die in this land, I shall not cross the Jordan, but you shall cross and take
possession of this good land.
23 "So watch yourselves, that you do not forget the covenant of the LORD your God
which He made with you, and make for yourselves a graven image in the form of anything *against* which the LORD your God has commanded you.

4:8 Ps 89:14; 97:2; 119:144, 160, 172
4:9 Deut 4:23; 6:12; 8:11, 14, 19; Prov 4:23; 23:19; Deut 6:2; 12:1; 16:3; Gen 18:19; Deut 4:10; 6:7, 20-25; 11:19; 32:46; Ps 78:5, 6; Prov 22:6; Eph 6:4
4:10 Deut 14:23; 17:19; 31:12, 13; Deut 4:9
4:11 Ex 19:18; Heb 12:18, 19
4:13 Ex 34:28; Deut 10:4; Ex 31:18; 34:1, 28
4:15 Josh 23:11; Is 40:18
4:16 Deut 4:25; 9:12; 31:29; Ex 20:4; Lev 26:1; Deut 5:8, 9; 27:15; Rom 1:23
4:17 Rom 1:23
4:19 Gen 2:1; Deut 17:3; 2 Kin 17:16; 21:3; Deut 13:5, 10; Job 31:26-28
4:20 1 Kin 8:51; Jer 11:4; Ex 19:5; Deut 7:6; 14:2; 26:18; Titus 2:14; 1 Pet 2:9
4:21 Num 20:12; Deut 1:37
4:22 Num 27:13, 14; Deut 3:25
4:23 Deut 4:9; Deut 4:16

5 Or *reverence*

4:8 Do the laws God gave to the Israelites still apply to Christians today? God's laws are designed to guide all people toward life-styles that are healthy, upright, and devoted to God. Their purpose was to point out sin (or potential sin) and show the proper way to deal with that sin. The Ten Commandments, the heart of God's law, are just as applicable today as they were 3,000 years ago because they proclaim a life-style endorsed by God. They are the perfect expression of who God is and how he wants people to live.

But God gave other laws besides the Ten Commandments. Are these just as important? God never issued a law that didn't have a purpose. However, many of the laws we read in the Pentateuch were directed specifically to people of that time and culture. Although a specific law may not apply to us, the timeless truth or principle behind the law does.

For example, Christians do not practice animal sacrifice in worship. However, the principles behind the sacrifices—forgiveness for sin and thankfulness to God—still apply. The sacrifices pointed to the ultimate sacrifice made for us by Jesus Christ. The New Testament says that with the death and resurrection of Jesus Christ the Old Testament laws were fulfilled. This means that while the Old Testament laws help us recognize our sins and correct our wrongdoings, it is Jesus Christ who takes our sins away. Jesus is now our primary example to follow because he alone perfectly obeyed the law and modeled its true intent.

4:9 Moses wanted to make sure that the people did not forget all they had seen God do, so he urged parents to teach their children about God's great miracles. This helped parents remember God's faithfulness and provided the means for passing on from one generation to the next the stories recounting God's great acts. It is easy to forget the wonderful ways God has worked in the lives of his people. But you can remember God's great acts of faithfulness by telling your children, friends, or associates what you have seen him do.

4:19 God was not excusing the other nations for their idol worship. He was simply saying that while judgment might be delayed for those other nations, it would be swift and complete for Israel because Israel knew God's laws. We must remember that idol worship was not just keeping statues around the house—harmless lumps of clay, wood, or iron. It was the commitment to the other evil qualities, beliefs, and practices the idol represented (such as murder, prostitution, cruelty in war, self-centeredness) or to strengths and attributes of mankind, the animal kingdom, or the orderliness of stars that were revered without reference to God who created them. Because God had so clearly revealed himself in Israel's history, the Israelites had no excuse for worshiping anyone but the true God.

24 "For the LORD your God is a consuming fire, a jealous God.
25 "When you become the father of children and children's children and have remained
long in the land, and act corruptly, and make an idol in the form of anything, and do that
which is evil in the sight of the LORD your God *so as* to provoke Him to anger,
26 I call heaven and earth to witness against you today, that you will surely perish quickly
from the land where you are going over the Jordan to possess it. You shall not live long
on it, but will be utterly destroyed.
27 "The LORD will scatter you among the peoples, and you will be left few in number
among the nations where the LORD drives you.
28 "There you will serve gods, the work of man's hands, wood and stone, which neither
see nor hear nor eat nor smell.
29 "But from there you will seek the LORD your God, and you will find *Him* if you search
for Him with all your heart and all your soul.
30 "When you are in distress and all these things have come upon you, in the latter days
you will return to the LORD your God and listen to His voice.
31 "For the LORD your God is a compassionate God; He will not fail you nor destroy
you nor forget the covenant with your fathers which He swore to them.
32 "Indeed, ask now concerning the former days which were before you, since the day
that God created man on the earth, and *inquire* from one end of the heavens to the other.
Has *anything* been done like this great thing, or has *anything* been heard like it?
33 "Has *any* people heard the voice of God speaking from the midst of the fire, as you
have heard *it,* and survived?
34 "Or has a god tried to go to take for himself a nation from within *another* nation by
trials, by signs and wonders and by war and by a mighty hand and by an outstretched arm
and by great terrors, as the LORD your God did for you in Egypt before your eyes?
35 "To you it was shown that you might know that the LORD, He is God; there is no
other besides Him.
36 "Out of the heavens He let you hear His voice to discipline you; and on earth He let
you see His great fire, and you heard His words from the midst of the fire.
37 "Because He loved your fathers, therefore He chose their descendants after them.
And He personally brought you from Egypt by His great power,
38 driving out from before you nations greater and mightier than you, to bring you in
and to give you their land for an inheritance, as it is today.
39 "Know therefore today, and take it to your heart, that the LORD, He is God in heav-
en above and on the earth below; there is no other.
40 "So you shall keep His statutes and His commandments which I am giving you today,
that it may go well with you and with your children after you, and that you may live long
on the land which the LORD your God is giving you for all time."
41 Then Moses set apart three cities across the Jordan to the east,

4:24 Ex 24:17; Deut 9:3; Is 30:27; 33:14; Heb 12:29; Deut 5:9

4:26 Deut 30:19; 31:28; 32:1; Is 1:2; Mic 6:2; Deut 7:4; 8:19, 20

4:28 Deut 28:36, 64; Jer 16:13; Deut 29:17; Ps 115:4-8; 135:15-18; Is 44:12-20

4:29 2 Chr 15:4; Is 55:6; Jer 29:13; Deut 6:5

4:30 Ps 18:6; 59:16; 107:6, 13; Deut 31:29; Jer 23:20; Hos 3:5; Heb 1:2; Jer 4:1, 2

4:31 Neh 9:31; Ps 103:8; 111:4; 116:5; Jon 4:2; Deut 31:6, 8; Josh 1:5; 1 Chr 28:20; Heb 13:5; Jer 30:11; Lev 26:45

4:32 Gen 1:27; Is 45:12; Deut 28:64; Matt 24:31; Deut 4:7; 2 Sam 7:23

4:34 Ex 14:30; Deut 33:29; Deut 7:19; Deut 5:15; 6:21; Ps 136:12

4:35 Ex 8:10; 9:14; Deut 4:39; 32:12, 39; 1 Sam 2:2; Is 43:10-12; 44:6-8; 45:5-7; Mark 12:32

4:36 Ex 19:9, 19; 20:18, 22; Deut 4:33; Neh 9:13; Heb 12:25

4:40 Ps 105:45; Deut 4:1; 5:16, 29, 33; 6:3, 18

4:24 God is a consuming fire. Because he is morally perfect, he hates sin and cannot accept those who practice it. Moses' sin kept him from entering the promised land, and no sacrifice could remove that judgment. Sin kept us from entering God's presence, but Jesus Christ paid the penalty for our sin and removed God's judgment forever by his death. Trusting in Jesus Christ will save you from God's anger and will allow you to begin a personal relationship with him.

4:24 Jealousy is a demand for someone else's exclusive affection or loyalty. Some jealousy is bad. It is destructive for a man to get upset when his wife talks pleasantly with another man. But other jealousy is good. It is right for a man to demand that his wife treat him, and only him, as her husband. Usually we use the word *jealousy* only for the bad reaction. But God's kind of jealousy is appropriate and good. He is defending his word and his high honor. He makes a strong, exclusive demand on us: We must treat only the Lord—and no one else in all the universe—as God.

4:29 Do you want to know God? God promised the Israelites that they would find him when they searched with all their hearts and souls. God is knowable and wants to be known—but we have to want to know him. Acts of service and worship must be accompanied by sincere devotion of the heart. As Hebrews 11:6 says, "He who comes to God must believe that He is and that He is a rewarder of those who seek Him." God will reward those who pursue a relationship with him.

4:32 How tempted we are to look everywhere else but to God for our guidance and leadership! We trust medical doctors, financial advisers, and news commentators, but do we trust God? Get God's advice first (4:39–40), and recognize his authority over every dimension of life.

4:40 Was Israel guaranteed prosperity for obeying God's laws? Yes—but we have to look carefully at what that means. God's laws were designed to make his chosen nation healthy, just, and merciful. When the people followed those laws, they prospered. This does not mean, however, that no sickness, no sadness, and no misunderstandings existed among them. Rather, it means that as a nation they prospered and that individuals' problems were handled as fairly as possible. Today God's promise of prosperity—his constant presence, comfort, and the resources to live as we should—extends to all believers. We will face trials; Jesus assured us of that. But we will avoid the misery that directly results from intentional sin, and we will know that a great treasure awaits us in heaven.

42 that a manslayer might flee there, who unintentionally slew his neighbor without
having enmity toward him in time past; and by fleeing to one of these cities he might
live:
43 Bezer in the wilderness on the plateau for the Reubenites, and Ramoth in Gilead **4:43**
for the Gadites, and Golan in Bashan for the Manassites. Josh 20:8

B. PRINCIPLES FOR GODLY LIVING: MOSES' SECOND ADDRESS (4:44—28:68)

After reviewing the history of Israel's journey, Moses recounts the Ten Commandments and the other laws given to the Israelites at Mount Sinai. He urges them to obey the law and reminds them of the consequences of disobeying God's laws. The Ten Commandments and all of God's laws point out to us where we fall short and show us how we should act as God's people.

44 Now this is the law which Moses set before the sons of Israel;
45 these are the testimonies and the statutes and the ordinances which Moses spoke
to the sons of Israel, when they came out from Egypt,
46 across the Jordan, in the valley opposite Beth-peor, in the land of Sihon king of the **4:46**
Amorites who lived at Heshbon, whom Moses and the sons of Israel defeated when they Deut 3:29; Num 21:21-25
came out from Egypt.
47 They took possession of his land and the land of Og king of Bashan, the two kings **4:47**
of the Amorites, *who were* across the Jordan to the east, Deut 1:4; 3:3, 4
48 from Aroer, which is on the edge of the valley of Arnon, even as far as Mount Sion **4:48**
(that is, Hermon), Deut 2:36; 3:12; Deut 3:9; Ps 133:3
49 with all the Arabah across the Jordan to the east, even as far as the sea of the Arabah, at the foot of the slopes of Pisgah.

1. The Ten Commandments

5:2 Ex 19:5; Mal 4:4

5 Then Moses summoned all Israel and said to them: **5:3**
"Hear, O Israel, the statutes and the ordinances which I am speaking today in your Jer 31:32; Heb 8:9
hearing, that you may learn them and observe them carefully. **5:4**
2 "The LORD our God made a covenant with us at Horeb. Num 14:14; Deut 34:10; Deut 4:33
3 "The LORD did not make this covenant with our fathers, but with us, *with* all those of
us alive here today. **5:5** Gal 3:19; Ex 19:16, 21-24; 20:18; Heb 12:18-21
4 "The LORD spoke to you face to face at the mountain from the midst of the fire,
5 *while* I was standing between the LORD and you at that time, to declare to you the
word of the LORD; for you were afraid because of the fire and did not go up the moun- **5:6**
tain. He said, Ex 20:2-17; Lev 26:1; Deut 6:4; Ps 81:10
6 'I am the LORD your God who brought you out of the land of Egypt, out of the house
of slavery. **5:7**
7 'You shall have no other gods before Me. Ex 20:3
8 'You shall not make for yourself an idol, *or* any likeness *of* what is in heaven above **5:8**
or on the earth beneath or in the water under the earth. Ex 20:4-6; Lev 26:1; Deut 4:15-18; 27:15; Ps 97:7
9 'You shall not worship them or serve them; for I, the LORD your God, am a jealous
God, visiting the iniquity of the fathers on the children, and on the third and the fourth **5:9**
generations of those who hate Me, Ex 34:7; Num 14:18; Deut 7:10

5:1 The people had entered into a covenant with God, and Moses commanded them to hear, learn, and observe (follow) his statutes. Christians also have entered into a covenant with God (through Jesus Christ) and should be responsive to what God expects. Moses' threefold command to the Israelites is excellent advice for all God's followers. *Hearing* is absorbing and accepting information about God. *Learning* is understanding its meaning and implications. *Following* is putting into action all we have learned and understood. All three parts are essential to a growing relationship with God.

5:7 A *god* is whatever people put first in their lives. Some people literally worship other gods by joining cults or strange religions. In a more subtle way, many of us worship other gods by building our lives around something other than the one true God. If your greatest desire is for popularity, power, or money, you are devoting yourself to something other than God. To put God first, (1) recognize what is taking his place in your life; (2) renounce this substitute god as unworthy of your devotion; (3) ask God for forgiveness; (4) restructure your priorities so that love for God is the motive for everything you do; (5) examine yourself daily to be sure you are giving God first place.

5:8–9 How would you feel if someone took a picture of you, framed it, stared at it a lot, showed it to others, but completely ignored the real you? God does not want to be treated this way either. He wants a genuine relationship with us, not mere ritual. He wants us to know him. God knows that if we put anything other than him at the center of our lives, we will not reach our potential and become all that he wants us to be.

5:10 Num 14:18; Deut 7:9; Jer 32:18

5:11 Ex 20:7; Lev 19:12; Deut 6:13; 10:20; Matt 5:33

5:12 Ex 16:23-30; 20:8-11; Mark 2:27f

5:14 Gen 2:2; Heb 4:4

5:16 Matt 15:4; 19:19; Mark 7:10; 10:19; Luke 18:20; Eph 6:2, 3; Col 3:20

5:17 Gen 9:6; Ex 20:13; Lev 24:17; Matt 5:21f; 19:18; Mark 10:19; Rom 13:9; James 2:11

5:18 Matt 5:27f; 19:18; Mark 10:19; Luke 18:20; Rom 13:9

10 but showing lovingkindness to thousands, to those who love Me and keep My commandments.
11 'You shall not take the name of the LORD your God in vain, for the LORD will not leave him unpunished who takes His name in vain.
12 'Observe the sabbath day to keep it holy, as the LORD your God commanded you.
13 'Six days you shall labor and do all your work,
14 but the seventh day is a sabbath of the LORD your God; *in it* you shall not do any work, you or your son or your daughter or your male servant or your female servant or your ox or your donkey or any of your cattle or your sojourner who stays with you, so that your male servant and your female servant may rest as well as you.
15 'You shall remember that you were a slave in the land of Egypt, and the LORD your God brought you out of there by a mighty hand and by an outstretched arm; therefore the LORD your God commanded you to observe the sabbath day.
16 'Honor your father and your mother, as the LORD your God has commanded you, that your days may be prolonged and that it may go well with you on the land which the LORD your God gives you.
17 'You shall not murder.
18 'You shall not commit adultery.
19 'You shall not steal.
20 'You shall not bear false witness against your neighbor.

BROKEN COMMANDMENTS
The Ten Commandments were God's standards for right living. To obey them was to obey God. Yet throughout the Old Testament, we can see how each commandment was broken. As you read the stories, notice the tragic consequences that occurred as a result of violating God's law.

Ten Commandments	*Notable Violations*
"You shall have no other gods before Me."	Solomon (1 Kings 11)
"You shall not make for yourself an idol . . . You shall not worship them or serve them."	The golden calf/idol incident (Exodus 32); generations after Joshua (Judges 2:10–14; 2 Kings 21:1–15; Jeremiah 1:16)
"You shall not take the name of the LORD your God in vain."	Zedekiah (Ezekiel 17:15–21)
"Observe the sabbath day to keep it holy."	Judah (2 Chronicles 36:21)
"Honor your father and your mother."	Eli's sons—Hophni and Phinehas (1 Samuel 2:12, 23–25)
"You shall not murder."	Hazael (2 Kings 8:15)
"You shall not commit adultery."	David (2 Samuel 11:2–5)
"You shall not steal."	Ahab (1 Kings 21:1–19)
"You shall not bear false witness against your neighbor."	Saul (1 Samuel 15:13–25)
"You shall not covet your neighbor's wife . . . your neighbor's house, his field or anything that belongs to your neighbor."	Achan (Joshua 7:19–26)

5:11 We are familar with the sin to be avoided in this commandment, that we should not take the name of the Lord in vain by saying it in an empty or worthless way. But there is also a good work that is commanded: to use God's name to praise him and ascribe to him glory. This is the opposite of misusing his name. While you might be able to keep yourself from swearing, how have you done at finding time to praise God and honor his name?

5:16 Obeying our parents is our main task when we are young, but *honoring* them should continue even beyond their death. One way to honor parents is to provide for them in times of financial need or when they are ill and unable to care for themselves. Perhaps the best way to honor them is to pass on their godly values to our children. Honoring involves all that sons and daughters do with their lives—the way they work and talk, the values they hold, and the morals they practice. What are you doing to show respect to your parents? Are you living in a way that brings honor to them?

5:17 "But I don't murder people," you may say. Good. That fulfills the letter of the law. But Jesus explained that hateful anger breaks this commandment (Matthew 5:21–22). Have you ever been so angry with someone who mistreated you that for a moment you wished that person were dead? Have you ever fantasized that you could do someone in? Jesus' teaching concerning this law demonstrates that we are capable of murder in our hearts. Even if we are legally innocent, we are all morally guilty of murder and need to ask God's forgiveness. We need to commit ourselves to the opposite of hatred and anger—love and reconciliation.

21 'You shall not covet your neighbor's wife, and you shall not desire your neighbor's
house, his field or his male servant or his female servant, his ox or his donkey or anything that belongs to your neighbor.'

5:21 Ex 20:17; Rom 7:7; 13:9

Moses Interceded

22 "These words the LORD spoke to all your assembly at the mountain from the midst
of the fire, *of* the cloud and *of* the thick gloom, with a great voice, and He added no more.
He wrote them on two tablets of stone and gave them to me.

5:22 Ex 24:12; 31:18; Deut 4:13

23 "And when you heard the voice from the midst of the darkness, while the mountain
was burning with fire, you came near to me, all the heads of your tribes and your elders.
24 "You said, 'Behold, the LORD our God has shown us His glory and His greatness,
and we have heard His voice from the midst of the fire; we have seen today that God
speaks with man, yet he lives.
25 'Now then why should we die? For this great fire will consume us; if we hear the voice
of the LORD our God any longer, then we will die.
26 'For who is there of all flesh who has heard the voice of the living God speaking from
the midst of the fire, as we *have,* and lived?
27 'Go near and hear all that the LORD our God says; then speak to us all that the LORD
our God speaks to you, and we will hear and do *it.*'

5:25 Ex 20:18, 19; Deut 18:16

5:26 Deut 4:33

28 "The LORD heard the voice of your words when you spoke to me, and the LORD said
to me, 'I have heard the voice of the words of this people which they have spoken to you.
They have done well in all that they have spoken.
29 'Oh that they had such a heart in them, that they would fear Me and keep all My
commandments always, that it may be well with them and with their sons forever!
30 'Go, say to them, "Return to your tents."
31 'But as for you, stand here by Me, that I may speak to you all the commandments
and the statutes and the judgments which you shall teach them, that they may observe
them in the land which I give them to possess.'
32 "So you shall observe to do just as the LORD your God has commanded you; you
shall not turn aside to the right or to the left.
33 "You shall walk in all the way which the LORD your God has commanded you, that
you may live and that it may be well with you, and that you may prolong *your* days in the
land which you will possess.

5:28 Deut 18:17

5:29 Ps 81:13; Is 48:18; Deut 11:1; Deut 5:16, 33

5:31 Ex 24:12

5:32 Deut 17:20; 28:14; Josh 1:7; 23:6; Prov 4:27

5:33 Deut 10:12; Jer 7:23; Luke 1:6; Deut 4:1, 40; 12:25, 28; 22:7; Eph 6:3

2. Love the LORD your God

Obey God and Prosper

6 "Now this is the commandment, the statutes and the judgments which the LORD your
God has commanded *me* to teach you, that you might do *them* in the land where you
are going over to possess it,
2 so that you and your son and your grandson might fear the LORD your God, to keep
all His statutes and His commandments which I command you, all the days of your life,
and that your days may be prolonged.
3 "O Israel, you should listen and be careful to do *it,* that it may be well with you and
that you may multiply greatly, just as the LORD, the God of your fathers, has promised
you, *in* a land flowing with milk and honey.

6:2 Ex 20:20; Deut 10:12; Ps 111:10; 128:1; Eccl 12:13; Deut 4:9

6:3 Deut 5:33; Ex 3:8, 17

5:21 To covet is to desire another person's prosperity. We are not to set our desires on anything that belongs to someone else. Not only can such desires make us miserable, they can also lead us to other sins such as adultery and stealing. Envying others is a useless exercise because God is able to provide everything we really need, even if he does not always give us everything we want. To stop coveting, we need to practice being content with what we have. The apostle Paul emphasizes the significance of contentment in Philippians 4:11. It's a matter of perspective. Instead of thinking about what we don't have, we should thank God for what he has given and strive to be content. After all, our most important possession is free and available to everyone—eternal life through Christ.

5:29 God told Moses that he wanted the people to incline their hearts to fear him—to *want* to respect and obey him. There is a difference between doing something because it is required and doing something because we want to. God is not interested in forced religious exercises and rule-keeping. He wants our hearts and lives completely dedicated to him. If we love him, obedience will follow.

6:3 For a nation that had wandered 40 years in a parched wilderness, a land flowing with milk and honey sounded like paradise. It brought to mind rich crops, rushing streams, gentle rains, and lush fields filled with livestock. The Israelites could have had all that 40 years earlier. Numbers 13 and 14 explain how the people missed their chance. Now Moses was determined to help the people avoid the same mistake by whetting their appetite for the beautiful land and then clearly explaining the conditions for entering the land.

6:4
Matt 22:37; Mark 12:29, 30; Luke 10:27; Deut 4:35, 39; John 10:30; 1 Cor 8:4; Eph 4:6

6:5
Matt 22:37; Mark 12:30; Luke 10:27; Deut 4:29; 10:12

6:7
Deut 4:9; 11:19; Eph 6:4

6:8
Ex 12:14; 13:9, 16; Deut 11:18; Prov 3:3; 6:21; 7:3

6:10
Deut 9:1; 19:1; Josh 24:13; Ps 105:44

4 "Hear, O Israel! The LORD is our God, the LORD is one!
5 "You shall love the LORD your God with all your heart and with all your soul and
with all your might.
6 "These words, which I am commanding you today, shall be on your heart.
7 "You shall teach them diligently to your sons and shall talk of them when you sit in
your house and when you walk by the way and when you lie down and when you rise up.
8 "You shall bind them as a sign on your hand and they shall be as frontals on your
forehead.
9 "You shall write them on the doorposts of your house and on your gates.
10 "Then it shall come about when the LORD your God brings you into the land which
He swore to your fathers, Abraham, Isaac and Jacob, to give you, great and splendid
cities which you did not build,
11 and houses full of all good things which you did not fill, and hewn cisterns which
you did not dig, vineyards and olive trees which you did not plant, and you eat and are
satisfied,
12 then watch yourself, that you do not forget the LORD who brought you from the
land of Egypt, out of the house of slavery.

DANGER IN PLENTY

God warned Israel, when "you eat and are satisfied, then watch yourself, that you do not forget the LORD" (Deuteronomy 6:11–12). It is often most difficult to follow God when life is easy—we can fall prey to temptation and fall away from God. Here are some notable examples of this truth.

Person	*Reference*	*Comment*
Adam	Genesis 3	Adam lived in a perfect world and had a perfect relationship with God. His needs were met; he had everything. But he fell to Satan's deception.
Noah	Genesis 9	Noah and his family had survived the flood and the whole world was theirs. They were prosperous, and life was easy. Noah shamed himself by becoming drunk and cursed his son Ham.
The nation of Israel	Judges 2	God had given Israel the promised land—rest at last with no more wandering. But as soon as brave and faithful Joshua died, they fell into the idolatrous practices of the Canaanites.
David	2 Samuel 11	David ruled well, and Israel was a dominant nation, politically, economically, and militarily. In the midst of prosperity and success, he committed adultery with Bathsheba and had her husband Uriah murdered.
Solomon	1 Kings 11	Solomon truly had it all: power, wealth, fame, and wisdom. But his very abundance was the source of his downfall. He loved his pagan, idolatrous wives so much that he allowed himself and Israel to copy their detestable religious rites.

6:4 Monotheism—belief in only one God—was a distinctive feature of Hebrew religion. Many ancient religions believed in many gods. But the God of Abraham, Isaac, and Jacob is the God of the whole earth, the only true God. This was an important insight for the nation of Israel because they were about to enter a land filled with people who believed in many gods. Both then and today, there are people who prefer to place their trust in many different "gods." But the day is coming when God will be recognized as the only one. He will be the king over the whole earth (Zechariah 14:9).

6:4–9 This passage provides the central theme of Deuteronomy. It sets a pattern that helps us relate the Word of God to our daily lives. We are to love God, think constantly about his commandments, teach his commandments to our children, and live each day by the guidelines in his Word. God emphasized the importance of parents' teaching the Bible to their children. The church and Christian schools cannot be used to escape from this responsibility. The Bible provides so many opportunities for object lessons and practical teaching that it would be a shame to study it only one day a week. Eternal truths are most effectively learned in the loving environment of a God-fearing home.

6:5 Jesus said that loving God with all of ourselves is the first and greatest commandment (Matthew 22:37–39). This command, combined with the command to love your neighbor (Leviticus 19:18), encompasses all the other Old Testament laws.

6:7 The Hebrews were extremely successful at making religion an integral part of life. The reason for their success was that religious education was life-oriented, not information-oriented. They used the context of daily life to teach about God. The key to teaching your children to love God is stated simply and clearly in these verses. If you want your children to follow God, you must make God a part of your everyday experiences. You must teach your children diligently to see God in all aspects of life, not just those that are church related.

6:10–13 Moses warned the people not to forget God when they entered the promised land and became prosperous. Prosperity, more than poverty, can dull our spiritual vision because it tends to make us self-sufficient and eager to acquire still more of everything—except God. The same thing can happen in our church. Once we become successful in terms of numbers, programs, and buildings, we can easily become self-sufficient and less sensitive to our need for God. This leads us to concentrate on self-preservation rather than thankfulness and service to God.

13 "You shall [6]fear *only* the LORD your God; and you shall worship Him and swear by
His name.
14 "You shall not follow other gods, any of the gods of the peoples who surround you,
15 for the LORD your God in the midst of you is a jealous God; otherwise the anger of
the LORD your God will be kindled against you, and He will wipe you off the face of the
earth.
16 "You shall not put the LORD your God to the test, as you tested *Him* at Massah.
17 "You should diligently keep the commandments of the LORD your God, and His testimonies and His statutes which He has commanded you.
18 "You shall do what is right and good in the sight of the LORD, that it may be well
with you and that you may go in and possess the good land which the LORD swore to *give*
your fathers,
19 by driving out all your enemies from before you, as the LORD has spoken.
20 "When your son asks you in time to come, saying, 'What *do* the testimonies and the
statutes and the judgments *mean* which the LORD our God commanded you?'
21 then you shall say to your son, 'We were slaves to Pharaoh in Egypt, and the LORD
brought us from Egypt with a mighty hand.
22 'Moreover, the LORD showed great and distressing signs and wonders before our
eyes against Egypt, Pharaoh and all his household;
23 He brought us out from there in order to bring us in, to give us the land which He
had sworn to our fathers.'
24 "So the LORD commanded us to observe all these statutes, to fear the LORD our God
for our good always and for our survival, as *it is* today.
25 "It will be righteousness for us if we are careful to observe all this commandment
before the LORD our God, just as He commanded us.

Warnings

7 "When the LORD your God brings you into the land where you are entering to possess it, and clears away many nations before you, the Hittites and the Girgashites
and the Amorites and the Canaanites and the Perizzites and the Hivites and the Jebusites, seven nations greater and stronger than you,
2 and when the LORD your God delivers them before you and you defeat them, then
you shall utterly destroy them. You shall make no covenant with them and show no favor to them.
3 "Furthermore, you shall not intermarry with them; you shall not give your daughters
to their sons, nor shall you take their daughters for your sons.
4 "For they will turn your sons away from following Me to serve other gods; then the
anger of the LORD will be kindled against you and He will quickly destroy you.
5 "But thus you shall do to them: you shall tear down their altars, and smash their *sacred* pillars, and hew down their [7]Asherim, and burn their graven images with fire.
6 "For you are a holy people to the LORD your God; the LORD your God has chosen
you to be a people for His own possession out of all the peoples who are on the face of
the earth.

6:13 Deut 13:4; Matt 4:10; Luke 4:8; Deut 5:11; 10:20; Ps 63:11; Matt 5:33
6:14 Jer 25:6
6:15 Deut 4:24; 5:9
6:16 Matt 4:7; Luke 4:12; Ex 17:7
6:17 Deut 11:22; Ps 119:4
6:18 Deut 4:40
6:20 Ex 13:8, 14
6:24 Deut 10:12; Jer 32:39; Ps 41:2; Luke 10:28
6:25 Deut 24:13; Rom 10:3
7:1 Deut 20:16-18; Acts 13:19
7:2 Num 31:17; Josh 11:11; Ex 23:32; Deut 7:16; 13:8
7:3 Ex 34:15, 16; Josh 23:12; Ezra 9:2
7:4 Deut 4:26
7:5 Ex 23:24; 34:13; Deut 12:3
7:6 Ex 19:6; Deut 14:2, 21; Ps 50:5; Jer 2:3; Ex 19:5; Deut 4:20; 14:2; 26:18; Ps 135:4; Titus 2:14; 1 Pet 2:9

6 Or *reverence* **7** I.e. wooden symbols of a female deity

6:24 Does the phrase "for our good always" mean that we can expect only prosperity and no suffering when we obey God? What is promised here is a right relationship with God for all those who love him with all their heart. It speaks of a good relationship with God and the ultimate benefit of knowing him. It is not blanket protection against poverty, adversity, or suffering. We can have this right relationship with God by obeying his command to love him with all that we are.

7:2 God told the Israelites to destroy their enemies totally. How can a God of love and mercy wipe out everyone, even children? Although God is loving and merciful, he is also just. These enemy nations were as much a part of God's creation as Israel was, and God does not allow evil to continue unchecked. God had punished Israel by keeping out of the promised land all those who had disobeyed. The command to destroy these nations was both a judgment (9:4–6) and a safety measure. On one hand, the people living in the land were being judged for their sin, and Israel was God's instrument of judgment—just as God would one day use other nations to judge Israel for its sin (2 Chronicles 36:17; Isaiah 10:12). On the other hand, God's command was designed to protect the nation of Israel from being ruined by the idolatry and immorality of its enemies. To think that God is too "nice" to judge sin would be to underestimate him.

7:5 Asherah was a Canaanite mother goddess of the sea, associated with Baal. The Asherim were idols of this goddess.

7:6 How did Israel deserve to be chosen above all of the other nations at that time? It was not a matter of Israel's merit, but of God keeping his promise to their ancestors. Just as God chose the nation of Israel, he has chosen all believers today to be a part of his treasured possession. Similarly, it is not because of our merit that we have come to faith in Christ. Instead God chose us out of his goodness and grace.

7 "The LORD did not set His love on you nor choose you because you were more in
number than any of the peoples, for you were the fewest of all peoples,
8 but because the LORD loved you and kept the oath which He swore to your fore
fathers, the LORD brought you out by a mighty hand and redeemed you from the house
of slavery, from the hand of Pharaoh king of Egypt.
9 "Know therefore that the LORD your God, He is God, the faithful God, who keeps
His covenant and His lovingkindness to a thousandth generation with those who love
Him and keep His commandments;
10 but repays those who hate Him to their faces, to destroy them; He will not delay
with him who hates Him, He will repay him to his face.
11 "Therefore, you shall keep the commandment and the statutes and the judgments
which I am commanding you today, to do them.

Promises of God

12 "Then it shall come about, because you listen to these judgments and keep and do
them, that the LORD your God will keep with you His covenant and His lovingkindness
which He swore to your forefathers.
13 "He will love you and bless you and multiply you; He will also bless the fruit of your
womb and the fruit of your ground, your grain and your new wine and your oil, the increase of your herd and the young of your flock, in the land which He swore to your forefathers to give you.
14 "You shall be blessed above all peoples; there will be no male or female barren among
you or among your cattle.
15 "The LORD will remove from you all sickness; and He will not put on you any of
the harmful diseases of Egypt which you have known, but He will lay them on all who
hate you.
16 "You shall consume all the peoples whom the LORD your God will deliver to you;
your eye shall not pity them, nor shall you serve their gods, for that *would be* a snare to you.
17 "If you should say in your heart, 'These nations are greater than I; how can I dispossess them?'
18 you shall not be afraid of them; you shall well remember what the LORD your God
did to Pharaoh and to all Egypt:
19 the great trials which your eyes saw and the signs and the wonders and the mighty
hand and the outstretched arm by which the LORD your God brought you out. So shall
the LORD your God do to all the peoples of whom you are afraid.
20 "Moreover, the LORD your God will send the hornet against them, until those who
are left and hide themselves from you perish.
21 "You shall not dread them, for the LORD your God is in your midst, a great and
awesome God.
22 "The LORD your God will clear away these nations before you little by little; you will
not be able to put an end to them quickly, for the wild beasts would grow too numerous
for you.
23 "But the LORD your God will deliver them before you, and will throw them into great
confusion until they are destroyed.
24 "He will deliver their kings into your hand so that you will make their name perish
from under heaven; no man will be able to stand before you until you have destroyed
them.
25 "The graven images of their gods you are to burn with fire; you shall not covet the
silver or the gold that is on them, nor take it for yourselves, or you will be snared by it,
for it is an abomination to the LORD your God.

7:7 Deut 4:37
7:8 Ex 32:13; Ex 13:3
7:9 Deut 4:35, 39; Is 49:7; 1 Cor 1:9; 1 Thess 5:24; 2 Tim 2:13; Ex 20:6; Dan 9:4; Deut 5:10
7:10 Is 59:18; Nah 1:2
7:12 Lev 26:3-13; Deut 28:1-14
7:13 Ps 146:8; Prov 15:9; John 14:21; Lev 26:9; Deut 13:17; 30:5
7:14 Ex 23:26
7:15 Ex 15:26
7:16 Deut 7:2; Ex 23:33; Judg 8:27; Ps 106:36
7:17 Num 33:53
7:18 Ps 105:5
7:19 Deut 4:34
7:20 Ex 23:28; Josh 24:12
7:21 Ex 29:45; Josh 3:10; Deut 10:17; Neh 1:5; 9:32
7:22 Ex 23:29, 30
7:23 Ex 23:27; Josh 10:10
7:24 Josh 6:2; 10:23-25; Deut 11:25; Josh 1:5; 10:8; 23:9
7:25 Ex 32:20; Deut 12:3; 1 Chr 14:12; Ex 20:17; Deut 7:16; Judg 8:27; Deut 17:1

7:21–24 Moses told the Israelites that God would destroy Israel's enemies, but not all at once. God had the power to destroy those nations instantly, but he chose to do it in stages. In the same way and with the same power, God could miraculously and instantaneously change your life. Usually, however, he chooses to help you gradually, teaching you one lesson at a time. Rather than expecting instant spiritual maturity and solutions to all your problems, slow down and work one step at a time, trusting God to make up the difference between where you should be and where you are now. You'll soon look back and see that a miraculous transformation has occurred.

7:25–26 Moses warned Israel against becoming ensnared by the idols of the defeated nations by coveting the silver or gold on them. We may think it's all right to be close to sin as long as we don't participate. "After all," we say, "I won't do anything wrong!" But being close can hurt us as we become attracted and finally give in. The only sure way to stay away from sin is to *stay away!*

26 "You shall not bring an abomination into your house, and like it come under the ban; you shall utterly detest it and you shall utterly abhor it, for it is something banned.

7:26 Lev 27:28f

God's Gracious Dealings

8 "All the commandments that I am commanding you today you shall be careful to do, that you may live and multiply, and go in and possess the land which the LORD swore *to give* to your forefathers.

8:1 Deut 4:1

2 "You shall remember all the way which the LORD your God has led you in the wilderness these forty years, that He might humble you, testing you, to know what was in your heart, whether you would keep His commandments or not.

8:2 Deut 8:16; Ps 136:16; Amos 2:10; Ex 15:25; 20:20; 2 Chr 32:31

3 "He humbled you and let you be hungry, and fed you with manna which you did not know, nor did your fathers know, that He might make you understand that man does not live by bread alone, but man lives by everything that proceeds out of the mouth of the LORD.

8:3 Matt 4:4; Luke 4:4

4 "Your clothing did not wear out on you, nor did your foot swell these forty years.

8:4 Deut 29:5; Neh 9:21

5 "Thus you are to know in your heart that the LORD your God was disciplining you just as a man disciplines his son.

8:5 Deut 4:36; 2 Sam 7:14; Prov 3:12; Heb 12:6; Rev 3:19

6 "Therefore, you shall keep the commandments of the LORD your God, to walk in His ways and to fear Him.

7 "For the LORD your God is bringing you into a good land, a land of brooks of water, of fountains and springs, flowing forth in valleys and hills;

8:7 Deut 11:9-12; Jer 2:7

8 a land of wheat and barley, of vines and fig trees and pomegranates, a land of olive oil and honey;

9 a land where you will eat food without scarcity, in which you will not lack anything; a land whose stones are iron, and out of whose hills you can dig copper.

10 "When you have eaten and are satisfied, you shall bless the LORD your God for the good land which He has given you.

8:10 Deut 6:11

11 "Beware that you do not forget the LORD your God by not keeping His commandments and His ordinances and His statutes which I am commanding you today;

8:11 Deut 4:9

12 otherwise, when you have eaten and are satisfied, and have built good houses and lived *in them,*

8:12 Prov 30:9; Hos 13:6

OBEDIENCE
Deut. 8:1 tells us to obey God's commandments. We do this by obeying God with . . .

OUR HEART	By loving him more than any relationship, activity, achievement, or possession.
OUR WILL	By committing ourselves completely to him.
OUR MIND	By seeking to know him and his Word, so his principles and values form the foundation of all we think and do.
OUR BODY	By recognizing that our strengths, talents, and sexuality are given to us by God to be used for pleasure and fulfillment according to his rules, not ours.
OUR FINANCES	By deciding that all of the resources we have ultimately come from God, and that we are to be managers of them and not owners.
OUR FUTURE	By deciding to make service to God and people the main purpose of our life's work.

8:3 Jesus quoted this verse when the devil tempted him to turn stones into bread (Matthew 4:4). Many people think that life is based on satisfying their appetites. If they can earn enough money to dress, eat, and play in high style, they think they are living "the good life." But such things do not satisfy our deepest longings. In the end they leave us empty and dissatisfied. Real life, according to Moses, comes from total commitment to God, the one who created life itself. It requires discipline, sacrifice, and hard work, and that's why most people never find it.

8:4 It's usually easy for us to take God's protection for granted. We seldom take notice or thank God when our car doesn't break down, our clothes don't rip, or our tools don't break. The people of Israel also failed to take notice, it seems, for they didn't even notice that in 40 years of wandering in the wilderness, their clothes didn't wear out and their feet didn't swell. Thus, they did not remember to give thanks to God for these blessings. What has been working well for you? What has been giving you good service? What has been lasting for a long time without breaking down or apart? Remember to thank God for these quiet blessings.

8:10 This verse is traditionally cited as the reason we say grace before or after meals. Its purpose, however, was to warn the Israelites not to forget God when their needs and wants were satisfied. Let your table prayers serve as a constant reminder of the Lord's goodness to you and your duty to those who are less fortunate.

8:11–20 In times of plenty, we often take credit for our prosperity and become proud that our own hard work and cleverness have made us rich. It is easy to get so busy collecting and managing wealth that we push God right out of our lives. But it is God who gives us everything we have, and it is God who asks us to manage it for him.

13 and when your herds and your flocks multiply, and your silver and gold multiply,
and all that you have multiplies,
14 then your heart will become proud and you will forget the LORD your God who
brought you out from the land of Egypt, out of the house of slavery.
15 "He led you through the great and terrible wilderness, *with its* fiery serpents and scorpions and thirsty ground where there was no water; He brought water for you out of the
rock of flint.
16 "In the wilderness He fed you manna which your fathers did not know, that He might
humble you and that He might test you, to do good for you in the end.
17 "Otherwise, you may say in your heart, 'My power and the strength of my hand made
me this wealth.'
18 "But you shall remember the LORD your God, for it is He who is giving you power to
make wealth, that He may confirm His covenant which He swore to your fathers, as *it is*
this day.
19 "It shall come about if you ever forget the LORD your God and go after other gods
and serve them and worship them, I testify against you today that you will surely perish.
20 "Like the nations that the LORD makes to perish before you, so you shall perish;
because you would not listen to the voice of the LORD your God.

Israel Provoked God

9 "Hear, O Israel! You are crossing over the Jordan today to go in to dispossess nations greater and mightier than you, great cities fortified to heaven,
2 a people great and tall, the sons of the Anakim, whom you know and of whom you
have heard *it said,* 'Who can stand before the sons of Anak?'
3 "Know therefore today that it is the LORD your God who is crossing over before you
as a consuming fire. He will destroy them and He will subdue them before you, so that
you may drive them out and destroy them quickly, just as the LORD has spoken to you.
4 "Do not say in your heart when the LORD your God has driven them out before you,
'Because of my righteousness the LORD has brought me in to possess this land,' but *it is*
because of the wickedness of these nations *that* the LORD is dispossessing them before
you.
5 "It is not for your righteousness or for the uprightness of your heart that you are going
to possess their land, but *it is* because of the wickedness of these nations *that* the LORD
your God is driving them out before you, in order to confirm the oath which the LORD
swore to your fathers, to Abraham, Isaac and Jacob.
6 "Know, then, *it is* not because of your righteousness *that* the LORD your God is giving you this good land to possess, for you are a stubborn people.
7 "Remember, do not forget how you provoked the LORD your God to wrath in the
wilderness; from the day that you left the land of Egypt until you arrived at this place,
you have been rebellious against the LORD.
8 "Even at Horeb you provoked the LORD to wrath, and the LORD was so angry with
you that He would have destroyed you.
9 "When I went up to the mountain to receive the tablets of stone, the tablets of the
covenant which the LORD had made with you, then I remained on the mountain forty
days and nights; I neither ate bread nor drank water.
10 "The LORD gave me the two tablets of stone written by the finger of God; and on
them *were* all the words which the LORD had spoken with you at the mountain from the
midst of the fire on the day of the assembly.
11 "It came about at the end of forty days and nights that the LORD gave me the two
tablets of stone, the tablets of the covenant.
12 "Then the LORD said to me, 'Arise, go down from here quickly, for your people whom
you brought out of Egypt have acted corruptly. They have quickly turned aside from the
way which I commanded them; they have made a molten image for themselves.'

8:14 Deut 8:11; Ps 106:21
8:15 Deut 1:19; Jer 2:6; Num 21:6; Ex 17:6; Num 20:11; Deut 32:13; Ps 78:15; 114:8
8:16 Ex 16:15; Deut 8:2
8:17 Deut 9:4
8:18 Prov 10:22; Hos 2:8
8:19 Deut 4:26; 30:18
8:20 Ezek 5:5-17
9:1 Deut 4:38; 7:1; 11:23; Deut 1:28
9:2 Num 13:22, 28, 33; Josh 11:21, 22
9:3 Deut 31:3; Josh 3:11; Deut 4:24; Heb 12:29; Ex 23:31; Deut 7:24
9:4 Deut 8:17; 9:7, 24; 31:27; Lev 18:3, 24-30; Deut 12:31; 18:9-14
9:5 Titus 3:5; Gen 12:7; 13:15; 15:7; 17:8; 26:4; 28:13
9:6 Deut 9:13; 10:16; 31:27
9:7 Ex 14:10f; Num 14:22
9:8 Ex 32:7-10; Ps 106:19
9:9 Ex 24:18; 34:28; Deut 8:3; 9:18
9:10 Deut 4:13
9:11 Deut 9:9
9:12 Ex 32:7, 8; Judg 2:17

9:2–3 The Anakim were enormous people, some seven to nine feet tall. Goliath, probably a descendant of this race, was over nine feet tall (1 Samuel 17:4–7). Unfortunately, these great men used their stature as a means of intimidation rather than for noble causes. Their appearance alone frightened the Israelite spies (Numbers 13:28), and their bad reputation may have been the deciding factor that had kept the Israelites out of the land 40 years earlier (Numbers 13—14). Moses used all his persuasive power to convince his people that God could handle these bullies. He used the illustration of God as a consuming fire, for not even a giant could stand up to that.

13 "The LORD spoke further to me, saying, 'I have seen this people, and indeed, it is a
stubborn people.
14 'Let Me alone, that I may destroy them and blot out their name from under heaven;
and I will make of you a nation mightier and greater than they.'
15 "So I turned and came down from the mountain while the mountain was burning
with fire, and the two tablets of the covenant were in my two hands.
16 "And I saw that you had indeed sinned against the LORD your God. You had made
for yourselves a molten calf; you had turned aside quickly from the way which the LORD
had commanded you.
17 "I took hold of the two tablets and threw them from my hands and smashed them
before your eyes.
18 "I fell down before the LORD, as at the first, forty days and nights; I neither ate bread
nor drank water, because of all your sin which you had committed in doing what was evil
in the sight of the LORD to provoke Him to anger.
19 "For I was afraid of the anger and hot displeasure with which the LORD was wrathful
against you in order to destroy you, but the LORD listened to me that time also.
20 "The LORD was angry enough with Aaron to destroy him; so I also prayed for Aaron
at the same time.
21 "I took your sinful *thing,* the calf which you had made, and burned it with fire and
crushed it, grinding it very small until it was as fine as dust; and I threw its dust into the
brook that came down from the mountain.
22 "Again at Taberah and at Massah and at Kibroth-hattaavah you provoked the LORD
to wrath.
23 "When the LORD sent you from Kadesh-barnea, saying, 'Go up and possess the land
which I have given you,' then you rebelled against the command of the LORD your God;
you neither believed Him nor listened to His voice.
24 "You have been rebellious against the LORD from the day I knew you.
25 "So I fell down before the LORD the forty days and nights, which I did because the
LORD had said He would destroy you.
26 "I prayed to the LORD and said, 'O Lord GOD, do not destroy Your people, even
Your inheritance, whom You have redeemed through Your greatness, whom You have
brought out of Egypt with a mighty hand.
27 'Remember Your servants, Abraham, Isaac, and Jacob; do not look at the stubbornness of this people or at their wickedness or their sin.
28 'Otherwise the land from which You brought us may say, "Because the LORD was
not able to bring them into the land which He had promised them and because He hated
them He has brought them out to slay them in the wilderness."
29 'Yet they are Your people, even Your inheritance, whom You have brought out by
Your great power and Your outstretched arm.'

The Tablets Rewritten

10 "At that time the LORD said to me, 'Cut out for yourself two tablets of stone like
the former ones, and come up to Me on the mountain, and make an ark of wood
for yourself.
2 'I will write on the tablets the words that were on the former tablets which you shattered, and you shall put them in the ark.'
3 "So I made an ark of acacia wood and cut out two tablets of stone like the former
ones, and went up on the mountain with the two tablets in my hand.
4 "He wrote on the tablets, like the former writing, the Ten Commandments which
the LORD had spoken to you on the mountain from the midst of the fire on the day of
the assembly; and the LORD gave them to me.

9:13 Ex 32:9; Deut 10:16; 31:27; 2 Kin 17:14
9:14 Ex 32:10; Ps 9:5; 109:13
9:15 Ex 32:15-19
9:18 Ex 34:28; Deut 10:10; Deut 9:9; Ex 34:9
9:19 Ex 32:10f; Heb 12:21; Ex 34:10; Deut 10:10
9:21 Ex 32:20
9:22 Num 11:3; Ex 17:7; Num 11:34
9:23 Deut 1:2; Deut 1:21; Deut 1:26; Ps 106:24
9:24 Deut 9:7; 31:27
9:25 Deut 9:18
9:26 Ex 32:11-13; 1 Sam 7:9; Jer 15:1
9:28 Ex 32:12; Num 14:16
9:29 Deut 4:20; 1 Kin 8:51; Neh 1:10; Ps 106:40; Deut 4:34
10:1 Ex 34:1; Ex 25:10
10:2 Deut 4:13; Ex 25:16
10:3 Ex 25:5; 37:1-9; Ex 34:4
10:4 Ex 34:28; Deut 4:13; Ex 20:1; Deut 9:10; 18:16

9:18 From the record of this event in Exodus 32, it seems as though Moses acted immediately, grinding the golden calf into powder, and forcing the people to drink water mixed with it. But evidently, Moses spent 40 days and nights interceding for the people.

9:23 Moses was reminding the people of the nation's unbelief 40 years earlier, when they were afraid to enter Canaan. The Israelites had not believed God would be able to help them in spite of all he had already done. They refused to follow because they looked only to their own limited resources instead of to God. Unbelief is the root of many sins and problems. When you feel lost, it may be because you're looking everywhere but to God for your help and guidance. (See Psalms 81:6–12; 95:8; 106:13–20; Hebrews 3.)

5 "Then I turned and came down from the mountain and put the tablets in the ark which
I had made; and there they are, as the LORD commanded me."
6 (Now the sons of Israel set out from Beeroth Bene-jaakan to Moserah. There Aaron
died and there he was buried and Eleazar his son ministered as priest in his place.
7 From there they set out to Gudgodah, and from Gudgodah to Jotbathah, a land of
brooks of water.
8 At that time the LORD set apart the tribe of Levi to carry the ark of the covenant
of the LORD, to stand before the LORD to serve Him and to bless in His name until
this day.
9 Therefore, Levi does not have a portion or inheritance with his brothers; the LORD
is his inheritance, just as the LORD your God spoke to him.)
10 "I, moreover, stayed on the mountain forty days and forty nights like the first time,
and the LORD listened to me that time also; the LORD was not willing to destroy you.
11 "Then the LORD said to me, 'Arise, proceed on your journey ahead of the people,
that they may go in and possess the land which I swore to their fathers to give them.'
12 "Now, Israel, what does the LORD your God require from you, but to fear the LORD
your God, to walk in all His ways and love Him, and to serve the LORD your God with all
your heart and with all your soul,
13 *and* to keep the LORD'S commandments and His statutes which I am commanding
you today for your good?
14 "Behold, to the LORD your God belong heaven and the highest heavens, the earth
and all that is in it.
15 "Yet on your fathers did the LORD set His affection to love them, and He chose their
descendants after them, *even* you above all peoples, as *it is* this day.
16 "So circumcise your heart, and stiffen your neck no longer.
17 "For the LORD your God is the God of gods and the Lord of lords, the great, the
mighty, and the awesome God who does not show partiality nor take a bribe.
18 "He executes justice for the orphan and the widow, and shows His love for the alien
by giving him food and clothing.
19 "So show your love for the alien, for you were aliens in the land of Egypt.
20 "You shall fear the LORD your God; you shall serve Him and cling to Him, and you
shall swear by His name.
21 "He is your praise and He is your God, who has done these great and awesome things
for you which your eyes have seen.
22 "Your fathers went down to Egypt seventy persons *in all,* and now the LORD your
God has made you as numerous as the stars of heaven.

Rewards of Obedience

11 "You shall therefore love the LORD your God, and always keep His charge,
His statutes, His ordinances, and His commandments.
2 "Know this day that I *am* not *speaking* with your sons who have not known and who
have not seen the [8]discipline of the LORD your God—His greatness, His mighty hand
and His outstretched arm,

8 Or *instruction*

10:5 Ex 34:29; Ex 40:20 1 Kin 8:9
10:6 Num 33:30, 31; Num 20:25-28; 33:38
10:8 Num 3:6; 18:1-7; Deut 31:9; Deut 17:12; 18:5; 21:5
10:9 Num 18:20, 24; Deut 18:1, 2; Ezek 44:28
10:10 Ex 34:28; Deut 9:18
10:12 Mic 6:8; Deut 6:5; Matt 22:37; 1 Tim 1:5; Deut 4:29
10:14 1 Kin 8:27; Neh 9:6; Ps 68:33; 115:16
10:16 Lev 26:41; Jer 4:4; Deut 9:6
10:17 Josh 22:22; Ps 136:2; Dan 2:47; 1 Tim 6:15; Rev 19:16; Rev 17:14; Deut 1:17; Acts 10:34; Rom 2:11; Gal 2:6; Eph 6:9; Deut 16:19
10:18 Ex 22:22-24; Ps 68:5; 146:9
10:19 Lev 19:34; Ezek 47:22, 23
10:20 Deut 11:22; 13:4; Deut 5:11; 6:13; Ps 63:11
10:21 Ps 109:1; 148:14; Jer 17:14
10:22 Gen 46:27; Gen 15:5; 22:17; Deut 1:10
11:1 Deut 6:5; 10:12; Lev 18:30; 22:9

10:5 The tablets of the law were still in the ark about 500 years later when Solomon put it in his newly built temple (1 Kings 8:9). The ark last appears in the Israelite's history during the reign of Josiah, about 300 years after Solomon (2 Chronicles 35:3).

10:12–13 Often we ask, "What does God expect of me?" Here Moses gives a summary that is simple in form and easy to remember. Here are the essentials: (1) Fear God (have reverence for him). (2) Walk in all his ways. (3) Love him. (4) Serve him with all your heart and soul. (5) Keep his commands. How often we complicate faith with man-made rules, regulations, and requirements. Are you frustrated and burned out from trying hard to please God? Concentrate on his real requirements and find peace. Respect, follow, love, serve, and obey.

10:16–19 God required all male Israelites to be circumcised, but he wanted them to go beyond performing the surgery to understanding its meaning. They needed to submit to God inside, in their hearts, as well as outside, in their bodies. Then they could begin to imitate God's love and justice in their relationships with others. If our hearts are right with God, then our relationships with other people can be made right too. When your heart has been cleansed and you have been reconciled to God, you will begin to see a difference in the way you treat others.

10:17 In saying that the Lord is God of gods and Lord of lords, Moses was distinguishing the true God from all the local gods worshiped throughout the land. Then Moses went a step further, calling God mighty and awesome. He has such awesome power and justice that people cannot stand before him without his mercy. Fortunately, his mercy toward his people is unlimited. When we begin to grasp the extent of God's mercy toward us, we see what true love is and how deeply God loves us. Although our sins deserve severe judgment, God has chosen to show love and mercy to all who seek him.

10:20 "Swear by His name" means that God alone should have their allegiance.

3 and His signs and His works which He did in the midst of Egypt to Pharaoh the king
of Egypt and to all his land;
4 and what He did to Egypt's army, to its horses and its chariots, when He made the
water of the Red Sea to engulf them while they were pursuing you, and the LORD completely destroyed them;
5 and what He did to you in the wilderness until you came to this place;
6 and what He did to Dathan and Abiram, the sons of Eliab, the son of Reuben, when
the earth opened its mouth and swallowed them, their households, their tents, and every
living thing that followed them, among all Israel—
7 but your own eyes have seen all the great work of the LORD which He did.
8 "You shall therefore keep every commandment which I am commanding you today,
so that you may be strong and go in and possess the land into which you are about to
cross to possess it;
9 so that you may prolong *your* days on the land which the LORD swore to your fathers to give to them and to their descendants, a land flowing with milk and honey.
10 "For the land, into which you are entering to possess it, is not like the land of Egypt
from which you came, where you used to sow your seed and water it with your [9]foot like
a vegetable garden.
11 "But the land into which you are about to cross to possess it, a land of hills and valleys, drinks water from the rain of heaven,
12 a land for which the LORD your God cares; the eyes of the LORD your God are always on it, from the beginning even to the end of the year.
13 "It shall come about, if you listen obediently to my commandments which I am commanding you today, to love the LORD your God and to serve Him with all your heart and
all your soul,
14 that He will give the rain for your land in its season, the [10]early and late rain, that
you may gather in your grain and your new wine and your oil.
15 "He will give grass in your fields for your cattle, and you will eat and be satisfied.
16 "Beware that your hearts are not deceived, and that you do not turn away and serve
other gods and worship them.
17 "Or the anger of the LORD will be kindled against you, and He will shut up the heavens so that there will be no rain and the ground will not yield its fruit; and you will perish
quickly from the good land which the LORD is giving you.
18 "You shall therefore impress these words of mine on your heart and on your soul;
and you shall bind them as a sign on your hand, and they shall be as frontals on your
forehead.
19 "You shall teach them to your sons, talking of them when you sit in your house and
when you walk along the road and when you lie down and when you rise up.
20 "You shall write them on the doorposts of your house and on your gates,
21 so that your days and the days of your sons may be multiplied on the land which the
LORD swore to your fathers to give them, as long as the heavens *remain* above the earth.
22 "For if you are careful to keep all this commandment which I am commanding you
to do, to love the LORD your God, to walk in all His ways and hold fast to Him,
23 then the LORD will drive out all these nations from before you, and you will dispossess nations greater and mightier than you.
24 "Every place on which the sole of your foot treads shall be yours; your border will be
from the wilderness to Lebanon, *and* from the river, the river Euphrates, as far as [11]the
western sea.
25 "No man will be able to stand before you; the LORD your God will lay the dread of
you and the fear of you on all the land on which you set foot, as He has spoken to you.
26 "See, I am setting before you today a blessing and a curse:

9 I.e. probably a treadmill **10** I.e. autumn **11** I.e. the Mediterranean

11:3 Ex 7:8-21
11:4 Ex 14:28; Deut 1:40; 2:1
11:6 Num 16:1-35; Ps 106:16-18; Num 26:10, 11
11:8 Deut 31:6, 7, 23; Josh 1:6, 7
11:9 Deut 4:40; 5:16, 33; 6:2; Prov 10:27; Ex 3:8
11:11 Deut 8:7
11:12 1 Kin 9:3
11:13 Lev 26:3; Deut 7:12; Deut 11:1; Deut 4:29
11:14 Lev 26:4; Deut 28:12; Joel 2:23; James 5:7
11:15 Ps 104:14; Deut 6:11
11:16 Job 31:27
11:17 Deut 6:15; 9:19 1 Kin 8:35; 2 Chr 6:26; 7:13; Deut 28:24; Deut 4:26
11:18 Ex 13:9, 16; Deut 6:8
11:19 Deut 4:9, 10; 6:7; Prov 22:6
11:20 Deut 6:9
11:21 Prov 3:2; 4:10; 9:11; Ps 72:5
11:22 Deut 6:17; Deut 11:1; Deut 10:20
11:23 Deut 4:38; Deut 9:1
11:24 Josh 1:3; 14:9; Gen 15:18; Ex 23:31; Deut 1:7, 8
11:25 Ex 23:27; Deut 7:24
11:26 Deut 30:1, 19

11:7 Israel had strong reasons to believe in God and obey his commands. They had witnessed a parade of mighty miracles that demonstrated God's love and care for them. Incredibly, they still had trouble remaining faithful. Because few of us have seen such dramatic miracles, it may seem even more difficult for us to obey God and remain faithful. But we have the Bible, the written record of God's acts throughout history. Reading God's Word gives us a panoramic view of both the miracles Israel saw and others they didn't see. The lessons from the past, the instructions for the present, and the glimpses into the future give us many opportunities to strengthen our faith in God.

11:26 What is God's curse? It is not a magician's spell. To understand it, we must remember the conditions of the covenant between God and Israel. Both parties had agreed to the terms. The blessings would benefit Israel if they kept their part of the covenant: They would receive the land, live there forever, have fruitful crops, and

11:27 Deut 28:1-14
27 the blessing, if you listen to the commandments of the LORD your God, which I am
commanding you today;
11:28 Deut 28:15-68
28 and the curse, if you do not listen to the commandments of the LORD your God, but
turn aside from the way which I am commanding you today, by following other gods which
you have not known.
11:29 Deut 27:12; Josh 8:33
29 "It shall come about, when the LORD your God brings you into the land where you
are entering to possess it, that you shall place the blessing on Mount Gerizim and the
curse on Mount Ebal.
11:30 Josh 4:19; Gen 12:6
30 "Are they not across the Jordan, west of the way toward the sunset, in the land of the
Canaanites who live in the Arabah, opposite Gilgal, beside the oaks of Moreh?
11:31 Deut 17:14; Josh 21:43
31 "For you are about to cross the Jordan to go in to possess the land which the LORD
your God is giving you, and you shall possess it and live in it,
32 and you shall be careful to do all the statutes and the judgments which I am setting
before you today.

3. Laws for proper worship

Laws of the Sanctuary

12:1 Deut 4:9, 10; 1 Kin 8:40
12 "These are the statutes and the judgments which you shall carefully observe in the
land which the LORD, the God of your fathers, has given you to possess as long as
you live on the earth.
12:2 2 Kin 16:4; 17:10, 11
2 "You shall utterly destroy all the places where the nations whom you shall dispossess
serve their gods, on the high mountains and on the hills and under every green tree.
12:3 Num 33:52; Deut 7:5; Judg 2:2; Ex 23:13; Ps 16:4; Zech 13:2
3 "You shall tear down their altars and smash their *sacred* pillars and burn their
[12]Asherim with fire, and you shall cut down the engraved images of their gods and oblit-
erate their name from that place.
4 "You shall not act like this toward the LORD your God.
12:5 Ex 20:24; Deut 12:11, 13; 2 Chr 7:12; Ps 78:68
5 "But you shall seek *the LORD* at the place which the LORD your God will choose from
all your tribes, to establish His name there for His dwelling, and there you shall come.
12:6 Deut 14:22
6 "There you shall bring your burnt offerings, your sacrifices, your tithes, the contribution of your hand, your votive offerings, your freewill offerings, and the firstborn of your
herd and of your flock.
12:7 Lev 23:40; Deut 12:12, 18; 14:26; 28:47; Eccl 3:12, 13; 5:18-20
7 "There also you and your households shall eat before the LORD your God, and rejoice in all your undertakings in which the LORD your God has blessed you.
8 "You shall not do at all what we are doing here today, every man *doing* whatever is
right in his own eyes;
12:9 Deut 3:20; 25:19; Ps 95:11; Deut 4:21
9 for you have not as yet come to the resting place and the inheritance which the LORD
your God is giving you.
12:10 Josh 11:23
10 "When you cross the Jordan and live in the land which the LORD your God is giving
you to inherit, and He gives you rest from all your enemies around *you* so that you live in
security,
12:11 Deut 12:5; 15:20; 16:2; 17:8; 18:6
11 then it shall come about that the place in which the LORD your God will choose for
His name to dwell, there you shall bring all that I command you: your burnt offerings
and your sacrifices, your tithes and the contribution of your hand, and all your choice
votive offerings which you will vow to the LORD.
12:12 Deut 12:7; Deut 12:18, 19; 26:11-13; Deut 10:9; 14:29
12 "And you shall rejoice before the LORD your God, you and your sons and daughters,

12 I.e. wooden symbols of a female deity

---

expel their enemies. The curse would fall on Israel only if they broke their agreement; then they would forfeit God's blessing and would be in danger of crop failure, invasion, and expulsion from their land. Joshua later reviewed these blessings and curses with the entire nation (Joshua 8:34).

11:26 It is amazing that God set before the Israelites a choice between blessings and curses. It is even more amazing that most of them, through their disobedience, chose the curses. We have the same fundamental choice today. We can live for ourselves or live in service to God. To choose our own way is to travel on a dead-end road, but to choose God's way is to receive eternal life (John 5:24).

12:2–3 When taking over a nation, the Israelites were supposed to destroy every pagan altar and idol in the land. God knew it would be easy for them to change their beliefs if they started using those altars, so nothing was to remain that might tempt them to worship idols. We too should ruthlessly find and remove any centers of false worship in our lives. These may be activities, attitudes, possessions, relationships, places, or habits—anything that tempts us to turn our hearts from God and do wrong. We should never flatter ourselves by thinking we're too strong to be tempted. Israel learned that lesson.

12:12, 18 The Hebrews placed great emphasis on family worship. Whether offering a sacrifice or attending a great feast, the family was often together. This gave the children a healthy attitude toward worship, and it put extra meaning into it for the adults. Watching a family member confess his or her sin was just as important as celebrating a great holiday together. Although there are appropriate times to separate people by ages, some of the most meaningful worship can be experienced only when shared by old and young.

your male and female servants, and the Levite who is within your gates, since he has no
portion or inheritance with you.
13 "Be careful that you do not offer your burnt offerings in every *cultic* place you see,
14 but in the place which the LORD chooses in one of your tribes, there you shall offer
your burnt offerings, and there you shall do all that I command you.
15 "However, you may slaughter and eat meat within any of your gates, whatever you
desire, according to the blessing of the LORD your God which He has given you; the
unclean and the clean may eat of it, as of the gazelle and the deer.
16 "Only you shall not eat the blood; you are to pour it out on the ground like water.
17 "You are not allowed to eat within your gates the tithe of your grain or new wine or
oil, or the firstborn of your herd or flock, or any of your votive offerings which you vow,
or your freewill offerings, or the contribution of your hand.
18 "But you shall eat them before the LORD your God in the place which the LORD your
God will choose, you and your son and daughter, and your male and female servants,
and the Levite who is within your gates; and you shall rejoice before the LORD your God
in all your undertakings.
19 "Be careful that you do not forsake the Levite as long as you live in your land.
20 "When the LORD your God extends your border as He has promised you, and you
say, 'I will eat meat,' because you desire to eat meat, *then* you may eat meat, whatever
you desire.
21 "If the place which the LORD your God chooses to put His name is too far from you,
then you may slaughter of your herd and flock which the LORD has given you, as I have
commanded you; and you may eat within your gates whatever you desire.
22 "Just as a gazelle or a deer is eaten, so you will eat it; the unclean and the clean alike
may eat of it.
23 "Only be sure not to eat the blood, for the blood is the life, and you shall not eat the
life with the flesh.
24 "You shall not eat it; you shall pour it out on the ground like water.
25 "You shall not eat it, so that it may be well with you and your sons after you, for you
will be doing what is right in the sight of the LORD.
26 "Only your holy things which you may have and your votive offerings, you shall take
and go to the place which the LORD chooses.
27 "And you shall offer your burnt offerings, the flesh and the blood, on the altar of the
LORD your God; and the blood of your sacrifices shall be poured out on the altar of the
LORD your God, and you shall eat the flesh.
28 "Be careful to listen to all these words which I command you, so that it may be well
with you and your sons after you forever, for you will be doing what is good and right in
the sight of the LORD your God.
29 "When the LORD your God cuts off before you the nations which you are going in to
dispossess, and you dispossess them and dwell in their land,
30 beware that you are not ensnared to follow them, after they are destroyed before
you, and that you do not inquire after their gods, saying, 'How do these nations serve
their gods, that I also may do likewise?'
31 "You shall not behave thus toward the LORD your God, for every abominable act
which the LORD hates they have done for their gods; for they even burn their sons and
daughters in the fire to their gods.
32 "Whatever I command you, you shall be careful to do; you shall not add to nor take
away from it.

12:13 Deut 12:5, 11
12:15 Deut 12:20-23; Deut 12:22; 14:5; 15:22
12:16 Gen 9:4; Lev 7:26; 17:10-12; 1 Sam 14:33f; Acts 15:20, 29; Deut 15:23
12:17 Deut 12:26
12:18 Deut 14:23; Deut 12:5; Deut 12:12; Deut 12:7; Eccl 3:12f; 5:18-20
12:19 Deut 14:27
12:20 Gen 15:18; Deut 11:24; 19:8
12:23 Gen 9:4; Lev 17:10-14; Deut 12:16
12:25 Deut 4:40; Is 3:10; Ex 15:26; 1 Kin 11:38
12:26 Num 5:9f; 18:19; Deut 12:17
12:27 Lev 1:9, 13; Lev 3:1-17
12:28 Deut 4:40; Eccl 8:12
12:29 Josh 23:4
12:31 Deut 9:5; Lev 18:21; Deut 18:10; Ps 106:37; Jer 32:35
12:32 Deut 4:2; Josh 1:7; Prov 30:6; Rev 22:18

12:13–14 While the pagans offered sacrifices to their gods, they offered them in many places. In contrast, the Israelites were only to offer sacrifices in the prescribed manner and in the prescribed places. This restriction was meant to ensure purity of worship for the nation of Israel. Later, they would neglect this injunction and offer sacrifices at the high places where pagan deities were worshiped. (See, for example, 2 Kings 23 where Josiah destroyed the other altars.) We should take steps to safeguard the purity of worship in our congregations. If we all individualized and customized worship to suit our own preferences, we would lose the benefit of worshiping as a body of believers.

12:16 Eating blood was forbidden for several reasons: (1) it was an integral part of the pagan practices of the land the Israelites were about to enter; (2) it represented life, which is sacred to God; (3) it was a symbol of the sacrifice that had to be made for sin. (For more on why eating blood was prohibited, see the note on Leviticus 17:14.)

12:30–31 God did not want the Israelites even to ask about the pagan religions surrounding them. Idolatry completely permeated the land of Canaan. It was too easy to get drawn into the subtle temptations of seemingly harmless practices. Sometimes curiosity can cause us to stumble. Knowledge of evil is harmful if the evil becomes too tempting to resist. To resist curiosity about harmful practices shows discretion and obedience.

Shun Idolatry

13 "If a prophet or a dreamer of dreams arises among you and gives you a sign or a
wonder,
2 and the sign or the wonder comes true, concerning which he spoke to you, saying,
'Let us go after other gods (whom you have not known) and let us serve them,'
3 you shall not listen to the words of that prophet or that dreamer of dreams; for the
LORD your God is testing you to find out if you love the LORD your God with all your
heart and with all your soul.
4 "You shall follow the LORD your God and fear Him; and you shall keep His commandments, listen to His voice, serve Him, and cling to Him.
5 "But that prophet or that dreamer of dreams shall be put to death, because he has
counseled rebellion against the LORD your God who brought you from the land of Egypt
and redeemed you from the house of slavery, to seduce you from the way in which the
LORD your God commanded you to walk. So you shall purge the evil from among you.
6 "If your brother, your mother's son, or your son or daughter, or the wife you cherish,
or your friend who is as your own soul, entice you secretly, saying, 'Let us go and serve
other gods' (whom neither you nor your fathers have known,
7 of the gods of the peoples who are around you, near you or far from you, from one
end of the earth to the other end),
8 you shall not yield to him or listen to him; and your eye shall not pity him, nor shall
you spare or conceal him.
9 "But you shall surely kill him; your hand shall be first against him to put him to death,
and afterwards the hand of all the people.
10 "So you shall stone him to death because he has sought to seduce you from the LORD
your God who brought you out from the land of Egypt, out of the house of slavery.
11 "Then all Israel will hear and be afraid, and will never again do such a wicked thing
among you.
12 "If you hear in one of your cities, which the LORD your God is giving you to live in,
anyone saying *that*
13 some worthless men have gone out from among you and have seduced the inhabitants of their city, saying, 'Let us go and serve other gods' (whom you have not known),
14 then you shall investigate and search out and inquire thoroughly. If it is true *and*
the matter established that this abomination has been done among you,
15 you shall surely strike the inhabitants of that city with the edge of the sword, utterly
destroying it and all that is in it and its cattle with the edge of the sword.
16 "Then you shall gather all its booty into the middle of its open square and burn the
city and all its booty with fire as a whole burnt offering to the LORD your God; and it
shall be a ruin forever. It shall never be rebuilt.
17 "Nothing from that which is put under the ban shall cling to your hand, in order that
the LORD may turn from His burning anger and show mercy to you, and have compassion on you and make you increase, just as He has sworn to your fathers,
18 if you will listen to the voice of the LORD your God, keeping all His commandments

13:1 Matt 24:24; Mark 13:22; 2 Thess 2:9
13:2 Deut 13:6, 13
13:3 Ex 20:20; Deut 8:2, 16; 1 Cor 11:19; Deut 6:5
13:4 2 Kin 23:3; 2 Chr 34:31; 2 John 6; Deut 10:20
13:5 Deut 13:9, 15; 17:5; 1 Kin 18:40; Deut 4:19; 13:10 1 Cor 5:13
13:6 Deut 17:2-7; 29:18; Deut 13:2
13:8 Prov 1:10; Deut 7:2
13:9 Deut 13:5; Lev 24:14; Deut 17:7
13:10 Deut 13:5
13:11 Deut 19:20
13:13 Deut 13:2
13:15 Deut 13:5
13:16 Deut 7:25, 26; Josh 8:28; Is 17:1; 25:2; Jer 49:2
13:17 Ex 32:12; Num 25:4; Deut 30:3; Deut 7:13; Gen 22:17; 26:4, 24; 28:14

13:1–3 Attractive leaders are not always led by God. Moses warned the Israelites against false prophets who encouraged worship of other gods. New ideas from inspiring people may sound good, but we must judge them by whether or not they are consistent with God's Word. When people claim to speak for God today, check them in these areas: Are they telling the truth? Is their focus on God? Are their words consistent with what you already know to be true? Some people speak the truth while directing you toward God, but others speak persuasively while directing you toward themselves. It is even possible to say the right words but still lead people in the wrong direction. God is not against new ideas, but he is for discernment. When you hear a new, attractive idea, examine it carefully before getting too excited. False prophets are still around today. The wise person will carefully test ideas against the truth of God's Word.

13:2–11 The Israelites were warned not to listen to false prophets or to anyone else who tried to get them to worship other gods—even if this person was a close friend or family member. The temptation to abandon God's commands often sneaks up on us. It may come not with a loud shout but in a whispering doubt. And whispers can be very persuasive, especially if they come from loved ones. But love for relatives should not take precedence over devotion to God. We can overcome whispered temptations by pouring out our hearts to God in prayer and by diligently studying his Word.

13:12–16 A city that completely rejected God was to be destroyed so as not to lead the rest of the nation astray. But Israel was not to take action against a city until the rumor about its rejecting God was proven true. This guideline saved many lives when the leaders of Israel wrongly accused three tribes of falling away from their faith (Joshua 22). If we hear of friends who have wandered from the Lord or of entire congregations that have fallen away, we should check the facts and find the truth before doing or saying anything that could prove harmful. There are times, of course, when God wants us to take action—to rebuke a wayward friend, to discipline a child, to reject false teaching—but first we must be sure we have all the facts straight.

which I am commanding you today, and doing what is right in the sight of the LORD
your God.

Clean and Unclean Animals

14 "You are the sons of the LORD your God; you shall not cut yourselves nor shave
your forehead for the sake of the dead.
2 "For you are a holy people to the LORD your God, and the LORD has chosen you to
be a people for His own possession out of all the peoples who are on the face of the
earth.
3 "You shall not eat any detestable thing.
4 "These are the animals which you may eat: the ox, the sheep, the goat,
5 the deer, the gazelle, the roebuck, the wild goat, the ibex, the antelope and the
mountain sheep.
6 "Any animal that divides the hoof and has the hoof split in two *and* chews the cud,
among the animals, that you may eat.
7 "Nevertheless, you are not to eat of these among those which chew the cud, or among
those that divide the hoof in two: the camel and the rabbit and the shaphan, for though
they chew the cud, they do not divide the hoof; they are unclean for you.
8 "The pig, because it divides the hoof but *does* not *chew* the cud, it is unclean for you.
You shall not eat any of their flesh nor touch their carcasses.
9 "These you may eat of all that are in water: anything that has fins and scales you
may eat,
10 but anything that does not have fins and scales you shall not eat; it is unclean for you.
11 "You may eat any clean bird.
12 "But these are the ones which you shall not eat: the eagle and the vulture and the
buzzard,
13 and the red kite, the falcon, and the kite in their kinds,
14 and every raven in its kind,
15 and the ostrich, the owl, the sea gull, and the hawk in their kinds,
16 the little owl, the great owl, the white owl,
17 the pelican, the carrion vulture, the cormorant,
18 the stork, and the heron in their kinds, and the hoopoe and the bat.
19 "And all the teeming life with wings are unclean to you; they shall not be eaten.
20 "You may eat any clean bird.
21 "You shall not eat anything which dies *of itself.* You may give it to the alien who is in
your town, so that he may eat it, or you may sell it to a foreigner, for you are a holy people to the LORD your God. You shall not boil a young goat in its mother's milk.
22 "You shall surely tithe all the produce from what you sow, which comes out of the
field every year.
23 "You shall eat in the presence of the LORD your God, at the place where He chooses
to establish His name, the tithe of your grain, your new wine, your oil, and the firstborn
of your herd and your flock, so that you may learn to fear the LORD your God always.
24 "If the distance is so great for you that you are not able to bring *the tithe,* since the

14:1 Rom 8:16; 9:8, 26; Gal 3:26; 1 John 3:1; Lev 19:28; 21:5; Jer 16:6; 41:5

14:2 Lev 20:26; Deut 7:6; Rom 12:1; Ex 19:5; Deut 4:20; 26:18; Titus 2:14; 1 Pet 2:9

14:3 Ezek 4:14

14:4 Lev 11:2-45; Acts 10:14

14:12 Lev 11:13

14:21 Lev 17:15; 22:8; Ezek 4:14; 44:31; Deut 14:2; Ex 23:19; 34:26

14:22 Lev 27:30; Deut 12:6, 17; Neh 10:37

14:23 Deut 12:5; Deut 4:10; Ps 2:11; 111:10; 147:11; Is 8:13; Jer 32:38-40

14:24 Deut 12:5, 21

14:1 The actions described here refer to a cult of the dead. Many other religions today have some kind of worship of or service to the dead. But Christianity and Judaism are very different from other religions because they focus on serving God in this life. Don't let concern or worry over the dead distract you from the tasks that God has for you while you are still alive.

14:3–21 Why was Israel forbidden to eat certain foods? There are several reasons: (1) Predatory animals ate the blood of other animals, and scavengers ate dead animals. Because the people could not eat blood or animals they found dead, they could not eat animals that did these things either. (2) Some forbidden animals had bad associations in the Israelite culture, as bats, snakes, and spiders do for some people today. Some may have been used in pagan religious practices (Isaiah 66:17). To the Israelites, the unclean animals represented sin or unhealthy habits. (3) Perhaps some restrictions were given to Israel just to remind them continually that they were a different and separate people committed to God. Although we no longer must follow these laws about food (Acts 10:9–16), we can still learn from them the lesson that holiness is to be carried into all parts of life. We can't restrict holiness only to the spiritual side; we must be holy in the everyday practical part of life as well. Health practices, finances, use of leisure—all provide opportunities to put holy living into daily living.

14:21 This prohibition against cooking a young goat in its mother's milk may reflect a Canaanite fertility rite. Or it may just mean that the Israelites were not to take what was intended to promote life and use it to kill or destroy life. This commandment is also given in Exodus 23:19.

14:22–23 The Bible makes the purpose of tithing very clear—to put God first in our lives. We are to give God the first and best of what we earn. For example, what we do first with our money shows what we value most. Giving the first part of our paycheck to God immediately focuses our attention on him. It also reminds us that all we have belongs to him. A habit of regular tithing can keep God at the top of our priority list and give us a proper perspective on everything else we have.

place where the LORD your God chooses to set His name is too far away from you when
the LORD your God blesses you,
25 then you shall exchange *it* for money, and bind the money in your hand and go to
the place which the LORD your God chooses.
26 "You may spend the money for whatever your heart desires: for oxen, or sheep, or
wine, or strong drink, or whatever your heart desires; and there you shall eat in the presence of the LORD your God and rejoice, you and your household.
27 "Also you shall not neglect the Levite who is in your town, for he has no portion or
inheritance among you.
28 "At the end of every third year you shall bring out all the tithe of your produce in
that year, and shall deposit *it* in your town.
29 "The Levite, because he has no portion or inheritance among you, and the alien, the
orphan and the widow who are in your town, shall come and eat and be satisfied, in order that the LORD your God may bless you in all the work of your hand which you do.

The Sabbatic Year

15 "At the end of *every* seven years you shall [13]grant a remission *of debts.*
2 "This is the manner of remission: every creditor shall release what he has loaned
to his neighbor; he shall not exact it of his neighbor and his brother, because the LORD'S
remission has been proclaimed.
3 "From a foreigner you may exact *it,* but your hand shall release whatever of yours is
with your brother.
4 "However, there will be no poor among you, since the LORD will surely bless you in
the land which the LORD your God is giving you as an inheritance to possess,
5 if only you listen obediently to the voice of the LORD your God, to observe carefully
all this commandment which I am commanding you today.
6 "For the LORD your God will bless you as He has promised you, and you will lend to
many nations, but you will not borrow; and you will rule over many nations, but they will
not rule over you.
7 "If there is a poor man with you, one of your brothers, in any of your towns in your
land which the LORD your God is giving you, you shall not harden your heart, nor close
your hand from your poor brother;
8 but you shall freely open your hand to him, and shall generously lend him sufficient
for his need *in* whatever he lacks.
9 "Beware that there is no base thought in your heart, saying, 'The seventh year, the
year of remission, is near,' and your eye is hostile toward your poor brother, and you
give him nothing; then he may cry to the LORD against you, and it will be a sin in you.
10 "You shall generously give to him, and your heart shall not be grieved when you give
to him, because for this thing the LORD your God will bless you in all your work and in
all your undertakings.
11 "For the poor will never cease *to be* in the land; therefore I command you, saying,
'You shall freely open your hand to your brother, to your needy and poor in your land.'

14:26 Deut 12:7
14:27 Deut 12:12; Num 18:20; Deut 10:9; 18:12
14:28 Deut 26:12
14:29 Deut 10:9; Deut 16:11, 14; 24:19-21; 26:12; Ps 94:6; Is 1:17; Deut 6:11; Deut 15:10; Mal 3:10
15:1 Deut 31:10
15:3 Deut 23:20
15:4 Deut 28:8
15:6 Deut 28:12, 13
15:7 Lev 25:35; Deut 15:11 1 John 3:17
15:8 Matt 5:42; Luke 6:34; Gal 2:10
15:9 Deut 15:1; Matt 20:15; Ex 22:23; Deut 24:15; Job 34:28; Ps 12:5; James 5:4
15:10 Deut 14:29; Ps 41:1; Prov 22:9
15:11 Matt 26:11; Mark 14:7; John 12:8

13 Lit *make a release*

14:28–29 The Bible supports an organized system of caring for the poor. God told his people to use their tithe every third year for those who were helpless, hungry, or poor. These regulations were designed to prevent the country from sinking under crushing poverty and oppression. It was everyone's responsibility to care for those less fortunate. Families were to help other family members, and towns were to help members of their community. National laws protected the rights of the poor, but helping the poor was also an active part of religious life. God counts on believers to provide for the needy, and we should use what God has given us to aid those less fortunate. Look beyond your regular giving and think of ways to help the needy. This will help you show your regard for God as Creator of all people, share God's goodness with others, and draw them to him. It is a practical and essential way to make faith work in everyday life.

15:7–11 God told the Israelites to help the poor among them when they arrived in the promised land. This was an important part of possessing the land. Many people conclude that people are poor through some fault of their own. This kind of reasoning makes it easy to close their hearts and hands to the needy. But we are not to invent reasons for ignoring the poor. We are to respond to their needs no matter who or what was responsible for their condition. Who are the poor in your community? How could your church help them? If your church does not have a program to identify the poor and assist in fulfilling their needs, why not help start one? What can you do to help someone in need?

12 "If your kinsman, a Hebrew man or woman, is sold to you, then he shall serve you six
years, but in the seventh year you shall set him free.
13 "When you set him free, you shall not send him away empty-handed.
14 "You shall furnish him liberally from your flock and from your threshing floor and
from your wine vat; you shall give to him as the LORD your God has blessed you.
15 "You shall remember that you were a slave in the land of Egypt, and the LORD your
God redeemed you; therefore I command you this today.
16 "It shall come about if he says to you, 'I will not go out from you,' because he loves
you and your household, since he fares well with you;
17 then you shall take an awl and pierce it through his ear into the door, and he shall
be your servant forever. Also you shall do likewise to your maidservant.
18 "It shall not seem hard to you when you set him free, for he has given you six years
with double the service of a hired man; so the LORD your God will bless you in whatever
you do.
19 "You shall consecrate to the LORD your God all the firstborn males that are born of
your herd and of your flock; you shall not work with the firstborn of your herd, nor shear
the firstborn of your flock.
20 "You and your household shall eat it every year before the LORD your God in the
place which the LORD chooses.
21 "But if it has any defect, *such as* lameness or blindness, *or* any serious defect, you
shall not sacrifice it to the LORD your God.
22 "You shall eat it within your gates; the unclean and the clean alike *may eat it,* as a
gazelle or a deer.
23 "Only you shall not eat its blood; you are to pour it out on the ground like water.

The Feasts of Passover, of Weeks, and of Booths

16 "Observe the month of Abib and celebrate the Passover to the LORD your God,
for in the month of Abib the LORD your God brought you out of Egypt by night.
2 "You shall sacrifice the Passover to the LORD your God from the flock and the herd,
in the place where the LORD chooses to establish His name.
3 "You shall not eat leavened bread with it; seven days you shall eat with it unleavened
bread, the bread of affliction (for you came out of the land of Egypt in haste), so that
you may remember all the days of your life the day when you came out of the land of
Egypt.
4 "For seven days no leaven shall be seen with you in all your territory, and none of
the flesh which you sacrifice on the evening of the first day shall remain overnight until
morning.
5 "You are not allowed to sacrifice the Passover in any of your towns which the LORD
your God is giving you;
6 but at the place where the LORD your God chooses to establish His name, you shall
sacrifice the Passover in the evening at sunset, at the time that you came out of Egypt.
7 "You shall cook and eat *it* in the place which the LORD your God chooses. In the
morning you are to return to your tents.
8 "Six days you shall eat unleavened bread, and on the seventh day there shall be a
solemn assembly to the LORD your God; you shall do no work *on it.*
9 "You shall count seven weeks for yourself; you shall begin to count seven weeks from
the time you begin to put the sickle to the standing grain.
10 "Then you shall celebrate the Feast of Weeks to the LORD your God with a tribute
of a freewill offering of your hand, which you shall give just as the LORD your God
blesses you;
11 and you shall rejoice before the LORD your God, you and your son and your daughter and your male and female servants and the Levite who is in your town, and the stranger
and the orphan and the widow who are in your midst, in the place where the LORD your
God chooses to establish His name.

15:12 Ex 21:2-6; Lev 25:39-43; Jer 34:14
15:16 Ex 21:5, 6
15:19 Ex 13:2, 12
15:20 Lev 7:15-18; Deut 12:5; 14:23
15:21 Lev 22:19-25; Deut 17:1
15:22 Deut 12:15, 16, 22
15:23 Gen 9:4; Lev 7:26; 17:10; 19:26; Deut 12:16, 23
16:1 Ex 12:2; Num 28:16
16:3 Ex 12:8, 15, 19, 39; 13:3; 34:18; Deut 4:9
16:4 Ex 12:8, 10; 34:25
16:6 Deut 12:5
16:7 Ex 12:8; 2 Chr 35:13
16:8 Num 28:25; Ex 12:16; 13:6; Lev 23:8, 36
16:9 Ex 23:16; 34:22; Lev 23:15; Num 28:26
16:11 Deut 12:7; Deut 12:12; Deut 14:29

15:12–15 The Israelites were to release their servants after six years, sending them away with enough food so that they would be amply supplied until their needs could be met by some other means. This humanitarian act recognized that God created each person with dignity and worth. It also reminded the Israelites that they, too, had once been slaves in Egypt, and that their present freedom was a gift from God. We do not have servants such as these today, but God's instructions still apply to us: We must still be sure to treat our employees with respect and economic fairness.

12 "You shall remember that you were a slave in Egypt, and you shall be careful to observe these statutes.
13 "You shall celebrate the Feast of Booths seven days after you have gathered in from
your threshing floor and your wine vat;
14 and you shall rejoice in your feast, you and your son and your daughter and your
male and female servants and the Levite and the stranger and the orphan and the widow
who are in your towns.
15 "Seven days you shall celebrate a feast to the LORD your God in the place which the
LORD chooses, because the LORD your God will bless you in all your produce and in all
the work of your hands, so that you will be altogether joyful.
16 "Three times in a year all your males shall appear before the LORD your God in the
place which He chooses, at the Feast of Unleavened Bread and at the Feast of Weeks
and at the Feast of Booths, and they shall not appear before the LORD empty-handed.
17 "Every man shall give as he is able, according to the blessing of the LORD your God
which He has given you.

4. Laws for ruling the nation

18 "You shall appoint for yourself judges and officers in all your towns which the LORD
your God is giving you, according to your tribes, and they shall judge the people with
righteous judgment.
19 "You shall not distort justice; you shall not be partial, and you shall not take a bribe,
for a bribe blinds the eyes of the wise and perverts the words of the righteous.
20 "Justice, *and only* justice, you shall pursue, that you may live and possess the land
which the LORD your God is giving you.
21 "You shall not plant for yourself an Asherah of any kind of tree beside the altar of
the LORD your God, which you shall make for yourself.
22 "You shall not set up for yourself a *sacred* pillar which the LORD your God hates.

Administration of Justice

17 "You shall not sacrifice to the LORD your God an ox or a sheep which has a blemish *or* any defect, for that is a detestable thing to the LORD your God.
2 "If there is found in your midst, in any of your towns, which the LORD your God is
giving you, a man or a woman who does what is evil in the sight of the LORD your God,
by transgressing His covenant,
3 and has gone and served other gods and worshiped them, or the sun or the moon or
any of the heavenly host, which I have not commanded,
4 and if it is told you and you have heard of it, then you shall inquire thoroughly. Behold,
if it is true and the thing certain that this detestable thing has been done in Israel,
5 then you shall bring out that man or that woman who has done this evil deed to your
gates, *that is,* the man or the woman, and you shall stone them to death.
6 "On the evidence of two witnesses or three witnesses, he who is to die shall be put to
death; he shall not be put to death on the evidence of one witness.

16:12 Deut 15:15
16:13 Lev 23:34-43
16:14 Deut 16:11
16:16 Ex 23:14-17; 34:23, 24; Ex 34:20
16:19 Ex 23:2; Lev 19:15; Deut 1:17; 10:17; Prov 24:23; Ex 23:8; Prov 17:23; Eccl 7:7
16:20 Deut 4:1
16:21 Deut 7:5; 2 Kin 17:16; 21:3; 2 Chr 33:3
16:22 Lev 26:1
17:1 Deut 15:21
17:2 Deut 13:6-11
17:3 Ex 22:20; Job 31:26-28; Jer 7:22
17:5 Lev 24:14; Josh 7:25
17:6 Num 35:30; Deut 19:15; Matt 18:16; John 8:17; 2 Cor 13:1; 1 Tim 5:19; Heb 10:28

16:16–17 Three times a year every male was to make a journey to the sanctuary in the city that would be designated as Israel's religious capital. At these feasts, each participant was encouraged to give what he could in proportion to what God had given him. God does not expect us to give more than we can, but we will be blessed when we give cheerfully. For some, 10 percent may be a burden. For most of us, that would be far too little. Look at what you have and then give in proportion to what you have been given.

16:18–20 These verses anticipated a great problem the Israelites would face when they arrived in the promised land. Although they had Joshua as their national leader, they failed to complete the task and choose other spiritual leaders who would lead the tribes, districts, and cities with justice and God's wisdom. Because they did not appoint wise judges and faithful administrators, rebellion and injustice plagued their communities. It is a serious responsibility to appoint or elect wise and just officials. In your sphere of influence—home, church, school, job—are you ensuring that justice and godliness prevail? Failing to choose leaders who uphold justice can lead to much trouble, as Israel would discover.

17:1 The fact that this command was included probably indicates that some Israelites were sacrificing imperfect or deformed animals to God. Then, as now, it is difficult and expensive to offer God our best (i.e., the first part of what we earn). It is always tempting to shortchange God because we think we won't get caught. But our giving shows our real priorities. When we give God the leftovers, it is obvious that he is not at the center of our lives. Give God the honor of having first claim on your money, time, and talents.

17:6–7 A person was not put to death on the testimony of only one witness. On the witness of two or three, a person could be condemned and then sentenced to death by stoning. The condemned person was taken outside the city gates, and the witnesses were the first to throw heavy stones down on him or her. Bystanders would then pelt the dying person with stones. This system would "purge the evil" by putting the idolater to death. At the same time, it protected the rights of accused persons two ways. First, by requiring several witnesses, it prevented any angry individual from giving "false testimony." Second, by requiring the accusers to throw the first stones, it made them think twice about accusing unjustly. They were responsible to finish what they had started.

7 "The hand of the witnesses shall be first against him to put him to death, and afterward the hand of all the people. So you shall purge the evil from your midst.
8 "If any case is too difficult for you to decide, between one kind of homicide or another, between one kind of lawsuit or another, and between one kind of assault or another,
being cases of dispute in your courts, then you shall arise and go up to the place which
the LORD your God chooses.
9 "So you shall come to the Levitical priest or the judge who is *in office* in those days,
and you shall inquire *of them* and they will declare to you the verdict in the case.
10 "You shall do according to the terms of the verdict which they declare to you from
that place which the LORD chooses; and you shall be careful to observe according to all
that they teach you.
11 "According to the terms of the law which they teach you, and according to the verdict which they tell you, you shall do; you shall not turn aside from the word which they
declare to you, to the right or the left.
12 "The man who acts presumptuously by not listening to the priest who stands there to
serve the LORD your God, nor to the judge, that man shall die; thus you shall purge the
evil from Israel.
13 "Then all the people will hear and be afraid, and will not act presumptuously again.
14 "When you enter the land which the LORD your God gives you, and you possess
it and live in it, and you say, 'I will set a king over me like all the nations who are
around me,'
15 you shall surely set a king over you whom the LORD your God chooses, *one* from
among your countrymen you shall set as king over yourselves; you may not put a foreigner over yourselves who is not your countryman.
16 "Moreover, he shall not multiply horses for himself, nor shall he cause the people to
return to Egypt to multiply horses, since the LORD has said to you, 'You shall never again
return that way.'
17 "He shall not multiply wives for himself, or else his heart will turn away; nor shall he
greatly increase silver and gold for himself.
18 "Now it shall come about when he sits on the throne of his kingdom, he shall write
for himself a copy of this law on a scroll in the presence of the Levitical priests.
19 "It shall be with him and he shall read it all the days of his life, that he may learn to
fear the LORD his God, by carefully observing all the words of this law and these statutes,
20 that his heart may not be lifted up above his countrymen and that he may not turn
aside from the commandment, to the right or the left, so that he and his sons may continue long in his kingdom in the midst of Israel.

Portion of the Levites

18 "The Levitical priests, the whole tribe of Levi, shall have no portion or inheritance
with Israel; they shall eat the LORD'S offerings by fire and His portion.

17:7 Lev 24:14; Deut 13:9 1 Cor 5:13
17:8 2 Chr 19:10; Hag 2:11; Deut 12:5; Ps 122:5
17:9 Deut 19:17
17:11 Deut 25:1
17:12 Num 15:30; Deut 1:43; 17:13; 18:20; Hos 4:4
17:13 Deut 17:12
17:14 Deut 11:31; Josh 21:43; 1 Sam 8:5, 19, 20; 10:19
17:15 Jer 30:21
17:16 1 Kin 4:26; 10:26-29; Ps 20:7; Is 31:1; Ezek 17:15; Ex 13:17, 18; Hos 11:5
17:17 2 Sam 5:13; 12:11; 1 Kin 11:3, 4
17:18 Deut 31:24-26
17:19 Deut 4:9, 10; Josh 1:8
17:20 Deut 5:32; 1 Kin 15:5
18:1 Deut 10:9; 1 Cor 9:13

17:14–20 God was not encouraging Israel to appoint a king to rule their nation. He was actually against the idea because he was their King, and the people were to obey and follow him. But God knew that the people would one day demand a king for selfish reasons—they would want to be like the nations around them (1 Samuel 8). If they insisted on having a king, he wanted to make sure they chose the right person. That is why he included these instructions both for the people's benefit as they chose their king and for the king himself as he sought to lead the nation according to God's laws.

17:16–17 Israel's kings did not heed this warning, and their behavior led to their downfall. Solomon had everything going for him, but when he became rich, built up a large army, and married many wives, his heart turned from God (1 Kings 11). Out of Solomon's sin came Israel's disobedience, division, and captivity.

17:18–20 The king was to be a man of God's Word. He was to (1) make a copy of the law for his personal use, (2) keep it with him all the time, (3) read from it every day, and (4) obey it completely. Through this process he would learn respect for God, keep himself from feeling more important than others, and avoid neglecting God in times of prosperity. We can't know what God wants except through his Word, and his Word won't affect our lives unless we read and think about it regularly. With the abundant availability of the Bible today, it is not difficult to gain access to the source of the king's wisdom. What is more of a challenge is following its directives.

18:1–8 The priests and Levites served much the same function as our ministers today. Their duties included (1) teaching the people about God, (2) setting an example of godly living, (3) caring for the sanctuary and its workers, and (4) distributing the offerings. Because priests could not own property or pursue outside business interests, God made special arrangements so that people would not take advantage of them. Often churches take advantage of the men and women God has brought to lead them. For example, ministers may not be paid in accordance with their skills or the time they put in. Or pastors may be expected to attend every evening meeting, even if this continual absence is harmful to their families. As you look at your own church in light of God's Word, what ways do you see to honor the leaders God has given you?

2 "They shall have no inheritance among their countrymen; the LORD is their inheritance, as He promised them.

3 "Now this shall be the priests' due from the people, from those who offer a sacrifice,
either an ox or a sheep, of which they shall give to the priest the shoulder and the two
cheeks and the stomach.

4 "You shall give him the first fruits of your grain, your new wine, and your oil, and the
first shearing of your sheep.

5 "For the LORD your God has chosen him and his sons from all your tribes, to stand
and serve in the name of the LORD forever.

6 "Now if a Levite comes from any of your towns throughout Israel where he resides,
and comes whenever he desires to the place which the LORD chooses,

7 then he shall serve in the name of the LORD his God, like all his fellow Levites who
stand there before the LORD.

8 "They shall eat equal portions, except *what they receive* from the sale of their fathers'
estates.

Spiritism Forbidden

9 "When you enter the land which the LORD your God gives you, you shall not learn to
imitate the detestable things of those nations.

10 "There shall not be found among you anyone who makes his son or his daughter pass
through the fire, one who uses divination, one who practices witchcraft, or one who interprets omens, or a sorcerer,

11 or one who casts a spell, or a medium, or a spiritist, or one who calls up the dead.

12 "For whoever does these things is detestable to the LORD; and because of these detestable things the LORD your God will drive them out before you.

13 "You shall be blameless before the LORD your God.

14 "For those nations, which you shall dispossess, listen to those who practice witchcraft and to diviners, but as for you, the LORD your God has not allowed you *to do* so.

15 "The LORD your God will raise up for you a prophet like me from among you, from
your countrymen, you shall listen to him.

16 "This is according to all that you asked of the LORD your God in Horeb on the day of
the assembly, saying, 'Let me not hear again the voice of the LORD my God, let me not
see this great fire anymore, or I will die.'

17 "The LORD said to me, 'They have spoken well.

18 'I will raise up a prophet from among their countrymen like you, and I will put My
words in his mouth, and he shall speak to them all that I command him.

19 'It shall come about that whoever will not listen to My words which he shall speak in
My name, I Myself will require *it* of him.

20 'But the prophet who speaks a word presumptuously in My name which I have not
commanded him to speak, or which he speaks in the name of other gods, that prophet
shall die.'

21 "You may say in your heart, 'How will we know the word which the LORD has not
spoken?'

18:2 Num 18:20
18:3 Lev 7:32-34; Num 18:11, 12
18:4 Num 18:12
18:5 Ex 29:9; Deut 10:8
18:6 Num 35:2, 3
18:8 Lev 27:30-33; Num 18:21-24; 2 Chr 31:4; Neh 12:44
18:9 Deut 9:5
18:10 Deut 12:31; Ex 22:18; Lev 19:26, 31; 20:6; Jer 27:9, 10; Mal 3:5
18:11 Lev 19:31
18:12 Lev 18:24
18:13 Gen 6:9; 17:1; Matt 5:48
18:14 2 Kin 21:6
18:15 Matt 21:11; Luke 2:25-34; 7:16; 24:19; John 1:21, 25; 4:19; Acts 3:22; 7:37
18:16 Ex 20:18, 19; Deut 5:23-27
18:17 Deut 5:28
18:18 Is 51:16; John 17:8; John 4:25; 8:28; 12:49, 50
18:19 Acts 3:23; Heb 12:25
18:20 Deut 13:5; 17:12; Deut 13:1, 2; Jer 14:14; Zech 13:3

18:10 Child sacrifice and occult practices were strictly forbidden by God. These practices were common among pagan religions. Israel's own neighbors actually sacrificed their children to the god Molech (Leviticus 20:2–5). Other neighboring religions used supernatural means, such as contacting the spirit world, to foretell the future and gain guidance. Because of these wicked practices, God would drive out the pagan nations (18:12). The Israelites were to replace their evil practices with the worship of the one true God.

18:10–13 The Israelites were naturally curious about the occult practices of the Canaanite religions. But Satan is behind the occult, and God flatly forbade Israel to have anything to do with it. Today people are still fascinated by horoscopes, fortune-telling, witchcraft, and bizarre cults. Often their interest comes from a desire to know and control the future. But Satan is no less dangerous today than he was in Moses' time. In the Bible, God tells us all we need to know about what is going to happen. The information Satan offers is likely to be distorted or completely false. With the trustworthy guidance of the Holy Spirit through the Bible and the church, we don't need to turn to occult sources for faulty information.

18:15 Who is this prophet? Stephen used this verse to support his claim that Jesus Christ is God's Son, the Messiah (Acts 7:37). The coming of Jesus Christ to earth was not an afterthought, but part of God's original plan.

18:21–22 As in the days of ancient Israel, some people today claim to have messages from God. God still speaks to his people, but we must be cautious before saying that someone is God's spokesman. How can we tell when people are speaking for the Lord? (1) We can see whether or not their prophecies come true—the ancient test for judging prophets. (2) We can check their words against the Bible. God never contradicts himself, so if someone says something contrary to the Bible, we can know that this is not God's word.

22 "When a prophet speaks in the name of the LORD, if the thing does not come about 18:22
or come true, that is the thing which the LORD has not spoken. The prophet has spoken Jer 28:9; Deut 18:20
it presumptuously; you shall not be afraid of him.

Cities of Refuge

19 "When the LORD your God cuts off the nations, whose land the LORD your God 19:1
gives you, and you dispossess them and settle in their cities and in their houses, Deut 6:10, 11
2 you shall set aside three cities for yourself in the midst of your land, which the LORD 19:2
your God gives you to possess. Deut 4:41; Josh 20:2
3 "You shall prepare the roads for yourself, and divide into three parts the territory of
your land which the LORD your God will give you as a possession, so that any manslayer
may flee there.
4 "Now this is the case of the manslayer who may flee there and live: when he kills his 19:4
friend unintentionally, not hating him previously— Num 35:9-34
5 as when *a man* goes into the forest with his friend to cut wood, and his hand swings
the axe to cut down the tree, and the iron *head* slips off the handle and strikes his friend
so that he dies—he may flee to one of these cities and live;
6 otherwise the avenger of blood might pursue the manslayer in the heat of his anger,
and overtake him, because the way is long, and take his life, though he was not deserving
of death, since he had not hated him previously.
7 "Therefore, I command you, saying, 'You shall set aside three cities for yourself.'
8 "If the LORD your God enlarges your territory, just as He has sworn to your fathers, 19:8
and gives you all the land which He promised to give your fathers— Gen 15:18
9 if you carefully observe all this commandment which I command you today, to love 19:9
the LORD your God, and to walk in His ways always—then you shall add three more Deut 6:5; Josh 20:7
cities for yourself, besides these three.
10 "So innocent blood will not be shed in the midst of your land which the LORD your 19:10
God gives you as an inheritance, and bloodguiltiness be on you. Num 35:33; Deut 21:1-9
11 "But if there is a man who hates his neighbor and lies in wait for him and rises up 19:11
against him and strikes him so that he dies, and he flees to one of these cities, Ex 21:12; Num
12 then the elders of his city shall send and take him from there and deliver him into 35:16; 1 John 3:15
the hand of the avenger of blood, that he may die.
13 "You shall not pity him, but you shall purge the blood of the innocent from Israel, 19:13 Deut 7:2
that it may go well with you. 1 Kin 2:31

Laws of Landmark and Testimony 19:14 Deut 27:17; Job 24:2; Prov 22:28;

14 "You shall not move your neighbor's boundary mark, which the ancestors have set, Hos 5:10
in your inheritance which you will inherit in the land that the LORD your God gives you 19:15
to possess. Num 35:30; Deut
15 "A single witness shall not rise up against a man on account of any iniquity or any sin 17:6; Matt 18:16; John 8:17; 2 Cor
which he has committed; on the evidence of two or three witnesses a matter shall be 13:1; 1 Tim 5:19;
confirmed. Heb 10:28
16 "If a malicious witness rises up against a man to accuse him of wrongdoing, 19:16 Ex 23:1; Ps 27:12
17 then both the men who have the dispute shall stand before the LORD, before the
priests and the judges who will be *in office* in those days. 19:17 Deut 17:9
18 "The judges shall investigate thoroughly, and if the witness is a false witness *and* he
has accused his brother falsely, 19:18 Deut 25:1

19:2–3 The Israelites were told to build roads because these cities of refuge would have been ineffective if the roads that led to them were in disrepair. Many who came to the cities were literally running for their lives. A well-maintained road could have meant the difference between life and death. This involved continued maintenance, because these were dirt roads that could easily be washed away, covered by sand, or crisscrossed with deep ruts. It was important not only to initiate this system of justice, but to provide the necessary means of maintaining it.

19:2–7 Every society must deal with the problem of murder. But how should society treat those who have innocently or accidentally killed someone? God had an answer for the Israelites. Since revenge was common and swift in Moses' day, God had the Israelites set apart several "cities of refuge." Anyone who claimed to have accidentally killed someone could flee to one of these cities until he could have a fair trial. If he was found innocent of intentional murder, he could remain in that city and be safe from those seeking revenge. This is a beautiful example of how God blended his justice and mercy toward his people. (For more information on cities of refuge, see the note on Numbers 35:6.)

19:12 The "avenger of blood" was the nearest male relative to the person killed. He acted as the family protector (see Numbers 35:19).

19 then you shall do to him just as he had intended to do to his brother. Thus you shall
purge the evil from among you.
20 “The rest will hear and be afraid, and will never again do such an evil thing among
you.
21 “Thus you shall not show pity: life for life, eye for eye, tooth for tooth, hand for hand,
foot for foot.

Laws of Warfare

20 “When you go out to battle against your enemies and see horses and chariots *and*
people more numerous than you, do not be afraid of them; for the LORD your
God, who brought you up from the land of Egypt, is with you.
2 “When you are approaching the battle, the priest shall come near and speak to the
people.
3 “He shall say to them, ‘Hear, O Israel, you are approaching the battle against your
enemies today. Do not be fainthearted. Do not be afraid, or panic, or tremble before
them,
4 for the LORD your God is the one who goes with you, to fight for you against your
enemies, to save you.’
5 “The officers also shall speak to the people, saying, ‘Who is the man that has built a
new house and has not dedicated it? Let him depart and return to his house, otherwise
he might die in the battle and another man would dedicate it.
6 ‘Who is the man that has planted a vineyard and has not begun to use its fruit? Let
him depart and return to his house, otherwise he might die in the battle and another
man would begin to use its fruit.
7 ‘And who is the man that is engaged to a woman and has not married her? Let him
depart and return to his house, otherwise he might die in the battle and another man
would marry her.’
8 “Then the officers shall speak further to the people and say, ‘Who is the man that is
afraid and fainthearted? Let him depart and return to his house, so that he might not
make his brothers’ hearts melt like his heart.’
9 “When the officers have finished speaking to the people, they shall appoint commanders of armies at the head of the people.
10 “When you approach a city to fight against it, you shall offer it terms of peace.
11 “If it agrees to make peace with you and opens to you, then all the people who are
found in it shall become your forced labor and shall serve you.
12 “However, if it does not make peace with you, but makes war against you, then you
shall besiege it.
13 “When the LORD your God gives it into your hand, you shall strike all the men in it
with the edge of the sword.
14 “Only the women and the children and the animals and all that is in the city, all its
spoil, you shall take as booty for yourself; and you shall use the spoil of your enemies
which the LORD your God has given you.
15 “Thus you shall do to all the cities that are very far from you, which are not of the
cities of these nations nearby.
16 “Only in the cities of these peoples that the LORD your God is giving you as an inheritance, you shall not leave alive anything that breathes.

19:19 Prov 19:5
19:20 Deut 17:13; 21:21
19:21 Deut 19:13; Ex 21:23; Lev 24:20; Matt 5:38
20:1 Deut 3:22; 7:18; 31:6, 8; Ps 20:7; Is 31:1; 2 Chr 32:7, 8; Ps 23:4; Is 41:10
20:3 Deut 20:1; Josh 23:10
20:4 Deut 1:30; 3:22; Josh 23:10
20:5 Neh 12:27
20:7 Deut 24:5
20:8 Judg 7:3
20:11 1 Kin 9:21
20:13 Num 31:7
20:14 Josh 8:2
20:16 Ex 23:31-33; Num 21:2, 3; Deut 7:1-5; Josh 11:14

19:21 This principle was for the judges to use, not a plan for personal vengeance. This attitude toward punishment may seem primitive, but it was actually a breakthrough for justice and fairness in ancient times when most nations used arbitrary methods to punish criminals. This guideline reflects a concern for evenhandedness and justice—ensuring that those who violated the law were not punished more severely than their particular crime deserved. In the same spirit of justice, a false witness was to receive the same punishment the accused person would have suffered. The principle of making the punishment fit the crime should still be observed today.

20:1 Just like the Israelites, we sometimes face overwhelming opposition. Whether at school, at work, or even at home, we can feel outnumbered and helpless. God bolstered the Israelites' confidence by reminding them that he was always with them and that he had already saved them from the potential danger. We too can feel secure when we consider that God is able to overcome even the most difficult odds.

20:13–18 To strike "with the edge of the sword" means to kill. How could a merciful and just God order the destruction of entire population centers? He did this to protect his people from idol worship, which was certain to bring ruin to Israel (20:18). In fact, because Israel did not completely destroy these evil people as God commanded, Israel was constantly oppressed by them and experienced greater bloodshed and destruction than if they had followed God's instructions in the first place.

17 "But you shall utterly destroy them, the Hittite and the Amorite, the Canaanite and
the Perizzite, the Hivite and the Jebusite, as the LORD your God has commanded you,
18 so that they may not teach you to do according to all their detestable things which
they have done for their gods, so that you would sin against the LORD your God.

20:18 Ex 34:12-16; Deut 7:4; 9:5; 12:30, 31; Ex 23:33; 2 Kin 21:3-15; Ps 106:34-41

19 "When you besiege a city a long time, to make war against it in order to capture it,
you shall not destroy its trees by swinging an axe against them; for you may eat from
them, and you shall not cut them down. For is the tree of the field a man, that it should
be besieged by you?
20 "Only the trees which you know are not fruit trees you shall destroy and cut down,
that you may construct siegeworks against the city that is making war with you until it
falls.

5. LAWS FOR HUMAN RELATIONSHIPS

Expiation of a Crime

21 "If a slain person is found lying in the open country in the land which the LORD
your God gives you to possess, *and* it is not known who has struck him,
2 then your elders and your judges shall go out and measure *the distance* to the cities
which are around the slain one.
3 "It shall be that the city which is nearest to the slain man, that is, the elders of that
city, shall take a heifer of the herd, which has not been worked and which has not pulled
in a yoke;
4 and the elders of that city shall bring the heifer down to a valley with running water,
which has not been plowed or sown, and shall break the heifer's neck there in the valley.
5 "Then the priests, the sons of Levi, shall come near, for the LORD your God has chosen
them to serve Him and to bless in the name of the LORD; and every dispute and every
assault shall be settled by them.

21:5 Deut 17:9-11; 19:17; 1 Chr 23:13

6 "All the elders of that city which is nearest to the slain man shall wash their hands
over the heifer whose neck was broken in the valley;

21:6 Matt 27:24

7 and they shall answer and say, 'Our hands did not shed this blood, nor did our eyes
see *it.*
8 '[14]Forgive Your people Israel whom You have redeemed, O LORD, and do not place
the guilt of innocent blood in the midst of Your people Israel.' And the bloodguiltiness
shall be forgiven them.

21:8 Num 35:33, 34; Jon 1:14

9 "So you shall remove the guilt of innocent blood from your midst, when you do what
is right in the eyes of the LORD.

21:9 Deut 19:13

Domestic Relations

10 "When you go out to battle against your enemies, and the LORD your God delivers
them into your hands and you take them away captive,

21:10 Josh 21:44

11 and see among the captives a beautiful woman, and have a desire for her and would
take her as a wife for yourself,
12 then you shall bring her home to your house, and she shall shave her head and trim
her nails.

21:12 Lev 14:8, 9; Num 6:9

13 "She shall also remove the clothes of her captivity and shall remain in your house,
and mourn her father and mother a full month; and after that you may go in to her and
be her husband and she shall be your wife.

21:13 Ps 45:10

14 "It shall be, if you are not pleased with her, then you shall let her go wherever she
wishes; but you shall certainly not sell her for money, you shall not mistreat her, because
you have humbled her.

21:14 Gen 34:2

15 "If a man has two wives, the one loved and the other unloved, and *both* the loved and
the unloved have borne him sons, if the firstborn son belongs to the unloved,

21:15 Gen 29:33

14 Lit *Cover over, atone for*

20:20 Archaeologists have uncovered the remnants of many well-fortified cities in Canaan. Some had tall walls (up to 30 feet high), ramparts, moats, and towers. Accustomed to fighting on the open plains, the Israelites were going to have to learn new battle strategies to conquer these massive fortresses.

21:1–9 When a crime was committed and the criminal got away, the whole community was held responsible. In much the same way, if a city has a dangerous intersection and someone is killed there, the community may be held responsible for both damages and repairs. God was pointing to the need for the whole community to feel a keen sense of responsibility for what was going on around them and to move to correct any situations that were potentially harmful—physically, socially, or morally.

16 then it shall be in the day he wills what he has to his sons, he cannot make the son of
the loved the firstborn before the son of the unloved, who is the firstborn.
17 "But he shall acknowledge the firstborn, the son of the unloved, by giving him a double portion of all that he has, for he is the beginning of his strength; to him belongs the
right of the firstborn.
18 "If any man has a stubborn and rebellious son who will not obey his father or his
mother, and when they chastise him, he will not even listen to them,
19 then his father and mother shall seize him, and bring him out to the elders of his
city at the gateway of his hometown.
20 "They shall say to the elders of his city, 'This son of ours is stubborn and rebellious,
he will not obey us, he is a glutton and a drunkard.'
21 "Then all the men of his city shall stone him to death; so you shall remove the evil
from your midst, and all Israel will hear *of it* and fear.
22 "If a man has committed a sin worthy of death and he is put to death, and you hang
him on a tree,
23 his corpse shall not hang all night on the tree, but you shall surely bury him on the
same day (for he who is hanged is accursed of God), so that you do not defile your land
which the LORD your God gives you as an inheritance.

Sundry Laws

22 "You shall not see your countryman's ox or his sheep straying away, and pay no
attention to them; you shall certainly bring them back to your countryman.
2 "If your countryman is not near you, or if you do not know him, then you shall bring
it home to your house, and it shall remain with you until your countryman looks for it;
then you shall restore it to him.
3 "Thus you shall do with his donkey, and you shall do the same with his garment, and
you shall do likewise with anything lost by your countryman, which he has lost and you
have found. You are not allowed to neglect *them.*
4 "You shall not see your countryman's donkey or his ox fallen down on the way, and
pay no attention to them; you shall certainly help him to raise *them* up.
5 "A woman shall not wear man's clothing, nor shall a man put on a woman's clothing;
for whoever does these things is an abomination to the LORD your God.
6 "If you happen to come upon a bird's nest along the way, in any tree or on the ground,
with young ones or eggs, and the mother sitting on the young or on the eggs, you shall
not take the mother with the young;
7 you shall certainly let the mother go, but the young you may take for yourself, in
order that it may be well with you and that you may prolong your days.
8 "When you build a new house, you shall make a parapet for your roof, so that you
will not bring bloodguilt on your house if anyone falls from it.
9 "You shall not sow your vineyard with two kinds of seed, or all the produce of the
seed which you have sown and the increase of the vineyard will become defiled.
10 "You shall not plow with an ox and a donkey together.
11 "You shall not wear a material mixed of wool and linen together.
12 "You shall make yourself tassels on the four corners of your garment with which you
cover yourself.

21:17 Gen 49:3; Gen 25:31
21:18 Ex 20:12; Lev 19:3; Prov 1:8; Eph 6:1-3
21:21 Lev 20:2, 27; 24:14-23; Num 15:25, 36; Deut 19:19; Deut 13:11
21:22 Deut 22:26; Matt 26:66; Mark 14:64; Acts 23:29
21:23 Josh 8:29; 10:26, 27; John 19:31; Gal 3:13; Lev 18:25; Num 35:34
22:1 Ex 23:4, 5; Prov 27:10; Zech 7:9
22:6 Lev 22:28
22:7 Deut 4:40
22:9 Lev 19:19
22:10 2 Cor 6:14-16
22:11 Lev 19:19
22:12 Num 15:37-41; Matt 23:5

21:18–21 Disobedient and rebellious children were to be brought before the elders of the city and stoned to death. There is no Biblical or archaeological evidence that this punishment was ever carried out, but the point was that disobedience and rebellion were not to be tolerated in the home or allowed to continue unchecked.

22:1–4 The Hebrews were to care for and return lost animals or possessions to their rightful owners. The way of the world, by contrast, is "Finders keepers, losers weepers." To go beyond the finders-keepers rule by protecting and returning the property of others keeps us from being envious and greedy.

22:5 This verse commands men and women not to reverse their sexual roles. It is not a statement about clothing styles. Today role rejections are common—there are men who want to become women and women who want to become men. It's not the clothing style that offends God, but using the style to act out a different sex role. God had a purpose in making us uniquely male and female.

22:8–11 These are practical laws, helpful for establishing good habits for everyday living. Verse 8: Since people used their flat roofs as porches, a guardrail (parapet) was a wise safety precaution. Verse 9: If you plant two different crops side by side, one of them will not survive, since the stronger, taller one will block the sunlight and take most of the vital nutrients from the soil. Verse 10: A donkey and an ox, due to differences in strength and size, cannot pull a plow evenly. Verse 11: Two different kinds of thread wear unevenly and wash differently. Combining them reduces the life of the garment. Don't think of God's laws as arbitrary restrictions. Look for the reasons behind the laws. They are not made just to teach or restrict, but also to protect.

Laws on Morality

13“If any man takes a wife and goes in to her and *then* turns against her,
14 and charges her with shameful deeds and publicly defames her, and says, ‘I took
this woman, *but* when I came near her, I did not find her a virgin,’
15 then the girl’s father and her mother shall take and bring out the *evidence* of the
girl’s virginity to the elders of the city at the gate.
16“The girl’s father shall say to the elders, ‘I gave my daughter to this man for a wife,
but he turned against her;
17 and behold, he has charged her with shameful deeds, saying, “I did not find your
daughter a virgin.” But this is the evidence of my daughter’s virginity.’ And they shall
spread the garment before the elders of the city.
18“So the elders of that city shall take the man and chastise him,
19 and they shall fine him a hundred *shekels* of silver and give it to the girl’s father,
because he publicly defamed a virgin of Israel. And she shall remain his wife; he cannot
divorce her all his days.
20“But if this charge is true, that the girl was not found a virgin,
21 then they shall bring out the girl to the doorway of her father’s house, and the men
of her city shall stone her to death because she has committed an act of folly in Israel by
playing the harlot in her father’s house; thus you shall purge the evil from among you.
22“If a man is found lying with a married woman, then both of them shall die, the man
who lay with the woman, and the woman; thus you shall purge the evil from Israel.
23“If there is a girl who is a virgin engaged to a man, and *another* man finds her in the
city and lies with her,
24 then you shall bring them both out to the gate of that city and you shall stone them
to death; the girl, because she did not cry out in the city, and the man, because he has
violated his neighbor’s wife. Thus you shall purge the evil from among you.
25“But if in the field the man finds the girl who is engaged, and the man forces her and
lies with her, then only the man who lies with her shall die.
26“But you shall do nothing to the girl; there is no sin in the girl worthy of death, for
just as a man rises against his neighbor and murders him, so is this case.
27“When he found her in the field, the engaged girl cried out, but there was no one to
save her.
28“If a man finds a girl who is a virgin, who is not engaged, and seizes her and lies with
her and they are discovered,
29 then the man who lay with her shall give to the girl’s father fifty *shekels* of silver, and
she shall become his wife because he has violated her; he cannot divorce her all his days.
30“A man shall not take his father’s wife so that he will not uncover his father’s skirt.

Persons Excluded from the Assembly

23 “No one who is emasculated or has his male organ cut off shall enter the assembly of the LORD.
2“No one of illegitimate birth shall enter the assembly of the LORD; none of his *descendants,* even to the tenth generation, shall enter the assembly of the LORD.
3“No Ammonite or Moabite shall enter the assembly of the LORD; none of their *descendants,* even to the tenth generation, shall ever enter the assembly of the LORD,
4 because they did not meet you with food and water on the way when you came out
of Egypt, and because they hired against you Balaam the son of Beor from Pethor of
Mesopotamia, to curse you.
5“Nevertheless, the LORD your God was not willing to listen to Balaam, but the LORD
your God turned the curse into a blessing for you because the LORD your God loves you.
6“You shall never seek their peace or their prosperity all your days.
7“You shall not detest an Edomite, for he is your brother; you shall not detest an
Egyptian, because you were an alien in his land.

22:13 Gen 29:21; Deut 24:1; Judg 15:1
22:18 Ex 18:21; Deut 1:9-18
22:20 Deut 17:4
22:21 Gen 34:7; Lev 19:29; 21:9; Deut 23:17, 18; Judg 20:5-10; 2 Sam 13:12, 13; Deut 13:5; 17:7; 19:19
22:22 Lev 20:10; Ezek 16:38; Matt 5:27, 28; John 8:5; 1 Cor 6:9; Heb 13:4
22:23 Lev 19:20-22; Matt 1:18, 19
22:28 Ex 22:16
22:30 Lev 18:8; 20:11; Deut 27:20; 1 Cor 5:1
23:1 Lev 21:20; 22:24
23:3 Neh 13:1, 2
23:4 Neh 13:2; Num 22:5; 23:7; Josh 24:9; 2 Pet 2:15; Jude 11
23:5 Prov 26:2; Deut 4:37
23:6 Ezra 9:12
23:7 Gen 25:24-26; Obad 10, 12; Ex 22:21; 23:9; Lev 19:34; Deut 10:19

22:13–30 Why did God include all these laws about sexual sins? Instructions about sexual behavior would have been vital for three million people on a 40-year camping trip. But they would be equally important when they entered the promised land and settled down as a nation. Paul, in Colossians 3:5–8, recognizes the importance of strong rules about sex for believers because sexual sins have the power to disrupt and destroy the church. Sins involving sex are not innocent dabblings in forbidden pleasures, as is so often portrayed, but powerful destroyers of relationships. They confuse and tear down the climate of respect, trust, and credibility so essential for solid marriages and secure children.

8 "The sons of the third generation who are born to them may enter the assembly of
the LORD.
9 "When you go out as an army against your enemies, you shall keep yourself from
every evil thing.
23:10 Lev 15:16
10 "If there is among you any man who is unclean because of a nocturnal emission, then
he must go outside the camp; he may not reenter the camp.
11 "But it shall be when evening approaches, he shall bathe himself with water, and at
sundown he may reenter the camp.
12 "You shall also have a place outside the camp and go out there,
13 and you shall have a spade among your tools, and it shall be when you sit down
outside, you shall dig with it and shall turn to cover up your excrement.
23:14 Lev 26:12; Ex 3:5
14 "Since the LORD your God walks in the midst of your camp to deliver you and to
defeat your enemies before you, therefore your camp must be holy; and He must not see
anything indecent among you or He will turn away from you.
23:15 1 Sam 30:15
15 "You shall not hand over to his master a slave who has escaped from his master
to you.
23:16 Ex 22:21; Prov 22:22
16 "He shall live with you in your midst, in the place which he shall choose in one of
your towns where it pleases him; you shall not mistreat him.
23:17 Lev 19:29; Deut 22:21; Gen 19:5; 2 Kin 23:7
17 "None of the daughters of Israel shall be a cult prostitute, nor shall any of the sons of
Israel be a cult prostitute.
18 "You shall not bring the hire of a harlot or the wages of a [15]dog into the house of the
23:18 Lev 18:22; 20:13
LORD your God for any votive offering, for both of these are an abomination to the LORD
your God.
23:19 Ex 22:25; Lev 25:35-37; Neh 5:2-7; Ps 15:5
19 "You shall not charge interest to your countrymen: interest on money, food, *or* anything that may be loaned at interest.
20 "You may charge interest to a foreigner, but to your countrymen you shall not charge
23:20 Deut 28:12; Deut 15:10
interest, so that the LORD your God may bless you in all that you undertake in the land
which you are about to enter to possess.
23:21 Num 30:1, 2; Job 22:27; Ps 61:8; Eccl 5:4, 5; Matt 5:33
21 "When you make a vow to the LORD your God, you shall not delay to pay it, for it
would be sin in you, and the LORD your God will surely require it of you.
22 "However, if you refrain from vowing, it would not be sin in you.
23 "You shall be careful to perform what goes out from your lips, just as you have voluntarily vowed to the LORD your God, what you have promised.
24 "When you enter your neighbor's vineyard, then you may eat grapes until you are
fully satisfied, but you shall not put any in your basket.
23:25 Matt 12:1; Mark 2:23; Luke 6:1
25 "When you enter your neighbor's standing grain, then you may pluck the heads with
your hand, but you shall not wield a sickle in your neighbor's standing grain.

Law of Divorce

24:1 Num 5:12, 28; Deut 22:13-21; Matt 5:31; 19:7-9; Mark 10:4, 5
24 "When a man takes a wife and marries her, and it happens that she finds no favor
in his eyes because he has found some indecency in her, and he writes her a certificate of divorce and puts *it* in her hand and sends her out from his house,
2 and she leaves his house and goes and becomes another man's *wife,*
3 and if the latter husband turns against her and writes her a certificate of divorce
and puts *it* in her hand and sends her out of his house, or if the latter husband dies who
took her to be his wife,

15 I.e. male prostitute, sodomite

23:17–18 Prostitution was not overlooked in God's law—it was strictly forbidden. To forbid this practice may seem obvious to us, but it may not have been so obvious to the Israelites. Almost every other religion known to them included cult prostitution as an integral part of its worship services. Prostitution makes a mockery of God's original idea for sex, treating sex as an isolated physical act rather than an act of commitment to another. Outside of marriage, sex destroys relationships. Within marriage, if approached with the right attitude, it can be a relationship builder. God frequently had to warn the people against the practice of extramarital sex. Today we still need to hear his warnings; young people need to be reminded about premarital sex, and adults need to be reminded about sexual fidelity.

23:24–25 This commandment guarded against selfishly holding on to one's possessions. It also ensured that no one had to go hungry. It was not, however, an excuse for taking advantage of one's neighbor. The Pharisees did not interpret this appropriately when they accused Jesus and the disciples of harvesting on the Sabbath (Matthew 12:1–2).

24:1–4 Some think this passage supports divorce, but that is not the case. It simply recognizes a practice that already existed in Israel. All four verses must be read to understand the point of the passage; it certainly is not suggesting that a man divorce his wife on a whim. Divorce was a permanent and final act for the couple. Once divorced and remarried to others, they could never be remarried to each other (24:4). This restriction was to prevent casual remarriage after a frivolous separation. The intention was to make people think twice before divorcing.

4 *then* her former husband who sent her away is not allowed to take her again to be
his wife, since she has been defiled; for that is an abomination before the LORD, and you
shall not bring sin on the land which the LORD your God gives you as an inheritance.
5 "When a man takes a new wife, he shall not go out with the army nor be charged with
any duty; he shall be free at home one year and shall give happiness to his wife whom he
has taken.

Sundry Laws

6 "No one shall take a handmill or an upper millstone in pledge, for he would be taking a life in pledge.
7 "If a man is caught kidnapping any of his countrymen of the sons of Israel, and he
deals with him violently or sells him, then that thief shall die; so you shall purge the evil
from among you.
8 "Be careful against an infection of leprosy, that you diligently observe and do according to all that the Levitical priests teach you; as I have commanded them, so you shall be
careful to do.
9 "Remember what the LORD your God did to Miriam on the way as you came out of
Egypt.
10 "When you make your neighbor a loan of any sort, you shall not enter his house to
take his pledge.
11 "You shall remain outside, and the man to whom you make the loan shall bring the
pledge out to you.
12 "If he is a poor man, you shall not sleep with his pledge.
13 "When the sun goes down you shall surely return the pledge to him, that he may
sleep in his cloak and bless you; and it will be righteousness for you before the LORD
your God.
14 "You shall not oppress a hired servant *who is* poor and needy, whether *he is* one of
your countrymen or one of your aliens who is in your land in your towns.
15 "You shall give him his wages on his day before the sun sets, for he is poor and sets
his heart on it; so that he will not cry against you to the LORD and it become sin in you.
16 "Fathers shall not be put to death for *their* sons, nor shall sons be put to death for
their fathers; everyone shall be put to death for his own sin.
17 "You shall not pervert the justice due an alien *or* [16]an orphan, nor take a widow's
garment in pledge.
18 "But you shall remember that you were a slave in Egypt, and that the LORD your
God redeemed you from there; therefore I am commanding you to do this thing.
19 "When you reap your harvest in your field and have forgotten a sheaf in the field,
you shall not go back to get it; it shall be for the alien, for the orphan, and for the widow,
in order that the LORD your God may bless you in all the work of your hands.
20 "When you beat your olive tree, you shall not go over the boughs again; it shall be for
the alien, for the orphan, and for the widow.
21 "When you gather the grapes of your vineyard, you shall not go over it again; it shall
be for the alien, for the orphan, and for the widow.
22 "You shall remember that you were a slave in the land of Egypt; therefore I am commanding you to do this thing.

16 Or *the fatherless*

24:4 Jer 3:1
24:5 Deut 20:7; Prov 5:18
24:7 Ex 21:16
24:8 Lev 13:1-14, 57
24:9 Num 12:10
24:10 Ex 22:26, 27
24:13 Ex 22:26; Deut 6:25; Ps 106:31; Dan 4:27
24:14 Lev 19:13; 25:35-43; Deut 15:7-18; Prov 14:31; Amos 4:1; 1 Tim 5:18
24:15 Lev 19:13; Jer 22:13; James 5:4; Ex 22:23; Deut 15:9; Job 35:9; James 5:4
24:16 2 Kin 14:6; 2 Chr 25:4; Jer 31:29, 30; Ezek 18:20
24:17 Ex 23:9; Lev 19:33; Deut 1:17; 10:17; 16:19; 27:19; Ex 22:22
24:19 Lev 19:9, 10; 23:22; Deut 14:29; Prov 19:17
24:20 Lev 19:10; Deut 24:19

24:5 Recently married couples were to remain together their first year. This was to avoid placing an excessive burden upon a new, unproven relationship and to give it a chance to mature and strengthen before confronting it with numerous responsibilities. A gardener starts a tiny seedling in a small pot and allows it to take root before planting it in the field. Let your marriage grow strong by protecting your relationship from too many outside pressures and distractions—especially in the beginning. And don't expect or demand so much from newlyweds that they have inadequate time or energy to establish their marriage.

24:10–22 Throughout the Old Testament God told his people to treat the poor with justice. The powerless and poverty-stricken are often looked upon as incompetent or lazy when, in fact, they may be victims of oppression and circumstance. God says we must do all we can to help these needy ones. His justice did not permit the Israelites to insist on profits or quick payment from those who were less fortunate. Instead, his laws gave the poor every opportunity to better their situation, while providing humane options for those who couldn't. None of us is completely isolated from the poor. God wants us to treat them fairly and do our part to see that their needs are met.

24:19–21 God's people were instructed to leave some of their harvest in the fields so travelers and the poor could gather it. This second gathering, called gleaning, was a way for them to provide food for themselves. Years later, Ruth obtained food for herself and Naomi by gleaning behind the reapers in Boaz's field, picking up the leftovers (Ruth 2:2). Because this law was being obeyed years after it was written, Ruth, a woman in Christ's lineage, was able to find food.

Sundry Laws

25 "If there is a dispute between men and they go to court, and the judges decide
their case, and they justify the righteous and condemn the wicked,
2 then it shall be if the wicked man deserves to be beaten, the judge shall then make
him lie down and be beaten in his presence with the number of stripes according to his
guilt.
3 "He may beat him forty times *but* no more, so that he does not beat him with many
more stripes than these and your brother is not degraded in your eyes.
4 "You shall not muzzle the ox while he is threshing.
5 "When brothers live together and one of them dies and has no son, the wife of the
deceased shall not be *married* outside *the family* to a strange man. Her husband's brother shall go in to her and take her to himself as wife and perform the duty of a husband's
brother to her.
6 "It shall be that the firstborn whom she bears shall assume the name of his dead brother, so that his name will not be blotted out from Israel.
7 "But if the man does not desire to take his brother's wife, then his brother's wife shall
go up to the gate to the elders and say, 'My husband's brother refuses to establish a name
for his brother in Israel; he is not willing to perform the duty of a husband's brother to me.'
8 "Then the elders of his city shall summon him and speak to him. And *if* he persists
and says, 'I do not desire to take her,'
9 then his brother's wife shall come to him in the sight of the elders, and pull his sandal off his foot and spit in his face; and she shall declare, 'Thus it is done to the man who
does not build up his brother's house.'
10 "In Israel his name shall be called, 'The house of him whose sandal is removed.'
11 "If *two* men, a man and his countryman, are struggling together, and the wife of one
comes near to deliver her husband from the hand of the one who is striking him, and
puts out her hand and seizes his genitals,
12 then you shall cut off her hand; you shall not show pity.
13 "You shall not have in your bag differing weights, a large and a small.
14 "You shall not have in your house differing measures, a large and a small.
15 "You shall have a full and just weight; you shall have a full and just measure, that
your days may be prolonged in the land which the LORD your God gives you.
16 "For everyone who does these things, everyone who acts unjustly is an abomination
to the LORD your God.
17 "Remember what Amalek did to you along the way when you came out from Egypt,
18 how he met you along the way and attacked among you all the stragglers at your
rear when you were faint and weary; and he did not [17]fear God.
19 "Therefore it shall come about when the LORD your God has given you rest from all
your surrounding enemies, in the land which the LORD your God gives you as an inheritance to possess, you shall blot out the memory of Amalek from under heaven; you must
not forget.

Offering First Fruits

26 "Then it shall be, when you enter the land which the LORD your God gives you as
an inheritance, and you possess it and live in it,

17 Or *reverence*

25:1 Deut 17:8-13; 19:17; Deut 1:16, 17
25:2 Prov 19:29; Luke 12:48
25:3 2 Cor 11:24; Job 18:3
25:4 Prov 12:10; 1 Cor 9:9; 1 Tim 5:18
25:5 Matt 22:24; Mark 12:19; Luke 20:28
25:6 Ruth 4:5, 10
25:7 Ruth 4:5, 6
25:9 Ruth 4:7, 8; Num 12:14
25:12 Deut 7:2; 19:13
25:13 Lev 19:35-37; Prov 11:1; 20:23; Ezek 45:10; Mic 6:11
25:15 Ex 20:12
25:16 Prov 11:1
25:17 Ex 17:8-16
25:18 Ps 36:1; Rom 3:18
25:19 Deut 12:9

25:1–3 At first glance these verses appear irrelevant today. But a closer look reveals some important principles about discipline. Are you responsible for the discipline of a child, a student, or an employee? Three important points will help you carry out your responsibility: (1) let the punishment follow quickly after the offense; (2) let the degree of punishment reflect the seriousness of the offense; and (3) don't overdo the punishment. Discipline that is swift, just, and restrained makes its point while preserving the dignity of the offender.

25:4 What is the point of this Old Testament regulation? Oxen were often used to tread out the grain on a threshing floor. The animal was attached by poles to a large millstone. As it walked around the millstone, its hooves trampled the grain, separating the kernels from the chaff. At the same time, the millstone ground the grain into flour. To muzzle the ox would prevent it from eating while it was working. Paul used this illustration in the New Testament to argue that people productive in Christian work should not be denied its benefits—they should receive financial support (2 Corinthians 9:10; 1 Timothy 5:17–18). The fact that a person is in Christian ministry doesn't mean he or she should be unfairly paid. There is also a broader application: Don't be stingy with those who work for you.

25:5–10 This law describes a "levirate" marriage, the marriage of a widow to the brother of her dead husband. The purpose of such a marriage was to carry on the dead man's name and inheritance. Family ties were an important aspect of Israelite culture. The best way to be remembered was through your line of descendants. If a widow married someone outside the family, her first husband's line would come to an end. Tamar fought for this right in Genesis 38.

2 that you shall take some of the first of all the produce of the ground which you bring
in from your land that the LORD your God gives you, and you shall put *it* in a basket and
go to the place where the LORD your God chooses to establish His name.
3 "You shall go to the priest who is in office at that time and say to him, 'I declare this
day to the LORD my God that I have entered the land which the LORD swore to our fathers to give us.'
4 "Then the priest shall take the basket from your hand and set it down before the altar
of the LORD your God.
5 "You shall answer and say before the LORD your God, 'My father was a wandering
Aramean, and he went down to Egypt and sojourned there, few in number; but there he
became a great, mighty and populous nation.
6 'And the Egyptians treated us harshly and afflicted us, and imposed hard labor on us.
7 'Then we cried to the LORD, the God of our fathers, and the LORD heard our voice
and saw our affliction and our toil and our oppression;
8 and the LORD brought us out of Egypt with a mighty hand and an outstretched arm
and with great terror and with signs and wonders;
9 and He has brought us to this place and has given us this land, a land flowing with
milk and honey.
10 'Now behold, I have brought the first of the produce of the ground which You,
O LORD have given me.' And you shall set it down before the LORD your God, and worship before the LORD your God;
11 and you and the Levite and the alien who is among you shall rejoice in all the good
which the LORD your God has given you and your household.
12 "When you have finished paying all the tithe of your increase in the third year, the
year of tithing, then you shall give it to the Levite, to the stranger, to the orphan and to
the widow, that they may eat in your towns and be satisfied.
13 "You shall say before the LORD your God, 'I have removed the sacred *portion* from
my house, and also have given it to the Levite and the alien, the orphan and the widow,
according to all Your commandments which You have commanded me; I have not transgressed or forgotten any of Your commandments.
14 'I have not eaten of it while mourning, nor have I removed any of it while I was unclean, nor offered any of it to the dead. I have listened to the voice of the LORD my God;
I have done according to all that You have commanded me.
15 'Look down from Your holy habitation, from heaven, and bless Your people Israel,
and the ground which You have given us, a land flowing with milk and honey, as You
swore to our fathers.'
16 "This day the LORD your God commands you to do these statutes and ordinances.
You shall therefore be careful to do them with all your heart and with all your soul.
17 "You have today declared the LORD to be your God, and that you would walk in His
ways and keep His statutes, His commandments and His ordinances, and listen to His
voice.
18 "The LORD has today declared you to be His people, a treasured possession, as He
promised you, and that you should keep all His commandments;
19 and that He will set you high above all nations which He has made, for praise, fame,
and honor; and that you shall be a consecrated people to the LORD your God, as He has
spoken."

6. Consequences of obedience and disobedience

The Curses of Mount Ebal

27 Then Moses and the elders of Israel charged the people, saying, "Keep all the commandments which I command you today.
2 "So it shall be on the day when you cross the Jordan to the land which the LORD

26:2 Ex 22:29; 23:16, 19; Num 18:13; Prov 3:9; Deut 12:5
26:5 Gen 43:1-14; Gen 46:27; Deut 1:10; 10:22
26:6 Ex 1:8-11
26:7 Ex 2:23-25; 3:9
26:8 Deut 4:34; 34:11, 12
26:9 Ex 3:8, 17
26:10 Deut 8:18; Prov 10:22
26:11 Deut 12:12; Deut 12:7; 16:11; Eccl 3:12, 13; 5:18-20
26:12 Lev 27:30; Num 18:24; Deut 14:28, 29; Heb 7:5, 9, 10
26:13 Ps 119:141, 153, 176
26:15 Ps 80:14; Is 63:15; Zech 2:13; Deut 26:9
26:16 Deut 4:29
26:17 Ps 48:14
26:18 Ex 6:7; 19:5; Deut 4:20; 7:6; 14:2; 28:9; 29:13; Titus 2:14; 1 Pet 2:9
26:19 Deut 4:7, 8; 28:1, 13; Ex 19:6; Deut 7:6; Is 62:12; Jer 2:3; 1 Pet 2:9
27:2 Josh 8:30-32

26:5–10 This recitation of God's dealings with his people helped the people remember what God had done for them. What is the history of your relationship with God? Can you put into clear and concise words what God has done for you? Find a friend with whom you can share your spiritual journey. Telling your stories to each other will help you clearly understand your personal spiritual history, as well as encouraging and inspiring you both. Note: *Wandering* can mean lost or dying. Also, Arameans were the people of northern Syria and among the ancestors of Abraham. This is also used as a reference to Jacob, who spent many years there (Genesis 29—31) and got his two wives in Aram.

26:18 Moses said that because the Israelites were now God's people, they needed to start obeying God's commands.

your God gives you, that you shall set up for yourself large stones and coat them with
lime
3 and write on them all the words of this law, when you cross over, so that you may
enter the land which the LORD your God gives you, a land flowing with milk and honey,
as the LORD, the God of your fathers, promised you.
4 "So it shall be when you cross the Jordan, you shall set up on Mount Ebal, these stones,
as I am commanding you today, and you shall coat them with lime.
5 "Moreover, you shall build there an altar to the LORD your God, an altar of stones;
you shall not wield an iron *tool* on them.
6 "You shall build the altar of the LORD your God of uncut stones, and you shall offer
on it burnt offerings to the LORD your God;
7 and you shall sacrifice peace offerings and eat there, and rejoice before the LORD
your God.
8 "You shall write on the stones all the words of this law very distinctly."
9 Then Moses and the Levitical priests spoke to all Israel, saying, "Be silent and listen, O Israel! This day you have become a people for the LORD your God.
10 "You shall therefore obey the LORD your God, and do His commandments and His
statutes which I command you today."
11 Moses also charged the people on that day, saying,
12 "When you cross the Jordan, these shall stand on Mount Gerizim to bless the people: Simeon, Levi, Judah, Issachar, Joseph, and Benjamin.
13 "For the curse, these shall stand on Mount Ebal: Reuben, Gad, Asher, Zebulun, Dan,
and Naphtali.
14 "The Levites shall then answer and say to all the men of Israel with a loud voice,
15 'Cursed is the man who makes an idol or a molten image, an abomination to the
LORD, the work of the hands of the craftsman, and sets *it* up in secret.' And all the people shall answer and say, 'Amen.'
16 'Cursed is he who dishonors his father or mother.' And all the people shall say, 'Amen.'
17 'Cursed is he who moves his neighbor's boundary mark.'
And all the people shall say, 'Amen.'
18 'Cursed is he who misleads a blind *person* on the road.' And all the people shall say,
'Amen.'
19 'Cursed is he who distorts the justice due an alien, orphan, and widow.' And all the
people shall say, 'Amen.'
20 'Cursed is he who lies with his father's wife, because he has uncovered his father's
skirt.' And all the people shall say, 'Amen.'
21 'Cursed is he who lies with any animal.' And all the people shall say, 'Amen.'
22 'Cursed is he who lies with his sister, the daughter of his father or of his mother.'
And all the people shall say, 'Amen.'
23 'Cursed is he who lies with his mother-in-law.' And all the people shall say, 'Amen.'
24 'Cursed is he who strikes his neighbor in secret.' And all the people shall say, 'Amen.'
25 'Cursed is he who accepts a bribe to strike down an innocent person.' And all the
people shall say, 'Amen.'
26 'Cursed is he who does not confirm the words of this law by doing them.' And all the
people shall say, 'Amen.'

27:3 Deut 26:9
27:4 Deut 11:29; Josh 8:30
27:5 Ex 20:25; Josh 8:31
27:7 Deut 26:11
27:12 Deut 11:29; Josh 8:33-35
27:15 Ex 20:4, 23; 34:17; Lev 19:4; 26:1; Deut 4:16, 23; 5:8; Is 44:9 1 Cor 14:16
27:16 Ex 20:12; 21:17; Lev 19:3; 20:9; Deut 5:16; Ezek 22:7
27:17 Deut 19:14; Prov 22:28
27:18 Lev 19:14
27:19 Ex 22:21; 23:9; Lev 19:33; Deut 10:18; 24:17
27:20 Lev 18:8; 20:11; Deut 22:30; 1 Cor 5:1
27:21 Ex 22:19; Lev 18:23; 20:15
27:22 Lev 18:9; 20:17
27:23 Lev 20:14
27:24 Ex 21:12; Lev 24:17; Num 35:30, 31
27:25 Ex 23:7; Deut 10:17; Ps 15:5; Ezek 22:12
27:26 Ps 119:21; Jer 11:3; Gal 3:10

27:5–6 The Lord had specified an altar made of uncut stones so that the people would not begin worshiping the altars as idols. To use an iron tool on a stone of the altar would be to profane it (Exodus 20:24–26). Additionally, because the Israelites did not have the capacity to work with iron at this time, using iron tools might mean using the cooperation and expertise of other nations.

27:9–10 Moses was reviewing the law with the new generation of people. When we decide to believe in God, we must also decide to follow his ways. What we do shows what we really believe. Can people tell that you are a member of God's family?

27:15–26 These curses were a series of oaths, spoken by the priests and affirmed by the people, by which the people promised to stay away from wrong actions. By saying *Amen,* "So be it," the people took responsibility for their actions. Sometimes looking at a list of curses like this gives us the idea that God has a bad temper and is out to crush anyone who steps out of line. But we need to see these restrictions not as threats, but as loving warnings about the plain facts of life. Just as we warn children to stay away from hot stoves and busy streets, so God warns us to stay away from dangerous actions. The natural law of his universe makes it clear that wrongdoing toward others or God has tragic consequences. God is merciful enough to tell us this truth plainly. Motivated by love and not anger, his strong words help us avoid the serious consequences that result from neglecting God or wronging others. But God does not leave us with only curses or consequences. Immediately following these curses, we discover the great blessings (positive consequences) that come from living for God (28:1–14). These give us extra incentive to obey God's laws. While all these blessings may not come in our lifetime on earth, those who obey God will experience the fullness of his blessing when he establishes the new heaven and the new earth.

Blessings at Gerizim

28 "Now it shall be, if you diligently obey the LORD your God, being careful to do all
His commandments which I command you today, the LORD your God will set you
high above all the nations of the earth.
2 "All these blessings will come upon you and overtake you if you obey the LORD
your God:
3 "Blessed *shall* you *be* in the city, and blessed *shall* you *be* in the country.
4 "Blessed *shall be* the offspring of your body and the produce of your ground and the
offspring of your beasts, the increase of your herd and the young of your flock.
5 "Blessed *shall be* your basket and your kneading bowl.
6 "Blessed *shall* you *be* when you come in, and blessed *shall* you *be* when you go out.
7 "The LORD shall cause your enemies who rise up against you to be defeated before
you; they will come out against you one way and will flee before you seven ways.
8 "The LORD will command the blessing upon you in your barns and in all that you put
your hand to, and He will bless you in the land which the LORD your God gives you.
9 "The LORD will establish you as a holy people to Himself, as He swore to you, if you
keep the commandments of the LORD your God and walk in His ways.
10 "So all the peoples of the earth will see that you are called by the name of the LORD,
and they will be afraid of you.
11 "The LORD will make you abound in prosperity, in the offspring of your body and in
the offspring of your beast and in the produce of your ground, in the land which the LORD
swore to your fathers to give you.
12 "The LORD will open for you His good storehouse, the heavens, to give rain to your
land in its season and to bless all the work of your hand; and you shall lend to many nations,
but you shall not borrow.
13 "The LORD will make you the head and not the tail, and you only will be above, and
you will not be underneath, if you listen to the commandments of the LORD your God,
which I charge you today, to observe *them* carefully,
14 and do not turn aside from any of the words which I command you today, to the
right or to the left, to go after other gods to serve them.

Consequences of Disobedience

15 "But it shall come about, if you do not obey the LORD your God, to observe to do all
His commandments and His statutes with which I charge you today, that all these curses
will come upon you and overtake you:
16 "Cursed *shall* you *be* in the city, and cursed *shall* you *be* in the country.
17 "Cursed *shall be* your basket and your kneading bowl.
18 "Cursed *shall be* the offspring of your body and the produce of your ground, the increase of your herd and the young of your flock.
19 "Cursed *shall* you *be* when you come in, and cursed *shall* you *be* when you go out.
20 "The LORD will send upon you curses, confusion, and rebuke, in all you undertake
to do, until you are destroyed and until you perish quickly, on account of the evil of your
deeds, because you have forsaken Me.
21 "The LORD will make the pestilence cling to you until He has consumed you from
the land where you are entering to possess it.
22 "The LORD will smite you with consumption and with fever and with inflammation
and with fiery heat and with [18]the sword and with blight and with mildew, and they will
pursue you until you perish.
23 "The heaven which is over your head shall be bronze, and the earth which is under
you, iron.
24 "The LORD will make the rain of your land powder and dust; from heaven it shall
come down on you until you are destroyed.
25 "The LORD shall cause you to be defeated before your enemies; you will go out one
way against them, but you will flee seven ways before them, and you will be *an example*
of terror to all the kingdoms of the earth.
26 "Your carcasses will be food to all birds of the sky and to the beasts of the earth, and
there will be no one to frighten *them* away.

18 Another reading is *drought*

28:1 Ex 15:26; 23:22-27; Lev 26:3-13; Deut 7:12-26; 11:13; Deut 28:13; 26:19; 1 Chr 14:2
28:2 Zech 1:6
28:3 Gen 39:5
28:6 Ps 121:8
28:8 Deut 15:10
28:9 Ex 19:5
28:10 2 Chr 7:14
28:11 Deut 28:4; Prov 10:22
28:12 Deut 23:20
28:13 Deut 28:1, 44
28:14 Deut 5:32; Josh 1:7
28:15 Lev 26:14-43; Josh 23:15; Dan 9:11
28:16 Deut 28:3
28:17 Deut 28:5
28:18 Deut 28:4
28:19 Deut 28:6
28:20 Deut 28:8; Mal 2:2; Ps 80:16; Is 51:20; 66:15; Deut 4:26
28:21 Lev 26:25; Num 14:12; Jer 24:10; Amos 4:10
28:22 Lev 26:16; Amos 4:9; Deut 4:26
28:24 Deut 11:17; 28:12
28:25 Deut 28:7; Is 30:17; 2 Chr 29:8; Jer 15:4; 24:9; Ezek 23:46
28:26 Jer 7:33; 16:4; 19:7; 34:20

28:23–24 This curse is referring to a drought.

28:27 Ex 9:9; Deut 7:15; 28:60, 61; 1 Sam 5:6
28:29 Ex 10:21
28:30 Job 31:10; Jer 8:10; Amos 5:11
28:32 Deut 28:41
28:33 Jer 5:15, 17
28:35 Deut 28:27
28:36 2 Kin 17:4, 6; 24:12, 14; 25:7, 11; 2 Chr 36:1-21; Jer 39:1-9; Deut 4:28; Jer 16:13
28:37 1 Kin 9:7, 8; Jer 19:8; 24:9; 25:9; 29:18
28:38 Is 5:10; Mic 6:15; Hag 1:6; Ex 10:4; Joel 1:4
28:39 Is 5:10; 17:10, 11
28:40 Jer 11:16; Mic 6:15
28:41 Deut 28:32
28:42 Deut 28:38
28:43 Deut 28:13
28:44 Deut 28:12; Deut 28:13
28:45 Deut 4:25, 26
28:46 Num 26:10; Is 8:18; Ezek 5:15; 14:8
28:47 Deut 12:7; Neh 9:35-37
28:48 Lam 4:4-6; Jer 28:13, 14
28:49 Is 5:26-30; 7:18-20; Jer 5:15; 6:22, 23; Jer 48:40; 49:22; Lam 4:19; Hos 8:1
28:50 Is 47:6

27 "The LORD will smite you with the boils of Egypt and with tumors and with the scab
and with the itch, from which you cannot be healed.
28 "The LORD will smite you with madness and with blindness and with bewilderment
of heart;
29 and you will grope at noon, as the blind man gropes in darkness, and you will not
prosper in your ways; but you shall only be oppressed and robbed continually, with none
to save you.
30 "You shall betroth a wife, but another man will violate her; you shall build a house,
but you will not live in it; you shall plant a vineyard, but you will not use its fruit.
31 "Your ox shall be slaughtered before your eyes, but you will not eat of it; your donkey shall be torn away from you, and will not be restored to you; your sheep shall be
given to your enemies, and you will have none to save you.
32 "Your sons and your daughters shall be given to another people, while your eyes look
on and yearn for them continually; but there will be nothing you can do.
33 "A people whom you do not know shall eat up the produce of your ground and all
your labors, and you will never be anything but oppressed and crushed continually.
34 "You shall be driven mad by the sight of what you see.
35 "The LORD will strike you on the knees and legs with sore boils, from which you cannot
be healed, from the sole of your foot to the crown of your head.
36 "The LORD will bring you and your king, whom you set over you, to a nation which
neither you nor your fathers have known, and there you shall serve other gods, wood
and stone.
37 "You shall become a horror, a proverb, and a taunt among all the people where the
LORD drives you.
38 "You shall bring out much seed to the field but you will gather in little, for the locust
will consume it.
39 "You shall plant and cultivate vineyards, but you will neither drink of the wine nor
gather *the grapes,* for the worm will devour them.
40 "You shall have olive trees throughout your territory but you will not anoint yourself
with the oil, for your olives will drop off.
41 "You shall have sons and daughters but they will not be yours, for they will go into
captivity.
42 "The cricket shall possess all your trees and the produce of your ground.
43 "The alien who is among you shall rise above you higher and higher, but you will go
down lower and lower.
44 "He shall lend to you, but you will not lend to him; he shall be the head, and you will
be the tail.
45 "So all these curses shall come on you and pursue you and overtake you until you are
destroyed, because you would not obey the LORD your God by keeping His commandments and His statutes which He commanded you.
46 "They shall become a sign and a wonder on you and your descendants forever.
47 "Because you did not serve the LORD your God with joy and a glad heart, for the
abundance of all things;
48 therefore you shall serve your enemies whom the LORD will send against you, in
hunger, in thirst, in nakedness, and in the lack of all things; and He will put an iron yoke
on your neck until He has destroyed you.
49 "The LORD will bring a nation against you from afar, from the end of the earth, as
the eagle swoops down, a nation whose language you shall not understand,
50 a nation of fierce countenance who will have no respect for the old, nor show favor
to the young.
51 "Moreover, it shall eat the offspring of your herd and the produce of your ground
until you are destroyed, who also leaves you no grain, new wine, or oil, nor the increase
of your herd or the young of your flock until they have caused you to perish.

28:34 One of the curses for those who rejected God was that they would go mad from seeing all the tragedy around them. Do you ever feel that you will go crazy if you hear about one more rape, kidnapping, murder, or war? Much of the world's evil is a result of people's failure to acknowledge and serve God. When you hear bad news, don't groan helplessly as do unbelievers who have no hope for the future. Remind yourself that in spite of it all, God has ultimate control and will one day come back to make everything right.

28:36 This happened when Assyria and Babylonia took the Israelites captive to their lands (2 Kings 17:23; 25:11).

52 "It shall besiege you in all your towns until your high and fortified walls in which you
trusted come down throughout your land, and it shall besiege you in all your towns
throughout your land which the LORD your God has given you.

28:52 Jer 10:17, 18; Zeph 1:15, 16

53 "Then you shall eat the offspring of your own body, the flesh of your sons and of
your daughters whom the LORD your God has given you, during the siege and the distress by which your enemy will oppress you.

28:53 Lev 26:29; 2 Kin 6:28, 29; Jer 19:9; Lam 2:20; 4:10

54 "The man who is refined and very delicate among you shall be hostile toward his
brother and toward the wife he cherishes and toward the rest of his children who remain,
55 so that he will not give *even* one of them any of the flesh of his children which he will
eat, since he has nothing *else* left, during the siege and the distress by which your enemy
will oppress you in all your towns.
56 "The refined and delicate woman among you, who would not venture to set the sole
of her foot on the ground for delicateness and refinement, shall be hostile toward the
husband she cherishes and toward her son and daughter,

28:56 Lam 4:10

57 and toward her afterbirth which issues from between her legs and toward her children whom she bears; for she will eat them secretly for lack of anything *else,* during the
siege and the distress by which your enemy will oppress you in your towns.

28:57 2 Kin 6:28, 29; Lam 4:10

58 "If you are not careful to observe all the words of this law which are written in this
book, to fear this honored and awesome name, the LORD your God,

28:58 Ps 99:3; Mal 1:14; Is 42:8

59 then the LORD will bring extraordinary plagues on you and your descendants, even
severe and lasting plagues, and miserable and chronic sicknesses.
60 "He will bring back on you all the diseases of Egypt of which you were afraid, and
they will cling to you.

28:60 Deut 28:27

61 "Also every sickness and every plague which, not written in the book of this law, the
LORD will bring on you until you are destroyed.

28:61 Deut 4:25, 26

62 "Then you shall be left few in number, whereas you were as numerous as the stars of
heaven, because you did not obey the LORD your God.

28:62 Deut 1:10; Neh 9:23

63 "It shall come about that as the LORD delighted over you to prosper you, and multiply you, so the LORD will delight over you to make you perish and destroy you; and you
will be torn from the land where you are entering to possess it.

28:63 Jer 32:41; Prov 1:26; Jer 12:14; 45:4

64 "Moreover, the LORD will scatter you among all peoples, from one end of the earth
to the other end of the earth; and there you shall serve other gods, wood and stone, which
you or your fathers have not known.

28:64 Lev 26:33; Deut 4:27; Neh 1:8; Deut 4:28; 29:26; 32:17

65 "Among those nations you shall find no rest, and there will be no resting place for
the sole of your foot; but there the LORD will give you a trembling heart, failing of eyes,
and despair of soul.

28:65 Lam 1:3; Lev 26:36

66 "So your life shall hang in doubt before you; and you will be in dread night and day,
and shall have no assurance of your life.
67 "In the morning you shall say, 'Would that it were evening!' And at evening you shall
say, 'Would that it were morning!' because of the dread of your heart which you dread,
and for the sight of your eyes which you will see.

28:67 Job 7:4

68 "The LORD will bring you back to Egypt in ships, by the way about which I spoke to
you, 'You will never see it again!' And there you will offer yourselves for sale to your
enemies as male and female slaves, but there will be no buyer."

C. A CALL FOR COMMITMENT TO GOD: MOSES' THIRD ADDRESS (29:1—30:20)

After reviewing God's laws, Moses calls for commitment, urging the people to honor the contract they had previously made with God. Knowing God's Word is not enough; we must obey it.

The Covenant in Moab

29 These are the words of the covenant which the LORD commanded Moses to make
with the sons of Israel in the land of Moab, besides the covenant which He had
made with them at Horeb.

29:1 Lev 26:46; 27:34; Deut 5:2, 3

28:64 This severe warning tragically came true when Israel was defeated and carried away into captivity by Assyria (722 B.C.), and Judah to Babylonia (586 B.C.). Later, in A.D. 70, Roman oppression forced many Jews to flee their homeland. Thus the people were dispersed throughout the various nations.

29:1ff At Mount Sinai, 40 years earlier, God and Israel had made a covenant (Exodus 19—20). Although there were many parts to the

2 And Moses summoned all Israel and said to them, "You have seen all that the LORD
did before your eyes in the land of Egypt to Pharaoh and all his servants and all his land;
3 the great trials which your eyes have seen, those great signs and wonders.
4 "Yet to this day the LORD has not given you a heart to know, nor eyes to see, nor
ears to hear.
5 "I have led you forty years in the wilderness; your clothes have not worn out on you,
and your sandal has not worn out on your foot.
6 "You have not eaten bread, nor have you drunk wine or strong drink, in order that
you might know that I am the LORD your God.
7 "When you reached this place, Sihon the king of Heshbon and Og the king of Bashan came out to meet us for battle, but we defeated them;
8 and we took their land and gave it as an inheritance to the Reubenites, the Gadites,
and the half-tribe of the Manassites.
9 "So keep the words of this covenant to do them, that you may prosper in all that
you do.
10 "You stand today, all of you, before the LORD your God: your chiefs, your tribes,
your elders and your officers, *even* all the men of Israel,
11 your little ones, your wives, and the alien who is within your camps, from the one
who chops your wood to the one who draws your water,
12 that you may enter into the covenant with the LORD your God, and into His oath
which the LORD your God is making with you today,
13 in order that He may establish you today as His people and that He may be your
God, just as He spoke to you and as He swore to your fathers, to Abraham, Isaac, and
Jacob.
14 "Now not with you alone am I making this covenant and this oath,
15 but both with those who stand here with us today in the presence of the LORD our
God and with those who are not with us here today
16 (for you know how we lived in the land of Egypt, and how we came through the
midst of the nations through which you passed;
17 moreover, you have seen their abominations and their idols *of* wood, stone, silver,
and gold, which *they had* with them);
18 so that there will not be among you a man or woman, or family or tribe, whose heart
turns away today from the LORD our God, to go and serve the gods of those nations;
that there will not be among you a root bearing poisonous fruit and wormwood.
19 "It shall be when he hears the words of this curse, that he will boast, saying, 'I have
peace though I walk in the stubbornness of my heart in order to destroy the watered
land with the dry.'
20 "The LORD shall never be willing to forgive him, but rather the anger of the LORD
and His jealousy will burn against that man, and every curse which is written in this book
will rest on him, and the LORD will blot out his name from under heaven.
21 "Then the LORD will single him out for adversity from all the tribes of Israel, according to all the curses of the covenant which are written in this book of the law.
22 "Now the generation to come, your sons who rise up after you and the foreigner who
comes from a distant land, when they see the plagues of the land and the diseases with
which the LORD has afflicted it, will say,

29:3 Deut 4:34; 7:19
29:4 Is 6:9, 10; Ezek 12:2; Matt 13:14; Acts 28:26, 27; Rom 11:8
29:5 Deut 8:4
29:6 Deut 8:3
29:7 Num 21:21-24, 33, 35; Deut 2:26-3:17
29:8 Num 32:32, 33; Deut 3:12, 13
29:9 Deut 4:6; 1 Kin 2:3; Josh 1:7
29:11 Josh 9:21, 23, 27
29:13 Gen 17:7; Ex 6:7
29:14 Jer 31:31; Heb 8:7, 8
29:15 Acts 2:39
29:17 Ex 20:23; Deut 4:28; 28:36
29:18 Deut 13:6; Deut 32:32; Heb 12:15
29:20 Ps 79:5; Ezek 23:25; Ps 74:1; 80:4; Ex 32:33; Deut 9:14; 2 Kin 14:27
29:21 Deut 30:10
29:22 Jer 19:8; 49:17; 50:13

---

covenant (read the books of Exodus, Leviticus, and Numbers), its purpose can be summed up in two sentences: God promised to bless the Israelites by making them the nation through whom the rest of the world could know God. In return, the Israelites promised to love and obey God in order to receive physical and spiritual blessings. Here Moses reviewed this covenant. God was still keeping his part of the bargain (and he always would), but the Israelites were already neglecting their part. Moses restated the covenant to warn the people that if they did not keep their part of the agreement, they would experience severe discipline.

29:5 Just as the people of Israel did not notice God's care for them along their journey, we sometimes do not notice all of the ways that God takes care of us—that all of our daily needs have been supplied and we have been well fed and well clothed. Worse yet, we mistakenly take the credit ourselves for being good providers instead of recognizing God's hand in the process.

29:9 What is the best way to prosper in life? For the Israelites, their first step was to keep their part of the covenant. They were to love God with all of their heart, soul, and might (6:4–5). We, too, are to seek first the kingdom of God and his righteousness (Matthew 6:33); then true success in life will follow as a blessing from the hand of God.

29:18 Moses cautioned that the day the Hebrews chose to turn from God, a root would be planted that would produce poisonous fruit (see Hebrews 12:15). When we decide to do what we know is wrong, we plant an evil seed that begins to grow out of control, eventually yielding a crop of sorrow and pain. But we can prevent those seeds of sin from taking root. If you have done something wrong, confess it to God and others immediately. If the seed never finds fertile soil, its poisonous fruit will never ripen.

23 'All its land is brimstone and salt, a burning waste, unsown and unproductive, and
no grass grows in it, like the overthrow of Sodom and Gomorrah, Admah and Zeboiim,
which the LORD overthrew in His anger and in His wrath.'
24 "All the nations will say, 'Why has the LORD done thus to this land? Why this great
outburst of anger?'
25 "Then *men* will say, 'Because they forsook the covenant of the LORD, the God of
their fathers, which He made with them when He brought them out of the land of Egypt.
26 'They went and served other gods and worshiped them, gods whom they have not
known and whom He had not allotted to them.
27 'Therefore, the anger of the LORD burned against that land, to bring upon it every
curse which is written in this book;
28 and the LORD uprooted them from their land in anger and in fury and in great wrath,
and cast them into another land, as *it is* this day.'
29 "The secret things belong to the LORD our God, but the things revealed belong to us
and to our sons forever, that we may observe all the words of this law.

29:23 Gen 19:24; Is 34:9; Jer 17:6; Zeph 2:9; Is 1:7; 64:11; Jude 7
29:24 1 Kin 9:8; Jer 22:8
29:25 2 Kin 17:9-23; 2 Chr 36:13-21
29:27 Dan 9:11
29:28 2 Chr 7:20; Ps 52:5; Prov 2:22; Ezek 19:12, 13
29:29 Acts 1:7; John 5:39; Acts 17:11; 2 Tim 3:16

Restoration Promised

30 "So it shall be when all of these things have come upon you, the blessing and the
curse which I have set before you, and you call *them* to mind in all nations where
the LORD your God has banished you,
2 and you return to the LORD your God and obey Him with all your heart and soul
according to all that I command you today, you and your sons,
3 then the LORD your God will restore you from captivity, and have compassion on
you, and will gather you again from all the peoples where the LORD your God has scattered you.
4 "If your outcasts are at the ends of the earth, from there the LORD your God will
gather you, and from there He will bring you back.
5 "The LORD your God will bring you into the land which your fathers possessed, and
you shall possess it; and He will prosper you and multiply you more than your fathers.
6 "Moreover the LORD your God will circumcise your heart and the heart of your descendants, to love the LORD your God with all your heart and with all your soul, so that
you may live.
7 "The LORD your God will inflict all these curses on your enemies and on those who
hate you, who persecuted you.
8 "And you shall again obey the LORD, and observe all His commandments which I
command you today.
9 "Then the LORD your God will prosper you abundantly in all the work of your hand,
in the offspring of your body and in the offspring of your cattle and in the produce of
your ground, for the LORD will again rejoice over you for good, just as He rejoiced over
your fathers;
10 if you obey the LORD your God to keep His commandments and His statutes which
are written in this book of the law, if you turn to the LORD your God with all your heart
and soul.
11 "For this commandment which I command you today is not too difficult for you, nor
is it out of reach.

30:1 Deut 11:26; 30:15, 19; Lev 26:40-45; Deut 28:64; 29:28; 1 Kin 8:47
30:2 Deut 4:29, 30; Neh 1:9; Deut 4:29
30:3 Gen 28:15; 48:21; Ps 126:1, 4; Jer 29:14; Ps 147:2; Jer 32:37; Ezek 34:13; Deut 4:27
30:4 Neh 1:9; Is 43:6; 48:20; 62:11
30:5 Jer 29:14; 30:3; Deut 7:13; 13:17
30:6 Deut 10:16; Deut 6:5
30:7 Deut 7:15
30:9 Jer 31:27, 28; Jer 32:41
30:10 Deut 29:21; Deut 4:29

29:29 There are some secrets God has chosen not to reveal to us, possibly for the following reasons: (1) our finite minds cannot fully understand the infinite aspects of God's nature and the universe (Ecclesiastes 3:11); (2) some things are unnecessary for us to know until we are more mature; (3) God is infinite and all-knowing, and we do not have the capacity to know everything he does. This verse shows that although God has not told us everything there is to know about obeying him, he has told us enough. Thus disobedience comes from an act of the will, not a lack of knowledge. Through God's Word we know enough about him to be saved by faith and to serve him. We must not use the limitation of our knowledge as an excuse to reject his claim on our life.

30:1–6 Moses told the Hebrews that when they were ready to return to God, he would be ready to receive them. God's mercy is unbelievable. It goes far beyond what we can imagine. Even if the Jews deliberately walked away from him and ruined their lives, God would still take them back. God would give them inward spiritual renewal (circumcise their hearts). God wants to forgive us and bring us back to himself too. Some people will not learn this until their world has crashed in around them. Then the sorrow and pain seem to open their eyes to what God has been saying all along. Are you separated from God by sin? No matter how far you have wandered, God promises a fresh beginning if only you will turn to him.

30:11–14 God has called us to keep his commands, while reminding us that his laws are not too difficult for us or beyond our reach. Have you ever said you would obey God if you knew what he wanted? Have you ever complained that obedience is too difficult for a mere human? These are unacceptable excuses. God's laws are written in the Bible and are clearly evident in the world around us. Obeying them is reasonable, sensible, and beneficial. The most difficult part of obeying God's laws is simply deciding to start now. Paul refers to this passage in Romans 10:5–8.

30:12 Rom 10:6-8

12 "It is not in heaven, that you should say, 'Who will go up to heaven for us to get it for
us and make us hear it, that we may observe it?'
13 "Nor is it beyond the sea, that you should say, 'Who will cross the sea for us to get it
for us and make us hear it, that we may observe it?'
14 "But the word is very near you, in your mouth and in your heart, that you may observe it.

Choose Life

30:15 Deut 11:26

30:16 Deut 6:5; Deut 4:1; 30:19

15 "See, I have set before you today life and prosperity, and death and adversity;
16 in that I command you today to love the LORD your God, to walk in His ways and to
keep His commandments and His statutes and His judgments, that you may live and
multiply, and that the LORD your God may bless you in the land where you are entering
to possess it.
17 "But if your heart turns away and you will not obey, but are drawn away and worship
other gods and serve them,

30:18 Deut 4:26; 8:19

18 I declare to you today that you shall surely perish. You will not prolong *your* days in
the land where you are crossing the Jordan to enter and possess it.

30:19 Deut 4:26; Deut 30:1

19 "I call heaven and earth to witness against you today, that I have set before you life
and death, the blessing and the curse. So choose life in order that you may live, you and
your descendants,

30:20 Deut 6:5; Deut 10:20; Deut 4:1; 32:47; Acts 17:25, 28; Gen 12:7; 17:1-8

20 by loving the LORD your God, by obeying His voice, and by holding fast to Him; for
this is your life and the length of your days, that you may live in the land which the LORD
swore to your fathers, to Abraham, Isaac, and Jacob, to give them."

D. THE CHANGE IN LEADERSHIP: MOSES' LAST DAYS (31:1—34:12)

Realizing that he is about to die, Moses commissions Joshua, records the laws in a permanent form, and teaches a special song to the Israelites. Thus Moses prepared the people for his departure. Similarly, we should not allow others to become dependent upon us for their spiritual growth, but help them to become dependent upon God.

Moses' Last Counsel

31:2 Deut 34:7; Num 27:17; 1 Kin 3:7; Deut 1:37; 3:27

31 So Moses went and spoke these words to all Israel.
2 And he said to them, "I am a hundred and twenty years old today; I am no
longer able to come and go, and the LORD has said to me, 'You shall not cross this
Jordan.'

31:3 Deut 9:3; Num 27:18

31:5 Deut 7:2

31:6 Josh 10:25; 1 Chr 22:13; Deut 1:29; 7:18; 20:1; Deut 20:4; Josh 1:5; Heb 13:5

3 "It is the LORD your God who will cross ahead of you; He will destroy these nations
before you, and you shall dispossess them. Joshua is the one who will cross ahead of you,
just as the LORD has spoken.
4 "The LORD will do to them just as He did to Sihon and Og, the kings of the Amorites, and to their land, when He destroyed them.
5 "The LORD will deliver them up before you, and you shall do to them according to
all the commandments which I have commanded you.
6 "Be strong and courageous, do not be afraid or tremble at them, for the LORD your
God is the one who goes with you. He will not fail you or forsake you."

31:7 Deut 1:38; 3:28

31:8 Ex 13:21; 33:14; Deut 31:6; Josh 1:5; Heb 13:5

7 Then Moses called to Joshua and said to him in the sight of all Israel, "Be strong
and courageous, for you shall go with this people into the land which the LORD has sworn
to their fathers to give them, and you shall give it to them as an inheritance.
8 "The LORD is the one who goes ahead of you; He will be with you. He will not fail
you or forsake you. Do not fear or be dismayed."

31:9 Num 4:5, 6, 15; Deut 10:8; 31:25, 26; Josh 3:3

9 So Moses wrote this law and gave it to the priests, the sons of Levi who carried the
ark of the covenant of the LORD, and to all the elders of Israel.

30:19–20 Moses challenged Israel to choose life, to obey God, and therefore continue to experience his blessings. God doesn't force his will on anyone. He lets us decide whether to follow him or reject him. This decision, however, is a life-or-death matter. God wants us to realize this, for he would like us all to choose life. Daily, in each new situation, we must affirm and reinforce this commitment.

10 Then Moses commanded them, saying, "At the end of *every* seven years, at the time
of the year of remission of debts, at the Feast of Booths,
11 when all Israel comes to appear before the LORD your God at the place which He
will choose, you shall read this law in front of all Israel in their hearing.
12 "Assemble the people, the men and the women and children and the alien who is in
your town, so that they may hear and learn and fear the LORD your God, and be careful
to observe all the words of this law.
13 "Their children, who have not known, will hear and learn to fear the LORD your God,
as long as you live on the land which you are about to cross the Jordan to possess."

Israel Will Fall Away

14 Then the LORD said to Moses, "Behold, the time for you to die is near; call Joshua,
and present yourselves at the tent of meeting, that I may commission him." So Moses
and Joshua went and presented themselves at the tent of meeting.
15 The LORD appeared in the tent in a pillar of cloud, and the pillar of cloud stood at
the doorway of the tent.
16 The LORD said to Moses, "Behold, you are about to lie down with your fathers; and
this people will arise and play the harlot with the strange gods of the land, into the midst
of which they are going, and will forsake Me and break My covenant which I have made
with them.
17 "Then My anger will be kindled against them in that day, and I will forsake them and
hide My face from them, and they will be consumed, and many evils and troubles will
come upon them; so that they will say in that day, 'Is it not because our God is not among
us that these evils have come upon us?'
18 "But I will surely hide My face in that day because of all the evil which they will do,
for they will turn to other gods.
19 "Now therefore, write this song for yourselves, and teach it to the sons of Israel; put
it on their lips, so that this song may be a witness for Me against the sons of Israel.
20 "For when I bring them into the land flowing with milk and honey, which I swore to
their fathers, and they have eaten and are satisfied and become prosperous, then they
will turn to other gods and serve them, and spurn Me and break My covenant.
21 "Then it shall come about, when many evils and troubles have come upon them, that
this song will testify before them as a witness (for it shall not be forgotten from the lips
of their descendants); for I know their intent which they are developing today, before I
have brought them into the land which I swore."
22 So Moses wrote this song the same day, and taught it to the sons of Israel.

Joshua Is Commissioned

23 Then He commissioned Joshua the son of Nun, and said, "Be strong and courageous,
for you shall bring the sons of Israel into the land which I swore to them, and I will be
with you."
24 It came about, when Moses finished writing the words of this law in a book until
they were complete,

31:10 Deut 15:1, 2; Lev 23:34; Deut 16:13

31:11 Deut 16:16; Deut 12:5; Josh 8:34; 2 Kin 23:2

31:12 Deut 4:10

31:14 Num 27:12, 13; Deut 4:22; 32:50; Ex 33:9-11

31:15 Ex 33:9

31:16 Gen 15:15; Ex 34:15; Deut 4:25-28; Judg 2:11, 12, 17; Judg 10:6; 1 Kin 18:18; 19:10; Jer 2:13

31:17 Judg 2:14; 6:13; 2 Chr 15:2; 24:20; Ps 104:29; Is 8:17; Num 14:42

31:19 Deut 31:22

31:20 Deut 6:10-12; 8:10, 19; 11:16, 17; Deut 32:15-17

31:21 Lev 26:41; Deut 4:30 1 Chr 28:9; John 2:24, 25

31:22 Deut 31:19

31:23 Num 27:23; Deut 31:7; Josh 1:6; Ex 3:12

31:10–13 The laws were to be read to the whole assembly so that everyone, including the children, could hear them. Every seven years the entire nation would gather together and listen as a priest read the law to them. There were no books, Bibles, or newsstands to spread God's word, so the people had to rely on word of mouth and an accurate memory. Memorization was an important part of worship because if everyone knew the law, ignorance would be no excuse for breaking it. To fulfill God's purpose and will in our lives, we need the content and substance of his Word in our hearts and minds. For the Hebrews, this process began in childhood. Teaching our children and new believers should be one of our top priorities. Our finest teachers, best resources, and most careful thought should be directed toward showing young believers how to follow God in all life's situations.

31:19–21 There is a place for music in Christian education, and for the building up of all believers. Some people memorize classic hymns of the church to help them think of what is true, right, and good. Others find tapes to play when they are in the car or at home. What creative ways can music be used to teach in your church? How might you maximize the benefit of music in your family?

31:23 Joshua had been appointed to take over the leadership of Israel and guide the people into the promised land (Moses could not enter the land due to his disobedience—Numbers 20:12). Joshua, first mentioned in Exodus 17:9, had been Moses' assistant for many years (Joshua 1:1). One of his key qualifications was his faith. As one of the 12 spies to first enter Canaan, only he and Caleb believed that God could help Israel conquer the land (Numbers 13:1—14:30). Moses told Joshua to be strong and courageous twice in this chapter (31:7, 23). Indeed, this was a frightening task with three million people to care for, settle disputes for, and lead into battle. Finding courage would be Joshua's greatest test. He was strong and courageous because he knew God was with him and because he had faith that God would do all he had promised Israel.

31:25 Deut 31:9

25 that Moses commanded the Levites who carried the ark of the covenant of the LORD,
saying,
26 "Take this book of the law and place it beside the ark of the covenant of the LORD
your God, that it may remain there as a witness against you.

31:27 Deut 9:7, 24; Ex 32:9; Deut 9:6, 13

27 "For I know your rebellion and your stubbornness; behold, while I am still alive with
you today, you have been rebellious against the LORD; how much more, then, after my
death?

31:28 Deut 4:26; 30:19; 32:1

28 "Assemble to me all the elders of your tribes and your officers, that I may speak these
words in their hearing and call the heavens and the earth to witness against them.

31:29 Judg 2:19

29 "For I know that after my death you will act corruptly and turn from the way which
I have commanded you; and evil will befall you in the latter days, for you will do that
which is evil in the sight of the LORD, provoking Him to anger with the work of your
hands."
30 Then Moses spoke in the hearing of all the assembly of Israel the words of this song,
until they were complete:

The Song of Moses

32:1 Deut 4:26; Ps 50:4; Is 1:2; Jer 6:19

32 "Give ear, O heavens, and let me speak;
And let the earth hear the words of my mouth.

32:2 Is 55:10, 11; Ps 72:6

2 "Let my teaching drop as the rain,
My speech distill as the dew,
As the droplets on the fresh grass
And as the showers on the herb.

32:3 Ex 33:19; 34:5, 6; Deut 3:24; 5:24

3 "For I proclaim the name of the LORD;
Ascribe greatness to our God!

32:4 Deut 32:15, 18, 30; 2 Sam 22:31; Gen 18:25; Dan 4:37; Deut 7:9

4 "The Rock! His work is perfect,
For all His ways are just;
A God of faithfulness and without injustice,
Righteous and upright is He.

32:5 Deut 4:25; 31:29; Matt 17:17

5 "They have acted corruptly toward Him,
They are not His children, because of their defect;
But are a perverse and crooked generation.

32:6 Ps 116:12; Deut 32:28; Deut 1:31; Ps 74:2; Is 63:16; Deut 32:15

6 "Do you thus repay the LORD,
O foolish and unwise people?
Is not He your Father who has bought you?
He has made you and established you.

32:7 Ex 12:26; Ps 78:5-8

7 "Remember the days of old,
Consider the years of all generations.
Ask your father, and he will inform you,
Your elders, and they will tell you.

VARIETY IN WORSHIP
Israel's worship used all of the senses. They reinforced the meaning of the ceremony. Every sense can be used to worship God.

SIGHT	the beauty and symbolism of the tabernacle; every color and hue had a meaning
HEARING	the use of music; there were instructions for the use of a variety of instruments, and the Bible records many songs
TOUCH	the head of the animal to be sacrificed was touched, symbolizing the fact that it was taking their place
SMELL	the sacrifices were burned, emitting a familiar aroma
TASTE	the feasts were celebrations and memorials—much of the food was symbolic

---

31:27–29 Moses knew that the Israelites, in spite of all they had seen of God's work, were rebellious at heart. They deserved God's punishment, although they often received his mercy instead. We too are stubborn and rebellious by nature. Throughout our lives we struggle with sin. Repentance once a month or once a week is not enough. We must constantly turn from our sins to God and let him, in his mercy, save us.

32:1ff Moses was not only a great prophet but also a song leader. After three sermons, he changed the form of his message to singing. Sometimes reciting something in a different form makes it easier to remember. This song gives a brief history of Israel. It reminds the people of their mistakes, warns them to avoid repetition of those mistakes, and offers the hope that comes only in trusting God.

8 "When the Most High gave the nations their inheritance,
When He separated the sons of man,
He set the boundaries of the peoples
According to the number of the sons of Israel.
9 "For the LORD'S portion is His people;
Jacob is the allotment of His inheritance.
10 "He found him in a desert land,
And in the howling waste of a wilderness;
He encircled him, He cared for him,
He guarded him as the pupil of His eye.
11 "Like an eagle that stirs up its nest,
That hovers over its young,
He spread His wings and caught them,
He carried them on His pinions.
12 "The LORD alone guided him,
And there was no foreign god with him.
13 "He made him ride on the high places of the earth,
And he ate the produce of the field;
And He made him suck honey from the rock,
And oil from the flinty rock,
14 Curds of cows, and milk of the flock,
With fat of lambs,
And rams, the breed of Bashan, and goats,
With the finest of the wheat—
And of the blood of grapes you drank wine.

15 "But [19]Jeshurun grew fat and kicked—
You are grown fat, thick, and sleek—
Then he forsook God who made him,
And scorned the Rock of his salvation.
16 "They made Him jealous with strange *gods;*
With abominations they provoked Him to anger.
17 "They sacrificed to demons who were not God,
To gods whom they have not known,
New *gods* who came lately,
Whom your fathers did not dread.
18 "You neglected the Rock who begot you,
And forgot the God who gave you birth.

19 "The LORD saw *this,* and spurned *them*
Because of the provocation of His sons and daughters.
20 "Then He said, 'I will hide My face from them,
I will see what their end *shall be;*
For they are a perverse generation,
Sons in whom is no faithfulness.
21 'They have made Me jealous with *what* is not God;
They have provoked Me to anger with their idols.
So I will make them jealous with *those who* are not a people;
I will provoke them to anger with a foolish nation,
22 For a fire is kindled in My anger,
And burns to the lowest part of Sheol,
And consumes the earth with its yield,
And sets on fire the foundations of the mountains.

19 I.e. Israel

32:8 Acts 17:26; Num 23:9; Deut 33:28

32:9 1 Sam 10:1; 1 Kin 8:51, 53; Jer 10:16

32:10 Deut 1:19; Ps 17:8; Prov 7:2; Zech 2:8

32:11 Ex 19:4; Deut 33:12; Ps 18:10-18

32:12 Deut 4:35, 39; Deut 32:39; Is 43:12

32:13 Is 58:14; Deut 8:8; Ps 81:16; Job 29:6

32:14 Ps 81:16; 147:14; Gen 49:11

32:15 Deut 31:20; Judg 10:6; Deut 32:6; Deut 32:4; Ps 89:26

32:16 Ps 78:58; Ps 106:29

32:17 Lev 17:7; 1 Cor 10:20; Deut 28:64; Judg 5:8

32:18 Deut 32:4; Ps 106:21

32:19 Lev 26:30; Ps 106:40; Jer 44:21-23

32:20 Deut 31:29; Deut 32:5; Deut 9:23

32:21 Deut 32:16; 1 Cor 10:22; Deut 32:17; 1 Kin 16:13, 26; Rom 10:19

32:22 Num 16:33-35; Ps 18:7, 8; Lam 4:11; Lev 26:20

32:10 The Israelites had no excuse for abandoning God. He had shielded them like a kindly shepherd. He had guarded them like a person protects the pupil of his eye. He had been the encircling protector, like a mother eagle who protects her young. The Lord alone had led them. And he alone leads us. Let us remember to trust in him.

32:23 Deut 29:21; Ps 18:14; 45:5

23 'I will heap misfortunes on them;
I will use My arrows on them.

32:24 Deut 28:22, 48; Ps 91:6; Lev 26:22; Amos 5:18, 19

24 '*They will be* wasted by famine, and consumed by plague
And bitter destruction;
And the teeth of beasts I will send upon them,
With the venom of crawling things of the dust.

32:25 Lam 1:20; Ezek 7:15; 2 Chr 36:17; Lam 2:21

25 'Outside the sword will bereave,
And inside terror—
Both young man and virgin,
The nursling with the man of gray hair.

32:26 Deut 4:27; 28:64; Deut 9:14

26 'I would have said, "I will cut them to pieces,
I will remove the memory of them from men,"

32:27 Num 15:30

27 Had I not feared the provocation by the enemy,
That their adversaries would misjudge,
That they would say, "Our hand is triumphant,
And the LORD has not done all this." '

32:28 Deut 32:6

28 "For they are a nation lacking in counsel,
And there is no understanding in them.

32:29 Deut 5:29; Deut 31:29

29 "Would that they were wise, that they understood this,
That they would discern their future!

32:30 Lev 26:7, 8; Deut 32:4; Ps 44:12

30 "How could one chase a thousand,
And two put ten thousand to flight,
Unless their Rock had sold them,
And the LORD had given them up?

32:31 Ex 14:25

31 "Indeed their rock is not like our Rock,
Even our enemies themselves judge this.

32:32 Deut 29:18

32 "For their vine is from the vine of Sodom,
And from the fields of Gomorrah;
Their grapes are grapes of poison,
Their clusters, bitter.
33 "Their wine is the venom of serpents,
And the deadly poison of cobras.

32:34 Job 14:17; Jer 44:21

34 'Is it not laid up in store with Me,
Sealed up in My treasuries?

32:35 Ps 94:1; Rom 12:19; Heb 10:30; Jer 23:12; Ezek 7:5-10

35 'Vengeance is Mine, and retribution,
In due time their foot will slip;
For the day of their calamity is near,
And the impending things are hastening upon them.'

32:36 Ps 135:14; Heb 10:30; Lev 26:43-45; Deut 30:1-3

36 "For the LORD will vindicate His people,
And will have compassion on His servants,
When He sees that *their* strength is gone,
And there is none *remaining,* bond or free.

32:37 Judg 10:14; Jer 2:28

37 "And He will say, 'Where are their gods,
The rock in which they sought refuge?

32:38 Num 25:1, 2; Jer 11:12

38 'Who ate the fat of their sacrifices,
And drank the wine of their drink offering?
Let them rise up and help you,
Let them be your hiding place!

32:39 Is 41:4; 43:10; Deut 32:12; Is 45:5 1 Sam 2:6; Ps 68:20; Ps 51:8; Ps 50:22

39 'See now that I, I am He,
And there is no god besides Me;
It is I who put to death and give life.
I have wounded and it is I who heal,
And there is no one who can deliver from My hand.

32:40 Ezek 20:5, 6; 21:4, 5

40 'Indeed, I lift up My hand to heaven,
And say, as I live forever,

32:41 Is 34:6-8; Jer 50:28-32

41 If I sharpen My flashing sword,
And My hand takes hold on justice,
I will render vengeance on My adversaries,
And I will repay those who hate Me.

42 'I will make My arrows drunk with blood,
And My sword will devour flesh,
With the blood of the slain and the captives,
From the long-haired leaders of the enemy.'
43 "Rejoice, O nations, *with* His people;
For He will avenge the blood of His servants,
And will render vengeance on His adversaries,
And will atone for His land *and* His people."
44 Then Moses came and spoke all the words of this song in the hearing of the people,
he, with Joshua the son of Nun.
45 When Moses had finished speaking all these words to all Israel,
46 he said to them, "Take to your heart all the words with which I am warning you today,
which you shall command your sons to observe carefully, *even* all the words of this law.
47 "For it is not an idle word for you; indeed it is your life. And by this word you will
prolong your days in the land, which you are about to cross the Jordan to possess."
48 The LORD spoke to Moses that very same day, saying,
49 "Go up to this mountain of the Abarim, Mount Nebo, which is in the land of Moab
opposite Jericho, and look at the land of Canaan, which I am giving to the sons of Israel
for a possession.
50 "Then die on the mountain where you ascend, and be gathered to your people, as
Aaron your brother died on Mount Hor and was gathered to his people,
51 because you broke faith with Me in the midst of the sons of Israel at the waters of
Meribah-kadesh, in the wilderness of Zin, because you did not treat Me as holy in the
midst of the sons of Israel.
52 "For you shall see the land at a distance, but you shall not go there, into the land
which I am giving the sons of Israel."

The Blessing of Moses

33 Now this is the blessing with which Moses the man of God blessed the sons of
Israel before his death.
2 He said,
"The LORD came from Sinai,
And dawned on them from Seir;
He shone forth from Mount Paran,
And He came from the midst of ten thousand holy ones;
At His right hand there was flashing lightning for them.
3 "Indeed, He loves the people;
All Your holy ones are in Your hand,
And they followed in Your steps;
Everyone receives of Your words.
4 "Moses charged us with a law,
A possession for the assembly of Jacob.
5 "And He was king in Jeshurun,
When the heads of the people were gathered,
The tribes of Israel together.

6 "May Reuben live and not die,
Nor his men be few."

7 And this regarding Judah; so he said,
"Hear, O LORD, the voice of Judah,
And bring him to his people.

32:42 Deut 32:23; Jer 12:12; 46:10, 14
32:43 Rom 15:10; 2 Kin 9:7; Rev 6:10; 19:2; Is 1:24, 25; Ps 65:3; 79:9; 85:1
32:44 Num 13:8, 16
32:46 Ezek 40:4; 44:5; Deut 4:9
32:47 Deut 8:3; 30:20; Deut 4:40; 33:25
32:48 Num 27:12
32:49 Num 27:12-14; Deut 3:27
32:50 Gen 25:8
32:51 Num 20:12; Num 27:14
32:52 Deut 34:1-3; Deut 1:37; 3:27
33:1 Josh 14:6
33:2 Ex 19:18, 20; Ps 68:8, 17; Judg 5:4; Num 10:12; Hab 3:3; Dan 7:10; Acts 7:53; Ex 23:20-22
33:3 Deut 4:37; Mal 1:2; Deut 7:6; 14:2; Deut 6:1-9; Luke 10:39
33:4 Deut 4:2; John 7:19; Ps 119:111
33:5 Num 23:21
33:6 Gen 49:3, 4
33:7 Gen 49:8-12

32:46–47 Moses urged the people to think about God's word and teach it to their children. The Bible can sit on your bookshelf and gather dust, or you can make it a vital part of your life by regularly setting aside time to study it. When you discover the wisdom of God's message, you will want to apply it to your life and pass it on to your family and others. The Bible is not merely good reading—it's real help for real life.

33:6–25 Note the difference in blessings God gave each tribe. To one he gave the best land, to another strength, to another safety. Too often we see someone with a particular blessing and think that God must love that person more than others. Think rather that God draws out in all people their unique talents. All these gifts are needed to complete his plan. Don't be envious of the gifts others have. Instead, look for the gifts God has given you, and resolve to do the tasks he has uniquely qualified you to do.

With his hands he contended for them,
And may You be a help against his adversaries."

33:8 Ex 28:30; Lev 8:8; Ps 106:16; Ex 17:7; Num 20:13, 24; Deut 6:16

8 Of Levi he said,
"*Let* Your Thummim and Your Urim *belong* to Your godly man,
Whom You proved at Massah,
With whom You contended at the waters of Meribah;

33:9 Ex 32:27-29; Mal 2:5

9 Who said of his father and his mother,
'I did not consider them';
And he did not acknowledge his brothers,
Nor did he regard his own sons,
For they observed Your word,
And kept Your covenant.

33:10 Lev 10:11; Deut 31:9-13; Lev 16:12, 13; Ps 51:19

10 "They shall teach Your ordinances to Jacob,
And Your law to Israel.
They shall put incense before You,
And whole burnt offerings on Your altar.
11 "O LORD, bless his substance,
And accept the work of his hands;
Shatter the loins of those who rise up against him,
And those who hate him, so that they will not rise *again*."

33:12 Deut 4:37f; 12:10; Deut 32:11; Ex 28:12

12 Of Benjamin he said,
"May the beloved of the LORD dwell in security by Him,
Who shields him all the day,
And he dwells between His shoulders."

33:13 Gen 27:27, 28; 49:22-26

13 Of Joseph he said,
"Blessed of the LORD *be* his land,
With the choice things of heaven, with the dew,
And from the deep lying beneath,
14 And with the choice yield of the sun,
And with the choice produce of the months.

33:15 Hab 3:6

15 "And with the best things of the ancient mountains,
And with the choice things of the everlasting hills,

33:16 Ex 2:2-6; 3:2, 4

16 And with the choice things of the earth and its fullness,
And the favor of Him who dwelt in the bush.
Let it come to the head of Joseph,
And to the crown of the head of the one distinguished among his brothers.

33:17 Num 23:22; 1 Kin 22:11; Ps 44:5

17 "As the firstborn of his ox, majesty is his,
And his horns are the horns of the wild ox;
With them he will push the peoples,
All at once, *to* the ends of the earth.
And those are the ten thousands of Ephraim,
And those are the thousands of Manasseh."

33:18 Gen 49:13-15

18 Of Zebulun he said,
"Rejoice, Zebulun, in your going forth,
And, Issachar, in your tents.

33:19 Ex 15:17; Ps 2:6; Is 2:3; Ps 4:5; 51:19; Is 60:5

19 "They will call peoples *to* the mountain;
There they will offer righteous sacrifices;
For they will draw out the abundance of the seas,
And the hidden treasures of the sand."

33:20 Gen 49:19; Gen 49:9

20 Of Gad he said,
"Blessed is the one who enlarges Gad;

33:20–21 The people of the tribe of Gad received the best of the new land because they obeyed God by punishing Israel's wicked enemies. Punishment is unpleasant for both the giver and the receiver, but it is a necessary part of growth. If you are in a position that sometimes requires you to correct others, don't hold back from fulfilling your task. Understand that realistic discipline is important to character development. Always strive to be both just and merciful, keeping in mind the best interests of the person who must receive the punishment.

He lies down as a lion,
And tears the arm, also the crown of the head.
21 "Then he provided the first *part* for himself,
For there the ruler's portion was reserved;
And he came *with* the leaders of the people;
He executed the justice of the LORD,
And His ordinances with Israel."

33:21 Num 32:1-5; Num 34:14; Josh 4:12; Josh 22:1-3

22 Of Dan he said,
"Dan is a lion's whelp,
That leaps forth from Bashan."

33:22 Gen 49:16; Ezek 19:2, 3

23 Of Naphtali he said,
"O Naphtali, satisfied with favor,
And full of the blessing of the LORD,
Take possession of the sea and the south."

33:23 Gen 49:21

24 Of Asher he said,
"More blessed than sons is Asher;
May he be favored by his brothers,
And may he dip his foot in oil.
25 "Your locks will be iron and bronze,
And according to your days, so will your leisurely walk be.

33:24 Gen 49:20; Job 29:6

33:25 Ps 147:13; Deut 4:40; 32:47

26 "There is none like the God of [20]Jeshurun,
Who rides the heavens to your help,
And through the skies in His majesty.
27 "The eternal God is a dwelling place,
And underneath are the everlasting arms;
And He drove out the enemy from before you,
And said, 'Destroy!'
28 "So Israel dwells in security,
The fountain of Jacob secluded,
In a land of grain and new wine;
His heavens also drop down dew.
29 "Blessed are you, O Israel;
Who is like you, a people saved by the LORD,
Who is the shield of your help
And the sword of your majesty!
So your enemies will cringe before you,
And you will tread upon their high places."

33:26 Ex 15:11; Deut 4:35; Ps 86:8; Jer 10:6; Deut 10:14; Ps 68:33, 34; 104:3; Hab 3:8

33:27 Ps 90:1, 2; Gen 49:24; Ex 34:11; Josh 24:18; Deut 7:2

33:28 Deut 33:12; Jer 23:6; Num 23:9; Deut 32:8; Gen 27:28, 37; Deut 33:13

33:29 Ps 1:1; 32:1, 2; Deut 4:32; 2 Sam 7:23; Gen 15:1; Ps 33:20; 115:9-11; Ps 68:34; Ps 66:3; Num 33:52

The Death of Moses

34 Now Moses went up from the plains of Moab to Mount Nebo, to the top of Pisgah, which is opposite Jericho. And the LORD showed him all the land, Gilead as
far as Dan,
2 and all Naphtali and the land of Ephraim and Manasseh, and all the land of Judah
as far as the [21]western sea,
3 and the Negev and the plain in the valley of Jericho, the city of palm trees, as far as
Zoar.
4 Then the LORD said to him, "This is the land which I swore to Abraham, Isaac, and
Jacob, saying, 'I will give it to your descendants'; I have let you see *it* with your eyes, but
you shall not go over there."

34:1 Deut 32:49; Deut 32:52

34:2 Deut 11:24

34:3 Judg 1:16; 3:13; 2 Chr 28:15

34:4 Gen 12:7; 26:3; 28:13

20 I.e. Israel **21** I.e. Mediterranean Sea

33:24 Dipping feet in oil was a sign of prosperity.

33:27 Moses' song declares that God is our dwelling place, a refuge, our only true security. How often we entrust our lives to other things—perhaps money, career, a noble cause, or a lifelong dream. But our only true refuge is the eternal God, who always holds out his arms to catch us when the shaky supports that we trust collapse and we fall. No storm can destroy us when we take refuge in him. Those without God, however, must forever be cautious. One mistake may wipe them out. Living for God in this world may look like risky business. But it is the godless who are on shaky ground. Because God is our refuge, we can dare to be bold.

34:5 Num 12:7; Josh 1:1, 2; Deut 32:50

34:6 Deut 3:29; 4:46; Jude 9

34:7 Deut 31:2; Gen 27:1; 48:10

34:9 Num 27:18, 23; Is 11:2

34:10 Deut 18:15, 18; Ex 33:11; Num 12:8; Deut 5:4

5 So Moses the servant of the LORD died there in the land of Moab, according to the
word of the LORD.
6 And He buried him in the valley in the land of Moab, opposite Beth-peor; but no
man knows his burial place to this day.
7 Although Moses was one hundred and twenty years old when he died, his eye was
not dim, nor his vigor abated.
8 So the sons of Israel wept for Moses in the plains of Moab thirty days; then the days
of weeping *and* mourning for Moses came to an end.
9 Now Joshua the son of Nun was filled with the spirit of wisdom, for Moses had laid
his hands on him; and the sons of Israel listened to him and did as the LORD had commanded Moses.
10 Since that time no prophet has risen in Israel like Moses, whom the LORD knew
face to face,
11 for all the signs and wonders which the LORD sent him to perform in the land of
Egypt against Pharaoh, all his servants, and all his land,
12 and for all the mighty power and for all the great terror which Moses performed in
the sight of all Israel.

34:4, 10 Moses was the only person who ever spoke with God face-to-face (Exodus 33:11; Numbers 12:8). He was called Israel's greatest prophet. Yet even this great man was not allowed to enter the promised land because he disobeyed God (Numbers 20:12). No matter how good we are, or how much we've done for God, we sometimes disobey him. The result of our disobedience is that we will be disciplined. God disciplined Moses severely, but still called him his friend. When you experience the sting of God's discipline, respond as Moses did. Don't turn away in anger, embarrassment, or resentment. Instead, turn toward God with love, openness, and a desire to do better.

34:10–12 Moses, the man who did not want to be sent to Egypt because he was "slow of speech" (Exodus 4:10), delivered the three addresses to Israel that make up the book of Deuteronomy. God gave him the power to develop from a stuttering shepherd into a national leader and powerful orator. His courage, humility, and wisdom molded the Hebrew slaves into a nation. But Moses was one person who did not let success go to his head. In the end, God was still Moses' best friend. His love, respect, and awe for God had grown daily throughout his life. Moses knew that it was not any greatness in himself that made him successful; it was the greatness of the all-powerful God in whom he trusted. There were many great and powerful prophets during the time of the kings. But it would be more than a thousand years before One greater than Moses would appear—Jesus.

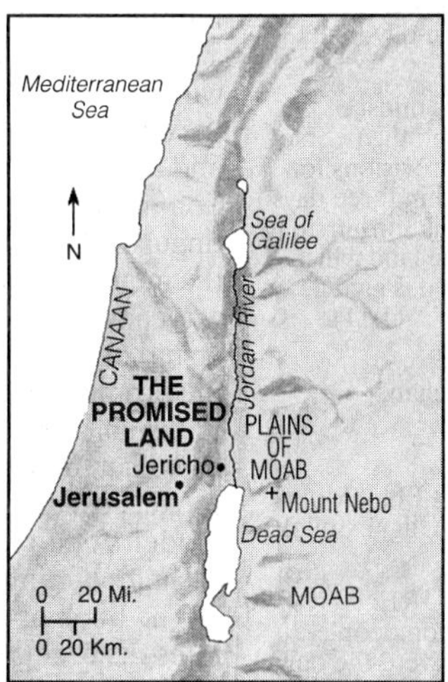

THE DEATH OF MOSES
Just before Moses died, he climbed Mount Nebo. Although he could not enter the promised land, God showed him its beauty from Mount Nebo's peak.

JOSHUA

Exodus from Egypt 1446 B.C. (1280 B.C.)	Israelites enter Canaan 1406 (1240)	Judges begin to rule 1375 (1220)	T H E D A Y S O F
	CONQUEST OF CANAAN		

VITAL STATISTICS

PURPOSE:
To give the history of Israel's conquest of the promised land

AUTHOR:
Joshua, except for the ending which may have been written by the high priest, Phinehas, an eyewitness to the events recounted there

SETTING:
Canaan, also called the promised land, which occupied the same general geographical territory of modern-day Israel

KEY VERSE:
" 'Pass through the midst of the camp and command the people, saying, "Prepare provisions for yourselves, for within three days you are to cross this Jordan, to go in to possess the land which the LORD your God is giving you, to possess it" ' " (1:11).

KEY PEOPLE:
Joshua, Rahab, Achan, Phinehas, Eleazar

KEY PLACES:
Jericho, Ai, Mount Ebal, Mount Gerizim, Gibeon, Gilgal, Shiloh, Shechem

SPECIAL FEATURE:
Out of over a million people, Joshua and Caleb were the only two who left Egypt and entered the promised land.

REMEMBER the childhood game "follow the leader"? The idea was to mimic the antics of the person in front of you in the line of boys and girls winding through the neighborhood. Being a follower was all right, but being leader was the most fun, creating imaginative routes and tasks for everyone else to copy.

In real life, great leaders are rare. Often, men and women are elected or appointed to leadership positions, but then falter or fail to act. Others abuse their power to satisfy their egos, crushing their subjects and squandering resources. But without faithful, ethical, and effective leaders, people wander.

For 40 years, Israel had journeyed a circuitous route through the wilderness, but *not* because they were following their leader. Quite the opposite was true—with failing faith, they had refused to obey God and to conquer Canaan. So they wandered. Finally, the new generation was ready to cross the Jordan and possess the land. Having distinguished himself as a man of faith and courage (he and Caleb gave the minority scout report recorded in Numbers 13:30—14:9), Joshua was chosen to be Moses' successor. This book records Joshua's leadership of the people of God as they finish their march and conquer the promised land.

Joshua was a brilliant military leader and a strong spiritual influence. But the key to his success was his submission to God. When God spoke, Joshua listened and obeyed. Joshua's obedience served as a model. As a result, Israel remained faithful to God throughout Joshua's lifetime.

The book of Joshua is divided into two main parts. The first narrates the events surrounding the conquest of Canaan. After crossing the Jordan River on dry ground, the Israelites camped near the mighty city of Jericho. God commanded the people to conquer Jericho by marching around the city 13 times, blowing trumpets, and shouting. Because they followed God's unique battle strategy, they won (chapter 6). After the destruction of Jericho, they set out against the small town of Ai. Their first attack was driven back because one of the Israelites (Achan) had sinned (chapter 7). After the men of Israel stoned Achan and his family—purging the community of its sin—the Israelites succeeded in capturing Ai (chapter 8). In their next battle against the Amorites, God even made the sun stand still to aid them in their victory (chapter 10). Finally, after defeating other assorted Canaanites led by Jabin and his allies (chapter 11), they possessed most of the land.

Part two of the book of Joshua records the assignment and settlement of the captured territory (chapters 13—22). The book concludes with Joshua's farewell address and his death (chapters 23–24).

Joshua was committed to obeying God, and this book is about obedience. Whether conquering enemies or settling the land, God's people were required to do it God's way. In his final message to the people, Joshua underscored the importance of obeying God. "So take diligent heed to yourselves to love the LORD your God" (23:11), and "choose

T H E J U D G E S

United Kingdom under Saul 1050 (1045)

David becomes king 1010

for yourselves today whom you will serve. . . . but as for me and my house, we will serve the LORD" (24:15). Read Joshua and make a fresh commitment to obey God today. Decide to follow your Lord wherever he leads and whatever it costs.

THE BLUEPRINT

A. ENTERING THE PROMISED LAND (1:1—5:12) 1. Joshua leads the nation 2. Crossing the Jordan	Joshua demonstrated his faith in God as he took up the challenge to lead the nation. The Israelites reaffirmed their commitment to God by obediently setting out across the Jordan River to possess the land. As we live the Christian life, we need to cross over from the old life to the new, put off our selfish desires, and press on to possess all God has planned for us. Like Joshua and Israel, we need courageous faith to live the new life.
B. CONQUERING THE PROMISED LAND (5:13—12:24) 1. Joshua attacks the center of the land 2. Joshua attacks the southern kings 3. Joshua attacks the northern kings 4. Summary of conquests	Joshua and his army moved from city to city, cleansing the land of its wickedness by destroying every trace of idol worship. Conflict with evil is inevitable, and we should be as merciless as Israel in destroying sin in our lives.
C. DIVIDING THE PROMISED LAND (13:1—24:33) 1. The tribes receive their land 2. Special cities are set aside 3. Eastern tribes return home 4. Joshua's farewell to the leaders	Joshua urged the Israelites to continue to follow the Lord and worship him alone. The people had seen God deliver them from many enemies and miraculously provide for all their needs, but they were prone to wander from the Lord. Even though we may have experienced God at work in our lives, we, too, must continually renew our commitment to obey him above all other authority and to worship him alone.

MEGATHEMES

THEME	EXPLANATION	IMPORTANCE
Success	God gave success to the Israelites when they obeyed his master plan, not when they followed their own desires. Victory came when they trusted in him rather than in their military power, money, muscle, or mental capacity.	God's work done in God's way will bring his success. The standard for success, however, is not to be set by the society around us but by God's Word. We must adjust our minds to God's way of thinking in order to see his standard for success.
Faith	The Israelites demonstrated their faith by trusting God daily to save and guide them. By noticing how God fulfilled his promises in the past, they developed strong confidence that he would be faithful in the future.	Our strength to do God's work comes from trusting him. His promises reassure us of his love and that he will be there to guide us in the decisions and struggles we face. Faith begins with believing he can be trusted.
Guidance	God gave instructions to Israel for every aspect of their lives. His law guided their daily living, and his specific marching orders gave them victory in battle.	Guidance from God for daily living can be found in his Word. By staying in touch with God, we will have the needed wisdom to meet the great challenges of life.
Leadership	Joshua was an example of an excellent leader. He was confident in God's strength, courageous in the face of opposition, and willing to seek God's advice.	To be a strong leader like Joshua, we must be ready to listen and to move quickly when God instructs us. Once we have his instructions, we must be diligent in carrying them out. Strong leaders are led by God.
Conquest	God commanded his people to conquer the Canaanites and take all their land. Completing this mission would have fulfilled God's promise to Abraham and brought judgment on the evil people living there. Unfortunately, Israel never finished the job.	The Israelites were faithful in accomplishing their mission at first, but their commitment faltered. To love God means more than being enthusiastic about him. We must complete all the work he gives us and apply his instructions to every corner of our lives.

KEY PLACES IN JOSHUA

1 Shittim The story of Joshua begins with the Israelites camping at Shittim. The Israelites under Joshua were ready to enter and conquer Canaan. But before the nation moved out, Joshua received instructions from God (1:1–18).

2 Jordan River The entire nation prepared to cross this river, which was swollen from spring rains. After the spies returned from Jericho with a positive report, Joshua prepared the priests and people for a miracle. As the priests carried the ark into the Jordan River, the water stopped flowing, and the entire nation crossed on dry ground into the promised land (2:1—4:24).

3 Gilgal After crossing the Jordan River, the Israelites camped at Gilgal, where they renewed their commitment to God and celebrated the Passover, the festival commemorating their deliverance from Egypt (see Exodus). As Joshua made plans for the attack on Jericho, an angel appeared to him (5:1–15).

4 Jericho The walled city of Jericho seemed a formidable enemy. But when Joshua followed God's plans, the great walls were no obstacle. The city was conquered with only the obedient marching of the people (6:1–27).

5 Ai Victory could not continue without obedience to God. That is why the disobedience of one man, Achan, brought defeat to the entire nation in the first battle against Ai. But once the sin was recognized and punished, God told Joshua to take heart and try Ai once again. This time the city was taken (7:1—8:29).

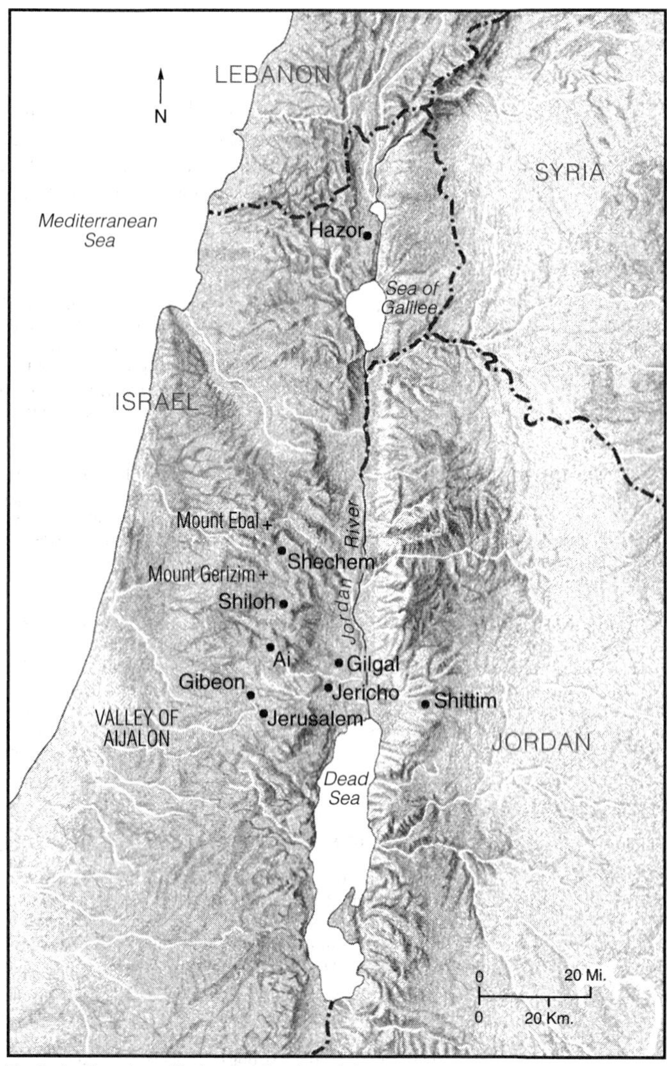

The broken lines (—·—·) indicate modern boundaries.

6 The Mountains of Ebal and Gerizim After the defeat of Ai, Joshua built an altar at Mount Ebal. Then the people divided themselves, half at the foot of Mount Ebal, half at the foot of Mount Gerizim. The priests stood between the mountains holding the ark of the covenant as Joshua read God's law to all the people (8:30–35).

7 Gibeon It was just after the Israelites reaffirmed their covenant with God that their leaders made a major mistake in judgment: They were tricked into making a peace treaty with the city of Gibeon. The Gibeonites pretended that they had traveled a long distance and asked the Israelites for a treaty. The leaders made the agreement without consulting God. The trick was soon discovered, but because the treaty had been made, Israel could not go back on its word. As a result, the Gibeonites saved their own lives, but they were forced to become Israel's slaves (9:1–27).

8 Valley of Aijalon The king of Jerusalem was very angry at Gibeon for making a peace treaty with the Israelites. He gathered armies from four other cities to attack the city. Gibeon summoned Joshua for help. Joshua took immediate action. Leaving Gilgal, he attacked the coalition by surprise. As the battle waged on and moved into the valley of Aijalon, Joshua prayed for the sun to stand still until the enemy could be destroyed (10:1–43).

9 Hazor Up north in Hazor, King Jabin mobilized the kings of the surrounding cities to unite and crush Israel. But God gave Joshua and Israel victory (11:1–23).

10 Shiloh After the armies of Canaan were conquered, Israel gathered at Shiloh to set up the tabernacle. This movable building had been the nation's center of worship during their years of wandering. The seven tribes who had not received their land were given their allotments (18:1—19:51).

11 Shechem Before Joshua died he called the entire nation together at Shechem to remind them that it was God who had given them their land and that only with God's help could they keep it. The people vowed to follow God. As long as Joshua was alive, the land was at rest from war and trouble (24:1–33).

A. ENTERING THE PROMISED LAND (1:1—5:12)

After wandering for 40 years in the desert, a new generation is ready to enter Canaan. But first God prepares both Joshua and the nation by teaching them the importance of courageous and consistent faith. The nation then miraculously crosses the Jordan River to begin the long-awaited conquest of the promised land. Like Joshua, we too need faith to begin and continue living the Christian life.

1. Joshua leads the nation

God's Charge to Joshua

1 Now it came about after the death of Moses the servant of the LORD, that the LORD
spoke to Joshua the son of Nun, Moses' [1]servant, saying,
2 "Moses My servant is dead; now therefore arise, cross this Jordan, you and all this
people, to the land which I am giving to them, to the sons of Israel.
3 "Every place on which the sole of your foot treads, I have given it to you, just as I
spoke to Moses.
4 "From the wilderness and this Lebanon, even as far as the great river, the river Euphrates, all the land of the Hittites, and as far as the Great Sea toward the setting of the
sun will be your territory.
5 "No man will *be able to* stand before you all the days of your life. Just as I have been
with Moses, I will be with you; I will not fail you or forsake you.

1:3 Deut 11:24

1:4 Gen 15:18; Num 34:3

1:5 Deut 7:24; Deut 31:6, 7; Heb 13:5

1 Or *minister*

TAKE THE LAND

God told Joshua to lead the Israelites into the promised land (also called Canaan) and conquer it. This was not an act of imperialism or aggression, but an act of judgment. Here are some of the earlier passages in the Bible where God promised to give this land to the Israelites and the reasons for doing so.

Passage	
Genesis 12:1–3	God promised to bless Abraham and make his descendants into a great nation
Genesis 15:16	God would choose the right time for Israel to enter Canaan because the nations living there then would be wicked and ripe for judgment (their sin would reach full measure)
Genesis 17:7–8	God promised to give all the land of Canaan to Abraham's descendants
Exodus 33:1–3	God promised to help the Israelites drive out all the evil nations from Canaan
Deuteronomy 4:5–8	The Israelites were to be an example of right living to the whole world; this would not work if they intermingled with the wicked Canaanites
Deuteronomy 7:1–5	The Israelites were to utterly wipe the Canaanites out because of their wickedness and because of Israel's call to purity
Deuteronomy 12:2	The Israelites were to completely destroy the Canaanite altars so nothing would tempt them away from worshiping God alone

---

1:1 As the book of Joshua opens, the Israelites are camped along the east bank of the Jordan River at the very edge of the promised land and are completing the mourning period for Moses, who has just died (Deuteronomy 34:7–8). Thirty-nine years earlier (after spending a year at Mount Sinai receiving God's law), the Israelites had an opportunity to enter the promised land, but they failed to trust God to give them victory. As a result, God did not allow them to enter the land, but made them wander in the wilderness until the disobedient generation had all died.

During their wilderness wanderings, the Israelites obeyed God's laws. They also taught the new generation to obey God's laws so that they might enter the promised land (also called Canaan). As the children grew, they were often reminded that faith and obedience to God brought victory, while unbelief and disobedience brought tragedy. When the last of the older generation had died and the new generation had become adults, the Israelites prepared to make their long-awaited claim on the promised land.

1:1–5 Joshua succeeded Moses as Israel's leader. What qualifications did he have to become the leader of a nation? (1) God appointed him (Numbers 27:18–23). (2) He was one of only two living eyewitnesses to the Egyptian plagues and the exodus from Egypt. (3) He was Moses' personal aide for 40 years. (4) Of the 12 spies, only he and Caleb showed complete confidence that God would help them conquer the land.

1:2 Because Joshua had assisted Moses for many years, he was well prepared to take over the leadership of the nation. Changes in leadership are common in many organizations. At such times, a smooth transition is essential for the establishment of the new administration. This doesn't happen unless new leaders are trained. If you are currently in a leadership position, begin preparing someone to take your place. Then, when you leave or are promoted, operations can continue to run efficiently. If you want to be a leader, learn from others so that you will be prepared when the opportunity comes.

1:5 Joshua's new job consisted of leading more than two million people into a strange new land and conquering it. What a challenge—even for a man of Joshua's caliber! Every new job is a challenge. Without God it can be frightening. With God it can be a great adventure. Just as God was with Joshua, so he is with us as we face our new challenges. We may not conquer nations, but every day we face tough situations, difficult people, and temptations. However, God promises that he will never abandon us or fail to help us. By asking God to direct us we can conquer many of life's challenges.

6 "Be strong and courageous, for you shall give this people possession of the land which 1:6
I swore to their fathers to give them. Deut 31:6, 7, 23
7 "Only be strong and very courageous; be careful to do according to all the law which 1:7
Moses My servant commanded you; do not turn from it to the right or to the left, so that Deut 5:32
you may have success wherever you go.
8 "This book of the law shall not depart from your mouth, but you shall meditate on it 1:8
day and night, so that you may be careful to do according to all that is written in it; for Deut 31:24; Josh 8:34; Deut 29:9; Ps
then you will make your way prosperous, and then you will have success. 1:1-3
9 "Have I not commanded you? Be strong and courageous! Do not tremble or be dis- 1:9
mayed, for the LORD your God is with you wherever you go." Josh 1:7; Deut 31:8

Joshua Assumes Command

10 Then Joshua commanded the officers of the people, saying,
11 "Pass through the midst of the camp and command the people, saying, 'Prepare pro- 1:11
visions for yourselves, for within three days you are to cross this Jordan, to go in to pos- Josh 3:2
sess the land which the LORD your God is giving you, to possess it.' "
12 To the Reubenites and to the Gadites and to the half-tribe of Manasseh, Joshua said, 1:12
13 "Remember the word which Moses the servant of the LORD commanded you, say- Num 32:20-22
ing, 'The LORD your God gives you rest and will give you this land.' 1:13
14 "Your wives, your little ones, and your cattle shall remain in the land which Moses Deut 3:18-20
gave you beyond the Jordan, but you shall cross before your brothers in battle array, all
your valiant warriors, and shall help them,
15 until the LORD gives your brothers rest, as *He gives* you, and they also possess the 1:15
land which the LORD your God is giving them. Then you shall return to your own land, Josh 22:4; Josh 1:1
and possess that which Moses the servant of the LORD gave you beyond the Jordan toward the sunrise."
16 They answered Joshua, saying, "All that you have commanded us we will do, and
wherever you send us we will go.
17 "Just as we obeyed Moses in all things, so we will obey you; only may the LORD your 1:17
God be with you as He was with Moses. Josh 1:5, 9
18 "Anyone who rebels against your command and does not obey your words in all that
you command him, shall be put to death; only be strong and courageous." 2:1 Num 25:1; Josh 3:1; Heb 11:31; James 2:25

Rahab Shelters Spies

2 Then Joshua the son of Nun sent two men as spies secretly from Shittim, saying, "Go,
view the land, especially Jericho." So they went and came into the house of a harlot
whose name was Rahab, and lodged there.

1:6–8 Many people think that prosperity and success come from having power, influential personal contacts, and a relentless desire to get ahead. But the strategy for gaining prosperity that God taught Joshua goes against such criteria. He said that to succeed Joshua must (1) be strong and courageous because the task ahead would not be easy, (2) obey God's law, and (3) constantly read and study the book of the law—God's Word. To be successful, follow God's words to Joshua. You may not succeed by the world's standards, but you will be a success in God's eyes—and his opinion lasts forever.

1:12–15 During the previous year, the tribes of Reuben and Gad and the half-tribe of Manasseh had asked Moses if they could settle just east of the promised land. The area was excellent pastureland for their large flocks. Moses agreed to give them the land on one condition—that they help their fellow tribes enter and conquer the promised land. Only after the land was conquered could they return to their homes. Now it was time for these three tribes to live up to their agreement.

1:13 God was giving the people rest. This was wonderful news to these people who had been on the move for their entire lives. The people who had no land would be given a land of their own, and they would be able to settle and to "rest."

1:16 If everyone had tried to conquer the promised land his own way, chaos would have resulted. In order to complete the enormous task of conquering the land, everyone had to agree to the leader's plan and be willing to support and obey him. If we are going to complete the tasks God has given us, we must fully agree to his plan, pledge ourselves to obey it, and put his principles into action. Agreeing to God's plan means both knowing what the plan is (as found in the Bible) and carrying it out daily.

1:18 When God commissioned Joshua, he was told three times to be strong and courageous (see 1:6–7, 9). Here, Joshua was given the same kind of encouragement from the people. Apparently, he took God's message to heart and found the strength and courage he needed in his relationship with God. The next time you are afraid to do what you know is right, remember that strength and courage are readily available from God.

2:1 Why did Joshua send the spies secretly? As far as he knew, he would be attacking a heavily fortified city using conventional warfare tactics. He needed strategic information about the city for the upcoming battle. But he also knew that this might draw criticism from the other leaders. After all, the last time spies were sent, the report they brought back caused disastrous problems (see Numbers 13:1—14:4). While he did not want to move ahead without information, he also did not want to cause the people to stumble and question his wisdom and ability to lead the nation.

2 It was told the king of Jericho, saying, "Behold, men from the sons of Israel have
come here tonight to search out the land."
3 And the king of Jericho sent *word* to Rahab, saying, "Bring out the men who have
come to you, who have entered your house, for they have come to search out all the land."
2:4 2 Sam 17:19 4 But the woman had taken the two men and hidden them, and she said, "Yes, the
men came to me, but I did not know where they were from.

JOSHUA

One of the greatest challenges facing leaders is to replace themselves, training others to become leaders. Many outstanding accomplishments have been started by someone with great ability whose life or career ended before the vision became reality. The fulfillment of that dream then became the responsibility of that person's successor. Death is the ultimate deadline for leadership. One of the best tests of our leadership is our willingness and ability to train another for our position.

Moses made an excellent decision when he chose Joshua as his assistant. That choice was later confirmed by God himself when he instructed Moses to commission Joshua as his successor (Numbers 27:15–23). Joshua had played a key role in the exodus from Egypt. Introduced as the field general of Israel's army, he was the only person allowed to accompany Moses partway up the mountain when Moses received the law. Joshua and Caleb were the only two among the 12 spies to bring back an encouraging report after being sent into the promised land the first time. Other references show him to have been Moses' constant shadow. His basic training was living with Moses—experiencing firsthand what it meant to lead God's people. This was modeling at its best!

Who is your Moses? Who is your Joshua? You are part of the chain of God's ongoing work in the world. You are modeling yourself after others, and others are patterning their lives after you. How important is God to those you want to be like? Do those who are watching you see God reflected in every area of your life? Ask God to lead you to a trustworthy Moses. Ask him to make you a good Joshua.

Strengths and accomplishments:
- Moses' assistant and successor
- One of only two adults who experienced Egyptian slavery and lived to enter the promised land
- Led the Israelites into their God-given homeland
- Brilliant military strategist
- Faithful to ask God's direction in the challenges he faced

Lessons from his life:
- Effective leadership is often the product of good preparation and encouragement
- The persons after whom we pattern ourselves will have a definite effect on us
- A person committed to God provides the best model for us

Vital statistics:
- Where: Egypt, the wilderness of Sinai, and Canaan (the promised land)
- Occupations: Special assistant to Moses, warrior, leader
- Relative: Father: Nun
- Contemporaries: Moses, Caleb, Miriam, Aaron

Key verses:
"Moses did just as the LORD commanded him; and he took Joshua and set him before Eleazar the priest and before all the congregation. Then he laid his hands on him and commissioned him, just as the LORD had spoken through Moses" (Numbers 27:22–23).

Joshua is also mentioned in Exodus 17:9–14; 24:13; 32:17; 33:11; Numbers 11:28; 13; 14; 26:65; 27:18–23; 32:11–12, 28; 34:17; Deuteronomy 1:38; 3:21, 28; 31:3, 7, 14, 23; 34:9; the book of Joshua; Judges 2:6–9; and 1 Kings 16:34.

2:1 Why would the spies stop at the house of Rahab, a harlot (prostitute)? (1) It was a good place to gather information and have no questions asked in return. (2) Rahab's house was in an ideal location for a quick escape because it was built into the city wall (2:15). (3) God directed the spies to Rahab's house because he knew her heart was open to him and that she would be instrumental in the Israelite victory over Jericho. God often uses people with simple faith to accomplish his great purposes, no matter what kind of past they have had or how insignificant they seem to be. Rahab didn't allow her past to keep her from the new role God had for her.

2:4–5 Was Rahab justified in lying to save the lives of the spies? Although the Bible does not speak negatively about her lie, it is clear that lying is sin. In Hebrews 11:31, however, Rahab is commended for her faith in God. Her lie is not mentioned. Several explanations have been offered: (1) God forgave Rahab's lie because of her faith; (2) Rahab was simply deceiving the enemy, a normal and acceptable practice in wartime; (3) because Rahab was not a Jew, she could not be held responsible for keeping the moral standards set forth in God's law; (4) Rahab broke a lesser principle—telling the truth—to uphold a higher principle—protecting God's people.

There may have been another way to save the lives of the Israelite spies. But under the pressure of the moment, Rahab had to make a choice. Most of us will face dilemmas at one time or another. We may feel that there is no perfect solution to our problem. Fortunately, God does not demand that our judgment be perfect in all situations. He simply asks us to put our trust in him and to do the best we know how. Rahab did that and was commended for her faith.

5 "It came about when *it was time* to shut the gate at dark, that the men went out; I do
not know where the men went. Pursue them quickly, for you will overtake them."
6 But she had brought them up to the roof and hidden them in the stalks of flax which **2:6**
she had laid in order on the roof. James 2:25
7 So the men pursued them on the road to the Jordan to the fords; and as soon as
those who were pursuing them had gone out, they shut the gate.
8 Now before they lay down, she came up to them on the roof,
9 and said to the men, "I know that the LORD has given you the land, and that the **2:9**
terror of you has fallen on us, and that all the inhabitants of the land have melted away Num 20:24; Josh 9:24; Ex 23:27; Deut
before you. 2:25; Josh 9:9, 10
10 "For we have heard how the LORD dried up the water of the Red Sea before you **2:10**
when you came out of Egypt, and what you did to the two kings of the Amorites who Ex 14:21; Num
were beyond the Jordan, to Sihon and Og, whom you utterly destroyed. 23:22; 24:8; Num 21:21-35
11 "When we heard *it,* our hearts melted and no courage remained in any man any longer **2:11**
because of you; for the LORD your God, He is God in heaven above and on earth be- Josh 5:1; 7:5; Ps
neath. 22:14; Is 13:7; 19:1; Deut 4:39
12 "Now therefore, please swear to me by the LORD, since I have dealt kindly with you, **2:12**
that you also will deal kindly with my father's household, and give me a pledge of truth, Josh 2:18, 19
13 and spare my father and my mother and my brothers and my sisters, with all who
belong to them, and deliver our [2]lives from death."
14 So the men said to her, "Our life for yours if you do not tell this business of ours; **2:14**
and it shall come about when the LORD gives us the land that we will deal kindly and Gen 24:49
faithfully with you."

The Promise to Rahab

15 Then she let them down by a rope through the window, for her house was on the
city wall, so that she was living on the wall.
16 She said to them, "Go to the hill country, so that the pursuers will not happen upon **2:16**
you, and hide yourselves there for three days until the pursuers return. Then afterward James 2:25
you may go on your way."
17 The men said to her, "We *shall be* free from this oath to you which you have made **2:17**
us swear, Gen 24:8
18 unless, when we come into the land, you tie this cord of scarlet thread in the win- **2:18**
dow through which you let us down, and gather to yourself into the house your father Josh 2:12
and your mother and your brothers and all your father's household.
19 "It shall come about that anyone who goes out of the doors of your house into the **2:19** Matt 27:25

2 Lit *souls*

SPY MISSION TO JERICHO
Two spies left the Israelite camp at Shittim, crossed the Jordan River, and slipped into Jericho. The city was built around an oasis in the midst of a hot and desolate valley 840 feet below sea level. Jericho was the first major city the Israelites set out to conquer.

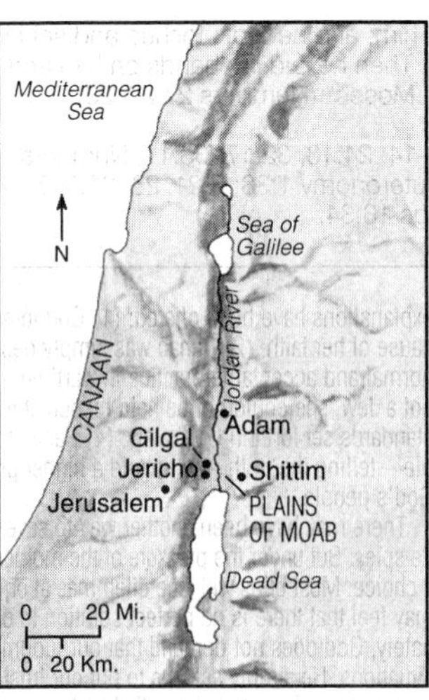

2:6 Flax was harvested in the fields and piled high on the rooftops to dry. It was then made into yarn which was used to make linen cloth. Flax grows to a height of three or four feet. Stacked on the roof, it made an excellent hiding place for the spies.

2:8–13 Many would assume that Rahab—a pagan, a Canaanite, and a prostitute—would never be interested in God. Yet Rahab was willing to risk everything she had for a God she barely knew. We must not gauge a person's interest in God by his or her background, life-style, or appearance. We should let nothing get in the way of our telling people about God.

2:11 Rahab recognized something that many of the Israelites did not—the God of heaven is not an ordinary god! He is all-powerful. The people of Jericho were afraid because they had heard the news of God's extraordinary power in defeating the armies across the Jordan River. Today we can worship this same powerful, miracle-working God. He is powerful enough to destroy mighty, wicked armies, as he did in Jericho. He is also powerful enough to save us from certain death, as he did with Rahab.

2:15 In Joshua's day it was common to build houses on city walls. Many cities had two walls about 12 to 15 feet apart. Houses were built on wooden logs laid across the tops of the two walls. Rahab may have lived in such a house with a window that looked out over the outside wall.

street, his blood *shall be* on his own head, and we *shall be* free; but anyone who is with
you in the house, his blood *shall be* on our head if a hand is *laid* on him.
20 "But if you tell this business of ours, then we shall be free from the oath which you
have made us swear."
21 She said, "According to your words, so be it." So she sent them away, and they departed; and she tied the scarlet cord in the window.
22 They departed and came to the hill country, and remained there for three days until
the pursuers returned. Now the pursuers had sought *them* all along the road, but had
not found *them*.
23 Then the two men returned and came down from the hill country and crossed over
and came to Joshua the son of Nun, and they related to him all that had happened to
them.
2:24 Josh 2:9 24 They said to Joshua, "Surely the LORD has given all the land into our hands; moreover, all the inhabitants of the land have melted away before us."

2. Crossing the Jordan

3:1 Josh 2:1 **3** Then Joshua rose early in the morning; and he and all the sons of Israel set out from
Shittim and came to the Jordan, and they lodged there before they crossed.
3:2 Josh 1:11 2 At the end of three days the officers went through the midst of the camp;

RAHAB

Rahab was a prostitute in the city of Jericho. As a prostitute, she lived on the edge of society, one stop short of rejection. Her house, built right into the city wall, provided both lodging and favors to travelers. It was a natural place for the Israelite spies to stay, as they would be mistaken for Rahab's customers.

Stories about the Israelites had been circulating for some time, but now it was evident that the Israelites were about to invade. Living on the wall, Rahab felt especially vulnerable. Yet while she shared the general mood of fear with the rest of Jericho's population, she alone turned to the Lord for her salvation. Her faith gave her the courage to hide the spies and lie to the authorities. Rahab knew her position was dangerous; she could have been killed if she were caught harboring the Israelites. Rahab took the risk, however, because she sensed that the Israelites relied on a God worth trusting. And God rewarded Rahab by promising safety for her and her family.

God works through people—like Rahab—whom we are inclined to reject. God remembers her because of her faith, not her profession. If at times you feel like a failure, remember that Rahab rose above her situation through her trust in God. You can do the same!

Strengths and accomplishments:
- Relative of Boaz, and thus an ancestor of David and Jesus
- One of only two women listed in the Hall of Faith in Hebrews 11
- Resourceful, willing to help others at great cost to herself

Weakness and mistake:
- She was a prostitute

Lesson from her life:
- She did not let fear affect her faith in God's ability to deliver

Vital statistics:
- Where: Jericho
- Occupations: Prostitute/innkeeper, later became a wife
- Relatives: Ancestor of David and Jesus (Matthew 1:5)
- Contemporary: Joshua

Key verse:
"By faith Rahab the harlot did not perish along with those who were disobedient, after she had welcomed the spies in peace" (Hebrews 11:31).

Rahab's story is told in Joshua 2 and 6:22–23. She is also mentioned in Matthew 1:5; Hebrews 11:31; and James 2:25.

3:2–4 The ark of the covenant was Israel's most sacred treasure. It was a symbol of God's presence and power. The ark was a golden rectangular box with two cherubim (angels) facing each other on the lid. Inside the ark were the tablets of the Ten Commandments Moses received from God, a jar of manna (the bread God miraculously sent from heaven during the wilderness wanderings), and Aaron's staff (the symbol of the high priest's authority). According to God's law, only the Levites could carry the ark. The ark was constructed at the same time as the tabernacle (Exodus 37:1–9) and placed in the sanctuary's most sacred room.

3 and they commanded the people, saying, "When you see the ark of the covenant of **3:3**
the LORD your God with the Levitical priests carrying it, then you shall set out from your Deut 31:9
place and go after it.
4 "However, there shall be between you and it a distance of about 2,000 cubits by
measure. Do not come near it, that you may know the way by which you shall go, for you
have not passed this way before."
5 Then Joshua said to the people, "Consecrate yourselves, for tomorrow the LORD **3:5**
will do wonders among you." Ex 19:10, 11; Josh 7:13
6 And Joshua spoke to the priests, saying, "Take up the ark of the covenant and cross
over ahead of the people." So they took up the ark of the covenant and went ahead of
the people.
7 Now the LORD said to Joshua, "This day I will begin to exalt you in the sight of all **3:7**
Israel, that they may know that just as I have been with Moses, I will be with you. Josh 4:14
8 "You shall, moreover, command the priests who are carrying the ark of the covenant,
saying, 'When you come to the edge of the waters of the Jordan, you shall stand *still* in
the Jordan.' "
9 Then Joshua said to the sons of Israel, "Come here, and hear the words of the LORD
your God."
10 Joshua said, "By this you shall know that the living God is among you, and that He **3:10**
will assuredly dispossess from before you the Canaanite, the Hittite, the Hivite, the Per- Deut 5:26; 1 Thess 1:9; Ex 33:2; Deut
izzite, the Girgashite, the Amorite, and the Jebusite. 7:1
11 "Behold, the ark of the covenant of the Lord of all the earth is crossing over ahead of **3:11**
you into the Jordan. Job 41:11; Ps 24:1; Zech 6:5
12 "Now then, take for yourselves twelve men from the tribes of Israel, one man for
each tribe. **3:12** Josh 4:2
13 "It shall come about when the soles of the feet of the priests who carry the ark of the
LORD, the Lord of all the earth, rest in the waters of the Jordan, the waters of the Jor- **3:13**
dan will be cut off, *and* the waters which are flowing down from above will stand in one Ex 15:8
heap."
14 So when the people set out from their tents to cross the Jordan with the priests carry- **3:14**
ing the ark of the covenant before the people, Ps 132:8; Acts 7:44f
15 and when those who carried the ark came into the Jordan, and the feet of the priests **3:15**
carrying the ark were dipped in the edge of the water (for the Jordan overflows all its 1 Chr 12:15; Jer
banks all the days of harvest), 12:5; 49:19

3:5 Before entering the promised land, the Israelites were to perform a consecration (purification) ceremony. This was often done before making a sacrifice or, as in this case, before witnessing a great act of God. God's law stated that a person could become unclean for many reasons—eating certain foods (Leviticus 11), childbirth (Leviticus 12), disease (Leviticus 13, 14), touching a dead person (Numbers 19:11–22). God used these various outward signs of uncleanness to illustrate people's inward uncleanness that comes as a result of sin. The consecration ceremony pictured the importance of approaching God with a pure heart. Like the Israelites, we need God's forgiveness before we approach him.

3:9 Just before crossing over into the promised land, Joshua gathered the people to hear the words of the Lord. Their excitement was high. No doubt they wanted to rush on, but Joshua made them stop and listen. We live in a fast-paced age where everyone rushes just to keep up. It is easy to get caught up in our tasks, becoming too busy for what God says is most important—listening to his words. Before making your schedule, take time to focus on what God wants from all your activities. Knowing what God has said before you rush into your day may help you avoid foolish mistakes.

3:10 Why would God help the Israelites drive out these nations from their native land? God had punished Israel first for its disobedience. He then turned to the rest of the nations. Genesis 15:16 implies that the people of Canaan were wicked and deserved to be punished for their terrible sins. Israel was to be a vehicle for this punishment. More important was the fact that Israel, as a holy nation, could not live among such evil and idolatrous people. To do so would be to invite sin into their lives. The only way to prevent Israel from being infected by evil religions was to drive out those who practiced them. Israel, however, failed to drive everyone out as God had told them to do. It wasn't long before Israel—the nation God chose to be his holy people—began following the evil practices of the Canaanites.

3:13–14 The Israelites were eager to enter the promised land, conquer nations, and live peacefully. But first they had to cross the flood-level waters of the Jordan River. God gave them specific instructions: in order to cross, the priests had to step into the water. What if these priests had been afraid to take that first step? Often God provides no solution to our problems until we trust him and move ahead with what we know we should do. What are the rivers, or obstacles, in your life? In obedience to God, take that first step into the water.

3:13–17 God had parted the waters of the Red Sea to let the people out of Egypt (Exodus 14), and here he parted the Jordan River to let them enter Canaan. These miracles showed Israel that God keeps his promises. God's presence among his people and his faithfulness to them made the entire journey from Egypt to the promised land possible. He was with them at the end of their wanderings just as he was with them in the beginning.

3:15–16 The Israelites crossed the Jordan River in the spring, when it was overflowing its banks. God chose the time when the river was at its highest to demonstrate his power—parting the waters so that the entire nation could cross on dry ground. Some say that God used a natural occurrence (such as a landslide) to stop the waters of the Jordan; others say he did it by a direct

3:16 Ps 66:6; 74:15; 114:3, 5; Josh 3:13; Deut 1:1

16 the waters which were flowing down from above stood *and* rose up in one heap, a great distance away at Adam, the city that is beside Zarethan; and those which were flowing down toward the sea of the Arabah, the Salt Sea, were completely cut off. So the people crossed opposite Jericho.

3:17 Ex 14:21, 22, 29

17 And the priests who carried the ark of the covenant of the LORD stood firm on dry ground in the middle of the Jordan while all Israel crossed on dry ground, until all the nation had finished crossing the Jordan.

Memorial Stones from Jordan

4:1 Deut 27:2; Josh 3:17

4 Now when all the nation had finished crossing the Jordan, the LORD spoke to Joshua, saying,

4:2 Josh 3:12

2 "Take for yourselves twelve men from the people, one man from each tribe,

4:3 Josh 4:20

3 and command them, saying, 'Take up for yourselves twelve stones from here out of the middle of the Jordan, from the place where the priests' feet are standing firm, and carry them over with you and lay them down in the lodging place where you will lodge tonight.' "

4 So Joshua called the twelve men whom he had appointed from the sons of Israel, one man from each tribe;

5 and Joshua said to them, "Cross again to the ark of the LORD your God into the middle of the Jordan, and each of you take up a stone on his shoulder, according to the number of the tribes of the sons of Israel.

4:6 Ex 12:26; 13:14; Josh 4:21

6 "Let this be a sign among you, so that when your children ask later, saying, 'What do these stones mean to you?'

4:7 Josh 3:13; Ex 12:14; Num 16:40

7 then you shall say to them, 'Because the waters of the Jordan were cut off before the ark of the covenant of the LORD; when it crossed the Jordan, the waters of the Jordan were cut off.' So these stones shall become a memorial to the sons of Israel forever."

4:8 Josh 4:20

8 Thus the sons of Israel did as Joshua commanded, and took up twelve stones from the middle of the Jordan, just as the LORD spoke to Joshua, according to the number of the tribes of the sons of Israel; and they carried them over with them to the lodging place and put them down there.

4:9 Gen 28:18; Josh 24:26f; 1 Sam 7:12

9 Then Joshua set up twelve stones in the middle of the Jordan at the place where the feet of the priests who carried the ark of the covenant were standing, and they are there to this day.

10 For the priests who carried the ark were standing in the middle of the Jordan until everything was completed that the LORD had commanded Joshua to speak to the people, according to all that Moses had commanded Joshua. And the people hurried and crossed;

11 and when all the people had finished crossing, the ark of the LORD and the priests crossed before the people.

4:12 Num 32:17

12 The sons of Reuben and the sons of Gad and the half-tribe of Manasseh crossed over in battle array before the sons of Israel, just as Moses had spoken to them;

13 about 40,000 equipped for war, crossed for battle before the LORD to the desert plains of Jericho.

4:14 Josh 3:7

14 On that day the LORD exalted Joshua in the sight of all Israel; so that they [3]revered him, just as they had revered Moses all the days of his life.

15 Now the LORD said to Joshua,

4:16 Ex 25:16

16 "Command the priests who carry the ark of the testimony that they come up from the Jordan."

3 Or *feared*

---

miracle. In either case, God showed his great power by working a miracle of timing and location to allow his people to cross the river on dry ground. This testimony of God's supernatural power served to build the Israelites' hope in God and to give them a great reputation with their enemies, who greatly outnumbered them.

4:1ff After the people safely crossed the river, what would be next? Conquering the land? Not yet. First, God directed them to build a memorial from 12 stones drawn from the river by 12 men, one from each tribe. This may seem like an insignificant step in their mission of conquering the land, but God did not want his people to plunge into their task unprepared. They were to focus on him and remember who was guiding them. As you are busy doing your God-given tasks, set aside quiet moments, times to build your own memorial to God's power. Too much activity may shift your focus away from God.

4:14 The Israelites revered Joshua for his role in leading them across the Jordan River. He, like Moses, would receive Israel's praises generation after generation. Although Israel was not a world power at that time, Joshua's reputation for handling his responsibilities God's way brought him greater glory than if he had been a hero in a "superpower" nation. Doing right is more important than doing well.

17 So Joshua commanded the priests, saying, "Come up from the Jordan."
18 It came about when the priests who carried the ark of the covenant of the LORD
had come up from the middle of the Jordan, and the soles of the priests' feet were lifted
up to the dry ground, that the waters of the Jordan returned to their place, and went
over all its banks as before.
19 Now the people came up from the Jordan on the tenth of the first month and camped
at Gilgal on the eastern edge of Jericho.
20 Those twelve stones which they had taken from the Jordan, Joshua set up at Gilgal.
21 He said to the sons of Israel, "When your children ask their fathers in time to come,
saying, 'What are these stones?'
22 then you shall inform your children, saying, 'Israel crossed this Jordan on dry ground.'
23 "For the LORD your God dried up the waters of the Jordan before you until you had
crossed, just as the LORD your God had done to the Red Sea, which He dried up before
us until we had crossed;
24 that all the peoples of the earth may know that the hand of the LORD is mighty, so
that you may fear the LORD your God forever."

4:19 Deut 1:3
4:20 Josh 4:8; Josh 4:3, 8
4:22 Josh 3:17
4:23 Ex 14:21
4:24 1 Kin 8:42; 2 Kin 19:19; Ps 106:8; Ex 15:16; 1 Chr 29:12; Ps 89:13; Ex 14:31; Ps 76:7f; Jer 10:7

Israel Is Circumcised

5 Now it came about when all the kings of the Amorites who *were* beyond the Jordan
to the west, and all the kings of the Canaanites who *were* by the sea, heard how the
LORD had dried up the waters of the Jordan before the sons of Israel until they had
crossed, that their hearts melted, and there was no spirit in them any longer because of
the sons of Israel.
2 At that time the LORD said to Joshua, "Make for yourself flint knives and circumcise again the sons of Israel the second time."
3 So Joshua made himself flint knives and circumcised the sons of Israel at [4]Gibeath-
haaraloth.
4 This is the reason why Joshua circumcised them: all the people who came out of
Egypt who were males, all the men of war, died in the wilderness along the way after
they came out of Egypt.
5 For all the people who came out were circumcised, but all the people who were born
in the wilderness along the way as they came out of Egypt had not been circumcised.
6 For the sons of Israel walked forty years in the wilderness, until all the nation, *that
is,* the men of war who came out of Egypt, perished because they did not listen to the
voice of the LORD, to whom the LORD had sworn that He would not let them see the
land which the LORD had sworn to their fathers to give us, a land flowing with milk and
honey.
7 Their children whom He raised up in their place, Joshua circumcised; for they were
uncircumcised, because they had not circumcised them along the way.
8 Now when they had finished circumcising all the nation, they remained in their places
in the camp until they were healed.

5:1 Num 13:29; Josh 2:10, 11
5:2 Ex 4:25
5:4 Deut 2:14
5:6 Deut 2:7, 14; Num 14:29-35; 26:63-65

4 I.e. the hill of the foreskins

4:21–24 The memorial of 12 stones was to be a constant reminder of the day the Israelites crossed the Jordan River on dry ground. Their children would see the stones, hear the story, and learn about God. Do you have traditions—special dates or special places—to help your children learn about God's work in your life? Do you take time to tell them what God has done for you—forgiving and saving you, answering your prayers, supplying your needs? Retelling your story will help keep memories of God's faithfulness alive in your family.

5:1 The Amorites and Canaanites were the two major groups living in Canaan at the time of Israel's invasion. The Canaanites worshiped a variety of gods, but Baal was their favorite. Canaanite culture was materialistic, and their religion, sensual. The Israelites continually turned to Baal after entering Canaan. The Amorite gods also infected Israel's worship and turned people away from worshiping the true God. Worshiping these false gods eventually brought about Israel's downfall.

5:1 The Israelites spent 39 years in the wilderness unnecessarily because they were terrified of the Canaanites. They underestimated God's ability. The Israelites' first attempt to enter the promised land had failed (Numbers 13—14). Here Israel saw that the Canaanites were terrified of their army. The Canaanites had heard about Israel's great victories through God (2:9–11), and they hoped that the Jordan River would slow Israel down or discourage them from entering Canaan. But news that the Israelites had crossed the Jordan on dry land caused any courage the Canaanites still had to melt away.

Don't underestimate God. If we are faithful to God, he will cause great opposition to disappear. God can change the attitudes of those who oppose him.

5:2–3 The rite of circumcision marked Israel's position as God's covenant people. When God made the original covenant with Abraham, he required that each male be circumcised as a sign of cutting off the old life and beginning a new life with God (Genesis 17:13). Other cultures at that time used circumcision as a sign of entry into adulthood, but only Israel used it as a sign of following God. A man would only be circumcised once. "The second time" here refers to the fact that many of the young men were uncircumcised at this time (see 5:5).

5:8–9 Located about two miles northeast of Jericho, Gilgal was Israel's base camp and their temporary center of government and worship during their invasion of Canaan. Here the people renewed

5:9 Zeph 2:8
9 Then the LORD said to Joshua, "Today I have rolled away the reproach of Egypt
from you." So the name of that place is called [5]Gilgal to this day.
5:10 Ex 12:18; Josh 4:19
10 While the sons of Israel camped at Gilgal they observed the Passover on the evening of the fourteenth day of the month on the desert plains of Jericho.
11 On the day after the Passover, on that very day, they ate some of the produce of the
land, unleavened cakes and parched *grain.*
5:12 Ex 16:35
12 The manna ceased on the day after they had eaten some of the produce of the land,
so that the sons of Israel no longer had manna, but they ate some of the yield of the land
of Canaan during that year.

B. CONQUERING THE PROMISED LAND (5:13—12:24)

After crossing the Jordan River, the Israelites begin to conquer Canaan. Jericho is the first to fall. Then Israel suffers its first defeat because of one man's disobedience. After the people remove the sin from their community, they strike again—this time with success. Soon great kings attack from the north and south, but they are defeated because God is with Israel. Evil could not be tolerated in the promised land, nor can it be tolerated in our lives. We, like Israel, must ruthlessly remove sin from our lives before it takes control of us.

1. Joshua attacks the center of the land

5:13 Gen 18:1, 2; 32:24, 30; Num 22:31
13 Now it came about when Joshua was by Jericho, that he lifted up his eyes and looked,
and behold, a man was standing opposite him with his sword drawn in his hand, and Joshua
went to him and said to him, "Are you for us or for our adversaries?"
5:14 Gen 17:3
14 He said, "No; rather I indeed come now *as* captain of the host of the LORD." And
Joshua fell on his face to the earth, and bowed down, and said to him, "What has my
lord to say to his servant?"
5:15 Ex 3:5
15 The captain of the LORD'S host said to Joshua, "Remove your sandals from your
feet, for the place where you are standing is holy." And Joshua did so.

The Conquest of Jericho

6 Now Jericho was tightly shut because of the sons of Israel; no one went out and no
one came in.
6:2 Deut 7:24
2 The LORD said to Joshua, "See, I have given Jericho into your hand, with its king
and the valiant warriors.

5 I.e. rolling

their commitment to God and covenant with him before attempting to conquer the new land. At Gilgal the angelic commander of the Lord's army appeared to Joshua with further instructions for battle and encouragement for the conquest (5:13–15). After the conquest, Gilgal continued to be an important place in Israel. It was here that Israel's first king, Saul, was crowned (1 Samuel 11:14–15).

5:10 This joyous Passover was the first to be celebrated in the promised land and only the third celebrated by Israel since the exodus from Egypt. The last time was at the foot of Mount Sinai, 39 years earlier. This celebration reminded Israel of God's mighty miracles that brought them out of Egypt. There they had to eat in fear and haste; here they ate in celebration of God's blessings and promises. (See Exodus 12 for a description of the night the angel "passed over" the Israelites' homes.)

5:11–12 God had miraculously supplied manna to the hungry Israelites during their 40 years in the wilderness (Exodus 16:14–31). In the bountiful promised land they no longer needed this daily food supply because the land was ready for planting and harvesting. God had miraculously provided food for the Israelites while they were in the wilderness; here he provided food from the land itself. Prayer is not an alternative to preparation, and faith is not a substitute for hard work. God can and does provide miraculously for his people as needed, but he also expects them to use their God-given talents and resources to provide for themselves. If your prayers have gone unanswered, perhaps what you need is within your reach. Pray instead for the wisdom to see it and the energy and motivation to do it.

5:14–15 This was an angel of superior rank, the commander of the Lord's army. Some say he was an appearance of God in human form. As a sign of respect, Joshua took off his sandals. Although Joshua was Israel's leader, he was still subordinate to God, the absolute Leader. Awe and respect are the responses due to our holy God. How can we show respect for God? By our attitudes and actions. We should recognize God's power, authority, and deep love, and our actions must model our attitudes before others. Respect for God is just as important today as it was in Joshua's day, even though removing shoes is no longer our cultural way of showing it.

6:1 The city of Jericho, built thousands of years before Joshua was born, was one of the oldest cities in the world. In some places it had fortified walls up to 25 feet high and 20 feet thick. Soldiers standing guard on top of the walls could see for miles. Jericho was a symbol of military power and strength—the Canaanites considered it invincible.

Israel would attack this city first, and its destruction would put the fear of Israel into the heart of every person in Canaan. The Canaanites saw Israel's God as a nature god because he parted the Jordan and as a war god because he defeated Sihon and Og. But the Canaanites did not consider him a fortress god—one who could prevail against a walled city. The defeat of Jericho showed not only that Israel's God was superior to the Canaanite gods, but also that he was invincible.

6:2–5 God told Joshua that Jericho was already delivered into his hands—the enemy was already defeated! What confidence Joshua must have had as he went into battle! Christians also fight against a defeated enemy. Our enemy, Satan, has been defeated by Christ (Romans 8:37–39; Hebrews 2:14, 15; 1 John 3:8). Although we still fight battles every day and sin runs rampant in the world, we have the assurance that the war has already been won. We do not have to be paralyzed by the power of a defeated enemy; we can overcome him through Christ's power.

3 "You shall march around the city, all the men of war circling the city once. You shall
do so for six days.
4 "Also seven priests shall carry seven trumpets of rams' horns before the ark; then on **6:4**
the seventh day you shall march around the city seven times, and the priests shall blow Lev 25:9
the trumpets.
5 "It shall be that when they make a long blast with the ram's horn, and when you hear
the sound of the trumpet, all the people shall shout with a great shout; and the wall of
the city will fall down flat, and the people will go up every man straight ahead."
6 So Joshua the son of Nun called the priests and said to them, "Take up the ark of
the covenant, and let seven priests carry seven trumpets of rams' horns before the ark
of the LORD."
7 Then he said to the people, "Go forward, and march around the city, and let the
armed men go on before the ark of the LORD."
8 And it was *so,* that when Joshua had spoken to the people, the seven priests carrying the seven trumpets of rams' horns before the LORD went forward and blew the trumpets; and the ark of the covenant of the LORD followed them.
9 The armed men went before the priests who blew the trumpets, and the rear guard **6:9**
came after the ark, while they continued to blow the trumpets. Josh 6:13; Is 52:12
10 But Joshua commanded the people, saying, "You shall not shout nor let your voice
be heard nor let a word proceed out of your mouth, until the day I tell you, 'Shout!' Then
you shall shout!"
11 So he had the ark of the LORD taken around the city, circling *it* once; then they came
into the camp and spent the night in the camp.
12 Now Joshua rose early in the morning, and the priests took up the ark of the LORD.
13 The seven priests carrying the seven trumpets of rams' horns before the ark of the **6:13**
LORD went on continually, and blew the trumpets; and the armed men went before them Josh 6:4; Josh 6:9
and the rear guard came after the ark of the LORD, while they continued to blow the
trumpets.
14 Thus the second day they marched around the city once and returned to the camp;
they did so for six days.
15 Then on the seventh day they rose early at the dawning of the day and marched
around the city in the same manner seven times; only on that day they marched around
the city seven times.
16 At the seventh time, when the priests blew the trumpets, Joshua said to the people, **6:16**
"Shout! For the LORD has given you the city. 2 Chr 13:14f
17 "The city shall be under the ban, it and all that is in it belongs to the LORD; only **6:17**
Rahab the harlot and all who are with her in the house shall live, because she hid the Lev 27:28; Deut 20:17
messengers whom we sent.
18 "But as for you, only keep yourselves from the things under the ban, so that you do **6:18**
not covet *them* and take some of the things under the ban, and make the camp of Israel Josh 7:1
accursed and bring trouble on it.
19 "But all the silver and gold and articles of bronze and iron are holy to the LORD; they **6:19**
shall go into the treasury of the LORD." Num 31:11, 12, 21-23
20 So the people shouted, and *priests* blew the trumpets; and when the people heard
the sound of the trumpet, the people shouted with a great shout and the wall fell down flat, **6:20** Heb 11:30
so that the people went up into the city, every man straight ahead, and they took the city.
21 They utterly destroyed everything in the city, both man and woman, young and old, **6:21**
and ox and sheep and donkey, with the edge of the sword. Deut 20:16

6:3–5 Why did God give Joshua all these complicated instructions for the battle? Several answers are possible: (1) God was making it undeniably clear that the battle would depend upon him, and not upon Israel's weapons and expertise. This is why priests carrying the ark, not soldiers, led the Israelites into battle. (2) God's method of taking the city accentuated the terror already felt in Jericho (2:9). (3) This strange military maneuver was a test of the Israelites' faith and their willingness to follow God completely. The blowing of the trumpets had a special significance. They had been instructed to blow the same trumpets used in the religious festivals in their battles to remind them that their victory would come from the Lord, not their own military might (Numbers 10:9).

6:21 Why did God demand that the Israelites destroy almost everyone and everything in Jericho? He was carrying out severe judgment against the wickedness of the Canaanites. This judgment, or *ban,* usually required that everything be destroyed (Deuteronomy 12:2–3; 13:12–18). Because of their evil practices and intense idolatry, the Canaanites were a stronghold of rebellion against God. This threat to the right kind of living that God required had to be removed. If not, it would affect all Israel like a cancerous growth (as it did in the sad story told in the book of Judges). A few people and some items in Jericho were not destroyed, but this was a special case. Rahab and her household were saved because she had faith in God and because she helped the Israelite spies. The silver and

6:22 Josh 2:12-19
22 Joshua said to the two men who had spied out the land, "Go into the harlot's house
and bring the woman and all she has out of there, as you have sworn to her."
6:23 Heb 11:31
23 So the young men who were spies went in and brought out Rahab and her father
and her mother and her brothers and all she had; they also brought out all her relatives
and placed them outside the camp of Israel.
6:24 Deut 20:16-18
24 They burned the city with fire, and all that was in it. Only the silver and gold, and
articles of bronze and iron, they put into the treasury of the [6]house of the LORD.
6:25 Heb 11:31; Josh 2:6
25 However, Rahab the harlot and her father's household and all she had, Joshua
spared; and she has lived in the midst of Israel to this day, for she hid the messengers
whom Joshua sent to spy out Jericho.
6:26 1 Kin 16:34
26 Then Joshua made them take an oath at that time, saying, "Cursed before the LORD
is the man who rises up and builds this city Jericho; with *the loss of* his firstborn he shall
lay its foundation, and with *the loss of* his youngest son he shall set up its gates."
6:27 Gen 39:2; Judg 1:19 Josh 9:1, 3
27 So the LORD was with Joshua, and his fame was in all the land.

Israel Is Defeated at Ai

7:1 Josh 6:17-19
7 But the sons of Israel acted unfaithfully in regard to the things under the ban, for
Achan, the son of Carmi, the son of Zabdi, the son of Zerah, from the tribe of Judah, took some of the things under the ban, therefore the anger of the LORD burned
against the sons of Israel.
7:2 Josh 18:12; 1 Sam 13:5; 14:23
2 Now Joshua sent men from Jericho to Ai, which is near Beth-aven, east of Bethel,
and said to them, "Go up and spy out the land." So the men went up and spied out Ai.
3 They returned to Joshua and said to him, "Do not let all the people go up; *only* about
two or three thousand men need go up to Ai; do not make all the people toil up there,
for they are few."
7:4 Lev 26:17; Deut 28:25
4 So about three thousand men from the people went up there, but they fled from the
men of Ai.
7:5 Lev 26:36; Josh 2:11; Ezek 21:7; Nah 2:10
5 The men of Ai struck down about thirty-six of their men, and pursued them from
the gate as far as Shebarim and struck them down on the descent, so the hearts of the
people melted and became as water.
7:6 Job 2:12; Job 42:6; Lam 2:10; Rev 18:19
6 Then Joshua tore his clothes and fell to the earth on his face before the ark of the
LORD until the evening, *both* he and the elders of Israel; and they put dust on their heads.
7 Joshua said, "Alas, O Lord GOD, why did You ever bring this people over the

6 I.e. tabernacle

---

gold and articles of bronze and iron were kept, not to enrich the people, but to beautify the tabernacle and its services.

God's purpose in all this was to keep the people's faith and religion uncontaminated. He did not want the plunder to remind Israel of Canaanite practices.

God also wants us to be pure. He wants us to clean up our behavior when we begin a new life with him. We must not let the desire for personal gain distract us from our spiritual purpose. We must also reject any objects that are reminders of a life of rebellion against God. (For more information on how Israel handled its plunder, see the note on Numbers 31:25–30.)

6:26 This curse was fulfilled in 1 Kings 16:34 when a man, Hiel, rebuilt Jericho and consequently lost his oldest and youngest sons. It is very possible that Hiel sacrificed his sons and placed them in the foundation and gate masonry to ward off evil.

7:1 "Things under the ban" refers to all the clothing, cattle, and other plunder that God said Israel should destroy when they conquered Jericho (see 6:17–19). It was not that they found a good use for something that was going to be thrown out anyway. This was a serious offense because it was in direct defiance to an explicit command of God (see Deuteronomy 20:16–18).

7:1ff Notice the results of Achan's sin: (1) many men died (7:5); (2) Israel's army melted in fear (7:5); (3) Joshua questioned God (7:7–9); (4) God threatened to withdraw his presence from the people (7:12); (5) Achan and his family had to be destroyed (7:24–26).

When Israel eliminated the sin from their community, these were the results: (1) encouragement from God (8:1); (2) God's presence in battle (8:1); (3) God's guidance and promise of victory (8:2); (4) God's permission to keep the plunder and livestock from the battle for themselves (8:2). Throughout Israel's history, blessings came when the people got rid of their sin. You will also experience victory when you turn from your sin and follow God's plan wholeheartedly.

7:6 Joshua and the elders tore their clothing and sprinkled dust on their heads as signs of deep mourning before God. They were confused by their defeat at the small city of Ai after the spectacular Jericho victory, so they went before God in deep humility and sorrow to receive his instructions. When our lives fall apart, we also should turn to God for direction and help. Like Joshua and the elders, we should humble ourselves so that we will be able to hear his words.

7:7 When Joshua first went against Ai (7:3), he did not consult God but relied on the strength of his army to defeat the small city. Only after Israel was defeated did they turn to God and ask what happened.

Too often we rely on our own skills and strength, especially when the task before us seems easy. We go to God only when the obstacles seem too great. However, only God knows what lies ahead. Consulting him, even when we are on a winning streak, may save us from grave mistakes or misjudgments. God may want us to learn lessons, remove pride, or consult others before he will work through us.

Jordan, *only* to deliver us into the hand of the Amorites, to destroy us? If only we had
been willing to dwell beyond the Jordan!
8 "O Lord, what can I say since Israel has turned *their* back before their enemies?
9 "For the Canaanites and all the inhabitants of the land will hear of it, and they will **7:9**
surround us and cut off our name from the earth. And what will You do for Your great Ex 32:12; Deut 9:28
name?"
10 So the LORD said to Joshua, "Rise up! Why is it that you have fallen on your face?
11 "Israel has sinned, and they have also transgressed My covenant which I command- **7:11**
ed them. And they have even taken some of the things under the ban and have both stolen Josh 6:18, 19
and deceived. Moreover, they have also put *them* among their own things.
12 "Therefore the sons of Israel cannot stand before their enemies; they turn *their* backs **7:12**
before their enemies, for they have become accursed. I will not be with you anymore Num 14:39, 45; Judg 2:14
unless you destroy the things under the ban from your midst.
13 "Rise up! Consecrate the people and say, 'Consecrate yourselves for tomorrow, for **7:13**
thus the LORD, the God of Israel, has said, "There are things under the ban in your midst, Josh 3:5; Josh 6:18
O Israel. You cannot stand before your enemies until you have removed the things un-
der the ban from your midst."
14 'In the morning then you shall come near by your tribes. And it shall be that the tribe **7:14**
which the LORD takes *by lot* shall come near by families, and the family which the LORD Prov 16:33
takes shall come near by households, and the household which the LORD takes shall come
near man by man.
15 'It shall be that the one who is taken with the things under the ban shall be burned **7:15**
with fire, he and all that belongs to him, because he has transgressed the covenant of the 1 Sam 14:38f; Gen 34:7; Judg 20:6
LORD, and because he has committed a disgraceful thing in Israel.' "

The Sin of Achan

16 So Joshua arose early in the morning and brought Israel near by tribes, and the tribe
of Judah was taken.
17 He brought the family of Judah near, and he took the family of the Zerahites; and
he brought the family of the Zerahites near man by man, and Zabdi was taken.
18 He brought his household near man by man; and Achan, son of Carmi, son of Zabdi, **7:18**
son of Zerah, from the tribe of Judah, was taken. Num 32:23; Acts 5:1-10
19 Then Joshua said to Achan, "My son, I implore you, give glory to the LORD, the
God of Israel, and give praise to Him; and tell me now what you have done. Do not hide **7:19**
it from me." 1 Sam 6:5; 2 Chr 30:22; Jer 13:16; John 9:24
20 So Achan answered Joshua and said, "Truly, I have sinned against the LORD, the
God of Israel, and this is what I did:
21 when I saw among the spoil a beautiful mantle from Shinar and two hundred shek- **7:21**
els of silver and a bar of gold fifty shekels in weight, then I coveted them and took them; Eph 5:5; 1 Tim 6:10
and behold, they are concealed in the earth inside my tent with the silver underneath it."
22 So Joshua sent messengers, and they ran to the tent; and behold, it was concealed
in his tent with the silver underneath it.
23 They took them from inside the tent and brought them to Joshua and to all the sons
of Israel, and they poured them out before the LORD.

7:7–9 Imagine praying this way to God. This is not a formal church prayer; it is the prayer of a man who is afraid and confused by what is happening around him. Joshua poured out his real thoughts to God. Hiding your needs from God is ignoring the only one who can really help. God welcomes your honest prayers and wants you to express your true feelings to him. Any believer can become more honest in prayer by remembering that God is all-knowing and all-powerful and that his love is everlasting.

7:10–12 Why did Achan's sin bring judgment on the entire nation? Although it was one man's failure, God saw it as national disobedience to a national law. God needed the entire nation to be committed to the job they had agreed to do—conquer the land. Thus, when one person failed, everyone failed. If Achan's sin went unpunished, unlimited looting could break out. The nation as a whole had to take responsibility for preventing this undisciplined disobedience.

Achan's sin was not merely his keeping some of the plunder (God allowed it in some cases), but his disobeying God's explicit command to destroy everything connected with Jericho. His sin was indifference to the evil and idolatry of the city, not just a desire for money and clothes. God would not protect Israel's army again until the sin was removed and the army returned to obeying him without reservation. God is not content with our doing what is right some of the time. He wants us to do what is right all the time. We are under his orders to eliminate any thoughts, practices, or possessions that hinder our devotion to him.

7:13 "Consecrate yourselves" meant that the Israelites were to undergo purification rites like those mentioned in 3:5 when they were preparing to cross the Jordan River. Such rites prepared the people to approach God and constantly reminded them of their sinfulness and his holiness.

7:24 Josh 15:7

24 Then Joshua and all Israel with him, took Achan the son of Zerah, the silver, the
mantle, the bar of gold, his sons, his daughters, his oxen, his donkeys, his sheep, his tent
and all that belonged to him, and they brought them up to the valley of [7]Achor.

7:25 Josh 6:18

25 Joshua said, "Why have you troubled us? The LORD will trouble you this day." And
all Israel stoned them with stones; and they burned them with fire after they had stoned
them with stones.

7:26 Is 65:10; Hos 2:15

26 They raised over him a great heap of stones that stands to this day, and the LORD
turned from the fierceness of His anger. Therefore the name of that place has been called
the valley of [7]Achor to this day.

The Conquest of Ai

8:1 Josh 1:9; 10:8; Josh 6:2

8:2 Deut 20:14; Josh 8:27

8:4 Judg 20:29

8:5 Judg 20:32

8 Now the LORD said to Joshua, "Do not fear or be dismayed. Take all the people of
war with you and arise, go up to Ai; see, I have given into your hand the king of Ai,
his people, his city, and his land.
2 "You shall do to Ai and its king just as you did to Jericho and its king; you shall
take only its spoil and its cattle as plunder for yourselves. Set an ambush for the city
behind it."
3 So Joshua rose with all the people of war to go up to Ai; and Joshua chose 30,000
men, valiant warriors, and sent them out at night.
4 He commanded them, saying, "See, you are going to ambush the city from behind
it. Do not go very far from the city, but all of you be ready.
5 "Then I and all the people who are with me will approach the city. And when they
come out to meet us as at the first, we will flee before them.
6 "They will come out after us until we have drawn them away from the city, for they
will say, '*They* are fleeing before us as at the first.' So we will flee before them.

7 I.e. trouble

7:24–25 Achan underestimated God and didn't take his commands seriously (6:18). It may have seemed a small thing to Achan, but the effects of his sin were felt by the entire nation, especially his family. Like Achan, our actions affect more people than just ourselves. Beware of the temptation to rationalize your sins by saying they are too small or too personal to hurt anyone but you.

7:24–26 Why did Achan's entire family pay for his sin? The Biblical record does not tell us if they were accomplices to his crime, but in the ancient world, the family was treated as a whole. Achan, as the head of his family, was like a tribal chief. If he prospered, the family prospered with him. If he suffered, so did they. Many Israelites had already died in battle because of Achan's sin. Now he was to be completely cut off from Israel.

Achan's entire family was to be stoned along with him so that no trace of the sin would remain in Israel. In our permissive and individualistic culture we have a hard time understanding such a decree, but in ancient cultures it was a common punishment. The punishment fit the crime: Achan had disobeyed God's command to destroy everything in Jericho; thus everything that belonged to Achan had to be destroyed. Sin has drastic consequences, so we should take drastic measures to avoid it.

8:1 After Israel had been cleansed from Achan's sin, Joshua prepared to attack Ai again—this time to win. Joshua had learned some lessons that we can follow: (1) confess your sins when God reveals them to you (7:19–21); (2) when you fail, refocus on God, deal with the problem, and move on (7:22–25; 8:1). God wants the cycle of sin, repentance, and forgiveness to strengthen us, not weaken us. The lessons we learn from our failures should make us better able to handle the same situation the second time around. Because God is eager to give us cleansing, forgiveness, and strength, the only way to lose is to give up. We can tell what kind of people we are by what we do on the second and third attempts.

8:2 Why did God allow the Israelites to keep the plunder and livestock this time? Israel's laws for handling the spoils of war covered two situations. (1) Cities like Jericho which were under God's *ban* (judgment for idolatry) could not be looted (see Deuteronomy 20:16–18). God's people were to be kept holy and separate from every influence of idolatry. (2) The distribution of plunder from cities not under the ban was a normal part of warfare. It provided the army and the nation with the necessary food, flocks, and weapons needed to sustain itself in wartime. Ai was not under the ban. The conquering army needed the food and equipment. Because soldiers were not paid, the loot was part of their incentive and reward for going to war.

8:3 The conquest of Ai was very important to the Israelites. Only 11 miles away from Jericho, Ai was a key stronghold for the Caananites and a buffer fortress for Bethel (8:12). If the Caananite kings got wind of an Israelite defeat at Ai, they could unite in a coordinated attack. They did not know that God had restored his power and protection to Joshua's troops. We must depend on God with absolute obedience to be sure of the victory he has promised.

THE BATTLE FOR AI
During the night, Joshua sent one detachment of soldiers to the west of Ai to lie in wait. The next morning he led a second group north of Ai. When the army of Ai attacked, the Israelites to the north pretended to scatter, only to turn on the enemy as the men lying in ambush moved in and burned the city.

7 "And you shall rise from *your* ambush and take possession of the city, for the LORD
your God will deliver it into your hand.
8 "Then it will be when you have seized the city, that you shall set the city on fire. You **8:8**
shall do *it* according to the word of the LORD. See, I have commanded you." Deut 20:16-18; Josh 8:2
9 So Joshua sent them away, and they went to the place of ambush and remained
between Bethel and Ai, on the west side of Ai; but Joshua spent that night among the
people.
10 Now Joshua rose early in the morning and mustered the people, and he went up **8:10**
with the elders of Israel before the people to Ai. Gen 22:3
11 Then all the people of war who *were* with him went up and drew near and arrived in
front of the city, and camped on the north side of Ai. Now *there was* a valley between
him and Ai.
12 And he took about 5,000 men and set them in ambush between Bethel and Ai, on **8:12**
the west side of the city. Gen 12:8; 28:19; Judg 1:22
13 So they stationed the people, all the army that was on the north side of the city, and
its rear guard on the west side of the city, and Joshua spent that night in the midst of the
valley.
14 It came about when the king of Ai saw *it,* that the men of the city hurried and rose
up early and went out to meet Israel in battle, he and all his people at the appointed
place before the desert plain. But he did not know that *there was* an ambush against him
behind the city.
15 Joshua and all Israel pretended to be beaten before them, and fled by the way of **8:15**
the wilderness. Josh 15:61; 16:1; 18:12
16 And all the people who were in the city were called together to pursue them, and **8:16**
they pursued Joshua and were drawn away from the city. Judg 20:31
17 So not a man was left in Ai or Bethel who had not gone out after Israel, and they
left the city unguarded and pursued Israel.
18 Then the LORD said to Joshua, "Stretch out the javelin that is in your hand toward **8:18**
Ai, for I will give it into your hand." So Joshua stretched out the javelin that was in his Ex 14:16; 17:9-13; Josh 8:26
hand toward the city.
19 The *men in* ambush rose quickly from their place, and when he had stretched out
his hand, they ran and entered the city and captured it, and they quickly set the city on
fire.
20 When the men of Ai turned back and looked, behold, the smoke of the city ascended to the sky, and they had no place to flee this way or that, for the people who had been
fleeing to the wilderness turned against the pursuers.
21 When Joshua and all Israel saw that the *men in* ambush had captured the city and
that the smoke of the city ascended, they turned back and slew the men of Ai.
22 The others came out from the city to encounter them, so that they were *trapped* in **8:22**
the midst of Israel, some on this side and some on that side; and they slew them until no Josh 8:8
one was left of those who survived or escaped.
23 But they took alive the king of Ai and brought him to Joshua.
24 Now when Israel had finished killing all the inhabitants of Ai in the field in the wilderness where they pursued them, and all of them were fallen by the edge of the sword
until they were destroyed, then all Israel returned to Ai and struck it with the edge of
the sword.
25 All who fell that day, both men and women, were 12,000—all the people of Ai. **8:25** Deut 20:16-18
26 For Joshua did not withdraw his hand with which he stretched out the javelin until
he had utterly destroyed all the inhabitants of Ai. **8:26** Ex 17:11, 12
27 Israel took only the cattle and the spoil of that city as plunder for themselves, according to the word of the LORD which He had commanded Joshua. **8:27** Josh 8:2
28 So Joshua burned Ai and made it a heap forever, a desolation until this day. **8:28**
29 He hanged the king of Ai on a tree until evening; and at sunset Joshua gave com- Deut 13:16
mand and they took his body down from the tree and threw it at the entrance of the city **8:29**
gate, and raised over it a great heap of stones *that stands* to this day. Deut 21:22, 23

8:18–19 The Lord gave Joshua the city. Yesterday's defeat became today's victory. Once sin is dealt with, forgiveness and victory lie ahead. With God's direction we need not stay discouraged or burdened with guilt. No matter how difficult a setback sin may bring, we must renew our efforts to carry out God's will.

30 Then Joshua built an altar to the LORD, the God of Israel, in Mount Ebal,
31 just as Moses the servant of the LORD had commanded the sons of Israel, as it is
written in the book of the law of Moses, an altar of uncut stones on which no man had
wielded an iron *tool;* and they offered burnt offerings on it to the LORD, and sacrificed
peace offerings.
32 He wrote there on the stones a copy of the law of Moses, which he had written, in
the presence of the sons of Israel.
33 All Israel with their elders and officers and their judges were standing on both sides
of the ark before the Levitical priests who carried the ark of the covenant of the LORD,
the stranger as well as the native. Half of them *stood* in front of Mount Gerizim and half
of them in front of Mount Ebal, just as Moses the servant of the LORD had given command at first to bless the people of Israel.
34 Then afterward he read all the words of the law, the blessing and the curse, according to all that is written in the book of the law.
35 There was not a word of all that Moses had commanded which Joshua did not read
before all the assembly of Israel with the women and the little ones and the strangers
who were living among them.

2. Joshua attacks the southern kings

Guile of the Gibeonites

9 Now it came about when all the kings who were beyond the Jordan, in the hill country and in the lowland and on all the coast of the Great Sea toward Lebanon, the
Hittite and the Amorite, the Canaanite, the Perizzite, the Hivite and the Jebusite, heard
of it,
2 that they gathered themselves together with one accord to fight with Joshua and
with Israel.
3 When the inhabitants of Gibeon heard what Joshua had done to Jericho and to Ai,
4 they also acted craftily and set out as envoys, and took worn-out sacks on their donkeys, and wineskins worn-out and torn and mended,
5 and worn-out and patched sandals on their feet, and worn-out clothes on themselves;
and all the bread of their provision was dry *and* had become crumbled.
6 They went to Joshua to the camp at Gilgal and said to him and to the men of Israel,
"We have come from a far country; now therefore, make a covenant with us."
7 The men of Israel said to the Hivites, "Perhaps you are living within our land; how
then shall we make a covenant with you?"
8 But they said to Joshua, "We are your servants." Then Joshua said to them, "Who
are you and where do you come from?"
9 They said to him, "Your servants have come from a very far country because of the
fame of the LORD your God; for we have heard the report of Him and all that He did in
Egypt,
10 and all that He did to the two kings of the Amorites who were beyond the Jordan,
to Sihon king of Heshbon and to Og king of Bashan who was at Ashtaroth.
11 "So our elders and all the inhabitants of our country spoke to us, saying, 'Take provisions in your hand for the journey, and go to meet them and say to them, "We are your
servants; now then, make a covenant with us." '
12 "This our bread *was* warm *when* we took it for our provisions out of our houses on
the day that we left to come to you; but now behold, it is dry and has become crumbled.
13 "These wineskins which we filled were new, and behold, they are torn; and these our
clothes and our sandals are worn out because of the very long journey."

8:30 Deut 27:2-8
8:31 Ex 20:25
8:32 Deut 27:2, 3, 8
8:33 Deut 27:11-14; Deut 11:29
8:34 Josh 1:8
8:35 Ex 12:38; Deut 31:12; Zech 8:23
9:1 Num 13:29; Josh 3:10; Num 34:6; Ex 3:17; 23:23
9:2 Ps 83:3, 5
9:3 Josh 9:17, 22; 10:2; 21:17
9:6 Josh 5:10
9:7 Josh 9:1; 11:19; Ex 23:32; Deut 7:2
9:8 Deut 20:11; 2 Kin 10:5
9:9 Josh 9:16, 17; Josh 2:9; 9:24
9:11 Josh 9:8

8:30–31 The altar was to be built out of uncut stones so it would not be profaned (see Exodus 20:25). This would prevent the people from worshiping altars like idols, or worshiping the craftsmanship of the workers rather than the great works of God.

8:32 It was most likely the Ten Commandments (recorded in Exodus 20) that Joshua copied on stones. These were the heart of all God's laws, and they are still relevant today.

9:1–6 As the news about their victory became widespread, the Israelites experienced opposition in two forms: direct (kings in the area began to unite against them); and indirect (the Gibeonites resorted to deception). We can expect similar opposition as we obey God's commands. To guard against these pressures, we must rely on God and communicate daily with him. He will give us strength to endure the direct pressures and wisdom to see through the trickery.

14 So the men *of Israel* took some of their provisions, and did not ask for the counsel of the LORD. 9:14 Num 27:21

15 Joshua made peace with them and made a covenant with them, to let them live; and the leaders of the congregation swore *an oath* to them. 9:15 Ex 23:32

16 It came about at the end of three days after they had made a covenant with them, that they heard that they were neighbors and that they were living within their land.

17 Then the sons of Israel set out and came to their cities on the third day. Now their cities *were* Gibeon and Chephirah and Beeroth and Kiriath-jearim. 9:17 Josh 18:25

18 The sons of Israel did not strike them because the leaders of the congregation had sworn to them by the LORD the God of Israel. And the whole congregation grumbled against the leaders.

19 But all the leaders said to the whole congregation, "We have sworn to them by the LORD, the God of Israel, and now we cannot touch them.

20 "This we will do to them, even let them live, so that wrath will not be upon us for the oath which we swore to them."

21 The leaders said to them, "Let them live." So they became hewers of wood and drawers of water for the whole congregation, just as the leaders had spoken to them. 9:21 Deut 29:11

22 Then Joshua called for them and spoke to them, saying, "Why have you deceived us, saying, 'We are very far from you,' when you are living within our land? 9:22 Josh 9:16

23 "Now therefore, you are cursed, and you shall never cease being slaves, both hewers of wood and drawers of water for the house of my God." 9:23 Gen 9:25

24 So they answered Joshua and said, "Because it was certainly told your servants that the LORD your God had commanded His servant Moses to give you all the land, and to destroy all the inhabitants of the land before you; therefore we feared greatly for our lives because of you, and have done this thing. 9:24 Josh 9:9

25 "Now behold, we are in your hands; do as it seems good and right in your sight to do to us." 9:25 Gen 16:6

26 Thus he did to them, and delivered them from the hands of the sons of Israel, and they did not kill them.

27 But Joshua made them that day hewers of wood and drawers of water for the congregation and for the altar of the LORD, to this day, in the place which He would choose. 9:27 Deut 12:5

Five Kings Attack Gibeon

10 Now it came about when Adoni-zedek king of Jerusalem heard that Joshua had captured Ai, and had utterly destroyed it (just as he had done to Jericho and its king, so he had done to Ai and its king), and that the inhabitants of Gibeon had made peace with Israel and were within their land, 10:1 Josh 8:21f; Josh 9:15

2 that he feared greatly, because Gibeon *was* a great city, like one of the royal cities, and because it was greater than Ai, and all its men *were* mighty. 10:2 Ex 15:14-16

3 Therefore Adoni-zedek king of Jerusalem sent *word* to Hoham king of Hebron and to Piram king of Jarmuth and to Japhia king of Lachish and to Debir king of Eglon, saying, 10:3 Josh 10:23

9:14–17 When the leaders sampled these men's provisions, they saw that the bread was dry and moldy, the wineskins were cracked, and the clothes and sandals worn out. But they did not see through the deception. After the promise had been made and the treaty ratified, the facts came out—Israel's leaders had been deceived. God had specifically instructed Israel to make no treaties with the inhabitants of Canaan (Exodus 23:32; 34:12; Numbers 33:55; Deuteronomy 7:2; 20:17–18). As a strategist, Joshua knew enough to talk to God before leading his troops into battle. But the peace treaty seemed innocent enough, so Joshua and the leaders made this decision on their own. By failing to seek God's guidance and rushing ahead with their own plans, they had to deal with angry people and an awkward alliance.

9:19–20 Joshua and the leaders had made a mistake. But because they had given an oath to protect the Gibeonites, they would keep their word. The oath was not nullified by the Gibeonites' trickery. God had commanded that oaths be kept (Leviticus 5:4; 27:1, 28), and breaking an oath was serious. This encourages us not to take our promises lightly.

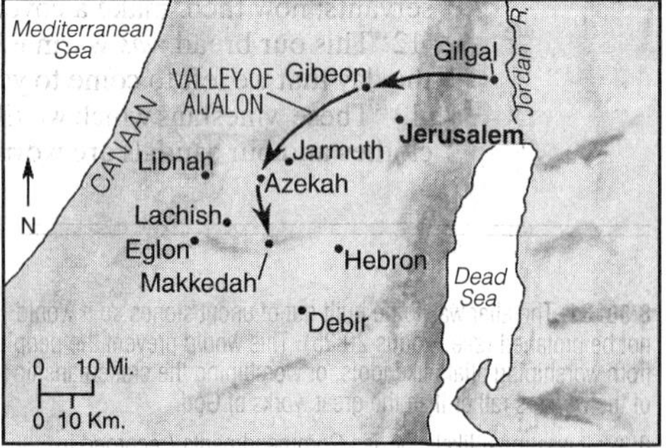

THE BATTLE FOR GIBEON Five Amorite kings conspired to destroy Gibeon. Israel came to the aid of the Gibeonites. The Israelites attacked the enemy armies outside of Gibeon and chased them through the valley of Aijalon as far as Makkedah and Azekah.

10:4 Josh 9:15
4 "Come up to me and help me, and let us attack Gibeon, for it has made peace with
Joshua and with the sons of Israel."
10:5 Num 13:29
5 So the five kings of the Amorites, the king of Jerusalem, the king of Hebron, the
king of Jarmuth, the king of Lachish, *and* the king of Eglon, gathered together and went
up, they with all their armies, and camped by Gibeon and fought against it.
6 Then the men of Gibeon sent *word* to Joshua to the camp at Gilgal, saying, "Do not
abandon your servants; come up to us quickly and save us and help us, for all the kings
of the Amorites that live in the hill country have assembled against us."
10:7 Josh 8:1
7 So Joshua went up from Gilgal, he and all the people of war with him and all the
valiant warriors.
10:8 Josh 1:5, 9
8 The LORD said to Joshua, "Do not fear them, for I have given them into your hands;
not one of them shall stand before you."
9 So Joshua came upon them suddenly by marching all night from Gilgal.
10:10 Deut 7:23
10 And the LORD confounded them before Israel, and He slew them with a great slaughter at Gibeon, and pursued them by the way of the ascent of Beth-horon and struck them
as far as Azekah and Makkedah.
10:11 Ps 18:12f; Is 28:2
11 As they fled from before Israel, *while* they were at the descent of Beth-horon, the
LORD threw large stones from heaven on them as far as Azekah, and they died; *there
were* more who died from the hailstones than those whom the sons of Israel killed with
the sword.
10:12 Hab 3:11
12 Then Joshua spoke to the LORD in the day when the LORD delivered up the Amorites before the sons of Israel, and he said in the sight of Israel,
"O sun, stand still at Gibeon,
And O moon in the valley of Aijalon."
10:13 Hab 3:11; 2 Sam 1:18; Is 38:8
13 So the sun stood still, and the moon stopped,
Until the nation avenged themselves of their enemies.
Is it not written in the book of Jashar? And the sun stopped in the middle of the sky and
did not hasten to go *down* for about a whole day.
10:14 Ex 14:14; Deut 1:30; Josh 10:42
14 There was no day like that before it or after it, when the LORD listened to the voice
of a man; for the LORD fought for Israel.
15 Then Joshua and all Israel with him returned to the camp to Gilgal.

Victory at Makkedah

10:16 Josh 10:5
16 Now these five kings had fled and hidden themselves in the cave at Makkedah.
17 It was told Joshua, saying, "The five kings have been found hidden in the cave at
Makkedah."
18 Joshua said, "Roll large stones against the mouth of the cave, and assign men by it
to guard them,
19 but do not stay *there* yourselves; pursue your enemies and attack them in the rear.
Do not allow them to enter their cities, for the LORD your God has delivered them into
your hand."
10:20 Deut 20:16
20 It came about when Joshua and the sons of Israel had finished slaying them with a
very great slaughter, until they were destroyed, and the survivors *who* remained of them
had entered the fortified cities,

10:5–8 This alliance of enemy kings from the south actually helped Joshua and his army. Because the enemies had united to attack Gibeon, Joshua didn't have to spend the time and resources required to wage separate campaigns against each fortified city represented in the coalition. Joshua confidently confronted this coalition of armies and defeated them in a single battle because he trusted God to give Israel the victory.

10:6–7 Joshua's response shows his integrity. After having been deceived by the Gibeonites, Joshua and the leaders could have been slow about their attempt to rescue them. Instead, they immediately responded to their call for help. How willing would you be to help someone who had deceived you, even though you had forgiven him or her? We should take our word just as seriously as Joshua did.

10:12–14 How did the sun stand still? Of course, in relation to the earth the sun always stands still—it is the earth that travels around the sun. But the terminology used in Joshua should not cause us to doubt the miracle. After all, we are not confused when someone tells us the sun rises or sets. The point is that the day was prolonged, not that God used a particular method to prolong it.

Two explanations have been given for how this event occurred: (1) A slowing of the earth's normal rotation gave Joshua more time, as the original Hebrew language seems to indicate. (2) Some unusual refraction of the sun's rays gave additional hours of light. Regardless of God's chosen method, the Bible is clear that the day was prolonged by a miracle and that God's intervention turned the tide of battle for his people.

10:13 The book of Jashar (also mentioned in 2 Samuel 1:18) was probably a collection of historical events put to music. Many parts of the Bible contain quotations from previous books, songs, poems, or other spoken and written materials. Because God guided the writer of this book to select this material, his message comes with divine authority.

21 that all the people returned to the camp to Joshua at Makkedah in peace. No one
uttered a word against any of the sons of Israel.
22 Then Joshua said, "Open the mouth of the cave and bring these five kings out to me
from the cave."
23 They did so, and brought these five kings out to him from the cave: the king of **10:23**
Jerusalem, the king of Hebron, the king of Jarmuth, the king of Lachish, *and* the king of Deut 7:24
Eglon.
24 When they brought these kings out to Joshua, Joshua called for all the men of Is- **10:24**
rael, and said to the chiefs of the men of war who had gone with him, "Come near, put Mal 4:3
your feet on the necks of these kings." So they came near and put their feet on their
necks.
25 Joshua then said to them, "Do not fear or be dismayed! Be strong and courageous, **10:25**
for thus the LORD will do to all your enemies with whom you fight." Josh 10:8
26 So afterward Joshua struck them and put them to death, and he hanged them on **10:26**
five trees; and they hung on the trees until evening. Josh 8:29
27 It came about at sunset that Joshua gave a command, and they took them down from **10:27**
the trees and threw them into the cave where they had hidden themselves, and put large Deut 21:22, 23
stones over the mouth of the cave, to this very day.
28 Now Joshua captured Makkedah on that day, and struck it and its king with the edge **10:28**
of the sword; he utterly destroyed it and every [8]person who was in it. He left no survivor. Deut 20:16; Josh
Thus he did to the king of Makkedah just as he had done to the king of Jericho. 6:21

Joshua's Conquest of Southern Palestine

29 Then Joshua and all Israel with him passed on from Makkedah to Libnah, and fought **10:29**
against Libnah. Josh 15:42; 21:13
30 The LORD gave it also with its king into the hands of Israel, and he struck it and
every person who *was* in it with the edge of the sword. He left no survivor in it. Thus he
did to its king just as he had done to the king of Jericho.
31 And Joshua and all Israel with him passed on from Libnah to Lachish, and they
camped by it and fought against it.
32 The LORD gave Lachish into the hands of Israel; and he captured it on the second
day, and struck it and every person who *was* in it with the edge of the sword, according
to all that he had done to Libnah.
33 Then Horam king of Gezer came up to help Lachish, and Joshua defeated him and **10:33**
his people until he had left him no survivor. Josh 16:3, 10; Judg 1:29; 1 Kin 9:16f
34 And Joshua and all Israel with him passed on from Lachish to Eglon, and they
camped by it and fought against it.
35 They captured it on that day and struck it with the edge of the sword; and he utterly
destroyed that day every person who *was* in it, according to all that he had done to Lachish.
36 Then Joshua and all Israel with him went up from Eglon to Hebron, and they fought **10:36**
against it. Num 13:22; Judg 1:10, 20; 2 Sam 5:1,
37 They captured it and struck it and its king and all its cities and all the persons who 3, 5, 13; 2 Chr 11:10
were in it with the edge of the sword. He left no survivor, according to all that he had
done to Eglon. And he utterly destroyed it and every person who *was* in it.
38 Then Joshua and all Israel with him returned to Debir, and they fought against it. **10:38**
39 He captured it and its king and all its cities, and they struck them with the edge of Josh 15:15; Judg 1:11; 1 Chr 6:58

8 Lit *soul,* and so throughout the ch

10:24 Placing a foot on the neck of a captive was a common military practice in the ancient Near East. It symbolized the victor's domination of his captives. These proud kings had boasted of their power. Now all Israel could see that God was superior to any earthly army.

10:25 With God's help, Israel won the battle against five Amorite armies. Such a triumph was part of God's daily business as he worked with his people for victory. Joshua told his men never to be afraid because God would give them similar victories over all their enemies. God has often protected us and won victories for us. The same God who empowered Joshua and who has led us in the past will help us with our present and future needs. Reminding ourselves of his help in the past will give us hope for the struggles that lie ahead.

10:32 Notice that in every Israelite victory, the text gives the credit to the Lord. All of Israel's victories came from God. When we are successful, the temptation is to take all the credit and glory as though we did it by ourselves, in our own strength. In reality, *God* gives us the victories; and he alone delivers us from our enemies. We should give him the credit and praise him for his goodness.

the sword, and utterly destroyed every person *who was* in it. He left no survivor. Just as
he had done to Hebron, so he did to Debir and its king, as he had also done to Libnah
and its king.

10:40 Deut 1:7; Deut 7:24; Deut 20:16

40 Thus Joshua struck all the land, the hill country and the [9]Negev and the lowland
and the slopes and all their kings. He left no survivor, but he utterly destroyed all who
breathed, just as the LORD, the God of Israel, had commanded.

10:41 Josh 11:16; 15:51

41 Joshua struck them from Kadesh-barnea even as far as Gaza, and all the country of
Goshen even as far as Gibeon.

10:42 Josh 10:14

42 Joshua captured all these kings and their lands at one time, because the LORD, the
God of Israel, fought for Israel.
43 So Joshua and all Israel with him returned to the camp at Gilgal.

3. Joshua attacks the northern kings

Northern Palestine Taken

11:1 Josh 11:10

11 Then it came about, when Jabin king of Hazor heard *of it,* that he sent to Jobab
king of Madon and to the king of Shimron and to the king of Achshaph,

11:2 Josh 12:3; 13:27

2 and to the kings who were of the north in the hill country, and in the Arabah—south
of [10]Chinneroth and in the lowland and on the heights of Dor on the west—

11:3 Deut 7:1; Judg 3:3, 5; 1 Kin 9:20; Josh 11:17; 13:5, 11; Josh 15:38; 18:26

3 to the Canaanite on the east and on the west, and the Amorite and the Hittite and
the Perizzite and the Jebusite in the hill country, and the Hivite at the foot of Hermon in
the land of Mizpeh.

11:4 Judg 7:12

4 They came out, they and all their armies with them, *as* many people as the sand that
is on the seashore, with very many horses and chariots.
5 So all of these kings having agreed to meet, came and encamped together at the
waters of Merom, to fight against Israel.

11:6 Josh 10:8; 2 Sam 8:4

6 Then the LORD said to Joshua, "Do not be afraid because of them, for tomorrow at
this time I will deliver all of them slain before Israel; you shall hamstring their horses
and burn their chariots with fire."
7 So Joshua and all the people of war with him came upon them suddenly by the waters
of Merom, and attacked them.

11:8 Josh 13:6; Josh 11:3

8 The LORD delivered them into the hand of Israel, so that they defeated them, and
pursued them as far as Great Sidon and Misrephoth-maim and the valley of Mizpeh to
the east; and they struck them until no survivor was left to them.

11:9 Josh 11:6

9 Joshua did to them as the LORD had told him; he hamstrung their horses and burned
their chariots with fire.

11:10 Josh 11:1

10 Then Joshua turned back at that time, and captured Hazor and struck its king with
the sword; for Hazor formerly was the head of all these kingdoms.

9 I.e. South country **10** I.e. Sea of Galilee

THE BATTLE FOR HAZOR
Kings from the north joined together to battle the Israelites who controlled the southern half of Canaan. They gathered by the water near Merom, but Joshua attacked them by surprise—the enemies' chariots were useless in the dense forests. Hazor, the largest Canaanite center in Galilee, was destroyed.

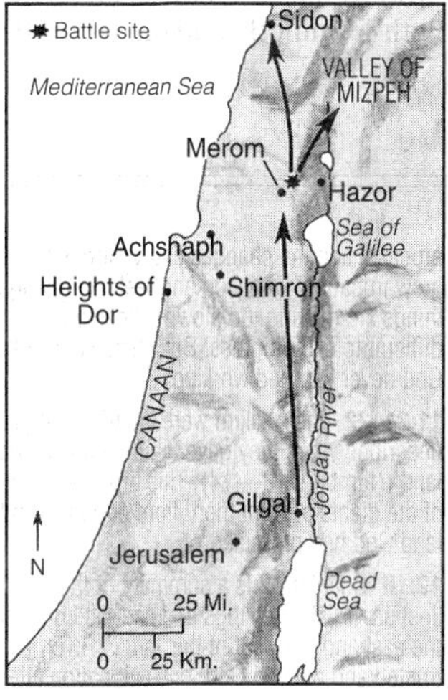

10:40–43 God had commanded Joshua to take the leadership in ridding the land of sin so God's people could occupy it. Joshua did his part thoroughly—leading the united army to weaken the inhabitants. When God orders us to stop sinning, we must not pause to debate, consider the options, negotiate a compromise, or rationalize. Instead, like Joshua, our response must be swift and complete. We must be ruthless in avoiding relationships and activities that can lead us into sin.

11:1–5 There were two kings of Hazor named Jabin. The other, apparently a weak ruler, is mentioned in Judges 4:2–3. The Jabin of this story was quite powerful because he was able to build an alliance with dozens of kings. By all appearances, Jabin had a clear advantage over Joshua and his outnumbered forces. But those who honor God can be victorious regardless of the odds.

11:10–13 Victorious invaders usually kept captured cities intact, moving into them and making them centers of commerce and defense. For example, Moses predicted in Deuteronomy 6:10–12 that Israel would occupy cities they themselves had not built. Hazor, however, was burned. As a former capital of the land, it symbolized the wicked culture that Israel had come to destroy. In addition, its capture and destruction broke the backbone of the federation and weakened the will of the people to resist.

11 They struck every person who was in it with the edge of the sword, utterly destroying *them;* there was no one left who breathed. And he burned Hazor with fire.
12 Joshua captured all the cities of these kings, and all their kings, and he struck them
with the edge of the sword, *and* utterly destroyed them; just as Moses the servant of the
LORD had commanded.
13 However, Israel did not burn any cities that stood on their mounds, except Hazor
alone, *which* Joshua burned.
14 All the spoil of these cities and the cattle, the sons of Israel took as their plunder;
but they struck every man with the edge of the sword, until they had destroyed them.
They left no one who breathed.
15 Just as the LORD had commanded Moses his servant, so Moses commanded Joshua, and so Joshua did; he left nothing undone of all that the LORD had commanded Moses.

11:11 Deut 20:16
11:12 Num 33:50-52; Deut 7:2; 20:16f
11:14 Num 31:11, 12

4. Summary of conquests

16 Thus Joshua took all that land: the hill country and all the Negev, all that land of
Goshen, the lowland, the Arabah, the hill country of Israel and its lowland
17 from Mount Halak, that rises toward Seir, even as far as Baal-gad in the valley of
Lebanon at the foot of Mount Hermon. And he captured all their kings and struck them
down and put them to death.
18 Joshua waged war a long time with all these kings.
19 There was not a city which made peace with the sons of Israel except the Hivites
living in Gibeon; they took them all in battle.
20 For it was of the LORD to harden their hearts, to meet Israel in battle in order that
he might utterly destroy them, that they might receive no mercy, but that he might destroy them, just as the LORD had commanded Moses.
21 Then Joshua came at that time and cut off the Anakim from the hill country, from
Hebron, from Debir, from Anab and from all the hill country of Judah and from all the
hill country of Israel. Joshua utterly destroyed them with their cities.
22 There were no Anakim left in the land of the sons of Israel; only in Gaza, in Gath,
and in Ashdod some remained.
23 So Joshua took the whole land, according to all that the LORD had spoken to Moses, and Joshua gave it for an inheritance to Israel according to their divisions by their
tribes. Thus the land had rest from war.

11:16 Josh 10:40, 41; Josh 11:2
11:17 Josh 12:7; Deut 7:24
11:19 Josh 9:3, 7
11:20 Ex 14:17; Deut 7:16
11:21 Num 13:33; Deut 9:2
11:22 1 Sam 17:4; 1 Kin 2:39; 1 Chr 8:13; Josh 15:46f; 1 Sam 5:1; Is 20:1
11:23 Deut 1:38; Deut 12:9, 10; 25:19; Heb 4:8

Kings Defeated by Israel

12 Now these are the kings of the land whom the sons of Israel defeated, and whose
land they possessed beyond the Jordan toward the sunrise, from the valley of the
Arnon as far as Mount Hermon, and all the Arabah to the east:
2 Sihon king of the Amorites, who lived in Heshbon, *and* ruled from Aroer, which is
on the edge of the valley of the Arnon, both the middle of the valley and half of Gilead,
even as far as the brook Jabbok, the border of the sons of Ammon;
3 and the Arabah as far as the Sea of [11]Chinneroth toward the east, and as far as the
sea of the Arabah, *even* the Salt Sea, eastward toward Beth-jeshimoth, and on the south,
at the foot of the slopes of Pisgah;

12:1 Num 32:33; Deut 3:8-17
12:2 Deut 2:36
12:3 Josh 11:2; Josh 13:20

11 I.e. Galilee

11:15 Joshua carefully obeyed all the instructions given by God. This theme of obedience is repeated frequently in the book of Joshua, partly because obedience is one aspect of life the individual believer can control. We can't always control our understanding because we may not have all the facts. We can't control what other people do or how they treat us. However, we can control our choice to obey God. Whatever new challenges we may face, the Bible contains relevant instructions that we can choose to ignore or choose to follow.

11:18 The conquest of much of the land of Canaan seems to have happened quickly (we can read about it in one sitting), but it actually took seven years. We often expect quick changes in our lives and quick victories over sin. But our journey with God is a lifelong process, and the changes and victories may take time. It is easy to grow impatient with God and feel like giving up hope because things are moving too slowly. When we are close to a situation, it is difficult to see progress. But when we look back we can see that God never stopped working.

11:21–22 The Anakim were the tribes of giants the Israelite spies described when they gave their negative report on the promised land (Numbers 13—14). This time the people did not let their fear of the giants prevent them from engaging in battle and claiming the land God had promised.

12:1ff Chapter 12 is a summary of the first half of the book of Joshua. It lists the kings and nations conquered by Joshua to both the east and the west of the Jordan River. As long as the people trusted and obeyed God, one evil nation after another fell in defeat.

12:4 Deut 3:11; Deut 1:4
12:5 Deut 3:10; Josh 13:11; 1 Chr 5:11; Deut 3:14; 1 Sam 27:8
12:6 Num 32:33; Deut 3:12
12:7 Josh 11:17
12:8 Josh 11:16
12:9 Josh 6:2; Josh 8:29

4 and the territory of Og king of Bashan, one of the remnant of Rephaim, who lived
at Ashtaroth and at Edrei,
5 and ruled over Mount Hermon and Salecah and all Bashan, as far as the border of
the Geshurites and the Maacathites, and half of Gilead, *as far as* the border of Sihon
king of Heshbon.
6 Moses the servant of the LORD and the sons of Israel defeated them; and Moses
the servant of the LORD gave it to the Reubenites and the Gadites and the half-tribe of
Manasseh as a possession.
7 Now these are the kings of the land whom Joshua and the sons of Israel defeated
beyond the Jordan toward the west, from Baal-gad in the valley of Lebanon even as far
as Mount Halak, which rises toward Seir; and Joshua gave it to the tribes of Israel as a
possession according to their divisions,
8 in the hill country, in the lowland, in the Arabah, on the slopes, and in the wilderness, and in the Negev; the Hittite, the Amorite and the Canaanite, the Perizzite, the
Hivite and the Jebusite:
9 the king of Jericho, one; the king of Ai, which is beside Bethel, one;

The broken lines (— · — ·) indicate modern boundaries.

THE CONQUERED LAND
Joshua displayed brilliant military strategy in the way he went about conquering the land of Canaan. He first captured the well-fortified Jericho to gain a foothold in Canaan and to demonstrate the awesome might of the God of Israel. Then he gained the hill country around Bethel and Gibeon. From there he subdued towns in the lowlands. Then his army conquered important cities in the north, such as Hazor. In all, Israel conquered land both east (12:1–6) and west (12:7–24) of the Jordan River; from Mount Hermon in the north to beyond the Negev to Mount Halak in the south. Thirty-one kings and their cities had been defeated. The Israelites had overpowered the Hittites, the Amorites, the Canaanites, the Perizzites, the Hivites, and the Jebusites. Other peoples living in Canaan were yet to be conquered.

10 the king of Jerusalem, one; the king of Hebron, one;
11 the king of Jarmuth, one; the king of Lachish, one;
12 the king of Eglon, one; the king of Gezer, one;
13 the king of Debir, one; the king of Geder, one;
14 the king of Hormah, one; the king of Arad, one;
15 the king of Libnah, one; the king of Adullam, one;
16 the king of Makkedah, one; the king of Bethel, one;
17 the king of Tappuah, one; the king of Hepher, one;
18 the king of Aphek, one; the king of Lasharon, one;
19 the king of Madon, one; the king of Hazor, one;
20 the king of Shimron-meron, one; the king of Achshaph, one;
21 the king of Taanach, one; the king of Megiddo, one;
22 the king of Kedesh, one; the king of Jokneam in Carmel, one;
23 the king of Dor in the heights of Dor, one; the king of Goiim in Gilgal, one;
24 the king of Tirzah, one: in all, thirty-one kings.

12:10 Josh 10:23
12:14 Num 21:1
12:17 1 Kin 4:10
12:18 Josh 13:4; 2 Kin 13:17
12:22 Josh 19:37; 20:7; 21:32
12:23 Gen 14:1
12:24 Deut 7:24

C. DIVIDING THE PROMISED LAND (13:1—24:33)

After seven years of battle, Israel gained control of the land, which was then divided and allotted to the tribes. Joshua dismissed the army, for it was now each tribe's responsibility to clear out the remaining enemies from their own areas. Joshua continued to encourage the people to remain faithful to God so they could remain in the land. The promised land was Israel's earthly inheritance. But Israel also had a spiritual inheritance in which we can share when we live a life of faithfulness to God.

1. The tribes receive their land

Canaan Divided among the Tribes

13 Now Joshua was old *and* advanced in years when the LORD said to him, "You are
old *and* advanced in years, and very much of the land remains to be possessed.
2 "This is the land that remains: all the regions *of* the Philistines and all *those of* the
Geshurites;
3 from the Shihor which is east of Egypt, even as far as the border of Ekron to
the north (it is counted as Canaanite); the five lords of the Philistines: the Gazite, the
Ashdodite, the Ashkelonite, the Gittite, the Ekronite; and the Avvite
4 to the south, all the land of the Canaanite, and Mearah that belongs to the Sidonians, as far as Aphek, to the border of the Amorite;
5 and the land of the Gebalite, and all of Lebanon, toward the east, from Baal-gad
below Mount Hermon as far as Lebo-hamath.
6 "All the inhabitants of the hill country from Lebanon as far as Misrephoth-maim, all
the Sidonians, I will drive them out from before the sons of Israel; only allot it to Israel
for an inheritance as I have commanded you.
7 "Now therefore, apportion this land for an inheritance to the nine tribes and the half-
tribe of Manasseh."

13:1 Josh 14:10
13:2 Josh 13:11; 1 Sam 27:8
13:3 1 Sam 6:4, 16
13:4 Josh 12:18; 19:30; 1 Sam 4:1; 1 Kin 20:26, 30; Ezek 16:3; Amos 2:10
13:5 1 Kin 5:18; Josh 12:7
13:6 Josh 11:8; Num 33:54

13—19 The following chapters describe how the promised land was to be divided among the 12 tribes. First, the tribe of Levi was not to have any land because they were to spend all their energies serving the people, not their own interests (13:14; 21). Second, the tribes of Reuben and Gad and the half-tribe of Manasseh had already received land east of the Jordan River, which had been given to them by Moses (Numbers 32). Third, the tribes of Judah and Joseph (Ephraim and the other half-tribe of Manasseh) had received land that their ancestor Jacob had promised them 450 years earlier (Genesis 48:22; Joshua 15—17). The rest of the tribes divided up the remaining land by casting lots (chapter 18).

Through Jacob's original blessing of his sons (Genesis 49) and Moses' blessing of the 12 tribes (Deuteronomy 33), the type of land each tribe would receive was already known. The two blessings were prophetic, for although Joshua cast lots to determine the land to be given to each of the remaining tribes, the allotments came out just as Jacob and Moses had predicted.

13:1 Joshua was getting old—he was between 85 and 100 years of age at this time. God, however, still had work for him to do. Our culture often glorifies the young and strong and sets aside those who are older. Yet older people are filled with the wisdom that comes with experience. They are very capable of serving if given the chance and should be encouraged to do so. Believers are never allowed to retire from God's service. Those past retirement age should not assume that age alone disqualifies or excuses them from serving God.

13:7 Much of the land was unconquered at this point, but God's plan was to go ahead and include it in the divisions among the tribes. God's desire was that it would eventually be conquered by the Israelites. God knows the future, and as he leads you he already knows about the victories that lie ahead. But just as the Israelites still had to go to battle and fight, so we must still face the trials and fight the battles of our unconquered land.

What are our unconquered lands? They may be overseas missionary territories, new languages in which to translate the Bible, new missionary areas in our neighborhoods, interest groups or institutions that need redemptive work, unchallenged public problems or ethical issues, unconfessed sin in our lives, or underdeveloped talents and resources. What territory has God given you to conquer? This territory is your "promised land." Our inheritance will be a new heaven and a new earth (Revelation 21:1) if we fulfill the mission God has given us to do.

13:8 Josh 12:1-6

8 With the other half-tribe, the Reubenites and the Gadites received their inheritance
which Moses gave them beyond the Jordan to the east, just as Moses the servant of the
LORD gave to them;
9 from Aroer, which is on the edge of the valley of the Arnon, with the city which is in
the middle of the valley, and all the plain of Medeba, as far as Dibon;
10 and all the cities of Sihon king of the Amorites, who reigned in Heshbon, as far as
the border of the sons of Ammon;

13:11 Gen 37:25; Num 32:29; Josh 13:25; 17:5f

11 and Gilead, and the territory of the Geshurites and Maacathites, and all Mount
Hermon, and all Bashan as far as Salecah;

13:12 Deut 3:11; Num 21:24

12 all the kingdom of Og in Bashan, who reigned in Ashtaroth and in Edrei (he alone
was left of the remnant of the Rephaim); for Moses struck them and dispossessed them.
13 But the sons of Israel did not dispossess the Geshurites or the Maacathites; for
Geshur and Maacath live among Israel until this day.

13:14 Deut 18:1, 2

14 Only to the tribe of Levi he did not give an inheritance; the offerings by fire to the
LORD, the God of Israel, are their inheritance, as He spoke to him.
15 So Moses gave *an inheritance* to the tribe of the sons of Reuben according to their
families.

13:16 Josh 13:9

16 Their territory was from Aroer, which is on the edge of the valley of the Arnon, with
the city which is in the middle of the valley and all the plain by Medeba;

13:18 Num 21:23; Judg 11:20; Is 15:4; Jer 48:34

17 Heshbon, and all its cities which are on the plain: Dibon and Bamoth-baal and Beth-
baal-meon,
18 and Jahaz and Kedemoth and Mephaath,

13:19 Num 32:37; Jer 48:1, 23; Ezek 25:9

19 and Kiriathaim and Sibmah and Zereth-shahar on the hill of the valley,
20 and Beth-peor and the slopes of Pisgah and Beth-jeshimoth,

13:21 Num 31:8

21 even all the cities of the plain and all the kingdom of Sihon king of the Amorites
who reigned in Heshbon, whom Moses struck with the chiefs of Midian, Evi and Rekem
and Zur and Hur and Reba, the princes of Sihon, who lived in the land.

13:22 Num 31:8

22 The sons of Israel also killed Balaam the son of Beor, the diviner, with the sword
among *the rest of* their slain.

THE LAND YET TO BE CONQUERED
Canaan was now controlled by the Israelites, although much land and several cities still needed to be conquered. Joshua told the people to include both conquered and unconquered lands in the territorial allotments (13:7). He was certain the people would complete the conquest as God had commanded.

13:13 One reason the Israelites encountered so many problems as they settled the land was that they failed to conquer *fully* the land and drive out all its inhabitants. The cancer-like presence of the remaining pagan peoples of Canaan caused unending difficulties for the Israelites, as the book of Judges records. Just as they failed to remove completely the sin from the land, believers today often fail to remove completely the sin from their lives—with equally disastrous results. As a self-test, reread the Ten Commandments in Exodus 20:1–17. Ask yourself, Am I tolerating sinful practices or thoughts? Have I accepted half-measures as good enough? Do I condemn the faults of others but condone my own?

13:15–23 There is often an interesting connection between the land a tribe received and the character of the tribe's founder. For example, because of Joseph's godly character (Genesis 49:22–26), the tribes descended from him—Ephraim and Manasseh—were given the richest, most fertile land in all of Canaan. Judah, who offered himself in exchange for his brother Benjamin's safety (Genesis 44:18–34), received the largest portion of land, which eventually became the southern kingdom and the seat of David's dynasty. Reuben, who slept with one of his father's wives (Genesis 49:4), was given desert land, the region described here.

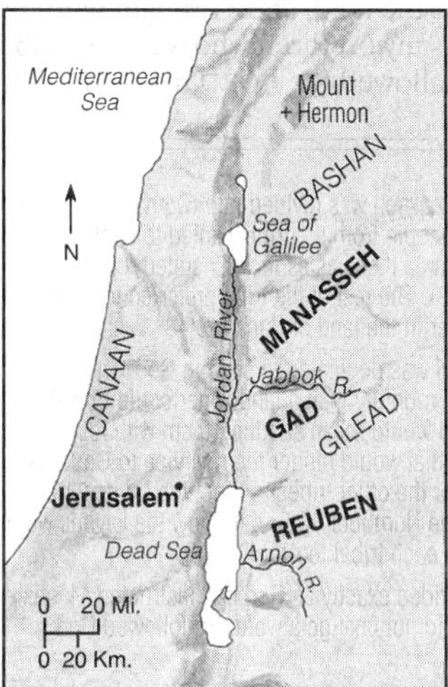

THE TRIBES EAST OF THE JORDAN
Joshua assigned territory to the tribes of Reuben, Gad, and the half-tribe of Manasseh on the east side of the Jordan where they had chosen to remain because of the wonderful livestock country (Numbers 32:1–5).

23 The border of the sons of Reuben was the Jordan. This was the inheritance of the
sons of Reuben according to their families, the cities and their villages.
24 Moses also gave *an inheritance* to the tribe of Gad, to the sons of Gad, according to
their families.
25 Their territory was Jazer, and all the cities of Gilead, and half the land of the sons
of Ammon, as far as Aroer which is before Rabbah;
26 and from Heshbon as far as Ramath-mizpeh and Betonim, and from Mahanaim as
far as the border of Debir;

13:25 Num 21:32; Josh 21:39; 2 Sam 24:5; 1 Chr 6:81; 26:31; Is 16:8f; Jer 48:32

27 and in the valley, Beth-haram and Beth-nimrah and Succoth and Zaphon, the rest
of the kingdom of Sihon king of Heshbon, with the Jordan as a border, as far as the *lower* end of the Sea of Chinnereth beyond the Jordan to the east.

13:27 Num 34:11; Deut 3:17

28 This is the inheritance of the sons of Gad according to their families, the cities and
their villages.
29 Moses also gave *an inheritance* to the half-tribe of Manasseh; and it was for the half-
tribe of the sons of Manasseh according to their families.
30 Their territory was from Mahanaim, all Bashan, all the kingdom of Og king of Bashan, and all the towns of Jair, which are in Bashan, sixty cities;

13:30 Num 32:41

31 also half of Gilead, with Ashtaroth and Edrei, the cities of the kingdom of Og in
Bashan, *were* for the sons of Machir the son of Manasseh, for half of the sons of Machir
according to their families.

13:31 Josh 9:10; 12:4; 13:12; Judg 10:6; 1 Sam 7:3f; 12:10; 1 Chr 6:71

32 These are *the territories* which Moses apportioned for an inheritance in the plains of
Moab, beyond the Jordan at Jericho to the east.
33 But to the tribe of Levi, Moses did not give an inheritance; the LORD, the God of
Israel, is their inheritance, as He had promised to them.

13:33 Deut 18:1f; Josh 13:14

Caleb's Request

14 Now these are *the territories* which the sons of Israel inherited in the land of Canaan, which Eleazar the priest, and Joshua the son of Nun, and the heads of the
households of the tribes of the sons of Israel apportioned to them for an inheritance,
2 by the lot of their inheritance, as the LORD commanded through Moses, for the nine
tribes and the half-tribe.

14:1 Num 34:16-29

14:2 Num 26:55; 33:54; 34:13

3 For Moses had given the inheritance of the two tribes and the half-tribe beyond the
Jordan; but he did not give an inheritance to the Levites among them.

14:3 Num 32:33; Josh 13:14

4 For the sons of Joseph were two tribes, Manasseh and Ephraim, and they did not
give a portion to the Levites in the land, except cities to live in, with their pasture lands
for their livestock and for their property.

14:4 Gen 41:51f; 46:20; 48:1, 5; Num 26:28; 2 Chr 30:1

5 Thus the sons of Israel did just as the LORD had commanded Moses, and they divided the land.

14:5 Num 35:1f; Josh 21:2

6 Then the sons of Judah drew near to Joshua in Gilgal, and Caleb the son of Jephunneh the Kenizzite said to him, "You know the word which the LORD spoke to Moses the
man of God concerning you and me in Kadesh-barnea.

14:6 Num 13:6, 30; 14:6, 24, 30

7 "I was forty years old when Moses the servant of the LORD sent me from Kadesh-
barnea to spy out the land, and I brought word back to him as *it was* in my heart.

14:7 Num 13:1-31

8 "Nevertheless my brethren who went up with me made the heart of the people melt
with fear; but I followed the LORD my God fully.

14:8 Num 14:24; Deut 1:36

13:29 The tribe of Manasseh was divided into two half-tribes. This occurred when many people from the tribe wanted to settle east of the Jordan River in an area that was especially suited for their flocks (Numbers 32:33). The rest of the tribe preferred to settle west of the Jordan River in the land of Canaan.

13:33 The tribe of Levi was dedicated to serving God. The Levites needed more time and mobility than a landowner could possibly have. Giving them land would mean saddling them with responsibilities and loyalties that would hinder their service to God. Instead, God arranged for the other tribes to meet the Levites' needs through donations. (See Numbers 35:2–4 for how the Levites were to receive cities within each tribal territory.)

14:5 The land was divided exactly as God had instructed Moses years before. Joshua did not change a word. He followed God's commands precisely. Often we believe that *almost* is close enough, and this idea can carry over into our spiritual lives. For example, we may follow God's Word as long as we agree with it, but ignore it when the demands seem harsh. But God is looking for leaders who follow instructions thoroughly.

14:6–12 Caleb was faithful from the start. As one of the original spies sent into the promised land (Numbers 13:30–33), he saw great cities and giants, yet he knew God would help the people conquer the land. Because of his faith, God promised him a personal inheritance of land (Numbers 14:24; Deuteronomy 1:34–36). Here, 45 years later, the land was given to him. His faith was still unwavering. Although his inherited land still had giants, Caleb knew the Lord would help him conquer them. Like Caleb, we must be faithful to God, not only at the start of our walk with him, but through our entire lives. We must never allow ourselves to rest on our past accomplishments or reputations.

14:9 Deut 1:36

9 "So Moses swore on that day, saying, 'Surely the land on which your foot has trodden will be an inheritance to you and to your children forever, because you have followed the LORD my God fully.'

10 "Now behold, the LORD has let me live, just as He spoke, these forty-five years, from the time that the LORD spoke this word to Moses, when Israel walked in the wilderness; and now behold, I am eighty-five years old today.

14:11 Deut 34:7; Deut 31:2

11 "I am still as strong today as I was in the day Moses sent me; as my strength was then, so my strength is now, for war and for going out and coming in.

14:12 Num 13:33

12 "Now then, give me this hill country about which the LORD spoke on that day, for you heard on that day that Anakim *were* there, with great fortified cities; perhaps the LORD will be with me, and I will drive them out as the LORD has spoken."

14:13 Josh 22:6; Judg 1:20; 1 Chr 6:55f

13 So Joshua blessed him and gave Hebron to Caleb the son of Jephunneh for an inheritance.

14 Therefore, Hebron became the inheritance of Caleb the son of Jephunneh the Kenizzite until this day, because he followed the LORD God of Israel fully.

14:15 Josh 11:23

15 Now the name of Hebron was formerly Kiriath-arba; *for Arba* was the greatest man among the Anakim. Then the land had rest from war.

Territory of Judah

15:1 Num 34:3, 4; Num 20:16; Deut 32:51

15 Now the lot for the tribe of the sons of Judah according to their families reached the border of Edom, southward to the wilderness of Zin at the extreme south.

2 Their south border was from the lower end of the Salt Sea, from the bay that turns to the south.

3 Then it proceeded southward to the ascent of Akrabbim and continued to Zin, then went up by the south of Kadesh-barnea and continued to Hezron, and went up to Addar and turned about to Karka.

15:4 Num 34:5; Gen 15:18; 1 Kin 8:65

4 It continued to Azmon and proceeded to the brook of Egypt, and the border ended at the sea. This shall be your south border.

15:5 Num 34:3, 10-12; Josh 18:15-19

5 The east border *was* the Salt Sea, as far as the mouth of the Jordan. And the border of the north side was from the bay of the sea at the mouth of the Jordan.

6 Then the border went up to Beth-hoglah, and continued on the north of Beth-arabah, and the border went up to the stone of Bohan the son of Reuben.

15:7 Josh 7:24

7 The border went up to Debir from the valley of Achor, and turned northward toward Gilgal which is opposite the ascent of Adummim, which is on the south of the valley; and the border continued to the waters of En-shemesh and it ended at En-rogel.

15:8 Josh 15:63

8 Then the border went up the valley of Ben-hinnom to the slope of the Jebusite on the south (that is, Jerusalem); and the border went up to the top of the mountain which is before the valley of Hinnom to the west, which is at the end of the valley of Rephaim toward the north.

15:9 1 Chr 13:6; Judg 18:12

9 From the top of the mountain the border curved to the spring of the waters of Nephtoah and proceeded to the cities of Mount Ephron, then the border curved to Baalah (that is, Kiriath-jearim).

15:10 Gen 38:13; Judg 14:1

10 The border turned about from Baalah westward to Mount Seir, and continued to the slope of Mount Jearim on the north (that is, Chesalon), and went down to Beth-shemesh and continued through Timnah.

11 The border proceeded to the side of Ekron northward. Then the border curved to Shikkeron and continued to Mount Baalah and proceeded to Jabneel, and the border ended at the sea.

15:12 Num 34:6

12 The west border *was* at the Great Sea, even *its* coastline. This is the border around the sons of Judah according to their families.

15:13 Josh 14:13-15; Num 13:6

13 Now he gave to Caleb the son of Jephunneh a portion among the sons of Judah, according to the command of the LORD to Joshua, *namely,* Kiriath-arba, *Arba being* the father of Anak (that is, Hebron).

15:14 Josh 11:21, 22; Num 13:33; Deut 9:2

14 Caleb drove out from there the three sons of Anak: Sheshai and Ahiman and Talmai, the children of Anak.

14:15 The Anakim were a race of giants who inhabited parts of the land before Joshua's conquest.

15:4 Notice that these boundaries and descriptions of the promised land are very specific. God was telling Israel exactly what to do, and he was giving them just what they needed. There was no excuse for disobedience.

15 Then he went up from there against the inhabitants of Debir; now the name of Debir **15:15**
formerly was Kiriath-sepher. Josh 10:38
16 And Caleb said, "The one who attacks Kiriath-sepher and captures it, I will give
him Achsah my daughter as a wife."
17 Othniel the son of Kenaz, the brother of Caleb, captured it; so he gave him Achsah **15:17**
his daughter as a wife. Judg 1:13; 3:9
18 It came about that when she came *to him,* she persuaded him to ask her father for **15:18**
a field. So she alighted from the donkey, and Caleb said to her, "What do you want?" Judg 1:14
19 Then she said, "Give me a blessing; since you have given me the land of the Negev,
give me also springs of water." So he gave her the upper springs and the lower springs.
20 This is the inheritance of the tribe of the sons of Judah according to their families.
21 Now the cities at the extremity of the tribe of the sons of Judah toward the border **15:21**
of Edom in the south were Kabzeel and Eder and Jagur, Gen 35:21
22 and Kinah and Dimonah and Adadah,
23 and Kedesh and Hazor and Ithnan,
24 Ziph and Telem and Bealoth,
25 and Hazor-hadattah and Kerioth-hezron (that is, Hazor),
26 Amam and Shema and Moladah,
27 and Hazar-gaddah and Heshmon and Beth-pelet,
28 and Hazar-shual and Beersheba and Biziothiah, **15:28**
29 Baalah and Iim and Ezem, Gen 21:31
30 and Eltolad and Chesil and Hormah,
31 and Ziklag and Madmannah and Sansannah,
32 and Lebaoth and Shilhim and Ain and Rimmon; in all, twenty-nine cities with their **15:31**
villages. 1 Sam 27:6; 30:1
33 In the lowland: Eshtaol and Zorah and Ashnah, **15:33**
34 and Zanoah and En-gannim, Tappuah and Enam, Judg 13:25; 16:31
35 Jarmuth and Adullam, Socoh and Azekah, **15:35**
36 and Shaaraim and Adithaim and Gederah and Gederothaim; fourteen cities with 1 Sam 22:1
their villages.
37 Zenan and Hadashah and Migdal-gad,
38 and Dilean and Mizpeh and Joktheel,
39 Lachish and Bozkath and Eglon, **15:39**
40 and Cabbon and Lahmas and Chitlish, Josh 10:3; 2 Kin 14:19
41 and Gederoth, Beth-dagon and Naamah and Makkedah; sixteen cities with their
villages.
42 Libnah and Ether and Ashan,
43 and Iphtah and Ashnah and Nezib,
44 and Keilah and Achzib and Mareshah; nine cities with their villages.
45 Ekron, with its towns and its villages;
46 from Ekron even to the sea, all that were by the side of Ashdod, with their villages.
47 Ashdod, its towns and its villages; Gaza, its towns and its villages; as far as the brook **15:47**
of Egypt and the Great Sea, even *its* coastline. Josh 15:4
48 In the hill country: Shamir and Jattir and Socoh,
49 and Dannah and Kiriath-sannah (that is, Debir),
50 and Anab and Eshtemoh and Anim,
51 and Goshen and Holon and Giloh; eleven cities with their villages.
52 Arab and Dumah and Eshan,
53 and Janum and Beth-tappuah and Aphekah,
54 and Humtah and Kiriath-arba (that is, Hebron), and Zior; nine cities with their villages.
55 Maon, Carmel and Ziph and Juttah,
56 and Jezreel and Jokdeam and Zanoah,
57 Kain, Gibeah and Timnah; ten cities with their villages.

15:16–19 Othniel became Israel's first judge after Joshua's death (Judges 1:13; 3:9–11). He played an important role in reforming Israel by chasing away an oppressive enemy army and bringing peace back to the land. Thus Caleb's legacy of faithfulness continued to the next generation.

15:19 Achsah asked Caleb for springs of water because her land was in the south and was very arid. Caleb probably granted her request as a wedding present (see 15:17).

58 Halhul, Beth-zur and Gedor,

59 and Maarath and Beth-anoth and Eltekon; six cities with their villages.

60 Kiriath-baal (that is, Kiriath-jearim), and Rabbah; two cities with their villages.

61 In the wilderness: Beth-arabah, Middin and Secacah,

62 and Nibshan and the City of Salt and Engedi; six cities with their villages.

15:63 Judg 1:21; 2 Sam 5:6; 1 Chr 11:4

63 Now as for the Jebusites, the inhabitants of Jerusalem, the sons of Judah could not drive them out; so the Jebusites live with the sons of Judah at Jerusalem until this day.

Territory of Ephraim

16:1 Josh 8:15; 18:12

16 Then the lot for the sons of Joseph went from the Jordan at Jericho to the waters of Jericho on the east into the wilderness, going up from Jericho through the hill country to Bethel.

16:2 Josh 18:13

2 It went from Bethel to Luz, and continued to the border of the Archites at Ataroth.

16:3 Josh 18:13; 1 Kin 9:17; Josh 10:33

3 It went down westward to the territory of the Japhletites, as far as the territory of lower Beth-horon even to Gezer, and it ended at the sea.

16:4 Josh 17:14

4 The sons of Joseph, Manasseh and Ephraim, received their inheritance.

16:5 Josh 18:13

5 Now *this* was the territory of the sons of Ephraim according to their families: the border of their inheritance eastward was Ataroth-addar, as far as upper Beth-horon.

16:6 Josh 17:7

6 Then the border went westward at Michmethath on the north, and the border turned about eastward to Taanath-shiloh and continued *beyond* it to the east of Janoah.

16:7 1 Chr 7:28

7 It went down from Janoah to Ataroth and to Naarah, then reached Jericho and came out at the Jordan.

16:8 Josh 17:8

8 From Tappuah the border continued westward to the brook of Kanah, and it ended at the sea. This is the inheritance of the tribe of the sons of Ephraim according to their families,

9 *together* with the cities which were set apart for the sons of Ephraim in the midst of the inheritance of the sons of Manasseh, all the cities with their villages.

16:10 Judg 1:29; 1 Kin 9:16; Josh 17:12, 13

10 But they did not drive out the Canaanites who lived in Gezer, so the Canaanites live in the midst of Ephraim to this day, and they became forced laborers.

Territory of Manasseh

17:1 Gen 41:51; 46:20; 48:17f

17 Now *this* was the lot for the tribe of Manasseh, for he was the firstborn of Joseph. To Machir the firstborn of Manasseh, the father of Gilead, were allotted Gilead and Bashan, because he was a man of war.

2 So *the lot* was *made* for the rest of the sons of Manasseh according to their families: for the sons of Abiezer and for the sons of Helek and for the sons of Asriel and for the sons of Shechem and for the sons of Hepher and for the sons of Shemida; these *were* the male descendants of Manasseh the son of Joseph according to their families.

17:3 Num 26:33; 27:1-7

3 However, Zelophehad, the son of Hepher, the son of Gilead, the son of Machir, the son of Manasseh, had no sons, only daughters; and these are the names of his daughters: Mahlah and Noah, Hoglah, Milcah and Tirzah.

17:4 Num 27:5-7

4 They came near before Eleazar the priest and before Joshua the son of Nun and before the leaders, saying, "The LORD commanded Moses to give us an inheritance among our brothers." So according to the command of the LORD he gave them an inheritance among their father's brothers.

5 Thus there fell ten portions to Manasseh, besides the land of Gilead and Bashan, which is beyond the Jordan,

17:6 Josh 13:30, 31

6 because the daughters of Manasseh received an inheritance among his sons. And the land of Gilead belonged to the rest of the sons of Manasseh.

16:1ff Although Joseph was one of Jacob's 12 sons, he did not have a tribe named after him. This was because Joseph, as the oldest son of Jacob's wife Rachel, received a double portion of the inheritance. This double portion was given to Joseph's two sons, Ephraim and Manasseh, whom Jacob considered as his own (Genesis 48:5). The largest territory and the greatest influence in the northern half of Israel belonged to their tribes.

16:10 Occasionally this short phrase appears: "They did not drive out" the people of the land (see also 15:63; 17:12). This was contrary to God's explicit desire and command (13:1–6). The failure to remove completely the pagan people and their gods from the land would cause many problems for the nation. The book of Judges records many of these struggles.

17:3–4 Although women did not traditionally inherit property in Israelite society, Moses put justice ahead of tradition and gave these five women the land they deserved (see Numbers 27:1–11). In fact, God told Moses to add a law that would help other women in similar circumstances inherit property as well. Joshua was now carrying out this law. It is easy to refuse to honor a reasonable request because "things have never been done that way before." But, like Moses and Joshua, it is best to look carefully at the purpose of the law and the merits of each case before deciding.

7 The border of Manasseh ran from Asher to Michmethath which was east of Shechem; then the border went southward to the inhabitants of En-tappuah.
8 The land of Tappuah belonged to Manasseh, but Tappuah on the border of Manas- **17:8**
seh *belonged* to the sons of Ephraim. Josh 16:8
9 The border went down to the brook of Kanah, southward of the brook (these cities **17:9**
belonged to Ephraim among the cities of Manasseh), and the border of Manasseh *was* Josh 16:8f
on the north side of the brook and it ended at the sea.
10 The south side *belonged* to Ephraim and the north side to Manasseh, and the sea
was their border; and they reached to Asher on the north and to Issachar on the east.
11 In Issachar and in Asher, Manasseh had Beth-shean and its towns and Ibleam and **17:11**
its towns, and the inhabitants of Dor and its towns, and the inhabitants of En-dor and its 1 Chr 7:29; Josh
towns, and the inhabitants of Taanach and its towns, and the inhabitants of Megiddo 11:2; 12:23
and its towns, the third is Napheth.
12 But the sons of Manasseh could not take possession of these cities, because the **17:12**
Canaanites persisted in living in that land. Judg 1:27
13 It came about when the sons of Israel became strong, they put the Canaanites to **17:13**
forced labor, but they did not drive them out completely. Josh 16:10
14 Then the sons of Joseph spoke to Joshua, saying, "Why have you given me only one **17:14**
lot and one portion for an inheritance, since I am a numerous people whom the LORD Num 13:7
has thus far blessed?"
15 Joshua said to them, "If you are a numerous people, go up to the forest and clear a
place for yourself there in the land of the Perizzites and of the Rephaim, since the hill
country of Ephraim is too narrow for you."
16 The sons of Joseph said, "The hill country is not enough for us, and all the Canaan- **17:16**
ites who live in the valley land have chariots of iron, both those who are in Beth-shean Josh 17:18; Judg
and its towns and those who are in the valley of Jezreel." 1:19; 4:3, 13
17 Joshua spoke to the house of Joseph, to Ephraim and Manasseh, saying, "You are
a numerous people and have great power; you shall not have one lot *only,*
18 but the hill country shall be yours. For though it is a forest, you shall clear it, and to **17:18**
its farthest borders it shall be yours; for you shall drive out the Canaanites, even though Josh 17:16
they have chariots of iron *and* though they are strong."

Rest of the Land Divided

18 Then the whole congregation of the sons of Israel assembled themselves at Shi- **18:1**
loh, and set up the tent of meeting there; and the land was subdued before them. Judg 21:19; Jer 7:12; 26:6, 9

17:14–15 Notice the two contrasting attitudes toward settling the promised land: Caleb took what God gave him and moved ahead to fulfill God's plan for him (14:12). He was confident that God would help him drive out the wicked inhabitants and that he would soon fully occupy his land (15:14–15). In contrast, the two tribes of Joseph were given rich land and lots of it, but they were afraid to drive out the inhabitants and take full possession of it. Instead they begged for more land. But Joshua asked them to prove their sincerity first by clearing the unclaimed forest areas. They agreed, but they failed to carry through (Judges 1:27).

18:1–2 With most of the conquest behind them, Israel moved their religious center from Gilgal (see the note on 5:8–9) to Shiloh. This was probably the first place where the tabernacle was set up permanently. The tent of meeting was part of the tabernacle and was where God lived among his people (Exodus 25:8). Its central location in the land made it easier for the people to attend the special worship services and yearly feasts.

The family of Samuel, a great priest and prophet, often traveled to Shiloh, and Samuel was taken there when he was a small boy (1 Samuel 1:3, 22). The tabernacle remained in Shiloh through the period of the judges (about 300 years). Apparently the city was destroyed by the Philistines when the ark of the covenant was captured (1 Samuel 4—5). Shiloh never lived up to its reputation as Israel's religious center, for later references in the Bible point to the wickedness and idolatry in the city (Psalm 78:56–60; Jeremiah 7:12–15).

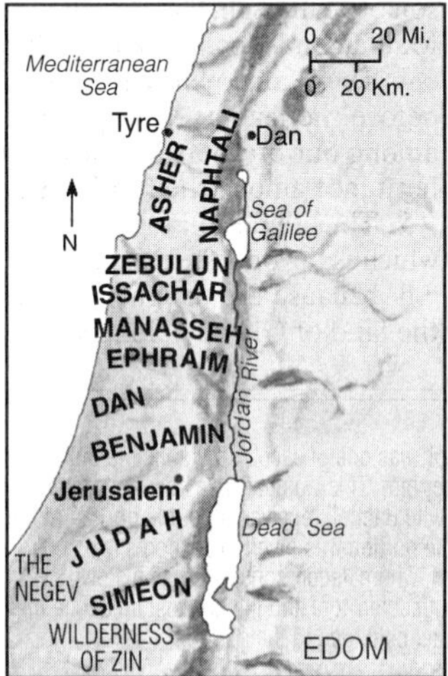

THE TRIBES WEST OF THE JORDAN
Judah, Ephraim, and the other half-tribe of Manasseh were the first tribes to receive land west of the Jordan because of their past acts of faith. The remaining seven tribes—Benjamin, Zebulun, Issachar, Asher, Naphtali, Simeon, and Dan—were slow to conquer and possess the land allotted to them.

2 There remained among the sons of Israel seven tribes who had not divided their
inheritance.

18:3 Judg 10.9

3 So Joshua said to the sons of Israel, "How long will you put off entering to take
possession of the land which the LORD, the God of your fathers, has given you?
4 "Provide for yourselves three men from each tribe that I may send them, and that
they may arise and walk through the land and write a description of it according to their
inheritance; then they shall return to me.

18:5 Josh 15:1

5 "They shall divide it into seven portions; Judah shall stay in its territory on the south,
and the house of Joseph shall stay in their territory on the north.

18:6 Josh 14:2

6 "You shall describe the land in seven divisions, and bring *the description* here to me.
I will cast lots for you here before the LORD our God.

18:7 Num 18:7, 20; Josh 13:33

7 "For the Levites have no portion among you, because the priesthood of the LORD
is their inheritance. Gad and Reuben and the half-tribe of Manasseh also have received
their inheritance eastward beyond the Jordan, which Moses the servant of the LORD gave
them."

18:8 Josh 18:1

8 Then the men arose and went, and Joshua commanded those who went to describe
the land, saying, "Go and walk through the land and describe it, and return to me; then
I will cast lots for you here before the LORD in Shiloh."
9 So the men went and passed through the land, and described it by cities in seven
divisions in a book; and they came to Joshua to the camp at Shiloh.

18:10 Num 34:16-29; Josh 19:51

10 And Joshua cast lots for them in Shiloh before the LORD, and there Joshua divided
the land to the sons of Israel according to their divisions.

The Territory of Benjamin

11 Now the lot of the tribe of the sons of Benjamin came up according to their families,
and the territory of their lot lay between the sons of Judah and the sons of Joseph.

18:12 Josh 16:1

12 Their border on the north side was from the Jordan, then the border went up to the
side of Jericho on the north, and went up through the hill country westward, and [12]it
ended at the wilderness of Beth-aven.

18:13 Gen 28:19; Judg 1:23; Josh 16:3

13 From there the border continued to Luz, to the side of Luz (that is, Bethel) southward;
and the border went down to Ataroth-addar, near the hill which *lies* on the south
of lower Beth-horon.
14 The border extended *from there* and turned round on the west side southward, from
the hill which *lies* before Beth-horon southward; and [12]it ended at Kiriath-baal (that is,
Kiriath-jearim), a city of the sons of Judah. This *was* the west side.

18:15 Josh 15:5-9

15 Then the south side *was* from the edge of Kiriath-jearim, and the border went westward
and went to the fountain of the waters of Nephtoah.

18:16 2 Kin 23:10

16 The border went down to the edge of the hill which is in the valley of Ben-hinnom,
which is in the valley of Rephaim northward; and it went down to the valley of Hinnom,
to the slope of the Jebusite southward, and went down to En-rogel.

12 Lit *the goings out of it were*

18:2ff Seven of the tribes had not yet been assigned their land. They gathered at Shiloh, where Joshua cast lots to determine which areas would be given to them. Using the sacred lottery, God would make the choice, not Joshua or any other human leader.

By this time, the Canaanites were, in most places, so weakened that they were no longer a threat. Instead of fulfilling God's command to destroy the remaining Canaanites, however, these seven tribes would often take the path of least resistance. As nomadic people, they may have been reluctant to settle down, preferring to depend economically on the people they were supposed to eliminate. Others may have feared the high cost of continued warfare. It was easier and more profitable to trade for goods than to destroy the suppliers and have to provide for themselves.

18:3–6 Joshua asked why some of the tribes were putting off the job of possessing the land. Often we delay doing jobs that seem large, difficult, boring, or disagreeable. But to continue putting them off shows lack of discipline, poor stewardship of time, and, in some cases, disobedience to God. Jobs we don't enjoy require concentration, teamwork, twice as much time, lots of encouragement, and accountability. Remember this when you are tempted to procrastinate.

18:8 Making decisions by casting lots was a common practice among the Hebrews. Little is known about the actual method used in Joshua's day. Dice may have been used. Another possibility is that two urns were used: one containing tribal names; the other, the divisions of the land. Drawing one name from each urn matched a tribe to a region. The Urim and Thummim (explained in the note on Leviticus 8:8) may also have been used. No matter how it was done, the process removed human choice from the decision-making process and allowed God to match tribes and lands as he saw fit.

18:11 The tribe of Benjamin was given a narrow strip of land that served as a buffer zone between Judah and Ephraim, the two tribes that would later dominate the land.

18:16 The valley of Ben-hinnom became associated with the worship of Molech (the Ammonite god) in Jeremiah's time. These terrible rites involved the sacrifice of children. Later the valley was used for burning garbage and the corpses of criminals and animals. Thus the name became a synonym for hell.

17 It extended northward and went to En-shemesh and went to Geliloth, which is 18:17
opposite the ascent of Adummim, and it went down to the stone of Bohan the son of Josh 15:6
Reuben.
18 It continued to the side in front of the Arabah northward and went down to the
Arabah.
19 The border continued to the side of Beth-hoglah northward; and the [13]border ended
at the north bay of the Salt Sea, at the south end of the Jordan. This *was* the south border.
20 Moreover, the Jordan was its border on the east side. This *was* the inheritance of
the sons of Benjamin, according to their families *and* according to its borders all around.
21 Now the cities of the tribe of the sons of Benjamin according to their families were
Jericho and Beth-hoglah and Emek-keziz,
22 and Beth-arabah and Zemaraim and Bethel,
23 and Avvim and Parah and Ophrah,
24 and Chephar-ammoni and Ophni and Geba; twelve cities with their villages. 18:24
25 Gibeon and Ramah and Beeroth, Ezra 2:26; Is 10:29
26 and Mizpeh and Chephirah and Mozah,
27 and Rekem and Irpeel and Taralah,
28 and Zelah, Haeleph and the Jebusite (that is, Jerusalem), Gibeah, Kiriath; four- 18:28
teen cities with their villages. This is the inheritance of the sons of Benjamin according 2 Sam 21:14; Num 26:38
to their families.

Territory of Simeon

19 Then the second lot fell to Simeon, to the tribe of the sons of Simeon according to
their families, and their inheritance was in the midst of the inheritance of the sons
of Judah.
2 So they had as their inheritance Beersheba or Sheba and Moladah,
3 and Hazar-shual and Balah and Ezem,
4 and Eltolad and Bethul and Hormah,
5 and Ziklag and Beth-marcaboth and Hazar-susah,
6 and Beth-lebaoth and Sharuhen; thirteen cities with their villages;
7 Ain, Rimmon and Ether and Ashan; four cities with their villages;
8 and all the villages which *were* around these cities as far as Baalath-beer, Ramah of
the Negev. This *was* the inheritance of the tribe of the sons of Simeon according to their
families.
9 The inheritance of the sons of Simeon *was taken* from the portion of the sons of
Judah, for the share of the sons of Judah was too large for them; so the sons of Simeon
received *an* inheritance in the midst of Judah's inheritance.

Territory of Zebulun

10 Now the third lot came up for the sons of Zebulun according to their families. And
the territory of their inheritance was as far as Sarid.
11 Then their border went up to the west and to Maralah, it then touched Dabbesheth
and reached to the brook that is before Jokneam.
12 Then it turned from Sarid to the east toward the sunrise as far as the border of
Chisloth-tabor, and it proceeded to Daberath and up to Japhia.
13 From there it continued eastward toward the sunrise to Gath-hepher, to Eth-kazin,
and it proceeded to Rimmon which stretches to Neah.
14 The border circled around it on the north to Hannathon, and it ended at the valley
of Iphtahel.
15 *Included* also *were* Kattah and Nahalal and Shimron and Idalah and Bethlehem;
twelve cities with their villages.
16 This *was* the inheritance of the sons of Zebulun according to their families, these
cities with their villages.

Territory of Issachar

17 The fourth lot fell to Issachar, to the sons of Issachar according to their families.
18 Their territory was to Jezreel and *included* Chesulloth and Shunem, 19:18
19 and Hapharaim and Shion and Anaharath, 1 Sam 28:4; 2 Kin 4:8
20 and Rabbith and Kishion and Ebez,
21 and Remeth and En-gannim and En-haddah and Beth-pazzez.

13 Lit *goings out of the border were*

19:22 Judg 4:6; Ps 89:12

22 The border reached to Tabor and Shahazumah and Beth-shemesh, and their border ended at the Jordan; sixteen cities with their villages.
23 This *was* the inheritance of the tribe of the sons of Issachar according to their families, the cities with their villages.

Territory of Asher

24 Now the fifth lot fell to the tribe of the sons of Asher according to their families.
25 Their territory was Helkath and Hali and Beten and Achshaph,
26 and Allammelech and Amad and Mishal; and it reached to Carmel on the west and
to Shihor-libnath.

19:27 1 Kin 9:13

27 It turned toward the east to Beth-dagon and reached to Zebulun, and to the valley
of Iphtahel northward to Beth-emek and Neiel; then it proceeded on north to Cabul,

19:28 Gen 10:19; Judg 1:31; Acts 27:3

28 and Ebron and Rehob and Hammon and Kanah, as far as Great Sidon.
29 The border turned to Ramah and to the fortified city of Tyre; then the border turned
to Hosah, and it ended at the sea by the region of Achzib.

19:29 Judg 1:31

30 *Included* also *were* Ummah, and Aphek and Rehob; twenty-two cities with their villages.
31 This *was* the inheritance of the tribe of the sons of Asher according to their families, these cities with their villages.

Territory of Naphtali

32 The sixth lot fell to the sons of Naphtali; to the sons of Naphtali according to their
families.
33 Their border was from Heleph, from the oak in Zaanannim and Adami-nekeb and
Jabneel, as far as Lakkum, and it ended at the Jordan.
34 Then the border turned westward to Aznoth-tabor and proceeded from there to
Hukkok; and it reached to Zebulun on the south and touched Asher on the west, and to
Judah at the Jordan toward the east.

19:35 Gen 10:18; 1 Kin 8:65; Deut 3:17

35 The fortified cities *were* Ziddim, Zer and Hammath, Rakkath and Chinnereth,
36 and Adamah and Ramah and Hazor,
37 and Kedesh and Edrei and En-hazor,
38 and Yiron and Migdal-el, Horem and Beth-anath and Beth-shemesh; nineteen cities with their villages.
39 This *was* the inheritance of the tribe of the sons of Naphtali according to their families, the cities with their villages.

Territory of Dan

40 The seventh lot fell to the tribe of the sons of Dan according to their families.
41 The territory of their inheritance was Zorah and Eshtaol and Ir-shemesh,
42 and Shaalabbin and Aijalon and Ithlah,
43 and Elon and Timnah and Ekron,
44 and Eltekeh and Gibbethon and Baalath,
45 and Jehud and Bene-berak and Gath-rimmon,
46 and Me-jarkon and Rakkon, with the territory over against Joppa.

19:47 Judg 18:1; Judg 18:29

47 The territory of the sons of Dan proceeded beyond them; for the sons of Dan went
up and fought with Leshem and captured it. Then they struck it with the edge of the
sword and possessed it and settled in it; and they called Leshem Dan after the name of
Dan their father.
48 This *was* the inheritance of the tribe of the sons of Dan according to their families,
these cities with their villages.
49 When they finished apportioning the land for inheritance by its borders, the sons of
Israel gave an inheritance in their midst to Joshua the son of Nun.

19:47–48 The tribe of Dan found that some of their land was difficult to conquer, so they chose to migrate to Leshem where they knew victory would be easier. Anyone can trust God when the going is easy. It is when everything looks impossible that our faith and courage are put to the test. Have faith that God is great enough to tackle your most difficult situations.

19:49 There were several good reasons for establishing these well-set boundaries instead of turning the promised land into a single undivided nation. (1) The boundaries gave each tribe ownership of an area, promoting loyalty and unity that would strengthen each tribe. (2) The boundaries delineated areas of responsibility and privilege, which would help each tribe develop and mature. (3) The boundaries reduced conflicts that might have broken out if everyone had wanted to live in the choicest areas. (4) The boundaries fulfilled the promised inheritance to each tribe that began to be given as early as the days of Jacob (Genesis 48:21–22).

50 In accordance with the command of the LORD they gave him the city for which he 19:50 Num 13:8; Josh 24:30
asked, Timnath-serah in the hill country of Ephraim. So he built the city and settled in it.
51 These are the inheritances which Eleazar the priest, and Joshua the son of Nun, 19:51 Josh 18:10
and the heads of the households of the tribes of the sons of Israel distributed by lot in
Shiloh before the LORD at the doorway of the tent of meeting. So they finished dividing
the land.

2. Special cities are set aside

Six Cities of Refuge

20 Then the LORD spoke to Joshua, saying,
2 "Speak to the sons of Israel, saying, 'Designate the cities of refuge, of which I 20:2 Num 35:6-34; Deut 4:41-43; 19:2ff
spoke to you through Moses,
3 that the manslayer who kills any person unintentionally, without premeditation, may
flee there, and they shall become your refuge from the avenger of blood.
4 'He shall flee to one of these cities, and shall stand at the entrance of the gate of the 20:4 Ruth 4:1; Job 5:4; Jer 38:7
city and state his case in the hearing of the elders of that city; and they shall take him
into the city to them and give him a place, so that he may dwell among them.
5 'Now if the avenger of blood pursues him, then they shall not deliver the manslayer 20:5 Num 35:12
into his hand, because he struck his neighbor without premeditation and did not hate
him beforehand.
6 'He shall dwell in that city until he stands before the congregation for judgment, until 20:6 Num 35:12
the death of the one who is high priest in those days. Then the manslayer shall return to
his own city and to his own house, to the city from which he fled.' "
7 So they set apart Kedesh in Galilee in the hill country of Naphtali and Shechem in 20:7 Josh 21:32; 1 Chr 6:76; Josh 21:11; Luke 1:39
the hill country of Ephraim, and Kiriath-arba (that is, Hebron) in the hill country of Judah.
8 Beyond the Jordan east of Jericho, they designated Bezer in the wilderness on the
plain from the tribe of Reuben, and Ramoth in Gilead from the tribe of Gad, and Golan
in Bashan from the tribe of Manasseh.
9 These were the appointed cities for all the sons of Israel and for the stranger who 20:9 Num 35:13ff
sojourns among them, that whoever kills any person unintentionally may flee there, and
not die by the hand of the avenger of blood until he stands before the congregation.

Forty-eight Cities of the Levites

21 Then the heads of households of the Levites approached Eleazar the priest, and 21:1 Num 35:1-8
Joshua the son of Nun, and the heads of households of the tribes of the sons of
Israel.
2 They spoke to them at Shiloh in the land of Canaan, saying, "The LORD command- 21:2 Num 35:2
ed through Moses to give us cities to live in, with their pasture lands for our cattle."

20:6 A new nation in a new land needed a new government. Many years earlier God had told Moses how this government should function. One of the tasks God wanted the Israelites to do when they entered the promised land was to designate certain cities as "cities of refuge." These were to be scattered throughout the land. Their purpose was to prevent injustice, especially in cases of revenge. For example, if someone accidentally killed another person, he could flee to a city of refuge where he was safe until he could have a fair trial. The Levites were in charge of these cities. They were to ensure that God's principles of justice and fairness were kept. (For more on cities of refuge, see the notes on Numbers 35:6; 35:11–28.)

21:2 The Levites were to minister before God on behalf of all the people, so they were given cities scattered throughout the land. Although Jerusalem was far away from the homes of many Israelites, almost no one lived more than a day's journey from a levitical city.

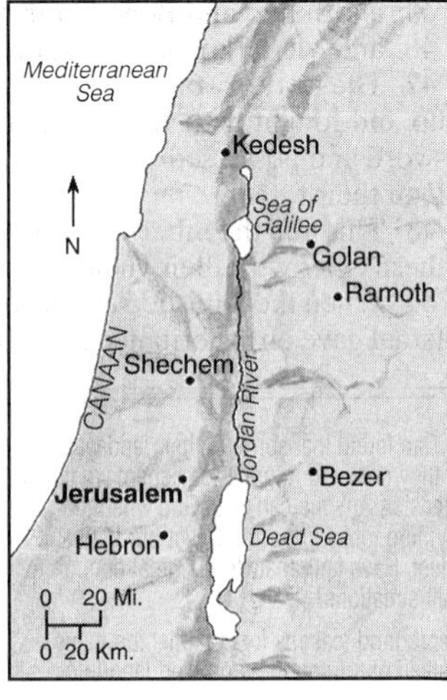

THE CITIES OF REFUGE
A city of refuge was just that—refuge for someone who committed an unintentional murder that would evoke revenge from the victim's friends and relatives. The six cities of refuge were spaced throughout the land so that a person was never too far from one.

3 So the sons of Israel gave the Levites from their inheritance these cities with their pasture lands, according to the command of the LORD.

4 Then the lot came out for the families of the Kohathites. And the sons of Aaron the priest, who were of the Levites, received thirteen cities by lot from the tribe of Judah and from the tribe of the Simeonites and from the tribe of Benjamin.

5 The rest of the sons of Kohath received ten cities by lot from the families of the tribe of Ephraim and from the tribe of Dan and from the half-tribe of Manasseh.

6 The sons of Gershon received thirteen cities by lot from the families of the tribe of Issachar and from the tribe of Asher and from the tribe of Naphtali and from the half-tribe of Manasseh in Bashan.

7 The sons of Merari according to their families received twelve cities from the tribe of Reuben and from the tribe of Gad and from the tribe of Zebulun.

21:8 Gen 49:5ff

8 Now the sons of Israel gave by lot to the Levites these cities with their pasture lands, as the LORD had commanded through Moses.

9 They gave these cities which are *here* mentioned by name from the tribe of the sons of Judah and from the tribe of the sons of Simeon;

10 and they were for the sons of Aaron, one of the families of the Kohathites, of the sons of Levi, for the lot was theirs first.

21:11 1 Chr 6:55; Josh 14:15; 15:13

11 Thus they gave them Kiriath-arba, *Arba being* the father of Anak (that is, Hebron), in the hill country of Judah, with its surrounding pasture lands.

12 But the fields of the city and its villages they gave to Caleb the son of Jephunneh as his possession.

21:13 1 Chr 6:57; Josh 15:54; Josh 15:42

13 So to the sons of Aaron the priest they gave Hebron, the city of refuge for the manslayer, with its pasture lands, and Libnah with its pasture lands,

14 and Jattir with its pasture lands and Eshtemoa with its pasture lands,

21:14 Josh 15:48; Josh 15:50

15 and Holon with its pasture lands and Debir with its pasture lands,

21:15 Josh 15:49

16 and Ain with its pasture lands and Juttah with its pasture lands *and* Beth-shemesh with its pasture lands; nine cities from these two tribes.

21:16 Josh 15:55; Josh 15:10

17 From the tribe of Benjamin, Gibeon with its pasture lands, Geba with its pasture lands,

21:17 Josh 18:25; Josh 18:24

18 Anathoth with its pasture lands and Almon with its pasture lands; four cities.

19 All the cities of the sons of Aaron, the priests, were thirteen cities with their pasture lands.

21:20 1 Chr 6:66

20 Then the cities from the tribe of Ephraim were allotted to the families of the sons of Kohath, the Levites, *even to* the rest of the sons of Kohath.

21:21 Josh 20:7

21 They gave them Shechem, the city of refuge for the manslayer, with its pasture lands, in the hill country of Ephraim, and Gezer with its pasture lands,

22 and Kibzaim with its pasture lands and Beth-horon with its pasture lands; four cities.

23 From the tribe of Dan, Elteke with its pasture lands, Gibbethon with its pasture lands,

24 Aijalon with its pasture lands, Gath-rimmon with its pasture lands; four cities.

25 From the half-tribe of Manasseh, *they allotted* Taanach with its pasture lands and Gath-rimmon with its pasture lands; two cities.

26 All the cities with their pasture lands for the families of the rest of the sons of Kohath were ten.

21:27 1 Chr 6:71

27 To the sons of Gershon, one of the families of the Levites, from the half-tribe of Manasseh, *they gave* Golan in Bashan, the city of refuge for the manslayer, with its pasture lands, and Be-eshterah with its pasture lands; two cities.

28 From the tribe of Issachar, *they gave* Kishion with its pasture lands, Daberath with its pasture lands,

29 Jarmuth with its pasture lands, En-gannim with its pasture lands; four cities.

30 From the tribe of Asher, *they gave* Mishal with its pasture lands, Abdon with its pasture lands,

31 Helkath with its pasture lands and Rehob with its pasture lands; four cities.

21:32 Josh 20:7

32 From the tribe of Naphtali, *they gave* Kedesh in Galilee, the city of refuge for the manslayer, with its pasture lands and Hammoth-dor with its pasture lands and Kartan with its pasture lands; three cities.

33 All the cities of the Gershonites according to their families were thirteen cities with their pasture lands.

21:34 1 Chr 6:77

34 To the families of the sons of Merari, the rest of the Levites, *they gave* from the tribe of Zebulun, Jokneam with its pasture lands and Kartah with its pasture lands.

35 Dimnah with its pasture lands, Nahalal with its pasture lands; four cities.
36 From the tribe of Reuben, *they gave* Bezer with its pasture lands and Jahaz with its
pasture lands,
37 Kedemoth with its pasture lands and Mephaath with its pasture lands; four cities.
38 From the tribe of Gad, *they gave* Ramoth in Gilead, the city of refuge for the
manslayer, with its pasture lands and Mahanaim with its pasture lands,
39 Heshbon with its pasture lands, Jazer with its pasture lands; four cities in all.
40 All *these were* the cities of the sons of Merari according to their families, the rest of
the families of the Levites; and their lot was twelve cities.
41 All the cities of the Levites in the midst of the possession of the sons of Israel were
forty-eight cities with their pasture lands.
42 These cities each had its surrounding pasture lands; thus *it was* with all these cities.
43 So the LORD gave Israel all the land which He had sworn to give to their fathers,
and they possessed it and lived in it.
44 And the LORD gave them rest on every side, according to all that He had sworn to
their fathers, and no one of all their enemies stood before them; the LORD gave all their
enemies into their hand.
45 Not one of the good promises which the LORD had made to the house of Israel failed;
all came to pass.

21:36 Deut 4:43; Josh 20:8
21:38 Deut 4:43; 1 Kin 4:13; Gen 32:2; 2 Sam 2:8
21:41 Num 35:7
21:43 Deut 34:4; Num 33:53; Deut 11:31; 17:14
21:44 Josh 1:13; 23:1; Deut 7:24; Ex 23:31
21:45 Josh 23:14; 1 Kin 8:56

3. Eastern tribes return home

Tribes beyond Jordan Return

22 Then Joshua summoned the Reubenites and the Gadites and the half-tribe of Manasseh,
2 and said to them, "You have kept all that Moses the servant of the LORD commanded
you, and have listened to my voice in all that I commanded you.
3 "You have not forsaken your brothers these many days to this day, but have kept the
charge of the commandment of the LORD your God.
4 "And now the LORD your God has given rest to your brothers, as He spoke to them;
therefore turn now and go to your tents, to the land of your possession, which Moses the
servant of the LORD gave you beyond the Jordan.
5 "Only be very careful to observe the commandment and the law which Moses the
servant of the LORD commanded you, to love the LORD your God and walk in all His
ways and keep His commandments and hold fast to Him and serve Him with all your
heart and with all your soul."
6 So Joshua blessed them and sent them away, and they went to their tents.
7 Now to the one half-tribe of Manasseh Moses had given *a possession* in Bashan, but
to the other half Joshua gave *a possession* among their brothers westward beyond the
Jordan. So when Joshua sent them away to their tents, he blessed them,
8 and said to them, "Return to your tents with great riches and with very much livestock, with silver, gold, bronze, iron, and with very many clothes; divide the spoil of your
enemies with your brothers."
9 The sons of Reuben and the sons of Gad and the half-tribe of Manasseh returned
home and departed from the sons of Israel at Shiloh which is in the land of Canaan, to
go to the land of Gilead, to the land of their possession which they had possessed, according to the command of the LORD through Moses.

22:1 Num 32:20-22
22:2 Josh 1:12-18
22:4 Num 32:18; Deut 3:20
22:5 Deut 5:10; Deut 4:29
22:6 Gen 47:7; Josh 14:13; 2 Sam 6:18; Luke 24:50
22:7 Num 32:33; Josh 17:1-13
22:8 Num 31:27; 1 Sam 30:16
22:9 Num 32:1, 26, 29

21:43–45 God proved faithful in fulfilling every promise he had given to Israel. Fulfillment of some promises took several years, but "all came to pass." His promises will be fulfilled according to his timetable, not ours, but we know that his word is sure. The more we learn of those promises God has fulfilled and continues to fulfill, the easier it is to hope for those yet to come. Sometimes we become impatient, wanting God to act in a certain way *now.* Instead, we should faithfully do what we know he wants us to do and trust him for the future.

22:2–4 Before the conquest had begun, these tribes were given land on the east side of the Jordan River. But before they could settle down, they had to first promise to help the other tribes conquer the land on the west side (Numbers 32:20–22). They had patiently and diligently carried out their promised duties. Joshua commended them for doing just that. At last they were permitted to return to their families and build their cities. Follow-through is vital in God's work. Beware of the temptation to quit early and leave God's work undone.

22:5 Here Joshua briefly restated the central message Moses gave the people in Deuteronomy: Obedience should be based on love for God. Although the Israelites had completed their military responsibility, Joshua reminded them of their spiritual responsibility. Sometimes we think so much about what we are to do that we neglect thinking about who we are to be. If we know we are God's children, we will love him and joyfully serve him. We must not let daily service take away from our love for God.

The Offensive Altar

10 When they came to the region of the Jordan which is in the land of Canaan, the
sons of Reuben and the sons of Gad and the half-tribe of Manasseh built an altar there
by the Jordan, a large altar in appearance.

22:11 Deut 12:5; Josh 22:19

11 And the sons of Israel heard *it* said, "Behold, the sons of Reuben and the sons of
Gad and the half-tribe of Manasseh have built an altar at the frontier of the land of
Canaan, in the region of the Jordan, on the side *belonging to* the sons of Israel."

22:12 Josh 18:1

12 When the sons of Israel heard *of it,* the whole congregation of the sons of Israel
gathered themselves at Shiloh to go up against them in war.

22:13 Num 25:7, 11; 31:6

13 Then the sons of Israel sent to the sons of Reuben and to the sons of Gad and to the
half-tribe of Manasseh, into the land of Gilead, Phinehas the son of Eleazar the priest,

22:14 Num 1:4

14 and with him ten chiefs, one chief for each father's household from each of the tribes
of Israel; and each one of them *was* the head of his father's household among the thousands of Israel.
15 They came to the sons of Reuben and to the sons of Gad and to the half-tribe of
Manasseh, to the land of Gilead, and they spoke with them saying,

22:16 Josh 22:11

16 "Thus says the whole congregation of the LORD, 'What is this unfaithful act which
you have committed against the God of Israel, turning away from following the LORD
this day, by building yourselves an altar, to rebel against the LORD this day?

22:17 Num 25:1-9

17 'Is not the iniquity of Peor enough for us, from which we have not cleansed ourselves
to this day, although a plague came on the congregation of the LORD,

22:18 Num 16:22

18 that you must turn away this day from following the LORD? If you rebel against the
LORD today, He will be angry with the whole congregation of Israel tomorrow.

22:19 Josh 22:11

19 'If, however, the land of your possession is unclean, then cross into the land of the
possession of the LORD, where the LORD'S tabernacle stands, and take possession among
us. Only do not rebel against the LORD, or rebel against us by building an altar for yourselves, besides the altar of the LORD our God.

22:20 Josh 7:1-26

20 'Did not Achan the son of Zerah act unfaithfully in the things under the ban, and
wrath fall on all the congregation of Israel? And that man did not perish alone in his
iniquity.' "
21 Then the sons of Reuben and the sons of Gad and the half-tribe of Manasseh answered and spoke to the heads of the families of Israel.

22:22 Deut 10:17; 1 Kin 8:39; Job 10:7; Ps 44:21

22 "The Mighty One, God, the LORD, the Mighty One, God, the LORD! He knows, and
may Israel itself know. If *it was* in rebellion, or if in an unfaithful act against the LORD
do not save us this day!

22:23 Deut 12:11

23 "If we have built us an altar to turn away from following the LORD, or if to offer a
burnt offering or grain offering on it, or if to offer sacrifices of peace offerings on it, may
the LORD Himself require it.
24 "But truly we have done this out of concern, for a reason, saying, 'In time to come
your sons may say to our sons, "What have you to do with the LORD, the God of Israel?
25 "For the LORD has made the Jordan a border between us and you, *you* sons of Reuben and sons of Gad; you have no portion in the LORD." So your sons may make our
sons stop fearing the LORD.'

22:27 Gen 31:48; Josh 24:27; Deut 12:6, 11, 26f

26 "Therefore we said, 'Let us build an altar, not for burnt offering or for sacrifice;
27 rather it shall be a witness between us and you and between our generations after
us, that we are to perform the service of the LORD before Him with our burnt offerings,

---

22:11–34 When the tribes of Reuben and Gad and the half-tribe of Manasseh built an altar at the Jordan River, the rest of Israel feared that these tribes were starting their own religion and rebelling against God. But before beginning an all-out war, Phinehas led a delegation to learn the truth, following the principle taught in Deuteronomy 13:12–19. He was prepared to negotiate rather than fight if a battle was not necessary. When he learned that the altar was for a memorial rather than for pagan sacrifice, war was averted and unity restored.

As nations and as individuals, we would benefit from a similar approach to resolving conflicts. Assuming the worst about the intentions of others only brings trouble. Israel averted the threat of civil war by asking before assaulting. Beware of reacting before you hear the whole story.

22:17 For the story of how Israel turned away from God and began to worship Baal at Peor, see Numbers 25:1–18.

22:20 For the story of Achan, a man who allowed greed to get the best of him, see chapter 7.

22:26–28 The tribes were concerned that, without some visible sign of unity between the people on the two sides of the Jordan, future generations might see conflict between them. The altar, patterned after the altar of the Lord, was to remind these people that they all worshiped the same God. Often we need to be reminded of the faith of our fathers. What actions demonstrate to your children your reliance on God and remind them of what he has done? Take the time to establish family traditions that will help your children remember.

and with our sacrifices and with our peace offerings, so that your sons will not say to our
sons in time to come, "You have no portion in the LORD." '
28 "Therefore we said, 'It shall also come about if they say *this* to us or to our generations in time to come, then we shall say, "See the copy of the altar of the LORD which
our fathers made, not for burnt offering or for sacrifice; rather it is a witness between us
and you." '
29 "Far be it from us that we should rebel against the LORD and turn away from follow- **22:29**
ing the LORD this day, by building an altar for burnt offering, for grain offering or for Deut 12:13f
sacrifice, besides the altar of the LORD our God which is before His [14]tabernacle."
30 So when Phinehas the priest and the leaders of the congregation, even the heads of
the families of Israel who *were* with him, heard the words which the sons of Reuben and
the sons of Gad and the sons of Manasseh spoke, it pleased them.
31 And Phinehas the son of Eleazar the priest said to the sons of Reuben and to the **22:31**
sons of Gad and to the sons of Manasseh, "Today we know that the LORD is in our midst, Ex 25:8; Lev 26:11f; 2 Chr 15:2
because you have not committed this unfaithful act against the LORD; now you have
delivered the sons of Israel from the hand of the LORD."
32 Then Phinehas the son of Eleazar the priest and the leaders returned from the sons
of Reuben and from the sons of Gad, from the land of Gilead to the land of Canaan, to
the sons of Israel, and brought back word to them.
33 The word pleased the sons of Israel, and the sons of Israel blessed God; and they **22:33**
did not speak of going up against them in war to destroy the land in which the sons of 1 Chr 29:20; Dan 2:19; Luke 2:28
Reuben and the sons of Gad were living.
34 The sons of Reuben and the sons of Gad called the altar *Witness;* "For," *they said,* **22:34**
"it is a witness between us that the LORD is God." Gen 31:47-49

4. Joshua's farewell to the leaders

Joshua's Farewell Address

23 Now it came about after many days, when the LORD had given rest to Israel from **23:1**
all their enemies on every side, and Joshua was old, advanced in years, Josh 21:44
2 that Joshua called for all Israel, for their elders and their heads and their judges **23:2**
and their officers, and said to them, "I am old, advanced in years. Josh 24:1
3 "And you have seen all that the LORD your God has done to all these nations be- **23:3**
cause of you, for the LORD your God is He who has been fighting for you. Deut 1:30
4 "See, I have apportioned to you these nations which remain as an inheritance for **23:4**
your tribes, with all the nations which I have cut off, from the Jordan even to the Great Ex 23:30
Sea toward the setting of the sun.
5 "The LORD your God, He will thrust them out from before you and drive them from **23:5**
before you; and you will possess their land, just as the LORD your God promised you. Ex 23:20; Num 33:53
6 "Be very firm, then, to keep and do all that is written in the book of the law of Moses,
so that you may not turn aside from it to the right hand or to the left, **23:6** Deut 5:32; Josh 1:7
7 so that you will not associate with these nations, these which remain among you, or
mention the name of their gods, or make *anyone* swear *by them,* or serve them, or bow **23:7** Ex 23:13; Ps 16:4;
down to them. Deut 6:13; 10:20; Ex 20:5
8 "But you are to cling to the LORD your God, as you have done to this day.
9 "For the LORD has driven out great and strong nations from before you; and as for **23:9**
you, no man has stood before you to this day. Ex 23:23, 30; Deut 7:24
10 "One of your men puts to flight a thousand, for the LORD your God is He who fights
for you, just as He promised you. **23:10** Lev 26:8; Deut 28:7;
11 "So take diligent heed to yourselves to love the LORD your God. 32:20; Deut 3:22; Josh 23:3

14 Lit *dwelling place*

23:6–13 Joshua knew the nation's weak spots. Before dying, he called the people together and gave commands to help them where they were most likely to slip: (1) follow all that is written in the book of the law of Moses without turning aside; (2) don't associate with the pagan nations or worship their gods; (3) don't intermarry with the pagan nations. These temptations were right in their backyard. Our associations and relationships can be temptations to us as well. It's wise to identify our weak spots *before* we break down. Then we can develop strategies to overcome these temptations instead of being overcome by them.

23:8 Joshua was dying and so he called all the leaders of the nation together to give them his final words of encouragement and instruction. His whole message can be summarized in this verse, "Cling to the LORD your God." Joshua had been a living example of those words, and he wanted that to be his legacy. For what do you want to be remembered, and what do you want to pass on to your children and associates? You can leave them nothing better than the admonition to hold on to God and to the memory of a person who did.

12 "For if you ever go back and cling to the rest of these nations, these which remain
among you, and intermarry with them, so that you associate with them and they
with you,
13 know with certainty that the LORD your God will not continue to drive these nations out from before you; but they will be a snare and a trap to you, and a whip on your
sides and thorns in your eyes, until you perish from off this good land which the LORD
your God has given you.
14 "Now behold, today I am going the way of all the earth, and you know in all your
hearts and in all your souls that not one word of all the good words which the LORD your
God spoke concerning you has failed; all have been fulfilled for you, not one of them
has failed.
15 "It shall come about that just as all the good words which the LORD your God spoke
to you have come upon you, so the LORD will bring upon you all the threats, until He has
destroyed you from off this good land which the LORD your God has given you.
16 "When you transgress the covenant of the LORD your God, which He commanded
you, and go and serve other gods and bow down to them, then the anger of the LORD
will burn against you, and you will perish quickly from off the good land which He has
given you."

Joshua Reviews Israel's History

24 Then Joshua gathered all the tribes of Israel to Shechem, and called for the elders of Israel and for their heads and their judges and their officers; and they
presented themselves before God.
2 Joshua said to all the people, "Thus says the LORD, the God of Israel, 'From ancient times your fathers lived beyond the [15]River, *namely,* Terah, the father of Abraham
and the father of Nahor, and they served other gods.
3 'Then I took your father Abraham from beyond the River, and led him through all
the land of Canaan, and multiplied his descendants and gave him Isaac.
4 'To Isaac I gave Jacob and Esau, and to Esau I gave Mount Seir to possess it; but
Jacob and his sons went down to Egypt.
5 'Then I sent Moses and Aaron, and I plagued Egypt by what I did in its midst; and
afterward I brought you out.
6 'I brought your fathers out of Egypt, and you came to the sea; and Egypt pursued
your fathers with chariots and horsemen to the Red Sea.
7 'But when they cried out to the LORD, He put darkness between you and the Egyptians, and brought the sea upon them and covered them; and your own eyes saw what I
did in Egypt. And you lived in the wilderness for a long time.
8 'Then I brought you into the land of the Amorites who lived beyond the Jordan, and

23:12 Ex 34:15, 16; Ps 106:34, 35; Deut 7:3, 4; Ezra 9:2; Neh 13:25
23:13 Ex 23:33; 34:12; Deut 7:16
23:14 1 Kin 2:2; Josh 21:45
23:15 Lev 26:14-33; Deut 28:15
23:16 Deut 4:25, 26
24:1 Josh 23:2
24:2 Gen 11:27-32
24:3 Gen 12:1; 24:7; Gen 15:5; Gen 21:3
24:4 Gen 25:25, 26; Gen 36:8; Deut 2:5; Gen 46:6, 7
24:5 Ex 4:14-17
24:6 Ex 14:2-31
24:7 Deut 1:46; 2:14
24:8 Num 21:21-32

15 I.e. Euphrates, and so throughout the ch

JOSHUA'S FINAL SPEECH
Joshua called all the Israelites to Shechem to hear his final words. He challenged the people to make a conscious choice to always serve God. Soon afterward, Joshua died and was buried in his hometown of Timnath-serah.

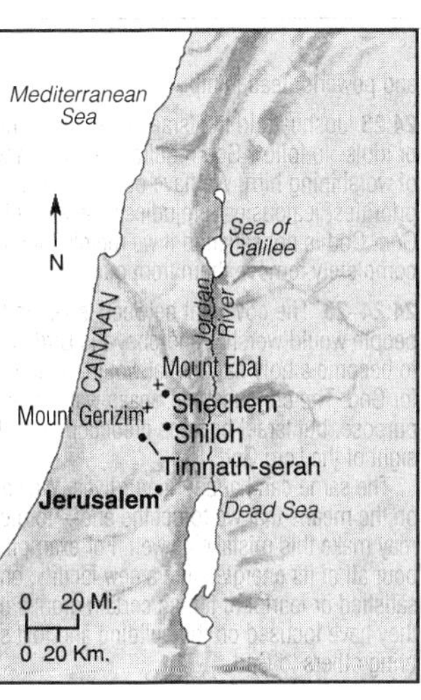

23:12–16 This chilling prediction about the consequences of intermarriage with the Canaanite nations eventually became a reality. Numerous stories in the book of Judges show what Israel had to suffer because of failure to follow God wholeheartedly. God was supremely loving and patient with Israel, just as he is today. But we must not confuse his patience with us as approval or indifference to our sin. Beware of demanding your own way because eventually you may get it—along with all its painful consequences.

they fought with you; and I gave them into your hand, and you took possession of their
land when I destroyed them before you.
9 'Then Balak the son of Zippor, king of Moab, arose and fought against Israel, and
he sent and summoned Balaam the son of Beor to curse you.
10 'But I was not willing to listen to Balaam. So he had to bless you, and I delivered you
from his hand.
11 'You crossed the Jordan and came to Jericho; and the citizens of Jericho fought
against you, *and* the Amorite and the Perizzite and the Canaanite and the Hittite and
the Girgashite, the Hivite and the Jebusite. Thus I gave them into your hand.
12 'Then I sent the hornet before you and it drove out the two kings of the Amorites
from before you, *but* not by your sword or your bow.
13 'I gave you a land on which you had not labored, and cities which you had not built,
and you have lived in them; you are eating of vineyards and olive groves which you did
not plant.'

"We Will Serve the LORD"

14 "Now, therefore, fear the LORD and serve Him in sincerity and truth; and put away
the gods which your fathers served beyond the River and in Egypt, and serve the LORD.
15 "If it is disagreeable in your sight to serve the LORD, choose for yourselves today
whom you will serve: whether the gods which your fathers served which were beyond the
River, or the gods of the Amorites in whose land you are living; but as for me and my
house, we will serve the LORD."
16 The people answered and said, "Far be it from us that we should forsake the LORD
to serve other gods;
17 for the LORD our God is He who brought us and our fathers up out of the land of
Egypt, from the house of bondage, and who did these great signs in our sight and preserved us through all the way in which we went and among all the peoples through whose
midst we passed.
18 "The LORD drove out from before us all the peoples, even the Amorites who lived in
the land. We also will serve the LORD, for He is our God."
19 Then Joshua said to the people, "You will not be able to serve the LORD, for He is
a holy God. He is a jealous God; He will not forgive your transgression or your sins.
20 "If you forsake the LORD and serve foreign gods, then He will turn and do you harm
and consume you after He has done good to you."
21 The people said to Joshua, "No, but we will serve the LORD."
22 Joshua said to the people, "You are witnesses against yourselves that you have chosen for yourselves the LORD, to serve Him." And they said, "We are witnesses."
23 "Now therefore, put away the foreign gods which are in your midst, and incline your
hearts to the LORD, the God of Israel."
24 The people said to Joshua, "We will serve the LORD our God and we will obey His
voice."

24:9 Num 22:2-6
24:10 Deut 23:5
24:11 Josh 3:14-17; Ex 23:23, 28; Deut 7:1; Ex 23:31
24:12 Ex 23:28; Deut 7:20; Ps 44:3
24:13 Deut 6:10, 11
24:14 Deut 10:12; 18:13; 1 Sam 12:24
24:15 Judg 6:10
24:19 Lev 19:2; 20:7, 26; Ex 20:5; 34:14; Ex 23:21
24:20 Deut 4:25, 26
24:22 Ps 119:173
24:23 1 Kin 8:57, 58; Ps 119:36; 141:4
24:24 Ex 19:8; 24:3, 7; Deut 5:27

24:15 The people had to decide whether they would obey the Lord, who had proven his trustworthiness, or obey the local gods, which were only man-made idols. It's easy to slip into a quiet rebellion—going about life in your own way. But the time comes when you have to choose who or what will control you. The choice is yours. Will it be God, your own limited personality, or another imperfect substitute? Once you have chosen to be controlled by God's Spirit, reaffirm your choice every day.

24:15 In taking a definite stand for the Lord, Joshua again displayed his spiritual leadership. Regardless of what others decided, Joshua had made a commitment to God, and he was willing to set the example of living by that decision. The way we live shows others the strength of our commitment to serving God.

24:16–18, 21 All the people boldly claimed that they would never forsake the Lord. But they did not keep that promise. Very soon God would charge them with breaking their contract with him (Judges 2:2–3). Talk is cheap. It is easy to say we will follow God, but it is much more important to live like it. Yet the nation followed God through Joshua's lifetime, a great tribute to Joshua's faith in God and powerful leadership.

24:23 Joshua told the Israelites to throw away their foreign gods, or idols. To follow God requires destroying whatever gets in the way of worshiping him. We have our own form of idols—greed, wrong priorities, jealousies, prejudices—that get in the way of worshiping God. God is not satisfied if we merely hide these idols. We must completely remove them from our lives.

24:24–26 The covenant between Israel and God was that the people would worship and obey the Lord alone. Their purpose was to become a holy nation that would influence the rest of the world for God. The conquest of Canaan was a means to achieve this purpose, but Israel became preoccupied with the land and lost sight of the Lord God.

The same can happen in our lives. We can spend so much time on the means that we forget the end—to glorify God. Churches may make this mistake as well. For example, the congregation may pour all of its energies into a new facility, only to become self-satisfied or fearful of letting certain groups use it. If this happens, they have focused on the building and lost sight of its purpose—to bring others to God.

24:25 Ex 24:8

25 So Joshua made a covenant with the people that day, and made for them a statute
and an ordinance in Shechem.

24:26 Deut 31:24

26 And Joshua wrote these words in the book of the law of God; and he took a large
stone and set it up there under the oak that was by the sanctuary of the LORD.

24:27 Josh 22:27, 34

27 Joshua said to all the people, "Behold, this stone shall be for a witness against us,
for it has heard all the words of the LORD which He spoke to us; thus it shall be for a
witness against you, so that you do not deny your God."
28 Then Joshua dismissed the people, each to his inheritance.

Joshua's Death and Burial

29 It came about after these things that Joshua the son of Nun, the servant of the LORD,
died, being one hundred and ten years old.

24:30 Josh 19:50

30 And they buried him in the territory of his inheritance in Timnath-serah, which is in
the hill country of Ephraim, on the north of Mount Gaash.

24:31 Judg 2:6f

31 Israel served the LORD all the days of Joshua and all the days of the elders who
survived Joshua, and had known all the deeds of the LORD which He had done for Israel.

24:32 Gen 50:24, 25; Ex 13:19; Gen 33:19; John 4:5; Acts 7:15f

32 Now they buried the bones of Joseph, which the sons of Israel brought up from Egypt,
at Shechem, in the piece of ground which Jacob had bought from the sons of Hamor the
father of Shechem for one hundred pieces of money; and they became the inheritance
of Joseph's sons.

24:33 Josh 22:13

33 And Eleazar the son of Aaron died; and they buried him at Gibeah of Phinehas his
son, which was given him in the hill country of Ephraim.

24:29–31 The book of Joshua opens with a new leader being handed a seemingly impossible task—to lead the nation in taking over the land of Canaan. By following God closely, Joshua led the people through military victories and faithful spiritual obedience. In 24:16 we read that the people were sure they would never forsake the Lord. The response of the whole nation during these many years is a tribute both to Joshua's leadership and to the God he faithfully served.

24:33 Joshua and Eleazar had died, but not before laying before the people the fundamentals of what it means to have faith in God. We are to fear and serve the Lord alone (24:14). This is based on a choice: to obey him instead of following other gods (24:15). We are incapable, however, of properly worshiping him because of our rebellion and sins (24:19). By choosing God as Lord we enter into a covenant with him (24:25) whereby he promises not only to forgive and love us, but also to enable us by his Spirit to do his work here on earth. This covenant requires us to renounce the principles and practices of the culture around us that are hostile to God's plan (24:23). This is not to be done alone, but by binding ourselves together with others who have faith in God. (See Deuteronomy 30:15–20 for a similar message from Moses.)

J U D G E S

Exodus from Egypt 1446 B.C. (1280 B.C.)	*Israelites enter Canaan 1406 (1240)*	*Period of the judges begins 1375 (1220)*	*Othniel 1367–1327 (1202–1162)*	*Ehud 1309–1229 (1184–1104)*	*Deborah 1209–1169 (1192–1152)*

VITAL STATISTICS

PURPOSE:
To show that God's judgment against sin is certain, and his forgiveness of sin and restoration to relationship are just as certain for those who repent

AUTHOR:
Possibly Samuel

SETTING:
The land of Canaan, later called Israel. God had helped the Israelites conquer Canaan, which had been inhabited by a host of wicked nations. But they were in danger of losing this promised land because they compromised their convictions and disobeyed God.

KEY VERSE:
"In those days there was no king in Israel; every man did what was right in his own eyes" (17:6).

KEY PEOPLE:
Othniel, Ehud, Deborah, Gideon, Abimelech, Jephthah, Samson, Delilah

SPECIAL FEATURE:
Records Israel's first civil war

REAL heroes are hard to find these days. Modern research and the media have made the foibles and weaknesses of our leaders very apparent; we search in vain for men and women to emulate. The music, movie, and sports industries produce a steady stream of "stars" who shoot to the top and then quickly fade from view.

Judges is a book about heroes—12 men and women who delivered Israel from its oppressors. These judges were not perfect; in fact, they included an assassin, a sexually promiscuous man, and a person who broke all the laws of hospitality. But they were submissive to God, and God used them.

Judges is also a book about sin and its consequences. Like a minor cut or abrasion that becomes infected when left untreated, sin grows and soon poisons the whole body. The book of Joshua ends with the nation taking a stand for God, ready to experience all the blessings of the promised land. After settling in Canaan, however, the Israelites lost their spiritual commitment and motivation. When Joshua and the elders died, the nation experienced a leadership vacuum, leaving them without a strong central government. Instead of enjoying freedom and prosperity in the promised land, Israel entered the dark ages of her history.

Simply stated, the reason for this rapid decline was sin—individual and corporate. The first step away from God was incomplete obedience (1:11—2:5); the Israelites refused to eliminate the enemy completely from the land. This led to intermarriage and idolatry (2:6—3:7) and everyone doing "what was right in his own eyes" (17:6). Before long the Israelites became captives. Out of their desperation they begged God to rescue them. In faithfulness to his promise and out of his loving-kindness, God would raise up a judge to deliver his people, and for a time there would be peace. Then complacency and disobedience would set in, and the cycle would begin again.

The book of Judges spans a period of over 325 years, recording six successive periods of oppression and deliverance, and the careers of 12 deliverers. Their captors included the Mesopotamians, Moabites, Philistines, Canaanites, Midianites, and Ammonites. A variety of deliverers—from Othniel to Samson—were used by God to lead his people to freedom and true worship. God's deliverance through the judges is a powerful demonstration of his love and mercy toward his people.

As you read the book of Judges, take a good look at these heroes from Jewish history. Take note of their dependence on God and obedience to his commands. Observe Israel's repeated downward spiral into sin, refusing to learn from history and living only for the moment. But most of all, stand in awe of God's mercy as he delivers his people over and over again.

Gideon 1162–1122 (1146–1106)	Samuel born 1105 (1083)	Samson 1075–1055 (1083–1063)	Saul anointed king 1050 (1045)	David becomes king 1010

THE BLUEPRINT

A. THE MILITARY FAILURE OF ISRAEL (1:1—3:6)
1. Incomplete conquest of the land
2. Disobedience and defeat

The tribes had compromised God's command to drive out the inhabitants of the land. Incomplete removal of evil often means disaster in the end. We must beware of compromising with wickedness.

B. THE RESCUE OF ISRAEL BY THE JUDGES (3:7—16:31)
1. First period: Othniel
2. Second period: Ehud and Shamgar
3. Third period: Deborah and Barak
4. Fourth period: Gideon, Tola, and Jair
5. Fifth period: Jephthah, Ibzan, Elon, and Abdon
6. Sixth period: Samson

Repeatedly we see the nation of Israel sinning against God and God allowing suffering to come upon the land and the people. Sin always has its consequences. Where there is sin we can expect suffering to follow. Rather than living in an endless cycle of abandoning God and then crying out to him for rescue, we should seek to live a consistent life of faithfulness.

C. THE MORAL FAILURE OF ISRAEL (17:1—21:25)
1. Idolatry in the tribe of Dan
2. War against the tribe of Benjamin

Despite the efforts of Israel's judges, the people still would not turn wholeheartedly to God. They all did whatever they thought was best for themselves. The result was the spiritual, moral, and political decline of the nation. Our lives will also fall into decline and decay unless we live by the guidelines God has given us.

MEGATHEMES

THEME	EXPLANATION	IMPORTANCE
Decline/ Compromise	Whenever a judge died, the people faced decline and failure because they compromised their high spiritual purpose in many ways. They abandoned their mission to drive all the people out of the land, and they adopted the customs of the people living around them.	Society has many rewards to offer those who compromise their faith: wealth, acceptance, recognition, power, and influence. When God gives us a mission, it must not be polluted by a desire for approval from society. We must keep our eyes on Christ, who is our Judge and Deliverer.
Decay/Apostasy	Israel's moral downfall had its roots in the fierce independence that each tribe cherished. It led to everyone doing whatever seemed good in his own eyes. There was no unity in government or in worship. Law and order broke down. Finally, idol worship and man-made religion led to the complete abandoning of faith in God.	We can expect decay when we value anything more highly than God. If we value our own independence more than dedication to God, we have placed an idol in our hearts. Soon our lives become temples to that god. We must constantly regard God's first claim on our lives and all our desires.
Defeat/ Oppression	God used evil oppressors to punish the Israelites for their sin, to bring them to the point of repentance, and to test their allegiance to him.	Rebellion against God leads to disaster. God may use defeat to bring wandering hearts back to him. When all else is stripped away, we recognize the importance of serving only him.
Repentance	Decline, decay, and defeat caused the people to cry out to God for help. They vowed to turn from idolatry and to turn to God for mercy and deliverance. When they repented, God delivered them.	Idolatry gains a foothold in our hearts when we make anything more important than God. We must identify modern idols in our hearts, renounce them, and turn to God for his love and mercy.

Deliverance/ Heroes	Because Israel repented, God raised up heroes to deliver his people from their path of sin and the oppression it brought. He used many kinds of people to accomplish this purpose by filling them with his Holy Spirit.	God's Holy Spirit is available to all people. Anyone who is dedicated to God can be used for his service. Real heroes recognize the futility of human effort without God's guidance and power.

KEY PLACES IN JUDGES

The broken lines (—·—·) indicate modern boundaries.

1 Bochim The book of Judges opens with the Israelites continuing their conquest of the promised land. Their failure to obey God and destroy all the evil inhabitants soon comes back to haunt them in two ways: (1) the enemies reorganized and counterattacked, and (2) Israel turned away from God, adopting the evil and idolatrous practices of the inhabitants of the land. The angel of the Lord appeared at Bochim to inform the Israelites that their sin and disobedience had broken their agreement with God and would result in punishment through oppression (1:1—3:11).

2 Jericho The nation of Moab was one of the first to oppress Israel. Moab's king Eglon conquered much of Israel—including the city of Jericho—and forced the people to pay unreasonable taxes. The messenger chosen to deliver this tax money to King Eglon was named Ehud. But he had more than money to deliver, for he drew his hidden sword and killed the Moabite king. Ehud then escaped, only to return with an army that chased out the Moabites and freed Israel from its oppressors (3:12–31).

3 Hazor After Ehud's death, King Jabin of Hazor conquered Israel and oppressed the people for 20 years. Then Deborah became Israel's leader. She summoned Barak to fight Commander Sisera, the leader of King Jabin's army. Together Deborah and Barak led their army into battle against Jabin's forces in the land between Mount Tabor and the Kishon River and conquered them (4:1—5:31).

4 Hill of Moreh After 40 years of peace, the Midianites began to harass the Israelites by destroying their flocks and crops. When the Israelites finally cried out to God, he chose Gideon, a poor and humble farmer, to be their deliverer. After struggling with doubt and feelings of inferiority, Gideon took courage and knocked down his town's altar to Baal, causing a great uproar among the citizens. Filled with the Spirit of God, he attacked the vast army of Midian, which was camped near the hill of Moreh. With just a handful of men he sent the enemy running away in confusion (6:1—7:25).

5 Shechem Even great leaders make mistakes. Gideon's relations with a concubine in Shechem resulted in the birth of a son named Abimelech. Abimelech turned out to be treacherous and power hungry—stirring up the people to proclaim him king. To carry out his plan, he went so far as to kill 69 of his 70 half brothers. Eventually some men of Shechem rebelled against Abimelech, but he gathered together an army and defeated them. His lust for power led him to ransack two other cities, but he was killed by a woman who dropped a millstone onto his head (8:28—9:57).

6 Land of Ammon Again Israel turned completely from God; so God turned from them. But when the Ammonites mobilized their army to attack, Israel threw away her idols and called upon God once again. Jephthah, a prostitute's son who had been run out of

Israel, was asked to return and lead Israel's forces against the enemy. After defeating the Ammonites, Jephthah became involved in a war with the tribe of Ephraim over a misunderstanding (10:1—12:15).

7 Timnah Israel's next judge, Samson, was a miracle child promised by God to a barren couple. He was the one who would begin to free Israel from their next and most powerful oppressor, the Philistines. According to God's command, Samson was to be a Nazirite—one who took a vow to be set apart for special service to God. One of the stipulations of the vow was that Samson's hair could never be cut. But when Samson grew up, he did not always take his special responsibility to God seriously. He even fell in love with a Philistine girl in Timnah and asked to marry her. Before the wedding, Samson held a party for some men in the city, using a riddle to place a bet with them. The men, however, forced Samson's fiancée into giving the answer. Furious at being tricked, Samson paid his bet with the lives of 30 Philistines who lived in the nearby city of Ashkelon (13:1—14:20).

8 Valley of Sorek Samson killed thousands of Philistines with his incredible strength. The nation's leaders looked for a way to stop him. They got their chance when another Philistine woman stole Samson's heart. Her name was Delilah, and she lived in the valley of Sorek. In exchange for a great sum of money, Delilah deceived Samson into confiding in her the secret of his strength. One night while he slept, Delilah had his hair cut off. As a result, Samson fell helplessly into the hands of the enemy (15:1—16:20).

9 Gaza Samson was blinded and led captive to a prison in Gaza. There his hair began to grow again. After a while, the Philistines held a great festival to celebrate Samson's imprisonment and to humiliate him before the crowds. When he was brought out as the entertainment, he literally brought down the house when he pushed on the main pillars of the banquet hall and killed the thousands trapped inside. The prophecy that he would begin to free Israel from the Philistines had come true (16:21–31).

10 Hill Country of Ephraim In the hill country of Ephraim lived a man named Micah. Micah hired his own priest to perform priestly duties in the shrine which housed his collection of idols. He thought he was pleasing God with all his religiosity! Like many of the Israelites, Micah assumed that his own opinions of what was right would agree with God's (17:1–13).

11 Dan The tribe of Dan migrated north in order to find new territory. They sent spies ahead of them to scout out the land. One night the spies stopped at Micah's home. Looking for some assurance of victory, the spies stole Micah's idols and priest. Rejoining the tribe, they came upon the city of Laish and slaughtered the unarmed and innocent citizens, renaming the conquered city Dan. Micah's idols were then set up in the city and became the focal point of the tribe's worship for many years (18:1–31).

12 Gibeah The extent to which many people had fallen away from God became clear in Gibeah, a village in the territory of Benjamin. A man and his concubine were traveling north toward the hill country of Ephraim. They stopped for the night in Gibeah, thinking they would be safe. But some perverts in the city gathered around the home where they were staying and demanded that the man come out to have sexual relations with them. Instead, the man and his host pushed the concubine out the door. She was raped and abused all night. When the man found her lifeless body the next morning, he cut it into 12 pieces and sent the parts to each tribe of Israel. This tragic event demonstrated that the nation had sunk to its lowest spiritual level (19:1–30).

13 Mizpah The leaders of Israel came to Mizpah to decide how to punish the wicked men from the city of Gibeah. When the city leaders refused to turn over the criminals, the whole nation of Israel took vengeance upon both Gibeah and the tribe of Benjamin where the city was located. When the battle ended, the entire tribe had been destroyed except for a handful of men who took refuge in the hills. Israel had become morally depraved. The stage was now set for the much-needed spiritual renewal that would come under the prophet Samuel (20:1—21:25).

A. THE MILITARY FAILURE OF ISRAEL (1:1—3:6)

By faithfully obeying the Lord, Joshua led the Israelites to military victory. After his death, however, the tribes failed to clear the inhabitants from the land, so the Lord withdrew his promise to help drive the people out and bless the Israelites in battle. The new generation abandoned God and worshiped idols. This part of Judges shows what can happen when we neglect to teach our children to follow the Lord.

1. Incomplete conquest of the land

Jerusalem Is Captured

1 Now it came about after the death of Joshua that the sons of Israel inquired of the **1:1**
LORD, saying, "Who shall go up first for us against the Canaanites, to fight against Num 27:21; Judg 1:27; 2:21-23; 3:1-6
them?"
2 The LORD said, "Judah shall go up; behold, I have given the land into his hand." **1:2**
3 Then Judah said to Simeon his brother, "Come up with me into the territory allot- Gen 49:8
ted me, that we may fight against the Canaanites; and I in turn will go with you into the
territory allotted you." So Simeon went with him.
4 Judah went up, and the LORD gave the Canaanites and the Perizzites into their hands, **1:4**
and they defeated ten thousand men at Bezek. Ps 44:2; 78:55
5 They found Adoni-bezek in Bezek and fought against him, and they defeated the
Canaanites and the Perizzites.
6 But Adoni-bezek fled; and they pursued him and caught him and cut off his thumbs
and big toes.
7 Adoni-bezek said, "Seventy kings with their thumbs and their big toes cut off used **1:7**
to gather up *scraps* under my table; as I have done, so God has repaid me." So they brought Lev 24:19
him to Jerusalem and he died there.
8 Then the sons of Judah fought against Jerusalem and captured it and struck it with **1:8**
the edge of the sword and set the city on fire. Josh 15:63; Judg 1:21
9 Afterward the sons of Judah went down to fight against the Canaanites living in the
hill country and in the [1]Negev and in the lowland.
10 So Judah went against the Canaanites who lived in Hebron (now the name of He- **1:10**
bron formerly *was* Kiriath-arba); and they struck Sheshai and Ahiman and Talmai. Josh 15:13-19

1 I.e. South country

1:1 The people of Israel had finally entered and taken control of the land promised to their ancestors (Genesis 12:7; Exodus 3:16–17). The book of Judges continues the story of this conquest that began in the book of Joshua. Through God's strength, the Israelites had conquered many enemies and overcome many difficulties, but their work was not yet finished. They had effectively met many political and military challenges, but facing spiritual challenges was more difficult. The unholy but attractive life-style of the Canaanites proved more dangerous than their military might. The Israelites gave in to the pressure and compromised their faith. If we attempt to meet life's challenges with human effort alone, we will find the pressures and temptations around us too great to resist.

1:1 Soon after Joshua died, Israel began to lose its firm grip on the land. Although Joshua was a great commander, the people missed his spiritual leadership even more than his military skill, for he had kept the people focused on God and his purposes. Joshua had been the obvious successor to Moses, but there was no obvious successor to Joshua. During this crisis of leadership, Israel had to learn that no matter how powerful and wise the current leader was, their real leader was God. We often focus our hope and confidence on some influential leader, failing to realize that in reality it is God who is in command. Acknowledge God as your commander in chief, and avoid the temptation of relying too heavily on human leaders, regardless of their spiritual wisdom.

1:1 The Canaanites were all the people who lived in Canaan (the promised land). They lived in city-states where each city had its own government, army, and laws. One reason Canaan was so difficult to conquer was that each city had to be defeated individually. There was no single king who could surrender the entire country into the hands of the Israelites.

Canaan's greatest threat to Israel was not its army, but its religion. Canaanite religion idealized evil traits: cruelty in war, sexual immorality, selfish greed, and materialism. It was a "me first, anything goes" society. Obviously, the religions of Israel and Canaan could not coexist.

1:2 The book of Joshua tells of a swift and thorough conquest of enemy armies and cities, while the book of Judges seems to suggest a more lengthy and gradual conquest. When the Israelites first entered the promised land (Joshua 1—12), they united as one army to crush the inhabitants until they were too weak to retaliate. Then, after the land was divided among the 12 tribes (Joshua 13—24), each tribe was responsible for driving out the remaining enemy from its own territory. The book of Judges tells of their failure to do this.

Some tribes were more successful than others. Under Joshua, they all began strong, but soon most were sidetracked by fear, weariness, lack of discipline, or pursuit of their own interests. As a result, their faith began to fade away, and "every man did what was right in his own eyes" (17:6). In order for our faith to survive, it must be practiced day by day. It must penetrate every aspect of our lives. Beware of starting out strong and then getting sidetracked from your real purpose—loving God and living for him.

1:6 The Israelites cut off the thumbs and big toes of Adoni-bezek to humiliate him and make him ineffective in battle. But according to God's instructions for conquering the promised land, he should have been killed.

1:8 Although the Israelites conquered Jerusalem, they did not occupy the city until the days of David (2 Samuel 5:6–10).

Capture of Other Cities

1:11 Josh 15:15

11 Then from there he went against the inhabitants of Debir (now the name of Debir
formerly *was* Kiriath-sepher).
12 And Caleb said, "The one who attacks Kiriath-sepher and captures it, I will even
give him my daughter Achsah for a wife."

1:13 Judg 3:9

13 Othniel the son of Kenaz, Caleb's younger brother, captured it; so he gave him his
daughter Achsah for a wife.

1:14 Josh 15:18

14 Then it came about when she came *to him,* that she persuaded him to ask her father
for a field. Then she alighted from her donkey, and Caleb said to her, "What do you
want?"
15 She said to him, "Give me a blessing, since you have given me the land of the
[2]Negev, give me also springs of water." So Caleb gave her the upper springs and the lower
springs.

1:16 Num 10:29-32; Judg 4:11; Deut 34:3; Judg 3:13; Num 21:1

16 The descendants of the Kenite, Moses' father-in-law, went up from the city of palms
with the sons of Judah, to the wilderness of Judah which is in the south of Arad; and
they went and lived with the people.

1:17 Num 21:3

17 Then Judah went with Simeon his brother, and they struck the Canaanites living in
Zephath, and utterly destroyed it. So the name of the city was called Hormah.

1:18 Josh 11:22

18 And Judah took Gaza with its territory and Ashkelon with its territory and Ekron
with its territory.

1:19 Josh 17:16; Judg 4:3, 13

19 Now the LORD was with Judah, and they took possession of the hill country; but
they could not drive out the inhabitants of the valley because they had iron chariots.

1:20 Josh 14:9; Josh 15:14; Judg 1:10

20 Then they gave Hebron to Caleb, as Moses had promised; and he drove out from
there the three sons of Anak.

1:21 Josh 15:63; Judg 1:8; 1 Chr 11:4

21 But the sons of Benjamin did not drive out the Jebusites who lived in Jerusalem; so
the Jebusites have lived with the sons of Benjamin in Jerusalem to this day.
22 Likewise the house of Joseph went up against Bethel, and the LORD was with them.

1:23 Gen 28:19

23 The house of Joseph spied out Bethel (now the name of the city was formerly Luz).

1:24 Josh 2:12

24 The spies saw a man coming out of the city and they said to him, "Please show us
the entrance to the city and we will treat you kindly."

2 I.e. South country

1:12–15 This same event is recorded in Joshua 15:16–19. Caleb was one of the original spies who scouted out the promised land (Numbers 13—14) and, with Joshua, encouraged the people to conquer it. For his faithfulness, he was given the land of his choice.

1:17 Why did God order the Israelites to drive the Canaanites from their land? Although the command seems cruel, the Israelites were under God's order to execute judgment on those wicked people. The other nations were to be judged for their sin as God had judged Israel by forcing them to wander for 40 years before they were allowed to enter the promised land. Over 700 years earlier, God had told Abraham that when the Israelites entered the promised land, the gross evil of the native people would be ready for judgment (Genesis 15:16). But God wasn't playing favorites with the Israelites because eventually they too would be severely punished for becoming as evil as the people they were ordered to drive out (2 Kings 17; 25; Jeremiah 6:18; 19; Ezekiel 8). God is not partial; all people are eligible for God's gracious forgiveness as well as for his firm justice.

1:19 Canaanite chariots pulled by horses were among the most sophisticated weapons of the day. Israelite foot soldiers were absolutely powerless when a speeding iron chariot bore down upon them. This is why Israel preferred to fight in the hills where chariots couldn't venture.

1:21ff Tribe after tribe failed to drive the evil Canaanites from their land. Why didn't they follow through and completely obey God's commands? (1) They had been fighting for a long time and were tired. Although the goal was in sight, they lacked the discipline and energy to reach it. (2) They were afraid the enemy was too strong—the iron chariots seemed invincible. (3) Since Joshua's death, power and authority had been decentralized to the tribal leaders, and the tribes were no longer unified in purpose. (4) Spiritual decay had infected them from within. They thought they could handle the temptation and be more prosperous by doing business with the Canaanites.

We, too, often fail to drive sin from our lives. Often we know what to do but just don't follow through. This results in a gradual deterioration of our relationship with God. In our battles, we may grow tired and want rest, but we need more than a break from our work. We need to know that God loves us and has given us a purpose for life. Victory comes from living according to his purpose.

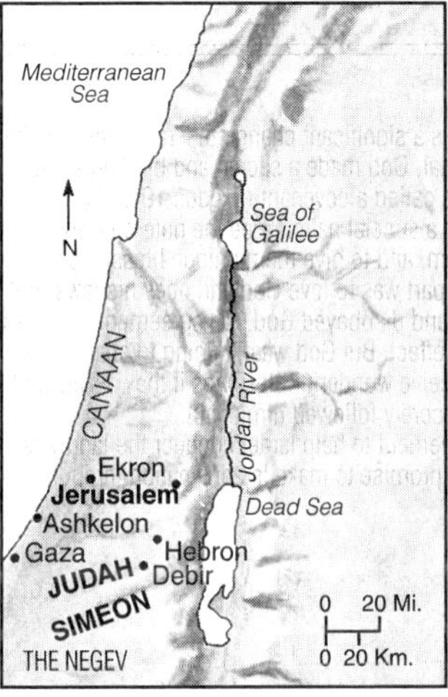

JUDAH FIGHTS FOR ITS LAND
The tribe of Judah wasted no time beginning their conquest of the territory allotted to them. With help from the tribe of Simeon, Jerusalem was conquered, as were the Canaanites in the Negev and along the coast. Hebron and Debir fell to Judah, and later Gaza, Ashkelon, and Ekron.

25 So he showed them the entrance to the city, and they struck the city with the edge of **1:25**
the sword, but they let the man and all his family go free. Josh 6:25
26 The man went into the land of the Hittites and built a city and named it Luz which
is its name to this day.

Places Not Conquered

27 But Manasseh did not take possession of Beth-shean and its villages, or Taanach **1:27**
and its villages, or the inhabitants of Dor and its villages, or the inhabitants of Ibleam Josh 17:12; Judg 1:1
and its villages, or the inhabitants of Megiddo and its villages; so the Canaanites persisted in living in that land.
28 It came about when Israel became strong, that they put the Canaanites to forced
labor, but they did not drive them out completely.
29 Ephraim did not drive out the Canaanites who were living in Gezer; so the Canaan- **1:29**
ites lived in Gezer among them. Josh 16:10
30 Zebulun did not drive out the inhabitants of Kitron, or the inhabitants of [3]Nahalol;
so the Canaanites lived among them and became subject to forced labor.
31 Asher did not drive out the inhabitants of Acco, or the inhabitants of Sidon, or of
Ahlab, or of Achzib, or of Helbah, or of Aphik, or of Rehob.
32 So the Asherites lived among the Canaanites, the inhabitants of the land; for they
did not drive them out.
33 Naphtali did not drive out the inhabitants of Beth-shemesh, or the inhabitants of
Beth-anath, but lived among the Canaanites, the inhabitants of the land; and the inhabitants of Beth-shemesh and Beth-anath became forced labor for them.
34 Then the Amorites forced the sons of Dan into the hill country, for they did not
allow them to come down to the valley;
35 yet the Amorites persisted in living in Mount Heres, in Aijalon and in Shaalbim;
but when the power of the house of Joseph grew strong, they became forced labor.
36 The border of the Amorites ran from the ascent of Akrabbim, from Sela and up- **1:36**
ward. Josh 15:3

Israel Rebuked

2 Now the angel of the LORD came up from Gilgal to Bochim. And he said, "I brought **2:1**
you up out of Egypt and led you into the land which I have sworn to your fathers; Judg 6:11; 13:2-21; Judg 2:5; Ex 20:2;
and I said, 'I will never break My covenant with you, Gen 17:7, 8; Lev
2 and as for you, you shall make no covenant with the inhabitants of this land; you 26:42, 44; Deut 7:9
shall tear down their altars.' But you have not obeyed Me; what is this you have done? **2:2**
3 "Therefore I also said, 'I will not drive them out before you; but they will [4]become *as* Ex 23:32; Deut 7:2-5; Ex 34:12, 13
thorns in your sides and their gods will be a snare to you.' " **2:3**
4 When the angel of the LORD spoke these words to all the sons of Israel, the people Josh 23:13; Num
lifted up their voices and wept. 33:55
5 So they named that place [5]Bochim; and there they sacrificed to the LORD.

3 Perhaps same as *Nahalal* **4** Some ancient mss read *be adversaries, and* **5** I.e. weepers

---

2:1–3 This event marks a significant change in Israel's relationship with God. At Mount Sinai, God made a sacred and binding agreement with the Israelites called a covenant (Exodus 19:5–8). God's part was to make Israel a special nation (see the note on Genesis 12:1–3), to protect them, and to give them unique blessings for following him. Israel's part was to love God and obey his laws. But because they rejected and disobeyed God, the agreement to protect them was no longer in effect. But God wasn't going to abandon his people. They would receive wonderful blessings if they asked God to forgive them and sincerely followed him again.

Although God's agreement to help Israel conquer the land was no longer in effect, his promise to make Israel a nation through whom the whole world would be blessed (fulfilled in the Messiah's coming) remained valid. God still wanted the Israelites to be a holy people (just as he wants us to be holy), and he often used oppression to bring them back to him, just as he warned he would (Leviticus 26; Deuteronomy 28). The book of Judges records a number of instances where God allowed his people to be oppressed so that they would repent of their sins and return to him.

Too often people want God to fulfill his promises while excusing themselves from their responsibilities. Before you claim God's promises, ask, "Have I done my part?"

2:4 The people of Israel knew they had sinned, and they wept aloud, responding with deep sorrow. Because we have a tendency to sin, repentance is the true measure of spiritual sensitivity. Repentance means asking God to forgive us, and then abandoning our sinful ways. But we cannot do this sincerely unless we are truly sorry for our sinful actions. When we are aware that we have done wrong, we should admit it plainly to God rather than try to cover it up or hope we can get away with it.

2. Disobedience and defeat

Joshua Dies

2:6 Josh 24:28-31

6 When Joshua had dismissed the people, the sons of Israel went each to his inheritance to possess the land.
7 The people served the LORD all the days of Joshua, and all the days of the elders
who survived Joshua, who had seen all the great work of the LORD which He had done
for Israel.
8 Then Joshua the son of Nun, the servant of the LORD, died at the age of one hundred and ten.

2:9 Josh 19:49f

9 And they buried him in the territory of his inheritance in Timnath-heres, in the hill
country of Ephraim, north of Mount Gaash.

2:10 Ex 5:2; 1 Sam 2:12

10 All that generation also were gathered to their fathers; and there arose another
generation after them who did not know the LORD, nor yet the work which He had done
for Israel.

2:11 Judg 3:7, 12; 4:1; 6:1; Judg 6:25; 8:33; 10:6

Israel Serves Baals

11 Then the sons of Israel did evil in the sight of the LORD and [6]served the Baals,

2:12 Deut 31:16

12 and they forsook the LORD, the God of their fathers, who had brought them out of

6 Or *worshiped*

THE JUDGES OF ISRAEL

Judge	*Years of Judging*	*Memorable Act(s)*	*Reference*
OTHNIEL	40	He captured a powerful Canaanite city	Judges 3:7–11
EHUD	80	He killed Eglon and defeated the Moabites	Judges 3:12–30
SHAMGAR	unrecorded	He killed 600 Philistines with an oxgoad	Judges 3:31
DEBORAH (w/Barak)	40	She defeated Sisera and the Canaanites and later sang a victory song with Barak	Judges 4—5
GIDEON	40	He destroyed his family idols, used a fleece to determine God's will, raised an army of 10,000, and defeated 135,000 Midianites with 300 soldiers	Judges 6—8
TOLA	23	He judged Israel for 23 years	Judges 10:1–2
JAIR	22	He had 30 sons	Judges 10:3–5
JEPHTHAH	6	He made a rash vow, defeated the Ammonites, and later battled jealous Ephraim	Judges 10:6—12:7
IBZAN	7	He had 30 sons and 30 daughters	Judges 12:8–10
ELON	10	unrecorded	Judges 12:11–12
ABDON	8	He had 40 sons and 30 grandsons, each of whom had his own donkey	Judges 12:13–15
SAMSON	20	He was a Nazirite, killed a lion with his bare hands, burned the Philistine wheat fields, killed 1,000 Philistines with a donkey's jawbone, tore off an iron gate, was betrayed by Delilah, and destroyed thousands of Philistines in one last mighty act	Judges 13—16

2:7–9 The account of Joshua's death is found here and at the end of the book of Joshua (24:29). Either this account is a summary of what happened earlier, or the account in the book of Joshua omitted the events in the first chapter of Judges. (For more on Joshua, see his Profile in Joshua 2.)

2:10ff One generation died, and the next did not follow God. Judges 2:10—3:7 is a brief preview of the cycle of sin, judgment, and repentance that Israel experienced again and again. Each generation failed to teach the next generation to love and follow God. Yet this was at the very center of God's law (Deuteronomy 6:4–9). It is tempting to leave the job of teaching the Christian faith to the church or Christian school. Yet God says that the responsibility for this task belongs primarily to the family. Because children learn so much by our example, faith must be a family matter.

2:11–15 Baal was the god of the storm and rains; therefore, he was thought to control vegetation and agriculture. Ashtaroth was the mother goddess of love, war, and fertility (she was also called Astarte or Ishtar). Temple prostitution and child sacrifice were a part of the worship of these Canaanite idols. This generation of Israelites abandoned the faith of their parents and began worshiping the gods of their neighbors. Many things can tempt us to abandon what we know is right. The desire to be accepted by our neighbors can lead us into behavior that is unacceptable to God. Don't be pressured into disobedience.

the land of Egypt, and followed other gods from *among* the gods of the peoples who
were around them, and bowed themselves down to them; thus they provoked the LORD
to anger.
13 So they forsook the LORD and served Baal and the Ashtaroth.
14 The anger of the LORD burned against Israel, and He gave them into the hands of
plunderers who plundered them; and He sold them into the hands of their enemies around
them, so that they could no longer stand before their enemies.
15 Wherever they went, the hand of the LORD was against them for evil, as the LORD
had spoken and as the LORD had sworn to them, so that they were severely distressed.
16 Then the LORD raised up judges who delivered them from the hands of those who
plundered them.
17 Yet they did not listen to their judges, for they played the harlot after other gods
and bowed themselves down to them. They turned aside quickly from the way in which
their fathers had walked in obeying the commandments of the LORD; they did not do as
their fathers.
18 When the LORD raised up judges for them, the LORD was with the judge and delivered them from the hand of their enemies all the days of the judge; for the LORD was
moved to pity by their groaning because of those who oppressed and afflicted them.
19 But it came about when the judge died, that they would turn back and act more
corruptly than their fathers, in following other gods to serve them and bow down to them;
they did not abandon their practices or their stubborn ways.
20 So the anger of the LORD burned against Israel, and He said, "Because this nation
has transgressed My covenant which I commanded their fathers and has not listened to
My voice,
21 I also will no longer drive out before them any of the nations which Joshua left when
he died,
22 in order to test Israel by them, whether they will keep the way of the LORD to walk
in it as their fathers did, or not."
23 So the LORD allowed those nations to remain, not driving them out quickly; and He
did not give them into the hand of Joshua.

Idolatry Leads to Servitude

3 Now these are the nations which the LORD left, to test Israel by them (*that is,* all
who had not experienced any of the wars of Canaan;

2:13 Judg 10:6
2:14 Deut 31:17; Ps 106:40-42; Deut 28:25; 32:30
2:15 Lev 26:14-39; Deut 28:15-68
2:16 Ps 106:43-45
2:17 Judg 2:7
2:18 Josh 1:5; Deut 32:36; Ps 106:44
2:20 Judg 2:14
2:21 Josh 23:4, 5, 13
2:22 Deut 8:2; 13:3
3:1 Judg 1:1; 2:21, 22

2:12–15 God often saved his harshest criticism and punishment for those who worshiped idols. Why were idols so bad in God's sight? To worship an idol violated the first two of the Ten Commandments (Exodus 20:3–6). The Canaanites had gods for almost every season, activity, or place. To them, the Lord was just another god to add to their collection of gods. Israel, by contrast, was to worship only the Lord. They could not possibly believe that God was the one true God and at the same time bow to an idol. Idol worshipers could not see their god as their creator because they created him. These idols represent sensual, carnal, and immoral aspects of human nature. God's nature is spiritual and moral. Adding the worship of idols to the worship of God could not be tolerated.

2:15–16 Despite Israel's disobedience, God showed his great mercy by raising up judges to save the people from their oppressors. Mercy has been defined as "not giving a person what he or she deserves." This is exactly what God did for Israel and what he does for us. Our disobedience demands judgment! But God shows mercy toward us by providing an escape from sin's penalty through Jesus Christ, who alone saves us from sin. When we pray for forgiveness, we are asking for what we do not deserve. Yet when we take this step and trust in Christ's saving work on our behalf, we can experience God's forgiveness.

2:16–19 Throughout this period of history Israel went through seven cycles of (1) rebelling against God, (2) being overrun by enemy nations, (3) being delivered by a God-fearing judge, (4) remaining loyal to God under that judge, and (5) again forgetting God when the judge died. We tend to follow the same cycle—remaining loyal to God as long as we are near those who are devoted to him. But when we are on our own, the pressure to be drawn away from God increases. Determine to be faithful to God despite the difficult situations you encounter.

2:17 Why would the people of Israel turn so quickly from their faith in God? Simply put, the Canaanite religion appeared more attractive to the sensual nature and offered more short-range benefits (sexual permissiveness and increased fertility in childbearing and farming). One of its most attractive features was that people could remain selfish and yet fulfill their religious requirements. They could do almost anything they wished and still be obeying at least one of the many Canaanite gods. Male and female prostitution were not only allowed, but encouraged as forms of worship.

Faith in the one true God, however, does not offer short-range benefits that appeal to our sinful human nature. The essence of sin is selfishness; the essence of God's way of life is selflessness. We must seek Christ's help to live God's way.

3:1–4 We learn from chapter 1 that these enemy nations were still in the land because the Israelites had failed to obey God and drive them out. Now God would allow the enemies to remain in order to "test" the Israelites; that is, to give them an opportunity to exercise faith and obedience. By now the younger generation that had not fought in the great battles of conquest was coming of age. It was their job to complete the conquest of the land. There were many obstacles yet to be overcome in their new homeland. How they would handle these obstacles would be a test of their faith.

Perhaps God has left obstacles in your life—hostile people, difficult situations, baffling problems—to allow you to develop faith and obedience.

2 only in order that the generations of the sons of Israel might be taught war, those
who had not experienced it formerly).

3:3 Josh 9:7; 11:19

3 *These nations are:* the five lords of the Philistines and all the Canaanites and the
Sidonians and the Hivites who lived in Mount Lebanon, from Mount Baal-hermon as
far as Lebo-hamath.

3:4 Deut 8:2

4 They were for testing Israel, to find out if they would obey the commandments of
the LORD, which He had commanded their fathers through Moses.

3:5 Ps 106:35

5 The sons of Israel lived among the Canaanites, the Hittites, the Amorites, the Perizzites, the Hivites, and the Jebusites;

3:6 Ex 34:15, 16; Deut 7:3, 4; Josh 23:12

6 and they took their daughters for themselves as wives, and gave their own daughters to their sons, and served their gods.

B. THE RESCUE OF ISRAEL BY THE JUDGES (3:7—16:31)

The Israelites began a series of cycles of sinning, worshiping idols, being punished, crying out for help, being rescued by a judge sent from God, obeying God for a while, then falling back into idolatry. They were conquered by Syria, Moab, Canaan, Midian, Ammon, and Philistia. They even faced the threat of civil war. Just as God sent help to the people when they cried out to him, so he will deliver us when we call on him.

1. First period: Othniel

3:7 Judg 2:11; Deut 4:9; Judg 2:13

7 The sons of Israel did what was evil in the sight of the LORD, and forgot the LORD
their God and served the Baals and the [7]Asheroth.
8 Then the anger of the LORD was kindled against Israel, so that He sold them into

7 I.e. wooden symbol of a female deity

WHY DID ISRAEL WANT TO WORSHIP IDOLS?

Worshiping God	*Worshiping idols*
long-range benefits	short-range benefits
gratification postponed	self-gratification immediate
morality required	sensuality approved
high ethical standards demanded	low ethical standards tolerated
neighbors' sins disapproved	neighbors' sins approved
unseen God worshiped	visible idols worshiped
unselfishness expected	selfishness condoned
business relations hindered	business relations improved
strict religious practices maintained	religious practices loosely regulated
changed life demanded	changed life not demanded
ethical stand expected	compromise and cooperation practiced
concern for others taught	no concern for others expected

The temptation to follow false gods because of short-term benefits, good feelings, easy "rules," or convenience was always present. But the benefits were deceptive because the gods were false. We worship God because he is the one and only true God.

3:5–7 The Israelites discovered that relationships affect faith. The men and women of the surrounding nations were attractive to the Israelites. Soon they intermarried, and the Israelites accepted their pagan gods. This was clearly prohibited by God (Exodus 34:15–17; Deuteronomy 7:1–4). By accepting these gods into their homes, the Israelites gradually began to accept the immoral practices associated with them. Most Israelites didn't start out determined to be idolaters; they just added the idols to the worship of God. But before long they found themselves absorbed in pagan worship.

A similar danger faces us. We want to befriend those who don't know God, but through those friendships we can become entangled in unhealthy practices. Friendships with unbelievers are important, but we must accept people without compromising or adopting their patterns of behavior.

3:7 Baal was the most worshiped god of the Canaanites. Most often cast in the form of a bull, he symbolized strength and fertility and was considered the god of agriculture. Asherah was Baal's female consort, mother goddess of the sea who was worshiped by means of wooden pillars that substituted for sacred trees. In times of famine, the Canaanites believed Baal was angry with them and was withholding rain as punishment. Archaeologists have uncovered many Baal idols in Israel. It is difficult to imagine the people of Israel trading worship of the Lord for worship of idols of wood, stone, and iron, but we do the same when we forsake worshiping God for other activities, hobbies, or priorities. Our idols are not made of wood or stone, but they are every bit as sinful.

the hands of Cushan-rishathaim king of Mesopotamia; and the sons of Israel served Cushan-rishathaim eight years.

The First Judge Delivers Israel

9 When the sons of Israel cried to the LORD, the LORD raised up a deliverer for the sons of Israel to deliver them, Othniel the son of Kenaz, Caleb's younger brother. **3:9** Judg 1:13
10 The Spirit of the LORD came upon him, and he judged Israel. When he went out to war, the LORD gave Cushan-rishathaim king of Mesopotamia into his hand, so that he prevailed over Cushan-rishathaim. **3:10** Num 11:25-29; 24:2
11 Then the land had rest forty years. And Othniel the son of Kenaz died.

2. Second period: Ehud and Shamgar

12 Now the sons of Israel again did evil in the sight of the LORD. So the LORD strengthened Eglon the king of Moab against Israel, because they had done evil in the sight of the LORD. **3:12** Judg 2:11; Judg 2:14
13 And he gathered to himself the sons of Ammon and Amalek; and he went and defeated Israel, and they possessed the city of the palm trees. **3:13** Deut 34:3; Judg 1:16
14 The sons of Israel served Eglon the king of Moab eighteen years.

Ehud Delivers from Moab

15 But when the sons of Israel cried to the LORD, the LORD raised up a deliverer for them, Ehud the son of Gera, the Benjamite, a left-handed man. And the sons of Israel sent tribute by him to Eglon the king of Moab. **3:15** Ps 78:34
16 Ehud made himself a sword which had two edges, a cubit in length, and he bound it on his right thigh under his cloak.
17 He presented the tribute to Eglon king of Moab. Now Eglon was a very fat man.
18 It came about when he had finished presenting the tribute, that he sent away the people who had carried the tribute.
19 But he himself turned back from the idols which were at Gilgal, and said, "I have a secret message for you, O king." And he said, "Keep silence." And all who attended him left him.
20 Ehud came to him while he was sitting alone in his cool roof chamber. And Ehud said, "I have a message from God for you." And he arose from his seat.
21 Ehud stretched out his left hand, took the sword from his right thigh and thrust it into his belly.

3:9 Othniel was Israel's first judge. In 1:13 we read that he volunteered to lead an attack against a fortified city. Here he was to lead the nation back to God. Othniel had a rich spiritual heritage—his uncle was Caleb, a man with unwavering faith in God (Numbers 13:30; 14:24). Othniel's leadership brought the people back to God and freed them from the oppression of the king of Mesopotamia. But after Othniel's death, it didn't take the Israelites long to fall back into their neighbors' comfortable but sinful ways.

3:10 This phrase, "The Spirit of the LORD came upon him," was also spoken of the judges Gideon, Jephthah, and Samson, among others. It expresses a temporary and spontaneous increase of physical, spiritual, or mental strength. This was an extraordinary and supernatural occurrence to prepare a person for a special task. The Holy Spirit is available to all believers today, but he will come upon believers in an extraordinary way for special tasks. We should ask the Holy Spirit's help as we face our daily problems as well as life's major challenges.

3:12–13 The Moabites, Ammonites, and Amalekites were nomadic tribes that lived near each other east and southeast of Canaan. These tribes were notorious raiders, possessing great military skill. This was the first time nations outside Canaan attacked the Israelites in their own land.

3:15 Ehud is called a *deliverer.* In the broadest sense, all the judges can be looked upon as foreshadowing the perfect Deliverer, Jesus Christ. While Ehud delivered Israel from its enemies, Jesus delivers us from sin, our greatest enemy.

3:15–30 This is a strange story, but it teaches us that God can use us just the way he made us. Being left-handed in Ehud's day was considered a handicap. Many Benjamites were left-handed (see 20:16). But God used Ehud's perceived weakness to give Israel victory. Let God use you the way you are to accomplish his work.

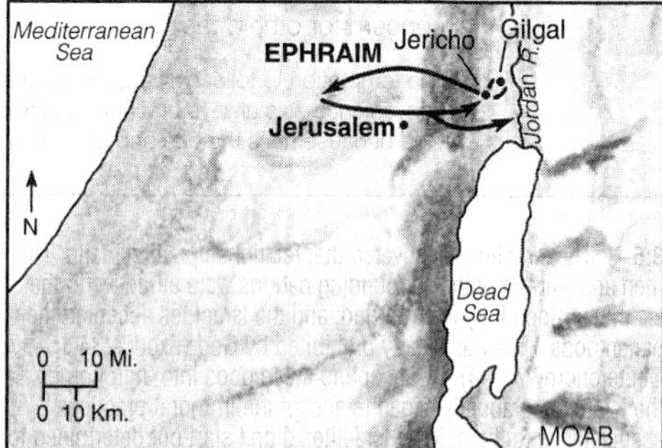

EHUD FREES ISRAEL FROM MOAB When King Eglon of Moab conquered part of Israel, he set up his throne in the city of Jericho. Ehud was chosen to take Israel's tribute there. After delivering Israel's tribute, Ehud killed King Eglon and escaped into the hill country of Ephraim. From there he gathered together an army to cut off any Moabites trying to escape across the Jordan River.

22 The handle also went in after the blade, and the fat closed over the blade, for he did not draw the sword out of his belly; and the refuse came out.
23 Then Ehud went out into the vestibule and shut the doors of the roof chamber behind him, and locked *them.*

3:24 1 Sam 24:3

24 When he had gone out, his servants came and looked, and behold, the doors of the roof chamber were locked; and they said, "He is only relieving himself in the cool room."
25 They waited until they became anxious; but behold, he did not open the doors of the roof chamber. Therefore they took the key and opened them, and behold, their master had fallen to the floor dead.
26 Now Ehud escaped while they were delaying, and he passed by the idols and escaped to Seirah.

3:27 Judg 6:34; 1 Sam 13:3

27 It came about when he had arrived, that he blew the trumpet in the hill country of Ephraim; and the sons of Israel went down with him from the hill country, and he *was* in front of them.

3:28 Judg 7:24; 12:5

28 He said to them, "Pursue *them,* for the LORD has given your enemies the Moabites into your hands." So they went down after him and seized the fords of the Jordan opposite Moab, and did not allow anyone to cross.
29 They struck down at that time about ten thousand Moabites, all robust and valiant men; and no one escaped.
30 So Moab was subdued that day under the hand of Israel. And the land was undisturbed for eighty years.

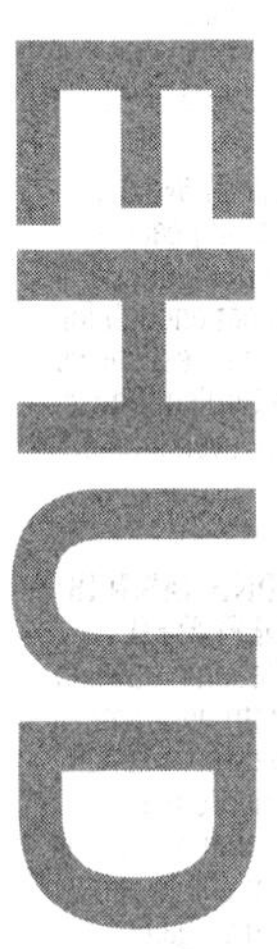

At first glance, Ehud's career as a judge in Israel may not seem relevant to us. He clearly lived in another time. He took radical and violent action to free his people. His murder of Eglon shocks us. His war on Moab was swift and deadly. His life is difficult to relate to. But our commitment to God's Word challenges us not to ignore this leader. As we read about his life, some questions come to mind: (1) When was the last time God showed me something wrong in my life and I took immediate and painful action to correct the error? (2) When was the last time I asked God to show me how he could use something unique about me (as he used Ehud's left-handedness)? (3) When was the last time I made a plan to obey God in some specific area of my life and then followed through on that plan? (4) When was the last time my life was an example to others of obedience to God?

The enemies we face are as real as Ehud's, but they are most often within ourselves. The battles we fight are not against other people but against the power of sin. We need God's help in doing battle against sin. We also need to remember that he has already won the war. He has defeated sin at the cross of his Son, Jesus. His help is the cause of each success, and his forgiveness is sufficient for each failure.

Strengths and accomplishments:
- Second judge of Israel
- A man of direct action, a frontline leader
- Used a perceived weakness (left-handedness) to do a great work for God
- Led the revolt against Moabite domination and gave Israel 80 years of peace

Lessons from his life:
- Some conditions call for radical action
- God responds to the cry of repentance
- God is ready to use our unique qualities to accomplish his work

Vital statistics:
- Where: Born during the last years of the wilderness wanderings or during Israel's early years in the promised land
- Occupation: Messenger, judge
- Relative: Father: Gera
- Contemporary: Eglon of Moab

Key verse:
"But when the sons of Israel cried to the LORD, the LORD raised up a deliverer for them, Ehud the son of Gera, the Benjamite, a left-handed man" (Judges 3:15).

His story is told in Judges 3:12–30.

3:31 To kill 600 Philistines with an oxgoad was quite a feat. An oxgoad was a long stick with a small flat piece of iron on one side and a sharp point on the other. The sharp side was used to drive the oxen during the times of plowing, and the flat end was used to clean the mud off the plow. Eight-foot-long ancient oxgoads have been found. In times of crisis they could easily have been used as spears, as in Shamgar's case. Oxgoads are still used in the Middle East to drive oxen.

Shamgar Delivers from Philistines

31 After him came Shamgar the son of Anath, who struck down six hundred Philis- **3:31**
tines with an oxgoad; and he also saved Israel. Judg 5:6

3. Third period: Deborah and Barak

Deborah and Barak Deliver from Canaanites

4 Then the sons of Israel again did evil in the sight of the LORD, after Ehud died. **4:1**
2 And the LORD sold them into the hand of Jabin king of Canaan, who reigned in Judg 2:19
Hazor; and the commander of his army was Sisera, who lived in Harosheth-hagoyim. **4:2**
3 The sons of Israel cried to the LORD; for he had nine hundred iron chariots, and he Josh 11:1, 10; Judg 4:13, 16
oppressed the sons of Israel severely for twenty years.
4 Now Deborah, a prophetess, the wife of Lappidoth, was judging Israel at that time. **4:3** Judg 1:19
5 She used to sit under the palm tree of Deborah between Ramah and Bethel in the **4:5**
hill country of Ephraim; and the sons of Israel came up to her for judgment. Gen 35:8
6 Now she sent and summoned Barak the son of Abinoam from Kedesh-naphtali, and **4:6**
said to him, "Behold, the LORD, the God of Israel, has commanded, 'Go and march to Heb 11:32
Mount Tabor, and take with you ten thousand men from the sons of Naphtali and from
the sons of Zebulun.
7 'I will draw out to you Sisera, the commander of Jabin's army, with his chariots and **4:7**
his many *troops* to the river Kishon, and I will give him into your hand.' " Ps 83:9
8 Then Barak said to her, "If you will go with me, then I will go; but if you will not go
with me, I will not go."
9 She said, "I will surely go with you; nevertheless, the honor shall not be yours on the **4:9** Judg 4:21

4:1 Israel sinned "in the sight of the LORD." Our sins harm both ourselves and others, but all sin is ultimately against God because it disregards his commands and his authority over us. When confessing his sin David prayed, "Against You, You only, I have sinned and done what is evil in Your sight" (Psalm 51:4). Recognizing the seriousness of sin is the first step toward removing it from our lives.

4:2–3 Nothing more is known about Jabin. Joshua had defeated a king by that name years earlier and burned the city of Hazor to the ground (Joshua 11:1–11). Either the city was rebuilt by this time, or Jabin was hoping to rebuild it.

This is the only time during the period of the judges when the Israelites' enemies came from within their land. The Israelites had failed to drive out all the Canaanites. These Canaanites had regrouped and were attempting to restore their lost power. If the Israelites had obeyed God in the first place and had driven the Canaanites from the land, this incident would not have happened.

4:2–3 Chariots were the tanks of the ancient world. Made of iron or wood, they were pulled by one or two horses and were the most feared and powerful weapons of the day. Some chariots even had razor-sharp knives extending from the wheels designed to mutilate helpless foot soldiers. The Canaanite army had 900 iron chariots. Israel was not powerful enough to defeat such an invincible army. Therefore, Jabin and Sisera had no trouble oppressing the people—until a faithful woman named Deborah called upon God.

4:3 After 20 years of unbearable circumstances, the Israelites finally cried to the Lord for help. But God should be the first place we turn when we are facing struggles or dilemmas. The Israelites chose to go their own way and got into a mess. We often do the same. Trying to control our own lives without God's help leads to struggle and confusion. By contrast, when we stay in daily contact with the Lord, we are less likely to create painful circumstances for ourselves. This is a lesson the Israelites never fully learned. When struggles come our way, God wants us to come to him first, seeking his strength and guidance.

4:4ff The Bible records several women who held national leadership positions, and Deborah was an exceptional woman. Obviously she was the best person for the job, and God chose her to lead Israel. God can choose anyone to lead his people, young or old, man or woman. Don't let your prejudices get in the way of those God may have chosen to lead you.

4:6–8 Was Barak cowardly or just in need of support? We don't know Barak's character, but we see the character of a great leader in Deborah, who took charge as God directed. Deborah told Barak that God would be with him in battle, but that was not enough for Barak. He wanted Deborah to go with him. Barak's request shows that at heart he trusted human strength more than God's promise. A person of real faith steps out at God's command, even if he or she must do so alone.

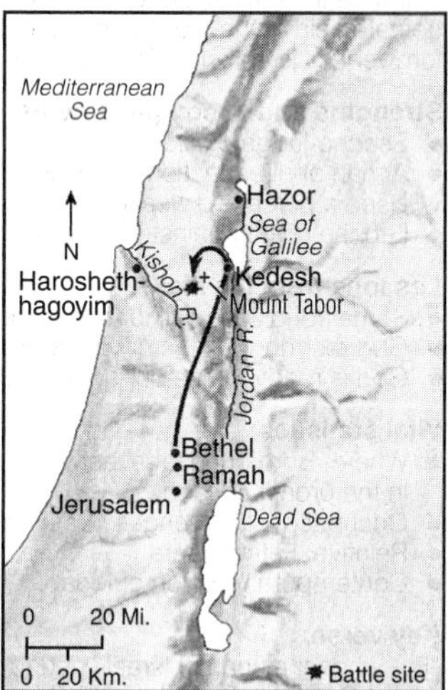

KING JABIN IS DEFEATED
Deborah traveled from her home between Ramah and Bethel to march with Barak and the Israelite army against Hazor. Sisera, commander of Hazor's army, assembled his men at Harosheth-hagoyim. In spite of Sisera's 900 chariots and expertly trained army, Israel was victorious.

4:9 How did Deborah command such respect? She was responsible for leading the people into battle, but more than that, she influenced them to live for God after the battle was over. Her personality drew people together and commanded the respect of even Barak, a military general. She was also a prophetess, whose main role was to encourage the people to obey God. Those who lead must not forget about the spiritual condition of those being led. A true leader is concerned for persons, not just success.

journey that you are about to take, for the LORD will sell Sisera into the hands of a
woman." Then Deborah arose and went with Barak to Kedesh.

4:10 Judg 5:18; Judg 4:14; 5:15

10 Barak called Zebulun and Naphtali together to Kedesh, and ten thousand men went
up with him; Deborah also went up with him.

4:11 Judg 1:16; Josh 19:33

11 Now Heber the Kenite had separated himself from the Kenites, from the sons of
Hobab the father-in-law of Moses, and had pitched his tent as far away as the oak in
Zaanannim, which is near Kedesh.
12 Then they told Sisera that Barak the son of Abinoam had gone up to Mount Tabor.

4:13 Judg 4:3; Judg 4:2

13 Sisera called together all his chariots, nine hundred iron chariots, and all the people who *were* with him, from Harosheth-hagoyim to the river Kishon.

4:14 Deut 9:3; 2 Sam 5:24; Ps 68:7

14 Deborah said to Barak, "Arise! For this is the day in which the LORD has given Sisera into your hands; [8]behold, the LORD has gone out before you." So Barak went down
from Mount Tabor with ten thousand men following him.

4:15 Deut 7:23; Josh 10:10

15 The LORD routed Sisera and all *his* chariots and all *his* army with the edge of the
sword before Barak; and Sisera alighted from *his* chariot and fled away on foot.

4:16 Ex 14:28; Ps 83:9

16 But Barak pursued the chariots and the army as far as Harosheth-hagoyim, and all
the army of Sisera fell by the edge of the sword; not even one was left.
17 Now Sisera fled away on foot to the tent of Jael the wife of Heber the Kenite, for
there was peace between Jabin the king of Hazor and the house of Heber the Kenite.
18 Jael went out to meet Sisera, and said to him, "Turn aside, my master, turn aside to
me! Do not be afraid." And he turned aside to her into the tent, and she covered him
with a rug.

4:19 Judg 5:24-27

19 He said to her, "Please give me a little water to drink, for I am thirsty." So she opened
a [9]bottle of milk and gave him a drink; then she covered him.
20 He said to her, "Stand in the doorway of the tent, and it shall be if anyone comes
and inquires of you, and says, 'Is there anyone here?' that you shall say, 'No.' "

4:21 Judg 5:26

21 But Jael, Heber's wife, took a tent peg and seized a hammer in her hand, and went
secretly to him and drove the peg into his temple, and it went through into the ground;
for he was sound asleep and exhausted. So he died.
22 And behold, as Barak pursued Sisera, Jael came out to meet him and said to him,
"Come, and I will show you the man whom you are seeking." And he entered with her,
and behold Sisera was lying dead with the tent peg in his temple.

4:23 Neh 9:24; Ps 18:47

23 So God subdued on that day Jabin the king of Canaan before the sons of Israel.
24 The hand of the sons of Israel pressed heavier and heavier upon Jabin the king of
Canaan, until they had destroyed Jabin the king of Canaan.

8 Or *has not the LORD gone...?* **9** I.e. skin container

THE JUDGES' FUNCTIONS

Regardless of an individual judge's leadership style, each one demonstrated that God's judgment follows apostasy, while repentance brings restoration.

Judges of Israel could be:

saviors (deliverers) and redeemers (Gideon)	or mediators and administrators (Tola)
providers of rest and peace (Ehud and Jair)	or rude, petty dictators (Jephthah)
famous and powerful (Samson)	or hardworking yet unsung (Elon and Abdon)
leaders of the nation (Othniel and Deborah)	or local heroes (Shamgar and Ibzan)

4:11 Heber was Jael's husband (4:17). He was from the Kenite tribe, a longtime ally of Israel. But for some reason, Heber decided to side with Jabin, maybe because Jabin's army appeared to have the military advantage. It was probably Heber who told Sisera that the Israelites were camped near Mount Tabor (4:12; see map). Although Heber threw in his lot with Jabin and his forces, his wife, Jael, did not (4:21).

4:18–21 Sisera couldn't have been more pleased when Jael offered him her tent as a hiding place. First, because Jael was the wife of Heber, a man loyal to Sisera's forces (see the note on 4:11), he thought she certainly could be trusted. Second, because men were never allowed to enter a woman's tent, no one would think to look for Sisera there.

Even though her husband, Heber, was loyal to Sisera's forces, Jael certainly was not. Because women of that day were in charge of pitching the tents, Jael had no problem driving the tent peg into Sisera's head while he slept. Deborah's prediction was thus fulfilled: The honor of conquering Sisera went to a brave and resourceful woman (4:9).

The Song of Deborah and Barak

5 Then Deborah and Barak the son of Abinoam sang on that day, saying,
2 "That the leaders led in Israel,
That the people volunteered,
Bless the LORD!
3 "Hear, O kings; give ear, O rulers!
I—to the LORD, I will sing,
I will sing praise to the LORD, the God of Israel.
4 "LORD, when You went out from Seir,
When You marched from the field of Edom,
The earth quaked, the heavens also dripped,
Even the clouds dripped water.
5 "The mountains quaked at the presence of the LORD,
This Sinai, at the presence of the LORD, the God of Israel.

6 "In the days of Shamgar the son of Anath,
In the days of Jael, the highways were deserted,
And travelers went by roundabout ways.
7 "The peasantry ceased, they ceased in Israel,
Until I, Deborah, arose,
Until I arose, a mother in Israel.
8 "New gods were chosen;
Then war *was* in the gates.
Not a shield or a spear was seen
Among forty thousand in Israel.
9 "My heart *goes out* to the commanders of Israel,
The volunteers among the people;
Bless the LORD!
10 "You who ride on white donkeys,
You who sit on *rich* carpets,
And you who travel on the road—sing!
11 "At the sound of those who divide *flocks* among the watering places,
There they shall recount the righteous deeds of the LORD,
The righteous deeds for His peasantry in Israel.
Then the people of the LORD went down to the gates.

12 "Awake, awake, Deborah;
Awake, awake, sing a song!
Arise, Barak, and take away your captives, O son of Abinoam.
13 "Then survivors came down to the nobles;
The people of the LORD came down to me as warriors.
14 "From Ephraim those whose root is in Amalek *came down,*
Following you, Benjamin, with your peoples;
From Machir commanders came down,
And from Zebulun those who wield the staff of office.
15 "And the princes of Issachar *were* with Deborah;
As *was* Issachar, so *was* Barak;

5:1 Ex 15:1
5:2 Judg 5:9; Ps 110:3
5:3 Ps 27:6
5:4 Deut 33:2; Ps 68:7; Ps 68:8, 9
5:5 Ex 19:18; Ps 68:8
5:6 Judg 3:31; Judg 4:17
5:8 Deut 32:17
5:9 Judg 5:2
5:10 Judg 10:4; 12:14
5:11 Gen 24:11; 29:2, 3; 1 Sam 12:7; Mic 6:5; Judg 5:8
5:12 Ps 57:8; Ps 68:18; Eph 4:8
5:14 Judg 12:15
5:15 Judg 4:10

5:1ff Music and singing were a cherished part of Israel's culture. Chapter 5 is a song, possibly composed and sung by Deborah and Barak. It sets to music the story of Israel's great victory recounted in chapter 4. This victory song was accompanied by joyous celebration. It proclaimed God's greatness by giving him credit for the victory. It was an excellent way to preserve and retell this wonderful story from generation to generation. (Other songs in the Bible are listed in the chart in Exodus 15.)

5:1ff In victory, Barak and Deborah sang praises to God. Songs of praise focus our attention on God, give us an outlet for spiritual celebration, and remind us of God's faithfulness and character. Whether you are experiencing a great victory or a major dilemma, singing praises to God can have a positive effect on your attitude.

5:8 War was the inevitable result when Israel chose to follow false gods. Although God had given Israel clear directions, the people failed to put his words into practice. Without God at the center of their national life, pressure from the outside soon became greater than power from within, and they were an easy prey for their enemies. If you are letting a desire for recognition, craving for power, or love of money rule your life, you may find yourself besieged by enemies—stress, anxiety, illness, fatigue. Keep God at the center of your life, and you will have the power you need to fight these destroyers.

5:15–17 Four tribes—Reuben, Gilead (either Gad or Manasseh), Dan, and Asher—were accused of not lending a helping hand in the battle. No reasons are given for their refusal to help their fellow

Into the valley they rushed at his heels;
Among the divisions of Reuben
There were great resolves of heart.

5:16 Num 32:1, 2, 24, 36
16 "Why did you sit among the [10]sheepfolds,
To hear the piping for the flocks?
Among the divisions of Reuben
There were great searchings of heart.

5:17 Josh 22:9
17 "Gilead remained across the Jordan;
And why did Dan stay in ships?
Asher sat at the seashore,
And remained by its landings.

5:18 Judg 4:6, 10
18 "Zebulun *was* a people who despised their lives *even* to death,
And Naphtali also, on the high places of the field.

5:19 Josh 11:1-5; Judg 4:13; Judg 1:27; Judg 5:30
19 "The kings came *and* fought;
Then fought the kings of Canaan
At Taanach near the waters of Megiddo;
They took no plunder in silver.

5:20 Josh 10:12-14
20 "The stars fought from heaven,
From their courses they fought against Sisera.

10 Or *saddlebags*

DEBORAH

Wise leaders are rare. They accomplish great amounts of work without direct involvement because they know how to work through other people. They are able to see the big picture that often escapes those directly involved, so they make good mediators, advisers, and planners. Deborah fit this description perfectly. She had all these leadership skills, and she had a remarkable relationship with God. The insight and confidence God gave this woman placed her in a unique position in the Old Testament. Deborah is among the outstanding women of history.

Her story shows that she was not power hungry. She wanted to serve God. Whenever praise came her way, she gave God the credit. She didn't deny or resist her position in the culture as a woman and wife, but she never allowed herself to be hindered by it either. Her story shows that God can accomplish great things through people who are willing to be led by him.

Deborah's life challenges us in several ways. She reminds us of the need to be available both to God and to others. She encourages us to spend our efforts on what we can do rather than on worrying about what we can't do. Deborah challenges us to be wise leaders. She demonstrates what a person can accomplish when God is in control.

Strengths and accomplishments:
- Fourth and only female judge of Israel
- Special abilities as a mediator, adviser, and counselor
- When called on to lead, was able to plan, direct, and delegate
- Known for her prophetic power
- A writer of songs

Lessons from her life:
- God chooses leaders by his standards, not ours
- Wise leaders choose good helpers

Vital statistics:
- Where: Canaan
- Occupations: Prophetess and judge
- Relative: Husband: Lappidoth
- Contemporaries: Barak, Jael, Jabin of Hazor, Sisera

Key verse:
"Now Deborah, a prophetess, the wife of Lappidoth, was judging Israel at that time" (Judges 4:4).

Her story is told in Judges 4—5.

Israelites, but they may be the same ones that stopped them from driving out the Canaanites in the first place: (1) lack of faith in God to help, (2) lack of effort, (3) fear of the enemy, and (4) fear of antagonizing those with whom they did business and thus from whom they prospered. This disobedience showed a lack of enthusiasm for God's plan.

21 "The torrent of Kishon swept them away,
The ancient torrent, the torrent Kishon.
O my soul, march on with strength.
22 "Then the horses' hoofs beat
From the dashing, the dashing of his valiant steeds.
23 'Curse Meroz,' said the angel of the LORD,
'Utterly curse its inhabitants;
Because they did not come to the help of the LORD,
To the help of the LORD against the warriors.'

5:21 Ex 15:2; Ps 44:5
5:22 Job 39:19-25
5:23 Judg 5:13

24 "Most blessed of women is Jael,
The wife of Heber the Kenite;
Most blessed is she of women in the tent.
25 "He asked for water *and* she gave him milk;
In a magnificent bowl she brought him curds.
26 "She reached out her hand for the tent peg,
And her right hand for the workmen's hammer.
Then she struck Sisera, she smashed his head;
And she shattered and pierced his temple.
27 "Between her feet he bowed, he fell, he lay;
Between her feet he bowed, he fell;
Where he bowed, there he fell dead.

5:24 Judg 4:19-21

28 "Out of the window she looked and lamented,
The mother of Sisera through the lattice,
'Why does his chariot delay in coming?
Why do the hoofbeats of his chariots tarry?'
29 "Her wise princesses would answer her,
Indeed she repeats her words to herself,
30 'Are they not finding, are they not dividing the spoil?
A maiden, two maidens for every warrior;
To Sisera a spoil of dyed work,
A spoil of dyed work embroidered,
Dyed work of double embroidery on the neck of the spoiler?'
31 "Thus let all Your enemies perish, O LORD;
But let those who love Him be like the rising of the sun in its might."
And the land was undisturbed for forty years.

5:30 Ex 15:9
5:31 Ps 68:2; 92:9; Ps 19:4-6; 89:36, 37

4. Fourth period: Gideon, Tola, and Jair

Israel Oppressed by Midian

6 Then the sons of Israel did what was evil in the sight of the LORD; and the LORD
gave them into the hands of Midian seven years.
2 The power of Midian prevailed against Israel. Because of Midian the sons of Israel
made for themselves the dens which were in the mountains and the caves and the strongholds.
3 For it was when Israel had sown, that the Midianites would come up with the Amalekites and the sons of the east and go against them.
4 So they would camp against them and destroy the produce of the earth as far as
Gaza, and leave no sustenance in Israel as well as no sheep, ox, or donkey.
5 For they would come up with their livestock and their tents, they would come in like
locusts for number, both they and their camels were innumerable; and they came into
the land to devastate it.

6:1 Judg 2:11; Num 22:4; 25:15-18; 31:1-3
6:2 1 Sam 13:6; Heb 11:38
6:4 Lev 26:16; Deut 28:31
6:5 Judg 7:12; 8:10

6:2 The Midianites were desert people descended from Abraham's second wife, Keturah (Genesis 25:1–2). From this relationship came a nation that was always in conflict with Israel. Years earlier the Israelites, while still wandering in the wilderness, battled the Midianites and almost totally destroyed them (Numbers 31:1–20). Because of their failure to completely destroy them, however, the tribe repopulated. Here they were once again oppressing Israel.

6:6 Deut 28:43

6 So Israel was brought very low because of Midian, and the sons of Israel cried to
the LORD.
7 Now it came about when the sons of Israel cried to the LORD on account of Midian,

6:8 Judg 2:1, 2

8 that the LORD sent a prophet to the sons of Israel, and he said to them, "Thus says
the LORD, the God of Israel, 'It was I who brought you up from Egypt and brought you
out from the house of slavery.
9 'I delivered you from the hands of the Egyptians and from the hands of all your
oppressors, and dispossessed them before you and gave you their land,

6:10 2 Kin 17:35; Jer 10:2

10 and I said to you, "I am the LORD your God; you shall not fear the gods of the
Amorites in whose land you live. But you have not obeyed Me." ' "

Gideon Is Visited

6:11 Judg 2:1; 6:14; 13:3; Josh 17:2; Judg 6:15; Heb 11:32

11 Then the angel of the LORD came and sat under the oak that was in Ophrah, which
belonged to Joash the Abiezrite as his son Gideon was beating out wheat in the wine
press in order to save *it* from the Midianites.
12 The angel of the LORD appeared to him and said to him, "The LORD is with you,
O valiant warrior."

6:13 Judg 6:1; Ps 44:9

13 Then Gideon said to him, "O my lord, if the LORD is with us, why then has all this
happened to us? And where are all His miracles which our fathers told us about, saying,
'Did not the LORD bring us up from Egypt?' But now the LORD has abandoned us and
given us into the hand of Midian."

6:14 Heb 11:32-34

14 The LORD looked at him and said, "Go in this your strength and deliver Israel from
the hand of Midian. Have I not sent you?"

6:15 Ex 3:11; Judg 6:11

15 He said to Him, "O Lord, how shall I deliver Israel? Behold, my family is the least
in Manasseh, and I am the youngest in my father's house."

6:16 Ex 3:12; Josh 1:5

16 But the LORD said to him, "Surely I will be with you, and you shall defeat Midian as
one man."

6:17 Judg 6:37; Is 38:7, 8

17 So Gideon said to Him, "If now I have found favor in Your sight, then show me a
sign that it is You who speak with me.
18 "Please do not depart from here, until I come *back* to You, and bring out my offering and lay it before You." And He said, "I will remain until you return."

6:19 Gen 18:6-8

19 Then Gideon went in and prepared a young goat and unleavened bread from an
[11]ephah of flour; he put the meat in a basket and the broth in a pot, and brought *them*
out to him under the oak and presented *them.*
20 The angel of God said to him, "Take the meat and the unleavened bread and lay
them on this rock, and pour out the broth." And he did so.

11 I.e. Approx one bu

6:6 Again the Israelites hit rock bottom before turning back to God. How much suffering they could have avoided if they had trusted him! Turning to God shouldn't be a last resort; we should look to him for help each day. This isn't to say life will always be easy. There will be struggles, but God will give us the strength to live through them. Don't wait until you're at the end of your rope. Call on God first in every situation.

6:11 The Old Testament records several appearances of the angel of the Lord: Genesis 16:7; 22:11; 31:11; Exodus 3:2; 14:19; Judges 2:1; 13:3; Zechariah 3:1–6. It is not known whether the same angel appeared in each case. The angel mentioned here appears to be separate from God in one place (6:12) and yet the same as God in another place (6:14). This has led some to believe that the angel was a special appearance of Jesus Christ prior to his mission on earth as recorded in the New Testament. It is also possible that as a special messenger from God, the angel had authority to speak for God. In either case, God sent a special messenger to deliver an important message to Gideon.

6:11 Beating out wheat is also called *threshing*—the process of separating the grains of wheat from the useless outer shell called chaff. This was normally done in a large area, often on a hill, where the wind could blow away the lighter chaff when the farmer tossed the beaten wheat into the air. If Gideon had done this, however, he would have been an easy target for the bands of raiders who were overrunning the land. Therefore, he was forced to thresh his wheat in a wine press, a pit that was probably hidden from view and that would not be suspected as a place to find a farmer's crops.

6:13 Gideon questioned God about the problems he and his nation faced and about God's apparent lack of help. What he didn't acknowledge was the fact that the people had brought calamity upon themselves when they decided to disobey and neglect God. How easy it is to overlook personal accountability and blame our problems on God and others. Unfortunately this does not solve our problems. It brings us no closer to God, and it escorts us to the very edge of rebellion and backsliding.

When problems come, the first place to look is within. Our first action should be confession to God of sins that may have created our problems.

6:14–16 "I will be with you," God told Gideon, and God promised to give him the strength he needed to overcome the opposition. In spite of this clear promise for strength, Gideon made excuses. Seeing only his limitations and weaknesses, he failed to see how God could work through him.

Like Gideon, we are called to serve God in specific ways. Although God promises us the tools and strength we need, we often make excuses. But reminding God of our limitations only implies that he does not know all about us or that he has made a mistake in evaluating our character. Don't spend time making excuses. Instead spend it doing what God wants.

21 Then the angel of the LORD put out the end of the staff that was in his hand and
touched the meat and the unleavened bread; and fire sprang up from the rock and consumed the meat and the unleavened bread. Then the angel of the LORD vanished from
his sight.

6:21 Lev 9:24

22 When Gideon saw that he was the angel of the LORD, he said, "Alas, O Lord GOD!
For now I have seen the angel of the LORD face to face."
23 The LORD said to him, "Peace to you, do not fear; you shall not die."

6:22 Gen 32:30; Ex 33:20; Judg 13:21, 22

24 Then Gideon built an altar there to the LORD and named it The LORD is Peace. To
this day it is still in Ophrah of the Abiezrites.

6:24 Judg 8:32

25 Now on the same night the LORD said to him, "Take your father's bull and a second
bull seven years old, and pull down the altar of Baal which belongs to your father, and
cut down the [12]Asherah that is beside it;
26 and build an altar to the LORD your God on the top of this stronghold in an orderly
manner, and take a second bull and offer a burnt offering with the wood of the Asherah
which you shall cut down."
27 Then Gideon took ten men of his servants and did as the LORD had spoken to him;
and because he was too afraid of his father's household and the men of the city to do it
by day, he did it by night.

6:25 Ex 34:13

The Altar of Baal Destroyed

28 When the men of the city arose early in the morning, behold, the altar of Baal was
torn down, and the Asherah which was beside it was cut down, and the second bull was
offered on the altar which had been built.
29 They said to one another, "Who did this thing?" And when they searched about
and inquired, they said, "Gideon the son of Joash did this thing."
30 Then the men of the city said to Joash, "Bring out your son, that he may die, for he
has torn down the altar of Baal, and indeed, he has cut down the Asherah which was
beside it."
31 But Joash said to all who stood against him, "Will you contend for Baal, or will you
deliver him? Whoever will plead for him shall be put to death by morning. If he is a god,
let him contend for himself, because someone has torn down his altar."
32 Therefore on that day he named him Jerubbaal, that is to say, "Let Baal contend
against him," because he had torn down his altar.

6:32 Judg 7:1

33 Then all the Midianites and the Amalekites and the sons of the east assembled themselves; and they crossed over and camped in the valley of Jezreel.

6:33 Josh 17:16

34 So the Spirit of the LORD came upon Gideon; and he blew a trumpet, and the Abiezrites were called together to follow him.

6:34 Judg 3:10; Judg 3:27

35 He sent messengers throughout Manasseh, and they also were called together to
follow him; and he sent messengers to Asher, Zebulun, and Naphtali, and they came up
to meet them.

6:35 Judg 4:6, 10; 5:18; Judg 7:3

Sign of the Fleece

36 Then Gideon said to God, "If You will deliver Israel through me, as You have spoken,
37 behold, I will put a fleece of wool on the threshing floor. If there is dew on the fleece

6:36 Judg 6:14, 16, 17

12 I.e. wooden symbol of a female deity, also vv 26, 28, 30

6:22–23 Why was Gideon afraid of seeing an angel? The Israelites believed that no one could see God and live (see God's words to Moses in Exodus 33:20). Evidently Gideon thought this also applied to angels.

6:25–30 After God called Gideon to be Israel's deliverer, he immediately asked him to tear down the altar of the pagan god, Baal—an act that would test Gideon's faith and commitment. Canaanite religion was very political, so an attack on a god was often seen as an attack on the local government supporting that god. If caught, Gideon would face serious social problems and probable physical attack. (For more on Baal and Asherah, see the notes on 2:11–15 and 3:7.)

Gideon took a great risk by following God's higher law, which specifically forbids idol worship (Exodus 20:1–5). After learning what Gideon had done, the townspeople wanted to kill him. Many of those people were fellow Israelites. This shows how immoral God's people had become. God said in Deuteronomy 13:6–11 that idolaters must be stoned to death, but these Israelites wanted to stone Gideon for tearing down an idol and worshiping God! When you begin to accomplish something for God, you may be criticized by the very people who should support you.

6:33 The armies of Midian and Amalek camped in the valley of Jezreel, the agricultural center for the area. Whoever controlled the valley's rich and fertile land controlled the people who lived in and around it. Because of the valley's vast resources, many major trade routes converged at the pass which led into it. This made it the site of many great battles. Gideon's men attacked the enemy armies from the hills, and the only escape route was through the pass toward the Jordan River. That is why Gideon urged some of his troops to take control of the river's crossing points (7:24).

only, and it is dry on all the ground, then I will know that You will deliver Israel through
me, as You have spoken."
38 And it was so. When he arose early the next morning and squeezed the fleece, he
drained the dew from the fleece, a bowl full of water.
6:39 Gen 18:32 39 Then Gideon said to God, "Do not let Your anger burn against me that I may speak
once more; please let me make a test once more with the fleece, let it now be dry only on
the fleece, and let there be dew on all the ground."
40 God did so that night; for it was dry only on the fleece, and dew was on all the ground.

Gideon's 300 Chosen Men

7:1 Judg 6:32; Gen 12:6; Deut 11:30 **7** Then Jerubbaal (that is, Gideon) and all the people who were with him, rose early
and camped beside the spring of Harod; and the camp of Midian was on the north
side of them by the hill of Moreh in the valley.
7:2 Deut 8:17, 18 **2** The LORD said to Gideon, "The people who are with you are too many for Me to
give Midian into their hands, for Israel would become boastful, saying, 'My own power
has delivered me.'
7:3 Deut 20:8 3 "Now therefore come, proclaim in the hearing of the people, saying, 'Whoever is afraid

GOD USES COMMON PEOPLE

God uses all sorts of people to do his work—like you and me!

Person	*Known as*	*Task*	*Reference*
JACOB	A deceiver	To "father" the Israelite nation	Genesis 27
JOSEPH	A slave	To save his family	Genesis 39—50
MOSES	Shepherd in exile (and murderer)	To lead Israel out of bondage, to the promised land	Exodus 3
GIDEON	A farmer	To deliver Israel from Midian	Judges 6:11
JEPHTHAH	Son of a prostitute	To deliver Israel from the Ammonites	Judges 11:1
HANNAH	A housewife	To be the mother of Samuel	1 Samuel 1
DAVID	A shepherd boy and last-born of the family	To be Israel's greatest king	1 Samuel 16
EZRA	A scribe	To lead the return to Judah and to write some of the Bible	Ezra, Nehemiah
ESTHER	A slave girl	To save her people from massacre	Esther
MARY	A peasant girl	To be the mother of Christ	Luke 1:27–38
MATTHEW	A tax collector	To be an apostle and Gospel writer	Matthew 9:9
LUKE	A Greek physician	To be a companion of Paul and a Gospel writer	Colossians 4:14
PETER	A fisherman	To be an apostle, a leader of the early church, and a writer of two New Testament letters	Matthew 4:18–20

6:37–39 Was Gideon testing God, or was he simply asking God for more encouragement? In either case, though his motive was right (to obey God and defeat the enemy), his method was less than ideal. Gideon seems to have known that his requests might displease God (6:39), and yet he demanded two miracles (6:37, 39) even after witnessing the miraculous fire from the rock (6:21). It is true that to make good decisions, we need facts. Gideon had all the facts, but still he hesitated. He delayed obeying God because he wanted even more proof.

Demanding extra signs was an indication of unbelief. Fear often makes us wait for more confirmation when we should be taking action. Visible signs are unnecessary if they only confirm what we already know is true.

Today the greatest means of God's guidance is his Word, the Bible. Unlike Gideon, we have God's complete, revealed Word. If you want to have more of God's guidance, don't ask for signs; study the Bible (2 Timothy 3:16–17).

6:39 After seeing the miracle of the wet fleece, why did Gideon ask for another miracle? Perhaps he thought the results of the first test could have happened naturally. A thick fleece could retain moisture long after the sun had dried the surrounding ground. "Putting out fleeces" is a poor decision-making method. Those who do this put limitations on God. They ask him to fit their expectations. The results of such experiments are usually inconclusive and thus fail to make us any more confident about our choices. Don't let a "fleece" become a substitute for God's wisdom that comes through Bible study and prayer.

7:2 Self-sufficiency is an enemy when it causes us to believe we can always do what needs to be done in our own strength. To prevent this attitude among Gideon's soldiers, God reduced their number from 32,000 to 300. With an army this small, there could be no doubt that victory was from God. The men could not take the credit. Like Gideon, we must recognize the danger of fighting in our own strength. We can be confident of victory only if we put our confidence in God and not ourselves.

and trembling, let him return and depart from Mount Gilead.' " So 22,000 people returned, but 10,000 remained.
4 Then the LORD said to Gideon, "The people are still too many; bring them down to the water and I will test them for you there. Therefore it shall be that he of whom I say to you, 'This one shall go with you,' he shall go with you; but everyone of whom I say to you, 'This one shall not go with you,' he shall not go."
5 So he brought the people down to the water. And the LORD said to Gideon, "You shall separate everyone who laps the water with his tongue as a dog laps, as well as everyone who kneels to drink."
6 Now the number of those who lapped, putting their hand to their mouth, was 300 men; but all the rest of the people kneeled to drink water.
7 The LORD said to Gideon, "I will deliver you with the 300 men who lapped and will give the Midianites into your hands; so let all the *other* people go, each man to his home."
8 So the 300 men took the people's provisions and their trumpets into their hands. And Gideon sent all the *other* men of Israel, each to his tent, but retained the 300 men; and the camp of Midian was below him in the valley.
9 Now the same night it came about that the LORD said to him, "Arise, go down against the camp, for I have given it into your hands.
10 "But if you are afraid to go down, go with Purah your servant down to the camp,
11 and you will hear what they say; and afterward your hands will be strengthened that you may go down against the camp." So he went with Purah his servant down to the outposts of the army that was in the camp.
12 Now the Midianites and the Amalekites and all the sons of the east were lying in the valley as numerous as locusts; and their camels were without number, as numerous as the sand on the seashore.
13 When Gideon came, behold, a man was relating a dream to his friend. And he said, "Behold, I had a dream; a loaf of barley bread was tumbling into the camp of Midian, and it came to the tent and struck it so that it fell, and turned it upside down so that the tent lay flat."
14 His friend replied, "This is nothing less than the sword of Gideon the son of Joash, a man of Israel; God has given Midian and all the camp into his hand."
15 When Gideon heard the account of the dream and its interpretation, he bowed in worship. He returned to the camp of Israel and said, "Arise, for the LORD has given the camp of Midian into your hands."
16 He divided the 300 men into three companies, and he put trumpets and empty pitchers into the hands of all of them, with torches inside the pitchers.
17 He said to them, "Look at me and do likewise. And behold, when I come to the outskirts of the camp, do as I do.

7:4 1 Sam 14:6
7:7 1 Sam 14:6
7:9 Josh 2:24; 10:8; 11:6
7:11 Judg 7:15; 1 Sam 14:9, 10
7:12 Judg 6:5; 8:10; Josh 11:4
7:14 Josh 2:9

GIDEON'S BATTLE
In spite of Deborah and Barak's victory, the Canaanites still caused trouble in this fertile region. God appeared to Gideon at Ophrah and called him to defeat them. With only 300 fighting men, Gideon routed thousands of Midianites, chasing them to Zererah and Abel-meholah.

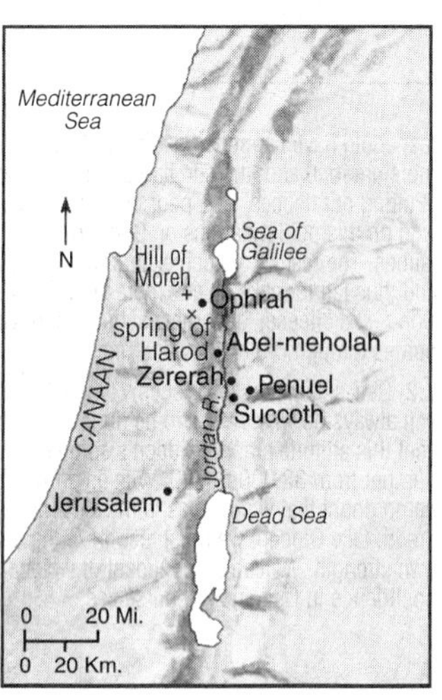

7:10–11 Facing overwhelming odds, Gideon was afraid. God understood his fear, but he didn't excuse Gideon from his task. Instead he allowed Gideon to slip into the enemy camp and overhear a conversation that would give him courage (7:12–15). Are you facing a battle? God can give you the strength you need for any situation. And don't be startled by the way he helps you. Like Gideon, you must listen to God and be ready to take the first step. Only after you begin to obey God will you find the courage to move ahead.

7:12 Midianites were camel-riding marauders composed of five families linked to Abraham through Midian, the son of Abraham's second wife, Keturah. They inhabited the desert regions from the Dead Sea to the Red Sea.

7:13 An enemy soldier dreamed of a loaf of barley bread tumbling into camp. Barley grain was only half the value of wheat, and the bread made from it was considered inferior. In the same way, Israel's tiny band of men was considered inferior to the vast forces of Midian and Amalek. But God would make the underdog Israelites seem invincible.

7:19 The night was divided equally into three watches. The beginning of the middle watch would have been around 10:00 p.m. Many in the camp would still have been awake.

18 "When I and all who are with me blow the trumpet, then you also blow the trumpets all around the camp and say, 'For the LORD and for Gideon.' "

Confusion of the Enemy

19 So Gideon and the hundred men who were with him came to the outskirts of the camp at the beginning of the middle watch, when they had just posted the watch; and they blew the trumpets and smashed the pitchers that were in their hands.
20 When the three companies blew the trumpets and broke the pitchers, they held the

Most of us want to know God's plan for our lives, but we're not always sure how to find it. One common misunderstanding is the idea that God's guidance will come to us out of the blue, that it has nothing to do with what we're doing now. But if we're always looking around for God's next assignment, we run the risk of ruining whatever we're working on right now. Fortunately, the Bible points to a kind of guidance that does not put our current projects in jeopardy. In the Bible's descriptions of how God guided many people, we can see that often God's call came while people were completely immersed in the challenge of the moment. A good example of this kind of guidance is seen in Gideon's life.

Gideon had a limited vision, but he was committed to it. His challenge was to obtain food for his family even though hostile invaders were making the growing, gathering, and preparation of the food almost impossible. Gideon was resourceful. He put a wine press to double duty by turning it into a sunken threshing floor. It lacked ventilation to blow the chaff away, but at least it was hidden from the Midianites. Gideon was working in his threshing floor when God sent him a messenger with a challenge.

Gideon was surprised by what God told him to do. He did not want to jump into a task for which he was ill prepared. The angel had to overcome three objections before Gideon was convinced: (1) Gideon's feelings of responsibility for his family's welfare, (2) his doubts about the call itself, and (3) his feelings of inadequacy for the job. Once Gideon was convinced, however, he obeyed with zest, resourcefulness, and speed. He dedicated those personality traits to God, with whom he was now personally acquainted.

Gideon had his weak moments and failures, but he was still God's servant. If you can easily see yourself in Gideon's weakness, can you also see yourself in being willing to serve? Remember Gideon as a man who obeyed God by giving his attention to the task at hand. Then give your full attention to believing God will prepare you for tomorrow when it comes.

Strengths and accomplishments:
- Israel's fifth judge. A military strategist who was expert at surprise
- A member of the Hall of Faith in Hebrews 11
- Defeated the Midianite army
- Was offered a hereditary kingship by the men of Israel
- Though slow to be convinced, acted on his convictions

Weaknesses and mistakes:
- Feared that his own limitations would prevent God from working
- Collected Midianite gold and made a symbol that became an evil object of worship
- Through a concubine, fathered a son who would bring great grief and tragedy to both Gideon's family and the nation of Israel
- Failed to establish the nation in God's ways; after he died they all went back to idol worship

Lessons from his life:
- God calls in the middle of our present obedience. As we are faithful, he gives us more responsibility
- God expands and uses the abilities he has already built into us
- God uses us in spite of our limitations and failures
- Even those who make great spiritual progress can easily fall into sin if they don't consistently follow God

Vital statistics:
- Where: Ophrah, valley of Jezreel, spring of Harod
- Occupations: Farmer, warrior, and judge
- Relatives: Father: Joash. Son: Abimelech
- Contemporaries: Zebah, Zalmunna

Key verses:
" 'O Lord, how shall I deliver Israel? Behold, my family is the least in Manasseh, and I am the youngest in my father's house.' But the LORD said to him, 'Surely I will be with you, and you shall defeat Midian as one man' " (Judges 6:15–16).

His story is told in Judges 6—8. He is also mentioned in Hebrews 11:32.

torches in their left hands and the trumpets in their right hands for blowing, and cried,
"A sword for the LORD and for Gideon!"
21 Each stood in his place around the camp; and all the [13]army ran, crying out as they **7:21**
fled. 2 Kin 7:7
22 When they blew 300 trumpets, the LORD set the sword of one against another even **7:22**
throughout the whole army; and the army fled as far as Beth-shittah toward Zererah, as 1 Sam 14:20; 1 Kin 4:12; 19:16
far as the edge of Abel-meholah, by Tabbath.
23 The men of Israel were summoned from Naphtali and Asher and all Manasseh, and **7:23**
they pursued Midian. Judg 6:35
24 Gideon sent messengers throughout all the hill country of Ephraim, saying, "Come **7:24**
down against Midian and take the waters before them, as far as Beth-barah and the Judg 3:28
Jordan." So all the men of Ephraim were summoned and they took the waters as far as
Beth-barah and the Jordan.
25 They captured the two leaders of Midian, Oreb and Zeeb, and they killed Oreb at **7:25**
the rock of Oreb, and they killed Zeeb at the wine press of Zeeb, while they pursued Ps 83:11; Is 10:26; Judg 8:4
Midian; and they brought the heads of Oreb and Zeeb to Gideon from across the
Jordan.

Zebah and Zalmunna Routed

8 Then the men of Ephraim said to him, "What is this thing you have done to us, not **8:1**
calling us when you went to fight against Midian?" And they contended with him Judg 12:1
vigorously.
2 But he said to them, "What have I done now in comparison with you? Is not the
gleaning *of the grapes* of Ephraim better than the vintage of Abiezer?
3 "God has given the leaders of Midian, Oreb and Zeeb into your hands; and what was
I able to do in comparison with you?" Then their anger toward him subsided when he
said that.
4 Then Gideon and the 300 men who were with him came to the Jordan *and* crossed **8:4**
over, weary yet pursuing. Judg 7:25
5 He said to the men of Succoth, "Please give loaves of bread to the people who are **8:5**
following me, for they are weary, and I am pursuing Zebah and Zalmunna, the kings of Gen 33:17
Midian."
6 The leaders of Succoth said, "Are the hands of Zebah and Zalmunna already in your **8:6**
hands, that we should give bread to your army?" Judg 8:15
7 Gideon said, "All right, when the LORD has given Zebah and Zalmunna into my **8:7**
hand, then I will thrash your bodies with the thorns of the wilderness and with briers." Judg 7:15
8 He went up from there to Penuel and spoke similarly to them; and the men of Pe- **8:8**
nuel answered him just as the men of Succoth had answered. Gen 32:31
9 So he spoke also to the men of Penuel, saying, "When I return safely, I will tear **8:9**
down this tower." Judg 8:17
10 Now Zebah and Zalmunna were in Karkor, and their armies with them, about 15,000 **8:10**
men, all who were left of the entire army of the sons of the east; for the fallen were 120,000 Judg 6:5; 7:12; Is 9:4
swordsmen.

13 Or *camp*

7:21 Gideon's army simply watched as the army of Midian fell into panic, confusion, and disordered retreat. Not one man had to draw a sword to defeat the enemy. Gideon's small army could never have brought about such a victory in their own strength. God wanted to demonstrate to Israel that victory depends not on strength or numbers, but on obedience and commitment to him.

8:1–3 Ephraim's leaders felt left out because Gideon had not called them to join the battle, but had left them in place to "clean up" (glean) the escaping Midianites, and so they angrily confronted him. Gideon assured the leaders of Ephraim that their accomplishment was even greater than his own clan's (Abiezer). His diplomatic explanation pointed out that this rear guard had managed to capture the enemy's generals, thus cutting off the leaders from their army. Not every necessary job is a highly visible leadership role. Much of the necessary labor of any effective enterprise is considered by many to be dirty work. But such work is vital to getting any big task done. Engineers and millionaires may design and finance an elegant building, but it is the bricklayers who get the work done. Pride causes us to want recognition. Are you content to be God's bricklayer, or do you resent the work God has given you?

8:5, 9 The leaders of Succoth and Penuel refused to help Gideon, probably fearing Midian's revenge should he fail (Gideon's army was 300 men chasing 15,000). They should have realized that victory was certain because God was with Gideon. But they were so worried about saving themselves that they never thought about God's power to save.

Because of fear for ourselves, we may not recognize God's presence in other people and therefore miss God's victory. Then we must face the often bitter consequences of failing to join forces with those God has chosen to do his work. Because God will prevail with or without you, be quick to join others who are engaged in his work. Lend support with your time, money, talents, and prayer.

11 Gideon went up by the way of those who lived in tents on the east of Nobah and
Jogbehah, and attacked the camp when the camp was unsuspecting.
12 When Zebah and Zalmunna fled, he pursued them and captured the two kings of
Midian, Zebah and Zalmunna, and routed the whole army.
13 Then Gideon the son of Joash returned from the battle by the ascent of Heres.
14 And he captured a youth from Succoth and questioned him. Then *the youth* wrote
down for him the princes of Succoth and its elders, seventy-seven men.

8:15 Judg 8:6

15 He came to the men of Succoth and said, "Behold Zebah and Zalmunna, concerning whom you taunted me, saying, 'Are the hands of Zebah and Zalmunna already in
your hand, that we should give bread to your men who are weary?' "
16 He took the elders of the city, and thorns of the wilderness and briers, and he disciplined the men of Succoth with them.

8:17 Judg 8:9

17 He tore down the tower of Penuel and killed the men of the city.
18 Then he said to Zebah and Zalmunna, "What kind of men *were* they whom you killed
at Tabor?" And they said, "They were like you, each one resembling the son of a king."
19 He said, "They *were* my brothers, the sons of my mother. *As* the LORD lives, if only
you had let them live, I would not kill you."
20 So he said to Jether his firstborn, "Rise, kill them." But the youth did not draw his
sword, for he was afraid, because he was still a youth.

8:21 Ps 83:11; Judg 8:26

21 Then Zebah and Zalmunna said, "Rise up yourself, and fall on us; for as the man,
so is his strength." So Gideon arose and killed Zebah and Zalmunna, and took the crescent ornaments which were on their camels' necks.
22 Then the men of Israel said to Gideon, "Rule over us, both you and your son, also
your son's son, for you have delivered us from the hand of Midian."

8:23 1 Sam 8:7; 10:19; 12:12; Ps 10:16

23 But Gideon said to them, "I will not rule over you, nor shall my son rule over you;
the LORD shall rule over you."

8:24 Gen 25:13-16

24 Yet Gideon said to them, "I would request of you, that each of you give me an earring from his spoil." (For they had gold earrings, because they were Ishmaelites.)
25 They said, "We will surely give *them.*" So they spread out a garment, and every one
of them threw an earring there from his spoil.
26 The weight of the gold earrings that he requested was 1,700 *shekels* of gold, besides
the crescent ornaments and the pendants and the purple robes which *were* on the kings
of Midian, and besides the neck bands that *were* on their camels' necks.

8:27 Ex 28:6-35; Judg 17:5; 18:14-20

27 Gideon made it into an ephod, and placed it in his city, Ophrah, and all Israel played
the harlot with it there, so that it became a snare to Gideon and his household.

Forty Years of Peace

28 So Midian was subdued before the sons of Israel, and they did not lift up their heads
anymore. And the land was undisturbed for forty years in the days of Gideon.

8:29 Judg 7:1

29 Then Jerubbaal the son of Joash went and lived in his own house.

8:11 The Midianites were escaping into the desert area, where the tent-dwelling nomads lived. They didn't expect Gideon to follow them that far.

8:15–17 Gideon carried out the threat he had made in 8:7. It is difficult to determine whether this act of revenge was justified or whether he should have left the punishment up to God. Gideon was God's appointed leader, but the officials of Succoth and Penuel refused to help him in any way because they feared the enemy. They showed neither faith nor respect for God or the man God had chosen to save them. We should help others because it is right, regardless of whether we will benefit personally.

8:20–21 For a king to be killed by a boy was humiliating because it would look as though he was no match for a boy ("for as the man, so is his strength"). The two men wanted to avoid that disgrace, as well as the slower and more painful death which an inexperienced swordsman might inflict.

8:23 The people wanted to make Gideon their king, but Gideon stressed that the Lord was to rule over them. Despite his inconsistencies, Gideon never lost sight of the importance, for both a nation and an individual, of putting God first. Is God first in your life? If he is, he must affect every dimension of your life, not just what you do in church.

8:26–27 Those who were very wealthy put ornaments on their camels as a way of displaying their riches. Women wore vast amounts of jewelry as well, often up to 15 pairs of earrings. Jewelry was also worn for good luck. After Gideon's rise to power, he seems to have become carried away with this accumulation of wealth. Eventually it led the Israelites to idolatry.

8:27 An ephod was a linen garment worn by priests over their chests. It was considered holy (Exodus 28:5–35; 39:2–24; Leviticus 8:7–8). Gideon probably had good motives for making the ephod (a visible remembrance commemorating the victory). Unfortunately, the people began to worship the ephod as an idol. Sadly, many decisions that stem from good motives produce negative results. Perhaps no one stops to ask, "What might go wrong?" or "Is there a possibility of negative consequences?" In your plans and decisions, take time to anticipate how a good idea might lead to a potential problem.

30 Now Gideon had seventy sons who were his direct descendants, for he had many **8:30** Judg 9:2, 5
wives.
31 His concubine who was in Shechem also bore him a son, and he named him Abimelech.
32 And Gideon the son of Joash died at a ripe old age and was buried in the tomb of
his father Joash, in Ophrah of the Abiezrites.
33 Then it came about, as soon as Gideon was dead, that the sons of Israel again played **8:33** Judg 2:11, 12; Judg 9:4, 27, 46
the harlot with the Baals, and made Baal-berith their god.
34 Thus the sons of Israel did not remember the LORD their God, who had delivered
them from the hands of all their enemies on every side; **8:34** Deut 4:9; Judg 3:7
35 nor did they show kindness to the household of Jerubbaal (*that is,* Gideon) in accord with all the good that he had done to Israel. **8:35** Judg 9:16-18

Abimelech's Conspiracy

9 And Abimelech the son of Jerubbaal went to Shechem to his mother's relatives, and **9:1** Judg 8:31, 35
spoke to them and to the whole clan of the household of his mother's father, saying,
2 "Speak, now, in the hearing of all the leaders of Shechem, 'Which is better for you, **9:2** Judg 8:30; 9:5, 18; Gen 29:14
that seventy men, all the sons of Jerubbaal, rule over you, or that one man rule over you?'
Also, remember that I am your bone and your flesh."
3 And his mother's relatives spoke all these words on his behalf in the hearing of all **9:3** Gen 29:15
the leaders of Shechem; and they were inclined to follow Abimelech, for they said, "He
is our relative."
4 They gave him seventy *pieces* of silver from the house of Baal-berith with which **9:4** Judg 8:33
Abimelech hired worthless and reckless fellows, and they followed him.
5 Then he went to his father's house at Ophrah and killed his brothers the sons of **9:5** 2 Kin 11:1, 2; Judg 8:30; 9:2, 18
Jerubbaal, seventy men, on one stone. But Jotham the youngest son of Jerubbaal was
left, for he hid himself.
6 All the men of Shechem and all [14]Beth-millo assembled together, and they went and
made Abimelech king, by the oak of the pillar which was in Shechem.
7 Now when they told Jotham, he went and stood on the top of Mount Gerizim, and **9:7** Deut 11:29, 30
lifted his voice and called out. Thus he said to them, "Listen to me, O men of Shechem,
that God may listen to you.
8 "Once the trees went forth to anoint a king over them, and they said to the olive tree,
'Reign over us!'

14 Or *the house of Millo*

8:31 This relationship between Gideon and a concubine produced a son who tore apart Gideon's family and caused tragedy for the nation. Gideon's story illustrates the fact that heroes in battle are not always heroes in daily life. Gideon led the nation but could not lead his family. No matter who you are, moral laxness will cause problems. Just because you have won a single battle with temptation does not mean you will automatically win the next one. We need to be constantly watchful against temptation. Sometimes Satan's strongest attacks come after a victory.

8:33 Baal-berith means "Baal (lord) of the covenant." Worship of the idol may have combined elements of both the Israelites and Canaanite religions.

9:1–3 With Gideon dead, Abimelech wanted to take his father's place. (Jerubbaal is another name for Gideon; see 6:32.) To set his plan in motion he went to the city of Shechem, his mother's hometown, to drum up support. Here he felt kinship with the residents. These relatives were Canaanites and would be glad to unite against Israel. Shechem was an important city, a crossroads for trade routes and a natural link between the coastal plain and the Jordan Valley. Whoever controlled Shechem would dominate the countryside.

9:2–5 Israel's king was to be the Lord and not a man. But Abimelech wanted to usurp the position reserved for God alone. In his selfish quest, he killed all but one of his 70 half brothers. People with selfish desires often seek to fulfill them in ruthless ways. Examine your ambitions to see if they are self-centered or God-centered. Be sure you always fulfill your desires in ways that God would approve.

9:4 Politics played a major part in pagan religions such as the worship of Baal-berith. Governments often went so far as to hire temple prostitutes to bring in additional money. In many cases a religious system was set up and supported by the government so the offerings could fund community projects. Religion became a profit-making business. In Israel's religion, this was strictly forbidden. God's system of religion was designed to come from an attitude of the heart, not from calculated plans and business opportunities. It was also designed to serve people and help those in need, not to oppress the needy. Is your faith genuine and sincere, or is it based on convenience, comfort, and availability?

9:6 Abimelech was declared ruler of Israel at Shechem, the site of other key Bible events. It was one of Abraham's first stops upon arriving in Canaan (Genesis 12:6–7). When Jacob lived there, two of his sons killed all the men in Shechem because the prince's son raped their sister (Genesis 34). Joseph's bones were buried in Shechem (Joshua 24:32); Israel renewed its covenant with God there (Joshua 24); and the kingdom of Israel split apart at this same city (1 Kings 12).

9:7–15 In Jotham's parable the trees represented Gideon's 70 sons, and the bramble represented Abimelech. Jotham's point was this: A productive person would be too busy doing good to want to bother with power politics. A worthless person, on the other hand, would be glad to accept the honor—but he would destroy the people he ruled. Abimelech, like a bramble, could offer Israel no real protection or security. Jotham's parable came true when Abimelech destroyed the city of Shechem (9:45), burned "the tower of Shechem" (9:46–49), and was finally killed at Thebez (9:53–54).

9 "But the olive tree said to them, 'Shall I leave my fatness with which God and men are honored, and go to wave over the trees?'
10 "Then the trees said to the fig tree, 'You come, reign over us!'
11 "But the fig tree said to them, 'Shall I leave my sweetness and my good fruit, and go to wave over the trees?'

ABIMELECH

People who desire power always outnumber those who are able to use power wisely once they have it. Perhaps this is because power has a way of taking over and controlling the person using it. This is especially true in cases of inherited but unmerited power. Abimelech's life shows us what happens when hunger for power corrupts judgment.

Abimelech's position in Gideon's family as the son of a concubine must have created great tension between him and Gideon's many other sons. One against 70: Such odds can either crush a person or make him ruthless. It is obvious which direction Abimelech chose. Gideon's position as warrior and judge had placed Abimelech in an environment of power; Gideon's death provided an opportunity for this son to seize power. Once the process began, the disastrous results were inevitable. A person's thirst for power is not satisfied when he gets power—it only becomes more intense. Abimelech's life was consumed by that thirst. Eventually, he could not tolerate any threat to his power.

By this time, ownership had changed: Abimelech no longer had power—power had him. One lesson we can learn from his life is that our goals control our actions. The amount of control is related to the importance of the goal. Abimelech's most important goal was to have power. His lust for power led him to wipe out not only his brothers, but also whole cities that refused to submit to him. Nothing but death could stop his bloodthirsty drive to conquer. How ironic that he was fatally injured by a woman! The contrast between Abimelech and the great people of the Bible is great. He wanted to control the nation; they were willing to be controlled by God.

Strengths and accomplishments:
- The first self-declared king of Israel
- Qualified tactical planner and organizer

Weaknesses and mistakes:
- Power hungry and ruthless
- Overconfident
- Took advantage of his father's position without imitating his character
- Had 69 of his 70 half brothers killed

Vital statistics:
- Where: Shechem, Arumah, Thebez
- Occupations: Self-acclaimed king, judge, political troublemaker
- Relatives: Father: Gideon. Only surviving brother: Jotham

Key verses:
"Thus God repaid the wickedness of Abimelech, which he had done to his father in killing his seventy brothers. Also God returned all the wickedness of the men of Shechem on their heads, and the curse of Jotham the son of Jerubbaal came on them" (Judges 9:56–57).

His story is told in Judges 8:31—9:57. He is also mentioned in 2 Samuel 11:21.

ABIMELECH'S FALL
Gideon's illegitimate son killed 69 of his half brothers in Ophrah and returned to Shechem to be acclaimed king. But three years later, Shechem rebelled. From Arumah, Abimelech attacked Shechem, the tower of Shechem, and Thebez, where he was killed.

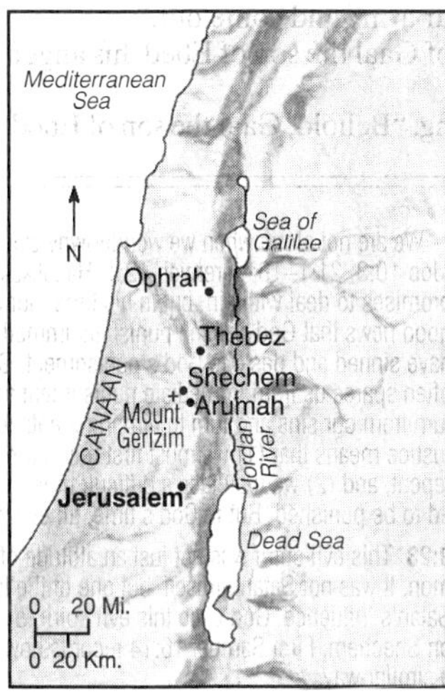

12 "Then the trees said to the vine, 'You come, reign over us!'
13 "But the vine said to them, 'Shall I leave my new wine, which cheers God and men,
and go to wave over the trees?'
14 "Finally all the trees said to the bramble, 'You come, reign over us!'
15 "The bramble said to the trees, 'If in truth you are anointing me as king over you,
come and take refuge in my shade; but if not, may fire come out from the bramble and
consume the cedars of Lebanon.'
16 "Now therefore, if you have dealt in truth and integrity in making Abimelech king, **9:16**
and if you have dealt well with Jerubbaal and his house, and have dealt with him as he Judg 8:35
deserved—
17 for my father fought for you and risked his life and delivered you from the hand of
Midian;
18 but you have risen against my father's house today and have killed his sons, seventy **9:18**
men, on one stone, and have made Abimelech, the son of his maidservant, king over the Judg 8:30; 9:2, 5; Judg 8:31
men of Shechem, because he is your relative—
19 if then you have dealt in truth and integrity with Jerubbaal and his house this day,
rejoice in Abimelech, and let him also rejoice in you.
20 "But if not, let fire come out from Abimelech and consume the men of Shechem and
Beth-millo; and let fire come out from the men of Shechem and from Beth-millo, and
consume Abimelech."
21 Then Jotham escaped and fled, and went to Beer and remained there because of
Abimelech his brother.

Shechem and Abimelech Fall

22 Now Abimelech ruled over Israel three years.
23 Then God sent an evil spirit between Abimelech and the men of Shechem; and the **9:23**
men of Shechem dealt treacherously with Abimelech, 1 Sam 16:14; Is 19:2, 14; Is 33:1
24 so that the violence done to the seventy sons of Jerubbaal might come, and their
blood might be laid on Abimelech their brother, who killed them, and on the men of **9:24**
Shechem, who strengthened his hands to kill his brothers. Deut 27:25; Judg 9:56, 57; Num 35:33
25 The men of Shechem set men in ambush against him on the tops of the mountains,
and they robbed all who might pass by them along the road; and it was told to Abimelech.
26 Now Gaal the son of Ebed came with his relatives, and crossed over into Shechem;
and the men of Shechem put their trust in him.
27 They went out into the field and gathered *the grapes of* their vineyards and trod *them,* **9:27**
and held a festival; and they went into the house of their god, and ate and drank and Judg 8:33; 9:46
cursed Abimelech.
28 Then Gaal the son of Ebed said, "Who is Abimelech, and who is Shechem, that we **9:28**
should serve him? Is he not the son of Jerubbaal, and *is* Zebul *not* his lieutenant? Serve Gen 34:2
the men of Hamor the father of Shechem; but why should we serve him?
29 "Would, therefore, that this people were under my authority! Then I would remove **9:29**
Abimelech." And he said to Abimelech, "Increase your army and come out." 2 Sam 15:4
30 When Zebul the ruler of the city heard the words of Gaal the son of Ebed, his anger
burned.
31 He sent messengers to Abimelech deceitfully, saying, "Behold, Gaal the son of Ebed

---

9:16 Jotham told the story about the trees in order to help the people set good priorities. He did not want them to appoint a leader of low character. As we serve in leadership positions, we should examine our motives. Do we just want praise, prestige, or power? In the parable, the good trees chose to be productive and to provide benefits to people. Make sure these are your priorities as you aspire to leadership.

9:22–24 Abimelech was the opposite of what God wanted in a judge, but it was three years before God moved against him, fulfilling Jotham's parable. Those three years must have seemed like forever to Jotham. Why wasn't Abimelech punished sooner for his evil ways?

We are not alone when we wonder why evil seems to prevail (Job 10:3; 21:1–18; Jeremiah 12:1; Habakkuk 1:2–4, 12–17). God promises to deal with sin, but in his time, not ours. Actually it is good news that God doesn't punish *us* immediately because we all have sinned and deserve God's punishment. God, in his mercy, often spares us from immediate punishment and allows us time to turn from our sins and turn to him in repentance. Trusting God for justice means that (1) we must first recognize our own sins and repent, and (2) we may face a difficult time of waiting for the wicked to be punished. But in God's time, all evil will be destroyed.

9:23 This evil spirit was not just an attitude of strife, it was a demon. It was not Satan himself, but one of the fallen angels under Satan's influence. God used this evil spirit to bring about judgment on Shechem. First Samuel 16:14 records how God judged Saul in a similar way.

and his relatives have come to Shechem; and behold, they are stirring up the city against
you.
32 "Now therefore, arise by night, you and the people who are with you, and lie in wait
in the field.
9:33 33 "In the morning, as soon as the sun is up, you shall rise early and rush upon the city;
1 Sam 10:7 and behold, when he and the people who are with him come out against you, you shall
do to them whatever you can."
34 So Abimelech and all the people who *were* with him arose by night and lay in wait
against Shechem in four companies.
35 Now Gaal the son of Ebed went out and stood in the entrance of the city gate; and
Abimelech and the people who *were* with him arose from the ambush.
36 When Gaal saw the people, he said to Zebul, "Look, people are coming down from
the tops of the mountains." But Zebul said to him, "You are seeing the shadow of the
mountains as *if they were* men."
9:37 37 Gaal spoke again and said, "Behold, people are coming down from the highest part
Ezek 38:12 of the land, and one company comes by the way of the diviners' oak."
38 Then Zebul said to him, "Where is your boasting now with which you said, 'Who is
Abimelech that we should serve him?' Is this not the people whom you despised? Go
out now and fight with them!"
39 So Gaal went out before the leaders of Shechem and fought with Abimelech.
40 Abimelech chased him, and he fled before him; and many fell wounded up to the
entrance of the gate.
41 Then Abimelech remained at Arumah, but Zebul drove out Gaal and his relatives
so that they could not remain in Shechem.
42 Now it came about the next day, that the people went out to the field, and it was
told to Abimelech.
43 So he took his people and divided them into three companies, and lay in wait in the
field; when he looked and saw the people coming out from the city, he arose against them
and slew them.
44 Then Abimelech and the company who was with him dashed forward and stood in
the entrance of the city gate; the other two companies then dashed against all who *were*
in the field and slew them.
9:45 45 Abimelech fought against the city all that day, and he captured the city and killed
2 Kin 3:25 the people who *were* in it; then he razed the city and sowed it with salt.
9:46 **46** When all the leaders of the tower of Shechem heard of *it,* they entered the inner
Judg 8:33 chamber of the temple of El-berith.
47 It was told Abimelech that all the leaders of the tower of Shechem were gathered
together.
9:48 48 So Abimelech went up to Mount Zalmon, he and all the people who *were* with him;
Ps 68:14 and Abimelech took an axe in his hand and cut down a branch from the trees, and lifted
it and laid *it* on his shoulder. Then he said to the people who *were* with him, "What you
have seen me do, hurry *and* do likewise."
49 All the people also cut down each one his branch and followed Abimelech, and put
them on the inner chamber and set the inner chamber on fire over those *inside,* so that
all the men of the tower of Shechem also died, about a thousand men and women.
50 Then Abimelech went to Thebez, and he camped against Thebez and captured it.
51 But there was a strong tower in the center of the city, and all the men and women
with all the leaders of the city fled there and shut themselves in; and they went up on the
roof of the tower.
52 So Abimelech came to the tower and fought against it, and approached the entrance
of the tower to burn it with fire.
9:53 53 But a certain woman threw an upper millstone on Abimelech's head, crushing his
2 Sam 11:21 skull.

9:45 To scatter salt over a conquered city was a ritual to symbolize the perpetual desolation of the city. It would not be rebuilt for 150 years.

9:53 In times of battle, women were sometimes asked to join the men at the city wall to drop heavy objects on the soldiers below. A millstone would have been an ideal object for this purpose. It was a round stone about 18 inches in diameter with a hole in the center. Millstones were used to grind grain into flour. The grain was placed between two millstones. The top millstone was turned, crushing the grain.

Abimelech's death was especially humiliating: he was killed by a woman, not by fighting; and he was killed by a farm implement instead of a weapon. Abimelech therefore asked his armor bearer to stab him with his sword before he died from the blow of the millstone.

54 Then he called quickly to the young man, his armor bearer, and said to him, "Draw your sword and kill me, so that it will not be said of me, 'A woman slew him.' " So the young man pierced him through, and he died.
55 When the men of Israel saw that Abimelech was dead, each departed to his home.
56 Thus God repaid the wickedness of Abimelech, which he had done to his father in killing his seventy brothers.
57 Also God returned all the wickedness of the men of Shechem on their heads, and the curse of Jotham the son of Jerubbaal came upon them.

9:54 1 Sam 31:4
9:56 Gen 9:5, 6; Ps 94:23

Oppression of Philistines and Ammonites

10 Now after Abimelech died, Tola the son of Puah, the son of Dodo, a man of Issachar, arose to save Israel; and he lived in Shamir in the hill country of Ephraim.
2 He judged Israel twenty-three years. Then he died and was buried in Shamir.
3 After him, Jair the Gileadite arose and judged Israel twenty-two years.
4 He had thirty sons who rode on thirty donkeys, and they had thirty cities in the land of Gilead that are called Havvoth-jair to this day.
5 And Jair died and was buried in Kamon.

10:1 Judg 2:16
10:4 Num 32:41

5. Fifth period: Jephthah, Ibzan, Elon, and Abdon

6 Then the sons of Israel again did evil in the sight of the LORD, served the Baals and
the Ashtaroth, the gods of Aram, the gods of Sidon, the gods of Moab, the gods of the
sons of Ammon, and the gods of the Philistines; thus they forsook the LORD and did not
serve Him.
7 The anger of the LORD burned against Israel, and He sold them into the hands of
the Philistines and into the hands of the sons of Ammon.
8 They afflicted and crushed the sons of Israel that year; for eighteen years they *afflicted* all the sons of Israel who were beyond the Jordan in Gilead in the land of the
Amorites.
9 The sons of Ammon crossed the Jordan to fight also against Judah, Benjamin, and
the house of Ephraim, so that Israel was greatly distressed.
10 Then the sons of Israel cried out to the LORD, saying, "We have sinned against You,
for indeed, we have forsaken our God and served the Baals."
11 The LORD said to the sons of Israel, *"Did I* not *deliver you* from the Egyptians, the
Amorites, the sons of Ammon, and the Philistines?
12 "Also when the Sidonians, the Amalekites and the Maonites oppressed you, you cried
out to Me, and I delivered you from their hands.
13 "Yet you have forsaken Me and served other gods; therefore I will no longer deliver you.

10:6 Judg 2:13; Judg 11:24; Deut 31:16, 17; 32:15
10:7 1 Sam 12:9
10:10 1 Sam 12:10
10:11 Judg 2:12; Num 21:21-25; Judg 3:13
10:12 Ps 106:42
10:13 Jer 2:13

9:56–57 Gideon, Abimelech's father, succeeded in military battles, but sometimes failed in his personal struggles. Gideon was not condemned for taking a concubine (8:31), but the family problems that resulted from this relationship are clearly stated.

In the end, Abimelech killed 69 of his 70 half brothers, tore apart a nation, and then was killed himself. From Gideon's life we learn that no matter how much good we do for God's kingdom, sin in our lives will still produce powerful, damaging consequences.

9:56–57 Jotham's curse is found in 9:16–20.

10:1–5 In five verses we read about two men who judged Israel for a total of 45 years, yet all we know about them besides the length of their rules is that one had 30 sons who rode around on 30 donkeys. What are you doing for God that is worth noting? When your life is over, will people remember more than just what was in your bank account or the number of years you lived?

10:6 Baal and Ashtaroth are explained in the notes on 2:11–15 and 3:7. The gods of Aram and Sidon are very similar. The gods of Moab and Ammon were Chemosh and Molech. The Philistine gods were Dagon, Ashtaroth, Asherah, and Baal-zebul.

10:9–10 Once again the Israelites suffered for many years before they gave up their sinful ways and called out to God for help (see 4:1–3; 6:1–7). Notice that when the Israelites were at the end of their rope they did not look to their pagan gods for help, but to the only One who was really able to help.

Is God your last resort? So much unnecessary suffering takes place because we don't call on God until we've used up all other resources. Rather than waiting until the situation becomes desperate, turn to God first. He has the necessary resources to meet every kind of problem.

10:11–16 These verses show how difficult it can be to follow God over the long haul. The Israelites always seemed to forget God when all was well. But despite being rejected by his own people, God never failed to rescue them when they called out to him in repentance. God never fails to rescue us either. We act just like the Israelites when we put God outside our daily events instead of at the center of them. Just as a loving parent feels rejected when a child rebels, so God feels great rejection when we ignore or neglect him (1 Samuel 8:4–9; 10:17–19; John 12:44–50). We should strive to stay close to God rather than see how far we can go before judgment comes.

10:14 Deut 32:37
14 "Go and cry out to the gods which you have chosen; let them deliver you in the time
of your distress."
10:15 1 Sam 3:18
15 The sons of Israel said to the LORD, "We have sinned, do to us whatever seems good
to You; only please deliver us this day."
10:16 Josh 24:23; Deut 32:36
16 So they put away the foreign gods from among them and served the LORD; and He
could bear the misery of Israel no longer.
10:17 Judg 11:29
17 Then the sons of Ammon were summoned and they camped in Gilead. And the sons
of Israel gathered together and camped in Mizpah.
18 The people, the leaders of Gilead, said to one another,
"Who is the man who will begin to fight against the sons of Ammon? He shall become
head over all the inhabitants of Gilead."

Jephthah the Ninth Judge

11:1 Heb 11:32
11 Now Jephthah the Gileadite was a valiant warrior, but he was the son of a harlot.
And Gilead was the father of Jephthah.
2 Gilead's wife bore him sons; and when his wife's sons grew up, they drove Jephthah
out and said to him, "You shall not have an inheritance in our father's house, for you are
the son of another woman."
11:3 2 Sam 10:6, 8
3 So Jephthah fled from his brothers and lived in the land of Tob; and worthless fellows gathered themselves about Jephthah, and they went out with him.

RASH VOWS

Ecclesiastes 5:2 says: "Do not be hasty in word or impulsive in thought to bring up a matter in the presence of God." Scripture records the vows of many men and women. Some of these vows proved to be rash and unwise, and others, though extreme, were kept to the letter by those who made them. Let us learn from the examples in God's Word not to make rash vows.

Person	*Reference*	*Vow*	*Result*
JACOB	Genesis 28:20	To "choose" the true God and to give back a tenth to him if he kept him safe	God protected Jacob, who kept his vow to follow God
JEPHTHAH	Judges 11:30–31	To offer to the Lord whomever came out to meet him after battle (it turned out to be his daughter)	He lost his daughter
HANNAH	1 Samuel 1:9–11	To give her son back to God, if God would give her a son	When Samuel was born, she dedicated him to God
SAUL	1 Samuel 14:24–45	To kill anyone who ate before evening (Jonathan, his son, had not heard the command and broke it)	Saul would have killed Jonathan if soldiers had not intervened
DAVID	2 Samuel 9:7	To be kind to Jonathan's family	Mephibosheth, Jonathan's son, was treated royally by David
ITTAI	2 Samuel 15:21	To remain loyal to David	He became one of the great men in David's army
MICAIAH	1 Kings 22:14	To say only what God told	He was put in prison
JOB	Job 27:2	That he was not rebelling against what God told him to say	His fortunes were restored
HEROD ANTIPAS	Mark 6:22–23	To give Herodias's daughter anything she requested	Herod was forced to order John the Baptist's death
PAUL	Acts 18:18	To offer a sacrifice of thanksgiving in Jerusalem	He made the sacrifice despite the danger

10:17–18 The power of the Ammonite nation was at its peak during the period of the judges. The people were descendants of Ammon, conceived when Lot's daughter slept with her drunk father (Genesis 19:30–38). The land of Ammon was located just east of the Jordan River across from Jerusalem. South of Ammon lay the land of Moab, the nation conceived when Lot's other daughter slept with her father. Moab and Ammon were usually allies. It was a formidable task to defeat these nations.

11:1–2 Jephthah, an illegitimate son of Gilead, was chased out of the country by his half brothers. He suffered as a result of another's decision and not for any wrong he had done. Yet in spite of his brothers' rejection, God used him. If you are suffering from unfair rejection, don't blame others and become discouraged. Remember how God used Jephthah despite his unjust circumstances, and realize that he is able to use you even if you feel rejected by some.

11:3 Circumstances beyond his control forced Jephthah away from his people and into life as an outcast. Today, both believers and nonbelievers may drive away those who do not fit the norms dictated by our society, neighborhoods, or churches. Often, as in Jephthah's case, great potential is wasted because of prejudice—a refusal to look beyond ill-conceived stereotypes. Look around you to see if there are potential Jephthahs being kept out due to factors beyond their control. As a Christian you know that everyone can have a place in God's family. Can you do anything to help these people gain acceptance for their character and abilities?

4 It came about after a while that the sons of Ammon fought against Israel.
5 When the sons of Ammon fought against Israel, the elders of Gilead went to get
Jephthah from the land of Tob;
6 and they said to Jephthah, "Come and be our chief that we may fight against the
sons of Ammon."
7 Then Jephthah said to the elders of Gilead, "Did you not hate me and drive me
from my father's house? So why have you come to me now when you are in trouble?"
8 The elders of Gilead said to Jephthah, "For this reason we have now returned to
you, that you may go with us and fight with the sons of Ammon and become head over
all the inhabitants of Gilead."
9 So Jephthah said to the elders of Gilead, "If you take me back to fight against the
sons of Ammon and the LORD gives them up to me, will I become your head?"
10 The elders of Gilead said to Jephthah, "The LORD is witness between us; surely we
will do as you have said."
11 Then Jephthah went with the elders of Gilead, and the people made him head and
chief over them; and Jephthah spoke all his words before the LORD at Mizpah.
12 Now Jephthah sent messengers to the king of the sons of Ammon, saying, "What is
between you and me, that you have come to me to fight against my land?"
13 The king of the sons of Ammon said to the messengers of Jephthah, "Because Israel took away my land when they came up from Egypt, from the Arnon as far as the
Jabbok and the Jordan; therefore, return them peaceably now."
14 But Jephthah sent messengers again to the king of the sons of Ammon,
15 and they said to him, "Thus says Jephthah, 'Israel did not take away the land of Moab
nor the land of the sons of Ammon.
16 'For when they came up from Egypt, and Israel went through the wilderness to the
Red Sea and came to Kadesh,
17 then Israel sent messengers to the king of Edom, saying, "Please let us pass through
your land," but the king of Edom would not listen. And they also sent to the king of Moab,
but he would not consent. So Israel remained at Kadesh.
18 'Then they went through the wilderness and around the land of Edom and the land
of Moab, and came to the east side of the land of Moab, and they camped beyond the
Arnon; but they did not enter the territory of Moab, for the Arnon *was* the border of
Moab.
19 'And Israel sent messengers to Sihon king of the Amorites, the king of Heshbon,
and Israel said to him, "Please let us pass through your land to our place."
20 'But Sihon did not trust Israel to pass through his territory; so Sihon gathered all his
people and camped in Jahaz and fought with Israel.
21 'The LORD, the God of Israel, gave Sihon and all his people into the hand of Israel,
and they defeated them; so Israel possessed all the land of the Amorites, the inhabitants
of that country.
22 'So they possessed all the territory of the Amorites, from the Arnon as far as the
Jabbok, and from the wilderness as far as the Jordan.
23 'Since now the LORD, the God of Israel, drove out the Amorites from before His
people Israel, are you then to possess it?
24 'Do you not possess what Chemosh your god gives you to possess? So whatever the
LORD our God has driven out before us, we will possess it.
25 'Now are you any better than Balak the son of Zippor, king of Moab? Did he ever
strive with Israel, or did he ever fight against them?

11:4 Judg 10:9, 17
11:7 Gen 26:27
11:8 Judg 10:18
11:10 Gen 31:50; Jer 29:23; 42:5; Mic 1:2
11:11 Judg 10:17; 11:29; 20:1; 1 Sam 10:17
11:13 Num 21:24; Gen 32:22
11:16 Num 14:25; Deut 1:40; Num 20:1, 4-21
11:17 Num 20:14-21; Josh 24:9
11:18 Num 21:4; Deut 2:8; Deut 2:9, 18, 19
11:19 Num 21:21-32; Deut 2:26-36
11:21 Num 21:24; Deut 2:32-34
11:22 Deut 2:36, 37
11:24 Num 21:29; 1 Kin 11:7
11:25 Num 22:2; Josh 24:9; Mic 6:5

11:11 What does it mean that Jephthah repeated all his words before the Lord? Those making covenants in ancient times often made them at shrines so that they would be witnessed by deities. Often a written copy was also deposited at the shrine. This was much like a coronation ceremony for Jephthah.

11:14ff Jephthah sent messengers to the Ammonite king wanting to know why the Israelites in the land of Gilead were being attacked (11:12). The king replied that Israel had stolen this land and he wanted it back (11:13).

Jephthah sent another message to the king (11:14–27). In it he gave three arguments against the king's claim: (1) Gilead was never the king's land in the first place because Israel took it from the Amorites, not the Ammonites (11:16–22); (2) Israel should possess land given by Israel's God, and Ammon should possess land given by Ammon's god; (3) no one had contested Israel's ownership of the land since its conquest 300 years earlier (11:25–26).

To Jephthah's credit, he tried to solve the problem without bloodshed. But the king of Ammon ignored his message and prepared his troops for battle.

11:26 Num 21:25, 26; Deut 2:36

26 'While Israel lived in Heshbon and its villages, and in Aroer and its villages, and in
all the cities that are on the banks of the Arnon, three hundred years, why did you not
recover them within that time?

11:27 Gen 16:5; 18:25; 31:53; 1 Sam 24:12, 15

27 'I therefore have not sinned against you, but you are doing me wrong by making war
against me; may the LORD, the Judge, judge today between the sons of Israel and the
sons of Ammon.' "
28 But the king of the sons of Ammon disregarded the message which Jephthah
sent him.

Jephthah's Tragic Vow

11:29 Judg 3:10

29 Now the Spirit of the LORD came upon Jephthah, so that he passed through Gilead
and Manasseh; then he passed through Mizpah of Gilead, and from Mizpah of Gilead
he went on to the sons of Ammon.
30 Jephthah made a vow to the LORD and said, "If You will indeed give the sons of
Ammon into my hand,
31 then it shall be that whatever comes out of the doors of my house to meet me when
I return in peace from the sons of Ammon, it shall be the LORD'S, and I will offer it up
as a burnt offering."
32 So Jephthah crossed over to the sons of Ammon to fight against them; and the LORD
gave them into his hand.

11:33 Ezek 27:17

33 He struck them with a very great slaughter from Aroer to the entrance of Minnith,
twenty cities, and as far as Abel-keramim. So the sons of Ammon were subdued before
the sons of Israel.

11:34 Judg 10:17; 11:11; Ex 15:20; 1 Sam 18:6; Jer 31:4

34 When Jephthah came to his house at Mizpah, behold, his daughter was coming out
to meet him with tambourines and with dancing. Now she was his one *and* only child;
besides her he had no son or daughter.

11:35 Num 30:2; Eccl 5:4, 5

35 When he saw her, he tore his clothes and said, "Alas, my daughter! You have brought
me very low, and you are among those who trouble me; for I have given my word to the
LORD, and I cannot take *it* back."

11:36 Num 30:2

36 So she said to him, "My father, you have given your word to the LORD; do to me as
you have said, since the LORD has avenged you of your enemies, the sons of Ammon."

11:37 Gen 30:23; Luke 1:25

37 She said to her father, "Let this thing be done for me; let me alone two months, that
I may go to the mountains and weep because of my virginity, I and my companions."
38 Then he said, "Go." So he sent her away for two months; and she left with her companions, and wept on the mountains because of her virginity.
39 At the end of two months she returned to her father, who did to her according to
the vow which he had made; and she had no relations with a man. Thus it became a custom in Israel,
40 that the daughters of Israel went yearly to commemorate the daughter of Jephthah
the Gileadite four days in the year.

11:27 Over the years, Israel had many judges to lead them. But Jephthah recognized the Lord as the people's true Judge, the only One who could really lead them and help them conquer the invading enemies.

11:30–31 In God's law, a vow was a promise to God that should not be broken (Numbers 30:1–2; Deuteronomy 23:21–23). It carried as much force as a written contract. Many people made vows in Biblical times. Some, like Jephthah's, were very foolish.

11:30–31 When Jephthah made his vow, did he stop to consider that a person, not a sheep or goat, might come out to meet him? Scholars are divided over the issue. Those who say Jephthah was considering human sacrifice use the following arguments: (1) He was from an area where pagan religion and human sacrifice were common. In his eyes, it may not have seemed like a sin. (2) Jephthah may not have had a background in religious law. Perhaps he was ignorant of God's command against human sacrifice.

Those who say Jephthah could not have been thinking about human sacrifice point to other evidence: (1) As leader of the people, Jephthah must have been familiar with God's laws; human sacrifice was clearly forbidden (Leviticus 18:21; 20:1–5). (2) No legitimate priest would have helped Jephthah carry out his vow if a person was to be the sacrifice.

Whatever Jephthah had in mind when he made the vow, did he or did he not sacrifice his daughter? Some think he did, because his vow was to make a burnt offering. Some think he did not, and they offer several reasons: (1) If the girl was to die, she would not have spent her last two months in the hills. (2) God would not have honored a vow based on a wicked practice. (3) Verse 39 says that she never married, not that she died, implying that she was set apart for service to God, not killed.

11:34–35 Jephthah's rash vow brought him unspeakable grief. In the heat of emotion or personal turmoil it is easy to make foolish promises to God. These promises may sound very spiritual when we make them, but they may produce only guilt and frustration when we are forced to fulfill them. Making spiritual "deals" only brings disappointment. God does not want promises for the future, but obedience for today.

Jephthah and His Successors

12 Then the men of Ephraim were summoned, and they crossed to Zaphon and said to Jephthah, "Why did you cross over to fight against the sons of Ammon without calling us to go with you? We will burn your house down on you." **12:1** Judg 8:1
2 Jephthah said to them, "I and my people were at great strife with the sons of Ammon; when I called you, you did not deliver me from their hand.
3 "When I saw that you would not deliver *me,* I took my life in my hands and crossed over against the sons of Ammon, and the LORD gave them into my hand. Why then have you come up to me this day to fight against me?" **12:3** 1 Sam 19:5; 28:21; Job 13:14
4 Then Jephthah gathered all the men of Gilead and fought Ephraim; and the men of Gilead defeated Ephraim, because they said, "You are fugitives of Ephraim, O Gileadites, in the midst of Ephraim *and* in the midst of Manasseh."
5 The Gileadites captured the fords of the Jordan opposite Ephraim. And it happened when *any of* the fugitives of Ephraim said, "Let me cross over," the men of Gilead would say to him, "Are you an Ephraimite?" If he said, "No," **12:5** Judg 3:28
6 then they would say to him, "Say now, 'Shibboleth.' "
But he said, "Sibboleth," for he could not pronounce it correctly. Then they seized him and slew him at the fords of the Jordan. Thus there fell at that time 42,000 of Ephraim.
7 Jephthah judged Israel six years. Then Jephthah the Gileadite died and was buried in *one of* the cities of Gilead.
8 Now Ibzan of Bethlehem judged Israel after him.
9 He had thirty sons, and thirty daughters *whom* he gave in marriage outside *the family,* and he brought in thirty daughters from outside for his sons. And he judged Israel seven years.
10 Then Ibzan died and was buried in Bethlehem.
11 Now Elon the Zebulunite judged Israel after him; and he judged Israel ten years.
12 Then Elon the Zebulunite died and was buried at Aijalon in the land of Zebulun.
13 Now Abdon the son of Hillel the Pirathonite judged Israel after him.
14 He had forty sons and thirty grandsons who rode on seventy donkeys; and he judged Israel eight years.
15 Then Abdon the son of Hillel the Pirathonite died and was buried at Pirathon in the land of Ephraim, in the hill country of the Amalekites.

6. Sixth period: Samson

Philistines Oppress Again

13 Now the sons of Israel again did evil in the sight of the LORD, so that the LORD gave them into the hands of the Philistines forty years. **13:1** Judg 2:11

JEPHTHAH'S VICTORY
The Ephraimites mobilized an army because they were angry at not being included in the battle against Ammon. They planned to attack Jephthah at his home in Gilead. Jephthah captured the fords of the Jordan at the Jabbok River and killed the Ephraimites who tried to cross.

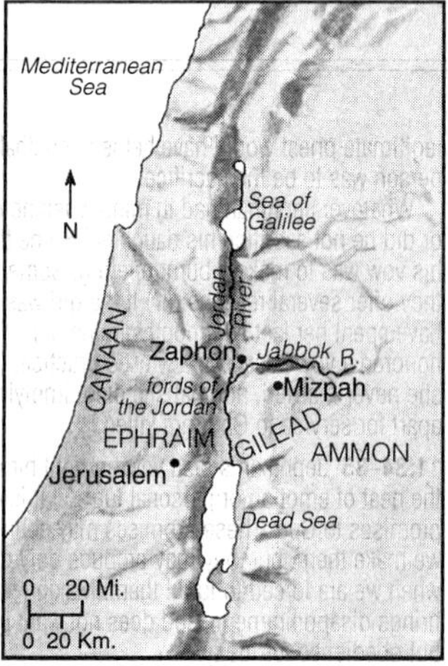

12:1ff Israel had just won a great battle, but instead of joy, there was pettiness and quarreling. The tribe of Ephraim was angry and jealous that they were not invited to join in the fighting (although Jephthah said he had invited them). The insults of the Ephraimites enraged Jephthah, who called out his troops and killed 42,000 men from Ephraim.

Jephthah usually spoke before he acted, but this time his revenge was swift. It cost Israel dearly, and it might have been avoided. Insulting others and being jealous are not right responses when we feel left out. But seeking revenge for an insult is just as wrong, and very costly.

12:4–7 The men of the tribe of Ephraim caused Jephthah trouble just as they had Gideon (8:1–3). Jephthah captured the fords of the Jordan, the boundary of Ephraim, and was able to defeat his countrymen as they crossed the river. He used a pronunciation test. *Shibboleth* is the word for stream. The Ephraimites pronounced "sh" as "s," so Jephthah's army could easily identify them.

12:8–15 There is little else known about these three judges or their importance. The large number of children and cattle are an indication of the wealth of these men.

13:1 The Philistines lived on the west side of Canaan, along the Mediterranean seacoast. From Samson's day until the time of David they were the major enemy force in the land and a constant threat to Israel. The Philistines were fierce warriors; they had the advantage over Israel in numbers, tactical expertise, and technology. They knew the secret of making weapons out of iron (1 Samuel 13:19–22). But none of that mattered when God was fighting for Israel.

13:2 Josh 19:41
13:3 Judg 6:11, 14; 13:6, 8, 10, 11; Luke 1:11-13
13:4 Num 6:2, 3; Luke 1:15
13:5 Luke 1:15; Num 6:2-5

2 There was a certain man of Zorah, of the family of the Danites, whose name was
Manoah; and his wife was barren and had borne no *children.*
3 Then the angel of the LORD appeared to the woman and said to her, "Behold now,
you are barren and have borne no *children,* but you shall conceive and give birth to a
son.
4 "Now therefore, be careful not to drink wine or strong drink, nor eat any unclean
thing.
5 "For behold, you shall conceive and give birth to a son, and no razor shall come upon
his head, for the boy shall be a Nazirite to God from the womb; and he shall begin to
deliver Israel from the hands of the Philistines."

JEPHTHAH

It's hard not to admire people whose word can be depended on completely and whose actions are consistent with their words. For such people, talking is not avoiding action; it is the beginning of action. People like this can make excellent negotiators. They approach a conflict with the full intention of settling issues verbally, but they do not hesitate to use other means if verbal attempts fail. Jephthah was this kind of person.

In most of his conflicts, Jephthah's first move was to talk. In the war with the Ammonites, his strategy was negotiation. He clarified the issues so that everyone knew the cause of the conflict. His opponent's response determined his next action.

The fate of Jephthah's daughter is difficult to understand. We are not sure what Jephthah meant by his vow recorded in Judges 11:31. In any case, his vow was unnecessary. We do not know what actually happened to his daughter—whether she was burned as an offering or set apart as a virgin, thus denying Jephthah any hope of descendants since she was his only child. What we do know is that Jephthah was a person of his word, even when it was a word spoken in haste, and even when keeping his word cost him great pain.

How do you approach conflicts? There is a big difference between trying to settle a conflict through words and simply counterattacking someone verbally. How dependable are the statements you make? Do your children, friends, and fellow workers know you to be a person of your word? The measure of your trustworthiness is your willingness to take responsibility, even if you must pay a painful price because of something you said.

Strengths and accomplishments:
- Listed in the Hall of Faith in Hebrews 11
- Controlled by God's Spirit
- Brilliant military strategist who negotiated before fighting

Weaknesses and mistakes:
- Was bitter over the treatment he received from his half brothers
- Made a rash and foolish vow that was costly

Lesson from his life:
- A person's background does not prevent God from working powerfully in his or her life

Vital statistics:
- Where: Gilead
- Occupations: Warrior, judge
- Relative: Father: Gilead

Key verse:
"So Jephthah crossed over to the sons of Ammon to fight against them; and the LORD gave them into his hand" (Judges 11:32).

His story is told in Judges 11:1—12:7. He is also mentioned in 1 Samuel 12:11 and Hebrews 11:32.

13:1ff Once again the cycle of sin, judgment, and repentance began (3:8–9, 14–15; 4:1–4; 6:1–14; 10:6—11:11). The Israelites would not turn to God unless they had been stunned by suffering, oppression, and death. This suffering was not caused by God but resulted from the fact that the people ignored God, their Judge and Ruler. What will it take for you to follow God? The warnings in God's Word are clear: If we continue to harden our hearts against God, we can expect the same fate as Israel.

13:5 Samson was to be a Nazirite—a person who took a vow to be set apart for God's service. Samson's parents made the vow for him. A Nazirite vow was sometimes temporary, but in Samson's case, it was for life. As a Nazirite, Samson could not cut his hair, touch a dead body, or drink anything containing alcohol.

Although Samson often used poor judgment and sinned terribly, he accomplished much when he determined to be set apart for God. In this way he was like the nation Israel. As long as the Israelites remained set apart for God, the nation thrived. But they fell into terrible sin when they ignored God.

13:5 Manoah's wife was told that her son would *begin* the deliverance of Israel from Philistine oppression. It wasn't until David's day that the Philistine opposition was completely crushed (2 Samuel 8:1). Samson's part in subduing the Philistines was just the beginning, but it was important nonetheless. It was the task God had given Samson to do. Be faithful in following God even if you don't see instant results, because you might be beginning an important job that others will finish.

6 Then the woman came and told her husband, saying, "A man of God came to me
and his appearance was like the appearance of the angel of God, very awesome. And I
did not ask him where he *came* from, nor did he tell me his name.
7 "But he said to me, 'Behold, you shall conceive and give birth to a son, and now you
shall not drink wine or strong drink nor eat any unclean thing, for the boy shall be a
Nazirite to God from the womb to the day of his death.' "
8 Then Manoah entreated the LORD and said, "O Lord, please let the man of God
whom You have sent come to us again that he may teach us what to do for the boy who
is to be born."
9 God listened to the voice of Manoah; and the angel of God came again to the woman as she was sitting in the field, but Manoah her husband was not with her.
10 So the woman ran quickly and told her husband, "Behold, the man who came the
other day has appeared to me."
11 Then Manoah arose and followed his wife, and when he came to the man he said to
him, "Are you the man who spoke to the woman?" And he said, "I am."
12 Manoah said, "Now when your words come *to pass,* what shall be the boy's mode of
life and his vocation?"
13 So the angel of the LORD said to Manoah, "Let the woman pay attention to all that
I said.
14 "She should not eat anything that comes from the vine nor drink wine or strong drink,
nor eat any unclean thing; let her observe all that I commanded."
15 Then Manoah said to the angel of the LORD, "Please let us detain you so that we
may prepare a young goat for you."
16 The angel of the LORD said to Manoah, "Though you detain me, I will not eat your
food, but if you prepare a burnt offering, *then* offer it to the LORD." For Manoah did not
know that he was the angel of the LORD.
17 Manoah said to the angel of the LORD, "What is your name, so that when your words
come *to pass,* we may honor you?"
18 But the angel of the LORD said to him, "Why do you ask my name, seeing it is [15]won-
derful?"
19 So Manoah took the young goat with the grain offering and offered it on the rock to
the LORD, and He performed wonders while Manoah and his wife looked on.
20 For it came about when the flame went up from the altar toward heaven, that the
angel of the LORD ascended in the flame of the altar. When Manoah and his wife saw
this, they fell on their faces to the ground.
21 Now the angel of the LORD did not appear to Manoah or his wife again. Then
Manoah knew that he was the angel of the LORD.
22 So Manoah said to his wife, "We will surely die, for we have seen God."
23 But his wife said to him, "If the LORD had desired to kill us, He would not have
accepted a burnt offering and a grain offering from our hands, nor would He have shown
us all these things, nor would He have let us hear *things* like this at this time."
24 Then the woman gave birth to a son and named him Samson; and the child grew up
and the LORD blessed him.
25 And the Spirit of the LORD began to stir him in [16]Mahaneh-dan, between Zorah
and Eshtaol.

15 I.e. incomprehensible **16** I.e. the camp of Dan

13:6 Judg 6:11; 13:8, 10, 11
13:8 Judg 13:3, 7
13:9 Judg 13:8
13:10 Judg 13:9
13:11 Judg 13:8
13:13 Judg 13:11; Judg 13:4
13:14 Num 6:4
13:15 Judg 13:3
13:16 Judg 6:20
13:17 Gen 32:29
13:18 Is 9:6
13:19 Judg 6:20, 21
13:20 Lev 9:24; 1 Chr 21:16; Ezek 1:28; Matt 17:6
13:21 Judg 13:16
13:22 Gen 32:30; Deut 5:26; Judg 6:22
13:23 Ps 25:14
13:24 1 Sam 3:19; Luke 1:80
13:25 Judg 3:10; Judg 18:11, 12

13:18 Why did the angel keep his name a secret? In those days people believed that if they knew someone's name, they knew his character and how to control him. By not giving his name, the angel was not allowing himself to be controlled by Manoah. He was also saying that his name was a mystery beyond understanding and too wonderful to imagine. Manoah asked the angel for an answer that he wouldn't have understood. Sometimes we ask God questions and then receive no answer. This may not be because God is saying no. We may have asked for knowledge beyond our ability to understand or accept.

13:19 Manoah sacrificed a grain offering to the Lord. A grain offering was grain, oil, and flour shaped into a cake and burned on the altar along with the *burnt offering* (the young goat). The grain offering, described in Leviticus 2, was offered to God as a sign of honor, respect, and worship. It was an acknowledgment that because the Israelites' food came from God, they owed their lives to him. With the grain offering, Manoah showed his desire to serve God and demonstrated his respect.

13:25 Samson's tribe, Dan, continued to wander in their inherited land (18:1), which was yet unconquered (Joshua 19:47–48). Samson must have grown up with his warlike tribe's yearnings for a permanent and settled territory. Thus his visits to the tribal army camp stirred his heart, and God's Spirit began preparing him for his role as judge and leader against the Philistines.

Perhaps there are things that stir your heart. These may indicate areas where God wants to use you. God uses a variety of means to develop and prepare us: hereditary traits, environmental influences, and personal experiences. As with Samson, this preparation often begins long before adulthood. Work at being sensitive to the Holy Spirit's leading and the tasks God has prepared for you. Your past may be more useful to you than you imagine.

Samson's Marriage

14 Then Samson went down to Timnah and saw a woman in Timnah, *one* of the daughters of the Philistines.
2 So he came back and told his father and mother, "I saw a woman in Timnah, *one* of
the daughters of the Philistines; now therefore, get her for me as a wife."
14:3 Gen 24:3, 4; Ex 34:16; Deut 7:3
3 Then his father and his mother said to him, "Is there no woman among the daughters of your relatives, or among all our people, that you go to take a wife from the uncircumcised Philistines?" But Samson said to his father, "Get her for me, for she looks good to me."
14:4 Josh 11:20
4 However, his father and mother did not know that it was of the LORD, for He was seeking an occasion against the Philistines. Now at that time the Philistines were ruling over Israel.

SAMSON

It is sad to be remembered for what one might have been. Samson had tremendous potential. Not many people have started life with credentials like his. Born as a result of God's plan in the lives of Manoah and his wife, Samson was to do a great work for God—to "begin to deliver Israel from the hands of the Philistines." To help him accomplish God's plan, he was given enormous physical strength.

Because Samson wasted his strength on practical jokes and getting out of scrapes, and because he eventually gave it up altogether to satisfy the woman he loved, we tend to see him as a failure. We remember him as the judge in Israel who spent his last days grinding grain in an enemy prison, and we say, "What wasted potential!"

Yes, Samson wasted his life. He could have strengthened his nation. He could have returned his people to the worship of God. He could have wiped out the Philistines. But even though he did none of those things, Samson still accomplished the purpose announced by the angel who visited his parents before his birth. In his final act, Samson began to rescue Israel from the Philistines.

Interestingly, the New Testament does not mention Samson's failures or his heroic feats of strength. In Hebrews, he is simply listed with others "who by faith conquered kingdoms, performed acts of righteousness, obtained promises," and in other ways were given superhuman aid. In the end, Samson recognized his dependence on God. When he died, God turned his failures and defeats into victory. Samson's story teaches us that it is never too late to start over. However badly we may have failed in the past, today is not too late for us to put our complete trust in God.

Strengths and accomplishments:
- Dedicated to God from birth as a Nazirite
- Known for his feats of strength
- Listed in the Hall of Faith in Hebrews 11
- Began to free Israel from Philistine oppression

Weaknesses and mistakes:
- Violated his vow and God's laws on many occasions
- Was controlled by sensuality
- Confided in the wrong people
- Used his gifts and abilities unwisely

Lessons from his life:
- Great strength in one area of life does not make up for great weaknesses in other areas
- God's presence does not overwhelm a person's will
- God can use a person of faith in spite of his or her mistakes

Vital statistics:
- Where: Zorah, Timnah, Ashkelon, Gaza, Valley of Sorek
- Occupation: Judge
- Relative: Father: Manoah
- Contemporaries: Delilah, Samuel (who might have been born while Samson was a judge)

Key verse:
"You shall conceive and give birth to a son, and no razor shall come upon his head, for the boy shall be a Nazirite to God from the womb; and he shall begin to deliver Israel from the hands of the Philistines" (Judges 13:5).

His story is told in Judges 13—16. He is also mentioned in Hebrews 11:32.

14:3 Samson's parents objected to his marrying the Philistine woman for several reasons: (1) It was against God's law (Exodus 34:15–17; Deuteronomy 7:1–4). A stark example of what happened when the Israelites married pagans can be found in 3:5–7. (2) The Philistines were Israel's greatest enemies. Marriage to a hated Philistine would be a disgrace to Samson's family. But Samson's father gave in to Samson's demand and allowed the marriage, even though he had the right to refuse his son.

5 Then Samson went down to Timnah with his father and mother, and came as far as
the vineyards of Timnah; and behold, a young lion *came* roaring toward him.
6 The Spirit of the LORD came upon him mightily, so that he tore him as one tears a
young goat though he had nothing in his hand; but he did not tell his father or mother
what he had done.
7 So he went down and talked to the woman; and she looked good to Samson.
8 When he returned later to take her, he turned aside to look at the carcass of the
lion; and behold, a swarm of bees and honey were in the body of the lion.
9 So he scraped the honey into his hands and went on, eating as he went. When he
came to his father and mother, he gave *some* to them and they ate *it;* but he did not tell
them that he had scraped the honey out of the body of the lion.
10 Then his father went down to the woman; and Samson made a feast there, for the
young men customarily did this.
11 When they saw him, they brought thirty companions to be with him.

14:6 Judg 3:10; 1 Sam 17:34-36

Samson's Riddle

12 Then Samson said to them, "Let me now propound a riddle to you; if you will indeed tell it to me within the seven days of the feast, and find it out, then I will give you
thirty linen wraps and thirty changes of clothes.
13 "But if you are unable to tell me, then you shall give me thirty linen wraps and thirty
changes of clothes." And they said to him, "Propound your riddle, that we may hear it."
14 So he said to them,
"Out of the eater came something to eat,
And out of the strong came something sweet."
But they could not tell the riddle in three days.
15 Then it came about on the fourth day that they said to Samson's wife, "Entice your
husband, so that he will tell us the riddle, or we will burn you and your father's house
with fire. Have you invited us to impoverish us? Is this not *so?*"
16 Samson's wife wept before him and said, "You only hate me, and you do not love me;
you have propounded a riddle to the sons of my people, and have not told *it* to me." And
he said to her, "Behold, I have not told *it* to my father or mother; so should I tell you?"
17 However she wept before him seven days while their feast lasted. And on the seventh day he told her because she pressed him so hard. She then told the riddle to the
sons of her people.
18 So the men of the city said to him on the seventh day before the sun went down,
"What is sweeter than honey?
And what is stronger than a lion?"
And he said to them,
"If you had not plowed with my heifer,
You would not have found out my riddle."
19 Then the Spirit of the LORD came upon him mightily, and he went down to Ashkelon and killed thirty of them and took their spoil and gave the changes *of clothes* to those
who told the riddle. And his anger burned, and he went up to his father's house.
20 But Samson's wife was *given* to his companion who had been his friend.

14:12 Ezek 17:2; Gen 45:22; 2 Kin 5:22

14:15 Judg 16:5; Judg 15:6

14:16 Judg 16:15

14:19 Judg 3:10; 13:25

14:20 Judg 15:2

Samson Burns Philistine Crops

15 But after a while, in the time of wheat harvest, Samson visited his wife with a young
goat, and said, "I will go in to my wife in *her* room." But her father did not let him
enter.

15:1 Gen 38:17

14:6 "The Spirit of the LORD came upon him mightily" refers to the unusual physical strength given him by the Spirit of the Lord. Samson did not seem to be affected in any other ways than increased physical strength.

14:18 "If you had not plowed with my heifer" means "If you had not manipulated my wife." If they hadn't threatened his wife, they wouldn't have learned the answer to his riddle.

14:19 Samson impulsively used the special gift God gave him for selfish purposes. Today, God distributes abilities and skills throughout the church (1 Corinthians 12:1ff). The apostle Paul states that these gifts are to be used "for the equipping of the saints for the work of service, to the building up of the body of Christ;" that is, to build up the church (Ephesians 4:12). To use these abilities for selfish purposes is to rob the church and fellow believers of strength. As you use the gifts God has given you, be sure you are helping others, not just yourself.

15:1ff Samson's reply in 15:11 tells the story of this chapter: "As they did to me, so I have done to them." Revenge is an uncontrollable monster. Each act of retaliation brings another. It is a boomerang that cannot be thrown without cost to the thrower. The revenge cycle can be halted only by forgiveness.

15:2 Judg 14:20
2 Her father said, "I really thought that you hated her intensely; so I gave her to your
companion. Is not her younger sister more beautiful than she? Please let her be yours
instead."
3 Samson then said to them, "This time I shall be blameless in regard to the Philistines when I do them harm."
4 Samson went and caught three hundred foxes, and took torches, and turned *the foxes*
tail to tail and put one torch in the middle between two tails.
5 When he had set fire to the torches, he released the foxes into the standing grain of
the Philistines, thus burning up both the shocks and the standing grain, along with the
vineyards *and* groves.
15:6 Judg 14:15
6 Then the Philistines said, "Who did this?" And they said, "Samson, the son-in-law
of the Timnite, because he took his wife and gave her to his companion." So the Philistines came up and burned her and her father with fire.
7 Samson said to them, "Since you act like this, I will surely take revenge on you, but
after that I will quit."
8 He struck them ruthlessly with a great slaughter; and he went down and lived in the
cleft of the rock of Etam.
9 Then the Philistines went up and camped in Judah, and spread out in Lehi.
10 The men of Judah said, "Why have you come up against us?"
And they said, "We have come up to bind Samson in order to do to him as he did to us."
15:11 Lev 26:25; Deut 28:43f; Judg 13:1; 14:4; Ps 106:40-42
11 Then 3,000 men of Judah went down to the cleft of the rock of Etam and said to
Samson, "Do you not know that the Philistines are rulers over us? What then is this that
you have done to us?" And he said to them, "As they did to me, so I have done to them."
12 They said to him, "We have come down to bind you so that we may give you into
the hands of the Philistines." And Samson said to them, "Swear to me that you will not
kill me."
13 So they said to him, "No, but we will bind you fast and give you into their hands; yet
surely we will not kill you." Then they bound him with two new ropes and brought him
up from the rock.
15:14 Judg 14:19; 1 Sam 11:6
14 When he came to Lehi, the Philistines shouted as they met him. And the Spirit of
the LORD came upon him mightily so that the ropes that were on his arms were as flax
that is burned with fire, and his bonds dropped from his hands.
15:15 Lev 26:8; Josh 23:10
15 He found a fresh jawbone of a donkey, so he reached out and took it and killed a
thousand men with it.
16 Then Samson said,
"With the jawbone of a donkey,
Heaps upon heaps,
With the jawbone of a donkey
I have killed a thousand men."

15:14–17 The Lord's strength came upon Samson, but he was proud and boasted only of his own strength. "With the jawbone of a donkey I have killed a thousand men," he said, and later asked God to refresh him because of *his* accomplishments (15:16–18). Pride can cause us to take credit for work we've done only because of God's strength.

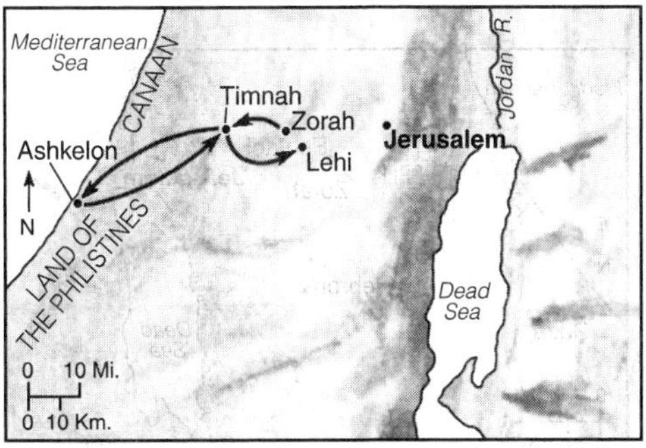

SAMSON'S VENTURES Samson grew up in Zorah and wanted to marry a Philistine girl from Timnah. Tricked at his own wedding feast, he went to Ashkelon and killed some Philistine men and stole their clothes to pay off a bet. Samson then let himself be captured and brought to Lehi, where he snapped his ropes and killed 1,000 people.

17 When he had finished speaking, he threw the jawbone from his hand; and he named
that place [17]Ramath-lehi.
18 Then he became very thirsty, and he called to the LORD and said, "You have given **15:18**
this great deliverance by the hand of Your servant, and now shall I die of thirst and fall Judg 16:28
into the hands of the uncircumcised?"
19 But God split the hollow place that is in Lehi so that water came out of it. When he **15:19**
drank, his strength returned and he revived. Therefore he named it En-hakkore, which Is 40:29
is in Lehi to this day.
20 So he judged Israel twenty years in the days of the Philistines. **15:20**
Judg 16:31; Heb 11:32; Judg 13:1

Samson's Weakness

16 Now Samson went to Gaza and saw a harlot there, and went in to her. **16:1**
2 *When it was told* to the Gazites, saying, "Samson has come here," they surround- Josh 15:47
ed *the place* and lay in wait for him all night at the gate of the city. And they kept silent **16:2**
all night, saying, "*Let us wait* until the morning light, then we will kill him." 1 Sam 23:26; Ps 118:10-12
3 Now Samson lay until midnight, and at midnight he arose and took hold of the doors
of the city gate and the two posts and pulled them up along with the bars; then he put
them on his shoulders and carried them up to the top of the mountain which is opposite
Hebron.
4 After this it came about that he loved a woman in the valley of Sorek, whose name
was Delilah.
5 The lords of the Philistines came up to her and said to her, "Entice him, and see **16:5**
where his great strength *lies* and how we may overpower him that we may bind him to Josh 13:3; Judg
afflict him. Then we will each give you eleven hundred *pieces* of silver." 14:15
6 So Delilah said to Samson, "Please tell me where your great strength is and how
you may be bound to afflict you."
7 Samson said to her, "If they bind me with seven fresh cords that have not been dried,
then I will become weak and be like any *other* man."
8 Then the lords of the Philistines brought up to her seven fresh cords that had not
been dried, and she bound him with them.
9 Now she had *men* lying in wait in an inner room. And she said to him, "The Philistines are upon you, Samson!" But he snapped the cords as a string of tow snaps when it
touches fire. So his strength was not discovered.
10 Then Delilah said to Samson, "Behold, you have deceived me and told me lies; now
please tell me how you may be bound."
11 He said to her, "If they bind me tightly with new ropes which have not been used,
then I will become weak and be like any *other* man."
12 So Delilah took new ropes and bound him with them and said to him, "The Philistines are upon you, Samson!" For the *men* were lying in wait in the inner room. But he
snapped the ropes from his arms like a thread.
13 Then Delilah said to Samson, "Up to now you have deceived me and told me lies;

17 I.e. the high place of the jawbone

15:18 Samson was physically and emotionally exhausted. After a great personal victory, his attitude declined quickly into self-pity—"Shall I die of thirst?" Emotionally, we are most vulnerable after a great effort or when faced with real physical needs. Severe depression often follows great achievements, so don't be surprised if you feel drained after a personal victory.

During these times of vulnerability, avoid the temptation to think that God owes you for your efforts. It was *his* strength that gave you victory. Concentrate on keeping your attitudes, actions, and words focused on God instead of yourself.

15:20 Apparently Samson was appointed Israel's judge after this victory over the Philistines.

16:5 The Philistines were ruled by five rulers, not just one. Each ruler ruled from a different city—Ashdod, Ashkelon, Ekron, Gath, or Gaza. Each of these cities was an important center for trade and commerce. Given Delilah's character, it is little wonder that she betrayed Samson when these rich and powerful men paid her a personal visit.

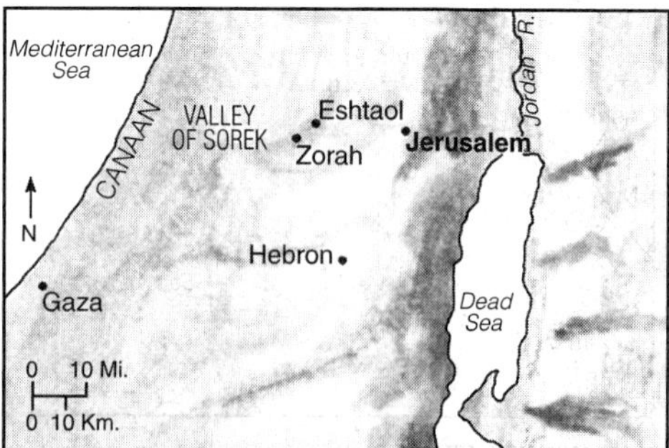

SAMSON AND DELILAH Samson was seduced by a Philistine woman named Delilah who lived in the valley of Sorek. She betrayed the secret of his strength to the Philistines, who captured him and led him away in chains to Gaza. There he died. His relatives buried him between Zorah and Eshtaol.

tell me how you may be bound." And he said to her, "If you weave the seven locks of my
hair with the web [18][and fasten it with a pin, then I will become weak and be like any
other man."
14 So while he slept, Delilah took the seven locks of his hair and wove them into the
web]. And she fastened *it* with the pin and said to him, "The Philistines are upon you,
Samson!" But he awoke from his sleep and pulled out the pin of the loom and the web.

Delilah Extracts His Secret

16:15 Judg 14:16 **15** Then she said to him, "How can you say, 'I love you,' when your heart is not with
me? You have deceived me these three times and have not told me where your great
strength is."
16 It came about when she pressed him daily with her words and urged him, that his
soul was annoyed to death.
16:17 Num 6:2, 5; Judg 13:5 17 So he told her all *that was* in his heart and said to her, "A razor has never come on
my head, for I have been a Nazirite to God from my mother's womb. If I am shaved,
then my strength will leave me and I will become weak and be like any *other* man."
18 When Delilah saw that he had told her all *that was* in his heart, she sent and called
the lords of the Philistines, saying, "Come up once more, for he has told me all *that is* in
his heart." Then the lords of the Philistines came up to her and brought the money in
their hands.

18 The passage in brackets is found in Gr but not in any Heb mss

---

DELILAH

A person's greatest accomplishment may well be helping others accomplish great things. Likewise, a person's greatest failure may be preventing others from achieving greatness. Delilah played a minor role in Samson's life, but her effect was devastating, for she influenced him to betray his special calling from God. Motivated by greed, Delilah used her persistence to wear down Samson. His infatuation with her made Samson a vulnerable target. For all his physical strength, he was no match for her, and he paid a great price for giving in to her. Delilah is never mentioned again in the Bible. Her unfaithfulness to Samson brought ruin to him and to her people.

Are people helped by knowing you? Do they find that knowing you challenges them to be the best they can be? Even more important, does knowing you help their relationship with God? What do your demands for their time and attention tell them about your real care for them? Are you willing to be God's instrument in the lives of others?

Strength and accomplishment:
- Persistent when faced with obstacles

Weaknesses and mistakes:
- Valued money more than relationships
- Betrayed the man who trusted her

Lesson from her life:
- We need to be careful to place our trust only in people who are trustworthy

Vital statistics:
- Where: Valley of Sorek
- Contemporary: Samson

Key verses:
"It came about when she pressed him daily with her words and urged him, that his soul was annoyed to death. So he told her all that was in his heart" (Judges 16:16–17).

Her story is told in Judges 16.

16:15 Samson was deceived because he wanted to believe Delilah's lies. Although he could strangle a lion, he could not smother his burning lust and see Delilah for who she really was. How can you keep your desire for love and sexual pleasure from deceiving you? (1) You must decide what kind of a person you will love *before* passion takes over. Determine whether a person's character and faith in God are as desirable as his or her physical appearance. (2) Because most of the time you spend with your spouse will *not* involve sex, your companion's personality, temperament, and commitment to solve problems must be as gratifying as his or her kisses. (3) Be patient. The second look often reveals what is beneath the pleasant appearance and attentive touch.

16:16–17 Delilah kept asking Samson for the secret of his strength until he finally grew tired of hearing her nagging and gave in. This was the second time that Samson allowed himself to be worn down by persistent nagging (14:17). What a pitiful excuse for disobedience. Don't allow anyone, no matter how attractive or persuasive, to talk you into doing wrong.

19 She made him sleep on her knees, and called for a man and had him shave off the
seven locks of his hair. Then she began to afflict him, and his strength left him.
20 She said, "The Philistines are upon you, Samson!" And he awoke from his sleep
and said, "I will go out as at other times and shake myself free." But he did not know
that the LORD had departed from him.

16:20 Num 14:42, 43; Josh 7:12; 1 Sam 16:14

21 Then the Philistines seized him and gouged out his eyes; and they brought him down
to Gaza and bound him with bronze chains, and he was a grinder in the prison.
22 However, the hair of his head began to grow again after it was shaved off.
23 Now the lords of the Philistines assembled to offer a great sacrifice to Dagon their
god, and to rejoice, for they said,
"Our god has given Samson our enemy into our hands."

16:23 1 Sam 5:2

24 When the people saw him, they praised their god, for they said,
"Our god has given our enemy into our hands,
Even the destroyer of our country,
Who has slain many of us."

16:24 1 Sam 31:9; 1 Chr 10:9; Ps 97:7

25 It so happened when they were in high spirits, that they said, "Call for Samson, that
he may amuse us." So they called for Samson from the prison, and he entertained them.
And they made him stand between the pillars.
26 Then Samson said to the boy who was holding his hand, "Let me feel the pillars on
which the house rests, that I may lean against them."
27 Now the house was full of men and women, and all the lords of the Philistines were
there. And about 3,000 men and women were on the roof looking on while Samson was
amusing *them.*

Samson Is Avenged

28 Then Samson called to the LORD and said, "O Lord GOD, please remember me and
please strengthen me just this time, O God, that I may at once be avenged of the Philistines for my two eyes."

16:28 Judg 15:18; Jer 15:15

29 Samson grasped the two middle pillars on which the house rested, and braced himself against them, the one with his right hand and the other with his left.
30 And Samson said, "Let me die with the Philistines!" And he bent with all his might
so that the house fell on the lords and all the people who were in it. So the dead whom
he killed at his death were more than those whom he killed in his life.
31 Then his brothers and all his father's household came down, took him, brought him

16:31 Judg 15:20

16:19 Delilah was a deceitful woman with honey on her lips and poison in her heart. Cold and calculating, she toyed with Samson, pretending to love him while looking for personal gain. How could Samson be so foolish? Four times Delilah took advantage of him. If he didn't realize what was happening after the first or second experience, surely he should have understood the situation by the fourth time! We think Samson is foolish, but how many times do we allow ourselves to be deceived by flattery and give in to temptation and wrong beliefs? Avoid falling prey to deceit by asking God to help you distinguish between deception and truth.

16:21 Samson, the mighty warrior, became a slave. Rather than kill him, the Philistines preferred to humiliate him by gouging out his eyes and making him grind grain. Samson now had plenty of time to wonder if Delilah's charms were worth spending the rest of his life in humiliation.

Although God did not completely abandon Samson (16:28–30), he allowed Samson's decision to stand, and the consequences of his decision followed naturally. We may choose to be close to God or to go our own way, but there are consequences resulting from our choice. Samson didn't choose to be captured, but he chose to be with Delilah, and he could not escape the consequences of his decision.

16:21 Blinded and without strength, Samson was taken to Gaza where he would spend the rest of his short life. Gaza was one of the five capital cities of the Philistines. Known for its many wells, Gaza was a vital stop along a great caravan route that connected Egypt to the south with Aram to the north. The Philistines probably showed off their prize captive, Samson, to many dignitaries passing through.

Ironically, it was in Gaza that Samson had earlier demonstrated his great strength by uprooting the city gates (16:1–3). Now he was an example of weakness.

16:23–24 Dagon was the chief god of the Philistines, the god of grain and harvest. Many temples were built to Dagon, and the worship there included human sacrifice. The temples were also the local entertainment centers. Just as people today crowd into theaters, Philistine townspeople crowded into the local temple. They sat on the flat temple roof and looked into the courtyard below. What they often saw was the torture and humiliation of prisoners.

Since the Philistines had control over the Israelites, they thought their god was stronger. But when the ark of God was placed before Dagon in a similar temple, the idol fell over and broke into pieces (1 Samuel 5:1–7). God's strength goes beyond numbers or physical might.

16:28–30 In spite of Samson's past, God still answered his prayer and destroyed the pagan temple and worshipers. God still loved him. He was willing to hear Samson's prayer of confession and repentance and use him this final time. One of the effects of sin in our lives is to keep us from feeling like praying. But perfect moral behavior is not a condition for prayer. Don't let guilt feelings over sin keep you from your only means of restoration. No matter how long you have been away from God, he is ready to hear from you and restore you to a right relationship. Every situation can be salvaged if you are willing to turn again to him. If God could still work in Samson's situation, he can certainly make something worthwhile out of yours.

up and buried him between Zorah and Eshtaol in the tomb of Manoah his father. Thus
he had judged Israel twenty years.

C. THE MORAL FAILURE OF ISRAEL (17:1—21:25)

This section shows Israel falling into idolatry, moral decline, and petty fighting. Israel, the nation that was to set the example for spiritual living, had instead become morally depraved. When Israel did serve God, and that was seldom, it was often from selfish motives. Selfish obedience does not bring us far. Genuine obedience is motivated by a love and reverence for God himself.

1. Idolatry in the tribe of Dan

Micah's Idolatry

17 Now there was a man of the hill country of Ephraim whose name was Micah.
2 He said to his mother, "The eleven hundred *pieces* of silver which were taken
from you, about which you uttered a curse in my hearing, behold, the silver is with me;
I took it." And his mother said, "Blessed be my son by the LORD."
17:3 Ex 20:4, 23; 34:17
3 He then returned the eleven hundred *pieces* of silver to his mother, and his mother
said, "I wholly dedicate the silver from my hand to the LORD for my son to make a graven
image and a molten image; now therefore, I will return them to you."
4 So when he returned the silver to his mother, his mother took two hundred *pieces*
of silver and gave them to the silversmith who made them into a graven image and a
molten image, and they were in the house of Micah.
17:5 Judg 18:24; Judg 8:27; 18:14; Gen 31:19; Num 3:10
5 And the man Micah had a [19]shrine and he made an ephod and household idols and
consecrated one of his sons, that he might become his priest.
17:6 Judg 18:1; 19:1; Deut 12:8; Judg 21:25
6 In those days there was no king in Israel; every man did what was right in his own
eyes.
17:7 Judg 19:1; Ruth 1:1, 2; Mic 5:2; Matt 2:1
7 Now there was a young man from Bethlehem in Judah, of the family of Judah, who
was a Levite; and he was staying there.
17:8 Josh 24:33
8 Then the man departed from the city, from Bethlehem in Judah, to stay wherever
he might find *a place;* and as he made his journey, he came to the hill country of Ephraim to the house of Micah.
9 Micah said to him, "Where do you come from?" And he said to him, "I am a Levite
from Bethlehem in Judah, and I am going to stay wherever I may find *a place.*"
17:10 Judg 18:19
10 Micah then said to him, "Dwell with me and be a father and a priest to me, and I
will give you ten *pieces* of silver a year, a suit of clothes, and your maintenance." So the
Levite went *in.*
11 The Levite agreed to live with the man, and the young man became to him like one
of his sons.
17:12 Num 16:10; 18:1-7
12 So Micah consecrated the Levite, and the young man became his priest and lived in
the house of Micah.
13 Then Micah said, "Now I know that the LORD will prosper me, seeing I have a Levite as priest."

19 Lit *house of gods*

17:2 Micah and his mother seemed to be good and moral and may have sincerely desired to worship God, but they disobeyed God by following their own desires instead of doing what God wanted. The attitude that prevailed in Micah's day was this: "Every man did what was right in his own eyes" (17:6). This is remarkably similar to today's prevailing attitudes. But God has given us standards. He has not left our conduct up to us and our opinions. We can avoid conforming to society's low standards by taking God's commands seriously and applying them to life. Independence and self-reliance are positive traits, but only within the framework of God's standards.

17:6 Today, as in Micah's day, everyone seems to put his or her own interests first. Time has not changed human nature. Most people still reject God's right way of living. The people in Micah's time replaced the true worship of God with a homemade version of worship. As a result, justice was soon replaced by revenge and chaos. Ignoring God's direction led to confusion and destruction. Anyone who has not submitted to God will end up doing whatever seems right at the time. This tendency is present in all of us. To know what is really right and to have the strength to do it, we need to draw closer to God and his Word.

17:7–12 Apparently the Israelites no longer supported the priests and Levites with their tithes because so many of the people no longer worshiped God. The young Levite in this story probably left his home in Bethlehem because the money he received from the people there was not enough to live on. But Israel's moral decay affected even the priests and Levites. This man accepted money (17:10–11), idols (18:20), and position (17:12) in a way that was inconsistent with God's laws. While Micah revealed the religious downfall of individual Israelites, this priest illustrated the religious downfall of priests and Levites.

Danites Seek Territory

18 In those days there was no king of Israel; and in those days the tribe of the Dan- **18:1**
ites was seeking an inheritance for themselves to live in, for until that day an Judg 17:6; 19:1; Josh 19:40-48
inheritance had not been allotted to them as a possession among the tribes of Israel.
2 So the sons of Dan sent from their family five men out of their whole number, val- **18:2**
iant men from Zorah and Eshtaol, to spy out the land and to search it; and they said to Judg 13:25; Judg 17:1
them, "Go, search the land." And they came to the hill country of Ephraim, to the house
of Micah, and lodged there.
3 When they were near the house of Micah, they recognized the voice of the young
man, the Levite; and they turned aside there and said to him, "Who brought you here?
And what are you doing in this *place?* And what do you have here?"
4 He said to them, "Thus and so has Micah done to me, and he has hired me and I **18:4**
have become his priest." Judg 17:12
5 They said to him, "Inquire of God, please, that we may know whether our way on
which we are going will be prosperous."
6 The priest said to them, "Go in peace; your way in which you are going has the
LORD'S approval."
7 Then the five men departed and came to Laish and saw the people who were in it **18:7**
living in security, after the manner of the Sidonians, quiet and secure; for there was no Josh 19:47; Judg 18:29
ruler humiliating *them* for anything in the land, and they were far from the Sidonians
and had no dealings with anyone.
8 When they came back to their brothers at Zorah and Eshtaol, their brothers said to
them, "What *do* you *report?*"
9 They said, "Arise, and let us go up against them; for we have seen the land, and
behold, it is very good. And will you sit still? Do not delay to go, to enter, to possess the
land.
10 "When you enter, you will come to a secure people with a spacious land; for God has **18:10**
given it into your hand, a place where there is no lack of anything that is on the earth." Deut 8:9
11 Then from the family of the Danites, from Zorah and from Eshtaol, six hundred
men armed with weapons of war set out.
12 They went up and camped at Kiriath-jearim in Judah. Therefore they called that **18:12**
place [20]Mahaneh-dan to this day; behold, it is west of Kiriath-jearim. Judg 13:25
13 They passed from there to the hill country of Ephraim and came to the house of
Micah.

20 I.e. the camp of Dan

THE TRIBE OF DAN MOVES NORTH
Troops from the tribe of Dan traveled from Zorah and Eshtaol into the hill country of Ephraim, where they persuaded Micah's priest to come with them. They continued north to Laish, where they ruthlessly butchered its citizens. The city was renamed Dan, and the priest's idols became the focus of their worship.

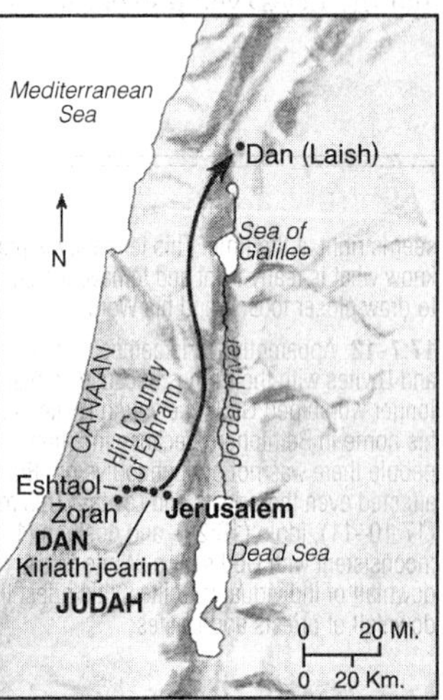

18:1 The Danites had been assigned enough land to meet their needs (Joshua 19:40–48). However, because they failed to trust God to help them conquer their territory, the Amorites forced them into the hill country and wouldn't let them settle in the plains (1:34). Rather than fight for their allotted territory, they preferred to look for new land in the north where resistance from the enemy wouldn't be so tough. It was while they were traveling north that some of their men passed Micah's home and stole some of his idols.

18:4–6 Priests and their assistants were all members of the tribe of Levi (Numbers 3:5–13). They were to serve the people, teach them how to worship God, and perform the rituals involved in the worship services both at the tabernacle in Shiloh and in the designated cities throughout the land. But this disobedient priest showed disrespect for God because (1) he performed his duties in a house. Priestly duties were to be performed only in the tabernacle or a designated city. This requirement was intended to prevent God's laws from being changed. (2) He carried idols with him (18:20). (3) He claimed to speak for God when God had not spoken through him (18:6).

18:11–26 Through this entire incident, no one desired to worship God; instead, they wanted to use God for selfish gain. Today some people go to church to feel better, be accepted, relieve guilt, and gain business contacts or friends. Beware of following God for selfish gain rather than selfless service.

Danites Take Micah's Idols

18:14 Judg 17:5

14 Then the five men who went to spy out the country of Laish said to their kinsmen, "Do you know that there are in these houses an ephod and [21]household idols and a graven image and a molten image? Now therefore, consider what you should do."

15 They turned aside there and came to the house of the young man, the Levite, to the house of Micah, and asked him of his welfare.

16 The six hundred men armed with their weapons of war, who were of the sons of Dan, stood by the entrance of the gate.

18:17 Gen 31:19, 30; Is 41:29; Mic 5:13

17 Now the five men who went to spy out the land went up *and* entered there, *and* took the graven image and the ephod and household idols and the molten image, while the priest stood by the entrance of the gate with the six hundred men armed with weapons of war.

18 When these went into Micah's house and took the graven image, the ephod and household idols and the molten image, the priest said to them, "What are you doing?"

18:19 Job 21:5; 29:9; 40:4; Judg 17:10

19 They said to him, "Be silent, put your hand over your mouth and come with us, and be to us a father and a priest. Is it better for you to be a priest to the house of one man, or to be priest to a tribe and a family in Israel?"

20 The priest's heart was glad, and he took the ephod and household idols and the graven image and went among the people.

21 Then they turned and departed, and put the little ones and the livestock and the valuables in front of them.

22 When they had gone some distance from the house of Micah, the men who *were* in the houses near Micah's house assembled and overtook the sons of Dan.

23 They cried to the sons of Dan, who turned around and said to Micah, "What is *the matter* with you, that you have assembled together?"

24 He said, "You have taken away my gods which I made, and the priest, and have gone away, and what do I have besides? So how can you say to me, 'What is *the matter* with you?' "

25 The sons of Dan said to him, "Do not let your voice be heard among us, or else fierce men will fall upon you and you will lose your life, with the lives of your household."

26 So the sons of Dan went on their way; and when Micah saw that they were too strong for him, he turned and went back to his house.

18:27 Josh 19:47; Judg 18:7

27 Then they took what Micah had made and the priest who had belonged to him, and came to Laish, to a people quiet and secure, and struck them with the edge of the sword; and they burned the city with fire.

18:28 2 Sam 10:6

28 And there was no one to deliver *them,* because it was far from Sidon and they had no dealings with anyone, and it was in the valley which is near Beth-rehob. And they rebuilt the city and lived in it.

18:29 Josh 19:47

29 They called the name of the city Dan, after the name of Dan their father who was born in Israel; however, the name of the city formerly was Laish.

18:30 Judg 17:3, 5; Ex 2:22; 18:3

30 The sons of Dan set up for themselves the graven image; and Jonathan, the son of

21 Heb *teraphim*

18:14 An ephod was a ceremonial vest worn by a priest.

18:24 Micah made idols and hired a priest to run his personal religion. When the men of Dan took his idols and priest, nothing remained. What an empty spiritual condition! An idol is anything that takes God's place in a person's life. Some people invest all their energy in pursuit of money, success, possessions, or a career. If these idols are taken away, only an empty shell is left. The only way to protect yourself against such loss is to invest your life in the living God, whom you can never lose.

18:27 Did the tribe of Dan have the right to kill the citizens of Laish? No. God had commanded Israel to clean out and destroy certain cities because of their idolatry and wickedness, but Laish did not fall under that judgment. It was not within the assigned boundaries of Dan, and its people were peaceful in contrast to the warlike Canaanites. But the tribe of Dan had no regard for God's law. God's law said to destroy a city for idolatry (Deuteronomy 13:12–15). The Danites themselves were guilty of this sin.
This story shows how far some of the tribes had wandered away from God.

18:27 Just because the Danites successfully defeated Laish doesn't mean their actions were right. Their idolatry showed that God was not guiding them. Today many justify their wrong actions by outward signs of success. They think that wealth, popularity, or lack of suffering is an indication of God's blessing. But many stories in the Bible indicate that evil and earthly success can go hand in hand (see, for example, 2 Kings 14:23–29). Success doesn't indicate God's approval. Don't allow personal success to become a measuring rod of whether or not you are pleasing God.

18:30–31 The tribe of Dan had stolen Micah's idols, and now they set them up in Laish. Although the Danites were actually denying God by worshiping these images (Exodus 20:1–5), they probably assumed they were worshiping God through them (see the note on Exodus 32:4, 5). Worshiping images of God is *not* worshiping God, even if it resembles true worship in some ways. People repeat the same mistake today when they claim to be Christians without really believing in God's power or changing their conduct to conform to his expectations. Godliness cannot be merely a claim. It must be a reality in our motives and in our actions.

Gershom, the son of [22]Manasseh, he and his sons were priests to the tribe of the Danites
until the day of the captivity of the land.
31 So they set up for themselves Micah's graven image which he had made, all the time **18:31**
that the house of God was at Shiloh. Josh 18:1

2. War against the tribe of Benjamin

A Levite's Concubine Degraded

19 Now it came about in those days, when there was no king in Israel, that there was **19:1**
a certain Levite staying in the remote part of the hill country of Ephraim, who took Judg 18:1
a concubine for himself from Bethlehem in Judah.
2 But his concubine played the harlot against him, and she went away from him to
her father's house in Bethlehem in Judah, and was there for a period of four months.
3 Then her husband arose and went after her to speak tenderly to her in order to bring **19:3**
her back, taking with him his servant and a pair of donkeys. So she brought him into her Gen 34:3; 50:21
father's house, and when the girl's father saw him, he was glad to meet him.
4 His father-in-law, the girl's father, detained him; and he remained with him three
days. So they ate and drank and lodged there.
5 Now on the fourth day they got up early in the morning, and he prepared to go; and **19:5**
the girl's father said to his son-in-law, "Sustain yourself with a piece of bread, and after- Gen 18:5; Judg 19:8
ward you may go."
6 So both of them sat down and ate and drank together; and the girl's father said to **19:6**
the man, "Please be willing to spend the night, and let your heart be merry." Judg 16:25; 19:9, 22; Ruth 3:7; 1 Kin
7 Then the man arose to go, but his father-in-law urged him so that he spent the night 21:7; Esth 1:10
there again.
8 On the fifth day he arose to go early in the morning, and the girl's father said, "Please
sustain yourself, and wait until afternoon"; so both of them ate.
9 When the man arose to go along with his concubine and servant, his father-in-law,
the girl's father, said to him, "Behold now, the day has drawn to a close; please spend
the night. Lo, the day is coming to an end; spend the night here that your heart may be
merry. Then tomorrow you may arise early for your journey so that you may go home."
10 But the man was not willing to spend the night, so he arose and departed and came **19:10**
to *a place* opposite Jebus (that is, Jerusalem). And there were with him a pair of saddled 1 Chr 11:4, 5
donkeys; his concubine also was with him.
11 When they *were* near Jebus, the day was almost gone; and the servant said to his **19:11**
master, "Please come, and let us turn aside into this city of the Jebusites and spend the Judg 19:19
night in it."
12 However, his master said to him, "We will not turn aside into the city of foreigners
who are not of the sons of Israel; but we will go on as far as Gibeah."
13 He said to his servant, "Come and let us approach one of these places; and we will
spend the night in Gibeah or Ramah."

22 Some ancient versions read *Moses*

18:31 Shiloh was probably destroyed during the events reported in 1 Samuel 4 and 5, not long after the time described here. Because Shiloh was the religious center for Israel, all adult males were required to travel there for certain religious feasts. The tribe of Dan, however, set up idols and priests in the new territory they conquered. The fact that they were over 80 miles away from Shiloh may have been their excuse for not fulfilling the law's requirements. This act was a further demonstration of their disregard for God.

18:31 The true worship of God should have been maintained through the Levitical priests scattered throughout the land and the influence of the tabernacle in Shiloh. This story shows how pagan influences and moral depravity had crept into every corner of Israelite culture. Although 300 years had passed since they entered the promised land, they still had not destroyed the idolatry and evil practices within it.

There may be a tendency in your life to allow "harmless" habits to have their own small corners, but they can become dominating forces. The values, attitudes, and practices you have adopted from the world's system can be exposed by applying the light of God's truth to them. Once you see them for what they are, you can begin to uproot them.

19:1—21:25 What is the significance of this tragic story? When the Israelites' faith in God disintegrated, their unity as a nation also disintegrated. They could have taken complete possession of the land if they had obeyed God and trusted him to keep his promises. But when they forgot him, they lost their purpose, and soon "every man did what was right in his own eyes" (21:25). When they stopped letting God lead them, they became no better than the evil people around them. When they made laws for their own benefit, they set standards far below God's. When you leave God out of your life you may be shocked at what you are capable of doing (19:30).

19:1 Having concubines was an accepted part of Israelite society although this is not what God intended (Genesis 2:24). A concubine had most of the duties but only some of the privileges of a wife. Although she was legally attached to one man, she and her children usually did not have the inheritance rights of the legal wife and legitimate children. Her primary purpose was giving the man sexual pleasure, bearing additional children, and contributing more help to the household or estate. Concubines were often foreign prisoners of war. But they could also be Israelites, as was probably the case in this story.

14 So they passed along and went their way, and the sun set on them near Gibeah which
belongs to Benjamin.
15 They turned aside there in order to enter *and* lodge in Gibeah. When they entered,
they sat down in the open square of the city, for no one took them into *his* house to spend
the night.

19:16 Judg 19:1; Judg 19:14

16 Then behold, an old man was coming out of the field from his work at evening. Now
the man was from the hill country of Ephraim, and he was staying in Gibeah, but the
men of the place were Benjamites.
17 And he lifted up his eyes and saw the traveler in the open square of the city; and the
old man said, "Where are you going, and where do you come from?"
18 He said to him, "We are passing from Bethlehem in Judah to the remote part of the
hill country of Ephraim, *for* I am from there, and I went to Bethlehem in Judah. But I
am *now* going to my house, and no man will take me into his house.

19:19 Judg 19:11

19 "Yet there is both straw and fodder for our donkeys, and also bread and wine for me,
your maidservant, and the young man who is with your servants; there is no lack of anything."

19:20 Gen 43:23; Judg 6:23

20 The old man said, "Peace to you. Only let me *take care of* all your needs; however,
do not spend the night in the open square."

19:21 Gen 24:32, 33

21 So he took him into his house and gave the donkeys fodder, and they washed their
feet and ate and drank.

19:22 Gen 19:4, 5; Ezek 16:46-48; Deut 13:13; 1 Sam 2:12; 1 Kin 21:10; 2 Cor 6:15

22 While they were celebrating, behold, the men of the city, certain worthless fellows,
surrounded the house, pounding the door; and they spoke to the owner of the house,
the old man, saying, "Bring out the man who came into your house that we may have
relations with him."

19:23 Gen 34:7; Deut 22:21; Judg 20:6; 2 Sam 13:12

23 Then the man, the owner of the house, went out to them and said to them, "No, my
fellows, please do not act so wickedly; since this man has come into my house, do not
commit this act of folly.

19:24 Gen 19:8

24 "Here is my virgin daughter and his concubine. Please let me bring them out that
you may ravish them and do to them whatever you wish. But do not commit such an act
of folly against this man."
25 But the men would not listen to him. So the man seized his concubine and brought
her out to them; and they raped her and abused her all night until morning, then let her
go at the approach of dawn.
26 As the day began to dawn, the woman came and fell down at the doorway of the
man's house where her master was, until *full* daylight.
27 When her master arose in the morning and opened the doors of the house and went
out to go on his way, then behold, his concubine was lying at the doorway of the house
with her hands on the threshold.

19:28 Judg 20:5

28 He said to her, "Get up and let us go," but there was no answer. Then he placed her
on the donkey; and the man arose and went to his home.

19:29 1 Sam 11:7

29 When he entered his house, he took a knife and laid hold of his concubine and cut
her in twelve pieces, limb by limb, and sent her throughout the territory of Israel.

19:30 Judg 20:7; Prov 13:10

30 All who saw *it* said, "Nothing like this has *ever* happened or been seen from the day
when the sons of Israel came up from the land of Egypt to this day. Consider it, take
counsel and speak up!"

19:24 Nowhere is the unwritten law of hospitality stronger than in the Middle East. Protecting a guest at any cost ranked at the top of a man's code of honor. But here the hospitality code turned to fanaticism. The rape and abuse of a daughter and companion was preferable to the *possibility* of a conflict between a guest and a neighbor. The two men were selfish (they didn't want to get hurt themselves); they lacked courage (they didn't want to face a conflict even when lives were at stake); and they disobeyed God's law (they allowed deliberate abuse and murder). What drastic consequences can result when social protocol carries more authority than moral convictions!

19:29–30 Although this was a terrible way to spread the news, it effectively communicated the horror of the crime and called the people to action. Saul used a similar method in 1 Samuel 11:7. Ironically, the man who alerted Israel to the murder of his concubine was just as guilty for her death as the men who actually killed her.

19:30 The horrible crime described in this chapter wasn't Israel's worst offense. Even worse was the nation's failure to establish a government based upon God's moral principles, where the law of God was the law of the land. As a result, laws were usually unenforced and crime was ignored. Sexual perversion and lawlessness were a by-product of Israel's disobedience to God. The Israelites weren't willing to speak up until events had gone too far.

Whenever we get away from God and his Word, all sorts of evil can follow. Our drifting away from God may be slow and almost imperceptible, with the ultimate results affecting a future generation. We must continually call our nation back to God and work toward the establishment of God's moral and spiritual reign in the heart of every person.

Resolve to Punish the Guilty

20 Then all the sons of Israel from Dan to Beersheba, including the land of Gilead, **20:1**
came out, and the congregation assembled as one man to the LORD at Mizpah. 1 Sam 7:5
2 The chiefs of all the people, *even* of all the tribes of Israel, took their stand in the **20:2**
assembly of the people of God, 400,000 foot soldiers who drew the sword. Judg 8:10
3 (Now the sons of Benjamin heard that the sons of Israel had gone up to Mizpah.)
And the sons of Israel said, "Tell *us*, how did this wickedness take place?"
4 So the Levite, the husband of the woman who was murdered, answered and said, "I
came with my concubine to spend the night at Gibeah which belongs to Benjamin.
5 "But the men of Gibeah rose up against me and surrounded the house at night be- **20:5**
cause of me. They intended to kill me; instead, they ravished my concubine so that she Judg 19:22; Judg 19:25f
died.
6 "And I took hold of my concubine and cut her in pieces and sent her throughout the **20:6**
land of Israel's inheritance; for they have committed a lewd and disgraceful act in Israel. Judg 19:29; Gen 34:7; Josh 7:15
7 "Behold, all you sons of Israel, give your advice and counsel here." **20:7**
8 Then all the people arose as one man, saying, "Not one of us will go to his tent, nor Judg 19:30
will any of us return to his house.
9 "But now this is the thing which we will do to Gibeah; *we will go up* against it by lot.
10 "And we will take 10 men out of 100 throughout the tribes of Israel, and 100 out of
1,000, and 1,000 out of 10,000 to supply food for the people, that when they come to
Gibeah of Benjamin, they may punish *them* for all the disgraceful acts that they have
committed in Israel."
11 Thus all the men of Israel were gathered against the city, united as one man.
12 Then the tribes of Israel sent men through the entire tribe of Benjamin, saying, "What
is this wickedness that has taken place among you?
13 "Now then, deliver up the men, the [23]worthless fellows in Gibeah, that we may put **20:13**
them to death and remove *this* wickedness from Israel." But the sons of Benjamin would 2 Cor 6:15; Deut 13:5; 17:12; 1 Cor 5:13
not listen to the voice of their brothers, the sons of Israel.
14 The sons of Benjamin gathered from the cities to Gibeah, to go out to battle against
the sons of Israel.
15 From the cities on that day the sons of Benjamin were numbered, 26,000 men who **20:15**
draw the sword, besides the inhabitants of Gibeah who were numbered, 700 choice men. Num 1:36, 37; 2:23; 26:41
16 Out of all these people 700 choice men were left-handed; each one could sling a
stone at a hair and not miss. **20:16** Judg 3:15; 1 Chr 12:2
17 Then the men of Israel besides Benjamin were numbered, 400,000 men who draw
the sword; all these were men of war.

Civil War, Benjamin Defeated

18 Now the sons of Israel arose, went up to Bethel, and inquired of God and said, "Who **20:18**
shall go up first for us to battle against the sons of Benjamin?" Then the LORD said, Num 27:21; Judg 20:23, 27
"Judah *shall go up* first."
19 So the sons of Israel arose in the morning and camped against Gibeah.
20 The men of Israel went out to battle against Benjamin, and the men of Israel arrayed for battle against them at Gibeah.
21 Then the sons of Benjamin came out of Gibeah and felled to the ground on that day **20:21**
22,000 men of Israel. Judg 20:25
22 But the people, the men of Israel, encouraged themselves and arrayed for battle
again in the place where they had arrayed themselves the first day.
23 The sons of Israel went up and wept before the LORD until evening, and inquired of **20:23**
the LORD, saying, "Shall we again draw near for battle against the sons of my brother Josh 7:6, 7; Judg 20:18
Benjamin?" And the LORD said, "Go up against him."

23 Lit *sons of Belial*

20:1 Dan was the northernmost city in Israel, and Beersheba, the southernmost. The two were often mentioned together as a reference to the entire nation.

20:13 Perhaps the Benjamite leaders had been given distorted facts about the serious crime in their territory, or perhaps they were too proud to admit that some of their people had stooped so low. In either case, they would not listen to the rest of Israel and hand over the accused criminals. They were more loyal to their own tribe than to God's law.

By covering for their kinsmen, the entire tribe of Benjamin sank to a level of immorality as low as the criminals'. Through this act, we get a glimpse of how thoroughly the nation's moral fabric had unraveled. The time period of the judges ends in a bloody civil war that sets the stage for the spiritual renewal to come under Samuel (see 1 Samuel).

24 Then the sons of Israel came against the sons of Benjamin the second day.
25 Benjamin went out against them from Gibeah the second day and felled to the ground
again 18,000 men of the sons of Israel; all these drew the sword.
20:26 Judg 20:23; 21:2
26 Then all the sons of Israel and all the people went up and came to Bethel and wept;
thus they remained there before the LORD and fasted that day until evening. And they
offered burnt offerings and peace offerings before the LORD.
20:27 Judg 20:18
27 The sons of Israel inquired of the LORD (for the ark of the covenant of God *was*
there in those days,
20:28 Judg 7:9
28 and Phinehas the son of Eleazar, Aaron's son, stood before it to *minister* in those
days), saying, "Shall I yet again go out to battle against the sons of my brother Benjamin, or shall I cease?" And the LORD said, "Go up, for tomorrow I will deliver them
into your hand."
20:29 Josh 8:4
29 So Israel set men in ambush around Gibeah.
30 The sons of Israel went up against the sons of Benjamin on the third day and arrayed themselves against Gibeah as at other times.
20:31 Josh 8:16
31 The sons of Benjamin went out against the people and were drawn away from the
city, and they began to strike and kill some of the people as at other times, on the highways, one of which goes up to Bethel and the other to Gibeah, *and* in the field, about
thirty men of Israel.
32 The sons of Benjamin said, "They are struck down before us, as at the first." But
the sons of Israel said, "Let us flee that we may draw them away from the city to the
highways."
20:33 Josh 8:19
33 Then all the men of Israel arose from their place and arrayed themselves at Baal-
tamar; and the men of Israel in ambush broke out of their place, even out of Maareh-
geba.
20:34 Josh 8:14; Job 21:13
34 When ten thousand choice men from all Israel came against Gibeah, the battle
became fierce; but Benjamin did not know that disaster was close to them.
35 And the LORD struck Benjamin before Israel, so that the sons of Israel destroyed
25,100 men of Benjamin that day, all who draw the sword.
20:36 Josh 8:15
36 So the sons of Benjamin saw that they were defeated. When the men of Israel gave
ground to Benjamin because they relied on the men in ambush whom they had set against
Gibeah,
20:37 Josh 8:19
37 the men in ambush hurried and rushed against Gibeah; the men in ambush also
deployed and struck all the city with the edge of the sword.
20:38 Josh 8:20
38 Now the appointed sign between the men of Israel and the men in ambush was that
they would make a great cloud of smoke rise from the city.
20:39 Judg 20:32
39 Then the men of Israel turned in the battle, and Benjamin began to strike and kill
about thirty men of Israel, for they said, "Surely they are defeated before us, as in the
first battle."
20:40 Josh 8:20
40 But when the cloud began to rise from the city in a column of smoke, Benjamin
looked behind them; and behold, the whole city was going up *in smoke* to heaven.
20:41 Prov 5:22; 11:5, 6; 29:6
41 Then the men of Israel turned, and the men of Benjamin were terrified; for they
saw that disaster was close to them.
20:42 Josh 8:15, 24
42 Therefore, they turned their backs before the men of Israel toward the direction of
the wilderness, but the battle overtook them while those who came out of the cities destroyed them in the midst of them.
20:43 Hos 9:9; 10:9
43 They surrounded Benjamin, pursued them without rest *and* trod them down opposite Gibeah toward the east.
44 Thus 18,000 men of Benjamin fell; all these were valiant warriors.
20:45 Judg 21:13
45 The rest turned and fled toward the wilderness to the rock of Rimmon, but they
caught 5,000 of them on the highways and overtook them at Gidom and killed 2,000 of
them.

20:27–28 This is the only place in Judges where the ark of the covenant is mentioned. This probably indicates how seldom the people consulted God.

Phinehas, the high priest, was also the high priest under Joshua (Joshua 22:13). The reference to Phinehas as high priest and the location of the tabernacle in Bethel instead of Shiloh probably indicate that the events of this story occurred during the early years of the judges.

46 So all of Benjamin who fell that day were 25,000 men who draw the sword; all these
were valiant warriors.
47 But 600 men turned and fled toward the wilderness to the rock of Rimmon, and
they remained at the rock of Rimmon four months.
48 The men of Israel then turned back against the sons of Benjamin and struck them
with the edge of the sword, both the entire city with the cattle and all that they found;
they also set on fire all the cities which they found.

Mourning Lost Tribe

21 Now the men of Israel had sworn in Mizpah, saying, "None of us shall give his 21:1
daughter to Benjamin in marriage." Judg 21:7, 18
2 So the people came to Bethel and sat there before God until evening, and lifted up 21:2
their voices and wept bitterly. Judg 20:26
3 They said, "Why, O LORD, God of Israel, has this come about in Israel, so that one
tribe should be *missing* today in Israel?"
4 It came about the next day that the people arose early and built an altar there and 21:4
offered burnt offerings and peace offerings. Deut 12:5; 2 Sam 24:25
5 Then the sons of Israel said, "Who is there among all the tribes of Israel who did
not come up in the assembly to the LORD?" For they had taken a great oath concerning 21:5 Judg 5:23
him who did not come up to the LORD at Mizpah, saying, "He shall surely be put to death."
6 And the sons of Israel were sorry for their brother Benjamin and said, "One tribe is
cut off from Israel today.
7 "What shall we do for wives for those who are left, since we have sworn by the LORD 21:7
not to give them any of our daughters in marriage?" Judg 21:1

Provision for Their Survival

8 And they said, "What one is there of the tribes of Israel who did not come up to the
LORD at Mizpah?" And behold, no one had come to the camp from Jabesh-gilead to the
assembly.
9 For when the people were numbered, behold, not one of the inhabitants of Jabesh-
gilead was there.
10 And the congregation sent 12,000 of the valiant warriors there, and commanded 21:10
them, saying, "Go and strike the inhabitants of Jabesh-gilead with the edge of the sword, Num 31:17; Judg 5:23; 1 Sam 11:7
with the women and the little ones.
11 "This is the thing that you shall do: you shall utterly destroy every man and every 21:11
woman who has lain with a man." Num 31:17
12 And they found among the inhabitants of Jabesh-gilead 400 young virgins who had
not known a man by lying with him; and they brought them to the camp at Shiloh, which
is in the land of Canaan.
13 Then the whole congregation sent *word* and spoke to the sons of Benjamin who were 21:13
at the rock of Rimmon, and proclaimed peace to them. Judg 20:47; Deut 20:10
14 Benjamin returned at that time, and they gave them the women whom they had kept
alive from the women of Jabesh-gilead; yet they were not enough for them.
15 And the people were sorry for Benjamin because the LORD had made a breach in
the tribes of Israel.

20:46–48 The effects of the horrible rape and murder should never have been felt outside the community where the crime happened. The local people should have brought the criminals to justice and corrected the laxness that originally permitted the crime. Instead, first the town and then the entire tribe defended this wickedness, even going to war over it.

To prevent unresolved problems from turning into major conflicts, firm action must be taken quickly, wisely, and forcefully *before* the situation gets out of hand.

20:48 The tribe of Benjamin eventually recovered from this slaughter. Saul, Israel's first king, was from this tribe (1 Samuel 9:21). So were Queen Esther (Esther 2:5–7) and the apostle Paul (Romans 11:1). But the tribe was always known for being smaller than the rest (as in Psalm 68:27).

21:8–12 The Israelites moved from one mess to another. Because of a rash vow made in the heat of emotion (21:5), here they destroyed another town. Israel probably justified their action with the following arguments: (1) An oath could not be broken, and Israel had vowed that anyone who did not help them fight the Benjamites would be killed. (2) Because all the women from Benjamin had been killed, the few remaining men needed wives to prevent the tribe from disappearing. To spare the unmarried women from Jabesh-gilead seemed the right solution.

We do not know all the circumstances behind the brutal massacre at Jabesh-gilead, but it seems that the rest of Israel followed Benjamin's pattern. They put tribal loyalties above God's commands, and they justified wrong actions to correct past mistakes.

16 Then the elders of the congregation said, "What shall we do for wives for those who
are left, since the women are destroyed out of Benjamin?"
17 They said, "*There must be* an inheritance for the survivors of Benjamin, so that a
tribe will not be blotted out from Israel.

21:18 Judg 21:1

18 "But we cannot give them wives of our daughters." For the sons of Israel had sworn,
saying, "Cursed is he who gives a wife to Benjamin."

21:19 Josh 18:1; Judg 18:31; 1 Sam 1:3

19 So they said, "Behold, there is a feast of the LORD from year to year in Shiloh, which
is on the north side of Bethel, on the east side of the highway that goes up from Bethel
to Shechem, and on the south side of Lebonah."
20 And they commanded the sons of Benjamin, saying, "Go and lie in wait in the vineyards,

21:21 Ex 15:20; Judg 11:34

21 and watch; and behold, if the daughters of Shiloh come out to take part in the dances,
then you shall come out of the vineyards and each of you shall catch his wife from the
daughters of Shiloh, and go to the land of Benjamin.

21:22 Judg 21:1, 18

22 "It shall come about, when their fathers or their brothers come to complain to us,
that we shall say to them, 'Give them to us voluntarily, because we did not take for each
man *of Benjamin* a wife in battle, nor did you give *them* to them, *else* you would now be
guilty.' "

21:23 Judg 20:48

21:25 Judg 17:6; 18:1; 19:1

23 The sons of Benjamin did so, and took wives according to their number from those
who danced, whom they carried away. And they went and returned to their inheritance
and rebuilt the cities and lived in them.
24 The sons of Israel departed from there at that time, every man to his tribe and family, and each one of them went out from there to his inheritance.
25 In those days there was no king in Israel; everyone did what was right in his own
eyes.

21:25 During the time of the judges, the people of Israel experienced trouble because everyone became his own authority and acted on his own opinions of right and wrong. This produced horrendous results. Our world is similar. Individuals, groups, and societies have made themselves the final authorities without reference to God. When people selfishly satisfy their personal desires at all costs, everyone pays the price.

It is the ultimate heroic act to submit all our plans, desires, and motives to God. Men like Gideon, Jephthah, and Samson are known for their heroism in battle. But their personal lives were far from heroic.

To be truly heroic, we must go into battle each day in our home, job, church, and society to make God's kingdom a reality. Our weapons are the standards, morals, truths, and convictions we receive from God's Word. We will lose the battle if we gather the spoils of earthly treasures rather than seeking the treasures of heaven.

RUTH

VITAL STATISTICS

PURPOSE:
To show how three people remained strong in character and true to God even when the society around them was collapsing

AUTHOR:
Unknown. Some think it was Samuel, but internal evidence suggests that it was written after Samuel's death.

DATE WRITTEN:
Sometime after the period of the judges (1375–1050 B.C.)

SETTING:
A dark time in Israel's history when people lived to please themselves, not God (Judges 17:6)

KEY VERSE:
"But Ruth said, 'Do not urge me to leave you or turn back from following you; for where you go, I will go, and where you lodge, I will lodge. Your people shall be my people, and your God, my God' " (1:16).

KEY PEOPLE:
Ruth, Naomi, Boaz

KEY PLACES:
Moab, Bethlehem

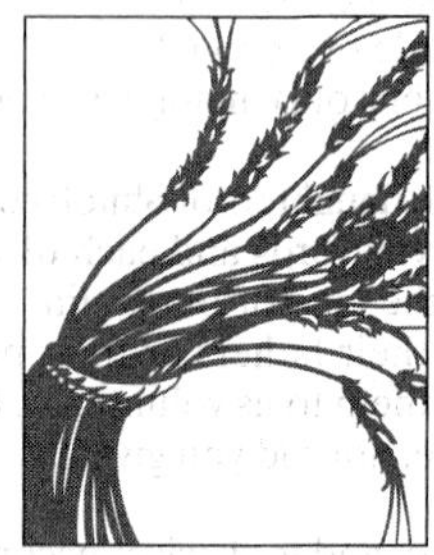

WHEN someone says, "Let me tell you about my mother-in-law," we expect some kind of negative statement or humorous anecdote because the mother-in-law caricature has been a standard centerpiece of ridicule or comedy. The book of Ruth, however, tells a different story. Ruth loved her mother-in-law, Naomi. Recently widowed, Ruth begged to stay with Naomi wherever she went, even though it would mean leaving her homeland. In heartfelt words, Ruth said, "Your people shall be my people, and your God, my God" (1:16). Naomi agreed, and Ruth traveled with her to Bethlehem.

Not much is said about Naomi except that she loved and cared for Ruth. Obviously, Naomi's life was a powerful witness to the reality of God. Ruth was drawn to her—and to the God she worshiped. In the succeeding months, God led this young Moabite widow to a man named Boaz, whom she eventually married. As a result, she became the great-grandmother of David and an ancestor in the line of the Messiah. What a profound impact Naomi's life made!

The book of Ruth is also the story of God's grace in the midst of difficult circumstances. Ruth's story occurred during the time of the judges—a period of disobedience, idolatry, and violence. Even in times of crisis and deepest despair, there are those who follow God and through whom God works. No matter how discouraging or antagonistic the world may seem, there are always people who follow God. He will use anyone who is open to him to achieve his purposes. Ruth was a Moabite, and Boaz was a descendant of Rahab, a former prostitute from Jericho. Nevertheless, their offspring continued the family line through which the Messiah came into our world.

Read this book and be encouraged. God is at work in the world, and he wants to use you. God could use you, as he used Naomi, to bring family and friends to him.

THE BLUEPRINT

1. Ruth remains loyal to Naomi (1:1–22)
2. Ruth gleans in Boaz's field (2:1–23)
3. Ruth follows Naomi's plan (3:1–18)
4. Ruth and Boaz are married (4:1–22)

When we first meet Ruth, she is a destitute widow. We follow her as she joins God's people, gleans in the grainfields, and risks her honor at the threshing floor of Boaz. In the end, we see Ruth becoming the wife of Boaz. What a picture of how we come to faith in Christ. We begin with no hope and are rebellious aliens with no part in the kingdom of God. Then as we risk everything by putting our faith in Christ, God saves us, forgives us, rebuilds our lives, and gives us blessings that will last through eternity. Boaz's redeeming of Ruth is a picture of Christ redeeming us.

MEGATHEMES

THEME	EXPLANATION	IMPORTANCE
Faithfulness	Ruth's faithfulness to Naomi as a daughter-in-law and friend is a great example of love and loyalty. Ruth, Naomi, and Boaz are also faithful to God and his laws. Throughout the story we see God's faithfulness to his people.	Ruth's life was guided by faithfulness toward God and showed itself in loyalty toward the people she knew. To be loyal and loving in relationships, we must imitate God's faithfulness in our relationships with others.
Kindness	Ruth showed great kindness to Naomi. In turn, Boaz showed kindness to Ruth—a despised Moabite woman with no money. God showed his kindness to Ruth, Naomi, and Boaz by bringing them together for his purposes.	Just as Boaz showed his kindness by buying back land to guarantee Ruth and Naomi's inheritance, so Christ showed his kindness by dying for us to guarantee our eternal life. God's kindness should motivate us to love and honor him.
Integrity	Ruth showed high moral character by being loyal to Naomi, by her clean break from her former land and customs, and by her hard work in the fields. Boaz showed integrity in his moral standards, his honesty, and by following through on his commitments.	When we have experienced God's faithfulness and kindness, we should respond by showing integrity. Just as the values by which Ruth and Boaz lived were in sharp contrast to those of the culture portrayed in Judges, so our lives should stand out from the world around us.
Protection	We see God's care and protection over the lives of Naomi and Ruth. His supreme control over circumstances brings them safety and security. He guides the minds and activities of people to fulfill his purposes.	No matter how devastating our present situation may be, our hope is in God. His resources are infinite. We must believe that he can work in the life of any person— whether that person is a king or a stranger in a foreign land. Trust his protection.
Prosperity/Blessing	Ruth and Naomi came to Bethlehem as poor widows, but they soon became prosperous through Ruth's marriage to Boaz. Ruth became the great-grandmother of King David. Yet the greatest blessing was not the money, the marriage, or the child; it was the quality of love and respect between Ruth, Boaz, and Naomi.	We tend to think of blessings in terms of prosperity rather than the high-quality relationships God makes possible for us. No matter what our economic situation, we can love and respect the people God has brought into our lives. In so doing, we give and receive blessings. Love is the greatest blessing.

1. Ruth remains loyal to Naomi

Naomi Widowed

1:1 Judg 2:16-18; Gen 12:10; 26:1; 2 Kin 8:1; Judg 17:8; Mic 5:2

1:2 Judg 3:30

1 Now it came about in the days when the judges governed, that there was a famine in
the land. And a certain man of Bethlehem in Judah went to sojourn in the land of
Moab with his wife and his two sons.
2 The name of the man *was* Elimelech, and the name of his wife, Naomi; and the names
of his two sons *were* Mahlon and Chilion, Ephrathites of Bethlehem in Judah. Now they
entered the land of Moab and remained there.

1:1 The story of Ruth takes place sometime during the period of the rule of the judges. These were dark days for Israel, when "every man did what was right in his own eyes" (Judges 17:6; 21:25). But during those dark and evil times, there were still some who followed God. Naomi and Ruth are beautiful examples of loyalty, friendship, and commitment—to God and to each other.

1:1–2 Moab was the land east of the Dead Sea. It was one of the nations that oppressed Israel during the period of the judges (Judges 3:12ff), so there was hostility between the two nations. The famine must have been quite severe in Israel for Elimelech to move his family here. They were called Ephrathites because Ephrath was an earlier name for Bethlehem. Even if Israel had already defeated Moab, there still would have been tensions between them.

3 Then Elimelech, Naomi's husband, died; and she was left with her two sons.
4 They took for themselves Moabite women *as* wives; the name of the one was Orpah
and the name of the other Ruth. And they lived there about ten years.
5 Then both Mahlon and Chilion also died, and the woman was bereft of her two
children and her husband.
6 Then she arose with her daughters-in-law that she might return from the land of **1:6**
Moab, for she had heard in the land of Moab that the LORD had visited His people in Ex 4:31; Jer 29:10; Zeph 2:7; Ps
giving them food. 132:15; Matt 6:11
7 So she departed from the place where she was, and her two daughters-in-law with
her; and they went on the way to return to the land of Judah.
8 And Naomi said to her two daughters-in-law, "Go, return each of you to her mother's **1:8**
house. May the LORD deal kindly with you as you have dealt with the dead and with me. 2 Tim 1:16
9 "May the LORD grant that you may find rest, each in the house of her husband." Then
she kissed them, and they lifted up their voices and wept.
10 And they said to her, "*No,* but we will surely return with you to your people."
11 But Naomi said, "Return, my daughters. Why should you go with me? Have I yet **1:11**
sons in my womb, that they may be your husbands? Gen 38:11; Deut 25:5
12 "Return, my daughters! Go, for I am too old to have a husband. If I said I have hope,
if I should even have a husband tonight and also bear sons,
13 would you therefore wait until they were grown? Would you therefore refrain from **1:13**
marrying? No, my daughters; for it is harder for me than for you, for the hand of the Judg 2:15; Job 19:21; Ps 32:4
LORD has gone forth against me."

Ruth's Loyalty

14 And they lifted up their voices and wept again; and Orpah kissed her mother-in-
law, but Ruth clung to her.
15 Then she said, "Behold, your sister-in-law has gone back to her people and her gods; **1:15**
return after your sister-in-law." Josh 24:15; Judg 11:24
16 But Ruth said, "Do not urge me to leave you *or* turn back from following you; for

---

1:4–5 Friendly relations with the Moabites were discouraged (Deuteronomy 23:3–6) but probably not forbidden, since the Moabites lived outside the promised land. Marrying a Canaanite (and all those living within the borders of the promised land), however, was against God's law (Deuteronomy 7:1–4). Moabites were not allowed to worship at the tabernacle because they had not let the Israelites pass through their land during the exodus from Egypt.

As God's chosen nation, Israel should have set the standards of high moral living for the other nations. Ironically it was Ruth, a Moabitess, whom God used as an example of genuine spiritual character. This shows just how bleak life had become in Israel during those days.

1:8–9 There was almost nothing worse than being a widow in the ancient world. Widows were taken advantage of or ignored. They were almost always poverty stricken. God's law, therefore, provided that the nearest relative of the dead husband should care for the widow; but Naomi had no relatives in Moab, and she did not know if any of her relatives were alive in Israel.

Even in her desperate situation, Naomi had a selfless attitude. Although she had decided to return to Israel, she encouraged Ruth and Orpah to stay in Moab and start their lives over, even though this would mean hardship for her. Like Naomi, we must consider the needs of others and not just our own. As Naomi discovered, when you act selflessly, others are encouraged to follow your example.

1:11 Naomi's comment here ("Have I yet sons in my womb, that they may be your husbands?") refers to *levirate marriage,* the obligation of a dead man's brother to care for the widow (Deuteronomy 25:5–10). This law kept the widow from poverty and provided a way for the family name of the dead husband to continue.

Naomi, however, had no other sons for Ruth or Orpah to marry, so she encouraged them to remain in their homeland and remarry.

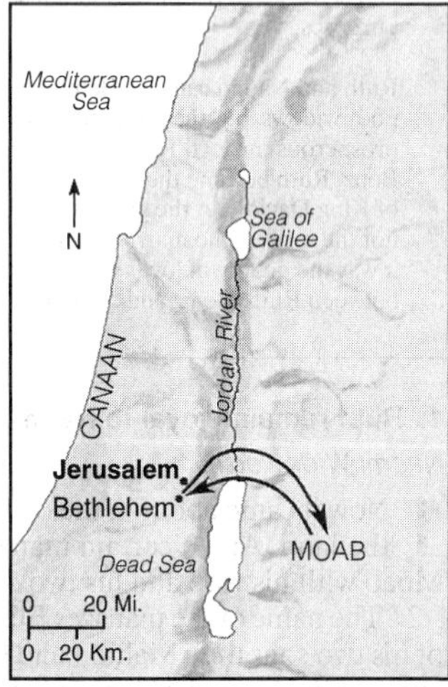

SETTING FOR THE STORY
Elimelech, Naomi, and their sons traveled from Bethlehem to Moab because of a famine. After her husband and sons died, Naomi returned to Bethlehem with her daughter-in-law Ruth.

Orpah agreed, which was her right. But Ruth was willing to give up the possibility of security and children in order to care for Naomi.

1:16 Ruth was a Moabitess, but that didn't stop her from worshiping the true God, nor did it stop God from accepting her worship and blessing her greatly. The Jews were not the only people God loved. God chose the Jews to be the people through whom the rest of the world would come to know him. This was fulfilled when Jesus Christ was born as a Jew. Through him, the entire world can come to know God. Acts 10:35 says that "In every nation the man who fears Him and does what is right is welcome to Him." God

where you go, I will go, and where you lodge, I will lodge. Your people *shall be* my peo-
1:17 1 Sam 3:17; 2 Kin 6:31 ple, and your God, my God.
17 "Where you die, I will die, and there I will be buried. Thus may the LORD do to me,
and worse, if *anything but* death parts you and me."
1:18 Acts 21:14 18 When she saw that she was determined to go with her, she said no more to her.
19 So they both went until they came to Bethlehem. And when they had come to Beth-
1:19 Matt 21:10 lehem, all the city was stirred because of them, and the women said, "Is this Naomi?"
20 She said to them, "Do not call me [1]Naomi; call me [2]Mara, for the Almighty has dealt
1:20 Ex 6:3; Job 6:4 very bitterly with me.
21 "I went out full, but the LORD has brought me back empty. Why do you call me Naomi,
1:21 Job 1:21 since the LORD has witnessed against me and the Almighty has afflicted me?"

1 I.e. pleasant **2** I.e. bitter

RUTH & NAOMI

The stories of several people in the Bible are woven together so closely that they are almost inseparable. We know more about their relationship than we know about them as individuals. And in an age that worships individualism, their stories become helpful models of good relationships. Naomi and Ruth are beautiful examples of this blending of lives. Their cultures, family backgrounds, and ages were very different. As mother-in-law and daughter-in-law, they probably had as many opportunities for tension as for tenderness. And yet they were bound to each other.

They shared deep sorrow, great affection for each other, and an overriding commitment to the God of Israel. And yet as much as they depended on each other, they also gave each other freedom in their commitment to one another. Naomi was willing to let Ruth return to her family. Ruth was willing to leave her homeland to go to Israel. Naomi even helped arrange Ruth's marriage to Boaz although it would change their relationship.

God was at the center of their intimate communication. Ruth came to know the God of Israel through Naomi. The older woman allowed Ruth to see, hear, and feel all the joy and anguish of her relationship to God. How often do you feel that your thoughts and questions about God should be left out of a close relationship? How often do you share your unedited thoughts about God with your spouse or friends? Sharing openly about our relationship with God can bring depth and intimacy to our relationships with others.

Strengths and accomplishments:
- A relationship where the greatest bond was faith in God
- A relationship of strong mutual commitment
- A relationship in which each person tried to do what was best for the other

Lesson from their lives:
- God's living presence in a relationship overcomes differences that might otherwise create division and disharmony

Vital statistics:
- Where: Moab, Bethlehem
- Occupation: Wives, widows
- Relatives: Elimelech, Mahlon, Chilion, Orpah, Boaz

Key verses:
"But Ruth said, 'Do not urge me to leave you or turn back from following you; for where you go, I will go, and where you lodge, I will lodge. Your people will be my people, and your God, my God. Where you die, I will die, and there I will be buried. Thus may the LORD do to me, and worse, if anything but death parts you and me' " (Ruth 1:16, 17).

Their story is told in the book of Ruth. Ruth is also mentioned in Matthew 1:5.

accepts all who worship him; he works through people regardless of their race, sex, or nationality. The book of Ruth is a perfect example of God's impartiality. Although Ruth belonged to a race often despised by Israel, she was blessed because of her faithfulness. She became a great-grandmother of King David and a direct ancestor of Jesus. No one should feel disqualified to serve God because of race, sex, or national background. And God can use every circumstance to build his kingdom.

1:20–21 Naomi had experienced severe hardships. She had left Israel married and secure; she returned widowed and poor. Naomi changed her name to express the bitterness and pain she felt. Naomi was not rejecting God by openly expressing her pain. However, she seems to have lost sight of the tremendous resources she had in her relationship with Ruth and with God. When you face bitter times, God welcomes your honest prayers, but be careful not to overlook the love, strength, and resources that he provides in your present relationships. And don't allow bitterness and disappointment to blind you to your opportunities.

22 So Naomi returned, and with her Ruth the Moabitess, her daughter-in-law, who
returned from the land of Moab. And they came to Bethlehem at the beginning of barley harvest.

1:22 Ex 9:31; Lev 23:10, 11

2. Ruth gleans in Boaz's field

2 Now Naomi had a kinsman of her husband, a man of great wealth, of the family of
Elimelech, whose name was Boaz.
2 And Ruth the Moabitess said to Naomi, "Please let me go to the field and glean
among the ears of grain after one in whose sight I may find favor." And she said to her,
"Go, my daughter."
3 So she departed and went and gleaned in the field after the reapers; and she happened to come to the portion of the field belonging to Boaz, who was of the family of
Elimelech.
4 Now behold, Boaz came from Bethlehem and said to the reapers, "May the LORD
be with you." And they said to him, "May the LORD bless you."
5 Then Boaz said to his servant who was in charge of the reapers, "Whose young
woman is this?"
6 The servant in charge of the reapers replied, "She is the young Moabite woman who
returned with Naomi from the land of Moab.
7 "And she said, 'Please let me glean and gather after the reapers among the sheaves.'
Thus she came and has remained from the morning until now; she has been sitting in the
house for a little while."
8 Then Boaz said to Ruth, "Listen carefully, my daughter. Do not go to glean in another field; furthermore, do not go on from this one, but stay here with my maids.
9 "Let your eyes be on the field which they reap, and go after them. Indeed, I have
commanded the servants not to touch you. When you are thirsty, go to the water jars
and drink from what the servants draw."
10 Then she fell on her face, bowing to the ground and said to him, "Why have I found
favor in your sight that you should take notice of me, since I am a foreigner?"
11 Boaz replied to her, "All that you have done for your mother-in-law after the death
of your husband has been fully reported to me, and how you left your father and your
mother and the land of your birth, and came to a people that you did not previously know.
12 "May the LORD reward your work, and your wages be full from the LORD, the God
of Israel, under whose wings you have come to seek refuge."
13 Then she said, "I have found favor in your sight, my lord, for you have comforted

2:1 Ruth 1:2

2:2 Lev 19:9, 10; 23:22; Deut 24:19; Ruth 2:7

2:4 Judg 6:12; Ps 129:8; Luke 1:28; 2 Thess 3:16

2:10 1 Sam 25:23

2:12 1 Sam 24:19; Ruth 1:16; Ps 17:8; 36:7; 57:1; 61:4; 63:7; 91:4

1:22 Bethlehem was about five miles southwest of Jerusalem. The town was surrounded by lush fields and olive groves. Its harvests were abundant.

Ruth and Naomi's return to Bethlehem was certainly part of God's plan because in this town David would be born (1 Samuel 16:1), and, as predicted by the prophet Micah (Micah 5:2), Jesus Christ would also be born there. This move, then, was more than merely convenient for Ruth and Naomi. It led to the fulfillment of Scripture.

1:22 Because Israel's climate is quite moderate, there are two harvests each year, in the spring and in the fall. The barley harvest took place in the spring, and it was during this time of hope and plenty that Ruth and Naomi returned to Bethlehem. Bethlehem was a farming community, and because it was the time of the harvest, there was plenty of leftover grain in the fields. This grain could be collected, or *gleaned,* and then made into food. (See the note on 2:2 for more information on gleaning.)

2:2 When the wheat and barley were ready to be harvested, reapers were hired to cut down the stalks and tie them into bundles. Israelite law demanded that the corners of the fields not be harvested. In addition, any grain that was dropped was to be left for poor people who picked it up (this was called *gleaning*) and used it for food (Leviticus 19:9; 23:22; Deuteronomy 24:19). The purpose of this law was to feed the poor and to prevent the owners from hoarding. This law served as a type of welfare program in Israel. Because she was a widow with no means of providing for herself, Ruth went into the fields to glean the grain.

2:2–3 Ruth made her home in a foreign land. Instead of depending on Naomi or waiting for good fortune to happen, she took the initiative. She went to work. She was not afraid of admitting her need or working hard to supply it. When Ruth went out to the fields, God provided for her. If you are waiting for God to provide, consider this: He may be waiting for you to take the first step to demonstrate just how important your need is.

2:7 Ruth's task, though menial, tiring, and perhaps degrading, was done faithfully. What is your attitude when the task you have been given is not up to your true potential? The task at hand may be all you can do, or it may be the work God wants you to do. Or, as in Ruth's case, it may be a test of your character that can open up new doors of opportunity.

2:10–12 Ruth's life exhibited admirable qualities: She was hardworking, loving, kind, faithful, and brave. These qualities gained for her a good reputation, but only because she displayed them *consistently* in all areas of her life. Wherever Ruth went or whatever she did, her character remained the same.

Your reputation is formed by the people who watch you at work, in town, at home, in church. A good reputation comes by *consistently* living out the qualities you believe in—no matter what group of people or surroundings you are in.

me and indeed have spoken kindly to your maidservant, though I am not like one of your
maidservants."
2:14 Ruth 2:18 **14** At mealtime Boaz said to her, "Come here, that you may eat of the bread and dip
your piece of bread in the vinegar." So she sat beside the reapers; and he served her
roasted grain, and she ate and was satisfied and had some left.
15 When she rose to glean, Boaz commanded his servants, saying,
"Let her glean even among the sheaves, and do not insult her.
16 "Also you shall purposely pull out for her *some grain* from the bundles and leave *it*
that she may glean, and do not rebuke her."
17 So she gleaned in the field until evening. Then she beat out what she had gleaned,
and it was about an ephah of barley.
2:18 Ruth 2:14 18 She took *it* up and went into the city, and her mother-in-law saw what she had
gleaned. She also took *it* out and gave Naomi what she had left after she was satisfied.
2:19 Ps 41:1 19 Her mother-in-law then said to her, "Where did you glean today and where did you
work? May he who took notice of you be blessed." So she told her mother-in-law with
whom she had worked and said, "The name of the man with whom I worked today is
Boaz."
2:20 2 Sam 2:5 20 Naomi said to her daughter-in-law, "May he be blessed of the LORD who has not
withdrawn his kindness to the living and to the dead." Again Naomi said to her, "The
man is our relative, he is one of our closest relatives."
21 Then Ruth the Moabitess said, "Furthermore, he said to me, 'You should stay close
to my servants until they have finished all my harvest.' "
22 Naomi said to Ruth her daughter-in-law, "It is good, my daughter, that you go out
with his maids, so that *others* do not fall upon you in another field."
2:23 Deut 16:9 23 So she stayed close by the maids of Boaz in order to glean until the end of the barley harvest and the wheat harvest. And she lived with her mother-in-law.

3. Ruth follows Naomi's plan

Boaz Will Redeem Ruth

3 Then Naomi her mother-in-law said to her, "My daughter, shall I not seek security
for you, that it may be well with you?
3:2 Deut 25:5-10 2 "Now is not Boaz our kinsman, with whose maids you were? Behold, he winnows
barley at the threshing floor tonight.

2:15–16 The characters in the book of Ruth are classic examples of good people in action. Boaz went far beyond the intent of the gleaners' law in demonstrating his kindness and generosity. Not only did he let Ruth glean in his field, but he also told his workers to let some of the grain fall in her path. Out of his abundance, he provided for the needy. How often do you go beyond the accepted patterns of providing for those less fortunate? Do more than the minimum for others.

2:19–20 Naomi had felt bitter (1:20–21), but her faith in God was still alive, and she praised God for Boaz's kindness to Ruth. In her sorrows, she still trusted God and acknowledged his goodness. We may feel bitter about a situation, but we must never despair. Today is always a new opportunity for experiencing God's care.

2:20 Though Ruth may not have always recognized God's guidance, he had been with her every step of the way. She went to glean and "just happened" to end up in the field owned by Boaz who "just happened" to be a close relative. This was more than mere coincidence. As you go about your daily tasks, God is working in your life in ways you may not even notice. We must not close the door on what God can do. Events do not occur by luck or coincidence. We should have faith that God is directing our lives for his purpose.

3:1–9 As widows, Ruth and Naomi could only look forward to difficult times. (See the note on 1:8–9 for more on a widow's life.) But when Naomi heard the news about Boaz, her hope for the future was renewed (2:20). Typical of her character, she thought first of Ruth, encouraging her to see if Boaz would take the responsibility of redeeming her (3:13).

A *kinsman-redeemer* was a relative who volunteered to take responsibility for the extended family. When a woman's husband died, the law (Deuteronomy 25:5–10) provided that she could marry a brother of her dead husband. But Naomi had no more sons. In such a case, the closest relative to the deceased husband could become a kinsman-redeemer and marry the widow. The closest relative did not have to marry the widow. If he chose not to, the next closest relative could take his place. If no one chose to help the widow, she would probably live in poverty the rest of her life because in Israelite culture the inheritance was passed on to the son or nearest male relative, not to the wife. To take the sting out of these inheritance rules, there were laws for gleaning and kinsman-redeemers.

We have a kinsman-redeemer in Jesus Christ, who though he was God, came to earth as a man in order to save us. By his death on the cross, he has redeemed us from sin and hopelessness and thereby purchased us to be his own possession (1 Peter 1:18–19). This guarantees our eternal inheritance.

3:2 The threshing floor was the place where the grain was separated from the harvested wheat. The wheat stalks were crushed, either by hand or by oxen, and the valuable grain (inner kernels) separated from the worthless chaff (the outside shell). The floor was made from rock or soil and located outside the village, usually on an elevated site where the winds would blow away the lighter chaff when the crushed wheat was thrown into the air (or winnowed). Boaz spent the night beside the threshing floor for two reasons: (1) to prevent theft and (2) to wait for his turn to thresh grain. (Threshing was often done at night because daylight hours were spent harvesting.)

3 "Wash yourself therefore, and anoint yourself and put on your *best* clothes, and go
down to the threshing floor; *but* do not make yourself known to the man until he has
finished eating and drinking.
4 "It shall be when he lies down, that you shall notice the place where he lies, and you
shall go and uncover his feet and lie down; then he will tell you what you shall do."
5 She said to her, "All that you say I will do."
6 So she went down to the threshing floor and did according to all that her mother-
in-law had commanded her.
7 When Boaz had eaten and drunk and his heart was merry, he went to lie down at
the end of the heap of grain; and she came secretly, and uncovered his feet and lay down.
8 It happened in the middle of the night that the man was startled and bent forward;
and behold, a woman was lying at his feet.
9 He said, "Who are you?" And she answered, "I am Ruth your maid. So spread your
covering over your maid, for you are a [3]close relative."
10 Then he said, "May you be blessed of the LORD, my daughter. You have shown your
last kindness to be better than the first by not going after young men, whether poor or
rich.
11 "Now, my daughter, do not fear. I will do for you whatever you ask, for all my people
in the city know that you are a woman of excellence.
12 "Now it is true I am a close relative; however, there is a relative closer than I.
13 "Remain this night, and when morning comes, if he will redeem you, good; let him
redeem you. But if he does not wish to redeem you, then I will redeem you, as the LORD
lives. Lie down until morning."
14 So she lay at his feet until morning and rose before one could recognize another;
and he said, "Let it not be known that the woman came to the threshing floor."
15 Again he said, "Give me the cloak that is on you and hold it." So she held it, and he
measured six *measures* of barley and laid *it* on her. Then she went into the city.
16 When she came to her mother-in-law, she said, "How did it go, my daughter?" And
she told her all that the man had done for her.
17 She said, "These six *measures* of barley he gave to me, for he said, 'Do not go to
your mother-in-law empty-handed.' "
18 Then she said, "Wait, my daughter, until you know how the matter turns out; for
the man will not rest until he has settled it today."

3:5 Eph 6:1; Col 3:20
3:7 Judg 19:6, 9; 2 Sam 13:28; 1 Kin 21:7; Esth 1:10
3:10 Ruth 2:20
3:11 Prov 12:4; 31:10
3:13 Deut 25:5; Matt 22:24; Judg 8:19; Jer 4:2; 12:16
3:14 Rom 14:16; 2 Cor 8:21

4. Ruth and Boaz are married

4 Now Boaz went up to the gate and sat down there, and behold, the close relative of
whom Boaz spoke was passing by, so he said, "Turn aside, friend, sit down here."
And he turned aside and sat down.

4:1 Ruth 3:12

3 Or *redeemer*

3:4 Naomi's advice seems strange, but she was not suggesting a seductive act. In reality, Naomi was telling Ruth to act in accordance with Israelite custom and law. It was common for a servant to lie at the feet of his master and even share a part of his covering. By observing this custom, Ruth would inform Boaz that he could be her kinsman-redeemer—that he could find someone to marry her or marry her himself. It was family business, nothing romantic. But the story later became beautifully romantic as Ruth and Boaz developed an unselfish love and deep respect for each other.

3:5 As a foreigner, Ruth may have thought that Naomi's advice was odd. But Ruth followed the advice because she knew Naomi was kind, trustworthy, and filled with moral integrity. Each of us knows a parent, older friend, or relative who is always looking out for our best interests. Be willing to listen to the advice of those older and wiser than you are. The experience and knowledge of such a person can be invaluable. Imagine what Ruth's life would have been like had she ignored her mother-in-law.

3:12 Ruth and Naomi must have assumed that Boaz was their closest relative. Boaz, too, must have already considered marrying Ruth because his answer to her shows he had been thinking about it. He couldn't have considered marrying Naomi because she was probably too old to bear any more children (1:11–12). One man in the city was a closer relative than Boaz, and this man had the first right to take Ruth as his wife. If he chose not to, then Boaz could marry Ruth (3:13).

3:18 Naomi implied that Boaz would follow through with his promise at once. He obviously had a reputation for keeping his word and would not rest until his task was completed. Such reliable people stand out in any age and culture. Do others regard you as one who will do what you say? Keeping your word and following through on assignments should be high on anyone's priority list. Building a reputation for integrity, however, must be done one brick, one act, at a time.

4:1 Boaz knew he could find his relative at the city gate. This was the center of activity. No one could enter or leave the town without traveling through the gate. Merchants set up their temporary shops near the gate, which also served as "city hall." Here city officials gathered to transact business. Because there was so much activity, it was a good place to find witnesses (4:2) and an appropriate place for Boaz to make his transaction.

4:2 1 Kin 21:8; Prov 31:23
4:3 Lev 25:25
4:4 Jer 32:7f; Lev 25:25
4:5 Gen 38:8; Deut 25:5f; Matt 22:24
4:6 Lev 25:25
4:7 Deut 25:8-10

2 He took ten men of the elders of the city and said, "Sit down here." So they sat down.
3 Then he said to the closest relative, "Naomi, who has come back from the land of
Moab, has to sell the piece of land which belonged to our brother Elimelech.
4 "So I thought to inform you, saying, 'Buy *it* before those who are sitting *here,* and
before the elders of my people. If you will redeem *it,* redeem *it;* but if not, tell me that I
may know; for there is no one but you to redeem *it,* and I am after you.' " And he said,
"I will redeem *it.*"
5 Then Boaz said, "On the day you buy the field from the hand of Naomi, you must
also acquire Ruth the Moabitess, the widow of the deceased, in order to raise up the
name of the deceased on his inheritance."
6 The closest relative said, "I cannot redeem *it* for myself, because I would jeopardize
my own inheritance. Redeem *it* for yourself; you *may have* my right of redemption, for I
cannot redeem *it.*"
7 Now this was *the custom* in former times in Israel concerning the redemption and
the exchange *of land* to confirm any matter: a man removed his sandal and gave it to
another; and this was the *manner of* attestation in Israel.

Heroes are easier to admire than to define. They are seldom conscious of their moments of heroism, and others may not recognize their acts as heroic. Heroes simply do the right thing at the right time, whether or not they realize the impact their action will have. Perhaps the one quality they share is a tendency to think of others before they think of themselves. Boaz was a hero.

In his dealings with other people, he was always sensitive to their needs. His words to his employees, relatives, and others were colored with kindness. He offered help openly, not grudgingly. When he discovered who Ruth was, he took several steps to help her because she had been faithful to his relative Naomi. When Naomi advised Ruth to request his protection, he was ready to marry her if the legal complications could be worked out.

Boaz not only did what was right; he also did it right away. Of course he could not foresee all that his actions would accomplish. He could not have known that the child he would have by Ruth would be an ancestor of both David and Jesus. He only met the challenge of taking the right action in the situation facing him.

We are faced with this challenge in our daily choices. Like Naomi's nearer relative, we are often more concerned with making the easy choice than with making the right one. Yet more often than not, the right choice is clear. Ask God to give you a special awareness in your choices today as well as renewed commitment to make the right ones.

Strengths and accomplishments:
- A man of his word
- Sensitive to those in need, caring for his workers
- A keen sense of responsibility, integrity
- A successful and shrewd businessman

Lessons from his life:
- It can be heroic to do what must be done and to do it right
- God often uses little decisions to carry out his big plan

Vital statistics:
- Where: Bethlehem
- Occupation: Wealthy farmer
- Relatives: Elimelech, Naomi, Ruth

Key verse:
"I have acquired Ruth the Moabitess, the widow of Mahlon, to be my wife in order to raise up the name of the deceased on his inheritance, so that the name of the deceased will not be cut off from his brothers or from the court of his birth place; you are witnesses today" (Ruth 4:10).

His story is told in the book of Ruth. He is also mentioned in Matthew 1:5.

4:3 Boaz cleverly presented his case to the relative. First he brought in new information not yet mentioned in the story—Elimelech, Naomi's former husband, still had some property in the area that was now for sale. As the closest relative, this man had the first right to buy the land, which he agreed to do (Leviticus 25:25). But then Boaz said that according to the law, if the relative bought the property he also had to marry the widow (probably because Mahlon, Ruth's former husband and Elimelech's son, had inherited the property). At this stipulation, the relative backed down. He did not want to complicate his inheritance. He may have feared that if he had a son through Ruth, some of his estate would transfer away from his family to the family of Elimelech. Whatever his reason, the way was now clear for Boaz to marry Ruth.

8 So the closest relative said to Boaz, "Buy *it* for yourself." And he removed his sandal.
9 Then Boaz said to the elders and all the people, "You are witnesses today that I
have bought from the hand of Naomi all that belonged to Elimelech and all that belonged
to Chilion and Mahlon.
10 "Moreover, I have acquired Ruth the Moabitess, the widow of Mahlon, to be my wife **4:10**
in order to raise up the name of the deceased on his inheritance, so that the name of the Deut 25:6
deceased will not be cut off from his brothers or from the court of his *birth* place; you are
witnesses today."
11 All the people who were in the court, and the elders, said, "*We are* witnesses. May **4:11**
the LORD make the woman who is coming into your home like Rachel and Leah, both Gen 29:25-30
of whom built the house of Israel; and may you achieve wealth in Ephrathah and become famous in Bethlehem.
12 "Moreover, may your house be like the house of Perez whom Tamar bore to Judah, **4:12**
through the offspring which the LORD will give you by this young woman." Gen 38:29; 46:12; Ruth 4:18
13 So Boaz took Ruth, and she became his wife, and he went in to her. And the LORD
enabled her to conceive, and she gave birth to a son. **4:13** Gen 29:31; 33:5
14 Then the women said to Naomi, "Blessed is the LORD who has not left you without
a redeemer today, and may his name become famous in Israel. **4:14** Luke 1:58
15 "May he also be to you a restorer of life and a sustainer of your old age; for your
daughter-in-law, who loves you and is better to you than seven sons, has given birth **4:15** Ruth 1:16, 17; 2:11, 12
to him."

The Line of David Began Here

16 Then Naomi took the child and laid him in her lap, and became his nurse.
17 The neighbor women gave him a name, saying, "A son has been born to Naomi!"
So they named him Obed. He is the father of Jesse, the father of David.
18 Now these are the generations of Perez: to Perez was born Hezron, **4:18** Matt 1:3-6
19 and to Hezron was born Ram, and to Ram, Amminadab,
20 and to Amminadab was born Nahshon, and to Nahshon, Salmon,
21 and to Salmon was born Boaz, and to Boaz, Obed,
22 and to Obed was born Jesse, and to Jesse, David.

4:15 Ruth's love for her mother-in-law was known and recognized throughout the town. From the beginning of the book of Ruth to the end, her kindness toward others remained unchanged.

4:15 God brought great blessings out of Naomi's tragedy, even greater than "seven sons," or an abundance of heirs. Throughout her tough times, Naomi continued to trust God. And God, in his time, blessed her greatly. Even in our sorrow and calamity, God can bring great blessings. Be like Naomi, and don't turn your back on God when tragedy strikes. Instead of asking "How can God allow this to happen to me?" trust him. He will be with you in the hard times.

4:16–17 To some, the book of Ruth may be just a nice story about a girl who was fortunate. But in reality, the events recorded in Ruth were part of God's preparations for the births of David and of Jesus, the promised Messiah. Just as Ruth was unaware of this larger purpose in her life, so we will not know the full purpose and importance of our lives until we are able to look back from the perspective of eternity. We must make our choices with God's eternal values in mind. Taking moral shortcuts and living for short-range pleasures are not good ways to move ahead. Because of Ruth's faithful obedience, her life and legacy were significant even though she couldn't see all the results. Live in faithfulness to God, knowing that the significance of your life will extend beyond your lifetime. The rewards will outweigh any sacrifice you may have made.

THE ANCESTORS OF JESUS
The book of Ruth is not just a nice story, or an inconsequential incident. The events recorded in Ruth were part of God's preparation for the births of David and eventually Jesus, the promised Messiah. In Matthew, the opening genealogy looks back to Ruth and Boaz as ancestors of Jesus (see Matthew 1:5).

"The record of the genealogy of Jesus the Messiah, the son of David, the son of Abraham:

"Abraham was the father of Isaac, Isaac the father of Jacob, and Jacob the father of Judah and his brothers. Judah was the father of Perez and Zerah by Tamar, Perez was the father of Hezron, and Hezron the father of Ram. Ram was the father of Amminadab, Amminadab the father of Nahshon, and Nahshon the father of Salmon. Salmon was the father of **Boaz** by Rahab, **Boaz** was the father of Obed by **Ruth**, and Obed the father of Jesse. Jesse was the father of David the king.

"David was the father of Solomon by Bathsheba who had been the wife of Uriah. Solomon was the father of Rehoboam, Rehoboam the father of Abijah, and Abijah the father of Asa. Asa was the father of Jehoshaphat, Jehoshaphat the father of Joram, and Joram the father of Uzziah. Uzziah was the father of Jotham, Jotham the father of Ahaz, and Ahaz the father of Hezekiah. Hezekiah was the father of Manasseh. Manasseh the father of Amon, and Amon the father of Josiah. Josiah became the father of Jeconiah and his brothers, at the time of the deportation to Babylon.

"After the deportation to Babylon: Jeconiah became the father of Shealtiel, and Shealtiel the father of Zerubbabel. Zerubbabel was the father of Abihud, Abihud the father of Eliakim, and Eliakim the father of Azor. Azor was the father of Zadok, Zadok the father of Achim, and Achim the father of Eliud. Eliud was the father of Eleazar, Eleazar the father of Matthan, and Matthan the father of Jacob. Jacob was the father of Joseph the husband of Mary, by whom Jesus was born, who is called the Messiah" (Matthew 1:1-16).

1 SAMUEL

Judges begin to rule 1375 B.C. (1220 B.C.)

Samuel born 1105 (1083)

Saul born 1080

VITAL STATISTICS

PURPOSE:
To record the life of Samuel, Israel's last judge; the reign and decline of Saul, the first king; and the choice and preparation of David, Israel's greatest king

AUTHOR:
Possibly Samuel, but also includes writings from the prophets Nathan and Gad (1 Chronicles 29:29)

SETTING:
The book begins in the days of the judges and describes Israel's transition from a theocracy (led by God) to a monarchy (led by a king)

KEY VERSES:
" The LORD said to Samuel, 'Listen to the voice of the people in regard to all that they say to you, for they have not rejected you, but they have rejected Me from being king over them .... Now then, listen to their voice; however, you shall solemnly warn them and tell them of the procedure of the king who will reign over them' " (8:7–9).

KEY PEOPLE:
Eli, Hannah, Samuel, Saul, Jonathan, David

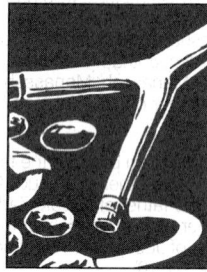

"RUNNERS, take your marks," the starter barks his signal, and the crowd turns quiet attention to the athletes walking toward the line. "Get set" . . . in position now, muscles tense, nervously anticipating the sound of the gun. It resounds! And the race begins. In any contest, the start is important, but the finish is even more crucial. Often a front-runner will lose strength and fade to the middle of the pack. And there is the tragedy of the brilliant beginner who sets the pace for a time, but does not even finish. He quits the race burned out, exhausted, injured.

First Samuel is a book of great beginnings . . . and tragic endings. It begins with Eli as high priest during the time of the judges. As a religious leader, Eli certainly must have begun his life with a close relationship to God. In his communication with Hannah, and in his training of her son Samuel, he demonstrated a clear understanding of God's purposes and call (chapters 1; 3). But his life ended in ignominy as his sacrilegious sons were judged by God and the sacred ark of the covenant fell into enemy hands (chapter 4). Eli's death marked the decline of the influence of the priesthood and the rise of the prophets in Israel.

Samuel was dedicated to God's service by his mother, Hannah. He became one of Israel's greatest prophets. He was a man of prayer who finished the work of the judges, began the school of the prophets, and anointed Israel's first kings. But even Samuel was not immune to finishing poorly. Like Eli's family, Samuel's sons turned away from God; they took bribes and perverted justice. The people rejected the leadership of the judges and priests and clamored for a king "like all the nations" (8:5).

Saul also started quickly. A striking figure, this handsome (9:2) and humble (9:21; 10:22) man was God's choice as Israel's first king (10:24). His early reign was marked by leadership (chapter 11) and bravery (14:46–48). But he disobeyed God (chapter 15), became jealous and paranoid (chapters 18–19), and finally had his kingship taken away from him by God (chapter 16). Saul's life continued steadily downward. Obsessed with killing David (chapters 19—30), he consulted a medium (chapter 28) and finally committed suicide (chapter 31).

Among the events of Saul's life is another great beginner—David. A man who followed God (13:14; 16:7), David ministered to Saul (chapter 16), killed Goliath (chapter 17), and became a great warrior. But we'll have to wait until the book of 2 Samuel to see how David finished.

As you read 1 Samuel, note the transition from theocracy to monarchy; exult in the classic stories of David and Goliath, David and Jonathan, David and Abigail; and watch the rise of the influence of the prophets. But in the midst of reading all the history and adventure, determine to run your race as God's person from start to finish.

Samson becomes judge 1075 (1083)	*Saul becomes king 1050 (1045)*	*David born 1040*	*David anointed; Goliath slain 1025*	*David becomes king over Judah 1010*	*David becomes king over all Israel 1003*	*Solomon becomes king 970*	*The kingdom is divided 930*

THE BLUEPRINT

A. ELI AND SAMUEL (1:1—7:17)
1. Samuel's birth and childhood
2. War with the Philistines

We see a vivid contrast between young Samuel and Eli's sons. Eli's sons were selfish, but Samuel was helpful. Eli's sons defrauded people, but Samuel grew in wisdom and gave the people messages from God. As an adult, Samuel became a prophet, priest, and judge over Israel. A person's actions reflect his character. This was true of Samuel and of Eli's sons. It is also true of us. Strive, like Samuel, to keep your heart pure before God.

B. SAMUEL AND SAUL (8:1—15:35)
1. Saul becomes king of Israel
2. God rejects Saul for disobedience

Saul showed great promise. He was strong, tall, and modest. God's Spirit came upon him, and Samuel was his counselor. But Saul deliberately disobeyed God and became an evil king. We must not base our hopes or future on our potential. Instead, we must consistently obey God in all areas of life. God evaluates obedience, not potential.

C. SAUL AND DAVID (16:1—31:13)
1. Samuel anoints David
2. David and Goliath
3. David and Jonathan become friends
4. Saul pursues David
5. Saul's defeat and death

David quickly killed Goliath but waited patiently for God to deal with Saul. Although David was anointed to be Israel's next king, he had to wait years to realize this promise. The difficult circumstances in life and the times of waiting often refine, teach, and prepare us for the future responsibilities God has for us.

MEGATHEMES

THEME	EXPLANATION	IMPORTANCE
King	Because Israel suffered from corrupt priests and judges, the people wanted a king. They wanted to be organized like the surrounding nations. Though it was against his original purpose, God chose a king for them.	Establishing a monarchy did not solve Israel's problems. What God desires is the genuine devotion of each person's mind and heart to him. No government or set of laws can substitute for the rule of God in your heart and life.
God's Control	Israel prospered as long as the people regarded God as their true king. When the leaders strayed from God's Law, God intervened in their personal lives and overruled their actions. In this way, God maintained ultimate control over Israel's history.	God is always at work in this world, even when we can't see what he is doing. No matter what kinds of pressures we must endure or how many changes we must face, God is ultimately in control of our situation. Being confident of God's sovereignty, we can face the difficult situations in our lives with boldness.
Leadership	God guided his people using different forms of leadership: judges, priests, prophets, kings. Those whom he chose for these different offices, such as Eli, Samuel, Saul, and David, portrayed different styles of leadership. Yet the success of each leader depended on his devotion to God, not his position, leadership style, wisdom, age, or strength.	When Eli, Samuel, Saul, and David disobeyed God, they faced tragic consequences. Sin affected what they accomplished for God and how some of them raised their children. Being a real leader means letting God guide all aspects of your activities, values, and goals, including the way you raise your children.
Obedience	For God, "to obey is better than sacrifice" (15:22). God wanted his people to obey, serve, and follow him with a whole heart rather than to maintain a superficial commitment based on tradition or ceremonial systems.	Although we are free from the sacrificial system of the Jewish Law, we may still rely on outward observances to substitute for inward commitment. God desires that all our work and worship be motivated by genuine, heartfelt devotion to him.

God's Faithfulness	God faithfully kept the promises he made to Israel. He responded to his people with tender mercy and swift justice. In showing mercy, he faithfully acted in the best interest of his people. In showing justice, he was faithful to his word and perfect moral nature.	Because God is faithful, he can be counted on to be merciful toward us. Yet God is also just, and he will not tolerate rebellion against him. His faithfulness and unselfish love should inspire us to dedicate ourselves to him completely. We must never take his mercy for granted.

KEY PLACES IN 1 SAMUEL

1 Ramah Samuel was born in Ramah. Before his birth, Samuel's mother Hannah made a promise to God that she would dedicate her son to serve God alongside the priests in the tabernacle at Shiloh (1:1—2:11).

2 Shiloh The focal point of Israel's worship was at Shiloh, where the tabernacle and the ark of the covenant resided. Eli was the high priest, but his sons, Hophni and Phinehas, were evil men who took advantage of the people. Samuel, however, served God faithfully, and God blessed him as he grew (2:12—3:21).

3 Kiriath-jearim Israel was constantly at odds with the Philistines, and another battle was brewing. Hophni and Phinehas brought the ark of the covenant from Shiloh to the battlefield, believing that its mere presence would bring the Israelites victory. The Israelites were defeated by the Philistines at Ebenezer, and the ark was captured. However, the Philistines soon found out that the ark was not quite the great battle trophy they expected. For God sent plagues upon every Philistine city into which the ark was brought. Finally, the Philistines sent it back to Kiriath-jearim in Israel (4:1—7:1).

4 Mizpah The Israelites' defeat made them realize that God was no longer blessing them. Samuel called the people together at Mizpah and asked them to fast and pray in sorrow for their sins. The assembly at Mizpah was a tempting target for the confident Philistines who advanced for an attack. But God intervened and routed their mighty army. Meanwhile, Samuel was judging cases throughout Israel. But as Samuel grew old, the people came to him at Ramah (his home base) demanding a king in order to be like the other nations. At Mizpah, Saul was chosen by sacred appointment to be Israel's first king with the blessing, but not the approval, of God and Samuel (7:2—10:27).

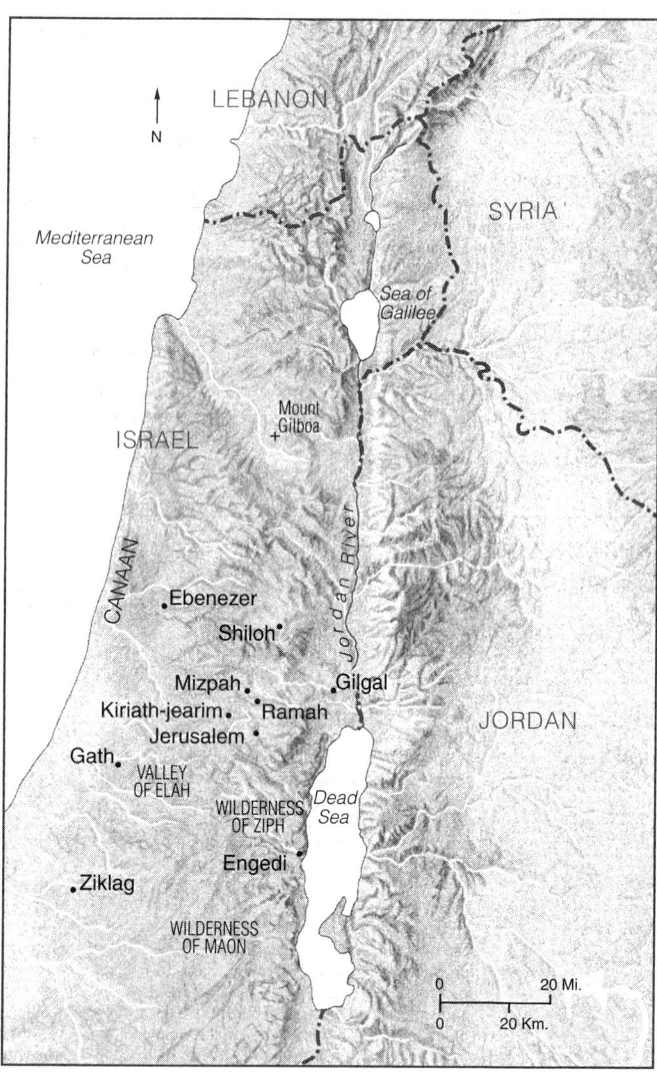

The broken lines (–·–·) indicate modern boundaries.

5 Gilgal A battle with the Ammonites proved Saul's leadership abilities to the people of Israel. He protected the people of Jabesh-gilead and scattered the Ammonite army. Samuel and the people crowned Saul as king of Israel at Gilgal (11:1–15).

6 Valley of Elah Saul won many other battles, but over time he proved to be arrogant, sinful, and rebellious, so God finally rejected him as king. Unknown to Saul, a young shepherd and musician named David was anointed to be Israel's next king. But it would be many years before David sat upon the throne. Ironically, Saul hired David to play the harp in his palace. Saul grew to like David so much that he made him his personal armor bearer. In one particular battle with the Philistines in the valley of Elah, David killed Goliath, the Philistines' mightiest soldier. But this victory was the beginning of the end of Saul's love for David. The Israelites praised David more than Saul, causing Saul to become so jealous that he plotted to kill David (12:1—22:23).

7 The Wilderness Even anointed kings are not exempt from troubles. David literally ran for his life from King Saul, hiding with his band of followers in the wilderness of Ziph (where the men of Ziph constantly betrayed him), the wilderness of Maon, and the wilderness of Engedi. Though he had opportunities to kill Saul, David refused to do so because Saul was God's anointed king (23:1—26:25).

8 Gath David moved his men and family to Gath, the Philistine city where King Achish lived. Saul then stopped chasing him. The Philistines seemed to welcome this famous fugitive from Israel (27:1–4).

9 Ziklag Desiring privacy in return for his pretended loyalty to King Achish, David asked for a city in which to house his men and family. Achish gave him Ziklag. From there David conducted raids against the cities of the Geshurites, Girzites, and Amalekites, making sure no one escaped to tell the tale (27:5–12). David later conquered the Amalekites after they raided Ziklag (30:1–31).

10 Mount Gilboa War with the Philistines broke out again in the north, near Mount Gilboa. Saul, who no longer relied on God, consulted a medium in a desperate attempt to contact Samuel for help. In the meantime, David was sent back to Ziklag because the Philistine commanders did not trust his loyalty in battle against Israel. The Philistines slaughtered the Israelites on Mount Gilboa, killing King Saul and his three sons, including David's loyal friend Jonathan. Without God, Saul led a bitter and misguided life. The consequences of his sinful actions affected not only him but hurt his family and the entire nation as well (28:1—31:13).

A. ELI AND SAMUEL (1:1—7:17)

Israel has been ruled by judges for over 200 years. Eli and Samuel are the last of those judges. Samuel is born near the end of Eli's life. He grows up in the tabernacle as a priest-in-training under Eli and is well qualified to serve Israel as both a priest and a judge. Although the nation has fallen away from God, it is clear that God is preparing Samuel from the very beginning to lead the nation back to right living. God is always in control; he is able to bring his people back to him.

1. Samuel's birth and childhood

Elkanah and His Wives

1:1 1 Sam 1:19; Josh 17:17, 18; 24:33; 1 Chr 6:22-28, 33-38
1:2 Deut 21:15-17; Luke 2:36
1:3 Ex 34:23; 1 Sam 1:21; Luke 2:41; Ex 23:14; Deut 12:5-7; 16:16; Josh 18:1
1:4 Deut 12:17, 18
1:5 Gen 16:1; 30:1
1:6 Job 24:21

1 Now there was a certain man from Ramathaim-zophim from the hill country of
Ephraim, and his name was Elkanah the son of Jeroham, the son of Elihu, the son
of Tohu, the son of Zuph, an Ephraimite.
2 He had two wives: the name of one was Hannah and the name of the other Peninnah; and Peninnah had children, but Hannah had no children.
3 Now this man would go up from his city yearly to worship and to sacrifice to the
LORD of hosts in Shiloh. And the two sons of Eli, Hophni and Phinehas, were priests to
the LORD there.
4 When the day came that Elkanah sacrificed, he would give portions to Peninnah his
wife and to all her sons and her daughters;
5 but to Hannah he would give a double portion, for he loved Hannah, but the LORD
had closed her womb.
6 Her rival, however, would provoke her bitterly to irritate her, because the LORD
had closed her womb.

1:1 The book of 1 Samuel begins in the days when the judges still ruled Israel, possibly during the closing years of Samson's life. Samuel was Israel's last judge and the first priest and prophet to serve during the time of a king. He was the best example of what a good judge should be, governing the people by God's word and not by his own impulses. Samuel was the man who anointed Saul as Israel's first king.

1:2 Although many great Old Testament leaders (such as Abraham, Jacob, and David) had more than one wife, this was not God's original intention for marriage. Genesis 2:24 states that in marriage, two people become one flesh. Why then did polygamy exist among God's people? First, it was to produce more offspring to help in the man's work and to assure the continuation of the man's family line. Numerous children were a symbol of status and wealth. Second, in societies where many young men were killed in battle, polygamy became an accepted way of supporting women who otherwise would have remained unmarried and, very likely, destitute. Nevertheless, polygamy often caused serious family problems, as we see in this story of Hannah and Peninnah.

1:3 The tabernacle (tent of meeting) was located at Shiloh, the religious center of the nation (see Joshua 18:1). Three times a year all Israelite men were required to attend a religious feast held at the tabernacle: the Passover with the Feast of Unleavened Bread, the Feast of Weeks, and the Feast of Booths (Deuteronomy 16:16). Elkanah made this pilgrimage regularly to fulfill God's commands. (See Exodus 23:14–17 for the regulations concerning the pilgrimage, and see the note on Exodus 40:34 for more on the tabernacle.)

1:6 Hannah had been unable to conceive children, and in Old Testament times a childless woman was considered a failure. Her barrenness was a social embarrassment for her husband. Children were a very important part of the society's economic structure. They were a source of labor for the family, and it was their duty to care for their parents in their old age. If a wife could not bear children she was often obligated, by ancient Middle Eastern custom, to give one of her servant girls to her husband to bear children for her. Although Elkanah could have left Hannah (a husband was permitted to divorce a barren wife), he remained lovingly devoted to her despite social criticism and his rights under civil law.

7 It happened year after year, as often as she went up to the house of the LORD, she
would provoke her; so she wept and would not eat.
8 Then Elkanah her husband said to her, "Hannah, why do you weep and why do you 1:8
not eat and why is your heart sad? Am I not better to you than ten sons?" Ruth 4:15
9 Then Hannah rose after eating and drinking in Shiloh. Now Eli the priest was sit- 1:9
ting on the seat by the doorpost of the temple of the LORD. 1 Sam 3:3
10 She, greatly distressed, prayed to the LORD and wept bitterly.
11 She made a vow and said, "O LORD of hosts, if You will indeed look on the afflic- 1:11
tion of Your maidservant and remember me, and not forget Your maidservant, but will Num 30:6-11; Gen 29:32; Num 6:5;
give Your maidservant a son, then I will give him to the LORD all the days of his life, and Judg 13:5
a razor shall never come on his head."
12 Now it came about, as she continued praying before the LORD, that Eli was watching her mouth.
13 As for Hannah, she was speaking in her heart, only her lips were moving, but her 1:13
voice was not heard. So Eli thought she was drunk. Gen 24:42-45
14 Then Eli said to her, "How long will you make yourself drunk? Put away your wine 1:14
from you." Acts 2:4, 13
15 But Hannah replied, "No, my lord, I am a woman oppressed in spirit; I have drunk 1:15
neither wine nor strong drink, but I have poured out my soul before the LORD. Job 30:16; Ps 42:4; 62:8; Lam 2:19
16 "Do not consider your maidservant as a worthless woman, for I have spoken until
now out of my great concern and provocation."
17 Then Eli answered and said, "Go in peace; and may the God of Israel grant your 1:17
petition that you have asked of Him." Judg 18:6; 1 Sam 25:35; 2 Kin 5:19;
18 She said, "Let your maidservant find favor in your sight." So the woman went her Mark 5:34; Luke 7:50; Ps 20:3-5
way and ate, and her face was no longer *sad*.

1:18 Gen 33:15; Ruth 2:13; Rom 15:13

Samuel Is Born to Hannah

19 Then they arose early in the morning and worshiped before the LORD, and returned 1:19
again to their house in Ramah. And Elkanah had relations with Hannah his wife, and 1 Sam 1:1; 2:11; Gen 21:1; 30:22
the LORD remembered her.

THE JOURNEY TO SHILOH
Each year Elkanah and his family traveled from their home at Ramah to Shiloh, where they worshiped and sacrificed at God's tabernacle.

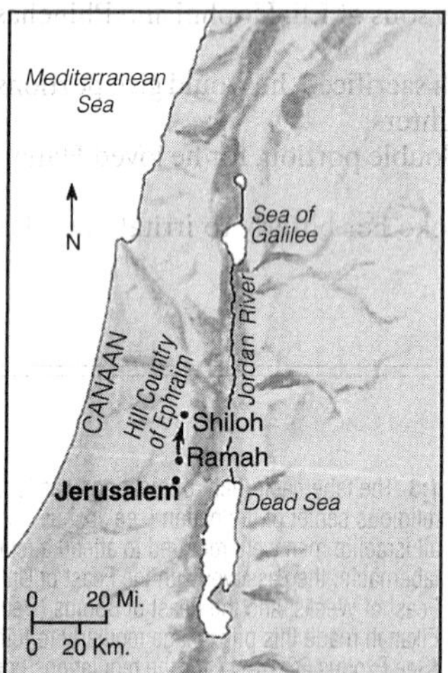

1:7 Part of God's plan for Hannah involved postponing her years of childbearing. While Peninnah and Elkanah looked at Hannah's outward circumstances, God was moving ahead with his plan. Think of those in your world who are struggling with God's timing in answering their prayers and who need your love and help. By supporting those who are struggling, you may help them remain steadfast in their faith and confident in his timing to bring fulfillment to their lives.

1:8 Hannah knew her husband loved her, but even his encouragement could not comfort her. She could not keep from listening to Peninnah's jeers and letting Peninnah's words erode her self-confidence. Although we cannot keep others from unjustly criticizing us, we can choose how we will react to their hurtful words. Rather than dwelling upon our problems, we can enjoy the loving relationships God has given us. By so doing, we can exchange self-pity for hope.

1:10 Hannah had good reason to feel discouraged and bitter. She was unable to bear children; she shared her husband with a woman who ridiculed her (1:7); her loving husband could not solve her problem (1:8); and even the high priest misunderstood her motives (1:14). But instead of retaliating or giving up hope, Hannah prayed. She brought her problem honestly before God.

Each of us may face times of barrenness when nothing "comes to birth" in our work, service, or relationships. It is difficult to pray in faith when we feel so ineffective. But, as Hannah discovered, prayer opens the way for God to work (1:19–20).

1:11 Be careful what you promise in prayer because God may take you up on it. Hannah so desperately wanted a child that she was willing to strike a bargain with God. God took her up on her promise, and to Hannah's credit, she did her part, even though it was painful (1:27–28).

Although we are not in a position to barter with God, he may still choose to answer a prayer that has an attached promise. When you pray, ask yourself, "Will I follow through on any promises I make to God if he grants my request?" It is dishonest and dangerous to ignore a promise, especially to God. God keeps his promises, and he expects you to keep yours.

1:18 Earlier Hannah had been discouraged to the point of being physically sick and unable to eat. At this point, she returned home well and happy. The change in her attitude may be attributed to three factors: (1) She honestly prayed to God (1:11); (2) she received encouragement from Eli (1:17); (3) she resolved to leave the problem with God (1:18). This is the antidote for discouragement: Tell God how you really feel and leave your problems with him. Then rely upon the support of good friends and counselors.

1:20 Gen 41:51, 52; Ex 2:10, 22; Matt 1:21
1:21 Deut 12:11; 1 Sam 1:3
1:22 Luke 2:22; 1 Sam 1:11, 28
1:23 Num 30:7, 10, 11; 1 Sam 1:17
1:24 Num 15:9, 10; Deut 12:5, 6; Josh 18:1; 1 Sam 4:3, 4
1:25 Lev 1:5; Luke 2:22
1:26 2 Kin 2:2, 4, 6; 4:30
1:27 1 Sam 1:11-13; Ps 6:9; 66:19, 20
1:28 1 Sam 1:11, 22; Gen 24:26, 52
2:1 1 Sam 2:1-10; Luke 1:46-55; Deut 33:17; Job 16:15; Ps 75:10; 89:17, 24; 92:10; 112:9; Ps 9:14; 13:5; 35:9; Is 12:2, 3
2:2 Ex 15:11; Lev 19:2; Ps 86:8; 2 Sam 22:32; Deut 32:30, 31
2:3 Prov 8:13; 1 Sam 16:7; 1 Kin 8:39; Prov 16:2; 24:12
2:4 Ps 37:15; 46:9; Ps 18:39; Heb 11:32-34
2:5 Ruth 4:15; Ps 113:9; Jer 15:9

20 It came about in due time, after Hannah had conceived, that she gave birth to a
son; and she named him Samuel, *saying*, "Because I have asked him of the LORD."
21 Then the man Elkanah went up with all his household to offer to the LORD the yearly
sacrifice and pay his vow.
22 But Hannah did not go up, for she said to her husband, "*I will not go up* until the
child is weaned; then I will bring him, that he may appear before the LORD and stay there
forever."
23 Elkanah her husband said to her, "Do what seems best to you. Remain until you
have weaned him; only may the LORD confirm His word." So the woman remained and
nursed her son until she weaned him.
24 Now when she had weaned him, she took him up with her, with a three-year-old
bull and one ephah of flour and a jug of wine, and brought him to the house of the LORD
in Shiloh, although the child was young.
25 Then they slaughtered the bull, and brought the boy to Eli.
26 She said, "Oh, my lord! As your soul lives, my lord, I am the woman who stood here
beside you, praying to the LORD.
27 "For this boy I prayed, and the LORD has given me my petition which I asked of Him.
28 "So I have also [1]dedicated him to the LORD; as long as he lives he is [1]dedicated to the
LORD." And he worshiped the LORD there.

Hannah's Song of Thanksgiving

2 Then Hannah prayed and said,
"My heart exults in the LORD;
My horn is exalted in the LORD,
My mouth speaks boldly against my enemies,
Because I rejoice in Your salvation.
2 "There is no one holy like the LORD,
Indeed, there is no one besides You,
Nor is there any rock like our God.
3 "Boast no more so very proudly,
Do not let arrogance come out of your mouth;
For the LORD is a God of knowledge,
And with Him actions are weighed.
4 "The bows of the mighty are shattered,
But the feeble gird on strength.
5 "Those who were full hire themselves out for bread,
But those who were hungry cease *to hunger.*
Even the barren gives birth to seven,
But she who has many children languishes.

1 Lit *lent*

1:26–28 To do what she promised (1:11), Hannah gave up what she wanted most—her son—and presented him to Eli to serve in the house of the Lord. In dedicating her only son to God, Hannah was dedicating her entire life and future to God. Because Samuel's life was from God, Hannah was not really giving him up. Rather, she was returning him to God who had given Samuel to Hannah in the first place. These verses illustrate the kind of gifts we should give to God. Do your gifts cost you little (Sunday mornings, a comfortable tithe), or are they gifts of sacrifice? Are you presenting God with tokens, or are you presenting him with your entire life?

1:28 Samuel was probably three years old—the customary age for weaning—when his mother left him at the tabernacle. By saying, "I have also dedicated him to the LORD," Hannah meant that she was dedicating Samuel to God for lifetime service. She did not, of course, forget her much-wanted son. She visited him regularly. And each year she brought him a robe just like Eli's (2:19). In later years, Samuel lived in Ramah (7:17), his parents' hometown (1:19–20).

2:1–10 Hannah praised God for his answer to her prayer for a son. The theme of her poetic prayer is her confidence in God's sovereignty and her thankfulness for everything he had done. Mary, the mother of Jesus, modeled her own praise song, called the Magnificat, after Hannah's prayer (Luke 1:46–55). Like Hannah and Mary, we should be confident of God's ultimate control over the events in our lives, and we should be thankful for the ways God has blessed us. By praising God for all good gifts, we acknowledge his ultimate control over all the affairs of life.

2:2 Hannah praised God for being a rock—firm, strong, and unchanging. In our fast-paced world, friends come and go, and circumstances change. It's difficult to find a solid foundation that will not change. Those who devote their lives to achievements, causes, or possessions have as their security that which is finite and changeable. The possessions that we work so hard to obtain will all pass away. But God is always present. Hope in him. He will never fail.

2:3 No doubt as Hannah said these words, she was thinking of Peninnah's arrogance and chiding. Hannah did not have to get even with Peninnah. She knew that God is all-knowing, and that he will judge all sin and pride. Hannah wisely left judgment up to God. Resist the temptation to take justice into your own hands. God will weigh your deeds as well as the deeds of those who have wronged you.

6 "The LORD kills and makes alive;
He brings down to Sheol and raises up.
7 "The LORD makes poor and rich;
He brings low, He also exalts.
8 "He raises the poor from the dust,
He lifts the needy from the ash heap
To make them sit with nobles,
And inherit a seat of honor;
For the pillars of the earth are the LORD'S,
And He set the world on them.
9 "He keeps the feet of His godly ones,
But the wicked ones are silenced in darkness;
For not by might shall a man prevail.
10 "Those who contend with the LORD will be shattered;
Against them He will thunder in the heavens,
The LORD will judge the ends of the earth;
And He will give strength to His king,
And will exalt the horn of His anointed."
11 Then Elkanah went to his home at Ramah. But the boy ministered to the LORD
before Eli the priest.

The Sin of Eli's Sons

12 Now the sons of Eli were [2]worthless men; they did not know the LORD
13 and the custom of the priests with the people. When any man was offering a sacrifice, the priest's servant would come while the meat was boiling, with a three-pronged
fork in his hand.
14 Then he would thrust it into the pan, or kettle, or caldron, or pot; all that the fork
brought up the priest would take for himself. Thus they did in Shiloh to all the Israelites
who came there.
15 Also, before they burned the fat, the priest's servant would come and say to the man
who was sacrificing, "Give the priest meat for roasting, as he will not take boiled meat
from you, only raw."
16 If the man said to him, "They must surely burn the fat first, and then take as much
as you desire," then he would say, "No, but you shall give *it to me* now; and if not, I will
take it by force."

2 Lit *sons of Belial*

2:6
Deut 32:39; 2 Kin 5:7; Rev 1:18; Is 26:19

2:7
Deut 8:17, 18; Job 5:11; Ps 75:7; James 4:10

2:8
Job 42:10-12; Ps 75:7; 113:7; 2 Sam 7:8; Dan 2:48; James 2:5; Job 36:7; Ps 113:8; Job 38:4-6; Ps 75:3; 104:5

2:9
Ps 91:11, 12; 121:3; Prov 3:26; 1 Pet 1:5; Matt 8:12; Ps 33:16, 17

2:10
Ex 15:6; Ps 2:9; 1 Sam 7:10; 2 Sam 22:14; Ps 18:13, 14; Ps 96:13; 98:9; Matt 25:31, 32; Ps 21:1, 7; Ps 89:24

2:11
1 Sam 1:1, 19; 1 Sam 1:28; 2:18; 3:1

2:12
Jer 2:8; 9:3, 6; 2 Cor 6:15

2:13
Lev 7:29-34

2:15
Lev 3:3-5, 16

2:10 Because we live in a world where evil abounds and a nuclear holocaust always threatens, we may forget that God is in control. Hannah saw God as (1) solid as a rock (2:2), (2) the one who knows what we do (2:3), (3) sovereign over all the affairs of people (2:4–8), and (4) the supreme judge who administers perfect justice (2:10). Remembering God's sovereign control helps us put both world and personal events in perspective.

2:11 Samuel "ministered to the LORD before Eli the priest." In other words, Samuel was Eli's helper or assistant. In this role, Samuel's responsibilities would have included opening the tabernacle doors each morning (3:15), cleaning the furniture, and sweeping the floors. As he grew older, Samuel would have assisted Eli in offering sacrifices. The fact that he was wearing a linen ephod (a garment worn only by priests) shows that he was a priest-in-training (2:18). Because Samuel was Eli's helper, he was God's helper too. When you serve others—even in carrying out ordinary tasks—you are serving God. Because ultimately we serve God, every job has dignity.

2:12ff The Law stipulated that the needs of all the Levites were to be met through the people's tithes (Numbers 18:20–24; Joshua 13:14, 33). Because Eli's sons were priests, they were to be taken care of this way. But Eli's sons took advantage of their position to satisfy their lust for power, possessions, and control. Their contempt and arrogance toward both people and worship undermined the integrity of the whole priesthood.

Eli knew that his sons were evil, but he did little to correct or stop them, even when the integrity of God's sanctuary was threatened. As the high priest, Eli should have responded by executing his sons (Numbers 15:22–31). No wonder he chose not to confront the situation. But by ignoring their selfish actions, Eli let his sons ruin their own lives and the lives of many others. There are times when serious problems must be confronted, even if the process and consequences could be painful.

2:13–14 This fork was a utensil used in the tabernacle for offering sacrifices. Made of bronze (Exodus 27:3), it usually had three prongs to hook the meat that was to be offered on the altar. Eli's sons used the fork to take more meat from the pot than was due them.

2:13–17 What were Eli's sons doing wrong? They were taking parts of the sacrifices *before* they were offered to God on the altar. They were also eating meat before the fat was burned off. This was against God's laws (Leviticus 3:3–5). In effect, Eli's sons were treating God's offerings with contempt. Offerings were given to show honor and respect to God while seeking forgiveness for sins, but through their irreverence, Eli's sons were actually sinning while making the offerings. To add to their sins, they were also sleeping with the women who served there (2:22).

Like Eli's sons, some religious leaders look down on the faith of ordinary people and treat their offerings to God casually or even with contempt. God harshly judges those who lead his people astray or scorn what is devoted to him (Numbers 18:32).

2:17 Mal 2:7-9

2:18 1 Sam 2:11; 3:1; 1 Sam 2:28; 22:18; 2 Sam 6:14; 1 Chr 15:27

2:19 Ex 28:31; 1 Sam 1:3, 21

2:20 Luke 2:34; 1 Sam 1:11, 27, 28

2:21 Gen 21:1; Judg 13:24; 1 Sam 2:26; 3:19-21; Luke 1:80; 2:40

2:22 1 Sam 2:13-17; Ex 38:8

17 Thus the sin of the young men was very great before the LORD, for the men despised the offering of the LORD.

Samuel before the LORD as a Boy

18 Now Samuel was ministering before the LORD, *as* a boy wearing a linen ephod.
19 And his mother would make him a little robe and bring it to him from year to year
when she would come up with her husband to offer the yearly sacrifice.
20 Then Eli would bless Elkanah and his wife and say, "May the LORD give you children from this woman in place of the one she dedicated to the LORD." And they went to
their own home.
21 The LORD visited Hannah; and she conceived and gave birth to three sons and two
daughters. And the boy Samuel grew before the LORD.

Eli Rebukes His Sons

22 Now Eli was very old; and he heard all that his sons were doing to all Israel, and
how they lay with the women who served at the doorway of the tent of meeting.

HANNAH

Hannah's prayer shows us that all we have and receive is on loan from God. Hannah might have had many excuses for being a possessive mother. But when God answered her prayer, she followed through on her promise to dedicate Samuel to God's service.

She discovered that the greatest joy in having a child is to give that child fully and freely back to God. She entered motherhood prepared to do what all mothers must eventually do—let go of their children.

When children are born, they are completely dependent upon their parents for all their basic necessities. This causes some parents to forget that those same children will grow toward independence within the span of a few short years. Being sensitive to the different stages of that healthy process will greatly strengthen family relationships; resisting or denying that process will cause great pain. We must gradually let go of our children in order to allow them to become mature, interdependent adults.

Strengths and accomplishments:
- Mother of Samuel, Israel's greatest judge
- Fervent in worship; effective in prayer
- Willing to follow through on even a costly commitment

Weakness and mistake:
- Struggled with her sense of self-worth because she was unable to have children

Lessons from her life:
- God hears and answers prayer
- Our children are gifts from God
- God is concerned for the oppressed and afflicted

Vital statistics:
- Where: Ephraim
- Occupation: Homemaker
- Relatives: Husband: Elkanah. Son: Samuel. Later, three other sons and two daughters
- Contemporary: Eli, the priest

Key verses:
"She said, 'Oh, my lord! As your soul lives, my lord, I am the woman who stood here beside you, praying to the LORD. For this boy I prayed, and the LORD has given me my petition which I asked of Him. So I have also dedicated him to the LORD; as long as he lives he is dedicated to the LORD' " (1 Samuel 1:26 28).

Her story is told in 1 Samuel 1; 2.

2:18 Samuel wore a linen ephod. *Ephods,* long sleeveless vests made of plain linen, were worn by all priests. The high priest's ephod carried special significance. It was embroidered with a variety of bright colors. Attached to it was the breastplate, a bib-like garment with gold embroidered shoulder straps. Twelve precious gemstones were attached to the breastplate, each stone representing one of the tribes of Israel. A pouch on the ephod held the Urim and the Thummim, two small objects used to determine God's will in certain national matters.

2:21 God honored the desires of faithful Hannah. We never hear about Peninnah or her children again, but Samuel was used mightily by God. God also gave Hannah five children in addition to Samuel. God often blesses us in ways we do not expect. Hannah never expected to have a child at her age, much less six children! Don't resent God's timing. His blessings might not be immediate, but they will come if we are faithful to do what he says in his Word.

23 He said to them, "Why do you do such things, the evil things that I hear from all
these people?
24 "No, my sons; for the report is not good which I hear the LORD'S people circulating.
25 "If one man sins against another, God will mediate for him; but if a man sins against
the LORD, who can intercede for him?" But they would not listen to the voice of their
father, for the LORD desired to put them to death.
26 Now the boy Samuel was growing in stature and in favor both with the LORD and
with men.
27 Then a man of God came to Eli and said to him, "Thus says the LORD, 'Did I *not*
indeed reveal Myself to the house of your father when they were in Egypt *in bondage* to
Pharaoh's house?
28 'Did I *not* choose them from all the tribes of Israel to be My priests, to go up to My
altar, to burn incense, to carry an ephod before Me; and did I *not* give to the house of
your father all the fire *offerings* of the sons of Israel?
29 'Why do you kick at My sacrifice and at My offering which I have commanded *in My*
dwelling, and honor your sons above Me, by making yourselves fat with the choicest of
every offering of My people Israel?'
30 "Therefore the LORD God of Israel declares, 'I did indeed say that your house and
the house of your father should walk before Me forever'; but now the LORD declares,
'Far be it from Me—for those who honor Me I will honor, and those who despise Me
will be lightly esteemed.
31 'Behold, the days are coming when I will break your strength and the strength of
your father's house so that there will not be an old man in your house.
32 'You will see the distress of *My* dwelling, in *spite of* all the good that I do for Israel;
and an old man will not be in your house forever.
33 'Yet I will not cut off every man of yours from My altar so that your eyes will fail
from weeping and your soul grieve, and all the increase of your house will die in the prime
of life.
34 'This will be the sign to you which will come concerning your two sons, Hophni and
Phinehas: on the same day both of them will die.
35 'But I will raise up for Myself a faithful priest who will do according to what is in My
heart and in My soul; and I will build him an enduring house, and he will walk before
My anointed always.
36 'Everyone who is left in your house will come and bow down to him for a piece of
silver or a loaf of bread and say, "Please assign me to one of the priest's offices so that I
may eat a piece of bread." ' "

The Prophetic Call to Samuel

3 Now the boy Samuel was ministering to the LORD before Eli. And word from the
LORD was rare in those days, visions were infrequent.

2:24 1 Kin 15:26

2:25 Deut 1:17; Num 15:30; 1 Sam 3:14; Heb 10:26, 27; Josh 11:20

2:26 1 Sam 2:21; Luke 2:52

2:27 Deut 33:1; Judg 13:6; Ex 4:14-16; 12:1, 43

2:28 Ex 28:1-4; 30:7, 8; Lev 8:7, 8; Lev 7:35, 36

2:29 1 Sam 2:13-17; Deut 12:5-9; Ps 26:8; Matt 10:37

2:30 Ex 29:9; Num 25:13; Ps 50:23; Mal 2:9

2:31 1 Sam 4:11-18; 22:17-20

2:32 1 Kin 2:26, 27; Zech 8:4

2:34 1 Sam 10:7-9; 1 Kin 13:3; 1 Sam 4:11, 17

2:35 1 Sam 3:1; 7:9; 9:12, 13; 1 Sam 8:3-5; 25:28; 2 Sam 7:11, 27; 1 Kin 11:38; 1 Sam 10:9, 10; 12:3; 16:13

3:1 1 Sam 2:11, 18; Ps 74:9; Ezek 7:26; Amos 8:11, 12

2:23–25 Eli's sons knew better, but they continued to disobey God deliberately by cheating, seducing, and robbing the people. Therefore, God planned to kill them. Any sin is wrong, but sin carried out deliberately and deceitfully is the worst kind. When we sin out of ignorance, we deserve punishment. But when we sin intentionally, the consequences will be more severe. Don't ignore God's warnings about sin. Abandon sin before it becomes a way of life.

2:25 Does a loving God really will or want to put people to death? Consider the situation in the tabernacle. A person made an offering in order to have his sins forgiven, and Eli's sons stole the offering and made a sham of the person's repentant attitude. God, in his love for Israel, could not permit this situation to continue. He allowed Eli's sons to die as a result of their own boastful presumption. They took the ark into battle, thinking it would protect them. But God withdrew his protection, and the wicked sons of Eli were killed (4:10–11).

2:29 Eli had a difficult time rearing his sons. He apparently did not take any strong disciplinary action with them when he became aware of their wrongdoing. But Eli was not just a father trying to handle his rebellious sons; he was the high priest ignoring the sins of priests under his jurisdiction. As a result, the Lord took the necessary disciplinary action that Eli would not.

Eli was guilty of honoring his sons above God by letting them continue in their sinful ways. Is there a situation in your life, family, or work that you allow to continue even though you know it is wrong? If so, you may become as guilty as those engaged in the wrong act.

2:31, 35–36 For the fulfillment of this prediction see 1 Kings 2:26–27. This is where Solomon removed Abiathar from his position, thus ending Eli's line. Then God raised up Zadok, a priest under David and then high priest under Solomon. Zadok's line was probably still in place as late as the days of Ezra.

2:35 "My anointed" refers to the king (see 2:10). God was saying that his faithful priest would serve his king forever.

3:1–5 Although God had spoken directly and audibly with Moses and Joshua, his word became rare during the three centuries of rule by judges. By Eli's time, no prophets were speaking God's messages to Israel. Why? Look at the attitude of Eli's sons. They either refused to listen to God or allowed greed to get in the way of any communication with him.

2 It happened at that time as Eli was lying down in his place (now his eyesight had
begun to grow dim *and* he could not see *well),*
3 and the lamp of God had not yet gone out, and Samuel was lying down in the temple of the LORD where the ark of God *was,*
4 that the LORD called Samuel; and he said, "Here I am."
5 Then he ran to Eli and said, "Here I am, for you called me." But he said, "I did not
call, lie down again." So he went and lay down.
6 The LORD called yet again, "Samuel!" So Samuel arose and went to Eli and said,
"Here I am, for you called me." But he answered, "I did not call, my son, lie down again."
7 Now Samuel did not yet know the LORD, nor had the word of the LORD yet been
revealed to him.
8 So the LORD called Samuel again for the third time. And he arose and went to Eli
and said, "Here I am, for you called me." Then Eli discerned that the LORD was calling
the boy.
9 And Eli said to Samuel, "Go lie down, and it shall be if He calls you, that you shall
say, 'Speak, LORD, for Your servant is listening.' " So Samuel went and lay down in his
place.
10 Then the LORD came and stood and called as at other times, "Samuel! Samuel!"
And Samuel said, "Speak, for Your servant is listening."
11 The LORD said to Samuel, "Behold, I am about to do a thing in Israel at which both
ears of everyone who hears it will tingle.
12 "In that day I will carry out against Eli all that I have spoken concerning his house,
from beginning to end.
13 "For I have told him that I am about to judge his house forever for the iniquity which
he knew, because his sons brought a curse on themselves and he did not rebuke them.
14 "Therefore I have sworn to the house of Eli that the iniquity of Eli's house shall not
be atoned for by sacrifice or offering forever."
15 So Samuel lay down until morning. Then he opened the doors of the house of the
LORD. But Samuel was afraid to tell the vision to Eli.
16 Then Eli called Samuel and said, "Samuel, my son." And he said, "Here I am."
17 He said, "What is the word that He spoke to you? Please do not hide it from me.
May God do so to you, and more also, if you hide anything from me of all the words that
He spoke to you."
18 So Samuel told him everything and hid nothing from him. And he said, "It is the
LORD; let Him do what seems good to Him."
19 Thus Samuel grew and the LORD was with him and let none of his words fail.
20 All Israel from Dan even to Beersheba knew that Samuel was confirmed as a prophet
of the LORD.
21 And the LORD appeared again at Shiloh, because the LORD revealed Himself to
Samuel at Shiloh by the word of the LORD.

3:2 Gen 27:1; 48:10; 1 Sam 4:15
3:3 Ex 25:31-37; Lev 24:2, 3
3:4 Is 6:8
3:7 Acts 19:2; 1 Cor 13:11
3:11 2 Kin 21:12; Jer 19:3
3:12 1 Sam 2:27-36
3:13 1 Sam 2:29-31; 1 Sam 2:22; 1 Sam 2:12, 17, 22; Deut 17:12; 21:18
3:14 Lev 15:31; Is 22:14
3:15 1 Chr 15:23; 1 Sam 3:10
3:17 2 Sam 3:35
3:18 Ex 34:5-7; Lev 10:3; Job 2:10; Is 39:8
3:19 1 Sam 2:21; Gen 21:22; 28:15; 39:2; 1 Sam 9:6
3:20 Judg 20:1
3:21 Gen 12:7; 1 Sam 3:10

Listening and responding is vital in a relationship with God. Although God does not always use the sound of a human voice, he always speaks clearly through his Word. To receive his messages, we must be ready to listen and to act upon what he tells us. Like Samuel, be ready to say "Here I am" when God calls you to action.

3:2–3 The ark of God was kept in the holy of holies, the innermost room of the tabernacle where only the high priest could enter once a year. In front of the holy of holies was the holy place, a small room where the other sacred furniture of the tabernacle was kept (the altar of incense, the bread of the Presence, the lampstand). Just outside the holy place was a court with small rooms where the priests were to stay. Samuel probably slept here with the other priests, only a few yards away from the ark.

3:8–9 One would naturally expect an audible message from God to be given to the priest Eli and not to the child Samuel. Eli was older and more experienced, and he held the proper position. But God's chain of command is based on faith, not on age or position. In finding faithful followers, God may use unexpected channels. Be prepared for the Lord to work at any place, at any time, and through anyone he chooses.

3:13 Eli had spent his entire life in service to God. His responsibility was to oversee all the worship in Israel. But in pursuing this great mission he neglected the responsibilities in his own home. Don't let your desire to do God's work cause you to neglect your family. If you do, your mission may degenerate into a quest for personal importance, and your family will suffer the consequences of your neglect.

3:14 *Atoned for* means "forgiven." God was saying that the sin of Eli's sons could not be covered by sacrifice and that they would be punished.

3:20 The phrase "from Dan even to Beersheba" was often used to describe the boundaries of the promised land. Dan was one of the northernmost cities in the land, and Beersheba one of the cities farthest south. In this context, it was a way of emphasizing that *everyone* in Israel knew that Samuel was called to be a prophet.

2. War with the Philistines

Philistines Take the Ark in Victory

4 Thus the word of Samuel came to all Israel. Now Israel went out to meet the Philistines in battle and camped beside Ebenezer while the Philistines camped in Aphek.
2 The Philistines drew up in battle array to meet Israel. When the battle spread, Israel
was defeated before the Philistines who killed about four thousand men on the battlefield.
3 When the people came into the camp, the elders of Israel said, "Why has the LORD
defeated us today before the Philistines? Let us take to ourselves from Shiloh the ark of
the covenant of the LORD, that it may come among us and deliver us from the power of
our enemies."
4 So the people sent to Shiloh, and from there they carried the ark of the covenant of
the LORD of hosts who sits *above* the cherubim; and the two sons of Eli, Hophni and
Phinehas, *were* there with the ark of the covenant of God.
5 As the ark of the covenant of the LORD came into the camp, all Israel shouted with
a great shout, so that the earth resounded.
6 When the Philistines heard the noise of the shout, they said, "What *does* the noise
of this great shout in the camp of the Hebrews *mean?*" Then they understood that the
ark of the LORD had come into the camp.
7 The Philistines were afraid, for they said, "God has come into the camp." And they
said, "Woe to us! For nothing like this has happened before.
8 "Woe to us! Who shall deliver us from the hand of these mighty gods? These are the
gods who smote the Egyptians with all *kinds of* plagues in the wilderness.
9 "Take courage and be men, O Philistines, or you will become slaves to the Hebrews,
as they have been slaves to you; therefore, be men and fight."
10 So the Philistines fought and Israel was defeated, and every man fled to his tent;
and the slaughter was very great, for there fell of Israel thirty thousand foot soldiers.
11 And the ark of God was taken; and the two sons of Eli, Hophni and Phinehas, died.

4:1 1 Sam 7:12; Josh 12:18; 1 Sam 29:1
4:3 Josh 7:7, 8; Num 10:35; Josh 6:6
4:4 Ex 25:22; 2 Sam 6:2; Ps 80:1
4:5 Josh 6:5, 20
4:7 Ex 15:14
4:9 1 Cor 16:13; Judg 13:1; 1 Sam 14:21
4:10 Deut 28:15, 25; 1 Sam 4:2; 2 Sam 18:17; 19:8; 2 Kin 14:12; 2 Chr 25:22
4:11 1 Sam 2:34; Ps 78:56-64

4:1 The Philistines, descendants of Noah's son Ham, settled along the southeastern Mediterranean coast between Egypt and Gaza. They were originally one of the "Sea Peoples" who had migrated to the Middle East in ships from Greece and Crete. By Samuel's time, these warlike people were well established in five of Gaza's cities in southwest Canaan and were constantly pressing inland against the Israelites. Throughout this time, the Philistines were Israel's major enemy.

4:3 The ark of the covenant contained the Ten Commandments given by God to Moses. The ark was supposed to be kept in the holy of holies, a sacred part of the tabernacle that only the high priest could enter once a year. Hophni and Phinehas desecrated the room by unlawfully entering it and removing the ark.

The Israelites rightly recognized the great holiness of the ark, but they thought that the ark itself—the wood and metal box—was their source of power. They began to use it as a good luck charm, expecting it to protect them from their enemies. A symbol of God does not guarantee his presence and power. Their attitude toward the ark came perilously close to idol worship. When the ark was captured by their enemies, they thought that Israel's glory was gone (4:19–22) and that God had deserted them (7:1–2). God uses his power according to his own wisdom and will. He responds to the faith of those who seek him.

4:4 "The LORD of hosts who sits above the cherubim" conveys that God's presence rested on the ark of the covenant between the two golden cherubim (or angels) attached to its lid. The people believed that the ark would bring victory when Hophni and Phinehas carried it into battle.

4:5–8 The Philistines were afraid because they remembered stories about God's intervention for Israel when they left Egypt. But Israel had turned away from God and was clinging to only a form of godliness, a symbol of former victories.

People (and churches) often try to live on the memories of God's blessings. The Israelites wrongly assumed that because God had given them victory in the past, he would do it again, even though they had strayed far from him. Today, as in Bible times, spiritual victories come through a continually renewed relationship with God. Don't live off the past. Keep your relationship with God new and fresh.

4:11 This event fulfills the prophecy in 2:34 stating that Eli's sons, Hophni and Phinehas, would die "on the same day."

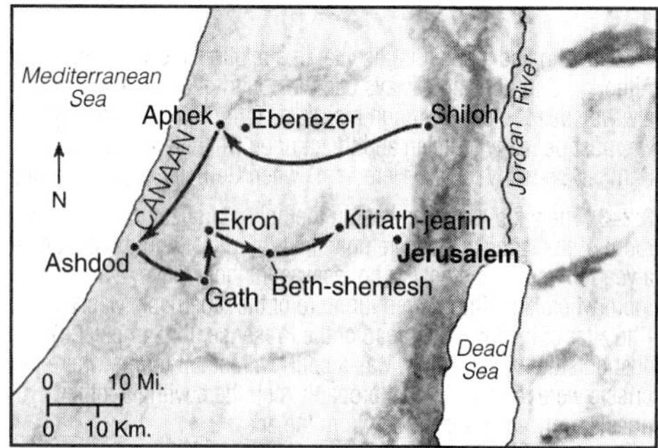

THE ARK'S TRAVELS Eli's sons took the ark from Shiloh to the battlefield on the lower plains at Ebenezer and Aphek. The Philistines captured the ark and took it to Ashdod, Gath, and Ekron. Plagues forced the people to send the ark back to Israel, where it finally was taken by cattle-driven carts to Beth-shemesh and on to the home of Eleazar in Kiriath-jearim.

4:12 Josh 7:6; 2 Sam 1:2; 15:32; Neh 9:1; Job 2:12
4:13 1 Sam 1:9; 4:18
4:15 1 Sam 3:2; 1 Kin 14:4
4:16 2 Sam 1:4
4:18 1 Sam 4:13

12 Now a man of Benjamin ran from the battle line and came to Shiloh the same day
with his clothes torn and dust on his head.
13 When he came, behold, Eli was sitting on *his* seat by the road eagerly watching,
because his heart was trembling for the ark of God. So the man came to tell *it* in the city,
and all the city cried out.
14 When Eli heard the noise of the outcry, he said, "What *does* the noise of this commotion *mean?*" Then the man came hurriedly and told Eli.
15 Now Eli was ninety-eight years old, and his eyes were set so that he could not see.
16 The man said to Eli, "I am the one who came from the battle line. Indeed, I escaped
from the battle line today." And he said, "How did things go, my son?"
17 Then the one who brought the news replied, "Israel has fled before the Philistines
and there has also been a great slaughter among the people, and your two sons also,
Hophni and Phinehas, are dead, and the ark of God has been taken."
18 When he mentioned the ark of God, Eli fell off the seat backward beside the gate,
and his neck was broken and he died, for he was old and heavy. Thus he judged Israel
forty years.

ISRAELITES VERSUS PHILISTINES
The Israelites and Philistines were arch-enemies and constantly fought. Here are some of their confrontations, found in 1 Samuel and 2 Samuel. When Israel trusted God for the victory, they always won.

Location of the Battle	*Winner*	*Comments*	*Reference*
Aphek to Ebenezer	Philistines	The ark was captured and Eli's sons killed	1 Samuel 4:1–11
Mizpah	Israelites	After the ark was returned, the Philistines planned to attack again, but God confused them. Israel chased the Philistines back to Beth-car	1 Samuel 7:7–14
Geba	Israelites under Jonathan	One detachment destroyed	1 Samuel 13:3–4
Gilgal	A standoff	The Israelites lost their nerve and hid	1 Samuel 13:6–17
Michmash	Israelites	Jonathan and his armor bearer said it didn't matter how many enemies there were. If God was with them, they would win. They began the battle, and the army completed it	1 Samuel 13:23—14:23
Valley of Elah	Israelites	David and Goliath	1 Samuel 17:1–58
?	Israelites	David killed 200 Philistines to earn a wife	1 Samuel 18:17–30
Keilah	Israelites under David	David protected the threshing floors from Philistine looters	1 Samuel 23:1–5
Aphek, Jezreel, to Mount Gilboa	Philistines	Saul and Jonathan killed	1 Samuel 29:1; 31:1–13
Baal-perazim	Israelites	The Philistines tried to capture King David	2 Samuel 5:17–25
Metheg-ammah ("the chief city," maybe near Gath)	Israelites	There was very little trouble with the Philistines after this defeat	2 Samuel 8:1
?	Israelites	Abishai saved David from a Philistine giant	2 Samuel 21:15–17
Gob	Israelites	Other giants were killed, including Goliath's brother	2 Samuel 21:18–22

4:12 At this time, the city of Shiloh was Israel's religious center (Joshua 18:1; 1 Samuel 4:3). The tabernacle was permanently set up there. Because Israel did not have a civil capital—a seat of national government—Shiloh was the natural place for a messenger to deliver the sad news from the battle. Many scholars believe that it was during this battle that Shiloh was destroyed (Jeremiah 7:12; 26:2–6; also see the note on 7:1).

4:18 Eli was Israel's judge and high priest. His death marked the end of the dark period of the judges when most of the nation ignored God. Although Samuel was also a judge, his career saw the transition from Israel's rule by judges to the nation's monarchy. He began the great revival that Israel would experience for the next century. The Bible does not say who became the next high priest (Samuel was not eligible because he was not a direct descendant of Aaron), but Samuel acted as high priest at this time by offering the important sacrifices throughout Israel.

19 Now his daughter-in-law, Phinehas's wife, was pregnant and about to give birth; and
when she heard the news that the ark of God was taken and that her father-in-law and
her husband had died, she kneeled down and gave birth, for her pains came upon her.
20 And about the time of her death the women who stood by her said to her, "Do not
be afraid, for you have given birth to a son." But she did not answer or pay attention.
21 And she called the boy [3]Ichabod, saying, "The glory has departed from Israel," because the ark of God was taken and because of her father-in-law and her husband.
22 She said, "The glory has departed from Israel, for the ark of God was taken."

Capture of the Ark Provokes God

5 Now the Philistines took the ark of God and brought it from Ebenezer to Ashdod.
2 Then the Philistines took the ark of God and brought it to the house of Dagon
and set it by Dagon.
3 When the Ashdodites arose early the next morning, behold, Dagon had fallen on
his face to the ground before the ark of the LORD. So they took Dagon and set him in his
place again.
4 But when they arose early the next morning, behold, Dagon had fallen on his face
to the ground before the ark of the LORD. And the head of Dagon and both the palms of
his hands *were* cut off on the threshold; only the trunk of Dagon was left to him.
5 Therefore neither the priests of Dagon nor all who enter Dagon's house tread on
the threshold of Dagon in Ashdod to this day.
6 Now the hand of the LORD was heavy on the Ashdodites, and He ravaged them and
smote them with tumors, both Ashdod and its territories.
7 When the men of Ashdod saw that it was so, they said, "The ark of the God of Israel must not remain with us, for His hand is severe on us and on Dagon our god."
8 So they sent and gathered all the lords of the Philistines to them and said, "What
shall we do with the ark of the God of Israel?" And they said, "Let the ark of the God of
Israel be brought around to Gath." And they brought the ark of the God of Israel *around.*
9 After they had brought it around, the hand of the LORD was against the city with
very great confusion; and He smote the men of the city, both young and old, so that tumors broke out on them.
10 So they sent the ark of God to Ekron. And as the ark of God came to Ekron the
Ekronites cried out, saying, "They have brought the ark of the God of Israel around to
us, to kill us and our people."
11 They sent therefore and gathered all the lords of the Philistines and said, "Send away
the ark of the God of Israel, and let it return to its own place, so that it will not kill us
and our people." For there was a deadly confusion throughout the city; the hand of God
was very heavy there.
12 And the men who did not die were smitten with tumors and the cry of the city went
up to heaven.

The Ark Returned to Israel

6 Now the ark of the LORD had been in the country of the Philistines seven months.
2 And the Philistines called for the priests and the diviners, saying, "What shall we
do with the ark of the LORD? Tell us how we shall send it to its place."

4:20 Gen 35:16-19
4:21 Ps 26:8; Jer 2:11; 1 Sam 4:11
5:1 1 Sam 4:1; 7:12; Josh 13:3
5:2 Judg 16:23-30; 1 Chr 10:8-10
5:3 Is 19:1; 46:1, 2; Is 46:7
5:4 Ezek 6:4, 6; Mic 1:7
5:5 Zeph 1:9
5:6 Ex 9:3; 1 Sam 5:7, 11; Ps 32:4; 145:20; 147:6; Acts 13:11; 1 Sam 6:5; Deut 28:27; Ps 78:66
5:8 1 Sam 5:11; 29:6-11
5:9 Deut 2:15; 1 Sam 5:11; 7:13; 12:15; 1 Sam 5:6
5:11 1 Sam 5:8; 1 Sam 5:6, 9
5:12 Ex 12:30; Is 15:3
6:2 Gen 41:8; Ex 7:11; Is 2:6

3 I.e. No glory

4:19–22 This incident illustrates the spiritual darkness and decline of Israel. This young boy, Ichabod, was supposed to succeed his father Phinehas in the priesthood, but his father had been killed because he was an evil man who desecrated the tabernacle. The terror of God's leaving his people overshadowed the joy of childbirth. When sin dominates our lives, even God-given joys and pleasures seem empty.

5:1ff Dagon was the chief god of the Philistines, whom they believed sent rain and assured a bountiful harvest. But the Philistines, like most of their pagan neighbors, worshiped many gods. The more gods they could have on their side, the more secure they felt. That was why they wanted the ark, thinking that if it helped the Israelites, it could help them too. But when the people living nearby began to get sick and die, the Philistines realized that the ark was not a good omen. It was a source of greater power than they had ever seen—power they could not control.

5:6–7 Although the Philistines had just witnessed a great victory by Israel's God over their god, Dagon, they didn't act upon that insight until they were afflicted with tumors (possibly bubonic plague). Similarly, today many people don't respond to Biblical truth until they experience pain. Are you willing to listen to God for truth's sake, or do you turn to him only when you are hurting?

5:8 The Philistines were governed by five rulers, or lords. Each lord lived in a different city—Gath, Ekron, Ashdod, Ashkelon, Gaza. The ark was taken to three of these capital cities, and each time it brought great trouble and chaos to the citizens.

6:4 1 Sam 5:6, 9, 12; 6:17; Josh 13:3; Judg 3:3; 1 Sam 6:17, 18

6:5 Josh 7:19; 1 Chr 16:28, 29; Is 42:12; Jer 13:16; John 9:24; Rev 14:7; 1 Sam 5:6, 11; 1 Sam 5:3, 4, 7

3 They said, "If you send away the ark of the God of Israel, do not send it empty; but you shall surely return to Him a guilt offering. Then you will be healed and it will be known to you why His hand is not removed from you."
4 Then they said, "What shall be the guilt offering which we shall return to Him?" And they said, "Five golden tumors and five golden mice *according to* the number of the lords of the Philistines, for one plague was on all of you and on your lords.
5 "So you shall make likenesses of your tumors and likenesses of your mice that ravage the land, and you shall give glory to the God of Israel; perhaps He will ease His hand from you, your gods, and your land.

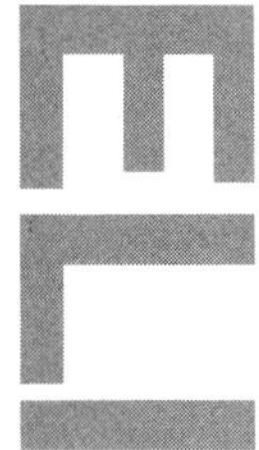

Eli was one Old Testament person with a very modern problem. The recognition and respect he earned in public did not extend to his handling of his private affairs. He may have been an excellent priest, but he was a poor parent. His sons brought him grief and ruin. He lacked two important qualities needed for effective parental discipline: firm resolve and corrective action.

Eli responded to situations rather than solving them. But even his responses tended to be weak. God pointed out his sons' errors, but Eli did little to correct them. The contrast between God's dealing with Eli and Eli's dealing with his sons is clear—God gave warning, spelled out the consequences of disobedience, and then acted. Eli only warned. Children need to learn that their parents' words and actions go together. Both love and discipline must be spoken as well as acted out.

But Eli had another problem. He was more concerned with the symbols of his religion than with the God they represented. For Eli, the ark of the covenant had become a relic to be protected rather than a reminder of the Protector. His faith shifted from the Creator to the created.

It may be easier to worship things we can see, whether buildings, people, or Scripture itself, but such tangible things have no power in themselves. This book you hold is either merely a respectable religious relic, or it is the sharp and effective Word of God. Your attitude toward it is largely shaped by your relationship to the God from whom it comes. A relic or antique has to be carefully stored away; God's Word has to be used and obeyed. Which attitude accurately describes your approach to the Word of God?

Strengths and accomplishments:
- Judged Israel for 40 years
- Spoke with Hannah, the mother of Samuel, and assured her of God's blessing
- Reared and trained Samuel, the greatest judge of Israel

Weaknesses and mistakes:
- Failed to discipline his sons or correct them when they sinned
- Tended to react to situations rather than take decisive action
- Saw the ark of the covenant as a relic to be cherished rather than as a symbol of God's presence with Israel

Lessons from his life:
- Parents need to discipline their children responsibly
- Life is more than simply reacting; it demands action
- Past victories cannot substitute for present trust

Vital statistics:
- Where: Shiloh
- Occupations: High priest and judge of Israel
- Relatives: Sons: Hophni and Phinehas
- Contemporary: Samuel

Key verses:
"The LORD said to Samuel, 'Behold, I am about to do a thing in Israel at which both ears of everyone who hears it will tingle. In that day I will carry out against Eli all that I have spoken concerning his house, from beginning to end. For I have told him that I am about to judge his house forever for the iniquity which he knew, because his sons brought a curse on themselves and he did not rebuke them. Therefore I have sworn to the house of Eli that the iniquity of Eli's house shall not be atoned for by sacrifice or offering forever' " (1 Samuel 3:11–14).

His story is told in 1 Samuel 1—4. He is also mentioned in 1 Kings 2:26–27.

6:3 What was this guilt offering supposed to accomplish? This was a normal reaction to trouble in the Canaanite religion. The Philistines thought their problems were the result of their gods being angry. They recognized their guilt in taking the ark and now were trying everything they could to placate Israel's God. The diviners (6:2) probably helped choose the gift they thought would placate Yahweh. But the offering consisted of images of tumors and mice, not the kind of guilt offering prescribed in God's laws (Leviticus 5:14—6:7; 7:1–10). How easy it is to design our own methods of acknowledging God rather than serving him in the way he requires.

6 "Why then do you harden your hearts as the Egyptians and Pharaoh hardened their
hearts? When He had severely dealt with them, did they not allow the people to go, and
they departed?
7 "Now therefore, take and prepare a new cart and two milch cows on which there has
never been a yoke; and hitch the cows to the cart and take their calves home, away from
them.
8 "Take the ark of the LORD and place it on the cart; and put the articles of gold which
you return to Him as a guilt offering in a box by its side. Then send it away that it may go.
9 "Watch, if it goes up by the way of its own territory to Beth-shemesh, then He has
done us this great evil. But if not, then we will know that it was not His hand that struck
us; it happened to us by chance."
10 Then the men did so, and took two milch cows and hitched them to the cart, and
shut up their calves at home.
11 They put the ark of the LORD on the cart, and the box with the golden mice and the
likenesses of their tumors.
12 And the cows took the straight way in the direction of Beth-shemesh; they went along
the highway, lowing as they went, and did not turn aside to the right or to the left. And
the lords of the Philistines followed them to the border of Beth-shemesh.
13 Now *the people of* Beth-shemesh were reaping their wheat harvest in the valley, and
they raised their eyes and saw the ark and were glad to see *it.*
14 The cart came into the field of Joshua the Beth-shemite and stood there where there
was a large stone; and they split the wood of the cart and offered the cows as a burnt
offering to the LORD.
15 The Levites took down the ark of the LORD and the box that was with it, in which
were the articles of gold, and put them on the large stone; and the men of Beth-shemesh
offered burnt offerings and sacrificed sacrifices that day to the LORD.
16 When the five lords of the Philistines saw it, they returned to Ekron that day.
17 These are the golden tumors which the Philistines returned for a guilt offering
to the LORD: one for Ashdod, one for Gaza, one for Ashkelon, one for Gath, one for
Ekron;
18 and the golden mice, *according* to the number of all the cities of the Philistines belonging to the five lords, both of fortified cities and of country villages. The large stone
on which they set the ark of the LORD *is a witness* to this day in the field of Joshua the
Beth-shemite.
19 He struck down some of the men of Beth-shemesh because they had looked into
the ark of the LORD. He struck down of all the people, 50,070 men, and the people
mourned because the LORD had struck the people with a great slaughter.
20 The men of Beth-shemesh said, "Who is able to stand before the LORD, this holy
God? And to whom shall He go up from us?"
21 So they sent messengers to the inhabitants of Kiriath-jearim, saying, "The Philistines have brought back the ark of the LORD; come down and take it up to you."

6:6 Ex 7:13; 8:15, 32; 9:34; 14:17; Ex 12:31
6:7 2 Sam 6:3; Num 19:2; Deut 21:3, 4
6:8 1 Sam 6:4, 5; 1 Sam 6:3
6:9 Josh 15:10; 21:16; 1 Sam 6:3
6:12 1 Sam 6:9; Num 20:19
6:14 2 Sam 24:22; 1 Kin 19:21
6:15 Josh 3:3
6:16 Josh 13:3; Judg 3:3
6:17 1 Sam 6:4
6:18 Deut 3:5; 1 Sam 6:14, 15
6:19 Ex 19:21; Num 4:5, 15, 20; 2 Sam 6:7
6:20 Lev 11:44, 45; 2 Sam 6:9; Mal 3:2; Rev 6:17
6:21 Josh 9:17; 15:9, 60; 1 Chr 13:5, 6

6:7–12 The Philistine priests and diviners devised a test to see if God was really the one who had caused all their recent troubles. Two cows who had just given birth were hitched to a cart and sent toward Israel's border carrying the ark of the covenant. For a cow to leave her nursing calf, she would have to go against all her motherly instincts. Only God, who has power over the natural order, could cause this to happen. God sent the cows to Israel, not to pass the Philistines' test, but to show them his mighty power.

6:9 The Philistines acknowledged the existence of the Hebrew God, but only as one of many deities whose favor they sought. Thinking of God in this way made it easy for them to ignore his demand that people worship him alone. Many people "worship" God this way. They see God as just one ingredient in a successful life. But God is far more than an ingredient—he is the source of life itself. Are you a "Philistine," seeing God's favor as only an ingredient of the good life?

6:19 Why were people killed for looking into the ark? The Israelites had made an idol of the ark. They had tried to harness God's power, to use it for their own purposes (victory in battle). But the Lord of the universe cannot be controlled by humans. To protect the Israelites from his power, he had warned them not even to look at the sacred sanctuary objects in the holy of holies or they would die (Numbers 4:20). Only Levites were allowed to move the ark. Because of their disobedience, God carried out his promised judgment.

God could not allow the people to think they could use his power for their own ends. He could not permit them to disregard his warnings and come into his presence lightly. He did not want the cycle of disrespect, disobedience, and defeat to start all over again. God did not kill the men of Beth-shemesh to be cruel. He killed them because overlooking their presumptuous sin would encourage the whole nation of Israel to ignore God.

Deliverance from the Philistines

7 And the men of Kiriath-jearim came and took the ark of the LORD and brought it
into the house of Abinadab on the hill, and consecrated Eleazar his son to keep the
ark of the LORD.
2 From the day that the ark remained at Kiriath-jearim, the time was long, for it was
twenty years; and all the house of Israel lamented after the LORD.
3 Then Samuel spoke to all the house of Israel, saying, "If you return to the LORD
with all your heart, remove the foreign gods and the Ashtaroth from among you and
direct your hearts to the LORD and serve Him alone; and He will deliver you from the
hand of the Philistines."
4 So the sons of Israel removed the Baals and the Ashtaroth and served the LORD
alone.
5 Then Samuel said, "Gather all Israel to Mizpah and I will pray to the LORD for you."
6 They gathered to Mizpah, and drew water and poured it out before the LORD, and
fasted on that day and said there, "We have sinned against the LORD." And Samuel judged
the sons of Israel at Mizpah.
7 Now when the Philistines heard that the sons of Israel had gathered to Mizpah, the
lords of the Philistines went up against Israel. And when the sons of Israel heard it, they
were afraid of the Philistines.
8 Then the sons of Israel said to Samuel, "Do not cease to cry to the LORD our God
for us, that He may save us from the hand of the Philistines."
9 Samuel took a suckling lamb and offered it for a whole burnt offering to the LORD;
and Samuel cried to the LORD for Israel and the LORD answered him.
10 Now Samuel was offering up the burnt offering, and the Philistines drew near to
battle against Israel. But the LORD thundered with a great thunder on that day against
the Philistines and confused them, so that they were routed before Israel.
11 The men of Israel went out of Mizpah and pursued the Philistines, and struck them
down as far as below Beth-car.
12 Then Samuel took a stone and set it between Mizpah and Shen, and named it [4]Eb-
enezer, saying, "Thus far the LORD has helped us."

4 I.e. The stone of help

7:1 2 Sam 6:3, 4

7:3 1 Kin 8:48; Is 55:7; Hos 6:1; Joel 2:12-14; Gen 35:2; Josh 24:14, 23; Judg 10:16; Judg 2:13; 1 Sam 31:10; Deut 13:4; 2 Chr 19:3; Deut 6:13; 10:20; 13:4; Josh 24:14; Matt 4:10; Luke 4:8

7:5 Judg 10:17; 20:1; 1 Sam 8:6; 12:17-19

7:6 1 Sam 1:15; Ps 62:8; Lam 2:19; Lev 16:29; Neh 9:1; Judg 10:10; 1 Kin 8:47; Ps 106:6

7:7 1 Sam 13:6; 17:11

7:8 1 Sam 12:19-24; Is 37:4

7:9 Lev 22:27; Ps 99:6; Jer 15:1

7:10 1 Sam 2:10; 2 Sam 22:14, 15; Ps 29:3, 4; Josh 10:10; Ps 18:14

7:12 Gen 35:14; Josh 4:9; 24:26

7:1 The ark was taken to Kiriath-jearim, a city near the battlefield, for safekeeping, and Eleazar was given the task of caring for it. Why wasn't it taken back to the tabernacle at Shiloh? Shiloh had probably been defeated and destroyed by the Philistines in an earlier battle (4:1–18; Jeremiah 26:2–6) because of the evil deeds of its priests (2:12–17). Apparently, the tabernacle and its furniture were saved because we read that the tabernacle was set up in Nob during Saul's reign (21:1–6) and in Gibeon during the reigns of David and Solomon (1 Chronicles 16:39; 21:29, 30; 2 Chronicles 1). Shiloh, however, is never again mentioned in the historical books of the Old Testament. Samuel's new home became Ramah (7:15–17; 8:4), his birthplace (further evidence of Shiloh's destruction).

7:2–3 Israel mourned and sorrow gripped the nation for 20 years. The ark was put away like an unwanted box in an attic, and it seemed as if the Lord had abandoned his people. Samuel, now a grown man, roused them to action by saying that if they were truly sorry, they should do something about it. How easy it is for us to complain about our problems, even to God, while we refuse to act, change, and do what he requires. We don't even take the advice he has already given us. Do you ever feel as if God has abandoned you? Check to see if there is anything he has already told you to do. You may not receive new guidance from God until you have acted on his previous directions.

7:3 Samuel urged the Israelites to get rid of their foreign gods. Idols today are much more subtle than gods of wood and stone, but they are just as dangerous. Whatever holds first place in our lives or controls us is our god. Money, success, material goods, pride, or anything else can be an idol if it takes the place of God in our lives. The Lord alone is worthy of our service and worship, and we must let nothing rival him. If we have "foreign gods," we need to ask God to help us dethrone them, making the true God our first priority.

7:4 Baal was believed to be the son of El, chief deity of the Canaanites. Baal was regarded as the god of thunder and rain, thus he controlled vegetation and agriculture. Ashtaroth was a goddess of love and war (she was called Ishtar in Babylon and Astarte or Aphrodite in Greece). She represented fertility. The Canaanites believed that by the sexual union of Baal and Ashtaroth, the earth would be magically rejuvenated and made fertile.

7:5 Mizpah held special significance for the Israelite nation. It was there that the Israelites had gathered to mobilize against the tribe of Benjamin (Judges 20:1). Samuel was appointed to be leader (7:6), and Saul, Israel's first king, was identified and presented to the people (10:17ff).

7:6 Pouring water on the ground "before the LORD" was a sign of repenting from sin, turning from idols, and determining to obey God alone.

7:6 Samuel became the last in the long line of Israel's judges (leaders), a line that began when Israel first conquered the promised land. For a list of these judges, see the chart in Judges 2. A judge was both a political and a religious leader. God was Israel's true leader, while the judge was to be God's spokesman to the people and administrator of justice throughout the land. While some of Israel's judges relied more on their own judgment than on God's, Samuel's obedience and dedication to God made him one of the greatest judges in Israel's history. (For more on Samuel as a judge, see the note on 4:18.)

7:12 The Israelites had great difficulty with the Philistines, but God rescued them. In response, the people set up a stone as a memorial of God's great help and deliverance. During tough times, we may need to remember the crucial turning points in our past to help us through the present. Memorials can help us remember God's past victories and gain confidence and strength for the present.

13 So the Philistines were subdued and they did not come anymore within the border
of Israel. And the hand of the LORD was against the Philistines all the days of Samuel.
14 The cities which the Philistines had taken from Israel were restored to Israel, from
Ekron even to Gath; and Israel delivered their territory from the hand of the Philistines.
So there was peace between Israel and the Amorites.

Samuel's Ministry

15 Now Samuel judged Israel all the days of his life.
16 He used to go annually on circuit to Bethel and Gilgal and Mizpah, and he judged
Israel in all these places.
17 Then his return *was* to Ramah, for his house *was* there, and there he judged Israel;
and he built there an altar to the LORD.

7:13 Judg 13:1-15; 1 Sam 13:5
7:14 Num 13:29; Josh 10:5-10
7:15 1 Sam 7:6
7:16 Gen 28:19; 35:6; Josh 5:9, 10; 1 Sam 7:5
7:17 1 Sam 1:1, 19; 2:11; Judg 21:4

B. SAMUEL AND SAUL (8:1—15:35)

Samuel judges Israel well, saves them from the Philistines, and leads them back to God. But when he retires, the nation does not want another judge. Instead they demand to be given a king in order to be like the nations around them. Although God is unhappy with their request, he tells Samuel to anoint Saul as Israel's first king. Saul is a skillful soldier who successfully leads the nation into many battles against their enemies. But in God's eyes Saul is a failure because he constantly disobeys and does things his own way. God eventually rejected Saul as king. Sometimes we want to go our own way rather than follow the ways of God. This will always end in ruin as it did for Saul.

1. Saul becomes king of Israel

Israel Demands a King

8 And it came about when Samuel was old that he appointed his sons judges over
Israel.
2 Now the name of his firstborn was Joel, and the name of his second, Abijah; *they*
were judging in Beersheba.
3 His sons, however, did not walk in his ways, but turned aside after dishonest gain
and took bribes and perverted justice.
4 Then all the elders of Israel gathered together and came to Samuel at Ramah;
5 and they said to him, "Behold, you have grown old, and your sons do not walk in
your ways. Now appoint a king for us to judge us like all the nations."
6 But the thing was displeasing in the sight of Samuel when they said, "Give us a king
to judge us." And Samuel prayed to the LORD.
7 The LORD said to Samuel, "Listen to the voice of the people in regard to all that
they say to you, for they have not rejected you, but they have rejected Me from being
king over them.
8 "Like all the deeds which they have done since the day that I brought them up from

8:1 Deut 16:18, 19
8:2 Gen 22:19; 1 Kin 19:3; Amos 5:5
8:3 Ex 23:6, 8; Deut 16:19
8:4 1 Sam 7:17
8:5 Deut 17:14, 15
8:6 1 Sam 12:17; 1 Sam 15:11
8:7 Ex 16:8; 1 Sam 10:19

7:14 In Joshua's time, the Amorites were a powerful tribe scattered throughout the hill country on both sides of the Jordan with a heavy concentration occupying the east side of the Jordan River opposite the Dead Sea. In the context of this verse, however, *Amorites* is another general name for all the inhabitants of Canaan who were not Israelites.

8:1–3 As an old man, Samuel appointed his sons to be judges over Israel in his place. But they turned out to be corrupt, much like Eli's sons (2:12). We don't know why Samuel's sons went wrong, but we do know that Eli was held responsible for his own sons' corruption (2:29–34).

It is impossible to know if Samuel was a bad parent. His children were old enough to be on their own. We must be careful not to blame ourselves for the sins of our children. On the other hand, parenthood is an awesome responsibility, and nothing is more important than molding and shaping our children's lives.

If your grown children are not following God, realize that you can't control them any longer. Don't blame yourself for something that is no longer your responsibility. But if your children are still in your care, know that what you do and teach can profoundly affect your children and lasts a lifetime.

8:4–9 Israel wanted a king for several reasons: (1) Samuel's sons were not fit to lead Israel. (2) The 12 tribes of Israel continually had problems working together because each tribe had its own leader and territory. It was hoped that a king would unite the tribes into one nation and one army. (3) The people wanted to be like the neighboring nations. This is exactly what God didn't want. Having a king would make it easy to forget that God was their real leader. It was not wrong for Israel to want a king; God had mentioned the possibility in Deuteronomy 17:14–20. Yet, in reality, the people were rejecting God as their leader. The Israelites wanted laws, an army, and a human monarch in the place of God. They wanted to run the nation through human strength, even though only God's strength could make them flourish in the hostile land of Canaan.

8:5–6 The people clamored for a king, thinking that a new system of government would bring about a change in the nation. But because their basic problem was disobedience to God, their other problems would only continue under the new administration. What they needed was a unified faith, not a uniform rule.

Had the Israelites submitted to God's leadership, they would have thrived beyond their expectations (Deuteronomy 28:1). Our obedience is weak if we ask God to lead our family or personal life but continue to live by the world's standards and values. Faith in God must touch all the practical areas of life.

Egypt even to this day—in that they have forsaken Me and served other gods—so they
are doing to you also.

8:9 Ezek 3:18; 1 Sam 8:11-18; 10:25

9 "Now then, listen to their voice; however, you shall solemnly warn them and tell them
of the [5]procedure of the king who will reign over them."

Warning concerning a King

8:10 1 Sam 8:4

10 So Samuel spoke all the words of the LORD to the people who had asked of him a
king.

8:11 Deut 17:14-20; 1 Sam 10:25; 1 Sam 14:52; 2 Sam 15:1

11 He said, "This will be the procedure of the king who will reign over you: he will take
your sons and place *them* for himself in his chariots and among his horsemen and they
will run before his chariots.

8:12 Num 31:14; 1 Sam 22:7

12 "He will appoint for himself commanders of thousands and of fifties, and *some* to do
his plowing and to reap his harvest and to make his weapons of war and equipment for
his chariots.
13 "He will also take your daughters for perfumers and cooks and bakers.

8:14 1 Kin 21:7; Ezek 46:18

14 "He will take the best of your fields and your vineyards and your olive groves and
give *them* to his servants.
15 "He will take a tenth of your seed and of your vineyards and give to his officers and
to his servants.
16 "He will also take your male servants and your female servants and your best young
men and your donkeys and use *them* for his work.
17 "He will take a tenth of your flocks, and you yourselves will become his servants.

5 Lit *custom*

SAMUEL

We often wonder about the childhoods of great people. We have little information about the early years of most of the people mentioned in the Bible. One delightful exception is Samuel; he came as a result of God's answer to Hannah's fervent prayer for a child. (In fact, the name *Samuel* comes from the Hebrew expression, "heard of God.") God shaped Samuel from the start. Like Moses, Samuel was called to fill many different roles: judge, priest, prophet, counselor, and God's man at a turning point in the history of Israel. God worked through Samuel because Samuel was willing to be one thing: God's servant.

Samuel showed that those whom God finds faithful in small things will be trusted with greater things. He grew up assisting the high priest (Eli) in the tabernacle until God directed him to other responsibilities. God was able to use Samuel because he was genuinely dedicated to God.

Samuel moved ahead because he was listening to God's directions. Too often we ask God to control our lives without making us give up the goals for which we strive. We ask God to help us get where *we* want to go. The first step in correcting this tendency is to turn over both the control and destination of our lives to him. The second step is to do what we *already know* God requires of us. The third step is to listen for further direction from his Word—God's map for life.

Strengths and accomplishments:
- Used by God to assist Israel's transition from a loosely governed tribal people to a monarchy
- Anointed the first two kings of Israel
- Was the last and most effective of Israel's judges
- Is listed in the Hall of Faith in Hebrews 11

Weakness and mistake:
- Was unable to lead his sons into a close relationship with God

Lessons from his life:
- The significance of what people accomplish is directly related to their relationship with God
- The kind of person we are is more important than anything we might do

Vital statistics:
- Where: Ephraim
- Occupations: Judge, prophet, priest
- Relatives: Mother: Hannah. Father: Elkanah. Sons: Joel and Abijah
- Contemporaries: Eli, Saul, David

Key verses:
"Thus Samuel grew and the LORD was with him and let none of his words fail. All Israel from Dan even to Beersheba knew that Samuel was confirmed as a prophet of the LORD" (1 Samuel 3:19–20).

His story is told in 1 Samuel 1—28. He is also mentioned in Psalm 99:6; Jeremiah 15:1; Acts 3:24; 13:20; Hebrews 11:32.

18 "Then you will cry out in that day because of your king whom you have chosen for
yourselves, but the LORD will not answer you in that day."
19 Nevertheless, the people refused to listen to the voice of Samuel, and they said, "No,
but there shall be a king over us,
20 that we also may be like all the nations, that our king may judge us and go out before us and fight our battles."
21 Now after Samuel had heard all the words of the people, he repeated them in the
LORD'S hearing.
22 The LORD said to Samuel, "Listen to their voice and appoint them a king." So Samuel said to the men of Israel, "Go every man to his city."

8:18 Is 8:21; Prov 1:25-28; Is 1:15; Mic 3:4
8:19 Is 66:4; Jer 44:16
8:20 1 Sam 8:5
8:21 Judg 11:11
8:22 1 Sam 8:7

Saul's Search

9 Now there was a man of Benjamin whose name was Kish the son of Abiel, the son of
Zeror, the son of Becorath, the son of Aphiah, the son of a Benjamite, a mighty man
of valor.
2 He had a son whose name was Saul, a choice and handsome *man,* and there was not
a more handsome person than he among the sons of Israel; from his shoulders and up
he was taller than any of the people.
3 Now the donkeys of Kish, Saul's father, were lost. So Kish said to his son Saul, "Take
now with you one of the servants, and arise, go search for the donkeys."
4 He passed through the hill country of Ephraim and passed through the land of Sha-
lishah, but they did not find *them.* Then they passed through the land of Shaalim, but
they were not *there.* Then he passed through the land of the Benjamites, but they did not
find *them.*
5 When they came to the land of Zuph, Saul said to his servant who was with him,
"Come, and let us return, or else my father will cease *to be concerned* about the donkeys
and will become anxious for us."
6 He said to him, "Behold now, there is a man of God in this city, and the man is held
in honor; all that he says surely comes true. Now let us go there, perhaps he can tell us
about our journey on which we have set out."
7 Then Saul said to his servant, "But behold, if we go, what shall we bring the man?

9:1 1 Sam 14:51; 1 Chr 8:33; 9:36-39
9:2 1 Sam 10:24; 1 Sam 10:23
9:4 Josh 24:33; 2 Kin 4:42; Josh 19:42
9:5 1 Sam 1:1; 1 Sam 10:2
9:6 Deut 33:1; 1 Kin 13:1; 2 Kin 5:8; 1 Sam 3:19; Gen 24:42
9:7 1 Kin 14:3; 2 Kin 5:15; 8:8, 9; Ezek 13:19

8:19–20 Samuel carefully explained all the negative consequences of having a king, but the Israelites refused to listen. When you have an important decision to make, weigh the positives and negatives carefully, considering everyone who might be affected by your choice. When you want something badly enough, it is difficult to see the potential problems. But don't discount the negatives. Unless you have a plan to handle each one, they will cause you great difficulty later.

8:19–20 Israel was called to be a holy nation, separate from and unique among all others (Leviticus 20:26). The Israelites' motive in asking for a king was to be like the nations around them. This was in total opposition to God's original plan. It was not their desire for a king that was wrong, but their reasons for wanting a king.

Often we let others' values and actions dictate our attitudes and behavior. Have you ever made a wrong choice because you wanted to be like everyone else? Be careful that the values of your friends or "heroes" don't pull you away from what God says is right. When God's people want to be like unbelievers, they are heading for spiritual disaster.

9:3 Saul was sent by his father on an important mission—to find their stray donkeys. Donkeys were all-purpose animals, the "pick-up trucks" of Bible times. Used for transportation, hauling, and farming, they were considered necessities. Even the poorest family owned one. To own many donkeys was a sign of wealth, and to lose them was a disaster. Saul's father was wealthy, and his many donkeys were evidence of that wealth.

9:3ff Often we think that events just happen to us, but as we learn from this story about Saul, God may use common occurrences to lead us where he wants. It is important to evaluate all situations as potential "divine appointments" designed to shape our lives. Think of all the good and bad circumstances that have affected you lately. Can you see God's purpose in them? Perhaps he is building a certain quality in you or leading you to serve him in a new area.

9:6 The city where the servant said the prophet lived was probably Ramah, where Samuel moved after the Philistine battle near Shiloh (7:17). Saul's lack of knowledge about Samuel showed his ignorance of spiritual matters. Saul and Samuel even lived in the same territory, Benjamin.

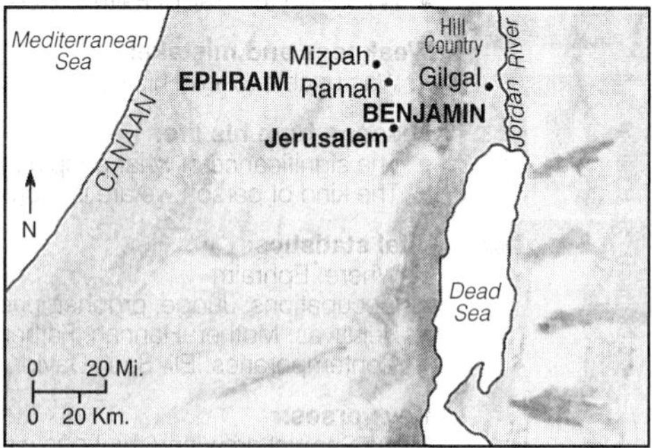

SAUL CHOSEN AS KING Saul and a servant searched for their lost donkeys in the hill country of Ephraim and the territory of Benjamin. They went to Ramah, looking for help from Samuel the prophet. While Saul was there, he found himself unexpectedly anointed by Samuel as Israel's first king. Samuel called Israel together at Mizpah to tell them God's choice for their king.

For the bread is gone from our sack and there is no present to bring to the man of God.
What do we have?"

9:8 1 Sam 9:6

8 The servant answered Saul again and said, "Behold, I have in my hand a fourth of a
shekel of silver; I will give *it* to the man of God and he will tell us our way."

9:9 2 Sam 24:11; 2 Kin 17:13; 1 Chr 9:22; 26:28; 29:29; Is 30:10; Amos 7:12

9 (Formerly in Israel, when a man went to inquire of God, he used to say, "Come,
and let us go to the seer"; for *he who is called* a prophet now was formerly called a seer.)
10 Then Saul said to his servant, "Well said; come, let us go." So they went to the city
where the man of God was.

9:11 Gen 24:11, 15; 29:8, 9; Ex 2:16

11 As they went up the slope to the city, they found young women going out to draw
water and said to them, "Is the seer here?"

9:12 Gen 31:54; Num 28:11-15; 1 Kin 3:2; 1 Sam 7:17; 10:5

12 They answered them and said, "He is; see, *he is* ahead of you. Hurry now, for he has
come into the city today, for the people have a sacrifice on the high place today.
13 "As soon as you enter the city you will find him before he goes up to the high place
to eat, for the people will not eat until he comes, because he must bless the sacrifice;

9:13 Luke 9:16; John 6:11

afterward those who are invited will eat. Now therefore, go up for you will find him at
once."
14 So they went up to the city. As they came into the city, behold, Samuel was coming
out toward them to go up to the high place.

God's Choice for King

9:15 1 Sam 15:1; Acts 13:21

15 Now a day before Saul's coming, the LORD had revealed *this* to Samuel saying,
16 "About this time tomorrow I will send you a man from the land of Benjamin, and

9:16 1 Sam 10:1; Ex 3:7, 9

you shall anoint him to be prince over My people Israel; and he will deliver My people
from the hand of the Philistines. For I have regarded My people, because their cry has
come to Me."

9:17 1 Sam 16:12

17 When Samuel saw Saul, the LORD said to him, "Behold, the man of whom I spoke
to you! This one shall rule over My people."
18 Then Saul approached Samuel in the gate and said, "Please tell me where the seer's
house is."
19 Samuel answered Saul and said, "I am the seer. Go up before me to the high place,
for you shall eat with me today; and in the morning I will let you go, and will tell you all
that is on your mind.

9:20 1 Sam 9:3; 1 Sam 8:5; 12:13

20 "As for your donkeys which were lost three days ago, do not set your mind on them,
for they have been found. And for whom is all that is desirable in Israel? Is it not for you
and for all your father's household?"

THE PROBLEMS WITH HAVING A KING

Problems (warned by Samuel)	*Reference*	*Fulfillment*
Drafting young men into the army	1 Samuel 8:11–12	1 Samuel 14:52—"When Saul saw any mighty man or any valiant man, he attached him to his staff."
Having the young men "run before his [the king's] chariots"	1 Samuel 8:11	2 Samuel 15:1—"Absalom provided for himself a chariot and horses and fifty men as runners before him."
Making slave laborers	1 Samuel 8:12, 17	2 Chronicles 2:17–18—Solomon assigned laborers to build the temple.
Taking the best of your fields and vineyards	1 Samuel 8:14	1 Kings 21:5–16—Jezebel stole Naboth's vineyard.
Using your property for his personal gain	1 Samuel 8:14–16	1 Kings 9:10–15—Solomon gave away 20 cities to Hiram of Tyre.
Demanding a tenth of your harvest and flocks	1 Samuel 8:15, 17	1 Kings 12:1–16—Rehoboam was going to demand heavier taxation than Solomon.

21 Saul replied, "Am I not a Benjamite, of the smallest of the tribes of Israel, and my family the least of all the families of the tribe of Benjamin? Why then do you speak to me in this way?"

9:21 1 Sam 15:17; Judg 20:46-48

22 Then Samuel took Saul and his servant and brought them into the hall and gave them a place at the head of those who were invited, who were about thirty men.

23 Samuel said to the cook, "Bring the portion that I gave you, concerning which I said to you, 'Set it aside.' "

24 Then the cook took up the leg with what was on it and set *it* before Saul. And *Samuel* said, "Here is what has been reserved! Set *it* before you *and* eat, because it has been kept for you until the appointed time, since I said I have invited the people." So Saul ate with Samuel that day.

9:24 Ex 29:22, 27; Lev 7:32, 33; Num 18:18

25 When they came down from the high place into the city, *Samuel* spoke with Saul on the [6]roof.

9:25 Deut 22:8; Luke 5:19; Acts 10:9

26 And they arose early; and at daybreak Samuel called to Saul on the roof, saying, "Get up, that I may send you away." So Saul arose, and both he and Samuel went out into the street.

27 As they were going down to the edge of the city, Samuel said to Saul, "Say to the servant that he might go ahead of us and pass on, but you remain standing now, that I may proclaim the word of God to you."

Saul among Prophets

10 Then Samuel took the flask of oil, poured it on his head, kissed him and said, "Has not the LORD anointed you a ruler over His inheritance?

2 "When you go from me today, then you will find two men close to Rachel's tomb in the territory of Benjamin at Zelzah; and they will say to you, 'The donkeys which you went to look for have been found. Now behold, your father has ceased to be concerned about the donkeys and is anxious for you, saying, "What shall I do about my son?" '

3 "Then you will go on further from there, and you will come as far as the oak of Tabor, and there three men going up to God at Bethel will meet you, one carrying three young goats, another carrying three loaves of bread, and another carrying a jug of wine;

4 and they will greet you and give you two *loaves* of bread, which you will accept from their hand.

5 "Afterward you will come to the hill of God where the Philistine garrison is; and it shall be as soon as you have come there to the city, that you will meet a group of prophets coming down from the high place with harp, tambourine, flute, and a lyre before them, and they will be prophesying.

6 "Then the Spirit of the LORD will come upon you mightily, and you shall prophesy with them and be changed into another man.

10:1 Ex 30:23-33; 1 Sam 16:13; 2 Kin 9:3, 6; Ps 2:12; 1 Sam 16:13; 26:9; 2 Sam 1:14; Deut 32:9; Ps 78:71

10:2 Gen 35:16-20; 48:7; 1 Sam 9:3-5

10:3 Gen 35:8; Gen 28:19; 35:1, 3, 7

10:5 1 Sam 13:2, 3; 1 Sam 19:20; 2 Kin 2:3, 5, 15; 2 Kin 3:15; 1 Chr 25:1-6; 1 Cor 14:1

10:6 Num 11:25, 29; Judg 14:6; 1 Sam 10:10; 19:23, 24

6 Gr adds *and they spread a bed for Saul on the roof and he slept*

9:21 "Why then do you speak to me in this way?" Saul's outburst reveals a problem he would face repeatedly—feeling inferior. Like a leaf tossed about by the wind, Saul vacillated between his feelings and his convictions. Everything he said and did was selfish because he was worried about himself. For example, Saul said his family was "the least" in the smallest tribe in Israel, but 9:1–3 pictures a family of wealth and prestige. (The tribe of Benjamin was the smallest because they were nearly wiped out as punishment for their immorality—see Judges 19—21.) Saul didn't want to face the responsibility God had given him. Later, Saul kept some war plunder that he shouldn't have and then tried to blame his soldiers (15:21) while claiming that they had really taken it to sacrifice to God (15:15).

Although Saul had been called by God and had a mission in life, he struggled constantly with jealousy, insecurity, arrogance, impulsiveness, and deceit. He did not decide to be wholeheartedly committed to God. Because Saul would not let God's love give rest to his heart, he never became God's man.

10:1 When an Israelite king took office he was not only crowned, he was anointed. The coronation was the political act of establishing the king as ruler; the anointing was the religious act of making the king God's representative to the people. A king was always anointed by a priest or prophet. The special anointing oil was a mixture of olive oil, myrrh, and other expensive spices. It was poured over the king's head to symbolize the presence and power of the Holy Spirit of God in his life. This anointing ceremony was to remind the king of his great responsibility to lead his people by God's wisdom and not his own.

10:6 How could Saul be so filled with the Spirit and yet later commit such evil acts? Throughout the Old Testament, God's Spirit would "come upon" a person temporarily so that God could use him or her for great acts. This happened frequently to Israel's judges when they were called by God to rescue the nation (Judges 3:8–10). This was not always a permanent, abiding influence, but sometimes a temporary manifestation of the Holy Spirit. Yet, at times in the Old Testament, the Spirit even came upon unbelievers to enable them to do unusual tasks (Numbers 24; 2 Chronicles 36:22–23). The Holy Spirit gave the person power to do what God asked, but it did not always produce the other fruits of the Spirit, such as self-control. Saul, in his early years as king, was a different person (10:1–10) as a result of the Holy Spirit's work in him. But as Saul's power grew, so did his pride. After a while he refused to seek God; the Spirit left him (16:14); and his good attitude melted away.

10:7 Eccl 9:10; Josh 1:5; Judg 6:12; Heb 13:5
10:8 1 Sam 11:14; 13:8; 1 Sam 11:15; 1 Sam 13:8
10:9 1 Sam 10:6
10:10 1 Sam 10:5, 6; 19:20
10:11 1 Sam 19:24; Amos 7:14, 15; Matt 13:54-57; John 7:15
10:12 1 Sam 19:23, 24
10:14 1 Sam 14:50; 1 Sam 9:3-6
10:16 1 Sam 9:20
10:17 Judg 20:1; 1 Sam 7:5
10:18 Judg 6:8, 9

7 "It shall be when these signs come to you, do for yourself what the occasion requires,
for God is with you.
8 "And you shall go down before me to Gilgal; and behold, I will come down to you to
offer burnt offerings and sacrifice peace offerings. You shall wait seven days until I come
to you and show you what you should do."
9 Then it happened when he turned his back to leave Samuel, God changed his heart;
and all those signs came about on that day.
10 When they came to the hill there, behold, a group of prophets met him; and the
Spirit of God came upon him mightily, so that he prophesied among them.
11 It came about, when all who knew him previously saw that he prophesied now with
the prophets, that the people said to one another, "What has happened to the son of
Kish? Is Saul also among the prophets?"
12 A man there said, "Now, who is their father?" Therefore it became a proverb: "Is
Saul also among the prophets?"
13 When he had finished prophesying, he came to the high place.
14 Now Saul's uncle said to him and his servant, "Where did you go?" And he said,
"To look for the donkeys. When we saw that they could not be found, we went to
Samuel."
15 Saul's uncle said, "Please tell me what Samuel said to you."
16 So Saul said to his uncle, "He told us plainly that the donkeys had been found." But
he did not tell him about the matter of the kingdom which Samuel had mentioned.

Saul Publicly Chosen King

17 Thereafter Samuel called the people together to the LORD at Mizpah;
18 and he said to the sons of Israel, "Thus says the LORD, the God of Israel, 'I brought
Israel up from Egypt, and I delivered you from the hand of the Egyptians and from the
power of all the kingdoms that were oppressing you.'

RELIGIOUS AND POLITICAL CENTERS OF ISRAEL

GILGAL	Joshua 4:19; Judges 2:1; Hosea 4:15; Micah 6:5
SHILOH	Joshua 18:1–10; 19:51; Judges 18:31; 1 Samuel 1:3; Jeremiah 7:12–14
SHECHEM	Joshua 24:1
RAMAH	1 Samuel 7:17; 8:4
MIZPAH	Judges 11:11; 20:1; 1 Samuel 10:17
BETHEL	Judges 20:18, 26; 1 Samuel 10:3
GIBEAH (political center only)	1 Samuel 10:26
GIBEON (religious center only)	1 Kings 3:4; 2 Chronicles 1:2–3
JERUSALEM	1 Kings 8:1ff; Psalm 51:16–19

During the period of the judges, Israel may have had more than one capital. This may explain why the Scriptures overlap with reference to some cities.

Samuel called the Israelites together at Mizpah, where he would anoint Saul as their first king. Up to this point, the political seat of the nation seems to have been the religious center of the nation as well. Above are the cities which probably served as both the religious and political centers of Israel since the days of Joshua. Saul may have been the first Israelite leader to separate the nation's religious center (probably Mizpah at this time) from its political center (Gibeah—1 Samuel 11:4; 1 Samuel 26:1). Politically, the nation grew strong for a while. But when Saul and his officials stopped seeking God's will, internal jealousies and strife soon began to decay the nation from within. When David became king he brought the ark of the covenant back to Jerusalem, his capital. King Solomon then completely united the religious and political centers at Jerusalem.

10:10–11 A prophet is someone who speaks God's words. While God told many prophets to predict certain events, what God wanted most was for them to instruct and inspire people to live in faithfulness to God. When Saul's friends heard inspired words coming from Saul they exclaimed, "Is Saul also among the prophets?" This was an expression of surprise at worldly Saul's becoming religious. It is equivalent to "What? Has he got religion?"

19 "But you have today rejected your God, who delivers you from all your calamities
and your distresses; yet you have said, 'No, but set a king over us!' Now therefore, present yourselves before the LORD by your tribes and by your clans."
20 Thus Samuel brought all the tribes of Israel near, and the tribe of Benjamin was
taken by lot.
21 Then he brought the tribe of Benjamin near by its families, and the Matrite family
was taken. And Saul the son of Kish was taken; but when they looked for him, he could
not be found.
22 Therefore they inquired further of the LORD, "Has the man come here yet?" So the
LORD said, "Behold, he is hiding himself by the baggage."
23 So they ran and took him from there, and when he stood among the people, he was
taller than any of the people from his shoulders upward.
24 Samuel said to all the people, "Do you see him whom the LORD has chosen? Surely
there is no one like him among all the people." So all the people shouted and said, "*Long*
live the king!"
25 Then Samuel told the people the ordinances of the kingdom, and wrote *them* in the
book and placed *it* before the LORD. And Samuel sent all the people away, each one to
his house.
26 Saul also went to his house at Gibeah; and the valiant *men* whose hearts God had
touched went with him.
27 But certain worthless men said, "How can this one deliver us?" And they despised
him and did not bring him any present. But he kept silent.

Saul Defeats the Ammonites

11 Now Nahash the Ammonite came up and besieged Jabesh-gilead; and all the men
of Jabesh said to Nahash, "Make a covenant with us and we will serve you."
2 But Nahash the Ammonite said to them, "I will make *it* with you on this condition,
that I will gouge out the right eye of every one of you, thus I will make it a reproach on
all Israel."
3 The elders of Jabesh said to him, "Let us alone for seven days, that we may send
messengers throughout the territory of Israel. Then, if there is no one to deliver us, we
will come out to you."

10:19 1 Sam 8:6, 7; 12:12; Josh 7:14-18; 24:1; Prov 16:33

10:22 1 Sam 23:2, 4

10:23 1 Sam 9:2

10:24 Deut 17:15; 2 Sam 21:6; 1 Kin 1:25, 34, 39

10:25 Deut 17:14-20; 1 Sam 8:11-18; Deut 31:26

10:26 1 Sam 11:4; 15:34

10:27 Deut 13:13; 1 Sam 25:17; 1 Kin 10:25; 2 Chr 17:5

11:1 1 Sam 12:12; Judg 21:8; 1 Sam 31:11; Gen 26:28; 1 Kin 20:34; Job 41:4; Ezek 17:13

11:2 Num 16:14; 1 Sam 17:26; Ps 44:13

11:3 1 Sam 8:4

10:19 Israel's true king was God, but the nation demanded another. Imagine wanting a human being instead of God as guide and leader! Throughout history, men and women have rejected God, and they continue to do it today. Are you rejecting God by pushing him aside and acknowledging someone or something else as your "king" or top priority? Learn from these stories of Israel's kings, and don't push God aside.

10:20 The Israelites chose their first king by casting lots or by using the Urim and Thummim, two plates or flat stones carried by the high priest. The fact that Saul was chosen may seem like luck, but it was really the opposite. God had instructed the Israelites to make the Urim and Thummim for the specific purpose of consulting him in times such as this (Exodus 28:30; Numbers 27:12–21). By using the Urim and Thummim, the Israelites were taking the decision out of their own hands and turning it over to God.

Only the high priest could use the Urim and Thummim, which were designed to give only yes or no answers.

10:22 When the Israelites assembled to choose a king, Saul already knew he was the one (10:1). Instead of coming forward, however, he hid among the baggage. Often we hide from important responsibilities because we are afraid of failure, afraid of what others will think, or perhaps unsure about how to proceed. Prepare now to step up to your future responsibilities. Count on God's provision rather than your feelings of adequacy.

10:25 The kings of Israel, unlike kings of other nations, had specific regulations outlined for them (Deuteronomy 17:14–20). Pagan kings were considered gods; they made their own laws and answered to no one. By contrast, Israel's king had to answer to a higher authority—the Lord of heaven and earth. The Israelites now had a king like everyone else, just as they wanted. But Samuel, in his charge to both the king and the people, wanted to make sure that the rule of Israel's king would be different from that of his pagan counterparts. "Placed it before the LORD" means that Samuel put the book, as a witness to the agreement, in a special place at Mizpah.

10:26–27 Some men became Saul's constant companions, while others despised him. Criticism will always be directed toward those who lead because they are out in front. At this time, Saul took no notice of those who seemed to be against him, although later he would become consumed with jealousy (19:1–3; 26:17–21). As you lead, listen to constructive criticism, but don't spend valuable time and energy worrying about those who may oppose you. Instead, focus your attention on those who are ready and willing to help.

11:1ff At this time, Israel was very susceptible to invasion by marauding tribes such as these Ammonites from east of the Jordan River. Saul's leadership in battle against this warlike tribe helped unify the nation and proved that he was a worthy military ruler. Saul's kingship was solidified when he saved the nation from disgrace and spared the people who had criticized him.

11:3 Why would Nahash give the city of Jabesh seven days to find an army to help them? Because Israel was still disorganized, Nahash was betting that no one would come to the city's aid. He was hoping to take the city without a fight and avoid a battle. He also may not have been prepared to attack the city because a siege against its walls could last weeks or months.

11:4 1 Sam 10:26; 15:34; Gen 27:38; Judg 2:4; 20:23, 26; 21:2; 1 Sam 30:4

11:5 1 Kin 19:19

11:6 Judg 3:10; 6:34; 11:29; 13:25; 14:6; 1 Sam 10:10; 16:13

11:7 Judg 19:29; Judg 21:5, 8; Judg 20:1

11:8 Judg 1:5; Judg 20:2

11:10 1 Sam 11:3

11:11 Judg 7:16, 20

11:12 1 Sam 10:27; Luke 19:27

11:13 1 Sam 10:27; 2 Sam 19:22; Ex 14:13, 30; 1 Sam 19:5

11:14 1 Sam 7:16; 10:8; 1 Sam 10:25

11:15 1 Sam 10:17; 1 Sam 10:8

4 Then the messengers came to Gibeah of Saul and spoke these words in the hearing
of the people, and all the people lifted up their voices and wept.
5 Now behold, Saul was coming from the field behind the oxen, and he said, "What is
the matter with the people that they weep?" So they related to him the words of the men
of Jabesh.
6 Then the Spirit of God came upon Saul mightily when he heard these words, and he
became very angry.
7 He took a yoke of oxen and cut them in pieces, and sent *them* throughout the territory of Israel by the hand of messengers, saying, "Whoever does not come out after Saul
and after Samuel, so shall it be done to his oxen." Then the dread of the LORD fell on
the people, and they came out as one man.
8 He numbered them in Bezek; and the sons of Israel were 300,000, and the men of
Judah 30,000.
9 They said to the messengers who had come, "Thus you shall say to the men of Jabesh-
gilead, 'Tomorrow, by the time the sun is hot, you will have deliverance.' " So the messengers went and told the men of Jabesh; and they were glad.
10 Then the men of Jabesh said, "Tomorrow we will come out to you, and you may do
to us whatever seems good to you."
11 The next morning Saul put the people in three companies; and they came into the
midst of the camp at the morning watch and struck down the Ammonites until the heat
of the day. Those who survived were scattered, so that no two of them were left together.
12 Then the people said to Samuel, "Who is he that said, 'Shall Saul reign over us?'
Bring the men, that we may put them to death."
13 But Saul said, "Not a man shall be put to death this day, for today the LORD has
accomplished deliverance in Israel."
14 Then Samuel said to the people, "Come and let us go to Gilgal and renew the kingdom there."
15 So all the people went to Gilgal, and there they made Saul king before the LORD in
Gilgal. There they also offered sacrifices of peace offerings before the LORD; and there
Saul and all the men of Israel rejoiced greatly.

SAUL DEFEATS THE AMMONITES
The Ammonites prepared to attack Jabesh-gilead. The people of Jabesh sent messengers to Saul in Gibeah asking for help. Saul mobilized an army at Bezek and then attacked the Ammonites. After the battle, the Israelites returned to Gilgal to crown Saul as king.

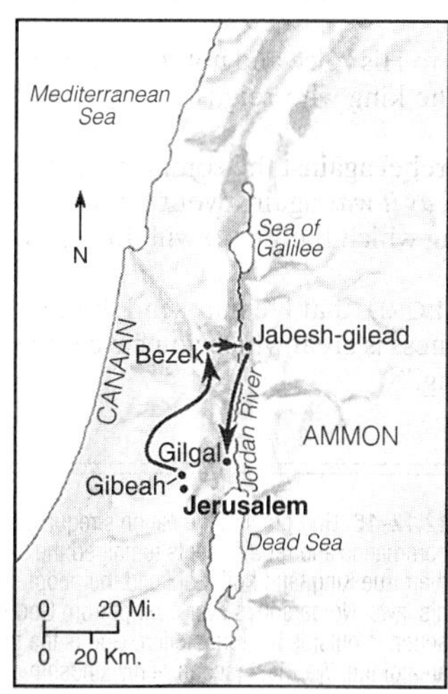

11:6 Anger is a powerful emotion. Often it may drive people to hurt others with words or physical violence. But anger directed at sin and the mistreatment of others is not wrong. Saul was angered by the Ammonites' threat to humiliate and mistreat his fellow Israelites. The Holy Spirit used Saul's anger to bring justice and freedom. When injustice or sin makes you angry, ask God how you can channel that anger in constructive ways to help bring about a positive change.

11:8 Judah, one of the 12 tribes of Israel, is often mentioned separately from the other 11. There are several reasons for this. Judah was the largest tribe (Numbers 1:20–46), and it was the tribe from which most of Israel's kings would come (Genesis 49:8–12). Later, Judah would be one of the few tribes to return to God after a century of captivity under a hostile foreign power. Judah would also be the tribe through which the Messiah would come (Micah 5:2).

11:14 Saul had been anointed by Samuel at Ramah (10:1); then Saul was publically chosen at Mizpah (10:17–27); his defeat of the Ammonites confirmed his kingship in the people's minds; at this time, all the people confirm his rule.

11:15 The Israelites sacrificed peace offerings to God as they made Saul their first king. The instructions for giving these offerings are given in Leviticus 3. The peace offering was an expression of gratitude and thanksgiving to God, symbolizing the peace that comes to those who know him and who live in accordance with his commands. Although God did not want his people to have a human king, the people were demonstrating through their offerings that he was still their true King. Unfortunately, this attitude did not last, just as God had predicted (8:7–19).

Samuel Addresses Israel

12 Then Samuel said to all Israel, "Behold, I have listened to your voice in all that
you said to me and I have appointed a king over you.
2 "Now, here is the king walking before you, but I am old and gray, and behold my
sons are with you. And I have walked before you from my youth even to this day.
3 "Here I am; bear witness against me before the LORD and His anointed. Whose ox
have I taken, or whose donkey have I taken, or whom have I defrauded? Whom have I
oppressed, or from whose hand have I taken a bribe to blind my eyes with it? I will restore *it* to you."
4 They said, "You have not defrauded us or oppressed us or taken anything from any
man's hand."
5 He said to them, "The LORD is witness against you, and His anointed is witness this
day that you have found nothing in my hand." And they said, "*He is* witness."
6 Then Samuel said to the people, "It is the LORD who appointed Moses and Aaron
and who brought your fathers up from the land of Egypt.
7 "So now, take your stand, that I may plead with you before the LORD concerning all
the righteous acts of the LORD which He did for you and your fathers.
8 "When Jacob went into Egypt and your fathers cried out to the LORD, then the LORD
sent Moses and Aaron who brought your fathers out of Egypt and settled them in this
place.
9 "But they forgot the LORD their God, so He sold them into the hand of Sisera, captain of the army of Hazor, and into the hand of the Philistines and into the hand of the
king of Moab, and they fought against them.
10 "They cried out to the LORD and said, 'We have sinned because we have forsaken
the LORD and have served the Baals and the Ashtaroth; but now deliver us from the
hands of our enemies, and we will serve You.'
11 "Then the LORD sent Jerubbaal and [7]Bedan and Jephthah and Samuel, and delivered you from the hands of your enemies all around, so that you lived in security.

The King Confirmed

12 "When you saw that Nahash the king of the sons of Ammon came against you, you
said to me, 'No, but a king shall reign over us,' although the LORD your God *was* your
king.
13 "Now therefore, here is the king whom you have chosen, whom you have asked for,
and behold, the LORD has set a king over you.
14 "If you will fear the LORD and serve Him, and listen to His voice and not rebel against
the command of the LORD, then both you and also the king who reigns over you will
follow the LORD your God.
15 "If you will not listen to the voice of the LORD, but rebel against the command of the
LORD, then the hand of the LORD will be against you, *as it was* against your fathers.
16 "Even now, take your stand and see this great thing which the LORD will do before
your eyes.
17 "Is it not the wheat harvest today? I will call to the LORD, that He may send thunder
and rain. Then you will know and see that your wickedness is great which you have done
in the sight of the LORD by asking for yourselves a king."

7 Gr and Syr read *Barak*

12:1 1 Sam 8:7, 9, 22; 1 Sam 10:24
12:2 1 Sam 8:20; 1 Sam 8:1, 5; 1 Sam 8:3, 5; 1 Sam 3:10, 19, 20
12:3 1 Sam 10:1; 24:6; 2 Sam 1:14; Ex 20:17; Num 16:15; Acts 20:33; Ex 23:8
12:5 Acts 23:9; 24:20
12:6 Ex 6:26; Mic 6:4
12:7 Ezek 20:35
12:8 Gen 46:5, 6; Ex 2:23-25; Ex 3:10; 4:14-16; 1 Sam 10:18
12:9 Deut 32:18; Judg 3:7; Judg 4:2; Judg 3:31; 10:7; 13:1; Judg 3:12-30
12:10 Judg 10:10; Judg 2:13; 3:7; Judg 10:15, 16
12:11 Judg 6:31, 32; 7:1; Judg 4:6; 11:1; Judg 11:29; 1 Sam 3:20
12:12 1 Sam 11:1, 2; 1 Sam 8:6, 19; Judg 8:23; 1 Sam 8:7
12:13 1 Sam 10:24; 1 Sam 8:5; 12:17, 19; Hos 13:11
12:14 Josh 24:14
12:15 Lev 26:14, 15; Josh 24:20; Is 1:20; 1 Sam 5:9; 1 Sam 12:9
12:17 Prov 26:1; 1 Sam 7:9, 10; James 5:16ff; 1 Sam 8:7

12:1ff Samuel continued to serve the people as their priest, prophet, and judge, but Saul exercised more and more political and military control over the tribes (see 7:15).

12:1–3 In his farewell speech, Samuel asked the Israelites to point out any wrongs he had committed during his time as Israel's judge. By doing so, Samuel was reminding them that he could be trusted to tell the truth. He was also reminding them that having a king was their idea, not his. Samuel was setting the stage for the miraculous thunderstorm recorded in 12:16–19, so that the people could not blame him when God punished them for their selfish motives.

12:10 "The Baals and the Ashtaroth" were pagan gods. See the note on 7:4 for more information.

12:11 Jerubbaal was the name given to Gideon when he demolished the altar of Baal (see Judges 6:32).

12:12–15 God granted the nation's request for a king, but his commands and requirements remained the same. God was to be their true King, and both Saul and the people were to be subject to his laws. No person is ever exempt from God's laws. No human action is outside his jurisdiction. God is the true King of every area of life. We must recognize his kingship and pattern our relationships, worklife, and homelife according to his principles.

12:17 The wheat harvest came near the end of the dry season during the months of May and June. Because rain rarely fell during this period, a great thunderstorm was considered a miraculous event. It was not a beneficial miracle, however, because rain during the wheat harvest could damage the crops and cause them to rot quickly. This unusual occurrence showed God's displeasure with Israel's demand for a king.

18 So Samuel called to the LORD, and the LORD sent thunder and rain that day; and
all the people greatly feared the LORD and Samuel.
19 Then all the people said to Samuel, "Pray for your servants to the LORD your God,
so that we may not die, for we have added to all our sins *this* evil by asking for ourselves
a king."
20 Samuel said to the people, "Do not fear. You have committed all this evil, yet do
not turn aside from following the LORD, but serve the LORD with all your heart.
21 "You must not turn aside, for *then you would go* after futile things which can not profit
or deliver, because they are futile.
22 "For the LORD will not abandon His people on account of His great name, because
the LORD has been pleased to make you a people for Himself.
23 "Moreover, as for me, far be it from me that I should sin against the LORD by ceasing to pray for you; but I will instruct you in the good and right way.
24 "Only [8]fear the LORD and serve Him in truth with all your heart; for consider what
great things He has done for you.
25 "But if you still do wickedly, both you and your king will be swept away."

2. God rejects Saul for disobedience

War with the Philistines

13 Saul was *thirty* years old when he began to reign, and he reigned *forty* two years
over Israel.
2 Now Saul chose for himself 3,000 men of Israel, of which 2,000 were with Saul in
Michmash and in the hill country of Bethel, while 1,000 were with Jonathan at Gibeah
of Benjamin. But he sent away the rest of the people, each to his tent.
3 Jonathan smote the garrison of the Philistines that was in Geba, and the Philistines
heard of *it.* Then Saul blew the trumpet throughout the land, saying, "Let the Hebrews
hear."
4 All Israel heard the news that Saul had smitten the garrison of the Philistines, and
also that Israel had become odious to the Philistines. The people were then summoned
to Saul at Gilgal.
5 Now the Philistines assembled to fight with Israel, 30,000 chariots and 6,000 horsemen, and people like the sand which is on the seashore in abundance; and they came up
and camped in Michmash, east of Beth-aven.
6 When the men of Israel saw that they were in a strait (for the people were hard-
pressed), then the people hid themselves in caves, in thickets, in cliffs, in cellars, and in
pits.
7 Also *some of* the Hebrews crossed the Jordan into the land of Gad and Gilead. But
as for Saul, he *was* still in Gilgal, and all the people followed him trembling.

8 Or *reverence*

12:18 Ex 14:31
12:19 Ex 9:28; 1 Sam 12:23; Jer 15:1; 1 John 5:16; 1 Sam 12:17, 20
12:20 Deut 11:16
12:21 Deut 11:16; Is 41:29; Hab 2:18
12:22 Deut 31:6; 1 Kin 6:13; Ex 32:12; Num 14:13; Josh 7:9; Ps 106:8; Jer 14:21; Deut 7:6-11; 1 Pet 2:9
12:23 Rom 1:9; 1 Cor 9:16; Col 1:9; 1 Thess 3:10; 2 Tim 1:3; 1 Kin 8:36; Ps 34:11; Prov 4:11
12:24 Eccl 12:13; Deut 10:21; Is 5:12
12:25 Is 1:20; 3:11; Josh 24:20; 1 Sam 31:1-5; Hos 10:3
13:2 1 Sam 13:5; 14:31; 1 Sam 10:26
13:3 1 Sam 10:5; 1 Sam 13:16; 14:5; Judg 3:27; 6:34
13:4 Gen 34:30; Ex 5:21; 2 Sam 10:6
13:5 Josh 11:4; Josh 18:12; 1 Sam 14:23
13:6 Judg 6:2
13:7 Num 32:33

12:22 Why did God make Israel "His people"? God did not choose them because they deserved it (Deuteronomy 7:7–8), but in order that they might become his channel of blessing to all people through the Messiah (Genesis 12:1–3). Because God chose the people of Israel, he would never abandon them; but because they were his special nation, he would often punish them for their disobedience in order to bring them back to a right relationship with him.

12:23 Is failing to pray for others a sin? Samuel's words seem to indicate that it is. His actions illustrate two of God's people's responsibilities: (1) they should pray consistently for others (Ephesians 6:18), and (2) they should teach others the right way to God (2 Timothy 2:2). Samuel disagreed with the Israelites' demand for a king, but he assured them that he would continue to pray for them and teach them. We may disagree with others, but we shouldn't stop praying for them.

12:24 This is the second time in his farewell speech that Samuel reminded the people to take time to consider what great things God had done for them (see 12:7). Taking time for reflection allows us to focus our attention upon God's goodness and strengthens our faith. Sometimes we are so progress- and future-oriented that we fail to take time to recall all that God has already done. Remember what God has done for you so that you may move ahead with gratitude.

13:3–4 Jonathan attacked and destroyed the Philistine outpost, but Saul took all the credit for it. Although this was normal in that culture, it didn't make his action right. Saul's growing pride started out small—taking credit for a battle that was won by his son. Left unchecked, his pride grew into an ugly obsession; thus it destroyed him, tore his family apart, and threatened the well-being of the nation. Taking credit for the accomplishments of others indicates that pride is controlling your life. When you notice pride taking a foothold, take immediate steps to put it in check by giving credit to those who deserve it.

13:6 When we forget who is on our side or see only our own resources, we tend to panic at the sight of the opposition. The Israelites became terrified and hid when they saw the mighty Philistine army. They forgot that God was on their side and that he couldn't be defeated. As you face problems and temptations, focus your attention on God and his resources, trusting him to help you (Romans 8:31–37).

8 Now he waited seven days, according to the appointed time set by Samuel, but Samuel
did not come to Gilgal; and the people were scattering from him.
9 So Saul said, "Bring to me the burnt offering and the peace offerings." And he offered the burnt offering.
10 As soon as he finished offering the burnt offering, behold, Samuel came; and Saul
went out to meet him *and* to greet him.
11 But Samuel said, "What have you done?" And Saul said, "Because I saw that the
people were scattering from me, and that you did not come within the appointed days,
and that the Philistines were assembling at Michmash,
12 therefore I said, 'Now the Philistines will come down against me at Gilgal, and
I have not asked the favor of the LORD.' So I forced myself and offered the burnt
offering."
13 Samuel said to Saul, "You have acted foolishly; you have not kept the commandment of the LORD your God, which He commanded you, for now the LORD would have
established your kingdom over Israel forever.
14 "But now your kingdom shall not endure. The LORD has sought out for Himself a
man after His own heart, and the LORD has appointed him as ruler over His people,
because you have not kept what the LORD commanded you."
15 Then Samuel arose and went up from Gilgal to Gibeah of Benjamin. And Saul
numbered the people who were present with him, about six hundred men.
16 Now Saul and his son Jonathan and the people who were present with them were
staying in Geba of Benjamin while the Philistines camped at Michmash.
17 And the raiders came from the camp of the Philistines in three companies: one
company turned toward Ophrah, to the land of Shual,
18 and another company turned toward Beth-horon, and another company turned
toward the border which overlooks the valley of Zeboim toward the wilderness.
19 Now no blacksmith could be found in all the land of Israel, for the Philistines said,
"Otherwise the Hebrews will make swords or spears."
20 So all Israel went down to the Philistines, each to sharpen his plowshare, his mat-
tock, his axe, and his hoe.
21 The charge was two-thirds of a shekel for the plowshares, the mattocks, the forks,
and the axes, and to fix the hoes.
22 So it came about on the day of battle that neither sword nor spear was found in the
hands of any of the people who *were* with Saul and Jonathan, but they were found with
Saul and his son Jonathan.
23 And the garrison of the Philistines went out to the pass of Michmash.

13:8 1 Sam 10:8
13:9 Deut 12:5-14; 2 Sam 24:25; 1 Kin 3:4
13:10 1 Sam 15:13
13:11 1 Sam 13:2, 5, 16, 23
13:13 2 Chr 16:9; 1 Sam 15:11, 22, 28; 1 Sam 1:22
13:14 1 Sam 15:28; Acts 7:46; 13:22
13:15 1 Sam 13:2; 1 Sam 13:2, 6, 7; 14:2
13:16 1 Sam 13:2, 3
13:17 1 Sam 14:15; Josh 18:23
13:18 Josh 16:3; 18:13, 14; Neh 11:34
13:19 Judg 5:8; 2 Kin 24:14; Jer 24:1; 29:2; Judg 5:8
13:22 Judg 5:8
13:23 1 Sam 14:1; 2 Sam 23:14; 1 Sam 14:4, 5; Is 10:28

Jonathan's Victory

14 Now the day came that Jonathan, the son of Saul, said to the young man who was
carrying his armor, "Come and let us cross over to the Philistines' garrison that is
on the other side." But he did not tell his father.

13:9 Rather than waiting for a priest, Saul offered the sacrifice himself. This was against God's laws (Deuteronomy 12:5–14) and against the specific instructions of Samuel (10:8). Under pressure from the approaching Philistines, he took matters into his own hands and disobeyed God. He was doing a good thing (offering a sacrifice to God before a crucial battle), but he did it in the wrong way. Like Saul, our true spiritual character is revealed under pressure. The methods we use to accomplish our goals are as important as the attainment of those goals.

13:11–12 It is difficult to trust God when you feel your resources slipping away. When Saul felt that time was running out, he became impatient with God's timing. In thinking that the ritual was all he needed, he substituted the ritual for faith in God.

When faced with a difficult decision, don't allow impatience to drive you to disobey God. When you know what God wants, follow his plan regardless of the consequences. God often uses delays to test our obedience and patience.

13:12–13 Saul had plenty of excuses for his disobedience. But Samuel zeroed in on the real issue: "You have not kept the commandment of the LORD your God." Like Saul, we often gloss over our mistakes and sins, trying to justify and spiritualize our actions because of our "special" circumstances. Our excuses, however, are nothing more than disobedience. God knows our true motives. He forgives, restores, and blesses only when we are honest about our sins. By trying to hide his sins behind excuses, Saul lost his kingship (13:14).

13:19–22 Israel was in no position to conquer anyone. The army had no iron weapons, and there were no facilities for turning their tools into weapons. In fact, if an Israelite wanted to sharpen his tools, he had to pay a Philistine blacksmith to do it because the Philistines had a carefully guarded monopoly on iron and blacksmithing. And they charged high prices for sharpening farm implements. The Philistines' tight control over the technology, along with their surprise raids, demoralized the Israelites and kept them in subjection.

Against such superiority, the Israelites were at a serious disadvantage. How could they hope to rout their oppressors? Only with God's help. God wanted to give Israel victory without swords, so they would realize their true source of strength.

First impressions can be deceiving, especially when the image created by a person's appearance is contradicted by his or her qualities and abilities. Saul presented the ideal visual image of a king, but the tendencies of his character often went contrary to God's commands for a king. Saul was God's chosen leader, but this did not mean he was capable of being king on his own.

During his reign, Saul had his greatest successes when he obeyed God. His greatest failures resulted from acting on his own. Saul had the raw materials to be a good leader—appearance, courage, and action. Even his weaknesses could have been used by God if Saul had recognized them and left them in God's hands. His own choices cut him off from God and eventually alienated him from his own people.

From Saul we learn that while our strengths and abilities make us useful, it is our weaknesses that make us usable. Our skills and talents make us tools, but our failures and shortcomings remind us that we need a Craftsman in control of our lives. Whatever we accomplish on our own is only a hint of what God could do through our lives. Does he control your life?

Strengths and accomplishments:
- First God-appointed king of Israel
- Known for his personal courage and generosity
- Stood tall, with a striking appearance

Weaknesses and mistakes:
- His leadership abilities did not match the expectations created by his appearance
- Impulsive by nature, he tended to overstep his bounds
- Jealous of David, he tried to kill him
- He specifically disobeyed God on several occasions

Lessons from his life:
- God wants obedience from the heart, not mere acts of religious ritual
- Obedience always involves sacrifice; but sacrifice is not always obedience
- God wants to make use of our strengths and weaknesses
- Weaknesses should help us remember our need for God's guidance and help

Vital statistics:
- Where: The land of Benjamin
- Occupation: King of Israel
- Relatives: Father: Kish. Sons: Jonathan and Ish-bosheth. Wife: Ahinoam. Daughters: Merab and Michal

Key verses:
"Samuel said, 'Has the LORD as much delight in burnt offerings and sacrifices as in obeying the voice of the LORD? Behold, to obey is better than sacrifice, and to heed than the fat of rams. For rebellion is as the sin of divination, and insubordination is as iniquity and idolatry. Because you have rejected the word of the LORD, He has also rejected you from being king' "
(1 Samuel 15:22–23).

His story is told in 1 Samuel 9—31. He is also mentioned in Acts 13:21.

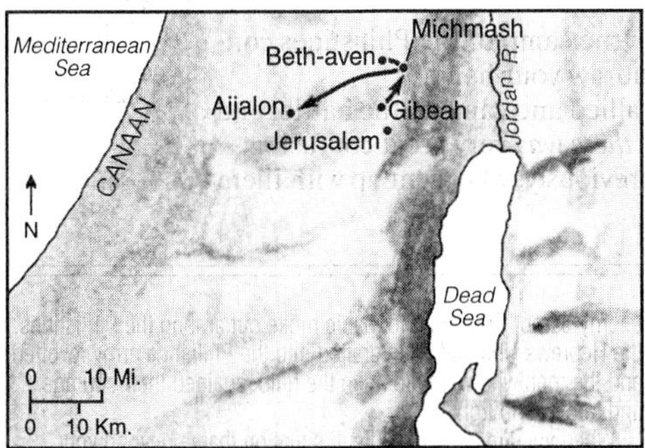

JONATHAN'S BRAVERY Jonathan, Saul's son, left the camp at Gibeah and crept to the Philistine camp at Michmash. With God's help, Jonathan and his armor bearer surprised the Philistines, who panicked and began killing each other! Saul's army heard the commotion and chased the Philistines as far as Beth-aven and Aijalon.

14:1 Why would Jonathan go alone to attack the Philistines? Jonathan may have been weary of the long, hopeless standoff in the battle; he trusted God to give the victory and wanted to act on that trust. He also knew that the number of Philistines was no problem for God. Perhaps he didn't tell his father about his mission because he thought Saul would not let him go.

14:1ff In this chapter we read about the miserable job Saul did as leader: he had no communication with Jonathan (14:1, 17); he made a foolish oath (14:24); and he ignored the well-being of his own soldiers (14:31). Saul's poor leadership was not a result of personality traits but of decaying spiritual character. What we do is often a direct result of our spiritual condition. We cannot ignore the importance of spiritual character in effective leadership.

2 Saul was staying in the outskirts of Gibeah under the pomegranate tree which is in
Migron. And the people who *were* with him *were* about six hundred men,
3 and Ahijah, the son of Ahitub, Ichabod's brother, the son of Phinehas, the son of
Eli, the priest of the LORD at Shiloh, was wearing an ephod. And the people did not
know that Jonathan had gone.
4 Between the passes by which Jonathan sought to cross over to the Philistines' garrison, there was a sharp crag on the one side and a sharp crag on the other side, and the
name of the one was Bozez, and the name of the other Seneh.
5 The one crag rose on the north opposite Michmash, and the other on the south
opposite Geba.
6 Then Jonathan said to the young man who was carrying his armor, "Come and let
us cross over to the garrison of these uncircumcised; perhaps the LORD will work for us,
for the LORD is not restrained to save by many or by few."
7 His armor bearer said to him, "Do all that is in your heart; turn yourself, *and* here
I am with you according to your desire."
8 Then Jonathan said, "Behold, we will cross over to the men and reveal ourselves to
them.
9 "If they say to us, 'Wait until we come to you'; then we will stand in our place and not
go up to them.
10 "But if they say, 'Come up to us,' then we will go up, for the LORD has given them
into our hands; and this shall be the sign to us."
11 When both of them revealed themselves to the garrison of the Philistines, the Philistines said, "Behold, Hebrews are coming out of the holes where they have hidden themselves."
12 So the men of the garrison hailed Jonathan and his armor bearer and said, "Come
up to us and we will tell you something." And Jonathan said to his armor bearer, "Come
up after me, for the LORD has given them into the hands of Israel."
13 Then Jonathan climbed up on his hands and feet, with his armor bearer behind him;
and they fell before Jonathan, and his armor bearer put some to death after him.
14 That first slaughter which Jonathan and his armor bearer made was about twenty
men within about half a furrow in an acre of land.
15 And there was a trembling in the camp, in the field, and among all the people. Even
the garrison and the raiders trembled, and the earth quaked so that it became a [9]great
trembling.
16 Now Saul's watchmen in Gibeah of Benjamin looked, and behold, the multitude
melted away; and they went here and *there.*
17 Saul said to the people who *were* with him, "Number now and see who has gone
from us." And when they had numbered, behold, Jonathan and his armor bearer were
not *there.*
18 Then Saul said to Ahijah, "Bring the ark of God here." For the ark of God was at
that time with the sons of Israel.
19 While Saul talked to the priest, the commotion in the camp of the Philistines continued and increased; so Saul said to the priest, "Withdraw your hand."
20 Then Saul and all the people who *were* with him rallied and came to the battle; and
behold, every man's sword was against his fellow, *and there was* very great confusion.
21 Now the Hebrews *who* were with the Philistines previously, who went up with them

14:2 1 Sam 13:15, 16; Is 10:28; 1 Sam 13:15
14:3 1 Sam 22:9-12, 20; 1 Sam 4:21; 1 Sam 1:3; 1 Sam 2:28
14:4 1 Sam 13:23
14:6 1 Sam 17:26, 36; Jer 9:25, 26; Judg 7:4, 7; 1 Sam 17:46, 47; Ps 115:3; 135:6; Zech 4:6; Matt 19:26
14:8 Judg 7:9-14
14:10 Gen 24:14; Judg 6:36
14:11 1 Sam 13:6; 14:22
14:12 1 Sam 17:43, 44; 2 Sam 5:24
14:15 1 Sam 13:17, 18; 1 Sam 7:10; Gen 35:5; 2 Kin 7:6
14:18 1 Sam 23:9; 30:7
14:19 Num 27:21
14:20 Judg 7:22; 2 Chr 20:23
14:21 1 Sam 29:4

9 Lit *trembling of God*

14:6 Jonathan and his armor bearer weren't much of a force to attack the huge Philistine army. But while everyone else was afraid, they trusted God, knowing that the size of the enemy army would not restrict God's ability to help them. God honored the faith and brave action of these two men with a tremendous victory.

Have you ever felt surrounded by the "enemy" or faced overwhelming odds? God is never intimidated by the size of the enemy or the complexity of a problem. With him, there are always enough resources to resist the pressures and win the battle. If God has called you to action, then bravely commit what resources you have to God, and rely upon him to lead you to victory.

14:12 Jonathan did not have the authority to lead all the troops into battle, but he could start a small skirmish in one corner of the enemy camp. When he did, panic broke out among the Philistines, the Hebrews who had been drafted into the Philistine army revolted, and the men who were hiding in the hills regained their courage and returned to fight.

When you are facing a difficult situation that is beyond your control, ask yourself, "What steps can I take now to work toward a solution?" A few small steps may be just what is needed to begin the chain of events leading to eventual victory.

14:19 "Withdraw your hand" refers to the use of the Urim and Thummim. They were withdrawn from the linen ephod (vest) as a way to determine God's will (see the note on 10:20). Saul was rushing the formalities of getting an answer from God so he could hurry and get into battle to take advantage of the confusion of the Philistines.

all around in the camp, even they also *turned* to be with the Israelites who *were* with Saul
and Jonathan.

14:22 1 Sam 13:6

22 When all the men of Israel who had hidden themselves in the hill country of Ephraim heard that the Philistines had fled, even they also pursued them closely in the battle.

14:23 Ex 14:30; 1 Sam 10:19; 14:23; 1 Chr 11:14; 2 Chr 32:22; Ps 44:7; 1 Sam 13:5

23 So the LORD delivered Israel that day, and the battle spread beyond Beth-aven.

Saul's Foolish Order

14:24 Josh 6:26

24 Now the men of Israel were hard-pressed on that day, for Saul had put the people
under oath, saying, "Cursed be the man who eats food before evening, and until I have
avenged myself on my enemies." So none of the people tasted food.
25 All *the people of* the land entered the forest, and there was honey on the ground.

14:26 Matt 3:4

26 When the people entered the forest, behold, *there was* a flow of honey; but no man
put his hand to his mouth, for the people feared the oath.

14:27 1 Sam 14:43; 1 Sam 30:12

27 But Jonathan had not heard when his father put the people under oath; therefore,
he put out the end of the staff that *was* in his hand and dipped it in the honeycomb, and
put his hand to his mouth, and his eyes brightened.
28 Then one of the people said, "Your father strictly put the people under oath, saying, 'Cursed be the man who eats food today.' " And the people were weary.

14:29 Josh 7:25; 1 Kin 18:18

29 Then Jonathan said, "My father has troubled the land. See now, how my eyes have
brightened because I tasted a little of this honey.
30 "How much more, if only the people had eaten freely today of the spoil of their enemies which they found! For now the slaughter among the Philistines has not been great."

14:31 1 Sam 14:5; Josh 10:12

31 They struck among the Philistines that day from Michmash to Aijalon. And the
people were very weary.

14:32 1 Sam 15:19; Gen 9:4; Lev 3:17; 17:10-14; 19:26; Deut 12:16, 23; Acts 15:20

32 The people rushed greedily upon the spoil, and took sheep and oxen and calves,
and slew *them* on the ground; and the people ate *them* with the blood.
33 Then they told Saul, saying, "Behold, the people are sinning against the LORD by
eating with the blood." And he said, "You have acted treacherously; roll a great stone to
me today."

14:33 Lev 7:26, 27; 19:26; Deut 12:16, 23-25; 15:23

34 Saul said, "Disperse yourselves among the people and say to them, 'Each one of
you bring me his ox or his sheep, and slaughter *it* here and eat; and do not sin against the
LORD by eating with the blood.' " So all the people that night brought each one his ox
with him and slaughtered *it* there.

GLOOM AND DOOM

Reference	*Message*
1 Samuel 3:11–14	Judgment will come to the house of Eli.
1 Samuel 7:1–4	The nation must turn from idol worship.
1 Samuel 8:10–22	Your kings will bring you nothing but trouble.
1 Samuel 12:25	If you continue in sin, you will be destroyed by God.
1 Samuel 13:13–14	Saul's kingdom will not continue.
1 Samuel 15:17–31	Saul, you have sinned before God.

It wasn't easy being a prophet. Most of the messages they had to give were very unpleasant to hear. They preached of repentance, judgment, impending destruction, sin, and in general, how displeased God was over the behavior of his people. Prophets were not the most popular people in town (unless they were false prophets and said just what the people wanted to hear). But popularity was not the bottom line for true prophets of God—it was obedience to God and faithfully proclaiming his word. Samuel is a good example of a faithful prophet.

God has words for us to proclaim as well. And although his messages are loaded with "good news," there is also "bad news" to give. May we, like true prophets, faithfully deliver all God's words, regardless of their popularity or lack of it.

14:24 Saul made an oath without thinking through the implications. The results? (1) His men were too tired to fight; (2) they were so hungry they ate meat that still contained blood, which was against God's Law (14:32); (3) Saul almost killed his own son (14:42–44).

Saul's impulsive oath sounded heroic, but it had disastrous side effects. If you are in the middle of a conflict, guard against impulsive statements that you may be forced to honor.

14:32–34 One of the oldest and strongest Hebrew food laws was the prohibition against eating meat containing the animal's blood (Leviticus 7:26–27). This law began in Noah's day (Genesis 9:4) and was still observed by the early Christians (Acts 15:27–29). It was wrong to eat blood because blood represented life and life belonged to God. (For a further explanation, see Leviticus 17:10–14.)

35 And Saul built an altar to the LORD; it was the first altar that he built to the LORD.
36 Then Saul said, "Let us go down after the Philistines by night and take spoil among
them until the morning light, and let us not leave a man of them." And they said, "Do
whatever seems good to you." So the priest said, "Let us draw near to God here."
37 Saul inquired of God, "Shall I go down after the Philistines? Will You give them
into the hand of Israel?" But He did not answer him on that day.
38 Saul said, "Draw near here, all you chiefs of the people, and investigate and see how
this sin has happened today.
39 "For as the LORD lives, who delivers Israel, though it is in Jonathan my son, he shall
surely die." But not one of all the people answered him.
40 Then he said to all Israel, "You shall be on one side and I and Jonathan my son will
be on the other side." And the people said to Saul, "Do what seems good to you."
41 Therefore, Saul said to the LORD, the God of Israel, "Give a perfect *lot*." And Jonathan and Saul were taken, but the people escaped.
42 Saul said, "Cast *lots* between me and Jonathan my son." And Jonathan was taken.
43 Then Saul said to Jonathan, "Tell me what you have done." So Jonathan told him
and said, "I indeed tasted a little honey with the end of the staff that was in my hand.
Here I am, I must die!"
44 Saul said, "May God do this *to me* and more also, for you shall surely die, Jonathan."
45 But the people said to Saul, "Must Jonathan die, who has brought about this great
deliverance in Israel? Far from it! As the LORD lives, not one hair of his head shall fall
to the ground, for he has worked with God this day." So the people rescued Jonathan
and he did not die.
46 Then Saul went up from pursuing the Philistines, and the Philistines went to their
own place.

14:35 1 Sam 7:12, 17; 2 Sam 24:25; James 4:8
14:36 1 Sam 14:3, 18, 19
14:37 1 Sam 10:22; 1 Sam 28:6
14:38 Josh 7:11, 12; 1 Sam 10:19, 20
14:39 1 Sam 14:24, 44; 2 Sam 12:5
14:41 Acts 1:24
14:43 Josh 7:19; 1 Sam 14:27
14:44 Ruth 1:17; 1 Sam 25:22; 1 Sam 14:39
14:45 2 Sam 14:11; 1 Kin 1:52; Luke 21:18; Acts 27:34; 2 Cor 6:1

Constant Warfare

47 Now when Saul had taken the kingdom over Israel, he fought against all his enemies on every side, against Moab, the sons of Ammon, Edom, the kings of Zobah, and
the Philistines; and wherever he turned, he inflicted punishment.
48 He acted valiantly and defeated the Amalekites, and delivered Israel from the hands
of those who plundered them.
49 Now the sons of Saul were Jonathan and Ishvi and Malchi-shua; and the names of
his two daughters *were these:* the name of the firstborn Merab and the name of the younger Michal.

14:47 1 Sam 11:1-13; 2 Sam 8:3-10; 1 Sam 14:52
14:48 1 Sam 15:3, 7
14:49 1 Sam 31:2; 1 Chr 8:33; 10:2; 1 Sam 18:17-19; 1 Sam 18:20, 27; 19:12; 2 Sam 6:20-23

14:35–36 After being king for several years, Saul finally built his first altar to God, but only as a last resort. Throughout Saul's reign he consistently approached God only after he had tried everything else. This was in sharp contrast to the priest, who suggested that God be consulted *first.* How much better if Saul had gone to God first, building an altar as his first official act as king. God is too great to be an afterthought. When we turn to him first, we will never have to turn to him as a last resort.

14:39 This is the second of Saul's foolish oaths. Saul made the first of his two oaths (14:24–26) because he was overly anxious to defeat the Philistines and wanted to give his soldiers an incentive to finish the battle quickly. In the Bible, God never asked people to make oaths or vows, but if they did, he expected them to keep them (Leviticus 5:4; Numbers 30).

Saul's curse was not something God would have condoned, but still it was an oath. And Jonathan, although he didn't know about Saul's oath, was nevertheless guilty of breaking it. Like Jephthah (Judges 11), Saul made an oath that risked the life of his own child. Fortunately, the people intervened and spared Jonathan's life.

14:39 Saul had issued a ridiculous command and had driven his men to sin, but still he wouldn't back down even if he had to kill his son. When we make ridiculous statements, it is difficult to admit we are wrong. Sticking to the story, just to save face, only compounds the problem. It takes more courage to admit a mistake than to hold resolutely to an error.

14:43 Jonathan's spiritual character was in striking contrast to Saul's. Jonathan admitted what he had done; he did not try to make excuses. Even though he was unaware of Saul's oath, Jonathan was willing to accept the consequences of his actions. When you do wrong, even unintentionally, respond like Jonathan, not like Saul.

14:44–45 Saul made another foolish statement, this time because he was more concerned about saving face than being right. To spare Jonathan's life would require him to admit he had acted foolishly, an embarrassment for a king. Saul was really more interested in protecting his image than in enforcing his vow. Fortunately, the people came to Jonathan's rescue. Don't be like Saul. Admit your mistakes, and show that you are more interested in doing what is right than in looking good.

14:47 Why was Saul so successful right after he had disobeyed God and been told that his reign would end (13:13–14)? Sometimes ungodly people win battles. Victory is neither guaranteed nor limited to the righteous. God provides according to his will. God might have given Saul success for the sake of the people, not for Saul. He may have left Saul on the throne for a while to utilize his military talents so that David, Israel's next king, could spend more time focusing on the nation's spiritual battles. Regardless of God's reasons for delaying Saul's demise, his reign ended exactly the way God had foretold. The timing of God's plans and promises are known only to him. Our task is to commit our ways to God and then trust him for the outcome.

50 The name of Saul's wife was Ahinoam the daughter of Ahimaaz. And the name of the captain of his army was Abner the son of Ner, Saul's uncle.

51 Kish *was* the father of Saul, and Ner the father of Abner *was* the son of Abiel.

52 Now the war against the Philistines was severe all the days of Saul; and when Saul saw any mighty man or any valiant man, he attached him to his staff.

Saul's Disobedience

15 Then Samuel said to Saul, "The LORD sent me to anoint you as king over His people, over Israel; now therefore, listen to the words of the LORD.

2 "Thus says the LORD of hosts, 'I will punish Amalek *for* what he did to Israel, how he set himself against him on the way while he was coming up from Egypt.

3 'Now go and strike Amalek and utterly destroy all that he has, and do not spare him; but put to death both man and woman, child and infant, ox and sheep, camel and donkey.' "

4 Then Saul summoned the people and numbered them in Telaim, 200,000 foot soldiers and 10,000 men of Judah.

5 Saul came to the city of Amalek and set an ambush in the valley.

6 Saul said to the Kenites, "Go, depart, go down from among the Amalekites, so that I do not destroy you with them; for you showed kindness to all the sons of Israel when they came up from Egypt." So the Kenites departed from among the Amalekites.

7 So Saul defeated the Amalekites, from Havilah as you go to Shur, which is east of Egypt.

8 He captured Agag the king of the Amalekites alive, and utterly destroyed all the people with the edge of the sword.

9 But Saul and the people spared Agag and the best of the sheep, the oxen, the fatlings, the lambs, and all that was good, and were not willing to destroy them utterly; but everything despised and worthless, that they utterly destroyed.

Samuel Rebukes Saul

10 Then the word of the LORD came to Samuel, saying,

11 "I regret that I have made Saul king, for he has turned back from following Me and has not carried out My commands." And Samuel was distressed and cried out to the LORD all night.

12 Samuel rose early in the morning to meet Saul; and it was told Samuel, saying, "Saul came to Carmel, and behold, he set up a monument for himself, then turned and proceeded on down to Gilgal."

13 Samuel came to Saul, and Saul said to him, "Blessed are you of the LORD! I have carried out the command of the LORD."

14:50 2 Sam 2:8
14:51 1 Sam 9:1, 21
14:52 1 Sam 8:11
15:1 1 Sam 9:16; 10:1
15:2 Ex 17:8-16; Num 24:20; Deut 25:17-19
15:3 Num 24:20; Deut 20:16-18; Josh 6:17-21; 1 Sam 22:19
15:4 Josh 15:24
15:6 Num 24:21; Judg 1:16; 4:11; Ex 18:9, 10; Num 10:29-32
15:7 1 Sam 14:48; Gen 25:18; Gen 16:7; Ex 15:22; 1 Sam 27:8
15:8 Num 24:7; 1 Sam 15:20; Esth 3:1; 1 Sam 27:8, 9; 30:1; 2 Sam 8:12
15:9 1 Sam 15:3, 15, 19
15:11 Gen 6:6, 7; Ex 32:14; 1 Sam 15:35; 2 Sam 24:16; Josh 22:16; 1 Sam 13:13; 1 Kin 9:6, 7; Ex 32:11-13; Luke 6:12
15:12 Josh 15:55; 1 Sam 25:2; 1 Sam 13:12, 15
15:13 Gen 14:19; Judg 17:2; Ruth 3:10; 2 Sam 2:5

15:2–3 Why did God command such utter destruction? The Amalekites were a band of guerrilla terrorists. They lived by attacking other nations and carrying off their wealth and their families. They were the first to attack the Israelites as they entered the promised land, and they continued to raid Israelite camps at every opportunity. God knew that the Israelites could never live peacefully in the promised land as long as the Amalekites existed. He also knew that their corrupt, idolatrous religious practices threatened Israel's relationship with him. The only way to protect the Israelites' bodies and souls was to utterly destroy the people of this warlike nation and all their possessions, including their idols.

15:9 Saul and his men did not destroy all the plunder from the battle as God commanded (15:3). The law of devoting something—setting it aside—entirely for destruction was well known to the Israelites. Anything under God's ban was to be completely destroyed (Deuteronomy 20:16–18). This was set up in order to prevent idolatry from taking hold in Israel because many of the valuables were idols. To break this law was punishable by death (Joshua 7). It showed disrespect and disregard for God because it directly violated his command.

When we gloss over sin in order to protect what we have or for material gain, we aren't being shrewd; we are disobeying God's law. Selective obedience is just another form of disobedience.

15:11 When God said he regretted that he had made Saul king, was he saying he had made a mistake? God's comment was an expression of sorrow, not an admission of error (Genesis 6:5–7). An omniscient God cannot make a mistake; therefore, God did not change his mind. He did, however, change his attitude toward Saul when Saul changed. Saul's heart no longer belonged to God, but to his own interests.

15:12 Saul built a monument in honor of himself. What a contrast to Moses and Joshua, who gave all the credit to God.

15:13–14 Saul thought he had won a great victory over the Amalekites, but God saw it as a great failure because Saul had disobeyed him and then lied to Samuel about the results of the battle. Saul may have thought his lie wouldn't be detected, or that what he did was not wrong. Saul was deceiving himself.

Dishonest people soon begin to believe the lies they construct around themselves. Then they lose the ability to tell the difference between truth and lies. By believing your own lies you deceive yourself, you will alienate yourself from God, and you will lose credibility in all your relationships. In the long run, honesty wins out.

14 But Samuel said, "What then is this bleating of the sheep in my ears, and the lowing
of the oxen which I hear?"
15 Saul said, "They have brought them from the Amalekites, for the people spared the
best of the sheep and oxen, to sacrifice to the LORD your God; but the rest we have utterly destroyed."
16 Then Samuel said to Saul, "Wait, and let me tell you what the LORD said to me last
night." And he said to him, "Speak!"
17 Samuel said, "Is it not true, though you were little in your own eyes, you were *made*
the head of the tribes of Israel? And the LORD anointed you king over Israel,
18 and the LORD sent you on a mission, and said, 'Go and utterly destroy the sinners,
the Amalekites, and fight against them until they are exterminated.'
19 "Why then did you not obey the voice of the LORD, but rushed upon the spoil and
did what was evil in the sight of the LORD?"
20 Then Saul said to Samuel, "I did obey the voice of the LORD, and went on the mission on which the LORD sent me, and have brought back Agag the king of Amalek, and
have utterly destroyed the Amalekites.
21 "But the people took *some* of the spoil, sheep and oxen, the choicest of the things
devoted to destruction, to sacrifice to the LORD your God at Gilgal."
22 Samuel said,
"Has the LORD as much delight in burnt offerings and sacrifices
As in obeying the voice of the LORD?
Behold, to obey is better than sacrifice,
And to heed than the fat of rams.
23 "For rebellion is as the sin of divination,
And insubordination is as iniquity and idolatry.
Because you have rejected the word of the LORD,
He has also rejected you from *being* king."
24 Then Saul said to Samuel, "I have sinned; I have indeed transgressed the command
of the LORD and your words, because I feared the people and listened to their voice.
25 "Now therefore, please pardon my sin and return with me, that I may worship the
LORD."
26 But Samuel said to Saul, "I will not return with you; for you have rejected the word
of the LORD, and the LORD has rejected you from being king over Israel."
27 As Samuel turned to go, *Saul* seized the edge of his robe, and it tore.
28 So Samuel said to him, "The LORD has torn the kingdom of Israel from you today
and has given it to your neighbor, who is better than you.
29 "Also the Glory of Israel will not lie or change His mind; for He is not a man that He
should change His mind."
30 Then he said, "I have sinned; *but* please honor me now before the elders of my people and before Israel, and go back with me, that I may worship the LORD your God."
31 So Samuel went back following Saul, and Saul worshiped the LORD.

15:14 Ex 32:21-24

15:15 Gen 3:12, 13; Ex 32:22, 23; 1 Sam 15:9, 21

15:17 1 Sam 9:21; 10:22

15:18 1 Sam 15:3

15:19 1 Sam 14:32

15:20 1 Sam 15:13

15:21 Ex 32:22, 23; 1 Sam 15:15

15:22 Ps 40:6-8; 51:16, 17; Is 1:11-15; Mic 6:6-8; Heb 10:6-9; Jer 7:22, 23; Hos 6:6; Matt 12:7; Mark 12:33

15:23 Deut 18:10; Gen 31:19, 34; 1 Sam 13:14

15:24 Num 22:34; 2 Sam 12:13; Ps 51:4; Prov 29:25; Is 51:12, 13

15:25 Ex 10:17

15:26 1 Sam 13:14; 16:1

15:27 1 Kin 11:30, 31

15:28 1 Sam 28:17, 18; 1 Kin 11:31

15:29 1 Chr 29:11; Num 23:19; Ezek 24:14; Titus 1:2

15:30 John 5:44; 12:43; Is 29:13

15:22–23 This is the first of numerous places in the Bible where the theme "to obey is better than sacrifice" is stated (Psalms 40:6–8; 51:16, 17; Proverbs 21:3; Isaiah 1:11–17; Jeremiah 7:21–23; Hosea 6:6; Micah 6:6–8; Matthew 12:7; Mark 12:33; Hebrews 10:8, 9). Was Samuel saying that sacrifice is unimportant? No, he was urging Saul to look at his reasons for making the sacrifice rather than at the sacrifice itself. A sacrifice was a ritual transaction between man and God that physically demonstrated a relationship between them. But if the person's heart was not truly repentant or if he did not truly love God, the sacrifice was a hollow ritual. Religious ceremonies or rituals are empty unless they are performed with an attitude of love and obedience. "Being religious" (going to church, serving on a committee, giving to charity) is not enough if we do not act out of devotion and obedience to God.

15:23 Rebellion and arrogance (insubordination) are serious sins. They involve far more than being independent and strong-minded. Scripture equates them with divination (witchcraft) and idolatry, sins worthy of death (Exodus 22:18; Leviticus 20:6; Deuteronomy 13:12–15; 18:10; Micah 5:10–14).

Saul became both rebellious and arrogant, so it is little wonder that God finally rejected him and took away his kingdom. Rebellion against God is perhaps the most serious sin of all because as long as a person rebels, he or she closes the door to forgiveness and restoration with God.

15:26 Saul's excuses had come to an end. It was the time of reckoning. God wasn't rejecting Saul as a person; the king could still seek forgiveness and restore his relationship with God, but it was too late to get his kingdom back. If you do not act responsibly with what God has entrusted to you, eventually you will run out of excuses. All of us must one day give an account for our actions (Romans 14:12; Revelation 22:12).

15:30 Saul was more concerned about what others would think of him than he was about the status of his relationship with God (15:24). He begged Samuel to go with him to worship as a public demonstration that Samuel still supported him. If Samuel had refused, the people probably would have lost all confidence in Saul.

15:33 Gen 9:6; Judg 1:7; Matt 7:2
15:34 1 Sam 7:17; 1 Sam 11:4
15:35 1 Sam 19:24; 1 Sam 16:1

32 Then Samuel said, "Bring me Agag, the king of the Amalekites." And Agag came
to him cheerfully. And Agag said, "Surely the bitterness of death is past."
33 But Samuel said, "As your sword has made women childless, so shall your mother
be childless among women." And Samuel hewed Agag to pieces before the LORD at
Gilgal.
34 Then Samuel went to Ramah, but Saul went up to his house at Gibeah of Saul.
35 Samuel did not see Saul again until the day of his death; for Samuel grieved over
Saul. And the LORD regretted that He had made Saul king over Israel.

C. SAUL AND DAVID (16:1—31:13)

While Saul is still on the throne, Samuel anoints David as Israel's next king. Young David then bravely conquers Goliath, the Philistine champion, and establishes a lifelong friendship with Jonathan, Saul's son. When Saul realizes that David will become king one day, he grows very jealous and tries to kill David on several occasions. David escapes into Philistine territory until Saul is killed in battle. When treated unjustly, we should not take matters into our own hands. God, who is faithful and just, sees all that is happening and will judge all evil.

1. Samuel anoints David

Samuel Goes to Bethlehem

16:1 1 Sam 15:35; 1 Sam 13:13, 14; 15:23; 1 Sam 9:16; 10:1; 2 Kin 9:1; Ruth 4:17-22; Ps 78:70, 71; Acts 13:22
16:2 1 Sam 20:29
16:3 Ex 4:15; Acts 9:6; Deut 17:14, 15; 1 Sam 9:16
16:4 Gen 48:7; Luke 2:4; 1 Kin 2:13; 2 Kin 9:22; 1 Chr 12:17, 18
16:5 Gen 35:2; Ex 19:10
16:6 1 Sam 17:13
16:7 1 Sam 2:3; 1 Kin 8:39; 1 Chr 28:9; Luke 16:15
16:8 1 Sam 17:13
16:9 1 Sam 17:13
16:11 1 Sam 17:12; 2 Sam 13:3
16:12 Gen 39:6; Ex 2:2; Acts 7:20; 1 Sam 9:17

16 Now the LORD said to Samuel, "How long will you grieve over Saul, since I have
rejected him from being king over Israel? Fill your horn with oil and go; I will send
you to Jesse the Bethlehemite, for I have selected a king for Myself among his sons."
2 But Samuel said, "How can I go? When Saul hears *of it,* he will kill me." And the
LORD said, "Take a heifer with you and say, 'I have come to sacrifice to the LORD.'
3 "You shall invite Jesse to the sacrifice, and I will show you what you shall do; and
you shall anoint for Me the one whom I designate to you."
4 So Samuel did what the LORD said, and came to Bethlehem. And the elders of the
city came trembling to meet him and said, "Do you come in peace?"
5 He said, "In peace; I have come to sacrifice to the LORD. Consecrate yourselves
and come with me to the sacrifice." He also consecrated Jesse and his sons and invited
them to the sacrifice.
6 When they entered, he looked at Eliab and thought, "Surely the LORD'S anointed
is before Him."
7 But the LORD said to Samuel, "Do not look at his appearance or at the height of his
stature, because I have rejected him; for God *sees* not as man sees, for man looks at the
outward appearance, but the LORD looks at the heart."
8 Then Jesse called Abinadab and made him pass before Samuel. And he said, "The
LORD has not chosen this one either."
9 Next Jesse made Shammah pass by. And he said, "The LORD has not chosen this
one either."
10 Thus Jesse made seven of his sons pass before Samuel. But Samuel said to Jesse,
"The LORD has not chosen these."
11 And Samuel said to Jesse, "Are these all the children?" And he said, "There remains
yet the youngest, and behold, he is tending the sheep." Then Samuel said to Jesse, "Send
and bring him; for we will not sit down until he comes here."

David Anointed

12 So he sent and brought him in. Now he was ruddy, with beautiful eyes and a handsome appearance. And the LORD said, "Arise, anoint him; for this is he."

16:5 Samuel "consecrated" Jesse and his sons to prepare them to come before God in worship or to offer a sacrifice. For more on this ceremony, see Genesis 35:2; Exodus 19:10, 14; and the note on Joshua 3:5.

16:7 Saul was tall and handsome; he was an impressive-looking man. Samuel may have been trying to find someone who looked like Saul to be Israel's next king, but God warned him against judging by appearance alone. When people judge by outward appearance, they may overlook quality individuals who lack the particular physical qualities society currently admires. Appearance doesn't reveal what people are really like or what their true value is.

Fortunately, God judges by faith and character, not appearances. And because only God can see on the inside, only he can accurately judge people. Most people spend hours each week maintaining their outward appearance; they should do even more to develop their inner character. While everyone can see your face, only you and God know what your heart really looks like. What steps are you taking to improve your heart's attitude?

13 Then Samuel took the horn of oil and anointed him in the midst of his brothers;
and the Spirit of the LORD came mightily upon David from that day forward. And Samuel arose and went to Ramah.
14 Now the Spirit of the LORD departed from Saul, and an evil spirit from the LORD
terrorized him.
15 Saul's servants then said to him, "Behold now, an evil spirit from God is terroriz-
ing you.
16 "Let our lord now command your servants who are before you. Let them seek a man
who is a skillful player on the harp; and it shall come about when the evil spirit from
God is on you, that he shall play *the harp* with his hand, and you will be well."
17 So Saul said to his servants, "Provide for me now a man who can play well and bring
him to me."
18 Then one of the young men said, "Behold, I have seen a son of Jesse the Bethlehemite who is a skillful musician, a mighty man of valor, a warrior, one prudent in speech,
and a handsome man; and the LORD is with him."
19 So Saul sent messengers to Jesse and said, "Send me your son David who is with the
flock."
20 Jesse took a donkey *loaded with* bread and a jug of wine and a young goat, and sent
them to Saul by David his son.
21 Then David came to Saul and attended him; and Saul loved him greatly, and he
became his armor bearer.
22 Saul sent to Jesse, saying, "Let David now stand before me, for he has found favor
in my sight."
23 So it came about whenever the *evil* spirit from God came to Saul, David would take
the harp and play *it* with his hand; and Saul would be refreshed and be well, and the evil
spirit would depart from him.

16:13 1 Sam 10:1; Num 27:18; 1 Sam 10:6, 9, 10
16:14 Judg 16:20; 1 Sam 11:6; 18:12; 28:15; Judg 9:23; 1 Sam 16:15, 16; 18:10; 19:9; 1 Kin 22:19-22
16:16 1 Sam 18:10; 19:9; 2 Kin 3:15
16:18 1 Sam 17:32-36; 1 Sam 3:19
16:20 1 Sam 10:4, 27; Prov 18:16
16:21 Gen 41:46; Prov 22:29
16:23 1 Sam 16:14-16

2. David and Goliath

Goliath's Challenge

17 Now the Philistines gathered their armies for battle; and they were gathered at
Socoh which belongs to Judah, and they camped between Socoh and Azekah, in
Ephes-dammim.
2 Saul and the men of Israel were gathered and camped in the valley of Elah, and
drew up in battle array to encounter the Philistines.
3 The Philistines stood on the mountain on one side while Israel stood on the mountain on the other side, with the valley between them.
4 Then a champion came out from the armies of the Philistines named Goliath, from
Gath, whose height was six [10]cubits and a span.
5 *He had* a bronze helmet on his head, and he was clothed with scale-armor which
weighed five thousand shekels of bronze.

17:1 1 Sam 13:5; Josh 15:35; 2 Chr 28:18; Josh 10:10; 1 Chr 11:13
17:2 1 Sam 21:9
17:4 2 Sam 21:19; Josh 11:22

10 I.e. One cubit equals approx 18 in.

16:13 David was anointed king, but it was done in secret; he was not publicly anointed until much later (2 Samuel 2:4; 5:3). Saul was still legally the king, but God was preparing David for his future responsibilities. The anointing oil poured over David's head stood for holiness. It was used to set people or objects apart for God's service. Each king and high priest of Israel was anointed with oil. This commissioned him as God's representative to the nation. Although God rejected Saul's kingship by not allowing any of his descendants to sit on Israel's throne, Saul himself remained in his position until his death.

16:14 What was this evil spirit the Lord sent? Perhaps Saul was simply depressed. Or perhaps the Holy Spirit had left Saul, and God allowed an evil spirit (a demon) to torment him as judgment for his disobedience (this would demonstrate God's power over the spirit world—1 Kings 22:19–23). Either way, Saul was driven to insanity, which led him to attempt to murder David.

16:15–16 Harps were popular musical instruments in Saul's day, and their music is still known for its soothing qualities. The simplest harps were merely two pieces of wood fastened at right angles to each other. The strings were stretched across the wood to give the harp a triangular shape. Simple strings could be made of twisted grasses, but better strings were made of dried animal intestine. Harps could have up to 40 strings and were louder than the smaller three- or four-stringed instruments called lyres. David, known for his shepherding skills and bravery, was also an accomplished harpist and musician who would eventually write many of the psalms found in the Bible.

16:19–21 When Saul asked David to be in his service, he obviously did not know that David had been secretly anointed king (16:12). Saul's invitation presented an excellent opportunity for the young man and future king to gain firsthand information about leading a nation ("David went back and forth from Saul," 17:15).

Sometimes our plans—even the ones we think God has approved—have to be put on hold indefinitely. Like David, we can use this waiting time profitably. We can choose to learn and grow in our present circumstances, whatever they may be.

17:4–7 In the days of the exodus, most of the Israelites had been afraid to enter the promised land because of the giants living there (Numbers 13:32, 33). King Og of Bashan needed a bed over 13

17:6 1 Sam 17:45
17:7 2 Sam 21:19; 1 Chr 11:23; 1 Sam 17:41
17:8 1 Sam 8:17
17:9 2 Sam 2:12-16
17:10 1 Sam 17:26, 36, 45; 2 Sam 21:21
17:12 Ruth 4:22; 1 Sam 16:18; Gen 35:19; 1 Sam 16:10, 11; 1 Chr 2:13-15
17:13 1 Sam 16:6, 8, 9
17:14 1 Sam 16:11
17:15 1 Sam 16:21-23; 1 Sam 16:11, 19
17:17 1 Sam 25:18
17:18 1 Sam 16:20; Gen 37:13, 14

6 *He* also *had* bronze [11]greaves on his legs and a bronze javelin *slung* between his
shoulders.
7 The shaft of his spear was like a weaver's beam, and the head of his spear *weighed*
six hundred shekels of iron; his shield-carrier also walked before him.
8 He stood and shouted to the ranks of Israel and said to them, "Why do you come
out to draw up in battle array? Am I not the Philistine and you servants of Saul? Choose
a man for yourselves and let him come down to me.
9 "If he is able to fight with me and kill me, then we will become your servants; but if
I prevail against him and kill him, then you shall become our servants and serve us."
10 Again the Philistine said, "I defy the ranks of Israel this day; give me a man that we
may fight together."
11 When Saul and all Israel heard these words of the Philistine, they were dismayed
and greatly afraid.
12 Now David was the son of the Ephrathite of Bethlehem in Judah, whose name was
Jesse, and he had eight sons. And Jesse was old in the days of Saul, advanced *in years*
among men.
13 The three older sons of Jesse had gone after Saul to the battle. And the names of
his three sons who went to the battle were Eliab the firstborn, and the second to him
Abinadab, and the third Shammah.
14 David was the youngest. Now the three oldest followed Saul,
15 but David went back and forth from Saul to tend his father's flock at Bethlehem.
16 The Philistine came forward morning and evening for forty days and took his stand.
17 Then Jesse said to David his son, "Take now for your brothers an ephah of this roasted grain and these ten loaves and run to the camp to your brothers.
18 "Bring also these ten cuts of cheese to the commander of *their* thousand, and look
into the welfare of your brothers, and bring back news of them.
19 "For Saul and they and all the men of Israel are in the valley of Elah, fighting with
the Philistines."

David Accepts the Challenge

17:20 1 Sam 26:5, 7
17:22 Judg 18:21; Is 10:28
17:23 1 Sam 17:8-10

20 So David arose early in the morning and left the flock with a keeper and took *the
supplies* and went as Jesse had commanded him. And he came to the circle of the camp
while the army was going out in battle array shouting the war cry.
21 Israel and the Philistines drew up in battle array, army against army.
22 Then David left his baggage in the care of the baggage keeper, and ran to the battle
line and entered in order to greet his brothers.
23 As he was talking with them, behold, the champion, the Philistine from Gath named
Goliath, was coming up from the army of the Philistines, and he spoke these same words;
and David heard *them.*
24 When all the men of Israel saw the man, they fled from him and were greatly afraid.

11 Or *shin guards*

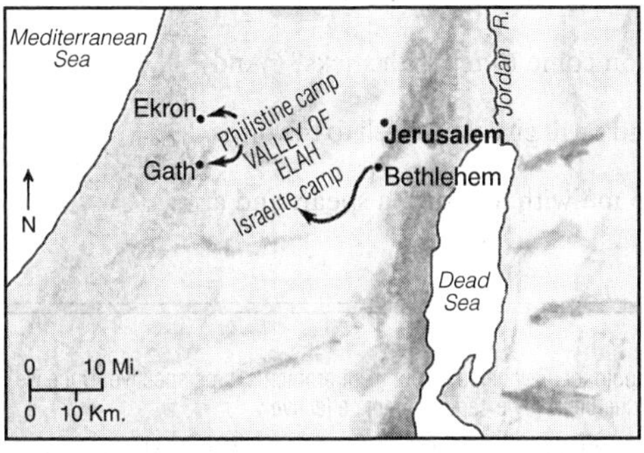

DAVID AND GOLIATH The armies of Israel and Philistia faced each other across the valley of Elah. David arrived from Bethlehem and offered to fight the giant Goliath. After David defeated Goliath, the Israelite army chased the Philistines to Ekron and Gath (Goliath's hometown).

feet long (Deuteronomy 3:11). Now Goliath, over nine feet tall, taunted Israel's soldiers and appeared invincible to them. Saul, the tallest of the Israelites, may have been especially worried because he was obviously the best match for Goliath. In God's eyes, however, Goliath was no different than anyone else.

17:9 An army often avoided the high cost of battle by pitting its strongest warrior against the strongest warrior of the enemy. This avoided great bloodshed because the winner of the fight was considered the winner of the battle. Goliath had the definite advantage against David from a human standpoint. But Goliath didn't realize that in fighting David, he also had to fight God.

17:16 Why would this go on for 40 days without one side attacking the other? They were camped on opposite sides of a valley with steep walls. Whoever would rush down the valley and up the steep cliffs would be at a disadvantage at the beginning of the battle and probably suffer great casualties. Each side was waiting for the other to attack first.

25 The men of Israel said, "Have you seen this man who is coming up? Surely he is
coming up to defy Israel. And it will be that the king will enrich the man who kills him
with great riches and will give him his daughter and make his father's house [12]free in
Israel."
26 Then David spoke to the men who were standing by him, saying, "What will be done
for the man who kills this Philistine and takes away the reproach from Israel? For who is
this uncircumcised Philistine, that he should taunt the armies of the living God?"
27 The people answered him in accord with this word, saying, "Thus it will be done for
the man who kills him."
28 Now Eliab his oldest brother heard when he spoke to the men; and Eliab's anger
burned against David and he said, "Why have you come down? And with whom have
you left those few sheep in the wilderness? I know your insolence and the wickedness of
your heart; for you have come down in order to see the battle."
29 But David said, "What have I done now? Was it not just a question?"
30 Then he turned away from him to another and said the same thing; and the people
answered the same thing as before.

David Kills Goliath

31 When the words which David spoke were heard, they told *them* to Saul, and he sent
for him.
32 David said to Saul, "Let no man's heart fail on account of him; your servant will go
and fight with this Philistine."
33 Then Saul said to David, "You are not able to go against this Philistine to fight with
him; for you are *but* a youth while he has been a warrior from his youth."
34 But David said to Saul, "Your servant was tending his father's sheep. When a lion
or a bear came and took a lamb from the flock,
35 I went out after him and attacked him, and rescued *it* from his mouth; and when he
rose up against me, I seized *him* by his beard and struck him and killed him.
36 "Your servant has killed both the lion and the bear; and this uncircumcised Philistine will be like one of them, since he has taunted the armies of the living God."
37 And David said, "The LORD who delivered me from the paw of the lion and from
the paw of the bear, He will deliver me from the hand of this Philistine." And Saul said
to David, "Go, and may the LORD be with you."
38 Then Saul clothed David with his garments and put a bronze helmet on his head,
and he clothed him with armor.
39 David girded his sword over his armor and tried to walk, for he had not tested *them.*
So David said to Saul, "I cannot go with these, for I have not tested *them.*" And David
took them off.
40 He took his stick in his hand and chose for himself five smooth stones from the brook,
and put them in the shepherd's bag which he had, even in *his* pouch, and his sling was in
his hand; and he approached the Philistine.
41 Then the Philistine came on and approached David, with the shield-bearer in front
of him.
42 When the Philistine looked and saw David, he disdained him; for he was *but* a youth,
and ruddy, with a handsome appearance.
43 The Philistine said to David, "Am I a dog, that you come to me with sticks?" And
the Philistine cursed David by his gods.
44 The Philistine also said to David, "Come to me, and I will give your flesh to the birds
of the sky and the beasts of the field."
45 Then David said to the Philistine, "You come to me with a sword, a spear, and a

17:25 Josh 15:16
17:26 1 Sam 11:2; 1 Sam 14:6; 17:36; Jer 9:25, 26; 1 Sam 17:10; Deut 5:26; 2 Kin 19:4; Jer 10:10
17:27 1 Sam 17:25
17:28 Gen 37:4, 8-36; Prov 18:19; Matt 10:36
17:30 1 Sam 17:26, 27
17:32 Deut 20:1-4; 1 Sam 16:18
17:33 Num 13:31
17:35 Amos 3:12
17:37 2 Cor 1:10; 2 Tim 4:17, 18; 1 Sam 20:13; 1 Chr 22:11, 16
17:40 Judg 20:16
17:42 Ps 123:4; Prov 16:18; 1 Sam 16:12
17:43 1 Sam 24:14; 2 Sam 3:8; 2 Kin 8:13; 1 Kin 20:10
17:44 1 Sam 17:46
17:45 2 Sam 22:35; 2 Chr 32:8; Ps 124:8; Heb 11:32-34

12 I.e. free from taxes and public service

17:26 What a difference perspective can make. Most of the onlookers saw only a giant. David, however, saw a mortal man defying almighty God. He knew he would not be alone when he faced Goliath; God would fight with him. He looked at his situation from God's point of view. Viewing impossible situations from God's point of view helps us put giant problems in perspective. Once we see clearly, we can fight more effectively.

17:28–32 Criticism couldn't stop David. While the rest of the army stood around, he knew the importance of taking action. With God to fight for him, there was no reason to wait. People may try to discourage you with negative comments or mockery, but continue to do what you know is right. By doing what is right, you will be pleasing God, whose opinion matters most.

javelin, but I come to you in the name of the LORD of hosts, the God of the armies of
Israel, whom you have taunted.

17:46 Deut 28:26; Josh 4:24; 1 Kin 8:43; 18:36; 2 Kin 19:19; Is 37:20

17:47 1 Sam 14:6; 2 Chr 14:11; 20:15; Ps 44:6; Hos 1:7; Zech 4:6; 2 Chr 20:15

17:48 Ps 27:3

46 "This day the LORD will deliver you up into my hands, and I will strike you down and
remove your head from you. And I will give the dead bodies of the army of the Philistines this day to the birds of the sky and the wild beasts of the earth, that all the earth
may know that there is a God in Israel,
47 and that all this assembly may know that the LORD does not deliver by sword or by
spear; for the battle is the LORD'S and He will give you into our hands."
48 Then it happened when the Philistine rose and came and drew near to meet David,
that David ran quickly toward the battle line to meet the Philistine.
49 And David put his hand into his bag and took from it a stone and slung *it,* and struck
the Philistine on his forehead. And the stone sank into his forehead, so that he fell on
his face to the ground.
50 Thus David prevailed over the Philistine with a sling and a stone, and he struck the
Philistine and killed him; but there was no sword in David's hand.

When we think of David, we think: shepherd, poet, giant-killer, king, ancestor of Jesus—in short, one of the greatest men in the Old Testament. But alongside that list stands another: betrayer, liar, adulterer, murderer. The first list gives qualities we all might like to have; the second, qualities that might be true of any one of us. The Bible makes no effort to hide David's failures. Yet he is remembered and respected for his heart for God. Knowing how much more we share in David's failures than in his greatness, we should be curious to find out what made God refer to David as "A MAN AFTER MY HEART" (Acts 13:22).

David, more than anything else, had an unchangeable belief in the faithful and forgiving nature of God. He was a man who lived with great zest. He sinned many times, but he was quick to confess his sins. His confessions were from the heart, and his repentance was genuine. David never took God's forgiveness lightly or his blessing for granted. In return, God never held back from David either his forgiveness or the consequences of his actions. David experienced the joy of forgiveness even when he had to suffer the consequences of his sins.

We tend to get these two reversed. Too often we would rather avoid the consequences than experience forgiveness. Another big difference between us and David is that while he sinned greatly, he did not sin repeatedly. He learned from his mistakes because he accepted the suffering they brought. Often we don't seem to learn from our mistakes or the consequences that result from those mistakes. What changes would it take for God to find this kind of obedience in you?

Strengths and accomplishments:
- Greatest king of Israel
- Ancestor of Jesus Christ
- Listed in the Hall of Faith in Hebrews 11
- A man described by God himself as a man after his own heart

Weaknesses and mistakes:
- Committed adultery with Bathsheba
- Arranged the murder of Uriah, Bathsheba's husband
- Directly disobeyed God in taking a census of the people
- Did not deal decisively with the sins of his children

Lessons from his life:
- Willingness to honestly admit our mistakes is the first step in dealing with them
- Forgiveness does not remove the consequences of sin
- God greatly desires our complete trust and worship

Vital statistics:
- Where: Bethlehem, Jerusalem
- Occupations: Shepherd, musician, poet, soldier, king
- Relatives: Father: Jesse. Wives: included Michal, Ahinoam, Bathsheba, Abigail. Sons: included Absalom, Amnon, Solomon, Adonijah. Daughters: included Tamar. Seven brothers
- Contemporaries: Saul, Jonathan, Samuel, Nathan

Key verses:
"Now, O Lord GOD, You are God, and Your words are truth, and You have promised this good thing to Your servant. Now therefore, may it please You to bless the house of Your servant, that it may continue forever before You. For You, O Lord GOD, have spoken; and with Your blessing may the house of Your servant be blessed forever" (2 Samuel 7:28–29).

His story is told in 1 Samuel 16—1 Kings 2. He is also mentioned in Amos 6:5; Matthew 1:1, 6; 22:43–45; Luke 1:32; Acts 13:22; Romans 1:3; Hebrews 11:32.

51 Then David ran and stood over the Philistine and took his sword and drew it out of
its sheath and killed him, and cut off his head with it. When the Philistines saw that their
champion was dead, they fled.
52 The men of Israel and Judah arose and shouted and pursued the Philistines as far
as the valley, and to the gates of Ekron. And the slain Philistines lay along the way to
Shaaraim, even to Gath and Ekron.
53 The sons of Israel returned from chasing the Philistines and plundered their camps.
54 Then David took the Philistine's head and brought it to Jerusalem, but he put his
weapons in his tent.
55 Now when Saul saw David going out against the Philistine, he said to Abner the
commander of the army, "Abner, whose son is this young man?" And Abner said, "By
your life, O king, I do not know."
56 The king said, "You inquire whose son the youth is."
57 So when David returned from killing the Philistine, Abner took him and brought
him before Saul with the Philistine's head in his hand.
58 Saul said to him, "Whose son are you, young man?" And David answered, "*I am*
the son of your servant Jesse the Bethlehemite."

17:51 1 Sam 21:9; 2 Sam 23:21; Heb 11:34
17:52 Josh 15:11; Josh 15:36
17:55 1 Sam 16:12, 21, 22
17:57 1 Sam 17:54
17:58 1 Sam 17:12

3. David and Jonathan become friends

Jonathan and David

18 Now it came about when he had finished speaking to Saul, that the soul of Jonathan was knit to the soul of David, and Jonathan loved him as himself.
2 Saul took him that day and did not let him return to his father's house.
3 Then Jonathan made a covenant with David because he loved him as himself.
4 Jonathan stripped himself of the robe that was on him and gave it to David, with his
armor, including his sword and his bow and his belt.
5 So David went out wherever Saul sent him, *and* prospered; and Saul set him over
the men of war. And it was pleasing in the sight of all the people and also in the sight of
Saul's servants.
6 It happened as they were coming, when David returned from killing the Philistine,
that the women came out of all the cities of Israel, singing and dancing, to meet King
Saul, with tambourines, with joy and with [13]musical instruments.
7 The women sang as they played, and said,
"Saul has slain his thousands,
And David his ten thousands."
8 Then Saul became very angry, for this saying displeased him; and he said, "They
have ascribed to David ten thousands, but to me they have ascribed thousands. Now what
more can he have but the kingdom?"
9 Saul looked at David with suspicion from that day on.

Saul Turns against David

10 Now it came about on the next day that an evil spirit from God came mightily upon
Saul, and he raved in the midst of the house, while David was playing *the harp* with his
hand, as usual; and a spear *was* in Saul's hand.

18:1 Gen 44:30; Deut 13:6; 1 Sam 20:17; 2 Sam 1:26
18:2 1 Sam 17:15
18:3 1 Sam 20:8-17
18:4 Gen 41:42; 1 Sam 17:38; Esth 6:8
18:6 Ex 15:20, 21; Judg 11:34; Ps 68:25; 149:3
18:7 Ex 15:21; 1 Sam 21:11; 29:5; 2 Sam 18:3
18:8 1 Sam 15:28
18:10 1 Sam 16:14; 1 Sam 19:23, 24; 1 Sam 16:23; 1 Sam 19:9

13 I.e. triangles; or three-stringed instruments

17:55–58 Although David had played his harp many times in front of Saul, Saul's question to Abner seems to show he didn't know David very well. Perhaps, since David was scheduled to marry Saul's daughter if he was successful (17:25), Saul wanted to know more about his family. Or possibly Saul's unstable mental condition (16:14) may have prevented him from recognizing David.

18:1–4 When David and Jonathan met, they became close friends at once. Their friendship is one of the deepest and closest recorded in the Bible: (1) they based their friendship on commitment to God, not just each other; (2) they let nothing come between them, not even career or family problems; (3) they drew closer together when their friendship was tested; (4) they remained friends to the end.

Jonathan, the prince of Israel, later realized that David, and not he, would be the next king (23:17). But that did not weaken his love for David. Jonathan would much rather lose the throne of Israel than lose his closest friend.

18:8 Saul's appreciation for David turned to jealousy as people began to applaud David's exploits. In a jealous rage, Saul attempted to murder David by hurling his spear at him (18:11–12).

Jealousy may not seem to be a major sin, but in reality, it is one step short of murder. Jealousy starts as you resent a rival; it leads to your wishing he or she were removed; then it manifests itself in your seeking ways to harm that person in word or action. Beware of letting jealousy get a foothold in your life.

18:10 The note on 16:14 explains what this evil spirit might have been.

18:11 1 Sam 19:10; 20:33
18:12 1 Sam 18:15, 29; 1 Sam 16:13, 18; 1 Sam 16:14; 28:15
18:13 Num 27:17; 1 Sam 18:16; 2 Sam 5:2
18:14 Gen 39:2, 3, 23; Josh 6:27; 1 Sam 16:18
18:16 1 Sam 18:5
18:17 1 Sam 17:25; Num 21:14; 1 Sam 17:36, 47; 25:28; 1 Sam 18:21, 25
18:18 1 Sam 9:21; 18:23; 2 Sam 7:18
18:19 2 Sam 21:8; Judg 7:22; 1 Kin 19:16
18:20 1 Sam 18:28
18:21 1 Sam 18:17; 1 Sam 18:26
18:23 Gen 29:20; 34:12

11 Saul hurled the spear for he thought, "I will pin David to the wall." But David escaped from his presence twice.
12 Now Saul was afraid of David, for the LORD was with him but had departed from
Saul.
13 Therefore Saul removed him from his presence and appointed him as his commander
of a thousand; and he went out and came in before the people.
14 David was prospering in all his ways for the LORD *was* with him.
15 When Saul saw that he was prospering greatly, he dreaded him.
16 But all Israel and Judah loved David, and he went out and came in before them.
17 Then Saul said to David, "Here is my older daughter Merab; I will give her to you
as a wife, only be a valiant man for me and fight the LORD'S battles." For Saul thought,
"My hand shall not be against him, but let the hand of the Philistines be against him."
18 But David said to Saul, "Who am I, and what is my life *or* my father's family in Israel, that I should be the king's son-in-law?"
19 So it came about at the time when Merab, Saul's daughter, should have been given
to David, that she was given to Adriel the Meholathite for a wife.

David Marries Saul's Daughter

20 Now Michal, Saul's daughter, loved David. When they told Saul, the thing was agreeable to him.
21 Saul thought, "I will give her to him that she may become a snare to him, and that
the hand of the Philistines may be against him." Therefore Saul said to David, "For a
second time you may be my son-in-law today."
22 Then Saul commanded his servants, "Speak to David secretly, saying, 'Behold, the
king delights in you, and all his servants love you; now therefore, become the king's son-
in-law.' "
23 So Saul's servants spoke these words to David. But David said, "Is it trivial in your
sight to become the king's son-in-law, since I am a poor man and lightly esteemed?"
24 The servants of Saul reported to him according to these words *which* David spoke.

SIMPLE OBJECTS

God often uses simple, ordinary objects to accomplish his tasks in the world. It is important only that they be dedicated to him for his use. What do you have that God can use? Anything and everything is a possible "instrument" for him.

Object	*Reference*	*Who used it?*	*How was it used?*
a staff	Exodus 4:2–4	Moses	To work miracles before Pharaoh
trumpets	Joshua 6:3–5	Joshua	To flatten the walls of Jericho
a fleece	Judges 6:36–40	Gideon	To confirm God's will
trumpets, pitchers, and torches	Judges 7:19–22	Gideon	To defeat the Midianites
jawbone	Judges 15:15	Samson	To kill 1,000 Philistines
small stone	1 Samuel 17:40	David	To kill Goliath
oil	2 Kings 4:1–7	Elisha	To demonstrate God's power to provide
a river	2 Kings 5:9–14	Elisha	To heal a man of leprosy
linen waistband	Jeremiah 13:1–11	Jeremiah	As an object lesson of God's wrath
jar	Jeremiah 19:1–13	Jeremiah	As an object lesson of God's wrath
iron plate, water, and food	Ezekiel 4:1–17	Ezekiel	As an object lesson of judgment
five loaves and two fish	Mark 6:30–44	Jesus	To feed a crowd of over 5,000 people

---

18:11–12 Saul tried to kill David because he was jealous of David's popularity, yet David continued to protect and comfort Saul. Perhaps people have been jealous of you and have even attacked you in some way. They may be intimidated by your strengths, which make them conscious of their own shortcomings. It would be natural to strike back or to avoid them. A better response is to befriend them (Matthew 5:43–44) and to ask God for the strength to continue to love them, as David kept on loving Saul.

18:15–18 While Saul's popularity made him proud and arrogant, David remained humble (18:23), even when the entire nation praised him. Although David succeeded in almost everything he tried and became famous throughout the land, he refused to use his popular support to his advantage against Saul. Don't allow popularity to twist your perception of your own importance. It's comparatively easy to be humble when you're not on center stage, but how will you react to praise and honor?

25 Saul then said, "Thus you shall say to David, 'The king does not desire any dowry
except a hundred foreskins of the Philistines, to take vengeance on the king's enemies.' "
Now Saul planned to make David fall by the hand of the Philistines.
26 When his servants told David these words, it pleased David to become the king's
son-in-law. Before the days had expired
27 David rose up and went, he and his men, and struck down two hundred men among
the Philistines. Then David brought their foreskins, and they gave them in full number
to the king, that he might become the king's son-in-law. So Saul gave him Michal his
daughter for a wife.
28 When Saul saw and knew that the LORD was with David, and *that* Michal, Saul's
daughter, loved him,
29 then Saul was even more afraid of David. Thus Saul was David's enemy continually.
30 Then the commanders of the Philistines went out *to battle,* and it happened as often
as they went out, that David behaved himself more wisely than all the servants of Saul.
So his name was highly esteemed.

David Protected from Saul

19 Now Saul told Jonathan his son and all his servants to put David to death. But
Jonathan, Saul's son, greatly delighted in David.
2 So Jonathan told David saying, "Saul my father is seeking to put you to death. Now
therefore, please be on guard in the morning, and stay in a secret place and hide yourself.
3 "I will go out and stand beside my father in the field where you are, and I will speak
with my father about you; if I find out anything, then I will tell you."
4 Then Jonathan spoke well of David to Saul his father and said to him, "Do not let
the king sin against his servant David, since he has not sinned against you, and since his
deeds *have been* very beneficial to you.
5 "For he took his life in his hand and struck the Philistine, and the LORD brought about
a great deliverance for all Israel; you saw *it* and rejoiced. Why then will you sin against
innocent blood by putting David to death without a cause?"
6 Saul listened to the voice of Jonathan, and Saul vowed, "As the LORD lives, he shall
not be put to death."
7 Then Jonathan called David, and Jonathan told him all these words. And Jonathan
brought David to Saul, and he was in his presence as formerly.
8 When there was war again, David went out and fought with the Philistines and defeated them with great slaughter, so that they fled before him.
9 Now there was an evil spirit from the LORD on Saul as he was sitting in his house
with his spear in his hand, and David was playing *the harp* with *his* hand.
10 Saul tried to pin David to the wall with the spear, but he slipped away out of Saul's
presence, so that he stuck the spear into the wall. And David fled and escaped that night.
11 Then Saul sent messengers to David's house to watch him, in order to put him to
death in the morning. But Michal, David's wife, told him, saying, "If you do not save
your life tonight, tomorrow you will be put to death."
12 So Michal let David down through a window, and he went out and fled and escaped.
13 Michal took the household idol and laid *it* on the bed, and put a quilt of goats' *hair*
at its head, and covered *it* with clothes.
14 When Saul sent messengers to take David, she said, "He is sick."
15 Then Saul sent messengers to see David, saying, "Bring him up to me on his bed,
that I may put him to death."
16 When the messengers entered, behold, the household idol *was* on the bed with the
quilt of goats' *hair* at its head.
17 So Saul said to Michal, "Why have you deceived me like this and let my enemy go,
so that he has escaped?" And Michal said to Saul, "He said to me, 'Let me go! Why should
I put you to death?' "

18:25 Gen 34:12; Ex 22:17; 1 Sam 14:24; 1 Sam 18:17
18:26 1 Sam 18:21
18:27 1 Sam 18:17; 2 Sam 3:14
18:30 2 Sam 11:1; 1 Sam 18:5
19:1 1 Sam 18:8, 9; 1 Sam 18:1-3
19:3 1 Sam 20:9, 13
19:4 1 Sam 20:32; Prov 31:8, 9; Gen 42:22; Prov 17:13; Jer 18:20
19:5 Judg 9:17; 1 Sam 17:49, 50; 28:21; Ps 119:109; 1 Sam 11:13; 1 Chr 11:14; Deut 19:10-13; 1 Sam 20:32; Ps 94:21; Matt 27:4
19:7 1 Sam 16:21; 18:2, 10, 13
19:9 1 Sam 16:14; 18:10, 11; 1 Sam 18:10; 1 Sam 16:16
19:10 1 Sam 18:11; 20:33; Prov 1:16
19:11 Judg 16:2; Ps 59: title
19:12 Josh 2:15; Acts 9:25; 2 Cor 11:33
19:13 Gen 31:19; Judg 18:14, 17
19:14 Josh 2:5
19:17 2 Sam 2:22

19:1–2 Is it ever right to disobey your father, as Jonathan did here? It is clearly a principle of Scripture that when a father instructs a son to break God's laws, the son should obey God rather than man. This principle assumes that the son is old enough to be accountable and to see through any deception. A son's role is to be respectful, helpful, and obedient to his father (Ephesians 6:1–3), but not to follow commands or advice that violate God's laws.

19:18 1 Sam 7:17; 1 Sam 19:22, 23

18 Now David fled and escaped and came to Samuel at Ramah, and told him all that
Saul had done to him. And he and Samuel went and stayed in Naioth.
19 It was told Saul, saying, "Behold, David is at Naioth in Ramah."

19:20 1 Sam 19:11, 14; John 7:32; 1 Sam 10:5, 6, 10; Num 11:25; Joel 2:28

20 Then Saul sent messengers to take David, but when they saw the company of the
prophets prophesying, with Samuel standing *and* presiding over them, the Spirit of God
came upon the messengers of Saul; and they also prophesied.
21 When it was told Saul, he sent other messengers, and they also prophesied. So Saul
sent messengers again the third time, and they also prophesied.
22 Then he himself went to Ramah and came as far as the large well that is in Secu;
and he asked and said, "Where are Samuel and David?" And *someone* said, "Behold,
they are at Naioth in Ramah."

19:23 1 Sam 10:10

23 He proceeded there to Naioth in Ramah; and the Spirit of God came upon him also,
so that he went along prophesying continually until he came to Naioth in Ramah.

19:24 2 Sam 6:20; Is 20:2; Mic 1:8; 1 Sam 10:10-12

24 He also stripped off his clothes, and he too prophesied before Samuel and lay
down naked all that day and all that night. Therefore they say, "Is Saul also among the
prophets?"

David and Jonathan Covenant

20:1 1 Sam 24:9

20 Then David fled from Naioth in Ramah, and came and said to Jonathan, "What
have I done? What is my iniquity? And what is my sin before your father, that he
is seeking my life?"
2 He said to him, "Far from it, you shall not die. Behold, my father does nothing either
great or small without disclosing it to me. So why should my father hide this thing from
me? It is not so!"

20:3 Deut 6:13; 1 Sam 25:26; 2 Kin 2:6

3 Yet David vowed again, saying, "Your father knows well that I have found favor in
your sight, and he has said, 'Do not let Jonathan know this, or he will be grieved.' But
truly as the LORD lives and as your soul lives, there is hardly a step between me and death."
4 Then Jonathan said to David, "Whatever you say, I will do for you."

20:5 Num 10:10; 28:11-15; Amos 8:5; 1 Sam 20:24, 27; 1 Sam 19:2

5 So David said to Jonathan, "Behold, tomorrow is the new moon, and I ought to sit
down to eat with the king. But let me go, that I may hide myself in the field until the
third evening.

20:6 1 Sam 17:58; Deut 12:5; 1 Sam 9:12

6 "If your father misses me at all, then say, 'David earnestly asked *leave* of me to run to
Bethlehem his city, because it is the yearly sacrifice there for the whole family.'

20:7 1 Sam 25:17

7 "If he says, 'It is good,' your servant *will be* safe; but if he is very angry, know that he
has decided on evil.

20:8 1 Sam 18:3; 23:18; 2 Sam 14:32

8 "Therefore deal kindly with your servant, for you have brought your servant into a
covenant of the LORD with you. But if there is iniquity in me, put me to death yourself;
for why then should you bring me to your father?"
9 Jonathan said, "Far be it from you! For if I should indeed learn that evil has been
decided by my father to come upon you, then would I not tell you about it?"

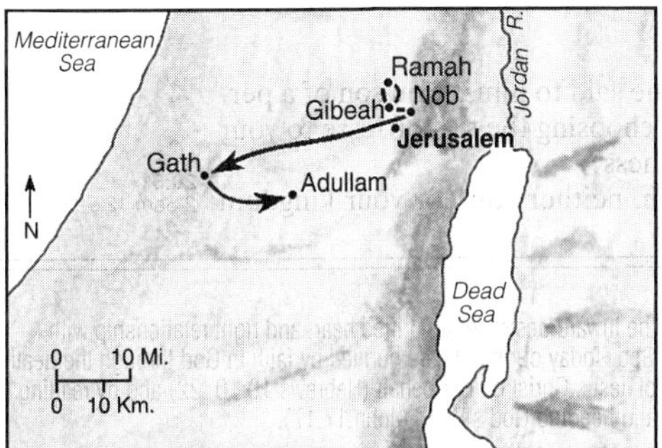

DAVID'S ESCAPE David learned of Saul's plans to kill him and fled to Samuel at Ramah. Returning to Gibeah to say good-bye to Jonathan, he then escaped to Nob, where he received food and a sword from the priest. He then fled to Gath in Philistine territory. When the Philistines became suspicious, he escaped to the cave of Adullam, where many men joined him.

19:20–24 This was the second time that Saul surprised everyone by joining a group of prophets and prophesying. The first time (chapter 10) happened right after he was anointed king and did not want to accept the responsibility. This time Saul was consumed with jealousy over David's growing popularity, but the Spirit of God immobilized him so he was unable to harm David. In both cases, Saul spoke God's words (he "prophesied"), although he was far from thinking God's thoughts.

20:5 At the beginning of each month, the Israelites gathered to celebrate the New Moon festival. While this was mainly a time to be enjoyed, it was also a way to dedicate the next month to God. Other nations had celebrations during the full moon and worshiped the moon itself. The Israelites, however, celebrated their festival at the time of the new moon, when the moon was not visible in the sky. This was an added precaution against false worship. Nothing in the creation is to be worshiped—only the Creator.

10 Then David said to Jonathan, "Who will tell me if your father answers you harshly?"
11 Jonathan said to David, "Come, and let us go out into the field." So both of them
went out to the field.
12 Then Jonathan said to David, "The LORD, the God of Israel, *be witness!* When I
have sounded out my father about this time tomorrow, *or* the third day, behold, if there
is good *feeling* toward David, shall I not then send to you and make it known to you?
13 "If it please my father *to do* you harm, may the LORD do so to Jonathan and more
also, if I do not make it known to you and send you away, that you may go in safety. And
may the LORD be with you as He has been with my father.
14 "If I am still alive, will you not show me the lovingkindness of the LORD, that I may
not die?
15 "You shall not cut off your lovingkindness from my house forever, not even when
the LORD cuts off every one of the enemies of David from the face of the earth."
16 So Jonathan made a *covenant* with the house of David, *saying,* "May the LORD require *it* at the hands of David's enemies."
17 Jonathan made David vow again because of his love for him, because he loved him
as he loved his own life.
18 Then Jonathan said to him, "Tomorrow is the new moon, and you will be missed
because your seat will be empty.
19 "When you have stayed for three days, you shall go down quickly and come to the
place where you hid yourself on that eventful day, and you shall remain by the stone Ezel.
20 "I will shoot three arrows to the side, as though I shot at a target.
21 "And behold, I will send the lad, *saying,* 'Go, find the arrows.' If I specifically say to
the lad, 'Behold, the arrows are on this side of you, get them,' then come; for there is
safety for you and no harm, as the LORD lives.
22 "But if I say to the youth, 'Behold, the arrows are beyond you,' go, for the LORD has
sent you away.
23 "As for the agreement of which you and I have spoken, behold, the LORD is between
you and me forever."
24 So David hid in the field; and when the new moon came, the king sat down to eat
food.
25 The king sat on his seat as usual, the seat by the wall; then Jonathan rose up and
Abner sat down by Saul's side, but David's place was empty.
26 Nevertheless Saul did not speak anything that day, for he thought, "It is an accident, he is not clean, surely *he is* not clean."
27 It came about the next day, the second *day* of the new moon, that David's place was
empty; so Saul said to Jonathan his son, "Why has the son of Jesse not come to the meal,
either yesterday or today?"
28 Jonathan then answered Saul, "David earnestly asked leave of me *to go* to Bethlehem,
29 for he said, 'Please let me go, since our family has a sacrifice in the city, and my
brother has commanded me to attend. And now, if I have found favor in your sight, please
let me get away that I may see my brothers.' For this reason he has not come to the king's
table."

Saul Is Angry with Jonathan

30 Then Saul's anger burned against Jonathan and he said to him, "You son of a perverse, rebellious woman! Do I not know that you are choosing the son of Jesse to your
own shame and to the shame of your mother's nakedness?
31 "For as long as the son of Jesse lives on the earth, neither you nor your kingdom

20:13 Ruth 1:17; 1 Sam 3:17; Josh 1:5; 1 Sam 17:37; 18:12; 1 Chr 22:11, 16

20:15 2 Sam 9:1, 3

20:16 Deut 23:21; 1 Sam 25:22

20:17 1 Sam 18:1

20:18 1 Sam 20:5, 25

20:22 1 Sam 20:37

20:23 1 Sam 20:14, 15; Gen 31:49, 53; 1 Sam 20:42

20:25 1 Sam 20:18

20:26 Lev 7:20, 21; 15:5; 1 Sam 16:5

20:28 1 Sam 20:6

20:31 2 Sam 12:5

20:15 Jonathan asked David to keep a promise to treat his children kindly in the future. Years later David took great pains to fulfill this promise: he invited Jonathan's son Mephibosheth into his palace to live (2 Samuel 9).

20:26 Because the New Moon festival involved making a sacrifice to God (Numbers 28:11–15), those attending the feast had to be ceremonially clean according to God's laws (Exodus 19:10; Leviticus 15; Numbers 19:11–22; also see the note on Joshua 3:5). This cleansing involved washing the body and clothes before approaching God to offer a sacrifice. The outward cleansing was a symbol of the inward desire for a purified heart and right relationship with God. Today our hearts are purified by faith in God through the death of Jesus Christ on our behalf (Hebrews 10:10, 22) and by reading and heeding God's Word (John 17:17).

20:31–32 Saul was still trying to secure his throne for future generations even though he had already been told his dynasty would end with him (13:13–14). Even worse, he was trying to do this by sinful human means, because he knew he would get no help from God. Jonathan could have made a move to become the next king by killing his rival, but he bypassed this opportunity because of his love for both God and David (23:16–18).

will be established. Therefore now, send and bring him to me, for he must surely die."

20:32 Gen 31:36; 1 Sam 19:5; Prov 31:9; Matt 27:23

32 But Jonathan answered Saul his father and said to him, "Why should he be put to
death? What has he done?"

20:33 1 Sam 18:11; 19:10; 1 Sam 20:7

33 Then Saul hurled his spear at him to strike him down; so Jonathan knew that his
father had decided to put David to death.
34 Then Jonathan arose from the table in fierce anger, and did not eat food on the
second day of the new moon, for he was grieved over David because his father had dishonored him.
35 Now it came about in the morning that Jonathan went out into the field for the
appointment with David, and a little lad *was* with him.

20:36 1 Sam 20:20, 21

36 He said to his lad, "Run, find now the arrows which I am about to shoot." As the lad
was running, he shot an arrow past him.

20:37 1 Sam 20:22

37 When the lad reached the place of the arrow which Jonathan had shot, Jonathan
called after the lad and said, "Is not the arrow beyond you?"
38 And Jonathan called after the lad, "Hurry, be quick, do not stay!" And Jonathan's
lad picked up the arrow and came to his master.
39 But the lad was not aware of anything; only Jonathan and David knew about the
matter.
40 Then Jonathan gave his weapons to his lad and said to him, "Go, bring *them* to the
city."

20:41 Gen 42:6; 1 Sam 18:3

41 When the lad was gone, David rose from the south side and fell on his face to the
ground, and bowed three times. And they kissed each other and wept together, but David
wept the more.

20:42 1 Sam 20:22; 1 Sam 20:15, 16, 23

42 Jonathan said to David, "Go in safety, inasmuch as we have sworn to each other in
the name of the LORD, saying, 'The LORD will be between me and you, and between my
descendants and your descendants forever.' " Then he rose and departed, while Jonathan went into the city.

JONATHAN

Loyalty is one of life's most costly qualities; it is the most selfless part of love. To be loyal, you cannot live only for yourself. Loyal people not only stand by their commitments; they are willing to suffer for them. Jonathan is a shining example of loyalty. Sometimes he was forced to deal with conflicting loyalties: to his father, Saul, and to his friend David. His solution to that conflict teaches us both how to be loyal and what must guide loyalty. In Jonathan, truth always guided loyalty.

Jonathan realized that the source of truth was God, who demanded his ultimate loyalty. It was his relationship with God that gave Jonathan the ability to deal effectively with the complicated situations in his life. He was loyal to Saul because Saul was his father and the king. He was loyal to David because David was his friend. His loyalty to God guided him through the conflicting demands of his human relationships.

The conflicting demands of our relationships challenge us as well. If we attempt to settle these conflicts only at the human level, we will be constantly dealing with a sense of betrayal. But if we communicate to our friends that our ultimate loyalty is to God and his truth, many of our choices will be much clearer. The truth in his Word, the Bible, will bring light to our decisions. Do those closest to you know who has your greatest loyalty?

Strengths and accomplishments:
- Brave, loyal, and a natural leader
- The closest friend David ever had
- Did not put his personal well-being ahead of those he loved
- Depended on God

Lessons from his life:
- Loyalty is one of the strongest parts of courage
- An allegiance to God puts all other relationships in perspective
- Great friendships are costly

Vital statistics:
- Occupation: Military leader
- Relatives: Father: Saul. Mother: Ahinoam. Brothers: Abinadab and Malchi-shua. Sisters: Merab and Michal. Son: Mephibosheth

Key verse:
"I am distressed for you, my brother Jonathan; you have been very pleasant to me. Your love to me was more wonderful than the love of women" (2 Samuel 1:26).

His story is told in 1 Samuel 13—31. He is also mentioned in 2 Samuel 9.

4. Saul pursues David

David Takes Consecrated Bread

21 Then David came to Nob to Ahimelech the priest; and Ahimelech came trembling to meet David and said to him, "Why are you alone and no one with you?"
2 David said to Ahimelech the priest, "The king has commissioned me with a matter
and has said to me, 'Let no one know anything about the matter on which I am sending
you and with which I have commissioned you; and I have directed the young men to a
certain place.'
3 "Now therefore, what do you have on hand? Give me five loaves of bread, or whatever can be found."
4 The priest answered David and said, "There is no ordinary bread on hand, but there
is consecrated bread; if only the young men have kept themselves from women."
5 David answered the priest and said to him, "Surely women have been kept from us
as previously when I set out and the vessels of the young men were holy, though it was an
ordinary journey; how much more then today will their vessels *be holy?*"
6 So the priest gave him consecrated *bread;* for there was no bread there but the bread
of the Presence which was removed from before the LORD, in order to put hot bread *in
its place* when it was taken away.
7 Now one of the servants of Saul was there that day, detained before the LORD; and
his name was Doeg the Edomite, the chief of Saul's shepherds.
8 David said to Ahimelech, "Now is there not a spear or a sword on hand? For I brought
neither my sword nor my weapons with me, because the king's matter was urgent."
9 Then the priest said, "The sword of Goliath the Philistine, whom you killed in the
valley of Elah, behold, it is wrapped in a cloth behind the ephod; if you would take it for
yourself, take *it.* For there is no other except it here." And David said, "There is none
like it; give it to me."
10 Then David arose and fled that day from Saul, and went to Achish king of Gath.
11 But the servants of Achish said to him, "Is this not David the king of the land? Did
they not sing of this one as they danced, saying,
'Saul has slain his thousands,
And David his ten thousands'?"
12 David took these words to heart and greatly feared Achish king of Gath.
13 So he disguised his sanity before them, and acted insanely in their hands, and
scribbled on the doors of the gate, and let his saliva run down into his beard.
14 Then Achish said to his servants, "Behold, you see the man behaving as a madman.
Why do you bring him to me?
15 "Do I lack madmen, that you have brought this one to act the madman in my presence? Shall this one come into my house?"

21:1 1 Sam 22:19; Neh 11:32; Is 10:32; 1 Sam 16:4

21:2 Ps 141:3

21:4 Ex 25:30; Lev 24:5-9; Matt 12:4; Ex 19:15

21:5 Ex 19:14, 15; 1 Thess 4:4

21:6 Matt 12:3, 4; Luke 6:3, 4; Lev 24:5-9

21:7 1 Sam 14:47; 22:9; Ps 52: title; 1 Chr 27:29, 31

21:9 1 Sam 17:51, 54; 1 Sam 17:2

21:10 Ps 34: title

21:11 Ps 56: title; 1 Sam 18:7; 29:5

21:12 Luke 2:19

21:13 Ps 34: title

21:1ff This is the first time Ahimelech is mentioned. Either he was the Ahijah mentioned in 14:3, 18, or, more likely, he was Ahijah's successor. In either case, Ahimelech had to go against the Law to give the consecrated bread to David because the bread was supposed to be given only to the priests (Leviticus 24:5–9). But Ahimelech put David's need and life ahead of religious ceremony and fed him the consecrated food. This upheld a higher law of love (Leviticus 19:18). Centuries later, Jesus would refer to this incident to show that God's laws should not be applied without compassion. To do good and to save life is God's greater law (Matthew 12:1–8; Luke 6:1–5).

21:2 David lied to protect himself from Saul (21:10). Some excuse this lie because a war was going on, and it is the duty of a good soldier to deceive the enemy. But nowhere is David's lie condoned. In fact, the opposite is true because his lie led to the death of 85 priests (22:9–19). David's small lie seemed harmless enough, but it led to tragedy. The Bible makes it very clear that lying is wrong (Leviticus 19:11). Lying, like every other sin, is serious in God's sight and may lead to all sorts of harmful consequences. Don't minimize or categorize sins. All sins must be avoided whether or not we can foresee their potential consequences.

21:5 The men's bodies were ceremonially clean because they had not had sexual intercourse during this journey. Therefore, the priest allowed them to eat the consecrated bread.

21:6 Once a week on the Sabbath, a priest entered the holy place in the tabernacle and placed 12 freshly baked loaves of bread on a small table. This bread, called the bread of the Presence, symbolized God's presence among his people as well as his loving care that met their physical needs. The bread that was replaced was to be eaten only by the priests on duty.

21:9 An ephod was a vest worn by the priest (see the second note on 2:18 for a more detailed explanation). David didn't know Goliath's sword was there probably because David was a young man when he killed the giant and he had spent much of his time at home.

21:10–15 Gath was one of the five major Philistine cities. Why did the Philistines accept their archenemy, David, into their camp? The Philistines may have been initially happy to accept a defector who was a high military leader. Any enemy of Saul would have been a friend of theirs. They could not have known that David had been anointed Israel's next king (16:13). Soon, however, the Philistines became nervous about David's presence. After all, he had slain thousands of their own people (18:7). David then protected himself by acting insane because it was the custom not to harm mentally unstable people.

The Priests Slain at Nob

22 So David departed from there and escaped to the cave of Adullam; and when his
brothers and all his father's household heard *of it,* they went down there to him.
2 Everyone who was in distress, and everyone who was in debt, and everyone who was
discontented gathered to him; and he became captain over them. Now there were about
four hundred men with him.
3 And David went from there to Mizpah of Moab; and he said to the king of Moab,
"Please let my father and my mother come *and stay* with you until I know what God will
do for me."
4 Then he left them with the king of Moab; and they stayed with him all the time that
David was in the stronghold.
5 The prophet Gad said to David, "Do not stay in the stronghold; depart, and go into
the land of Judah." So David departed and went into the forest of Hereth.
6 Then Saul heard that David and the men who were with him had been discovered.
Now Saul was sitting in Gibeah, under the tamarisk tree on the height with his spear in
his hand, and all his servants were standing around him.
7 Saul said to his servants who stood around him, "Hear now, O Benjamites! Will the
son of Jesse also give to all of you fields and vineyards? Will he make you all commanders of thousands and commanders of hundreds?
8 "For all of you have conspired against me so that there is no one who discloses to me
when my son makes *a covenant* with the son of Jesse, and there is none of you who is
sorry for me or discloses to me that my son has stirred up my servant against me to lie in
ambush, as *it is* this day."
9 Then Doeg the Edomite, who was standing by the servants of Saul, said, "I saw the
son of Jesse coming to Nob, to Ahimelech the son of Ahitub.
10 "He inquired of the LORD for him, gave him provisions, and gave him the sword of
Goliath the Philistine."
11 Then the king sent someone to summon Ahimelech the priest, the son of Ahitub,
and all his father's household, the priests who were in Nob; and all of them came to the
king.
12 Saul said, "Listen now, son of Ahitub." And he answered, "Here I am, my lord."
13 Saul then said to him, "Why have you and the son of Jesse conspired against me, in
that you have given him bread and a sword and have inquired of God for him, so that he
would rise up against me by lying in ambush as *it is* this day?"
14 Then Ahimelech answered the king and said, "And who among all your servants is
as faithful as David, even the king's son-in-law, who is captain over your guard, and is
honored in your house?
15 "Did I *just* begin to inquire of God for him today? Far be it from me! Do not let the
king impute anything to his servant *or* to any of the household of my father, for your
servant knows nothing at all of this whole affair."

22:1 Ps 57: title; Josh 12:15; 15:35; 2 Sam 23:13; Ps 142: title
22:2 1 Sam 23:13; 25:13
22:5 2 Sam 24:11; 1 Chr 21:9; 29:29; 2 Chr 29:25
22:6 Judg 4:5; 1 Sam 14:2
22:7 1 Sam 8:12; 1 Chr 12:16-18
22:8 1 Sam 18:3; 20:16; 1 Sam 23:21
22:9 Ps 52: title
1 Sam 21:1; 1 Sam 14:3; 21:1
22:10 Num 27:21; 1 Sam 10:22; 1 Sam 21:6; 1 Sam 21:9
22:13 1 Sam 22:8
22:14 1 Sam 19:4, 5; 20:32
22:15 2 Sam 5:19, 23; 2 Sam 19:18, 19

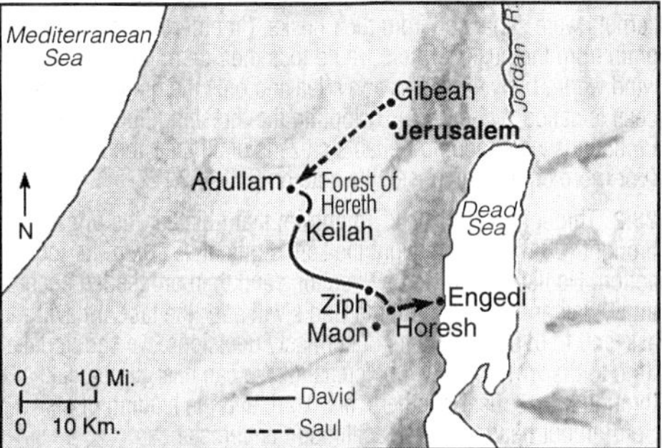

DAVID FLEES FROM SAUL David and his men attacked the Philistines at Keilah from the forest of Hereth. Saul came from Gibeah to attack David, but David escaped into the wilderness of Ziph. At Horesh he met Jonathan, who encouraged him. Then he fled into the wilderness of Maon and into the strongholds of Engedi.

22:2 Those in distress, in debt, or discontented joined David, who himself was an outlaw. These people were outcasts themselves and could only improve their lot by helping David become king. David's control over this band of men again shows his resourcefulness and ability to lead and motivate others. It is difficult enough to build an army out of good men, but it takes even greater leadership to build one out of the kind of men that followed David. This group eventually formed the core of his military leadership and produced several "mighty men" (2 Samuel 23:8ff).

22:7–8 Apparently Saul's key officers were from the tribe of Benjamin, just as he was. David was from the neighboring tribe of Judah. Saul was appealing to tribal loyalty to maintain his hold on the throne.

16 But the king said, "You shall surely die, Ahimelech, you and all your father's household!"
17 And the king said to the guards who were attending him, "Turn around and put the **22:17**
priests of the LORD to death, because their hand also is with David and because they 2 Kin 10:25; Ex 1:17
knew that he was fleeing and did not reveal it to me." But the servants of the king were
not willing to put forth their hands to attack the priests of the LORD.
18 Then the king said to Doeg, "You turn around and attack the priests." And Doeg **22:18**
the Edomite turned around and attacked the priests, and he killed that day eighty-five 1 Sam 2:31; 1 Sam 2:18
men who wore the linen ephod.
19 And he struck Nob the city of the priests with the edge of the sword, both men and **22:19**
women, children and infants; also oxen, donkeys, and sheep *he struck* with the edge of 1 Sam 15:3
the sword.
20 But one son of Ahimelech the son of Ahitub, named Abiathar, escaped and fled **22:20**
after David. 1 Sam 23:6, 9; 30:7; 1 Kin 2:26, 27;
21 Abiathar told David that Saul had killed the priests of the LORD. 1 Sam 23:6
22 Then David said to Abiathar, "I knew on that day, when Doeg the Edomite was **22:22**
there, that he would surely tell Saul. I have brought about *the death* of every person in 1 Sam 21:7
your father's household.
23 "Stay with me; do not be afraid, for he who seeks my life seeks your life, for you are **22:23**
safe with me." 1 Kin 2:26

David Delivers Keilah

23 Then they told David, saying, "Behold, the Philistines are fighting against Keilah **23:1**
and are plundering the threshing floors." Josh 15:44; Neh 3:17, 18
2 So David inquired of the LORD, saying, "Shall I go and attack these Philistines?" **23:2**
And the LORD said to David, "Go and attack the Philistines and deliver Keilah." 1 Sam 23:4, 6, 9-12;
3 But David's men said to him, "Behold, we are afraid here in Judah. How much more 2 Sam 5:19, 23
then if we go to Keilah against the ranks of the Philistines?"
4 Then David inquired of the LORD once more. And the LORD answered him and **23:4**
said, "Arise, go down to Keilah, for I will give the Philistines into your hand." Josh 8:7; Judg 7:7
5 So David and his men went to Keilah and fought with the Philistines; and he led
away their livestock and struck them with a great slaughter. Thus David delivered the
inhabitants of Keilah.
6 Now it came about, when Abiathar the son of Ahimelech fled to David at Keilah, **23:6**
that he came down *with* an ephod in his hand. 1 Sam 22:20
7 When it was told Saul that David had come to Keilah, Saul said, "God has deliv-

---

22:18 Why would Saul have his own priests killed? Saul suspected a conspiracy among Jonathan, David, and the priests. His suspicion came from Doeg's report of seeing David talking to Ahimelech, the high priest, and receiving food and a weapon from him (22:9–10). Saul's action showed his mental and emotional instability and how far he had strayed from God.

By destroying everything in Nob, Saul was placing the city under the ban (declaring it to be utterly destroyed) described in Deuteronomy 13:12–17, which was supposed to be used only in cases of idolatry and rebellion against God. But it was Saul, not the priests, who had rebelled against God.

22:18–19 Why did God allow 85 innocent priests to be killed? Their deaths served to dramatize to the nation how a king could become an evil tyrant. Where were Saul's advisers? Where were the elders of Israel? Sometimes God allows evil to develop to teach us not to let evil systems flourish. Serving God is not a ticket to wealth, success, or health. God does not promise to protect good people from evil in this world, but he does promise that ultimately all evil will be abolished. Those who have remained faithful through their trials will experience great rewards in the age to come (Matthew 5:11, 12; Revelation 21:1–7; 22:1–21).

22:20 Abiathar escaped to David with an ephod (23:6), a priestly garment containing the Urim and Thummim, two objects David used to consult God. The ephod was probably the only symbol of the priesthood that survived Saul's raid and made it into David's camp (23:6). Saul destroyed Israel's priesthood, but when David became king, he installed Abiathar as the new high priest. Abiathar remained in that position during David's entire reign.

23:1 Threshing floors were open, circular areas where the grain kernels were separated from their husks. (In order to separate the grain from the husk, farmers would toss their grain into the air. The wind would blow the husks away, leaving only the grain. This process is called *winnowing.*) By looting the threshing floors, the Philistines were robbing Keilah's citizens of all their food supplies. (For more on threshing, see the note on Ruth 3:2.)

23:2 Through the Urim and Thummim that Abiathar the priest brought (23:6), David sought the Lord's guidance *before* he took action. He listened to God's directions and then proceeded accordingly. Rather than trying to find God's will *after* the fact or having to ask God to undo the results of our hasty decisions, we should take time to discern God's will beforehand. We can hear him speak through the counsel of others, his Word, and the leading of his Spirit in our hearts, as well as through circumstances.

23:6 An ephod was a sleeveless linen vest worn by priests. The high priest's ephod was brightly colored and had a breastplate with 12 gemstones representing each tribe. The Urim and Thummim were kept in a pouch of the high priest's ephod. (See the note on 2:18 for a more detailed explanation of the ephod.)

23:7 When Saul heard that David was trapped in a walled town

ered him into my hand, for he shut himself in by entering a city with double gates and
bars."
8 So Saul summoned all the people for war, to go down to Keilah to besiege David
and his men.

23:9 1 Sam 22:20; 1 Sam 23:6; 30:7

9 Now David knew that Saul was plotting evil against him; so he said to Abiathar the
priest, "Bring the ephod here."
10 Then David said, "O LORD God of Israel, Your servant has heard for certain that
Saul is seeking to come to Keilah to destroy the city on my account.
11 "Will the men of Keilah surrender me into his hand? Will Saul come down just as
Your servant has heard? O LORD God of Israel, I pray, tell Your servant." And the LORD
said, "He will come down."

23:12 Judg 15:10-13; 1 Sam 23:20

12 Then David said, "Will the men of Keilah surrender me and my men into the hand
of Saul?" And the LORD said, "They will surrender you."

23:13 1 Sam 22:2; 25:13; 2 Sam 15:20

13 Then David and his men, about six hundred, arose and departed from Keilah, and
they went wherever they could go. When it was told Saul that David had escaped from
Keilah, he gave up the pursuit.

23:14 Josh 15:55; 2 Chr 11:8; Ps 32:7

14 David stayed in the wilderness in the strongholds, and remained in the hill country
in the wilderness of Ziph. And Saul sought him every day, but God did not deliver him
into his hand.

Saul Pursues David

15 Now David became aware that Saul had come out to seek his life while David was
in the wilderness of Ziph at Horesh.

23:16 1 Sam 30:6; Neh 2:18

16 And Jonathan, Saul's son, arose and went to David at Horesh, and [14]encouraged
him in God.

23:17 Ps 27:1, 3; 118:6; Is 54:17; Heb 13:6; 1 Sam 20:31; 24:20

17 Thus he said to him, "Do not be afraid, because the hand of Saul my father will not
find you, and you will be king over Israel and I will be next to you; and Saul my father
knows that also."

23:18 1 Sam 18:3; 20:12-17, 42; 2 Sam 9:1; 21:7

18 So the two of them made a covenant before the LORD; and David stayed at Horesh
while Jonathan went to his house.

23:19 1 Sam 26:1; Ps 54: title; 1 Sam 26:3

19 Then Ziphites came up to Saul at Gibeah, saying, "Is David not hiding with us in
the strongholds at Horesh, on the hill of Hachilah, which is on the south of [15]Jeshimon?

23:20 1 Sam 23:12

20 "Now then, O king, come down according to all the desire of your soul to do so; and
our part *shall be* to surrender him into the king's hand."

23:21 1 Sam 22:8

21 Saul said, "May you be blessed of the LORD, for you have had compassion on me.
22 "Go now, make more sure, and investigate and see his place where his haunt is, *and*
who has seen him there; for I am told that he is very cunning.
23 "So look, and learn about all the hiding places where he hides himself and return to
me with certainty, and I will go with you; and if he is in the land, I will search him out
among all the thousands of Judah."

23:24 Josh 15:55; 1 Sam 25:2

24 Then they arose and went to Ziph before Saul. Now David and his men were in the
wilderness of Maon, in the Arabah to the south of Jeshimon.
25 When Saul and his men went to seek *him,* they told David, and he came down to the
rock and stayed in the wilderness of Maon. And when Saul heard *it,* he pursued David in
the wilderness of Maon.

23:26 Ps 17:9

26 Saul went on one side of the mountain, and David and his men on the other side of
the mountain; and David was hurrying to get away from Saul, for Saul and his men were
surrounding David and his men to seize them.

14 Lit *strengthened his hand* **15** Or *the desert*

(one with gates and bars), he thought God was putting David at his mercy. Saul wanted to kill David so badly that he would have interpreted any sign as God's approval to move ahead with his plan. Had Saul known God better, he would have known what God wanted and would not have misread the situation as God's approval for murder.

Not every opportunity is sent from God. We may want something so much that we assume any opportunity to obtain it is of divine origin. As we see from Saul's case, however, this may not be true. An opportunity to do something against God's will can never be from God because God does not tempt us. When opportunities come your way, double-check your motives. Make sure you are following God's desires, and not just your own.

23:16–18 This may have been the last time David and Jonathan were together. As true friends they were more than just companions who enjoyed each other's company. They encouraged each other's faith in God and trusted each other with their deepest thoughts and closest confidences. These are the marks of true friendship.

27 But a messenger came to Saul, saying, "Hurry and come, for the Philistines have
made a raid on the land."
28 So Saul returned from pursuing David and went to meet the Philistines; therefore
they called that place the Rock of Escape.
29 David went up from there and stayed in the strongholds of Engedi.

David Spares Saul's Life

24 Now when Saul returned from pursuing the Philistines, he was told, saying, "Behold, David is in the wilderness of Engedi."
2 Then Saul took three thousand chosen men from all Israel and went to seek David
and his men in front of the Rocks of the Wild Goats.
3 He came to the sheepfolds on the way, where there *was* a cave; and Saul went in to
relieve himself. Now David and his men were sitting in the inner recesses of the cave.
4 The men of David said to him, "Behold, *this is* the day of which the LORD said to
you, 'Behold; I am about to give your enemy into your hand, and you shall do to him as
it seems good to you.' " Then David arose and cut off the edge of Saul's robe secretly.
5 It came about afterward that David's conscience bothered him because he had cut
off the edge of Saul's *robe.*
6 So he said to his men, "Far be it from me because of the LORD that I should do this
thing to my lord, the LORD'S anointed, to stretch out my hand against him, since he is
the LORD'S anointed."
7 David persuaded his men with *these* words and did not allow them to rise up against
Saul. And Saul arose, left the cave, and went on *his* way.
8 Now afterward David arose and went out of the cave and called after Saul, saying,
"My lord the king!" And when Saul looked behind him, David bowed with his face to
the ground and prostrated himself.
9 David said to Saul, "Why do you listen to the words of men, saying, 'Behold, David
seeks to harm you'?
10 "Behold, this day your eyes have seen that the LORD had given you today into my
hand in the cave, and some said to kill you, but *my eye* had pity on you; and I said, 'I will
not stretch out my hand against my lord, for he is the LORD'S anointed.'
11 "Now, my father, see! Indeed, see the edge of your robe in my hand! For in that I cut
off the edge of your robe and did not kill you, know and perceive that there is no evil or
rebellion in my hands, and I have not sinned against you, though you are lying in wait for
my life to take it.
12 "May the LORD judge between you and me, and may the LORD avenge me on you;
but my hand shall not be against you.
13 "As the proverb of the ancients says, 'Out of the wicked comes forth wickedness';
but my hand shall not be against you.
14 "After whom has the king of Israel come out? Whom are you pursuing? A dead dog,
a single flea?
15 "The LORD therefore be judge and decide between you and me; and may He see and
plead my cause and deliver me from your hand."
16 When David had finished speaking these words to Saul, Saul said, "Is this your voice,
my son David?" Then Saul lifted up his voice and wept.

23:29 Josh 15:62; 2 Chr 20:2
24:1 1 Sam 23:28, 29; 1 Sam 23:19
24:2 1 Sam 26:2
24:3 Judg 3:24; Ps 57: title; 142: title
24:4 1 Sam 23:17; 25:28-30; 1 Sam 26:8, 11
24:5 2 Sam 24:10
24:6 1 Sam 26:11
24:8 1 Sam 25:23, 24; 1 Kin 1:31
24:10 Ps 7:3, 4; 1 Sam 24:4
24:11 2 Kin 5:13; 1 Sam 23:14, 23; 26:20
24:12 Gen 16:5; 31:53; Judg 11:27; 1 Sam 26:10, 23
24:13 Matt 7:16-20
24:14 2 Sam 9:8; 1 Sam 26:20
24:15 1 Sam 24:12; Ps 35:1; 43:1; 119:154; Mic 7:9
24:16 1 Sam 26:17

24:3 David and his 600 men found the wilderness of Engedi a good place to hide because of the many caves in the area. These caves were used by local people for housing and as tombs. For David's men they were places of refuge. These caves can still be seen today. Some are large enough to hold thousands of people.

24:4 Scripture does not record that God made any such statement to David or his men. The men were probably offering their own interpretation of some previous event such as David's anointing (16:13) or Jonathan's prediction that David would become king (23:17). When David's men saw Saul entering their cave, they wrongly assumed that this was an indication from God that they should act.

24:5–6 David had great respect for Saul, in spite of the fact that Saul was trying to kill him. Although Saul was sinning and rebelling against God, David still respected the position he held as God's anointed king. David knew he would one day be king, and he also knew it was not right to strike down the man God had placed on the throne. If he assassinated Saul, he would be setting a precedent for his own opponents to remove him some day.

Romans 13:1–7 teaches that God has placed the government and its leaders in power. We may not know why, but, like David, we are to respect the positions and roles of those to whom God has given authority. There is one exception, however. Because God is our highest authority, we should not allow a leader to pressure us to violate God's Law.

24:16–19 The means we use to accomplish a goal are just as important as the goal we are trying to accomplish. David's goal was to become king, so his men urged him to kill Saul when he had the chance. David's refusal was not an example of cowardice but of courage—the courage to stand against the group and do what he knew was right. Don't compromise your moral standards by giving in to group pressure or taking the easy way out.

24:17 1 Sam 26:21; Matt 5:44
24:18 1 Sam 26:23
24:19 1 Sam 23:17
24:20 1 Sam 23:17; 1 Sam 13:14
24:21 Gen 21:23; 1 Sam 20:14-17; 2 Sam 21:6-8
24:22 1 Sam 23:29

17 He said to David, "You are more righteous than I; for you have dealt well with me,
while I have dealt wickedly with you.
18 "You have declared today that you have done good to me, that the LORD delivered
me into your hand and *yet* you did not kill me.
19 "For if a man finds his enemy, will he let him go away safely? May the LORD therefore reward you with good in return for what you have done to me this day.
20 "Now, behold, I know that you will surely be king, and that the kingdom of Israel will
be established in your hand.
21 "So now swear to me by the LORD that you will not cut off my descendants after me
and that you will not destroy my name from my father's household."
22 David swore to Saul. And Saul went to his home, but David and his men went up to
the stronghold.

25:1 1 Sam 28:3; Num 20:29; Deut 34:8; 2 Kin 21:18; 2 Chr 33:20; Gen 21:21; Num 10:12; 13:3

Samuel's Death

25 Then Samuel died; and all Israel gathered together and mourned for him, and
buried him at his house in Ramah. And David arose and went down to the wilderness of Paran.

25:2 1 Sam 23:24; Josh 15:55; Gen 38:13; 2 Sam 13:23
25:3 Prov 31:10; Josh 15:13; 1 Sam 30:14

Nabal and Abigail

2 Now *there was* a man in Maon whose business was in Carmel; and the man was very
rich, and he had three thousand sheep and a thousand goats. And it came about while
he was shearing his sheep in Carmel
3 (now the man's name was Nabal, and his wife's name was Abigail. And the woman
was intelligent and beautiful in appearance, but the man was harsh and evil in *his* dealings, and he was a Calebite),
4 that David heard in the wilderness that Nabal was shearing his sheep.
5 So David sent ten young men; and David said to the young men, "Go up to Carmel,
visit Nabal and greet him in my name;

LIFE OF DAVID VERSUS LIFE OF SAUL

Life of David	*Life of Saul*
David was God's kind of king (2 Samuel 7:8–16)	Saul was man's kind of king (1 Samuel 10:23–24)
David was a man after God's heart (Acts 13:22)	Saul was a man after people's praise (1 Samuel 18:6–8)
David's kingship was eternal (through Jesus) (2 Samuel 7:29)	Saul's kingship was rejected (1 Samuel 15:23)
David was kind and benevolent (2 Samuel 9; 1 Chronicles 19:2)	Saul was cruel (1 Samuel 20:30–34; 22:11–19)
David was forgiving (1 Samuel 26)	Saul was unforgiving (1 Samuel 14:44; 18:9)
David repented (2 Samuel 12:13; 24:10)	When confronted, Saul lied (1 Samuel 15:10–31)
David was courageous (1 Samuel 17; 1 Chronicles 18)	Saul was fearful (1 Sam. 17:11; 18:12)
David was at peace with God (Psalms 4:8; 37:11)	Saul was separated from God (1 Samuel 16:14)

24:21–22 David kept his promise—he never took revenge on Saul's family or descendants. Most of Saul's sons were killed later, however, by the Philistines (31:2) and the Gibeonites (2 Samuel 21:1–14). David had promised to be kind to the descendants of Saul's son Jonathan (20:14–15), and he kept this promise when he invited Mephibosheth to live in his palace (2 Samuel 9).

25:1 Saul was king, but Samuel had been the nation's spiritual leader. As a young boy and an older man, Samuel was always careful to listen to (3:10; 9:14–17) and obey (3:21; 10:1–2) the Lord. With Samuel gone, Israel would be without this spiritual leadership until David became king. (For more on Samuel, read his Profile in chapter 8.)

25:2–11 Nabal rudely refused David's request to feed his 600 men. If we sympathize with Nabal, it is because customs are so different today. First, simple hospitality demanded that travelers—any number of them—be fed. Nabal was very rich and could have easily afforded to meet David's request. Second, David wasn't asking for a handout. He and his men had been protecting Nabal's work force, and part of Nabal's prosperity was due to David's vigilance. We should be generous with those who protect us and help us prosper, even if we are not obligated to do so by law or custom.

6 and thus you shall say, 'Have a long life, peace be to you, and peace be to your house, **25:6**
and peace be to all that you have. 1 Chr 12:18; Ps 122:7; Luke 10:5
7 'Now I have heard that you have shearers; now your shepherds have been with us
and we have not insulted them, nor have they missed anything all the days they were in **25:7** 2 Sam 13:23, 24;
Carmel. 1 Sam 25:15, 21
8 'Ask your young men and they will tell you. Therefore let *my* young men find favor **25:8**
in your eyes, for we have come on a festive day. Please give whatever you find at hand to Neh 8:10-12; Esth 9:19, 22
your servants and to your son David.' "
9 When David's young men came, they spoke to Nabal according to all these words
in David's name; then they waited.
10 But Nabal answered David's servants and said, "Who is David? And who is the son **25:10**
of Jesse? There are many servants today who are each breaking away from his master. Judg 9:28
11 "Shall I then take my bread and my water and my meat that I have slaughtered for **25:11**
my shearers, and give it to men whose origin I do not know?" Judg 8:6, 15
12 So David's young men retraced their way and went back; and they came and told
him according to all these words.
13 David said to his men, "Each *of you* gird on his sword." So each man girded on his **25:13**
sword. And David also girded on his sword, and about four hundred men went up be- 1 Sam 23:13; 1 Sam 30:24
hind David while two hundred stayed with the baggage.
14 But one of the young men told Abigail, Nabal's wife, saying, "Behold, David sent **25:14**
messengers from the wilderness to greet our master, and he scorned them. 1 Sam 13:10; 15:13
15 "Yet the men were very good to us, and we were not insulted, nor did we miss any- **25:15**
thing as long as we went about with them, while we were in the fields. 1 Sam 25:7, 21
16 "They were a wall to us both by night and by day, all the time we were with them **25:16**
tending the sheep. Ex 14:22; Job 1:10
17 "Now therefore, know and consider what you should do, for evil is plotted against
our master and against all his household; and he is such a worthless man that no one can
speak to him."

Abigail Intercedes

18 Then Abigail hurried and took two hundred *loaves* of bread and two jugs of wine **25:18**
and five sheep already prepared and five measures of roasted grain and a hundred clus- 2 Sam 16:1; 1 Chr 12:40
ters of raisins and two hundred cakes of figs, and loaded *them* on donkeys.
19 She said to her young men, "Go on before me; behold, I am coming after you." But **25:19**
she did not tell her husband Nabal. Gen 32:16, 20
20 It came about as she was riding on her donkey and coming down by the hidden part
of the mountain, that behold, David and his men were coming down toward her; so she
met them.
21 Now David had said, "Surely in vain I have guarded all that this *man* has in the wil- **25:21**
derness, so that nothing was missed of all that belonged to him; and he has returned me Ps 109:5; Prov 17:13
evil for good.
22 "May God do so to the enemies of David, and more also, if by morning I leave *as* **25:22**
much as one male of any who belong to him." 1 Sam 3:17; 20:13; 1 Kin 14:10
23 When Abigail saw David, she hurried and dismounted from her donkey, and fell on
her face before David and bowed herself to the ground. **25:23** 1 Sam 20:41
24 She fell at his feet and said, "On me alone, my lord, be the blame. And please let
your maidservant speak to you, and listen to the words of your maidservant.
25 "Please do not let my lord pay attention to this worthless man, Nabal, for as his name
is, so is he. Nabal is his name and folly is with him; but I your maidservant did not see the
young men of my lord whom you sent.
26 "Now therefore, my lord, as the LORD lives, and as your soul lives, since the LORD **25:26**
has restrained you from shedding blood, and from avenging yourself by your own hand, Heb 10:30; 2 Sam 18:32
now then let your enemies and those who seek evil against my lord, be as Nabal.

25:24 David was in no mood to listen when he set out for Nabal's property (25:13, 22). Nevertheless, he stopped to hear what Abigail had to say. If he had ignored her, he would have been guilty of taking vengeance into his own hands. No matter how right we think we are, we must always be careful to stop and listen to others. The extra time and effort can save us pain and trouble in the long run.

25:27 Gen 30:11; 1 Sam 30:26
25:28 1 Sam 25:24; 1 Sam 22:14; 2 Sam 7:11, 16; 1 Sam 18:17; 1 Sam 24:11; Ps 7:3
25:29 Jer 10:18
25:30 1 Sam 13:14
25:31 Gen 40:14; 1 Sam 25:30
25:32 Ex 18:10; 1 Kin 1:48; Ps 41:13; 72:18; 106:48; Luke 1:68
25:33 1 Sam 25:26
25:34 1 Sam 25:26
25:35 1 Sam 20:42; 2 Kin 5:19; Gen 19:21
25:36 2 Sam 13:28; Prov 20:1; Is 5:11; Hos 4:11; 1 Sam 25:19

27 "Now let this gift which your maidservant has brought to my lord be given to the young
men who accompany my lord.
28 "Please forgive the transgression of your maidservant; for the LORD will certainly
make for my lord an enduring house, because my lord is fighting the battles of the LORD,
and evil will not be found in you all your days.
29 "Should anyone rise up to pursue you and to seek your life, then the life of my lord
shall be bound in the bundle of the living with the LORD your God; but the lives of your
enemies He will sling out as from the hollow of a sling.
30 "And when the LORD does for my lord according to all the good that He has spoken
concerning you, and appoints you ruler over Israel,
31 this will not cause grief or a troubled heart to my lord, both by having shed blood
without cause and by my lord having avenged himself. When the LORD deals well with
my lord, then remember your maidservant."
32 Then David said to Abigail, "Blessed be the LORD God of Israel, who sent you this
day to meet me,
33 and blessed be your discernment, and blessed be you, who have kept me this day
from bloodshed and from avenging myself by my own hand.
34 "Nevertheless, as the LORD God of Israel lives, who has restrained me from harming you, unless you had come quickly to meet me, surely there would not have been left
to Nabal until the morning light *as much as* one male."
35 So David received from her hand what she had brought him and said to her, "Go up
to your house in peace. See, I have listened to you and granted your request."
36 Then Abigail came to Nabal, and behold, he was holding a feast in his house, like
the feast of a king. And Nabal's heart was merry within him, for he was very drunk; so
she did not tell him anything at all until the morning light.

Some men don't deserve their wives. Abigail was probably the best woman Nabal could afford, and he got even more than he bargained for when he arranged to marry her. She was beautiful and more suited than he was to manage his wealth. But Nabal took this wife for granted.

In spite of his shortcomings, Nabal's household did what they could to keep him out of trouble. This loyalty must have been inspired by Abigail. Although her culture and her husband placed a low value on her, she made the most of her skills and opportunities. David was impressed with her abilities, and when Nabal died, he married her.

Abigail was an effective counselor to both of the men in her life, working hard to prevent them from making rash moves. By her swift action and skillful negotiation, she kept David from taking vengeance upon Nabal. She saw the big picture and left plenty of room for God to get involved.

Do you, like Abigail, look beyond the present crisis to the big picture? Do you use your skills to promote peace? Are you loyal without being blind? What challenge or responsibility do you face today that needs a person under God's control?

Strengths and accomplishments:
- Sensible and capable
- A persuasive speaker, able to see beyond herself

Lessons from her life:
- Life's tough situations can bring out the best in people
- One does not need a prestigious title to play a significant role

Vital statistics:
- Where: Carmel
- Occupation: Homemaker
- Relatives: First husband: Nabal. Second husband: David. Son: Chileab (Daniel)
- Contemporaries: Saul, Michal, Ahinoam

Key verses:
"Then David said to Abigail, 'Blessed be the LORD God of Israel, who sent you this day to meet me, and blessed be your discernment, and blessed be you, who have kept me this day from bloodshed and from avenging myself by my own hand' " (1 Samuel 25:32–33).

Her story is told in 1 Samuel 25—2 Samuel 2. She is also mentioned in 1 Chronicles 3:1.

25:36 Because Nabal was drunk, Abigail waited until morning to tell him what she had done. Abigail knew that Nabal, in his drunkenness, may not have understood her or may have reacted foolishly. When discussing difficult matters with people, especially family members, timing is everything. Ask God for wisdom to know the best time for confrontation and for bringing up touchy subjects.

37 But in the morning, when the wine had gone out of Nabal, his wife told him these
things, and his heart died within him so that he became *as* a stone.
38 About ten days later, the LORD struck Nabal and he died.

25:38 1 Sam 26:10; 2 Sam 6:7; Ps 104:29

David Marries Abigail

39 When David heard that Nabal was dead, he said, "Blessed be the LORD, who has
pleaded the cause of my reproach from the hand of Nabal and has kept back His servant
from evil. The LORD has also returned the evildoing of Nabal on his own head." Then
David sent a proposal to Abigail, to take her as his wife.
40 When the servants of David came to Abigail at Carmel, they spoke to her, saying,
"David has sent us to you to take you as his wife."
41 She arose and bowed with her face to the ground and said, "Behold, your maidservant is a maid to wash the feet of my lord's servants."
42 Then Abigail quickly arose, and rode on a donkey, with her five maidens who attended her; and she followed the messengers of David and became his wife.
43 David had also taken Ahinoam of Jezreel, and they both became his wives.
44 Now Saul had given Michal his daughter, David's wife, to Palti the son of Laish,
who was from Gallim.

25:39 1 Sam 24:15; Prov 22:23; 1 Sam 25:26, 34; Song 8:8

25:41 1 Sam 25:23; Mark 1:7

25:42 Gen 24:61-67

25:43 Josh 15:56; 1 Sam 27:3; 30:5

25:44 1 Sam 18:27; 2 Sam 3:14; Is 10:30

David Again Spares Saul

26 Then the Ziphites came to Saul at Gibeah, saying, "Is not David hiding on the hill
of Hachilah, *which is* before [16]Jeshimon?"
2 So Saul arose and went down to the wilderness of Ziph, having with him three thousand chosen men of Israel, to search for David in the wilderness of Ziph.
3 Saul camped in the hill of Hachilah, which is before [16]Jeshimon, beside the road,
and David was staying in the wilderness. When he saw that Saul came after him into the
wilderness,
4 David sent out spies, and he knew that Saul was definitely coming.
5 David then arose and came to the place where Saul had camped. And David saw
the place where Saul lay, and Abner the son of Ner, the commander of his army; and
Saul was lying in the circle of the camp, and the people were camped around him.
6 Then David said to Ahimelech the Hittite and to Abishai the son of Zeruiah, Joab's
brother, saying, "Who will go down with me to Saul in the camp?" And Abishai said, "I
will go down with you."
7 So David and Abishai came to the people by night, and behold, Saul lay sleeping
inside the circle of the camp with his spear stuck in the ground at his head; and Abner
and the people were lying around him.
8 Then Abishai said to David, "Today God has delivered your enemy into your hand;
now therefore, please let me strike him with the spear to the ground with one stroke,
and I will not strike him the second time."

26:1 1 Sam 23:19; Ps 54: title

26:2 1 Sam 13:2; 24:2

26:3 1 Sam 24:3; 1 Sam 23:15

26:5 1 Sam 14:50, 51; 17:55

26:6 Gen 23:3; 26:34; Josh 3:10; 1 Kin 10:29; 2 Kin 7:6; 1 Chr 2:16; Judg 7:10, 11

16 Or *the desert*

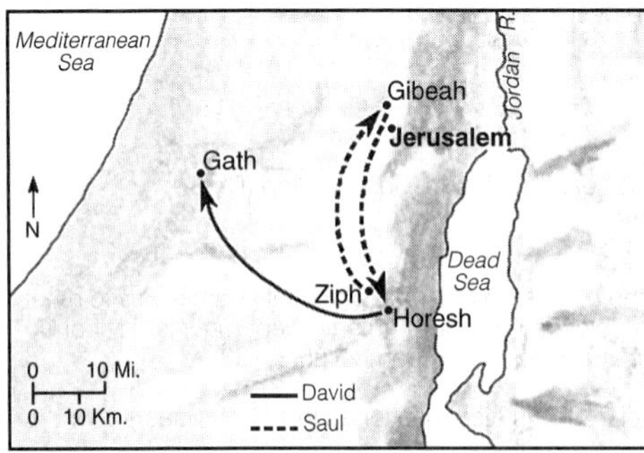

SAUL CHASES DAVID The men of Ziph again betrayed David to Saul, who was in his palace in Gibeah. Saul took 3,000 troops to the area around Horesh in order to find David. David could have killed Saul, but he refused. Saul, feeling foolish at David's kindness, returned to Gibeah, and David went to Gath.

25:44 The story of David and Michal does not end here. (See 2 Samuel 3:12–16 for the next episode.)

26:5–9 Abishai showed great courage when he volunteered to go into Saul's camp with David. In the heat of emotion, Abishai wanted to kill Saul, but David restrained him. Although Abishai was only trying to protect David, his leader, David could not hurt Saul because of his respect for Saul's authority and position as God's anointed king. Abishai may have disagreed with David, but he also respected the one in authority over him. Eventually he became the greatest warrior in David's army (2 Samuel 23:18–19).

26:8ff The strongest moral decisions are the ones we make before temptation strikes. David was determined to follow God, and this carried over into his decision not to murder God's anointed king, Saul, even when his men and the circumstances seemed to make it a feasible option. Who would you have been like in such a situation—David or David's men? To be like David and follow God, we must realize that we can't do wrong in order to execute justice. Even when our closest friends counsel us to do something that seems right, we must always put God's commands first.

9 But David said to Abishai, "Do not destroy him, for who can stretch out his hand
against the LORD'S anointed and be without guilt?"
10 David also said, "As the LORD lives, surely the LORD will strike him, or his day will
come that he dies, or he will go down into battle and perish.
11 "The LORD forbid that I should stretch out my hand against the LORD'S anointed;
but now please take the spear that is at his head and the jug of water, and let us go."
12 So David took the spear and the jug of water from *beside* Saul's head, and they went
away, but no one saw or knew *it,* nor did any awake, for they were all asleep, because a
sound sleep from the LORD had fallen on them.
13 Then David crossed over to the other side and stood on top of the mountain at a
distance *with* a large area between them.
14 David called to the people and to Abner the son of Ner, saying, "Will you not answer, Abner?" Then Abner replied, "Who are you who calls to the king?"
15 So David said to Abner, "Are you not a man? And who is like you in Israel? Why
then have you not guarded your lord the king? For one of the people came to destroy
the king your lord.
16 "This thing that you have done is not good. As the LORD lives, *all* of you must surely
die, because you did not guard your lord, the LORD'S anointed. And now, see where the
king's spear is and the jug of water that was at his head."
17 Then Saul recognized David's voice and said, "Is this your voice, my son David?"
And David said, "It is my voice, my lord the king."
18 He also said, "Why then is my lord pursuing his servant? For what have I done? Or
what evil is in my hand?
19 "Now therefore, please let my lord the king listen to the words of his servant. If the
LORD has stirred you up against me, let Him accept an offering; but if it is men, cursed
are they before the LORD, for they have driven me out today so that I would have no
attachment with the inheritance of the LORD, saying, 'Go, serve other gods.'
20 "Now then, do not let my blood fall to the ground away from the presence of the
LORD; for the king of Israel has come out to search for a single flea, just as one hunts a
partridge in the mountains."
21 Then Saul said, "I have sinned. Return, my son David, for I will not harm you again
because my life was precious in your sight this day. Behold, I have played the fool and
have committed a serious error."
22 David replied, "Behold the spear of the king! Now let one of the young men come
over and take it.
23 "The LORD will repay each man *for* his righteousness and his faithfulness; for the
LORD delivered you into *my* hand today, but I refused to stretch out my hand against the
LORD'S anointed.
24 "Now behold, as your life was highly valued in my sight this day, so may my life be
highly valued in the sight of the LORD, and may He deliver me from all distress."
25 Then Saul said to David, "Blessed are you, my son David; you will both accomplish
much and surely prevail." So David went on his way, and Saul returned to his place.

26:9 1 Sam 24:6, 7; 2 Sam 1:14, 16
26:10 Deut 32:35; 1 Sam 25:26, 38; Rom 12:19; Heb 10:30; Gen 47:29; Deut 31:14; Ps 37:13; 1 Sam 31:6
26:11 1 Sam 24:6, 12; Rom 12:17, 19; 1 Pet 3:9
26:12 Gen 2:21; 15:12; Is 29:10
26:16 1 Sam 20:31
26:17 1 Sam 24:16
26:18 1 Sam 24:9, 11-14
26:19 2 Sam 16:11; Gen 8:21; 1 Sam 24:9; Josh 22:25-27
26:20 1 Sam 24:14
26:21 Ex 9:27; 1 Sam 15:24, 30; 24:17
26:23 1 Sam 24:19; Ps 7:8; 18:20; 62:12; 1 Sam 24:12
26:24 1 Sam 18:30; Ps 54:7
26:25 1 Sam 24:19; 1 Sam 24:22

26:9 Why did David refuse to kill Saul? God had placed Saul in power and had not yet removed him. David did not want to run ahead of God's timing. We are in similar situations when we have leaders in church or government who are unfaithful or incompetent. It may be easy for us to criticize or move against a leader oblivious to God's hidden purposes and timing. Determining not to do wrong, David left Saul's destiny in God's hands. While we should not ignore sin or sit back and allow evil leaders to carry on their wickedness, neither should we take actions that are against God's laws. We should work for righteousness while trusting God.

26:15–16 David could have killed Saul and Abner, but he would have disobeyed God and set into motion unknown consequences. Instead, he took a spear and water jug, showing that he could have killed the king, but had not done it. And he made the point that he had great respect for both God and God's anointed king. When you need to make a point, look for creative, God-honoring ways to do so. It will have a more significant impact.

26:25 Saul had opportunities to kill David, but he never did. Why? First, every time David and Saul were face-to-face, David did something generous for Saul. The king did not want to respond to David's kindness with cruelty in front of all his men. Second, David had a large following in Israel. By killing him, Saul would risk his hold on the kingdom. Third, God had appointed David to become king of Israel and was protecting him.

5. Saul's defeat and death

David Flees to the Philistines

27 Then David said to himself, "Now I will perish one day by the hand of Saul. There 27:1
is nothing better for me than to escape into the land of the Philistines. Saul then 1 Sam 26:19
will despair of searching for me anymore in all the territory of Israel, and I will escape
from his hand."
2 So David arose and crossed over, he and the six hundred men who were with him, 27:2
to Achish the son of Maoch, king of Gath. 1 Sam 25:13; 1 Sam 21:10; 1 Kin 2:39
3 And David lived with Achish at Gath, he and his men, each with his household, *even*
David with his two wives, Ahinoam the Jezreelitess, and Abigail the Carmelitess, Nabal's 27:3 1 Sam 30:3; 2 Sam
widow. 2:3; 1 Sam 25:42, 43
4 Now it was told Saul that David had fled to Gath, so he no longer searched for him.
5 Then David said to Achish, "If now I have found favor in your sight, let them give
me a place in one of the cities in the country, that I may live there; for why should your
servant live in the royal city with you?"
6 So Achish gave him Ziklag that day; therefore Ziklag has belonged to the kings of 27:6
Judah to this day. Josh 15:31; 19:5; Neh 11:28
7 The number of days that David lived in the country of the Philistines was a year and
four months. 27:7 1 Sam 29:3
8 Now David and his men went up and raided the Geshurites and the Girzites and
the Amalekites; for they were the inhabitants of the land from ancient times, as you come 27:8 Josh 13:2, 13; Ex
to Shur even as far as the land of Egypt. 17:8; 1 Sam 15:7, 8; Ex 15:22
9 David attacked the land and did not leave a man or a woman alive, and he took
away the sheep, the cattle, the donkeys, the camels, and the clothing. Then he returned 27:9 1 Sam 15:3; Job 1:3
and came to Achish.
10 Now Achish said, "Where have you made a raid today?" And David said, "Against 27:10
the [17]Negev of Judah and against the Negev of the Jerahmeelites and against the Negev 1 Sam 23:27; 1 Sam 30:29; 1 Chr 2:9, 25;
of the Kenites." Judg 1:16; 4:11
11 David did not leave a man or a woman alive to bring to Gath, saying, "Otherwise
they will tell about us, saying, 'So has David done and so *has been* his practice all the
time he has lived in the country of the Philistines.' "

17 I.e. South country

THE BATTLE AT GILBOA
David pretended loyalty to Achish, but when war broke out with Israel, he was sent to Ziklag from Aphek. The Philistines defeated the Israelites at Mount Gilboa. David returned to Ziklag to find that the Amalekites had destroyed Ziklag. So David and his men pursued the Amalekite raiders and slaughtered them, recovering all that was taken.

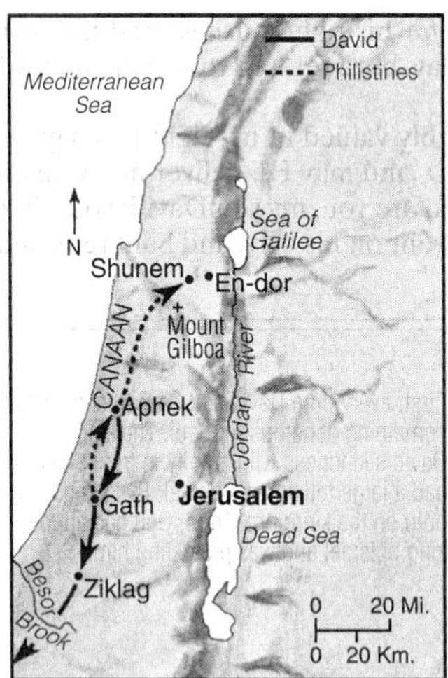

27:1–3 For the second time, David sought refuge from Saul in Philistine territory (21:10–15). The once-great conqueror of Philistines now had permission to live under the protection of King Achish of Gath. Previously David had acted insane in front of this king. Evidently Achish had forgotten that incident or had overlooked it in light of David's current situation. Achish certainly would have known about the split between Saul and David and would have been glad to shelter this Israelite traitor. In return, Achish would have expected military support from David and his 600 warriors. David further strengthened his position with Achish by leading Achish to believe that he was conducting raids on Israel and by pretending loyalty to the Philistine ruler.

27:4 Saul finally stopped pursuing David. His army was not strong enough to invade Philistine territory just to seek one man. Besides, the immediate threat to Saul's throne was gone while David was out of the country.

27:5–7 Gath was one of five principal cities in Philistia, and Achish was one of five co-rulers. David may have wanted to move out of this important city to avoid potential skirmishes or attacks upon his family. He may also have wanted to escape the close scrutiny of the Philistine officials. Achish let David move to Ziklag, where he lived until Saul's death (2 Samuel 2:1).

27:8–9 David probably conducted these guerrilla-style raids because these three tribes were known for their surprise attacks and cruel treatment of innocent people. These desert tribes were a danger not just to the Philistines, but especially to the Israelites, the people David would one day lead.

27:10–12 Was David wrong in falsely reporting his activities to Achish? No doubt David was lying, but he may have felt his strategy was justified in a time of war against a pagan enemy. David knew he would one day be Israel's king. The Philistines were still his enemies, but this was an excellent place to hide from Saul. When Achish asked David to go into battle against Israel, David agreed, once again pretending loyalty to the Philistines (28:1ff). Whether he would have actually fought Saul's army we can't know, but we can be sure that his ultimate loyalty was to God and not to Achish or Saul.

12 So Achish believed David, saying, "He has surely made himself odious among his
people Israel; therefore he will become my servant forever."

Saul and the Spirit Medium

28:1 1 Sam 29:1

28 Now it came about in those days that the Philistines gathered their armed camps
for war, to fight against Israel. And Achish said to David, "Know assuredly that
you will go out with me in the camp, you and your men."

28:2 1 Sam 1:22, 28

2 David said to Achish, "Very well, you shall know what your servant can do." So Achish
said to David, "Very well, I will make you my bodyguard for life."

28:3 1 Sam 25:1; 1 Sam 7:17; Lev 19:31; 20:27; Deut 18:10; 1 Sam 15:23

3 Now Samuel was dead, and all Israel had lamented him and buried him in Ramah,
his own city. And Saul had removed from the land those who were mediums and spiritists.
4 So the Philistines gathered together and came and camped in Shunem; and Saul
gathered all Israel together and they camped in Gilboa.

28:4 Josh 19:18; 1 Sam 28:4; 1 Kin 1:3; 2 Kin 4:8; 1 Sam 31:1

5 When Saul saw the camp of the Philistines, he was afraid and his heart trembled
greatly.
6 When Saul inquired of the LORD, the LORD did not answer him, either by dreams

28:6 1 Chr 10:13, 14; 1 Sam 14:37; Prov 1:24-31; Num 12:6; Joel 2:28; Ex 28:30; Num 27:21

or by Urim or by prophets.
7 Then Saul said to his servants, "Seek for me a woman who is a medium, that I may
go to her and inquire of her." And his servants said to him, "Behold, there is a woman
who is a medium at En-dor."

28:7 Acts 16:16; Josh 17:11; Ps 83:10

8 Then Saul disguised himself by putting on other clothes, and went, he and two men
with him, and they came to the woman by night; and he said, "Conjure up for me, please,
and bring up for me whom I shall name to you."

28:8 2 Chr 18:29; 35:22; 1 Chr 10:13; Is 8:19; Deut 18:10, 11

9 But the woman said to him, "Behold, you know what Saul has done, how he has cut
off those who are mediums and spiritists from the land. Why are you then laying a snare
for my life to bring about my death?"

28:9 1 Sam 28:3

10 Saul vowed to her by the LORD, saying, "As the LORD lives, no punishment shall
come upon you for this thing."
11 Then the woman said, "Whom shall I bring up for you?" And he said, "Bring up
Samuel for me."
12 When the woman saw Samuel, she cried out with a loud voice; and the woman spoke
to Saul, saying, "Why have you deceived me? For you are Saul."
13 The king said to her, "Do not be afraid; but what do you see?" And the woman said
to Saul, "I see a divine being coming up out of the earth."

28:14 1 Sam 15:27; 1 Sam 24:8

14 He said to her, "What is his form?" And she said, "An old man is coming up, and he
is wrapped with a robe." And Saul knew that it was Samuel, and he bowed with his face
to the ground and did homage.

28:1–2 Achish's request put David in a difficult position. To refuse to help Achish fight the Israelites would give away David's loyalty to Israel and endanger the lives of his soldiers and family. But to fight his own people would hurt the very people he loved and would soon lead. David, however, never had to solve his dilemma because God protected him. The other Philistine leaders objected to his presence in battle; thus, he did not have to fight his countrymen.

28:3–8 It was Saul who had banned all mediums and spiritists (those who consult with the dead) from Israel, but in desperation he turned to one for counsel. Although he had removed the sin of witchcraft from the land, he did not remove it from his heart. We may make a great show of denouncing sin, but if our hearts do not change, the sins will return. Knowing what is right and condemning what is wrong does not take the place of *doing* what is right.

28:5–6 The Urim, along with the Thummim, was used by the high priest to determine God's guidance in certain matters. (See the notes on 2:18 and 10:20 for further information on the use of the Urim and Thummim.)

28:5–7 Saul was overwhelmed at the sight of the Philistine army, and so he turned to the occult. Let life's difficulties and obstacles push you in God's direction and make you depend upon him. As we see from Saul's story, turning to anything or anyone else leads only to disaster.

28:7–8 God had strictly forbidden the Israelites to have anything to do with divination, sorcery, witchcraft, mediums, spiritists, or anyone who consults the dead (Deuteronomy 18:9–14). In fact, sorcerers were to be put to death (Exodus 22:18). Occult practices were carried on in the name of pagan gods, and people turned to the occult for answers that God would not give.

Practitioners of the occult have Satan and demons as the source of their information; God does not reveal his will to them. Instead he speaks through his own channels: the Bible, his Son Jesus Christ, and the Holy Spirit.

28:12 Did Samuel really come back from the dead at the medium's call? The medium shrieked at the appearance of Samuel—she knew too well that the spirits she usually contacted were either contrived or satanic. Somehow Samuel's appearance revealed to her that she was dealing with a power far greater than she had known. She did not call up Samuel by trickery or by the power of Satan; God brought Samuel back to give Saul a prediction regarding his fate, a message Saul already knew. This in no way justifies efforts to contact the dead or communicate with persons or spirits from the past. God is against all such practices (Galatians 5:19–21).

15 Then Samuel said to Saul, "Why have you disturbed me by bringing me up?" And
Saul answered, "I am greatly distressed; for the Philistines are waging war against me,
and God has departed from me and no longer answers me, either through prophets
or by dreams; therefore I have called you, that you may make known to me what I
should do."
16 Samuel said, "Why then do you ask me, since the LORD has departed from you and
has become your adversary?
17 "The LORD has done accordingly as He spoke through me; for the LORD has torn
the kingdom out of your hand and given it to your neighbor, to David.
18 "As you did not obey the LORD and did not execute His fierce wrath on Amalek, so
the LORD has done this thing to you this day.
19 "Moreover the LORD will also give over Israel along with you into the hands of the
Philistines, therefore tomorrow you and your sons will be with me. Indeed the LORD
will give over the army of Israel into the hands of the Philistines!"
20 Then Saul immediately fell full length upon the ground and was very afraid because
of the words of Samuel; also there was no strength in him, for he had eaten no food all
day and all night.
21 The woman came to Saul and saw that he was terrified, and said to him, "Behold,
your maidservant has obeyed you, and I have taken my life in my hand and have listened
to your words which you spoke to me.
22 "So now also, please listen to the voice of your maidservant, and let me set a piece of
bread before you that *you may* eat and have strength when you go on *your* way."
23 But he refused and said, "I will not eat." However, his servants together with
the woman urged him, and he listened to them. So he arose from the ground and sat on
the bed.
24 The woman had a fattened calf in the house, and she quickly slaughtered it; and she
took flour, kneaded it and baked unleavened bread from it.
25 She brought *it* before Saul and his servants, and they ate. Then they arose and went
away that night.

The Philistines Mistrust David

29 Now the Philistines gathered together all their armies to Aphek, while the Israelites were camping by the spring which is in Jezreel.
2 And the lords of the Philistines were proceeding on by hundreds and by thousands,
and David and his men were proceeding on in the rear with Achish.
3 Then the commanders of the Philistines said, "What *are* these Hebrews *doing here?*"
And Achish said to the commanders of the Philistines, "Is this not David, the servant of
Saul the king of Israel, who has been with me these days, or *rather* these years, and I
have found no fault in him from the day he deserted *to me* to this day?"
4 But the commanders of the Philistines were angry with him, and the commanders
of the Philistines said to him, "Make the man go back, that he may return to his place
where you have assigned him, and do not let him go down to battle with us, or in the
battle he may become an adversary to us. For with what could this *man* make himself
acceptable to his lord? *Would it* not *be* with the heads of these men?
5 "Is this not David, of whom they sing in the dances, saying,
'Saul has slain his thousands,
And David his ten thousands'?"
6 Then Achish called David and said to him, "*As* the LORD lives, you *have been* upright, and your going out and your coming in with me in the army are pleasing in my
sight; for I have not found evil in you from the day of your coming to me to this day.
Nevertheless, you are not pleasing in the sight of the lords.

28:15 1 Sam 16:14; 18:12; 1 Sam 28:6
28:17 1 Sam 15:28
28:18 1 Sam 15:20, 26; 1 Kin 20:42
28:19 1 Sam 31:2; Job 3:17-19
28:21 Judg 12:3; 1 Sam 19:5; Job 13:14
28:23 1 Kin 21:4; 2 Kin 5:13; Esth 1:6; Ezek 23:41
28:24 Gen 18:7; Luke 15:23, 27, 30; Gen 18:6
29:1 1 Sam 28:1; Josh 12:18; 19:30; 1 Sam 4:1; 1 Kin 20:30; 1 Kin 21:1; 2 Kin 9:30
29:2 1 Sam 28:1, 2
29:3 1 Sam 27:7; 1 Sam 27:1-6; 1 Chr 12:19, 20; Dan 6:5
29:4 1 Sam 27:6; 1 Sam 14:21
29:5 1 Sam 18:7; 21:11
29:6 2 Sam 3:25; 2 Kin 19:27; Is 37:28; 1 Sam 27:8-12; 29:3

28:15 God did not answer Saul's appeals because Saul had not followed God's previous directions. Sometimes people wonder why their prayers are not answered. But if they don't fulfill the responsibilities God has already given them, they should not be surprised when he does not give further guidance.

29:4 The other Philistine commanders knew that David was the one who, as a young man, had killed their champion, Goliath (17:32–54), had killed hundreds of Philistine soldiers (18:27), and was the hero of Israelite victory songs (21:11). They were afraid that, in the heat of battle, David might turn against them. Although David was upset at this at first, God used the commanders' suspicion to keep him from having to fight against Saul and his countrymen.

7 "Now therefore return and go in peace, that you may not displease the lords of the
Philistines."
8 David said to Achish, "But what have I done? And what have you found in your
servant from the day when I came before you to this day, that I may not go and fight
against the enemies of my lord the king?"
9 But Achish replied to David, "I know that you are pleasing in my sight, like an angel
of God; nevertheless the commanders of the Philistines have said, 'He must not go up
with us to the battle.'
10 "Now then arise early in the morning with the servants of your lord who have come
with you, and as soon as you have arisen early in the morning and have light, depart."
11 So David arose early, he and his men, to depart in the morning to return to the land
of the Philistines. And the Philistines went up to Jezreel.

David's Victory over the Amalekites

30 Then it happened when David and his men came to Ziklag on the third day, that
the Amalekites had made a raid on the Negev and on Ziklag, and had overthrown
Ziklag and burned it with fire;
2 and they took captive the women *and all* who were in it, both small and great, without killing anyone, and carried *them* off and went their way.
3 When David and his men came to the city, behold, it was burned with fire, and their
wives and their sons and their daughters had been taken captive.
4 Then David and the people who were with him lifted their voices and wept until
there was no strength in them to weep.
5 Now David's two wives had been taken captive, Ahinoam the Jezreelitess and Abigail the widow of Nabal the Carmelite.
6 Moreover David was greatly distressed because the people spoke of stoning him,
for all the people were embittered, each one because of his sons and his daughters. But
David strengthened himself in the LORD his God.
7 Then David said to Abiathar the priest, the son of Ahimelech, "Please bring me the
ephod." So Abiathar brought the ephod to David.
8 David inquired of the LORD, saying, "Shall I pursue this band? Shall I overtake
them?" And He said to him, "Pursue, for you will surely overtake them, and you will
surely rescue *all.*"
9 So David went, he and the six hundred men who were with him, and came to the
brook Besor, *where* those left behind remained.
10 But David pursued, he and four hundred men, for two hundred who were too exhausted to cross the brook Besor remained *behind.*
11 Now they found an Egyptian in the field and brought him to David, and gave him
bread and he ate, and they provided him water to drink.
12 They gave him a piece of fig cake and two clusters of raisins, and he ate; then his
spirit revived. For he had not eaten bread or drunk water for three days and three nights.
13 David said to him, "To whom do you belong? And where are you from?" And he
said, "I am a young man of Egypt, a servant of an Amalekite; and my master left me
behind when I fell sick three days ago.
14 "We made a raid on the Negev of the Cherethites, and on that which belongs to Judah, and on the Negev of Caleb, and we burned Ziklag with fire."
15 Then David said to him, "Will you bring me down to this band?" And he said, "Swear

29:8 1 Sam 27:10-12
29:9 2 Sam 14:17, 20; 19:27; 1 Sam 29:4
29:10 1 Chr 12:19, 22
30:1 1 Sam 29:4, 11; 1 Sam 15:7; 27:8-10; 1 Sam 27:6, 8
30:2 1 Sam 27:11
30:4 Num 14:1
30:5 1 Sam 25:42, 43; 2 Sam 2:2
30:6 Ex 17:4; John 8:59; 1 Sam 23:16; Ps 18:2; 27:14; 31:24; 71:4, 5; Rom 4:20
30:7 1 Sam 23:6, 9; 1 Sam 22:20-23
30:8 1 Sam 23:2, 4; Ps 50:15; 91:15; Ex 15:9; 1 Sam 30:18
30:9 1 Sam 27:2
30:10 1 Sam 30:9, 21
30:12 Judg 15:19
30:14 1 Sam 30:1, 16; 2 Sam 8:18; 1 Kin 1:38, 44; Ezek 25:16; Zeph 2:5; Josh 14:13; 15:13; 21:12; 1 Sam 30:1

30:6 Faced with the tragedy of losing their families, David's soldiers began to turn against him and even talked about killing him. Instead of planning a rescue, they looked for someone to blame. But David found his strength in God and began looking for a solution instead of a scapegoat. When facing problems, remember that it is useless to look for someone to blame or criticize. Instead, consider how you can help find a solution.

30:7 David couldn't go to the tabernacle to ask the Lord for guidance because it was in Saul's territory. Therefore he called for the ephod, the only tabernacle-related object he possessed. In the presence of the priest and this priestly garment, he asked God for direction. When David called for the ephod, he was really asking the priest to bring him the Urim and Thummim, which were kept in a pouch attached to the ephod. Only the high priest could carry and use the Urim and Thummim. (For more information on the ephod and its contents, see the note on Exodus 39:1–21.)

30:11–15 The Amalekites cruelly left this slave to die, but God used him to lead David and his men to the Amalekite camp. David and his men treated the young man kindly, and he returned the kindness by leading them to the enemy. Treat those you meet with respect and dignity no matter how insignificant they may seem. You never know how God will use them to help you or haunt you, depending upon your response to them.

to me by God that you will not kill me or deliver me into the hands of my master, and I
will bring you down to this band."
16 When he had brought him down, behold, they were spread over all the land, eating
and drinking and dancing because of all the great spoil that they had taken from the land
of the Philistines and from the land of Judah.
17 David slaughtered them from the twilight until the evening of the next day; and not
a man of them escaped, except four hundred young men who rode on camels and fled.
18 So David recovered all that the Amalekites had taken, and rescued his two wives.
19 But nothing of theirs was missing, whether small or great, sons or daughters, spoil
or anything that they had taken for themselves; David brought *it* all back.
20 So David had captured all the sheep and the cattle *which the people* drove ahead of
the *other* livestock, and they said, "This is David's spoil."

30:16 Luke 12:19; 17:27f; 1 Sam 30:14
30:17 1 Sam 11:11; Judg 7:12; 1 Sam 15:3
30:18 Gen 14:16
30:19 1 Sam 30:8
30:20 1 Sam 30:26-31

The Spoils Are Divided

21 When David came to the two hundred men who were too exhausted to follow David, who had also been left at the brook Besor, and they went out to meet David and to
meet the people who were with him, then David approached the people and greeted them.
22 Then all the wicked and worthless men among those who went with David said,
"Because they did not go with us, we will not give them any of the spoil that we have
recovered, except to every man his wife and his children, that they may lead *them* away
and depart."
23 Then David said, "You must not do so, my brothers, with what the LORD has given
us, who has kept us and delivered into our hand the band that came against us.
24 "And who will listen to you in this matter? For as his share is who goes down to the
battle, so shall his share be who stays by the baggage; they shall share alike."
25 So it has been from that day forward, that he made it a statute and an ordinance for
Israel to this day.
26 Now when David came to Ziklag, he sent *some* of the spoil to the elders of Judah,
to his friends, saying, "Behold, a gift for you from the spoil of the enemies of the LORD:
27 to those who were in Bethel, and to those who were in Ramoth of the Negev, and to
those who were in Jattir,
28 and to those who were in Aroer, and to those who were in Siphmoth, and to those
who were in Eshtemoa,
29 and to those who were in Racal, and to those who were in the cities of the Jerahmeelites, and to those who were in the cities of the Kenites,
30 and to those who were in Hormah, and to those who were in Bor-ashan, and to those
who were in Athach,
31 and to those who were in Hebron, and to all the places where David himself and his
men were accustomed to go."

30:21 1 Sam 30:10
30:24 Num 31:27; Josh 22:8
30:26 1 Sam 25:27; 1 Sam 18:17; 25:28
30:27 Gen 12:8; Josh 7:2; 8:9; 16:1; Josh 19:8; Josh 15:48; 21:14
30:28 Josh 13:16; 1 Chr 11:44; Josh 15:50
30:29 1 Sam 27:10; Judg 1:16; 1 Sam 15:6
30:30 Num 14:45; 21:3; Josh 12:14; 15:30; 19:4; Judg 1:17; Josh 15:42; 19:7
30:31 Num 13:22; Josh 14:13-15; 21:11-13; 2 Sam 2:1; 1 Sam 23:22

Saul and His Sons Slain

31 Now the Philistines were fighting against Israel, and the men of Israel fled from
before the Philistines and fell slain on Mount Gilboa.
2 The Philistines overtook Saul and his sons; and the Philistines killed Jonathan and
Abinadab and Malchi-shua the sons of Saul.
3 The battle went heavily against Saul, and the archers hit him; and he was badly
wounded by the archers.

31:1 1 Chr 10:1-12; 1 Sam 28:4
31:2 1 Chr 8:33f
31:3 2 Sam 1:6

30:24–25 David made a law that those who stayed with the supplies were to be treated equally with those who fought in battle. Today it takes several people to provide the support services needed for every soldier in battle. In the church and other organizations, we need to treat those who provide support services equally with those on the front lines. Without bookkeepers, secretaries, trainers, and administrators, those with a public ministry would be unable to do their jobs. Are you on the front lines? Don't forget those who are backing you up. Are you in the support group? Realize that your position, although it may be less glamorous or exciting, is vital to the work of the entire group.

31:3–4 The Philistines had a well-earned reputation for torturing their captives. Saul no doubt knew about Samson's fate (Judges 16:18–31) and did not want to risk physical mutilation or other abuse. When his armor bearer refused to kill him, he took his own life.

31:3–4 Saul was tall, handsome, strong, rich, and powerful, but all of this was not enough to make him someone we should emulate. He was tall physically, but he was small in God's eyes. He was handsome, but his sin made him ugly. He was strong, but his lack of faith made him weak. He was rich, but he was spiritually bankrupt. He could give orders to many, but he couldn't command their respect or allegiance. Saul looked good on the outside, but he was decaying on the inside. A right relationship with God and a strong character are much more valuable than a good-looking exterior.

31:4 Judg 9:54; 1 Chr 10:4; Judg 14:3; 1 Sam 14:6; 17:26, 36; 2 Sam 1:6, 10

4 Then Saul said to his armor bearer, "Draw your sword and pierce me through with
it, otherwise these uncircumcised will come and pierce me through and make sport of
me." But his armor bearer would not, for he was greatly afraid. So Saul took his sword
and fell on it.
5 When his armor bearer saw that Saul was dead, he also fell on his sword and died
with him.
6 Thus Saul died with his three sons, his armor bearer, and all his men on that day
together.
7 When the men of Israel who were on the other side of the valley, with those who
were beyond the Jordan, saw that the men of Israel had fled and that Saul and his sons
were dead, they abandoned the cities and fled; then the Philistines came and lived in
them.

31:9 2 Sam 1:20; Judg 16:23, 24

31:10 Judg 2:13; 1 Sam 7:3; 1 Sam 31:12; 2 Sam 21:12; Josh 17:11

31:11 1 Sam 11:1-13

31:12 2 Sam 2:4-7; 2 Chr 16:14

31:13 2 Sam 21:12-14; 1 Sam 22:6; 2 Sam 1:12

8 It came about on the next day when the Philistines came to strip the slain, that they
found Saul and his three sons fallen on Mount Gilboa.
9 They cut off his head and stripped off his weapons, and sent *them* throughout the
land of the Philistines, to carry the good news to the house of their idols and to the
people.
10 They put his weapons in the temple of Ashtaroth, and they fastened his body to the
wall of Beth-shan.
11 Now when the inhabitants of Jabesh-gilead heard what the Philistines had done to
Saul,
12 all the valiant men rose and walked all night, and took the body of Saul and the bodies
of his sons from the wall of Beth-shan, and they came to Jabesh and burned them there.
13 They took their bones and buried them under the tamarisk tree at Jabesh, and fasted
seven days.

31:3–4 Saul's armor bearer faced a moral dilemma—should he carry out a sinful order from a man he was supposed to obey? He knew he should obey his master, the king, but he also knew murder was wrong. He decided not to kill Saul.

There is a difference between following an order with which you don't agree and following one you know is wrong. It is never right or ethical to carry out a wrong act, no matter who gives the order or what the consequences for disobedience may be. What shapes your choice when you face a moral dilemma? Have the courage to follow God's law above human commands.

31:4 Saul faced death the same way he faced life. He took matters into his own hands without thinking of God or asking for his guidance. If our lives aren't the way we would like them to be now, we can't assume that change will come more easily later. When nearing death, we will respond to God the same way we have been responding all along. Coming face-to-face with death only shows us what we are *really* like. How do you want to face death? Start facing life that way right now.

31:10 To put Saul's armor in the Philistine temple gave credit to a pagan goddess for victory over Saul. Ashtaroth was a goddess of fertility and sex. Beth-shan was a town on the eastern slopes of Mount Gilboa, overlooking the Jordan Valley.

31:13 Consider the difference between the last judge of Israel and its first king. Saul, the king, was characterized by inconsistency, disobedience, and self-will. He did not have a heart for God. Samuel, the judge, was characterized by consistency, obedience, and a deep desire for God's will. He had a genuine desire for God.

When God called Samuel, he said, "Speak, LORD, for Your servant is listening" (3:9). But when God, through Samuel, called Saul, Saul replied, "Why then do you speak to me in this way?" (9:21). Saul was dedicated to himself; Samuel was dedicated to God.

31:13 Saul's death was also the death of an ideal—Israel could no longer believe that having a king like the other nations would solve all their troubles. The real problem was not the form of government, but the sinful king. Saul tried to please God by spurts of religiosity, but real spirituality takes a lifetime of consistent obedience.

Heroic spiritual lives are built by stacking days of obedience one on top of the other. Like a brick, each obedient act is small in itself, but in time the acts will pile up, and a huge wall of strong character will be built—a great defense against temptation. We should strive for consistent obedience each day.

2 SAMUEL

Judges begin to rule 1375 B.C. (1220 B.C.)

Saul becomes king 1050 (1045)

VITAL STATISTICS

PURPOSES:
(1) to record the history of David's reign;
(2) to demonstrate effective leadership under God;
(3) to reveal that one person can make a difference;
(4) to show the personal qualities that please God;
(5) to depict David as an ideal leader of an imperfect kingdom, and to foreshadow Christ, who will be the ideal leader of a new and perfect kingdom (chapter 7)

AUTHOR:
Unknown. Some have suggested that Nathan's son Zabud may have been the author (1 Kings 4:5). The book also includes the writings of Nathan and Gad (1 Chronicles 29:29).

DATE WRITTEN:
930 B.C.; written soon after David's reign, 1050–970 B.C.

SETTING:
The land of Israel under David's rule

KEY VERSE:
"And David realized that the LORD had established him as king over Israel, and that He had exalted his kingdom for the sake of His people Israel" (5:12).

KEY PEOPLE:
David, Joab, Bathsheba, Nathan, Absalom

SPECIAL FEATURES:
This book was named after the prophet who anointed David and guided him in living for God.

THE CHILD enters the room with long gown flowing, trailing well behind her high-heeled shoes. The wide-brimmed hat rests precariously atop her head, tilted to the right, and the long necklace swings like a pendulum as she walks. Following close is the "man." His fingernails peek out of the coat sleeves that are already pushed upward six inches. With feet shuffling in the double-sized boots, his unsteady steps belie his confident smile. Children at play, dressing up—they copy Mom and Dad, having watched them dress and walk. Models . . . everyone has them . . . people we emulate, people who are our ideals. Unconsciously, perhaps, we copy their actions and adopt their ideas.

Among all the godly role models mentioned in the Bible, there is probably no one who stands out more than King David. Born halfway between Abraham and Jesus, he became God's leader for all of Israel and the ancestor of the Messiah. David was "a man after [God's] own heart" (1 Samuel 13:14). What are the personal qualities that David possessed that pleased God?

The book of 2 Samuel tells David's story. As you read, you will be filled with excitement as he is crowned king over Judah and then king over all of Israel (5:1–5), praising God as he brings the ark of the covenant back to the tabernacle (6:1–23) and exulting as he leads his armies to victory over all their enemies and completes the conquest of the promised land begun by Joshua (8—10). David was a man who accomplished much.

But David was human, and there were those dark times when he stumbled and fell into sin. The record of lust, adultery, and murder is not easy to read (11—13) and reveals that even great people who try to follow God are susceptible to temptation and sin.

Godliness does not guarantee an easy and carefree life. David had family problems—his own son incited the entire nation to rebellion and crowned himself king (14:1—18:33). And greatness can cause pride, as we see in David's sinful act of taking a census in order to glory in the strength of his nation (24:1–25). But the story of this fallen hero does not end in tragedy. Through repentance, his fellowship and peace with God were restored, but he had to face the consequences of the sins he committed (12—20). These consequences stayed with him the rest of his life as a reminder of his sinful deeds and his need for God.

As you read 2 Samuel, look for David's godlike characteristics—his faithfulness, patience, courage, generosity, commitment, honesty—as well as other God-honoring characteristics, such as modesty and penitence. Valuable lessons can be learned from his sins and from his repentance. You, like David, can become a person after God's own heart.

Saul dies; David is king over Judah 1010	David becomes king over all Israel 1003	David and Bathsheba sin 997(?)	Solomon born 991	David's census 980(?)	David dies; Solomon made king 970	The kingdom is divided 930

THE BLUEPRINT

A. DAVID'S SUCCESSES (1:1—10:19)
1. David becomes king over Judah
2. David becomes king over Israel
3. David conquers the surrounding nations

David took the fractured kingdom that Saul had left behind and built a strong, united power. Forty years later, David would turn this kingdom over to his son Solomon. David had a heart for God. He was a king who governed God's people by God's principles, and God blessed him greatly. We may not have David's earthly success, but following God is, ultimately, the most successful decision we can make.

B. DAVID'S STRUGGLES (11:1—24:25)
1. David and Bathsheba
2. Turmoil in David's family
3. National rebellion against David
4. The later years of David's rule

David sinned with Bathsheba and then tried to cover his sin by having her husband killed. Although he was forgiven for his sin, the consequences remained—he experienced trouble and distress, both with his family and with the nation. God is always ready to forgive, but we must live with the consequences of our actions. Covering up our sin will only multiply sin's painful consequences.

MEGATHEMES

THEME	EXPLANATION	IMPORTANCE
Kingdom Growth	Under David's leadership, Israel's kingdom grew rapidly. With the growth came many changes: from tribal independence to centralized government, from the leadership of judges to a monarchy, from decentralized worship to worship at Jerusalem.	No matter how much growth or how many changes we experience, God provides for us if we love him and highly regard his principles. God's work done in God's way never lacks God's supply of wisdom and energy.
Personal Greatness	David's popularity and influence increased greatly. He realized that the Lord was behind his success because he wanted to pour out his kindness on Israel. David regarded God's interests as more important than his own.	God graciously pours out his favor on us because of what Christ has done. God does not regard personal greatness as something to be used selfishly, but as an instrument to carry out his work among his people. The greatness we should desire is to love others as God loves us.
Justice	King David showed justice, mercy, and fairness to Saul's family, enemies, rebels, allies, and close friends alike. His just rule was grounded in his faith in and knowledge of God. God's perfect moral nature is the standard for justice.	Although David was the most just of all Israel's kings, he was still imperfect. His use of justice offered hope for a heavenly, ideal kingdom. This hope will never be satisfied in the heart of man until Christ, the Son of David, comes to rule in perfect justice forever.
Consequences of Sin	David abandoned his purpose as leader and king in time of war. His desire for prosperity and ease led him from triumph to trouble. Because David committed adultery with Bathsheba, he experienced consequences of his sin that destroyed both his family and the nation.	Temptation quite often comes when a person's life is aimless. We sometimes think that sinful pleasures and freedom from God's restraint will bring us a feeling of vitality; but sin creates a cycle of suffering that is not worth the fleeting pleasures it offers.
Feet of Clay	David not only sinned with Bathsheba, he murdered an innocent man. He neglected to discipline his sons when they got involved in rape and murder. This great hero showed a lack of character in some of his most important personal decisions. The man of iron had feet of clay.	Sin should never be considered as a mere weakness or flaw. Sin is fatal and must be eradicated from our lives. David's life teaches us to have compassion for all people, including those whose sinful nature leads them into sinful acts. It serves as a warning to us not to excuse sin in our own lives, even in times of success.

KEY PLACES IN 2 SAMUEL

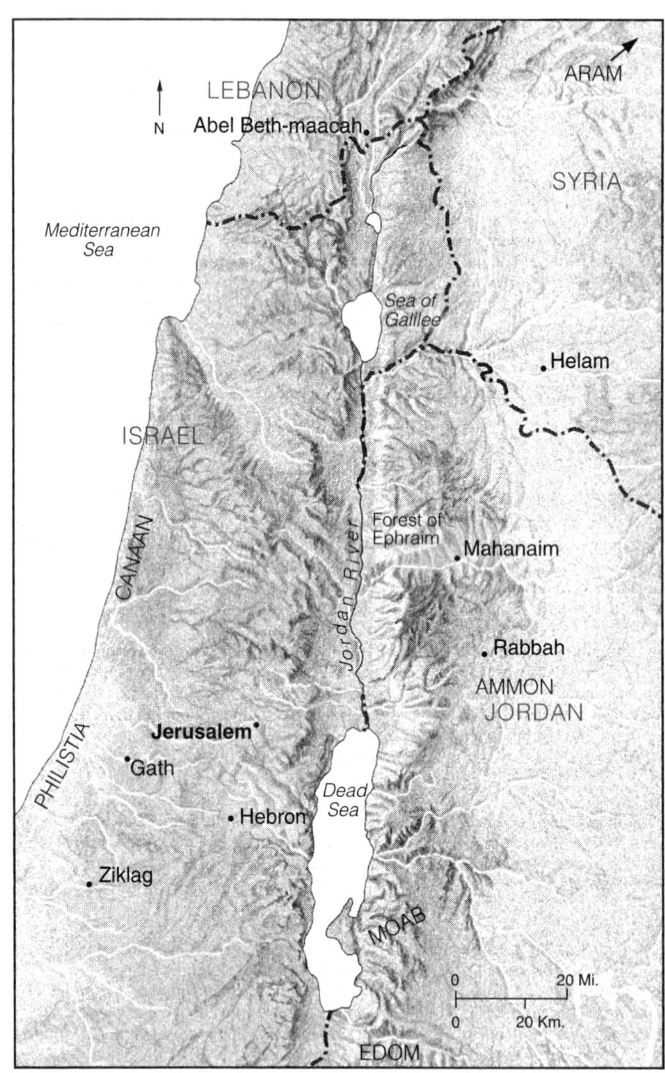

The broken lines (–·–·) indicate modern boundaries.

1 Hebron After Saul's death, David moved from the Philistine city of Ziklag to Hebron, where the tribe of Judah crowned him king. But the rest of Israel's tribes backed Saul's son Ish-bosheth and crowned him king at Mahanaim. As a result, there was war between Judah and the rest of the tribes of Israel until Ish-bosheth was assassinated. Then all of Israel pledged loyalty to David as their king (1:1—5:5).

2 Jerusalem One of David's first battles as king occurred at the stronghold of Zion (Jerusalem). David and his troops took the city by surprise, and it became his capital. It was here that David brought the ark of the covenant and made a special agreement with God (5:6—7:29).

3 Gath The Philistines were Israel's constant enemy, though they did give David sanctuary when he was hiding from Saul (1 Samuel 27). But when Saul died and David became king, the Philistines planned to defeat him. In a battle near Jerusalem, David and his troops routed the Philistines (5:17–25), but they were not completely subdued until David conquered their largest city (8:1).

4 Moab During the time of the judges, Moab controlled many cities in Israel and demanded heavy taxes (Judges 3:12–30). David conquered Moab and, in turn, levied tribute from them (8:2).

5 Edom Though the Edomites and the Israelites traced their ancestry back to the same man, Isaac (Genesis 25:19–23), they were long-standing enemies. David defeated Edom and forced them to pay tribute also (8:14).

6 Rabbah The Ammonites insulted David's delegation and turned a peace-making mission into angry warfare. The Ammonites called troops from Aram, but David defeated this alliance first at Helam, then at Rabbah, the capital city (10:1—12:31).

7 Mahanaim David had victory in the field, but problems at home. His son Absalom incited a rebellion and crowned himself king at Hebron. David and his men fled to Mahanaim. Acting on bad advice, Absalom mobilized his army to fight David (13:1—17:29).

8 Forest of Ephraim The armies of Absalom and David fought in the forest of Ephraim. Absalom's hair got caught in a tree, and Joab, David's general, found and killed him. With Absalom's death the rebellion died, and David was welcomed back to Jerusalem (18:1—19:43).

9 Abel Beth-maacah A man named Sheba also incited a rebellion against David. He fled to Abel Beth-maacah, but Joab and a small troop besieged the city. The citizens of Abel Beth-maacah killed Sheba themselves (20:1–26). David's victories laid the foundation for the peaceful reign of his son Solomon.

A. DAVID'S SUCCESSES (1:1—10:19)

After years of running from Saul, David is finally crowned king over the tribe of Judah. The rest of Israel, however, followed Ish-Bosheth, Saul's son. David did not attempt to take the tribes by force, but placed the matter in God's hands. After a few years Ish-Bosheth was assassinated and the rest of the tribes finally put their support behind David. David moved the capital to Jerusalem, defeated the surrounding nations, and even showed kindness to Saul's family. We may not understand why God seems to move slowly at times, but we must trust him and be faithful with what he has given us.

1. David becomes king over Judah

David Learns of Saul's Death

1 Now it came about after the death of Saul, when David had returned from the slaughter of the Amalekites, that David remained two days in Ziklag.
2 On the third day, behold, a man came out of the camp from Saul, with his clothes
torn and dust on his head. And it came about when he came to David that he fell to the
ground and prostrated himself.
3 Then David said to him, "From where do you come?" And he said to him, "I have
escaped from the camp of Israel."
4 David said to him, "How did things go? Please tell me." And he said, "The people
have fled from the battle, and also many of the people have fallen and are dead; and
Saul and Jonathan his son are dead also."
5 So David said to the young man who told him, "How do you know that Saul and his
son Jonathan are dead?"
6 The young man who told him said, "By chance I happened to be on Mount Gilboa,
and behold, Saul was leaning on his spear. And behold, the chariots and the horsemen
pursued him closely.
7 "When he looked behind him, he saw me and called to me. And I said, 'Here I am.'
8 "He said to me, 'Who are you?' And I answered him, 'I am an Amalekite.'
9 "Then he said to me, 'Please stand beside me and kill me, for agony has seized me
because my life still lingers in me.'
10 "So I stood beside him and killed him, because I knew that he could not live after he
had fallen. And I took the crown which *was* on his head and the bracelet which *was* on
his arm, and I have brought them here to my lord."
11 Then David took hold of his clothes and tore them, and *so* also *did* all the men who
were with him.
12 They mourned and wept and fasted until evening for Saul and his son Jonathan and
for the people of the LORD and the house of Israel, because they had fallen by the sword.
13 David said to the young man who told him, "Where are you from?" And he answered,
"I am the son of an alien, an Amalekite."

1:1 1 Sam 31:6; 1 Sam 30:1, 17, 26
1:2 2 Sam 4:10; 1 Sam 4:12; 1 Sam 25:23
1:4 1 Sam 4:16
1:6 1 Sam 28:4; 31:1-6; 1 Chr 10:4-10; 1 Sam 31:2-4
1:8 1 Sam 15:3; 30:1, 13, 17
1:10 Judg 9:54; 2 Kin 11:12
1:11 Gen 37:29, 34; Josh 7:6; 2 Chr 34:27; Ezra 9:3
1:12 2 Sam 3:35
1:13 2 Sam 1:8

1:1 David was a man who had great faith in God. He waited for God to fulfill his promises. The book of 1 Samuel tells of David's struggles as he waited to become king of Israel (Samuel had anointed David as king of Israel many years earlier). King Saul became jealous of David because the people were praising him for his accomplishments. Eventually, Saul's jealousy became so intense that he tried to kill David. As a result, David had to run and hide. For many years David hid from Saul in enemy territory and in the barren wilderness south and east of Jerusalem. David may have wondered when God's promise that he would be king would come true, but his struggles prepared him for the great responsibilities he would later face. The book of 2 Samuel tells how David was finally rewarded for his patience and consistent faith in God.

1:1 When Saul died, David and his men were still living in Ziklag, a Philistine city. Because Saul had driven him out of Israel, David had pretended to be loyal to Achish, a Philistine ruler (1 Samuel 27). There he was safe from Saul.

1:11–12 "They mourned and wept and fasted until evening." David and his men were visibly shaken over Saul's death. Their actions showed their genuine sorrow over the loss of their king, their friend Jonathan, and the other soldiers of Israel who died that day. They were not ashamed to grieve. Today, some people consider expressing emotions to be a sign of weakness. Those who wish to appear strong try to hide their feelings. But expressing our grief can help us deal with our intense sorrow when a loved one dies.

1:13 The man identified himself as an Amalekite from Saul's camp (1:2). He may have been an Amalekite under Israelite jurisdiction, but more likely he was a battlefield scavenger. Obviously the man was lying both about his identity and about what happened on the battlefield. (Compare his story with the account in 1 Samuel 31:3–4.) Because he had Saul's crown with him, something the Philistines wouldn't have left behind, we can infer that he found Saul dead on the battlefield before the Philistines arrived (1 Samuel 31:8).

A life of deceit leads to disaster. The man lied to gain some personal reward for killing David's rival, but he misread David's character. If David had rewarded him for murdering the king, David would have shared his guilt. Instead, David had the messenger killed. Lying can bring disaster upon the liar, even for something he or she has not done.

1:13 The Amalekites were a fierce nomadic tribe that frequently conducted surprise raids on Canaanite villages. They had been Israel's enemies since Moses' time. David had just destroyed an Amalekite band of raiders who had burned his city and kidnapped its women and children (1 Samuel 30:1–20). This man was probably unaware of David's recent confrontations with Amalekites, or he may not have come. Instead, he incurred David's wrath by posing as an enemy of Israel and claiming to have killed God's chosen king.

14 Then David said to him, "How is it you were not afraid to stretch out your hand to
destroy the LORD'S anointed?"
15 And David called one of the young men and said, "Go, cut him down." So he struck
him and he died.
16 David said to him, "Your blood is on your head, for your mouth has testified against
you, saying, 'I have killed the LORD'S anointed.' "

1:14 1 Sam 24:6; 26:9, 11, 16

1:15 2 Sam 4:10, 12

1:16 1 Sam 26:9; 2 Sam 3:28, 29; 1 Kin 2:32; 2 Sam 1:10; Luke 19:22

David's Dirge for Saul and Jonathan

17 Then David chanted with this lament over Saul and Jonathan his son,
18 and he told *them* to teach the sons of Judah *the song of* the bow; behold, it is written
in the book of Jashar.
19 "Your beauty, O Israel, is slain on your high places!
How have the mighty fallen!
20 "Tell *it* not in Gath,
Proclaim it not in the streets of Ashkelon,
Or the daughters of the Philistines will rejoice,
The daughters of the uncircumcised will exult.
21 "O mountains of Gilboa,
Let not dew or rain be on you, nor fields of offerings;
For there the shield of the mighty was defiled,
The shield of Saul, not anointed with oil.
22 "From the blood of the slain, from the fat of the mighty,
The bow of Jonathan did not turn back,
And the sword of Saul did not return empty.
23 "Saul and Jonathan, beloved and pleasant in their life,
And in their death they were not parted;
They were swifter than eagles,
They were stronger than lions.
24 "O daughters of Israel, weep over Saul,
Who clothed you luxuriously in scarlet,
Who put ornaments of gold on your apparel.
25 "How have the mighty fallen in the midst of the battle!
Jonathan is slain on your high places.
26 "I am distressed for you, my brother Jonathan;
You have been very pleasant to me.
Your love to me was more wonderful
Than the love of women.
27 "How have the mighty fallen,
And the weapons of war perished!"

1:17 2 Chr 35:25

1:18 Josh 10:13

1:19 2 Sam 1:25, 27

1:20 1 Sam 31:8-13; Mic 1:10; Ex 15:20, 21; 1 Sam 18:6; 1 Sam 14:6

1:21 1 Sam 31:1; Ezek 31:15; Is 21:5

1:22 Deut 32:42; Is 34:6; 1 Sam 18:4

1:23 Jer 4:13; Judg 14:18

1:25 2 Sam 1:19, 27

1:26 1 Sam 18:1-4

1:27 2 Sam 1:19, 25; Is 13:5

1:15–16 Why did David consider it a crime to kill the king, even though Saul was his enemy? David believed that God anointed Saul, and only God could remove him from office. If it became casual or commonplace to assassinate the king, the whole society would become chaotic. It was God's job, not David's, to judge Saul's sins (Leviticus 19:18). We must realize that God has placed rulers in authority over us, and we should respect their positions (Romans 13:1–5).

1:17–18 David was a talented musician. He played the harp (1 Samuel 16:23), he brought music into the worship services of the temple (1 Chronicles 25), and he wrote many of the psalms. Here we are told that he wrote a lament in memory of Saul and his son Jonathan, David's closest friend. Music played an important role in Israel's history. (For other famous songs in the Bible, see the chart in Exodus 15.)

1:17–27 Saul had caused much trouble for David, but when he died, David composed a lament for the king and his son. David had every reason to hate Saul, but he chose not to. Instead, he chose to look at the good Saul had done and to ignore the times when Saul had attacked him. It takes courage to lay aside hatred and hurt and to respect the positive side of another person, especially an enemy.

1:26 By saying that Jonathan's love was "more wonderful than the love of women," David was not implying that he had a sexual relationship with Jonathan. Homosexual acts were absolutely forbidden in Israel. Leviticus 18:22 calls homosexuality an "abomination," and Leviticus 20:13 decrees the death penalty for those who practice homosexuality. David was simply restating the deep brotherhood and faithful friendship he had with Jonathan. (For more on their friendship, see the note on 1 Samuel 18:1–4.)

David Made King over Judah

2:1 1 Sam 23:2, 4, 9-12; Josh 14:13; 1 Sam 30:31

2 Then it came about afterwards that David inquired of the LORD, saying, "Shall I go
up to one of the cities of Judah?" And the LORD said to him, "Go up." So David
said, "Where shall I go up?" And He said, "To Hebron."

2:2 1 Sam 25:42, 43

2 So David went up there, and his two wives also, Ahinoam the Jezreelitess and Abigail the widow of Nabal the Carmelite.

2:3 1 Sam 30:9; 1 Chr 12:1

3 And David brought up his men who *were* with him, each with his household; and
they lived in the cities of Hebron.

2:4 1 Sam 16:13; 2 Sam 5:3, 5; 1 Sam 31:11-13

4 Then the men of Judah came and there anointed David king over the house of Judah.
And they told David, saying, "It was the men of Jabesh-gilead who buried Saul."

2:5 1 Sam 23:21; Ps 115:15

5 David sent messengers to the men of Jabesh-gilead, and said to them, "May you be
blessed of the LORD because you have shown this kindness to Saul your lord, and have
buried him.

2:6 Ex 34:6; 2 Tim 1:16

6 "Now may the LORD show lovingkindness and truth to you; and I also will show this
goodness to you, because you have done this thing.
7 "Now therefore, let your hands be strong and be valiant; for Saul your lord is dead,
and also the house of Judah has anointed me king over them."

Ish-bosheth Made King over Israel

2:8 1 Sam 14:50; Gen 32:2; 2 Sam 17:24

8 But Abner the son of Ner, commander of Saul's army, had taken [1]Ish-bosheth the
son of Saul and brought him over to Mahanaim.

2:9 Josh 22:9; Judg 1:32; 1 Sam 29:1

9 He made him king over Gilead, over the Ashurites, over Jezreel, over Ephraim, and
over Benjamin, even over all Israel.
10 Ish-bosheth, Saul's son, was forty years old when he became king over Israel, and
he was king for two years. The house of Judah, however, followed David.

2:11 2 Sam 5:5

11 The time that David was king in Hebron over the house of Judah was seven years
and six months.

1 I.e. man of shame; cf 1 Chr 8:33, *Eshbaal*

2:1 Although David knew he would become king (1 Samuel 16:13; 23:17; 24:20), and although the time seemed right now that Saul was dead, David still asked God if he should move back to Judah, the home territory of his tribe. Before moving ahead with what seems obvious, first bring the matter to God, who alone knows the best timing.

2:1 God told David to return to Hebron, where he would soon be crowned king of Judah. David made Hebron his capital because (1) it was the largest city in Judah at that time; (2) it was secure against attack; (3) it was located near the center of Judah's territory, an ideal location for a capital city; (4) many key trade routes converged at Hebron, making it difficult for supply lines to be cut off in wartime.

2:4 The men of Judah publicly anointed David as their king. David had been anointed king by Samuel years earlier (1 Samuel 16:13), but that ceremony had taken place in private. This one was like inaugurating a public official who has already been elected to office. The rest of Israel, however, didn't accept David's kingship for seven-and-a-half years (2:10–11).

2:4–7 David sent a message thanking the men of Jabesh-gilead who had risked their lives to bury Saul's body (1 Samuel 31:11–13). Saul had rescued Jabesh-gilead from certain defeat when Nahash the Ammonite surrounded the city (1 Samuel 11), so these citizens showed their gratitude and kindness. In his message, he also suggested that they follow Judah's lead and acknowledge him as their king. Jabesh-gilead was to the north in the land of Gilead, and David was seeking to gain support among the 10 remaining tribes who had not yet recognized him as king.

2:10–11 David ruled over Judah for seven-and-a-half years, while Ish-bosheth reigned in Israel for only two years. The five-year gap may be due to Ish-bosheth's not assuming the throne immediately after Saul's death. Because of constant danger from the Philistines in the northern part of Israel, five years may have passed before Ish-bosheth could begin his reign. During that time, Abner, commander of his army, probably played a principal role in driving out the Philistines and leading the northern confederacy. Regardless of when Ish-bosheth began to rule, his control was weak and limited. The Philistines still dominated the area, and Ish-bosheth was intimidated by Abner (3:11).

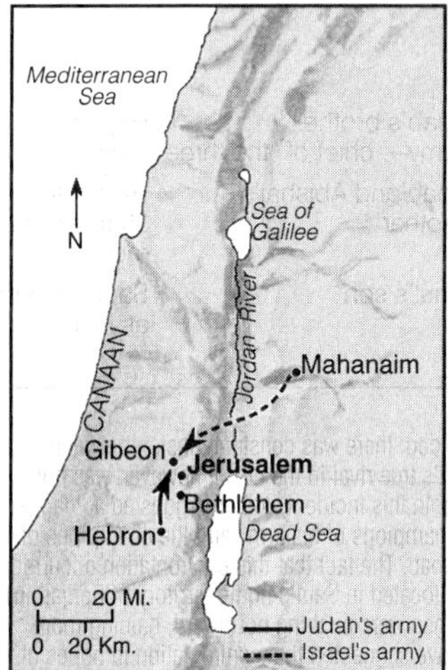

JOAB VERSUS ABNER
David was crowned king of Judah in Hebron; Ish-bosheth was crowned king of Israel in Mahanaim. The opposing armies of Judah and Israel met at Gibeon for battle—Judah under Joab, Israel under Abner.

Civil War

12 Now Abner the son of Ner, went out from Mahanaim to Gibeon with the servants **2:12** Josh 10:12; 18:25
of Ish-bosheth the son of Saul.
13 And Joab the son of Zeruiah and the servants of David went out and met them by **2:13** 2 Sam 8:16; 1 Chr 2:16; 11:6
the pool of Gibeon; and they sat down, one on the one side of the pool and the other on
the other side of the pool.
14 Then Abner said to Joab, "Now let the young men arise and [2]hold a contest before **2:14** 2 Sam 2:16, 17
us." And Joab said, "Let them arise."
15 So they arose and went over by count, twelve for Benjamin and Ish-bosheth the son
of Saul, and twelve of the servants of David.
16 Each one of them seized his opponent by the head and *thrust* his sword in his
opponent's side; so they fell down together. Therefore that place was called [3]Helkath-
hazzurim, which is in Gibeon.
17 That day the battle was very severe, and Abner and the men of Israel were beaten **2:17** 2 Sam 3:1
before the servants of David.
18 Now the three sons of Zeruiah were there, Joab and Abishai and Asahel; and Asa- **2:18** 1 Chr 2:16; 1 Chr 12:8; Hab 3:19
hel *was as* swift-footed as one of the gazelles which is in the field.
19 Asahel pursued Abner and did not turn to the right or to the left from following
Abner.
20 Then Abner looked behind him and said, "Is that you, Asahel?" And he answered,
"It is I."
21 So Abner said to him, "Turn to your right or to your left, and take hold of one of the
young men for yourself, and take for yourself his spoil." But Asahel was not willing to
turn aside from following him.
22 Abner repeated again to Asahel, "Turn aside from following me. Why should I strike **2:22** 2 Sam 3:27
you to the ground? How then could I lift up my face to your brother Joab?"
23 However, he refused to turn aside; therefore Abner struck him in the belly with the **2:23** 2 Sam 20:12
butt end of the spear, so that the spear came out at his back. And he fell there and died
on the spot. And it came about that all who came to the place where Asahel had fallen
and died, stood still.

2 Lit *make sport* **3** I.e. the field of sword-edges

CHARACTERS IN THE DRAMA
It can be confusing to keep track of all the characters introduced in the first few chapters of 2 Samuel. Here is some help.

Character	*Relation*	*Position*	*Whose side?*
Joab	Son of Zeruiah, David's half sister	One of David's military leaders and, later, commander in chief	David's
Abner	Saul's cousin	Saul's commander in chief	Saul and Ish-bosheth's, but made overtures to David
Abishai	Joab's brother	High officer in David's army— chief of "the three"	Joab and David's
Asahel	Joab and Abishai's brother	High officer—one of David's 30 select warriors ("mighty men")	Joab and David's
Ish-bosheth	Saul's son	Saul and Abner's selection as king	Saul's

2:12ff With Israel divided, there was constant tension between north and south. David's true rival in the north, however, was not Ish-bosheth but Abner. In this incident, Abner suggested a "dagger match" between the champions of his army and the champions of David's army, led by Joab. The fact that this confrontation occurred at the pool of Gibeon (located in Saul's home territory of Benjamin) suggests that Joab's men were pushing northward, gaining more territory. Abner may have suggested this confrontation in hopes of stopping Joab's advance.

Twelve men from each side were supposed to fight each other, and the side with the most survivors would be declared the winner. The confrontation between David and Goliath (1 Samuel 17) was a similar battle strategy—a way to avoid terrible bloodshed from an all-out war. In this case, however, all 24 champions were killed before either side could claim victory. Nothing was accomplished, and the civil war continued.

2:21–23 Abner repeatedly warned Asahel to turn back or risk losing his life, but Asahel refused to turn from his self-imposed duty. Persistence is a good trait if it is for a worthy cause. But if the goal is only personal honor or gain, persistence may be no more than stubbornness. Asahel's stubbornness not only cost his life, but it also spurred unfortunate disunity in David's army for years to come (3:26, 27; 1 Kings 2:28–35). Before you decide to pursue a goal, make sure it is worthy of your devotion.

24 But Joab and Abishai pursued Abner, and when the sun was going down, they came
to the hill of Ammah, which is in front of Giah by the way of the wilderness of Gibeon.
25 The sons of Benjamin gathered together behind Abner and became one band, and
they stood on the top of a certain hill.
26 Then Abner called to Joab and said, "Shall the sword devour forever? Do you not
know that it will be bitter in the end? How long will you refrain from telling the people
to turn back from following their brothers?"
27 Joab said, "As God lives, if you had not spoken, surely then the people would have
gone away in the morning, each from following his brother."

2:28 2 Sam 3:1

28 So Joab blew the trumpet; and all the people halted and pursued Israel no longer,
nor did they continue to fight anymore.

2:29 2 Sam 2:8

29 Abner and his men then went through the Arabah all that night; so they crossed the
Jordan, walked all morning, and came to Mahanaim.
30 Then Joab returned from following Abner; when he had gathered all the people
together, nineteen of David's servants besides Asahel were missing.
31 But the servants of David had struck down many of Benjamin and Abner's men, *so
that* three hundred and sixty men died.

2:32 Gen 47:29, 30; Judg 8:32

32 And they took up Asahel and buried him in his father's tomb which was in Bethlehem. Then Joab and his men went all night until the day dawned at Hebron.

The House of David Strengthened

3:1 1 Kin 14:30; Ps 46:9

3 Now there was a long war between the house of Saul and the house of David; and
David grew steadily stronger, but the house of Saul grew weaker continually.

3:2 1 Chr 3:1-3; 1 Sam 25:42, 43

2 Sons were born to David at Hebron: his firstborn was Amnon, by Ahinoam the
Jezreelitess;

3:3 1 Sam 27:8; 1 Chr 3:2; 2 Sam 14:32; 15:8

3 and his second, Chileab, by Abigail the widow of Nabal the Carmelite; and the third,
Absalom the son of Maacah, the daughter of Talmai, king of Geshur;
4 and the fourth, Adonijah the son of Haggith; and the fifth, Shephatiah the son of
Abital;

3:4 1 Kin 1:5

5 and the sixth, Ithream, by David's wife Eglah. These were born to David at Hebron.

Abner Joins David

3:6 2 Sam 2:8, 9

6 It came about while there was war between the house of Saul and the house of David
that Abner was making himself strong in the house of Saul.

3:7 2 Sam 21:8-11

7 Now Saul had a concubine whose name was Rizpah, the daughter of Aiah; and Ish-
bosheth said to Abner, "Why have you gone in to my father's concubine?"

3:8 1 Sam 24:14; 2 Sam 9:8

8 Then Abner was very angry over the words of Ish-bosheth and said, "Am I a dog's
head that belongs to Judah? Today I show kindness to the house of Saul your father, to

---

2:28 This battle ended with a victory for Joab's troops (2:17), but war in the divided nation continued until David was finally crowned king over all Israel (5:1–5).

3:1 The events recorded in chapter 2 led to a long war between David's followers and the troops loyal to Abner and Ish-bosheth. Civil war rocked the country at great cost to both sides. This war occurred because Israel and Judah had lost sight of God's vision and purpose: to settle the land (Genesis 12:7), to drive out the Canaanites (Deuteronomy 7:1–4), and to obey God's laws (Deuteronomy 8:1). Instead of uniting to accomplish these goals, they fought each other. When you face conflict, step back from the hostilities and consider whether you and your enemy have common goals that are bigger than your differences. Appeal to those interests as you work for a settlement.

3:2–5 David suffered much heartache because of his many wives. Polygamy was a socially acceptable practice for kings at this time, although God specifically warned against it (Deuteronomy 17:14–17). Sadly, the numerous sons born to David's wives caused him great trouble. Rape (13:14), murder (13:28), rebellion (15:13), and greed (1 Kings 1:5–6) all resulted from the jealous rivalries among the half brothers. Solomon, one of David's sons and his successor to the throne, also took many wives who eventually turned him away from God (1 Kings 11:3–4).

3:6–7 To sleep with any of the king's wives or concubines was to make a claim to the throne, and it was considered treason. Because Ish-bosheth was a weak ruler, Abner was running the country; thus he may have felt justified in sleeping with Saul's concubine. Ish-bosheth, however, saw that Abner's power was becoming too great.

3:7 Ish-bosheth may have been right to speak out against Abner's behavior, but he didn't have the moral strength to maintain his authority (3:11). Lack of moral backbone became the root of Israel's troubles over the next four centuries. Only 4 of the next 40 kings of Israel were called "good." It takes courage and strength to stand firm in your convictions and to confront wrongdoing in the face of opposition. When you believe something is wrong, do not let yourself be talked out of your position. Firmly attack the wrong and uphold the right.

3:8 By saying, "Am I a dog's head?" Abner meant, "Am I a traitor for Judah?" He may have been refuting the accusation that he was trying to take over the throne, or he may have been angry that Ish-bosheth scolded him after Abner had helped put him on the throne in the first place. Prior to this conversation, Abner realized that he could not keep David from eventually taking over Israel. Because he was angry at Ish-bosheth, Abner devised a plan to turn over the kingdom of Israel to David.

his brothers and to his friends, and have not delivered you into the hands of David; and
yet today you charge me with a guilt concerning the woman.
9 "May God do so to Abner, and more also, if as the LORD has sworn to David, I do **3:9**
not accomplish this for him, 1 Kin 19:2; 1 Sam 15:28
10 to transfer the kingdom from the house of Saul and to establish the throne of David
over Israel and over Judah, from Dan even to Beersheba." **3:10** 1 Sam 15:28; 1 Sam
11 And he could no longer answer Abner a word, because he was afraid of him. 3:20
12 Then Abner sent messengers to David in his place, saying, "Whose is the land? Make
your covenant with me, and behold, my hand shall be with you to bring all Israel over
to you."
13 He said, "Good! I will make a covenant with you, but I demand one thing of you, **3:13**
namely, you shall not see my face unless you first bring Michal, Saul's daughter, when Gen 43:3; 1 Sam 18:20; 19:11
you come to see me."
14 So David sent messengers to Ish-bosheth, Saul's son, saying, "Give me my wife **3:14**
Michal, to whom I was betrothed for a hundred foreskins of the Philistines." 1 Sam 18:25, 27
15 Ish-bosheth sent and took her from *her* husband, from Paltiel the son of Laish.
16 But her husband went with her, weeping as he went, and followed her as far as **3:16**
Bahurim. Then Abner said to him, "Go, return." So he returned. 2 Sam 16:5; 19:16
17 Now Abner had consultation with the elders of Israel, saying, "In times past you **3:17**
were seeking for David to be king over you. 1 Sam 8:4
18 "Now then, do *it!* For the LORD has spoken of David, saying, 'By the hand of My **3:18**
servant David I will save My people Israel from the hand of the Philistines and from the 1 Sam 9:16; 15:28
hand of all their enemies.' "
19 Abner also spoke in the hearing of Benjamin; and in addition Abner went to speak **3:19**
in the hearing of David in Hebron all that seemed good to Israel and to the whole house 1 Sam 10:20, 21; 1 Chr 12:29
of Benjamin.
20 Then Abner and twenty men with him came to David at Hebron. And David made
a feast for Abner and the men who were with him.
21 Abner said to David, "Let me arise and go and gather all Israel to my lord the king, **3:21**
that they may make a covenant with you, and that you may be king over all that your soul 2 Sam 3:10, 12; 1 Kin 11:37
desires." So David sent Abner away, and he went in peace.
22 And behold, the servants of David and Joab came from a raid and brought much **3:22**
spoil with them; but Abner was not with David in Hebron, for he had sent him away, and 1 Sam 27:8
he had gone in peace.
23 When Joab and all the army that was with him arrived, they told Joab, saying, "Abner the son of Ner came to the king, and he has sent him away, and he has gone in peace."
24 Then Joab came to the king and said, "What have you done? Behold, Abner came
to you; why then have you sent him away and he is already gone?
25 "You know Abner the son of Ner, that he came to deceive you and to learn of your **3:25**
going out and coming in and to find out all that you are doing." Deut 28:6; 1 Sam 29:6; Is 37:28

Joab Murders Abner

26 When Joab came out from David, he sent messengers after Abner, and they brought
him back from the well of Sirah; but David did not know *it.* **3:27**
27 So when Abner returned to Hebron, Joab took him aside into the middle of the gate 2 Sam 2:23; 20:9, 10; 1 Kin 2:5

3:13–14 Michal had been married to David. Saul had arranged the marriage as a reward for David's acts of bravery (1 Samuel 17:25; 18:24–27). Later, however, in one of his jealous fits, Saul took Michal away from David and forced her to marry Palti (1 Samuel 25:44). Now David wanted his wife back before he would begin to negotiate peace with the northern tribes. Perhaps David still loved her (but see 6:20–23 for the tension in their relationship). More likely, he thought that marriage to Saul's daughter would strengthen his claim to rule all Israel and demonstrate that he had no animosity toward Saul's house. Palti (Paltiel) was the unfortunate victim caught in the web of Saul's jealousy.

3:19 Because Saul, Ish-bosheth, and Abner were all from the tribe of Benjamin, the support of the elders of that tribe meant that Abner was serious about his offer. There was a strong possibility of overcoming tribal jealousies and uniting the kingdom.

3:26–29 Joab took revenge for the death of his brother instead of leaving justice to God. But that revenge backfired on him (1 Kings 2:31–34). God will repay those who deserve it (Romans 12:19). Refuse to rejoice when your enemies suffer, and don't try to get revenge. Seeking revenge will ruin your own peace of mind and increase the chances of further retaliation.

3:27 Abner killed Joab's brother Asahel in self-defense. Joab then killed Abner to avenge his brother's death and also to save his position of military leadership. People who killed in self-defense were supposed to be safe in cities of refuge (Numbers 35:22–25). Joab showed his disrespect for God's laws by killing Abner out of revenge in Hebron, a city of refuge (Joshua 20:7).

to speak with him privately, and there he struck him in the belly so that he died on account of the blood of Asahel his brother.

28 Afterward when David heard it, he said, "I and my kingdom are innocent before the LORD forever of the blood of Abner the son of Ner.

3:29 Deut 21:6-9; 1 Kin 2:31-33; Lev 13:46

29 "May it fall on the head of Joab and on all his father's house; and may there not fail from the house of Joab one who has a discharge, or who is a leper, or who takes hold of a distaff, or who falls by the sword, or who lacks bread."

3:30 2 Sam 2:23

30 So Joab and Abishai his brother killed Abner because he had put their brother Asahel to death in the battle at Gibeon.

David Mourns Abner

3:31 Gen 37:34; Judg 11:35

31 Then David said to Joab and to all the people who were with him, "Tear your clothes and gird on sackcloth and lament before Abner." And King David walked behind the bier.

The honest compliments of an opponent are often the best measure of someone's greatness. Although Abner and David frequently saw each other across battle lines, the Bible gives a glimpse of the respect they had for each other. As a young man, David had served under Abner. But later, Saul's campaign to kill David was carried out by Abner. After Saul's death, Abner temporarily upheld the power of the king's family. But the struggle between Abner and Saul's heir, Ish-bosheth, brought about Abner's decision to support David's claim to the throne. It was during his efforts to unite the kingdom that Abner was murdered by Joab.

Several years earlier, in a battle between Ish-bosheth's army under Abner and David's forces under Joab, Abner fled and was pursued by Joab's brother, Asahel. Abner told Asahel twice to stop following him. But the eager young soldier refused, so Abner killed him. Joab was determined to avenge his brother.

Abner realized Saul's family was doomed to defeat and that David would be the next king, so he decided to change sides. He hoped that in exchange for his delivering Saul's kingdom, David would make him commander in chief of his army. David's willingness to accept this proposal was probably another reason for Joab's action.

Abner lived by his wits and his will. To him, God was someone with whom he would cooperate if it suited his plans. Otherwise he did what seemed best for him at the time. We can identify with Abner's tendency to give God conditional cooperation. Obedience is easy when the instructions in God's Word fit in with our plans. But our allegiance to God is tested when his plans are contrary to ours. What action should you take today in obedience to God's Word?

Strengths and accomplishments:
- Commander in chief of Saul's army and a capable military leader
- Held Israel together for several years under the weak king Ish-bosheth
- Recognized and accepted God's plan to make David king over all Israel and Judah

Weaknesses and mistakes:
- He had selfish motives in his effort to reunite Judah and Israel rather than godly conviction
- He slept with one of the royal concubines after Saul's death

Lesson from his life:
- God requires more than conditional, halfhearted cooperation

Vital statistics:
- Where: Territory of Benjamin
- Occupation: Commander of the armies under Saul and Ish-bosheth
- Relatives: Father: Ner. Cousin: Saul. Son: Jaasiel
- Contemporaries: David, Asahel, Joab, Abishai

Key verse:
"Then the king said to his servants, 'Do you not know that a prince and a great man has fallen this day in Israel?' " (2 Samuel 3:38).

Abner's story is told in 1 Samuel 14:50—2 Samuel 4:12. He is also mentioned in 1 Kings 2:5, 32; 1 Chronicles 26:28; 27:16–22.

3:29 David was saying that Joab's descendants would be unclean, unhealthy, and in want. Why did David say such harsh words about Joab? David was upset over Abner's death for several reasons. (1) He was grieved over the loss of a skilled military officer. (2) He wanted to place the guilt of Abner's murder on Joab, not himself. (3) He was on the verge of becoming king over the entire nation, and utilizing Abner was the key to winning over the northern tribes. Abner's death could have revived the civil war. (4) Joab violated David's agreement to protect Abner. Joab's murderous act ruined David's plans, and David was especially angry that his own commander had committed the crime.

3:31 By walking behind the bier, or casket, David was leading the mourning.

3:31ff David ordered Joab to mourn, possibly because few people were aware that Joab had committed the crime and because David did not want any further trouble. If this is true, David was thinking more about strengthening his kingdom than about justice.

32 Thus they buried Abner in Hebron; and the king lifted up his voice and wept at the
grave of Abner, and all the people wept.
33 The king chanted a *lament* for Abner and said,
"Should Abner die as a fool dies?
34 "Your hands were not bound, nor your feet put in fetters;
As one falls before the wicked, you have fallen."
And all the people wept again over him.
35 Then all the people came to persuade David to eat bread while it was still day; but
David vowed, saying, "May God do so to me, and more also, if I taste bread or anything
else before the sun goes down."
36 Now all the people took note *of it,* and it pleased them, just as everything the king
did pleased all the people.
37 So all the people and all Israel understood that day that it had not been *the will* of
the king to put Abner the son of Ner to death.
38 Then the king said to his servants, "Do you not know that a prince and a great man
has fallen this day in Israel?
39 "I am weak today, though anointed king; and these men the sons of Zeruiah are too
difficult for me. May the LORD repay the evildoer according to his evil."

3:32 Job 31:28, 29; Prov 24:17
3:33 2 Sam 1:17; 2 Chr 35:25
3:35 2 Sam 12:17; 1 Sam 3:17; 2 Sam 1:12
3:39 1 Chr 29:1; 2 Chr 13:7; 2 Sam 19:5-7; 1 Kin 2:32-34

Ish-bosheth Murdered

4 Now when Ish-bosheth, Saul's son, heard that Abner had died in Hebron, he lost
courage, and all Israel was disturbed.
2 Saul's son *had* two men who were commanders of bands: the name of the one was
Baanah and the name of the other Rechab, sons of Rimmon the Beerothite, of the sons
of Benjamin (for Beeroth is also considered *part* of Benjamin,
3 and the Beerothites fled to Gittaim and have been aliens there until this day).
4 Now Jonathan, Saul's son, had a son crippled in his feet. He was five years old when
the report of Saul and Jonathan came from Jezreel, and his nurse took him up and fled.
And it happened that in her hurry to flee, he fell and became lame. And his name was
Mephibosheth.
5 So the sons of Rimmon the Beerothite, Rechab and Baanah, departed and came to
the house of Ish-bosheth in the heat of the day while he was taking his midday rest.
6 They came to the middle of the house as if to get wheat, and they struck him in the
belly; and Rechab and Baanah his brother escaped.
7 Now when they came into the house, as he was lying on his bed in his bedroom, they
struck him and killed him and beheaded him. And they took his head and traveled by
way of the Arabah all night.
8 Then they brought the head of Ish-bosheth to David at Hebron and said to the king,
"Behold, the head of Ish-bosheth the son of Saul, your enemy, who sought your life; thus
the LORD has given my lord the king vengeance this day on Saul and his descendants."
9 David answered Rechab and Baanah his brother, sons of Rimmon the Beerothite,
and said to them, "As the LORD lives, who has redeemed my life from all distress,
10 when one told me, saying, 'Behold, Saul is dead,' and thought he was bringing good
news, I seized him and killed him in Ziklag, which was the reward I gave him for *his* news.
11 "How much more, when wicked men have killed a righteous man in his own house

4:1 2 Sam 3:27; Ezra 4:4
4:2 Josh 9:17; Josh 18:25
4:3 Neh 11:33
4:4 2 Sam 9:3, 6; 1 Sam 31:1-4; 1 Chr 8:34; 9:40
4:5 2 Sam 2:8
4:6 2 Sam 2:23
4:7 2 Sam 2:29
4:8 1 Sam 24:4; 25:29
4:9 Gen 48:16; 1 Kin 1:29; Ps 31:7
4:10 2 Sam 1:2, 4, 15
4:11 Gen 9:5; Ps 9:12

3:39 Joab and Abishai were the two sons of Zeruiah David mentioned. David had an especially hard time controlling Joab because, although he was intensely loyal, he was strong willed, preferring to do things his own way. In exchange for his loyalty, however, David was willing to give him the flexibility he craved.

Joab's murder of Abner is an example of his fierce independence. While David opposed the murder, he allowed it to remain unpunished because (1) to punish Joab could cause the troops to rebel; (2) Joab was David's nephew, and any harsh treatment could cause family problems; (3) Joab was from the tribe of Judah, and David didn't want rebellion from his own tribe; (4) to get rid of Joab would mean losing a skilled and competent commander who had been invaluable in strengthening his army.

4:1 Ish-bosheth was a man who took his courage from another man (Abner) rather than from God. When Abner died, Ish-bosheth was left with nothing. In crisis and under pressure, he collapsed in fear. Fear can paralyze us, but faith and trust in God can overcome fear (2 Timothy 1:6–8; Hebrews 13:6). If we trust in God, we will be free to respond boldly to the events around us.

4:4 The rest of Mephibosheth's story is told in chapters 9; 16:1–4; and 19:24–30.

4:11 David called Ish-bosheth a "righteous man." As Saul's son, Ish-bosheth had reason to think he was in line for the throne. He was not wicked for wanting to be king; rather, he was simply too weak to stand against injustice. Although David knew Ish-bosheth was not the strong leader needed to unite Israel, he had no intention of killing him. God had promised the kingdom to David, and he knew that God would fulfill his promise.

When David learned of Ish-bosheth's death, he was angry. He had never harmed Saul, and he thought the assassins' method was cowardly. David wanted to unite Israel, not drive a permanent wedge between him and Ish-bosheth's supporters. To show that he

on his bed, shall I not now require his blood from your hand and destroy you from the earth?"

4:12 2 Sam 1:15; 2 Sam 3:32

12 Then David commanded the young men, and they killed them and cut off their hands
and feet and hung them up beside the pool in Hebron. But they took the head of Ish-
bosheth and buried it in the grave of Abner in Hebron.

2. David becomes king over Israel

5:1 1 Chr 11:1-3; 2 Sam 19:13

5:2 1 Sam 18:5, 13, 16; Gen 49:24; 2 Sam 7:7; 1 Sam 25:30

5:4 Gen 41:46; Num 4:3; Luke 3:23; 1 Kin 2:11; 1 Chr 26:31

5:5 2 Sam 2:11; 1 Chr 3:4; 29:27

5:6 1 Chr 11:4-9; Josh 15:63; 18:28; Judg 1:21

5:7 2 Sam 6:12, 16; 1 Kin 2:10; 9:24

5:9 2 Sam 5:7; 1 Kin 9:15, 24

5:11 1 Kin 5:1, 10, 18; 1 Chr 14:1

5 Then all the tribes of Israel came to David at Hebron and said, "Behold, we are your
bone and your flesh.
2 "Previously, when Saul was king over us, you were the one who led Israel out and in.
And the LORD said to you, 'You will shepherd My people Israel, and you will be a ruler
over Israel.' "
3 So all the elders of Israel came to the king at Hebron, and King David made a covenant with them before the LORD at Hebron; then they anointed David king over Israel.
4 David was thirty years old when he became king, *and* he reigned forty years.
5 At Hebron he reigned over Judah seven years and six months, and in Jerusalem he
reigned thirty-three years over all Israel and Judah.
6 Now the king and his men went to Jerusalem against the Jebusites, the inhabitants
of the land, and they said to David, "You shall not come in here, but the blind and lame
will turn you away"; thinking, "David cannot enter here."
7 Nevertheless, David captured the stronghold of Zion, that is the city of David.
8 David said on that day, "Whoever would strike the Jebusites, let him reach the lame
and the blind, who are hated by David's soul, through the water tunnel." Therefore they
say, "The blind or the lame shall not come into the house."
9 So David lived in the stronghold and called it the city of David. And David built all
around from the [4]Millo and inward.
10 David became greater and greater, for the LORD God of hosts was with him.
11 Then Hiram king of Tyre sent messengers to David with cedar trees and carpenters
and stonemasons; and they built a house for David.

4 I.e. citadel

had nothing to do with the extermination of Saul's royal line, he ordered the assassins killed and gave Ish-bosheth a proper burial. All the tribes of Israel, recognizing in David the strong leader they needed, pledged their loyalty to him. No doubt the Philistine threat and David's military reputation (1 Samuel 18:7) also helped unify the people.

5:3–5 This was the third time David was anointed king. First he was privately anointed by Samuel (1 Samuel 16:13). Then he was made king over the tribe of Judah (2:4). Finally he was crowned king over all Israel. As an outlaw, life had looked bleak, but God's promise to make him king over all Israel was now being fulfilled. Although the kingdom would be divided again in less than 75 years, David's dynasty would reign over Judah, the southern kingdom, for over 400 years.

5:4–5 David did not become king over all Israel until he was 37 years old, although he had been promised the kingdom many years earlier (1 Samuel 16:13). During those years, David had to wait patiently for the fulfillment of God's promise. If you feel pressured to achieve instant results and success, remember David's patience. Just as his time of waiting prepared him for his important task, a waiting period may help prepare you by strengthening your character.

5:6 The fortress city of Jerusalem was located on a high ridge near the center of the united Israelite kingdom. It was considered neutral territory because it stood on the border of the territory of the tribes of Benjamin and Judah and it was still occupied by the Jebusites, a Canaanite tribe that had never been expelled from the land (Judges 1:21). Because of its strategic advantages, David made Jerusalem his capital.

5:6–7 The Jebusites had a clear military advantage, and they boasted of their security behind the impregnable walls of Jerusalem, also called Zion. But they soon discovered that their walls would not protect them. David caught them by surprise by entering the city through the water tunnel.

Only in God are we truly safe and secure. Anything else is false security. Whether you are surrounded by mighty walls of stone, a comfortable home, or a secure job, no one can predict what tomorrow may bring. Our relationship with God is the only security that cannot be taken away.

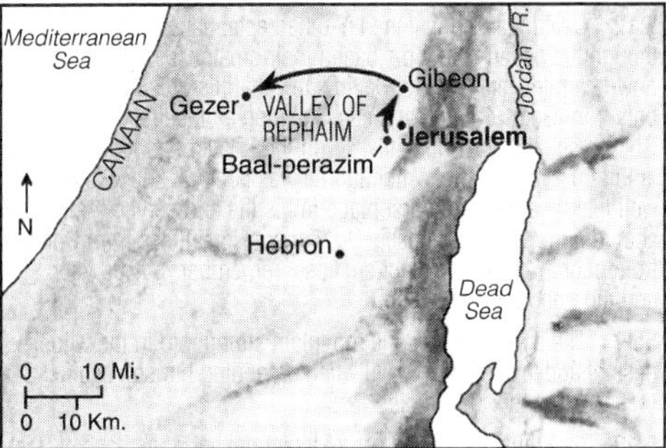

DAVID DEFEATS THE PHILISTINES The Philistines camped in the valley of Rephaim. David defeated them at Baal-perazim, but they remained in the valley. He attacked again and chased them from Gibeon to Gezer.

12 And David realized that the LORD had established him as king over Israel, and that
He had exalted his kingdom for the sake of His people Israel.
13 Meanwhile David took more concubines and wives from Jerusalem, after he came
from Hebron; and more sons and daughters were born to David.
14 Now these are the names of those who were born to him in Jerusalem: Shammua,
Shobab, Nathan, Solomon,
15 Ibhar, Elishua, Nepheg, Japhia,
16 Elishama, Eliada and Eliphelet.

War with the Philistines

17 When the Philistines heard that they had anointed David king over Israel, all the
Philistines went up to seek out David; and when David heard *of it,* he went down to the
stronghold.
18 Now the Philistines came and spread themselves out in the valley of Rephaim.
19 Then David inquired of the LORD, saying, "Shall I go up against the Philistines?
Will You give them into my hand?"
And the LORD said to David, "Go up, for I will certainly give the Philistines into your
hand."
20 So David came to Baal-perazim and defeated them there; and he said, "The LORD
has broken through my enemies before me like the breakthrough of waters." Therefore
he named that place [5]Baal-perazim.
21 They abandoned their idols there, so David and his men carried them away.
22 Now the Philistines came up once again and spread themselves out in the valley of
Rephaim.
23 When David inquired of the LORD, He said, "You shall not go *directly* up; circle
around behind them and come at them in front of the [6]balsam trees.
24 "It shall be, when you hear the sound of marching in the tops of the [6]balsam trees,
then you shall act promptly, for then the LORD will have gone out before you to strike
the army of the Philistines."
25 Then David did so, just as the LORD had commanded him, and struck down the
Philistines from Geba as far as Gezer.

Peril in Moving the Ark

6 Now David again gathered all the chosen men of Israel, thirty thousand.
2 And David arose and went with all the people who were with him to Baale-judah,
to bring up from there the ark of God which is called by the Name, the very name of the
LORD of hosts who is enthroned *above* the cherubim.

5:13 Deut 17:17; 1 Chr 3:9
5:14 1 Chr 3:5-8
5:17 1 Sam 29:1; 2 Sam 23:14; 1 Chr 11:16
5:18 Gen 14:5; Josh 15:8; 17:15; 18:16
5:19 1 Sam 23:2; 2 Sam 2:1
5:20 1 Chr 14:11; Is 28:21
5:21 1 Chr 14:12
5:22 2 Sam 5:18
5:23 2 Sam 5:19
5:24 2 Kin 7:6; Judg 4:14
5:25 Is 28:21; Josh 12:12; 21:21
6:1 1 Chr 13:5-14
6:2 Josh 15:9, 10; 1 Sam 7:1; Lev 24:16; Ex 25:22

5 I.e. the master of breakthrough 6 Or *baka-shrubs*

5:12 "David realized that the LORD had established him . . ." Although the pagan kingdoms based their greatness on conquest, power, armies, and wealth, David knew that his greatness came only from God. To be great means keeping a close relationship with God personally and nationally. To do this, David had to keep his ambition under control. Although he was famous, successful, and well liked, he gave God first place in his life and served the people according to God's purposes. Do you seek greatness from God or from people? In the drive for success, remember to keep your ambition under God's control.

5:17 "The stronghold" is the mountain stronghold in the wilderness of Judah that David used when defending himself against Saul (see 23:14 and 1 Chronicles 12:8).

5:17 The Philistine oppression of Israel began in the days of Samson (Judges 13—16). The Philistines were still Israel's most powerful enemy although David was once considered a friend and ally (1 Samuel 27; 29). Because they occupied much of Israel's northern territory, they apparently did not bother David while he was king of Judah to the south. But when they learned that David was planning to unite all Israel, they tried to stop him.

5:19 How could David get such a clear message from God? He may have prayed and been urged to action by the Holy Spirit. He may have asked God through a prophet. Most likely, however, he went to the high priest, who consulted God through the Urim and Thummim that God had told the Israelites to use for just such a purpose. (For more on the Urim and Thummim, see the notes on Leviticus 8:8 and 1 Samuel 10:20.)

5:19–25 David fought his battles the way God instructed him. In each instance he (1) asked if he should fight or not, (2) followed instructions carefully, and (3) gave God the glory. We can err in our "battles" when we ignore these steps and instead: (1) do what we want without considering God's will, (2) do things our way and ignore advice in the Bible or from other wise people, and (3) take the glory ourselves or give it to someone else without acknowledging the help we received from God. All these responses are sinful.

5:25 After David became king, his first order of business was to subdue his enemies—a task the nation had failed to complete when they first entered the land (Judges 2:1–4). David knew this had to be done in order to (1) protect the nation, (2) unify the kingdom, and (3) prepare for building the temple (which would unify religion under God and help abolish idolatrous influences).

6:3 Num 7:4-9; 1 Sam 6:7

6:4 1 Sam 7:1; 1 Chr 13:7

6:5 1 Sam 18:6, 7; 1 Chr 13:8

3 They placed the ark of God on a new cart that they might bring it from the house of Abinadab which was on the hill; and Uzzah and Ahio, the sons of Abinadab, were leading the new cart.
4 So they brought it with the ark of God from the house of Abinadab, which was on the hill; and Ahio was walking ahead of the ark.
5 Meanwhile, David and all the house of Israel were celebrating before the LORD with all kinds of *instruments made of* fir wood, and with lyres, harps, tambourines, castanets and cymbals.

MICHAL

Sometimes love is not enough—especially if that love is little more than the strong emotional attraction that grows between a hero and an admirer. To Michal, Saul's daughter, the courageous young David must have seemed like a dream come true. Her feelings about this hero gradually became obvious to others, and eventually, her father heard about her love for David. He saw this as an opportunity to get rid of his rival for the people's loyalty. He promised Michal's hand in marriage in exchange for David's success in the impossible task of killing 100 Philistines. But David was victorious, and so Saul lost a daughter and saw his rival become even more popular with the people.

Michal's love for David did not have time to be tested by the realities of marriage. Instead, she became involved in saving David's life. Her quick thinking helped him escape, but it cost her Saul's anger and her separation from David. Her father gave her to another man, Palti, but David eventually took her back.

Unlike her brother Jonathan, Michal did not have the kind of deep relationship with God that would have helped her through the difficulties in her life. Instead she became bitter. She could not share David's joyful worship of God, so she hated it. As a result, she never bore David any children.

Beyond feeling sorry for her, we need to see Michal as a person mirroring our own tendencies. How quickly and easily we become bitter with life's unexpected turns. But bitterness cannot remove or change the bad things that have happened. Often bitterness only makes a bad situation worse. On the other hand, a willingness to respond to God gives him the opportunity to bring good out of the difficult situations. That willingness has two parts: asking God for his guidance and looking for that guidance in his Word.

Strengths and accomplishments:
- Loved David and became his first wife
- Saved David's life
- Could think and act quickly when it was needed

Weaknesses and mistakes:
- Lied under pressure
- Allowed herself to become bitter over her circumstances
- In her unhappiness, she hated David for loving God

Lessons from her life:
- We are not as responsible for what happens to us as we are for how we respond to our circumstances
- Disobedience to God almost always harms us as well as others

Vital statistics:
- Occupations: Daughter of one king, Saul, and wife of another, David
- Relatives: Parents: Saul and Ahinoam. Brothers: Abinadab, Jonathan, Malchi-shua. Sister: Merab. Husbands: David and Palti

Key verse:
"Then it happened as the ark of the LORD came into the city of David that Michal the daughter of Saul looked out of the window and saw King David leaping and dancing before the LORD; and she despised him in her heart" (2 Samuel 6:16).

Michal's story is told in 1 Samuel 14—2 Samuel 6. She is also mentioned in 1 Chronicles 15:29.

6:3 The ark of God was Israel's national treasure and was ordinarily kept in the tabernacle. When the ark was returned to Israel after a brief Philistine captivity (1 Samuel 4:1—7:2), it was kept in Abinadab's home for 20 years. David saw how God blessed Abinadab, and he wanted to bring the ark to Jerusalem to ensure God's blessing on the entire nation. (See the notes on Exodus 37:1 and Joshua 3:2–4 for more information on the ark.)

6 But when they came to the threshing floor of Nacon, Uzzah reached out toward the
ark of God and took hold of it, for the oxen nearly upset *it.*
7 And the anger of the LORD burned against Uzzah, and God struck him down there
for his irreverence; and he died there by the ark of God.
8 David became angry because of the LORD'S outburst against Uzzah, and that place
is called [7]Perez-uzzah to this day.
9 So David was afraid of the LORD that day; and he said, "How can the ark of the
LORD come to me?"
10 And David was unwilling to move the ark of the LORD into the city of David with
him; but David took it aside to the house of Obed-edom the Gittite.
11 Thus the ark of the LORD remained in the house of Obed-edom the Gittite three
months, and the LORD blessed Obed-edom and all his household.

The Ark Is Brought to Jerusalem

12 Now it was told King David, saying, "The LORD has blessed the house of Obed-
edom and all that belongs to him, on account of the ark of God." David went and brought
up the ark of God from the house of Obed-edom into the city of David with gladness.
13 And so it was, that when the bearers of the ark of the LORD had gone six paces, he
sacrificed an ox and a fatling.
14 And David was dancing before the LORD with all *his* might, and David was wearing
a linen ephod.
15 So David and all the house of Israel were bringing up the ark of the LORD with
shouting and the sound of the trumpet.
16 Then it happened *as* the ark of the LORD came into the city of David that Michal
the daughter of Saul looked out of the window and saw King David leaping and dancing
before the LORD; and she despised him in her heart.
17 So they brought in the ark of the LORD and set it in its place inside the tent which
David had pitched for it; and David offered burnt offerings and peace offerings before
the LORD.
18 When David had finished offering the burnt offering and the peace offering, he
blessed the people in the name of the LORD of hosts.
19 Further, he distributed to all the people, to all the multitude of Israel, both to men
and women, a cake of bread and one of dates and one of raisins to each one. Then all the
people departed each to his house.
20 But when David returned to bless his household, Michal the daughter of Saul came
out to meet David and said, "How the king of Israel distinguished himself today! He
uncovered himself today in the eyes of his servants' maids as one of the foolish ones
shamelessly uncovers himself!"

6:6 1 Chr 13:9; Num 4:15, 19, 20
6:7 1 Sam 6:19
6:9 Ps 119:120; Luke 5:8
6:10 1 Chr 26:4-8
6:11 Gen 30:27; 39:5
6:12 1 Chr 15:25-16:3; 1 Kin 8:1
6:13 Num 4:15; Josh 3:3; 1 Chr 15:2, 15; 1 Kin 8:5
6:14 Ex 15:20, 21; Judg 11:34; Ex 19:6; 1 Sam 2:18, 28
6:16 2 Sam 3:14
6:17 1 Chr 15:1; 2 Chr 1:4; 1 Kin 8:62-65
6:18 1 Kin 8:14, 15
6:20 2 Sam 6:14, 16; Eccl 7:17; Judg 9:4

7 I.e. the breakthrough of Uzzah

6:6–7 Uzzah was only trying to protect the ark, so was God's anger against Uzzah just? According to Numbers 4:5–15, the ark was to be moved only by the Levites, who were to carry it using the carrying poles—they were *never* to touch the ark itself. To touch it was a capital offense under Hebrew law (Numbers 4:15). God's action was directed against both David and Uzzah. David placed the ark on a cart, following the Philistines' example (1 Samuel 6:7–8) rather than God's commands. Uzzah, though sincere in his desire to protect the ark, had to face the consequences of the sin of touching it. Also, Uzzah may not have been a Levite. As David sought to bring Israel back into a relationship with God, God had to remind the nation dramatically that enthusiasm must be accompanied by obedience to his laws. The next time David tried to bring the ark to Jerusalem, he was careful to handle it correctly (1 Chronicles 15:1–15).

6:8–12 David was angry that a well-meaning man had been killed and that his plans for a joyous return of the ark had been spoiled (6:8). He undoubtedly knew that the fault was his own for transporting the ark carelessly. After cooling down, he had the ark put into temporary storage while he waited to see if the Lord would allow him to bring it to Jerusalem. This also gave David time to consider the right way to transport the ark. The fact that God blessed the home of Obed-edom was a sign to David that he could try once again to move the ark to Jerusalem.

6:14 David wore a linen ephod, the priest's apron, possibly because it was a religious celebration.

6:16ff Michal was David's first wife, but here she is called daughter of Saul, possibly to show how similar her attitude was to her father's. Her contempt for David probably did not start with David's grand entrance into the city. Perhaps she thought it was undignified to be so concerned with public worship at a time when it was so unimportant in the kingdom. Or maybe she thought it was not fitting for a king to display such emotion. She may have resented David's taking her from Palti (see the note on 3:13–14). Whatever the reason, this contempt she felt toward her husband escalated into a difficult confrontation, and Michal ended up childless for life. Feelings of bitterness and resentment that go unchecked will destroy a relationship. Deal with your feelings before they escalate into open warfare.

6:17 Only a priest could place the sacrifices on the altar. Leviticus 1:2–13 indicates that anyone who was ceremonially clean could assist a priest in offering the sacrifice (see the notes on Joshua 3:5; 1 Samuel 20:26). So David probably offered these sacrifices to God with the aid of a priest. Solomon did the same (1 Kings 8:62–65).

6:21 1 Sam 13:14; 15:28

21 So David said to Michal, "*It was* before the LORD, who chose me above your father
and above all his house, to appoint me ruler over the people of the LORD, over Israel;
therefore I will celebrate before the LORD.
22 "I will be more lightly esteemed than this and will be humble in my own eyes, but
with the maids of whom you have spoken, with them I will be distinguished."
23 Michal the daughter of Saul had no child to the day of her death.

David Plans to Build a Temple

7:1 1 Chr 17:1-27
7:2 2 Sam 7:17; 12:1; 1 Kin 1:22; 1 Chr 29:29; 2 Chr 9:29; 2 Sam 5:11; Ex 26:1
7:3 1 Kin 8:17, 18; 1 Chr 22:7
7:5 1 Kin 5:3, 4; 8:19
7:6 Josh 18:1; 1 Kin 8:16; Ex 40:18, 34
7:7 Lev 26:11, 12; 2 Sam 5:2

7 Now it came about when the king lived in his house, and the LORD had given him
rest on every side from all his enemies,
2 that the king said to Nathan the prophet, "See now, I dwell in a house of cedar, but
the ark of God dwells within tent curtains."
3 Nathan said to the king, "Go, do all that is in your mind, for the LORD is with you."
4 But in the same night the word of the LORD came to Nathan, saying,
5 "Go and say to My servant David, 'Thus says the LORD, "Are you the one who should
build Me a house to dwell in?
6 "For I have not dwelt in a house since the day I brought up the sons of Israel from
Egypt, even to this day; but I have been moving about in a tent, even in a tabernacle.
7 "Wherever I have gone with all the sons of Israel, did I speak a word with one of the
tribes of Israel, which I commanded to shepherd My people Israel, saying, 'Why have
you not built Me a house of cedar?' " '

God's Covenant with David

7:8 1 Sam 16:11, 12; Ps 78:70, 71; 2 Sam 6:21

8 "Now therefore, thus you shall say to My servant David, 'Thus says the LORD of hosts,
"I took you from the pasture, from following the sheep, to be ruler over My people Israel.

CRITICIZING GOD'S LEADERS
It is dangerous to criticize God's leaders. Consider the consequences for these men and women.

Person/Situation	*Result*	*Reference*
Miriam: Mocked Moses because he had a Cushite wife	Stricken with leprosy	Numbers 12
Korah and followers: Led the people of Israel to rebel against Moses' leadership	Swallowed by the earth	Numbers 16
Michal: Despised David because he danced before the Lord	Remained childless	2 Samuel 6
Shimei: Cursed and threw stones at David	Executed at Solomon's order	2 Samuel 16 1 Kings 2
Youths: Mocked Elisha and laughed at his baldness	Killed by bears	2 Kings 2
Sanballat and Tobiah: Spread rumors and lies to stop the building of Jerusalem's walls	Frightened and humiliated	Nehemiah 2; 4; 6
Hananiah: Contradicted Jeremiah's prophecies with false predictions	Died two months later	Jeremiah 28
Bar-Jesus, a sorcerer: Lied about Paul in an attempt to turn the proconsul against him	Stricken with blindness	Acts 13

7:1ff This chapter records the covenant God made with David, promising to carry on David's line forever. This promise would be fully realized in the birth of Jesus Christ. Although the word *covenant* is not specifically stated here, it is used elsewhere to describe this occasion (23:5; Psalm 89:3–4, 28, 34–37).

7:2 This is the first time Nathan the prophet is mentioned. God made certain that a prophet was living during the reign of each of the kings of Israel. The prophet's main tasks were to urge the people to follow God and to communicate God's laws and plans to the king. Most of the kings rejected the prophets God sent. But at least God had given them the opportunity to listen and obey. In earlier years, judges and priests had the role of prophets. Samuel served as judge, priest, and prophet, bridging the gap between the period of the judges and the monarchy.

7:5 In this message from Nathan, God is saying that he doesn't want David to build a "house" for him. Why didn't God want David to build the temple? God told David that his job was to unify and lead Israel and to destroy its enemies. This huge task would require David to shed a great deal of blood. In 1 Chronicles 28:3, we learn that God did not want his temple built by a warrior. Therefore, David made the plans and collected the materials so that his son Solomon could begin work on the temple as soon as he became king (1 Kings 5—7). David accepted his part in God's plan and did not try to go beyond it. Sometimes God says no to our plans. When he does, we should utilize the other opportunities he gives us.

7:8–16 David's request was good, but God said no. This does not mean that God rejected David. In fact, God was planning to do

9"I have been with you wherever you have gone and have cut off all your enemies from
before you; and I will make you a great name, like the names of the great men who are
on the earth.
10"I will also appoint a place for My people Israel and will plant them, that they may
live in their own place and not be disturbed again, nor will the wicked afflict them any
more as formerly,
11 even from the day that I commanded judges to be over My people Israel; and I will
give you rest from all your enemies. The LORD also declares to you that the LORD will
make a house for you.
12"When your days are complete and you lie down with your fathers, I will raise up
your descendant after you, who will come forth from you, and I will establish his kingdom.
13"He shall build a house for My name, and I will establish the throne of his kingdom
forever.
14"I will be a father to him and he will be a son to Me; when he commits iniquity, I will
correct him with the rod of men and the strokes of the sons of men,
15 but My lovingkindness shall not depart from him, as I took *it* away from Saul, whom
I removed from before you.
16"Your house and your kingdom shall endure before Me forever; your throne shall be
established forever." ' "
17 In accordance with all these words and all this vision, so Nathan spoke to David.

David's Prayer

18 Then David the king went in and sat before the LORD, and he said, "Who am I,
O Lord GOD, and what is my house, that You have brought me this far?
19"And yet this was insignificant in Your eyes, O Lord GOD, for You have spoken also
of the house of Your servant concerning the distant future. And this is the custom of
man, O Lord GOD.
20"Again what more can David say to You? For You know Your servant, O Lord GOD!
21"For the sake of Your word, and according to Your own heart, You have done all
this greatness to let Your servant know.
22"For this reason You are great, O Lord GOD; for there is none like You, and there is
no God besides You, according to all that we have heard with our ears.
23"And what one nation on the earth is like Your people Israel, whom God went to
redeem for Himself as a people and to make a name for Himself, and to do a great thing
for You and awesome things for Your land, before Your people whom You have redeemed
for Yourself from Egypt, *from* nations and their gods?
24"For You have established for Yourself Your people Israel as Your own people forever, and You, O LORD, have become their God.
25"Now therefore, O LORD God, the word that You have spoken concerning Your servant and his house, confirm *it* forever, and do as You have spoken,
26 that Your name may be magnified forever, by saying, 'The LORD of hosts is God
over Israel'; and may the house of Your servant David be established before You.
27"For You, O LORD of hosts, the God of Israel, have made a revelation to Your servant, saying, 'I will build you a house'; therefore Your servant has found courage to pray
this prayer to You.
28"Now, O Lord GOD, You are God, and Your words are truth, and You have promised this good thing to Your servant.
29"Now therefore, may it please You to bless the house of Your servant, that it may
continue forever before You. For You, O Lord GOD, have spoken; and with Your blessing may the house of Your servant be blessed forever."

7:9 1 Sam 5:10; Ps 18:37-42
7:10 Ex 15:17; Is 5:2, 7; Ps 89:22, 23; Is 60:18
7:11 Judg 2:14-16; 1 Sam 12:9-11; 2 Sam 7:1; 1 Sam 25:28; 2 Sam 7:27
7:12 1 Kin 2:1; Deut 31:16; Acts 13:36; 1 Kin 8:20; Ps 132:11
7:13 1 Kin 6:12; 8:19; Is 9:7; 49:8
7:14 Ps 89:26, 27; 2 Cor 6:18; Heb 1:5; 1 Kin 11:34; Ps 89:30-33
7:15 1 Sam 15:23; 16:14
7:16 2 Sam 7:13; Ps 89:36, 37
7:18 Ex 3:11; 1 Sam 18:18
7:19 2 Sam 7:11-16; 1 Chr 17:17; Is 55:8, 9
7:20 1 Sam 16:7; John 21:17
7:21 1 Chr 17:19; Eph 4:32
7:22 Deut 3:24; Ps 48:1; 86:10; Ex 15:11; 1 Sam 2:2; Ex 10:2; Ps 44:1
7:23 Deut 4:32-38; Deut 10:21; Deut 15:15; Deut 9:26
7:24 Deut 32:6; Gen 17:7, 8; Ex 6:7
7:26 Ps 72:18, 19; Matt 6:9
7:27 2 Sam 7:13
7:28 Ex 34:6; John 17:17
7:29 Num 6:24-26

---

something even greater in David's life than allowing him the prestige of building the temple. Although God turned down David's request, he promised to continue the house (or dynasty) of David forever. David's earthly dynasty ended four centuries later, but Jesus Christ, a direct descendant of David, was the ultimate fulfillment of this promise (Acts 2:22–36). Christ will reign for eternity—now in his spiritual kingdom and in heaven, and later, on earth, in the new Jerusalem (Luke 1:30–33; Revelation 21). Have you prayed with good intentions, only to have God say no? This is God's way of directing you to a greater purpose in your life. Accepting God's no requires as great a faith as carrying out his yes.

7:18ff This section records David's prayer expressing his humble acceptance of God's promise to extend his dynasty forever. David realized that these blessings were given to him and his descendants in order that Israel might benefit from them. They would help fulfill God's greater purpose and promises that through the nation the whole world would be blessed (Genesis 12:1–3).

3. David conquers the surrounding nations

David's Triumphs

8 Now after this it came about that David defeated the Philistines and subdued them;
and David took control of the chief city from the hand of the Philistines.
2 He defeated Moab, and measured them with the line, making them lie down on the
ground; and he measured two lines to put to death and one full line to keep alive. And
the Moabites became servants to David, bringing tribute.
3 Then David defeated Hadadezer, the son of Rehob king of Zobah, as he went to
restore his rule at the [8]River.
4 David captured from him 1,700 horsemen and 20,000 foot soldiers; and David hamstrung the chariot horses, but reserved *enough* of them for 100 chariots.
5 When the Arameans of Damascus came to help Hadadezer, king of Zobah, David
killed 22,000 Arameans.
6 Then David put garrisons among the Arameans of Damascus, and the Arameans
became servants to David, bringing tribute. And the LORD helped David wherever he
went.
7 David took the shields of gold which were carried by the servants of Hadadezer and
brought them to Jerusalem.
8 From Betah and from Berothai, cities of Hadadezer, King David took a very large
amount of bronze.
9 Now when Toi king of Hamath heard that David had defeated all the army of Hadadezer,
10 Toi sent Joram his son to King David to greet him and bless him, because he had
fought against Hadadezer and defeated him; for Hadadezer had been at war with Toi.
And *Joram* brought with him articles of silver, of gold and of bronze.
11 King David also dedicated these to the LORD, with the silver and gold that he had
dedicated from all the nations which he had subdued:

8 I.e. Euphrates

8:1 1 Chr 18
8:2 Num 24:17; 1 Sam 22:3, 4; 2 Sam 8:6; 1 Kin 4:21; 2 Kin 3:4; 17:3
8:3 1 Sam 14:47; 2 Sam 10:16, 19; 2 Sam 10:15-19
8:4 Josh 11:6, 9
8:5 1 Kin 11:23-25
8:6 2 Sam 8:2; 2 Sam 3:18
8:8 Ezek 47:16
8:9 1 Kin 8:65; 2 Chr 8:4
8:11 1 Kin 7:51

COVENANTS

A covenant is a legally binding obligation (promise). Throughout history God has made covenants with his people—he would keep his side if they would keep theirs. Here are seven covenants found in the Bible.

Name and Reference	*God's Promise*	*Sign*
In Eden Genesis 3:15	Satan and mankind will be enemies	Pain of childbirth
Noah Genesis 9:8–17	God would never again destroy the earth with a flood	Rainbow
Abraham Genesis 15:12–21; 17:1–14	Abraham's descendants would become a great nation if they obeyed God. God would be their God forever	Smoking oven and flaming torch
At Mount Sinai Exodus 19:5–6	Israel would be God's special people, a holy nation. But they would have to keep their part of the covenant—obedience	The exodus
The Priesthood Numbers 25:10–13	Aaron's descendants would be priests forever	The Aaronic priesthood
David 2 Samuel 7:13; 23:5	Salvation would come through David's line through the birth of the Messiah	David's line continued and the Messiah was born a descendant of David
New Covenant Hebrews 8:6–13	Forgiveness and salvation are available through faith in Christ	Christ's resurrection

8:1–5 Part of God's covenant with David included the promise that the Israelites' enemies would be defeated and would no longer oppress them (7:10–11). God fulfilled this promise by helping David defeat the opposing nations. Several enemies are listed in this chapter: (1) *The Moabites,* descendants of Lot who lived east of the Dead Sea. They posed a constant military and religious threat to Israel (Numbers 25:1–3; Judges 3:12–30; 1 Samuel 14:47). David seemed to have a good relationship with the Moabites at one time. (2) *King Hadadezer of Zobah.* His defeat at David's hands fulfilled God's promise to Abraham that Israel would control the land as far north as the Euphrates River (Genesis 15:18). (3) *The Edomites,* descendants of Esau (Genesis 36:1) who were also archenemies of Israel (see 2 Kings 8:20; Jeremiah 49:7–22; Ezekiel 25:12–14; and the note on Genesis 36:9).

8:6 The *tribute* was the tax levied on conquered nations. The tax helped to support Israel's government and demonstrated that the conquered nation was under Israel's control.

12 from [9]Aram and Moab and the sons of Ammon and the Philistines and Amalek,
and from the spoil of Hadadezer, son of Rehob, king of Zobah.
13 So David made a name *for himself* when he returned from killing 18,000 [9]Arameans
in the Valley of Salt.
14 He put garrisons in Edom. In all Edom he put garrisons, and all the Edomites became servants to David. And the LORD helped David wherever he went.
15 So David reigned over all Israel; and David administered justice and righteousness
for all his people.
16 Joab the son of Zeruiah *was* over the army, and Jehoshaphat the son of Ahilud *was*
recorder.
17 Zadok the son of Ahitub and Ahimelech the son of Abiathar *were* priests, and Seraiah *was* secretary.
18 Benaiah the son of Jehoiada was over the Cherethites and the Pelethites; and David's
sons were chief ministers.

David's Kindness to Mephibosheth

9 Then David said, "Is there yet anyone left of the house of Saul, that I may show him
kindness for Jonathan's sake?"
2 Now there was a servant of the house of Saul whose name was Ziba, and they called
him to David; and the king said to him, "Are you Ziba?" And he said, "*I am* your servant."
3 The king said, "Is there not yet anyone of the house of Saul to whom I may show the
kindness of God?" And Ziba said to the king, "There is still a son of Jonathan who is
crippled in both feet."
4 So the king said to him, "Where is he?" And Ziba said to the king, "Behold, he is in
the house of Machir the son of Ammiel in Lo-debar."
5 Then King David sent and brought him from the house of Machir the son of Ammiel, from Lo-debar.
6 Mephibosheth, the son of Jonathan the son of Saul, came to David and fell on his
face and prostrated himself. And David said, "Mephibosheth." And he said, "Here is
your servant!"

9 Some mss read *Edom*

8:12 2 Sam 8:2; 2 Sam 10:14; 2 Sam 5:17-25; 1 Sam 27:8; 30:17-20
8:13 2 Sam 7:9; 2 Kin 14:7
8:14 Gen 27:37-40; Num 24:17, 18; 2 Sam 8:6
8:16 1 Chr 11:6; 1 Kin 4:3; 2 Kin 18:18, 37
8:17 1 Chr 6:4-8; 1 Chr 16:39, 40; 2 Kin 18:18
8:18 1 Kin 4:4; 1 Sam 30:14; 2 Sam 15:18; 20:7, 23; 1 Kin 1:38, 44; 1 Chr 18:17
9:1 1 Sam 20:14-17, 42
9:2 2 Sam 16:1-4; 19:17, 29
9:3 1 Sam 20:14; 2 Sam 4:4
9:4 2 Sam 17:27-29
9:6 2 Sam 16:4; 19:24-30; 1 Sam 25:23

DAVID'S ENEMIES
David wanted to complete the conquest of Canaan begun by Joshua. He defeated the Jebusites at Jerusalem and the Philistines in the vicinity of Gath. The Ammonites, Arameans, and Moabites became his subjects. He put garrisons in Edom and levied a tax upon them.

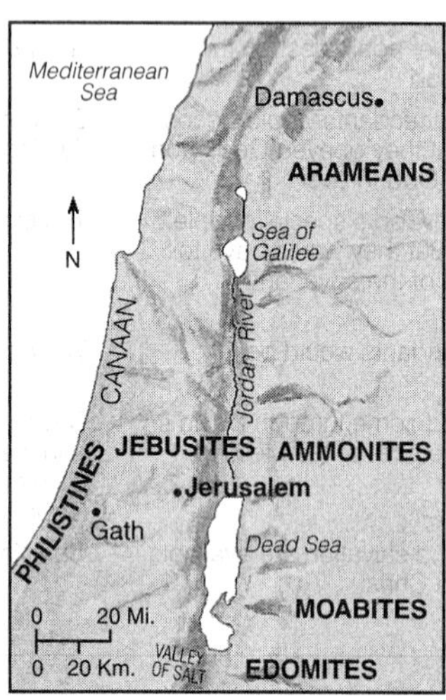

8:15 David pleased the people (3:36), not because he tried to please them, but because he tried to please God. Often those who try the hardest to become popular never make it. But the praise of people is not that important. Don't spend your time devising ways to become accepted in the public eye. Instead strive to do what is right, and both God and people will respect your convictions.

8:15 King David's reign was characterized by administering justice and righteousness. Justice means fairness in interpreting the law, administering punishment with mercy, respect for people's rights, and recognition of people's duty toward God. Is it any wonder that almost everyone trusted and followed David? Why was it good for David to pursue justice? (1) It was God's command (Deuteronomy 16:18–20) and his character (Deuteronomy 32:4). God's laws were meant to establish a just society. (2) It was in the nation's best interest because times would arise when each individual would need justice. Justice should characterize the way you relate to people. Make sure you are fair in the way you treat them.

9:1ff Most kings in David's day tried to wipe out the families of their rivals in order to prevent any descendants from seeking the throne. But David showed kindness to Mephibosheth, whose father was Jonathan and whose grandfather was King Saul. David was kind, partly because of his loyalty to God's previously anointed king (see the note on 1 Samuel 24:5–6); partly for political reasons—to unite Judah and Israel (see the notes on 3:13–14 and 3:29); and mainly because of his vow to show kindness to all of Jonathan's descendants (1 Samuel 20:14–17).

9:3 How Mephibosheth became crippled is recorded in 4:4. Mephibosheth was five years old when Saul and Jonathan died.

9:5–6 Mephibosheth was afraid to visit the king, who wanted to treat him like a prince. Although Mephibosheth feared for his life and may have felt unworthy, that didn't mean he should refuse David's gifts. When God graciously offers us forgiveness of sins and a place in heaven, we may feel unworthy, but we will receive these gifts if we accept them. A reception even warmer than the one David gave Mephibosheth waits for all who receive God's gifts through trusting Jesus Christ, not because we deserve it, but because of God's promise (Ephesians 2:8–9).

9:7 2 Sam 9:1, 3; 2 Sam 12:8; 2 Sam 19:28; 1 Kin 2:7; 2 Kin 25:29

7 David said to him, "Do not fear, for I will surely show kindness to you for the sake
of your father Jonathan, and will restore to you all the land of your grandfather Saul;
and you shall eat at my table regularly."

9:8 2 Sam 16:9; 24:14

8 Again he prostrated himself and said, "What is your servant, that you should regard a dead dog like me?"

9:9 2 Sam 16:4; 19:29

9 Then the king called Saul's servant Ziba and said to him,
"All that belonged to Saul and to all his house I have given to your master's grandson.

9:10 2 Sam 9:7, 11, 13; 2 Sam 19:28; 1 Kin 2:7

10 "You and your sons and your servants shall cultivate the land for him, and you shall
bring in *the produce* so that your master's grandson may have food; nevertheless Mephibosheth your master's grandson shall eat at my table regularly." Now Ziba had fifteen sons and twenty servants.

9:11 2 Sam 16:1-4; 19:24-30

11 Then Ziba said to the king, "According to all that my lord the king commands his
servant so your servant will do." So Mephibosheth ate at David's table as one of the king's
sons.
12 Mephibosheth had a young son whose name was Mica. And all who lived in the house
of Ziba were servants to Mephibosheth.

9:13 2 Sam 9:7, 11; 2 Sam 9:3

13 So Mephibosheth lived in Jerusalem, for he ate at the king's table regularly. Now
he was lame in both feet.

Ammon and Aram Defeated

10:1 1 Chr 19:1-19; 1 Sam 11:1

10 Now it happened afterwards that the king of the Ammonites died, and Hanun his
son became king in his place.

10:2 1 Sam 11:1

2 Then David said, "I will show kindness to Hanun the son of Nahash, just as his father showed kindness to me." So David sent some of his servants to console him concerning his father. But when David's servants came to the land of the Ammonites,

10:3 Gen 42:9, 16

3 the princes of the Ammonites said to Hanun their lord, "Do you think that David is
honoring your father because he has sent consolers to you? Has David not sent his servants to you in order to search the city, to spy it out and overthrow it?"

10:4 Is 15:2; Jer 41:5; Is 20:4

4 So Hanun took David's servants and shaved off half of their beards, and cut off their
garments in the middle as far as their hips, and sent them away.
5 When they told *it* to David, he sent to meet them, for the men were greatly humiliated. And the king said, "Stay at Jericho until your beards grow, and *then* return."

10:6 Gen 34:30; 1 Sam 27:12; 2 Sam 8:3, 5; 2 Kin 7:6; Judg 18:28; 2 Sam 8:3; Deut 3:14

6 Now when the sons of Ammon saw that they had become odious to David, the sons
of Ammon sent and hired the Arameans of Beth-rehob and the Arameans of Zobah,
20,000 foot soldiers, and the king of Maacah with 1,000 men, and the men of Tob with
12,000 men.
7 When David heard *of it,* he sent Joab and all the army, the mighty men.

10:8 1 Chr 19:9; Judg 11:3, 5

8 The sons of Ammon came out and drew up in battle array at the entrance of the
city, while the Arameans of Zobah and of Rehob and the men of Tob and Maacah *were*
by themselves in the field.

DAVID AND THE AMMONITES
Ammon gathered together its troops from the north; Joab brought the Israelite army to attack them near Rabbah. Joab returned to Jerusalem victorious, but the enemy recruited additional forces and regrouped at Helam. David himself led the next victorious attack.

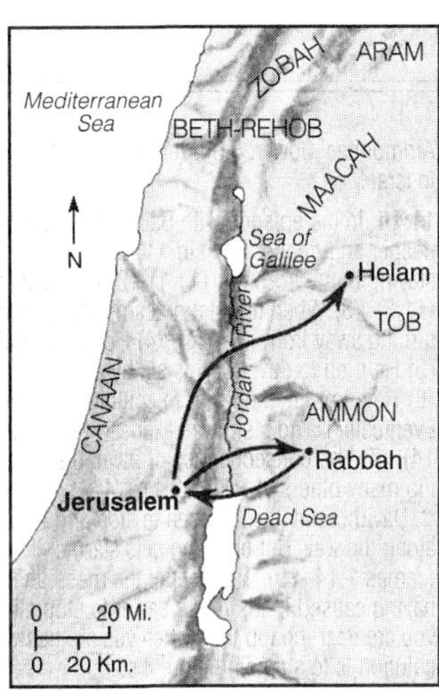

9:7 His treatment of Mephibosheth shows David's integrity as a leader who accepted his obligation to show love and mercy. His generous provision for Jonathan's son goes beyond any political benefit he might have received. Are you able to forgive those who have wronged you? Can you be generous with those less deserving? Each time we show compassion, our character is strengthened.

10:4–5 In Israelite culture, all men wore full beards. It was a sign of maturity and authority. Thus when these ambassadors had their beards half shaved, they suffered great indignity. Cutting off their garments also exposed them to ridicule.

10:6 Because Hanun took the wrong advice, he suspected the motives of the ambassadors and humiliated them. Then he realized that David was angry and immediately marshaled his forces for battle. Hanun should have thought through the advice more carefully; but even if he had not, he should have tried to negotiate with David. Instead, he refused to admit any fault and got ready for war. Often we respond angrily and defensively rather than admitting our mistakes, apologizing, and trying to diffuse the other person's anger. Instead of fighting, we should seek peace.

9 Now when Joab saw that the battle was set against him in front and in the rear, he
selected from all the choice men of Israel, and arrayed *them* against the Arameans.
10 But the remainder of the people he placed in the hand of Abishai his brother, and
he arrayed *them* against the sons of Ammon.
11 He said, "If the Arameans are too strong for me, then you shall help me, but if the
sons of Ammon are too strong for you, then I will come to help you.
12 "Be strong, and let us show ourselves courageous for the sake of our people and for
the cities of our God; and may the LORD do what is good in His sight."
13 So Joab and the people who were with him drew near to the battle against the Arameans, and they fled before him.
14 When the sons of Ammon saw that the Arameans fled, they *also* fled before Abishai and entered the city. Then Joab returned from *fighting* against the sons of Ammon
and came to Jerusalem.
15 When the Arameans saw that they had been defeated by Israel, they gathered themselves together.
16 And Hadadezer sent and brought out the Arameans who were beyond the [10]River,
and they came to Helam; and Shobach the commander of the army of Hadadezer led
them.
17 Now when it was told David, he gathered all Israel together and crossed the Jordan, and came to Helam. And the Arameans arrayed themselves to meet David and
fought against him.
18 But the Arameans fled before Israel, and David killed 700 charioteers of the Arameans and 40,000 horsemen and struck down Shobach the commander of their army,
and he died there.
19 When all the kings, servants of Hadadezer, saw that they were defeated by Israel,
they made peace with Israel and served them. So the Arameans feared to help the sons
of Ammon anymore.

10:12 Deut 31:6; Josh 1:6; 1 Cor 16:13; 1 Sam 3:18

10:13 1 Kin 20:13-21

10:14 2 Sam 11:1

10:16 2 Sam 8:3-8; 1 Chr 19:16

10:18 1 Chr 19:18

10:19 2 Sam 8:6

B. DAVID'S STRUGGLES (11:1—24:25)

After restoring the nation to peace and great military power, David's personal life becomes entangled in sin. He commits adultery with Bathsheba and then orders her husband killed in an attempted cover-up. David deeply regretted what he had done and sought God's forgiveness, but the child of his sinful act died. We may be forgiven by God for our sins, but we will often experience harsh consequences.

1. David and Bathsheba

Bathsheba, David's Great Sin

11 Then it happened in the spring, at the time when kings go out *to battle,* that David
sent Joab and his servants with him and all Israel, and they destroyed the sons of
Ammon and besieged Rabbah. But David stayed at Jerusalem.
2 Now when evening came David arose from his bed and walked around on the roof
of the king's house, and from the roof he saw a woman bathing; and the woman was very
beautiful in appearance.

11:1 1 Chr 20:1; 2 Sam 10:14; 1 Kin 20:22, 26; 2 Sam 12:26-29; Jer 49:2, 3; Amos 1:14

11:2 Deut 22:8; 1 Sam 9:25; Matt 24:17; Acts 10:9

10 I.e. Euphrates

10:12 There must be a balance in life between our actions and our faith in God. David said, "Let us show ourselves courageous." In other words, they should do what they could, using their minds to figure out the best techniques and using their resources. But he also said, "May the LORD do what is good in His sight." He knew that the outcome was in God's hands. We should use our minds and our resources to obey God, while at the same time trusting God for the outcome.

11:1 Winter is the rainy season in Israel, the time when crops are planted. Spring was a good time to go to war because the roads were dry, making travel easier for troop movements, supply wagons, and chariots. In Israel, wheat and barley were ready to be harvested in the spring. These crops were an important food source for traveling armies.

11:1 This successful siege (see 12:26–27) put an end to the Ammonites' power. From this time on, the Ammonites were subject to Israel.

11:1ff In the episode with Bathsheba, David allowed himself to fall deeper and deeper into sin. (1) David abandoned his purpose by staying home from war (11:1). (2) He focused on his own desires (11:3). (3) When temptation came, he looked into it instead of turning away from it (11:4). (4) He sinned deliberately (11:4). (5) He tried to cover up his sin by deceiving others (11:6–15). (6) He committed murder to continue the cover-up (11:15, 17). Eventually David's sin was exposed (12:9) and punished (12:10–14). (7) The consequences of David's sin were far-reaching, affecting many others (11:17; 12:11, 14–15).

David could have chosen to stop and turn from evil at any stage along the way. But once sin gets started, it is difficult to stop (James 1:14–15). The deeper the mess, the less we want to admit having caused it. It's much easier to stop sliding down a hill when you are near the top than when you are halfway down. The best solution is to stop sin before it starts.

11:3 1 Chr 3:5; 2 Sam 23:39
11:4 Ps 51: title; James 1:14, 15; Lev 12:2-5; 15:18-28; 18:19
11:5 Lev 20:10; Deut 22:22
11:7 Gen 37:14; 1 Sam 17:22
11:8 Gen 43:24; Luke 7:44
11:9 1 Kin 14:27, 28
11:11 2 Sam 7:2, 6; 2 Sam 20:6
11:12 Job 20:12-14
11:13 Prov 20:1; 23:29-35; 2 Sam 11:9
11:14 1 Kin 21:8-10
11:15 Eccl 8:11; Jer 17:9; 2 Sam 12:9
11:17 2 Sam 11:21
11:21 Judg 9:50-54

3 So David sent and inquired about the woman. And one said, "Is this not Bathsheba,
the daughter of Eliam, the wife of Uriah the Hittite?"
4 David sent messengers and took her, and when she came to him, he lay with her;
and when she had purified herself from her uncleanness, she returned to her house.
5 The woman conceived; and she sent and told David, and said, "I am pregnant."
6 Then David sent to Joab, *saying,* "Send me Uriah the Hittite." So Joab sent Uriah
to David.
7 When Uriah came to him, David asked concerning the welfare of Joab and the people and the state of the war.
8 Then David said to Uriah, "Go down to your house, and wash your feet." And Uriah went out of the king's house, and a present from the king was sent out after him.
9 But Uriah slept at the door of the king's house with all the servants of his lord, and
did not go down to his house.
10 Now when they told David, saying, "Uriah did not go down to his house," David
said to Uriah, "Have you not come from a journey? Why did you not go down to your
house?"
11 Uriah said to David, "The ark and Israel and Judah are staying in temporary shelters, and my lord Joab and the servants of my lord are camping in the open field. Shall I
then go to my house to eat and to drink and to lie with my wife? By your life and the life
of your soul, I will not do this thing."
12 Then David said to Uriah, "Stay here today also, and tomorrow I will let you go."
So Uriah remained in Jerusalem that day and the next.
13 Now David called him, and he ate and drank before him, and he made him drunk;
and in the evening he went out to lie on his bed with his lord's servants, but he did not go
down to his house.
14 Now in the morning David wrote a letter to Joab and sent *it* by the hand of Uriah.
15 He had written in the letter, saying, "Place Uriah in the front line of the fiercest
battle and withdraw from him, so that he may be struck down and die."
16 So it was as Joab kept watch on the city, that he put Uriah at the place where he
knew there *were* valiant men.
17 The men of the city went out and fought against Joab, and some of the people among
David's servants fell; and Uriah the Hittite also died.
18 Then Joab sent and reported to David all the events of the war.
19 He charged the messenger, saying, "When you have finished telling all the events
of the war to the king,
20 and if it happens that the king's wrath rises and he says to you, 'Why did you go so
near to the city to fight? Did you not know that they would shoot from the wall?
21 'Who struck down Abimelech the son of Jerubbesheth? Did not a woman throw an
upper millstone on him from the wall so that he died at Thebez? Why did you go so near
the wall?'—then you shall say, 'Your servant Uriah the Hittite is dead also.' "
22 So the messenger departed and came and reported to David all that Joab had sent
him *to tell.*
23 The messenger said to David, "The men prevailed against us and came out against
us in the field, but we pressed them as far as the entrance of the gate.
24 "Moreover, the archers shot at your servants from the wall; so some of the king's
servants are dead, and your servant Uriah the Hittite is also dead."

11:3 See 1 Kings 1 for Bathsheba's Profile.

11:3–4 As David looked from the roof of the palace, he saw a beautiful woman bathing, and he was filled with lust. David should have left the roof and fled the temptation. Instead, he entertained the temptation by inquiring about Bathsheba. The results were devastating.

To flee temptation, (1) ask God in earnest prayer to help you stay away from people, places, and situations that may tempt you. (2) Memorize and meditate on portions of Scripture that combat your specific weaknesses. At the root of most temptation is a real need or desire that God can fill, but we must trust in his timing. (3) Find another believer with whom you can openly share your struggles, and call this person for help when temptation strikes.

11:4 The phrase "she had purified herself from her uncleanness" means that Bathsheba had just completed the purification rites following menstruation. Thus she could not have already been pregnant by her own husband when David slept with her. Leviticus 15:19–30 gives more information on the purification rites Bathsheba had to perform.

11:15 David put both Bathsheba and Joab in difficult situations. Bathsheba knew it was wrong to commit adultery, but to refuse a king's request could mean punishment or death. Joab did not know why Uriah had to die, but it was obvious the king wanted him killed. We sometimes face situations with only two apparent choices, and both seem wrong. When that happens, we must not lose sight of what God wants. The answer may be to seek out more choices. By doing this, we are likely to find a choice that honors God.

25 Then David said to the messenger, "Thus you shall say to Joab, 'Do not let this thing
displease you, for the sword devours one as well as another; make your battle against
the city stronger and overthrow it'; and *so* encourage him."
26 Now when the wife of Uriah heard that Uriah her husband was dead, she mourned
for her husband.

11:26 Gen 50:10; Deut 34:8; 1 Sam 31:13

27 When the *time of* mourning was over, David sent and brought her to his house and
she became his wife; then she bore him a son. But the thing that David had done was evil
in the sight of the LORD.

11:27 2 Sam 12:9; Ps 51:4, 5

Nathan Rebukes David

12 Then the LORD sent Nathan to David. And he came to him and said,
"There were two men in one city, the one rich and the other poor.

12:1 2 Sam 7:2, 4, 17; Ps 51: title

2 "The rich man had a great many flocks and herds.
3 "But the poor man had nothing except one little ewe lamb
Which he bought and nourished;
And it grew up together with him and his children.
It would eat of his bread and drink of his cup and lie in his bosom,
And was like a daughter to him.

12:3 2 Sam 11:3

4 "Now a traveler came to the rich man,
And he was unwilling to take from his own flock or his own herd,
To prepare for the wayfarer who had come to him;
Rather he took the poor man's ewe lamb and prepared it for the man who had
come to him."
5 Then David's anger burned greatly against the man, and he said to Nathan, "As the
LORD lives, surely the man who has done this deserves to die.

12:5 1 Sam 26:16

6 "He must make restitution for the lamb fourfold, because he did this thing and had
no compassion."

12:6 Ex 22:1; Luke 19:8

7 Nathan then said to David, "You are the man! Thus says the LORD God of Israel,
'It is I who anointed you king over Israel and it is I who delivered you from the hand of
Saul.

12:7 1 Kin 20:42; 1 Sam 16:13

8 'I also gave you your master's house and your master's wives into your care, and I
gave you the house of Israel and Judah; and if *that had been* too little, I would have added
to you many more things like these!

12:8 2 Sam 9:7

9 'Why have you despised the word of the LORD by doing evil in His sight? You have
struck down Uriah the Hittite with the sword, have taken his wife to be your wife, and
have killed him with the sword of the sons of Ammon.

12:9 1 Sam 15:23, 26; 2 Sam 11:14-17; 2 Sam 11:27

10 'Now therefore, the sword shall never depart from your house, because you have
despised Me and have taken the wife of Uriah the Hittite to be your wife.'

12:10 2 Sam 13:28; 18:14; 1 Kin 2:25

11 "Thus says the LORD, 'Behold, I will raise up evil against you from your own household; I will even take your wives before your eyes and give *them* to your companion, and
he will lie with your wives in broad daylight.

12:11 Deut 28:30; 2 Sam 16:21, 22

12 'Indeed you did it secretly, but I will do this thing before all Israel, and under
the sun.' "

12:12 2 Sam 11:4-15; 2 Sam 16:22

11:25 David's response to Uriah's death seems flippant and insensitive. While he grieved deeply for Saul and Abner, his rivals (chapter 1; 3:31–39), he showed no grief for Uriah, a good man with strong spiritual character. Why? David had become callous to his own sin. The only way he could cover up his first sin (adultery) was to sin again, and soon he no longer felt guilty for what he had done. Feelings are not reliable guides for determining right and wrong. Deliberate, repeated sinning had dulled David's sensitivity to God's laws and others' rights. The more you try to cover up a sin, the more insensitive you become toward it. Don't become hardened to sin, as David did. Confess your wrong actions to God before you forget they are sins.

12:1ff As a prophet, Nathan was required to confront sin, even the sin of a king. It took great courage, skill, and tact to speak to David in a way that would make him aware of his wrong actions. When you have to confront someone with unpleasant news, pray for courage, skill, and tact. If you want that person to respond constructively, think through what you are going to say. How you present your message may be as important as what you say. Season your words with wisdom.

12:5–6 It was a year later, and by then David had become so insensitive to his own sins that he didn't realize he was the villain in Nathan's story. The qualities we condemn in others are often our own character flaws. Which friends, associates, or family members do you find easy to criticize and hard to accept? Instead of trying to change them, ask God to help you understand their feelings and see your own flaws more clearly. You may discover that in condemning others, you have been condemning yourself.

12:10–14 The predictions in these verses came true. Because David murdered Uriah and stole his wife, (1) murder was a constant threat in his family (13:26–30; 18:14–15; 1 Kings 2:23–25); (2) his household rebelled against him (15:13); (3) his wives were given to another in public view (16:20–23); (4) his first child by Bathsheba died (12:18). If David had known the painful consequences of his sin, he might not have pursued the pleasures of the moment.

12:13 1 Sam 15:24, 30; 2 Sam 24:10; Luke 18:13; Lev 20:10; 24:17; Prov 28:13; Mic 7:18

12:14 Is 52:5; Rom 2:24

12:16 Neh 1:4; 2 Sam 13:31

12:17 Gen 24:2

13 Then David said to Nathan, "I have sinned against the LORD." And Nathan said to
David, "The LORD also has taken away your sin; you shall not die.
14 "However, because by this deed you have given occasion to the enemies of the LORD
to blaspheme, the child also that is born to you shall surely die."
15 So Nathan went to his house.

Loss of a Child

Then the LORD struck the child that Uriah's widow bore to David, so that he was
very sick.
16 David therefore inquired of God for the child; and David fasted and went and lay
all night on the ground.
17 The elders of his household stood beside him in order to raise him up from the
ground, but he was unwilling and would not eat food with them.
18 Then it happened on the seventh day that the child died. And the servants of David
were afraid to tell him that the child was dead, for they said, "Behold, while the child
was *still* alive, we spoke to him and he did not listen to our voice. How then can we tell
him that the child is dead, since he might do *himself* harm!"
19 But when David saw that his servants were whispering together, David perceived
that the child was dead; so David said to his servants, "Is the child dead?" And they said,
"He is dead."

DAVID'S FAMILY TROUBLES

David's many wives caused him much grief. And as a result of David's sin with Bathsheba, God said that murder would be a constant threat in his family, his family would rebel, and someone else would sleep with his wives. All this happened as the prophet Nathan had predicted. The consequences of sin affect not only us, but those we know and love. Remember that the next time you are tempted to sin.

Wife	*Children*	*What happened*
Michal (Saul's daughter)	She was childless	David gave her five nephews to the Gibeonites to be killed because of Saul's sins
Ahinoam (from Jezreel)	Amnon, David's firstborn	He raped Tamar, his half sister, and was later murdered by Absalom in revenge
Maacah (daughter of King Talmai of Geshur)	Absalom, third son; Tamar, the only daughter mentioned by name	Absalom killed Amnon for raping Tamar, and then fled to Geshur. Later he returned, only to rebel against David. He set up a tent on his roof and slept with ten of his father's concubines there. His pride led to his death
Haggith	Adonijah, fourth son. He was very handsome but it is recorded that he was never disciplined	He set himself up as king before David's death. His plot was exposed and David spared his life, but his half brother Solomon later had him executed
Bathsheba	Unnamed son	Died in fulfillment of God's punishment for David and Bathsheba's adultery
Bathsheba	Solomon	Became the next king of Israel. Ironically, Solomon's many wives caused his downfall

12:13 During this incident, David wrote Psalm 51, giving valuable insight into his character and offering hope for us as well. No matter how miserable guilt makes you feel or how terribly you have sinned, you can pour out your heart to God and seek his forgiveness as David did. There is forgiveness for us when we sin. David also wrote Psalm 32 to express the joy he felt after he was forgiven.

12:14 David confessed and repented of his sin (12:13), but God's judgment was that his child would die. The consequences of David's sin were irreversible. Sometimes an apology isn't enough. When God forgives us and restores our relationship with him, he doesn't eliminate all the consequences of our wrongdoing. We may be tempted to say, "If this is wrong, I can always apologize to God," but we must remember that we may set into motion events with irreversible consequences.

12:14 Why did this child have to die? This was not a judgment on the child for being conceived out of wedlock, but a judgment on David for his sin. David and Bathsheba deserved to die, but God spared their lives and took the child instead. God still had work for David to do in building the kingdom. Perhaps the child's death was a greater punishment for David than his own death would have been.

It is also possible that had the child lived, God's name would have been dishonored among Israel's pagan neighbors. What would they have thought of a God who rewards murder and adultery by giving a king a new heir? A baby's death is tragic, but despising God brings death to entire nations. While God readily forgave David's sin, he did not negate all its consequences.

20 So David arose from the ground, washed, anointed *himself,* and changed his clothes;
and he came into the house of the LORD and worshiped. Then he came to his own house,
and when he requested, they set food before him and he ate.

12:20 Ruth 3:3; Matt 6:17; Ps 95:6-8; 103:1, 8-17; Prov 3:7

21 Then his servants said to him, "What is this thing that you have done? While the
child was alive, you fasted and wept; but when the child died, you arose and ate food."
22 He said, "While the child was *still* alive, I fasted and wept; for I said, 'Who knows,
the LORD may be gracious to me, that the child may live.'

12:22 Is 38:1-3; Jon 3:9

23 "But now he has died; why should I fast? Can I bring him back again? I will go to
him, but he will not return to me."

12:23 Gen 37:35; Job 7:8-10

Solomon Born

24 Then David comforted his wife Bathsheba, and went in to her and lay with her; and
she gave birth to a son, and he named him Solomon. Now the LORD loved him

12:24 1 Chr 22:9; Matt 1:6

25 and sent *word* through Nathan the prophet, and he named him [11]Jedidiah for the
LORD'S sake.

War Again

26 Now Joab fought against Rabbah of the sons of Ammon and captured the royal city.
27 Joab sent messengers to David and said, "I have fought against Rabbah, I have even
captured the city of waters.

12:26 1 Chr 20:1-3; Deut 3:11

28 "Now therefore, gather the rest of the people together and camp against the city and
capture it, or I will capture the city myself and it will be named after me."
29 So David gathered all the people and went to Rabbah, fought against it and captured it.
30 Then he took the crown of their king from his head; and its weight *was* a talent of
gold, and *in it was* a precious stone; and it was *placed* on David's head. And he brought
out the spoil of the city in great amounts.

12:30 1 Chr 20:2

31 He also brought out the people who were in it, and set *them* under saws, sharp iron
instruments, and iron axes, and made them pass through the brickkiln. And thus he did
to all the cities of the sons of Ammon. Then David and all the people returned *to* Jerusalem.

12:31 1 Chr 20:3; Heb 11:37

2. Turmoil in David's family

Amnon and Tamar

13 Now it was after this that Absalom the son of David had a beautiful sister whose
name was Tamar, and Amnon the son of David loved her.
2 Amnon was so frustrated because of his sister Tamar that he made himself ill, for
she was a virgin, and it seemed hard to Amnon to do anything to her.

13:1 2 Sam 3:2, 3; 1 Chr 3:2; 1 Chr 3:9; 2 Sam 3:2

3 But Amnon had a friend whose name was Jonadab, the son of Shimeah, David's
brother; and Jonadab was a very shrewd man.

13:3 1 Sam 16:9

4 He said to him, "O son of the king, why are you so depressed morning after morning? Will you not tell me?" Then Amnon said to him, "I am in love with Tamar, the sister of my brother Absalom."
5 Jonadab then said to him, "Lie down on your bed and pretend to be ill; when your
father comes to see you, say to him, 'Please let my sister Tamar come and give me *some*
food to eat, and let her prepare the food in my sight, that I may see *it* and eat from her
hand.' "

11 I.e. beloved of the LORD

12:20–24 David did not continue to dwell on his sin. He returned to God, and God forgave him, opening the way to begin life anew. Even the name God gave Solomon (*Jedidiah,* "loved by the LORD"; 12:25) was a reminder of God's grace. When we return to God, accept his forgiveness, and change our ways, he gives us a fresh start. To feel forgiven as David did, admit your sins to God and turn to him. Then move ahead with a new and fresh approach to life.

12:22–23 Perhaps the most bitter experience in life is the death of one's child. For comfort in such difficult circumstances, see Psalms 16:9–11; 17:15; 139; Isaiah 40:11.

12:24 Solomon was the fourth son of David and Bathsheba (1 Chronicles 3:5). Therefore several years passed between the death of their first child and Solomon's birth. Bathsheba may still have been grieving over the child's death.

13:3–5 Amnon was encouraged by his cousin Jonadab to commit sexual sin. We may be more vulnerable to the advice of our relatives because we are close to them. However, we must make sure to evaluate every piece of advice by God's standards, even when it comes from relatives.

13:6 Gen 18:6 6 So Amnon lay down and pretended to be ill; when the king came to see him, Amnon said to the king, "Please let my sister Tamar come and make me a couple of cakes in
my sight, that I may eat from her hand."
7 Then David sent to the house for Tamar, saying, "Go now to your brother Amnon's
house, and prepare food for him."
8 So Tamar went to her brother Amnon's house, and he was lying down. And she took
dough, kneaded *it,* made cakes in his sight, and baked the cakes.
13:9 Gen 45:1 9 She took the pan and dished *them* out before him, but he refused to eat. And Amnon said, "Have everyone go out from me." So everyone went out from him.
10 Then Amnon said to Tamar, "Bring the food into the bedroom, that I may eat from
your hand." So Tamar took the cakes which she had made and brought them into the
bedroom to her brother Amnon.
13:11 Gen 39:12 11 When she brought *them* to him to eat, he took hold of her and said to her, "Come,
lie with me, my sister."
13:12 Lev 20:17; Judg 19:23; 20:6 12 But she answered him, "No, my brother, do not violate me, for such a thing is not
done in Israel; do not do this disgraceful thing!
13:13 Gen 20:12 13 "As for me, where could I get rid of my reproach? And as for you, you will be like
one of the fools in Israel. Now therefore, please speak to the king, for he will not withhold me from you."

NATHAN

This prophet lived up to the meaning of his name, "He [God] has given." He was a necessary and helpful gift from God to David. He served as God's spokesman to David and proved himself a fearless friend and counselor, always willing to speak the truth, even when he knew great pain would result.

In confronting David's multiple sin of coveting, theft, adultery, and murder in his affair with Bathsheba, Nathan was able to help David see his own wrongdoing by showing that he would not have tolerated such actions from anyone else. David's repentance allowed Nathan to comfort him with the reality of God's forgiveness, and at the same time remind him of the painful consequences his sin would bring.

Nathan's approach helps us judge our actions. How often do we make choices that we would condemn others for making? It is helpful to ask ourselves how God and others see our actions. Unfortunately, we have a huge capacity to lie to ourselves. God still provides two safeguards against self-deception: his Word and true friends. In each case, we get a view beyond ourselves. You are holding God's Word. Let it speak to you about yourself, even if the truth is painful. If you don't have a friend like Nathan, ask God for one. And ask God to use you as a suitable Nathan for someone else.

Strengths and accomplishments:
- A trusted adviser to David
- A prophet of God
- A fearless, but careful confronter
- One of God's controls in David's life

Weakness and mistake:
- His eagerness to see David build a temple for God in Jerusalem made him speak without God's instruction

Lessons from his life:
- We should not be afraid to tell the truth to those we care about
- A trustworthy companion is one of God's greatest gifts
- God cares enough to find a way to communicate to us when we are in the wrong

Vital statistics:
- Occupations: Prophet, royal adviser
- Contemporaries: David, Bathsheba, Solomon, Zadok, Adonijah

Key verse:
"In accordance with all these words and all this vision, so Nathan spoke to David" (2 Samuel 7:17).

Nathan's story is told in 2 Samuel 7—1 Kings 1. He is also mentioned in 1 Chronicles 17:15; 2 Chronicles 9:29; 29:25.

14 However, he would not listen to her; since he was stronger than she, he violated her
and lay with her.

13:14 Lev 18:9; Deut 22:25; 27:22; 2 Sam 12:11

15 Then Amnon hated her with a very great hatred; for the hatred with which he hated
her was greater than the love with which he had loved her. And Amnon said to her, "Get
up, go away!"
16 But she said to him, "No, because this wrong in sending me away is greater than the
other that you have done to me!" Yet he would not listen to her.
17 Then he called his young man who attended him and said, "Now throw this woman
out of my *presence,* and lock the door behind her."
18 Now she had on a long-sleeved garment; for in this manner the virgin daughters of
the king dressed themselves in robes. Then his attendant took her out and locked the
door behind her.

13:18 Gen 37:3, 23

19 Tamar put ashes on her head and tore her long-sleeved garment which *was* on her;
and she put her hand on her head and went away, crying aloud as she went.

13:19 1 Sam 4:12; Esth 4:1; Gen 37:29; 2 Sam 1:11; Jer 2:37

20 Then Absalom her brother said to her, "Has Amnon your brother been with you?
But now keep silent, my sister, he is your brother; do not take this matter to heart." So
Tamar remained and was desolate in her brother Absalom's house.
21 Now when King David heard of all these matters, he was very angry.
22 But Absalom did not speak to Amnon either good or bad; for Absalom hated Amnon because he had violated his sister Tamar.

13:22 Gen 31:24; Lev 19:17; 1 John 2:9, 11; 3:10, 12, 15

23 Now it came about after two full years that Absalom had sheepshearers in Baal-
hazor, which is near Ephraim, and Absalom invited all the king's sons.

13:23 1 Sam 25:7

Absalom Avenges Tamar

24 Absalom came to the king and said, "Behold now, your servant has sheepshearers;
please let the king and his servants go with your servant."
25 But the king said to Absalom, "No, my son, we should not all go, for we will be
burdensome to you." Although he urged him, he would not go, but blessed him.
26 Then Absalom said, "If not, please let my brother Amnon go with us." And the king
said to him, "Why should he go with you?"

13:26 2 Sam 3:27; 11:13-15

27 But when Absalom urged him, he let Amnon and all the king's sons go with him.
28 Absalom commanded his servants, saying, "See now, when Amnon's heart is merry
with wine, and when I say to you, 'Strike Amnon,' then put him to death. Do not fear;
have not I myself commanded you? Be courageous and be valiant."

13:28 Judg 19:6, 9, 22; 1 Sam 25:36-38

29 The servants of Absalom did to Amnon just as Absalom had commanded. Then all
the king's sons arose and each mounted his mule and fled.

13:29 2 Sam 18:9; 1 Kin 1:33, 38

30 Now it was while they were on the way that the report came to David, saying, "Absalom has struck down all the king's sons, and not one of them is left."
31 Then the king arose, tore his clothes and lay on the ground; and all his servants were
standing by with clothes torn.

13:31 2 Sam 1:11; 2 Sam 12:16

32 Jonadab, the son of Shimeah, David's brother, responded, "Do not let my lord suppose they have put to death all the young men, the king's sons, for Amnon alone is dead;
because by the intent of Absalom this has been determined since the day that he violated his sister Tamar.

13:32 2 Sam 13:3-5

33 "Now therefore, do not let my lord the king take the report to heart, namely, 'all the
king's sons are dead,' for only Amnon is dead."

13:33 2 Sam 19:19

13:14–15 Love and lust are very different. After Amnon raped his half sister, his "love" turned to hate. Although he had claimed to be in love, he was actually overcome by lust. Love is patient; lust requires immediate satisfaction. Love is kind; lust is harsh. Love does not demand its own way; lust does. You can read about the characteristics of real love in 1 Corinthians 13. Lust may feel like love at first, but when physically expressed, it results in self-disgust and hatred of the other person. If you just can't wait, what you feel is not true love.

13:16 Rape was strictly forbidden by God (Deuteronomy 22:28–29). Why was sending Tamar away an even greater crime? By throwing her out, Amnon made it look as if Tamar had made a shameful proposition to him, and there were no witnesses on her behalf because he had gotten rid of the servants. His crime destroyed her chances of marriage—because she was no longer a virgin, she could not be given in marriage.

13:20 Absalom tried to comfort Tamar and persuade her not to turn the incident into a public scandal. Secretly, he planned to take revenge against Amnon himself. This he did two years later (13:23–33). Absalom told Tamar the crime was only a family matter. But God's standards for moral conduct are not suspended when we deal with family matters.

13:21–24 David was angry with Amnon for raping Tamar, but David did not punish him. David probably hesitated because (1) he didn't want to cross Amnon, who was his firstborn son (1 Chronicles 3:1) and therefore next in line to be king, and (2) David was guilty of a similar sin himself in his adultery with Bathsheba. While David was unsurpassed as a king and military leader, he lacked skill and sensitivity as a husband and father.

13:34 2 Sam 13:37, 38; 2 Sam 18:24

34 Now Absalom had fled. And the young man who was the watchman raised his eyes
and looked, and behold, many people were coming from the road behind him by the
side of the mountain.
35 Jonadab said to the king, "Behold, the king's sons have come; according to your
servant's word, so it happened."
36 As soon as he had finished speaking, behold, the king's sons came and lifted their
voices and wept; and also the king and all his servants wept very bitterly.

13:37 2 Sam 13:34; 2 Sam 3:3; 2 Sam 14:23, 32

37 Now Absalom fled and went to Talmai the son of Ammihud, the king of Geshur.
And *David* mourned for his son every day.

13:38 2 Sam 13:34

38 So Absalom had fled and gone to Geshur, and was there three years.

13:39 2 Sam 12:19-23

39 *The heart of* King David longed to go out to Absalom; for he was comforted concerning Amnon, since he was dead.

The Woman of Tekoa

14:1 2 Sam 13:39

14 Now Joab the son of Zeruiah perceived that the king's heart *was inclined* toward
Absalom.

14:2 2 Sam 23:26; 2 Chr 11:6; Amos 1:1; 2 Sam 12:20

2 So Joab sent to Tekoa and brought a wise woman from there and said to her, "Please
pretend to be a mourner, and put on mourning garments now, and do not anoint yourself with oil, but be like a woman who has been mourning for the dead many days;

14:3 2 Sam 14:19

3 then go to the king and speak to him in this manner." So Joab put the words in her
mouth.

14:4 1 Sam 25:23; 2 Kin 6:26-28

4 Now when the woman of Tekoa [12]spoke to the king, she fell on her face to the ground
and prostrated herself and said, "Help, O king."
5 The king said to her, "What is your trouble?" And she answered, "Truly I am a widow, for my husband is dead.
6 "Your maidservant had two sons, but the two of them struggled together in the field,
and there was no [13]one to separate them, so one struck the other and killed him.

14:7 Num 35:19; Deut 19:12, 13; Matt 21:38

7 "Now behold, the whole family has risen against your maidservant, and they say, 'Hand
over the one who struck his brother, that we may put him to death for the life of his brother
whom he killed, and destroy the heir also.' Thus they will extinguish my coal which is
left, so as to leave my husband neither name nor remnant on the face of the earth."
8 Then the king said to the woman, "Go to your house, and I will give orders concerning you."

14:9 Gen 43:9; 1 Sam 25:24; 1 Kin 2:33

9 The woman of Tekoa said to the king, "O my lord, the king, the iniquity is on me
and my father's house, but the king and his throne are guiltless."
10 So the king said, "Whoever speaks to you, bring him to me, and he will not touch
you anymore."

14:11 Num 35:19, 21; Deut 19:4-10; 1 Sam 14:45; 1 Kin 1:52; Matt 10:30

11 Then she said, "Please let the king remember the LORD your God, *so that* the avenger
of blood will not continue to destroy, otherwise they will destroy my son." And he said,
"As the LORD lives, not one hair of your son shall fall to the ground."
12 Then the woman said, "Please let your maidservant speak a word to my lord the
king." And he said, "Speak."

14:13 2 Sam 12:7; 1 Kin 20:40-42; 2 Sam 13:37, 38

13 The woman said, "Why then have you planned such a thing against the people of
God? For in speaking this word the king is as one who is guilty, *in that* the king does not
bring back his banished one.

14:14 Job 30:23; 34:15; Heb 9:27; Ps 58:7; Num 35:15, 25, 28

14 "For we will surely die and are like water spilled on the ground which cannot be gathered up again. Yet God does not take away life, but plans ways so that the banished one
will not be cast out from him.
15 "Now the reason I have come to speak this word to my lord the king is that the peo-

14:16 Deut 32:9; 1 Sam 26:19

ple have made me afraid; so your maidservant said, 'Let me now speak to the king, perhaps the king will perform the request of his maidservant.
16 'For the king will hear and deliver his maidservant from the hand of the man who

14:17 1 Sam 29:9; 2 Sam 14:20; 19:27

would destroy both me and my son from the inheritance of God.'
17 "Then your maidservant said, 'Please let the word of my lord the king be comforting,

12 Many mss and ancient versions read *came* **13** Lit *deliverer between*

13:37–39 Absalom fled to Geshur because King Talmai was his grandfather (1 Chronicles 3:2), and he would be welcomed.

14:11 The Law provided for a way to avenge murder. Numbers 35:9–21 records how cities of refuge protected people from revenge and how blood avengers were to pursue murderers. This woman was asking for the king's protection against any claim against her.

for as the angel of God, so is my lord the king to discern good and evil. And may the
LORD your God be with you.' "
18 Then the king answered and said to the woman, "Please do not hide anything from
me that I am about to ask you." And the woman said, "Let my lord the king please speak."
19 So the king said, "Is the hand of Joab with you in all this?" And the woman replied, **14:19**
"As your soul lives, my lord the king, no one can turn to the right or to the left from 2 Sam 14:3
anything that my lord the king has spoken. Indeed, it was your servant Joab who commanded me, and it was he who put all these words in the mouth of your maidservant;
20 in order to change the appearance of things your servant Joab has done this thing. **14:20**
But my lord is wise, like the wisdom of the angel of God, to know all that is in the earth." 2 Sam 14:17; 19:27

Absalom Is Recalled

21 Then the king said to Joab, "Behold now, I will surely do this thing; go therefore, **14:21**
bring back the young man Absalom." 2 Sam 14:11
22 Joab fell on his face to the ground, prostrated himself and blessed the king; then
Joab said, "Today your servant knows that I have found favor in your sight, O my lord,
the king, in that the king has performed the request of his servant."
23 So Joab arose and went to Geshur and brought Absalom to Jerusalem. **14:23**
24 However the king said, "Let him turn to his own house, and let him not see my face." Deut 3:14; 2 Sam 13:37, 38
So Absalom turned to his own house and did not see the king's face.
25 Now in all Israel was no one as handsome as Absalom, so highly praised; from the **14:24** 2 Sam 13:20
sole of his foot to the crown of his head there was no defect in him.
26 When he cut the hair of his head (and it was at the end of every year that he cut *it,* **14:25** Deut 28:35; Job 2:7;
for it was heavy on him so he cut it), he weighed the hair of his head at 200 shekels by the Is 1:6
king's weight. **14:26**
27 To Absalom there were born three sons, and one daughter whose name was Tamar; Ezek 44:20
she was a woman of beautiful appearance. **14:27**
28 Now Absalom lived two full years in Jerusalem, and did not see the king's face. 2 Sam 18:18; 2 Sam 13:1
29 Then Absalom sent for Joab, to send him to the king, but he would not come to **14:28**
him. So he sent again a second time, but he would not come. 2 Sam 14:24
30 Therefore he said to his servants, "See, Joab's [14]field is next to mine, and he has **14:30**
barley there; go and set it on fire." So Absalom's servants set the field on fire. Judg 15:3-5
31 Then Joab arose, came to Absalom at his house and said to him, "Why have your
servants set my [14]field on fire?"
32 Absalom answered Joab, "Behold, I sent for you, saying, 'Come here, that I may **14:32**
send you to the king, to say, "Why have I come from Geshur? It would be better for me 1 Sam 20:8; Prov 28:13
still to be there." ' Now therefore, let me see the king's face, and if there is iniquity in
me, let him put me to death."
33 So when Joab came to the king and told him, he called for Absalom. Thus he came **14:33**
to the king and prostrated himself on his face to the ground before the king, and the Gen 33:4; Luke 15:20
king kissed Absalom.

3. National rebellion against David

Absalom's Conspiracy

15 Now it came about after this that Absalom provided for himself a chariot and horses **15:1**
and fifty men as runners before him. 1 Kin 1:5

14 Lit *portion*

14:27 By naming his daughter Tamar, Absalom was showing his love and respect for his sister Tamar. This was also a reminder to everyone of the Amnon/Tamar incident.

14:30 Already we can see the seeds of rebellion in Absalom. As an independent and scheming young man, he took matters into his own hands and killed his brother (13:22–29). Without his father or anyone else to keep him in check, he probably did whatever he wanted, as evidenced by his setting Joab's field on fire to get his attention (14:30). Undoubtedly his good looks also added to his self-centeredness (14:25). Children need discipline, especially those with natural abilities and beauty. Otherwise, like Absalom, they will grow up thinking they can do whatever they want whenever they want to.

14:33 David only made halfhearted efforts to correct his children. He did not punish Amnon for his sin against Tamar, nor did he deal decisively with Absalom's murder of Amnon. Such indecisiveness became David's undoing. When we ignore sin, we experience greater pain than if we deal with it immediately.

15:1ff David wrote several psalms during the days of Absalom's rebellion. Some of them are Psalms 39, 41, 55, 61, and 63.

15:2 Ruth 4:1; 2 Sam 19:8
15:3 Prov 12:2
15:4 Judg 9:29
15:5 2 Sam 14:33; 20:9
15:6 Rom 16:18
15:7 2 Sam 3:2, 3
15:8 2 Sam 13:37, 38; Gen 28:20, 21
15:10 1 Kin 1:34; 2 Kin 9:13
15:11 1 Sam 9:13; 1 Sam 22:15
15:12 2 Sam 15:31; Josh 15:51; Ps 3:1
15:13 Judg 9:3; 2 Sam 15:6
15:14 2 Sam 12:11; Ps 3: title

2 Absalom used to rise early and stand beside the way to the gate; and when any man
had a suit to come to the king for judgment, Absalom would call to him and say, "From
what city are you?" And he would say, "Your servant is from one of the tribes of Israel."
3 Then Absalom would say to him, "See, your claims are good and right, but no man
listens to you on the part of the king."
4 Moreover, Absalom would say, "Oh that one would appoint me judge in the land,
then every man who has any suit or cause could come to me and I would give him justice."
5 And when a man came near to prostrate himself before him, he would put out his
hand and take hold of him and kiss him.
6 In this manner Absalom dealt with all Israel who came to the king for judgment; so
Absalom stole away the hearts of the men of Israel.
7 Now it came about at the end of [15]forty years that Absalom said to the king, "Please
let me go and pay my vow which I have vowed to the LORD, in Hebron.
8 "For your servant vowed a vow while I was living at Geshur in Aram, saying, 'If the
LORD shall indeed bring me back to Jerusalem, then I will serve the LORD.' "
9 The king said to him, "Go in peace." So he arose and went to Hebron.
10 But Absalom sent spies throughout all the tribes of Israel, saying, "As soon as you
hear the sound of the trumpet, then you shall say, 'Absalom is king in Hebron.' "
11 Then two hundred men went with Absalom from Jerusalem, who were invited and
went innocently, and they did not know anything.
12 And Absalom sent for Ahithophel the Gilonite, David's counselor, from his city
Giloh, while he was offering the sacrifices. And the conspiracy was strong, for the people increased continually with Absalom.

David Flees Jerusalem

13 Then a messenger came to David, saying, "The hearts of the men of Israel are with
Absalom."
14 David said to all his servants who were with him at Jerusalem, "Arise and let us flee,
for *otherwise* none of us will escape from Absalom. Go in haste, or he will overtake us
quickly and bring down calamity on us and strike the city with the edge of the sword."

15 Some ancient versions render *four*

15:2 The city gate was like city hall and a shopping center combined. Because Jerusalem was the nation's capital, both local and national leaders met there daily to transact business and conduct government affairs. The city gate was the perfect spot for this because government and business transactions needed witnesses to be legitimate, and anyone entering or leaving the city had to enter through the gate. Merchants set up their tent-shops near the gate for the same reason. Absalom, therefore, went to the city gate to win the hearts of Israel's leaders as well as those of the common people.

15:5–6 Absalom's political strategy was to steal the hearts of the people with his good looks, grand entrances, apparent concern for justice, and friendly embraces. Many were fooled and switched their allegiance. Later, however, Absalom proved to be an evil ruler.

We need to evaluate our leaders to make sure their charisma is not a mask covering graft, deception, or hunger for power. Make sure that underneath their style and charm, they are able to make good decisions and handle people wisely.

15:9 Absalom went to Hebron because it was his hometown (3:2–3). Hebron was David's first capital as well, and there Absalom could expect to find loyal friends who would be proud of him.

15:14 Had David not escaped from Jerusalem, the ensuing fight might have killed both him and many innocent inhabitants of the city. Some fights that we think necessary can be costly and destructive to those around us. In such cases, it may be wise to back down and save the fight for another day—even if doing so hurts our pride. It takes courage to stand and fight, but it also takes courage to back down for the sake of others.

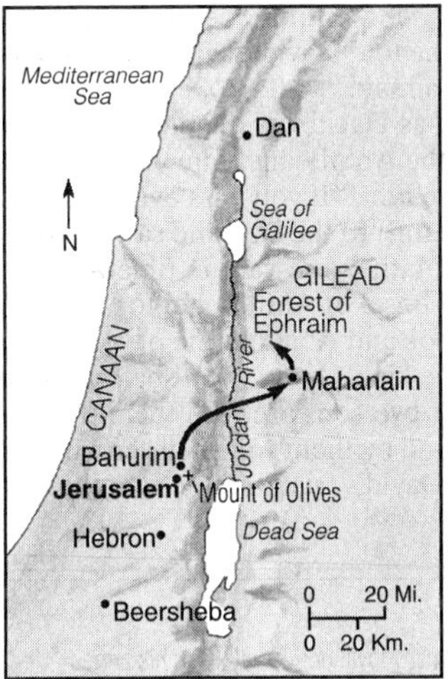

ABSALOM'S REBELLION
Absalom crowned himself king in Hebron. David and his men fled from Jerusalem, crossed the Jordan, and went to Mahanaim. Absalom and his army followed, only to be defeated in the forest of Ephraim, where Absalom was killed.

15:14 Why couldn't David just crush this rebellion? There were several reasons he chose to flee: (1) The rebellion was widespread (15:10–13) and would not have been easily suppressed; (2) David did not want the city of Jerusalem to be destroyed; (3) David still cared for his son and did not want to hurt him. We know that David expected to return to Jerusalem soon because he left ten of his concubines to take care of the palace (15:16).

15 Then the king's servants said to the king, "Behold, your servants *are ready to do*
whatever my lord the king chooses."
16 So the king went out and all his household with him. But the king left ten concubines to keep the house.
17 The king went out and all the people with him, and they stopped at the last house.
18 Now all his servants passed on beside him, all the Cherethites, all the Pelethites and
all the Gittites, six hundred men who had come with him from Gath, passed on before
the king.
19 Then the king said to Ittai the Gittite, "Why will you also go with us? Return and
remain with the king, for you are a foreigner and also an exile; *return* to your own place.
20 "You came *only* yesterday, and shall I today make you wander with us, while I go
where I will? Return and take back your brothers; mercy and truth be with you."
21 But Ittai answered the king and said, "As the LORD lives, and as my lord the king
lives, surely wherever my lord the king may be, whether for death or for life, there also
your servant will be."
22 Therefore David said to Ittai, "Go and pass over." So Ittai the Gittite passed over
with all his men and all the little ones who *were* with him.
23 While all the country was weeping with a loud voice, all the people passed over. The
king also passed over the brook Kidron, and all the people passed over toward the way
of the wilderness.
24 Now behold, Zadok also *came,* and all the Levites with him carrying the ark of the
covenant of God. And they set down the ark of God, and Abiathar came up until all the
people had finished passing from the city.
25 The king said to Zadok, "Return the ark of God to the city. If I find favor in the
sight of the LORD, then He will bring me back again and show me both it and His habitation.
26 "But if He should say thus, 'I have no delight in you,' behold, here I am, let Him do
to me as seems good to Him."
27 The king said also to Zadok the priest, "Are you *not* a seer? Return to the city in
peace and your two sons with you, your son Ahimaaz and Jonathan the son of Abiathar.
28 "See, I am going to wait at the fords of the wilderness until word comes from you to
inform me."
29 Therefore Zadok and Abiathar returned the ark of God to Jerusalem and remained
there.
30 And David went up the ascent of the *Mount of* Olives, and wept as he went, and his
head was covered and he walked barefoot. Then all the people who were with him each
covered his head and went up weeping as they went.
31 Now someone told David, saying, "Ahithophel is among the conspirators with Absalom." And David said, "O LORD, I pray, make the counsel of Ahithophel foolishness."
32 It happened as David was coming to the summit, where God was worshiped, that
behold, Hushai the Archite met him with his coat torn and dust on his head.
33 David said to him, "If you pass over with me, then you will be a burden to me.
34 "But if you return to the city, and say to Absalom, 'I will be your servant, O king; as
I have been your father's servant in time past, so I will now be your servant,' then you
can thwart the counsel of Ahithophel for me.
35 "Are not Zadok and Abiathar the priests with you there? So it shall be that whatever
you hear from the king's house, you shall report to Zadok and Abiathar the priests.
36 "Behold their two sons are with them there, Ahimaaz, Zadok's son and Jonathan,
Abiathar's son; and by them you shall send me everything that you hear."
37 So Hushai, David's friend, came into the city, and Absalom came into Jerusalem.

15:16 2 Sam 16:21, 22
15:18 2 Sam 8:18; 1 Sam 23:13; 25:13; 30:1, 9
15:19 2 Sam 18:2
15:20 1 Sam 23:13; 2 Sam 2:6
15:21 Ruth 1:16, 17; Prov 17:17
15:23 1 Kin 15:13; 2 Chr 29:16; 2 Sam 15:28; 16:2
15:24 2 Sam 8:17; 20:25; Num 4:15; 1 Sam 4:4, 5; 1 Sam 22:20
15:25 Ps 43:3; Ex 15:13; Jer 25:30
15:26 2 Sam 11:27; 1 Chr 21:7; 1 Sam 3:18
15:27 1 Sam 9:6-9; 2 Sam 17:17
15:28 Josh 5:10; 2 Sam 17:16
15:30 Esth 6:12; Ezek 24:17, 23; Is 20:2-4
15:31 2 Sam 15:12; 2 Sam 16:23; 17:14, 23
15:32 Josh 16:2
15:33 2 Sam 19:35
15:34 2 Sam 16:19
15:35 2 Sam 17:15, 16
15:36 2 Sam 15:27; 2 Sam 17:17
15:37 2 Sam 16:16; 1 Chr 27:33; 2 Sam 16:15

15:17–18 David had many loyal non-Israelites in his armed forces. The Gittites, from the Philistine city of Gath, were apparently friends David had acquired while hiding from Saul. The Cherethites and Pelethites were also from Philistine territory. Although Israel was supposed to destroy wicked enemies, the nation was to welcome foreigners who came on friendly terms (Exodus 23:9; Deuteronomy 10:19) and to try to show them the importance of obeying God.

15:24–25 The priests and Levites were also loyal to David.

15:27–37 David needed spies in Absalom's court to inform him of Absalom's decisions. By sending Hushai to Absalom as a supposed traitor to David, Hushai could offer advice contradictory to Ahithophel's advice. Ahithophel was Absalom's adviser (he was also Bathsheba's grandfather).

Ziba, a False Servant

16:1 2 Sam 15:32; 2 Sam 9:2-13; 1 Sam 25:18

16:2 Judg 10:4; 2 Sam 17:29

16:3 2 Sam 9:9, 10; 2 Sam 19:26, 27

16 Now when David had passed a little beyond the summit, behold, Ziba the servant
of Mephibosheth met him with a couple of saddled donkeys, and on them *were*
two hundred loaves of bread, a hundred clusters of raisins, a hundred summer fruits,
and a jug of wine.
2 The king said to Ziba, "Why do you have these?" And Ziba said, "The donkeys are
for the king's household to ride, and the bread and summer fruit for the young men to
eat, and the wine, for whoever is faint in the wilderness to drink."
3 Then the king said, "And where is your master's son?" And Ziba said to the king,
"Behold, he is staying in Jerusalem, for he said, 'Today the house of Israel will restore
the kingdom of my father to me.' "
4 So the king said to Ziba, "Behold, all that belongs to Mephibosheth is yours." And
Ziba said, "I prostrate myself; let me find favor in your sight, O my lord, the king!"

ABSALOM

A father's mistakes are often reflected in the lives of his children. In Absalom, David saw a bitter replay and amplification of many of his own past sins. God had predicted that David's family would suffer because of his sin against Bathsheba and Uriah. David's heart was broken as he realized that God's predictions were coming true. God forgave David, but he did not cancel the consequences of his sin. David was horrified as he saw his son's strengths run wild without the controls God had built into his own life.

By most casual evaluations, Absalom would have made an excellent king, and the people loved him. But he lacked the inner character and control needed in a good leader. His appearance, skill, and position did not make up for his lack of personal integrity.

David's sins took him away from God, but repentance brought him back. In contrast, Absalom sinned and kept on sinning. Although he relied heavily on the advice of others, he was not wise enough to evaluate the counsel he received.

Can you identify with Absalom? Do you find yourself on a fast track toward self-destruction? Absalom wasn't able to say, "I was wrong. I need forgiveness." God offers forgiveness, but we will not experience that forgiveness until we genuinely admit our sins and confess them to God. Absalom rejected his father's love and ultimately God's love. How often do you miss entering back into God's love through the door of forgiveness?

Strength and accomplishment:
- Was handsome and charismatic like his father, David

Weaknesses and mistakes:
- Avenged the rape of his sister Tamar by killing his half brother Amnon
- Plotted against his father to take away the throne
- Consistently listened to the wrong advice

Lessons from his life:
- The sins of parents are often repeated and amplified in the children
- A smart man gets a lot of advice; a wise man evaluates the advice he gets
- Actions against God's plans will fail, sooner or later

Vital statistics:
- Where: Hebron
- Occupation: Prince
- Relatives: Father: David. Mother: Maacah. Brothers: Amnon, Chileab, Solomon, and others. Sister: Tamar
- Contemporaries: Nathan, Jonadab, Joab, Ahithophel, Hushai

Key verse:
"Absalom sent spies throughout all the tribes of Israel, saying, 'As soon as you hear the sound of the trumpet, then you shall say, "Absalom is king in Hebron" ' " (2 Samuel 15:10).

Absalom's story is told in 2 Samuel 3:3; 13—19.

16:3 Saul was Mephibosheth's grandfather. Most likely Ziba was lying, hoping to receive a reward from David. (See 19:24–30 for Mephibosheth's side of the story.) For the story of Mephibosheth, see chapter 9.

16:4 David believed Ziba's charge against Mephibosheth without checking into it or even being skeptical. Don't be hasty to accept someone's condemnation of another, especially when the accuser may profit from the other's downfall. David should have been skeptical of Ziba's comments until he checked them out for himself.

David Is Cursed

5 When King David came to Bahurim, behold, there came out from there a man of
the family of the house of Saul whose name was Shimei, the son of Gera; he came out
cursing continually as he came.
6 He threw stones at David and at all the servants of King David; and all the people
and all the mighty men were at his right hand and at his left.
7 Thus Shimei said when he cursed, "Get out, get out, you man of bloodshed, and
worthless fellow!
8 "The LORD has returned upon you all the bloodshed of the house of Saul, in whose
place you have reigned; and the LORD has given the kingdom into the hand of your son
Absalom. And behold, you are *taken* in your own evil, for you are a man of bloodshed!"
9 Then Abishai the son of Zeruiah said to the king, "Why should this dead dog curse
my lord the king? Let me go over now and cut off his head."
10 But the king said, "What have I to do with you, O sons of Zeruiah? If he curses, and
if the LORD has told him, 'Curse David,' then who shall say, 'Why have you done so?' "
11 Then David said to Abishai and to all his servants, "Behold, my son who came out
from me seeks my life; how much more now this Benjamite? Let him alone and let him
curse, for the LORD has told him.
12 "Perhaps the LORD will look on my affliction and return good to me instead of his
cursing this day."
13 So David and his men went on the way; and Shimei went along on the hillside parallel with him and as he went he cursed and cast stones and threw dust at him.
14 The king and all the people who were with him arrived weary and he refreshed himself there.

16:5 2 Sam 3:16; 17:18; 2 Sam 19:16-23; 1 Kin 2:8, 9, 44; Ex 22:28; 1 Sam 17:43

16:7 2 Sam 12:9

16:8 2 Sam 21:1-9; 2 Sam 1:16; 3:28, 29; 4:11, 12

16:9 1 Sam 26:8; 2 Sam 19:21; Luke 9:54; 2 Sam 9:8; Ex 22:28

16:10 2 Sam 3:39; 19:22; John 18:11; Rom 9:20

16:11 2 Sam 12:11; Gen 45:5; 1 Sam 26:19

16:12 Deut 23:5; Rom 8:28

Absalom Enters Jerusalem

15 Then Absalom and all the people, the men of Israel, entered Jerusalem, and Ahithophel with him.
16 Now it came about when Hushai the Archite, David's friend, came to Absalom, that
Hushai said to Absalom, "*Long* live the king! *Long* live the king!"
17 Absalom said to Hushai, "Is this your loyalty to your friend? Why did you not go
with your friend?"
18 Then Hushai said to Absalom, "No! For whom the LORD, this people, and all the
men of Israel have chosen, his I will be, and with him I will remain.
19 "Besides, whom should I serve? *Should I* not *serve* in the presence of his son? As I
have served in your father's presence, so I will be in your presence."
20 Then Absalom said to Ahithophel, "Give your advice. What shall we do?"
21 Ahithophel said to Absalom, "Go in to your father's concubines, whom he has left
to keep the house; then all Israel will hear that you have made yourself odious to your
father. The hands of all who are with you will also be strengthened."
22 So they pitched a tent for Absalom on the roof, and Absalom went in to his father's
concubines in the sight of all Israel.
23 The advice of Ahithophel, which he gave in those days, *was* as if one inquired of the
word of God; so was all the advice of Ahithophel *regarded* by both David and Absalom.

16:15 2 Sam 15:12, 37

16:16 2 Sam 15:37; 2 Sam 15:34; 1 Sam 10:24; 2 Kin 11:12

16:17 2 Sam 19:25

16:19 2 Sam 15:34

16:21 2 Sam 15:16; 20:3

16:22 2 Sam 15:16; 20:3; 2 Sam 12:11, 12

16:23 2 Sam 17:14, 23; 2 Sam 15:12

Hushai's Counsel

17 Furthermore, Ahithophel said to Absalom, "Please let me choose 12,000 men that
I may arise and pursue David tonight.
2 "I will come upon him while he is weary and exhausted and terrify him, so that all the
people who are with him will flee. Then I will strike down the king alone,

17:2 2 Sam 16:14; 1 Kin 22:31

16:5–14 Shimei kept up a steady tirade against David. Although his curses were unjustified because David had had no part in Saul's death, David and his followers quietly tolerated the abuse. Maintaining your composure in the face of unjustified criticism can be a trying experience and an emotional drain, but if you can't stop criticism, it is best just to ignore it. Remember that God knows what you are enduring, and he will vindicate you if you are in the right.

16:21–22 This incident fulfilled Nathan's prediction that because of David's sin, another man would sleep with his wives (12:11–12). (See the note on 3:6–7 for the cultural significance of this act.)

16:23 Ahithophel was an adviser to Absalom. Most rulers had advisers to help them make decisions about governmental and political matters. They probably arranged the king's marriages as well because these were usually politically motivated unions. But God made Ahithophel's advice seem foolish, just as David had prayed (15:31).

17:3 Jer 6:14

3 and I will bring back all the people to you. The return of everyone depends on the
man you seek; *then* all the people will be at peace."
4 So the plan pleased Absalom and all the elders of Israel.

17:5 2 Sam 15:32-34

5 Then Absalom said, "Now call Hushai the Archite also, and let us hear what he has
to say."
6 When Hushai had come to Absalom, Absalom said to him, "Ahithophel has spoken thus. Shall we carry out his plan? If not, you speak."

17:7 2 Sam 16:21

7 So Hushai said to Absalom, "This time the advice that Ahithophel has given is not
good."

17:8 Hos 13:8

8 Moreover, Hushai said, "You know your father and his men, that they are mighty
men and they are fierce, like a bear robbed of her cubs in the field. And your father is an
expert in warfare, and will not spend the night with the people.
9 "Behold, he has now hidden himself in one of the caves or in another place; and it
will be when he falls on them at the first attack, that whoever hears *it* will say, 'There has
been a slaughter among the people who follow Absalom.'

17:10 Josh 2:9-11

10 "And even the one who is valiant, whose heart is like the heart of a lion, will completely lose heart; for all Israel knows that your father is a mighty man and those who
are with him are valiant men.

17:11 1 Sam 3:20; Gen 22:17; 1 Sam 13:5

11 "But I counsel that all Israel be surely gathered to you, from Dan even to Beersheba,
as the sand that is by the sea in abundance, and that you personally go into battle.

17:12 Ps 110:3; Mic 5:7

12 "So we shall come to him in one of the places where he can be found, and we will fall
on him as the dew falls on the ground; and of him and of all the men who are with him,
not even one will be left.

17:13 Mic 1:6

13 "If he withdraws into a city, then all Israel shall bring ropes to that city, and we will
drag it into the valley until not even a small stone is found there."

17:14 2 Sam 15:31, 34; Ps 9:15, 16

14 Then Absalom and all the men of Israel said, "The counsel of Hushai the Archite is
better than the counsel of Ahithophel." For the LORD had ordained to thwart the good
counsel of Ahithophel, so that the LORD might bring calamity on Absalom.

Hushai's Warning Saves David

17:15 2 Sam 15:35, 36

15 Then Hushai said to Zadok and to Abiathar the priests, "This is what Ahithophel
counseled Absalom and the elders of Israel, and this is what I have counseled.

HIGHS AND LOWS OF DAVID'S LIFE

The Bible calls David a man after God's own heart (1 Samuel 13:14, Acts 13:22), but that didn't mean his life was free of troubles. David's life was full of highs and lows. Some of David's troubles were a result of his sins; some were a result of the sins of others. We can't always control our ups and downs, but we can trust God every day. We can be certain that he will help us through our trials, just as he helped David. In the end, he will reward us for our consistent faith.

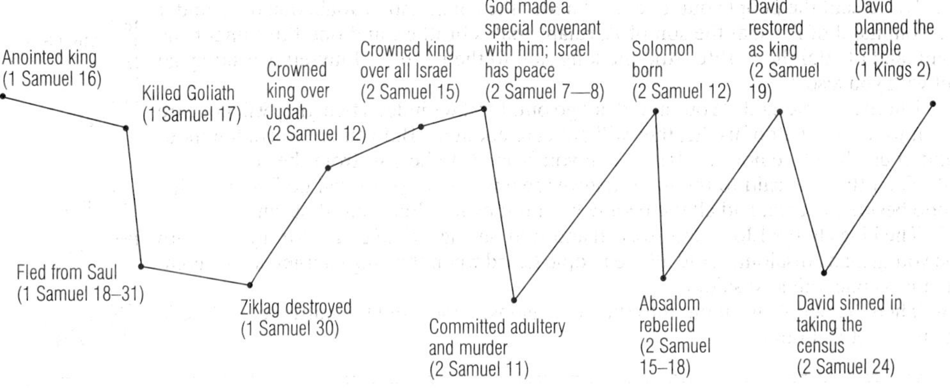
Anointed king (1 Samuel 16)
Killed Goliath (1 Samuel 17)
Fled from Saul (1 Samuel 18–31)
Ziklag destroyed (1 Samuel 30)
Crowned king over Judah (2 Samuel 12)
Crowned king over all Israel (2 Samuel 15)
God made a special covenant with him; Israel has peace (2 Samuel 7—8)
Committed adultery and murder (2 Samuel 11)
Solomon born (2 Samuel 12)
Absalom rebelled (2 Samuel 15–18)
David restored as king (2 Samuel 19)
David sinned in taking the census (2 Samuel 24)
David planned the temple (1 Kings 2)

17:11 Hushai appealed to Absalom through flattery, and Absalom's vanity became his own trap. Hushai predicted great glory for Absalom if he personally led the entire army against David. "Pride goes before destruction" (Proverbs 16:18) is an appropriate comment on Absalom's ambitions.

16 "Now therefore, send quickly and tell David, saying, 'Do not spend the night at the
fords of the wilderness, but by all means cross over, or else the king and all the people
who are with him will be destroyed.' "
17 Now Jonathan and Ahimaaz were staying at En-rogel, and a maidservant would go
and tell them, and they would go and tell King David, for they could not be seen entering the city.
18 But a lad did see them and told Absalom; so the two of them departed quickly and
came to the house of a man in Bahurim, who had a well in his courtyard, and they went
down into it.
19 And the woman took a covering and spread it over the well's mouth and scattered
grain on it, so that nothing was known.
20 Then Absalom's servants came to the woman at the house and said, "Where are
Ahimaaz and Jonathan?" And the woman said to them, "They have crossed the brook
of water." And when they searched and could not find *them,* they returned to Jerusalem.
21 It came about after they had departed that they came up out of the well and went
and told King David; and they said to David, "Arise and cross over the water quickly for
thus Ahithophel has counseled against you."
22 Then David and all the people who *were* with him arose and crossed the Jordan;
and by dawn not even one remained who had not crossed the Jordan.
23 Now when Ahithophel saw that his counsel was not followed, he saddled *his* donkey and arose and went to his home, to his city, and set his house in order, and strangled
himself; thus he died and was buried in the grave of his father.
24 Then David came to Mahanaim. And Absalom crossed the Jordan, he and all the
men of Israel with him.
25 Absalom set Amasa over the army in place of Joab. Now Amasa was the son of a
man whose name was Ithra the Israelite, who went in to Abigail the daughter of Nahash,
sister of Zeruiah, Joab's mother.
26 And Israel and Absalom camped in the land of Gilead.
27 Now when David had come to Mahanaim, Shobi the son of Nahash from Rabbah
of the sons of Ammon, Machir the son of Ammiel from Lo-debar, and Barzillai the
Gileadite from Rogelim,
28 brought beds, basins, pottery, wheat, barley, flour, parched *grain,* beans, lentils,
parched *seeds,*
29 honey, curds, sheep, and cheese of the herd, for David and for the people who *were*
with him, to eat; for they said, "The people are hungry and weary and thirsty in the wilderness."

17:16 2 Sam 15:28
17:17 2 Sam 15:27, 36; Josh 15:7; 18:16
17:18 2 Sam 3:16; 16:5
17:19 Josh 2:4-6
17:20 Lev 19:11; Josh 2:3-5; 1 Sam 19:12-17
17:21 2 Sam 17:15, 16
17:23 2 Sam 15:12; 2 Kin 20:1; Matt 27:5
17:24 Gen 32:2, 10; 2 Sam 2:8
17:25 2 Sam 19:13; 20:9-12; 1 Kin 2:5, 32; 1 Chr 2:16
17:27 1 Sam 11:1; 2 Sam 10:1, 2; 2 Sam 12:26, 29; 2 Sam 9:4; 2 Sam 19:31-39; 1 Kin 2:7
17:28 Prov 11:25; Matt 5:7
17:29 2 Sam 16:2, 14; Prov 21:26; Eccl 11:1; Rom 12:13

Absalom Slain

18 Then David numbered the people who were with him and set over them commanders of thousands and commanders of hundreds.
2 David sent the people out, one third under the command of Joab, one third under
the command of Abishai the son of Zeruiah, Joab's brother, and one third under the
command of Ittai the Gittite. And the king said to the people, "I myself will surely go
out with you also."
3 But the people said, "You should not go out; for if we indeed flee, they will not care
about us; even if half of us die, they will not care about us. But you are worth ten thousand of us; therefore now it is better that you *be ready* to help us from the city."
4 Then the king said to them, "Whatever seems best to you I will do." So the king
stood beside the gate, and all the people went out by hundreds and thousands.
5 The king charged Joab and Abishai and Ittai, saying, "*Deal* gently for my sake with
the young man Absalom." And all the people heard when the king charged all the commanders concerning Absalom.
6 Then the people went out into the field against Israel, and the battle took place in
the forest of Ephraim.

18:1 Ex 18:25; Num 31:14; 1 Sam 22:7
18:2 Judg 7:16; 1 Sam 11:11; 2 Sam 15:19-22
18:3 2 Sam 21:17
18:4 2 Sam 18:24
18:5 2 Sam 18:12
18:6 Josh 17:15, 18; 2 Sam 17:26

17:25 Joab and Amasa were David's nephews and Absalom's cousins. Because Joab had left Jerusalem with David (see 18:5, 10ff), Amasa took his place as commander of Israel's troops.

18:1 David took command as he had in former days. In recent years, his life had been characterized by indecisiveness and moral paralysis. At this time he began to take charge and do his duty.

7 The people of Israel were defeated there before the servants of David, and the slaughter there that day was great, 20,000 men.
8 For the battle there was spread over the whole countryside, and the forest devoured more people that day than the sword devoured.

18:9
2 Sam 14:26

9 Now Absalom happened to meet the servants of David. For Absalom was riding on *his* mule, and the mule went under the thick branches of a great oak. And his head caught fast in the oak, so he was left hanging between heaven and earth, while the mule that was under him kept going.
10 When a certain man saw *it,* he told Joab and said, "Behold, I saw Absalom hanging in an oak."
11 Then Joab said to the man who had told him, "Now behold, you saw *him!* Why then did you not strike him there to the ground? And I would have given you ten *pieces* of silver and a belt."

REBELLION
The Bible records many rebellions. Many were against God's chosen leaders. They were doomed for failure. Others were begun by wicked men against wicked men. While these were sometimes successful, the rebel's life usually came to a violent end. Still other rebellions were made by good people against the wicked or unjust actions of others. This kind of rebellion is sometimes good in freeing the common people from oppression and giving them the freedom to turn back to God.

Who rebelled?	*Who they rebelled against*	*What happened*	*Reference*
Adam and Eve	God	Expelled from Eden	Genesis 3
Israelites	God, Moses	Forced to wander in wilderness for 40 years	Numbers 14
Korah	Moses	Swallowed by the earth	Numbers 16
Israelites	God	God took away his special promise of protection	Judges 2
Absalom (David's son)	David	Killed in battle	2 Samuel 15–18
Sheba	David	Killed in battle	2 Samuel 20
Adonijah (David's son)	David, Solomon	Killed for treason	1 Kings 1–2
Joab	David, Solomon	Supported Adonijah's kingship without seeking God's choice. Killed for treason	1 Kings 1–2
Ten tribes of Israel	Rehoboam	The kingdom was divided. The ten tribes forgot about God, sinned, and were eventually taken into captivity	1 Kings 12:16–20
Baasha king of Israel	Nadab king of Israel	Overthrew the throne and became king. God destroyed his descendants	1 Kings 15:27–16:7
Zimri king of Israel	Elah king of Israel	Overthrew the throne, but killed himself when his rule was not accepted	1 Kings 16:9–16
Jehu king of Israel	Joram king of Israel Ahaziah king of Judah	Killed both kings. Later turned from God and his dynasty was wiped out	2 Kings 9–10
Joash king of Judah Jehoiada, a priest	Athaliah queen of Judah	Athaliah, a wicked queen, was overthrown. This was a "good" rebellion	2 Kings 11
Shallum king of Israel	Zechariah king of Israel	Overthrew the throne, but then was assassinated	2 Kings 15:8–15
Menahem king of Israel	Shallum king of Israel	Overthrew the throne, but then was invaded by Assyrian army	2 Kings 15:16–22
Hoshea king of Israel	Assyria	The city of Samaria was destroyed, the nation of Israel taken into captivity	2 Kings 17
Zedekiah king of Judah	Nebuchadnezzar king of Babylon	The city of Jerusalem destroyed, the nation of Judah taken into captivity	2 Kings 24–25

12 The man said to Joab, "Even if I should receive a thousand *pieces of* silver in my
hand, I would not put out my hand against the king's son; for in our hearing the king
charged you and Abishai and Ittai, saying, 'Protect for me the young man Absalom!'
13 "Otherwise, if I had dealt treacherously against his life (and there is nothing hidden
from the king), then you yourself would have stood aloof."
14 Then Joab said, "I will not waste time here with you." So he took three spears in his
hand and thrust them through the heart of Absalom while he was yet alive in the midst
of the oak.
15 And ten young men who carried Joab's armor gathered around and struck Absalom and killed him.
16 Then Joab blew the trumpet, and the people returned from pursuing Israel, for Joab
restrained the people.
17 They took Absalom and cast him into a deep pit in the forest and erected over him
a very great heap of stones. And all Israel fled, each to his tent.
18 Now Absalom in his lifetime had taken and set up for himself a pillar which is in the
King's Valley, for he said, "I have no son to preserve my name." So he named the pillar
after his own name, and it is called Absalom's Monument to this day.

18:12 2 Sam 18:5
18:13 2 Sam 14:19, 20
18:14 2 Sam 14:30
18:16 2 Sam 2:28; 20:22
18:17 Deut 21:20, 21; Josh 7:26; 8:29; 2 Sam 19:8; 20:1, 22
18:18 1 Sam 15:12; Gen 14:17; 2 Sam 14:27

David Is Grief-stricken

19 Then Ahimaaz the son of Zadok said, "Please let me run and bring the king news
that the LORD has freed him from the hand of his enemies."
20 But Joab said to him, "You are not the man to carry news this day, but you shall
carry news another day; however, you shall carry no news today because the king's son is
dead."
21 Then Joab said to the Cushite, "Go, tell the king what you have seen." So the Cushite bowed to Joab and ran.
22 Now Ahimaaz the son of Zadok said once more to Joab, "But whatever happens,
please let me also run after the Cushite." And Joab said, "Why would you run, my son,
since you will have no reward for going?"
23 "But whatever happens," *he said,* "I will run." So he said to him, "Run." Then Ahimaaz ran by way of the plain and passed up the Cushite.
24 Now David was sitting between the two gates; and the watchman went up to the
roof of the gate by the wall, and raised his eyes and looked, and behold, a man running
by himself.
25 The watchman called and told the king. And the king said, "If he is by himself there
is good news in his mouth." And he came nearer and nearer.
26 Then the watchman saw another man running; and the watchman called to the gatekeeper and said, "Behold, *another* man running by himself." And the king said, "This
one also is bringing good news."
27 The watchman said, "I think the running of the first one is like the running of Ahimaaz the son of Zadok." And the king said, "This is a good man and comes with good
news."
28 Ahimaaz called and said to the king, "[16]All is well." And he prostrated himself before the king with his face to the ground. And he said, "Blessed is the LORD your God,
who has delivered up the men who lifted their hands against my lord the king."
29 The king said, "Is it well with the young man Absalom?" And Ahimaaz answered,
"When Joab sent the king's servant, and your servant, I saw a great tumult, but I did not
know what *it was.*"
30 Then the king said, "Turn aside and stand here." So he turned aside and stood still.
31 Behold, the Cushite arrived, and the Cushite said, "Let my lord the king receive
good news, for the LORD has freed you this day from the hand of all those who rose up
against you."
32 Then the king said to the Cushite, "Is it well with the young man Absalom?" And

18:19 2 Sam 15:36; 2 Sam 18:31
18:22 2 Sam 18:29
18:24 2 Sam 19:8; 2 Sam 13:34; 2 Kin 9:17
18:27 2 Kin 9:20; 1 Kin 1:42
18:28 1 Sam 25:23; 2 Sam 14:4; 1 Sam 17:46
18:29 2 Sam 20:9; 2 Kin 4:26; 2 Sam 18:22
18:31 Judg 5:31; 2 Sam 18:19
18:32 2 Sam 18:29; 1 Sam 25:26

16 Lit *Peace*

18:12–14 This man had caught Joab in his hypocrisy. He knew Joab would have turned on him for killing the man if the king had found out about it. Joab could not answer, but only dismissed him. Those about to do evil often do not take the time to consider what they are about to do. They don't care whether or not it is right or lawful. Don't rush into action without thinking. Consider whether what you are about to do is right or wrong.

18:29 Although he reached the city first, Ahimaaz was afraid to tell the king the truth about the death of his son Absalom.

the Cushite answered, "Let the enemies of my lord the king, and all who rise up against
you for evil, be as that young man!"
18:33 2 Sam 19:4; Ex 32:32; Rom 9:3
33 The king was deeply moved and went up to the chamber over the gate and wept.
And thus he said as he walked, "O my son Absalom, my son, my son Absalom! Would I
had died instead of you, O Absalom, my son, my son!"

Joab Reproves David's Lament

19:1 2 Sam 18:5, 14
19 Then it was told Joab, "Behold, the king is weeping and mourns for Absalom."
2 The victory that day was turned to mourning for all the people, for the people
heard *it* said that day, "The king is grieved for his son."
3 So the people went by stealth into the city that day, as people who are humiliated
steal away when they flee in battle.
19:4 2 Sam 15:30; 2 Sam 18:33
4 The king covered his face and cried out with a loud voice, "O my son Absalom,
O Absalom, my son, my son!"
5 Then Joab came into the house to the king and said, "Today you have covered with
shame the faces of all your servants, who today have saved your life and the lives of your
sons and daughters, the lives of your wives, and the lives of your concubines,
6 by loving those who hate you, and by hating those who love you. For you have shown
today that princes and servants are nothing to you; for I know this day that if Absalom
were alive and all of us were dead today, then you would be pleased.
19:7 Prov 14:28
7 "Now therefore arise, go out and speak kindly to your servants, for I swear by the
LORD, if you do not go out, surely not a man will pass the night with you, and this will be
worse for you than all the evil that has come upon you from your youth until now."

David Restored as King

19:8 2 Sam 15:2; 18:24; 2 Sam 18:17
8 So the king arose and sat in the gate. When they told all the people, saying, "Behold, the king is sitting in the gate," then all the people came before the king.
Now Israel had fled, each to his tent.
19:9 2 Sam 8:1-14; 2 Sam 5:20; 8:1; 2 Sam 15:14
9 All the people were quarreling throughout all the tribes of Israel, saying, "The king
delivered us from the hand of our enemies and saved us from the hand of the Philistines,
but now he has fled out of the land from Absalom.
10 "However, Absalom, whom we anointed over us, has died in battle. Now then, why
are you silent about bringing the king back?"
19:11 2 Sam 15:29
11 Then King David sent to Zadok and Abiathar the priests, saying, "Speak to the el-
19:12 2 Sam 5:1
ders of Judah, saying, 'Why are you the last to bring the king back to his house, since the
word of all Israel has come to the king, *even* to his house?
19:13 2 Sam 17:25; 1 Kin 19:2; 2 Sam 8:16; 2 Sam 3:27-39; 19:5-7
12 'You are my brothers; you are my bone and my flesh. Why then should you be the
last to bring back the king?'
13 "Say to Amasa, 'Are you not my bone and my flesh? May God do so to me, and more
also, if you will not be commander of the army before me continually in place of Joab.' "
19:14 Judg 20:1
14 Thus he turned the hearts of all the men of Judah as one man, so that they sent
word to the king, *saying,* "Return, you and all your servants."
19:15 Josh 5:9; 1 Sam 11:14, 15
15 The king then returned and came as far as the Jordan. And Judah came to Gilgal in
order to go to meet the king, to bring the king across the Jordan.
19:16 2 Sam 16:5-13; 1 Kin 2:8
16 Then Shimei the son of Gera, the Benjamite who was from Bahurim, hurried and
came down with the men of Judah to meet King David.

18:33 Why was David so upset over the death of his rebel son? (1) David realized that he, in part, was responsible for Absalom's death. Nathan, the prophet, had said that because David had killed Uriah, his own sons would rebel against him. (2) David was angry at Joab and his officers for killing Absalom against his wishes. (3) David truly loved his son, even though Absalom did nothing to deserve his love. It would have been kinder and more loving to deal with Absalom and his runaway ego when he was younger.

19:4–7 At times we must reprove those in authority over us. Joab knew he was risking the king's displeasure by confronting him, but he saw what had to be done. Joab told David that there would be dreadful consequences if he didn't commend the troops for their victory. Joab's actions are a helpful example to us when personal confrontation is necessary.

19:8 David sat at the city gate because that was where business was conducted and judgment rendered. His presence there showed that he was over his mourning and back in control.

19:8–10 Just a few days before, most of Israel was supporting the rebel ruler Absalom. Now the people wanted David back as their king. Because crowds are often fickle, there must be a higher moral code to follow than the pleasure of the majority. Following the moral principles given in God's Word will help you avoid being swayed by the popular opinions of the crowd.

19:13 David's appointment of Amasa was a shrewd political move. First, Amasa had been commander of Absalom's army; by making Amasa his commander, David would secure the allegiance of the rebel army. Second, by replacing Joab as commander in chief, David punished him for his previous crimes (3:26–29). Third, Amasa had a great deal of influence over the leaders of Judah (19:14). All of these moves would help to unite the kingdom.

17 There were a thousand men of Benjamin with him, with Ziba the servant of the house
of Saul, and his fifteen sons and his twenty servants with him; and they rushed to the
Jordan before the king.
18 Then they kept crossing the ford to bring over the king's household, and to do what
was good in his sight. And Shimei the son of Gera fell down before the king as he was
about to cross the Jordan.
19 So he said to the king, "Let not my lord consider me guilty, nor remember what
your servant did wrong on the day when my lord the king came out from Jerusalem, so
that the king would take *it* to heart.
20 "For your servant knows that I have sinned; therefore behold, I have come today,
the first of all the house of Joseph to go down to meet my lord the king."
21 But Abishai the son of Zeruiah said, "Should not Shimei be put to death for this,
because he cursed the LORD'S anointed?"
22 David then said, "What have I to do with you, O sons of Zeruiah, that you should
this day be an adversary to me? Should any man be put to death in Israel today? For do
I not know that I am king over Israel today?"
23 The king said to Shimei, "You shall not die." Thus the king swore to him.
24 Then Mephibosheth the [17]son of Saul came down to meet the king; and he had neither cared for his feet, nor trimmed his mustache, nor washed his clothes, from the day
the king departed until the day he came *home* in peace.
25 It was when he came from Jerusalem to meet the king, that the king said to him,
"Why did you not go with me, Mephibosheth?"
26 So he answered, "O my lord, the king, my servant deceived me; for your servant
said, 'I will saddle a donkey for myself that I may ride on it and go with the king,' because your servant is lame.
27 "Moreover, he has slandered your servant to my lord the king; but my lord the king
is like the angel of God, therefore do what is good in your sight.
28 "For all my father's household was nothing but dead men before my lord the king;
yet you set your servant among those who ate at your own table. What right do I have yet
that I should complain anymore to the king?"
29 So the king said to him, "Why do you still speak of your affairs? I have decided,
'You and Ziba shall divide the land.' "
30 Mephibosheth said to the king, "Let him even take it all, since my lord the king has
come safely to his own house."
31 Now Barzillai the Gileadite had come down from Rogelim; and he went on to the
Jordan with the king to escort him over the Jordan.
32 Now Barzillai was very old, being eighty years old; and he had sustained the king
while he stayed at Mahanaim, for he was a very great man.
33 The king said to Barzillai, "You cross over with me and I will sustain you in Jerusalem with me."
34 But Barzillai said to the king, "How long have I yet to live, that I should go up with
the king to Jerusalem?
35 "I am now eighty years old. Can I distinguish between good and bad? Or can your
servant taste what I eat or what I drink? Or can I hear anymore the voice of singing men
and women? Why then should your servant be an added burden to my lord the king?
36 "Your servant would merely cross over the Jordan with the king. Why should the king
compensate me *with* this reward?
37 "Please let your servant return, that I may die in my own city near the grave of my
father and my mother. However, here is your servant Chimham, let him cross over with
my lord the king, and do for him what is good in your sight."
38 The king answered, "Chimham shall cross over with me, and I will do for him what
is good in your sight; and whatever you require of me, I will do for you."

17 I.e. grandson

19:17 2 Sam 16:1-4; 19:26, 27
19:19 1 Sam 22:15; 2 Sam 16:6-8
19:20 2 Sam 16:5
19:21 2 Sam 16:7, 8; Ex 22:28
19:22 2 Sam 3:39; 16:9, 10; 1 Sam 11:13
19:23 1 Kin 2:8
19:24 2 Sam 9:6-10; 2 Sam 12:20; Ex 19:10
19:25 2 Sam 16:17
19:26 2 Sam 9:3
19:27 2 Sam 16:3, 4; 2 Sam 14:17, 20
19:28 2 Sam 21:6-9; 2 Sam 9:7, 10, 13
19:31 2 Sam 17:27-29; 1 Kin 2:7
19:32 2 Sam 17:27-29
19:34 Gen 47:8
19:35 Ps 90:10; Eccl 2:8; Is 5:11, 12; 2 Sam 15:33
19:37 2 Sam 19:40; 1 Kin 2:7; Jer 41:17

19:19–20 By admitting his wrong and asking David's forgiveness, Shimei was trying to save his own life. His plan worked for a while. This was a day of celebration, not execution. But we read in 1 Kings 2:8–9 that David advised Solomon to execute Shimei.

19:21ff David showed tremendous mercy and generosity as he returned to Jerusalem. He spared Shimei, restored Mephibosheth, and rewarded faithful Barzillai. David's fairness sets a standard for government that will be fully realized in Christ's righteous rule in the coming kingdom.

19:24–30 David could not be certain if Mephibosheth or Ziba was in the right, and Scripture leaves the question unanswered. (For the whole story on Mephibosheth, see also 9:1–13 and 16:1–4.)

19:39 Gen 31:55; Ruth 1:14; 2 Sam 14:33
19:40 2 Sam 19:9, 10
19:41 Judg 8:1; 12:1; 2 Sam 19:11, 12
19:42 2 Sam 19:12
19:43 2 Sam 5:1; 1 Kin 11:30, 31

39 All the people crossed over the Jordan and the king crossed too. The king then kissed
Barzillai and blessed him, and he returned to his place.
40 Now the king went on to Gilgal, and Chimham went on with him; and all the people
of Judah and also half the people of Israel accompanied the king.
41 And behold, all the men of Israel came to the king and said to the king, "Why had
our brothers the men of Judah stolen you away, and brought the king and his household
and all David's men with him over the Jordan?"
42 Then all the men of Judah answered the men of Israel, "Because the king is a close
relative to us. Why then are you angry about this matter? Have we eaten at all at the
king's *expense,* or has anything been taken for us?"
43 But the men of Israel answered the men of Judah and said, "We have ten parts in
the king, therefore we also have more *claim* on David than you. Why then did you treat
us with contempt? Was it not our advice first to bring back our king?" Yet the words of
the men of Judah were harsher than the words of the men of Israel.

JOAB

Joab, the great military leader, had two brothers who were also famous soldiers: Abishai and Asahel. Joab proved to be the greatest leader of the three and was the commander of David's army throughout most of David's reign. There is no record that his troops ever lost a battle.

Joab was a fearless fighter like his brothers. Unlike them, he was also a brilliant and ruthless strategist. His plans usually worked, but he was seldom concerned about those hurt or killed by them. He did not hesitate to use treachery or murder to achieve his goals. His career is a story of great accomplishments and shameful acts. He conquered Jerusalem and the surrounding nations, defeated Abner, and reconciled Absalom and David. But he also murdered Abner, Amasa, and Absalom, took part in Uriah's murder, and plotted with Adonijah against Solomon. That plot led to his execution.

Joab set his own standards—he lived by them and died because of them. There is little evidence that Joab ever acknowledged God's standards. On one occasion he confronted David about the danger of taking a census without God's command, but this may have been little more than a move to protect himself. Joab's self-centeredness eventually destroyed him. He was loyal only to himself, even willing to betray his lifelong relationship with David to preserve his power.

Joab's life illustrates the disastrous results of having no source of direction outside oneself. Brilliance and power are self-destructive without God's guidance. Only God can give the direction we need. For that reason, he has made available his Word, the Bible, and he is willing to be personally present in the lives of those who admit their need for him.

Strengths and accomplishments:
- Brilliant planner and strategist
- Fearless fighter and resourceful commander
- Confident leader who did not hesitate to confront even the king
- Helped reconcile David and Absalom
- Masterminded the conquest of Jerusalem

Weaknesses and mistakes:
- Was repeatedly ruthless, violent, and vengeful
- Carried out David's scheme to have Uriah, Bathsheba's husband, killed
- Avenged his brother's murder by murdering Abner
- Killed Absalom against David's orders
- Plotted with Adonijah against David and Solomon

Lessons from his life:
- Those who live by violence often die by violence
- Even brilliant leaders need guidance

Vital statistics:
- Occupation: Commander in chief of David's army
- Relatives: Mother: Zeruiah. Brothers: Abishai, Asahel. Uncle: David
- Contemporaries: Saul, Abner, Absalom

Key verse:
"The king said to [Benaiah], 'Do as he has spoken and fall upon him and bury him, that you may remove from me and from my father's house the blood which Joab shed without cause' " (1 Kings 2:31).

Joab's story is told in 2 Samuel 2—1 Kings 2. He is also mentioned in 1 Chronicles 2:16; 11:5–9, 20, 26; 19:8–15; 20:1; 21:2–6; 26:28; and in the title of Psalm 60.

Sheba's Revolt

20 Now a worthless fellow happened to be there whose name was Sheba, the son of
Bichri, a Benjamite; and he blew the trumpet and said,
"We have no portion in David,
Nor do we have inheritance in the son of Jesse;
Every man to his tents, O Israel!"

20:1 2 Sam 16:7; Gen 46:21; 2 Sam 19:43; 1 Kin 12:16; 1 Sam 22:7-9; 1 Sam 13:2; 2 Sam 18:17; 2 Chr 10:16

2 So all the men of Israel withdrew from following David *and* followed Sheba the son
of Bichri; but the men of Judah remained steadfast to their king, from the Jordan even
to Jerusalem.
3 Then David came to his house at Jerusalem, and the king took the ten women, the
concubines whom he had left to keep the house, and placed them under guard and provided them with sustenance, but did not go in to them. So they were shut up until the day
of their death, living as widows.

20:3 2 Sam 15:16; 16:21, 22

4 Then the king said to Amasa, "Call out the men of Judah for me within three days,
and be present here yourself."

20:4 2 Sam 17:25; 19:13

5 So Amasa went to call out *the men of* Judah, but he delayed longer than the set time
which he had appointed him.

20:5 1 Sam 13:8

6 And David said to Abishai, "Now Sheba the son of Bichri will do us more harm than
Absalom; take your lord's servants and pursue him, so that he does not find for himself
fortified cities and escape from our sight."

20:6 2 Sam 21:17; 2 Sam 11:11; 1 Kin 1:33

7 So Joab's men went out after him, along with the Cherethites and the Pelethites
and all the mighty men; and they went out from Jerusalem to pursue Sheba the son of
Bichri.

20:7 2 Sam 8:18; 1 Kin 1:38

8 When they were at the large stone which is in Gibeon, Amasa came to meet them.
Now Joab was dressed in his military attire, and over it was a belt with a sword in its
sheath fastened at his waist; and as he went forward, it fell out.

20:8 2 Sam 2:13; 3:30

9 Joab said to Amasa, "Is it well with you, my brother?" And Joab took Amasa by the
beard with his right hand to kiss him.

20:9 Matt 26:49

Amasa Murdered

10 But Amasa was not on guard against the sword which was in Joab's hand so he struck
him in the belly with it and poured out his inward parts on the ground, and did not *strike*
him again, and he died. Then Joab and Abishai his brother pursued Sheba the son of
Bichri.

20:10 2 Sam 2:23; 3:27; 1 Kin 2:5

11 Now there stood by him one of Joab's young men, and said, "Whoever favors Joab
and whoever is for David, *let him* follow Joab."

20:11 2 Sam 20:13

12 But Amasa lay wallowing in *his* blood in the middle of the highway. And when the
man saw that all the people stood still, he removed Amasa from the highway into the field
and threw a garment over him when he saw that everyone who came by him stood still.

Revolt Put Down

13 As soon as he was removed from the highway, all the men passed on after Joab to
pursue Sheba the son of Bichri.
14 Now he went through all the tribes of Israel to Abel, even Beth-maacah, and all the
Berites; and they were gathered together and also went after him.
15 They came and besieged him in Abel Beth-maacah, and they cast up a siege ramp
against the city, and it stood by the rampart; and all the people who were with Joab were
wreaking destruction in order to topple the wall.

20:15 1 Kin 15:20; 2 Kin 15:29; 2 Kin 19:32; Ezek 4:2

16 Then a wise woman called from the city, "Hear, hear! Please tell Joab, 'Come here
that I may speak with you.' "

20:16 2 Sam 14:2

20:1 Although Israel was a united kingdom, it was still made up of 12 separate tribes. These tribes often had difficulty agreeing on the goals of the nation as a whole. Tribal jealousies had originally kept Israel from completely conquering the promised land (read the book of Joshua), and now tribal jealousies were threatening the stability of David's reign by giving Sheba an opportunity to rebel (20:1ff).

20:7–10 Once again Joab's murderous act went unpunished, just as it did when he killed Abner (3:26–27). Eventually, however, justice caught up with him (1 Kings 2:28–35). It may seem that sin and treachery often go unpunished, but God's justice is not limited to this life's rewards. Even if Joab had died of old age, he would have to face the day of judgment.

20:16ff Joab's men were attacking the city, and it looked as if it would be destroyed. Though women in that society were usually quiet in public, this woman spoke out. She stopped Joab's attack, not with weapons, but with wise words and a plan of action. Often the courage to speak a few sensible words can prevent great disaster.

17 So he approached her, and the woman said, "Are you Joab?" And he answered, "I am." Then she said to him, "Listen to the words of your maidservant." And he answered, "I am listening."
18 Then she spoke, saying, "Formerly they used to say, 'They will surely ask *advice* at Abel,' and thus they ended *the dispute*.

20:19 Deut 20:10; 1 Sam 26:19; 2 Sam 14:16; 21:3

19 "I am of those who are peaceable *and* faithful in Israel. You are seeking to destroy a city, even a mother in Israel. Why would you swallow up the inheritance of the LORD?"
20 Joab replied, "Far be it, far be it from me that I should swallow up or destroy!

20:21 Josh 24:33; 2 Sam 20:2

21 "Such is not the case. But a man from the hill country of Ephraim, Sheba the son of Bichri by name, has lifted up his hand against King David. Only hand him over, and I will depart from the city." And the woman said to Joab, "Behold, his head will be thrown to you over the wall."

20:22 2 Sam 20:16; Eccl 9:13-16; 2 Sam 20:1

22 Then the woman wisely came to all the people. And they cut off the head of Sheba the son of Bichri and threw it to Joab. So he blew the trumpet, and they were dispersed from the city, each to his tent. Joab also returned to the king at Jerusalem.

20:23 2 Sam 8:16-18; 1 Kin 4:3-6

23 Now Joab was over the whole army of Israel, and Benaiah the son of Jehoiada was over the Cherethites and the Pelethites;

20:24 1 Kin 4:3

24 and Adoram was over the forced labor, and Jehoshaphat the son of Ahilud was the recorder;

20:25 1 Kin 4:4

25 and Sheva was scribe, and Zadok and Abiathar were priests;
26 and Ira the Jairite was also a priest to David.

4. The later years of David's rule

Gibeonite Revenge

21:1 Gen 12:10; 26:1; 42:5; Num 27:21

21 Now there was a famine in the days of David for three years, year after year; and David sought the presence of the LORD. And the LORD said, "It is for Saul and his bloody house, because he put the Gibeonites to death."

21:2 Josh 9:3, 15-20

2 So the king called the Gibeonites and spoke to them (now the Gibeonites were not of the sons of Israel but of the remnant of the Amorites, and the sons of Israel made a covenant with them, but Saul had sought to kill them in his zeal for the sons of Israel and Judah).

21:3 1 Sam 26:19; 2 Sam 20:19

3 Thus David said to the Gibeonites, "What should I do for you? And how can I make atonement that you may bless the inheritance of the LORD?"

21:4 Num 35:31, 32

4 Then the Gibeonites said to him, "We have no *concern* of silver or gold with Saul or his house, nor is it for us to put any man to death in Israel." And he said, "I will do for you whatever you say."

SHEBA'S REBELLION
After defeating Absalom, David returned to Jerusalem from Mahanaim. But Sheba incited a rebellion against David, so David sent Joab, Abishai, and a small army after him. Joab and his troops besieged Abel Beth-maacah, Sheba's hideout, until the people of Abel Beth-maacah killed Sheba themselves.

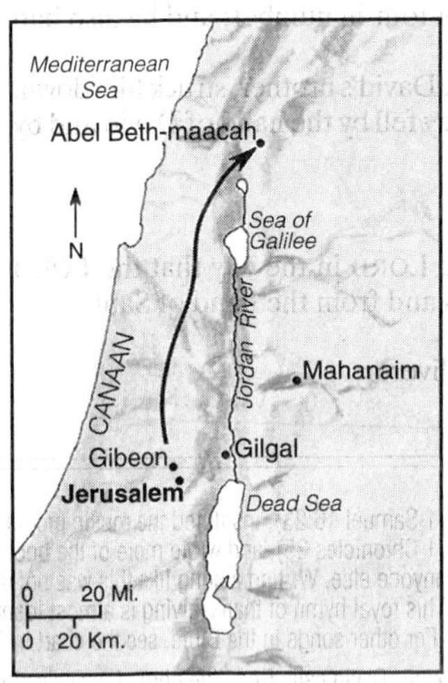

20:23 Benaiah was the captain of David's bodyguard and a famous member of that special group of mighty men called "the thirty" (23:24). He remained loyal to David during Absalom's rebellion. Later he helped establish Solomon as king (1 Kings 1:32–40; 2:28–34) and eventually replaced Joab as commander of Israel's army (1 Kings 2:35).

21:1 Farmers relied heavily on spring and fall rains for their crops. If the rains stopped or came at the wrong time, or if the plants became insect infested, there would be drastic food shortages in the coming year. Agriculture at that time was completely dependent upon natural conditions. There were no irrigation sprinklers, fertilizers, or pesticides. Even moderate variations in rainfall or insect activity could destroy an entire harvest.

21:1ff The next four chapters are an appendix to the book. The events described are not presented in chronological order. They tell of David's exploits at various times during his reign.

21:1–14 Although the Bible does not record Saul's act of vengeance against the Gibeonites, it was apparently a serious crime making him guilty of their blood. Still, why were Saul's sons killed for the murders their father committed? In many Near Eastern cultures, including Israel's, an entire family was held guilty for the crime of the father because the family was considered an indissoluble unit. Saul broke the vow that the Israelites had made to the Gibeonites (Joshua 9:16–20). This was a serious offense against God's Law (Numbers 30:1–2). Either David was following the custom of treating the family as a unit, or Saul's sons were guilty of helping Saul kill the Gibeonites.

5 So they said to the king, "The man who consumed us and who planned to exterminate us from remaining within any border of Israel,
6 let seven men from his sons be given to us, and we will hang them before the LORD
in Gibeah of Saul, the chosen of the LORD." And the king said, "I will give *them.*"
7 But the king spared Mephibosheth, the son of Jonathan the son of Saul, because of
the oath of the LORD which was between them, between David and Saul's son Jonathan.
8 So the king took the two sons of Rizpah the daughter of Aiah, Armoni and Mephibosheth whom she had borne to Saul, and the five sons of Merab the daughter of
Saul, whom she had borne to Adriel the son of Barzillai the Meholathite.
9 Then he gave them into the hands of the Gibeonites, and they hanged them in the
mountain before the LORD, so that the seven of them fell together; and they were put to
death in the first days of harvest at the beginning of barley harvest.
10 And Rizpah the daughter of Aiah took sackcloth and spread it for herself on the
rock, from the beginning of harvest until it rained on them from the sky; and she allowed
neither the birds of the sky to rest on them by day nor the beasts of the field by night.
11 When it was told David what Rizpah the daughter of Aiah, the concubine of Saul,
had done,
12 then David went and took the bones of Saul and the bones of Jonathan his son from
the men of Jabesh-gilead, who had stolen them from the open square of Beth-shan, where
the Philistines had hanged them on the day the Philistines struck down Saul in Gilboa.
13 He brought up the bones of Saul and the bones of Jonathan his son from there, and
they gathered the bones of those who had been hanged.
14 They buried the bones of Saul and Jonathan his son in the country of Benjamin in
Zela, in the grave of Kish his father; thus they did all that the king commanded, and
after that God was moved by prayer for the land.
15 Now when the Philistines were at war again with Israel, David went down and his
servants with him; and as they fought against the Philistines, David became weary.
16 Then Ishbi-benob, who was among the descendants of the giant, the weight of whose
spear was three hundred *shekels* of bronze in weight, was girded with a new *sword,* and
he intended to kill David.
17 But Abishai the son of Zeruiah helped him, and struck the Philistine and killed him.
Then the men of David swore to him, saying, "You shall not go out again with us to battle, so that you do not extinguish the lamp of Israel."
18 Now it came about after this that there was war again with the Philistines at Gob; then
Sibbecai the Hushathite struck down Saph, who was among the descendants of the giant.
19 There was war with the Philistines again at Gob, and Elhanan the son of Jaare-oregim
the Bethlehemite killed Goliath the Gittite, the shaft of whose spear was like a weaver's
beam.
20 There was war at Gath again, where there was a man of *great* stature who had six
fingers on each hand and six toes on each foot, twenty-four in number; and he also had
been born to the giant.
21 When he defied Israel, Jonathan the son of Shimei, David's brother, struck him down.
22 These four were born to the giant in Gath, and they fell by the hand of David and by
the hand of his servants.

David's Psalm of Deliverance

22 And David spoke the words of this song to the LORD in the day that the LORD
delivered him from the hand of all his enemies and from the hand of Saul.
2 He said,
"The LORD is my rock and my fortress and my deliverer;
3 My God, my rock, in whom I take refuge,

21:5 2 Sam 21:1
21:6 Num 25:4; 1 Sam 10:24
21:7 2 Sam 4:4; 9:10; 1 Sam 18:3; 20:12-17; 23:18; 2 Sam 9:1-7
21:8 2 Sam 3:7; 1 Sam 18:19; 1 Kin 19:16
21:9 Ex 9:31, 32
21:10 Deut 21:23; 1 Sam 17:44, 46
21:12 1 Sam 31:11-13; Josh 17:11; 1 Sam 31:10; 1 Sam 31:3, 4
21:14 Josh 18:28; Josh 7:26; 2 Sam 24:25
21:15 2 Sam 5:17-25
21:16 Num 13:22, 28; Josh 15:14; 2 Sam 21:18-22
21:17 2 Sam 20:6-10; 2 Sam 18:3; 2 Sam 22:29 1 Kin 11:36
21:18 1 Chr 20:4-8; 1 Chr 11:29; 27:11
21:19 1 Sam 17:7
21:20 2 Sam 21:16, 18
21:22 1 Chr 20:8
22:1 Ps 18:2-50; Ex 15:1; Deut 31:30
22:2 1 Sam 23:25; 24:2; Ps 31:3; 71:3
22:3 Deut 32:4, 37; 1 Sam 2:2; Gen 15:1; Deut 33:29; Luke 1:69; Ps 9:9

21:9–10 The barley harvest was in late April and early May. Barley was similar to wheat but less suitable for breadmaking. Rizpah guarded the men's bodies during the entire harvest season, which lasted from April to October.

21:16–18 For more information on giants, see 1 Samuel 17:4–7 and the note on Genesis 6:4.

22:1ff David was a skilled musician who played his harp for Saul (1 Samuel 16:23), instituted the music programs in the temple (1 Chronicles 25), and wrote more of the book of Psalms than anyone else. Writing a song like this was not unusual for David. This royal hymn of thanksgiving is almost identical to Psalm 18. (For other songs in the Bible, see the chart in Exodus 15.)

22:3 David calls God "the horn of my salvation," referring to the strength and defensive protection animals have in their horns. God had helped David overcome his enemies and rescued him from his foes.

My shield and the horn of my salvation, my stronghold and my refuge;
My savior, You save me from violence.
4 "I call upon the LORD, who is worthy to be praised,
And I am saved from my enemies.
5 "For the waves of death encompassed me;
The torrents of destruction overwhelmed me;
6 The cords of Sheol surrounded me;
The snares of death confronted me.
7 "In my distress I called upon the LORD,
Yes, I cried to my God;
And from His temple He heard my voice,
And my cry for help *came* into His ears.
8 "Then the earth shook and quaked,
The foundations of heaven were trembling
And were shaken, because He was angry.
9 "Smoke went up out of His nostrils,
Fire from His mouth devoured;
Coals were kindled by it.
10 "He bowed the heavens also, and came down
With thick darkness under His feet.
11 "And He rode on a cherub and flew;
And He appeared on the wings of the wind.

22:4 Ps 48:1; 96:4
22:5 Ps 93:4; Jon 2:3; Ps 69:14, 15
22:6 Ps 116:3
22:7 Ps 116:4; 120:1
22:8 Judg 5:4; Ps 97:4; Job 26:11
22:9 Ps 97:3; Heb 12:29; 2 Sam 22:13
22:10 Ex 19:16; 1 Kin 8:12; Ps 97:2; Nah 1:3
22:11 2 Sam 6:2; Ps 104:3

ABISHAI

Most great leaders struggle with a few followers who try too hard. For David, Abishai was that kind of follower. His fierce loyalty to David had to be kept from becoming destructive—he was too willing to leap to his leader's defense. David never put down Abishai's eager loyalty. Instead, he patiently tried to direct its powerful energy. This approach, while not completely successful, saved David's life on at least one occasion. At three other times, however, Abishai would have killed for the king if David had not stopped him.

Abishai was an excellent soldier, but he was better at taking orders than giving them. When he wasn't carrying out David's orders, Abishai was usually under the command of his younger brother Joab. The two brothers helped each other accomplish great military feats as well as shameful acts of violence—Abishai helped Joab murder Abner and Amasa. When he was effective as a leader, he led mostly by example. But all too often he did not think before he acted.

We should be challenged by Abishai's admirable qualities of fearlessness and loyalty, but we should be warned by his tendency to act without thinking. It is not enough to be strong and effective; we must also have the self-control and wisdom that God can give us. We are to follow and obey with our hearts and our minds.

Strengths and accomplishments:
- Known as one of the heroes among David's fighting men
- A fearless and willing volunteer, fiercely loyal to David
- Saved David's life

Weaknesses and mistakes:
- Tended to act without thinking
- Helped Joab murder Abner and Amasa

Lessons from his life:
- The most effective followers combine careful thought and action
- Blind loyalty can cause great evil

Vital statistics:
- Occupation: Soldier
- Relatives: Mother: Zeruiah. Brothers: Joab and Asahel. Uncle: David

Key verses:
"Abishai, the brother of Joab, the son of Zeruiah, was chief of the thirty. And he swung his spear against three hundred and killed them, and had a name as well as the three. He was most honored of the thirty, therefore he became their commander; however, he did not attain to the three" (2 Samuel 23:18–19).

Abishai's story is told in 2 Samuel 2:18—23:19. He is also mentioned in 1 Samuel 26:1–13; 1 Chronicles 2:16; 11:20; 18:12; 19:11, 15.

22:11 Cherubim (plural of cherub) are mighty angels.

12 "And He made darkness canopies around Him,
A mass of waters, thick clouds of the sky.
13 "From the brightness before Him
Coals of fire were kindled.
14 "The LORD thundered from heaven,
And the Most High uttered His voice.
15 "And He sent out arrows, and scattered them,
Lightning, and routed them.
16 "Then the channels of the sea appeared,
The foundations of the world were laid bare
By the rebuke of the LORD,
At the blast of the breath of His nostrils.
17 "He sent from on high, He took me;
He drew me out of many waters.
18 "He delivered me from my strong enemy,
From those who hated me, for they were too strong for me.
19 "They confronted me in the day of my calamity,
But the LORD was my support.
20 "He also brought me forth into a broad place;
He rescued me, because He delighted in me.
21 "The LORD has rewarded me according to my righteousness;
According to the cleanness of my hands He has recompensed me.
22 "For I have kept the ways of the LORD,
And have not acted wickedly against my God.
23 "For all His ordinances *were* before me,
And *as for* His statutes, I did not depart from them.
24 "I was also blameless toward Him,
And I kept myself from my iniquity.
25 "Therefore the LORD has recompensed me according to my righteousness,
According to my cleanness before His eyes.
26 "With the kind You show Yourself kind,
With the blameless You show Yourself blameless;
27 With the pure You show Yourself pure,
And with the perverted You show Yourself astute.
28 "And You save an afflicted people;
But Your eyes are on the haughty *whom* You abase.
29 "For You are my lamp, O LORD;
And the LORD illumines my darkness.
30 "For by You I can [18]run upon a troop;
By my God I can leap over a wall.
31 "As for God, His way is blameless;
The word of the LORD is tested;
He is a shield to all who take refuge in Him.
32 "For who is God, besides the LORD?
And who is a rock, besides our God?
33 "God is my strong fortress;
And He sets the blameless in His way.
34 "He makes my feet like hinds' *feet,*
And sets me on my high places.
35 "He trains my hands for battle,
So that my arms can bend a bow of bronze.
36 "You have also given me the shield of Your salvation,
And Your help makes me great.

22:12 Job 36:29
22:13 2 Sam 22:9
22:14 Job 37:2-5; Ps 29:3
22:15 Deut 32:23; Josh 10:10; 1 Sam 7:10
22:16 Ex 15:8; Nah 1:4
22:17 Ps 144:7; Ex 2:10
22:19 Ps 23:4
22:20 Ps 31:8; 118:5; 2 Sam 15:26
22:21 1 Sam 26:23; 1 Kin 8:32; Ps 24:4
22:22 Gen 18:19; Ps 128:1; Prov 8:32
22:23 Deut 6:6-9; Ps 119:30, 102
22:24 Gen 6:9; 7:1; Eph 1:4; Col 1:21, 22
22:25 2 Sam 22:21
22:26 Matt 5:7
22:27 Matt 5:8; 1 John 3:3; Lev 26:23, 24
22:28 Ex 3:7, 8; Ps 72:12, 13; Is 2:11, 12, 17; 5:15
22:29 2 Sam 21:17; 1 Kin 11:36; Ps 27:1
22:30 2 Sam 5:6-8
22:31 Deut 32:4; Matt 5:48; Ps 12:6; 119:140; Prov 30:5; 2 Sam 22:3; Ps 84:9
22:32 1 Sam 2:2
22:33 2 Sam 22:2
22:34 2 Sam 2:18; Hab 3:19; Deut 32:13
22:35 Ps 144:1; Job 20:24
22:36 Eph 6:16, 17

18 Or *crush a troop*

22:22–24 David was not denying that he had ever sinned. Psalm 51 shows his tremendous anguish over his sin against Uriah and Bathsheba. But David understood God's faithfulness and was writing this hymn from God's perspective. He knew that God had made him clean again—"whiter than snow," (Psalm 51:7) with a "clean heart" (Psalm 51:10). Through the death and resurrection of Jesus Christ, we also are made clean and perfect. God replaces our sin with his purity, and he no longer sees our sin.

22:27 "With the perverted You show Yourself astute" means that to those who sin, God is a judge who will punish them for their sins. God destroys those who are evil.

22:37
2 Sam 22:20; Prov 4:12

22:39
Mal 4:3

22:40
Ps 44:5

22:41
Ex 23:27; Josh 10:24

22:42
Is 17:7, 8; 1 Sam 28:6; Is 1:15

22:43
2 Kin 13:7; Is 10:6; Mic 7:10

22:44
2 Sam 3:1; 19:9, 14; 2 Sam 8:1-14; Is 55:5

22:45
Ps 66:3; 81:15

22:46
1 Sam 14:11; Mic 7:17

22:47
2 Sam 22:3; Ps 89:26

22:48
1 Sam 24:12; 25:39; 2 Sam 4:8; Ps 94:1; Ps 144:2

22:49
Ps 44:5; Ps 140:1, 4

22:50
Rom 15:9

22:51
Ps 144:10; Ps 89:24; 2 Sam 7:12-16

37 "You enlarge my steps under me,
And my feet have not slipped.
38 "I pursued my enemies and destroyed them,
And I did not turn back until they were consumed.
39 "And I have devoured them and shattered them, so that they did not rise;
And they fell under my feet.
40 "For You have girded me with strength for battle;
You have subdued under me those who rose up against me.
41 "You have also made my enemies turn *their* backs to me,
And I destroyed those who hated me.
42 "They looked, but there was none to save;
Even to the LORD, but He did not answer them.
43 "Then I pulverized them as the dust of the earth;
I crushed *and* stamped them as the mire of the streets.
44 "You have also delivered me from the contentions of my people;
You have kept me as head of the nations;
A people whom I have not known serve me.
45 "Foreigners pretend obedience to me;
As soon as they hear, they obey me.
46 "Foreigners lose heart,
And come trembling out of their fortresses.
47 "The LORD lives, and blessed be my rock;
And exalted be God, the rock of my salvation,
48 The God who executes vengeance for me,
And brings down peoples under me,
49 Who also brings me out from my enemies;
You even lift me above those who rise up against me;
You rescue me from the violent man.
50 "Therefore I will give thanks to You, O LORD, among the nations,
And I will sing praises to Your name.
51 "*He* is a tower of [19]deliverance to His king,
And shows lovingkindness to His anointed,
To David and his descendants forever."

David's Last Song

23:1
2 Sam 7:8, 9; Ps 78:70, 71; 1 Sam 16:12, 13; Ps 89:20

23:2
Matt 22:43; 2 Pet 1:21

23:3
2 Sam 22:2, 3, 32; Ps 72:1-3; Is 11:1-5; 2 Chr 19:7, 9

23 Now these are the last words of David.
David the son of Jesse declares,
The man who was raised on high declares,
The anointed of the God of Jacob,
And the sweet psalmist of Israel,
2 "The Spirit of the LORD spoke by me,
And His word was on my tongue.
3 "The God of Israel said,
The Rock of Israel spoke to me,
'He who rules over men righteously,

19 I.e. victories; lit *salvation*

David reveals many truths about God in his song of praise.

David says, "The LORD is my . . ."	rock, fortress, deliverer, refuge, shield, horn of salvation, stronghold, savior, lamp
David names these characteristics of God. He is:	saving, worthy of praise, hearing, angry (against enemies), rescuing, rewarding, seeing, faithful, showing (revealing) himself, shrewd, powerful, strong, perfect, pure, flawless, shielding (us from enemies), giving, gentle, preserving, living

---

23:3 In the style of a prophet, David spoke of a just and righteous ruler. This will be fulfilled in Jesus Christ when he returns to rule in perfect justice and peace. For similar prophecies, see Isaiah 11:1–10; Jeremiah 23:5, 6; 33:15–18; Zechariah 9:9, 10. For the fulfillment of some of these prophecies, see Matthew 4:14–16; Luke 24:25–27, 44–49; John 5:45–47; 8:28–29.

Who rules in the fear of God,
4 Is as the light of the morning *when* the sun rises,
A morning without clouds,
When the tender grass *springs* out of the earth,
Through sunshine after rain.'
5 "Truly is not my house so with God?
For He has made an everlasting covenant with me,
Ordered in all things, and secured;
For all my salvation and all *my* desire,
Will He not indeed make *it* grow?
6 "But the worthless, every one of them will be thrust away like thorns,
Because they cannot be taken in hand;
7 But the man who touches them
Must be armed with iron and the shaft of a spear,
And they will be completely burned with fire in *their* place."

23:4 Judg 5:31; Ps 72:6
23:5 2 Sam 7:12-16; Ps 89:29; Is 55:3
23:6 Matt 13:41
23:7 Matt 3:10; 13:30; Heb 6:8

His Mighty Men

8 These are the names of the mighty men whom David had: Josheb-basshebeth a
Tahchemonite, chief of the captains, he was *called* Adino the Eznite, because of eight
hundred slain *by him* at one time;
9 and after him was Eleazar the son of Dodo the Ahohite, one of the three mighty
men with David when they defied the Philistines who were gathered there to battle and
the men of Israel had withdrawn.
10 He arose and struck the Philistines until his hand was weary and clung to the sword,
and the LORD brought about a great victory that day; and the people returned after him
only to strip *the slain.*
11 Now after him was Shammah the son of Agee a Hararite. And the Philistines were
gathered into a troop where there was a plot of ground full of lentils, and the people fled
from the Philistines.
12 But he took his stand in the midst of the plot, defended it and struck the Philistines;
and the LORD brought about a great victory.
13 Then three of the thirty chief men went down and came to David in the harvest time
to the cave of Adullam, while the troop of the Philistines was camping in the valley of
Rephaim.
14 David was then in the stronghold, while the garrison of the Philistines was then in
Bethlehem.
15 David had a craving and said, "Oh that someone would give me water to drink from
the well of Bethlehem which is by the gate!"
16 So the three mighty men broke through the camp of the Philistines, and drew water
from the well of Bethlehem which was by the gate, and took *it* and brought *it* to David.
Nevertheless he would not drink it, but poured it out to the LORD;
17 and he said, "Be it far from me, O LORD, that I should do this. *Shall I drink* the
blood of the men who went in *jeopardy* of their lives?" Therefore he would not drink it.
These things the three mighty men did.
18 Abishai, the brother of Joab, the son of Zeruiah, was chief of the thirty. And he
swung his spear against three hundred and killed *them,* and had a name as well as the
three.
19 He was most honored of the thirty, therefore he became their commander; however, he did not attain to the three.
20 Then Benaiah the son of Jehoiada, the son of a valiant man of Kabzeel, who had
done mighty deeds, killed the two *sons of* Ariel of Moab. He also went down and killed
a lion in the middle of a pit on a snowy day.

23:8 1 Chr 11:11-47
23:9 1 Chr 27:4; 1 Chr 8:4
23:10 1 Chr 11:13; 1 Sam 11:13; 19:5
23:11 2 Sam 23:33
23:12 2 Sam 23:10
23:13 1 Sam 22:1; 2 Sam 5:18
23:14 1 Sam 22:4, 5
23:15 1 Chr 11:17
23:16 1 Chr 11:18; Gen 35:14
23:17 Lev 17:10
23:18 2 Sam 10:10, 14; 18:2; 1 Chr 11:20, 21
23:20 2 Sam 8:18; 20:23; Josh 15:21

23:8–39 These verses tell of some of the exploits that the special corps of David's army carried out. There were two elite groups of men: "the thirty" and "the three" (23:18, 23; 1 Chronicles 11:11–25). To become a member of such a group a man had to show unparalleled courage in battle as well as wisdom in leadership. "The three" was the most elite group. The list of "the thirty" actually contains 37 names, but it mentions some warriors known to be dead (Uriah, for example, in 23:39). Apparently, new members were appointed to replace those who had fallen in battle.

23:16 David poured out the water as an offering to God because he was so moved by the sacrifice it represented. When Hebrews offered sacrifices, they never consumed the blood. It represented life, and they poured it out before God. David would not drink this water that represented the lives of his soldiers. Instead, he offered it to God.

23:24 2 Sam 2:18
23:25 1 Chr 11:27; Judg 7:1
23:26 2 Sam 14:2
23:27 Josh 21:18
23:29 1 Chr 11:30
23:30 Judg 12:13, 15; Josh 24:30
23:31 2 Sam 3:16
23:32 Josh 19:42
23:33 2 Sam 23:11
23:34 2 Sam 10:6, 8; 20:14; 2 Sam 11:3
23:35 1 Chr 11:37

21 He killed an Egyptian, an impressive man. Now the Egyptian *had* a spear in his hand,
but he went down to him with a club and snatched the spear from the Egyptian's hand
and killed him with his own spear.
22 These *things* Benaiah the son of Jehoiada did, and had a name as well as the three
mighty men.
23 He was honored among the thirty, but he did not attain to the three. And David
appointed him over his guard.
24 Asahel the brother of Joab was among the thirty; Elhanan the son of Dodo of Bethlehem,
25 Shammah the Harodite, Elika the Harodite,
26 Helez the Paltite, Ira the son of Ikkesh the Tekoite,
27 Abiezer the Anathothite, Mebunnai the Hushathite,
28 Zalmon the Ahohite, Maharai the Netophathite,
29 Heleb the son of Baanah the Netophathite, Ittai the son of Ribai of Gibeah of the
sons of Benjamin,
30 Benaiah a Pirathonite, Hiddai of the brooks of Gaash,
31 Abi-albon the Arbathite, Azmaveth the Barhumite,
32 Eliahba the Shaalbonite, the sons of Jashen, Jonathan,
33 Shammah the Hararite, Ahiam the son of Sharar the Ararite,
34 Eliphelet the son of Ahasbai, the son of the Maacathite, Eliam the son of Ahithophel the Gilonite,
35 Hezro the Carmelite, Paarai the Arbite,
36 Igal the son of Nathan of Zobah, Bani the Gadite,

DAVID'S MIGHTY MEN

One way to understand David's success is to notice the kind of men who followed him. During the time he was being hunted by Saul, David gradually built a fighting force of several hundred men. Some were relatives; others were outcasts of society; many were in trouble with the law. They all had at least one trait in common—complete devotion to David. Their achievements made them famous. Among these men were elite military groups like "the three" and "the thirty." They were true heroes.

Scripture gives the impression that these men were motivated to greatness by the personal qualities of their leader. David inspired them to achieve beyond their goals and meet their true potential. Likewise, the leaders we follow and the causes to which we commit ourselves will affect our lives. David's effectiveness was clearly connected with his awareness of God's leading. He was a good leader when he was following *his* Leader. Do you know whom the people you respect most are following? Your answer should help you decide whether they deserve your loyalty. Do you also recognize God's leading in your life? No one can lead you to excellence as your Creator can.

Strengths and accomplishments:
- Able soldiers and military leaders
- Shared many special skills
- Though frequently outnumbered, were consistently victorious
- Loyal to David

Weakness and mistake:
- Often had little in common beyond their loyalty to David and their military expertise

Lessons from their lives:
- Greatness is often inspired by the quality and character of leadership
- Even a small force of able and loyal men can accomplish great feats

Vital statistics:
- Where: They came from all over Israel (primarily Judah and Benjamin), and from some of the other surrounding nations as well
- Occupations: Various backgrounds—almost all were fugitives

Key verses:
"So David departed from [Gath] and escaped to the cave of Adullam; and when his brothers and all his father's household heard of it, they went down there to him. Everyone who was in distress, and everyone who was in debt, and everyone who was discontented gathered to him; and he became captain over them. Now there were about four hundred men with him" (1 Samuel 22:1–2).

Their stories are told in 1 Samuel 22—2 Samuel 23:39. They are also mentioned in 1 Chronicles 11—12.

37 Zelek the Ammonite, Naharai the Beerothite, armor bearers of Joab the son of
Zeruiah,
38 Ira the Ithrite, Gareb the Ithrite,
39 Uriah the Hittite; thirty-seven in all.

The Census Taken

24 Now again the anger of the LORD burned against Israel, and it incited David against
them to say, "Go, number Israel and Judah."
2 The king said to Joab the commander of the army who was with him, "Go about
now through all the tribes of Israel, from Dan to Beersheba, and register the people,
that I may know the number of the people."
3 But Joab said to the king, "Now may the LORD your God add to the people a hundred times as many as they are, while the eyes of my lord the king *still* see; but why does
my lord the king delight in this thing?"
4 Nevertheless, the king's word prevailed against Joab and against the commanders
of the army. So Joab and the commanders of the army went out from the presence of the
king to register the people of Israel.
5 They crossed the Jordan and camped in Aroer, on the right side of the city that is in
the middle of the valley of Gad and toward Jazer.
6 Then they came to Gilead and to [20]the land of Tahtim-hodshi, and they came to
Dan-jaan and around to Sidon,
7 and came to the fortress of Tyre and to all the cities of the Hivites and of the Canaanites, and they went out to the south of Judah, *to* Beersheba.
8 So when they had gone about through the whole land, they came to Jerusalem at
the end of nine months and twenty days.
9 And Joab gave the number of the registration of the people to the king; and there
were in Israel eight hundred thousand valiant men who drew the sword, and the men of
Judah were five hundred thousand men.
10 Now David's heart troubled him after he had numbered the people. So David said
to the LORD, "I have sinned greatly in what I have done. But now, O LORD, please take
away the iniquity of Your servant, for I have acted very foolishly."
11 When David arose in the morning, the word of the LORD came to the prophet Gad,
David's seer, saying,
12 "Go and speak to David, 'Thus the LORD says, "I am offering you three things; choose
for yourself one of them, which I will do to you." ' "
13 So Gad came to David and told him, and said to him, "Shall seven years of famine
come to you in your land? Or will you flee three months before your foes while they pursue
you? Or shall there be three days' pestilence in your land? Now consider and see what
answer I shall return to Him who sent me."
14 Then David said to Gad, "I am in great distress. Let us now fall into the hand of the
LORD for His mercies are great, but do not let me fall into the hand of man."

23:37 2 Sam 4:2
23:38 1 Chr 2:53
23:39 2 Sam 11:3, 6
24:1 1 Chr 21:1; 2 Sam 21:1, 2; 1 Chr 27:23, 24
24:2 Judg 20:1; 2 Sam 3:10
24:3 Deut 1:11
24:5 Deut 2:36; Josh 13:9, 16; Num 21:32; 32:35
24:6 Josh 19:28; Judg 1:31
24:7 Josh 19:29; Josh 11:3; Judg 3:3; Gen 21:22-33
24:9 Num 1:44-46; 1 Chr 21:5
24:10 1 Sam 24:5; 2 Sam 12:13; 1 Sam 13:13; 2 Chr 16:9
24:11 1 Sam 22:5; 1 Chr 29:29; 1 Sam 9:9
24:13 1 Chr 21:12; Ezek 14:21
24:14 Ps 51:1; 130:4, 7

20 Or *Kadesh in the land of the Hittite*

24:1 Did God cause David to sin? God does not cause people to sin, but he does allow sinners to reveal the sinfulness of their hearts by their actions. God presented the opportunity to David in order to deal with a disastrous national tendency, and he wanted this desire to show itself. First Chronicles 21:1 says Satan incited David to do it. Hebrew writers do not always distinguish between primary and secondary causes. So if God allowed Satan to tempt David, to them it is as if God did it.

24:1–3 What was wrong with taking a census (numbering the people of Israel and Judah)? A census was commanded in Numbers to prepare an army for conquering the promised land (Numbers 1:2; 26:2). A census amounted to a draft or conscription for the army. The land was now at peace, so there was no need to enlist troops. Israel had extended its borders and become a recognized power. David's sin was pride and ambition in counting the people so that he could glory in the size of his nation and army, its power and defenses. By doing this, he put his faith in the size of his army rather than in God's ability to protect them regardless of their number. Even Joab knew a census was wrong, but David did not heed his advice. We sin in a similar way when we place our security in money, possessions, or the might of our nation.

24:12–14 Both David and the Israelites were guilty of sin (24:1). David's sin was pride, but the Bible does not say why God was angry with the people of Israel. Perhaps it was due to their support of the rebellions of Absalom (chapters 15—18) and Sheba (chapter 20), or perhaps they put their security in military and financial prosperity rather than God, as David did. God dealt with the whole nation through David who exemplified the national sin of pride.

God gave David three choices. Each was a form of punishment God had told the people they could expect if they disobeyed his laws (pestilence, disease—Deuteronomy 28:20–22; famine—28:23–24; war—28:25–26). David wisely chose the form of punishment that came most directly from God. He knew how brutal and harsh men in war could be, and he also knew God's great mercy. When you sin greatly, turn back to God. To be punished by him is far better than to take your chances without him.

Pestilence Sent

24:15 1 Chr 21:14; 27:24; 2 Sam 24:2

15 So the LORD sent a pestilence upon Israel from the morning until the appointed
time, and seventy thousand men of the people from Dan to Beersheba died.

24:16 Ex 12:23; 2 Kin 19:35; Acts 12:23; Ex 32:14; 1 Sam 15:11

16 When the angel stretched out his hand toward Jerusalem to destroy it, the LORD
relented from the calamity and said to the angel who destroyed the people, "It is enough!
Now relax your hand!" And the angel of the LORD was by the threshing floor of Araunah the Jebusite.

24:17 2 Sam 24:10; 2 Sam 7:8; Ps 74:1

17 Then David spoke to the LORD when he saw the angel who was striking down the
people, and said, "Behold, it is I who have sinned, and it is I who have done wrong; but
these sheep, what have they done? Please let Your hand be against me and against my
father's house."

David Builds an Altar

24:18 1 Chr 21:18

18 So Gad came to David that day and said to him, "Go up, erect an altar to the LORD
on the threshing floor of Araunah the Jebusite."
19 David went up according to the word of Gad, just as the LORD had commanded.
20 Araunah looked down and saw the king and his servants crossing over toward him;
and Araunah went out and bowed his face to the ground before the king.

24:21 Num 16:44-50

21 Then Araunah said, "Why has my lord the king come to his servant?" And David
said, "To buy the threshing floor from you, in order to build an altar to the LORD, that
the plague may be held back from the people."

24:22 1 Sam 6:14; 1 Kin 19:21

22 Araunah said to David, "Let my lord the king take and offer up what is good in his
sight. Look, the oxen for the burnt offering, the threshing sledges and the yokes of the
oxen for the wood.

24:23 Ezek 20:40, 41

23 "Everything, O king, Araunah gives to the king." And Araunah said to the king, "May
the LORD your God accept you."

24:24 Mal 1:13, 14; 1 Chr 21:24, 25

24 However, the king said to Araunah, "No, but I will surely buy *it* from you for a price,
for I will not offer burnt offerings to the LORD my God which cost me nothing." So David
bought the threshing floor and the oxen for fifty shekels of silver.

24:25 2 Sam 21:14

25 David built there an altar to the LORD and offered burnt offerings and peace offerings. Thus the LORD was moved by prayer for the land, and the plague was held back
from Israel.

24:18 Many believe that this threshing floor where David built the altar is the location where Abraham nearly sacrificed his son Isaac (Genesis 22:1–18). After David's death, Solomon built the temple on this spot. Centuries later, Jesus would teach and preach here.

24:25 The book of 2 Samuel describes David's reign. Since the Israelites first entered the promised land under Joshua, they had been struggling to unite the nation and drive out the wicked inhabitants. Now, after more than 400 years, Israel was finally at peace. David had accomplished what no leader before him, judge or king, had done. His administration was run on the principle of dedication to God and to the well-being of the people. Yet David also sinned. Despite his sins, however, the Bible calls David a man after God's own heart (1 Samuel 13:14; Acts 13:22) because when he sinned, he recognized it and confessed his sins to God. David committed his life to God and remained loyal to him throughout his lifetime. Psalms gives an even deeper insight into David's love for God.

1 KINGS

David becomes king 1010 B.C. | *Solomon becomes king 970* | *Temple completed 959* | *The kingdom divides 930* | *Shishak invades Jerusalem 925*

VITAL STATISTICS

PURPOSE:
To contrast the lives of those who live for God and those who refuse to do so through the history of the kings of Israel and Judah

AUTHOR:
Unknown. Possibly Jeremiah or a group of prophets

SETTING:
The once great nation of Israel turned into a land divided, not only physically, but also spiritually.

KEY VERSES:
"As for you, if you will walk before Me as your father David walked, in integrity of heart and uprightness, doing according to all that I have commanded you and will keep My statutes and My ordinances, then I will establish the throne of your kingdom over Israel forever, just as I promised to your father David, saying, 'You shall not lack a man on the throne of Israel' " (9:4–5).

KEY PEOPLE:
David, Solomon, Rehoboam, Jeroboam, Elijah, Ahab, Jezebel

SPECIAL FEATURE:
The books of 1 and 2 Kings were originally one book.

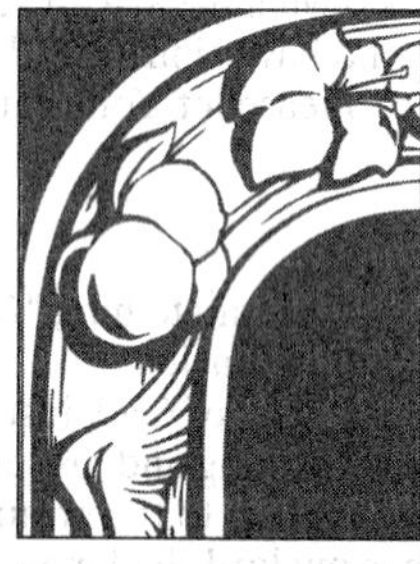

"I DON'T CARE what anyone says, I'm going to do it!" he yells at his mother as he storms out of the house.

This is a familiar scene in our society. The words change, but the essential message is the same: A person is *not* open to advice because his mind is closed. Some advice may be sought, but it is heeded only if it reinforces the decision already made or is an easier path to take. It is human nature to reject help and to do things *our* way.

A much wiser approach is to seek, hear, and heed the advice of good counselors. Solomon, the world's wisest man, urges this in Proverbs (see 11:14; 15:22; 24:6). How ironic that his son and successor, Rehoboam, listened instead to foolish advice, with devastating results. At Rehoboam's inauguration, he was petitioned by the people to be a kind and generous ruler. The older men counseled him to "serve them and grant them their petition" (12:7). But Rehoboam agreed to the cruel words of his peers who urged him to be harsh. As a result, Rehoboam split the kingdom. Learn from Rehoboam's mistake. Commit yourself to seeking and following wise counsel.

The main events of 1 Kings are David's death, Solomon's reign, the division of the kingdom, and Elijah's ministry. As Solomon ascended the throne, David charged him to obey God's laws and to "walk in His ways" (2:3). This Solomon did; and when given the choice of gifts from God, he humbly asked for wisdom (3:9). As a result, Solomon's reign began with great success, including the construction of the temple—his greatest achievement. Unfortunately, Solomon took many pagan wives and concubines who eventually turned his heart away from the Lord to their false gods (11:1–4).

Rehoboam succeeded Solomon and had the opportunity to be a wise, compassionate, and just king. Instead, he accepted the poor advice of his young friends and attempted to rule with an iron hand. But the people rebelled, and the kingdom split with 10 tribes in the north (Israel) ruled by Jeroboam, and only Judah and Benjamin remaining with Rehoboam. Both kingdoms wove a path through the reigns of corrupt and idolatrous kings with only the clear voice of the prophets continuing to warn and call the nation back to God.

Elijah is surely one of the greatest prophets, and chapters 17 through 22 feature his conflict with wicked Ahab and Jezebel in Israel. In one of the most dramatic confrontations in history, Elijah defeated the prophets of Baal at Mount Carmel. In spite of incredible opposition, Elijah stood for God and proves that *one plus God* is a majority. If God is on our side, no one can stand against us (Romans 8:31).

Asa becomes king of Judah 910	*Elijah begins his ministry 875*	*Ahab becomes king of Israel 874*	*Jehoshaphat becomes king of Judah 872*	*Ben-hadad attacks Samaria 857*	*Ahab dies in battle 853*

THE BLUEPRINT

A. THE UNITED KINGDOM (1:1—11:43)
1. Solomon becomes king
2. Solomon's wisdom
3. Solomon builds the temple
4. Solomon's greatness and downfall

Solomon was a botanist, zoologist, architect, poet, and philosopher. He was the wisest king in the history of Israel, but his wives led to the introduction of false gods and false worship in Israel. It is good for us to have wisdom, but that is not enough. The highest goal in life is to obey the Lord. Patient obedience to God should characterize our lives.

B. THE DIVIDED KINGDOM (12:1—22:53)
1. Revolt of the northern tribes
2. Kings of Israel and Judah
3. Elijah's ministry
4. Kings of Israel and Judah

When the northern kingdom of Israel was being led by wicked kings, God raised up a prophet to proclaim his messages. Elijah single-handedly challenged the priesthood of the state religion and had them removed in one day. Through the dividing of the kingdom and the sending of Elijah, God dealt with the people's sin in powerful ways. Sin in our lives is graciously forgiven by God. However, the sin of an unrepentant person will be handled harshly. We must turn from sin and turn to God to be saved from judgment.

MEGATHEMES

THEME	EXPLANATION	IMPORTANCE
The King	Solomon's wisdom, power, and achievements brought honor to the Israelite nation and to God. All the kings of Israel and Judah were told to obey God and to govern according to his laws. But their tendency to abandon God's commands and to worship other gods led them to change the religion and government to meet their personal desires. This neglect of God's Law led to their downfall.	Wisdom, power, and achievement do not ultimately come from any human source; they are from God. No matter what we lead or govern, we can't do well when we ignore God's guidelines. Whether or not we are leaders, effectiveness depends upon listening and obeying God's Word. Don't let your personal desires distort God's Word.
The Temple	Solomon's temple was a beautiful place of worship and prayer. This sanctuary was the center of Jewish religion. It was the place of God's special presence and housed the ark of the covenant containing the Ten Commandments.	A beautiful house of worship doesn't always guarantee heartfelt worship of God. Providing opportunities for true worship doesn't ensure that it will happen. God wants to live in our hearts, not just meet us in a sanctuary.
Other Gods	Although the Israelites had God's Law and experienced his presence among them, they became attracted to other gods. When this happened, their hearts became cold to God's Law, resulting in the ruin of families and government, and eventually leading to the destruction of the nation.	Through the years, the people took on the false qualities of the false gods they worshiped. They became cruel, power-hungry, and sexually perverse. We tend to become what we worship. Unless we serve the true God, we will become slaves to whatever takes his place.
The Prophet's Message	The prophet's responsibility was to confront and correct any deviation from God's Law. Elijah was a bolt of judgment against Israel. His messages and miracles were a warning to the evil and rebellious kings and people.	The Bible, the truth in sermons, and the wise counsel of believers are warnings to us. Anyone who points out how we deviate from obeying God's Word is a blessing to us. Changing our lives in order to obey God and get back on track often takes painful discipline and hard work.
Sin and Repentance	Each king had God's commands, a priest or prophet, and the lessons of the past to draw him back to God. All the people had the same resources. Whenever they repented and returned to God, God heard their prayers and forgave them.	God hears and forgives us when we pray—if we are willing to trust him and turn from sin. Our desire to forsake our sin must be heartfelt and sincere. Then he will give us a fresh start and a desire to live for him.

KEY PLACES IN 1 KINGS

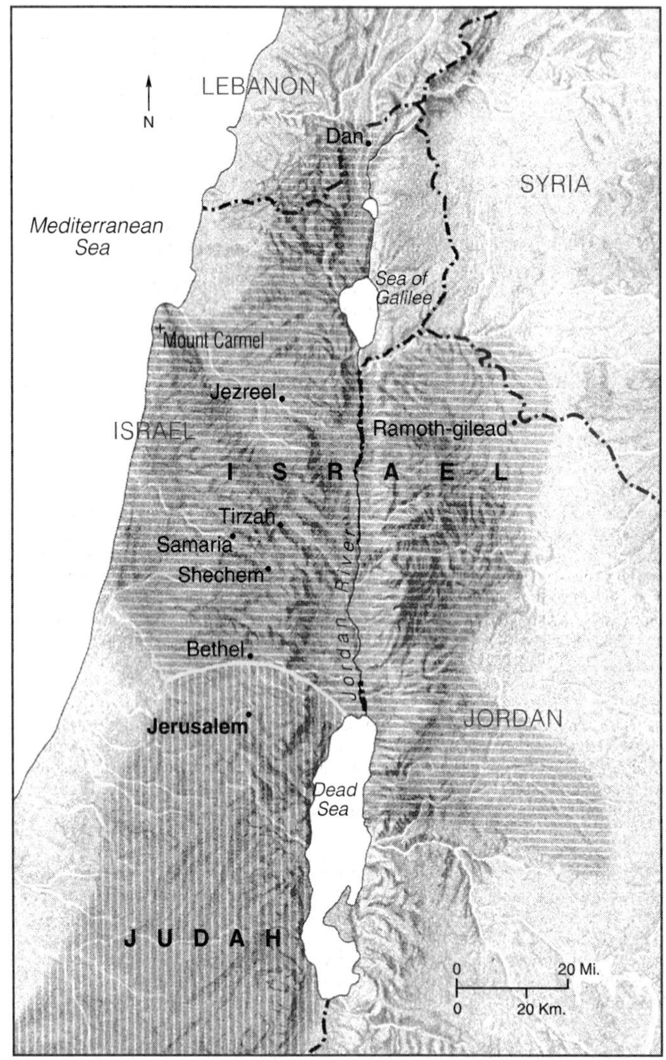

The broken lines (—·—·) indicate modern boundaries.

Solomon, David's son, brought Israel into its golden age. His wealth and wisdom were acclaimed worldwide. But he ignored God in his later years (1:1—11:43).

1 Shechem After Solomon's death, Israel assembled at Shechem to inaugurate his son Rehoboam. However, Rehoboam foolishly angered the people by threatening even heavier burdens, causing a revolt (12:1–19).

2 Israel Jeroboam, leader of the rebels, was made king of Israel, now called the northern kingdom. Jeroboam made Shechem his capital city (12:20, 25).

3 Judah Only the tribes of Judah and part of Benjamin remained loyal to Rehoboam. These two tribes became the southern kingdom. Rehoboam returned to Judah from Shechem and prepared to force the rebels into submission, but a prophet's message halted these plans (12:21–24).

4 Jerusalem Jerusalem was the capital city of Judah. Its temple, built by Solomon, was the focal point of Jewish worship. This worried Jeroboam. How could he keep his people loyal if they were constantly going to Rehoboam's capital to worship (12:26–27)?

5 Dan Jeroboam's solution was to set up his own worship centers. Two golden calves were made and proclaimed to be Israel's gods. One was placed in Dan, and the people were told that they could go there instead of to Jerusalem to worship (12:28–29).

6 Bethel The other golden calf was placed in Bethel. The people of the northern kingdom had two convenient locations for worship in their own country, but their sin displeased God. In Jerusalem, meanwhile, Rehoboam was also allowing idolatry to creep in. The two nations were constantly at war (12:29—15:26).

7 Tirzah Jeroboam had moved the capital city to Tirzah (1 Kings 14:17). Next, Baasha became king of Israel after assassinating Nadab (15:27—16:22).

8 Samaria Israel continued to gain and lose kings through plots, assassinations, and warfare. When Omri became king, he bought a hill on which he built a new capital city, Samaria. Omri's son, Ahab, became the most wicked king of Israel. His wife, Jezebel, worshiped Baal. Ahab erected a temple to Baal in Samaria (16:23–34).

9 Mount Carmel Great evil often brings great people who oppose it. Elijah challenged the prophets of Baal and Asherah at Mount Carmel, where he would prove that they were false prophets. There Elijah humiliated these prophets and then executed them (17:1—18:46).

10 Jezreel Elijah returned to Jezreel. But Queen Jezebel, furious at the execution of her prophets, vowed to kill Elijah. He ran for his life, but God cared for and encouraged him. During his travels he anointed the future kings of Aram and Israel, as well as Elisha, his own replacement (19:1–21).

11 Ramoth-gilead The king of Aram declared war on Israel and was defeated in two battles. But the Arameans occupied Ramoth-gilead. Ahab and Jehoshaphat joined forces to recover the city. In this battle, Ahab was killed. Jehoshaphat later died (20:1—22:53).

A. THE UNITED KINGDOM (1:1—11:43)

When Solomon is anointed king, he eliminates all opposition to the throne, builds the temple, establishes a strong army, and becomes the richest and wisest king in the history of Israel. But his pagan wives lead him into idolatry and, as a result, he leads the nation into spiritual decline. No matter what position in life we attain, we are always ripe for a downfall and must never let our guard down against sin and temptation.

1. Solomon becomes king

David in Old Age

1 Now King David was old, advanced in age; and they covered him with clothes, but
he could not keep warm.
2 So his servants said to him, "Let them seek a young virgin for my lord the king, and
let her attend the king and become his nurse; and let her lie in your bosom, that my lord
the king may keep warm."
1:3 Josh 19:18; 1 Sam 28:4 — 3 So they searched for a beautiful girl throughout all the territory of Israel, and found
Abishag the Shunammite, and brought her to the king.
4 The girl was very beautiful; and she became the king's nurse and served him, but
the king did not cohabit with her.
1:5 2 Sam 3:4; 2 Sam 15:1 — 5 Now Adonijah the son of Haggith exalted himself, saying, "I will be king." So he
prepared for himself chariots and horsemen with fifty men to run before him.
1:6 2 Sam 3:3, 4 — 6 His father had never crossed him at any time by asking, "Why have you done so?"
And he was also a very handsome man, and he was born after Absalom.

1:1 Israel was near the end of the golden years of David's reign. The book of 1 Kings begins with a unified kingdom, glorious and God-centered; it ends with a divided kingdom, degraded and idolatrous. The reason for Israel's decline appears simple to us—they failed to obey God. But we are vulnerable to the same forces that brought about Israel's decay—greed, jealousy, lust for power, weakening of marriage vows, and superficiality in our devotion to God. As we read about these tragic events in Israel's history, we must see ourselves in the mirror of their experiences.

1:4 David was about 70 years old. His health had deteriorated from years of hardship. Abishag served as his nurse and to help keep him warm. In times when polygamy was accepted and kings had harems, this action was not considered offensive.

1:5 Adonijah was David's fourth son and the logical choice to succeed him as king. David's first son, Amnon, had been killed by Absalom for having raped his sister (2 Samuel 13:20–33). His second son, Daniel, is mentioned only in the genealogy of 1 Chronicles 3:1 and had probably died by this time. David's third son, Absalom, died in an earlier rebellion (2 Samuel 18:1–18). Although many people expected Adonijah to be the next king (2:13–25), David (and God) had other plans (1:29–30).

1:5 Adonijah decided to seize the throne without David's knowledge. He knew that Solomon, not he, was David's first choice to be the next king (1:17). This was why he did not invite Solomon and David's loyal advisers when he declared himself king (1:9–10). But his deceptive plans to gain the throne were unsuccessful. The proud Adonijah was self-exalted and self-defeated.

1:6 God-fearing people like David and Samuel were used by God to lead nations, but nevertheless they had problems in family relationships. God-fearing leaders cannot take for granted the spiritual well-being of their children. They are used to having others follow their orders, but they cannot expect their children to manufacture faith upon request. Moral and spiritual character takes years to build, and it requires constant attention and patient discipline.

David served God well as a king, but as a parent he often failed both God and his children. Don't let your service to God even in leadership positions take up so much of your time and energy that you neglect your other God-given responsibilities.

1:6 Because David had never interfered by opposing or even questioning his son, Adonijah did not know how to work within limits. The result was that he always wanted his own way, regardless of how it affected others. Adonijah did whatever he wanted and paid no respect to God's wishes. An undisciplined child may look cute to his or her parents, but an undisciplined adult destroys himself and others. As you set limits for your children, you make it possible for them to develop the self-restraint they will need in order to control themselves later. Discipline your children carefully while they are young, so that they will grow into self-disciplined adults.

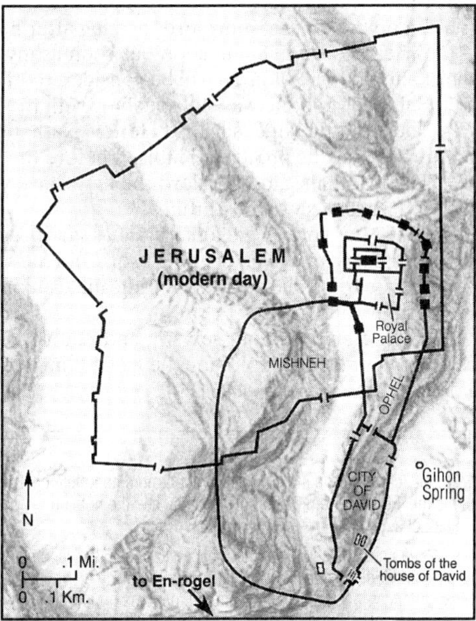

TWO CORONATIONS As David lay on his deathbed, his son Adonijah crowned himself king at En-rogel outside Jerusalem. When the news reached David, he declared that Solomon was to be the next ruler. Solomon was anointed at Gihon. It may have been more than coincidence that Gihon was not only within shouting distance of En-rogel but also closer to the royal palace.

7 He had conferred with Joab the son of Zeruiah and with Abiathar the priest; and
following Adonijah they helped him.
8 But Zadok the priest, Benaiah the son of Jehoiada, Nathan the prophet, Shimei,
Rei, and the mighty men who belonged to David, were not with Adonijah.
9 Adonijah sacrificed sheep and oxen and fatlings by the [1]stone of Zoheleth, which is
beside En-rogel; and he invited all his brothers, the king's sons, and all the men of Judah, the king's servants.
10 But he did not invite Nathan the prophet, Benaiah, the mighty men, and Solomon
his brother.

Nathan and Bathsheba

11 Then Nathan spoke to Bathsheba the mother of Solomon, saying, "Have you not
heard that Adonijah the son of Haggith has become king, and David our lord does not
know *it?*
12 "So now come, please let me give you counsel and save your life and the life of your
son Solomon.
13 "Go at once to King David and say to him, 'Have you not, my lord, O king, sworn to
your maidservant, saying, "Surely Solomon your son shall be king after me, and he shall
sit on my throne"? Why then has Adonijah become king?'
14 "Behold, while you are still there speaking with the king, I will come in after you and
confirm your words."
15 So Bathsheba went in to the king in the bedroom. Now the king was very old, and
Abishag the Shunammite was ministering to the king.
16 Then Bathsheba bowed and prostrated herself before the king. And the king said,
"What do you wish?"
17 She said to him, "My lord, you swore to your maidservant by the LORD your God,
saying, 'Surely your son Solomon shall be king after me and he shall sit on my throne.'
18 "Now, behold, Adonijah is king; and now, my lord the king, you do not know *it.*
19 "He has sacrificed oxen and fatlings and sheep in abundance, and has invited all the
sons of the king and Abiathar the priest and Joab the commander of the army, but he
has not invited Solomon your servant.
20 "As for you now, my lord the king, the eyes of all Israel are on you, to tell them who
shall sit on the throne of my lord the king after him.
21 "Otherwise it will come about, as soon as my lord the king sleeps with his fathers,
that I and my son Solomon will be considered offenders."
22 Behold, while she was still speaking with the king, Nathan the prophet came in.
23 They told the king, saying, "Here is Nathan the prophet." And when he came in
before the king, he prostrated himself before the king with his face to the ground.
24 Then Nathan said, "My lord the king, have you said, 'Adonijah shall be king after
me, and he shall sit on my throne'?
25 "For he has gone down today and has sacrificed oxen and fatlings and sheep in abundance, and has invited all the king's sons and the commanders of the army and Abiathar
the priest, and behold, they are eating and drinking before him; and they say, '*Long* live
King Adonijah!'
26 "But me, *even* me your servant, and Zadok the priest and Benaiah the son of Jehoiada and your servant Solomon, he has not invited.

1:7 1 Chr 11:6; 1 Sam 22:20, 23; 2 Sam 20:25; 1 Kin 2:22
1:8 2 Sam 20:25; 1 Chr 16:39; 2 Sam 8:18; 2 Sam 12:1; 1 Kin 4:18; 2 Sam 23:8-39
1:9 Josh 15:7; 18:16; 2 Sam 17:17
1:10 2 Sam 12:24
1:11 2 Sam 12:24
1:12 Prov 15:22
1:13 1 Kin 1:30; 1 Chr 22:9-13
1:15 1 Kin 1:1
1:17 1 Kin 1:13
1:19 1 Kin 1:9
1:21 Deut 31:16; 2 Sam 7:12; 1 Kin 2:10
1:25 1 Kin 1:9; 1 Sam 10:24
1:26 1 Kin 1:8, 10

1 Or *Gliding* or *Serpent Stone*

1:7 See Joab's Profile in 2 Samuel 19 for a more complete picture of his life. For more information on Abiathar, see the note on 1 Samuel 22:20.

1:9 When Saul was anointed king, peace offerings were sacrificed as a reminder of the nation's covenant with God given at Mount Sinai. Adonijah wanted sacrifices offered, perhaps hoping to legitimize his takeover. But Adonijah was not God's choice to succeed David. Sealing an action with religious ceremony does not make it God's will.

1:11 For more on Bathsheba, David's wife, read 2 Samuel 11—12. As mother of the king, Bathsheba was highly influential in the royal palace.

1:11–14 When Nathan learned of Adonijah's conspiracy, he immediately tried to stop it. He was a man of both faith and action. He knew that Solomon should rightly be king, and he moved quickly when he saw someone else trying to take the throne. We often know what is right but don't act on it. Perhaps we don't want to get involved, or maybe we are fearful or lazy. Don't stop with prayer, good intentions, or angry feelings. Take the action needed to correct the situation.

1:13 The Bible does not record David's promise that Solomon would be Israel's next king, but it is clear that Solomon was the choice of both David (1:17, 30) and God (1 Chronicles 22:9–10).

27 "Has this thing been done by my lord the king, and you have not shown to your servants who should sit on the throne of my lord the king after him?"
28 Then King David said, "Call Bathsheba to me." And she came into the king's presence and stood before the king.
29 The king vowed and said, "As the LORD lives, who has redeemed my life from all
distress,
30 surely as I vowed to you by the LORD the God of Israel, saying, 'Your son Solomon
shall be king after me, and he shall sit on my throne in my place'; I will indeed do so this
day."
31 Then Bathsheba bowed with her face to the ground, and prostrated herself before
the king and said, "May my lord King David live forever."
32 Then King David said, "Call to me Zadok the priest, Nathan the prophet, and Benaiah the son of Jehoiada." And they came into the king's presence.
33 The king said to them, "Take with you the servants of your lord, and have my son
Solomon ride on my own mule, and bring him down to Gihon.
34 "Let Zadok the priest and Nathan the prophet anoint him there as king over Israel,
and blow the trumpet and say, '*Long* live King Solomon!'
35 "Then you shall come up after him, and he shall come and sit on my throne and be
king in my place; for I have appointed him to be ruler over Israel and Judah."

1:29 2 Sam 4:9

1:30 1 Kin 1:13, 17

1:31 Dan 2:4; 3:9

1:32 1 Kin 1:8

1:33 2 Sam 20:6, 7; 2 Chr 32:30; 33:14

1:34 1 Sam 10:1; 16:3, 12; 2 Sam 5:3; 1 Kin 19:16; 2 Kin 9:3; 2 Sam 15:10; 1 Kin 1:25

BATHSHEBA

Bathsheba was the unlikely link between Israel's two most famous kings—David and Solomon. She was lover and wife to one, mother to the other. Her adultery with David almost brought an end to the family through which God planned to physically enter his world. Out of the ashes of that sin, however, God brought good. Eventually Jesus Christ, the salvation of mankind, was born to a descendant of David and Bathsheba.

David and Bathsheba's story shows that little wrong decisions often lead to big mistakes. It is likely that neither was where he or she should have been. Bathsheba may have been rash in bathing where she might be seen; David should have been at war with his army. Each decision contributed to the beginning of a very sad series of events.

Bathsheba must have been devastated by the chain of events—unfaithfulness to her husband, discovery of pregnancy, death of her husband, death of her child. We are told that David comforted her (2 Samuel 12:24), and she lived to see another son, Solomon, sit on the throne.

From her life we see that the little, day-to-day choices we make are very important. They prepare us to make the right choices when the big decisions come. The wisdom to make right choices in small and large matters is a gift from God. Understanding this should make us more conscious of the decisions we make and more willing to include God in our decision making. Have you asked for his help with today's decisions?

Strengths and accomplishments:
- Became influential in the palace alongside her son, Solomon
- Was the mother of Israel's wisest king and an ancestor of Jesus Christ

Weakness and mistake:
- Committed adultery

Lessons from her life:
- Although we may feel caught up in a chain of events, we are still responsible for the way we participate in those events
- A sin may seem like one small seed, but the harvest of consequences is beyond measure
- In the worst possible situations, God is still able to bring about good when people truly turn to him
- While we must live with the natural consequences of our sins, God's forgiveness of sin is total

Vital statistics:
- Where: Jerusalem
- Occupations: Queen and queen mother
- Relatives: Father: Elim. Husbands: Uriah and David. Son: Solomon
- Contemporaries: Nathan, Joab, Adonijah

Key verses:
"Now when the wife of Uriah heard that Uriah her husband was dead, she mourned for her husband. When the time of mourning was over, David sent and brought her to his house and she became his wife; then she bore him a son. But the thing that David had done was evil in the sight of the LORD" (2 Samuel 11:26–27).

Her story is told in 2 Samuel 11; 12 and 1 Kings 1; 2. A related passage is Psalm 51.

36 Benaiah the son of Jehoiada answered the king and said, "Amen! Thus may the
LORD, the God of my lord the king, say.
37 "As the LORD has been with my lord the king, so may He be with Solomon, and make **1:37**
his throne greater than the throne of my lord King David!" Josh 1:5, 17; 1 Sam 20:13; 1 Kin 1:47

Solomon Anointed King

38 So Zadok the priest, Nathan the prophet, Benaiah the son of Jehoiada, the **1:38**
Cherethites, and the Pelethites went down and had Solomon ride on King David's mule, 1 Kin 1:8; 2 Sam 8:18; 1 Kin 1:33
and brought him to Gihon.
39 Zadok the priest then took the horn of oil from the tent and anointed Solomon. **1:39**
Then they blew the trumpet, and all the people said, "*Long* live King Solomon!" Ex 30:23-32; Ps 89:20; 1 Chr 29:22;
40 All the people went up after him, and the people were playing on flutes and rejoic- 1 Kin 1:34; 1 Sam
ing with great joy, so that the earth shook at their noise. 10:24
41 Now Adonijah and all the guests who *were* with him heard *it* as they finished eating.
When Joab heard the sound of the trumpet, he said, "Why is the city making such an
uproar?"
42 While he was still speaking, behold, Jonathan the son of Abiathar the priest came. **1:42**
Then Adonijah said, "Come in, for you are a valiant man and bring good news." 2 Sam 15:27, 36; 17:17; 2 Sam 18:27
43 But Jonathan replied to Adonijah, "No! Our lord King David has made Solomon
king.
44 "The king has also sent with him Zadok the priest, Nathan the prophet, Benaiah the
son of Jehoiada, the Cherethites, and the Pelethites; and they have made him ride on
the king's mule.
45 "Zadok the priest and Nathan the prophet have anointed him king in Gihon, and **1:45**
they have come up from there rejoicing, so that the city is in an uproar. This is the noise 1 Kin 1:40
which you have heard.
46 "Besides, Solomon has even taken his seat on the throne of the kingdom. **1:46**
47 "Moreover, the king's servants came to bless our lord King David, saying, 'May your 1 Chr 29:23
God make the name of Solomon better than your name and his throne greater than your **1:47**
throne!' And the king bowed himself on the bed. 1 Kin 1:37; Gen 47:31
48 "The king has also said thus, 'Blessed be the LORD, the God of Israel, who has granted one to sit on my throne today while my own eyes see *it*.' " **1:48** 2 Sam 7:12; 1 Kin
49 Then all the guests of Adonijah were terrified; and they arose and each went on 3:6
his way.
50 And Adonijah was afraid of Solomon, and he arose, went and took hold of the horns **1:50**
of the altar. Ex 27:2; 30:10; 1 Kin 2:28
51 Now it was told Solomon, saying, "Behold, Adonijah is afraid of King Solomon, for
behold, he has taken hold of the horns of the altar, saying, 'Let King Solomon swear to
me today that he will not put his servant to death with the sword.' "
52 Solomon said, "If he is a worthy man, not one of his hairs will fall to the ground; but **1:52**
if wickedness is found in him, he will die." 1 Sam 14:45; 2 Sam 14:11; Acts 27:34
53 So King Solomon sent, and they brought him down from the altar. And he came
and prostrated himself before King Solomon, and Solomon said to him, "Go to your
house."

1:39 The sacred anointing oil was used to anoint Israel's kings and high priests, as well as to dedicate certain objects to God. The tent where the oil was kept was probably the tent David set up to shelter the ark of the covenant (2 Samuel 6:17). It was not the tabernacle Moses carried in the wilderness; that tabernacle was still at Gibeon (see the note on 1 Samuel 7:1 for more details). The recipe and uses for the sacred oil are found in Exodus 30:22–33. For more on anointing, see the notes on 1 Samuel 10:1 and 16:13.

1:49–50 Sometimes it takes getting caught before someone is willing to give up his scheme. When Adonijah learned that his plans were doomed to fail, he ran in panic to the altar, the place of God's mercy and forgiveness. He went there, however, *after* his plans for treason were exposed. If Adonijah had first considered what God wanted, he might have avoided trouble. Don't wait until you have made a mess of your life before you run to God. Seek God's guidance *before* you act.

1:49–51 Both Adonijah and his commander, Joab, thought they would be safe by clutching the horns (or corner posts) of the sacred altar of burnt offering in the tabernacle court. They hoped to place themselves under God's protection. Solomon granted Adonijah a reprieve, but later he had Joab killed right at the altar (2:28–34). This punishment was appropriate justice for a cold-blooded murderer such as Joab (Exodus 21:14).

1:52–53 While Adonijah feared for his life and expected the severest punishment, Solomon simply dismissed his brother and sent him home. As a new king, Solomon had the power to kill his rivals, something Adonijah would have done had his conspiracy succeeded. But Solomon acted as if he had nothing to prove, thus demonstrating his authority and power. Sometimes forgiving a personal attack shows more strength than lashing out in revenge. Trying to prove one's power and authority often proves only one's fear and self-doubt. Only after Adonijah made another attempt to secure royal power was Solomon forced to have him executed (2:13–25).

2:1 Gen 47:29
2:2 Josh 23:14; Deut 31:7, 23; Josh 1:6, 7
2:3 Deut 17:18-20; 1 Chr 22:12, 13
2:4 2 Sam 7:25; Ps 132:12; 2 Kin 20:3; 2 Sam 7:12, 13; 1 Kin 8:25; 9:5
2:5 2 Sam 2:13, 18; 2 Sam 3:27; 1 Kin 2:32; 2 Sam 20:10

David's Charge to Solomon

2 As David's time to die drew near, he charged Solomon his son, saying,
2 "I am going the way of all the earth. Be strong, therefore, and show yourself a
man.
3 "Keep the charge of the LORD your God, to walk in His ways, to keep His statutes,
His commandments, His ordinances, and His testimonies, according to what is written
in the Law of Moses, that you may succeed in all that you do and wherever you turn,
4 so that the LORD may carry out His promise which He spoke concerning me, saying, 'If your sons are careful of their way, to walk before Me in [2]truth with all their heart
and with all their soul, you shall not lack a man on the throne of Israel.'
5 "Now you also know what Joab the son of Zeruiah did to me, what he did to the two
commanders of the armies of Israel, to Abner the son of Ner, and to Amasa the son of

2 Or *faithfulness*

Who joined Adonijah's conspiracy and who remained loyal to David? Contrast the fate of those who rebelled and those who remained loyal to David, God's appointed leader. Adonijah, the leader of the conspiracy, met a violent death (1 Kings 2:25). Those who rebel against God's leaders rebel against God.

Joined Adonijah

JOAB (1:7)
Brilliant military general and commander of David's army. He continually demonstrated his belief that cold-blooded murder was as acceptable as a fairly fought battle. Solomon later had him executed.

ABIATHAR (1:7)
One of two high priests under David. He was a son of Ahimelech who had helped David, and David promised to protect him. Abiathar repaid David with his treachery. Solomon later had him banished, fulfilling the prophecy that Eli's priestly line would end (1 Samuel 2:31).

JONATHAN (1:42)
Abiathar's son. He helped David stop Absalom's rebellion (2 Sam. 17:17–22), but supported this rebellion by another of David's sons.

CHARIOTS AND HORSEMEN (1:5)
Hired by Adonijah, apparently more loyal to money than to their king.

50 RUNNERS (1:5)
Recruited to give Adonijah a "royal" appearance.

Remained with David

ZADOK (1:8)
The other high priest under David. His loyalty gave him the privilege of crowning Solomon. He became the sole high priest under King Solomon.

BENAIAH (1:8)
Distinguished himself as a great warrior. Commanded a division of David's army—over 24,000 men. One of the thirty, he was also placed in charge of David's bodyguard. Solomon later made him chief commander of the army.

NATHAN (1:8)
God's prominent prophet during David's reign. The Bible says he wrote a history of David and Solomon.

SHIMEI (1:8)
This man was probably the Shimei who was rewarded by Solomon and appointed district governor in Benjamin (1 Kings 4:18). (He was not the same person who cursed David at Bahurim and brought on his own death under Solomon.)

REI (1:8)
Only mentioned here. Possibly he was an army officer. The word means "and his friends."

MIGHTY MEN (1:8, 10)
David's army was highly organized with several different divisions of troops. It is enough to know that many of his leaders remained true to their king.

2:3–4 David stressed to Solomon the need to make God and his laws the center of personal life and government in order to preserve the kingdom, as God had promised to do (2 Samuel 7). This promise from God had two parts. One part was conditional and depended upon the kings' actions. The other part was unconditional.

God's conditional promise was that David and his descendants would remain in office as kings *only* when they honored and obeyed him. When David's descendants failed to do this, they lost the throne (2 Kings 25). God's unconditional promise was that David's line would go on forever. This was fulfilled in the birth of Jesus Christ, a descendant of David who was also the eternal Son of God (Romans 1:3–4). David, whose life exemplified obedience, gave well-seasoned advice to his son, the next king. It would be up to Solomon to follow it.

2:5–7 Joab epitomizes those who are ruthless in accomplishing their goals. His strength was his only code, and winning the battle his only law. He wanted to get power for himself and protect it. In contrast, Barzillai stands for those who are loyal to God and live by his standards. When offered glory, for example, he unselfishly asked that it be given to his son. Is your leadership self-serving or God-serving?

2:5–9 David had some harsh advice for Solomon concerning his enemies. This advice was designed to help the young king establish and secure his throne, and it was directed only toward blatant enemies—those who opposed God by opposing God's appointed king. Legally, David was asking Solomon to give his enemies the punishment they deserved. It was against both civil law and God's laws for Shimei to curse a king (Exodus 22:28).

Jether, whom he killed; he also shed the blood of war in peace. And he put the blood of
war on his belt about his waist, and on his sandals on his feet.
6 "So act according to your wisdom, and do not let his gray hair go down to Sheol in
peace.
7 "But show kindness to the sons of Barzillai the Gileadite, and let them be among
those who eat at your table; for they assisted me when I fled from Absalom your brother.
8 "Behold, there is with you Shimei the son of Gera the Benjamite, of Bahurim; now it
was he who cursed me with a violent curse on the day I went to Mahanaim. But when he
came down to me at the Jordan, I swore to him by the LORD, saying, 'I will not put you
to death with the sword.'
9 "Now therefore, do not let him go unpunished, for you are a wise man; and you will
know what you ought to do to him, and you will bring his gray hair down to Sheol with
blood."

Death of David

10 Then David slept with his fathers and was buried in the city of David.
11 The days that David reigned over Israel *were* forty years: seven years he reigned in
Hebron and thirty-three years he reigned in Jerusalem.
12 And Solomon sat on the throne of David his father, and his kingdom was firmly
established.
13 Now Adonijah the son of Haggith came to Bathsheba the mother of Solomon. And
she said, "Do you come peacefully?" And he said, "Peacefully."
14 Then he said, "I have something *to say* to you." And she said, "Speak."
15 So he said, "You know that the kingdom was mine and that all Israel expected me
to be king; however, the kingdom has turned about and become my brother's, for it was
his from the LORD.
16 "Now I am making one request of you; do not [3]refuse me." And she said to him,
"Speak."
17 Then he said, "Please speak to Solomon the king, for he will not refuse you, that he
may give me Abishag the Shunammite as a wife."
18 Bathsheba said, "Very well; I will speak to the king for you."

Adonijah Executed

19 So Bathsheba went to King Solomon to speak to him for Adonijah. And the king
arose to meet her, bowed before her, and sat on his throne; then he had a throne set for
the king's mother, and she sat on his right.
20 Then she said, "I am making one small request of you; do not refuse me." And the
king said to her, "Ask, my mother, for I will not refuse you."
21 So she said, "Let Abishag the Shunammite be given to Adonijah your brother as a
wife."
22 King Solomon answered and said to his mother, "And why are you asking Abishag
the Shunammite for Adonijah? Ask for him also the kingdom—for he is my older brother—even for him, for Abiathar the priest, and for Joab the son of Zeruiah!"
23 Then King Solomon swore by the LORD, saying, "May God do so to me and more
also, if Adonijah has not spoken this word against his own life.
24 "Now therefore, as the LORD lives, who has established me and set me on the throne
of David my father and who has made me a house as He promised, surely Adonijah shall
be put to death today."
25 So King Solomon sent Benaiah the son of Jehoiada; and he fell upon him so that he
died.
26 Then to Abiathar the priest the king said, "Go to Anathoth to your own field, for

2:6 1 Kin 2:9
2:7 2 Sam 19:31-38; 2 Sam 9:7, 10; 2 Sam 17:27-29
2:8 2 Sam 16:5-8; 2 Sam 19:18-23
2:9 1 Kin 2:6
2:10 Acts 2:29; 13:36; 2 Sam 5:7; 1 Kin 3:1
2:11 2 Sam 5:4, 5; 1 Chr 3:4; 29:26, 27; 2 Sam 5:5
2:12 1 Chr 29:23; 2 Chr 1:1
2:13 1 Sam 16:4
2:15 2 Sam 3:3, 4; 1 Kin 2:22; 1 Kin 1:5-25; 1 Kin 1:38-50; 1 Chr 22:9, 10; 28:5-7
2:17 1 Kin 1:3, 4
2:19 1 Kin 15:13; Ps 45:9
2:20 1 Kin 2:16
2:21 1 Kin 1:3, 4
2:22 2 Sam 12:8; 1 Kin 1:6; 2:15; 1 Chr 3:2, 5; 1 Kin 1:7
2:23 Ruth 1:17
2:24 2 Sam 7:11, 13; 1 Chr 22:10
2:25 2 Sam 8:18
2:26 Josh 21:18; Jer 1:1; 1 Sam 26:16; 1 Sam 23:6; 2 Sam 15:24-29; 1 Sam 22:20-23; 23:8, 9

3 Lit *turn away my face*

2:10 David died at about age 70 (2 Samuel 5:4–5). See David's Profile in 1 Samuel 17 for more on his life.

2:15–22 This was not a case of thwarted love, although Adonijah probably hoped Bathsheba would think so. Although she was still a virgin, Abishag was considered part of David's harem. Adonijah wanted Abishag because possessing the king's harem was equivalent to claiming the throne. Absalom had done the same thing in his rebellion against David (2 Samuel 16:20–23). Solomon well understood what Adonijah was trying to do.

2:26–27 As a young man, Abiathar was the only one to escape when King Saul massacred all the priests in the city of Nob (1 Samuel 22:11–23). Abiathar then became the high priest under David and remained loyal to David throughout his reign. When he

you deserve to die; but I will not put you to death at this time, because you carried the
ark of the Lord GOD before my father David, and because you were afflicted in everything with which my father was afflicted."

2:27 1 Sam 2:27-36

27 So Solomon dismissed Abiathar from being priest to the LORD, in order to fulfill
the word of the LORD, which He had spoken concerning the house of Eli in Shiloh.

Joab Executed

2:28 1 Kin 1:7; 2 Sam 17:25; 18:2; 1 Kin 1:50

28 Now the news came to Joab, for Joab had followed Adonijah, although he had not
followed Absalom. And Joab fled to the tent of the LORD and took hold of the horns of
the altar.

2:29 1 Kin 2:25; Ex 21:14

29 It was told King Solomon that Joab had fled to the tent of the LORD, and behold,
he is beside the altar. Then Solomon sent Benaiah the son of Jehoiada, saying, "Go, fall
upon him."
30 So Benaiah came to the tent of the LORD and said to him, "Thus the king has said,
'Come out.' " But he said, "No, for I will die here." And Benaiah brought the king word
again, saying, "Thus spoke Joab, and thus he answered me."

2:31 Ex 21:14; Num 35:33; Deut 19:13; 21:8, 9

31 The king said to him, "Do as he has spoken and fall upon him and bury him, that
you may remove from me and from my father's house the blood which Joab shed without cause.

2:32 Gen 9:6; Judg 9:24, 57; Ps 7:16; 2 Chr 21:13, 14; 2 Sam 3:27; 2 Sam 20:9, 10

32 "The LORD will return his blood on his own head, because he fell upon two men more
righteous and better than he and killed them with the sword, while my father David did
not know *it:* Abner the son of Ner, commander of the army of Israel, and Amasa the son
of Jether, commander of the army of Judah.

2:33 2 Sam 3:29

33 "So shall their blood return on the head of Joab and on the head of his descendants
forever; but to David and his descendants and his house and his throne, may there be
peace from the LORD forever."

2:34 1 Kin 2:25; Josh 15:61; Matt 3:1

34 Then Benaiah the son of Jehoiada went up and fell upon him and put him to death,
and he was buried at his own house in the wilderness.

2:35 1 Kin 4:4; 1 Chr 6:53; 24:3; 29:22; 1 Kin 2:27

35 The king appointed Benaiah the son of Jehoiada over the army in his place, and the
king appointed Zadok the priest in the place of Abiathar.

Shimei Executed

2:36 2 Sam 16:5; 1 Kin 2:8

36 Now the king sent and called for Shimei and said to him, "Build for yourself a house
in Jerusalem and live there, and do not go out from there to any place.

2:37 2 Sam 15:23; 2 Kin 23:6; John 18:1; Josh 2:19; 2 Sam 1:16; Ezek 18:13

37 "For on the day you go out and cross over the brook Kidron, you will know for certain that you shall surely die; your blood shall be on your own head."
38 Shimei then said to the king, "The word is good. As my lord the king has said, so
your servant will do." So Shimei lived in Jerusalem many days.

2:39 1 Sam 27:2

39 But it came about at the end of three years, that two of the servants of Shimei ran
away to Achish son of Maacah, king of Gath. And they told Shimei, saying, "Behold,
your servants are in Gath."
40 Then Shimei arose and saddled his donkey, and went to Gath to Achish to look for
his servants. And Shimei went and brought his servants from Gath.
41 It was told Solomon that Shimei had gone from Jerusalem to Gath, and had returned.
42 So the king sent and called for Shimei and said to him, "Did I not make you swear
by the LORD and solemnly warn you, saying, 'You will know for certain that on the day
you depart and go anywhere, you shall surely die'? And you said to me, 'The word which
I have heard is good.'

---

supported Adonijah's wrongful claim to the throne after David's death (1:7), Solomon forced him to give up the priesthood, fulfilling the prophecy of 1 Samuel 2:27–36 that Eli's descendants would not continue to serve as priests.

2:31 Joab had spent his life trying to defend his position as David's commander. Twice David tried to replace him, and both times Joab treacherously killed his rivals before they could assume command (2 Samuel 3:17–30; 19:13; 20:4–10). Because Joab was in his service, David was ultimately responsible for these senseless deaths. But for political and military reasons (see the note on 2 Samuel 3:39), David decided not to publicly punish Joab. Instead he put a curse on Joab and his family (2 Samuel 3:29). Solomon, in punishing Joab, was publicly declaring that David was not part of Joab's crimes, thus removing the guilt from David and placing it on Joab where it belonged.

2:35 Abiathar the high priest and Joab the army commander were key men in David's kingdom. But when they conspired against Solomon, they were replaced with Zadok and Benaiah. Zadok, a descendant of Aaron, had been a prominent priest during David's reign, and he was also loyal to Solomon after David's death. He was put in charge of the ark of the covenant (2 Samuel 15:24ff). His descendants were in charge of the temple until its destruction. At one time, Benaiah was one of David's mighty men (2 Samuel 23:20–23) and the captain of David's bodyguard.

43 "Why then have you not kept the oath of the LORD, and the command which I have
laid on you?"
44 The king also said to Shimei, "You know all the evil which you acknowledge in your
heart, which you did to my father David; therefore the LORD shall return your evil on
your own head.
45 "But King Solomon shall be blessed, and the throne of David shall be established
before the LORD forever."
46 So the king commanded Benaiah the son of Jehoiada, and he went out and fell upon
him so that he died.
Thus the kingdom was established in the hands of Solomon.

2. Solomon's wisdom

Solomon's Rule Consolidated

3 Then Solomon formed a marriage alliance with Pharaoh king of Egypt, and took
Pharaoh's daughter and brought her to the city of David until he had finished building his own house and the house of the LORD and the wall around Jerusalem.
2 The people were still sacrificing on the high places, because there was no house built
for the name of the LORD until those days.
3 Now Solomon loved the LORD, walking in the statutes of his father David, except
he sacrificed and burned incense on the high places.
4 The king went to Gibeon to sacrifice there, for that was the great high place; Solomon offered a thousand burnt offerings on that altar.
5 In Gibeon the LORD appeared to Solomon in a dream at night; and God said, "Ask
what *you wish* me to give you."

Solomon's Prayer

6 Then Solomon said, "You have shown great lovingkindness to Your servant David
my father, according as he walked before You in [4]truth and righteousness and uprightness of heart toward You; and You have reserved for him this great lovingkindness, that
You have given him a son to sit on his throne, as *it is* this day.
7 "Now, O LORD my God, You have made Your servant king in place of my father
David, yet I am but a little child; I do not know how to go out or come in.
8 "Your servant is in the midst of Your people which You have chosen, a great people
who are too many to be numbered or counted.
9 "So give Your servant an understanding heart to judge Your people to discern between good and evil. For who is able to judge this great people of Yours?"

God's Answer

10 It was pleasing in the sight of the Lord that Solomon had asked this thing.
11 God said to him, "Because you have asked this thing and have not asked for your-

4 Or *faithfulness*

2:44 2 Sam 16:5-13; 1 Sam 25:39; 2 Kin 11:1, 12-16; Ps 7:16

2:45 2 Sam 7:13; Prov 25:5

2:46 1 Kin 2:25, 34; 1 Kin 2:12; 2 Chr 1:1

3:1 1 Kin 7:8; 9:16, 24; 2 Chr 8:11; 1 Kin 9:24; 1 Kin 7:1; 9:10; 1 Kin 9:15

3:2 Lev 17:3-5; Deut 12:2, 13, 14; 1 Kin 22:43

3:3 Deut 6:5; 10:12, 13; 11:13; 30:16; Ps 31:23; 145:20; 1 Cor 8:3; 1 Kin 2:3; 9:4; 11:4, 6, 38

3:4 2 Chr 1:3; Josh 18:21-25; 1 Chr 16:39; 21:29

3:5 1 Kin 9:2; 11:9; Num 12:6; Matt 1:20; 2:13; John 15:7

3:6 2 Sam 7:8-17; 2 Chr 1:8; 1 Kin 9:4; 1 Kin 1:48

3:7 1 Chr 22:9-13; 1 Chr 29:1; Jer 1:6, 7; Num 27:17

3:8 Ex 19:6; Deut 7:6; Gen 15:5; 22:17

3:9 2 Chr 1:10; Ps 72:1, 2; Prov 2:3-9; James 1:5; 2 Sam 14:17; Heb 5:14

3:11 James 4:3

2:46 Solomon ordered the executions of Adonijah, Joab, and Shimei, forced Abiathar out as priest, and then appointed new men to take their places. He did these things swiftly, securing his grip on the kingdom. By executing justice and tying up loose ends that could affect the future stability of his kingdom, Solomon was promoting peace, not bloodshed. He was a man of peace in two ways: he did not go to war, and he put an end to internal rebellion.

3:1 Marriage between royal families was a common practice in the ancient Near East because it secured peace. Although Solomon's marital alliances built friendships with surrounding nations, they were also the beginning of his downfall. These relationships became inroads for pagan ideas and practices. Solomon's foreign wives brought their gods to Jerusalem and eventually lured him into idolatry (11:1–6).

It is easy to minimize religious differences in order to encourage the development of a friendship, but seemingly small differences can have an enormous impact upon a relationship. God gives us standards to follow for all our relationships, including marriage. If we follow God's will, we will not be lured away from our true focus.

3:2–3 God's laws said that the Israelites could make sacrifices only in specified places (Deuteronomy 12:13–14). This was to prevent the people from instituting their own methods of worship and allowing pagan practices to creep into their worship. But many Israelites, including Solomon, made sacrifices in the surrounding hills. Solomon loved God, but this act was sin. It took the offerings out of the watchful care of priests and ministers loyal to God and opened the way for false teaching to be tied to these sacrifices. God appeared to Solomon to grant him wisdom, but at night, not during the sacrifice. God honored his prayer but did not condone the sacrifice.

3:6–9 When given a chance to have anything in the world, Solomon asked for wisdom—"an understanding heart"—in order to lead well and to make right decisions. We can ask God for this same wisdom (James 1:5). Notice that Solomon asked for discernment to carry out his job; he did not ask God to do the job for him. We should not ask God to do *for* us what he wants to do *through* us. Instead we should ask God to give us the wisdom to know what to do and the courage to follow through on it.

3:11–14 Solomon asked for wisdom ("discernment"), not wealth, but God gave him riches and long life as well. While God does not

self long life, nor have asked riches for yourself, nor have you asked for the life of your
enemies, but have asked for yourself discernment to understand justice,

3:12 1 John 5:14, 15; 1 Kin 4:29-31; 5:12; 10:23, 24; Eccl 1:16

12 behold, I have done according to your words. Behold, I have given you a wise and
discerning heart, so that there has been no one like you before you, nor shall one like
you arise after you.

3:13 1 Kin 4:21-24; 10:23, 27; Matt 6:33; Eph 3:20; Prov 3:16

13 "I have also given you what you have not asked, both riches and honor, so that there
will not be any among the kings like you all your days.

3:14 1 Kin 3:6; Ps 91:16; Prov 3:2

14 "If you walk in My ways, keeping My statutes and commandments, as your father
David walked, then I will prolong your days."

3:15 Gen 41:7; 1 Kin 8:65

15 Then Solomon awoke, and behold, it was a dream. And he came to Jerusalem and
stood before the ark of the covenant of the Lord, and offered burnt offerings and made
peace offerings, and made a feast for all his servants.

Solomon Wisely Judges

16 Then two women who were harlots came to the king and stood before him.
17 The one woman said, "Oh, my lord, this woman and I live in the same house; and I
gave birth to a child while she *was* in the house.
18 "It happened on the third day after I gave birth, that this woman also gave birth to a
child, and we were together. There was no stranger with us in the house, only the two of
us in the house.
19 "This woman's son died in the night, because she lay on it.
20 "So she arose in the middle of the night and took my son from beside me while your
maidservant slept, and laid him in her bosom, and laid her dead son in my bosom.
21 "When I rose in the morning to nurse my son, behold, he was dead; but when I looked
at him carefully in the morning, behold, he was not my son, whom I had borne."
22 Then the other woman said, "No! For the living one is my son, and the dead one is
your son." But the first woman said, "No! For the dead one is your son, and the living
one is my son." Thus they spoke before the king.
23 Then the king said, "The one says, 'This is my son who is living, and your son is the
dead one'; and the other says, 'No! For your son is the dead one, and my son is the living
one.' "
24 The king said, "Get me a sword." So they brought a sword before the king.
25 The king said, "Divide the living child in two, and give half to the one and half to
the other."

3:26 Gen 43:30; Is 49:15; Jer 31:20; Hos 11:8

26 Then the woman whose child *was* the living one spoke to the king, for she was deeply stirred over her son and said, "Oh, my lord, give her the living child, and by no means
kill him." But the other said, "He shall be neither mine nor yours; divide *him!*"
27 Then the king said, "Give the first woman the living child, and by no means kill him.
She is his mother."

3:28 1 Kin 3:9, 11, 12; Dan 1:17; Col 2:2, 3

28 When all Israel heard of the judgment which the king had handed down, they feared
the king, for they saw that the wisdom of God was in him to administer justice.

Solomon's Officials

4 Now King Solomon was king over all Israel.

4:2 1 Chr 6:10

2 These were his officials: Azariah the son of Zadok *was* the priest;

4:3 2 Sam 8:16

3 Elihoreph and Ahijah, the sons of Shisha *were* secretaries; Jehoshaphat the son of
Ahilud *was* the recorder;

---

promise riches to those who follow him, he gives us what we need if we put his kingdom, his interests, and his principles first (Matthew 6:31–33). Setting your sights on riches will only leave you dissatisfied because even if you get the riches you crave, you will still want something more. But if you put God and his work first, he will satisfy your deepest needs.

3:12 Solomon received "a wise and discerning heart" from God, but it was up to Solomon to apply that wisdom to all areas of his life. Solomon was obviously wise in governing the nation, but he was foolish in running his household. Wisdom is both the ability to discern what is best and the strength of character to act upon that knowledge. While Solomon remained wise all his life, he did not always act upon his wisdom (11:6).

3:13–18 Solomon's settlement of this dispute was a classic example of his wisdom. This wise ruling was verification that God had answered Solomon's prayer and given him a discerning heart. We have God's wisdom available to us as we pray and request it. But, like Solomon, we must put it into action. Applying wisdom to life demonstrates our discernment.

4:1ff Solomon was well organized, with 11 officials with specific responsibilities, 12 deputies, and a manager in charge of the district officers. Each person had a specific responsibility or territory to manage. This organization was essential to maintain the government's effectiveness: it was a wise move by a wise man. It is good stewardship to be well organized. Good organization helps people work together in harmony and ensures that the desired goal will be reached.

4 and Benaiah the son of Jehoiada *was* over the army; and Zadok and Abiathar *were*
priests;
5 and Azariah the son of Nathan *was* over the deputies; and Zabud the son of Nathan, a priest, *was* the king's friend;
6 and Ahishar was over the household; and Adoniram the son of Abda *was* over the
men subject to forced labor.
7 Solomon had twelve deputies over all Israel, who provided for the king and his
household; each man had to provide for a month in the year.
8 These are their names: Ben-hur, in the hill country of Ephraim;
9 Ben-deker in Makaz and Shaalbim and Beth-shemesh and Elonbeth-hanan;
10 Ben-hesed, in Arubboth (Socoh *was* his and all the land of Hepher);
11 Ben-abinadab, *in* all the height of Dor (Taphath the daughter of Solomon was his
wife);
12 Baana the son of Ahilud, *in* Taanach and Megiddo, and all Beth-shean which is beside
Zarethan below Jezreel, from Beth-shean to Abel-meholah as far as the other side of
Jokmeam;
13 Ben-geber, in Ramoth-gilead (the towns of Jair, the son of Manasseh, which are in
Gilead were his: the region of Argob, which is in Bashan, sixty great cities with walls and
bronze bars *were* his);
14 Ahinadab the son of Iddo, *in* Mahanaim;
15 Ahimaaz, in Naphtali (he also married Basemath the daughter of Solomon);
16 Baana the son of Hushai, in Asher and Bealoth;
17 Jehoshaphat the son of Paruah, in Issachar;
18 Shimei the son of Ela, in Benjamin;
19 Geber the son of Uri, in the land of Gilead, the country of Sihon king of the Amorites and of Og king of Bashan; and *he was* the only deputy who *was* in the land.

Solomon's Power, Wealth and Wisdom

20 Judah and Israel *were* as numerous as the sand that is on the seashore in abundance;
they were eating and drinking and rejoicing.
21 Now Solomon ruled over all the kingdoms from the [5]River *to* the land of the Philistines and to the border of Egypt; *they* brought tribute and served Solomon all the days of
his life.
22 Solomon's provision for one day was thirty [6]kors of fine flour and sixty kors of meal,
23 ten fat oxen, twenty pasture-fed oxen, a hundred sheep besides deer, gazelles, roe-
bucks, and fattened fowl.
24 For he had dominion over everything west of the River, from Tiphsah even to Gaza,
over all the kings west of the River; and he had peace on all sides around about him.
25 So Judah and Israel lived in safety, every man under his vine and his fig tree, from
Dan even to Beersheba, all the days of Solomon.
26 Solomon had [7]40,000 stalls of horses for his chariots, and 12,000 horsemen.

5 I.e. Euphrates 6 I.e. One kor equals approx 10 bu 7 One ms reads *4000,* cf 2 Chr 9:25

4:4 1 Kin 2:35; 1 Kin 2:27
4:5 1 Kin 4:7
4:8 Josh 24:33
4:9 Judg 1:35; Josh 21:16
4:10 Josh 15:35; Josh 12:17
4:11 Josh 11:1, 2
4:12 Judg 5:19; Josh 17:11; Josh 3:16; 1 Kin 19:16; 1 Chr 6:68
4:13 1 Kin 22:3-15; Num 32:41; Deut 3:4
4:14 Josh 13:26
4:15 2 Sam 15:27
4:16 2 Sam 15:32
4:18 1 Kin 1:8
4:19 Deut 3:8-10
4:20 Gen 22:17; 32:12; 1 Kin 3:8
4:21 2 Chr 9:26; Gen 15:18; Josh 1:4; 2 Sam 8:2, 6
4:24 Judg 1:18; Ps 72:11; 1 Chr 22:9
4:25 Jer 23:6; Mic 4:4; Zech 3:10; 1 Sam 3:20
4:26 1 Kin 10:26; 2 Chr 1:14

4:20–25 Throughout most of his reign, Solomon applied his wisdom well because he sought God. The fruits of this wisdom were peace, security, and prosperity for the nation. Solomon's era is often looked upon as the ideal of what any nation can become when united in trust in and obedience to God.

SOLOMON'S KINGDOM Solomon's kingdom spread from the Euphrates River in the north to the borders of Egypt. The entire land was at peace under his rule.

4:29 1 Kin 3:12; 1 Kin 4:20

4:30 Gen 29:1; Judg 6:33; Is 19:11; Acts 7:22

4:31 1 Kin 3:12; 1 Chr 15:19; Ps 89: title; 1 Chr 2:6

4:32 Prov 1:1; 10:1; 25:1; Eccl 12:9; Song 1:1

27 Those deputies provided for King Solomon and all who came to King Solomon's
table, each in his month; they left nothing lacking.
28 They also brought barley and straw for the horses and swift steeds to the place where
it should be, each according to his charge.
29 Now God gave Solomon wisdom and very great discernment and breadth of mind,
like the sand that is on the seashore.
30 Solomon's wisdom surpassed the wisdom of all the sons of the east and all the wisdom of Egypt.
31 For he was wiser than all men, than Ethan the Ezrahite, Heman, Calcol and Darda,
the sons of Mahol; and his fame was *known* in all the surrounding nations.
32 He also spoke 3,000 proverbs, and his songs were 1,005.

SOLOMON

Wisdom is only effective when it is put into action. Early in his life, Solomon had the sense to recognize his need for wisdom. But by the time Solomon asked for wisdom to rule his kingdom, he had already started a habit that would make his wisdom ineffective for his own life—he sealed a pact with Egypt by marrying Pharaoh's daughter. She was the first of hundreds of wives married for political reasons. In doing this, Solomon went against not only his father's last words, but also God's direct commands. His action reminds us how easy it is to know what is right and yet not do it.

It is clear that God's gift of wisdom to Solomon did not mean that he couldn't make mistakes. He had been given great possibilities as the king of God's chosen people, but with them came great responsibilities; unfortunately, he tended to pursue the former and neglect the latter. While becoming famous as the builder of the temple and the palace, he became infamous as a leader who excessively taxed and worked his people. Visitors from distant lands came to admire this wise king, while his own people were gradually alienated from him.

Little is mentioned in the Bible about the last decade of Solomon's reign. Ecclesiastes probably records his last reflections on life. In that book we find a man proving through bitter experience that finding meaning in life apart from God is a vain pursuit. Security and contentment are found only in a personal relationship with God. The contentment we find in the opportunities and successes of this life is temporary. The more we expect our successes to be permanent, the more quickly they are gone. Be sure to balance your pursuit of life's possibilities with reliable fulfillment of your responsibilities.

Strengths and accomplishments:
- Third king of Israel, David's chosen heir
- The wisest man who ever lived
- Author of Ecclesiastes and Song of Solomon, as well as many of the proverbs and a couple of the psalms
- Built God's temple in Jerusalem
- Diplomat, trader, collector, patron of the arts

Weaknesses and mistakes:
- Sealed many foreign agreements by marrying pagan women
- Allowed his wives to affect his loyalty to God
- Excessively taxed his people and drafted them into a labor and military force

Lessons from his life:
- Effective leadership can be nullified by an ineffective personal life
- Solomon failed to obey God, but did not learn the lesson of repentance until late in life
- Knowing what actions are required of us means little without the will to do those actions

Vital statistics:
- Where: Jerusalem
- Occupation: King of Israel
- Relatives: Father: David. Mother: Bathsheba. Brothers: Absalom, Adonijah. Sister: Tamar. Son: Rehoboam

Key verse:
"Did not Solomon king of Israel sin regarding these things? Yet among the many nations there was no king like him, and he was loved by his God, and God made him king over all Israel; nevertheless the foreign women caused even him to sin" (Nehemiah 13:26).

Solomon's story is told in 2 Samuel 12:24—1 Kings 11:43. He is also mentioned in 1 Chronicles 28—29; 2 Chronicles 1—10; Nehemiah 13:26; Psalm 72; and Matthew 6:29; 12:42.

4:32 The book of Proverbs records many of these 3,000 wise proverbs. Other Biblical writings of Solomon include Psalms 72 and 127 and the books of Ecclesiastes and Song of Solomon. Solomon's wisdom was known throughout the world.

33 He spoke of trees, from the cedar that is in Lebanon even to the hyssop that grows
on the wall; he spoke also of animals and birds and creeping things and fish.
34 Men came from all peoples to hear the wisdom of Solomon, from all the kings of
the earth who had heard of his wisdom.

4:34 1 Kin 10:1; 2 Chr 9:23

3. Solomon builds the temple

Alliance with King Hiram

5 Now Hiram king of Tyre sent his servants to Solomon, when he heard that they had
anointed him king in place of his father, for Hiram had always been a friend of David.
2 Then Solomon sent *word* to Hiram, saying,
3 "You know that David my father was unable to build a house for the name of the
LORD his God because of the wars which surrounded him, until the LORD put them under
the soles of his feet.
4 "But now the LORD my God has given me rest on every side; there is neither adversary nor misfortune.
5 "Behold, I intend to build a house for the name of the LORD my God, as the LORD
spoke to David my father, saying, 'Your son, whom I will set on your throne in your place,
he will build the house for My name.'
6 "Now therefore, command that they cut for me cedars from Lebanon, and my servants will be with your servants; and I will give you wages for your servants according to
all that you say, for you know that there is no one among us who knows how to cut timber like the Sidonians."
7 When Hiram heard the words of Solomon, he rejoiced greatly and said, "Blessed
be the LORD today, who has given to David a wise son over this great people."
8 So Hiram sent *word* to Solomon, saying, "I have heard *the message* which you have
sent me; I will do what you desire concerning the cedar and cypress timber.
9 "My servants will bring *them* down from Lebanon to the sea; and I will make them
into rafts *to go* by sea to the place where you direct me, and I will have them broken up
there, and you shall carry *them* away. Then you shall accomplish my desire by giving food
to my household."
10 So Hiram gave Solomon as much as he desired of the cedar and cypress timber.
11 Solomon then gave Hiram 20,000 kors of wheat as food for his household, and twenty
kors of beaten oil; thus Solomon would give Hiram year by year.
12 The LORD gave wisdom to Solomon, just as He promised him; and there was peace
between Hiram and Solomon, and the two of them made a covenant.

5:1 2 Chr 2:3; 2 Sam 5:11; 1 Chr 14:1
5:2 2 Chr 2:3
5:3 2 Sam 7:5; 1 Chr 28:2, 3
5:4 1 Kin 4:24; 1 Chr 22:9
5:5 2 Sam 7:12, 13; 1 Chr 17:12; 22:10; 28:6; 2 Chr 2:4
5:6 2 Chr 2:8
5:9 2 Chr 2:16; Ezra 3:7; Ezek 27:17
5:11 2 Chr 2:10
5:12 1 Kin 3:12

Conscription of Laborers

13 Now King Solomon levied forced laborers from all Israel; and the forced laborers
numbered 30,000 men.
14 He sent them to Lebanon, 10,000 a month in relays; they were in Lebanon a month
and two months at home. And Adoniram *was* over the forced laborers.
15 Now Solomon had 70,000 transporters, and 80,000 hewers *of stone* in the mountains,
16 besides Solomon's 3,300 chief deputies who *were* over the project *and* who ruled
over the people who were doing the work.
17 Then the king commanded, and they quarried great stones, costly stones, to lay the
foundation of the house with cut stones.
18 So Solomon's builders and Hiram's builders and the Gebalites cut them, and prepared the timbers and the stones to build the house.

5:13 1 Kin 4:6; 9:15
5:14 1 Kin 4:6; 12:18
5:15 1 Kin 9:20-22; 2 Chr 2:17, 18
5:16 1 Kin 9:23
5:17 1 Kin 6:7; 1 Chr 22:2
5:18 Josh 13:5; Ezek 27:9

5:2–3 When David offered to build a temple, God said no through the prophet Nathan (2 Samuel 7:1–17). God wanted a peacemaker, not a warrior, to build his house of prayer (1 Chronicles 28:2–3).

5:13–14 Solomon drafted three times the number of workers needed for the temple project and then arranged their schedules so they didn't have to be away from home for long periods of time. This showed his concern for the welfare of his workers and the importance he placed on family life. The strength of a nation is in direct proportion to the strength of its families. Solomon wisely recognized that family should always be a top priority. As you structure your own work or arrange the schedules of others, watch for the impact of your plans on families.

5:18 Gebal, also called Byblos, was located north of what is now Beirut, near the cedar forest. These men were Phoenicians, probably skilled as shipbuilders, but employed for this project.

The Building of the Temple

6 Now it came about in the four hundred and eightieth year after the sons of Israel
came out of the land of Egypt, in the fourth year of Solomon's reign over Israel, in
the month of Ziv which is the second month, that he began to build the house of the
LORD.
2 As for the house which King Solomon built for the LORD, its length *was* sixty [8]cu-
bits and its width twenty *cubits* and its height thirty cubits.
3 The porch in front of the nave of the house *was* twenty cubits in length, corresponding to the width of the house, *and* its depth along the front of the house *was* ten cubits.
4 Also for the house he made windows with *artistic* frames.
5 Against the wall of the house he built stories encompassing the walls of the house
around both the nave and the inner sanctuary; thus he made side chambers all around.
6 The lowest story *was* five cubits wide, and the middle *was* six cubits wide, and the
third *was* seven cubits wide; for on the outside he made offsets *in the wall* of the house
all around in order that *the beams* would not be inserted in the walls of the house.
7 The house, while it was being built, was built of stone prepared at the quarry, and
there was neither hammer nor axe nor any iron tool heard in the house while it was being built.
8 The doorway for the [9]lowest side chamber *was* on the right side of the house; and
they would go up by winding stairs to the middle *story,* and from the middle to the third.
9 So he built the house and finished it; and he covered the house with beams and planks
of cedar.
10 He also built the stories against the whole house, each five cubits high; and they
were fastened to the house with timbers of cedar.
11 Now the word of the LORD came to Solomon saying,
12 "*Concerning* this house which you are building, if you will walk in My statutes and
execute My ordinances and keep all My commandments by walking in them, then I will
carry out My word with you which I spoke to David your father.
13 "I will dwell among the sons of Israel, and will not forsake My people Israel."
14 So Solomon built the house and finished it.
15 Then he built the walls of the house on the inside with boards of cedar; from the
floor of the house to the ceiling he overlaid *the walls* on the inside with wood, and he
overlaid the floor of the house with boards of cypress.
16 He built twenty cubits on the rear part of the house with boards of cedar from the
floor to the ceiling; he built *them* for it on the inside as an inner sanctuary, *even* as the
most holy place.
17 The house, that is, the nave in front of *the inner sanctuary,* was forty cubits *long.*
18 There was cedar on the house within, carved *in the shape* of gourds and open flowers; all was cedar, there was no stone seen.
19 Then he prepared an inner sanctuary within the house in order to place there the
ark of the covenant of the LORD.
20 The inner sanctuary *was* twenty cubits in length, twenty cubits in width, and twenty
cubits in height, and he overlaid it with pure gold. He also overlaid the altar with cedar.
21 So Solomon overlaid the inside of the house with pure gold. And he drew chains of
gold across the front of the inner sanctuary, and he overlaid it with gold.

8 I.e. One cubit equals approx 18 in. **9** So with Gr and versions; M.T. *middle*

6:1 2 Chr 3:1, 2
6:4 Ezek 40:16; 41:16
6:5 Ezek 41:6; 1 Kin 6:16, 19, 20; Ezek 41:5
6:7 Ex 20:25; Deut 27:5, 6
6:9 1 Kin 6:14, 38
6:12 2 Sam 7:5-16; 1 Kin 9:4
6:13 Ex 25:8; 29:45; Lev 26:11; Deut 31:6; Josh 1:5; Heb 13:5
6:14 1 Kin 6:9, 38
6:15 1 Kin 7:7
6:16 2 Chr 3:8; Ex 26:33, 34; Lev 16:2; 1 Kin 8:6; Heb 9:3
6:18 1 Kin 7:24

6:1ff For more information on the purpose of the temple, see the note on 2 Chronicles 5:1ff.

6:7 In honor of God, the temple in Jerusalem was built without the sound of a hammer or any other tool at the building site. This meant that the stone had to be "dressed" (cut and shaped) miles away at the quarry. The people's honor and respect for God extended to every aspect of constructing this house of worship. This detail is recorded not to teach us how to build a church, but to show us the importance of demonstrating care, concern, honor, and respect for God and his sanctuary.

6:13 This verse summarizes the temple's main purpose. God promised that his eternal presence would never leave the temple as long as one condition was met: the Israelites had to obey God's Law. Knowing how many laws they had to follow, we may think this condition was difficult. But the Israelites' situation was much like ours today: They were not cut off from God for failing to keep some small subpoint of a law. Forgiveness was amply provided for all their sins, no matter how large or small. As you read the history of the kings, you will see that lawbreaking was the result, not the cause, of estrangement from God. The kings abandoned God in their hearts first and *then* failed to keep his laws. When we close our hearts to God, his power and presence soon leave us.

6:14 The concept of Solomon's temple was more like a palace for God than a place of worship. As a dwelling place for God, it was fitting for it to be ornate and beautiful. It had small inside dimensions because most worshipers gathered outside.

22 He overlaid the whole house with gold, until all the house was finished. Also the
whole altar which was by the inner sanctuary he overlaid with gold.
23 Also in the inner sanctuary he made two cherubim of olive wood, each ten cubits
high.
24 Five cubits *was* the one wing of the cherub and five cubits the other wing of the
cherub; from the end of one wing to the end of the other wing *were* ten cubits.
25 The other cherub *was* ten cubits; both the cherubim were of the same measure and
the same form.
26 The height of the one cherub *was* ten cubits, and so *was* the other cherub.
27 He placed the cherubim in the midst of the inner house, and the wings of the cherubim were spread out, so that the wing of the one was touching the *one* wall, and the
wing of the other cherub was touching the other wall. So their wings were touching each
other in the center of the house.
28 He also overlaid the cherubim with gold.
29 Then he carved all the walls of the house round about with carved engravings of
cherubim, palm trees, and open flowers, inner and outer *sanctuaries.*
30 He overlaid the floor of the house with gold, inner and outer *sanctuaries.*
31 For the entrance of the inner sanctuary he made doors of olive wood, the lintel *and*
five-sided doorposts.
32 So *he made* two doors of olive wood, and he carved on them carvings of cherubim,
palm trees, and open flowers, and overlaid them with gold; and he spread the gold on
the cherubim and on the palm trees.
33 So also he made for the entrance of the nave four-sided doorposts of olive wood
34 and two doors of cypress wood; the two leaves of the one door turned on pivots,
and the two leaves of the other door turned on pivots.
35 He carved *on it* cherubim, palm trees, and open flowers; and he overlaid *them* with
gold evenly applied on the engraved work.
36 He built the inner court with three rows of cut stone and a row of cedar beams.
37 In the fourth year the foundation of the house of the LORD was laid, in the month
of Ziv.
38 In the eleventh year, in the month of Bul, which is the eighth month, the house was
finished throughout all its parts and according to all its plans. So he was seven years in
building it.

6:22 Ex 30:1, 3, 6
6:23 Ex 37:7-9; 2 Chr 3:10-12
6:27 Ex 25:20; 37:9; 1 Kin 8:7
6:34 Ezek 41:23-25
6:36 1 Kin 7:12; Jer 36:10
6:37 1 Kin 6:1

Solomon's Palace

7 Now Solomon was building his own house thirteen years, and he finished all his house.
2 He built the house of the forest of Lebanon; its length was 100 [10]cubits and its
width 50 cubits and its height 30 cubits, on four rows of cedar pillars with cedar beams
on the pillars.
3 It was paneled with cedar above the side chambers which were on the 45 pillars, 15
in each row.
4 *There were artistic window* frames in three rows, and window was opposite window
in three ranks.
5 All the doorways and doorposts *had* squared *artistic* frames, and window was opposite window in three ranks.
6 Then he made the hall of pillars; its length was 50 cubits and its width 30 cubits, and
a porch *was* in front of them and pillars and a threshold in front of them.
7 He made the hall of the throne where he was to judge, the hall of judgment, and it
was paneled with cedar from floor to floor.
8 His house where he was to live, the other court inward from the hall, was of the
same workmanship. He also made a house like this hall for Pharaoh's daughter, whom
Solomon had married.
9 All these were of costly stones, of stone cut according to measure, sawed with saws,
inside and outside; even from the foundation to the coping, and so on the outside to the
great court.

7:1 1 Kin 3:1; 9:10; 2 Chr 8:1
7:2 1 Kin 10:17, 21; 2 Chr 9:16
7:6 1 Kin 7:12; Ezek 41:25, 26
7:7 Ps 122:5; Prov 20:8; 1 Kin 6:15, 16
7:8 1 Kin 9:24; 2 Chr 8:11; 1 Kin 3:1

10 I.e. One cubit equals approx 18 in.

7:1 That Solomon took longer to build his palace than to build the temple is not a comment on his priorities. His palace project took longer because it was part of a huge civic building project including barracks and housing for his harem.

10 The foundation was of costly stones, *even* large stones, stones of ten cubits and stones
of eight cubits.
11 And above were costly stones, stone cut according to measure, and cedar.

7:12 1 Kin 6:36; 1 Kin 7:6

12 So the great court all around *had* three rows of cut stone and a row of cedar beams
even as the inner court of the house of the LORD, and the porch of the house.

Hiram's Work in the Temple

7:13 2 Chr 2:13, 14; 4:11
7:14 2 Chr 2:14; Ex 28:3; 31:3-5; 35:31; 36:1; 2 Chr 4:11-16
7:15 2 Kin 25:17; 2 Chr 3:15; 4:12; Jer 52:21; 1 Kin 7:41

13 Now King Solomon sent and brought Hiram from Tyre.
14 He was a widow's son from the tribe of Naphtali, and his father was a man of Tyre,
a worker in bronze; and he was filled with wisdom and understanding and skill for doing
any work in bronze. So he came to King Solomon and performed all his work.
15 He fashioned the two pillars of bronze; eighteen cubits was the height of one pillar,
and a line of twelve cubits measured the circumference of both.
16 He also made two capitals of molten bronze to set on the tops of the pillars; the
height of the one capital was five cubits and the height of the other capital was five
cubits.
17 *There were* nets of network and twisted threads of chainwork for the capitals which
were on the top of the pillars; seven for the one capital and seven for the other capital.
18 So he made the pillars, and two rows around on the one network to cover the capitals which were on the top of the pomegranates; and so he did for the other capital.
19 The capitals which *were* on the top of the pillars in the porch were of lily design,
four cubits.

7:20 1 Kin 7:42; 2 Chr 3:16; 4:13; Jer 52:23
7:21 2 Chr 3:17; 1 Kin 6:3

20 *There were* capitals on the two pillars, even above *and* close to the rounded projection which was beside the network; and the pomegranates *numbered* two hundred in rows
around both capitals.
21 Thus he set up the pillars at the porch of the nave; and he set up the right pillar and
named it [11]Jachin, and he set up the left pillar and named it [12]Boaz.
22 On the top of the pillars was lily design. So the work of the pillars was finished.

7:23 2 Chr 4:2; 2 Kin 16:17; 25:13
7:24 1 Kin 6:18; 2 Chr 4:3
7:25 2 Chr 4:4, 5; Jer 52:20

23 Now he made the sea of cast *metal* ten cubits from brim to brim, circular in form,
and its height was five cubits, and thirty cubits in circumference.
24 Under its brim gourds went around encircling it ten to a cubit, completely surrounding the sea; the gourds were in two rows, cast with the rest.
25 It stood on twelve oxen, three facing north, three facing west, three facing south,
and three facing east; and the sea *was set* on top of them, and all their rear parts *turned*
inward.
26 It was a handbreadth thick, and its brim was made like the brim of a cup, *as* a lily
blossom; it could hold two thousand baths.

7:27 1 Kin 7:38; 2 Kin 25:13; 2 Chr 4:14

27 Then he made the ten stands of bronze; the length of each stand was four cubits
and its width four cubits and its height three cubits.
28 This was the design of the stands: they had borders, even borders between the
[13]frames,
29 and on the borders which were between the [13]frames *were* lions, oxen and cherubim; and on the [13]frames there *was* a pedestal above, and beneath the lions and oxen
were wreaths of hanging work.
30 Now each stand had four bronze wheels with bronze axles, and its four feet had
supports; beneath the basin *were* cast supports with wreaths at each side.
31 Its opening inside the crown at the top *was* a cubit, and its opening *was* round like
the design of a pedestal, a cubit and a half; and also on its opening *there were* engravings,
and their borders were square, not round.
32 The four wheels *were* underneath the borders, and the axles of the wheels *were* on
the stand. And the height of a wheel *was* a cubit and a half.

11 I.e. he shall establish **12** I.e. in it is strength **13** Or *crossbars*

7:14 Hiram was an expert craftsman. Solomon chose only the best.

7:23 The "sea" was an enormous tank. Designed and used for the priests' ceremonial washings, it was placed in the temple court near the altar of burnt offering. There the priests washed themselves before offering sacrifices or entering the temple (Exodus 30:17–21).

7:27–39 These "ten stands of bronze" held basins of water. The basins were used for washing the various parts of the animal sacrifices. The basins were movable so they could be used where needed.

33 The workmanship of the wheels *was* like the workmanship of a chariot wheel. Their
axles, their rims, their spokes, and their hubs *were* all cast.
34 Now *there were* four supports at the four corners of each stand; its supports *were*
part of the stand itself.
35 On the top of the stand *there was* a circular form half a cubit high, and on the top of
the stand its stays and its borders *were* part of it.
36 He engraved on the plates of its stays and on its borders, cherubim, lions and palm
trees, according to the clear space on each, with wreaths *all* around.
37 He made the ten stands like this: all of them had one casting, one measure and one
form.
38 He made ten basins of bronze, one basin held forty baths; each basin *was* four cubits, *and* on each of the ten stands *was* one basin.
39 Then he set the stands, five on the right side of the house and five on the left side of
the house; and he set the sea *of cast metal* on the right side of the house eastward toward
the south.
40 Now Hiram made the basins and the shovels and the bowls. So Hiram finished doing all the work which he performed for King Solomon *in* the house of the LORD:
41 the two pillars and the *two* bowls of the capitals which *were* on the top of the two
pillars, and the two networks to cover the two bowls of the capitals which *were* on the top
of the pillars;
42 and the four hundred pomegranates for the two networks, two rows of pomegranates for each network to cover the two bowls of the capitals which *were* on the tops of the
pillars;
43 and the ten stands with the ten basins on the stands;
44 and the one sea and the twelve oxen under the sea;
45 and the pails and the shovels and the bowls; even all these utensils which Hiram
made for King Solomon *in* the house of the LORD *were* of polished bronze.
46 In the plain of the Jordan the king cast them, in the clay ground between Succoth
and Zarethan.
47 Solomon left all the utensils *unweighed,* because *they were* too many; the weight of
the bronze could not be ascertained.
48 Solomon made all the furniture which *was in* the house of the LORD: the golden
altar and the golden table on which *was* the bread of the Presence;
49 and the lampstands, five on the right side and five on the left, in front of the inner
sanctuary, of pure gold; and the flowers and the lamps and the tongs, of gold;
50 and the cups and the snuffers and the bowls and the spoons and the firepans, of
pure gold; and the hinges both for the doors of the inner house, the most holy place, *and*
for the doors of the house, *that is,* of the nave, of gold.
51 Thus all the work that King Solomon performed *in* the house of the LORD was finished. And Solomon brought in the things dedicated by his father David, the silver and
the gold and the utensils, *and* he put them in the treasuries of the house of the LORD.

The Ark Brought into the Temple

8 Then Solomon assembled the elders of Israel and all the heads of the tribes, the leaders of the fathers' *households* of the sons of Israel, to King Solomon in Jerusalem, to
bring up the ark of the covenant of the LORD from the city of David, which is Zion.
2 All the men of Israel assembled themselves to King Solomon at the feast, in the
month Ethanim, which is the seventh month.
3 Then all the elders of Israel came, and the priests took up the ark.

7:37 2 Chr 4:14
7:38 Ex 30:18; 2 Chr 4:6
7:41 1 Kin 7:17, 18
7:42 1 Kin 7:20
7:44 1 Kin 7:23, 25
7:45 Ex 27:3; 2 Chr 4:16
7:46 2 Chr 4:17; Gen 33:17; Josh 13:27; Josh 3:16
7:47 1 Chr 22:3, 14
7:48 Ex 30:1-3; 37:10-29; 2 Chr 4:8; Ex 25:30
7:49 Ex 25:31-38
7:50 Ex 27:3; 2 Kin 25:15
7:51 2 Chr 5:1; 2 Sam 8:11; 1 Chr 18:11; 2 Chr 5:1
8:1 2 Chr 5:2-10; Num 1:4; 7:2; 2 Sam 6:12-17; 1 Chr 15:25-29; 2 Sam 5:7
8:2 Lev 23:34; 1 Kin 8:65; 2 Chr 7:8-10
8:3 Num 7:9; Deut 31:9; Josh 3:3, 6

7:40–47 Hiram's items of bronze would look strange in today's churches, but we use other articles to enhance worship. Stained-glass windows, crosses, pulpits, hymnbooks, and communion tables serve as aids to worship. While the instruments of worship may change, the purpose of worship should never change—to give honor and praise to God.

8:1ff Solomon gathered the people not just to dedicate the temple, but to rededicate themselves to God's service. Solomon could well be speaking these words to us today: "Let your heart therefore be wholly devoted to the LORD our God, to walk in His statutes and to keep His commandments, as at this day" (8:61).

8:1ff What was the difference between the tabernacle and the temple, and why did the Israelites change from one to the other? As a tent, the tabernacle was a portable place of worship designed for the people as they were traveling toward the promised land. The temple was a permanent place to worship God after the Israelites were at peace in their land. To bring the ark of the Lord's covenant to the temple signified God's actual presence there.

8:4
1 Kin 3:4; 2 Chr 1:3

8:5
2 Sam 6:13; 2 Chr 1:6

8:6
1 Kin 8:3; 1 Kin 6:19; 1 Kin 6:27

4 They brought up the ark of the LORD and the tent of meeting and all the holy utensils, which were in the tent, and the priests and the Levites brought them up.
5 And King Solomon and all the congregation of Israel, who were assembled to him, were with him before the ark, sacrificing so many sheep and oxen they could not be counted or numbered.
6 Then the priests brought the ark of the covenant of the LORD to its place, into the inner sanctuary of the house, to the most holy place, under the wings of the cherubim.
7 For the cherubim spread *their* wings over the place of the ark, and the cherubim made a covering over the ark and its poles from above.

SOLOMON'S TEMPLE 960–586 B.C.

Solomon's temple was a beautiful sight. It took over seven years to build and was a magnificent building containing gold, silver, bronze, and cedar. This house for God was without equal. The description is found in 1 Kings 6—7 and 2 Chronicles 2—4.

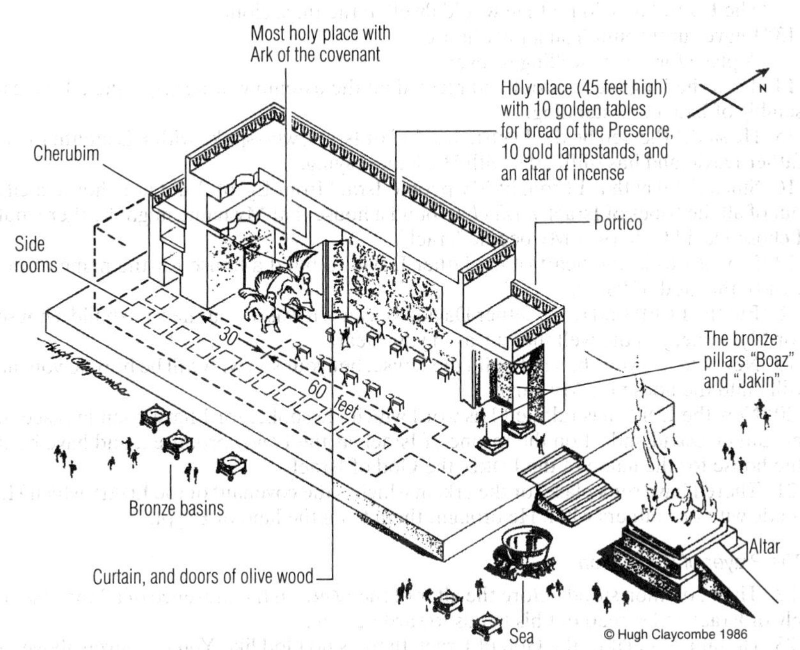

FURNISHINGS

Cherubim: represented heavenly beings, symbolized God's presence and holiness (gold-plated, 15 feet wide)

Ark of the covenant: contained the law written on two tablets, symbolized God's presence with Israel (wood overlaid with gold)

Curtain: separated the holy place and most holy place (blue, purple, and crimson yarn and fine linen, with cherubim worked into it)

Doors: between holy place and most holy place (wood overlaid with gold)

Golden tables (wood overlaid with gold), *gold lampstands* (with seven lamps on each stand), and *altar of incense* (wood overlaid with gold): instruments for priestly functions in the holy place

Bronze pillars: named Jakin (meaning "he establishes") and Boaz (meaning "in him is strength")—taken together they could mean "God provides the strength"

Altar: for burning of sacrifices (bronze)

Sea: for priests' washing (had 12,000 gallon capacity)

Bronze basins: for washing the sacrifices (water basins on wheeled bases)

This reconstruction uses known archaeological parallels to supplement the text, and assumes interior dimensions for 1 Kings 6:17–20. © Hugh Claycombe.

8:6 Cherubim are mighty angels.

8 But the poles were so long that the ends of the poles could be seen from the holy
place before the inner sanctuary, but they could not be seen outside; they are there to
this day.
9 There was nothing in the ark except the two tablets of stone which Moses put there
at Horeb, where the LORD made a covenant with the sons of Israel, when they came out
of the land of Egypt.
10 It happened that when the priests came from the holy place, the cloud filled the
house of the LORD,
11 so that the priests could not stand to minister because of the cloud, for the glory of
the LORD filled the house of the LORD.

Solomon Addresses the People

12 Then Solomon said,
"The LORD has said that He would dwell in the thick cloud.
13 "I have surely built You a lofty house,
A place for Your dwelling forever."
14 Then the king faced about and blessed all the assembly of Israel, while all the assembly of Israel was standing.
15 He said, "Blessed be the LORD, the God of Israel, who spoke with His mouth to my
father David and has fulfilled *it* with His hand, saying,
16 'Since the day that I brought My people Israel from Egypt, I did not choose a city
out of all the tribes of Israel *in which* to build a house that My name might be there, but
I chose David to be over My people Israel.'
17 "Now it was in the heart of my father David to build a house for the name of the
LORD, the God of Israel.
18 "But the LORD said to my father David, 'Because it was in your heart to build a house
for My name, you did well that it was in your heart.
19 'Nevertheless you shall not build the house, but your son who will be born to you, he
will build the house for My name.'
20 "Now the LORD has fulfilled His word which He spoke; for I have risen in place of
my father David and sit on the throne of Israel, as the LORD promised, and have built
the house for the name of the LORD, the God of Israel.
21 "There I have set a place for the ark, in which is the covenant of the LORD, which He
made with our fathers when He brought them from the land of Egypt."

The Prayer of Dedication

22 Then Solomon stood before the altar of the LORD in the presence of all the assembly of Israel and spread out his hands toward heaven.
23 He said, "O LORD, the God of Israel, there is no God like You in heaven above or
on earth beneath, keeping covenant and *showing* lovingkindness to Your servants who
walk before You with all their heart,
24 who have kept with Your servant, my father David, that which You have promised
him; indeed, You have spoken with Your mouth and have fulfilled it with Your hand as
it is this day.
25 "Now therefore, O LORD, the God of Israel, keep with Your servant David my father that which You have promised him, saying, 'You shall not lack a man to sit on the
throne of Israel, if only your sons take heed to their way to walk before Me as you have
walked.'
26 "Now therefore, O God of Israel, let Your word, I pray, be confirmed which You
have spoken to Your servant, my father David.
27 "But will God indeed dwell on the earth? Behold, heaven and the highest heaven
cannot contain You, how much less this house which I have built!

8:8 Ex 25:13-15; 37:4, 5
8:9 Ex 25:16, 21; Deut 10:2-5; Heb 9:4; Ex 24:7, 8; 40:20; Deut 4:13
8:10 Ex 40:34, 35; 2 Chr 7:1, 2
8:12 2 Chr 6:1; Lev 16:2; Ps 18:11; 97:2
8:13 2 Sam 7:13; Ex 15:17; Ps 132:14
8:14 2 Sam 6:18; 1 Kin 8:55
8:15 1 Chr 29:10, 20; Neh 9:5; Luke 1:68; 2 Sam 7:12, 13; 1 Chr 22:10
8:16 2 Sam 7:4, 5; 1 Chr 17:3-10; 2 Chr 6:5; Deut 12:5, 11; 1 Sam 16:1; 2 Sam 7:8
8:17 2 Sam 7:2, 3; 1 Chr 17:1, 2
8:19 2 Sam 7:5, 12, 13; 1 Kin 5:3, 5; 1 Chr 17:11, 12; 22:8-10
8:20 1 Chr 28:5, 6
8:21 Deut 31:26; 1 Kin 8:9
8:22 1 Kin 8:54; 2 Chr 6:12; Ex 9:33; Ezra 9:5
8:23 1 Sam 2:2; 2 Sam 7:22; Deut 7:9; Neh 1:5; 9:32; Dan 9:4
8:25 1 Kin 2:4
8:26 2 Sam 7:25
8:27 2 Chr 2:6; Ps 139:7-16; Is 66:1; Jer 23:24; Acts 7:49

8:15–21 For 480 years after Israel's escape from Egypt, God did not ask them to build a temple for him. Instead he emphasized the importance of his presence among them and their need for spiritual leaders. It is easy to think of a building as the focus of God's presence and power, but God chooses and uses *people* to do his work. He can use you more than he can use a building of wood and stone. Building or enlarging our place of worship may be necessary, but it should never take priority over developing spiritual leaders.

8:24 Solomon was referring to the promise God made to David in 2 Samuel 7:12–15 that one of David's sons would build the temple.

8:27 In his prayer of dedication, Solomon declared that even the highest heaven cannot contain God. Isn't it amazing that, though the heavens can't contain God, he is willing to live in the hearts of those who love him? The God of the universe takes up residence in his people.

28 "Yet have regard to the prayer of Your servant and to his supplication, O LORD my
God, to listen to the cry and to the prayer which Your servant prays before You today;
29 that Your eyes may be open toward this house night and day, toward the place of
which You have said, 'My name shall be there,' to listen to the prayer which Your servant shall pray toward this place.
30 "Listen to the supplication of Your servant and of Your people Israel, when they pray
toward this place; hear in heaven Your dwelling place; hear and forgive.
31 "If a man sins against his neighbor and is made to take an oath, and he comes *and*
takes an oath before Your altar in this house,
32 then hear in heaven and act and judge Your servants, condemning the wicked by
bringing his way on his own head and justifying the righteous by giving him according to
his righteousness.
33 "When Your people Israel are defeated before an enemy, because they have sinned
against You, if they turn to You again and confess Your name and pray and make supplication to You in this house,
34 then hear in heaven, and forgive the sin of Your people Israel, and bring them back
to the land which You gave to their fathers.
35 "When the heavens are shut up and there is no rain, because they have sinned against
You, and they pray toward this place and confess Your name and turn from their sin
when You afflict them,
36 then hear in heaven and forgive the sin of Your servants and of Your people Israel,
indeed, teach them the good way in which they should walk. And send rain on Your land,
which You have given Your people for an inheritance.
37 "If there is famine in the land, if there is pestilence, if there is blight *or* mildew, locust *or* grasshopper, if their enemy besieges them in the land of their cities, whatever
plague, whatever sickness *there is,*
38 whatever prayer or supplication is made by any man *or* by all Your people Israel,
each knowing the affliction of his own heart, and spreading his hands toward this house;
39 then hear in heaven Your dwelling place, and forgive and act and render to each
according to all his ways, whose heart You know, for You alone know the hearts of all
the sons of men,
40 that they may [14]fear You all the days that they live in the land which You have given
to our fathers.
41 "Also concerning the foreigner who is not of Your people Israel, when he comes from
a far country for Your name's sake
42 (for they will hear of Your great name and Your mighty hand, and of Your outstretched arm); when he comes and prays toward this house,
43 hear in heaven Your dwelling place, and do according to all for which the foreigner
calls to You, in order that all the peoples of the earth may know Your name, to [15]fear
You, as *do* Your people Israel, and that they may know that this house which I have built
is called by Your name.
44 "When Your people go out to battle against their enemy, by whatever way You shall
send them, and they pray to the LORD toward the city which You have chosen and the
house which I have built for Your name,
45 then hear in heaven their prayer and their supplication, and maintain their cause.
46 "When they sin against You (for there is no man who does not sin) and You are angry with them and deliver them to an enemy, so that they take them away captive to the
land of the enemy, far off or near;

14 Or *revere* **15** Or *reverence*

8:28 Phil 4:6
8:29 2 Chr 7:15; Neh 1:6; Deut 12:11
8:30 Neh 1:6; Dan 6:10; Ex 34:6, 7; Ps 85:2; Dan 9:9; 1 John 1:9
8:31 Ex 22:8-11
8:32 Deut 25:1
8:33 Lev 26:17, 25; Deut 28:25, 48; Lev 26:40-42
8:35 Lev 26:19; Deut 11:16, 17; 2 Sam 24:10-13
8:36 1 Sam 12:23; Ps 5:8; 25:4, 5; 27:11; 86:11; 119:133; Jer 6:16; 1 Kin 18:1, 41-45; Jer 14:22
8:37 Lev 26:16, 25, 26; Deut 28:21-23, 38-42
8:39 1 Sam 2:3; 16:7; 1 Chr 28:9; Ps 11:4; Jer 17:10; John 2:24, 25; Acts 1:24
8:42 Ex 13:3; Deut 3:24
8:43 Josh 4:23, 24; 1 Sam 17:46; Ps 67:2
8:44 2 Chr 14:11
8:46 Ps 130:3, 4; 143:2; Prov 20:9; Eccl 7:20; Rom 3:23; 1 John 1:8-10; Lev 26:34-39; 2 Kin 17:6, 18; 25:21

8:33–34 After Solomon's reign, the people continually turned away from God. The rest of the kingdom era is a vivid fulfillment of Solomon's description in these verses. As a result of the people's sin, God let them be overrun by enemies several times. Then, in desperation, they cried out to God for forgiveness, and God restored them.

8:41–43 God chose Israel to be a blessing to the whole world (Genesis 12:1–3). This blessing found its fulfillment in Jesus—a descendant of Abraham and David (Galatians 3:8–9)—who became the Messiah for all people, Jews and non-Jews. When the Israelites first entered the promised land, they were ordered to clear out several wicked nations; thus we read in the Old Testament of many wars. But we should not conclude that war was Israel's first duty. After subduing the evil people, Israel was to become a light to the surrounding nations. Sadly, Israel's own sin and spiritual blindness prevented them from reaching out to the rest of the world with God's love. Jesus came to do what the nation of Israel failed to do.

8:46–53 Solomon, who seemed to have prophetic insight into the future captivities of his people (2 Kings 17; 25), asked God to be merciful to them when they cried out to him, to forgive them, and to return them to their homeland. Reference to their return is made in Ezra 1—2; Nehemiah 1—2.

47 if they take thought in the land where they have been taken captive, and repent and
make supplication to You in the land of those who have taken them captive, saying, 'We
have sinned and have committed iniquity, we have acted wickedly';
48 if they return to You with all their heart and with all their soul in the land of their
enemies who have taken them captive, and pray to You toward their land which You
have given to their fathers, the city which You have chosen, and the house which I have
built for Your name;
49 then hear their prayer and their supplication in heaven Your dwelling place, and
maintain their cause,
50 and forgive Your people who have sinned against You and all their transgressions
which they have transgressed against You, and make them *objects of* compassion before
those who have taken them captive, that they may have compassion on them
51 (for they are Your people and Your inheritance which You have brought forth from
Egypt, from the midst of the iron furnace),
52 that Your eyes may be open to the supplication of Your servant and to the supplication of Your people Israel, to listen to them whenever they call to You.
53 "For You have separated them from all the peoples of the earth as Your inheritance,
as You spoke through Moses Your servant, when You brought our fathers forth from
Egypt, O Lord GOD."

Solomon's Benediction

54 When Solomon had finished praying this entire prayer and supplication to the LORD,
he arose from before the altar of the LORD, from kneeling on his knees with his hands
spread toward heaven.
55 And he stood and blessed all the assembly of Israel with a loud voice, saying:
56 "Blessed be the LORD, who has given rest to His people Israel, according to all that
He promised; not one word has failed of all His good promise, which He promised
through Moses His servant.
57 "May the LORD our God be with us, as He was with our fathers; may He not leave us
or forsake us,
58 that He may incline our hearts to Himself, to walk in all His ways and to keep His
commandments and His statutes and His ordinances, which He commanded our fathers.
59 "And may these words of mine, with which I have made supplication before the LORD,
be near to the LORD our God day and night, that He may maintain the cause of His servant and the cause of His people Israel, as each day requires,
60 so that all the peoples of the earth may know that the LORD is God; there is no one
else.
61 "Let your heart therefore be wholly devoted to the LORD our God, to walk in His
statutes and to keep His commandments, as at this day."

Dedicatory Sacrifices

62 Now the king and all Israel with him offered sacrifice before the LORD.
63 Solomon offered for the sacrifice of peace offerings, which he offered to the LORD,
22,000 oxen and 120,000 sheep. So the king and all the sons of Israel dedicated the house
of the LORD.
64 On the same day the king consecrated the middle of the court that *was* before the
house of the LORD, because there he offered the burnt offering and the grain offering
and the fat of the peace offerings; for the bronze altar that *was* before the LORD *was* too
small to hold the burnt offering and the grain offering and the fat of the peace offerings.
65 So Solomon observed the feast at that time, and all Israel with him, a great assembly from the entrance of Hamath to the brook of Egypt, before the LORD our God, for
seven days and seven *more* days, *even* fourteen days.
66 On the eighth day he sent the people away and they blessed the king. Then they

8:47 Lev 26:40-42; Neh 9:2; Ezra 9:6, 7; Neh 1:6; Ps 106:6; Dan 9:5

8:48 Deut 4:29; 1 Sam 7:3, 4; Neh 1:9; Dan 6:10; Jon 2:4

8:50 2 Chr 30:9; Ps 106:46; Acts 7:10

8:51 Ex 32:11, 12; Deut 9:26-29; Deut 4:20; Jer 11:4

8:52 1 Kin 8:29

8:53 Ex 19:5, 6; Deut 9:26-29

8:54 2 Chr 7:1; 2 Chr 6:13

8:55 Num 6:23-26; 2 Sam 6:18; 1 Kin 8:14

8:56 Deut 12:10; Josh 21:45; 23:14, 15

8:57 Deut 31:6, 17; Josh 1:5; 1 Sam 12:22; Rom 8:31; Heb 13:5

8:58 Ps 119:36; Jer 31:33

8:60 Josh 4:24; 1 Sam 17:46; 1 Kin 8:43; 2 Kin 19:19; Deut 4:35; 1 Kin 18:39; Jer 10:10-12

8:61 Deut 18:13; 1 Kin 11:4; 2 Kin 20:3

8:62 2 Chr 7:4-10; 2 Sam 6:17-19; Ezra 6:16, 17

8:63 Ezra 6:15-18; Neh 12:27

8:64 2 Chr 4:1

8:65 Lev 23:34-42; 1 Kin 8:2; Num 34:8; Josh 13:5; Judg 3:3; 2 Kin 14:25; Gen 15:18; Ex 23:31; Num 34:5; Josh 13:3

8:56-60 Solomon praised the Lord and prayed for the people. His prayer can be a pattern for our prayers. He had five basic requests: (1) for God's presence (8:57); (2) for the desire to do God's will in everything; ("incline our hearts to Himself," 8:58); (3) for help with each day's need (8:59); (4) for the desire and ability to obey God's decrees and commands (8:58); (5) for the spread of God's kingdom to the entire world (8:60). These prayer requests are just as important today. When you pray for your church or family, you can make these same requests to God.

went to their tents joyful and glad of heart for all the goodness that the LORD had shown
to David His servant and to Israel His people.

4. Solomon's greatness and downfall

God's Promise and Warning

9 Now it came about when Solomon had finished building the house of the LORD, and
the king's house, and all that Solomon desired to do,
2 that the LORD appeared to Solomon a second time, as He had appeared to him at
Gibeon.
3 The LORD said to him, "I have heard your prayer and your supplication, which you
have made before Me; I have consecrated this house which you have built by putting My
name there forever, and My eyes and My heart will be there perpetually.
4 "As for you, if you will walk before Me as your father David walked, in integrity of
heart and uprightness, doing according to all that I have commanded you *and* will keep
My statutes and My ordinances,
5 then I will establish the throne of your kingdom over Israel forever, just as I promised to your father David, saying, 'You shall not lack a man on the throne of Israel.'
6 "But if you or your sons indeed turn away from following Me, and do not keep My
commandments and My statutes which I have set before you, and go and serve other
gods and worship them,
7 then I will cut off Israel from the land which I have given them, and the house which
I have consecrated for My name, I will cast out of My sight. So Israel will become a proverb and a byword among all peoples.
8 "And this house will become a heap of ruins; everyone who passes by will be astonished and hiss and say, 'Why has the LORD done thus to this land and to this house?'
9 "And they will say, 'Because they forsook the LORD their God, who brought their
fathers out of the land of Egypt, and adopted other gods and worshiped them and served
them, therefore the LORD has brought all this adversity on them.' "

Cities Given to Hiram

10 It came about at the end of twenty years in which Solomon had built the two houses,
the house of the LORD and the king's house
11 (Hiram king of Tyre had supplied Solomon with cedar and cypress timber and gold
according to all his desire), then King Solomon gave Hiram twenty cities in the land of
Galilee.
12 So Hiram came out from Tyre to see the cities which Solomon had given him, and
they did not please him.
13 He said, "What are these cities which you have given me, my brother?" So they were
called the land of [16]Cabul to this day.
14 And Hiram sent to the king 120 talents of gold.
15 Now this is the account of the forced labor which King Solomon levied to build the
house of the LORD, his own house, the [17]Millo, the wall of Jerusalem, Hazor, Megiddo,
and Gezer.
16 *For* Pharaoh king of Egypt had gone up and captured Gezer and burned it with fire,
and killed the Canaanites who lived in the city, and had given it *as* a dowry to his daughter, Solomon's wife.

9:1 2 Chr 7:11; 1 Kin 7:1, 2; 2 Chr 8:6
9:2 1 Kin 3:5; 11:9; 2 Chr 1:7
9:3 2 Kin 20:5; Ps 10:17; 34:17; 1 Kin 8:29; Deut 11:12; 2 Chr 6:40
9:4 1 Kin 3:6, 14; 11:4, 6, 8; 2 Kin 20:3; Ps 128:1
9:5 2 Sam 7:12, 16; 1 Kin 2:4; 6:12; 1 Chr 22:10
9:6 2 Sam 7:14-16; 1 Chr 28:9; Ps 89:30ff
9:7 Lev 18:24-29; Deut 4:26; 2 Kin 17:23; Jer 7:4-14; Deut 28:37; Ps 44:14; Jer 24:9
9:8 2 Kin 25:9; 2 Chr 36:19; Deut 29:24-26; 2 Chr 7:21; Jer 22:8, 9, 28
9:9 Deut 29:25-28; Jer 2:10-13
9:10 2 Chr 8:1; 1 Kin 6:37, 38; 7:1; 9:1
9:13 Josh 19:27
9:14 1 Kin 9:11
9:15 1 Kin 5:13; 2 Sam 5:9; 1 Kin 9:24; Josh 11:1; 19:36; Josh 17:11; Judg 1:29
9:16 Josh 16:10; 1 Kin 3:1; 7:8

16 I.e. as good as nothing **17** I.e. citadel

9:4–9 God appeared to Solomon a second time; the first was at Gibeon (3:4–15). For more on the conditions of God's great promise to David and his descendants, see the note on 2:3–4.

9:11–14 Was Solomon being unfair to Hiram? It is not clear from these verses whether Solomon gave these towns to Hiram, or whether they were collateral until he could repay Hiram for the gold he had borrowed. Second Chronicles 8:1–2 implies that the towns were returned to Solomon. In either case, Hiram probably preferred a piece of land on the coast more suitable for trade (the name he gave these cities, *Cabul,* sounds like the Hebrew word for "good-for-nothing"). In the end, Hiram was repaid many times over through his trade partnerships with Solomon (2 Chronicles 9:10, 21). Because Phoenicia was on friendly terms with Israel and dependent on it for grain and oil, Hiram's relationship with Solomon was more important than a feud over some cities.

9:16 At this time, Israel and Egypt were the major powers in the Near East. For many years Egypt had retained control of Gezer, even though it was in Israelite territory. In Solomon's time the pharaoh gave the city to his daughter, whom Solomon married, putting Gezer under Israelite control. Intermarriage among royal families was common, but it was not endorsed by God (Deuteronomy 17:17).

17 So Solomon rebuilt Gezer and the lower Beth-horon
18 and Baalath and Tamar in the wilderness, in the land *of Judah,*
19 and all the storage cities which Solomon had, even the cities for his chariots and the
cities for his horsemen, and all that it pleased Solomon to build in Jerusalem, in Lebanon, and in all the land under his rule.
20 *As for* all the people who were left of the Amorites, the Hittites, the Perizzites, the
Hivites and the Jebusites, who were not of the sons of Israel,
21 their descendants who were left after them in the land whom the sons of Israel were
unable to destroy utterly, from them Solomon levied forced laborers, even to this day.
22 But Solomon did not make slaves of the sons of Israel; for they were men of war, his
servants, his princes, his captains, his chariot commanders, and his horsemen.
23 These *were* the chief officers who *were* over Solomon's work, five hundred and fifty,
who ruled over the people doing the work.
24 As soon as Pharaoh's daughter came up from the city of David to her house which
Solomon had built for her, then he built the Millo.
25 Now three times in a year Solomon offered burnt offerings and peace offerings on
the altar which he built to the LORD, burning incense with them *on the altar* which *was*
before the LORD. So he finished the house.
26 King Solomon also built a fleet of ships in Ezion-geber, which is near Eloth on the
shore of the Red Sea, in the land of Edom.
27 And Hiram sent his servants with the fleet, sailors who knew the sea, along with the
servants of Solomon.
28 They went to Ophir and took four hundred and twenty talents of gold from there,
and brought *it* to King Solomon.

The Queen of Sheba

10 Now when the queen of Sheba heard about the fame of Solomon concerning the
name of the LORD, she came to test him with difficult questions.
2 So she came to Jerusalem with a very large retinue, with camels carrying spices and
very much gold and precious stones. When she came to Solomon, she spoke with him
about all that was in her heart.
3 Solomon answered all her questions; nothing was hidden from the king which he
did not explain to her.
4 When the queen of Sheba perceived all the wisdom of Solomon, the house that he
had built,
5 the food of his table, the seating of his servants, the attendance of his waiters and
their attire, his cupbearers, and his stairway by which he went up to the house of the
LORD, there was no more spirit in her.
6 Then she said to the king, "It was a true report which I heard in my own land about
your words and your wisdom.

9:17 Josh 10:10; 16:3; 21:22; 2 Chr 8:5
9:18 Josh 19:44
9:19 1 Kin 10:26; 2 Chr 1:14; 1 Kin 4:26; 1 Kin 9:1
9:21 Judg 1:21-29; 3:1; Josh 15:63; 17:12, 13; Judg 1:28, 35; Gen 9:25, 26; Ezra 2:55, 58
9:22 Lev 25:39
9:23 2 Chr 8:10; 1 Kin 5:16
9:24 1 Kin 3:1; 7:8; 2 Sam 5:9; 1 Kin 9:15; 11:27; 2 Chr 32:5
9:25 Ex 23:14-17; Deut 16:16
9:26 1 Kin 22:48; Num 33:35; Deut 2:8; 1 Kin 22:48
9:27 1 Kin 5:6, 9; 10:11
9:28 1 Chr 29:4; 2 Chr 8:18
10:1 2 Chr 9:1; Matt 12:42; Luke 11:31; Gen 10:7, 28; Ps 72:10, 15; Judg 14:12-14; Ps 49:4
10:2 1 Kin 10:10

10:1–5 The queen of Sheba came to see for herself if everything she had heard about Solomon was true. Contests using riddles or proverbs were often used to test wisdom. The queen may have used some of these as she questioned Solomon (10:1, 3). When she realized the extent of his riches and wisdom, she was overwhelmed and no longer questioned his power or wisdom. No longer a competitor, she became an admirer. Her experience was repeated by many kings and foreign dignitaries who paid honor to Solomon (4:34).

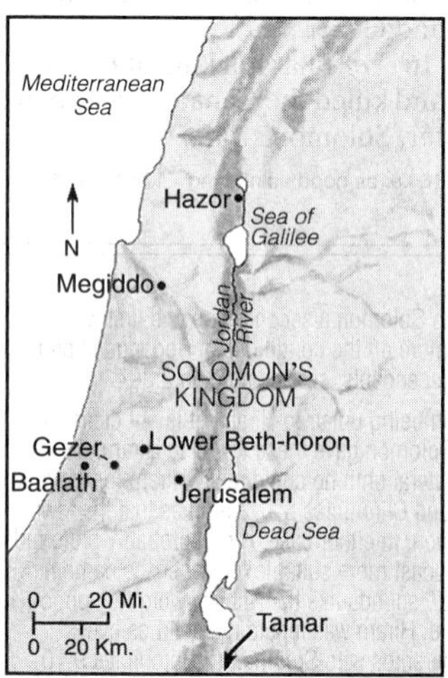

SOLOMON'S BUILDING PROJECTS
Solomon became known as one of the great builders in Israel's history. He built Hazor, Megiddo, and Gezer as fortress cities at key points during his reign. He also rebuilt the cities of lower Beth-horon, Baalath, and Tamar.

7 "Nevertheless I did not believe the reports, until I came and my eyes had seen it. And behold, the half was not told me. You exceed *in* wisdom and prosperity the report which I heard.

10:8 Prov 8:34

8 "How blessed are your men, how blessed are these your servants who stand before you continually *and* hear your wisdom.

10:9 1 Kin 5:7; 1 Chr 17:22; 2 Chr 2:11; 2 Sam 8:15; 23:3; Ps 72:2

9 "Blessed be the LORD your God who delighted in you to set you on the throne of Israel; because the LORD loved Israel forever, therefore He made you king, to do justice and righteousness."

10:10 1 Kin 10:2

10 She gave the king a hundred and twenty talents of gold, and a very great *amount* of spices and precious stones. Never again did such abundance of spices come in as that which the queen of Sheba gave King Solomon.

10:11 1 Kin 9:27, 28; Job 22:24

11 Also the ships of Hiram, which brought gold from Ophir, brought in from Ophir a very great *number of* almug trees and precious stones.

10:12 2 Chr 9:11

12 The king made of the almug trees supports for the house of the LORD and for the king's house, also lyres and harps for the singers; such almug trees have not come in *again* nor have they been seen to this day.

13 King Solomon gave to the queen of Sheba all her desire which she requested, besides what he gave her according to his royal bounty. Then she turned and went to her own land together with her servants.

Wealth, Splendor and Wisdom

10:14 2 Chr 9:13-28

14 Now the weight of gold which came in to Solomon in one year was 666 talents of gold,

10:15 2 Chr 9:14

15 besides *that* from the traders and the [18]wares of the merchants and all the kings of the Arabs and the governors of the country.

10:16 1 Kin 14:26-28; 2 Chr 12:9, 10

16 King Solomon made 200 large shields of beaten gold, using 600 *shekels of* gold on each large shield.

10:17 1 Kin 14:26; 1 Kin 7:2

17 *He made* 300 shields of beaten gold, using three minas of gold on each shield, and the king put them in the house of the forest of Lebanon.

10:18 1 Kin 10:22; 2 Chr 9:17; Ps 45:8

18 Moreover, the king made a great throne of ivory and overlaid it with refined gold.

19 *There were* six steps to the throne and a round top to the throne at its rear, and arms on each side of the seat, and two lions standing beside the arms.

20 Twelve lions were standing there on the six steps on the one side and on the other; nothing like *it* was made for any other kingdom.

21 All King Solomon's drinking vessels *were* of gold, and all the vessels of the house of the forest of Lebanon *were* of pure gold. None was of silver; it was not considered [19]valuable in the days of Solomon.

10:22 1 Kin 9:26-28; 22:48; 2 Chr 20:36

22 For the king had at sea the ships of Tarshish with the ships of Hiram; once every three years the ships of Tarshish came bringing gold and silver, ivory and apes and peacocks.

10:23 1 Kin 3:12, 13; 4:30

23 So King Solomon became greater than all the kings of the earth in riches and in wisdom.

10:24 1 Kin 3:9, 12, 28

24 All the earth was seeking the presence of Solomon, to hear his wisdom which God had put in his heart.

10:25 Ps 68:29

25 They brought every man his gift, articles of silver and gold, garments, weapons, spices, horses, and mules, so much year by year.

18 Or *traffic* **19** Lit *anything*

10:14ff When Solomon asked for wisdom, God promised him riches and honor as well (3:13). These verses show just how extensive his wealth became. Israel was no longer a second-rate nation, but at the height of its power and wealth. Solomon's riches became legendary. Great men came from many nations to listen to Israel's powerful king. Jesus would later refer to "Solomon in all his glory" (Matthew 6:29).

10:23 Why does the Bible place so much emphasis on Solomon's material possessions? In the Old Testament, riches were considered tangible evidence of God's blessing. Prosperity was seen as a proof of right living. In the books of Ecclesiastes and Job this concept is placed in a broader perspective. In ideal conditions, people prosper when God runs their lives, but prosperity is not guaranteed. Wealth does not prove that a person is living rightly before God, and poverty does not indicate sin.

In fact, a greater evidence that a person is living for God is the presence of suffering and persecution (Mark 10:29–31; 13:13). The most important "treasure" is not earthly, but heavenly (Matthew 6:19–21; 19:21; 1 Timothy 6:17–19). The gift of greatest worth has no price tag—it is the gift of salvation freely offered by God.

26 Now Solomon gathered chariots and horsemen; and he had 1,400 chariots and 12,000
horsemen, and he stationed them in the chariot cities and with the king in Jerusalem.
27 The king made silver *as common* as stones in Jerusalem, and he made cedars as
plentiful as sycamore trees that are in the [20]lowland.
28 Also Solomon's import of horses was from Egypt and Kue, *and* the king's merchants
procured *them* from Kue for a price.
29 A chariot was imported from Egypt for 600 *shekels* of silver, and a horse for 150;
and by the same means they exported them to all the kings of the Hittites and to the
kings of the Arameans.

10:26 1 Kin 4:26; 2 Chr 1:14-17; 9:25; 1 Kin 9:19

10:27 Deut 17:17; 2 Chr 1:15

10:28 Deut 17:16; 2 Chr 1:16; 9:28

10:29 2 Kin 7:6, 7

Solomon Turns from God

11 Now King Solomon loved many foreign women along with the daughter of Pharaoh: Moabite, Ammonite, Edomite, Sidonian, and Hittite women,
2 from the nations concerning which the LORD had said to the sons of Israel, "You
shall not associate with them, nor shall they associate with you, *for* they will surely turn
your heart away after their gods." Solomon held fast to these in love.
3 He had seven hundred wives, princesses, and three hundred concubines, and his wives
turned his heart away.
4 For when Solomon was old, his wives turned his heart away after other gods; and
his heart was not [21]wholly devoted to the LORD his God, as the heart of David his father
had been.
5 For Solomon went after Ashtoreth the goddess of the Sidonians and after Milcom
the detestable idol of the Ammonites.
6 Solomon did what was evil in the sight of the LORD, and did not follow the LORD
fully, as David his father *had done.*
7 Then Solomon built a high place for Chemosh the detestable idol of Moab, on the
mountain which is east of Jerusalem, and for Molech the detestable idol of the sons of
Ammon.
8 Thus also he did for all his foreign wives, who burned incense and sacrificed to their
gods.
9 Now the LORD was angry with Solomon because his heart was turned away from
the LORD, the God of Israel, who had appeared to him twice,
10 and had commanded him concerning this thing, that he should not go after other
gods; but he did not observe what the LORD had commanded.

11:1 Deut 17:17; Neh 13:23-27

11:2 Ex 23:31-33; 34:12-16; Deut 7:3

11:3 2 Sam 5:13-16

11:4 1 Kin 9:4

11:5 Judg 2:13; 10:6; 1 Sam 7:3, 4; 1 Kin 11:7

11:7 Num 21:29; Judg 11:24; 2 Kin 23:13; Lev 20:2-5; 2 Kin 23:10; Acts 7:43

11:9 Ps 90:7; 1 Kin 11:2, 4; 1 Kin 3:5; 9:2

11:10 1 Kin 6:12; 9:6, 7

20 Heb *Shephelah* 21 Lit *complete with*

10:26—11:3 In accumulating chariots and horsemen, a huge harem, and incredible wealth, Solomon was violating God's commands for a king (Deuteronomy 17:14–20). Why were they prohibited? God knew how these activities would hurt the nation both politically and spiritually (1 Samuel 8:11–18). The more luxurious Solomon's court became, the more the people were taxed. Excessive taxation created unrest, and soon conditions became ripe for a revolution. With everything he wanted, Solomon forgot God and allowed pagan influences to enter his court through his pagan wives, thus accelerating the spiritual corruption of the nation.

11:2 Although Solomon had clear instructions from God *not* to marry women from foreign nations, he chose to disregard God's commands. He married not one, but many foreign women, who subsequently led him away from God. God knows our strengths and weaknesses, and his commands are always for our good. When people ignore God's commands, negative consequences inevitably result. It is not enough to know God's Word or even to believe it; we must follow it and apply it to our daily activities and decisions. Take God's commands seriously. Like Solomon, the wisest man who ever lived, we are not as strong as we may think.

11:3 For all his wisdom, Solomon had some weak spots. He could not say no to compromise or to lustful desires. Whether he married to strengthen political alliances or to gain personal pleasure, these foreign wives led him into idolatry. You may have strong faith, but you also have weak spots—and that is where temptation usually strikes. Strengthen and protect your weaker areas because a chain is only as strong as its weakest link. If Solomon, the wisest man, could fall, so can you.

11:4 Solomon handled great pressures in running the government, but he could not handle the pressure from his wives who wanted him to worship their gods. In marriage and close friendships, it is difficult to resist pressure to compromise. Our love leads us to identify with the desires of those we care about.

Faced with such pressure, Solomon at first *resisted* it, maintaining pure faith. Then he *tolerated* a more widespread practice of idolatry. Finally he became involved in idolatrous worship, *rationalizing* away the potential danger to himself and to the kingdom. It is because we want to please and identify with our loved ones that God asks us not to marry those who do not share our commitment to him.

11:5–8 Ashtoreth was a goddess that symbolized reproductive power—a mistress of the god Baal. Milcom was the national god of the Ammonites, called "detestable" because its worship rites included child sacrifice. Chemosh was the Moabites' national god. The Israelites were warned against worshiping all other gods in general and Molech in particular (Exodus 20:1–6; Leviticus 18:21; 20:1–5).

11:9–10 Solomon didn't turn away from God all at once or in a brief moment. His spiritual coldness started with a minor departure from God's laws (3:1). Over the years, that little sin grew until it resulted in Solomon's downfall. A little sin can be the first step in turning away from God. It is not the sins we don't know about, but the sins we excuse, that cause us the greatest trouble. We must never let any sin go unchallenged. In your life, is an unchallenged sin spreading like a deadly cancer? Don't excuse it. Confess this sin to God and ask him for strength to resist temptation.

11:11 1 Sam 2:30; 1 Kin 11:29-31; 12:15, 16, 20; 2 Kin 17:15, 21

11 So the LORD said to Solomon, "Because you have done this, and you have not kept
My covenant and My statutes, which I have commanded you, I will surely tear the kingdom from you, and will give it to your servant.
12 "Nevertheless I will not do it in your days for the sake of your father David, *but* I will
tear it out of the hand of your son.

11:13 2 Sam 7:15; 1 Chr 17:13; Ps 89:33; 1 Kin 11:32, 36; 12:20; 1 Kin 8:29

13 "However, I will not tear away all the kingdom, *but* I will give one tribe to your son
for the sake of My servant David and for the sake of Jerusalem which I have chosen."

God Raises Adversaries

14 Then the LORD raised up an adversary to Solomon, Hadad the Edomite; he was of
the royal line in Edom.

11:15 2 Sam 8:14; 1 Chr 18:12, 13; Deut 20:13

15 For it came about, when David was in Edom, and Joab the commander of the army
had gone up to bury the slain, and had struck down every male in Edom
16 (for Joab and all Israel stayed there six months, until he had cut off every male in
Edom),
17 that Hadad fled to Egypt, he and certain Edomites of his father's servants with him,
while Hadad *was* a young boy.

11:18 Num 10:12; Deut 1:1

18 They arose from Midian and came to Paran; and they took men with them from
Paran and came to Egypt, to Pharaoh king of Egypt, who gave him a house and assigned
him food and gave him land.
19 Now Hadad found great favor before Pharaoh, so that he gave him in marriage the
sister of his own wife, the sister of Tahpenes the queen.
20 The sister of Tahpenes bore his son Genubath, whom Tahpenes weaned in Pharaoh's
house; and Genubath was in Pharaoh's house among the sons of Pharaoh.

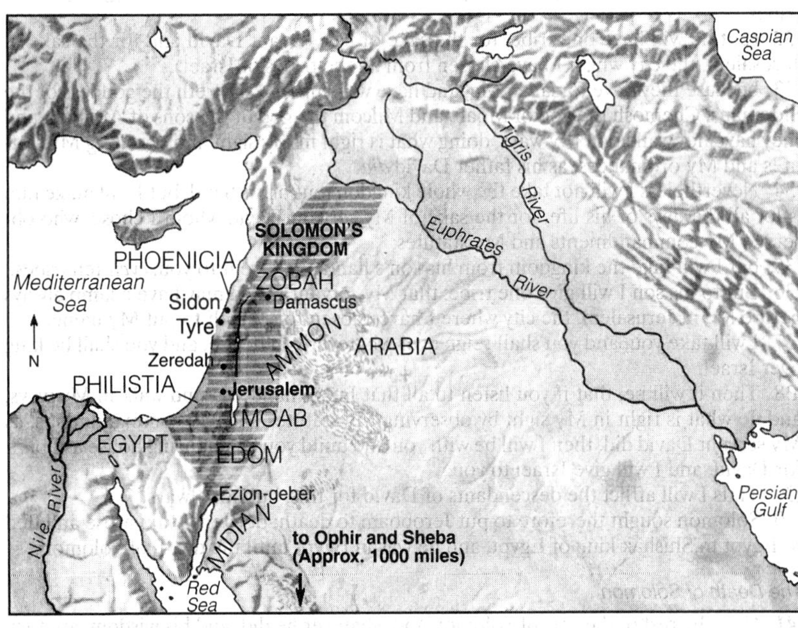

FRIENDS AND ENEMIES Solomon's reputation brought acclaim and riches from many nations, but he disobeyed God, marrying pagan women and worshiping their gods. So God raised up enemies like Hadad from Edom and Rezon from Zobah (modern-day Syria). Jeroboam from Zeredah was another enemy who would eventually divide this mighty kingdom.

11:11–13 Solomon's powerful and glorious kingdom could have been blessed for all time; instead, it was approaching its end. Solomon had God's promises, guidance, and answers to prayer, and yet he allowed sin to remain all around him. Eventually it corrupted him so much that he was no longer interested in God. Psalm 127, written by Solomon, says, "Unless the LORD builds the house, they labor in vain who build it." Solomon had begun by laying the foundation with God, but he did not follow through in his later years. As a result, he lost everything. It is not enough to get off to a right start in building our marriage, career, or church on God's principles; we must remain faithful to God to the end (Mark 13:13). God must be in control of our lives from start to finish.

11:14–22 Edom was the kingdom southeast of the Dead Sea. David had added this nation to his empire (2 Samuel 8:13–14). It was of strategic importance because it controlled the route to the Red Sea. Edom's revolt was disturbing the peace of Solomon's kingdom.

21 But when Hadad heard in Egypt that David slept with his fathers and that Joab the
commander of the army was dead, Hadad said to Pharaoh, "Send me away, that I may
go to my own country."
22 Then Pharaoh said to him, "But what have you lacked with me, that behold, you are
seeking to go to your own country?" And he answered, "Nothing; nevertheless you must
surely let me go."
23 God also raised up *another* adversary to him, Rezon the son of Eliada, who had fled
from his lord Hadadezer king of Zobah.
24 He gathered men to himself and became leader of a marauding band, after David
slew them of *Zobah;* and they went to Damascus and stayed there, and reigned in Damascus.
25 So he was an adversary to Israel all the days of Solomon, along with the evil that
Hadad *did;* and he abhorred Israel and reigned over Aram.
26 Then Jeroboam the son of Nebat, an Ephraimite of Zeredah, Solomon's servant,
whose mother's name was Zeruah, a widow, also rebelled against the king.
27 Now this was the reason why he rebelled against the king: Solomon built the Millo,
and closed up the breach of the city of his father David.
28 Now the man Jeroboam was a valiant warrior, and when Solomon saw that the young
man was industrious, he appointed him over all the forced labor of the house of Joseph.
29 It came about at that time, when Jeroboam went out of Jerusalem, that the prophet
Ahijah the Shilonite found him on the road. Now Ahijah had clothed himself with a new
cloak; and both of them were alone in the field.
30 Then Ahijah took hold of the new cloak which was on him and tore it into twelve
pieces.
31 He said to Jeroboam, "Take for yourself ten pieces; for thus says the LORD, the God
of Israel, 'Behold, I will tear the kingdom out of the hand of Solomon and give you ten
tribes
32 (but he will have one tribe, for the sake of My servant David and for the sake of
Jerusalem, the city which I have chosen from all the tribes of Israel),
33 because they have forsaken Me, and have worshiped Ashtoreth the goddess of the
Sidonians, Chemosh the god of Moab, and Milcom the god of the sons of Ammon; and
they have not walked in My ways, doing what is right in My sight and *observing* My statutes and My ordinances, as his father David *did.*
34 'Nevertheless I will not take the whole kingdom out of his hand, but I will make him
ruler all the days of his life, for the sake of My servant David whom I chose, who observed My commandments and My statutes;
35 but I will take the kingdom from his son's hand and give it to you, *even* ten tribes.
36 'But to his son I will give one tribe, that My servant David may have a lamp always
before Me in Jerusalem, the city where I have chosen for Myself to put My name.
37 'I will take you, and you shall reign over whatever you desire, and you shall be king
over Israel.
38 'Then it will be, that if you listen to all that I command you and walk in My ways,
and do what is right in My sight by observing My statutes and My commandments, as
My servant David did, then I will be with you and build you an enduring house as I built
for David, and I will give Israel to you.
39 'Thus I will afflict the descendants of David for this, but not always.' "
40 Solomon sought therefore to put Jeroboam to death; but Jeroboam arose and fled
to Egypt to Shishak king of Egypt, and he was in Egypt until the death of Solomon.

The Death of Solomon

41 Now the rest of the acts of Solomon and whatever he did, and his wisdom, are they
not written in the book of the acts of Solomon?
42 Thus the time that Solomon reigned in Jerusalem over all Israel was forty years.

11:21 1 Kin 2:10
11:23 1 Kin 11:14; 2 Sam 8:3; 10:16
11:24 2 Sam 10:8, 18
11:26 1 Kin 11:11, 28; 12:2, 20; 2 Chr 13:6; 2 Sam 20:21
11:27 1 Kin 9:15, 24
11:28 Prov 22:29
11:29 1 Kin 12:15; 14:2; 2 Chr 9:29
11:30 1 Sam 15:27, 28
11:31 1 Kin 11:11, 12
11:32 1 Kin 11:13; 12:21; 1 Kin 11:13; 14:21
11:33 1 Sam 7:3; 1 Kin 11:5-8; Num 21:29; Jer 48:7, 13
11:35 1 Kin 11:12; 12:16, 17
11:36 1 Kin 11:13; 1 Kin 15:4; 2 Kin 8:19; Ps 132:17
11:38 Deut 31:8; Josh 1:5; 2 Sam 7:11, 27
11:40 1 Kin 14:25; 2 Chr 12:2-9
11:41 2 Chr 9:29
11:42 2 Chr 9:30

11:29–39 The prophet Ahijah predicted the division of the kingdom of Israel. After Solomon's death, 10 of Israel's 12 tribes would follow Jeroboam. The other two tribes, Judah and the area of Benjamin around Jerusalem, would remain loyal to David. Judah, the largest tribe, and Benjamin, the smallest, were often mentioned as one tribe because they shared the same border. Both Jeroboam and Ahijah were from Ephraim, the most prominent of the 10 rebel tribes. (For more on the divided kingdom, see the note on 12:20.)

11:41 Nothing is known of "the book of the acts of Solomon." See also the note on 14:19.

11:43 1 Kin 2:10; 2 Chr 9:31; 1 Kin 14:21; Matt 1:7

43 And Solomon slept with his fathers and was buried in the city of his father David,
and his son Rehoboam reigned in his place.

B. THE DIVIDED KINGDOM (12:1—22:53)

After Solomon's death, the northern tribes revolt, forming two separate nations. Each nation experiences disastrous consequences from having evil kings. Elijah appears on the scene, confronting these kings for their sin. God deals with sin in powerful ways. Although judgment may appear to be slow, God will judge evil harshly.

1. Revolt of the northern tribes

King Rehoboam Acts Foolishly

12:1 2 Chr 10:1; Judg 9:6

12 Then Rehoboam went to Shechem, for all Israel had come to Shechem to make
him king.

12:2 1 Kin 11:26, 40

2 Now when Jeroboam the son of Nebat heard *of it,* he was living in Egypt (for he was
yet in Egypt, where he had fled from the presence of King Solomon).
3 Then they sent and called him, and Jeroboam and all the assembly of Israel came
and spoke to Rehoboam, saying,

12:4 1 Sam 8:11-18; 1 Kin 4:7, 21-25; 9:15

4 "Your father made our yoke hard; now therefore lighten the hard service of your
father and his heavy yoke which he put on us, and we will serve you."
5 Then he said to them, "Depart for three days, then return to me." So the people
departed.

12:5 1 Kin 12:12

12:6 1 Kin 4:1-6; Job 12:12; 32:7

6 King Rehoboam consulted with the elders who had served his father Solomon while
he was still alive, saying, "How do you counsel *me* to answer this people?"
7 Then they spoke to him, saying, "If you will be a servant to this people today, and
will serve them and grant them their petition, and speak good words to them, then they
will be your servants forever."

12:7 2 Chr 10:7; Prov 15:1

8 But he forsook the counsel of the elders which they had given him, and consulted
with the young men who grew up with him and served him.
9 So he said to them, "What counsel do you give that we may answer this people who
have spoken to me, saying, 'Lighten the yoke which your father put on us'?"
10 The young men who grew up with him spoke to him, saying, "Thus you shall say to
this people who spoke to you, saying, 'Your father made our yoke heavy, now you make
it lighter for us!' But you shall speak to them, 'My little finger is thicker than my father's
loins!
11 'Whereas my father loaded you with a heavy yoke, I will add to your yoke; my father
disciplined you with whips, but I will discipline you with scorpions.' "

12:12 1 Kin 12:5

12 Then Jeroboam and all the people came to Rehoboam on the third day as the king
had directed, saying, "Return to me on the third day."
13 The king answered the people harshly, for he forsook the advice of the elders which
they had given him,

12:14 Ex 1:13, 14; 5:5-9, 16-18

14 and he spoke to them according to the advice of the young men, saying, "My father

---

THE KINGDOM DIVIDES
Rehoboam's threat of heavier burdens caused a rebellion and divided the nation. Rehoboam ruled the southern kingdom; Jeroboam ruled the northern kingdom. Jeroboam set up idols in Dan and Bethel to discourage worship in Jerusalem. At the same time Aram, Ammon, Moab, and Edom claimed independence from the divided nation.

12:1 Rehoboam was made king at Shechem, about 35 miles north of Jerusalem. It would have been normal to anoint the new king in Jerusalem, the capital city, but Rehoboam saw trouble brewing with Jeroboam and went north to try to maintain good relations with the northern tribes. He probably chose Shechem because it was an ancient location for making covenants (Joshua 24:1). When the kingdom divided, Shechem became the capital of the northern kingdom for a short time (12:25).

12:6–14 Rehoboam asked for advice, but he didn't carefully evaluate what he was told. If he had, he would have realized that the advice offered by the elders was wiser than that of his peers. To evaluate advice, ask if it is realistic, workable, and consistent with Biblical principles. Determine if the results of following the advice will be fair, make improvements, and give a positive solution or direction. Seek counsel from those more experienced and wiser. Advice is helpful only if it is consistent with God's standards.

made your yoke heavy, but I will add to your yoke; my father disciplined you with whips,
but I will discipline you with scorpions."
15 So the king did not listen to the people; for it was a turn *of events* from the LORD,
that He might establish His word, which the LORD spoke through Ahijah the Shilonite
to Jeroboam the son of Nebat.

The Kingdom Divided, Jeroboam Rules Israel

16 When all Israel *saw* that the king did not listen to them, the people answered the
king, saying,
"What portion do we have in David?
We have no inheritance in the son of Jesse;
To your tents, O Israel!
Now look after your own house, David!"
So Israel departed to their tents.
17 But as for the sons of Israel who lived in the cities of Judah, Rehoboam reigned
over them.
18 Then King Rehoboam sent Adoram, who was over the forced labor, and all Israel
stoned him to death. And King Rehoboam made haste to mount his chariot to flee to
Jerusalem.
19 So Israel has been in rebellion against the house of David to this day.
20 It came about when all Israel heard that Jeroboam had returned, that they sent and
called him to the assembly and made him king over all Israel. None but the tribe of Judah followed the house of David.
21 Now when Rehoboam had come to Jerusalem, he assembled all the house of Judah
and the tribe of Benjamin, 180,000 chosen men who were warriors, to fight against the
house of Israel to restore the kingdom to Rehoboam the son of Solomon.
22 But the word of God came to Shemaiah the man of God, saying,
23 "Speak to Rehoboam the son of Solomon, king of Judah, and to all the house of Judah
and Benjamin and to the rest of the people, saying,
24 'Thus says the LORD, "You must not go up and fight against your relatives the sons
of Israel; return every man to his house, for this thing has come from Me."'" So they
listened to the word of the LORD, and returned and went *their way* according to the word
of the LORD.

Jeroboam's Idolatry

25 Then Jeroboam built Shechem in the hill country of Ephraim, and lived there. And
he went out from there and built Penuel.
26 Jeroboam said in his heart, "Now the kingdom will return to the house of David.
27 "If this people go up to offer sacrifices in the house of the LORD at Jerusalem, then
the heart of this people will return to their lord, *even* to Rehoboam king of Judah; and
they will kill me and return to Rehoboam king of Judah."
28 So the king consulted, and made two golden calves, and he said to them, "It is too
much for you to go up to Jerusalem; behold your gods, O Israel, that brought you up
from the land of Egypt."

12:15 Deut 2:30; Judg 14:4; 1 Kin 12:24; 2 Chr 10:15; 1 Kin 11:11, 31
12:16 2 Sam 20:1
12:17 1 Kin 11:13, 36
12:18 2 Sam 20:24; 1 Kin 4:6; 5:14
12:19 2 Kin 17:21
12:20 1 Kin 11:13, 32, 36
12:21 2 Chr 11:1
12:22 2 Chr 11:2; 12:5-7
12:23 1 Kin 12:17
12:24 1 Kin 12:15
12:25 Gen 12:6; Judg 9:45-49; Gen 32:30, 31; Judg 8:8, 17
12:27 Deut 12:5-7, 14
12:28 2 Kin 10:29; 17:16; Hos 8:4-7; Hos 10:5; Ex 32:4, 8

12:15–19 Both Jeroboam and Rehoboam did what was good for themselves, not what was good for their people. Rehoboam was harsh and did not listen to what the people said; Jeroboam established new places of worship to keep his people from traveling to Jerusalem, Rehoboam's capital. Both actions backfired. Rehoboam's move divided the nation, and Jeroboam's turned the people from God. Good leaders put the best interests of the "followers" above their own. Making decisions only for yourself will backfire and cause you to lose more than if you had kept the welfare of others in mind.

12:20 This marks the beginning of the division of the kingdom that lasted for centuries. Ten of Israel's 12 tribes followed Jeroboam and called their new nation Israel (the northern kingdom). The other two tribes remained loyal to Rehoboam and called their nation Judah (the southern kingdom). The kingdom did not split overnight. It was already dividing as early as the days of the judges because of tribal jealousies, especially between Ephraim, the most influential tribe of the north, and Judah, the chief tribe of the south.

Before the days of Saul and David, the religious center of Israel was located, for the most part, in the territory of Ephraim. When Solomon built the temple, he moved the religious center of Israel to Jerusalem. This eventually brought tribal rivalries to the breaking point. (For more information on tribal jealousies and how they affected Israel, see Judges 12:1ff; 2 Samuel 2:4ff; 19:41–43.)

12:28 All Jewish men were required to travel to the temple three times each year (Deuteronomy 16:16), but Jeroboam set up his own worship centers and told his people it was too much trouble to travel all the way to Jerusalem. Those who obeyed Jeroboam were disobeying God. Some ideas, though practical, may include suggestions that lead you away from God. Don't let anyone talk you out of doing what is right by telling you that moral actions are not worth the effort. Do what God wants, no matter what the cost in time, energy, reputation, or resources.

12:29 Hos 10:5; Gen 28:19; Judg 18:26-31

12:30 1 Kin 13:34; 2 Kin 17:21

12:31 1 Kin 13:32; 1 Kin 13:33; 2 Kin 17:32; 2 Chr 11:15; 13:9

12:32 Lev 23:33, 34; Num 29:12; 1 Kin 8:2, 5; Amos 7:10-13

12:33 Num 15:39; 1 Kin 13:1

29 He set one in Bethel, and the other he put in Dan.
30 Now this thing became a sin, for the people went *to worship* before the one as far as
Dan.
31 And he made houses on high places, and made priests from among all the people
who were not of the sons of Levi.
32 Jeroboam instituted a feast in the eighth month on the fifteenth day of the month,
like the feast which is in Judah, and he went up to the altar; thus he did in Bethel, sacrificing to the calves which he had made. And he stationed in Bethel the priests of the
high places which he had made.
33 Then he went up to the altar which he had made in Bethel on the fifteenth day in
the eighth month, even in the month which he had devised in his own heart; and he instituted a feast for the sons of Israel and went up to the altar to burn incense.

2. Kings of Israel and Judah

Jeroboam Warned, Stricken

13:1 1 Kin 12:22; 2 Kin 23:17; 1 Kin 12:33

13:2 1 Kin 13:32; 2 Kin 23:15, 16

13 Now behold, there came a man of God from Judah to Bethel by the word of the
LORD, while Jeroboam was standing by the altar to burn incense.
2 He cried against the altar by the word of the LORD, and said, "O altar, altar, thus
says the LORD, 'Behold, a son shall be born to the house of David, Josiah by name; and
on you he shall sacrifice the priests of the high places who burn incense on you, and human
bones shall be burned on you.' "

TRIBAL JEALOUSIES

Although the kingdom of Israel was "united" under David and Solomon, the tensions between north and south were never resolved. The jealousy and animosity behind this civil war didn't begin with Rehoboam and Jeroboam, but had its roots in the days of the judges, when the people were more interested in tribal loyalty than in national unity. Note how easily tension arose between Ephraim, the most prominent tribe in the north, and Judah, the prominent tribe of the south.

- Ephraim claimed the promises in Genesis 48:17–22 and Genesis 49:22–26 for its leadership role.
- Joshua, who conquered the promised land, was an Ephraimite (Numbers 13:8).
- Samuel, Israel's greatest judge, was from Ephraim (1 Samuel 1:1–28).
- Ephraim allied with Ish-bosheth in revolt against David, who was from the tribe of Judah (2 Samuel 2:8–11).
- David, a shepherd from the tribe of Judah, became king over all Israel, including Ephraim, which no longer had a claim to leadership.
- Although David helped to smooth over the bad feelings, the heavy yoke under Solomon and Rehoboam led the northern tribes to the breaking point.

Such tension developed because Ephraim was the key tribe in the north. They resented Judah's role in leadership under David and resented that the nation's capital and center of worship were located in Jerusalem.

12:28–29 Calves were used as idols to symbolize fertility and strength. Pagan gods of the Canaanites were often depicted as standing on calves or bulls. Jeroboam shrewdly placed the golden calves in Bethel and Dan, strategic locations. Bethel was just 10 miles north of Jerusalem on the main road, enticing the citizens from the north to stop there instead of traveling the rest of the way to Jerusalem. Dan was the northernmost city in Israel, so people living in the north far from Jerusalem were attracted to its convenient location. As leader of the northern kingdom, Jeroboam wanted to establish his own worship centers; otherwise his people would make regular trips to Jerusalem, and his authority would be undermined. Soon this substitute religion had little in common with true faith in God.

12:30 Jeroboam and his advisers did not learn from Israel's previous disaster with a golden calf (Exodus 32). Perhaps they were ignorant of Scripture, or maybe they knew about the event and decided to ignore it. Study the Bible to become aware of God's acts in history, and then apply the important lessons to your life. If you learn from the past, you will not face disaster as a result of repeating others' mistakes (Isaiah 42:23; 1 Corinthians 10:11).

12:32–33 In the days of Israel's founding fathers, the city of Bethel was a symbol of commitment to God because it was there that Jacob had rededicated himself to God (Genesis 28:16–22). But Jeroboam turned the city into Israel's chief religious center, intending it to compete with Jerusalem. Bethel's religion, however, centered on an idol, and this led to Israel's eventual downfall. Bethel developed a reputation as a wicked and idolatrous city. The prophets Hosea and Amos recognized the sins of Bethel and condemned the city for its godless ways (Hosea 4:15–17; 10:8; Amos 5:4–6).

13:2 Three hundred years later, this prophecy was fulfilled in every detail when Josiah killed the pagan priests at their own altars. The story is found in 2 Kings 23:1–20.

3 Then he gave a sign the same day, saying, "This is the sign which the LORD has
spoken, 'Behold, the altar shall be split apart and the ashes which are on it shall be
poured out.' "
4 Now when the king heard the saying of the man of God, which he cried against the
altar in Bethel, Jeroboam stretched out his hand from the altar, saying, "Seize him." But
his hand which he stretched out against him dried up, so that he could not draw it back
to himself.
5 The altar also was split apart and the ashes were poured out from the altar, according to the sign which the man of God had given by the word of the LORD.
6 The king said to the man of God, "Please [22]entreat the LORD your God, and pray
for me, that my hand may be restored to me." So the man of God [23]entreated the LORD,
and the king's hand was restored to him, and it became as it was before.
7 Then the king said to the man of God, "Come home with me and refresh yourself,
and I will give you a reward."
8 But the man of God said to the king, "If you were to give me half your house I would
not go with you, nor would I eat bread or drink water in this place.
9 "For so it was commanded me by the word of the LORD, saying, 'You shall eat no
bread, nor drink water, nor return by the way which you came.' "
10 So he went another way and did not return by the way which he came to Bethel.

13:3 Ex 4:1-5; Judg 6:17; Is 38:7; John 2:18; 1 Cor 1:22

13:6 Ex 8:8, 28; 9:28; 10:17; Acts 8:24; James 5:16; Luke 6:27, 28

13:7 1 Sam 9:7, 8; 2 Kin 5:15

13:8 Num 22:18; 24:13; 1 Kin 13:16, 17

The Disobedient Prophet

11 Now an old prophet was living in Bethel; and his sons came and told him all the
deeds which the man of God had done that day in Bethel; the words which he had spoken to the king, these also they related to their father.
12 Their father said to them, "Which way did he go?" Now his sons had seen the way
which the man of God who came from Judah had gone.
13 Then he said to his sons, "Saddle the donkey for me." So they saddled the donkey
for him and he rode away on it.
14 So he went after the man of God and found him sitting under an oak; and he said to
him, "Are you the man of God who came from Judah?" And he said, "I am."
15 Then he said to him, "Come home with me and eat bread."
16 He said, "I cannot return with you, nor go with you, nor will I eat bread or drink
water with you in this place.
17 "For a command *came* to me by the word of the LORD, 'You shall eat no bread, nor
drink water there; do not return by going the way which you came.' "
18 He said to him, "I also am a prophet like you, and an angel spoke to me by the word
of the LORD, saying, 'Bring him back with you to your house, that he may eat bread and
drink water.' " *But* he lied to him.
19 So he went back with him, and ate bread in his house and drank water.
20 Now it came about, as they were sitting down at the table, that the word of the LORD
came to the prophet who had brought him back;
21 and he cried to the man of God who came from Judah, saying, "Thus says the LORD,
'Because you have disobeyed the command of the LORD, and have not observed the
commandment which the LORD your God commanded you,
22 but have returned and eaten bread and drunk water in the place of which He said to
you, "Eat no bread and drink no water"; your body shall not come to the grave of your
fathers.' "
23 It came about after he had eaten bread and after he had drunk, that he saddled the
donkey for him, for the prophet whom he had brought back.
24 Now when he had gone, a lion met him on the way and killed him, and his body was

13:11 1 Kin 13:25; 2 Kin 23:18

13:16 1 Kin 13:8, 9

13:17 1 Kin 20:35

13:18 Matt 7:15; 1 John 4:1; Gal 1:8; Prov 12:19, 22; 19:5; Jer 29:31, 32; Ezek 13:8, 9; 1 Tim 4:1, 2

13:24 1 Kin 20:36

22 Lit *soften the face of* **23** Lit *softened the face of*

13:7–32 This prophet had been given strict orders from God not to eat or drink anything while on his mission (13:9). He died because he listened to a man who claimed to have a message from God, rather than to God himself. This prophet should have followed God's word instead of hearsay. Trust what God's Word says rather than what someone claims is true. And disregard what others claim to be messages from God if their words contradict the Bible.

13:24–25 Lions are mentioned frequently in the Old Testament. They were common enough to be a threat both to people and to their flocks. Samson (Judges 14:5–6), David (1 Samuel 17:34–37), and Benaiah (2 Samuel 23:20) all faced wild lions. The fact that the lion and the donkey were standing by the prophet's body showed that this was a divine judgment. Normally, the lion would have attacked the donkey and/or devoured the man.

thrown on the road, with the donkey standing beside it; the lion also was standing beside
the body.
13:25 1 Kin 13:11 25 And behold, men passed by and saw the body thrown on the road, and the lion standing beside the body; so they came and told *it* in the city where the old prophet lived.
26 Now when the prophet who brought him back from the way heard *it,* he said, "It is
the man of God, who disobeyed the command of the LORD; therefore the LORD has
given him to the lion, which has torn him and killed him, according to the word of the
LORD which He spoke to him."
27 Then he spoke to his sons, saying, "Saddle the donkey for me." And they saddled *it.*
28 He went and found his body thrown on the road with the donkey and the lion standing beside the body; the lion had not eaten the body nor torn the donkey.

JEROBOAM

Even clear warnings are hard to obey. The Bible is filled with stories of people who had direction from God and yet chose their own way. Their disobedience was rarely due to ignorance of what God wanted; rather, it grew out of stubborn selfishness. Jeroboam was a consistent example of this all-too-human trait.

During his construction activities, Solomon noticed young Jeroboam's natural leadership skills and made him a special project foreman. Shortly after this, God contacted Jeroboam through the prophet Ahijah. He told Jeroboam that God would punish David's dynasty by tearing the kingdom from Solomon's son and that Jeroboam would rule the ten northern tribes. And God made it clear that the same fate would destroy Jeroboam's family if they refused to obey God. Apparently Solomon heard about these events and tried to have Jeroboam killed. The future king escaped to Egypt, where he stayed until Solomon died.

When Rehoboam, Solomon's heir, took the throne, Jeroboam returned. He represented the people in demanding that the new king be more lenient than his father. Rehoboam's unwise choice to reject his people's request led to their rejecting him as king. Only Judah and the annexed tribe of Benjamin remained loyal to David's dynasty. The other ten tribes made Jeroboam king.

Rather than seeing this fulfillment of God's promise as motivation to obey God, Jeroboam decided to do whatever he could to secure his position. He led his kingdom away from the God who had allowed him to reign. God had already warned him of the consequences of this action—his family was eventually wiped out. And Jeroboam set into motion events that would lead to the destruction of the northern kingdom.

Sin's consequences are guaranteed in God's Word, but the timing of those consequences is hard to predict. When we do something directly opposed to God's commands and there isn't immediate disaster, we are often fooled into believing we got away with disobedience. But that is a dangerous assumption. Jeroboam's life should make us recognize our frequent need to admit our disobedience and ask God to forgive us.

Strengths and accomplishments:
- An effective leader and organizer
- First king of the ten tribes of Israel in the divided kingdom
- A charismatic leader with much popular support

Weaknesses and mistakes:
- Erected idols in Israel to keep people away from the temple in Jerusalem
- Appointed priests from outside the tribe of Levi
- Depended more on his own cunning than on God's promises

Lessons from his life:
- Great opportunities are often destroyed by small decisions
- Careless efforts to correct another's errors often lead to the same errors
- Mistakes always occur when we attempt to take over God's role in a situation

Vital statistics:
- Where: The northern kingdom of Israel
- Occupations: Project foreman, king of Israel
- Relatives: Father: Nebat. Mother: Zeruah. Sons: Abijah, Nadab
- Contemporaries: Solomon, Nathan, Ahijah, Rehoboam

Key verses:
"After this event Jeroboam did not return from his evil way, but again he made priests of the high places from among all the people; any who would, he ordained, to be priests of the high places. This event became sin to the house of Jeroboam, even to blot it out and destroy it from off the face of the earth" (1 Kings 13:33–34).

Jeroboam's story is told in 1 Kings 11:26—14:20. He is also mentioned in 2 Chronicles 10—13.

29 So the prophet took up the body of the man of God and laid it on the donkey and
brought it back, and he came to the city of the old prophet to mourn and to bury him.
30 He laid his body in his own grave, and they mourned over him, *saying,* "Alas, my
brother!"
31 After he had buried him, he spoke to his sons, saying, "When I die, bury me in the
grave in which the man of God is buried; lay my bones beside his bones.
32 "For the thing shall surely come to pass which he cried by the word of the LORD against
the altar in Bethel and against all the houses of the high places which are in the cities of
Samaria."
33 After this event Jeroboam did not return from his evil way, but again he made priests
of the high places from among all the people; any who would, he ordained, to be priests
of the high places.
34 This event became sin to the house of Jeroboam, even to blot *it* out and destroy *it*
from off the face of the earth.

Ahijah Prophesies against the King

14 At that time Abijah the son of Jeroboam became sick.
2 Jeroboam said to his wife, "Arise now, and disguise yourself so that they will
not know that you are the wife of Jeroboam, and go to Shiloh; behold, Ahijah the prophet
is there, who spoke concerning me *that I would be* king over this people.
3 "Take ten loaves with you, *some* cakes and a jar of honey, and go to him. He will tell
you what will happen to the boy."
4 Jeroboam's wife did so, and arose and went to Shiloh, and came to the house of
Ahijah. Now Ahijah could not see, for his eyes were dim because of his age.
5 Now the LORD had said to Ahijah, "Behold, the wife of Jeroboam is coming to inquire of you concerning her son, for he is sick. You shall say thus and thus to her, for it
will be when she arrives that she will pretend to be another woman."
6 When Ahijah heard the sound of her feet coming in the doorway, he said, "Come
in, wife of Jeroboam, why do you pretend to be another woman? For I am sent to you
with a harsh *message.*
7 "Go, say to Jeroboam, 'Thus says the LORD God of Israel, "Because I exalted you
from among the people and made you leader over My people Israel,
8 and tore the kingdom away from the house of David and gave it to you—yet you
have not been like My servant David, who kept My commandments and who followed
Me with all his heart, to do only that which was right in My sight;
9 you also have done more evil than all who were before you, and have gone and made
for yourself other gods and molten images to provoke Me to anger, and have cast Me
behind your back—
10 therefore behold, I am bringing calamity on the house of Jeroboam, and will cut off
from Jeroboam every male person, both bond and free in Israel, and I will make a clean
sweep of the house of Jeroboam, as one sweeps away dung until it is all gone.
11 "Anyone belonging to Jeroboam who dies in the city the dogs will eat. And he who
dies in the field the birds of the heavens will eat; for the LORD has spoken *it.*" '
12 "Now you, arise, go to your house. When your feet enter the city the child will die.
13 "All Israel shall mourn for him and bury him, for he alone of Jeroboam's *family* will
come to the grave, because in him something good was found toward the LORD God of
Israel in the house of Jeroboam.
14 "Moreover, the LORD will raise up for Himself a king over Israel who will cut off the
house of Jeroboam this day and from now on.

13:30 Jer 22:18
13:31 Ruth 1:17; 2 Kin 23:17, 18
13:32 1 Kin 13:2; Lev 26:30; 1 Kin 12:31; 1 Kin 16:24; John 4:5; Acts 8:14
13:33 1 Kin 12:31, 32; Judg 17:5
13:34 1 Kin 12:30; 2 Kin 17:21; 1 Kin 14:10; 15:29, 30
14:2 1 Sam 28:8; 2 Sam 14:2; 2 Chr 18:29; Josh 18:1; 1 Kin 11:29-31
14:3 1 Sam 9:7, 8; 1 Kin 13:7; 2 Kin 4:42
14:4 1 Kin 14:2; 1 Kin 11:29; 1 Sam 3:2; 4:15
14:5 2 Sam 14:2
14:7 2 Sam 12:7; 1 Kin 11:28-31; 16:2
14:8 1 Kin 11:31; 1 Kin 11:33, 38; 1 Kin 15:5
14:9 1 Kin 12:28; 2 Chr 11:15; Ex 34:17; Neh 9:26; Ps 50:17; Ezek 23:35
14:10 1 Kin 21:21; 2 Kin 9:8; Deut 32:36; 2 Kin 14:26; 1 Kin 15:29
14:11 1 Kin 16:4; 21:24
14:12 1 Kin 14:17
14:13 2 Chr 19:3
14:14 1 Kin 15:27-29

13:33–34 Under penalty of death, God had forbidden anyone to be a priest who was not from the tribe of Levi (Numbers 3:10). Levites were assured of lifetime support from the tithe, so they did not have to spend time farming, worrying about tribal interests, or fearing for their financial futures. Jeroboam's new priests were financed by the king and his fees. They had to mix priestly and secular duties, and they quickly fell into party politics. Because they didn't have job security, they were easily corrupted by bribes. Jeroboam's disobedience was the downfall of true religion in the northern kingdom.

14:10–11 These disasters were practical applications to Israel of the specific teachings of Deuteronomy (see Deuteronomy 28:15–19, 36–68; 30:15–20). Ahijah is prophesying the downfall of Israel for its flagrant violation of God's commands.

14:14 Who was this king who would "cut off the house of Jeroboam"? His name was Baasha, and he would kill all of Jeroboam's descendants (15:27–30).

15 "For the LORD will strike Israel, as a reed is shaken in the water; and He will uproot
Israel from this good land which He gave to their fathers, and will scatter them beyond
the *Euphrates* River, because they have made their [24]Asherim, provoking the LORD to
anger.
16 "He will give up Israel on account of the sins of Jeroboam, which he committed and
with which he made Israel to sin."
17 Then Jeroboam's wife arose and departed and came to Tirzah. As she was entering
the threshold of the house, the child died.
18 All Israel buried him and mourned for him, according to the word of the LORD which
He spoke through His servant Ahijah the prophet.
19 Now the rest of the acts of Jeroboam, how he made war and how he reigned, behold, they are written in the Book of the Chronicles of the Kings of Israel.
20 The time that Jeroboam reigned *was* twenty-two years; and he slept with his fathers,
and Nadab his son reigned in his place.

Rehoboam Misleads Judah

21 Now Rehoboam the son of Solomon reigned in Judah. Rehoboam was forty-one
years old when he became king, and he reigned seventeen years in Jerusalem, the city
which the LORD had chosen from all the tribes of Israel to put His name there. And his
mother's name was Naamah the Ammonitess.
22 Judah did evil in the sight of the LORD, and they provoked Him to jealousy more
than all that their fathers had done, with the sins which they committed.
23 For they also built for themselves high places and *sacred* pillars and Asherim on every
high hill and beneath every luxuriant tree.
24 There were also male cult prostitutes in the land. They did according to all the abominations of the nations which the LORD dispossessed before the sons of Israel.

24 I.e. wooden symbols of a female deity

14:15 Deut 29:28; 2 Kin 17:6; Ps 52:5; Josh 23:15, 10; 2 Kin 15:29; Ex 34:13, 14; Deut 12:3, 4

14:16 1 Kin 12:30; 13:34; 15:30, 34; 16:2

14:17 1 Kin 15:21, 33; 16:6-9, 15, 23; Song 6:4; 1 Kin 14:12

14:18 1 Kin 14:13

14:19 1 Kin 14:30; 2 Chr 13:2-20

14:21 2 Chr 12:13; 1 Kin 11:32, 36

14:22 2 Chr 12:1, 14; Deut 32:21; Ps 78:58; 1 Cor 10:22

14:23 Deut 12:2; Ezek 16:24; Deut 16:22; 1 Kin 14:15; 2 Kin 17:10; Is 57:5; Jer 2:20

14:24 Gen 19:5; Deut 23:17; 1 Kin 15:12; 22:46; 2 Kin 23:7

THE APPEAL OF IDOLS

On the surface, the lives of the kings don't make sense. How could they run to idolatry so fast when they had God's Word (at least some of it), prophets, and the example of David? Here are some of the reasons for the enticement of idols:

	The appeal of Idols	*Modern parallel*
POWER	The people wanted freedom from the authority of both God and the priests. They wanted their religion to fit their life-style, not their life-style to fit their religion.	People do not want to answer to a greater authority. Instead of having power over others, God wants us to have the Holy Spirit's power to help others.
PLEASURE	Idol worship exalted sensuality without responsibility or guilt. People acted out the vicious and sensuous personalities of the gods they worshiped, thus gaining approval for their degraded lives.	People deify pleasure, seeking it at the expense of everything else. Instead of seeking pleasure that leads to long-range disaster, God calls us to seek the kind of pleasure that leads to long-range rewards.
PASSION	Mankind was reduced to little more than animals. The people did not have to be viewed as unique individuals, but could be exploited sexually, politically, and economically.	Like animals, people let physical drives and passion rule them. Instead of seeking passion that exploits others, God calls us to redirect our passions to areas that build others up.
PRAISE AND POPULARITY	The high and holy nature of God was replaced by gods who were more a reflection of human nature, thus more culturally suitable to the people. These gods no longer required sacrifice, just a token of appeasement.	Sacrifice is seen as self-inflicted punishment, making no sense. Success is to be sought at all costs. Instead of seeking praise for ourselves, God calls us to praise him and those who honor him.

As societies change, they often throw out norms and values no longer considered necessary or acceptable. Believers must be careful not to follow society's example if it discards God's Word. When society does that, only godlessness and evil remain.

14:15 "Asherim" refers to idol worship. Wooden images were made for the worship of Asherah, a Canaanite mother-goddess.

14:19 Three books are mentioned in 1 and 2 Kings—the Book of the Chronicles of the Kings of Israel (14:19), the Book of the Chronicles of the Kings of Judah (14:29), and the book of the acts of Solomon (11:41). These historical records of Israel and Judah were the main sources of material God directed the author to use to write 1 and 2 Kings. No copies of these books have been found.

14:23 "Sacred pillars" were pillars of stone placed next to pagan altars. These pillars were supposed to represent deity.

25 Now it happened in the fifth year of King Rehoboam, that Shishak the king of Egypt
came up against Jerusalem.
26 He took away the treasures of the house of the LORD and the treasures of the king's
house, and he took everything, even taking all the shields of gold which Solomon had
made.
27 So King Rehoboam made shields of bronze in their place, and committed them to
the care of the commanders of the [25]guard who guarded the doorway of the king's house.
28 Then it happened as often as the king entered the house of the LORD, that the
[26]guards would carry them and would bring them back into the guards' room.
29 Now the rest of the acts of Rehoboam and all that he did, are they not written in the
Book of the Chronicles of the Kings of Judah?
30 There was war between Rehoboam and Jeroboam continually.
31 And Rehoboam slept with his fathers and was buried with his fathers in the city of
David; and his mother's name was Naamah the Ammonitess. And Abijam his son became king in his place.

Abijam Reigns over Judah

15 Now in the eighteenth year of King Jeroboam, the son of Nebat, Abijam became
king over Judah.
2 He reigned three years in Jerusalem; and his mother's name was Maacah the daughter of Abishalom.
3 He walked in all the sins of his father which he had committed before him; and his
heart was not wholly devoted to the LORD his God, like the heart of his father David.
4 But for David's sake the LORD his God gave him a lamp in Jerusalem, to raise up
his son after him and to establish Jerusalem;
5 because David did what was right in the sight of the LORD, and had not turned aside
from anything that He commanded him all the days of his life, except in the case of Uriah
the Hittite.
6 There was war between Rehoboam and Jeroboam all the days of his life.
7 Now the rest of the acts of Abijam and all that he did, are they not written in the
Book of the Chronicles of the Kings of Judah? And there was war between Abijam and
Jeroboam.

Asa Succeeds Abijam

8 And Abijam slept with his fathers and they buried him in the city of David; and Asa
his son became king in his place.
9 So in the twentieth year of Jeroboam the king of Israel, Asa began to reign as king
of Judah.
10 He reigned forty-one years in Jerusalem; and his mother's name was Maacah the
daughter of Abishalom.
11 Asa did what was right in the sight of the LORD, like David his father.
12 He also put away the male cult prostitutes from the land and removed all the idols
which his fathers had made.
13 He also removed Maacah his mother from *being* queen mother, because she had
made a horrid image as an Asherah; and Asa cut down her horrid image and burned *it* at
the brook Kidron.
14 But the high places were not taken away; nevertheless the heart of Asa was wholly
devoted to the LORD all his days.

25 Lit *runner* **26** Lit *runners*

14:25 1 Kin 11:40; 2 Chr 12:2, 9
14:26 1 Kin 15:18; 2 Chr 12:9; 1 Kin 10:17; 2 Chr 9:15, 16
14:27 1 Sam 8:11; 22:17
14:29 2 Chr 12:15, 16
14:30 1 Kin 12:21; 15:6
14:31 1 Kin 14:21
15:1 2 Chr 13:1
15:2 2 Chr 13:2; 2 Chr 11:21
15:3 1 Kin 11:4; Ps 119:80
15:4 2 Sam 21:17; 1 Kin 11:36; 2 Chr 21:7
15:5 1 Kin 9:4; 14:8; Luke 1:6; 2 Sam 11:3f, 15-17; 12:9, 10
15:6 1 Kin 14:30; 2 Chr 12:15-13:20
15:7 2 Chr 13:2, 21, 22; 2 Chr 13:3-20
15:8 2 Chr 14:1
15:10 1 Kin 15:2
15:11 2 Chr 14:2
15:12 Deut 23:17; 1 Kin 14:24; 22:46; 1 Kin 11:7, 8; 14:23; 2 Chr 14:2-5
15:13 2 Chr 15:16-18; Ex 32:20
15:14 1 Kin 22:43; 2 Kin 12:3; 1 Kin 8:61; 15:3

14:25 When Rehoboam came to power, he inherited a mighty kingdom. Everything he could ever want was given to him. But apparently he did not recognize why he had so much or how it had been obtained. To teach Rehoboam a lesson, God allowed Shishak of Egypt to invade Judah and Israel. Egypt was no longer the world power it had once been, and Shishak, possibly resenting Solomon's enormous success, was determined to change that. Shishak's army was not strong enough to destroy Judah and Israel, but he weakened them so much that they were never the same again.

14:25–26 Just five years after Solomon died, the temple and palace were ransacked by foreign invaders. How quickly the glory, power, and money disappeared! When the people became spiritually corrupt and immoral (14:24), it was just a short time until they lost everything. Wealth, idol worship, and immorality had become more important to them than God. When God is gone from our lives, everything else becomes useless, no matter how valuable it seems.

15:5 See 2 Samuel 11 for the story of David and Uriah the Hittite.

15:9 See Asa's Profile in 2 Chronicles 14 for more information on this king.

15:15 1 Kin 7:51
15:16 1 Kin 15:32
15:17 2 Chr 16:1-6; Josh 18:25; 1 Kin 15:21, 22; 1 Kin 12:26-29
15:18 1 Kin 14:26; 15:15; 2 Kin 12:17, 18; 2 Chr 16:2; Gen 14:15; 1 Kin 11:23, 24
15:19 2 Chr 16:7
15:20 2 Kin 15:29; Judg 18:29; 1 Kin 12:29; 2 Sam 20:15; 2 Kin 15:29; Josh 11:2; 12:3
15:21 1 Kin 15:17; 1 Kin 14:17; 16:15-18
15:22 Josh 18:24; 21:17
15:23 2 Chr 16:11-14
15:24 1 Kin 22:41-44; 2 Chr 17:1; Matt 1:8

15 He brought into the house of the LORD the dedicated things of his father and his
own dedicated things: silver and gold and utensils.
16 Now there was war between Asa and Baasha king of Israel all their days.
17 Baasha king of Israel went up against Judah and fortified Ramah in order to prevent *anyone* from going out or coming in to Asa king of Judah.
18 Then Asa took all the silver and the gold which were left in the treasuries of the
house of the LORD and the treasuries of the king's house, and delivered them into the
hand of his servants. And King Asa sent them to Ben-hadad the son of Tabrimmon, the
son of Hezion, king of Aram, who lived in Damascus, saying,
19 "*Let there be* a treaty between you and me, *as* between my father and your father.
Behold, I have sent you a present of silver and gold; go, break your treaty with Baasha
king of Israel so that he will withdraw from me."
20 So Ben-hadad listened to King Asa and sent the commanders of his armies against
the cities of Israel, and conquered Ijon, Dan, Abel-beth-maacah and all Chinneroth,
besides all the land of Naphtali.
21 When Baasha heard *of it,* he ceased fortifying Ramah and remained in Tirzah.
22 Then King Asa made a proclamation to all Judah—none was exempt—and they
carried away the stones of Ramah and its timber with which Baasha had built. And King
Asa built with them Geba of Benjamin and Mizpah.

Jehoshaphat Succeeds Asa

23 Now the rest of all the acts of Asa and all his might and all that he did and the cities
which he built, are they not written in the Book of the Chronicles of the Kings of Judah?
But in the time of his old age he was diseased in his feet.
24 And Asa slept with his fathers and was buried with his fathers in the city of David
his father; and Jehoshaphat his son reigned in his place.

KINGS TO DATE AND THEIR ENEMIES (930 B.C. – 853 B.C.)

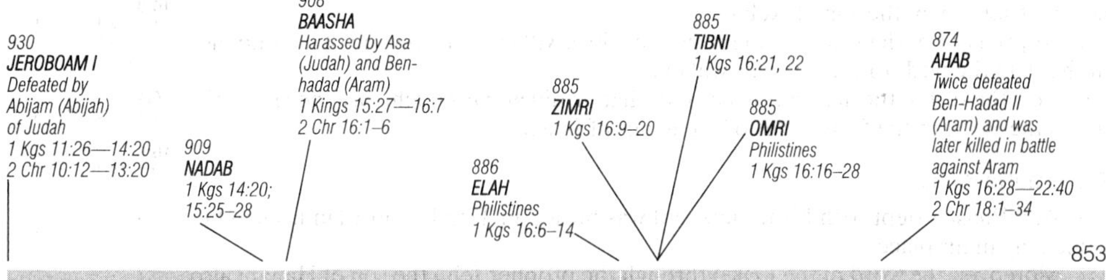

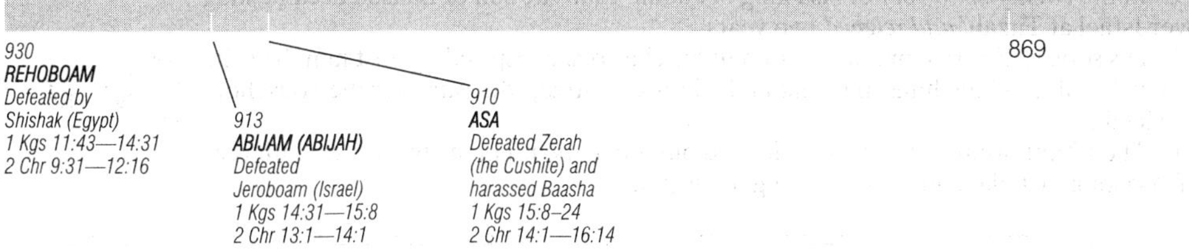

All dates are B.C.
For all the kings of Israel and Judah, see the chart at the end of 1 Kings.

15:15 These gifts for the temple were articles devoted to God as sacred offerings that Abijah had taken in his war with Jeroboam (2 Chronicles 13:16–17) and Asa had taken when he defeated the Cushites (2 Chronicles 14:12–13).

15:16 Baasha seized the throne from Nadab (15:27–28), who had replaced his father, Jeroboam, as king.

Nadab, then Baasha, Rules over Israel

25 Now Nadab the son of Jeroboam became king over Israel in the second year of Asa
king of Judah, and he reigned over Israel two years.
26 He did evil in the sight of the LORD, and walked in the way of his father and in his
sin which he made Israel sin.
27 Then Baasha the son of Ahijah of the house of Issachar conspired against him, and
Baasha struck him down at Gibbethon, which belonged to the Philistines, while Nadab
and all Israel were laying siege to Gibbethon.
28 So Baasha killed him in the third year of Asa king of Judah and reigned in his place.
29 It came about as soon as he was king, he struck down all the household of Jeroboam. He did not leave to Jeroboam any persons alive, until he had destroyed them, according to the word of the LORD, which He spoke by His servant Ahijah the Shilonite,
30 *and* because of the sins of Jeroboam which he sinned, and which he made Israel sin,
because of his provocation with which he provoked the LORD God of Israel to anger.
31 Now the rest of the acts of Nadab and all that he did, are they not written in the
Book of the Chronicles of the Kings of Israel?

War with Judah

32 There was war between Asa and Baasha king of Israel all their days.
33 In the third year of Asa king of Judah, Baasha the son of Ahijah became king over
all Israel at Tirzah, *and reigned* twenty-four years.
34 He did evil in the sight of the LORD, and walked in the way of Jeroboam and in his
sin which he made Israel sin.

Prophecy against Baasha

16 Now the word of the LORD came to Jehu the son of Hanani against Baasha,
saying,
2 "Inasmuch as I exalted you from the dust and made you leader over My people Israel,
and you have walked in the way of Jeroboam and have made My people Israel sin, provoking Me to anger with their sins,
3 behold, I will consume Baasha and his house, and I will make your house like the
house of Jeroboam the son of Nebat.
4 "Anyone of Baasha who dies in the city the dogs will eat, and anyone of his who dies
in the field the birds of the heavens will eat."
5 Now the rest of the acts of Baasha and what he did and his might, are they not written in the Book of the Chronicles of the Kings of Israel?

The Israelite Kings

6 And Baasha slept with his fathers and was buried in Tirzah, and Elah his son became king in his place.
7 Moreover, the word of the LORD through the prophet Jehu the son of Hanani also
came against Baasha and his household, both because of all the evil which he did in the
sight of the LORD, provoking Him to anger with the work of his hands, in being like the
house of Jeroboam, and because he struck it.
8 In the twenty-sixth year of Asa king of Judah, Elah the son of Baasha became king
over Israel at Tirzah, *and reigned* two years.
9 His servant Zimri, commander of half his chariots, conspired against him. Now he
was at Tirzah drinking himself drunk in the house of Arza, who *was* over the household
at Tirzah.
10 Then Zimri went in and struck him and put him to death in the twenty-seventh year
of Asa king of Judah, and became king in his place.

15:25 1 Kin 14:20
15:26 1 Kin 12:28-33; 13:33, 34; 1 Kin 14:16; 15:30, 34
15:27 1 Kin 14:14; Josh 19:44; 21:23; 1 Kin 16:15
15:29 1 Kin 14:9-16
15:30 1 Kin 15:26
15:31 1 Kin 14:19
15:32 1 Kin 15:16
15:34 1 Kin 15:26
16:1 1 Kin 16:7; 2 Chr 19:2; 20:34; 2 Chr 16:7-10
16:2 1 Sam 2:8; 1 Kin 14:7; 1 Kin 15:34
16:3 1 Kin 14:10; 21:21; 1 Kin 16:11; 1 Kin 15:29
16:4 1 Kin 14:11; 21:24
16:5 1 Kin 14:19; 15:31
16:6 1 Kin 14:17; 15:21
16:7 1 Kin 16:1; Ps 115:4; Is 2:8; 1 Kin 14:14; 15:27, 29
16:9 2 Kin 9:30-33; Gen 24:2; 39:4; 1 Kin 18:3

15:29 See 1 Kings 14:12–14 for Ahijah's prediction of this event.

15:30 All the descendants of Jeroboam were killed because Jeroboam had led Israel into sin. Sin is always judged harshly, but the worst sinners are those who lead others into doing wrong. Jesus said it would be better if such people had millstones tied around their necks and were thrown into the sea (Mark 9:42). If you have taken the responsibility for leading others, remember the consequences of leading them astray. Teaching the truth is a responsibility that goes with the privilege of leadership.

16:1–7 God destroyed Jeroboam's descendants for their flagrant sins, and yet Baasha repeated the same mistakes. He did not learn from the example of those who went before him; he did not stop to think that his sin would be punished. Make sure you learn from your past, the experiences of others, and the lives of those whose stories are told in the Bible. Don't repeat mistakes.

16:11 1 Kin 15:29; 16:3
16:12 1 Kin 16:3; 2 Chr 19:2; 20:34
16:13 Deut 32:21; 1 Kin 15:30
16:14 1 Kin 16:5
16:15 1 Kin 15:27
16:18 1 Sam 31:4, 5; 2 Sam 17:23
16:19 1 Kin 12:28; 14:16; 15:26
16:20 1 Kin 16:5, 14, 27
16:23 1 Kin 15:21
16:24 1 Kin 16:28, 29, 32
16:25 Mic 6:16; 1 Kin 14:9; 16:30-33
16:26 1 Kin 16:19
16:30 1 Kin 14:9; 16:25
16:31 Deut 7:1-5; Judg 18:7; 1 Kin 11:1-5; 2 Kin 10:18; 17:16
16:32 2 Kin 10:21, 26, 27
16:33 2 Kin 13:6; 1 Kin 14:9; 16:29, 30; 21:25

11 It came about when he became king, as soon as he sat on his throne, that he killed
all the household of Baasha; he did not leave a single male, neither of his relatives nor of
his friends.
12 Thus Zimri destroyed all the household of Baasha, according to the word of the
LORD, which He spoke against Baasha through Jehu the prophet,
13 for all the sins of Baasha and the sins of Elah his son, which they sinned and which
they made Israel sin, provoking the LORD God of Israel to anger with their idols.
14 Now the rest of the acts of Elah and all that he did, are they not written in the Book
of the Chronicles of the Kings of Israel?
15 In the twenty-seventh year of Asa king of Judah, Zimri reigned seven days at Tirzah. Now the people were camped against Gibbethon, which belonged to the Philistines.
16 The people who were camped heard it said, "Zimri has conspired and has also struck
down the king." Therefore all Israel made Omri, the commander of the army, king over
Israel that day in the camp.
17 Then Omri and all Israel with him went up from Gibbethon and besieged Tirzah.
18 When Zimri saw that the city was taken, he went into the citadel of the king's house
and burned the king's house over him with fire, and died,
19 because of his sins which he sinned, doing evil in the sight of the LORD, walking in
the way of Jeroboam, and in his sin which he did, making Israel sin.
20 Now the rest of the acts of Zimri and his conspiracy which he carried out, are they
not written in the Book of the Chronicles of the Kings of Israel?
21 Then the people of Israel were divided into two parts: half of the people followed
Tibni the son of Ginath, to make him king; the *other* half followed Omri.
22 But the people who followed Omri prevailed over the people who followed Tibni
the son of Ginath. And Tibni died and Omri became king.
23 In the thirty-first year of Asa king of Judah, Omri became king over Israel *and reigned*
twelve years; he reigned six years at Tirzah.
24 He bought the hill Samaria from Shemer for two talents of silver; and he built on
the hill, and named the city which he built Samaria, after the name of Shemer, the owner of the hill.
25 Omri did evil in the sight of the LORD, and acted more wickedly than all who *were*
before him.
26 For he walked in all the way of Jeroboam the son of Nebat and in his sins which he
made Israel sin, provoking the LORD God of Israel with their idols.
27 Now the rest of the acts of Omri which he did and his might which he showed, are
they not written in the Book of the Chronicles of the Kings of Israel?
28 So Omri slept with his fathers and was buried in Samaria; and Ahab his son became
king in his place.
29 Now Ahab the son of Omri became king over Israel in the thirty-eighth year of Asa
king of Judah, and Ahab the son of Omri reigned over Israel in Samaria twenty-two years.
30 Ahab the son of Omri did evil in the sight of the LORD more than all who were before
him.
31 It came about, as though it had been a trivial thing for him to walk in the sins of
Jeroboam the son of Nebat, that he married Jezebel the daughter of Ethbaal king of the
Sidonians, and went to serve Baal and worshiped him.
32 So he erected an altar for Baal in the house of Baal which he built in Samaria.
33 Ahab also made the [27]Asherah. Thus Ahab did more to provoke the LORD God of
Israel than all the kings of Israel who were before him.

27 I.e. wooden symbol of a female deity

16:21–22 Omri began his reign as political dissension brewed in Israel. After Zimri killed himself, the Israelite army chose Omri, their commander, as the next ruler. Tibni, Omri's chief rival to the throne, died, and Omri then began his evil reign. During his 12-year rule over Israel, he was a shrewd and capable leader. He organized the building of his new capital city, Samaria, while strengthening the nation politically and militarily. But he did not care about the nation's spiritual condition (Micah 6:16), and he purposely led Israel farther from God in order to put more power in his own hands.

16:24 Omri's new capital, Samaria, offered some political advantages. The city was his personal property, so he had total control over it. Samaria also commanded a hilltop position, which made it easy to defend. Omri died before completing the city. So his son, Ahab, completed it, building not only the beautiful ivory palace (1 Kings 22:39; Amos 3:13–15), but also a temple to the god Baal. Samaria served as the capital city for the rest of Israel's dynasties until it fell to the Assyrians in 722 B.C. (2 Kings 17:5).

16:31 Ahab's evil wife, Jezebel, came from the Phoenician city of Tyre where her father had been a high priest and eventually king. Jezebel worshiped the god Baal. In order to please her, Ahab built a temple and an altar for Baal (16:32), thus promoting idolatry and leading the entire nation into sin. (For more about Baal, see the note on 18:18.)

34 In his days Hiel the Bethelite built Jericho; he laid its foundations with the *loss of* **16:34** Josh 6:26
Abiram his firstborn, and set up its gates with the *loss of* his youngest son Segub, according to the word of the LORD, which He spoke by Joshua the son of Nun.

3. Elijah's ministry

Elijah Predicts Drought

17 Now Elijah the Tishbite, who was of the settlers of Gilead, said to Ahab, "As the **17:1** Judg 12:4; 1 Kin 18:10; 22:14; 2 Kin 3:14; 5:20; 1 Kin 18:1; Luke 4:25; James 5:17
LORD, the God of Israel lives, before whom I stand, surely there shall be neither
dew nor rain these years, except by my word."
2 The word of the LORD came to him, saying,
3 "Go away from here and turn eastward, and hide yourself by the brook Cherith, which
is east of the Jordan.
4 "It shall be that you will drink of the brook, and I have commanded the ravens to **17:4** 1 Kin 17:9
provide for you there."
5 So he went and did according to the word of the LORD, for he went and lived by the
brook Cherith, which is east of the Jordan.
6 The ravens brought him bread and meat in the morning and bread and meat in the
evening, and he would drink from the brook.
7 It happened after a while that the brook dried up, because there was no rain in the
land.
8 Then the word of the LORD came to him, saying,
9 "Arise, go to Zarephath, which belongs to Sidon, and stay there; behold, I have com- **17:9** Obad 20; Luke 4:26; 1 Kin 17:4
manded a widow there to provide for you."
10 So he arose and went to Zarephath, and when he came to the gate of the city, be-
hold, a widow was there gathering sticks; and he called to her and said, "Please get me a **17:10** Gen 24:17; John 4:7
little water in a jar, that I may drink."
11 As she was going to get *it,* he called to her and said, "Please bring me a piece of
bread in your hand."
12 But she said, "As the LORD your God lives, I have no bread, only a handful of flour **17:12** 1 Kin 17:1; 2 Kin 4:2-7; Gen 21:15, 16
in the bowl and a little oil in the jar; and behold, I am gathering a few sticks that I may
go in and prepare for me and my son, that we may eat it and die."
13 Then Elijah said to her, "Do not fear; go, do as you have said, but make me a little
bread cake from it first and bring *it* out to me, and afterward you may make *one* for yourself
and for your son.
14 "For thus says the LORD God of Israel, 'The bowl of flour shall not be exhausted, nor

---

17:1 Elijah was the first in a long line of important prophets God sent to Israel and Judah. Israel, the northern kingdom, had no faithful kings throughout its history. Each king was wicked, actually leading the people in worshiping pagan gods. There were few priests left from the tribe of Levi (most had gone to Judah), and the priests appointed by Israel's kings were corrupt and ineffective. With no king or priests to bring God's word to the people, God called prophets to try to rescue Israel from its moral and spiritual decline. For the next 300 years these men and women would play vital roles in both nations, encouraging the people and leaders to turn back to God.

17:1 Those who worshiped Baal believed he was the god who brought the rains and bountiful harvests. So when Elijah walked into the presence of this Baal-worshiping king and told him there would be no rain for several years, Ahab was shocked. Ahab had built a strong military defense, but it would be no help against drought. He had many priests of Baal, but they could not bring rain. Elijah bravely confronted the man who led his people into evil, and he told of a power far greater than any pagan god—the Lord God of Israel. When rebellion and heresy were at an all-time high in Israel, God responded not only with words but with action.

17:10ff In a nation that was required by law to care for its prophets, it is ironic that God turned to ravens (unclean birds) and a widow (a foreigner from Jezebel's home territory) to care for Elijah. God has help where we least expect it. He provides for us in ways that go beyond our narrow definitions or expectations. No matter how bitter our trials or how seemingly hopeless our situation, we should look for God's caring touch. We may find his providence in some strange places!

17:13–16 When the widow of Zarephath met Elijah, she thought she was preparing her last meal. But a simple act of faith produced

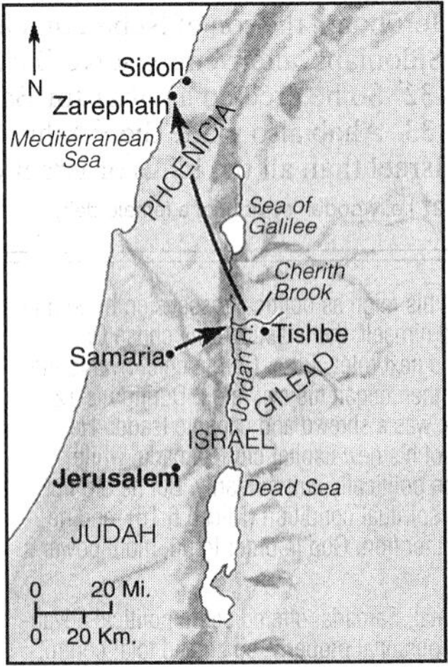

ELIJAH HIDES FROM AHAB
Elijah prophesied a drought and then hid from King Ahab by the Cherith Brook, where he was fed by ravens. When the brook dried up, God sent him to Zarephath in Phoenicia, where a widow and her son fed him and gave him lodging.

shall the jar of oil be empty, until the day that the LORD sends rain on the face of the
earth.' "
15 So she went and did according to the word of Elijah, and she and he and her household ate for *many* days.
16 The bowl of flour was not exhausted nor did the jar of oil become empty, according
to the word of the LORD which He spoke through Elijah.

Elijah Raises the Widow's Son

17 Now it came about after these things that the son of the woman, the mistress of the
house, became sick; and his sickness was so severe that there was no breath left in him.
17:18 2 Sam 16:10; 2 Kin 3:13; Luke 4:34; John 2:4; 1 Kin 12:22
18 So she said to Elijah, "What do I have to do with you, O man of God? You have
come to me to bring my iniquity to remembrance and to put my son to death!"
19 He said to her, "Give me your son." Then he took him from her bosom and carried
him up to the upper room where he was living, and laid him on his own bed.
20 He called to the LORD and said, "O LORD my God, have You also brought calamity
to the widow with whom I am staying, by causing her son to die?"
17:21 2 Kin 4:34, 35; Acts 20:10
21 Then he stretched himself upon the child three times, and called to the LORD and
said, "O LORD my God, I pray You, let this child's life return to him."
17:22 Luke 7:14; Heb 11:35
22 The LORD heard the voice of Elijah, and the life of the child returned to him and he
revived.
23 Elijah took the child and brought him down from the upper room into the house
and gave him to his mother; and Elijah said, "See, your son is alive."
17:24 John 2:11; 3:2; 16:30
24 Then the woman said to Elijah, "Now I know that you are a man of God and that
the word of the LORD in your mouth is truth."

Obadiah Meets Elijah

18:1 1 Kin 17:1; Luke 4:25; James 5:17; Deut 28:12
18 Now it happened *after* many days that the word of the LORD came to Elijah in the
third year, saying, "Go, show yourself to Ahab, and I will send rain on the face of
the earth."
2 So Elijah went to show himself to Ahab. Now the famine *was* severe in Samaria.
18:3 1 Kin 16:9; Neh 7:2; Job 28:28
3 Ahab called Obadiah who *was* over the household. (Now Obadiah [28]feared the LORD
greatly;
18:4 1 Kin 18:13; Matt 10:40-42
4 for when Jezebel destroyed the prophets of the LORD, Obadiah took a hundred
prophets and hid them by fifties in a cave, and provided them with bread and water.)
5 Then Ahab said to Obadiah, "Go through the land to all the springs of water and to
all the valleys; perhaps we will find grass and keep the horses and mules alive, and not
have to kill some of the cattle."
6 So they divided the land between them to survey it; Ahab went one way by himself
and Obadiah went another way by himself.
18:7 2 Kin 1:6-8
7 Now as Obadiah was on the way, behold, Elijah met him, and he recognized him
and fell on his face and said, "Is this you, Elijah my master?"
8 He said to him, "It is I. Go, say to your master, 'Behold, Elijah *is here.*' "
9 He said, "What sin have I committed, that you are giving your servant into the hand
of Ahab to put me to death?
18:10 1 Kin 17:1
10 "As the LORD your God lives, there is no nation or kingdom where my master has
not sent to search for you; and when they said, 'He is not *here,*' he made the kingdom or
nation swear that they could not find you.
11 "And now you are saying, 'Go, say to your master, "Behold, Elijah *is here.*" '
18:12 2 Kin 2:16; Ezek 3:12, 14; Acts 8:39
12 "It will come about when I leave you that the Spirit of the LORD will carry you where
I do not know; so when I come and tell Ahab and he cannot find you, he will kill me,
although *I* your servant have feared the LORD from my youth.

28 Or *revered*

a miracle. She trusted Elijah and gave all she had to eat to him. Faith is the step between promise and assurance. Miracles seem so out of reach for our feeble faith. But every miracle, large or small, begins with an act of obedience. We may not see the solution until we take the first step of faith.

17:17 Even when God has done a miracle in our lives, our troubles may not be over. The famine was a terrible experience, but the worst was yet to come. God's provision is never given in order to let us rest upon it. We need to depend on him as each new trial faces us.

18:3–4 Although Elijah was alone in his confrontation with Ahab and Jezebel, he was not the only one in Israel who believed in God. Obadiah had been faithful in hiding 100 prophets still true to the Lord.

13 "Has it not been told to my master what I did when Jezebel killed the prophets of the
LORD, that I hid a hundred prophets of the LORD by fifties in a cave, and provided them
with bread and water?
14 "And now you are saying, 'Go, say to your master, "Behold, Elijah *is here*" '; he will
then kill me."
15 Elijah said, "As the LORD of hosts lives, before whom I stand, I will surely show
myself to him today."
16 So Obadiah went to meet Ahab and told him; and Ahab went to meet Elijah.
17 When Ahab saw Elijah, Ahab said to him, "Is this you, you troubler of Israel?"
18 He said, "I have not troubled Israel, but you and your father's house *have,* because
you have forsaken the commandments of the LORD and you have followed the Baals.
19 "Now then send *and* gather to me all Israel at Mount Carmel, *together* with 450
prophets of Baal and 400 prophets of the Asherah, who eat at Jezebel's table."

God or Baal on Mount Carmel

20 So Ahab sent *a message* among all the sons of Israel and brought the prophets together at Mount Carmel.
21 Elijah came near to all the people and said, "How long *will* you hesitate between
two opinions? If the LORD is God, follow Him; but if Baal, follow him." But the people
did not answer him a word.
22 Then Elijah said to the people, "I alone am left a prophet of the LORD, but Baal's
prophets are 450 men.
23 "Now let them give us two oxen; and let them choose one ox for themselves and cut
it up, and place it on the wood, but put no fire *under it;* and I will prepare the other ox
and lay it on the wood, and I will not put a fire *under it.*
24 "Then you call on the name of your god, and I will call on the name of the LORD, and
the God who answers by fire, He is God." And all the people said, "[29]That is a good idea."
25 So Elijah said to the prophets of Baal, "Choose one ox for yourselves and prepare
it first for you are many, and call on the name of your god, but put no fire *under it.*"
26 Then they took the ox which was given them and they prepared it and called on the
name of Baal from morning until noon saying, "O Baal, answer us." But there was no
voice and no one answered. And they leaped about the altar which they made.
27 It came about at noon, that Elijah mocked them and said, "Call out with a loud voice,
for he is a god; either he is occupied or gone aside, or is on a journey, or perhaps he is
asleep and needs to be awakened."
28 So they cried with a loud voice and cut themselves according to their custom with
swords and lances until the blood gushed out on them.

18:13 1 Kin 18:4

18:15 1 Kin 17:1

18:17 Josh 7:25; 1 Kin 21:20

18:18 1 Kin 9:9; 2 Chr 15:2; 1 Kin 16:31; 21:25, 26

18:19 Josh 19:26; 2 Kin 2:25; 1 Kin 18:22; 1 Kin 16:33

18:21 2 Kin 17:41; Matt 6:24; Josh 24:15

18:22 1 Kin 19:10, 14; 1 Kin 18:19

18:24 1 Kin 18:38

18:26 Ps 115:4, 5; Jer 10:5

18:28 Lev 19:28; Deut 14:1

29 Lit *The matter is good*

18:18 Instead of worshiping the true God, Ahab and his wife Jezebel worshiped Baal, the most popular Canaanite god. Baal idols were often made in the shape of a bull, representing strength and fertility and reflecting lust for power and sexual pleasure.

18:19 Ahab brought 850 pagan prophets to Mount Carmel to match wits and power with Elijah. Evil kings hated God's prophets because they spoke against sin and idolatry and undermined their control over the people. With the wicked kings' backing, many pagan prophets sprang up to counter the words of God's prophets. But Elijah showed the people that speaking a prophecy wasn't enough. One needed the power of a living God to fulfill it.

18:21 Elijah challenged the people to take a stand—to follow whoever was the true God. Why did so many people waver between the two choices? Perhaps some were not sure. Many, however, knew that the Lord was God, but they enjoyed the sinful pleasures and other benefits that came with following Ahab in his idolatrous worship. It is important to take a stand for the Lord. If we just drift along with whatever is pleasant and easy, we will someday discover that we have been worshiping a false god—ourselves.

THE SHOWDOWN AT CARMEL
In a showdown with the false prophets of Baal at Mount Carmel, Elijah set out to prove to evil Ahab that only the Lord is God. Elijah then killed the false prophets by the Kishon Brook and fled back to Jezreel.

18:29 Ex 29:39, 41

18:30 1 Kin 19:10, 14; 2 Chr 33:16

29 When midday was past, they raved until the time of the offering of the *evening* sacrifice; but there was no voice, no one answered, and no one paid attention.
30 Then Elijah said to all the people, "Come near to me." So all the people came near
to him. And he repaired the altar of the LORD which had been torn down.

Elijah's single-minded commitment to God shocks and challenges us. He was sent to confront, not comfort, and he spoke God's words to a king who often rejected his message just because he brought it. Elijah chose to carry out his ministry for God alone and paid for that decision by experiencing isolation from others who were also faithful to God.

It is interesting to think about the amazing miracles God accomplished through Elijah, but we would do well to focus on the relationship they shared. All that happened in Elijah's life began with the same miracle that is available to us—he responded to the miracle of being able to know God.

For example, after God worked an overwhelming miracle through Elijah in defeating the prophets of Baal, Queen Jezebel retaliated by threatening Elijah's life. And Elijah ran. He felt afraid, depressed, and abandoned. Despite God's provision of food and shelter in the wilderness, Elijah wanted to die. So God presented Elijah with an "audio-visual display" and a message he needed to hear. Elijah witnessed a windstorm, an earthquake, and fire. But the Lord was not in any of those powerful things. Instead, God displayed his presence in a gentle whisper.

Elijah, like us, struggled with his feelings even after this comforting message from God. So God confronted Elijah's emotions and commanded action. He told Elijah what to do next and informed him that part of his loneliness was based on ignorance: 7,000 others in Israel were still faithful to God.

Even today, God often speaks through the gentle and obvious rather than the spectacular and unusual. God has work for us to do even when we feel fear and failure. And God always has more resources and people than we know about. Although we might wish to do amazing miracles for God, we should instead focus on developing a relationship with him. The real miracle of Elijah's life was his very personal relationship with God. And that miracle is available to us.

Strengths and accomplishments:
- Was the most famous and dramatic of Israel's prophets
- Predicted the beginning and end of a three-year drought
- Was used by God to restore a dead child to his mother
- Represented God in a showdown with priests of Baal and Asherah
- Appeared with Moses and Jesus in the New Testament transfiguration scene

Weaknesses and mistakes:
- Chose to work alone and paid for it with isolation and loneliness
- Fled in fear from Jezebel when she threatened his life

Lessons from his life:
- We are never closer to defeat than in our moments of greatest victory
- We are never as alone as we may feel; God is always there
- God speaks more frequently in persistent whispers than in shouts

Vital statistics:
- Where: Gilead
- Occupation: Prophet
- Contemporaries: Ahab, Jezebel, Ahaziah, Obadiah, Jehu, Hazael

Key verses:
"At the time of the offering of the evening sacrifice, Elijah the prophet came near and said, 'O LORD, the God of Abraham, Isaac and Israel, today let it be known that You are God in Israel and that I am Your servant and I have done all these things at Your word. Answer me, O LORD, answer me, that this people may know that You, O LORD, are God, and that You have turned their heart back again.' Then the fire of the LORD fell and consumed the burnt offering and the wood and the stones and the dust, and licked up the water that was in the trench" (1 Kings 18:36–38).

Elijah's story is told in 1 Kings 17:1—2 Kings 2:11. He is also mentioned in 2 Chronicles 21:12–15; Malachi 4:5–6; Matthew 11:14; 16:14; 17:3–13; 27:47–49; Luke 1:17; 4:25, 26; John 1:19–25; Romans 11:2–4; James 5:17–18.

18:29 Although the prophets of Baal raved all afternoon, no one answered them. Their god was silent because it was not real. The gods we may be tempted to follow are not idols of wood or stone, but they are just as false and dangerous because they cause us to depend on something other than God. Power, status, appearance, or material possessions can become our gods if we devote our lives to them. But when we reach times of crisis and desperately call out to these gods, there will only be silence. They can offer no true answers, no guidance, and no wisdom.

31 Elijah took twelve stones according to the number of the tribes of the sons of Jacob,
to whom the word of the LORD had come, saying, "Israel shall be your name."
32 So with the stones he built an altar in the name of the LORD, and he made a trench
around the altar, large enough to hold two measures of seed.
33 Then he arranged the wood and cut the ox in pieces and laid *it* on the wood.
34 And he said, "Fill four pitchers with water and pour *it* on the burnt offering and on
the wood." And he said, "Do it a second time," and they did it a second time. And he
said, "Do it a third time," and they did it a third time.
35 The water flowed around the altar and he also filled the trench with water.

Elijah's Prayer

36 At the time of the offering of the *evening* sacrifice, Elijah the prophet came near
and said, "O LORD, the God of Abraham, Isaac and Israel, today let it be known that
You are God in Israel and that I am Your servant and I have done all these things at
Your word.
37 "Answer me, O LORD, answer me, that this people may know that You, O LORD, are
God, and *that* You have turned their heart back again."
38 Then the fire of the LORD fell and consumed the burnt offering and the wood and
the stones and the dust, and licked up the water that was in the trench.
39 When all the people saw it, they fell on their faces; and they said, "The LORD, He is
God; the LORD, He is God."
40 Then Elijah said to them, "Seize the prophets of Baal; do not let one of them escape." So they seized them; and Elijah brought them down to the brook Kishon, and
slew them there.
41 Now Elijah said to Ahab, "Go up, eat and drink; for there is the sound of the roar
of a *heavy* shower."
42 So Ahab went up to eat and drink. But Elijah went up to the top of Carmel; and he
crouched down on the earth and put his face between his knees.
43 He said to his servant, "Go up now, look toward the sea."
So he went up and looked and said, "There is nothing." And he said, "Go back" seven
times.
44 It came about at the seventh *time,* that he said, "Behold, a cloud as small as a man's
hand is coming up from the sea." And he said, "Go up, say to Ahab, 'Prepare *your chariot* and go down, so that the *heavy* shower does not stop you.' "
45 In a little while the sky grew black with clouds and wind, and there was a heavy shower. And Ahab rode and went to Jezreel.
46 Then the hand of the LORD was on Elijah, and he girded up his loins and outran
Ahab to Jezreel.

Elijah Flees from Jezebel

19 Now Ahab told Jezebel all that Elijah had done, and how he had killed all the prophets with the sword.
2 Then Jezebel sent a messenger to Elijah, saying, "So may the gods do to me and
even more, if I do not make your [30]life as the life of one of them by tomorrow about this
time."

18:31 Gen 32:28; 35:10; 2 Kin 17:34
18:32 Col 3:17
18:33 Gen 22:9; Lev 1:7, 8
18:36 1 Kin 18:29; Gen 28:13; Ex 3:6; 4:5; Matt 22:32; 1 Kin 8:43; Num 16:28-32
18:38 Gen 15:17; Lev 9:24; 10:1, 2; Judg 6:21; 2 Kin 1:12; 1 Chr 21:26; 2 Chr 7:1; Job 1:16
18:39 1 Kin 18:21, 24
18:40 Judg 4:7; 5:21; Deut 13:5; 18:20; 2 Kin 10:24, 25
18:42 1 Kin 18:19, 20; James 5:18
18:44 Luke 12:54
18:45 Josh 17:16; Judg 6:33
18:46 2 Kin 3:15; Is 8:11; Ezek 3:14; 2 Kin 4:29; Jer 1:17; 1 Pet 1:13
19:1 1 Kin 18:40
19:2 Ruth 1:17; 1 Kin 20:10; 2 Kin 6:31

30 Lit *soul*

18:31 Using 12 stones to build the altar took courage. This would have angered some of the people because it was a silent reminder of the split between the tribes. While the 10 tribes of the north called themselves Israel, it was a name originally given to all 12 of the tribes together.

18:36–38 God flashed fire from heaven for Elijah, and he will help us accomplish what he commands us to do. The proof may not be as dramatic in our lives as in Elijah's, but God will make resources available to us in creative ways to accomplish his purposes. He will give us the wisdom to raise a family, the courage to take a stand for truth, or the means to provide help for someone in need. Like Elijah, we can have faith that whatever God commands us to do, he will provide what we need to carry it through.

18:46 Elijah ran the six miles back to the city in order to give Ahab a last chance to turn from his sin before joining Jezebel in Jezreel. His run also ensured that the correct story of what happened would reach Jezreel.

19:2 Jezebel was enraged about the death of her prophets because they had told her everything *she* wanted to hear, prophesying her future power and glory. Their job was to deify the king and queen and help perpetuate their kingdom. Jezebel was also angry because her supporters had been eliminated and her pride and authority damaged. The money she had invested in these prophets was now lost.

Elijah, who caused the prophets' deaths, was a constant thorn in Jezebel's side because he was always predicting gloom and doom. Because she could not control his actions, she vowed to kill him. As long as God's prophet was around, she could not carry out all the evil she wanted.

19:3 Gen 21:31
19:4 Num 11:15; Jer 20:14-18; Jon 4:3, 8
19:5 Gen 28:12
19:8 Ex 24:18; 34:28; Deut 9:9-11, 18; Matt 4:2; Ex 3:1; 4:27
19:9 Ex 33:21, 22
19:10 Ex 20:5; 34:14; Rom 11:3, 4; 1 Kin 18:22

3 And he was afraid and arose and ran for his [31]life and came to Beersheba, which belongs to Judah, and left his servant there.
4 But he himself went a day's journey into the wilderness, and came and sat down under a juniper tree; and he requested for himself that he might die, and said, "It is enough; now, O LORD, take my [31]life, for I am not better than my fathers."
5 He lay down and slept under a juniper tree; and behold, there was an angel touching him, and he said to him, "Arise, eat."
6 Then he looked and behold, there was at his head a bread cake *baked on* hot stones, and a jar of water. So he ate and drank and lay down again.
7 The angel of the LORD came again a second time and touched him and said, "Arise, eat, because the journey is too great for you."
8 So he arose and ate and drank, and went in the strength of that food forty days and forty nights to Horeb, the mountain of God.

Elijah at Horeb

9 Then he came there to a cave and lodged there; and behold, the word of the LORD *came* to him, and He said to him, "What are you doing here, Elijah?"
10 He said, "I have been very zealous for the LORD, the God of hosts; for the sons of Israel have forsaken Your covenant, torn down Your altars and killed Your prophets with the sword. And I alone am left; and they seek my life, to take it away."

31 Lit *soul*

PROPHETS—FALSE AND TRUE

False Prophets	*True Prophets*
Worked for political purposes to benefit themselves	Worked for spiritual purposes to serve God and the people
Held positions of great wealth	Owned little or nothing
Gave false messages	Spoke only true messages
Spoke only what the people wanted to hear	Spoke only what God told them to say—no matter how unpopular

The false prophets were an obstacle to bringing God's word to the people. They would bring messages that contradicted the words of the true prophets. They gave "messages" that appealed to the people's sinful natures and comforted their fears. False prophets told people what they wanted to hear. True prophets told God's truth.

19:3ff Elijah experienced the depths of fatigue and discouragement just after his two great spiritual victories: the defeat of the prophets of Baal and the answered prayer for rain. Often discouragement sets in after great spiritual experiences, especially those requiring physical effort or involving great emotion. To lead him out of depression, God first let Elijah rest and eat. Then God confronted him with the need to return to his mission—to speak God's words in Israel. Elijah's battles were not over; there was still work for him to do. When you feel let down after a great spiritual experience, remember that God's purpose for your life is not yet over.

19:8 When Elijah fled to Mount Horeb, he was returning to the sacred place where God had met Moses and had given his laws to the people. Obviously, God gave Elijah special strength to travel this great distance—over 200 miles—without additional food. Like Moses before him and Jesus after him, Elijah fasted for 40 days and 40 nights (Deuteronomy 9:9; Matthew 4:1–2). Centuries later, Moses, Elijah, and Jesus would meet together on a mountaintop (Luke 9:28–36).

19:10 Elijah thought he was the only person left who was still true to God. He had seen both the king's court and the priesthood become corrupt. After experiencing great victory at Mount Carmel, he had to run for his life. Lonely and discouraged, he forgot that others had remained faithful during the nation's wickedness. When you are tempted to think that you are the only one remaining faithful to a task, don't stop to feel sorry for yourself. Self-pity will dilute the good you are doing. Be assured that even if you don't know who they are, others are faithfully obeying God and fulfilling their duties.

ELIJAH FLEES FROM JEZEBEL
After killing Baal's prophets, Elijah ran from the furious Queen Jezebel. He fled to Beersheba, then into the wilderness, and finally to Mount Horeb (Sinai). There, like Moses centuries earlier, he talked with God.

11 So He said, "Go forth and stand on the mountain before the LORD." And behold,
the LORD was passing by! And a great and strong wind was rending the mountains and
breaking in pieces the rocks before the LORD; *but* the LORD *was* not in the wind. And
after the wind an earthquake, *but* the LORD *was* not in the earthquake.
12 After the earthquake a fire, *but* the LORD *was* not in the fire; and after the fire a
sound of a gentle blowing.
13 When Elijah heard *it,* he wrapped his face in his mantle and went out and stood in
the entrance of the cave. And behold, a voice *came* to him and said, "What are you doing here, Elijah?"
14 Then he said, "I have been very zealous for the LORD, the God of hosts; for the
sons of Israel have forsaken Your covenant, torn down Your altars and killed Your prophets with the sword. And I alone am left; and they seek my life, to take it away."
15 The LORD said to him, "Go, return on your way to the wilderness of Damascus, and
when you have arrived, you shall anoint Hazael king over Aram;
16 and Jehu the son of Nimshi you shall anoint king over Israel; and Elisha the son of
Shaphat of Abel-meholah you shall anoint as prophet in your place.
17 "It shall come about, the one who escapes from the sword of Hazael, Jehu shall put
to death, and the one who escapes from the sword of Jehu, Elisha shall put to death.
18 "Yet I will leave 7,000 in Israel, all the knees that have not bowed to Baal and every
mouth that has not kissed him."
19 So he departed from there and found Elisha the son of Shaphat, while he was plowing with twelve pairs *of oxen* before him, and he with the twelfth. And Elijah passed over
to him and threw his mantle on him.
20 He left the oxen and ran after Elijah and said, "Please let me kiss my father and my
mother, then I will follow you." And he said to him, "Go back again, for what have I
done to you?"
21 So he returned from following him, and took the pair of oxen and sacrificed them
and boiled their flesh with the implements of the oxen, and gave *it* to the people and
they ate. Then he arose and followed Elijah and ministered to him.

War with Aram

20 Now Ben-hadad king of Aram gathered all his army, and there *were* thirty-two
kings with him, and horses and chariots. And he went up and besieged Samaria
and fought against it.
2 Then he sent messengers to the city to Ahab king of Israel and said to him, "Thus
says Ben-hadad,
3 'Your silver and your gold are mine; your most beautiful wives and children are also
mine.' "

19:11 Ex 19:20; 24:12, 18; Ezek 1:4
19:12 Job 4:16; Zech 4:6
19:13 Ex 3:6; 1 Kin 19:9
19:14 1 Kin 19:10
19:15 2 Kin 8:8-15
19:16 2 Kin 9:1-10; 1 Kin 19:19-21; 2 Kin 2:9, 15
19:17 2 Kin 8:12; 13:3, 22; 2 Kin 9:14-10:25
19:18 Rom 11:4; Hos 13:2
19:19 1 Sam 28:14; 2 Kin 2:8, 13, 14
19:20 Matt 8:21, 22; Luke 9:61, 62; Acts 20:37
19:21 2 Sam 24:22
20:1 1 Kin 15:18, 20; 2 Kin 6:24; 1 Kin 22:31; 1 Kin 16:24; 2 Kin 6:24

19:11–13 Elijah knew that the sound of gentle blowing was God's voice. He realized that God doesn't reveal himself only in powerful, miraculous ways. To look for God only in something big (rallies, churches, conferences, highly visible leaders) may be to miss him because he is often found gently whispering in the quietness of a humbled heart. Are you listening for God? Step back from the noise and activity of your busy life and listen humbly and quietly for his guidance. It may come when you least expect it.

19:15–16 God asked Elijah to anoint three different people. The first was Hazael, as king of Aram. Elijah was told to anoint an enemy king because God was going to use Aram as his instrument to punish Israel for its sin. Aram brought Israel's *external* punishment.

Israel's *internal* punishment came from Jehu, the next man Elijah was to anoint. As king of Israel, Jehu would destroy those who worshiped the false god Baal (2 Kings 9—10).

The third person Elijah was told to anoint was Elisha, the prophet who would succeed him. Elisha's job was to work in Israel, the northern kingdom, to help point the people back to God. At this time, the southern kingdom was ruled by Jehoshaphat, a king devoted to God.

19:18 Kissing Baal meant kissing some object representing him to show loyalty to him.

19:19 The mantle (cloak) was the most important article of clothing a person could own. It was used as protection against the weather, as bedding, as a place to sit, and as luggage. It could be given as a pledge for a debt or torn into pieces to show grief. Elijah put his mantle on Elisha's shoulders to show that he would become Elijah's successor. Later, when the transfer of authority was complete, Elijah left his mantle for Elisha (2 Kings 2:11–14).

19:21 By killing his oxen, Elisha made a strong commitment to follow Elijah. Without them, he could not return to his life as a wealthy farmer. This meal was more than a feast among farmers. It was an offering of thanks to the Lord who chose Elisha to be his prophet.

20:1ff With two evil and two good kings up to this point, the southern kingdom, Judah, wavered between godly and ungodly living. But the northern kingdom, Israel, had eight evil kings in succession. To punish both kingdoms for living their own way instead of following God, God allowed other nations to gain strength and become their enemies. Three main enemies threatened Israel and Judah during the next two centuries—Aram, Assyria, and Babylon. Aram, the first to rise to power, presented an immediate threat to Ahab and Israel.

4 The king of Israel replied, "It is according to your word, my lord, O king; I am yours,
and all that I have."
5 Then the messengers returned and said, "Thus says Ben-hadad, 'Surely, I sent to
you saying, "You shall give me your silver and your gold and your wives and your children,"
6 but about this time tomorrow I will send my servants to you, and they will search
your house and the houses of your servants; and whatever is desirable in your eyes, they
will take in their hand and carry away.' "
20:7 2 Kin 5:7 **7** Then the king of Israel called all the elders of the land and said, "Please observe
and see how this man is looking for trouble; for he sent to me for my wives and my children and my silver and my gold, and I did not refuse him."
8 All the elders and all the people said to him, "Do not listen or consent."

AHAB

The kings of Israel and Judah, both good and evil, had prophets sent by God to advise, confront, and aid them. King David had a faithful friend in God's prophet, Nathan; Ahab could have had an equally faithful friend in Elijah. But while David listened to Nathan and was willing to repent of his sins, Ahab saw Elijah as his enemy. Why? Because Elijah always brought bad news to Ahab, and Ahab refused to acknowledge that it was his own constant disobedience to God and persistent idol worship, not Elijah's prophecies, that brought the evil on his nation. He blamed Elijah for bringing the prophecies of judgment, rather than taking his advice and changing his evil ways.

Ahab was trapped by his own choices, and he was unwilling to take the right action. As king, he was responsible to God and his prophet Elijah, but he was married to an evil woman who drew him into idol worship. He was a childish man who brooded for days if unable to get his own way. He took his evil wife's advice, listened only to the "prophets" who gave good news, and surrounded himself with people who encouraged him to do whatever he wanted. But the value of advice cannot be judged by the number of people for or against it. Ahab consistently chose to follow the majority opinion of those who surrounded him, and that led to his death.

It may seem nice to have someone encourage us to do whatever we want because advice that goes against our wishes is difficult to accept. However, our decisions must be based on the quality of the advice, not its attractiveness or the majority opinion of our peers. God encourages us to get advice from wise counselors, but how can we test the advice we receive? Advice that agrees with the principles in God's Word is reliable. We must always separate advice from our own desires, the majority opinion, or whatever seems best in our limited perspective, and weigh it against God's commands. He will never lead us to do what he has forbidden in his Word—even in principle. Unlike Ahab, we should trust godly counselors and have the courage to stand against those who would have us do otherwise.

Strengths and accomplishments:
- Eighth king of Israel
- Capable leader and military strategist

Weaknesses and mistakes:
- Was the most evil king of Israel
- Married Jezebel, a pagan woman, and allowed her to promote Baal worship
- Brooded about not being able to get a piece of land, and so his wife had its owner, Naboth, killed
- Was used to getting his own way, and got depressed when he didn't

Lessons from his life:
- The choice of a mate will have a significant effect on life—physically, spiritually, and emotionally
- Selfishness, left unchecked, can lead to great evil

Vital statistics:
- Where: Northern kingdom of Israel
- Occupation: King
- Relatives: Wife: Jezebel. Father: Omri. Sons: Ahaziah, Jehoram
- Contemporaries: Elijah, Naboth, Jehu, Ben-hadad, Jehoshaphat

Key verses:
"Ahab the son of Omri did evil in the sight of the LORD more than all who were before him . . . He married Jezebel the daughter of Ethbaal king of the Sidonians, and went to serve Baal and worshiped him. So he erected an altar for Baal in the house of Baal which he built in Samaria. Ahab also made the Asherah. Thus Ahab did more to provoke the LORD God of Israel than all the kings of Israel who were before him" (1 Kings 16:30–33).

Ahab's story is told in 1 Kings 16:28—22:40. He is also mentioned in 2 Chronicles 18—22; Micah 6:16.

9 So he said to the messengers of Ben-hadad, "Tell my lord the king, 'All that you sent
for to your servant at the first I will do, but this thing I cannot do.' " And the messengers
departed and brought him word again.
10 Ben-hadad sent to him and said, "May the gods do so to me and more also, if the
dust of Samaria will suffice for handfuls for all the people who follow me."
11 Then the king of Israel replied, "Tell *him,* 'Let not him who girds on *his armor* boast
like him who takes *it* off.' "
12 When *Ben-hadad* heard this message, as he was drinking with the kings in the temporary shelters, he said to his servants, "Station *yourselves.*" So they stationed *themselves*
against the city.

20:10 1 Kin 19:2; 2 Kin 6:31
20:11 Prov 27:1
20:12 1 Kin 16:9; Prov 31:4, 5

Ahab Victorious

13 Now behold, a prophet approached Ahab king of Israel and said, "Thus says the
LORD, 'Have you seen all this great multitude? Behold, I will deliver them into your hand
today, and you shall know that I am the LORD.' "
14 Ahab said, "By whom?" So he said, "Thus says the LORD, 'By the young men of the
rulers of the provinces.' " Then he said, "Who shall begin the battle?" And he answered,
"You."
15 Then he mustered the young men of the rulers of the provinces, and there were 232;
and after them he mustered all the people, *even* all the sons of Israel, 7,000.
16 They went out at noon, while Ben-hadad was drinking himself drunk in the temporary shelters with the thirty-two kings who helped him.
17 The young men of the rulers of the provinces went out first; and Ben-hadad sent
out and they told him, saying, "Men have come out from Samaria."
18 Then he said, "If they have come out for peace, take them alive; or if they have come
out for war, take them alive."
19 So these went out from the city, the young men of the rulers of the provinces, and
the army which followed them.
20 They killed each his man; and the Arameans fled and Israel pursued them, and Ben-hadad king of Aram escaped on a horse with horsemen.
21 The king of Israel went out and struck the horses and chariots, and killed the Arameans with a great slaughter.
22 Then the prophet came near to the king of Israel and said to him, "Go, strengthen
yourself and observe and see what you have to do; for at the turn of the year the king of
Aram will come up against you."
23 Now the servants of the king of Aram said to him, "Their gods are gods of the mountains, therefore they were stronger than we; but rather let us fight against them in the
plain, *and* surely we will be stronger than they.
24 "Do this thing: remove the kings, each from his place, and put captains in their place,

20:13 1 Kin 20:28; 1 Kin 18:36
20:16 1 Kin 16:9; 20:12; Prov 20:1
20:18 2 Kin 14:8-12
20:22 1 Kin 20:13; 2 Sam 11:1; 1 Kin 20:26
20:23 1 Kin 14:23; Jer 16:19-21; Rom 1:21-23

20:23 Since the days of Joshua, Israel's soldiers had a reputation for being superior fighters in the hills, but ineffective in the open plains and valleys because they did not use chariots in battle. Horse-drawn chariots, useless in hilly terrain and dense forests, could easily run down great numbers of foot soldiers on the plains. What Ben-hadad's officers did not understand was that it was God, not chariots, that made the difference in battle.

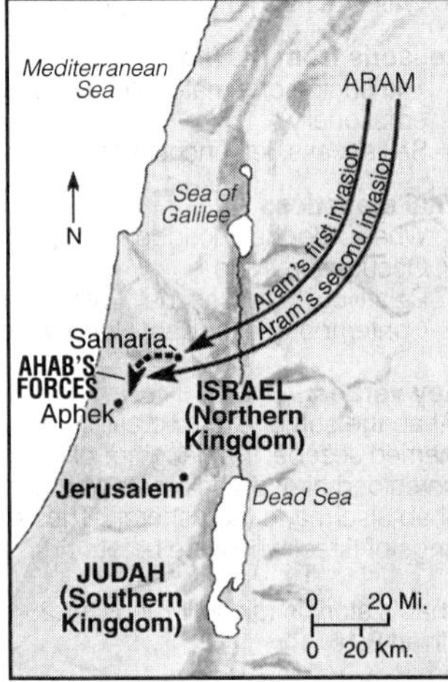

GOD DELIVERS AHAB
Despite Ahab's wickedness, God approached him in love. When Samaria was surrounded by Aramean forces, God miraculously delivered the city. But Ahab refused to give God credit. A year later, the Arameans attacked near Aphek. Again God gave Ahab victory, but again the king refused to acknowledge God's help.

25 and muster an army like the army that you have lost, horse for horse, and chariot
for chariot. Then we will fight against them in the plain, and surely we will be stronger
than they." And he listened to their voice and did so.

Another Aramean War

20:26 1 Kin 20:22; 2 Kin 13:17

26 At the turn of the year, Ben-hadad mustered the Arameans and went up to Aphek
to fight against Israel.

20:27 Judg 6:3-5; 1 Sam 13:5-8

27 The sons of Israel were mustered and were provisioned and went to meet them; and
the sons of Israel camped before them like two little flocks of goats, but the Arameans
filled the country.

20:28 1 Kin 17:18; 1 Kin 20:23; 1 Kin 20:13

28 Then a man of God came near and spoke to the king of Israel and said, "Thus says
the LORD, 'Because the Arameans have said, "The LORD is a god of *the* mountains, but
He is not a god of *the* valleys," therefore I will give all this great multitude into your hand,
and you shall know that I am the LORD.' "
29 So they camped one over against the other seven days. And on the seventh day the
battle was joined, and the sons of Israel killed *of* the Arameans 100,000 foot soldiers in
one day.

20:30 1 Kin 20:26; 1 Kin 22:25; 2 Chr 18:24

30 But the rest fled to Aphek into the city, and the wall fell on 27,000 men who were
left. And Ben-hadad fled and came into the city into an inner chamber.

20:31 1 Kin 20:23-26; Gen 37:34; 2 Sam 3:31

31 His servants said to him, "Behold now, we have heard that the kings of the house of
Israel are merciful kings, please let us put sackcloth on our loins and ropes on our heads,
and go out to the king of Israel; perhaps he will save your life."

20:32 1 Kin 20:31; 1 Kin 20:3-6

32 So they girded sackcloth on their loins and *put* ropes on their heads, and came to
the king of Israel and said, "Your servant Ben-hadad says, 'Please let me live.' " And he
said, "Is he still alive? He is my brother."
33 Now the men took this as an omen, and quickly catching his word said, "Your brother
Ben-hadad." Then he said, "Go, bring him." Then Ben-hadad came out to him, and he
took him up into the chariot.

20:34 1 Kin 15:20

34 *Ben-hadad* said to him, "The cities which my father took from your father I will
restore, and you shall make streets for yourself in Damascus, as my father made in Samaria." *Ahab said,* "And I will let you go with this covenant." So he made a covenant
with him and let him go.

20:35 2 Kin 2:3-7; 1 Kin 13:17, 18

35 Now a certain man of the sons of the prophets said to another by the word of the
LORD, "Please strike me." But the man refused to strike him.

20:36 1 Kin 13:24

36 Then he said to him, "Because you have not listened to the voice of the LORD, behold, as soon as you have departed from me, a lion will kill you." And as soon as he had
departed from him a lion found him and killed him.
37 Then he found another man and said, "Please strike me." And the man struck him,
wounding him.

20:38 1 Kin 14:2

38 So the prophet departed and waited for the king by the way, and disguised himself
with a bandage over his eyes.

20:39 2 Kin 10:24

39 As the king passed by, he cried to the king and said, "Your servant went out into the
midst of the battle; and behold, a man turned aside and brought a man to me and said,
'Guard this man; if for any reason he is missing, then your life shall be for his life, or else
you shall pay a talent of silver.'
40 "While your servant was busy here and there, he was gone."
And the king of Israel said to him, "So shall your judgment be; you yourself have decided *it.*"
41 Then he hastily took the bandage away from his eyes, and the king of Israel recognized him that he was of the prophets.

20:31 Sackcloth was coarse cloth usually made of goat's hair and worn as a symbol of mourning for the dead or for natural disaster. Wearing ropes around the head may have been a symbol of putting oneself at another's disposal. In other words, Ahab could have hung them if he wished. Wearing ropes around the head, therefore, was a sign of submission.

20:35–36 The prophet needed a wound so he would look like an injured soldier and could effectively deliver his prophecy to Ahab. The first man was killed by a lion because he refused to obey the Lord's instructions through the prophet.

20:41–42 It is difficult to explain why Ahab let Ben-hadad go, especially after all the trouble the Arameans had caused him. God helped Ahab destroy the Aramean army to prove to Ahab and to Aram that he alone was God. But Ahab failed to destroy the king, his greatest enemy. Ben-hadad was under God's judgment to die, and Ahab had no authority to let him live. For this, God told Ahab that he must now die instead. This prophet's message soon came true when Ahab was killed on the battlefield (22:35).

42 He said to him, "Thus says the LORD, 'Because you have let go out of *your* hand the
man whom I had devoted to destruction, therefore your life shall go for his life, and your
people for his people.' "
43 So the king of Israel went to his house sullen and vexed, and came to Samaria.

Ahab Covets Naboth's Vineyard

21 Now it came about after these things that Naboth the Jezreelite had a vineyard
which *was* in Jezreel beside the palace of Ahab king of Samaria.
2 Ahab spoke to Naboth, saying, "Give me your vineyard, that I may have it for a
vegetable garden because it is close beside my house, and I will give you a better vineyard than it in its place; if you like, I will give you the price of it in money."
3 But Naboth said to Ahab, "The LORD forbid me that I should give you the inheritance of my fathers."
4 So Ahab came into his house sullen and vexed because of the word which Naboth
the Jezreelite had spoken to him; for he said, "I will not give you the inheritance of my
fathers." And he lay down on his bed and turned away his face and ate no food.
5 But Jezebel his wife came to him and said to him, "How is it that your spirit is so
sullen that you are not eating food?"
6 So he said to her, "Because I spoke to Naboth the Jezreelite and said to him, 'Give
me your vineyard for money; or else, if it pleases you, I will give you a vineyard in its
place.' But he said, 'I will not give you my vineyard.' "
7 Jezebel his wife said to him, "Do you now reign over Israel? Arise, eat bread, and
let your heart be joyful; I will give you the vineyard of Naboth the Jezreelite."
8 So she wrote letters in Ahab's name and sealed them with his seal, and sent letters
to the elders and to the nobles who were living with Naboth in his city.
9 Now she wrote in the letters, saying, "Proclaim a fast and seat Naboth at the head
of the people;
10 and seat two worthless men before him, and let them testify against him, saying,
'You cursed God and the king.' Then take him out and stone him to death."

Jezebel's Plot

11 So the men of his city, the elders and the nobles who lived in his city, did as Jezebel
had sent *word* to them, just as it was written in the letters which she had sent them.
12 They proclaimed a fast and seated Naboth at the head of the people.
13 Then the two worthless men came in and sat before him; and the worthless men
testified against him, even against Naboth, before the people, saying, "Naboth cursed
God and the king." So they took him outside the city and stoned him to death with stones.
14 Then they sent *word* to Jezebel, saying, "Naboth has been stoned and is dead."
15 When Jezebel heard that Naboth had been stoned and was dead, Jezebel said to
Ahab, "Arise, take possession of the vineyard of Naboth, the Jezreelite, which he refused to give you for money; for Naboth is not alive, but dead."
16 When Ahab heard that Naboth was dead, Ahab arose to go down to the vineyard of
Naboth the Jezreelite, to take possession of it.
17 Then the word of the LORD came to Elijah the Tishbite, saying,
18 "Arise, go down to meet Ahab king of Israel, who is in Samaria; behold, he is in the
vineyard of Naboth where he has gone down to take possession of it.
19 "You shall speak to him, saying, 'Thus says the LORD, "Have you murdered and also
taken possession?" ' And you shall speak to him, saying, 'Thus says the LORD, "In the
place where the dogs licked up the blood of Naboth the dogs will lick up your blood,
even yours." ' "

20:42 1 Kin 20:39
20:43 1 Kin 21:4
21:1 Judg 6:33; 1 Kin 18:45, 46
21:2 1 Sam 8:14
21:3 Lev 25:23; Num 36:7; Ezek 46:18
21:4 1 Kin 20:43
21:7 1 Sam 8:14
21:8 Esth 3:12; 8:8, 10; 1 Kin 20:7
21:10 1 Sam 2:12; 2 Sam 20:1; Ex 22:28; Lev 24:15, 16; Acts 6:11; Lev 24:14
21:12 Is 58:4
21:13 2 Kin 9:26; 2 Chr 24:21; Acts 7:58, 59; Heb 11:37
21:18 1 Kin 16:29
21:19 2 Sam 12:9; 1 Kin 22:38; 2 Kin 9:26

21:4 After hearing God's judgment (20:42), Ahab went home to pout. Driven by anger and rebellion against God, he had a fit of rage when Naboth refused to sell his vineyard. The same feelings that led him to a career of power grabbing drove him to resent Naboth. Rage turned to hatred and led to murder. Naboth, however, wanted to uphold God's laws: it was considered a duty to keep ancestral land in the family. This incident shows the cruel interplay between Ahab and Jezebel, two of the most wicked leaders in Israel's history.

21:13 Jezebel devised a scheme that appeared legal to get the land for her husband. Two witnesses were required to establish guilt, and the punishment for blasphemy was death by stoning. Those who twist the law and legal procedures to get what they want today may be more sophisticated in how they go about it, but they are still guilty of the same sin.

21:19, 23 For the fulfillment of these verses, see 22:38 where dogs licked Ahab's blood, and 2 Kings 9:30—10:28 where Jezebel and the rest of Ahab's family were destroyed.

21:20 1 Kin 18:17; 1 Kin 21:25; 2 Kin 17:17; Rom 7:14
21:21 1 Kin 14:10; 2 Kin 9:8
21:22 1 Kin 15:29; 1 Kin 16:3, 11; 1 Kin 12:30; 13:34; 14:16
21:23 2 Kin 9:10, 30-37
21:24 1 Kin 14:11; 16:4
21:25 1 Kin 16:30-33; 21:20

20 Ahab said to Elijah, "Have you found me, O my enemy?" And he answered, "I have
found *you,* because you have sold yourself to do evil in the sight of the LORD.
21 "Behold, I will bring evil upon you, and will utterly sweep you away, and will cut off
from Ahab every male, both bond and free in Israel;
22 and I will make your house like the house of Jeroboam the son of Nebat, and like
the house of Baasha the son of Ahijah, because of the provocation with which you have
provoked *Me* to anger, and *because* you have made Israel sin.
23 "Of Jezebel also has the LORD spoken, saying, 'The dogs will eat Jezebel in the district of Jezreel.'
24 "The one belonging to Ahab, who dies in the city, the dogs will eat, and the one who
dies in the field the birds of heaven will eat."
25 Surely there was no one like Ahab who sold himself to do evil in the sight of the
LORD, because Jezebel his wife incited him.

The Bible is as honest about the lives of its heroes as it is about those who rejected God. Some Bible characters found out what God can do with failures when they turned to him. Many, however, neither admitted their failures nor turned to God.

Jezebel ranks as the most evil woman in the Bible. The Bible even uses her name as an example of people who completely reject God (Revelation 2:20–21). Many pagan women married into Israel without acknowledging the God their husbands worshiped. They brought their religions with them. But no one was as determined as Jezebel to make all Israel worship *her* gods. To the prophet Elijah, she seemed to have succeeded. He felt he was the only one still faithful to God until God told him there were still 7,000 who had not turned from the faith. Jezebel's one outstanding "success" was in contributing to the cause of the eventual downfall of the northern kingdom—idolatry. God punished the northern tribes for their idolatry by having them carried off into captivity.

Jezebel held great power. She not only managed her husband, Ahab, but she also had 850 assorted pagan priests under her control. She was committed to her gods and to getting what she wanted. She believed that the king had the right to possess anything he wanted. When Naboth refused to sell Ahab his vineyard, Jezebel ruthlessly had Naboth killed and took ownership of the land. Jezebel's plan to wipe out worship of God in Israel led to painful consequences. Before she died, Jezebel suffered the loss of her husband in combat and her son at the hand of Jehu, who took the throne by force. She died in the defiant and scornful way she had lived.

When comparing Jezebel and Elijah, we have to admire each one's strength of commitment. The big difference was *to whom* they were committed. Jezebel was committed to herself and her false gods; Elijah was totally committed to the one true God. In the end, God proved Elijah right. To what or to whom are you most committed? How would God evaluate your commitment?

Weaknesses and mistakes:
- Systematically eliminated the representatives of God in Israel
- Promoted and funded Baal worship
- Threatened to have Elijah killed
- Believed kings and queens could rightfully do or have anything they wanted
- Used her strong convictions to get her own way

Lessons from her life:
- It is not enough to be committed or sincere. Where our commitment lies makes a great difference
- Rejecting God always leads to disaster

Vital statistics:
- Where: Sidon, Samaria
- Occupation: Queen of Israel
- Relatives: Husband: Ahab. Father: Ethbaal. Sons: Jehoram, Ahaziah
- Contemporaries: Elijah, Jehu

Key verse:
"Surely there was no one like Ahab who sold himself to do evil in the sight of the LORD, because Jezebel his wife incited him" (1 Kings 21:25).

Jezebel's story is told in 1 Kings 16:31—2 Kings 9:37. Her name is used as a synonym for great evil in Revelation 2:20.

21:20 Ahab still refused to admit his sin against God. Instead he accused Elijah of being his enemy. When we are blinded by envy and hatred, it is almost impossible to see our own sin.

26 He acted very abominably in following idols, according to all that the Amorites had
done, whom the LORD cast out before the sons of Israel.
27 It came about when Ahab heard these words, that he tore his clothes and put on
sackcloth and fasted, and he lay in sackcloth and went about despondently.
28 Then the word of the LORD came to Elijah the Tishbite, saying,
29 "Do you see how Ahab has humbled himself before Me? Because he has humbled
himself before Me, I will not bring the evil in his days, *but* I will bring the evil upon his
house in his son's days."

21:26 1 Kin 15:12; 2 Kin 17:12; Gen 15:16; Lev 18:25-30; 2 Kin 21:11

21:27 Gen 37:34; 2 Sam 3:31; 2 Kin 6:30

21:29 2 Kin 9:25-37

4. Kings of Israel and Judah

Ahab's Third Campaign against Aram

22 Three years passed without war between Aram and Israel.
2 In the third year Jehoshaphat the king of Judah came down to the king of
Israel.
3 Now the king of Israel said to his servants, "Do you know that Ramoth-gilead belongs to us, and we are still doing nothing to take it out of the hand of the king of Aram?"
4 And he said to Jehoshaphat, "Will you go with me to battle at Ramoth-gilead?" And
Jehoshaphat said to the king of Israel, "I am as you are, my people as your people, my
horses as your horses."
5 Moreover, Jehoshaphat said to the king of Israel, "Please inquire first for the word
of the LORD."
6 Then the king of Israel gathered the prophets together, about four hundred men,
and said to them, "Shall I go against Ramoth-gilead to battle or shall I refrain?" And
they said, "Go up, for the Lord will give *it* into the hand of the king."
7 But Jehoshaphat said, "Is there not yet a prophet of the LORD here that we may
inquire of him?"
8 The king of Israel said to Jehoshaphat, "There is yet one man by whom we may
inquire of the LORD, but I hate him, because he does not prophesy good concerning me,
but evil. *He is* Micaiah son of Imlah." But Jehoshaphat said, "Let not the king say so."
9 Then the king of Israel called an officer and said, "Bring quickly Micaiah son of
Imlah."
10 Now the king of Israel and Jehoshaphat king of Judah were sitting each on his throne,
arrayed in *their* robes, at the threshing floor at the entrance of the gate of Samaria; and
all the prophets were prophesying before them.
11 Then Zedekiah the son of Chenaanah made horns of iron for himself and said, "Thus
says the LORD, 'With these you will gore the Arameans until they are consumed.' "
12 All the prophets were prophesying thus, saying, "Go up to Ramoth-gilead and prosper, for the LORD will give *it* into the hand of the king."

Micaiah Predicts Defeat

13 Then the messenger who went to summon Micaiah spoke to him saying, "Behold
now, the words of the prophets are uniformly favorable to the king. Please let your word
be like the word of one of them, and speak favorably."
14 But Micaiah said, "As the LORD lives, what the LORD says to me, that I shall speak."
15 When he came to the king, the king said to him, "Micaiah, shall we go to Ramoth-

22:2 2 Chr 18:2; 1 Kin 15:24

22:3 Deut 4:43; Josh 21:38; 1 Kin 4:13

22:4 2 Kin 3:7

22:6 1 Kin 18:19

22:7 2 Kin 3:11

22:10 1 Kin 22:6

22:11 Zech 1:18-21; Deut 33:17

22:14 1 Kin 18:10, 15; Num 22:18; 24:13

22:15 1 Kin 22:12

21:29 Ahab was more wicked than any other king of Israel (16:30; 21:25), but when he repented in deep humility, God took notice and reduced his punishment. The same Lord who was merciful to Ahab wants to be merciful to you. No matter how evil you have been, it is never too late to humble yourself, turn to God, and ask for forgiveness.

22:6 These 400 prophets may have been the 400 Asherah priests left alive by Elijah at Carmel, although 450 prophets of Baal were killed (see 18:19–40).

22:7 Jehoshaphat knew there was a difference between these pagan prophets and the "prophet of the LORD," so he asked if one was available. Evidently Jehoshaphat wanted to do what was right although Ahab didn't. However, both kings disregarded God's message and listened only to the pagan prophets.

22:10 Threshing floors were placed in elevated areas to allow the wind to blow away the discarded hulls of grain.

22:15–16 Why did Micaiah tell Ahab to attack when he had previously vowed to speak only what God had told him? Perhaps he was speaking sarcastically, making fun of the messages from the pagan prophets by showing that they were telling the king only what he wanted to hear. Somehow, Micaiah's tone of voice let everyone know he was mocking the pagan prophets. When confronted, he predicted that the king would die and the battle would be lost. Although Ahab repented temporarily (21:27), he still maintained the system of false prophets. These false prophets would be instrumental in leading him to his own ruin.

gilead to battle, or shall we refrain?" And he answered him, "Go up and succeed, and the LORD will give *it* into the hand of the king."

16 Then the king said to him, "How many times must I adjure you to speak to me nothing but the truth in the name of the LORD?"

17 So he said,

"I saw all Israel
Scattered on the mountains,
Like sheep which have no shepherd.
And the LORD said, 'These have no master.
Let each of them return to his house in peace.' "

18 Then the king of Israel said to Jehoshaphat, "Did I not tell you that he would not
prophesy good concerning me, but evil?"

19 Micaiah said, "Therefore, hear the word of the LORD. I saw the LORD sitting on
His throne, and all the host of heaven standing by Him on His right and on His left.
20 "The LORD said, 'Who will entice Ahab to go up and fall at Ramoth-gilead?' And
one said this while another said that.

22:17 Num 27:17; 1 Kin 22:34-36; 2 Chr 18:16; Matt 9:36; Mark 6:34

22:18 1 Kin 22:8

22:19 Is 6:1; Ezek 1:26-28; Dan 7:9, 10; Job 1:6; 2:1; Ps 103:20, 21; Dan 7:10; Matt 18:10; Heb 1:7, 14

KINGS AND THEIR ENEMIES (910 B.C. – 841 B.C.)

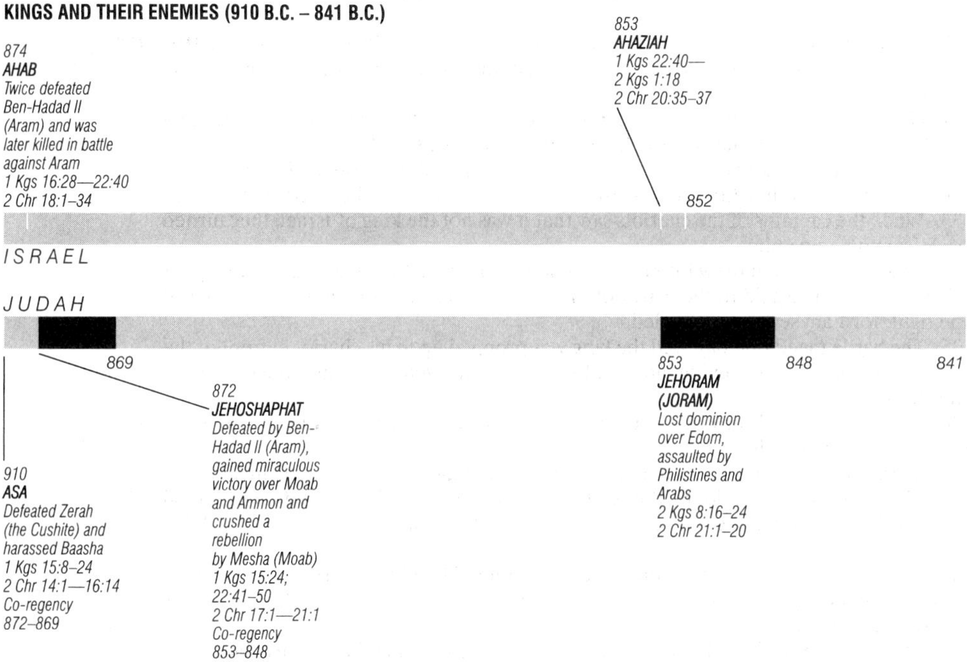

874
AHAB
Twice defeated Ben-Hadad II (Aram) and was later killed in battle against Aram
1 Kgs 16:28—22:40
2 Chr 18:1–34

853
AHAZIAH
1 Kgs 22:40—
2 Kgs 1:18
2 Chr 20:35–37

852

ISRAEL

JUDAH

869

910
ASA
Defeated Zerah (the Cushite) and harassed Baasha
1 Kgs 15:8–24
2 Chr 14:1—16:14
Co-regency 872–869

872
JEHOSHAPHAT
Defeated by Ben-Hadad II (Aram), gained miraculous victory over Moab and Ammon and crushed a rebellion by Mesha (Moab)
1 Kgs 15:24; 22:41–50
2 Chr 17:1—21:1
Co-regency 853–848

853
JEHORAM (JORAM)
Lost dominion over Edom, assaulted by Philistines and Arabs
2 Kgs 8:16–24
2 Chr 21:1–20

848

841

All dates are B.C.
Solid section of the timeline indicates co-regency.
For all the kings of Israel and Judah, see the chart at the end of 1 Kings.

22:19–22 The vision Micaiah saw was either a picture of a real incident in heaven or a parable of what was happening on earth, illustrating that the seductive influence of the false prophets would be part of God's judgment upon Ahab (22:23). Whether or not God sent an angel in disguise, he used the system of false prophets to snare Ahab in his sin. The deceiving spirit (22:22) symbolized the way of life for these prophets, who told the king only what he wanted to hear.

22:20–22 Does God allow angels to entice people to do evil? To understand evil one must first understand God. (1) God himself is good (Psalm 11:7). (2) God created a good world that fell because of man's sin (Romans 5:12). (3) Someday God will recreate the world and it will be good again (Revelation 21:1). (4) God is stronger than evil (Matthew 13:41–43; Revelation 19:11–21). (5) God allows evil, and thus he has control over it. God did not create evil, and he offers help to those who wish to overcome it (Matthew 11:28–30). (6) God uses everything—both good and evil—for his good purposes (Genesis 50:20; Romans 8:28).

The Bible shows us a God who hates all evil and will one day do away with it completely and forever (Revelation 20:10–15). God does not entice anyone to become evil. Those committed to evil, however, may be used by God to sin even more in order to hurry their deserved judgment (Exodus 11:10). We don't need to understand every detail of how God works in order to have perfect confidence in his absolute power over evil and his total goodness toward us.

21 "Then a spirit came forward and stood before the LORD and said, 'I will entice him.'
22 "The LORD said to him, 'How?' And he said, 'I will go out and be a deceiving spirit
in the mouth of all his prophets.' Then He said, 'You are to entice *him* and also prevail.
Go and do so.'
23 "Now therefore, behold, the LORD has put a deceiving spirit in the mouth of all these
your prophets; and the LORD has proclaimed disaster against you."
24 Then Zedekiah the son of Chenaanah came near and struck Micaiah on the cheek
and said, "How did the Spirit of the LORD pass from me to speak to you?"
25 Micaiah said, "Behold, you shall see on that day when you enter an inner room to
hide yourself."
26 Then the king of Israel said, "Take Micaiah and return him to Amon the governor
of the city and to Joash the king's son;
27 and say, 'Thus says the king, "Put this man in prison and feed him sparingly with
bread and water until I return safely." ' "
28 Micaiah said, "If you indeed return safely the LORD has not spoken by me." And he
said, "Listen, all you people."

22:22 Judg 9:23; 1 Sam 16:14; 18:10; 19:9; Ezek 14:9; 2 Thess 2:11
22:23 Ezek 14:9
22:24 1 Kin 22:11; Matt 5:39; Acts 23:2, 3; 2 Chr 18:23
22:25 1 Kin 20:30
22:27 2 Chr 16:10; 18:25-27
22:28 Deut 18:22; Mic 1:2

Defeat and Death of Ahab

29 So the king of Israel and Jehoshaphat king of Judah went up against Ramoth-
gilead.
30 The king of Israel said to Jehoshaphat, "I will disguise myself and go into the battle,
but you put on your robes." So the king of Israel disguised himself and went into the
battle.
31 Now the king of Aram had commanded the thirty-two captains of his chariots, saying, "Do not fight with small or great, but with the king of Israel alone."
32 So when the captains of the chariots saw Jehoshaphat, they said, "Surely it is the
king of Israel," and they turned aside to fight against him, and Jehoshaphat cried out.
33 When the captains of the chariots saw that it was not the king of Israel, they turned
back from pursuing him.
34 Now a certain man drew his bow at random and struck the king of Israel in a joint
of the armor. So he said to the driver of his chariot, "Turn around and take me out of
the fight; for I am severely wounded."
35 The battle raged that day, and the king was propped up in his chariot in front of the
Arameans, and died at evening, and the blood from the wound ran into the bottom of
the chariot.
36 Then a cry passed throughout the army close to sunset, saying, "Every man to his
city and every man to his country."
37 So the king died and was brought to Samaria, and they buried the king in Samaria.
38 They washed the chariot by the pool of Samaria, and the dogs licked up his blood
(now the harlots bathed themselves *there*), according to the word of the LORD which He
spoke.
39 Now the rest of the acts of Ahab and all that he did and the ivory house which he
built and all the cities which he built, are they not written in the Book of the Chronicles
of the Kings of Israel?
40 So Ahab slept with his fathers, and Ahaziah his son became king in his place.

22:29 1 Kin 22:3, 4
22:30 2 Chr 35:22
22:31 1 Kin 20:1, 16, 24; 2 Chr 18:30
22:34 2 Chr 35:23
22:36 2 Kin 14:12
22:38 1 Kin 21:19
22:39 Amos 3:15

The New Rulers

41 Now Jehoshaphat the son of Asa became king over Judah in the fourth year of Ahab
king of Israel.
42 Jehoshaphat was thirty-five years old when he became king, and he reigned twenty-
five years in Jerusalem. And his mother's name was Azubah the daughter of Shilhi.

22:41 2 Chr 20:31

22:34 Ahab could not escape God's judgment. The king of Aram sent 32 of his best chariot captains with the sole purpose of killing Ahab. Thinking he could escape, Ahab tried a disguise, but a random arrow struck him while the chariots chased the wrong king, Jehoshaphat. It was foolish for Ahab to think he could escape by wearing a disguise. Sometimes people try to escape reality by disguising themselves—changing jobs, moving to a new town, even changing spouses. But God sees and evaluates the motives of each person. Any attempted disguise is futile.

22:35 Just as the prophet had predicted (20:42), Ahab was killed. See Ahab's Profile in chapter 19 for more of Ahab's sad story.

22:41–50 For more details on Jehoshaphat, see the other account of his reign in 2 Chronicles 17—20.

22:43 2 Chr 17:3; 1 Kin 15:14; 2 Kin 12:3

22:44 1 Kin 22:2; 2 Kin 8:16, 18; 2 Chr 19:2

22:45 2 Chr 20:34

22:46 Gen 19:5; Deut 23:17; 1 Kin 14:24; 15:12; Jude 7

22:47 2 Sam 8:14

22:48 1 Kin 10:22; 2 Chr 20:36; 1 Kin 9:28; 2 Chr 20:37; 1 Kin 9:26

22:51 1 Kin 22:40

22:52 1 Kin 15:26; 21:25

22:53 Judg 2:11; 1 Kin 16:30-32

43 He walked in all the way of Asa his father; he did not turn aside from it, doing right
in the sight of the LORD. However, the high places were not taken away; the people still
sacrificed and burnt incense on the high places.
44 Jehoshaphat also made peace with the king of Israel.
45 Now the rest of the acts of Jehoshaphat, and his might which he showed and how he
warred, are they not written in the Book of the Chronicles of the Kings of Judah?
46 The remnant of the sodomites who remained in the days of his father Asa, he expelled from the land.
47 Now there was no king in Edom; a deputy was king.
48 Jehoshaphat made ships of Tarshish to go to Ophir for gold, but they did not go for
the ships were broken at Ezion-geber.
49 Then Ahaziah the son of Ahab said to Jehoshaphat, "Let my servants go with your
servants in the ships." But Jehoshaphat was not willing.
50 And Jehoshaphat slept with his fathers and was buried with his fathers in the city of
his father David, and Jehoram his son became king in his place.
51 Ahaziah the son of Ahab became king over Israel in Samaria in the seventeenth
year of Jehoshaphat king of Judah, and he reigned two years over Israel.
52 He did evil in the sight of the LORD and walked in the way of his father and in the
way of his mother and in the way of Jeroboam the son of Nebat, who caused Israel to
sin.
53 So he served Baal and worshiped him and provoked the LORD God of Israel to anger,
according to all that his father had done.

22:43 Just like his ancestors Solomon and Asa, Jehoshaphat followed God, but he didn't remove the high places—the pagan shrines in the hills (2 Chronicles 20:33). It was against God's laws to worship idols in the shrines (Numbers 33:52), and at first Jehoshaphat attempted to remove them (2 Chronicles 17:6). They were so popular, however, that this proved difficult. In spite of Jehoshaphat's many contributions to the spiritual, moral, and material health of his country, he did not succeed in eradicating the hill shrines.

22:52–53 The book of 1 Kings begins with a nation united under David, the most devout king in Israel's history. The book ends with a divided kingdom and the death of Ahab, the most wicked king of all. What happened? The people forgot to acknowledge God as their ultimate leader; they appointed human leaders who ignored God; and then they conformed to the life-styles of these evil leaders. Occasional wrongdoing gradually turned into a way of life. Their blatant wickedness could be met only with judgment from God, who allowed enemy nations to arise and defeat Israel and Judah in battle as punishment for their sins. Failing to acknowledge God as our ultimate leader is the first step toward ruin.

DIVIDED KINGDOM OF ISRAEL

AHIJAH 934-909

ELIJAH 875–848

930
JEROBOAM I
(22 years)
Fortified a capital city (Shechem), set up two golden calf-idols, led the nation into sin,allowed anyone to be a priest
1 Kgs 11:26—14:20
2 Chr 10:12—13:20

909
NADAB
(2 years)
1 Kgs 14:20; 15:25-28

908
BAASHA
(24 years)
Led people into idol worship
1 Kgs 15:27—16:7
2 Chr 16:1-6

886
ELAH
(2 years)
Continued idol worship
1 Kgs 16:6-14

885
ZIMRI
(7 days)
1 Kgs 16:9-20

885
TIBNI
(4 years)
1 Kgs 16:21–22

885
OMRI
(12 years)
Built the capital city of Samaria, had great military power, but continued to lead Israel into idolatry
1 Kgs 16:16-28

874
AHAB
(22 years)
Married Jezebel (a non-Jew and extremely wicked woman), worshiped Baal, and suffered three years of famine caused by his consistent disobedience to God
1 Kgs 16:28—22:40
2 Chr 18:1-34

CAPITAL: SHECHEM, THEN TIRZAH, THEN SAMARIA
THE NORTHERN KINGDOM OF ISRAEL (TEN TRIBES)

THE SOUTHERN KINGDOM OF JUDAH (TWO TRIBES)
CAPITAL: JERUSALEM

930
REHOBOAM
(17 years)
Built many fortified cities, strengthened the economy (despite the tribute paid to Egypt), followed God for three years, but then set up idols and shrines to foreign gods
1 Kgs 11:43—14:31
2 Chr 9:31—12:16

913
ABIJAM (ABIJAH)
(3 years)
Despite his wickedness, he called for God's help to win the battle against Israel
1 Kgs 14:31—15:8
2 Chr 13:1—14:1

910
ASA
(41 years)
Destroyed pagan altars and rebuilt altar of God, built fortified cities, gained much wealth from plunder of foreign conquest, removed the queen mother for worshiping Asherah, led the people to worship God with their hearts, provided peace on home soil, was greatly loved and given a beautiful funeral
1 Kgs 15:8-24
2 Chr 14:1—16:14

872
JEHOSHAPHAT
(25 years)
Arranged for the marriage of his son to a daughter of Ahab (who made trouble later on), had a strong military (kept troops in cities of Israel his father had conquered), collected tribute from the Philistines, worshiped the Lord and destroyed idols, established education, and appointed judges and courts
1 Kgs 15:24; 22:41-50
2 Chr 17:1—21:1

All dates are B.C. The total years of reign sometimes include years of co-regency. (See charts, "Kings to Date," throughout 1 and 2 Kings.)

ELISHA 848–797

JONAH 793–753(?)

853
AHAZIAH
(2 years)
Proposed a joint trade venture with Judah
1 Kgs 22:40—2 Kgs 1:18
2 Chr 20:35-37

852
JEHORAM (JORAM)
(12 years)
Suffered famine and war during most of his reign
2 Kgs 1:17; 3:1—8:25
2 Chr 22:5-7

841
JEHU
(28 years)
Was responsible for the deaths of Jehoram (king of Israel), Ahaziah (king of Judah), and Jezebel (wicked mother of Jehoram); destroyed the priests and temples of Baal but did not consistently follow God
2 Kgs 9:1—10:36
2 Chr 22:7-12

814
JEHOAHAZ
(17 years)
Evil reign included worship of Asherah
2 Kgs 10:35; 13:1-9

798
JEHOASH (JOASH)
(16 years)
Even though he was evil, he recognized the authority of Elisha as a prophet of God
2 Kgs 13:10—14:16
2 Chr 25:17-24

793
JEROBOAM II
(41 years)
Very evil but politically powerful; his nation enjoyed economic prosperity and military peace
2 Kgs 14:16-29

853
JEHORAM (JORAM)
(8 years)
Married a wicked daughter of Ahab, compelled the people to worship idols, and killed all his brothers
2 Kgs 8:16-24
2 Chr 21:1-20

841
AHAZIAH
(1 year)
Friend of Jehoram of Israel
2 Kgs 8:24—9:29
2 Chr 22:1-9

841
ATHALIAH (QUEEN)
(6 years)
Killed all her grandchildren except Joash, who was hidden by his nurse for six years, and ravaged the temple to furnish Baal's temple
2 Kgs 11:1-20
2 Chr 22:10—23:21

835
JOASH (JEHOASH)
(40 years)
Was crowned king at the age of seven by Jehoiada (the high priest), promoted peace and prosperity, repaired the temple, and smashed the altars to Baal; but abandoned God after Jehoiada died, and even had Jehoiada's son killed
2 Kgs 11:2—12:21
2 Chr 22:11—24:27

796
AMAZIAH
(29 years)
Was basically good but did not completely wipe out idol worship; organized and mustered the army
2 Kgs 14:1-20
2 Chr 24:27—25:28

792
AZARIAH (UZZIAH)
(52 years)
Rebuilt a city named Eloth, owned many farms and vineyards, constructed water reservoirs and fortified towers, reorganized the army (so powerful that his fame spread to Egypt), but violated God's laws for priestly function—so God struck him with leprosy
2 Kgs 15:1-7
2 Chr 26:1-23

OBADIAH 855–840(?)

JOEL 835–796(?)

HOSEA 753–715

AMOS 760–750

753
ZECHARIAH
(6 months)
Encouraged idol worship
2 Kgs 14:29—15:12

752
SHALLUM
(1 month)
2 Kgs 15:10-15

752
MENAHEM
(10 years)
Imposed heavy taxes and oppressed his people
2 Kgs 15:14-22

742
PEKAHIAH
(2 years)
Continued idol worship
2 Kgs 15:22-26

740
PEKAH
(8 years)
During his reign many of the people were taken captive to Assyria
2 Kgs 15:25-31
2 Chr 28:5-8

732
HOSHEA
(9 years)
Suffered heavy taxation by Assyria and eventual conquest—bringing about Israelite captivity and resettlement of foreigners in Israel
2 Kgs 15:30; 17:1-6

722
END OF THE NORTHERN KINGDOM—Israel taken to Assyria by Shalmaneser

ISRAEL

JUDAH

750
JOTHAM
(16 years)
Rebuilt the upper gate of the temple, rebuilt walls and cities, but still permitted idol worship
2 Kgs 15:32-38
2 Chr 26:23—27:9

735
AHAZ
(16 years)
Sacrificed his own son to pagan gods, nailed the temple doors shut
2 Kgs 15:38—16:20
2 Chr 27:9—28:27

715
HEZEKIAH
(29 years)
Was a devoted follower of God, reopened the temple doors, purified the temple, reinstated priests and their duties, organized an orchestra to aid worship, destroyed idols (including the bronze serpent of Moses because people had begun to worship it), celebrated the Passover and even invited people who were living in the north to participate, constructed large public waterworks, was given 15 extra years of life, foolishly showed messengers the wealth in the temple
2 Kgs 16:20; 18:1—20:21
2 Chr 28:7—32:33

697
MANASSEH
(55 years)
Rebuilt all the pagan shrines, sacrificed one of his own sons, practiced sorcery, set up an idol right in the temple, murdered many of his own people, but repented during his Assyrian captivity
2 Kgs 20:21—21:18
2 Chr 32:33—33:20

MICAH 742–687

ISAIAH 740–681)

586
END OF THE SOUTHERN KINGDOM—carried off captive to Babylon by Nebuchadnezzar

642
AMON
(2 years)
2 Kgs 21:18-26
2 Chr 33:20-25

640
JOSIAH
(31 years)
Loved God with all his heart, repaired the temple, found a lost scroll of the law (he promised to obey it; thus God delayed destruction for Judah until after his death), personally oversaw the major project of destroying idol shrines, reinstated the priests of God, celebrated the Passover with greater zeal than had been since Samuel's day, was greatly loved by his people
2 Kgs 21:26—23:30
2 Chr 33:25—35:27

609
JEHOAHAZ (JOAHAZ)
(3 months)
Jailed and taken to Egypt, where he died
2 Kgs 23:30-34
2 Chr 36:1-4

609
JEHOIAKIM
(11 years)
Burned part of God's Word given to Jeremiah, was a puppet king for Egypt and then Babylon, watched gold and articles taken from the temple to Babylon, saw first exile (in which Daniel was taken)
2 Kgs 23:34—24:6
2 Chr 36:4-8

598
JEHOIACHIN
(3 months)
Saw next exile to Babylon
2 Kgs 24:6-15; 25:27-30
2 Chr 36:8-10

597
ZEDEKIAH
(11 years)
Saw the temple burned and Jerusalem destroyed, was tortured and carried away in the final exile to Babylon
2 Kgs 24:17—25:21
2 Chr 36:10-21

HABAKKUK 612–589

NAHUM 663–654

ZEPHANIAH 640–621

HULDAH 632

JEREMIAH 627–586

2 KINGS

Kingdom divides 930 B.C.	*Ahab dies in battle 853*	*Elijah's ministry transfers to Elisha 848*	*Jehu becomes king of Israel 841*	*Joash becomes king of Judah 835*	*Elisha's ministry ends 797*	*Jeroboam II becomes king of Israel 793*	*Amos's ministry begins 760*	*Hosea's ministry begins 753*

VITAL STATISTICS

PURPOSE:
To demonstrate the fate that awaits all who refuse to make God their true leader

AUTHOR:
Unknown. Possibly Jeremiah or a group of prophets

SETTING:
The once-united nation of Israel has been divided into two kingdoms, Israel and Judah, for over a century.

KEY VERSES:
"Yet the LORD warned Israel and Judah through all His prophets and every seer, saying, 'Turn from your evil ways and keep My commandments, My statutes according to all the law which I commanded your fathers, and which I sent to you through My servants the prophets.' However, they did not listen, but stiffened their neck like their fathers, who did not believe in the LORD their God" (17:13–14).

KEY PEOPLE:
Elijah, Elisha, the woman from Shunem, Naaman, Jezebel, Jehu, Joash, Hezekiah, Sennacherib, Isaiah, Manasseh, Josiah, Jehoiakim, Zedekiah, Nebuchadnezzar

SPECIAL FEATURES:
The 17 prophetic books at the end of the Old Testament give great insights into the time period of 2 Kings.

SPARKLING as it crashes against boulders along its banks, the river swiftly cascades toward the sea. The current grabs, pushes, and tugs at leaves and logs, carrying them along for the ride. Here and there a sportsman is spotted in a kayak or a canoe, going with the flow. Gravity pulls the water, and the river pulls the rest . . . downward. Suddenly, a silver missile breaks the surface and darts upstream, and then another. Oblivious to the swirling opposition, the shining salmon swim against the stream. They must go upstream, and nothing will stop them from reaching their destination.

The current of society's river is flowing fast and furious, pulling downward everything in its way. It would be easy to float along with the current. But God calls us to swim against the flow. It will not be easy, and we may be alone, but it will be right.

In the book of 2 Kings, we read of evil rulers, rampant idolatry, and a complacent populace—certainly pulling downward. Despite the pressure to conform, to turn from the Lord and to serve only self, a minority of chosen people moved in the opposite direction, toward God. The Bethel prophets and others, as well as two righteous kings, spoke God's word and stood for him. As you read 2 Kings, watch these courageous individuals. Catch the strength and force of Elijah and Elisha and the commitment of Hezekiah and Josiah, and determine to be one who swims against the current!

Second Kings continues the history of Israel, halfway between the death of David and the death of the nation. Israel had been divided (1 Kings 12), and the two kingdoms had begun to slide into idolatry and corruption toward collapse and captivity. Second Kings relates the sordid stories of the 12 kings of the northern kingdom (called Israel) and the 16 kings of the southern kingdom (called Judah). For 130 years Israel endured the succession of evil rulers until they were conquered by Shalmaneser of Assyria and led into captivity in 722 B.C. (17:6). Of all the kings in both the north and south, only two—Hezekiah and Josiah—were called good. Because of their obedience to God and the spiritual revivals during their reigns, Judah stood for an additional 136 years until falling to Nebuchadnezzar and the Babylonians in 586 B.C.

Throughout this dark period, the Bible mentions 30 prophets who proclaimed God's message to the people and their leaders. Most notable of these fearless people of God are Elijah and Elisha. As Elijah neared the end of his earthly ministry, Elisha asked that he might become Elijah's rightful successor (2:9). Soon after, Elijah was taken to heaven in a whirlwind (2:11), and Elisha became God's spokesman to the northern kingdom. Elisha's life was filled with signs, proclamations, warnings, and miracles. Four of the most memorable are the flowing oil (4:1–7), the healing of the Shunammite woman's son (4:8–37), the healing of Naaman's leprosy (5:1–27), and the floating axe head (6:1–7).

Even in the midst of terrible situations, God will have his faithful minority, his remnant (19:31). He desires courageous men and women to proclaim his truth.

Micah's ministry begins 742	Isaiah's ministry begins 740	Israel (northern kingdom) falls 722	Hezekiah becomes king of Judah 715	Josiah becomes king of Judah 640	Jeremiah's ministry begins 627	Book of the law found in the temple 622	First captivity of Judah; Daniel taken 605	Second captivity of Judah; Ezekiel taken 597	Judah (southern kingdom) falls 586

THE BLUEPRINT

A. THE DIVIDED KINGDOM (1:1—17:41)
1. Elisha's ministry
2. Kings of Israel and Judah
3. Israel is exiled to Assyria

Although Israel had the witness and power of Elisha, the nation turned from God and was exiled to Assyria. Assyria filled the northern kingdom with people from other lands. There has been no return from this captivity—it was permanent. Such is the end of all who shut God out of their lives.

B. THE SURVIVING KINGDOM (18:1—25:30)
1. Kings of Judah
2. Judah is exiled to Babylon

The northern kingdom was destroyed, and prophets were predicting the same fate for Judah. What more could cause the nation to repent? Hezekiah and Josiah were able to stem the tide of evil. They both repaired the temple and gathered the people for the Passover. Josiah eradicated idolatry from the land, but as soon as these good kings were gone, the people returned again to living their own way instead of God's way. Each individual must believe and live for God in his or her family, church, and nation.

MEGATHEMES

THEME	EXPLANATION	IMPORTANCE
Elisha	The purpose of Elisha's ministry was to restore respect for God and his message, and he stood firmly against the evil kings of Israel. By faith, with courage and prayer, he revealed not only God's judgment on sin but also his mercy, love, and tenderness toward faithful people.	Elisha's mighty miracles showed that God controls not only great armies but also events in everyday life. When we listen to and obey God, he shows us his power to transform any situation. God's care is for all who are willing to follow him. He can perform miracles in our lives.
Idolatry	Every evil king in both Israel and Judah encouraged idolatry. These false gods represented war, cruelty, power, and sex. Although they had God's law, priests, and prophets to guide them, these kings sought priests and prophets whom they could manipulate to their own advantage.	An idol is any idea, ability, possession, or person that we regard more highly than God. We condemn Israel and Judah for foolishly worshiping idols, but we also worship other gods—power, money, physical attractiveness. Those who believe in God must resist the lure of these attractive idols.
Evil Kings/ Good Kings	Only 20 percent of Israel's and Judah's kings followed God. The evil kings were shortsighted. They thought they could control their nations' destinies by importing other religions, forming alliances with pagan nations, and enriching themselves. The good kings had to spend most of their time undoing the evil done by their predecessors.	Although the evil kings led the people into sin, the priests, princes, heads of families, and military leaders all had to cooperate with the evil plans and practices in order for them to be carried out. We cannot discharge our responsibility to obey God by blaming our leaders. We are responsible to know God's Word and obey it.
God's Patience	God told his people that if they obeyed him, they would live successfully; if they disobeyed, they would be judged and destroyed. God had been patient with the people for hundreds of years. He sent many prophets to guide them. And he gave ample warning of coming destruction. But even God's patience has limits.	God is patient with us. He gives us many chances to hear his message, to turn from sin, and to believe him. His patience does not mean he is indifferent to how we live, nor does it mean we can ignore his warnings. His patience should make us want to come to him now.
Judgment	After King Solomon's reign, Israel lasted 209 years before the Assyrians destroyed it; Judah lasted 345 years before the Babylonians took Jerusalem. After repeated warnings to his people, God used these evil nations as instruments for his justice.	The consequences of rejecting God's commands and purpose for our lives are severe. He will not ignore unbelief or rebellion. We must believe in him and accept Christ's sacrificial death on our behalf, or we will be judged also.

KEY PLACES IN 2 KINGS

The history of both Israel and Judah was much affected by the prophet Elisha's ministry. He served Israel for 50 years, fighting the idolatry of its kings and calling its people back to God.

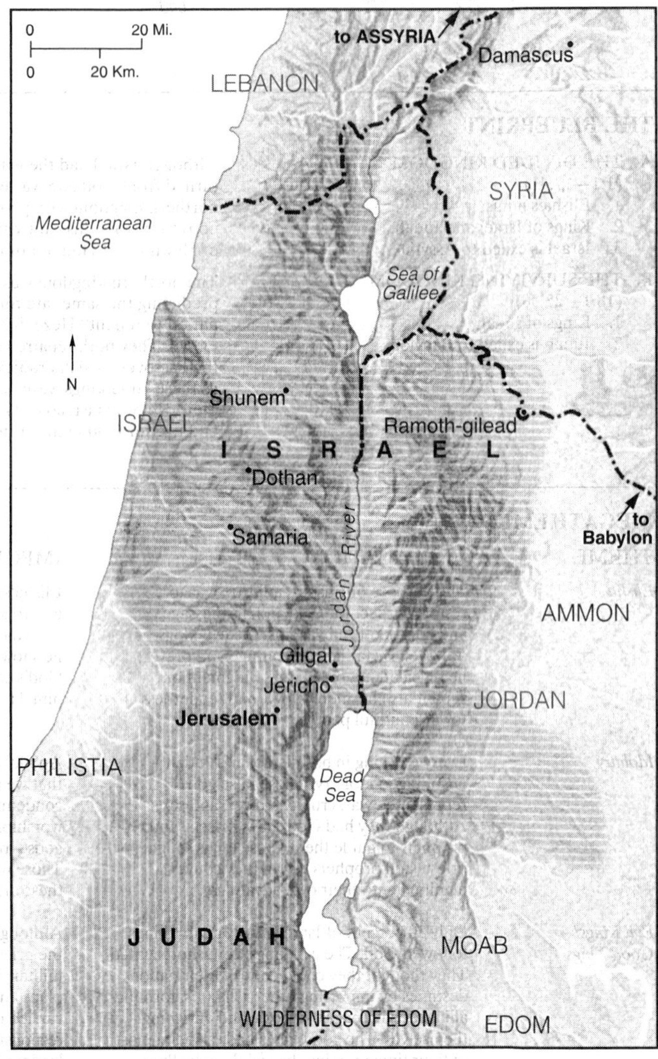

The broken lines (—·—·) indicate modern boundaries.

1 Jericho Elijah's ministry had come to an end. He touched his mantle to the Jordan River, and he and Elisha crossed on dry ground. Elijah was taken by God in a whirlwind, and Elisha returned alone with the mantle. The prophets in Jericho realized that Elisha was Elijah's replacement (1:1—2:25).

2 Wilderness of Edom The king of Moab rebelled against Israel, so the nations of Israel, Judah, and Edom decided to attack from the wilderness of Edom but ran out of water. The kings consulted Elisha, who said God would send both water and victory (3:1–27).

3 Shunem Elisha cared for individuals and their needs. He helped a woman clear a debt by giving her a supply of oil to sell. For another family in Shunem, he raised a son from the dead (4:1–37).

4 Gilgal Elisha cared for the young prophets in Gilgal—he removed poison from a stew, made a small amount of food feed everyone, and even caused an axe head to float so it could be retrieved. It was to Elisha that Naaman, a commander in the Aramean army, came to be healed of leprosy (4:38—6:7).

5 Dothan Although he cured an Aramean commander's leprosy, Elisha was loyal to Israel. He knew the Aramean army's battle plans and kept Israel's king informed. The Aramean king tracked Elisha down in Dothan and surrounded the city, hoping to kill him. But Elisha prayed that the Arameans would be blinded; then he led the blinded army into Samaria, Israel's capital city (6:8–23).

6 Samaria But the Arameans didn't learn their lesson. They later besieged Samaria. Ironically, Israel's king thought it was Elisha's fault, but Elisha said food would be available in abundance the next day. True to Elisha's word, the Lord caused panic in the Aramean camp, and the enemy ran, leaving their supplies to Samaria's starving people (6:24—7:20).

7 Damascus Despite Elisha's loyalty to Israel, he obeyed God and traveled to Damascus, the capital of Aram. King Ben-hadad was sick, and he sent Hazael to ask Elisha if he would recover. Elisha knew the king would die and told this to Hazael. But Hazael then murdered Ben-hadad, making himself king. Later, Israel and Judah joined forces to fight this new Aramean threat (8:1–29).

8 Ramoth-gilead As Israel and Judah warred with Aram, Elisha sent a young prophet to Ramoth-gilead to anoint Jehu as Israel's next king. Jehu set out to destroy the wicked dynasties of Israel and Judah, killing kings Joram and Ahaziah, and wicked Queen Jezebel. He then destroyed King Ahab's family and all the Baal worshipers in Israel (9:1—11:1).

9 Jerusalem Power-hungry Athaliah became queen of Judah when her son Ahaziah was killed. She had all her grandsons killed except Joash, who was hidden by his aunt. Joash was crowned king at the age of seven and overthrew Athaliah. Meanwhile in Samaria, the Arameans continued to harass Israel. Israel's new king met with Elisha and was told that he would be victorious over Aram three times (11:2—13:19).

Following Elisha's death came a series of evil kings in Israel. Their idolatry and rejection of God caused their downfall. The Assyrian empire captured Samaria and took most of the Israelites into captivity (13:20—17:41). Judah had a short reprieve because of a few good kings who destroyed idols and worshiped God. But many strayed from God. So Jerusalem fell to the next world power, Babylon (18:1—25:30).

A. THE DIVIDED KINGDOM (1:1—17:41)

Elisha begins his ministry to the northern kingdom after Elijah is taken away by a chariot of fire. Elisha performs many miracles and calls Israel to return to God, but they persist in their wickedness. Israel is defeated by Assyria and the people of the northern kingdom are exiled, never to return. Such is the end of all those who ignore God's warnings and demand their own way in their desire to sin.

Ahaziah's Messengers Meet Elijah

1 Now Moab rebelled against Israel after the death of Ahab.
2 And Ahaziah fell through the lattice in his upper chamber which *was* in Samaria,
and became ill. So he sent messengers and said to them, "Go, inquire of Baal-zebub, the
god of Ekron, whether I will recover from this sickness."
3 But the angel of the LORD said to Elijah the Tishbite, "Arise, go up to meet the
messengers of the king of Samaria and say to them, 'Is it because there is no God in Israel *that* you are going to inquire of Baal-zebub, the god of Ekron?'
4 "Now therefore thus says the LORD, 'You shall not come down from the bed where
you have gone up, but you shall surely die.' " Then Elijah departed.
5 When the messengers returned to him he said to them, "Why have you returned?"
6 They said to him, "A man came up to meet us and said to us, 'Go, return to the king
who sent you and say to him, "Thus says the LORD, 'Is it because there is no God in Israel *that* you are sending to inquire of Baal-zebub, the god of Ekron? Therefore you shall
not come down from the bed where you have gone up, but shall surely die.' " ' "
7 He said to them, "What kind of man was he who came up to meet you and spoke
these words to you?"
8 They answered him, "*He was* a hairy man with a leather girdle bound about his loins."
And he said, "It is Elijah the Tishbite."
9 Then *the king* sent to him a captain of fifty with his fifty. And he went up to him, and
behold, he was sitting on the top of the hill. And he said to him, "O man of God, the king
says, 'Come down.' "
10 Elijah replied to the captain of fifty, "If I am a man of God, let fire come down from
heaven and consume you and your fifty." Then fire came down from heaven and consumed him and his fifty.
11 So he again sent to him another captain of fifty with his fifty. And he said to him,
"O man of God, thus says the king, 'Come down quickly.' "
12 Elijah replied to them, "If I am a man of God, let fire come down from heaven and
consume you and your fifty." Then the fire of God came down from heaven and consumed him and his fifty.
13 So he again sent the captain of a third fifty with his fifty. When the third captain of
fifty went up, he came and bowed down on his knees before Elijah, and begged him and
said to him, "O man of God, please let my life and the lives of these fifty servants of
yours be precious in your sight.
14 "Behold fire came down from heaven and consumed the first two captains of fifty
with their fifties; but now let my life be precious in your sight."

1:1 2 Sam 8:2; 2 Kin 3:5
1:2 2 Kin 1:3, 6, 16; Matt 10:25; Mark 3:22; 2 Kin 8:7-10
1:3 1 Kin 17:1; 21:17; 2 Kin 1:2
1:4 2 Kin 1:6, 16
1:6 2 Kin 1:2
1:8 Zech 13:4; Matt 3:4; Mark 1:6
1:9 2 Kin 6:13, 14
1:10 1 Kin 18:36-38; Luke 9:54; Job 1:16
1:13 Is 1:5; Jer 5:3

1:1 Because 1 and 2 Kings were originally one book, 2 Kings continues where 1 Kings ended. The once great nation of Israel was split in two because the people forgot God. The book begins with Elijah, a prophet of God, being carried away to heaven. It ends with the people of Israel and Judah being carried away into captivity. In 1 Kings, the beautiful temple of God was built. In 2 Kings, it is desecrated and destroyed.

Our world is strikingly similar to the world described in 2 Kings. National and local governments do not seek God, and countries are tormented by war. Many people follow the false gods of technology, materialism, and war. True worship of God is rare on the earth.

In our chaotic and corrupt world, we can turn to examples such as David, Elijah, and Elisha, who were devoted to God's high honor and moral law and who brought about renewal and change in their society. More important, we can look to Jesus Christ, the perfect example. For nations to do God's will, they need individuals who will do God's work. If your heart is committed to God, he can work through you to accomplish the work he has called you to do.

1:2 Baal-zebub was not the same god as Baal, the Canaanite god worshiped by Ahab and Jezebel (1 Kings 16:31–33). Baal-zebub was another popular god whose temple was located in the city of Ekron. Because this god was thought to have the power of prophecy, King Ahaziah sent messengers to Ekron to learn of his fate. Supernatural power and mystery were associated with this god. Ahaziah's action showed the king's disrespect for God.

1:8 For more information on Elijah, see his Profile in 1 Kings 18.

1:13–15 Notice how the third captain went to Elijah. Although the first two captains called Elijah "man of God," they were not being genuine—God was not in their hearts. The third captain also called him "man of God," but he humbly begged for mercy. His attitude showed respect for God and his power and saved the lives of his men. Effective living begins with a right attitude toward God. Before religious words come to your mouth, make sure they are from your heart. Let respect, humility, and servanthood characterize your attitude toward God and others.

15 The angel of the LORD said to Elijah, "Go down with him; do not be afraid of him."
So he arose and went down with him to the king.
16 Then he said to him, "Thus says the LORD, 'Because you have sent messengers to
inquire of Baal-zebub, the god of Ekron—is it because there is no God in Israel to inquire of His word?—therefore you shall not come down from the bed where you have
gone up, but shall surely die.' "

1:15 2 Kin 1:3; Is 51:12; Jer 1:17; Ezek 2:6
1:16 2 Kin 1:3

Jehoram Reigns over Israel

17 So Ahaziah died according to the word of the LORD which Elijah had spoken. And
because he had no son, Jehoram became king in his place in the second year of Jehoram
the son of Jehoshaphat, king of Judah.
18 Now the rest of the acts of Ahaziah which he did, are they not written in the Book
of the Chronicles of the Kings of Israel?

1:17 2 Kin 3:1; 8:16

1. Elisha's ministry

Elijah Taken to Heaven

2 And it came about when the LORD was about to take up Elijah by a whirlwind to
heaven, that Elijah went with Elisha from Gilgal.
2 Elijah said to Elisha, "Stay here please, for the LORD has sent me as far as Bethel."
But Elisha said, "As the LORD lives and as you yourself live, I will not leave you." So
they went down to Bethel.
3 Then the sons of the prophets who *were at* Bethel came out to Elisha and said to
him, "Do you know that the LORD will take away your master from over you today?"
And he said, "Yes, I know; be still."
4 Elijah said to him, "Elisha, please stay here, for the LORD has sent me to Jericho."
But he said, "As the LORD lives, and as you yourself live, I will not leave you." So they
came to Jericho.
5 The sons of the prophets who *were* at Jericho approached Elisha and said to him,
"Do you know that the LORD will take away your master from over you today?" And he
answered, "Yes, I know; be still."
6 Then Elijah said to him, "Please stay here, for the LORD has sent me to the Jordan." And he said, "As the LORD lives, and as you yourself live, I will not leave you." So
the two of them went on.
7 Now fifty men of the sons of the prophets went and stood opposite *them* at a distance, while the two of them stood by the Jordan.
8 Elijah took his mantle and folded it together and struck the waters, and they were
divided here and there, so that the two of them crossed over on dry ground.
9 When they had crossed over, Elijah said to Elisha, "Ask what I shall do for you before
I am taken from you." And Elisha said, "Please, let a double portion of your spirit be
upon me."
10 He said, "You have asked a hard thing. *Nevertheless,* if you see me when I am taken
from you, it shall be so for you; but if not, it shall not be *so.*"

2:1 Gen 5:24; Heb 11:5; 1 Kin 19:16-21; Josh 4:19
2:2 Ruth 1:15; 1 Kin 12:28, 29; 1 Sam 1:26; 2 Kin 2:4, 6
2:3 2 Kin 4:1, 38; 5:22
2:4 2 Kin 2:2; Josh 6:26
2:5 2 Kin 2:3; 2 Kin 2:3
2:6 2 Kin 2:2; Josh 3:8, 15-17
2:7 2 Kin 2:15, 16
2:8 1 Kin 19:13, 19; Ex 14:21, 22; 2 Kin 2:14
2:9 Num 11:17-25; Deut 21:17
2:10 Acts 1:10

1:18 The Book of the Chronicles of the Kings of Israel and the Book of the Chronicles of the Kings of Judah (8:23) were history books. The inspired writer of 2 Kings selected facts from these books to retell the story of Israel and Judah from God's perspective. God directed the writer's thoughts and selection process to make sure that the truth, God's Word, would be written.

2:3 The "sons of the prophets" were a school, a gathering of disciples around a recognized prophet, such as Elijah or Elisha. These companies of prophets, located throughout the country, helped stem the tide of spiritual and moral decline in the nation begun under Jeroboam. The students at Bethel were eyewitnesses to the succession of the prophetic ministry from Elijah to Elisha.

2:8 Elijah's mantle (cloak) was a symbol of his authority as a prophet.

2:9 Elisha asked for a double portion of Elijah's spirit (prophetic ministry). Deuteronomy 21:17 helps explain Elisha's request. According to custom, the firstborn son received a double portion of the father's inheritance (see the note on Genesis 25:31). He was asking to be Elijah's heir, or successor, the one who would continue Elijah's work as leader of the prophets. But the decision to grant Elisha's request was up to God. Elijah only told him how he would know if his request had been granted.

2:9 God granted Elisha's request because Elisha's motives were pure. His main goal was not to be better or more powerful than Elijah, but to accomplish more for God. If our motives are pure, we don't have to be afraid to ask great things from God. When we ask God for great power or ability, we need to examine our desires and get rid of any selfishness we find. To have the Holy Spirit's help, we must be willing to ask.

2:11 2 Kin 6:17

11 As they were going along and talking, behold, *there appeared* a chariot of fire and
horses of fire which separated the two of them. And Elijah went up by a whirlwind to
heaven.

2:12 2 Kin 13:14; Gen 37:34; Job 1:20

12 Elisha saw *it* and cried out, "My father, my father, the chariots of Israel and its horsemen!" And he saw Elijah no more. Then he took hold of his own clothes and tore them
in two pieces.
13 He also took up the mantle of Elijah that fell from him and returned and stood by
the bank of the Jordan.

2:14 2 Kin 2:8

14 He took the mantle of Elijah that fell from him and struck the waters and said,
"Where is the LORD, the God of Elijah?" And when he also had struck the waters, they
were divided here and there; and Elisha crossed over.

Elisha Succeeds Elijah

2:15 2 Kin 2:7

15 Now when the sons of the prophets who *were* at Jericho opposite *him* saw him, they
said, "The spirit of Elijah rests on Elisha." And they came to meet him and bowed themselves to the ground before him.

2:16 1 Kin 18:12; Acts 8:39

16 They said to him, "Behold now, there are with your servants fifty strong men, please
let them go and search for your master; perhaps the Spirit of the LORD has taken him up
and cast him on some mountain or into some valley." And he said, "You shall not send."

2:17 2 Kin 8:11

17 But when they urged him until he was ashamed, he said, "Send." They sent therefore fifty men; and they searched three days but did not find him.
18 They returned to him while he was staying at Jericho; and he said to them, "Did I
not say to you, 'Do not go'?"

KINGS TO DATE AND THEIR ENEMIES

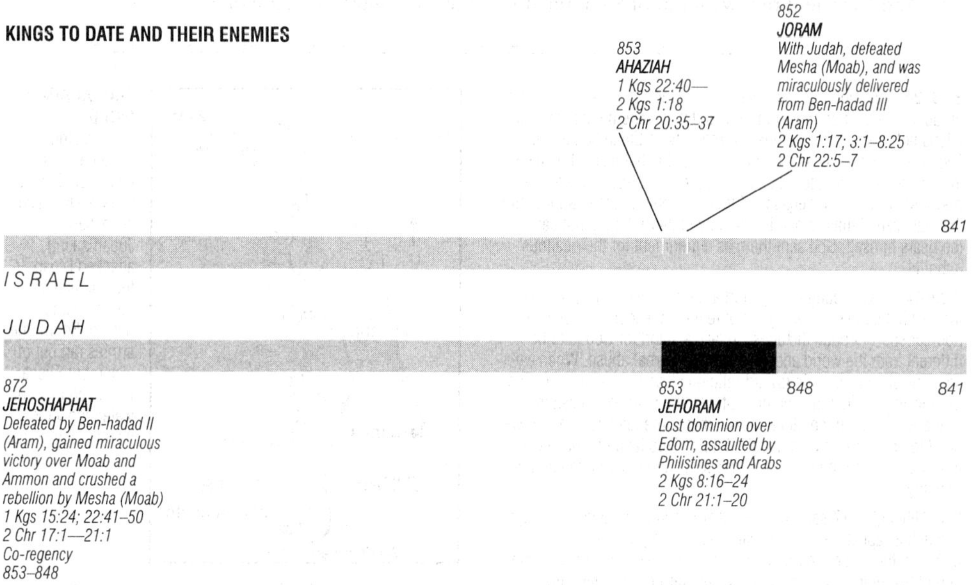

853
AHAZIAH
1 Kgs 22:40—
2 Kgs 1:18
2 Chr 20:35–37

852
JORAM
With Judah, defeated Mesha (Moab), and was miraculously delivered from Ben-hadad III (Aram)
2 Kgs 1:17; 3:1–8:25
2 Chr 22:5–7

841

ISRAEL

JUDAH

872
JEHOSHAPHAT
Defeated by Ben-hadad II (Aram), gained miraculous victory over Moab and Ammon and crushed a rebellion by Mesha (Moab)
1 Kgs 15:24; 22:41–50
2 Chr 17:1—21:1
Co-regency
853–848

853
JEHORAM
Lost dominion over Edom, assaulted by Philistines and Arabs
2 Kgs 8:16–24
2 Chr 21:1–20

848

841

All dates are B.C.
Solid section of the timeline indicates co-regency.
For all the kings of Israel and Judah, see the chart at the end of 1 Kings.

2:11 Elijah was taken to heaven without dying. He is the second person mentioned in Scripture to do so. Enoch was the first (Genesis 5:21–24). The other prophets may not have seen God take Elijah, or they may have had a difficult time believing what they saw. In either case, they wanted to search for Elijah (2:16–18). Finding no physical trace of him would confirm what had happened and strengthen their faith. The only other person taken to heaven in bodily form was Jesus after his resurrection from the dead (Acts 1:9).

2:13–25 These three incidents were testimonies to Elisha's commission as a prophet of God. They are recorded to demonstrate Elisha's new power and authority as Israel's chief prophet under God's ultimate power and authority.

2:14 When Elisha struck the water, it was not out of disrespect to God or Elijah. It was a plea by Elisha to God to confirm his appointment as Elijah's successor.

19 Then the men of the city said to Elisha, "Behold now, the situation of this city is
pleasant, as my lord sees; but the water is bad and the land is unfruitful."
20 He said, "Bring me a new jar, and put salt in it." So they brought *it* to him.
21 He went out to the spring of water and threw salt in it and said, "Thus says the LORD,
'I have purified these waters; there shall not be from there death or unfruitfulness any
longer.'"
22 So the waters have been purified to this day, according to the word of Elisha which
he spoke.
23 Then he went up from there to Bethel; and as he was going up by the way, young
lads came out from the city and mocked him and said to him, "Go up, you baldhead; go
up, you baldhead!"
24 When he looked behind him and saw them, he cursed them in the name of the LORD.
Then two female bears came out of the woods and tore up forty-two lads of their number.
25 He went from there to Mount Carmel, and from there he returned to Samaria.

2:21 Ex 15:25, 26; 2 Kin 4:41; 6:6
2:23 2 Chr 36:16; Ps 31:17, 18
2:24 Neh 13:25-27
2:25 1 Kin 18:19, 20; 2 Kin 4:25

Jehoram Meets Moab Rebellion

3 Now Jehoram the son of Ahab became king over Israel at Samaria in the eighteenth
year of Jehoshaphat king of Judah, and reigned twelve years.
2 He did evil in the sight of the LORD, though not like his father and his mother; for
he put away the *sacred* pillar of Baal which his father had made.
3 Nevertheless, he clung to the sins of Jeroboam the son of Nebat, which he made
Israel sin; he did not depart from them.
4 Now Mesha king of Moab was a sheep breeder, and used to pay the king of Israel
100,000 lambs and the wool of 100,000 rams.
5 But when Ahab died, the king of Moab rebelled against the king of Israel.
6 And King Jehoram went out of Samaria at that time and mustered all Israel.

3:1 2 Kin 1:17
3:2 Ex 23:24; 2 Kin 10:18, 26-28; 1 Kin 16:31, 32
3:3 1 Kin 12:28-32; 1 Kin 14:9, 16
3:4 2 Sam 8:2; Is 16:1, 2
3:5 2 Kin 1:1

2:23–24 This mob of youths was from Bethel, the religious center of idolatry in the northern kingdom, and they were probably warning Elisha not to speak against their immorality as Elijah had done. They were not merely teasing Elisha about his baldness, but showing severe disrespect for Elisha's message and God's power. They may also have jeered because of their disbelief in the chariot of fire that had taken Elijah. When Elisha cursed them, he did not call out the bears himself. God sent them as a judgment for their callous unbelief.

2:23–24 These young men jeered at God's messenger and paid for it with their lives. Making fun of religious leaders has been a popular sport through the ages. To take a stand for God is to be different from the world and vulnerable to verbal abuse. When we are cynical and sarcastic toward religious leaders, we are in danger of mocking not just the person, but also the spiritual message. While we are not to condone the sin that some leaders commit, we need to pray for them, not laugh at them. True leaders, those who follow God, need to be heard with respect and encouraged in their ministry.

3:1 Although 1:17 says that Jehoram was king of Judah, 3:1 says that Jehoshaphat was Judah's king. As a king grew older, it was common for his son to rule beside him. Jehoshaphat, nearing the end of his reign, appointed his son Jehoram to rule with him. Jehoram served as co-ruler with Jehoshaphat for five years (853–848 B.C.; he is mentioned again in 8:16–24). Another Jehoram, king of Israel, was Ahab's son and Ahaziah's brother (1:17). Both Ahab (1 Kings 16:29—22:40) and Ahaziah (1:2–18) served as kings of Israel before Jehoram. Both kings of Judah and Israel are called Jehoram in some places, and Joram in other places.

3:3 The sins of Israel's kings are often compared to "the sins of Jeroboam," the first ruler of the northern kingdom of Israel. His great sin was to institute idol worship throughout his kingdom, causing people to turn away from God (1 Kings 12:25–33). By ignoring God and allowing idol worship, Jehoram clung to Jeroboam's sins.

3:4–5 Israel and Judah held some of the most fertile land and strategic positions in the ancient Near East. It is no wonder that neighboring nations like Moab envied them and constantly attempted to seize the land. Moab lay just southeast of Israel. The country had been under Israel's control for some time due to Ahab's strong military leadership. When Ahab died, Mesha, the Moabite king, took the opportunity to rebel. While Israel's next king, Ahaziah, did nothing about the revolt, his successor, Jehoram, decided to take action. He joined forces with Jehoshaphat, king of Judah, and went to fight the Moabites. Together, Israel and Judah brought the Moabites to the brink of surrender. But when they saw the Moabite king sacrifice his own son and successor (3:27), they withdrew even though they had won the battle. Moab fought many other battles with both Israel and Judah. Some of them, in fact, were recorded by Mesha (c. 840 B.C.), who carved his exploits on a plaque called the Moabite Stone (discovered in 1868).

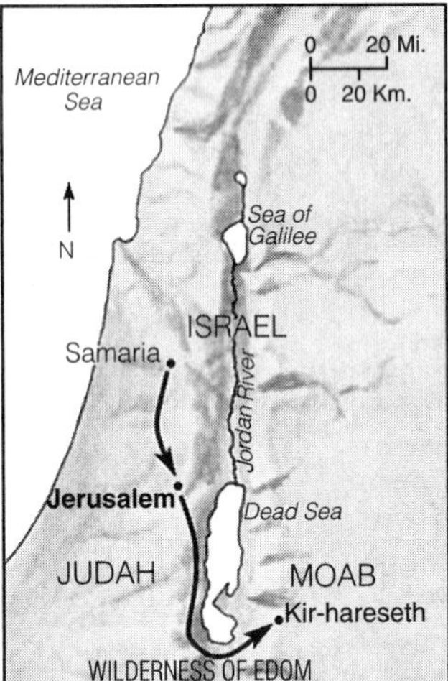

WAR AGAINST MOAB
Moab's king rebelled against Israel. So Jehoram, Israel's king, and Jehoshaphat, Judah's king, attacked Moab. In the parched and rugged wilderness of Edom, the armies ran out of water, but Elisha promised that both water and victory would soon come.

3:7 1 Kin 22:4

7 Then he went and sent *word* to Jehoshaphat the king of Judah, saying, "The king of
Moab has rebelled against me. Will you go with me to fight against Moab?" And he said,
"I will go up; I am as you are, my people as your people, my horses as your horses."
8 He said, "Which way shall we go up?" And he answered, "The way of the wilderness of Edom."

3:9 2 Kin 3:1; 2 Kin 3:7; 1 Kin 22:47

9 So the king of Israel went with the king of Judah and the king of Edom; and they
made a circuit of seven days' journey, and there was no water for the army or for the
cattle that followed them.
10 Then the king of Israel said, "Alas! For the LORD has called these three kings to
give them into the hand of Moab."

3:11 1 Kin 22:7; 2 Kin 2:25; 1 Kin 19:21; John 13:4, 5, 13, 14

11 But Jehoshaphat said, "Is there not a prophet of the LORD here, that we may inquire of the LORD by him?" And one of the king of Israel's servants answered and said,
"Elisha the son of Shaphat is here, who used to pour water on the hands of Elijah."
12 Jehoshaphat said, "The word of the LORD is with him." So the king of Israel and
Jehoshaphat and the king of Edom went down to him.

3:13 1 Kin 18:19; 22:6-11, 22-25

13 Now Elisha said to the king of Israel, "What do I have to do with you? Go to the
prophets of your father and to the prophets of your mother." And the king of Israel said
to him, "No, for the LORD has called these three kings *together* to give them into the
hand of Moab."

3:14 1 Kin 17:1; 2 Kin 5:16

14 Elisha said, "As the LORD of hosts lives, before whom I stand, were it not that I
regard the presence of Jehoshaphat the king of Judah, I would not look at you nor see
you.

3:15 1 Sam 16:23; 1 Chr 25:1; 1 Kin 18:46; Ezek 1:3

15 "But now bring me a minstrel." And it came about, when the minstrel played, that
the hand of the LORD came upon him.
16 He said, "Thus says the LORD, 'Make this valley full of trenches.'

3:17 Ps 107:35

17 "For thus says the LORD, 'You shall not see wind nor shall you see rain; yet that

MIRACLES OF ELIJAH AND ELISHA

Baal, the false god worshiped by many Israelites, was the god of rain, fire, and farm crops. He also demanded child sacrifice. Elijah's and Elisha's miracles repeatedly show the power of the true God over the purported realm of Baal, as well as the value God places on the life of a child.

Miracle	*Found where?*	*Factors*
ELIJAH		
1. Food brought by ravens	1 Kings 17:5–6	Food
2. Widow's food multiplied	1 Kings 17:12–16	Flour and oil
3. Widow's son raised to life	1 Kings 17:17–24	Life of a child
4. Altar and sacrifice consumed	1 Kings 18:16–46	Fire and water
5. Ahaziah's soldiers consumed	2 Kings 1:9–14	Fire
6. Jordan River parted	2 Kings 2:6–8	Water
7. Transported to heaven	2 Kings 2:11–12	Fire and wind
ELISHA		
1. Jordan River parted	2 Kings 2:13–14	Water
2. Spring purified at Jericho	2 Kings 2:19–22	Water
3. Widow's oil multiplied	2 Kings 4:1–7	Oil
4. Dead boy raised to life	2 Kings 4:18–37	Life of a child
5. Poison in stew purified	2 Kings 4:38–41	Flour
6. Prophets' food multiplied	2 Kings 4:42–44	Bread and grain
7. Naaman healed of leprosy	2 Kings 5:1–14	Water
8. Gehazi became leprous	2 Kings 5:15–27	Words alone
9. Axe head floated	2 Kings 6:1–7	Water
10. Aramean army blinded	2 Kings 6:8–23	Elisha's prayer

3:10 Edom was under Judah's control; thus they marched with them, making three kings.

3:11–20 Jehoshaphat's request for "a prophet of the LORD" shows how true worship and religious experience in both Israel and Judah had declined. In David's day, both the high priest and the prophets gave the king advice. But most of the priests had left Israel (see the first note on 1 Kings 17:1), and God's prophets were seen as messengers of doom (1 Kings 22:18). This miracle predicted by Elisha affirmed God's power and authority and validated Elisha's ministry. In 2 Chronicles 18, King Jehoshaphat of Judah and King Ahab of Israel gave the prophet Micaiah a similar request. But they ignored God's advice—with disastrous results.

3:15 In Old Testament times music often accompanied prophecy (1 Chronicles 25:1).

valley shall be filled with water, so that you shall drink, both you and your cattle and
your beasts.
18 'This is but a slight thing in the sight of the LORD; He will also give the Moabites
into your hand.
19 'Then you shall strike every fortified city and every choice city, and fell every good
tree and stop all springs of water, and mar every good piece of land with stones.' "
20 It happened in the morning about the time of offering the sacrifice, that behold,
water came by the way of Edom, and the country was filled with water.
21 Now all the Moabites heard that the kings had come up to fight against them. And
all who were able to put on armor and older were summoned and stood on the border.
22 They rose early in the morning, and the sun shone on the water, and the Moabites
saw the water opposite *them* as red as blood.
23 Then they said, "This is blood; the kings have surely fought together, and they have
slain one another. Now therefore, Moab, to the spoil!"
24 But when they came to the camp of Israel, the Israelites arose and struck the Moabites, so that they fled before them; and they went forward into the land, slaughtering the
Moabites.
25 Thus they destroyed the cities; and each one threw a stone on every piece of good
land and filled it. So they stopped all the springs of water and felled all the good
trees, until in Kir-hareseth *only* they left its stones; however, the slingers went about *it*
and struck it.
26 When the king of Moab saw that the battle was too fierce for him, he took with him
700 men who drew swords, to break through to the king of Edom; but they could not.
27 Then he took his oldest son who was to reign in his place, and offered him as a burnt
offering on the wall. And there came great wrath against Israel, and they departed from
him and returned to their own land.

3:18 Jer 32:17, 27; Mark 10:27; Luke 1:37
3:19 2 Kin 3:25
3:20 Ex 29:39, 40
3:25 2 Kin 3:19; Is 16:7; Jer 48:31, 36
3:27 Amos 2:1; Mic 6:7

The Widow's Oil

4 Now a certain woman of the wives of the sons of the prophets cried out to Elisha,
"Your servant my husband is dead, and you know that your servant feared the LORD;
and the creditor has come to take my two children to be his slaves."
2 Elisha said to her, "What shall I do for you? Tell me, what do you have in the house?"
And she said, "Your maidservant has nothing in the house except a jar of oil."
3 Then he said, "Go, borrow vessels at large for yourself from all your neighbors, *even*
empty vessels; do not get a few.
4 "And you shall go in and shut the door behind you and your sons, and pour out into
all these vessels, and you shall set aside what is full."
5 So she went from him and shut the door behind her and her sons; they were bringing *the vessels* to her and she poured.
6 When the vessels were full, she said to her son, "Bring me another vessel." And he
said to her, "There is not one vessel more." And the oil stopped.
7 Then she came and told the man of God. And he said, "Go, sell the oil and pay your
debt, and you *and* your sons can live on the rest."

4:1 2 Kin 2:3; Lev 25:39-41, 48; 1 Sam 22:2; Neh 5:2-5
4:2 1 Kin 17:12
4:6 Matt 14:20
4:7 1 Kin 12:22

3:20 The morning sacrifice was one of two sacrifices that the priests were required to offer each day.

4:1 Poor people and debtors were allowed to pay their debts by selling themselves or their children as slaves. God ordered rich people and creditors not to take advantage of these people during their time of extreme need (see Deuteronomy 15:1–18 for an explanation of these practices). This woman's creditor was not acting in the spirit of God's Law. Elisha's kind deed demonstrates that God wants us to go beyond simply keeping the Law. We must also show compassion.

4:1ff This chapter records four of God's miracles through Elisha: providing money for a poverty-stricken widow (4:1–7); raising a dead boy to life (4:32–37); purifying poisonous food (4:38–41); and providing food for 100 men (4:42–44). These miracles show God's tenderness and care for those who are faithful to him.

When reading the Old Testament, it is easy to focus on God's harsh judgment of the rebellious and to minimize his tender care for those who love and serve him. To see him at work providing for his followers helps us keep his severe justice toward the unrepentant in proper perspective.

4:6 The woman and her sons collected vessels from their neighbors, pouring oil into them from their one pot. The oil was probably olive oil and was used for cooking, for lamps, and for fuel. The oil stopped pouring only when they ran out of containers. The number of vessels they gathered was an indication of their faith. God's provision was as large as their faith and willingness to obey. Beware of limiting God's blessings by a lack of faith and obedience. God is able to do immeasurably more than all we ask or imagine (Ephesians 3:20).

The Shunammite Woman

4:8 Josh 19:18

8 Now there came a day when Elisha passed over to Shunem, where there was a prominent woman, and she persuaded him to eat food. And so it was, as often as he passed by, he turned in there to eat food.

4:9 2 Kin 4:7

9 She said to her husband, "Behold now, I perceive that this is a holy man of God passing by us continually.

4:10 Matt 10:41, 42; 25:40; Rom 12:13

10 "Please, let us make a little walled upper chamber and let us set a bed for him there, and a table and a chair and a lampstand; and it shall be, when he comes to us, *that* he can turn in there."

11 One day he came there and turned in to the upper chamber and rested.

4:12 2 Kin 4:29-31; 5:20-27; 8:4, 5

12 Then he said to Gehazi his servant, "Call this Shunammite." And when he had called her, she stood before him.

13 He said to him, "Say now to her, 'Behold, you have been careful for us with all this care; what can I do for you? Would you be spoken for to the king or to the captain of the army?' " And she answered, "I live among my own people."

14 So he said, "What then is to be done for her?" And Gehazi answered, "Truly she has no son and her husband is old."

15 He said, "Call her." When he had called her, she stood in the doorway.

4:16 Gen 18:14; 2 Kin 4:28

16 Then he said, "At this season next year you will embrace a son." And she said, "No, my lord, O man of God, do not lie to your maidservant."

17 The woman conceived and bore a son at that season the next year, as Elisha had said to her.

The Shunammite's Son

18 When the child was grown, the day came that he went out to his father to the reapers.

19 He said to his father, "My head, my head." And he said to his servant, "Carry him to his mother."

20 When he had taken him and brought him to his mother, he sat on her lap until noon, and *then* died.

4:21 2 Kin 4:32; 2 Kin 4:7

21 She went up and laid him on the bed of the man of God, and shut *the door* behind him and went out.

22 Then she called to her husband and said, "Please send me one of the servants and one of the donkeys, that I may run to the man of God and return."

4:23 Num 10:10; 28:11; 1 Chr 23:31

23 He said, "Why will you go to him today? It is neither new moon nor sabbath." And she said, "*It will be* well."

24 Then she saddled a donkey and said to her servant, "Drive and go forward; do not slow down the pace for me unless I tell you."

4:25 2 Kin 2:25

25 So she went and came to the man of God to Mount Carmel.

When the man of God saw her at a distance, he said to Gehazi his servant, "Behold, there is the Shunammite.

THE FAMILY IN SHUNEM
Elisha often stayed with a kind family in Shunem. When the son suddenly died, his mother traveled to Mount Carmel to find Elisha. He returned with her and raised the boy from the dead. Elisha then went to his home in Gilgal.

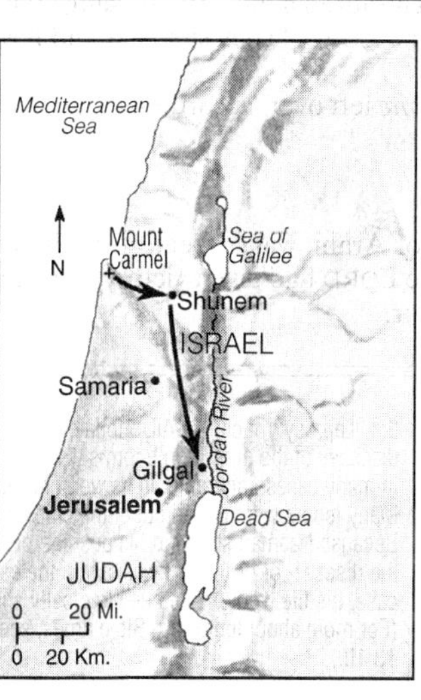

4:9 The woman from Shunem realized that Elisha was a man of God, and so she prepared a room for him to use whenever he was in town. She did this out of kindness and because she sensed a need, not for any selfish motives. Soon, however, her kindness would be rewarded far beyond her wildest dreams. How sensitive are you to those who pass by your home and flow through your life—especially those who teach and preach God's Word? What special needs do they have that you could meet? Look for ways to serve and help.

26 "Please run now to meet her and say to her, 'Is it well with you? Is it well with your
husband? Is it well with the child?' " And she answered, "It is well."
27 When she came to the man of God to the hill, she caught hold of his feet. And Gehazi
came near to push her away; but the man of God said, "Let her alone, for her soul is
troubled within her; and the LORD has hidden it from me and has not told me."
28 Then she said, "Did I ask for a son from my lord? Did I not say, 'Do not deceive
me'?"
29 Then he said to Gehazi, "Gird up your loins and take my staff in your hand, and go
your way; if you meet any man, do not salute him, and if anyone salutes you, do not answer him; and lay my staff on the lad's face."
30 The mother of the lad said, "As the LORD lives and as you yourself live, I will not
leave you." And he arose and followed her.
31 Then Gehazi passed on before them and laid the staff on the lad's face, but there
was no sound or response. So he returned to meet him and told him, "The lad has not
awakened."
32 When Elisha came into the house, behold the lad was dead and laid on his bed.
33 So he entered and shut the door behind them both and prayed to the LORD.
34 And he went up and lay on the child, and put his mouth on his mouth and his eyes
on his eyes and his hands on his hands, and he stretched himself on him; and the flesh of
the child became warm.
35 Then he returned and walked in the house once back and forth, and went up and
stretched himself on him; and the lad sneezed seven times and the lad opened his eyes.
36 He called Gehazi and said, "Call this Shunammite." So he called her. And when
she came in to him, he said, "Take up your son."
37 Then she went in and fell at his feet and bowed herself to the ground, and she took
up her son and went out.

4:27 2 Kin 4:25
4:28 2 Kin 4:16
4:29 1 Kin 18:46; 2 Kin 9:1; Ex 4:17; 2 Kin 2:14; Luke 10:4; Ex 7:19, 20; 14:16
4:30 2 Kin 2:2, 4
4:31 John 11:11
4:33 2 Kin 4:4; Matt 6:6; Luke 8:51
4:34 1 Kin 17:21-23
4:35 1 Kin 17:21
4:37 Heb 11:35

The Poisonous Stew

38 When Elisha returned to Gilgal, *there was* a famine in the land. As the sons of the
prophets were sitting before him, he said to his servant, "Put on the large pot and boil
stew for the sons of the prophets."
39 Then one went out into the field to gather herbs, and found a wild vine and gathered from it his lap full of wild gourds, and came and sliced them into the pot of stew, for
they did not know *what they were.*
40 So they poured *it* out for the men to eat. And as they were eating of the stew, they
cried out and said, "O man of God, there is death in the pot." And they were unable to eat.
41 But he said, "Now bring meal." He threw it into the pot and said, "Pour *it* out for
the people that they may eat." Then there was no harm in the pot.
42 Now a man came from Baal-shalishah, and brought the man of God bread of the
first fruits, twenty loaves of barley and fresh ears of grain in his sack. And he said, "Give
them to the people that they may eat."
43 His attendant said, "What, will I set this before a hundred men?" But he said, "Give
them to the people that they may eat, for thus says the LORD, 'They shall eat and have
some left over.' "
44 So he set *it* before them, and they ate and had *some* left over, according to the word
of the LORD.

4:38 2 Kin 2:1; 2 Kin 8:1; 2 Kin 2:3; Luke 10:39; Acts 22:3; Ezek 11:3, 7, 11; 24:3
4:40 Ex 10:17
4:41 Ex 15:25; 2 Kin 2:21
4:42 Matt 14:16-21; 15:32-38
4:43 Luke 9:13; John 6:9
4:44 Matt 14:20; 15:37; John 6:13

Naaman Is Healed

5 Now Naaman, captain of the army of the king of Aram, was a great man with his
master, and highly respected, because by him the LORD had given victory to Aram.
The man was also a valiant warrior, *but he was* a leper.

5:1 Luke 4:27

4:32–36 Elisha's prayer and method of raising the dead boy show God's personal care for hurting people. We must express genuine concern for others as we carry God's message to them. Only then will we faithfully represent our Father in heaven.

4:40 "Death in the pot" means that the food was poisonous. Perhaps a poisonous wild vegetable or herb had been mixed in with the edible plants.

5:1 Leprosy, much like AIDS today, was one of the most feared diseases of the time. Some forms were extremely contagious and, in many cases, incurable. In its worst forms, leprosy led to death. Many lepers were forced out of the cities into quarantined camps. Because Naaman still held his post, he probably had a mild form of the disease, or perhaps it was still in the early stages. In either case, his life would have been tragically shortened by his disease. (For more about leprosy in Bible times, see the note on Leviticus 13:1ff.)

5:2 2 Kin 6:23; 13:20

2 Now the Arameans had gone out in bands and had taken captive a little girl from
the land of Israel; and she waited on Naaman's wife.
3 She said to her mistress, "I wish that my master were with the prophet who is in
Samaria! Then he would cure him of his leprosy."
4 Naaman went in and told his master, saying, "Thus and thus spoke the girl who is
from the land of Israel."

5:5 1 Sam 9:7; 2 Kin 4:42; Judg 14:12; 2 Kin 5:22, 23

5 Then the king of Aram said, "Go now, and I will send a letter to the king of Israel."
He departed and took with him ten talents of silver and six thousand *shekels* of gold and
ten changes of clothes.
6 He brought the letter to the king of Israel, saying, "And now as this letter comes to
you, behold, I have sent Naaman my servant to you, that you may cure him of his leprosy."

5:7 Gen 37:29; Gen 30:2; 1 Sam 2:6; 1 Kin 20:7; Luke 11:54

7 When the king of Israel read the letter, he tore his clothes and said, "Am I God, to
kill and to make alive, that this man is sending *word* to me to cure a man of his leprosy?
But consider now, and see how he is seeking a quarrel against me."

5:8 1 Kin 12:22

8 It happened when Elisha the man of God heard that the king of Israel had torn his
clothes, that he sent *word* to the king, saying, "Why have you torn your clothes? Now let
him come to me, and he shall know that there is a prophet in Israel."
9 So Naaman came with his horses and his chariots and stood at the doorway of the
house of Elisha.

5:10 John 9:7

10 Elisha sent a messenger to him, saying, "Go and wash in the Jordan seven times,
and your flesh will be restored to you and *you will* be clean."
11 But Naaman was furious and went away and said, "Behold, I thought, 'He will surely come out to me and stand and call on the name of the LORD his God, and wave his
hand over the place and cure the leper.'

5:12 Prov 14:17; 16:32; 19:11

12 "Are not Abanah and Pharpar, the rivers of Damascus, better than all the waters of
Israel? Could I not wash in them and be clean?" So he turned and went away in a rage.

5:13 1 Sam 28:23; 2 Kin 2:12; 6:21; 8:9

13 Then his servants came near and spoke to him and said, "My father, had the prophet told you *to do some* great thing, would you not have done *it?* How much more *then,*
when he says to you, 'Wash, and be clean'?"

5:14 2 Kin 5:10; Job 33:25; Luke 4:27; 5:13

14 So he went down and dipped *himself* seven times in the Jordan, according to the
word of the man of God; and his flesh was restored like the flesh of a little child and he
was clean.

Gehazi's Greed

5:15 Josh 2:11; 1 Sam 17:46, 47; 2 Kin 5:8; 1 Sam 25:27

15 When he returned to the man of God with all his company, and came and stood
before him, he said, "Behold now, I know that there is no God in all the earth, but in
Israel; so please take a present from your servant now."

5:16 2 Kin 3:14; Gen 14:22, 23; 2 Kin 5:20, 26

16 But he said, "As the LORD lives, before whom I stand, I will take nothing." And he
urged him to take *it,* but he refused.

5:2 Aram was Israel's neighbor to the northeast, but the two nations were rarely on friendly terms. Under David, Aram paid tribute to Israel. In Elisha's day, Aram was growing in power and frequently conducted raids on Israel, trying to frustrate the people and bring about political confusion. Israelite captives were often taken back to Aram after successful raids. Naaman's servant girl was an Israelite, kidnapped from her home and family. Ironically, Naaman's only hope of being cured came from Israel.

5:3–4 The little girl's faith and Naaman's quest contrast with the stubbornness of Israel's king (5:7). A leader in mighty Aram sought the God of Israel; Israel's own king would not. We don't know the little girl's name or much about her, but her brief word to her mistress brought healing and faith in God to a powerful Aramean captain. God had placed her for a purpose, and she was faithful. Where has God put you? No matter how humble or small your position, God can use you to spread his Word. Look for opportunities to tell others what God can do. There's no telling who will hear your message!

5:9–15 Naaman, a great hero, was used to getting respect, and he was outraged when Elisha treated him like an ordinary person. A proud man, he expected royal treatment. To wash in a great river would be one thing, but the Jordan was small and dirty. To wash in the Jordan, Naaman thought, was beneath a man of his position. But Naaman had to humble himself and obey Elisha's commands in order to be healed.

Obedience to God begins with humility. We must believe that his way is better than our own. We may not always understand his ways of working, but by humbly obeying, we will receive his blessings. We must remember that (1) God's ways are best; (2) God wants our obedience more than anything else; (3) God can use anything to accomplish his purposes.

5:12 Naaman left in a rage because the cure for his disease seemed too simple. He was a hero, and he expected a heroic cure. Full of pride and self-will, he could not accept the simple cure of faith. Sometimes people react to God's offer of forgiveness in the same way. Just to *believe* in Jesus Christ somehow doesn't seem significant enough to bring eternal life. To obey God's commands doesn't seem heroic. What Naaman had to do to have his leprosy washed away is similar to what we must do to have our sin washed away—humbly accept God's mercy. Don't let your reaction to the way of faith keep you from the cure you need the most.

5:16 Elisha refused Naaman's money to show that God's favor cannot be purchased. Our money, like Naaman's, is useless when we face death. No matter how much wealth we accumulate in this life, it will evaporate when we stand before God, our Creator. It will be our faith in Jesus Christ that saves us, not our bank accounts.

17 Naaman said, "If not, please let your servant at least be given two mules' load of
earth; for your servant will no longer offer burnt offering nor will he sacrifice to other
gods, but to the LORD.
18 "In this matter may the LORD pardon your servant: when my master goes into the
house of Rimmon to worship there, and he leans on my hand and I bow myself in the
house of Rimmon, when I bow myself in the house of Rimmon, the LORD pardon your
servant in this matter."
19 He said to him, "Go in peace." So he departed from him some distance.
20 But Gehazi, the servant of Elisha the man of God, thought, "Behold, my master has
spared this Naaman the Aramean, by not receiving from his hands what he brought. As
the LORD lives, I will run after him and take something from him."
21 So Gehazi pursued Naaman. When Naaman saw one running after him, he came
down from the chariot to meet him and said, "Is all well?"
22 He said, "All is well. My master has sent me, saying, 'Behold, just now two young
men of the sons of the prophets have come to me from the hill country of Ephraim. Please
give them a talent of silver and two changes of clothes.' "
23 Naaman said, "Be pleased to take two talents." And he urged him, and bound two
talents of silver in two bags with two changes of clothes and gave them to two of his servants; and they carried *them* before him.
24 When he came to the hill, he took them from their hand and deposited them in the
house, and he sent the men away, and they departed.
25 But he went in and stood before his master. And Elisha said to him, "Where have
you been, Gehazi?" And he said, "Your servant went nowhere."
26 Then he said to him, "Did not my heart go *with you,* when the man turned from his
chariot to meet you? Is it a time to receive money and to receive clothes and olive groves
and vineyards and sheep and oxen and male and female servants?
27 "Therefore, the leprosy of Naaman shall cling to you and to your descendants forever." So he went out from his presence a leper *as white* as snow.

5:17 Ex 20:24
5:18 2 Kin 7:2, 17
5:19 Ex 4:18; 1 Sam 1:17; Mark 5:34
5:20 2 Kin 4:12, 31, 36; Ex 20:7; 2 Kin 6:31
5:22 2 Kin 4:26; Josh 24:33; 2 Kin 5:5
5:23 2 Kin 6:3
5:24 Josh 7:1, 11, 12, 21; 1 Kin 21:16
5:25 2 Kin 5:22
5:26 2 Kin 5:16
5:27 Ex 4:6; Num 12:10

The Axe Head Recovered

6 Now the sons of the prophets said to Elisha, "Behold now, the place before you where
we are living is too limited for us.
2 "Please let us go to the Jordan and each of us take from there a beam, and let us
make a place there for ourselves where we may live." So he said, "Go."
3 Then one said, "Please be willing to go with your servants." And he answered, "I
shall go."
4 So he went with them; and when they came to the Jordan, they cut down trees.
5 But as one was felling a beam, the axe head fell into the water; and he cried out and
said, "Alas, my master! For it was borrowed."
6 Then the man of God said, "Where did it fall?" And when he showed him the place,
he cut off a stick and threw *it* in there, and made the iron float.
7 He said, "Take it up for yourself." So he put out his hand and took it.

6:1 2 Kin 2:3
6:6 Ex 15:25; 2 Kin 2:21; 4:41

5:18–19 How could Naaman be forgiven for bowing to a pagan idol? Naaman was not asking for permission to worship the god Rimmon, but to do his civil duty, helping the king get down and up as he bowed. Also known as Hadad, Rimmon, the god of Damascus, was believed to be a god of rain and thunder. Naaman, unlike most of his contemporaries, showed a keen awareness of God's power. Instead of adding God to his nation's collection of idols, he acknowledged that there was only one true God. He did not intend to worship other gods. His asking for pardon in this one area shows the marked contrast between Naaman and the Israelites, who were continually worshiping many idols.

5:20–27 Gehazi saw a perfect opportunity to get rich by selfishly asking for the reward Elisha had refused. Unfortunately, there were three problems with his plan: (1) He willingly accepted money that had been offered to someone else; (2) he wrongly implied that money could be exchanged for God's free gift of healing and mercy; (3) he lied and tried to cover up his motives for accepting the money. Although Gehazi had been a helpful servant, personal gain had become more important to him than serving God.

This passage is not teaching that money is evil or that ministers should not get paid; instead, it is warning against greed and deceit. True service is motivated by love and devotion to God and seeks no personal gain. As you serve God, check your motives—you can't serve both God and money (Matthew 6:24).

6:1–7 The incident of the floating axe head is recorded to show God's care and provision for those who trust him, even in the insignificant events of everyday life. God is always present. Placed in the Bible between the healing of an Aramean general and the deliverance of Israel's army, this miracle also shows Elisha's personal contact with the students in the companies of the prophets. Although he had the respect of kings, Elisha never forgot to care for the faithful. Don't let the importance of your work drive out your concern for human need.

The Arameans Plot to Capture Elisha

8 Now the king of Aram was warring against Israel; and he counseled with his servants saying, "In such and such a place shall be my camp."

6:9 2 Kin 4:1, 7; 6:12

9 The man of God sent *word* to the king of Israel saying, "Beware that you do not pass this place, for the Arameans are coming down there."
10 The king of Israel sent to the place about which the man of God had told him; thus he warned him, so that he guarded himself there, more than once or twice.
11 Now the heart of the king of Aram was enraged over this thing; and he called his servants and said to them, "Will you tell me which of us is for the king of Israel?"
12 One of his servants said, "No, my lord, O king; but Elisha, the prophet who is in Israel, tells the king of Israel the words that you speak in your bedroom."

6:13 Gen 37:17

13 So he said, "Go and see where he is, that I may send and take him." And it was told him, saying, "Behold, he is in Dothan."
14 He sent horses and chariots and a great army there, and they came by night and surrounded the city.
15 Now when the attendant of the man of God had risen early and gone out, behold, an army with horses and chariots was circling the city. And his servant said to him, "Alas, my master! What shall we do?"

Few "replacements" in Scripture were as effective as Elisha, who was Elijah's replacement as God's prophet to Israel. But Elisha had a great example to follow in the prophet Elijah. He remained with Elijah until the last moments of his teacher's life on earth. He was willing to follow and learn in order to gain power to do the work to which God had called him.

Both Elijah and Elisha concentrated their efforts on the particular needs of the people around them. The fiery Elijah confronted and exposed idolatry, helping to create an atmosphere where people could freely and publicly worship God. Elisha then moved in to demonstrate God's powerful, yet caring, nature to all who came to him for help. He spent less time in conflict with evil and more in compassionate care of people. The Bible records 18 encounters between Elisha and needy people.

Elisha saw more *in* life than most people because he recognized that with God there was more *to* life. He knew that all we are and have comes to us from God. The miracles that occurred during Elisha's ministry put people in touch with the personal and all-powerful God. Elijah would have been proud of his replacement's work.

We too have great examples to follow—both people in Scripture and those who have positively influenced our lives. We must resist the tendency to think about the limitations that our family background or environment create for us. Instead, we should ask God to use us for his purposes—perhaps, like Elijah, to take a stand against great wrongs or, like Elisha, to show compassion for the daily needs of those around us. Ask him to use you as only he can.

Strengths and accomplishments:
- Was Elijah's successor as a prophet of God
- Had a ministry that lasted over 50 years
- Had a major impact on four nations: Israel, Judah, Moab, and Aram
- Was a man of integrity who did not try to enrich himself at others' expense
- Did many miracles to help those in need

Lessons from his life:
- In God's eyes, one measure of greatness is the willingness to serve the poor as well as the powerful
- An effective replacement not only learns from his master, but also builds upon his master's achievements

Vital statistics:
- Where: Prophesied to the northern kingdom
- Occupations: Farmer, prophet
- Relative: Father: Shaphat
- Contemporaries: Elijah, Ahab, Jezebel, Jehu

Key verse:
"When they had crossed over, Elijah said to Elisha, 'Ask what I shall do for you before I am taken from you.' And Elisha said, 'Please, let a double portion of your spirit be upon me' " (2 Kings 2:9).

Elisha's story is told in 1 Kings 19:16—2 Kings 13:20. He is also mentioned in Luke 4:27.

16 So he answered, "Do not fear, for those who are with us are more than those who 6:16
are with them." Ex 14:13; 2 Chr 32:7, 8; Rom 8:31
17 Then Elisha prayed and said, "O LORD, I pray, open his eyes that he may see." And
the LORD opened the servant's eyes and he saw; and behold, the mountain was full of 6:17
horses and chariots of fire all around Elisha. 2 Kin 6:20; 2 Kin 2:11; Ps 68:17; Zech 6:1-7
18 When they came down to him, Elisha prayed to the LORD and said, "Strike this
people with blindness, I pray." So He struck them with blindness according to the word 6:18 Gen 19:11
of Elisha.
19 Then Elisha said to them, "This is not the way, nor is this the city; follow me and I
will bring you to the man whom you seek." And he brought them to Samaria.
20 When they had come into Samaria, Elisha said, "O LORD, open the eyes of these 6:20
men, that they may see." So the LORD opened their eyes and they saw; and behold, they 2 Kin 6:17
were in the midst of Samaria.
21 Then the king of Israel when he saw them, said to Elisha, "My father, shall I kill 6:21
them? Shall I kill them?" 2 Kin 2:12; 5:13; 8:9
22 He answered, "You shall not kill *them.* Would you kill those you have taken captive 6:22
with your sword and with your bow? Set bread and water before them, that they may eat Deut 20:11-16; 2 Chr 28:8-15; Rom
and drink and go to their master." 12:20
23 So he prepared a great feast for them; and when they had eaten and drunk he sent 6:23
them away, and they went to their master. And the marauding bands of Arameans did 2 Kin 5:2; 24:2
not come again into the land of Israel.

The Siege of Samaria—Cannibalism

24 Now it came about after this, that Ben-hadad king of Aram gathered all his army 6:24
and went up and besieged Samaria. 1 Kin 20:1
25 There was a great famine in Samaria; and behold, they besieged it, until a donkey's 6:25
head was sold for eighty *shekels* of silver, and a fourth of a [1]kab of dove's dung for five Lev 26:26
shekels of silver.
26 As the king of Israel was passing by on the wall a woman cried out to him, saying,
"Help, my lord, O king!"
27 He said, "If the LORD does not help you, from where shall I help you? From the
threshing floor, or from the wine press?"
28 And the king said to her, "What is the matter with you?" And she answered, "This 6:28
woman said to me, 'Give your son that we may eat him today, and we will eat my son Judg 18:23
tomorrow.'
29 "So we boiled my son and ate him; and I said to her on the next day, 'Give your son, 6:29 Lev 26:27-29; Deut 28:52, 53, 57; Lam
that we may eat him'; but she has hidden her son." 4:10

1 I.e. One kab equals approx 2 qts

6:16–17 Elisha's servant was no longer afraid when he saw God's mighty heavenly army. Faith reveals that God is doing more for his people than we can ever realize through sight alone. When you face difficulties that seem insurmountable, remember that spiritual resources are there even if you can't see them. Look through the eyes of faith and let God show you his resources. If you don't see God working in your life, the problem may be your spiritual eyesight, not God's power.

6:21–22 Elisha told the king not to kill the Arameans. The king was not to take credit for what God alone had done. In setting food and water before them, he was heaping "burning coals" on their heads (Proverbs 25:21–22).

6:23 How long the Arameans stayed away from Israel is not known, but a number of years probably passed before the invasion recorded in 6:24 occurred. The Arameans must have forgotten the time their army was supernaturally blinded and sent home.

6:24 This was probably Ben-hadad II, whose father ruled Aram in the days of Baasha (1 Kings 15:18). Elisha constantly frustrated Ben-hadad II in his attempts to take control of Israel.

6:25 When a city like Samaria faced famine, it was no small matter. Although its farmers grew enough food to feed the people for a specific season, they did not have enough to maintain them in prolonged times of emergency when all supplies were cut off. This famine was so severe that mothers resorted to eating their children (6:26–30). Deuteronomy 28:49–57 predicted that this would happen when the people of Israel rejected God's leadership.

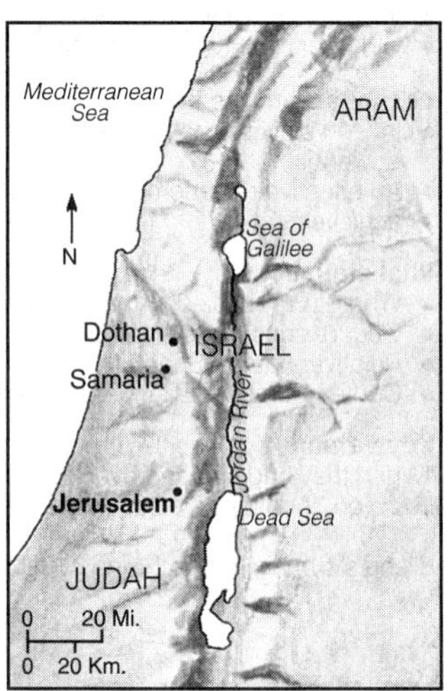

ELISHA AND THE ARAMEANS
Elisha knew Aram's battle plans and kept Israel's king informed. The Aramean king tracked down Elisha at Dothan, but Elisha prayed that the Aramean army would be blinded. He then led the blind army into Samaria, Israel's capital city!

6:30 1 Kin 21:27

30 When the king heard the words of the woman, he tore his clothes—now he was
passing by on the wall—and the people looked, and behold, he had sackcloth beneath
on his body.

6:31 Ruth 1:17; 1 Kin 19:2

31 Then he said, "May God do so to me and more also, if the head of Elisha the son of
Shaphat remains on him today."

6:32 Ezek 8:1; 14:1; 20:1; 1 Kin 18:4, 13, 14; 21:10, 13

32 Now Elisha was sitting in his house, and the elders were sitting with him. And *the*
king sent a man from his presence; but before the messenger came to him, he said to the
elders, "Do you see how this son of a murderer has sent to take away my head? Look,
when the messenger comes, shut the door and hold the door shut against him. Is not the
sound of his master's feet behind him?"

6:33 Is 8:21

33 While he was still talking with them, behold, the messenger came down to him and
he said, "Behold, this evil is from the LORD; why should I wait for the LORD any longer?"

Elisha Promises Food

7:1 2 Kin 7:18

7 Then Elisha said, "Listen to the word of the LORD; thus says the LORD, 'Tomorrow
about this time a measure of fine flour will be *sold* for a shekel, and two measures of
barley for a shekel, in the gate of Samaria.' "

7:2 2 Kin 5:18; 7:17, 19; Gen 7:11; Mal 3:10

2 The royal officer on whose hand the king was leaning answered the man of God
and said, "Behold, if the LORD should make windows in heaven, could this thing be?"
Then he said, "Behold, you will see it with your own eyes, but you will not eat of it."

Four Lepers Relate Arameans' Flight

7:3 Lev 13:45, 46; Num 5:2-4; 12:10-14

7:4 2 Kin 6:24

3 Now there were four leprous men at the entrance of the gate; and they said to one
another, "Why do we sit here until we die?
4 "If we say, 'We will enter the city,' then the famine is in the city and we will die there;
and if we sit here, we die also. Now therefore come, and let us go over to the camp of the
Arameans. If they spare us, we will live; and if they kill us, we will but die."
5 They arose at twilight to go to the camp of the Arameans; when they came to the
outskirts of the camp of the Arameans, behold, there was no one there.

7:6 2 Sam 5:24; 1 Kin 10:29; 2 Chr 12:2, 3; Is 31:1; 36:9

6 For the Lord had caused the army of the Arameans to hear a sound of chariots and
a sound of horses, *even* the sound of a great army, so that they said to one another, "Behold, the king of Israel has hired against us the kings of the Hittites and the kings of the
Egyptians, to come upon us."

PEOPLE RAISED FROM THE DEAD

God is all-powerful. Nothing in life is beyond his control, not even death.

Elijah raised a boy from the dead	1 Kings 17:22
Elisha raised a boy from the dead	2 Kings 4:34–35
Elisha's bones raised a man from the dead	2 Kings 13:20–21
Jesus raised a boy from the dead	Luke 7:14–15
Jesus raised a girl from the dead	Luke 8:52–56
Jesus raised Lazarus from the dead	John 11:38–44
Peter raised a woman from the dead	Acts 9:40–41
Paul raised a man from the dead	Acts 20:9–20

6:31–33 Why did the king blame Elisha for the famine and troubles of the siege? Here are some possible reasons: (1) Some commentators say that Elisha must have told the king to trust God for deliverance. The king did this and even wore sackcloth (6:30), but at this point the situation seemed hopeless. Apparently the king thought Elisha had given him bad advice and not even God could help them. (2) For years there was conflict between the kings of Israel and the prophets of God. The prophets often predicted doom because of the kings' evil, so the kings saw them as troublemakers. Thus Israel's king was striking out in frustration at Elisha. (3) The king may have remembered when Elijah helped bring an end to a famine (1 Kings 18:41–46). Knowing Elisha was a man of God, perhaps the king thought he could do any miracle he wanted and was angry that he had not come to Israel's rescue.

7:1–2 When Elisha prophesied God's deliverance, the king's officer said it couldn't happen. The officer's faith and hope were gone, but God's words came true anyway (7:14–16)! Sometimes we become preoccupied with problems when we should be looking for opportunities. Instead of focusing on the negatives, develop an attitude of expectancy. To say that God *cannot* rescue someone or that a situation is *impossible* demonstrates a lack of faith.

7:3 According to the law, lepers were not allowed in the city, but were to depend on charity outside the gate (Leviticus 13:45–46; Numbers 5:1–4). Because of the famine and the presence of the Aramean army, their situation was desperate.

7:3–10 The lepers discovered the deserted camp and realized their lives had been spared. At first they kept the good news to themselves, forgetting their fellow citizens who were starving in the city. The Good News about Jesus Christ must be shared too, for no news is more important. We must not forget those who are dying without it. We must not become so preoccupied with our own faith that we neglect sharing it with those around us. Our "good news," like that of the lepers, will not "wait until morning light."

7 Therefore they arose and fled in the twilight, and left their tents and their horses and their donkeys, *even* the camp just as it was, and fled for their life.

7:7 Ps 48:4-6; Prov 28:1

8 When these lepers came to the outskirts of the camp, they entered one tent and ate and drank, and carried from there silver and gold and clothes, and went and hid *them;* and they returned and entered another tent and carried from there *also,* and went and hid *them.*

7:8 Josh 7:21

9 Then they said to one another, "We are not doing right. This day is a day of good news, but we are keeping silent; if we wait until morning light, punishment will overtake us. Now therefore come, let us go and tell the king's household."

10 So they came and called to the gatekeepers of the city, and they told them, saying, "We came to the camp of the Arameans, and behold, there was no one there, nor the voice of man, only the horses tied and the donkeys tied, and the tents just as they were."

11 The gatekeepers called and told *it* within the king's household.

12 Then the king arose in the night and said to his servants, "I will now tell you what the Arameans have done to us. They know that we are hungry; therefore they have gone from the camp to hide themselves in the field, saying, 'When they come out of the city, we will capture them alive and get into the city.' "

7:12 2 Kin 6:25-29; Josh 8:4-12

13 One of his servants said, "Please, let some *men* take five of the horses which remain, which are left in the city. Behold, they *will be in any case* like all the multitude of Israel who are left in it; behold, they *will be in any case* like all the multitude of Israel who have already perished, so let us send and see."

14 They took therefore two chariots with horses, and the king sent after the army of the Arameans, saying, "Go and see."

The Promise Fulfilled

15 They went after them to the Jordan, and behold, all the way was full of clothes and equipment which the Arameans had thrown away in their haste. Then the messengers returned and told the king.

16 So the people went out and plundered the camp of the Arameans. Then a measure of fine flour *was sold* for a shekel and two measures of barley for a shekel, according to the word of the LORD.

7:16 2 Kin 7:1

17 Now the king appointed the royal officer on whose hand he leaned to have charge of the gate; but the people trampled on him at the gate, and he died just as the man of God had said, who spoke when the king came down to him.

7:17 2 Kin 7:2; 2 Kin 6:32

18 It happened just as the man of God had spoken to the king, saying, "Two measures of barley for a shekel and a measure of fine flour for a shekel, will be *sold* tomorrow about this time at the gate of Samaria."

7:18 2 Kin 7:1

19 Then the royal officer answered the man of God and said, "Now behold, if the LORD should make windows in heaven, could such a thing be?" And he said, "Behold, you will see it with your own eyes, but you will not eat of it."

7:19 2 Kin 7:2

20 And so it happened to him, for the people trampled on him at the gate and he died.

Jehoram Restores the Shunammite's Land

8 Now Elisha spoke to the woman whose son he had restored to life, saying, "Arise and go with your household, and sojourn wherever you can sojourn; for the LORD has called for a famine, and it will even come on the land for seven years."

8:1 2 Kin 4:18, 31-35; Ps 105:16; Hag 1:11; Gen 41:27, 54

2 So the woman arose and did according to the word of the man of God, and she went with her household and sojourned in the land of the Philistines seven years.

3 At the end of seven years, the woman returned from the land of the Philistines; and she went out to appeal to the king for her house and for her field.

4 Now the king was talking with Gehazi, the servant of the man of God, saying, "Please relate to me all the great things that Elisha has done."

8:4 2 Kin 4:12; 5:20-27

5 As he was relating to the king how he had restored to life the one who was dead,

8:5 2 Kin 4:35

7:19–20 It is God, not worthless idols, who provides our daily food. Although our faith may be weak or very small, we must avoid becoming skeptical of God's provision. When our resources are low and our doubts are the strongest, remember God can open the floodgates of heaven.

8:1–6 This story must have happened before the events recorded in chapter 5, because the seven-year famine must have ended before Gehazi was struck with leprosy. This shows Elijah's long-term concern for this widow and contrasts his miraculous public ministry with his private ministry to this family. Elisha's life exemplifies the kind of concern we should have for others.

behold, the woman whose son he had restored to life appealed to the king for her house
and for her field. And Gehazi said, "My lord, O king, this is the woman and this is her
son, whom Elisha restored to life."
6 When the king asked the woman, she related *it* to him. So the king appointed for
her a certain officer, saying, "Restore all that was hers and all the produce of the field
from the day that she left the land even until now."

Elisha Predicts Evil from Hazael

7 Then Elisha came to Damascus. Now Ben-hadad king of Aram was sick, and it was
told him, saying, "The man of God has come here."
8 The king said to Hazael, "Take a gift in your hand and go to meet the man of God,
and inquire of the LORD by him, saying, 'Will I recover from this sickness?' "
9 So Hazael went to meet him and took a gift in his hand, even every kind of good
thing of Damascus, forty camels' loads; and he came and stood before him and said, "Your
son Ben-hadad king of Aram has sent me to you, saying, 'Will I recover from this sickness?' "
10 Then Elisha said to him, "Go, say to him, 'You will surely recover,' but the LORD
has shown me that he will certainly die."
11 He fixed his gaze steadily *on him* until he was ashamed, and the man of God wept.
12 Hazael said, "Why does my lord weep?" Then he answered, "Because I know the
evil that you will do to the sons of Israel: their strongholds you will set on fire, and their
young men you will kill with the sword, and their little ones you will dash in pieces, and
their women with child you will rip up."
13 Then Hazael said, "But what is your servant, *who is but* a dog, that he should do this
great thing?" And Elisha answered, "The LORD has shown me that you will be king over
Aram."
14 So he departed from Elisha and returned to his master, who said to him, "What did
Elisha say to you?" And he answered, "He told me that you would surely recover."
15 On the following day, he took the cover and dipped it in water and spread it on his
face, so that he died. And Hazael became king in his place.

8:7 1 Kin 11:24; 2 Kin 6:24; 2 Kin 5:20
8:8 1 Kin 19:15, 17; 1 Kin 14:3; 2 Kin 1:2
8:9 2 Kin 5:13
8:10 2 Kin 8:14; 2 Kin 8:15
8:11 2 Kin 2:17; Luke 19:41
8:12 2 Kin 10:32, 33; 12:17; 13:3, 7; 2 Kin 15:16; Nah 3:10
8:13 1 Sam 17:43; 2 Sam 9:8; 1 Kin 19:15
8:14 2 Kin 8:10
8:15 2 Kin 8:10

2. Kings of Israel and Judah

Another Jehoram Reigns in Judah

16 Now in the fifth year of Joram the son of Ahab king of Israel, Jehoshaphat being
then the king of Judah, Jehoram the son of Jehoshaphat king of Judah became king.
17 He was thirty-two years old when he became king, and he reigned eight years in
Jerusalem.
18 He walked in the way of the kings of Israel, just as the house of Ahab had done, for
the daughter of Ahab became his wife; and he did evil in the sight of the LORD.
19 However, the LORD was not willing to destroy Judah, for the sake of David His
servant, since He had promised him to give a lamp to him through his sons always.
20 In his days Edom revolted from under the hand of Judah, and made a king over
themselves.

8:16 2 Kin 1:17; 3:1
8:17 2 Chr 21:5-10
8:18 2 Kin 8:27
8:19 2 Sam 7:12-15; 1 Kin 11:36
8:20 1 Kin 22:47; 2 Kin 3:9, 26, 27; 8:22

8:12–13 When Elisha told Hazael he would sin greatly, Hazael protested that he would never do that sort of thing. He did not acknowledge his personal potential for evil. In our enlightened society, it is easy to think we are above gross sin and can control our actions. We think that we would never sink so low. Instead, we should take a more Biblical and realistic look at ourselves and admit our sinful potential. Then we will ask for God's strength to resist such evil.

8:12–15 Elisha's words about Hazael's treatment of Israel were partially fulfilled in 10:32–33. Apparently Hazael had known he would be king because Elijah had anointed him (1 Kings 19:15). But he was impatient and, instead of waiting for God's timing, took matters into his own hands, killing Ben-hadad. God used Hazael as an instrument of judgment against the disobedient Israelites.

8:18 King Jehoshaphat arranged the marriage between Jehoram, his son, and Athaliah, the daughter of wicked Ahab and Jezebel. Athaliah followed the idolatrous ways of the northern kingdom, bringing Baal worship into Judah and starting the southern kingdom's decline. When Jehoram died, his son Ahaziah became king. Then, when Ahaziah was killed in battle, Athaliah murdered all her grandsons except Joash and made herself queen (11:1–3). Jehoram's marriage may have been politically advantageous, but spiritually it was deadly.

8:20–22 Although Judah and Edom shared a common border and a common ancestor (Isaac), the two nations fought continually. Edom had been a vassal of the united kingdom of Israel and then the southern kingdom of Judah since the days of David (2 Samuel 8:13–14). Here Edom rebelled against Jehoram (Joram) and declared independence. Immediately Jehoram marched out to attack Edom, but his ambush failed. Thus Jehoram lost some of his borderlands as punishment for his failure to honor God.

21 Then Joram crossed over to Zair, and all his chariots with him. And he arose by
night and struck the Edomites who had surrounded him and the captains of the chariots; but *his* army fled to their tents.
22 So Edom revolted against Judah to this day. Then Libnah revolted at the same time.
23 The rest of the acts of Joram and all that he did, are they not written in the Book of
the Chronicles of the Kings of Judah?

Ahaziah Succeeds Jehoram in Judah

24 So Joram slept with his fathers and was buried with his fathers in the city of David;
and Ahaziah his son became king in his place.
25 In the twelfth year of Joram the son of Ahab king of Israel, Ahaziah the son of Jehoram king of Judah began to reign.
26 Ahaziah *was* twenty-two years old when he became king, and he reigned one year
in Jerusalem. And his mother's name *was* Athaliah the granddaughter of Omri king of
Israel.
27 He walked in the way of the house of Ahab and did evil in the sight of the LORD,
like the house of Ahab *had done,* because he was a son-in-law of the house of Ahab.
28 Then he went with Joram the son of Ahab to war against Hazael king of Aram at
Ramoth-gilead, and the Arameans wounded Joram.
29 So King Joram returned to be healed in Jezreel of the wounds which the Arameans
had inflicted on him at Ramah when he fought against Hazael king of Aram. Then Ahaziah the son of Jehoram king of Judah went down to see Joram the son of Ahab in Jezreel because he was sick.

Jehu Reigns over Israel

9 Now Elisha the prophet called one of the sons of the prophets and said to him, "Gird
up your loins, and take this flask of oil in your hand and go to Ramoth-gilead.
2 "When you arrive there, search out Jehu the son of Jehoshaphat the son of Nimshi,
and go in and bid him arise from among his brothers, and bring him to an inner room.
3 "Then take the flask of oil and pour it on his head and say, 'Thus says the LORD, "I
have anointed you king over Israel." ' Then open the door and flee and do not wait."
4 So the young man, the servant of the prophet, went to Ramoth-gilead.
5 When he came, behold, the captains of the army were sitting, and he said, "I have a
word for you, O captain." And Jehu said, "For which *one* of us?" And he said, "For you,
O captain."
6 He arose and went into the house, and he poured the oil on his head and said to
him, "Thus says the LORD, the God of Israel, 'I have anointed you king over the people
of the LORD, *even* over Israel.
7 'You shall strike the house of Ahab your master, that I may avenge the blood of My
servants the prophets, and the blood of all the servants of the LORD, at the hand of Jezebel.
8 'For the whole house of Ahab shall perish, and I will cut off from Ahab every male
person both bond and free in Israel.
9 'I will make the house of Ahab like the house of Jeroboam the son of Nebat, and
like the house of Baasha the son of Ahijah.

8:21 2 Sam 18:17; 19:8
8:22 Gen 27:40; Josh 21:13; 2 Kin 19:8
8:24 2 Chr 21:20; 2 Chr 21:1, 7
8:25 2 Chr 22:1-6
8:26 2 Chr 22:2
8:27 2 Chr 22:3
8:28 2 Kin 8:15; 1 Kin 22:3, 29
8:29 2 Kin 9:15; 2 Kin 8:28; 2 Chr 22:5, 6; 2 Kin 9:16
9:1 2 Kin 2:3; 2 Kin 4:29; 1 Sam 10:1; 16:1; 1 Kin 1:39; 2 Kin 8:28, 29
9:2 1 Kin 19:16, 17; 2 Kin 9:14, 20; 2 Kin 9:5, 11
9:3 2 Chr 22:7
9:4 2 Kin 9:1
9:6 1 Sam 2:7, 8; 1 Kin 19:16; 2 Kin 9:3; 2 Chr 22:7
9:7 Deut 32:35, 43; 1 Kin 18:4; 21:15, 21, 25; 2 Kin 9:32-37
9:8 1 Kin 21:21; 2 Kin 10:17; 1 Sam 25:22; Deut 32:36; 2 Kin 14:26
9:9 1 Kin 14:10, 11; 15:29; 1 Kin 16:3-5, 11, 12

8:26 Ahaziah was the only remaining son of Jehoram of Judah. Although he was the youngest son, he took the throne because the rest of his brothers had been taken captive in a raid by the Philistines and Arabs (2 Chronicles 21:16–17).

8:26–27 Ahaziah's mother was Athaliah, daughter of Ahab and Jezebel, former king and queen of Israel, and granddaughter of Omri, Ahab's father and predecessor. The evil of Ahab and Jezebel spread to Judah through Athaliah.

8:29 Jezreel was the location of the summer palace of the kings of Israel.

9:1 "Gird up your loins" means tucking the cloak into the belt to make it easier to run.

9:3 Elijah had prophesied that many people would be killed when Jehu became king (1 Kings 19:16–17). Thus Elisha advised the young prophet to get out of the area as soon as he delivered his message, before the slaughter began. Jehu's actions seem harsh, as he hunted down relatives and friends of Ahab (2 Chronicles 22:8–9), but unchecked Baal worship was destroying the nation. If Israel was to survive, the followers of Baal had to be eliminated. Jehu fulfilled the need of the hour—justice.

9:7 Elisha's statement fulfilled Elijah's prophecy made 20 years earlier: All of Ahab's family would be killed (1 Kings 21:17–24). Jezebel's death, predicted by Elijah, is described in 9:30–37.

9:9 Ahab's dynasty would end as had those of Jeroboam and Baasha. Ahijah had prophesied the end of Jeroboam's dynasty (1 Kings 14:1–11), and this was fulfilled by Baasha (1 Kings 15:29). The prophet Jehu—not King Jehu—then foretold the end of Baasha's family (1 Kings 16:1–7), and this too was fulfilled (1 Kings 16:11–12). The end of Ahab's family, therefore, was certain—Elijah had predicted it (1 Kings 21:17–24), and God brought it to pass.

9:10 1 Kin 21:23; 2 Kin 9:35, 36

9:11 2 Kin 9:17, 19, 22; Jer 29:26; Hos 9:7; Mark 3:21

9:13 Matt 21:7, 8; Mark 11:7, 8; 2 Sam 15:10; 1 Kin 1:34, 39

9:14 1 Kin 22:3; 2 Kin 8:28

9:15 2 Kin 8:29

9:16 2 Kin 8:29

10 'The dogs shall eat Jezebel in the territory of Jezreel, and none shall bury *her.*' " Then
he opened the door and fled.
11 Now Jehu came out to the servants of his master, and one said to him, "Is all well?
Why did this mad fellow come to you?" And he said to them, "You know *very well* the
man and his talk."
12 They said, "It is a lie, tell us now." And he said, "Thus and thus he said to me, 'Thus
says the LORD, "I have anointed you king over Israel." ' "
13 Then they hurried and each man took his garment and placed it under him on the
bare steps, and blew the trumpet, saying, "Jehu is king!"

Jehoram (Joram) Is Assassinated

14 So Jehu the son of Jehoshaphat the son of Nimshi conspired against Joram. Now
Joram with all Israel was defending Ramoth-gilead against Hazael king of Aram,
15 but King [2]Joram had returned to Jezreel to be healed of the wounds which the Arameans had inflicted on him when he fought with Hazael king of Aram. So Jehu said, "If
this is your mind, *then* let no one escape *or* leave the city to go tell *it* in Jezreel."
16 Then Jehu rode in a chariot and went to Jezreel, for Joram was lying there. Ahaziah
king of Judah had come down to see Joram.
17 Now the watchman was standing on the tower in Jezreel and he saw the company of
Jehu as he came, and said, "I see a company." And Joram said, "Take a horseman and
send him to meet them and let him say, 'Is it peace?' "

2 Heb *Jehoram*

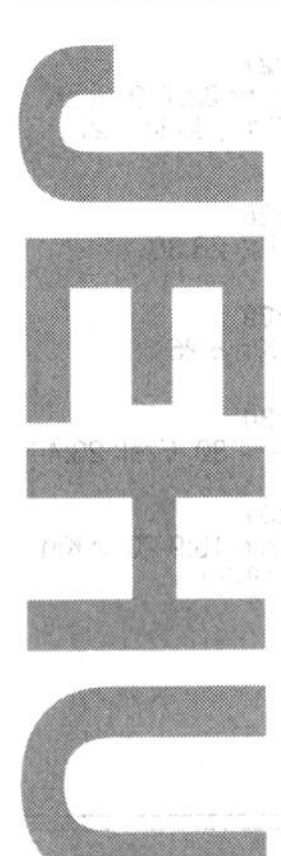

Jehu had the basic qualities that could have made him a great success. From a human perspective, in fact, he was a successful king. His family ruled the northern kingdom longer than any other. He was used by God as an instrument of punishment to Ahab's evil dynasty, and he fiercely attacked Baal worship. He came close to being God's kind of king, but he recklessly went beyond God's commands and failed to follow through on the obedient actions that began his reign. Within sight of victory, he settled for mediocrity.

Jehu was a man of immediate action but without ultimate purpose. His kingdom moved, but its destination was unclear. He eliminated one form of idolatry, Baal worship, only to uphold another by continuing to worship the golden calves Jeroboam had set up. He could have accomplished much for God if he had been obedient to the One who made him king. Even when he was carrying out God's directions, Jehu's style showed he was not fully aware of who was directing him.

As he did with Jehu, God gives each person strengths and abilities that will find their greatest usefulness only under his control. Outside that control, however, they don't accomplish what they could and often become tools for evil. One way to make sure this does not happen is to tell God of your willingness to be under his control. With his presence in your life, your natural strengths and abilities will be used to their greatest potential for the greatest good.

Strengths and accomplishments:
- Took the throne from Ahab's family and destroyed his evil influence
- Founded the longest-lived dynasty of the northern kingdom
- Was anointed by Elijah and confirmed by Elisha
- Destroyed Baal worship

Weaknesses and mistakes:
- Had a reckless outlook on life that made him bold and prone to error
- Worshiped Jeroboam's golden calves
- Was devoted to God only to the point that obedience served his own interests

Lessons from his life:
- Fierce commitment needs control because it can result in recklessness
- Obedience involves both action and direction

Vital statistics:
- Where: The northern kingdom of Israel
- Occupations: Commander in the army of Jehoram, king of Israel
- Relatives: Grandfather: Nimshi. Father: Jehoshaphat. Son: Jehoahaz
- Contemporaries: Elijah, Elisha, Ahab, Jezebel, Jehoram, Ahaziah

Key verse:
"But Jehu was not careful to walk in the law of the LORD, the God of Israel, with all his heart; he did not depart from the sins of Jeroboam, which he made Israel sin" (2 Kings 10:31).

Jehu's story is told in 1 Kings 19:16—2 Kings 10:36. He is also mentioned in 2 Kings 15:12; 2 Chronicles 22:7–9; Hosea 1:4–5.

18 So a horseman went to meet him and said, "Thus says the king, 'Is it peace?' " And
Jehu said, "What have you to do with peace? Turn behind me." And the watchman reported, "The messenger came to them, but he did not return."
19 Then he sent out a second horseman, who came to them and said, "Thus says
the king, 'Is it peace?' " And Jehu answered, "What have you to do with peace? Turn
behind me."
20 The watchman reported, "He came even to them, and he did not return; and the
driving is like the driving of Jehu the son of Nimshi, for he drives furiously."
21 Then Joram said, "Get ready." And they made his chariot ready. Joram king of Israel and Ahaziah king of Judah went out, each in his chariot, and they went out to meet
Jehu and found him in the property of Naboth the Jezreelite.
22 When Joram saw Jehu, he said, "Is it peace, Jehu?" And he answered, "What peace,
so long as the harlotries of your mother Jezebel and her witchcrafts are so many?"
23 So Joram reined about and fled and said to Ahaziah, "*There is* treachery, O Ahaziah!"
24 And Jehu drew his bow with his full strength and shot Joram between his arms; and
the arrow went through his heart and he sank in his chariot.
25 Then *Jehu* said to Bidkar his officer, "Take *him* up and cast him into the [3]property
of the field of Naboth the Jezreelite, for I remember when you and I were riding together
after Ahab his father, that the LORD laid this oracle against him:
26 'Surely I have seen yesterday the blood of Naboth and the blood of his sons,' says
the LORD, 'and I will repay you in this [3]property,' says the LORD. Now then, take and
cast him into the property, according to the word of the LORD."

Jehu Assassinates Ahaziah

27 When Ahaziah the king of Judah saw *this,* he fled by the way of the garden house.
And Jehu pursued him and said, "Shoot him too, in the chariot." *So they shot him* at the
ascent of Gur, which is at Ibleam. But he fled to Megiddo and died there.
28 Then his servants carried him in a chariot to Jerusalem and buried him in his grave
with his fathers in the city of David.
29 Now in the eleventh year of Joram, the son of Ahab, Ahaziah became king over
Judah.
30 When Jehu came to Jezreel, Jezebel heard *of it,* and she painted her eyes and adorned
her head and looked out the window.
31 As Jehu entered the gate, she said, "Is it well, Zimri, your master's murderer?"
32 Then he lifted up his face to the window and said, "Who is on my side? Who?" And
two or three officials looked down at him.

9:18 2 Kin 9:19, 22
9:20 2 Sam 18:27; 1 Kin 19:17
9:21 2 Chr 22:7; 1 Kin 21:1-7, 15-19; 2 Kin 9:26
9:22 1 Kin 16:30-33; 18:19; 2 Chr 21:13
9:23 2 Kin 11:14
9:24 1 Kin 22:34
9:25 1 Kin 21:1; 1 Kin 21:19, 24-29; Is 13:1
9:26 1 Kin 21:13, 19; 2 Kin 9:21, 25
9:27 2 Chr 22:7, 9; Josh 17:11; Judg 1:27
9:28 2 Kin 23:30
9:29 2 Kin 8:25
9:30 Jer 4:30; Ezek 23:40
9:31 1 Kin 16:9-20; 2 Kin 9:18-22

3 Lit *portion*

9:18–19 The horsemen met Jehu and asked if he came in peace. But Jehu responded, "What have you to do with peace?" Peace, properly understood, comes from God. It is not genuine except when rooted in belief in God and love for him. Jehu knew the men represented a disobedient, wicked king. Don't seek peace and friendship with those who are enemies of the good and the true. Lasting peace can come only from knowing God who gives it to us.

9:26 Joram of Israel was wicked like his father and mother, Ahab and Jezebel; therefore, his body was thrown into the field that his parents had unlawfully taken. Jezebel had arranged the murder of Naboth, the previous owner, because he would not sell his vineyard—which Ahab wanted for a garden (1 Kings 21:1–24). Little did Ahab know that it would become a burial plot for his evil son.

9:31 Why did Jezebel refer to Zimri? Zimri was an army commander who, some 40 years earlier, had killed Elah and then had declared himself king of Israel (1 Kings 16:8–10). Jezebel was accusing Jehu of trying the same treachery.

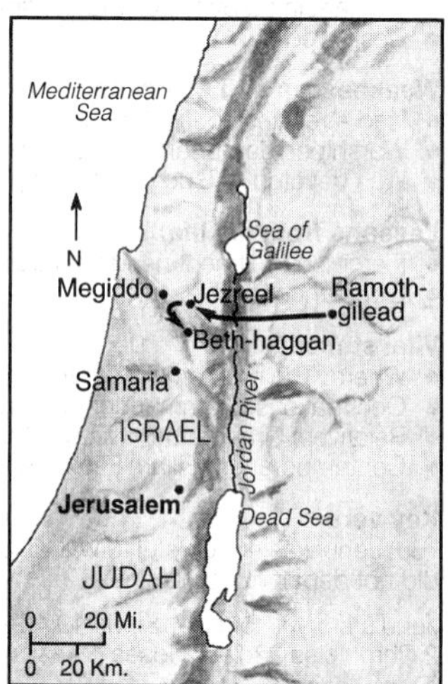

JEHU TAKES OVER ISRAEL
Elisha sent a prophet to Ramoth-gilead to anoint Jehu as Israel's new king. Jehu immediately rode to Jezreel to find and kill King Joram of Israel and King Ahaziah of Judah. Jehu killed Joram; Ahaziah fled toward Beth-haggan (the garden house), where he was wounded. He later died at Megiddo. Back in Jezreel, Jehu had Jezebel killed.

Jezebel Is Slain

33 He said, "Throw her down." So they threw her down, and some of her blood was
sprinkled on the wall and on the horses, and he trampled her under foot.
9:34 1 Kin 21:25; 1 Kin 16:31
34 When he came in, he ate and drank; and he said, "See now to this cursed woman
and bury her, for she is a king's daughter."
35 They went to bury her, but they found nothing more of her than the skull and the
feet and the palms of her hands.
9:36 1 Kin 21:23
36 Therefore they returned and told him. And he said, "This is the word of the LORD,
which He spoke by His servant Elijah the Tishbite, saying, 'In the property of Jezreel the
dogs shall eat the flesh of Jezebel;
9:37 Jer 8:1-3
37 and the corpse of Jezebel will be as dung on the face of the field in the property of
Jezreel, so they cannot say, "This is Jezebel." ' "

Judgment upon Ahab's House

10:1 1 Kin 16:24-29
10 Now Ahab had seventy sons in Samaria. And Jehu wrote letters and sent *them* to
Samaria, to the rulers of Jezreel, the elders, and to the guardians of *the children of*
Ahab, saying,
10:2 2 Kin 5:6
2 "Now, when this letter comes to you, since your master's sons are with you, as well as
the chariots and horses and a fortified city and the weapons,
3 select the best and [4]fittest of your master's sons, and set *him* on his father's throne,
and fight for your master's house."
10:4 2 Kin 9:24, 27
4 But they feared greatly and said, "Behold, the two kings did not stand before him;
how then can we stand?"
10:5 Josh 9:8, 11; 1 Kin 20:4, 32; 2 Kin 18:14
5 And the one who *was* over the household, and he who *was* over the city, the elders,
and the guardians of *the children,* sent *word* to Jehu, saying, "We are your servants, all
that you say to us we will do, we will not make any man king; do what is good in your
sight."
6 Then he wrote a letter to them a second time saying, "If you are on my side, and you
will listen to my voice, take the heads of the men, your master's sons, and come to me at
Jezreel tomorrow about this time." Now the king's sons, seventy persons, *were* with the
great men of the city, *who* were rearing them.
10:7 Judg 9:5; 2 Kin 11:1
7 When the letter came to them, they took the king's sons and slaughtered *them,* seventy persons, and put their heads in baskets, and sent *them* to him at Jezreel.
8 When the messenger came and told him, saying, "They have brought the heads
of the king's sons," he said, "Put them in two heaps at the entrance of the gate until
morning."
10:9 2 Kin 9:14-24; 2 Kin 10:6
9 Now in the morning he went out and stood and said to all the people, "You are innocent; behold, I conspired against my master and killed him, but who killed all these?
10:10 2 Kin 9:7-10; 1 Kin 21:19-29
10 "Know then that there shall fall to the earth nothing of the word of the LORD, which
the LORD spoke concerning the house of Ahab, for the LORD has done what He spoke
through His servant Elijah."
10:11 Hos 1:4
11 So Jehu killed all who remained of the house of Ahab in Jezreel, and all his great
men and his acquaintances and his priests, until he left him without a survivor.
12 Then he arose and departed and went to Samaria. On the way while he was at [5]Beth-
eked of the shepherds,
10:13 2 Kin 8:24, 29; 2 Chr 21:17; 22:8
13 Jehu met the relatives of Ahaziah king of Judah and said, "Who are you?" And they
answered, "We are the relatives of Ahaziah; and we have come down to greet the sons
of the king and the sons of the queen mother."

4 Lit *most upright* **5** I.e. house of binding

9:35 Jezebel's skull, feet, and hands were all that remained of her evil life—no power, no money, no prestige, no royal finery, no family, no spiritual heritage. In the end, her life of luxury and treachery amounted to nothing. Power, health, and wealth may make you feel as if you can live forever. But death strips everyone of all external security. The time to set your life's course is now, while you still have time and before your heart becomes hardened. The end will come soon enough.

10:7 This fulfilled Elijah's prophecy that not one of Ahab's male descendants would survive (1 Kings 21:17–24).

10:11 In his zeal, Jehu went far beyond the Lord's command with this bloodbath. The prophet Hosea later announced punishment upon Jehu's dynasty for this senseless slaughter (Hosea 1:4–5). Many times in history, "religious" people have mixed faith with personal ambition, power, or cruelty, without God's consent or blessing. To use God or the Bible to condone oppression is wrong. When people attack Christianity because of atrocities that "Christians" carried out, help them to see that these men and women were using faith to their own political ends and not following Christ.

14 He said, "Take them alive." So they took them alive and killed them at the pit of
Beth-eked, forty-two men; and he left none of them.
15 Now when he had departed from there, he met Jehonadab the son of Rechab *coming* to meet him; and he greeted him and said to him, "Is your heart right, as my heart is
with your heart?" And Jehonadab answered, "It is." *Jehu said,* "If it is, give *me* your hand."
And he gave him his hand, and he took him up to him into the chariot.
16 He said, "Come with me and see my zeal for the LORD." So he made him ride in his
chariot.
17 When he came to Samaria, he killed all who remained to Ahab in Samaria, until he
had destroyed him, according to the word of the LORD which He spoke to Elijah.

Jehu Destroys Baal Worshipers

18 Then Jehu gathered all the people and said to them, "Ahab served Baal a little; Jehu
will serve him much.
19 "Now, summon all the prophets of Baal, all his worshipers and all his priests; let no
one be missing, for I have a great sacrifice for Baal; whoever is missing shall not live."
But Jehu did it in cunning, so that he might destroy the worshipers of Baal.
20 And Jehu said, "Sanctify a solemn assembly for Baal." And they proclaimed *it.*
21 Then Jehu sent throughout Israel and all the worshipers of Baal came, so that there
was not a man left who did not come. And when they went into the house of Baal, the
house of Baal was filled from one end to the other.
22 He said to the one who *was* in charge of the wardrobe, "Bring out garments for all
the worshipers of Baal." So he brought out garments for them.
23 Jehu went into the house of Baal with Jehonadab the son of Rechab; and he said to
the worshipers of Baal, "Search and see that there is here with you none of the servants
of the LORD, but only the worshipers of Baal."
24 Then they went in to offer sacrifices and burnt offerings.
Now Jehu had stationed for himself eighty men outside, and he had said, "The one
who permits any of the men whom I bring into your hands to escape shall give up his life
in exchange."
25 Then it came about, as soon as he had finished offering the burnt offering, that Jehu
said to the guard and to the royal officers, "Go in, kill them; let none come out." And
they killed them with the edge of the sword; and the guard and the royal officers threw
them out, and went to the inner room of the house of Baal.
26 They brought out the *sacred* pillars of the house of Baal and burned them.
27 They also broke down the *sacred* pillar of Baal and broke down the house of Baal,
and made it a latrine to this day.
28 Thus Jehu eradicated Baal out of Israel.
29 However, *as for* the sins of Jeroboam the son of Nebat, which he made Israel sin, from
these Jehu did not depart, *even* the golden calves that *were* at Bethel and that *were* at Dan.
30 The LORD said to Jehu, "Because you have done well in executing what is right in

10:15 Jer 35:6-19; 1 Chr 2:55; Ezra 10:19; Ezek 17:18
10:16 1 Kin 19:10
10:17 2 Kin 9:8; 2 Kin 10:10
10:18 1 Kin 16:31, 32
10:19 1 Kin 18:19; 22:6
10:20 Joel 1:14; Ex 32:4-6
10:21 1 Kin 16:32; 2 Kin 11:18
10:24 1 Kin 20:30-42
10:25 1 Sam 22:17; 1 Kin 18:40
10:26 1 Kin 14:23; 2 Kin 3:2
10:27 Ezra 6:11; Dan 2:5; 3:29
10:29 1 Kin 12:28-30; 13:33, 34; 1 Kin 12:29
10:30 2 Kin 15:12

10:15 Jehonadab was a man who, like Jehu, was zealous in following God. Jehonadab, however, demonstrated his zeal by separating himself and his family from the materialistic, idol-worshiping culture. He founded a group called the Rechabites (named after his father Rechab), who strove to keep their lives pure by living apart from society's pressures and temptations. Jeremiah 35 gives us an example of their dedication to God. Because of their dedication, God promised that they would always have descendants who would worship him.

10:24 Israel was supposed to be intolerant of any religion that did not worship the true God. The religions of surrounding nations were evil and corrupt. They were designed to destroy life, not uphold it. Israel was God's special nation, chosen to be an example of what was right. But Israel's kings, priests, and elders first tolerated, then incorporated surrounding pagan beliefs, and thus became apathetic to God's way. We are to be completely intolerant of sin and remove it from our lives. We should be tolerant of people who hold differing views, but we should not condone beliefs or practices that lead people away from God's standards of living.

10:28–29 Why did Jehu destroy the idols of Baal but not the golden calves in Bethel and Dan? Jehu's motives may have been more political than spiritual. (1) If Jehu had destroyed the golden calves, his people would have traveled to the temple in Jerusalem, in the rival southern kingdom, and worshiped there (which is why Jeroboam set them up in the first place; see 1 Kings 12:25–33). (2) Baal worship was associated with the dynasty of Ahab, so it was politically advantageous to destroy Baal. The golden calves, on the other hand, had a longer history in the northern kingdom and were valued by all political factions. (3) Baal worship was anti-God, but the golden calves were thought by many to be visible representations of God himself, even though God's Law stated clearly that such worship was idolatrous (Exodus 20:3–6). Like Jehu, it is easy for us to denounce the sins of others while excusing sin in our own lives.

10:30–31 Jehu did much of what the Lord told him to, but he did not obey him with all his heart. He had become God's *instrument* for carrying out justice, but he had not become God's *servant.* As a result, he gave only lip service to God while permitting the worship of the golden calves. Check the condition of your heart toward God. We can be very active in our work for God and still not give the heartfelt obedience he desires.

My eyes, *and* have done to the house of Ahab according to all that *was* in My heart, your
sons of the fourth generation shall sit on the throne of Israel."
31 But Jehu was not careful to walk in the law of the LORD, the God of Israel, with all
his heart; he did not depart from the sins of Jeroboam, which he made Israel sin.
32 In those days the LORD began to cut off *portions* from Israel; and Hazael defeated
them throughout the territory of Israel:
33 from the Jordan eastward, all the land of Gilead, the Gadites and the Reubenites
and the Manassites, from Aroer, which is by the valley of the Arnon, even Gilead and
Bashan.

Jehoahaz Succeeds Jehu

34 Now the rest of the acts of Jehu and all that he did and all his might, are they not
written in the Book of the Chronicles of the Kings of Israel?
35 And Jehu slept with his fathers, and they buried him in Samaria. And Jehoahaz his
son became king in his place.
36 Now the time which Jehu reigned over Israel in Samaria *was* twenty-eight years.

Athaliah Queen of Judah

11 When Athaliah the mother of Ahaziah saw that her son was dead, she rose and
destroyed all the royal offspring.
2 But Jehosheba, the daughter of King Joram, sister of Ahaziah, took Joash the son
of Ahaziah and stole him from among the king's sons who were being put to death, and
placed him and his nurse in the bedroom. So they hid him from Athaliah, and he was not
put to death.
3 So he was hidden with her in the house of the LORD six years, while Athaliah was
reigning over the land.
4 Now in the seventh year Jehoiada sent and brought the captains of hundreds of the
Carites and of the [6]guard, and brought them to him in the house of the LORD. Then he
made a covenant with them and put them under oath in the house of the LORD, and
showed them the king's son.
5 He commanded them, saying, "This is the thing that you shall do: one third of you,
who come in on the sabbath and keep watch over the king's house
6 (one third also *shall be* at the gate Sur, and one third at the gate behind the [6]guards),
shall keep watch over the house for defense.
7 "Two parts of you, *even* all who go out on the sabbath, shall also keep watch over the
house of the LORD for the king.
8 "Then you shall surround the king, each with his weapons in his hand; and whoever
comes within the ranks shall be put to death. And be with the king when he goes out and
when he comes in."
9 So the captains of hundreds did according to all that Jehoiada the priest commanded. And each one of them took his men who were to come in on the sabbath, with those
who were to go out on the sabbath, and came to Jehoiada the priest.
10 The priest gave to the captains of hundreds the spears and shields that *had been*
King David's, which *were* in the house of the LORD.
11 The guards stood each with his weapons in his hand, from the right side of the house
to the left side of the house, by the altar and by the house, around the king.
12 Then he brought the king's son out and put the crown on him and *gave him* the testimony; and they made him king and anointed him, and they clapped their hands and
said, "*Long* live the king!"
13 When Athaliah heard the noise of the guard *and of* the people, she came to the
people in the house of the LORD.
14 She looked and behold, the king was standing by the pillar, according to the
custom, with the captains and the trumpeters beside the king; and all the people of the

10:31 Prov 4:23; 2 Kin 10:29
10:32 2 Kin 13:25; 14:25; 1 Kin 19:17; 2 Kin 8:12; 13:22
10:33 Deut 2:36; Amos 1:3-5
11:1 2 Chr 22:10-12
11:2 2 Kin 11:21; 12:1
11:4 2 Chr 23:1-21; 2 Sam 20:23; 2 Kin 11:19
11:5 1 Chr 9:25
11:8 Num 27:16, 17
11:9 2 Chr 23:8
11:10 2 Sam 8:7; 1 Chr 18:7
11:12 2 Sam 1:10; Ex 25:16; 31:18; 1 Sam 10:24
11:13 2 Chr 23:12
11:14 2 Kin 23:3; 2 Chr 34:31; 1 Kin 1:39, 40; Gen 37:29; 44:13; 2 Kin 9:23

6 Lit *runners*

11:1 This story is continued from 9:27, where Ahaziah, Athaliah's son, had been killed by Jehu. Athaliah's attempt to kill all of Ahaziah's sons was futile because God had promised that the Messiah would be born through David's descendants (2 Samuel 7).

11:2–3 Jehosheba was the wife of Jehoiada, the high priest, so the temple was a practical and natural place to hide baby Joash. Athaliah, who loved idolatry, would have had no interest in the temple.

11:4 The Carites were mercenary troops possibly associated with the Philistines. Some scholars believe they settled in southern Palestine from Crete.

land rejoiced and blew trumpets. Then Athaliah tore her clothes and cried, "Treason!
Treason!"
15 And Jehoiada the priest commanded the captains of hundreds who were appointed
over the army and said to them, "Bring her out between the ranks, and whoever follows
her put to death with the sword." For the priest said, "Let her not be put to death in the
house of the LORD."
16 So they seized her, and when she arrived at the horses' entrance of the king's house,
she was put to death there.
17 Then Jehoiada made a covenant between the LORD and the king and the people,
that they would be the LORD'S people, also between the king and the people.
18 All the people of the land went to the house of Baal, and tore it down; his altars and
his images they broke in pieces thoroughly, and killed Mattan the priest of Baal before
the altars. And the priest appointed officers over the house of the LORD.
19 He took the captains of hundreds and the Carites and the guards and all the people
of the land; and they brought the king down from the house of the LORD, and came by
the way of the gate of the guards to the king's house. And he sat on the throne of the
kings.
20 So all the people of the land rejoiced and the city was quiet. For they had put Athaliah to death with the sword at the king's house.
21 Jehoash was seven years old when he became king.

11:16 Gen 9:6; Lev 24:17
11:17 Josh 24:25; 2 Chr 15:12-14; 34:31; 1 Sam 10:25; 2 Sam 5:3
11:18 2 Kin 10:26, 27; Deut 12:2, 3; 1 Kin 18:40
11:19 2 Kin 11:4; 2 Kin 11:6
11:20 Prov 11:10
11:21 2 Chr 24:1-14

Joash (Jehoash) Reigns over Judah

12 In the seventh year of Jehu, Jehoash became king, and he reigned forty years in
Jerusalem; and his mother's name was Zibiah of Beersheba.
2 Jehoash did right in the sight of the LORD all his days in which Jehoiada the priest
instructed him.
3 Only the high places were not taken away; the people still sacrificed and burned
incense on the high places.

12:1 2 Chr 24:1
12:3 2 Kin 14:4; 15:35

The Temple to Be Repaired

4 Then Jehoash said to the priests, "All the money of the sacred things which is brought
into the house of the LORD, in current money, *both* the money of each man's assessment
and all the money which any man's heart prompts him to bring into the house of the
LORD,
5 let the priests take it for themselves, each from his acquaintance; and they shall repair
the [7]damages of the house wherever any damage may be found."
6 But it came about that in the twenty-third year of King Jehoash the priests had not
repaired the damages of the house.
7 Then King Jehoash called for Jehoiada the priest, and for the *other* priests and said
to them, "Why do you not repair the damages of the house? Now therefore take no *more*
money from your acquaintances, but pay it for the damages of the house."

12:4 2 Kin 22:4; Ex 30:13-16; 35:5, 22, 29; 1 Chr 29:3-9
12:6 2 Chr 24:5

7 Lit *breaches,* and so through v 12

11:17 This covenant was in fact a recommitment to a very old covenant—the one set up in the book of Deuteronomy for the righteous rule of the nation. It was meant to function as a constitution for the people. This covenant, however, had been virtually ignored for over 100 years. Unfortunately, with Jehoiada's death, the reforms were discontinued.

11:21 If Joash became king at only seven years of age, who really ran the country? Although the answer is not spelled out in the Bible, Judah was probably run during the first seven years of Joash's reign by the king's mother, the high priest Jehoiada, and other advisers.

12:2ff Joash (Jehoash) didn't go far enough in removing sin from the nation, but he did much that was good and right. When we aren't sure if we've gone far enough in correcting our actions, we can ask: (1) Does the Bible expressly prohibit this action? (2) Does this action take me away from loving, worshiping, or serving God? (3) Does it make me its slave? (4) Is it bringing out the best in me, consistent with God's purpose? (5) Does it benefit other believers?

12:3 The Israelites were supposed to offer sacrifices to God only in designated areas under supervision of the priests, not just anywhere (Deuteronomy 12:13–14). Making sacrifices on the hilltops (high places) copied pagan customs and encouraged other pagan practices to enter into their worship. By blending in these beliefs, people were custom-making their religion, and it led them far away from God. (For more information on these high places, see the note on 1 Kings 22:43.)

12:4–5 The temple needed repair because it had been damaged and neglected by previous evil leaders, especially Athaliah (2 Chronicles 24:7). The temple was to be a holy place, set apart for worship of God. Thanks to Joash's (Jehoash's) fund-raising program, it could be restored. The dirt and filth that had collected inside over the years were cleaned out; joints were remortared; pagan idols and other traces of idol worship were removed; and the gold and bronze were polished. The neglected condition of the temple reveals how far the people had strayed from God.

8 So the priests agreed that they would take no *more* money from the people, nor repair
the damages of the house.

12:9 Mark 12:41; Luke 21:1

9 But Jehoiada the priest took a chest and bored a hole in its lid and put it beside the
altar, on the right side as one comes into the house of the LORD; and the priests who
guarded the threshold put in it all the money which was brought into the house of the
LORD.

12:10 2 Sam 8:17; 2 Kin 19:2; 22:3, 4, 12

10 When they saw that there was much money in the chest, the king's scribe and the
high priest came up and tied *it* in bags and counted the money which was found in the
house of the LORD.
11 They gave the money which was weighed out into the hands of those who did the
work, who had the oversight of the house of the LORD; and they paid it out to the carpenters and the builders who worked on the house of the LORD;

12:12 2 Kin 22:5, 6

12 and to the masons and the stonecutters, and for buying timber and hewn stone to
repair the damages to the house of the LORD, and for all that was laid out for the house
to repair it.

12:13 2 Chr 24:14; 1 Kin 7:48, 50

13 But there were not made for the house of the LORD silver cups, snuffers, bowls,
trumpets, any vessels of gold, or vessels of silver from the money which was brought into
the house of the LORD;
14 for they gave that to those who did the work, and with it they repaired the house of
the LORD.

12:15 2 Kin 22:7; 1 Cor 4:2; 2 Cor 8:20

15 Moreover, they did not require an accounting from the men into whose hand they
gave the money to pay to those who did the work, for they dealt faithfully.

12:16 Lev 5:15-18; Lev 4:24, 29; Lev 7:7; Num 18:19

16 The money from the guilt offerings and the money from the sin offerings was not
brought into the house of the LORD; it was for the priests.

12:17 1 Kin 19:17; 2 Kin 8:12; 10:32, 33; 2 Chr 24:23, 24

17 Then Hazael king of Aram went up and fought against Gath and captured it, and
Hazael set his face to go up to Jerusalem.

12:18 1 Kin 14:26; 15:18; 2 Kin 16:8; 18:15, 16; 2 Kin 12:4

18 Jehoash king of Judah took all the sacred things that Jehoshaphat and Jehoram and
Ahaziah, his fathers, kings of Judah, had dedicated, and his own sacred things and all
the gold that was found among the treasuries of the house of the LORD and of the king's
house, and sent *them* to Hazael king of Aram. Then he went away from Jerusalem.

Joash (Jehoash) Succeeded by Amaziah in Judah

19 Now the rest of the acts of Joash and all that he did, are they not written in the Book
of the Chronicles of the Kings of Judah?

12:20 2 Chr 24:25-27; 2 Kin 14:5; Judg 9:6; 2 Sam 5:9; 1 Kin 11:27

20 His servants arose and made a conspiracy and struck down Joash at the house of
Millo *as he was* going down to Silla.
21 For Jozacar the son of Shimeath and Jehozabad the son of Shomer, his servants,
struck *him* and he died; and they buried him with his fathers in the city of David, and

12:21 2 Chr 24:26; 2 Kin 14:1

Amaziah his son became king in his place.

Kings of Israel: Jehoahaz and Jehoash

13 In the twenty-third year of Joash the son of Ahaziah, king of Judah, Jehoahaz the
son of Jehu became king over Israel at Samaria, *and he reigned* seventeen years.

13:2 1 Kin 12:26-33

2 He did evil in the sight of the LORD, and followed the sins of Jeroboam the son of
Nebat, with which he made Israel sin; he did not turn from them.

13:3 Judg 2:14; 2 Kin 12:17; 2 Kin 13:24, 25

3 So the anger of the LORD was kindled against Israel, and He gave them continually
into the hand of Hazael king of Aram, and into the hand of Ben-hadad the son of
Hazael.

12:15 What a contrast between the workmen who needed no accounting of their use of the money, and the priests who couldn't be trusted to handle their funds well enough to set some aside for the temple (12:8). As trained men of God, the Levites should have been responsible and concerned. After all, the temple was their life's work. Though the priests were not dishonest, they did not have the commitment or energy needed to finish the work. Sometimes God's work is better accomplished by devoted laypeople. Don't let your lack of training or position stop you from contributing to God's kingdom. Everyone's energy is needed to carry out God's work.

12:16 To read more about guilt and sin offerings, see Leviticus 4; 5; 6:24—7:10.

12:20 The reasons for the officials' plot against Joash are listed in 2 Chronicles 24:17–26. Joash had begun to worship idols, had killed the prophet Zechariah, and had been conquered by the Arameans. When Joash turned away from God, his life began to unravel. The officials didn't kill Joash because he turned from God; they killed him because his kingdom was out of control. In the end he became an evil man and was killed by evil people.

4 Then Jehoahaz entreated the favor of the LORD, and the LORD listened to him; for
He saw the oppression of Israel, how the king of Aram oppressed them.
5 The LORD gave Israel a [8]deliverer, so that they escaped from under the hand of the
Arameans; and the sons of Israel lived in their tents as formerly.
6 Nevertheless they did not turn away from the sins of the house of Jeroboam, with
which he made Israel sin, but walked in them; and the Asherah also remained standing
in Samaria.
7 For he left to Jehoahaz of the army not more than fifty horsemen and ten chariots
and 10,000 footmen, for the king of Aram had destroyed them and made them like the
dust at threshing.
8 Now the rest of the acts of Jehoahaz, and all that he did and his might, are they not
written in the Book of the Chronicles of the Kings of Israel?
9 And Jehoahaz slept with his fathers, and they buried him in Samaria; and Joash his
son became king in his place.
10 In the thirty-seventh year of Joash king of Judah, Jehoash the son of Jehoahaz became king over Israel in Samaria, *and reigned* sixteen years.
11 He did evil in the sight of the LORD; he did not turn away from all the sins of Jeroboam the son of Nebat, with which he made Israel sin, but he walked in them.
12 Now the rest of the acts of Joash and all that he did and his might with which he
fought against Amaziah king of Judah, are they not written in the Book of the Chronicles of the Kings of Israel?
13 So Joash slept with his fathers, and Jeroboam sat on his throne; and Joash was buried in Samaria with the kings of Israel.

Death of Elisha

14 When Elisha became sick with the illness of which he was to die, Joash the king of
Israel came down to him and wept over him and said, "My father, my father, the chariots of Israel and its horsemen!"
15 Elisha said to him, "Take a bow and arrows." So he took a bow and arrows.
16 Then he said to the king of Israel, "Put your hand on the bow." And he put his hand
on it, then Elisha laid his hands on the king's hands.
17 He said, "Open the window toward the east," and he opened *it.* Then Elisha said,
"Shoot!" And he shot. And he said, "The LORD'S arrow of victory, even the arrow of
victory over Aram; for you will defeat the Arameans at Aphek until you have destroyed
them."
18 Then he said, "Take the arrows," and he took them. And he said to the king of Israel, "Strike the ground," and he struck *it* three times and stopped.
19 So the man of God was angry with him and said, "You should have struck five or six
times, then you would have struck Aram until you would have destroyed *it.* But now you
shall strike Aram *only* three times."

13:4 Num 21:7-9; Ex 3:7, 9; 2 Kin 14:26
13:5 2 Kin 13:25; 14:25, 27; Neh 9:27
13:6 2 Kin 13:2; 1 Kin 16:33
13:7 Amos 1:3
13:12 2 Kin 13:14-19; 14:8-15
13:14 2 Kin 2:12
13:17 1 Kin 20:26
13:19 2 Kin 5:20; 2 Kin 13:25

8 Or *savior*

13:4–6 The Lord heard Jehoahaz's prayer for help. God delayed his judgment on Israel when they turned to him for help, but they did not sustain their dependence on God for long. Although there were periodic breaks in their idol worship, there was rarely evidence of genuine faith. It is not enough to say no to sin; we must also say yes to a life of commitment to God. An occasional call for help is not a substitute for a daily life of trust in God.

13:5 Aram, which lay to the north of Israel, was always Israel's enemy. This was partly because Israel blocked most of Aram's trade from the south, and Aram cut off most of Israel's from the north. If one nation could conquer the other, all its trade routes would be open and its economy would flourish. Israel and Aram were so busy fighting each other that they didn't notice the rapidly growing strength of the Assyrians to the far north. Soon both nations would be surprised (16:9; 17:6).

13:9–10 Jehoash assumed the throne of Israel in 798 B.C. At that time, the king of Judah, Joash, was nearing the end of his reign. In Hebrew, Jehoash and Joash were two forms of the same name. Thus two kings named with the same name, one in the south and one in the north, reigned at approximately the same time. While Joash of Judah began as a good king, Jehoash of Israel was evil.

13:14 Elisha was highly regarded for his prophetic powers and miracles on Israel's behalf. Joash called him, "The chariots of Israel and its horsemen!" This recalls the title Elisha gave to Elijah in 2:12. Joash feared Elisha's death because he ascribed the nation's well-being to Elisha rather than to God. Joash's fear reveals his lack of spiritual understanding. At least 43 years had passed since Elisha was last mentioned in Scripture (9:1), when he anointed Jehu king (841 B.C.). Joash's reign began in 798 B.C.

13:15–19 When Joash was told to strike the ground with the arrows, he did it only halfheartedly. As a result, Elisha told the king that his victory over Aram would not be complete. Receiving the full benefits of God's plan for our lives requires us to receive and obey God's commands fully. If we don't follow God's complete instructions, we should not be surprised that his full benefits and blessings are not present.

20 Elisha died, and they buried him. Now the bands of the Moabites would invade the
land in the spring of the year.
21 As they were burying a man, behold, they saw a marauding band, and they cast the
man into the grave of Elisha. And when the man touched the bones of Elisha he revived
and stood up on his feet.
22 Now Hazael king of Aram had oppressed Israel all the days of Jehoahaz.
23 But the LORD was gracious to them and had compassion on them and turned to
them because of His covenant with Abraham, Isaac, and Jacob, and would not destroy
them or cast them from His presence until now.
24 When Hazael king of Aram died, Ben-hadad his son became king in his place.
25 Then Jehoash the son of Jehoahaz took again from the hand of Ben-hadad the son
of Hazael the cities which he had taken in war from the hand of Jehoahaz his father.
Three times Joash defeated him and recovered the cities of Israel.

Amaziah Reigns over Judah

14 In the second year of Joash son of Joahaz king of Israel, Amaziah the son of Joash
king of Judah became king.
2 He was twenty-five years old when he became king, and he reigned twenty-nine years
in Jerusalem. And his mother's name was Jehoaddin of Jerusalem.
3 He did right in the sight of the LORD, yet not like David his father; he did according
to all that Joash his father had done.
4 Only the high places were not taken away; the people still sacrificed and burned
incense on the high places.
5 Now it came about, as soon as the kingdom was firmly in his hand, that he killed his
servants who had slain the king his father.
6 But the sons of the slayers he did not put to death, according to what is written in
the book of the Law of Moses, as the LORD commanded, saying, "The fathers shall not
be put to death for the sons, nor the sons be put to death for the fathers; but each shall
be put to death for his own sin."
7 He killed *of* Edom in the Valley of Salt 10,000 and took Sela by war, and named it
Joktheel to this day.
8 Then Amaziah sent messengers to Jehoash, the son of Jehoahaz son of Jehu, king
of Israel, saying, "Come, let us face each other."
9 Jehoash king of Israel sent to Amaziah king of Judah, saying, "The thorn bush which
was in Lebanon sent to the cedar which was in Lebanon, saying, 'Give your daughter to

13:20 2 Kin 3:7; 24:2
13:21 Matt 27:52
13:22 2 Kin 8:12, 13
13:23 2 Kin 14:27; 1 Kin 8:28; Gen 13:16, 17; 17:2-5
13:25 2 Kin 10:32, 33; 14:25; 2 Kin 13:18, 19
14:1 2 Chr 25:1; 2 Kin 13:10
14:4 2 Kin 12:3; 2 Kin 16:4
14:5 2 Kin 12:20
14:6 Deut 24:16; Jer 31:30; Ezek 18:4, 20
14:7 2 Sam 8:13; 1 Chr 18:12; 2 Chr 25:11; Is 16:1; Josh 15:38
14:8 2 Chr 25:17-24; 2 Sam 2:14-17
14:9 Judg 9:8-15

GOD OR IDOLS
Why did people continually turn to idols instead of to God?

Idols were:	*God is:*
Tangible	Intangible—no physical form
Morally similar—had human characteristics	Morally dissimilar—had divine characteristics
Comprehensible	Incomprehensible
Able to be manipulated	Not able to be manipulated
Worshiping idols involved:	*Worshiping God involved:*
Materialism	Sacrifice
Sexual immorality	Purity and commitment
Doing whatever a person wanted	Doing what God wants
Focusing on self	Focusing on others

13:20–21 Elisha was dead, but his good influence remained, even causing miracles. This demonstrated that Elisha was indeed a prophet of God. It also attested to God's power—no pagan idol ever raised anyone from the dead. This miracle served as one more reminder to Israel that it had rejected God's word as given through Elisha.

14:7 Sela was the ancient stronghold of Petra, a city carved into a rock cliff. It was not only a stronghold for Edom, but also a wealthy outpost for trade with India.

14:9–10 In this parable, Judah is compared to a thorn bush. King Amaziah of Judah had become proud after defeating the Edomites. Here he was trying to pick a fight with Israel because he was sure his army was stronger. Jehoash tried to warn Amaziah not to attack by comparing his army to a thorn bush and Israel's army to a cedar tree. Amaziah had overrated his strength; his ambition was greater than his ability. He didn't listen to Jehoash and was soundly defeated.

my son in marriage.' But there passed by a wild beast that was in Lebanon, and trampled
the thorn bush.
10 "You have indeed defeated Edom, and your heart has become proud. Enjoy your
glory and stay at home; for why should you provoke trouble so that you, even you, would
fall, and Judah with you?"
11 But Amaziah would not listen. So Jehoash king of Israel went up; and he and Amaziah king of Judah faced each other at Beth-shemesh, which belongs to Judah.
12 Judah was defeated by Israel, and they fled each to his tent.
13 Then Jehoash king of Israel captured Amaziah king of Judah, the son of Jehoash
the son of Ahaziah, at Beth-shemesh, and came to Jerusalem and tore down the wall of
Jerusalem from the Gate of Ephraim to the Corner Gate, 400 cubits.
14 He took all the gold and silver and all the utensils which were found in the house of
the LORD, and in the treasuries of the king's house, the hostages also, and returned to
Samaria.

Jeroboam II Succeeds Jehoash in Israel

15 Now the rest of the acts of Jehoash which he did, and his might and how he fought
with Amaziah king of Judah, are they not written in the Book of the Chronicles of the
Kings of Israel?
16 So Jehoash slept with his fathers and was buried in Samaria with the kings of Israel;
and Jeroboam his son became king in his place.

Azariah (Uzziah) Succeeds Amaziah in Judah

17 Amaziah the son of Joash king of Judah lived fifteen years after the death of Jehoash son of Jehoahaz king of Israel.
18 Now the rest of the acts of Amaziah, are they not written in the Book of the Chronicles of the Kings of Judah?
19 They conspired against him in Jerusalem, and he fled to Lachish; but they sent after
him to Lachish and killed him there.
20 Then they brought him on horses and he was buried at Jerusalem with his fathers in
the city of David.
21 All the people of Judah took Azariah, who *was* sixteen years old, and made him king
in the place of his father Amaziah.
22 He built Elath and restored it to Judah after the king slept with his fathers.
23 In the fifteenth year of Amaziah the son of Joash king of Judah, Jeroboam the son
of Joash king of Israel became king in Samaria, *and reigned* forty-one years.
24 He did evil in the sight of the LORD; he did not depart from all the sins of Jeroboam
the son of Nebat, which he made Israel sin.
25 He restored the border of Israel from the entrance of Hamath as far as the Sea of
the Arabah, according to the word of the LORD, the God of Israel, which He spoke
through His servant Jonah the son of Amittai, the prophet, who was of Gath-hepher.
26 For the LORD saw the affliction of Israel, *which was* very bitter; for there was neither bond nor free, nor was there any helper for Israel.
27 The LORD did not say that He would blot out the name of Israel from under heav-
en, but He saved them by the hand of Jeroboam the son of Joash.

Zechariah Reigns over Israel

28 Now the rest of the acts of Jeroboam and all that he did and his might, how he fought
and how he recovered for Israel, Damascus and Hamath, *which had belonged* to Judah,
are they not written in the Book of the Chronicles of the Kings of Israel?

14:10 2 Kin 14:7; Deut 8:14; 2 Chr 26:16
14:11 Josh 19:38
14:12 2 Sam 18:17
14:13 Neh 8:16; 12:39; 2 Chr 25:23
14:14 1 Kin 14:26; 2 Kin 12:18
14:15 2 Kin 13:12, 13
14:17 2 Chr 25:25-28
14:19 Josh 10:31; 2 Kin 18:14, 17
14:22 1 Kin 9:26; 2 Kin 16:6; 2 Chr 8:17
14:25 2 Kin 10:32; 13:25; 1 Kin 8:65; Deut 3:17; Jon 1:1; Matt 12:39, 40; Josh 19:13
14:26 2 Kin 13:4; Deut 32:36
14:27 2 Kin 13:23
14:28 1 Kin 11:24; 2 Chr 8:3

14:13 A broken-down city wall disgraced the citizens and left them defenseless against future invasions.

14:25 During this period of history, many prophets—such as Hosea, Amos, Jonah, Micah, and Isaiah—began collecting their prophecies and writing them under God's direction. They continued to preach about the worldwide significance of God's work as they looked forward to the future spiritual kingdom. God would use Israel's moral and spiritual decline to prepare the way for the Messiah's coming. Because the kingdom and military power of Israel was stripped away, many people would be ready to turn to the Good News that Jesus would bring.

14:25 For more information about the prophet Jonah, see the book of Jonah.

14:28 Jeroboam II had no devotion to God, yet under his warlike policies and skillful administration Israel enjoyed more national power and material prosperity than at any time since the days of Solomon. The prophets Amos and Hosea, however, tell us what was

29 And Jeroboam slept with his fathers, even with the kings of Israel, and Zechariah
his son became king in his place.

Series of Kings: Azariah (Uzziah) over Judah

15:1 2 Kin 14:17 **15** In the twenty-seventh year of Jeroboam king of Israel, Azariah son of Amaziah
king of Judah became king.
15:2 2 Chr 26:3, 4 2 He was sixteen years old when he became king, and he reigned fifty-two years in
Jerusalem; and his mother's name was Jecoliah of Jerusalem.
3 He did right in the sight of the LORD, according to all that his father Amaziah had
done.
15:4 2 Kin 12:3 4 Only the high places were not taken away; the people still sacrificed and burned
incense on the high places.

KINGS AND THEIR ENEMIES (841 B.C. – 753 B.C.)

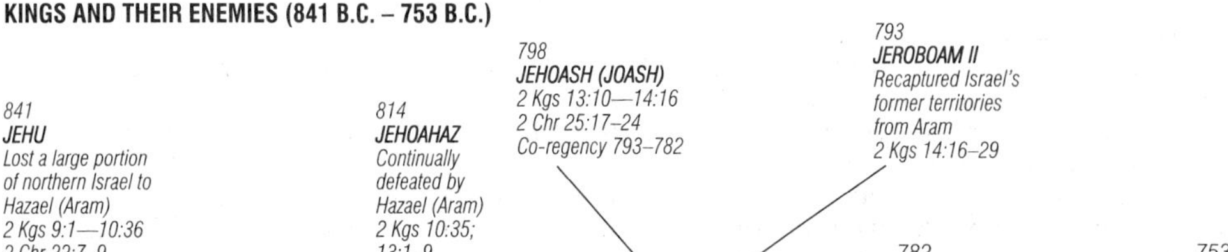

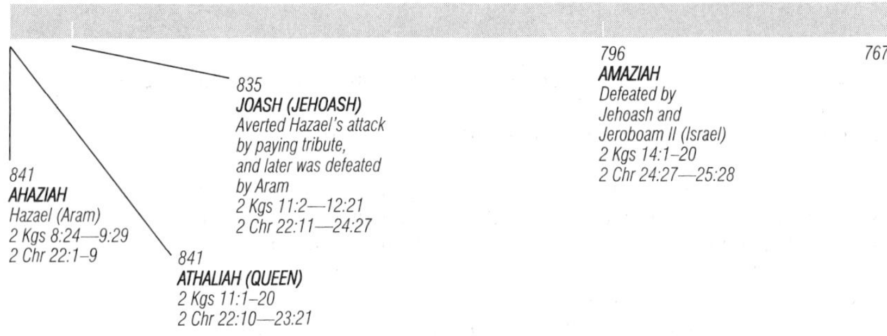

All dates are B.C.
Solid section of the timeline indicates co-regency.
For all the kings of Israel and Judah, see the chart at the end of 1 Kings.

really happening within the kingdom (Hosea 13:4–8; Amos 6:11–14). Jeroboam's administration ignored policies of justice and fairness. As a result, the rich became richer, and the poor, poorer. The people became self-centered, relying more on their power, security, and possessions than on God. The poor were so oppressed that it was hard for them to believe God noticed their plight. Material prosperity is not always an indication of God's blessing. It can also be a result of self-centeredness. If you are experiencing prosperity, remember that God holds us accountable for how we attain success and how we use our wealth. Everything we have really belongs to him. We must use God's gifts with his interests in mind.

15:1 Azariah was also known as Uzziah. His story is given in greater detail in 2 Chronicles 26. He is also mentioned in Isaiah 1:1 and 6:1. Before the beginning of Azariah's reign, Israel broke down 200 yards of Jerusalem's walls after defeating Judah and carrying off their king, Amaziah (14:13; 2 Chronicles 25:23–24). But during Azariah's 52-year reign, Judah rebuilt the wall, refortified the city with anti-siege weapons, and gained independence from Israel. Azariah's devotion to God helped Judah enjoy peace and prosperity such as it had not experienced since the days of Solomon. During this time, however, Israel declined drastically and would soon be overthrown.

15:4 Although Azariah accomplished a great deal, he failed to destroy the high places, the location of pagan shrines in Judah, just as his father Amaziah and grandfather Joash had failed to do. Azariah imitated the kings he had heard stories about and had watched while growing up. Although Azariah's father and grandfather were basically good kings, they were poor models in some important areas. To rise above the influence of poor models, we must seek better ones. Christ provides a perfect model. No matter how you were raised or who has influenced your life, you can move beyond those limitations by taking Christ as your example and consciously trying to live as he did.

5 The LORD struck the king, so that he was a leper to the day of his death. And he
lived in a separate house, while Jotham the king's son was over the household, judging
the people of the land.

15:5 2 Chr 26:21-23; Lev 13:46; Num 12:14

6 Now the rest of the acts of Azariah and all that he did, are they not written in the
Book of the Chronicles of the Kings of Judah?
7 And Azariah slept with his fathers, and they buried him with his fathers in the city
of David, and Jotham his son became king in his place.

Zechariah over Israel

8 In the thirty-eighth year of Azariah king of Judah, Zechariah the son of Jeroboam
became king over Israel in Samaria *for* six months.

15:8 2 Kin 15:1

9 He did evil in the sight of the LORD, as his fathers had done; he did not depart from
the sins of Jeroboam the son of Nebat, which he made Israel sin.
10 Then Shallum the son of Jabesh conspired against him and struck him before the
people and killed him, and reigned in his place.

15:10 Amos 7:9

11 Now the rest of the acts of Zechariah, behold they are written in the Book of the
Chronicles of the Kings of Israel.
12 This is the word of the LORD which He spoke to Jehu, saying, "Your sons to the
fourth generation shall sit on the throne of Israel." And so it was.

15:12 2 Kin 10:30

13 Shallum son of Jabesh became king in the thirty-ninth year of Uzziah king of Judah, and he reigned one month in Samaria.

15:13 2 Kin 15:1, 8; 1 Kin 16:24

14 Then Menahem son of Gadi went up from Tirzah and came to Samaria, and struck
Shallum son of Jabesh in Samaria, and killed him and became king in his place.

15:14 1 Kin 14:17

15 Now the rest of the acts of Shallum and his conspiracy which he made, behold they
are written in the Book of the Chronicles of the Kings of Israel.
16 Then Menahem struck Tiphsah and all who were in it and its borders from Tirzah,
because they did not open *to him;* therefore he struck *it* and ripped up all its women who
were with child.

15:16 2 Kin 8:12; Hos 13:16

Menahem over Israel

17 In the thirty-ninth year of Azariah king of Judah, Menahem son of Gadi became
king over Israel *and reigned* ten years in Samaria.

15:17 2 Kin 15:1, 8, 13

18 He did evil in the sight of the LORD; he did not depart all his days from the sins of
Jeroboam the son of Nebat, which he made Israel sin.
19 Pul, king of Assyria, came against the land, and Menahem gave Pul a thousand talents of silver so that his hand might be with him to strengthen the kingdom under his rule.

15:19 1 Chr 5:25, 26; 2 Kin 14:5

20 Then Menahem exacted the money from Israel, even from all the mighty men of
wealth, from each man fifty shekels of silver to pay the king of Assyria. So the king of
Assyria returned and did not remain there in the land.
21 Now the rest of the acts of Menahem and all that he did, are they not written in the
Book of the Chronicles of the Kings of Israel?
22 And Menahem slept with his fathers, and Pekahiah his son became king in his place.

15:5 For 10 years Jotham was the co-ruler with his father, Azariah. A father and son would rule together for any of the following reasons: (1) The father was very old and needed help; (2) the father wanted to train his son in leading the nation; (3) the father was sick or exiled. There were many co-regents during the period of the kings—Asa/Jehoshaphat; Jehoshaphat/Jehoram; Azariah/Jotham; Jehoash/Jeroboam II; Hezekiah/Manasseh.

15:8 Zechariah was an evil king because he encouraged Israel to sin by worshiping idols. Sin in our lives is serious. But it is even more serious to encourage others to disobey God. We are responsible for the way we influence others. Beware of double sins: ones that not only hurt us, but also hurt others by encouraging them to sin.

15:10 Zechariah was warned by the prophet Amos of his impending death and the subsequent end of Jeroboam's dynasty (Amos 7:9).

15:14 Ancient historical documents say that Menahem was the commander in chief of Jeroboam's army (see 14:23–29 for an account of Jeroboam II's reign). After Jeroboam's son was assassinated (15:8–10), Menahem probably saw himself, and not Shallum, as the rightful successor to Israel's throne.

15:18 Menahem, like the kings before him, led his people into sin—"He did evil in the sight of the LORD." What a horrible epitaph for a leader! Leaders profoundly affect the people they serve. They can either encourage or discourage devotion to God both by their example and by the structure they give their organization. Good leaders put up no obstacles to faith in God or to right living.

15:19–20 When King Pul of Assyria (also called Tiglath-pileser in 15:29) took the throne, the Assyrian empire was becoming a world power, and the nations of Aram, Israel, and Judah were in decline. This is the first mention of Assyria in 2 Kings. Pul's invasion occurred in 743 B.C. Assyria made Israel a vassal, and Menahem was forced to pay tribute to Assyria. This was the first of three Assyrian invasions (15:29 and 17:6 tell of the other ones).

Pekahiah over Israel

15:23 2 Kin 15:1, 8, 13, 17

23 In the fiftieth year of Azariah king of Judah, Pekahiah son of Menahem became king over Israel in Samaria, *and reigned* two years.

24 He did evil in the sight of the LORD; he did not depart from the sins of Jeroboam son of Nebat, which he made Israel sin.

15:25 1 Kin 16:18

25 Then Pekah son of Remaliah, his officer, conspired against him and struck him in Samaria, in the castle of the king's house with Argob and Arieh; and with him were fifty men of the Gileadites, and he killed him and became king in his place.

26 Now the rest of the acts of Pekahiah and all that he did, behold they are written in the Book of the Chronicles of the Kings of Israel.

Pekah over Israel

15:27 2 Kin 15:23; 2 Chr 28:6; Is 7:1

27 In the fifty-second year of Azariah king of Judah, Pekah son of Remaliah became king over Israel in Samaria, *and reigned* twenty years.

28 He did evil in the sight of the LORD; he did not depart from the sins of Jeroboam son of Nebat, which he made Israel sin.

15:29 2 Kin 15:19; 2 Kin 17:6

29 In the days of Pekah king of Israel, Tiglath-pileser king of Assyria came and captured Ijon and Abel-beth-maacah and Janoah and Kedesh and Hazor and Gilead and Galilee, all the land of Naphtali; and he carried them captive to Assyria.

30 And Hoshea the son of Elah made a conspiracy against Pekah the son of Remaliah, and struck him and put him to death and became king in his place, in the twentieth year of Jotham the son of Uzziah.

31 Now the rest of the acts of Pekah and all that he did, behold, they are written in the Book of the Chronicles of the Kings of Israel.

Jotham over Judah

32 In the second year of Pekah the son of Remaliah king of Israel, Jotham the son of Uzziah king of Judah became king.

15:33 2 Chr 27:1

33 He was twenty-five years old when he became king, and he reigned sixteen years in Jerusalem; and his mother's name *was* Jerusha the daughter of Zadok.

15:34 2 Kin 15:3, 4; 2 Chr 26:4, 5

34 He did what was right in the sight of the LORD; he did according to all that his father Uzziah had done.

15:35 2 Kin 12:3; 2 Chr 23:20; 27:3

35 Only the high places were not taken away; the people still sacrificed and burned incense on the high places. He built the upper gate of the house of the LORD.

36 Now the rest of the acts of Jotham and all that he did, are they not written in the Book of the Chronicles of the Kings of Judah?

15:37 2 Kin 16:5; Is 7:1

37 In those days the LORD began to send Rezin king of Aram and Pekah the son of Remaliah against Judah.

38 And Jotham slept with his fathers, and he was buried with his fathers in the city of David his father; and Ahaz his son became king in his place.

Ahaz Reigns over Judah

16:1 2 Chr 28:1

16 In the seventeenth year of Pekah the son of Remaliah, Ahaz the son of Jotham, king of Judah, became king.

16:2 2 Chr 28:1-4

2 Ahaz *was* twenty years old when he became king, and he reigned sixteen years in Jerusalem; and he did not do what was right in the sight of the LORD his God, as his father David *had done.*

16:3 Lev 18:21; 2 Kin 17:17; 21:6; Deut 12:31; 2 Kin 21:2, 11

3 But he walked in the way of the kings of Israel, and even made his son pass through the fire, according to the abominations of the nations whom the LORD had driven out from before the sons of Israel.

15:30 Hoshea was Israel's last king.

15:32 A year after Pekah became king, Uzziah (also called Azariah) of Judah died, and Isaiah the prophet had a vision of God's holiness and Israel's future destruction. See Isaiah 6 for more details on what Isaiah saw.

15:34–35 Much good can be said of Jotham and his reign as king of Judah, but he failed in a most important area: He didn't destroy the high places, although leaving them clearly violated the first commandment (Exodus 20:3). Like Jotham, we may live basically good lives and yet miss doing what is most important. A lifetime of doing good is not enough if we make the crucial mistake of not following God with all our hearts. A true follower of God puts God first in all areas of life.

16:3 Ahaz was so depraved that he sacrificed his own son to the pagan gods. This was a practice of the Canaanites whom the Israelites were supposed to drive out of the land.

4 He sacrificed and burned incense on the high places and on the hills and under every
green tree.
5 Then Rezin king of Aram and Pekah son of Remaliah, king of Israel, came up to
Jerusalem to *wage* war; and they besieged Ahaz, but could not overcome him.
6 At that time Rezin king of Aram recovered Elath for Aram, and cleared the Judeans
out of Elath entirely; and the Arameans came to Elath and have lived there to this day.

Ahaz Seeks Help of Aram

7 So Ahaz sent messengers to Tiglath-pileser king of Assyria, saying, "I am your servant and your son; come up and deliver me from the hand of the king of Aram and from
the hand of the king of Israel, who are rising up against me."
8 Ahaz took the silver and gold that was found in the house of the LORD and in the
treasuries of the king's house, and sent a present to the king of Assyria.
9 So the king of Assyria listened to him; and the king of Assyria went up against Damascus and captured it, and carried *the people of* it away into exile to Kir, and put Rezin
to death.

Damascus Falls

10 Now King Ahaz went to Damascus to meet Tiglath-pileser king of Assyria, and saw
the altar which *was* at Damascus; and King Ahaz sent to Urijah the priest the pattern of
the altar and its model, according to all its workmanship.
11 So Urijah the priest built an altar; according to all that King Ahaz had sent from
Damascus, thus Urijah the priest made *it,* before the coming of King Ahaz from Damascus.
12 When the king came from Damascus, the king saw the altar; then the king approached the altar and went up to it,
13 and burned his burnt offering and his meal offering, and poured his drink offering
and sprinkled the blood of his peace offerings on the altar.
14 The bronze altar, which *was* before the LORD, he brought from the front of the house,
from between *his* altar and the house of the LORD, and he put it on the north side of *his*
altar.
15 Then King Ahaz commanded Urijah the priest, saying, "Upon the great altar burn
the morning burnt offering and the evening meal offering and the king's burnt offering
and his meal offering, with the burnt offering of all the people of the land and their meal
offering and their drink offerings; and sprinkle on it all the blood of the burnt offering
and all the blood of the sacrifice. But the bronze altar shall be for me to inquire *by.*"
16 So Urijah the priest did according to all that King Ahaz commanded.
17 Then King Ahaz cut off the borders of the stands, and removed the laver from them;
he also took down the sea from the bronze oxen which were under it and put it on a
pavement of stone.
18 The covered way for the sabbath which they had built in the house, and the outer
entry of the king, he removed from the house of the LORD because of the king of Assyria.

16:4 Deut 12:2; 2 Kin 14:4
16:5 2 Kin 15:37; Is 7:1; 2 Chr 28:5, 6
16:6 2 Kin 14:22; 2 Chr 26:2
16:7 2 Chr 28:16; 2 Kin 15:29
16:8 2 Kin 12:17, 18; 18:15
16:9 2 Chr 28:21; Amos 1:3-5; Is 22:6; Amos 9:7
16:10 2 Kin 15:29; Is 8:2
16:12 2 Chr 26:16, 19
16:14 Ex 27:1, 2; 40:6, 29; 2 Chr 4:1; 2 Kin 16:11
16:15 Ex 29:39-41; 2 Kin 16:14
16:17 1 Kin 7:27, 28, 38; 1 Kin 7:23, 25

16:5 Israel and Aram were both under Assyria's control. They joined forces against Judah, hoping to force the southern kingdom to join their revolt against Assyria and strengthen their western alliance. But the plan backfired when King Ahaz of Judah unexpectedly asked Assyria to come to his aid (16:8–9).

16:10 Ahaz went to Damascus to express gratitude and loyalty to Tiglath-pileser. Because the Assyrians had captured Damascus, the capital of Aram (732 B.C.), Ahaz was afraid of a southern sweep. But he was relying more on money than on God to keep the powerful king out of his land, and his plan failed. Although Tiglath-pileser did not conquer Judah, he caused much trouble, and Ahaz regretted asking for his help (2 Chronicles 28:20–21).

16:10–16 Evil King Ahaz copied pagan religious customs, changed the temple services, and used the temple altar for his personal benefit. In so doing, he demonstrated a callous disregard for God's commands. We condemn Ahaz for his action, but we act the same way if we try to mold God's message to fit our personal preferences. We must worship God for who he is, not what we would selfishly like him to be.

16:14–18 Ahaz replaced the altar of burnt offering with a replica of the pagan altar he had seen in Damascus. (The original bronze altar was not thrown out, but was kept for use in divination. The lavers were where the sacrifices were washed. The sea was a huge reservoir of water for temple use.) This was extremely serious because God had given specific directions on how the altar should look and be used (Exodus 27:1–8). Building this new altar was like installing an idol. But because Judah was Assyria's vassal, Ahaz was eager to please the Assyrian king. Sadly, Ahaz allowed the king of Assyria to replace God as Judah's leader. No one, no matter how attractive or powerful, should replace God's leadership in our lives.

16:18 Ahaz had become a weak king with a weak and compromising high priest. Judah's religious system was in shambles. It was now built on pagan customs, and its chief aim was only to please those in power. If we are quick to copy others in order to please them, we risk making them more important than God in our lives.

Hezekiah Reigns over Judah

16:19 2 Chr 28:26 19 Now the rest of the acts of Ahaz which he did, are they not written in the Book of
the Chronicles of the Kings of Judah?
16:20 Is 14:28; 2 Chr 28:27 20 So Ahaz slept with his fathers, and was buried with his fathers in the city of David;
and his son Hezekiah reigned in his place.

3. Israel is exiled to Assyria

Hoshea Reigns over Israel

17:1 2 Kin 15:30 **17** In the twelfth year of Ahaz king of Judah, Hoshea the son of Elah became king
over Israel in Samaria, *and reigned* nine years.
2 He did evil in the sight of the LORD, only not as the kings of Israel who were before him.
17:3 Hos 10:14; 2 Kin 18:9-12 3 Shalmaneser king of Assyria came up against him, and Hoshea became his servant
and paid him tribute.
4 But the king of Assyria found conspiracy in Hoshea, who had sent messengers to So
king of Egypt and had offered no tribute to the king of Assyria, as *he had done* year by
year; so the king of Assyria shut him up and bound him in prison.

KINGS AND THEIR ENEMIES (796 B.C. – 715 B.C.)

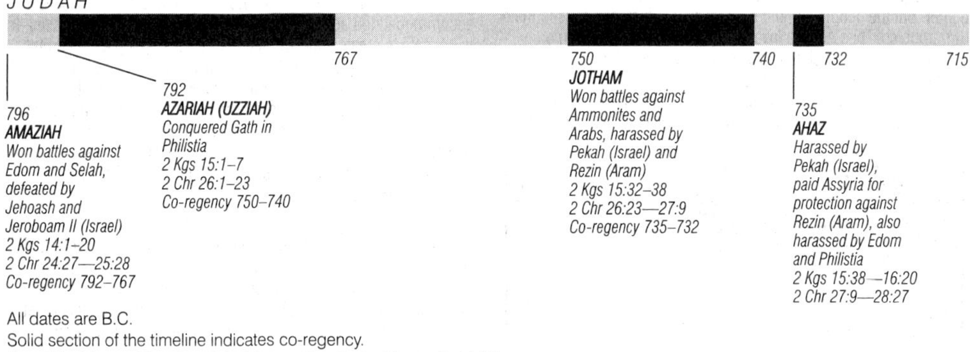

All dates are B.C.
Solid section of the timeline indicates co-regency.
For all the kings of Israel and Judah, see the chart at the end of 1 Kings.

17:3 This was probably Shalmaneser V, who became king of Assyria after Tiglath-pileser (727–722 B.C.). He continued to demand heavy tribute from Israel. Israel's King Hoshea decided to rebel against Assyria and join forces with King So of Egypt (17:4). This was not only foolish, but also against God's commands. To destroy this conspiracy, Shalmaneser attacked and besieged Samaria for three years. But just before Samaria fell, Shalmaneser died. His successor, Sargon II, took credit for capturing the city, destroying the nation of Israel, and carrying away its people.

5 Then the king of Assyria invaded the whole land and went up to Samaria and besieged it three years.

Israel Captive

6 In the ninth year of Hoshea, the king of Assyria captured Samaria and carried Israel away into exile to Assyria, and settled them in Halah and Habor, *on* the river of
Gozan, and in the cities of the Medes.

Why Israel Fell

7 Now *this* came about because the sons of Israel had sinned against the LORD their
God, who had brought them up from the land of Egypt from under the hand of Pharaoh, king of Egypt, and they had [9]feared other gods
8 and walked in the customs of the nations whom the LORD had driven out before
the sons of Israel, and *in the customs* of the kings of Israel which they had introduced.
9 The sons of Israel did things secretly which were not right against the LORD their
God. Moreover, they built for themselves high places in all their towns, from watchtower
to fortified city.
10 They set for themselves *sacred* pillars and [10]Asherim on every high hill and under
every green tree,
11 and there they burned incense on all the high places as the nations *did* which the
LORD had carried away to exile before them; and they did evil things provoking the LORD.
12 They served idols, concerning which the LORD had said to them, "You shall not do
this thing."
13 Yet the LORD warned Israel and Judah through all His prophets *and* every seer,
saying, "Turn from your evil ways and keep My commandments, My statutes according
to all the law which I commanded your fathers, and which I sent to you through My servants the prophets."
14 However, they did not listen, but stiffened their neck like their fathers, who did not
believe in the LORD their God.

17:5 Hos 13:16

17:6 Hos 13:16; Deut 28:64; 29:27, 28; 2 Kin 18:11; 1 Chr 5:26; Is 37:12; Is 13:17; 21:2

17:7 Josh 23:16; Ex 14:15-30; Judg 6:10

17:8 Lev 18:3; Deut 18:9; 2 Kin 16:3; 17:19

17:9 2 Kin 18:8

17:10 Ex 34:12-14; 1 Kin 14:23; Mic 5:14

17:12 Ex 20:4

17:13 Neh 9:29, 30; 2 Kin 17:23; 1 Sam 9:9; Jer 7:3-7; 18:11; Ezek 18:31

17:14 Ex 32:9; 33:3; Acts 7:51

9 Lit *revered,* and so throughout the ch **10** I.e. wooden symbols of a female deity

---

17:5-6 This was the third and final invasion of Assyria into Israel. (The first two invasions are recorded in 15:19 and 15:29.) The first wave was merely a warning to Israel—to avoid further attack, pay money and not rebel. The people should have learned their lesson and returned to God. When they didn't, God allowed Assyria to invade again, this time carrying off some captives from the northern border. But the people still did not realize that they had caused their own troubles. Thus Assyria invaded for the third and final time, destroying Israel completely, carrying away most of the people, and resettling the land with foreigners.

God was doing what he had said he would do (Deuteronomy 28). He had given Israel ample warning; they knew what would come, but they still ignored God. Israel was now no better than the pagan nations it had destroyed in the days of Joshua. The nation had turned sour and rejected its original purpose—to honor God and be a light to the world.

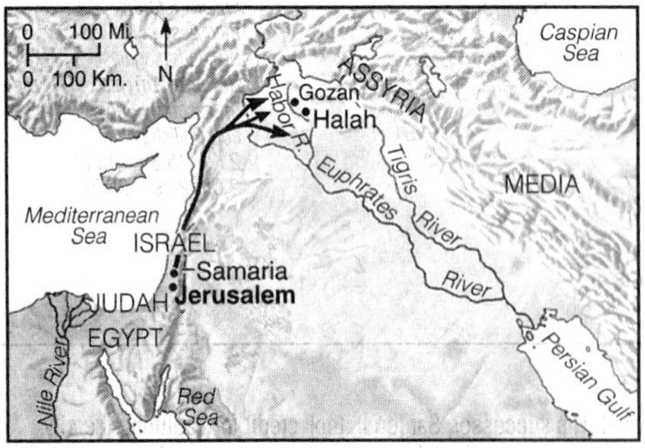

ISRAEL TAKEN CAPTIVE Finally the sins of Israel's people caught up with them. God allowed Assyria to defeat and disperse the people. They were led into captivity, swallowed up by the mighty, evil Assyrian empire. Sin always brings discipline, and the consequences of that sin are sometimes irreversible.

17:7-17 The Lord judged the people of Israel because they copied the evil customs of the surrounding nations, worshiping false gods, accommodating pagan customs, and following their own desires. It is not safe to create your own religion because people who do tend to live selfishly. And to live for yourself, as Israel learned, brings serious consequences from God. Sometimes it is difficult and painful to follow God, but consider the alternative. You can live for God or die for yourself. Determine to be God's person and do what he says regardless of the cost. What God thinks of you is infinitely more important than what those around you think. (See Romans 12:1–2; 1 John 2:15–17.)

17:9 Ruin came upon Israel for both their public sins and their secret sins. Not only did they condone wickedness and idolatry in public, but they committed even worse sins in private. Secret sins are the ones we don't want others to know about because they are embarrassing or incriminating. Sins done in private are not secret to God, and secret defiance of him is just as damaging as open rebellion.

17:13-15 The people took on the characteristics of the idols and imitated the godless nations around them. Israel had forgotten the importance and benefits of obeying God's word. The king and the people were mired in wickedness. Time and again God had sent prophets to warn them of how far they had turned away from him and to call them to turn back.

God's patience and mercy are beyond our ability to understand. He will pursue us until we either respond to him or, by our own choice and hardness of heart, make ourselves unreachable. Then God's judgment is swift and sure. The only safe course is to turn to God before our stubbornness puts us out of his reach.

17:15 Jer 8:9; Ex 24:6-8; Deut 29:25; Deut 32:21; Jer 2:5; Rom 1:21-23; Deut 12:30, 31

17:16 1 Kin 12:28; 1 Kin 14:15, 23; Deut 4:19; 2 Kin 21:3; 1 Kin 16:31

17:17 2 Kin 16:3; Lev 19:26; Deut 18:10-12; 1 Kin 21:20

17:18 2 Kin 17:6; 1 Kin 11:13, 32, 36

17:19 1 Kin 14:22, 23; 2 Kin 16:3

17:20 2 Kin 15:29

17:21 1 Kin 11:11, 31; 1 Kin 12:20; 1 Kin 12:28-33

17:23 2 Kin 17:6; 2 Kin 17:13

15 They rejected His statutes and His covenant which He made with their fathers and
His warnings with which He warned them. And they followed vanity and became vain,
and *went* after the nations which surrounded them, concerning which the LORD had
commanded them not to do like them.
16 They forsook all the commandments of the LORD their God and made for themselves molten images, *even* two calves, and made an Asherah and worshiped all the host
of heaven and served Baal.
17 Then they made their sons and their daughters pass through the fire, and practiced
divination and enchantments, and sold themselves to do evil in the sight of the LORD,
provoking Him.
18 So the LORD was very angry with Israel and removed them from His sight; none
was left except the tribe of Judah.
19 Also Judah did not keep the commandments of the LORD their God, but walked in
the customs which Israel had introduced.
20 The LORD rejected all the descendants of Israel and afflicted them and gave them
into the hand of plunderers, until He had cast them out of His sight.
21 When He had torn Israel from the house of David, they made Jeroboam the son of
Nebat king. Then Jeroboam drove Israel away from following the LORD and made them
commit a great sin.
22 The sons of Israel walked in all the sins of Jeroboam which he did; they did not depart
from them
23 until the LORD removed Israel from His sight, as He spoke through all His servants
the prophets. So Israel was carried away into exile from their own land to Assyria until
this day.

Cities of Israel Filled with Strangers

17:24 Ezra 4:2, 10; 2 Kin 18:34; 1 Kin 8:65

17:25 2 Kin 17:32-41

17:29 1 Kin 12:31; 13:32

24 The king of Assyria brought *men* from Babylon and from Cuthah and from Avva
and from Hamath and Sephar-vaim, and settled *them* in the cities of Samaria in place of
the sons of Israel. So they possessed Samaria and lived in its cities.
25 At the beginning of their living there, they did not fear the LORD; therefore the LORD
sent lions among them which killed some of them.
26 So they spoke to the king of Assyria, saying, "The nations whom you have carried
away into exile in the cities of Samaria do not know the custom of the god of the land; so
he has sent lions among them, and behold, they kill them because they do not know the
custom of the god of the land."
27 Then the king of Assyria commanded, saying, "Take there one of the priests whom
you carried away into exile and let him go and live there; and let him teach them the
custom of the god of the land."
28 So one of the priests whom they had carried away into exile from Samaria came and
lived at Bethel, and taught them how they should fear the LORD.
29 But every nation still made gods of its own and put them in the houses of the high

---

17:16 The "host of heaven" refers to the Canaanite practice of worshiping the sun, moon, and constellations. These were Assyrian gods that were being added to their religion. (See also 21:1–6; 23:4–5.)

17:17 Divination means witchcraft, and enchantment is consulting evil spirits. Forms of witchcraft, fortune-telling, and black magic were forbidden by God (Deuteronomy 18:9–14). They were wrong because they sought power and guidance totally apart from God, his law, and his Word. Isaiah echoed this law and prophesied of the complete destruction these occult practices would bring to those who participated in them (Isaiah 8:19–22).

17:23 Israel was taken into exile, just as God's prophets had warned. Whatever God predicts will come to pass. This, of course, is good news to those who trust and obey him—they can be confident of his promises; but it is bad news to those who ignore or disobey him. Both the promises and warnings God has given in his Word will surely come true.

17:24 Moving the Israelites out and moving foreigners in was Assyria's resettlement policy to prevent revolt. Spreading the captives across Assyria prevented their uniting, and repopulating Israel with foreign captives made it difficult for the remaining Israelites to unite as well. This mixture of peoples resettled in Israel came to be known as *Samaritans.* They were despised by the Jews, even through the time of Christ (John 4:9).

17:27–29 The new settlers in Israel worshiped God without giving up their pagan customs. They worshiped God to appease him rather than to please him, treating him as a good luck charm or just another idol to add to their collection. A similar attitude is common today. Many people claim to believe in God while refusing to give up attitudes and actions that God denounces. God cannot be added to the values we already have. He must come first, and his Word must shape all our actions and attitudes.

17:29–31 Israel was conquered because it had lost sight of the only true God and why it was important to follow him. When conquering the land, the Israelites were told to destroy the pagan influences that could lead them away from God. Their failure to do so brought about their ruin. Here they faced an even greater influx of gods from the many pagan peoples moving into the land.

places which the people of Samaria had made, every nation in their cities in which they lived.

30 The men of Babylon made Succoth-benoth, the men of Cuth made Nergal, the men of Hamath made Ashima,

17:30
2 Kin 17:24

WHO WERE

Who?	*When?(B.C.)*	*Ministered during the reign of these kings:*	*Main message*	*Significance*
AHIJAH	934–909	Jeroboam of Israel (1 Kings 11:29–39)	Israel would split in two and God had chosen Jeroboam to lead the ten tribes. Warned him to be obedient to God.	We should not take lightly our God-given responsibilities. Jeroboam did and lost his kingdom.
ELIJAH	875–848	Ahab of Israel (1 Kings 17:1—2 Kings 2:11)	In fiery style, urged wicked Ahab to turn back to God. On Mount Carmel, he proved who is the one true God (1 Kings 18).	Even giants of faith can't force sinners to change. But those who remain faithful to God have a great impact for him.
MICAIAH	865–853	Ahab of Israel Jehoshaphat of Judah (1 Kings 22:8; 2 Chronicles 18:28)	Ahab would be unsuccessful in fighting the Arameans.	It is foolish to move ahead with plans that are contrary to God's Word.
JEHU	853	Jehoshaphat of Judah (2 Chronicles 19:1–3)	Jehoshaphat should never have allied himself with wicked Ahab.	Partnerships with immoral people can lead us into trouble.
OBADIAH	855–840 (?)	Jehoram of Judah (The book of Obadiah)	God would judge the Edomites for taking advantage of God's people.	Pride is one of the most dangerous sins because it causes us to take advantage of others.
ELISHA	848–797	Jehoram, Jehu, Jehoahaz, and Jehoash, all of Israel (2 Kings 2:1—9:1; 13:10–21)	Expressed by his actions the importance of helping ordinary people in need.	God is concerned about the everyday needs of his people.
JOEL	835–796 (?)	Joash of Judah (The book of Joel)	Because a plague of locusts had come to punish the nation, he called the people to turn back to God before an even greater judgment occurred.	While God judges all people for their sins, he gives eternal salvation only to those who have turned to him.
JONAH	793–753	Jeroboam II of Israel (2 Kings 14:25, the book of Jonah)	Nineveh, the capital of Assyria, should repent of its sins.	God wants all nations to turn to him. His love reaches out to all peoples.
AMOS	760–750	Jeroboam II of Israel (The book of Amos)	Warned against those who exploited or ignored the needy. (In Amos's day, Israel was an affluent and materialistic society.)	Believing in God is more than a personal matter. God calls all believers to work against injustices in society and to aid those less fortunate.
HOSEA	753–715	The last seven kings of Israel; Azariah (Uzziah), Jotham, Ahaz, and Hezekiah of Judah (The book of Hosea)	Condemned the people of Israel because they had sinned against God as an adulterous woman sins against her husband.	When we sin, we sever our relationship to God, breaking our commitment to him. While all must answer to God for their sins, those who seek God's forgiveness are spared from eternal judgment.

"Yet the LORD warned Israel and Judah through all His prophets *and* every seer, saying, 'Turn from your evil ways and keep My commandments . . .' " (2 Kings 17:13). Who were these prophets? Here are some of those who tried to turn their nations back to God. Predicting the future as revealed by God was just one part of a prophet's job; his

17:31 2 Kin 17:17; 2 Kin 19:37; 2 Kin 17:24

17:32 Zeph 1:5; 1 Kin 12:31

31 and the Avvites made Nibhaz and Tartak; and the Sepharvites burned their children in the fire to Adrammelech and Anammelech the gods of Sepharvaim.
32 They also feared the LORD and appointed from among themselves priests of the
high places, who acted for them in the houses of the high places.

THESE PROPHETS?

Who?	When? (B.C.)	*Ministered during the reign of these kings:*	*Main message*	*Significance*
MICAH	742–687	Jotham, Ahaz, and Hezekiah of Judah (The book of Micah)	Predicted the fall of both the northern and southern kingdoms. This was God's discipline on the people, actually showing how much he cared for them.	Choosing to live a life apart from God is making a commitment to sin. Sin leads to judgment and death. God alone shows us the way to eternal peace. His discipline often keeps us on the right path.
ISAIAH	740–681	Azariah (Uzziah), Jotham, Ahaz, Hezekiah, and Manasseh of Judah (The book of Isaiah)	Called the people back to a special relationship with God—although judgment through other nations was inevitable.	Sometimes we must suffer judgment and discipline before we are restored to God.
NAHUM	663–654	Manasseh of Judah (The book of Nahum)	The mighty empire of Assyria that oppressed God's people would soon tumble.	Those who do evil and oppress others will one day meet a bitter end.
ZEPHANIAH	640–621	Josiah of Judah (The book of Zephaniah)	A day will come when God, as Judge, will severely punish all nations; but afterwards, he will show mercy to his people.	We will all be judged for our disobedience to God, but if we remain faithful to him, he will show us mercy.
JEREMIAH	627–586	Josiah, Jehoahaz, Jehoiakim, Jehoiachin, Zedekiah of Judah (The book of Jeremiah)	Repentance would postpone Judah's coming judgment at the hands of Babylon.	Repentance is one of the greatest needs in our world of immorality. God's promises to the faithful shine brightly.
HABAKKUK	612–589	Josiah, Jehoahaz, Jehoiakim, Jehoiachin, Zedekiah of Judah (The book of Habakkuk)	Habakkuk couldn't understand why God seemed to do nothing about the wickedness in society. Then he realized that faith in God alone would one day supply the answer.	Instead of questioning the ways of God, we should realize that he is completely just, and we should have faith that he is in control and that one day evil will be utterly destroyed.
DANIEL	605–536	Prophesied as an exile in Babylon during the reigns of Nebuchadnezzar, Darius the Mede, and Cyrus of Persia (The book of Daniel)	Describes both near and distant future events—throughout it all, God is sovereign and triumphant.	We should spend less time wondering when these events will happen and more time learning how we should live *now* so we won't be victims of those events.
EZEKIEL	593–571	Prophesied as an exile in Babylon during the reign of Nebuchadnezzar (The book of Ezekiel)	Sent messages back to Jerusalem urging the people to turn back to God before they were all forced to join him in exile. After Jerusalem fell, Ezekiel urged his fellow exiles to turn back to God so they could eventually return to their homeland.	God disciplines his people to draw them closer to him.

main role was to preach God's word to the people—warning, instructing, and encouraging them to live as they ought.

The prophets Haggai, Zechariah, and Malachi were prophets to the people of Judah after they returned from exile. For more information, see the chart in Ezra 7.

33 They feared the LORD and served their own gods according to the custom of the
nations from among whom they had been carried away into exile.
34 To this day they do according to the earlier customs: they do not fear the LORD, nor **17:34**
do they follow their statutes or their ordinances or the law, or the commandments which Gen 32:28; 35:10
the LORD commanded the sons of Jacob, whom He named Israel;
35 with whom the LORD made a covenant and commanded them, saying, "You shall **17:35**
not fear other gods, nor bow down yourselves to them nor serve them nor sacrifice to Judg 6:10; Ex 20:5; Deut 5:9
them.
36 "But the LORD, who brought you up from the land of Egypt with great power and **17:36**
with an outstretched arm, Him you shall fear, and to Him you shall bow yourselves down, Ex 14:15-30; Ex 6:6; 9:15; Lev 19:32;
and to Him you shall sacrifice. Deut 6:13
37 "The statutes and the ordinances and the law and the commandment which He wrote **17:37**
for you, you shall observe to do forever; and you shall not fear other gods. Deut 5:32
38 "The covenant that I have made with you, you shall not forget, nor shall you fear **17:38**
other gods. Deut 4:23; 6:12
39 "But the LORD your God you shall fear; and He will deliver you from the hand of all
your enemies."
40 However, they did not listen, but they did according to their earlier custom.
41 So while these nations feared the LORD, they also served their idols; their children **17:41**
likewise and their grandchildren, as their fathers did, so they do to this day. Zeph 1:5; Matt 6:24

B. THE SURVIVING KINGDOM (18:1—25:30)

After seeing their brothers and sisters carried away into exile, Judah still lapses into sin. Hezekiah and Josiah begin many reforms, but this is not enough to permanently turn the nation back to God. Judah is defeated by the Babylonians, who exile many of them, but they are not scattered and the land is not repopulated. Sometimes we do not learn from the examples of sin and foolishness around us.

1. Kings of Judah

Hezekiah Reigns over Judah

18 Now it came about in the third year of Hoshea, the son of Elah king of Israel, that **18:1** 2 Kin 16:2; 17:1;
Hezekiah the son of Ahaz king of Judah became king. 2 Chr 28:27
2 He was twenty-five years old when he became king, and he reigned twenty-nine years **18:2**
in Jerusalem; and his mother's name was Abi the daughter of Zechariah. 2 Chr 29:1, 2
3 He did right in the sight of the LORD, according to all that his father David had **18:3** 2 Kin 20:3; 2 Chr
done. 31:20
4 He removed the high places and broke down the *sacred* pillars and cut down the **18:4**
[11]Asherah. He also broke in pieces the bronze serpent that Moses had made, for until 2 Kin 18:22; 2 Chr
those days the sons of Israel burned incense to it; and it was called [12]Nehushtan. 31:1; Num 21:8, 9
5 He trusted in the LORD, the God of Israel; so that after him there was none like **18:5** 2 Kin 19:10; 2 Kin
him among all the kings of Judah, nor *among those* who were before him. 23:25

11 I.e. a wooden symbol of a female deity **12** I.e. a piece of bronze

18:4 The bronze serpent had been made to cure the Israelites of the bite of fiery serpents (Numbers 21:4–9). It demonstrated God's presence and power and reminded the people of his mercy and forgiveness. But it had become an object of worship instead of a reminder of *whom* to worship, so Hezekiah was forced to destroy it. We must be careful that aids to our worship don't become objects of worship themselves. Most objects are not made to be idols—they become idols by the way people use them.

18:5 "There was none like him . . ." In dramatic contrast to his father, Ahaz, Hezekiah followed God more closely and sincerely than any other king of Judah or Israel. This statement refers to the kings after the division of the kingdom and so does not include David, considered the king most devoted to God.

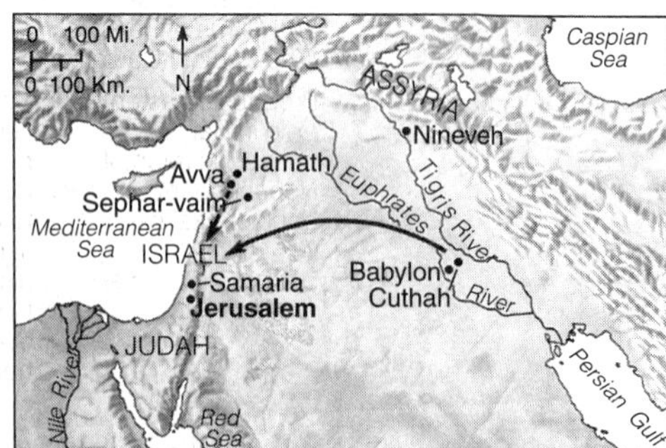

ISRAEL RESETTLED BY FOREIGNERS After the Israelites were deported, foreigners from the Assyrian empire were sent to resettle the land. This policy helped Assyria keep peace in conquered territories.

6 For he clung to the LORD; he did not depart from following Him, but kept His commandments, which the LORD had commanded Moses.

Hezekiah Victorious

7 And the LORD was with him; wherever he went he prospered. And he rebelled against
the king of Assyria and did not serve him.
8 He defeated the Philistines as far as Gaza and its territory, from watchtower to fortified city.
9 Now in the fourth year of King Hezekiah, which was the seventh year of Hoshea
son of Elah king of Israel, Shalmaneser king of Assyria came up against Samaria and
besieged it.
10 At the end of three years they captured it; in the sixth year of Hezekiah, which was
the ninth year of Hoshea king of Israel, Samaria was captured.
11 Then the king of Assyria carried Israel away into exile to Assyria, and put them in
Halah and on the Habor, the river of Gozan, and in the cities of the Medes,
12 because they did not obey the voice of the LORD their God, but transgressed His
covenant, *even* all that Moses the servant of the LORD commanded; they would neither
listen nor do *it*.

Invasion of Judah

13 Now in the fourteenth year of King Hezekiah, Sennacherib king of Assyria came up
against all the fortified cities of Judah and seized them.
14 Then Hezekiah king of Judah sent to the king of Assyria at Lachish, saying, "I have
done wrong. Withdraw from me; whatever you impose on me I will bear." So the king of
Assyria required of Hezekiah king of Judah three hundred talents of silver and thirty
talents of gold.
15 Hezekiah gave *him* all the silver which was found in the house of the LORD, and in
the treasuries of the king's house.
16 At that time Hezekiah cut off *the gold from* the doors of the temple of the LORD,
and *from* the doorposts which Hezekiah king of Judah had overlaid, and gave it to the
king of Assyria.
17 Then the king of Assyria sent Tartan and Rab-saris and Rabshakeh from Lachish
to King Hezekiah with a large army to Jerusalem. So they went up and came to Jerusalem. And when they went up, they came and stood by the conduit of the upper pool,
which is on the highway of the [13]fuller's field.
18 When they called to the king, Eliakim the son of Hilkiah, who was over the household, and Shebnah the scribe and Joah the son of Asaph the recorder, came out to them.
19 Then Rabshakeh said to them, "Say now to Hezekiah, 'Thus says the great king, the
king of Assyria, "What is this confidence that you have?

18:6 Deut 10:20; Josh 23:8
18:7 Gen 39:2, 3; 1 Sam 18:14; 2 Kin 16:7
18:8 2 Chr 28:18; Is 14:29; 2 Kin 17:9
18:9 2 Kin 17:3-7
18:10 2 Kin 17:6
18:11 1 Chr 5:26
18:12 1 Kin 9:6; Dan 9:6, 10
18:13 2 Chr 32:1; Is 36:1-39:8
18:14 2 Kin 18:7
18:15 1 Kin 15:18, 19; 2 Kin 12:18; 16:8
18:17 Is 20:1; 2 Kin 20:20; Is 7:3
18:18 2 Kin 19:2; Is 22:20; Is 22:15
18:19 2 Chr 32:10

13 I.e. launderer's

18:7 Judah was sandwiched between two world powers, Egypt and Assyria. Both wanted to control Judah and Israel because they lay at the vital crossroads of all ancient Near East trade. The nation who controlled Judah would have a military and economic advantage over its rivals. When Hezekiah became king, Assyria controlled Judah. Acting with great courage, Hezekiah rebelled against this mighty empire to whom his father had submitted. He placed his faith in God's strength rather than his own, and he obeyed God's commands in spite of the obstacles and dangers that, from a purely human standpoint, looked overwhelming.

18:9–12 These verses flash back to the days just before Israel's destruction. Hezekiah reigned with his father Ahaz for 14 years (729–715 B.C.), by himself for 18 years (715–697 B.C.), and with his son Manasseh for 11 years (697–686 B.C.), a total of 43 years. The 29 years listed in 18:2 indicate only those years in which Hezekiah had complete control of the kingdom. While Hezekiah was on the throne, the nation of Israel to the north was destroyed (722 B.C.). Knowing Israel's fate probably caused Hezekiah to reform his own nation. (For more on Hezekiah, see 2 Chronicles 29—32 and Isaiah 36—39.)

18:13 This event occurred in 701 B.C., four years after Sennacherib had become Assyria's king. Sennacherib was the son of Sargon II, the king who had deported Israel's people into captivity (see the note on 17:3). To keep Assyria from attacking, the southern kingdom paid tribute annually. But when Sennacherib became king, Hezekiah stopped paying this money, hoping Assyria would ignore him. When Sennacherib and his army retaliated, Hezekiah realized his mistake and paid the tribute money (18:14), but Sennacherib attacked anyway (18:19ff). Although Sennacherib attacked Judah, he was not as war-hungry as the previous Assyrian kings, preferring to spend most of his time building and beautifying his capital city, Nineveh. With less frequent invasions, Hezekiah was able to institute many reforms and strengthen the nation.

18:17 Sending the supreme commander (Tartan), the chief officer (Rab-saris), and the field commander (Rabshakeh) was like sending the vice president, secretary of state, and the head general of the army to speak to the enemy prior to a battle. All of these men were sent in an effort to impress and discourage the Israelites.

20 "You say (but *they are* only empty words), '*I have* counsel and strength for the war.' **18:20**
Now on whom do you rely, that you have rebelled against me? 2 Kin 18:7
21 "Now behold, you rely on the staff of this crushed reed, *even* on Egypt; on which if a **18:21**
man leans, it will go into his hand and pierce it. So is Pharaoh king of Egypt to all who Is 30:2, 3, 7; Ezek 29:6, 7
rely on him.
22 "But if you say to me, 'We trust in the LORD our God,' is it not He whose high places **18:22**
and whose altars Hezekiah has taken away, and has said to Judah and to Jerusalem, 'You 2 Kin 18:4; 2 Chr 31:1
shall worship before this altar in Jerusalem'?
23 "Now therefore, come, make a bargain with my master the king of Assyria, and I will
give you two thousand horses, if you are able on your part to set riders on them.
24 "How then can you repulse one official of the least of my master's servants, and rely
on Egypt for chariots and for horsemen?
25 "Have I now come up without the LORD'S approval against this place to destroy it?
The LORD said to me, 'Go up against this land and destroy it.' " ' "
26 Then Eliakim the son of Hilkiah, and Shebnah and Joah, said to Rabshakeh, "Speak **18:26**
now to your servants in Aramaic, for we understand *it;* and do not speak with us in Jude- Ezra 4:7; Dan 2:4
an in the hearing of the people who are on the wall."
27 But Rabshakeh said to them, "Has my master sent me only to your master and to
you to speak these words, *and* not to the men who sit on the wall, *doomed* to eat their
own dung and drink their own urine with you?"
28 Then Rabshakeh stood and cried with a loud voice in Judean, saying, "Hear the word
of the great king, the king of Assyria.
29 "Thus says the king, 'Do not let Hezekiah deceive you, for he will not be able to de- **18:29**
liver you from my hand; 2 Chr 32:15
30 nor let Hezekiah make you trust in the LORD, saying, "The LORD will surely deliver
us, and this city will not be given into the hand of the king of Assyria."
31 'Do not listen to Hezekiah, for thus says the king of Assyria, "Make your peace with **18:31**
me and come out to me, and eat each of his vine and each of his fig tree and drink each 1 Kin 4:20, 25
of the waters of his own cistern,
32 until I come and take you away to a land like your own land, a land of grain and new **18:32**
wine, a land of bread and vineyards, a land of olive trees and honey, that you may live Deut 8:7-9; 11:12
and not die." But do not listen to Hezekiah when he misleads you, saying, "The LORD
will deliver us."
33 'Has any one of the gods of the nations delivered his land from the hand of the king **18:33**
of Assyria? 2 Kin 19:12; Is 10:10, 11
34 'Where are the gods of Hamath and Arpad? Where are the gods of Sepharvaim, Hena
and Ivvah? Have they delivered Samaria from my hand? **18:34** 2 Kin 19:13; Is 10:9;
35 'Who among all the gods of the lands have delivered their land from my hand, that 2 Kin 17:24
the LORD should deliver Jerusalem from my hand?' " **18:35**
36 But the people were silent and answered him not a word, for the king's command- Ps 2:1-3; 59:7
ment was, "Do not answer him."
37 Then Eliakim the son of Hilkiah, who was over the household, and Shebna the scribe **18:37**
and Joah the son of Asaph, the recorder, came to Hezekiah with their clothes torn and 2 Kin 18:26; 2 Kin 6:30
told him the words of Rabshakeh.

Isaiah Encourages Hezekiah **19:1**

19 And when King Hezekiah heard *it,* he tore his clothes, covered himself with sack- 2 Chr 32:20-22; Is 37:1; 2 Kin 18:37;
cloth and entered the house of the LORD. 1 Kin 21:27
2 Then he sent Eliakim who was over the household with Shebna the scribe and the **19:2**
elders of the priests, covered with sackcloth, to Isaiah the prophet the son of Amoz. 2 Sam 3:31; Is 1:1; 2:1

19:1–7 Sennacherib, whose armies had captured all the fortified cities of Judah, sent a message to Hezekiah to surrender. Realizing the situation was hopeless, Hezekiah went to the temple and prayed. God answered Hezekiah's prayer and delivered Judah by sending an army to attack the Assyrian camp, forcing Sennacherib to leave at once. Prayer should be our first response in any crisis. Don't wait until things appear hopeless. Pray daily for his guidance. Our problems are God's opportunities.

19:2 Isaiah the prophet had been working for God since the days of Uzziah—40 years (Isaiah 6:1). Although Assyria was a world power, it could not conquer Judah as long as Isaiah counseled the kings. Isaiah prophesied during the reigns of Uzziah (Azariah), Jotham, Ahaz, and Hezekiah. Ahaz ignored Isaiah, but Hezekiah listened to his advice. To read his prophecies, see the book of Isaiah.

3 They said to him, "Thus says Hezekiah, 'This day is a day of distress, rebuke, and
rejection; for children have come to birth and there is no strength to *deliver.*
19:4 Josh 14:12; 2 Sam 16:12; 2 Kin 18:35; Is 1:9
4 'Perhaps the LORD your God will hear all the words of Rabshakeh, whom his master
the king of Assyria has sent to reproach the living God, and will rebuke the words which
the LORD your God has heard. Therefore, offer a prayer for the remnant that is left.' "
5 So the servants of King Hezekiah came to Isaiah.
19:6 2 Kin 18:17; 2 Kin 18:22-25, 30, 35
6 Isaiah said to them, "Thus you shall say to your master, 'Thus says the LORD, "Do
not be afraid because of the words that you have heard, with which the servants of the
king of Assyria have blasphemed Me.

The past is an important part of today's actions and tomorrow's plans. The people and kings of Judah had a rich past, filled with God's action, guidance, and commands. But with each passing generation, they also had a growing list of tragedies that occurred when the people forgot that their God, who had cared for them in the past, also cared about the present and the future—and demanded their continued obedience. Hezekiah was one of the few kings of Judah who was constantly aware of God's acts in the past and his interest in the events of every day. The Bible describes him as a king who had a close relationship with God.

As a reformer, Hezekiah was most concerned with present obedience. Judah was filled with visual reminders of the people's lack of trust in God, and Hezekiah boldly cleaned house. Altars, idols, and pagan temples were destroyed. Even the bronze serpent Moses had made in the wilderness was not spared because it had ceased to point the people to God and had also become an idol. The temple in Jerusalem, whose doors had been nailed shut by Hezekiah's own father, was cleaned out and reopened. The Passover was reinstituted as a national holiday, and there was revival in Judah.

Although he had a natural inclination to respond to present problems, Hezekiah's life shows little evidence of concern about the future. He took few actions to preserve the effects of his sweeping reforms. His successful efforts made him proud. His unwise display of wealth to the Babylonian delegation got Judah included on Babylon's "Nations to Conquer" list. When Isaiah informed Hezekiah of the foolishness of his act, the king's answer displayed his persistent lack of foresight—he was thankful that any evil consequences would be delayed until after he died. And the lives of three kings who followed him—Manasseh, Amon, and Josiah—were deeply affected by both Hezekiah's accomplishments *and* his weaknesses.

The past affects your decisions and actions today, and these, in turn, affect the future. There are lessons to learn and errors to avoid repeating. Remember that part of the success of your past will be measured by what you do with it now and how well you use it to prepare for the future.

Strengths and accomplishments:
- Was the king of Judah who instigated civil and religious reforms
- Had a personal, growing relationship with God
- Developed a powerful prayer life
- Noted as the patron of several chapters in the book of Proverbs (Proverbs 25:1)

Weaknesses and mistakes:
- Showed little interest or wisdom in planning for the future and protecting for others the spiritual heritage he enjoyed
- Rashly showed all his wealth to messengers from Babylon

Lessons from his life:
- Sweeping reforms are short-lived when little action is taken to preserve them for the future
- Past obedience to God does not remove the possibility of present disobedience
- Complete dependence on God yields amazing results

Vital statistics:
- Where: Jerusalem
- Occupation: 13th king of Judah, the southern kingdom
- Relatives: Father: Ahaz. Mother: Abijah. Son: Manasseh
- Contemporaries: Isaiah, Hoshea, Micah, Sennacherib

Key verses:
"He trusted in the LORD, the God of Israel; so that after him there was none like him among all the kings of Judah, nor among those who were before him. For he clung to the LORD; he did not depart from following Him, but kept His commandments, which the LORD had commanded Moses" (2 Kings 18:5–6).

Hezekiah's story is told in 2 Kings 16:20—20:21; 2 Chronicles 28:27—32:33; Isaiah 36:1—39:8. He is also mentioned in Proverbs 25:1; Isaiah 1:1; Jeremiah 15:4; 26:18–19; Hosea 1:1; Micah 1:1.

7 "Behold, I will put a spirit in him so that he will hear a rumor and return to his own
land. And I will make him fall by the sword in his own land." ' "

19:7 2 Kin 7:6; 2 Kin 19:37

Sennacherib Defies God

8 Then Rabshakeh returned and found the king of Assyria fighting against Libnah,
for he had heard that the king had left Lachish.
9 When he heard *them* say concerning Tirhakah king of Cush, "Behold, he has come
out to fight against you," he sent messengers again to Hezekiah saying,
10 "Thus you shall say to Hezekiah king of Judah, 'Do not let your God in whom you
trust deceive you saying, "Jerusalem will not be given into the hand of the king of Assyria."
11 'Behold, you have heard what the kings of Assyria have done to all the lands, destroying them completely. So will you be spared?
12 'Did the gods of those nations which my fathers destroyed deliver them, *even* Gozan
and Haran and Rezeph and the sons of Eden who *were* in Telassar?
13 'Where is the king of Hamath, the king of Arpad, the king of the city of Sepharvaim,
and *of* Hena and Ivvah?' "

19:8 Josh 10:29; 2 Kin 18:14
19:10 2 Kin 18:5; 2 Kin 18:30
19:12 2 Kin 18:33; 2 Kin 17:6; Gen 11:31; Is 37:12
19:13 2 Kin 18:34

Hezekiah's Prayer

14 Then Hezekiah took the letter from the hand of the messengers and read it, and he
went up to the house of the LORD and spread it out before the LORD.
15 Hezekiah prayed before the LORD and said, "O LORD, the God of Israel, who are
enthroned *above* the cherubim, You are the God, You alone, of all the kingdoms of the
earth. You have made heaven and earth.
16 "Incline Your ear, O LORD, and hear; open Your eyes, O LORD, and see; and listen
to the words of Sennacherib, which he has sent to reproach the living God.
17 "Truly, O LORD, the kings of Assyria have devastated the nations and their lands
18 and have cast their gods into the fire, for they were not gods but the work of men's
hands, wood and stone. So they have destroyed them.
19 "Now, O LORD our God, I pray, deliver us from his hand that all the kingdoms of the
earth may know that You alone, O LORD, are God."

19:14 Is 37:14
19:15 Ex 25:22; Is 37:14; 2 Kin 5:15
19:16 Ps 31:2; Is 37:17; 1 Kin 8:29; 2 Chr 6:40; 2 Kin 19:4
19:18 Is 44:9-20; Acts 17:29
19:19 1 Kin 8:42, 43; 2 Kin 19:15

God's Answer through Isaiah

20 Then Isaiah the son of Amoz sent to Hezekiah saying, "Thus says the LORD, the
God of Israel, 'Because you have prayed to Me about Sennacherib king of Assyria, I have
heard *you.*'
21 "This is the word that the LORD has spoken against him:
'She has despised you and mocked you,
The virgin daughter of Zion;
She has shaken *her* head behind you,
The daughter of Jerusalem!
22 'Whom have you reproached and blasphemed?
And against whom have you raised *your* voice,
And haughtily lifted up your eyes?
Against the Holy One of Israel!
23 'Through your messengers you have reproached the Lord,
And you have said, "With my many chariots
I came up to the heights of the mountains,
To the remotest parts of Lebanon;
And I cut down its tall cedars *and* its choice cypresses.
And I entered its farthest lodging place, its thickest forest.

19:20 2 Kin 20:5
19:21 Jer 14:17; Lam 2:13; Ps 109:25; Matt 27:39
19:22 2 Kin 19:4; 2 Kin 19:6; Is 5:24; 30:11-15
19:23 2 Kin 18:17; 2 Chr 26:10; Is 10:18

19:15 Cherubim are mighty angels.

19:15–19 Although Hezekiah came boldly to God, he did not take God for granted or approach him flippantly. Instead, Hezekiah acknowledged God's sovereignty and Judah's total dependence on him. Hezekiah's prayer provides a good model for us. We should not be afraid to approach God with our prayers, but we must come to him with respect for who he is and what he can do.

19:21–34 God replied to Sennacherib's taunting words (18:19–25), indicting him for arrogance. Sennacherib believed his kingdom had grown because of his own efforts and strength. In reality, said God, he succeeded only because of what God had allowed and caused. It is arrogance to think we are solely responsible for our achievements. God, as Creator, rules over nations and people.

19:24 Is 19:6

24 "I dug *wells* and drank foreign waters,
And with the sole of my feet I dried up
All the rivers of Egypt."

19:25 Is 45:7; Is 10:5

25 'Have you not heard?
Long ago I did it;
From ancient times I planned it.
Now I have brought it to pass,
That you should turn fortified cities into ruinous heaps.

19:26 Ps 129:6

26 'Therefore their inhabitants were short of strength,
They were dismayed and put to shame;
They were as the vegetation of the field and as the green herb,
As grass on the housetops is scorched before it is grown up.

19:27 Ps 139:1

27 'But I know your sitting down,
And your going out and your coming in,
And your raging against Me.

19:28 Ezek 19:9; 29:4; 2 Kin 19:33, 36

28 'Because of your raging against Me,
And because your arrogance has come up to My ears,
Therefore I will put My hook in your nose,
And My bridle in your lips,
And I will turn you back by the way which you came.

19:29 Ex 3:12; 2 Kin 20:8, 9; **19:30** 2 Kin 19:4; 2 Chr 32:22, 23; **19:31** Is 10:20; Is 9:7; **19:32** Is 8:7-10; **19:33** 2 Kin 19:28; **19:34** 2 Kin 20:6; Is 31:5; 1 Kin 11:12, 13; **19:35** 2 Sam 24:16; 2 Chr 32:21; **19:36** 2 Kin 19:7, 28, 33; Jon 1:2; **19:37** 2 Kin 19:17, 31; Gen 8:4; Jer 51:27; Ezra 4:2

29 'Then this shall be the sign for you: you will eat this year what grows of itself, in the
second year what springs from the same, and in the third year sow, reap, plant vineyards,
and eat their fruit.
30 'The surviving remnant of the house of Judah will again take root downward and
bear fruit upward.
31 'For out of Jerusalem will go forth a remnant, and out of Mount Zion survivors. The
zeal of [14]the LORD will perform this.
32 'Therefore thus says the LORD concerning the king of Assyria, "He will not come to
this city or shoot an arrow there; and he will not come before it with a shield or throw up
a siege ramp against it.
33 "By the way that he came, by the same he will return, and he shall not come to this
city," ' declares the LORD.
34 'For I will defend this city to save it for My own sake and for My servant David's
sake.' "
35 Then it happened that night that the angel of the LORD went out and struck 185,000
in the camp of the Assyrians; and when men rose early in the morning, behold, all of
them were dead.
36 So Sennacherib king of Assyria departed and returned *home,* and lived at Nineveh.
37 It came about as he was worshiping in the house of Nisroch his god, that Adrammelech and Sharezer killed him with the sword; and they escaped into the land of Ararat.
And Esarhaddon his son became king in his place.

Hezekiah's Illness and Recovery

20:1 2 Chr 32:24; Is 38:1-22; 2 Sam 17:23; **20:3** Neh 5:19; 13:14, 22, 31; 2 Kin 18:3-6; 2 Sam 12:21, 22

20 In those days Hezekiah became mortally ill. And Isaiah the prophet the son of
Amoz came to him and said to him, "Thus says the LORD, 'Set your house in order, for you shall die and not live.' "
2 Then he turned his face to the wall and prayed to the LORD, saying,
3 "Remember now, O LORD, I beseech You, how I have walked before You in truth
and with a whole heart and have done what is good in Your sight." And Hezekiah wept
bitterly.

14 Some ancient mss read *the LORD of hosts*

19:28 The Assyrians treated captives with cruelty. They tortured them for entertainment by blinding them, cutting them, or pulling off strips of their skin until they died. If they wished to make a captive a slave, they would often put a hook in his nose. God was saying that the Assyrians would be treated the way they had treated others.

19:31 As long as a tiny spark remains, a fire can be rekindled and fanned into a roaring blaze. Similarly, if just the smallest remnant of true believers retains the spark of faith, God can rebuild it into a strong nation. And if only a glimmer of faith remains in a heart, God can use it to restore blazing faith in that believer. If you feel that only a spark of faith remains in you, ask God to use it to rekindle a blazing fire of commitment to him.

4 Before Isaiah had gone out of the middle court, the word of the LORD came to him,
saying,
5 "Return and say to Hezekiah the leader of My people, 'Thus says the LORD, the God
of your father David, "I have heard your prayer, I have seen your tears; behold, I will
heal you. On the third day you shall go up to the house of the LORD.
6 "I will add fifteen years to your life, and I will deliver you and this city from the hand
of the king of Assyria; and I will defend this city for My own sake and for My servant
David's sake." ' "
7 Then Isaiah said, "Take a cake of figs." And they took and laid *it* on the boil, and he
recovered.
8 Now Hezekiah said to Isaiah, "What will be the sign that the LORD will heal me,
and that I shall go up to the house of the LORD the third day?"
9 Isaiah said, "This shall be the sign to you from the LORD, that the LORD will do the
thing that He has spoken: shall the shadow go forward ten steps or go back ten steps?"
10 So Hezekiah answered, "It is easy for the shadow to decline ten steps; no, but let
the shadow turn backward ten steps."
11 Isaiah the prophet cried to the LORD, and He brought the shadow on the stairway
back ten steps by which it had gone down on the stairway of Ahaz.

20:5 1 Sam 9:16; 10:1; 2 Kin 19:20; Ps 39:12
20:6 2 Kin 19:34
20:9 Is 38:7
20:11 Josh 10:12-14; Is 38:8

Hezekiah Shows Babylon His Treasures

12 At that time Berodach-baladan a son of Baladan, king of Babylon, sent letters and
a present to Hezekiah, for he heard that Hezekiah had been sick.
13 Hezekiah listened to them, and showed them all his treasure house, the silver and
the gold and the spices and the precious oil and the house of his armor and all that was
found in his treasuries. There was nothing in his house nor in all his dominion that Hezekiah did not show them.
14 Then Isaiah the prophet came to King Hezekiah and said to him, "What did these
men say, and from where have they come to you?" And Hezekiah said, "They have come
from a far country, from Babylon."
15 He said, "What have they seen in your house?" So Hezekiah answered, "They have
seen all that is in my house; there is nothing among my treasuries that I have not shown
them."
16 Then Isaiah said to Hezekiah, "Hear the word of the LORD.
17 'Behold, the days are coming when all that is in your house, and all that your fathers
have laid up in store to this day will be carried to Babylon; nothing shall be left,' says the
LORD.
18 'Some of your sons who shall issue from you, whom you will beget, will be taken away;
and they will become officials in the palace of the king of Babylon.' "
19 Then Hezekiah said to Isaiah, "The word of the LORD which you have spoken is
good." For he thought, "Is it not so, if there will be peace and truth in my days?"
20 Now the rest of the acts of Hezekiah and all his might, and how he made the pool

20:12 2 Chr 32:31; Is 39:1-8
20:13 2 Chr 32:27
20:17 2 Kin 24:13; 25:13-15; 2 Chr 36:10; Jer 52:17-19
20:18 2 Kin 24:12; 2 Chr 33:11; Dan 1:3-7
20:19 1 Sam 3:18
20:20 2 Chr 32:32; Neh 3:16

20:5–6 Over a 100-year period of Judah's history (732–640 B.C.), Hezekiah was the only faithful king; but what a difference he made! Because of Hezekiah's faith and prayer, God healed him and saved his city from the Assyrians. You can make a difference too, even if your faith puts you in the minority. Faith and prayer, if they are sincere and directed toward the one true God, can change any situation.

20:11 The stairway of Ahaz was a sundial. Egyptian sundials in this period were sometimes made in the form of miniature staircases so that the shadows moved up and down the steps.

20:12–19 Hezekiah had been a good and faithful king. But when Isaiah asked him what he had shown the messengers from Babylon, he replied, "They have seen all that is in my house." From the account in 2 Chronicles 32:24–31, it appears that Hezekiah's prosperity, success, and deliverance from sickness had made him proud. Rather than giving credit to God for all his blessings, he tried to impress the foreigners. When God helps us, we must not use his blessings to impress others. A testimony of victory can quickly degenerate into vanity and self-congratulations.

20:14 Babylon, a city that had rebelled against the Assyrian empire, was destroyed by Sennacherib in 689 B.C. This story probably occurred shortly before that date. When Sennacherib died in 681 B.C., his son, Esarhaddon, foolishly rebuilt the city of Babylon. Assyria, whose rulers at that time were weak, allowed Babylon plenty of opportunity to become strong. As the Assyrian army marched off to conquer and oppress faraway lands, the city of Babylon grew and expanded into a small nation. After some years, Babylon was strong enough to rebel again. It eventually crushed Assyria (612 B.C.) and became the next world power.

20:19 Hezekiah was saying that it was good that these terrible events foretold by Isaiah wouldn't happen during his lifetime. Hezekiah's statement seems selfish, shortsighted, and proud. However, he knew that his nation would be punished for its sins, so he may have been acknowledging and thanking God for choosing not to destroy Judah during his lifetime.

20:20 The pool and the conduit refer to a 1,777-foot tunnel built from the Gihon spring to the Pool of Siloam (see 2 Chronicles 32:30). It was from a water source outside the wall of Jerusalem to a secure reservoir inside the city. This was done so the Assyrian army would not cut off the city's water supply.

and the conduit and brought water into the city, are they not written in the Book of the
Chronicles of the Kings of Judah?
21 So Hezekiah slept with his fathers, and Manasseh his son became king in his place.

Manasseh Succeeds Hezekiah

21 Manasseh was twelve years old when he became king, and he reigned fifty-five
years in Jerusalem; and his mother's name was Hephzibah.
2 He did evil in the sight of the LORD, according to the abominations of the nations
whom the LORD dispossessed before the sons of Israel.
3 For he rebuilt the high places which Hezekiah his father had destroyed; and he erected altars for Baal and made an Asherah, as Ahab king of Israel had done, and worshiped
all the host of heaven and served them.
4 He built altars in the house of the LORD, of which the LORD had said, "In Jerusalem I will put My name."
5 For he built altars for all the host of heaven in the two courts of the house of the
LORD.
6 He made his son pass through the fire, practiced witchcraft and used divination, and
dealt with mediums and spiritists. He did much evil in the sight of the LORD provoking
Him to anger.
7 Then he set the carved image of Asherah that he had made, in the house of which
the LORD said to David and to his son Solomon, "In this house and in Jerusalem, which
I have chosen from all the tribes of Israel, I will put My name forever.
8 "And I will not make the feet of Israel wander anymore from the land which I gave
their fathers, if only they will observe to do according to all that I have commanded them,
and according to all the law that My servant Moses commanded them."
9 But they did not listen, and Manasseh seduced them to do evil more than the nations whom the LORD destroyed before the sons of Israel.

The King's Idolatries Rebuked

10 Now the LORD spoke through His servants the prophets, saying,
11 "Because Manasseh king of Judah has done these abominations, having done wickedly more than all the Amorites did who *were* before him, and has also made Judah sin
with his idols;
12 therefore thus says the LORD, the God of Israel, 'Behold, I am bringing *such* calamity on Jerusalem and Judah, that whoever hears of it, both his ears will tingle.
13 'I will stretch over Jerusalem the line of Samaria and the plummet of the house of
Ahab, and I will wipe Jerusalem as one wipes a dish, wiping it and turning it upside down.
14 'I will abandon the remnant of My inheritance and deliver them into the hand of
their enemies, and they will become as plunder and spoil to all their enemies;
15 because they have done evil in My sight, and have been provoking Me to anger since
the day their fathers came from Egypt, even to this day.' "
16 Moreover, Manasseh shed very much innocent blood until he had filled Jerusalem
from one end to another; besides his sin with which he made Judah sin, in doing evil in
the sight of the LORD.

20:21 2 Chr 32:33
21:1 2 Chr 33:1-9
21:2 Jer 15:4; 2 Kin 16:3
21:3 2 Kin 18:4; 1 Kin 16:31-33; Deut 17:2-5; 2 Kin 17:16; 23:5
21:4 2 Kin 16:10-16; 2 Sam 7:13; 1 Kin 8:29
21:5 2 Kin 23:4, 5; 1 Kin 7:12; 2 Kin 23:12
21:6 Lev 18:21; 2 Kin 16:3; 17:17; Lev 19:26, 31; Deut 18:10-14
21:7 Deut 16:21; 2 Kin 23:6; 1 Kin 8:29; 9:3; 2 Chr 7:12, 16
21:8 2 Sam 7:10; 2 Kin 18:11, 12
21:9 Prov 29:12
21:11 2 Kin 21:2; 24:3, 4; Gen 15:16; 1 Kin 21:26; 2 Kin 21:16; 2 Kin 21:21
21:12 1 Sam 3:11; Jer 19:3
21:13 Is 34:11; Amos 7:7, 8
21:16 2 Kin 24:4; 2 Kin 21:11

21:1ff Manasseh followed the example of his grandfather Ahaz more than that of his father. He adopted the wicked practices of the Babylonians and Canaanites, including sacrificing his own son (21:6). He did not listen to the words of God's prophets, but willfully led his people into sin. (See his Profile in 2 Chronicles 34 for more information about his life. The "high places" were shrines in the hills for worshiping idols.)

21:6 Manasseh was an evil king, and he angered God with his sin. Listed among his sins are occult practices—witchcraft and divination, and consulting mediums and spiritists. These acts were strictly forbidden by God (Leviticus 19:31; Deuteronomy 18:9–13) because they demonstrate a lack of faith in him, involve sinful actions, and open the door to demonic influences. Today, many books, television shows, and games emphasize fortune-telling, seances, and other occult practices. Don't let desire to know the future or the belief that superstition is harmless lead you into condoning occult practices. They are counterfeits of God's power and have at their root a system of beliefs totally opposed to God.

21:7 Asherah was a Canaanite mother-goddess, a mistress of Baal. Her images were made of wood. In Exodus 34:13 and Deuteronomy 12:3, the Israelites were expressly forbidden to associate with Asherah practices in any way.

21:13 The line and the plummet (plumb line) symbolize the judgment process. These measuring instruments used in construction measured Jerusalem, and the city was found lacking. God was saying that he would destroy Jerusalem as he had done Samaria and the house of Ahab.

21:16 Tradition says that during Manasseh's massive slaughter, Isaiah was sawed in two when trying to hide in a hollow log (see Hebrews 11:37–38). Other prophets may also have been killed at this time.

17 Now the rest of the acts of Manasseh and all that he did and his sin which he committed, are they not written in the Book of the Chronicles of the Kings of Judah?
21:17 2 Chr 33:11-19
18 And Manasseh slept with his fathers and was buried in the garden of his own house,
in the garden of Uzza, and Amon his son became king in his place.
21:18 2 Chr 33:20; 2 Kin 21:26

Amon Succeeds Manasseh

19 Amon was twenty-two years old when he became king, and he reigned two years in
Jerusalem; and his mother's name *was* Meshullemeth the daughter of Haruz of Jotbah.
21:19 2 Chr 33:21-23
20 He did evil in the sight of the LORD, as Manasseh his father had done.
21:20 2 Kin 21:2-6, 11, 16
21 For he walked in all the way that his father had walked, and served the idols that his
father had served and worshiped them.
22 So he forsook the LORD, the God of his fathers, and did not walk in the way of the
LORD.
21:22 2 Kin 22:17; 1 Chr 28:9
23 The servants of Amon conspired against him and killed the king in his own house.
21:23 2 Kin 12:20; 14:19
24 Then the people of the land killed all those who had conspired against King Amon,
and the people of the land made Josiah his son king in his place.
21:24 2 Kin 14:5
25 Now the rest of the acts of Amon which he did, are they not written in the Book of
the Chronicles of the Kings of Judah?
26 He was buried in his grave in the garden of Uzza, and Josiah his son became king in
his place.
21:26 2 Kin 21:18

Josiah Succeeds Amon

22 Josiah was eight years old when he became king, and he reigned thirty-one years
in Jerusalem; and his mother's name *was* Jedidah the daughter of Adaiah of
Bozkath.
22:1 2 Chr 34:1; Josh 15:39
2 He did right in the sight of the LORD and walked in all the way of his father David,
nor did he turn aside to the right or to the left.
22:2 Deut 5:32; Josh 1:7
3 Now in the eighteenth year of King Josiah, the king sent Shaphan, the son of Azaliah the son of Meshullam the scribe, to the house of the LORD saying,
22:3 2 Chr 34:8
4 "Go up to Hilkiah the high priest that he may count the money brought in to the
house of the LORD which the doorkeepers have gathered from the people.
22:4 2 Kin 12:4, 9, 10
5 "Let them deliver it into the hand of the workmen who have the oversight of the house
of the LORD, and let them give it to the workmen who are in the house of the LORD to
repair the damages of the house,
22:5 2 Kin 12:11-14
6 to the carpenters and the builders and the masons and for buying timber and hewn
stone to repair the house.
7 "Only no accounting shall be made with them for the money delivered into their hands,
for they deal faithfully."
22:7 2 Kin 12:15; 1 Cor 4:2

The Lost Book

8 Then Hilkiah the high priest said to Shaphan the scribe, "I have found the book of
the law in the house of the LORD." And Hilkiah gave the book to Shaphan who read it.
22:8 Deut 31:24-26; 2 Chr 34:14, 15
9 Shaphan the scribe came to the king and brought back word to the king and said,
"Your servants have emptied out the money that was found in the house, and have delivered it into the hand of the workmen who have the oversight of the house of the LORD."
10 Moreover, Shaphan the scribe told the king saying, "Hilkiah the priest has given
me a book." And Shaphan read it in the presence of the king.

22:1–2 In reading the Biblical lists of kings, it is rare to find one who obeyed God completely. Josiah was such a person, and he was only eight years old when he began to reign. For 18 years he reigned obediently; then, when he was 26, he began the reforms based on God's laws. Children are the future leaders of our churches and our world. A person's major work for God may have to wait until he is an adult, but no one is ever too young to take God seriously and obey him. Josiah's early years laid the base for his later task of reforming Judah.

22:4 The doorkeepers controlled who entered the temple and supervised the collection of the money.

22:8 This book may have been the entire Pentateuch (Genesis—Deuteronomy) or just the book of Deuteronomy. Because of the long line of evil kings, the record of God's laws had been lost. Josiah, who was about 26 years old at this time, wanted religious reform throughout the nation. When God's Word was found, drastic changes had to be made to bring the kingdom in line with God's commands. Today you have God's Word at your fingertips. How much change must you make in order to bring your life into line with God's Word?

22:11 Gen 37:34; Josh 7:6
22:12 2 Kin 25:22; Jer 26:24; 2 Chr 34:20
22:13 Deut 29:23-28; 31:17, 18

11 When the king heard the words of the book of the law, he tore his clothes.
12 Then the king commanded Hilkiah the priest, Ahikam the son of Shaphan, Achbor
the son of Micaiah, Shaphan the scribe, and Asaiah the king's servant saying,
13 "Go, inquire of the LORD for me and the people and all Judah concerning the words
of this book that has been found, for great is the wrath of the LORD that burns against
us, because our fathers have not listened to the words of this book, to do according to all
that is written concerning us."

Huldah Predicts

22:14 2 Chr 34:22; Zeph 1:10

14 So Hilkiah the priest, Ahikam, Achbor, Shaphan, and Asaiah went to Huldah the
prophetess, the wife of Shallum the son of Tikvah, the son of Harhas, keeper of the
wardrobe (now she lived in Jerusalem in the Second Quarter); and they spoke to her.
15 She said to them, "Thus says the LORD God of Israel, 'Tell the man who sent you
to me,

22:16 Deut 29:27; Dan 9:11-14
22:17 Deut 29:25, 26; 2 Kin 21:22
22:18 2 Chr 34:26
22:19 1 Sam 24:5; Ps 51:17; Ex 10:3; 1 Kin 21:29; Lev 26:31; Jer 26:6; 2 Kin 22:11
22:20 2 Kin 23:30

16 thus says the LORD, "Behold, I bring evil on this place and on its inhabitants, *even*
all the words of the book which the king of Judah has read.
17 "Because they have forsaken Me and have burned incense to other gods that they
might provoke Me to anger with all the work of their hands, therefore My wrath burns
against this place, and it shall not be quenched." '
18 "But to the king of Judah who sent you to inquire of the LORD thus shall you say to
him, 'Thus says the LORD God of Israel, "*Regarding* the words which you have heard,
19 because your heart was tender and you humbled yourself before the LORD when
you heard what I spoke against this place and against its inhabitants that they should
become a desolation and a curse, and you have torn your clothes and wept before Me, I
truly have heard you," declares the LORD.
20 "Therefore, behold, I will gather you to your fathers, and you will be gathered to your
grave in peace, and your eyes will not see all the evil which I will bring on this place." ' "
So they brought back word to the king.

Josiah's Covenant

23:1 2 Chr 34:29-32
23:2 Deut 31:10-13; 2 Kin 22:8
23:3 2 Kin 11:14, 17; Deut 13:4

23 Then the king sent, and they gathered to him all the elders of Judah and of Jerusalem.
2 The king went up to the house of the LORD and all the men of Judah and all the
inhabitants of Jerusalem with him, and the priests and the prophets and all the people,
both small and great; and he read in their hearing all the words of the book of the covenant which was found in the house of the LORD.
3 The king stood by the pillar and made a covenant before the LORD, to walk after
the LORD, and to keep His commandments and His testimonies and His statutes with
all *his* heart and all *his* soul, to carry out the words of this covenant that were written in
this book. And all the people entered into the covenant.

Reforms under Josiah

23:4 2 Kin 25:18; Jer 52:24; 2 Kin 21:3, 7; 2 Chr 33:3; 2 Kin 23:15

4 Then the king commanded Hilkiah the high priest and the priests of the second order
and the doorkeepers, to bring out of the temple of the LORD all the vessels that were
made for Baal, for [15]Asherah, and for all the host of heaven; and he burned them outside Jerusalem in the fields of the Kidron, and carried their ashes to Bethel.

15 I.e. a wooden symbol of a female deity, and so throughout the ch

---

22:11ff When Josiah heard the Law, he tore his clothes in grief. He immediately instituted reforms. With just one reading of God's Law, he changed the course of the nation. Today many people own Bibles, but few are affected by the truths found in God's Word. The Word of God should cause us, like Josiah, to take action immediately to reform our lives and bring them into harmony with God's will.

22:14 Huldah was a prophetess, as were Miriam (Exodus 15:20) and Deborah (Judges 4:4). God freely selects his servants to carry out his will—rich or poor, male or female, king or slave (Joel 2:28–30). Huldah was obviously highly regarded by the people of her time.

22:19 When Josiah realized how corrupt his nation had become, he tore his clothes and wept before God. Then God had mercy on him. Josiah used the customs of his day to show his repentance. When we repent today, we are unlikely to tear our clothing, but weeping, fasting, making restitution or apologies (if our sin has involved others) demonstrate our sincerity when we repent. The hardest part of repentance is changing the attitudes that originally produced the sinful behavior.

23:1–2 For more about the importance and operation of the temple, see 1 Kings 5—8 and 2 Chronicles 2—7.

23:4–8 When Josiah realized the terrible state of Judah's religious life, he did something about it. It is not enough to say we believe what is right; we must respond with action, doing what faith requires. This is what James was emphasizing when he wrote, "faith without works is useless" (James 2:20). This means acting differently at home, school, work, and church. Simply talking about obedience is not enough.

5 He did away with the idolatrous priests whom the kings of Judah had appointed to
burn incense in the high places in the cities of Judah and in the surrounding area of Jerusalem, also those who burned incense to Baal, to the sun and to the moon and to the
constellations and to all the host of heaven.
6 He brought out the Asherah from the house of the LORD outside Jerusalem to the
brook Kidron, and burned it at the brook Kidron, and ground *it* to dust, and threw its
dust on the graves of the common people.
7 He also broke down the houses of the *male* cult prostitutes which *were* in the house
of the LORD, where the women were weaving hangings for the Asherah.
8 Then he brought all the priests from the cities of Judah, and defiled the high places
where the priests had burned incense, from Geba to Beersheba; and he broke down the
high places of the gates which *were* at the entrance of the gate of Joshua the governor of
the city, which *were* on one's left at the city gate.
9 Nevertheless the priests of the high places did not go up to the altar of the LORD in
Jerusalem, but they ate unleavened bread among their brothers.
10 He also defiled [16]Topheth, which is in the valley of the son of Hinnom, that no man
might make his son or his daughter pass through the fire for Molech.
11 He did away with the horses which the kings of Judah had given to the sun, at the
entrance of the house of the LORD, by the chamber of Nathan-melech the official, which
was in the precincts; and he burned the chariots of the sun with fire.
12 The altars which *were* on the roof, the upper chamber of Ahaz, which the kings of
Judah had made, and the altars which Manasseh had made in the two courts of the house
of the LORD, the king broke down; and he [17]smashed them there and threw their dust
into the brook Kidron.
13 The high places which *were* before Jerusalem, which *were* on the right of the mount
of destruction which Solomon the king of Israel had built for Ashtoreth the abomination of the Sidonians, and for Chemosh the abomination of Moab, and for Milcom the
abomination of the sons of Ammon, the king defiled.
14 He broke in pieces the *sacred* pillars and cut down the Asherim and filled their places
with human bones.
15 Furthermore, the altar that *was* at Bethel *and* the high place which Jeroboam the
son of Nebat, who made Israel sin, had made, even that altar and the high place he broke
down. Then he demolished its stones, ground them to dust, and burned the Asherah.
16 Now when Josiah turned, he saw the graves that *were* there on the mountain, and
he sent and took the bones from the graves and burned *them* on the altar and defiled it
according to the word of the LORD which the man of God proclaimed, who proclaimed
these things.
17 Then he said, "What is this monument that I see?" And the men of the city told
him, "It is the grave of the man of God who came from Judah and proclaimed these things
which you have done against the altar of Bethel."
18 He said, "Let him alone; let no one disturb his bones." So they left his bones undisturbed with the bones of the prophet who came from Samaria.
19 Josiah also removed all the houses of the high places which *were* in the cities of
Samaria, which the kings of Israel had made provoking the LORD; and he did to them
just as he had done in Bethel.
20 All the priests of the high places who *were* there he slaughtered on the altars and
burned human bones on them; then he returned to Jerusalem.

23:5 2 Kin 21:3
23:6 2 Kin 23:15; 2 Chr 34:4
23:7 1 Kin 14:24; 15:12; Ex 35:25, 26; Ezek 16:16
23:8 Josh 21:17; 1 Kin 15:22
23:9 Ezek 44:10-14
23:10 Is 30:33; Jer 7:31, 32; 19:4-6; Lev 18:21; 1 Kin 11:7
23:11 Deut 4:19; Job 31:26; Ezek 8:16
23:12 Jer 19:13; Zeph 1:5; 2 Kin 21:5; 2 Chr 33:5; 2 Kin 23:4, 6
23:13 1 Kin 11:7; 1 Kin 11:5; Num 21:29
23:14 Deut 7:5, 25; 2 Kin 23:16
23:15 1 Kin 13:1; 1 Kin 12:28-33; 2 Kin 23:6
23:16 1 Kin 13:2
23:17 1 Kin 13:1, 30, 31
23:18 1 Kin 13:11, 31
23:19 2 Chr 34:6, 7
23:20 2 Kin 10:25; 11:18

16 I.e. place of burning **17** Or *ran from there*

23:6 This shameful Asherah (an idol) had been set up in God's temple by the evil King Manasseh (21:7). Asherah is most often identified as a sea goddess and the mistress of Baal. She was a chief goddess of the Canaanites. Her worship glorified sex and war and was accompanied by male prostitution.

23:11 These horses were used in processions honoring the sun.

23:13 The Mount of Olives is here called the mount of destruction because it had become a favorite spot to build pagan shrines. Solomon built a pagan shrine, and other kings built places of idol worship there. But God-fearing kings such as Hezekiah and Josiah destroyed these pagan worship centers. In New Testament times, Jesus often sat on the Mount of Olives and taught his disciples about serving only God (Matthew 24:3). For more background on Ashtoreth, Chemosh, and Milcom, see the note on 1 Kings 11:5–8.

23:16–18 The prophecies mentioned in this passage appear in 1 Kings 13:20–32.

Passover Reinstituted

21 Then the king commanded all the people saying, "Celebrate the Passover to the
LORD your God as it is written in this book of the covenant."
22 Surely such a Passover had not been celebrated from the days of the judges who
judged Israel, nor in all the days of the kings of Israel and of the kings of Judah.
23 But in the eighteenth year of King Josiah, this Passover was observed to the LORD
in Jerusalem.
24 Moreover, Josiah removed the mediums and the spiritists and the teraphim and the
idols and all the abominations that were seen in the land of Judah and in Jerusalem, that
he might confirm the words of the law which were written in the book that Hilkiah the
priest found in the house of the LORD.
25 Before him there was no king like him who turned to the LORD with all his heart
and with all his soul and with all his might, according to all the law of Moses; nor did any
like him arise after him.
26 However, the LORD did not turn from the fierceness of His great wrath with which
His anger burned against Judah, because of all the provocations with which Manasseh
had provoked Him.
27 The LORD said, "I will remove Judah also from My sight, as I have removed Israel.
And I will cast off Jerusalem, this city which I have chosen, and the temple of which I
said, 'My name shall be there.' "

Jehoahaz Succeeds Josiah

28 Now the rest of the acts of Josiah and all that he did, are they not written in the
Book of the Chronicles of the Kings of Judah?
29 In his days Pharaoh Neco king of Egypt went up to the king of Assyria to the river
Euphrates. And King Josiah went to meet him, and when *Pharaoh Neco* saw him he killed
him at Megiddo.
30 His servants drove his body in a chariot from Megiddo, and brought him to Jerusalem and buried him in his own tomb. Then the people of the land took Jehoahaz the son
of Josiah and anointed him and made him king in place of his father.
31 Jehoahaz was twenty-three years old when he became king, and he reigned three
months in Jerusalem; and his mother's name was Hamutal the daughter of Jeremiah of
Libnah.
32 He did evil in the sight of the LORD, according to all that his fathers had done.
33 Pharaoh Neco imprisoned him at Riblah in the land of Hamath, that he might not
reign in Jerusalem; and he imposed on the land a fine of one hundred talents of silver
and a talent of gold.

23:21 2 Chr 35:1-17; Num 9:2-4; Deut 16:2-8

23:22 2 Chr 35:18, 19

23:24 Lev 19:31; 2 Kin 21:6; Gen 31:19; 2 Kin 21:11, 21; Deut 18:10-22; 2 Kin 22:8

23:25 2 Kin 18:5

23:26 2 Kin 21:11-13; Jer 15:4

23:27 2 Kin 18:11; 2 Kin 21:13, 14

23:29 2 Chr 35:20-24; Jer 46:2; Judg 5:19

23:30 2 Kin 9:28; 2 Chr 36:1-4

23:31 1 Chr 3:15; Jer 22:11; 2 Kin 24:18

23:32 2 Kin 21:2-7

23:33 2 Kin 23:29; 2 Kin 25:6; 1 Kin 8:65

23:21–23 When Josiah rediscovered the Passover in the book of the covenant, he ordered everyone to observe the ceremonies exactly as prescribed. This Passover celebration was to have been a yearly holiday celebrated in remembrance of the entire nation's deliverance from slavery in Egypt (Exodus 12), but it had not been kept for many years. As a result, "surely such a Passover had not been celebrated from the days of the judges who judged Israel, nor in all the days of the kings of Israel and of the kings of Judah." It is a common misconception that God is against celebration, wanting to take all the fun out of life. In reality, God wants to give us life in its fullness (John 10:10), and those who love him have the most to celebrate.

23:25 Josiah is remembered as Judah's most obedient king. His obedience followed this pattern: (1) He recognized sin; (2) he eliminated sinful practices; (3) he attacked the causes of sin. This approach for dealing with sin is still effective today. Not only must we remove sinful actions, we must also eliminate causes for sin—those situations, relationships, routines, and patterns of life that lead us to the door of temptation.

23:25 Both Josiah and Hezekiah (18:5) are praised for their reverence toward God. Hezekiah was said to be greatest in trusting God (faith), while Josiah is said to be greatest in following the law of Moses (obedience). May we follow their example through our trust in God and our obedient actions.

23:29 Pharaoh Neco of Egypt was marching through Judah to Assyria. Egypt and Assyria had formed an alliance to battle Babylon, which was threatening to become the dominant world power. Josiah may have thought that both nations would turn on him after the battle with Babylon, so he tried to stop Egypt's army from marching through his land. But Josiah was killed, his army was defeated, and the nation of Judah became a vassal of Egypt (609 B.C.). A more detailed account of this story is found in 2 Chronicles 35:20–25.

23:31–34 The people appointed Jehoahaz, one of Josiah's sons, to be Judah's next king. But Neco was not happy with their choice, and he exiled Jehoahaz to Egypt, where he died. Neco then appointed Eliakim, another of Josiah's sons, king of Judah, changing his name to Jehoiakim. Jehoiakim was little more than a puppet ruler. In 605 B.C., Egypt was defeated by Babylon. Judah then became a vassal of Babylon (24:1).

Jehoiakim Made King by Pharaoh

34 Pharaoh Neco made Eliakim the son of Josiah king in the place of Josiah his father,
and changed his name to Jehoiakim. But he took Jehoahaz away and brought *him* to
Egypt, and he died there.
35 So Jehoiakim gave the silver and gold to Pharaoh, but he taxed the land in order to
give the money at the command of Pharaoh. He exacted the silver and gold from the
people of the land, each according to his valuation, to give it to Pharaoh Neco.

23:34 1 Chr 3:15; 2 Kin 24:17; 2 Chr 36:4; Jer 22:11, 12; Ezek 19:3, 4

23:35 2 Kin 23:33

2. Judah is exiled to Babylon

36 Jehoiakim was twenty-five years old when he became king, and he reigned eleven
years in Jerusalem; and his mother's name *was* Zebidah the daughter of Pedaiah of
Rumah.
37 He did evil in the sight of the LORD, according to all that his fathers had done.

23:36 2 Chr 36:5; Jer 22:18, 19; 26:1

23:37 2 Kin 23:32

Babylon Controls Jehoiakim

24 In his days Nebuchadnezzar king of Babylon came up, and Jehoiakim became his
servant *for* three years; then he turned and rebelled against him.
2 The LORD sent against him bands of Chaldeans, bands of Arameans, bands of
Moabites, and bands of Ammonites. So He sent them against Judah to destroy it, according to the word of the LORD which He had spoken through His servants the prophets.
3 Surely at the command of the LORD it came upon Judah, to remove *them* from His
sight because of the sins of Manasseh, according to all that he had done,
4 and also for the innocent blood which he shed, for he filled Jerusalem with innocent blood; and the LORD would not forgive.
5 Now the rest of the acts of Jehoiakim and all that he did, are they not written in the
Book of the Chronicles of the Kings of Judah?

24:1 2 Chr 36:6; Jer 25:1; Dan 1:1, 2

24:2 Jer 35:11f; 2 Kin 6:23; 2 Kin 13:20; 2 Kin 23:27

24:3 2 Kin 18:25; 2 Kin 23:26

24:4 2 Kin 21:16

Jehoiachin Reigns

6 So Jehoiakim slept with his fathers, and Jehoiachin his son became king in his place.
7 The king of Egypt did not come out of his land again, for the king of Babylon had
taken all that belonged to the king of Egypt from the brook of Egypt to the river Euphrates.
8 Jehoiachin was eighteen years old when he became king, and he reigned three months
in Jerusalem; and his mother's name *was* Nehushta the daughter of Elnathan of Jerusalem.
9 He did evil in the sight of the LORD, according to all that his father had done.

24:6 Jer 22:18, 19

24:7 Jer 37:5-7; Jer 46:2; Gen 15:18

24:8 1 Chr 3:16; 2 Chr 36:9

24:9 2 Kin 21:2-7

23:36–37 Josiah followed God, but Jehoiakim, his son, was evil. He killed the prophet Uriah (Jeremiah 26:20–23) and was dishonest, greedy, and unjust with the people (Jeremiah 22:13–19). Jehoiakim also rebelled against Babylon, switching his allegiance to Egypt. This proved to be a crucial mistake. Nebuchadnezzar crushed Jehoiakim's rebellion and took him to Babylon (2 Chronicles 36:6), but he was eventually allowed to return to Jerusalem, where he died. The Bible does not record the cause of Jehoiakim's death.

23:37 Many good kings had children who did not turn out to follow God. Perhaps it was because of neglect or preoccupation with political and military affairs or because these kings delegated the religious education to others. No doubt many of the children simply rebelled at the way they were raised. Being a strong believer as a parent doesn't guarantee that your children will pick up your beliefs. Children must be taught about faith, and parents dare not leave that task for others to do. Make sure you practice, explain, and teach what you preach.

24:1 Babylon became the new world power after overthrowing Assyria in 612 B.C. and defeating Egypt at the battle of Carchemish in 605 B.C. After defeating Egypt, the Babylonians invaded Judah and brought it under their control. This was the first of three Babylonian invasions of Judah over the next 20 years. The other two invasions occurred in 597 and 586 B.C. With each invasion, captives were taken back to Babylon. Daniel, who wrote the book of Daniel, was one of the captives taken during this first invasion (605 B.C.; Daniel 1:1–6).

24:1 For more information on Nebuchadnezzar, see his Profile in Daniel 3.

24:1–4 Nebuchadnezzar took control as king of Babylon in 605 B.C. Earlier that year Nebuchadnezzar had defeated the Egyptians led by Pharaoh Neco at Carchemish. Thus Babylon took control of all Egypt's vassals (including Judah). Nebuchadnezzar invaded the land later in order to establish his rule by force.

Deportation to Babylon

10 At that time the servants of Nebuchadnezzar king of Babylon went up to Jerusalem, and the city came under siege.
11 And Nebuchadnezzar the king of Babylon came to the city, while his servants were
besieging it.
12 Jehoiachin the king of Judah went out to the king of Babylon, he and his mother
and his servants and his captains and his officials. So the king of Babylon took him captive in the eighth year of his reign.
13 He carried out from there all the treasures of the house of the LORD, and the treasures of the king's house, and cut in pieces all the vessels of gold which Solomon king of
Israel had made in the temple of the LORD, just as the LORD had said.

24:12 Jer 22:24-30; 24:1; 29:1, 2; 2 Chr 36:10

24:13 2 Kin 20:17; Is 39:6; 2 Kin 25:13-15; 1 Kin 7:48-50

JOSIAH

Josiah never knew his great-grandfather Hezekiah, but they were alike in many ways. Both had close, personal relationships with God. Both were passionate reformers, making valiant efforts to lead their people back to God. Both were bright flashes of obedience to God among kings with darkened consciences, who seemed bent on outdoing each other in disobedience and evil.

Although Josiah's father and grandfather were exceptionally wicked, his life is an example of God's willingness to provide ongoing guidance to those who set out to be obedient. At a young age, Josiah already understood that there was spiritual sickness in his land. Idols were sprouting in the countryside faster than crops. In a sense, Josiah began his search for God by destroying and cleaning up whatever he recognized as not belonging to the worship of the true God. In the process, God's Word was rediscovered. The king's intentions and the power of God's written revelation were brought together.

As the book of God's law was read to Josiah, he was shocked, frightened, and humbled. He realized what a great gap existed between his efforts to lead his people to God and God's expectations for his chosen nation. He was overwhelmed by God's holiness and immediately tried to expose his people to that holiness. The people did respond, but the Bible makes it clear that their renewed worship of God was much more out of respect for Josiah than out of personal understanding of their own guilt before God.

How would you describe your relationship with God? Are your feeble efforts at holiness based mostly on a desire to "go along" with a well-liked leader or popular opinion? Or are you, like Josiah, deeply humbled by God's Word, realizing that great gap between your life and the kind of life God expects, realizing your deep need to be cleansed and renewed by him? Humble obedience pleases God. Good intentions, even reforms, are not enough. You must allow God's Word to truly humble you and change your life.

Strengths and accomplishments:
- Was king of Judah
- Sought after God and was open to him
- Was a reformer like his great-grandfather Hezekiah
- Cleaned out the temple and revived obedience to God's law

Weakness and mistake:
- Became involved in a military conflict that he had been warned against

Lessons from his life:
- God consistently responds to those with repentant and humble hearts
- Even sweeping outward reforms are of little lasting value if there are no changes in people's lives

Vital statistics:
- Where: Jerusalem
- Occupation: 16th king of Judah, the southern kingdom
- Relatives: Father: Amon. Mother: Jedidah. Son: Jehoahaz
- Contemporaries: Jeremiah, Huldah, Hilkiah, Zephaniah

Key verse:
"Before him there was no king like him who turned to the LORD with all his heart and with all his soul and with all his might, according to all the law of Moses" (2 Kings 23:25).

Josiah's story is told in 2 Kings 21:24—23:30; 2 Chronicles 33:25—35:26. He is also mentioned in Jeremiah 1:1–3; 22:11, 18.

24:10 Babylonian troops were already on the march to crush Jehoiakim's rebellion when he died. After Jehoiakim's death, his son Jehoiachin became king of Judah, only to face the mightiest army on earth just weeks after he was crowned (597 B.C.). During this second of three invasions, the Babylonians looted the temple and took most of the leaders captive, including the king. Then Nebuchadnezzar placed Zedekiah, another son of Josiah, on the throne. The Jews, however, didn't recognize him as their true king as long as Jehoiachin was still alive, even though he was a captive in Babylon.

14 Then he led away into exile all Jerusalem and all the captains and all the mighty men of valor, ten thousand captives, and all the craftsmen and the smiths. None remained except the poorest people of the land.
15 So he led Jehoiachin away into exile to Babylon; also the king's mother and the king's wives and his officials and the leading men of the land, he led away into exile from Jerusalem to Babylon.
16 All the men of valor, seven thousand, and the craftsmen and the smiths, one thousand, all strong and fit for war, and these the king of Babylon brought into exile to Babylon.

24:14 Jer 24:1; 2 Kin 24:16; Jer 52:28; Jer 24:1; 29:2; 2 Kin 25:12

24:15 2 Chr 36:10; Jer 22:24-28; Ezek 17:12

24:16 2 Kin 24:14

Zedekiah Made King

17 Then the king of Babylon made his uncle Mattaniah king in his place, and changed his name to Zedekiah.
18 Zedekiah was twenty-one years old when he became king, and he reigned eleven years in Jerusalem; and his mother's name was Hamutal the daughter of Jeremiah of Libnah.
19 He did evil in the sight of the LORD, according to all that Jehoiakim had done.
20 For through the anger of the LORD *this* came about in Jerusalem and Judah until He cast them out from His presence. And Zedekiah rebelled against the king of Babylon.

24:17 2 Chr 36:10-13; Jer 37:1

24:18 Jer 27:1; 28:1; 52:1; 2 Kin 23:31

24:19 2 Kin 23:37

24:20 Deut 4:24; 29:27; 2 Kin 23:26; 2 Chr 36:13; Ezek 17:15

Nebuchadnezzar Besieges Jerusalem

25 Now in the ninth year of his reign, on the tenth day of the tenth month, Nebuchadnezzar king of Babylon came, he and all his army, against Jerusalem, camped against it and built a siege wall all around it.
2 So the city was under siege until the eleventh year of King Zedekiah.
3 On the ninth day of the *fourth* month the famine was so severe in the city that there was no food for the people of the land.
4 Then the city was broken into, and all the men of war *fled* by night by way of the gate between the two walls beside the king's garden, though the Chaldeans were all around the city. And they went by way of the Arabah.
5 But the army of the Chaldeans pursued the king and overtook him in the plains of Jericho and all his army was scattered from him.
6 Then they captured the king and brought him to the king of Babylon at Riblah, and he passed sentence on him.
7 They slaughtered the sons of Zedekiah before his eyes, then put out the eyes of Zedekiah and bound him with bronze fetters and brought him to Babylon.

25:1 2 Chr 36:17-20; Jer 39:1-7; Jer 21:2; 34:1, 2; Ezek 24:2; Ezek 21:22

25:3 2 Kin 6:24, 25; Lam 4:9, 10

25:4 Ezek 33:21; Neh 3:15

25:6 Jer 34:21, 22; Jer 32:4; 2 Kin 23:33

25:7 Jer 39:6, 7; Ezek 12:13

Jerusalem Burned and Plundered

8 Now on the seventh day of the fifth month, which was the nineteenth year of King Nebuchadnezzar, king of Babylon, Nebuzaradan the captain of the guard, a servant of the king of Babylon, came to Jerusalem.

25:8 Jer 52:12; Jer 39:8-12

24:14 The Babylonian policy for taking captives was different from that of the Assyrians who moved most of the people out and resettled the land with foreigners (see the note on 17:24). The Babylonians took only the strong and skilled, leaving the poor and weak to rule the land, thus elevating them to positions of authority and winning their loyalty. The leaders were taken to Babylonian cities where they were permitted to live together, find jobs, and become an important part of the society. This policy kept the Jews united and faithful to God throughout the captivity and made it possible for their return in the days of Zerubbabel and Ezra as recorded in the book of Ezra.

25:1 Judah was invaded by the Babylonians three times (24:1; 24:10; 25:1), just as Israel was invaded by the Assyrians three times. Once again, God demonstrated his mercy in the face of deserved judgment by giving the people repeated opportunities to repent.

JUDAH EXILED Evil permeated Judah, and God's anger flared against his rebellious people. Babylon conquered Assyria and became the new world power. The Babylonian army marched into Jerusalem, burned the temple, tore down the city's massive walls, and carried off the people into captivity.

25:9 1 Kin 9:8; 2 Chr 36:19; Ps 74:3-7; Amos 2:5

9 He burned the house of the LORD, the king's house, and all the houses of Jerusalem; even every great house he burned with fire.

25:10 2 Kin 14:13; Neh 1:3

10 So all the army of the Chaldeans who *were with* the captain of the guard broke down
the walls around Jerusalem.

25:11 2 Chr 36:20

11 Then the rest of the people who were left in the city and the deserters who had
deserted to the king of Babylon and the rest of the people, Nebuzaradan the captain of
the guard carried away into exile.

25:12 2 Kin 24:14; Jer 40:7

12 But the captain of the guard left some of the poorest of the land to be vinedressers
and plowmen.

25:13 1 Kin 7:15-22; 2 Kin 20:17; 2 Chr 3:15-17; 36:18; 1 Kin 7:23-26; 2 Chr 4:2-4

13 Now the bronze pillars which were in the house of the LORD, and the stands and
the bronze sea which were in the house of the LORD, the Chaldeans broke in pieces and
carried the bronze to Babylon.

25:14 Ex 27:3; 1 Kin 7:47-50; 2 Chr 4:16

14 They took away the pots, the shovels, the snuffers, the spoons, and all the bronze
vessels which were used in *temple* service.
15 The captain of the guard also took away the firepans and the basins, what was fine
gold and what was fine silver.

25:16 1 Kin 7:47

16 The two pillars, the one sea, and the stands which Solomon had made for the house
of the LORD—the bronze of all these vessels was beyond weight.

25:17 1 Kin 7:15-22

17 The height of the one pillar was eighteen cubits, and a bronze capital was on it; the
height of the capital was three cubits, with a network and pomegranates on the capital
all around, all of bronze. And the second pillar was like these with network.

25:18 1 Chr 6:14; Ezra 7:1; Jer 21:1; 29:25, 29

18 Then the captain of the guard took Seraiah the chief priest and Zephaniah the second priest, with the three officers of the temple.

25:19 Esth 1:14

19 From the city he took one official who was overseer of the men of war, and five of
the king's advisers who were found in the city; and the scribe of the captain of the army
who mustered the people of the land; and sixty men of the people of the land who were
found in the city.

25:20 2 Kin 23:33

20 Nebuzaradan the captain of the guard took them and brought them to the king of
Babylon at Riblah.

25:21 Deut 28:64; 2 Kin 23:27

21 Then the king of Babylon struck them down and put them to death at Riblah in the
land of Hamath. So Judah was led away into exile from its land.

Gedaliah Made Governor

25:22 Jer 39:14; 40:7-9

22 Now *as for* the people who were left in the land of Judah, whom Nebuchadnezzar
king of Babylon had left, he appointed Gedaliah the son of Ahikam, the son of Shaphan
over them.

25:23 Jer 40:7-9; Josh 18:26

23 When all the captains of the forces, they and *their* men, heard that the king of
Babylon had appointed Gedaliah *governor,* they came to Gedaliah to Mizpah, namely,
Ishmael the son of Nethaniah, and Johanan the son of Kareah, and Seraiah the son
of Tanhumeth the Netophathite, and Jaazaniah the son of the Maacathite, they and
their men.
24 Gedaliah swore to them and their men and said to them, "Do not be afraid of the
servants of the Chaldeans; live in the land and serve the king of Babylon, and it will be
well with you."

25:25 Jer 41:1, 2

25 But it came about in the seventh month, that Ishmael the son of Nethaniah, the son
of Elishama, of the royal family, came with ten men and struck Gedaliah down so that
he died along with the Jews and the Chaldeans who were with him at Mizpah.

25:13 The bronze sea was used to contain the huge reservoir of water for ritual cleansing for the priests. The bronze in the sea, the pillars, and the movable stands were so valuable that it was broken up and carried off to Babylon.

25:21 Judah, like Israel, was unfaithful to God. So God, as he had warned, allowed Judah to be destroyed and taken away (Deuteronomy 28). The book of Lamentations records the prophet Jeremiah's sorrow at seeing Jerusalem destroyed.

25:22 In place of the king (Zedekiah) who was deported to Babylon, Nebuchadnezzar appointed a governor (Gedaliah) who would faithfully administer the Babylonian policies.

25:22–30 This story shows that Israel's last hope of gaining back its land was gone—even the captains (now guerrilla rebels) had fled. Judah's earthly kingdom was absolutely demolished. But through prophets like Ezekiel and Daniel, who were also captives, God was able to keep his spiritual kingdom alive in the hearts of many of the exiles.

26 Then all the people, both small and great, and the captains of the forces arose and went to Egypt; for they were afraid of the Chaldeans.
27 Now it came about in the thirty-seventh year of the exile of Jehoiachin king of Ju-
dah, in the twelfth month, on the twenty-seventh *day* of the month, that Evil-merodach
king of Babylon, in the year that he became king, released Jehoiachin king of Judah from
prison;
28 and he spoke kindly to him and set his throne above the throne of the kings who
were with him in Babylon.
29 Jehoiachin changed his prison clothes and had his meals in the king's presence regularly all the days of his life;
30 and for his allowance, a regular allowance was given him by the king, a portion for
each day, all the days of his life.

25:26 Jer 43:4-7
25:27 Jer 52:31-34; 2 Kin 24:12, 15; Gen 40:13, 20
25:28 Dan 2:37; 5:18, 19
25:29 2 Sam 9:7
25:30 Neh 11:23; 12:47

KINGS AND THEIR ENEMIES (735 B.C. – 586 B.C.)

722
Captivity in Assyria

ISRAEL

JUDAH

686

586

735
AHAZ
Harassed by Pekah (Israel), paid Assyria for protection against Rezin (Aram), also harassed by Edom and Philistia
2 Kgs 15:38—16:20
2 Chr 27:9—28:27

715
HEZEKIAH
Miraculously delivered from Sennacherib's (Assyria) attack, conquered Gaza in Philistia
2 Kgs 16:20; 18:1—20:21
2 Chr 28:27—32:33
Co–regency 697–686

697
MANASSEH
Taken captive by Assyria, imprisoned in Babylon and later released
2 Kgs 20:21—21:18
2 Chr 32:33—33:20

642
AMON
2 Kgs 21:18–26
2 Chr 33:20–25

640
JOSIAH
Died in battle against Neco (Egypt)
2 Kgs 21:26—23:30
2 Chr 33:25—35:27

609
JEHOAHAZ (JOAHAZ)
Neco (Egypt)
2 Kgs 23:30–34
2 Chr 36:1–4

609
JEHOIAKIM
2 Kgs 23:34—24:6
2 Chr 36:4–8

598
JEHOIACHIN
Rebelled against Babylon and was taken captive
2 Kgs 24:6–16; 25:27–30
2 Chr 36:8–10

597
ZEDEKIAH
Rebelled, completely conquered by Babylon
2 Kgs 24:17—25:21
2 Chr 36:10–21

All dates are B.C.
Solid section of the timeline indicates co-regency.
For all the kings of Israel and Judah, see the chart at the end of 1 Kings.

25:27 Evil-merodach, the son of Nebuchadnezzar, became king of the Babylonian empire in 562 B.C., 24 years after the beginning of the general captivity and 37 years after Jehoiachin was removed from Jerusalem. The new king treated Jehoiachin with kindness, even allowing him to eat at his table (25:29). Evil-merodach was later killed in a plot by his brother-in-law, Nergal-sharezer, who succeeded him to the throne.

25:30 The book of 2 Kings opens with Elijah being carried to heaven—the destination awaiting those who follow God. But the book ends with the people of Judah being carried off to foreign lands as humiliated slaves—the result of failing to follow God.

Second Kings is an illustration of what happens when we make anything more important than God, when we make ruinous alliances, when our consciences become desensitized to right and wrong, and when we are no longer able to discern God's purpose for our lives. We may fail, like the people of Judah and Israel, but God's promises do not. He is always there to help us straighten out our lives and start over. And that is just what would happen in the book of Ezra. When the people acknowledged their sins, God was ready and willing to help them return to their land and start again.

KEY PLACES IN 1 CHRONICLES

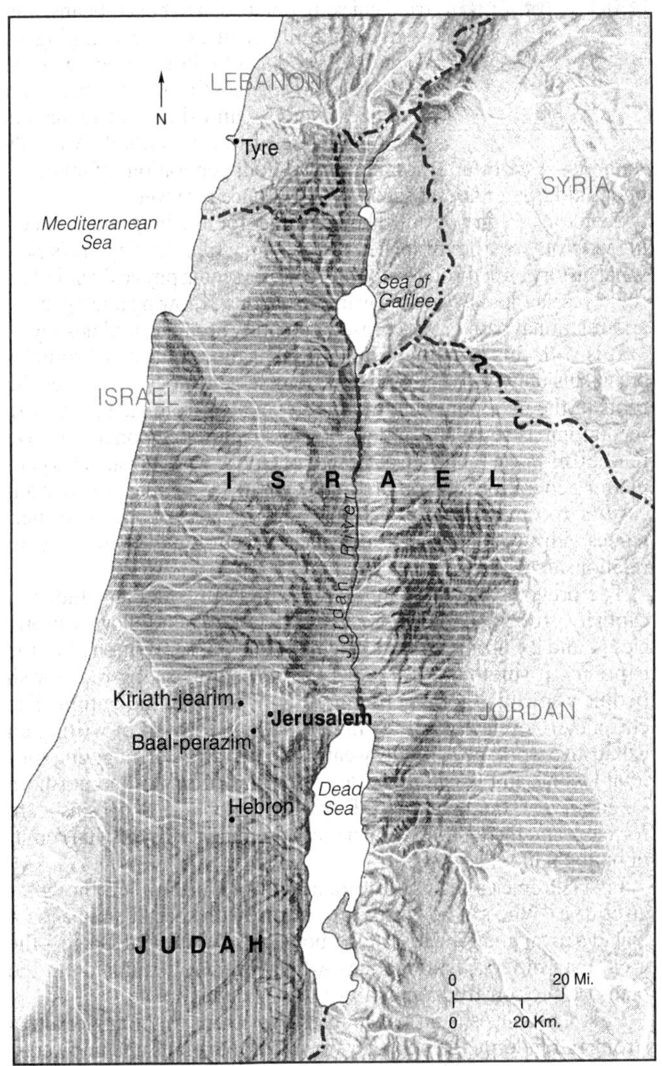

The broken lines (—·—·) indicate modern boundaries.

1 Hebron Although David had been anointed king years earlier, his reign began when the leaders of Israel accepted him as king at Hebron (11:1–3).

2 Jerusalem David set out to complete the conquest of the land begun by Joshua. He attacked Jerusalem, captured it, and made it his capital (11:4—12:40).

3 Kiriath-jearim The ark of the covenant, which had been captured by the Philistines in battle and returned (1 Samuel 4—6), was in safekeeping in Kiriath-jearim. David summoned all Israel to this city to join in bringing the ark to Jerusalem. Unfortunately, it was not moved according to God's instructions, and as a result, one man died. David left the ark in the home of Obed-edom until he could discover how to transport it correctly (13:1–14).

4 Tyre David did much building in Jerusalem. King Hiram of Tyre sent workers and supplies to help build David's palace. Cedar, abundant in the mountains north of Israel, was a valuable and hardy wood for the beautiful buildings in Jerusalem (14:1—17:27).

5 Baal-perazim David was not very popular with the Philistines because he had slain Goliath, one of their greatest warriors (1 Samuel 17). When David began to rule over a united Israel, the Philistines set out to capture him. But as David and his army approached Jerusalem, they attacked the Philistines at Baal-perazim. His army defeated the mighty Philistines twice, causing all the surrounding nations to fear David's power (14:11–17). After these battles, David moved the ark to Jerusalem (this time in accordance with God's instructions for transporting the ark).There was great celebration as the ark was brought into Jerusalem (15:1—17:27). David spent the remainder of his life making preparations for the building of the temple, a central place for the worship of God (18:1—29:30).

The genealogies of 1 Chronicles present an overview of Israel's history. The first nine chapters are filled with genealogies tracing the lineages of people from the creation to the exile in Babylon. Saul's death is recorded in chapter 10. Chapter 11 begins the history of David's reign over Israel.

1 CHRONICLES

Saul becomes king 1050 B.C. (1045 B.C.)	Saul dies; David becomes king over Judah 1010	David becomes king over all Israel 1003	David captures Jerusalem 1000	David captures Rabbah 997(?)

VITAL STATISTICS

PURPOSE:
To unify God's people, to trace the Davidic line, and to teach that genuine worship ought to be the center of individual and national life

AUTHOR:
Ezra, according to Jewish tradition

TO WHOM WRITTEN:
All Israel

DATE WRITTEN:
Approximately 430 B.C., recording events that occurred from about 1000–960 B.C.

SETTING:
First Chronicles parallels 2 Samuel and serves as a commentary on it. Written after the exile from a priestly point of view, 1 Chronicles emphasizes the religious history of Judah and Israel.

KEY VERSE:
"And David realized that the LORD had established him as king over Israel, and that his kingdom was highly exalted, for the sake of His people Israel" (14:2).

KEY PEOPLE:
David, Solomon

KEY PLACES:
Hebron, Jerusalem, the temple

IN the wide shade of the ageless oak, a mother watches her toddler discover acorns, leaves, and dandelions. Nearby, her mother, aunt, and uncle spread the checkerboard cloth over park tables and cover it with bowls and platters of fried chicken, potato salad, baked beans, and assorted family recipes. The clanging of Grandpa's and Dad's horseshoes against stakes regularly pierces the air and mixes with the cheers, laughs, and shouts of teenagers playing a game of touch football. A family reunion—a sunny afternoon filled with four generations of miscellaneous kids, parents, and second cousins once removed.

Reunions are important. They are times for touching and connecting with others from branches of the family tree, tracing one's personal history back through time and culture, seeing physical reminders (her eyes, his nose), recalling warm traditions. Knowing one's genetic and relational path gives a sense of identity, heritage, and destiny.

It is with this same high purpose that the writer of Chronicles begins his unifying work with an extensive genealogy. He traces the roots of the nation in a literary family reunion from Adam onward, recounting its royal line and the loving plan of a personal God. We read 1 Chronicles and gain a glimpse of God at work through his people for generations. If you are a believer, these people are your ancestors, too. As you approach this part of God's Word, read their names with awe and respect, and gain new security and identity in your relationship with God.

The previous book, 2 Kings, ends with both Israel and Judah in captivity, surely a dark age for God's people. Then follows Chronicles (1 and 2 Chronicles were originally one book). Written after the captivity, it summarizes Israel's history, emphasizing the Jewish people's spiritual heritage in an attempt to unify the nation. The chronicler is selective in his history telling. Instead of writing an exhaustive work, he carefully weaves the narrative, highlighting spiritual lessons and teaching moral truths. In Chronicles the northern kingdom is virtually ignored, David's triumphs—not his sins—are recalled, and the temple is given great prominence as the vital center of national life.

First Chronicles begins with Adam, and for nine chapters the writer gives us a "Who's Who" of Israel's history with special emphasis on David's royal line. The rest of the book tells the story of David—the great man of God, Israel's king—who served God and laid out the plans for the construction of and worship in the temple.

First Chronicles is an invaluable supplement to 2 Samuel and a strong reminder of the necessity for tracing our roots and thus rediscovering our spiritual foundation. As you read 1 Chronicles, trace your own godly heritage, thank God for your spiritual forefathers, and recommit yourself to passing on God's truth to the next generation.

David's census 980(?)	Solomon becomes king 970	The kingdom divides 930

THE BLUEPRINT

A. THE GENEALOGIES OF ISRAEL (1:1—9:44)
1. Ancestry of the nation
2. The tribes of Israel
3. Returnees from exile in Babylon

The long list of names that follows presents a history of God's work in the world from Adam through Zerubbabel. Some of these names remind us of stories of great faith, and others, of tragic failure. About most of the people named, however, we know nothing. But those who died unknown to us are known by God. God will also remember us when we die.

B. THE REIGN OF DAVID (10:1—29:30)
1. David becomes king over all of Israel
2. David brings the ark to Jerusalem
3. David's military exploits
4. David arranges for the building of the temple

David loved the Lord and wanted to build a temple to replace the tabernacle, but God denied his request. David's greatest contribution to the temple would not be the construction but the preparation. We may be unable to see the results of our labors for God in our lifetime, but David's example helps us understand that we serve God so *he* will see *his* results, not so we will see ours.

MEGATHEMES

THEME	EXPLANATION	IMPORTANCE
Israel's History	By retelling Israel's history in the genealogies and the stories of the kings, the writer laid down the true spiritual foundation for the nation. God kept his promises, and we are reminded of them in the historical record of his people, leaders, prophets, priests, and kings.	Israel's past formed a reliable basis for reconstructing the nation after the exile. Because God's promises are revealed in the Bible, we can know God and trust him to keep his word. Like Israel, we should have no higher goal in life than devoted service to God.
God's People	By listing the names of people in Israel's past, God established Israel's true heritage. They were all one family in Adam, one nation in Abraham, one priesthood under Levi, and one kingdom under David. The national and spiritual unity of the people was important to the rebuilding of the nation.	God is always faithful to his people. He protects them in every generation and provides leaders to guide them. Because God has been at work throughout the centuries, his people can trust him to work in the present. You can rely on his presence today.
David, the King	The story of David's life and his relationship with God showed that he was God's appointed leader. David's devotion to God, the Law, the temple, true worship, the people, and justice sets the standard for what God's chosen king should be.	Jesus Christ came to earth as a descendant of David. One day he will rule as King over all the earth. His strength and justice will fulfill God's ideal for the king. He is our hope. We can experience God's kingdom now by giving Christ complete control of our lives.
True Worship	David brought the ark of the covenant to the tabernacle at Jerusalem to restore true worship to the people. God gave the plans for building the temple, and David organized the priests to make worship central to all Israel.	The temple stood as the throne of God on earth, the place of true worship. God's true throne is in the hearts of his people. When we acknowledge him as the true King over our lives, true worship takes place.
The Priests	God ordained the priests and Levites to guide the people in faithful worship according to his Law. By leading the people in worship according to God's design, the priests and Levites were an important safeguard to Israel's faith.	For true worship to remain central in our lives, God's people need to take a firm stand for the ways of God recorded in the Bible. Today, all believers are priests for one another, and we should encourage each other to faithful worship.

A. THE GENEALOGIES OF ISRAEL (1:1—9:44)

These genealogies are the official family records of the nation of Israel. They give us an overview of the history of God's work from creation through the captivity of his people. These records served to teach the exiles returning from Babylon about their spiritual heritage as a nation and to inspire them to renew their faithfulness to God. Although these lists show the racial heritage of the Jews, they contain the spiritual heritage for every believer. We are a part of the community of faith that has existed from generation to generation since the dawn of human history.

1. Ancestry of the nation

Genealogy from Adam

1 Adam, Seth, Enosh, 1:1 Gen 4:25-5:32
2 Kenan, Mahalalel, Jared,
3 Enoch, Methuselah, Lamech,
4 Noah, Shem, Ham and Japheth.
5 The sons of Japheth *were* Gomer, Magog, Madai, Javan, Tubal, Meshech and Tiras. 1:5 Gen 10:2-4
6 The sons of Gomer *were* Ashkenaz, Diphath, and Togarmah.
7 The sons of Javan *were* Elishah, Tarshish, Kittim and Rodanim.
8 The sons of Ham *were* Cush, Mizraim, Put, and Canaan.
9 The sons of Cush *were* Seba, Havilah, Sabta, Raama and Sabteca; and the sons of
Raamah *were* Sheba and Dedan.
10 Cush became the father of Nimrod; he began to be a mighty one in the earth.
11 Mizraim became the father of the people of Lud, Anam, Lehab, Naphtuh, 1:11 Gen 10:13-18
12 Pathrus, Casluh, from which the Philistines came, and Caphtor.
13 Canaan became the father of Sidon, his firstborn, Heth,
14 and the Jebusites, the Amorites, the Girgashites,
15 the Hivites, the Arkites, the Sinites,
16 the Arvadites, the Zemarites and the Hamathites.
17 The sons of Shem *were* Elam, Asshur, Arpachshad, Lud, Aram, Uz, Hul, Gether 1:17 Gen 10:22-29
and Meshech.
18 Arpachshad became the father of Shelah and Shelah became the father of Eber.
19 Two sons were born to Eber, the name of the one was Peleg, for in his days the earth
was divided, and his brother's name was Joktan.
20 Joktan became the father of Almodad, Sheleph, Hazarmaveth, Jerah,
21 Hadoram, Uzal, Diklah,

1:1 This record of names demonstrates that God is interested not only in nations, but also in individuals. Although billions of people have lived since Adam, God knows and remembers the face and name of each person. Each of us is more than a name on a list; we are special persons whom God knows and loves. As we recognize and accept his love, we discover both our uniqueness as individuals and our solidarity with the rest of his family.

1:1ff This long list of names was compiled after the people of Judah, the southern kingdom, were taken captive to Babylon. As the exiles looked forward to the day when they would return to their homeland, one of their biggest fears was that the records of their heritage would be lost. The Jews placed great importance upon their heritage because each person wanted to be able to prove that he was a descendant of Abraham, the father of the Jewish people. Only then could he enjoy the benefits of the special blessings God had promised to Abraham and his descendants (see the notes on Genesis 12:1–3 and 17:2–8 for what these special blessings were).

This list reconstructed the family tree for both Judah, the southern kingdom, and Israel, the northern kingdom, before their captivities and served as proof for those who claimed to be Abraham's descendants. (For more information about why the Bible includes genealogies, read the notes on Genesis 5:1ff, Matthew 1:1, and Luke 3:23–38.)

1:1ff There is more to this long genealogy than meets the eye. It holds importance for us today because it supports the Old Testament promise that Jesus the Messiah would be a descendant of Abraham and David. This promise is recorded in Genesis 12:1–3 and 2 Samuel 7:12–13.

1:1, 4 Adam's story and Profile are found in Genesis 1—5. Noah's story and Profile are found in Genesis 6—9.

1:5–9 *Sons* can also mean *descendants;* thus a Biblical genealogy may skip several generations. These lists were not meant to be exhaustive, but to give adequate information about the various family lines.

1:10 Nimrod is also mentioned in Genesis 10:8–9.

1:11–12 The Philistines had been Israel's constant enemy from the days of the judges. King David finally weakened them, and by this time they were no longer a threat. (For more information on the Philistines, see the notes on Judges 13:1 and 1 Samuel 4:1.)

1:13–16 Canaan was the ancestor of the Canaanites, who inhabited the promised land (also called Canaan) before the Israelites entered under Joshua's leadership. God helped the Israelites drive out the Canaanites, a wicked and idolatrous people. The land's name was then changed to Israel. The book of Joshua tells that story.

1:19 "The earth was divided" refers to the time when the earth was divided into different language groups. At one time, everyone spoke a single language. But some people became proud of their accomplishments and gathered to build a monument to themselves—the tower of Babel. The building project was brought to an abrupt conclusion when God caused the people to speak different languages. Without the ability to communicate with one another, the people could not be unified. God showed them that their great efforts were useless without him. Pride in our achievements must not lead us to conclude that we no longer need God. This story is told in Genesis 11:1–9.

22 Ebal, Abimael, Sheba,
23 Ophir, Havilah and Jobab; all these *were* the sons of Joktan.
1:24 Gen 11:10-26; Luke 3:34-36
24 Shem, Arpachshad, Shelah,
25 Eber, Peleg, Reu,
26 Serug, Nahor, Terah,
27 Abram, that is Abraham.

Descendants of Abraham

28 The sons of Abraham *were* Isaac and Ishmael.
1:29 Gen 25:13-16
29 These are their genealogies: the firstborn of Ishmael *was* Nebaioth, then Kedar,
Adbeel, Mibsam,
30 Mishma, Dumah, Massa, Hadad, Tema,
31 Jetur, Naphish and Kedemah; these *were* the sons of Ishmael.
1:32 Gen 25:1-4
32 The sons of Keturah, Abraham's concubine, *whom* she bore, *were* Zimran, Jokshan,
Medan, Midian, Ishbak and Shuah. And the sons of Jokshan *were* Sheba and Dedan.
33 The sons of Midian were Ephah, Epher, Hanoch, Abida and Eldaah. All these were
the sons of Keturah.
1:34 1 Chr 1:28; Gen 25:25, 26; 32:28
34 Abraham became the father of Isaac. The sons of Isaac *were* Esau and Israel.
35 The sons of Esau *were* Eliphaz, Reuel, Jeush, Jalam and Korah.
1:35 Gen 36:4-10
36 The sons of Eliphaz *were* Teman, Omar, Zephi, Gatam, Kenaz, Timna and
Amalek.
37 The sons of Reuel *were* Nahath, Zerah, Shammah and Mizzah.
1:38 Gen 36:20-28
38 The sons of Seir *were* Lotan, Shobal, Zibeon, Anah, Dishon, Ezer and Dishan.
39 The sons of Lotan *were* Hori and Homam; and Lotan's sister *was* Timna.
40 The sons of Shobal *were* Alian, Manahath, Ebal, Shephi and Onam. And the sons
of Zibeon *were* Aiah and Anah.
41 The son of Anah *was* Dishon. And the sons of Dishon *were* Hamran, Eshban, Ithran and Cheran.
42 The sons of Ezer *were* Bilhan, Zaavan and Jaakan. The sons of Dishan *were* Uz and
Aran.
1:43 Gen 36:31-43
43 Now these are the kings who reigned in the land of Edom before any king of the
sons of Israel reigned. Bela was the son of Beor, and the name of his city was Dinhabah.
1:44 Is 34:6
44 When Bela died, Jobab the son of Zerah of Bozrah became king in his place.
45 When Jobab died, Husham of the land of the Temanites became king in his place.
1:45 Job 2:11
46 When Husham died, Hadad the son of Bedad, who defeated Midian in the field of
Moab, became king in his place; and the name of his city *was* Avith.
47 When Hadad died, Samlah of Masrekah became king in his place.
48 When Samlah died, Shaul of Rehoboth by the River became king in his place.
49 When Shaul died, Baal-hanan the son of Achbor became king in his place.
50 When Baal-hanan died, Hadad became king in his place; and the name of his city
was Pai, and his wife's name was Mehetabel, the daughter of Matred, the daughter of
Mezahab.
51 Then Hadad died.
Now the chiefs of Edom were: chief Timna, chief Aliah, chief Jetheth,
52 chief Oholibamah, chief Elah, chief Pinon,
53 chief Kenaz, chief Teman, chief Mibzar,
54 chief Magdiel, chief Iram. These *were* the chiefs of Edom.

1:24–27 Abraham's story and Profile are found in Genesis 11:26—25:10.

1:28–31 Ishmael's story and Profile are found in Genesis 17 and 21.

1:34 Israel is another name for Jacob because Jacob's 12 sons became the nation of Israel. Esau's descendants became the nation of Edom, a constant enemy of Israel. To learn more about the lives of Isaac and his two sons, Jacob and Esau, read their stories and Profiles in Genesis 21—36 and 46—49.

1:36 Amalek, Esau's grandson, was the son of his father's concubine (Genesis 36:12). He was the ancestor of the wicked tribe known as Amalekites, the first people to attack the Israelites on their way to the promised land. (For more about the Amalekites, read the note on Exodus 17:8.)

1:43–54 Why are we given information in this genealogy about the descendants of Edom who were Israel's enemies? Esau, ancestor of the Edomites, was Isaac's oldest son and thus a direct descendant of Abraham. As Abraham's first grandson, he deserved a place in the Jewish records. It was through Esau's marriages to pagan women, however, that the nation of Edom began. This genealogy shows the ancestry of enemy nations; they were *not* a part of the direct lineage of King David, and thus of the Messiah. This listing further identified Israel's special identity and role.

Genealogy: Twelve Sons of Jacob (Israel)

2 These are the sons of Israel: Reuben, Simeon, Levi, Judah, Issachar, Zebulun, **2:1** Gen 35:22-26; 46:8-25
2 Dan, Joseph, Benjamin, Naphtali, Gad and Asher.
3 The sons of Judah *were* Er, Onan and Shelah; *these* three were born to him by Bath-
shua the Canaanitess. And Er, Judah's firstborn, was wicked in the sight of the LORD, so **2:3** Gen 38:2-10
He put him to death.
4 Tamar his daughter-in-law bore him Perez and Zerah. Judah had five sons in all. **2:4** Gen 38:13-30
5 The sons of Perez *were* Hezron and Hamul.
6 The sons of Zerah *were* Zimri, Ethan, Heman, Calcol and Dara; five of them in all.
7 The son of Carmi *was* Achar, the troubler of Israel, who violated the ban. **2:7** Josh 7:1
8 The son of Ethan *was* Azariah.

Genealogy of David

9 Now the sons of Hezron, who were born to him *were* Jerahmeel, Ram and Chelubai.
10 Ram became the father of Amminadab, and Amminadab became the father of
Nahshon, leader of the sons of Judah;
11 Nahshon became the father of Salma, Salma became the father of Boaz,
12 Boaz became the father of Obed, and Obed became the father of Jesse;
13 and Jesse became the father of Eliab his firstborn, then Abinadab the second, Shimea
the third,
14 Nethanel the fourth, Raddai the fifth,
15 Ozem the sixth, David the seventh;
16 and their sisters *were* Zeruiah and Abigail. And the three sons of Zeruiah *were*
Abshai, Joab and Asahel.
17 Abigail bore Amasa, and the father of Amasa was Jether the Ishmaelite.
18 Now Caleb the son of Hezron had sons by Azubah *his* wife, and by Jerioth; and these
were her sons: Jesher, Shobab, and Ardon.
19 When Azubah died, Caleb married Ephrath, who bore him Hur.
20 Hur became the father of Uri, and Uri became the father of Bezalel.
21 Afterward Hezron went in to the daughter of Machir the father of Gilead, whom
he married when he was sixty years old; and she bore him Segub.
22 Segub became the father of Jair, who had twenty-three cities in the land of Gilead.
23 But Geshur and Aram took the towns of Jair from them, with Kenath and its villages, *even* sixty cities. All these were the sons of Machir, the father of Gilead.
24 After the death of Hezron in Caleb-ephrathah, Abijah, Hezron's wife, bore him
Ashhur the father of Tekoa.
25 Now the sons of Jerahmeel the firstborn of Hezron *were* Ram the firstborn, then
Bunah, Oren, Ozem *and* Ahijah.
26 Jerahmeel had another wife, whose name was Atarah; she was the mother of Onam.
27 The sons of Ram, the firstborn of Jerahmeel, were Maaz, Jamin and Eker.
28 The sons of Onam were Shammai and Jada. And the sons of Shammai *were* Nadab
and Abishur.
29 The name of Abishur's wife *was* Abihail, and she bore him Ahban and Molid.

2:1–2 The story of Israel's (Jacob's) sons is found in Genesis 29:32—50:26. Profiles of Reuben, Judah, and Joseph are found in the same section.

2:3 This long genealogy not only lists names, but gives us insights into some of the people. Here, almost as an epitaph, the genealogy states that Er "was wicked in the sight of the LORD, so He put him to death." Now, thousands of years later, this is all we know of the man. Each of us is forging a reputation, developing personal qualities by which we will be remembered. How would God summarize your life up to now? Some defiantly claim that how they live is their own business. But Scripture teaches that the way you live today will determine how you will be remembered by others and how you will be judged by God. What you do now *does* matter.

2:7 Achar is called Achan in Joshua 7. This is the man who kept for himself some of the plunder that was devoted to the Lord for destruction.

2:12 Boaz was Ruth's husband and an ancestor of both David and Jesus. Boaz's story and Profile are found in the book of Ruth.

2:15 David is one of the best-known people of the Bible. He was certainly not perfect, but he exemplified what it means to seek God first in all areas of life. God called David "a man after My heart" (Acts 13:22) because David's greatest desire was to serve and worship God. We can please God in the same way by making God our first consideration in all our desires and plans. David's story is found in 1 Samuel 16:1—1 Kings 2:10 and 1 Chronicles 10:14—29:30. David's Profile is found in 1 Samuel 17.

2:16 Joab's story is found in 2 Samuel 2; 3; 10—20; 24; 1 Kings 1—3; 1 Chronicles 11:4-9; 19—21. His Profile is found in 2 Samuel 19. Abishai's story is found in 1 Samuel 26; 2 Samuel 2; 3; 10; 15—21; 23; 1 Chronicles 18:12; 19. Abishai's Profile is found in 2 Samuel 21.

2:18 This is not the Caleb who spied out the promised land with Joshua. Caleb, the spy, is listed in 4:15.

30 The sons of Nadab *were* Seled and Appaim, and Seled died without sons.
31 The son of Appaim *was* Ishi. And the son of Ishi *was* Sheshan. And the son of Sheshan *was* Ahlai.
32 The sons of Jada the brother of Shammai *were* Jether and Jonathan, and Jether died
without sons.
33 The sons of Jonathan *were* Peleth and Zaza. These were the sons of Jerahmeel.
34 Now Sheshan had no sons, only daughters. And Sheshan had an Egyptian servant
whose name was Jarha.
35 Sheshan gave his daughter to Jarha his servant in marriage, and she bore him Attai.
36 Attai became the father of Nathan, and Nathan became the father of Zabad,
37 and Zabad became the father of Ephlal, and Ephlal became the father of Obed,
38 and Obed became the father of Jehu, and Jehu became the father of Azariah,
39 and Azariah became the father of Helez, and Helez became the father of Eleasah,
40 and Eleasah became the father of Sismai, and Sismai became the father of Shallum,
41 and Shallum became the father of Jekamiah, and Jekamiah became the father of
Elishama.
42 Now the sons of Caleb, the brother of Jerahmeel, *were* Mesha his firstborn, who
was the father of Ziph; and his son was Mareshah, the father of Hebron.
43 The sons of Hebron *were* Korah and Tappuah and Rekem and Shema.
44 Shema became the father of Raham, the father of Jorkeam; and Rekem became
the father of Shammai.
45 The son of Shammai was Maon, and Maon *was* the father of Bethzur.
46 Ephah, Caleb's concubine, bore Haran, Moza and Gazez; and Haran became the
father of Gazez.
47 The sons of Jahdai *were* Regem, Jotham, Geshan, Pelet, Ephah and Shaaph.
48 Maacah, Caleb's concubine, bore Sheber and Tirhanah.
49 She also bore Shaaph the father of Madmannah, Sheva the father of Machbena and
the father of Gibea; and the daughter of Caleb *was* Achsah.
50 These were the sons of Caleb.
The sons of Hur, the firstborn of Ephrathah, *were* Shobal the father of Kiriath-jearim,
51 Salma the father of Bethlehem *and* Hareph the father of Beth-gader.
52 Shobal the father of Kiriath-jearim had sons: Haroeh, half of the Manahathites,
53 and the families of Kiriath-jearim: the Ithrites, the Puthites, the Shumathites and
the Mishraites; from these came the Zorathites and the Eshtaolites.
54 The sons of Salma *were* Bethlehem and the Netophathites, Atroth-beth-joab and
half of the Manahathites, the Zorites.
55 The families of scribes who lived at Jabez *were* the Tirathites, the Shimeathites *and*
the Sucathites. Those are the Kenites who came from Hammath, the father of the house
of Rechab.

Family of David

3:1 2 Sam 3:2-5

3 Now these were the sons of David who were born to him in Hebron: the firstborn
was Amnon, by Ahinoam the Jezreelitess; the second *was* Daniel, by Abigail the
Carmelitess;
2 the third *was* Absalom the son of Maacah, the daughter of Talmai king of Geshur;
the fourth *was* Adonijah the son of Haggith;
3 the fifth *was* Shephatiah, by Abital; the sixth *was* Ithream, by his wife Eglah.

3:4 2 Sam 2:11; 5:4, 5; 1 Kin 2:11; 1 Chr 29:27

4 Six were born to him in Hebron, and there he reigned seven years and six months.
And in Jerusalem he reigned thirty-three years.
5 These were born to him in Jerusalem: Shimea, Shobab, Nathan and Solomon, four,
by Bath-shua the daughter of Ammiel;

3:5 2 Sam 5:14-16; 1 Chr 14:4-7; 2 Sam 12:24, 25; 2 Sam 11:3

6 and Ibhar, Elishama, Eliphelet,
7 Nogah, Nepheg and Japhia,
8 Elishama, Eliada and Eliphelet, nine.

3:1 For more about David's wife Abigail, see 1 Samuel 25; her Profile is also in 1 Samuel 25.

3:2 David's son Absalom is introduced in 2 Samuel 13—18; his Profile is in 2 Samuel 16.

3:5 Bath-shua is Bathsheba. Her story is found in 2 Samuel 11; 12; 1 Kings 1, and her Profile is in 1 Kings 1. The story of her son, Solomon, who became Israel's third king, is found in 1 Kings 1—11 and 2 Chronicles 1—9. Solomon's Profile is found in 1 Kings 4.

9 All *these were* the sons of David, besides the sons of the concubines; and Tamar *was* 3:9 2 Sam 13:1
their sister.
10 Now Solomon's son *was* Rehoboam, Abijah *was* his son, Asa his son, Jehoshaphat
his son,
11 Joram his son, Ahaziah his son, Joash his son,
12 Amaziah his son, Azariah his son, Jotham his son,
13 Ahaz his son, Hezekiah his son, Manasseh his son,
14 Amon his son, Josiah his son.
15 The sons of Josiah *were* Johanan the firstborn, and the second *was* Jehoiakim, the
third Zedekiah, the fourth Shallum.
16 The sons of Jehoiakim *were* Jeconiah his son, Zedekiah his son.
17 The sons of Jeconiah, the prisoner, *were* Shealtiel his son,
18 and Malchiram, Pedaiah, Shenazzar, Jekamiah, Hoshama and Nedabiah.
19 The sons of Pedaiah *were* Zerubbabel and Shimei. And the sons of Zerubbabel *were*
Meshullam and Hananiah, and Shelomith *was* their sister;
20 and Hashubah, Ohel, Berechiah, Hasadiah and Jushab-hesed, five.
21 The sons of Hananiah *were* Pelatiah and Jeshaiah, the sons of Rephaiah, the sons of
Arnan, the sons of Obadiah, the sons of Shecaniah.
22 The [1]descendants of Shecaniah *were* Shemaiah, and the sons of Shemaiah: Hattush,
Igal, Bariah, Neariah and Shaphat, six.
23 The sons of Neariah *were* Elioenai, Hizkiah and Azrikam, three.
24 The sons of Elioenai *were* Hodaviah, Eliashib, Pelaiah, Akkub, Johanan, Delaiah
and Anani, seven.

2. The tribes of Israel

Line of Hur, Asher

4 The sons of Judah *were* Perez, Hezron, Carmi, Hur and Shobal. 4:1 1 Chr 2:3
2 Reaiah the son of Shobal became the father of Jahath, and Jahath became the
father of Ahumai and Lahad. These *were* the families of the Zorathites.
3 These *were* the sons of Etam: Jezreel, Ishma and Idbash; and the name of their sister *was* Hazzelelponi.
4 Penuel *was* the father of Gedor, and Ezer the father of Hushah. These *were* the sons
of Hur, the firstborn of Ephrathah, the father of Bethlehem.
5 Ashhur, the father of Tekoa, had two wives, Helah and Naarah.
6 Naarah bore him Ahuzzam, Hepher, Temeni and Haahashtari. These were the sons
of Naarah.
7 The sons of Helah *were* Zereth, Izhar and Ethnan.
8 Koz became the father of Anub and Zobebah, and the families of Aharhel the son
of Harum.
9 Jabez was more honorable than his brothers, and his mother named him Jabez saying, "Because I bore *him* with pain."
10 Now Jabez called on the God of Israel, saying, "Oh that You would bless me indeed
and enlarge my border, and that Your hand might be with me, and that You would keep
me from harm that *it* may not pain me!" And God granted him what he requested.

1 Lit *sons*

3:9 The tragic story of Tamar, David's daughter, is found in 2 Samuel 13; 14.

3:10–14 Many of Solomon's descendants ruled the nation of Judah. For Rehoboam's story and Profile, see 2 Chronicles 10—12. For Jehoshaphat's story and Profile, see 2 Chronicles 17—20. Azariah's (Uzziah's) story and Profile are found in 2 Chronicles 28. Hezekiah's story and Profile are in 2 Kings 18—20. For Josiah's story, see 2 Kings 22; 23. His Profile is in 2 Kings 24.

3:15 Jehoiakim's story is found in Jeremiah 22—28; 35; 36. Zedekiah's story is found in Jeremiah 21—39.

3:19–20 Zerubbabel was the leader of the first exiles to return from Babylon. His story and Profile are found in the book of Ezra.

4:9–10 Jabez is remembered for a prayer request rather than a heroic act. In his prayer, he asked God to (1) bless him, (2) help him in his work ("enlarge my border"), (3) be with him in all he did, and (4) keep him from evil and harm. Jabez acknowledged God as the true center of his work. When we pray for God's blessing, we should also pray that he will take his rightful position as Lord over our work, our family time, and our recreation. Obeying him in daily responsibilities *is* heroic living.

4:10 Jabez prayed specifically to be protected from harm and pain. We live in a fallen world filled with sin, and it is important to ask God to keep us safe from the unavoidable evil that comes our way. But we must also avoid evil motives, desires, and actions that begin within us. Therefore, not only must we seek God's protection from evil, but we must also ask God to guard our thoughts and actions. We can begin to utilize his protection by filling our minds with positive thoughts and attitudes.

11 Chelub the brother of Shuhah became the father of Mehir, who was the father of
Eshton.
12 Eshton became the father of Beth-rapha and Paseah, and Tehinnah the father of
Ir-nahash. These are the men of Recah.
13 Now the sons of Kenaz *were* Othniel and Seraiah. And the sons of Othniel *were*
Hathath and Meonothai.
14 Meonothai became the father of Ophrah, and Seraiah became the father of Joab
the father of Ge-harashim, for they were craftsmen.
15 The sons of Caleb the son of Jephunneh *were* Iru, Elah and Naam; and the son of
Elah *was* Kenaz.
16 The sons of Jehallelel *were* Ziph and Ziphah, Tiria and Asarel.
17 The sons of Ezrah *were* Jether, Mered, Epher and Jalon. (And these are the sons of
Bithia the daughter of Pharaoh, whom Mered took) and she conceived *and bore* Miriam, Shammai and Ishbah the father of Eshtemoa.
18 His Jewish wife bore Jered the father of Gedor, and Heber the father of Soco, and
Jekuthiel the father of Zanoah.
19 The sons of the wife of Hodiah, the sister of Naham, *were* the fathers of Keilah the
Garmite and Eshtemoa the Maacathite.
20 The sons of Shimon *were* Amnon and Rinnah, Benhanan and Tilon. And the sons
of Ishi *were* Zoheth and Ben-zoheth.
21 The sons of Shelah the son of Judah *were* Er the father of Lecah and Laadah the
father of Mareshah, and the families of the house of the linen workers at Beth-ashbea;
22 and Jokim, the men of Cozeba, Joash, Saraph, who ruled in Moab, and Jashubi-
lehem. And the records are ancient.
23 These were the potters and the inhabitants of Netaim and Gederah; they lived there
with the king for his work.

Descendants of Simeon

24 The sons of Simeon *were* Nemuel and Jamin, Jarib, Zerah, Shaul;
25 Shallum his son, Mibsam his son, Mishma his son.
26 The sons of Mishma *were* Hammuel his son, Zaccur his son, Shimei his son.
27 Now Shimei had sixteen sons and six daughters; but his brothers did not have many
sons, nor did all their family multiply like the sons of Judah.
28 They lived at Beersheba, Moladah and Hazar-shual,
29 at Bilhah, Ezem, Tolad,
30 Bethuel, Hormah, Ziklag,
31 Beth-marcaboth, Hazar-susim, Beth-biri and Shaaraim. These *were* their cities until the reign of David.
32 Their villages *were* Etam, Ain, Rimmon, Tochen and Ashan, five cities;
33 and all their villages that *were* around the same cities as far as Baal. These *were* their
settlements, and they have their genealogy.
34 Meshobab and Jamlech and Joshah the son of Amaziah,
35 and Joel and Jehu the son of Joshibiah, the son of Seraiah, the son of Asiel,
36 and Elioenai, Jaakobah, Jeshohaiah, Asaiah, Adiel, Jesimiel, Benaiah,
37 Ziza the son of Shiphi, the son of Allon, the son of Jedaiah, the son of Shimri, the
son of Shemaiah;
38 these mentioned by name *were* leaders in their families; and their fathers' houses
increased greatly.
39 They went to the entrance of Gedor, even to the east side of the valley, to seek pasture for their flocks.
4:40 Judg 18:7-10
40 They found rich and good pasture, and the land was broad and quiet and peaceful;
for those who lived there formerly *were* Hamites.
4:41 1 Chr 4:33-38
41 These, recorded by name, came in the days of Hezekiah king of Judah, and attacked
their tents and the Meunites who were found there, and destroyed them utterly to this
day, and lived in their place, because there was pasture there for their flocks.

4:13 Othniel was Israel's first judge. He reformed the nation and brought peace to the land. His story is found in Judges 1:9–15 and 3:5–14.

4:15 Caleb was one of the 12 spies sent into the promised land by Moses. He and Joshua were the only two spies to return with a positive report, believing in God's promise to help the Israelites conquer the land. Caleb's story is told in Numbers 13; 14 and Joshua 14; 15. His Profile is found in Numbers 15.

42 From them, from the sons of Simeon, five hundred men went to Mount Seir, with
Pelatiah, Neariah, Rephaiah and Uzziel, the sons of Ishi, as their leaders.
43 They destroyed the remnant of the Amalekites who escaped, and have lived there
to this day.

Genealogy from Reuben

5 Now the sons of Reuben the firstborn of Israel (for he was the firstborn, but because
he defiled his father's bed, his birthright was given to the sons of Joseph the son of
Israel; so that he is not enrolled in the genealogy according to the birthright.
2 Though Judah prevailed over his brothers, and from him *came* the leader, yet the
birthright belonged to Joseph),
3 the sons of Reuben the firstborn of Israel *were* Hanoch and Pallu, Hezron and
Carmi.
4 The sons of Joel *were* Shemaiah his son, Gog his son, Shimei his son,
5 Micah his son, Reaiah his son, Baal his son,
6 Beerah his son, whom Tilgath-pilneser king of Assyria carried away into exile; he
was leader of the Reubenites.
7 His kinsmen by their families, in the genealogy of their generations, *were* Jeiel the
chief, then Zechariah
8 and Bela the son of Azaz, the son of Shema, the son of Joel, who lived in Aroer,
even to Nebo and Baal-meon.
9 To the east he settled as far as the entrance of the wilderness from the river Euphrates, because their cattle had increased in the land of Gilead.
10 In the days of Saul they made war with the Hagrites, who fell by their hand, so that
they occupied their tents throughout all the land east of Gilead.
11 Now the sons of Gad lived opposite them in the land of Bashan as far as Salecah.
12 Joel *was* the chief and Shapham the second, then Janai and Shaphat in Bashan.
13 Their kinsmen of their fathers' households *were* Michael, Meshullam, Sheba, Jorai,
Jacan, Zia and Eber, seven.
14 These *were* the sons of Abihail, the son of Huri, the son of Jaroah, the son of Gilead, the son of Michael, the son of Jeshishai, the son of Jahdo, the son of Buz;
15 Ahi the son of Abdiel, the son of Guni, *was* head of their fathers' households.
16 They lived in Gilead, in Bashan and in its towns, and in all the pasture lands of Sharon,
as far as their borders.
17 All of these were enrolled in the genealogies in the days of Jotham king of Judah
and in the days of Jeroboam king of Israel.
18 The sons of Reuben and the Gadites and the half-tribe of Manasseh, *consisting* of
valiant men, men who bore shield and sword and shot with bow and *were* skillful in battle, *were* 44,760, who went to war.
19 They made war against the Hagrites, Jetur, Naphish and Nodab.
20 They were helped against them, and the Hagrites and all who *were* with them were
given into their hand; for they cried out to God in the battle, and He answered their
prayers because they trusted in Him.
21 They took away their cattle: their 50,000 camels, 250,000 sheep, 2,000 donkeys; and
100,000 men.
22 For many fell slain, because the war *was* of God. And they settled in their place until
the exile.

4:42 Gen 36:8, 9
4:43 1 Sam 15:7, 8; 30:17
5:1 Gen 29:32; 1 Chr 2:1; Gen 35:22; 49:4; Gen 48:15-22
5:2 Gen 49:8-10; Ps 60:7; 108:8; Mic 5:2; Matt 2:6
5:3 Gen 46:9; Ex 6:14; Num 26:5-9
5:4 1 Chr 5:8
5:7 1 Chr 5:17
5:8 Num 32:34; Josh 12:2
5:9 Josh 22:8, 9
5:10 1 Chr 5:18-21
5:11 Josh 13:11; Deut 3:10
5:16 1 Chr 27:29; Song 2:1; Is 35:2; 65:10
5:17 2 Kin 15:5, 32; 2 Kin 14:16, 28
5:18 Num 1:3
5:19 1 Chr 5:10; Gen 25:15; 1 Chr 1:31
5:20 2 Chr 14:11-13; Ps 9:10; 20:7, 8; 22:4, 5
5:22 Josh 23:10; 2 Chr 32:8; Rom 8:31; 1 Chr 4:41; 2 Kin 15:29; 17:6

5:1 Reuben's sin of incest was recorded for all future generations to read. The purpose of this epitaph was not to smear Reuben's name, but to show that painful memories aren't the only results of sin. The real consequences of sin are ruined lives. As the oldest son, Reuben was the rightful heir to both a double portion of his father's estate and the leadership of Abraham's descendants, who had grown into a large tribe. But his sin stripped away his rights and privileges and ruined his family. Before you give in to temptation, take a close look at the disastrous consequences sin may produce in your life and the lives of others.

5:2 This leader from the tribe of Judah refers to David and his royal line, and to Jesus the Messiah, David's greatest descendant.

5:18–22 The armies of Reuben, Gad, and Manasseh succeeded in battle because they trusted God. Although they had instinct and skill as soldiers, they prayed and sought God's direction. The natural and developed abilities God gives us are meant to be used for him, but they should never replace our dependence on him. When we trust in our own cleverness, skill, and strength rather than in God, we open the door for pride. When facing difficult situations, seek God's purpose and ask for his guidance and strength. Psalm 20:7 says, "Some boast in chariots and some in horses, but we will boast in the name of the LORD, our God."

5:22 The exile mentioned here refers to the exile of the ten northern tribes (the northern kingdom of Israel) to Assyria in 722 B.C. These tribes never returned to their homeland. This story is found in 2 Kings 15:29—17:41.

WHO'S WHO IN THE BIBLE
Here are some of the people mentioned in this genealogy who are also mentioned elsewhere in the Bible. The writer of Chronicles reproduced a thorough history of Israel in one list of people. Many of the people in this list have exciting stories that can be traced through the Bible. Look up some of the names below that intrigue you. You may be surprised what you discover!

Name	*Key life lesson*	*Story told in:*
Adam (1:1)	Our sins have far greater implications than we realize.	Genesis 2—3
Noah (1:4)	Great rewards come from obeying God.	Genesis 6—9
Abraham (1:27)	Faith alone makes one right in God's eyes.	Genesis 11:26—25:10
Isaac (1:28)	Seeking peace brings true respect.	Genesis 21—35
Esau (1:35)	It is never too late to put away bitterness and forgive.	Genesis 25:20—36:43
Amalek (1:36)	There are evil men and nations who seek to harm God's people.	Exodus 17:8–16
Israel (Jacob) (2:1)	While our sins may haunt us, God will honor our faith.	Genesis 25:20—50:13
Judah (2:3)	God can change the hearts of even the most wicked people.	Genesis 37—50
Tamar (2:4)	God works his purposes even through sinful events.	Genesis 38
Perez (2:5)	Your background does not matter to God.	Genesis 38:27–30
Boaz (2:12)	Those who are kind to others will receive kindness themselves.	The book of Ruth
Jesse (2:13)	Never take lightly the impact you may have on your children.	1 Samuel 16
David (2:15)	True greatness is having a heart for God.	1 Samuel—2 Samuel
Joab (2:16)	Those who seek power die with nothing.	2 Samuel 2:13—1 Kings 2:34
Amnon (3:1)	Giving in to lust leads only to tragedy.	2 Samuel 13
Absalom (3:2)	Those seeking to oust a God-appointed leader will have a difficult battle.	2 Samuel 13—18
Adonijah (3:2)	God must determine what is rightfully ours.	1 Kings 1—2
Bathsheba (3:5)	One wrong act does not disqualify us from accomplishing things for God.	2 Samuel 11—12; 1 Kings 1—2
Solomon (3:5)	Man's wisdom is foolishness without God.	1 Kings 1—11
Reuben (5:1)	What is gained from a moment of passion is only perceived; what is lost is real and permanent.	Genesis 35:22; 37; 49:3–4
Aaron (6:3)	Don't expect God's leaders to be perfect, but don't let them get away with sin either.	Exodus 4—Numbers 20
Nadab (6:3)	Pretending to be God's representative is dangerous business.	Leviticus 10
Eleazar (6:3)	Those who are consistent in their faith are the best models to follow.	Numbers 20:25–29; 26—34; Joshua 24:33
Korah (6:22)	Rebelling against God's leaders is rebelling against God and will always be unsuccessful.	Numbers 16
Joshua (7:27)	Real courage comes from God.	The book of Joshua
Saul (8:33)	Those who say they follow God but don't live like it waste their God-given potential.	1 Samuel 8—31
Jonathan (8:33)	True friends always think of the other person, not just themselves.	1 Samuel 14—31

23 Now the sons of the half-tribe of Manasseh lived in the land; from Bashan to Baal- **5:23**
hermon and Senir and Mount Hermon they were numerous. Deut 3:9
24 These were the heads of their fathers' households, even Epher, Ishi, Eliel, Azriel,
Jeremiah, Hodaviah and Jahdiel, mighty men of valor, famous men, heads of their fathers' households.
25 But they acted treacherously against the God of their fathers and played the harlot **5:25**
after the gods of the peoples of the land, whom God had destroyed before them. Deut 32:15-18; Ex 34:15; 2 Kin 17:7
26 So the God of Israel stirred up the spirit of Pul, king of Assyria, even the spirit of
Tilgath-pilneser king of Assyria, and he carried them away into exile, namely the Reu- **5:26**
benites, the Gadites and the half-tribe of Manasseh, and brought them to Halah, Ha- 2 Kin 15:19, 29; 2 Chr 28:20; 2 Kin 17:6
bor, Hara and to the river of Gozan, to this day.

Genealogy: The Priestly Line

6 The sons of Levi *were* Gershon, Kohath and Merari. **6:1**
2 The sons of Kohath *were* Amram, Izhar, Hebron and Uzziel. Gen 46:11; Ex 6:16-25
3 The children of Amram *were* Aaron, Moses and Miriam. And the sons of Aaron
were Nadab, Abihu, Eleazar and Ithamar.
4 Eleazar became the father of Phinehas, *and* Phinehas became the father of
Abishua,
5 and Abishua became the father of Bukki, and Bukki became the father of Uzzi,
6 and Uzzi became the father of Zerahiah, and Zerahiah became the father of Meraioth,
7 Meraioth became the father of Amariah, and Amariah became the father of Ahitub,
8 and Ahitub became the father of Zadok, and Zadok became the father of Ahimaaz, **6:8**
9 and Ahimaaz became the father of Azariah, and Azariah became the father of Jo- 2 Sam 8:17; 2 Sam 15:27
hanan,
10 and Johanan became the father of Azariah (it was he who served as the priest in the **6:10**
house which Solomon built in Jerusalem), 2 Chr 26:17; 1 Kin 6:1; 2 Chr 3:1
11 and Azariah became the father of Amariah, and Amariah became the father of **6:11**
Ahitub, Ezra 7:3
12 and Ahitub became the father of Zadok, and Zadok became the father of Shallum,
13 and Shallum became the father of Hilkiah, and Hilkiah became the father of Azariah,
14 and Azariah became the father of Seraiah, and Seraiah became the father of Jehoz- **6:14**
adak; Neh 11:11
15 and Jehozadak went *along* when the LORD carried Judah and Jerusalem away into
exile by Nebuchadnezzar.
16 The sons of Levi *were* Gershom, Kohath and Merari. **6:16**
17 These are the names of the sons of Gershom: Libni and Shimei. Gen 46:11; Ex 6:16
18 The sons of Kohath *were* Amram, Izhar, Hebron and Uzziel.
19 The sons of Merari *were* Mahli and Mushi. And these are the families of the Levites **6:19**
according to their fathers' *households.* Num 3:33; 1 Chr 23:21
20 Of Gershom: Libni his son, Jahath his son, Zimmah his son,
21 Joah his son, Iddo his son, Zerah his son, Jeatherai his son.
22 The sons of Kohath *were* Amminadab his son, Korah his son, Assir his son,
23 Elkanah his son, Ebiasaph his son and Assir his son,
24 Tahath his son, Uriel his son, Uzziah his son and Shaul his son.

5:24–25 As warriors and leaders, these men had established excellent reputations for their great skill and leadership qualities. But in God's eyes they failed in the most important quality—being faithful to God. If you try to measure up to society's standards for fame and success, you may neglect your true purpose—to please and obey God. In the end, God alone examines our hearts and determines our final standing.

6:1ff The tribe of Levi was set apart to serve God in the tabernacle (Numbers 3; 4), and later in the temple (1 Chronicles 23—26). Aaron, Levi's descendant (6:3), became Israel's first high priest. God required all future priests to be descendants of Aaron. The rest of the Levites assisted the priests in the various tabernacle or temple duties and assisted the people by teaching them God's word and encouraging them to obey it.

6:3 The people listed here played major roles in the drama of the exodus. Aaron's story is found in the books of Exodus, Leviticus, and Numbers. His Profile is found in Exodus 32. Moses was one of the greatest prophets and leaders in Israel's history. His story is found in the books of Exodus, Leviticus, Numbers, and Deuteronomy. His Profile is found in Exodus 14. The story of Miriam, Moses and Aaron's sister, is found in Exodus 2; 15:20–21; and Numbers 12; 20:1. Her Profile is found in Numbers 13. Nadab and Abihu were killed for disobeying God (Leviticus 10). Eleazar became Israel's high priest after Aaron (Numbers 20:24–28), and Ithamar played an important role in organizing the worship services of the tabernacle (Numbers 4:28, 33; 7:8).

25 The sons of Elkanah *were* Amasai and Ahimoth.
26 *As for* Elkanah, the sons of Elkanah *were* Zophai his son and Nahath his son,
27 Eliab his son, Jeroham his son, Elkanah his son.

6:28 1 Sam 8:2; 1 Chr 6:33

28 The sons of Samuel *were* Joel the firstborn, and Abijah the second.
29 The sons of Merari *were* Mahli, Libni his son, Shimei his son, Uzzah his son,
30 Shimea his son, Haggiah his son, Asaiah his son.

6:31 1 Chr 15:16-22, 27; 16:4-6; 2 Sam 6:17; 1 Kin 8:4; 1 Chr 15:25-16:1

31 Now these are those whom David appointed over the service of song in the house
of the LORD, after the ark rested *there.*
32 They ministered with song before the tabernacle of the tent of meeting, until Solomon had built the house of the LORD in Jerusalem; and they served in their office according to their order.
33 These are those who served with their sons: From the sons of the Kohathites *were*
Heman the singer, the son of Joel, the son of Samuel,
34 the son of Elkanah, the son of Jeroham, the son of Eliel, the son of Toah,
35 the son of Zuph, the son of Elkanah, the son of Mahath, the son of Amasai,
36 the son of Elkanah, the son of Joel, the son of Azariah, the son of Zephaniah,
37 the son of Tahath, the son of Assir, the son of Ebiasaph, the son of Korah,
38 the son of Izhar, the son of Kohath, the son of Levi, the son of Israel.
39 *Heman's* brother Asaph stood at his right hand, even Asaph the son of Berechiah,
the son of Shimea,
40 the son of Michael, the son of Baaseiah, the son of Malchijah,
41 the son of Ethni, the son of Zerah, the son of Adaiah,
42 the son of Ethan, the son of Zimmah, the son of Shimei,
43 the son of Jahath, the son of Gershom, the son of Levi.
44 On the left hand *were* their kinsmen the sons of Merari: Ethan the son of Kishi, the
son of Abdi, the son of Malluch,
45 the son of Hashabiah, the son of Amaziah, the son of Hilkiah,
46 the son of Amzi, the son of Bani, the son of Shemer,
47 the son of Mahli, the son of Mushi, the son of Merari, the son of Levi.
48 Their kinsmen the Levites were appointed for all the service of the tabernacle of
the house of God.

6:49 Ex 27:1-8; Ex 30:1-7; Ex 30:10-16

49 But Aaron and his sons offered on the altar of burnt offering and on the altar of
incense, for all the work of the most holy place, and to make atonement for Israel, according to all that Moses the servant of God had commanded.

6:50 1 Chr 6:4-8; Ezra 7:5

50 These are the sons of Aaron: Eleazar his son, Phinehas his son, Abishua his son,
51 Bukki his son, Uzzi his son, Zerahiah his son,
52 Meraioth his son, Amariah his son, Ahitub his son,
53 Zadok his son, Ahimaaz his son.

6:54 Josh 21:4, 10

54 Now these are their settlements according to their camps within their borders. To
the sons of Aaron of the families of the Kohathites (for theirs was the *first* lot),

---

6:28 When Samuel became God's leader and spokesman, Israel was on the brink of collapse. The last few chapters of the book of Judges give a vivid picture of the moral decay and the resulting decline of the nation. But with God's help, Samuel almost single-handedly brought the nation from ruin to revival. He unified the people by showing them that God was their common leader and that any nation that focused on him would find and fulfill its true purpose. For the rest of Samuel's story, and to see how he set up rules for governing a nation based on spiritual principles, read the book of 1 Samuel and his Profile in 1 Samuel 8.

6:31 David did much to bring music into worship. He established songleaders and choirs to perform regularly at the temple (chapter 25). As a young man, David was hired to play the harp for King Saul (1 Samuel 16:15–23). He also wrote many of the songs found in the book of Psalms.

6:31ff The builders and craftsmen had completed the temple, and the priests and Levites had been given their responsibilities for taking care of it. Then it was time for another group of people—the musicians—to exercise their talents for God. The names of some of those who served with music are recorded here. You don't have to be an ordained minister to have an important place in the body of believers. Builders, craftsmen, worship assistants, choir members, and songleaders all have significant contributions to make. God has given you a unique combination of talents. Use them to serve and honor him.

6:49 Aaron and his descendants strictly followed the details of worship commanded by God through Moses. They did not choose only those commands they *wanted* to obey. Note what happened to Uzza when important details in handling the ark of the covenant were neglected (13:6–10). We should not try to obey God selectively, choosing those commands we will obey and those we will ignore. God's Word has authority over every aspect of our lives, not just selected portions.

6:49 For more information on priests, see the note on Leviticus 8:1ff.

6:54 The tribe of Levi was not given a specific area of land as were the other tribes. Instead, the Levites were to live throughout the land in order to aid the people of *every* tribe in their worship of God. Thus the Levites were given towns or pasturelands within the allotted areas of the other tribes (Joshua 13:14, 33).

55 to them they gave Hebron in the land of Judah and its pasture lands around it;
56 but the fields of the city and its villages, they gave to Caleb the son of Jephunneh.
57 To the sons of Aaron they gave the *following* cities of refuge: Hebron, Libnah also
with its pasture lands, Jattir, Eshtemoa with its pasture lands,
58 Hilen with its pasture lands, Debir with its pasture lands,
59 Ashan with its pasture lands and Beth-shemesh with its pasture lands;
60 and from the tribe of Benjamin: Geba with its pasture lands, Allemeth with its pasture lands, and Anathoth with its pasture lands. All their cities throughout their families
were thirteen cities.
61 Then to the rest of the sons of Kohath *were given* by lot, from the family of the tribe,
from the half-tribe, the half of Manasseh, ten cities.
62 To the sons of Gershom, according to their families, *were given* from the tribe of
Issachar and from the tribe of Asher, the tribe of Naphtali, and the tribe of Manasseh,
thirteen cities in Bashan.
63 To the sons of Merari *were given* by lot, according to their families, from the tribe of
Reuben, the tribe of Gad and the tribe of Zebulun, twelve cities.
64 So the sons of Israel gave to the Levites the cities with their pasture lands.
65 They gave by lot from the tribe of the sons of Judah, the tribe of the sons of Simeon
and the tribe of the sons of Benjamin, these cities which are mentioned by name.
66 Now some of the families of the sons of Kohath had cities of their territory from the
tribe of Ephraim.
67 They gave to them the *following* cities of refuge: Shechem in the hill country of
Ephraim with its pasture lands, Gezer also with its pasture lands,
68 Jokmeam with its pasture lands, Beth-horon with its pasture lands,
69 Aijalon with its pasture lands and Gath-rimmon with its pasture lands;
70 and from the half-tribe of Manasseh: Aner with its pasture lands and Bileam with
its pasture lands, for the rest of the family of the sons of Kohath.
71 To the sons of Gershom *were given,* from the family of the half-tribe of Manasseh:
Golan in Bashan with its pasture lands and Ashtaroth with its pasture lands;
72 and from the tribe of Issachar: Kedesh with its pasture lands, Daberath with its
pasture lands
73 and Ramoth with its pasture lands, Anem with its pasture lands;
74 and from the tribe of Asher: Mashal with its pasture lands, Abdon with its pasture
lands,
75 Hukok with its pasture lands and Rehob with its pasture lands;
76 and from the tribe of Naphtali: Kedesh in Galilee with its pasture lands, Hammon
with its pasture lands and Kiriathaim with its pasture lands.
77 To the rest of *the Levites,* the sons of Merari, *were given,* from the tribe of Zebulun:
Rimmono with its pasture lands, Tabor with its pasture lands;
78 and beyond the Jordan at Jericho, on the east side of the Jordan, *were given them,*
from the tribe of Reuben: Bezer in the wilderness with its pasture lands, Jahzah with its
pasture lands,
79 Kedemoth with its pasture lands and Mephaath with its pasture lands;
80 and from the tribe of Gad: Ramoth in Gilead with its pasture lands, Mahanaim with
its pasture lands,
81 Heshbon with its pasture lands and Jazer with its pasture lands.

Genealogy from Issachar

7 Now the sons of Issachar *were* four: Tola, Puah, Jashub and Shimron.
2 The sons of Tola *were* Uzzi, Rephaiah, Jeriel, Jahmai, Ibsam and Samuel, heads
of their fathers' households. *The sons* of Tola *were* mighty men of valor in their generations; their number in the days of David was 22,600.

6:55 Josh 14:13; 21:11f
6:56 Josh 15:13
6:57 Josh 21:13, 19
6:61 Josh 21:5; 1 Chr 6:66-70
6:63 Josh 21:7, 34-40
6:64 Num 35:1-8; Josh 21:3, 41, 42
6:65 1 Chr 6:57-60
6:66 Josh 21:20-26
7:2 2 Sam 24:1-9

6:57ff God had told the tribes to designate specific cities to be cities of refuge (Numbers 35). These cities were to provide refuge for a person who accidentally killed someone. This instruction may have seemed unimportant when it was given—the Israelites hadn't even entered the promised land. Sometimes God gives us instructions that do not seem relevant to us at the moment. But later we can see the importance of those instructions. Don't discard the lessons of the Bible because certain details seem irrelevant. Obey God now—in the future you will have a clearer understanding of the reasons for his instructions.

6:61 The Israelites cast lots in order to take the decision-making process out of man's hands and put it into God's hands. Casting lots was like drawing straws or throwing dice. Lots were cast only after seeking God's guidance in prayer. (For more information on casting lots, see the note on Joshua 18:8.)

7:3 1 Chr 5:24

3 The son of Uzzi *was* Izrahiah. And the sons of Izrahiah *were* Michael, Obadiah, Joel,
Isshiah; all five of them *were* chief men.
4 With them by their generations according to their fathers' households were 36,000
troops of the army for war, for they had many wives and sons.
5 Their relatives among all the families of Issachar *were* mighty men of valor, enrolled
by genealogy, in all 87,000.

Descendants of Benjamin

7:6 1 Chr 8:1-40

6 *The sons of* Benjamin *were* three: Bela and Becher and Jediael.
7 The sons of Bela were five: Ezbon, Uzzi, Uzziel, Jerimoth and Iri. They *were* heads
of fathers' households, mighty men of valor, and were 22,034 enrolled by genealogy.
8 The sons of Becher *were* Zemirah, Joash, Eliezer, Elioenai, Omri, Jeremoth, Abijah, Anathoth and Alemeth. All these *were* the sons of Becher.
9 They were enrolled by genealogy, according to their generations, heads of their
fathers' households, 20,200 mighty men of valor.
10 The son of Jediael *was* Bilhan. And the sons of Bilhan *were* Jeush, Benjamin, Ehud,
Chenaanah, Zethan, Tarshish and Ahishahar.
11 All these *were* sons of Jediael, according to the heads of their fathers' households,
17,200 mighty men of valor, who were ready to go out with the army to war.
12 Shuppim and Huppim *were* the sons of Ir; Hushim *was* the son of Aher.

Sons of Naphtali

13 The sons of Naphtali *were* Jahziel, Guni, Jezer, and Shallum, the sons of Bilhah.

Descendants of Manasseh

14 The sons of Manasseh *were* Asriel, whom his Aramean concubine bore; she bore
Machir the father of Gilead.
15 Machir took a wife for Huppim and Shuppim, whose sister's name was Maacah. And
the name of the second was Zelophehad, and Zelophehad had daughters.
16 Maacah the wife of Machir bore a son, and she named him Peresh; and the name of
his brother *was* Sheresh, and his sons *were* Ulam and Rakem.
17 The son of Ulam *was* Bedan. These *were* the sons of Gilead the son of Machir, the
son of Manasseh.
18 His sister Hammolecheth bore Ishhod and Abiezer and Mahlah.
19 The sons of Shemida were Ahian and Shechem and Likhi and Aniam.

Descendants of Ephraim

7:20 Num 26:35, 36

20 The sons of Ephraim *were* Shuthelah and Bered his son, Tahath his son, Eleadah
his son, Tahath his son,
21 Zabad his son, Shuthelah his son, and Ezer and Elead whom the men of Gath who
were born in the land killed, because they came down to take their livestock.

7:22 Gen 37:34; Job 2:11; John 11:19

22 Their father Ephraim mourned many days, and his relatives came to comfort him.
23 Then he went in to his wife, and she conceived and bore a son, and he named him
Beriah, because misfortune had come upon his house.

7:24 Josh 16:3, 5; 2 Chr 8:5

24 His daughter was Sheerah, who built lower and upper Beth-horon, also Uzzen-
sheerah.
25 Rephah was his son *along* with Resheph, Telah his son, Tahan his son,
26 Ladan his son, Ammihud his son, Elishama his son,

7:27 Ex 17:9-14; 24:13

27 Non his son and Joshua his son.

7:28 Josh 16:2

28 Their possessions and settlements *were* Bethel with its towns, and to the east Naa-
ran, and to the west Gezer with its towns, and Shechem with its towns as far as Ayyah
with its towns,

7:29 Judg 1:22-29

29 and along the borders of the sons of Manasseh, Beth-shean with its towns, Taanach
with its towns, Megiddo with its towns, Dor with its towns. In these lived the sons of Joseph
the son of Israel.

7:27 Joshua was one of Israel's great leaders, leading the people into the promised land. His story is told in the book of Joshua. His Profile is found in Joshua 2.

Descendants of Asher

30 The sons of Asher *were* Imnah, Ishvah, Ishvi and Beriah, and Serah their sister. **7:30** Gen 46:17; Num 26:44-46
31 The sons of Beriah *were* Heber and Malchiel, who was the father of Birzaith.
32 Heber became the father of Japhlet, Shomer and Hotham, and Shua their sister.
33 The sons of Japhlet *were* Pasach, Bimhal and Ashvath. These were the sons of
Japhlet.
34 The sons of Shemer *were* Ahi and Rohgah, Jehubbah and Aram.
35 The sons of his brother Helem *were* Zophah, Imna, Shelesh and Amal.
36 The sons of Zophah *were* Suah, Harnepher, Shual, Beri and Imrah,
37 Bezer, Hod, Shamma, Shilshah, Ithran and Beera.
38 The sons of Jether *were* Jephunneh, Pispa and Ara.
39 The sons of Ulla *were* Arah, Hanniel and Rizia.
40 All these *were* the sons of Asher, heads of the fathers' houses, choice and mighty
men of valor, heads of the princes. And the number of them enrolled by genealogy for
service in war was 26,000 men.

Genealogy from Benjamin

8 And Benjamin became the father of Bela his firstborn, Ashbel the second, Aharah **8:1** Gen 46:21; 1 Chr 7:6-12; 1 Chr 7:12
the third,
2 Nohah the fourth and Rapha the fifth.
3 Bela had sons: Addar, Gera, Abihud,
4 Abishua, Naaman, Ahoah,
5 Gera, Shephuphan and Huram.
6 These are the sons of Ehud: these are the heads of fathers' *households* of the inhabitants of Geba, and they carried them into exile to Manahath,
7 namely, Naaman, Ahijah and Gera—he carried them into exile; and he became the
father of Uzza and Ahihud.
8 Shaharaim became the father of children in the country of Moab after he had sent
away Hushim and Baara his wives.
9 By Hodesh his wife he became the father of Jobab, Zibia, Mesha, Malcam,
10 Jeuz, Sachia, Mirmah. These were his sons, heads of fathers' *households.*
11 By Hushim he became the father of Abitub and Elpaal.
12 The sons of Elpaal *were* Eber, Misham, and Shemed, who built Ono and Lod, with
its towns;
13 and Beriah and Shema, who were heads of fathers' *households* of the inhabitants of
Aijalon, who put to flight the inhabitants of Gath;
14 and Ahio, Shashak and Jeremoth.
15 Zebadiah, Arad, Eder,
16 Michael, Ishpah and Joha *were* the sons of Beriah.
17 Zebadiah, Meshullam, Hizki, Heber,
18 Ishmerai, Izliah and Jobab *were* the sons of Elpaal.
19 Jakim, Zichri, Zabdi,
20 Elienai, Zillethai, Eliel,
21 Adaiah, Beraiah and Shimrath *were* the sons of Shimei.
22 Ishpan, Eber, Eliel,
23 Abdon, Zichri, Hanan,
24 Hananiah, Elam, Anthothijah,
25 Iphdeiah and Penuel *were* the sons of Shashak.
26 Shamsherai, Shehariah, Athaliah,
27 Jaareshiah, Elijah and Zichri *were* the sons of Jeroham.
28 These were heads of the fathers' *households* according to their generations, chief
men who lived in Jerusalem.

8:8–10 These verses list Shaharaim's children by Hodesh after he had divorced his first two wives, Hushim and Baara. Divorce and polygamy are sometimes recorded in the Old Testament without critical comments. This does not mean that God takes divorce lightly. Malachi 2:15–16 says, "Let no one deal treacherously against the wife of your youth. 'For I hate divorce,' says the LORD, the God of Israel." Jesus explained that, although divorce was allowed, it was not God's will: " 'Because of your hardness of heart Moses permitted you to divorce your wives; but from the beginning it has not been this way ' " (Matthew 19:8). Don't assume that God approves of an act simply because it isn't vigorously condemned in every related Bible reference.

8:29 1 Chr 9:35-38

29 Now in Gibeon, *Jeiel,* the father of Gibeon lived, and his wife's name was Maacah;
30 and his firstborn son *was* Abdon, then Zur, Kish, Baal, Nadab,
31 Gedor, Ahio and Zecher.
32 Mikloth became the father of Shimeah. And they also lived with their relatives in Jerusalem opposite their *other* relatives.

Genealogy from King Saul

8:33 1 Chr 9:39-44

33 Ner became the father of Kish, and Kish became the father of Saul, and Saul became the father of Jonathan, Malchi-shua, Abinadab and Eshbaal.
34 The son of Jonathan *was* Merib-baal, and Merib-baal became the father of Micah.
35 The sons of Micah *were* Pithon, Melech, Tarea and Ahaz.
36 Ahaz became the father of Jehoaddah, and Jehoaddah became the father of Alemeth, Azmaveth and Zimri; and Zimri became the father of Moza.
37 Moza became the father of Binea; Raphah *was* his son, Eleasah his son, Azel his son.
38 Azel had six sons, and these *were* their names: Azrikam, Bocheru, Ishmael, Sheariah, Obadiah and Hanan. All these *were* the sons of Azel.
39 The sons of Eshek his brother *were* Ulam his firstborn, Jeush the second and Eliphelet the third.
40 The sons of Ulam were mighty men of valor, archers, and had many sons and grandsons, 150 *of them.* All these *were* of the sons of Benjamin.

3. Returnees from exile in Babylon

People of Jerusalem

9:1 1 Chr 5:25, 26

9 So all Israel was enrolled by genealogies; and behold, they are written in the Book of the Kings of Israel. And Judah was carried away into exile to Babylon for their unfaithfulness.

9:2 Ezra 2:70; Neh 7:73; 11:3-22; Ezra 2:43, 58; 8:20

2 Now the first who lived in their possessions in their cities *were* Israel, the priests, the Levites and the temple servants.

9:3 Neh 11:1

3 Some of the sons of Judah, of the sons of Benjamin and of the sons of Ephraim and Manasseh lived in Jerusalem:

9:4 Gen 46:12; Num 26:20

4 Uthai the son of Ammihud, the son of Omri, the son of Imri, the son of Bani, from the sons of Perez the son of Judah.
5 From the Shilonites *were* Asaiah the firstborn and his sons.
6 From the sons of Zerah *were* Jeuel and their relatives, 690 *of them.*
7 From the sons of Benjamin *were* Sallu the son of Meshullam, the son of Hodaviah, the son of Hassenuah,
8 and Ibneiah the son of Jeroham, and Elah the son of Uzzi, the son of Michri, and Meshullam the son of Shephatiah, the son of Reuel, the son of Ibnijah;

9:9 Neh 11:8

9 and their relatives according to their generations, 956. All these *were* heads of fathers' *households* according to their fathers' houses.

9:10 Neh 11:10-14

10 From the priests *were* Jedaiah, Jehoiarib, Jachin,

9:11 Jer 20:1

11 and Azariah the son of Hilkiah, the son of Meshullam, the son of Zadok, the son of Meraioth, the son of Ahitub, the chief officer of the house of God;
12 and Adaiah the son of Jeroham, the son of Pashhur, the son of Malchijah, and Maasai

---

8:33 Saul, Israel's first king, was very inconsistent. His story is found in 1 Samuel 9—31, and his Profile is in 1 Samuel 14. Saul's son Jonathan was the opposite. Although Jonathan was the rightful heir to the throne, he realized that David was God's choice to be Israel's next king. Instead of being jealous, Jonathan was David's friend and even helped him escape from Saul's attempts at murder. Jonathan's story is told in 1 Samuel 14—31. His Profile is found in 1 Samuel 20.

9:1 Although not every person in Judah was unfaithful, the entire nation was carried away into captivity. Everyone was affected by the sin of some. Even if we don't participate in a certain widespread wrongdoing, we will still be affected by those who do. It is not enough to say, "I didn't do it." We must speak out against the sins of our society.

9:1ff Chronologically, this chapter could be placed at the end of 2 Chronicles because it records the names of the exiles who returned from the Babylonian captivity. The writer included it here to show his concern for their need, as a nation, to return to what made them great in the first place—obedience to God.

9:10–11 When we think of doing God's work, usually preaching, teaching, singing, and other kinds of up-front leadership come to mind. Azariah, however, was in charge of the house of God, and he was singled out for special mention. Whatever role you have in church, it is important to God. He appreciates your service and the positive attitude you have as you do it.

the son of Adiel, the son of Jahzerah, the son of Meshullam, the son of Meshillemith,
the son of Immer;
13 and their relatives, heads of their fathers' households, 1,760 very able men for the
work of the service of the house of God.
14 Of the Levites *were* Shemaiah the son of Hasshub, the son of Azrikam, the son of
Hashabiah, of the sons of Merari;
15 and Bakbakkar, Heresh and Galal and Mattaniah the son of Mica, the son of Zichri,
the son of Asaph,
16 and Obadiah the son of Shemaiah, the son of Galal, the son of Jeduthun, and
Berechiah the son of Asa, the son of Elkanah, who lived in the villages of the Netophathites.
17 Now the gatekeepers *were* Shallum and Akkub and Talmon and Ahiman and their
relatives (Shallum the chief
18 *being stationed* until now at the king's gate to the east). These *were* the gatekeepers
for the camp of the sons of Levi.
19 Shallum the son of Kore, the son of Ebiasaph, the son of Korah, and his relatives of
his father's house, the Korahites, *were* over the work of the service, keepers of the thresholds of the tent; and their fathers had been over the camp of the LORD, keepers of the
entrance.
20 Phinehas the son of Eleazar was ruler over them previously, *and* the LORD was
with him.
21 Zechariah the son of Meshelemiah was gatekeeper of the entrance of the tent of
meeting.
22 All these who were chosen to be gatekeepers at the thresholds were 212. These were
enrolled by genealogy in their villages, whom David and Samuel the seer appointed in
their office of trust.
23 So they and their sons had charge of the gates of the house of the LORD, *even* the
house of the tent, as guards.
24 The gatekeepers were on the four sides, to the east, west, north and south.
25 Their relatives in their villages *were* to come in every seven days from time to time
to be with them;
26 for the four chief gatekeepers who *were* Levites, were in an office of trust, and were
over the chambers and over the treasuries in the house of God.
27 They spent the night around the house of God, because the watch was committed
to them; and they *were* in charge of opening *it* morning by morning.
28 Now some of them had charge of the utensils of service, for they counted them when
they brought them in and when they took them out.
29 Some of them also were appointed over the furniture and over all the utensils of
the sanctuary and over the fine flour and the wine and the oil and the frankincense and
the spices.
30 Some of the sons of the priests prepared the mixing of the spices.
31 Mattithiah, one of the Levites, who was the firstborn of Shallum the Korahite, had
the responsibility over the things which were baked in pans.
32 Some of their relatives of the sons of the Kohathites *were* over the showbread to
prepare it every sabbath.

9:14 Neh 11:15-19
9:18 Ezek 44:1; 46:1, 2
9:20 Num 25:7-13
9:21 1 Chr 26:2, 14
9:22 1 Chr 26:1; 2 Chr 31:15, 18
9:25 2 Kin 11:5, 7; 2 Chr 23:8
9:27 1 Chr 23:30-32
9:29 1 Chr 23:29
9:30 Ex 30:23-25
9:31 1 Chr 9:22
9:32 Lev 24:5-8

9:17–18 Gatekeepers guarded the four main entrances to the temple and opened the gates each morning for those who wanted to worship. In addition, they did other day-to-day chores to keep the temple running smoothly—cleaning, preparing the offerings for sacrifice, and accounting for the gifts designated to the temple (9:22–32).

Gatekeepers had to be reliable, honest, and trustworthy. The people in our churches who handle the offerings and care for the materials and functions of the building follow in a great tradition, and we should honor them for their reliability and service.

9:22–32 The priests and Levites put a great deal of time and care into worship. Not only did they perform rather complicated tasks (described in Leviticus 1—9), but they also took care of many pieces of equipment. Everything relating to worship was carefully prepared and maintained so they and all the people could enter worship with their minds and hearts focused on God.

In our busy world, it is easy to rush into our one-hour-a-week worship services without preparing ourselves for worship beforehand. We reflect and worry about the week's problems; we pray about whatever comes into our minds; and we do not meditate on the words we are singing. But God wants our worship to be conducted "properly and in an orderly manner" (1 Corinthians 14:40). Just as we prepare to meet a business associate or invited guests, we should carefully prepare to meet our King in worship.

9:33 1 Chr 6:31-47; 25:1; Ps 134:1
33 Now these are the singers, heads of fathers' *households* of the Levites, *who lived* in
the chambers *of the temple* free *from other service;* for they were engaged in their work
day and night.
34 These were heads of fathers' *households* of the Levites according to their generations, chief men, who lived in Jerusalem.

Ancestry and Descendants of Saul

9:35 1 Chr 8:29-32
35 In Gibeon Jeiel the father of Gibeon lived, and his wife's name was Maacah,
36 and his firstborn son *was* Abdon, then Zur, Kish, Baal, Ner, Nadab,
37 Gedor, Ahio, Zechariah and Mikloth.
38 Mikloth became the father of Shimeam. And they also lived with their relatives in
Jerusalem opposite their *other* relatives.
9:39 1 Chr 8:33-38
39 Ner became the father of Kish, and Kish became the father of Saul, and Saul became the father of Jonathan, Malchi-shua, Abinadab and Eshbaal.
40 The son of Jonathan *was* Merib-baal; and Merib-baal became the father of Micah.
9:41 1 Chr 8:35-37
41 The sons of Micah *were* Pithon, Melech, Tahrea *and Ahaz.*
42 Ahaz became the father of Jarah, and Jarah became the father of Alemeth, Azmaveth and Zimri; and Zimri became the father of Moza,
43 and Moza became the father of Binea and Rephaiah his son, Eleasah his son, Azel
his son.
44 Azel had six sons whose names are these: Azrikam, Bocheru and Ishmael and Sheariah and Obadiah and Hanan. These were the sons of Azel.

B. THE REIGN OF DAVID (10:1—29:30)

David becomes king over all Israel and captures the city of Jerusalem. God promises blessings to him and the nation, but David is not allowed to build the temple. Instead, he begins to make preparations for its construction. Although stumbling and falling occasionally, David walks step-by-step with God, sincerely wanting to be obedient. Through David's successes and his failures, we learn the importance of giving our whole heart to God and letting him be the focus of our lives, striving each day to be consistent in our obedience to his will.

1. David becomes king over all of Israel

Defeat and Death of Saul and His Sons

10:1 1 Sam 31:1-13
10 Now the Philistines fought against Israel; and the men of Israel fled before the
Philistines and fell slain on Mount Gilboa.
10:2 1 Sam 31:2
2 The Philistines closely pursued Saul and his sons, and the Philistines struck down
Jonathan, Abinadab and Malchi-shua, the sons of Saul.
3 The battle became heavy against Saul, and the archers overtook him; and he was
wounded by the archers.
10:4 1 Sam 31:4
4 Then Saul said to his armor bearer, "Draw your sword and thrust me through with
it, otherwise these uncircumcised will come and abuse me." But his armor bearer would
not, for he was greatly afraid. Therefore Saul took his sword and fell on it.
5 When his armor bearer saw that Saul was dead, he likewise fell on his sword and
died.
10:6 1 Sam 31:6
6 Thus Saul died with his three sons, and all *those* of his house died together.
7 When all the men of Israel who were in the valley saw that they had fled, and that
Saul and his sons were dead, they forsook their cities and fled; and the Philistines came
and lived in them.
8 It came about the next day, when the Philistines came to strip the slain, that they
found Saul and his sons fallen on Mount Gilboa.
10:9 1 Sam 31:9
9 So they stripped him and took his head and his armor and sent *messengers* around
the land of the Philistines to carry the good news to their idols and to the people.

9:33–34 Worship was the primary focus of many Israelites, whose vocation centered on the house of the Lord. Worship (appreciating God for his nature and worth) should occupy the core of our lives and not just a few minutes once a week. We too can worship at all hours if we stay aware of God's presence and guidance in all situations and if we maintain an attitude of serving him. Build your life around the worship of God rather than making worship just another activity in a busy schedule.

10:1 The chronology of chapters 1—9 covers Israelite history from creation to the exile in Babylon (586 B.C.). At this point, the narrative goes back to the beginning of Israel's kingdom period, picking up with Israel's first king, Saul. 1 Chronicles begins with Saul's death; to learn about his reign, read 1 Samuel.

10 They put his armor in the house of their gods and fastened his head in the house of
Dagon.

Jabesh-gilead's Tribute to Saul

11 When all Jabesh-gilead heard all that the Philistines had done to Saul,
12 all the valiant men arose and took away the body of Saul and the bodies of his sons **10:12**
and brought them to Jabesh, and they buried their bones under the oak in Jabesh, and 1 Sam 31:12f
fasted seven days.
13 So Saul died for his trespass which he committed against the LORD, because of the **10:13**
word of the LORD which he did not keep; and also because he asked counsel of a medi- 1 Sam 13:13, 14; 15:23; Lev 19:31;
um, making inquiry *of it,* 20:6; 1 Sam 28:7
14 and did not inquire of the LORD. Therefore He killed him and turned the kingdom **10:14**
to David the son of Jesse. 1 Sam 15:28; 1 Chr 12:23

David Made King over All Israel

11 Then all Israel gathered to David at Hebron and said, "Behold, we are your bone **11:1**
and your flesh. 2 Sam 5:1, 3, 6-10
2 "In times past, even when Saul was king, you *were* the one who led out and brought **11:2**
in Israel; and the LORD your God said to you, 'You shall shepherd My people Israel, 2 Sam 5:2; 7:7
and you shall be prince over My people Israel.' "
3 So all the elders of Israel came to the king at Hebron, and David made a covenant **11:3**
with them in Hebron before the LORD; and they anointed David king over Israel, ac- 2 Sam 2:4; 5:3, 5; 1 Sam 16:1, 3, 12,
cording to the word of the LORD through Samuel. 13

Jerusalem, Capital City

4 Then David and all Israel went to Jerusalem (that is, Jebus); and the Jebusites, the **11:4**
inhabitants of the land, *were* there. Josh 15:8, 63; Judg 1:21

10:10 Dagon, the most important god of the Philistines, was believed to bring rain and provide rich harvests. The Philistines built temples to him when they settled in the grain-producing land of Canaan. In times of drought, people begged Dagon for pity, even to the point of sacrificing their children in his temples. In times of plenty, the temples were used for twisted forms of entertainment, such as the humiliation of captives (see Judges 16:23–30). But Dagon, like the other pagan gods, was powerless against the one true God (1 Samuel 5:1–7).

10:11–12 The actions of the valiant warriors who brought back and buried the bodies of King Saul and his sons should encourage us to respect our God-given leaders. David showed respect for Saul's position, even when Saul was chasing him to kill him (1 Samuel 26). How easy it is to be critical of those in authority over us, focusing only on their weaknesses. We cannot excuse sin, but we should respect the positions of those in authority, whether at work, at church, or in government. First Thessalonians 5:12, 13 gives instructions for honoring church leaders. Romans 13:1ff gives instructions for relating to government leaders.

10:13–14 Saul's unfaithfulness was both active and passive; he not only did wrong, but he also *failed to do right.* He actively disobeyed by attempting murder, ignoring God's instructions, and seeking guidance from a medium. He passively disobeyed by neglecting to ask God for guidance as he ran the kingdom. Obedience, too, is both passive and active. It is not enough just to avoid what is wrong, we need to actively pursue what is right.

10:13–14 In the account in 1 Samuel 28, Saul asked the Lord for guidance but received no answer; this account says he "did not inquire of the LORD." The answer to this apparent contradiction lies in understanding Saul's motives and the timing of his request to God. His frantic requests came only when he had tried everything his own way. He never went to God unless there was nowhere else to turn. When he finally asked, God refused to answer. Saul sought God only when it suited him, and God rejected him for his constant stubbornness and rebellion.

10:14 Throughout much of Saul's reign, David was forced to hide from him (1 Samuel 19—30). During this time David had opportunities to kill Saul (1 Samuel 24; 26) and to assume the throne that God had promised him (1 Samuel 16:1–13). But David trusted in God's promise that he would be king in God's good timing. It was not up to David to decide when Saul's reign would end. During this battle, God ended Saul's reign just as he had promised.

10:14 Why does this verse say that the Lord put Saul to death, when Saul took his own life (1 Samuel 31:3–4)? God had rejected Saul because of his stubbornness and rebellion (1 Samuel 15:22–26) and had judged him for his sins (1 Samuel 28:16–19). God arranged a defeat in battle so that Saul would die and his kingdom would be taken from his family. If Saul had not taken his own life, the Philistine soldiers would have killed him.

11:1–2 The details of how David came to power are given more completely in 2 Samuel. Chronicles emphasizes that *God,* declared David to be the ruler, although he used the efforts of many people, even some of Saul's own family. God is still sovereign over history, directing events to accomplish his will. The books of Chronicles demonstrate that no matter what people may do to try to hinder God's work, God still controls all events and works his will in them.

11:3–4 David was king over Judah for seven-and-a-half years before he captured Jerusalem. When David was finally anointed king over all Israel, 20 years had passed since Samuel had anointed him (1 Samuel 16:1–13). God's promises are worth waiting for, even when his timetable doesn't match our expectations or desires.

11:4 David chose Jerusalem as his capital for both political and military reasons. Jerusalem was near the center of the kingdom and, because it rested on a tribal border, was in neutral territory. Thus its location decreased tribal jealousies. Jerusalem also sat on a high ridge, making it difficult to attack. (For more information on the city of Jerusalem, see the note on 2 Samuel 5:6.)

5 The inhabitants of Jebus said to David, "You shall not enter here." Nevertheless David captured the stronghold of Zion (that is, the city of David).

11:6 2 Sam 8:16

6 Now David had said, "Whoever strikes down a Jebusite first shall be chief and commander." Joab the son of Zeruiah went up first, so he became chief.

7 Then David dwelt in the stronghold; therefore it was called the city of David.

8 He built the city all around, from the [2]Millo even to the surrounding area; and Joab repaired the rest of the city.

11:9 2 Sam 3:1

9 David became greater and greater, for the LORD of hosts *was* with him.

David's Mighty Men

11:10 2 Sam 23:8-39; 1 Chr 11:3

10 Now these are the heads of the mighty men whom David had, who gave him strong support in his kingdom, together with all Israel, to make him king, according to the word of the LORD concerning Israel.

11:11 2 Sam 23:8; 1 Chr 12:18

11 These *constitute* the list of the mighty men whom David had: Jashobeam, the son of a Hachmonite, the chief of the thirty; he lifted up his spear against three hundred whom he killed at one time.

11:12 1 Chr 27:4

12 After him was Eleazar the son of Dodo, the Ahohite, who *was* one of the three mighty men.

11:13 2 Sam 23:11, 12

13 He was with David at Pasdammim when the Philistines were gathered together there to battle, and there was a plot of ground full of barley; and the people fled before the Philistines.

14 They took their stand in the midst of the plot and defended it, and struck down the Philistines; and the LORD saved them by a great victory.

11:15 1 Chr 14:9

15 Now three of the thirty chief men went down to the rock to David, into the cave of Adullam, while the army of the Philistines was camping in the valley of Rephaim.

11:16 1 Sam 10:5

16 David was then in the stronghold, while the garrison of the Philistines *was* then in Bethlehem.

17 David had a craving and said, "Oh that someone would give me water to drink from the well of Bethlehem, which is by the gate!"

18 So the three broke through the camp of the Philistines and drew water from the well of Bethlehem which *was* by the gate, and took *it* and brought *it* to David; nevertheless David would not drink it, but poured it out to the LORD;

19 and he said, "Be it far from me before my God that I should do this. Shall I drink the blood of these men *who went* at the risk of their lives? For at the risk of their lives they brought it." Therefore he would not drink it. These things the three mighty men did.

20 As for Abshai the brother of Joab, he was chief of the thirty, and he swung his spear against three hundred and killed them; and he had a name as well as the thirty.

21 Of the three in the second *rank* he was the most honored and became their commander; however, he did not attain to the *first* three.

11:22 2 Sam 8:18

22 Benaiah the son of Jehoiada, the son of a valiant man of Kabzeel, mighty in deeds, struck down the two *sons of* Ariel of Moab. He also went down and killed a lion inside a pit on a snowy day.

11:23 1 Sam 17:7

23 He killed an Egyptian, a man of *great* stature five cubits tall. Now in the Egyptian's hand *was* a spear like a weaver's beam, but he went down to him with a club and snatched the spear from the Egyptian's hand and killed him with his own spear.

2 I.e. citadel

11:9 David's power increased as a direct result of his consistent trust in God. By contrast, Saul's power decreased because he wanted all the credit for himself and ignored God (1 Samuel 15:17–26). Those who are concerned about building a name for themselves risk losing the very recognition they crave. Like David, we should be concerned about righteousness, honesty, and excellence, and then leave the results to God.

11:12–14 Eleazar's action changed the course of a battle. When everyone around him ran, he held his ground and was saved by the Lord. In any struggle, fear can keep us from taking a stand for God and from participating in God's victories. Face your fear head on. If you are grounded in God, victory will come when you hold that ground.

11:15 The 30 chief men were the most courageous and highest-ranking officers of David's army.

11:15–19 These three men risked their lives just to serve and please David. David recognized that their devotion to him was inspired by their devotion to God, so he poured out the water as a drink offering, demonstrating that only God is worthy of such devotion. They gave the water to David and he, in turn, gave it to God. Just as these men gave of themselves to serve David, we should put aside our own interests to serve other Christians (Romans 12:10). When we serve others, we are also serving God.

24 These *things* Benaiah the son of Jehoiada did, and had a name as well as the three
mighty men.
25 Behold, he was honored among the thirty, but he did not attain to the three; and
David appointed him over his guard.
26 Now the mighty men of the armies *were* Asahel the brother of Joab, Elhanan the
son of Dodo of Bethlehem,
27 Shammoth the Harorite, Helez the Pelonite,
28 Ira the son of Ikkesh the Tekoite, Abiezer the Anathothite,
29 Sibbecai the Hushathite, Ilai the Ahohite,
30 Maharai the Netophathite, Heled the son of Baanah the Netophathite,
31 Ithai the son of Ribai of Gibeah of the sons of Benjamin, Benaiah the Pirathonite,
32 Hurai of the brooks of Gaash, Abiel the Arbathite,
33 Azmaveth the Baharumite, Eliahba the Shaalbonite,
34 the sons of Hashem the Gizonite, Jonathan the son of Shagee the Hararite,
35 Ahiam the son of Sacar the Hararite, Eliphal the son of Ur,
36 Hepher the Mecherathite, Ahijah the Pelonite,
37 Hezro the Carmelite, Naarai the son of Ezbai,
38 Joel the brother of Nathan, Mibhar the son of Hagri,
39 Zelek the Ammonite, Naharai the Berothite, the armor bearer of Joab the son of
Zeruiah,
40 Ira the Ithrite, Gareb the Ithrite,
41 Uriah the Hittite, Zabad the son of Ahlai,
42 Adina the son of Shiza the Reubenite, a chief of the Reubenites, and thirty
with him,
43 Hanan the son of Maacah and Joshaphat the Mithnite,
44 Uzzia the Ashterathite, Shama and Jeiel the sons of Hotham the Aroerite,
45 Jediael the son of Shimri and Joha his brother, the Tizite,
46 Eliel the Mahavite and Jeribai and Joshaviah, the sons of Elnaam, and Ithmah the
Moabite,
47 Eliel and Obed and Jaasiel the Mezobaite.

David's Supporters in Ziklag

12 Now these are the ones who came to David at Ziklag, while he was still restricted **12:1**
because of Saul the son of Kish; and they were among the mighty men who helped 1 Sam 27:2-6
him in war.
2 They were equipped with bows, using both the right hand and the left *to sling* stones **12:2**
and *to shoot* arrows from the bow; *they were* Saul's kinsmen from Benjamin. Judg 3:15; 20:16; 1 Chr 12:29
3 The chief was Ahiezer, then Joash, the sons of Shemaah the Gibeathite; and Jeziel
and Pelet, the sons of Azmaveth, and Beracah and Jehu the Anathothite,
4 and Ishmaiah the Gibeonite, a mighty man among the thirty, and over the thirty.
Then Jeremiah, Jahaziel, Johanan, Jozabad the Gederathite,
5 Eluzai, Jerimoth, Bealiah, Shemariah, Shephatiah the Haruphite,
6 Elkanah, Isshiah, Azarel, Joezer, Jashobeam, the Korahites,
7 and Joelah and Zebadiah, the sons of Jeroham of Gedor.

12:1 Ziklag was a city in Philistia where David had escaped to hide from Saul. Achish, the Philistine ruler of the area, was happy to have a famous Israelite warrior defect to his land. He did not know, however, that David was only pretending loyalty. Achish gave the city of Ziklag to David, his family, and his army (1 Samuel 27:5–7). David's whereabouts was not a great secret, and many loyal followers joined him there.

12:1ff David surrounded himself with great warriors, the best of the Israelite army. What qualities made them worthy to be David's warriors and servants? (1) They had practiced long and hard to perfect their skills (with bow, sling, and spear); (2) they were mentally tough and determined (their "faces were like the faces of lions," 12:8); (3) they were physically in shape ("as swift as the gazelles on the mountains," 12:8); (4) they were dedicated to serving God and David. Weak leaders are easily threatened by competent subordinates, but strong leaders surround themselves with the best. They are not intimidated by able and competent followers.

12:1–7 All the warriors mentioned here were from the tribe of Benjamin. Even members of Saul's own tribe (1 Samuel 9:1–2) were deserting him to help David become king over all Israel. It was clear to them that God had chosen David to be Israel's next leader.

12:2 Archers and slingers had special weapons. The sling was unassuming in appearance but deadly in battle. A shallow leather pouch with a cord of leather or goat's hair attached to each side, the sling was whirled around the head. When one side was released, it sent a stone to its target. The bow and arrow had been in use for thousands of years. Arrowheads were made of stone, wood, or bone because the Philistines still had a monopoly on metalworking (1 Samuel 13:19–20). Arrow shafts were made of reed or wood, and bowstrings were made of animal gut.

12:8 2 Sam 2:18
8 From the Gadites there came over to David in the stronghold in the wilderness,
mighty men of valor, men trained for war, who could handle shield and spear, and whose
faces were like the faces of lions, and *they were* as swift as the gazelles on the mountains.
9 Ezer *was* the first, Obadiah the second, Eliab the third,
10 Mishmannah the fourth, Jeremiah the fifth,
11 Attai the sixth, Eliel the seventh,
12 Johanan the eighth, Elzabad the ninth,
13 Jeremiah the tenth, Machbannai the eleventh.
12:14 Deut 32:30
14 These of the sons of Gad were captains of the army; he who was least was equal to
a hundred and the greatest to a thousand.
12:15 Josh 3:15; 4:18
15 These are the ones who crossed the Jordan in the first month when it was overflowing all its banks and they put to flight all those in the valleys, both to the east and to the
west.
16 Then some of the sons of Benjamin and Judah came to the stronghold to David.
17 David went out to meet them, and said to them, "If you come peacefully to me to
help me, my heart shall be united with you; but if to betray me to my adversaries, since
there is no wrong in my hands, may the God of our fathers look on *it* and decide."
12:18 Judg 3:10; 6:34; 1 Chr 2:17; 1 Sam 25:5, 6
18 Then the Spirit came upon Amasai, who was the chief of the thirty, *and he said,*
"*We* are yours, O David,
And with you, O son of Jesse!
Peace, peace to you,
And peace to him who helps you;
Indeed, your God helps you!"
Then David received them and made them captains of the band.
12:19 1 Sam 29:2-9
19 From Manasseh also some defected to David when he was about to go to battle with
the Philistines against Saul. But they did not help them, for the lords of the Philistines
after consultation sent him away, saying, "At *the cost of* our heads he may defect to his
master Saul."
20 As he went to Ziklag there defected to him from Manasseh: Adnah, Jozabad, Jediael, Michael, Jozabad, Elihu and Zillethai, captains of thousands who belonged to Manasseh.
12:21 1 Sam 30:1
21 They helped David against the band of raiders, for they were all mighty men of valor,
and were captains in the army.
12:22 Gen 32:2; Josh 5:13-15
22 For day by day *men* came to David to help him, until there was a great army like the
army of God.

Supporters Gathered at Hebron

12:23 2 Sam 2:3, 4; 1 Chr 10:14; 1 Chr 11:10
23 Now these are the numbers of the divisions equipped for war, who came to David
at Hebron, to turn the kingdom of Saul to him, according to the word of the LORD.
24 The sons of Judah who bore shield and spear *were* 6,800, equipped for war.
25 Of the sons of Simeon, mighty men of valor for war, 7,100.
26 Of the sons of Levi 4,600.
27 Now Jehoiada was the leader of *the house of* Aaron, and with him were 3,700,
12:28 2 Sam 8:17; 1 Chr 6:8, 53
28 also Zadok, a young man mighty of valor, and of his father's house twenty-two
captains.

12:8 While the men of Benjamin were expert archers and slingers, the warriors of Gad were experts with the shield and spear. Israelite spears had wood shafts and spearheads of bone or stone and were often thrown through the air toward their mark. Philistine spears had bronze shafts and iron spearheads, and their shields were made of wood and overlaid with leather. Large shields were often carried by an armor bearer, whose main task was to protect the warrior.

12:18 How did the Holy Spirit work in Old Testament times? When there was an important job to be done, God chose a person to do it, and the Spirit gave that person the needed power and ability. The Spirit gave Bezalel artistic ability (Exodus 31:1–5), Jephthah military prowess (Judges 11:29), David power to rule (1 Samuel 16:13), and Zechariah an authoritative word of prophecy (2 Chronicles 24:20). Here the Holy Spirit came upon David's warriors. The Spirit came upon individuals in order to accomplish specific goals. Beginning at Pentecost, however, the Spirit came upon all believers, not only to empower them to do God's will, but also to dwell within them day by day (Acts 2:14–21).

12:22 David had "a great army like the army of God." Men were drawn to David by the reputation of his great warriors, the news of their victories, and their desire to see God's will done in making David king. People are often drawn to a great cause and the brave, determined people who support it. As believers, we have the greatest cause—the salvation of mankind. If we are brave, determined, and faithful, others will be drawn to work with us.

12:26–29 In Numbers 1:47–50, God said that the Levites were to be exempt from military service. Why then are they listed as part of David's army? Although they were exempt from the draft, they strongly supported David and volunteered their services to help install him as king.

29 Of the sons of Benjamin, Saul's kinsmen, 3,000; for until now the greatest part of **12:29**
them had kept their allegiance to the house of Saul. 1 Chr 12:2; 2 Sam
30 Of the sons of Ephraim 20,800, mighty men of valor, famous men in their fathers' 2:8, 9
households.
31 Of the half-tribe of Manasseh 18,000, who were designated by name to come and
make David king.
32 Of the sons of Issachar, men who understood the times, with knowledge of what **12:32**
Israel should do, their chiefs *were* two hundred; and all their kinsmen *were* at their com- Esth 1:13
mand.
33 Of Zebulun, there were 50,000 who went out in the army, who could draw up in **12:33**
battle formation with all kinds of weapons of war and helped *David* with an undivided Ps 12:2
heart.
34 Of Naphtali *there were* 1,000 captains, and with them 37,000 with shield and spear.
35 Of the Danites who could draw up in battle formation, *there were* 28,600.
36 Of Asher *there were* 40,000 who went out in the army to draw up in battle formation.
37 From the other side of the Jordan, of the Reubenites and the Gadites and of the
half-tribe of Manasseh, *there were* 120,000 with all *kinds* of weapons of war for the
battle.
38 All these, being men of war who could draw up in battle formation, came to He- **12:38**
bron with a perfect heart to make David king over all Israel; and all the rest also of Isra- 2 Sam 5:1-3; 1 Chr
el were of one mind to make David king. 12:33
39 They were there with David three days, eating and drinking, for their kinsmen had
prepared for them.
40 Moreover those who were near to them, even as far as Issachar and Zebulun and **12:40**
Naphtali, brought food on donkeys, camels, mules and on oxen, great quantities of flour 1 Sam 25:18
cakes, fig cakes and bunches of raisins, wine, oil, oxen and sheep. There was joy indeed
in Israel.

2. David brings the ark to Jerusalem

Peril in Transporting the Ark

13 Then David consulted with the captains of the thousands and the hundreds, even
with every leader.
2 David said to all the assembly of Israel, "If it seems good to you, and if it is from the
LORD our God, let us send everywhere to our kinsmen who remain in all the land of
Israel, also to the priests and Levites who are with them in their cities with pasture lands,
that they may meet with us;
3 and let us bring back the ark of our God to us, for we did not seek it in the days of **13:3**
Saul." 1 Sam 7:1, 2

12:32 The 200 chiefs from the tribe of Issachar "understood the times." As a result, their knowledge and judgment provided needed help in making decisions for the nation. For leaders today, it is equally necessary to know what is happening in society in order to plan the best course of action for the church. Knowledge of current events, trends, and needs helps us understand people's thoughts and attitudes. This gives leaders information to help them make wise decisions for the church and make God's message relevant to people's lives.

12:40 The people were ready for change. They had suffered under Saul's leadership because of his disobedience to God (see 10:13). They were so overjoyed with David's coronation that they contributed lavishly to the celebration. It is right and proper to give generously for celebration and joyous worship. God is the author of joy, and he will join us in our celebrations.

13:1 David took time to confer with all his captains and leaders. As king, he had ultimate authority and could have given orders on his own, but he chose to involve others in leadership. Perhaps this is why there was unanimous support for his decisions (13:1–5). When we are in charge, it is tempting to make unilateral decisions, pushing through our own opinions. But effective leaders listen carefully to others' opinions, and they encourage others to participate in making decisions. Of course, we should always consult God first. We can run into big problems if we don't talk to him (see the note on 13:10).

13:1ff The parallel account of moving the ark (2 Samuel 5; 6) shows that David's building projects were completed *before* he brought the ark to Jerusalem. The writer of Chronicles puts the moving of the ark first in order to highlight David's spiritual accomplishments and relationship to God.

13:3 The ark of God is also called the ark of the covenant. The most sacred object of the Hebrew faith, it was a large box containing the stone tablets on which God had written the Ten Commandments (Exodus 25:10–22). David had already made Jerusalem his political capital (11:4–9). At this time, David brought the ark there in order to make Jerusalem the nation's center for worship.

13:3 The ark of God had been in Kiriath-jearim for many years. The neglect of the ark symbolized Israel's neglect of God. Bringing the ark back to the center of Israel's life reflected David's desire to remind the nation of its true foundation—God. Neglecting those things that remind us of God—the Bible, the church, and contact with Christians—will cause us also to neglect God. We must keep God at the center of our lives.

4 Then all the assembly said that they would do so, for the thing was right in the eyes
of all the people.
5 So David assembled all Israel together, from the Shihor of Egypt even to the entrance of Hamath, to bring the ark of God from Kiriath-jearim.
6 David and all Israel went up to Baalah, *that is,* to Kiriath-jearim, which belongs to
Judah, to bring up from there the ark of God, the LORD who is enthroned *above* the
cherubim, where His name is called.
7 They carried the ark of God on a new cart from the house of Abinadab, and Uzza
and Ahio drove the cart.
8 David and all Israel were celebrating before God with all *their* might, even with songs
and with lyres, harps, tambourines, cymbals and with trumpets.
9 When they came to the threshing floor of Chidon, Uzza put out his hand to hold
the ark, because the oxen nearly upset *it.*
10 The anger of the LORD burned against Uzza, so He struck him down because he
put out his hand to the ark; and he died there before God.
11 Then David became angry because of the LORD'S outburst against Uzza; and he
called that place [3]Perez-uzza to this day.
12 David was afraid of God that day, saying, "How can I bring the ark of God *home*
to me?"
13 So David did not take the ark with him to the city of David, but took it aside to the
house of Obed-edom the Gittite.
14 Thus the ark of God remained with the family of Obed-edom in his house three
months; and the LORD blessed the family of Obed-edom with all that he had.

David's Family Enlarged

14 Now Hiram king of Tyre sent messengers to David with cedar trees, masons and
carpenters, to build a house for him.
2 And David realized that the LORD had established him as king over Israel, *and* that
his kingdom was highly exalted, for the sake of His people Israel.
3 Then David took more wives at Jerusalem, and David became the father of more
sons and daughters.

3 I.e. the breakthrough of Uzza

13:5 2 Sam 6:1; 1 Kin 8:65; 1 Chr 15:3; 1 Sam 6:21; 7:1

13:6 2 Sam 6:2-11; Josh 15:9; Ex 25:22; 2 Kin 19:15

13:7 1 Sam 7:1

13:8 1 Chr 15:16

13:9 2 Sam 6:6

13:10 1 Chr 15:13, 15; Lev 10:2

13:13 1 Chr 15:25

13:14 1 Chr 26:4, 5

14:1 2 Sam 5:11

13:6 Cherubim are mighty angels.

13:8 Worship in the Old Testament was more than a sober religious exercise. David's exuberance as he worshiped God with dancing and music is approved in Scripture. Our worship should reflect a healthy balance: Sometimes we should be reflective and serious (see Exodus 19:14ff), and sometimes we should show enthusiasm and jubilation. What do you need—more serious reflection or more joyous celebration?

13:10 Why did Uzza die? He touched the ark, and that offense was punishable by death. God had given specific instructions about how the ark was to be moved and carried (Numbers 4:5–15), and those instructions were neglected. The Levites were responsible to move the ark (there is no record that Uzza was a Levite), and it was to be carried on their shoulders with poles through its rings (Numbers 7:9). It was *never* to be touched. Bringing the ark on a cart followed the Philistines' example (1 Samuel 6:1ff). Uzza, though sincere in his desire to protect the ark, had to face the consequences of his sin, and David was reminded that his obedience to God's laws was more important than his enthusiasm. Also, David had "consulted with the captains" (13:1) but had neglected to ask God. The advice of our friends and colleagues is no substitute for God's direction.

13:10–14 Uzza died instantly for touching the ark, but God blessed Obed-edom's home where the ark was stored. This demonstrates the two-edged aspect of God's power: He is perfectly loving and perfectly just. Great blessings come to those who obey his commands, but severe punishment comes to those who disobey him. This punishment may come swiftly or over time, but it will come. Sometimes we focus only on the blessings God gives us, while forgetting that when we sin, "It is a terrifying thing to fall into the hands of the living God" (Hebrews 10:31). At other times, however, we concentrate so much on judgment that we miss his blessings. Don't fall into a one-sided view of God. Along with God's blessings comes the responsibility to live up to his demands for fairness, honesty, and justice.

13:11 David was angry at both God and himself. David knew that he had done something wrong in transporting the ark, and he was angry that his plans for the joyous return of the ark had ended in a man's death. But David's anger cooled, and he left the ark in Obed-edom's home until he could consider how to get it to Jerusalem. This allowed David to discover God's instructions for transporting the ark. The next trip would be carried out according to God's commands.

14:1 King Hiram also sent lumber and craftsmen to help Solomon build the temple (2 Chronicles 2:1ff).

14:2 God gave David honor and success ("his kingdom was highly exalted"), but not simply for David's personal gain. David realized that God had prospered him for a special reason—for the sake of God's people! Often we are tempted to use our position or possessions only for our own good. Instead, we must remember that God has placed us where we are and given us all we have so that we may encourage others and give to those in need.

14:3 Accumulating wives and concubines in a harem was the custom of the day among Middle Eastern royalty, but it was not God's ideal (Genesis 2:24). David's marriages brought him greater power and influence, but they also caused strife, jealousy, and even murder within his family. (See the chart in 2 Samuel 12 for other consequences of polygamy.)

4 These are the names of the children born *to him* in Jerusalem: Shammua, Shobab, 14:4 1 Chr 3:5-8
Nathan, Solomon,
5 Ibhar, Elishua, Elpelet,
6 Nogah, Nepheg, Japhia,
7 Elishama, Beeliada and Eliphelet.

Philistines Defeated

8 When the Philistines heard that David had been anointed king over all Israel, all the
Philistines went up in search of David; and David heard of it and went out against them.
9 Now the Philistines had come and made a raid in the valley of Rephaim. 14:9 1 Chr 11:15; 14:13
10 David inquired of God, saying, "Shall I go up against the Philistines? And will You
give them into my hand?" Then the LORD said to him, "Go up, for I will give them into
your hand."
11 So they came up to Baal-perazim, and David defeated them there; and David said,
"God has broken through my enemies by my hand, like the breakthrough of waters."
Therefore they named that place [4]Baal-perazim.
12 They abandoned their gods there; so David gave the order and they were burned
with fire.
13 The Philistines made yet another raid in the valley. 14:13 1 Chr 14:9
14 David inquired again of God, and God said to him, "You shall not go up after them;
circle around behind them and come at them in front of the balsam trees.
15 "It shall be when you hear the sound of marching in the tops of the balsam trees,
then you shall go out to battle, for God will have gone out before you to strike the army
of the Philistines."
16 David did just as God had commanded him, and they struck down the army of the
Philistines from Gibeon even as far as Gezer.
17 Then the fame of David went out into all the lands; and the LORD brought the fear 14:17 Ex 15:14-16; Deut 2:25
of him on all the nations.

Plans to Move the Ark to Jerusalem

15 Now *David* built houses for himself in the city of David; and he prepared a place 15:1 1 Chr 15:3; 16:1; 17:1-5
for the ark of God and pitched a tent for it.
2 Then David said, "No one is to carry the ark of God but the Levites; for the LORD
chose them to carry the ark of God and to minister to Him forever." 15:2 Num 4:15; Deut 10:8
3 And David assembled all Israel at Jerusalem to bring up the ark of the LORD to its
place which he had prepared for it. 15:3 1 Kin 8:1; 1 Chr 13:5; Ex 40:20f; 2 Sam 6:12, 17; 1 Chr 15:1, 12
4 David gathered together the sons of Aaron and the Levites:
5 of the sons of Kohath, Uriel the chief, and 120 of his relatives;
6 of the sons of Merari, Asaiah the chief, and 220 of his relatives; 15:4 1 Chr 6:16-30; 12:26
7 of the sons of Gershom, Joel the chief, and 130 of his relatives;
8 of the sons of Elizaphan, Shemaiah the chief, and 200 of his relatives;
9 of the sons of Hebron, Eliel the chief, and 80 of his relatives;
10 of the sons of Uzziel, Amminadab the chief, and 112 of his relatives.
11 Then David called for Zadok and Abiathar the priests, and for the Levites, for Uriel, 15:11 1 Chr 12:28; 1 Sam 22:20-23; 1 Kin 2:26, 35
Asaiah, Joel, Shemaiah, Eliel and Amminadab,

4 I.e. the master of breakthrough

14:8–16 A map of this battle is in 2 Samuel 5.

14:10 Before David went to battle, he inquired of God, asking for his presence and guidance. Too often we wait until we are in trouble before turning to God. By then the consequences of our actions are already unfolding. Do you ask for God's help only as a desperate last resort? Instead, go to him first! Like David, you may receive incredible help and avoid serious trouble.

14:12 David's quick and decisive action against idols helped unify his kingdom and focus the people on worshiping the one true God. He was obeying the law that said, "But thus you shall do to them: you shall tear down their altars, and smash their sacred pillars, and hew down their Asherim, and burn their graven images with fire" (Deuteronomy 7:5). Most of David's successors failed to destroy idols, and this led to unbelievable moral corruption in Israel.

14:12 Often the soldiers wanted to keep souvenirs from the battle (and 2 Samuel 5:21 states that some of the men kept some of these idols), but David ordered them to burn the idols. The only proper response to sin is to get rid of it completely. You cannot be a follower of God while continuing to hold on to parts of your past life that push God out of the center of your thoughts and actions. Eliminate whatever takes God's rightful place in your life, and follow him with complete devotion.

12 and said to them, "You are the heads of the fathers' *households* of the Levites; consecrate yourselves both you and your relatives, that you may bring up the ark of the LORD
God of Israel to *the place* that I have prepared for it.
13 "Because you did not *carry it* at the first, the LORD our God made an outburst on us,
for we did not seek Him according to the ordinance."
14 So the priests and the Levites consecrated themselves to bring up the ark of the LORD
God of Israel.
15 The sons of the Levites carried the ark of God on their shoulders with the poles
thereon, as Moses had commanded according to the word of the LORD.
16 Then David spoke to the chiefs of the Levites to appoint their relatives the singers,
with instruments of music, harps, lyres, loud-sounding cymbals, to raise sounds of joy.
17 So the Levites appointed Heman the son of Joel, and from his relatives, Asaph the
son of Berechiah; and from the sons of Merari their relatives, Ethan the son of Ku-
shaiah,
18 and with them their relatives of the second rank, Zechariah, Ben, Jaaziel, Shemiramoth, Jehiel, Unni, Eliab, Benaiah, Maaseiah, Mattithiah, Eliphelehu, Mikneiah, Obed-
edom and Jeiel, the gatekeepers.
19 So the singers, Heman, Asaph and Ethan *were appointed* to sound aloud cymbals of
bronze;
20 and Zechariah, Aziel, Shemiramoth, Jehiel, Unni, Eliab, Maaseiah and Benaiah,
with harps *tuned* to alamoth;
21 and Mattithiah, Eliphelehu, Mikneiah, Obed-edom, Jeiel and Azaziah, to lead with
lyres tuned to the sheminith.
22 Chenaniah, chief of the Levites, was *in charge of* the singing; he gave instruction in
singing because he was skillful.
23 Berechiah and Elkanah were gatekeepers for the ark.
24 Shebaniah, Joshaphat, Nethanel, Amasai, Zechariah, Benaiah and Eliezer, the
priests, blew the trumpets before the ark of God. Obed-edom and Jehiah also *were* gatekeepers for the ark.
25 So *it was* David, with the elders of Israel and the captains over thousands, who went
to bring up the ark of the covenant of the LORD from the house of Obed-edom with joy.
26 Because God was helping the Levites who were carrying the ark of the covenant of
the LORD, they sacrificed seven bulls and seven rams.
27 Now David was clothed with a robe of fine linen with all the Levites who were carrying the ark, and the singers and Chenaniah the leader of the singing *with* the singers.
David also wore an ephod of linen.
28 Thus all Israel brought up the ark of the covenant of the LORD with shouting, and
with sound of the horn, with trumpets, with loud-sounding cymbals, with harps and lyres.

15:12 Ex 19:14, 15; 2 Chr 35:6; 1 Chr 15:1, 3
15:13 2 Sam 6:3; 1 Chr 13:7
15:14 1 Chr 15:12
15:15 Ex 25:14; Num 4:5f
15:16 1 Chr 13:8; 25:1
15:17 1 Chr 25:1
15:20 Ps 46: title
15:21 Ps 6: title
15:24 1 Chr 15:28; 16:6
15:25 2 Sam 6:12, 15; 1 Chr 13:13
15:26 Num 23:1-4, 29
15:27 2 Sam 6:14

15:12 The priests consecrated themselves so they would be prepared to carry the ark. To *consecrate* literally means to separate, to set apart for sacred purposes, to purify. The priests symbolically separated themselves from sin and evil. This was done by washing themselves and their clothing in a special ceremony (Numbers 8:5–8). While we are not required to carry out this ceremony today, we can purify ourselves by reading God's Word and preparing our hearts to participate in worship.

15:13 David refers to the incident recorded in 13:8–11 and 2 Samuel 6:1–11. As the ark was being brought back to Israel on a cart, the oxen stumbled. Uzza, trying to steady the ark with his hand, was killed instantly for touching it. The mistake was not in David's desire to move the ark, but in his method for its return. David either ignored or was unaware of the specific instructions in God's law about how the ark was to be moved. Obviously he had discovered his mistake and was now preparing to correct it. This incident was a divine object lesson to all Israel that God governed the king and not the other way around. If David had been allowed to handle the ark of God carelessly, what would that have said to the people about their faith?

15:13–15 When David's first attempt to move the ark failed (13:8–14), he learned an important lesson: When God gives specific instructions, it is wise to follow them precisely. This time David saw to it that the Levites carried the ark (Numbers 4:5–15). We may not fully understand the reasons behind God's instructions, but we do know that his wisdom is complete and his judgment infallible. The way to know God's instructions is to know his Word. But just as children do not understand the reasons for all their parents' instructions until they are older, we may not understand all of God's reasons in this life. It is far better to obey God first, and then discover the reasons. We are never free to disobey God just because we don't understand.

15:16–25 The great musical procession was designed as a worthy accompaniment to the great occasion. It heightened the excitement, elevated the people's hearts and minds, and focused their attention on the event. It also helped seal it in their memory for years to come. Beginning any task by praising God can inspire us to give him our best. Develop the practice of giving praise to God, and you will experience greater joy and strength to face anything.

29 It happened when the ark of the covenant of the LORD came to the city of David, **15:29**
that Michal the daughter of Saul looked out of the window and saw King David leaping 2 Sam 3:13f; 6:16
and celebrating; and she despised him in her heart.

A Tent for the Ark

16 And they brought in the ark of God and placed it inside the tent which David had **16:1**
pitched for it, and they offered burnt offerings and peace offerings before God. 1 Chr 15:1
2 When David had finished offering the burnt offering and the peace offerings, he
blessed the people in the name of the LORD.
3 He distributed to everyone of Israel, both man and woman, to everyone a loaf of
bread and a portion *of meat* and a raisin cake.
4 He appointed some of the Levites *as* ministers before the ark of the LORD, even to
celebrate and to thank and praise the LORD God of Israel:
5 Asaph the chief, and second to him Zechariah, *then* Jeiel, Shemiramoth, Jehiel,
Mattithiah, Eliab, Benaiah, Obed-edom and Jeiel, with musical instruments, harps, lyres;
also Asaph *played* loud-sounding cymbals,
6 and Benaiah and Jahaziel the priests *blew* trumpets continually before the ark of
the covenant of God.
7 Then on that day David first assigned Asaph and his relatives to give thanks to the **16:7**
LORD. 2 Sam 22:1; 23:1

Psalm of Thanksgiving

8 Oh give thanks to the LORD, call upon His name; **16:8**
Make known His deeds among the peoples. 1 Chr 16:8-36; Ps 105:1-15; 1 Kin 8:43; 2 Kin 19:19
9 Sing to Him, sing praises to Him;
[5]Speak of all His wonders.
10 Glory in His holy name;
Let the heart of those who seek the LORD be glad.
11 Seek the LORD and His strength; **16:11**
Seek His face continually. Ps 24:6
12 Remember His wonderful deeds which He has done, **16:12**
His marvels and the judgments from His mouth, Ps 103:2; Ps 78:43-68
13 O seed of Israel His servant,
Sons of Jacob, His chosen ones!
14 He is the LORD our God; **16:14**
His judgments are in all the earth. Ps 48:10
15 Remember His covenant forever,
The word which He commanded to a thousand generations,
16 *The covenant* which He made with Abraham, **16:16**
And His oath to Isaac. Gen 12:7; 17:2; 22:16-18; 26:3
17 He also confirmed it to Jacob for a statute, **16:17**
To Israel as an everlasting covenant, Gen 35:11, 12
18 Saying, "To you I will give the land of Canaan, **16:18**
As the portion of your inheritance." Gen 13:15

5 Or *Meditate on*

15:29 David was willing to look foolish in the eyes of some people in order to express his thankfulness to God fully and honestly. By contrast, Michal was so disgusted by his "undignified" actions that she could not rejoice in the ark's return to Jerusalem. Worship had so deteriorated under her father Saul's reign that it had become stilted and ritualistic. Michal could accept David as a military conqueror and as a king, but she could not accept his free and spontaneous expression of praise to God. Some devoted people may look foolish to us in their heartfelt expressions of worship, but we must accept them. In the same way, we should not be afraid to worship God with whatever expressions seem appropriate.

16:4 Certain Levites were appointed to give continual praise and thanks to God. Praise and thanksgiving should be a regular part of our routine, not reserved only for celebrations. Praise God continually, and you will find that you won't take his blessings for granted.

16:7–36 Four elements of true thanksgiving are found in this song (psalm): (1) *remembering* what God has done, (2) *telling* others about it, (3) *showing* God's glory to others, and (4) *offering* gifts of self, time, and resources. If you are truly thankful, your life will show it.

16:8ff Several parts of this psalm are parallel to songs in the book of Psalms: 16:8–22 with Psalm 105:1–15; 16:23–33 with Psalm 96; 16:34–36 with Psalm 106:1, 47–48.

16:15–18 This covenant was given to Abraham (Genesis 15:18–21), and then passed on to Isaac (Genesis 26:24–25) and Jacob (Genesis 28:13–15). God promised to give the land of Canaan (present-day Israel) to their descendants. He also promised that the Messiah would come from their line.

16:19 Gen 31:30; Deut 7:7

16:21 Gen 12:17; 20:3; Ex 7:15-18

16:22 Gen 20:7

16:23 Ps 96:1-13

16:25 Ps 144:3-6; Ps 89:7

16:26 Lev 19:4; Ps 102:25

16:29 Ps 29:2

16:31 Is 44:23; 49:13; Ps 93:1; 96:10

16:32 Ps 98:7

16:34 2 Chr 5:13; 7:3; Ezra 3:11; Ps 106:1; 136:1; Jer 33:11

16:35 Ps 106:47, 48

16:36 1 Kin 8:15, 56; Ps 72:18; Deut 27:15; Neh 8:6

16:37 1 Chr 16:4, 5; 2 Chr 8:14; Ezra 3:4

16:38 1 Chr 13:14; 1 Chr 26:10

16:39 1 Chr 15:11; 1 Kin 3:4

19 When they were only a few in number,
Very few, and strangers in it,
20 And they wandered about from nation to nation,
And from *one* kingdom to another people,
21 He permitted no man to oppress them,
And He reproved kings for their sakes, *saying,*
22 "Do not touch My anointed ones,
And do My prophets no harm."
23 Sing to the LORD, all the earth;
Proclaim good tidings of His salvation from day to day.
24 Tell of His glory among the nations,
His wonderful deeds among all the peoples.
25 For great is the LORD, and greatly to be praised;
He also is to be feared above all gods.
26 For all the gods of the peoples are idols,
But the LORD made the heavens.
27 Splendor and majesty are before Him,
Strength and joy are in His place.
28 Ascribe to the LORD, O families of the peoples,
Ascribe to the LORD glory and strength.
29 Ascribe to the LORD the glory due His name;
Bring an offering, and come before Him;
Worship the LORD in holy array.
30 Tremble before Him, all the earth;
Indeed, the world is firmly established, it will not be moved.
31 Let the heavens be glad, and let the earth rejoice;
And let them say among the nations, "The LORD reigns."
32 Let the sea roar, and all it contains;
Let the field exult, and all that is in it.
33 Then the trees of the forest will sing for joy before the LORD;
For He is coming to judge the earth.
34 O give thanks to the LORD, for *He is* good;
For His lovingkindness is everlasting.
35 Then say, "Save us, O God of our salvation,
And gather us and deliver us from the nations,
To give thanks to Your holy name,
And glory in Your praise."
36 Blessed be the LORD, the God of Israel,
From everlasting even to everlasting.
Then all the people said, "Amen," and praised the LORD.

Worship before the Ark

37 So he left Asaph and his relatives there before the ark of the covenant of the LORD
to minister before the ark continually, as every day's work required;
38 and Obed-edom with his 68 relatives; Obed-edom, also the son of Jeduthun, and
Hosah as gatekeepers.
39 *He left* Zadok the priest and his relatives the priests before the tabernacle of the
LORD in the high place which *was* at Gibeon,

16:25 The basis of praise is declaring God's character and attributes in the presence of others. When we recognize and affirm his goodness we are holding up his perfect moral nature for all to see. Praise benefits us because it takes our minds off our problems and needs and focuses on God's power, mercy, majesty, and love.

16:29 Genuine praise also involves ascribing glory to God. Remember this in your worship—give God all the glory.

16:37 Asaph and his fellow Levites ministered in the temple, doing each day whatever was needed. To carry out God's work is not merely to engage in religious exercises. It includes other necessary tasks. Even if you don't have the opportunity to teach or preach, God can use you in the ministry. What needs to be done? Cleaning, serving, singing, planning, administering? Look for ways to minister each day.

16:39 David brought the ark to Jerusalem although the tabernacle was still at Gibeon. His plan was to reunite the tabernacle and ark in a new temple at Jerusalem that would then become Israel's only worship center. The temple, however, was not built until Solomon's time. In the meantime, Israel had two worship centers and two high priests (15:11), one at Gibeon and one at Jerusalem.

40 to offer burnt offerings to the LORD on the altar of burnt offering continually morn- 16:40 Ex 29:38-42; Num 28:3, 4
ing and evening, even according to all that is written in the law of the LORD, which He
commanded Israel.
41 With them *were* Heman and Jeduthun, and the rest who were chosen, who were 16:41 1 Chr 6:33; 1 Chr 25:1-6; 2 Chr 5:13
designated by name, to give thanks to the LORD, because His lovingkindness is ever-
lasting.
42 And with them *were* Heman and Jeduthun *with* trumpets and cymbals for those who 16:42 1 Chr 25:7; 2 Chr 7:6; 29:27
should sound aloud, and *with* instruments *for* the songs of God, and the sons of Jedu-
thun for the gate.
43 Then all the people departed each to his house, and David returned to bless his 16:43 2 Sam 6:19
household.

God's Covenant with David

17 And it came about, when David dwelt in his house, that David said to Nathan the 17:1 2 Sam 7:1-29
prophet, "Behold, I am dwelling in a house of cedar, but the ark of the covenant
of the LORD is under curtains."
2 Then Nathan said to David, "Do all that is in your heart, for God is with you."
3 It came about the same night that the word of God came to Nathan, saying,
4 "Go and tell David My servant, 'Thus says the LORD, "You shall not build a house 17:4 1 Chr 28:2, 3
for Me to dwell in;
5 for I have not dwelt in a house since the day that I brought up Israel to this day, but 17:5 Ex 40:2, 3; 2 Sam 7:6
I have gone from tent to tent and from *one* dwelling place *to another.*
6 "In all places where I have walked with all Israel, have I spoken a word with any of 17:6 2 Sam 7:7
the judges of Israel, whom I commanded to shepherd My people, saying, 'Why have you
not built for Me a house of cedar?' " '
7 "Now, therefore, thus shall you say to My servant David, 'Thus says the LORD of hosts,
"I took you from the pasture, from following the sheep, to be leader over My people
Israel.
8 "I have been with you wherever you have gone, and have cut off all your enemies
from before you; and I will make you a name like the name of the great ones who are in
the earth.
9 "I will appoint a place for My people Israel, and will plant them, so that they may
dwell in their own place and not be moved again; and the wicked will not waste them
anymore as formerly,
10 even from the day that I commanded judges *to be* over My people Israel. And I will
subdue all your enemies.
Moreover, I tell you that the LORD will build a house for you.
11 "When your days are fulfilled that you must go *to be* with your fathers, that I will set
up *one of* your descendants after you, who will be of your sons; and I will establish his
kingdom.
12 "He shall build for Me a house, and I will establish his throne forever.
13 "I will be his father and he shall be My son; and I will not take My lovingkindness 17:13 2 Cor 6:18; Heb 1:5; 1 Chr 10:14
away from him, as I took it from him who was before you.
14 "But I will settle him in My house and in My kingdom forever, and his throne shall
be established forever." ' "
15 According to all these words and according to all this vision, so Nathan spoke to
David.

17:1 David felt disturbed that the ark, the symbol of God's presence, sat in a tent while he lived in a beautiful palace. David's desire was right, but his timing was wrong. God told David *not* to build a temple (17:3–4), and David was willing to abide by God's timing. If you live in comparative luxury while God's work, house, or ministers go lacking, perhaps God wants you to change the situation. Like David, take action to correct the imbalance, but be willing to move according to God's timing.

17:3–14 God did not want a warrior to build his temple (28:3; 1 Kings 5:3), and David had shed much blood in unifying the nation. So the honor of building the temple would go to David's son Solomon. David would pass on to Solomon a peaceful and united kingdom, ready to begin work on a beautiful temple.

17:10 God promised to subdue David's enemies. Chapters 18—20 tell how God kept that promise.

17:12–14 Why, after this eternal promise, were the Israelites eventually taken from the promised land into captivity? The promise to David had two parts. The first part was conditional: As long as David's descendants followed God's laws and honored him, they would continually be on the throne of Israel. The second part was unconditional: A son of David would occupy his throne forever. This was Jesus the Messiah. The first part of the promise was based on the faithful obedience of David's descendants. The second part would come true regardless of the way his descendants acted.

David's Prayer in Response

17:16 2 Sam 7:18 **16** Then David the king went in and sat before the LORD and said, "Who am I, O LORD
God, and what is my house that You have brought me this far?
17 "This was a small thing in Your eyes, O God; but You have spoken of Your servant's
house for a great while to come, and have regarded me according to the standard of a
man of high degree, O LORD God.
18 "What more can David still *say* to You concerning the honor *bestowed* on Your servant? For You know Your servant.
17:19 2 Sam 7:21; Is 37:35 19 "O LORD, for Your servant's sake, and according to Your own heart, You have
wrought all this greatness, to make known all these great things.
20 "O LORD, there is none like You, nor is there any God besides You, according to all
that we have heard with our ears.
21 "And what one nation in the earth is like Your people Israel, whom God went to
redeem for Himself *as* a people, to make You a name by great and terrible things, in
driving out nations from before Your people, whom You redeemed out of Egypt?
17:22 Ex 19:5, 6 22 "For Your people Israel You made Your own people forever, and You, O LORD,
became their God.
23 "Now, O LORD, let the word that You have spoken concerning Your servant and
concerning his house be established forever, and do as You have spoken.
24 "Let Your name be established and magnified forever, saying, 'The LORD of hosts is
the God of Israel, *even* a God to Israel; and the house of David Your servant is established before You.'
25 "For You, O my God, have revealed to Your servant that You will build for him a
house; therefore Your servant has found *courage* to pray before You.
26 "Now, O LORD, You are God, and have promised this good thing to Your servant.
27 "And now it has pleased You to bless the house of Your servant, that it may continue
forever before You; for You, O LORD, have blessed, and it is blessed forever."

3. David's military exploits

David's Kingdom Strengthened

18:1 2 Sam 8:1-18 **18** Now after this it came about that David defeated the Philistines and subdued them
and took Gath and its towns from the hand of the Philistines.
2 He defeated Moab, and the Moabites became servants to David, bringing tribute.
3 David also defeated Hadadezer king of Zobah *as far as* Hamath, as he went to establish his rule to the Euphrates River.

17:16–20 God told David that Solomon would be given the honor of building the temple. David responded with deep humility, not resentment. This king who had conquered his enemies and was loved by his people said, "Who am I . . . that You have brought me this far?" David recognized that God was the *true* king. God has done just as much for us, and he plans to do even more! Like David, we should humble ourselves and give glory to God, saying, "O LORD, there is none like You." When God chooses someone else to implement your ideas, will you respond with such humility?

17:16–27 David prayed by humbling himself (17:16–18), praising God (17:19–20), recognizing God's blessings (17:21–22), and accepting God's decisions, promises, and commands (17:23–24). Sometimes we are quick to make requests to God and to tell him our troubles, but these other dimensions of prayer can deepen our spiritual life. Take time to praise God, to count his blessings, and to affirm your commitment to do what he has already said to do.

17:21 David's reference to Israel's exodus from Egypt would have had special significance to the original readers of 1 Chronicles who were either beginning or had just completed a second great exodus back to Israel from captivity in Babylon. Remembering God's promises, mercy, and protection during the first exodus would have encouraged the exiles returning once again to Israel, just as God had promised.

18:2 In 2 Samuel 8:1–2, it is recorded that David killed two-thirds of the people of Moab. His ancestor Ruth was originally from the land of Moab.

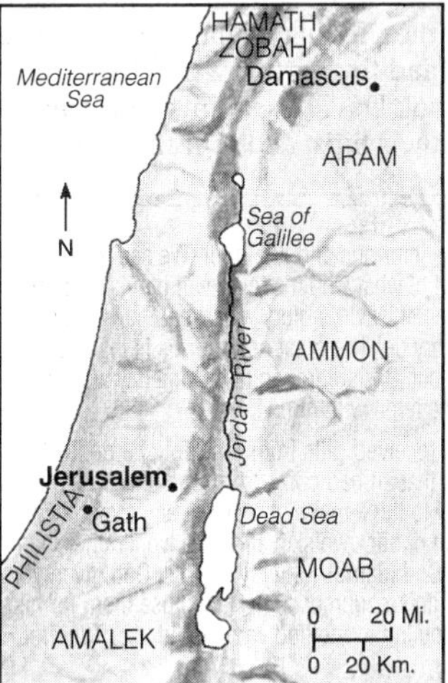

DAVID SUBDUES HIS ENEMIES
David expanded his kingdom as the Lord continued to give him victory. He subdued the Philistines by taking Gath, conquered Moab, won battles as far north as Zobah and Hamath (conquering Aram when they came to help these enemy nations), and subdued the other surrounding nations of Ammon and Amalek.

4 David took from him 1,000 chariots and 7,000 horsemen and 20,000 foot soldiers,
and David hamstrung all the chariot horses, but reserved *enough* of them for 100 chariots.
5 When the Arameans of Damascus came to help Hadadezer king of Zobah, David **18:5**
killed 22,000 men of the Arameans. 1 Chr 19:6
6 Then David put *garrisons* among the Arameans of Damascus; and the Arameans became servants to David, bringing tribute. And the LORD helped David wherever he went.
7 David took the shields of gold which were carried by the servants of Hadadezer and
brought them to Jerusalem.
8 Also from Tibhath and from Cun, cities of Hadadezer, David took a very large **18:8**
amount of bronze, with which Solomon made the bronze sea and the pillars and the 1 Kin 7:40-47; 2 Chr 4:11-18
bronze utensils.
9 Now when Tou king of Hamath heard that David had defeated all the army of Hadadezer king of Zobah,
10 he sent Hadoram his son to King David to greet him and to bless him, because he
had fought against Hadadezer and had defeated him; for Hadadezer had been at war
with Tou. And *Hadoram brought* all kinds of articles of gold and silver and bronze.
11 King David also dedicated these to the LORD with the silver and the gold which he
had carried away from all the nations: from Edom, Moab, the sons of Ammon, the Philistines, and from Amalek.
12 Moreover Abishai the son of Zeruiah defeated 18,000 Edomites in the Valley of Salt.
13 Then he put garrisons in Edom, and all the Edomites became servants to David.
And the LORD helped David wherever he went.
14 So David reigned over all Israel; and he administered justice and righteousness for
all his people.
15 Joab the son of Zeruiah *was* over the army, and Jehoshaphat the son of Ahilud *was* **18:15**
recorder; 1 Chr 11:6
16 and Zadok the son of Ahitub and Abimelech the son of Abiathar *were* priests, and
Shavsha *was* secretary;
17 and Benaiah the son of Jehoiada *was* over the Cherethites and the Pelethites, and
the sons of David *were* chiefs at the king's side.

David's Messengers Abused

19 Now it came about after this, that Nahash the king of the sons of Ammon died, **19:1**
and his son became king in his place. 2 Sam 10:1-19
2 Then David said, "I will show kindness to Hanun the son of Nahash, because his
father showed kindness to me." So David sent messengers to console him concerning
his father. And David's servants came into the land of the sons of Ammon to Hanun to
console him.
3 But the princes of the sons of Ammon said to Hanun, "Do you think that David is
honoring your father, in that he has sent comforters to you? Have not his servants come
to you to search and to overthrow and to spy out the land?"
4 So Hanun took David's servants and shaved them and cut off their garments in the
middle as far as their hips, and sent them away.

18:6, 14 David was a victorious and just ruler. We see in David's glowing success a hint of what Christ's reign will be like—complete victory and justice. If David's glory was great, how much greater will Christ's glory be! The great news for us is that we can be rightly related to Jesus Christ through faith. One day we will share in his glory as we reign with him.

18:9–11 When David received gifts from King Tou, he dedicated them to God, realizing that all had come from God and was to be used for him. It is easy to think that our financial and material blessings are the result of our own skill and hard work rather than coming from a loving God (James 1:17). What has God given you? Dedicate all your gifts and resources to him, and use them for his service. He will lead you in the method you should use. The first step is to be willing.

18:13 The list of battles in this chapter shows how God gave David victory after victory. Unbelieving people think that victory comes from their own skill plus a little luck. Just as David acknowledged God's role in his success, so should we. Don't take credit for the work God does.

18:17 The Cherethites and Pelethites were probably a group of foreign soldiers who had joined David during his flight from Saul. They remained loyal to David throughout his reign (2 Samuel 15:17–18) and became part of his bodyguard.

19:1 The land of Ammon bordered Israel to the east. The nation had a sordid beginning—its founding ancestor, Ben-ammi, was conceived through incest between Lot and his daughter (Genesis 19:30–38). The Ammonites, who were constant enemies of Israel, reached their greatest strength in the days of the judges. David was the first military leader of Israel to crush them. They were unable to cause further trouble for many years.

19:2–3 Hanun misread David's intentions. Because he was overly suspicious, he brought disaster upon himself. Because of past experiences, it is easy to be overly suspicious of others, questioning every move and second-guessing their motives. But while we should be cautious and wise as we deal with others, we should not assume their every action is ill-intended.

5 Then *certain persons* went and told David about the men. And he sent to meet them,
for the men were greatly humiliated. And the king said, "Stay at Jericho until your beards
grow, and *then* return."

19:6 1 Chr 18:5, 9

6 When the sons of Ammon saw that they had made themselves odious to David,
Hanun and the sons of Ammon sent 1,000 talents of silver to hire for themselves chariots and horsemen from Mesopotamia, from Aram-maacah and from Zobah.

19:7 Num 21:30; Josh 13:9, 16

7 So they hired for themselves 32,000 chariots, and the king of Maacah and his people, who came and camped before Medeba. And the sons of Ammon gathered together
from their cities and came to battle.
8 When David heard *of it,* he sent Joab and all the army, the mighty men.
9 The sons of Ammon came out and drew up in battle array at the entrance of the
city, and the kings who had come were by themselves in the field.

Ammon and Aram Defeated

10 Now when Joab saw that the battle was set against him in front and in the rear, he
selected from all the choice men of Israel and they arrayed themselves against the Arameans.
11 But the remainder of the people he placed in the hand of Abshai his brother; and
they arrayed themselves against the sons of Ammon.
12 He said, "If the Arameans are too strong for me, then you shall help me; but if the
sons of Ammon are too strong for you, then I will help you.
13 "Be strong, and let us show ourselves courageous for the sake of our people and for
the cities of our God; and may the LORD do what is good in His sight."
14 So Joab and the people who were with him drew near to the battle against the Arameans, and they fled before him.
15 When the sons of Ammon saw that the Arameans fled, they also fled before Abshai
his brother and entered the city. Then Joab came to Jerusalem.
16 When the Arameans saw that they had been defeated by Israel, they sent messengers and brought out the Arameans who were beyond the [6]River, with Shophach the
commander of the army of Hadadezer leading them.
17 When it was told David, he gathered all Israel together and crossed the Jordan, and
came upon them and drew up in formation against them. And when David drew up in
battle array against the Arameans, they fought against him.
18 The Arameans fled before Israel, and David killed of the Arameans 7,000 charioteers and 40,000 foot soldiers, and put to death Shophach the commander of the
army.
19 So when the servants of Hadadezer saw that they were defeated by Israel, they made
peace with David and served him. Thus the Arameans were not willing to help the sons
of Ammon anymore.

War with Philistine Giants

20:1 2 Sam 11:1; 2 Sam 12:26

20 Then it happened in the spring, at the time when kings go out *to battle,* that Joab
led out the army and ravaged the land of the sons of Ammon, and came and besieged Rabbah. But David stayed at Jerusalem. And Joab struck Rabbah and overthrew it.

6 I.e. Euphrates

19:4–5 Israelite men always wore beards. To be forcibly shaven was embarrassing enough, but these men were also left half naked. Hanun's actions humiliated these men and insulted Israel.

19:6 Rather than admit his mistake and seek forgiveness and reconciliation, Hanun spent an enormous amount of money to cover up his error. His cover-up cost him dearly (20:1–4). It often costs more to cover up an error than to admit it honestly. Rather than compound an error through defensiveness, seek forgiveness and reconciliation as soon as you realize your mistake. You will save yourself and others a lot of pain and trouble.

20:1 David's adultery occurred at this time, while he remained in Jerusalem instead of going to battle (2 Samuel 11–12). This story may have been excluded from 1 Chronicles because the book was written to focus on God's long-term interest in Israel and on the temple as a symbol of God's presence among them. The story of David and Bathsheba did not fit this purpose. The story of Absalom's rebellion, which occurred between this chapter and the next, was probably omitted for the same reason (2 Samuel 15—18).

20:1 Kings went out to battle following the spring harvest. At this time, farm work eased off, and the armies could live off the land. During the winter, they plotted and planned future conquests. Then, when the fair weather permitted it, their armies went into war. But David ignored this opportunity. He stayed home and sent Joab out to lead the army. It was during this time of inactivity that he sinned with Bathsheba. Look for the "springs" in your life, the times when God wants you to respond, take the initiative, and move out to do his will. It is during these critical times that we may be most sensitive to temptation. Resolve to take the action God has prescribed. Don't give temptation a foothold in your inactivity.

20:1 Rabbah was the capital of the Ammonites and is the site of modern Amman in Jordan.

2 David took the crown of their king from his head, and he found it to weigh a talent **20:2**
of gold, and there was a precious stone in it; and it was placed on David's head. And he 2 Sam 12:30, 31
brought out the spoil of the city, a very great amount.
3 He brought out the people who *were* in it, and cut *them* with saws and with sharp **20:3**
instruments and with axes. And thus David did to all the cities of the sons of Ammon. 2 Sam 12:31
Then David and all the people returned *to* Jerusalem.
4 Now it came about after this, that war broke out at Gezer with the Philistines; then **20:4**
Sibbecai the Hushathite killed Sippai, one of the descendants of the giants, and they were 2 Sam 21:18-22
subdued.
5 And there was war with the Philistines again, and Elhanan the son of Jair killed **20:5**
Lahmi the brother of Goliath the Gittite, the shaft of whose spear *was* like a weaver's 2 Sam 21:19; 1 Sam 17:7; 1 Chr 11:23
beam.
6 Again there was war at Gath, where there was a man of *great* stature who had twenty-
four fingers and toes, six *fingers on each hand* and six *toes on each foot;* and he also was
descended from the giants.
7 When he taunted Israel, Jonathan the son of Shimea, David's brother, killed him.
8 These were descended from the giants in Gath, and they fell by the hand of David
and by the hand of his servants.

Census Brings Pestilence

21 Then Satan stood up against Israel and moved David to number Israel. **21:1**
2 So David said to Joab and to the princes of the people, "Go, number Israel 2 Sam 24:1-25
from Beersheba even to Dan, and bring me *word* that I may know their number." **21:2**
3 Joab said, "May the LORD add to His people a hundred times as many as they are! 1 Chr 27:23, 24
But, my lord the king, are they not all my lord's servants? Why does my lord seek this **21:3**
thing? Why should he be a cause of guilt to Israel?" Deut 1:11
4 Nevertheless, the king's word prevailed against Joab. Therefore, Joab departed and
went throughout all Israel, and came to Jerusalem.
5 Joab gave the number of the census of *all* the people to David. And all Israel were **21:5**
1,100,000 men who drew the sword; and Judah *was* 470,000 men who drew the sword. 2 Sam 24:9
6 But he did not number Levi and Benjamin among them, for the king's command **21:6**
was abhorrent to Joab. 1 Chr 27:24
7 God was displeased with this thing, so He struck Israel.
8 David said to God, "I have sinned greatly, in that I have done this thing. But now, **21:8**
please take away the iniquity of Your servant, for I have done very foolishly." 2 Sam 12:13
9 The LORD spoke to Gad, David's seer, saying, **21:9**
10 "Go and speak to David, saying, 'Thus says the LORD, "I offer you three things; choose 2 Sam 24:11; 1 Chr 29:29; 1 Sam 9:9
for yourself one of them, which I will do to you." ' "
11 So Gad came to David and said to him, "Thus says the LORD, 'Take for yourself
12 either three years of famine, or three months to be swept away before your foes, **21:12**
while the sword of your enemies overtakes *you,* or else three days of the sword of the 2 Sam 24:13
LORD, even pestilence in the land, and the angel of the LORD destroying throughout all

---

21:1 David's census brought disaster because, unlike the census taken in the book of Numbers (Numbers 1; 2) that God had ordered, this census was taken so David could take pride in the strength of his army. In determining his military strength, he was beginning to trust more in military power than in God. There is a thin line between feeling confident because you rely on God's power and becoming proud because you have been used by God for great purposes.

21:1 The Bible text says Satan *moved* David to take a census. Can Satan force people to do wrong? No, Satan only *tempted* David with the idea, but David *decided to act* on the temptation. Ever since the Garden of Eden, Satan has been tempting people to sin. David's census was not against God's Law, but his reason for the census was wrong—pride in his mighty army while forgetting that his real strength came from God. Even Joab, not known for his high moral ideals, recognized the census as sin. From David's example we learn that an action that may not be wrong in itself can be sinful if it is motivated by greed, arrogance, or selfishness. Often our motives, not the action itself, contain the sin. We must constantly weigh our motives before we act.

21:1–3 David fell to Satan's temptation. God provided a way out in Joab's counsel, but David's curiosity was spurred on by arrogance. His faith was in his own strength rather than in God's. If we feel self-sufficient and put confidence in ourselves apart from God, we soon fall to Satan's schemes. Self-sufficiency pulls us away from God. When you are tempted, examine your inner desires to understand why the external temptation is so appealing. (See 1 Corinthians 10:13 for more about escaping temptation.)

21:8 When David realized his sin, he took full responsibility, admitted he was wrong, and asked God to forgive him. Many people want to add God and the benefits of Christianity to their lives without acknowledging their personal sin and guilt. But confession and repentance must come before receiving forgiveness. Like David, we must take full responsibility for our actions and confess them to God before we can expect him to forgive us and continue his work in us.

the territory of Israel.' Now, therefore, consider what answer I shall return to Him who
sent me."
21:13 Ps 51:1; 130:4, 7 13 David said to Gad, "I am in great distress; please let me fall into the hand of the
LORD, for His mercies are very great. But do not let me fall into the hand of man."
21:14 1 Chr 27:24 **14** So the LORD sent a pestilence on Israel; 70,000 men of Israel fell.
15 And God sent an angel to Jerusalem to destroy it; but as he was about to destroy *it,*
21:15 Ex 32:14; 1 Sam 15:11; Jon 3:10 the LORD saw and was sorry over the calamity, and said to the destroying angel, "It is
enough; now relax your hand." And the angel of the LORD was standing by the thresh-
ing floor of Ornan the Jebusite.
21:16 1 Kin 21:27 16 Then David lifted up his eyes and saw the angel of the LORD standing between earth
and heaven, with his drawn sword in his hand stretched out over Jerusalem. Then David
and the elders, covered with sackcloth, fell on their faces.
21:17 2 Sam 7:8; Ps 74:1 17 David said to God, "Is it not I who commanded to count the people? Indeed, I am
the one who has sinned and done very wickedly, but these sheep, what have they done?
O LORD my God, please let Your hand be against me and my father's household, but
not against Your people that they should be plagued."

David's Altar

21:18 2 Chr 3:1 **18** Then the angel of the LORD commanded Gad to say to David, that David should go
up and build an altar to the LORD on the threshing floor of Ornan the Jebusite.
19 So David went up at the word of Gad, which he spoke in the name of the LORD.
20 Now Ornan turned back and saw the angel, and his four sons *who were* with him hid
themselves. And Ornan was threshing wheat.
21 As David came to Ornan, Ornan looked and saw David, and went out from the
threshing floor and prostrated himself before David with his face to the ground.
22 Then David said to Ornan, "Give me the site of *this* threshing floor, that I may build
on it an altar to the LORD; for the full price you shall give it to me, that the plague may
be restrained from the people."
23 Ornan said to David, "Take *it* for yourself; and let my lord the king do what is good
in his sight. See, I will give the oxen for burnt offerings and the threshing sledges for
wood and the wheat for the grain offering; I will give *it* all."
24 But King David said to Ornan, "No, but I will surely buy *it* for the full price; for I
will not take what is yours for the LORD, or offer a burnt offering which costs me
nothing."
21:25 2 Sam 24:24 25 So David gave Ornan 600 shekels of gold by weight for the site.
26 Then David built an altar to the LORD there and offered burnt offerings and peace
21:26 Lev 9:24; Judg 6:21 offerings. And he called to the LORD and He answered him with fire from heaven on the
altar of burnt offering.
27 The LORD commanded the angel, and he put his sword back in its sheath.
28 At that time, when David saw that the LORD had answered him on the threshing
floor of Ornan the Jebusite, he offered sacrifice there.

21:13–14 Sin has a domino effect; once a sin is committed, a series of consequences follows. God will forgive our sin if we ask him, but the consequences of that sin have already been set in motion. David pled for mercy, and God responded by stopping the angel before his mission of death was complete. The consequences of David's sin, however, had already caused severe damage. God will always forgive our sins and will often intervene to make their bitter consequences less severe, but the scars will remain. Thinking through the possible consequences before we act can stop us and thus save us much sorrow and suffering.

21:14 Why did 70,000 innocent people die for David's sin? Our society places great emphasis upon the individual. In ancient times, however, the family leaders, tribal leaders, and kings represented the people they led, and all expected to share in their successes as well as in their failures and punishments. David deserved punishment for his sin, but his death could have resulted in political chaos and invasion by enemy armies, leaving hundreds of thousands dead. Instead, God graciously spared David's life. He also put a stop to the plague so that most of the people of Jerusalem were spared.

God made us to work together interdependently. Whether or not we think it is fair, our actions always affect other people. We cannot fully know the mind of God in this severe judgment. We don't know where the prophets, the tribal leaders, and the other advisers were during this incident or whether or not they chose to go along with the king. We do know that putting confidence in military might alone is idolatry. To allow anything to take God's place is sinful, and it may cause disastrous consequences.

21:22–24 When David wanted to buy Ornan's land to build an altar, Ornan generously offered it as a gift. But David refused, saying, "I will not take what is yours for the LORD, or offer a burnt offering which costs me nothing." David wanted to offer a sacrifice to God. The word *sacrifice* implies giving something that costs the giver in terms of self, time, or money. To give sacrificially requires more than a token effort or gift. God wants us to give voluntarily, but he wants it to mean something. Giving to God what costs you nothing does not demonstrate commitment.

29 For the tabernacle of the LORD, which Moses had made in the wilderness, and the
altar of burnt offering *were* in the high place at Gibeon at that time.
30 But David could not go before it to inquire of God, for he was terrified by the sword
of the angel of the LORD.

21:29 1 Kin 3:4; 1 Chr 16:39

4. David arranges for the building of the temple

David Prepares for Temple Building

22 Then David said, "This is the house of the LORD God, and this is the altar of burnt
offering for Israel."
2 So David gave orders to gather the foreigners who were in the land of Israel, and he
set stonecutters to hew out stones to build the house of God.
3 David prepared large quantities of iron to make the nails for the doors of the gates
and for the clamps, and more bronze than could be weighed;
4 and timbers of cedar logs beyond number, for the Sidonians and Tyrians brought
large quantities of cedar timber to David.
5 David said, "My son Solomon is young and inexperienced, and the house that is to
be built for the LORD shall be exceedingly magnificent, famous and glorious throughout
all lands. *Therefore* now I will make preparation for it." So David made ample preparations before his death.

22:1 1 Chr 21:18-28; 2 Chr 3:1
22:2 1 Kin 9:20, 21; 2 Chr 2:17; 1 Kin 5:17, 18
22:3 1 Chr 29:2, 7; 1 Chr 22:14
22:4 1 Kin 5:6-10
22:5 1 Kin 3:7; 1 Chr 29:1

Solomon Charged with the Task

6 Then he called for his son Solomon, and charged him to build a house for the LORD
God of Israel.
7 David said to Solomon, "My son, I had intended to build a house to the name of the
LORD my God.
8 "But the word of the LORD came to me, saying, 'You have shed much blood and have
waged great wars; you shall not build a house to My name, because you have shed *so*
much blood on the earth before Me.
9 'Behold, a son will be born to you, who shall be a man of rest; and I will give him rest
from all his enemies on every side; for his name shall be [7]Solomon, and I will give peace
and quiet to Israel in his days.
10 'He shall build a house for My name, and he shall be My son and I will be his father;
and I will establish the throne of his kingdom over Israel forever.'
11 "Now, my son, the LORD be with you that you may be successful, and build the house
of the LORD your God just as He has spoken concerning you.
12 "Only the LORD give you discretion and understanding, and give you charge over
Israel, so that you may keep the law of the LORD your God.
13 "Then you will prosper, if you are careful to observe the statutes and the ordinances
which the LORD commanded Moses concerning Israel. Be strong and courageous, do
not fear nor be dismayed.
14 "Now behold, with great pains I have prepared for the house of the LORD 100,000
talents of gold and 1,000,000 talents of silver, and bronze and iron beyond weight, for they
are in great quantity; also timber and stone I have prepared, and you may add to them.
15 "Moreover, there are many workmen with you, stonecutters and masons of stone and
carpenters, and all men who are skillful in every kind of work.
16 "Of the gold, the silver and the bronze and the iron there is no limit. Arise and work,
and may the LORD be with you."

22:6 1 Kin 2:1
22:7 2 Sam 7:2, 3; 1 Chr 17:1
22:8 1 Chr 28:3
22:9 1 Kin 4:20, 25; 2 Sam 12:24, 25
22:10 2 Sam 7:13, 14; 1 Chr 17:12
22:11 1 Chr 22:16
22:12 1 Kin 3:9-12; 2 Chr 1:10; 1 Kin 2:3
22:13 1 Chr 28:7; Josh 1:6-9
22:14 1 Chr 29:4; 1 Chr 22:3
22:16 1 Chr 22:11

7 I.e. peaceful

21:29—22:1 Gibeon was a Benjaminite city. After the defeat of Nob by Saul, who was a Benjaminite, Saul moved the tabernacle to Gibeon. Gibeon was about two hours journey northwest of Jerusalem.

22:1 Out of David's tragic mistake came the purchase of a plot of land that would become the site of God's temple, the symbol of God's presence among his people. Every time the people went to the temple they would remember that God is their true King and that everyone, including their human king, is fallible and subject to sin. God can use our sins for good purposes if we are sorry for them and seek his forgiveness. When we confess our sins, the way is opened for God to bring good from a bad situation.

22:7–10 God told David he would not be the one to build the temple. Instead the task would be left to his son Solomon. David graciously accepted this "no" from God. He was not jealous of the fact that his son would have the honor of building God's temple, but instead made preparations for Solomon to carry out his task. Similarly, we should take steps now to prepare the way for our children to find and fulfill God's purpose. Sooner or later our children will have to make their own decisions, but we can help by supplying them with the proper tools: showing them how to pray and study God's Word, the difference between right and wrong, and the importance of church involvement.

22:17 1 Chr 28:1-6

22:18 1 Chr 22:9; 23:25

22:19 1 Chr 28:9; 1 Kin 8:6, 21; 2 Chr 5:7; 1 Chr 22:7

17 David also commanded all the leaders of Israel to help his son Solomon, *saying,*
18 "Is not the LORD your God with you? And has He not given you rest on every side?
For He has given the inhabitants of the land into my hand, and the land is subdued before the LORD and before His people.
19 "Now set your heart and your soul to seek the LORD your God; arise, therefore, and
build the sanctuary of the LORD God, so that you may bring the ark of the covenant of
the LORD and the holy vessels of God into the house that is to be built for the name of
the LORD."

Solomon Reigns

23:1 1 Chr 29:28; 1 Kin 1:1-40; 2:12; 1 Chr 28:5; 29:22

23 Now when David reached old age, he made his son Solomon king over Israel.
2 And he gathered together all the leaders of Israel with the priests and the
Levites.

Offices of the Levites

23:3 Num 4:3-49; Num 4:48; 1 Chr 23:24

23:4 Ezra 3:8, 9; 1 Chr 26:29

3 The Levites were numbered from thirty years old and upward, and their number by
census of men was 38,000.
4 Of these, 24,000 were to oversee the work of the house of the LORD; and 6,000 *were*
officers and judges,

DUTIES ASSIGNED IN THE TEMPLE
King David charged all these people to do their jobs "for the name of the LORD" (1 Chronicles 22:17–19). God needs people of every talent—not just prophets and priests—to obey him.

Administrative Duties	Overseers	23:4–5
	Officers	23:4–5
	Judges	23:4–5
	Public administrators	26:29–30
Ministerial Duties	Priests	24:1
	Prophets	25:1
	Assistants for sacrifices	23:29–31
	Assistants for purification ceremonies	23:28
Service Duties	Bakers of the showbread	23:29
	Those who made the measurements	23:29
	Caretakers	23:28
Financial Duties	Those who cared for the treasuries	26:20
	Those who cared for the dedicated things	26:26–28
Artistic Duties	Musicians	25:6
	Singers	25:7
Protective Duties	Gatekeepers	26:12–18
Individual Assignments	Chief of the gatekeepers	9:19–21
	Scribe	24:6
	Seer	25:5
	Prophet under the king	25:2
	Chief officer of the treasuries	26:23–24

23:1 For more information on Solomon's coronation and the attempts to seize his throne, see 1 Kings 1; 2.

23:1ff Although David couldn't build the temple, he could make preparations, and he took that job seriously. He not only gathered funds and materials for God's house, but he also planned much of the administration and arranged the worship services. The original readers of Chronicles were rebuilding the temple after it had been destroyed by invading armies, and this information about its procedures was invaluable to them. The next five chapters demonstrate that organization is essential for smooth and effective service.

23:3 Why was this census acceptable when the other was not (chapter 21)? This census counted only the Levites—those set apart to serve God—and was used to organize the work in the temple. The census was not based on pride or self-sufficiency as was the previous census of fighting men.

5 and 4,000 *were* gatekeepers, and 4,000 *were* praising the LORD with the instruments **23:5**
which David made for giving praise. 1 Chr 15:16
6 David divided them into divisions according to the sons of Levi: Gershon, Kohath, **23:6**
and Merari. 1 Chr 6:1

Gershonites

7 Of the Gershonites *were* Ladan and Shimei.
8 The sons of Ladan *were* Jehiel the first and Zetham and Joel, three.
9 The sons of Shimei *were* Shelomoth and Haziel and Haran, three. These were the
heads of the fathers' *households* of Ladan.
10 The sons of Shimei *were* Jahath, Zina, Jeush and Beriah. These four *were* the sons
of Shimei.
11 Jahath was the first and Zizah the second; but Jeush and Beriah did not have many
sons, so they became a father's household, one class.

Kohathites

12 The sons of Kohath were four: Amram, Izhar, Hebron and Uzziel.
13 The sons of Amram were Aaron and Moses. And Aaron was set apart to sanctify **23:13**
him as most holy, he and his sons forever, to burn incense before the LORD, to minister Ex 6:20; Ex 28:1; Ex
to Him and to bless in His name forever. 30:6-10
14 But *as for* Moses the man of God, his sons were named among the tribe of Levi. **23:14**
15 The sons of Moses *were* Gershom and Eliezer. Deut 33:1; Ps 90:
16 The son of Gershom *was* Shebuel the chief. title
17 The son of Eliezer was Rehabiah the chief; and Eliezer had no other sons, but the
sons of Rehabiah were very many.
18 The son of Izhar was Shelomith the chief.
19 The sons of Hebron *were* Jeriah the first, Amariah the second, Jahaziel the third
and Jekameam the fourth.
20 The sons of Uzziel *were* Micah the first and Isshiah the second.

Merarites

21 The sons of Merari were Mahli and Mushi. The sons of Mahli *were* Eleazar and Kish.
22 Eleazar died and had no sons, but daughters only, so their brothers, the sons of Kish,
took them *as wives.*
23 The sons of Mushi *were* three: Mahli, Eder and Jeremoth.

Duties Revised

24 These were the sons of Levi according to their fathers' households, *even* the heads **23:24**
of the fathers' *households* of those of them who were counted, in the number of names Num 10:17, 21;
by their census, doing the work for the service of the house of the LORD, from twenty 1 Chr 23:3
years old and upward.
25 For David said, "The LORD God of Israel has given rest to His people, and He dwells **23:25**
in Jerusalem forever. 1 Chr 22:18
26 "Also, the Levites will no longer need to carry the tabernacle and all its utensils for **23:26**
its service." Num 4:5, 15; 7:9;
27 For by the last words of David the sons of Levi *were* numbered from twenty years Deut 10:8
old and upward.
28 For their office is to assist the sons of Aaron with the service of the house of the
LORD, in the courts and in the chambers and in the purifying of all holy things, even the
work of the service of the house of God,

23:14 All that is stated here about Moses is that he was "the man of God." What a profound description of a person! A man or woman of God is one whose life reflects God's presence, priorities, and power.

23:28–32 Priests and Levites had different jobs in and around the temple. Priests were authorized to perform the sacrifices. Levites were set apart to help the priests. They did the work of elders, deacons, custodians, assistants, musicians, moving men, and repairmen. Both priests and Levites came from the tribe of Levi, but priests also had to be descendants of Aaron, Israel's first high priest (Exodus 28:1–3). Priests and Levites were supported by Israel's tithes and by revenues from certain cities that had been given to them. Worship in the temple could not have taken place without the combined efforts of the priests and Levites. Their responsibilities were different, but they were equally important to God's plan. No matter what place of service you have in the church, you are important to the healthy functioning of the congregation.

23:29 Lev 24:5-9; Lev 6:20; 1 Chr 9:31; Lev 6:21; Lev 19:35, 36

29 and with the showbread, and the fine flour for a grain offering, and unleavened wafers, or *what is baked in* the pan or what is well-mixed, and all measures of volume and size.

30 They are to stand every morning to thank and to praise the LORD, and likewise at evening,

23:31 Is 1:13, 14; Lev 23:2-4

31 and to offer all burnt offerings to the LORD, on the sabbaths, the new moons and the fixed festivals in the number *set* by the ordinance concerning them, continually before the LORD.

23:32 Num 1:53; 1 Chr 9:27; Num 3:6-9, 38

32 Thus they are to keep charge of the tent of meeting, and charge of the holy place, and charge of the sons of Aaron their relatives, for the service of the house of the LORD.

Divisions of Levites

24:1 Ex 6:23

24 Now the divisions of the descendants of Aaron *were these:* the sons of Aaron *were* Nadab, Abihu, Eleazar and Ithamar.

24:2 Lev 10:2

2 But Nadab and Abihu died before their father and had no sons. So Eleazar and Ithamar served as priests.

24:3 1 Chr 6:8

3 David, with Zadok of the sons of Eleazar and Ahimelech of the sons of Ithamar, divided them according to their offices for their ministry.

4 Since more chief men were found from the descendants of Eleazar than the descendants of Ithamar, they divided them thus: *there were* sixteen heads of fathers' households of the descendants of Eleazar and eight of the descendants of Ithamar, according to their fathers' households.

24:5 1 Chr 24:31

5 Thus they were divided by lot, the one as the other; for they were officers of the sanctuary and officers of God, both from the descendants of Eleazar and the descendants of Ithamar.

24:6 1 Chr 18:16

6 Shemaiah, the son of Nethanel the scribe, from the Levites, recorded them in the presence of the king, the princes, Zadok the priest, Ahimelech the son of Abiathar, and the heads of the fathers' *households* of the priests and of the Levites; one father's household taken for Eleazar and one taken for Ithamar.

7 Now the first lot came out for Jehoiarib, the second for Jedaiah,
8 the third for Harim, the fourth for Seorim,
9 the fifth for Malchijah, the sixth for Mijamin,

24:10 Neh 12:4; Luke 1:5

10 the seventh for Hakkoz, the eighth for Abijah,
11 the ninth for Jeshua, the tenth for Shecaniah,
12 the eleventh for Eliashib, the twelfth for Jakim,
13 the thirteenth for Huppah, the fourteenth for Jeshebeab,
14 the fifteenth for Bilgah, the sixteenth for Immer,
15 the seventeenth for Hezir, the eighteenth for Happizzez,
16 the nineteenth for Pethahiah, the twentieth for Jehezkel,
17 the twenty-first for Jachin, the twenty-second for Gamul,
18 the twenty-third for Delaiah, the twenty-fourth for Maaziah.

24:19 1 Chr 9:25

19 These were their offices for their ministry when *they* came in to the house of the LORD according to the ordinance *given* to them through Aaron their father, just as the LORD God of Israel had commanded him.

20 Now for the rest of the sons of Levi: of the sons of Amram, Shubael; of the sons of Shubael, Jehdeiah.

24:1ff The temple service was highly structured, but this did not hinder the Spirit of God. Rather, it provided an orderly context for worship. (Compare 1 Corinthians 14:40.) Sometimes we feel that planning and structure are unspiritual activities that may hinder spontaneity in worship. But order and structure can free us to respond to God. Order brings glory to God as we experience the joy, freedom, and calm that come when we have wisely prepared in advance.

24:3 This Ahimelech was the son of Abiathar and the grandson of another Ahimelech, one of the priests massacred by Saul (1 Samuel 22:11–18). Abiathar and Zadok were co-high priests under David: One was at Jerusalem where the ark of God was kept, and one was at Gibeon serving at the tabernacle. It appears from this verse and 18:16 that Ahimelech began to assume some of Abiathar's duties as his father grew old.

24:4 Eleazar's descendants were divided into 16 groups (as opposed to Ithamar's eight) for three reasons. (1) Eleazar had received the birthright since his two older brothers, Nadab and Abihu, had been killed (Leviticus 10). The birthright included a double portion of the father's estate. (2) His descendants were greater in number than Ithamar's. (3) His descendants had greater leadership ability. These 24 groups gave order to the functioning of the temple.

24:7–18 Each of these 24 groups of priests served two-week shifts each year at the temple. The rest of the time they served in their hometowns. This system was still in place in Jesus' day (Luke 1:5–9). Zacharias was a member of the Abijah division. During his shift at the temple, an angel appeared to him and predicted that he would have a son, John.

21 Of Rehabiah: of the sons of Rehabiah, Isshiah the first.
22 Of the Izharites, Shelomoth; of the sons of Shelomoth, Jahath.
23 The sons *of Hebron:* Jeriah *the first,* Amariah the second, Jahaziel the third, Jeka- **24:23** 1 Chr 23:19
meam the fourth.
24 *Of* the sons of Uzziel, Micah; of the sons of Micah, Shamir.
25 The brother of Micah, Isshiah; of the sons of Isshiah, Zechariah.
26 The sons of Merari, Mahli and Mushi; the sons of Jaaziah, Beno.
27 The sons of Merari: by Jaaziah *were* Beno, Shoham, Zaccur and Ibri.
28 By Mahli: Eleazar, who had no sons.
29 By Kish: the sons of Kish, Jerahmeel.
30 The sons of Mushi: Mahli, Eder and Jerimoth. These *were* the sons of the Levites
according to their fathers' households.
31 These also cast lots just as their relatives the sons of Aaron in the presence of David **24:31** 1 Chr 24:5, 6; 1 Chr 24:6
the king, Zadok, Ahimelech, and the heads of the fathers' *households* of the priests and
of the Levites—the head of fathers' *households* as well as those of his younger brother.

Number and Services of Musicians

25 Moreover, David and the commanders of the army set apart for the service *some* **25:1** 1 Chr 6:33, 39; 2 Kin 3:15; 1 Chr 15:16
of the sons of Asaph and of Heman and of Jeduthun, who *were* to prophesy with
lyres, harps and cymbals; and the number of those who performed their service was:
2 Of the sons of Asaph: Zaccur, Joseph, Nethaniah and Asharelah; the sons of Asaph
were under the direction of Asaph, who prophesied under the direction of the king.
3 Of Jeduthun, the sons of Jeduthun: Gedaliah, Zeri, Jeshaiah, Shimei, Hashabiah **25:3** 1 Chr 16:41, 42
and Mattithiah, six, under the direction of their father Jeduthun with the harp, who prophesied in giving thanks and praising the LORD.
4 Of Heman, the sons of Heman: Bukkiah, Mattaniah, Uzziel, Shebuel and Jerimoth,
Hananiah, Hanani, Eliathah, Giddalti and Romamti-ezer, Joshbekashah, Mallothi,
Hothir, Mahazioth.
5 All these *were* the sons of Heman the king's seer to exalt him according to the words **25:5** 2 Sam 24:11; 1 Chr 21:9
of God, for God gave fourteen sons and three daughters to Heman.
6 All these were under the direction of their father to sing in the house of the LORD,
with cymbals, harps and lyres, for the service of the house of God. Asaph, Jeduthun and **25:6** 1 Chr 15:16; 1 Chr 15:19
Heman *were* under the direction of the king.
7 Their number who were trained in singing to the LORD, with their [8]relatives, all who **25:7** 1 Chr 23:5
were skillful, *was* 288.

Divisions of Musicians

8 They cast lots for their duties, all alike, the small as well as the great, the teacher as **25:8** 1 Chr 26:13
well as the pupil.
9 Now the first lot came out for Asaph to Joseph, the second for Gedaliah, he with
his relatives and sons were twelve;
10 the third to Zaccur, his sons and his relatives, twelve;
11 the fourth to Izri, his sons and his relatives, twelve;
12 the fifth to Nethaniah, his sons and his relatives, twelve;
13 the sixth to Bukkiah, his sons and his relatives, twelve;
14 the seventh to Jesharelah, his sons and his relatives, twelve;
15 the eighth to Jeshaiah, his sons and his relatives, twelve;
16 the ninth to Mattaniah, his sons and his relatives, twelve;
17 the tenth to Shimei, his sons and his relatives, twelve;
18 the eleventh to Azarel, his sons and his relatives, twelve;

8 Lit *brothers,* and so throughout the ch

25:1 There is more to prophesying than predicting the future. Prophecy also involves singing God's praises and preaching God's messages (1 Corinthians 14:1ff). Prophets could be musicians, farmers (Amos 1:1), wives (2 Kings 22:14), or leaders (Deuteronomy 34:10)—anyone who boldly and accurately spoke out for God and tried to bring people back to worshiping him. From a large group of musicians David chose those who showed an unusual ability to tell about God and to encourage others in song.

25:1–7 There were many ways to contribute to the worship in the tabernacle. Some prophesied (25:1), some led in thanksgiving and praise (25:3), and others played instruments (25:6–7). God wants all his people to participate in worship. You may not be a master musician, a prophet, or a teacher, but God appreciates whatever you have to offer. Develop your special gifts to offer in service to God (Romans 12:3–8; 1 Corinthians 12:29–31).

19 the twelfth to Hashabiah, his sons and his relatives, twelve;
20 for the thirteenth, Shubael, his sons and his relatives, twelve;
21 for the fourteenth, Mattithiah, his sons and his relatives, twelve;
22 for the fifteenth to Jeremoth, his sons and his relatives, twelve;
23 for the sixteenth to Hananiah, his sons and his relatives, twelve;
24 for the seventeenth to Joshbekashah, his sons and his relatives, twelve;
25 for the eighteenth to Hanani, his sons and his relatives, twelve;
26 for the nineteenth to Mallothi, his sons and his relatives, twelve;
27 for the twentieth to Eliathah, his sons and his relatives, twelve;
28 for the twenty-first to Hothir, his sons and his relatives, twelve;
29 for the twenty-second to Giddalti, his sons and his relatives, twelve;
30 for the twenty-third to Mahazioth, his sons and his relatives, twelve;
31 for the twenty-fourth to Romamti-ezer, his sons and his relatives, twelve.

Divisions of the Gatekeepers

26 For the divisions of the gatekeepers *there were* of the Korahites, Meshelemiah the
son of Kore, of the sons of Asaph.
2 Meshelemiah had sons: Zechariah the firstborn, Jediael the second, Zebadiah the
third, Jathniel the fourth,
3 Elam the fifth, Johanan the sixth, Eliehoenai the seventh.
4 Obed-edom had sons: Shemaiah the firstborn, Jehozabad the second, Joah the third,
Sacar the fourth, Nethanel the fifth,
5 Ammiel the sixth, Issachar the seventh *and* Peullethai the eighth; God had indeed
blessed him.

26:4 2 Sam 6:11; 1 Chr 13:14

MUSIC IN BIBLE TIMES
Paul clearly puts forth the Christian's view that things are not good or bad in and of themselves (see Romans 14 and 1 Corinthians 14:7–8, 26). The point should always be to worship the Lord or help others by means of the things of this world, including music. Music was created by God and can be returned to him in praise. Does the music you play or listen to have a negative or positive impact upon your relationship with God?

Highlights of musical use in Scripture	*References*
Jubal was father of all musicians	Genesis 4:21
Miriam and other women sang and danced to praise God	Exodus 15:1–21
The priest was to have bells on his robes	Exodus 28:34–35
Jericho fell to the sound of trumpets	Joshua 6:4–20
Saul experienced the soothing effect of music	1 Samuel 16:14–23
The king's coronation was accompanied by music	1 Kings 1:39–40
The ark was accompanied by trumpeters	1 Chronicles 16:6
There were musicians for the king's court	Ecclesiastes 2:8
From David's time on, the use of music in worship was much more organized. Music for the temple became refined.	1 Chronicles 15:16–24 1 Chronicles 16:4–7 2 Chronicles 5:11–14
Everything was to be used by everyone to praise the Lord	Psalm 150

In the New Testament, worship continued in the synagogues until the Christians became unwelcome there, so there was a rich musical heritage already established. The fact that music is mentioned less often in the New Testament does not mean it was less important.

Jesus and the disciples sang a hymn	Matthew 26:30
Paul and Silas sang in jail	Acts 16:25
We are to sing to the Lord as a response to what he has done in our lives	Ephesians 5:19–20 Colossians 3:16 James 5:13

25:9–31 The musicians were divided into 24 groups to match the 24 groups of Levites (24:7–25). This division of labor gave order to the planning of temple work, promoted excellence by making training easier, gave variety to worship because each group worked a term, and provided opportunities for many to be involved.

26:1 There were 4,000 gatekeepers (23:4–5). They were all Levites and did many other jobs as well. Some of their duties included (1) checking out the equipment and utensils used each day and making sure they were returned, (2) storing, ordering, and maintaining the food supplies for the priests and sacrifices, (3) caring for the furniture, (4) mixing the incense that was burned daily, and (5) accounting for the gifts brought. (For more on gatekeepers, see the note on 9:17–18.)

26:5 "God had indeed blessed" Obed-edom. The status of children in society has fluctuated throughout history; sometimes they are highly esteemed, and sometimes abused and cheated. But Scripture shows no such vacillation—children are called a blessing from God, and God never views them as a burden (Psalm 127:3–5; Mark 10:13–15).

6 Also to his son Shemaiah sons were born who ruled over the house of their father,
for they were mighty men of valor.
7 The sons of Shemaiah *were* Othni, Rephael, Obed and Elzabad, whose brothers,
Elihu and Semachiah, were valiant men.
8 All these *were* of the sons of Obed-edom; they and their sons and their relatives *were*
able men with strength for the service, 62 from Obed-edom.
9 Meshelemiah had sons and relatives, 18 valiant men.
10 Also Hosah, *one* of the sons of Merari had sons: Shimri the first (although he was **26:10**
not the firstborn, his father made him first), 1 Chr 16:38
11 Hilkiah the second, Tebaliah the third, Zechariah the fourth; all the sons and relatives of Hosah *were* 13.
12 To these divisions of the gatekeepers, the chief men, *were given* duties like their relatives to minister in the house of the LORD.
13 They cast lots, the small and the great alike, according to their fathers' households, **26:13**
for every gate. 1 Chr 24:5, 31; 25:8
14 The lot to the east fell to Shelemiah. Then they cast lots *for* his son Zechariah, a
counselor with insight, and his lot came out to the north.
15 For Obed-edom *it fell* to the south, and to his sons went the storehouse.
16 For Shuppim and Hosah *it was* to the west, by the gate of Shallecheth, on the ascending highway. Guard corresponded to guard.
17 On the east there were six Levites, on the north four daily, on the south four daily,
and at the storehouse two by two.
18 At the [9]Parbar on the west *there were* four at the highway and two at the Parbar. **26:18**
19 These were the divisions of the gatekeepers of the sons of Korah and of the sons of 2 Kin 23:11
Merari.

Keepers of the Treasure

20 [10]The Levites, their relatives, had charge of the treasures of the house of God and **26:20**
of the treasures of the dedicated gifts. 1 Chr 26:22, 24, 26; 28:12; Ezra 2:69
21 The sons of Ladan, the sons of the Gershonites belonging to Ladan, *namely,* the
Jehielites, *were* the heads of the fathers' *households,* belonging to Ladan the Gershonite.
22 The sons of Jehieli, Zetham and Joel his brother, had charge of the treasures of the
house of the LORD.
23 As for the Amramites, the Izharites, the Hebronites and the Uzzielites,
24 Shebuel the son of Gershom, the son of Moses, was officer over the treasures.
25 His relatives by Eliezer *were* Rehabiah his son, Jeshaiah his son, Joram his son, Zichri
his son and Shelomoth his son.
26 This Shelomoth and his relatives had charge of all the treasures of the dedicated **26:26**
gifts which King David and the heads of the fathers' *households,* the commanders of 2 Sam 8:11
thousands and hundreds, and the commanders of the army, had dedicated.
27 They dedicated part of the spoil won in battles to repair the house of the LORD.
28 And all that Samuel the seer had dedicated and Saul the son of Kish, Abner the son
of Ner and Joab the son of Zeruiah, everyone who had dedicated *anything, all of this* was
in the care of Shelomoth and his relatives.

Outside Duties

29 As for the Izharites, Chenaniah and his sons were *assigned* to outside duties for Is- **26:29**
rael, as officers and judges. Neh 11:16; 1 Chr 23:4
30 As for the Hebronites, Hashabiah and his relatives, 1,700 capable men, had charge
of the affairs of Israel west of the Jordan, for all the work of the LORD and the service of **26:30** 1 Chr 27:17
the king.
31 As for the Hebronites, Jerijah the chief (these Hebronites were investigated accord- **26:31**
ing to their genealogies and fathers' *households,* in the fortieth year of David's reign, 1 Chr 23:19; 1 Chr 6:81
and men of outstanding capability were found among them at Jazer of Gilead)

9 Possibly *court* or *colonnade* **10** So Gr; Heb *As for the Levites, Ahijah had*

26:27 War spoil rightfully belonged to the victorious army. These soldiers, however, gave their portion of all the spoil to the temple to express their dedication to God. Like these commanders, we should think of what we *can* give, rather than what we are obligated to give. Is your giving a matter of rejoicing rather than duty? Give as a response of joy and love for God.

26:32 2 Chr 19:11
32 and his relatives, capable men, *were* 2,700 in number, heads of fathers' *households.* And King David made them overseers of the Reubenites, the Gadites and the half-tribe of the Manassites concerning all the affairs of God and of the king.

Commanders of the Army

27 Now *this is* the enumeration of the sons of Israel, the heads of fathers' *households,* the commanders of thousands and of hundreds, and their officers who served the king in all the affairs of the divisions which came in and went out month by month throughout all the months of the year, each division *numbering* 24,000:

27:2 2 Sam 23:8-30; 1 Chr 11:11-31
2 Jashobeam the son of Zabdiel [11]had charge of the first division for the first month; and in his division *were* 24,000.
3 *He was* from the sons of Perez, *and was* chief of all the commanders of the army for the first month.
4 Dodai the Ahohite and his division had charge of the division for the second month, Mikloth *being* the chief officer; and in his division *were* 24,000.
5 The third commander of the army for the third month *was* Benaiah, the son of Jehoiada the priest, *as* chief; and in his division *were* 24,000.
6 This Benaiah *was* the mighty man of the thirty, and had charge of thirty; and over his division was Ammizabad his son.
7 The fourth for the fourth month *was* Asahel the brother of Joab, and Zebadiah his son after him; and in his division *were* 24,000.
8 The fifth for the fifth month *was* the commander Shamhuth the Izrahite; and in his division *were* 24,000.
9 The sixth for the sixth month *was* Ira the son of Ikkesh the Tekoite; and in his division *were* 24,000.
10 The seventh for the seventh month *was* Helez the Pelonite of the sons of Ephraim; and in his division *were* 24,000.
11 The eighth for the eighth month *was* Sibbecai the Hushathite of the Zerahites; and in his division *were* 24,000.
12 The ninth for the ninth month *was* Abiezer the Anathothite of the Benjamites; and in his division *were* 24,000.
13 The tenth for the tenth month *was* Maharai the Netophathite of the Zerahites; and in his division *were* 24,000.
14 The eleventh for the eleventh month *was* Benaiah the Pirathonite of the sons of Ephraim; and in his division *were* 24,000.
15 The twelfth for the twelfth month *was* Heldai the Netophathite of Othniel; and in his division *were* 24,000.

Chief Officers of the Tribes

16 Now in charge of the tribes of Israel: chief officer for the Reubenites was Eliezer the son of Zichri; for the Simeonites, Shephatiah the son of Maacah;
17 for Levi, Hashabiah the son of Kemuel; for Aaron, Zadok;
18 for Judah, Elihu, *one* of David's brothers; for Issachar, Omri the son of Michael;
19 for Zebulun, Ishmaiah the son of Obadiah; for Naphtali, Jeremoth the son of Azriel;
20 for the sons of Ephraim, Hoshea the son of Azaziah; for the half-tribe of Manasseh, Joel the son of Pedaiah;
21 for the half-tribe of Manasseh in Gilead, Iddo the son of Zechariah; for Benjamin, Jaasiel the son of Abner;

27:22 1 Chr 28:1
22 for Dan, Azarel the son of Jeroham. These *were* the princes of the tribes of Israel.

27:23 1 Chr 21:2-5; Gen 15:5; 22:17; 26:4
23 But David did not count those twenty years of age and under, because the LORD had said He would multiply Israel as the stars of heaven.

27:24 2 Sam 24:12-15; 1 Chr 21:1-7
24 Joab the son of Zeruiah had begun to count *them,* but did not finish; and because of this, wrath came upon Israel, and the number was not included in the account of the chronicles of King David.

11 Lit *was over,* and so throughout the ch

27:24 The account of the chronicles of King David was a historical document kept in the royal archives with other official records. It no longer exists. See 1 Kings 14:19.

Various Overseers

25 Now Azmaveth the son of Adiel had charge of the king's storehouses. And Jonathan the son of Uzziah had charge of the storehouses in the country, in the cities, in the
villages and in the towers.
26 Ezri the son of Chelub had charge of the agricultural workers who tilled the soil.
27 Shimei the Ramathite had charge of the vineyards; and Zabdi the Shiphmite had
charge of the produce of the vineyards *stored* in the wine cellars.
28 Baal-hanan the Gederite had charge of the olive and sycamore trees in the [12]Shep-
helah; and Joash had charge of the stores of oil.
29 Shitrai the Sharonite had charge of the cattle which were grazing in Sharon; and
Shaphat the son of Adlai had charge of the cattle in the valleys.
30 Obil the Ishmaelite had charge of the camels; and Jehdeiah the Meronothite had
charge of the donkeys.
31 Jaziz the Hagrite had charge of the flocks. All these were overseers of the property
which belonged to King David.

Counselors

32 Also Jonathan, David's uncle, *was* a counselor, a man of understanding, and a scribe;
and Jehiel the son of Hachmoni tutored the king's sons.
33 Ahithophel *was* counselor to the king; and Hushai the Archite *was* the king's friend.
34 Jehoiada the son of Benaiah, and Abiathar succeeded Ahithophel; and Joab was
the commander of the king's army.

David's Address about the Temple

28 Now David assembled at Jerusalem all the officials of Israel, the princes of the
tribes, and the commanders of the divisions that served the king, and the commanders of thousands, and the commanders of hundreds, and the overseers of all the
property and livestock belonging to the king and his sons, with the officials and the mighty
men, even all the valiant men.
2 Then King David rose to his feet and said, "Listen to me, my brethren and my people; I *had* [13]intended to build a [14]permanent home for the ark of the covenant of the
LORD and for the footstool of our God. So I had made preparations to build *it.*
3 "But God said to me, 'You shall not build a house for My name because you are a
man of war and have shed blood.'
4 "Yet, the LORD, the God of Israel, chose me from all the house of my father to be
king over Israel forever. For He has chosen Judah to be a leader; and in the house of
Judah, my father's house, and among the sons of my father He took pleasure in me to
make *me* king over all Israel.
5 "Of all my sons (for the LORD has given me many sons), He has chosen my son Solomon to sit on the throne of the kingdom of the LORD over Israel.
6 "He said to me, 'Your son Solomon is the one who shall build My house and My
courts; for I have chosen him to be a son to Me, and I will be a father to him.
7 'I will establish his kingdom forever if he resolutely performs My commandments
and My ordinances, as is done now.'
8 "So now, in the sight of all Israel, the assembly of the LORD, and in the hearing of

27:28 1 Kin 10:27; 2 Chr 1:15
27:29 1 Chr 5:16
27:31 1 Chr 5:10
27:33 2 Sam 15:12; 2 Sam 15:32, 37
27:34 1 Chr 27:5; 1 Kin 1:7; 1 Chr 11:6
28:1 1 Chr 23:2; 27:1-31; 1 Chr 11:10-47
28:2 1 Chr 17:1, 2; Ps 132:7; Is 66:1
28:3 1 Chr 22:8
28:4 1 Sam 16:6-13; 1 Chr 17:23, 27; Gen 49:8-10; 1 Chr 5:2; 1 Sam 16:1
28:5 1 Chr 3:1-9; 14:3-7; 1 Chr 22:9, 10
28:6 2 Sam 7:13, 14
28:7 1 Chr 22:13

12 Or *lowlands* **13** Lit *in my heart* **14** Lit *house of rest*

27:33–34 When Absalom rebelled against David, Ahithophel betrayed David and joined the rebellion. Hushai pretended loyalty to Absalom, and his advice caused Absalom's downfall (2 Samuel 15:31—17:23).

28:1 The last two chapters of 1 Chronicles present the transition from David to Solomon as king of Israel. The writer doesn't mention Adonijah's conspiracy or David's frailty (1 Kings 1; 2). Instead, he focuses on the positive—God's plans for Israel and his promise to David's descendants.

28:5 The kingdom of Israel belonged to the Lord, not to David or anyone else. Israel's king, then, was God's deputy, commissioned to carry out God's will for the nation. Thus God could choose the person he wanted as king without following customary lines of succession. David was not Saul's heir, and Solomon was not David's oldest son, but this did not matter because God appointed them.

28:8 David told Solomon to be careful to follow every one of God's commands to ensure Israel's prosperity and the continuation of David's descendants upon the throne. It was the king's solemn duty to study and obey God's laws. The teachings of Scripture are the keys to security, happiness, and justice, but you'll never discover them unless you search God's Word. If we ignore God's will and neglect his teaching, anything we attempt to build, even if it has God's name on it, will be headed for collapse. Get to know God's commands through regular Bible study, and find ways to apply them consistently.

our God, observe and seek after all the commandments of the LORD your God so that
you may possess the good land and bequeath *it* to your sons after you forever.

28:9 1 Kin 8:61; 1 Chr 29:17-19; 1 Sam 16:7; 2 Chr 15:2; Jer 29:13

9 "As for you, my son Solomon, know the God of your father, and serve Him with a
whole heart and a willing mind; for the LORD searches all hearts, and understands every
intent of the thoughts. If you seek Him, He will let you find Him; but if you forsake Him,
He will reject you forever.

28:10 1 Chr 22:13

10 "Consider now, for the LORD has chosen you to build a house for the sanctuary; be
courageous and act."

28:11 Ex 25:40; 1 Chr 28:12, 19; 1 Kin 6:3; Ex 25:17-22

28:12 1 Chr 26:20, 28

28:13 1 Chr 24:1; 1 Chr 23:6

11 Then David gave to his son Solomon the plan of the porch *of the temple,* its buildings, its storehouses, its upper rooms, its inner rooms and the room for the mercy seat;
12 and the plan of all that he had in mind, for the courts of the house of the LORD, and
for all the surrounding rooms, for the storehouses of the house of God and for the storehouses of the dedicated things;
13 also for the divisions of the priests and the Levites and for all the work of the service of the house of the LORD and for all the utensils of service in the house of the LORD;
14 for the golden *utensils,* the weight of gold for all utensils for every kind of service;
for the silver utensils, the weight *of silver* for all utensils for every kind of service;

28:15 Ex 25:31-39

15 and the weight *of gold* for the golden lampstands and their golden lamps, with the
weight of each lampstand and its lamps; and *the weight of silver* for the silver lampstands,
with the weight of each lampstand and its lamps according to the use of each lampstand;
16 and the gold by weight for the tables of showbread, for each table; and silver for the
silver tables;
17 and the forks, the basins, and the pitchers of pure gold; and for the golden bowls
with the weight for each bowl; and for the silver bowls with the weight for each bowl;

28:18 Ex 30:1-10; Ex 25:18-22

18 and for the altar of incense refined gold by weight; and gold for the model of the
chariot, *even* the cherubim that spread out *their wings* and covered the ark of the covenant of the LORD.

28:19 1 Chr 28:11, 12

19 "All *this,*" *said David,* "the LORD made me understand in writing by His hand upon
me, all the details of this pattern."

28:20 1 Chr 22:13; Josh 1:5; Heb 13:5

20 Then David said to his son Solomon, "Be strong and courageous, and act; do not
fear nor be dismayed, for the LORD God, my God, is with you. He will not fail you nor
forsake you until all the work for the service of the house of the LORD is finished.

28:21 1 Chr 28:13; Ex 35:25-35; 36:1, 2

21 "Now behold, *there are* the divisions of the priests and the Levites for all the service
of the house of God, and every willing man of any skill will be with you in all the work for
all kinds of service. The officials also and all the people will be entirely at your command."

PRINCIPLES TO LIVE BY

King David gave his son Solomon principles to guide him through life (see 1 Chronicles 28:9–10). These same ideas are ones that any Christian parent would want to present to a child:

1. Get to know God personally.
2. Learn God's commands and discover what he wants you to do.
3. Worship God with wholehearted devotion.
4. Serve God with a willing mind.
5. Be faithful.
6. Don't become discouraged.

28:9 "The LORD searches all hearts." Nothing can be hidden from God. He sees and understands everything in our hearts. David found this out the hard way when God sent Nathan to expose David's sins of adultery and murder (2 Samuel 12). David told Solomon to be completely open with God and dedicated to him. It makes no sense to try to hide any thoughts or actions from an all-knowing God. This should cause us joy, not fear, because God knows even the worst about us and loves us anyway.

28:13 Some of the instructions about the work of the priests and Levites are in chapters 23 and 24.

28:20 David advised Solomon not to be frightened about the size of his task as king and builder of the temple. Fear can immobilize us. The size of a job, its risks, or the pressure of the situation can cause us to freeze and do nothing. One remedy for fear is found here—don't focus on the fear; instead, get to work. Getting started is often the most difficult and frightening part of a job.

Offerings for the Temple

29 Then King David said to the entire assembly, "My son Solomon, whom alone God 29:1 1 Chr 22:5; 1 Chr
has chosen, is still young and inexperienced and the work is great; for the temple 29:19
is not for man, but for the LORD God.
2 "Now with all my ability I have provided for the house of my God the gold for the 29:2
things of gold, and the silver for the *things of* silver, and the bronze for the *things of* bronze, 1 Chr 22:3-5
the iron for the *things of* iron, and wood for the *things of* wood, onyx stones and inlaid
stones, stones of antimony and stones of various colors, and all kinds of precious stones
and alabaster in abundance.
3 "Moreover, in my delight in the house of my God, the treasure I have of gold and
silver, I give to the house of my God, over and above all that I have already provided for
the holy [15]temple,
4 *namely,* 3,000 talents of gold, of the gold of Ophir, and 7,000 talents of refined sil- 29:4
ver, to overlay the walls of the buildings; 1 Chr 22:14; 1 Kin 9:28
5 of gold for the *things of* gold and of silver for the *things of* silver, that is, for all the
work done by the craftsmen. Who then is willing to consecrate himself this day to the
LORD?"
6 Then the rulers of the fathers' *households,* and the princes of the tribes of Israel, 29:6
and the commanders of thousands and of hundreds, with the overseers over the king's 1 Chr 27:1; 28:1;
work, offered willingly; 1 Chr 27:25-31
7 and for the service for the house of God they gave 5,000 talents and 10,000 darics of 29:7
gold, and 10,000 talents of silver, and 18,000 talents of brass, and 100,000 talents of iron. Ezra 2:69; Neh 7:70
8 Whoever possessed *precious* stones gave them to the treasury of the house of the 29:8
LORD, in care of Jehiel the Gershonite. 1 Chr 23:8
9 Then the people rejoiced because they had offered so willingly, for they made their 29:9
offering to the LORD with a whole heart, and King David also rejoiced greatly. 1 Kin 8:61; 2 Cor 9:7

David's Prayer

10 So David blessed the LORD in the sight of all the assembly; and David said, "Blessed
are You, O LORD God of Israel our father, forever and ever.
11 "Yours, O LORD, is the greatness and the power and the glory and the victory and 29:11
the majesty, indeed everything that is in the heavens and the earth; Yours is the domin- Matt 6:13; Rev 5:13
ion, O LORD, and You exalt Yourself as head over all.
12 "Both riches and honor *come* from You, and You rule over all, and in Your hand is 29:12
power and might; and it lies in Your hand to make great and to strengthen everyone. 2 Chr 1:12; 2 Chr
13 "Now therefore, our God, we thank You, and praise Your glorious name. 20:6
14 "But who am I and who are my people that we should be able to offer as generously
as this? For all things come from You, and from Your hand we have given You.
15 "For we are sojourners before You, and tenants, as all our fathers were; our days on 29:15
the earth are like a shadow, and there is no hope. Lev 25:23; Job 14:2,
16 "O LORD our God, all this abundance that we have provided to build You a house 10-12
for Your holy name, it is from Your hand, and all is Yours.

15 Lit *house*

29:1 Solomon became king in 970 B.C.

29:1 It is possible to be obsessed with a church building to the neglect of the real church—the people of God. But the opposite response, neglecting the church building, is also wrong. David makes this point when he says that the temple is "not for man, but for the LORD God." Although we should avoid wasteful extravagance, we must remember that every church building can be a visible witness for God. How can your church building be better used to tell the world about God?

29:3–5 David gave from his personal fortune for the temple. He encouraged others to follow his example, and they willingly did. Both the tabernacle (Exodus 35:5—36:7) and the temple were built from the voluntary gifts of the people. Like David, we can acknowledge that all we have comes from God (29:14–16). We may not have David's wealth, but we can develop his willingness to give. It is not what we have that counts with God, but our willingness to give it.

29:6–9 These leaders displayed a right attitude toward their money by giving willingly to God's work. This attitude is described by Paul in 2 Corinthians 9:7: "Each one must do just as he has purposed in his heart, not grudgingly or under compulsion, for God loves a cheerful giver." When we are generous because we are thankful, our attitude can inspire others. Give generously to God's work.

29:15 David contrasts God's everlasting nature with the fleeting lives of his people. Nothing lasts unless it is rooted in God's unchanging character. If our most impressive deeds fade as dust before God, where should we place our confidence? Only in a relationship with God can we find anything permanent. His love never fades and nothing can take it away.

29:17 1 Chr 28:9; Ps 15:2
17 "Since I know, O my God, that You try the heart and delight in uprightness, I, in the
integrity of my heart, have willingly offered all these *things;* so now with joy I have seen
Your people, who are present here, make *their* offerings willingly to You.
18 "O LORD, the God of Abraham, Isaac and Israel, our fathers, preserve this forever
in the intentions of the heart of Your people, and direct their heart to You;

29:19 1 Chr 28:9; Ps 72:1; 1 Chr 29:1, 2
19 and give to my son Solomon a perfect heart to keep Your commandments, Your
testimonies and Your statutes, and to do *them* all, and to build the temple, for which I
have made provision."

29:20 Josh 22:33; Ex 4:31
20 Then David said to all the assembly, "Now bless the LORD your God." And all the
assembly blessed the LORD, the God of their fathers, and bowed low and did homage to
the LORD and to the king.

Sacrifices

29:21 1 Kin 8:62, 63
21 On the next day they made sacrifices to the LORD and offered burnt offerings to
the LORD, 1,000 bulls, 1,000 rams *and* 1,000 lambs, with their drink offerings and sacrifices in abundance for all Israel.

29:22 1 Chr 23:1; 1 Kin 1:33-39
22 So they ate and drank that day before the LORD with great gladness.

Solomon Again Made King

And they made Solomon the son of David king a second time, and they anointed *him*
as ruler for the LORD and Zadok as priest.

29:23 1 Kin 2:12
23 Then Solomon sat on the throne of the LORD as king instead of David his father;
and he prospered, and all Israel obeyed him.
24 All the officials, the mighty men, and also all the sons of King David pledged allegiance to King Solomon.

29:25 2 Chr 1:1; 1 Kin 3:13; 2 Chr 1:12
25 The LORD highly exalted Solomon in the sight of all Israel, and bestowed on him
royal majesty which had not been on any king before him in Israel.

29:26 1 Chr 18:14
26 Now David the son of Jesse reigned over all Israel.

29:27 2 Sam 5:4, 5; 1 Kin 2:11; 1 Chr 3:4
27 The period which he reigned over Israel *was* forty years; he reigned in Hebron sev-
en years and in Jerusalem thirty-three *years.*

Death of David

29:28 Gen 15:15; Acts 13:36; 1 Chr 23:1
28 Then he died in a ripe old age, full of days, riches and honor; and his son Solomon
reigned in his place.

29:29 1 Sam 9:9; 2 Sam 7:2-4; 12:1-7; 1 Sam 22:5
29 Now the acts of King David, from first to last, are written in the chronicles of Samuel the seer, in the chronicles of Nathan the prophet and in the chronicles of Gad the
seer,
30 with all his reign, his power, and the circumstances which came on him, on Israel,
and on all the kingdoms of the lands.

29:19 "A perfect heart" means to be entirely dedicated to God. This is what David wished for Solomon—that he would desire, above all else, to serve God. Do you find it hard to do what God wants, or even harder to want to do it? God can give you wholehearted devotion. If you believe in Jesus Christ, this is already happening in you. Paul wrote that God works within us "to will and to work for His good pleasure" (Philippians 2:13).

29:21 Drink offerings of wine were poured out as sacrifices to God to acknowledge his role in providing for his people.

29:25 Solomon surpassed his father's wealth and splendor. David's legacy resulted from his vital relationship with the Lord, and he passed his spiritual values on to Solomon. Any money or power we leave to our children is far less valuable than the spiritual legacy we pass on. What spiritual inheritance will your children receive?

29:29 A seer was someone who received messages from God for the nation in visions or dreams.

29:30 First Chronicles vividly illustrates the importance of maintaining a relationship with God. The genealogies in chapters 1—9 emphasize the importance of a spiritual heritage. The second part of the book details the life of David. Few men or women in the Bible were as close to God as David was. His daily contact with God increased his capacity to worship and strengthened his desire to build God's temple. David's life shows us the importance of staying close to God—through studying and obeying his Word and communicating with him daily. Second Chronicles, on the other hand, reveals how quickly our lives can deteriorate (spiritually, mentally, and socially) when we fail to stay well grounded in God.

2 CHRONICLES

Solomon becomes king 970 B.C.	Temple built 966–959	The kingdom divides 930	Asa becomes king of Judah 910	Jehoshaphat becomes king of Judah 872	Ahab killed in battle 853	Athaliah seizes the throne 841	Uzziah becomes king of Judah 792

VITAL STATISTICS

PURPOSE:
To unify the nation around true worship of God by showing his standard for judging kings. The righteous kings of Judah and the religious revivals under their rule are highlighted, and the sins of the evil kings are exposed.

AUTHOR:
Ezra, according to Jewish tradition

TO WHOM WRITTEN:
All Israel

DATE WRITTEN:
Approximately 430 B.C., recording events from the beginning of Solomon's reign (970 B.C.) to the beginning of the Babylonian captivity (586 B.C.)

SETTING:
Second Chronicles parallels 1 and 2 Kings and serves as their commentary. Originally 1 and 2 Chronicles were one book. It was written after the exile from a priestly perspective, highlighting the importance of the temple and the religious revivals in Judah. The northern kingdom, Israel, is virtually ignored in this history.

KEY VERSE:
"If My people who are called by My name humble themselves and pray and seek My face and turn from their wicked ways, then I will hear from heaven, will forgive their sin and will heal their land" (7:14).

KEY PEOPLE:
Solomon, the queen of Sheba, Rehoboam, Asa, Jehoshaphat, Jehoram, Joash, Uzziah (Azariah), Ahaz, Hezekiah, Manasseh, Josiah

KEY PLACES:
Jerusalem, the temple

SPECIAL FEATURES:
Includes a detailed record of the temple's construction

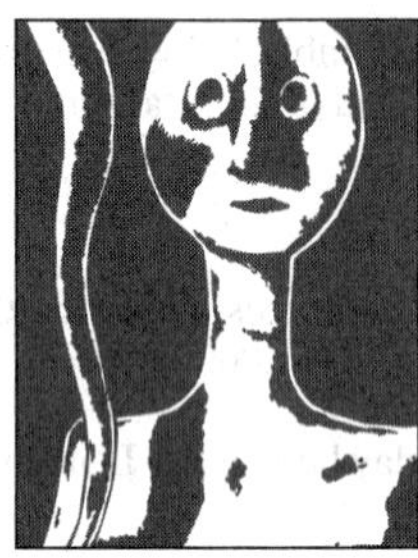

THE SLIDE clicks, and our eyes focus on the image flashed onto the screen in the darkened sanctuary. "This idol," explains the missionary, "is made of stone and is worshiped daily. The natives believe that this will guarantee good crops and healthy children." With condescending smiles, we wonder at their ignorance. How could anyone worship an object? Idols are for the naive and the superstitious! But after the presentation, we return home to *our* idols of wealth, prestige, or self-fulfillment. If we put anything in God's place, we worship it, despite what we profess with our lips.

Our experience parallels Israel's. They were chosen by God to represent him on earth. But too often they forgot the truth and their calling, stumbling blindly after idols as the neighboring nations did. Then prophets, priests, and judgment would push them abruptly back to the one true God. Second Chronicles relates this sordid history of Judah's corrupt and idolatrous kings. Here and there a good king would arise in Judah, and for a time there would be revival, but the downward spiral would continue—ending in chaos, destruction, and captivity.

The chronicler writes this volume to bring the people of Israel back to God by reminding them of their past. Only by following God would they prosper! As you read 2 Chronicles, you will catch a vivid glimpse of Judah's history (the history of Israel, the northern kingdom, is virtually ignored), and you will see the tragic results of idolatry. Learn the lessons of the past: Determine to get rid of any idols in your life and to worship God alone.

Second Chronicles continues the history of 1 Chronicles. David's son Solomon was inaugurated as king. Solomon built the magnificent temple in Jerusalem, thus fulfilling his father's wish and last request (chapters 2—5). Solomon enjoyed a peaceful and prosperous reign of 40 years that made him world famous. After Solomon died, his son Rehoboam assumed the throne, and his immaturity divided the kingdom.

In Judah there were a few good kings and many evil ones. The writer of Chronicles faithfully records their achievements and failures, noting how each king measured up to God's standard for success. Clearly a good king obeyed God's laws, eliminated the places of idol worship, and made no alliances with other nations. Judah's good kings include Asa, Jehoshaphat, Uzziah (Azariah), Hezekiah, and Josiah. Of its many evil ones, Ahaz and Manasseh were perhaps the worst. Eventually the nation was conquered and taken captive, and the temple was destroyed.

The writer's purpose was to reunite the nation around the true worship of God after the captivity. In these pages, he reminds the people of their past. He clearly broadcasts his message through one of the best-known verses in Scripture, "If My people who are called by My name humble themselves and pray and seek My face and turn from their wicked ways, then I will hear from heaven, will forgive their sin and will heal their land" (7:14). As you read 2 Chronicles, listen to God's voice and obey him; and receive his redemptive, healing touch.

Israel (northern kingdom) falls 722	*Hezekiah becomes king of Judah 715*	*Sennacherib taunts Hezekiah 701*	*Josiah becomes king 640*	*Book of the law found 622*	*Judah (southern kingdom) falls 586*	*Cyrus's decree 538*

THE BLUEPRINT

A. THE REIGN OF SOLOMON (1:1—9:31)
1. Solomon asks for wisdom
2. Solomon builds the temple
3. Solomon dedicates the temple
4. Solomon's riches and wisdom

Solomon achieved much in business and government, but most important, he was the man God used to build the glorious temple. This beautiful building was the religious center of the nation. It symbolized the unity of all the tribes, the presence of God among them, and the nation's high calling. We may achieve great things in life, but we must not neglect any effort that will help nurture God's people or bring others into God's kingdom. It is easy for us to get the wrong perspective on what's really important in life.

B. THE KINGDOM OF JUDAH (10:1—36:23)
1. The northern tribes revolt
2. History of apostasy and reform
3. Judah is exiled to Babylon

Throughout the reigns of 20 kings, the nation of Judah wavered between obedience to God and apostasy. The reigning king's response to God determined the spiritual climate of the nation and whether or not God would send judgment upon his people. Our personal history is shaped by our response to God. Just as Judah's failure to repent brought them captivity in Babylon, so the abuse of our high calling by sinful living will ultimately bring us catastrophe and destruction.

MEGATHEMES

THEME	EXPLANATION	IMPORTANCE
Temple	The temple was the symbol of God's presence and the place set aside for worship and prayer. Built by Solomon from the plans God gave to David, the temple was the spiritual center of the nation.	As Christians meet together to worship God, they experience the presence of God in a way that no individual believer can, for the dwelling place of God is the people of God. The body of Christ is God's temple.
Peace	As Solomon and his descendants were faithful to God, they experienced victory in battle, success in government, and peace with other nations. Peace was the result of the people being unified and loyal to God and his law.	Only God can bring true peace. God is greater than any enemy, army, or nation. Just as Israel's faithful response was key to her peace and survival as a nation, so our obedience to God as individuals and nations is vital to peace today.
Prayer	After Solomon died, David's kingdom was divided. When a king led the Israelites into idolatry, the nation suffered. When the king and his people prayed to God for deliverance and they turned from their sinful ways, God delivered them.	God still answers prayer today. We have God's promise that if we humble ourselves, seek him, turn from our sin, and pray, God will hear, heal, and forgive us. If we are alert, we can pray for God's guidance before we get into trouble.
Reform	Although idolatry and injustice were common, some kings turned to God and led the people in spiritual revival—renewing their commitment to God and reforming their society. Revival included the destruction of idols, obedience to the Law, and the restoration of the priesthood.	We must constantly commit ourselves to obeying God. We are never secure in what others have done before us. Believers in each generation must dedicate themselves to the task of carrying out God's will in their own lives as well as in society.
National Collapse	In 586 B.C. the Babylonians completely destroyed Solomon's beautiful temple. The formal worship of God was ended. The Israelites had abandoned God. As a result, God brought judgment upon his people, and they were carried off into captivity.	Although our disobedience may not be as blatant as Israel's, quite often our commitment to God is insincere and casual. When we forget that all our power, wisdom, and wealth come from God and not ourselves, we are in danger of the same spiritual and moral collapse that Israel experienced.

KEY PLACES IN 2 CHRONICLES

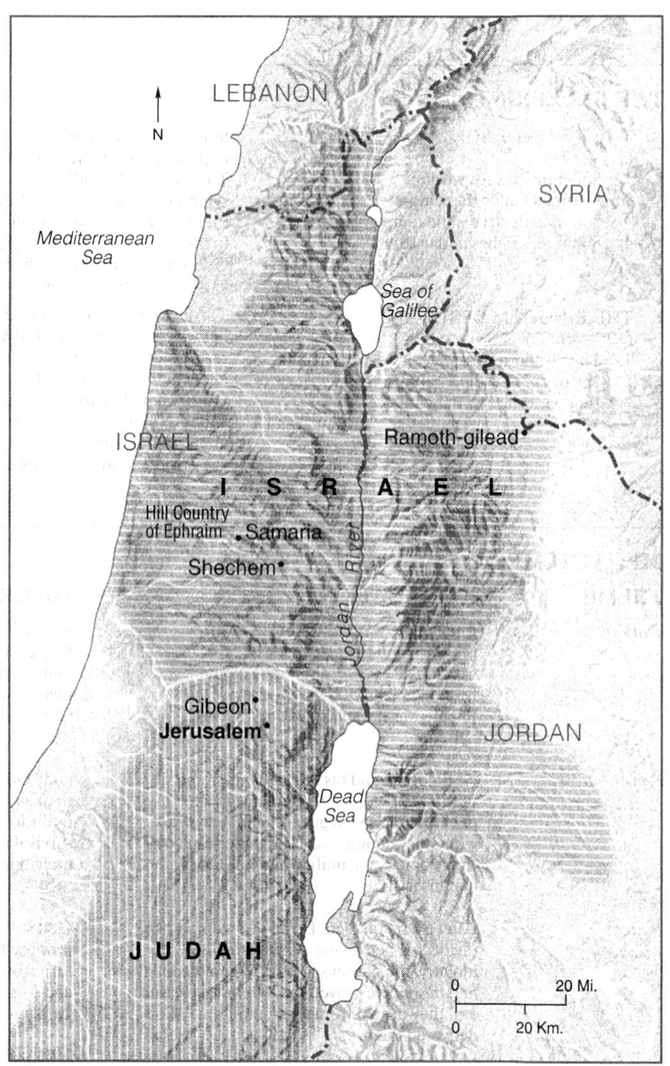

The broken lines (—·—·) indicate modern boundaries.

1 Gibeon David's son Solomon became king over Israel. He summoned the nation's leaders to a ceremony in Gibeon. Here God told Solomon to ask for whatever he desired. Solomon asked for wisdom and knowledge to rule Israel (1:1–12).

2 Jerusalem After the ceremony in Gibeon, Solomon returned to the capital city, Jerusalem. His reign began a golden age for Israel. Solomon implemented the plans for the temple, which had been drawn up by his father, David. It was a magnificent construction. It symbolized Solomon's wealth and wisdom, which became known worldwide (1:13—9:31).

3 Shechem After Solomon's death, his son Rehoboam was ready to be crowned in Shechem. However, his promise of higher taxes and harder work for the people led to rebellion. Everyone but the tribes of Judah and Benjamin deserted Rehoboam and set up their own kingdom to the north called Israel. Rehoboam returned to Jerusalem as ruler over the southern kingdom called Judah (10:1—12:16). The remainder of 2 Chronicles records the history of Judah.

4 Hill Country of Ephraim Abijah became the next king of Judah, and soon war broke out between Israel and Judah. When the armies of the two nations arrived for battle in the hill country of Ephraim, Israel had twice as many troops as Judah. It looked like Judah's defeat was certain. But they cried out to God, and God gave them victory over Israel. In their history as separate nations, Judah had a few godly kings, who instituted reforms and brought the people back to God. Israel, however, had a succession of only evil kings (13:1–22).

5 Aram (Syria) Asa, a godly king, removed every trace of pagan worship from Judah and renewed the people's covenant with God in Jerusalem. But King Baasha of Israel built a fortress to control traffic into Judah. Instead of looking to God for guidance, Asa took the silver and gold from the temple and sent it to the king of Aram, requesting his help against King Baasha. As a result, God became angry with Judah (14:1—16:14).

6 Samaria Although Jehoshaphat was a godly king, he allied himself with Israel's most evil king, Ahab. Ahab's capital was Samaria. Ahab wanted help fighting against Ramoth-gilead. Jehoshaphat wanted advice, but rather than listening to God's prophet who had promised defeat, he joined Ahab in battle (17:1—18:27).

7 Ramoth-gilead The alliance with Israel against Ramoth-gilead ended in defeat and Ahab's death. Shaken by his defeat, Jehoshaphat returned to Jerusalem and to God. But his son Jehoram was a wicked king, as was his son Ahaziah, and history repeated itself. Ahaziah formed an alliance with Israel's king Joram to do battle with the Arameans at Ramoth-gilead. This led to the death of both kings (18:28—22:9).

8 Jerusalem The rest of Judah's history recorded in 2 Chronicles centers on Jerusalem. Some kings caused Judah to sin by bringing idol worship into their midst. Others cleaned up the idol worship, reopened and restored the temple, and in the case of Josiah, tried to follow God's laws as they were written by Moses. In spite of the few good influences, a series of evil kings sent Judah into a downward spiral that ended with the Babylonian empire overrunning the country. The temple was burned, the walls of the city were broken down, and the people were deported to Babylon.

A. THE REIGN OF SOLOMON (1:1—9:31)

In response to Solomon's request, God gives to Solomon great wisdom. Solomon launches great building programs, including the temple, his greatest achievement. In the midst of the celebration dedicating the temple, fire flashes down from heaven and God's glory fills the temple. God wants to live among his people and to be central in their lives. Today, our bodies are God's temple, the place where God, through his Holy Spirit, lives and reigns.

1. Solomon asks for wisdom

Solomon Worships at Gibeon

1 Now Solomon the son of David established himself securely over his kingdom, and
the LORD his God *was* with him and exalted him greatly.
2 Solomon spoke to all Israel, to the commanders of thousands and of hundreds and
to the judges and to every leader in all Israel, the heads of the fathers' *households.*
3 Then Solomon and all the assembly with him went to the high place which was at
Gibeon, for God's tent of meeting was there, which Moses the servant of the LORD had
made in the wilderness.
4 However, David had brought up the ark of God from Kiriath-jearim to the place he
had prepared for it, for he had pitched a tent for it in Jerusalem.
5 Now the bronze altar, which Bezalel the son of Uri, the son of Hur, had made, was
there before the tabernacle of the LORD, and Solomon and the assembly sought it out.
6 Solomon went up there before the LORD to the bronze altar which *was* at the tent
of meeting, and offered a thousand burnt offerings on it.
7 In that night God appeared to Solomon and said to him, "Ask what I shall give you."

Solomon's Prayer for Wisdom

8 Solomon said to God, "You have dealt with my father David with great
lovingkindness, and have made me king in his place.
9 "Now, O LORD God, Your promise to my father David is fulfilled, for You have made
me king over a people as numerous as the dust of the earth.
10 "Give me now wisdom and knowledge, that I may go out and come in before this
people, for who can rule this great people of Yours?"
11 God said to Solomon, "Because you had this in mind, and did not ask for riches,
wealth or honor, or the life of those who hate you, nor have you even asked for long life,
but you have asked for yourself wisdom and knowledge that you may rule My people
over whom I have made you king,
12 wisdom and knowledge have been granted to you. And I will give you riches and

1:1 1 Kin 2:12, 46; 1 Chr 29:25
1:2 1 Chr 28:1
1:3 1 Kin 3:4; Ex 36:8
1:4 1 Chr 15:25-28; 2 Chr 6:2
1:5 Ex 31:9; 38:1-7
1:6 1 Kin 3:4
1:7 1 Kin 3:5-14
1:8 1 Chr 28:5
1:9 2 Sam 7:12-16; Gen 13:16; 22:17; 28:14
1:10 1 Kin 3:9; Num 27:17; 2 Sam 5:2
1:11 1 Kin 3:11
1:12 1 Chr 29:25; 2 Chr 9:22

1:1 While the book of 1 Chronicles focuses mainly on David's life, 2 Chronicles focuses on the lives of the rest of the kings of Judah, the southern kingdom. Very little is mentioned about Israel, the northern kingdom, because (1) Chronicles was written for Judeans who had returned from captivity in Babylon, and (2) Judah represented David's family, from which the Messiah would come. Israel was in a state of constant turmoil, anarchy, and rebellion against God, but Judah, at least, made sporadic efforts to follow God.

1:1 More details about Solomon's rise to the throne can be read in 1 Kings 1; 2. Solomon's Profile is found in 1 Kings 4.

1:2–5 The tent of meeting, or tabernacle, that Moses had built centuries earlier (Exodus 35—40) was still in operation, although it had been moved several times. When Solomon became king, the tabernacle was located at Gibeon, a town about six miles northwest of Jerusalem. All the tabernacle furniture was kept at Gibeon except the ark of God, which David had moved to Jerusalem (1 Chronicles 13; 15; 16). David wanted the ark, the symbol of God's presence, to reside in the city where he ruled the people. The tabernacle at Gibeon, however, was still considered Israel's main religious center until Solomon built the temple in Jerusalem.

1:10 Wisdom is the ability to make good decisions based on proper discernment and judgment. Knowledge, in this verse, refers to the practical know-how necessary for handling everyday matters. Solomon used his wisdom and knowledge not only to build the temple from his father's plans, but also to put the nation on firm economic footing.

1:10 God's offer to Solomon stretches the imagination: "Ask what I shall give you" (1:7). But Solomon put the needs of his people first and asked for wisdom rather than riches. He realized that wisdom would be the most valuable asset he could have as king. Later he wrote, wisdom "is more precious than jewels; and nothing you desire compares with her" (Proverbs 3:15). The same wisdom that was given to Solomon is available to us; the same God offers it. How can we acquire wisdom? First, we must ask God, who "gives to all generously and without reproach" (James 1:5). Second, we must devote ourselves wholeheartedly to studying and applying God's Word, the source of divine wisdom. (For more on Solomon's wisdom, read the notes on 1 Kings 3:6–9 and 3:12.)

1:11–12 Solomon could have had anything, but he asked for wisdom to rule the nation. Because God approved of the way Solomon ordered his priorities, he gave Solomon wealth, riches, and honor as well. Jesus also spoke about priorities. He said that when we put God first, everything we really need will be given to us as well (Matthew 6:33). This does not guarantee that we will be wealthy and famous like Solomon, but it means that when we put God first, the wisdom he gives will enable us to have richly rewarding lives. When we have a purpose for living and learn to be content with what we have, we will have greater wealth than we could ever accumulate.

wealth and honor, such as none of the kings who were before you has possessed nor those
who will come after you."
13 So Solomon went from the high place which was at Gibeon, from the tent of meeting, to Jerusalem, and he reigned over Israel.

1:13 2 Chr 1:3

Solomon's Wealth

14 Solomon amassed chariots and horsemen. He had 1,400 chariots and 12,000 horsemen, and he stationed them in the chariot cities and with the king at Jerusalem.
15 The king made silver and gold as plentiful in Jerusalem as stones, and he made cedars as plentiful as sycamores in the lowland.
16 Solomon's horses were imported from Egypt and from Kue; the king's traders procured them from Kue for a price.
17 They imported chariots from Egypt for 600 *shekels* of silver apiece and horses for
150 apiece, and by the same means they exported them to all the kings of the Hittites
and the kings of Aram.

1:14 1 Kin 10:26-29; 1 Kin 4:26; 1 Kin 9:19

1:15 1 Kin 10:27; Deut 17:17

1:16 Deut 17:16

2. Solomon builds the temple

Solomon Will Build a Temple and Palace

2 Now Solomon decided to build a house for the name of the LORD and a royal palace
for himself.
2 So Solomon assigned 70,000 men to carry loads and 80,000 men to quarry *stone* in
the mountains and 3,600 to supervise them.
3 Then Solomon sent *word* to Huram the king of Tyre, saying, "As you dealt with David
my father and sent him cedars to build him a house to dwell in, so do for me.
4 "Behold, I am about to build a house for the name of the LORD my God, dedicating
it to Him, to burn fragrant incense before Him and *to set out* the showbread continually,
and to offer burnt offerings morning and evening, on sabbaths and on new moons and
on the appointed feasts of the LORD our God, this *being required* forever in Israel.
5 "The house which I am about to build *will be* great, for greater is our God than all
the gods.
6 "But who is able to build a house for Him, for the heavens and the highest heavens
cannot contain Him? So who am I, that I should build a house for Him, except to [1]burn
incense before Him?
7 "Now send me a skilled man to work in gold, silver, brass and iron, and in purple,

2:1 1 Kin 5:5

2:2 1 Kin 5:15, 16; 2 Chr 2:18

2:3 1 Kin 5:2-11; 1 Chr 14:1

2:4 Ex 30:7; Ex 25:30; Ex 29:38-42; Num 28:9, 10

2:5 Ex 15:11; 1 Chr 16:25

2:6 1 Kin 8:27; 2 Chr 6:18

2:7 Ex 31:3-5; 2 Chr 2:13, 14; 1 Chr 22:15

1 Lit *offer up in smoke*

2:1 David had wanted to build a temple for God (2 Samuel 7). God denied his request because David had been a warrior, but God said that David's son Solomon would build the temple. God allowed David to make the plans and preparations for the temple (1 Chronicles 23—26; 28:11–13). David bought the land (2 Samuel 24:18–25; 1 Chronicles 22:1), gathered most of the construction materials (1 Chronicles 22:14–16), and received the plans from God (1 Chronicles 28:11–12). It was Solomon's responsibility to make the plans a reality. His job was made easier by his father's exhaustive preparations. God's work can be moved forward when the older generation paves the way for the younger.

2:3–12 Although Huram was one of David's and Solomon's friendly allies, he was the ruler of a nation that worshiped many different gods. Huram was happy to send materials for the temple, and both David and Solomon used this occasion to testify about the one true God.

2:5–6 We should try our best to build beautiful and helpful places of worship to be a testimony and credit to God. In so doing, however, we must remember that God cannot be contained in our building or beautiful setting. He is far greater than any building, so we must focus our praise on him and not merely on the place of worship.

2:7 Why use foreign craftsmen? The Israelites had great knowledge of agriculture, but knew little about metalworking. So they found people who were experts in this area. It is not a sin to obtain secular expertise for God's work. He distributes natural talents as he chooses, and he often decides to give skill to non-Christians. When we hire secular contractors to build or repair our church buildings, we are recognizing that God gives gifts liberally. We may also be gaining an opportunity to tell the workers about God.

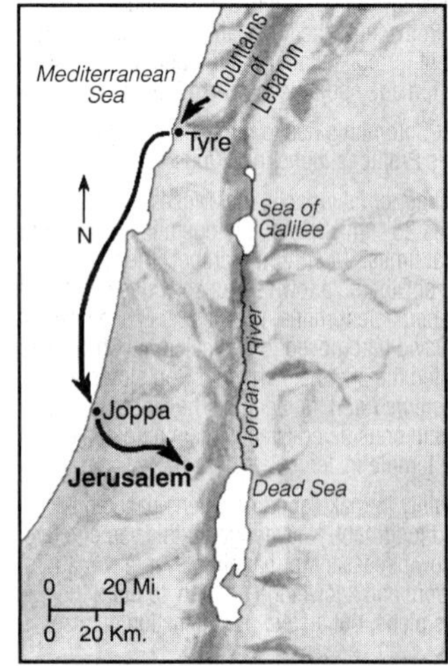

SHIPPING RESOURCES FOR THE TEMPLE
Solomon asked King Huram of Tyre to provide supplies and skilled workmen to help build God's temple in Jerusalem. The plan was to cut the cedar logs in the mountains of Lebanon, float them by sea to Joppa, then bring them inland to Jerusalem by the shortest and easiest route.

crimson and violet *fabrics,* and who knows how to make engravings, to *work* with the skilled
men whom I have in Judah and Jerusalem, whom David my father provided.

2:8 1 Kin 5:6; 2 Chr 9:10, 11

8 "Send me also cedar, cypress and algum timber from Lebanon, for I know that your
servants know how to cut timber of Lebanon; and indeed my servants *will work* with your
servants,
9 to prepare timber in abundance for me, for the house which I am about to build *will
be* great and wonderful.

2:10 1 Kin 5:11

10 "Now behold, I will give to your servants, the woodsmen who cut the timber, 20,000
[2]kors of crushed wheat and 20,000 kors of barley, and 20,000 baths of wine and 20,000
baths of oil."

Huram to Assist

2:11 1 Kin 10:9; 2 Chr 9:8

11 Then Huram, king of Tyre, answered in a letter sent to Solomon: "Because the LORD
loves His people, He has made you king over them."

2:12 Ps 33:6; 102:25; 2 Chr 2:1

12 Then Huram continued, "Blessed be the LORD, the God of Israel, who has made
heaven and earth, who has given King David a wise son, endowed with discretion and
understanding, who will build a house for the LORD and a royal palace for himself.
13 "Now I am sending Huram-abi, a skilled man, endowed with understanding,

2:14 1 Kin 7:14

14 the son of a Danite woman and a Tyrian father, who knows how to work in gold,
silver, bronze, iron, stone and wood, *and* in purple, violet, linen and crimson fabrics, and
who knows how to make all kinds of engravings and to execute any design which may be
assigned to him, *to work* with your skilled men and with those of my lord David your
father.

2:15 2 Chr 2:10

15 "Now then, let my lord send to his servants wheat and barley, oil and wine, of which
he has spoken.

2:16 1 Kin 5:8, 9

16 "We will cut whatever timber you need from Lebanon and bring it to you on rafts by
sea to Joppa, so that you may carry it up to Jerusalem."

2:17 1 Chr 22:2

17 Solomon numbered all the aliens who *were* in the land of Israel, following the census which his father David had taken; and 153,600 were found.

2:18 2 Chr 2:2

18 He appointed 70,000 of them to carry loads and 80,000 to quarry *stones* in the mountains and 3,600 supervisors to make the people work.

The Temple Construction in Jerusalem

3:1 1 Kin 6:1; 1 Chr 21:18

3 Then Solomon began to build the house of the LORD in Jerusalem on Mount Moriah,
where *the LORD* had appeared to his father David, at the place that David had prepared on the threshing floor of Ornan the Jebusite.
2 He began to build on the second *day* in the second month of the fourth year of his
reign.

Dimensions and Materials of the Temple

3:3 1 Kin 6:2

3 Now these are the foundations which Solomon laid for building the house of God.
The length in [3]cubits, according to the old standard *was* sixty cubits, and the width twenty cubits.

2 I.e. One kor equals approx 10 bu **3** I.e. One cubit equals approx 18 in.

2:8–9 Israel did not have much wood, but Lebanon, a small nation on the seacoast, had some of the finest cedar forests in the ancient Near East. Lebanon also imported a great deal of food from Israel. Thus the two kings made a trade agreement that was beneficial to both nations.

2:17–18 Why would Solomon force aliens (foreigners) living in Israel to do the work of slaves? These aliens were descendants of the pagan nations who had not been driven out of the land in Joshua's day (Joshua 9:23–27; Judges 1:21–33; 1 Kings 9:20–21). Scripture has specific laws about treating slaves fairly (Leviticus 25:39–55), so Solomon would not have treated them harshly as other nations might. Solomon's action was probably only in force during the construction of the temple.

3:1 Solomon built a permanent temple on Mount Moriah to replace the movable tabernacle (now at Gibeon) that had accompanied Israel in the wilderness. Mount Moriah was also the place where God had stopped Abraham from sacrificing Isaac (Genesis 22:1–18). David purchased the land when it was a threshing floor (see 2 Samuel 24:15–25 and the note on 1 Chronicles 21:22–24).

3:1ff Why was the temple decorated so ornately? Although no one can build God a worthy home (2:6), this temple was going to be the best that humans could design. The care and craftsmanship were acts of worship in themselves. Although a simple chapel is an adequate place to pray and meet God, it is not wrong to want to make a beautiful place of worship.

3:3 A cubit "according to the old standard" was equal to 20.5 inches and was the one used by Ezekiel in the temple he envisioned.

4 The porch which was in front of the house was as long as the width of the house,
twenty cubits, and the height 120; and inside he overlaid it with pure gold.
5 He overlaid the main room with cypress wood and overlaid it with fine gold, and
ornamented it with palm trees and chains.
6 Further, he adorned the house with precious stones; and the gold was gold from
Parvaim.
7 He also overlaid the house with gold—the beams, the thresholds and its walls and
its doors; and he carved cherubim on the walls.
8 Now he made the room of the holy of holies: its length across the width of the house
was twenty cubits, and its width *was* twenty cubits; and he overlaid it with fine gold,
amounting to 600 talents.
9 The weight of the nails was fifty shekels of gold. He also overlaid the upper rooms
with gold.
10 Then he made two sculptured cherubim in the room of the holy of holies and overlaid them with gold.
11 The wingspan of the cherubim *was* twenty cubits; the wing of one, of five cubits,
touched the wall of the house, and *its* other wing, of five cubits, touched the wing of the
other cherub.
12 The wing of the other cherub, of five cubits, touched the wall of the house; and *its*
other wing of five cubits was attached to the wing of the first cherub.
13 The wings of these cherubim extended twenty cubits, and they stood on their feet
facing the *main* room.
14 He made the veil of violet, purple, crimson and fine linen, and he worked cherubim
on it.
15 He also made two pillars for the front of the house, thirty-five cubits high, and the
capital on the top of each *was* five cubits.
16 He made chains in the inner sanctuary and placed *them* on the tops of the pillars;
and he made one hundred pomegranates and placed *them* on the chains.
17 He erected the pillars in front of the temple, one on the right and the other on the
left, and named the one on the right Jachin and the one on the left Boaz.

Furnishings of the Temple

4 Then he made a bronze altar, twenty cubits in length and twenty cubits in width and
ten cubits in height.
2 Also he made the cast *metal* sea, ten cubits from brim to brim, circular in form, and
its height *was* five cubits and its circumference thirty cubits.
3 Now figures like oxen *were* under it *and* all around it, ten cubits, entirely encircling
the sea. The oxen *were* in two rows, cast in one piece.
4 It stood on twelve oxen, three facing the north, three facing west, three facing south
and three facing east; and the sea *was set* on top of them and all their hindquarters turned
inwards.
5 It was a handbreadth thick, and its brim was made like the brim of a cup, *like* a lily
blossom; it could hold 3,000 baths.
6 He also made ten basins in which to wash, and he set five on the right side and
five on the left to rinse things for the burnt offering; but the sea *was* for the priests to
wash in.
7 Then he made the ten golden lampstands in the way prescribed for them and he set
them in the temple, five on the right side and five on the left.
8 He also made ten tables and placed them in the temple, five on the right side and
five on the left. And he made one hundred golden bowls.
9 Then he made the court of the priests and the great court and doors for the court,
and overlaid their doors with bronze.
10 He set the sea on the right side *of the house* toward the southeast.

3:4 1 Kin 6:3
3:5 1 Kin 6:17
3:7 1 Kin 6:20-22; 1 Kin 6:29-35
3:8 Ex 26:33; 1 Kin 6:16
3:9 1 Chr 28:11
3:10 Ex 25:18-20; 1 Kin 6:23-28
3:14 Ex 26:31
3:15 1 Kin 7:15-20
3:17 1 Kin 7:21
4:1 Ex 27:1, 2; 2 Kin 16:14
4:2 1 Kin 7:23-26
4:5 1 Kin 7:26
4:6 Ex 30:17-21; 1 Kin 7:38, 40
4:7 Ex 25:31-40; 1 Kin 7:49
4:8 1 Kin 7:48
4:9 1 Kin 6:36; 2 Kin 21:5
4:10 1 Kin 7:39

3:10 Cherubim are mighty angels.

4:6 Why was everything in the temple built on such a grand scale? The great size and numbers were necessary to accommodate the huge crowds that would visit for the feasts, such as the Passover (30:13). The numerous daily sacrifices (5:6) required many priests and much equipment.

4:7 The craftsmen followed God's specifications carefully—with spectacular results. When God gives specific instructions, they must be followed to the letter. There is a time to be creative and to put forth our own ideas, but not when the ideas add to, alter, or contradict any specific directions God has already given to us in the Bible. For best results in your spiritual life, carefully seek and follow God's instructions.

4:11 1 Kin 7:40-51

11 Huram also made the pails, the shovels and the bowls. So Huram finished doing the
work which he performed for King Solomon in the house of God:
12 the two pillars, the bowls and the two capitals on top of the pillars, and the two
networks to cover the two bowls of the capitals which were on top of the pillars,

4:13 1 Kin 7:20

13 and the four hundred pomegranates for the two networks, two rows of pomegranates for each network to cover the two bowls of the capitals which were on the pillars.

4:14 1 Kin 7:27-43

14 He also made the stands and he made the basins on the stands,
15 *and* the one sea with the twelve oxen under it.

4:16 1 Kin 7:14; 2 Chr 2:13

16 The pails, the shovels, the forks and all its utensils, Huram-abi made of polished
bronze for King Solomon for the house of the LORD.
17 On the plain of the Jordan the king cast them in the clay ground between Succoth
and Zeredah.

4:18 1 Kin 7:47

18 Thus Solomon made all these utensils in great quantities, for the weight of the bronze
could not be found out.

4:19 2 Chr 4:8

19 Solomon also made all the things that *were* in the house of God: even the golden
altar, the tables with the bread of the Presence on them,

4:20 Ex 25:31-37; 2 Chr 5:7

20 the lampstands with their lamps of pure gold, to burn in front of the inner sanctuary
in the way prescribed;
21 the flowers, the lamps, and the tongs of gold, of purest gold;
22 and the snuffers, the bowls, the spoons and the firepans of pure gold; and the entrance of the house, its inner doors for the holy of holies and the doors of the house, *that
is,* of the nave, of gold.

CAREFUL OBEDIENCE
Solomon and his workers carefully followed God's instructions. As a result, the temple work was blessed by God and completed in every detail. Here are a few examples of people in the Bible who did not carefully follow one of God's instructions, and the resulting consequences. It is not enough to obey God halfheartedly.

Who?	*God's instruction*	*Disobedience*	*Result*
Adam and Eve	Don't eat fruit from the tree of the knowledge of good and evil (Genesis 2:16–17)	Satan tempted them, and they ate (Genesis 3:1–6)	They were banished from the Garden of Eden; pain and death were inflicted on all mankind (Genesis 3:24; Romans 5:12)
Nadab and Abihu	Fire for the sacrifice must come from the proper source (Leviticus 6:12–13)	They used unauthorized fire for their sacrifice (Leviticus 10:1)	They were struck dead (Leviticus 10:2)
Moses	"Speak to the rock before their eyes, that it may yield its waters"(Numbers 20:8)	He spoke to the rock, but also struck it with his staff (Numbers 20:11)	He was not allowed to enter the promised land (Numbers 20:12)
Saul	Completely destroy the evil Amalekites (1 Samuel 15:3)	He spared the king and kept some of the plunder (1 Samuel 15:8–9)	God promised to end his reign (1 Samuel 15:16–26)
Uzzah	Only a priest can touch the holy furnishings and articles (Numbers 4:15)	He touched the ark of the covenant (2 Samuel 6:6)	He died instantly (2 Samuel 6:7)
Uzziah	Only the priests could offer incense in the temple or tabernacle sanctuary (Numbers 16:39–40; 18:7)	He entered the holy place in the temple where only priests were allowed to go (2 Chronicles 26:16–18)	He became a leper (2 Chronicles 26:19)

4:11–16 Pails, shovels, and bowls—these are implements of worship unfamiliar to us. Although the articles we use to aid our worship have changed, the purpose of worship remains the same—to give honor and praise to God. We must never let our worship of God be overshadowed by things we use to help us worship him.

4:22 All these details about the temple demonstrated the care Israel gave to acts of worship (see the note on 3:1ff). The instructions also served as a manual to the original readers of 2 Chronicles, those who would rebuild a new temple on its original site (Ezra 3:8—6:15) after Solomon's temple was destroyed by the Babylonians (2 Kings 25).

3. Solomon dedicates the temple

The Ark Is Brought into the Temple

5 Thus all the work that Solomon performed for the house of the LORD was finished.
And Solomon brought in the things that David his father had dedicated, even the
silver and the gold and all the utensils, *and* put *them* in the treasuries of the house
of God.

5:1 1 Kin 7:51; 2 Sam 8:11; 1 Chr 18:11

2 Then Solomon assembled to Jerusalem the elders of Israel and all the heads of the
tribes, the leaders of the fathers' *households* of the sons of Israel, to bring up the ark of
the covenant of the LORD out of the city of David, which is Zion.

5:2 1 Kin 8:1-9; 2 Sam 6:12-15; 1 Chr 15:25-28; 2 Chr 1:4

3 All the men of Israel assembled themselves to the king at the feast, that is *in* the
seventh month.

5:3 1 Kin 8:2; 2 Chr 7:8-10

4 Then all the elders of Israel came, and the Levites took up the ark.
5 They brought up the ark and the tent of meeting and all the holy utensils which *were*
in the tent; the Levitical priests brought them up.

5:4 Josh 3:6; 2 Chr 5:7

6 And King Solomon and all the congregation of Israel who were assembled with him
before the ark, were sacrificing so many sheep and oxen that they could not be counted
or numbered.
7 Then the priests brought the ark of the covenant of the LORD to its place, into the
inner sanctuary of the house, to the holy of holies, under the wings of the cherubim.
8 For the cherubim spread their wings over the place of the ark, so that the cherubim
made a covering over the ark and its poles.
9 The poles were so long that the ends of the poles of the ark could be seen in front of
the inner sanctuary, but they could not be seen outside; and they are there to this day.

5:9 1 Kin 8:8, 9

10 There was nothing in the ark except the two tablets which Moses put *there* at Horeb, where the LORD made a covenant with the sons of Israel, when they came out of
Egypt.

5:10 Deut 10:2-5; Heb 9:4

The Glory of God Fills the Temple

5:11 1 Chr 24:1-5

11 When the priests came forth from the holy place (for all the priests who were present had sanctified themselves, without regard to divisions),
12 and all the Levitical singers, Asaph, Heman, Jeduthun, and their sons and kinsmen,

5:12 1 Chr 25:1-4; 1 Chr 13:8; 15:16, 24; 2 Chr 7:6

5:1ff Why is there so much emphasis on the temple in the Old Testament?

(1) *It was a symbol of religious authority.* The temple was God's way of centralizing worship at Jerusalem in order to ensure that correct belief would be kept intact through many generations.

(2) *It was a symbol of God's holiness.* The temple's beautiful atmosphere inspired respect and awe for God; it was the setting for many of the great visions of the prophets.

(3) *It was a symbol of God's covenant with Israel.* The temple kept the people focused upon God's Law (the tablets of the Ten Commandments were kept in the temple) rather than on the kings' exploits. It was a place where God was especially present to his people.

(4) *It was a symbol of forgiveness.* The temple's design, furniture, and customs were great object lessons for all the people, reminding them of the seriousness of sin, the penalty that sin incurred, and their need of forgiveness.

(5) *It prepared the people for the Messiah.* In the New Testament, Christ said he came to fulfill the Law, not destroy it. Hebrews 8:1–2 and 9:11–12 use temple customs to explain what Christ did when he died for us.

(6) *It was a testimony to human effort and creativity.* Inspired by the beauty of God's character, people devoted themselves to high achievements in engineering, science, and art in order to praise him.

(7) *It was a place of prayer.* In the temple, people could spend time in prayer to God.

5:1–3 The temple took seven years to build. 1 Kings 6:38 says that the temple was completed in the eighth month (November) of Solomon's eleventh year as king (959 B.C.). Because 5:3 states that the dedication ceremonies were held in the seventh month, they must have occurred either one month before or eleven months after the temple's completion.

5:3 The feast in the seventh month was the Feast of Booths, celebrating God's protection of Israel as they wandered in the wilderness before entering the promised land. The purpose of this annual festival was to renew Israel's commitment to God and their trust in his guidance and protection. The festival beautifully coincided with the dedication of the temple. As the people remembered the wanderings in the wilderness when their ancestors had lived in tents, they were even more thankful for the permanence of this glorious temple.

5:9 Under God's inspiration, some books of the Bible were compiled and edited from other sources. Because 1 and 2 Chronicles cover many centuries, they were compiled from several sources by a single person. The phrase "they are there to this day" (see also 1 Kings 8:8) was taken from material written before Judah's exile in 586 B.C. Although 1 and 2 Chronicles were compiled after the exile and after Solomon's temple was destroyed, the writer thought it best to leave this phrase in the narrative.

5:7–12 The priests came out of the holy place after having placed the ark in the holy of holies of the temple. The holy place is the outer room, where the bread of the Presence, altar of incense, and lampstand were kept. Ordinarily the holy of holies could be entered only once a year by the high priest on the day of atonement. On this unique occasion, however, several priests had to enter the holy of holies to carry the ark to its new resting place. The Levites praised God when these priests emerged from the holy place because they then knew God had accepted this new home for the ark (5:13).

clothed in fine linen, with cymbals, harps and lyres, standing east of the altar, and with them one hundred and twenty priests blowing trumpets

5:13 1 Chr 16:42; 1 Chr 16:34; 2 Chr 7:3; Ezra 3:11; Ps 100:5; Jer 33:11

13 in unison when the trumpeters and the singers were to make themselves heard with one voice to praise and to glorify the LORD, and when they lifted up their voice accompanied by trumpets and cymbals and instruments of music, and when they praised the LORD *saying, "He* indeed is good for His lovingkindness is everlasting," then the house, the house of the LORD, was filled with a cloud,

5:14 Ex 40:35; 1 Kin 8:11

14 so that the priests could not stand to minister because of the cloud, for the glory of the LORD filled the house of God.

Solomon's Dedication

6:1 1 Kin 8:12-50

6 Then Solomon said,
"The LORD has said that He would dwell in the thick cloud.
2 "I have built You a lofty house,
And a place for Your dwelling forever."

3 Then the king faced about and blessed all the assembly of Israel, while all the assembly of Israel was standing.

4 He said, "Blessed be the LORD, the God of Israel, who spoke with His mouth to my father David and has fulfilled *it* with His hands, saying,

5 'Since the day that I brought My people from the land of Egypt, I did not choose a city out of all the tribes of Israel *in which* to build a house that My name might be there, nor did I choose any man for a leader over My people Israel;

6:6 2 Chr 12:13; 1 Chr 28:4

6 but I have chosen Jerusalem that My name might be there, and I have chosen David to be over My people Israel.'

6:7 1 Kin 5:3; 1 Chr 28:2

7 "Now it was in the heart of my father David to build a house for the name of the LORD, the God of Israel.

8 "But the LORD said to my father David, 'Because it was in your heart to build a house for My name, you did well that it was in your heart.

9 'Nevertheless you shall not build the house, but your son who will be born to you, he shall build the house for My name.'

10 "Now the LORD has fulfilled His word which He spoke; for I have risen in the place of my father David and sit on the throne of Israel, as the LORD promised, and have built the house for the name of the LORD, the God of Israel.

6:11 2 Chr 5:7, 10

11 "There I have set the ark in which is the covenant of the LORD, which He made with the sons of Israel."

Solomon's Prayer of Dedication

12 Then he stood before the altar of the LORD in the presence of all the assembly of Israel and spread out his hands.

6:13 Neh 8:4; 1 Kin 8:54

13 Now Solomon had made a bronze platform, five cubits long, five cubits wide and three cubits high, and had set it in the midst of the court; and he stood on it, knelt on his knees in the presence of all the assembly of Israel and spread out his hands toward heaven.

6:14 Ex 15:11; Deut 3:24; Deut 7:9

14 He said, "O LORD, the God of Israel, there is no god like You in heaven or on earth, keeping covenant and *showing* lovingkindness to Your servants who walk before You with all their heart;

6:15 1 Chr 22:9, 10

15 who has kept with Your servant David, my father, that which You have promised him; indeed You have spoken with Your mouth and have fulfilled it with Your hand, as it is this day.

6:16 1 Kin 2:4; 2 Chr 7:18

16 "Now therefore, O LORD, the God of Israel, keep with Your servant David, my

---

5:13 The first service at the temple began with honoring God and acknowledging his presence and goodness. In the same way, our worship should begin by acknowledging God's love. Praise God first; then you will be prepared to present your needs to him. Recalling God's love and mercy will inspire you to worship him daily. Psalm 107 is an example of how David recalled God's enduring love.

6:3 As the people received Solomon's blessing, they stood; as Solomon prayed, he knelt (6:13). Both standing and kneeling are acts of reverence. Acts of reverence make us feel more worshipful, and they let others see that we are honoring God. When you stand or kneel in church or at prayer, make these actions more than mere forms prescribed by tradition. Let them indicate your love for God.

6:12–13 It was unusual for a king to kneel before someone else in front of his own people because kneeling meant submitting to a higher authority. Solomon demonstrated his great love and respect for God by kneeling before him. His action showed that he acknowledged God as the ultimate king and authority, and it encouraged the people to do the same.

father, that which You have promised him, saying, 'You shall not lack a man to sit on
the throne of Israel, if only your sons take heed to their way, to walk in My law as you
have walked before Me.'
17 "Now therefore, O LORD, the God of Israel, let Your word be confirmed which You
have spoken to Your servant David.
18 "But will God indeed dwell with mankind on the earth? Behold, heaven and the high- **6:18** Ps 113:5, 6; 2 Chr
est heaven cannot contain You; how much less this house which I have built. 2:6; Is 66:1; Acts
19 "Yet have regard to the prayer of Your servant and to his supplication, O LORD my 7:49
God, to listen to the cry and to the prayer which Your servant prays before You;
20 that Your eye may be open toward this house day and night, toward the place of **6:20** Ps 33:18; 34:15;
which You have said that *You would* put Your name there, to listen to the prayer which Deut 12:11
Your servant shall pray toward this place.
21 "Listen to the supplications of Your servant and of Your people Israel when they **6:21** Is 43:25; 44:22; Mic
pray toward this place; hear from Your dwelling place, from heaven; hear and forgive. 7:18
22 "If a man sins against his neighbor and is made to take an oath, and he comes *and*
takes an oath before Your altar in this house,
23 then hear from heaven and act and judge Your servants, punishing the wicked by **6:23** Is 3:11; Rom 2:8, 9
bringing his way on his own head and justifying the righteous by giving him according to
his righteousness.
24 "If Your people Israel are defeated before an enemy because they have sinned against **6:24** Ps 51:4
You, and they return *to You* and confess Your name, and pray and make supplication
before You in this house,
25 then hear from heaven and forgive the sin of Your people Israel, and bring them
back to the land which You have given to them and to their fathers.
26 "When the heavens are shut up and there is no rain because they have sinned against **6:26** 1 Kin 17:1
You, and they pray toward this place and confess Your name, and turn from their sin
when You afflict them;
27 then hear in heaven and forgive the sin of Your servants and Your people Israel, **6:27** Ps 94:12
indeed, teach them the good way in which they should walk. And send rain on Your land
which You have given to Your people for an inheritance.
28 "If there is famine in the land, if there is pestilence, if there is blight or mildew, if **6:28** 2 Chr 20:9
there is locust or grasshopper, if their enemies besiege them in the land of their cities,
whatever plague or whatever sickness *there is,*
29 whatever prayer or supplication is made by any man or by all Your people Israel,
each knowing his own affliction and his own pain, and spreading his hands toward this
house,
30 then hear from heaven Your dwelling place, and forgive, and render to each ac- **6:30** 1 Sam 16:7; 1 Chr
cording to all his ways, whose heart You know for You alone know the hearts of the 28:9
sons of men,
31 that they may [4]fear You, to walk in Your ways as long as they live in the land which
You have given to our fathers.
32 "Also concerning the foreigner who is not from Your people Israel, when he comes **6:32** Is 56:3-8
from a far country for Your great name's sake and Your mighty hand and Your outstretched arm, when they come and pray toward this house,

4 Or *reverence*

6:18 Solomon marveled that the temple could contain the power of God and that God would be willing to live on earth among sinful people. We marvel that God, through his Son, Jesus, lived among us in human form to reveal his eternal purposes to us. In doing so, God was reaching out to us in love. God wants us to reach out to him in return in order to know him and to love him with all our hearts. Don't simply marvel at his power; take time to get to know him.

6:19–42 As Solomon led the people in prayer, he asked God to hear their prayers concerning a variety of situations: (1) crime (6:22–23); (2) enemy attacks (6:24–25); (3) drought (6:26–27); (4) famine (6:28–31); (5) the influx of foreigners (6:32–33); (6) war (6:34–35); (7) sin (6:36–39). God is concerned with whatever we face, even the difficult consequences we bring upon ourselves. He wants us to turn to him in prayer. When you pray, remember that God hears you. Don't let the extremity of your situation cause you to doubt his care for you.

6:26 Why would Solomon assume that drought would come as a result of sin? Sin is not necessarily the direct cause of natural disasters today, but this was a special case. God had made a specific agreement with the Israelites that drought could be a consequence of their sins (Deuteronomy 28:20–24).

6:30 Have you ever felt far from God, separated by feelings of failure and personal problems? In his prayer, Solomon underscored the fact that God stands ready to hear his people, to forgive their sins, and to restore their relationship with him. God is waiting and listening for our confessions of guilt and our recommitment to obey him. He hears us when we pour out our needs and problems to him and is ready to forgive us and restore us to fellowship with him. Don't wait to experience his loving forgiveness.

6:33 2 Chr 7:14

33 then hear from heaven, from Your dwelling place, and do according to all for which
the foreigner calls to You, in order that all the peoples of the earth may know Your name,
and [5]fear You as *do* Your people Israel, and that they may know that this house which I
have built is called by Your name.
34 "When Your people go out to battle against their enemies, by whatever way You shall
send them, and they pray to You toward this city which You have chosen and the house
which I have built for Your name,
35 then hear from heaven their prayer and their supplication, and maintain their cause.

6:36 Job 15:14-16; James 3:2; 1 John 1:8-10

36 "When they sin against You (for there is no man who does not sin) and You are angry with them and deliver them to an enemy, so that they take them away captive to a
land far off or near,
37 if they take thought in the land where they are taken captive, and repent and make
supplication to You in the land of their captivity, saying, 'We have sinned, we have committed iniquity and have acted wickedly';

6:38 Jer 29:12, 13

38 if they return to You with all their heart and with all their soul in the land of their
captivity, where they have been taken captive, and pray toward their land which You
have given to their fathers and the city which You have chosen, and toward the house
which I have built for Your name,
39 then hear from heaven, from Your dwelling place, their prayer and supplications,
and maintain their cause and forgive Your people who have sinned against You.

6:40 2 Chr 7:15; Neh 1:6, 11; Ps 17:1

40 "Now, O my God, I pray, let Your eyes be open and Your ears attentive to the prayer
offered in this place.

6:41 Ps 132:8, 9

41 "Now therefore arise, O LORD God, to Your resting place, You and the ark of Your
might; let Your priests, O LORD God, be clothed with salvation and let Your godly ones
rejoice in what is good.

6:42 Ps 89:24, 28; 132:10-12; Is 55:3

42 "O LORD God, do not turn away the face of Your anointed; remember *Your*
lovingkindness to Your servant David."

The Shekinah Glory

7:1 1 Kin 8:54; Lev 9:23f; 1 Kin 18:24, 38

7 Now when Solomon had finished praying, fire came down from heaven and consumed
the burnt offering and the sacrifices, and the glory of the LORD filled the house.

7:2 2 Chr 5:14

2 The priests could not enter into the house of the LORD because the glory of the
LORD filled the LORD'S house.

7:3 2 Chr 5:13; 20:21

3 All the sons of Israel, seeing the fire come down and the glory of the LORD upon
the house, bowed down on the pavement with their faces to the ground, and they worshiped and gave praise to the LORD, *saying,* "Truly He is good, truly His lovingkindness
is everlasting."

Sacrifices Offered

7:4 1 Kin 8:62, 63

4 Then the king and all the people offered sacrifice before the LORD.
5 King Solomon offered a sacrifice of 22,000 oxen and 120,000 sheep. Thus the king
and all the people dedicated the house of God.

7:6 1 Chr 15:16-21; 2 Chr 5:12

6 The priests stood at their posts, and the Levites also, with the instruments of music
to the LORD, which King David had made for giving praise to the LORD—"for His
lovingkindness is everlasting"—whenever he gave praise by their means, while the priests
on the other side blew trumpets; and all Israel was standing.

7:7 1 Kin 8:64-66

7 Then Solomon consecrated the middle of the court that *was* before the house of the
LORD, for there he offered the burnt offerings and the fat of the peace offerings because

5 Or *reverence*

6:36 "For there is no man who does not sin"—the Bible makes it clear that no one is exempt from sin, not even God's appointed kings. Sin is a condition we all share, and we all should acknowledge it as Solomon did. When we realize we have sinned, we should quickly ask God for forgiveness and restoration. Knowing we have a tendency to sin should keep us close to God, seeking his guidance and strength. This truth is also mentioned in Psalm 14:3, Ecclesiastes 7:20, and Romans 3:23.

7:1–2 God sent fire from heaven to consume the offering and to begin the fire that was to burn continuously under the altar of burnt offering (see Leviticus 6:8–13). This perpetual fire symbolized God's presence. God also sent fire when inaugurating the tabernacle (Leviticus 9:22–24). This was the real dedication of the temple because only God's purifying power can make something holy.

7:4–5 The temple was dedicated to God, and Solomon and the people prepared to worship him. Dedication means setting apart a place, an object, or a person for an exclusive purpose. The purpose of this dedication was to set apart the temple as a place to worship God. Today, our bodies are God's temple (2 Corinthians 6:16). Solomon's dedication of the temple shows us that we should dedicate ourselves to carry out God's special purpose (Ephesians 1:11–12).

the bronze altar which Solomon had made was not able to contain the burnt offering,
the grain offering and the fat.

The Feast of Dedication

8 So Solomon observed the feast at that time for seven days, and all Israel with him, **7:8** 1 Kin 8:65; Gen 15:18
a very great assembly *who came* from the entrance of Hamath to the brook of Egypt.
9 On the eighth day they held a solemn assembly, for the dedication of the altar they
observed seven days and the feast seven days. **7:9** Lev 23:36
10 Then on the twenty-third day of the seventh month he sent the people to their tents,
rejoicing and happy of heart because of the goodness that the LORD had shown to David and to Solomon and to His people Israel.

God's Promise and Warning

11 Thus Solomon finished the house of the LORD and the king's palace, and success- **7:11** 1 Kin 9:1-9
fully completed all that he had planned on doing in the house of the LORD and in his palace.
12 Then the LORD appeared to Solomon at night and said to him, "I have heard your **7:12** Deut 12:5, 11
prayer and have chosen this place for Myself as a house of sacrifice.
13 "If I shut up the heavens so that there is no rain, or if I command the locust to de- **7:13** 2 Chr 6:26-28
vour the land, or if I send pestilence among My people,
14 and My people who are called by My name humble themselves and pray and seek **7:14** 2 Chr 6:37-39; James 4:10
My face and turn from their wicked ways, then I will hear from heaven, will forgive their
sin and will heal their land.
15 "Now My eyes will be open and My ears attentive to the prayer *offered* in this place. **7:15** 2 Chr 6:20, 40
16 "For now I have chosen and consecrated this house that My name may be there for-
ever, and My eyes and My heart will be there perpetually. **7:16** 2 Chr 7:12
17 "As for you, if you walk before Me as your father David walked, even to do according to all that I have commanded you, and will keep My statutes and My ordinances,
18 then I will establish your royal throne as I covenanted with your father David, say- **7:18** 1 Kin 2:4; 2 Chr 6:16
ing, 'You shall not lack a man *to be* ruler in Israel.'
19 "But if you turn away and forsake My statutes and My commandments which I have **7:19** Lev 26:14, 33; Deut 28:15
set before you, and go and serve other gods and worship them,
20 then I will uproot you from My land which I have given you, and this house which I
have consecrated for My name I will cast out of My sight and I will make it a proverb **7:20** Deut 29:28; 1 Kin 14:15; Deut 28:37
and a byword among all peoples.
21 "As for this house, which was exalted, everyone who passes by it will be astonished **7:21** Deut 29:24-27
and say, 'Why has the LORD done thus to this land and to this house?'
22 "And they will say, 'Because they forsook the LORD, the God of their fathers who **7:22** Judg 2:13
brought them from the land of Egypt, and they adopted other gods and worshiped them
and served them; therefore He has brought all this adversity on them.' "

7:12 Months, maybe years, had passed since Solomon's prayer of dedication (chapter 6). Several other building projects had been completed after the temple (7:11; 8:1). Then after all this time, God told Solomon that he had heard Solomon's prayer. How often do we look for immediate answers to our prayers and, when nothing happens, wonder if God has heard us? God does hear, and he will provide for us. We must trust that God will answer at the proper time.

7:14 In chapter 6, Solomon asked God to make provisions for the people when they sinned. God answered with four conditions for forgiveness: (1) humble yourself by admitting your sins, (2) pray to God, asking for forgiveness, (3) seek God continually, and (4) turn from sinful behavior. True repentance is more than talk—it is changed behavior. Whether we sin individually, as a group, or as a nation, following these steps will lead to forgiveness. God will answer our earnest prayers.

7:17–22 God plainly set forth certain conditions for Solomon to meet if he wanted the kingdom to continue. If Solomon followed God, he and his descendants would prosper; if Solomon did not, he and the nation would be destroyed. In Deuteronomy 27 and 28, these conditions were outlined before all the people.

But sin is deceptively attractive, and Solomon eventually turned from God. As a result, his son and heir lost most of the kingdom. Following God brings benefits and rewards (not necessarily material). Turning away from God brings suffering, punishment, and ultimately destruction. Today, God's conditions are just as clear as they were in Solomon's day. Choose to obey God and live.

7:21–22 Soon after Solomon's reign, the temple was ransacked (12:9). It is difficult for us to imagine that such a great and wise king could become corrupted by idols—symbols of power, prosperity, and sexuality. But even today these idols lure us into their traps. When we allow any desire to rival God's proper place, we have taken the first step toward moral and spiritual decay.

4. Solomon's riches and wisdom

Solomon's Activities and Accomplishments

8:1 1 Kin 9:10-28

8 Now it came about at the end of the twenty years in which Solomon had built the
house of the LORD and his own house
2 that he built the cities which Huram had given to him, and settled the sons of Israel
there.
3 Then Solomon went to Hamath-zobah and captured it.
4 He built Tadmor in the wilderness and all the storage cities which he had built in
Hamath.

8:5 1 Chr 7:24; 2 Chr 14:7

5 He also built upper Beth-horon and lower Beth-horon, fortified cities *with* walls,
gates and bars;
6 and Baalath and all the storage cities that Solomon had, and all the cities for his
chariots and cities for his horsemen, and all that it pleased Solomon to build in Jerusalem, in Lebanon, and in all the land under his rule.

8:7 Gen 15:18-21; 1 Kin 9:20

8:8 1 Kin 4:6; 9:21

7 All of the people who were left of the Hittites, the Amorites, the Perizzites, the
Hivites and the Jebusites, who were not of Israel,
8 *namely,* from their descendants who were left after them in the land whom the sons
of Israel had not destroyed, them Solomon raised as forced laborers to this day.
9 But Solomon did not make slaves for his work from the sons of Israel; they were
men of war, his chief captains and commanders of his chariots and his horsemen.
10 These were the chief officers of King Solomon, two hundred and fifty who ruled
over the people.

8:11 1 Kin 3:1; 7:8

11 Then Solomon brought Pharaoh's daughter up from the city of David to the house
which he had built for her, for he said, "My wife shall not dwell in the house of David
king of Israel, because the places are holy where the ark of the LORD has entered."

8:12 2 Chr 4:1

8:13 Ex 29:38-42; Num 28:3; Num 28:9, 10; Num 28:11; Ex 23:14-17; 34:22, 23; Deut 16:16

8:14 1 Chr 24:1; 1 Chr 25:1; 1 Chr 26:1; Neh 12:24, 36

12 Then Solomon offered burnt offerings to the LORD on the altar of the LORD which
he had built before the porch;
13 and *did so* according to the daily rule, offering *them* up according to the commandment of Moses, for the sabbaths, the new moons and the three annual feasts—the Feast
of Unleavened Bread, the Feast of Weeks and the Feast of Booths.
14 Now according to the ordinance of his father David, he appointed the divisions of
the priests for their service, and the Levites for their duties of praise and ministering
before the priests according to the daily rule, and the gatekeepers by their divisions at
every gate; for David the man of God had so commanded.
15 And they did not depart from the commandment of the king to the priests and Levites
in any manner or concerning the storehouses.
16 Thus all the work of Solomon was carried out from the day of the foundation of the
house of the LORD, and until it was finished. So the house of the LORD was completed.

8:17 1 Kin 9:26; 2 Kin 14:22

8:18 2 Chr 9:10, 13

17 Then Solomon went to Ezion-geber and to Eloth on the seashore in the land of Edom.
18 And Huram by his servants sent him ships and servants who knew the sea; and they
went with Solomon's servants to Ophir, and took from there four hundred and fifty talents of gold and brought them to King Solomon.

Visit of the Queen of Sheba

9:1 1 Kin 10:1-13; Matt 12:42; Luke 11:31

9 Now when the queen of Sheba heard of the fame of Solomon, she came to Jerusalem to test Solomon with difficult questions. She had a very large retinue, with
camels carrying spices and a large amount of gold and precious stones; and when she
came to Solomon, she spoke with him about all that was on her heart.

8:11 Solomon married Pharaoh's daughter to secure a military alliance with Egypt. He did not let the woman live in David's palace, however, where the ark of God had once been kept. This implies that Solomon knew his pagan marriage would not please God. Solomon married many other foreign women, and this was contrary to God's Law (Deuteronomy 7:3–4). These women worshiped false gods and were certain to contaminate Israel with their beliefs and practices. Eventually Solomon's pagan wives caused his downfall (1 Kings 11:1–11).

8:15 Although Solomon carefully followed God's instructions for building the temple and offering sacrifices (8:13), he paid no attention to what God said about marrying pagan women. His sin in marrying a foreign wife (8:11) began his slide away from God. No matter how good or spiritual we are in most areas of life, one unsurrendered area can begin a downfall. Guard carefully *every* area of your life, especially your relationships. Don't give sin any foothold.

9:1–8 The queen of Sheba had heard about Solomon's wisdom, but she was overwhelmed when she saw for herself the fruits of that wisdom. Although Solomon had married Pharaoh's daughter, he still sincerely tried to follow God at this stage in his life. When people get to know you and ask hard questions, will your responses reflect God? Your life can be a powerful witness; let others see God at work in you.

2 Solomon answered all her questions; nothing was hidden from Solomon which he
did not explain to her.
3 When the queen of Sheba had seen the wisdom of Solomon, the house which he
had built,
4 the food at his table, the seating of his servants, the attendance of his ministers and
their attire, his cupbearers and their attire, and his stairway by which he went up to the
house of the LORD, she was breathless.
5 Then she said to the king, "It was a true report which I heard in my own land about
your words and your wisdom.
6 "Nevertheless I did not believe their reports until I came and my eyes had seen it.
And behold, the half of the greatness of your wisdom was not told me. You surpass the
report that I heard.
7 "How blessed are your men, how blessed are these your servants who stand before
you continually and hear your wisdom.
8 "Blessed be the LORD your God who delighted in you, setting you on His throne as **9:8**
king for the LORD your God; because your God loved Israel establishing them forever, 1 Chr 28:5; 29:23; Deut 7:8; 2 Chr 2:11
therefore He made you king over them, to do justice and righteousness."
9 Then she gave the king one hundred and twenty talents of gold and a very great
amount of spices and precious stones; there had never been spice like that which the queen
of Sheba gave to King Solomon.
10 The servants of Huram and the servants of Solomon who brought gold from Ophir, **9:10**
also brought algum trees and precious stones. 1 Kin 10:11; 2 Chr 8:18
11 From the algum trees the king made steps for the house of the LORD and for the
king's palace, and lyres and harps for the singers; and none like that was seen before in
the land of Judah.
12 King Solomon gave to the queen of Sheba all her desire which she requested besides *a return for* what she had brought to the king. Then she turned and went to her own
land with her servants.

Solomon's Wealth and Power

13 Now the weight of gold which came to Solomon in one year was 666 talents of gold, **9:13**
14 besides that which the traders and merchants brought; and all the kings of Arabia 1 Kin 10:14-28
and the governors of the country brought gold and silver to Solomon. **9:14**
15 King Solomon made 200 large shields of beaten gold, using 600 *shekels of* beaten Ps 68:29; 72:10
gold on each large shield.
16 *He made* 300 shields of beaten gold, using three hundred shekels of gold on each
shield, and the king put them in the house of the forest of Lebanon.
17 Moreover, the king made a great throne of ivory and overlaid it with pure gold.
18 *There were* six steps to the throne and a footstool in gold attached to the throne, and
arms on each side of the seat, and two lions standing beside the arms.
19 Twelve lions were standing there on the six steps on the one side and on the other;
nothing like *it* was made for any *other* kingdom.
20 All King Solomon's drinking vessels *were* of gold, and all the vessels of the house of
the forest of Lebanon *were* of pure gold; silver was not considered valuable in the days
of Solomon.
21 For the king had ships which went to Tarshish with the servants of Huram; once **9:21**
every three years the ships of Tarshish came bringing gold and silver, ivory and apes and 2 Chr 20:36, 37
peacocks.
22 So King Solomon became greater than all the kings of the earth in riches and **9:22**
wisdom. 1 Kin 3:13; 2 Chr 1:12
23 And all the kings of the earth were seeking the presence of Solomon, to hear his
wisdom which God had put in his heart.

9:8 The queen of Sheba marveled at Solomon, claiming that God must love his people greatly to give them such a king. Israel greatly prospered during Solomon's reign, witnessing to God's power and love for his people. The good times show God's love and faithfulness. But hard times come to believers, too, and our perseverance and steadfast hope during those times will demonstrate our love and faithfulness to God. How we live will help others see our love for God.

9:11 Algum wood was probably sandalwood, a smooth, red-colored wood that accepts a high polish. This beautiful wood was extremely expensive.

9:24 Ps 72:10
9:25 Deut 17:16; 1 Kin 4:26; 10:26; 2 Chr 1:14
9:26 Gen 15:18; 1 Kin 4:21, 24
9:27 2 Chr 1:15-17
9:28 2 Chr 1:16
9:29 1 Kin 11:41-43; 1 Chr 29:29
9:30 1 Kin 11:42, 43
9:31 1 Kin 2:10

24 They brought every man his gift, articles of silver and gold, garments, weapons, spices,
horses and mules, so much year by year.
25 Now Solomon had 4,000 stalls for horses and chariots and 12,000 horsemen, and he
stationed them in the chariot cities and with the king in Jerusalem.
26 He was the ruler over all the kings from the Euphrates River even to the land of the
Philistines, and as far as the border of Egypt.
27 The king made silver *as common* as stones in Jerusalem, and he made cedars as
plentiful as sycamore trees that are in the lowland.
28 And they were bringing horses for Solomon from Egypt and from all countries.
29 Now the rest of the acts of Solomon, from first to last, are they not written in the
records of Nathan the prophet, and in the prophecy of Ahijah the Shilonite, and in the
visions of Iddo the seer concerning Jeroboam the son of Nebat?
30 Solomon reigned forty years in Jerusalem over all Israel.

Death of Solomon

31 And Solomon slept with his fathers and was buried in the city of his father David;
and his son Rehoboam reigned in his place.

B. THE KINGDOM OF JUDAH (10:1—36:23)

After Solomon's death, the northern tribes revolt, and we read little more about them in 2 Chronicles. The remainder of 2 Chronicles recounts the alternating periods of apostasy and reform in Judah. In the end, Judah would not turn from its sin, and the tragic result was a 70-year captivity in Babylon. Sin in our lives will also lead to judgment and devastation. Although God's judgment may seem slow, it is nevertheless certain.

1. The northern tribes revolt

Rehoboam's Reign of Folly

10:1 1 Kin 12:1-20
10:2 1 Kin 11:40
10:4 1 Kin 5:13-16
10:6 Job 8:8, 9; 32:7
10:7 Prov 15:1
10:8 2 Sam 17:14; Prov 13:20

10 Then Rehoboam went to Shechem, for all Israel had come to Shechem to make
him king.
2 When Jeroboam the son of Nebat heard *of it* (for he was in Egypt where he had fled
from the presence of King Solomon), Jeroboam returned from Egypt.
3 So they sent and summoned him. When Jeroboam and all Israel came, they spoke
to Rehoboam, saying,
4 "Your father made our yoke hard; now therefore lighten the hard service of your
father and his heavy yoke which he put on us, and we will serve you."
5 He said to them, "Return to me again in three days." So the people departed.
6 Then King Rehoboam consulted with the elders who had served his father Solomon while he was still alive, saying, "How do you counsel *me* to answer this people?"
7 They spoke to him, saying, "If you will be kind to this people and please them and
speak good words to them, then they will be your servants forever."
8 But he forsook the counsel of the elders which they had given him, and consulted
with the young men who grew up with him and served him.
9 So he said to them, "What counsel do you give that we may answer this people, who
have spoken to me, saying, 'Lighten the yoke which your father put on us'?"
10 The young men who grew up with him spoke to him, saying, "Thus you shall say to
the people who spoke to you, saying, 'Your father made our yoke heavy, but you make
it lighter for us.' Thus you shall say to them, 'My little finger is thicker than my father's
loins!

9:29 For the rest of Solomon's story, see 1 Kings 10:26—11:43. In his later years, Solomon turned away from God and led the nation into worshiping idols.

10:1 The crowning of an Israelite king would normally have taken place in Jerusalem, the capital city. But Rehoboam saw that there was the possibility of trouble in the north; so to maintain his hold on the country, he chose Shechem, a city about 35 miles north of Jerusalem. Shechem was an ancient site for making covenants (Joshua 24:1).

10:1–15 Following bad advice can cause disaster. Rehoboam lost the chance to rule a peaceful, united kingdom because he rejected the advice of Solomon's older counselors, preferring the counsel of his peers. Rehoboam made two errors in seeking advice: (1) He did not give extra consideration to the suggestions of those who knew the situation better than he, and (2) he did not ask God for wisdom to discern which was the better option.

It is easy to follow the advice of our peers because they often feel as we do. But their view may be limited. It is important to listen carefully to those who have more experience than we do—they can see the bigger picture.

10:2–3 Why was Jeroboam in Egypt? Ahijah the prophet had predicted that Israel would split in two and that Jeroboam would become king of the northern section. When Solomon learned of this prophecy, he tried to kill Jeroboam, and Jeroboam was forced to flee to Egypt (1 Kings 11:26–40).

11 'Whereas my father loaded you with a heavy yoke, I will add to your yoke; my father
disciplined you with whips, but I *will discipline you* with scorpions.' "
12 So Jeroboam and all the people came to Rehoboam on the third day as the king
had directed, saying, "Return to me on the third day."
13 The king answered them harshly, and King Rehoboam forsook the counsel of the
elders.
14 He spoke to them according to the advice of the young men, saying, "My father made
your yoke heavy, but I will add to it; my father disciplined you with whips, but I *will discipline you* with scorpions."
15 So the king did not listen to the people, for it was a turn *of events* from God that the
LORD might establish His word, which He spoke through Ahijah the Shilonite to Jeroboam the son of Nebat.
16 When all Israel *saw* that the king did not listen to them the people answered the
king, saying,

"What portion do we have in David?
We have no inheritance in the son of Jesse.
Every man to your tents, O Israel;
Now look after your own house, David."

So all Israel departed to their tents.
17 But as for the sons of Israel who lived in the cities of Judah, Rehoboam reigned
over them.
18 Then King Rehoboam sent Hadoram, who was over the forced labor, and the sons
of Israel stoned him to death. And King Rehoboam made haste to mount his chariot to
flee to Jerusalem.
19 So Israel has been in rebellion against the house of David to this day.

10:15 2 Chr 25:16-20; 1 Kin 11:29-39
10:16 2 Sam 20:1; 2 Chr 10:19
10:18 1 Kin 4:6; 5:14
10:19 1 Kin 12:19

Rehoboam Reigns over Judah and Builds Cities

11 Now when Rehoboam had come to Jerusalem, he assembled the house of Judah
and Benjamin, 180,000 chosen men who were warriors, to fight against Israel to
restore the kingdom to Rehoboam.
2 But the word of the LORD came to Shemaiah the man of God, saying,
3 "Speak to Rehoboam the son of Solomon, king of Judah, and to all Israel in Judah
and Benjamin, saying,
4 'Thus says the LORD, "You shall not go up or fight against your relatives; return every
man to his house, for this thing is from Me." ' " So they listened to the words of the LORD
and returned from going against Jeroboam.
5 Rehoboam lived in Jerusalem and built cities for defense in Judah.
6 Thus he built Bethlehem, Etam, Tekoa,
7 Beth-zur, Soco, Adullam,
8 Gath, Mareshah, Ziph,
9 Adoraim, Lachish, Azekah,

11:1 1 Kin 12:21-24
11:2 2 Chr 12:5-7, 15
11:4 2 Chr 28:8-11; 2 Chr 10:15
11:5 2 Chr 8:2-6; 11:23

10:14 Rehoboam must have gotten an unbalanced picture of leadership from his father, Solomon. Apparently Rehoboam saw only the difficulty of leading the nation, not the opportunities. He mentioned only the harsher aspects of Solomon's rule, and he himself decided to be very harsh toward the people. As you discuss your responsibilities with your children, be sure that you temper words of complaint with words of joy. Otherwise you may sour their attitudes toward the work you do and those you serve.

10:16–19 In trying to have it all, Rehoboam lost almost everything. Motivated by greed and power, he pressed too hard and divided his kingdom. He didn't need more money or power because he had inherited the richest kingdom in the world. He didn't need more control because he was the king. His demands were based on selfishness rather than reason or spiritual discernment. Those who insist on having it all often wind up with little or nothing.

10:16–19 This is the beginning of the divided kingdom. The peaceful united kingdom under Solomon divided into two parts. Ten of the tribes followed Jeroboam and called their nation Israel, or the northern kingdom. The other two tribes, Judah and Benjamin, remained loyal to David's line and accepted Rehoboam's rule. They called their nation Judah, or the southern kingdom.

11:1 Rehoboam's foolishness divided his kingdom, and he tried to reunite it by force. True unity, however, cannot be forced—it must be the free response of willing hearts. If you want the loyalty of employees, children, or anyone else in your charge, win their respect through love instead of trying to gain their submission through force.

11:4 Why would God support this rebellion? It was part of the nation's punishment for turning away from God (1 Kings 11:11). It may also have been God's way of saving Rehoboam's smaller kingdom from defeat. In doing so, God preserved David's line and kept intact his plan for the Messiah to be a descendant of David (see 2 Samuel 7:16). When we see division, especially in a church that splits, we wonder what God would have us do. God desires unity, but while we should always work toward reconciliation, we must recognize that only God knows the future. He may allow a division in order to fulfill his greater purposes.

10 Zorah, Aijalon and Hebron, which are fortified cities in Judah and in Benjamin.
11 He also strengthened the fortresses and put officers in them and stores of food, oil and wine.
12 *He put* shields and spears in every city and strengthened them greatly. So he held Judah and Benjamin.
13 Moreover, the priests and the Levites who were in all Israel stood with him from all their districts.

REHOBOAM

Settling for cheap imitations in exchange for the real thing is a poor way to live. In every area of his life, Rehoboam consistently traded away what was real for what was counterfeit. Given wise and unwise counsel by his advisers at his coronation, he chose to grab for power and control rather than to take patiently the counsel of those older and wiser than he and treat his people with kindness. Although his position came from God, he chose to abandon God. These unwise decisions made him weaker rather than stronger. As a result, he was invaded by the Egyptians and stripped of the riches he had inherited from David and Solomon. To replace them, he had cheap bronze copies made.

Throughout the early part of his reign, Rehoboam fluctuated between obeying God and going his own way. Outward appearances were kept up, but his inward attitudes were evil. Following in the tradition of David gave Rehoboam many opportunities for real greatness. Instead, he ended up with a divided and broken kingdom.

How much of real living have we traded away for the things that do not last? We trade healthy bodies for momentary excitement, personal integrity for fast-fading wealth, honesty for lies, God's wise guidance for our selfish ways. We sin when we willingly give little value to "the real thing" God has already given us.

Our counterfeit lives may fool some people, but they never fool God. Yet in spite of what he sees in us, God offers mercy. Are you a self-managed enterprise, counterfeit at best? Or have you placed yourself in God's care? Do the decisions you must make today need a second consideration in light of Rehoboam's example?

Strengths and accomplishments:
- Fourth and last king of the united nation of Israel, but only for a short time
- Fortified his kingdom and achieved a measure of popularity

Weaknesses and mistakes:
- Followed unwise advice and divided his kingdom
- Married foreign women, as his father Solomon had done
- Abandoned the worship of God and allowed idolatry to flourish

Lessons from his life:
- Thoughtless decisions often lead to exchanging what is most valuable for something of far less value
- Every choice we make has real and long-lasting consequences

Vital statistics:
- Where: Jerusalem
- Occupation: King of the united kingdom of Israel, and later of the southern kingdom of Judah
- Relatives: Father: Solomon. Mother: Naamah. Son: Abijah. Wife: Maacah
- Contemporaries: Jeroboam, Shishak, Shemaiah

Key verse:
"When the kingdom of Rehoboam was established and strong, he and all Israel with him forsook the law of the LORD" (2 Chronicles 12:1).

Rehoboam's story is told in 1 Kings 11:43—14:31 and 2 Chronicles 9:31—13:7. He is also mentioned in Matthew 1:7.

11:13–14 Before the nation split, the center of worship was in Jerusalem, and people flocked there for the three great annual religious festivals. During the rest of the year, other worship services and rituals were conducted in the tribal territories by priests and Levites who lived throughout the land. They offered sacrifices, taught God's laws, and encouraged the people to continue to follow God and avoid pagan influences.

After the nation split, Jeroboam, the new king of Israel, saw these priests and Levites as threats to his new government because they retained loyalty to Jerusalem, now the capital of Judah. So he appointed his own priests, effectively banning the Levites from their duties and forcing them to move to the southern kingdom. Jeroboam's pagan priests encouraged idol worship. With the absence of spiritual leaders, the new northern kingdom was in danger of abandoning God.

Jeroboam Appoints False Priests

14 For the Levites left their pasture lands and their property and came to Judah and Jerusalem, for Jeroboam and his sons had excluded them from serving as priests to the LORD.

11:14 Num 35:2-5; 1 Kin 12:28-33; 2 Chr 13:9

15 He set up priests of his own for the high places, for the satyrs and for the calves which he had made.

11:15 1 Kin 12:31; 13:33

16 Those from all the tribes of Israel who set their hearts on seeking the LORD God of Israel followed them to Jerusalem, to sacrifice to the LORD God of their fathers.

11:16 2 Chr 15:9

17 They strengthened the kingdom of Judah and supported Rehoboam the son of Solomon for three years, for they walked in the way of David and Solomon for three years.

11:17 2 Chr 12:1

2. History of apostasy and reform

Rehoboam's Family

18 Then Rehoboam took as a wife Mahalath the daughter of Jerimoth the son of David *and of* Abihail the daughter of Eliab the son of Jesse,

11:18 1 Sam 16:6

19 and she bore him sons: Jeush, Shemariah and Zaham.

20 After her he took Maacah the daughter of Absalom, and she bore him Abijah, Attai, Ziza and Shelomith.

11:20 1 Kin 15:2; 2 Chr 13:2

21 Rehoboam loved Maacah the daughter of Absalom more than all his *other* wives and concubines. For he had taken eighteen wives and sixty concubines and fathered twenty-eight sons and sixty daughters.

11:21 Deut 17:17

22 Rehoboam appointed Abijah the son of Maacah as head and leader among his brothers, for he *intended* to make him king.

11:22 Deut 21:15-17

23 He acted wisely and distributed some of his sons through all the territories of Judah and Benjamin to all the fortified cities, and he gave them food in abundance. And he sought many wives *for them.*

Shishak of Egypt Invades Judah

12 When the kingdom of Rehoboam was established and strong, he and all Israel with him forsook the law of the LORD.

12:1 2 Chr 11:17; 12:13; 2 Chr 26:13-16

2 And it came about in King Rehoboam's fifth year, because they had been unfaithful to the LORD, that Shishak king of Egypt came up against Jerusalem

12:2 1 Kin 14:25; 1 Kin 11:40

3 with 1,200 chariots and 60,000 horsemen. And the people who came with him from Egypt were without number: the Lubim, the Sukkiim and the Ethiopians.

12:3 2 Chr 16:8; Nah 3:9

4 He captured the fortified cities of Judah and came as far as Jerusalem.

12:4 2 Chr 11:5-12

5 Then Shemaiah the prophet came to Rehoboam and the princes of Judah who had gathered at Jerusalem because of Shishak, and he said to them, "Thus says the LORD, 'You have forsaken Me, so I also have forsaken you to Shishak.' "

12:5 2 Chr 11:2; Deut 28:15; 2 Chr 15:2

6 So the princes of Israel and the king humbled themselves and said, "The LORD is righteous."

12:6 Ex 9:27; Dan 9:14

7 When the LORD saw that they humbled themselves, the word of the LORD came to Shemaiah, saying, "They have humbled themselves *so* I will not destroy them, but I will grant them some *measure* of deliverance, and My wrath shall not be poured out on Jerusalem by means of Shishak.

12:7 1 Kin 21:29; 2 Chr 34:25-27; Ps 78:38

11:16 These people obeyed God rather than Jeroboam. By their actions, they preserved their integrity and strengthened the southern kingdom. In the future, most of the people in the northern kingdom would go along with the evil designs of the kings, hoping to benefit by cooperating. Don't follow their example and rationalize away God's teachings in order to gain earthly reward.

12:1–2 Here "Israel" refers to Judah, the southern kingdom. During his first three years on the throne, Rehoboam made an attempt to obey God, and as a result Judah prospered. But then, at his peak of popularity and power, he abandoned God. The result was destruction because God allowed Judah to be conquered by Egypt. How could this happen? Often it is more difficult to be a believer in good times than in bad. Tough times push us toward God; but easy times can make us feel self-sufficient and self-satisfied. When everything is going right, guard your faith closely.

12:2 A record of this invasion has been found on an Egyptian stone that says Shishak's army penetrated as far north as the Sea of Galilee, in the northern kingdom. Egypt was not the world power it had once been, and Shishak wanted to restore his nation to its former greatness. He was not strong enough to conquer both Israel and Judah, but he managed to destroy key cities in Judah in an effort to regain control of the trade routes and create dissension among the people.

12:6–8 God eased his judgment when Israel's leaders confessed their sins, humbled themselves, and recognized God's justice in punishing them. It's never too late to repent, even in the midst of punishment. Regardless of what we have done, God is willing to receive us back into fellowship. Are you struggling and alone because sin has broken your fellowship with God? Confession and humility will open the door to receiving God's mercy.

12:8 Deut 28:47, 48

8 “But they will become his slaves so that they may learn *the difference between* My
service and the service of the kingdoms of the countries.”

Plunder Impoverishes Judah

12:9 1 Kin 14:26-28; 1 Kin 10:16, 17; 2 Chr 9:15, 16

9 So Shishak king of Egypt came up against Jerusalem, and took the treasures of the
house of the LORD and the treasures of the king’s palace. He took everything; he even
took the golden shields which Solomon had made.
10 Then King Rehoboam made shields of bronze in their place and committed them
to the care of the commanders of the guard who guarded the door of the king’s house.
11 As often as the king entered the house of the LORD, the guards came and carried
them and *then* brought them back into the guards’ room.

12:12 2 Chr 12:6, 7; 2 Chr 19:3

12 And when he humbled himself, the anger of the LORD turned away from him, so as
not to destroy *him* completely; and also conditions were good in Judah.

12:13 1 Kin 14:21

13 So King Rehoboam strengthened himself in Jerusalem and reigned. Now Rehoboam was forty-one years old when he began to reign, and he reigned seventeen years in
Jerusalem, the city which the LORD had chosen from all the tribes of Israel, to put His
name there. And his mother’s name was Naamah the Ammonitess.

12:14 2 Chr 19:3

14 He did evil because he did not set his heart to seek the LORD.

12:15 1 Kin 14:29; 2 Chr 12:5; 2 Chr 9:29

15 Now the acts of Rehoboam, from first to last, are they not written in the records of
Shemaiah the prophet and of Iddo the seer, according to genealogical enrollment? And
there were wars between Rehoboam and Jeroboam continually.

12:16 2 Chr 11:20

16 And Rehoboam slept with his fathers and was buried in the city of David; and his
son Abijah became king in his place.

Abijah Succeeds Rehoboam

13:1 1 Kin 15:1, 2

13:2 1 Kin 15:7

13 In the eighteenth year of King Jeroboam, Abijah became king over Judah.
2 He reigned three years in Jerusalem; and his mother’s name was Micaiah the
daughter of Uriel of Gibeah.
Now there was war between Abijah and Jeroboam.
3 Abijah began the battle with an army of valiant warriors, 400,000 chosen men, while
Jeroboam drew up in battle formation against him with 800,000 chosen men *who were*
valiant warriors.

Civil War

13:4 Josh 18:22

4 Then Abijah stood on Mount Zemaraim, which is in the hill country of Ephraim,
and said, “Listen to me, Jeroboam and all Israel:

13:5 2 Sam 7:12-16; Lev 2:13; Num 18:19

5 “Do you not know that the LORD God of Israel gave the rule over Israel forever to
David and his sons by a covenant of salt?

13:6 1 Kin 11:26

6 “Yet Jeroboam the son of Nebat, the servant of Solomon the son of David, rose up
and rebelled against his master,

13:7 2 Chr 12:13

7 and worthless men gathered about him, scoundrels, who proved too strong for Rehoboam, the son of Solomon, when he was young and timid and could not hold his own
against them.

13:8 1 Kin 12:28; 2 Chr 11:15

8 “So now you intend to resist the kingdom of the LORD through the sons of David,
being a great multitude and *having* with you the golden calves which Jeroboam made for
gods for you.

12:8 “Service of the kingdoms of the countries” was the price Judah had to pay for disobeying God. The nation’s leaders thought they could succeed in their own strength, but they were wrong. When we rebel against God, we always pay for it. When we leave God out of our lives, we lose more spiritually than we ever gain financially.

12:10–11 How ironic that the pure gold of Solomon’s temple was replaced by cheaper bronze. Rehoboam tried to maintain the trappings and appearance of former glory, but he couldn’t measure up. When God is no longer central in our lives, maintaining the appearance of a Christian life becomes superficial. Outer beauty must come from inner strength.

12:14 Rehoboam’s story is tragic because he “did not set his heart to seek the LORD.” It is dangerous to put off responding to God. God asks us for a firm commitment, and unless we respond by trusting him completely, we will find ourselves alienated from him.

13:1ff 1 Kings 15:3 says Abijah (Abijam) committed many sins, but the Chronicles account has only positive comments about him. For the most part, Abijah was, no doubt, a wicked king. The writer of Chronicles chose to highlight the little good he did in order to show that he was still under God’s covenant promise to David. Because of Abijah’s fiery speech to Jeroboam (13:4–12), he was spared the immediate consequences of his sin.

13:8 Jeroboam’s army was cursed because of the golden calves they carried with them. It was as though they had put sin into a physical form so they could haul it around. Consider carefully the things you cherish. If you value anything more than God, it becomes your golden calf and will one day drag you down. Let go of anything that interferes with your relationship with God.

9 "Have you not driven out the priests of the LORD, the sons of Aaron and the Levites,
and made for yourselves priests like the peoples of *other* lands? Whoever comes to consecrate himself with a young bull and seven rams, even he may become a priest of *what*
are no gods.

13:9 2 Chr 11:14, 15; Ex 29:29-33; Jer 2:11; 5:7

10 "But as for us, the LORD is our God, and we have not forsaken Him; and the sons of
Aaron are ministering to the LORD as priests, and the Levites attend to their work.
11 "Every morning and evening they burn to the LORD burnt offerings and fragrant
incense, and the showbread is *set* on the clean table, and the golden lampstand with its
lamps is *ready* to light every evening; for we keep the charge of the LORD our God, but
you have forsaken Him.

13:11 Ex 29:38; 2 Chr 2:4; Ex 25:30-39; Lev 24:5-9

12 "Now behold, God is with us at *our* head and His priests with the signal trumpets to
sound the alarm against you. O sons of Israel, do not fight against the LORD God of your
fathers, for you will not succeed."

13:12 Num 10:8, 9

13 But Jeroboam had set an ambush to come from the rear, so that *Israel* was in front
of Judah and the ambush was behind them.

13:13 Josh 8:4-9

14 When Judah turned around, behold, they were attacked both front and rear; so they
cried to the LORD, and the priests blew the trumpets.

13:14 2 Chr 14:11

15 Then the men of Judah raised a war cry, and when the men of Judah raised the war
cry, then it was that God routed Jeroboam and all Israel before Abijah and Judah.

13:15 2 Chr 14:12

16 When the sons of Israel fled before Judah, God gave them into their hand.
17 Abijah and his people defeated them with a great slaughter, so that 500,000 chosen
men of Israel fell slain.

13:16 2 Chr 16:8

18 Thus the sons of Israel were subdued at that time, and the sons of Judah conquered
because they trusted in the LORD, the God of their fathers.

13:18 2 Chr 14:11

19 Abijah pursued Jeroboam and captured from him *several* cities, Bethel with its villages, Jeshanah with its villages and Ephron with its villages.

Death of Jeroboam

20 Jeroboam did not again recover strength in the days of Abijah; and the LORD struck
him and he died.

13:20 1 Sam 25:38; 1 Kin 14:20

21 But Abijah became powerful; and took fourteen wives to himself, and became the
father of twenty-two sons and sixteen daughters.
22 Now the rest of the acts of Abijah, and his ways and his words are written in the
treatise of the prophet Iddo.

13:22 2 Chr 24:27; 2 Chr 9:29

14:1 1 Kin 15:8

Asa Succeeds Abijah in Judah

14 So Abijah slept with his fathers, and they buried him in the city of David, and his
son Asa became king in his place. The land was undisturbed for ten years during
his days.
2 Asa did good and right in the sight of the LORD his God,
3 for he removed the foreign altars and high places, tore down the *sacred* pillars, cut
down the [6]Asherim,

14:3 Deut 7:5; 1 Kin 15:12-14; Ex 34:13

6 I.e. wooden symbols of a female deity

13:9 Abijah criticized Jeroboam's low standards in appointing priests. Anyone is qualified to represent a god that is worthless. To represent the Lord God Almighty, however, a person must live by God's standards, not man's. Those appointed to positions of responsibility in your church should not be selected merely because they volunteer, are influential, or are highly educated. Instead they should demonstrate sound doctrine, dedication to God, and strong spiritual character (see 2 Timothy 3).

13:18–19 Although outnumbered by Israel, Judah won this conflict by depending on God's help. Some kings in Judah's history focused on God, but not one Israelite king consistently followed God—all followed Jeroboam's idolatry or served Baal. As a result, Israel experienced God's punishment many years before Judah did.

Judah had an advantage—the temple, with its sacrifices and the loyal priests and prophets, was in the southern kingdom. Many of Judah's kings were good, at least for parts of their reigns. Whenever an idolatrous king reigned, his rule was followed by that of a God-honoring king who reformed religious life. Also, the idolatrous kings usually served for a much shorter time than the good ones. The result was that true faith in God ran stronger and deeper in Judah than in Israel, but it was still not up to God's standards.

14:1–6 Asa's reign was marked by peace because he "did good and right in the sight of the LORD his God." This refrain is often repeated in Chronicles—*obedience* to God leads to *peace* with God and others. In the case of Judah's kings, obedience to God led to national peace, just as God had promised centuries earlier. In our case, obedience may not always bring peace with our enemies, but it will bring peace with God and complete peace in his future kingdom. Obeying God is the first step on the path to peace.

14:3–5 Simply attending worship services is not enough to secure God's peace. Like Asa, we must also actively remove anything that is offensive to God. Becoming more active in church attendance or good deeds will still leave us in turmoil if we have failed to eliminate sinful practices from our lives. We should continually ask God to help us remove any source of temptation from our lives.

4 and commanded Judah to seek the LORD God of their fathers and to observe the law and the commandment.

14:5 2 Chr 34:4, 7
5 He also removed the high places and the incense altars from all the cities of Judah. And the kingdom was undisturbed under him.

14:6 2 Chr 11:5; 2 Chr 15:15
6 He built fortified cities in Judah, since the land was undisturbed, and there was no one at war with him during those years, because the LORD had given him rest.

14:7 2 Chr 8:5
7 For he said to Judah, "Let us build these cities and surround *them* with walls and towers, gates and bars. The land is still ours because we have sought the LORD our God; we have sought Him, and He has given us rest on every side." So they built and prospered.

God has never accepted the idea that "the ends justify the means." He is just and perfect in all his ways. People, on the other hand, are far from perfect. That a bond can exist between a loving and merciful Creator and a resisting and rebellious creation is as great a miracle as creation itself! As a king, Asa came very close to being good. He traveled a long way with God before getting off track. His sin was not so much deliberate disobedience as choosing the *easy* way rather than the *right* way.

When the odds seemed impossible in the battle with the Cushites, Asa recognized his need to depend on God. Following that victory, God's promise of peace based on obedience spurred the king and people to many years of right living. But Asa was to face a tougher test.

Years of animosity between Asa and Israel's king Baasha took an ugly turn. Baasha, king of the rival northern kingdom, was building a fort that threatened both the peace and the economy of Judah. Asa thought he saw a way out—he bribed King Ben-hadad of Aram to break his alliance with King Baasha. The plan worked brilliantly, but it wasn't God's way. When Asa was confronted by God's prophet Hanani, he flew into a rage, jailed Hanani, and took out his anger on his people. Asa rejected correction and refused to admit his error to God. His greatest failure was missing what God could have done with his life if he had been willing to be humble. His pride ruined the health of his reign. He stubbornly held on to his failure until his death.

Does this attitude sound familiar? Can you identify failures in your life that you have continued to rationalize rather than admit them to God and accept his forgiveness? The ends do not justify the means. Such a belief leads to sin and failure. The stubborn refusal to admit a failure due to sin can become a big problem because it makes you spend time rationalizing rather than learning from your mistakes and moving on.

Strengths and accomplishments:
- Obeyed God during the first ten years of his reign
- Carried out a partially successful effort to abolish idolatry
- Deposed his idolatrous mother Maacah
- Defeated Cush's mighty army

Weaknesses and mistakes:
- Responded with rage when confronted about his sin
- Made alliances with foreign nations and evil people

Lessons from his life:
- God not only reinforces good, but he also confronts evil
- Efforts to follow God's plans and rules yield positive results
- How well a plan works is no measure of its rightness or approval by God

Vital statistics:
- Where: Jerusalem
- Occupation: King of Judah
- Relatives: Mother: Maacah. Father: Abijah. Son: Jehoshaphat
- Contemporaries: Hanani, Ben-hadad, Zerah, Azariah, Baasha

Key verse:
"For the eyes of the LORD move to and fro throughout the earth that he may strongly support those whose heart is completely His. You have acted foolishly in this. Indeed, from now on you will surely have wars" (2 Chronicles 16:9).

Asa's story is told in 1 Kings 15:8-24 and 2 Chronicles 14—16. He is also mentioned in Jeremiah 41:9; Matthew 1:7.

14:7 "Rest on every side" means that Judah had peace with all her neighbors. Times of peace are not just for resting. They allow us to prepare for times of trouble. King Asa recognized the period of peace as the right time to build his defenses—the moment of attack would be too late. It is also difficult to withstand spiritual attack unless defenses are prepared beforehand. Decisions about how to face temptations must be made with cool heads long before we feel the heat of temptation. Build your defenses now before temptation strikes.

8 Now Asa had an army of 300,000 from Judah, bearing large shields and spears, and
280,000 from Benjamin, bearing shields and wielding bows; all of them were valiant
warriors.
9 Now Zerah the Ethiopian came out against them with an army of a million men
and 300 chariots, and he came to Mareshah.
10 So Asa went out to meet him, and they drew up in battle formation in the valley of
Zephathah at Mareshah.
11 Then Asa called to the LORD his God and said, "LORD, there is no one besides You
to help *in the battle* between the powerful and those who have no strength; so help us,
O LORD our God, for we trust in You, and in Your name have come against this multitude. O LORD, You are our God; let not man prevail against You."
12 So the LORD routed the Ethiopians before Asa and before Judah, and the Ethiopians fled.
13 Asa and the people who *were* with him pursued them as far as Gerar; and so many
Ethiopians fell that they could not recover, for they were shattered before the LORD and
before His army. And they carried away very much plunder.
14 They destroyed all the cities around Gerar, for the dread of the LORD had fallen on
them; and they despoiled all the cities, for there was much plunder in them.
15 They also struck down those who owned livestock, and they carried away large numbers of sheep and camels. Then they returned to Jerusalem.

14:8 2 Chr 13:3
14:9 2 Chr 12:2, 3; 16:8; 2 Chr 11:8
14:11 2 Chr 13:14; 2 Chr 13:18
14:12 2 Chr 13:15
14:13 Gen 10:19
14:14 2 Chr 17:10

The Prophet Azariah Warns Asa

15 Now the Spirit of God came on Azariah the son of Oded,
2 and he went out to meet Asa and said to him, "Listen to me, Asa, and all Judah
and Benjamin: the LORD is with you when you are with Him. And if you seek Him, He
will let you find Him; but if you forsake Him, He will forsake you.
3 "For many days Israel was without the true God and without a teaching priest and
without law.
4 "But in their distress they turned to the LORD God of Israel, and they sought Him,
and He let them find Him.
5 "In those times there was no peace to him who went out or to him who came in, for
many disturbances afflicted all the inhabitants of the lands.
6 "Nation was crushed by nation, and city by city, for God troubled them with every
kind of distress.
7 "But you, be strong and do not lose courage, for there is reward for your work."

15:1 2 Chr 20:14; 24:20
15:2 2 Chr 20:17; 2 Chr 15:4, 15
15:3 1 Kin 12:28-33; Lev 10:8-11; 2 Chr 17:9
15:4 Deut 4:29
15:5 Judg 5:6
15:6 Matt 24:7
15:7 Josh 1:7, 9; Ps 58:11

ASA'S BATTLES
A huge army from Ethiopia under Zerah advanced toward Mareshah, greatly outnumbering King Asa's army. Asa sent his troops to meet them, and the battle took place in the valley north of Mareshah. Asa prayed to God, and the Ethiopians were defeated and chased as far as Gerar.

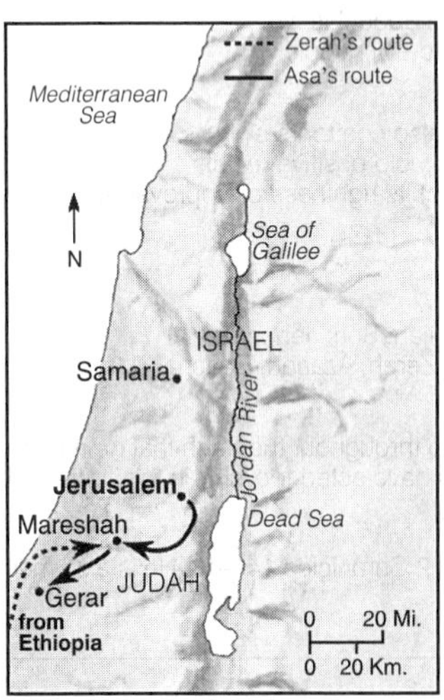

14:11 If you are facing battles you feel you can't possibly win, don't give up. In the face of vast hordes of enemy soldiers, Asa prayed for God's help, recognizing his powerlessness against such a mighty army. The secret of victory is first to admit the futility of unaided human effort and then to trust God to save. His power works best through those who recognize their limitations (2 Corinthians 12:9). It is those who think they can do it all on their own who are in the greatest danger.

15:1–2 Asa wisely welcomed people who had a close relationship with God, and he listened to their messages. Azariah gave the armies an important warning and encouraged them to stay close to God. Keep in contact with people who are filled with God's Spirit, and you will learn God's counsel. Spend regular time in discussion and prayer with those who can help explain and apply God's message.

15:3 Azariah said that Israel, the northern kingdom, was "without the true God." Eight kings reigned in Israel during the 41-year rule of Asa in Judah, and all eight were evil. Jeroboam, the first ruler of Israel, began this wicked trend by setting up idols and expelling God's priests (11:13–15). Azariah used Israel's problems as an example of the evil that would come to Judah if they turned away from God as their northern brothers and sisters had.

15:7 Azariah encouraged the men of Judah to keep up the good work, "for there is reward for your work." This is an inspiration for us too. Recognition and reward are great motivators that have two dimensions: (1) *The temporal dimension.* Living by God's standards may result in acclaim here on earth. (2) *The eternal dimension.* Permanent recognition and reward will be given in the next life. Don't be discouraged if you feel your faith in God is going unrewarded here on earth. The best rewards are not in this life but in the life to come.

Asa's Reforms

15:8 2 Chr 13:19; 2 Chr 4:1; 8:12

8 Now when Asa heard these words and the prophecy which Azariah the son of Oded the prophet spoke, he took courage and removed the abominable idols from all the land of Judah and Benjamin and from the cities which he had captured in the hill country of Ephraim. He then restored the altar of the LORD which was in front of the porch of the LORD.

15:9 2 Chr 11:16

9 He gathered all Judah and Benjamin and those from Ephraim, Manasseh and Simeon who resided with them, for many defected to him from Israel when they saw that the LORD his God was with him.

10 So they assembled at Jerusalem in the third month of the fifteenth year of Asa's reign.

15:11 2 Chr 14:13-15

11 They sacrificed to the LORD that day 700 oxen and 7,000 sheep from the spoil they had brought.

15:12 2 Chr 23:16

12 They entered into the covenant to seek the LORD God of their fathers with all their heart and soul;

15:13 Ex 22:20; Deut 13:6-9

13 and whoever would not seek the LORD God of Israel should be put to death, whether small or great, man or woman.

14 Moreover, they made an oath to the LORD with a loud voice, with shouting, with trumpets and with horns.

15:15 2 Chr 14:7

15 All Judah rejoiced concerning the oath, for they had sworn with their whole heart and had sought Him earnestly, and He let them find Him. So the LORD gave them rest on every side.

15:16 1 Kin 15:13-15; Ex 34:13; 2 Chr 14:2-5

16 He also removed Maacah, the mother of King Asa, from the *position of* queen mother, because she had made a horrid image as an Asherah, and Asa cut down her horrid image, crushed *it* and burned *it* at the brook Kidron.

17 But the high places were not removed from Israel; nevertheless Asa's heart was blameless all his days.

18 He brought into the house of God the dedicated things of his father and his own dedicated things: silver and gold and utensils.

19 And there was no more war until the thirty-fifth year of Asa's reign.

Asa Wars against Baasha

16:1 1 Kin 15:17-22

16 In the thirty-sixth year of Asa's reign Baasha king of Israel came up against Judah and fortified Ramah in order to prevent *anyone* from going out or coming in to Asa king of Judah.

2 Then Asa brought out silver and gold from the treasuries of the house of the LORD and the king's house, and sent them to Ben-hadad king of Aram, who lived in Damascus, saying,

3 "*Let there be* a treaty between you and me, *as* between my father and your father. Behold, I have sent you silver and gold; go, break your treaty with Baasha king of Israel so that he will withdraw from me."

16:4 Ex 1:11

4 So Ben-hadad listened to King Asa and sent the commanders of his armies against the cities of Israel, and they conquered Ijon, Dan, Abel-maim and all the store cities of Naphtali.

5 When Baasha heard *of it,* he ceased fortifying Ramah and stopped his work.

6 Then King Asa brought all Judah, and they carried away the stones of Ramah and its timber with which Baasha had been building, and with them he fortified Geba and Mizpah.

15:14–15 Many people find it difficult to commit themselves to anything. They are tentative, indecisive, and afraid of responsibility. Asa and his people were different—they had clearly declared themselves for God. Their oath of allegiance was punctuated with shouts and trumpet blasts! This decisive and wholehearted commitment pleased God and resulted in peace for the nation. If you want peace, check to see if there is some area where you lack total commitment to God. Peace comes as a by-product of giving your life wholeheartedly to God.

15:16 The Ten Commandments tell us to honor our fathers and mothers, and yet Asa removed his mother from the throne. While honoring parents is God's command, maintaining loyalty to God is an even higher priority. Jesus warned that respect for parents should never keep us from following him (Luke 14:26). If you have unbelieving parents, you must respect and honor them, but you must make devotion to God an even higher priority.

Asa Imprisons the Prophet

7 At that time Hanani the seer came to Asa king of Judah and said to him, "Because
you have relied on the king of Aram and have not relied on the LORD your God, therefore the army of the king of Aram has escaped out of your hand.
8 "Were not the Ethiopians and the Lubim an immense army with very many chariots
and horsemen? Yet because you relied on the LORD, He delivered them into your hand.
9 "For the eyes of the LORD move to and fro throughout the earth that He may strongly support those whose heart is completely His. You have acted foolishly in this. Indeed,
from now on you will surely have wars."
10 Then Asa was angry with the seer and put him in prison, for he was enraged at him
for this. And Asa oppressed some of the people at the same time.
11 Now, the acts of Asa from first to last, behold, they are written in the Book of the
Kings of Judah and Israel.
12 In the thirty-ninth year of his reign Asa became diseased in his feet. His disease was
severe, yet even in his disease he did not seek the LORD, but the physicians.
13 So Asa slept with his fathers, having died in the forty-first year of his reign.
14 They buried him in his own tomb which he had cut out for himself in the city of
David, and they laid him in the resting place which he had filled with spices of various
kinds blended by the perfumers' art; and they made a very great fire for him.

16:7 1 Kin 16:1; 2 Chr 19:2; 2 Chr 14:11; 32:7, 8
16:8 2 Chr 14:9; 2 Chr 12:3; 2 Chr 13:16, 18
16:9 Prov 15:3; Jer 16:17; Zech 4:10; 2 Chr 15:17
16:11 1 Kin 15:23, 24
16:12 Jer 17:5
16:14 Gen 50:2; John 19:39, 40; 2 Chr 21:19

Jehoshaphat Succeeds Asa

17 Jehoshaphat his son then became king in his place, and made his position over
Israel firm.
2 He placed troops in all the fortified cities of Judah, and set garrisons in the land of
Judah and in the cities of Ephraim which Asa his father had captured.

17:1 1 Kin 15:24
17:2 2 Chr 11:5; 2 Chr 15:8

His Good Reign

3 The LORD was with Jehoshaphat because he followed the example of his father
David's earlier days and did not seek the Baals,
4 but sought the God of his father, followed His commandments, and did not act as
Israel did.
5 So the LORD established the kingdom in his control, and all Judah brought tribute
to Jehoshaphat, and he had great riches and honor.
6 He took great pride in the ways of the LORD and again removed the high places and
the Asherim from Judah.
7 Then in the third year of his reign he sent his officials, Ben-hail, Obadiah, Zechariah, Nethanel and Micaiah, to teach in the cities of Judah;
8 and with them the Levites, Shemaiah, Nethaniah, Zebadiah, Asahel, Shemiramoth,
Jehonathan, Adonijah, Tobijah and Tobadonijah, the Levites; and with them Elishama
and Jehoram, the priests.
9 They taught in Judah, *having* the book of the law of the LORD with them; and they
went throughout all the cities of Judah and taught among the people.
10 Now the dread of the LORD was on all the kingdoms of the lands which *were* around
Judah, so that they did not make war against Jehoshaphat.

17:4 1 Kin 12:28
17:5 2 Chr 18:1
17:6 2 Chr 15:17
17:7 2 Chr 15:3; 35:3
17:8 2 Chr 19:8
17:9 Deut 6:4-9
17:10 2 Chr 14:14

16:7–10 Judah and Israel never learned! Although God had delivered them even when they were outnumbered (13:3ff; 14:9ff), they repeatedly sought help from pagan nations rather than from God. That Asa sought help from Aram was evidence of national spiritual decline. With help from God alone, Asa had defeated the Cushites in open battle. But his confidence in God had slipped, and now he sought only a human solution to his problem. When confronted by the prophet Hanani, Asa threw him in prison, revealing the true condition of his heart. It is not sin to use human means to solve our problems, but it is sin to trust them more than God, to think they are better than God's ways, or to leave God completely out of the problem-solving process.

16:12 The criticism of Asa's visit to the physicians was not a general indictment of medicine. Asa's problem was that he completely ignored God's help. The medicine practiced at this time was a mixture of superstition and folk remedies. We should certainly avoid any pseudo-medical treatment derived from occult sources. Asa's experience should also encourage us to follow the New Testament practice of receiving prayer for our sickness (James 5:14) as we seek responsible medical help.

17:7–9 The people of Judah were Biblically illiterate. They had never taken time to listen to and discuss God's Law and understand how it could change them. Jehoshaphat realized that knowing God's commands was the first step to getting people to live as they should, so he initiated a nationwide religious education program. He reversed the religious decline that had occurred at the end of Asa's reign by putting God first in the people's minds and instilling in them a sense of commitment and mission. Because of this action, the nation began to follow God. Churches and Christian schools today need solid Christian education programs. Exposure to good Bible teaching through church school, church, Bible study, and personal and family devotions is essential for living as God intended.

17:11 2 Chr 9:14; 26:8

11 Some of the Philistines brought gifts and silver as tribute to Jehoshaphat; the Arabians also brought him flocks, 7,700 rams and 7,700 male goats.
12 So Jehoshaphat grew greater and greater, and he built fortresses and store cities in
Judah.
13 He had large supplies in the cities of Judah, and warriors, valiant men, in Jerusalem.
14 This was their muster according to their fathers' households: of Judah, commanders of thousands, Adnah *was* the commander, and with him 300,000 valiant warriors;
15 and next to him *was* Johanan the commander, and with him 280,000;

17:16 Judg 5:2, 9; 1 Chr 29:9

16 and next to him Amasiah the son of Zichri, who volunteered for the LORD, and with
him 200,000 valiant warriors;
17 and of Benjamin, Eliada a valiant warrior, and with him 200,000 armed with bow
and shield;
18 and next to him Jehozabad, and with him 180,000 equipped for war.

17:19 2 Chr 17:2

19 These are they who served the king, apart from those whom the king put in the fortified cities through all Judah.

JEHOSHAPHAT

Are children more likely to learn from their parents' mistakes or to simply repeat them? In the lives of the people in the Bible, we find that the effects of parental examples are powerful and long-lasting. For much of his life, Jehoshaphat seems to have been a son who learned from his father Asa's mistakes and followed his positive actions. But on several occasions, his decisions reveal the negative aspects of his father's example.

When the challenges were obvious, like the need for religious education of the people or the threat of war with a vast army, Jehoshaphat turned to God for guidance and made the right choices. His dependence on God was consistent when the odds were clearly against him. It was in depending on God for the day-to-day plans and actions that Jehoshaphat was weak. He allowed his son to marry Athaliah, the daughter of the wicked Ahab and Jezebel of Israel, who did her best to be as evil as her parents. Jehoshaphat was almost killed when, without asking God, he made an alliance with Ahab. Later, he got involved in an unwise shipbuilding venture with Ahab's son, Ahaziah—a venture that was shipwrecked by God.

God's faithfulness when the issues are clear and the enemy overwhelming is more than enough reason to seek his guidance when the issues are unclear and the enemy unseen. Jehoshaphat knew this, yet he made little use of that knowledge.

We repeat Jehoshaphat's error when we relegate God to the background in the "easy" decisions of life. Then, when things get out of hand, we want him to get us out of the mess we got ourselves into. God wants us to give him not only the major decisions, but also our daily lives—the things we are most often fooled into believing we can control. Perhaps there is nothing major facing you today. Have you paused long enough to give your day to God anyway?

Strengths and accomplishments:
- A bold follower of God, he reminded the people of the early years of his father, Asa
- Carried out a national program of religious education
- Had many military victories
- Developed an extensive legal structure throughout the kingdom

Weaknesses and mistakes:
- Failed to recognize the long-term results of his decisions
- Did not completely destroy idolatry in the land
- Became entangled with evil King Ahab through alliances
- Allowed his son Jehoram to marry Athaliah, Ahab's daughter
- Became Ahaziah's business partner in an ill-fated shipping venture

Vital statistics:
- Where: Jerusalem
- Occupation: King of Judah
- Relatives: Father: Asa. Mother: Azubah. Son: Jehoram. Daughter-in-law: Athaliah
- Contemporaries: Ahab, Jezebel, Micaiah, Ahaziah, Jehu

Key verses:
"He walked in the way of his father Asa and did not depart from it, doing right in the sight of the LORD. The high places, however, were not removed; the people had not yet directed their hearts to the God of their fathers" (2 Chronicles 20:32–33).

Jehoshaphat's story is told in 1 Kings 15:24—22:50 and 2 Chronicles 17:1—21:1. He is also mentioned in 2 Kings 3:1–14 and Joel 3:2, 12.

Jehoshaphat Allies with Ahab

18 Now Jehoshaphat had great riches and honor; and he allied himself by marriage **18:1**
with Ahab. 2 Chr 17:5
2 Some years later he went down to *visit* Ahab at Samaria. And Ahab slaughtered many **18:2**
sheep and oxen for him and the people who were with him, and induced him to go up 1 Kin 22:2-35
against Ramoth-gilead.
3 Ahab king of Israel said to Jehoshaphat king of Judah, "Will you go with me *against*
Ramoth-gilead?" And he said to him, "I am as you are, and my people as your people,
and *we will be* with you in the battle."
4 Moreover, Jehoshaphat said to the king of Israel, "Please inquire first for the word
of the LORD."
5 Then the king of Israel assembled the prophets, four hundred men, and said to them,
"Shall we go against Ramoth-gilead to battle, or shall I refrain?" And they said, "Go up,
for God will give *it* into the hand of the king."
6 But Jehoshaphat said, "Is there not yet a prophet of the LORD here that we may
inquire of him?"
7 The king of Israel said to Jehoshaphat, "There is yet one man by whom we may
inquire of the LORD, but I hate him, for he never prophesies good concerning me but
always evil. He is Micaiah, son of Imla." But Jehoshaphat said, "Let not the king say so."

Ahab's False Prophets Assure Victory

8 Then the king of Israel called an officer and said, "Bring quickly Micaiah, Imla's
son."
9 Now the king of Israel and Jehoshaphat the king of Judah were sitting each on his **18:9**
throne, arrayed in *their* robes, and *they* were sitting at the threshing floor at the entrance Ruth 4:1
of the gate of Samaria; and all the prophets were prophesying before them.
10 Zedekiah the son of Chenaanah made horns of iron for himself and said, "Thus says
the LORD, 'With these you shall gore the Arameans until they are consumed.' "
11 All the prophets were prophesying thus, saying, "Go up to Ramoth-gilead and succeed, for the LORD will give *it* into the hand of the king."

18:1ff Although Jehoshaphat was deeply committed to God, he arranged for his son to marry Athaliah, the daughter of wicked King Ahab of Israel, and then made a military alliance with him. Jehoshaphat's popularity and power made him attractive to the cunning and opportunistic Ahab. This alliance had three devastating consequences: (1) Jehoshaphat incurred God's wrath (19:2); (2) when Jehoshaphat died and Athaliah became queen, she seized the throne and almost destroyed all of David's descendants (22:10–12); (3) Athaliah brought the evil practices of Israel into Judah, which eventually led to the nation's downfall.

When believers in leadership positions become allied with unbelievers, values can be compromised and spiritual awareness dulled. The Bible often warns against teaming with unbelievers (2 Corinthians 6:14). (See the note on 20:37 for more on alliances.)

18:3–8 Evil kings did not like God's prophets bringing messages of doom (18:17; Jeremiah 5:13). Many, therefore, hired prophets who told them only what they wanted to hear (Isaiah 30:10–11; Jeremiah 14:13–16; 23:16, 21, 30–36). These men were false prophets because they extolled the greatness of the king and predicted victory regardless of the real situation.

18:3–8 Wicked Ahab asked Jehoshaphat to join forces with him in battle (18:2–3). Before making that commitment, Jehoshaphat rightly sought God's advice. However, when God gave his answer through the prophet Micaiah (18:16), Jehoshaphat ignored it (18:28). It does us no good to seek God's advice if we ignore it when it is given. Real love for God is shown not by merely asking for direction, but by following that direction once it is given.

18:5–16 When you want to please or impress someone, it is tempting to lie to make yourself look good. Ahab's 400 prophets did just that, telling Ahab only what he wanted to hear. They were then rewarded for making Ahab happy. Micaiah, however, told the truth and got arrested (18:25–26). Obeying God doesn't always protect us from evil consequences. Obedience may, in fact, provoke them. But it is better to suffer from man's displeasure than from God's wrath (Matthew 10:28). If you are ridiculed for being honest, remember that this can be a sign that you are indeed doing what is right in God's eyes (Matthew 5:10–12; Romans 8:17, 35–39).

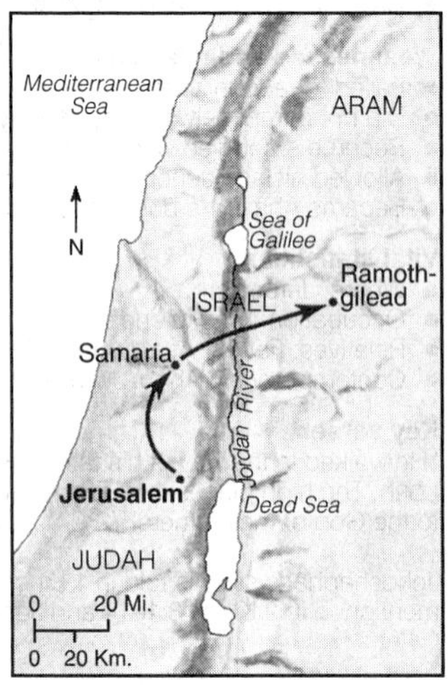

BATTLE WITH ARAM
King Jehoshaphat made an alliance with evil King Ahab of Israel. Together they decided to attack Ramoth-gilead and rout the Arameans who had occupied the city. But Jehoshaphat first wanted to seek the advice of a prophet. Ahab's prophets predicted victory, but Micaiah predicted defeat. The two kings were defeated, and Ahab was killed.

Micaiah Brings Word from God

12 Then the messenger who went to summon Micaiah spoke to him saying, "Behold,
the words of the prophets are uniformly favorable to the king. So please let your word
be like one of them and speak favorably."

18:13 Num 22:18-20, 35

13 But Micaiah said, "As the LORD lives, what my God says, that I will speak."
14 When he came to the king, the king said to him, "Micaiah, shall we go to Ramoth-
gilead to battle, or shall I refrain?" He said, "Go up and succeed, for they will be given
into your hand."
15 Then the king said to him, "How many times must I adjure you to speak to me nothing
but the truth in the name of the LORD?"

18:16 Num 27:17; 1 Kin 22:17; Ezek 34:5; 35:4-8; Matt 9:36; Mark 6:34

16 So he said,
"I saw all Israel
Scattered on the mountains,
Like sheep which have no shepherd;
And the LORD said,
'These have no master.
Let each of them return to his house in peace.' "
17 Then the king of Israel said to Jehoshaphat, "Did I not tell you that he would not
prophesy good concerning me, but evil?"

18:18 Is 6:1-5; Dan 7:9, 10

18 Micaiah said, "Therefore, hear the word of the LORD. I saw the LORD sitting on
His throne, and all the host of heaven standing on His right and on His left.
19 "The LORD said, 'Who will entice Ahab king of Israel to go up and fall at Ramoth-
gilead?' And one said this while another said that.

18:20 Job 1:6; 2 Thess 2:9

20 "Then a spirit came forward and stood before the LORD and said, 'I will entice him.'
And the LORD said to him, 'How?'

18:21 John 8:44

21 "He said, 'I will go and be a deceiving spirit in the mouth of all his prophets.' Then
He said, 'You are to entice *him* and prevail also. Go and do so.'

18:22 Is 19:14; Ezek 14:9

22 "Now therefore, behold, the LORD has put a deceiving spirit in the mouth of these
your prophets, for the LORD has proclaimed disaster against you."

18:23 Jer 20:2; Mark 14:65; Acts 23:2

23 Then Zedekiah the son of Chenaanah came near and struck Micaiah on the cheek
and said, "How did the Spirit of the LORD pass from me to speak to you?"
24 Micaiah said, "Behold, you will see on that day when you enter an inner room to
hide yourself."

18:25 2 Chr 18:8; 2 Chr 34:8

25 Then the king of Israel said, "Take Micaiah and return him to Amon the governor
of the city and to Joash the king's son;

18:26 2 Chr 16:10

26 and say, 'Thus says the king, "Put this *man* in prison and feed him sparingly with
bread and water until I return safely." ' "

18:27 Mic 1:2

27 Micaiah said, "If you indeed return safely, the LORD has not spoken by me." And
he said, "Listen, all you people."

Ahab's Defeat and Death

28 So the king of Israel and Jehoshaphat king of Judah went up against Ramoth-
gilead.
29 The king of Israel said to Jehoshaphat, "I will disguise myself and go into battle,
but you put on your robes." So the king of Israel disguised himself, and they went into
battle.
30 Now the king of Aram had commanded the captains of his chariots, saying, "Do not
fight with small or great, but with the king of Israel alone."

18:31 2 Chr 13:14, 15

31 So when the captains of the chariots saw Jehoshaphat, they said, "It is the king of

---

18:22 God used the seductive influence of false prophets to judge Ahab. They were determined to tell Ahab what he wanted to hear. God confirmed their plans to lie as a means to remove Ahab from the throne. These prophets, supported by Ahab, snared him in his sin. Because he listened to them instead of God, he was killed in battle. The deceiving spirit is a picture of the prophets' entire way of life—telling the king only what he wanted to hear, not what he needed to hear. Leaders will only find trouble if they surround themselves with advisers whose only thought is to please them.

18:31 Jehoshaphat's troubles began when he joined forces with the evil King Ahab. Almost at once he found himself the target for soldiers who mistakenly identified him as Ahab. He could have accepted this fate because he deserved it, but instead he cried out to God, who miraculously saved him. When we sin and the inevitable consequences follow, we may be tempted to give up. "I chose to sin," we may think. "It's my fault, and I must accept the consequences." While we may deserve what comes to us, that is no reason to avoid calling on God for urgent help. Had Jehoshaphat given up, he might have died. No matter how greatly you have sinned, you can still call upon God.

Israel," and they turned aside to fight against him. But Jehoshaphat cried out, and the
LORD helped him, and God diverted them from him.
32 When the captains of the chariots saw that it was not the king of Israel, they turned
back from pursuing him.
33 A certain man drew his bow at random and struck the king of Israel in a joint of the
armor. So he said to the driver of the chariot, "Turn around and take me out of the fight,
for I am severely wounded."
34 The battle raged that day, and the king of Israel propped himself up in his chariot
in front of the Arameans until the evening; and at sunset he died.

Jehu Rebukes Jehoshaphat

19 Then Jehoshaphat the king of Judah returned in safety to his house in Jerusalem.
2 Jehu the son of Hanani the seer went out to meet him and said to King Jehosh- **19:2** 1 Kin 16:1; 2 Chr 20:34; 2 Chr 18:1, 3; 2 Chr 24:18
aphat, "Should you help the wicked and love those who hate the LORD and so *bring* wrath
on yourself from the LORD?

BIBLE

The Persecuted	*The Persecutors*	*Why the Persecution*	*Result*	*Reference*
Isaac	Philistines	God was blessing Isaac, and they envied him	The Philistines could not subdue Isaac, so they made peace with him	Genesis 26:12–33
Moses	Israelites	The Israelites wanted water	God provided water, thanks to Moses' prayer	Exodus 17:1–7
David	Saul and others	David was becoming a powerful leader, threatening Saul's position as king	David endured the persecution and became king	1 Samuel 20—27; Psalms 31:13; 59:1–4
Priests of Nob	Saul and Doeg	Saul and Doeg thought the priests helped David escape	85 priests were killed	1 Samuel 22
Prophets	Jezebel	Jezebel didn't like to have her evil ways pointed out	Many prophets were killed	1 Kings 18:3–4
Elijah	Ahab and Jezebel	Elijah confronted their sins	Elijah had to flee for his life	1 Kings 18:10—19:2
Micaiah	Ahab	Ahab thought Micaiah was stirring up trouble rather than prophesying from God	Micaiah was thrown into prison	2 Chronicles 18:12–26
Elisha	A king of Israel (Probably Joram)	The king thought Elisha had caused the famine	Elisha ignored the threatened persecution and prophesied the famine's end	2 Kings 6:31
Hanani	Asa	Hanani criticized Asa for trusting in Aram's help more than in God's help	Hanani was thrown in prison	2 Chronicles 16:7–10
Zechariah	Joash	Zechariah confronted the people of Judah for disregarding God's commands	Zechariah was executed	2 Chronicles 24:20–22
Uriah	Jehoiakim	Uriah confronted Jehoiakim about his evil ways	Uriah was butchered to death	Jeremiah 26:20–23
Jeremiah	Zedekiah	Zedekiah thought Jeremiah was a traitor for prophesying Jerusalem's fall	Jeremiah was thrown in prison, then into a muddy cistern	Jeremiah 37:1—38:13
Shadrach, Meshach, Abednego	Nebuchadnezzar	The three men refused to bow down to anyone but God	They were thrown into a fiery furnace, but God miraculously saved them	Daniel 3

18:33 Micaiah prophesied death for Ahab (18:16, 27), so Ahab disguised himself to fool the enemy. Apparently the disguise worked, but that didn't change the prophecy. A random Aramean arrow found a crack in his armor and killed him. God fulfills his will despite the defenses people try to erect. God can use anything, even an error, to bring his will to pass. This is good news for God's followers because we can trust him to work his plans and keep his promises no matter how desperate our circumstances are.

19:5–10 Jehoshaphat delegated some of the responsibilities for ruling and judging the people, but he warned his appointees that they were accountable to God for the standards they used to judge others. Jehoshaphat's advice is helpful for all leaders: (1) Realize

19:3 2 Chr 12:12; 2 Chr 17:6; 2 Chr 12:14
19:4 2 Chr 15:8-13
19:5 Deut 16:18-20
19:6 Lev 19:15; Deut 1:17
19:7 Gen 18:25; Deut 32:4; Deut 10:17, 18
19:8 2 Chr 17:8, 9

3 "But there is *some* good in you, for you have removed the Asheroth from the land
and you have set your heart to seek God."
4 So Jehoshaphat lived in Jerusalem and went out again among the people from Beersheba to the hill country of Ephraim and brought them back to the LORD, the God of
their fathers.

Reforms Instituted

5 He appointed judges in the land in all the fortified cities of Judah, city by city.
6 He said to the judges, "Consider what you are doing, for you do not judge for man
but for the LORD who is with you when you render judgment.
7 "Now then let the fear of the LORD be upon you; be very careful what you do, for the
LORD our God will have no part in unrighteousness or partiality or the taking of a bribe."
8 In Jerusalem also Jehoshaphat appointed some of the Levites and priests, and some
of the heads of the fathers' *households* of Israel, for the judgment of the LORD and to
judge disputes among the inhabitants of Jerusalem.

PERSECUTIONS

The Persecuted	*The Persecutors*	*Why the Persecution*	*Result*	*Reference*
Daniel	National leaders	Daniel was praying	Daniel was thrown into a den of lions, but God miraculously saved him	Daniel 6
Job	Satan	Satan wanted to prove that pain and suffering would make a person abandon God	Job remained faithful to God and was restored	Job 1:8–12; 2:3–7
John the Baptist	Herod and Herodias	John confronted King Herod's adultery	John was beheaded	Matthew 14:3–13
Jesus	Religious leaders	Jesus exposed their sinful motives	Jesus was crucified, but rose Jagain from the dead to show his authority over all evil	Mark 7:1–16; Luke 22:63—24:7
Peter and John	Religious leaders	Peter and John preached that Jesus was God's Son and the only way to salvation	They were thrown into prison, but later released	Acts 4:1–31
Stephen	Religious leaders	Stephen ex posed their guilt in crucifying Jesus	Stephen was stoned to death	Acts 6—7
The church	Paul and others	The Christians preached Jesus as the Messiah	Believers faced death, prison, torture, exile	Acts 8:1–3; 9:1–9
James	Herod Agrippa I	To please the Jewish leaders	James was executed	Acts 12:1–2
Peter	Herod Agrippa I	To please the Jewish leaders	Peter was thrown into prison	Acts 12:3–17
Paul	Jews, city officials	Paul preached about Jesus and confronted those who made money by manipulating others	Paul was stoned; thrown into prison	Acts 14:19; 16:16–24
Timothy	Unknown	Unknown	Timothy was thrown into prison	Hebrews 13:23
John	Probably the Romans	John told others about Jesus	John was sent into exile on a remote island	Revelation 1:9

Micaiah, like thousands of believers before and after him, was persecuted for his faith. The chart shows that persecution comes from a variety of people and is given in a variety of ways. Sometimes God protects us from it, sometimes he doesn't. But as long as we remain faithful to God alone, we must expect persecution (see also Luke 6:22; 2 Corinthians 6:4–10; 2 Timothy 2:9–12; Revelation 2:10). God also seems to have a special reward for those who endure such persecution (Revelation 6:9–11; 20:4).

you are judging for God (19:6); (2) be impartial and honest (19:7); (3) be faithful (19:9); (4) act only out of fear of God, not men (19:9). God holds us accountable for the authority we exercise.

19:8 Jehoshaphat appointed priests and Levites to help in administering civil laws. Many years earlier, Moses had chosen men who were capable, faithful, and honest to help him judge disputes among the people (Exodus 18:21–22). Obviously the best kind of leader is one who always acts with reverence for God. Effective leaders get the job done; faithful leaders make sure the job is done in God's way with God's timing. They are careful to instill God's wisdom in future leaders and build God's values into the entire community.

9 Then he charged them saying, "Thus you shall do in the fear of the LORD, faithfully
and wholeheartedly.
10 "Whenever any dispute comes to you from your brethren who live in their cities, **19:10**
between blood and blood, between law and commandment, statutes and ordinances, you Deut 17:8; 2 Chr 19:2
shall warn them so that they may not be guilty before the LORD, and wrath may *not* come
on you and your brethren. Thus you shall do and you will not be guilty.
11 "Behold, Amariah the chief priest will be over you in all that pertains to the LORD, **19:11**
and Zebadiah the son of Ishmael, the ruler of the house of Judah, in all that pertains to 2 Chr 19:8; 1 Chr 28:20
the king. Also the Levites shall be officers before you. Act resolutely, and the LORD be
with the upright."

Judah Invaded

20 Now it came about after this that the sons of Moab and the sons of Ammon, to- **20:1** 1 Chr 4:41; 2 Chr 26:7
gether with some of the Meunites, came to make war against Jehoshaphat.
2 Then some came and reported to Jehoshaphat, saying, "A great multitude is coming against you from beyond the sea, out of Aram and behold, they are in Hazazon- **20:2** Gen 14:7
tamar (that is Engedi)."
3 Jehoshaphat was afraid and turned his attention to seek the LORD, and proclaimed **20:3**
a fast throughout all Judah. 2 Chr 19:3; 1 Sam 7:6; Ezra 8:21
4 So Judah gathered together to seek help from the LORD; they even came from all
the cities of Judah to seek the LORD. **20:4** Joel 1:14

Jehoshaphat's Prayer

5 Then Jehoshaphat stood in the assembly of Judah and Jerusalem, in the house of
the LORD before the new court,
6 and he said, "O LORD, the God of our fathers, are You not God in the heavens? **20:6**
And are You not ruler over all the kingdoms of the nations? Power and might are in Deut 4:39; 1 Chr 29:11
Your hand so that no one can stand against You.
7 "Did You not, O our God, drive out the inhabitants of this land before Your people **20:7**
Israel and give it to the descendants of Abraham Your friend forever? Is 41:8; James 2:23
8 "They have lived in it, and have built You a sanctuary there for Your name, saying,
9 'Should evil come upon us, the sword, *or* judgment, or pestilence, or famine, we will **20:9**
stand before this house and before You (for Your name is in this house) and cry to You 2 Chr 6:28-30; 2 Chr 6:20
in our distress, and You will hear and deliver *us*.'
10 "Now behold, the sons of Ammon and Moab and Mount Seir, whom You did not let **20:10**
Israel invade when they came out of the land of Egypt (they turned aside from them and 2 Chr 20:1, 22; Num 20:17-21
did not destroy them),
11 see *how* they are rewarding us by coming to drive us out from Your possession which **20:11**
You have given us as an inheritance. Ps 83:12
12 "O our God, will You not judge them? For we are powerless before this great multi- **20:12**
tude who are coming against us; nor do we know what to do, but our eyes are on You." Judg 11:27; Ps 25:15; 121:1, 2
13 All Judah was standing before the LORD, with their infants, their wives and their
children.

Jahaziel Answers the Prayer

14 Then in the midst of the assembly the Spirit of the LORD came upon Jahaziel the **20:14** 2 Chr 15:1; 24:20
son of Zechariah, the son of Benaiah, the son of Jeiel, the son of Mattaniah, the Levite **20:15**
of the sons of Asaph; Ex 14:13; Deut 20:1-4; 2 Chr 32:7, 8;
15 and he said, "Listen, all Judah and the inhabitants of Jerusalem and King Jehosha- 1 Sam 17:47

20:3 When the nation was faced with disaster, Jehoshaphat called upon the people to get serious with God by going without food (fasting) for a designated time. By separating themselves from the daily routine of food preparation and eating, they could devote that extra time to considering their sin and praying to God for help. Hunger pangs would reinforce their feelings of penitence and remind them of their weakness and their dependence upon God. Fasting still can be helpful today as we seek God's will in special situations.

20:6ff Jehoshaphat's prayer had several essential ingredients. (1) He committed the situation to God, acknowledging that only God could save the nation. (2) He sought God's favor because his people were God's people. (3) He acknowledged God's sovereignty over the current situation. (4) He praised God's glory and took comfort in his promises. (5) He professed complete dependence on God, not himself, for deliverance. To be God's kind of leader today, follow Jehoshaphat's example—focus entirely on God's power rather than your own.

20:15 As the enemy bore down on Judah, God spoke through Jahaziel: "Do not fear or be dismayed . . . . for the battle is not yours but God's." We may not fight an enemy army, but every day we battle temptation, pressure, and "rulers . . . of this darkness"

phat: thus says the LORD to you, 'Do not fear or be dismayed because of this great multitude, for the battle is not yours but God's.
16 'Tomorrow go down against them. Behold, they will come up by the ascent of Ziz,
and you will find them at the end of the valley in front of the wilderness of Jeruel.
20:17 Ex 14:13; 2 Chr 15:2
17 'You *need* not fight in this *battle;* station yourselves, stand and see the salvation of
the LORD on your behalf, O Judah and Jerusalem.' Do not fear or be dismayed; tomorrow go out to face them, for the LORD is with you."
20:18 Ex 4:31
18 Jehoshaphat bowed his head with *his* face to the ground, and all Judah and the inhabitants of Jerusalem fell down before the LORD, worshiping the LORD.
19 The Levites, from the sons of the Kohathites and of the sons of the Korahites, stood
up to praise the LORD God of Israel, with a very loud voice.

Enemies Destroy Themselves

20:20 Is 7:9
20 They rose early in the morning and went out to the wilderness of Tekoa; and when
they went out, Jehoshaphat stood and said, "Listen to me, O Judah and inhabitants of
Jerusalem, put your trust in the LORD your God and you will be established. Put your
trust in His prophets and succeed."
20:21 1 Chr 16:29; Ps 29:2; 1 Chr 16:34
21 When he had consulted with the people, he appointed those who sang to the LORD
and those who praised *Him* in holy attire, as they went out before the army and said,
"Give thanks to the LORD, for His lovingkindness is everlasting."
20:22 2 Chr 13:13; 2 Chr 20:10
22 When they began singing and praising, the LORD set ambushes against the sons of
Ammon, Moab and Mount Seir, who had come against Judah; so they were routed.
20:23 Judg 7:22; 1 Sam 14:20
23 For the sons of Ammon and Moab rose up against the inhabitants of Mount Seir
destroying *them* completely; and when they had finished with the inhabitants of Seir, they
helped to destroy one another.
24 When Judah came to the lookout of the wilderness, they looked toward the multitude, and behold, they *were* corpses lying on the ground, and no one had escaped.
25 When Jehoshaphat and his people came to take their spoil, they found much among
them, *including* goods, garments and valuable things which they took for themselves, more
than they could carry. And they were three days taking the spoil because there was so
much.

Triumphant Return to Jerusalem

26 Then on the fourth day they assembled in the valley of Beracah, for there they blessed
the LORD. Therefore they have named that place "The Valley of [7]Beracah" until today.
20:27 Neh 12:43
27 Every man of Judah and Jerusalem returned with Jehoshaphat at their head, returning to Jerusalem with joy, for the LORD had made them to rejoice over their enemies.
28 They came to Jerusalem with harps, lyres and trumpets to the house of the LORD.
20:29 2 Chr 14:14; 17:10
29 And the dread of God was on all the kingdoms of the lands when they heard that
the LORD had fought against the enemies of Israel.
20:30 2 Chr 14:6, 7; 15:15
30 So the kingdom of Jehoshaphat was at peace, for his God gave him rest on all sides.
20:31 1 Kin 22:41-43
31 Now Jehoshaphat reigned over Judah. He *was* thirty-five years old when he became
king, and he reigned in Jerusalem twenty-five years. And his mother's name *was* Azubah the daughter of Shilhi.
32 He walked in the way of his father Asa and did not depart from it, doing right in the
sight of the LORD.
20:33 2 Chr 17:6; 2 Chr 19:3
33 The high places, however, were not removed; the people had not yet directed their
hearts to the God of their fathers.
20:34 2 Chr 19:2
34 Now the rest of the acts of Jehoshaphat, first to last, behold, they are written in the
annals of Jehu the son of Hanani, which is recorded in the Book of the Kings of Israel.

7 I.e. blessing

(Ephesians 6:12) who want us to rebel against God. Remember, as believers, we have God's Spirit in us. If we ask for God's help when we face struggles, God will fight for us. And God always triumphs.

How do we let God fight for us? (1) By realizing the battle is not ours, but God's; (2) by recognizing human limitations and allowing God's strength to work through our fears and weaknesses; (3) by making sure we are pursuing God's interests and not just our own selfish desires; (4) by asking God for help in our daily battles.

20:33 This verse says that Jehoshaphat did not remove the corrupt high places (idol shrines), while 17:6 and 19:3 say he did remove them. Jehoshaphat destroyed most of the Baal and Asherah idols, but he did not succeed in wiping out the corrupt religions practiced at the high places.

Alliance Displeases God

35 After this Jehoshaphat king of Judah allied himself with Ahaziah king of Israel. He **20:35** 1 Kin 22:48, 49
acted wickedly in so doing.
36 So he allied himself with him to make ships to go to Tarshish, and they made the **20:36** 2 Chr 9:21
ships in Ezion-geber.
37 Then Eliezer the son of Dodavahu of Mareshah prophesied against Jehoshaphat
saying, "Because you have allied yourself with Ahaziah, the LORD has destroyed your
works." So the ships were broken and could not go to Tarshish.

Jehoram Succeeds Jehoshaphat in Judah

21 Then Jehoshaphat slept with his fathers and was buried with his fathers in the city **21:1** 1 Kin 22:50
of David, and Jehoram his son became king in his place.
2 He had brothers, the sons of Jehoshaphat: Azariah, Jehiel, Zechariah, Azaryahu, **21:2** 2 Chr 12:6; 23:2
Michael and Shephatiah. All these *were* the sons of Jehoshaphat king of Israel.
3 Their father gave them many gifts of silver, gold and precious things, with fortified **21:3** 2 Chr 11:5
cities in Judah, but he gave the kingdom to Jehoram because he was the firstborn.
4 Now when Jehoram had taken over the kingdom of his father and made himself **21:4** Gen 4:8; Judg 9:5
secure, he killed all his brothers with the sword, and some of the rulers of Israel also.
5 Jehoram *was* thirty-two years old when he became king, and he reigned eight years **21:5** 2 Kin 8:17-22
in Jerusalem.
6 He walked in the way of the kings of Israel, just as the house of Ahab did (for Ahab's **21:6** 1 Kin 12:28-30; 2 Chr 18:1
daughter was his wife), and he did evil in the sight of the LORD.
7 Yet the LORD was not willing to destroy the house of David because of the covenant
which He had made with David, and since He had promised to give a lamp to him and **21:7** 2 Sam 7:12-17; 1 Kin 11:13, 36
his sons forever.

Revolt against Judah

8 In his days Edom revolted [8]against the rule of Judah and set up a king over them- **21:8** 2 Chr 20:22, 23; 21:10
selves.
9 Then Jehoram crossed over with his commanders and all his chariots with him. And
he arose by night and struck down the Edomites who were surrounding him and the
commanders of the chariots.
10 So Edom revolted [8]against Judah to this day. Then Libnah revolted at the same time
against his rule, because he had forsaken the LORD God of his fathers. **21:11** 1 Kin 11:7; Lev 20:5
11 Moreover, he made high places in the mountains of Judah, and caused the inhabitants of Jerusalem to play the harlot and led Judah astray. **21:12** 2 Chr 17:3, 4; 2 Chr 14:2-5
12 Then a letter came to him from Elijah the prophet saying, "Thus says the LORD

8 Lit *from under the hand of*

20:37 Jehoshaphat met disaster when he joined forces with wicked King Ahaziah. He did not learn from his disastrous alliance with Ahab (18:28–34) or from his father's alliance with Aram (16:2–9). The partnership stood on unequal footing because one man served the Lord and the other worshiped idols. We court disaster when we enter into partnership with unbelievers, because our very foundations differ (2 Corinthians 6:14–18). While one serves the Lord, the other does not recognize God's authority. Inevitably, the one who serves God is faced with the temptation to compromise values. When that happens, spiritual disaster results.

Before entering into partnerships, ask: (1) What are my motives? (2) What problems am I avoiding by seeking this partnership? (3) Is this partnership the best solution, or is it only a quick solution to my problem? (4) Have I prayed or asked others to pray for guidance? (5) Are my partner and I really working toward the same goals? (6) Am I willing to settle for less financial gain in order to do what God wants?

21:6 Jehoram, the new king of Judah, married Athaliah, one of the daughters of King Ahab of Israel. She became the mother of Judah's next king, Ahaziah (22:2). Athaliah's mother was Jezebel, the most wicked woman Israel had ever known. Jehoram's marriage to Athaliah was Judah's downfall, for Athaliah brought her mother's wicked influence into Judah, causing the nation to forget God and turn to Baal worship (22:3).

21:7 God promised that a descendant of David would always sit on the throne (2 Samuel 7:8–16). What happened to this promise when the nation was destroyed and carried away? There were two parts to God's promise. (1) In the physical sense, as long as there was an actual throne in Judah, a descendant of David would sit upon it. But this part of the promise depended on the obedience of these kings. When they disobeyed, God was not bound to continue David's temporal line. (2) In the spiritual sense, this promise was completely fulfilled in the coming of Jesus the Messiah, a descendant of David, who would sit on the throne of David forever.

21:8–11 Jehoram's reign was marked by sin and cruelty. He married a woman who worshiped idols; he killed his six brothers; he allowed and even promoted idol worship. Yet he was not killed in battle or by treachery—he died by a lingering and painful disease (21:18–19). Punishment for sin is not always immediate or dramatic. But if we ignore God's laws, we will eventually suffer the consequences of our sin.

21:12 Chronicles mentions Elijah only here. Much more about this great prophet can be found in 1 Kings 17:1—2 Kings 2:11. Elijah's Profile is found in 1 Kings 18.

God of your father David, 'Because you have not walked in the ways of Jehoshaphat
your father and the ways of Asa king of Judah,

21:13 2 Chr 21:6; 1 Kin 16:31-33; 2 Chr 21:4

13 but have walked in the way of the kings of Israel, and have caused Judah and the
inhabitants of Jerusalem to play the harlot as the house of Ahab played the harlot, and
you have also killed your brothers, your own family, who were better than you,
14 behold, the LORD is going to strike your people, your sons, your wives and all your
possessions with a great calamity;

21:15 2 Chr 21:18, 19

15 and you will suffer severe sickness, a disease of your bowels, until your bowels come
out because of the sickness, day by day.' "

21:16 2 Chr 33:11; 2 Chr 17:11; 22:1

16 Then the LORD stirred up against Jehoram the spirit of the Philistines and the Arabs
who bordered the Ethiopians;

21:17 2 Chr 25:23

17 and they came against Judah and invaded it, and carried away all the possessions
found in the king's house together with his sons and his wives, so that no son was left to
him except Jehoahaz, the youngest of his sons.

21:18 2 Chr 21:15

18 So after all this the LORD smote him in his bowels with an incurable sickness.

21:19 2 Chr 16:14

19 Now it came about in the course of time, at the end of two years, that his bowels
came out because of his sickness and he died in great pain. And his people made no fire
for him like the fire for his fathers.

21:20 Jer 22:18, 28; 2 Chr 24:25; 28:27

20 He was thirty-two years old when he became king, and he reigned in Jerusalem eight
years; and he departed with no one's regret, and they buried him in the city of David,
but not in the tombs of the kings.

Ahaziah Succeeds Jehoram in Judah

22:1 2 Kin 8:24-29; 2 Chr 21:16

22 Then the inhabitants of Jerusalem made Ahaziah, his youngest son, king in his
place, for the band of men who came with the Arabs to the camp had slain all the
older *sons.* So Ahaziah the son of Jehoram king of Judah began to reign.
2 Ahaziah *was* twenty-two years old when he became king, and he reigned one year in
Jerusalem. And his mother's name was Athaliah, the granddaughter of Omri.
3 He also walked in the ways of the house of Ahab, for his mother was his counselor
to do wickedly.

22:4 Prov 13:20

4 He did evil in the sight of the LORD like the house of Ahab, for they were his counselors after the death of his father, to his destruction.

Ahaziah Allies with Jehoram of Israel

22:5 2 Kin 8:28

5 He also walked according to their counsel, and went with Jehoram the son of Ahab
king of Israel to wage war against Hazael king of Aram at Ramoth-gilead. But the Arameans wounded Joram.
6 So he returned to be healed in Jezreel of the wounds which they had inflicted on
him at Ramah, when he fought against Hazael king of Aram. And Ahaziah, the son of
Jehoram king of Judah, went down to see Jehoram the son of Ahab in Jezreel, because
he was sick.

22:7 2 Chr 10:15; 2 Kin 9:21; 2 Kin 9:6, 7

7 Now the destruction of Ahaziah was from God, in that he went to Joram. For when
he came, he went out with Jehoram against Jehu the son of Nimshi, whom the LORD
had anointed to cut off the house of Ahab.

Jehu Murders Princes of Judah

22:8 2 Kin 10:11-14

8 It came about when Jehu was executing judgment on the house of Ahab, he found
the princes of Judah and the sons of Ahaziah's brothers ministering to Ahaziah, and slew
them.

22:9 2 Kin 9:27; 2 Kin 9:28; 2 Chr 17:4

9 He also sought Ahaziah, and they caught him while he was hiding in Samaria; they
brought him to Jehu, put him to death and buried him. For they said, "He is the son of
Jehoshaphat, who sought the LORD with all his heart." So there was no one of the house
of Ahaziah to retain the power of the kingdom.

22:4–5 Although it is wise to seek advice, we must also carefully weigh the advice we receive. Ahaziah had advisers, but the advisers he chose to listen to were wicked and led him to ruin. When you seek advice, listen carefully and use God's Word to "examine everything carefully; hold fast to that which is good" (1 Thessalonians 5:21).

22:7 Jehu's Profile and a more complete story of his reign are found in 2 Kings 9:1—10:36.

10 Now when Athaliah the mother of Ahaziah saw that her son was dead, she rose and **22:10**
destroyed all the royal offspring of the house of Judah. 2 Kin 11:1-3
11 But Jehoshabeath the king's daughter took Joash the son of Ahaziah, and stole him
from among the king's sons who were being put to death, and placed him and his nurse
in the bedroom. So Jehoshabeath, the daughter of King Jehoram, the wife of Jehoiada
the priest (for she was the sister of Ahaziah), hid him from Athaliah so that she would
not put him to death.
12 He was hidden with them in the house of God six years while Athaliah reigned over
the land.

Jehoiada Sets Joash on the Throne of Judah

23 Now in the seventh year Jehoiada strengthened himself, and took captains of hun- **23:1**
dreds: Azariah the son of Jeroham, Ishmael the son of Johanan, Azariah the son 2 Kin 11:4-20
of Obed, Maaseiah the son of Adaiah, and Elishaphat the son of Zichri, *and they entered*
into a covenant with him.
2 They went throughout Judah and gathered the Levites from all the cities of Judah, **23:2**
and the heads of the fathers' *households* of Israel, and they came to Jerusalem. 2 Chr 11:13-17; 21:2
3 Then all the assembly made a covenant with the king in the house of God. And **23:3**
Jehoiada said to them, "Behold, the king's son shall reign, as the LORD has spoken con- 2 Sam 7:12; 2 Chr 21:7
cerning the sons of David.
4 "This is the thing which you shall do: one third of you, of the priests and Levites who **23:4**
come in on the sabbath, *shall be* gatekeepers, 1 Chr 9:25
5 and one third *shall be* at the king's house, and a third at the Gate of the Foundation;
and all the people *shall be* in the courts of the house of the LORD.
6 "But let no one enter the house of the LORD except the priests and the ministering **23:6**
Levites; they may enter, for they are holy. And let all the people keep the charge of the 1 Chr 23:28-32
LORD.
7 "The Levites will surround the king, each man with his weapons in his hand; and
whoever enters the house, let him be killed. Thus be with the king when he comes in and
when he goes out."
8 So the Levites and all Judah did according to all that Jehoiada the priest command- **23:8**
ed. And each one of them took his men who were to come in on the sabbath, with those 1 Chr 24:1
who were to go out on the sabbath, for Jehoiada the priest did not dismiss *any of* the
divisions.
9 Then Jehoiada the priest gave to the captains of hundreds the spears and the large
and small shields which had been King David's, which were in the house of God.
10 He stationed all the people, each man with his weapon in his hand, from the right
side of the house to the left side of the house, by the altar and by the house, around the
king.
11 Then they brought out the king's son and put the crown on him, and *gave him* the **23:11**
testimony and made him king. And Jehoiada and his sons anointed him and said, "*Long* Ex 25:16, 21; 1 Sam 10:24
live the king!"

Athaliah Murdered

12 When Athaliah heard the noise of the people running and praising the king, she
came into the house of the LORD to the people.
13 She looked, and behold, the king was standing by his pillar at the entrance, and the
captains and the trumpeters *were* beside the king. And all the people of the land rejoiced

---

23:1 After seven years of rule by Athaliah, the queen mother, Jehoiada the priest finally got up his courage and took action to get rid of the idolatrous ruler. To confront the king (or queen) with the demands of God's law was supposed to be the role of every priest in every generation. Tragically, many priests shied away from this duty, and thus only a few made a difference in the nation.

23:1 Although it could have cost him his life, this priest did what was right, restoring the temple worship and anointing the new king. There are times when we must correct a wrong or speak out for what is right. When such a situation arises, gather up your courage and act.

23:12–15 Athaliah thought she had it made. After assuming the throne, she killed all potential heirs to it—so she thought. But even the best plans for evil go sour. When the truth was revealed, she was overthrown immediately. It is much safer to live according to the truth, even if it means not obtaining everything you want.

and blew trumpets, the singers with *their* musical instruments leading the praise. Then
Athaliah tore her clothes and said, "Treason! Treason!"
14 Jehoiada the priest brought out the captains of hundreds who were appointed over
the army and said to them, "Bring her out between the ranks; and whoever follows her,
put to death with the sword." For the priest said, "Let her not be put to death in the
house of the LORD."

23:15 Neh 3:28; Jer 31:40; 2 Chr 22:10

15 So they seized her, and when she arrived at the entrance of the Horse Gate of the
king's house, they put her to death there.

Reforms Carried Out

23:16 2 Kin 11:17

16 Then Jehoiada made a covenant between himself and all the people and the king,
that they would be the LORD'S people.

23:17 Deut 13:6-9; 1 Kin 18:40

17 And all the people went to the house of Baal and tore it down, and they broke in
pieces his altars and his images, and killed Mattan the priest of Baal before the altars.

23:18 2 Chr 5:5; 1 Chr 23:6, 25-31; 1 Chr 25:1

18 Moreover, Jehoiada placed the offices of the house of the LORD under the authority of the Levitical priests, whom David had assigned over the house of the LORD, to
offer the burnt offerings of the LORD, as it is written in the law of Moses—with rejoicing
and singing according to the order of David.

23:19 1 Chr 9:22

19 He stationed the gatekeepers of the house of the LORD, so that no one would enter
who was in any way unclean.

23:20 2 Kin 11:19

20 He took the captains of hundreds, the nobles, the rulers of the people and all the people
of the land, and brought the king down from the house of the LORD, and came through
the upper gate to the king's house. And they placed the king upon the royal throne.

23:21 2 Kin 11:20

21 So all of the people of the land rejoiced and the city was quiet. For they had put
Athaliah to death with the sword.

Young Joash Influenced by Jehoiada

24:1 2 Kin 11:21; 12:1-15

24 Joash *was* seven years old when he became king, and he reigned forty years in
Jerusalem; and his mother's name *was* Zibiah from Beersheba.

24:2 2 Chr 26:4, 5

2 Joash did what was right in the sight of the LORD all the days of Jehoiada the priest.
3 Jehoiada took two wives for him, and he became the father of sons and daughters.

Faithless Priests

24:4 2 Chr 24:7

4 Now it came about after this that Joash decided to restore the house of the LORD.

24:5 2 Chr 21:2

5 He gathered the priests and Levites and said to them, "Go out to the cities of Judah
and collect money from all Israel to repair the house of your God annually, and you shall
do the matter quickly." But the Levites did not act quickly.

24:6 Ex 30:12-16; Num 1:50

6 So the king summoned Jehoiada the chief *priest* and said to him, "Why have you not
required the Levites to bring in from Judah and from Jerusalem the levy *fixed by* Moses
the servant of the LORD on the congregation of Israel for the tent of the testimony?"

24:7 2 Chr 21:17

7 For the sons of the wicked Athaliah had broken into the house of God and even
used the holy things of the house of the LORD for the Baals.

Temple Repaired

24:8 2 Kin 12:9

8 So the king commanded, and they made a chest and set it outside by the gate of the
house of the LORD.

24:9 2 Chr 36:22; 2 Chr 24:6

9 They made a proclamation in Judah and Jerusalem to bring to the LORD the levy
fixed by Moses the servant of God on Israel in the wilderness.
10 All the officers and all the people rejoiced and brought in their levies and dropped
them into the chest until they had finished.

23:15–17 Athaliah's life ended as her mother Jezebel's had—by execution. Her life of idolatry and treachery was cut short by God's judgment of her sin. By this time Judah had slipped so far away from God that Baal was worshiped in Jerusalem.

23:18 Jehoiada restored the temple procedures and its worship services according to David's original plans, recorded in 1 Chronicles 24; 25.

24:5 The Levites took their time carrying out the king's order, even though he told them not to delay. A tax for keeping the temple in order was not just the king's wish, but God's command (Exodus 30:11–16). The Levites, therefore, were not only disregarding the king, but disregarding God. When it comes to following God's commands, a slow response may be little better than disobedience. Obey God willingly and immediately.

24:10 Evidently the Levites weren't convinced that the people would want to contribute to the rebuilding of the temple (24:5), but the people were glad to give of what they had for this project. Don't underestimate people's desire to be faithful to God. When challenged to do God's work, they will often respond willingly and generously.

11 It came about whenever the chest was brought in to the king's officer by the Le- **24:11**
vites, and when they saw that there was much money, then the king's scribe and the chief 2 Kin 12:10
priest's officer would come, empty the chest, take it, and return it to its place. Thus they
did daily and collected much money.
12 The king and Jehoiada gave it to those who did the work of the service of the house
of the LORD; and they hired masons and carpenters to restore the house of the LORD,
and also workers in iron and bronze to repair the house of the LORD.
13 So the workmen labored, and the repair work progressed in their hands, and they
restored the house of God according to its specifications and strengthened it.
14 When they had finished, they brought the rest of the money before the king and
Jehoiada; and it was made into utensils for the house of the LORD, utensils for the service and the burnt offering, and pans and utensils of gold and silver. And they offered
burnt offerings in the house of the LORD continually all the days of Jehoiada.
15 Now when Jehoiada reached a ripe old age he died; he was one hundred and thirty
years old at his death.
16 They buried him in the city of David among the kings, because he had done well in **24:16** 2 Chr 21:20; 2 Chr
Israel and to God and His house. 21:2
17 But after the death of Jehoiada the officials of Judah came and bowed down to the
king, and the king listened to them.
18 They abandoned the house of the LORD, the God of their fathers, and served the **24:18**
[9]Asherim and the idols; so wrath came upon Judah and Jerusalem for this their guilt. 2 Chr 24:4; Ex 34:12-14; Josh
19 Yet He sent prophets to them to bring them back to the LORD; though they testi- 22:20
fied against them, they would not listen. **24:19** Jer 7:25

Joash Murders Son of Jehoiada

20 Then the Spirit of God came on Zechariah the son of Jehoiada the priest; and he **24:20**
stood above the people and said to them, "Thus God has said, 'Why do you transgress 2 Chr 20:14; Num 14:41; 2 Chr 15:2
the commandments of the LORD and do not prosper? Because you have forsaken the
LORD, He has also forsaken you.' "
21 So they conspired against him and at the command of the king they stoned him to **24:21**
death in the court of the house of the LORD. Neh 9:26; Matt 23:34, 35
22 Thus Joash the king did not remember the kindness which his father Jehoiada had
shown him, but he murdered his son. And as he died he said, "May the LORD see and **24:22** Gen 9:5
avenge!"

Aram Invades and Defeats Judah

23 Now it happened at the turn of the year that the army of the Arameans came up **24:23**
against him; and they came to Judah and Jerusalem, destroyed all the officials of the 2 Kin 12:17
people from among the people, and sent all their spoil to the king of Damascus.
24 Indeed the army of the Arameans came with a small number of men; yet the LORD **24:24**
delivered a very great army into their hands, because they had forsaken the LORD, the 2 Chr 16:7, 8; 2 Chr 24:20
God of their fathers. Thus they executed judgment on Joash.
25 When they had departed from him (for they left him very sick), his own servants **24:25**
conspired against him because of the blood of the son of Jehoiada the priest, and mur- 2 Kin 12:20, 21
dered him on his bed. So he died, and they buried him in the city of David, but they did
not bury him in the tombs of the kings.

9 I.e. wooden symbols of a female deity

24:18 If everything went so well in Judah when the people worshiped God, why did they turn away from him? Prosperity can be both a blessing and a curse. While it can be a sign of God's blessing to those who follow him, it carries with it the potential for moral and spiritual decline. Prosperous people are tempted to become self-sufficient and proud—to take God for granted. In our prosperity, we must not forget that God is the source of our blessings. See Deuteronomy 6:10–12; 8:11–14.

24:18–20 When King Joash and the nation of Judah abandoned God, God sent Zechariah to call them to repentance. Before dispensing judgment and punishment, God gave them another chance. In the same way, God does not abandon us or lash out in revenge when we sin. Instead, he aggressively pursues us through his Word, his Spirit in us, the words of others, and sometimes discipline. He does not intend to destroy us, but to urge us to return to him. When you are moving away from God, remember that he is pursuing you. Stop and listen. Allow him to point out your sin so you can repent and follow him again.

24:19 God sent many prophets to Joash and the people to warn them that they were headed for destruction. Joel may have been one of these prophets. Read the book of Joel for more information about the political and spiritual climate of the times.

24:22 Zechariah asked God to call the people to account for their sins. He was not seeking revenge, but pleading for justice. When we feel like despairing over the wickedness around us, we can rest assured that in the end God will bring complete justice to the earth.

26 Now these are those who conspired against him: Zabad the son of Shimeath the
Ammonitess, and Jehozabad the son of Shimrith the Moabitess.

24:27 2 Chr 24:12; 2 Chr 13:22

27 As to his sons and the many oracles against him and the rebuilding of the house of
God, behold, they are written in the treatise of the Book of the Kings. Then Amaziah
his son became king in his place.

Amaziah Succeeds Joash in Judah

25:1 2 Kin 14:1-6

25 Amaziah was twenty-five years old when he became king, and he reigned twenty-nine years in Jerusalem. And his mother's name was Jehoaddan of Jerusalem.

JOASH

All parents want their children to make the right decisions. But to do this, children must first learn to make *their own* decisions. Making bad ones helps them learn to make good ones. If parents make all the decisions for their children, they leave their children without the skills for wise decision making when they are on their own. This problem seriously affected Joash. He had great advice, but he never grew up. He became so dependent on what he was told that his effectiveness was limited to the quality of his advisers.

When Joash was one year old, his grandmother Athaliah decided to slaughter all her descendants in a desperate bid for power. Joash was the only survivor, rescued and hidden by his aunt and uncle, Jehosheba and Jehoiada. Jehoiada's work as a priest made it possible to keep Joash hidden in the temple for six years. At that point, Jehoiada arranged for the overthrow of Athaliah and the crowning of Joash. For many years following, Jehoiada made most of the kingdom's decisions for Joash. When the old priest died, he was buried in the royal cemetery as a tribute to his role.

But after Jehoiada's death, Joash didn't know what to do. He listened to counsel that carried him into evil. Within a short time he even ordered the death of Jehoiada's son Zechariah. After a few months, Joash's army had been soundly defeated by the Arameans. Jerusalem was saved only because Joash stripped the temple of its treasures as a bribe. Finally, the king's own officials assassinated him. In contrast to Jehoiada, Joash was not buried among the kings; he is not even listed in Jesus' genealogy in the New Testament.

As dependent as Joash was on Jehoiada, there is little evidence that he ever established a real dependence on the God Jehoiada obeyed. Like many children, Joash's knowledge of God was secondhand. It was a start, but the king needed his own relationship with God that would outlast and overrule the changes in the advice he received.

It would be easy to criticize Joash's failure were it not for the fact that we often fall into the same traps. How often have we acted on poor advice without considering God's Word?

Strengths and accomplishments:
- Carried out extensive repairs on the temple
- Was faithful to God as long as Jehoiada lived

Weaknesses and mistakes:
- Allowed idolatry to continue among his people
- Used the temple treasures to bribe King Hazael of Aram
- Killed Jehoiada's son Zechariah
- Allowed his advisers to lead the people away from God

Lessons from his life:
- A good and hopeful start can be ruined by an evil end
- Even the best counsel is ineffective if it does not help us make wise decisions
- As helpful or hurtful as others may be, we are individually responsible for what we do

Vital statistics:
- Where: Jerusalem
- Occupation: King of Judah
- Relatives: Father: Ahaziah. Mother: Zibiah. Grandmother: Athaliah. Aunt: Jehosheba. Uncle: Jehoiada. Son: Amaziah. Cousin: Zechariah
- Contemporaries: Jehu, Hazael

Key verses:
"But after the death of Jehoiada the officials of Judah came and bowed down to the king, and the king listened to them. They abandoned the house of the LORD, the God of their fathers, and served the Asherim and the idols; so wrath came upon Judah and Jerusalem for this their guilt" (2 Chronicles 24:17–18).

Joash's story is told in 2 Kings 11:1—14:23 and 2 Chronicles 22:11—25:25.

2 He did right in the sight of the LORD, yet not with a whole heart. 25:2
3 Now it came about as soon as the kingdom was firmly in his grasp, that he killed his 2 Chr 25:14
servants who had slain his father the king. 25:3
4 However, he did not put their children to death, but *did* as it is written in the law in 2 Kin 14:5
the book of Moses, which the LORD commanded, saying, “Fathers shall not be put to 25:4
death for sons, nor sons be put to death for fathers, but each shall be put to death for his Deut 24:16
own sin.”

Amaziah Defeats Edomites

5 Moreover, Amaziah assembled Judah and appointed them according to *their* fathers’ 25:5
households under commanders of thousands and commanders of hundreds throughout Num 1:3; 2 Chr 26:13
Judah and Benjamin; and he took a census of those from twenty years old and upward
and found them to be 300,000 choice men, *able* to go to war *and* handle spear and shield.
6 He hired also 100,000 valiant warriors out of Israel for one hundred talents of
silver.
7 But a man of God came to him saying, “O king, do not let the army of Israel go with 25:7
you, for the LORD is not with Israel *nor with* any of the sons of Ephraim. 2 Kin 4:9
8 “But if you do go, do *it,* be strong for the battle; *yet* God will bring you down before 25:8
the enemy, for God has power to help and to bring down.” 2 Chr 14:11; 20:6
9 Amaziah said to the man of God, “But what *shall we* do for the hundred talents which 25:9
I have given to the troops of Israel?” And the man of God answered, “The LORD has Deut 8:18; Prov 10:22
much more to give you than this.”
10 Then Amaziah dismissed them, the troops which came to him from Ephraim, to go
home; so their anger burned against Judah and they returned home in fierce anger.
11 Now Amaziah strengthened himself and led his people forth, and went to the Val- 25:11
ley of Salt and struck down 10,000 of the sons of Seir. 2 Kin 14:7
12 The sons of Judah also captured 10,000 alive and brought them to the top of the
cliff and threw them down from the top of the cliff, so that they were all dashed to pieces.
13 But the troops whom Amaziah sent back from going with him to battle, raided the
cities of Judah, from Samaria to Beth-horon, and struck down 3,000 of them and plundered much spoil.

Amaziah Rebuked for Idolatry

14 Now after Amaziah came from slaughtering the Edomites, he brought the gods of 25:14
the sons of Seir, set them up as his gods, bowed down before them and burned incense 2 Chr 28:23
to them.
15 Then the anger of the LORD burned against Amaziah, and He sent him a prophet 25:15
who said to him, “Why have you sought the gods of the people who have not delivered 2 Chr 25:11, 12
their own people from your hand?”
16 As he was talking with him, the king said to him, “Have we appointed you a royal
counselor? Stop! Why should you be struck down?” Then the prophet stopped and said,
“I know that God has planned to destroy you, because you have done this and have not
listened to my counsel.”

25:2 Amaziah did what was right on the outside, but inside he often resented what he had to do. His obedience was at best half-hearted. When the prophet promised God’s deliverance, Amaziah first complained about the money that had been lost (25:9). And he valued military success more than God’s will. We must search our own hearts and root out any resistance to obeying God. Grudging compliance is not true obedience.

25:9–10 Amaziah made a financial agreement with Israelite soldiers, offering to pay them to fight for him (25:6). But before they could go to battle, Amaziah sent them home with their pay because of the prophet’s warning. Although it cost him plenty, he wisely realized that the money was not worth the ruin the alliance could cause. How would you have reacted? Money must never stand in the way of making right decisions. The Lord’s favor is priceless, worth more than any amount of money.

25:14 After the victory, Amaziah returned and sacrificed to idols. We are very susceptible to sin after great victories. It is then that we feel confident, relaxed, and ready to celebrate. If, in that excitement, we let our defenses down, Satan can attack with all sorts of temptations. When you win, watch out. After the mountain peaks come the valleys.

25:15 Amaziah made a foolish mistake by worshiping the gods of the nation he had just conquered. Impressed by the accomplishments of the Edomites, Amaziah worshiped their idols! How foolish to serve the gods of a defeated enemy. We make the same mistake as Amaziah when we run after money, power, or recognition. By recognizing the emptiness of these worldly pursuits, we can free ourselves from the desire to follow them.

Amaziah Defeated by Joash of Israel

25:17 2 Kin 14:8-14

17 Then Amaziah king of Judah took counsel and sent to Joash the son of Jehoahaz
the son of Jehu, the king of Israel, saying, "Come, let us face each other."

25:18 Judg 9:8-15

18 Joash the king of Israel sent to Amaziah king of Judah, saying, "The thorn bush which
was in Lebanon sent to the cedar which was in Lebanon, saying, 'Give your daughter to
my son in marriage.' But there passed by a wild beast that was in Lebanon and trampled
the thorn bush.

25:19 2 Chr 26:16; 32:25

19 "You said, 'Behold, you have defeated Edom.' And your heart has become proud in
boasting. Now stay at home; for why should you provoke trouble so that you, even you,
would fall and Judah with you?"
20 But Amaziah would not listen, for it was from God, that He might deliver them into
the hand *of Joash* because they had sought the gods of Edom.
21 So Joash king of Israel went up, and he and Amaziah king of Judah faced each other
at Beth-shemesh, which belonged to Judah.
22 Judah was defeated by Israel, and they fled each to his tent.

25:23 2 Chr 21:17; 22:1

23 Then Joash king of Israel captured Amaziah king of Judah, the son of Joash the son
of Jehoahaz, at Beth-shemesh, and brought him to Jerusalem and tore down the wall of
Jerusalem from the Gate of Ephraim to the Corner Gate, 400 cubits.

25:24 1 Chr 26:15

24 *He took* all the gold and silver and all the utensils which were found in the house of
God with Obed-edom, and the treasures of the king's house, the hostages also, and returned to Samaria.

25:25 2 Kin 14:17-22

25 And Amaziah, the son of Joash king of Judah, lived fifteen years after the death of
Joash, son of Jehoahaz, king of Israel.
26 Now the rest of the acts of Amaziah, from first to last, behold, are they not written
in the Book of the Kings of Judah and Israel?
27 From the time that Amaziah turned away from following the LORD they conspired
against him in Jerusalem, and he fled to Lachish; but they sent after him to Lachish and
killed him there.
28 Then they brought him on horses and buried him with his fathers in the city of
Judah.

Uzziah Succeeds Amaziah in Judah

26 And all the people of Judah took Uzziah, who *was* sixteen years old, and made
him king in the place of his father Amaziah.
2 He built Eloth and restored it to Judah after the king slept with his fathers.

26:3 2 Kin 15:2, 3

3 Uzziah was sixteen years old when he became king, and he reigned fifty-two years
in Jerusalem; and his mother's name was Jechiliah of Jerusalem.
4 He did right in the sight of the LORD according to all that his father Amaziah had
done.

26:5 2 Chr 24:2; Dan 1:17; 2 Chr 15:2

5 He continued to seek God in the days of Zechariah, who had understanding through
the vision of God; and as long as he sought the LORD, God prospered him.

Uzziah Succeeds in War

26:6 Is 14:29

6 Now he went out and warred against the Philistines, and broke down the wall of
Gath and the wall of Jabneh and the wall of Ashdod; and he built cities in *the area of*
Ashdod and among the Philistines.

26:7 2 Chr 21:16

7 God helped him against the Philistines, and against the Arabians who lived in Gur-
baal, and the Meunites.

26:8 2 Chr 17:11

8 The Ammonites also gave tribute to Uzziah, and his fame extended to the border
of Egypt, for he became very strong.

26:9 2 Chr 25:23; Neh 2:13, 15; 3:13

9 Moreover, Uzziah built towers in Jerusalem at the Corner Gate and at the Valley
Gate and at the corner buttress and fortified them.

26:10 Gen 26:18-21

10 He built towers in the wilderness and hewed many cisterns, for he had much livestock, both in the lowland and in the plain. *He also had* plowmen and vinedressers in the
hill country and the fertile fields, for he loved the soil.
11 Moreover, Uzziah had an army ready for battle, which entered combat by divisions

---

25:18 In this parable, Judah is the thorn bush and Israel's army is the cedar tree. Amaziah was proud after defeating Edom. He wanted to defeat Israel, but Joash warned him not to attack. Amaziah had more ambition than ability, and he paid for it when he was soundly defeated. Don't let ambition and pride into your life, for they will cause you to forget God.

according to the number of their muster, prepared by Jeiel the scribe and Maaseiah the
official, under the direction of Hananiah, one of the king's officers.
12 The total number of the heads of the households, of valiant warriors, was 2,600.
13 Under their direction was an elite army of 307,500, who could wage war with great
power, to help the king against the enemy.
14 Moreover, Uzziah prepared for all the army shields, spears, helmets, body armor,
bows and sling stones.
15 In Jerusalem he made engines *of war* invented by skillful men to be on the towers
and on the corners for the purpose of shooting arrows and great stones. Hence his fame
spread afar, for he was marvelously helped until he *was* strong.

Pride Is Uzziah's Undoing

16 But when he became strong, his heart was so proud that he acted corruptly, and he
was unfaithful to the LORD his God, for he entered the temple of the LORD to burn incense on the altar of incense.
17 Then Azariah the priest entered after him and with him eighty priests of the LORD,
valiant men.
18 They opposed Uzziah the king and said to him, "It is not for you, Uzziah, to burn
incense to the LORD, but for the priests, the sons of Aaron who are consecrated to burn
incense. Get out of the sanctuary, for you have been unfaithful and will have no honor
from the LORD God."
19 But Uzziah, with a censer in his hand for burning incense, was enraged; and while
he was enraged with the priests, the leprosy broke out on his forehead before the priests
in the house of the LORD, beside the altar of incense.
20 Azariah the chief priest and all the priests looked at him, and behold, he *was* leprous on his forehead; and they hurried him out of there, and he himself also hastened to
get out because the LORD had smitten him.
21 King Uzziah was a leper to the day of his death; and he lived in a separate house,
being a leper, for he was cut off from the house of the LORD. And Jotham his son *was*
over the king's house judging the people of the land.
22 Now the rest of the acts of Uzziah, first to last, the prophet Isaiah, the son of Amoz,
has written.
23 So Uzziah slept with his fathers, and they buried him with his fathers in the field of
the grave which belonged to the kings, for they said, "He is a leper." And Jotham his son
became king in his place.

Jotham Succeeds Uzziah in Judah

27 Jotham was twenty-five years old when he became king, and he reigned sixteen
years in Jerusalem. And his mother's name was Jerushah the daughter of Zadok.
2 He did right in the sight of the LORD, according to all that his father Uzziah had
done; however he did not enter the temple of the LORD. But the people continued acting corruptly.
3 He built the upper gate of the house of the LORD, and he built extensively the wall
of Ophel.

26:13 2 Chr 25:5
26:16 Deut 32:15; 2 Chr 25:19; 1 Kin 13:1-4
26:17 1 Chr 6:10
26:18 2 Chr 19:2; Num 3:10; 16:39, 40; Ex 30:7, 8
26:19 2 Kin 5:25-27
26:21 2 Kin 15:5-7; Lev 13:46
26:22 Is 1:1
26:23 2 Chr 21:20; 28:27; Is 6:1
27:1 2 Kin 15:33-35
27:2 2 Chr 26:16
27:3 2 Chr 33:14; Neh 3:26

26:15 These machines were similar to the catapults later used by the Romans and were capable of slinging stones or arrows a great distance.

26:16 After God gave Uzziah great prosperity and power, he became proud and corrupt. It is true that "pride goes before destruction" (Proverbs 16:18). If God has given you wealth, influence, popularity, and power, be thankful, but be careful. God hates pride. While it is normal to feel elation when we accomplish something, it is wrong to be disdainful of God or to look down on others. Check your attitudes and remember to give God the credit for what you have. Use your gifts in ways that please him.

26:17–21 When people have power, they often think they can live above the law. But even rulers are subject to God, as Uzziah discovered. No matter what your position in society, God expects you to honor, worship, and obey him.

26:21 For much of his life, Uzziah "did right in the sight of the LORD" (26:4). But Uzziah turned away from God, and he was struck with leprosy and remained leprous until his death. He is remembered more for his arrogant act and subsequent punishment than for his great reforms. God requires lifelong obedience. Spurts of obedience are not enough. Only "the one who endure to the end" will be rewarded (Mark 13:13). Be remembered for your consistent faith; otherwise you, too, may become more famous for your downfall than for your success.

26:23 This was the year that God called Isaiah to be a prophet (Isaiah 6:1).

27:2 Jotham was generally a good king (27:6), but his people became corrupt. Those you lead will not always follow your example, but that should not affect the way you live for God. This sinfulness of Jotham's kingdom is vividly portrayed in Isaiah 1—5.

27:4 2 Chr 11:5
4 Moreover, he built cities in the hill country of Judah, and he built fortresses and
towers on the wooded *hills.*
5 He fought also with the king of the Ammonites and prevailed over them so that the
Ammonites gave him during that year one hundred talents of silver, ten thousand [10]kors
of wheat and ten thousand of barley. The Ammonites also paid him this *amount* in the
second and in the third year.
27:6 2 Chr 26:5
6 So Jotham became mighty because he ordered his ways before the LORD his God.
27:7 2 Kin 15:36
7 Now the rest of the acts of Jotham, even all his wars and his acts, behold, they are
written in the Book of the Kings of Israel and Judah.
27:8 2 Chr 27:1
8 He was twenty-five years old when he became king, and he reigned sixteen years in
Jerusalem.
9 And Jotham slept with his fathers, and they buried him in the city of David; and
Ahaz his son became king in his place.

Ahaz Succeeds Jotham in Judah

28:1 2 Kin 16:2-4; 2 Chr 27:2
28 Ahaz *was* twenty years old when he became king, and he reigned sixteen years in
Jerusalem; and he did not do right in the sight of the LORD as David his father
had done.

10 I.e. One kor equals approx 10 bu

UZZIAH

We are never closer to failure than during our greatest successes. If we fail to recognize God's part in our achievements, they are no better than failures. Uzziah (also called Azariah) was a remarkably successful king. His achievements brought him fame. He was successful in war and peace, in planning and execution, in building and planting.

Uzziah overestimated his own importance in bringing about the great achievements he experienced. He did so many things well that a consuming pride gradually invaded his life like the leprous disease that finally destroyed his body. In trying to act like a priest, he took on a role that God did not mean for him to have. He had forgotten not only how much God had given him, but also that God had certain roles for others that he needed to respect.

Uzziah's pride was rooted in his lack of thankfulness. We have no accounts of this king's ever showing appreciation to God for the marvelous gifts he received. Our accomplishments may not compare with Uzziah's, but we still owe a debt of thanksgiving to God for our very lives. If God is not getting the credit for your successes, shouldn't you start looking at your life differently?

Strengths and accomplishments:
- Pleased God during his early years as king
- Successful warrior and city builder
- Skillful in organizing and delegating
- Reigned for 52 years

Weaknesses and mistakes:
- Developed a prideful attitude due to his great success
- Tried to perform the priests' duties, in direct disobedience to God
- Failed to remove many of the symbols of idolatry in the land

Lessons from his life:
- Lack of thankfulness to God can lead to pride
- Even successful people must acknowledge the role God has for others in their lives

Vital statistics:
- Where: Jerusalem
- Occupation: King of Judah
- Relatives: Father: Amaziah. Mother: Jecoliah. Son: Jotham
- Contemporaries: Isaiah, Amos, Hosea, Jeroboam, Zechariah, Azariah

Key verses:
"In Jerusalem he made engines of war invented by skillful men to be on the towers and on the corners for the purpose of shooting arrows and great stones. Hence his fame spread afar, for he was marvelously helped until he was strong. But when he became strong, his heart was so proud that he acted corruptly, and he was unfaithful to the LORD his God, for he entered the temple of the LORD to burn incense on the altar of incense" (2 Chronicles 26:15–16).

Uzziah's story is told in 2 Kings 15:1-7 (where he is called Azariah), and in 2 Chronicles 26:1-23. He is also mentioned in Isaiah 1:1; 6:1; 7:1; Hosea 1:1; Amos 1:1; Zechariah 14:5.

27:5 The tribute he received amounted to 3 3/4 tons of silver and 62,000 bushels each of wheat and barley.

2 But he walked in the ways of the kings of Israel; he also made molten images for the
Baals.

28:2 2 Chr 22:3; Ex 34:17

3 Moreover, he burned incense in the valley of Ben-hinnom and burned his sons in
fire, according to the abominations of the nations whom the LORD had driven out before the sons of Israel.

28:3 Josh 15:8; Lev 18:21; 2 Chr 33:6; 2 Chr 33:2

4 He sacrificed and burned incense on the high places, on the hills and under every
green tree.

28:4 2 Chr 28:25

Judah Is Invaded

5 Wherefore, the LORD his God delivered him into the hand of the king of Aram;
and they defeated him and carried away from him a great number of captives and brought
them to Damascus. And he was also delivered into the hand of the king of Israel, who
inflicted him with heavy casualties.

28:5 2 Kin 16:5; 2 Chr 24:24; Is 7:1

6 For Pekah the son of Remaliah slew in Judah 120,000 in one day, all valiant men,
because they had forsaken the LORD God of their fathers.

28:6 2 Kin 16:5

7 And Zichri, a mighty man of Ephraim, slew Maaseiah the king's son and Azrikam
the ruler of the house and Elkanah the second to the king.
8 The sons of Israel carried away captive of their brethren 200,000 women, sons and
daughters; and they took also a great deal of spoil from them, and brought the spoil to
Samaria.

28:8 Deut 28:25, 41; 2 Chr 11:4

9 But a prophet of the LORD was there, whose name *was* Oded; and he went out to
meet the army which came to Samaria and said to them, "Behold, because the LORD,
the God of your fathers, was angry with Judah, He has delivered them into your hand,
and you have slain them in a rage *which* has even reached heaven.

28:9 2 Chr 25:15; Is 47:6; Ezra 9:6; Rev 18:5

10 "Now you are proposing to subjugate for yourselves the people of Judah and Jerusalem for male and female slaves. Surely, *do* you not *have* transgressions of your own against
the LORD your God?

28:10 Lev 25:39

11 "Now therefore, listen to me and return the captives whom you captured from your
brothers, for the burning anger of the LORD is against you."

28:11 2 Chr 28:8; James 2:13

12 Then some of the heads of the sons of Ephraim—Azariah the son of Johanan,
Berechiah the son of Meshillemoth, Jehizkiah the son of Shallum, and Amasa the son of
Hadlai—arose against those who were coming from the battle,
13 and said to them, "You must not bring the captives in here, for you are proposing *to*
bring upon us guilt against the LORD adding to our sins and our guilt; for our guilt is
great so that *His* burning anger is against Israel."
14 So the armed men left the captives and the spoil before the officers and all the assembly.
15 Then the men who were designated by name arose, took the captives, and they
clothed all their naked ones from the spoil; and they gave them clothes and sandals, fed
them and gave them drink, anointed them *with oil,* led all their feeble ones on donkeys,
and brought them to Jericho, the city of palm trees, to their brothers; then they returned
to Samaria.

28:15 2 Chr 28:12; 2 Kin 6:22; Prov 25:21, 22; Deut 34:3

Compromise with Assyria

16 At that time King Ahaz sent to the [11]kings of Assyria for help.

28:16 2 Kin 16:7

17 For again the Edomites had come and attacked Judah and carried away captives.

28:17 Obad 10, 14

18 The Philistines also had invaded the cities of the lowland and of the Negev of Judah,
and had taken Beth-shemesh, Aijalon, Gederoth, and Soco with its villages, Timnah with
its villages, and Gimzo with its villages, and they settled there.

28:18 Ezek 16:57

19 For the LORD humbled Judah because of Ahaz king of Israel, for he had brought
about a lack of restraint in Judah and was very unfaithful to the LORD.

28:19 2 Chr 21:2

20 So Tilgath-pilneser king of Assyria came against him and afflicted him instead of
strengthening him.

28:20 1 Chr 5:26

21 Although Ahaz took a portion out of the house of the LORD and out of the pal-

28:21 2 Kin 16:8, 9

11 Ancient versions read *king*

28:3 Imagine the monstrous evil of a religion that offers young children as sacrifices. God allowed the nation to be conquered in response to Ahaz's evil practices. Even today the practice hasn't abated. The sacrifice of children to the harsh gods of convenience, economy, and whim continues in sterile medical facilities in numbers that would astound the wicked Ahaz. If we are to allow children to come to Christ (Matthew 19:14), we must first allow them to come into the world.

ace of the king and of the princes, and gave *it* to the king of Assyria, it did not help him.
28:22 Is 1:5; Jer 5:3; Rev 16:11
22 Now in the time of his distress this same King Ahaz became yet more unfaithful to
the LORD.
28:23 2 Chr 25:14; Jer 44:17, 18
23 For he sacrificed to the gods of Damascus which had defeated him, and said, "Because the gods of the kings of Aram helped them, I will sacrifice to them that they may
help me." But they became the downfall of him and all Israel.
28:24 2 Kin 16:17; 2 Chr 29:7; 2 Chr 30:14; 33:3-5
24 Moreover, when Ahaz gathered together the utensils of the house of God, he cut
the utensils of the house of God in pieces; and he closed the doors of the house of the
LORD and made altars for himself in every corner of Jerusalem.
25 In every city of Judah he made high places to burn incense to other gods, and provoked the LORD, the God of his fathers, to anger.
28:26 2 Kin 16:19, 20
26 Now the rest of his acts and all his ways, from first to last, behold, they are written
in the Book of the Kings of Judah and Israel.
28:27 2 Kin 16:20; 2 Chr 24:25; Is 14:28; 2 Chr 21:2
27 So Ahaz slept with his fathers, and they buried him in the city, in Jerusalem, for
they did not bring him into the tombs of the kings of Israel; and Hezekiah his son reigned
in his place.

Hezekiah Succeeds Ahaz in Judah

29:1 2 Kin 18:1-3
29 Hezekiah became king *when he was* twenty-five years old; and he reigned twenty-
nine years in Jerusalem. And his mother's name *was* Abijah, the daughter of
Zechariah.
29:2 2 Chr 28:1; 34:2
2 He did right in the sight of the LORD, according to all that his father David had
done.
29:3 2 Chr 28:24; 29:7
3 In the first year of his reign, in the first month, he opened the doors of the house of
the LORD and repaired them.
4 He brought in the priests and the Levites and gathered them into the square on
the east.

Reforms Begun

29:5 2 Chr 29:15, 34; 35:6
5 Then he said to them, "Listen to me, O Levites. Consecrate yourselves now, and
consecrate the house of the LORD, the God of your fathers, and carry the uncleanness
out from the holy place.
29:6 Ezek 8:16
6 "For our fathers have been unfaithful and have done evil in the sight of the LORD
our God, and have forsaken Him and turned their faces away from the dwelling place of
the LORD, and have turned *their* backs.
29:7 2 Chr 28:24
7 "They have also shut the doors of the porch and put out the lamps, and have not
burned incense or offered burnt offerings in the holy place to the God of Israel.
29:8 2 Chr 24:20; Jer 25:9, 18
8 "Therefore the wrath of the LORD was against Judah and Jerusalem, and He has made
them an object of terror, of horror, and of hissing, as you see with your own eyes.
29:9 2 Chr 28:5-8, 17
9 "For behold, our fathers have fallen by the sword, and our sons and our daughters
and our wives are in captivity for this.
29:10 2 Chr 23:16
10 "Now it is in my heart to make a covenant with the LORD God of Israel, that His
burning anger may turn away from us.
29:11 Num 3:6; 8:6
11 "My sons, do not be negligent now, for the LORD has chosen you to stand before
Him, to minister to Him, and to be His ministers and burn incense."
29:12 2 Chr 31:13; Num 3:19, 20
12 Then the Levites arose: Mahath, the son of Amasai and Joel the son of Azariah,
from the sons of the Kohathites; and from the sons of Merari, Kish the son of Abdi and
Azariah the son of Jehallelel; and from the Gershonites, Joah the son of Zimmah and
Eden the son of Joah;

28:22 Difficulties and struggles can devastate people, or they can stimulate growth and maturity. For Ahaz, deep troubles led to spiritual collapse. We do not need to respond like Ahaz. When facing problems or tragedy, we must remember that rough times give us a chance to grow (James 1:2–4). When you are facing trials, don't turn away from God; turn *to* him. See these times as an opportunity for you to claim God's help.

29:1 Hezekiah's Profile is found in 2 Kings 19.

29:11 The Levites, chosen by God to serve in the temple, had been kept from their duties by Ahaz's wickedness (28:24). But Hezekiah called them back into service, reminding them that the Lord had chosen them to minister.

We may not have to face a wicked king, but pressures or responsibilities can render us inactive and ineffective. When you have been given the responsibility to minister, don't neglect your duty. If you have become inactive in Christian service, either by choice or by circumstance, look for opportunities (and listen to the "Hezekiahs") God will send your way to help you resume your responsibilities. Then, like the Levites, be ready for action (29:12–15).

13 and from the sons of Elizaphan, Shimri and Jeiel; and from the sons of Asaph, Zechariah and Mattaniah;

14 and from the sons of Heman, Jehiel and Shimei; and from the sons of Jeduthun, Shemaiah and Uzziel.

15 They assembled their brothers, consecrated themselves, and went in to cleanse the house of the LORD, according to the commandment of the king by the words of the LORD.

16 So the priests went in to the inner part of the house of the LORD to cleanse *it,* and every unclean thing which they found in the temple of the LORD they brought out to the court of the house of the LORD. Then the Levites received *it* to carry out to the Kidron valley.

17 Now they began the consecration on the first *day* of the first month, and on the eighth day of the month they entered the porch of the LORD. Then they consecrated the house of the LORD in eight days, and finished on the sixteenth day of the first month.

18 Then they went in to King Hezekiah and said, "We have cleansed the whole house of the LORD, the altar of burnt offering with all of its utensils, and the table of showbread with all of its utensils.

19 "Moreover, all the utensils which King Ahaz had discarded during his reign in his unfaithfulness, we have prepared and consecrated; and behold, they are before the altar of the LORD."

Hezekiah Restores Temple Worship

20 Then King Hezekiah arose early and assembled the princes of the city and went up to the house of the LORD.

21 They brought seven bulls, seven rams, seven lambs and seven male goats for a sin offering for the kingdom, the sanctuary, and Judah. And he ordered the priests, the sons of Aaron, to offer *them* on the altar of the LORD.

22 So they slaughtered the bulls, and the priests took the blood and sprinkled it on the altar. They also slaughtered the rams and sprinkled the blood on the altar; they slaughtered the lambs also and sprinkled the blood on the altar.

23 Then they brought the male goats of the sin offering before the king and the assembly, and they laid their hands on them.

24 The priests slaughtered them and purged the altar with their blood to atone for all Israel, for the king ordered the burnt offering and the sin offering for all Israel.

25 He then stationed the Levites in the house of the LORD with cymbals, with harps and with lyres, according to the command of David and of Gad the king's seer, and of Nathan the prophet; for the command was from the LORD through His prophets.

26 The Levites stood with the *musical* instruments of David, and the priests with the trumpets.

27 Then Hezekiah gave the order to offer the burnt offering on the altar. When the burnt offering began, the song to the LORD also began with the trumpets, *accompanied* by the instruments of David, king of Israel.

28 While the whole assembly worshiped, the singers also sang and the trumpets sounded; all this *continued* until the burnt offering was finished.

29 Now at the completion of the burnt offerings, the king and all who were present with him bowed down and worshiped.

30 Moreover, King Hezekiah and the officials ordered the Levites to sing praises to the LORD with the words of David and Asaph the seer. So they sang praises with joy, and bowed down and worshiped.

31 Then Hezekiah said, "Now *that* you have consecrated yourselves to the LORD, come near and bring sacrifices and thank offerings to the house of the LORD." And the assembly brought sacrifices and thank offerings, and all those who were willing *brought* burnt offerings.

29:15 2 Chr 29:5; 1 Chr 23:28; 2 Chr 30:12

29:16 2 Chr 15:16

29:17 2 Chr 29:3

29:19 2 Chr 28:24

29:21 Lev 4:3-14

29:22 Lev 4:18

29:23 Lev 4:15

29:24 Lev 4:26

29:25 1 Chr 25:6; 2 Chr 8:14; 2 Sam 24:11; 2 Sam 7:2

29:26 1 Chr 23:5; 2 Chr 5:12

29:27 2 Chr 23:18

29:29 2 Chr 20:18

29:30 Ps 100:1; 106:12

29:31 2 Chr 13:9; Ex 35:5, 22

29:21 Throughout the Old Testament, the sacrifice was God's appointed way of approaching him and restoring a right relationship with him. The sin offering made by Hezekiah was one such sacrifice, given to ask God's forgiveness for unintentional sins. (For more information on why God required sacrifices and how they were carried out, see the notes in Leviticus 1.)

29:22 The blood sprinkled on the altar represented the innocence of the sacrificed animal taking the place of the guilt of the person making the offering. The animal died so the sinner could live. This ritual looked forward to the day when Jesus Christ, God's perfect Son, would sacrifice his innocent life on the cross in order that the sinful and guilty human race might be spared the punishment it deserves (Hebrews 10:1–14).

29:30 A seer was someone who received messages from God for the nation through visions or dreams.

32 The number of the burnt offerings which the assembly brought was 70 bulls, 100
rams, and 200 lambs; all these were for a burnt offering to the LORD.
33 The consecrated things were 600 bulls and 3,000 sheep.
34 But the priests were too few, so that they were unable to skin all the burnt offerings;
therefore their brothers the Levites helped them until the work was completed and until
the *other* priests had consecrated themselves. For the Levites were more conscientious
to consecrate themselves than the priests.
35 There *were* also many burnt offerings with the fat of the peace offerings and with
the libations for the burnt offerings. Thus the service of the house of the LORD was established *again*.
36 Then Hezekiah and all the people rejoiced over what God had prepared for the
people, because the thing came about suddenly.

29:34 2 Chr 35:11; 2 Chr 30:3

29:35 2 Chr 29:32; Lev 3:16; Num 15:5-10

All Israel Invited to the Passover

30 Now Hezekiah sent to all Israel and Judah and wrote letters also to Ephraim and
Manasseh, that they should come to the house of the LORD at Jerusalem to celebrate the Passover to the LORD God of Israel.
2 For the king and his princes and all the assembly in Jerusalem had decided to celebrate the Passover in the second month,
3 since they could not celebrate it at that time, because the priests had not consecrated themselves in sufficient numbers, nor had the people been gathered to Jerusalem.
4 Thus the thing was right in the sight of the king and all the assembly.
5 So they established a decree to circulate a proclamation throughout all Israel from
Beersheba even to Dan, that they should come to celebrate the Passover to the LORD
God of Israel at Jerusalem. For they had not celebrated *it* in great numbers as it was
prescribed.

30:2 Num 9:10, 11; 2 Chr 30:13, 15

30:3 2 Chr 29:17, 34

30:5 Judg 20:1

GREAT REVIVALS IN THE BIBLE

The Bible records several great revivals where people in great numbers turned to God and gave up their sinful ways of living. Each revival was characterized by a leader who recognized his nation's spiritual dryness. And in each case, the leader took action and was not afraid to make his desires known to the people.

Leader	*Reference*	*How the People Responded*
Moses	Exodus 32—33	Accepted God's laws and built the tabernacle
Samuel	1 Samuel 7:2–13	Promised to make God first in their lives by destroying their idols
David	2 Samuel 6	Brought the ark of the covenant to Jerusalem; praised God with singing and musical instruments
Jehoshaphat	2 Chronicles 20	Decided to trust in God alone to help them, and their discouragement turned to joy
Hezekiah	2 Chronicles 29—31	Purified the temple; got rid of idols; brought tithes to God's house
Josiah	2 Chronicles 34—35	Made a commitment to obey God's commands and remove sinful influences from their lives
Ezra	Ezra 9—10 Haggai 1	Stopped associating with those who caused them to compromise their faith; renewed their commitment to God's commands; began rebuilding the temple
Nehemiah (with Ezra)	Nehemiah 8—10	Fasted, confessed their sins, read God's Word publicly, and promised in writing to again serve God wholeheartedly

29:31 A thank offering, one type of peace offering (see Leviticus 7:12–15), was given as an expression of gratitude toward God. As a peace offering, it symbolized restored peace and fellowship with God.

30:1 The Passover celebration commemorated the time that God spared the lives of Israel's firstborn sons in Egypt. God had promised to send a plague to kill all the firstborn sons except in those homes where the blood of a slain lamb had been painted on the doorposts. The Israelites obeyed, and when the destroyer saw the blood, he "passed over" the house and did not harm anyone in it (Exodus 12:23). After this plague, Pharaoh freed the Israelites from slavery. This celebration was to be a yearly reminder of how God delivered his people. The careful preparations, both in the temple and for the feast, show that this was not a temporary or impulsive revival, but a deep-seated change of heart and life.

30:2–3 God's law had a provision that, under certain circumstances, the Passover could be celebrated one month later (Numbers 9:10–11).

6 The couriers went throughout all Israel and Judah with the letters from the hand of
the king and his princes, even according to the command of the king, saying, "O sons of
Israel, return to the LORD God of Abraham, Isaac and Israel, that He may return to
those of you who escaped *and* are left from the hand of the kings of Assyria.
7 "Do not be like your fathers and your brothers, who were unfaithful to the LORD
God of their fathers, so that He made them a horror, as you see.
8 "Now do not stiffen your neck like your fathers, but yield to the LORD and enter His
sanctuary which He has consecrated forever, and serve the LORD your God, that His
burning anger may turn away from you.
9 "For if you return to the LORD, your brothers and your sons *will find* compassion
before those who led them captive and will return to this land. For the LORD your God
is gracious and compassionate, and will not turn *His* face away from you if you return
to Him."
10 So the couriers passed from city to city through the country of Ephraim and Manasseh, and as far as Zebulun, but they laughed them to scorn and mocked them.
11 Nevertheless some men of Asher, Manasseh and Zebulun humbled themselves and
came to Jerusalem.
12 The hand of God was also on Judah to give them one heart to do what the king and
the princes commanded by the word of the LORD.

30:6 Esth 8:14; Job 9:25; Jer 51:31; 2 Chr 28:20
30:7 Ezek 20:13; 2 Chr 29:8
30:8 Ex 32:9; 2 Chr 29:10
30:9 Deut 30:2; Ex 34:6, 7; Mic 7:18
30:10 2 Chr 36:16
30:11 2 Chr 30:18, 21, 25
30:12 2 Cor 3:5; Phil 2:13; Heb 13:20, 21

Passover Reinstituted

13 Now many people were gathered at Jerusalem to celebrate the Feast of Unleavened
Bread in the second month, a very large assembly.
14 They arose and removed the altars which *were* in Jerusalem; they also removed all
the incense altars and cast *them* into the brook Kidron.
15 Then they slaughtered the Passover *lambs* on the fourteenth of the second month.
And the priests and Levites were ashamed of themselves, and consecrated themselves
and brought burnt offerings to the house of the LORD.
16 They stood at their stations after their custom, according to the law of Moses the
man of God; the priests sprinkled the blood *which they received* from the hand of the
Levites.
17 For *there were* many in the assembly who had not consecrated themselves; therefore, the Levites *were* over the slaughter of the Passover *lambs* for everyone who *was*
unclean, in order to consecrate *them* to the LORD.
18 For a multitude of the people, *even* many from Ephraim and Manasseh, Issachar
and Zebulun, had not purified themselves, yet they ate the Passover otherwise than prescribed. For Hezekiah prayed for them, saying, "May the good LORD pardon
19 everyone who prepares his heart to seek God, the LORD God of his fathers, though
not according to the purification *rules* of the sanctuary."
20 So the LORD heard Hezekiah and healed the people.

30:13 2 Chr 30:2
30:14 2 Chr 28:24; 2 Chr 29:16
30:15 2 Chr 30:2, 3; 2 Chr 29:34
30:16 2 Chr 35:10, 15
30:17 2 Chr 29:34
30:18 2 Chr 30:11, 25; Num 9:10; Ex 12:43-49
30:19 2 Chr 19:3
30:20 James 5:16

30:6–9 Hezekiah was a king dedicated to God and to the spiritual progress of the nation. He sent letters throughout Judah and Israel urging everyone to return to God. He told them not to be stubborn, but to submit to the Lord. To yield means to obey him first, yielding our bodies, minds, wills, and emotions to him. His Holy Spirit must guide and renew every part of us. Only then will we be able to temper our stubborn selfishness.

30:10 The northern kingdom of Israel had recently been conquered by Assyria, and most of the people had been carried away to foreign lands. Hezekiah sent a proclamation to the few people who remained, inviting them to come to the Passover (30:1), but most responded with scorn and ridicule. People may mock you when you try to promote spiritual renewal and growth. Are you prepared to be ridiculed for your faith? When it comes your way, do not waver. Stand strong in your faith, as Hezekiah did, and God will honor you.

30:11 These people invited to the Passover scorned Hezekiah's messengers, but some accepted the invitation. Our efforts to tell others about God often meet with similar reactions. Many people will laugh at an invitation to accept Christ. But this must not stop us from reaching out. If you know and understand that rejecting the gospel is common, you can guard against feelings of personal rejection. Remember that the Holy Spirit convicts and convinces. Our task is to invite others to consider God's actions, his claims, and his promises.

30:14 Just as the priests had consecrated the temple (29:4–5), so the people cleared the city of pagan idols and then consecrated themselves to prepare for worship (30:17–19). Even the good kings of Judah found it difficult to get rid of the pagan idols and altars in the high places (2 Kings 14:4; 2 Chronicles 20:33). Finally Hezekiah, with the help of his people, completed this task.

30:15 The people were so zealous to celebrate the Passover and bring offerings to the temple that the priests and Levites were ashamed they did not share the same enthusiasm. The zeal of common people's faith motivated the ministers to take action. The devoted faith of laypersons today should motivate professional church staff to rekindle their enthusiasm for God's work. Laypersons should never be shut out of church government or decision making. The church needs their good examples of faith.

30:21 Ex 12:15, 13:6

21 The sons of Israel present in Jerusalem celebrated the Feast of Unleavened Bread *for* seven days with great joy, and the Levites and the priests praised the LORD day after day with loud instruments to the LORD.

30:22 2 Chr 32:6; Ezra 10:11

22 Then Hezekiah spoke encouragingly to all the Levites who showed good insight *in the things* of the LORD. So they ate for the appointed seven days, sacrificing peace offerings and giving thanks to the LORD God of their fathers.

30:23 1 Kin 8:65

23 Then the whole assembly decided to celebrate *the feast* another seven days, so they celebrated the seven days with joy.

30:24 2 Chr 35:7, 8; 2 Chr 29:34; 30:3

24 For Hezekiah king of Judah had contributed to the assembly 1,000 bulls and 7,000 sheep, and the princes had contributed to the assembly 1,000 bulls and 10,000 sheep; and a large number of priests consecrated themselves.

30:25 2 Chr 30:11, 18

25 All the assembly of Judah rejoiced, with the priests and the Levites and all the assembly that came from Israel, both the sojourners who came from the land of Israel and those living in Judah.

30:26 2 Chr 7:8-10

26 So there was great joy in Jerusalem, because there was nothing like this in Jerusalem since the days of Solomon the son of David, king of Israel.

30:27 2 Chr 23:18; Num 6:23; Deut 26:15; Ps 68:5

27 Then the Levitical priests arose and blessed the people; and their voice was heard and their prayer came to His holy dwelling place, to heaven.

Idols Are Destroyed

31:1 2 Kin 18:4

31 Now when all this was finished, all Israel who were present went out to the cities of Judah, broke the pillars in pieces, cut down the [12]Asherim and pulled down the high places and the altars throughout all Judah and Benjamin, as well as in Ephraim and Manasseh, until they had destroyed them all. Then all the sons of Israel returned to their cities, each to his possession.

31:2 1 Chr 24:1; 1 Chr 23:28-31

2 And Hezekiah appointed the divisions of the priests and the Levites by their divisions, each according to his service, *both* the priests and the Levites, for burnt offerings and for peace offerings, to minister and to give thanks and to praise in the gates of the camp of the LORD.

Reforms Continued

31:3 2 Chr 35:7; Num 28:1-29:40

3 *He* also *appointed* the king's portion of his goods for the burnt offerings, *namely,* for the morning and evening burnt offerings, and the burnt offerings for the sabbaths and for the new moons and for the fixed festivals, as it is written in the law of the LORD.

31:4 Num 18:8; Mal 2:7

4 Also he commanded the people who lived in Jerusalem to give the portion due to the priests and the Levites, that they might devote themselves to the law of the LORD.

31:5 Neh 13:12

5 As soon as the order spread, the sons of Israel provided in abundance the first fruits of grain, new wine, oil, honey and of all the produce of the field; and they brought in abundantly the tithe of all.

31:6 Lev 27:30; Deut 14:28

6 The sons of Israel and Judah who lived in the cities of Judah also brought in the tithe of oxen and sheep, and the tithe of sacred gifts which were consecrated to the LORD their God, and placed *them* in heaps.

7 In the third month they began to make the heaps, and finished *them* by the seventh month.

12 I.e. wooden symbols of a female deity

30:22 One important purpose of the peace offering was to express gratitude to God for health or for safety in times of crisis.

30:26 It had been more than 200 years since there had been such a celebration in Jerusalem.

31:1ff Why was idol worship so bad? The Israelites had access to the one true God, but they constantly fell into worshiping lifeless idols made of wood or stone. They put aside worshiping the Creator in order to worship the creation. We are just as guilty when God no longer holds first place in our lives. When we think more about wealth, pleasure, prestige, or material possessions than about God, we are actually worshiping them as gods. Because of idol worship, the people of Judah were eventually sent into captivity in foreign lands (36:14–17). We may not be sent into captivity, but discipline awaits all those who continually put earthly desires above spiritual priorities.

31:2–21 The priests had not been supported by the government during the evil kings' reigns. Now that the temple was repaired, Hezekiah organized the priests and resumed the work of the temple according to a plan originally set up by David (1 Chronicles 23:6–23; 24:3–19).

31:4–8 Hezekiah reinstated the practice of tithing—giving a tenth of one's income to the priests and Levites so they could be free to serve God and minister to the people. The people responded immediately and generously. God's work needs the support of God's people. Does God receive a regular percentage of your income? Generosity makes our giving delightful to us and to God (2 Corinthians 8; 9). How different the church would be today if all believers consistently followed this pattern.

8 When Hezekiah and the rulers came and saw the heaps, they blessed the LORD and
His people Israel.
9 Then Hezekiah questioned the priests and the Levites concerning the heaps.
10 Azariah the chief priest of the house of Zadok said to him, "Since the contributions
began to be brought into the house of the LORD, we have had enough to eat with plenty
left over, for the LORD has blessed His people, and this great quantity is left over."
11 Then Hezekiah commanded *them* to prepare rooms in the house of the LORD, and
they prepared *them.*
12 They faithfully brought in the contributions and the tithes and the consecrated things;
and Conaniah the Levite *was* the officer in charge of them and his brother Shimei *was*
second.
13 Jehiel, Azaziah, Nahath, Asahel, Jerimoth, Jozabad, Eliel, Ismachiah, Mahath and
Benaiah *were* overseers under the authority of Conaniah and Shimei his brother by the
appointment of King Hezekiah, and Azariah *was* the *chief* officer of the house of God.
14 Kore the son of Imnah the Levite, the keeper of the eastern *gate, was* over the freewill offerings of God, to apportion the contributions for the LORD and the most holy
things.
15 Under his authority *were* Eden, Miniamin, Jeshua, Shemaiah, Amariah and Secaniah in the cities of the priests, to distribute faithfully *their portions* to their brothers by
divisions, whether great or small,
16 without regard to their genealogical enrollment, to the males from thirty years old
and upward—everyone who entered the house of the LORD for his daily obligations—
for their work in their duties according to their divisions;
17 as well as the priests who were enrolled genealogically according to their fathers'
households, and the Levites from twenty years old and upwards, by their duties *and* their
divisions.
18 The genealogical enrollment *included* all their little children, their wives, their sons
and their daughters, for the whole assembly, for they consecrated themselves faithfully
in holiness.
19 Also for the sons of Aaron the priests *who were* in the pasture lands of their cities,
or in each and every city, *there were* men who were designated by name to distribute
portions to every male among the priests and to everyone genealogically enrolled among
the Levites.
20 Thus Hezekiah did throughout all Judah; and he did what *was* good, right and true
before the LORD his God.
21 Every work which he began in the service of the house of God in law and in commandment, seeking his God, he did with all his heart and prospered.

31:8 Deut 33:29; Ps 33:12; 144:15
31:10 1 Chr 6:8, 9; Mal 3:10
31:11 1 Kin 6:5, 8
31:12 2 Chr 35:9
31:13 2 Chr 31:10
31:15 2 Chr 29:12; Josh 21:9-19
31:16 1 Chr 23:3; Ezra 3:4
31:17 1 Chr 23:24
31:19 Lev 25:34; Num 35:2-5; 2 Chr 31:12-15
31:20 2 Kin 20:3; 22:2
31:21 Deut 29:9; Prov 3:9, 10

Sennacherib Invades Judah

32 After these acts of faithfulness Sennacherib king of Assyria came and invaded Judah and besieged the fortified cities, and thought to break into them for himself.
2 Now when Hezekiah saw that Sennacherib had come and that he intended to make
war on Jerusalem,
3 he decided with his officers and his warriors to cut off the *supply of* water from the
springs which *were* outside the city, and they helped him.

32:1 2 Kin 18:13-19, 37; Is 36:1-37:38

31:20–21 Because Hezekiah did "what was good, right and true before the LORD," he led the people of Judah in spiritual renewal. His actions serve as a model of renewal for us: (1) He remembered God's compassion (30:9); (2) he kept going despite ridicule (30:10); (3) he aggressively removed evil influences from his life (30:14; 31:1); (4) he interceded for the people, asking for the Lord's pardon (30:15–20); (5) he was open to spontaneity in worship (30:23); (6) he contributed generously to God's work (31:3). If any of these are lacking in your life, consider how they might apply, and renew your commitment to God.

32:1 Assyria was a great empire by Hezekiah's time, controlling most of the Middle East. From a small strip of land located in present-day Iran and Iraq, it began to establish its power under Ashurnasirpal II (883–859 B.C.) and his son Shalmaneser III (859–824). Under Tiglath-pileser III (745–727), Assyria's boundaries extended to the borders of Israel, making it one of the largest empires in ancient history. Shalmaneser V destroyed the northern kingdom in 722, and his grandson, Sennacherib (705–681), tried to bring Judah, the southern kingdom, under his control. Less than a century later, Assyria would lie in ruins (612).

32:1 Sennacherib wanted to "break into them for himself" so he could force the cities to pay tribute. Forcing captured cities to pay tribute was a way for kings to build their income base. Often Assyria would require an oath of allegiance from a country, including the promise to pay taxes in the form of livestock, wine, battle equipment (horses, chariots, weapons), gold, silver, and anything else that pleased the invading king. Tribute was more important to Assyria than captives because captives cost money. Thus captives were taken only in cases of extreme rebellion or to repopulate cities that had been destroyed.

32:1ff When Hezekiah was confronted with the frightening prospect of an Assyrian invasion, he made two important decisions. He

32:4 2 Kin 20:20; 2 Chr 32:30

4 So many people assembled and stopped up all the springs and the stream which flowed through the region, saying, "Why should the kings of Assyria come and find abundant water?"

32:5 2 Chr 25:23; 2 Kin 25:4; 1 Kin 9:24

5 And he took courage and rebuilt all the wall that had been broken down and erected towers on it, and *built* another outside wall and strengthened the Millo *in* the city of David, and made weapons and shields in great number.

32:6 2 Chr 30:22

6 He appointed military officers over the people and gathered them to him in the square at the city gate, and spoke encouragingly to them, saying,

32:7 1 Chr 22:13; 2 Kin 6:16

7 "Be strong and courageous, do not fear or be dismayed because of the king of Assyria nor because of all the horde that is with him; for the one with us is greater than the one with him.

32:8 Jer 17:5; 2 Chr 20:17

8 "With him is *only* an arm of flesh, but with us is the LORD our God to help us and to fight our battles." And the people relied on the words of Hezekiah king of Judah.

Sennacherib Undermines Hezekiah

32:9 2 Kin 18:17

9 After this Sennacherib king of Assyria sent his servants to Jerusalem while he *was* besieging Lachish with all his forces with him, against Hezekiah king of Judah and against all Judah who *were* at Jerusalem, saying,

10 "Thus says Sennacherib king of Assyria, 'On what are you trusting that you are remaining in Jerusalem under siege?

11 'Is not Hezekiah misleading you to give yourselves over to die by hunger and by thirst, saying, "The LORD our God will deliver us from the hand of the king of Assyria"?

32:12 2 Chr 31:1

12 'Has not the same Hezekiah taken away His high places and His altars, and said to Judah and Jerusalem, "You shall worship before one altar, and on it you shall burn incense"?

32:13 2 Kin 18:33-35

13 'Do you not know what I and my fathers have done to all the peoples of the lands? Were the gods of the nations of the lands able at all to deliver their land from my hand?

32:14 Is 10:9-11

14 'Who *was there* among all the gods of those nations which my fathers utterly destroyed who could deliver his people out of my hand, that your God should be able to deliver you from my hand?

32:15 Ex 5:2; Is 36:18-20; Dan 3:15

15 'Now therefore, do not let Hezekiah deceive you or mislead you like this, and do not believe him, for no god of any nation or kingdom was able to deliver his people from my hand or from the hand of my fathers. How much less will your God deliver you from my hand?' "

16 His servants spoke further against the LORD God and against His servant Hezekiah.

32:17 2 Chr 32:14

17 He also wrote letters to insult the LORD God of Israel, and to speak against Him, saying, "As the gods of the nations of the lands have not delivered their people from my hand, so the God of Hezekiah will not deliver His people from my hand."

---

did everything he could to deal with the situation, and he trusted God for the outcome. That is exactly what we must do when faced with difficult or frightening situations. Take all the steps you possibly can to solve the problem or improve the situation. But also commit the situation to God in prayer, trusting him for the solution.

32:3–4 Cities had to be built near reliable water sources. Natural springs were some of Jerusalem's major sources of water. In a brilliant military move, Hezekiah plugged the springs outside the city and channeled the water through an underground tunnel (32:30); therefore, Jerusalem would have water even through a long siege. Hezekiah's tunnel has been discovered along with an inscription describing how it was built: two groups of workers started digging underground, one in Jerusalem and one at the Gihon spring, and they met in the middle.

32:7–8 Hezekiah could see with eyes of faith. The number of his opponents meant nothing as long as he was on the Lord's side. Victory is " 'not by might nor by power, but by My Spirit,' says the LORD of hosts" (Zechariah 4:6). Hezekiah could confidently encourage his men because he had no doubt about where he stood with God. Are you on the Lord's side? You may never face an enemy army, but the battles you face every day can be won with God's strength.

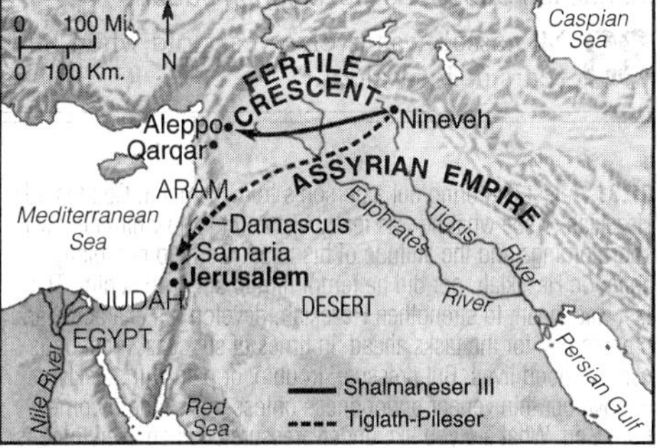

THE ASSYRIAN EMPIRE The mighty Assyrian empire extended from the Persian Gulf, across the Fertile Crescent, and south to Egypt. Shalmaneser III extended the empire toward the Mediterranean Sea by conquering cities as far west as Qarqar. Tiglath-pileser extended the empire south into Aram, Israel, Judah, and Philistia. It was Shalmaneser V who destroyed Samaria, Israel's capital.

18 They called this out with a loud voice in the language of Judah to the people of **32:18**
Jerusalem who were on the wall, to frighten and terrify them, so that they might take the 2 Kin 18:28
city.
19 They spoke of the God of Jerusalem as of the gods of the peoples of the earth, the **32:19**
work of men's hands. Ps 115:4-8

Hezekiah's Prayer Is Answered

20 But King Hezekiah and Isaiah the prophet, the son of Amoz, prayed about this and
cried out to heaven.
21 And the LORD sent an angel who destroyed every mighty warrior, commander and
officer in the camp of the king of Assyria. So he returned in shame to his own land. And
when he had entered the temple of his god, some of his own children killed him there
with the sword.
22 So the LORD saved Hezekiah and the inhabitants of Jerusalem from the hand of **32:22**
Sennacherib the king of Assyria and from the hand of all *others,* and guided them on Is 31:5
every side.
23 And many were bringing gifts to the LORD at Jerusalem and choice presents to **32:23**
Hezekiah king of Judah, so that he was exalted in the sight of all nations thereafter. 2 Sam 8:10; 2 Chr 1:1
24 In those days Hezekiah became mortally ill; and he prayed to the LORD, and the
LORD spoke to him and gave him a sign. **32:24** 2 Kin 20:1-11; Is
25 But Hezekiah gave no return for the benefit he received, because his heart was proud; 38:1-8
therefore wrath came on him and on Judah and Jerusalem. **32:25**
26 However, Hezekiah humbled the pride of his heart, both he and the inhabitants of 2 Chr 26:16; 32:31; 2 Chr 24:18
Jerusalem, so that the wrath of the LORD did not come on them in the days of Hezekiah.
27 Now Hezekiah had immense riches and honor; and he made for himself treasuries **32:26** Jer 26:18, 19
for silver, gold, precious stones, spices, shields and all kinds of valuable articles,
28 storehouses also for the produce of grain, wine and oil, pens for all kinds of cattle
and sheepfolds for the flocks.
29 He made cities for himself and acquired flocks and herds in abundance, for God **32:29**
had given him very great wealth. 1 Chr 29:12
30 It was Hezekiah who stopped the upper outlet of the waters of Gihon and directed **32:30**
them to the west side of the city of David. And Hezekiah prospered in all that he did. 2 Kin 20:20; 1 Kin 1:33
31 Even *in the matter of* the envoys of the rulers of Babylon, who sent to him to inquire
of the wonder that had happened in the land, God left him *alone only* to test him, that **32:31** 2 Kin 20:12; Is 39:1;
He might know all that was in his heart. 2 Chr 32:24; Is 38:7,
32 Now the rest of the acts of Hezekiah and his deeds of devotion, behold, they are 8; Deut 8:16
written in the vision of Isaiah the prophet, the son of Amoz, in the Book of the Kings of
Judah and Israel.
33 So Hezekiah slept with his fathers, and they buried him in the upper section of the **32:33**
tombs of the sons of David; and all Judah and the inhabitants of Jerusalem honored him Ps 112:6; Prov 10:7
at his death. And his son Manasseh became king in his place.

Manasseh Succeeds Hezekiah in Judah

33 Manasseh was twelve years old when he became king, and he reigned fifty-five **33:1**
years in Jerusalem. 2 Kin 21:1-9

32:31 A test can bring out a person's true character. God tested Hezekiah to see what he was really like and to show him his own shortcomings and the attitude of his heart. God did not totally abandon Hezekiah, nor did he tempt him to sin or trick him. The test was meant to strengthen Hezekiah, develop his character, and prepare him for the tasks ahead. In times of success, most of us can live good lives. But pressure, trouble, or pain will quickly remove our thin veneer of goodness unless our strength comes from God. What are you like under pressure or when everything is going wrong? Do you give in or turn to God? Those who are consistently in touch with God don't have to worry about what pressure may reveal about them.

32:31 Babylon was slowly and quietly rising to become a world power. At the same time, the Assyrian empire was slowly declining due to internal strife and a succession of weak kings. When Assyria was finally crushed in 612 B.C., Babylon under Nebuchadnezzar moved into its place of prominence. (For more information on Babylon, see the note on 2 Kings 20:14.)

32:31 Why did God leave Hezekiah to himself? After Hezekiah was healed of his sickness, he developed excessive pride. When envoys came to inquire about his miraculous healing, God stepped back to see how Hezekiah would respond. Unfortunately, Hezekiah's actions revealed his runaway pride. He pointed to his own accomplishments rather than to God (see 2 Kings 20:12–19). Pride is any attitude that elevates our effort or abilities above God's, or treats with disdain his work in us. It causes us to congratulate ourselves for our successes and to look down on other people. God does not object to self-confidence, healthy self-esteem, or good feelings about our accomplishments. He objects to the foolish attitude of taking full credit for what he has done or for setting ourselves up as superior to others.

33:2 2 Chr 28:3; Jer 15:4
33:3 2 Chr 31:1; Deut 16:21; 2 Kin 23:5, 6
33:4 2 Chr 28:24; 2 Sam 7:13; 2 Chr 7:16
33:5 2 Chr 4:9
33:6 2 Chr 28:3; Lev 19:31; 20:27
33:7 2 Chr 33:15; 1 Kin 9:3-5; 2 Chr 7:16; 33:4
33:8 2 Sam 7:10
33:10 Neh 9:29; Jer 25:4
33:11 Deut 28:36; 2 Chr 36:6
33:12 Ps 118:5; 120:1; 130:1, 2; 2 Chr 32:26
33:13 1 Chr 5:20; Ezra 8:23; Dan 4:32

2 He did evil in the sight of the LORD according to the abominations of the nations
whom the LORD dispossessed before the sons of Israel.
3 For he rebuilt the high places which Hezekiah his father had broken down; he also
erected altars for the Baals and made [13]Asherim, and worshiped all the host of heaven
and served them.
4 He built altars in the house of the LORD of which the LORD had said, "My name
shall be in Jerusalem forever."
5 For he built altars for all the host of heaven in the two courts of the house of the
LORD.
6 He made his sons pass through the fire in the valley of Ben-hinnom; and he practiced witchcraft, used divination, practiced sorcery and dealt with mediums and spiritists. He did much evil in the sight of the LORD, provoking Him *to anger.*
7 Then he put the carved image of the idol which he had made in the house of God,
of which God had said to David and to Solomon his son, "In this house and in Jerusalem, which I have chosen from all the tribes of Israel, I will put My name forever;
8 and I will not again remove the foot of Israel from the land which I have appointed
for your fathers, if only they will observe to do all that I have commanded them according to all the law, the statutes and the ordinances *given* through Moses."
9 Thus Manasseh misled Judah and the inhabitants of Jerusalem to do more evil than
the nations whom the LORD destroyed before the sons of Israel.

Manasseh's Idolatry Rebuked

10 The LORD spoke to Manasseh and his people, but they paid no attention.
11 Therefore the LORD brought the commanders of the army of the king of Assyria
against them, and they captured Manasseh with [14]hooks, bound him with bronze *chains*
and took him to Babylon.
12 When he was in distress, he entreated the LORD his God and humbled himself greatly
before the God of his fathers.
13 When he prayed to Him, He was moved by his entreaty and heard his supplication,

13 I.e. wooden symbols of a female deity **14** I.e. thongs put through the nose

THE DAVIDIC DYNASTY

The Lord promised David that his kingdom would endure and his throne would be established forever (2 Samuel 7:16). As a partial fulfillment of this promise, David and his descendants ruled Judah for over 400 years. Jesus Christ was a direct descendant of David, and was the ultimate fulfillment of this promise (Acts 2:22–36).

David (40 years, 1 Chr. 10—29)	Uzziah (Azariah) (52 years, 2 Chr. 26)
Solomon (40 years, 2 Chr. 1—9)	Jotham (16 years, 2 Chr. 27)
Rehoboam (17 years, 2 Chr. 10—12)	Ahaz (16 years, 2 Chr. 28)
Abijah (3 years, 2 Chr. 13)	Hezekiah (29 years, 2 Chr. 29—32)
Asa (41 years, 2 Chr. 14—16)	Manasseh (55 years, 2 Chr. 33:1–20)
Jehoshaphat (25 years, 2 Chr. 17—20)	Amon (2 years, 2 Chr. 33:21–25)
Jehoram (8 years, 2 Chr. 21)	Josiah (31 years, 2 Chr. 34—35)
Ahaziah (1 year, 2 Chr. 22:1–9)	Jehoahaz (3 months, 2 Chr. 36:1–4)
Athaliah (6 years, 2 Chr. 22:10—23:21)	Jehoiakim (11 years, 2 Chr. 36:5–8)
Joash (40 years, 2 Chr. 24)	Jehoiachin (3 months, 2 Chr. 36:9–10)
Amaziah (29 years, 2 Chr. 25)	Zedekiah (11 years, 2 Chr. 36:11–16)

33:6 Sorcery is using power gained from evil spirits. Divination is predicting the future through omens.

33:11 Between 652 and 648 B.C., the city of Babylon rebelled against Assyria. The rebellion was crushed, but Assyria may have suspected that Manasseh supported it. That may explain why Manasseh was taken to Babylon for trial rather than to the Assyrian capital of Nineveh.

33:12–13 In a list of corrupt kings, Manasseh would rank near the

and brought him again to Jerusalem to his kingdom. Then Manasseh knew that the LORD
was God.
14 Now after this he built the outer wall of the city of David on the west side of Gihon,
in the valley, even to the entrance of the Fish Gate; and he encircled the Ophel *with it*
and made it very high. Then he put army commanders in all the fortified cities of Judah.
15 He also removed the foreign gods and the idol from the house of the LORD, as well
as all the altars which he had built on the mountain of the house of the LORD and in
Jerusalem, and he threw *them* outside the city.
16 He set up the altar of the LORD and sacrificed peace offerings and thank offerings
on it; and he ordered Judah to serve the LORD God of Israel.
17 Nevertheless the people still sacrificed in the high places, *although* only to the LORD
their God.
18 Now the rest of the acts of Manasseh even his prayer to his God, and the words of
the seers who spoke to him in the name of the LORD God of Israel, behold, they are
among the records of the kings of Israel.
19 His prayer also and *how God* was entreated by him, and all his sin, his unfaithfulness, and the sites on which he built high places and erected the Asherim and the carved
images, before he humbled himself, behold, they are written in the records of the Hozai.
20 So Manasseh slept with his fathers, and they buried him in his own house. And Amon
his son became king in his place.

33:14 1 Kin 1:33; Neh 3:3; 2 Chr 27:3
33:15 2 Chr 33:3-7
33:16 Lev 7:11-18
33:17 2 Chr 32:12
33:18 2 Chr 33:12, 13; 2 Chr 33:10; 2 Chr 21:2
33:19 2 Chr 33:13; 2 Chr 33:3

Amon Becomes King in Judah

21 Amon *was* twenty-two years old when he became king, and he reigned two years in
Jerusalem.
22 He did evil in the sight of the LORD as Manasseh his father had done, and Amon sacrificed to all the carved images which his father Manasseh had made, and he served them.
23 Moreover, he did not humble himself before the LORD as his father Manasseh had
done, but Amon multiplied guilt.
24 Finally his servants conspired against him and put him to death in his own house.
25 But the people of the land killed all the conspirators against King Amon, and the
people of the land made Josiah his son king in his place.

33:21 2 Kin 21:19-24
33:22 2 Chr 33:2-7; 2 Chr 34:3, 4
33:23 2 Chr 33:12, 19
33:24 2 Chr 25:27

Josiah Succeeds Amon in Judah

34 Josiah *was* eight years old when he became king, and he reigned thirty-one years
in Jerusalem.
2 He did right in the sight of the LORD, and walked in the ways of his father David
and did not turn aside to the right or to the left.
3 For in the eighth year of his reign while he was still a youth, he began to seek the
God of his father David; and in the twelfth year he began to purge Judah and Jerusalem
of the high places, the Asherim, the carved images and the molten images.
4 They tore down the altars of the Baals in his presence, and the incense altars that
were high above them he chopped down; also the Asherim, the carved images and the
molten images he broke in pieces and ground to powder and scattered *it* on the graves
of those who had sacrificed to them.
5 Then he burned the bones of the priests on their altars and purged Judah and Jerusalem.
6 In the cities of Manasseh, Ephraim, Simeon, even as far as Naphtali, in their surrounding ruins,

34:1 2 Kin 22:1, 2; Jer 1:2; 3:6
34:2 2 Chr 29:2
34:3 2 Chr 15:2; Prov 8:17; 1 Kin 13:2; 2 Chr 33:22
34:4 2 Kin 23:4, 5, 11; Ex 32:20
34:5 1 Kin 13:2; 2 Kin 23:20
34:6 2 Kin 23:15, 19

---

top. His life was a catalog of evil deeds including idol worship, sacrificing his own children, and temple desecration. Eventually, however, he realized his sins and cried out to God for forgiveness. And God listened. If God can forgive Manasseh, surely he can forgive anyone. Are you burdened by overpowering guilt? Do you doubt that anyone could forgive what you have done? Take heart—until death, no one is beyond the reach of God's forgiveness.

33:17 Although the people worshiped God alone, they worshiped him in the wrong way. God had told them to make their sacrifices only in certain places (Deuteronomy 12:13–14). This kept them from changing their way of worship and protected them against the dangerous influence of pagan religious practices. Unfortunately, the people continued to use these places of worship, not realizing that (1) they were adopting practices God opposed, and (2) these places were against God's law. They were mixing pagan beliefs with worship of God. Blending religious ideas leads to confusion about who God really is. We must take care that subtle secular influences do not distort our worship practices.

34:1 Josiah's Profile is found in 2 Kings 24.

34:3 In Josiah's day, boys were considered men at age 12. By 16, Josiah understood the responsibility of his office. Even at this young age, he showed greater wisdom than many of the older kings who came before him because he had decided to seek the Lord God and his wisdom. Don't let your age disqualify you from serving God.

34:7 2 Chr 31:1

7 he also tore down the altars and beat the Asherim and the carved images into powder, and chopped down all the incense altars throughout the land of Israel. Then he
returned to Jerusalem.

Josiah Repairs the Temple

34:8 2 Kin 22:3-20; 2 Chr 18:25

8 Now in the eighteenth year of his reign, when he had purged the land and the house,
he sent Shaphan the son of Azaliah, and Maaseiah an official of the city, and Joah the
son of Joahaz the recorder, to repair the house of the LORD his God.

34:9 2 Chr 35:8; 2 Chr 30:10, 18

9 They came to Hilkiah the high priest and delivered the money that was brought into
the house of God, which the Levites, the doorkeepers, had collected from Manasseh and
Ephraim, and from all the remnant of Israel, and from all Judah and Benjamin and the
inhabitants of Jerusalem.
10 Then they gave *it* into the hands of the workmen who had the oversight of the house
of the LORD, and the workmen who were working in the house of the LORD used it to
restore and repair the house.

34:11 2 Chr 33:4-7

11 They in turn gave *it* to the carpenters and to the builders to buy quarried stone and
timber for couplings and to make beams for the houses which the kings of Judah had let
go to ruin.

34:12 2 Kin 12:15; 1 Chr 25:1

12 The men did the work faithfully with foremen over them to supervise: Jahath and
Obadiah, the Levites of the sons of Merari, Zechariah and Meshullam of the sons of the
Kohathites, and the Levites, all who were skillful with musical instruments.

34:13 Neh 4:10

13 *They were* also over the burden bearers, and supervised all the workmen from job to
job; and *some* of the Levites *were* scribes and officials and gatekeepers.

MANASSEH

Even a brief outline of King Manasseh's evil sickens us, and we wonder how God could ever forgive him. Not only did he intentionally offend God by desecrating Solomon's temple with idols, but he also worshiped pagan gods and even sacrificed his children to them! Child sacrifice is a vile act of pagan idolatry, an act against both God and people. Such blatant sins require severe correction.

God showed justice to Manasseh in warning and punishing him. He showed mercy in responding to Manasseh's heartfelt repentance by forgiving and restoring him. Given the nature of Manasseh's rebellion, we are not surprised by God's punishment—defeat and exile at the hands of the Assyrians. But Manasseh's repentance and God's forgiveness are unexpected. Manasseh's life was changed. He was given a new start.

How far has God gone to get your attention? Have you ever, like Manasseh, come to your senses and cried out to God for help? Only your repentance and a prayer for a new attitude stand between you and God's complete forgiveness.

Strengths and accomplishments:
- Despite the bitter consequences of his sins, he learned from them
- Humbly repented of his sins before God

Weaknesses and mistakes:
- Challenged God's authority and was defeated
- Reversed many of the positive effects of his father Hezekiah's rule
- Sacrificed his children to idols

Lessons from his life:
- God will go a long way to get someone's attention
- Forgiveness is limited not by the amount of sin, but by our willingness to repent

Vital statistics:
- Where: Jerusalem
- Occupation: King of Judah
- Relatives: Father: Hezekiah. Mother: Hephzibah. Son: Amon

Key verses:
"When he was in distress, he entreated the LORD his God and humbled himself greatly before the God of his fathers. When he prayed to Him, He was moved by his entreaty and heard his supplication, and brought him again to Jerusalem to his kingdom. Then Manasseh knew that the LORD was God" (2 Chronicles 33:12–13).

Manasseh's story is told in 2 Kings 21:1-18 and 2 Chronicles 32:33—33:20. He is also mentioned in Jeremiah 15:4.

Hilkiah Discovers Lost Book of the Law

14 When they were bringing out the money which had been brought into the house of **34:14**
the LORD, Hilkiah the priest found the book of the law of the LORD *given* by Moses. 2 Chr 34:9
15 Hilkiah responded and said to Shaphan the scribe, "I have found the book of the
law in the house of the LORD." And Hilkiah gave the book to Shaphan.
16 Then Shaphan brought the book to the king and reported further word to the king,
saying, "Everything that was entrusted to your servants they are doing.
17 "They have also emptied out the money which was found in the house of the LORD,
and have delivered it into the hands of the supervisors and the workmen."
18 Moreover, Shaphan the scribe told the king saying, "Hilkiah the priest gave me a
book." And Shaphan read from it in the presence of the king.
19 When the king heard the words of the law, he tore his clothes. **34:19**
20 Then the king commanded Hilkiah, Ahikam the son of Shaphan, Abdon the son of Deut 28:3-68; Josh
Micah, Shaphan the scribe, and Asaiah the king's servant, saying, 7:6
21 "Go, inquire of the LORD for me and for those who are left in Israel and in Judah, **34:21**
concerning the words of the book which has been found; for great is the wrath of the 2 Chr 29:8
LORD which is poured out on us because our fathers have not observed the word of the
LORD, to do according to all that is written in this book."

Huldah, the Prophetess, Speaks

22 So Hilkiah and *those* whom the king had told went to Huldah the prophetess, the
wife of Shallum the son of Tokhath, the son of Hasrah, the keeper of the wardrobe (now
she lived in Jerusalem in the Second Quarter); and they spoke to her regarding this.
23 She said to them, "Thus says the LORD, the God of Israel, 'Tell the man who sent
you to Me,
24 thus says the LORD, "Behold, I am bringing evil on this place and on its inhabitants, **34:24**
even all the curses written in the book which they have read in the presence of the king 2 Chr 36:14-20;
of Judah. Deut 28:15-68
25 "Because they have forsaken Me and have burned incense to other gods, that they **34:25**
might provoke Me to anger with all the works of their hands; therefore My wrath will be 2 Chr 33:3
poured out on this place and it shall not be quenched." '
26 "But to the king of Judah who sent you to inquire of the LORD, thus you will say to
him, 'Thus says the LORD God of Israel *regarding* the words which you have heard,
27 "Because your heart was tender and you humbled yourself before God when you heard **34:27**
His words against this place and against its inhabitants, and *because* you humbled your- 2 Kin 22:19; 2 Chr
self before Me, tore your clothes and wept before Me, I truly have heard you," declares 12:7; 32:26
the LORD.
28 "Behold, I will gather you to your fathers and you shall be gathered to your grave in
peace, so your eyes will not see all the evil which I will bring on this place and on its
inhabitants." ' " And they brought back word to the king.
29 Then the king sent and gathered all the elders of Judah and Jerusalem. **34:29**
30 The king went up to the house of the LORD and all the men of Judah, the inhabi- 2 Kin 23:1-3
tants of Jerusalem, the priests, the Levites and all the people, from the greatest to the **34:30**
least; and he read in their hearing all the words of the book of the covenant which was Neh 8:1-3
found in the house of the LORD.

Josiah's Good Reign

34:31 2 Kin 11:14; 23:3; 2 Chr 30:16; 2 Chr 23:16; 29:10
31 Then the king stood in his place and made a covenant before the LORD to walk after

---

34:14–15 The book of the law of the Lord that Hilkiah found was probably the book of Deuteronomy that had been lost during the reigns of the evil kings. Now that it was found, Josiah realized that drastic changes had to be made in order to bring the nation back in line with God's commands. This account is also recorded in 2 Kings 22:8–13.

34:19 It is human nature to treat sin lightly—to make excuses, blame somebody else, or minimize the harm done. Not so with Josiah. He was so appalled at the people's neglect of the Law that he tore his clothing to express his grief. True understanding of our sins should lead to godly sorrow that "produces a repentance without regret, leading to salvation" (2 Corinthians 7:10). Are you always excusing your sin, blaming others, and pretending that it's not so bad? God does not take sin lightly, and he wants us to respond with true remorse as Josiah did.

the LORD, and to keep His commandments and His testimonies and His statutes with all
his heart and with all his soul, to perform the words of the covenant written in this book.
32 Moreover, he made all who were present in Jerusalem and Benjamin to stand *with*
him. So the inhabitants of Jerusalem did according to the covenant of God, the God of
their fathers.

34:33 2 Chr 34:3-7

33 Josiah removed all the abominations from all the lands belonging to the sons of Israel,
and made all who were present in Israel to serve the LORD their God. Throughout his
lifetime they did not turn from following the LORD God of their fathers.

The Passover Observed Again

35:1 2 Kin 23:21; Ex 12:6; Num 9:3

35:2 2 Chr 29:11

35:3 2 Chr 17:8, 9; Neh 8:7; 1 Chr 23:26

35 Then Josiah celebrated the Passover to the LORD in Jerusalem, and they slaughtered the Passover *animals* on the fourteenth *day* of the first month.
2 He set the priests in their offices and encouraged them in the service of the house
of the LORD.
3 He also said to the Levites who taught all Israel *and* who were holy to the LORD,
"Put the holy ark in the house which Solomon the son of David king of Israel built; it will
be a burden on *your* shoulders no longer. Now serve the LORD your God and His people
Israel.

35:4 1 Chr 9:10-13; 2 Chr 8:14

35:5 Ezra 6:18

4 "Prepare *yourselves* by your fathers' households in your divisions, according to the
writing of David king of Israel and according to the writing of his son Solomon.
5 "Moreover, stand in the holy place according to the sections of the fathers' households of your brethren the lay people, and according to the Levites, by division of a father's
household.

35:6 2 Chr 35:1; 2 Chr 29:5

6 "Now slaughter the Passover *animals,* sanctify yourselves and prepare for your brethren to do according to the word of the LORD by Moses."
7 Josiah contributed to the lay people, to all who were present, flocks of lambs and
young goats, all for the Passover offerings, numbering 30,000 plus 3,000 bulls; these were
from the king's possessions.

35:8 2 Chr 31:13

8 His officers also contributed a freewill offering to the people, the priests and the
Levites. Hilkiah and Zechariah and Jehiel, the officials of the house of God, gave to the
priests for the Passover offerings 2,600 *from the flocks* and 300 bulls.

35:9 2 Chr 31:12

35:10 2 Chr 35:5

35:11 2 Chr 35:1, 6; 2 Chr 29:22; 2 Chr 29:34

9 Conaniah also, and Shemaiah and Nethanel, his brothers, and Hashabiah and Jeiel
and Jozabad, the officers of the Levites, contributed to the Levites for the Passover offerings 5,000 *from the flocks* and 500 bulls.
10 So the service was prepared, and the priests stood at their stations and the Levites
by their divisions according to the king's command.
11 They slaughtered the Passover *animals,* and while the priests sprinkled the blood
received from their hand, the Levites skinned *them.*

THE BATTLE AT CARCHEMISH A world war was brewing in 609 B.C. when Pharaoh Neco of Egypt set out for the city of Carchemish to join the Assyrians in an attempt to defeat the Babylonians, who were rising to great power. Neco marched his armies through Judah, where King Josiah tried to stop him at Megiddo, but was killed. The battle began at Carchemish in 605 B.C., and the Egyptians and Assyrians were soundly defeated, chased to Hamath, and defeated again. Babylon was now the new world power.

34:31 When Josiah read the book that Hilkiah discovered (34:14), he responded with repentance and humility and promised to follow God's commands as written in the book. The Bible is God's Word to us, "living and active" (Hebrews 4:12), but we cannot know what God wants us to do if we do not read it. And even reading God's Word is not enough; we must be willing to do what it says. There is not much difference between the book hidden in the temple and the Bible hidden on the bookshelf. An unread Bible is as useless as a lost one.

35:3 In Moses' day, one of the duties of the Levites was to carry the ark of the covenant whenever Israel traveled. "Put the holy ark in the house which Solomon the son of David king of Israel built" implies that it may have been moved during the reigns of the previous evil kings, Manasseh and Amon. The ark was now permanently housed in the temple and would no longer be carried about in procession as it was in the wilderness. Josiah was telling the Levites that they were now free to take on other responsibilities (1 Chronicles 24).

12 Then they removed the burnt offerings that *they* might give them to the sections of
the fathers' households of the lay people to present to the LORD, as it is written in the
book of Moses. *They did* this also with the bulls.
13 So they roasted the Passover *animals* on the fire according to the ordinance, and
they boiled the holy things in pots, in kettles, in pans, and carried *them* speedily to all the
lay people.
14 Afterwards they prepared for themselves and for the priests, because the priests,
the sons of Aaron, *were* offering the burnt offerings and the fat until night; therefore the
Levites prepared for themselves and for the priests, the sons of Aaron.
15 The singers, the sons of Asaph, *were* also at their stations according to the command
of David, Asaph, Heman, and Jeduthun the king's seer; and the gatekeepers at each gate
did not have to depart from their service, because the Levites their brethren prepared
for them.
16 So all the service of the LORD was prepared on that day to celebrate the Passover,
and to offer burnt offerings on the altar of the LORD according to the command of King
Josiah.
17 Thus the sons of Israel who were present celebrated the Passover at that time, and
the Feast of Unleavened Bread seven days.
18 There had not been celebrated a Passover like it in Israel since the days of Samuel
the prophet; nor had any of the kings of Israel celebrated such a Passover as Josiah did
with the priests, the Levites, all Judah and Israel who were present, and the inhabitants
of Jerusalem.
19 In the eighteenth year of Josiah's reign this Passover was celebrated.

Josiah Dies in Battle

20 After all this, when Josiah had set the temple in order, Neco king of Egypt came up
to make war at Carchemish on the Euphrates, and Josiah went out to engage him.
21 But Neco sent messengers to him, saying, "What have we to do with each other,
O King of Judah? *I am* not *coming* against you today but against the house with which I
am at war, and God has ordered me to hurry. Stop for your own sake from *interfering
with* God who is with me, so that He will not destroy you."
22 However, Josiah would not turn away from him, but disguised himself in order to
make war with him; nor did he listen to the words of Neco from the mouth of God, but
came to make war on the plain of Megiddo.
23 The archers shot King Josiah, and the king said to his servants, "Take me away, for
I am badly wounded."
24 So his servants took him out of the chariot and carried him in the second chariot
which he had, and brought him to Jerusalem where he died and was buried in the tombs
of his fathers. All Judah and Jerusalem mourned for Josiah.
25 Then Jeremiah chanted a lament for Josiah. And all the male and female singers
speak about Josiah in their lamentations to this day. And they made them an ordinance
in Israel; behold, they are also written in the Lamentations.

35:13 Ex 12; Is 9; Lev 6:28
35:15 1 Chr 25:1; 1 Chr 26:12-19
35:17 Ex 12:1-20; 2 Chr 30:21
35:18 2 Kin 23:21; 2 Chr 30:5
35:20 2 Kin 23:29, 30; Is 10:9; Jer 46:2
35:21 2 Chr 25:19
35:22 2 Chr 18:29; 2 Chr 35:21; Judg 5:19
35:24 Zech 12:11
35:25 Jer 22:10; Lam 4:20

35:15 The temple gatekeepers, who were all Levites, guarded the four main entrances to the temple and opened the gates each morning. They also did other day-to-day chores such as cleaning and preparing the offerings for sacrifice and accounting for the gifts given to the temple. (For more on gatekeepers, see 1 Chronicles 26:1ff.)

35:17 The Feast of Unleavened Bread was a seven-day celebration beginning the day after Passover. Like Passover, it commemorated the exodus from Egypt. For seven days the people ate bread without yeast, just as their ancestors did while leaving Egypt because it could be made quickly in preparation for their swift departure (Exodus 12:14–20). This feast reminded the people that they had left slavery behind and had come to the land God promised them.

35:20 This event occurred in 609 B.C. Nineveh, the Assyrian capital, had been destroyed three years earlier by the Babylonians. The defeated Assyrians regrouped at Haran and Carchemish, but Babylon sent its army to destroy them once and for all. Pharaoh Neco, who wanted to make Egypt a world power, was worried about Babylon's growing strength, so he marched his army north through Judah to help the Assyrians at Carchemish. But King Josiah of Judah tried to prevent Neco from passing through his land on his way to Carchemish. Josiah was killed, and Judah became subject to Egypt. (Second Kings 23:25–30 helps explain the tragedy. Even though Josiah followed the Lord, God did not turn from his judgment on Judah because of Manasseh's sin and Israel's superficial repentance.) Neco went on to Carchemish and held off the Babylonians for four years, but in 605 he was soundly defeated, and Babylon moved into the spotlight as the dominant world power.

35:21–24 Josiah ignored Neco's message because of who Neco was—king of a pagan nation. The mistaken assumption that Neco could not be part of God's larger plan cost Josiah his life. While not everyone who claims to have a message from God really does, God's messages may come in unexpected ways. God had spoken to pagan kings in the past (Genesis 12:17–20; 20:3–7; see also Daniel 4:1–3). Don't let prejudice or false assumptions blind you to God's message.

35:25 Though Jeremiah recorded these laments for the death of Josiah, they are not the same as the book of Lamentations.

26 Now the rest of the acts of Josiah and his deeds of devotion as written in the law of
the LORD,
27 and his acts, first to last, behold, they are written in the Book of the Kings of Israel
and Judah.

3. Judah is exiled to Babylon

Jehoahaz, Jehoiakim, then Jehoiachin Rule

36:1 2 Kin 23:30-34; Jer 22:11

36 Then the people of the land took [15]Joahaz the son of Josiah, and made him king
in place of his father in Jerusalem.
2 Joahaz was twenty-three years old when he became king, and he reigned three
months in Jerusalem.
3 Then the king of Egypt deposed him at Jerusalem, and imposed on the land a fine
of one hundred talents of silver and one talent of gold.

36:4 Jer 22:10-12

4 The king of Egypt made Eliakim his brother king over Judah and Jerusalem, and
changed his name to Jehoiakim. But Neco took Joahaz his brother and brought him to
Egypt.

36:5 2 Kin 23:36, 37; Jer 22:13-19; 26:1; 35:1

5 Jehoiakim was twenty-five years old when he became king, and he reigned eleven
years in Jerusalem; and he did evil in the sight of the LORD his God.

36:6 2 Kin 24:1; Jer 25:1-9; 2 Chr 33:11

6 Nebuchadnezzar king of Babylon came up against him and bound him with bronze
chains to take him to Babylon.

36:7 2 Kin 24:13

7 Nebuchadnezzar also brought *some* of the articles of the house of the LORD to
Babylon and put them in his temple at Babylon.

36:8 2 Kin 24:5

8 Now the rest of the acts of Jehoiakim and the abominations which he did, and what
was found against him, behold, they are written in the Book of the Kings of Israel and
Judah. And Jehoiachin his son became king in his place.

36:9 2 Kin 24:8-17

9 Jehoiachin was eight years old when he became king, and he reigned three months
and ten days in Jerusalem, and he did evil in the sight of the LORD.

Captivity in Babylon Begun

36:10 2 Sam 11:1; Jer 22:25; 24:1; 29:1; Ezek 17:12; Jer 37:1

10 At the turn of the year King Nebuchadnezzar sent and brought him to Babylon with
the valuable articles of the house of the LORD, and he made his kinsman Zedekiah king
over Judah and Jerusalem.

Zedekiah Rules in Judah

36:11 2 Kin 24:18-20; Jer 27:1; 28:1; 52:1

11 Zedekiah was twenty-one years old when he became king, and he reigned eleven
years in Jerusalem.

36:12 2 Chr 33:23; Jer 21:3-7

12 He did evil in the sight of the LORD his God; he did not humble himself before Jeremiah the prophet who spoke for the LORD.

36:13 Jer 52:3; Ezek 17:15; 2 Chr 30:8

13 He also rebelled against King Nebuchadnezzar who had made him swear *allegiance*
by God. But he stiffened his neck and hardened his heart against turning to the LORD
God of Israel.
14 Furthermore, all the officials of the priests and the people were very unfaithful *following* all the abominations of the nations; and they defiled the house of the LORD which
He had sanctified in Jerusalem.

36:15 Jer 7:13; 25:3

15 The LORD, the God of their fathers, sent *word* to them again and again by His
messengers, because He had compassion on His people and on His dwelling place;

36:16 2 Chr 30:10; Jer 5:12, 13; Prov 1:24-32; Ezra 5:12

16 but they *continually* mocked the messengers of God, despised His words and scoffed
at His prophets, until the wrath of the LORD arose against His people, until there was
no remedy.

15 I.e. short form of Jehoahaz

36:6 Nebuchadnezzar was the son of the founder of the new Babylonian empire. In 605 B.C., the year he became king, Nebuchadnezzar won the battle of Carchemish. That loss crushed Assyria (see the note on 35:20). (For more information about Nebuchadnezzar, read his Profile in Daniel 5.)

36:9–10 In 2 Kings 24:8, Jehoiachin is listed as 18 years old. Many Hebrew manuscripts list him as eight years old. The age given in 2 Kings 24:8 is most likely accurate because he had wives at that time (see 2 Kings 24:15).

36:16 God warned Judah about its sin and continually restored the people to his favor, only to have them turn away. Eventually the situation was beyond remedy. Beware of harboring sin in your heart. The day will come when remedy is no longer possible and God's judgment replaces his mercy. Sin often repeated, but never repented of, invites disaster.

17 Therefore He brought up against them the king of the Chaldeans who slew their
young men with the sword in the house of their sanctuary, and had no compassion on
young man or virgin, old man or infirm; He gave *them* all into his hand.
18 All the articles of the house of God, great and small, and the treasures of the house
of the LORD, and the treasures of the king and of his officers, he brought *them* all to
Babylon.
19 Then they burned the house of God and broke down the wall of Jerusalem, and
burned all its fortified buildings with fire and destroyed all its valuable articles.
20 Those who had escaped from the sword he carried away to Babylon; and they were
servants to him and to his sons until the rule of the kingdom of Persia,
21 to fulfill the word of the LORD by the mouth of Jeremiah, until the land had enjoyed its sabbaths. All the days of its desolation it kept sabbath until seventy years were
complete.

36:17 2 Kin 25:1-7; Jer 21:1-10
36:18 2 Chr 36:7, 10
36:19 1 Kin 9:8; 2 Kin 25:9; Jer 52:13
36:20 2 Kin 25:11; Jer 27:7
36:21 Jer 29:10; Lev 26:34; Lev 25:4; Jer 25:11

Cyrus Permits Return

22 Now in the first year of Cyrus king of Persia—in order to fulfill the word of the LORD
by the mouth of Jeremiah—the LORD stirred up the spirit of Cyrus king of Persia, so
that he sent a proclamation throughout his kingdom, and also *put it* in writing, saying,
23 "Thus says Cyrus king of Persia, 'The LORD, the God of heaven, has given me all the
kingdoms of the earth, and He has appointed me to build Him a house in Jerusalem,
which is in Judah. Whoever there is among you of all His people, may the LORD his God
be with him, and let him go up!' "

36:22 Ezra 1:1-3; Jer 25:12; 29:10; Is 44:28

36:21 Leviticus 26:27–45 strikingly predicts the captivity, telling how God's people would be torn from their land for disobeying him. One of the laws they had ignored stated that one year in every seven the land should lie fallow, resting from producing crops (Exodus 23:10–11). The 70-year captivity allowed the land to rest, making up for all the years the Israelites had not observed this law. We know that God keeps all his promises—not only his promises of blessing, but also his promises of judgment.

36:22–23 Cyrus made this proclamation 48 years after the temple was destroyed (36:18–19), the year after he had conquered Babylon. The book of Ezra tells the story of this proclamation and the return of the exiles to Judah.

36:22–23 Second Chronicles focuses on the rise and fall of the worship of God as symbolized by the Jerusalem temple. David planned the temple; Solomon built it and then put on the greatest dedication service the world had ever seen. Worship in the temple was superbly organized.

But several evil kings defiled the temple and degraded worship so that the people revered idols more highly than God. Finally, King Nebuchadnezzar of Babylon destroyed the temple (36:19). The kings were gone, the temple was destroyed, and the people were removed. The nation was stripped to its very foundation. But fortunately there was a greater foundation—God himself. When everything in life seems stripped away from us, we too still have God—his Word, his presence, and his promises.

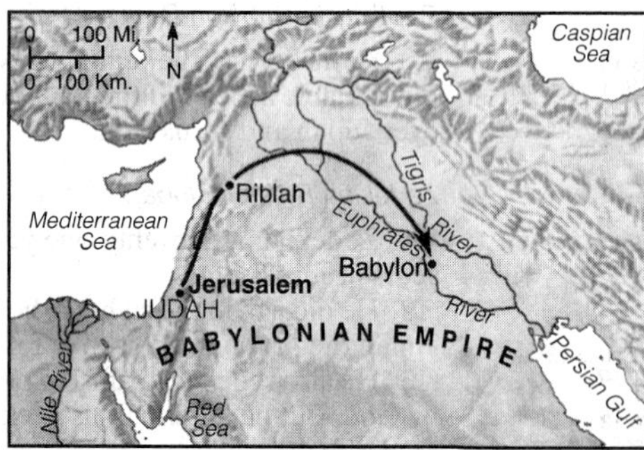

EXILE TO BABYLON Despite Judah's few good kings and timely reforms, the people never truly changed. Their evil continued, and finally God used the Babylonian empire, under Nebuchadnezzar, to conquer Judah, destroy Jerusalem, and take the people captive to Babylon.

NAMES OF GOD

Name of God	*Meaning*	*Reference*	*Significance*
Elohim	God	Genesis 1:1; Numbers 23:19; Psalm 19:1	Refers to God's power and might. He is the only supreme and true God.
Yahweh	The Lord	Genesis 2:4; Exodus 6:2–3	The proper name of the divine person.
El Elyon	God Most High	Genesis 14:17-20; Numbers 24:16; Psalm 7:17; Isaiah 14:13–14	He is above all gods; nothing in life is more sacred.
El Roi	God Who Sees	Genesis 16:12	God oversees all creation and the affairs of people.
El Shaddai	God Almighty	Genesis 17:1; Psalm 91:1	God is all-powerful.
Yahweh Yireh	The Lord will Provide	Genesis 22:13–14	God will provide our real needs.
Yahweh Nissi	The Lord is my Banner	Exodus 17:15	We should remember God for helping us.
Adonai	Lord	Deuteronomy 6:4	God alone is the head over all.
Yahweh Elohe Yisrae	LORD God of Israel	Judges 5:3; Psalm 58:5; Isaiah 17:6; Zephaniah 2:9	He is the God of the nation.
Yahweh Shalom	The Lord is Peace	Judges 6:24	God gives us peace, so we need not fear.
Quedosh Yisrael	Holy One of Israel	Isaiah 1:4	God is morally perfect.
Yahweh Sabaoth Isaiah 6:1-3	LORD of Hosts Host refers to armies but also to all the heavenly powers.	1 Samuel 1:3	God is our Savior and Protector.
El Olam	The Everlasting God	Isaiah 40:28-31	God is eternal. He will never die.
Yahweh Tsidkenu	The Lord is Our Righteousness	Jeremiah 23:6; 33:16	God is our standard for right behavior. He alone can make us righteous.
Yahweh Shammah	The Lord is There	Ezekiel 48:35	God is always present with us.
Attiq Yomin	Ancient of Days	Daniel 7:9; 13:12	God is the ultimate authority. He will one day judge all nations.

EZRA

Jerusalem destroyed; exiles go to Babylon 586 B.C.

Babylon overthrown by Cyrus 539

Exiles return to Jerusalem 538

Temple construction begins 536

Temple work halted 530

VITAL STATISTICS

PURPOSE:
To show God's faithfulness and the way he kept his promise to restore his people to their land

AUTHOR:
Not stated, but probably Ezra

DATE WRITTEN:
Around 450 B.C., recording events from about 538–450 B.C. (omitting 516–458 B.C.); possibly begun earlier in Babylon and finished in Jerusalem

SETTING:
Ezra follows 2 Chronicles as a history of the Jewish people, recording their return to the land after the captivity.

KEY VERSES:
"The sons of Israel who returned from exile and all those who had separated themselves from the impurity of the nations of the land to join them, to seek the LORD God of Israel, ate the Passover. And they observed the Feast of Unleavened Bread seven days with joy, for the LORD had caused them to rejoice, and had turned the heart of the king of Assyria toward them to encourage them in the work of the house of God, the God of Israel" (6:21–22).

KEY PEOPLE:
Cyrus, Zerubbabel, Haggai, Zechariah, Darius I, Artaxerxes I, Ezra

KEY PLACES:
Babylon, Jerusalem

SPECIAL FEATURES:
Ezra and Nehemiah were one book in the Hebrew Bible, and, with Esther, they comprise the post-captivity historical books. The post-captivity prophetic books are Haggai, Zechariah, and Malachi. Haggai and Zechariah should be studied with Ezra because they prophesied during the period of the reconstruction.

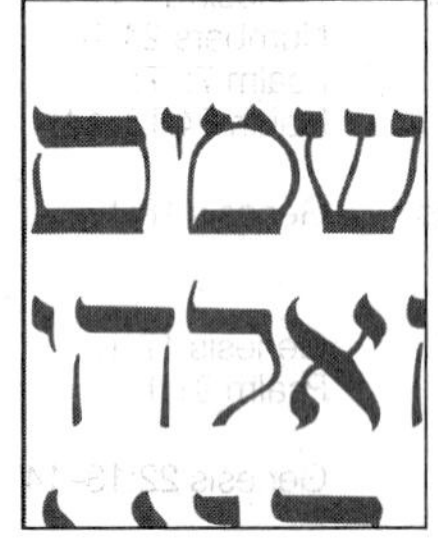

NAME the truly great men and women of your lifetime. Celebrities, including politicians, war heroes, sports figures, and maybe your parents and special friends come to mind. You remember them because of certain acts or character qualities. Now, name some Biblical heroes—figures etched in your mind through countless sermons and church school lessons. This list undoubtedly includes many who served God faithfully and courageously. Does your list include Ezra? Far from being well known, this unheralded man of God deserves to be mentioned in any discussion of greatness.

Ezra was a priest, a scribe, and a great leader. His name means "help," and his whole life was dedicated to serving God and God's people. Tradition says that Ezra wrote most of 1 and 2 Chronicles, Ezra, Nehemiah, and Psalm 119 and that he led the council of 120 men who formed the Old Testament canon. The narrative of the book of Ezra is centered on God and his promise that the Jews would return to their land, as prophesied by Jeremiah (see the third note on 1:1). This message formed the core of Ezra's life. The last half of the book gives a very personal glimpse of Ezra. His knowledge of Scripture and his God-given wisdom were so obvious to the king that he appointed Ezra to lead the second emigration to Jerusalem, to teach the people God's Word, and to administer national life (7:14–26).

Ezra not only knew God's Word, but he believed and obeyed it. Upon learning of the Israelites' sins of intermarriage and idolatry, Ezra fell in humility before God and prayed for the nation (9:1–15). Their disobedience touched him deeply (10:1). His response helped lead the people back to God.

Second Chronicles ends with Cyrus, king of Persia, asking for volunteers to return to Jerusalem to build a house for God. Ezra continues this account (1:1–3 is almost identical to 2 Chronicles 36:22–23) as two caravans of God's people were returning to Jerusalem. Zerubbabel, the leader of the first trip, was joined by 42,360 pilgrims who journeyed homeward (chapter 2). After arriving, they began to build the altar and the temple foundations (chapter 3). But opposition arose from the local inhabitants, and a campaign of accusations and rumors temporarily halted the project (chapter 4). During this time, the prophets Haggai and Zechariah encouraged the people (chapter 5). Finally, Darius decreed that the work should proceed unhindered (chapter 6).

After a 58-year gap, Ezra led a group of Jews from Persia. Armed with decrees and authority from Artaxerxes I, Ezra's task was to administer the affairs of the land (chapters 7—8). Upon arriving, he learned of intermarriage between God's people and their pagan neighbors. He wept and prayed for the nation (chapter 9). Ezra's example of humble confession led to national revival (chapter 10). Ezra, a man of God and a true hero, was a model for Israel, and he is a fitting model for us.

Read Ezra, the book, and remember Ezra, the man—a humble, obedient helper. Commit yourself to serving God as he did, with your whole life.

Darius I becomes king of Persia 522	Temple work resumed/ messages of Haggai, Zechariah 520	Temple completed 515	Ezra comes to Jerusalem 458	Nehemiah comes to Jerusalem 445

THE BLUEPRINT

A. THE RETURN LED BY ZERUBBABEL (1:1—6:22) 1. The first group of exiles returns to the land 2. The people rebuild the temple	Finally given the chance to return to their homeland, the people started to rebuild the temple, only to be stopped by opposition from their enemies. God's work in the world is not without opposition. We must not get discouraged and quit, as the returning people did at first, but continue on boldly in the face of difficulties, as they did later with the encouragement from the prophets.
B. THE RETURN LED BY EZRA (7:1—10:44) 1. The second group of exiles returns to the land 2. Ezra opposes intermarriage	Ezra returned to Jerusalem almost 80 years after Zerubbabel, only to discover that the people had married pagan or foreign spouses. This polluted the religious purity of the people and endangered the future of the nation. Believers today must be careful not to threaten their walk with God by taking on the practices of unbelievers.

MEGATHEMES

THEME	EXPLANATION	IMPORTANCE
The Jews Return	By returning to the land of Israel from Babylon, the Jews showed their faith in God's promise to restore them as a people. They returned not only to their homeland but also to the place where their forefathers had promised to follow God.	God shows his mercy to every generation. He compassionately restores his people. No matter how difficult our present "captivity," we are never far from his love and mercy. He restores us when we return to him.
Rededication	In 536 B.C., Zerubbabel led the people in rebuilding the altar and laying the temple foundation. They reinstated daily sacrifices and annual festivals, and rededicated themselves to a new spiritual worship of God.	In rededicating the altar, the people were recommitting themselves to God and his service. To grow spiritually, our commitment must be reviewed and renewed often. As we rededicate ourselves to God, our lives become altars to him.
Opposition	Opposition came soon after the altar was built and the temple foundation laid. Enemies of the Jews used deceit to hinder the building for over six years. Finally, there was a decree to stop the building altogether. This opposition severely tested their wavering faith.	There will always be adversaries who oppose God's work. The life of faith is never easy. But God can overrule all opposition to his service. When we face opposition, we must not falter or withdraw, but keep active and patient.
God's Word	When the people returned to the land, they were also returning to the influence of God's Word. The prophets Haggai and Zechariah helped encourage them, while Ezra's preaching of Scripture built them up. God's Word gave them what they needed to do God's work.	We also need the encouragement and direction of God's Word. We must make it the basis for our faith and actions to finish God's work and fulfill our obligations. We must never waver in our commitment to hear and obey his Word.
Faith and Action	The urging of Israel's leaders motivated the people to complete the temple. Over the years they had intermarried with idol-worshipers and adopted their pagan practices. Their faith, tested and revived, also led them to remove these sins from their lives.	Faith led them to complete the temple and to remove sin from their society. As we trust God with our hearts and minds, we must also act by completing our daily responsibilities. It is not enough to say we believe; we must make the changes God requires.

A. THE RETURN LED BY ZERUBBABEL (1:1—6:22)

After 70 years in exile, the captives from Judah were allowed to return to their homeland. Nearly 50,000 people made this journey. Upon arrival they began to rebuild the temple, but became discouraged by opposition. After encouragement from Haggai and Zechariah, they returned to the task and completed the temple. The message of the prophets still speaks to us today, encouraging us to continue building up God's church.

1. The first group of exiles returns to the land

Cyrus's Proclamation

1 Now in the first year of Cyrus king of Persia, in order to fulfill the word of the LORD **1:1**
by the mouth of Jeremiah, the LORD stirred up the spirit of Cyrus king of Persia, so 2 Chr 36:22; Jer 25:12; 29:10; Ezra
that he sent a proclamation throughout all his kingdom, and also *put it* in writing, saying: 5:13
2 "Thus says Cyrus king of Persia, 'The LORD, the God of heaven, has given me all the **1:2**
kingdoms of the earth and He has appointed me to build Him a house in Jerusalem, Is 44:28; 45:1, 12, 13
which is in Judah.
3 'Whoever there is among you of all His people, may his God be with him! Let him **1:3**
go up to Jerusalem which is in Judah and rebuild the house of the LORD, the God of 1 Kin 8:23; 18:39; Is 37:16; Dan 6:26
Israel; He is the God who is in Jerusalem.
4 'Every survivor, at whatever place he may live, let the men of that place support him
with silver and gold, with goods and cattle, together with a freewill offering for the house
of God which is in Jerusalem.' "

Holy Vessels Restored

5 Then the heads of fathers' *households* of Judah and Benjamin and the priests and **1:5**
the Levites arose, even everyone whose spirit God had stirred to go up and rebuild the Ezra 1:1, 2
house of the LORD which is in Jerusalem.

1:1 The book of Ezra opens in 538 B.C., 48 years after Nebuchadnezzar destroyed Jerusalem, defeated the southern kingdom of Judah, and carried the Jews away to Babylon as captives (2 Kings 25; 2 Chronicles 36). Nebuchadnezzar died in 562, and because his successors were not strong, Babylon was overthrown by Persia in 539, just prior to the events recorded in this book. Both the Babylonians and the Persians had a relaxed policy toward their captives, allowing them to own land and homes and to take ordinary jobs. Many Jews such as Daniel, Mordecai, and Esther rose to prominent positions within the nation. King Cyrus of Persia went a step further: He allowed many groups of exiles, including the Jews, to return to their homelands. By doing this, he hoped to win their loyalty and thus provide buffer zones around the borders of his empire. For the Jews this was a day of hope, a new beginning.

1:1 Cyrus, king of Persia (559–530 B.C.), had already begun his rise to power in the Near East by unifying the Medes and Persians into a strong empire. As he conquered cities, he treated the inhabitants with mercy. Although not a servant of Yahweh, Cyrus was used by God to return the Jews to their homeland. Cyrus may have been shown the prophecy of Isaiah 44:28—45:6, written over a century earlier, which predicted that Cyrus himself would help the Jews return to Jerusalem. Daniel, a prominent government official (Daniel 5:29; 6:28), would have been familiar with the prophecy. The book of Daniel has more to say about Cyrus.

1:1 Jeremiah prophesied that the Jews would remain in captivity for 70 years (Jeremiah 25:11; 29:10). The 70-year period has been calculated two different ways: (1) from the first captivity in 605 B.C. (2 Kings 24:1) until the altar was rebuilt by the returned exiles in 536 (Ezra 3:1–6), or (2) from the destruction of the temple in 586 until the exiles finished rebuilding it in 516. Many scholars prefer the second approach because the temple was the focus and heartbeat of the nation. Without the temple, the Jews did not consider themselves reestablished as a nation.

1:2 Cyrus was not a Jew, but God worked through him to return the exiled Jews to their homeland. Cyrus gave the proclamation allowing their return, and he gave them protection, money, and the temple articles taken by Nebuchadnezzar. When you face difficult situations and feel surrounded, outnumbered, overpowered, or outclassed, remember that God's power is not limited to your resources. He is able to use anyone to carry out his plans.

1:2–4 This proclamation permitted the Jews to work together to accomplish the huge task of rebuilding the temple. Some did the actual building, while others operated the supply lines. Significant ventures require teamwork, with certain people serving in the forefront and others providing support. Each function is vital to accomplishing the task. When you're asked to serve, do so faithfully as a team member, no matter who gets the credit.

1:5 Cyrus was king over the entire region that had once been Assyria and Babylon. Assyria had deported the Israelites from the northern kingdom (Israel) in 722 B.C. Babylon, the next world power, had taken Israelites captive from the southern kingdom (Judah) in 586 B.C. Therefore, when the Medo-Persian empire came to power, King Cyrus's proclamation of freedom went to all the original 12 tribes, but only Judah and Benjamin responded and returned to rebuild God's temple. The ten tribes of the northern kingdom had been so fractured and dispersed by Assyria, and so much time had elapsed since their captivity, that many may have been unsure of their real heritage. Thus they were unwilling to share in the vision of rebuilding the temple.

1:5 God moved the hearts of the leaders, family heads, priests, and Levites and gave them a great desire to return to Jerusalem to rebuild the temple. Major changes begin on the inside as God works on our attitudes, beliefs, and desires. These inner changes lead to faithful actions. After 48 years of captivity, the arrogant Jewish nation had been humbled. When the people's attitudes and desires changed, God ended their punishment and gave them another opportunity to go home and try again. Paul reminds us that "for it is God who is at work in you, both to will and to work for His good pleasure" (Philippians 2:13). Doing God's will begins with your desires. Are you willing to be humble, to be open to his opportunities, and to move at his direction? Ask God to give you the desire to follow him more closely.

1:5–6 Many Jews chose to go to Jerusalem, but many more chose to remain in Babylon rather than return to their homeland. The journey back to Jerusalem was difficult, dangerous, and expensive, lasting over four months. Travel conditions were poor; Jerusalem

1:6 Neh 6:9; Is 35:3
1:7 Ezra 5:14; 6:5; 2 Kin 24:13; 2 Chr 36:7
1:8 Ezra 5:14
1:9 Ezra 8:27

6 All those about them encouraged them with articles of silver, with gold, with goods,
with cattle and with valuables, aside from all that was given as a freewill offering.
7 Also King Cyrus brought out the articles of the house of the LORD, which Nebuchadnezzar had carried away from Jerusalem and put in the house of his gods;
8 and Cyrus, king of Persia, had them brought out by the hand of Mithredath the treasurer, and he counted them out to Sheshbazzar, the prince of Judah.
9 Now this *was* their number: 30 gold dishes, 1,000 silver dishes, 29 duplicates;
10 30 gold bowls, 410 silver bowls of a second *kind and* 1,000 other articles.
11 All the articles of gold and silver *numbered* 5,400. Sheshbazzar brought them all up
with the exiles who went up from Babylon to Jerusalem.

Number of Those Returning

2:1 2 Kin 24:14-16; 25:11; 2 Chr 36:20; Neh 7:6-73

2 Now these are the people of the province who came up out of the captivity of the
exiles whom Nebuchadnezzar the king of Babylon had carried away to Babylon, and
returned to Jerusalem and Judah, each to his city.

PROPHECIES FULFILLED BY THE RETURN OF ISRAEL FROM EXILE

Reference	*Prophecy*	*Approximate Date*	*Fulfillment Date*	*Significance*
Isaiah 44:28	Cyrus would be used by God to guarantee the return of a remnant. Jerusalem would be rebuilt and the temple restored.	688 B.C.	539 B.C.	As God named Cyrus even before he was born, God knows what will happen—he is in control.
Jeremiah 25:12	Babylon would be punished for destroying Jerusalem and exiling God's people.	605 B.C.	539 B.C.	Babylon was conquered by Cyrus the Great. God may seem to allow evil to go unpunished, but consequences for wrongdoing are inevitable. God will punish evil.
Jeremiah 29:10	The people would spend 70 years in Babylon, then God would bring them back to their homeland.	594 B.C.	538 B.C.	The 70 years of captivity passed (see the third note on 1:1), and God provided the opportunity for Zerubbabel to lead the first group of captives home. God's plans may allow for hardship, but his desire is for our good.
Daniel 5:17–30	God had judged the Babylonian empire. It would be given to the Medes and the Persians, forming a new world power.	539 B.C.	539 B.C.	Belshazzar was killed and Babylon was conquered the same night. God's judgment is accurate and swift. God knows the point of no return in each of our lives. Until then he allows the freedom for us to repent and seek his forgiveness.

God, through his faithful prophets, predicted that the people of Judah would be taken into captivity because of their sinfulness. But he also predicted that they would return to Jerusalem and rebuild the city, the temple, and the nation.

and the surrounding countryside were in ruins; and the people living in the area were hostile.

Persian records indicate that many Jews in captivity had accumulated great wealth. Returning to Jerusalem would have meant giving up everything they had and starting over. Many people couldn't bring themselves to do that; they preferred wealth and security to the sacrifice that God's work would require. Their priorities were upside down (Mark 4:18–19). We must not let our comfort, security, or material possessions prevent us from doing what God wants.

1:7 When King Nebuchadnezzar ransacked the temple, he took many of the valuable furnishings with him. What he did not take, he burned (2 Chronicles 36:18–19). Most of the captured items were made of solid gold (1 Kings 7:48–50), and Cyrus kindly returned them to the Jews for the temple they would soon rebuild.

1:8 Either Sheshbazzar was the Babylonian name for Zerubbabel, one of the Jewish leaders during the first return (2:2; 3:8; 4:3), or he was a government official with responsibility for the returning party. The reasons Sheshbazzar may be identified with Zerubbabel are as follows: (1) Both were called governors (5:14; Haggai 1:1); (2) both laid the temple foundation (3:8; 5:16); (3) Jews in exile were often given Babylonian names (see Daniel 1:7 where Daniel and his companions were given new names).

1:9–11 Every article of gold and silver was a witness to God's protection and care. Although many years had passed, God delivered these temple articles back to his people. We may be discouraged by events in life, but we must never give up our hope in God's promises to us. The turning point may be just ahead.

2 These came with Zerubbabel, Jeshua, Nehemiah, Seraiah, Reelaiah, Mordecai, Bilshan, Mispar, Bigvai, Rehum *and* Baanah.
The number of the men of the people of Israel:
3 the sons of Parosh, 2,172;
4 the sons of Shephatiah, 372;
5 the sons of Arah, 775;
6 the sons of Pahath-moab of the sons of Jeshua *and* Joab, 2,812;
7 the sons of Elam, 1,254;
8 the sons of Zattu, 945;
9 the sons of Zaccai, 760;
10 the sons of Bani, 642;
11 the sons of Bebai, 623;
12 the sons of Azgad, 1,222;
13 the sons of Adonikam, 666;
14 the sons of Bigvai, 2,056;
15 the sons of Adin, 454;
16 the sons of Ater of Hezekiah, 98;
17 the sons of Bezai, 323;
18 the sons of Jorah, 112;
19 the sons of Hashum, 223;
20 the sons of Gibbar, 95;
21 the men of Bethlehem, 123;
22 the men of Netophah, 56;
23 the men of Anathoth, 128;
24 the sons of Azmaveth, 42;
25 the sons of Kiriath-arim, Chephirah and Beeroth, 743;
26 the sons of Ramah and Geba, 621;
27 the men of Michmas, 122;
28 the men of Bethel and Ai, 223;
29 the sons of Nebo, 52;
30 the sons of Magbish, 156;
31 the sons of the other Elam, 1,254;
32 the sons of Harim, 320;
33 the sons of Lod, Hadid and Ono, 725;
34 the men of Jericho, 345;
35 the sons of Senaah, 3,630.

Priests Returning

36 The priests: the sons of Jedaiah of the house of Jeshua, 973;
37 the sons of Immer, 1,052;
38 the sons of Pashhur, 1,247;
39 the sons of Harim, 1,017.

2:5 Neh 7:10
2:6 Neh 7:11
2:13 Ezra 8:13
2:21 Gen 35:19; Matt 2:6
2:26 Josh 18:25
2:34 1 Kin 16:34; 2 Chr 28:15
2:36 1 Chr 24:7-18
2:37 1 Chr 24:14
2:38 1 Chr 9:12
2:39 1 Chr 24:8

2:2 The Nehemiah listed here is a different person from the one who rebuilt Jerusalem's walls 80 years later, and the Mordecai listed here is not the one who appears in the book of Esther.

2:2 This first list is made up of men who were leaders. The same list occurs in Nehemiah 7:7.

2:2–35 These people were from the tribes of Judah and Benjamin (1:5).

2:3–35 This list is the major group of those returning, divided by families (2:3–20) or by cities (2:21–35). Verse 36 begins listing priests, Levites, and other temple servants.

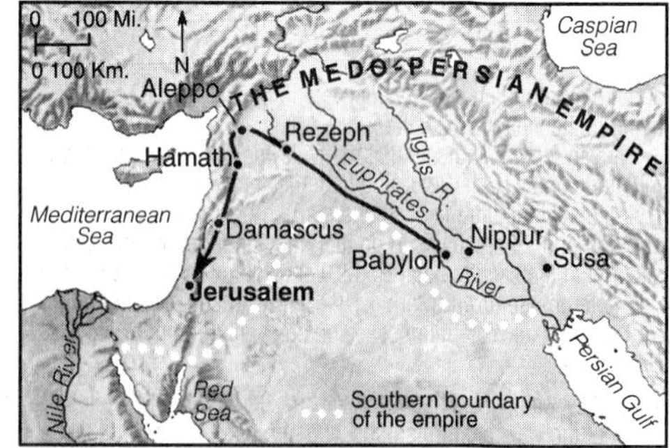

THE JOURNEY HOME The vast Medo-Persian empire included all the area on this map and more. A group of exiles began the long trip back to their homeland. Many exiles, however, preferred the comfort and security they had in Babylon to the dangerous trip back to Jerusalem, and so they decided to stay in Babylon.

Levites Returning

40 The Levites: the sons of Jeshua and Kadmiel, of the sons of Hodaviah, 74.
41 The singers: the sons of Asaph, 128.
42 The sons of the gatekeepers: the sons of Shallum, the sons of Ater, the sons of Talmon, the sons of Akkub, the sons of Hatita, the sons of Shobai, in all 139.

2:43 1 Chr 9:2

43 The temple servants: the sons of Ziha, the sons of Hasupha, the sons of Tabbaoth,
44 the sons of Keros, the sons of Siaha, the sons of Padon,
45 the sons of Lebanah, the sons of Hagabah, the sons of Akkub,
46 the sons of Hagab, the sons of Shalmai, the sons of Hanan,
47 the sons of Giddel, the sons of Gahar, the sons of Reaiah,
48 the sons of Rezin, the sons of Nekoda, the sons of Gazzam,
49 the sons of Uzza, the sons of Paseah, the sons of Besai,
50 the sons of Asnah, the sons of Meunim, the sons of Nephisim,
51 the sons of Bakbuk, the sons of Hakupha, the sons of Harhur,
52 the sons of Bazluth, the sons of Mehida, the sons of Harsha,
53 the sons of Barkos, the sons of Sisera, the sons of Temah,
54 the sons of Neziah, the sons of Hatipha.

2:55 1 Kin 9:21

55 The sons of Solomon's servants: the sons of Sotai, the sons of Hassophereth, the sons of Peruda,
56 the sons of Jaalah, the sons of Darkon, the sons of Giddel,
57 the sons of Shephatiah, the sons of Hattil, the sons of Pochereth-hazzebaim, the sons of Ami.

2:58 1 Chr 9:2; 1 Kin 9:21

58 All the temple servants and the sons of Solomon's servants were 392.
59 Now these are those who came up from Tel-melah, Tel-harsha, Cherub, Addan *and* Immer, but they were not able to give evidence of their fathers' households and their descendants, whether they were of Israel:
60 the sons of Delaiah, the sons of Tobiah, the sons of Nekoda, 652.

THE RETURN FROM EXILE

Year	*Number of People Returned*	*Persian King*	*Jewish Leader*	*Main Accomplishment*
538 B.C.	50,000	Cyrus	Zerubbabel	They rebuilt the temple, but only after a 20-year struggle. The work was halted for several years but was finally finished.
458 B.C.	2,000 men and their families	Artaxerxes	Ezra	Ezra confronted the spiritual disobedience of the people, and they repented and established worship at the temple. But the wall of Jerusalem remained in ruins.
445 B.C.	Small group	Artaxerxes	Nehemiah	The city was rebuilt, and a spiritual awakening followed. But the people still struggled with ongoing disobedience.

Babylon, the once-mighty nation that had destroyed Jerusalem and carried the people of Judah into captivity, had itself become a defeated nation. Persia was the new world power, and under its new foreign policy, captured peoples were allowed to return to their homelands. The people of Judah and Israel returned to their land in three successive waves.

2:59–63 Genealogies were very important credentials to the Hebrew people. If they could not prove they had descended from Abraham, they were not considered true Jews and were excluded from full participation in Jewish community life. In addition, some privileges were restricted to members of certain tribes. For example, only descendants of Levi (Abraham's great-grandson) could serve in the temple.

Priests Removed

61 Of the sons of the priests: the sons of Habaiah, the sons of Hakkoz, the sons of
Barzillai, who took a wife from the daughters of Barzillai the Gileadite, and he was called
by their name.
62 These searched *among* their ancestral registration, but they could not be located;
therefore they were considered unclean *and excluded* from the priesthood.
63 The governor said to them that they should not eat from the most holy things until
a priest stood up with Urim and Thummim.
64 The whole assembly numbered 42,360,
65 besides their male and female servants who numbered 7,337; and they had 200 singing
men and women.
66 Their horses were 736; their mules, 245;
67 their camels, 435; *their* donkeys, 6,720.
68 Some of the heads of fathers' *households,* when they arrived at the house of the LORD
which is in Jerusalem, offered willingly for the house of God to restore it on its foundation.
69 According to their ability they gave to the treasury for the work 61,000 gold drachmas and 5,000 silver minas and 100 priestly garments.
70 Now the priests and the Levites, some of the people, the singers, the gatekeepers
and the temple servants lived in their cities, and all Israel in their cities.

2:61 2 Sam 17:27; 1 Kin 2:7
2:62 Num 16:39, 40
2:63 Lev 2:3, 10; Ex 28:30; Num 27:21
2:65 2 Chr 35:25
2:69 Ezra 8:25-34
2:70 1 Chr 9:2; Neh 11:3

2. The people rebuild the temple

Altar and Sacrifices Restored

3 Now when the seventh month came, and the sons of Israel *were* in the cities, the people
gathered together as one man to Jerusalem.
2 Then Jeshua the son of Jozadak and his brothers the priests, and Zerubbabel the
son of Shealtiel and his brothers arose and built the altar of the God of Israel to offer
burnt offerings on it, as it is written in the law of Moses, the man of God.
3 So they set up the altar on its foundation, for they were terrified because of the
peoples of the lands; and they offered burnt offerings on it to the LORD, burnt offerings
morning and evening.
4 They celebrated the Feast of [1]Booths, as it is written, and *offered* the fixed number
of burnt offerings daily, according to the ordinance, as each day required;
5 and afterward *there was* a continual burnt offering, also for the new moons and for

3:1 Neh 7:73; 8:1
3:2 Neh 12:1, 8; Ezra 2:2; Hag 1:1; 2:2; 1 Chr 3:17; Ex 27:1; Deut 12:5, 6
3:3 Ezra 4:4; Num 28:2
3:4 Neh 8:14; Zech 14:16; Ex 23:16; Num 29:12
3:5 Ex 29:38; Num 28:3; Num 28:11; Num 29:39

1 Or *Tabernacles*

2:63 The governor mentioned here was probably Zerubbabel. The Urim and Thummim were two objects, probably shaped like flat stones, originally carried in the garment worn by the high priest. They were used to determine God's will in important matters. (For more on the Urim and Thummim, see the note on Leviticus 8:8.) The "most holy things" were the food that only the priests could eat. It was their allotted portion of meat that was sacrificed on the altar.

2:68–69 As the temple reconstruction progressed, everyone contributed freewill offerings according to his or her ability. Some were able to give huge gifts and did so generously. Everyone's effort and cooperation was required, and the people gave as much as they could. Often we limit our giving to ten percent of our income. The Bible, however, emphasizes that we should give from the heart *all* that we are able (2 Corinthians 8:12; 9:6). Let the amount of your gift be decided by God's call to give generously, not by the amount of your leftovers.

2:69 Drachmas and minas were gold and silver coins. The money given was enough to start rebuilding the temple. The people put what resources they had to their best use. They were enthusiastic and sincere, but this temple would never match the splendor of Solomon's. The money David gathered to start the building of Solomon's temple was a thousand times more (1 Chronicles 22:14). Some people wept as they remembered the glorious temple that had been destroyed (3:12).

3:2–3 The Jews built the altar as one of their first official acts. It symbolized God's presence and protection. It also demonstrated their purpose as a nation and their commitment to serve God alone. Zerubbabel sacrificed burnt offerings as the law of Moses instructed (Leviticus 1—7). The sacrifices were essential because they demonstrated that the people were seeking God's guidance, rededicating themselves to living as he commanded, and daily asking him to forgive their sins.

3:3 The Jews were afraid they were going to be attacked by the surrounding people—a mixed group whose ancestors had been conquered by the Assyrians. Foreigners had been forced to resettle in the northern kingdom of Israel after Israel was defeated and her people taken captive in 722 B.C. (4:1–2). This resettlement procedure was a common tactic of the Assyrians to prevent strong nationalistic uprisings by conquered peoples. Some of the resettled people in Israel had migrated south near Jerusalem, and they may have thought the returning exiles threatened their claim on the land.

3:4 The Feast of Booths lasted seven days. During this time the people lived in temporary dwellings (tents, booths, lean-tos) as their ancestors had done years before as they journeyed through the wilderness on their way to thc promised land. The feast reminded the people of God's past protection and guidance in the wilderness and of his continued love for them. The Feast of Booths is described in detail in Leviticus 23:33–36.

3:5 Almost immediately after arriving in the new land, the returning exiles built an altar. The people began worshiping God through sacrifices even before the temple foundations were laid. After many years in captivity, they had learned their lesson—they knew that God does not offer special protection to people who ignore him.

all the fixed festivals of the LORD that were consecrated, and from everyone who offered a freewill offering to the LORD.
6 From the first day of the seventh month they began to offer burnt offerings to the
LORD, but the foundation of the temple of the LORD had not been laid.

3:7 2 Chr 2:10; Acts 12:20; 2 Chr 2:16; Acts 9:36; Ezra 1:2; 6:3

7 Then they gave money to the masons and carpenters, and food, drink and oil to the
Sidonians and to the Tyrians, to bring cedar wood from Lebanon to the sea at Joppa,
according to the permission they had from Cyrus king of Persia.

Temple Restoration Begun

3:8 Ezra 3:2; 4:3; 1 Chr 23:4, 24

8 Now in the second year of their coming to the house of God at Jerusalem in the
second month, Zerubbabel the son of Shealtiel and Jeshua the son of Jozadak and the
rest of their brothers the priests and the Levites, and all who came from the captivity to
Jerusalem, began *the work* and appointed the Levites from twenty years and older to
oversee the work of the house of the LORD.

3:9 Ezra 2:40

9 Then Jeshua *with* his sons and brothers stood united *with* Kadmiel and his sons, the
sons of Judah *and* the sons of Henadad *with* their sons and brothers the Levites, to oversee the workmen in the temple of God.

3:10 Zech 4:6-10; 1 Chr 6:31; 25:1

10 Now when the builders had laid the foundation of the temple of the LORD, the priests
stood in their apparel with trumpets, and the Levites, the sons of Asaph, with cymbals,
to praise the LORD according to the directions of King David of Israel.

3:11 2 Chr 7:3; Neh 12:24, 40; 1 Chr 16:34; 2 Chr 5:13; Ps 100:5; 106:1; 107:1; 118:1; 131:1; Jer 33:11

3:12 Hag 2:3

11 They sang, praising and giving thanks to the LORD, *saying,* "For He is good, for His
lovingkindness is upon Israel forever." And all the people shouted with a great shout
when they praised the LORD because the foundation of the house of the LORD was laid.
12 Yet many of the priests and Levites and heads of fathers' *households,* the old men
who had seen the first temple, wept with a loud voice when the foundation of this house
was laid before their eyes, while many shouted aloud for joy,
13 so that the people could not distinguish the sound of the shout of joy from the sound
of the weeping of the people, for the people shouted with a loud shout, and the sound
was heard far away.

They had been carried off by the Babylonians when they were relatively strong; here they were few, weak, and surrounded by enemies. If ever they needed to rely on God's power, it was at this time. They realized the importance of obeying God from the heart, and not merely out of habit. If we want God's help when we undertake large tasks, we must make staying close to him our top priority.

3:5 These sacrifices were originally set up under the Law of Moses in Leviticus 1 and 6:8–13. The feasts are described in Leviticus 23. Every month on the day of the new moon, they held a special observance (Numbers 10:10).

3:7 When Solomon built the first temple (2 Chronicles 2), he also exchanged food and olive oil—plentiful resources in Israel—for wood, a resource Israel lacked. The wood came from Sidon and Tyre that time too.

3:8 Why was the Lord's temple begun first, even before the city wall? The temple was used for spiritual purposes; the wall, for military and political purposes. God had always been the nation's protector, and the Jews knew that the strongest stone wall would not protect them if God was not with them. They knew that putting their spiritual lives in order was a far higher priority than assuring the national defense.

3:8 It took from September (3:1; September was the seventh month because the year began in March) to June just to *prepare* to build the temple. The exiles took time to make plans because the project was important to them. Preparation may not feel heroic or spiritual, but it is vital to any project meant to be done well.

3:10–11 David had given clear instructions concerning the use of music in worship services in the temple (1 Chronicles 16; 25).

3:10–11 Completing the foundation for the temple required great effort on the part of all involved. But no one tried to get praise for himself and his own hard work. Instead, everyone praised God for what had been done. All good gifts come from God—talents, abilities, strength, and leadership. We should thank God for what has been done in and through us!

3:11 The Bible records many songs and musical events. For a list of such events, see the chart in Exodus 16.

3:12 Fifty years after its destruction, the temple was being rebuilt (536 B.C.). Some of the older people remembered Solomon's temple, and they wept because the new temple would not be as glorious as the first one. But the beauty of the building was not nearly as important to God as were the attitudes of the builders and worshipers. God cares more about who we are than what we accomplish. Our world is always changing, and once-magnificent accomplishments decay and disappear. Seek to serve God wholeheartedly. Then you won't need to compare your work with anyone else's.

3:12 Because the new temple was built on the foundation of Solomon's temple, the two structures were not that different in size. But the old temple was far more elaborate and ornate, and was surrounded by many buildings and a vast courtyard. Both temples were constructed of imported cedar wood, but Solomon's was decorated with vast amounts of gold and precious stones. Solomon's temple took over seven years to build; Zerubbabel's took about four years. Solomon's temple was at the hub of a thriving city; Zerubbabel's was surrounded by ruins. No wonder the people wept.

3:13 The celebration after laying the temple foundation was marked by contrasts of emotion—shouts of joy and sounds of weeping. Both were appropriate. The Holy Spirit can stimulate us both to rejoice over the goodness of his grace and to grieve over the sins that required him to correct us. When we come into the presence of Almighty God, we may feel full of joy and thanksgiving, yet at the same time feel sobered by our shortcomings.

Adversaries Hinder the Work

4 Now when the enemies of Judah and Benjamin heard that the people of the exile **4:1**
were building a temple to the LORD God of Israel, Ezra 4:7-10; Ezra 1:11
2 they approached Zerubbabel and the heads of fathers' *households,* and said to them,
"Let us build with you, for we, like you, seek your God; and we have been sacrificing to **4:2** 2 Kin 17:32; 2 Kin
Him since the days of Esarhaddon king of Assyria, who brought us up here." 19:37
3 But Zerubbabel and Jeshua and the rest of the heads of fathers' *households* of Is- **4:3**
rael said to them, "You have nothing in common with us in building a house to our God; Neh 2:20; Ezra 1:1, 2
but we ourselves will together build to the LORD God of Israel, as King Cyrus, the king
of Persia has commanded us."
4 Then the people of the land discouraged the people of Judah, and frightened them **4:4**
from building, Ezra 3:3
5 and hired counselors against them to frustrate their counsel all the days of Cyrus
king of Persia, even until the reign of Darius king of Persia.
6 Now in the reign of [2]Ahasuerus, in the beginning of his reign, they wrote an accusa- **4:6**
tion against the inhabitants of Judah and Jerusalem. Esth 1:1; Dan 9:1
7 And in the days of Artaxerxes, Bishlam, Mithredath, Tabeel and the rest of his col- **4:7**
leagues wrote to Artaxerxes king of Persia; and the text of the letter was written in Ara- 2 Kin 18:26; Dan 2:4
maic and translated *from* Aramaic.

The Letter to King Artaxerxes

8 Rehum the commander and Shimshai the scribe wrote a letter against Jerusalem to
King Artaxerxes, as follows—
9 then *wrote* Rehum the commander and Shimshai the scribe and the rest of their **4:9**
colleagues, the judges and the lesser governors, the officials, the secretaries, the men of 2 Kin 17:24; Ezra 5:6; 6:6
Erech, the Babylonians, the men of Susa, that is, the Elamites,
10 and the rest of the nations which the great and honorable Osnappar deported and **4:10**
settled in the city of Samaria, and in the rest of the region beyond the [3]River. Now Ezra 4:11, 17; 7:12
11 this is the copy of the letter which they sent to him:
"To King Artaxerxes: Your servants, the men in the region beyond the River, and now
12 let it be known to the king that the Jews who came up from you have come to us at **4:12**
Jerusalem; they are rebuilding the rebellious and evil city and are finishing the walls and 2 Chr 36:13; Ezra 5:3, 9
repairing the foundations.
13 "Now let it be known to the king, that if that city is rebuilt and the walls are finished, **4:13**
they will not pay tribute, custom or toll, and it will damage the revenue of the kings. Ezra 4:20; 7:24

2 Or *Xerxes;* Heb *Ahash-verosh* **3** I.e. Euphrates River, and so throughout the ch

4:1–3 The enemies of Judah and Benjamin were people who had been relocated in the northern kingdom when Assyria conquered Israel (see 2 Kings 17 and the note on 3:3). In an attempt to infiltrate and disrupt the project, these people offered to help in the rebuilding project. They wanted to keep a close eye on what the Jews were doing. They were hoping to keep Jerusalem from becoming strong again. The Jews, however, saw through their ploy. Such a partnership with unbelievers would have led God's people to compromise their faith.

4:1–6 Believers can expect opposition when they do God's work (2 Timothy 3:12). Unbelievers and evil spiritual forces are always working against God and his people. The opposition may offer compromising alliances (4:2), attempt to discourage and intimidate us (4:4–5), or accuse us unjustly (4:6). If you expect these tactics, you won't be halted by them. Move ahead with the work God has planned for you, and trust him to show you how to overcome the obstacles.

4:2 These enemies claimed to worship the same God as Zerubbabel and the rest of the Jews. In one sense, this was true; they worshiped God, but they also worshiped many other gods (see 2 Kings 17:27–29, 32–34, 41). In God's eyes, this was not worship—it was sin and rebellion. True worship involves devotion to God alone (Exodus 20:3–5). To these foreigners, God was just another "idol" to be added to their collection. Their real motive was to disrupt the temple project. Believers today must beware of those who claim to be Christians but whose actions clearly reveal that they are using Christianity to serve their own interests.

4:4–5 Discouragement and fear are two of the greatest obstacles to completing God's work. Most often they come where and when you least expect them. Discouragement eats away at our motivation and fear paralyzes us so we don't act at all. Recognize these common barriers. Remember that God's people in every age have faced these problems and with God's help overcome them. By standing together with other believers, you can overcome fear and discouragement and complete God's will.

4:6–23 In these verses, Ezra summarizes the entire story of the opposition to building the temple, the walls, and other important buildings in Jerusalem. Chronologically, 4:6 fits between chapters 6 and 7; 4:7–23 refers to the events between Ezra 7 and Nehemiah 1. Ezra grouped them here to highlight the persistent opposition to God's people over the years and God's ability to overcome it.

4:7 This letter sent to King Artaxerxes may have been inscribed on a clay tablet, a fragment of pottery, or sheets of parchment.

4:10 Osnapper (669–627 B.C.) was the Assyrian king who completed the relocation of Israelite captives. He was the last of the strong Assyrian kings. After his death the nation quickly declined. Assyria was conquered by Babylon in 612.

14 "Now because we are in the service of the palace, and it is not fitting for us to see the
king's dishonor, therefore we have sent and informed the king,
15 so that a search may be made in the record books of your fathers. And you will dis-
cover in the record books and learn that that city is a rebellious city and damaging to kings and provinces, and that they have incited revolt within it in past days; therefore that city was laid waste.

ZERUBBABEL

Sometimes God's ownership of a project is only recognized after *our* best efforts have failed. It is dangerous to think of God as responsible for the insignificant details while we take charge of the larger aspects of a project. Instead, it is God who is in control, and we only play a part in his overall plan. When God gives us important jobs to do, it isn't because he needs our help. Zerubbabel learned this lesson.

God's people had been exiled in Babylon for many years. Many had settled into comfortable life-styles there and wanted to stay. There were, however, almost 60,000 who had not forgotten Judah. When Babylon was defeated in 539 B.C., the Persian ruler, Cyrus, allowed the Jews to return to Jerusalem and rebuild their temple. Zerubbabel led the first and largest group back to the promised land.

Zerubbabel's leadership was by right and recognition. Not only was he a descendant of David, he also had personal leadership qualities. When the people arrived in Judah, they were given time to establish living quarters, and then were called to begin the work. They began not by laying the city walls or constructing government buildings, but by rebuilding the altar, worshiping God together, and celebrating a feast. Under Zerubbabel's leadership, they established a spiritual foundation for their building efforts.

The temple foundation was then quickly completed, and another round of celebration followed. But soon, two problems arose. A few old men remembered Solomon's glorious temple and were saddened at how much smaller and less glorious this one was. Also, some enemies of the Jews tried to infiltrate the work force and stop the building with political pressure. Fear caused the work to grind to a halt. The people went to their homes, and 16 years passed.

We do not know what Zerubbabel did during this time. His discouragement, following those first months of excitement and accomplishment, must have been deep. Those feelings eventually hardened into hopelessness. So God sent the prophets Haggai and Zechariah to be Zerubbabel's encouraging companions. They confronted the people's reluctance and comforted their fears. The work began once again with renewed energy and was completed in four years.

Zerubbabel, like many of us, knew how to start well but found it hard to keep going. His successes depended on the quality of encouragement he received. Zerubbabel let discouragement get the better of him. But when he let God take control, the work was finished. God is always in control. We must not let circumstances or lack of encouragement slow us from doing the tasks God has given us.

Strengths and accomplishments:
- Led the first group of Jewish exiles back to Jerusalem from Babylon
- Completed the rebuilding of God's temple
- Demonstrated wisdom in the help he accepted and refused
- Started his building project with worship as the focal point

Weaknesses and mistakes:
- Needed constant encouragement
- Allowed problems and resistance to stop the rebuilding work

Lessons from his life:
- A leader needs to provide not only the initial motivation for a project, but the continued encouragement necessary to keep the project going
- A leader must find his/her own dependable source of encouragement
- God's faithfulness is shown in the way he preserved David's line

Vital statistics:
- Where: Babylon, Jerusalem
- Occupation: Recognized leader of the exiles
- Relatives: Father: Shealtiel. Grandfather: Jehoiachin
- Contemporaries: Cyrus, Darius, Zechariah, Haggai

Key verses:
"This is the word of the LORD to Zerubbabel saying, 'Not by might nor by power, but by My Spirit,' says the LORD of hosts. 'What are you, O great mountain? Before Zerubbabel you will become a plain; and he will bring forth the top stone with shouts of "Grace, grace to it" ' " (Zechariah 4:6–7).

Zerubbabel's story is told in Ezra 2:2—5:2. He is also mentioned in 1 Chronicles 3:19; Nehemiah 7:7; 12:1, 47; Haggai 1:1, 12, 14; 2:4, 21, 23; Zechariah 4:6–10; Matthew 1:12–13; Luke 3:27.

16 "We inform the king that if that city is rebuilt and the walls finished, as a result you
will have no possession in *the province* beyond the River."

The King Replies and Work Stops

17 *Then* the king sent an answer to Rehum the commander, to Shimshai the scribe,
and to the rest of their colleagues who live in Samaria and in the rest of *the provinces*
beyond the River: "Peace. And now
18 the document which you sent to us has been translated and read before me. **4:18**
19 "A decree has been issued by me, and a search has been made and it has been dis- Neh 8:8
covered that that city has risen up against the kings in past days, that rebellion and revolt have been perpetrated in it,
20 that mighty kings have ruled over Jerusalem, governing all *the provinces* beyond the **4:20**
River, and that tribute, custom and toll were paid to them. 1 Kin 4:21; 1 Chr 18:3; Gen 15:18;
21 "So, now issue a decree to make these men stop *work,* that this city may not be re- Josh 1:4; Ezra 4:13;
built until a decree is issued by me. 7:24
22 "Beware of being negligent in carrying out this *matter;* why should damage increase
to the detriment of the kings?"
23 Then as soon as the copy of King Artaxerxes' document was read before Rehum
and Shimshai the scribe and their colleagues, they went in haste to Jerusalem to the Jews
and stopped them by force of arms.
24 Then work on the house of God in Jerusalem ceased, and it was stopped until the
second year of the reign of Darius king of Persia.

Temple Work Resumed

5 When the prophets, Haggai the prophet and Zechariah the son of Iddo, prophesied **5:1**
to the Jews who were in Judah and Jerusalem in the name of the God of Israel, who Hag 1:1; Zech 1:1
was over them,
2 then Zerubbabel the son of Shealtiel and Jeshua the son of Jozadak arose and be- **5:2**
gan to rebuild the house of God which is in Jerusalem; and the prophets of God were Ezra 3:2; Hag 1:12; Zech 4:6-9; Ezra
with them supporting them. 6:14; Hag 2:4; Zech 3:1
3 At that time Tattenai, the governor of *the province* beyond the River, and Shethar-
bozenai and their colleagues came to them and spoke to them thus, "Who issued you a **5:3**
decree to rebuild this [4]temple and to finish this structure?" Ezra 6:6, 13; Ezra 1:3; 5:9
4 Then we told them accordingly what the names of the men were who were reconstructing this building. **5:4** Ezra 5:10
5 But the eye of their God was on the elders of the Jews, and they did not stop them **5:5**
until a report could come to Darius, and then a written reply be returned concerning it. Ezra 7:6, 28

4 Lit *house,* and so in vv 9, 11, 12

4:19–20 Artaxerxes said that Jerusalem "has risen up against the kings in past days . . . rebellion and revolt have been perpetrated in it." By reading the historical records, he learned that mighty kings had come from Jerusalem, and he may have feared that another would arise if the city were rebuilt. Solomon had ruled a huge empire (1 Kings 4:21), and Jerusalem's kings had rebelled against mighty powers—for example, Zedekiah rebelled against Nebuchadnezzar despite his oath of loyalty (2 Chronicles 36:13). Artaxerxes did not want to aid the rebuilding of a rebellious city and nation.

4:23 Setbacks and standstills are painful and discouraging to God's workers. These exiles had received a double dose (see 4:1–5 and 4:6–22). Leaders should do everything to keep work from grinding to a halt; yet circumstances sometimes really are beyond our control. When you have been brought to a standstill, remember to still stand strong in the Lord.

4:24 Ezra resumes his chronological account here. It may have been ten years since the Israelites had worked on the temple. It did not begin again until 520 B.C., the second year of Darius's reign (5:1ff).

5:1 More details about the work and messages of Haggai and Zechariah are found in the books of the Bible that bear their names.

5:1–2 "The prophets of God were with them supporting them." God sometimes sends prophets to encourage and strengthen his people. To accomplish this, Haggai and Zechariah not only preached, but also got involved in the labor. In the church today, God appoints prophetic voices to help us with our work (Ephesians 4:11–13). Their ministry should have the same effect upon us as Haggai's and Zechariah's had on Israel. "But one who prophesies speaks to men for edification and exhortation and consolation" (1 Corinthians 14:3). In turn, we should encourage those who bring God's words to us.

5:3–5 The non-Jews who lived nearby attempted to hinder the construction of the temple. But while the legal debate went on and the decision was under appeal, the Jews continued to rebuild. When we are doing God's work, others may try to delay, confuse, or frustrate us, but we can proceed confidently. God will accomplish his purposes in our world, no matter who attempts to block them. Just as he watched over the Jewish elders, so he watches over you. Concentrate on God's purpose, and don't be sidetracked by intrigues or slander.

Adversaries Write to Darius

5:6 Ezra 5:3; Ezra 4:9 **6** *This is* the copy of the letter which Tattenai, the governor of *the province* beyond the
River, and Shethar-bozenai and his colleagues the officials, who were beyond the River,
sent to Darius the king.
7 They sent a report to him in which it was written thus: "To Darius the king, all peace.
8 "Let it be known to the king that we have gone to the province of Judah, to the house
of the great God, which is being built with huge stones, and beams are being laid in the
walls; and this work is going on with great care and is succeeding in their hands.
9 "Then we asked those elders and said to them thus, 'Who issued you a decree to
rebuild this temple and to finish this structure?'
10 "We also asked them their names so as to inform you, and that we might write down
the names of the men who were at their head.
5:11 1 Kin 6:1, 38 11 "Thus they answered us, saying, 'We are the servants of the God of heaven and earth
and are rebuilding the temple that was built many years ago, which a great king of Israel
built and finished.
5:12 2 Chr 36:16, 17; 12 'But because our fathers had provoked the God of heaven to wrath, He gave them
2 Kin 25:8-11; Jer into the hand of Nebuchadnezzar king of Babylon, the Chaldean, *who* destroyed this
52:12-15 temple and deported the people to Babylon.
5:13 13 'However, in the first year of Cyrus king of Babylon, King Cyrus issued a decree to
Ezra 1:1; Ezra 1:1-4 rebuild this house of God.
5:14 14 'Also the gold and silver utensils of the house of God which Nebuchadnezzar had
Ezra 1:7; 6:5; Dan taken from the temple in Jerusalem, and brought them to the temple of Babylon, these
5:2; Ezra 1:8; 5:16 King Cyrus took from the temple of Babylon and they were given to one whose name
was Sheshbazzar, whom he had appointed governor.
15 'He said to him, "Take these utensils, go *and* deposit them in the temple in Jerusalem and let the house of God be rebuilt in its place."
5:16 16 'Then that Sheshbazzar came *and* laid the foundations of the house of God in Jeru-
Ezra 3:8, 10; Ezra salem; and from then until now it has been under construction and it is not *yet* com-
6:15 pleted.'
5:17 17 "Now if it pleases the king, let a search be conducted in the king's treasure house,
Ezra 6:1, 2 which is there in Babylon, if it be that a decree was issued by King Cyrus to rebuild this
house of God at Jerusalem; and let the king send to us his decision concerning this
matter."

THE PERSIAN KINGS OF EZRA'S DAY

Name	*Date of Reign*	*Relationship to Israel*
Cyrus	559–530 B.C.	Conquered Babylon. Established a policy of returning exiles to their homelands. Sent Zerubbabel to Jerusalem, financed his project, and returned the gold and silver articles that Nebuchadnezzar had taken from the temple. He probably knew Daniel.
Darius	522–486 B.C.	Stopped construction of the temple in Jerusalem.
Ahasuerus (Xerxes)	486–465 B.C.	Was Esther's husband. Allowed the Jews to protect themselves against Haman's attempt to eliminate their people.
Artaxerxes I	465–424 B.C.	Had Nehemiah as his cupbearer. Allowed both Ezra and Nehemiah to return to Jerusalem.

5:11 While rebuilding the temple, the workers were confronted by the Persia-appointed governor, demanding to know who gave permission for their construction project (5:3). This could have been intimidating, but, as we learn from the letter, they boldly replied, "We are the servants of the God of heaven and earth."

It is not always easy to speak up for our faith in an unbelieving world, but we must. The way to deal with pressure and intimidation is to recognize that we are workers for God. Our allegiance is to him first, people second. When we contemplate the reactions and criticisms of hostile people, we can become paralyzed with fear. If we try to offend no one or to please everyone, we won't be effective. God is our leader, and his rewards are most important. So don't be intimidated. Let others know by your words and actions whom you really serve.

5:13–17 Cyrus is called king of Persia in 1:1 and king of Babylon in 5:13. Because Persia had just conquered Babylon, Cyrus was king of both nations. Babylon is more important to this story because it was the location of the Hebrews' 70-year captivity. The Babylon in 5:17 may refer to the city of Babylon, which was the capital of the nation of Babylon.

Darius Finds Cyrus's Decree

6 Then King Darius issued a decree, and search was made in the [5]archives, where the
treasures were stored in Babylon.
2 In [6]Ecbatana in the fortress, which is in the province of Media, a scroll was found
and there was written in it as follows: "Memorandum—
3 "In the first year of King Cyrus, Cyrus the king issued a decree: '*Concerning* the house
of God at Jerusalem, let the temple, the place where sacrifices are offered, be rebuilt
and let its foundations be retained, its height being 60 cubits and its width 60 cubits;
4 with three layers of huge stones and one layer of timbers. And let the cost be paid
from the royal treasury.
5 'Also let the gold and silver utensils of the house of God, which Nebuchadnezzar
took from the temple in Jerusalem and brought to Babylon, be returned and brought to
their places in the temple in Jerusalem; and you shall put *them* in the house of God.'
6 "Now *therefore,* Tattenai, governor of *the province* beyond the River, Shethar-
bozenai and your colleagues, the officials of *the provinces* beyond the River, keep away
from there.
7 "Leave this work on the house of God alone; let the governor of the Jews and the
elders of the Jews rebuild this house of God on its site.
8 "Moreover, I issue a decree concerning what you are to do for these elders of Judah
in the rebuilding of this house of God: the full cost is to be paid to these people from the
royal treasury out of the taxes of *the provinces* beyond the River, and that without delay.
9 "Whatever is needed, both young bulls, rams, and lambs for a burnt offering to the
God of heaven, and wheat, salt, wine and anointing oil, as the priests in Jerusalem request, *it* is to be given to them daily without fail,
10 that they may offer [7]acceptable sacrifices to the God of heaven and pray for the life
of the king and his sons.
11 "And I issued a decree that any man who violates this edict, a timber shall be drawn
from his house and he shall be impaled on it and his house shall be made a refuse heap
on account of this.
12 "May the God who has caused His name to dwell there overthrow any king or people who attempts to change *it,* so as to destroy this house of God in Jerusalem. I, Darius,
have issued *this* decree, let *it* be carried out with all diligence!"

The Temple Completed and Dedicated

13 Then Tattenai, the governor of *the province* beyond the River, Shethar-bozenai and
their colleagues carried out *the decree* with all diligence, just as King Darius had sent.
14 And the elders of the Jews were successful in building through the prophesying of
Haggai the prophet and Zechariah the son of Iddo. And they finished building according to the command of the God of Israel and the decree of Cyrus, Darius, and Artaxerxes king of Persia.
15 This temple was completed on the third day of the month Adar; it was the sixth year
of the reign of King Darius.
16 And the sons of Israel, the priests, the Levites and the rest of the exiles, celebrated
the dedication of this house of God with joy.
17 They offered for the dedication of this temple of God 100 bulls, 200 rams, 400 lambs,
and as a sin offering for all Israel 12 male goats, corresponding to the number of the
tribes of Israel.

6:1 Ezra 5:17
6:2 2 Kin 17:6
6:3 Ezra 1:1; 5:13
6:4 1 Kin 6:36
6:5 Ezra 1:7; 5:14
6:6 Ezra 5:3; 6:13
6:8 Ezra 6:4; 7:14-22
6:10 Ezra 7:23; Jer 29:7; 1 Tim 2:1, 2
6:11 Ezra 7:26; Dan 2:5; 3:29
6:12 Deut 12:5, 11; 1 Kin 9:3
6:13 Ezra 6:6
6:14 Ezra 5:1, 2; Ezra 1:1; 5:13; Ezra 4:24; 6:12; Ezra 7:1
6:15 Esth 3:7
6:16 1 Kin 8:63; 2 Chr 7:5
6:17 Ezra 8:35

5 Lit *house of the books* 6 Aram *Achmetha* 7 Lit *pleasing;* or *sweet-smelling sacrifices*

6:1–2 Many clay and papyrus documents recording business transactions and historical data have been discovered in this area (near present-day Syria). A great library and archives with thousands of such records have been discovered at Ebla in Syria.

6:14 Ezra carefully pointed out that rebuilding the temple was commanded first by God and then by the kings, who were his instruments. How ironic and wonderful that God's work was carried on by the discovery of a lost paragraph in a pagan library. All the opposition of powerful forces was stopped by a clause in a legal document. God's will is supreme over all rulers, all historical events, and all hostile forces. He can deliver us in ways we can't imagine. If we trust in his power and love, no opposition can stop us.

6:15 The temple was completed in 516 B.C.

6:16–22 Feasting and celebration were in order at the great temple dedication. This celebration was similar to the one that Solomon had when he dedicated the temple in 1 Kings 8:63, although Solomon offered more than 200 times as many cattle and sheep. This book of Moses was probably Leviticus. The priests and Levites were organized into groups in order to do "the service of God . . . as it is written in the book of Moses." There is time to celebrate, but there is also a time to work. Both are proper and necessary when worshiping God, and both are pleasing to him.

6:18 1 Chr 24:1; 2 Chr 35:5; 1 Chr 23:6; Num 3:6; 8:9

18 Then they appointed the priests to their divisions and the Levites in their orders for
the service of God in Jerusalem, as it is written in the book of Moses.

The Passover Observed

6:19 Ezra 1:11; Ex 12:6

6:20 2 Chr 29:34; 30:15; 2 Chr 35:11

6:21 Neh 9:2; 10:28; Ezra 9:11

6:22 Ex 12:15; Ezra 7:27; Prov 21:1; Ezra 1:1; 6:1

19 The exiles observed the Passover on the fourteenth of the first month.
20 For the priests and the Levites had purified themselves together; all of them were
pure. Then they slaughtered the Passover *lamb* for all the exiles, both for their brothers
the priests and for themselves.
21 The sons of Israel who returned from exile and all those who had separated themselves from the impurity of the nations of the land to *join* them, to seek the LORD God
of Israel, ate *the Passover.*
22 And they observed the Feast of Unleavened Bread seven days with joy, for the LORD
had caused them to rejoice, and had turned the heart of the king of Assyria toward them
to encourage them in the work of the house of God, the God of Israel.

B. THE RETURN LED BY EZRA (7:1—10:44)

Ezra returned to the land with a second group of exiles, 80 years after Zerubbabel. Ezra found the temple rebuilt, but the lives of the people in shambles. Intermarriage with foreigners opposed to God threatened the spiritual future of the nation. So Ezra prayed for guidance and then followed through with action. Christians today must also strive to keep their lives pure, refusing to let the sinful allurements of the world around them compromise their life-style.

1. The second group of exiles returns to the land

Ezra Journeys from Babylon to Jerusalem

7:1 1 Chr 6:4-14; Ezra 7:12, 21; Neh 2:1

7 Now after these things, in the reign of Artaxerxes king of Persia, *there went up* Ezra
son of Seraiah, son of Azariah, son of Hilkiah,
2 son of Shallum, son of Zadok, son of Ahitub,

THE POSTEXILIC PROPHETS

God used these men to confront and comfort his people after their return to their homeland from exile in Babylon.

Who?	*When?*	*Ministered to These Contemporary Leaders*	*Main Message*	*Significance*
Haggai	520 B.C.	Zerubbabel Joshua	• Encouraged the leaders and the people to continue rebuilding the temple, which God would bless • Challenged the people's careless worship, which God would not bless	Disobedience and careless obedience of God's commands lead to judgment.
Zechariah	520 B.C.	Zerubbabel Joshua	• Emphasized God's command to rebuild his temple • Gave the people another look at God's plan to bless the world through Israel and its coming king—the Messiah (Zechariah 9:9–10)	Encouragement for today's effort sometimes requires that we remember God has a plan and purpose for tomorrow. Meanwhile, the challenge is to live for him today.
Malachi	430 B.C.	The priests are the only leaders mentioned	• Confronted the people and priests with God's promises of judgment on those who reject him and God's blessing on those who live as he desires	God expects our obedience to him to affect our attitude toward him and our treatment of one another.

6:19 The Passover was an annual celebration commemorating Israel's deliverance from Egypt. After a series of plagues failed to convince Pharaoh to free the Israelites, God said that he would send the destroying angel to kill the firstborn in every household. But the angel would pass over every home that had the blood of a specified type of lamb on the sides and top of the doorpost. See Exodus 12:1–30 for the story of this event and the establishment of the Passover celebration.

6:22 There are many ways to pray for God's help. Have you ever considered that God would change the attitude of a person or group of people? God is infinitely powerful; his insight and wisdom transcend the laws of human nature. While you must always change your attitude as a first step, remember that he can change the attitude of others.

7:1 There is a gap of almost 60 years between the events of chapters six and seven. The story in the book of Esther occurred during this time, in the reign of Ahasuerus, who ruled from 486–465 B.C. Artaxerxes, his son, became king in 465, and Ezra returned to Jerusalem in 458.

3 son of Amariah, son of Azariah, son of Meraioth,
4 son of Zerahiah, son of Uzzi, son of Bukki,
5 son of Abishua, son of Phinehas, son of Eleazar, son of Aaron the chief priest.
6 This Ezra went up from Babylon, and he was a scribe skilled in the law of Moses,
which the LORD God of Israel had given; and the king granted him all he requested
because the hand of the LORD his God *was* upon him.
7 Some of the sons of Israel and some of the priests, the Levites, the singers, the gatekeepers and the temple servants went up to Jerusalem in the seventh year of King Artaxerxes.
8 He came to Jerusalem in the fifth month, which was in the seventh year of the king.
9 For on the first of the first month he began to go up from Babylon; and on the
first of the fifth month he came to Jerusalem, because the good hand of his God *was*
upon him.
10 For Ezra had set his heart to study the law of the LORD and to practice *it,* and to
teach *His* statutes and ordinances in Israel.

7:6 Ezra 7:11, 12, 21; Ezra 7:9, 28; 8:22
7:7 Ezra 8:1-20
7:9 Ezra 7:6; Neh 2:8
7:10 Deut 33:10; Ezra 7:25; Neh 8:1

King's Decree on Behalf of Ezra

11 Now this is the copy of the decree which King Artaxerxes gave to Ezra the priest,
the scribe, learned in the words of the commandments of the LORD and His statutes to
Israel:
12 "Artaxerxes, king of kings, to Ezra the priest, the scribe of the law of the God of
heaven, perfect *peace.* And now
13 I have issued a decree that any of the people of Israel and their priests and the Levites
in my kingdom who are willing to go to Jerusalem, may go with you.
14 "Forasmuch as you are sent by the king and his seven counselors to inquire concerning Judah and Jerusalem according to the law of your God which is in your hand,
15 and to bring the silver and gold, which the king and his counselors have freely offered to the God of Israel, whose dwelling is in Jerusalem,
16 with all the silver and gold which you find in the whole province of Babylon, along
with the freewill offering of the people and of the priests, who offered willingly for the
house of their God which is in Jerusalem;
17 with this money, therefore, you shall diligently buy bulls, rams and lambs, with their
grain offerings and their drink offerings and offer them on the altar of the house of your
God which is in Jerusalem.
18 "Whatever seems good to you and to your brothers to do with the rest of the silver
and gold, you may do according to the will of your God.
19 "Also the utensils which are given to you for the service of the house of your God,
deliver in full before the God of Jerusalem.
20 "The rest of the needs for the house of your God, for which you may have occasion
to provide, provide *for it* from the royal treasury.
21 "I, even I, King Artaxerxes, issue a decree to all the treasurers who are *in the provinces* beyond the River, that whatever Ezra the priest, the scribe of the law of the God of
heaven, may require of you, it shall be done diligently,
22 *even* up to 100 talents of silver, 100 kors of wheat, 100 baths of wine, 100 baths of
oil, and salt as needed.

7:12 Ezek 26:7; Dan 2:37
7:13 Ezra 6:1
7:14 Ezra 7:15, 28; 8:25
7:15 2 Chr 6:2; Ezra 6:12; Ps 135:21
7:16 Ezra 8:25; Ezra 1:4, 6; 1 Chr 29:6
7:17 Num 15:4-13; Deut 12:5-11
7:20 Ezra 6:4
7:21 Ezra 7:6

7:6 Eighty years after the first exiles returned to Jerusalem (2:1), Ezra himself returned. This was his first trip, and it took four months. The temple had been standing for about 58 years. Up to this point in the narrative, Ezra had remained in Babylon, probably compiling a record of the events that had taken place.

Why did he have to ask the king if he could return? Ezra wanted to lead many Jews back to Jerusalem, and he needed a decree from the king stating that any Jew who wanted to return could do so. This decree would be like a passport in case they ran into opposition along the way. The king's generous decree showed that God was blessing Ezra (7:6, 28). It also indicated that Ezra was probably a prominent man in Artaxerxes' kingdom. He was willing to give up this position in order to return to his homeland and teach the Israelites God's laws.

7:6–10 Ezra demonstrates how a gifted Bible teacher can move God's people forward. He was effective because he was a well-versed student of the law of the Lord and because he was determined to obey those laws. He taught through both his speaking and his example. Like Ezra, we should determine both to study and to obey God's Word.

7:14 The seven counselors were Artaxerxes' supreme court (see Esther 1:14).

7:14 When Nebuchadnezzar destroyed the temple, he took a vast amount of plunder that may have included a copy of the book of the law (2 Chronicles 36:18). It is also possible that this book was brought by the Jews into exile and was confiscated and read by their conquerors. Foreign leaders who worshiped many gods liked to have records of the gods of other nations for military and political reasons.

7:23 Ezra 6:10

7:24 Ezra 4:13, 20; Ezra 7:7

7:25 Ex 18:21; Deut 16:18; Ezra 7:10; Mal 2:7; Col 1:28

7:26 Ezra 6:11, 12

7:27 Ezra 6:22

7:28 Ezra 9:9; Ezra 5:5

23 "Whatever is commanded by the God of heaven, let it be done with zeal for the house
of the God of heaven, so that there will not be wrath against the kingdom of the king
and his sons.
24 "We also inform you that it is not allowed to impose tax, tribute or toll *on* any of the
priests, Levites, singers, doorkeepers, Nethinim or servants of this house of God.
25 "You, Ezra, according to the wisdom of your God which is in your hand, appoint
magistrates and judges that they may judge all the people who are in *the province* beyond the River, *even* all those who know the laws of your God; and you may teach anyone who is ignorant *of them.*
26 "Whoever will not observe the law of your God and the law of the king, let judgment
be executed upon him strictly, whether for death or for banishment or for confiscation
of goods or for imprisonment."

The King's Kindness

27 Blessed be the LORD, the God of our fathers, who has put *such a thing* as this in the
king's heart, to adorn the house of the LORD which is in Jerusalem,
28 and has extended lovingkindness to me before the king and his counselors and before all the king's mighty princes. Thus I was strengthened according to the hand of the
LORD my God upon me, and I gathered leading men from Israel to go up with me.

People Who Went with Ezra

8 Now these are the heads of their fathers' *households* and the genealogical enrollment of those who went up with me from Babylon in the reign of King Artaxerxes:

THE MEDO-PERSIAN EMPIRE
The Medo-Persian empire included the lands of Media and Persia, much of the area shown on this map and more. The Jewish exiles were concentrated in the area around Nippur in the Babylonian province. The decree by King Cyrus that allowed the Israelites to return to their homeland and rebuild the temple was discovered in the palace at Ecbatana.

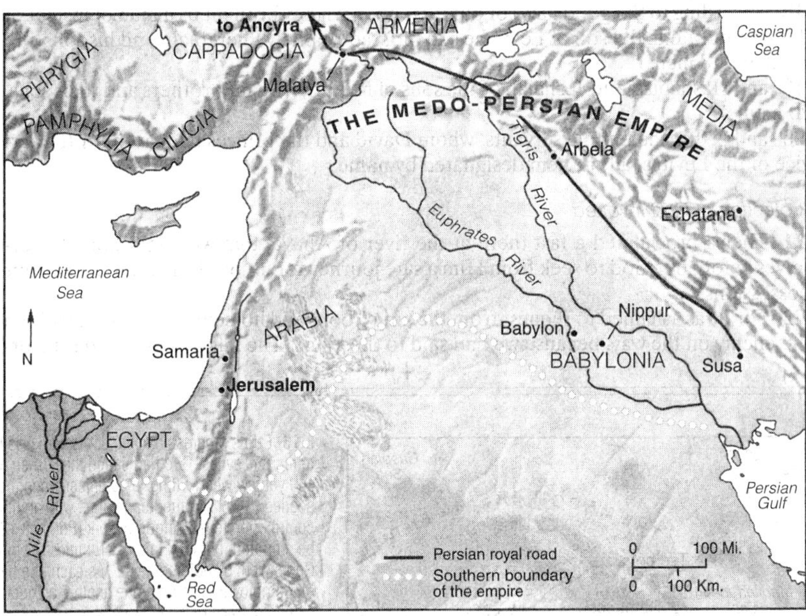

7:24 Why did Artaxerxes exempt temple workers from paying taxes? He recognized that the priests and Levites filled an important role in society as spiritual leaders, so he freed them of tax burdens. While the Bible does not teach tax exemption for religious employees, Artaxerxes, a pagan king, recognized and supported the principle. Today, churches have the responsibility to keep worldly burdens off the shoulders of spiritual workers.

7:27 In Ezra's doxology, he acknowledges that God "put such a thing as this in the king's heart." God can change a king's heart (see Proverbs 21:1). When we face life's challenges, we often must work diligently and with extraordinary effort, realizing that God oversees all our work. Recognize his hand in your success, and remember to praise him for his help and protection.

7:27–28 Ezra praised God for all that God had done for him and through him. Ezra had honored God throughout his life, and God chose to honor him. Ezra could have assumed that his own greatness and charisma had won over the king and his princes, but he gave the credit to God. We, too, should be grateful to God for our success and not think that we did it in our own power.

7:28 The speaker here is Ezra. He writes in the first person for the remainder of the book.

2 of the sons of Phinehas, Gershom; of the sons of Ithamar, Daniel; of the sons of **8:2**
David, Hattush; 1 Chr 3:22
3 of the sons of Shecaniah *who was* of the sons of Parosh, Zechariah and with him 150 **8:3**
males *who were in* the genealogical list; Ezra 2:3
4 of the sons of Pahath-moab, Eliehoenai the son of Zerahiah and 200 males with him;
5 of the sons of Zattu, Shecaniah, the son of Jahaziel and 300 males with him;
6 and of the sons of Adin, Ebed the son of Jonathan and 50 males with him; **8:6**
7 and of the sons of Elam, Jeshaiah the son of Athaliah and 70 males with him; Ezra 2:15; Neh 7:20;
8 and of the sons of Shephatiah, Zebadiah the son of Michael and 80 males with him; 10:16
9 of the sons of Joab, Obadiah the son of Jehiel and 218 males with him;
10 and of the sons of Bani, Shelomith, the son of Josiphiah and 160 males with him;
11 and of the sons of Bebai, Zechariah the son of Bebai and 28 males with him;
12 and of the sons of Azgad, Johanan the son of Hakkatan and 110 males with him;
13 and of the sons of Adonikam, the last ones, these being their names, Eliphelet, Jeuel and Shemaiah, and 60 males with them;
14 and of the sons of Bigvai, Uthai and Zabbud, and 70 males with them.

Ezra Sends for Levites

15 Now I assembled them at the river that runs to Ahava, where we camped for three **8:15**
days; and when I observed the people and the priests, I did not find any Levites there. Ezra 8:21, 31; Ezra 7:7; 8:2
16 So I sent for Eliezer, Ariel, Shemaiah, Elnathan, Jarib, Elnathan, Nathan, Zechari-
ah and Meshullam, leading men, and for Joiarib and Elnathan, teachers.
17 I sent them to Iddo the leading man at the place Casiphia; and I told them what to **8:17**
say to Iddo *and* his brothers, the temple servants at the place Casiphia, *that is,* to bring Ezra 2:43
ministers to us for the house of our God.
18 According to the good hand of our God upon us they brought us a man of insight of **8:18**
the sons of Mahli, the son of Levi, the son of Israel, namely Sherebiah, and his sons and Ezra 7:6, 28; 2 Chr 30:22
brothers, 18 men;
19 and Hashabiah and Jeshaiah of the sons of Merari, with his brothers and their sons,
20 men;
20 and 220 of the temple servants, whom David and the princes had given for the ser- **8:20**
vice of the Levites, all of them designated by name. Ezra 2:43; 7:7

Protection of God Invoked

8:21
21 Then I proclaimed a fast there at the river of Ahava, that we might humble our- 1 Sam 7:6; 2 Chr 20:3; Ezra 8:15, 31;
selves before our God to seek from Him a safe journey for us, our little ones, and all our Lev 16:29; 23:29; Is
possessions. 58:3, 5
22 For I was ashamed to request from the king troops and horsemen to protect us from **8:22**
the enemy on the way, because we had said to the king, "The hand of our God is favor- Ezra 7:6, 9, 28; Josh 22:16; 2 Chr 15:2

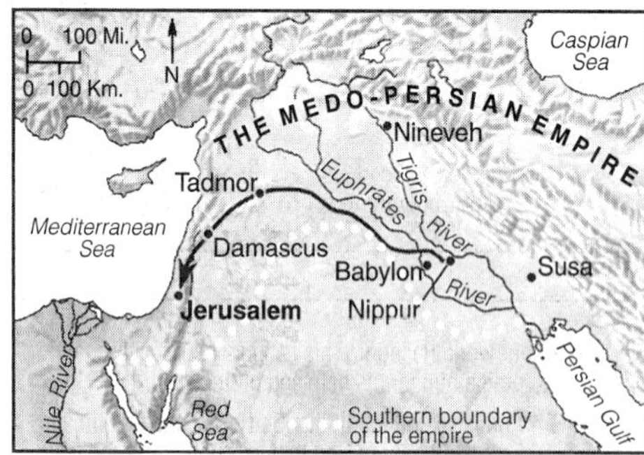

EZRA'S JOURNEY Ezra led a second group of exiles back to Judah and Jerusalem about 80 years after the first group. He traveled the dangerous route without military escort (8:22), but the people prayed and, under Ezra's godly leadership, arrived safely in Jerusalem after several months.

8:15 Ezra's progress back to Jerusalem was halted while he waited to recruit Levites. God had called these men to a special service, and yet few were willing to volunteer when their services were needed. God has gifted each of us with abilities so we can make a contribution to his kingdom work (Romans 12:4–8). Don't wait to be recruited, but look for opportunities to volunteer. Don't hinder God's work by holding back. "As each one has received a special gift, employ it in serving one another as good stewards of the manifold grace of God" (1 Peter 4:10).

8:21 Ezra and the people traveled approximately 900 miles on foot. The trip took them through dangerous and difficult territory and lasted about four months. They prayed that God would give them a safe journey. Our journeys today may not be as difficult and dangerous as Ezra's, but we should recognize our need to ask God for guidance and protection.

8:21–23 Before making all the physical preparations for the journey, Ezra made spiritual preparations. Their prayers and fasting prepared them spiritually by showing their dependence on God for protection, their faith that God was in control, and their affirmation that they were not strong enough to make the trip without him. When we take time to put God first in any endeavor, we are preparing well for whatever lies ahead.

ably disposed to all those who seek Him, but His power and His anger are against all those who forsake Him."

8:23 1 Chr 5:20; 2 Chr 33:13

23 So we fasted and sought our God concerning this *matter*, and He listened to our entreaty.

8:24 Ezra 8:18, 19

24 **Then I set apart twelve of the leading priests, Sherebiah, Hashabiah, and with them ten of their brothers;**

8:25 Ezra 8:33; Ezra 7:15, 16; Ezra 7:14

25 and I weighed out to them the silver, the gold and the utensils, the offering for the house of our God which the king and his counselors and his princes and all Israel present *there* had offered.

It is not personal achievement, but personal commitment to live for God, that is important. Achievements are simply examples of what God can do through someone's life. The most effective leaders spoken of in the Bible had little awareness of the impact their lives had on others. They were too busy obeying God to keep track of their successes. Ezra fits that description.

About 80 years after the rebuilding of the temple under Zerubbabel, Ezra returned to Judah with about 2,000 men and their families. He was given a letter from Artaxerxes instructing him to carry out a program of religious education. Along with the letter came significant power. But long before Ezra's mission began, God had shaped him in three important ways so that he would use the power well. First, as a scribe, Ezra dedicated himself to carefully studying God's Word. Second, he intended to apply and obey personally the commands he discovered in God's Word. Third, he was committed to teaching others both God's Word and its application to life.

Knowing Ezra's priorities, it is not surprising to note his actions when he arrived in Jerusalem. The people had disobeyed God's command not to marry women of foreign nations. On a cold and rainy day, Ezra addressed the people and made it clear they had sinned. Because of the sins of many, all were under God's condemnation. Confession, repentance, and action were needed. The people admitted their sin and devised a plan to deal with the problem.

This initial effort on Ezra's part set the stage for what Nehemiah would later accomplish. Ezra continued his ministry under Nehemiah, and the two were used by God to start a spiritual movement that swept the nation following the rebuilding of Jerusalem.

Ezra achieved great things and made a significant impact because he had the right starting place for his actions and his life: God's Word. He studied it seriously and applied it faithfully. He taught others what he learned. He is, therefore, a great model for anyone who wants to live for God.

Strengths and accomplishments:
- Committed to study, follow, and teach God's Word
- Led the second group of exiles from Babylon to Jerusalem
- May have written 1 and 2 Chronicles
- Concerned about keeping the details of God's commands
- Sent by King Artaxerxes to Jerusalem to evaluate the situation, set up a religious education system, and return with a firsthand report
- Worked alongside Nehemiah during the last spiritual awakening recorded in the Old Testament

Lessons from his life:
- A person's willingness to know and practice God's Word will have a direct effect on how God uses his/her life
- The starting place for serving God is a personal commitment to serve him today, even before knowing what that service will be

Vital statistics:
- Where: Babylon, Jerusalem
- Occupations: Scribe among the exiles in Babylon, king's envoy, teacher
- Relative: Father: Seriah
- Contemporaries: Nehemiah, Artaxerxes

Key verse:
"For Ezra had set his heart to the study the law of the LORD and to practice it, and to teach His statutes and ordinances in Israel" (Ezra 7:10).

Ezra's story is told in Ezra 7:1—10:16 and Nehemiah 8:1—12:36.

8:23 Ezra knew God's promises to protect his people, but he didn't take them for granted. He also knew that God's blessings are appropriated through prayer; so Ezra and the people humbled themselves by fasting and praying. And their prayers were answered. Fasting humbled them because going without food was a reminder of their complete dependence on God. Fasting also gave them more time to pray and meditate on God.

Too often we pray glibly and superficially. Serious prayer, by contrast, requires concentration. It puts us in touch with God's will and can really change us. Without serious prayer, we reduce God to a quick-service pharmacist with painkillers for our every ailment.

26 Thus I weighed into their hands 650 talents of silver, and silver utensils *worth* 100 talents, *and* 100 gold talents,
27 and 20 gold bowls *worth* 1,000 darics, and two utensils of fine shiny bronze, precious as gold.
28 Then I said to them, "You are holy to the LORD, and the utensils are holy; and the silver and the gold are a freewill offering to the LORD God of your fathers.
29 "Watch and keep *them* until you weigh *them* before the leading priests, the Levites and the heads of the fathers' *households* of Israel at Jerusalem, *in* the chambers of the house of the LORD."
30 So the priests and the Levites accepted the weighed out silver and gold and the utensils, to bring *them* to Jerusalem to the house of our God.
31 Then we journeyed from the river Ahava on the twelfth of the first month to go to Jerusalem; and the hand of our God was over us, and He delivered us from the hand of the enemy and the ambushes by the way.
32 Thus we came to Jerusalem and remained there three days.

8:26 Ezra 1:9-11
8:28 Lev 21:6-8; Lev 22:2, 3
8:29 Ezra 8:33, 34
8:30 Ezra 1:9
8:31 Ezra 8:15, 21; Ezra 7:9; Ezra 8:22
8:32 Neh 2:11

Treasure Placed in the Temple

33 On the fourth day the silver and the gold and the utensils were weighed out in the house of our God into the hand of Meremoth the son of Uriah the priest, and with him *was* Eleazar the son of Phinehas; and with them *were* the Levites, Jozabad the son of Jeshua and Noadiah the son of Binnui.
34 Everything *was* numbered and weighed, and all the weight was recorded at that time.
35 The exiles who had come from the captivity offered burnt offerings to the God of Israel: 12 bulls for all Israel, 96 rams, 77 lambs, 12 male goats for a sin offering, all as a burnt offering to the LORD.
36 Then they delivered the king's edicts to the king's satraps and to the governors *in the provinces* beyond the River, and they supported the people and the house of God.

8:33 Ezra 8:30; Neh 3:4, 21
8:35 Ezra 2:1; Ezra 6:17
8:36 Ezra 7:21-24; Ezra 4:7; 5:6

2. Ezra opposes intermarriage

Mixed Marriages

9 Now when these things had been completed, the princes approached me, saying, "The people of Israel and the priests and the Levites have not separated themselves from the peoples of the lands, according to their abominations, *those* of the Canaanites, the Hittites, the Perizzites, the Jebusites, the Ammonites, the Moabites, the Egyptians and the Amorites.
2 "For they have taken some of their daughters *as wives* for themselves and for their sons, so that the holy race has intermingled with the peoples of the lands; indeed, the hands of the princes and the rulers have been foremost in this unfaithfulness."
3 When I heard about this matter, I tore my garment and my robe, and pulled some of the hair from my head and my beard, and sat down appalled.
4 Then everyone who trembled at the words of the God of Israel on account of the unfaithfulness of the exiles gathered to me, and I sat appalled until the evening offering.

9:1 Ezra 6:21; Neh 9:2; Lev 18:24-30
9:2 Deut 7:3; Ezra 10:2, 18; Ex 22:31; Deut 14:2; 2 Cor 6:14; Neh 13:3
9:3 2 Kin 18:37; Neh 1:4
9:4 Ezra 10:3; Is 66:2; Ex 29:39

8:26 Six hundred fifty talents of silver would be about 25 tons. This was a large amount of treasure to transport, with or without a detachment of soldiers for protection.

8:28–29 Every object used in temple service was consecrated to God; each was considered a holy treasure to be guarded carefully and set apart for his special use. Stewardship means taking special care of whatever God has entrusted to you. This means considering what God has given to you as being *from* him and *for* his use. What has God entrusted to your care?

9:1, 2 Since the time of the judges, Israelite men had married pagan women and then adopted their religious practices (Judges 3:5–7). Even Israel's great King Solomon was guilty of this sin (1 Kings 11:1–8). Although this practice was forbidden in God's Law (Exodus 34:11–16; Deuteronomy 7:1–4), it happened in Ezra's day, and again only a generation after him (Nehemiah 13:23–27). Opposition to mixed marriage was not racial prejudice because Jews and non-Jews of this area were of the same Semitic background. The reasons were strictly spiritual. A person who married a pagan was inclined to adopt that person's pagan beliefs and practices. If the Israelites were insensitive enough to disobey God in something as important as marriage, they wouldn't be strong enough to stand firm against their spouses' idolatry. Until the Israelites finally stopped this practice, idolatry remained a constant problem.

9:2 Some Israelites had married pagan spouses and lost track of God's purpose for them. The New Testament says that believers should not "be bound together with unbelievers" (2 Corinthians 6:14). Such marriages cannot have unity in the most important issue in life—commitment and obedience to God. Because marriage involves two people becoming one, faith may become an issue, and one spouse may have to compromise beliefs for the sake of unity. Many people discount this problem only to regret it later. Don't allow emotion or passion to blind you to the ultimate importance of marrying someone with whom you can be united spiritually.

9:3–5 Tearing one's clothes or pulling hair from one's head or beard were signs of self-abasement or humility. They expressed sorrow for sin.

Prayer of Confession

9:5 Ex 9:29

5 But at the evening offering I arose from my humiliation, even with my garment and
my robe torn, and I fell on my knees and stretched out my hands to the LORD my God;

9:6 2 Chr 28:9; Ezra 9:13, 15; Rev 18:5

6 and I said, "O my God, I am ashamed and embarrassed to lift up my face to You,
my God, for our iniquities have risen above our heads and our guilt has grown even to
the heavens.

9:7 2 Chr 29:6; Ps 106:6; Dan 9:7

7 "Since the days of our fathers to this day we *have been* in great guilt, and on account
of our iniquities we, our kings *and* our priests have been given into the hand of the kings
of the lands, to the sword, to captivity and to plunder and to open shame, as *it is* this day.

9:8 Ezra 9:13-15; Is 22:23; Ps 13:3

8 "But now for a brief moment grace has been *shown* from the LORD our God, to leave
us an escaped remnant and to give us a peg in His holy place, that our God may enlight-
en our eyes and grant us a little reviving in our bondage.

9:9 Neh 9:36; Ezra 7:28

9 "For we are slaves; yet in our bondage our God has not forsaken us, but has extended lovingkindness to us in the sight of the kings of Persia, to give us reviving to raise up
the house of our God, to restore its ruins and to give us a wall in Judah and Jerusalem.
10 "Now, our God, what shall we say after this? For we have forsaken Your commandments,

9:11 Ezra 6:21

11 which You have commanded by Your servants the prophets, saying, 'The land which
you are entering to possess is an unclean land with the uncleanness of the peoples of the
lands, with their abominations which have filled it from end to end *and* with their impurity.

9:12 Ex 34:15, 16; Deut 7:3; Ezra 9:2; Deut 23:6; Prov 13:22

12 'So now do not give your daughters to their sons nor take their daughters to your
sons, and never seek their peace or their prosperity, that you may be strong and eat the
good *things* of the land and leave *it* as an inheritance to your sons forever.'

9:13 Ezra 9:6, 7; Ezra 9:8

13 "After all that has come upon us for our evil deeds and our great guilt, since You our
God have requited *us* less than our iniquities *deserve,* and have given us an escaped remnant as this,

9:14 Ezra 9:2; Deut 9:8, 14

14 shall we again break Your commandments and intermarry with the peoples who
commit these abominations? Would You not be angry with us to the point of destruction, until there is no remnant nor any who escape?

9:15 Neh 9:33; Dan 9:7; Ezra 9:6; Job 9:2; Ps 130:3

15 "O LORD God of Israel, You are righteous, for we have been left an escaped remnant, as *it is* this day; behold, we are before You in our guilt, for no one can stand before
You because of this."

Reconciliation with God

10:1 Dan 9:4, 20; 2 Chr 20:9

10 Now while Ezra was praying and making confession, weeping and prostrating himself before the house of God, a very large assembly, men, women and children,
gathered to him from Israel; for the people wept bitterly.

10:2 Ezra 9:2; Neh 13:27

2 Shecaniah the son of Jehiel, one of the sons of Elam, said to Ezra, "We have been
unfaithful to our God and have married foreign women from the peoples of the land;
yet now there is hope for Israel in spite of this.

9:5–15 After learning about the sins of the people, Ezra fell to his knees in prayer. His heartfelt prayer provides a good perspective on sin. He recognized: (1) that sin is serious (9:6); (2) that no one sins without affecting others (9:7); (3) that he was not sinless, although he didn't have a pagan wife (9:10ff); (4) that God's love and mercy had spared the nation when they did nothing to deserve it (9:8–9, 15). It is easy to view sin lightly in a world that sees sin as inconsequential, but we should view sin as seriously as Ezra did.

9:5–15 Ezra's prayer confessed the sins of his people. Although he had not sinned in the way his people had, he identified with their sins. With weeping, he expressed shame for sin, fear of the consequences, and desire that the people would come to their senses and repent. His prayer moved the people to tears (10:1). Ezra demonstrated the need for a holy community around the rebuilt temple. We need a holy community in our local churches too. Even when we sin in the worst imaginable way, we can turn to God with prayers of repentance.

9:9 Building a wall was not only a matter of civic pride or architectural beauty, it was essential for security and defense against robbers and marauders (see 9:7). God in his kindness had given them new life and protection.

9:15 Ezra recognized that if God gave the people the justice they deserved, they would not be able to stand before him. Often we cry out for justice when we feel abused and unfairly treated. In those moments, we forget the reality of our own sin and the righteous judgment we deserve. How fortunate we are that God gives us mercy and grace rather than only justice. The next time you ask God for fair and just treatment, pause to think what would happen if God gave you what you really deserve. Plead instead for his mercy.

3 "So now let us make a covenant with our God to put away all the wives and their
children, according to the counsel of [8]my lord and of those who tremble at the commandment of our God; and let it be done according to the law.

10:3 2 Chr 34:31; Ezra 10:44; Ezra 9:4; Deut 7:2, 3

4 "Arise! For *this* matter is your responsibility, but we will be with you; be courageous
and act."

10:4 1 Chr 28:10

5 Then Ezra rose and made the leading priests, the Levites and all Israel, take oath
that they would do according to this proposal; so they took the oath.

10:5 Neh 5:12; 13:25

6 Then Ezra rose from before the house of God and went into the chamber of Jehohanan the son of Eliashib. Although he went there, he did not eat bread nor drink water, for he was mourning over the unfaithfulness of the exiles.

10:6 Ezra 10:1; Deut 9:18

7 They made a proclamation throughout Judah and Jerusalem to all the exiles, that
they should assemble at Jerusalem,
8 and that whoever would not come within three days, according to the counsel of the
leaders and the elders, all his possessions should be forfeited and he himself excluded
from the assembly of the exiles.
9 So all the men of Judah and Benjamin assembled at Jerusalem within the three days.
It was the ninth month on the twentieth of the month, and all the people sat in the open
square *before* the house of God, trembling because of this matter and the heavy rain.

10:9 1 Sam 12:18; Ezra 9:4; 10:3

10 Then Ezra the priest stood up and said to them, "You have been unfaithful and have
married foreign wives adding to the guilt of Israel.
11 "Now therefore, make confession to the LORD God of your fathers and do His will;
and separate yourselves from the peoples of the land and from the foreign wives."

10:11 Lev 26:40; Prov 28:13; Rom 12:2; Ezra 10:3

12 Then all the assembly replied with a loud voice, "That's right! As you have said, so
it is our duty to do.
13 "But there are many people; it is the rainy season and we are not able to stand in the
open. Nor *can* the task *be done* in one or two days, for we have transgressed greatly in
this matter.
14 "Let our leaders represent the whole assembly and let all those in our cities who have
married foreign wives come at appointed times, together with the elders and judges of each
city, until the fierce anger of our God on account of this matter is turned away from us."

10:14 2 Kin 23:26; 2 Chr 28:11-13; 29:10; 30:8

15 Only Jonathan the son of Asahel and Jahzeiah the son of Tikvah opposed this, with
Meshullam and Shabbethai the Levite supporting them.
16 But the exiles did so. And Ezra the priest selected men *who were* heads of fathers'
households for *each of* their father's households, all of them by name. So they convened
on the first day of the tenth month to investigate the matter.
17 They finished *investigating* all the men who had married foreign wives by the first
day of the first month.

List of Offenders

18 Among the sons of the priests who had married foreign wives were found of the
sons of Jeshua the son of Jozadak, and his brothers: Maaseiah, Eliezer, Jarib and Gedaliah.

10:18 Ezra 5:2; Hag 1:1, 12; 2:4; Zech 3:1; 6:11

8 Or *the Lord*

10:3 Why were the men commanded to send away their wives and children? Although the measure was extreme, intermarriage to pagans was strictly forbidden (Deuteronomy 7:3–4), and even the priests and Levites had intermarried. This could be compared today to a Christian marrying a devil worshiper. Although a severe solution, it only involved 113 of the approximately 29,000 families.

Ezra's strong act, though very difficult for some, was necessary to preserve Israel as a nation committed to God. Some of the exiles of the northern kingdom of Israel had lost both their spiritual and physical identity through intermarriage. Their pagan spouses had caused the people to worship idols. Ezra did not want this to happen to the exiles of the southern kingdom of Judah.

10:3–4, 11 Following Ezra's earnest prayer, the people confessed their sin to God. Then they asked for direction in restoring their relationship with God. True repentance does not end with words of confession—that would be mere lip service. It must lead to corrected behavior and changed attitudes. When you sin and are truly sorry, confess this to God, ask his forgiveness, and accept his grace and mercy. Then, as an act of thankfulness for your forgiveness, make the needed corrections.

10:8 To forfeit one's property meant to be disinherited: to lose one's legal right to own land. This was to ensure that no pagan children would inherit Israel's land. In addition, the person who refused to come to Jerusalem would be expelled from the assembly of the exiles and not allowed to worship in the temple. The Jews considered this a horrible punishment.

10:11 As believers in Christ, all our sins are forgiven. His death cleansed us from all sin. Why do we then still confess our sins? Confession is more than appropriating Christ's forgiveness for what we have done wrong, and we do not have to confess again sins that were previously confessed. Confession is agreeing with God that our thoughts, words, and actions are wrong and contrary to his will. It is recommitting ourselves to do his will and to renounce any acts of disobedience. Confession is turning away from sin and asking God for fresh power to live for him.

10:19 Lev 5:15; 6:6

19 They pledged to put away their wives, and being guilty, *they offered* a ram of the flock
for their offense.
20 Of the sons of Immer *there were* Hanani and Zebadiah;
21 and of the sons of Harim: Maaseiah, Elijah, Shemaiah, Jehiel and Uzziah;
22 and of the sons of Pashhur: Elioenai, Maaseiah, Ishmael, Nethanel, Jozabad and
Elasah.
23 Of Levites *there were* Jozabad, Shimei, Kelaiah (that is, Kelita), Pethahiah, Judah
and Eliezer.
24 Of the singers *there was* Eliashib; and of the gatekeepers: Shallum, Telem and Uri.
25 Of Israel, of the sons of Parosh *there were* Ramiah, Izziah, Malchijah, Mijamin, Eleazar, Malchijah and Benaiah;
26 and of the sons of Elam: Mattaniah, Zechariah, Jehiel, Abdi, Jeremoth and Elijah;
27 and of the sons of Zattu: Elioenai, Eliashib, Mattaniah, Jeremoth, Zabad and
Aziza;
28 and of the sons of Bebai: Jehohanan, Hananiah, Zabbai *and* Athlai;
29 and of the sons of Bani: Meshullam, Malluch and Adaiah, Jashub, Sheal *and* Jeremoth;
30 and of the sons of Pahath-moab: Adna, Chelal, Benaiah, Maaseiah, Mattaniah,
Bezalel, Binnui and Manasseh;
31 and *of* the sons of Harim: Eliezer, Isshijah, Malchijah, Shemaiah, Shimeon,
32 Benjamin, Malluch *and* Shemariah;
33 of the sons of Hashum: Mattenai, Mattattah, Zabad, Eliphelet, Jeremai, Manasseh
and Shimei;
34 of the sons of Bani: Maadai, Amram, Uel,
35 Benaiah, Bedeiah, Cheluhi,
36 Vaniah, Meremoth, Eliashib,
37 Mattaniah, Mattenai, Jaasu,
38 Bani, Binnui, Shimei,
39 Shelemiah, Nathan, Adaiah,
40 Machnadebai, Shashai, Sharai,
41 Azarel, Shelemiah, Shemariah,
42 Shallum, Amariah *and* Joseph.
43 Of the sons of Nebo *there were* Jeiel, Mattithiah, Zabad, Zebina, Jaddai, Joel *and*
Benaiah.
44 All these had married foreign wives, and some of them had wives *by whom* they had
children.

10:25 Ezra 2:3; 8:3; Neh 7:8
10:27 Ezra 2:8; Neh 7:13
10:31 Neh 3:11
10:43 Num 32:38; Ezra 2:29
10:44 1 Kin 11:1-3; Ezra 10:3

10:44 The book of Ezra opens with God's temple in ruins and the people of Judah captive in Babylon. Ezra tells of the return of God's people, the rebuilding of the temple, and the restoration of the sacrificial worship system. Similarly, God is able to restore and rebuild the lives of people today. No one is so far away from God that he or she cannot be restored. Repentance is all that is required. No matter how far we have strayed or how long it has been since we have worshiped God, he is able to restore our relationship to him and rebuild our lives.

NEHEMIAH

Jerusalem destroyed; exiles go to Babylon 586 B.C.

First exiles return to Jerusalem 538

Temple completed 515

VITAL STATISTICS

PURPOSE:
Nehemiah is the last of the Old Testament historical books. It records the history of the third return to Jerusalem after captivity, telling how the walls were rebuilt and the people were renewed in their faith.

AUTHOR:
Much of the book is written in the first person, suggesting Nehemiah as the author. Nehemiah probably wrote the book with Ezra serving as editor.

DATE WRITTEN:
Approximately 445–432 B.C.

SETTING:
Zerubbabel led the first return to Jerusalem in 538 B.C. In 458, Ezra led the second return. Finally, in 445, Nehemiah returned with the third group of exiles to rebuild the city walls.

KEY VERSES:
"So the wall was completed on the twenty-fifth of the month Elul, in fifty-two days. When all our enemies heard of it, and all the nations surrounding us saw it, they lost their confidence; for they recognized that this work had been accomplished with the help of our God" (6:15–16).

KEY PEOPLE:
Nehemiah, Ezra, Sanballat, Tobiah

KEY PLACE:
Jerusalem

SPECIAL FEATURES:
The book shows the fulfillment of the prophecies of Zechariah and Daniel concerning the rebuilding of Jerusalem's walls.

"WHAT this church needs is . . . !" "I can't believe our government officials. If I were there I would . . . !" "Our schools are really in bad shape. Someone ought to do something!"

Gripers, complainers, self-proclaimed prophets, and "armchair quarterbacks" abound. It is easy to analyze, scrutinize, and *talk* about all the problems in the world. But what we really need are people who will not just discuss a situation but who will *do* something about it!

Nehemiah saw a problem and was distressed. Instead of complaining or wallowing in self-pity and grief, he took action. Nehemiah knew that God wanted him to motivate the Jews to rebuild Jerusalem's walls, so he left a responsible position in the Persian government to do what God wanted. Nehemiah knew God could use his talents to get the job done. From the moment he arrived in Jerusalem, everyone knew who was in charge. He organized, managed, supervised, encouraged, met opposition, confronted injustice, and kept going until the walls were built. Nehemiah was a man of action.

As the story begins, Nehemiah was talking with fellow Jews who reported that the walls and gates of Jerusalem were in disrepair. This was disturbing news, and rebuilding those walls became Nehemiah's burden. At the appropriate time, Nehemiah asked King Artaxerxes for permission to go to Jerusalem to rebuild its fallen walls. The king approved.

Armed with royal letters, Nehemiah traveled to Jerusalem. He organized the people into groups and assigned them to specific sections of the wall (chapter 3). The construction project was not without opposition, however. Sanballat, Tobiah, and others tried to halt the work with insults, ridicule, threats, and sabotage. Some of the workers became fearful; others became weary. In each case, Nehemiah employed a strategy to frustrate the enemies—prayer, encouragement, guard duty, consolidation (chapter 4). But a different problem arose—an internal one. Rich Jews were profiteering off the plight of their working countrymen. Hearing of their oppression and greed, Nehemiah confronted the extortioners face to face (chapter 5). Then, with the walls almost complete, Sanballat, Tobiah, and company tried one last time to stop Nehemiah. But Nehemiah stood firm, and the wall was finished in just 52 days. What a tremendous monument to God's love and faithfulness. Enemies and friends alike knew that God had helped (chapter 6).

After building the walls, Nehemiah continued to organize the people, taking a registration and appointing gatekeepers, Levites, and other officials (chapter 7). Ezra led the city in worship and Bible instruction (chapters 8; 9). This led to a reaffirmation of faith and religious revival as the people promised to serve God faithfully (chapters 10; 11).

Nehemiah closes with the listing of the clans and their leaders, the dedication of the new wall of Jerusalem, and the purging of sin from the land (chapters 12; 13). As you read this book, watch Nehemiah in action—and determine to be a person on whom God can depend to *act* for him in the world.

Ahasuerus becomes king of Persia 486	Artaxerxes I becomes king of Persia 465	Ezra comes to Jerusalem 458	Nehemiah comes to Jerusalem; wall completed 445	Nehemiah returns to Babylon 433	Nehemiah goes back to Jerusalem 432	Malachi begins his ministry 430(?)

THE BLUEPRINT

A. REBUILDING THE WALL (1:1—7:73)
1. Nehemiah returns to Jerusalem
2. Nehemiah leads the people

Nehemiah's life is an example of leadership and organization. Giving up a comfortable and wealthy position in Persia, he returned to the fractured homeland of his ancestors and rallied the people to rebuild Jerusalem's wall. In the face of opposition, he used wise defense measures to care for the people and to keep the project moving. To accomplish more for the sake of God's kingdom, we must pray, persevere, and sacrifice, as did Nehemiah.

B. REFORMING THE PEOPLE (7:73—13:31)
1. Ezra renews the covenant
2. Nehemiah establishes policies

After the wall was rebuilt, Ezra read the Law to the people, bringing about national repentance. Nehemiah and Ezra were very different people, yet God used them both to lead the nation. Remember, there is a place for you in God's work even if you're different from most other people. God uses each person in a unique way to accomplish his purposes.

MEGATHEMES

THEME	EXPLANATION	IMPORTANCE
Vision	Although the Jews completed the temple in 515 B.C., the city walls remained in shambles for the next 70 years. These walls represented power, protection, and beauty to the city of Jerusalem. They were also desperately needed to protect the temple from attack and to ensure the continuity of worship. God put the desire to rebuild the walls in Nehemiah's heart, giving him a vision for the work.	Does God have a vision for us? Are there "walls" that need to be built today? God still wants his people to be united and trained to do his work. As we recognize deep needs in our world, God can give us the vision and desire to "build." With that vision, we can mobilize others to pray and put together a plan of action.
Prayer	Both Nehemiah and Ezra responded to problems with prayer. When Nehemiah began his work, he recognized the problem, immediately prayed, and then acted on the problem.	Prayer is still God's mighty force in solving problems today. Prayer and action go hand in hand. Through prayer, God guides our preparation, teamwork, and diligent efforts to carry out his will.
Leadership	Nehemiah demonstrated excellent leadership. He was spiritually ready to heed God's call. He used careful planning, teamwork, problem solving, and courage to get the work done. Although he had tremendous faith, he never avoided the extra work necessary for good leadership.	Being God's leader is not just gaining recognition, holding a position, or being the boss. It requires planning, hard work, courage, and perseverance. Positive expectations are never a substitute for doing the difficult work. And in order to lead others, you need to listen for God's direction in your own life.
Problems	After the work began, Nehemiah faced scorn, slander, and threats from enemies, as well as fear, conflict, and discouragement from his own workers. Although these problems were difficult, they did not stop Nehemiah from finishing the work.	When difficulties come, there is a tendency for conflict and discouragement to set in. We must recognize that there are no triumphs without troubles. When problems arise, we must face them squarely and press on to complete God's work.
Repentance/ Revival	Although God had enabled them to build the wall, the work wasn't complete until the people rebuilt their lives spiritually. Ezra instructed the people in God's Word. As they listened, they recognized the sin in their lives, admitted it, and took steps to remove it.	Recognizing and admitting sin are not enough; revival must result in reform, or it is merely the expression of enthusiasm. God does not want halfhearted measures. We must not only remove sin from our lives but also ask God to move into the center of all we do.

A. REBUILDING THE WALL (1:1—7:73)

Despite the fact that the returned exiles had been in Jerusalem for many years, the walls of the city remained unrepaired, leaving its people defenseless and vulnerable. Upon hearing this news, Nehemiah seeks permission from the Persian king to go to Jerusalem. Arriving in Jerusalem, he mobilizes the people to begin rebuilding the wall. Faced with opposition, both from without and from within, Nehemiah perseveres until the project is complete and the city resettled. Seemingly impossible tasks can be accomplished when God is helping those who honor him and when their efforts are united.

1. Nehemiah returns to Jerusalem

Nehemiah's Grief for the Exiles

1 The words of Nehemiah the son of Hacaliah.
Now it happened in the month Chislev, *in* the twentieth year, while I was in Susa the
[1]capitol,
2 that Hanani, one of my brothers, and some men from Judah came; and I asked them
concerning the Jews who had escaped *and* had survived the captivity, and about Jerusalem.
3 They said to me, "The remnant there in the province who survived the captivity are
in great distress and reproach, and the wall of Jerusalem is broken down and its gates
are burned with fire."
4 When I heard these words, I sat down and wept and mourned for days; and I was
fasting and praying before the God of heaven.
5 I said, "I beseech You, O LORD God of heaven, the great and awesome God, who
preserves the covenant and lovingkindness for those who love Him and keep His commandments,
6 let Your ear now be attentive and Your eyes open to hear the prayer of Your servant which I am praying before You now, day and night, on behalf of the sons of Israel
Your servants, confessing the sins of the sons of Israel which we have sinned against You;
I and my father's house have sinned.
7 "We have acted very corruptly against You and have not kept the commandments,
nor the statutes, nor the ordinances which You commanded Your servant Moses.
8 "Remember the word which You commanded Your servant Moses, saying, 'If you
are unfaithful I will scatter you among the peoples;

1:1 Neh 10:1; Zech 7:1; Neh 2:1; Esth 1:2; Dan 8:2
1:2 Neh 7:2
1:3 Neh 7:6; Neh 2:17; Neh 2:3
1:4 Ezra 9:3; 10:1; Neh 2:4
1:5 Neh 4:14; 9:32; Dan 9:4; Ex 20:6; Ps 89:2, 3
1:6 Dan 9:17; Ezra 10:1; Dan 9:20; 2 Chr 29:6
1:7 Dan 9:5; Deut 28:14
1:8 Lev 26:33

1 Or *palace* or *citadel*

1:1 Nehemiah wasn't the first of the exiles to return to Jerusalem. Zerubbabel had led the first group back in 538 B.C., more than 90 years earlier (Ezra 1–2). Ezra followed with a second group in 458 B.C. (Ezra 7), and here Nehemiah was ready to lead the third major return to Jerusalem (445 B.C.). When he arrived after a three-month journey, he saw the completed temple and became acquainted with others who had returned to their homeland.

But Nehemiah also found a disorganized group of people and a defenseless city with no walls to protect it. Before the exile, Israel had its own language, king, army, and identity. At this time it had none of these. What the Jews lacked most was leadership; there was no one to show them where to start and what direction to take as they tried to rebuild their city. As soon as Nehemiah arrived he began a back to the basics program. He helped care for the people's physical needs by setting up a fair system of government and rebuilding Jerusalem's walls. He also cared for their spiritual needs by rebuilding broken lives. Nehemiah is a model of committed, God-honoring leadership, and his book contains many useful lessons for today.

1:2–4 Nehemiah was concerned about Jerusalem because it was the Jews' holy city. As Judah's capital city, it represented Jewish national identity, and it was blessed with God's special presence in the temple. Jewish history centered around the city from the time of Abraham's gifts to Melchizedek, king of Salem (Genesis 14:17–20), to the days when Solomon built the glorious temple (1 Kings 7:51), and throughout the history of the kings. Nehemiah loved his homeland even though he had lived his whole life in Babylon. He wanted to return to Jerusalem to reunite the Jews and to remove the shame of Jerusalem's broken-down walls. This would bring glory to God and restore the reality and power of God's presence among his people.

1:4 Nehemiah broke down and wept when he heard that Jerusalem's walls still had not been rebuilt. Why did this upset him? Walls mean little in most present-day cities, but in Nehemiah's day they were essential. They offered safety from raids and symbolized strength and peace. Nehemiah also mourned for his people, the Jews, who had been stifled by a previous edict that kept them from rebuilding their walls (Ezra 4:6–23).

1:4 Nehemiah was deeply grieved about the condition of Jerusalem, but he didn't just brood about it. After his initial grief, he prayed, pouring his heart out to God (1:5–11), and he looked for ways to improve the situation. Nehemiah put all his resources of knowledge, experience, and organization into determining what should be done. When tragic news comes to you, first pray. Then seek ways to move beyond grief to specific action that helps those who need it.

1:5 God's covenant refers to God's promise to love the descendants of Abraham. It is also mentioned in Deuteronomy 7:7–9.

1:5ff Nehemiah fasted and prayed for several days, expressing his sorrow for Israel's sin and his desire that Jerusalem would again come alive with the worship of the one true God. Nehemiah demonstrated the elements of effective prayer: (1) praise, (2) thanksgiving, (3) repentance, (4) specific request, and (5) commitment.

Heartfelt prayers like Nehemiah's can help clarify (1) any problem you may be facing, (2) God's great power to help you, and (3) the job you have to do. By the end of his prayer time, Nehemiah knew what action he had to take (1:11). When God's people pray, difficult decisions fall into proper perspective, and appropriate actions follow.

1:9 Deut 30:2, 3; Deut 30:4; Deut 12:5

9 but *if* you return to Me and keep My commandments and do them, though those of
you who have been scattered were in the most remote part of the heavens, I will gather
them from there and will bring them to the place where I have chosen to cause My name
to dwell.'

1:10 Ex 32:11; Deut 9:29

10 "They are Your servants and Your people whom You redeemed by Your great power
and by Your strong hand.

1:11 Neh 1:6; Gen 40:21; Neh 2:1

11 "O Lord, I beseech You, may Your ear be attentive to the prayer of Your servant and
the prayer of Your servants who delight to revere Your name, and make Your servant
successful today and grant him compassion before this man."

Now I was the cupbearer to the king.

Nehemiah's Prayer Answered

2:1 Neh 1:1; Ezra 7:1; Neh 1:11

2 And it came about in the month Nisan, in the twentieth year of King Artaxerxes,
that wine *was* before him, and I took up the wine and gave it to the king. Now I had
not been sad in his presence.

2:2 Prov 15:13

2 So the king said to me, "Why is your face sad though you are not sick? This is nothing but sadness of heart." Then I was very much afraid.

2:3 Dan 2:4; 2 Kin 25:8-10; 2 Chr 36:19; Neh 1:3; Jer 52:12-14

3 I said to the king, "Let the king live forever. Why should my face not be sad when the
city, the place of my fathers' tombs, lies desolate and its gates have been consumed by fire?"

HOW NEHEMIAH USED PRAYER

Reference	*Occasion*	*Summary of his Prayer*	*What Prayer Accomplished*	*Our Prayers*
1:4–11	After receiving the bad news about the state of Jerusalem's walls	Recognized God's holiness. Asked for a hearing. Confessed sin. Asked for specific help in approaching the king	Included God in Nehemiah's plans and concerns. Prepared Nehemiah's heart and gave God room to work	How often do you pour out your heart to God? How often do you give him a specific request to answer?
2:4	During his conversation with the king	"Here's where you can help, God!"	Put the expected results in God's hands	Giving God credit for what happens before it happens keeps us from taking more credit than we should.
4:4–5	After being taunted and ridiculed by Tobiah and Sanballat	"They're mocking you, God. You decide what to do with them."	Expressed anger to God, but Nehemiah did not take matters into his own hands	We are prone to do exactly the opposite— take matters into our hands and not tell God how we feel.
4:9	After threats of attack by enemies	"We are in your hands, God. We'll keep our weapons handy in case you want us to use them."	Showed trust in God even while taking necessary precautions	Trusting God does not mean we do nothing. Action does not mean we do not trust.
6:9	Responding to threats	"Oh Lord God, please strengthen me!"	Showed Nehemiah's reliance on God for emotional and mental stability	How often do you ask God for help when under pressure?
13:29	Reflecting on the actions of his enemies	Asked God to deal with the enemies and their evil plans	Took away the compulsion to get revenge, and entrusted justice to God	When did you last settle a desire for revenge by turning the matter over to God?
5:19; 13:14, 22, 31	Reflecting on his own efforts to serve God	"Remember me, God."	Kept clear in Nehemiah's mind his own motives for action	How many of your actions today will be done with the purpose of pleasing God?

1:11 Nehemiah was in a unique position to speak to the king. He was the trusted cupbearer who ensured the safety and quality of the king's food and drink. Nehemiah was concerned, prayerful, and prepared as he looked for the right opportunity to tell the king about God's people. Each of us is unique and capable of serving no matter what our position. Just as Nehemiah used his place as the king's trusted servant to intercede for his people, so we can use our present positions to serve God.

1:11 Nehemiah prayed for success in this venture, not just for the strength to cope with his problems (see also 2:20). Yet the success he prayed for was not for personal advantage, position, or acclaim. He requested success for God's work. When God's purposes are at work, don't hesitate to ask for success.

2:2 The king noticed Nehemiah's sad appearance. This frightened Nehemiah because it was dangerous to show sorrow before the king, who could execute anyone who displeased him. Anyone wearing sackcloth (mourning clothes) was barred from the palace (Esther 4:2).

2:2–3 Nehemiah wasn't ashamed to admit his fear, but he refused to allow fear to stop him from doing what God had called him to do. When we allow our fears to rule us, we make fear more powerful than God. Is there a task God wants you to do, but fear is holding you back? God is greater than all your fears. Recognizing why you are afraid is the first step in committing it to God. Realize that if God has called you to a task, he will help you accomplish it.

4 Then the king said to me, "What would you request?" So I prayed to the God of heaven. **2:4** Neh 1:4
5 I said to the king, "If it please the king, and if your servant has found favor before you, send me to Judah, to the city of my fathers' tombs, that I may rebuild it."
6 Then the king said to me, the queen sitting beside him, "How long will your journey be, and when will you return?" So it pleased the king to send me, and I gave him a definite time. **2:6** Neh 13:6
7 And I said to the king, "If it please the king, let letters be given me for the governors *of the provinces* beyond the River, that they may allow me to pass through until I come to Judah, **2:7** Ezra 7:21; 8:36
8 and a letter to Asaph the keeper of the king's forest, that he may give me timber to make beams for the gates of the fortress which is by the [2]temple, for the wall of the city and for the house to which I will go." And the king granted *them* to me because the good hand of my God *was* on me. **2:8** Eccl 2:5, 6; Neh 7:2; Ezra 7:6; Neh 2:18
9 Then I came to the governors *of the provinces* beyond the River and gave them the king's letters. Now the king had sent with me officers of the army and horsemen. **2:9** Neh 2:7; Ezra 8:22
10 When Sanballat the Horonite and Tobiah the Ammonite official heard *about it,* it was very displeasing to them that someone had come to seek the welfare of the sons of Israel. **2:10** Neh 2:19; 4:1

2. Nehemiah leads the people

Nehemiah Inspects Jerusalem's Walls

11 So I came to Jerusalem and was there three days. **2:11** Ezra 8:32
12 And I arose in the night, I and a few men with me. I did not tell anyone what my

2 Lit *house*

2:4 With little time to think, Nehemiah immediately prayed. Eight times in this book we read that he prayed spontaneously (2:4; 4:4–5, 9; 5:19; 6:14; 13:14, 22, 29). Nehemiah prayed at any time, even while talking with others. He knew that God is always in charge, is always present, and hears and answers every prayer. Nehemiah could confidently pray throughout the day because he had established an intimate relationship with God during times of extended prayer (1:4–7). If we want to reach God with our emergency prayers, we need to take time to cultivate a strong relationship with God through times of in-depth prayer.

2:6 The king asked Nehemiah how long he would be gone. The Bible does not record Nehemiah's immediate answer, but he ended up staying in Jerusalem 12 years (5:14; 13:6).

2:7–8 After his prayer, Nehemiah asked the king for permission to go to Judah. As soon as he got a positive answer, he began asking for additional help. Sometimes when we have needs, we hesitate to ask the right people for help because we are afraid to approach them. Not Nehemiah! He went directly to the person who could help him the most. Don't be reluctant to ask those who are most able to help. They may be more interested and approachable than you think. God's answers to prayer may come as a result of our asking others.

2:8 Nehemiah had position, power, and many good organizational skills, but he acknowledged that God's gracious hand was upon him. He knew that without God's strength his efforts would be in vain. Do you acknowledge God as your power source and the giver of your gifts?

2:9–10, 19 When Nehemiah arrived in Judah, he was greeted with opposition. Opposition to the rebuilding of Jerusalem had been going on for 90 years by those who had settled in the area when the Jews were taken captive. In every generation there are those who hate God's people and try to block God's purpose. When you attempt to do God's work, some will oppose you; some will even hope you fail. If you expect opposition, you will be prepared rather than surprised (1 John 3:13). Knowing that God is behind your task is the best incentive to move ahead in the face of opposition.

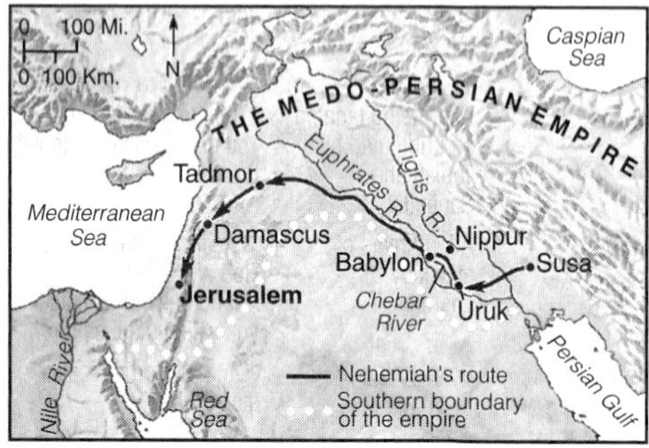

NEHEMIAH GOES TO JERUSALEM Nehemiah worked in Susa as a personal assistant for the king of the vast Medo-Persian Empire. When he heard that the rebuilding projects in Jerusalem were progressing slowly, he asked the king if he could go there to help his people complete the task of rebuilding their city's walls. The king agreed to let him go; so he left as soon as possible, traveling along much the same route Ezra had taken.

2:10 Sanballat was governor of Samaria, and Tobiah was probably governor of Transjordan under the Persians. Why were these government officials so concerned about the arrival of Nehemiah and his small band of exiles? There are several possible reasons. (1) When Zerubbabel first returned with his group (Ezra 1; 2), his refusal to accept help from the Samaritans had caused bad relations. (2) Nehemiah was no ordinary exile; he was the king's personal adviser and cupbearer, arriving in Jerusalem with the king's approval to build and fortify the city. If anyone could rebuild Jerusalem, he could. A rebuilt Jerusalem was a threat to the authority of the Samaritan officials who had been in charge of the land since Judah's exile. (3) This was the third group to return from exile. The increasing number of people in Jerusalem made Sanballat and

God was putting into my mind to do for Jerusalem and there was no animal with me
except the animal on which I was riding.

2:13 Neh 3:13; Neh 1:3; Neh 2:3, 17

13 So I went out at night by the Valley Gate in the direction of the Dragon's Well and
on to the Refuse Gate, inspecting the walls of Jerusalem which were broken down and
its gates which were consumed by fire.

2:14 Neh 3:15; 2 Kin 20:20

14 Then I passed on to the Fountain Gate and the King's Pool, but there was no place
for my mount to pass.

2:15 John 18:1

15 So I went up at night by the ravine and inspected the wall. Then I entered the Valley
Gate again and returned.
16 The officials did not know where I had gone or what I had done; nor had I as yet
told the Jews, the priests, the nobles, the officials or the rest who did the work.

2:17 Neh 1:3

17 Then I said to them, "You see the bad situation we are in, that Jerusalem is desolate
and its gates burned by fire. Come, let us rebuild the wall of Jerusalem so that we will no
longer be a reproach."

2:18 2 Sam 2:7

18 I told them how the hand of my God had been favorable to me and also about the
king's words which he had spoken to me. Then they said, "Let us arise and build." So
they put their hands to the good *work.*

2:19 Neh 6:6; Neh 4:1

19 But when Sanballat the Horonite and Tobiah the Ammonite official, and Geshem
the Arab heard *it,* they mocked us and despised us and said, "What is this thing you are
doing? Are you rebelling against the king?"

2:20 Ezra 4:3; Neh 2:4; Acts 8:21

20 So I answered them and said to them, "The God of heaven will give us success; therefore we His servants will arise and build, but you have no portion, right or memorial in
Jerusalem."

3:1 Neh 3:20; 13:28; Neh 3:32; 12:39; Neh 6:1; 7:1; Neh 12:39; Jer 31:38

Builders of the Walls

3 Then Eliashib the high priest arose with his brothers the priests and built the Sheep
Gate; they consecrated it and hung its doors. They consecrated the wall to the Tower
of the Hundred *and* the Tower of Hananel.

3:2 Neh 7:36

2 Next to him the men of Jericho built, and next to them Zaccur the son of Imri built.

Tobiah angry. They did not want returned exiles taking control of the land and threatening their secure position.

2:11–17 Nehemiah arrived quietly in Jerusalem and spent several days carefully observing and assessing the damage to the walls. Following this time of thoughtful consideration, he confidently presented his plan. Nehemiah demonstrated an excellent approach to problem solving. He got firsthand information and carefully considered the situation. Then he presented a realistic strategy. Before jumping into a project, follow Nehemiah's example and plan ahead. Check your information to make sure your ideas will work—be realistic. Then you will be able to present your plan with confidence.

2:14 The walls were so broken down that Nehemiah's mount couldn't get through, so Nehemiah had to inspect that section on foot.

2:15–16 Nehemiah kept his mission a secret and surveyed the walls by moonlight to avoid unhealthy gossip about his arrival and to prevent enemies from being alerted to his plans. Only after planning carefully would he be ready to go public with his mission from God. A premature announcement could have caused rivalry among the Jews as to the best way to begin. In this case, Nehemiah didn't need tedious planning sessions; he needed one plan that would bring quick action.

2:17–18 Spiritual renewal often begins with one person's vision. Nehemiah had a vision, and he shared it with enthusiasm, inspiring Jerusalem's leaders to rebuild the walls.

We frequently underestimate people and don't challenge them with our dreams for God's work in the world. When God plants an idea in your mind to accomplish something for him, share it with others and trust the Holy Spirit to impress them with similar thoughts. Don't regard yourself as the only one through whom God is working. Often God uses one person to express the vision and others to turn it into reality. When you encourage and inspire others, you put teamwork into action to accomplish God's goals.

2:19 Sanballat and Tobiah labeled the rebuilding of Jerusalem's walls as rebellion against the king, probably threatening to report the builders as traitors. These enemies also ridiculed Nehemiah, saying that the walls could never be rebuilt because the damage was too extensive. Nehemiah did not tell them he already had permission from the king to rebuild. Instead, he simply said he had God's approval—that was enough.

3:1 The high priest is the first person mentioned who pitched in and helped with the work. Spiritual leaders must lead not only by word, but also by action. The Sheep Gate was the gate used to bring sheep into the city to the temple for sacrifices. Nehemiah had the priests repair this gate and section of the wall, respecting the priests' area of interest and at the same time emphasizing the priority of worship.

3:1ff All the citizens of Jerusalem did their part on the huge job of rebuilding the city wall. Similarly, the work of the church requires every member's effort in order for the body of Christ to function effectively (1 Corinthians 12:12–27). The body needs you! Are you doing your part? Find a place to serve God, and start contributing whatever time, talent, and money is needed.

3:1ff Jerusalem was a large city, and because many roads converged there, it required many gates. The wall on each side of these heavy wooden gates was taller and thicker so soldiers could stand guard to defend the gates against attack. Sometimes two stone towers guarded the gate. In times of peace, the city gates were hubs of activity—city council was held there, and shopkeepers set up their wares at the entrance. Building the city walls and gates was not only a military priority, but also a boost for trade and commerce.

3 Now the sons of Hassenaah built the Fish Gate; they laid its beams and hung its **3:3**
doors with its bolts and bars. Neh 12:39
4 Next to them Meremoth the son of Uriah the son of Hakkoz made repairs. And
next to him Meshullam the son of Berechiah the son of Meshezabel made repairs. And
next to him Zadok the son of Baana *also* made repairs.
5 Moreover, next to him the Tekoites made repairs, but their nobles did not support
the work of their masters.
6 Joiada the son of Paseah and Meshullam the son of Besodeiah repaired the Old **3:6**
Gate; they laid its beams and hung its doors with its bolts and its bars. Neh 12:39
7 Next to them Melatiah the Gibeonite and Jadon the Meronothite, the men of Gib- **3:7**
eon and of Mizpah, also made repairs for the official seat of the governor *of the province* Neh 2:7
beyond the River.
8 Next to him Uzziel the son of Harhaiah of the goldsmiths made repairs. And next **3:8**
to him Hananiah, one of the perfumers, made repairs, and they restored Jerusalem as Neh 3:31, 32; Neh
far as the Broad Wall. 12:38
9 Next to them Rephaiah the son of Hur, the official of half the district of Jerusalem, **3:9**
made repairs. Neh 3:12, 17
10 Next to them Jedaiah the son of Harumaph made repairs opposite his house. And
next to him Hattush the son of Hashabneiah made repairs.
11 Malchijah the son of Harim and Hasshub the son of Pahath-moab repaired another **3:11**
section and the Tower of Furnaces. Neh 12:38
12 Next to him Shallum the son of Hallohesh, the official of half the district of Jerusa- **3:12**
lem, made repairs, he and his daughters. Neh 3:9
13 Hanun and the inhabitants of Zanoah repaired the Valley Gate. They built it and **3:13**
hung its doors with its bolts and its bars, and a thousand cubits of the wall to the Refuse Neh 2:13
Gate.
14 Malchijah the son of Rechab, the official of the district of Beth-haccherem repaired **3:14**
the Refuse Gate. He built it and hung its doors with its bolts and its bars. Jer 6:1; Neh 2:13
15 Shallum the son of Col-hozeh, the official of the district of Mizpah, repaired the **3:15**
Fountain Gate. He built it, covered it and hung its doors with its bolts and its bars, and Neh 2:17; 2 Kin 25:4; Neh 12:37

3:3 One of the main roads through Jerusalem entered the city through the Fish Gate (2 Chronicles 33:14). The fish market was near the gate, and merchants from Tyre, the Sea of Galilee, and other fishing areas entered this gate to sell their goods.

3:5 The nobles of Tekoa were lazy and wouldn't help. These men were the only ones who did not support the building project in Jerusalem. Every group, even churches, will have those who think they are too wise or important to work hard. Gentle encouragement doesn't seem to help. Sometimes the best policy is to ignore them. They may think they are getting away with something, but their inactivity will be remembered by all who worked hard.

3:12 Shallum's daughters helped with the difficult work of repairing the city walls. Rebuilding Jerusalem's walls was a matter of national emergency for the Jews, not just a civic beautification project. Nearly everyone was dedicated to the task and willing to work at it.

3:14 The Refuse Gate was the gate through which the people carried their garbage to be burned in the valley of Hinnom.

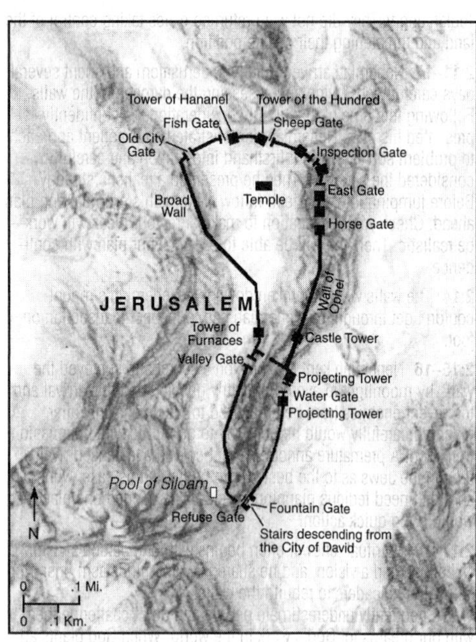

THE RESTORATION OF THE CITY WALLS Nehemiah takes us on a counterclockwise tour around Jerusalem (beginning with the Sheep Gate). He describes for us each section, gate, and tower on the wall and who worked to rebuild it.

the wall of the Pool of Shelah at the king's garden as far as the steps that descend from
the city of David.

3:16 Neh 3:9, 12, 17; 2 Kin 20:20; Is 7:3

16 After him Nehemiah the son of Azbuk, official of half the district of Beth-zur, made
repairs as far as *a point* opposite the tombs of David, and as far as the artificial pool and
the house of the mighty men.
17 After him the Levites carried out repairs *under* Rehum the son of Bani. Next to him
Hashabiah, the official of half the district of Keilah, carried out repairs for his district.
18 After him their brothers carried out repairs *under* Bavvai the son of Henadad, official of *the other* half of the district of Keilah.

3:19 Neh 3:15; 2 Chr 26:9

19 Next to him Ezer the son of Jeshua, the official of Mizpah, repaired another section
in front of the ascent of the armory at the Angle.

3:20 Neh 3:1

20 After him Baruch the son of Zabbai zealously repaired another section, from the
Angle to the doorway of the house of Eliashib the high priest.
21 After him Meremoth the son of Uriah the son of Hakkoz repaired another section,
from the doorway of Eliashib's house even as far as the end of his house.

3:22 Neh 12:28

22 After him the priests, the men of the [3]valley, carried out repairs.
23 After them Benjamin and Hasshub carried out repairs in front of their house. After
them Azariah the son of Maaseiah, son of Ananiah, carried out repairs beside his house.

3:24 Neh 3:19

24 After him Binnui the son of Henadad repaired another section, from the house of
Azariah as far as the Angle and as far as the corner.

3:25 Jer 32:2

25 Palal the son of Uzai *made repairs* in front of the Angle and the tower projecting
from the upper house of the king, which is by the court of the guard. After him Pedaiah
the son of Parosh *made repairs.*

3:26 Neh 7:46; Neh 11:21; Neh 8:1

26 The temple servants living in Ophel *made repairs* as far as the front of the Water
Gate toward the east and the projecting tower.

3:27 Neh 3:5

27 After them the Tekoites repaired another section in front of the great projecting
tower and as far as the wall of Ophel.

3:28 2 Kin 11:16; 2 Chr 23:15; Jer 31:40

28 Above the Horse Gate the priests carried out repairs, each in front of his house.
29 After them Zadok the son of Immer carried out repairs in front of his house. And
after him Shemaiah the son of Shecaniah, the keeper of the East Gate, carried out repairs.
30 After him Hananiah the son of Shelemiah, and Hanun the sixth son of Zalaph, repaired another section. After him Meshullam the son of Berechiah carried out repairs
in front of his own quarters.

3:31 Neh 3:8, 32

31 After him Malchijah, one of the goldsmiths, carried out repairs as far as the house
of the temple servants and of the merchants, in front of the Inspection Gate and as far
as the upper room of the corner.

3:32 Neh 3:1; 12:39

32 Between the upper room of the corner and the Sheep Gate the goldsmiths and the
merchants carried out repairs.

Work Is Ridiculed

4:1 Neh 2:10

4 Now it came about that when Sanballat heard that we were rebuilding the wall, he
became furious and very angry and mocked the Jews.

3 Lit *circle;* i.e. lower Jordan valley

3:28 The Horse Gate was at the far eastern point of the wall, facing the Kidron valley.

3:28 Each priest also repaired the wall in front of his own house, in addition to other sections. If each person was responsible for the part of the wall closest to his own house, (1) he would be more motivated to build it quickly and properly, (2) he wouldn't waste time traveling to more distant parts of the wall, (3) he would defend his own home if the wall were attacked, and (4) he would be able to make the building a family effort. Nehemiah blended self-interest with the group's objectives, helping everyone to feel that the wall project was his own. If you are part of a group working on a large project, make sure each person sees the importance and meaning of the job that he or she has to do. This will ensure high-quality work and personal satisfaction.

3:31 The Inspection Gate was in the northern part of the eastern wall.

4:1 Sanballat was governor of Samaria, the region just north of Judea where Jerusalem was located. Sanballat may have hoped to become governor of Judea as well, but Nehemiah's arrival spoiled his plans. (For his other reasons for opposing Nehemiah, see the note on 2:10.) Sanballat tried to scare Nehemiah away or at least discourage him by scorn (4:2; 6:6), threats (4:8), and bluffs (6:7).

4:1–2 Almost 300 years before Nehemiah's time, the northern kingdom of Israel was conquered, and most of the people were carried away captive (722 B.C.). Sargon of Assyria repopulated Israel with captives from other lands. These captives eventually intermarried with the few Israelites who remained in the land to form a mixed race of people who became known as Samaritans. The Jews who returned to Jerusalem and the southern region of Judea during the days of Ezra and Nehemiah would have nothing to do with Samaritans, whom they considered to be racially impure. Relations between both groups grew progressively worse—400 years later, the Jews and Samaritans hated each other (John 4:9).

2 He spoke in the presence of his brothers and the wealthy *men* of Samaria and said, 4:2 Ezra 4:9, 10; Neh 4:10
"What are these feeble Jews doing? Are they going to restore *it* for themselves? Can
they offer sacrifices? Can they finish in a day? Can they revive the stones from the dusty
rubble even the burned ones?"
3 Now Tobiah the Ammonite *was* near him and he said, "Even what they are build- 4:3 Lam 5:18
ing—if a fox should jump on *it,* he would break their stone wall down!"
4 Hear, O our God, how we are despised! Return their reproach on their own heads 4:4 Ps 123:3, 4; Ps 79:12
and give them up for plunder in a land of captivity.
5 Do not forgive their iniquity and let not their sin be blotted out before You, for they 4:5 Ps 69:27, 28; Jer 18:23
have demoralized the builders.
6 So we built the wall and the whole wall was joined together to half its *height,* for the
people had a mind to work.
7 Now when Sanballat, Tobiah, the Arabs, the Ammonites and the Ashdodites heard
that the repair of the walls of Jerusalem went on, *and* that the breaches began to be closed,
they were very angry.
8 All of them conspired together to come *and* fight against Jerusalem and to cause a 4:8 Ps 83:3
disturbance in it.

Discouragement Overcome

9 But we prayed to our God, and because of them we set up a guard against them day 4:9 Neh 4:11
and night.
10 Thus in Judah it was said,
"The strength of the burden bearers is failing,
Yet there is much rubbish;
And we ourselves are unable
To rebuild the wall."
11 Our enemies said, "They will not know or see until we come among them, kill them
and put a stop to the work."
12 When the Jews who lived near them came and told us ten times, "They will come up
against us from every place where you may turn,"
13 then I stationed *men* in the lowest parts of the space behind the wall, the exposed 4:13 Neh 4:17, 18
places, and I stationed the people in families with their swords, spears and bows.
14 When I saw *their fear,* I rose and spoke to the nobles, the officials and the rest of the 4:14 Num 14:9; Deut 1:29, 30; 2 Sam 10:12
people: "Do not be afraid of them; remember the Lord who is great and awesome, and
fight for your brothers, your sons, your daughters, your wives and your houses."
15 When our enemies heard that it was known to us, and that God had frustrated their 4:15 2 Sam 17:14
plan, then all of us returned to the wall, each one to his work.
16 From that day on, half of my servants carried on the work while half of them held
the spears, the shields, the bows and the breastplates; and the captains *were* behind the
whole house of Judah.

4:1–5 Ridicule can cut deeply, causing discouragement and despair. Sanballat and Tobiah used ridicule to try to dissuade the Jews from building the wall. Instead of trading insults, however, Nehemiah prayed, and the work continued. When you are mocked for your faith or criticized for doing what you know is right, refuse to respond in the same way or to become discouraged. Tell God how you feel and remember his promise to be with you. This will give you encouragement and strength to carry on.

4:4–5 Nehemiah is not praying for revenge but that God's justice would be carried out. His prayer is similar to many of David's (see the note in Psalm 7:1–6).

4:6 The work of rebuilding the wall progressed well because the people had set their hearts and minds on accomplishing the task. They did not lose faith or give up, but they persevered in the work. If God has called you to a task, determine to complete it, even if you face opposition or discouragement. The rewards of work well done will be worth the effort.

4:9 Nehemiah constantly combined prayer with preparation and planning. His people trusted God and at the same time kept vigilant watch over what had been entrusted to them. Too often we pray without looking for what God wants us to do. We show God we are serious when we combine prayer with thought, preparation, and effort.

4:10–14 Accomplishing any large task is tiring. There are always pressures that foster discouragement—the task seems impossible, it can never be finished, or too many factors are working against us. The only cure for fatigue and discouragement is focusing on God's purposes. Nehemiah reminded the workers of their calling, their goal, and God's protection. If you are overwhelmed by an assignment, tired, and discouraged, remember God's purpose for your life and his special purpose for the project.

4:16 The workers were spread out along the wall, so Nehemiah devised a plan of defense that would unite and protect his people—half the men worked while the other half stood guard. Christians need to help one another in the same way because we can become so afraid of possible dangers that we can't get anything done. By looking out for each other, we will be free to put forth our best efforts, confident that others are ready to offer help when needed. Don't cut yourself off from others; instead, join together for mutual benefit. You need them as much as they need you.

17 Those who were rebuilding the wall and those who carried burdens took *their* load
with one hand doing the work and the other holding a weapon.
18 As for the builders, each *wore* his sword girded at his side as he built, while the trum-
peter *stood* near me.
19 I said to the nobles, the officials and the rest of the people, "The work is great and
extensive, and we are separated on the wall far from one another.
4:20 Ex 14:14; Deut 1:30 20 "At whatever place you hear the sound of the trumpet, rally to us there. Our God
will fight for us."
21 So we carried on the work with half of them holding spears from dawn until the stars
appeared.

NEHEMIAH

God is in the business of working through his people to accomplish seemingly impossible tasks. God often shapes people with personality characteristics, experiences, and training that prepare them for his purpose, and usually the people have no idea what God has in store for them. God prepared and positioned Nehemiah to accomplish one of the Bible's "impossible" tasks.

Nehemiah was a common man in a unique position. He was secure and successful as cupbearer to the Persian king Artaxerxes. Nehemiah had little power, but he had great influence. He was trusted by the king. He was also a man of God, concerned about the fate of Jerusalem.

Seventy years earlier, Zerubbabel had managed to rebuild God's temple. Thirteen years had passed since Ezra had returned to Jerusalem and helped the people with their spiritual needs. Now Nehemiah was needed. Jerusalem's wall was still in ruins, and the news broke his heart. As he talked to God, a plan began to take form in Nehemiah's mind about his own role in the rebuilding of the city walls. He willingly left the security of his home and job in Persia to follow God on an "impossible" mission. And the rest is history.

From beginning to end, Nehemiah prayed for God's help. He never hesitated to ask God to remember him, closing his autobiography with these words: "Remember me, O my God, for good." Throughout the "impossible" task, Nehemiah displayed unusual leadership. The wall around Jerusalem was rebuilt in record time, despite resistance. Even Israel's enemies grudgingly and fearfully admitted that God was with these builders. Not only that, but God worked through Nehemiah to bring about a spiritual awakening among the people of Judah.

You may not have Nehemiah's unique abilities or feel that you are in a position where you can do anything great for God, but there are two ways you can become useful to God. First, be a person who *talks* to God. Welcome him into your thoughts and share yourself with him—your concerns, feelings, and dreams. Second, be a person who [walks] with God. Put what you learn from his Word into action. God may have an "impossible" mission that he wants to do through you.

Strengths and accomplishments:
- A man of character, persistence, and prayer
- Brilliant planner, organizer, and motivator
- Under his leadership, the wall around Jerusalem was rebuilt in 52 days
- As political leader, led the nation to religious reform and spiritual awakening
- Was calm under opposition
- Was capable of being bluntly honest with his people when they were sinning

Lessons from his life:
- The first step in any venture is to pray
- People under God's direction can accomplish impossible tasks
- There are two parts to real service for God: talking with him, and walking with him

Vital statistics:
- Where: Persia, Jerusalem
- Occupations: King's cupbearer, city builder, governor of Judah
- Relative: Father: Hacaliah
- Contemporaries: Ezra, Artaxerxes, Tobiah, Sanballat

Key verse:
"I told them how the hand of my God had been favorable to me and also about the king's words which he had spoken to me. They they said, 'Let us arise and build.' So they put their hands to the good work" (Nehemiah 2:18).

Nehemiah's story is told in the book of Nehemiah.

4:18–20 To further relieve the anxieties of the people, Nehemiah set up a communication system. The man who sounded the trumpet stayed with Nehemiah, and the people knew what to do if they heard it. We have no record that the trumpet was ever used, but simply knowing it would issue a warning when needed was reassuring. The promise of open, immediate communication helped the group accomplish its task.

22 At that time I also said to the people, "Let each man with his servant spend the night
within Jerusalem so that they may be a guard for us by night and a laborer by day."
23 So neither I, my brothers, my servants, nor the men of the guard who followed me,
none of us removed our clothes, each *took* his weapon *even to* the water.

Usury Abolished

5 Now there was a great outcry of the people and of their wives against their Jewish **5:1**
brothers. Lev 25:35; Deut 15:7
2 For there were those who said, "We, our sons and our daughters are many; there- **5:2**
fore let us get grain that we may eat and live." Hag 1:6
3 There were others who said, "We are mortgaging our fields, our vineyards and our
houses that we might get grain because of the famine."
4 Also there were those who said, "We have borrowed money for the king's tax *on* **5:4**
our fields and our vineyards. Ezra 4:13; 7:24
5 "Now our flesh is like the flesh of our brothers, our children like their children. Yet **5:5**
behold, we are forcing our sons and our daughters to be slaves, and some of our daugh- Gen 37:27; Lev 25:39
ters are forced into bondage *already,* and we are helpless because our fields and vineyards belong to others."
6 Then I was very angry when I had heard their outcry and these words. **5:6**
7 I consulted with myself and contended with the nobles and the rulers and said to Ex 11:8
them, "You are exacting usury, each from his brother!" Therefore, I held a great assem- **5:7**
bly against them. Ex 22:25; Lev 25:36; Deut 23:19, 20
8 I said to them, "We according to our ability have redeemed our Jewish brothers who
were sold to the nations; now would you even sell your brothers that they may be sold to **5:8** Lev 25:48
us?" Then they were silent and could not find a word *to say.*
9 Again I said, "The thing which you are doing is not good; should you not walk in the **5:9**
fear of our God because of the reproach of the nations, our enemies? Neh 4:4
10 "And likewise I, my brothers and my servants are lending them money and grain.
Please, let us leave off this usury.
11 "Please, give back to them this very day their fields, their vineyards, their olive groves
and their houses, also the hundredth *part* of the money and of the grain, the new wine
and the oil that you are exacting from them."
12 Then they said, "We will give *it* back and will require nothing from them; we will do **5:12**
exactly as you say." So I called the priests and took an oath from them that they would 2 Chr 28:15; Neh 10:31; Ezra 10:5
do according to this promise.
13 I also shook out the front of my garment and said, "Thus may God shake out every **5:13**
man from his house and from his possessions who does not fulfill this promise; even thus Acts 18:6; Neh 8:6
may he be shaken out and emptied." And all the assembly said, "Amen!" And they praised
the LORD. Then the people did according to this promise.

4:23 Although the exact meaning of the Hebrew phrase, "even to the water" is unclear (it has been translated, "in his right hand" or "at his right hand at night"), the point is that each man always had his weapon close at hand. The guards were prepared and took their responsibilities seriously.

5:1–5 Who were these bitterly resented Jews? They were either (1) Jews who had become wealthy in exile and brought this wealth with them to Jerusalem, or (2) descendants of Jews who had arrived almost a century earlier during the first return under Zerubbabel (Ezra 1; 2) and had established lucrative businesses.

5:7–9 Many of the returned exiles were suffering at the hands of some of their rich countrymen. These people would lend large sums of money; then, when the debtors missed a payment, they would take over their fields. Left with no means of income, the debtors were forced to sell their children into slavery, a common practice of this time. Nehemiah was angry with these Jews who were taking advantage of their own people in order to enrich themselves. Usury is the practice of charging excessive interest. These practices violated the law set forth in Exodus 22:25.

5:9–11 God's concern for the poor is revealed in almost every book of the Bible. Here, Nehemiah insisted that fairness to the poor and oppressed was central to following God. The books of Moses clearly spelled out the Israelites' responsibility to care for the poor (Exodus 22:22–27; Leviticus 25:35–37; Deuteronomy 14:28–29; 15:7–11). The way we help those in need ought to mirror God's love and concern.

5:10 Nehemiah told the rich Jews to stop charging interest ("usury") on their loans to their needy brothers. God never intended people to profit from others' misfortunes. In contrast to the values of this world, God says that caring for one another is more important than personal gain. When a Christian brother or sister suffers, we all suffer (1 Corinthians 12:26). We should help needy believers, not exploit them. The Jerusalem church was praised for working together to eliminate poverty (Acts 4:34–35). Remember, "He who gives to the poor will never want" (Proverbs 28:27). Make it a practice to help those in need around you.

5:13 This symbolic act was a curse. Nehemiah shook out the front of his garment and pronounced that anyone who did not keep his promise would likewise be "shaken out and emptied," losing all he had.

Nehemiah's Example

5:14 Neh 1:1; Neh 13:6

14 Moreover, from the day that I was appointed to be their governor in the land of Judah, from the twentieth year to the thirty-second year of King Artaxerxes, *for* twelve years, neither I nor my kinsmen have eaten the governor's food *allowance.*

5:15 Neh 5:9; Job 31:23

15 But the former governors who were before me laid burdens on the people and took from them bread and wine besides forty shekels of silver; even their servants domineered the people. But I did not do so because of the fear of God.

16 I also [4]applied myself to the work on this wall; we did not buy any land, and all my servants were gathered there for the work.

5:17 1 Kin 18:19

17 Moreover, *there were* at my table one hundred and fifty Jews and officials, besides those who came to us from the nations that were around us.

5:18 1 Kin 4:22, 23; 2 Thess 3:8

18 Now that which was prepared for each day was one ox *and* six choice sheep, also birds were prepared for me; and once in ten days all sorts of wine *were furnished* in abundance. Yet for all this I did not demand the governor's food *allowance,* because the servitude was heavy on this people.

5:19 Neh 13:14, 22, 31

19 Remember me, O my God, for good, *according to* all that I have done for this people.

The Enemy's Plot

6:1 Neh 3:1, 3

6 Now when it was reported to Sanballat, Tobiah, to Geshem the Arab and to the rest of our enemies that I had rebuilt the wall, and *that* no breach remained in it, although at that time I had not set up the doors in the gates,

6:2 1 Chr 8:12

2 then Sanballat and Geshem sent *a message* to me, saying, "Come, let us meet together at [5]Chephirim in the plain of Ono." But they were planning to harm me.

3 So I sent messengers to them, saying, "I am doing a great work and I cannot come down. Why should the work stop while I leave it and come down to you?"

4 They sent *messages* to me four times in this manner, and I answered them in the same way.

5 Then Sanballat sent his servant to me in the same manner a fifth time with an open letter in his hand.

6:6 Neh 2:19

6 In it was written, "It is reported among the nations, and Gashmu says, that you and the Jews are planning to rebel; therefore you are rebuilding the wall. And you are to be their king, according to these reports.

7 "You have also appointed prophets to proclaim in Jerusalem concerning you, 'A king is in Judah!' And now it will be reported to the king according to these reports. So come now, let us take counsel together."

6:8 Job 13:4; Ps 52:2

8 Then I sent *a message* to him saying, "Such things as you are saying have not been done, but you are inventing them in your own mind."

6:9 Ps 138:3

9 For all of them were *trying* to frighten us, thinking, "They will become discouraged with the work and it will not be done." But now, *O God,* strengthen my hands.

4 Or *held fast* **5** Another reading is, one of *the villages*

5:14–15 This comment by Nehemiah is a parenthetical statement, comparing his 12 years as governor with the unjust proceedings in the land before he arrived. The governor was appointed by the Persian king, not elected by the people.

5:16 Nehemiah led the entire construction project, but he also worked on the wall alongside the others. He was not a bureaucrat in a well-guarded office, but a leader who got involved in the day-to-day work. He did not use his position to lord it over his people. A good leader keeps in touch with the work to be done. Those who lead best lead by what they *do* as well as by what they say.

6:1ff Sanballat and Tobiah were desperate. The wall was almost complete, and their efforts to stop its construction were failing. So they tried a new approach, centering their attacks on Nehemiah's character. They attacked him personally with rumors (6:6), deceit (6:10–13), and false reports (6:17). Personal attacks hurt, and when the criticism is unjustified, it is easy to despair. When you are doing God's work, you may receive attacks on your character. Follow Nehemiah's example by trusting God to accomplish the task and by overlooking unjustified abuse.

6:2 The plain of Ono was about 20 miles northwest of Jerusalem. If Sanballat and Geshem could get Nehemiah to agree to meet them there, they could ambush him on the way.

6:7 During these days, prophets such as Malachi proclaimed the coming of the Messiah (Malachi 3:1–3). Sanballat, with his usual flair for stirring up trouble, tried to turn Nehemiah's people against him by saying that Nehemiah was trying to set himself up as the king. Sanballat also tried to turn the local officials against Nehemiah by threatening to report to the king of Persia that Nehemiah was starting a revolt. The fact that Sanballat had an open, or unsealed, letter delivered to Nehemiah shows that he wanted to make sure the letter's contents were made public. But Sanballat's accusations were untrue and did not divert Nehemiah from his task.

6:9 When opposition builds up against you or God's work, it is tempting to pray, "God, get me out of this situation." But Nehemiah prayed, "Strengthen my hands." He showed tremendous determination and character to remain steadfast in his responsibility. When we pray for strength, God always answers.

10 When I entered the house of Shemaiah the son of Delaiah, son of Mehetabel, who **6:10**
was confined at home, he said, "Let us meet together in the house of God, within the Jer 36:5
temple, and let us close the doors of the temple, for they are coming to kill you, and they
are coming to kill you at night."
11 But I said, "Should a man like me flee? And could one such as I go into the temple **6:11**
to save his life? I will not go in." Prov 28:1
12 Then I perceived that surely God had not sent him, but he uttered *his* prophecy
against me because Tobiah and Sanballat had hired him.
13 He was hired for this reason, that I might become frightened and act accordingly **6:13**
and sin, so that they might have an evil report in order that they could reproach me. Neh 6:6
14 Remember, O my God, Tobiah and Sanballat according to these works of theirs, **6:14**
and also Noadiah the prophetess and the rest of the prophets who were *trying* to fright- Neh 13:29; Ezek 13:17
en me.

The Wall Is Finished

15 So the wall was completed on the twenty-fifth of *the month* Elul, in fifty-two days. **6:15**
16 When all our enemies heard *of it,* and all the nations surrounding us saw *it,* they lost Neh 4:1, 2
their confidence; for they recognized that this work had been accomplished with the help **6:16**
of our God. Neh 2:10; 4:1, 7; Ex 14:25
17 Also in those days many letters went from the nobles of Judah to Tobiah, and Tobiah's
letters came to them.
18 For many in Judah were bound by oath to him because he was the son-in-law of
Shecaniah the son of Arah, and his son Jehohanan had married the daughter of Meshullam the son of Berechiah.
19 Moreover, they were speaking about his good deeds in my presence and reported
my words to him. Then Tobiah sent letters to frighten me.

Census of First Returned Exiles

7 Now when the wall was rebuilt and I had set up the doors, and the gatekeepers and **7:1**
the singers and the Levites were appointed, Neh 6:1, 15
2 then I put Hanani my brother, and Hananiah the commander of the fortress, in **7:2**
charge of Jerusalem, for he was a faithful man and feared God more than many. Neh 1:2; Neh 10:23; Neh 2:8; Neh 13:13
3 Then I said to them, "Do not let the gates of Jerusalem be opened until the sun is
hot, and while they are standing *guard,* let them shut and bolt the doors. Also appoint
guards from the inhabitants of Jerusalem, each at his post, and each in front of his own
house."

6:10 Shemaiah warned Nehemiah of danger and told him to hide in the temple. Nehemiah wisely tested the message, exposing it as another trick of the enemy. People may misuse God's name by saying they know God's will when they have other motives. Examine self-proclaimed messengers from God to see if they stand up to the test of being consistent with what is revealed in God's Word.

6:10–13 Nehemiah did not have the full support of the people. Shemaiah (6:10), Noadiah (6:14), and many of the nobles (6:17) were working against him. When Nehemiah was attacked personally, he refused to give in to fear and flee to the temple. According to God's law, it would have been wrong for Nehemiah to go into the temple to hide because he wasn't a priest (Numbers 18:22). If he had run for his life, he would have undermined the courage he was trying to instill in the people. Leaders are targets for attacks. Make it a practice to pray for those in authority (1 Timothy 2:1–2). Request God to give them strength to stand against personal attacks and temptation. They need God-given courage to overcome fear.

6:15 Daniel, who was among the first group of captives taken from Jerusalem to Babylon (605 B.C.), predicted the rebuilding of the city (Daniel 9:25). Here his prophecy comes true. He, like Nehemiah, was a Jew who held a prominent position in the kingdom where he had been exiled (Daniel 5:29—6:3). The twenty-fifth of the month Elul corresponds to October 2.

6:15 They said it couldn't be done. The job was too big, and the problems were too great. But God's men and women, joined together for special tasks, can solve huge problems and accomplish great goals. Don't let the size of a task or the length of time needed to accomplish it keep you from doing it. With God's help, it can be done.

7:2 Integrity and fear of God were the key character traits that qualified these men to govern Jerusalem. People of integrity can be trusted to carry out their work; God-fearing people can be expected to do so in line with God's priorities. These men had both qualities. If you are in a position of selecting leaders, look for integrity and reverence as two of the most important qualifications. Although other qualities may seem more impressive, integrity and reverence pass the test of time.

7:3 City gates were usually opened at sunrise, enabling merchants to enter and set up their tent-stores. Nehemiah didn't want Jerusalem to be caught unprepared by an enemy attack, so he ordered the gates closed until well after sunrise when the people were sure to be awake and alert.

7:3 The wall was complete, but the work was not finished. Nehemiah assigned each family the task of protecting the section of wall next to their home. It is tempting to relax our guard and rest on past accomplishments after we have completed a large task. But we must continue to serve and to take care of all that God has entrusted to us. Following through after a project is completed is as vital as doing the project itself.

4 Now the city was large and spacious, but the people in it were few and the houses
were not built.

7:5 Prov 2:6; 3:6

5 Then my God put it into my heart to assemble the nobles, the officials and the people to be enrolled by genealogies. Then I found the book of the genealogy of those who
came up first in which I found the following record:

7:6 Ezra 2:1-70

6 These are the people of the province who came up from the captivity of the exiles
whom Nebuchadnezzar the king of Babylon had carried away, and who returned to Jerusalem and Judah, each to his city,
7 who came with Zerubbabel, Jeshua, Nehemiah, Azariah, Raamiah, Nahamani,
Mordecai, Bilshan, Mispereth, Bigvai, Nehum, Baanah.
The number of men of the people of Israel:
8 the sons of Parosh, 2,172;
9 the sons of Shephatiah, 372;
10 the sons of Arah, 652;
11 the sons of Pahath-moab of the sons of Jeshua and Joab, 2,818;
12 the sons of Elam, 1,254;
13 the sons of Zattu, 845;
14 the sons of Zaccai, 760;
15 the sons of Binnui, 648;
16 the sons of Bebai, 628;
17 the sons of Azgad, 2,322;
18 the sons of Adonikam, 667;
19 the sons of Bigvai, 2,067;
20 the sons of Adin, 655;
21 the sons of Ater, of Hezekiah, 98;
22 the sons of Hashum, 328;
23 the sons of Bezai, 324;
24 the sons of Hariph, 112;
25 the sons of Gibeon, 95;
26 the men of Bethlehem and Netophah, 188;
27 the men of Anathoth, 128;
28 the men of Beth-azmaveth, 42;
29 the men of Kiriath-jearim, Chephirah and Beeroth, 743;
30 the men of Ramah and Geba, 621;
31 the men of Michmas, 122;
32 the men of Bethel and Ai, 123;
33 the men of the other Nebo, 52;
34 the sons of the other Elam, 1,254;
35 the sons of Harim, 320;
36 the men of Jericho, 345;
37 the sons of Lod, Hadid and Ono, 721;
38 the sons of Senaah, 3,930.
39 The priests: the sons of Jedaiah of the house of Jeshua, 973;
40 the sons of Immer, 1,052;
41 the sons of Pashhur, 1,247;
42 the sons of Harim, 1,017.
43 The Levites: the sons of Jeshua, of Kadmiel, of the sons of Hodevah, 74.
44 The singers: the sons of Asaph, 148.
45 The gatekeepers: the sons of Shallum, the sons of Ater, the sons of Talmon, the sons
of Akkub, the sons of Hatita, the sons of Shobai, 138.
46 The temple servants: the sons of Ziha, the sons of Hasupha, the sons of Tabbaoth,
47 the sons of Keros, the sons of Sia, the sons of Padon,
48 the sons of Lebana, the sons of Hagaba, the sons of Shalmai,
49 the sons of Hanan, the sons of Giddel, the sons of Gahar,
50 the sons of Reaiah, the sons of Rezin, the sons of Nekoda,
51 the sons of Gazzam, the sons of Uzza, the sons of Paseah,
52 the sons of Besai, the sons of Meunim, the sons of Nephushesim,

7:5ff Nehemiah found the genealogical record. Because this genealogy is almost identical to Ezra's (Ezra 2), most likely Ezra's list was stored in the temple archives and was the one Nehemiah found.

53 the sons of Bakbuk, the sons of Hakupha, the sons of Harhur,
54 the sons of Bazlith, the sons of Mehida, the sons of Harsha,
55 the sons of Barkos, the sons of Sisera, the sons of Temah,
56 the sons of Neziah, the sons of Hatipha.
57 The sons of Solomon's servants: the sons of Sotai, the sons of Sophereth, the sons
of Perida,
58 the sons of Jaala, the sons of Darkon, the sons of Giddel,
59 the sons of Shephatiah, the sons of Hattil, the sons of Pochereth-hazzebaim, the
sons of Amon.
60 All the temple servants and the sons of Solomon's servants *were* 392.
61 These *were* they who came up from Tel-melah, Tel-harsha, Cherub, Addon and
Immer; but they could not show their fathers' houses or their descendants, whether they
were of Israel:
62 the sons of Delaiah, the sons of Tobiah, the sons of Nekoda, 642.
63 Of the priests: the sons of Hobaiah, the sons of Hakkoz, the sons of Barzillai, who
took a wife of the daughters of Barzillai, the Gileadite, and was named after them.
64 These searched *among* their ancestral registration, but it could not be located; therefore they were considered unclean *and excluded* from the priesthood.
65 The governor said to them that they should not eat from the most holy things until
a priest arose with Urim and Thummim.

7:65 Neh 8:9; 10:1; Ex 28:30; Deut 33:8

Total of People and Gifts

66 The whole assembly together *was* 42,360,
67 besides their male and their female servants, of whom *there were* 7,337; and they
had 245 male and female singers.
68 Their horses were 736; their mules, 245;
69 *their* camels, 435; *their* donkeys, 6,720.
70 Some from among the heads of fathers' *households* gave to the work. The governor
gave to the treasury 1,000 gold drachmas, 50 basins, 530 priests' garments.
71 Some of the heads of fathers' *households* gave into the treasury of the work 20,000
gold drachmas and 2,200 silver minas.
72 That which the rest of the people gave was 20,000 gold drachmas and 2,000 silver
minas and 67 priests' garments.
73 Now the priests, the Levites, the gatekeepers, the singers, some of the people, the
temple servants and all Israel, lived in their cities.
And when the seventh month came, the sons of Israel *were* in their cities.

7:68 Ezra 2:66

7:70 Neh 7:65; 8:9

7:73 1 Chr 9:2; Ezra 3:1

B. REFORMING THE PEOPLE (8:1—13:31)

When Nehemiah arrived in Jerusalem he found more than just broken walls; he found broken lives. In response, Nehemiah gathers the people together to hear Ezra read God's law. The people repent and promise to change their lives by obeying God's words. No matter where we live, backsliding is an ever-present danger. We must constantly check our behavior against God's standards in the Bible so that we do not slide back into sinful ways of living.

1. Ezra renews the covenant

Ezra Reads the Law

8 And all the people gathered as one man at the square which was in front of the Water
Gate, and they asked Ezra the scribe to bring the book of the law of Moses which
the LORD had given to Israel.

8:1 Neh 3:26; Ezra 7:6; 2 Chr 34:15

7:61 Genealogies were greatly valued because it was vitally important for a Jew to be able to prove that he or she was a descendant of Abraham and was, therefore, part of God's people (Genesis 12:1–3; 15; Exodus 19:5, 6; Deuteronomy 11:22–28). A lost genealogy put one's status as a Jew at risk.

7:64–65 The Urim and Thummim were a means of learning God's will (Exodus 28:30). If someone's name wasn't in the genealogies, he could still be admitted as a priest if the Urim and Thummim proved him to be a Jew and a Levite. It is not clear whether the Urim and Thummim were the originals that had survived the destruction of Jerusalem or if they were new. The "most holy things" were meat dedicated to God as part of the sacrifice. Only true priests could eat it.

8:1 This is the first mention of Ezra in this book. He had arrived in Jerusalem from Babylon 13 years before Nehemiah (458 B.C., see Ezra 7:6–9).

8:1 Ezra and Nehemiah were contemporaries (8:9), although Ezra was probably much older. Nehemiah, as governor, was the political leader; and Ezra, as priest and scribe, was the religious leader. A scribe in these days was a combination lawyer, notary public, scholar, and consultant. Scribes were among the most educated people, so they were teachers. No doubt the Jews would have liked to set up the kingdom again as in the days of David, but this would have signaled rebellion against the king of Persia to whom they were subject. The best alternative was to divide the leadership between Nehemiah and Ezra.

8:2 Deut 31:9-11; Neh 8:9; Lev 23:24
8:3 Neh 8:1

2 Then Ezra the priest brought the law before the assembly of men, women and all
who *could* listen with understanding, on the first day of the seventh month.
3 He read from it before the square which was in front of the Water Gate from early
morning until midday, in the presence of men and women, those who could understand;
and all the people were attentive to the book of the law.
4 Ezra the scribe stood at a wooden podium which they had made for the purpose.
And beside him stood Mattithiah, Shema, Anaiah, Uriah, Hilkiah, and Maaseiah on his
right hand; and Pedaiah, Mishael, Malchijah, Hashum, Hashbaddanah, Zechariah *and*
Meshullam on his left hand.

8:5 Neh 8:3; Judg 3:20; 1 Kin 8:12-14
8:6 Neh 5:13; Ex 4:31

5 Ezra opened the book in the sight of all the people for he was standing above all the
people; and when he opened it, all the people stood up.
6 Then Ezra blessed the LORD the great God. And all the people answered, "Amen,
Amen!" while lifting up their hands; then they bowed low and worshiped the LORD with
their faces to the ground.
7 Also Jeshua, Bani, Sherebiah, Jamin, Akkub, Shabbethai, Hodiah, Maaseiah, Kelita, Azariah, Jozabad, Hanan, Pelaiah, the Levites, explained the law to the people while
the people *remained* in their place.
8 They read from the book, from the law of God, translating to give the sense so that
they understood the reading.

"This Day Is Holy"

8:9 Neh 7:65, 70; Neh 12:26; Neh 8:2; Deut 12:7, 12

9 Then Nehemiah, who was the governor, and Ezra the priest *and* scribe, and the
Levites who taught the people said to all the people, "This day is holy to the LORD your
God; do not mourn or weep." For all the people were weeping when they heard the words
of the law.

8:10 Deut 26:11-13

10 Then he said to them, "Go, eat of the fat, drink of the sweet, and send portions to
him who has nothing prepared; for this day is holy to our Lord. Do not be grieved, for
the joy of the LORD is your strength."
11 So the Levites calmed all the people, saying, "Be still, for the day is holy; do not be
grieved."

8:12 Neh 8:10; Neh 8:7, 8

12 All the people went away to eat, to drink, to send portions and to celebrate a great
festival, because they understood the words which had been made known to them.

Feast of Booths Restored

13 Then on the second day the heads of fathers' *households* of all the people, the priests
and the Levites were gathered to Ezra the scribe that they might gain insight into the
words of the law.

8:14 Lev 23:34, 40, 42
8:15 Lev 23:4; Deut 16:16; Lev 23:40

14 They found written in the law how the LORD had commanded through Moses that
the sons of Israel should live in booths during the feast of the seventh month.
15 So they proclaimed and circulated a proclamation in all their cities and in Jerusalem,

---

8:1–5 The book of the law of Moses was probably the Pentateuch, the first five books of the Bible. The people listened attentively to Ezra as he read God's Word, and their lives were changed. Because we hear the Bible so often, we can become dulled to its words and immune to its teachings. Instead, we should *listen carefully* to every verse and ask the Holy Spirit to help us answer the question, "How does this apply to *my* life?"

8:9 Ezra, not Nehemiah, was the official religious leader. It is significant that Nehemiah was a layman, not a member of the religious establishment or a prophet. He was motivated by his relationship with God, and he devoted his life to doing God's will in a secular world. Such people are crucial to God's work in all aspects of life. No matter what your work or role in life, view it as God's special calling to serve him.

8:9–10 The people wept openly when they heard God's laws and realized how far they were from obeying them. But Ezra told them they should be filled with joy because the day was holy. It was time to celebrate and to give gifts to those in need.

Celebration is not to be self-centered. Ezra connected celebration with giving. This gave those in need an opportunity to celebrate as well. Often when we celebrate and give to others (even when we don't feel like it), we are strengthened spiritually and filled with joy. Enter into celebrations that honor God, and allow him to fill you with his joy.

8:13ff After Ezra read God's laws to the people, they studied them further and then acted upon them. A careful reading of Scripture always calls for a response to these questions: What should I *do* with this knowledge? How should my life change? We must *do* something about what we have learned if it is to have real significance for our lives.

8:14–17 During the seven-day Feast of Booths, the people lived in booths made of branches. This practice was instituted as a reminder of their rescue from Egypt and the time spent in shelters in the wilderness (Leviticus 23:43). They were to think about God's protection and guidance during their years of wandering and the fact that God would still protect and guide them if they obeyed him. This was a time to remember their origins, where they had come from. It is helpful to remember our beginnings in order to appreciate where we are today. Think back on your life to see where God has led you. Then thank God for his continuing work to protect you and provide for your needs.

saying, "Go out to the hills, and bring olive branches and wild olive branches, myrtle
branches, palm branches and branches of *other* leafy trees, to make booths, as it is written."
16 So the people went out and brought *them* and made booths for themselves, each on
his roof, and in their courts and in the courts of the house of God, and in the square at
the Water Gate and in the square at the Gate of Ephraim.
17 The entire assembly of those who had returned from the captivity made booths and
lived in them. The sons of Israel had indeed not done so from the days of Joshua the son
of Nun to that day. And there was great rejoicing.
18 He read from the book of the law of God daily, from the first day to the last day.
And they celebrated the feast seven days, and on the eighth day *there was* a solemn assembly according to the ordinance.

8:16 Jer 32:29; Neh 8:1; 2 Kin 14:13; Neh 12:39

8:17 2 Chr 7:8; 8:13; 2 Chr 30:21

8:18 Deut 31:11; Lev 23:36; Num 29:35

The People Confess Their Sin

9 Now on the twenty-fourth day of this month the sons of Israel assembled with fasting, in sackcloth and with dirt upon them.
2 The descendants of Israel separated themselves from all foreigners, and stood and
confessed their sins and the iniquities of their fathers.
3 While they stood in their place, they read from the book of the law of the LORD
their God for a fourth of the day; and for *another* fourth they confessed and worshiped
the LORD their God.
4 Now on the Levites' platform stood Jeshua, Bani, Kadmiel, Shebaniah, Bunni, Sherebiah, Bani *and* Chenani, and they cried with a loud voice to the LORD their God.
5 Then the Levites, Jeshua, Kadmiel, Bani, Hashabneiah, Sherebiah, Hodiah, Sheb-
aniah *and* Pethahiah, said, "Arise, bless the LORD your God forever and ever!
O may Your glorious name be blessed
And exalted above all blessing and praise!
6 "You alone are the LORD.
You have made the heavens,
The heaven of heavens with all their host,
The earth and all that is on it,
The seas and all that is in them.
You give life to all of them
And the heavenly host bows down before You.
7 "You are the LORD God,
Who chose Abram
And brought him out from Ur of the Chaldees,
And gave him the name Abraham.
8 "You found his heart faithful before You,
And made a covenant with him
To give *him* the land of the Canaanite,
Of the Hittite and the Amorite,
Of the Perizzite, the Jebusite and the Girgashite—
To give *it* to his descendants.
And You have fulfilled Your promise,
For You are righteous.

9 "You saw the affliction of our fathers in Egypt,
And heard their cry by the Red Sea.
10 "Then You performed signs and wonders against Pharaoh,

9:1 Neh 8:2; Ezra 8:23; 1 Sam 4:12

9:2 Ezra 10:11; Neh 13:3; Prov 28:13; Jer 3:13

9:3 Neh 8:4

9:4 Neh 8:7

9:6 Deut 6:4; 2 Kin 19:15; Gen 1:1; Col 1:16f

9:7 Gen 12:1; Gen 11:31; Gen 17:5

9:8 Gen 15:6, 18-21; Josh 21:43-45

9:9 Ex 3:7; Ex 14:10-14, 31

9:10 Ex 7:8-12:32; Ex 5:2; Ex 9:16

9:1 Fasting, wearing sackcloth, and putting dirt on the head were public signs of sorrow and repentance.

9:2–3 The Hebrews practiced open confession, admitting their sins to one another. Reading and studying God's Word should precede confession (see 8:18) because God can show us where we are sinning. Honest confession should precede worship, because we cannot have a right relationship with God if we hold on to certain sins.

9:7–38 Many prayers and speeches in the Bible include a long summary of Israel's history because individuals did not have their own copies of the Bible as we do today. This summary of God's past works reminded the people of their great heritage and God's promises.

We should also remember our history to avoid repeating our mistakes so that we can serve God better. Reviewing our past helps us understand how to improve our behavior. It shows us the pattern to our spiritual growth. Learn from your past so that you will become the kind of person God wants you to be.

Against all his servants and all the people of his land;
For You knew that they acted arrogantly toward them,
And made a name for Yourself as *it is* this day.

9:11 Ex 14:21; Ex 15:1, 5, 10

11 "You divided the sea before them,
So they passed through the midst of the sea on dry ground;
And their pursuers You hurled into the depths,
Like a stone into raging waters.

9:12 Ex 13:21, 22

12 "And with a pillar of cloud You led them by day,
And with a pillar of fire by night
To light for them the way
In which they were to go.

9:13 Ex 19:11, 18-20; Ex 20:1; Ps 19:7-9

13 "Then You came down on Mount Sinai,
And spoke with them from heaven;
You gave them just ordinances and true laws,
Good statutes and commandments.

9:14 Ex 16:23; 20:8

14 "So You made known to them Your holy sabbath,
And laid down for them commandments, statutes and law,
Through Your servant Moses.

9:15 Ex 16:4, 14, 15; Ex 17:6; Num 20:7-13; Deut 1:8, 21

15 "You provided bread from heaven for them for their hunger,
You brought forth water from a rock for them for their thirst,
And You told them to enter in order to possess
The land which You swore to give them.

9:16 Neh 9:10; Deut 1:26-33; 31:27; Neh 9:29

16 "But they, our fathers, acted arrogantly;
They [6]became stubborn and would not listen to Your commandments.

9:17 Ps 78:11, 42-55; Num 14:4; Ex 34:6, 7; Num 14:18

17 "They refused to listen,
And did not remember Your wondrous deeds which You had performed among them;
So they became stubborn and appointed a leader to return to their slavery in Egypt.

6 Lit *stiffened their neck;* so also v 17

GOING HOME: TWO GREAT JOURNEYS OF ISRAEL

What about the Journeys?	*The Exodus*	*The Return from Exile*
Where were they?	Egypt (430 years)	Babylon (70 years)
How many?	About 1 million	60,000
How long did the journey take them?	40 years and 2 attempts	100 years and 3 journeys
Who led them?	Moses/Aaron/Joshua	Zerubbabel/Ezra/Nehemiah
What was their purpose?	To reclaim the promised land	To rebuild the temple and city of Jerusalem
What obstacles did they face?	Red Sea/Wilderness/Enemies	Ruins/Limited Resources/Enemies
What failures did they experience?	Complaining/Disobedience/Retreat—all of which turned a journey of a few weeks into a 40-year ordeal	Fear/Discouragement/Apathy—all of which turned a project of a few months into one that required a century to complete
What successes did they have?	Eventually entered the promised land	Eventually rebuilt Jerusalem's temple and wall
What lessons did they learn?	God will build his nation. God is both faithful and just. God will accomplish great acts to make his promises come true.	God will preserve his nation. God will continue to have a chosen people, a home for them, and a plan to offer himself to mankind.

9:16–21 Seeing how God continued to be with his people shows that his patience is amazing! In spite of our repeated failings, pride, and stubbornness, he is always ready to pardon (9:17), and his Spirit is always ready to instruct (9:20). Realizing the extent of God's forgiveness helps us forgive those who fail us, even "seventy times seven" if necessary (Matthew 18:21–22).

But You are a God of forgiveness,
Gracious and compassionate,
Slow to anger and abounding in lovingkindness;
And You did not forsake them.
18 "Even when they made for themselves
A calf of molten metal
And said, 'This is your God
Who brought you up from Egypt,'
And committed great [7]blasphemies,
19 You, in Your great compassion,
Did not forsake them in the wilderness;
The pillar of cloud did not leave them by day,
To guide them on their way,
Nor the pillar of fire by night, to light for them the way in which they were to go.
20 "You gave Your good Spirit to instruct them,
Your manna You did not withhold from their mouth,
And You gave them water for their thirst.
21 "Indeed, forty years You provided for them in the wilderness *and* they were not in want;
Their clothes did not wear out, nor did their feet swell.
22 "You also gave them kingdoms and peoples,
And allotted *them* to them as a boundary.
They took possession of the land of Sihon the king of Heshbon
And the land of Og the king of Bashan.
23 "You made their sons numerous as the stars of heaven,
And You brought them into the land
Which You had told their fathers to enter and possess.
24 "So their sons entered and possessed the land.
And You subdued before them the inhabitants of the land, the Canaanites,
And You gave them into their hand, with their kings and the peoples of the land,
To do with them as they desired.
25 "They captured fortified cities and a fertile land.
They took possession of houses full of every good thing,
Hewn cisterns, vineyards, olive groves,
Fruit trees in abundance.
So they ate, were filled and grew fat,
And reveled in Your great goodness.

26 "But they became disobedient and rebelled against You,
And cast Your law behind their backs
And killed Your prophets who had admonished them
So that they might return to You,
And they committed great [7]blasphemies.
27 "Therefore You delivered them into the hand of their oppressors who oppressed them,
But when they cried to You in the time of their distress,
You heard from heaven, and according to Your great compassion
You gave them deliverers who delivered them from the hand of their oppressors.
28 "But as soon as they had rest, they did evil again before You;
Therefore You abandoned them to the hand of their enemies, so that they ruled over them.
When they cried again to You, You heard from heaven,
And many times You rescued them according to Your compassion,

9:18 Ex 32:4-8, 31
9:19 Deut 8:2-4; Neh 9:27, 31; Neh 9:12
9:20 Num 11:17; Neh 9:30; Is 63:11-14
9:21 Deut 2:7
9:22 Num 21:21-35
9:23 Gen 15:5; 22:17
9:24 Josh 11:23; 21:43; Josh 18:1
9:25 Deut 3:5; Num 13:27; Deut 6:11; Deut 32:15; 1 Kin 8:66
9:26 Judg 2:11; 1 Kin 14:9; 2 Chr 36:16; Neh 9:30; Neh 9:18
9:27 Judg 2:14; Deut 4:29; Judg 2:16
9:28 Judg 3:11; Ps 106:43

7 Lit *acts of contempt*

9:28–31 Israel was devastated by times of intense rebellion and sin. Yet when the people repented and returned to God, he delivered them. God puts no limit on the number of times we can come to him to obtain mercy, but we must *come* in order to obtain it, recognizing our need and asking him for help. This miracle of grace should inspire us to say, "You are a gracious and compassionate God." If there is a recurring problem or difficulty in your life, continue to ask God for help, and be willing and ready to make changes in your attitude and behavior that will correct that situation.

9:29 Neh 9:26, 30; Neh 9:10, 16; Lev 18:5, Zech 7:11

29 And admonished them in order to turn them back to Your law.
Yet they acted arrogantly and did not listen to Your commandments but sinned against Your ordinances,
By which if a man observes them he shall live.
And they turned a stubborn shoulder and stiffened their neck, and would not listen.

9:30 Ps 95:10; Acts 13:18; 2 Kin 17:13-18; 2 Chr 36:15, 16; Neh 9:26, 29; Neh 9:20

30 "However, You bore with them for many years,
And admonished them by Your Spirit through Your prophets,
Yet they would not give ear.
Therefore You gave them into the hand of the peoples of the lands.

9:31 Jer 4:27; Neh 9:17

31 "Nevertheless, in Your great compassion You did not make an end of them or forsake them,
For You are a gracious and compassionate God.

9:32 Neh 1:5; 2 Kin 15:19, 29; 2 Kin 17:3-6; Ezra 4:2, 10

32 "Now therefore, our God, the great, the mighty, and the awesome God, who keeps covenant and lovingkindness,
Do not let all the hardship seem insignificant before You,
Which has come upon us, our kings, our princes, our priests, our prophets, our fathers and on all Your people,
From the days of the kings of Assyria to this day.

9:33 Gen 18:25; Jer 12:1

33 "However, You are just in all that has come upon us;
For You have dealt faithfully, but we have acted wickedly.
34 "For our kings, our leaders, our priests and our fathers have not kept Your law
Or paid attention to Your commandments and Your admonitions with which You have admonished them.

9:35 Deut 28:47; Neh 9:25

35 "But they, in their own kingdom,
With Your great goodness which You gave them,
With the broad and rich land which You set before them,
Did not serve You or turn from their evil deeds.

9:36 Deut 28:48

36 "Behold, we are slaves today,
And as to the land which You gave to our fathers to eat of its fruit and its bounty,
Behold, we are slaves in it.

9:37 Deut 28:33

37 "Its abundant produce is for the kings
Whom You have set over us because of our sins;
They also rule over our bodies
And over our cattle as they please,
So we are in great distress.

A Covenant Results

9:38 Neh 10:29; Neh 10:1

38 "Now because of all this
We are making an agreement in writing;
And on the sealed document *are the names of* our leaders, our Levites *and* our priests."

Signers of the Document

10:1 Neh 9:38

10 Now on the sealed document *were the names of:* Nehemiah the governor, the son of Hacaliah, and Zedekiah,
2 Seraiah, Azariah, Jeremiah,
3 Pashhur, Amariah, Malchijah,
4 Hattush, Shebaniah, Malluch,

9:35 Sometimes the very blessings God has showered on us make us forget him (9:28). We are often tempted to rely on wealth for security rather than on God. As you see what happened to the Israelites, look at your own life. Do your blessings make you thankful to God and draw you closer to him, or do they make you feel self-sufficient and forgetful of God?

9:36 The Israelites were in the strange position of being slaves in their own land, having to turn over a part of their resources each year to a foreign king. How ironic, since God had given the land to them.

9:38 This binding agreement or covenant between the people and God had six provisions. They agreed to: (1) not marry non-Jewish neighbors (10:30), (2) observe the sabbath (10:31), (3) observe every seventh year as a sabbath year (10:31), (4) pay a temple tax (10:32–33), (5) supply wood for the burnt offerings in the temple (10:34), and (6) give dues to the temple (10:35–38). After years of decadence and exile, the people once again took seriously their responsibility to follow God and keep his laws wholeheartedly.

5 Harim, Meremoth, Obadiah,
6 Daniel, Ginnethon, Baruch,
7 Meshullam, Abijah, Mijamin,
8 Maaziah, Bilgai, Shemaiah. These *were* the priests.
9 And the Levites: Jeshua the son of Azaniah, Binnui of the sons of Henadad,
Kadmiel;
10 also their brothers Shebaniah, Hodiah, Kelita, Pelaiah, Hanan,
11 Mica, Rehob, Hashabiah,
12 Zaccur, Sherebiah, Shebaniah,
13 Hodiah, Bani, Beninu.
14 The leaders of the people: Parosh, Pahath-moab, Elam, Zattu, Bani,
15 Bunni, Azgad, Bebai,
16 Adonijah, Bigvai, Adin,
17 Ater, Hezekiah, Azzur,
18 Hodiah, Hashum, Bezai,
19 Hariph, Anathoth, Nebai,
20 Magpiash, Meshullam, Hezir,
21 Meshezabel, Zadok, Jaddua,
22 Pelatiah, Hanan, Anaiah,
23 Hoshea, Hananiah, Hasshub,
24 Hallohesh, Pilha, Shobek,
25 Rehum, Hashabnah, Maaseiah,
26 Ahiah, Hanan, Anan,
27 Malluch, Harim, Baanah.

Obligations of the Document

28 Now the rest of the people, the priests, the Levites, the gatekeepers, the singers,
the temple servants and all those who had separated themselves from the peoples of the
lands to the law of God, their wives, their sons and their daughters, all those who had
knowledge and understanding,
29 are joining with their kinsmen, their nobles, and are taking on themselves a curse
and an oath to walk in God's law, which was given through Moses, God's servant, and to
keep and to observe all the commandments of GOD our Lord, and His ordinances and
His statutes;
30 and that we will not give our daughters to the peoples of the land or take their daughters for our sons.
31 As for the peoples of the land who bring wares or any grain on the sabbath day to
sell, we will not buy from them on the sabbath or a holy day; and we will forego *the crops*
the seventh year and the exaction of every debt.
32 We also placed ourselves under obligation to contribute yearly one third of a shekel
for the service of the house of our God:
33 for the showbread, for the continual grain offering, for the continual burnt offering, the sabbaths, the new moon, for the appointed times, for the holy things and for the
sin offerings to make atonement for Israel, and all the work of the house of our God.

10:28 Ezra 2:36-58; Neh 9:2
10:29 Neh 5:12
10:30 Ex 34:16; Deut 7:3
10:31 Neh 13:15-22; Ex 23:10, 11; Lev 25:1-7; Deut 15:1, 2
10:32 Ex 30:11-16; Matt 17:24
10:33 Lev 24:5, 6; 2 Chr 2:4

10:28ff The wall was completed, and the agreement God made with his people in the days of Moses was restored (Deuteronomy 8). This covenant has principles that are important for us today. Our relationship with God must go far beyond church attendance and regular devotions. It should affect our relationships (10:30), our time (10:31), and our material resources (10:32–39). When you chose to follow God, you promised to serve him in this way. The Israelites had fallen away from their original commitment. We must keep our promise to God in times of adversity or prosperity.

10:30 If God's chosen people were going to witness for him in a pagan world, they needed united, God-fearing families. They also needed to avoid any enticements to worship the idols of the people who lived around them. This was why God prohibited marriage between Israelites and the pagan inhabitants of the land (Deuteronomy 7:3–4). But Israelites and pagans often intermarried anyway, and the results were disastrous for the families and for the nation. Time after time, marrying foreigners led God's people into idolatry (1 Kings 11:1–11). Whenever the nation turned its back on God, it also lost its prosperity and influence for good.

10:31 God recognized that the lure of money would conflict with the need for a day of rest, so trade was forbidden inside the city on the sabbath. By deciding to honor God first, the Israelites would be refusing to make money their god. Our culture often makes us choose between convenience and profit on the one hand, and putting God first on the other. Look at your work and worship habits: is God really first?

10:31 Forgoing all debts every seventh year was a part of the Law (see Exodus 23:10 and Deuteronomy 15:1, 2). The people were reciting and promising to obey God's Law and keep the covenant.

10:32 The temple had been rebuilt under Ezra's leadership about 70 years earlier (Ezra 6:14–15). So the temple tax, offerings, and feasts had been restored.

10:34
Neh 11:1; Neh 13:31

34 Likewise we cast lots for the supply of wood *among* the priests, the Levites and the
people so that they might bring it to the house of our God, according to our fathers'
households, at fixed times annually, to burn on the altar of the LORD our God, as it is
written in the law;

10:35
Ex 23:19; 34:26; Deut 26:2

35 and that they might bring the first fruits of our ground and the first fruits of all the
fruit of every tree to the house of the LORD annually,

10:36
Ex 13:2

36 and bring to the house of our God the firstborn of our sons and of our cattle, and
the firstborn of our herds and our flocks as it is written in the law, for the priests who are
ministering in the house of our God.

10:37
Lev 23:17; Neh 13:5, 9; Lev 27:30; Num 18:21

37 We will also bring the first of our dough, our contributions, the fruit of every tree,
the new wine and the oil to the priests at the chambers of the house of our God, and the
tithe of our ground to the Levites, for the Levites are they who receive the tithes in all
the rural towns.

10:38
Num 18:26; Neh 13:12, 13

38 The priest, the son of Aaron, shall be with the Levites when the Levites receive tithes,
and the Levites shall bring up the tenth of the tithes to the house of our God, to the
chambers of the storehouse.

10:39
Deut 12:6; Neh 13:10, 11

39 For the sons of Israel and the sons of Levi shall bring the contribution of the grain,
the new wine and the oil to the chambers; there are the utensils of the sanctuary, the
priests who are ministering, the gatekeepers and the singers. Thus we will not neglect
the house of our God.

2. Nehemiah establishes policies

Time Passes; Heads of Provinces

11:1
Neh 7:4; Neh 10:34; Neh 11:18; Is 48:2

11 Now the leaders of the people lived in Jerusalem, but the rest of the people cast
lots to bring one out of ten to live in Jerusalem, the holy city, while nine-tenths
remained in the *other* cities.

11:2
Judg 5:9

2 And the people blessed all the men who volunteered to live in Jerusalem.

11:3
1 Chr 9:2-34; Neh 7:73; 11:20; Ezra 2:43; Neh 7:57

3 Now these are the heads of the provinces who lived in Jerusalem, but in the cities of
Judah each lived on his own property in their cities—the Israelites, the priests, the Levites, the temple servants and the descendants of Solomon's servants.
4 Some of the sons of Judah and some of the sons of Benjamin lived in Jerusalem.
From the sons of Judah: Athaiah the son of Uzziah, the son of Zechariah, the son of
Amariah, the son of Shephatiah, the son of Mahalalel, of the sons of Perez;
5 and Maaseiah the son of Baruch, the son of Col-hozeh, the son of Hazaiah, the son
of Adaiah, the son of Joiarib, the son of Zechariah, the son of the Shilonite.
6 All the sons of Perez who lived in Jerusalem were 468 able men.
7 Now these are the sons of Benjamin: Sallu the son of Meshullam, the son of Joed,
the son of Pedaiah, the son of Kolaiah, the son of Maaseiah, the son of Ithiel, the son of
Jeshaiah;
8 and after him Gabbai *and* Sallai, 928.
9 Joel the son of Zichri was their overseer, and Judah the son of Hassenuah was second in command of the city.
10 From the priests: Jedaiah the son of Joiarib, Jachin,

10:36 This practice was instituted at the time of the exodus from Egypt (see the note on Exodus 13:12–14). The people needed to relearn the importance of dedicating the firstfruits of their yield to God. Nehemiah was simply reinstating this practice from the early days of the nation (Exodus 13:1–2; Numbers 3:40–51). Although this principle was not carried over to New Testament times, the concept of giving God the first portion of our time, treasure, and talent still remains. Do you give God your first and best, or merely what is left over?

10:37–39 According to God's Law, the people were to give a tenth of their produce to the temple for the support of the Levites (those who cared for the temple and the religious observances). A tenth of what the Levites received or produced went to the priests for their support. The principle at work was to ensure the support of the house of God and his workers. We must not overlook our responsibility to God's workers today.

11:1ff The exiles who returned were few in number compared to Jerusalem's population in the days of the kings. And because the walls had been rebuilt on their original foundations, the city seemed sparsely populated. Nehemiah asked one-tenth of the people from the outlying areas to move inside the city walls to keep large areas of the city from being vacant. Apparently these people did not want to move into the city. Only a few people volunteered (11:1–2), and Nehemiah cast lots to determine who among the remaining people would have to move.

Many of them may not have wanted to live in the city because (1) non-Jews attached a stigma to Jerusalem residents, often excluding them from trade because of their religious beliefs; (2) moving into the city meant rebuilding their homes and reestablishing their businesses, a major investment of time and money; (3) living in Jerusalem required stricter obedience to God's Word because of greater social pressure and proximity to the temple.

11 Seraiah the son of Hilkiah, the son of Meshullam, the son of Zadok, the son of
Meraioth, the son of Ahitub, the leader of the house of God,
12 and their [8]kinsmen who performed the work of the temple, 822; and Adaiah the son
of Jeroham, the son of Pelaliah, the son of Amzi, the son of Zechariah, the son of Pashhur, the son of Malchijah,
13 and his kinsmen, heads of fathers' *households,* 242; and Amashsai the son of Azarel, the son of Ahzai, the son of Meshillemoth, the son of Immer,
14 and their brothers, valiant warriors, 128. And their overseer was Zabdiel, the son of
Haggedolim.
15 Now from the Levites: Shemaiah the son of Hasshub, the son of Azrikam, the son
of Hashabiah, the son of Bunni;
16 and Shabbethai and Jozabad, from the leaders of the Levites, who were in charge **11:16**
of the outside work of the house of God; 1 Chr 26:29
17 and Mattaniah the son of Mica, the son of Zabdi, the son of Asaph, who was the
leader in beginning the thanksgiving at prayer, and Bakbukiah, the second among his
brethren; and Abda the son of Shammua, the son of Galal, the son of Jeduthun.
18 All the Levites in the holy city *were* 284. **11:18**
19 Also the gatekeepers, Akkub, Talmon and their brethren who kept watch at the gates, Neh 11:1
were 172.

Outside Jerusalem

20 The rest of Israel, of the priests *and* of the Levites, *were* in all the cities of Judah, **11:20**
each on his own inheritance. Neh 11:3
21 But the temple servants were living in Ophel, and Ziha and Gishpa were in charge **11:21**
of the temple servants. Neh 3:26
22 Now the overseer of the Levites in Jerusalem was Uzzi the son of Bani, the son of **11:22**
Hashabiah, the son of Mattaniah, the son of Mica, from the sons of Asaph, who were Neh 11:9, 14
the singers for the service of the house of God.
23 For *there was* a commandment from the king concerning them and a firm regula- **11:23**
tion for the song leaders day by day. Ezra 6:8; 7:20; Neh 12:47
24 Pethahiah the son of Meshezabel, of the sons of Zerah the son of Judah, was the
king's representative in all matters concerning the people. **11:24** Gen 38:30; 1 Chr 18:17
25 Now as for the villages with their fields, some of the sons of Judah lived in Kiriath-
arba and its [9]towns, in Dibon and its towns, and in Jekabzeel and its villages, **11:25**
26 and in Jeshua, in Moladah and Beth-pelet, Josh 14:15; Josh 13:9, 17
27 and in Hazar-shual, in Beersheba and its towns,
28 and in Ziklag, in Meconah and in its towns,
29 and in En-rimmon, in Zorah and in Jarmuth,
30 Zanoah, Adullam, and their villages, Lachish and its fields, Azekah and its towns.
So they encamped from Beersheba as far as the valley of Hinnom.
31 The sons of Benjamin also *lived* from Geba *onward,* at Michmash and Aija, at Bethel and its towns,
32 at Anathoth, Nob, Ananiah,
33 Hazor, Ramah, Gittaim,
34 Hadid, Zeboim, Neballat,
35 Lod and Ono, the valley of craftsmen.
36 From the Levites, *some* divisions in Judah belonged to Benjamin.

Priests and Levites Who Returned to Jerusalem with Zerubbabel

12 Now these are the priests and the Levites who came up with Zerubbabel the son **12:1**
of Shealtiel, and Jeshua: Seraiah, Jeremiah, Ezra, Ezra 2:1; 7:7
2 Amariah, Malluch, Hattush,
3 Shecaniah, Rehum, Meremoth,
4 Iddo, Ginnethoi, Abijah,
5 Mijamin, Maadiah, Bilgah,
6 Shemaiah and Joiarib, Jedaiah,
7 Sallu, Amok, Hilkiah and Jedaiah. These were the heads of the priests and their
kinsmen in the days of Jeshua.
8 The Levites *were* Jeshua, Binnui, Kadmiel, Sherebiah, Judah, *and* Mattaniah *who*
was in charge of the songs of thanksgiving, he and his brothers.

8 Lit *brothers,* and so throughout the ch **9** Lit *daughters,* and so throughout the ch

12:9 Neh 12:24
9 Also Bakbukiah and Unni, their brothers, stood opposite them in *their* service divisions.
10 Jeshua became the father of Joiakim, and Joiakim became the father of Eliashib,
and Eliashib became the father of Joiada,
11 and Joiada became the father of Jonathan, and Jonathan became the father of
Jaddua.
12 Now in the days of Joiakim, the priests, the heads of fathers' *households* were: of
Seraiah, Meraiah; of Jeremiah, Hananiah;
13 of Ezra, Meshullam; of Amariah, Jehohanan;
14 of Malluchi, Jonathan; of Shebaniah, Joseph;
15 of Harim, Adna; of Meraioth, Helkai;
16 of Iddo, Zechariah; of Ginnethon, Meshullam;
17 of Abijah, Zichri; of Miniamin, of Moadiah, Piltai;
18 of Bilgah, Shammua; of Shemaiah, Jehonathan;
19 of Joiarib, Mattenai; of Jedaiah, Uzzi;
20 of Sallai, Kallai; of Amok, Eber;
21 of Hilkiah, Hashabiah; of Jedaiah, Nethanel.

The Chief Levites

22 As for the Levites, the heads of fathers' *households* were registered in the days of
Eliashib, Joiada, and Johanan and Jaddua; so *were* the priests in the reign of Darius the
Persian.
23 The sons of Levi, the heads of fathers' *households,* were registered in the Book of
the Chronicles up to the days of Johanan the son of Eliashib.
12:24 Neh 11:17; Neh 12:9
24 The heads of the Levites *were* Hashabiah, Sherebiah and Jeshua the son of Kadmiel, with their brothers opposite them, to praise *and* give thanks, as prescribed by David
the man of God, division corresponding to division.
12:25 1 Chr 26:15
25 Mattaniah, Bakbukiah, Obadiah, Meshullam, Talmon *and* Akkub *were* gatekeepers
keeping watch at the storehouses of the gates.
12:26 Neh 8:9
26 These *served* in the days of Joiakim the son of Jeshua, the son of Jozadak, and in
the days of Nehemiah the governor and of Ezra the priest *and* scribe.

Dedication of the Wall

12:27 1 Chr 15:16, 28
27 Now at the dedication of the wall of Jerusalem they sought out the Levites from all
their places, to bring them to Jerusalem so that they might celebrate the dedication with
gladness, with hymns of thanksgiving and with songs *to the accompaniment* of cymbals,
harps and lyres.
12:28 1 Chr 9:16
28 So the sons of the singers were assembled from the district around Jerusalem, and
from the villages of the Netophathites,
29 from Beth-gilgal and from *their* fields in Geba and Azmaveth, for the singers had
built themselves villages around Jerusalem.
12:30 Neh 13:22, 30
30 The priests and the Levites purified themselves; they also purified the people, the
gates and the wall.

Procedures for the Temple

12:31 Neh 12:38; Neh 2:13
31 Then I had the leaders of Judah come up on top of the wall, and I appointed two
great choirs, the first proceeding to the right on top of the wall toward the Refuse Gate.
32 Hoshaiah and half of the leaders of Judah followed them,
33 with Azariah, Ezra, Meshullam,
34 Judah, Benjamin, Shemaiah, Jeremiah,
35 and some of the sons of the priests with trumpets; *and* Zechariah the son of Jonathan, the son of Shemaiah, the son of Mattaniah, the son of Micaiah, the son of Zaccur,
the son of Asaph,
12:36 Neh 12:24
36 and his kinsmen, Shemaiah, Azarel, Milalai, Gilalai, Maai, Nethanel, Judah *and*

12:35–36 How could the priests have used musical instruments? David had instituted music as a part of worship in the temple, and so his instruments had probably been stored there. Although Nebuchadnezzar destroyed the temple, he took many temple items back to Babylon with him (2 Chronicles 36:18). These were most likely preserved in Babylon and given back to the Israelites by Cyrus when they returned to their land (Ezra 1:7–11).

Hanani, with the musical instruments of David the man of God. And Ezra the scribe
went before them.
37 At the Fountain Gate they went directly up the steps of the city of David by the stairway of the wall above the house of David to the Water Gate on the east.
38 The second choir proceeded to the left, while I followed them with half of the people on the wall, above the Tower of Furnaces, to the Broad Wall,
39 and above the Gate of Ephraim, by the Old Gate, by the Fish Gate, the Tower of
Hananel and the Tower of the Hundred, as far as the Sheep Gate; and they stopped at
the Gate of the Guard.
40 Then the two choirs took their stand in the house of God. So did I and half of the
officials with me;
41 and the priests, Eliakim, Maaseiah, Miniamin, Micaiah, Elioenai, Zechariah and
Hananiah, with the trumpets;
42 and Maaseiah, Shemaiah, Eleazar, Uzzi, Jehohanan, Malchijah, Elam and Ezer. And
the singers sang, with Jezrahiah *their* leader,
43 and on that day they offered great sacrifices and rejoiced because God had given
them great joy, even the women and children rejoiced, so that the joy of Jerusalem was
heard from afar.
44 On that day men were also appointed over the chambers for the stores, the contributions, the first fruits and the tithes, to gather into them from the fields of the cities the
portions required by the law for the priests and Levites; for Judah rejoiced over the priests
and Levites who served.
45 For they performed the worship of their God and the service of purification, together
with the singers and the gatekeepers in accordance with the command of David *and* of
his son Solomon.
46 For in the days of David and Asaph, in ancient times, *there were* leaders of the singers, songs of praise and hymns of thanksgiving to God.
47 So all Israel in the days of Zerubbabel and Nehemiah gave the portions due the singers and the gatekeepers as each day required, and set apart the consecrated *portion* for
the Levites, and the Levites set apart the consecrated *portion* for the sons of Aaron.

12:37 Neh 2:14; Neh 3:15; Neh 3:26
12:38 Neh 12:31; Neh 3:11; Neh 3:8
12:39 Neh 8:16; Neh 3:6; Neh 3:3; Neh 3:1; Neh 3:25
12:43 Ps 9:2; 92:4
12:44 Neh 13:4, 5, 12, 13
12:45 1 Chr 25:1
12:46 2 Chr 29:30; 1 Chr 9:33
12:47 Neh 11:23; Num 18:21

Foreigners Excluded

13 On that day they read aloud from the book of Moses in the hearing of the people;
and there was found written in it that no Ammonite or Moabite should ever enter
the assembly of God,
2 because they did not meet the sons of Israel with bread and water, but hired Balaam against them to curse them. However, our God turned the curse into a blessing.
3 So when they heard the law, they excluded all foreigners from Israel.

Tobiah Expelled and the Temple Cleansed

4 Now prior to this, Eliashib the priest, who was appointed over the chambers of the
house of our God, being related to Tobiah,
5 had prepared a large room for him, where formerly they put the grain offerings, the
frankincense, the utensils and the tithes of grain, wine and oil prescribed for the Levites,
the singers and the gatekeepers, and the contributions for the priests.

13:1 Neh 9:3; Deut 23:3-5; Neh 13:23
13:2 Num 22:3-11; Deut 23:5
13:3 Neh 9:2; 10:28; Ex 12:38
13:4 Neh 12:44; Neh 2:10; 6:1, 17, 18
13:5 Num 18:21

12:44 Further arrangements were made for supporting those who served at the temple. The storage chambers were administered by men who made sure the tithes and contributions were collected and distributed appropriately. These chambers had to be large to hold all the grain presented by the people. This chamber administration was an important responsibility.

12:44–47 The dedication of the city wall was characterized by joy, praise, and singing (12:24, 27–29, 35–36, 40–43). Nehemiah repeatedly mentioned David, who began the custom of using choirs in worship. In David's day, Israel was a vigorous, God-fearing nation. These exiles who had returned wanted their rebuilt Jerusalem to be the hub of a renewed nation, strengthened by God; therefore, they dedicated themselves and their city to God.

13:3 "All foreigners" refers to the Moabites and Ammonites, two nations who were bitter enemies of Israel (13:1). God's law clearly stated that these two peoples should never be allowed in the temple (Deuteronomy 23:3–5). This had nothing to do with racial prejudice, because God clearly loved all people, including foreigners (Deuteronomy 10:18). He allowed foreigners to make sacrifices (Numbers 15:15–16), and he desires all nations to know and love him (Isaiah 42:6). But while God wants all to come to him, he warns believers to stay away from those bent on evil (Proverbs 24:1). The relationships established between Jews and pagans had caused their captivity in the first place. In their celebration and rededication, they had to show they were serious about following God's law.

6 But during all this *time* I was not in Jerusalem, for in the thirty-second year of Artaxerxes king of Babylon I had gone to the king. After some time, however, I asked leave
from the king,
7 and I came to Jerusalem and learned about the evil that Eliashib had done for Tobiah, by preparing a room for him in the courts of the house of God.
8 It was very displeasing to me, so I threw all of Tobiah's household goods out of the
room.
9 Then I gave an order and they cleansed the rooms; and I returned there the utensils
of the house of God with the grain offerings and the frankincense.

Tithes Restored

10 I also discovered that the portions of the Levites had not been given *them,* so that
the Levites and the singers who performed the service had gone away, each to his own
field.
11 So I reprimanded the officials and said, "Why is the house of God forsaken?" Then
I gathered them together and restored them to their posts.
12 All Judah then brought the tithe of the grain, wine and oil into the storehouses.
13 In charge of the storehouses I appointed Shelemiah the priest, Zadok the scribe,
and Pedaiah of the Levites, and in addition to them was Hanan the son of Zaccur, the
son of Mattaniah; for they were considered reliable, and it was their task to distribute to
their kinsmen.
14 Remember me for this, O my God, and do not blot out my loyal deeds which I have
performed for the house of my God and its services.

Sabbath Restored

15 In those days I saw in Judah some who were treading wine presses on the sabbath,
and bringing in sacks of grain and loading *them* on donkeys, as well as wine, grapes, figs
and all kinds of loads, and they brought *them* into Jerusalem on the sabbath day. So I
admonished *them* on the day they sold food.
16 Also men of Tyre were living there *who* imported fish and all kinds of merchandise,
and sold *them* to the sons of Judah on the sabbath, even in Jerusalem.
17 Then I reprimanded the nobles of Judah and said to them, "What is this evil thing
you are doing, by profaning the sabbath day?
18 "Did not your fathers do the same, so that our God brought on us and on this city all
this trouble? Yet you are adding to the wrath on Israel by profaning the sabbath."
19 It came about that just as it grew dark at the gates of Jerusalem before the sabbath,
I commanded that the doors should be shut and that they should not open them until
after the sabbath. Then I stationed some of my servants at the gates *so that* no load would
enter on the sabbath day.
20 Once or twice the traders and merchants of every kind of merchandise spent the
night outside Jerusalem.
21 Then I warned them and said to them, "Why do you spend the night in front of the
wall? If you do so again, I will use force against you." From that time on they did not
come on the sabbath.
22 And I commanded the Levites that they should purify themselves and come as

13:6 Neh 5:14; Ezra 6:22
13:7 Neh 13:5
13:8 John 2:13-16
13:9 2 Chr 29:5, 15, 16
13:10 Deut 12:19; Neh 10:37; Neh 12:28, 29
13:11 Neh 13:17, 25; Neh 10:39
13:12 Neh 10:37; 12:44; Mal 3:10
13:13 Neh 7:2
13:14 Neh 5:19; 13:22, 31
13:15 Ex 20:8; 34:21; Deut 5:12-14; Jer 17:22; Neh 10:31; Jer 17:21; Neh 9:29; 13:21
13:17 Neh 13:11, 25
13:18 Ezra 9:13; Jer 17:21
13:19 Lev 23:32
13:21 Neh 13:15
13:22 1 Chr 15:12; Neh 12:30; Neh 13:14, 31

13:6–7 Nehemiah had to return to Babylon in 433 B.C., 12 years after he had arrived in Jerusalem. Either he was recalled by Artaxerxes, or he was fulfilling an agreement to return. It is not known exactly how long he remained in Babylon, but when he returned to Jerusalem (13:7), he found that one of his major opponents in rebuilding the wall, Tobiah, had been given his own room at the temple. He was an Ammonite (4:3), and thus forbidden to enter the temple. Eliashib, the priest, had married Tobiah's daughter, so Tobiah used his influence with his son-in-law to get this special room. Chapters 2, 4, and 6 tell about Tobiah's opposition to Nehemiah and Nehemiah's appropriate action.

13:10 Because the Levites were no longer supported, they had returned to their farms to support themselves, neglecting their temple duties and the spiritual welfare of the people. Spiritual workers deserve their pay, and their support ought to be enough to care for their needs. They shouldn't have to suffer (or leave) because believers don't adequately assess and meet the needs of their ministers.

13:16 Tyre was a large Phoenician city and port on the Mediterranean Sea.

13:17 God had commanded Israel not to work on the sabbath, but to rest in remembrance of creation and the exodus (Exodus 20:8–11; Deuteronomy 5:12–15). The sabbath rest, lasting from sunset Friday to sunset Saturday, was to be honored and observed by all Jews, servants, visiting foreigners, and even farm animals. Jerusalem's busy sabbath trade directly violated God's Law, so Nehemiah commanded that the city gates be shut and traders be sent home every Friday afternoon as the Sabbath hours approached.

gatekeepers to sanctify the sabbath day. *For* this also remember me, O my God, and have compassion on me according to the greatness of Your lovingkindness.

Mixed Marriages Forbidden

23 In those days I also saw that the Jews had married women from Ashdod, Ammon *and* Moab.
24 As for their children, half spoke in the language of Ashdod, and none of them was able to speak the language of Judah, but the language of his own people.
25 So I contended with them and cursed them and struck some of them and pulled out their hair, and made them swear by God, "You shall not give your daughters to their sons, nor take of their daughters for your sons or for yourselves.
26 "Did not Solomon king of Israel sin regarding these things? Yet among the many nations there was no king like him, and he was loved by his God, and God made him king over all Israel; nevertheless the foreign women caused even him to sin.
27 "Do we then hear about you that you have committed all this great evil by acting unfaithfully against our God by marrying foreign women?"
28 Even one of the sons of Joiada, the son of Eliashib the high priest, was a son-in-law of Sanballat the Horonite, so I drove him away from me.
29 Remember them, O my God, because they have defiled the priesthood and the covenant of the priesthood and the Levites.
30 Thus I purified them from everything foreign and appointed duties for the priests and the Levites, each in his task,
31 and *I arranged* for the supply of wood at appointed times and for the first fruits. Remember me, O my God, for good.

13:23 Ex 34:11-16; Deut 7:1-5; Ezra 9:2; Neh 10:30; Neh 4:7; Ezra 9:1; Neh 13:1

13:25 Neh 13:11, 17; Deut 25:2; Neh 10:29, 30

13:26 1 Kin 11:1; 1 Kin 3:13; 2 Chr 1:12; 2 Sam 12:24, 25

13:27 Ezra 10:2; Neh 13:23

13:28 Neh 2:10, 19; 4:1

13:29 Neh 6:14; Num 25:13

13:30 Neh 10:30

13:31 Neh 10:34; Neh 13:14, 22

13:24 Ashdod was on the Mediterranean coast, in the region controlled by the Philistines. Ammon and Moab were across the Jordan to the east. These nations were abhorrent to those who knew Israel's history.

13:25 Nehemiah was filled with righteous indignation at the blatant way the Jews were breaking God's laws and disregarding the covenant they had previously reaffirmed (10:30). The people had promised not to allow their children to marry pagans. But during Nehemiah's absence, the people had been intermarrying, breaking their solemn covenant with God. Nehemiah's severe treatment of these people shows the contrast between his great faithfulness to God and the people's neglect, disobedience, and disloyalty (see also Ezra 10:3).

13:26 Nehemiah used the example of Solomon's mistakes to teach his people. If one of the greatest kings of Israel fell because of the influence of unbelievers, others could too. Nehemiah saw this principle in Solomon's example: Your gifts and strengths won't be of much benefit if you fail to deal with your weaknesses. Although Solomon was a great king, his marriages to foreign women brought tragedy to the whole kingdom. A tendency to sin must be recognized and dealt with swiftly; otherwise, it may overpower you and bring you down. One of the strongest reasons for reading the Bible is to learn from the mistakes of God's people.

13:31 "Remember me . . . for good" means "look favorably upon me for all that I have done."

13:31 Nehemiah's life story provides many principles of effective leadership that are still valid today. (1) *Have a clear purpose and keep evaluating it in light of God's will.* Nothing prevented Nehemiah from staying on track. (2) *Be straightforward and honest.* Everyone knew exactly what Nehemiah needed, and he spoke the truth even when it made his goal harder to achieve. (3) *Live above reproach.* The accusations against Nehemiah were empty and false. (4) *Be a person of constant prayer,* deriving power and wisdom from your contact with God. Everything Nehemiah did glorified God.

Leadership appears glamorous at times, but it is often lonely, thankless, and filled with pressures to compromise values and standards. Nehemiah was able to accomplish a huge task against incredible odds because he learned that there is no success without risk of failure, no reward without hard work, no opportunity without criticism, and no true leadership without trust in God. This book is about rebuilding the wall of a great city, but it is also about spiritual renewal, rebuilding a people's dependence on God. When we take our eyes off God, our lives begin to crumble.

ESTHER

Jerusalem destroyed/ exiles go to Babylon 586 B.C.	First exiles return to Jerusalem 538	Temple completed 515	Ahasuerus becomes king of Persia 486	Esther becomes queen 479	Haman's decree to destroy the Jews 474	First Feast of Purim 473

DRAMA, power, romance, intrigue—this is the stuff of which best-selling novels are made. But far from a modern piece of fiction, those words describe a true story, lived and written centuries ago. More than entertaining reading, it is a story of the profound interplay of God's sovereignty and human will. God prepared the place and the opportunity, and his people, Esther and Mordecai, chose to act.

The book of Esther begins with Queen Vashti refusing to obey an order from her husband, King Ahasuerus. She was subsequently banished, and the search began for a new queen. The king sent out a decree to gather together all the beautiful women in the empire and bring them into the royal harem. Esther, a young Jewish woman, was one of those chosen to be in the royal harem. King Ahasuerus was so pleased with Esther that he made her his queen.

Meanwhile, Mordecai, Esther's older cousin, became a government official and during his tenure foiled an assassination plot. But the ambitious and self-serving Haman was appointed second-in-command in the empire. When Mordecai refused to bow in reverence to him, Haman became furious and determined to destroy Mordecai and all the Jews along with him.

To accomplish his vengeful deed, Haman deceived the king and persuaded him to issue an edict condemning the Jews to death. Mordecai told Queen Esther about this edict, and she decided to risk her life to save her people. Esther asked King Ahasuerus and Haman to be her guests at a banquet. During the feast, the king asked Esther what she really wanted, and he promised to give her anything. Esther simply invited both men to another banquet the next day.

That night, unable to sleep, the king was flipping through some records in the royal archives when he read of the assassination plot that Mordecai thwarted. Surprised to learn that Mordecai had never been rewarded for this deed, the king asked Haman what should be done to properly thank a hero. Haman thought the king must be talking about him, and so he described a lavish reward. The king agreed, but to Haman's shock and utter humiliation, he learned that Mordecai was the person to be so honored.

During the second banquet, the king again asked Esther what she desired. She replied that someone had plotted to destroy her and her people, and she named Haman as the culprit. Immediately the king sentenced Haman to die on the gallows that he had built for Mordecai.

In the final act of this true-life drama, Mordecai was appointed to Haman's position, and the Jews were guaranteed protection throughout the land. To celebrate this historic occasion, the Feast of Purim was established.

Because of Queen Esther's courageous act, a whole nation was saved. Seeing her God-given opportunity, she seized it! Her life made a difference. Read Esther and watch for God at work in *your* life. Perhaps he has prepared you to act in "such a time as this" (4:14).

VITAL STATISTICS

PURPOSE:
To demonstrate God's sovereignty and his loving care for his people

AUTHOR:
Unknown. Possibly Mordecai (9:29). Some have suggested Ezra or Nehemiah because of the similarity of the writing style.

DATE WRITTEN:
Approximately 470 B.C. (Esther became queen in 479)

SETTING:
Although Esther follows Nehemiah in the Bible, its events are about 30 years prior to those recorded in Nehemiah. The story is set in the Persian empire, and most of the action takes place in the king's palace in Susa, the Persian capital.

KEY VERSE:
"For if you remain silent at this time, relief and deliverance will arise for the Jews from another place and you and your father's house will perish. And who knows whether you have not attained royalty for such a time as this?" (4:14).

KEY PEOPLE:
Esther, Mordecai, King Ahasuerus, Haman

KEY PLACE:
The king's palace in Susa, Persia

SPECIAL FEATURES:
Esther is one of only two books named for women (Ruth is the other). The book is unusual in that in the original version no name, title, or pronoun for God appears in it (see the note on 4:14). This caused some church fathers to question its inclusion in the canon. But God's presence is clear throughout the book.

THE BLUEPRINT

1. Esther becomes queen (1:1—2:23)
2. The Jews are threatened (3:1—4:17)
3. Esther intercedes for the Jews (5:1—8:17)
4. The Jews are delivered (9:1—10:3)

The book of Esther is an example of God's divine guidance and care over our lives. God's sovereignty and power are seen throughout this book. Although we may question certain circumstances in our lives, we must have faith that God is in control, working through both the pleasant and difficult times so that we can serve him effectively.

MEGATHEMES

THEME	EXPLANATION	IMPORTANCE
God's Sovereignty	The book of Esther tells of the circumstances that were essential to the survival of God's people in Persia. These "circumstances" were not the result of chance but of God's grand design. God is sovereign over every area of life.	With God in charge, we can take courage. He can guide us through the circumstances we face in our lives. We should expect God to display his power in carrying out his will. As we unite our life's purposes to God's purpose, we benefit from his sovereign care.
Racial Hatred	The Jews in Persia had been a minority since their deportation from Judah 100 years earlier. Haman was a descendant of King Agag, an enemy of the Jews. Lust for power and pride drove Haman to hate Mordecai, Esther's cousin. Haman convinced the king to kill all the Jews.	Racial hatred is always sinful. We must never condone it in any form. Every person on earth has intrinsic worth because God created people in his own image. Therefore, God's people must stand against racism whenever and wherever it occurs.
Deliverance	In February or March, the Jews celebrate the Feast of Purim, which symbolizes God's deliverance. *Purim* means "lots," such as those used by Haman to set the date for the extermination of all Jews from Persia. But God overruled, using Queen Esther to intercede on behalf of the Jews.	Because God is in control of history, he is never frustrated by any turn of events or human action. He is able to save us from the evil of this world and deliver us from sin and death. Because we trust God, we are not to fear what people may do to us; instead, we are to be confident in God's control.
Action	Faced with death, Esther and Mordecai set aside their own fear and took action. Esther risked her life by asking King Ahasuerus to save the Jews. They were not paralyzed by fear.	When outnumbered and powerless, it is natural for us to feel helpless. Esther and Mordecai resisted this temptation and acted with courage. It is not enough to know that God is in control; we must act with self-sacrifice and courage to follow God's guidance.
Wisdom	The Jews were a minority in a world hostile to them. It took great wisdom for Mordecai to survive. Serving as a faithful official of the king, Mordecai took steps to understand and work with the Persian law. Yet he did not compromise his integrity.	It takes great wisdom to survive in a non-believing world. In a setting which is for the most part hostile to Christianity, we can demonstrate wisdom by giving respect to what is true and good and by humbly standing against what is wrong.

1. Esther becomes queen

The Banquets of the King

1 Now it took place in the days of Ahasuerus, the Ahasuerus who reigned from India
to Ethiopia over 127 provinces,
2 in those days as King Ahasuerus sat on his royal throne which *was* at the citadel in
Susa,

1:1 Ezra 4:6; Dan 9:1; Esth 8:9; Esth 9:30

1:2 1 Kin 1:46; Neh 1:1; Dan 8:2

1:1 Esther's story begins in 483 B.C., 103 years after Nebuchadnezzar had taken the Jews into captivity (2 Kings 25), 54 years after Zerubbabel led the first group of exiles back to Jerusalem (Ezra 1; 2), and 25 years before Ezra led the second group to Jerusalem (Ezra 7). Esther lived in the kingdom of Persia, the dominant kingdom in the Middle East after Babylon's fall in 539 B.C. Esther's parents must have been among those exiles who chose not to return to Jerusalem, even though Cyrus, the Persian king, had issued a decree allowing them to do so. The Jewish exiles had great freedom in Persia, and many remained because they had established themselves there or were fearful of the dangerous journey back to their homeland.

1:1 Ahasuerus the Great (also called Xerxes) was Persia's fifth king (486–465 B.C.). He was proud and impulsive, as we see from the

1:3 Esth 2:18

1:5 Esth 7:7, 8

1:6 Ezek 23:41; Amos 6:4

1:7 Esth 2:18

3 in the third year of his reign he gave a banquet for all his princes and attendants,
the army *officers* of Persia and Media, the nobles and the princes of his provinces being
in his presence.
4 And he displayed the riches of his royal glory and the splendor of his great majesty
for many days, 180 days.
5 When these days were completed, the king gave a banquet lasting seven days for all
the people who were present at the citadel in Susa, from the greatest to the least, in the
court of the garden of the king's palace.
6 *There were hangings of* fine white and violet linen held by cords of fine purple linen
on silver rings and marble columns, *and* couches of gold and silver on a mosaic pavement of porphyry, marble, mother-of-pearl and precious stones.
7 Drinks were served in golden vessels of various kinds, and the royal wine was plentiful according to the king's bounty.
8 The drinking was *done* according to the law, there was no compulsion, for so the
king had given orders to each official of his household that he should do according to
the desires of each person.
9 Queen Vashti also gave a banquet for the women in the palace which belonged to
King Ahasuerus.

THE WORLD OF ESTHER'S DAY
Esther lived in the capital of the vast Medo-Persian empire, which incorporated the provinces of Media and Persia, as well as the previous empires of Assyria and Babylon. Esther, a Jewess, was chosen by King Ahasuerus to be his queen. The story of how she saved her people takes place in the palace in Susa.

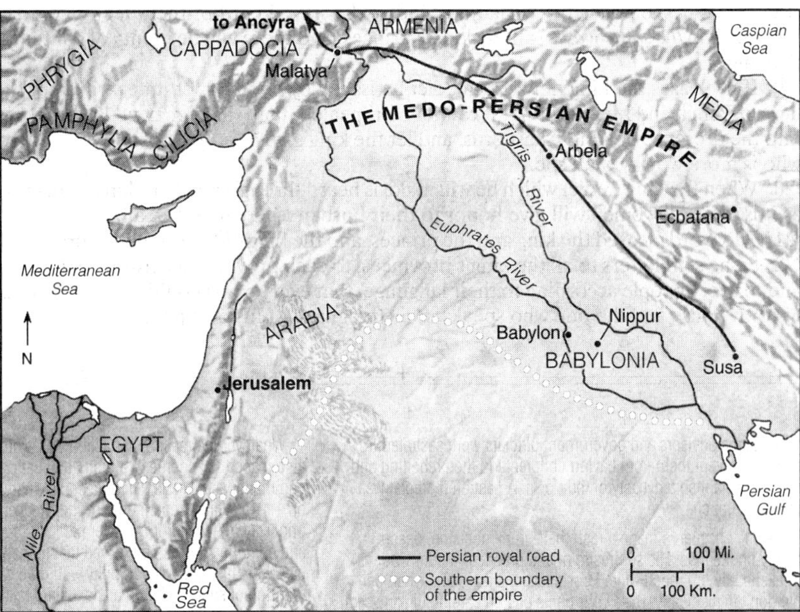

events in chapter 1. His winter palace was in Susa, where he held the banquet described in 1:3–7. Persian kings often held great banquets before going to war. In 481, Ahasuerus launched an attack against Greece. After his fleet won a great victory at Thermopylae, he was defeated at Salamis in 480 and had to return to Persia. Esther became queen in 479.

1:2 In this context, "citadel" means "palace."

1:4 The celebration lasted 180 days (about six months) because its real purpose was to plan the battle strategy for invading Greece and to demonstrate that the king had sufficient wealth to carry it out. Waging war was not only for survival; it was a means of acquiring more wealth, territory, and power.

1:5–7 Persia was a world power, and the king, as the center of that power, was one of the wealthiest people in the world. Persian kings loved to flaunt their wealth, even wearing precious gemstones in their beards. Jewelry was a sign of rank for Persian men. Even soldiers wore great amounts of gold jewelry into battle.

1:8 The guests at this banquet could drink as much or as little as they wished. (Usually the king controlled how much his guests could drink.)

1:9 Ancient Greek documents call Ahasuerus's wife Amestris, probably a Greek form of Vashti. Vashti was deposed in 484/483 B.C., but she is mentioned again in ancient records as the queen mother during the reign of her son, Artaxerxes, who succeeded Ahasuerus. Toward the end of Ahasuerus' reign, either Esther died or Vashti was able through her son to regain the influence she had lost.

Queen Vashti's Refusal

10 On the seventh day, when the heart of the king was merry with wine, he commanded Mehuman, Biztha, Harbona, Bigtha, Abagtha, Zethar and Carkas, the seven eunuchs
who served in the presence of King Ahasuerus,
11 to bring Queen Vashti before the king with *her* royal crown in order to display her
beauty to the people and the princes, for she was beautiful.
12 But Queen Vashti refused to come at the king's command delivered by the eunuchs.
Then the king became very angry and his wrath burned within him.
13 Then the king said to the wise men who understood the times—for it was the custom of the king so *to speak* before all who knew law and justice
14 and were close to him: Carshena, Shethar, Admatha, Tarshish, Meres, Marsena and
Memucan, the seven princes of Persia and Media who had access to the king's presence
and sat in the first place in the kingdom—
15 "According to law, what is to be done with Queen Vashti, because she did not obey
the command of King Ahasuerus *delivered* by the eunuchs?"
16 In the presence of the king and the princes, Memucan said, "Queen Vashti has
wronged not only the king but *also* all the princes and all the peoples who are in all the
provinces of King Ahasuerus.
17 "For the queen's conduct will become known to all the women causing them to look
with contempt on their husbands by saying, 'King Ahasuerus commanded Queen Vashti
to be brought in to his presence, but she did not come.'
18 "This day the ladies of Persia and Media who have heard of the queen's conduct
will speak in *the same way* to all the king's princes, and there will be plenty of contempt
and anger.
19 "If it pleases the king, let a royal edict be issued by him and let it be written in the
laws of Persia and Media so that it cannot be repealed, that Vashti may no longer come
into the presence of King Ahasuerus, and let the king give her royal position to another
who is more worthy than she.
20 "When the king's edict which he will make is heard throughout all his kingdom, great
as it is, then all women will give honor to their husbands, great and small."
21 *This* word pleased the king and the princes, and the king did as Memucan proposed.
22 So he sent letters to all the king's provinces, to each province according to its script
and to every people according to their language, that every man should be the master in
his own house and the one who speaks in the language of his own people.

1:10 Judg 16:25

1:11 Esth 2:17; 6:8

1:13 Jer 10:7; Dan 2:2; 1 Chr 12:32

1:14 2 Kin 25:19; Matt 18:10

1:19 Esth 8:8; Dan 6:8

1:20 Eph 5:22; Col 3:18

1:22 Esth 3:12; 8:9; Eph 5:22-24

1:10 Some advisers and government officials were castrated in order to prevent them from having children and then rebelling and trying to establish a dynasty of their own. A castrated official was called a eunuch.

1:10–11 Ahasuerus made a rash, half-drunk decision, based purely on feelings. His self-restraint and practical wisdom were weakened by too much wine. Poor decisions are made when people don't think clearly. Base your decisions on careful thinking, not on the emotions of the moment. Impulsive decision making leads to severe complications.

1:12 Queen Vashti refused to parade before the king's all-male party, possibly because it was against Persian custom for a woman to appear before a public gathering of men. This conflict between Persian custom and the king's command put her in a difficult situation, and she chose to refuse her half-drunk husband, hoping he would come to his senses later. Some have suggested that Vashti was pregnant with Artaxerxes, who was born in 483 B.C., and that she did not want to be seen in public in that state.

Whatever the reason, her action was a breach of protocol that also placed Ahasuerus in a difficult situation. Once he made the command, as a Persian king he could not reverse it (see the note on 1:19). While preparing to invade Greece, Ahasuerus had invited important officials from all over his land to see his power, wealth, and authority. If it was perceived that he had no authority over his own wife, his military credibility would be damaged—the greatest criterion of success for an ancient king. In addition, King Ahasuerus was accustomed to getting what he wanted.

1:15 Middle Eastern kings often did not have close personal relationships with their wives. Ahasuerus demonstrates this because (1) he had a harem (2:3); (2) he showed no respect for Vashti's personhood (1:10–12); (3) Esther, when she became queen, did not see him for long periods of time (4:11).

1:16–21 Perhaps the men's thinking had been clouded by drinking. Obviously this law would not cause the women of the country to respect their husbands. Respect between men and women comes from mutual regard and appreciation for each other as those created in God's image, not from legal pronouncements and orders. Forced obedience is a poor substitute for the love and respect wives and husbands should have for each other.

1:19 A Persian king was thought to be a god by many of his people; therefore, when he issued a law or command, it stood forever (see the notes on 8:8 and Daniel 6:8). The law could never be canceled, even if it was ill-advised; but if necessary, a new law could be issued to neutralize the effects of the old law.

Vashti's Successor Sought

2:1 Esth 7:10; Esth 1:19, 20

2 After these things when the anger of King Ahasuerus had subsided, he remembered
Vashti and what she had done and what had been decreed against her.

2:2 1 Kin 1:2

2 Then the king's attendants, who served him, said, "Let beautiful young virgins be
sought for the king.

2:3 Esth 1:1, 2; Esth 2:8, 15; Esth 2:9, 12

3 "Let the king appoint overseers in all the provinces of his kingdom that they may
gather every beautiful young virgin to the citadel of Susa, to the harem, into the custody
of Hegai, the king's eunuch, who is in charge of the women; and let their cosmetics be
given *them.*
4 "Then let the young lady who pleases the king be queen in place of Vashti." And the
matter pleased the king, and he did accordingly.

2:5 Esth 3:2

5 *Now* there was at the citadel in Susa a Jew whose name was Mordecai, the son of
Jair, the son of Shimei, the son of Kish, a Benjamite,

2:6 2 Kin 24:14, 15; 2 Chr 36:10

6 who had been taken into exile from Jerusalem with the captives who had been
exiled with Jeconiah king of Judah, whom Nebuchadnezzar the king of Babylon had
exiled.

2:7 Esth 2:15

7 He was bringing up Hadassah, that is Esther, his uncle's daughter, for she had no
father or mother. Now the young lady was beautiful of form and face, and when her father and her mother died, Mordecai took her as his own daughter.

Esther Finds Favor

2:8 Esth 2:3; Esth 2:3, 15

8 So it came about when the command and decree of the king were heard and many
young ladies were gathered to the citadel of Susa into the custody of Hegai, that Esther
was taken to the king's palace into the custody of Hegai, who was in charge of the
women.

2:9 Esth 2:3, 12

9 Now the young lady pleased him and found favor with him. So he quickly provided
her with her cosmetics and food, gave her seven choice maids from the king's palace and
transferred her and her maids to the best place in the harem.

2:10 Esth 2:20

10 Esther did not make known her people or her kindred, for Mordecai had instructed
her that she should not make *them* known.
11 Every day Mordecai walked back and forth in front of the court of the harem to
learn how Esther was and how she fared.
12 Now when the turn of each young lady came to go in to King Ahasuerus, after the
end of her twelve months under the regulations for the women—for the days of their
beautification were completed as follows: six months with oil of myrrh and six months
with spices and the cosmetics for women—
13 the young lady would go in to the king in this way: anything that she desired was
given her to take with her from the harem to the king's palace.
14 In the evening she would go in and in the morning she would return to the second
harem, to the custody of Shaashgaz, the king's eunuch who was in charge of the concubines. She would not again go in to the king unless the king delighted in her and she was
summoned by name.

2:1 The phrase, "he remembered Vashti," may mean that the king began to miss his queen and what she had done for him. But he also remembered that in his anger he had banished her from his presence with a decree that couldn't be rescinded.

2:3, 14–17 Persian kings collected not only vast amounts of jewelry, but also great numbers of women. These young virgins were taken from their homes and were required to live in a separate building near the palace, called a harem. Their sole purpose was to serve the king and to await his call for sexual pleasure. They rarely saw the king, and their lives were restricted and boring. If rejected, Esther would be one of many girls the king had seen once and forgotten. But Esther's presence and beauty pleased the king enough that he crowned her queen in place of Vashti. The queen held a more influential position than a concubine, and she was given more freedom and authority than others in the harem. But even as queen, Esther had few rights—especially because she had been chosen to replace a woman who had become too assertive.

2:5–6 Mordecai was a Jew. The Jewish population had increased since their exile over 100 years earlier. They had been given great freedom and were allowed to run their own businesses and hold positions in government (2:19; Daniel 6:3).

2:6 The Bible says that Mordecai was carried into exile from Jerusalem by Nebuchadnezzar. If this referred to Mordecai himself, he would have been over 100 years old at the time of this story. This difficult phrase can be resolved by understanding that the word "who," referring to Mordecai, can also mean "whose family." It is likely that Mordecai's great-grandparents were carried into captivity rather than Mordecai himself.

2:10 With virtually no rights and little access to the king, it was better for Esther not to reveal her identity. While boldness in stating our identity as God's people is our responsibility, at times a good strategy is to keep quiet until we have won the right to be heard. This is especially true when dealing with those in authority over us. But we can always let them see the difference God makes in our lives.

15 Now when the turn of Esther, the daughter of Abihail the uncle of Mordecai who 2:15
had taken her as his daughter, came to go in to the king, she did not request anything Esth 2:7; 9:29; Esth 2:3, 8
except what Hegai, the king's eunuch who was in charge of the women, advised. And
Esther found favor in the eyes of all who saw her.
16 So Esther was taken to King Ahasuerus to his royal palace in the tenth month which
is the month Tebeth, in the seventh year of his reign.

Esther Becomes Queen

17 The king loved Esther more than all the women, and she found favor and kindness 2:17
with him more than all the virgins, so that he set the royal crown on her head and made Esth 1:11
her queen instead of Vashti.
18 Then the king gave a great banquet, Esther's banquet, for all his princes and his 2:18
servants; he also made a holiday for the provinces and gave gifts according to the king's Esth 1:3; Esth 1:7
bounty.
19 When the virgins were gathered together the second time, then Mordecai was sit- 2:19
ting at the king's gate. Esth 2:3, 4; Esth 2:21; 3:2
20 Esther had not yet made known her kindred or her people, even as Mordecai had com- 2:20
manded her; for Esther did what Mordecai told her as she had done when under his care. Esth 2:10; Esth 2:7

Mordecai Saves the King

21 In those days, while Mordecai was sitting at the king's gate, Bigthan and Teresh, 2:21
two of the king's officials from those who guarded the door, became angry and sought to Esth 6:2
lay hands on King Ahasuerus.
22 But the plot became known to Mordecai and he told Queen Esther, and Esther 2:22
informed the king in Mordecai's name. Esth 6:1, 2
23 Now when the plot was investigated and found *to be so,* they were both hanged on 2:23
a [1]gallows; and it was written in the Book of the Chronicles in the king's presence. Esth 10:2

2. The Jews are threatened

Haman's Plot against the Jews

3 After these events King Ahasuerus promoted Haman, the son of Hammedatha the 3:1
Agagite, and advanced him and established his authority over all the princes who Esth 5:11; Esth 3:10; 8:3
were with him.
2 All the king's servants who were at the king's gate bowed down and paid homage to 3:2
Haman; for so the king had commanded concerning him. But Mordecai neither bowed Esth 2:19; 5:9
down nor paid homage.
3 Then the king's servants who were at the king's gate said to Mordecai, "Why are 3:3
you transgressing the king's command?" Esth 2:19; Esth 3:2
4 Now it was when they had spoken daily to him and he would not listen to them, that
they told Haman to see whether Mordecai's reason would stand; for he had told them
that he was a Jew.
5 When Haman saw that Mordecai neither bowed down nor paid homage to him, 3:5
Haman was filled with rage. Esth 5:9

1 Lit *tree*

2:17 God placed Esther on the throne even before the Jews faced the possibility of complete destruction (3:5ff), so that when trouble came, a person would already be in the position to help. No human effort could thwart God's plan to send the Messiah to earth as a Jew. If you are changing jobs, position, or location and can't see God's purpose in your situation, understand that God is in control. He may be placing you in a position so you can help when the need arises.

3:2 Mordecai's determination came from his faith in God. He did not take a poll first to determine the safest or most popular course of action; he had the courage to stand alone. Doing what is right will not always make you popular. Those who do right will be in the minority, but to obey God is more important than to obey people (Acts 5:29).

3:2–4 Mordecai refused to bow down before Haman. Jews did bow down to government authorities, at times, as a sign of respect (Genesis 23:7; 1 Samuel 24:8), but Haman's ancestors were ancient enemies of the Jews. Israel had been commanded by God to "blot out the memory of Amalek from under heaven" (Deuteronomy 25:17–19; see also Exodus 17:16). Mordecai was not about to bow before wicked Haman and, by his act, acknowledge Haman as a god. Daniel's three friends had the same convictions (Daniel 3). We must worship God alone. We should never let any person, institution, or government take God's place. When people demand loyalties or duties from you that do not honor God, don't give in. It may be time to take a stand.

3:5–6 Why did Haman want to destroy all Jews just because of one man's action? (1) Haman was an Agagite (3:1), a descendant of Agag, king of the Amalekites (1 Samuel 15:20). The Amalekites were ancient enemies of the Israelites (see Exodus 17:16; Deuteronomy 25:17–19). Haman's hatred was directed not just at

3:6 Ps 83:4
3:7 Esth 9:24-26; Ezra 6:15

6 But he disdained to lay hands on Mordecai alone, for they had told him *who* the
people of Mordecai *were;* therefore Haman sought to destroy all the Jews, the people of
Mordecai, who *were* throughout the whole kingdom of Ahasuerus.
7 In the first month, which is the month Nisan, in the twelfth year of King Ahasuerus,

---

MORDECAI

Following Jerusalem's last stand against Nebuchadnezzar, Mordecai's family was deported to the Babylonian empire. He was probably born in Susa, a city that became one of Persia's capitals after Cyrus conquered Babylon, and inherited an official position among the Jewish captives that kept him around the palace even after the Babylonians were driven out. At one time, when he overheard plans to assassinate Ahasuerus, he reported the plot and saved the king's life.

Mordecai's life was filled with challenges that he turned into opportunities. When his aunt and uncle died, he adopted Esther, their daughter and his young cousin, probably because his own parents were dead and he felt responsible for her. Later, when she was drafted into Ahasuerus's harem and chosen to be queen, Mordecai continued to advise her. Shortly after this, he found himself in conflict with Ahasuerus's recently appointed second-in-command, Haman. Although willing to serve the king, Mordecai refused to worship the king's representative. Haman was furious with Mordecai. So he planned to have Mordecai and all the Jews killed. His plan became a law of the Medes and Persians, and it looked as though the Jews were doomed.

Mordecai, willing to be God's servant wherever he was, responded by contacting Esther and telling her that one reason God had allowed her to be queen might well be to save her people from this threat. But God had also placed *him* in the right place years earlier. God revealed to the king through his nighttime reading of historical documents that Mordecai had once saved his life, and the king realized he had never thanked Mordecai. The great honor then given to Mordecai ruined Haman's plan to hang him on the gallows. God had woven an effective counter-strategy against which Haman's plan could not stand.

Later, Mordecai instituted the Jewish Feast of Purim. He had a lengthy career of service to the king on behalf of the Jews. In Mordecai's life, God blended both character and circumstances to accomplish great things. He has not changed the way he works. God is using the situations you face each day to weave a pattern of godliness into your character. Pause and ask God to help you respond appropriately to the situations you find yourself in today.

Strengths and accomplishments:
- Exposed an assassination plot against the king
- Cared enough to adopt his cousin
- Refused to bow to anyone except God
- Took Haman's place as second-in-command under Ahasuerus

Lessons from his life:
- The opportunities we have are more important than the ones we wish we had
- We can trust God to weave together the events of life for our best, even though we may not be able to see the overall pattern
- The rewards for doing right are sometimes delayed, but they are guaranteed by God himself

Vital statistics:
- Where: Susa, one of several capital cities in Persia
- Occupation: Jewish official who became second in rank to Ahasuerus
- Relatives: Adopted daughter: Esther. Father: Jair
- Contemporaries: Ahasuerus, Haman

Key verse:
"For Mordecai the Jew was second only to King Ahasuerus, and great among the Jews and in favor with his many kinsmen, one who sought the good of his people and one who spoke for the welfare of his whole nation" (Esther 10:3).

Mordecai's story is told in the book of Esther.

Mordecai, but at all the Jews. (2) As second-in-command in the Persian empire (3:1), Haman loved his power and authority and the reverence shown him. The Jews, however, looked to God as their final authority, not to any man. Haman realized that the only way to fulfill his self-centered desires was to kill all those who disregarded his authority. His quest for personal power and his hatred of the Jewish race consumed him.

3:5–6 Haman enjoyed the power and prestige of his position, and he was enraged when Mordecai did not respond with the expected reverential bow. Haman's anger was not directed just toward Mordecai, but toward what Mordecai stood for—the Jews' dedication to God as the only authority worthy of reverence. Haman's attitude was prejudiced: He hated a group of people because of a difference in belief or culture. Prejudice grows out of personal pride—considering oneself better than others. In the end, Haman was punished for his arrogant attitude (7:9–10). God will harshly judge those who are prejudiced or whose pride causes them to look down on others.

3:7 Haman cast lots to determine the best day to carry out his decree. Little did he know that he was playing into the hands of God, for the day of death was set for almost a year away, giving Esther time to make her plea to the king. The Persian word for lots was *purim*, which became the name for the holiday celebrated by the Jews when they were delivered, not killed, on the day appointed by Haman.

Pur, that is the lot, was cast before Haman from day to day and from month *to month,*
until the twelfth month, that is the month Adar.
8 Then Haman said to King Ahasuerus, "There is a certain people scattered and dispersed among the peoples in all the provinces of your kingdom; their laws are different
from *those* of all *other* people and they do not observe the king's laws, so it is not in the
king's interest to let them remain.

3:8 Ezra 4:12-15; Acts 16:20, 21

9 "If it is pleasing to the king, let it be decreed that they be destroyed, and I will pay
ten thousand talents of silver into the hands of those who carry on the *king's* business, to
put into the king's treasuries."
10 Then the king took his signet ring from his hand and gave it to Haman, the son of
Hammedatha the Agagite, the enemy of the Jews.

3:10 Gen 41:42; Esth 8:2; Esth 3:1; Esth 7:6

11 The king said to Haman, "The silver is yours, and the people *also,* to do with them
as you please."
12 Then the king's scribes were summoned on the thirteenth day of the first month,
and it was written just as Haman commanded to the king's satraps, to the governors who
were over each province and to the princes of each people, each province according to
its script, each people according to its language, being written in the name of King
Ahasuerus and sealed with the king's signet ring.

3:12 Esth 8:9; Ezra 8:36; 1 Kin 21:8; Esth 8:8, 10

13 Letters were sent by couriers to all the king's provinces to destroy, to kill and to
annihilate all the Jews, both young and old, women and children, in one day, the thirteenth *day* of the twelfth month, which is the month Adar, and to seize their possessions
as plunder.

3:13 2 Chr 30:6; Esth 8:10, 14; Esth 7:4; Esth 8:12; Esth 8:11; 9:10

14 A copy of the edict to be issued as law in every province was published to all the
peoples so that they should be ready for this day.

3:14 Esth 8:13, 14

15 The couriers went out impelled by the king's command while the decree was issued
at the citadel in Susa; and while the king and Haman sat down to drink, the city of Susa
was in confusion.

3:15 Esth 8:15

Esther Learns of Haman's Plot

4 When Mordecai learned all that had been done, he tore his clothes, put on sackcloth and ashes, and went out into the midst of the city and wailed loudly and
bitterly.

4:1 2 Sam 1:11; Esth 3:8-10; Jon 3:5, 6

2 He went as far as the king's gate, for no one was to enter the king's gate clothed in
sackcloth.
3 In each and every province where the command and decree of the king came, there
was great mourning among the Jews, with fasting, weeping and wailing; and many lay on
sackcloth and ashes.

4:3 Esth 4:16

4 Then Esther's maidens and her eunuchs came and told her, and the queen writhed
in great anguish. And she sent garments to clothe Mordecai that he might remove his
sackcloth from him, but he did not accept *them.*
5 Then Esther summoned Hathach from the king's eunuchs, whom the king had appointed to attend her, and ordered him *to go* to Mordecai to learn what this *was* and why
it *was.*
6 So Hathach went out to Mordecai to the city square in front of the king's gate.
7 Mordecai told him all that had happened to him, and the exact amount of money
that Haman had promised to pay to the king's treasuries for the destruction of the Jews.

4:7 Esth 3:9

8 He also gave him a copy of the text of the edict which had been issued in Susa for
their destruction, that he might show Esther and inform her, and to order her to go in to
the king to implore his favor and to plead with him for her people.

4:8 Esth 3:14

9 Hathach came back and related Mordecai's words to Esther.
10 Then Esther spoke to Hathach and ordered him *to reply* to Mordecai:

3:9 Haman must have hoped to acquire this tremendous sum of money by plundering the homes and businesses of the Jews who would be killed through his decree. A large number of Jews were living in the kingdom at this time. Little did Haman know that his treachery would backfire.

3:10–12 Officials in the ancient world used signet rings as personal signatures. The ring's surface had a raised imprint made of metal, wood, or bone; Ahasuerus's was probably made of silver or gold. Each individual had his own imprint. Letters were sealed by pressing the ring into soft wax, and official documents were certified by using the royal signet. By giving Haman his signet ring, Ahasuerus gave him his personal signature and with it the authority to do whatever he wished. Little did the king realize that his own ring would sign the death warrant for his queen, Esther.

4:11 Esth 5:1; 6:4; Dan 2:9; Esth 5:2; 8:4

11 "All the king's servants and the people of the king's provinces know that for any man
or woman who comes to the king to the inner court who is not summoned, he has but
one law, that he be put to death, unless the king holds out to him the golden scepter so
that he may live. And I have not been summoned to come to the king for these thirty
days."
12 They related Esther's words to Mordecai.
13 Then Mordecai told *them* to reply to Esther, "Do not imagine that you in the king's
palace can escape any more than all the Jews.

4:14 Lev 26:42; 2 Kin 13:5

14 "For if you remain silent at this time, relief and deliverance will arise for the Jews
from another place and you and your father's house will perish. And who knows whether
you have not attained royalty for such a time as this?"

Esther Plans to Intercede

4:16 Joel 1:14; 2:12; Esth 5:1

15 Then Esther told *them* to reply to Mordecai,
16 "Go, assemble all the Jews who are found in Susa, and fast for me; do not eat or drink

---

GOD BEHIND THE SCENES IN ESTHER
Although God's name is not mentioned in the Hebrew text of Esther, he makes himself known in these ways:

	Reference	
Indirect References	2:17	Esther, who worshiped God, became queen
	4:14	God's existence and his power over the affairs of people are assumed.
	4:16	Fasting was a distinct spiritual activity usually connected with prayer.
	2:21, 23	Mordecai overhears a death plot and saves the king's life
Divine Incidents (The book of Esther is filled with divine interventions)	6:1	Ahasuerus can't sleep and decides to read a history book
	6:2	Ahasuerus reads the exact page needed for the moment, reminding him of an unpaid reward to Mordecai
	7:9–10	Haman's plan is exactly reversed—the intended victims are the victors

Why was God's name hidden in the book of Esther? There were many gods in the Middle East and Persian empire. Usually, their names were mentioned in official documents in order to control the people who worshiped those particular gods. The Jews were unique in being the people of one God. A story about them was naturally a story about God, for even the name "Jew" carried with it the connotation of one who worshiped Yahweh.

4:11—5:2 Esther risked her life by coming before the king. Her courageous act gives us a model to follow in approaching a difficult or dangerous task. Like Esther, we can: (1) *Calculate the cost.* Esther realized her life was at stake. (2) *Set priorities.* She believed that the safety of the Jewish race was more important than her life. (3) *Prepare.* She gathered support and fasted. (4) *Determine a course of action and move ahead boldly.* She didn't think too long about it, allowing the interlude to lessen her commitment to what she had to do.

Do you have to face a hostile audience, confront a friend on a delicate subject, or talk to your family about changes to be made? Rather than dreading difficult situations or putting them off, take action with confidence by following Esther's inspiring example.

4:13 Although Esther was the queen and shared some of the king's power and wealth, she still needed God's protection and wisdom. No one is secure in his or her own strength in any political system. It is foolish to believe that wealth or position can make us impervious to danger. Deliverance only comes from God.

4:13–14 After the decree to kill the Jews was given, Mordecai and Esther could have despaired, decided to save only themselves, or just waited for God's intervention. Instead, they saw that God had placed them in their positions for a purpose, so they seized the moment and acted. When it is within our reach to save others, we must do so. In a life-threatening situation, don't withdraw, behave selfishly, wallow in despair, or wait for God to fix everything. Instead, ask God for his direction, and *act* God may have placed you where you are "for such a time as this."

4:14 God is not specifically mentioned in the book of Esther, but it is obvious that Mordecai expected God to deliver his people. While the book of Esther does not mention God directly, his presence fills the pages. Esther and Mordecai believed in God's care, and because they acted at the right time, God used them to save his people.

4:16 By calling for a fast, Esther was asking the Jews to pray for God's help on her dangerous mission. In the Old Testament, prayer always accompanies fasting (see Exodus 34:28; Deuteronomy 9:9; Ezra 8:21–23). An important function of a community of believers is mutual support in difficult times. When you are experiencing struggles, turn to fellow believers for support by sharing your trials with them and gaining strength from the bond that unites you. Ask them to pray for you. And when others need your support, give it willingly.

4:16 *Save your own skin* and *Watch out for number one* are mottoes that reflect our world's selfish outlook on life. Esther's attitude stands in bold contrast to this. She knew what she had to do, and she knew it could cost her her life. And yet she responded, "If I perish, I perish." We should have the same commitment to do what is right despite the possible consequences. Do you try to save yourself by remaining silent rather than standing up for what is right? Decide to do what God wants, and trust him for the outcome.

for three days, night or day. I and my maidens also will fast in the same way. And thus I
will go in to the king, which is not according to the law; and if I perish, I perish."
17 So Mordecai went away and did just as Esther had commanded him.

3. Esther intercedes for the Jews

Esther Plans a Banquet

5 Now it came about on the third day that Esther put on her royal robes and stood in
the inner court of the king's palace in front of the king's rooms, and the king was
sitting on his royal throne in the throne room, opposite the entrance to the palace.

5:1 Esth 4:16; Esth 4:11; 6:4

2 When the king saw Esther the queen standing in the court, she obtained favor in his
sight; and the king extended to Esther the golden scepter which *was* in his hand. So Esther came near and touched the top of the scepter.

5:2 Esth 2:9; Esth 4:11; 8:4

3 Then the king said to her, "What is *troubling* you, Queen Esther? And what is your
request? Even to half of the kingdom it shall be given to you."

5:3 Esth 7:2; Mark 6:23

4 Esther said, "If it pleases the king, may the king and Haman come this day to the
banquet that I have prepared for him."
5 Then the king said, "Bring Haman quickly that we may do as Esther desires." So
the king and Haman came to the banquet which Esther had prepared.

5:5 Esth 6:14

6 As they drank their wine at the banquet, the king said to Esther, "What is your
petition, for it shall be granted to you. And what is your request? Even to half of the
kingdom it shall be done."

5:6 Esth 7:2; Esth 5:3

7 So Esther replied, "My petition and my request is:
8 if I have found favor in the sight of the king, and if it pleases the king to grant my
petition and do what I request, may the king and Haman come to the banquet which I
will prepare for them, and tomorrow I will do as the king says."

5:8 Esth 7:3; 8:5; Esth 6:14

Haman's Pride

9 Then Haman went out that day glad and pleased of heart; but when Haman saw
Mordecai in the king's gate and that he did not stand up or tremble before him, Haman
was filled with anger against Mordecai.

5:9 Esth 2:19; Esth 3:5

10 Haman controlled himself, however, went to his house and sent for his friends and
his wife Zeresh.

5:10 Esth 6:13

11 Then Haman recounted to them the glory of his riches, and the number of his sons,
and every *instance* where the king had magnified him and how he had promoted him
above the princes and servants of the king.

5:11 Esth 9:7-10; Esth 3:1

12 Haman also said, "Even Esther the queen let no one but me come with the king to
the banquet which she had prepared; and tomorrow also I am invited by her with the
king.

5:12 Esth 5:8

13 "Yet all of this does not satisfy me every time I see Mordecai the Jew sitting at the
king's gate."

5:13 Esth 5:9

14 Then Zeresh his wife and all his friends said to him, "Have a gallows fifty cubits
high made and in the morning ask the king to have Mordecai hanged on it; then go joyfully with the king to the banquet." And the advice pleased Haman, so he had the gallows made.

5:14 Esth 6:4; 7:9, 10

4:17—5:1 God was in control, yet Mordecai and Esther had to act. We cannot understand how both can be true at the same time, and yet they are. God chooses to work through those *willing* to act for him. We should pray as if all depended on God and act as if all depended on us. We should avoid two extremes: doing nothing, and feeling that we must do everything.

5:9 Hatred and bitterness are like weeds with long roots that grow in the heart and corrupt all of life. Haman was so consumed with hatred toward Mordecai that he could not even enjoy the honor of being invited to Esther's party. Hebrews 12:15 warns us to watch out "that no root of bitterness springing up causes trouble, and by it many be defiled." Don't let hatred and its resulting bitterness build in your heart. Like Haman, you will find it backfiring against you (see 6:13; 7:9–10). If the mere mention of someone's name provokes you to anger, confess your bitterness as sin. Ignoring bitterness, hiding it from others, or making superficial changes in behavior is not enough. If bitterness isn't completely removed, it will grow back, making matters worse.

5:14 Haman's family and friends, who were as arrogant as he, suggested that the gallows be fifty cubits (75 feet) high, probably built on the city wall or some prominent building. They wanted to make sure that all the people of the city saw Mordecai's death and would be reminded of the consequences of disobeying Haman. Ironically, these high gallows allowed everyone to see Haman's death.

The King Plans to Honor Mordecai

6:1 Dan 6:18; Esth 2:23; 10:2

6:2 Esth 2:21, 22

6:4 Esth 4:11; Esth 5:14

6 During that night the king could not sleep so he gave an order to bring the book of
records, the chronicles, and they were read before the king.
2 It was found written what Mordecai had reported concerning Bigthana and Teresh,
two of the king's eunuchs who were doorkeepers, that they had sought to lay hands on
King Ahasuerus.
3 The king said, "What honor or dignity has been bestowed on Mordecai for this?"
Then the king's servants who attended him said, "Nothing has been done for him."
4 So the king said, "Who is in the court?" Now Haman had just entered the outer
court of the king's palace in order to speak to the king about hanging Mordecai on the
gallows which he had prepared for him.
5 The king's servants said to him, "Behold, Haman is standing in the court." And the
king said, "Let him come in."

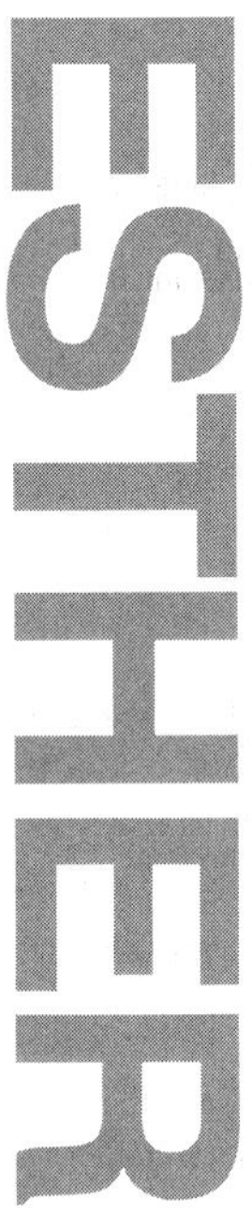

We treasure security, even though we know that security in this life carries no guarantees—possessions can be destroyed, beauty fades, relationships can be broken, death is inevitable. Real security, then, must be found beyond this life. Only when our security rests on God and his unchanging nature can we face the challenges that life is sure to bring our way.

Esther's beauty and character won Ahasuerus's heart, and he made her his queen. Even in her favored position, however, she would risk her life by attempting to see the king when he had not requested her presence. There was no guarantee that the king would even see her. Although she was queen, she was still not secure. But, cautiously and courageously, Esther decided to risk her life by approaching the king on behalf of her people.

She made her plans carefully. The Jews were asked to fast and pray with her before she went to the king. Then on the chosen day she went before him, and he *did* ask her to come forward and speak. But instead of issuing her request directly, she invited him and Haman to a banquet. He was astute enough to realize she had something on her mind, yet she conveyed the importance of the matter by insisting on a second banquet.

In the meantime, God was working behind the scenes. He caused Ahasuerus to read the historical records of the kingdom late one night, and the king discovered that Mordecai had once saved his life. Ahasuerus lost no time in honoring Mordecai for that act. During the second banquet, Esther told the king of Haman's plot against the Jews, and Haman was doomed. There is grim justice in Haman's death on the gallows he had built for Mordecai, and it seems fitting that the day on which the Jews were to be slaughtered became the day their enemies died. Esther's risk confirmed that God was the source of her security.

How much of your security lies in your possessions, position, or reputation? God has not placed you in your present position for your own benefit. He put you there *to serve him.* As in Esther's case, this may involve risking your security. Are you willing to let God be your ultimate security?

Strengths and accomplishments:
- Her beauty and character won the heart of Persia's king
- She combined courage with careful planning
- She was open to advice and willing to act
- She was more concerned for others than for her own security

Lessons from her life:
- Serving God often demands that we risk our own security
- God has a purpose for the situations in which he places us
- Courage, while often vital, does not replace careful planning

Vital statistics:
- Where: Persian empire
- Occupation: Ahasuerus's wife, queen of Persia
- Relatives: Cousin: Mordecai. Husband: Ahasuerus. Father: Abihail

Key verse:
"Go, assemble all the Jews who are found in Susa, and fast for me; do not eat or drink for three days, night or day. I and my maidens also will fast in the same way. And thus I will go in to the king, which is not according to the law; and if I perish, I perish" (Esther 4:16).

Esther's story is told in the book of Esther.

6:1–2 Unable to sleep, the king decided to review the history of his reign, and his servants read to him about Mordecai's good deed. This seems coincidental, but God is *always* at work. God has been working quietly and patiently throughout your life as well. The events that have come together for good are not mere coincidence; they are the result of God's sovereign control over the course of people's lives (Romans 8:28).

6 So Haman came in and the king said to him, "What is to be done for the man whom **6:6**
the king desires to honor?" And Haman said to himself, "Whom would the king desire Esth 6:7, 9, 11
to honor more than me?"
7 Then Haman said to the king, "For the man whom the king desires to honor,
8 let them bring a royal robe which the king has worn, and the horse on which the **6:8**
king has ridden, and on whose head a royal crown has been placed; 1 Kin 1:33; Esth 1:11; 2:17
9 and let the robe and the horse be handed over to one of the king's most noble princes
and let them array the man whom the king desires to honor and lead him on horseback **6:9**
through the city square, and proclaim before him, 'Thus it shall be done to the man whom Gen 41:43
the king desires to honor.' "

Haman Must Honor Mordecai

10 Then the king said to Haman, "Take quickly the robes and the horse as you have
said, and do so for Mordecai the Jew, who is sitting at the king's gate; do not fall short in
anything of all that you have said."
11 So Haman took the robe and the horse, and arrayed Mordecai, and led him *on*
horseback through the city square, and proclaimed before him, "Thus it shall be done to
the man whom the king desires to honor."
12 Then Mordecai returned to the king's gate. But Haman hurried home, mourning, **6:12**
with *his* head covered. 2 Sam 15:30
13 Haman recounted to Zeresh his wife and all his friends everything that had hap- **6:13**
pened to him. Then his wise men and Zeresh his wife said to him, "If Mordecai, before Esth 5:10
whom you have begun to fall, is of Jewish origin, you will not overcome him, but will
surely fall before him."
14 While they were still talking with him, the king's eunuchs arrived and hastily brought **6:14**
Haman to the banquet which Esther had prepared. Esth 5:8

Esther's Plea

7 Now the king and Haman came to drink *wine* with Esther the queen.
2 And the king said to Esther on the second day also as they drank their wine at the **7:2**
banquet, "What is your petition, Queen Esther? It shall be granted you. And what is Esth 5:6; 9:12; Esth 5:3
your request? Even to half of the kingdom it shall be done."
3 Then Queen Esther replied, "If I have found favor in your sight, O king, and if it **7:3**
pleases the king, let my life be given me as my petition, and my people as my request; Esth 5:8; 8:5
4 for we have been sold, I and my people, to be destroyed, to be killed and to be an- **7:4**
nihilated. Now if we had only been sold as slaves, men and women, I would have remained Esth 3:9; Esth 3:13
silent, for the trouble would not be commensurate with the annoyance to the king."
5 Then King Ahasuerus asked Queen Esther, "Who is he, and where is he, who would
presume to do thus?"
6 Esther said, "A foe and an enemy is this wicked Haman!" Then Haman became **7:6**
terrified before the king and queen. Esth 3:10

Haman Is Hanged

7 The king arose in his anger from drinking wine *and went* into the palace garden; but **7:7**
Haman stayed to beg for his life from Queen Esther, for he saw that harm had been Esth 1:12; Esth 1:5
determined against him by the king.
8 Now when the king returned from the palace garden into the place where they were **7:8**
drinking wine, Haman was falling on the couch where Esther was. Then the king said, Esth 1:6

6:7–9 Haman had wealth, but he craved something even his money couldn't buy—respect. He could buy the trappings of success and power, but his lust for popularity had become an obsession. Don't let your desire for approval, applause, and popularity drive you to immoral actions.

6:10–13 Mordecai had exposed a plot to assassinate Ahasuerus—thus he had saved the king's life (2:21–23). Although his good deed was recorded in the history books, Mordecai had gone unrewarded. But God was saving Mordecai's reward for the right time. Just as Haman was about to hang Mordecai unjustly, the king was ready to give the reward. Although God promises to reward our good deeds, we sometimes feel our "payoff" is too far away. Be patient. God steps in when it will do the most good.

7:6–10 Haman's hatred and evil plotting turned against him when the king discovered his true intentions. He was hanged on the gallows he had built for someone else. Proverbs 26:27 teaches that a person who digs a pit for others will fall into it himself. What happened to Haman shows the often violent results of setting any kind of trap for others.

7:8 "They covered Haman's face." A veil was placed over the face of someone condemned to death because Persian kings refused to look upon the face of a condemned person.

"Will he even assault the queen with me in the house?" As the word went out of the
king's mouth, they covered Haman's face.

7:9 Esth 5:14; Esth 2:22

9 Then Harbonah, one of the eunuchs who *were* before the king said, "Behold indeed,
the gallows standing at Haman's house fifty cubits high, which Haman made for Mordecai who spoke good on behalf of the king!" And the king said, "Hang him on it."

7:10 Ps 7:16; 94:23; Esth 7:7, 8

10 So they hanged Haman on the gallows which he had prepared for Mordecai, and
the king's anger subsided.

Mordecai Promoted

8:1 Esth 7:6; Esth 2:7, 15

8 On that day King Ahasuerus gave the house of Haman, the enemy of the Jews, to
Queen Esther; and Mordecai came before the king, for Esther had disclosed what
he was to her.

HAMAN

The most arrogant people are often those who must measure their self-worth by the power or influence they think they have over others. Haman was an extremely arrogant leader. He recognized the king as his superior, but could not accept anyone as an equal. When one man, Mordecai, refused to bow in submission to him, Haman wanted to destroy him. He became consumed with hatred for Mordecai. He was already filled with racial hatred for all the Jewish people because of the long-standing hatred between the Jews and Haman's ancestors, the Amalekites. Mordecai's dedication to God and his refusal to give homage to any human person challenged Haman's self-centered religion. Haman saw the Jews as a threat to his power, and he decided to kill them all.

God was preparing Haman's downfall and the protection of his people long before Haman came to power under Ahasuerus. Esther, a Jew, became queen, and Mordecai's role in exposing an assassination plot indebted the king to him. Not only was Haman prevented from killing Mordecai, he also had to suffer the humiliation of publicly honoring him. Within hours, Haman died on the gallows he had built to hang Mordecai, and his plan to wipe out the Jews was thwarted. In contrast to Esther, who risked everything for God and won, Haman risked everything for an evil purpose and lost.

Our initial response to the story about Haman is to say that he got what he deserved. But the Bible leads us to ask deeper questions: "How much of Haman is in me?" "Do I desire to control others?" "Am I threatened when others don't appreciate me as I think they should?" "Do I want revenge when my pride is attacked?" Confess these attitudes to God, and ask him to replace them with an attitude of forgiveness. Otherwise, God's justice will settle the matter.

Strength and accomplishment:
- Achieved great power, second in rank to Persia's King Ahasuerus

Weaknesses and mistakes:
- The desire to control others and receive honor was his highest goal
- Was blinded by arrogance and self-importance
- Planned to murder Mordecai and built a gallows for him
- Orchestrated the plan to slaughter God's people throughout the empire

Lessons from his life:
- Hatred will be punished
- God has an amazing record for making evil plans backfire on the planners
- Pride and self-importance will be punished
- An insatiable thirst for power and prestige is self-destructive

Vital statistics:
- Where: Susa, the capital of Persia
- Occupation: Second in rank in the empire
- Relative: Wife: Zeresh
- Contemporaries: Ahasuerus, Mordecai, Esther

Key verses:
"When Haman saw that Mordecai neither bowed down nor paid homage to him, Haman was filled with rage. But he disdained to lay hands on Mordecai alone, for they had told him who the people of Mordecai were; therefore Haman sought to destroy all the Jews, the people of Mordecai, who were throughout the whole kingdom of Ahasuerus" (Esther 3:5, 6).

Haman's story is told in the book of Esther.

8:1–7 While we should not expect earthly rewards for being faithful to God, they often come. Esther and Mordecai were faithful, even to the point of risking their lives to save others. When they were willing to give up everything, God gave them a reward in proportion to their all-out commitment.

2 The king took off his signet ring which he had taken away from Haman, and gave it **8:2**
to Mordecai. And Esther set Mordecai over the house of Haman. Esth 3:10
3 Then Esther spoke again to the king, fell at his feet, wept and implored him to avert
the evil *scheme* of Haman the Agagite and his plot which he had devised against the Jews.
4 The king extended the golden scepter to Esther. So Esther arose and stood before **8:4**
the king. Esth 4:11; 5:2
5 Then she said, "If it pleases the king and if I have found favor before him and the **8:5**
matter *seems* proper to the king and I am pleasing in his sight, let it be written to revoke Esth 5:8; 7:3; Esth 3:13
the letters devised by Haman, the son of Hammedatha the Agagite, which he wrote to
destroy the Jews who are in all the king's provinces.
6 "For how can I endure to see the calamity which will befall my people, and how can **8:6**
I endure to see the destruction of my kindred?" Esth 7:4; 9:1
7 So King Ahasuerus said to Queen Esther and to Mordecai the Jew, "Behold, I have **8:7**
given the house of Haman to Esther, and him they have hanged on the gallows because Esth 8:1
he had stretched out his hands against the Jews.

The King's Decree Avenges the Jews

8 "Now you write to the Jews as you see fit, in the king's name, and seal *it* with the **8:8**
king's signet ring; for a decree which is written in the name of the king and sealed with Esth 3:12; 8:10; Esth 1:19
the king's signet ring may not be revoked."
9 So the king's scribes were called at that time in the third month (that is, the month **8:9**
Sivan), on the twenty-third day; and it was written according to all that Mordecai com- Esth 3:12; Esth 1:1; Esth 1:22; 3:12
manded to the Jews, the satraps, the governors and the princes of the provinces which
extended from India to Ethiopia, 127 provinces, to every province according to its script,
and to every people according to their language as well as to the Jews according to their
script and their language.
10 He wrote in the name of King Ahasuerus, and sealed it with the king's signet ring, **8:10**
and sent letters by couriers on horses, riding on steeds sired by the royal stud. 1 Kin 4:28
11 In them the king granted the Jews who were in each and every city *the right* to as- **8:11**
semble and to defend their lives, to destroy, to kill and to annihilate the entire army of Esth 9:2; Esth 3:13; Esth 9:10
any people or province which might attack them, including children and women, and to
plunder their spoil,
12 on one day in all the provinces of King Ahasuerus, the thirteenth *day* of the twelfth **8:12**
month (that is, the month Adar). Esth 3:13; 9:1
13 A copy of the edict to be issued as law in each and every province was published to **8:13**
all the peoples, so that the Jews would be ready for this day to avenge themselves on Esth 3:14
their enemies.
14 The couriers, hastened and impelled by the king's command, went out, riding on
the royal steeds; and the decree was given out at the citadel in Susa.
15 Then Mordecai went out from the presence of the king in royal robes of blue and **8:15**
white, with a large crown of gold and a garment of fine linen and purple; and the city of Esth 5:11; Gen 41:42; Esth 3:15
Susa shouted and rejoiced.
16 For the Jews there was light and gladness and joy and honor. **8:16**
17 In each and every province and in each and every city, wherever the king's com- Ps 97:11; 112:4
mandment and his decree arrived, there was gladness and joy for the Jews, a feast and a **8:17**
holiday. And many among the peoples of the land became Jews, for the dread of the Esth 9:19; Esth 9:27
Jews had fallen on them.

8:8 Haman's message had been sealed with the king's signet ring and could not be reversed, even by the king. It was part of the famed "law of the Medes and Persians." Now the king gave permission for whatever other decree Mordecai could devise that would offset the first, without actually canceling it.

8:12 This was the day set by Haman for the extermination of the Jews.

8:15–17 Everyone wants to be a hero and receive praise, honor, and wealth. But few are willing to pay the price. Mordecai served the government faithfully for years, bore Haman's hatred and oppression, and risked his life for his people. The price to be paid by God's heroes is long-term commitment. Are you ready and willing to pay the price?

4. The Jews are delivered

The Jews Destroy Their Enemies

9:1 Esth 8:12; Esth 9:17; Esth 3:13

9 Now in the twelfth month (that is, the month Adar), on the thirteenth day when the
king's command and edict were about to be executed, on the day when the enemies
of the Jews hoped to gain the mastery over them, it was turned to the contrary so that
the Jews themselves gained the mastery over those who hated them.

9:2 Esth 8:11; 9:15-18; Esth 8:17

2 The Jews assembled in their cities throughout all the provinces of King Ahasuerus
to lay hands on those who sought their harm; and no one could stand before them, for
the dread of them had fallen on all the peoples.

9:3 Ezra 8:36

3 Even all the princes of the provinces, the satraps, the governors and those who were
doing the king's business assisted the Jews, because the dread of Mordecai had fallen on
them.

9:4 2 Sam 3:1; 1 Chr 11:9

4 Indeed, Mordecai was great in the king's house, and his fame spread throughout all
the provinces; for the man Mordecai became greater and greater.

9:5 Esth 3:13

5 Thus the Jews struck all their enemies with the sword, killing and destroying; and
they did what they pleased to those who hated them.

HOW GOD WORKS IN THE WORLD

God's Will	*What God wants done—he works through...*		
	▼*Natural order*	▼*Miracles*	▼*Providence*
God's Action	▼God set into action through creation a normal working of his universe. He also revealed his expectations of man through his Word and man's conscience.	▼God breaks into the natural order to respond to the expressed needs of people.	▼God overrules the natural order to accomplish an act that people may or may not have requested.
Examples From Esther	▼God gave Esther natural beauty.	▼God allowed Esther to speak to the king.	▼God allowed Mordecai to overhear a plot.
	▲Esther planned a way to save her people.	▲The people prayed and fasted.	▲Mordecai trusted God to accomplish what was impossible in human terms.
People's Will	*What people want done—we either...*		
	▲*Plan*	▲*Pray*	▲*Trust and Obey*
Action We Can Take	▲Can make plans based on the order and dependability of God's creation. Know and obey his words.	▲Can ask God to intervene in certain affairs while realizing that our knowledge and perspective are limited.	▲Can trust that God is in control even when the circumstances may seem to indicate that he is not.
	or...		
	▼*Disobey*	▼*Demand*	▼*Despair*
Mistakes We Can Make	▼Can violate the natural order, disobey God's commands.	▼Can assume that we understand what is needed and expect God to agree and answer our prayers that way.	▼Can assume God doesn't answer prayer or respond to our needs and live as though there is nothing but the natural order.

9:5–16 Haman had decreed that on the 13th day of the 12th month anyone could kill the Jews and take their property. Mordecai's decree could not reverse Haman's because no law signed by the king could be repealed. Instead, Mordecai had the king sign a new law giving Jews the right to fight back. When the dreaded day arrived, there was much fighting, but the Jews killed only those who wanted to kill them, and they did not take their enemies' possessions, even though they could have (8:11; 9:10, 16). There were no additional riots after the two-day slaughter, so obviously selfish gain or revenge were not primary motives of the Jews. They simply wanted to defend themselves and their families from those who hated them.

6 At the citadel in Susa the Jews killed and destroyed five hundred men,
7 and Parshandatha, Dalphon, Aspatha,
8 Poratha, Adalia, Aridatha,
9 Parmashta, Arisai, Aridai and Vaizatha,
10 the ten sons of Haman the son of Hammedatha, the Jews' **9:10**
enemy; but they did not lay their hands on the plunder. Esth 5:11; Esth 8:11
11 On that day the number of those who were killed at the citadel in Susa was reported
to the king.
12 The king said to Queen Esther, "The Jews have killed and destroyed five hundred **9:12**
men and the ten sons of Haman at the citadel in Susa. What then have they done in the Esth 5:6; 7:2
rest of the king's provinces! Now what is your petition? It shall even be granted you. And
what is your further request? It shall also be done."
13 Then said Esther, "If it pleases the king, let tomorrow also be granted to the Jews **9:13**
who are in Susa to do according to the edict of today; and let Haman's ten sons be hanged Esth 8:11; 9:15
on the gallows."
14 So the king commanded that it should be done so; and an edict was issued in Susa,
and Haman's ten sons were hanged.
15 The Jews who were in Susa assembled also on the fourteenth day of the month Adar **9:15**
and killed three hundred men in Susa, but they did not lay their hands on the plunder. Esth 9:12; Esth 9:10
16 Now the rest of the Jews who *were* in the king's provinces assembled, to defend their **9:16**
lives and rid themselves of their enemies, and kill 75,000 of those who hated them; but Esth 9:2; Lev 26:7,
they did not lay their hands on the plunder. 8; Esth 8:11
17 *This was done* on the thirteenth day of the month Adar, and on the fourteenth day **9:17**
they rested and made it a day of feasting and rejoicing. Esth 9:1; Esth 9:21
18 But the Jews who were in Susa assembled on the thirteenth and the fourteenth of **9:18**
the same month, and they rested on the fifteenth day and made it a day of feasting and Esth 8:11; 9:2; Esth
rejoicing. 9:21
19 Therefore the Jews of the rural areas, who live in the rural towns, make the four- **9:19**
teenth day of the month Adar *a* holiday for rejoicing and feasting and sending portions Deut 3:5; Zech 2:4;
of food to one another. Esth 9:22; Neh 8:10

The Feast of Purim Instituted

20 Then Mordecai recorded these events, and he sent letters to all the Jews who were
in all the provinces of King Ahasuerus, both near and far,
21 obliging them to celebrate the fourteenth day of the month Adar, and the fifteenth
day of the same month, annually,
22 because on those days the Jews rid themselves of their enemies, and *it was a* month **9:22**
which was turned for them from sorrow into gladness and from mourning into a holiday; Ps 30:11; Neh 8:12
that they should make them days of feasting and rejoicing and sending portions *of food*
to one another and gifts to the poor.
23 Thus the Jews undertook what they had started to do, and what Mordecai had written to them.
24 For Haman the son of Hammedatha, the Agagite, the adversary of all the Jews, had **9:24**
schemed against the Jews to destroy them and had cast Pur, that is the lot, to disturb Esth 3:7
them and destroy them.
25 But when it came to the king's attention, he commanded by letter that his wicked **9:25**
scheme which he had devised against the Jews, should return on his own head and that Esth 7:4-10; Esth
he and his sons should be hanged on the gallows. 3:6-15; Ps 7:16
26 Therefore they called these days Purim after the name of Pur. And because of the **9:26**
instructions in this letter, both what they had seen in this regard and what had happened Esth 9:20
to them,

9:11 Here the word "citadel" seems to refer to the fortified city of Susa. The king appears to be more concerned about Esther's wishes than the slaughter of his subjects.

9:19–22 People tend to have short memories when it comes to God's faithfulness. To help counter this, Mordecai wrote down these events and encouraged an annual holiday to commemorate the historic days of Purim. Jews still celebrate Purim today. Celebrations of feasting, gladness, and gift-giving are important ways to remember God's specific acts. Today the festivities of Christmas and Easter help us remember the birth and resurrection of Jesus Christ. Don't let the celebration or the exchanging of gifts hide the meaning of these great events.

9:27 Esth 8:17; Esth 9:20, 21

27 the Jews established and made a custom for themselves and for their descendants
and for all those who allied themselves with them, so that they would not fail to celebrate these two days according to their regulation and according to their appointed time
annually.
28 So these days were to be remembered and celebrated throughout every generation,
every family, every province and every city; and these days of Purim were not to fail from
among the Jews, or their memory fade from their descendants.

9:29 Esth 2:15; Esth 9:20, 21

29 Then Queen Esther, daughter of Abihail, with Mordecai the Jew, wrote with full
authority to confirm this second letter about Purim.

9:30 Esth 1:1

30 He sent letters to all the Jews, to the 127 provinces of the kingdom of Ahasuerus,
namely, words of peace and truth,

9:31 Esth 4:3

31 to establish these days of Purim at their appointed times, just as Mordecai the Jew
and Queen Esther had established for them, and just as they had established for themselves and for their descendants with instructions for their times of fasting and their lamentations.

9:32 Esth 9:26

32 The command of Esther established these customs for Purim, and it was written in
the book.

Mordecai's Greatness

10:1 Is 11:11; 24:15

10:2 Esth 8:15; 9:4; Esth 2:23

10:3 Gen 41:43, 44; Neh 2:10

10 Now King Ahasuerus laid a tribute on the land and on the coastlands of the sea.
2 And all the accomplishments of his authority and strength, and the full account
of the greatness of Mordecai to which the king advanced him, are they not written in the
Book of the Chronicles of the Kings of Media and Persia?
3 For Mordecai the Jew was second *only* to King Ahasuerus, and great among the Jews
and in favor with his many kinsmen, one who sought the good of his people and one who
spoke for the welfare of his whole nation.

9:29–31 Among Jews, women were expected to be quiet, to serve in the home, and to stay on the fringe of religious and political life. But Esther was a Jewish woman who broke through the cultural norms, stepping outside her expected role to risk her life to help God's people. Whatever your place in life, God can use you. Be open, available, and ready because God may use you to do what others are afraid even to consider.

10:3 Mordecai enjoyed a good reputation among the Jews because he was still their friend when he rose to a place of power. Corruption and abuse of authority often characterize those in power. But power used to lift the fallen and ease the burden of the oppressed is power used well. People placed by God in positions of power or political influence must not turn their backs on those in need.

10:3 No archaeological records of Mordecai's being second-in-command have been discovered, but during this time there is a strange gap in ancient Persian records. The records indicate that another man held that position in 465 B.C., about seven years after Mordecai was first appointed. One tablet has been discovered naming Mardukaya as an official in the early years of Ahasuerus' reign; some believe this was Mordecai.

10:3 In the book of Esther, we clearly see God at work in the lives of individuals and in the affairs of a nation. Even when it looks as if the world is in the hands of evil people, God is still in control, protecting those who are his. Although we may not understand everything happening around us, we must trust in God's protection and retain our integrity by doing what we know is right. Esther, who risked her life appearing before the king, became a hero. Mordecai, who was effectively condemned to death, rose to become the second highest ranking official in the nation. No matter how hopeless our condition, or how much we would like to give up, we need not despair. God is in control of our world.

JOB

VITAL STATISTICS

PURPOSE:
To demonstrate God's sovereignty and the meaning of true faith. It addresses the question, "Why do the righteous suffer?"

AUTHOR:
Unknown, possibly Job. Some have suggested Moses, Solomon, or Elihu.

DATE WRITTEN:
Unknown. Records events that probably occurred during the time of the patriarchs, approximately 2000–1800 B.C.

SETTING:
The land of Uz, probably located northeast of Palestine, near desert land between Damascus and the Euphrates River

KEY VERSE:
"The LORD said to Satan, 'Have you considered My servant Job? For there is no one like him on the earth, a blameless and upright man fearing God and turning away from evil. And he still holds fast his integrity, although you incited Me against him to ruin him without cause' " (2:3).

KEY PEOPLE:
Job, Eliphaz the Temanite, Bildad the Shuhite, Zophar the Naamathite, Elihu the Buzite

SPECIAL FEATURES:
Job is the first of the poetic books in the Hebrew Bible. Some believe this was the first book of the Bible to be written. The book gives us insights into the work of Satan. Ezekiel 14:14, 20 and James 5:11 mention Job as a historical character.

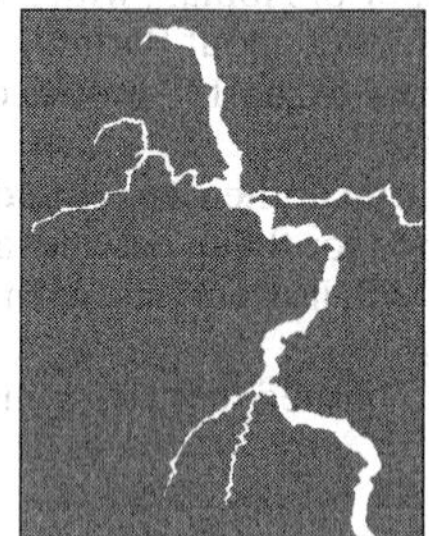

TREES snap like toothpicks or fly upward, wrenched from the earth. Whole rooftops sail, cars tumble like toys, houses collapse, and a wall of water obliterates the shore and inundates the land. A hurricane cuts and tears, and only solid foundations survive its unbridled fury. But those foundations can be used for rebuilding after the storm.

For any building, the foundation is critical. It must be deep enough and solid enough to withstand the weight of the building and other stresses. Lives are like buildings, and the quality of their foundation will determine the quality of the whole. Too often inferior materials are used, and when tests come, lives crumble.

Job was tested. With a life filled with prestige, possessions, and people, he was suddenly assaulted on every side, devastated, stripped down to his foundation. But his life was built on God, and he endured.

Job, the book, tells the story of Job, the man of God. It is a gripping drama of riches-to-rags-to-riches, a theological treatise about suffering and divine sovereignty and a picture of faith that endures. As you read Job, analyze your life and check your foundation. And may you be able to say that when all is gone but God, he is enough.

Job was a prosperous farmer living in the land of Uz. He had thousands of sheep, camels, and other livestock, a large family, and many servants. Suddenly, Satan the Accuser came before God claiming that Job was trusting God only because he was wealthy and everything was going well for him. And so the testing of Job's faith began.

Satan was allowed to destroy Job's children, servants, livestock, herdsmen, and home; but Job continued to trust in God. Next Satan attacked Job physically, covering him with painful sores. Job's wife told him to curse God and die (2:9), but Job suffered in silence.

Three of Job's friends, Eliphaz, Bildad, and Zophar, came to visit him. At first they silently grieved with Job. But when they began to talk about the reasons for Job's tragedies, they told him that sin had caused his suffering. They told him to confess his sins and turn back to God. But Job maintained his innocence.

Unable to convince Job of his sin, the three men fell silent (32:1). At this point, another voice—the young Elihu—entered the debate. Although his argument also failed to convince Job, it prepared the way for God to speak.

Finally, God spoke out of a mighty storm. Confronted with the great power and majesty of God, Job fell in humble reverence before God—speechless. God rebuked Job's friends, and the drama ended with Job restored to happiness and wealth.

It is easy to think that we have all the answers. In reality, only God knows exactly why things happen as they do, and we must submit to him as our Sovereign. As you read this book, emulate Job and decide to trust God no matter what happens.

THE BLUEPRINT

A. JOB IS TESTED (1:1—2:13)	Job, a wealthy and upright man, lost his possessions, his children, and his health. Job did not understand why he was suffering. Why does God allow his children to suffer? Although there is an explanation, we may not know it while we are here on earth. In the meantime, we must always be ready for testing in our lives.
B. THREE FRIENDS ANSWER JOB (3:1—31:40) 1. First round of discussion 2. Second round of discussion 3. Third round of discussion	Job's friends wrongly assumed that suffering always came as a result of sin. With this in mind, they tried to persuade Job to repent of his sin. But the three friends were wrong. Suffering is not always a direct result of personal sin. When we experience severe suffering, it may not be our fault, so we don't have to add to our pain by feeling guilty that some hidden sin is causing our trouble.
C. A YOUNG MAN ANSWERS JOB (32:1—37:24)	A young man named Elihu, who had been listening to the entire conversation, criticized the three friends for being unable to answer Job. He said that although Job was a good man, he had allowed himself to become proud, and God was punishing him in order to humble him. This answer was partially true because suffering does purify our faith. But God is beyond our comprehension, and we cannot know why he allows each instance of suffering to come into our lives. Our part is simply to remain faithful.
D. GOD ANSWERS JOB (38:1—41:34)	God himself finally answered Job. God is in control of the world, and only he understands why the good are allowed to suffer. This only becomes clear to us when we see God for who he is. We must courageously accept what God allows to happen in our lives and remain firmly committed to him.
E. JOB IS RESTORED (42:1–17)	Job finally learned that when nothing else was left, he had God, and that was enough. Through suffering, we learn that God is enough for our lives and our future. We must love God regardless of whether he allows blessing or suffering to come to us. Testing is difficult, but the result is often a deeper relationship with God. Those who endure the testing of their faith will experience God's great rewards in the end.

MEGATHEMES

THEME	EXPLANATION	IMPORTANCE
Suffering	Through no fault of his own, Job lost his wealth, children, and health. Even his friends were convinced that Job had brought this suffering upon himself. For Job, the greatest trial was not the pain or the loss; it was not being able to understand why God allowed him to suffer.	Suffering can be, but is not always, a penalty for sin. In the same way, prosperity is not always a reward for being good. Those who love God are not exempt from trouble. Although we may not be able to understand fully the pain we experience, it can lead us to rediscover God.
Satan's Attacks	Satan attempted to drive a wedge between Job and God by getting Job to believe that God's governing of the world was not just and good. Satan had to ask God for permission to take Job's wealth, children, and health away. Satan was limited to what God allowed.	We must learn to recognize but not fear Satan's attacks because Satan cannot exceed the limits that God sets. Don't let any experience drive a wedge between you and God. Although you can't control how Satan may attack, you can always choose how you will respond when it happens.

God's Goodness	God is all-wise and all-powerful. His will is perfect, yet he doesn't always act in ways that we understand. Job's suffering didn't make sense because everyone believed good people were supposed to prosper. When Job was at the point of despair, God spoke to him, showing him his great power and wisdom.	Although God is present everywhere, at times he may seem far away. This may cause us to feel alone and to doubt his care for us. We should serve God for who he is, not what we feel. He is never insensitive to our suffering. Because God is sufficient, we must hold on to him.
Pride	Job's friends were certain that they were correct in their judgment of him. God rebuked them for their pride and arrogance. Human wisdom is always partial and temporary, so undue pride in our own conclusions is sin.	We must be careful not to judge others who are suffering. We may be demonstrating the sin of pride. We must be cautious in maintaining the certainty of our own conclusions about how God treats us. When we congratulate ourselves for being right, we become proud.
Trusting	God alone knew the purpose behind Job's suffering, and yet he never explained it to Job. In spite of this, Job never gave up on God—even in the midst of suffering. He never placed his hope in his experience, his wisdom, his friends, or his wealth. Job focused on God.	Job showed the kind of trust we are to have. When everything is stripped away, we are to recognize that God is all we ever really had. We should not demand that God explain everything. God gives us himself, but not all the details of his plans. We must remember that this life, with all its pain, is not our final destiny.

A. JOB IS TESTED (1:1—2:13)

Job is portrayed as a wealthy man of upright character who loves God. Yet God allows Satan to destroy his flocks, his possessions, his children, and his health. Job refuses to give up on God, even though he does not understand why this is happening to him. We, too, must trust God when we do not understand the difficulties we face.

Job's Character and Wealth

1 There was a man in the land of Uz whose name was Job; and that man was blameless, upright, fearing God and turning away from evil.
2 Seven sons and three daughters were born to him.
3 His possessions also were 7,000 sheep, 3,000 camels, 500 yoke of oxen, 500 female
donkeys, and very many servants; and that man was the greatest of all the men of the
east.
4 His sons used to go and hold a feast in the house of each one on his day, and they
would send and invite their three sisters to eat and drink with them.
5 When the days of feasting had completed their cycle, Job would send and consecrate them, rising up early in the morning and offering burnt offerings *according to* the

1:1 Jer 25:20; Lam 4:21; Ezek 14:14, 20; James 5:11; Gen 6:9; 17:1; Deut 18:13; Gen 22:12; 42:18; Ex 18:21; Prov 8:13; Job 28:28

1:2 Job 42:13

1:3 Job 42:12; Job 29:25

1:5 Gen 8:20; Job 42:8; Job 8:4; 1 Kin 21:10, 13

1:1 As we read the book of Job, we have information that the characters of the story do not. Job, the main character of the book, lost all he had through no fault of his own. As he struggled to understand why all this was happening to him, it became clear that he was not meant to know the reasons. He would have to face life with the answers and explanations held back. Only then would his faith fully develop.

We must experience life as Job did—one day at a time and without complete answers to all of life's questions. Will we, like Job, trust God no matter what? Or will we give in to the temptation to say that God doesn't really care?

1:1 The location of the land of Uz is uncertain. We only know that Uz had plentiful pastures and crops (1:3), was located near a wilderness (1:19), and was close enough to the Sabeans and Chaldeans to be raided (1:14–17). Uz is also mentioned in Jeremiah 25:19–20. Most scholars believe Uz was located east of the Jordan River near Canaan (Israel), where the Jews (those to whom God first revealed himself) lived. Job probably knew about God because he knew God's people.

1:1ff As we see calamity and suffering in the book of Job, we must remember that we live in a fallen world where good behavior is not always rewarded and bad behavior is not always punished. When we see a notorious criminal prospering or an innocent child in pain, we say, "That's wrong." And it is. Sin has twisted justice and made our world unpredictable and ugly.

The book of Job shows a good man suffering for no apparent fault of his own. Sadly, our world is like that. But Job's story does not end in despair. Through Job's life we can see that faith in God is justified even when our situations look hopeless. Faith based on rewards or prosperity is hollow. To be unshakable, faith must be built on the confidence that God's ultimate purpose will come to pass.

1:5 It is not known for sure, but Job probably lived during the days of the patriarchs (Abraham, Isaac, Jacob) before God gave his written Law or appointed priests to be religious leaders. During Job's day, the father was the family's religious leader. Because there were no priests to instruct him in God's laws, Job acted as the priest and offered sacrifices to God to ask for forgiveness for sins he and his family had committed. This demonstrated that Job did not consider himself sinless. Job did this out of conviction and love for God, not just because it was his role as head of the house. Do you carry out your spiritual duties because they are expected, or spontaneously from a heart of devotion?

1:6 Job 2:1; Job 38:7

1:7 1 Pet 5:8

1:8 Num 12:7; Josh 1:2, 7; Job 42:7, 8; Job 1:1

1:9 Rev 12:9f

1:10 Job 29:2-6; Ps 34:7; Job 31:25; Job 1:3; 31:25

1:11 Job 2:5; Job 19:21

number of them all; for Job said, "Perhaps my sons have sinned and cursed God in their
hearts." Thus Job did continually.
6 Now there was a day when the sons of God came to present themselves before the
LORD, and [1]Satan also came among them.
7 The LORD said to Satan, "From where do you come?" Then Satan answered the
LORD and said, "From roaming about on the earth and walking around on it."
8 The LORD said to Satan, "Have you considered My servant Job? For there is no
one like him on the earth, a blameless and upright man, fearing God and turning away
from evil."
9 Then Satan answered the LORD, "Does Job fear God for nothing?
10 "Have You not made a hedge about him and his house and all that he has, on every
side? You have blessed the work of his hands, and his possessions have increased in the
land.
11 "But put forth Your hand now and touch all that he has; he will surely curse You to
Your face."
12 Then the LORD said to Satan, "Behold, all that he has is in your power, only do not
put forth your hand on him." So Satan departed from the presence of the LORD.

Satan Allowed to Test Job

13 Now on the day when his sons and his daughters were eating and drinking wine in
their oldest brother's house,
14 a messenger came to Job and said, "The oxen were plowing and the donkeys feeding beside them,

1 I.e. the adversary, and so throughout chs 1 and 2

1:5 Job showed deep concern for the spiritual welfare of his children. Fearful that they might have sinned unknowingly, he offered sacrifices for them. Parents today can show the same concern by praying for their children. This means "sacrificing" some time each day to ask God to forgive them, to help them grow, to protect them, and to help them please him.

1:6 The Bible speaks of other heavenly councils where God and the angels (sons of God) plan their activities on earth and where angels are required to give account of themselves (see 1 Kings 22:19–23). Because God is Creator of all angels—both of those who serve him and of those who rebelled—he has complete power and authority over them.

1:6–7 Satan, originally an angel of God, became corrupt through his own pride. He has been evil since his rebellion against God (1 John 3:8). Satan considers God as his enemy. He tries to hinder God's work in people, but he is limited by God's power and can do only what he is permitted (Luke 22:31–32; 1 Timothy 1:19–20; 2 Timothy 2:23–26). Satan is called the enemy because he actively looks for people to attack with temptation (1 Peter 5:8–9) and because he wants to make people hate God. He does this through lies and deception (Genesis 3:1–6). Job, a blameless and upright man who had been greatly blessed, was a perfect target for Satan. Any person who is committed to God should expect Satan's attacks. Satan, who hates God, also hates God's people.

1:6–12 From this conversation, we learn a great deal about Satan. (1) He is accountable to God. All angelic beings, good and evil, are compelled to present themselves before God (1:6). God knew that Satan was intent on attacking Job. (2) Satan can be at only one place at a time (1:6–7). His demons aid him in his work; but as a created being, he is limited. (3) Satan cannot see into our minds or foretell the future (1:9–11). If he could, he would have known that Job would not break under pressure. (4) Because Satan can do nothing without God's permission (1:12), God's people can overcome his attacks through God's power. (5) God puts limitations on what Satan can do (1:12; 2:6). Satan's response to the Lord's question (1:7) tells us that Satan is real and active on earth. Knowing this about Satan should cause us to remain close to the One who is greater than Satan—God himself.

1:7ff Some people suggest that this dialogue was made up by the author of this book. Could this conversation between God and Satan really have happened? Other Bible passages tell us that Satan does indeed have access to God (see Revelation 12:10). He even went into God's presence to make accusations against Joshua the high priest (Zechariah 3:1–2). If this conversation didn't take place, then the reasons for Job's suffering become meaningless and the book of Job is reduced to fiction rather than fact.

1:8, 12 Job was a model of trust and obedience to God, yet God permitted Satan to attack him in an especially harsh manner. Although God loves us, believing and obeying him do not shelter us from life's calamities. Setbacks, tragedies, and sorrows strike Christians and non-Christians alike. But in our tests and trials, God expects us to express our faith to the world. How do you respond to your troubles? Do you ask God, "Why me?" or do you say, "Use me!"?

1:9 Satan attacked Job's motives, saying that Job was blameless and upright only because he had no reason to turn against God. Ever since he had started following God, everything had gone well for Job. Satan wanted to prove that Job worshiped God, not out of love, but because God had given him so much.

Satan accurately analyzed why many people trust God. They are fair-weather believers, following God only when everything is going well or for what they can get. Adversity destroys this superficial faith. But adversity strengthens real faith by causing believers to dig their roots deeper into God in order to withstand the storms. How deep does your faith go? Put the roots of your faith down deep into God so that you can withstand any storm you may face.

1:12 This conversation between God and Satan teaches us an important fact about God—he is fully aware of every attempt by Satan to bring suffering and difficulty upon us. While God may allow us to suffer for a reason beyond our understanding, he is never caught by surprise by our troubles and is always compassionate.

15 and the Sabeans attacked and took them. They also slew the servants with the edge **1:15** Gen 10:7; Job 6:19
of the sword, and I alone have escaped to tell you."
16 While he was still speaking, another also came and said, "The fire of God fell from **1:16** Gen 19:24; Lev 10:2; Num 11:1-3
heaven and burned up the sheep and the servants and consumed them, and I alone have
escaped to tell you."
17 While he was still speaking, another also came and said, "The Chaldeans formed **1:17** Gen 11:28, 31
three bands and made a raid on the camels and took them and slew the servants with the
edge of the sword, and I alone have escaped to tell you."
18 While he was still speaking, another also came and said, "Your sons and your daughters were eating and drinking wine in their oldest brother's house,
19 and behold, a great wind came from across the wilderness and struck the four corners of the house, and it fell on the young people and they died, and I alone have escaped to tell you."
20 Then Job arose and tore his robe and shaved his head, and he fell to the ground and **1:20** Gen 37:29, 34; Josh 7:6
worshiped.
21 He said,
"Naked I came from my mother's womb, **1:21** Eccl 5:15; 1 Sam 2:7, 8; Job 2:10
And naked I shall return there.
The LORD gave and the LORD has taken away.
Blessed be the name of the LORD."
22 Through all this Job did not sin nor did he blame God. **1:22** Job 2:10

Job Loses His Health

2 Again there was a day when the sons of God came to present themselves before the **2:1** Job 1:6-8
LORD, and Satan also came among them to present himself before the LORD.
2 The LORD said to Satan, "Where have you come from?" Then Satan answered the
LORD and said, "From roaming about on the earth and walking around on it."
3 The LORD said to Satan, "Have you considered My servant Job? For there is no **2:3** Job 27:5, 6
one like him on the earth, a blameless and upright man fearing God and turning away
from evil. And he still holds fast his integrity, although you incited Me against him to
ruin him without cause."
4 Satan answered the LORD and said, "Skin for skin! Yes, all that a man has he will
give for his life.
5 "However, put forth Your hand now, and touch his bone and his flesh; he will curse **2:5** Job 1:11; Job 19:20
You to Your face."
6 So the LORD said to Satan, "Behold, he is in your power, only spare his life."
7 Then Satan went out from the presence of the LORD and smote Job with sore boils **2:7** Deut 28:35; Job 7:5; 13:28; 30:17, 18, 30
from the sole of his foot to the crown of his head.
8 And he took a potsherd to scrape himself while he was sitting among the ashes. **2:8** Job 42:6; Jer 6:26; Ezek 27:30; Jon 3:6
9 Then his wife said to him, "Do you still hold fast your integrity? Curse God
and die!"

1:15–17 The Sabeans were from southwest Arabia, while the Chaldeans were from the region north of the Persian Gulf.

1:16 "The fire of God" was a poetic way to describe lightning (1 Kings 18:38; 2 Kings 1:10–14). In this case, it had to be unusually powerful to kill 7,000 sheep.

1:20–22 Job did not hide his overwhelming grief. He had not lost his faith in God; instead, his emotions showed that he was human and that he loved his family. God created our emotions, and it is not sinful or inappropriate to express them as Job did. If you have experienced a deep loss, a disappointment, or a heartbreak, admit your feelings to yourself and others, and grieve.

1:20–22 Job had lost his possessions and family in this first of Satan's tests, but he reacted rightly toward God by acknowledging God's sovereign authority over everything God had given him. Satan lost this first round. Job passed the test and proved that people can love God for who he is, not for what he gives.

2:3–6 Can Satan persuade God to change his plans? At first God said he did not want Job harmed physically, but then he decided to allow it. Satan is unable to persuade God to go against his character: God is completely and eternally good. But God was willing to go along with Satan's plan because God knew the eventual outcome of Job's story. God cannot be fooled by Satan. Job's suffering was a test for Job, Satan, and us—not God.

2:4–5 "Skin for skin" was Satan's comment concerning Job's response to the loss of his family. Satan still held to his opinion that Job was faithful only because of God's blessings. Satan believed that Job was willing to accept the loss of family and property as long as his own skin was safe. Satan's next step was to inflict physical suffering upon Job to prove his original accusation (1:9).

2:6 Again Satan had to seek permission from God to inflict pain upon Job. God limits Satan, and in this case, he did not allow Satan to destroy Job.

2:9 Why was Job's wife spared when the rest of his family was killed? It is possible that her very presence caused Job even more suffering through her chiding or sorrow over all they had lost.

2:10
Job 1:21; Job 1:22;
Ps 39:1; James 1:12

10 But he said to her, "You speak as one of the foolish women speaks. Shall we indeed accept good from God and not accept adversity?" In all this Job did not sin with his lips.

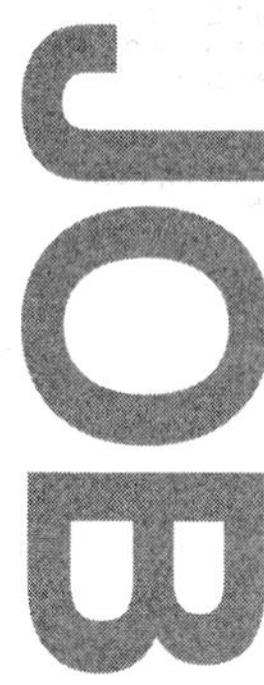

Children never tire of asking "Why?" Yet the question produces a bitter taste the older we get. Children wonder about everything; adults wonder about suffering. We notice that the world seems to run by a system of cause and effect, yet there are some effects for which we can't find a clear cause, and some causes that don't lead to the expected effects. We would expect Job's wealth and family to give him a very happy life, and, for a while, they did. But the loss and pain he experienced shock us. The first two chapters of his story are more than we can bear. To those so quick to ask "Why?" at the smallest misfortune, Job's faithfulness seems incredible. But even Job had something to learn. We can learn with him.

Our age of "instant" everything has caused us to lose the ability to wait. We expect to learn patience instantly, and in our hurry, we miss the contradiction. Of all that we want now, relief from pain is at the top of our list. We want an instant cure for everything from toothaches to heartbreaks.

Although some pains have been cured, we still live in a world where many people suffer. Job was not expecting instant answers for the intense emotional and physical pain he endured. But in the end, what broke Job's patience was not the suffering, but not knowing *why* he suffered.

When Job expressed his frustration, his friends were ready with their answers. They believed that the law of cause and effect applied to all people's experiences. Their view of life boiled down to this: good things happen to good people, and bad things happen to bad people. Because of this, they felt their role was to help Job admit to whatever sin was causing his suffering.

Job actually looked at life almost the same way as his friends. What he couldn't understand was why he was suffering so much when he was sure he had done nothing to deserve such punishment. The last friend, Elihu, did offer another explanation for the pain by pointing out that God might be allowing it to purify Job. But this was only partly helpful. When God finally spoke, he didn't offer Job an answer. Instead, he drove home the point that it is better to know God than to know answers.

Often we suffer consequences for bad decisions and actions. Job's willingness to repent and confess known wrongs is a good guideline for us. Sometimes suffering shapes us for special service to others. Sometimes suffering is an attack by Satan on our lives. And sometimes we don't know why we suffer. At those times, are we willing to trust God in spite of unanswered questions?

Strengths and accomplishments:
- Was a man of faith, patience, and endurance
- Was known as a generous and caring person
- Was very wealthy

Weakness and mistake:
- Allowed his desire to understand why he was suffering to overwhelm him and make him question God

Lessons from his life:
- Knowing God is better than knowing answers
- God is not arbitrary or uncaring
- Pain is not always punishment

Vital statistics:
- Where: Uz
- Occupation: Wealthy landowner and livestock owner
- Relatives: Wife and first ten children not named. Daughters from the second set of children: Jemimah, Keziah, Keren-happuch
- Contemporaries: Eliphaz, Bildad, Zophar, Elihu

Key verses:
"As an example, brethren, of suffering and patience, take the prophets who spoke in the name of the Lord. We count those blessed who endured. You have heard of the endurance of Job and have seen the outcome of the Lord's dealings, that the Lord is full of compassion and is merciful" (James 5:10–11).

Job's story is told in the book of Job. He is also referred to in Ezekiel 14:14, 20 and James 5:11.

2:10 Many people think that believing in God protects them from trouble, so when calamity comes, they question God's goodness and justice. But the message of Job is that you should not give up on God because he allows you to have bad experiences. Faith in God does not guarantee personal prosperity, and lack of faith does not guarantee troubles in this life. If this were so, people would believe in God simply to get rich. God is capable of rescuing us from suffering, but he may also allow suffering to come for reasons we cannot understand. It is Satan's strategy to get us to doubt God at exactly this moment. Here Job shows a perspective broader than seeking his own personal comfort. If we always knew why we were suffering, our faith would have no room to grow.

11 Now when Job's three friends heard of all this adversity that had come upon him, they came each one from his own place, Eliphaz the Temanite, Bildad the Shuhite and Zophar the Naamathite; and they made an appointment together to come to sympathize with him and comfort him.
12 When they lifted up their eyes at a distance and did not recognize him, they raised their voices and wept. And each of them tore his robe and they threw dust over their heads toward the sky.
13 Then they sat down on the ground with him for seven days and seven nights with no one speaking a word to him, for they saw that *his* pain was very great.

2:11 Gen 36:11; Job 6:19; Jer 49:7; Gen 25:2; Job 42:11; Rom 12:15

2:12 Job 1:20; Josh 7:6; Neh 9:1; Lam 2:10; Ezek 27:30

2:13 Gen 50:10; Ezek 3:15

B. THREE FRIENDS ANSWER JOB (3:1—31:40)

Job agonizes over his situation. His three friends explain that he must be suffering because of some terrible sin he committed. They try to persuade Job to repent of his sin. When Job argues that he has not sinned enough to deserve such suffering, his friends respond with even harsher accusations. While there are elements of truth in the speeches of Job's three friends, they are based on wrong assumptions. We must be careful what we assume to be true in the lives of others. We cannot assume that suffering is their own fault or a result of their sin.

1. First round of discussion

Job's Lament

3 Afterward Job opened his mouth and cursed the day of his *birth.*
2 And Job said,
3 "Let the day perish on which I was to be born,
And the night *which* said, 'A boy is conceived.'
4 "May that day be darkness;
Let not God above care for it,
Nor light shine on it.
5 "Let darkness and black gloom claim it;
Let a cloud settle on it;
Let the blackness of the day terrify it.
6 "*As for* that night, let darkness seize it;
Let it not rejoice among the days of the year;
Let it not come into the number of the months.
7 "Behold, let that night be barren;
Let no joyful shout enter it.
8 "Let those curse it who curse the day,
Who are prepared to rouse Leviathan.
9 "Let the stars of its twilight be darkened;
Let it wait for light but have none,
And let it not see the breaking dawn;
10 Because it did not shut the opening of my *mother's* womb,
Or hide trouble from my eyes.

3:3 Jer 20:14-18

3:5 Jer 13:16

3:8 Job 41:1, 25

2:11 Eliphaz, Bildad, and Zophar were not only Job's friends; they were also known for their wisdom. In the end, however, their wisdom was shown to be narrow-minded and incomplete.

2:11 Upon learning of Job's difficulties, three of his friends came to sympathize with him and and comfort him. Later we learn that their words of comfort were not helpful—but at least they came. While God rebuked them for what they said (42:7), he did not rebuke them for what they did—making the effort to come to someone who was in need. Unfortunately, when they came, they did a poor job of comforting Job because they were proud of their own advice and insensitive to Job's needs. When someone is in need, go to that person, but be sensitive in how you comfort him or her.

2:13 Why did the friends arrive and then just sit quietly? According to Jewish tradition, people who come to comfort someone in mourning should not speak until the mourner speaks. Often the best response to another person's suffering is silence. Job's friends realized that his pain was too deep to be healed with mere words, so they said nothing. (If only they had continued to sit quietly!) Often, we feel we must say something spiritual and insightful to a hurting friend. Perhaps what he or she needs most is just our presence, showing that we care. Pat answers and trite quotations say much less than empathetic silence and loving companionship.

3:1ff Job's response to his second test—physical affliction—contrasts greatly to his attitude after the first test (1:20–22). Job still did not curse God, but he cursed the day of his birth. He felt it would be better never to be born than to be forsaken by God. Job was struggling emotionally, physically, and spiritually; his misery was pervasive and deep. Never underestimate how vulnerable we are during times of suffering and pain. We must hold on to our faith even if there is no relief.

3:8 In Job's day, people were hired to pronounce curses. Job desires that those who are experts at cursing would call up the sea monster, Leviathan, to swallow up the day of Job's birth.

11 "Why did I not die at birth,
Come forth from the womb and expire?
12 "Why did the knees receive me,
And why the breasts, that I should suck?
13 "For now I would have lain down and been quiet;
I would have slept then, I would have been at rest,
14 With kings and *with* counselors of the earth,
Who rebuilt ruins for themselves;
15 Or with princes who had gold,
Who were filling their houses *with* silver.
16 "Or like a miscarriage which is discarded, I would not be,
As infants that never saw light.
17 "There the wicked cease from raging,
And there the weary are at rest.
18 "The prisoners are at ease together;
They do not hear the voice of the taskmaster.
19 "The small and the great are there,
And the slave is free from his master.

20 "Why is light given to him who suffers,
And life to the bitter of soul,
21 Who long for death, but there is none,
And dig for it more than for hidden treasures,
22 Who rejoice greatly,
And exult when they find the grave?
23 "*Why is light given* to a man whose way is hidden,
And whom God has hedged in?
24 "For my groaning comes at the sight of my food,
And my cries pour out like water.
25 "For what I fear comes upon me,
And what I dread befalls me.
26 "I am not at ease, nor am I quiet,
And I am not at rest, but turmoil comes."

Eliphaz: Innocent Do Not Suffer

4 Then Eliphaz the Temanite answered,
2 "If one ventures a word with you, will you become impatient?
But who can refrain from speaking?
3 "Behold you have admonished many,
And you have strengthened weak hands.
4 "Your words have helped the tottering to stand,
And you have strengthened feeble knees.

3:11 Job 10:18, 19
3:13 Job 3:13-19; 7:8-10, 21; 10:21, 22; 14:10-15, 20-22; 16:22; 17:13-16; 19:25-27; 21:13, 23-26; 24:19, 20; 26:5, 6; 34:22
3:14 Job 12:18; Job 12:17; Job 15:28; Is 58:12
3:15 Job 12:21; Job 27:16, 17
3:17 Job 17:16
3:20 Jer 20:18
3:21 Rev 9:6; Prov 2:4
3:23 Job 19:6, 8, 12; Job 19:8; Ps 88:8; Lam 3:7
3:24 Job 6:7; 33:20; Job 30:16; Ps 42:4
3:25 Job 9:28; 30:15
3:26 Job 7:13, 14
4:2 Job 32:18-20
4:3 Job 4:3, 4; 29:15, 16, 21, 25

3:11 Job was experiencing extreme physical pain as well as grief over the loss of his family and possessions. He can't be blamed for wishing he were dead. Job's grief placed him at the crossroads of his faith, shattering many misconceptions about God (such as: He makes you rich, always keeps you from trouble and pain, or protects your loved ones). Job was driven back to the basics of his faith in God. He had only two choices: (1) He could curse God and give up, or (2) he could trust God and draw strength from him to continue.

3:23–26 Job had been careful not to worship material possessions but to worship God alone. Here he was overwhelmed by calamities that mocked his caution, and he complained about trials that came despite his right living. All the principles by which he had lived were crumbling, and Job began to lose his perspective. Trials and grief, whether temporary or enduring, do not destroy the real purpose of life. Life is not given merely for happiness and personal fulfillment, but for us to serve and honor God. The worth and meaning of life are not based on what we feel, but on the one reality no one can take away—God's love for us. Don't assume that because God truly loves you, he will always prevent suffering. The opposite may be true. God's love cannot be measured or limited by how great or how little we may suffer. Romans 8:38–39 teaches us that nothing can separate us from God's love.

4:1ff Eliphaz claimed to have been given secret knowledge through a special revelation from God (4:12–16) and that he had learned much from personal experience (4:8). He argued that suffering is a direct result of sin, so if Job would only confess his sin, his suffering would end. Eliphaz saw suffering as God's punishment, which should be welcomed in order to bring a person back to God. In some cases, of course, this may be true (Galatians 6:7–8), but it was not true with Job. Although Eliphaz had many good and true comments, he made three wrong assumptions: (1) A good and innocent person never suffers; (2) those who suffer are being punished for their past sins; and (3) Job, because he was suffering, had done something wrong in God's eyes. (For more about Eliphaz, see the chart in chapter 28. Teman was a trading city in Edom, noted as a place of wisdom; see Jeremiah 49:7.)

5 "But now it has come to you, and you are impatient;
It touches you, and you are dismayed.
6 "Is not your [2]fear *of God* your confidence,
And the integrity of your ways your hope?

7 "Remember now, who *ever* perished being innocent?
Or where were the upright destroyed?
8 "According to what I have seen, those who plow iniquity
And those who sow trouble harvest it.
9 "By the breath of God they perish,
And by the blast of His anger they come to an end.
10 "The roaring of the lion and the voice of the *fierce* lion,
And the teeth of the young lions are broken.
11 "The lion perishes for lack of prey,
And the whelps of the lioness are scattered.

12 "Now a word was brought to me stealthily,
And my ear received a whisper of it.
13 "Amid disquieting thoughts from the visions of the night,
When deep sleep falls on men,
14 Dread came upon me, and trembling,
And made all my bones shake.
15 "Then a [3]spirit passed by my face;
The hair of my flesh bristled up.
16 "It stood still, but I could not discern its appearance;
A form *was* before my eyes;
There was silence, then I heard a voice:
17 'Can mankind be just before God?
Can a man be pure before his Maker?
18 'He puts no trust even in His servants;
And against His angels He charges error.
19 'How much more those who dwell in houses of clay,
Whose foundation is in the dust,
Who are crushed before the moth!
20 'Between morning and evening they are broken in pieces;
Unobserved, they perish forever.
21 'Is not their tent-cord plucked up within them?
They die, yet without wisdom.'

God Is Just

5 "Call now, is there anyone who will answer you?
And to which of the holy ones will you turn?

4:5 Job 6:14; Job 19:21
4:6 Job 1:1; Prov 3:26
4:7 Job 8:20; 36:6, 7; Ps 37:25
4:8 Job 15:31, 35; Prov 22:8; Hos 10:13; Gal 6:7
4:9 Job 15:30; Is 11:4; 30:33; 2 Thess 2:8; Job 40:11-13
4:10 Job 5:15; Ps 58:6
4:11 Job 29:17; Ps 34:10; Job 5:4; 20:10; 27:14
4:12 Job 4:12-17; 33:15-18; Job 26:14
4:13 Job 33:15
4:17 Job 9:2; 25:4; Job 31:15; 32:22; 35:10; 36:3
4:18 Job 15:15
4:19 Job 10:9; 33:6; Gen 2:7; 3:19; Job 22:16
4:20 Job 14:2; Job 14:20; 20:7
4:21 Job 8:22; Job 18:21; 36:12
5:1 Job 15:15

2 Or *reverence* **3** Or *breath passed over*

4:7–8 Part of what Eliphaz said is true, and part is false. It is true that those who promote sin and trouble eventually will be punished; it is false that anyone who is good and innocent will never suffer.

All the material recorded and quoted in the Bible is there by God's choice. Some is a record of what people said and did but is not an example to follow. The sins, the defeats, the evil thoughts, and misconceptions about God are all part of God's divinely inspired Word, but we should not follow those wrong examples just because they are in the Bible. The Bible gives us teachings and examples of what we *should* do as well as what we *should not* do. Eliphaz's comments are an example of what we should try to avoid—making false assumptions about others based on our own experiences.

4:12–13 Although Eliphaz claimed that his vision was divinely inspired, it is doubtful that it came from God because later God criticized Eliphaz for misrepresenting him (42:7). Whatever the vision's source, it is summarized in 4:17. On the surface, this statement is completely true—a mere mortal cannot compare to God and should not try to question God's motives and actions. Eliphaz, however, took this thought and expounded on it later, expressing his own opinions. His conclusion (5:8) reveals a very shallow understanding of Job and his suffering. It is easy for teachers, counselors, and well-meaning friends to begin with a portion of God's truth but then go off on a tangent. Don't limit God to your perspective and finite understanding of life.

4:18–19 Do angels really make errors? Remember that Eliphaz was speaking, not God, so we must be careful about building our knowledge of the spiritual world from Eliphaz's opinions. In addition, the word translated *error* is used only here, and its meaning is unclear. We could save Eliphaz's credibility by saying he meant fallen angels, but this passage is not meant to teach about angels. Eliphaz was saying that sinful human beings are far beneath God and the angels. Eliphaz was right about God's greatness, but he did not understand God's greater purposes concerning suffering.

5:2 Prov 12:16; 27:3
5:3 Jer 12:2; Job 24:18; 31:30
5:4 Job 4:11
5:5 Job 18:8-10; 22:10
5:6 Job 15:35
5:7 Job 14:1
5:8 Job 13:2, 3; Ps 50:15

2 "For anger slays the foolish man,
And jealousy kills the simple.
3 "I have seen the foolish taking root,
And I cursed his abode immediately.
4 "His sons are far from safety,
They are even [4]oppressed in the gate,
And there is no deliverer.
5 "His harvest the hungry devour
And take it to a *place of* thorns,
And the schemer is eager for their wealth.
6 "For affliction does not come from the dust,
Nor does trouble sprout from the ground,
7 For man is born for trouble,
As sparks fly upward.

8 "But as for me, I would seek God,
And I would place my cause before God;

4 Lit *crushed*

ADVICE FROM FRIENDS

Overwhelmed by suffering, Job was not comforted, but condemned by his friends. Each of their views represents a well-known way to understand suffering. God proves that each explanation given by Job's friends has less than the whole answer.

Who They Were	*Reference*	*How They Helped*	*Their Reasoning*	*Their Advice*	*Job's Response*	*God's Response*
Eliphaz the Temanite	Job 4, 5, 15, 22	They sat in silence with Job for seven days (2:11–13)	Job is suffering because he has sinned.	Go to God and place your cause before him. (5:8)	Desist now; take back your false accusations. (6:29)	God rebukes Job's friends (42:7)
Bildad the Shuhite	Job 8, 18, 25		Job won't admit he sinned, so he's still suffering.	How long will you say these things? (8:2)	"I will say to God . . . 'let me know why You contend with me.' " (10:2)	
Zophar the Naamathite	Job 11—20		Job's sin deserves even more suffering than he's experienced.	Put your sin far away. (11:13–14)	I know that I will be vindicated. (13:18)	
Elihu the Buzite	Job 32—37		God is using suffering to mold and train Job.	Keep silent, and I will teach you wisdom. (33:33)	No response	God does not directly address Elihu.
God	Job 38—41	Confronted Job with the need to be content even though he didn't know why he was suffering	Did not explain the reason for the pain	Do you still want to contend with the Almighty? (40:2)	I have declared that which I did not understand. (42:3–5)	

5:8 All three of Job's friends made the mistake of assuming that Job had committed some great sin that had caused his suffering. Neither they nor Job knew of Satan's conversation with God (1:6—2:8). It is human nature to blame people for their own troubles, but Job's story makes it clear that blame cannot always be attached to those whom trouble strikes.

9 Who does great and unsearchable things,
Wonders without number.
10 "He gives rain on the earth
And sends water on the fields,
11 So that He sets on high those who are lowly,
And those who mourn are lifted to safety.
12 "He frustrates the plotting of the shrewd,
So that their hands cannot attain success.
13 "He captures the wise by their own shrewdness,
And the advice of the cunning is quickly thwarted.
14 "By day they meet with darkness,
And grope at noon as in the night.
15 "But He saves from the sword of their mouth,
And the poor from the hand of the mighty.
16 "So the helpless has hope,
And unrighteousness must shut its mouth.

17 "Behold, how happy is the man whom God reproves,
So do not despise the discipline of the Almighty.
18 "For He inflicts pain, and gives relief;
He wounds, and His hands *also* heal.
19 "From six troubles He will deliver you,
Even in seven evil will not touch you.
20 "In famine He will redeem you from death,
And in war from the power of the sword.
21 "You will be hidden from the scourge of the tongue,
And you will not be afraid of violence when it comes.
22 "You will laugh at violence and famine,
And you will not be afraid of wild beasts.
23 "For you will be in league with the stones of the field,
And the beasts of the field will be at peace with you.
24 "You will know that your tent is secure,
For you will visit your abode and fear no loss.
25 "You will know also that your descendants will be many,
And your offspring as the grass of the earth.
26 "You will come to the grave in full vigor,
Like the stacking of grain in its season.
27 "Behold this; we have investigated it, *and* so it is.
Hear it, and know for yourself."

Job's Friends Are No Help

6 Then Job answered,
2 "Oh that my grief were actually weighed
And laid in the balances together with my calamity!
3 "For then it would be heavier than the sand of the seas;
Therefore my words have been rash.

5:9 Job 9:10; 37:14, 16; 42:3
5:10 Job 36:27-29; 37:6-11; 38:26
5:11 Job 22:29; 36:7
5:12 Ps 33:10
5:13 Job 37:24; 1 Cor 3:19
5:14 Job 12:25; 15:30; 18:18; 20:26; 24:13
5:15 Job 4:10, 11; Ps 35:10; Job 29:17; 34:28; 36:6, 15; 38:15
5:16 Ps 107:42
5:17 Ps 94:12; Job 36:15, 16; Prov 3:11; Heb 12:5-11; James 1:12
5:18 Deut 32:39; 1 Sam 2:6; Is 30:26; Hos 6:1
5:19 Ps 34:19; Ps 91:10
5:20 Ps 33:19; 37:19; Ps 144:10
5:21 Job 5:15; Ps 31:20; Ps 91:5, 6
5:22 Job 8:21; Ps 91:13; Ezek 34:25; Hos 2:18
5:23 Is 11:6-9; 65:25
5:24 Job 8:6
5:25 Ps 112:2; Is 44:3, 4; 48:19
5:26 Job 42:17
6:2 Job 31:6
6:3 Job 23:2

5:13 Paul later quoted part of this verse (1 Corinthians 3:19)—the only time Job is clearly quoted in the New Testament. Although God rebuked Eliphaz for being wrong in his advice to Job (42:7), not all he said was in error. The part Paul quoted was correct—people are often caught in their own traps ("by their own shrewdness"). This illustrates how Scripture must be used to explain and comment on itself. We must be familiar with the entire scope of God's Word to properly understand the difficult portions of it.

5:17 Eliphaz was correct—it is a blessing to be disciplined by God when we do wrong. Eliphaz's advice, however, did not apply to Job. As we know from the beginning of the book, Job's suffering was not a result of some great sin. We sometimes give people excellent advice only to learn that it does not apply to them and is therefore not very helpful. All who offer counsel from God's Word should take care to thoroughly understand a person's situation *before* giving advice.

5:17–26 Eliphaz's words in 5:17–18 show a view of discipline that has been almost forgotten: Pain can help us grow. These are good words to remember when we face hardship and loss. Because Job did not understand why he suffered, his faith in God had a chance to grow. On the other hand, we must not make Eliphaz's mistake. God does not eliminate all hardship when we are following him closely, and good behavior is not always rewarded by prosperity. Rewards for good and punishment for evil are in God's hands and given out according to his timetable. Satan's ploy is to get us to doubt God's goodwill toward us.

6:4 Job 16:13; Ps 38:2; Job 20:16; 21:20; Job 30:15

4 "For the arrows of the Almighty are within me,
Their poison my spirit drinks;
The terrors of God are arrayed against me.

6:5 Job 39:5-8

5 "Does the wild donkey bray over *his* grass,
Or does the ox low over his fodder?
6 "Can something tasteless be eaten without salt,
Or is there any taste in the white of an egg?

6:7 Job 3:24; 33:20

7 "My soul refuses to touch *them;*
They are like loathsome food to me.

8 "Oh that my request might come to pass,
And that God would grant my longing!

6:9 Num 11:15; 1 Kin 19:4; Job 7:16; 9:21; 10:1

9 "Would that God were willing to crush me,
That He would loose His hand and cut me off!
10 "But it is still my consolation,
And I rejoice in unsparing pain,
That I have not denied the words of the Holy One.

6:10 Job 22:22; 23:11, 12

6:11 Job 21:4

11 "What is my strength, that I should wait?
And what is my end, that I should endure?
12 "Is my strength the strength of stones,
Or is my flesh bronze?

6:13 Job 26:2; Job 26:3

13 "Is it that my help is not within me,
And that deliverance is driven from me?

6:14 Job 4:5; Job 1:5; 15:4

14 "For the despairing man *there should be* kindness from his friend;
So that he does not forsake the fear of the Almighty.

6:15 Jer 15:18

15 "My brothers have acted deceitfully like a wadi,
Like the torrents of wadis which vanish,
16 Which are turbid because of ice
And into which the snow melts.

6:17 Job 24:19

17 "When they become waterless, they are silent,
When it is hot, they vanish from their place.
18 "The paths of their course wind along,
They go up into nothing and perish.

6:19 Gen 25:15; Is 21:14; Jer 25:23; Job 1:15

19 "The caravans of Tema looked,
The travelers of Sheba hoped for them.

6:20 Jer 14:3

20 "They were disappointed for they had trusted,
They came there and were confounded.

6:21 Ps 38:11

21 "Indeed, you have now become such,
You see a terror and are afraid.
22 "Have I said, 'Give me *something,*'
Or, 'Offer a bribe for me from your wealth,'
23 Or, 'Deliver me from the hand of the adversary,'
Or, 'Redeem me from the hand of the tyrants'?

6:24 Ps 39:1

24 "Teach me, and I will be silent;
And show me how I have erred.
25 "How painful are honest words!
But what does your argument prove?

6:26 Job 8:2; 15:2; 16:3

26 "Do you intend to reprove *my* words,
When the words of one in despair belong to the wind?

6:6–7 Job said that Eliphaz's advice was like eating the tasteless white of an egg. When people are going through severe trials, ill-advised counsel is distasteful. They may listen politely, but inside they are upset. Be slow to give advice to those who are hurting. They often need compassion more than they need advice.

6:8–9 In his grief, Job wanted to give in, to be freed from his discomfort, and to die. But God did not grant Job's request. He had a greater plan for him. Our tendency, like Job's, is to want to give up and get out when the going gets rough. To trust God in the good times is commendable, but to trust him during the difficult times tests us to our limits and exercises our faith. In your struggles, large or small, trust that God is in control and that he will take care of you (Romans 8:28).

27 "You would even cast *lots* for the orphans
And barter over your friend.
28 "Now please look at me,
And *see* if I lie to your face.
29 "Desist now, let there be no injustice;
Even desist, my righteousness is yet in it.
30 "Is there injustice on my tongue?
Cannot my palate discern calamities?

Job's Life Seems Futile

7 "Is not man forced to labor on earth,
And *are not* his days like the days of a hired man?
2 "As a slave who pants for the shade,
And as a hired man who eagerly waits for his wages,
3 So am I allotted months of vanity,
And nights of trouble are appointed me.
4 "When I lie down I say,
'When shall I arise?'
But the night continues,
And I am continually tossing until dawn.
5 "My flesh is clothed with worms and a crust of dirt,
My skin hardens and runs.
6 "My days are swifter than a weaver's shuttle,
And come to an end without hope.

7 "Remember that my life is *but* breath;
My eye will not again see good.
8 "The eye of him who sees me will behold me no longer;
Your eyes *will be* on me, but I will not be.
9 "When a cloud vanishes, it is gone,
So he who goes down to Sheol does not come up.
10 "He will not return again to his house,
Nor will his place know him anymore.

11 "Therefore I will not restrain my mouth;
I will speak in the anguish of my spirit,
I will complain in the bitterness of my soul.
12 "Am I the sea, or the sea monster,
That You set a guard over me?
13 "If I say, 'My bed will comfort me,
My couch will ease my complaint,'
14 Then You frighten me with dreams
And terrify me by visions;
15 So that my soul would choose suffocation,
Death rather than my pains.
16 "I waste away; I will not live forever.
Leave me alone, for my days are *but* a breath.

6:27 Joel 3:3; Nah 3:10; Job 22:9; 24:3, 9; 2 Pet 2:3
6:28 Job 27:4; 33:3; 36:4
6:29 Job 13:18; 19:6; 23:10; 27:5, 6; 34:5; 42:1-6
6:30 Job 12:11
7:1 Job 5:7; 10:17; 14:1, 14; Job 14:6
7:3 Job 16:7
7:4 Deut 28:67; Job 7:13, 14
7:5 Job 2:7; 17:14
7:6 Job 9:25; Job 13:15; 14:19; 17:15, 16; 19:10
7:7 Job 7:16; Ps 78:39; James 4:14; Job 9:25
7:8 Job 8:18; 20:9; Job 7:21
7:9 Job 30:15; Job 3:13-19; 2 Sam 12:23; Job 11:8; 14:13; 17:13, 16
7:10 Job 8:18; 20:9; 27:21, 23
7:11 Job 10:1; 21:4; 23:2; Ps 40:9
7:12 Ezek 32:2, 3
7:13 Job 7:4; Ps 6:6
7:16 Job 6:9; 9:21; 10:1; Job 7:7

6:29–30 Job referred to his own integrity, not because he was sinless, but because he had a right relationship with God. He was not guilty of the sins his friends accused him of (see chapter 31 for his summary of the life he had led). Another rendering of this verse could read, "My righteousness still stands." *Righteousness* is not the same as *sinlessness* (Romans 3:23). No one but Jesus Christ has ever been sinless—free from all wrong thoughts and actions. Even Job needed to make some changes in his attitude toward God, as we will see by the end of the book. Nevertheless, Job was righteous (1:8). He carefully obeyed God to the best of his ability in all aspects of his life.

7:11 Job felt deep anguish and bitterness, and he spoke honestly to God about his feelings to let out his frustrations. If we express our feelings to God, we can deal with them without exploding in harsh words and actions, possibly hurting ourselves and others. The next time strong emotions threaten to overwhelm you, express them openly to God in prayer. This will help you gain an eternal perspective on the situation and give you greater ability to deal with it constructively.

7:12 Job stopped talking to Eliphaz and spoke directly to God. Although Job had lived a blameless life, he was beginning to doubt the value of living in such a way. By doing this, he was coming dangerously close to suggesting that God didn't care about him and was not being fair. Later God reproved Job for this attitude (38:2). Satan always exploits these thoughts to get us to forsake God. Our suffering, like Job's, may not be the result of our sin, but we must be careful not to sin as a result of our suffering.

7:17 Job 22:2; Ps 8:4; 144:3; Heb 2:6

7:18 Job 14:3

7:19 Job 9:18; 10:20; 14:6

7:20 Job 35:3, 6; Ps 36:6

7:21 Job 9:28; 10:14; Job 10:9; Job 7:8

17 "What is man that You magnify him,
And that You are concerned about him,
18 That You examine him every morning
And try him every moment?
19 "Will You never turn Your gaze away from me,
Nor let me alone until I swallow my spittle?
20 "Have I sinned? What have I done to You,
O watcher of men?
Why have You set me as Your target,
So that I am a burden to myself?
21 "Why then do You not pardon my transgression
And take away my iniquity?
For now I will lie down in the dust;
And You will seek me, but I will not be."

Bildad Says God Rewards the Good

8:2 Job 6:26

8:3 Gen 18:25; Deut 32:4; 2 Chr 19:7; Job 34:10, 12; 36:23; 37:23; Rom 3:5

8:4 Job 1:5, 18, 19

8:5 Job 5:17-27

8:6 Job 22:27; 34:28; Ps 7:6; Job 5:24

8:7 Job 42:12

8:8 Deut 4:32; 32:7; Job 15:18; 20:4

8:9 Job 14:2

8:13 Ps 9:17; Job 11:20; 13:16; 15:34; 20:5; 27:8

8:14 Is 59:5, 6

8:15 Job 8:22; 27:18; Ps 49:11

8 Then Bildad the Shuhite answered,
2 "How long will you say these things,
And the words of your mouth be a mighty wind?
3 "Does God pervert justice?
Or does the Almighty pervert what is right?
4 "If your sons sinned against Him,
Then He delivered them into the power of their transgression.
5 "If you would seek God
And implore the compassion of the Almighty,
6 If you are pure and upright,
Surely now He would rouse Himself for you
And restore your righteous estate.
7 "Though your beginning was insignificant,
Yet your end will increase greatly.

8 "Please inquire of past generations,
And consider the things searched out by their fathers.
9 "For we are *only* of yesterday and know nothing,
Because our days on earth are as a shadow.
10 "Will they not teach you *and* tell you,
And bring forth words from their minds?

11 "Can the papyrus grow up without a marsh?
Can the rushes grow without water?
12 "While it is still green *and* not cut down,
Yet it withers before any *other* plant.
13 "So are the paths of all who forget God;
And the hope of the godless will perish,
14 Whose confidence is fragile,
And whose trust a spider's web.
15 "He trusts in his house, but it does not stand;
He holds fast to it, but it does not endure.

7:20 Job referred to God as a watcher or observer of humanity. He was expressing his feeling that God seemed like an enemy to him—someone who mercilessly watched him squirm in his misery. We know that God does watch over everything that happens to us. We must never forget that he sees us with compassion, not merely with critical scrutiny. His eyes are eyes of love.

8:1ff Bildad was upset that Job still claimed innocence while questioning God's justice. The basis of Bildad's argument (the justice of God) was correct, but his idea of God's justice was not. Bildad's argument went like this: God could not be unjust, and God would not punish a just man; therefore Job must be unjust. Bildad felt there were no exceptions to his theory. Like Eliphaz, Bildad wrongly assumed that people suffer only as a result of their sins. Bildad was even less sensitive and compassionate, saying that Job's children died because of *their* wickedness. (For more information about Bildad, see the chart in chapter 28.)

8:14–15 Bildad wrongly assumed that Job was trusting in something other than God for security, so he pointed out that such supports will collapse. One of man's basic needs is security, and people will do almost anything to feel secure. Eventually, however, our money, possessions, knowledge, and relationships will fail or be gone. Only God can give lasting security. What have you trusted for your security? How lasting is it? If you have a secure foundation with God, feelings of insecurity will not undermine you.

16 "He thrives before the sun,
And his shoots spread out over his garden.
17 "His roots wrap around a rock pile,
He grasps a house of stones.
18 "If he is removed from his place,
Then it will deny him, *saying,* 'I never saw you.'
19 "Behold, this is the joy of His way;
And out of the dust others will spring.
20 "Lo, God will not reject *a man of* integrity,
Nor will He support the evildoers.
21 "He will yet fill your mouth with laughter
And your lips with shouting.
22 "Those who hate you will be clothed with shame,
And the tent of the wicked will be no longer."

Job Says There Is No Arbitrator between God and Man

9 Then Job answered,
2 "In truth I know that this is so;
But how can a man be in the right before God?
3 "If one wished to dispute with Him,
He could not answer Him once in a thousand *times.*
4 "Wise in heart and mighty in strength,
Who has defied Him without harm?
5 "*It is God* who removes the mountains, they know not *how,*
When He overturns them in His anger;
6 Who shakes the earth out of its place,
And its pillars tremble;
7 Who commands the sun not to shine,
And sets a seal upon the stars;
8 Who alone stretches out the heavens
And tramples down the waves of the sea;
9 Who makes the Bear, Orion and the Pleiades,
And the chambers of the south;
10 Who does great things, unfathomable,
And wondrous works without number.
11 "Were He to pass by me, I would not see Him;
Were He to move past *me,* I would not perceive Him.
12 "Were He to snatch away, who could restrain Him?
Who could say to Him, 'What are You doing?'

13 "God will not turn back His anger;
Beneath Him crouch the helpers of Rahab.
14 "How then can I answer Him,
And choose my words before Him?
15 "For though I were right, I could not answer;
I would have to implore the mercy of my judge.
16 "If I called and He answered me,
I could not believe that He was listening to my voice.
17 "For He bruises me with a tempest
And multiplies my wounds without cause.

8:16 Ps 37:35; Jer 11:16; Ps 80:11
8:18 Job 7:10; Job 7:8
8:19 Job 20:5
8:20 Job 4:7; Job 21:30
8:21 Job 5:22; Ps 126:1, 2
8:22 Ps 132:18; Job 8:15; 15:34; 18:14; 21:28
9:2 Job 4:17; 25:4
9:3 Job 10:2; 13:19; 23:6; 40:2
9:4 Job 11:6; 12:13; 28:23; 38:36, 37; Job 9:19; 23:6; 2 Chr 13:12; Prov 29:1
9:5 Job 9:5-10; 26:6-14; 41:11
9:6 Is 2:19, 21; 13:13; Hag 2:6; Ps 75:3
9:7 Is 13:10; Ezek 32:7, 8
9:8 Gen 1:1; Job 37:18; Ps 104:2; Is 40:22; Job 38:16; Ps 77:19
9:9 Job 38:31, 32; Amos 5:8; Job 37:9
9:10 Job 5:9
9:11 Job 23:8, 9; 35:14
9:12 Job 10:7; 11:10; Is 45:9
9:13 Job 26:12; Ps 89:10; Is 30:7; 51:9
9:14 Job 9:3, 32
9:15 Job 9:20, 21; 10:15; Job 8:5
9:17 Job 16:12, 14; 30:22

9:1ff Bildad said nothing new to Job. Job knew that the wicked ultimately perish, but his situation confused him. Why, then, was *he* perishing? Job didn't think his life warranted such suffering, so he wanted his case presented before God (9:32–35). He recognized, however, that arguing with God would be futile and unproductive (9:4). Job didn't claim to be perfect (7:20, 21; 9:20), but he did claim to be good and faithful (6:29–30). While Job showed impatience toward God, he did not reject or curse God.

9:9 The Bear, Orion, and Pleiades are constellations of stars.

9:13 Rahab is the name of a legendary sea monster. According to a Babylonian creation myth, Marduk defeated Tiamat (another name for Rahab), then captured her helpers. Job's friends would have known this myth and understood Job's meaning. God is sovereign over all the forces.

9:18 Job 7:10; 10:20; Job 13:26; 27:2
9:19 Job 9:4
9:20 Job 9:15; Job 9:29; 15:6
9:21 Job 1:1; 12:4; 13:18; Job 7:16
9:22 Job 10:7, 8
9:23 Job 24:12
9:24 Job 10:3; 12:6; 16:11; Job 12:17

18 "He will not allow me to get my breath,
But saturates me with bitterness.
19 "If *it is a matter* of power, behold, *He is* the strong one!
And if *it is a matter* of justice, who can summon Him?
20 "Though I am righteous, my mouth will condemn me;
Though I am guiltless, He will declare me guilty.
21 "I am guiltless;
I do not take notice of myself;
I despise my life.
22 "It is *all* one; therefore I say,
'He destroys the guiltless and the wicked.'
23 "If the scourge kills suddenly,
He mocks the despair of the innocent.
24 "The earth is given into the hand of the wicked;
He covers the faces of its judges.
If *it is* not *He,* then who is it?

9:25 Job 7:6; Job 7:7
9:26 Is 18:2; Job 39:29; Hab 1:8
9:27 Job 7:11
9:28 Job 3:25; Job 7:21; 10:14
9:29 Job 10:2; Ps 37:33
9:30 Jer 2:22; Job 31:7
9:32 Eccl 6:10; Job 9:3; Rom 9:20
9:33 1 Sam 2:25; Job 9:19; Is 1:18
9:34 Job 13:21
9:35 Job 13:22

25 "Now my days are swifter than a runner;
They flee away, they see no good.
26 "They slip by like reed boats,
Like an eagle that swoops on its prey.
27 "Though I say, 'I will forget my complaint,
I will leave off my *sad* countenance and be cheerful,'
28 I am afraid of all my pains,
I know that You will not acquit me.
29 "I am accounted wicked,
Why then should I toil in vain?
30 "If I should wash myself with snow
And cleanse my hands with lye,
31 Yet You would plunge me into the pit,
And my own clothes would abhor me.
32 "For *He is* not a man as I am that I may answer Him,
That we may go to court together.
33 "There is no umpire between us,
Who may lay his hand upon us both.
34 "Let Him remove His rod from me,
And let not dread of Him terrify me.
35 "*Then* I would speak and not fear Him;
But I am not like that in myself.

Job Despairs of God's Dealings

10:1 Job 7:16; Job 7:11
10:2 Job 9:29
10:3 Job 9:22-24; 16:11; 19:6; 27:2; Job 10:8; 14:15; Ps 138:8; Is 64:8; Job 21:16; 22:18
10:4 1 Sam 16:7; Job 28:24; 34:21

10 "I loathe my own life;
I will give full vent to my complaint;
I will speak in the bitterness of my soul.
2 "I will say to God, 'Do not condemn me;
Let me know why You contend with me.
3 'Is it right for You indeed to oppress,
To reject the labor of Your hands,
And to look favorably on the schemes of the wicked?
4 'Have You eyes of flesh?
Or do You see as a man sees?

9:20–21 "Though I am righteous, my mouth will condemn me." Job was saying, "In spite of my good life, God is determined to condemn me." As his suffering continued, he became more impatient. Although Job remained loyal to God, he made statements he would later regret. In times of extended sickness or prolonged pain, it is natural for people to doubt, to despair, or to become impatient. During those times, people need someone to listen to them, to help them work through their feelings and frustrations. Your patience with their impatience will help them.

10:1 Job began to wallow in self-pity. When we face baffling affliction, our pain lures us toward feeling sorry for ourselves. At this point we are only one step from self-righteousness, where we keep track of life's injustices and say, "Look what happened to me; how unfair it is!" We may feel like blaming God. Remember that life's trials, whether allowed by God or sent by God, can be the means for development and refinement. When facing trials, ask, "What can I learn and how can I grow?" rather than "Who did this to me and how can I get out of it?"

5 'Are Your days as the days of a mortal,
Or Your years as man's years,
6 That You should seek for my guilt
And search after my sin?
7 'According to Your knowledge I am indeed not guilty,
Yet there is no deliverance from Your hand.

8 'Your hands fashioned and made me altogether,
And would You destroy me?
9 'Remember now, that You have made me as clay;
And would You turn me into dust again?
10 'Did You not pour me out like milk
And curdle me like cheese;
11 Clothe me with skin and flesh,
And knit me together with bones and sinews?
12 'You have granted me life and lovingkindness;
And Your care has preserved my spirit.
13 'Yet these things You have concealed in Your heart;
I know that this is within You:
14 If I sin, then You would take note of me,
And would not acquit me of my guilt.
15 'If I am wicked, woe to me!
And if I am righteous, I dare not lift up my head.
I am sated with disgrace and conscious of my misery.
16 'Should *my head* be lifted up, You would hunt me like a lion;
And again You would show Your power against me.
17 'You renew Your witnesses against me
And increase Your anger toward me;
Hardship after hardship is with me.

18 'Why then have You brought me out of the womb?
Would that I had died and no eye had seen me!
19 'I should have been as though I had not been,
Carried from womb to tomb.'
20 "Would He not let my few days alone?
Withdraw from me that I may have a little cheer
21 Before I go—and I shall not return—
To the land of darkness and deep shadow,
22 The land of utter gloom as darkness *itself,*
Of deep shadow without order,
And which shines as the darkness."

10:5 Job 36:26
10:6 Job 14:16
10:7 Job 9:21; 13:18; Job 9:12; 23:13; 27:22
10:8 Job 10:3; Ps 119:73; Job 9:22
10:9 Job 4:19; 33:6; Job 7:21
10:12 Job 33:4
10:13 Job 23:13
10:14 Job 7:20; Job 7:21; 9:28
10:15 Job 10:7; Is 3:11; Job 6:29
10:16 Is 38:13; Lam 3:10; Hos 13:7; Job 5:9
10:17 Ruth 1:21; Job 16:8; Job 7:1
10:18 Job 3:11-13
10:20 Job 14:1; Job 7:16, 19
10:21 2 Sam 12:23; Job 3:13-19; 16:22; Ps 88:12; Job 10:22; 34:22; 38:17; Ps 23:4

Zophar Rebukes Job

11 Then Zophar the Naamathite answered,
2 "Shall a multitude of words go unanswered,
And a talkative man be acquitted?
3 "Shall your boasts silence men?
And shall you scoff and none rebuke?

11:2 Job 8:2; 15:2; 18:2
11:3 Job 17:2; 21:3

10:13–14 In frustration, Job jumped to the false conclusion that God was out to get him. Wrong assumptions lead to wrong conclusions. We dare not take our limited experiences and jump to conclusions about life in general. If you find yourself doubting God, remember that you don't have all the facts. God wants only the very best for your life. Many people endure great pain, but ultimately they find some greater good came from it. When you're struggling, don't assume the worst.

10:20–22 Job was expressing the view of death common in Old Testament times, that the dead went to a joyless, dark place. There was no punishment or reward there, and no escape from it. (See the note on 19:26 for a broader picture of Job's view of death.)

11:1ff Zophar is the third of Job's friends to speak, and the least courteous. Full of anger, he lashed out at Job, saying that Job deserved more punishment, not less. Zophar took the same position as Eliphaz (chapters 4–5) and Bildad (chapter 8)—that Job was suffering because of sin—but his speech was by far the most arrogant. Zophar was the kind of person who has an answer for everything; he was totally insensitive to Job's unique situation. (For more on Zophar, see the chart in chapter 28.)

11:4 Job 6:10; Job 10:7

4 "For you have said, 'My teaching is pure,
And I am innocent in your eyes.'
5 "But would that God might speak,
And open His lips against you,

11:6 Job 9:4; Job 15:5; 22:5

6 And show you the secrets of wisdom!
For sound wisdom has two sides.
Know then that God forgets a part of your iniquity.

11:7 Job 33:12, 13; 36:26; 37:5, 23; Rom 11:33

7 "Can you discover the depths of God?
Can you discover the limits of the Almighty?
8 "*They are* high as the heavens, what can you do?

11:8 Job 22:12; 35:5; Job 26:6; 38:17

Deeper than Sheol, what can you know?
9 "Its measure is longer than the earth
And broader than the sea.

11:10 Job 9:12

10 "If He passes by or shuts up,
Or calls an assembly, who can restrain Him?

11:11 Job 34:21-23; Job 24:23; 28:24; 31:4

11 "For He knows false men,
And He sees iniquity without investigating.
12 "An idiot will become intelligent

11:12 Ps 39:5, 11; 62:9; 144:4; Eccl 1:2; 11:10; Job 39:5

When the foal of a wild donkey is born a man.

11:13 Job 5:17-27; 11:13-20; 1 Sam 7:3; Ps 78:8; Job 22:27; Ps 88:9; 143:6

13 "If you would direct your heart right
And spread out your hand to Him,
14 If iniquity is in your hand, put it far away,
And do not let wickedness dwell in your tents;

11:14 Job 22:23

15 "Then, indeed, you could lift up your face without *moral* defect,
And you would be steadfast and not fear.

11:15 Job 22:26; Ps 27:3; 46:2

16 "For you would forget *your* trouble,
As waters that have passed by, you would remember *it.*
17 "Your life would be brighter than noonday;

11:16 Is 65:16; Job 22:11

Darkness would be like the morning.
18 "Then you would trust, because there is hope;

11:17 Job 22:26

And you would look around and rest securely.
19 "You would lie down and none would disturb *you,*

11:19 Lev 26:6; Is 17:2; Mic 4:4; Zeph 3:13; Is 45:14

And many would entreat your favor.
20 "But the eyes of the wicked will fail,
And there will be no escape for them;

11:20 Deut 28:65; Job 17:5; Job 27:22; 34:22; Job 8:13; Job 6:9

And their hope is to breathe their last."

Job Chides His Accusers

12 Then Job responded,
2 "Truly then you are the people,

12:2 Job 17:10

And with you wisdom will die!

12:3 Job 13:2

3 "But I have intelligence as well as you;
I am not inferior to you.
And who does not know such things as these?

12:4 Job 17:6; 30:1, 9, 10; 34:7; Job 6:29

4 "I am a joke to my friends,
The one who called on God and He answered him;
The just *and* blameless *man* is a joke.
5 "He who is at ease holds calamity in contempt,
As prepared for those whose feet slip.

11:11 By calling Job "false," Zophar was accusing Job of hiding secret faults and sins. Although Zophar's assumption was wrong, he explained quite accurately that God knows and sees everything. We are often tempted by the thought, "No one will ever know!" Perhaps we can hide some sin from others, but we can do *nothing* without God knowing about it. Because our very thoughts are known to God, of course he will notice our sins. Job understood this as well as Zophar did, but it didn't apply to his current dilemma.

12:1ff Job answered Zophar's argument with great sarcasm: "With you wisdom will die!" He went on to say that his three friends didn't need to explain God to him—they were saying nothing he didn't already know (12:7–9; 13:1–2). Job continued to maintain that his friends had completely misunderstood the reason for his suffering. Job did not know it either, but he was certain that his friends' reasons were both narrow-minded and incorrect. Once again Job appealed to God to give him an answer (13:3).

6 "The tents of the destroyers prosper,
And those who provoke God are secure,
Whom God brings into their power.

7 "But now ask the beasts, and let them teach you;
And the birds of the heavens, and let them tell you.
8 "Or speak to the earth, and let it teach you;
And let the fish of the sea declare to you.
9 "Who among all these does not know
That the hand of the LORD has done this,
10 In whose hand is the life of every living thing,
And the breath of all mankind?
11 "Does not the ear test words,
As the palate tastes its food?
12 "Wisdom is with aged men,
With long life is understanding.

Job Speaks of the Power of God

13 "With Him are wisdom and might;
To Him belong counsel and understanding.
14 "Behold, He tears down, and it cannot be rebuilt;
He imprisons a man, and there can be no release.
15 "Behold, He restrains the waters, and they dry up;
And He sends them out, and they inundate the earth.
16 "With Him are strength and sound wisdom,
The misled and the misleader belong to Him.
17 "He makes counselors walk barefoot
And makes fools of judges.
18 "He loosens the bond of kings
And binds their loins with a girdle.
19 "He makes priests walk barefoot
And overthrows the secure ones.
20 "He deprives the trusted ones of speech
And takes away the discernment of the elders.
21 "He pours contempt on nobles
And loosens the belt of the strong.
22 "He reveals mysteries from the darkness
And brings the deep darkness into light.
23 "He makes the nations great, then destroys them;
He enlarges the nations, then leads them away.
24 "He deprives of intelligence the chiefs of the earth's people
And makes them wander in a pathless waste.
25 "They grope in darkness with no light,
And He makes them stagger like a drunken man.

Job Says His Friends' Proverbs Are Ashes

13 "Behold, my eye has seen all *this,*
My ear has heard and understood it.
2 "What you know I also know;
I am not inferior to you.

3 "But I would speak to the Almighty,
And I desire to argue with God.

12:6 Job 9:24; 21:7-9; Job 24:23; Job 22:18
12:9 Is 41:20
12:10 Acts 17:28; Job 27:3; 33:4
12:11 Job 34:3
12:12 Job 15:10; 32:7
12:13 Job 9:4; Job 11:6; 26:12; 32:8; 36:5; 38:36
12:14 Job 19:10; Is 25:2; Job 37:7
12:15 Deut 11:17; 1 Kin 8:35; 17:1; Gen 7:11-24
12:16 Job 13:7, 9
12:17 Job 3:14; Job 9:24
12:18 Ps 116:16
12:19 Job 24:22; 34:24-28; 35:9
12:20 Job 17:4; 32:9
12:21 Job 34:19; Ps 107:40; Job 12:18
12:22 Dan 2:22; 1 Cor 4:5
12:23 Is 9:3; 26:15
12:24 Job 12:20
12:25 Job 5:14; Is 24:20
13:1 Job 12:9
13:2 Job 12:3
13:3 Job 13:22; 23:4; Job 13:15

12:24–25 Job affirmed that no leader has any real wisdom apart from God. No research or report can outweigh God's opinion. No scientific discovery or medical advance takes him by surprise. When we look for guidance for our decisions, we must recognize that God's wisdom is superior to any the world has to offer. Don't let earthly advisers dampen your desire to know God better.

13:4 Ps 119:69; Jer 23:32
13:5 Job 13:13; 21:5; Prov 17:28
13:7 Job 27:4
13:8 Lev 19:15; Prov 24:23
13:9 Job 12:16
13:10 Job 13:8; 32:21; 34:19
13:11 Job 31:23

4 "But you smear with lies;
You are all worthless physicians.
5 "O that you would be completely silent,
And that it would become your wisdom!
6 "Please hear my argument
And listen to the contentions of my lips.
7 "Will you speak what is unjust for God,
And speak what is deceitful for Him?
8 "Will you show partiality for Him?
Will you contend for God?
9 "Will it be well when He examines you?
Or will you deceive Him as one deceives a man?
10 "He will surely reprove you
If you secretly show partiality.
11 "Will not His majesty terrify you,
And the dread of Him fall on you?
12 "Your memorable sayings are proverbs of ashes,
Your defenses are defenses of clay.

Job Is Sure He Will Be Vindicated

13:13 Job 13:5
13:14 Ps 119:109
13:15 Job 7:6; Job 27:5
13:16 Job 23:7; Is 12:1, 2; Job 34:21-23
13:18 Job 23:4; Job 9:21; 10:7; 12:4
13:19 Is 50:8; Job 7:21; 10:8

13 "Be silent before me so that I may speak;
Then let come on me what may.
14 "Why should I take my flesh in my teeth
And put my life in my hands?
15 "Though He slay me,
I will hope in Him.
Nevertheless I will argue my ways before Him.
16 "This also will be my salvation,
For a godless man may not come before His presence.
17 "Listen carefully to my speech,
And let my declaration *fill* your ears.
18 "Behold now, I have prepared my case;
I know that I will be vindicated.
19 "Who will contend with me?
For then I would be silent and die.

13:21 Job 9:34; Ps 39:10
13:22 Job 9:16; 14:15
13:23 Job 7:21
13:24 Ps 13:1; 44:24; 88:14; Is 8:17; Job 19:11; 33:10; Lam 2:5
13:25 Lev 26:36; Job 21:18
13:26 Job 9:18; Ps 25:7
13:27 Job 33:11

20 "Only two things do not do to me,
Then I will not hide from Your face:
21 Remove Your hand from me,
And let not the dread of You terrify me.
22 "Then call, and I will answer;
Or let me speak, then reply to me.
23 "How many are my iniquities and sins?
Make known to me my rebellion and my sin.
24 "Why do You hide Your face
And consider me Your enemy?
25 "Will You cause a driven leaf to tremble?
Or will You pursue the dry chaff?
26 "For You write bitter things against me
And make me to inherit the iniquities of my youth.
27 "You put my feet in the stocks
And watch all my paths;
You set a limit for the soles of my feet,

13:4 Job compared his three friends to physicians who did not know what they were doing. They were like eye surgeons trying to perform open-heart surgery. Many of their ideas about God were true, but they did not apply to Job's situation. They were right to say that God is just. They were right to say God punishes sin. But they were wrong to assume that Job's suffering was a just punishment for his sin. They took a true principle and applied it wrongly, ignoring the vast differences in human circumstances. We must be careful and compassionate in how we apply Biblical condemnations to others; we must be slow to judge.

28 While I am decaying like a rotten thing,
Like a garment that is moth-eaten.

13:28
Job 2:7

Job Speaks of the Finality of Death

14 "Man, who is born of woman,
Is short-lived and full of turmoil.
2 "Like a flower he comes forth and withers.
He also flees like a shadow and does not remain.
3 "You also open Your eyes on him
And bring him into judgment with Yourself.
4 "Who can make the clean out of the unclean?
No one!
5 "Since his days are determined,
The number of his months is with You;
And his limits You have set so that he cannot pass.
6 "Turn Your gaze from him that he may rest,
Until he fulfills his day like a hired man.

7 "For there is hope for a tree,
When it is cut down, that it will sprout again,
And its shoots will not fail.
8 "Though its roots grow old in the ground
And its stump dies in the dry soil,
9 At the scent of water it will flourish
And put forth sprigs like a plant.
10 "But man dies and lies prostrate.
Man expires, and where is he?
11 "*As* water evaporates from the sea,
And a river becomes parched and dried up,
12 So man lies down and does not rise.
Until the heavens are no longer,
He will not awake nor be aroused out of his sleep.

13 "Oh that You would hide me in Sheol,
That You would conceal me until Your wrath returns *to You,*
That You would set a limit for me and remember me!
14 "If a man dies, will he live *again?*
All the days of my struggle I will wait
Until my change comes.
15 "You will call, and I will answer You;
You will long for the work of Your hands.
16 "For now You number my steps,
You do not observe my sin.
17 "My transgression is sealed up in a bag,
And You wrap up my iniquity.

18 "But the falling mountain crumbles away,
And the rock moves from its place;

14:1
Job 5:7; Eccl 2:23

14:2
Ps 90:5, 6; 103:15; Is 40:6, 7; James 1:10; 1 Pet 1:24; Job 8:9

14:3
Ps 8:4; 144:3; Ps 143:2

14:4
Job 15:14; 25:4; Ps 51:5

14:5
Job 21:21

14:6
Job 7:19; Ps 39:13

14:10
Job 3:13; 14:10-15; Job 13:9

14:11
Is 19:5

14:12
Job 3:13

14:13
Is 26:20

14:15
Job 10:3

14:16
Job 31:4; 34:21; Ps 139:1-3; Prov 5:21; Job 10:6

14:17
Deut 32:32-34

14:1ff Life is brief and full of trouble, Job laments in his closing remarks. Sickness, loneliness, disappointment, and death cause Job to say that life is not fair. Some understand verses 14 and 15 to mean that, even in his gloom, Job hoped for the resurrection of the dead. If this is true, then Job understood the one truth that could put his suffering in perspective. God's solution to believers who live in an unfair world is to guarantee life with him forever. No matter how unfair your present world seems, God offers the hope of being in his presence eternally. Have you accepted this offer?

14:7–22 The Old Testament does not say much about the resurrection of the dead. This is not surprising because Jesus had not yet conquered death. Job's pessimism about death is understandable. What is remarkable is his budding hope (14:14). If only God would hide him with the dead and then bring him out again! If only he could die and live again! When we must endure suffering, we have an advantage over Job. We *know* that the dead will rise. Christ arose, and we have hope based on Christ's promise in John 14:19.

14:19 Job 7:6

19 Water wears away stones,
Its torrents wash away the dust of the earth;
So You destroy man's hope.

14:20 Job 4:20; 20:7

20 "You forever overpower him and he departs;
You change his appearance and send him away.

14:21 Eccl 9:5

21 "His sons achieve honor, but he does not know *it;*
Or they become insignificant, but he does not perceive it.
22 "But his body pains him,
And he mourns only for himself."

2. Second round of discussion

Eliphaz Says Job Presumes Much

15:2 Job 6:26

15 Then Eliphaz the Temanite responded,
2 "Should a wise man answer with windy knowledge
And fill himself with the east wind?
3 "Should he argue with useless talk,
Or with words which are not profitable?
4 "Indeed, you do away with reverence
And hinder meditation before God.

15:5 Job 22:5; Job 5:12, 13

5 "For your guilt teaches your mouth,
And you choose the language of the crafty.

15:6 Job 18:7

6 "Your own mouth condemns you, and not I;
And your own lips testify against you.

15:7 Job 38:4, 21; Prov 8:25

7 "Were you the first man to be born,
Or were you brought forth before the hills?

15:8 Job 29:4; Rom 11:34; 1 Cor 2:11

8 "Do you hear the secret counsel of God,
And limit wisdom to yourself?

15:9 Job 12:3; 13:2

9 "What do you know that we do not know?
What do you understand that we do not?

15:10 Job 12:12; 32:6, 7

10 "Both the gray-haired and the aged are among us,
Older than your father.

15:11 Job 5:17-19; 36:15, 16; Job 6:10; 23:12

11 "Are the consolations of God too small for you,
Even the word *spoken* gently with you?
12 "Why does your heart carry you away?

15:12 Job 11:13; 36:13

And why do your eyes flash,
13 That you should turn your spirit against God
And allow *such* words to go out of your mouth?

15:14 Job 14:4; Prov 20:9; Eccl 7:20; Job 25:4

14 "What is man, that he should be pure,
Or he who is born of a woman, that he should be righteous?

15:15 Job 5:1; Job 25:5

15 "Behold, He puts no trust in His holy ones,
And the heavens are not pure in His sight;

15:16 Ps 14:1; Job 34:7; Prov 19:28

16 How much less one who is detestable and corrupt,
Man, who drinks iniquity like water!

What Eliphaz Has Seen of Life

17 "I will tell you, listen to me;
And what I have seen I will also declare;

14:22 Job's profound speech in this chapter illustrates a great truth: To have a right set of doctrines is not enough. To know what to believe is not all that is required to please God. Truth untested by life's experiences may become static and stagnant. Suffering can bring a dynamic quality to life. Just as drought drives the roots of a tree deeper to find water, so suffering can drive us beyond superficial acceptance of truth to dependence on God for hope and life.

15:1ff With the first round of talks concluded, each friend, in the same order, pressed the argument further. Again Job answered each argument (chapters 15—31). This time Eliphaz was more rude, more intense, and more threatening, but he said nothing new. (See his first speech in chapters 4—5.) He began by saying that Job's words were empty and useless; then he restated his opinion that Job must be a great sinner. According to Eliphaz, the experience and wisdom of their ancestors were more valuable than Job's individual thoughts. Eliphaz assumed that his words were as true as God's. It is easy to spot his arrogance.

15:15–16 "The heavens are not pure in His sight." Eliphaz was repeating his argument that anything created, whether angels (holy ones) or man, is not a sufficient basis for trust and hope. Only in God can we be sure. (See the note on 4:18–19.)

18 What wise men have told,
And have not concealed from their fathers,
19 To whom alone the land was given,
And no alien passed among them.
20 "The wicked man writhes in pain all *his* days,
And numbered are the years stored up for the ruthless.
21 "Sounds of terror are in his ears;
While at peace the destroyer comes upon him.
22 "He does not believe that he will return from darkness,
And he is destined for the sword.
23 "He wanders about for food, saying, 'Where is it?'
He knows that a day of darkness is at hand.
24 "Distress and anguish terrify him,
They overpower him like a king ready for the attack,
25 Because he has stretched out his hand against God
And conducts himself arrogantly against the Almighty.
26 "He rushes headlong at Him
With his massive shield.
27 "For he has covered his face with his fat
And made his thighs heavy with flesh.
28 "He has lived in desolate cities,
In houses no one would inhabit,
Which are destined to become ruins.
29 "He will not become rich, nor will his wealth endure;
And his grain will not bend down to the ground.
30 "He will not escape from darkness;
The flame will wither his shoots,
And by the breath of His mouth he will go away.
31 "Let him not trust in emptiness, deceiving himself;
For emptiness will be his reward.
32 "It will be accomplished before his time,
And his palm branch will not be green.
33 "He will drop off his unripe grape like the vine,
And will cast off his flower like the olive tree.
34 "For the company of the godless is barren,
And fire consumes the tents of the corrupt.
35 "They conceive mischief and bring forth iniquity,
And their mind prepares deception."

15:18 Job 8:8; 20:4
15:20 Job 15:24; Job 24:1; 27:13
15:21 Job 15:24; 18:11; 20:25; 24:17; 27:20; Job 20:21; 1 Thess 5:3
15:22 Job 15:30; Job 19:29; 27:14; 33:18; 36:12
15:23 Job 15:22, 30
15:25 Job 36:9
15:27 Ps 73:7; 119:70
15:28 Job 3:14; Is 5:8, 9
15:29 Job 27:16, 17
15:30 Job 5:14; 15:22; Job 15:34; 20:26; 22:20; 31:12; Job 4:9
15:31 Job 35:13; Is 59:4
15:32 Job 22:16; Eccl 7:17; Job 18:16
15:33 Job 14:2
15:34 Job 8:13; Job 8:22
15:35 Ps 7:14; Is 59:4

Job Says Friends Are Sorry Comforters

16 Then Job answered,
2 "I have heard many such things;
Sorry comforters are you all.
3 "Is there *no* limit to windy words?
Or what plagues you that you answer?
4 "I too could speak like you,
If I were in your place.
I could compose words against you
And shake my head at you.
5 "I could strengthen you with my mouth,
And the solace of my lips could lessen *your pain.*

16:2 Job 13:4; 21:34
16:3 Job 6:26
16:4 Ps 22:7; 109:25; Zeph 2:15; Matt 27:39

Job Says God Shattered Him

6 "If I speak, my pain is not lessened,
And if I hold back, what has left me?

16:6 Job 9:27, 28

16:1ff Job's friends were supposed to be comforting him in his grief. Instead they condemned him for causing his own suffering. Job began his reply to Eliphaz by calling him and his friends "sorry comforters." Job's words reveal several ways to become a better comforter to those in pain: (1) Don't talk just for the sake of talking; (2) don't sermonize by giving pat answers; (3) don't accuse or criticize; (4) put yourself in the other person's place; and (5) offer help and encouragement. Try Job's suggestions, knowing that they are given by a person who needed great comfort. The best comforters are those who know something about personal suffering.

7 "But now He has exhausted me;
You have laid waste all my company.
8 "You have shriveled me up,
It has become a witness;
And my leanness rises up against me,
It testifies to my face.
9 "His anger has torn me and hunted me down,
He has gnashed at me with His teeth;
My adversary glares at me.
10 "They have gaped at me with their mouth,
They have slapped me on the cheek with contempt;
They have massed themselves against me.
11 "God hands me over to ruffians
And tosses me into the hands of the wicked.
12 "I was at ease, but He shattered me,
And He has grasped me by the neck and shaken me to pieces;
He has also set me up as His target.
13 "His arrows surround me.
Without mercy He splits my kidneys open;
He pours out my gall on the ground.
14 "He breaks through me with breach after breach;
He runs at me like a warrior.
15 "I have sewed sackcloth over my skin
And thrust my horn in the dust.
16 "My face is flushed from weeping,
And deep darkness is on my eyelids,
17 Although there is no violence in my hands,
And my prayer is pure.

18 "O earth, do not cover my blood,
And let there be no *resting* place for my cry.
19 "Even now, behold, my witness is in heaven,
And my advocate is on high.
20 "My friends are my scoffers;
My eye weeps to God.
21 "O that a man might plead with God
As a man with his neighbor!
22 "For when a few years are past,
I shall go the way of no return.

Job Says He Has Become a Byword

17 "My spirit is broken, my days are extinguished,
The grave is *ready* for me.
2 "Surely mockers are with me,
And my eye gazes on their provocation.

3 "Lay down, now, a pledge for me with Yourself;
Who is there that will be my guarantor?
4 "For You have kept their heart from understanding,
Therefore You will not exalt *them.*
5 "He who informs against friends for a share *of the spoil,*
The eyes of his children also will languish.

6 "But He has made me a byword of the people,
And I am one at whom men spit.

16:7 Job 7:3; Job 16:20; 19:13-15
16:8 Job 10:17; Job 19:20; Ps 109:24
16:9 Job 19:11; Hos 6:1; Ps 35:16; Lam 2:16; Acts 7:54; Job 13:24; 33:10
16:10 Ps 22:13; Is 50:6; Lam 3:30; Acts 23:2; Job 30:12; Ps 35:15
16:12 Job 9:17; Job 7:20; Lam 3:12
16:13 Job 6:4; 19:12; 25:3; Job 20:25
16:14 Job 9:17; Joel 2:7
16:15 Gen 37:34; Ps 69:11; Ps 7:5
16:16 Job 16:20; Job 24:17
16:17 Is 59:6; Jon 3:8; Job 27:4
16:19 Gen 31:50; Job 19:25-27; Rom 1:9; Phil 1:8; 1 Thess 2:5; Job 31:2
16:20 Job 17:7
16:22 Job 3:13
17:1 Ps 88:3, 4
17:2 Job 12:4; 17:6
17:3 Ps 119:122; Is 38:14
17:4 Job 12:20
17:5 Lev 19:13, 16; Job 11:20
17:6 Job 17:2; Job 30:10

16:19 Job was afraid that God had abandoned him. Yet he appealed directly to God (his witness and advocate) and to God's knowledge of his innocence. A *witness* is someone who has seen what has happened, and an *advocate* is like a lawyer who speaks on behalf of the plaintiff. By using these terms, Job showed he had cast all his hope for any fair defense upon God in heaven because he would probably die before it happened on earth. In the New Testament we learn that Jesus Christ intercedes on our behalf (Hebrews 7:25; 1 John 2:1); therefore, we have nothing to fear.

7 "My eye has also grown dim because of grief,
And all my members are as a shadow.
8 "The upright will be appalled at this,
And the innocent will stir up himself against the godless.
9 "Nevertheless the righteous will hold to his way,
And he who has clean hands will grow stronger and stronger.
10 "But come again all of you now,
For I do not find a wise man among you.
11 "My days are past, my plans are torn apart,
Even the wishes of my heart.
12 "They make night into day, *saying,*
'The light is near,' in the presence of darkness.
13 "If I look for Sheol as my home,
I make my bed in the darkness;
14 If I call to the pit, 'You are my father';
To the worm, 'my mother and my sister';
15 Where now is my hope?
And who regards my hope?
16 "Will it go down with me to Sheol?
Shall we together go down into the dust?"

Bildad Speaks of the Wicked

18 Then Bildad the Shuhite responded,
2 "How long will you hunt for words?
Show understanding and then we can talk.
3 "Why are we regarded as beasts,
As stupid in your eyes?
4 "O you who tear yourself in your anger—
For your sake is the earth to be abandoned,
Or the rock to be moved from its place?

5 "Indeed, the light of the wicked goes out,
And the flame of his fire gives no light.
6 "The light in his tent is darkened,
And his lamp goes out above him.
7 "His vigorous stride is shortened,
And his own scheme brings him down.
8 "For he is thrown into the net by his own feet,
And he steps on the webbing.
9 "A snare seizes *him* by the heel,
And a trap snaps shut on him.
10 "A noose for him is hidden in the ground,
And a trap for him on the path.
11 "All around terrors frighten him,
And harry him at every step.
12 "His strength is famished,
And calamity is ready at his side.

17:7 Job 16:16; Job 16:8
17:8 Job 22:19
17:9 Prov 4:18; Job 22:30; 31:7
17:10 Job 12:2
17:11 Job 7:6
17:13 Job 3:13
17:14 Job 7:5; 13:28; 30:30; Job 21:26; 25:6
17:15 Job 7:6
17:16 Job 3:17; 21:33
18:3 Ps 73:22
18:5 Job 21:17; Prov 13:9; 20:20; 24:20
18:6 Job 12:25
18:7 Job 15:6
18:8 Job 22:10; Ps 9:15; 35:8; Is 24:17, 18
18:11 Job 15:21; Job 18:18; 20:8
18:12 Is 8:21

17:10 Job's three friends had a reputation for being wise, but Job could not find wisdom in any of them. God backed up Job's claim in 42:7, when he condemned these men for their false portrayal of him. Obviously these men had a faulty view of wisdom. They assumed that because they were prosperous and successful, God must be pleased with the way they were living and thinking. Job, however, told his friends that they were starting with the wrong idea because earthly success and prosperity are not proof of faith in God. Likewise, trouble and affliction do not prove faithlessness. The truly wise man knows that wisdom comes from God alone, not from human successes or failures. And the truly wise man never forsakes God. God's wisdom proved superior to Job and to all his friends.

17:15 Job was giving up hope of any future restoration of wealth and family and wrapping himself in thoughts of death and the rest from grief and pain it promised. The rewards that Job's friends described were all related to this present life. They were silent about the possibility of life after death. We must not evaluate life only in terms of this present world because God promises a never-ending, wonderful future to those who are faithful to him.

18:1ff Bildad thought he knew how the universe should be run, and he saw Job as an illustration of the consequences of sin. Bildad rejected Job's side of the story because it did not fit in with his outlook on life. It is easy to condemn Bildad because his errors are obvious; unfortunately, however, we often act the same way when our ideas are threatened.

18:13 Zech 14:12

18:14 Job 8:22; 18:6; Job 15:21

18:15 Ps 11:6

18:16 Is 5:24; Hos 9:16; Amos 2:9; Mal 4:1; Job 15:30, 32

18:17 Job 24:20; Ps 34:16; Prov 10:7

18:18 Job 5:14; Is 8:22; Job 20:8; 27:21-23

18:19 Job 27:14, 15; Is 14:22

18:20 Ps 37:13; Jer 50:27; Obad 12

18:21 Job 21:28

13 "His skin is devoured by disease,
The firstborn of death devours his limbs.
14 "He is torn from the security of his tent,
And they march him before the king of terrors.
15 "There dwells in his tent nothing of his;
Brimstone is scattered on his habitation.
16 "His roots are dried below,
And his branch is cut off above.
17 "Memory of him perishes from the earth,
And he has no name abroad.
18 "He is driven from light into darkness,
And chased from the inhabited world.
19 "He has no offspring or posterity among his people,
Nor any survivor where he sojourned.
20 "Those in the west are appalled at his fate,
And those in the east are seized with horror.
21 "Surely such are the dwellings of the wicked,
And this is the place of him who does not know God."

Job Feels Insulted

19 Then Job responded,
2 "How long will you torment me
And crush me with words?
3 "These ten times you have insulted me;
You are not ashamed to wrong me.
4 "Even if I have truly erred,
My error lodges with me.
5 "If indeed you vaunt yourselves against me
And prove my disgrace to me,
6 Know then that God has wronged me
And has closed His net around me.

19:5 Ps 35:26; 38:16; 55:12, 13

19:6 Job 16:11; 27:2; Job 18:8-10; Ps 66:11; Lam 1:13

Everything Is against Him

7 "Behold, I cry, 'Violence!' but I get no answer;
I shout for help, but there is no justice.
8 "He has walled up my way so that I cannot pass,
And He has put darkness on my paths.
9 "He has stripped my honor from me
And removed the crown from my head.
10 "He breaks me down on every side, and I am gone;
And He has uprooted my hope like a tree.
11 "He has also kindled His anger against me
And considered me as His enemy.
12 "His troops come together,
And build up their way against me
And camp around my tent.

13 "He has removed my brothers far from me,
And my acquaintances are completely estranged from me.

19:7 Job 9:24; 30:20, 24; Hab 1:2

19:8 Job 3:23; Lam 3:7, 9; Job 30:26

19:9 Job 12:17, 19; Ps 89:44; Job 16:15; Ps 89:39; Lam 5:16

19:10 Job 12:14; Job 7:6; Job 24:20

19:11 Job 16:9; Job 13:24; 33:10

19:12 Job 16:13; Job 30:12

19:13 Job 16:7; Ps 69:8; Job 16:20; Ps 88:8, 18

18:14 The "king of terrors" is a figure of speech referring to death. Bildad viewed death as a great devourer (18:13), but the Bible teaches that God has the power to devour even death (Psalm 49:15; Isaiah 25:8; 1 Corinthians 15:54–56).

19:3–5 It is easy to point out someone else's faults or sins. Job's friends accused him of sin to make him feel guilty, not to encourage or correct him. If we feel we must admonish someone, we should be sure we are confronting that person because we love him, not because we are annoyed, inconvenienced, or seeking to blame him.

19:6 Job felt that God was treating him as an enemy when, in fact, God was his friend and thought highly of him (1:8; 2:3). In his difficulty, Job pointed at the wrong person. It was Satan, not God, who was Job's enemy. Because they stressed ultimate causes, most Israelites believed that both good and evil came from God; they also thought people were responsible for their own destinies. But the evil power loose in this world accounts for much of the suffering we experience. In verse 7, Job continued to cry out to be heard by God.

14 "My relatives have failed,
And my intimate friends have forgotten me.
15 "Those who live in my house and my maids consider me a stranger.
I am a foreigner in their sight.
16 "I call to my servant, but he does not answer;
I have to implore him with my mouth.
17 "My breath is offensive to my wife,
And I am loathsome to my own brothers.
18 "Even young children despise me;
I rise up and they speak against me.
19 "All my associates abhor me,
And those I love have turned against me.
20 "My bone clings to my skin and my flesh,
And I have escaped *only* by the skin of my teeth.
21 "Pity me, pity me, O you my friends,
For the hand of God has struck me.
22 "Why do you persecute me as God *does,*
And are not satisfied with my flesh?

19:14 Job 19:19
19:19 Ps 38:11; 55:12, 13
19:20 Job 16:8; 33:21; Ps 102:5; Lam 4:8
19:21 Job 1:11; Ps 38:2
19:22 Job 13:24, 25; 16:11; 19:6; Ps 69:26

Job Says, "My Redeemer Lives"

23 "Oh that my words were written!
Oh that they were inscribed in a book!
24 "That with an iron stylus and lead
They were engraved in the rock forever!
25 "As for me, I know that my Redeemer lives,
And at the last He will take His stand on the earth.
26 "Even after my skin is destroyed,
Yet from my flesh I shall see God;
27 Whom I myself shall behold,
And whom my eyes will see and not another.
My heart faints within me!
28 "If you say, 'How shall we persecute him?'
And 'What pretext for a case against him can we find?'
29 "*Then* be afraid of the sword for yourselves,
For wrath *brings* the punishment of the sword,
So that you may know there is judgment."

19:23 Is 30:8; Jer 36:2
19:25 Job 16:19; Ps 78:35; Prov 23:11; Is 43:14; Jer 50:34
19:26 Ps 17:15; Matt 5:8; 1 Cor 13:12; 1 John 3:2
19:27 Ps 73:26
19:28 Job 19:22
19:29 Job 15:22; Job 22:4; Ps 1:5; 9:7; Eccl 12:14

Zophar Says, "The Triumph of the Wicked Is Short"

20 Then Zophar the Naamathite answered,
2 "Therefore my disquieting thoughts make me respond,
Even because of my inward agitation.
3 "I listened to the reproof which insults me,
And the spirit of my understanding makes me answer.
4 "Do you know this from of old,
From the establishment of man on earth,
5 That the triumphing of the wicked is short,
And the joy of the godless momentary?

20:3 Job 19:3
20:4 Job 8:8
20:5 Job 8:12, 13; Ps 37:35, 36; Job 8:13

19:25–27 At the heart of the book of Job comes his ringing affirmation of confidence: "I know that my Redeemer lives." In ancient Israel a *redeemer* was a family member who bought a slave's way to freedom or who took care of a widow (see the note on Ruth 3:1). What tremendous faith Job had, especially in light of the fact that he was unaware of the conference between God and Satan. Job thought that God had brought all these disasters upon him! Faced with death and decay, Job still expected to see God—and he expected to do so in his body. When the book of Job was written, Israel did not have a well-developed doctrine of the resurrection. Although Job struggled with the idea that God was presently against him, he firmly believed that in the end God would be on his side. This belief was so strong that Job became one of the first to talk about the resurrection of the body (see also Psalm 16:10; Isaiah 26:19; Daniel 12:2, 13).

19:26 Job said: "from my flesh I shall see God." In Job's situation, it seemed unlikely to him that he would, in his flesh, see God. And that's just the point of Job's faith! He was confident that God's justice would triumph, even if it would take a miracle like resurrection to accomplish this.

20:1ff Zophar's speech again revealed his false assumption because he based his arguments purely on the idea that Job was an evil hypocrite. Zophar said that although Job had it good for a while, he didn't live righteously, so God took his wealth from him. According to Zophar, Job's calamities *proved* his wickedness.

20:6 Is 14:13, 14; Obad 3, 4
20:7 Job 4:20; 14:20; Job 7:10; 8:18
20:8 Ps 73:20; 90:5; Job 18:18; 27:21-23
20:9 Job 7:8; 8:18; Job 7:10
20:10 Job 5:4; 27:14; Job 20:18; 27:16, 17
20:11 Job 21:23, 24
20:12 Job 15:16
20:13 Num 11:18-20, 33; Job 20:23
20:15 Job 20:10, 20, 21
20:16 Deut 32:24, 33
20:17 Deut 32:13, 14; Job 29:6
20:18 Job 20:10, 15
20:19 Job 24:2-4; 35:9
20:20 Eccl 5:13-15
20:21 Job 15:29
20:22 Job 5:5
20:23 Job 20:13, 14; Num 11:18-20, 33; Ps 78:30, 31
20:24 Is 24:18; Amos 5:19
20:25 Job 16:13; Job 18:11, 14
20:26 Job 18:18; Job 15:30; Ps 21:9
20:27 Deut 31:28; Is 26:21

6 "Though his loftiness reaches the heavens,
And his head touches the clouds,
7 He perishes forever like his refuse;
Those who have seen him will say, 'Where is he?'
8 "He flies away like a dream, and they cannot find him;
Even like a vision of the night he is chased away.
9 "The eye which saw him sees him no longer,
And his place no longer beholds him.
10 "His sons favor the poor,
And his hands give back his wealth.
11 "His bones are full of his youthful vigor,
But it lies down with him in the dust.

12 "Though evil is sweet in his mouth
And he hides it under his tongue,
13 *Though* he desires it and will not let it go,
But holds it in his mouth,
14 *Yet* his food in his stomach is changed
To the venom of cobras within him.
15 "He swallows riches,
But will vomit them up;
God will expel them from his belly.
16 "He sucks the poison of cobras;
The viper's tongue slays him.
17 "He does not look at the streams,
The rivers flowing with honey and curds.
18 "He returns what he has attained
And cannot swallow *it;*
As to the riches of his trading,
He cannot even enjoy *them.*
19 "For he has oppressed *and* forsaken the poor;
He has seized a house which he has not built.

20 "Because he knew no quiet within him,
He does not retain anything he desires.
21 "Nothing remains for him to devour,
Therefore his prosperity does not endure.
22 "In the fullness of his plenty he will be cramped;
The hand of everyone who suffers will come *against* him.
23 "When he fills his belly,
God will send His fierce anger on him
And will rain *it* on him while he is eating.
24 "He may flee from the iron weapon,
But the bronze bow will pierce him.
25 "It is drawn forth and comes out of his back,
Even the glittering point from his gall.
Terrors come upon him,
26 Complete darkness is held in reserve for his treasures,
And unfanned fire will devour him;
It will consume the survivor in his tent.
27 "The heavens will reveal his iniquity,
And the earth will rise up against him.

20:6–7 Although Zophar was wrong in directing this tirade against Job, he was correct in talking about the final end of evil people. At first, sin seems enjoyable and attractive. Lying, stealing, or oppressing others often brings temporary gain to those who practice these sins. Some live a long time with ill-gotten gain. But in the end, God's justice will prevail. What Zophar missed is that judgment for these sins may not come in the lifetime of the sinner. Punishment may be deferred until the last judgment, when sinners will be eternally cut off from God. We should not be impressed with the success and power of evil people. God's judgment on them is certain.

28 "The increase of his house will depart;
His possessions will flow away in the day of His anger.
29 "This is the wicked man's portion from God,
Even the heritage decreed to him by God."

20:28 Deut 28:31; Job 20:15; 21:30

20:29 Job 27:13; 31:2, 3

Job Says God Will Deal with the Wicked

21 Then Job answered,
2 "Listen carefully to my speech,
And let this be your *way of* consolation.
3 "Bear with me that I may speak;
Then after I have spoken, you may mock.
4 "As for me, is my complaint to man?
And why should I not be impatient?
5 "Look at me, and be astonished,
And put *your* hand over *your* mouth.
6 "Even when I remember, I am disturbed,
And horror takes hold of my flesh.
7 "Why do the wicked *still* live,
Continue on, also become very powerful?
8 "Their descendants are established with them in their sight,
And their offspring before their eyes,
9 Their houses are safe from fear,
And the rod of God is not on them.
10 "His ox mates without fail;
His cow calves and does not abort.
11 "They send forth their little ones like the flock,
And their children skip about.
12 "They sing to the timbrel and harp
And rejoice at the sound of the flute.
13 "They spend their days in prosperity,
And suddenly they go down to Sheol.
14 "They say to God, 'Depart from us!
We do not even desire the knowledge of Your ways.
15 'Who is the Almighty, that we should serve Him,
And what would we gain if we entreat Him?'
16 "Behold, their prosperity is not in their hand;
The counsel of the wicked is far from me.

17 "How often is the lamp of the wicked put out,
Or does their calamity fall on them?
Does God apportion destruction in His anger?
18 "Are they as straw before the wind,
And like chaff which the storm carries away?
19 "*You say,* 'God stores away a man's iniquity for his sons.'
Let God repay him so that he may know *it.*
20 "Let his own eyes see his decay,
And let him drink of the wrath of the Almighty.
21 "For what does he care for his household [5]after him,
When the number of his months is cut off?
22 "Can anyone teach God knowledge,
In that He judges those on high?

21:3 Job 11:3; 17:2

21:4 Job 7:11; Job 6:11

21:5 Judg 18:19; Job 13:5; 29:9; 40:4

21:6 Ps 55:5

21:7 Job 9:24; Ps 73:3; Jer 12:1; Hab 1:13; Job 12:19

21:8 Ps 17:14

21:9 Job 12:6

21:13 Job 21:23; 36:11

21:14 Job 22:17

21:15 Job 22:17; 34:9

21:16 Job 22:18

21:17 Job 18:5, 6; Job 31:2, 3

21:18 Job 13:25; Ps 83:13; Ps 1:4; 35:5; Is 17:13; Hos 13:3

21:19 Ex 20:5; Jer 31:29; Ezek 18:2

21:20 Num 14:28-32; Jer 31:30; Ezek 18:4; Ps 60:3; Is 51:17; Jer 25:15; Rev 14:10

21:22 Job 35:11; 36:22; Is 40:14; Rom 11:34; Job 4:18; 15:15; Ps 82:1

5 I.e. after he dies

21:1ff Job refuted Zophar's idea that evil people never experience wealth and happiness, pointing out that in the real world the wicked do indeed prosper. God does as he wills to individuals (21:22–25), and people cannot use their circumstances to measure their own goodness or God's—they are sometimes (but not always) related. Success to Job's friends was based on outward performance; success to God, however, is based on a person's heart.

21:22 Although baffled by the reasons for his suffering, Job affirmed God's superior understanding by asking, "Can anyone teach God knowledge?" The way you respond to your personal struggles shows your attitude toward God. Rather than becoming angry with God, continue to trust him, no matter what your circumstances may be. Although it is sometimes difficult to see, God *is* in control. We must commit ourselves to him so we will not resent his timing.

21:23 Job 20:11; 21:13
21:24 Prov 3:8
21:26 Job 3:13; 20:11; Eccl 9:2; Job 24:20; Is 14:11
21:28 Job 1:3; 31:37; Job 8:22; 18:21
21:30 Job 20:29; Prov 16:4; 2 Pet 2:9; Job 21:17, 20; 40:11
21:33 Job 3:22; 17:16; Job 3:19; 24:24
21:34 Job 16:2

23 "One dies in his full strength,
Being wholly at ease and satisfied;
24 His sides are filled out with fat,
And the marrow of his bones is moist,
25 While another dies with a bitter soul,
Never even tasting *anything* good.
26 "Together they lie down in the dust,
And worms cover them.

27 "Behold, I know your thoughts,
And the plans by which you would wrong me.
28 "For you say, 'Where is the house of the nobleman,
And where is the tent, the dwelling places of the wicked?'
29 "Have you not asked wayfaring men,
And do you not recognize their witness?
30 "For the wicked is reserved for the day of calamity;
They will be led forth at the day of fury.
31 "Who will confront him with his actions,
And who will repay him for what he has done?
32 "While he is carried to the grave,
Men will keep watch over *his* tomb.
33 "The clods of the valley will gently cover him;
Moreover, all men will follow after him,
While countless ones *go* before him.
34 "How then will you vainly comfort me,
For your answers remain *full of* falsehood?"

3. Third round of discussion

Eliphaz Accuses and Exhorts Job

22:2 Job 35:7; Luke 17:10
22:4 Job 14:3; 19:29
22:5 Job 11:6; 15:5
22:6 Ex 22:26; Deut 24:6, 17; Job 24:3, 9; Ezek 18:16; Job 31:19, 20
22:7 Job 31:16, 17; Job 31:31
22:8 Job 9:24; Job 12:19; Is 3:3; 9:15
22:9 Job 24:3, 21; 29:13; 31:16, 18; Job 6:27
22:10 Job 18:8; Job 15:21
22:11 Job 5:14; Job 38:34; Ps 69:2; 124:5; Lam 3:54

22 Then Eliphaz the Temanite responded,
2 "Can a vigorous man be of use to God,
Or a wise man be useful to himself?
3 "Is there any pleasure to the Almighty if you are righteous,
Or profit if you make your ways perfect?
4 "Is it because of your reverence that He reproves you,
That He enters into judgment against you?
5 "Is not your wickedness great,
And your iniquities without end?
6 "For you have taken pledges of your brothers without cause,
And stripped men naked.
7 "To the weary you have given no water to drink,
And from the hungry you have withheld bread.
8 "But the earth belongs to the mighty man,
And the honorable man dwells in it.
9 "You have sent widows away empty,
And the strength of the orphans has been crushed.
10 "Therefore snares surround you,
And sudden dread terrifies you,
11 Or darkness, so that you cannot see,
And an abundance of water covers you.

21:29–33 If wicked people become wealthy despite their sin, why should we try to be good? The wicked may *seem* to get away with sin, but there is a higher Judge and a future judgment (Revelation 20:11–15). The final settlement of justice will come not in this life, but in the next. What is important is how a person views God in prosperity or poverty, not the prosperity or poverty itself.

22:1ff This is Eliphaz's third and final speech to Job. When he first spoke to Job (chapters 4—5), he commended Job's good deeds and gently suggested that Job might need to repent of some sin. While he said nothing new in this speech, he did get more specific. He couldn't shake his belief that suffering is God's punishment for evil deeds, so he suggested several possible sins that Job might have committed. Eliphaz wasn't trying to destroy Job; at the end of his speech he promised that Job would receive peace and restoration if he would only admit his sin and repent.

12 "Is not God *in* the height of heaven?
Look also at the distant stars, how high they are!
13 "You say, 'What does God know?
Can He judge through the thick darkness?
14 'Clouds are a hiding place for Him, so that He cannot see;
And He walks on the vault of heaven.'
15 "Will you keep to the ancient path
Which wicked men have trod,
16 Who were snatched away before their time,
Whose foundations were washed away by a river?
17 "They said to God, 'Depart from us!'
And 'What can the Almighty do to them?'
18 "Yet He filled their houses with good *things;*
But the counsel of the wicked is far from me.
19 "The righteous see and are glad,
And the innocent mock them,
20 *Saying,* 'Truly our adversaries are cut off,
And their abundance the fire has consumed.'

21 "Yield now and be at peace with Him;
Thereby good will come to you.
22 "Please receive instruction from His mouth
And establish His words in your heart.
23 "If you return to the Almighty, you will be restored;
If you remove unrighteousness far from your tent,
24 And place *your* gold in the dust,
And *the gold of* Ophir among the stones of the brooks,
25 Then the Almighty will be your gold
And choice silver to you.
26 "For then you will delight in the Almighty
And lift up your face to God.
27 "You will pray to Him, and He will hear you;
And you will pay your vows.
28 "You will also decree a thing, and it will be established for you;
And light will shine on your ways.
29 "When you are cast down, you will speak with confidence,
And the humble person He will save.
30 "He will deliver one who is not innocent,
And he will be delivered through the cleanness of your hands."

Job Says He Longs for God

23 Then Job replied,
2 "Even today my complaint is rebellion;
His hand is heavy despite my groaning.
3 "Oh that I knew where I might find Him,
That I might come to His seat!
4 "I would present *my* case before Him
And fill my mouth with arguments.

22:12 Job 11:7-9
22:13 Ps 10:11; 59:7; 64:5; 94:7; Is 29:15; Ezek 8:12
22:14 Job 26:9
22:15 Job 34:36
22:16 Job 15:32; 21:13, 18; Job 14:19; Ps 90:5; Is 28:2; Matt 7:26, 27
22:17 Job 21:14, 15
22:18 Job 12:6; Job 21:16
22:19 Ps 52:6; 58:10; 107:42
22:20 Job 15:30
22:21 Ps 34:10
22:22 Job 6:10; 23:12; Prov 2:6
22:23 Job 8:5; 11:13; Is 19:22; 31:6; Zech 1:3; Job 11:14
22:24 Job 31:24, 25
22:25
22:26 Job 27:10; Ps 37:4; Is 58:14
22:27 Job 11:13; 33:26; Is 58:9; Job 34:28
22:28 Job 11:17; Ps 112:4
22:29 Job 5:11; 36:7; Matt 23:12; James 4:6; 1 Pet 5:5
22:30 Job 42:7, 8; Ps 18:20; 24:3, 4
23:2 Job 7:11; Job 6:2, 3; Ps 32:4
23:4 Job 13:18

22:12–14 Eliphaz declared that Job's view of God was too small, and he criticized Job for thinking that God was too far removed from earth to care about him. If Job knew of God's intense, personal interest in him, Eliphaz said, he wouldn't dare take his sins so lightly. Eliphaz had a point—some people do take sin lightly because they think God is far away and doesn't notice all we do. But his point did not apply to Job.

22:21–30 Several times Job's friends showed a partial knowledge of God's truth and character, but they had trouble accurately applying this truth to life. Such was the case with Eliphaz, who gave a beautiful summary of repentance. He was correct in saying that we must ask for God's forgiveness when we sin, but his statement did not apply to Job, who had already sought God's forgiveness (7:20, 21; 9:20; 13:23) and had lived closely in touch with God all along.

23:1—24:25 Job continued his questioning, saying that his suffering would be more bearable if only he knew why it was happening. If there was sin for which he could repent, he would! He knew about the wicked and the fact that they would be punished; he knew God could vindicate him if he so chose. In all his examples of the wicked in the world, his overriding desire was for God to clear his name, prove his righteousness, and explain why he was chosen to receive all this calamity. Job tried to make his friends see that questions about God, life, and justice are not as simple as they assumed.

5 "I would learn the words *which* He would answer,
And perceive what He would say to me.
6 "Would He contend with me by the greatness of *His* power?
No, surely He would pay attention to me.
7 "There the upright would reason with Him;
And I would be delivered forever from my Judge.

23:6 Job 9:4
23:7 Job 13:3; Job 13:16; 23:10

8 "Behold, I go forward but He is not *there,*
And backward, but I cannot perceive Him;
9 When He acts on the left, I cannot behold *Him;*
He turns on the right, I cannot see Him.
10 "But He knows the way I take;
When He has tried me, I shall come forth as gold.
11 "My foot has held fast to His path;
I have kept His way and not turned aside.
12 "I have not departed from the command of His lips;
I have treasured the words of His mouth more than my necessary food.
13 "But He is unique and who can turn Him?
And *what* His soul desires, that He does.
14 "For He performs what is appointed for me,
And many such *decrees* are with Him.
15 "Therefore, I would be dismayed at His presence;
When I consider, I am terrified of Him.
16 "*It is* God *who* has made my heart faint,
And the Almighty *who* has dismayed me,
17 But I am not silenced by the darkness,
Nor deep gloom *which* covers me.

23:8 Job 9:11; 35:14
23:10 Job 7:18; Ps 7:9; 11:5; 66:10; Zech 13:9; 1 Pet 1:7
23:11 Job 31:7; Ps 17:5; 44:18
23:12 Job 6:10; 22:22
23:16 Deut 20:3; Job 27:2; Jer 51:46
23:17 Job 10:18, 19; Job 19:8

Job Says God Seems to Ignore Wrongs

24 "Why are times not stored up by the Almighty,
And why do those who know Him not see His days?
2 "Some remove the landmarks;
They seize and devour flocks.
3 "They drive away the donkeys of the orphans;
They take the widow's ox for a pledge.
4 "They push the needy aside from the road;
The poor of the land are made to hide themselves altogether.
5 "Behold, as wild donkeys in the wilderness
They go forth seeking food in their activity,
As bread for *their* children in the desert.
6 "They harvest their fodder in the field
And glean the vineyard of the wicked.
7 "They spend the night naked, without clothing,
And have no covering against the cold.
8 "They are wet with the mountain rains
And hug the rock for want of a shelter.
9 "Others snatch the orphan from the breast,
And against the poor they take a pledge.
10 "They cause *the poor* to go about naked without clothing,
And they take away the sheaves from the hungry.

24:1 Acts 1:7; Is 2:12; Jer 46:10; Obad 15; Zeph 1:7
24:2 Deut 19:14; 27:17; Prov 23:10
24:3 Job 6:27; Deut 24:17; Job 22:9
24:4 Job 24:14; 29:16; 30:25; 31:19; Job 29:12; Ps 41:1; Prov 14:31; 28:28; Amos 8:4
24:5 Job 39:5-8; Ps 104:23
24:7 Ex 22:26; Job 22:6
24:9 Job 6:27

23:10 In chapter 22, Eliphaz had tried to condemn Job by identifying some secret sin which he may have committed. Here Job declares his confidence in his integrity and God's justice. We are always likely to have hidden sin in our lives, sin we don't even know about because God's standards are so high and our performance is so imperfect. If we are true believers, however, all our sins are forgiven because of what Christ did on the cross in our behalf (Romans 5:1; 8:1). The Bible also teaches that even if our hearts condemn us, God is greater than our hearts (1 John 3:20). His forgiveness and cleansing are sufficient; they overrule our nagging doubts. The Holy Spirit in us is our proof that we are forgiven in God's eyes even though we may *feel* guilty. If we, like Job, are truly seeking God, we can stand up to others' accusations as well as our own nagging doubts. If God has forgiven and accepted us, we are forgiven indeed.

11 "Within the walls they produce oil;
They tread wine presses but thirst.
12 "From the city men groan,
And the souls of the wounded cry out;
Yet God does not pay attention to folly.

13 "Others have been with those who rebel against the light;
They do not want to know its ways
Nor abide in its paths.
14 "The murderer arises at dawn;
He kills the poor and the needy,
And at night he is as a thief.
15 "The eye of the adulterer waits for the twilight,
Saying, 'No eye will see me.'
And he disguises his face.
16 "In the dark they dig into houses,
They shut themselves up by day;
They do not know the light.
17 "For the morning is the same to him as thick darkness,
For he is familiar with the terrors of thick darkness.

18 "They are insignificant on the surface of the water;
Their portion is cursed on the earth.
They do not turn toward the vineyards.
19 "Drought and heat consume the snow waters,
So does Sheol *those who* have sinned.
20 "A mother will forget him;
The worm feeds sweetly till he is no longer remembered.
And wickedness will be broken like a tree.
21 "He wrongs the barren woman
And does no good for the widow.
22 "But He drags off the valiant by His power;
He rises, but no one has assurance of life.
23 "He provides them with security, and they are supported;
And His eyes are on their ways.
24 "They are exalted a little while, then they are gone;
Moreover, they are brought low and like everything gathered up;
Even like the heads of grain they are cut off.
25 "Now if it is not so, who can prove me a liar,
And make my speech worthless?"

Bildad Says Man Is Inferior

25 Then Bildad the Shuhite answered,
2 "Dominion and awe belong to Him
Who establishes peace in His heights.
3 "Is there any number to His troops?
And upon whom does His light not rise?
4 "How then can a man be just with God?
Or how can he be clean who is born of woman?
5 "If even the moon has no brightness
And the stars are not pure in His sight,

24:12 Job 9:23, 24
24:14 Mic 2:1; Ps 10:8
24:15 Prov 7:9
24:16 Ex 22:2; Matt 6:19; John 3:20
24:17 Job 15:21
24:18 Job 22:11, 16; 27:20; Job 5:3; Job 24:6, 11
24:19 Job 6:16, 17; Job 21:13
24:20 Is 49:15; Job 21:26; Job 18:17; Ps 34:16; Prov 10:7; Job 19:10; Dan 4:14
24:21 Job 22:9
24:22 Job 9:4; Job 18:20
24:23 Job 12:6; Job 10:4; 11:11
24:24 Ps 37:10; Job 14:21
24:25 Job 6:28; 27:4
25:2 Job 9:4; 36:5, 22; 37:23; 42:2; Job 16:19; 31:2
25:3 Job 16:13
25:4 Job 4:17; 9:2; Job 14:4
25:5 Job 31:26; Job 15:15

24:18–21 Job suddenly seemed to be arguing on his friends' side. For this reason, some commentators think one of Job's friends said these words. But we shouldn't expect Job to present a unified argument. He was confused. He was not arguing that, in every case, God rewards the wicked and punishes the righteous; he was simply asserting that in his case, a righteous man was suffering.

25:1ff Bildad's final reply was weak. It ignored Job's examples of the prosperity of the wicked. Instead of attempting to refute Job, Bildad accused Job of pride because he was claiming that his suffering was not the result of sin. Job never claimed to be without sin, but only that his sin could not have caused his present trouble.

6 How much less man, *that* maggot,
And the son of man, *that* worm!"

Job Rebukes Bildad

26 Then Job responded,
2 "What a help you are to the weak!
How you have saved the arm without strength!
3 "What counsel you have given to *one* without wisdom!
What helpful insight you have abundantly provided!
4 "To whom have you uttered words?
And whose spirit was expressed through you?

The Greatness of God

5 "The departed spirits tremble
Under the waters and their inhabitants.
6 "Naked is Sheol before Him,
And [6]Abaddon has no covering.
7 "He stretches out the north over empty space
And hangs the earth on nothing.
8 "He wraps up the waters in His clouds,
And the cloud does not burst under them.
9 "He obscures the face of the full moon
And spreads His cloud over it.
10 "He has inscribed a circle on the surface of the waters
At the boundary of light and darkness.
11 "The pillars of heaven tremble
And are amazed at His rebuke.
12 "He quieted the sea with His power,
And by His understanding He shattered Rahab.
13 "By His breath the heavens are cleared;
His hand has pierced the fleeing serpent.
14 "Behold, these are the fringes of His ways;
And how faint a word we hear of Him!
But His mighty thunder, who can understand?"

Job Affirms His Righteousness

27 Then Job continued his discourse and said,
2 "As God lives, who has taken away my right,
And the Almighty, who has embittered my soul,
3 For as long as life is in me,
And the breath of God is in my nostrils,
4 My lips certainly will not speak unjustly,
Nor will my tongue mutter deceit.
5 "Far be it from me that I should declare you right;
Till I die I will not put away my integrity from me.

25:6 Job 7:17; Job 17:14
26:2 Job 6:11, 12; Ps 71:9
26:5 Job 3:13; Ps 88:10
26:6 Job 9:5-10; 26:6-14; 38:17; 41:11; Job 28:22; 31:12
26:7 Job 9:8
26:8 Job 37:11; Prov 30:4
26:9 Job 22:14; Ps 97:2; 105:39
26:10 Job 38:1-11; Prov 8:29; Job 38:19, 20, 24
26:12 Is 51:15; Jer 31:35; Job 12:13; Job 9:13
26:13 Job 9:8; Is 27:1
26:14 Job 4:12; Job 36:29; 37:4, 5
27:1 Job 13:12; 29:1
27:2 Job 16:11; 34:5; Job 9:18
27:3 Job 32:8; 33:4
27:4 Job 6:28; 33:3
27:5 Job 6:29

6 I.e. place of destruction

25:6 It is important to understand that Bildad, not God, was calling man a worm. Human beings are created in God's image (Genesis 1:26–27). Psalm 8:5 says that man is "a little lower than God." Bildad may have simply been using a poetic description to contrast our worth to the worth and power of God. To come to God, we need not crawl like worms. We can approach him boldly in faith (Hebrews 4:16).

26:1ff Job has the distinction of giving the longest speech in the book—six chapters—weaving together pictures of God's mystery and power in a beautiful poem of trust. Beginning by brushing off Bildad's latest reply as irrelevant (chapter 25), Job then told Bildad and his friends that they could not possibly know everything about God. Wisdom does not originate from this life or from the human mind—it comes from God (28:27–28). Job then defended his upright and honest life. He had effectively sought to follow God's way of living. While admitting that he was not perfect, Job maintained that his motives were right.

26:2–4 With great sarcasm, Job attacked Bildad's comments. Their theological explanations failed to bring any relief because they were unable to turn their knowledge into helpful counsel. When dealing with people, it is more important to love and understand them than to analyze them or give advice. Compassion produces greater results than criticism or blame.

6 "I hold fast my righteousness and will not let it go.
My heart does not reproach any of my days.

27:6 Job 2:3; 13:18

The State of the Godless

7 "May my enemy be as the wicked
And my opponent as the unjust.
8 "For what is the hope of the godless when he is cut off,
When God requires his life?
9 "Will God hear his cry
When distress comes upon him?
10 "Will he take delight in the Almighty?
Will he call on God at all times?
11 "I will instruct you in the power of God;
What is with the Almighty I will not conceal.
12 "Behold, all of you have seen *it;*
Why then do you act foolishly?

27:8 Job 8:13; 11:20; Job 12:10
27:9 Job 35:12, 13; Ps 18:41; Prov 1:28; Is 1:15; Jer 14:12; Mic 3:4; Prov 1:27
27:10 Job 22:26, 27; Ps 37:4; Is 58:14

13 "This is the portion of a wicked man from God,
And the inheritance *which* tyrants receive from the Almighty.
14 "Though his sons are many, they are destined for the sword;
And his descendants will not be satisfied with bread.
15 "His survivors will be buried because of the plague,
And their widows will not be able to weep.
16 "Though he piles up silver like dust
And prepares garments as *plentiful as* the clay,
17 He may prepare *it,* but the just will wear *it*
And the innocent will divide the silver.
18 "He has built his house like the spider's web,
Or as a hut *which* the watchman has made.
19 "He lies down rich, but never again;
He opens his eyes, and it is no longer.
20 "Terrors overtake him like a flood;
A tempest steals him away in the night.
21 "The east wind carries him away, and he is gone,
For it whirls him away from his place.
22 "For it will hurl at him without sparing;
He will surely try to flee from its power.
23 "*Men* will clap their hands at him
And will hiss him from his place.

27:13 Job 20:29; Job 15:20
27:14 Job 15:22; 18:19; Job 20:10
27:15 Ps 78:64
27:17 Job 20:18-21
27:18 Job 8:15; 18:14
27:19 Job 7:8, 21; 20:7
27:20 Job 15:21; Job 20:8; 34:20
27:21 Job 21:18; Job 7:10
27:22 Jer 13:14; Ezek 5:11; 24:14; Job 11:20
27:23 Job 18:18; 20:8

Job Tells of Earth's Treasures

28 "Surely there is a [7]mine for silver
And a place where they refine gold.
2 "Iron is taken from the dust,
And copper is smelted from rock.
3 "*Man* puts an end to darkness,
And to the farthest limit he searches out
The rock in gloom and deep shadow.
4 "He sinks a shaft far from habitation,
Forgotten by the foot;
They hang and swing to and fro far from men.

28:3 Eccl 1:13

7 Or *source*

27:6 In the midst of all the accusations, Job was able to declare that his conscience was clear. Only God's forgiveness and the determination to live rightly before God can bring a clear conscience. How important Job's record became as he was being accused. Like Job, we can't claim sinless lives, but we *can* claim forgiven lives. When we confess our sins to God, he forgives us. Then we can live with clear consciences (1 John 1:9).

27:13–23 Job agreed with his friends that the end of the wicked will be disaster, but he did not agree that *he* was wicked and deserving of punishment. Most of the punishments Job listed never happened to him. So he wasn't including himself as one of the wicked. On the contrary, he continually pleaded for God to vindicate him.

5 "The earth, from it comes food,
And underneath it is turned up as fire.
6 "Its rocks are the source of sapphires,
And its dust *contains* gold.
7 "The path no bird of prey knows,
Nor has the falcon's eye caught sight of it.
8 "The proud beasts have not trodden it,
Nor has the *fierce* lion passed over it.
9 "He puts his hand on the flint;
He overturns the mountains at the base.
10 "He hews out channels through the rocks,
And his eye sees anything precious.
11 "He dams up the streams from flowing,
And what is hidden he brings out to the light.

The Search for Wisdom Is Harder

28:12 Job 28:23, 28; Eccl 7:24
28:13 Matt 13:44-46
28:15 Prov 3:13, 14; 8:10, 11; 16:16
28:17 Prov 8:10; 16:16
28:18 Prov 8:11
28:19 Prov 8:19

12 "But where can wisdom be found?
And where is the place of understanding?
13 "Man does not know its value,
Nor is it found in the land of the living.
14 "The deep says, 'It is not in me';
And the sea says, 'It is not with me.'
15 "Pure gold cannot be given in exchange for it,
Nor can silver be weighed as its price.
16 "It cannot be valued in the gold of Ophir,
In precious onyx, or sapphire.
17 "Gold or glass cannot equal it,
Nor can it be exchanged for articles of fine gold.
18 "Coral and crystal are not to be mentioned;
And the acquisition of wisdom is above *that of* pearls.
19 "The topaz of Ethiopia cannot equal it,
Nor can it be valued in pure gold.

WHERE CAN WISDOM BE FOUND?
Job and his friends differed in their ideas of how people become wise.

Person	*His Source of Wisdom*	*Attitude toward God*
Eliphaz	Wisdom is learned by observing and experiencing life. He based his advice to Job on his confident, firsthand knowledge (4:7–8; 5:3, 27).	"I have personally observed how God works and have figured him out."
Bildad	Wisdom is inherited from the past. Trustworthy knowledge is secondhand. He based his advice to Job on traditional proverbs and sayings that he frequently quoted (8:8–9; 18:5–21).	"Those who have gone before us figured God out and all we have to do is use that knowledge."
Zophar	Wisdom belongs to the wise. He based his advice on his wisdom that had no other source than himself (11:6; 20:1–29).	"The wise know what God is like, but there aren't many of us around."
Job	God is the source of wisdom, and the first step toward wisdom is to fear God (28:20–28).	"God reveals his wisdom to those who humbly trust him."

28:13 Job stated that wisdom cannot be found among the living. It is natural for people who do not understand the importance of God's Word to seek wisdom here on earth. They look to philosophers and other leaders to give them direction for living. Yet Job said that wisdom is not found there. No leader or group of leaders can produce enough knowledge or insight to explain the totality of human experience. The ultimate interpretation of life, of who we are and where we are going, must come from outside and above our mortal life. When looking for guidance, seek God's wisdom as revealed in the Bible. To be lifted above and beyond the boundaries of life, we must know and trust the Lord of life.

28:16 Gold of Ophir was considered the finest gold available. Ophir may have been located in Africa, along the Arabian coast, or in India. Wherever it was, it was a good distance from Israel, for it took Solomon's ships three years to make the voyage (1 Kings 9:28; 10:22).

20 "Where then does wisdom come from?
And where is the place of understanding?
21 "Thus it is hidden from the eyes of all living
And concealed from the birds of the sky.
22 "[8]Abaddon and Death say,
'With our ears we have heard a report of it.'

23 "God understands its way,
And He knows its place.
24 "For He looks to the ends of the earth
And sees everything under the heavens.
25 "When He imparted weight to the wind
And meted out the waters by measure,
26 When He set a limit for the rain
And a course for the thunderbolt,
27 Then He saw it and declared it;
He established it and also searched it out.
28 "And to man He said, 'Behold, the fear of the Lord, that is wisdom;
And to depart from evil is understanding.' "

28:20 Job 28:23, 28
28:22 Job 26:6; Prov 8:32-36
28:23 Job 9:4; Prov 8:22-36
28:24 Ps 11:4; 33:13, 14; 66:7; Prov 15:3
28:25 Ps 135:7; Job 12:15; 38:8-11
28:26 Job 37:6, 11, 12; 38:26-28; Job 37:3; 38:25
28:28 Ps 111:10; Prov 1:7; 9:10; Eccl 12:13

Job's Past Was Glorious

29 And Job again took up his discourse and said,
2 "Oh that I were as in months gone by,
As in the days when God watched over me;
3 When His lamp shone over my head,
And by His light I walked through darkness;
4 As I was in [9]the prime of my days,
When the friendship of God *was* over my tent;
5 When the Almighty was yet with me,
And my children were around me;
6 When my steps were bathed in butter,
And the rock poured out for me streams of oil!
7 "When I went out to the gate of the city,
When I took my seat in the square,
8 The young men saw me and hid themselves,
And the old men arose *and* stood.
9 "The princes stopped talking
And put *their* hands on their mouths;
10 The voice of the nobles was hushed,
And their tongue stuck to their palate.
11 "For when the ear heard, it called me blessed,
And when the eye saw, it gave witness of me,
12 Because I delivered the poor who cried for help,
And the orphan who had no helper.
13 "The blessing of the one ready to perish came upon me,
And I made the widow's heart sing for joy.

29:1 Num 23:7; 24:3; Job 13:12; 27:1
29:2 Jer 31:28
29:3 Job 18:6; Job 11:17
29:4 Job 15:8; Ps 25:14; Prov 3:32
29:6 Deut 32:14; Job 20:17; Deut 32:13; Ps 81:16
29:7 Job 31:21
29:9 Job 29:21; Job 21:5
29:10 Job 29:22; Ps 137:6
29:11 Job 4:3, 4
29:12 Job 24:4, 9; 34:28; Ps 72:12; Prov 21:13; Job 31:17, 21
29:13 Job 31:19; Job 22:9

8 I.e. Destruction **9** Lit *the days of my autumn*

28:28 "The fear of the Lord" is a key theme in the wisdom literature of the Bible (Job through Song of Solomon). It means to have respect and reverence for God and to be in awe of his majesty and power. This is the starting point to finding real wisdom (see Proverbs 1:7–9).

29:6 Butter and oil were symbols of material prosperity in an agricultural society. Job's flocks and olive trees were so plentiful that everything seemed to overflow.

29:7ff Job was walking a fine line between bragging about past accomplishments and recalling good deeds in order to answer the charges against him. Job's one weakness throughout his conversations is that he came dangerously close to pride. Pride is especially deceptive when we are doing right. But it separates us from God by making us think we're better than we really are. Then comes the tendency to trust our own opinions, which leads to other kinds of sin. While it is not wrong to recount past deeds, it is far better to recount God's blessings to us. This will help keep us from inadvertently falling into pride.

29:7–17 Because of this description of Job's work, many commentators believe that Job was a judge. In Job's day, a judge served as both a city councilman and a magistrate, helping to manage the community and settle disputes. In most cases, this was not a full-time position but a part-time post held on the basis of one's respect and standing in the area.

29:14 Job 27:5, 6; Ps 132:9; Is 59:17, 61:10; Eph 6:14
29:15 Num 10:31
29:16 Job 24:4; Prov 29:7
29:17 Ps 3:7
29:19 Jer 17:8; Hos 14:5
29:20 Gen 49:24; Ps 18:34
29:21 Job 4:3; 29:9
29:22 Job 29:10; Deut 32:2
29:25 Job 1:3; 31:37; Job 4:4; 16:5
30:1 Job 12:4
30:9 Job 12:4; Job 17:6; Ps 69:11; Lam 3:14, 63
30:10 Num 12:14; Deut 25:9; Job 17:6; Is 50:6; Matt 26:67
30:11 Ruth 1:21; Ps 88:7; Ps 32:9
30:12 Ps 140:4, 5; Job 19:12
30:13 Is 3:12

14 "I put on righteousness, and it clothed me;
My justice was like a robe and a turban.
15 "I was eyes to the blind
And feet to the lame.
16 "I was a father to the needy,
And I investigated the case which I did not know.
17 "I broke the jaws of the wicked
And snatched the prey from his teeth.
18 "Then I thought, 'I shall die in my nest,
And I shall multiply *my* days as the sand.
19 'My root is spread out to the waters,
And dew lies all night on my branch.
20 'My glory is *ever* new with me,
And my bow is renewed in my hand.'

21 "To me they listened and waited,
And kept silent for my counsel.
22 "After my words they did not speak again,
And my speech dropped on them.
23 "They waited for me as for the rain,
And opened their mouth as for the spring rain.
24 "I smiled on them when they did not believe,
And the light of my face they did not cast down.
25 "I chose a way for them and sat as chief,
And dwelt as a king among the troops,
As one who comforted the mourners.

Job's Present State Is Humiliating

30 "But now those younger than I mock me,
Whose fathers I disdained to put with the dogs of my flock.
2 "Indeed, what *good was* the strength of their hands to me?
Vigor had perished from them.
3 "From want and famine they are gaunt
Who gnaw the dry ground by night in waste and desolation,
4 Who pluck [10]mallow by the bushes,
And whose food is the root of the broom shrub.
5 "They are driven from the community;
They shout against them as *against* a thief,
6 So that they dwell in dreadful valleys,
In holes of the earth and of the rocks.
7 "Among the bushes they cry out;
Under the nettles they are gathered together.
8 "Fools, even those without a name,
They were scourged from the land.

9 "And now I have become their taunt,
I have even become a byword to them.
10 "They abhor me *and* stand aloof from me,
And they do not refrain from spitting at my face.
11 "Because He has loosed His bowstring and afflicted me,
They have cast off the bridle before me.
12 "On the right hand their brood arises;
They thrust aside my feet and build up against me their ways of destruction.
13 "They break up my path,

10 I.e. plant of the salt marshes

30:1ff To suffer extreme loss, as Job did, was humiliating. But to face abuse at the hands of young upstarts added insult to injury. Job had lost his family, possessions, health, position, and good name. He was not even respected for suffering bravely. Unfortunately, young people sometimes mock and take advantage of older people and those who are limited in some way. Instead, they should realize that their own physical abilities and attributes are short-lived and that God loves all people equally.

They profit from my destruction;
No one restrains them.
14 "As *through* a wide breach they come,
Amid the tempest they roll on.
15 "Terrors are turned against me;
They pursue my honor as the wind,
And my prosperity has passed away like a cloud.

30:15 Job 3:25; 31:23; Ps 55:3-5; Job 7:9; Hos 13:3

16 "And now my soul is poured out within me;
Days of affliction have seized me.
17 "At night it pierces my bones within me,
And my gnawing *pains* take no rest.
18 "By a great force my garment is distorted;
It binds me about as the collar of my coat.
19 "He has cast me into the mire,
And I have become like dust and ashes.
20 "I cry out to You for help, but You do not answer me;
I stand up, and You turn Your attention against me.
21 "You have become cruel to me;
With the might of Your hand You persecute me.
22 "You lift me up to the wind *and* cause me to ride;
And You dissolve me in a storm.
23 "For I know that You will bring me to death
And to the house of meeting for all living.

30:16 1 Sam 1:15; Job 3:24; Ps 22:14; 42:4; Is 53:12
30:17 Job 30:30
30:18 Job 2:7
30:19 Ps 69:2, 14
30:20 Job 19:7
30:21 Job 10:3; 16:9, 14; 19:6, 22
30:22 Job 9:17; 27:21
30:23 Job 9:22; 10:8; Job 3:19; Eccl 12:5

24 "Yet does not one in a heap of ruins stretch out *his* hand,
Or in his disaster therefore cry out for help?
25 "Have I not wept for the one whose life is hard?
Was not my soul grieved for the needy?
26 "When I expected good, then evil came;
When I waited for light, then darkness came.
27 "I am seething within and cannot relax;
Days of affliction confront me.
28 "I go about mourning without comfort;
I stand up in the assembly *and* cry out for help.
29 "I have become a brother to jackals
And a companion of ostriches.
30 "My skin turns black on me,
And my bones burn with fever.
31 "Therefore my harp is turned to mourning,
And my flute to the sound of those who weep.

30:24 Job 19:7
30:25 Ps 35:13, 14; Rom 12:15; Job 24:4
30:26 Job 3:25, 26; Jer 8:15; Job 19:8
30:27 Lam 2:11
30:28 Job 30:31; Ps 38:6; 42:9; 43:2; Job 19:7
30:29 Ps 44:19; Mic 1:8
30:30 Job 2:7; Ps 102:3
30:31 Is 24:8

Job Asserts His Integrity

31 "I have made a covenant with my eyes;
How then could I gaze at a virgin?
2 "And what is the portion of God from above
Or the heritage of the Almighty from on high?
3 "Is it not calamity to the unjust
And disaster to those who work iniquity?
4 "Does He not see my ways
And number all my steps?

5 "If I have walked with falsehood,
And my foot has hastened after deceit,

31:1 Matt 5:28
31:2 Job 20:29
31:3 Job 18:12; 21:30; Job 34:22
31:4 2 Chr 16:9; Job 24:23; 28:24; 34:21; 36:7; Prov 5:21; 15:3; Job 14:16; 31:37
31:5 Job 15:31; Mic 2:11

31:1–4 Job had not only avoided committing the great sin of adultery; he had not even taken the first step toward that sin by looking at a woman with lust. Job said he was innocent of both outward and inward sins. In chapter 29, Job reviewed his good deeds. Here in chapter 31 he listed sins he had not committed—in his heart (31:1–12), against his neighbors (31:13–23), or against God (31:24–34).

31:6 Job 6:2, 3; Job 23:10; 27:5, 6
31:7 Job 23:11; Job 9:30
31:8 Lev 26:16; Job 20:18; Mic 6:15; Job 31:12

6 Let Him weigh me with accurate scales,
And let God know my integrity.
7 "If my step has turned from the way,
Or my heart followed my eyes,
Or if any spot has stuck to my hands,
8 Let me sow and another eat,
And let my crops be uprooted.

31:9 Job 24:15; 31:1
31:10 Is 47:2; Deut 28:30; Jer 8:10
31:11 Lev 20:10; Deut 22:24; Job 31:28
31:12 Job 15:30; Job 26:6; Job 20:28; 31:8

9 "If my heart has been enticed by a woman,
Or I have lurked at my neighbor's doorway,
10 May my wife grind for another,
And let others kneel down over her.
11 "For that would be a lustful crime;
Moreover, it would be an iniquity *punishable by* judges.
12 "For it would be fire that consumes to Abaddon,
And would uproot all my increase.

31:13 Deut 24:14, 15
31:15 Job 10:3

13 "If I have despised the claim of my male or female slaves
When they filed a complaint against me,
14 What then could I do when God arises?
And when He calls me to account, what will I answer Him?
15 "Did not He who made me in the womb make him,
And the same one fashion us in the womb?

31:16 Job 5:16; 20:19; Ex 22:22-24; Job 22:9
31:17 Job 22:7; Job 29:12
31:19 Job 22:6; 29:13; Job 24:4
31:21 Job 29:12; 31:17; Job 29:7
31:22 Job 38:15
31:23 Job 31:3; Job 13:11

16 "If I have kept the poor from *their* desire,
Or have caused the eyes of the widow to fail,
17 Or have eaten my morsel alone,
And the orphan has not shared it
18 (But from my youth he grew up with me as with a father,
And from infancy I guided her),
19 If I have seen anyone perish for lack of clothing,
Or that the needy had no covering,
20 If his loins have not thanked me,
And if he has not been warmed with the fleece of my sheep,
21 If I have lifted up my hand against the orphan,
Because I saw I had support in the gate,
22 Let my shoulder fall from the socket,
And my arm be broken off at the elbow.
23 "For calamity from God is a terror to me,
And because of His majesty I can do nothing.

31:24 Job 22:24; Mark 10:23-25
31:25 Job 1:3, 10; Ps 62:10
31:26 Deut 4:19; 17:3; Ezek 8:16
31:28 Deut 17:2-7; Job 31:11; Josh 24:27; Is 59:13

24 "If I have put my confidence *in* gold,
And called fine gold my trust,
25 If I have gloated because my wealth was great,
And because my hand had secured *so* much;
26 If I have looked at the sun when it shone
Or the moon going in splendor,
27 And my heart became secretly enticed,
And my hand threw a kiss from my mouth,
28 That too would have been an iniquity *calling for* judgment,
For I would have denied God above.

31:29 Prov 17:5; 24:17; Obad 12

29 "Have I rejoiced at the extinction of my enemy,
Or exulted when evil befell him?

31:24–28 Job affirmed that depending on wealth for happiness is idolatry and denies the God of heaven. We excuse our society's obsession with money and possessions as a necessary evil or "the way it works" in the modern world. But every society in every age has valued the power and prestige that money brings. True believers must purge themselves of the deep-seated desire for more power, prestige, and possessions. They must also not withhold their resources from neighbors near and far who have desperate physical needs.

30 "No, I have not allowed my mouth to sin
By asking for his life in a curse.
31 "Have the men of my tent not said,
'Who can find one who has not been satisfied with his meat'?
32 "The alien has not lodged outside,
For I have opened my doors to the traveler.
33 "Have I covered my transgressions like Adam,
By hiding my iniquity in my bosom,
34 Because I feared the great multitude,
And the contempt of families terrified me,
And kept silent and did not go out of doors?
35 "Oh that I had one to hear me!
Behold, here is my signature;
Let the Almighty answer me!
And the indictment which my adversary has written,
36 Surely I would carry it on my shoulder,
I would bind it to myself like a crown.
37 "I would declare to Him the number of my steps;
Like a prince I would approach Him.

38 "If my land cries out against me,
And its furrows weep together;
39 If I have eaten its fruit without money,
Or have caused its owners to lose their lives,
40 Let briars grow instead of wheat,
And stinkweed instead of barley."
The words of Job are ended.

31:30 Ps 7:4; Job 5:3
31:31 Job 22:7
31:33 Gen 3:10; Prov 28:13
31:34 Ex 23:2
31:35 Job 19:7; 30:20, 24, 28; 35:14; Job 27:7
31:37 Job 31:4; Job 1:3; 29:25
31:38 Job 24:2
31:39 Job 24:6, 10-12; James 5:4; 1 Kin 21:19
31:40 Job 32:13; Is 5:6

C. A YOUNG MAN ANSWERS JOB (32:1—37:24)

Young Elihu rebukes the three friends for being unable to give Job a reasonable answer for why he was suffering. But he only gives a partial answer to Job's question by saying that man cannot understand all that God allows, but must trust him. This was the best answer that man could give, yet it was incomplete. Often the best human answers are incomplete because we do not have all the facts.

Elihu in Anger Rebukes Job

32 Then these three men ceased answering Job, because he was righteous in his own
eyes.
2 But the anger of Elihu the son of Barachel the Buzite, of the family of Ram burned;
against Job his anger burned because he justified himself before God.
3 And his anger burned against his three friends because they had found no answer,
and yet had condemned Job.
4 Now Elihu had waited to speak to Job because they were years older than he.
5 And when Elihu saw that there was no answer in the mouth of the three men his
anger burned.

32:1 Job 10:7; 13:18; 27:5, 6; 31:6
32:2 Gen 22:21; Job 27:5, 6; Job 30:21

31:33–34 Job declared that he did not try to hide his sin as men often do. The fear that our sins will be discovered leads us to patterns of deception. We cover up with lies so that we will appear good to others. But we cannot hide from God. Do you try to keep people from seeing the real you? When you acknowledge your sins, you free yourself to receive forgiveness and a new life.

32:1 If Job was really a good man, his three friends would have to drop their theory that suffering is always God's punishment for evil actions. Instead of considering another viewpoint, however, they cut off the discussion. They were convinced that Job had some hidden fault or sin, so there was no point in talking if Job would not confess it. But Job knew he had lived uprightly before God and others (chapter 29) and had avoided wrong thoughts and actions (chapter 31). He wasn't about to invent a sin to satisfy his friends!

32:2ff When Eliphaz, Bildad, and Zophar had nothing more to say, Elihu became the fourth person to speak to Job. This was the first and only time he spoke. Apparently he was a bystander and much younger than the others (32:6–7), but he introduced a new viewpoint. While Job's three friends said he was suffering from some past sins, Elihu said Job's suffering would not go away until he realized his *present* sin. He maintained that Job wasn't suffering because of sin, he was sinning because of suffering. Elihu pointed out that Job's attitude had become arrogant as he tried to defend his innocence. Elihu also said that suffering is not meant to punish us as much as it is meant to correct and restore us, to keep us on the right path.

There is much truth in Elihu's speech. He was urging Job to look at his suffering from a different perspective and with a greater purpose in mind. While his speech is on a higher spiritual plateau than the others, Elihu still wrongly assumed that a correct response to suffering always brings healing and restoration (33:23–30) and that suffering is always in some way connected to sin (34:11).

32:6 Job 15:10
6 So Elihu the son of Barachel the Buzite spoke out and said,
"I am young in years and you are old;
Therefore I was shy and afraid to tell you what I think.
32:7 Job 8:8, 9
7 "I thought age should speak,
And increased years should teach wisdom.
32:8 Job 33:4; Job 38:36
8 "But it is a spirit in man,
And the breath of the Almighty gives them understanding.
32:9 Job 32:7
9 "The abundant *in years* may not be wise,
Nor may elders understand justice.
10 "So I say, 'Listen to me,
I too will tell what I think.'

11 "Behold, I waited for your words,
I listened to your reasonings,
While you pondered what to say.
12 "I even paid close attention to you;
Indeed, there was no one who refuted Job,
Not one of you who answered his words.
32:13 Jer 9:23
13 "Do not say,
'We have found wisdom;
God will rout him, not man.'
14 "For he has not arranged *his* words against me,
Nor will I reply to him with your arguments.

15 "They are dismayed, they no longer answer;
Words have failed them.
16 "Shall I wait, because they do not speak,
Because they stop *and* no longer answer?
17 "I too will answer my share,
I also will tell my opinion.
18 "For I am full of words;
The spirit within me constrains me.
19 "Behold, my belly is like unvented wine,
Like new wineskins it is about to burst.
20 "Let me speak that I may get relief;
Let me open my lips and answer.
32:21 Lev 19:15; Job 13:8, 10; 34:19
21 "Let me now be partial to no one,
Nor flatter *any* man.
22 "For I do not know how to flatter,
Else my Maker would soon take me away.

Elihu Claims to Speak for God

33:1 Job 13:6
33 "However now, Job, please hear my speech,
And listen to all my words.
2 "Behold now, I open my mouth,
My tongue in my mouth speaks.
33:3 Job 6:28; 27:4; 36:4
3 "My words are *from* the uprightness of my heart,
And my lips speak knowledge sincerely.
33:4 Gen 2:7; Job 10:3; 32:8; Job 27:3
4 "The Spirit of God has made me,
And the breath of the Almighty gives me life.
33:5 Job 33:32
5 "Refute me if you can;
Array yourselves before me, take your stand.
33:6 Job 4:19
6 "Behold, I belong to God like you;
I too have been formed out of the clay.

32:7–9 "The breath of the Almighty gives them understanding." It is not enough to recognize a great truth; it must be lived out each day. Elihu recognized the truth that God was the only source of real wisdom, but he did not use God's wisdom to help Job. While he recognized where wisdom came from, he did not seek to acquire it. Becoming wise is an ongoing, lifelong pursuit. Don't be content just to know about wisdom; make it part of your life.

7 "Behold, no fear of me should terrify you,
Nor should my pressure weigh heavily on you.

8 "Surely you have spoken in my hearing,
And I have heard the sound of *your* words:
9 'I am pure, without transgression;
I am innocent and there is no guilt in me.
10 'Behold, He invents pretexts against me;
He counts me as His enemy.
11 'He puts my feet in the stocks;
He watches all my paths.'
12 "Behold, let me tell you, you are not right in this,
For God is greater than man.

13 "Why do you complain against Him
That He does not give an account of all His doings?
14 "Indeed God speaks once,
Or twice, *yet* no one notices it.
15 "In a dream, a vision of the night,
When sound sleep falls on men,
While they slumber in their beds,
16 Then He opens the ears of men,
And seals their instruction,
17 That He may turn man aside *from his* conduct,
And keep man from pride;
18 He keeps back his soul from the pit,
And his life from passing over into Sheol.

19 "Man is also chastened with pain on his bed,
And with unceasing complaint in his bones;
20 So that his life loathes bread,
And his soul favorite food.
21 "His flesh wastes away from sight,
And his bones which were not seen stick out.
22 "Then his soul draws near to the pit,
And his life to those who bring death.

23 "If there is an angel *as* mediator for him,
One out of a thousand,
To remind a man what is right for him,
24 Then let him be gracious to him, and say,
'Deliver him from going down to the pit,
I have found a ransom';
25 Let his flesh become fresher than in youth,
Let him return to the days of his youthful vigor;
26 Then he will pray to God, and He will accept him,
That he may see His face with joy,
And He may restore His righteousness to man.
27 "He will sing to men and say,
'I have sinned and perverted what is right,

33:7 Job 13:21

33:9 Job 9:21; 10:7; 13:18; 16:17; Job 7:21; 13:23; 14:17; Job 10:14

33:10 Job 13:24

33:11 Job 13:27

33:12 Eccl 7:20

33:13 Job 40:2; Is 45:9

33:14 Job 33:29; 40:5; Ps 62:11

33:15 Job 4:12-17; 33:15-18

33:16 Job 36:10, 15

33:18 Job 33:22, 24, 28, 30; Job 15:22

33:19 Job 30:17

33:20 Job 3:24; 6:7; Ps 107:18

33:21 Job 16:8; Job 19:20; Ps 22:17; 102:5

33:22 Job 33:18, 28

33:23 Gen 40:8

33:24 Job 33:18, 28; Is 38:17; Job 36:18; Ps 49:7

33:26 Job 22:27; 34:28; Ps 50:14, 15; Job 22:26

33:27 2 Sam 12:13; Luke 15:21; Rom 6:21

33:13 Being informed brings a sense of security. It's natural to want to know what's happening in our lives. Job wanted to know what was going on, why he was suffering. In previous chapters, we sense his frustration. Elihu claimed to have the answer for Job's biggest question, "Why doesn't God tell me what is happening?" Elihu told Job that God was trying to answer him, but he was not listening. Elihu misjudged God on this point. If God were to answer all our questions, we would not be adequately tested. What if God had said, "Job, Satan's going to test you and afflict you, but in the end you'll be healed and get everything back"? Job's greatest test was not the pain, but that he did not know *why* he was suffering. Our greatest test may be that we must trust God's goodness even though we don't understand why our lives are going a certain way. We must learn to trust in *God* who is good and not in the goodness of life.

33:14–24 Elihu's point was that God had spoken again and again. He spoke in dreams and visions (33:15–18), through suffering (33:19–22), and by mediating angels (33:23–24). Job already knew that. Elihu accused Job of not listening to God, which was not true.

And it is not proper for me.
28 'He has redeemed my soul from going to the pit,
And my life shall see the light.'

33:28 Job 22:28

29 "Behold, God does all these oftentimes with men,
30 To bring back his soul from the pit,
That he may be enlightened with the light of life.
31 "Pay attention, O Job, listen to me;
Keep silent, and let me speak.
32 "*Then* if you have anything to say, answer me;
Speak, for I desire to justify you.
33 "If not, listen to me;
Keep silent, and I will teach you wisdom."

33:29 Eph 1:11; Phil 2:13
33:30 Job 33:18; Zech 9:11
33:33 Ps 34:11

Elihu Vindicates God's Justice

34 Then Elihu continued and said,
2 "Hear my words, you wise men,
And listen to me, you who know.
3 "For the ear tests words
As the palate tastes food.
4 "Let us choose for ourselves what is right;
Let us know among ourselves what is good.
5 "For Job has said, 'I am righteous,
But God has taken away my right;
6 Should I lie concerning my right?
My wound is incurable, *though I am* without transgression.'
7 "What man is like Job,
Who drinks up derision like water,
8 Who goes in company with the workers of iniquity,
And walks with wicked men?
9 "For he has said, 'It profits a man nothing
When he is pleased with God.'

10 "Therefore, listen to me, you men of understanding.
Far be it from God to do wickedness,
And from the Almighty to do wrong.
11 "For He pays a man according to his work,
And makes him find it according to his way.

34:3 Job 12:11
34:5 Job 13:18; 33:9; Job 27:2
34:6 Job 6:4
34:7 Job 15:16
34:8 Job 22:15
34:9 Job 21:15; 35:3; Ps 50:18
34:10 Gen 18:25; Deut 32:4; Job 8:3; 34:12; Rom 9:14
34:11 Job 34:25; Ps 62:12; Prov 24:12; Jer 32:19; Ezek 33:20; Matt 16:27; Rom 2:6; 2 Cor 5:10; Rev 22:12

HOW SUFFERING AFFECTS US

Suffering is helpful when:	*Suffering is harmful when:*
We turn to God for understanding, endurance and deliverance	We become hardened and reject God
We ask important questions we might not take time to think about in our normal routine	We refuse to ask any questions and miss any lessons that might be good for us
We are prepared by it to identify with and comfort others who suffer	We allow it to make us self-centered and selfish
We are open to being helped by others who are obeying God	We withdraw from the help others can give
We are ready to learn from a trustworthy God	We reject the fact that God can bring good out of calamity
We realize we can identify with what Christ suffered on the cross for us	We accuse God of being unjust and perhaps lead others to reject him
We are sensitized to the amount of suffering in the world	We refuse to be open to any changes in our lives

34:10–15 God doesn't sin and is never unjust, Elihu claimed. Throughout this book, Eliphaz, Bildad, Zophar, and Elihu all have elements of truth in their speeches. Unfortunately, the nuggets of truth are buried under layers of false assumptions and conclusions. Although we might have a wealth of Bible knowledge and life experiences, we must make sure our conclusions are consistent with all of God's Word, not just parts of it.

12 "Surely, God will not act wickedly,
And the Almighty will not pervert justice.
13 "Who gave Him authority over the earth?
And who has laid *on Him* the whole world?
14 "If He should determine to do so,
If He should gather to Himself His spirit and His breath,
15 All flesh would perish together,
And man would return to dust.

16 "But if *you have* understanding, hear this;
Listen to the sound of my words.
17 "Shall one who hates justice rule?
And will you condemn the righteous mighty One,
18 Who says to a king, 'Worthless one,'
To nobles, 'Wicked ones';
19 Who shows no partiality to princes
Nor regards the rich above the poor,
For they all are the work of His hands?
20 "In a moment they die, and at midnight
People are shaken and pass away,
And the mighty are taken away without a hand.

21 "For His eyes are upon the ways of a man,
And He sees all his steps.
22 "There is no darkness or deep shadow
Where the workers of iniquity may hide themselves.
23 "For He does not *need to* consider a man further,
That he should go before God in judgment.
24 "He breaks in pieces mighty men without inquiry,
And sets others in their place.
25 "Therefore He knows their works,
And He overthrows *them* in the night,
And they are crushed.
26 "He strikes them like the wicked
In a public place,
27 Because they turned aside from following Him,
And had no regard for any of His ways;
28 So that they caused the cry of the poor to come to Him,
And that He might hear the cry of the afflicted—
29 When He keeps quiet, who then can condemn?
And when He hides His face, who then can behold Him,
That is, in regard to both nation and man?—
30 So that godless men would not rule
Nor be snares of the people.

31 "For has anyone said to God,
'I have borne *chastisement;*
I will not offend *anymore;*
32 Teach me what I do not see;
If I have done iniquity,
I will not do it again'?
33 "Shall He recompense on your terms, because you have rejected *it?*
For you must choose, and not I;
Therefore declare what you know.
34 "Men of understanding will say to me,
And a wise man who hears me,
35 'Job speaks without knowledge,
And his words are without wisdom.
36 'Job ought to be tried to the limit,
Because he answers like wicked men.
37 'For he adds rebellion to his sin;

34:12 Job 34:10

34:13 Job 38:4; Job 38:5

34:14 Job 12:10; Ps 104:29; Eccl 12:7

34:15 Gen 7:21; Job 9:22; Gen 3:19; Job 10:9

34:17 2 Sam 23:3; Job 34:30; Job 40:8

34:19 Lev 19:15; Deut 10:17; 2 Chr 19:7; Acts 10:34; Rom 2:11; Gal 2:6; Eph 6:9; Col 3:25; 1 Pet 1:17; Job 10:3

34:20 Ex 12:29; Job 34:25; 36:20; Job 12:19

34:21 Job 24:23; 31:4; Prov 5:21; 15:3; Jer 16:17

34:22 Ps 139:11, 12; Amos 9:2, 3

34:23 Job 11:11

34:24 Job 12:19

34:25 Job 34:11; Job 34:20

34:26 Ps 9:5; 11:5

34:27 1 Sam 15:11; Job 21:14

34:28 Job 35:9; James 5:4; Ex 22:23; Job 22:27

34:30 Job 5:15; 20:5; 34:17; Prov 29:2-12

34:32 Job 33:27

34:33 Job 41:11

34:35 Job 35:16; 38:2

34:36 Job 22:15

34:37 Job 23:2; Job 27:23

He claps his hands among us,
And multiplies his words against God.' "

Elihu Sharply Reproves Job

35 Then Elihu continued and said,
2 "Do you think this is according to justice?
Do you say, 'My righteousness is more than God's'?
3 "For you say, 'What advantage will it be to You?
What profit will I have, more than if I had sinned?'
4 "I will answer you,
And your friends with you.
5 "Look at the heavens and see;
And behold the clouds—they are higher than you.
6 "If you have sinned, what do you accomplish against Him?
And if your transgressions are many, what do you do to Him?
7 "If you are righteous, what do you give to Him,
Or what does He receive from your hand?
8 "Your wickedness is for a man like yourself,
And your righteousness is for a son of man.

9 "Because of the multitude of oppressions they cry out;
They cry for help because of the arm of the mighty.
10 "But no one says, 'Where is God my Maker,
Who gives songs in the night,
11 Who teaches us more than the beasts of the earth
And makes us wiser than the birds of the heavens?'
12 "There they cry out, but He does not answer
Because of the pride of evil men.
13 "Surely God will not listen to an empty *cry,*
Nor will the Almighty regard it.
14 "How much less when you say you do not behold Him,
The case is before Him, and you must wait for Him!
15 "And now, because He has not visited *in* His anger,
Nor has He acknowledged transgression well,
16 So Job opens his mouth emptily;
He multiplies words without knowledge."

35:2 Job 27:2
35:3 Job 34:9; Job 9:30, 31
35:5 Gen 15:5; Ps 8:3; Job 22:12
35:6 Job 7:20; Prov 8:36; Jer 7:19
35:7 Job 22:2, 3; Prov 9:12; Luke 17:10; Rom 11:35
35:9 Ex 2:23; Job 12:19
35:10 Job 21:14; 27:10; 36:13; Is 51:13; Job 8:21; Ps 42:8; 77:6; 149:5; Acts 16:25
35:11 Job 36:22; Ps 94:12; Jer 32:33
35:12 Prov 1:28
35:13 Job 27:9; Prov 15:29; Is 1:15; Jer 11:11; Mic 3:4
35:14 Job 9:11; 23:8, 9; Job 31:35
35:16 Job 34:35; 38:2

Elihu Speaks of God's Dealings with Men

36 Then Elihu continued and said,
2 "Wait for me a little, and I will show you
That there is yet more to be said in God's behalf.
3 "I will fetch my knowledge from afar,
And I will ascribe righteousness to my Maker.
4 "For truly my words are not false;
One who is perfect in knowledge is with you.
5 "Behold, God is mighty but does not despise *any;*
He is mighty in strength of understanding.
6 "He does not keep the wicked alive,
But gives justice to the afflicted.
7 "He does not withdraw His eyes from the righteous;
But with kings on the throne
He has seated them forever, and they are exalted.
8 "And if they are bound in fetters,
And are caught in the cords of affliction,
9 Then He declares to them their work
And their transgressions, that they have magnified themselves.

36:3 Job 8:3; 37:23
36:4 Job 33:3; Job 37:16
36:5 Ps 22:24; 69:33; 102:17; Job 12:13
36:6 Job 8:22; 34:26; Job 5:15
36:7 Ps 33:18; 34:15; Job 5:11; Ps 113:8
36:8 Job 36:15, 21
36:9 Job 15:25

35:1ff Sometimes we wonder if being faithful to our convictions really does any good at all. Elihu spoke to this very point. His conclusion was that God is still concerned even though he doesn't intervene immediately in every situation. In the broad scope of time God executes justice. We have his promise on that. Don't lose hope. Wait upon God. He notices your right living and your faith.

10 "He opens their ear to instruction,
And commands that they return from evil.
11 "If they hear and serve *Him,*
They will end their days in prosperity
And their years in pleasures.
12 "But if they do not hear, they shall perish by the sword
And they will die without knowledge.
13 "But the godless in heart lay up anger;
They do not cry for help when He binds them.
14 "They die in youth,
And their life *perishes* among the cult prostitutes.
15 "He delivers the afflicted in their affliction,
And opens their ear in *time of* oppression.
16 "Then indeed, He enticed you from the mouth of distress,
Instead of it, a broad place with no constraint;
And that which was set on your table was full of fatness.

17 "But you were full of judgment on the wicked;
Judgment and justice take hold *of you.*
18 "*Beware* that wrath does not entice you to scoffing;
And do not let the greatness of the ransom turn you aside.
19 "Will your riches keep you from distress,
Or all the forces of *your* strength?
20 "Do not long for the night,
When people vanish in their place.
21 "Be careful, do not turn to evil,
For you have preferred this to affliction.
22 "Behold, God is exalted in His power;
Who is a teacher like Him?
23 "Who has appointed Him His way,
And who has said, 'You have done wrong'?

24 "Remember that you should exalt His work,
Of which men have sung.
25 "All men have seen it;
Man beholds from afar.
26 "Behold, God is exalted, and we do not know *Him;*
The number of His years is unsearchable.
27 "For He draws up the drops of water,
They distill rain from the mist,
28 Which the clouds pour down,
They drip upon man abundantly.
29 "Can anyone understand the spreading of the clouds,
The thundering of His pavilion?
30 "Behold, He spreads His lightning about Him,
And He covers the depths of the sea.
31 "For by these He judges peoples;
He gives food in abundance.
32 "He covers *His* hands with the lightning,
And commands it to strike the mark.
33 "Its noise declares His presence;
The cattle also, concerning what is coming up.

36:10 Job 33:16; 36:15; 2 Kin 17:13; Job 36:21; Jon 3:8

36:11 1 Tim 4:8; Ps 16:11

36:12 Job 15:22; Job 4:21

36:14 Deut 23:17

36:15 Job 36:8, 21; Job 36:10

36:16 Hos 2:14

36:17 Job 22:5, 10, 11

36:18 Jon 4:4, 9; Job 33:24

36:20 Job 34:20, 25

36:21 Job 36:10; Ps 31:6; 66:18; Job 36:8, 15; Heb 11:25

36:22 Job 35:11

36:23 Deut 32:4; Job 8:3

36:24 Ps 92:5; Rev 15:3; Ex 15:1; Judg 5:1; 1 Chr 16:9; Ps 59:16; 138:5

36:26 Job 11:7-9; 37:23; 1 Cor 13:12; Job 10:5; Ps 90:2; 102:24, 27; Heb 1:12

36:27 Job 5:10; 36:26-29; 37:6, 11; 38:28; Ps 147:8

36:29 Job 37:11, 16; Job 26:14

36:31 Job 37:13; Ps 104:27; 136:25; Acts 14:17

36:32 Job 37:11, 12, 15

36:33 Job 37:2

36:26 One theme in the poetic literature of the Bible is that God is incomprehensible; we cannot know him completely. We can have some knowledge about him, for the Bible is full of details about who God is, how we can know him, and how we can have an eternal relationship with him. But we can never know enough to answer all of life's questions (Ecclesiastes 3:11), to predict our own future, or to manipulate God for our own ends. Life always creates more questions than we have answers, and we must constantly go to God for fresh insights into life's dilemmas. (See 37:19–24.)

Elihu Says God Is Back of the Storm

37 "At this also my heart trembles,
And leaps from its place.
2 "Listen closely to the thunder of His voice,
And the rumbling that goes out from His mouth.
3 "Under the whole heaven He lets it loose,
And His lightning to the ends of the earth.
4 "After it, a voice roars;
He thunders with His majestic voice,
And He does not restrain the lightnings when His voice is heard.
5 "God thunders with His voice wondrously,
Doing great things which we cannot comprehend.
6 "For to the snow He says, 'Fall on the earth,'
And to the downpour and the rain, 'Be strong.'
7 "He seals the hand of every man,
That all men may know His work.
8 "Then the beast goes into its lair
And remains in its den.
9 "Out of the south comes the storm,
And out of the north the cold.
10 "From the breath of God ice is made,
And the expanse of the waters is frozen.
11 "Also with moisture He loads the thick cloud;
He disperses the cloud of His lightning.
12 "It changes direction, turning around by His guidance,
That it may do whatever He commands it
On the face of the inhabited earth.
13 "Whether for correction, or for His world,
Or for lovingkindness, He causes it to happen.

14 "Listen to this, O Job,
Stand and consider the wonders of God.
15 "Do you know how God establishes them,
And makes the lightning of His cloud to shine?
16 "Do you know about the layers of the thick clouds,
The wonders of one perfect in knowledge,
17 You whose garments are hot,
When the land is still because of the south wind?
18 "Can you, with Him, spread out the skies,
Strong as a molten mirror?
19 "Teach us what we shall say to Him;
We cannot arrange *our case* because of darkness.
20 "Shall it be told Him that I would speak?
Or should a man say that he would be swallowed up?

21 "Now men do not see the light which is bright in the skies;
But the wind has passed and cleared them.
22 "Out of the north comes golden *splendor;*
Around God is awesome majesty.

37:2 Job 36:33; 37:4, 5; Ps 29:3-9
37:3 Job 28:24; 37:11, 12; 38:13
37:5 Job 26:14; Job 5:9; 37:14, 16, 23
37:6 Job 38:22; Job 36:27
37:7 Job 12:14; Ps 111:2
37:8 Job 38:40; Ps 104:21, 22
37:9 Job 9:9
37:10 Job 38:29; Ps 147:17
37:11 Job 36:27; Job 36:29; Job 37:15
37:12 Job 36:32; Ps 148:8; Is 14:21; 27:6
37:13 Ex 9:18, 23; 1 Sam 12:18, 19; Job 38:26, 27; 1 Kin 18:41-46
37:16 Job 37:5, 14, 23; Job 36:4
37:18 Job 9:8; Ps 104:2; Is 44:24; 45:12; Jer 10:12; Zech 12:1
37:19 Job 9:14; Rom 8:26

37:2 Nothing can compare to God. His power and presence are awesome, and when he speaks, we must listen. Too often we presume to speak for God (as did Job's friends), to put words in his mouth, to take him for granted, or to interpret his silence to mean that he is absent or unconcerned. But God cares. He is in control, and he will speak. Be ready to hear his message—in the Bible, in your life through the Holy Spirit, and through circumstances and relationships.

37:21–24 Elihu concluded his speech with the tremendous truth that faith in God is far more important than Job's desire for an explanation for his suffering. He came so close to helping Job but then went down the wrong path. Significantly, it is here that God himself breaks into the discussion to draw the right conclusions from this important truth (38:1ff).

23 "The Almighty—we cannot find Him;
He is exalted in power
And He will not do violence to justice and abundant righteousness.
24 "Therefore men fear Him;
He does not regard any who are wise of heart."

37:23 Job 11:7, 8; Rom 11:33; 1 Tim 6:16; Job 9:4; 36:5; Is 63:9; Lam 3:33; Ezek 18:23, 32; 33:11; Job 8:3

37:24 Matt 10:28; Job 5:13; Matt 11:25; 1 Cor 1:26

D. GOD ANSWERS JOB (38:1—41:34)

Instead of answering Job's question directly, God asks Job a series of questions that no human could possibly answer. Job responds by recognizing that God's ways are best. During difficult times, we, too, must humbly remember our position before the eternal, holy, incomprehensible God.

God Speaks Now to Job

38 Then the LORD answered Job out of the whirlwind and said,
2 "Who is this that darkens counsel
By words without knowledge?
3 "Now gird up your loins like a man,
And I will ask you, and you instruct Me!
4 "Where were you when I laid the foundation of the earth?
Tell *Me,* if you have understanding,
5 Who set its measurements? Since you know.
Or who stretched the line on it?
6 "On what were its bases sunk?
Or who laid its cornerstone,
7 When the morning stars sang together
And all the sons of God shouted for joy?

8 "Or *who* enclosed the sea with doors
When, bursting forth, it went out from the womb;
9 When I made a cloud its garment
And thick darkness its swaddling band,
10 And I placed boundaries on it
And set a bolt and doors,
11 And I said, 'Thus far you shall come, but no farther;
And here shall your proud waves stop'?

38:1 Job 40:6

38:2 Job 35:16; 42:3

38:3 Job 40:7; Job 42:4

38:4 Job 15:7; Ps 104:5; Prov 8:29; 30:4

38:5 Prov 8:29; Is 40:12

38:6 Job 26:7

38:7 Job 1:6

38:8 Gen 1:9; Ps 104:6-9; Prov 8:29; Jer 5:22

38:10 Gen 1:9; Ps 33:7; 104:9; Prov 8:29; Jer 5:22

God's Mighty Power

12 "Have you ever in your life commanded the morning,
And caused the dawn to know its place,
13 That it might take hold of the ends of the earth,
And the wicked be shaken out of it?
14 "It is changed like clay *under* the seal;
And they stand forth like a garment.
15 "From the wicked their light is withheld,
And the uplifted arm is broken.

16 "Have you entered into the springs of the sea
Or walked in the recesses of the deep?
17 "Have the gates of death been revealed to you,
Or have you seen the gates of deep darkness?
18 "Have you understood the expanse of the earth?
Tell *Me,* if you know all this.

38:13 Job 28:24; 37:3; Job 34:25, 26; 36:6

38:15 Job 5:14; Num 15:30; Ps 10:15; 37:17

38:16 Gen 7:11; 8:2; Prov 8:24, 28

38:17 Job 10:21; 26:6; 34:22

38:18 Job 28:24

37:23 Elihu stressed God's sovereignty over all of nature as a reminder of his sovereignty over our lives. God is in control—he directs, preserves, and maintains his created order. Although we can't see it, God is divinely governing the moral and political affairs of people as well. By spending time observing the majestic and intricate parts of God's creation, we can be reminded of his power in every aspect of our lives.

38:1ff Out of a whirlwind, God spoke. Surprisingly, he didn't answer any of Job's questions; Job's questions were not at the heart of the issue. Instead, God used Job's ignorance of the earth's natural order to reveal his ignorance of God's moral order. If Job did not understand the workings of God's physical creation, how could he possibly understand God's mind and character? There is no standard or criterion higher than God himself by which to judge. God himself is the standard. Our only option is to submit to his authority and rest in his care.

19 "Where is the way to the dwelling of light?
And darkness, where is its place,
20 That you may take it to its territory
And that you may discern the paths to its home?
21 "You know, for you were born then,
And the number of your days is great!
22 "Have you entered the storehouses of the snow,
Or have you seen the storehouses of the hail,
23 Which I have reserved for the time of distress,
For the day of war and battle?
24 "Where is the way that the light is divided,
Or the east wind scattered on the earth?

25 "Who has cleft a channel for the flood,
Or a way for the thunderbolt,
26 To bring rain on a land without people,
On a desert without a man in it,
27 To satisfy the waste and desolate land
And to make the seeds of grass to sprout?
28 "Has the rain a father?
Or who has begotten the drops of dew?
29 "From whose womb has come the ice?
And the frost of heaven, who has given it birth?
30 "Water becomes hard like stone,
And the surface of the deep is imprisoned.

38:20 Job 26:10
38:21 Job 15:7
38:22 Job 37:6; Ex 9:18; Josh 10:11; Is 30:30; Ezek 13:11, 13; Rev 16:21
38:24 Job 26:10
38:26 Job 36:27
38:27 Ps 104:13, 14; 107:35
38:28 Job 36:27, 28; Ps 147:8; Jer 14:22
38:29 Job 37:10; Ps 147:17

GOD SPEAKS
On various occasions in the Old Testament, God chose to communicate audibly with individuals. God will always find a way to make contact with those who want to know him. Some of those occasions are listed here.

Whom he spoke to	*What he said*	*Reference*
Adam and Eve	Confronted them about sin	Genesis 3:8–13
Noah	Gave him directions about building the ark	Genesis 6:13–22; 7:1; 8:15–17
Abraham	Commanded him to follow God's leading and promised to bless him	Genesis 12:1–9
	Tested his obedience by commanding him to sacrifice his son	Genesis 22:1–14
Jacob	Permitted him to go to Egypt	Genesis 46:1–4
Moses	Sent him to lead the people out of Egypt	Exodus 3:1–10
	Gave him the Ten Commandments	Exodus 19:1—20:20
Moses, Aaron, Miriam	Pronounced judgment on a family conflict	Numbers 12:1–15
Joshua	Promised to be with him as he was with Moses	Joshua 1:1–9
Samuel	Chose him to be his spokesman	1 Samuel 3:1–18
Isaiah	Sent him to the people with his message	Isaiah 6:1–13
Jeremiah	Encouraged him to be his prophet	Jeremiah 1:4–10
Ezekiel	Sent him to Israel to warn them of coming judgment	Ezekiel 2:1–8

38:22–23 God said he was reserving the storehouses of the snow and hail for times of trouble. God used hail to help Joshua and the Israelites win a battle (Joshua 10:11). Just as armies keep weapons in the armory, God has all the forces of nature in his control. Sometimes he uses them to confound those opposed to him or his people. Job couldn't even begin to know all of God's resources.

38:22–35 God stated that he has all the forces of nature at his command and that he can unleash or restrain them at will. No one completely understands such common occurrences as rain or snow, and no one can command them—only God who created them has that power. God's point was that if Job could not explain such common events in nature, how could he possibly explain or question God? And if nature is beyond our grasp, God's moral purposes may not be what we imagine either.

31 "Can you bind the chains of the Pleiades,
Or loose the cords of Orion?
32 "Can you lead forth a constellation in its season,
And guide the Bear with her satellites?
33 "Do you know the ordinances of the heavens,
Or fix their rule over the earth?

34 "Can you lift up your voice to the clouds,
So that an abundance of water will cover you?
35 "Can you send forth lightnings that they may go
And say to you, 'Here we are'?
36 "Who has put wisdom in the innermost being
Or given understanding to the mind?
37 "Who can count the clouds by wisdom,
Or tip the water jars of the heavens,
38 When the dust hardens into a mass
And the clods stick together?

39 "Can you hunt the prey for the lion,
Or satisfy the appetite of the young lions,
40 When they crouch in *their* dens
And lie in wait in *their* lair?
41 "Who prepares for the raven its nourishment
When its young cry to God
And wander about without food?

38:31 Job 9:9; Amos 5:8
38:33 Ps 148:6; Jer 31:35, 36
38:34 Job 22:11; 36:27, 28; 38:37
38:35 Job 36:32; 37:3
38:36 Job 9:4; Ps 51:6; Eccl 2:26; Job 32:8
38:37 Job 38:34
38:39 Ps 104:21
38:40 Job 37:8
38:41 Ps 147:9; Matt 6:26; Luke 12:24

God Speaks of Nature and Its Beings

39 "Do you know the time the mountain goats give birth?
Do you observe the calving of the deer?
2 "Can you count the months they fulfill,
Or do you know the time they give birth?
3 "They kneel down, they bring forth their young,
They get rid of their labor pains.
4 "Their offspring become strong, they grow up in the open field;
They leave and do not return to them.

5 "Who sent out the wild donkey free?
And who loosed the bonds of the swift donkey,
6 To whom I gave the wilderness for a home
And the salt land for his dwelling place?
7 "He scorns the tumult of the city,
The shoutings of the driver he does not hear.
8 "He explores the mountains for his pasture
And searches after every green thing.
9 "Will the wild ox consent to serve you,
Or will he spend the night at your manger?
10 "Can you bind the wild ox in a furrow with ropes,
Or will he harrow the valleys after you?
11 "Will you trust him because his strength is great
And leave your labor to him?
12 "Will you have faith in him that he will return your grain
And gather *it from* your threshing floor?

39:1 Deut 14:5; 1 Sam 24:2; Ps 104:18; Ps 29:9
39:5 Job 6:5; 11:12; 24:5; Ps 104:11
39:6 Job 24:5; Jer 2:24; Hos 8:9
39:9 Num 23:22; Deut 33:17; Ps 22:21; 29:6; 92:10; Is 34:7

38:31–32 These are star constellations, and they are all under God's control.

39:1ff God asked Job several questions about the animal kingdom in order to demonstrate how limited Job's knowledge really was. God was not seeking answers from Job. Instead, he was getting Job to recognize and submit to God's power and sovereignty. Only then could he hear what God was really saying to him.

13 "The ostriches' wings flap joyously
With the pinion and plumage of [11]love,
14 For she abandons her eggs to the earth
And warms them in the dust,
15 And she forgets that a foot may crush them,
Or that a wild beast may trample them.
16 "She treats her young cruelly, as if *they* were not hers;
Though her labor be in vain, *she* is unconcerned;
17 Because God has made her forget wisdom,
And has not given her a share of understanding.
18 "When she lifts herself on high,
She laughs at the horse and his rider.

19 "Do you give the horse *his* might?
Do you clothe his neck with a mane?
20 "Do you make him leap like the locust?
His majestic snorting is terrible.
21 "He paws in the valley, and rejoices in *his* strength;
He goes out to meet the weapons.
22 "He laughs at fear and is not dismayed;
And he does not turn back from the sword.
23 "The quiver rattles against him,
The flashing spear and javelin.
24 "With shaking and rage he races over the ground,
And he does not stand still at the voice of the trumpet.
25 "As often as the trumpet *sounds* he says, 'Aha!'
And he scents the battle from afar,
And the thunder of the captains and the war cry.

26 "Is it by your understanding that the hawk soars,
Stretching his wings toward the south?
27 "Is it at your command that the eagle mounts up
And makes his nest on high?
28 "On the cliff he dwells and lodges,
Upon the rocky crag, an inaccessible place.
29 "From there he spies out food;
His eyes see *it* from afar.
30 "His young ones also suck up blood;
And where the slain are, there is he."

39:16 Lam 4:3
39:20 Joel 2:5; Jer 8:16
39:21 Jer 8:6
39:27 Jer 49:16; Obad 4
39:29 Job 9:26
39:30 Matt 24:28; Luke 17:37

11 Or *a stork*

GOD'S JUSTICE

Wrong view	*Correct view*
LAW OF FAIRNESS / GOD	GOD / JUSTICE
There is a law of fairness or justice that is higher and more absolute than God. It is binding even for God. God must act in response to that law in order to be fair. Our response is to appeal to that law.	God himself is the standard of justice. He uses his power according to his own moral perfection. Thus, whatever he does is fair, is to appeal directly to him.

Job: What Can I Say?

40 Then the LORD said to Job,
2 "Will the faultfinder contend with the Almighty?
Let him who reproves God answer it."

40:2 Job 9:3; 10:2; 33:13; Is 45:9; Job 13:3; 23:4; 31:35

3 Then Job answered the LORD and said,
4 "Behold, I am insignificant; what can I reply to You?
I lay my hand on my mouth.
5 "Once I have spoken, and I will not answer;
Even twice, and I will add nothing more."

40:4 Job 21:5; 29:9

40:5 Job 9:3, 15

God Questions Job

6 Then the LORD answered Job out of the storm and said,
7 "Now gird up your loins like a man;
I will ask you, and you instruct Me.
8 "Will you really annul My judgment?
Will you condemn Me that you may be justified?
9 "Or do you have an arm like God,
And can you thunder with a voice like His?

40:6 Job 38:1

40:7 Job 38:3; Job 38:3; 42:4

40:8 Rom 3:4; Job 10:3, 7; 16:11; 19:6; 27:2; Job 13:18; 27:6

40:9 Job 37:5; Ps 29:3

10 "Adorn yourself with eminence and dignity,
And clothe yourself with honor and majesty.
11 "Pour out the overflowings of your anger,
And look on everyone who is proud, and make him low.
12 "Look on everyone who is proud, *and* humble him,
And tread down the wicked where they stand.
13 "Hide them in the dust together;
Bind them in the hidden *place.*
14 "Then I will also confess to you,
That your own right hand can save you.

40:10 Ps 93:1; 104:1

40:11 Is 42:25; Nah 1:6, 8; Is 2:12; Dan 4:37

40:12 1 Sam 2:7; Is 2:12; 13:11; Dan 4:37; Is 63:3

40:13 Is 2:10-12

God's Power Shown in Creatures

15 "Behold now, [12]Behemoth, which I made as well as you;
He eats grass like an ox.
16 "Behold now, his strength in his loins
And his power in the muscles of his belly.
17 "He bends his tail like a cedar;
The sinews of his thighs are knit together.

40:15 Job 40:19

12 Or *the hippopotamus*

FOUR VIEWS OF SUFFERING

Satan's view	People believe in God only when they are prospering and not suffering. This is wrong.
The view of Job's three friends	Suffering is God's judgment for sin. This is not always true.
Elihu's view	Suffering is God's way to teach, discipline, and refine. This is true, but an incomplete explanation.
God's view	Suffering causes us to trust God for who he is, not what he does.

40:2–5 How do you contend with or reprove Almighty God? Do you demand answers when things don't go your way, you lose a job, someone close to you is ill or dies, finances are tight, you fail, or unexpected changes occur? The next time you are tempted to complain to God, consider how much he loves you. And remember Job's reaction when he had his chance to speak. Are you worse off than Job or more righteous than he? Give God a chance to reveal his greater purposes for you, but remember that they may unfold over the course of your life and not at the moment you desire.

40:4 Throughout his time of suffering, Job longed to have an opportunity to plead his innocence before God. Here God appeared to Job and gave him that opportunity. But Job decided to remain quiet because it was no longer necessary for him to speak. God had shown Job that, as a limited human being, he had neither the ability to judge the God who created the universe nor the right to ask why. God's actions do not depend on ours. He will do what he knows is best, regardless of what we think is fair. It is important to note, however, that God came to Job, demonstrating his love and care for him.

40:15 The Behemoth was a large land animal, possibly an elephant or hippopotamus.

18 "His bones are tubes of bronze;
His limbs are like bars of iron.

40:19 Job 41:33; Job 40:15

40:20 Ps 104:14; Ps 104:26

19 "He is the first of the ways of God;
Let his maker bring near his sword.
20 "Surely the mountains bring him food,
And all the beasts of the field play there.
21 "Under the lotus plants he lies down,
In the covert of the reeds and the marsh.
22 "The lotus plants cover him with shade;
The willows of the brook surround him.

40:23 Gen 13:10

23 "If a river rages, he is not alarmed;
He is confident, though the Jordan rushes to his mouth.
24 "Can anyone capture him when he is on watch,
With barbs can anyone pierce *his* nose?

God's Power Shown in Creatures

41:1 Job 3:8; Ps 74:14; 104:26; Is 27:1

41:2 2 Kin 19:28; Is 37:29

41 "Can you draw out [13]Leviathan with a fishhook?
Or press down his tongue with a cord?
2 "Can you put a rope in his nose
Or pierce his jaw with a hook?
3 "Will he make many supplications to you,
Or will he speak to you soft words?
4 "Will he make a covenant with you?
Will you take him for a servant forever?
5 "Will you play with him as with a bird,
Or will you bind him for your maidens?
6 "Will the traders bargain over him?
Will they divide him among the merchants?
7 "Can you fill his skin with harpoons,
Or his head with fishing spears?
8 "Lay your hand on him;
Remember the battle; you will not do it again!
9 "Behold, your expectation is false;
Will you be laid low even at the sight of him?

41:10 Job 3:8

41:11 Rom 11:35; Ex 19:5; Deut 10:14; Job 9:5-10; 26:6-14; 28:24; Ps 24:1; 50:12; 1 Cor 10:26

10 "No one is so fierce that he dares to arouse him;
Who then is he that can stand before Me?
11 "Who has given to Me that I should repay *him?*
Whatever is under the whole heaven is Mine.

12 "I will not keep silence concerning his limbs,
Or his mighty strength, or his orderly frame.

13 Or *the crocodile*

JOB AND JESUS
The book of Job is intimately tied to the New Testament because Job's questions and problems are answered perfectly in Jesus Christ.

Subject	*Reference in Job*	*How Jesus is the Answer*
Someone must help us approach God	9:32–33	1 Timothy 2:5
Is there life after death?	14:14	John 11:25
There is one in heaven working on our behalf	16:19	Hebrews 9:24
There is one who can save us from judgment	19:25	Hebrews 7:24–25
What is important in life?	21:7–15	Matthew 16:26; John 3:16
Where do we find God?	23:3–5	John 14:9

41:1 While *Leviathan* usually refers to a seven-headed sea monster in old Canaanite myths, it probably means crocodile here.

41:9–11 It is foolish for people to think they can stand up against God when they are afraid to confront even a crocodile. How much more powerful is God! It is better to submit to God's loving authority than to face his wrath.

13 "Who can strip off his outer armor?
Who can come within his double mail?
14 "Who can open the doors of his face?
Around his teeth there is terror.
15 "*His* strong scales are *his* pride,
Shut up *as with* a tight seal.
16 "One is so near to another
That no air can come between them.
17 "They are joined one to another;
They clasp each other and cannot be separated.
18 "His sneezes flash forth light,
And his eyes are like the eyelids of the morning. **41:18** Job 3:9
19 "Out of his mouth go burning torches;
Sparks of fire leap forth.
20 "Out of his nostrils smoke goes forth
As *from* a boiling pot and *burning* rushes.
21 "His breath kindles coals,
And a flame goes forth from his mouth.
22 "In his neck lodges strength,
And dismay leaps before him.
23 "The folds of his flesh are joined together,
Firm on him and immovable.
24 "His heart is as hard as a stone,
Even as hard as a lower millstone.
25 "When he raises himself up, the mighty fear;
Because of the crashing they are bewildered.
26 "The sword that reaches him cannot avail,
Nor the spear, the dart or the javelin.
27 "He regards iron as straw,
Bronze as rotten wood.
28 "The arrow cannot make him flee;
Slingstones are turned into stubble for him.
29 "Clubs are regarded as stubble;
He laughs at the rattling of the javelin.
30 "His underparts are *like* sharp potsherds;
He spreads out *like* a threshing sledge on the mire.
31 "He makes the depths boil like a pot;
He makes the sea like a jar of ointment.
32 "Behind him he makes a wake to shine;
One would think the deep to be gray-haired.

WHEN WE SUFFER

Here are six questions to ask ourselves when we suffer, and what to do if the answer is yes.

Questions	*Our responses*
Am I being punished by God for sin?	Confess known sin.
Is Satan attacking me as I try to survive as a Christian?	Call on God for strength.
Am I being prepared for a special service, learning to be compassionate to those who suffer?	Resist self-pity. Ask God to open up doors of opportunity and help you discover others who suffer as you do.
Am I specifically selected for testing, like Job?	Accept help from the body of believers. Trust God to work his purpose through you.
Is my suffering a result of natural consequences for which I am not directly responsible?	Recognize that in a sinful world, both good and evil people will suffer. But the good person has a promise from God that his or her suffering will one day come to an end.
Is my suffering due to some unknown reason?	Don't draw inward from the pain. Proclaim your faith in God, know that he cares, and wait patiently for his aid.

41:33 Job 40:19
41:34 Job 28:8

33 "Nothing on earth is like him,
One made without fear.
34 "He looks on everything that is high;
He is king over all the sons of pride."

E. JOB IS RESTORED (42:1—17)

In response to God's speech, Job humbles himself. God rebukes the three friends for adding to Job's suffering by their false assumptions and critical attitudes. Job's material possessions and family are restored, and he receives even greater blessings than he had before. Those who persist in trusting God will be rewarded.

Job's Confession

42:2 Gen 18:14; Matt 19:26
42:3 Job 38:2; Ps 40:5; 131:1; 139:6
42:4 Job 38:3; 40:7
42:5 Job 26:14; Rom 10:17; Is 6:5; Eph 1:17, 18

42 Then Job answered the LORD and said,
2 "I know that You can do all things,
And that no purpose of Yours can be thwarted.
3 'Who is this that hides counsel without knowledge?'
"Therefore I have declared that which I did not understand,
Things too wonderful for me, which I did not know."
4 'Hear, now, and I will speak;
I will ask You, and You instruct me.'
5 "I have heard of You by the hearing of the ear;
But now my eye sees You;
6 Therefore I retract,
And I repent in dust and ashes."

God Displeased with Job's Friends

42:7 Job 40:3-5; 42:1-6
42:8 Num 23:1; Job 1:5; Gen 20:17; James 5:16; 1 John 5:16; Job 22:30

7 It came about after the LORD had spoken these words to Job, that the LORD said to
Eliphaz the Temanite, "My wrath is kindled against you and against your two friends,
because you have not spoken of Me what is right as My servant Job has.
8 "Now therefore, take for yourselves seven bulls and seven rams, and go to My servant Job, and offer up a burnt offering for yourselves, and My servant Job will pray for
you. For I will accept him so that I may not do with you *according to your* folly, because
you have not spoken of Me what is right, as My servant Job has."
9 So Eliphaz the Temanite and Bildad the Shuhite *and* Zophar the Naamathite went
and did as the LORD told them; and the LORD accepted Job.

God Restores Job's Fortunes

42:10 Deut 30:3; Job 1:2, 3; Ps 14:7; 85:1-3; 126:1-6
42:11 Job 19:13; Job 2:11
42:12 Job 1:10; 8:7; James 5:11; Job 1:3
42:13 Job 1:2

10 The LORD restored the fortunes of Job when he prayed for his friends, and the LORD
increased all that Job had twofold.
11 Then all his brothers and all his sisters and all who had known him before came to
him, and they ate bread with him in his house; and they consoled him and comforted
him for all the adversities that the LORD had brought on him. And each one gave him
one piece of money, and each a ring of gold.
12 The LORD blessed the latter *days* of Job more than his beginning; and he had 14,000
sheep and 6,000 camels and 1,000 yoke of oxen and 1,000 female donkeys.
13 He had seven sons and three daughters.
14 He named the first Jemimah, and the second Keziah, and the third Keren-happuch.

42:1ff Throughout the book, Job's friends had asked him to admit his sin and ask for forgiveness, and eventually Job did indeed repent. Ironically, Job's repentance was not the kind called for by his friends. He did not ask for forgiveness for committing secret sins, but for questioning God's sovereignty and justice. Job repented of his attitude and acknowledged God's great power and perfect justice. We sin when we angrily ask, "If God is in control, how could he let this happen?" Because we are locked into time, unable to see beyond today, we cannot know the reasons for everything that happens. Will you trust God with your unanswered questions?

42:2-4 Job was quoting the Lord's earlier questions to him (38: 2-3). He openly and honestly faced God and admitted that he was the one who had been foolish. Are you using what you can't understand as an excuse for your lack of trust? Admit to God that you don't even have enough faith to trust him. True faith begins in such humility.

42:7-8 God made it clear that Job's friends were wrong. The fact that God did not mention any specific sins shows that God confirmed Job's claim to have led a devout and obedient life. Job's friends had made the error of assuming that Job's suffering was caused by some great sin. They were judging Job without knowing what God was doing. We must be careful to avoid making judgments about a person because God may be working in ways we know nothing about.

15 In all the land no women were found so fair as Job's daughters; and their father
gave them inheritance among their brothers.
16 After this, Job lived 140 years, and saw his sons and his grandsons, four generations.
17 And Job died, an old man and full of days.

42:17 Gen 15:15; 25:8; Job 5:26

THE SOURCES OF SUFFERING

Sources	*Who is Responsible*	*Who is Affected*	*Needed Response*
My sin	I am	Myself and others	Repentance and confession to God
Others' sin	Person who sinned and others who allowed the sin	Probably many people, including those who sinned	Active resistance to the sinful behavior, while accepting the sinner
Avoidable physical (or natural) disaster	Persons who ignore the facts or refuse to take precautions	Most of those exposed to the cause	Prevent them if possible; be prepared if they can't be prevented
Unavoidable physical (or natural) disaster	God, Satan	Most of those present	Ongoing trust in God's faithfulness

When suffering or troubles happen, do they always come from Satan? In Job's story, his series of tragedies did come from Satan, but this is not always the case. The chart above demonstrates the four main causes of suffering. Any one of these or a combination of them may create suffering. If knowing why we are suffering will teach us to avoid the cause, then the causes are worth knowing. However, it is most important to know how to respond during suffering.

PSALMS

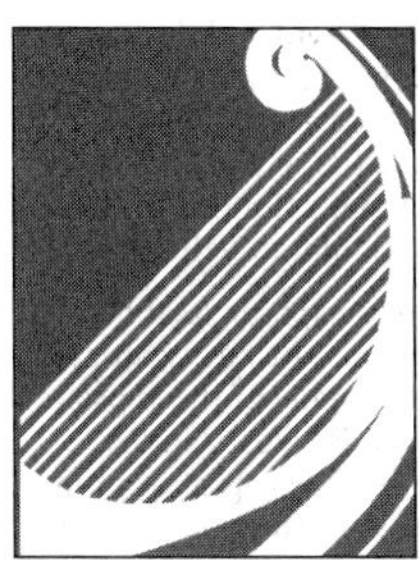

"HI, how are you?" "Fine." Not exactly an "in-depth" discussion, this brief interchange is normal as friends and acquaintances pass and briefly touch each other with a cliché or two. Actually, clichés are a way of life, saturating sentences and permeating paragraphs. But if this is the essence of our communication, our relationships will stall on a superficial plateau. Facts and opinions also fill our verbiage. These words go deeper, but the true person still lies hidden beneath them. In reality, it is only when honest feelings and emotions are shared that real people can be known, loved, and helped.

Often, patterns of superficial communication spill over into our talks with God. We easily slide through well-worn lines recited for decades, or we quickly toss a cliché or two at God and call it prayer. There is no doubt that God hears and understands these feeble attempts, but by limiting the depth of our communication, we become shallow in our relationship with him. But God knows us, and he wants to have genuine communication with us.

At the center of the Bible is the book of Psalms. This great collection of songs and prayers expresses the heart and soul of humanity. In them, the whole range of human experiences is expressed. There are no clichés in this book. Instead, David and the other writers honestly pour out their true feelings, reflecting a dynamic, powerful, and life-changing friendship with God. The psalmists confess their sins, express their doubts and fears, ask God for help in times of trouble, and praise and worship him.

As you read the book of Psalms, you will hear believers crying out to God from the depths of despair, and you will hear them singing to him in the heights of celebration. But whether the psalmists are despairing or rejoicing, you will always hear them sharing honest feelings with their God. Because of the honesty expressed by the psalmists, men and women throughout history have come, again and again, to the book of Psalms for comfort during times of struggle and distress. And with the psalmists, they have risen from the depths of despair to new heights of joy and praise as they also discovered the power of God's everlasting love and forgiveness. Let the honesty of the psalmists guide you into a deep and genuine relationship with God.

VITAL STATISTICS

PURPOSE:
To provide poetry for the expression of praise, worship, and confession to God

AUTHORS:
David wrote 73 psalms; Asaph wrote 12; the sons of Korah wrote 9; Solomon wrote 2; Heman (with the sons of Korah), Ethan, and Moses each wrote one; and 51 psalms are anonymous. The New Testament ascribes two of the anonymous psalms (Psalms 2 and 95) to David (see Acts 4:25; Hebrews 4:7).

DATE WRITTEN:
Between the time of Moses (approximately 1440 B.C.) and the Babylonian captivity (586 B.C.)

SETTING:
For the most part, the psalms were not intended to be narrations of historical events. However, they often parallel events in history, such as David's flight from Saul and his sin with Bathsheba.

KEY VERSE:
"Let everything that has breath praise to the LORD. Praise the LORD!" (150:6).

KEY PERSON:
David

KEY PLACE:
God's holy temple

THE BLUEPRINT

BOOK 1 PSALMS 1:1—41:13	While the psalms are not organized by topic, it is helpful to compare the dominant themes in each section of the Psalms to the five books of Moses. This first collection of psalms, mainly written by David, is similar to the book of Genesis. Just as Genesis tells how mankind was created, fell into sin, and was then promised redemption, many of these psalms discuss humans as blessed, fallen, and redeemed by God.
BOOK 2 PSALMS 42:1—72:20	This collection of psalms, mainly written by David and the sons of Korah, is similar to the book of Exodus. Just as Exodus describes the nation of Israel, many of these psalms describe the nation as ruined and then recovered. As God rescued the nation of Israel, he also rescues us. We do not have to work out solutions first, but we can go to God with our problems and ask him to help.
BOOK 3 PSALMS 73:1—89:52	This collection of psalms, mainly written by Asaph or Asaph's descendants, is similar to the book of Leviticus. Just as Leviticus discusses the tabernacle and God's holiness, many of these psalms discuss the temple and God's enthronement. Because God is almighty, we can turn to him for deliverance. These psalms praise God because he is holy, and his perfect holiness deserves our worship and reverence.
BOOK 4 PSALMS 90:1—106:48	This collection of psalms, mainly written by unknown authors, is similar to the book of Numbers. Just as Numbers discusses the relationship of the nation of Israel to surrounding nations, these psalms often mention the relationship of God's overruling kingdom to the other nations. Because we are citizens of the kingdom of God, we can keep the events and troubles of earth in their proper perspective.
BOOK 5 PSALMS 107:1—150:6	This collection of psalms, mainly written by David, is similar to the book of Deuteronomy. Just as Deuteronomy was concerned with God and his Word, these psalms are anthems of praise and thanksgiving for God and his Word. Most of the psalms were originally set to music and used in worship. We can use these psalms today as they were used in the past, as a hymnbook of praise and worship. This is a book that ought to make our hearts sing.

MEGATHEMES

THEME	EXPLANATION	IMPORTANCE
Praise	Psalms are songs of praise to God as our Creator, Sustainer, and Redeemer. Praise is recognizing, appreciating, and expressing God's greatness.	Focusing our thoughts on God moves us to praise him. The more we know him, the more we can appreciate what he has done for us.
God's power	God is all-powerful; and he always acts at the right time. He is sovereign over every situation. God's power is shown by the ways he reveals himself in creation, history, and his Word.	When we feel powerless, God can help us. His strength can overcome the despair of any pain or trial. We can always pray that he will deliver, protect, and sustain us.
Forgiveness	Many psalms are intense prayers asking God for forgiveness. God forgives us when we confess our sin and turn from it.	Because God forgives us, we can pray to him honestly and directly. When we receive his forgiveness, we move from alienation to intimacy, from guilt to love.
Thankfulness	We are grateful to God for his personal concern, help, and mercy. Not only does he protect, guide, and forgive us, but his creation provides everything we need.	When we realize how we benefit from knowing God, we can fully express our thanks to him. By thanking him often, we develop spontaneity in our prayer life.
Trust	God is faithful and just. When we put our trust in him, he quiets our hearts. Because he has been faithful throughout history, we can trust him in times of trouble.	People can be unfair and friends may desert us. But we can trust God. Knowing God intimately drives away doubt, fear, and loneliness.

The following expressions occur often in the Psalms:

Selah	May mean *Pause, Crescendo* or *Musical Interlude*
Maskil	Possibly, *Contemplative,* or *Didactic,* or *Skillful Psalm*
Mikhtam	Possibly, *Epigrammatic Poem,* or *Atonement Psalm*
Sheol	The nether world

BOOK 1
PSALMS 1:1—41:13

In this book, the psalmists praise God for his justice, express confidence in God's compassion, recount the depravity of man, plead for vindication, ask God to deliver them from their enemies, speak of the blessedness of the forgiven sinner, and portray God as a shepherd. We should worship God with the same sense of adoration found in these psalms.

PSALM 1

Theme: Life's two roads. The life of the faithful person is contrasted with the life of the faithless person.
Author: Anonymous

1 How blessed is the man who does not walk in the counsel of the wicked,
Nor stand in the path of sinners,
Nor sit in the seat of scoffers!
2 But his delight is in the law of the LORD,
And in His law he meditates day and night.
3 He will be like a tree *firmly* planted by streams of water,
Which yields its fruit in its season
And its leaf does not wither;
And in whatever he does, he prospers.

4 The wicked are not so,
But they are like chaff which the wind drives away.

1:1 Prov 4:14; Ps 5:9, 10; 10:2-11; 36:1-4; Ps 17:4; 119:104; Ps 26:4, 5; Jer 15:17

1:2 Ps 119:14, 16, 35; Josh 1:8; Ps 25:5; Ps 63:5, 6

1:3 Ps 92:12-14; Jer 17:8; Ezek 19:10; Gen 39:2, 3, 23; Ps 128:2

1:4 Job 21:18; Ps 35:5; Is 17:13

1:1 The writer begins his psalm extolling the joys of obeying God and refusing to listen to those who discredit or ridicule him. Our friends and associates can have a profound influence on us, often in very subtle ways. If we insist on friendships with those who mock what God considers important, we might sin by becoming indifferent to God's will. This attitude is the same as mocking. Do your friends build up your faith, or do they tear it down? True friends should help, not hinder, you to draw closer to God.

1:1ff God doesn't judge people on the basis of race, sex, or national origin. He judges them on the basis of their faith in him and their response to his revealed will. Those who diligently try to obey God's will are blessed. Their happy condition is like healthy, fruit-bearing trees with strong roots (Jeremiah 17:5–8), and God promises to watch over them. God's wisdom guides their lives. In contrast, those who don't trust and obey God have meaningless lives that blow away like dust.

There are only two paths of life before us—God's way of obedience or the way of rebellion and destruction. Be sure to choose God's path because the path you choose determines how you will spend eternity.

1:2 You can learn how to follow God by meditating on his Word. Meditating means spending time reading and thinking about what you have read. It means asking yourself how you should change so you're living as God wants. Knowing and meditating on God's Word are the first steps toward applying it to your everyday life. If you want to follow God more closely, you must know what he says.

1:2 This "law of the LORD" means all of Scripture: The first five books of Moses, the Prophets, and the other writings. The more we know of the whole scope of God's Word, the more resources we will have to guide us in our daily decisions.

1:2–3 There is simple wisdom in these two verses—the more we delight in God's presence, the more fruitful we are. On the other hand, the more we allow those who ridicule God to affect our thoughts and attitudes, the more we separate ourselves from our source of nourishment. We must have contact with unbelievers if we are to witness to them, but we must not join in or imitate their sinful behavior. If you want despair, spend time with mocking sinners; but if you want God's happiness, make friends with those who love God and his Word.

1:3 When Scripture says, "In whatever he does, he prospers," it does not mean immunity from failure or difficulties. Nor is it a guarantee of health, wealth, and happiness. What the Bible means by prosperity is this: When we apply God's wisdom, the fruit (results or by-products) we bear will be good and receive God's approval. Just as a tree soaks up water and bears luscious fruit, so we also are to soak up God's Word, producing actions and attitudes that honor God. To achieve anything worthwhile, we must have God's Word in our hearts.

1:4 Chaff is the outer shell (or husk) that must be removed to get at the valuable kernels of grain inside. Chaff was removed by a process called threshing and winnowing. After the plants were cut, they were crushed, and then the pieces were thrown into the air. Chaff is very light and is carried away by even the slightest wind, while the good grain falls back to the earth. Chaff is a symbol of a faithless life that drifts along without direction. Good grain is a symbol of a faithful life that can be used by God. Unlike grain, however, we can choose the direction we will take.

5 Therefore the wicked will not stand in the judgment,
Nor sinners in the assembly of the righteous.
6 For the LORD knows the way of the righteous,
But the way of the wicked will perish.

1:5 Ps 5:5; Ps 9:7, 8, 16; Ps 89:5, 7

1:6 Ps 37:18; Nah 1:7; John 10:14; 2 Tim 2:19; Ps 9:5, 6; 11:6

PSALM 2

Theme: God's ultimate rule. A psalm written to celebrate the coronation of an Israelite king, but also written for the coronation of Christ, the eternal King.
Author: Acts 4:25–26 attributes this psalm to David.

1 Why are the nations in an uproar
And the peoples devising a vain thing?
2 The kings of the earth take their stand
And the rulers take counsel together
Against the LORD and against His [1]Anointed, saying,
3 "Let us tear their fetters apart
And cast away their cords from us!"

4 He who [2]sits in the heavens laughs,
The Lord scoffs at them.
5 Then He will speak to them in His anger
And terrify them in His fury, saying,
6 "But as for Me, I have installed My King
Upon Zion, My holy mountain."

7 "I will surely tell of the decree of the LORD:
He said to Me, 'You are My Son,
Today I have begotten You.
8 'Ask of Me, and I will surely give the nations as Your inheritance,
And the *very* ends of the earth as Your possession.
9 'You shall [3]break them with a rod of iron,
You shall shatter them like earthenware.' "

10 Now therefore, O kings, show discernment;
Take warning, O [4]judges of the earth.
11 Worship the LORD with reverence

2:1 Ps 46:6; 83:2-5; Acts 4:25, 26; Ps 21:11

2:2 Ps 48:4-6; Ps 74:18, 23; John 1:41

2:3 Jer 5:5

2:4 Ps 37:13; Ps 59:8

2:5 Ps 21:8, 9; 76:7; Ps 78:49, 50

2:6 Ps 45:6; Ps 48:1, 2

2:7 Acts 13:33; Heb 1:5; 5:5

2:8 Ps 21:1, 2; Ps 22:27; Ps 67:7

2:9 Ps 89:23; 110:5, 6; Rev 2:26, 27; 12:5; 19:15; Ps 28:5; 52:5; 72:4

2:10 Prov 8:15; 27:11

2:11 Ps 5:7; Ps 119:119, 120

1 Or *Messiah* 2 Or *is enthroned* 3 Another reading is *rule* 4 Or *leaders*

2:1ff Several psalms are called *Messianic* because of their prophetic descriptions of Jesus the Messiah (Christ)—his life, death, resurrection, and future reign. David, who may have been the author of this psalm, was a shepherd, soldier, and king. We can see that he was also a prophet (Acts 2:29–30) because this psalm describes the rebellion of the nations and the coming of Christ to establish his eternal reign. This psalm is often mentioned in the New Testament (see Acts 4:25–26; 13:33; Hebrews 1:5–6; 5:5; Revelation 2:26–27; 12:5; 19:15).

2:1ff David may have written these words during a conspiracy against Israel by some of the surrounding pagan nations. Chosen and anointed by God, David knew that God would fulfill his promise to bring the Messiah into the world through his bloodline (2 Samuel 7:16; 1 Chronicles 17:11–12).

2:3 People often think they will be free if they can get away from God. Yet we all inevitably serve somebody or something, whether a human king, an organization, or even our own selfish desires. Just as a fish is not free when it leaves the water and a tree is not free when it leaves the soil, so we are not free when we leave the Lord. We can find the one sure route to freedom by wholeheartedly serving God the Creator. God can set you free to be the person he created you to be.

2:4 God laughs, not at the nations, but at their confused thoughts about power. It is the laughter of a father when his three-year-old boasts that he or she can outrun him or beat him in a wrestling match. The father knows the boundaries of power of his little child, and God knows the boundaries of power of the nations. Every nation is limited, but God is transcendent. If you have to choose between confidence in God and confidence in any nation, choose God!

2:4 God is all-powerful. He created the world, and knew about the empires of the earth long before they came into being (Daniel 2:26–45). But pride and power cause nations and leaders to rebel against God and try to break free of him. Our world has many leaders who boast of their power, who rant and rave against God and his people, who promise to take over and form their own empires. But God laughs because any power they have comes from him, and he can also take it from them. We need not fear the boasts of tyrants—they are in God's hands.

2:11–12 "Do homage to the Son" means to surrender fully and submit to him. Christ is not only God's chosen King; he is also the rightful King of our hearts and lives. To be ready for his coming, we must submit to his leadership every day.

2:12 Ps 2:7; Rev 6:16, 17; Ps 5:11; 34:22

And rejoice with trembling.
12 Do homage to the Son, that He not become angry, and you perish *in* the way,
For His wrath may [5]soon be kindled.
How blessed are all who take refuge in Him!

PSALM 3

A Psalm of David, when he fled from Absalom his son.

Theme: Confidently trusting God for protection and peace.
Author: David

3:1 2 Sam 15:12; Ps 69:4

3:2 Ps 22:7, 8; 71:11

3:3 Ps 5:12; 28:7; Ps 62:7; Ps 9:13; 27:6

3:4 Ps 4:3; 34:4; Ps 2:6; 15:1; 43:3

1 O LORD, how my adversaries have increased!
Many are rising up against me.
2 Many are saying of my soul,
"There is no deliverance for him in God." [6]Selah.

3 But You, O LORD, are a shield about me,
My glory, and the One who lifts my head.
4 I was crying to the LORD with my voice,

5 Or *quickly, suddenly, easily* 6 *Selah* may mean: *Pause, Crescendo* or *Musical interlude*

REASONS TO READ PSALMS

When you want. . .	*Read . . .*
to find comfort	Psalm 23
to meet God intimately	Psalm 103
to learn a new prayer	Psalm 136
to learn a new song	Psalm 92
to learn more about God	Psalm 24
to understand yourself more clearly	Psalm 8
to know how to come to God each day	Psalm 5
to be forgiven for your sins	Psalm 51
to feel worthwhile	Psalm 139
to understand why you should read the Bible	Psalm 119
to give praise to God	Psalm 145
to know that God is in control	Psalm 146
to give thanks to God	Psalm 136
to please God	Psalm 15
to know why you should worship God	Psalm 104

God's Word was written to be studied, understood, and applied, and the book of Psalms lends itself most directly to application. We understand the psalms best when we "stand under" them and allow them to flow over us like a rain shower. We may turn to Psalms looking for something, but sooner or later we will meet Someone. As we read and memorize the psalms, we will gradually discover how much they are already part of us. They put into words our deepest hurts, longings, thoughts, and prayers. They gently push us toward being what God designed us to be—people loving and living for him.

3:1–2 David felt like he was in the minority. There may have been as many as 10,000 soldiers surrounding him at this time (3:6). Not only did David's enemies view life differently; they actively sought to harm him. As king, David could have trusted his army to defeat Absalom. Instead, he depended upon God's mercy (3:4); therefore, he was at peace with whatever outcome occurred, knowing that God's great purposes would prevail. We can overcome fear by trusting God for his protection in our darkest hour.

3:1–3 David was not sitting on his throne in a place of power, but he was running for his life from his rebellious son Absalom and a host of traitors. When circumstances go against us, it is tempting to think that God also is against us. But David reminds us that the opposite is true. When everything seems to go against us, God is still for us. If circumstance has turned against you, don't blame God—seek him!

3:2 The word "Selah" occurs 71 times in Psalms and three times in Habakkuk (3:3, 9, 13). Though its precise use is unknown, it was most likely a musical sign. Three suggestions are: (1) It was a musical direction to the singers and orchestra to play *forte* or *crescendo.* (2) It was a signal to lift up the hands or voice in worship, or to the priest to give a benediction. (3) It was a phrase like "Amen" meaning "So be it," or "Hallelujah" meaning "Praise the Lord."

3:4 God's holy mountain was Mount Moriah in Jerusalem, the place where David's son Solomon would build the temple (2 Chronicles 3:1). David knew that God could not be confined to any space, but he wrote poetically, expressing confidence that God would hear him when he prayed. God responds to us when we urgently pray to him.

And He answered me from His holy mountain. Selah.
5 I lay down and slept;
I awoke, for the LORD sustains me.
6 I will not be afraid of ten thousands of people
Who have set themselves against me round about.

7 Arise, O LORD; save me, O my God!
For You have smitten all my enemies on the cheek;
You have shattered the teeth of the wicked.
8 Salvation belongs to the LORD;
Your blessing *be* upon Your people! Selah.

3:5
Lev 26:6; Ps 4:8; Prov 3:24

3:6
Ps 23:4; 27:3; Ps 118:10-13

3:7
Ps 7:6; Ps 6:4; 22:21; Job 16:10; Ps 57:4; 58:6

3:8
Ps 28:8; 35:3; Is 43:11; Ps 29:11

PSALM 4

For the choir director; on stringed instruments. A Psalm of David.

Theme: Rejoicing in God's protection and peace. We can place our confidence in God because he will listen when we call on him.
Author: David

1 Answer me when I call, O God of my righteousness!
You have relieved me in my distress;
Be gracious to me and hear my prayer.

2 O sons of men, how long will my honor become a reproach?
How long will you love what is worthless and aim at deception? Selah.
3 But know that the LORD has set apart the godly man for Himself;
The LORD hears when I call to Him.

4 Tremble, and do not sin;
Meditate in your heart upon your bed, and be still. Selah.
5 Offer the sacrifices of righteousness,
And trust in the LORD.

6 Many are saying, "Who will show us *any* good?"
Lift up the light of Your countenance upon us, O LORD!
7 You have put gladness in my heart,
More than when their grain and new wine abound.

4:1
Ps 3:4; 17:6; Ps 18:6; Ps 18:18, 19; Ps 25:16; Ps 17:6; 39:12

4:2
Ps 3:3; Ps 69:7-10, 19, 20; Ps 12:2; 31:6; Ps 31:18

4:3
Ps 135:4; Ps 31:23; 50:5; 79:2; Ps 6:8, 9; 17:6

4:4
Ps 99:1; Ps 119:11; Eph 4:26; Ps 77:6

4:5
Deut 33:19; Ps 51:19; Ps 37:3, 5; 62:8

4:6
Job 7:7; 9:25; Num 6:26; Ps 80:3, 7, 19

4:7
Ps 97:11, 12; Is 9:3; Acts 14:17

3:5 Sleep does not come easily during a crisis. David could have had sleepless nights when his son Absalom rebelled and gathered an army to kill him. But he slept peacefully, even during the rebellion. What made the difference? David cried out to the Lord, and the Lord heard him. The assurance of answered prayer brings peace. It is easier to sleep well when we have full assurance that God is in control of circumstances. If you are lying awake at night worrying about circumstances you can't change, pour out your heart to God, and thank him that he is in control. Then sleep will come.

3:7 This description of God's anger reveals David's desire for justice against his persecutors. David himself was slapped and insulted, and here he simply asked for equal treatment for his enemies. He did this, not out of personal revenge, but for the sake of God's justice. Verse 8 shows the humility behind David's words—he realized that faith in God's timing was the answer to his question about the success the wicked had unfairly achieved.

4:1ff This psalm may have been written as David was asking his enemies to reconsider their support of Absalom. Others see this psalm as a prayer for relief from a calamity such as a drought (see 4:7). It was probably written shortly after Psalm 3.

4:3 The godly are those who are faithful and devoted to God. David knew that God would hear him when he called and would answer him. We too can be confident that God listens to our prayers and answers when we call on him. Sometimes we think that God will not hear us because we have fallen short of his high standards for holy living. But if we have trusted Christ for salvation, God has forgiven us, and he will listen to us. When you feel as though your prayers are bouncing off the ceiling, remember that as a believer you have been set apart by God and that he loves you. He hears and answers, although his answers may not be what you expect. Look at your problems in the light of God's power instead of looking at God in the shadow of your problems.

4:5 Worship in David's day included animal sacrifices by the priests in the tabernacle. The animal's blood covered the sins of the one who offered the animal. There were specific rules for offering sacrifices, but more important to God than ceremony was the offerer's attitude of submission and obedience (1 Samuel 15:22–23). Today, a "sacrifice of righteousness," one that is pleasing to God, is still the same. He wants our obedience and our praise before our gifts (Hebrews 13:15). Offer God your sacrifice of total obedience and heartfelt praise.

4:7 Two kinds of joy are contrasted here—inward joy that comes from knowing and trusting God and happiness that comes as a result of pleasant circumstances. Inward joy is steady as long as we trust God; happiness is unpredictable. Inward joy defeats discouragement; happiness covers it up. Inward joy is lasting; happiness is temporary.

4:8 Job 11:19; Ps 3:5; Lev 25:18; Deut 12:10; Ps 16:9

8 In peace I will both lie down and sleep,
For You alone, O LORD, make me to dwell in safety.

PSALM 5

For the choir director; for flute accompaniment. A Psalm of David.

Theme: The lies of enemies. God is able to defend us from lies spoken against us.
Author: David

5:1 Ps 54:2; Ps 104:34
5:2 Ps 140:6; Ps 84:3
5:3 Ps 88:13; Ps 130:5
5:4 Ps 11:5; 34:16; Ps 92:15
5:5 Ps 73:3; 75:4; Ps 1:5; Ps 11:5; 45:7

1 Give ear to my words, O LORD,
Consider my [7]groaning.
2 Heed the sound of my cry for help, my King and my God,
For to You I pray.
3 In the morning, O LORD, You will hear my voice;
In the morning I will order *my prayer* to You and *eagerly* watch.

4 For You are not a God who takes pleasure in wickedness;
No evil dwells with You.
5 The boastful shall not stand before Your eyes;

7 Or *meditation*

PSALMS FROM DAVID'S LIFE
Of the more than 70 psalms attributed to David, at least 14 of them are connected with specific events in his life. From them we see an outline of a growing relationship with God. They are listed here, roughly in chronological order.

Event in David's life	*Reference*	*Psalm*	*What David learned about God*
When Saul sent men to David's home to kill him	1 Samuel 19	59	God is my stronghold.
While running from Saul	1 Samuel 21	34	I will bless the Lord at all times.
While running from Saul	1 Samuel 21	56	When I am afraid, I will put my trust in God.
While hiding in the cave of Adullam	1 Samuel 22	142	God is my refuge.
After learning that Doeg had murdered 85 priests and their families	1 Samuel 22	52	God will break down evil people forever.
When the Ziphites tried to betray him	1 Samuel 23	54	Behold, God is my helper.
While hiding in a cave	1 Samuel 24	57	In the shadow of your wings I will take refuge until destruction passes by.
While hiding in the wilderness of Engedi	1 Samuel 24	63	My soul clings to God; his right hand upholds me.
When Saul's pursuit was over	2 Samuel 22	18	With the blameless God shows himself blameless.
After being confronted about his adultery with Bathsheba	2 Samuel 12	51	The sacrifices of God are a broken spirit; a broken and a contrite heart he will not despise.
During Absalom's rebellion	2 Samuel 15	3	Salvation belongs to the Lord.
During Absalom's rebellion	2 Samuel 15	7	He is a righteous God who tries hearts and minds; he saves the upright in heart.

5:1–3 The secret of a close relationship with God is to pray to him earnestly *in the morning.* In the morning our minds are more free from problems and then we can commit the whole day to God. Regular communication helps any friendship and is certainly necessary for a strong relationship with God. We need to communicate with him daily. Do you have a regular time to pray and read God's Word?

5:5 God cannot condone or excuse even the smallest sin. Therefore we cannot excuse ourselves for sinning only a little bit. As we grow spiritually, our sensitivity to sin increases. What is your reaction to sin in your life? Are you insensitive, unconcerned, disappointed, or comfortable? As God makes us aware of sin, we must be intolerant toward it and be willing to change. All believers should strive to be more tolerant of people but less tolerant of the sin in others and in themselves.

You hate all who do iniquity.
6 You destroy those who speak falsehood;
The LORD abhors the man of bloodshed and deceit.
7 But as for me, by Your abundant lovingkindness I will enter Your house,
At Your holy temple I will bow in reverence for You.

8 O LORD, lead me in Your righteousness because of my foes;
Make Your way straight before me.
9 There is nothing reliable in what they say;
Their inward part is destruction *itself.*
Their throat is an open grave;
They flatter with their tongue.
10 Hold them guilty, O God;
By their own devices let them fall!
In the multitude of their transgressions thrust them out,
For they are rebellious against You.

11 But let all who take refuge in You be glad,
Let them ever sing for joy;
And may You shelter them,
That those who love Your name may exult in You.
12 For it is You who blesses the righteous man, O LORD,
You surround him with favor as with a shield.

5:6 Ps 52:4, 5; Ps 55:23
5:7 Ps 69:13; Ps 138:2; Ps 115:11, 13
5:8 Ps 31:3; Ps 31:1; Ps 27:11
5:9 Ps 52:3; Ps 7:14; Rom 3:13
5:10 Ps 9:16; Ps 36:12; Ps 107:10, 11
5:11 Ps 2:12; Ps 33:1; 64:10; Ps 12:7; Ps 69:36
5:12 Ps 29:11; Ps 32:7, 10

PSALM 6

For the choir director; with stringed instruments, upon an eight-string lyre. A Psalm of David.

Theme: Deliverance in trouble. God is able to rescue us.
Author: David

1 O LORD, do not rebuke me in Your anger,
Nor chasten me in Your wrath.
2 Be gracious to me, O LORD, for I *am* pining away;
Heal me, O LORD, for my bones are dismayed.
3 And my soul is greatly dismayed;
But You, O LORD—how long?

4 Return, O LORD, rescue my [8]soul;
Save me because of Your lovingkindness.
5 For there is no [9]mention of You in death;
In Sheol who will give You thanks?

6 I am weary with my sighing;
Every night I make my bed swim,
I dissolve my couch with my tears.
7 My eye has wasted away with grief;
It has become old because of all my adversaries.

6:1 Ps 38:1; 118:18
6:2 Ps 102:4, 11; Ps 41:4; 147:3; Hos 6:1; Ps 22:14; 31:10
6:3 Ps 88:3; John 12:27; Ps 90:13
6:4 Ps 17:13
6:5 Ps 30:9; 88:10-12; 115:17; Eccl 9:10; Is 38:18
6:6 Ps 69:3; Ps 42:3
6:7 Job 17:7; Ps 31:9; 38:10

8 Or *life* **9** Or *remembrance*

6:1ff This is the first of seven "penitential" psalms, where the writer humbly realizes his predicament (usually the result of sin), expresses sorrow over it, and demonstrates a fresh commitment to remain close to God. We don't know the cause of David's pain, but whatever the cause, he sought God for the remedy.

6:1–3 David accepted God's punishment, but he begged God not to discipline him in anger. Jeremiah also asked God to correct him gently and not in anger (Jeremiah 10:24). David recognized that if God treated him with justice alone and not with mercy, he would be wiped out by God's wrath. Often we want God to show mercy to us and justice to everyone else. God in his kindness forgives us instead of giving us what we deserve.

6:6 Pouring out his heart with tears, David was completely honest with God. We can be honest with God even when we are filled with anger or despair because God knows us thoroughly and wants the very best for us. Anger may result in rash outward acts or turning inward in depression. But because we trust in our all-powerful God, we don't have to be victims of circumstance or be weighed down by the guilt of sin. Be honest with God, and he will help you turn your attention from yourself to him and his mercy.

6:8 Ps 119:115; Matt 7:23; Luke 13:27; Ps 3:4; 28:6
6:9 Ps 116:1; Ps 66:19, 20
6:10 Ps 71:13, 24; Ps 73:19

8 Depart from me, all you who do iniquity,
For the LORD has heard the voice of my weeping.
9 The LORD has heard my supplication,
The LORD receives my prayer.
10 All my enemies will be ashamed and greatly dismayed;
They shall turn back, they will suddenly be ashamed.

PSALM 7

A [10]Shiggaion of David, which he sang to the LORD concerning Cush, a Benjamite.

Theme: A request for justice against those who make slanderous comments. God is the perfect judge and will punish those who persecute the innocent.
Author: David

7:1 Ps 31:1; 71:1; Ps 31:15
7:2 Ps 57:4; Is 38:13
7:3 1 Sam 24:11
7:4 Ps 109:4, 5; 1 Sam 24:7; 26:9
7:6 Ps 3:7; Ps 94:2; Ps 138:7; Ps 35:23; 44:23
7:7 Ps 22:27
7:8 Ps 96:13; 98:9; Ps 18:20; 26:1; 35:24; 43:1
7:9 Ps 34:21; 94:23; Ps 37:23; 40:2; Ps 11:4, 5; Jer 11:20; Rev 2:23
7:10 Ps 18:2, 30; Ps 97:10, 11; 125:4
7:11 Ps 50:6; Ps 90:9
7:12 Ps 58:5; Deut 32:41; Ps 64:7
7:13 Ps 18:14; 45:5

1 O LORD my God, in You I have taken refuge;
Save me from all those who pursue me, and deliver me,
2 Or he will tear my soul like a lion,
Dragging me away, while there is none to deliver.

3 O LORD my God, if I have done this,
If there is injustice in my hands,
4 If I have rewarded evil to my friend,
Or have plundered him who without cause was my adversary,
5 Let the enemy pursue my soul and overtake *it;*
And let him trample my life down to the ground
And lay my glory in the dust. Selah.

6 Arise, O LORD, in Your anger;
Lift up Yourself against the rage of my adversaries,
And arouse Yourself for me; You have appointed judgment.
7 Let the assembly of the peoples encompass You,
And over them return on high.
8 The LORD judges the peoples;
Vindicate me, O LORD, according to my righteousness and my integrity that is in me.
9 O let the evil of the wicked come to an end, but establish the righteous;
For the righteous God tries the hearts and [11]minds.
10 My shield is with God,
Who saves the upright in heart.
11 God is a righteous judge,
And a God who has indignation every day.

12 If a man does not repent, He will sharpen His sword;
He has bent His bow and made it ready.
13 He has also prepared for Himself deadly weapons;
He makes His arrows fiery shafts.

10 I.e. Dithyrambic rhythm; or wild passionate song **11** Lit *kidneys,* figurative for inner man

---

7 title *Shiggaion* may be a term derived from the verb "to err" or "to wander;" it might also mean "wild" or "ecstatic." It is a poem written with intense feeling, a lament to stir the emotions.

7:1–6 Have you ever been falsely accused or so badly hurt that you wanted revenge? David wrote this psalm in response to the slanderous accusations of those who claimed he was trying to kill Saul and seize the throne (1 Samuel 24:9–11). Instead of taking matters into his own hands and striking back, David cried out to God for justice. The proper response to slander is prayer, not revenge, because God says, "Vengeance is Mine, I will repay" (Romans 12:19; see also Deuteronomy 32:35–36; Hebrews 10:30). Instead of striking back, ask God to take your case, bring justice, and restore your reputation.

7:9 God "tries the hearts and minds." Nothing is hidden from God—this can be either terrifying or comforting. Our thoughts are an open book to him. Because he knows even our motives, we have no place to hide, no way to pretend we can get away with sin. But that very knowledge also gives us great comfort. We don't have to impress God or put up a false front. Instead, we can trust God to help us work through our weaknesses in order to serve him as he has planned. When we truly follow God, he rewards our effort.

14 Behold, he travails with wickedness,
And he conceives mischief and brings forth falsehood.
15 He has dug a pit and hollowed it out,
And has fallen into the hole which he made.
16 His mischief will return upon his own head,
And his violence will descend upon [12]his own pate.

17 I will give thanks to the LORD according to His righteousness
And will sing praise to the name of the LORD Most High.

7:14 Job 15:35; Is 59:4; James 1:15

7:15 Job 4:8; Ps 57:6

7:16 Esth 9:25; Ps 140:9; Ps 140:11

7:17 Ps 71:15, 16; Ps 9:2; 66:1, 2, 4

PSALM 8

For the choir director; on the Gittith. A Psalm of David.

Theme: The greatness of God assures the worth of mankind. God, the all-powerful Creator, cares for his most valuable creation—people.
Author: David

1 O LORD, our Lord,
How majestic is Your name in all the earth,
Who have displayed Your splendor above the heavens!
2 From the mouth of infants and nursing babes You have established strength
Because of Your adversaries,
To make the enemy and the revengeful cease.

3 When I consider Your heavens, the work of Your fingers,
The moon and the stars, which You have ordained;
4 What is man that You take thought of him,
And the son of man that You care for him?
5 Yet You have made him a little lower than God,
And You crown him with glory and majesty!
6 You make him to rule over the works of Your hands;
You have put all things under his feet,
7 All sheep and oxen,
And also the beasts of the field,
8 The birds of the heavens and the fish of the sea,
Whatever passes through the paths of the seas.

8:1 Ps 57:5, 11; 113:4; 148:13

8:2 Matt 21:16; 1 Cor 1:27; Ps 29:1; 118:14; Ps 44:16

8:3 Ps 111:2; Ps 89:11; 144:5; Ps 136:9

8:4 Job 7:17; Ps 144:3; Heb 2:6-8

8:5 Gen 1:26; Ps 82:6; Ps 103:4; Ps 21:5

8:6 Gen 1:26, 28; 1 Cor 15:27; Eph 1:22; Heb 2:8

12 I.e. the crown of his own head

7:14–16 When allowed to run its course, evil destroys itself. Violent people become victims of violence, and liars become victims of others' deceit (9:15–16). But in the process, innocent people are hurt. Sometimes God intervenes and stops evildoers in their tracks in order to protect his followers. At other times, for reasons known only to him, God allows evil to continue even though innocent people are hurt. It is during these times that we must ask God to protect us. Remember that God will execute final justice, even if it is not during our lifetime.

7:17 During a time of great evil and injustice, David was grateful that God is righteous (see also 7:11). When we wonder if anyone is honest or fair, we can be assured that God will continue to bring justice and fairness when we involve him in our activities. If you ever feel that you are being treated unfairly, ask the one who is always fair and just to be with you. Then thank him for his presence (see Isaiah 42:1–6).

8:1ff Portions of this psalm are quoted in the New Testament and applied to Christ (1 Corinthians 15:27; Hebrews 2:6–8). Jesus became human, just a little lower than God (8:5), and he will raise all who belong to him above the heavenly beings when he comes to reign over the new heaven and new earth. Jesus is the only person who perfectly reflects God's image (Galatians 2:20; Colossians 1:15).

8:2 Children are able to trust and praise God without doubts or reservations. As we get older, many of us find this more and more difficult to do. Ask God to give you childlike faith, removing any barriers to having a closer walk with him. Get in touch with this childlike quality in yourself so that you can be more expressive.

8:3–4 To respect God's majesty, we must compare ourselves to his greatness. When we look at creation, we often feel small by comparison. To feel small is a healthy way to get back to reality, but God does not want us to dwell on our smallness. Humility means proper respect for God, not self-depreciation.

8:3–5 When we look at the vast expanse of creation, we wonder how God could be concerned for people who constantly disappoint him. Yet God created us only a little lower than himself or the angels! The next time you question your worth as a person, remember that God considers you highly valuable. We have great worth because we bear the stamp of the Creator. (See Genesis 1:26–27 for the extent of worth God places on all people.) Because God has already declared how valuable we are to him, we can be set free from feelings of worthlessness.

8:6 God gave human beings tremendous authority—to be in charge of the whole earth. But with great authority comes great responsibility. If we own a pet, we have the legal authority to do with it as we wish, but we also have the responsibility to feed and care for it. How do you treat God's creation? Use your resources wisely because God holds you accountable for your stewardship.

9 O LORD, our Lord,
How majestic is Your name in all the earth!

PSALM 9

For the choir director; on [13]Muth-labben. A Psalm of David.

Theme: God never ignores our cries for help.
Author: David, probably written after a victory over the Philistines

1 I will give thanks to the LORD with all my heart;
I will tell of all Your wonders.
2 I will be glad and exult in You;
I will sing praise to Your name, O Most High.

3 When my enemies turn back,
They stumble and perish before You.
4 For You have maintained my just cause;
You have sat on the throne judging righteously.
5 You have rebuked the nations, You have destroyed the wicked;
You have blotted out their name forever and ever.
6 The enemy has come to an end in perpetual ruins,
And You have uprooted the cities;
The very memory of them has perished.

7 But the LORD [14]abides forever;
He has established His throne for judgment,
8 And He will judge the world in righteousness;
He will execute judgment for the peoples with equity.
9 The LORD also will be a stronghold for the oppressed,
A stronghold in times of trouble;
10 And those who know Your name will put their trust in You,
For You, O LORD, have not forsaken those who seek You.

11 Sing praises to the LORD, who dwells in Zion;
Declare among the peoples His deeds.
12 For He who [15]requires blood remembers them;
He does not forget the cry of the afflicted.
13 Be gracious to me, O LORD;
See my affliction from those who hate me,
You who lift me up from the gates of death,
14 That I may tell of all Your praises,

8:9 Ps 8:1
9:1 Ps 86:12; Ps 26:7
9:2 Ps 5:11; 104:34; Ps 66:2, 4; Ps 83:18; 92:1
9:3 Ps 27:2
9:4 Ps 140:12; Ps 50:6
9:5 Ps 119:21; Ps 69:28; Prov 10:7
9:6 Ps 34:16
9:7 Ps 10:16; Ps 89:14
9:8 Ps 96:13; 98:9
9:9 Ps 32:7; 59:9, 16, 17
9:10 Ps 91:14; Ps 37:28; 94:14
9:11 Ps 76:2; Ps 105:1; 107:22
9:12 Gen 9:5; Ps 72:14; Ps 9:18
9:13 Ps 38:19; Ps 30:3; 86:13
9:14 Ps 106:2; Ps 13:5; 20:5; 35:9; 51:12

13 I.e. "Death to the Son" **14** Or *sits* as king **15** I.e. avenges bloodshed

---

9:1ff Praise is expressing to God our appreciation and understanding of his worth. It is saying "thank you" for each aspect of his divine nature. Our inward attitude becomes outward expression. When we praise God, we help ourselves by expanding our awareness of who he is. In each psalm you read, look for an attribute or characteristic of God for which you can thank him.

9:4 God upholds our just cause; he is our vindicator (one who clears us from criticism and justifies us before others). In this life, we may face many injustices: (1) We may be falsely accused and misunderstood by friends and enemies; (2) we may not be truly appreciated by others for the love we show; (3) the true value of our work and service may not be duly rewarded; (4) our ideas may be ignored. But God is to be praised, for he sees and remembers all the good we do, and it is up to him to decide the timing and the appropriateness of our rewards. If we do not trust him to vindicate us, then we will be susceptible to hatred and self-pity. If we do trust him, we can experience God's peace and be free from the worry of how others perceive us and treat us.

9:10 God will never forsake those who seek him. To forsake someone is to abandon that person. God's promise does not mean that if we trust in him we will escape loss or suffering; it means that God himself will never leave us no matter what we face.

9:11 God does not live only in Zion (another name for Mount Moriah, the hill on which the temple was built); he is everywhere all the time. The focal point of Israelite worship, however, came to be Jerusalem and its beautiful temple. God was present in the tabernacle (Exodus 25:8–9) and in the temple built by Solomon (2 Chronicles 7:16). From this central place of worship, the Jews were to tell the world about the one true God.

9:13–14 All of us want God to help us when we are in trouble, but often for different reasons. Some want God's help so that they will be successful and other people will like them. Others want God's help so that they will be comfortable and feel good about themselves. David, however, wanted help from God so that justice would be restored to Israel and so that he could show others God's power. When you call to God for help, consider your motive. Is it to save yourself pain and embarrassment or to bring God glory and honor?

That in the gates of the daughter of Zion
I may rejoice in Your salvation.
15 The nations have sunk down in the pit which they have made;
In the net which they hid, their own foot has been caught.
16 The LORD has made Himself known;
He has executed judgment.
In the work of his own hands the wicked is snared. Higgaion Selah.

17 The wicked will return to Sheol,
Even all the nations who forget God.
18 For the needy will not always be forgotten,
Nor the hope of the afflicted perish forever.
19 Arise, O LORD, do not let man prevail;
Let the nations be judged before You.
20 Put them in fear, O LORD;
Let the nations know that they are but men. Selah.

9:15 Ps 7:15, 16; Ps 57:6
9:16 Ex 7:5; Ps 9:4
9:17 Ps 49:14; Job 8:13; Ps 50:22
9:18 Ps 9:12; 12:5; Ps 62:5; 71:5; Prov 23:18
9:19 Num 10:35; Ps 9:5
9:20 Ps 14:5; Ps 62:9

PSALM 10

Theme: Why do the wicked succeed? Although God may seem to be hidden at times, we can be assured that he is aware of every injustice.
Author: Anonymous, but probably David. Many ancient manuscripts combine Psalms 9 and 10, and Psalm 9 was written by David.

1 Why do You stand afar off, O LORD?
Why do You hide *Yourself* in times of trouble?
2 In pride the wicked hotly pursue the afflicted;
Let them be caught in the plots which they have devised.

3 For the wicked boasts of his heart's desire,
And [16]the greedy man curses *and* spurns the LORD.
4 The wicked, in the haughtiness of his countenance, does not seek *Him*.
All his thoughts are, "There is no God."

5 His ways prosper at all times;
Your judgments are on high, out of his sight;
As for all his adversaries, he snorts at them.
6 He says to himself, "I will not be moved;
Throughout all generations I will not be in adversity."
7 His mouth is full of curses and deceit and oppression;
Under his tongue is mischief and wickedness.
8 He sits in the lurking places of the villages;
In the hiding places he kills the innocent;
His eyes stealthily watch for the unfortunate.
9 He lurks in a hiding place as a lion in his lair;
He lurks to catch the afflicted;

10:1 Ps 22:1; Ps 13:1; 55:1
10:2 Ps 73:6, 8; Ps 7:16; 9:16
10:3 Ps 49:6; 94:3, 4; Ps 112:10; Ps 10:13
10:4 Ps 10:13; 36:2; Ps 14:1; 36:1
10:5 Ps 52:7; Ps 28:5
10:6 Ps 49:11; Eccl 8:11; Rev 18:7
10:7 Rom 3:14; Ps 73:8; Job 20:12; Ps 140:3
10:8 Ps 11:2; Ps 94:6; Ps 72:12
10:9 Ps 17:12; Ps 59:3; Mic 7:2; Ps 10:2; Ps 140:5

16 Or *blesses the greedy man*

9:16 "Higgaion" is a musical direction and probably means to use the quieter instruments.

9:18 The world may ignore the plight of the needy, crushing any earthly hope they may have. But God, the champion of the weak, promises that this will not be the case forever. The wicked nations who forget the Lord and refuse to help their people will be judged by God. He knows our needs, he knows our tendency to despair, and he has promised to care for us (see also 9:9, 12). Even when others forget us, he will remember.

10:1 "Why do You hide Yourself in times of trouble?" To the psalmist, God seemed far away. But even though the writer had honest doubts, he did not stop praying or conclude that God no longer cared. He was not complaining, but simply asking God to hurry to his aid. It is during those times when we feel most alone or oppressed that we need to keep praying, telling God about our troubles.

10:4–6 Some people succeed in everything they do, and they brag that no one, not even God, can keep them down. We may wonder why God allows these people to amass great wealth while they despise him as they do. But why are we upset when the wicked prosper? Are we angry about the damage they are doing or just jealous of their success? To answer these questions we must gain the right perspective on wickedness and wealth. The wicked will surely be punished because God hates their evil deeds. Wealth is only temporary. It is not necessarily a sign of God's approval on a person's life; nor is lack of it a sign of God's disapproval. Don't let wealth or lack of it become your obsession. See Proverbs 30:7–8 for a prayer you can pray.

He catches the afflicted when he draws him into his net.
10 He crouches, he bows down,
And the unfortunate fall [17]by his mighty ones.
11 He says to himself, "God has forgotten;
He has hidden His face; He will never see it."

12 Arise, O LORD; O God, lift up Your hand.
Do not forget the afflicted.
13 Why has the wicked spurned God?
He has said to himself, "You will not require *it.*"
14 You have seen *it,* for You have beheld mischief and vexation to take it into Your hand.
The unfortunate commits *himself* to You;
You have been the helper of the orphan.
15 Break the arm of the wicked and the evildoer,
Seek out his wickedness until You find none.

16 The LORD is King forever and ever;
Nations have perished from His land.
17 O LORD, You have heard the desire of the [18]humble;
You will strengthen their heart, You will incline Your ear
18 To [19]vindicate the orphan and the oppressed,
So that man who is of the earth will no longer cause terror.

10:11 Ps 10:4
10:12 Ps 17:7; Mic 5:9; Ps 9:12
10:13 Ps 10:3
10:14 Ps 10:7; Ps 22:11; Ps 68:5
10:15 Ps 37:17; Ps 140:11
10:16 Ps 29:10; Deut 8:20
10:17 Ps 9:18; 1 Chr 29:18; Ps 34:15
10:18 Ps 146:9; Ps 9:9; 74:21; Is 29:20

PSALM 11

For the choir director. *A Psalm* of David.

Theme: God's rule provides stability in the midst of panic. Because we can trust him, we can face our problems.
Author: David

1 In the LORD I take refuge;
How can you say to my soul, "Flee *as* a bird to your mountain;
2 For, behold, the wicked bend the bow,
They make ready their arrow upon the string
To shoot in darkness at the upright in heart.
3 If the foundations are destroyed,
What can the righteous do?"

4 The LORD is in His holy temple; the LORD'S throne is in heaven;
His eyes behold, His eyelids test the sons of men.
5 The LORD tests the righteous and the wicked,

11:1 Ps 2:12; Ps 121:1
11:2 Ps 7:12; 37:14; Ps 64:3; Ps 64:4
11:3 Ps 82:5; 87:1; 119:152
11:4 Ps 18:6; Mic 1:2; Hab 2:20; Ps 103:19; Is 66:1; Matt 5:34; Rev 4:2; Ps 33:18; 34:15, 16
11:5 Gen 22:1; Ps 34:19; James 1:12; Ps 5:5

17 Or *into his claws* 18 Or *afflicted* 19 Lit *judge*

10:11 There is an incompatibility between blind arrogance and the presence of God in our hearts. The proud person depends on himself rather than on God. This causes God's guiding influences to leave his life. When God's presence is welcome, there is no room for pride because he makes us aware of our true selves.

10:14 God sees and takes note of each evil deed, encourages us, and listens to our cries (10:17). He is always with us. We can face the wicked because we do not face them alone. God is by our side.

11:1–4 David was forced to flee for safety several times. Being God's anointed king did not make him immune to injustice and hatred from others. This psalm may have been written when he was being hunted by Saul (1 Samuel 18—31) or during the days of Absalom's rebellion (2 Samuel 15—18). In both instances, David fled, but not as if all was lost. He knew God was in control. While David wisely avoided trouble, he did not fearfully run away from his troubles.

11:1–4 David seems to be speaking to those who are advising him to run from his enemies. David's faith contrasts dramatically with the fear of the advisers who tell him to flee. Faith in God keeps us from losing hope and helps us resist fear. David's advisers were afraid because they saw only frightening circumstances and crumbling foundations. David was comforted and optimistic because he knew God was greater than anything his enemies could bring against him (7:10; 16:1; 31:2–3).

11:4 When the foundations are shaking and you wish you could hide, remember that God is still in control. His power is not diminished by any turn of events. Nothing happens without his knowledge and permission. When you feel like running away—run to God. He will restore justice and goodness on the earth in his good time.

11:5 God does not preserve believers from difficult circumstances, but he tests both the righteous and the wicked. For some, God's tests become a refining fire, while for others, they become an incinerator for destruction. Don't ignore or defy the tests and challenges that come your way. Use them as opportunities for you to grow.

And the one who loves violence His soul hates.
6 Upon the wicked He will rain [20]snares;
Fire and brimstone and burning wind will be the portion of their cup.
7 For the LORD is righteous, He loves righteousness;
The upright will behold His face.

11:6 Ps 18:13, 14; Gen 19:24; Ezek 38:22; Jer 4:11, 12; Ps 75:8

11:7 Ps 7:9, 11; Ps 33:5; 45:7; Ps 16:11; 17:15

PSALM 12

For the choir director; upon an eight-stringed lyre. A Psalm of David.

Theme: The proud and lying words of people versus the true and pure words of God. A call for protection against those who try to manipulate us.
Author: David

1 Help, LORD, for the godly man ceases to be,
For the faithful disappear from among the sons of men.
2 They speak falsehood to one another;
With flattering lips and with a double heart they speak.
3 May the LORD cut off all flattering lips,
The tongue that speaks great things;
4 Who have said, "With our tongue we will prevail;
Our lips are our own; who is lord over us?"
5 "Because of the devastation of the afflicted, because of the groaning of the needy,
Now I will arise," says the LORD; "I will set him in the safety for which he longs."

6 The words of the LORD are pure words;
As silver tried in a furnace on the earth, refined seven times.
7 You, O LORD, will keep them;
You will preserve him from this generation forever.
8 The wicked strut about on every side
When [21]vileness is exalted among the sons of men.

12:1 Is 57:1; Mic 7:2

12:2 Ps 10:7; 41:6; Ps 28:3; 55:21; Jer 9:8; Rom 16:18

12:3 Dan 7:8; Rev 13:5

12:4 Ps 73:8, 9

12:5 Ps 9:9; 10:18; Is 33:10; Ps 34:6; 35:10

12:6 2 Sam 22:31; Ps 18:30; 19:8, 10; 119:140; Prov 30:5

12:7 Ps 37:28; 97:10

12:8 Ps 55:10, 11; Is 32:5

PSALM 13

For the choir director. A Psalm of David.

Theme: Praying for relief from despair. We must continue to trust God even when he doesn't answer us immediately.
Author: David

1 How long, O LORD? Will You forget me forever?
How long will You hide Your face from me?

13:1 Ps 44:24; Job 13:24; Ps 89:46

20 Or *coals of fire* **21** Or *worthlessness*

12:1 Living for God in a deceitful world can be a difficult and lonely battle. At one time the great prophet Elijah felt so lonely he wanted to die. But God told him that there were 7,000 other faithful servants (1 Kings 19:4, 14, 18). We are never alone in our battle against evil. When you feel alone, seek out other believers for strength and support.

12:2–4 We may be tempted to believe that lies are relatively harmless, even useful at times. But God does not overlook lies, flattery, deception, or boasting. Each of these sins originates from a bad attitude that is eventually expressed in our speech. The tongue can be our greatest enemy because, though small, it can do great damage (James 3:5). Be careful how you use yours.

12:5 God cares for the weak and the needy. Here he promises to protect the downtrodden and confront their oppressors. We should identify with God's attitude. His work is not done until we care for the needs of the poor.

12:6 Sincerity and truth are extremely valuable because they are so rare. Many people are deceivers, liars, flatterers; they think they will get what they want by deception. As a king, David certainly faced his share of such people, who hoped to win his favor and gain advancement through flattery. When we feel as though sincerity and truth have nearly gone out of existence, we have one hope—the Word of God. God's words are as flawless as refined silver. So listen carefully when he speaks.

13:1 Sometimes all we need to do is talk over a problem with a friend to help put it in perspective. In this psalm, the phrase "how long" occurs four times in the first two verses, indicating the depth of David's distress. David expressed his feelings to God and found strength. By the end of his prayer, he was able to express hope and trust in God. Through prayer we can express our feelings and talk our problems out with God. He helps us regain the right perspective, and this gives us peace (Habakkuk 3:17–19).

13:1–5 David frequently claimed that God was slow to act on his behalf. We often feel this same impatience. It seems that evil and suffering go unchecked, and we wonder when God is going to stop them. David affirmed that he would continue to trust God no matter how long he had to wait for God's justice to be realized. When you feel impatient, remember David's steadfast faith in God's unfailing love.

13:2
Ps 42:4; Ps 42:9

2 How long shall I take counsel in my soul,
Having sorrow in my heart all the day?
How long will my enemy be exalted over me?

13:3
Ps 5:1; 1 Sam 14:29; Ezra 9:8; Job 33:30; Ps 18:28; Jer 51:39

13:4
Ps 12:4; Ps 25:2; 38:16

13:5
Ps 52:8; Ps 9:14

13:6
Ps 96:1, 2; Ps 116:7; 119:17; 142:7

3 Consider *and* answer me, O LORD my God;
Enlighten my eyes, or I will sleep the *sleep of* death,
4 And my enemy will say, "I have overcome him,"
And my adversaries will rejoice when I am shaken.

5 But I have trusted in Your lovingkindness;
My heart shall rejoice in Your salvation.
6 I will sing to the LORD,
Because He has dealt bountifully with me.

PSALM 14

For the choir director. *A Psalm* of David.

Theme: Only the fool denies God. How foolish it must seem to God when people say there is no God.
Author: David

14:1
Ps 10:4; 53:1; Ps 14:1-3; 130:3; Rom 3:10-12

14:2
Ps 33:13, 14; 102:19; Ps 92:6; 1 Chr 22:19

14:3
Ps 58:3; Ps 143:2

1 The fool has said in his heart, "There is no God."
They are corrupt, they have committed abominable deeds;
There is no one who does good.
2 The LORD has looked down from heaven upon the sons of men
To see if there are any who understand,
Who seek after God.
3 They have all turned aside, together they have become corrupt;
There is no one who does good, not even one.

TROUBLES AND COMPLAINTS IN THE PSALMS

We can relate to the psalms because they express our feelings. We all face troubles, as did the psalm writers hundreds of years ago, and we often respond as they did. In Psalm 3, David told God how he felt about the odds against him. But within three verses, the king realized that God's presence and care made the odds meaningless. This experience is repeated in many of the psalms. Usually, the hope and confidence in God outweigh the fear and suffering; sometimes they do not. Still, the psalm writers consistently poured out their thoughts and emotions to God. When they felt abandoned by God, they told him so. When they were impatient with how slowly God seemed to be answering their prayers, they also told him so. Because they recognized the difference between themselves and God, they were free to be men and to be honest with their Creator. That is why so many of the dark psalms end in the light. The psalmists started by expressing their feelings and ended up remembering to whom they were speaking!

Although we have much in common with the psalmists, we may differ in two ways: we might not tell God what we are really thinking and feeling; and therefore we also might not recognize, even faintly, who is listening to our prayers!

Notice this pattern as you read Psalms, and put the psalmists' insight to the test. You may well find that your awareness and appreciation of God will grow as you are honest with him. (See Psalms 3; 6; 13; 31; 37; 64; 77; 102; 121; 142.)

14:1–3 The true atheist is either foolish or wicked—foolish because he ignores the evidence that God exists or wicked because he refuses to live by God's truths. We become atheists in practice when we rely more on ourselves than on God. The fool mentioned here is someone who is aggressively perverse in his actions. To speak in direct defiance of God is utterly foolish according to the Bible.

14:3 No one but God is perfect; all of us stand guilty before him (see Romans 3:23) and need his forgiveness. No matter how well we perform or how much we achieve compared to others, none of us can boast of his or her goodness when compared to God's standard. God not only expects us to obey his guidelines, but he wants us to love him with all our heart. No one except Jesus Christ has done that perfectly. Because we all fall short we must turn to Christ to save us (Romans 10:9–11). Have you asked him to save you?

14:3–4 David applies these observations to his enemies when he says the evildoers "eat up my people as they eat bread": "Together they have become corrupt; there is no one who does good, not even one." By contrast, David said, "You have tried my heart; . . . You find nothing" (17:3).

There is a clear distinction between those who worship God and those who refuse to worship him. David worshiped God, and under his leadership Israel obeyed God and prospered. Several hundred years later, however, Israel forgot God, and it became difficult to distinguish between God's followers and those who worshiped idols. When Isaiah called Israel to repentance, he, like David, spoke of people who had gone astray (Isaiah 53:6). But Isaiah was talking about the Israelites themselves. Paul quoted Psalm 14 in Romans 3:10–12. He made the image of straying sheep even more general, referring to all people. The whole human race—Jew and Gentile alike—has turned away from God.

4 Do all the workers of wickedness not know,
Who eat up my people *as* they eat bread,
And do not call upon the Lord?
5 There they are in great dread,
For God is with the righteous generation.
6 You would put to shame the counsel of the afflicted,
But the LORD is his refuge.

7 Oh, that the salvation of Israel would come out of Zion!
When the LORD [22]restores His captive people,
Jacob will rejoice, Israel will be glad.

14:4 Ps 82:5; Ps 27:2; Jer 10:25; Mic 3:3; Ps 79:6; Is 64:7
14:5 Ps 73:15; 112:2
14:6 Ps 9:9; 40:17; 46:1; 142:5
14:7 Ps 53:6; Ps 85:1, 2

PSALM 15

A Psalm of David.

Theme: Guidelines for living a blameless life.
Author: David

1 O LORD, who may abide in Your tent?
Who may dwell on Your holy hill?
2 He who walks with integrity, and works righteousness,
And speaks truth in his heart.
3 He does not slander with his tongue,
Nor does evil to his neighbor,
Nor takes up a reproach against his friend;
4 In whose eyes a reprobate is despised,
But who honors those who fear the LORD;
He swears to his own hurt and does not change;
5 He does not put out his money [23]at interest,
Nor does he take a bribe against the innocent.
He who does these things will never be shaken.

15:1 Ps 27:5, 6; 61:4; Ps 24:3
15:2 Ps 24:4; Is 33:15; Zech 8:16; Eph 4:25
15:3 Ps 50:20; Ps 28:3; Ex 23:1
15:4 Acts 28:10; Judg 11:35
15:5 Ex 22:25; Lev 25:36; Deut 23:20; Ezek 18:8; Ex 23:8; Deut 16:19; 2 Pet 1:10

PSALM 16

A [24]Mikhtam of David.

Theme: The joys and benefits of a life lived in companionship with God. We enjoy these benefits now and eternally.
Author: David

1 Preserve me, O God, for I take refuge in You.
2 I said to the LORD, "You are my Lord;
I have no good besides You."

16:1 Ps 17:8; Ps 7:1
16:2 Ps 73:25

22 Or *restores the fortunes of His people* **23** I.e. to a fellow Israelite **24** Possibly *Epigrammatic Poem,* or *Atonement Psalm*

14:5 If God is "with the righteous generation," then those who attack God's followers may be attacking God. To attack God is utterly futile (see 2:4–5, 10–12). Thus, while we may feel we are losing the battle, there can be absolutely no doubt that our ultimate victory is in God.

15:1 *Tent* and *holy hill* are interchangeable words describing the focal point of Israelite worship—the dwelling place of God. In Hebrew poetry the repeating pattern is found more in the thought than in the sound or rhythm.

15:1ff God calls his people to be morally upright, and, in this psalm, he gives us ten standards to determine how we are doing. We live among evil people whose standards and morals are eroding. Our standards for living should not come from our evil society, but from God. For other references where righteous conduct is summarized, see Isaiah 33:15; 56:1; Micah 6:8; Habakkuk 2:4; and Mark 12:29–31.

15:3–4 Words are powerful, and how you use them reflects on your relationship with God. Perhaps nothing so identifies Christians as their ability to control their speech—speaking the truth, refusing to slander, and keeping promises. Watch out for what you say. (See James 3:1–12 for more on the importance of controlling your tongue.)

15:5 God was against the Jews' charging interest or making a profit on loans to needy, fellow Jews (see also Exodus 22:25; Leviticus 25:35–37), although charging interest on loans to foreigners was allowed (Deuteronomy 23:20). Interest was also allowable for business purposes, as long as it wasn't exorbitant (Proverbs 28:8).

15:5 Some people are so obsessed with money that they will change their God-given standards and lifestyle to get it. If money is a controlling force in your life, it must be curbed, or it will harm others and destroy your relationship with God.

16 title *Mikhtam* comes from a term that may mean "to cover." It could mean a covering of the lips (a silent prayer), or a prayer that someone might be covered with protection. *Mikhtam* may mean a psalm of atonement.

16:3
Ps 101:6; Ps 119:63

16:4
Ps 32:10; Ps 106:37, 38; Ex 23:13; Josh 23:7

16:5
Ps 73:26; 119:57; 142:5; Lam 3:24; Ps 23:5; Ps 125:3

16:6
Ps 78:55; Jer 3:19

16:7
Ps 73:24; Ps 77:6

16:8
Ps 16:8-11; Acts 2:25-28; Ps 27:8; 123:1, 2; Ps 73:23; 110:5; 121:5; Ps 112:6

16:9
Ps 4:7; 13:5; Ps 30:12; 57:8; 108:1; Ps 4:8

16:10
Ps 49:15; 86:13; Acts 13:35

16:11
Ps 139:24; Matt 7:14; Ps 21:6; 43:4; Job 36:11; Ps 36:7, 8; 46:4

3 As for the saints who are in the earth,
They are the majestic ones in whom is all my delight.
4 The sorrows of those who have bartered for another *god* will be multiplied;
I shall not pour out their drink offerings of blood,
Nor will I take their names upon my lips.

5 The LORD is the portion of my inheritance and my cup;
You support my lot.
6 The lines have fallen to me in pleasant places;
Indeed, my heritage is beautiful to me.

7 I will bless the LORD who has counseled me;
Indeed, my mind instructs me in the night.
8 I have set the LORD continually before me;
Because He is at my right hand, I will not be shaken.
9 Therefore my heart is glad and my glory rejoices;
My flesh also will dwell securely.
10 For You will not abandon my soul to Sheol;
Nor will You allow Your Holy One to [25]undergo decay.
11 You will make known to me the path of life;
In Your presence is fullness of joy;
In Your right hand there are pleasures forever.

PSALM 17

A Prayer of David.

Theme: A plea for justice in the face of false accusations and persecution. David urges us to realize the true goal of life—to know God—and the true reward of life—to see God one day.
Author: David, written while he was being persecuted by Saul

17:1
Ps 9:4; Ps 61:1; 142:6; Ps 88:2; Is 29:13

17:2
Ps 103:6; Ps 98:9; 99:4

17:3
Ps 26:1, 2; Job 23:10; Ps 66:10; Zech 13:9; 1 Pet 1:7; Jer 50:20; Ps 39:1

1 Hear a just cause, O LORD, give heed to my cry;
Give ear to my prayer, which is not from deceitful lips.
2 Let my judgment come forth from Your presence;
Let Your eyes look with equity.
3 You have tried my heart;
You have visited *me* by night;
You have tested me and You find [26]nothing;
I have purposed that my mouth will not transgress.

25 Or *see corruption* or *the pit* **26** Or *no evil device in me; My mouth*

16:7–8 It is human nature to make our own plans and *then* ask God to bless them. Instead, we should seek God's will first. By constantly thinking about the Lord and his way of living, we will gain insights that will help us make right decisions and live the way God desires. Communicating with God allows him to counsel us and give us wisdom.

16:8 By saying that he "will not be shaken," David was talking about the unique sense of security felt by believers. God does not exempt believers from the day-to-day circumstances of life. Believers and unbelievers alike experience pain, trouble, and failure at times (Matthew 5:45). Unbelievers have a sense of hopelessness about life and confusion over their true purpose on earth. Those who seek God, however, can move ahead confidently with what they know is right and important in God's eyes. They know that God will keep them from being moved off of his chosen path.

16:8–11 This psalm is often called a Messianic psalm because it is quoted in the New Testament as referring to the resurrection of Jesus Christ. Both Peter and Paul quoted from this psalm when speaking of Christ's bodily resurrection (see Acts 2:25–28, 31; 13:35–37).

16:9 David's heart was glad—he had found the secret to joy. True joy is far deeper than happiness; we can feel joy in spite of our deepest troubles. Happiness is temporary because it is based on external circumstances, but joy is lasting because it is based on God's presence within us. As we contemplate his daily presence, we will find contentment. As we understand the future he has for us, we will experience joy. Don't base your life on circumstances, but on God.

16:10 David stated confidently that God would not leave him in the grave (Sheol). Many people fear death because they can neither control nor understand it. As believers, we can be assured that God will not forget us when we die. He will bring us to life again to live with him forever. This provides *real* security. For other passages about resurrection, see Job 19:25–26; Isaiah 26:19; Daniel 12:2, 13; Mark 13:27; 1 Corinthians 15:12–58; 1 Thessalonians 4:13–18; Revelation 20:11—21:4.

17:3 Was David saying he was sinless? Far from a proud assumption of purity, David's claim was an understanding of his relationship with God. In Psalms 32 and 51, David freely acknowledged his own sins. Nevertheless, his relationship with God was one of close fellowship and constant repentance and forgiveness. His claim to goodness, therefore, was based on his continual seeking after God.

4 As for the deeds of men, by the word of Your lips
I have kept from the paths of the violent.
5 My steps have held fast to Your paths.
My feet have not slipped.

6 I have called upon You, for You will answer me, O God;
Incline Your ear to me, hear my speech.
7 Wondrously show Your lovingkindness,
O Savior of those who take refuge at Your right hand
From those who rise up *against them.*
8 Keep me as [27]the apple of the eye;
Hide me in the shadow of Your wings
9 From the wicked who despoil me,
My deadly enemies who surround me.
10 They have closed their unfeeling *heart,*
With their mouth they speak proudly.
11 They have now surrounded us in our steps;
They set their eyes to cast *us* down to the ground.
12 He is like a lion that is eager to tear,
And as a young lion lurking in hiding places.

13 Arise, O LORD, confront him, bring him low;
Deliver my soul from the wicked with Your sword,
14 From men with Your hand, O LORD,
From men of the world, whose portion is in *this* life,
And whose belly You fill with Your treasure;
They are satisfied with children,
And leave their abundance to their babes.
15 As for me, I shall behold Your face in righteousness;
I will be satisfied with Your likeness when I awake.

17:4
Ps 119:9, 101; Ps 10:5-11

17:5
Job 23:11; Ps 44:18; 119:133; Ps 18:36; 37:31

17:6
Ps 86:7; 116:2; Ps 88:2

17:7
Ps 31:21; Ps 20:6

17:8
Deut 32:10; Zech 2:8; Ruth 2:12; Ps 36:7; 57:1; 61:4; 63:7; 91:1, 4

17:9
Ps 31:20; Ps 27:12

17:10
Job 15:27; Ps 73:7; 1 Sam 2:3; Ps 31:18; 73:8

17:11
Ps 88:17; Ps 37:14

17:12
Ps 7:2; Ps 10:9

17:13
Ps 3:7; Ps 55:23; Ps 22:20; Ps 7:12

17:14
Ps 17:7; Ps 73:3-7; Luke 16:25; Ps 49:6

17:15
Ps 11:7; 16:11; 140:13; 1 John 3:2; Ps 4:6, 7; Num 12:8

PSALM 18

For the choir director. A *Psalm* of David the servant of the LORD,
who spoke to the LORD the words of this song in the day
that the LORD delivered him from the hand of all his enemies
and from the hand of Saul. And he said,

Theme: Gratitude for deliverance and victory. The only sure way to be delivered from surrounding evil is to call upon God for help and strength.
Author: David

1 "I love You, O LORD, my strength."
2 The LORD is my rock and my fortress and my deliverer,
My God, my rock, in whom I take refuge;

18:1
Ps 59:17

18:2
Deut 32:18; 1 Sam 2:2; Ps 18:31, 46; 28:1; 31:3; 42:9; 71:3; 78:15; Ps 144:2; Ps 19:14; Ps 28:7; 33:20; 59:11; 84:9, 11; Prov 30:5; Ps 75:10; Ps 59:9

27 Lit *the pupil, the daughter of the eye*

17:8 Just as we protect the pupils ("apples") of our eyes, so God will protect us. We must not conclude, however, that we have somehow missed God's protection if we experience troubles. God's protection has far greater purposes than helping us avoid pain; it is to make us better servants for him. God also protects us by guiding us through painful circumstances, not only by helping us escape them.

17:8 The "shadow of Your wings" is a figure of speech symbolizing God's protection. He guards us just as a mother bird protects her young by covering them with her wings. Moses used this same metaphor in Deuteronomy 32:11.

17:13–15 We deceive ourselves when we measure our happiness or contentment in life by the amount of wealth we possess. When we put riches at the top of our value system, we let power, pleasure, and financial security overshadow the eternal value of our relationship with God. We think we will be happy or content when we get riches, only to discover that they don't really satisfy, and the pleasures fade away. The true measurement of happiness or contentment is found in God's love and in doing his will. You will find true happiness if you put your relationship with God above earthly riches.

17:15 The word *awake* shows that David believed in life after death. Although belief in resurrection was not widespread in Old Testament times, several verses show that it was partially understood. Some of these are Job 19:25–27; Psalms 16:10; 49:15; 139:17–18; Isaiah 26:19; and Daniel 12:2, 13.

18:1ff This psalm is almost a duplicate of 2 Samuel 22. It may have been written toward the end of David's life when there was peace. God is praised for his glorious works and blessings through the years.

18:2–3 God's protection of his people is limitless and can take many forms. David characterized God's care with five military symbols. God is like (1) a *rock* that can't be moved by any who would harm us, (2) a *fortress* or place of safety where the enemy

18:3 Ps 48:1; 96:4; 145:3; Ps 34:6
18:4 Ps 116:3; Ps 69:2; 124:3, 4
18:5 Ps 116:3
18:6 Ps 50:15; 120:1; Ps 3:4; Ps 34:15
18:7 Judg 5:4; Ps 68:7, 8; Is 13:13; Hag 2:6; Ps 114:4, 6
18:8 Ps 50:3
18:9 Ps 144:5; Ps 97:2
18:10 Ps 80:1; 99:1; Ps 104:3
18:11 Deut 4:11; Ps 97:2
18:12 Ps 104:2; Ps 97:3; 140:10; Hab 3:4
18:13 Ps 29:3; 104:7
18:14 Ps 144:6; Hab 3:11
18:15 Ps 106:9; Ps 76:6; Ps 18:8
18:16 Ps 144:7; Ps 32:6
18:17 Ps 59:1; Ps 35:10; 142:6
18:18 Ps 59:16; Ps 16:8
18:19 Ps 4:1; 31:8; 118:5; Ps 37:23; 41:11

My shield and the horn of my salvation, my stronghold.
3 I call upon the LORD, who is worthy to be praised,
And I am saved from my enemies.

4 The cords of death encompassed me,
And the torrents of [28]ungodliness terrified me.
5 The cords of Sheol surrounded me;
The snares of death confronted me.
6 In my distress I called upon the LORD,
And cried to my God for help;
He heard my voice out of His temple,
And my cry for help before Him came into His ears.

7 Then the earth shook and quaked;
And the foundations of the mountains were trembling
And were shaken, because He was angry.
8 Smoke went up out of His nostrils,
And fire from His mouth devoured;
Coals were kindled by it.
9 He bowed the heavens also, and came down
With thick darkness under His feet.
10 He rode upon a cherub and flew;
And He sped upon the wings of the wind.
11 He made darkness His hiding place, His canopy around Him,
Darkness of waters, thick clouds of the skies.
12 From the brightness before Him passed His thick clouds,
Hailstones and coals of fire.
13 The LORD also thundered in the heavens,
And the Most High uttered His voice,
Hailstones and coals of fire.
14 He sent out His arrows, and scattered them,
And lightning flashes in abundance, and routed them.
15 Then the channels of water appeared,
And the foundations of the world were laid bare
At Your rebuke, O LORD,
At the blast of the breath of Your nostrils.

16 He sent from on high, He took me;
He drew me out of many waters.
17 He delivered me from my strong enemy,
And from those who hated me, for they were too mighty for me.
18 They confronted me in the day of my calamity,
But the LORD was my stay.
19 He brought me forth also into a broad place;
He rescued me, because He delighted in me.

28 Or *destruction;* Heb *Belial*

---

can't follow, (3) a *shield* that comes between us and harm, (4) a *horn* of salvation, a symbol of might and power, (5) a *stronghold* high above our enemies. If you need protection, look to God.

18:10 A cherub is a mighty angel. One of the functions of the cherubim was to serve as guardians. These angels guarded the entrances to both the tree of life (Genesis 3:24) and the holy of holies (Exodus 26:31–33). Two cherubim of hammered gold were part of the ark of the covenant (Exodus 25:18–22). The living creatures carrying God's throne in Ezekiel 1 may have been cherubim.

18:13 The "Most High" was an important designation for David to make. Pagan idol worship was deeply rooted in the land, and each region had its own deity. But these images of wood and stone were powerless. David was placing the Lord alone in a superior category: He is by far the Most High.

18:16 Do your troubles, like "many waters," threaten to drown you? David, helpless and weak, knew that God alone had rescued him from his enemies when he was defenseless. When you wish that God would quickly rescue you from your troubles, remember that he can either deliver you or be your support as you go through them (18:18). Either way, his protection is best for you. When you feel like you're drowning in troubles, ask God to help you, hold you steady, and protect you. In his care, you are never helpless.

20 The LORD has rewarded me according to my righteousness;
According to the cleanness of my hands He has recompensed me.
21 For I have kept the ways of the LORD,
And have not wickedly departed from my God.
22 For all His ordinances were before me,
And I did not put away His statutes from me.
23 I was also [29]blameless with Him,
And I kept myself from my iniquity.
24 Therefore the LORD has recompensed me according to my righteousness,
According to the cleanness of my hands in His eyes.

25 With the kind You show Yourself kind;
With the blameless You show Yourself blameless;
26 With the pure You show Yourself pure,
And with the crooked You show Yourself [30]astute.
27 For You save an afflicted people,
But haughty eyes You abase.
28 For You light my lamp;
The LORD my God illumines my darkness.
29 For by You I can [31]run upon a troop;
And by my God I can leap over a wall.

30 As for God, His way is blameless;
The word of the LORD is tried;
He is a shield to all who take refuge in Him.
31 For who is God, but the LORD?
And who is a rock, except our God,
32 The God who girds me with strength
And makes my way blameless?
33 He makes my feet like hinds' *feet,*
And sets me upon my high places.
34 He trains my hands for battle,
So that my arms can bend a bow of bronze.
35 You have also given me the shield of Your salvation,
And Your right hand upholds me;
And Your gentleness makes me great.
36 You enlarge my steps under me,
And my feet have not slipped.

37 I pursued my enemies and overtook them,
And I did not turn back until they were consumed.
38 I shattered them, so that they were not able to rise;
They fell under my feet.
39 For You have girded me with strength for battle;
You have subdued under me those who rose up against me.
40 You have also made my enemies turn their backs to me,
And I [32]destroyed those who hated me.

29 Lit *complete;* or *having integrity;* or *perfect* **30** Lit *twisted* **31** Or *crush a troop* **32** Or *silenced*

18:20 1 Sam 24:19; Job 33:26; Ps 7:8; Job 22:30; Ps 24:4
18:21 Ps 37:34; 119:33; Prov 8:32; 2 Chr 34:33; Ps 119:102
18:22 Ps 119:30; Ps 119:83
18:23 Ps 18:32; Ps 19:12, 13; 25:11; 66:18
18:24 1 Sam 26:23
18:25 Ps 62:12; Matt 5:7
18:26 Job 25:5; Hab 1:13; Lev 26:23, 24, 27, 28; Prov 3:34
18:27 Ps 72:12; Ps 101:5; Prov 6:17
18:28 1 Kin 15:4; Job 18:6; Ps 132:17; Ps 27:1
18:29 Ps 118:10-12; Ps 18:33; 40:2
18:30 Deut 32:4; Ps 19:7; 145:17; Rev 15:3; Ps 12:6; Ps 17:7; 91:4
18:31 Deut 32:39; 1 Sam 2:2; Ps 86:8-10; Is 45:5; Deut 32:31; Ps 18:2; 62:2
18:32 Ps 18:39; Is 45:5; Ps 18:23
18:33 Hab 3:19
18:35 Ps 33:20; Ps 63:8; 119:117; Ps 138:6
18:36 Ps 18:33; Ps 66:9; Prov 4:12
18:38 Ps 36:12; Ps 47:3
18:39 Ps 18:32; Ps 18:47
18:40 Ps 21:12; Ps 94:23

18:30 Some people think that belief in God is a crutch for weak people who cannot make it on their own. God is indeed a shield to protect us when we are too weak to face certain trials by ourselves, but he does not want us to remain weak. He strengthens, protects, and guides us in order to send us back into an evil world to fight for him. And then he continues to work with us because the strongest person on earth is infinitely weaker than God and needs his help. David was not a coward; he was a mighty warrior who, even with all his armies and weapons, knew that only God could ultimately protect and save him.

18:32–34 God promises to give us strength to meet challenges, but he doesn't promise to eliminate them. If he gave us no rough roads to walk, no mountains to climb, and no battles to fight, we would not grow. He does not leave us alone with our challenges, however. Instead he stands beside us, teaches us, and strengthens us to face them.

18:40–42 David was a merciful man. He spared the lives of Saul (1 Samuel 24:1–8), Nabal (1 Samuel 25:21–35), and Shimei (2 Samuel 16:5–12) and showed great kindness to Mephibosheth (2 Samuel 9). In asking God to destroy his enemies, David was simply asking him to give the wicked the punishment they deserved.

18:41
Ps 50:22; Job 27:9; Prov 1:28

18:42
Ps 83:13

41 They cried for help, but there was none to save,
Even to the LORD, but He did not answer them.
42 Then I beat them fine as the dust before the wind;
I emptied them out as the mire of the streets.

18:43
2 Sam 3:1; 19:9; Ps 35:1; 2 Sam 8:1-18; Ps 89:27; Is 55:5

18:44
Ps 66:3

18:45
Ps 37:2; Mic 7:17

43 You have delivered me from the contentions of the people;
You have placed me as head of the nations;
A people whom I have not known serve me.
44 As soon as they hear, they obey me;
Foreigners [33]submit to me.
45 Foreigners fade away,
And come trembling out of their fortresses.

18:46
Job 19:25; Ps 18:2; Ps 51:14

18:47
Ps 94:1; Ps 18:43; 47:3; 144:2

18:48
Ps 3:7; Ps 27:6; 59:1; Ps 11:5

18:49
Rom 15:9; Ps 108:1

18:50
Ps 21:1; 144:10; Ps 28:8; Ps 89:4

46 The LORD lives, and blessed be my rock;
And exalted be the God of my salvation,
47 The God who executes vengeance for me,
And subdues peoples under me.
48 He delivers me from my enemies;
Surely You lift me above those who rise up against me;
You rescue me from the violent man.
49 Therefore I will give thanks to You among the nations, O LORD,
And I will sing praises to Your name.
50 He gives great [34]deliverance to His king,
And shows lovingkindness to His anointed,
To David and his descendants forever.

PSALM 19

For the choir director. A Psalm of David.

Theme: Both God's creation and his Word reveal his greatness.
Author: David

19:1
Ps 8:1; 50:6; Rom 1:19, 20; Gen 1:6, 7

19:2
Ps 74:16; Ps 139:12

19:4
Rom 10:18; Ps 104:2

1 The heavens are telling of the glory of God;
And their expanse is declaring the work of His hands.
2 Day to day pours forth speech,
And night to night reveals knowledge.
3 There is no speech, nor are there words;
Their voice is not heard.
4 Their [35]line has gone out through all the earth,
And their utterances to the end of the world.
In them He has placed a tent for the sun,
5 Which is as a bridegroom coming out of his chamber;
It rejoices as a strong man to run his course.

33 Lit *deceive me;* i.e. give feigned obedience 34 I.e. victories; lit *salvations* 35 Another reading is *sound*

18:43–45 David's great power had become legendary. God gave him victory in every battle. The book of 2 Samuel records victories over the Jebusites (5:6–10), the Philistines (5:17–25; 8:1–2), Hadadezer of Zobah (8:3–4), the Arameans (8:5–6; 10), the Edomites (8:13–14), and the Ammonites (12:26–31). In addition, the king of Tyre sent supplies and workmen to help David build his palace (5:11). But David did not attribute his victories to himself. He fully realized that the purpose of his position was to bless God's people (1 Chronicles 14:2).

19:1ff In this psalm, David's steps of meditation take him from creation, through God's Word, through David's own sinfulness, to salvation. As God reveals himself through nature (19:1–6), we learn about his power and our finiteness. As God reveals himself through Scripture (19:7–11), we learn about his holiness and our sinfulness. As God reveals himself through daily experiences (19:12–14), we learn about his gracious forgiveness and our salvation.

19:1–6 We are surrounded by fantastic displays of God's craftsmanship—the heavens give dramatic evidence of his existence, his power, his love, his care. To say that the universe happened by chance is absurd. Its design, intricacy, and orderliness point to a personally involved Creator. As you look at God's handiwork in nature and the heavens, thank him for such magnificent beauty and the truth it reveals about the Creator.

19:3–4 The apostle Paul referred to this psalm when he explained that everyone knows about God because nature proclaims God's existence and power (Romans 1:19–20). This does not cancel the need for missions because the message of God's salvation found in his Word, the Bible, must still be told to the ends of the earth. While nature points to the existence of God, the Bible tells us about salvation. God's people must explain to others how they can have a relationship with God. Although people everywhere should already believe in a Creator by just looking at the evidence of nature around them, God needs us to explain his love, mercy, and grace. What are you doing to take God's message to the world?

6 Its rising is from one end of the heavens,
And its circuit to the other end of them;
And there is nothing hidden from its heat.

7 The law of the LORD is [36]perfect, restoring the soul;
The testimony of the LORD is sure, making wise the simple.
8 The precepts of the LORD are right, rejoicing the heart;
The commandment of the LORD is pure, enlightening the eyes.
9 The fear of the LORD is clean, enduring forever;
The judgments of the LORD are true; they are righteous altogether.
10 They are more desirable than gold, yes, than much fine gold;
Sweeter also than honey and the drippings of the honeycomb.
11 Moreover, by them Your servant is warned;
In keeping them there is great reward.
12 Who can discern *his* errors? Acquit me of hidden *faults.*
13 Also keep back Your servant from presumptuous *sins;*
Let them not rule over me;
Then I will be [37]blameless,
And I shall be acquitted of great transgression.
14 Let the words of my mouth and the meditation of my heart
Be acceptable in Your sight,
O LORD, my rock and my Redeemer.

19:6 Ps 113:3; Eccl 1:5

19:7 Ps 111:7; Ps 119:160; Ps 23:3; Ps 93:5; Ps 119:98-100

19:8 Ps 119:128; Ps 119:14; Ps 12:6; Ps 36:9

19:9 Ps 119:142; Ps 119:138

19:10 Ps 119:72, 127; Ps 119:103

19:11 Ps 17:4; Ps 24:5, 6; Prov 29:18

19:12 Ps 40:12; 139:6; Ps 51:1, 2; Ps 90:8; 139:23, 24

19:13 Num 15:30; Ps 119:133; Ps 18:32; Ps 25:11

19:14 Ps 104:34; Ps 18:2; Ps 31:5; Is 47:4

PSALM 20

For the choir director. A Psalm of David.

Theme: A prayer for victory in battle. Such a prayer can help us prepare for any great challenge. David knew that trust should be placed in the Lord more than in human power.
Author: David. The events in 2 Samuel 10 may have prompted this prayer.

1 May the LORD answer you in the day of trouble!
May the name of the God of Jacob set you *securely* on high!
2 May He send you help from the sanctuary
And support you from Zion!
3 May He remember all your meal offerings
And find your burnt offering acceptable! Selah.

4 May He grant you your heart's desire
And fulfill all your [38]counsel!
5 We will sing for joy over your victory,
And in the name of our God we will set up our banners.
May the LORD fulfill all your petitions.

6 Now I know that the LORD saves His anointed;
He will answer him from His holy heaven

20:1 Ps 50:15; Ps 91:14; Ps 46:7, 11

20:2 Ps 3:4; Ps 110:2

20:3 Acts 10:4; Ps 51:19

20:4 Ps 21:2; Ps 145:19

20:5 Ps 9:14; Ps 60:4; 1 Sam 1:17

20:6 Ps 41:11; Is 58:9; Ps 28:8

36 I.e. blameless **37** Lit *complete* **38** Or *purpose*

19:7–11 When we think of the law, we often think of something that keeps us from having fun. But here we see the opposite—law that revives us, makes us wise, gives joy to the heart, gives light to the eyes, warns us, and rewards us. That's because God's laws are guidelines and lights for our path, rather than chains on our hands and feet. They point at danger and warn us, then point at success and guide us.

19:12–13 Many Christians are plagued by guilt. They worry that they may have committed a sin unknowingly, done something good with selfish intentions, failed to put their whole heart into a task, or neglected what they should have done. Guilt can play an important role in bringing us to Christ and in keeping us behaving properly, but it should not cripple us or make us fearful. God fully and completely forgives us—even for those sins we do unknowingly.

19:14 Would you change the way you live if you knew that every word and thought would be examined by God first? David asks that God approve his words and thoughts as though they were offerings brought to the altar. As you begin each day, determine that God's love will guide what you say and how you think.

20:6–8 As long as there have been armies and weapons, nations have boasted of their power, but such power does not last. Throughout history, empires and kingdoms have risen to great power only to vanish in the dust. David, however, knew that the true might of his nation was not in weaponry but in worship; not in firepower but in God's power. Because God alone can preserve a nation or an individual, be sure your confidence is in God, who gives eternal victory. Whom do you trust?

With the saving strength of His right hand.
7 Some *boast* in chariots and some in horses,
But we will boast in the name of the LORD, our God.
8 They have bowed down and fallen,
But we have risen and stood upright.
9 Save, O LORD;
May the King answer us in the day we call.

20:7 Ps 33:17; 2 Chr 32:8
20:8 Is 2:11, 17; Ps 37:24; Mic 7:8
20:9 Ps 3:7; Ps 17:6

PSALM 21

For the choir director. A Psalm of David.

Theme: Praising God after victory in battle. When God answers our prayers for victory, we must quickly and openly thank him for his help.
Author: David

1 O LORD, in Your strength the king will be glad,
And in Your [39]salvation how greatly he will rejoice!
2 You have given him his heart's desire,
And You have not withheld the request of his lips. Selah.
3 For You meet him with the blessings of good things;
You set a crown of fine gold on his head.
4 He asked life of You,
You gave it to him,
Length of days forever and ever.
5 His glory is great through Your [39]salvation,
Splendor and majesty You place upon him.
6 For You make him most blessed forever;
You make him joyful with gladness in Your presence.

7 For the king trusts in the LORD,
And through the lovingkindness of the Most High he will not be shaken.
8 Your hand will find out all your enemies;
Your right hand will find out those who hate you.
9 You will make them as a fiery oven in the time of your anger;
The LORD will swallow them up in His wrath,
And fire will devour them.
10 Their [40]offspring You will destroy from the earth,
And their [41]descendants from among the sons of men.
11 Though they intended evil against You
And devised a plot,
They will not succeed.
12 For You will make them turn their back;
You will aim with Your bowstrings at their faces.
13 Be exalted, O LORD, in Your strength;
We will sing and praise Your power.

21:1 Ps 59:16, 17
21:2 Ps 20:4; 37:4
21:3 Ps 59:10; 2 Sam 12:30
21:4 Ps 61:6; 133:3; Ps 91:16
21:5 Ps 9:14; 20:5; Ps 8:5; 96:6
21:6 1 Chr 17:27; Ps 43:4
21:7 Ps 125:1; Ps 112:6
21:8 Is 10:10
21:9 Mal 4:1; Lam 2:2; Ps 50:3
21:10 Ps 37:28
21:11 Ps 2:1-3; Ps 10:2
21:12 Ps 18:40; Ps 7:12, 13
21:13 Ps 59:16; 81:1

39 Or *victory* **40** Lit *fruit* **41** Lit *seed*

21:1–6 David described all that he had as gifts from God: "his heart's desire," rich blessings, a crown of pure gold, long life, splendor and majesty, eternal blessings, gladness. We too must look upon all we have—position, family, wealth, talent—as gifts from God. Only then will we use them to give glory back to him.

21:7 A good leader trusts the Lord and depends upon his unfailing love. Too often leaders trust in their own cleverness, popular support, or military power. But God is above all these "gods." If you aspire to leadership, keep the Lord God at the center of your life and depend on him. His wisdom is the best strength you can have.

21:7 Because David trusted in God, God would not let him be shaken (removed from the throne). When we trust in God, we have permanence and stability. We may lose a great deal—families, jobs, material possessions—but we cannot be shaken from God's favor. He will be our foundation of solid rock. He will never leave or desert us.

21:11 When you see people succeeding with evil acts, remember that they will not succeed forever. Their power is only temporary, and God's very presence would send them scattering in a moment. God, according to his plan and purpose, will intervene for his people and give the wicked the judgment they deserve. We should not be dismayed when we see the temporary advantage God's enemies have.

PSALM 22

For the choir director; upon
[42]Aijeleth Hashshahar. A Psalm of David.

Theme: A prayer that carries us from great suffering to great joy. Despite apparent rejection by his friends and God, David believed that God would lead him out of despair. He looked forward to that future day when God would rule over the entire earth.
Author: David

1 My God, my God, why have You forsaken me?
Far from my deliverance are the words of my groaning.
2 O my God, I cry by day, but You do not answer;
And by night, but I have no rest.
3 Yet You are holy,
O You who are enthroned upon the praises of Israel.
4 In You our fathers trusted;
They trusted and You delivered them.
5 To You they cried out and were delivered;
In You they trusted and were not disappointed.

6 But I am a worm and not a man,
A reproach of men and despised by the people.
7 All who see me sneer at me;
They [43]separate with the lip, they wag the head, *saying,*
8 "[44]Commit *yourself* to the LORD; let Him deliver him;
Let Him rescue him, because He delights in him."

9 Yet You are He who brought me forth from the womb;
You made me trust *when* upon my mother's breasts.
10 Upon You I was cast from birth;
You have been my God from my mother's womb.

11 Be not far from me, for trouble is near;
For there is none to help.
12 Many bulls have surrounded me;
Strong *bulls* of Bashan have encircled me.
13 They open wide their mouth at me,
As a ravening and a roaring lion.
14 I am poured out like water,
And all my bones are out of joint;
My heart is like wax;
It is melted within me.
15 My strength is dried up like a potsherd,
And my tongue cleaves to my jaws;
And You lay me in the dust of death.
16 For dogs have surrounded me;
A band of evildoers has encompassed me;

22:1 Matt 27:46; Mark 15:34; Ps 10:1; Job 3:24; Ps 6:6; 32:3; 38:8
22:2 Ps 42:3; 88:1
22:3 Ps 99:9; Deut 10:21; Ps 148:14
22:4 Ps 78:53; Ps 107:6
22:5 Is 49:23
22:6 Job 25:6; Is 41:14; Ps 31:11; Is 49:7; 53:3
22:7 Ps 79:4; Is 53:3; Luke 23:35; Matt 27:39; Mark 15:29
22:8 Ps 91:14; Matt 27:43
22:9 Ps 71:5, 6
22:10 Is 46:3; 49:1
22:11 Ps 71:12; 2 Kin 14:26; Ps 72:12; Is 63:5
22:12 Ps 22:21; 68:30; Deut 32:14; Amos 4:1
22:13 Job 16:10; Ps 35:21; Lam 2:16; 3:46; Ps 10:9; 17:12
22:14 Job 30:16; Ps 31:10; Dan 5:6; Josh 7:5; Job 23:16; Ps 73:26; Nah 2:10
22:15 Ps 38:10; John 19:28; Ps 104:29
22:16 Ps 59:6, 7; Matt 27:35; John 20:25

42 Lit *the hind of the morning* **43** I.e. make mouths at me **44** Lit *Roll;* another reading is *He committed* himself

22:1 David gave an amazingly accurate description of the suffering the Messiah would endure hundreds of years later. David was obviously enduring some great trial, but through his suffering he, like the Messiah to come, gained victory. Jesus, the Messiah, quoted this verse while hanging on the cross carrying our burden of sin (Matthew 27:46). It was not a cry of doubt, but an urgent appeal to God.

22:6 When others despise us and heap scorn upon us, they treat us as less than human. After much degradation, we, like David, could begin to feel like worms. When we feel the sting of rejection, we must keep in mind the hope and victory that God promises us (22:22ff).

22:9–11 God's loving concern does not begin on the day we are born and conclude on the day we die. It reaches back to those days before we were born, and reaches ahead along the unending path of eternity. Our only sure help comes from a God whose concern for us reaches beyond our earthly existence. When faced with such love, how could anyone reject it?

22:12 The land of Bashan, located east of the Sea of Galilee, was known for its strong and well-fed cattle (Amos 4:1). Because of its grain fields, it was often called the breadbasket of Palestine.

22:15 A "potsherd" is a pottery fragment or a piece of sun-baked clay.

They pierced my hands and my feet.
17 I can count all my bones.
They look, they stare at me;
18 They divide my garments among them,
And for my clothing they cast lots.

19 But You, O LORD, be not far off;
O You my help, hasten to my assistance.
20 Deliver my soul from the sword,
My only *life* from the power of the dog.
21 Save me from the lion's mouth;
From the horns of the wild oxen You answer me.

22 I will tell of Your name to my brethren;
In the midst of the assembly I will praise You.
23 You who fear the LORD, praise Him;
All you descendants of Jacob, glorify Him,
And stand in awe of Him, all you descendants of Israel.

22:17 Luke 23:27, 35
22:18 Matt 27:35; Mark 15:24; Luke 23:34; John 19:24
22:19 Ps 22:11; Ps 70:5
22:20 Ps 37:14; Ps 35:17
22:21 Ps 22:13; Ps 22:12; Ps 34:4; 118:5; 120:1
22:22 Ps 40:10; Heb 2:12
22:23 Ps 135:19, 20; Ps 86:12; Ps 33:8

CHRIST IN THE PSALMS

Both the Jewish and Christian faiths have long believed that many psalms referred as much to the promised Messiah as they did to events at the time. Because the Messiah was to be a descendant of David, it was expected that many of the royal psalms would apply to him. Christians noted how many of the passages seemed to describe in detail events from Christ's life and death. Jesus himself frequently quoted from Psalms. Almost everything that happened at the crucifixion and most of Jesus' words during his final hours are prophesied in Psalms.

The following is a list of the main references in Psalms pertaining to Christ.

Reference in Psalms	*Reference to Christ*	*Fulfillment in the New Testament*
2:7	The Messiah will be God's Son	Hebrews 1:5–6
16:8–10	He will rise from the dead	Luke 24:5–7
22:1–21	He will experience agony on the cross	Matthew 26—27
22:18	Evil men cast lots for his clothing	Matthew 27:35; John 19:23–24
22:15	He thirsts while on the cross	John 19:28
22:22	He will declare God's name	Hebrews 2:12
34:20	His bones would not be broken	John 19:36–37
40:6–8	He came to do God's will	Hebrews 10:5–7
41:9	His close friend would betray him	Luke 22:48
45:6–7	His throne will last forever	Hebrews 1:8–9
68:18	He ascended into heaven	Ephesians 4:8–10
69:9	He is zealous for God	John 2:17
69:21	He was offered vinegar for his thirst on the cross	Matthew 27:48
89:3–4, 35–36	He will be a descendant of David	Luke 1:31–33
96:13	He will return to judge the world	1 Thessalonians 1:10
110:1	He is David's son and David's Lord	Matthew 22:44
110:4	He is the eternal priest-king	Hebrews 6:20
118:22	He is rejected by many but accepted by God	1 Peter 2:7–8

22:18 It is a great insult to human dignity to rob a person of everything, even his clothing, leaving him naked and destitute. Jesus the Messiah would suffer this humiliating experience on the cross (Matthew 27:35). Most of us will never know the shame and suffering of being penniless and virtually naked in a public place, as many of the Jews experienced during the Nazi holocaust or even the homeless on the streets of our cities today. But most of us would feel equally exposed and naked when some sin, secret or not-so-secret, would be uncovered. At that time, we will need to cry out with David, "O You my help, hasten to my assistance" (22:19).

22:22 David would praise God in the assembly because his private deliverance deserved a public testimony. God wonderfully delivers us in the quiet moments when we are hurting, and we must be prepared to offer public praise for his care.

24 For He has not despised nor abhorred the affliction of the afflicted;
Nor has He hidden His face from him;
But when he cried to Him for help, He heard.

25 From You *comes* my praise in the great assembly;
I shall pay my vows before those who fear Him.
26 The [45]afflicted will eat and be satisfied;
Those who seek Him will praise the LORD.
Let your heart live forever!
27 All the ends of the earth will remember and turn to the LORD,
And all the families of the nations will worship before You.
28 For the kingdom is the LORD'S
And He rules over the nations.
29 All the prosperous of the earth will eat and worship,
All those who go down to the dust will bow before Him,
Even he who cannot keep his soul alive.
30 Posterity will serve Him;
It will be told of the Lord to the *coming* generation.
31 They will come and will declare His righteousness
To a people who will be born, that He has performed *it*.

22:24 Ps 69:33; Ps 27:9; 69:17; 102:2; Ps 31:22; Heb 5:7

22:25 Ps 35:18; 40:9, 10; Ps 61:8; Eccl 5:4

22:26 Ps 107:9; Ps 40:16; Ps 69:32

22:27 Ps 2:8; 82:8; Ps 86:9

22:28 Ps 47:7; Obad 21; Zech 14:9; Matt 6:13; Ps 47:8

22:29 Ps 17:10; 45:12; Hab 1:16; Ps 28:1; Is 26:19; Ps 89:48

22:30 Ps 102:28; Ps 102:18

22:31 Ps 40:9; 71:18; Ps 78:6

PSALM 23

A Psalm of David.

Theme: God is seen as a caring shepherd and a dependable guide. We must follow God and obey his commands. He is our only hope for eternal life and security.
Author: David

1 The LORD is my shepherd,
I shall not want.
2 He makes me lie down in green pastures;
He leads me beside quiet waters.
3 He restores my soul;
He guides me in the paths of righteousness
For His name's sake.

4 Even though I walk through the [46]valley of the shadow of death,
I fear no [47]evil, for You are with me;
Your rod and Your staff, they comfort me.

23:1 Ps 78:52; 80:1; Is 40:11; Jer 31:10; Ezek 34:11-13; John 10:11; 1 Pet 2:25; Ps 34:9, 10; Phil 4:19

23:2 Ps 65:11-13; Ezek 34:14; Rev 7:17; Ps 36:8; 46:4

23:3 Ps 19:7; Ps 5:8; 31:3; Ps 85:13; Prov 4:11; 8:20

23:4 Job 10:21, 22; Ps 107:14; Ps 3:6; 27:1; Ps 16:8; Is 43:2; Mic 7:14

45 Or *poor* **46** Or *valley of deep darkness* **47** Or *harm*

22:30–31 Unborn generations are depending on our faithfulness today. As we teach our children about the Lord, so they will teach their children and their children's children. If we fail to tell our children about the Lord, we may well be breaking the chain of God's influence in generations to come. We must view our children and all the young people we meet as God's future leaders. If we are faithful in opportunities today, we may well be affecting the future.

22:30–31 If we want our children to serve the Lord, they must hear about him from us. It is not enough to rely on the church or those with more knowledge to provide all their Christian education. We must reinforce the lessons of the Bible in our homes.

23:1 In describing the Lord as a shepherd, David wrote out of his own experience because he had spent his early years caring for sheep (1 Samuel 16:10–11). Sheep are completely dependent on the shepherd for provision, guidance, and protection. The New Testament calls Jesus the good shepherd (John 10:11); the great Shepherd (Hebrews 13:20); and the Chief Shepherd (1 Peter 5:4). As the Lord is the good shepherd, so we are his sheep—not frightened, passive animals, but obedient followers, wise enough to follow one who will lead us in the right places and in right ways. This psalm does not focus on the animal-like qualities of sheep, but on the discipleship qualities of those who follow. When you recognize the good shepherd, follow him!

23:2–3 When we allow God our shepherd to guide us, we have contentment. When we choose to sin, however, we go our own way and cannot blame God for the environment we create for ourselves. Our shepherd knows the "green pastures" and "quiet waters" that will restore us. We will reach these places only by following him obediently. Rebelling against the shepherd's leading is actually rebelling against our own best interests. We must remember this the next time we are tempted to go our own way rather than the shepherd's way.

23:4 Death casts a frightening shadow over us because we are entirely helpless in its presence. We can struggle with other enemies—pain, suffering, disease, injury—but strength and courage cannot overcome death. It has the final word. Only one person can walk with us through death's dark valley and bring us safely to the other side—the God of life, our shepherd. Because life is uncertain, we should follow this shepherd who offers us eternal comfort.

23:5 Ps 78:19; Ps 92:10; Luke 7:46; Ps 16:5

5 You prepare a table before me in the presence of my enemies;
You have anointed my head with oil;
My cup overflows.

23:6 Ps 25:7, 10; Ps 27:4-6

6 Surely goodness and lovingkindness will follow me all the days of my life,
And I will [48]dwell in the house of the LORD forever.

PSALM 24

A Psalm of David.

Theme: Everything belongs to God—the glorious eternal King. Let us worship him and welcome his glorious reign.
Author: David

24:1 1 Cor 10:26; Ps 89:11

1 The earth is the LORD'S, and [49]all it contains,
The world, and those who dwell in it.

24:2 Ps 104:3, 5; 136:6

2 For He has founded it upon the seas
And established it upon the rivers.

24:3 Ps 15:1; Ps 2:6; Ps 65:4

3 Who may ascend into the hill of the LORD?
And who may stand in His holy place?

24:4 Job 17:9; Ps 22:30; 26:6; Ps 51:10; 73:1; Matt 5:8; Ezek 18:15; Ps 15:4

4 He who has clean hands and a pure heart,
Who has not lifted up his soul to falsehood
And has not sworn deceitfully.

24:5 Ps 115:13; Ps 36:10

5 He shall receive a blessing from the LORD
And righteousness from the God of his salvation.

24:6 Ps 27:4, 8

6 This is the generation of those who seek Him,
Who seek Your face—*even* Jacob. Selah.

48 Another reading is *return to* **49** Lit *its fullness*

PSALMS TO LEARN AND LOVE

Almost everyone, whether religious or not, has heard Psalm 23 because it is quoted so frequently. Many other psalms are also familiar because they are quoted in music, in literature, or in the words of the worship service.

The psalms we know and love are the ones that come into our minds when we need them. They inspire us, comfort us, correct us just when we need a word from the Lord. If you want to begin memorizing psalms, start with some of these favorites. Memorize the whole psalm or just the verses that speak most directly to you. Or read the psalm aloud several times a day until it is part of you.

Psalms to bring us into God's presence	29; 95:1–7; 96; 100
Psalms about goodness	1; 19; 24; 133; 136; 139
Psalms of praise	8; 97; 103; 107; 113; 145; 150
Psalms of repentance and forgiveness	32:1–5; 51; 103
Psalms for times of trouble	3; 14; 22; 37:1–11; 42; 46; 53; 116:1–7
Psalms of confidence and trust	23; 40:1–4; 91; 119:11; 121; 127

23:5–6 In ancient Near Eastern culture, at a banquet it was customary to anoint a person with fragrant oil as a lotion. Hosts were also expected to protect their guests at all costs. God offers the protection of a host even when enemies surround us. In the final scene of this psalm, we see that believers will dwell with God. God, the perfect shepherd and host, promises to guide and protect us through life to bring us into his house forever.

24:1 Because "the earth is the LORD'S," all of us are stewards, or caretakers. We should be committed to the proper management of this world and its resources, but we are not to become devoted to anything created or act as sole proprietors because this world will pass away (1 John 2:17).

24:1ff This psalm may have been written to celebrate the moving of the ark of the covenant from Obed-edom's house to Jerusalem (2 Samuel 6:10–12). Tradition says that this psalm was sung on the first day of each week in the temple services. Verses 1–6 tell who is worthy to join in such a celebration of worship.

24:4 Swearing deceitfully means telling lies under oath. How greatly God values honesty! Dishonesty comes easily, especially when complete truthfulness could cost us something, make us uncomfortable, or put us in an unfavorable light. Dishonest communication hinders relationships. Without honesty, a relationship with God is impossible. If we lie to others, we will begin to deceive ourselves. God cannot hear us or speak to us if we are building a wall of self-deception.

7 Lift up your heads, O gates,
And be lifted up, O [50]ancient doors,
That the King of glory may come in!
8 Who is the King of glory?
The LORD strong and mighty,
The LORD mighty in battle.
9 Lift up your heads, O gates,
And lift *them* up, O [50]ancient doors,
That the King of glory may come in!
10 Who is this King of glory?
The LORD of hosts,
He is the King of glory. Selah.

24:7 Ps 118:20; Is 26:2; Ps 29:2, 9; 97:6; Acts 7:2; 1 Cor 2:8

24:8 Deut 4:34; Ps 96:7; Ex 15:3, 6; Ps 76:3-6

24:9 Ps 26:8; 57:11

24:10 Gen 32:2; Josh 5:14; 2 Sam 5:10; Neh 9:6

PSALM 25

A Psalm of David.

Theme: A prayer for defense, guidance, and pardon. As we trust in God, he grants these same requests for us.
Author: David

1 To You, O LORD, I lift up my soul.
2 O my God, in You I trust,
Do not let me be ashamed;
Do not let my enemies exult over me.
3 Indeed, none of those who wait for You will be ashamed;
Those who deal treacherously without cause will be ashamed.

4 Make me know Your ways, O LORD;
Teach me Your paths.
5 Lead me in Your truth and teach me,
For You are the God of my salvation;
For You I wait all the day.
6 Remember, O LORD, Your compassion and Your lovingkindnesses,
For they have been [50]from of old.
7 Do not remember the sins of my youth or my transgressions;
According to Your lovingkindness remember me,
For Your goodness' sake, O LORD.

8 Good and upright is the LORD;
Therefore He instructs sinners in the way.

25:1 Ps 86:4; 143:8

25:2 Ps 31:1; Ps 25:20; 31:1; Ps 13:4; 41:11

25:3 Ps 37:9; 40:1; Is 49:23; Ps 119:158; Is 21:2; Hab 1:13

25:4 Ex 33:13; Ps 27:11; 86:11

25:5 Ps 25:10; 43:3; Ps 79:9; Ps 40:1

25:6 Ps 98:3; Ps 103:17

25:7 Job 13:26; 20:11; Ps 51:1; Ps 31:19

25:8 Ps 86:5; Ps 92:15; Ps 32:8

50 Lit *everlasting*

24:7 Who is this King of glory? The King of glory, identified also as the Lord of hosts, or the commander of heaven's armies, is the Messiah himself, eternal, holy, and mighty. This psalm is not only a battle cry for the church; it also looks forward to Christ's future entry into the new Jerusalem to reign forever (Revelation 19:11–21).

24:7–10 This psalm, often set to music, was probably used in corporate worship. It may have been re-enacted many times at the temple. The people outside would call out to the temple gates to open up and let the King of glory in. From inside, the priests or another group would ask, "Who is the King of glory?" Outside, the people would respond in unison, "The LORD strong and mighty, the LORD mighty in battle," proclaiming his great power and strength. The exchange was then repeated (24:9–10), and the temple gates would swing open, symbolizing the people's desire to have God's presence among them. This would have been an important lesson for children who were participating.

25:2 Seventy-two psalms—almost half the book—speak about enemies. Enemies are those who oppose not only us, but also God's way of living. We can view temptations—money, success, prestige, lust—as our enemies. And our greatest enemy is Satan. David asked God to keep his enemies from overcoming him because they opposed what God stood for. If his enemies succeeded, David feared that many would think that living for God was futile. David did not question his own faith—he knew that God would triumph. But he didn't want his enemies' success to be an obstacle to the faith of others.

25:4 David expressed his desire for guidance. How do we receive God's guidance? The first step is to *want* to be guided and to realize that God's primary guidance system is in his Word, the Bible. Psalm 119 tells of the endless knowledge found in God's Word. By reading it and constantly learning from it, we will gain the wisdom to perceive God's direction for our lives. We may be tempted to demand answers from God, but David asked for direction. When we are willing to seek God, learn from his Word, and obey his commands, then will we receive his specific guidance.

25:8–11 We are bombarded today with relentless appeals to go in various directions. Television advertising alone places hundreds of options before us, in addition to appeals made by political parties, cults, false religions, and dozens of other groups. Numerous organizations, including Christian organizations, seek to motivate us to support a cause. Add to that the dozens of decisions we must make

25:9 Ps 23:3; Ps 27:11
25:10 Ps 40:11; Ps 103:18
25:11 Ps 31:3; 79:9; Ex 34:9
25:12 Ps 31:19; Ps 25:8; 37:23
25:13 Prov 1:33; Jer 23:6; Ps 37:11; 69:36; Matt 5:5
25:14 Prov 3:32; John 7:17; Gen 17:1, 2
25:15 Ps 123:2; 141:8; Ps 31:4; 124:7
25:16 Ps 69:16; Ps 143:4
25:17 Ps 40:12; Ps 107:6
25:18 2 Sam 16:12; Ps 31:7; Ps 103:3
25:19 Ps 3:1; Ps 9:13
25:20 Ps 86:2; Ps 25:2
25:21 Ps 41:12; Ps 25:3
25:22 Ps 130:8

9 He leads the humble in justice,
And He teaches the humble His way.
10 All the paths of the LORD are lovingkindness and truth
To those who keep His covenant and His testimonies.
11 For Your name's sake, O LORD,
Pardon my iniquity, for it is great.

12 Who is the man who fears the LORD?
He will instruct him in the way he should choose.
13 His soul will abide in prosperity,
And his [51]descendants will inherit the land.
14 The secret of the LORD is for those who fear Him,
And He will make them know His covenant.
15 My eyes are continually toward the LORD,
For He will pluck my feet out of the net.

16 Turn to me and be gracious to me,
For I am lonely and afflicted.
17 The troubles of my heart are enlarged;
Bring me out of my distresses.
18 Look upon my affliction and my [52]trouble,
And forgive all my sins.
19 Look upon my enemies, for they are many,
And they hate me with violent hatred.
20 Guard my soul and deliver me;
Do not let me be ashamed, for I take refuge in You.
21 Let integrity and uprightness preserve me,
For I wait for You.
22 Redeem Israel, O God,
Out of all his troubles.

PSALM 26

A Psalm of David.

Theme: Declaring loyalty to God. If we are genuinely committed to God, we can stand up to opposition and examination.
Author: David, possibly written during the days of Absalom's rebellion.

26:1 Ps 7:8; 2 Kin 20:3; Prov 20:7; Ps 13:5; 28:7; Heb 10:23
26:2 Ps 17:3; 139:23; Ps 7:9

1 [53]Vindicate me, O LORD, for I have walked in my integrity,
And I have trusted in the LORD without wavering.
2 Examine me, O LORD, and try me;

51 Lit *seed* **52** Lit *toil* **53** Lit *Judge*

concerning our job, our family, our money, our society, and we become desperate for someone to show us the right way. If you find yourself pulled in several directions, remember that God teaches the humble his way.

25:12 To fear the Lord is to recognize God for who he is: holy, almighty, righteous, pure, all-knowing, all-powerful, and all-wise. When we regard God correctly, we gain a clearer picture of ourselves: sinful, weak, frail, and needy. When we recognize who God is and who we are, we will fall at his feet in humble respect. Only then will he show us how to choose his way.

25:14 "The LORD is for those who fear Him." God offers intimate and lasting friendship to those who revere him, who hold him in highest honor. What relationship could ever compare with having the Lord of all creation for a friend? Your everlasting friendship with God will grow as you revere him.

25:16–17 Do life's problems always seem to go from bad to worse? God is the only one who can reverse this downward spiral. He can take our problems and turn them into glorious victories. There is one necessary requirement—we, like David, must cry out, "Turn to me and be gracious to me." When you are willing to do that, God can turn the worst into something wonderful. The next step is yours—God has already made his offer.

25:21 If ever we needed two powerful forces to preserve us along life's way, they are integrity and uprightness. The psalmist asks for these to protect him step-by-step. Uprightness makes us learn God's requirements and strive to fulfill them. Integrity—being what we say we are—keeps us from claiming to be upright while living as if we do not know God. Uprightness says, "This is the Shepherd's way," and integrity says, "I will walk consistently in it."

26:1–3 By saying that he had walked in "integrity," David was not claiming to be sinless—that is impossible for any human being to achieve. But he was consistently in fellowship with God, clearing his record when he sinned by asking for forgiveness. Here he pleads with God to clear his name of the false charges made against him by his enemies. We also can ask God to examine us, trusting him to forgive our sins and clear our record according to his mercy.

Test my [54]mind and my heart.
3 For Your lovingkindness is before my eyes,
And I have walked in Your truth.
4 I do not sit with [55]deceitful men,
Nor will I go with pretenders.
5 I hate the assembly of evildoers,
And I will not sit with the wicked.
6 I shall wash my hands in innocence,
And I will go about Your altar, O LORD,
7 That I may proclaim with the voice of thanksgiving
And declare all Your wonders.

8 O LORD, I love the habitation of Your house
And the place where Your glory dwells.
9 Do not take my soul away *along* with sinners,
Nor my life with men of bloodshed,
10 In whose hands is a wicked scheme,
And whose right hand is full of bribes.
11 But as for me, I shall walk in my integrity;
Redeem me, and be gracious to me.
12 My foot stands on a level place;
In the congregations I shall bless the LORD.

26:3 Ps 48:9; 2 Kin 20:3; Ps 86:11
26:4 Ps 1:1; Ps 28:3
26:5 Ps 31:6; 139:21
26:6 Ps 73:13; Ps 43:3, 4
26:7 Ps 9:1
26:8 Ps 27:4; Ps 24:7
26:9 Ps 28:3; Ps 139:19
26:10 Ps 37:7; Ps 15:5
26:11 Ps 26:1; Ps 44:26; 69:18
26:12 Ps 40:2; Ps 27:11; Ps 22:22

PSALM 27

A Psalm of David.

Theme: God offers help for today and hope for the future.
Unwavering confidence in God is our antidote for fear and loneliness.
Author: David

1 The LORD is my light and my salvation;
Whom shall I fear?
The LORD is the defense of my life;
Whom shall I dread?
2 When evildoers came upon me to devour my flesh,
My adversaries and my enemies, they stumbled and fell.
3 Though a host encamp against me,
My heart will not fear;
Though war arise against me,
In *spite of* this I shall be confident.

4 One thing I have asked from the LORD, that I shall seek:
That I may dwell in the house of the LORD all the days of my life,

27:1 Ps 18:28; Is 60:20; Mic 7:8; Ex 15:2; Ps 62:7; 118:14; Is 33:2; Jon 2:9; Ps 28:8; Ps 118:6
27:2 Ps 14:4; Ps 9:3
27:3 Ps 3:6; Job 4:6
27:4 Ps 26:8; Ps 23:6; Ps 90:17; Ps 18:6

54 Lit *kidneys,* figurative for inner man **55** Or *worthless men;* lit *men of falsehood*

26:4–5 Should we stay away from unbelievers? No. Although there are some places Christians should avoid, Jesus demonstrated that we must go among unbelievers to help them. But there is a difference between being *with* unbelievers and being *one of* them. Trying to be one of them harms our witness for God. Ask about the people you enjoy, "If I am with them often, will I become less obedient to God in outlook or action?" If the answer is yes, carefully monitor how you spend your time with these people and what effect it has on you.

26:8 God's house in this verse can mean either the tabernacle in Gibeon (the one constructed in the days of Moses; see Exodus 40:35) or the temporary dwelling David built to house the ark of the covenant (2 Samuel 6:17). David exclaimed how he loved to worship God at this place. We should worship God with the same love and reverence as David did.

26:12 Too often we complain about our problems to anyone who will listen and praise God only in private. How much better it would be for us to complain privately and to praise God publicly.

27:1 Fear is a dark shadow that envelops us and ultimately imprisons us within ourselves. Each of us has been a prisoner of fear at one time or another—fear of rejection, misunderstanding, uncertainty, sickness, or even death. But we can conquer fear by using the bright liberating light of the Lord who brings salvation. If we want to dispel the darkness of fear, let us remember with the psalmist that "the LORD is my light and my salvation."

27:4 By the "house of the LORD" and "His temple," David could be referring to the tabernacle in Gibeon, to the sanctuary he had put up to house the ark of the covenant, or to the temple that his son Solomon was to build. David probably had the temple in mind because he made many of the plans for it (1 Chronicles 22). But David may also have used the word *temple* to mean "the presence of the Lord." His greatest desire was to live in God's presence each day of his life. Sadly, this is not the greatest desire of many who claim to be believers. But those who desire to live in God's presence each day will be able to enjoy that relationship forever.

To behold the [56]beauty of the LORD
And to [57]meditate in His temple.

27:5 Ps 50:15; Ps 31:20; Ps 17:8; Ps 40:2

5 For in the day of trouble He will conceal me in His tabernacle;
In the secret place of His tent He will hide me;
He will lift me up on a rock.

27:6 Ps 3:3; Ps 107:22; Ps 13:6

6 And now my head will be lifted up above my enemies around me,
And I will offer in His tent sacrifices with shouts of joy;
I will sing, yes, I will sing praises to the LORD.

27:7 Ps 4:3; 61:1; Ps 13:3

7 Hear, O LORD, when I cry with my voice,
And be gracious to me and answer me.

27:8 Ps 105:4; Amos 5:6; Ps 34:4

8 *When You said,* "Seek My face," my heart said to You,
"Your face, O LORD, I shall seek."

27:9 Ps 69:17; Ps 6:1; Ps 40:17; Ps 94:14; Ps 37:28

9 Do not hide Your face from me,
Do not turn Your servant away in anger;
You have been my help;
Do not abandon me nor forsake me,
O God of my salvation!

27:10 Is 49:15; Is 40:11

10 For my father and my mother have forsaken me,
But the LORD will take me up.

27:11 Ps 25:4; 86:11; Ps 5:8; 26:12

11 Teach me Your way, O LORD,
And lead me in a level path
Because of my foes.

27:12 Ps 41:2; Deut 19:18; Ps 35:11; Matt 26:60; Acts 9:1

12 Do not deliver me over to the desire of my adversaries,
For false witnesses have risen against me,
And such as breathe out violence.

27:13 Ps 31:19; Job 28:13; Ps 52:5; 116:9; 142:5; Is 38:11; Jer 11:19; Ezek 26:20

13 *I would have despaired* unless I had believed that I would see the goodness of the LORD
In the land of the living.

27:14 Ps 25:3; 37:34; 40:1; 62:5; 130:5; Prov 20:22; Is 25:9; Ps 31:24

14 Wait for the LORD;
Be strong and let your heart take courage;
Yes, wait for the LORD.

PSALM 28

A Psalm of David.

Theme: Prayer when surrounded by trouble or wickedness. God is our only real source of safety. Prayer is our best help when trials come our way because it keeps us in communion with God.
Author: David

28:1 Ps 18:2; Ps 35:22; 39:12; 83:1; Ps 88:4; 143:7; Prov 1:12

1 To You, O LORD, I call;
My rock, do not be deaf to me,
For if You are silent to me,
I will become like those who go down to the pit.

28:2 Ps 140:6; Ps 134:2; 141:2; Lam 2:19; 1 Tim 2:8; Ps 5:7; 138:2; 1 Kin 6:5

2 Hear the voice of my supplications when I cry to You for help,
When I lift up my hands toward [58]Your holy sanctuary.

56 Lit *delightfulness* **57** Lit *inquire* **58** Lit *the innermost place of Your sanctuary*

27:10 Many have had the sad experience of being forsaken by father or mother. Broken homes, differences of belief, addiction to drugs or alcohol, even psychological isolation can leave children crippled by this loss. Even as adults, the pain may linger. God can take that place in our life, fill that void, and heal that hurt. He can direct us to adults who may take the role of father or mother for us. His love is sufficient for all our needs.

27:13 The "land of the living" simply means "this life." David was obviously going through a trial, but he was confident that in this present life God would see him through it.

27:14 David knew from experience what it meant to wait for the Lord. He had been anointed king at age 16, but didn't become king until he was 30. During the interim, he was chased through the wilderness by jealous King Saul. David had to wait on God for the fulfillment of his promise to reign. Later, after becoming king, he was chased by his rebellious son, Absalom.

Waiting for God is not easy. Often it seems that he isn't answering our prayers or doesn't understand the urgency of our situation. That kind of thinking implies that God is not in control or is not fair. But God is worth waiting for. Lamentations 3:24–26 calls us to hope in and wait for the Lord because often God uses waiting to refresh, renew, and teach us. Make good use of your waiting times by discovering what God may be trying to teach you in them.

3 Do not drag me away with the wicked
And with those who work iniquity,
Who speak peace with their neighbors,
While evil is in their hearts.
4 Require them according to their work and according to the evil of their practices;
Requite them according to the deeds of their hands;
Repay them their [59]recompense.
5 Because they do not regard the works of the LORD
Nor the deeds of His hands,
He will tear them down and not build them up.

6 Blessed be the LORD,
Because He has heard the voice of my supplication.
7 The LORD is my strength and my shield;
My heart trusts in Him, and I am helped;
Therefore my heart exults,
And with my song I shall thank Him.
8 The LORD is their strength,
And He is a saving defense to His anointed.
9 Save Your people and bless Your inheritance;
Be their shepherd also, and carry them forever.

28:3 Ps 26:9; Ps 12:2; 55:21; 62:4; Jer 9:8
28:4 Ps 62:12; 2 Tim 4:14; Rev 18:6; 22:12
28:5 Is 5:12
28:6 Ps 28:2
28:7 Ps 18:2; 59:17; Ps 3:3; Ps 13:5; 112:7; Ps 16:9; Ps 40:3; 69:30
28:8 Ps 20:6; 89:17; Ps 27:1; 140:7
28:9 Ps 106:47; Deut 9:29; 32:9; 1 Kin 8:51; Ps 33:12; 106:40; Ps 80:1; Deut 1:31; Is 40:11; 46:3; 63:9

PSALM 29

A Psalm of David.

Theme: God reveals his great power in nature. We can trust God to give us both the peace and the strength to weather the storms of life.
Author: David

1 Ascribe to the LORD, O sons of the mighty,
Ascribe to the LORD glory and strength.
2 Ascribe to the LORD the glory due to His name;
Worship the LORD in holy array.

3 The voice of the LORD is upon the waters;
The God of glory thunders,
The LORD is over many waters.
4 The voice of the LORD is powerful,
The voice of the LORD is majestic.
5 The voice of the LORD breaks the cedars;
Yes, the LORD breaks in pieces the cedars of Lebanon.
6 He makes Lebanon skip like a calf,
And Sirion like a young wild ox.
7 The voice of the LORD hews out flames of fire.
8 The voice of the LORD shakes the wilderness;
The LORD shakes the wilderness of Kadesh.
9 The voice of the LORD makes the deer to calve
And strips the forests bare;
And in His temple everything says, "Glory!"

10 The LORD sat *as King* at the flood;
Yes, the LORD sits as King forever.

29:1 1 Chr 16:28, 29; Ps 96:7-9
29:2 2 Chr 20:21; Ps 110:3
29:3 Ps 104:7; Job 37:4, 5; Ps 18:13; Ps 18:16; 107:23
29:4 Ps 68:33
29:5 Judg 9:15; 1 Kin 5:6; Ps 104:16; Is 2:13; 14:8
29:6 Ps 114:4, 6; Deut 3:9
29:8 Num 13:26
29:9 Job 39:1; Ps 26:8
29:10 Gen 6:17; Ps 10:16

59 Or *dealings*

28:3–5 It's easy to pretend friendship. Wicked people often put on a show of kindness or friendship in order to gain their own ends. David, in his royal position, may have met many who pretended friendship only to meet their own goals. David knew that God would punish them eventually, but he prayed that their punishment would come swiftly. True believers should be straightforward and sincere in all their relationships.

29:5–6 The cedars of Lebanon were giant trees that could grow to 120 feet tall and 30 feet in circumference. A voice that could break the cedars of Lebanon would be a truly powerful voice—the voice of God. "Sirion" means Mount Hermon. All that was impressive to people was under God's complete control.

29:10–11 Throughout history, God has revealed his power through mighty miracles over nature, such as the great flood

29:11 Ps 28:8; 68:35; Is 40:29; Ps 37:11; 72:3

11 The LORD will give strength to His people;
The LORD will bless His people with peace.

PSALM 30

A Psalm; a Song at the Dedication of the House. *A Psalm* of David.

Theme: A celebration of God's deliverance. Earthly security is uncertain, but God is always faithful.
Author: David

30:1 Ps 118:28; 145:1; Ps 3:3; Ps 25:2; 35:19, 24
30:2 Ps 88:13; Ps 6:2; 103:3; Is 53:5
30:3 Ps 86:13; Ps 28:1
30:4 Ps 149:1; Ps 50:5; Ps 97:12; Ex 3:15; Ps 135:13; Hos 12:5
30:5 Ps 103:9; Is 26:20; 54:7, 8; Ps 118:1; Ps 126:5; 2 Cor 4:17

1 I will extol You, O LORD, for You have lifted me up,
And have not let my enemies rejoice over me.
2 O LORD my God,
I cried to You for help, and You healed me.
3 O LORD, You have brought up my soul from Sheol;
You have kept me alive, that I would not go down to the pit.
4 Sing praise to the LORD, you His godly ones,
And give thanks to His holy name.
5 For His anger is but for a moment,
His favor is for a lifetime;
Weeping may last for the night,
But a shout of joy *comes* in the morning.

30:6 Ps 10:6; 62:2, 6
30:7 Deut 31:17; Ps 104:29; 143:7
30:9 Ps 28:1; Ps 6:5

6 Now as for me, I said in my prosperity,
"I will never be moved."
7 O LORD, by Your favor You have made my mountain to stand strong;
You hid Your face, I was dismayed.
8 To You, O LORD, I called,
And to the Lord I made supplication:
9 "What profit is there in my blood, if I go down to the pit?
Will the dust praise You? Will it declare Your faithfulness?

30:10 Ps 4:1; 27:7; Ps 27:9; 54:4
30:11 Eccl 3:4; Jer 31:4, 13; Is 20:2; Ps 4:7
30:12 Ps 16:9; 57:8; 108:1; Ps 44:8

10 "Hear, O LORD, and be gracious to me;
O LORD, be my helper."
11 You have turned for me my mourning into dancing;
You have loosed my sackcloth and girded me with gladness,
12 That *my* soul may sing praise to You and not be silent.
O LORD my God, I will give thanks to You forever.

PSALM 31

For the choir director. A Psalm of David.

Theme: In times of stress, depending upon God requires complete commitment.
Author: David, although same say Jeremiah

31:1 Ps 31:1-3; 71:1-3; Ps 25:2; Ps 143:1

1 In You, O LORD, I have taken refuge;
Let me never be ashamed;

(Genesis 6—9). He promises to continue to reveal his power. Paul urged us to understand how great God's power is (Ephesians 1:18–23). The same power that raised Christ from the dead is available to help us with our daily problems. When you feel weak and limited, don't despair. Remember that God can give you strength. The power that controls creation and raises the dead is available to you.

30:1ff David may have written this psalm when he dedicated Ornan's threshing floor (which became the future site of the temple) and after God stopped the great plague he had used to discipline David (1 Chronicles 21:1—22:6). The serious illness mentioned in 30:2–3 may refer to an illness David experienced or to the plague itself.

30:5 Like a shot given by a doctor, the discomfort of God's anger lasts only a moment, but the good effects go on for a long time. Let God's anger be a sharp pain that warns you to turn from sin.

30:6–7 Security had made David feel invincible. Although he knew that his riches and power had come from God, they had gone to his head, making him proud. Wealth, power, and fame have an intoxicating effect on people, making them feel self-reliant, self-secure, and independent of God. But this false security can be easily shattered. Don't be trapped by the false security of prosperity. Depend on God for your security, and you won't be shaken when worldly possessions disappear.

30:11 *Sackcloth* refers to clothes worn as a sign of mourning.

31:1 David called upon God to deliver him. He wanted God to stop those who were unjustly causing trouble. Therefore, David made his request based upon what he knew of God's name, or character. Because God is righteous and loving, he loves to deliver his people.

In Your righteousness deliver me.
2 Incline Your ear to me, rescue me quickly;
Be to me a rock of strength,
A stronghold to save me.
3 For You are my rock and my fortress;
For Your name's sake You will lead me and guide me.
4 You will pull me out of the net which they have secretly laid for me,
For You are my strength.
5 Into Your hand I commit my spirit;
You have ransomed me, O LORD, God of truth.

6 I hate those who regard vain idols,
But I trust in the LORD.
7 I will rejoice and be glad in Your lovingkindness,
Because You have seen my affliction;
You have known the troubles of my soul,
8 And You have not given me over into the hand of the enemy;
You have set my feet in a large place.

9 Be gracious to me, O LORD, for I am in distress;
My eye is wasted away from grief, my soul and my body *also*.
10 For my life is spent with sorrow
And my years with sighing;
My strength has failed because of my iniquity,
And my body has wasted away.
11 Because of all my adversaries, I have become a reproach,
Especially to my neighbors,
And an object of dread to my acquaintances;
Those who see me in the street flee from me.
12 I am forgotten as a dead man, out of mind;
I am like a broken vessel.
13 For I have heard the slander of many,
Terror is on every side;
While they took counsel together against me,
They schemed to take away my life.

14 But as for me, I trust in You, O LORD,
I say, "You are my God."
15 My times are in Your hand;
Deliver me from the hand of my enemies and from those who persecute me.

31:2 Ps 17:6; 71:2; 86:1; 102:2; Ps 18:2; 71:3

31:3 Ps 18:2; Ps 23:3; 25:11

31:4 Ps 25:15; Ps 46:1

31:5 Luke 23:46; Acts 7:59; Ps 55:18; 71:23; Deut 32:4; Ps 71:22

31:6 Jon 2:8; Ps 52:8

31:7 Ps 90:14; Ps 10:14

31:8 Deut 32:30; Ps 37:33

31:9 Ps 66:14; 69:17; Ps 6:7; Ps 63:1

31:10 Ps 13:2; Ps 39:11; Ps 32:3; 38:3; 102:3

31:11 Ps 69:19; Job 19:13; Ps 38:11; 88:8, 18

31:12 Ps 88:5

31:13 Ps 50:20; Jer 20:10; Lam 2:22; Ps 62:4; Matt 27:1; Ps 41:7

31:14 Ps 140:6

31:15 Job 14:5; 24:1; Ps 143:9

31:1–6 We say we have faith in God, but do we really trust him? David's words, "Into Your hand I commit my spirit," convey his complete trust in God. Jesus used this phrase as he was dying on the cross—showing his absolute dependence on God the Father (Luke 23:46). Stephen repeated these words as he was being stoned to death (Acts 7:59), confident that in death he was simply passing from God's earthly care to God's eternal care. We should commit our possessions, our families, and our vocations to God. But first and foremost, we should commit *ourselves* completely to him.

31:6 Why did David suddenly bring up the subject of idol worship? He wanted to contrast his total devotion to God with the diluted worship offered by many Israelites. Pagan religious rituals were never completely banished from Israel and Judah, despite the efforts of David and a few other kings. Obviously a person who clung to idols could not commit his spirit into God's hands. When we put today's idols (wealth, material possessions, success) first in our lives, we cannot expect God's Spirit to guide us. God is our highest authority and requires our first allegiance.

31:8 In David's day, armies needed large areas of land for their military maneuvers. David praised God for the "large place"—the open spaces that gave him the freedom to move within God's boundaries. If you feel restrained by God's moral boundaries, remember that God has given you much freedom, far more than you need to move within those boundaries. Use the opportunities he gives you to make proper decisions. Use them wisely and they will lead to victory.

31:9–13 In describing his own feelings, David writes of the helplessness and hopelessness everyone feels when hated or rejected. But adversity is easier to accept when we recognize our true relationship with the sovereign God (31:14–18). Although our enemies may seem to have the upper hand, they are ultimately the helpless and hopeless ones. Those who know God will be victorious in the end (31:23). We can have courage today because God will preserve us.

31:14–15 In saying, "My times are in Your hand," David was expressing his belief that all of life's circumstances are under God's control. Knowing that God loves and cares for us enables us to keep steady in our faith regardless of our circumstances. It keeps us from sinning foolishly by taking matters into our own hands or resenting God's timetable.

16 Make Your face to shine upon Your servant;
Save me in Your lovingkindness.
17 Let me not be put to shame, O LORD, for I call upon You;
Let the wicked be put to shame, let them be silent in Sheol.
18 Let the lying lips be mute,
Which speak arrogantly against the righteous
With pride and contempt.

19 How great is Your goodness,
Which You have stored up for those who fear You,
Which You have wrought for those who take refuge in You,
Before the sons of men!
20 You hide them in the secret place of Your presence from the conspiracies of man;
You keep them secretly in a shelter from the strife of tongues.
21 Blessed be the LORD,
For He has made marvelous His lovingkindness to me in a besieged city.
22 As for me, I said in my alarm,
"I am cut off from before Your eyes";
Nevertheless You heard the voice of my supplications
When I cried to You.

23 O love the LORD, all you His godly ones!
The LORD preserves the faithful
And fully recompenses the proud doer.
24 Be strong and let your heart take courage,
All you who hope in the LORD.

31:16 Num 6:25; Ps 4:6; 80:3; Ps 6:4
31:17 Ps 25:2, 20; Ps 25:3; 1 Sam 2:9; Ps 94:17; 115:17
31:18 Ps 109:2; 120:2; 1 Sam 2:3; Ps 94:4; Jude 15
31:19 Ps 65:4; 145:7; Is 64:4; Rom 2:4; 11:22; Ps 5:11; Ps 23:5
31:20 Ps 27:5; Ps 37:12; Job 5:21; Ps 31:13
31:21 Ps 28:6; Ps 17:7; 1 Sam 23:7; Ps 87:5
31:22 Ps 116:11; Ps 88:5; Is 38:11, 12; Lam 3:54; Ps 18:6; 66:19; 145:19
31:23 Ps 30:4; 37:28; 50:5; Ps 145:20; Rev 2:10; Deut 32:41; Ps 94:2
31:24 Ps 27:14

PSALM 32

A Psalm of David. A [60]Maskil.

Theme: Forgiveness brings true joy. Only when we ask God to forgive our sins will he give us real happiness and relief from guilt.
Author: David

1 How blessed is he whose transgression is forgiven,
Whose sin is covered!
2 How blessed is the man to whom the LORD does not impute iniquity,
And in whose spirit there is no deceit!

3 When I kept silent *about my sin,* my body wasted away
Through my groaning all day long.
4 For day and night Your hand was heavy upon me;
My vitality was drained away *as* with the fever heat of summer. Selah.
5 I acknowledged my sin to You,
And my iniquity I did not hide;
I said, "I will confess my transgressions to the LORD";
And You forgave the guilt of my sin. Selah.
6 Therefore, let everyone who is godly pray to You in a time when You may be
found;

32:1 Ps 85:2; 103:3; Rom 4:7, 8
32:2 2 Cor 5:19; John 1:47
32:3 Ps 39:2, 3; Ps 31:10; Ps 38:8
32:4 1 Sam 5:6; Job 23:2; 33:7; Ps 38:2; 39:10; Ps 22:15
32:5 Lev 26:40; Job 31:33; Ps 38:18; Prov 28:13; 1 John 1:9; Ps 103:12
32:6 Ps 69:13; Is 55:6; Ps 46:1-3; 69:1; 124:5; 144:7; Is 43:2

60 Possibly *Contemplative,* or *Didactic,* or *Skillful Psalm*

---

32 title *Maskil* is a term perhaps denoting psalms written to make a person wise or prudent, to increase a person's success or skill.

32:1ff Read this psalm in conjunction with Psalm 51—both are penitential psalms. Here David expresses the joy of forgiveness. God had forgiven him for the sins he had committed against Bath-sheba and Uriah (2 Samuel 11–12). This is another of the penitential (repentance) psalms where the writer confesses his sin to God.

32:1–2 God *wants* to forgive sinners. Forgiveness has always been part of his loving nature. He announced this to Moses (Exodus 34:7); he revealed it to David; and he dramatically showed it to the world through Jesus Christ. These verses convey several aspects of God's forgiveness: He forgives transgression, covers sin, doesn't count our sins against us. Paul quoted these verses in Romans 4:7–8 and showed that we can have this joyous experience of forgiveness through faith in Christ.

32:5 What is confession? To confess our sin is to agree with God, acknowledging that he is right to declare what we have done as sinful, and that we are wrong to desire or to do it. It is to affirm our intention of abandoning that sin in order to follow him more faithfully.

Surely in a flood of great waters they will not reach him.
7 You are my hiding place; You preserve me from trouble;
You surround me with songs of deliverance. Selah.

8 I will instruct you and teach you in the way which you should go;
I will counsel you with My eye upon you.
9 Do not be as the horse or as the mule which have no understanding,
Whose trappings include bit and bridle to hold them in check,
Otherwise they will not come near to you.
10 Many are the sorrows of the wicked,
But he who trusts in the LORD, lovingkindness shall surround him.
11 Be glad in the LORD and rejoice, you righteous ones;
And shout for joy, all you who are upright in heart.

32:7 Ps 9:9; 31:20; 91:1; 119:114; Ps 121:7; Ex 15:1; Judg 5:1; Ps 40:3

32:8 Ps 25:8; Ps 33:18

32:9 Prov 26:3

32:10 Ps 16:4; Prov 13:21; Rom 2:9; Ps 5:11, 12; Prov 16:20

32:11 Ps 64:10; 68:3; 97:12; Ps 7:10; 64:10

PSALM 33

Theme: Because God is Creator, Lord, Savior, and Deliverer, he is worthy of our trust and praise. Because he is faithful, and his word is dependable, we can rejoice and sing, giving thanks and praise.
Author: Anonymous

1 Sing for joy in the LORD, O you righteous ones;
Praise is becoming to the upright.
2 Give thanks to the LORD with the lyre;
Sing praises to Him with a harp of ten strings.
3 Sing to Him a new song;
Play skillfully with a shout of joy.
4 For the word of the LORD is upright,
And all His work is *done* in faithfulness.
5 He loves righteousness and justice;
The earth is full of the lovingkindness of the LORD.

6 By the word of the LORD the heavens were made,
And by the breath of His mouth all their host.

33:1 Ps 32:11; Phil 3:1; 4:4; Ps 92:1; 147:1

33:2 Ps 71:22; 147:7; Ps 144:9

33:3 Ps 40:3; 96:1; 98:1; 144:9; Is 42:10; Rev 5:9; Ps 98:4

33:4 Ps 19:8; Ps 119:90

33:5 Ps 11:7; 37:28; Ps 119:64

33:6 Gen 1:6; Ps 148:5; Heb 11:3; Ps 104:30; Gen 2:1

CONFESSION, REPENTANCE, AND FORGIVENESS IN PSALMS

Over the centuries, many believers, overcome by an awareness of their own sins, have found in the words of the penitential (confession) psalms a ray of hope. The psalmists shared with God both the depth of their sorrow and repentance, as well as the height of joy at being forgiven. They rejoiced in the knowledge that God would respond to confession and repentance with complete forgiveness. We, who live on the other side of the cross of Christ, can rejoice even more because we understand more. God has shown us that he is willing to forgive because his judgment on sin was satisfied by Christ's death on the cross.

As you read these psalms, note the pattern followed by the psalmists in responding to God: (1) they recognized their sinfulness and tendency to do wrong; (2) they realized that sin was rebellion against God himself; (3) they admitted their sins to God; (4) they trusted in God's willingness to forgive; and (5) they accepted his forgiveness. Use these psalms as a reminder of how easy it is to drift away from God and fall into sin, and what is needed to reestablish that fellowship.

Selected psalms that emphasize these themes are Psalms 6; 14; 31; 32; 38; 41; 51; 102; 130; 143.

32:8–9 God describes some people as being like horses or mules that have to be controlled by bits and bridles. Rather than letting God guide them step-by-step, they stubbornly leave God only one option. If God wants to keep them useful for him, he must use discipline and punishment. God longs to guide us with love and wisdom rather than punishment. He offers to teach us the *best* way to go. Accept the advice written in God's Word and don't let your stubbornness keep you from obeying God.

33:2–3 David, who some believe wrote this psalm, was an accomplished harpist (1 Samuel 16:15–25). He frequently spoke about musical instruments throughout his psalms. He undoubtedly composed music for many of the psalms, and he commissioned music for temple worship (1 Chronicles 25).

33:4 All God's words are right and true—they can be trusted. The Bible is reliable because, unlike people, God does not lie, forget, change his words, or leave his promises unfulfilled. We can trust the Bible because it contains the words of a holy, trustworthy, and unchangeable God.

33:6–9 This is a poetic summary of the first chapter of Genesis. God is not just the coordinator of natural forces; he is the Lord of creation, the almighty God. Because he is all-powerful, we should revere him in all we do.

33:7 Ex 15:8; Josh 3:16; Ps 78:13

7 He gathers the waters of the sea together as a heap;
He lays up the deeps in storehouses.

33:8 Ps 67:7; Ps 96:9

8 Let all the earth fear the LORD;
Let all the inhabitants of the world stand in awe of Him.

33:9 Gen 1:3; Ps 148:5

9 For He spoke, and it was done;
He commanded, and it stood fast.

33:10 Ps 2:1-3; Is 8:10; 19:3

10 The LORD nullifies the counsel of the nations;
He frustrates the plans of the peoples.

33:11 Job 23:12; Prov 19:21; Ps 40:5; 92:5; 139:17; Is 55:8

11 The counsel of the LORD stands forever,
The plans of His heart from generation to generation.

33:12 Ps 144:15; Ex 19:5; Deut 7:6; Ps 28:9

12 Blessed is the nation whose God is the LORD,
The people whom He has chosen for His own inheritance.

33:13 Job 28:24; Ps 14:2; Ps 11:4

13 The LORD looks from heaven;
He sees all the sons of men;

33:14 1 Kin 8:39, 43; Ps 102:19

14 From His dwelling place He looks out
On all the inhabitants of the earth,

33:15 Job 10:8; Ps 119:73; 2 Chr 16:9; Job 34:21; Jer 32:19

15 He who fashions the hearts of them all,
He who understands all their works.

33:16 Ps 44:6; 60:11

16 The king is not saved by a mighty army;
A warrior is not delivered by great strength.

33:17 Ps 20:7; 147:10; Prov 21:31

17 A horse is a false hope for victory;
Nor does it deliver anyone by its great strength.

33:18 Job 36:7; Ps 32:8; 34:15; 1 Pet 3:12; Ps 32:10; 147:11

18 Behold, the eye of the LORD is on those who fear Him,
On those who hope for His lovingkindness,

33:19 Ps 56:13; Acts 12:11; Job 5:20; Ps 37:19

19 To deliver their soul from death
And to keep them alive in famine.

33:20 Ps 62:1; 130:6; Is 8:17; Ps 115:9

20 Our soul waits for the LORD;
He is our help and our shield.

33:21 Ps 13:5; 28:7; Zech 10:7; John 16:22

21 For our heart rejoices in Him,
Because we trust in His holy name.
22 Let Your lovingkindness, O LORD, be upon us,
According as we have hoped in You.

PSALM 34

A Psalm of David when he feigned madness before Abimelech,
who drove him away and he departed.

Theme: God pays attention to those who call on him. Whether God offers escape from trouble or help in times of trouble, we can be certain that he always hears and acts on behalf of those who love him.
Author: David, after pretending to be insane in order to escape from King Achish (1 Samuel 21:10-15)

34:1 Eph 5:20; 1 Thess 5:18; Ps 71:6

1 I will bless the LORD at all times;
His praise shall continually be in my mouth.

33:11 "The counsel of the LORD stands forever." Are you frustrated by inconsistencies you see in others, or even in yourself? God is completely trustworthy—his intentions never change. There is a promise that good and perfect gifts come to us from the Creator who never changes (James 1:17). When you wonder if there is anyone in whom you can trust, remember that God is completely consistent. Let him counsel you, and trust in his plans for your life.

33:16–17 *Horse* refers to military strength. Because God rules and overrules every nation, leaders should never put their trust in their physical power. Military might is not the ground of our hope. Our hope is in God and in his gracious offer to save us if we will trust in him.

33:18–19 This is not an ironclad guarantee that all believers will be delivered from death and starvation. Thousands of Christian saints have been beaten to death, whipped, fed to lions, or executed (Romans 8:35–36; Hebrews 11:32–40). God can (and often miraculously does) deliver his followers from pain and death, though sometimes, for purposes known only to him, he chooses not to. When faced with these harsh realities, we must focus on the wise judgments of God. The writer was pleading for God's watchful care and protection. In times of crisis, we can place our hope in God.

34:1ff God promises great blessings to his people, but many of these blessings require our active participation. He will deliver us from fear (34:4), save us out of our troubles (34:6), rescue us (34:7), show us goodness (34:8), supply our needs (34:9), listen when we talk to him (34:15), and redeem us (34:22), but we must do our part. We can appropriate his blessings when we seek him (34:4, 10), cry out to him (34:6, 17), trust him (34:8), fear him (34:7, 9), refrain from deceit (34:13), depart from evil, do good and seek peace (34:14), are humble (34:18), and serve him (34:22).

2 My soul will make its boast in the LORD;
The humble will hear it and rejoice.
3 O magnify the LORD with me,
And let us exalt His name together.

4 I sought the LORD, and He answered me,
And delivered me from all my fears.
5 They looked to Him and were radiant,
And their faces will never be ashamed.
6 This poor man cried, and the LORD heard him
And saved him out of all his troubles.
7 The angel of the LORD encamps around those who fear Him,
And rescues them.

8 O taste and see that the LORD is good;
How blessed is the man who takes refuge in Him!
9 O fear the LORD, you His saints;
For to those who fear Him there is no want.
10 The young lions do lack and suffer hunger;
But they who seek the LORD shall not be in want of any good thing.
11 Come, you children, listen to me;
I will teach you the fear of the LORD.
12 Who is the man who desires life
And loves *length of* days that he may see good?
13 Keep your tongue from evil
And your lips from speaking deceit.
14 Depart from evil and do good;
Seek peace and pursue it.

15 The eyes of the LORD are toward the righteous
And His ears are *open* to their cry.
16 The face of the LORD is against evildoers,
To cut off the memory of them from the earth.
17 *The righteous* cry, and the LORD hears
And delivers them out of all their troubles.

34:2 Ps 44:8; Jer 9:24; 1 Cor 1:31; Ps 69:32

34:3 Ps 35:27; 69:30; Luke 1:46; Ps 18:46

34:4 2 Chr 15:2; Ps 9:10; Matt 7:7

34:5 Ps 36:9; Is 60:5

34:7 Ps 91:11; Dan 6:22

34:8 Ps 119:103; Heb 6:5; 1 Pet 2:3; Ps 2:12

34:9 Ps 31:23; Ps 23:1

34:10 Ps 84:11

34:11 Ps 66:16; Ps 32:8; Ps 111:10

34:12 1 Pet 3:10-12

34:13 Ps 141:3; Prov 13:3; James 1:26; 1 Pet 2:22

34:14 Ps 37:27; Is 1:16, 17; Rom 14:19; Heb 12:14

34:15 Job 36:7; Ps 33:18

34:17 Ps 34:6; 145:19

34:8 "Taste and see" does not mean, "Check out God's credentials." Instead it is a warm invitation: "Try this; I know you'll like it." When we take that first step of obedience in following God, we cannot help discovering that he is good and kind. When we begin the Christian life, our knowledge of God is partial and incomplete. As we trust him daily, we experience how good he is.

34:9 You say you belong to the Lord, but do you fear him? To fear the Lord means to show deep respect and honor to him. We demonstrate true reverence by our humble attitude and genuine worship. Reverence was shown by Abraham (Genesis 17:2–4), Moses (Exodus 3:5–6), and the Israelites (Exodus 19:16–24). Their reactions to God's presence varied, but all deeply respected him.

34:9, 10 At first we may question David's statement, because we seem to lack many good things. This is not a blanket promise that all Christians will have everything they want. Instead, this is David's praise for God's goodness—all those who call upon God in their need will be answered, sometimes in unexpected ways.

Remember, God knows what we need, and our deepest needs are spiritual. Many Christians, even though they face unbearable poverty and hardship, still have enough spiritual nourishment to live for God. David was saying that to have God is to have all you really need. God is enough.

If you feel you don't have everything you need, ask: (1) Is this really a need? (2) Is this really good for me? (3) Is this the best time for me to have what I desire? Even if you answer yes to all three questions, God may allow you to go without to help you grow more dependent on him. He may want you to learn that you need *him* more than you need to achieve your immediate desires.

34:11–14 The Bible often connects the fear of the Lord (love and reverence for him) with obedience. "Fear God and keep His commandments" (Ecclesiastes 12:13); "If anyone loves Me, he will keep My word" (John 14:23). David said that a person who fears the Lord doesn't lie, turns from evil, does good, and promotes peace. Reverence is much more than sitting quietly in church. It includes obeying God in the way we speak and the way we treat others.

34:14 Somehow we think that peace should come to us with no effort. But David explained that we are to seek and pursue peace. Paul echoed this thought in Romans 12:18. A person who wants peace cannot be argumentative and contentious. Because peaceful relationships come from our efforts at peacemaking, work hard at living in peace with others each day.

34:18 Ps 145:18; Ps 147:3; Is 61:1; Ps 51:17; Is 57:15
34:19 Prov 24:16; Ps 71:20; 2 Tim 3:11f; Ps 34:4, 6, 17
34:20 John 19:33, 36
34:21 Ps 94:23; 140:11; Prov 24:16
34:22 1 Kin 1:29; Ps 71:23; Ps 37:40

18 The LORD is near to the brokenhearted
And saves those who are [61]crushed in spirit.

19 Many are the afflictions of the righteous,
But the LORD delivers him out of them all.
20 He keeps all his bones,
Not one of them is broken.
21 Evil shall slay the wicked,
And those who hate the righteous will be condemned.
22 The LORD redeems the soul of His servants,
And none of those who take refuge in Him will be condemned.

PSALM 35

A Psalm of David.

Theme: A prayer to God for help against those who try to inflict injury for no reason. When our enemies are unjust and lie about us, even when we do good to them, we can appeal to God who is always just.
Author: David, possibly written when he was being hunted by Saul (1 Samuel 24)

35:1 Ps 18:43; Is 49:25; Ps 56:2
35:2 Ps 91:4; Ps 44:26
35:3 Ps 62:2
35:4 Ps 70:2; Ps 40:14; 129:5
35:5 Job 21:18; Ps 83:13; Is 29:5
35:6 Ps 73:18; Jer 23:12
35:7 Ps 69:4; 109:3; 140:5; Ps 9:15
35:8 Ps 55:23; Is 47:11; 1 Thess 5:3; Ps 9:15; Ps 73:18
35:9 Is 61:10; Ps 9:14; 13:5; Luke 1:47
35:10 Ps 51:8; Ex 15:11; Ps 86:8; Mic 7:18; Ps 18:17; Ps 37:14; 109:16
35:11 Ps 27:12

1 Contend, O LORD, with those who contend with me;
Fight against those who fight against me.
2 Take hold of [62]buckler and shield
And rise up for my help.
3 Draw also the spear and the battle-axe to meet those who pursue me;
Say to my soul, "I am your salvation."
4 Let those be ashamed and dishonored who seek my life;
Let those be turned back and humiliated who devise evil against me.
5 Let them be like chaff before the wind,
With the angel of the LORD driving *them* on.
6 Let their way be dark and slippery,
With the angel of the LORD pursuing them.
7 For without cause they hid their net for me;
Without cause they dug a pit for my soul.
8 Let destruction come upon him unawares,
And let the net which he hid catch himself;
Into that very destruction let him fall.

9 And my soul shall rejoice in the LORD;
It shall exult in His salvation.
10 All my bones will say, "LORD, who is like You,
Who delivers the afflicted from him who is too strong for him,
And the afflicted and the needy from him who robs him?"
11 Malicious witnesses rise up;

61 Or *contrite* **62** I.e. small shield

34:18–19 We often wish we could escape troubles—the pain of grief, loss, sorrow, and failure; or even the small daily frustrations that constantly wear us down. God promises to be "near to the brokenhearted," to be our source of power, courage, and wisdom, helping us through our problems. Sometimes he chooses to deliver us from those problems. When trouble strikes, don't get frustrated with God. Instead, admit that you need God's help and thank him for being by your side.

34:20 This is a prophecy about Christ when he was crucified. Although it was the Roman custom to break the legs of the victim to speed death, not one of Jesus' bones was broken (John 19:32–37). In addition to the prophetic meaning, David was pleading for God's protection in times of crisis.

35:1ff This is one of the "imprecatory" (cursing) psalms that call upon God to deal with enemies. These psalms sound extremely harsh, but we must remember: (1) David could not understand why he was forced to flee from men who were unjustly seeking to kill him. He was God's anointed king over a nation called to annihilate the evil people of the land. (2) David's call for justice was sincere; it was not a cover for his own personal vengeance. He truly wanted to seek God's perfect ideal for his nation. (3) David did not say that *he* would take revenge, but he gave the matter to God. These are merely his suggestions. (4) These psalms use hyperbole (or overstatement). They were meant to motivate others to take a strong stand against sin and evil.

Cruelty may be far removed from some people's experience, but it is a daily reality to others. God promises to help the persecuted and to bring judgment on unrepentant sinners. When we pray for justice to be done, we are praying as David did. When Christ returns, the wicked will be punished.

They ask me of things that I do not know.
12 They repay me evil for good,
To the bereavement of my soul.
13 But as for me, when they were sick, my clothing was sackcloth;
I humbled my soul with fasting,
And my prayer kept returning to my bosom.
14 I went about as though it were my friend or brother;
I bowed down mourning, as one who sorrows for a mother.
15 But at my [63]stumbling they rejoiced and gathered themselves together;
The smiters whom I did not know gathered together against me,
They slandered me without ceasing.
16 Like godless jesters at a feast,
They gnashed at me with their teeth.

17 Lord, how long will You look on?
Rescue my soul from their ravages,
My only *life* from the lions.
18 I will give You thanks in the great congregation;
I will praise You among a mighty throng.
19 Do not let those who are wrongfully my enemies rejoice over me;
Nor let those who hate me without cause wink maliciously.
20 For they do not speak peace,
But they devise deceitful words against those who are quiet in the land.
21 They opened their mouth wide against me;
They said, "Aha, aha, our eyes have seen it!"

22 You have seen it, O LORD, do not keep silent;
O Lord, do not be far from me.
23 Stir up Yourself, and awake to my right
And to my cause, my God and my Lord.
24 Judge me, O LORD my God, according to Your righteousness,
And do not let them rejoice over me.
25 Do not let them say in their heart, "Aha, our desire!"
Do not let them say, "We have swallowed him up!"
26 Let those be ashamed and humiliated altogether who rejoice at my distress;
Let those be clothed with shame and dishonor who magnify themselves over me.

27 Let them shout for joy and rejoice, who favor my vindication;
And let them say continually, "The LORD be magnified,
Who delights in the prosperity of His servant."
28 And my tongue shall declare Your righteousness
And Your praise all day long.

35:12 Ps 38:20; 109:5; Jer 18:20; John 10:32
35:13 Job 30:25; Ps 69:11; Ps 69:10; Matt 10:13; Luke 10:6
35:14 Ps 38:6
35:15 Obad 12; Job 30:1, 8, 12; Ps 7:2
35:16 Job 16:9; Ps 37:12; Lam 2:16
35:17 Ps 13:1; Hab 1:13; Ps 35:7; Ps 22:20, 21
35:18 Ps 22:22; Ps 22:25
35:19 Ps 13:4; 30:1; 38:16; Ps 38:19; 69:4; John 15:25; Prov 6:13; 10:10
35:20 Ps 55:21; Jer 9:8; Mic 6:12
35:21 Job 16:10; Ps 22:13; Ps 40:15; 70:3
35:22 Ex 3:7; Ps 10:14; Ps 28:1; Ps 10:1; 22:11; 38:21; 71:12
35:23 Ps 7:6; 44:23; 59:4; 80:2
35:24 Ps 9:4; 26:1; 43:1; Ps 35:19
35:25 Ps 35:21; Ps 56:1; 124:3; Prov 1:12; Lam 2:16
35:26 Ps 40:14; Ps 109:29; Job 19:5; Ps 38:16
35:27 Ps 32:11; Ps 9:4; Ps 40:16; 70:4; Ps 147:11; 149:4
35:28 Ps 51:14; 71:15, 24

PSALM 36

For the choir director. *A Psalm* of David the servant of the LORD.

Theme: God's faithfulness, justice, and love are contrasted with the sinful hearts of men and women. In spite of our fallen condition, God pours out his love on those who know him.
Author: David

1 Transgression speaks to the ungodly within his heart;
There is no fear of God before his eyes.

36:1 Rom 3:18

63 Or *limping*

35:13 David was sad when his prayers seemed unanswered. When our deliverance is delayed, it is easy to assume that God hasn't answered our prayers. God hears every prayer, but he answers according to his wisdom. Don't let the absence of an immediate answer cause you to doubt or resent God. Instead let it be an occasion to deepen your faith.

35:21–23 David cried out to God to defend him when people wrongly accused him. If you are unjustly accused, your natural reaction may be to lash out in revenge or to give a detailed defense of your every move. Instead, ask God to fight the battle for you. He will clear your name in the eyes of those who really matter.

36:1 Because the wicked have no fear of God, nothing restrains them from sinning. They plunge ahead as if nothing will happen to

36:2 Deut 29:19; Ps 10:11; 49:18

36:3 Ps 10:7; 12:2; Ps 94:8; Jer 4:22

36:4 Prov 4:16; Mic 2:1; Is 65:2; Ps 52:3; Rom 12:9

36:5 Ps 57:10; 103:11; 108:4

36:6 Ps 71:19; Job 11:8; Ps 77:19; Rom 11:33; Neh 9:6; Ps 104:14, 15; 145:16

36:7 Ps 40:5; 139:17; Ruth 2:12; Ps 17:8; 57:1; 91:4

36:8 Ps 63:5; 65:4; Is 25:6; Jer 31:12-14; Job 20:17; Ps 46:4; Rev 22:1

36:9 Jer 2:13

36:10 Jer 22:16; Ps 24:5

36:12 Ps 140:10; Is 26:14

2 For it flatters him in his *own* eyes
Concerning the discovery of his iniquity *and* the hatred *of it.*
3 The words of his mouth are wickedness and deceit;
He has ceased to be wise *and* to do good.
4 He plans wickedness upon his bed;
He sets himself on a path that is not good;
He does not despise evil.

5 Your lovingkindness, O LORD, extends to the heavens,
Your faithfulness *reaches* to the skies.
6 Your righteousness is like the mountains of God;
Your judgments are *like* a great deep.
O LORD, You preserve man and beast.
7 How precious is Your lovingkindness, O God!
And the children of men take refuge in the shadow of Your wings.
8 They drink their fill of the abundance of Your house;
And You give them to drink of the river of Your delights.
9 For with You is the fountain of life;
In Your light we see light.

10 O continue Your lovingkindness to those who know You,
And Your righteousness to the upright in heart.
11 Let not the foot of pride come upon me,
And let not the hand of the wicked drive me away.
12 There the doers of iniquity have fallen;
They have been thrust down and cannot rise.

PSALM 37

A Psalm of David.

37:1 Prov 23:17; 24:19; Ps 73:3; Prov 3:31

37:2 Job 14:2; Ps 90:6; 92:7; James 1:11; Ps 129:6

37:3 Ps 62:8; Deut 30:20; Is 40:11; Ezek 34:13, 14

37:4 Job 22:26; Ps 94:19; Is 58:14; Ps 21:2; 145:19; Matt 7:7, 8

Theme: Trust in the Lord and wait patiently for him to act. This psalm vividly contrasts the wicked person with the righteous.
Author: David

1 Do not fret because of evildoers,
Be not envious toward wrongdoers.
2 For they will wither quickly like the grass
And fade like the green herb.
3 Trust in the LORD and do good;
Dwell in the land and [64]cultivate faithfulness.
4 Delight yourself in the LORD;
And He will give you the desires of your heart.

64 Or *feed securely* or *feed on His faithfulness*

them. But God is just and is only delaying their punishment. This knowledge should hold us back from sinning. Let the fear of God do its work in you to keep you from sin. In your gratitude for God's love, don't ignore his justice.

36:5–8 In contrast to evil people and their wicked plots that end in failure, God is faithful, righteous, and just. His love reaches to the heavens; his faithfulness reaches to the skies; his righteousness is as solid as mighty mountains; and his judgments are as full of wisdom as the oceans with water (the "great deep"). We need not fear evil people because we know God loves us, judges evil, and will care for us throughout eternity.

36:9 This vivid image—"fountain of life"—gives us a sense of fresh, cleansing water that gives life to the spiritually thirsty. This same picture is used in Jeremiah 2:13, where God is called the "fountain of living waters." Jesus spoke of himself as living water that could quench thirst forever and give eternal life (John 4:14).

37:1 We should never envy evil people, even though some may be extremely popular or excessively rich. No matter how much they have, it will fade and vanish like grass that withers and dies. Those who follow God live differently from the wicked and, in the end, will have far greater treasures in heaven. What the unbeliever gets may last a lifetime, if he is lucky. What you get from following God lasts forever.

37:4–5 David calls us to take delight in the Lord and to commit everything we have and do (our "way") to him. But how do we do this? To *delight* in someone means to experience great pleasure and joy in his or her presence. This happens only when we know that person well. Thus, to delight in the Lord, we must know him better. Knowledge of God's great love for us will indeed give us delight.

To *commit* ourselves to the Lord means entrusting everything—our lives, families, jobs, possessions—to his control and guidance. To commit ourselves to the Lord means to trust in him (37:5), believing that he can care for us better than we can ourselves. We should be willing to wait patiently (37:7) for him to work out what is best for us.

5 Commit your way to the LORD,
Trust also in Him, and He will do it.
6 He will bring forth your righteousness as the light
And your judgment as the noonday.

7 [65]Rest in the LORD and wait [66]patiently for Him;
Do not fret because of him who prospers in his way,
Because of the man who carries out wicked schemes.
8 Cease from anger and forsake wrath;
Do not fret; *it leads* only to evildoing.
9 For evildoers will be cut off,
But those who wait for the LORD, they will inherit the land.
10 Yet a little while and the wicked man will be no more;
And you will look carefully for his place and he will not be *there.*
11 But the humble will inherit the land
And will delight themselves in abundant prosperity.

12 The wicked plots against the righteous
And gnashes at him with his teeth.
13 The Lord laughs at him,
For He sees his day is coming.
14 The wicked have drawn the sword and bent their bow
To cast down the afflicted and the needy,
To slay those who are upright in conduct.
15 Their sword will enter their own heart,
And their bows will be broken.

16 Better is the little of the righteous
Than the abundance of many wicked.
17 For the arms of the wicked will be broken,
But the LORD sustains the righteous.
18 The LORD knows the days of the blameless,
And their inheritance will be forever.
19 They will not be ashamed in the time of evil,
And in the days of famine they will have abundance.
20 But the wicked will perish;
And the enemies of the LORD will be like the [67]glory of the pastures,
They vanish—like smoke they vanish away.
21 The wicked borrows and does not pay back,
But the righteous is gracious and gives.
22 For those blessed by Him will inherit the land,
But those cursed by Him will be cut off.

23 The steps of a man are established by the LORD,
And He delights in his way.
24 When he falls, he will not be hurled headlong,
Because the LORD is the One who holds his hand.

65 Or *Be still* **66** Or *longingly* **67** I.e. flowers

37:5 Ps 55:22; Prov 16:3; 1 Pet 5:7

37:6 Ps 97:11; Is 58:8, 10; Mic 7:9; Job 11:17

37:7 Ps 40:1; 62:5; Lam 3:26; Ps 37:1, 8; Jer 12:1

37:8 Eph 4:31; Col 3:8

37:9 Ps 25:13; Prov 2:21; Is 57:13; 60:21; Matt 5:5

37:10 Job 24:24; Job 7:10; Ps 37:35, 36

37:11 Matt 5:5; Ps 72:7

37:12 Ps 31:13, 20; Ps 35:16

37:13 Ps 2:4; 1 Sam 26:10; Job 18:20

37:14 Ps 11:2; Lam 2:4; Ps 35:10; 86:1; Ps 11:2

37:15 1 Sam 2:4; Ps 46:9

37:16 Prov 15:16; 16:8

37:17 Job 38:15; Ps 10:15; Ezek 30:21; Ps 71:6; 145:14

37:18 Ps 1:6; 31:7

37:19 Job 5:20; Ps 33:19

37:20 Ps 73:27; Ps 68:2; 102:3

37:21 Ps 112:5, 9

37:22 Prov 3:33; Job 5:3

37:23 1 Sam 2:9; Ps 40:2; 66:9; 119:5; Ps 147:11

37:24 Ps 145:14; Prov 24:16; Ps 147:6

37:8–9 Anger and worry (fretting) are two very destructive emotions. They reveal a lack of faith that God loves us and is in control. We should not worry; instead, we should trust in God, giving ourselves to him for his use and safekeeping. When you dwell on your problems, you will become anxious and angry. But if you concentrate on God and his goodness, you will find peace. Where do you focus your attention?

37:11 Humbleness hardly seems the proper weapon to deal with enemies. God's warfare must be carried out with calm faith, humility before God, and hope in his deliverance. Jesus also promises a sure reward for those with humble attitudes (Matthew 5:5).

37:21 You can tell a lot about a person's character by the way he or she handles money. The wicked person steals under the guise of borrowing. The righteous person gives generously to the needy. The wicked person, therefore, focuses on himself, while the righteous person looks to the welfare of others.

37:23–24 The person in whom God delights is one who follows God, trusts him, and tries to do his will. God watches over and makes firm every step that person takes. If you would like to have God direct your way, then seek his advice before you step out.

25 I have been young and now I am old,
Yet I have not seen the righteous forsaken
Or his descendants begging bread.
26 All day long he is gracious and lends,
And his descendants are a blessing.

27 Depart from evil and do good,
So you will abide forever.
28 For the LORD loves justice
And does not forsake His godly ones;
They are preserved forever,
But the descendants of the wicked will be cut off.
29 The righteous will inherit the land
And dwell in it forever.
30 The mouth of the righteous utters wisdom,
And his tongue speaks justice.
31 The law of his God is in his heart;
His steps do not slip.
32 The wicked spies upon the righteous
And seeks to kill him.
33 The LORD will not leave him in his hand
Or let him be condemned when he is judged.
34 Wait for the LORD and keep His way,
And He will exalt you to inherit the land;
When the wicked are cut off, you will see it.

35 I have seen a wicked, violent man
Spreading himself like a luxuriant tree in its native soil.
36 Then he passed away, and lo, he was no more;
I sought for him, but he could not be found.
37 Mark the blameless man, and behold the upright;
For the man of peace will have a posterity.
38 But transgressors will be altogether destroyed;
The posterity of the wicked will be cut off.
39 But the salvation of the righteous is from the LORD;
He is their strength in time of trouble.
40 The LORD helps them and delivers them;
He delivers them from the wicked and saves them,
Because they take refuge in Him.

37:25 Ps 37:28; Is 41:17; Heb 13:5; Ps 109:10

37:26 Deut 15:8; Ps 37:21; Ps 147:13

37:27 Ps 34:14; Ps 37:18; 102:28

37:28 Ps 11:7; 33:5; Ps 37:25; Ps 31:23; Ps 21:10; 37:9; Prov 2:22; Is 14:20

37:29 Ps 37:9; Prov 2:21; Ps 37:18

37:30 Ps 49:3; Prov 10:13; Ps 101:1; 119:13

37:31 Deut 6:6; Ps 40:8; 119:11; Is 51:7; Jer 31:33; Ps 26:1; 37:23

37:33 Ps 31:8; 2 Pet 2:9; Ps 34:22; 109:31

37:34 Ps 27:14; 37:9; Ps 52:5, 6; 91:8

37:35 Job 5:3; Jer 12:2

37:36 Job 20:5; Ps 37:10

37:37 Ps 37:18; Ps 7:10; Is 57:1, 2

37:38 Ps 1:4-6; 73:17

37:39 Ps 3:8; 62:1; Ps 9:9; 37:19

37:40 Ps 54:4; Ps 22:4; Is 31:5; Dan 3:17; 6:23; 1 Chr 5:20; Ps 34:22

37:25 Because some people have to beg for bread today, as they did in David's time, what did David mean by these words? David is observing God's provision over a lifetime. Though there are unfortunate exceptions to this general principle, God provides for his own people. The children of the righteous need not go hungry because other believers can help out in their time of need. In David's day, Israel obeyed God's laws that ensured that the poor were treated fairly and mercifully. As long as Israel was obedient, there was enough food for everyone. When Israel forgot God, the rich took care only of themselves, and the poor suffered (Amos 2:6, 7).

When we see a Christian brother or sister suffering today, we can respond in one of three ways. (1) We can say, as Job's friends did, that the afflicted person brought this on himself. (2) We can say that this is a test to help the poor develop more patience and trust in God. (3) We can help the person in need. David would approve of only the last option. Although many governments today have their own programs for helping those in need, this is no excuse for ignoring the poor and needy within our reach.

37:34 It is difficult to wait patiently for God to act when we want change right away. But God promises that if we submit to his timing, he will honor us. Peter said, "Humble yourselves under the mighty hand of God, that He may exalt you at the proper time" (1 Peter 5:6). Be patient, steadily doing the work God has given you to do, and allow God to choose the best time to change your circumstances.

PSALM 38

A Psalm of David, for a memorial.

Theme: Sorrow for sin brings hope. God alone is the true source of healing and protection for those who confess their sins to him.
Author: David

1 O LORD, rebuke me not in Your wrath,
And chasten me not in Your burning anger.
2 For Your arrows have sunk deep into me,
And Your hand has pressed down on me.
3 There is no soundness in my flesh because of Your indignation;
There is no health in my bones because of my sin.
4 For my iniquities are gone over my head;
As a heavy burden they weigh too much for me.
5 My wounds grow foul *and* fester
Because of my folly.
6 I am bent over and greatly bowed down;
I go mourning all day long.
7 For my loins are filled with burning,
And there is no soundness in my flesh.
8 I am benumbed and badly crushed;
I groan because of the agitation of my heart.

9 Lord, all my desire is before You;
And my sighing is not hidden from You.
10 My heart throbs, my strength fails me;
And the light of my eyes, even that has gone from me.
11 My loved ones and my friends stand aloof from my plague;
And my kinsmen stand afar off.
12 Those who seek my life lay snares *for me;*
And those who seek to injure me have threatened destruction,
And they devise treachery all day long.

13 But I, like a deaf man, do not hear;
And *I am* like a mute man who does not open his mouth.
14 Yes, I am like a man who does not hear,
And in whose mouth are no arguments.
15 For I hope in You, O LORD;
You will answer, O Lord my God.
16 For I said, "May they not rejoice over me,
Who, when my foot slips, would magnify themselves against me."
17 For I am ready to fall,
And my [68]sorrow is continually before me.
18 For I confess my iniquity;
I am full of anxiety because of my sin.

38:1 Ps 6:1
38:2 Job 6:4; Ps 32:4
38:3 Is 1:6; Ps 102:10; Job 33:19; Ps 6:2; 31:10
38:4 Ezra 9:6; Ps 40:12
38:5 Ps 69:5
38:6 Ps 35:14; Job 30:28; Ps 42:9; 43:2
38:7 Ps 102:3; Ps 38:3
38:8 Lam 1:13, 20f; 2:11; 5:17; Job 3:24; Ps 22:1; 32:3
38:9 Ps 10:17; Ps 6:6; 102:5
38:10 Ps 31:10; Ps 6:7; 69:3; 88:9
38:11 Ps 31:11; 88:18; Luke 23:49
38:12 Ps 54:3; Ps 140:5; Ps 35:4; Ps 35:20
38:13 Ps 39:2, 9
38:15 Ps 39:7; Ps 17:6
38:16 Ps 35:26
38:17 Ps 35:15; Ps 13:2
38:18 Ps 32:5; 2 Cor 7:9, 10

68 Lit *pain*

38:1 As a child might cry to his father, so David cried to God. David was not saying, "Don't punish me," but, "Don't punish me while you are angry." He acknowledged that he deserved to be punished, but he asked that God temper his discipline with mercy. Like children, we are free to ask for mercy, but we should not deny that we deserve punishment.

38:1ff This is called a penitential psalm because David expressed sorrow for his sin (38:18). He stated that his sin led to health problems (38:1–8) and separated him from God and others, causing extreme loneliness (38:9–14). He then confessed his sin and repented (38:15–22).

38:2–4 David saw his anguish as judgment from God for his sins. Although God does not always send physical illness to punish us for sin, this verse and others in Scripture (Acts 12:21–23; 1 Corinthians 11:30–32) indicate that he does in certain circumstances. Our sin can have physical or mental side effects that can cause great suffering. Sometimes God has to punish his children in order to bring them back to himself (Hebrews 12:5–11). When we repent of our sin, God promises to forgive us. He delivers us from sin's eternal consequences although he does not promise to undo all of sin's earthly consequences.

38:13–14 It is extremely difficult to be silent when others tear us down because we want to protect our reputation. We find it difficult to do nothing while they assault something so precious to us. But we don't need to lash back in revenge or justify our position; we can trust God to protect our reputation. Jesus was silent before his accusers (Luke 23:9–10); he left his case in God's hands (1 Peter 2:21–24). That is a good place to leave our case too!

38:19 Ps 18:17; Ps 35:19

38:20 Ps 35:12; Ps 109:5; 1 John 3:12

38:21 Ps 22:19; 35:22

38:22 Ps 40:13, 17; Ps 27:1

19 But my enemies are vigorous *and* [69]strong,
And many are those who hate me wrongfully.
20 And those who repay evil for good,
They oppose me, because I follow what is good.
21 Do not forsake me, O LORD;
O my God, do not be far from me!
22 Make haste to help me,
O Lord, my salvation!

PSALM 39

For the choir director, for Jeduthun. A Psalm of David.

Theme: Apart from God, life is fleeting and empty.
This is an appeal for God's mercy because life is so brief.
Author: David

39:1 1 Kin 2:4; 2 Kin 10:31; Ps 119:9; Job 2:10; Ps 34:13; James 3:5-12; Ps 141:3; James 3:2

39:2 Ps 38:13

39:3 Ps 32:4; Jer 20:9; Luke 24:32

39:4 Job 6:11; Ps 90:12; 119:84; Ps 78:39; 103:14

39:5 Ps 89:47; Ps 144:4; Job 14:2; Ps 62:9; Eccl 6:12

39:6 1 Cor 7:31; James 1:10, 11; 1 Pet 1:24; Ps 127:2; Eccl 5:17; Ps 49:10; Eccl 2:26; 5:14; Luke 12:20

39:7 Ps 38:15

39:8 Ps 51:9, 14; 79:9; Ps 44:13; 79:4; 119:22

39:9 Ps 39:2; 2 Sam 16:10; Job 2:10

39:10 Job 9:34; 13:21; Ps 32:4

1 I said, "I will guard my ways
That I may not sin with my tongue;
I will guard my mouth as with a muzzle
While the wicked are in my presence."
2 I was mute and silent,
I [70]refrained *even* from good,
And my [71]sorrow grew worse.
3 My heart was hot within me,
While I was musing the fire burned;
Then I spoke with my tongue:
4 "LORD, make me to know my end
And what is the extent of my days;
Let me know how transient I am.
5 "Behold, You have made my days *as* handbreadths,
And my lifetime as nothing in Your sight;
Surely every man at his best is a mere breath. Selah.
6 "Surely every man walks about as [72]a phantom;
Surely they make an uproar for nothing;
He amasses *riches* and does not know who will gather them.

7 "And now, Lord, for what do I wait?
My hope is in You.
8 "Deliver me from all my transgressions;
Make me not the reproach of the foolish.
9 "I have become mute, I do not open my mouth,
Because it is You who have done *it.*
10 "Remove Your plague from me;

69 Or *numerous* **70** Lit *kept silence* **71** Lit *pain* **72** Lit *an image*

39:1–3 David resolved to keep his tongue from sin; that is, he decided not to complain to other people about God's treatment of him. David certainly had reason to complain. David was the anointed king of Israel, but he had to wait many years before taking the throne. Then one of his sons tried to kill him and become king instead. But when David could not keep still any longer, he took his complaints directly to God. We all have complaints about our job, money, or situations, but complaining to others may make them think that God cannot take care of us. It may also look as if we blame God for our troubles. Instead, like David, we should take our complaints directly to God.

39:4 Life is short no matter how long we live. If there is something important we want to do, we must not put it off for a better day. Ask yourself, "If I had only six months to live, what would I do?" Tell someone that you love him or her? Deal with an undisciplined area in your life? Tell someone about Jesus? Because life is short, don't neglect what is truly important.

39:5–6 The brevity of life is a theme throughout the books of Psalms, Proverbs, and Ecclesiastes. Jesus also spoke about it (Luke 12:20). It is ironic that people spend so much time securing their lives on earth and spend little or no thought about where they will spend eternity. David realized that amassing riches and busily accomplishing worldly tasks would make no difference in eternity. Few people understand that their only hope is in the Lord. (For other verses on the brevity of life, see Ecclesiastes 2:18 and James 4:14.)

39:10 What did David mean when he asked God to remove the "plague" because he was overcome by the "opposition" of God's hand? It may be a picture of the difficulties David was facing that caused him to feel as if he were being struck. Just as a loving father carefully disciplines his children, so God corrects us (Hebrews 12:5–9).

Because of the opposition of Your hand I am perishing.
11 "With reproofs You chasten a man for iniquity;
You consume as a moth what is precious to him;
Surely every man is a mere breath. Selah.

39:11 Ezek 5:15; 2 Pet 2:16; Job 13:28; Ps 90:7; Is 50:9; Ps 39:5

12 "Hear my prayer, O LORD, and give ear to my cry;
Do not be silent at my tears;
For I am a stranger with You,
A sojourner like all my fathers.
13 "Turn Your gaze away from me, that I may [73]smile *again*
Before I depart and am no more."

39:12 Ps 102:1; 143:1; 2 Kin 20:5; Ps 56:8; Lev 25:23; 1 Chr 29:15; Ps 119:19; Heb 11:13; 1 Pet 2:11; Gen 47:9

39:13 Job 7:19; 10:20, 21; 14:6; Ps 102:24

PSALM 40

For the choir director. A Psalm of David.

Theme: Doing God's will sometimes means waiting patiently. While we wait, we can love God, serve others, and tell others about him.
Author: David

1 I waited [74]patiently for the LORD;
And He inclined to me and heard my cry.
2 He brought me up out of the pit of destruction, out of the miry clay,
And He set my feet upon a rock making my footsteps firm.
3 He put a new song in my mouth, a song of praise to our God;
Many will see and fear
And will trust in the LORD.

40:1 Ps 25:5; 27:14; 37:7; Ps 34:15

40:2 Ps 69:2, 14; Jer 38:6; Ps 27:5; Ps 37:23

40:3 Ps 32:7; 33:3; Ps 52:6; 64:9

4 How blessed is the man who has made the LORD his trust,
And has not turned to the proud, nor to those who lapse into falsehood.
5 Many, O LORD my God, are the wonders which You have done,
And Your thoughts toward us;
There is none to compare with You.
If I would declare and speak of them,
They would be too numerous to count.

40:4 Ps 34:8; 84:12; Job 37:24; Ps 125:5

40:5 Job 5:9; Ps 136:4; Ps 139:17; Is 55:8; Ps 71:15; 139:18

6 Sacrifice and meal offering You have not desired;
My ears You have [75]opened;
Burnt offering and sin offering You have not required.
7 Then I said, "Behold, I come;
In the scroll of the book it is written of me.
8 I delight to do Your will, O my God;
Your Law is within my heart."

40:6 1 Sam 15:22; Ps 51:16; Is 1:11; Jer 6:20; 7:22, 23; Amos 5:22; Mic 6:6-8; Heb 10:5-7

40:8 John 4:34; Ps 37:31; Jer 31:33; 2 Cor 3:3

9 I have proclaimed glad tidings of righteousness in the great congregation;
Behold, I will not restrain my lips,
O LORD, You know.

40:9 Ps 22:22, 25; Ps 119:13; Josh 22:22; Ps 139:4

73 Or *become cheerful* **74** Or *intently* **75** Lit *dug;* or possibly *pierced*

40:1–4 Waiting for God to help us is not easy, but David received four benefits from waiting: God (1) lifted him out of his despair, (2) set his feet on a rock, (3) gave him a firm place to stand, and (4) put a new song of praise in his mouth. Often blessings cannot be received unless we go through the trial of waiting.

40:6 "Sacrifice and meal offering You have not desired." The religious ritual of David's day involved sacrificing animals in the tabernacle. David says these acts were meaningless unless done for the right reasons. Today we often make rituals of going to church, taking communion, or paying tithes. These activities are also empty if our reasons for doing them are selfish. God doesn't want these sacrifices and offerings without an attitude of devotion to him. The prophet Samuel told Saul, "To obey is better than sacrifice" (1 Samuel 15:22). Make sure that you give God the obedience and lifelong service he desires from you.

40:7–8 "I delight to do Your will, O my God." Jesus portrayed this attitude of obeying and serving God (John 4:34; 5:30). He came as the prophets foretold, proclaiming the Good News of God's righteousness and forgiveness of sins. In Hebrews 10:5–10, verses 6–8 are applied to Jesus.

40:9–10 David said he would speak of God's faithfulness and salvation to those around him. When we feel the impact of God's righteousness on our lives, we cannot keep it hidden. We want to tell other people what God has done for us. If God's faithfulness has changed your life, don't be timid. It is natural to share a good bargain with others or recommend a skillful doctor, so it should also feel natural to share what God has done for us.

40:10 Acts 20:20, 27; Ps 89:1

10 I have not hidden Your righteousness within my heart;
I have spoken of Your faithfulness and Your salvation;
I have not concealed Your lovingkindness and Your truth from the great congregation.

40:11 Ps 43:3; 57:3; 61:7; Prov 20:28

40:12 Ps 18:5; 116:3; Ps 38:4; 65:3; Ps 69:4; Ps 73:26

11 You, O LORD, will not withhold Your compassion from me;
Your lovingkindness and Your truth will continually preserve me.
12 For evils beyond number have surrounded me;
My iniquities have overtaken me, so that I am not able to see;
They are more numerous than the hairs of my head,
And my heart has failed me.

40:13 Ps 70:1; Ps 22:19; 71:12

40:14 Ps 35:4, 26; 70:2; 71:13; Ps 63:9

40:15 Ps 70:3; Ps 35:21; 70:3

40:16 Ps 70:4; Ps 35:27

40:17 Ps 70:5; 86:1; 109:22; Ps 40:5; 1 Pet 5:7

13 Be pleased, O LORD, to deliver me;
Make haste, O LORD, to help me.
14 Let those be ashamed and humiliated together
Who seek my [76]life to destroy it;
Let those be turned back and dishonored
Who delight [77]in my hurt.
15 Let those be appalled because of their shame
Who say to me, "Aha, aha!"
16 Let all who seek You rejoice and be glad in You;
Let those who love Your salvation say continually,
"The LORD be magnified!"
17 Since I am afflicted and needy,
Let the Lord be mindful of me.
You are my help and my deliverer;
Do not delay, O my God.

PSALM 41

For the choir director. A Psalm of David.

Theme: A prayer for God's mercy when feeling sick or abandoned. When we're sick or when everyone deserts us, God remains at our side.
Author: David

41:1 Ps 82:3, 4; Prov 14:21; Ps 27:5; 37:19

41:2 Ps 37:28; Ps 37:22; Ps 27:12

1 How blessed is he who considers the helpless;
The LORD will deliver him in a day of trouble.
2 The LORD will protect him and keep him alive,
And he shall be called blessed upon the earth;
And do not give him over to the desire of his enemies.
3 The LORD will sustain him upon his sickbed;
In his illness, You [78]restore him to health.

41:4 Ps 6:2; 103:3; 147:3; Ps 51:4

41:5 Ps 38:12

41:6 Ps 12:2; 62:4; Prov 26:24-26

41:7 Ps 56:5

4 As for me, I said, "O LORD, be gracious to me;
Heal my soul, for I have sinned against You."
5 My enemies speak evil against me,
"When will he die, and his name perish?"
6 And when he comes to see *me,* he speaks falsehood;
His heart gathers wickedness to itself;
When he goes outside, he tells it.
7 All who hate me whisper together against me;
Against me they devise my hurt, *saying,*

76 Or *soul* **77** Or *to injure me* **78** Lit *turn all his bed*

40:10 When we think of faithfulness, a friend or a spouse may come to mind. People who are faithful to us accept and love us, even when we are unlovable. Faithful people keep their promises, whether promises of support or promises made in our marriage vows. God's faithfulness is like human faithfulness, only perfect. His love is absolute, and his promises are irrevocable. He loves us in spite of our constant bent toward sin, and he keeps all the promises he has made to us, even when we break our promises to him.

41:1 The Bible often speaks of God's care for the weak, poor, and needy, and of his blessing on those who share this concern. God wants our generosity to reflect his own free giving. As he has blessed us, we should bless others.

8 "A wicked thing is poured out upon him,
That when he lies down, he will not rise up again."
9 Even my close friend in whom I trusted,
Who ate my bread,
Has lifted up his heel against me.

10 But You, O LORD, be gracious to me and raise me up,
That I may repay them.
11 By this I know that You are pleased with me,
Because my enemy does not shout in triumph over me.
12 As for me, You uphold me in my integrity,
And You set me in Your presence forever.

13 Blessed be the LORD, the God of Israel,
From everlasting to everlasting.
Amen and Amen.

41:8 Ps 71:10, 11

41:9 2 Sam 15:12; Job 19:13, 19; Ps 55:12, 13, 20; Jer 20:10; Mic 7:5; Matt 26:23; Luke 22:21; John 13:18

41:10 Ps 3:3

41:11 Ps 37:23; 147:11; Ps 25:2

41:12 Ps 18:32; 37:17; 63:8; Job 36:7; Ps 21:6

41:13 Ps 72:18, 19; 89:52; 106:48; 150:6

BOOK 2
PSALMS 42:1—72:20

These psalms include a prayer for rescue, a call to worship, a confession of sin, an encouragement to trust God, a psalm for those hurt by friends, a prayer for those who have been slandered, and a missionary psalm. These psalms can help us retain a sense of wonder in our worship.

PSALM 42

For the choir director. A Maskil of the sons of Korah.

Theme: A thirst for God. When you feel lonely or depressed, meditate on God's kindness and love.
Author: The sons of Korah, who were temple musicians and assistants

1 As the deer [79]pants for the water brooks,
So my soul pants for You, O God.
2 My soul thirsts for God, for the living God;
When shall I come and appear before God?
3 My tears have been my food day and night,
While *they* say to me all day long, "Where is your God?"
4 These things I remember and I pour out my soul within me.
For I used to go along with the throng *and* lead them in procession to the house of God,
With the voice of joy and thanksgiving, a multitude keeping festival.

5 Why are you in despair, O my soul?
And *why* have you become disturbed within me?

79 Lit *longs for*

42:1 Ps 119:131

42:2 Ps 63:1; 84:2; 143:6; Josh 3:10; Ps 84:2; Jer 10:10; Dan 6:26; Matt 26:63; Rom 9:26; 1 Thess 1:9; Ex 23:17; Ps 43:4; 84:7

42:3 Ps 80:5; 102:9; Ps 79:10; 115:2; Joel 2:17; Mic 7:10

42:4 1 Sam 1:15; Job 30:16; Ps 62:8; Lam 2:19; Ps 55:14; 122:1; Is 30:29; Ps 100:4

42:5 Ps 42:11; 43:5; Ps 38:6; Matt 26:38; Ps 77:3; Ps 71:14; Lam 3:24; Ps 44:3

41:9 This verse is viewed in the New Testament as a prophecy of Christ's betrayal (John 13:18). Judas, one of Jesus' 12 disciples, had spent three years learning from Jesus, traveling and eating with him (Mark 3:14–19), and handling the finances for the group. Eventually Judas, who knew Jesus extremely well, betrayed him (Matthew 26:14–16, 20–25).

41:13 Psalms is divided into five books, and each one ends with a doxology or an expression of praise to God. The first book of the psalms, chapters 1 through 41, takes us on a journey through suffering, sorrow, and great joy. It teaches us much about God's eternal love and care for us and how we should trust him even in the day-to-day experiences of life.

42:1ff Psalms 42—49 were written by the sons of Korah. Korah was a Levite who led a rebellion against Moses (Numbers 16:1–35). He was killed, but his descendants remained faithful to God and continued to serve God in the temple. David appointed men from the clan of Korah to serve as choir leaders (1 Chronicles 6:31–38), and they continued to be temple musicians for hundreds of years (2 Chronicles 20:18–19).

42:1–2 As the life of a deer depends upon water, so our lives depend upon God. Those who seek him and long to understand him find never-ending life. Feeling separated from God, this psalmist wouldn't rest until he restored his relationship with God because he knew that his very life depended on it.

42:4–5 The writer of this psalm was discouraged because he was exiled to a place far from Jerusalem and could not worship in the temple. During these God-given holidays, the nation was to remember all that God had done for them. Many of these festivals are explained in the chart in Leviticus 23.

Hope in God, for I shall again praise Him
For the help of His presence.

42:6 Ps 61:2; 2 Sam 17:22; Deut 3:8

6 O my God, my soul is in despair within me;
Therefore I remember You from the land of the Jordan
And the peaks of Hermon, from Mount Mizar.

42:7 Ps 69:1, 2; 88:7; Jon 2:3

7 Deep calls to deep at the sound of Your waterfalls;
All Your breakers and Your waves have rolled over me.

42:8 Ps 57:3; 133:3; Job 35:10; Ps 16:7; 63:6; 77:6; 149:5; Eccl 5:18; 8:15

8 The LORD will command His lovingkindness in the daytime;
And His song will be with me in the night,
A prayer to the God of my life.

42:9 Ps 18:2; Ps 38:6; Ps 17:9

9 I will say to God my rock, "Why have You forgotten me?
Why do I go mourning because of the oppression of the enemy?"

42:10 Ps 42:3; Joel 2:17

10 As a shattering of my bones, my adversaries revile me,
While they say to me all day long, "Where is your God?"

42:11 Ps 42:5; 43:5

11 Why are you in despair, O my soul?
And why have you become disturbed within me?
Hope in God, for I shall yet praise Him,
The help of my countenance and my God.

PSALM 43

Theme: Hope in a time of discouragement. In the face of discouragement, our only hope is in God.
Author: The sons of Korah (temple assistants)

43:1 Ps 26:1; 35:24; 1 Sam 24:15; Ps 35:1; Ps 5:6; 38:12

1 Vindicate me, O God, and plead my case against an ungodly nation;
O deliver me from the deceitful and unjust man!

43:2 Ps 18:1; 28:7; 31:4; Ps 44:9; 88:14; Ps 42:9

2 For You are the God of my strength; why have You rejected me?
Why do I go mourning because of the oppression of the enemy?

43:3 Ps 36:9; Ps 2:6; 3:4; 42:4; 46:4; Ps 84:1

3 O send out Your light and Your truth, let them lead me;
Let them bring me to Your holy hill
And to Your dwelling places.

43:4 Ps 26:6; Ps 21:6; Ps 33:2; 49:4; 57:8; 71:22

4 Then I will go to the altar of God,
To God my exceeding joy;
And upon the lyre I shall praise You, O God, my God.

43:5 Ps 42:5, 11

5 Why are you in despair, O my soul?
And why are you disturbed within me?
Hope in God, for I shall again praise Him,
The help of my countenance and my God.

42:5–6 Depression is one of the most common emotional ailments. One antidote for depression is to meditate on the record of God's goodness to his people. This will take your mind off the present situation and give hope that it will improve. It will focus your thoughts on God's ability to help you rather than on your inability to help yourself. When you feel depressed, take advantage of this psalm's antidepressant. Read the Bible's accounts of God's goodness, and meditate on them.

42:6 Hermon refers to Mount Hermon. *Mizar* means smallness, so Mount Mizar could be a smaller mountain in that mountain range.

43:3 The "holy hill" is Mount Zion, in Jerusalem, the city that David named as Israel's capital. The temple was built there as the place for the people to meet God in worship and prayer.

43:3–4 The psalmist asked God to send his light and truth to guide him to the holy mountain, the temple, where he would meet God. God's truth (see 1 John 2:27) provides the right path to follow, and God's light (see 1 John 1:5) provides the clear vision to follow it. If you feel surrounded by darkness and uncertainty, follow God's light and truth. He will guide you.

PSALM 44

For the choir director. A Maskil of the sons of Korah.

Theme: A plea for victory by the battle-weary and defeated. When it seems that God has let you down, don't despair. Instead, remember God's past deliverance and be confident that he will restore you.
Author: The sons of Korah (temple assistants)

1 O God, we have heard with our ears,
Our fathers have told us
The work that You did in their days,
In the days of old.
2 You with Your own hand drove out the nations;
Then You planted them;
You afflicted the peoples,
Then You spread them abroad.
3 For by their own sword they did not possess the land,
And their own arm did not save them,
But Your right hand and Your arm and the light of Your presence,
For You favored them.

4 You are my King, O God;
Command victories for Jacob.
5 Through You we will push back our adversaries;
Through Your name we will trample down those who rise up against us.
6 For I will not trust in my bow,
Nor will my sword save me.
7 But You have saved us from our adversaries,
And You have put to shame those who hate us.
8 In God we have boasted all day long,
And we will give thanks to Your name forever. Selah.

9 Yet You have rejected *us* and brought us to dishonor,
And do not go out with our armies.
10 You cause us to turn back from the adversary;
And those who hate us have taken spoil for themselves.
11 You give us as sheep to be eaten
And have scattered us among the nations.
12 You sell Your people cheaply,
And have not [80]profited by their sale.
13 You make us a reproach to our neighbors,
A scoffing and a derision to those around us.
14 You make us a byword among the nations,
A laughingstock among the peoples.
15 All day long my dishonor is before me
And my humiliation has overwhelmed me,

80 Or *set a high price on them*

44:1
Ex 12:26, 27; Deut 6:20; Judg 6:13; Ps 78:3; Ps 78:12; Deut 32:7; Ps 77:5; Is 51:9; 63:9

44:2
Josh 3:10; Neh 9:24; Ps 78:55; 80:8; Ex 15:17; 2 Sam 7:10; Jer 24:6; Amos 9:15; Ps 135:10-12; Ps 80:9-11; Zech 2:6

44:3
Deut 8:17, 18; Josh 24:12; Ps 77:15; Ps 4:6; 89:15; Deut 4:37; 7:7, 8; 10:15; Ps 106:4

44:4
Ps 74:12; Ps 42:8

44:5
Deut 33:17; Ps 60:12; Dan 8:4; Ps 108:13; Zech 10:5

44:6
1 Sam 17:47; Ps 33:16; Hos 1:7

44:7
Ps 136:24; Ps 53:5

44:8
Ps 34:2; Ps 30:12

44:9
Ps 43:2; 60:1, 10; 74:1; 89:38; 108:11; Ps 69:19; Ps 60:10; 108:11

44:10
Lev 26:17; Josh 7:8, 12; Ps 89:43; Ps 89:41

44:11
Ps 44:22; Rom 8:36; Lev 26:33; Deut 4:27; 28:64; Ps 106:27; Ezek 20:23

44:12
Deut 32:30; Judg 2:14; 3:8; Is 52:3, 4; Jer 15:13

44:13
Deut 28:37; Ps 79:4; 89:41; Ps 80:6; Ezek 23:32

44:14
Job 17:6; Ps 69:11; Jer 24:9; 2 Kin 19:21; Ps 109:25

44:15
2 Chr 32:21; Ps 69:7

44:1ff This psalm may have been sung at an occasion like the one in 2 Chronicles 20:18–19, where the faithful Jehoshaphat was surrounded by enemies and the Levites sang to the Lord before the battle.

44:1–3 Driving out the nations refers to the conquest of Canaan (the promised land) described in the book of Joshua. God gave the land to Israel—they were supposed to enter and drive out anyone who was wicked and opposed to God. Israel was told to settle the land and to be a witness to the world of God's power and love. Surrounded by enemies, the psalmist remembered what God had done for his people and took heart. We can have this same confidence in God when we feel attacked.

44:6–7 In whom or in what do you trust? Only God is trustworthy—he will never let you down.

44:9–22 Israel had been defeated despite their faith (44:17) and obedience (44:18) to God. The psalmist could not understand why God allowed this to happen, but he did not give up hope of discovering the answer (44:17–22). Although he felt his suffering was undeserved, he revealed the real reason for it: He suffered because he was *committed to the Lord.* Paul quoted the psalmist's complaint (Romans 8:36) to show that we must always be ready to face death for the cause of Christ. Thus, our suffering may not be a punishment, but a battle scar that demonstrates our loyalty.

44:16
Ps 74:10; Ps 8:2

44:17
Ps 78:7; 119:61, 83, 109, 141, 153, 176; Ps 78:57

44:18
Ps 78:57; Job 23:11; Ps 119:51, 157

44:19
Ps 51:8; 94:5; Job 30:29; Is 13:22; Jer 9:11; Job 3:5; Ps 23:4

44:20
Ps 78:11; Deut 6:14; Ps 81:9

44:21
Ps 139:1, 2; Jer 17:10

44:22
Rom 8:36; Is 53:7; Jer 12:3

44:23
Ps 7:6; Ps 78:65; Ps 77:7

44:24
Job 13:24; Ps 88:14; Ps 42:9; Lam 5:20

44:25
Ps 119:25

44:26
Ps 35:2; Ps 6:4; 25:22

16 Because of the voice of him who reproaches and reviles,
Because of the presence of the enemy and the avenger.

17 All this has come upon us, but we have not forgotten You,
And we have not dealt falsely with Your covenant.
18 Our heart has not turned back,
And our steps have not deviated from Your way,
19 Yet You have crushed us in a place of jackals
And covered us with the shadow of death.

20 If we had forgotten the name of our God
Or extended our hands to a strange god,
21 Would not God find this out?
For He knows the secrets of the heart.
22 But for Your sake we are killed all day long;
We are considered as sheep to be slaughtered.
23 Arouse Yourself, why do You sleep, O Lord?
Awake, do not reject us forever.
24 Why do You hide Your face
And forget our affliction and our oppression?
25 For our soul has sunk down into the dust;
Our body cleaves to the earth.
26 Rise up, be our help,
And redeem us for the sake of Your lovingkindness.

PSALM 45

For the choir director; according to the [81]Shoshannim.
A Maskil of the sons of Korah. A Song of Love.

Theme: A poem to the king (possibly Solomon) on the occasion of his wedding. While this psalm was written for a historic occasion, it is also seen as a prophecy about Christ and his bride, the church, who will praise him throughout all generations.
Author: The sons of Korah (temple assistants)

45:1
Ezra 7:6

45:2
Luke 4:22; Ps 21:6

45:3
Heb 4:12; Rev 1:16; Is 9:6

45:4
Zeph 2:3; Ps 21:8

45:5
Ps 18:14; 120:4; Is 5:28; 7:13; Ps 92:9; 2 Sam 18:14

1 My heart [82]overflows with a good theme;
I address my verses to the King;
My tongue is the pen of a ready writer.
2 You are fairer than the sons of men;
Grace is poured upon Your lips;
Therefore God has blessed You forever.

3 Gird Your sword on *Your* thigh, O Mighty One,
In Your splendor and Your majesty!
4 And in Your majesty ride on victoriously,
For the cause of truth and meekness *and* righteousness;
Let Your right hand teach You awesome things.
5 Your arrows are sharp;
The peoples fall under You;
Your arrows are in the heart of the King's enemies.

81 Or possibly *Lilies* **82** Lit *is astir*

44:22–26 The writer cried out to God to redeem his people because of his unfailing love. Nothing can separate us from God's love, not even death (Romans 8:36–39). When you fear for your life, ask God for deliverance, and remember that even death cannot separate you from him.

44:23–25 The psalmist's words suggest that he did not believe God had left him. God was still the Ruler, but he seemed to be asleep, and the psalmist wondered why. In the New Testament, the disciples wondered why Jesus was asleep when they needed his help during a storm (Mark 4:35–41). In both cases, of course, God was ready to help, but he wished first to build faith in his followers.

45:1ff This is called a Messianic psalm because it prophetically describes the Messiah's future relationship to the church, his body of believers. Verse 2 expresses God's abundant blessing on his Messiah; verses 6–8 find their true fulfillment in Christ (Hebrews 1:8–9). The church is described as the bride of Christ in Revelation 19:7–8; 21:9; 22:17.

6 Your throne, O God, is forever and ever;
A scepter of uprightness is the scepter of Your kingdom.
7 You have loved righteousness and hated wickedness;
Therefore God, Your God, has anointed You
With the oil of joy above Your fellows.
8 All Your garments are *fragrant with* myrrh and aloes *and* cassia;
Out of ivory palaces stringed instruments have made You glad.
9 Kings' daughters are among Your noble ladies;
At Your right hand stands the queen in gold from Ophir.

10 Listen, O daughter, give attention and incline your ear:
Forget your people and your father's house;
11 Then the King will desire your beauty.
Because He is your Lord, bow down to Him.
12 The daughter of Tyre *will come* with a gift;
The rich among the people will seek your favor.

13 The King's daughter is all glorious within;
Her clothing is interwoven with gold.
14 She will be led to the King in embroidered work;
The virgins, her companions who follow her,
Will be brought to You.
15 They will be led forth with gladness and rejoicing;
They will enter into the King's palace.

16 In place of your fathers will be your sons;
You shall make them princes in all the earth.
17 I will cause Your name to be remembered in all generations;
Therefore the peoples will give You thanks forever and ever.

45:6 Ps 93:2; Heb 1:8, 9; Ps 98:9
45:7 Ps 11:7; 33:5; Ps 2:2
45:8 Song 4:14; John 19:39; Ps 150:4
45:9 Song 6:8; 1 Kin 2:19; 1 Kin 9:28; Is 13:12
45:10 Deut 21:13; Ruth 1:16, 17
45:11 Gen 18:12; 1 Pet 3:6; Eph 5:33
45:12 Ps 87:4; Ps 22:29; 68:29; 72:10, 11; Is 49:23
45:13 Ex 39:2, 3
45:14 Song 1:4; Judg 5:30; Ezek 16:10; Ps 45:9
45:17 Mal 1:11; Ps 138:4

PSALM 46

For the choir director. *A Psalm* of the sons of Korah, [83]set to Alamoth. A Song.

Theme: God is always there to help, providing refuge, security, and peace. God's power is complete and his ultimate victory is certain. He will not fail to rescue those who love him.
Author: The sons of Korah (temple assistants)

1 God is our refuge and strength,
[84]A very present help in trouble.
2 Therefore we will not fear, though the earth should change
And though the mountains slip into the heart of the sea;
3 Though its waters roar *and* foam,
Though the mountains quake at its swelling pride. Selah.

4 There is a river whose streams make glad the city of God,
The holy dwelling places of the Most High.

46:1 Ps 14:6; 62:7, 8; Deut 4:7; Ps 145:18; Ps 9:9
46:2 Ps 23:4; 27:1; Ps 82:5; Ps 18:7
46:3 Ps 93:3, 4; Jer 5:22
46:4 Ps 36:8; 65:9; Is 8:6; Rev 22:1; Ps 48:1; 87:3; 101:8; Is 60:14; Rev 3:12; Ps 43:3

83 Possibly *for soprano voices* **84** Or *Abundantly available for help*

45:8–9 Myrrh is a fragrant gum of an Arabian tree, generally used in perfumes. Aloes, a spice, may have come from sandalwood, a close-grained and fragrant wood often used for storage boxes or chests (see also Proverbs 7:14–17; Song of Solomon 4:13–14). Cassia was probably made from flowers of the cinnamon tree. These expensive fragrances were appropriate for a king's wedding. The location of Ophir is unknown, but believed to be in either Arabia or Africa. It was famous as a source of gold.

45:13–17 This beautiful section of poetry pictures Christ's bride, the church, with the richest blessings as she unites forever with him (see Revelation 19:6–8; 21:2).

46—48 Psalms 46—48 are hymns of praise, celebrating deliverance from some great foe. Psalm 46 may have been written when the Assyrian army invaded the land and surrounded Jerusalem (2 Kings 18:13—19:37).

46:1–3 The fear of mountains or cities suddenly crumbling into the sea as the result of a nuclear blast haunts many people today. But the psalmist says that even if the world ends, we need not fear. In the face of utter destruction, the writer expressed a quiet confidence in God's ability to save him. It seems impossible to consider the end of the world without becoming consumed by fear, but the Bible is clear—God is our refuge even in the face of total destruction. He is not merely a temporary retreat; he is our eternal refuge and can provide strength in any circumstance.

46:4–5 Many great cities have rivers flowing through them, sustaining people's lives by making agriculture possible and facilitat-

46:5
Deut 23:14; Is 12:6; Ezek 43:7, 9; Hos 11:9; Joel 2:27; Zech 2:5; Ps 37:40; Is 41:14; Luke 1:54

46:6
Ps 2:1, 2; Ps 18:13; 68:33; Jer 25:30; Joel 2:11; Amos 1:2; Amos 9:5; Mic 1:4; Nah 1:5

46:7
Num 14:9; 2 Chr 13:12; Ps 9:9; 48:3

46:8
Ps 66:5; Is 61:4; Jer 51:43

46:9
Is 2:4; Mic 4:3; 1 Sam 2:4; Ps 76:3; Is 9:5; Ezek 39:9

46:10
Ps 100:3; Is 2:11, 17

5 God is in the midst of her, she will not be moved;
God will help her when morning dawns.
6 The nations made an uproar, the kingdoms tottered;
He raised His voice, the earth melted.
7 The LORD of hosts is with us;
The God of Jacob is our stronghold. Selah.

8 Come, behold the works of the LORD,
Who has wrought desolations in the earth.
9 He makes wars to cease to the end of the earth;
He breaks the bow and cuts the spear in two;
He burns the chariots with fire.
10 "Cease *striving* and know that I am God;
I will be exalted among the nations, I will be exalted in the earth."
11 The LORD of hosts is with us;
The God of Jacob is our stronghold. Selah.

PSALM 47

For the choir director. A Psalm of the sons of Korah.

Theme: God is still King of the world. All nations of the earth will eventually recognize his lordship.
Author: The sons of Korah (temple assistants)

47:1
Ps 98:8; Ps 106:47

47:2
Deut 7:21; Neh 1:5; Ps 66:3, 5; 68:35; Mal 1:14

47:3
Ps 18:47

47:4
1 Pet 1:4; Amos 6:8; 8:7; Nah 2:2

47:5
Ps 68:18; Ps 98:6

1 O clap your hands, all peoples;
Shout to God with the voice of joy.
2 For the LORD Most High is to be feared,
A great King over all the earth.
3 He subdues peoples under us
And nations under our feet.
4 He chooses our inheritance for us,
The glory of Jacob whom He loves. Selah.

5 God has ascended with a shout,
The LORD, with the sound of a trumpet.

PSALMS THAT HAVE INSPIRED HYMNS

Psalm 23	The King of Love My Shepherd Is My Shepherd Shall Supply My Need The Lord Is My Shepherd
Psalm 46	A Mighty Fortress Is Our God
Psalm 61	Hiding in Thee (O Safe to the Rock That Is Higher Than I...)
Psalm 87	Glorious Things of Thee Are Spoken
Psalm 90	O God, Our Help in Ages Past
Psalm 100	All People That on Earth Do Dwell Before Jehovah's Awful Throne
Psalm 103	Praise to the Lord, the Almighty
Psalm 104	O Worship the King, All Glorious Above
Psalm 126	Bringing in the Sheaves

ing trade with other cities. Jerusalem had no river, but it had God who, like a river, sustained the people's lives. As long as God lived among the people, the city was invincible. But when the people abandoned him, God no longer protected them, and Jerusalem fell to the Babylonian army.

46:10 War and destruction are inevitable, but so is God's final victory. At that time, all will stand quietly before the Lord Almighty. How proper, then, for us to be still now, reverently honoring him and his power and majesty. Take time each day to be still and to exalt God.

47:1ff This psalm may have been written about the same event as Psalm 46—the Assyrian invasion of Judah by Sennacherib (2 Kings 18:13—19:37).

47:2 The Lord Most High is awesome beyond words, but this didn't keep Bible writers from trying to describe him. And it shouldn't keep us from talking about him either. We can't describe God completely, but we can tell others what he has done for us. Don't let the indescribable aspects of God's greatness prevent you from telling others what you know about him.

6 Sing praises to God, sing praises;
Sing praises to our King, sing praises.
7 For God is the King of all the earth;
Sing praises with a skillful psalm.
8 God reigns over the nations,
God sits on His holy throne.
9 The princes of the people have assembled themselves *as* the people of the God of Abraham,
For the shields of the earth belong to God;
He is highly exalted.

47:6 Ps 68:4; Ps 89:18

47:7 Zech 14:9; 1 Cor 14:15

47:8 1 Chr 16:31; Ps 22:28; Ps 97:2

47:9 Ps 72:11; 102:22; Is 49:7, 23; Rom 4:11, 12; Ps 89:18; Ps 97:9

PSALM 48

A Song; a Psalm of the sons of Korah.

Theme: God's presence is our joy, security, and salvation. God is praised as the defender of Jerusalem, the holy city of the Jews. He is also our defender and guide forever.
Author: The sons of Korah (temple assistants)

1 Great is the LORD, and greatly to be praised,
In the city of our God, His holy mountain.
2 Beautiful in elevation, the joy of the whole earth,
Is Mount Zion *in* the far north,
The city of the great King.
3 God, in her palaces,
Has made Himself known as a stronghold.

4 For, lo, the kings assembled themselves,
They passed by together.
5 They saw *it,* then they were amazed;
They were terrified, they fled in alarm.
6 Panic seized them there,
Anguish, as of a woman in childbirth.
7 With the east wind
You break the ships of Tarshish.
8 As we have heard, so have we seen
In the city of the LORD of hosts, in the city of our God;
God will establish her forever. Selah.

9 We have thought on Your lovingkindness, O God,
In the midst of Your temple.
10 As is Your name, O God,
So is Your praise to the ends of the earth;
Your right hand is full of righteousness.
11 Let Mount Zion be glad,
Let the daughters of Judah rejoice
Because of Your judgments.
12 Walk about Zion and go around her;
Count her towers;

48:1 1 Chr 16:25; Ps 96:4; 145:3; Ps 46:4; Ps 2:6; 87:1; Is 2:3; Mic 4:1; Zech 8:3

48:2 Ps 50:2; Lam 2:15; Matt 5:35

48:3 Ps 46:7

48:4 2 Sam 10:6-19

48:5 Ex 15:15

48:6 Is 13:8

48:7 Jer 18:17; 1 Kin 22:48; 1 Kin 10:22; Ezek 27:25

48:8 Ps 87:5

48:9 Ps 26:3; 40:10

48:10 Deut 28:58; Josh 7:9; Mal 1:11; Ps 65:1, 2; 100:1; Is 41:10

48:11 Ps 97:8

48:12 Neh 3:1, 11, 25-27

47:9 Abraham was the father of the Israelite nation. The one true God was sometimes called the "God of Abraham" (Exodus 3:6; 1 Kings 18:36). In a spiritual sense, God's promises to Abraham apply to all who believe in God, Jew or Gentile (Romans 4:11–12; Galatians 3:7–9). Thus the God of Abraham is our God too.

48:2 Why is Mount Zion—Jerusalem—"the city of the great King"? Because the temple was located in Jerusalem, the city was seen as the center of God's presence in the world. The Bible pictures Jerusalem as the place where believers will gather in the "last days" (Isaiah 2:2ff), and as the spiritual home of all believers where God will live among them (Revelation 21:2–3).

48:8 Because Jerusalem has been destroyed several times since this psalm was written, the phrase, "God will establish her forever" may refer prophetically to the new Jerusalem where God will judge all nations and live with all believers (Revelation 21).

48:11 The people of Judah were from Israel's largest tribe, which settled in the southern part of Canaan where Jerusalem was located (Joshua 15:1–12). David was from Judah, and he made Jerusalem his capital and the center of the nation's worship. Jesus was also a member of the tribe of Judah. The psalmist was saying that the day would come when God would bring justice to the land, and God's people would get the respect they deserved.

48:12–13 After an enemy army had unsuccessfully besieged Jerusalem, it was important for the people to make a tour of the city, inspecting its defenses and praising God for the protection it had offered. In times of great joy or after God has brought us

48:13 Ps 122:7; Ps 78:5-7

13 Consider her ramparts;
Go through her palaces,
That you may tell *it* to the next generation.

48:14 Ps 23:4; Is 58:11

14 For such is God,
Our God forever and ever;
He will guide us [85]until death.

PSALM 49

For the choir director. A Psalm of the sons of Korah.

Theme: Trusting in worldly possessions is futile. You cannot take possessions with you when you die, and they cannot buy forgiveness from sin.
Author: The sons of Korah (temple assistants)

49:1 Ps 78:1; Is 1:2; Mic 1:2; Ps 33:8

1 Hear this, all peoples;
Give ear, all inhabitants of the world,

49:2 Ps 62:9

2 Both low and high,
Rich and poor together.

49:3 Ps 37:30; Ps 119:130

3 My mouth will speak wisdom,
And the meditation of my heart *will be* understanding.

49:4 Ps 78:2; 2 Kin 3:15; Num 12:8

4 I will incline my ear to a proverb;
I will express my riddle on the harp.

49:5 Ps 23:4; 27:1

5 Why should I fear in days of adversity,
When the iniquity of my foes surrounds me,

49:6 Job 31:24; Ps 52:7; Prov 11:28; Mark 10:24

6 Even those who trust in their wealth
And boast in the abundance of their riches?

49:7 Matt 25:8, 9; Job 36:18, 19

7 No man can by any means redeem *his* brother
Or give to God a ransom for him—

49:8 Matt 16:26

8 For the redemption of his soul is costly,
And he should cease *trying* forever—

49:9 Ps 22:29; Ps 16:10; 89:48

9 That he should live on eternally,
That he should not [86]undergo decay.

49:10 Eccl 2:16; Ps 92:6; 94:8; Ps 39:6; Eccl 2:18, 21; Luke 12:20

10 For he sees *that even* wise men die;
The stupid and the senseless alike perish
And leave their wealth to others.

49:11 Ps 64:6; Ps 10:6; Gen 4:17; Deut 3:14

11 Their [87]inner thought is *that* their houses are forever
And their dwelling places to all generations;
They have called their lands after their own names.

85 Lit *upon;* some mss and the Gr read *forever* **86** Or *see corruption* or *the pit* **87** Some versions read *graves are their houses*

---

through some great trial, we ought to inspect our defenses to make sure that the foundations—faith in God, knowledge of his Word, and the fellowship and prayers of the body of believers—remain strong (Ephesians 2:20–22). Then we should praise God for his protection!

48:14 We often pray for God's guidance as we struggle with decisions. What we need is both guidance and a guide—a map that gives us landmarks and directions and a constant companion who has an intimate knowledge of the way and will make sure we interpret the map correctly. The Bible will be such a map, and the Holy Spirit will be the constant companion and guide. As you make your way through life, use both the map and your Guide.

49:1ff The futility of worldliness—riches, pride, fame—resounds from this psalm. Comparable in form to the book of Ecclesiastes, this psalm is one of the few written more to instruct than to give praise.

49:7–8, 15 In the slave market of the ancient world, a slave had to be redeemed or ransomed (someone had to pay the price) in order to go free. In Mark 10:45, Ephesians 1:7, and Hebrews 9:12, we learn that Jesus paid such a price so that we could be set free from slavery to sin in order to begin a new life with him.

There is no way for a person to buy eternal life with God. God alone can redeem a soul. Don't count on wealth and physical comforts to keep you happy because you will never have enough wealth to keep from dying.

49:10–14 The rich and poor have one similarity—when they die, they leave all they own here on earth. At the moment of death (and all of us will face that moment), both rich and poor are naked and empty-handed before God. The only riches we have at that time are those we have already invested in our eternal heritage. At the time of death, each of us will wish we had invested less on earth, where we must leave it, and more in heaven, where we will retain it forever. To have treasure in heaven, we must place our faith in God, pledge ourselves to obey him, and utilize our resources for the good of his kingdom. This is a good time to check up on your investments and see where you have invested the most. Then do whatever it takes to place your investments where they really count.

12 But man in *his* pomp will not endure;
He is like the beasts that perish.

13 This is the way of those who are foolish,
And of those after them who approve their words. Selah.
14 As sheep they are appointed for Sheol;
Death shall be their shepherd;
And the upright shall rule over them in the morning,
And their form shall be for Sheol to consume
So that they have no habitation.
15 But God will redeem my soul from the power of Sheol,
For He will receive me. Selah.

16 Do not be afraid when a man becomes rich,
When the [88]glory of his house is increased;
17 For when he dies he will carry nothing away;
His [88]glory will not descend after him.
18 Though while he lives he congratulates himself—
And though *men* praise you when you do well for yourself—
19 He shall go to the generation of his fathers;
They will never see the light.
20 Man in *his* pomp, yet without understanding,
Is like the beasts that perish.

49:12 Ps 49:20
49:13 Jer 17:11; Ps 49:18
49:14 Ps 9:17; Dan 7:18; Mal 4:3; 1 Cor 6:2; Rev 2:26; Job 24:19
49:15 Ps 16:10; 56:13; Hos 13:14; Gen 5:24; Ps 16:11; 73:24
49:16 Ps 37:7
49:17 Ps 17:14; 1 Tim 6:7
49:18 Deut 29:19; Ps 10:3, 6; Luke 12:19
49:19 Gen 15:15; Job 33:30; Ps 56:13
49:20 Ps 49:12; Eccl 3:19

PSALM 50

A Psalm of Asaph.

Theme: The contrast between true and false faith. God desires sincere thanks, trust, and praise.
Author: Asaph, one of David's chief musicians

1 The Mighty One, God, the LORD, has spoken,
And summoned the earth from the rising of the sun to its setting.
2 Out of Zion, the perfection of beauty,
God has shone forth.
3 May our God come and not keep silence;
Fire devours before Him,
And it is very tempestuous around Him.
4 He summons the heavens above,
And the earth, to judge His people:
5 "Gather My godly ones to Me,
Those who have made a covenant with Me by sacrifice."
6 And the heavens declare His righteousness,
For God Himself is judge. Selah.

7 "Hear, O My people, and I will speak;
O Israel, I will testify against you;
I am God, your God.

88 Or *wealth*

50:1 Josh 22:22; Ps 113:3
50:2 Ps 48:2; Lam 2:15; Deut 33:2; Ps 80:1; 94:1
50:3 Ps 96:13; Lev 10:2; Num 16:35; Ps 97:3; Dan 7:10; Ps 18:12, 13
50:4 Deut 4:26; 31:28; 32:1; Is 1:2
50:5 Ps 30:4; 37:28; 52:9; Ex 24:7; 2 Chr 6:11; Ps 25:10; Ps 50:8
50:6 Ps 89:5; 97:6; Ps 75:7; 96:13
50:7 Ps 49:1; 81:8; Ex 20:2; Ps 48:14

50:1ff God judges people for treating him lightly. First, he speaks to the superficially religious people who bring their sacrifices but are only going through the motions (50:1–15). They do not honor God with true praise and thankfulness. Second, he chides wicked, hardhearted people for their evil words and immoral lives (50:16–22). He asks the superficially religious for genuine thanksgiving and trust, and he warns the evil people to consider their deeds, lest he destroy them in his anger.

50:1–4 This psalm begins as though God is finally ready to judge the evil people on earth. But surprisingly, we read that God's great fury is leveled against his own people (or at least those who claim to be his). God's judgment must begin with his own people (1 Peter 4:17).

50:5–9 God's perfect moral nature demands that the penalty for sin be death; however, a person could offer an animal to God as a substitute for himself, symbolizing the person's faith in the merciful, forgiving God. But, the people were offering sacrifices and forgetting their significance! The very act of sacrifice showed that they had once agreed to follow God wholeheartedly. But at this time their hearts were not in it. We may fall into the same pattern when we participate in religious activities, tithe, or attend church out of habit or conformity rather than out of heartfelt love and obedience. God wants righteousness, not empty ritual. (See the note on 40:6.)

50:8 Ps 40:6; 51:16; Is 1:11; Hos 6:6
50:9 Ps 69:31
50:10 Ps 104:24
50:11 Matt 6:26
50:12 Ex 19:5; Deut 10:14; Ps 24:1; 1 Cor 10:26
50:13 Ps 50:9
50:14 Ps 27:6; 69:30; 107:22; 116:17; Hos 14:2; Rom 12:1; Heb 13:15; Num 30:2; Deut 23:21; Ps 22:25; 56:12; 61:8; 65:1; 76:11
50:15 Ps 91:15; 107:6, 13; Zech 13:9; Ps 81:7; Ps 22:23
50:16 Is 29:13
50:17 Prov 5:12; 12:1; Rom 2:21, 22; 1 Kin 14:9; Neh 9:26
50:18 Rom 1:32; 1 Tim 5:22
50:19 Ps 10:7; Ps 36:3; 52:2
50:20 Job 19:18; Matt 10:21
50:21 Eccl 8:11; Is 42:14; 57:11; Ps 90:8
50:22 Job 8:13; Ps 9:17; Ps 7:2
50:23 Ps 50:14; Ps 85:13; Ps 91:16

8 "I do not reprove you for your sacrifices,
And your burnt offerings are continually before Me.
9 "I shall take no young bull out of your house
Nor male goats out of your folds.
10 "For every beast of the forest is Mine,
The cattle on a thousand hills.
11 "I know every bird of the mountains,
And everything that moves in the field is [89]Mine.
12 "If I were hungry I would not tell you,
For the world is Mine, and all it contains.
13 "Shall I eat the flesh of bulls
Or drink the blood of male goats?
14 "Offer to God a sacrifice of thanksgiving
And pay your vows to the Most High;
15 Call upon Me in the day of trouble;
I shall rescue you, and you will honor Me."

16 But to the wicked God says,
"What right have you to tell of My statutes
And to take My covenant in your mouth?
17 "For you hate discipline,
And you cast My words behind you.
18 "When you see a thief, you are pleased with him,
And you associate with adulterers.
19 "You let your mouth loose in evil
And your tongue frames deceit.
20 "You sit and speak against your brother;
You slander your own mother's son.
21 "These things you have done and I kept silence;
You thought that I was just like you;
I will reprove you and state *the case* in order before your eyes.

22 "Now consider this, you who forget God,
Or I will tear *you* in pieces, and there will be none to deliver.
23 "He who offers a sacrifice of thanksgiving honors Me;
And to him who orders *his* way *aright*
I shall show the salvation of God."

PSALM 51

For the choir director. A Psalm of David, when Nathan the prophet came to him, after he had gone in to Bathsheba.

Theme: David's plea for mercy, forgiveness, and cleansing. God wants our hearts to be right with him.
Author: David

51:1 Ps 4:1; 109:26; Ps 69:16; 106:45; Ps 51:9; Is 43:25; 44:22; Acts 3:19; Col 2:14

1 Be gracious to me, O God, according to Your lovingkindness;
According to the greatness of Your compassion blot out my transgressions.

89 Or *in My mind;* lit *with Me*

50:16–22 Some people glibly recite God's laws but are filled with deceit and evil. They claim his promises but refuse to obey him. This is sin, and God will judge people for it. We too are hypocrites when we are not what we claim to be. To let this inconsistency remain shows that we are not true followers of God.

50:21 At times God seems silent. By his silence he is not condoning sin, nor is he indifferent to it. Instead, he is withholding deserved punishment, giving time for people to repent (2 Peter 3:9). God takes no pleasure in the death of the wicked and wants them to turn from evil (Ezekiel 33:11). But his silence does not last forever—a time of punishment will surely come.

51:1–7 David was truly sorry for his adultery with Bathsheba and for murdering her husband to cover it up. He knew that his actions had hurt many people. But because David repented of those sins, God mercifully forgave him. No sin is too great to be forgiven! Do you feel that you could never come close to God because you have done something terrible? God can and will forgive you of any sin. While God forgives us, however, he does not always erase the natural consequences of our sin—David's life and family were never the same as a result of what he had done (see 2 Samuel 12:1–23).

2 Wash me thoroughly from my iniquity
And cleanse me from my sin.
3 For I know my transgressions,
And my sin is ever before me.
4 Against You, You only, I have sinned
And done what is evil in Your sight,
So that You [90]are justified when You speak
And blameless when You judge.

5 Behold, I was brought forth in iniquity,
And in sin my mother conceived me.
6 Behold, You desire truth in the innermost being,
And in the hidden part You will make me know wisdom.
7 Purify me with hyssop, and I shall be clean;
Wash me, and I shall be whiter than snow.
8 Make me to hear joy and gladness,
Let the bones which You have broken rejoice.
9 Hide Your face from my sins
And blot out all my iniquities.

10 Create in me a clean heart, O God,
And renew a steadfast spirit within me.
11 Do not cast me away from Your presence
And do not take Your Holy Spirit from me.
12 Restore to me the joy of Your salvation
And sustain me with a willing spirit.
13 *Then* I will teach transgressors Your ways,
And sinners will [91]be converted to You.

14 Deliver me from bloodguiltiness, O God, the God of my salvation;
Then my tongue will joyfully sing of Your righteousness.
15 O Lord, open my lips,
That my mouth may declare Your praise.
16 For You do not delight in sacrifice, otherwise I would give it;
You are not pleased with burnt offering.
17 The sacrifices of God are a broken spirit;
A broken and a contrite heart, O God, You will not despise.

90 Or *may be in the right* **91** Or *turn back*

51:2 Jer 4:14; Acts 22:16; Ezek 36:33; Heb 9:14; 1 John 1:7, 9

51:4 Gen 20:6; 39:9; 2 Sam 12:13; Ps 41:4; Luke 15:21; Rom 3:4

51:5 Job 14:4; 15:14; Ps 58:3; Eph 2:3

51:6 Job 38:36; Ps 15:2; Prov 2:6; Eccl 2:26; James 1:5

51:7 Ex 12:22; Lev 14:4; Num 19:18; Heb 9:19; Is 1:18

51:8 Is 35:10; Joel 1:16; Ps 35:10

51:9 Jer 16:17

51:10 Ezek 18:31; Eph 2:10; Ps 24:4; Matt 5:8; Acts 15:9; Ps 78:37

51:11 2 Kin 13:23; 24:20; Jer 7:15; Is 63:10, 11

51:12 Ps 13:5; Ps 110:3

51:13 Acts 9:21, 22; Ps 22:27

51:14 2 Sam 12:9; Ps 26:9; Ps 25:5; Ps 35:28; 71:15

51:15 Ex 4:15; Ps 9:14

51:16 1 Sam 15:22

51:17 Ps 34:18

51:4 Although David had sinned with Bathsheba, David said that he had sinned against God. When someone steals, murders, or slanders, it is against someone else—a victim. According to the world's standards, extramarital sex between two consenting adults is acceptable if nobody gets hurt. But people *do* get hurt—in David's case, a man was murdered, and a baby died. All sin hurts us and others, but ultimately it offends God because sin in any form is a rebellion against God's way of living. When tempted to do wrong, remember that you will be sinning against God. That may help you stay on the right track.

51:7 Hyssop branches were used by the Israelites in Egypt to place the blood of a lamb on the doorposts of their homes. This would keep them safe from death (Exodus 12:22). This act demonstrated the Israelites' faith and secured their release from slavery in Egypt. This verse calls for cleansing from sin and readiness to serve the Lord.

51:10 Because we are born as sinners (51:5), our natural inclination is to please ourselves rather than God. David followed that inclination when he took another man's wife. We also follow it when we sin in any way. Like David, we must ask God to purify us from within (51:7), clearing our hearts and spirits for new thoughts and desires. Right conduct can come only from a clean heart and spirit. Ask God to create a pure heart and spirit in you.

51:12 Do you ever feel stagnant in your faith, as though you are just going through the motions? Has sin ever driven a wedge between you and God, making him seem distant? David felt this way. He had sinned with Bathsheba and had just been confronted by Nathan the prophet. In his prayer he cried, "Restore to me the joy of Your salvation." God wants us to be close to him and to experience his full and complete life. But sin that remains unconfessed makes such intimacy impossible. Confess your sin to God. You may still have to face some earthly consequences, as David did, but God will give back the joy of your relationship with him.

51:13 When God forgives our sin and restores us to a relationship with him, we want to reach out to others who need this forgiveness and reconciliation. The more you have felt God's forgiveness, the more you will desire to tell others about it.

51:17 God wants a broken spirit and a broken and contrite heart. You can never please God by outward actions—no matter how good—if your inward heart attitude is not right. Are you sorry for your sin? Do you genuinely intend to stop? God is pleased by this kind of humility.

51:18 Ps 69:35; Is 51:3; Ps 102:16; 147:2
51:19 Ps 4:5; Ps 66:13, 15

18 By Your favor do good to Zion;
Build the walls of Jerusalem.
19 Then You will delight in righteous sacrifices,
In burnt offering and whole burnt offering;
Then young bulls will be offered on Your altar.

PSALM 52

For the choir director. A Maskil of David, when Doeg the Edomite came and told Saul and said to him, "David has come to the house of Ahimelech."

Theme: God will judge the evildoer. Our anger must not block our confidence in God's ability to defeat evil.
Author: David

52:1 Ps 94:4; Ps 52:8
52:2 Ps 5:9; Ps 57:4; 59:7; Ps 101:7
52:3 Ps 36:4; Ps 58:3; Jer 9:5
52:4 Ps 120:3

1 Why do you boast in evil, O mighty man?
The lovingkindness of God *endures* all day long.
2 Your tongue devises destruction,
Like a sharp razor, O worker of deceit.
3 You love evil more than good,
Falsehood more than speaking what is right. Selah.
4 You love all words that devour,
O deceitful tongue.

52:5 Is 22:18, 19; Prov 2:22; Ps 27:13
52:6 Ps 37:34; 40:3; Job 22:19
52:7 Ps 49:6; Ps 10:6

5 But God will break you down forever;
He will snatch you up and tear you away from *your* tent,
And uproot you from the land of the living. Selah.
6 The righteous will see and fear,
And will laugh at him, *saying,*
7 "Behold, the man who would not make God his refuge,
But trusted in the abundance of his riches
And was strong in his *evil* desire."

52:8 Ps 92:12; 128:3; Jer 11:16; Ps 13:5
52:9 Ps 30:12; Ps 54:6

8 But as for me, I am like a green olive tree in the house of God;
I trust in the lovingkindness of God forever and ever.
9 I will give You thanks forever, because You have done *it,*
And I will wait on Your name, for *it is* good, in the presence of Your godly ones.

PSALM 53

For the choir director; according to [92]Mahalath. A Maskil of David.

Theme: All have sinned. Because of sin, no person can find God on his or her own. Only God can save us.
Author: David

53:1 Ps 10:4; 14:1-7; 53:1-6; Rom 3:10
53:2 Rom 3:11; 2 Chr 15:2

1 The fool has said in his heart, "There is no God,"
They are corrupt, and have committed abominable injustice;
There is no one who does good.
2 God has looked down from heaven upon the sons of men
To see if there is anyone who understands,

92 I.e. sickness, a sad tone

52:1 This psalm was written about Doeg, the Edomite who had betrayed Ahimelech and David and then killed God's priests (see 1 Samuel 21:7; 22:9–23). Doeg thought he was a great hero—even boasting about his deed. In reality, his deed was evil, an offense to God. It is easy to mistake "accomplishment" with goodness. Just because something is done well or thoroughly doesn't mean it is good (for example, someone may be a great gambler or a skillful liar). Measure all you do by the rule of God's Word, not by how proficiently you do it.

52:8 With God by his side, David compared himself to an olive tree flourishing in the house of God. Not only is an olive tree one of the longest-living trees, but a flourishing tree has even greater longevity. David was contrasting God's eternal protection of his faithful servants with the sudden destruction of the wicked (52:5–7).

53:1 Echoing the message of Psalm 14, this psalm proclaims the foolishness of atheism (see also Romans 3:10). People may say there is no God in order to cover their sin, to have an excuse to continue in sin, and/or to ignore the Judge in order to avoid the judgment. A "fool" does not necessarily lack intelligence; many atheists and unbelievers are highly educated. Fools are people who reject God, the only One who can save them.

Who seeks after God.
3 Every one of them has turned aside; together they have become corrupt;
There is no one who does good, not even one.

4 Have the workers of wickedness no knowledge,
Who eat up My people *as though* they ate bread
And have not called upon God?
5 There they were in great fear *where* no fear had been;
For God scattered the bones of him who encamped against you;
You put *them* to shame, because God had rejected them.
6 Oh, that the salvation of Israel would come out of Zion!
When God restores His captive people,
Let Jacob rejoice, let Israel be glad.

53:3 Rom 3:12

53:4 Jer 4:22

53:5 Lev 26:17, 36; Prov 28:1; Ps 141:7; Jer 8:1, 2; Ezek 6:5; Ps 44:7; 2 Kin 17:20; Jer 6:30; Lam 5:22

53:6 Ps 14:7

PSALM 54

For the choir director; on stringed instruments. A Maskil of David, when the Ziphites came and said to Saul, "Is not David hiding himself among us?"

Theme: A call for God to overcome enemies. God is our helper, even in times of hurt and betrayal.
Author: David

1 Save me, O God, by Your name,
And [93]vindicate me by Your power.
2 Hear my prayer, O God;
Give ear to the words of my mouth.
3 For strangers have risen against me
And violent men have sought my life;
They have not set God before them. Selah.

4 Behold, God is my helper;
The Lord is the sustainer of my soul.
5 [94]He will recompense the evil to my foes;
Destroy them in Your faithfulness.

6 Willingly I will sacrifice to You;
I will give thanks to Your name, O LORD, for it is good.
7 For He has delivered me from all trouble,
And my eye has looked *with satisfaction* upon my enemies.

54:1 Ps 20:1; 2 Chr 20:6

54:2 Ps 17:6; 55:1; Ps 5:1

54:3 Ps 86:14; Ps 18:48; 86:14; 140:1, 4, 11; 1 Sam 20:1; 25:29; Ps 40:14; 63:9; 70:2; Ps 36:1

54:4 Ps 30:10; 37:40; 118:7; Ps 37:17, 24; 41:12; 51:12; 145:14; Is 41:10

54:5 Ps 94:23; Ps 143:12; Ps 89:49; 96:13; Is 42:3

54:6 Num 15:3; Ps 116:17; Ps 50:14

54:7 Ps 34:6; Ps 59:10; 92:11; 112:8; 118:7

PSALM 55

For the choir director; on stringed instruments. A Maskil of David.

Theme: Expressing deep dismay over the treachery of a close friend. When friends hurt us, the burden is too difficult to carry alone.
Author: David

1 Give ear to my prayer, O God;
And do not hide Yourself from my supplication.
2 Give heed to me and answer me;
I am restless in my complaint and [95]am surely distracted,

55:1 Ps 54:2; 61:1; 86:6; Ps 27:9

55:2 Ps 66:19; 86:6, 7; 1 Sam 1:16; Job 9:27; Ps 64:1; 77:3; 142:2; Is 38:14; 59:11; Ezek 7:16

93 Lit *judge* **94** Lit *The evil will return* **95** Or *I must moan*

54:3–4 Many of David's psalms follow the pattern found in these two verses—a transition from prayer to praise. David was not afraid to come to God and express his true feelings and needs. Thus his spirit was lifted, and he praised God, his helper, protector, and friend.

54:5 David said that God repays evil to his enemies. Proverbs 26:27 warns that those who cause trouble will reap trouble. What we have intended for others may blow up in our own faces. To be honest and straightforward before God and others is simpler, easier, and safer in the long run.

55:1ff This psalm was most likely written during the time of Absalom's rebellion and Ahithophel's betrayal (2 Samuel 15—17). Some say verses 12–14 are Messianic because they also describe Judas's betrayal of Christ (Matthew 26:14–16, 20–25).

55:3 Ps 17:9; 2 Sam 16:7, 8; Ps 71:11; 143:3

3 Because of the voice of the enemy,
Because of the pressure of the wicked;
For they bring down trouble upon me
And in anger they bear a grudge against me.

55:4 Ps 38:8; Ps 18:4, 5; 116:3

55:5 Ps 119:120; Job 21:6; Is 21:4; Ezek 7:18

55:6 Job 3:13

55:7 1 Sam 23:14

55:8 Is 4:6; 25:4; 29:6

4 My heart is in anguish within me,
And the terrors of death have fallen upon me.
5 Fear and trembling come upon me,
And horror has overwhelmed me.
6 I said, "Oh, that I had wings like a dove!
I would fly away and [96]be at rest.
7 "Behold, I would wander far away,
I would lodge in the wilderness. Selah.
8 "I would hasten to my place of refuge
From the stormy wind *and* tempest."

55:9 Gen 11:9; Ps 11:5; Jer 6:7

55:11 Ps 5:9; Ps 10:7; 17:9

9 Confuse, O Lord, divide their tongues,
For I have seen violence and strife in the city.
10 Day and night they go around her upon her walls,
And iniquity and mischief are in her midst.
11 Destruction is in her midst;
Oppression and deceit do not depart from her streets.

55:12 Ps 41:9; Ps 35:26

55:13 2 Sam 15:12; Job 19:14; Ps 41:9

55:14 Ps 42:4

55:15 Ps 64:7; Prov 6:15; Is 47:11; 1 Thess 5:3; Num 16:30, 33

12 For it is not an enemy who reproaches me,
Then I could bear *it;*
Nor is it one who hates me who has exalted himself against me,
Then I could hide myself from him.
13 But it is you, a man my equal,
My companion and my familiar friend;
14 We who had sweet [97]fellowship together
Walked in the house of God in the throng.
15 Let death come deceitfully upon them;
Let them go down alive to Sheol,
For evil is in their dwelling, in their midst.

55:16 Ps 57:2, 3

55:17 Ps 141:2; Dan 6:10; Acts 3:1; 10:3, 30; Ps 5:3; 88:13; 92:2; Acts 10:9

55:18 Ps 103:4; Ps 56:2

55:19 Ps 78:59; Deut 33:27; Ps 90:2; 93:2; Ps 36:1

55:20 Ps 7:4; 120:7; Num 30:2; Ps 89:34

55:21 Ps 12:2; 28:3; Prov 5:3, 4; Ps 57:4; 59:7

16 As for me, I shall call upon God,
And the LORD will save me.
17 Evening and morning and at noon, I will complain and murmur,
And He will hear my voice.
18 He will redeem my soul in peace from the battle *which is* against me,
For they are many *who strive* with me.
19 God will hear and answer them—
Even the one who sits enthroned from of old— Selah.
With whom there is no change,
And who do not fear God.
20 He has put forth his hands against those who were at peace with him;
He has [98]violated his covenant.
21 His speech was smoother than butter,
But his heart was war;

96 Lit *settle down* **97** Lit *counsel;* or *intimacy* **98** Lit *profaned*

55:6–8 Even those who are especially close to God, as David was, have moments when they want to escape from their problems and pressures.

55:9–11 The city that was supposed to be holy was plagued by internal problems: violence, strife, malice, abuse, destruction, threats, and lies. External enemies, though a constant threat, were not nearly as dangerous as the corruption inside. Even today, churches often look to defend themselves against troubles from the sinful world while failing to see that their own sins are causing their troubles.

55:12–14 Nothing hurts more than a wound from a friend. There may be times when friends will lovingly confront you in order to help you. Real friends stick by you in times of trouble and bring healing, love, acceptance, and understanding. What kind of friend are you? Don't betray those you love.

55:17 Praying evening, morning, and noon is certainly an excellent way to maintain correct priorities throughout every day. Daniel followed this pattern (Daniel 6:10), as did Peter (Acts 10:9–10). The prayers of God's people are effective against the overwhelming evil in the world.

His words were softer than oil,
Yet they were drawn swords.

22 Cast your burden upon the LORD and He will sustain you;
He will never allow the righteous to be shaken.
23 But You, O God, will bring them down to the pit of destruction;
Men of bloodshed and deceit will not live out half their days.
But I will trust in You.

55:22 Ps 37:5; 1 Pet 5:7; Ps 37:24; Ps 15:5; 112:6

55:23 Ps 73:18; Is 38:17; Ezek 28:8; Ps 5:6; Job 15:32; Prov 10:27; Ps 25:2; 56:3

PSALM 56

For the choir director; according to Jonath elem rehokim.
A Mikhtam of David, when the Philistines seized him in Gath.

Theme: Trusting in God's care in the midst of fear. When all seems dark, one truth still shines bright: When God is for us, those against us will never succeed.
Author: David

1 Be gracious to me, O God, for man has trampled upon me;
Fighting all day long he oppresses me.
2 My foes have trampled upon me all day long,
For they are many who fight proudly against me.
3 When I am afraid,
I will put my trust in You.
4 In God, whose word I praise,
In God I have put my trust;
I shall not be afraid.
What can *mere* man do to me?
5 All day long they [99]distort my words;
All their thoughts are against me for evil.
6 They [100]attack, they lurk,
They watch my steps,
As they have waited *to take* my life.
7 Because of wickedness, cast them forth,
In anger put down the peoples, O God!

8 You have taken account of my wanderings;
Put my tears in Your bottle.
Are *they* not in Your book?
9 Then my enemies will turn back in the day when I call;
This I know, [101]that God is for me.
10 In God, *whose* word I praise,
In the LORD, *whose* word I praise,
11 In God I have put my [102]trust, I shall not be afraid.
What can man do to me?
12 Your vows are *binding* upon me, O God;
I will render thank offerings to You.

56:1 Ps 57:3; Ps 17:9

56:2 Ps 35:25; 57:3; 124:3; Ps 35:1

56:3 Ps 55:4, 5; Ps 11:1

56:4 Ps 56:10, 11; Ps 118:6; Heb 13:6

56:5 2 Pet 3:16; Ps 41:7

56:6 Ps 59:3; 140:2; Is 54:15; Ps 17:11; Ps 71:10

56:7 Ps 36:12; Prov 19:5; Ezek 17:15; Rom 2:3; Ps 55:23

56:8 Ps 139:3; 2 Kin 20:5; Ps 39:12; Mal 3:16

56:9 Ps 9:3; Ps 102:2; Ps 41:11; 118:6; Rom 8:31

56:12 Ps 50:14

99 Or *trouble my affairs* **100** Or *stir up strife* **101** Or *because* **102** Or *trust without fear*

55:22 God wants us to cast our cares on him, but often we continue to bear them ourselves even when we say we are trusting in him. Trust the same strength that sustains you to carry your cares also.

56:1ff This was probably written on the same occasion as Psalm 34, when David fled from Saul to Philistine territory. He had to pretend insanity before Achish when some servants grew suspicious of him (1 Samuel 21:10–15).

56:3, 4 David stated, "What can mere man do to me?" How much harm can people do to us? They can inflict pain, suffering, and death. But no person can rob us of our souls or our future beyond this life. How much harm can we do to ourselves? The worst thing we can do is to reject God and lose our eternal future. Jesus said, "Do not fear those who kill the body, but are unable to kill the soul" (Matthew 10:28). Instead, we should fear God, who controls this life and the next.

56:8 Even in our deepest sorrow, God cares! Jesus reminded us further of how much God understands us—he knows even the number of hairs on our heads (Matthew 10:30). Often we waver between faith and fear. When you feel so discouraged that you are sure no one understands, remember that God knows every problem and sees every tear.

56:13 Ps 33:19; 49:15; 86:13; Ps 116:8; Ps 116:9; Job 33:30

13 For You have delivered my soul from death,
Indeed my feet from stumbling,
So that I may walk before God
In the light of the living.

PSALM 57

For the choir director; *set to* [103]Al-tashheth. A Mikhtam of David, when he fled from Saul in the cave.

Theme: God's faithful help and love in times of trouble. When we face trials, God will quiet our hearts and give us confidence.
Author: David

57:1 Ps 2:12; 34:22; Ruth 2:12; Ps 17:8; 36:7; 63:7; 91:4; Is 26:20

1 Be gracious to me, O God, be gracious to me,
For my soul takes refuge in You;
And in the shadow of Your wings I will take refuge
Until destruction passes by.

57:2 Ps 138:8

2 I will cry to God Most High,
To God who accomplishes *all things* for me.

57:3 Ps 18:16; 144:5, 7; Ps 56:2; Ps 25:10; 40:11

3 He will send from heaven and save me;
He reproaches him who tramples upon me. Selah.
God will send forth His lovingkindness and His truth.

57:4 Ps 35:17; 58:6; Prov 30:14; Ps 55:21; 59:7; 64:3; Prov 12:18

4 My soul is among lions;
I must lie among those who breathe forth fire,
Even the sons of men, whose teeth are spears and arrows
And their tongue a sharp sword.

57:5 Ps 57:11; 108:5

5 Be exalted above the heavens, O God;
Let Your glory *be* above all the earth.

57:6 Ps 10:9; 31:4; 35:7; 140:5; Ps 145:14; Ps 7:15; Prov 26:27; 28:10; Eccl 10:8

6 They have [104]prepared a net for my steps;
My soul is bowed down;
They dug a pit before me;
They *themselves* have fallen into the midst of it. Selah.

57:7 Ps 57:7-11; 108:1-5; Ps 112:7

7 My heart is steadfast, O God, my heart is steadfast;
I will sing, yes, I will sing praises!

57:8 Ps 16:9; 30:12; Ps 150:3

8 Awake, my glory!
Awake, harp and lyre!
I will awaken the dawn.

57:9 Ps 108:3

9 I will give thanks to You, O Lord, among the peoples;
I will sing praises to You among the nations.

57:10 Ps 36:5; 103:11; 108:4

10 For Your lovingkindness is great to the heavens
And Your truth to the clouds.

57:11 Ps 57:5; 108:5

11 Be exalted above the heavens, O God;
Let Your glory *be* above all the earth.

103 Lit *Do Not Destroy* **104** Or *spread*

57:1ff This psalm was probably written when David was hiding in a cave from Saul (see 1 Samuel 22—24).

57:4 At times, we may be surrounded by people who gossip about us or criticize us. Verbal cruelty can damage us as badly as physical abuse. Rather than answering with hateful words, we, like David, can talk with God about the problem.

57:7 David's firm faith in God contrasted sharply with his enemies' loud lying and boasting. When confronted with verbal attacks, the best defense is simply to be quiet and praise God, realizing that our confidence is in his love and faithfulness (57:10). In times of great suffering, don't turn inward to self-pity or outward to revenge, but upward to God.

PSALM 58

For the choir director; *set to* Al-tashheth. A Mikhtam of David.

Theme: A prayer for God's justice. When no justice can be found, rejoice in knowing that justice will triumph because there is a God who will judge with complete fairness.
Author: David, at a time when men in authority were twisting justice

1 Do you indeed speak righteousness, O [105]gods?
Do you judge [106]uprightly, O sons of men?
2 No, in heart you work unrighteousness;
On earth you weigh out the violence of your hands.
3 The wicked are estranged from the womb;
These who speak lies go astray from birth.
4 They have venom like the venom of a serpent;
Like a deaf cobra that stops up its ear,
5 So that it does not hear the voice of charmers,
Or a skillful caster of spells.

6 O God, shatter their teeth in their mouth;
Break out the fangs of the young lions, O LORD.
7 Let them flow away like water that runs off;
When he aims his arrows, let them be as headless shafts.
8 *Let them be* as a snail which melts away as it goes along,
Like the miscarriages of a woman which never see the sun.
9 Before your pots can feel *the fire of* thorns
He will sweep them away with a whirlwind, the green and the burning alike.

10 The righteous will rejoice when he sees the vengeance;
He will wash his feet in the blood of the wicked.
11 And men will say, "Surely there is a reward for the righteous;
Surely there is a God who judges on earth!"

PSALM 59

For the choir director; *set to* Al-tashheth. A Mikhtam of David, when Saul sent *men* and they watched the house in order to kill him.

Theme: Prayer and praise for God's saving help.
God's constant love is our place of safety in a wicked world.
Author: David

1 Deliver me from my enemies, O my God;
Set me *securely* on high away from those who rise up against me.
2 Deliver me from those who do iniquity
And save me from men of bloodshed.
3 For behold, they have set an ambush for my life;
Fierce men [107]launch an attack against me,
Not for my transgression nor for my sin, O LORD,
4 For no guilt of *mine,* they run and set themselves against me.
Arouse Yourself to help me, and see!
5 You, O LORD God of hosts, the God of Israel,

58:1 Ps 82:2
58:2 Mal 3:15; Ps 94:20; Is 10:1
58:3 Ps 51:5; Is 48:8; Ps 53:3
58:4 Deut 32:33; Ps 140:3
58:5 Jer 8:17; Eccl 10:11
58:6 Job 4:10; Ps 3:7
58:7 Josh 2:11; 7:5; Ps 112:10; Is 13:7; Ezek 21:7; Ps 64:3
58:8 Job 3:16; Eccl 6:3
58:9 Ps 118:12; Eccl 7:6; Job 27:21; Ps 83:15; Prov 10:25
58:10 Job 22:19; Ps 32:11; 64:10; 107:42; Deut 32:43; Ps 91:8; Jer 11:20; 20:12; Ps 68:23
58:11 Ps 18:20; 19:11; Is 3:10; Luke 6:23, 35; Ps 9:8; 67:4; 75:7; 94:2
59:1 Ps 143:9; Ps 20:1; 69:29
59:2 Ps 28:3; 36:12; 53:4; 92:7; 94:16; Ps 26:9; 139:19; Prov 29:10
59:3 Ps 56:6; 1 Sam 24:11; Ps 7:3, 4; 69:4
59:4 Ps 35:19; Ps 7:6; 35:23
59:5 Ps 69:6; 80:4; 84:8; Ps 9:5; Is 26:14; Is 2:9; Jer 18:23

105 Or *mighty ones* or *judges* **106** Or *uprightly the sons of men* **107** Or *stir up strife*

58:1ff This is called an imprecatory psalm (see the note on 35:1ff). It is a cry for justice so intense that it seems, at first glance, to be a call for revenge.

58:1ff The Old Testament is filled with references to justice, and it is a key topic in the psalms. Unfortunately, many judges and rulers in ancient times took justice into their own hands. They had complete authority with no accountability and the power to make their own laws. When earth's judges are corrupt, there is little hope of justice in this life. But God loves justice, and those who obey him will experience perfect justice in eternity.

58:11 Of all people, our national leaders should be just and fair. When they are unjust and unfair, people suffer. The rich get richer, the poor get poorer, politicians wrest power from the people, national morality deteriorates, and God is ignored. When right triumphs at last, "the righteous will rejoice" (58:10). Be assured that there will be a day of accountability and that God judges fairly. Be careful never to side with injustice, lest you find yourself standing before an angry Judge.

59:6
Ps 59:14; Ps 22:16

59:7
Ps 94:4; Prov 15:2, 28; Ps 57:4; Prov 12:18; Job 22:13; Ps 10:11; 73:11; 94:7

59:8
Ps 37:13; Prov 1:26; Ps 2:4

59:9
Ps 18:17; Ps 9:9; 62:2

59:10
Ps 21:3; Ps 54:7

59:11
Deut 4:9; 6:12; Ps 106:27; 144:6; Is 33:3; Ps 84:9

59:12
Prov 12:13; Zeph 3:11; Ps 10:7

59:13
Ps 104:35; Ps 83:18

59:14
Ps 59:6

59:15
Job 15:23

59:16
Ps 21:13; Ps 101:1; Ps 5:3; 88:13; Ps 59:9; 2 Sam 22:3; Ps 46:1

59:17
Ps 59:9; Ps 59:10

Awake to punish all the nations;
Do not be gracious to any *who are* treacherous in iniquity. Selah.
6 They return at evening, they howl like a dog,
And go around the city.
7 Behold, they belch forth with their mouth;
Swords are in their lips,
For, *they say,* "Who hears?"
8 But You, O LORD, laugh at them;
You scoff at all the nations.

9 *Because of* [108]his strength I will watch for You,
For God is my stronghold.
10 My God in His lovingkindness will meet me;
God will let me look *triumphantly* upon my foes.
11 Do not slay them, or my people will forget;
Scatter them by Your power, and bring them down,
O Lord, our shield.
12 *On account of* the sin of their mouth *and* the words of their lips,
Let them even be caught in their pride,
And on account of curses and lies which they utter.
13 [109]Destroy *them* in wrath, [109]destroy *them* that they may be no more;
That *men* may know that God rules in Jacob
To the ends of the earth. Selah.
14 They return at evening, they howl like a dog,
And go around the city.
15 They wander about [110]for food
And growl if they are not satisfied.

16 But as for me, I shall sing of Your strength;
Yes, I shall joyfully sing of Your lovingkindness in the morning,
For You have been my stronghold
And a refuge in the day of my distress.
17 O my strength, I will sing praises to You;
For God is my stronghold, the God who shows me lovingkindness.

PSALM 60

For the choir director; according to [111]Shushan Eduth.
A Mikhtam of David, to teach; when he struggled with Aram-naharaim
and with Aram-zobah, and Joab returned, and smote
twelve thousand of Edom in the Valley of Salt.

Theme: Real help comes from God alone. When a situation seems out of control, we can trust God to do mighty things.
Author: David, when Israel was away at war with Aram in the north, and Edom invaded Israel from the south (2 Samuel 8).

60:1
Ps 44:9; 2 Sam 5:20; Ps 79:5; Ps 80:3

60:2
Ps 18:7; 2 Chr 7:14; Is 30:26

1 O God, You have rejected us. You have broken us;
You have been angry; O, restore us.
2 You have made the land quake, You have split it open;

108 Many mss and some ancient versions read *My strength* **109** Lit *Bring to an end* **110** Or *to devour* **111** Lit *The lily of testimony*

59:7–8 Vile men curse God as if he cannot hear and will not respond. But God scoffs at them. Evil people live as if God cannot see and will not punish. But God watches patiently until that day when their deeds will rise up to accuse them. As believers we must be careful not to follow the same foolish practices as evil people. We must remember that God hears and sees all we do.

59:10 David was hunted by those whose love had turned to jealousy, and this was driving them to try to murder him. Trusted friends, and even his son, had turned against him. What changeable love! But David knew that God's love for him was *changeless.* "His lovingkindness is everlasting" (100:5). God's mercy to all who trust him is just as permanent as his mercy to David. When the love of others fails or disappoints us, we can rest in God's enduring love.

60:1ff This psalm gives us information about David's reign not found in the books of 1 and 2 Samuel or 1 and 2 Chronicles. Although the setting of the psalm is found in 2 Samuel 8, that passage makes no reference to the fact that David's forces had met stiff resistance (60:1–3) and apparently even a temporary defeat (60:9–10). The closer we get to God, the more our enemies will attack us because we threaten their evil and selfish way of living.

Heal its breaches, for it totters.
3 You have made Your people experience hardship;
You have given us wine to drink that makes us stagger.
4 You have given a banner to those who fear You,
That it may be displayed because of the truth. Selah.
5 That Your beloved may be delivered,
Save with Your right hand, and answer us!

6 God has spoken in His [112]holiness:
"I will exult, I will portion out Shechem and measure out the valley of Succoth.
7 "Gilead is Mine, and Manasseh is Mine;
Ephraim also is the helmet of My head;
Judah is My [113]scepter.
8 "Moab is My washbowl;
Over Edom I shall throw My shoe;
Shout loud, O Philistia, because of Me!"

9 Who will bring me into the besieged city?
Who will lead me to Edom?
10 Have not You Yourself, O God, rejected us?
And will You not go forth with our armies, O God?
11 O give us help against the adversary,
For deliverance by man is in vain.
12 Through God we shall do valiantly,
And it is He who will tread down our adversaries.

60:3 Ps 66:12; 71:20; Ps 75:8; Is 51:17, 22; Jer 25:15

60:4 Ps 20:5; Is 5:26; 11:12; 13:2

60:5 Ps 60:5-12; 108:6-13; Deut 33:12; Ps 127:2; Is 5:1; Jer 11:15; Ps 17:7

60:6 Ps 89:35; Gen 12:6; 33:18; Josh 17:7; Gen 33:17; Josh 13:27

60:7 Josh 13:31; Deut 33:17; Gen 49:10

60:8 2 Sam 8:2; 2 Sam 8:14; 2 Sam 8:1

60:10 Ps 60:1; 108:11; Josh 7:12; Ps 44:9

60:11 Ps 146:3

60:12 Num 24:18; Ps 118:16; Ps 44:5; Is 63:3

PSALM 61

For the choir director; on a stringed instrument. *A Psalm* of David.

Theme: Prayer for security and assurance. Wherever we are, we can trust that God will be there to answer our cries for help.
Author: David, written when he was forced to escape during the days of Absalom's rebellion (2 Samuel 15—18), or after he had narrowly escaped one of Saul's efforts to kill him while hiding in the desert

1 Hear my cry, O God;
Give heed to my prayer.
2 From the end of the earth I call to You when my heart is faint;
Lead me to the rock that is higher than I.
3 For You have been a refuge for me,
A tower of strength against the enemy.
4 Let me dwell in Your tent forever;
Let me take refuge in the shelter of Your wings. Selah.

5 For You have heard my vows, O God;
You have given *me* the inheritance of those who fear Your name.
6 You will prolong the king's life;
His years will be as many generations.

61:1 Ps 64:1; Ps 86:6

61:2 Ps 42:6; Ps 77:3; Ps 18:2; 94:22

61:3 Ps 62:7; Ps 59:9; Prov 18:10

61:4 Ps 23:6; 27:4; Ps 17:8; 91:4

61:5 Job 22:27; Ps 56:12; Deut 28:58; Neh 1:11; Ps 86:11; 102:15; Is 59:19; Mal 2:5; 4:2

61:6 Ps 21:4

112 Or *sanctuary* **113** Or *lawgiver*

60:3 Instead of the wine of blessing God had given them the cup of his judgment. God's rejection was intended to bring them back to himself.

60:6–10 God said the cities and territories of Israel were his, and he knew the future of each of the nations. When the world seems out of control, we must remind ourselves that God owns the cities and knows the future of every nation. God is in control. In and through him we will gain the victory.

60:8 David mentioned the enemy nations that surrounded Israel. Moab lay directly to the east, Edom to the south, and Philistia to the west. At the time this psalm was written, David was fighting Aram to the north. Although he was surrounded by enemies, David believed that God would help him triumph.

61:1–2 David must have been far from home when he wrote this psalm. Fortunately, God is not limited to any geographic location. Even when we are among unknown people and surroundings, God never abandons us. A "higher" rock would be a plain of refuge and safety. God's all-surpassing strength is always with us.

61:7 Ps 41:12; Ps 40:11

7 He will abide before God forever;
Appoint lovingkindness and truth that they may preserve him.

61:8 Judg 5:3; Ps 30:4; 33:2; 71:22; Ps 65:1; Is 19:21

8 So I will sing praise to Your name forever,
That I may pay my vows day by day.

PSALM 62

For the choir director; according to Jeduthun. A Psalm of David.

Theme: Placing all hope in God. Knowing that God is in control allows us to wait patiently for him to rescue us. True relief does not come when the problem is resolved because more problems are on the way! True relief comes from an enduring hope in God's ultimate salvation. Only then will all trials be resolved.
Author: David, possibly written during the days of Absalom's rebellion (2 Samuel 15—18).

62:1 Ps 33:20; Ps 37:39

1 My soul *waits* in silence for God only;
From Him is my salvation.

62:2 Ps 89:26; Ps 59:17; 62:6

2 He only is my rock and my salvation,
My stronghold; I shall not be greatly shaken.

62:3 Is 30:13

3 How long will you assail a man,
That you may murder *him,* all of you,
Like a leaning wall, like a tottering fence?

62:4 Ps 4:2; Ps 28:3; 55:21

4 They have counseled only to thrust him down from his high position;
They delight in falsehood;
They bless with their mouth,
But inwardly they curse. Selah.

62:5 Ps 62:1

5 My soul, wait in silence for God only,
For my hope is from Him.

62:6 Ps 62:2

6 He only is my rock and my salvation,
My stronghold; I shall not be shaken.

62:7 Ps 85:9; Jer 3:23; Ps 46:1

7 On God my salvation and my glory *rest;*
The rock of my strength, my refuge is in God.

62:8 Ps 37:3, 5; 52:8; Is 26:4; 1 Sam 1:15; Ps 42:4; Lam 2:19

8 Trust in Him at all times, O people;
Pour out your heart before Him;
God is a refuge for us. Selah.

62:9 Ps 49:2; Job 7:16; Ps 39:5; Is 40:17; Ps 116:11; Is 40:15

9 Men of low degree are only vanity and men of rank are a lie;
In the balances they go up;
They are together lighter than breath.

62:10 Is 30:12; Is 61:8; Ezek 22:29; Nah 3:1; Job 31:25; Ps 49:6; 52:7; Mark 10:24; Luke 12:15; 1 Tim 6:10

10 Do not trust in oppression
And do not vainly hope in robbery;
If riches increase, do not set *your* heart *upon them.*

62:11 Job 33:14; 40:5; Ps 59:17; Rev 19:1

11 [114]Once God has spoken;
[115]Twice I have heard this:
That power belongs to God;

62:12 Ps 86:5; 103:8; 130:7; Job 34:11; Ps 28:4; Jer 17:10; Matt 16:27; Rom 2:6; 1 Cor 3:8; Rev 2:23

12 And lovingkindness is Yours, O Lord,
For You recompense a man according to his work.

114 Or *One thing* **115** Or *These two things I have heard*

61:8 David made a vow to praise God each day. David continually praised God through both the good and difficult times of his life. Do you find something to praise God for each day? As you do, you will find your heart elevated from daily distractions to lasting confidence.

62:3–6 David expressed his feelings to God and then reaffirmed his faith. Prayer can release our tensions in times of emotional stress. Trusting God to be our rock, salvation, and stronghold (62:2) will change our entire outlook on life. No longer must we be held captive by resentment toward others when they hurt us. When we are resting in God's strength, nothing can shake us.

62:9–12 It is tempting to use honor, power, wealth, or prestige to measure people. We may even think that such people are really getting ahead in life. But on God's scales, these people are a "breath," a puff of air. What, then, can tilt the scales when God weighs us? Trusting God and working for him (62:12). Wealth, honor, power, or prestige add nothing to our value in God's eyes, but the faithful work we do for him has eternal value.

PSALM 63

A Psalm of David, when he was in the wilderness of Judah.

Theme: Our desire for God's presence, provision, and protection. No matter where we are, our desire should be for God because only he satisfies fully.
Author: David

1 O God, You are my God; I shall seek You [116]earnestly;
My soul thirsts for You, my flesh yearns for You,
In a dry and weary land where there is no water.
2 Thus I have seen You in the sanctuary,
To see Your power and Your glory.
3 Because Your lovingkindness is better than life,
My lips will praise You.
4 So I will bless You as long as I live;
I will lift up my hands in Your name.
5 My soul is satisfied as with [117]marrow and fatness,
And my mouth offers praises with joyful lips.

6 When I remember You on my bed,
I meditate on You in the night watches,
7 For You have been my help,
And in the shadow of Your wings I sing for joy.
8 My soul clings to You;
Your right hand upholds me.

9 But those who seek my life to destroy it,
Will go into the depths of the earth.
10 They will be delivered over to the power of the sword;
They will be a prey for foxes.
11 But the king will rejoice in God;
Everyone who swears by Him will glory,
For the mouths of those who speak lies will be stopped.

63:1 Ps 118:28; Ps 42:2; 84:2; Matt 5:6; Ps 143:6
63:2 Ps 27:4
63:3 Ps 69:16
63:4 Ps 104:33; 146:2; Ps 28:2; 143:6
63:5 Ps 36:8; Ps 71:23
63:6 Ps 4:4; Ps 16:7; 42:8; 119:55
63:7 Ps 27:9; Ps 17:8
63:8 Num 32:12; Deut 1:36; Hos 6:3; Ps 18:35; 41:12
63:9 Ps 40:14; Ps 55:15
63:10 Jer 18:21; Ezek 35:5; Lam 5:18
63:11 Ps 21:1; Deut 6:13; Is 45:23; 65:16; Job 5:16; Ps 107:42; Rom 3:19

PSALM 64

For the choir director. A Psalm of David.

Theme: A complaint against conspiracy. When others conspire against us, we can ask God for protection because he knows everything.
Author: David

1 Hear my voice, O God, in my [118]complaint;
Preserve my life from dread of the enemy.
2 Hide me from the secret counsel of evildoers,
From the tumult of those who do iniquity,

64:1 Ps 55:2; Ps 140:1
64:2 Ps 56:6; Ps 59:2

116 Lit *early* **117** Lit *fat* **118** Or *concern*

63:1ff Psalms 61, 62, and 63 were probably written when David was seeking refuge during Absalom's rebellion (2 Samuel 15—18).

63:1–5 Hiding from his enemies in the barren wilderness of Judah, David was intensely lonely. He longed for a friend he could trust to ease his loneliness. No wonder he cried out, "O God, . . . my soul thirsts for You, . . . in a dry and weary land." If you are lonely or thirsty for something lasting in your life, remember David's prayer. God alone can satisfy our deepest longings!

63:6 The night was divided into three watches. Someone aware of all three would be having a sleepless night. A cure for sleepless nights is to turn our thoughts to God. There are many reasons we can't sleep—illness, stress, worry—but sleepless nights can be turned into quiet times of reflection and worship. Use them to review how God has guided and helped you.

64:1ff Evil can come in the form of a secret conspiracy or an ambush because Satan wants to catch us unprepared. He tempts us in our weakest areas when we least expect it. But God himself will strike down our enemies (64:7), whether they are physical or spiritual. Wickedness is widespread and affects us in many ways, but the final victory already belongs to God and those who trust and believe in him.

64:1–2 We may believe that God wants to hear only certain requests from us. While it is true that we should offer praise, confession, and respectful petitions, it is true also that God is willing to listen to *anything* we want to tell him. David expressed himself honestly, knowing that God would hear his voice. God will always listen to us, and he will fully understand what we say.

64:3
Ps 140:3; Ps 58:7

64:4
Ps 10:8; 11:2; Ps 55:19

64:5
Ps 140:5; Job 22:13; Ps 10:11

64:6
Ps 49:11

3 Who have sharpened their tongue like a sword.
They aimed bitter speech *as* their arrow,
4 To shoot from concealment at the blameless;
Suddenly they shoot at him, and do not fear.
5 They hold fast to themselves an evil purpose;
They talk of laying snares secretly;
They say, "Who can see them?"
6 They [119]devise injustices, *saying,*
"We are ready with a well-conceived plot";
For the inward thought and the heart of a man are [120]deep.

64:7
Ps 7:12, 13

64:8
Ps 9:3; Prov 12:13; 18:7; Ps 22:7; 44:14; Jer 18:16; 48:27; Lam 2:15

64:9
Ps 40:3; Jer 51:10

64:10
Job 22:19; Ps 32:11; Ps 11:1; 25:20

7 But God will shoot at them with an arrow;
Suddenly they will be wounded.
8 So they will make him stumble;
Their own tongue is against them;
All who see them will shake the head.
9 Then all men will fear,
And they will declare the work of God,
And will consider what He has done.
10 The righteous man will be glad in the LORD and will take refuge in Him;
And all the upright in heart will glory.

PSALM 65

For the choir director. A Psalm of David. A Song.

Theme: God provides abundantly. We can be thankful to God for his many blessings.
Author: David

65:1
Ps 116:18

65:2
Ps 86:9; 145:21; Is 66:23

65:3
Ps 38:4; 40:12; Ps 79:9

65:4
Ps 33:12; 84:4; Ps 4:3; Ps 36:8

65:5
Ps 45:4; 66:3; Ps 85:4; Ps 22:27; 48:10; Ps 107:23

65:6
Ps 95:4; Ps 93:1

65:7
Ps 89:9; 93:3, 4; 107:29; Matt 8:26; Ps 2:1; 74:23; Is 17:12, 13

1 There will be silence before You, *and* praise in Zion, O God,
And to You the vow will be performed.
2 O You who hear prayer,
To You all men come.
3 Iniquities prevail against me;
As for our transgressions, You forgive them.
4 How blessed is the one whom You choose and bring near *to You*
To dwell in Your courts.
We will be satisfied with the goodness of Your house,
Your holy temple.

5 By awesome *deeds* You answer us in righteousness, O God of our salvation,
You who are the trust of all the ends of the earth and of the farthest sea;
6 Who establishes the mountains by His strength,
Being girded with might;
7 Who stills the roaring of the seas,
The roaring of their waves,

119 Or *search out* **120** Or *unsearchable*

64:3–10 The words spoken against us are among the most painful attacks we may have to face. If we trust in God, these attacks will not hurt us.

65:1–2 In Old Testament times, vows were taken seriously and fulfilled completely. No one had to make a vow, but once made, it was binding (Deuteronomy 23:21–23). The vow that is being fulfilled here is the promise to praise God for his answers to prayer.

65:3 Although we may feel overwhelmed by the multitude of our sins, God will forgive them all if we ask sincerely. Do you feel as though God could never forgive you, that your sins are too many, or that some of them are too great? The good news is that God can and will forgive them all. Nobody is beyond redemption, and nobody is so full of sin that he or she cannot be made clean.

65:4 Access to God, the joy of living in the temple courts, was a great honor. God had chosen a special group of Israelites, the tribe of Levi, to serve as priests in the tabernacle (Numbers 3:5–51). They were the only ones who could enter the sacred rooms where God's presence resided. Because of Jesus' death on the cross, all believers today have personal access to God's presence everywhere and at any time.

65:6–13 This harvest psalm glorifies God the Creator as reflected in the beauty of nature. Nature helps us understand something of God's character. The Jews believed that God's care of nature was a sign of his love and provision for them. Nature shows God's generosity—giving us more than we need or deserve. Understanding God's abundant generosity should make us grateful to God and generous to others.

And the tumult of the peoples.
8 They who dwell in the ends *of the earth* stand in awe of Your signs;
You make the dawn and the sunset shout for joy.

9 You visit the earth and cause it to overflow;
You greatly enrich it;
The stream of God is full of water;
You prepare their grain, for thus You prepare the earth.
10 You water its furrows abundantly,
You settle its ridges,
You soften it with showers,
You bless its growth.
11 You have crowned the year with Your bounty,
And Your paths drip *with* fatness.
12 The pastures of the wilderness drip,
And the hills gird themselves with rejoicing.
13 The meadows are clothed with flocks
And the valleys are covered with grain;
They shout for joy, yes, they sing.

65:8 Ps 2:8; 139:9; Is 24:16

65:9 Lev 26:4; Job 5:10; Ps 68:9; 104:13; 147:8; Jer 5:24; Ps 104:24; Ps 46:4; Ps 104:14; 147:14

65:10 Deut 32:2; Ps 72:6; 147:8

65:11 Ps 104:28; Job 36:28; Ps 147:14

65:12 Job 38:26, 27; Joel 2:22; Ps 98:8; Is 55:12

65:13 Ps 144:13; Is 30:23; Ps 72:16; Ps 98:8; Is 44:23; 55:12

PSALM 66

For the choir director. A Song. A Psalm.

Theme: God answers prayer. Individually and as a body of believers, we should praise and worship God.
Author: Anonymous, written after a great victory in battle

1 Shout joyfully to God, all the earth;
2 Sing the glory of His name;
Make His praise glorious.
3 Say to God, "How awesome are Your works!
Because of the greatness of Your power Your enemies will give feigned obedience to You.
4 "All the earth will worship You,
And will sing praises to You;
They will sing praises to Your name." Selah.

5 Come and see the works of God,
Who is awesome in *His* deeds toward the sons of men.
6 He turned the sea into dry land;
They passed through the river on foot;
There let us rejoice in Him!
7 He rules by His might forever;
His eyes keep watch on the nations;
Let not the rebellious exalt themselves. Selah.

8 Bless our God, O peoples,
And sound His praise abroad,
9 Who keeps us in life
And does not allow our feet to slip.
10 For You have tried us, O God;
You have refined us as silver is refined.
11 You brought us into the net;
You laid an oppressive burden upon our loins.

66:1 Ps 81:1; 95:1; 98:4; 100:1

66:2 Ps 79:9; Is 42:8; Is 42:12

66:3 Ps 47:2; 65:5; 145:6; Ps 18:44; 81:15

66:4 Ps 22:27; 67:7; 86:9; 117:1; Zech 14:16; Ps 67:4

66:5 Ps 46:8; Ps 106:22

66:6 Ex 14:21; Ps 106:9; Josh 3:16; Ps 114:3; Ps 105:43

66:7 Ps 145:13; Ps 11:4; Ps 140:8

66:8 Ps 98:4

66:9 Ps 30:3; Ps 121:3

66:10 Job 23:10; Ps 7:9; 17:3; 26:2; Is 48:10; Zech 13:9; Mal 3:3; 1 Pet 1:7

66:11 Lam 1:13; Ezek 12:13

66:5–7 The writer was remembering the famous story about God's rescue of the Israelites by parting the Red Sea. God saved the Israelites then, and he continues to save his people today.

66:10–12 Just as fire refines silver in the smelting process, trials refine our character. They bring us a new and deeper wisdom, helping us discern truth from falsehood and giving us the discipline to do what we know is right. Above all, these trials help us realize that life is a gift from God to be cherished, not a right to be taken for granted.

66:12 Is 51:23; Ps 78:21; Is 43:2; Ps 18:19

66:13 Ps 96:8; Jer 17:26; Ps 22:25; 116:14; Eccl 5:4

66:14 Ps 18:6

66:15 Ps 51:19; Num 6:14

12 You made men ride over our heads;
We went through fire and through water,
Yet You brought us out into *a place of* abundance.
13 I shall come into Your house with burnt offerings;
I shall pay You my vows,
14 Which my lips uttered
And my mouth spoke when I was in distress.
15 I shall offer to You burnt offerings of fat beasts,
With the smoke of rams;
I shall make *an offering of* bulls with male goats. Selah.

66:16 Ps 34:11; Ps 71:15, 24

66:17 Ps 30:1

66:18 Job 36:21; John 9:31; Job 27:9; Ps 18:41; Prov 1:28; 28:9; Is 1:15; James 4:3

66:19 Ps 18:6; 116:1, 2

66:20 Ps 68:35; Ps 22:24

16 Come *and* hear, all who [121]fear God,
And I will tell of what He has done for my soul.
17 I cried to Him with my mouth,
And He was extolled with my tongue.
18 If I [122]regard wickedness in my heart,
The Lord will not hear;
19 But certainly God has heard;
He has given heed to the voice of my prayer.
20 Blessed be God,
Who has not turned away my prayer
Nor His lovingkindness from me.

PSALM 67

For the choir director; with stringed instruments. A Psalm. A Song.

Theme: Joy comes from spreading the news about God around the world.
Author: Anonymous, possibly written for one of the harvest feasts

67:1 Num 6:25; Ps 4:6; 31:16; 80:3, 7, 19; 119:135

67:2 Ps 98:2; Acts 18:25; Titus 2:11; Is 52:10

67:3 Ps 66:4

67:4 Ps 100:1, 2; Ps 9:8; 96:10, 13; 98:9; Ps 47:8

67:5 Ps 67:3

67:6 Lev 26:4; Ps 85:12; Ezek 34:27; Zech 8:12; Ps 29:11; 115:12

67:7 Ps 22:27; 33:8

1 God be gracious to us and bless us,
And cause His face to shine upon us— Selah.
2 That Your way may be known on the earth,
Your salvation among all nations.
3 Let the peoples praise You, O God;
Let all the peoples praise You.
4 Let the nations be glad and sing for joy;
For You will judge the peoples with uprightness
And guide the nations on the earth. Selah.
5 Let the peoples praise You, O God;
Let all the peoples praise You.
6 The earth has yielded its produce;
God, our God, blesses us.
7 God blesses us,
[123]That all the ends of the earth may fear Him.

121 Or *revere* **122** Or *had regarded* **123** Or *And let all...earth fear Him*

66:13–15 People sometimes make bargains with God, saying, "If you heal me (or get me out of this mess), I'll obey you for the rest of my life." However, soon after they recover, the vow is forgotten and the old lifestyle is resumed. This writer made a promise to God, but he remembered the promise and was prepared to carry it out. God always keeps his promises and wants us to follow his example. Be careful to follow through on whatever you promise to do.

66:18 Our confession of sin must be continual because we continue to do wrong. But true confession requires us to listen to God and to want to stop doing what is wrong. David confessed his sin and prayed, "Acquit me of hidden faults. Also keep back Your servant from presumptuous sins" (19:12–13). When we *refuse* to repent or when we harbor and cherish certain sins, we place a wall between us and God. We may not be able to remember *every* sin we have ever committed, but our attitude should be one of confession and obedience.

67:2 Could the psalmist have looked across the years to see the gospel go throughout the earth? This psalm surely speaks of the fulfillment of the Great Commission (Matthew 28:18–20), when Jesus commanded that the gospel be taken to all nations. Count yourself among that great crowd of believers worldwide who know the Savior; praise him for his Good News; and share that gospel so that the harvest will be abundant.

PSALM 68

For the choir director. A Psalm of David. A Song.

Theme: Remembering God's glory and power. Times and cultures change, but God is always majestically present as defender and provider.
Author: David

1 Let God arise, let His enemies be scattered,
And let those who hate Him flee before Him.
2 As smoke is driven away, *so* drive *them* away;
As wax melts before the fire,
So let the wicked perish before God.
3 But let the righteous be glad; let them exult before God;
Yes, let them rejoice with gladness.
4 Sing to God, sing praises to His name;
Lift up *a song* for Him who rides through the deserts,
Whose name is the LORD, and exult before Him.

5 A father of the fatherless and a judge [124]for the widows,
Is God in His holy habitation.
6 God makes a home for the lonely;
He leads out the prisoners into prosperity,
Only the rebellious dwell in a parched land.

7 O God, when You went forth before Your people,
When You marched through the wilderness, Selah.
8 The earth quaked;
The heavens also dropped *rain* at the presence of God;
Sinai itself *quaked* at the presence of God, the God of Israel.
9 You shed abroad a plentiful rain, O God;
You confirmed Your inheritance when it was parched.
10 Your creatures settled in it;
You provided in Your goodness for the poor, O God.

11 The Lord gives the command;
The women who proclaim the *good* tidings are a great host:
12 "Kings of armies flee, they flee,
And she who remains at home will divide the spoil!"
13 [125]When you lie down among the [126]sheepfolds,
You are like the wings of a dove covered with silver,
And its pinions with glistening gold.
14 When the Almighty scattered the kings there,
It was snowing in Zalmon.

124 Lit *of* **125** Lit *If* **126** Or *cooking stones* or *saddle bags*

68:1 Num 10:35; Ps 12:5; 132:8
68:2 Ps 9:3; 37:20; 80:16
68:3 Ps 32:11; 64:10; 97:12
68:4 Ps 66:2; Is 57:14; 62:10; Deut 33:26; Ps 18:10; 68:33; Is 40:3; Ex 6:3; Ps 83:18
68:5 Ps 10:14; 146:9; Deut 10:18; Deut 26:15
68:6 Ps 107:4-7; 113:9; Ps 69:33; 102:20; 107:10, 14; 146:7; Acts 12:7; 16:26; Ps 78:17; 107:34, 40
68:7 Ex 13:21; Ps 78:14; Hab 3:13; Judg 5:4; Ps 78:52
68:8 Ex 19:18; Judg 5:4; 2 Sam 22:8; Ps 77:18; Jer 10:10; Judg 5:4; Ps 18:9; Is 45:8; Ex 19:18; Judg 5:5
68:9 Lev 26:4; Deut 11:11; Job 5:10; Ezek 34:26
68:10 Ps 65:9; 74:19; 78:20; 107:9
68:11 Ex 15:20; 1 Sam 18:6
68:12 Josh 10:16; Judg 5:19; Ps 135:11; Judg 5:30; 1 Sam 30:24
68:13 Gen 49:14; Judg 5:16
68:14 Josh 10:10; Judg 9:48

68:1ff This psalm begins just like Moses' cry in Numbers 10:35 as the Israelites followed the ark of the covenant. It undoubtedly brought to mind the time when David led a joyous procession that brought the ark from the house of Obed-edom to Jerusalem (2 Samuel 6:11–15).

68:3–6 With shouts of praise and the sound of trumpets, David and his people took the holy ark toward Mount Zion (2 Samuel 6:15). It was a time to sing praises to the Lord, whose presence brings great joy. Only in God is there hope for the orphans, widows, prisoners, and all other lonely people. If you are lonely or disadvantaged, join David in praise, and discover great joy from loving and praising God.

68:4–6 David praised God for his protection and provision. When we see God's true majesty, our response should be to praise him. This was a song of faith because many of these benefits had not yet come true in David's time. It should also be our song of faith. We must continue to trust God because, in time, he will fulfill all his promises.

68:8 Mount Sinai had a prominent role in Israelite history. It was at Mount Sinai that God met Moses and commissioned him to lead Israel out of Egypt (Exodus 3:1–10). It was to Mount Sinai that the nation of Israel returned and received God's laws (Exodus 19:1–3), and God's presence made the entire mountain tremble (Exodus 19:18). This sacred mountain was a constant reminder of God's words and promises.

68:13 The dove is a symbol of God's beloved Israel, who is so protected and blessed that it has taken silver and gold from its enemies, even though it stayed in camp.

68:15 Ps 36:6
68:16 Deut 12:5; Ps 87:1, 2; 132:13; Ps 132:14
68:17 2 Kin 6:17; Hab 3:8; Deut 33:2; Dan 7:10
68:18 Ps 7:7; 47:5; Eph 4:8; Judg 5:12
68:19 Ps 55:22; Is 46:4; Ps 65:5
68:20 Ps 106:43; Deut 32:39; Ps 49:15; 56:13
68:21 Ps 110:6; Hab 3:13
68:22 Num 21:33; Amos 9:1-3
68:23 Ps 58:10; 1 Kin 21:19; Jer 15:3
68:24 Ps 77:13; Ps 63:2
68:25 1 Chr 13:8; 15:6; Ps 47:6; Ex 15:20; Judg 11:34
68:26 Ps 22:22, 23; 26:12; Deut 33:28; Is 48:1
68:27 Judg 5:14; 1 Sam 9:21; Judg 5:18
68:28 Ps 29:11; 44:4; Is 26:12
68:29 1 Kin 10:10, 25; 2 Chr 32:23; Ps 45:12; 72:10; Is 18:7
68:30 Job 40:21; Ezek 29:3; Ps 22:12; Ps 18:14; 89:10
68:31 Is 19:19, 21; Is 45:14; Zeph 3:10
68:32 Ps 102:22; Ps 67:4
68:33 Deut 33:26; Ps 18:10; 104:3; Deut 10:14; 1 Kin 8:27; Ps 46:6; Ps 29:4

15 A mountain of God is the mountain of Bashan;
A mountain *of many* peaks is the mountain of Bashan.
16 Why do you look with envy, O mountains with *many* peaks,
At the mountain which God has desired for His abode?
Surely the LORD will dwell *there* forever.
17 The chariots of God are [127]myriads, thousands upon thousands;
The Lord is among them *as at* Sinai, in holiness.
18 You have ascended on high, You have led captive *Your* captives;
You have received gifts among men,
Even *among* the rebellious also, that the LORD God may dwell *there.*

19 Blessed be the Lord, who daily bears our burden,
The God *who* is our salvation. Selah.
20 God is to us a God of deliverances;
And to GOD the Lord belong escapes from death.
21 Surely God will shatter the head of His enemies,
The hairy crown of him who goes on in his guilty deeds.
22 The Lord said, "I will bring *them* back from Bashan.
I will bring *them* back from the depths of the sea;
23 That your foot may shatter *them* in blood,
The tongue of your dogs *may have* its portion from *your* enemies."

24 They have seen Your procession, O God,
The procession of my God, my King, into the sanctuary.
25 The singers went on, the musicians after *them,*
In the midst of the maidens beating tambourines.
26 Bless God in the congregations,
Even the LORD, *you who are* of the fountain of Israel.
27 There is Benjamin, the youngest, ruling them,
The princes of Judah *in* their throng,
The princes of Zebulun, the princes of Naphtali.

28 Your God has commanded your strength;
Show Yourself strong, O God, who have acted on our behalf.
29 Because of Your temple at Jerusalem
Kings will bring gifts to You.
30 Rebuke the beasts in the reeds,
The herd of bulls with the calves of the peoples,
Trampling under foot the pieces of silver;
He has scattered the peoples who delight in war.
31 Envoys will come out of Egypt;
Ethiopia will quickly stretch out her hands to God.

32 Sing to God, O kingdoms of the earth,
Sing praises to the Lord, Selah.
33 To Him who rides upon the highest heavens, which are from ancient times;
Behold, He speaks forth with His voice, a mighty voice.

127 Lit *twice ten thousand*

68:15–16 Bashan, the land northeast of Israel, was the home of mighty mountains, including Mount Hermon, the tallest and most awesome mountain in the region. God's choice of Mount Zion, a foothill by comparison, for the site of the temple led the psalmist to write poetically of the envy of the mountains of Bashan.

68:17 This psalm celebrates the final stages of a journey that began at Mount Sinai with the construction of the ark of the covenant and finally ended at Mount Zion (site of the sanctuary), the chosen dwelling place of God among his people. It may describe the moving of the ark of the covenant into Jerusalem.

68:18 This verse, quoted in Ephesians 4:8, is applied to the ministry of the ascended Christ. It celebrates his victory over evil. It assures all of us who believe in Christ that by trusting him, we can overcome evil.

68:19–21 God sets his people free and crushes his enemies. Salvation is freedom from sin and death. Those who refuse to turn to God will be crushed by sin and death. They will be trapped by the sin they loved and destroyed by the death they feared. How much better it will be for those who love God and fear the consequences of sin.

34 Ascribe strength to God;
His majesty is over Israel
And His strength is in the skies.
35 O God, *You are* awesome from Your sanctuary.
The God of Israel Himself gives strength and power to the people.
Blessed be God!

68:34 Ps 29:1; Ps 150:1
68:35 Deut 7:21; 10:17; Ps 47:2; 66:5; Ps 29:11; Is 40:29; Ps 66:20; 2 Cor 1:3

PSALM 69

For the choir director; according to [128]Shoshannim. *A Psalm* of David.

Theme: A cry of distress in a sea of trouble. We may have to suffer severely for our devotion to God, but that should cause us to look forward with joy to the day when evil and injustice will be gone forever.
Author: David

1 Save me, O God,
For the waters have threatened my life.
2 I have sunk in deep mire, and there is no foothold;
I have come into deep waters, and a flood overflows me.
3 I am weary with my crying; my throat is parched;
My eyes fail while I wait for my God.
4 Those who hate me without a cause are more than the hairs of my head;
Those who would destroy me are powerful, being wrongfully my enemies;
What I did not steal, I then have to restore.

5 O God, it is You who knows my folly,
And my wrongs are not hidden from You.
6 May those who wait for You not be ashamed through me, O Lord GOD of hosts;
May those who seek You not be dishonored through me, O God of Israel,
7 Because for Your sake I have borne reproach;
Dishonor has covered my face.
8 I have become estranged from my brothers
And an alien to my mother's sons.
9 For zeal for Your house has consumed me,
And the reproaches of those who reproach You have fallen on me.
10 When I wept in my soul with fasting,
It became my reproach.
11 When I made sackcloth my clothing,
I became a byword to them.
12 Those who sit in the gate talk about me,
And I *am* the song of the drunkards.

13 But as for me, my prayer is to You, O LORD, at an acceptable time;
O God, in the greatness of Your lovingkindness,

69:1 Job 22:11; Ps 32:6; 42:7; 69:14, 15; Jon 2:5
69:2 Ps 40:2; Jon 2:3
69:3 Ps 6:6; Deut 28:32; Ps 38:10; 119:82, 123; Is 38:14
69:4 Ps 35:19; John 15:25; Ps 35:19; 38:19; 59:3; Ps 35:11; Jer 15:10
69:5 Ps 38:5; Ps 44:21
69:6 2 Sam 12:14
69:7 Jer 15:15; Ps 44:15; Is 50:6; Jer 51:51
69:8 Job 19:13-15; Ps 31:11; 38:11
69:9 Ps 119:139; John 2:17; Ps 89:41, 50; Rom 15:3
69:10 Ps 35:13
69:11 1 Kin 20:31; Ps 35:13; 1 Kin 9:7; Job 17:6; Ps 44:14; Jer 24:9
69:12 Gen 19:1; Ruth 4:1; Job 30:9
69:13 Ps 32:6; Is 49:8; 2 Cor 6:2; Ps 51:1

128 Or possibly *Lilies*

68:34–35 When we consider all God has done for us, we should feel an overwhelming sense of awe as we kneel before the Lord in his sanctuary. Nature surrounds us with countless signs of God's wonderful power. His unlimited power and unspeakable majesty leave us breathless in his presence. How fortunate we are that God cares for us.

69:1ff This is one of the most quoted psalms in the New Testament, and it is often applied to the ministry and suffering of Jesus. Verse 4, like John 15:25, speaks of Jesus' many enemies. The experience of being scorned by his brothers (69:8) is expressed in John 7:5. Verse 9 portrays David's zeal for God; Christ showed great zeal when he threw the money changers out of the temple (John 2:14–17). Paul quoted part of 69:9 in Romans 15:3. Christ's great suffering is portrayed in 69:20–21 (Matthew 27:24; Mark 15:23; Luke 23:36; John 19:28–30). Verses 22 through 28 are quoted in Romans 11:9, 10; and Peter applied 69:25 to Judas (Acts 1:20).

69:3 David cried out until he was physically exhausted, with a parched throat and blurred vision. Yet he still trusted God to save him. When devastated by death or tragedy, we need not collapse or despair because we can turn to God and ask him to save us and help us. The tears will still come, but we will not be crying in vain.

69:13 What problems David faced! He was scoffed at, mocked, insulted, humiliated, and made the object of city-wide gossip. But still he prayed. When we are completely beaten down, we are tempted to turn from God, give up, and quit trusting him. When your situation seems hopeless, determine that no matter how bad things become you will continue to pray. God will hear your prayer, and he will rescue you. When others reject us, we need God most. Don't turn from your most faithful friend.

Answer me with Your saving truth.
14 Deliver me from the mire and do not let me sink;
May I be delivered from my foes and from the deep waters.
15 May the flood of water not overflow me
Nor the deep swallow me up,
Nor the pit shut its mouth on me.

16 Answer me, O LORD, for Your lovingkindness is good;
According to the greatness of Your compassion, turn to me,
17 And do not hide Your face from Your servant,
For I am in distress; answer me quickly.
18 Oh draw near to my soul *and* redeem it;
Ransom me because of my enemies!
19 You know my reproach and my shame and my dishonor;
All my adversaries are [129]before You.

20 Reproach has broken my heart and I am so sick.
And I looked for sympathy, but there was none,
And for comforters, but I found none.
21 They also gave me [130]gall for my food
And for my thirst they gave me vinegar to drink.

22 May their table before them become a snare;
And when they are in peace, *may it become* a trap.
23 May their eyes grow dim so that they cannot see,
And make their loins shake continually.
24 Pour out Your indignation on them,
And may Your burning anger overtake them.
25 May their camp be desolate;
May none dwell in their tents.
26 For they have persecuted him whom You Yourself have smitten,
And they tell of the pain of those whom You have wounded.
27 Add iniquity to their iniquity,
And may they not come into Your righteousness.
28 May they be blotted out of the book of life
And may they not be recorded with the righteous.

29 But I am afflicted and in pain;
May Your salvation, O God, set me *securely* on high.
30 I will praise the name of God with song
And magnify Him with thanksgiving.
31 And it will please the LORD better than an ox
Or a young bull with horns and hoofs.
32 The humble have seen *it and* are glad;
You who seek God, let your heart revive.
33 For the LORD hears the needy
And does not despise His *who are* prisoners.

34 Let heaven and earth praise Him,
The seas and everything that moves in them.

129 Or known *to You* **130** Or *poison*

69:14 Ps 69:2; Ps 144:7
69:15 Ps 124:4, 5; Ps 28:1; 141:7
69:16 Ps 63:3; 109:21; Ps 51:1; 106:45; Ps 25:16; 86:16
69:17 Ps 27:9; 102:2; 143:7; Ps 31:9; 66:14
69:18 2 Sam 4:9; Ps 26:11; 49:15
69:19 Ps 22:6; 31:11
69:20 Jer 23:9; Ps 142:4; Is 63:5; Job 16:2
69:21 Mark 15:23, 36; John 19:28-30
69:22 Rom 11:9, 10; 1 Thess 5:3
69:23 Is 6:10; Dan 5:6
69:24 Ps 79:6; Jer 10:25; Ezek 20:8; Hos 5:10
69:25 Matt 23:38; Luke 13:35; Acts 1:20
69:26 2 Chr 28:9; Zech 1:15; Is 53:4; Ps 109:22
69:27 Neh 4:5; Ps 109:14; Rom 1:28; Is 26:10; Ps 103:17
69:28 Rev 3:5; Rev 13:8; 17:8; 20:15; Ps 87:6; Luke 10:20; Heb 12:23
69:29 Ps 70:5; Ps 20:1; 59:1
69:30 Ps 28:7; Ps 34:3; Ps 50:14
69:31 Ps 50:13, 14; 51:16
69:32 Ps 34:2; Ps 22:26
69:33 Ps 12:5; Ps 68:6
69:34 Ps 96:11; 98:7

69:28 The book of life is God's list of those who are in right relationship to him and who remain faithful (1:3; 7:9; 11:7; 34:12; 37:17, 29; 55:22; 75:10; 92:12–14; 140:13). The New Testament use of "book of life" indicates those who will receive eternal life (see Philippians 4:3; Revelation 3:5; 13:8; 20:15).

69:32 When David says, "Let your heart revive!" he means, "You will feel glad and joyful." Most people want lasting joy and will try almost anything to obtain it, from scrambling for more money to being involved in sexual escapades. The only genuine source of happiness is God, and we receive lasting joy only by seeking him. How are you trying to find happiness? Seek God and live as he directs you (Matthew 6:33–34), and true joy will soon follow.

35 For God will save Zion and build the cities of Judah,
That they may dwell there and possess it.
36 The descendants of His servants will inherit it,
And those who love His name will dwell in it.

69:35 Ps 46:5; 51:18; Ps 147:2; Is 44:26; Obad 17

69:36 Ps 25:13; 102:28; Ps 37:29

PSALM 70

For the choir director. *A Psalm* of David; for a memorial.

Theme: An urgent prayer for help. It can be your prayer when you're short on time and long on need.
Author: David

1 O God, *hasten* to deliver me;
O LORD, hasten to my help!
2 Let those be ashamed and humiliated
Who seek my life;
Let those be turned back and dishonored
Who delight in my hurt.
3 Let those be turned back because of their shame
Who say, "Aha, aha!"

4 Let all who seek You rejoice and be glad in You;
And let those who love Your salvation say continually,
"Let God be magnified."
5 But I am afflicted and needy;
Hasten to me, O God!
You are my help and my deliverer;
O LORD, do not delay.

70:1 Ps 40:13-17; 70:1-5

70:2 Ps 35:4, 26

70:3 Ps 40:15

70:5 Ps 40:17; Ps 141:1

PSALM 71

Theme: God's constant help—from childhood to old age. Our lives are a testimony of what God has done for us.
Author: Anonymous

1 In You, O LORD, I have taken refuge;
Let me never be ashamed.
2 In Your righteousness deliver me and rescue me;
Incline Your ear to me and save me.
3 Be to me a rock of habitation to which I may continually come;
You have given commandment to save me,
For You are my rock and my fortress.
4 Rescue me, O my God, out of the hand of the wicked,
Out of the grasp of the wrongdoer and ruthless man,
5 For You are my hope;
O Lord GOD, *You are* my confidence from my youth.
6 By You I have been sustained from *my* birth;

71:1 Ps 25:2, 3; 31:1-3; 71:1-3

71:2 Ps 31:1; Ps 17:6

71:3 Ps 31:2, 3; Deut 33:27; Ps 90:1; 91:9; Ps 7:6; 42:8; Ps 18:2

71:4 Ps 140:1, 4

71:5 Ps 39:7; Jer 14:8; 17:7, 13, 17; 50:7; Ps 22:9

71:6 Ps 22:10; Is 46:3; Job 10:18; Ps 22:9; Ps 34:1

70:1–5 When others disappoint and threaten us, we feel empty, as though a vital part of ourselves has been stolen. When others break the trust we have placed in them, they also break our spirits. At those empty, broken moments, we must join the psalmist in begging God to rush to our aid. He alone can fill our lives with his joy (70:4). With the psalmist we should cry out, "O LORD, do not delay."

70:4 This short psalm (similar in content to 40:13–17) was David's plea for God to come quickly with his help. Yet even in his moment of panic, he did not forget praise. Praise is important because it helps us remember who God is. Often our prayers are filled with requests for ourselves and others, and we forget to thank God for what he has done and to worship him for who he is. Don't take God for granted and treat him as a vending machine. Even when David was afraid, he praised God.

71:1ff The psalmist was old and saw his life as a solemn sign or testimony to others of all God had done for him (71:7, 18). Remembering God's lifetime of blessing will help us see the consistency of his grace throughout the years, trust him for the future, and share with others the benefits of following him.

You are He who took me from my mother's womb;
My praise is continually of You.

7 I have become a marvel to many,
For You are my strong refuge.
8 My mouth is filled with Your praise
And with Your glory all day long.
9 Do not cast me off in the time of old age;
Do not forsake me when my strength fails.
10 For my enemies have spoken against me;
And those who watch for my life have consulted together,
11 Saying, "God has forsaken him;
Pursue and seize him, for there is no one to deliver."

12 O God, do not be far from me;
O my God, hasten to my help!
13 Let those who are adversaries of my soul be ashamed *and* consumed;
Let them be covered with reproach and dishonor, who seek to injure me.
14 But as for me, I will hope continually,
And will praise You yet more and more.
15 My mouth shall tell of Your righteousness
And of Your salvation all day long;
For I do not know the sum *of them.*
16 I will come with the mighty deeds of the Lord GOD;
I will make mention of Your righteousness, Yours alone.

17 O God, You have taught me from my youth,
And I still declare Your wondrous deeds.
18 And even when *I am* old and gray, O God, do not forsake me,
Until I declare Your strength to *this* generation,
Your power to all who are to come.
19 For Your righteousness, O God, *reaches* to the heavens,
You who have done great things;
O God, who is like You?
20 You who have shown [131]me many troubles and distresses
Will revive [131]me again,
And will bring [131]me up again from the depths of the earth.
21 May You increase my greatness
And turn *to* comfort me.

22 I will also praise You with a harp,
Even Your truth, O my God;
To You I will sing praises with the lyre,
O Holy One of Israel.
23 My lips will shout for joy when I sing praises to You;
And my soul, which You have redeemed.
24 My tongue also will utter Your righteousness all day long;
For they are ashamed, for they are humiliated who seek my hurt.

131 Another reading is *us*

71:7 Is 8:18; 1 Cor 4:9; Ps 61:3
71:8 Ps 35:28; 63:5; Ps 96:6; 104:1
71:9 Ps 71:18; 92:14; Is 46:4
71:10 Ps 56:6; Ps 31:13; 83:3; Matt 27:1
71:11 Ps 3:2; Ps 7:2
71:12 Ps 10:1; 22:11; 35:22; 38:21; Ps 38:22; 40:13; 70:1, 5
71:13 Ps 35:4, 26; 40:14; Ps 109:29; Esth 9:2; Ps 71:24
71:14 Ps 130:7; Ps 71:8
71:15 Ps 35:28; Ps 96:2; Ps 40:5
71:16 Ps 106:2; Ps 51:14
71:17 Deut 4:5; 6:7; Ps 26:7; 40:5; 119:27
71:18 Ps 71:9; Ps 22:31; 78:4, 6
71:19 Ps 36:6; 57:10; Ps 126:2; Luke 1:49; Deut 3:24; Ps 35:10
71:20 Ps 60:3; Ps 80:18; 85:6; 119:25; 138:7; Hos 6:1, 2; Ps 86:13
71:21 Ps 18:35; Ps 23:4; 86:17; Is 12:1; 49:13
71:22 Ps 33:2; 81:2; 92:1-3; 144:9; Ps 33:2; 147:7; 2 Kin 19:22; Ps 78:41; 89:18; Is 1:4
71:23 Ps 5:11; 32:11; 132:9, 16; Ps 34:22; 55:18; 103:4
71:24 Ps 35:28; Ps 71:13

71:14 As we face the sunset years, we recognize that God has been our constant help in the past. As physical powers wane, we need God even more, and we realize he is still our constant help. We must never despair, but keep on expecting his help no matter how severe our limitations. Hope in him helps us to keep going, to keep serving him.

71:18 A person is never too old to serve God, never too old to pray. Though age may stop us from certain physical activities, it need not end our desire to tell others (especially children) about all we have seen God do in the many years we've lived.

PSALM 72

A Psalm of Solomon.

Theme: The perfect king. In this psalm, a king asks God to help his son rule the nation justly and wisely. It looks forward to the endless reign of the Messiah, who alone can rule with perfect justice and whose citizens will enjoy perfect peace.
Author: Solomon

1 Give the king Your judgments, O God,
And Your righteousness to the king's son.
2 May he judge Your people with righteousness
And [132]Your afflicted with justice.
3 Let the mountains bring peace to the people,
And the hills, in righteousness.
4 May he vindicate the afflicted of the people,
Save the children of the needy
And crush the oppressor.

5 Let them fear You while the sun *endures,*
And as long as the moon, throughout all generations.
6 May he come down like rain upon the mown grass,
Like showers that water the earth.
7 In his days may the righteous flourish,
And abundance of peace till the moon is no more.

8 May he also rule from sea to sea
And from the River to the ends of the earth.
9 Let the nomads of the desert bow before him,
And his enemies lick the dust.
10 Let the kings of Tarshish and of the islands bring presents;
The kings of Sheba and Seba offer gifts.
11 And let all kings bow down before him,
All nations serve him.

12 For he will deliver the needy when he cries for help,
The afflicted also, and him who has no helper.
13 He will have compassion on the poor and needy,
And the lives of the needy he will save.
14 He will rescue their life from oppression and violence,
And their blood will be precious in his sight;
15 So may he live, and may the gold of Sheba be given to him;
And let them pray for him continually;
Let them bless him all day long.

16 May there be abundance of grain in the earth on top of the mountains;
Its fruit will wave like *the cedars of* Lebanon;
And may those from the city flourish like vegetation of the earth.
17 May his name endure forever;
May his name increase as long as the sun *shines;*
And let *men* bless themselves by him;
Let all nations call him blessed.

132 Or *Your humble*

72:1
1 Kin 3:9; 1 Chr 22:13; Ps 24:5

72:2
Is 9:7; 11:2-5; 32:1; Ps 82:3

72:3
Is 2:4; 9:5, 6; Mic 4:3, 4; Zech 9:10

72:4
Is 11:4

72:5
Ps 72:17; 89:36, 37

72:6
Deut 32:2; 2 Sam 23:4; Hos 6:3; Ps 65:10

72:7
Ps 92:12; Is 2:4

72:8
Ex 23:31; Zech 9:10

72:9
Ps 74:14; Is 23:13; Ps 22:29; Is 49:23; Mic 7:17

72:10
2 Chr 9:21; Ps 48:7; Ps 97:1; Is 42:4, 10; Zeph 2:11; 1 Kin 10:1; Job 6:19; Is 60:6; Gen 10:7; Is 43:3; Ps 45:12; 68:29

72:11
Ps 138:4; Is 49:23; Ps 86:9

72:12
Job 29:12; Ps 72:4

72:13
Prov 19:17; 28:8

72:14
Ps 69:18; 1 Sam 26:21; Ps 116:15

72:15
Is 60:6

72:16
Ps 104:16; Job 5:25

72:17
Ex 3:15; Ps 135:13; Ps 89:36; Gen 12:3; 22:18; Luke 1:48

72:1–2 What qualities do we want most in our leaders? God desires all who rule under him to be righteous and just. Think how the world would change if world leaders would commit themselves to these two qualities. Let us pray that they will (see 1 Timothy 2:1–2).

72:12–14 God cares for the needy, the afflicted, and the weak because they are precious to him. If God feels so strongly about these needy ones and loves them so deeply, how can we ignore their plight? Examine what you are doing to reach out with God's love—are you ignoring their plight or are you meeting their needs?

72:17 Solomon, David's son, reigned in Israel's golden age. He built the magnificent temple, and the land rested in peace. This psalm, though written by Solomon, looks beyond Solomon's reign to that of Jesus the Messiah, whose kingdom extends "to the ends of the earth" (72:8) and is greater than any human empire. This will be fulfilled when Christ returns to reign forever (Revelation 11:15). When we anticipate his worldwide rule, it fills our hearts with hope.

72:18 1 Chr 29:10; Ps 41:13; 89:52; 106:48; Ex 15:11; Job 5:9; Ps 77:14; 86:10; 136:4

72:19 Neh 9:5; Ps 96:8; Num 14:21; Ps 41:13

18 Blessed be the LORD God, the God of Israel,
Who alone works wonders.
19 And blessed be His glorious name forever;
And may the whole earth be filled with His glory.
Amen, and Amen.

20 The prayers of David the son of Jesse are ended.

BOOK 3
PSALMS 73:1—89:52

These psalms celebrate the sovereignty of God, God's hand in history, God's faithfulness, and God's covenant with David. These psalms remind us that our worship of the almighty God should be continual.

PSALM 73

A Psalm of Asaph.

Theme: The temporary prosperity of the wicked and the lasting rewards of the righteous. We should live holy lives and trust God for our future rewards.
Author: Asaph, a leader of one of the temple choirs (see 1 Chronicles 25:1)

73:1 Ps 86:5; Ps 24:4; 51:10; Matt 5:8

73:2 Ps 94:18

73:3 Ps 37:1; Prov 23:17; Job 21:7; Ps 37:7; Jer 12:1

73:5 Job 21:9; Ps 73:12; Ps 73:14

73:6 Gen 41:42; Prov 1:9; Ps 109:18

73:7 Job 15:27; Ps 17:10; Jer 5:28

73:8 Ps 1:1; Ps 17:10; 2 Pet 2:18; Jude 16

73:9 Rev 13:6

73:10 Ps 23:5

73:11 Job 22:13

73:12 Ps 49:6; 52:7; Jer 49:31; Ezek 23:42

73:13 Job 21:15; 34:9; 35:3; Ps 26:6

1 Surely God is good to Israel,
To those who are pure in heart!
2 But as for me, my feet came close to stumbling,
My steps had almost slipped.
3 For I was envious of the arrogant
As I saw the prosperity of the wicked.
4 For there are no pains in their death,
And their body is fat.
5 They are not in trouble *as other* men,
Nor are they plagued like mankind.
6 Therefore pride is their necklace;
The garment of violence covers them.
7 Their eye bulges from fatness;
The imaginations of *their* heart run riot.
8 They mock and wickedly speak of oppression;
They speak from on high.
9 They have set their mouth against the heavens,
And their tongue parades through the earth.

10 Therefore his people return to this place,
And waters of abundance are drunk by them.
11 They say, "How does God know?
And is there knowledge with the Most High?"
12 Behold, these are the wicked;
And always at ease, they have increased *in* wealth.
13 Surely in vain I have kept my heart pure
And washed my hands in innocence;

72:19–20 Book 2 ends with "Amen, and Amen," as did Psalm 41, which closed Book 1 This last verse does not mean that David wrote this psalm, but that he wrote most of the psalms in Book 2.

73:1ff Asaph was the leader of one of David's Levitical choirs. He collected Psalms 73—83 but may not have written all of them. In this psalm, Asaph explains that until he entered God's sanctuary, he could not understand the justice in allowing the wicked to thrive while the righteous endured hardship. But when he saw that one day justice would be done, he acknowledged God's wisdom.

73:1–20 Two strong themes wind their way through these verses: (1) The wicked prosper, leaving faithful people wondering why they bother to be good, and (2) the wealth of the wicked looks so inviting that faithful people may wish they could trade places. But these two themes come to unexpected ends, for the wealth of the wicked suddenly loses its power at death and the rewards for the good suddenly take on eternal value. What seemed like wealth is now waste, and what seemed worthless now lasts forever. Don't wish you could trade places with evil people to get their wealth. One day they will wish they could trade places with you and have your eternal wealth.

14 For I have been stricken all day long
And chastened every morning.

15 If I had said, "I will speak thus,"
Behold, I would have betrayed the generation of Your children.
16 When I pondered to understand this,
It was troublesome in my sight
17 Until I came into the sanctuary of God;
Then I perceived their end.
18 Surely You set them in slippery places;
You cast them down to destruction.
19 How they are destroyed in a moment!
They are utterly swept away by sudden terrors!
20 Like a dream when one awakes,
O Lord, when aroused, You will despise their form.

21 When my heart was embittered
And I was pierced within,
22 Then I was senseless and ignorant;
I was *like* a beast before You.
23 Nevertheless I am continually with You;
You have taken hold of my right hand.
24 With Your counsel You will guide me,
And afterward receive me to glory.

25 Whom have I in heaven *but You?*
And besides You, I desire nothing on earth.
26 My flesh and my heart may fail,
But God is the strength of my heart and my portion forever.
27 For, behold, those who are far from You will perish;
You have destroyed all those who are unfaithful to You.
28 But as for me, the nearness of God is my good;
I have made the Lord GOD my refuge,
That I may tell of all Your works.

73:14 Ps 38:6; Job 33:19; Ps 118:18
73:16 Eccl 8:17
73:17 Ps 27:4; 77:13; Ps 37:38
73:18 Ps 35:6; Ps 35:8; 36:12
73:19 Num 16:21; Is 47:11; Job 18:11
73:20 Job 20:8; Ps 78:65; 1 Sam 2:30
73:21 Judg 10:16; Acts 2:37
73:22 Ps 49:10; 92:6; Job 18:3; Ps 49:20; Eccl 3:18
73:23 Ps 16:8
73:24 Ps 32:8; 48:14; Is 58:11; Gen 5:24; Ps 49:15
73:25 Ps 16:2; Phil 3:8
73:26 Ps 38:10; 40:12; 84:2; 119:81; Ps 16:5
73:27 Ps 119:155; Ps 37:20; Ex 34:15; Num 15:39; Ps 106:39; Hos 4:12; 9:1
73:28 Ps 65:4; Heb 10:22; James 4:8; Ps 14:6; 71:7; Ps 40:5; 107:22; 118:17

PSALM 74

A Maskil of Asaph.

Theme: A plea for God to help his people defend his cause and remember his promises. When we feel devastated or forgotten, we can plead to God for help, knowing that he hears.
Author: Asaph (or one of his descendants, since many believe this to be written after Jerusalem's fall in 586 B.C.)

1 O God, why have You rejected *us* forever?
Why does Your anger smoke against the sheep of Your pasture?
2 Remember Your congregation, which You have purchased of old,
Which You have redeemed to be the tribe of Your inheritance;
And this Mount Zion, where You have dwelt.
3 Turn Your footsteps toward the perpetual ruins;
The enemy has damaged everything within the sanctuary.

74:1 Ps 44:9; 77:7; Deut 29:20; Ps 18:8; 89:46; Ps 79:13; 95:7; 100:3
74:2 Ex 15:16; Deut 32:6; Ex 15:13; Ps 77:15; 106:10; Is 63:9; Deut 32:9; Is 63:17; Jer 10:16; 51:19; Ps 9:11; 68:16
74:3 Is 61:4; Ps 79:1

73:20 Asaph realized that the rich who put their hope, joy, and confidence in their wealth live in a dreamworld. A dream exists only in the mind of the dreamer. Don't let your life's goals be so unreal that you awaken too late and miss the reality of God's truth. Happiness and hope can be a reality, but only when they are based on God, not on riches. Because reality is in God, we should get as close to him as we can in order to be realistic about life.

73:23–24 Asaph declares his confidence in God's presence and guidance. From birth to death God has us continually in his grip. But far more, we have the hope of the resurrection. Though our courage and strength may fail, we know that one day we will be raised to life to serve him forever. He is our security, and we must cling to him.

74:1–2 God's anger against Israel had grown hot during the many years of their sin and idolatry. His patience endured for generations, but at last it was set aside for judgment. If you fall into sin and quickly seek God's forgiveness, his mercy may come quickly and his anger may leave quickly. If you persist in sinning against him, don't be surprised when his patience runs out.

74:4 Lam 2:7; Num 2:2
74:6 1 Kin 6:18, 29, 32, 35
74:7 2 Kin 25:9; Ps 89:39; Lam 2:2
74:9 Ps 78:43; 1 Sam 3:1; Lam 2:9; Ezek 7:26; Amos 8:11; Ps 6:3; 79:5; 80:4
74:10 Ps 44:16; 79:12; 89:51; Lev 24:16
74:11 Lam 2:3; Ps 59:13
74:12 Ps 44:4
74:13 Ex 14:21; Ps 78:13; Is 51:9; Ps 148:7; Jer 51:34
74:14 Job 41:1; Ps 104:26; Is 27:1; Ps 72:9
74:15 Ps 78:15; 105:41; 114:8; Is 48:21; Ex 14:21, 22
74:16 Gen 1:14-18; Ps 104:19; 136:7, 8
74:17 Deut 32:8; Acts 17:26; Gen 8:22; Ps 147:16-18
74:18 Ps 74:10; Deut 32:6; Ps 14:1; 39:8; 53:1
74:19 Song 2:14; Ps 9:18
74:20 Gen 17:7; Ps 106:45; Ps 88:6
74:21 Ps 103:6; Ps 35:10; Is 41:17
74:22 Ps 43:1; Is 3:13; 43:26; Ezek 20:35; Ps 14:1; 53:1; 74:18
74:23 Ps 74:10; Ps 65:7

4 Your adversaries have roared in the midst of Your meeting place;
They have set up their own standards for signs.
5 It seems as if one had lifted up
His axe in a forest of trees.
6 And now all its carved work
They smash with hatchet and hammers.
7 They have burned Your sanctuary to the ground;
They have defiled the dwelling place of Your name.
8 They said in their heart, "Let us completely subdue them."
They have burned all the meeting places of God in the land.
9 We do not see our signs;
There is no longer any prophet,
Nor is there any among us who knows how long.
10 How long, O God, will the adversary revile,
And the enemy spurn Your name forever?
11 Why do You withdraw Your hand, even Your right hand?
From within Your bosom, destroy *them!*

12 Yet God is my king from of old,
Who works deeds of deliverance in the midst of the earth.
13 [133]You divided the sea by Your strength;
You broke the heads of the sea monsters in the waters.
14 You crushed the heads of Leviathan;
You gave him as food for the creatures of the wilderness.
15 You broke open springs and torrents;
You dried up ever-flowing streams.
16 Yours is the day, Yours also is the night;
You have prepared the light and the sun.
17 You have established all the boundaries of the earth;
You have made summer and winter.

18 Remember this, O LORD, that the enemy has reviled,
And a foolish people has spurned Your name.
19 Do not deliver the soul of Your turtledove to the wild beast;
Do not forget the life of Your afflicted forever.
20 Consider the covenant;
For the dark places of the land are full of the habitations of violence.
21 Let not the oppressed return dishonored;
Let the afflicted and needy praise Your name.

22 Arise, O God, *and* plead Your own cause;
Remember how the foolish man reproaches You all day long.
23 Do not forget the voice of Your adversaries,
The uproar of those who rise against You which ascends continually.

133 Or *You Yourself*

74:8 When enemy armies defeated Israel, they sacked and burned Jerusalem, trying to wipe out every trace of God. This has often been the response of people who hate God. Today many are trying to erase God from traditions in our society and from subjects taught in our schools. Do what you can to maintain a Christian influence, but don't become discouraged when others appear to make great strides in eliminating all traces of God—they cannot eliminate his presence among believers.

74:10–18 From our perspective, God sometimes seems slow to intervene on our behalf. But what might appear slow to us is good timing from God's perspective. It's easy to become impatient while waiting for God to act, but we must never give up on him. When God is silent and you are in deep anguish, follow the method in this psalm. Review the great acts of God throughout Biblical history; then review what he has done for you. This will remind you that God is at work, not only in history, but also in your life today.

74:13–14 "Sea monsters in the waters" recalls the Lord's words to Egypt (Ezekiel 32:2ff). "Leviathan" refers to the Canaanite seven-headed serpent, Lotan. In their legends, Baal defeated these creatures. This psalm praised God for doing in reality what the Canaanite gods could only do in legends.

PSALM 75

For the choir director; *set to* Al-tashheth.
A Psalm of Asaph, a Song.

Theme: Because God is the final judge, the tables will be turned upon the wicked. When arrogant people threaten our security, we can be confident that God will ultimately overrule and destroy them.
Author: Asaph

1 We give thanks to You, O God, we give thanks,
For Your name is near;
Men declare Your wondrous works.
2 "When I select an appointed time,
It is I who judge with equity.
3 "The earth and all who dwell in it [134]melt;
It is I who have firmly set its pillars. Selah.
4 "I said to the boastful, 'Do not boast,'
And to the wicked, 'Do not lift up the horn;
5 Do not lift up your horn on high,
Do not speak with insolent pride.' "

6 For not from the east, nor from the west,
Nor from the desert *comes* exaltation;
7 But God is the Judge;
He puts down one and exalts another.
8 For a cup is in the hand of the LORD, and the wine foams;
It is well mixed, and He pours out of this;
Surely all the wicked of the earth must drain *and* drink down its dregs.

9 But as for me, I will declare *it* forever;
I will sing praises to the God of Jacob.
10 And all the horns of the wicked He will cut off,
But the horns of the righteous will be lifted up.

75:1 Ps 79:13; Ps 145:18; Ps 26:7; 44:1; 71:17
75:2 Ps 102:13; Ps 9:8; 67:4; Is 11:4
75:3 Ps 46:6; Is 24:19; 1 Sam 2:8
75:4 Zech 1:21
75:5 1 Sam 2:3; Ps 94:4
75:6 Ps 3:3
75:7 Ps 50:6; 1 Sam 2:7; Ps 147:6; Dan 2:21
75:8 Job 21:20; Ps 11:6; 60:3; Jer 25:15; Prov 23:30; Obad 16
75:9 Ps 22:22; 40:10
75:10 Ps 101:8; Jer 48:25; 1 Sam 2:1; Ps 89:17; 92:10; 148:14

PSALM 76

For the choir director; on stringed instruments.
A Psalm of Asaph, a Song.

Theme: A call for God to punish evildoers. Even man's angry revolt will be used by God to bring glory to himself.
Author: Asaph

1 God is known in Judah;
His name is great in Israel.
2 His tabernacle is in Salem;
His dwelling place also is in Zion.
3 There He broke the flaming arrows,
The shield and the sword and the weapons of war. Selah.

76:1 Ps 48:3; Ps 99:3
76:2 Ps 27:5; Lam 2:6; Gen 14:18; Ps 9:11; 132:13; 135:21
76:3 Ps 46:9

134 Or *totter*

75:2 God will act when he is ready. Children have difficulty grasping the concept of time. "It's not time yet" is not a reason they easily understand because they only comprehend the present. As limited human beings, we can't understand God's perspective about time. We want everything now, unaware that God's timing is better. When God is ready, he will do what needs to be done, not what we would like him to do. We may be as impatient as children, but we must not doubt the wisdom of God's timing. Wait for God to reveal his plan. Don't take matters into your own hands.

75:8 The cup of wine represents God's judgment. The judgment of God is coming against the wicked. God will pour out his fury on his enemies, and they will be forced to drink it. Drinking the cup of God's judgment is a picture used frequently in Scripture (Isaiah 51:17, 22; Jeremiah 25:15; 49:12; Habakkuk 2:16; Revelation 14:10; 16:19; 18:6). It gives the impression of taking a dose of one's own medicine. To drink it down to the dregs means to be punished completely.

76:1ff This psalm praises God for his awesome power. It was most likely written to celebrate the defeat of Sennacherib's army after he invaded Judah (see 2 Kings 18:13–19, 37).

4 You are resplendent,
More majestic than the mountains of prey.
5 The stouthearted were plundered,
They sank into sleep;
And none of the warriors could use his hands.
6 At Your rebuke, O God of Jacob,
Both rider and horse were cast into a dead sleep.
7 You, even You, are to be feared;
And who may stand in Your presence when once You are angry?

8 You caused judgment to be heard from heaven;
The earth feared and was still
9 When God arose to judgment,
To save all the humble of the earth. Selah.
10 For the wrath of man shall praise You;
With a remnant of wrath You will gird Yourself.

11 Make vows to the LORD your God and fulfill *them;*
Let all who are around Him bring gifts to Him who is to be feared.
12 He will cut off the spirit of princes;
He is feared by the kings of the earth.

76:5 Is 10:12; 46:12
76:6 Ps 80:16; Ex 15:1, 21; Ps 78:53
76:7 1 Chr 16:25; Ps 89:7; 96:4; Ezra 9:15; Ps 130:3; Nah 1:6; Mal 3:2; Rev 6:17
76:8 1 Chr 16:30; 2 Chr 20:29, 30; Ps 33:8
76:9 Ps 9:7, 8; 74:22; 82:8
76:10 Ex 9:16; Rom 9:17
76:11 Eccl 5:4-6; Ps 50:14; 2 Chr 32:23; Ps 68:29
76:12 Ps 47:2

PSALM 77

For the choir director; according to Jeduthun. A Psalm of Asaph.

Theme: We are comforted through the hard times by remembering God's help in the past. Recalling God's miracles and previous works can give us courage to continue.
Author: Asaph

1 My voice *rises* to God, and I will cry aloud;
My voice *rises* to God, and He will hear me.
2 In the day of my trouble I sought the Lord;
In the night my hand was stretched out [135]without weariness;
My soul refused to be comforted.
3 *When* I remember God, then I am disturbed;
When I sigh, then my spirit grows faint. Selah.
4 You have held my eyelids *open;*
I am so troubled that I cannot speak.
5 I have considered the days of old,
The years of long ago.
6 I will remember my song in the night;
I will meditate with my heart,
And my spirit ponders:

7 Will the Lord reject forever?
And will He never be favorable again?
8 Has His lovingkindness ceased forever?
Has *His* promise come to an end forever?
9 Has God forgotten to be gracious,

77:1 Ps 3:4; 142:1
77:2 Ps 50:15; 86:7; Ps 63:6; Is 26:9; Job 11:13; Ps 88:9; Gen 37:35
77:3 Ps 42:5, 11; 43:5; Ps 55:2; 142:2; Ps 61:2; 143:4
77:4 Ps 39:9
77:5 Deut 32:7; Ps 44:1; 143:5; Is 51:9
77:6 Ps 42:8; Ps 4:4
77:7 Ps 44:9; Ps 85:1, 5
77:8 Ps 89:49; 2 Pet 3:9
77:9 Is 49:15; Ps 25:6; 40:11; 51:1

135 Lit *and did not grow numb*

76:10 How can wrath bring praise to God? Hostility to God and his people gives God the opportunity to do great deeds. For example, the Pharaoh of Egypt refused to free the Hebrew slaves (Exodus 5:1–2) and thus allowed God to work mighty miracles for his people (Exodus 11:9). God turns the tables on evildoers and brings glory to himself from the foolishness of those who deny him or revolt against him. God's wrath expressed in judgment brings praise from those who have been delivered.

77:1–12 Asaph cried out to God for courage during a time of deep distress. The source of Asaph's distress (77:4) was his doubt (77:7–9). He pled, "My voice rises to God, and I will cry aloud." But in 77:13–20, the "I" is gone. As Asaph expressed his requests to God, his focus changed from thinking of himself to worshiping God: "You are the God who works wonders" (77:14). Only after he put aside his doubts about God's holiness and care for him (77:13–14) did he eliminate his distress (77:20). As we pray to God, he shifts our focus from ourselves to him.

Or has He in anger withdrawn His compassion? Selah.
10 Then I said, "It is my grief,
That the right hand of the Most High has changed."

11 I shall remember the deeds of the LORD;
Surely I will remember Your wonders of old.
12 I will meditate on all Your work
And muse on Your deeds.
13 Your way, O God, is holy;
What god is great like our God?
14 You are the God who works wonders;
You have made known Your strength among the peoples.
15 You have by Your power redeemed Your people,
The sons of Jacob and Joseph. Selah.

16 The waters saw You, O God;
The waters saw You, they were in anguish;
The deeps also trembled.
17 The clouds poured out water;
The skies gave forth a sound;
Your arrows flashed here and there.
18 The sound of Your thunder was in the whirlwind;
The lightnings lit up the world;
The earth trembled and shook.
19 Your way was in the sea
And Your paths in the mighty waters,
And Your footprints may not be known.
20 You led Your people like a flock
By the hand of Moses and Aaron.

77:10 Ps 31:22; 73:14; Ps 44:2, 3
77:11 Ps 105:5; 143:5
77:12 Ps 145:5
77:13 Ps 63:2; 73:17; Ex 15:11; Ps 71:19; 86:8
77:14 Ps 72:18; Ps 106:8
77:15 Ex 6:6; Deut 9:29; Ps 74:2; 78:42; Ps 80:1
77:16 Ex 14:21; Ps 114:3; Hab 3:8, 10
77:17 Judg 5:4; Ps 68:33; Ps 18:14
77:18 Ps 18:13; 104:7; Ps 97:4; Judg 5:4; Ps 18:7
77:19 Is 51:10; Hab 3:15
77:20 Ex 13:21; 14:19; Ps 78:52; 80:1; Is 63:11-13; Ex 6:26; Ps 105:26

PSALM 78

A Maskil of Asaph.

Theme: Lessons from history. Asaph retells the history of the Jewish nation from the time of slavery in Egypt to David's reign. It was told over and over to each generation so they would not forget God and make the same mistakes as their ancestors.
Author: Asaph

1 Listen, O my people, to my instruction;
Incline your ears to the words of my mouth.
2 I will open my mouth in a parable;
I will utter dark sayings of old,
3 Which we have heard and known,
And our fathers have told us.
4 We will not conceal them from their children,
But tell to the generation to come the praises of the LORD,
And His strength and His wondrous works that He has done.

5 For He established a testimony in Jacob
And appointed a law in Israel,

78:1 Is 51:4; Is 55:3
78:2 Ps 49:4; Matt 13:35; Prov 1:6
78:3 Ps 44:1
78:4 Ex 12:26; Deut 6:7; 11:19; Job 15:18; Ps 145:4; Is 38:19; Joel 1:3; Ex 13:8, 14; Ps 22:30; Job 37:16; Ps 26:7; 71:17
78:5 Ps 19:7; 81:5; Is 8:20; Ps 147:19; Deut 6:4-9; Deut 4:9

77:11–12 Memories of God's miracles and faithfulness sustained Israel through their difficulties. They knew that God was capable and trustworthy. When you meet new trials, review how good God has been to you, and this will strengthen your faith.

77:16 This statement refers to the miraculous parting of the Red Sea. This great event is mentioned many times in the Old Testament (Exodus 14:21–22; Joshua 24:6; Nehemiah 9:9; Psalm 74:13; 106:9; 136:13–15). The story of this incredible miracle was handed down from generation to generation, reminding the Israelites of God's power, protection, and love.

78:1ff The people of Israel rebelled and were not faithful to God (78:8); forgot about the wonders God had done (78:11–12); put God to the test by making demands of him (78:18); lied to him and tried to flatter him (78:36); and continued to turn away from him even after he did great works on their behalf (78:42–56). This is recorded in God's Word so that we can avoid the same errors. In 1 Corinthians 10:5–12, Paul used this classic story of Israel's unfaithfulness to warn the early Christians to be faithful.

78:5 God commanded that the stories of his mighty acts in Israel's history and his laws be passed on from parents to children. This shows the purpose and importance of religious education—to help

78:6 Ps 22:31; Deut 11:19
78:7 Deut 4:9; 6:12; 8:14; Deut 4:2; 5:1, 29; 27:1; Josh 22:5
78:8 2 Kin 17:14; 2 Chr 30:7; Ezek 20:18; Ex 32:9; Deut 9:7, 24; 31:27; Judg 2:19; Is 30:9; Job 11:13; Ps 78:37; Ps 51:10
78:9 1 Chr 12:2
78:10 Judg 2:20; 1 Kin 11:11; 2 Kin 17:15; 18:12; Ps 119:1; Jer 32:23; 44:10, 23
78:11 Ps 106:13
78:12 Ex chs 7-12; Ps 106:22; Num 13:22
78:13 Ex 14:21; Ps 74:13; 136:13; Ex 15:8; Ps 33:7
78:14 Ex 13:21; Ps 105:39; Ex 14:24
78:15 Ex 17:6; Num 20:11; Ps 105:41; 114:8; Is 48:21; 1 Cor 10:4
78:16 Num 20:8, 10, 11
78:17 Deut 9:22; Is 63:10; Heb 3:16
78:18 Ex 17:6; Deut 6:16; 1 Cor 10:9; Num 11:4
78:19 Ex 16:3; Num 11:4; 20:3; 21:5; Ps 23:5
78:20 Num 20:11; Num 11:18
78:21 Num 11:1
78:22 Deut 1:32; 9:23; Heb 3:18
78:23 Gen 7:11; Mal 3:10
78:24 Ex 16:4; Ps 105:40; John 6:31
78:25 Ex 16:3

Which He commanded our fathers
That they should teach them to their children,
6 That the generation to come might know, *even* the children *yet* to be born,
That they may arise and tell *them* to their children,
7 That they should put their confidence in God
And not forget the works of God,
But keep His commandments,
8 And not be like their fathers,
A stubborn and rebellious generation,
A generation that did not [136]prepare its heart
And whose spirit was not faithful to God.

9 The sons of Ephraim were archers equipped with bows,
Yet they turned back in the day of battle.
10 They did not keep the covenant of God
And refused to walk in His law;
11 They forgot His deeds
And His miracles that He had shown them.
12 He wrought wonders before their fathers
In the land of Egypt, in the field of Zoan.
13 He divided the sea and caused them to pass through,
And He made the waters stand up like a heap.
14 Then He led them with the cloud by day
And all the night with a light of fire.
15 He split the rocks in the wilderness
And gave *them* abundant drink like the ocean depths.
16 He brought forth streams also from the rock
And caused waters to run down like rivers.

17 Yet they still continued to sin against Him,
To rebel against the Most High in the desert.
18 And in their heart they put God to the test
By asking food according to their desire.
19 Then they spoke against God;
They said, "Can God prepare a table in the wilderness?
20 "Behold, He struck the rock so that waters gushed out,
And streams were overflowing;
Can He give bread also?
Will He provide meat for His people?"

21 Therefore the LORD heard and was full of wrath;
And a fire was kindled against Jacob
And anger also mounted against Israel,
22 Because they did not believe in God
And did not trust in His salvation.
23 Yet He commanded the clouds above
And opened the doors of heaven;
24 He rained down manna upon them to eat
And gave them food from heaven.
25 Man did eat the bread of angels;
He sent them food in abundance.

136 Or *put right*

each generation obey God and set their hope on him. It is important to keep children from repeating the same mistakes as their ancestors. What are you doing to pass on the history of God's work to the next generation?

78:9–10 Ephraim was the most prominent tribe of Israel from the days of Moses to Saul's time. The tabernacle was set up in its territory. There is no other Biblical record of Ephraim's soldiers turning back from battle, so this is probably a metaphor referring to Ephraim's failure to provide strong leadership during those years. When David became king, the tribe of Judah gained prominence. Because of David's faith and obedience, God chose Jerusalem in Judah to be the place for the new temple and rejected Ephraim (78:67). This caused tension between the two tribes. This psalm may have been written because of that tension in order to demonstrate once again why God chose Judah. God works through those who are faithful to him.

26 He caused the east wind to blow in the heavens
And by His power He directed the south wind.
27 When He rained meat upon them like the dust,
Even winged fowl like the sand of the seas,
28 Then He let *them* fall in the midst of their camp,
Round about their dwellings.
29 So they ate and were well filled,
And their desire He gave to them.
30 Before they had satisfied their desire,
While their food was in their mouths,
31 The anger of God rose against them
And killed some of their stoutest ones,
And subdued the choice men of Israel.
32 In spite of all this they still sinned
And did not believe in His wonderful works.
33 So He brought their days to an end in futility
And their years in sudden terror.

34 When He killed them, then they sought Him,
And returned and searched diligently for God;
35 And they remembered that God was their rock,
And the Most High God their Redeemer.
36 But they deceived Him with their mouth
And lied to Him with their tongue.
37 For their heart was not steadfast toward Him,
Nor were they faithful in His covenant.
38 But He, being compassionate, forgave *their* iniquity and did not destroy *them;*
And often He restrained His anger
And did not arouse all His wrath.
39 Thus He remembered that they were but flesh,
A wind that passes and does not return.

40 How often they rebelled against Him in the wilderness
And grieved Him in the desert!
41 Again and again they [137]tempted God,
And pained the Holy One of Israel.
42 They did not remember His power,
The day when He redeemed them from the adversary,
43 When He performed His signs in Egypt
And His marvels in the field of Zoan,
44 And turned their rivers to blood,
And their streams, they could not drink.
45 He sent among them swarms of flies which devoured them,
And frogs which destroyed them.
46 He gave also their crops to the grasshopper
And the product of their labor to the locust.
47 He destroyed their vines with hailstones
And their sycamore trees with frost.
48 He gave over their cattle also to the hailstones
And their herds to bolts of lightning.
49 He sent upon them His burning anger,
Fury and indignation and trouble,
A band of destroying angels.
50 He leveled a path for His anger;

137 Or *put God to the test*

78:26 Num 11:31
78:27 Ex 16:13; Ps 105:40
78:29 Num 11:19, 20
78:30 Num 11:33
78:31 Num 11:33, 34
78:32 Num chs 14, 16, 17; Num 14:11; Ps 78:11
78:33 Num 14:29, 35
78:34 Num 21:7; Hos 5:15
78:35 Deut 32:4; Ex 15:13; Deut 9:26; Ps 74:2; Is 41:14
78:36 Ex 24:7, 8; Ezek 33:31; Ex 32:7, 8; Is 57:11
78:37 Ps 51:10; 78:8; Acts 8:21
78:38 Ex 34:6; Num 14:18-20; Is 48:9
78:39 Job 10:9; Ps 103:14; Ps 103:14; James 4:14
78:40 Ps 95:8, 9; 106:43; 107:11; Heb 3:16; Ps 95:10; Is 63:10
78:41 Num 14:22; 2 Kin 19:22; Ps 89:18
78:42 Judg 8:34; Ps 44:3; Ps 106:10
78:43 Ps 105:27; Ex 4:21; 7:3
78:44 Ex 7:20; Ps 105:29
78:45 Ex 8:24; Ps 105:31; Ex 8:6; Ps 105:30
78:46 1 Kin 8:37; Ps 105:34; Ex 10:14
78:47 Ex 9:23-25
78:48 Ex 9:19
78:49 Ex 15:7
78:50 Ex 12:29, 30

78:36–37 Over and over the children of Israel claimed that they would follow God, but then they turned away from him. The problem was that they followed God with words and not with their hearts; thus their repentance was empty. Talk is cheap. God wants our conduct to back up our spiritual claims and promises.

78:51 Ex 12:29; Ps 105:36; 135:8; 136:10; Gen 49:3; Ps 105:23, 27; 106:22
78:52 Ex 15:22; Ps 77:20
78:53 Ex 14:19, 20; Ex 14:27, 28; Ps 106:11
78:54 Ex 15:17; Ps 68:16; Is 11:9; Ps 44:3
78:55 Josh 11:16-23; Ps 44:2; Josh 13:7; 23:4; Ps 105:11
78:56 Judg 2:11-13
78:57 Ezek 20:27, 28; Hos 7:16
78:58 Deut 4:25; Judg 2:12; 1 Kin 14:9; Deut 32:16, 21; 1 Kin 14:22; Ex 20:4
78:59 Deut 1:34; 9:19; Ps 106:40; Lev 26:30; Deut 32:19; Amos 6:8
78:60 1 Sam 4:11; Ps 78:67; Jer 7:12, 14
78:61 Ps 63:2; 132:8; 1 Sam 4:17
78:62 Judg 20:21; 1 Sam 4:10
78:64 1 Sam 4:17; 22:18; Job 27:15; Ezek 24:23
78:65 Ps 44:23; 73:20
78:66 1 Sam 5:6
78:68 Ps 87:2; 132:13
78:69 1 Kin 6:1-38
78:70 1 Sam 16:11, 12
78:71 2 Sam 7:8; 2 Sam 5:2; 1 Chr 11:2; Ps 28:9; 1 Sam 10:1
78:72 1 Kin 9:4

He did not spare their soul from death,
But gave over their life to the plague,
51 And smote all the firstborn in Egypt,
The first *issue* of their virility in the tents of Ham.
52 But He led forth His own people like sheep
And guided them in the wilderness like a flock;
53 He led them safely, so that they did not fear;
But the sea engulfed their enemies.

54 So He brought them to His holy land,
To this hill country which His right hand had gained.
55 He also drove out the nations before them
And apportioned them for an inheritance by measurement,
And made the tribes of Israel dwell in their tents.
56 Yet they [138]tempted and rebelled against the Most High God
And did not keep His testimonies,
57 But turned back and acted treacherously like their fathers;
They turned aside like a treacherous bow.
58 For they provoked Him with their high places
And aroused His jealousy with their graven images.
59 When God heard, He was filled with wrath
And greatly abhorred Israel;
60 So that He abandoned the dwelling place at Shiloh,
The tent which He had pitched among men,
61 And gave up His strength to captivity
And His glory into the hand of the adversary.
62 He also delivered His people to the sword,
And was filled with wrath at His inheritance.
63 Fire devoured His young men,
And His virgins had no wedding songs.
64 His priests fell by the sword,
And His widows could not weep.

65 Then the Lord awoke as *if from* sleep,
Like a warrior overcome by wine.
66 He drove His adversaries backward;
He put on them an everlasting reproach.
67 He also rejected the tent of Joseph,
And did not choose the tribe of Ephraim,
68 But chose the tribe of Judah,
Mount Zion which He loved.
69 And He built His sanctuary like the heights,
Like the earth which He has founded forever.
70 He also chose David His servant
And took him from the sheepfolds;
71 From the care of the ewes with suckling lambs He brought him
To shepherd Jacob His people,
And Israel His inheritance.
72 So he shepherded them according to the integrity of his heart,
And guided them with his skillful hands.

138 Or *put to the test*

78:51 This was the Passover described in Exodus 12:29, 30 when all the firstborn of the Egyptians were slain. The "tents of Ham" refers to Noah's second son, who was the ancestor of the Egyptians. Ham is sometimes used as a synonym for Egypt.

78:71–72 Although David had been on the throne when this psalm was written, he is called a shepherd and not a king. Shepherding, a common profession in Biblical times, was a highly responsible job. The flocks were completely dependent upon shepherds for guidance, provision, and protection. David had spent his early years as a shepherd (1 Samuel 16:10–11). This was a training ground for the future responsibilities God had in store for him. When he was ready, God took him from caring for sheep to caring for Israel, God's people. Don't treat your present situation lightly or irresponsibly; it may be God's training ground for your future.

PSALM 79

A Psalm of Asaph.

Theme: When outraged by injustice, cry out to God, not against him. In times of disaster, our mood may be anger, but our trust must remain in God.
Author: Asaph (or one of his descendants), probably written after the Babylonians had leveled Jerusalem (see 2 Kings 25)

1 O God, the nations have invaded Your inheritance;
They have defiled Your holy temple;
They have laid Jerusalem in ruins.
2 They have given the dead bodies of Your servants for food to the birds of the heavens,
The flesh of Your godly ones to the beasts of the earth.
3 They have poured out their blood like water round about Jerusalem;
And there was no one to bury them.
4 We have become a reproach to our neighbors,
A scoffing and derision to those around us.
5 How long, O LORD? Will You be angry forever?
Will Your jealousy burn like fire?
6 Pour out Your wrath upon the nations which do not know You,
And upon the kingdoms which do not call upon Your name.
7 For they have devoured Jacob
And laid waste his habitation.

8 Do not remember the iniquities of *our* forefathers against us;
Let Your compassion come quickly to meet us,
For we are brought very low.
9 Help us, O God of our salvation, for the glory of Your name;
And deliver us and forgive our sins for Your name's sake.

79:1 Lam 1:10; Ps 74:2; Ps 74:3, 7; 2 Kin 25:9, 10; 2 Chr 36:17-19; Jer 26:18; 52:12-14; Mic 3:12

79:2 Deut 28:26; Jer 7:33; 16:4; 19:7; 34:20

79:3 Jer 14:16; 16:4

79:4 Ps 44:13; 80:6; Dan 9:16

79:5 Ps 13:1; 74:1, 9, 10; 85:5; 89:46; Deut 29:20; Ezek 36:5; 38:19; Ps 89:46; Zeph 3:8

79:6 Ps 69:24; Jer 10:25; Ezek 21:31; Zeph 3:8; 1 Thess 4:5; 2 Thess 1:8; Ps 14:4; 53:4

79:7 Ps 53:4; 2 Chr 36:19; Jer 39:8

79:8 Ps 106:6; Is 64:9; Ps 21:3; Deut 28:43; Ps 116:6; 142:6; Is 26:5

79:9 2 Chr 14:11; Ps 31:3; Ps 25:11; 65:3; Jer 14:7

PRAYER IN THE BOOK OF PSALMS

Prayer is human communication with God. Psalms could be described as a collection of song-prayers. Probably the most striking feature of these prayers is their unedited honesty. The words often express our own feelings—feelings that we would prefer no one, much less God, ever knew. Making these psalms our prayers can teach us a great deal about how God wants us to communicate with him. Too often we give God a watered-down version of our feelings, hoping we won't offend him or make him curious about our motives. As we use the psalms to express our feelings, we learn that honesty, openness, and sincerity are valuable to God.

Following are several types of prayers with examples from Psalms. Note that the psalm writers communicated with God in a variety of ways for a variety of reasons. Each of us is invited to communicate with God. Using the psalms will enrich your personal prayer life.

Prayers of:	*Psalms:*
Praise to God	100; 113; 117
Thanksgiving by a community	67; 75; 136
Thanksgiving by an individual	18; 30; 32
Request by the community	79; 80; 123
Request by an individual	3; 55; 86
Sorrow by the community	44; 74; 137
Sorrow by an individual	5; 6; 120
Anger	35; 109; 140
Confession	6; 32; 51
Faith	11; 16; 23

79:6 According to the Old Testament, God's wrath and judgment often fell on entire nations because of the sins of people within those nations. Here Asaph pled for judgment on kingdoms that refused to acknowledge God's authority. Ironically, Asaph's own nation of Judah was being judged by God for refusing to do this very thing (2 Chronicles 36:14–20). These were people who had sworn allegiance to God but were now rejecting him. This made their judgment even worse.

79:10 Ps 42:10; 115:2; Ps 94:1, 2
79:11 Ps 102:20
79:12 Gen 4:15; Lev 26:21, 28; Ps 12:6; 119:164; Prov 6:31; 24:16; Is 30:26; Ps 35:13; Is 65:6, 7; Jer 32:18; Luke 6:38; Ps 74:10, 18, 22
79:13 Ps 74:1; 95:7; 100:3; Ps 44:8; Ps 89:1; Is 43:21

10 Why should the nations say, "Where is their God?"
Let there be known among the nations in our sight,
Vengeance for the blood of Your servants which has been shed.
11 Let the groaning of the prisoner come before You;
According to the greatness of Your power preserve those who are doomed to die.
12 And return to our neighbors sevenfold into their bosom
The reproach with which they have reproached You, O Lord.
13 So we Your people and the sheep of Your pasture
Will give thanks to You forever;
To all generations we will tell of Your praise.

PSALM 80

For the choir director; *set to* El Shoshannim; Eduth.
A Psalm of Asaph.

Theme: A prayer for revival and restoration after experiencing destruction. God is our only hope for salvation.
Author: Asaph (or one of his descendants), probably written after the northern kingdom of Israel was defeated and its people deported to Assyria.

80:1 Ps 23:1; Ps 77:15; 78:67; Amos 5:15; Ex 25:22; 1 Sam 4:4; 2 Sam 6:2; Ps 99:1
80:2 Num 2:18-24; Ps 35:23
80:3 Ps 60:1; 80:7, 19; 85:4; 126:1; Lam 5:21; Num 6:25; Ps 4:6; 31:16
80:4 Ps 59:5; 84:8; Ps 79:5; 85:5
80:5 Ps 42:3; 102:9; Is 30:20
80:6 Ps 44:13; 79:4
80:8 Ps 80:15; Is 5:1, 2, 7; Jer 2:21; 12:10; Ezek 17:6; 19:10; Josh 13:6; 2 Chr 20:7; Ps 44:2; Acts 7:45; Jer 11:17; 32:41; Ezek 17:23; Amos 9:15
80:9 Ex 23:28; Josh 24:12; Is 5:2; Hos 14:5
80:10 Gen 49:22
80:11 Ps 72:8
80:12 Ps 89:40; Is 5:5
80:13 Jer 5:6
80:14 Ps 90:13; Ps 102:19; Is 63:15

1 Oh, give ear, Shepherd of Israel,
You who lead Joseph like a flock;
You who are enthroned *above* the cherubim, shine forth!
2 Before Ephraim and Benjamin and Manasseh, stir up Your power
And come to save us!
3 O God, restore us
And cause Your face to shine *upon us,* and we will be saved.

4 O LORD God *of* hosts,
How long will You be angry with the prayer of Your people?
5 You have fed them with the bread of tears,
And You have made them to drink tears in large measure.
6 You make us [139]an object of contention to our neighbors,
And our enemies laugh among themselves.
7 O God *of* hosts, restore us
And cause Your face to shine *upon us,* [140]and we will be saved.

8 You removed a vine from Egypt;
You drove out the nations and planted it.
9 You cleared *the ground* before it,
And it took deep root and filled the land.
10 The mountains were covered with its shadow,
And the cedars of God with its boughs.
11 It was sending out its branches to the sea
And its shoots to the River.
12 Why have You broken down its hedges,
So that all who pass *that* way pick its *fruit?*
13 A boar from the forest eats it away
And whatever moves in the field feeds on it.

14 O God *of* hosts, turn again now, we beseech You;
Look down from heaven and see, and take care of this vine,

139 Lit *a strife to* **140** Or *that we may*

79:10 In the end, God's glory will be evident to all people, but in the meantime, we must endure suffering with patience and allow God to strengthen our character through it. For reasons that we do not know, pagan people often are allowed to scoff at believers. We should be prepared for criticism, jokes, and unkind remarks because God does not place us beyond the attacks of scoffers.

80:1 Cherubim are mighty angels.

80:3, 7, 19 Three times the writer calls on God to "restore us." Before restoration must come repentance, turning away from sin. Repentance involves humbling ourselves and turning to God to receive his forgiveness. As we turn to God, he helps us see ourselves, including our sin, more clearly. Then, as we see our sin, we must repeat the process of repentance. Only then can we constantly be restored to fellowship with God.

15 Even the shoot which Your right hand has planted,
And on the son whom You have strengthened for Yourself.
16 It is burned with fire, it is cut down;
They perish at the rebuke of Your countenance.
17 Let Your hand be upon the man of Your right hand,
Upon the son of man whom You made strong for Yourself.
18 Then we shall not turn back from You;
Revive us, and we will call upon Your name.
19 O LORD God of hosts, restore us;
Cause Your face to shine *upon us,* and we will be saved.

80:15 Ps 80:8
80:16 2 Chr 36:19; Ps 74:8; Jer 52:13; Ps 39:11; 76:6
80:17 Ps 89:21; Ps 80:15
80:18 Is 50:5; Ps 71:20
80:19 Ps 80:3

PSALM 81

For the choir director; on the Gittith. *A Psalm* of Asaph.

Theme: A holiday hymn. This hymn celebrates the exodus from Egypt—God's goodness versus Israel's waywardness. God is our deliverer in spite of our wanderings.
Author: Asaph, probably written to be used during the Feast of Tabernacles

1 Sing for joy to God our strength;
Shout joyfully to the God of Jacob.
2 Raise a song, strike the timbrel,
The sweet sounding lyre with the harp.
3 Blow the trumpet at the new moon,
At the full moon, on our feast day.
4 For it is a statute for Israel,
An ordinance of the God of Jacob.
5 He established it for a testimony in Joseph
When he went throughout the land of Egypt.
I heard a language that I did not know:

6 "I relieved his shoulder of the burden,
His hands were freed from the basket.
7 "You called in trouble and I rescued you;
I answered you in the hiding place of thunder;
I proved you at the waters of Meribah. Selah.
8 "Hear, O My people, and I will admonish you;
O Israel, if you would listen to Me!
9 "Let there be no strange god among you;
Nor shall you worship any foreign god.
10 "I, the LORD, am your God,
Who brought you up from the land of Egypt;
Open your mouth wide and I will fill it.

11 "But My people did not listen to My voice,
And Israel did not obey Me.
12 "So I gave them over to the stubbornness of their heart,
To walk in their own devices.

81:1 Ps 51:14; 59:16; 95:1; Ps 46:1; Ps 66:1; 95:2; 98:4; Ps 84:8
81:2 Ex 15:20; Ps 149:3; Ps 92:3; 98:5; 147:7; Ps 108:2; 144:9
81:3 Num 10:10; Lev 23:24
81:5 Ex 11:4; Deut 28:49; Ps 114:1; Jer 5:15
81:6 Is 9:4; 10:27
81:7 Ex 2:23; 14:10; Ps 50:15; Ex 19:19; 20:18; Ex 17:6, 7; Num 20:13; Ps 95:8
81:8 Ps 50:7; Ps 95:7
81:9 Ex 20:3; Deut 5:7; 32:12; Ps 44:20; Is 43:12
81:10 Ex 20:2; Deut 5:6; Job 29:23; Ps 37:4; 78:25; 107:9
81:11 Deut 32:15; Ps 106:25
81:12 Job 8:4; Acts 7:42; Rom 1:24, 26

80:17 "The man of Your right hand" is probably not the Messiah, but Israel, whom God calls elsewhere his "firstborn" son (Exodus 4:22). The psalmist is making a plea that God would restore his mercy to Israel, the people he chose to bring his message into the world.

81:1–5 Israel's holidays reminded the nation of God's great miracles. They were times of rejoicing and times to renew one's strength for life's daily struggles. At Christmas, do your thoughts revolve mostly around presents? Is Easter only a warm anticipation of spring and Thanksgiving only a good meal? Remember the spiritual origins of these special days, and use them as opportunities to worship God for his goodness to you, your family, and your nation.

81:2–4 David instituted music for the temple worship services (1 Chronicles 25). Music and worship go hand in hand. Worship should involve the whole person, and music helps lift a person's thoughts and emotions to God. Through music we can reflect upon our needs and shortcomings as well as celebrate God's greatness.

81:11–12 God let the Israelites go on blindly, stubbornly, and selfishly, when they should have been obeying and pursuing God's desires. God sometimes lets us continue in our stubbornness to bring us to our senses. He does not keep us from rebelling, because he wants us to learn the consequences of sin. He uses these experiences to turn people away from greater sin to faith in him.

81:13 Deut 5:29; Ps 81:8; Is 48:18; Ps 128:1; Is 42:24; Jer 7:23

81:14 Ps 18:47; 47:3; Amos 1:8

81:15 Rom 1:30; Ps 18:44; 66:3

81:16 Deut 32:14; Ps 147:14; Deut 32:13

13 "Oh that My people would listen to Me,
That Israel would walk in My ways!
14 "I would quickly subdue their enemies
And turn My hand against their adversaries.
15 "Those who hate the LORD would pretend obedience to Him,
And their time *of punishment* would be forever.
16 "But I would feed you with the finest of the wheat,
And with honey from the rock I would satisfy you."

PSALM 82

A Psalm of Asaph.

Theme: A fair judge, God will judge the wicked who have unfairly treated others.
Author: Asaph

82:1 Is 3:13; 2 Chr 19:6; Ps 58:11; Ex 21:6; 22:8, 28

82:2 Ps 58:1; Deut 1:17; Prov 18:5

82:3 Deut 24:17; Ps 10:18; Is 11:4; Jer 22:16

82:4 Job 29:12

82:5 Ps 14:4; Jer 4:22; Mic 3:1; Prov 2:13; Is 59:9; Jer 23:12; Ps 11:3

82:6 Ps 82:1; John 10:34; Ps 89:26

82:7 Job 21:32; Ps 49:12; Ezek 31:14; Ps 83:11

82:8 Ps 12:5; Ps 58:11; 96:13; Ps 2:8; Rev 11:15

1 God takes His stand in His own congregation;
He judges in the midst of the rulers.
2 How long will you judge unjustly
And show partiality to the wicked? Selah.
3 Vindicate the weak and fatherless;
Do justice to the afflicted and destitute.
4 Rescue the weak and needy;
Deliver *them* out of the hand of the wicked.

5 They do not know nor do they understand;
They walk about in darkness;
All the foundations of the earth are shaken.
6 I said, "You are gods,
And all of you are sons of the Most High.
7 "Nevertheless you will die like men
And fall like *any* one of the princes."
8 Arise, O God, judge the earth!
For it is You who possesses all the nations.

PSALM 83

A Song, a Psalm of Asaph.

Theme: Combating God's enemies. This psalm is a prayer for God to do whatever it takes to convince the world that he is indeed God. Someday all will recognize and admit that God is in charge.
Author: Asaph (or one of his descendants)

83:1 Ps 28:1; 35:22; Ps 109:1

83:2 Ps 2:1; Is 17:12; Ps 81:15; Judg 8:28; Zech 1:21

83:3 Ps 64:2; Is 29:15; Ps 27:5; 31:20

83:4 Esth 3:6; Ps 74:8; Jer 48:2; Ps 41:5; Jer 11:19

83:5 Ps 2:2; Dan 6:7

1 O God, do not remain quiet;
Do not be silent and, O God, do not be still.
2 For behold, Your enemies make an uproar,
And those who hate You have exalted themselves.
3 They make shrewd plans against Your people,
And conspire together against Your treasured ones.
4 They have said, "Come, and let us wipe them out as a nation,
That the name of Israel be remembered no more."
5 For they have conspired together with one mind;

81:13–16 God had provided in his covenant that he would restore his people if they would listen to him and return to him (Exodus 23:22–27; Leviticus 26:3–13; Deuteronomy 7:12–26; 28:1–14).

82:6 This psalm calls the rulers and judges of Israel "gods" and "sons of the Most High." They were called gods because they represented God in executing judgment. John 10:34–36 records Jesus using this passage to defend his claims to be God. His argument was as follows: If God would call mere men "gods," why was it blasphemous for him, the true Son of God, to declare himself equal with God?

83:5–8 This alliance against God may refer to the gathering of certain kings to fight against Jehoshaphat and the people of Judah (2 Chronicles 20). The psalm's author is called Asaph, but this can mean Asaph or one of his descendants. A descendant of Asaph named Jahaziel prophesied victory for Judah in the battle against Jehoshaphat (2 Chronicles 20:13–17). The psalmist says the alliance against Judah is really against God. Thus Jahaziel exclaimed, "The battle is not yours but God's" (2 Chronicles 20:15). God is "the Most High over all the earth" (83:18), and the enemies of Israel were considered God's enemies.

Against You they make a covenant:
6 The tents of Edom and the Ishmaelites,
Moab and the Hagrites;
7 Gebal and Ammon and Amalek,
Philistia with the inhabitants of Tyre;
8 Assyria also has joined with them;
They have become a help to the children of Lot. Selah.

9 Deal with them as with Midian,
As with Sisera *and* Jabin at the torrent of Kishon,
10 Who were destroyed at En-dor,
Who became as dung for the ground.
11 Make their nobles like Oreb and Zeeb
And all their princes like Zebah and Zalmunna,
12 Who said, "Let us possess for ourselves
The pastures of God."

13 O my God, make them like the [141]whirling dust,
Like chaff before the wind.
14 Like fire that burns the forest
And like a flame that sets the mountains on fire,
15 So pursue them with Your tempest
And terrify them with Your storm.
16 Fill their faces with dishonor,
That they may seek Your name, O LORD.
17 Let them be ashamed and dismayed forever,
And let them be humiliated and perish,
18 That they may know that You alone, whose name is the LORD,
Are the Most High over all the earth.

83:6 2 Chr 20:10; Ps 137:7; Gen 25:12-16; 2 Chr 20:10; 1 Chr 5:10

83:7 Josh 13:5; Ezek 27:9; 2 Chr 20:10; 1 Sam 15:2; 1 Sam 4:1; 29:1; Ezek 27:3; Amos 1:9

83:8 2 Kin 15:19; Deut 2:9

83:9 Judg 7:1-24; Judg 4:7, 15, 21-24

83:10 Zeph 1:17

83:11 Judg 7:25; Judg 8:12, 21

83:12 2 Chr 20:11; Ps 132:13

83:13 Is 17:13; Job 21:18; Ps 35:5; Is 40:24; Jer 13:24

83:14 Is 9:18; Ex 19:18; Deut 32:22

83:15 Job 9:17; Ps 58:9

83:16 Job 10:15; Ps 109:29; 132:18

83:17 Ps 35:4; 70:2

83:18 Ps 59:13; Ps 86:10; Is 45:21; Ps 9:2; 18:13; 97:9

PSALM 84

For the choir director; on the Gittith.
A Psalm of the sons of Korah.

Theme: God's living presence is our greatest joy. His radiant presence helps us grow in strength, grace, and glory.
Author: The sons of Korah (temple assistants)

1 How lovely are Your dwelling places,
O LORD of hosts!
2 My soul longed and even yearned for the courts of the LORD;
My heart and my flesh sing for joy to the living God.
3 The bird also has found a house,
And the swallow a nest for herself, where she may lay her young,
Even Your altars, O LORD of hosts,
My King and my God.
4 How blessed are those who dwell in Your house!
They are ever praising You. Selah.

84:1 Ps 43:3; 132:5

84:2 Ps 42:1, 2; 63:1; Ps 42:2

84:3 Ps 43:4; Ps 5:2

84:4 Ps 65:4; Ps 42:5, 11

141 Or *tumbleweed*

83:6 The Hagrites may have been the descendants of Hagar (Genesis 21:8–21).

83:8–11 The "children of Lot" refers to the Moabites and Ammonites (Genesis 19:36–38). Sisera was the commander of the army of the oppressive Canaanite King Jabin. He was killed by a woman (see Judges 4 for the complete story). (For the story of Oreb and Zeeb, see Judges 7:25; for Zebah and Zalmunna, see Judges 8:21.)

83:13–18 Surrounding Judah were pagan nations that sought Judah's downfall. The psalmist prayed that God would blow these nations away like chaff before the wind until they recognized that the Lord is above all rulers of the earth. Sometimes we must be humbled by adversity before we will look up and see the Lord; we must be defeated before we can have the ultimate victory. Wouldn't it be better to seek the Lord in times of prosperity than to wait until his judgment is upon us?

84:1, 4 The writer longed to get away from the bustling world to meet God inside his dwelling place, his holy temple. We can meet God anywhere, at any time. But we know that going into a church building can help us step aside from the busy mainstream of life so we can quietly meditate and pray. We find joy not only in the beautiful building but also in the prayers, music, lessons, sermons, and fellowship.

5 How blessed is the man whose strength is in You,
In whose heart are the highways *to Zion!*
6 Passing through the valley of [142]Baca they make it a spring;
The early rain also covers it with blessings.
7 They go from strength to strength,
Every one of them appears before God in Zion.

8 O LORD God of hosts, hear my prayer;
Give ear, O God of Jacob! Selah.
9 Behold our shield, O God,
And look upon the face of Your anointed.
10 For a day in Your courts is better than a thousand *outside.*
I would rather stand at the threshold of the house of my God
Than dwell in the tents of wickedness.
11 For the LORD God is a sun and shield;
The LORD gives grace and glory;
No good thing does He withhold from those who walk uprightly.
12 O LORD of hosts,
How blessed is the man who trusts in You!

PSALM 85

For the choir director. A Psalm of the sons of Korah.

Theme: From reverence to restoration. Reverence leads to forgiveness, restoring our love and joy for God.
Author: The sons of Korah (temple assistants)

1 O LORD, You showed favor to Your land;
You [143]restored the captivity of Jacob.
2 You forgave the iniquity of Your people;
You covered all their sin. Selah.
3 You withdrew all Your fury;
You turned away from Your burning anger.

4 Restore us, O God of our salvation,
And cause Your indignation toward us to cease.
5 Will You be angry with us forever?
Will You prolong Your anger to all generations?
6 Will You not Yourself revive us again,
That Your people may rejoice in You?
7 Show us Your lovingkindness, O LORD,
And grant us Your salvation.

8 I will hear what God the LORD will say;
For He will speak peace to His people, to His godly ones;
But let them not turn back to folly.
9 Surely His salvation is near to those who [144]fear Him,
That glory may dwell in our land.

84:5 Ps 81:1; Ps 86:11; 122:1; Jer 31:6
84:6 Ps 107:35; Joel 2:23
84:7 Prov 4:18; Is 40:31; John 1:16; 2 Cor 3:18; Ex 34:23; Deut 16:16; Ps 42:2
84:8 Ps 59:5; 80:4; 84:1; Ps 81:1
84:9 Gen 15:1; Ps 3:3; 28:7; 59:11; 115:9-11; 1 Sam 16:6; 2 Sam 19:21; Ps 2:2; 132:17
84:10 Ps 27:4
84:11 Is 60:19, 20; Mal 4:2; Rev 21:23; Gen 15:1; Ps 85:9; Ps 34:9, 10
84:12 Ps 2:12; 40:4
85:1 Ps 77:7; 106:4; Ezra 1:11; Ps 14:7; 126:1; Jer 30:18; Ezek 39:25; Hos 6:11; Joel 3:1
85:2 Num 14:19; 1 Kin 8:34; Ps 78:38; 103:3; Jer 31:34; Ps 32:1
85:3 Ps 78:38; 106:23; Ex 32:12; Deut 13:17; Ps 106:23; Jon 3:9
85:4 Ps 80:3,7; Dan 9:16
85:5 Ps 74:1; 79:5; 80:4
85:6 Ps 71:20; 80:18; Ps 33:1; 90:14; 149:2
85:7 Ps 106:4
85:8 Ps 29:11; Hag 2:9; Zech 9:10; Ps 78:57; 2 Pet 2:21
85:9 Ps 34:18; Is 46:13; Ps 84:11; Hag 2:7; Zech 2:5; John 1:14

142 Probably, *Weeping;* or *Balsam trees* **143** Or *restore the fortunes* **144** Or *reverence*

84:5–7 The pilgrimage to the temple passed through the barren valley of Baca. No specific valley has been identified with Baca. Because *Baca* can mean "weeping," it may have been a symbolic reference to the times of struggles and tears through which people must pass on their way to meet God. Growing strong in God's presence is often preceded by a journey through barren places in our lives. The person who loves to spend time with God will see his or her adversity as an opportunity to re-experience God's faithfulness. If you are walking through your own valley of Baca today, be sure your pilgrimage leads toward God, not away from him.

84:11 God does not promise to give us everything *we* think is good, but he will not withhold what is permanently good. He will give us the means to walk along his paths, but we must do the walking. When we obey him, he will not hold anything back that will help us serve him.

85:6–7 The psalmist was asking God to revive his people, bringing them back to spiritual life. God is capable of reviving both churches and individuals. He can pour out his love on us, renewing our love for him. If you need revival in your church, family, or personal spiritual life, ask God to give you a fresh touch of his love.

10 Lovingkindness and truth have met together;
Righteousness and peace have kissed each other.
11 Truth springs from the earth,
And righteousness looks down from heaven.
12 Indeed, the LORD will give what is good,
And our land will yield its produce.
13 Righteousness will go before Him
And will make His footsteps into a way.

85:10 Ps 25:10; 89:14; Prov 3:3; Ps 72:3; Is 32:17
85:11 Is 45:8
85:12 Ps 84:11; James 1:17; Lev 26:4; Ps 67:6; Ezek 34:27; Zech 8:12
85:13 Ps 89:14

PSALM 86

A Prayer of David.

Theme: Devoted trust in times of deep trouble.
Author: David

1 Incline Your ear, O LORD, *and* answer me;
For I am afflicted and needy.
2 Preserve my soul, for I am a godly man;
O You my God, save Your servant who trusts in You.
3 Be gracious to me, O Lord,
For to You I cry all day long.
4 Make glad the soul of Your servant,
For to You, O Lord, I lift up my soul.
5 For You, Lord, are good, and ready to forgive,
And abundant in lovingkindness to all who call upon You.
6 Give ear, O LORD, to my prayer;
And give heed to the voice of my supplications!
7 In the day of my trouble I shall call upon You,
For You will answer me.
8 There is no one like You among the gods, O Lord,
Nor are there any works like Yours.
9 All nations whom You have made shall come and worship before You, O Lord,
And they shall glorify Your name.
10 For You are great and do wondrous deeds;
You alone are God.

11 Teach me Your way, O LORD;
I will walk in Your truth;
Unite my heart to fear Your name.
12 I will give thanks to You, O Lord my God, with all my heart,
And will glorify Your name forever.
13 For Your lovingkindness toward me is great,
And You have delivered my soul from the depths of Sheol.

14 O God, arrogant men have risen up against me,
And a band of violent men have sought my life,
And they have not set You before them.
15 But You, O Lord, are a God merciful and gracious,
Slow to anger and abundant in lovingkindness and truth.
16 Turn to me, and be gracious to me;
Oh grant Your strength to Your servant,
And save the son of Your handmaid.

86:1 Ps 17:6; 31:2; 71:2; Ps 40:17; 70:5
86:2 Ps 25:20; Ps 4:3; 50:5; Ps 25:2; 31:14; 56:4
86:3 Ps 4:1; 57:1; Ps 25:5; 88:9
86:4 Ps 25:1; 143:8
86:5 Ps 25:8; Ps 130:4; Ex 34:6; Neh 9:17; Ps 103:8; 145:8; Joel 2:13; Jon 4:2
86:6 Ps 55:1
86:7 Ps 50:15; 77:2; Ps 17:6
86:8 Ex 15:11; 2 Sam 7:22; 1 Kin 8:23; Ps 89:6; Jer 10:6; Deut 3:24
86:9 Ps 22:27; 66:4; Is 66:23; Rev 15:4
86:10 Ps 77:13; Ex 15:11; Ps 72:18; 77:14; 136:4; Deut 6:4; 32:39; Ps 83:18; Is 37:16; 44:6, 8; Mark 12:29; 1 Cor 8:4
86:11 Ps 25:5; Jer 32:39
86:12 Ps 111:1
86:13 Ps 30:3
86:14 Ps 54:3
86:15 Ps 86:5
86:16 Ps 25:16; Ps 68:35; Ps 116:16

86:7 Sometimes our trouble or pain is so great that all we can do is cry out to God, "Preserve my soul" (86:2). And often, when there is no relief in sight, all we can do is acknowledge the greatness of God and wait for better days ahead. The conviction that God answers prayer will sustain us in such difficult times.

86:8–10 "There is no one like You among the gods, O LORD." The God of the Bible is unique! He is alive and able to do mighty deeds for those who love him. All human-created deities are powerless because they are merely inventions of the mind, not living beings. The Lord alone is "worthy . . . to receive glory and honor and power" (Revelation 4:11). Although people believe in many gods, you need never fear that God is only one among many or that you may be worshiping the wrong God. The Lord alone is God.

86:17 Judg 6:17; Ps 119:122; Ps 112:10; Ps 118:13

17 Show me a sign for good,
That those who hate me may see *it* and be ashamed,
Because You, O LORD, have helped me and comforted me.

PSALM 87

A Psalm of the sons of Korah. A Song.

Theme: The city of God, where all believers will one day gather.
Author: The sons of Korah (temple assistants)

87:1 Ps 78:69; Is 28:16
87:2 Ps 78:67, 68
87:3 Is 60:1; Ps 46:4; 48:8
87:4 Job 9:13; Ps 89:10; Is 19:23-25; Ps 45:12; Ps 68:31
87:5 Ps 48:8
87:6 Ps 69:28; Is 4:3; Ezek 13:9
87:7 Ps 68:25; 149:3; 2 Sam 6:14; Ps 30:11; Ps 36:9

1 His foundation is in the holy mountains.
2 The LORD loves the gates of Zion
More than all the *other* dwelling places of Jacob.
3 Glorious things are spoken of you,
O city of God. Selah.
4 "I shall mention [145]Rahab and Babylon among those who know Me;
Behold, Philistia and Tyre with Ethiopia:
'This one was born there.' "
5 But of Zion it shall be said, "This one and that one were born in her";
And the Most High Himself will establish her.
6 The LORD will count when He registers the peoples,
"This one was born there." Selah.
7 Then those who sing as well as those who play the flutes *shall say,*
"All my springs *of joy* are in you."

PSALM 88

A Song. A Psalm of the sons of Korah. For the choir director; according to Mahalath Leannoth. A Maskil of Heman the Ezrahite.

Theme: When there is no relief in sight. God understands even our deepest misery.
Author: Herman, one of the sons of Korah (possibly the same man mentioned in 1 Chronicles 15:19; 16:41; 25:4–5 as a musician and the king's seer)

88:1 Ps 24:5; 27:9; Ps 22:2; 86:3; Luke 18:7
88:2 Ps 18:6; Ps 31:2; 86:1
88:3 Ps 107:26; Ps 107:18; 116:3
88:4 Ps 28:1; 143:7; Job 29:12; Ps 22:11
88:5 Ps 31:12; Ps 31:22; Is 53:8
88:6 Ps 86:13; Lam 3:55; Ps 143:3; Ps 69:15

1 O LORD, the God of my salvation,
I have cried out by day and in the night before You.
2 Let my prayer come before You;
Incline Your ear to my cry!
3 For my soul has had enough troubles,
And my life has drawn near to Sheol.
4 I am reckoned among those who go down to the pit;
I have become like a man without strength,
5 Forsaken among the dead,
Like the slain who lie in the grave,
Whom You remember no more,
And they are cut off from Your hand.
6 You have put me in the lowest pit,
In dark places, in the depths.

145 I.e. Egypt

86:17 It is right to pray for a sign of God's goodness. As David found, it may be just what we need. But let us not overlook the signs he has already given: the support of family and friends, the fellowship of other Christians, the light of each new day. And we can be confident that he knows our situation no matter how desperate it becomes, and that he cares.

87:1ff Zion (the holy mountain, Jerusalem) and its temple here represent the future community of all believers. This psalm looks ahead to the Holy City of God described in Revelation 21:10–27. The honor of living there will be granted to all whose names are recorded in the Lamb's book of life (Revelation 21:27). It is God's grace that forms and sustains this wonderful community. How could anyone refuse God's offer to be part of this celebration?

87:4 Rahab is a name for a monster known in ancient Near Eastern poetry as an enemy of God. Here the name is used to represent Egypt, a traditional enemy of God's people.

88:1ff Have you ever felt as though you have hit bottom? The psalmist is so low that he even despairs of life itself. Although everything is bad and getting worse, he is able to tell it all to God. This is one of the few psalms that gives no answer or expression of hope. Don't think that you must always be cheerful and positive. Grief and depression take time to heal. No matter how low we feel, we can always take our problems to God and express our anguish to him.

7 Your wrath has rested upon me,
And You have afflicted me with all Your waves. Selah.
8 You have removed my acquaintances far from me;
You have made me an [146]object of loathing to them;
I am shut up and cannot go out.
9 My eye has wasted away because of affliction;
I have called upon You every day, O LORD;
I have spread out my hands to You.

10 Will You perform wonders for the dead?
Will the departed spirits rise *and* praise You? Selah.
11 Will Your lovingkindness be declared in the grave,
Your faithfulness in Abaddon?
12 Will Your wonders be made known in the darkness?
And Your righteousness in the land of forgetfulness?

13 But I, O LORD, have cried out to You for help,
And in the morning my prayer comes before You.
14 O LORD, why do You reject my soul?
Why do You hide Your face from me?
15 I was afflicted and about to die from my youth on;
I suffer Your terrors; I am overcome.
16 Your burning anger has passed over me;
Your terrors have destroyed me.
17 They have surrounded me like water all day long;
They have encompassed me altogether.
18 You have removed lover and friend far from me;
My acquaintances are *in* darkness.

88:7 Ps 32:4; 39:10; Ps 42:7
88:8 Job 19:13, 19; Ps 31:11; 142:4; Job 30:10; Ps 142:7; Jer 32:2; 36:5
88:9 Ps 6:7; 31:9; Ps 22:2; 86:3; Job 11:13; Ps 143:6
88:10 Ps 6:5; 30:9
88:12 Job 10:21; Ps 88:6
88:13 Ps 30:2; Ps 5:3; 119:147
88:14 Ps 43:2; 44:9; Job 13:24; Ps 13:1; 44:24
88:15 Prov 24:11; Job 6:4; 31:23
88:16 2 Chr 28:11; Is 13:13; Lam 1:12; Lam 3:54; Ezek 37:11
88:17 Ps 118:10-12; Ps 124:4; Ps 17:11; 22:12, 16
88:18 Job 19:13; Ps 88:8; 31:11; 38:11

PSALM 89

A Maskil of Ethan the Ezrahite.

Theme: God's promise to preserve David's descendants. God's promise is fulfilled in Jesus Christ, who will reign for eternity. The love and kindness promised to David is ours in Christ.
Author: Ethan (a Levite leader and possibly one of the head musicians in the temple, 1 Chronicles 15:17, 19), or one of his descendants

1 I will sing of the lovingkindness of the LORD forever;
To all generations I will make known Your faithfulness with my mouth.
2 For I have said, "Lovingkindness will be built up forever;
In the heavens You will establish Your faithfulness."
3 "I have made a covenant with My chosen;
I have sworn to David My servant,
4 I will establish your seed forever
And build up your throne to all generations." Selah.

5 The heavens will praise Your wonders, O LORD;
Your faithfulness also in the assembly of the holy ones.

89:1 Ps 59:16; 101:1; Ps 40:10; Ps 36:5; 88:11; 89:5, 8, 24, 33, 49; 92:2; 119:90; Is 25:1; Lam 3:23
89:2 Ps 103:17; Ps 36:5; 119:90
89:3 1 Kin 8:16; Ps 132:11
89:4 2 Sam 7:16; 2 Sam 7:13; Is 9:7; Luke 1:33
89:5 Ps 19:1; 97:6; Ps 149:1; Job 5:1

146 Lit *abomination to them*

88:13–14 When writing this, the psalmist was close to death, perhaps debilitated by disease, and forsaken by friends. But he could still pray. Perhaps you are not so afflicted, but you know someone who is. Consider being a prayer companion for that person. This psalm can be a prayer you can lift to God on his or her behalf.

89:1ff This psalm was written to describe the glorious reign of David. God had promised to make David the mightiest king on earth and to keep his descendants on the throne forever (2 Samuel 7:8–16). But Jerusalem was destroyed, and kings no longer reign there. So these verses can only look forward, prophetically, to the future reign of Jesus Christ, David's descendant. Verse 27 is a prophecy concerning David's never-ending dynasty, which will reach its fulfillment and highest expression in Christ's future reign over the world (see Revelation 22:5).

89:5 The "assembly of the holy ones" generally refers to angels. In the courts of heaven, a host of angels praises the Lord. This scene is one of majesty and grandeur to show that God is beyond compare. His power and purity place him high above nature and angels. See Deuteronomy 33:2, Luke 2:13, and Hebrews 12:22 for more about angels.

6 For who in the skies is comparable to the LORD?
Who among the sons of the mighty is like the LORD,
7 A God greatly feared in the council of the holy ones,
And awesome above all those who are around Him?
8 O LORD God of hosts, who is like You, O mighty LORD?
Your faithfulness also surrounds You.
9 You rule the swelling of the sea;
When its waves rise, You still them.
10 You Yourself crushed Rahab like one who is slain;
You scattered Your enemies with Your mighty arm.

11 The heavens are Yours, the earth also is Yours;
The world and [147]all it contains, You have founded them.
12 The north and the south, You have created them;
Tabor and Hermon shout for joy at Your name.
13 You have a strong arm;
Your hand is mighty, Your right hand is exalted.
14 Righteousness and justice are the foundation of Your throne;
Lovingkindness and truth go before You.
15 How blessed are the people who know the [148]joyful sound!
O LORD, they walk in the light of Your countenance.
16 In Your name they rejoice all the day,
And by Your righteousness they are exalted.
17 For You are the glory of their strength,
And by Your favor our horn is exalted.
18 For our shield belongs to the LORD,
[149]And our king to the Holy One of Israel.

19 Once You spoke in vision to Your godly ones,
And said, "I have given help to one who is mighty;
I have exalted one chosen from the people.
20 "I have found David My servant;
With My holy oil I have anointed him,
21 With whom My hand will be established;
My arm also will strengthen him.
22 "The enemy will not [150]deceive him,
Nor the son of wickedness afflict him.
23 "But I shall crush his adversaries before him,
And strike those who hate him.
24 "My faithfulness and My lovingkindness will be with him,
And in My name his horn will be exalted.
25 "I shall also set his hand on the sea
And his right hand on the rivers.
26 "He will cry to Me, 'You are my Father,
My God, and the rock of my salvation.'
27 "I also shall make him *My* firstborn,
The highest of the kings of the earth.
28 "My lovingkindness I will keep for him forever,

89:6 Ps 86:8; 113:5; Ps 29:1; 82:1
89:7 Ps 47:2; 68:35; 76:7
89:8 Ps 35:10; 71:19
89:9 Ps 65:7; 107:29
89:10 Ps 87:4; Is 30:7; 51:9; Ps 18:14; 68:1
89:11 Gen 1:1; 1 Chr 29:11; Ps 96:5
89:12 Job 26:7; Josh 19:22; Judg 4:6; Jer 46:18
89:13 Ps 98:1; 118:16
89:14 Ps 97:2; Ps 85:13
89:15 Lev 23:24; Num 10:10; Ps 98:6; Ps 4:6; 44:3; 67:1; 80:3
89:16 Ps 105:3
89:17 Ps 28:8; Ps 75:10; 92:10; 148:14
89:18 Ps 47:9; Ps 71:22; 78:41
89:19 2 Sam 17:10; 1 Kin 11:34; Ps 78:70
89:20 1 Sam 13:14; 16:1-12; Acts 13:22
89:21 Ps 18:35; 80:17
89:22 2 Sam 7:10; Ps 125:3
89:23 2 Sam 7:9; Ps 18:40
89:25 Ps 72:8
89:26 1 Chr 22:10; Jer 3:19; 2 Sam 22:47; Ps 95:1
89:27 Ps 2:7; Jer 31:9; Col 1:15, 18; Ps 72:11; Rev 19:16

147 Lit *its fullness* **148** Or *blast of the trumpet, shout of joy* **149** Or *Even to the Holy One of Israel our King* **150** Or *exact usury from him*

89:12 This refers to Mount Tabor and Mount Hermon. Mount Tabor, though low in elevation (1,900 feet), was the scene of Deborah's victory in Judges 4. Mount Hermon (9,000 feet) was tall and majestic.

89:14–15 Righteousness, justice, lovingkindness, and truth are the foundation of God's throne; they are fundamental aspects of the way God rules. As God's ambassadors, we should deal with people similarly. Make sure your actions flow out of righteousness, justice, love, and faithfulness because any unfair, unloving, or dishonest action cannot come from God.

89:17, 24 *Horn* refers to the horn of an animal, the symbol of its power. In verse 17, *horn* means our strong one, our hope for the Messiah. In verse 24, David is promised to have God's power to accomplish God's will. Without God's help, we are weak and powerless, inadequate for even the simplest spiritual tasks. But when we are filled with God's Spirit, his power flows through us and our accomplishments will exceed our expectations.

And My covenant shall be confirmed to him.
29 "So I will establish his descendants forever
And his throne as the days of heaven.

30 "If his sons forsake My law
And do not walk in My judgments,
31 If they [151]violate My statutes
And do not keep My commandments,
32 Then I will punish their transgression with the rod
And their iniquity with stripes.
33 "But I will not break off My lovingkindness from him,
Nor deal falsely in My faithfulness.
34 "My covenant I will not violate,
Nor will I alter the utterance of My lips.
35 "[152]Once I have sworn by My holiness;
I will not lie to David.
36 "His descendants shall endure forever
And his throne as the sun before Me.
37 "It shall be established forever like the moon,
And the witness in the sky is faithful." Selah.

38 But You have cast off and rejected,
You have been full of wrath against Your anointed.
39 You have spurned the covenant of Your servant;
You have profaned his crown in the dust.
40 You have broken down all his walls;
You have brought his strongholds to ruin.
41 All who pass along the way plunder him;
He has become a reproach to his neighbors.
42 You have exalted the right hand of his adversaries;
You have made all his enemies rejoice.
43 You also turn back the edge of his sword
And have not made him stand in battle.
44 You have made his splendor to cease
And cast his throne to the ground.
45 You have shortened the days of his youth;
You have covered him with shame. Selah.

46 How long, O LORD?
Will You hide Yourself forever?
Will Your wrath burn like fire?
47 Remember what my span of life is;
For what vanity You have created all the sons of men!
48 What man can live and not see death?
Can he deliver his soul from the power of Sheol? Selah.

49 Where are Your former lovingkindnesses, O Lord,
Which You swore to David in Your faithfulness?
50 Remember, O Lord, the reproach of Your servants;
How I bear in my bosom *the reproach of* all the many peoples,
51 With which Your enemies have reproached, O LORD,
With which they have reproached the footsteps of Your anointed.

89:29 Ps 18:50; 89:4, 36; 1 Kin 2:4; Ps 89:4; 132:12; Is 9:7; Jer 33:17; Deut 11:21
89:30 2 Sam 7:14; Ps 119:53
89:32 Job 9:34; 21:9
89:33 2 Sam 7:15
89:34 Deut 7:9; Jer 33:20, 21; Num 23:19
89:35 Ps 60:6; Amos 4:2
89:36 Ps 89:29; Luke 1:33; Ps 72:5; Ps 72:17
89:37 Ps 72:5; Job 16:19
89:38 Ps 44:9; Deut 32:19; 1 Chr 28:9; Ps 20:6; 89:20, 51
89:39 Ps 78:59; Lam 2:7; Ps 74:7; Lam 5:16
89:40 Ps 80:12; Lam 2:2, 5
89:41 Ps 80:12; Ps 44:13; 69:9, 19; 79:4
89:42 Ps 13:2; Ps 80:6
89:43 Ps 44:10
89:44 Ezek 28:7
89:45 Ps 102:23; Ps 44:15; 71:13; 109:29
89:46 Ps 13:1; 44:24; Ps 79:5; 80:4
89:47 Job 7:7; 10:9; 14:1; Ps 39:5; 62:9; Eccl 1:2; 2:11
89:48 Ps 22:29; 49:9; Ps 49:15
89:49 2 Sam 7:15; Jer 30:9; Ezek 34:23
89:50 Ps 69:9; 74:18, 22
89:51 Ps 74:10, 18, 22; Ps 89:38

151 Lit *profane* **152** Or *One thing*

89:34–37 In light of Israel's continual disobedience throughout history, this is an amazing promise. God promised that David's descendants would always sit on the throne (89:29), but that if the people disobeyed, they would be punished (89:30–32). Yet, even through their disobedience and punishment, God would never break faith with them (89:33). Israel *did* disobey, evil ran rampant, the nation was divided, exile came—but through it all, a remnant of God's people remained faithful. Centuries later, the Messiah arrived, the eternal King from David's line, just as God had promised. All that God promises, he fulfills. He will not take back even one word of what he says. God can also be trusted to save us as he promised he would (Hebrews 6:13–18). God is completely reliable.

89:52 Ps 41:13; 72:19; 106:48

52 Blessed be the LORD forever!
Amen and Amen.

BOOK 4
PSALMS 90:1—106:48

These psalms include a prayer of Moses, a psalm about oppressors, and a psalm praising God as our King. These psalms remind us that we should remember our place and be submissive before the almighty God.

PSALM 90

A Prayer of Moses, the man of God.

Theme: God's eternal nature is contrasted with man's frailty. Our time on earth is limited and we are to use it wisely, not living for the moment, but with our eternal home in mind.
Author: Moses, making this the oldest of the psalms

90:1 Deut 33:27; Ps 71:3; 91:1; Ezek 11:16
90:2 Job 15:7; Prov 8:25; Gen 1:1; Ps 102:25; 104:5; Ps 93:2; 102:24, 27; Jer 10:10
90:3 Gen 3:19; Job 34:14, 15; Ps 104:29
90:4 2 Pet 3:8; Ps 39:5; Ex 14:24; Judg 7:19
90:5 Job 22:16; 27:20; Job 14:12; 20:8; Ps 76:5; Ps 103:15; Is 40:6
90:6 Job 14:2; Ps 92:7; Matt 6:30; James 1:11

1 Lord, You have been our [153]dwelling place in all generations.
2 Before the mountains were born
Or You gave birth to the earth and the world,
Even from everlasting to everlasting, You are God.

3 You turn man back into dust
And say, "Return, O children of men."
4 For a thousand years in Your sight
Are like yesterday when it passes by,
Or *as* a watch in the night.
5 You have swept them away like a flood, they fall asleep;
In the morning they are like grass which sprouts anew.
6 In the morning it flourishes and sprouts anew;
Toward evening it fades and withers away.

90:7 Ps 39:11
90:8 Ps 50:21; Jer 16:17; Ps 19:12; Eccl 12:14
90:9 Ps 78:33
90:10 2 Kin 19:35; Eccl 12:2-7; Jer 20:18; Job 20:8; Ps 78:39
90:11 Ps 76:7; Neh 5:9
90:12 Deut 32:29; Ps 39:4; Prov 2:1-6
90:13 Ps 6:4; 80:14; Ps 6:3; 74:10; Ex 32:12; Deut 32:36; Ps 106:45; 135:14; Amos 7:3, 6; Jon 3:9
90:14 Ps 36:8; 65:4; 103:5; Jer 31:14; Ps 31:7; 85:6

7 For we have been consumed by Your anger
And by Your wrath we have been dismayed.
8 You have placed our iniquities before You,
Our secret *sins* in the light of Your presence.
9 For all our days have declined in YoYour fury;
We have finished our years like a sigh.
10 As for the days of our life, they contain seventy years,
Or if due to strength, eighty years,
Yet their pride is *but* labor and sorrow;
For soon it is gone and we fly away.
11 Who understands the power of Your anger
And Your fury, according to the fear that is due You?
12 So teach us to number our days,
That we may present to You a heart of wisdom.

13 Do return, O LORD; how long *will it be?*
And be sorry for Your servants.
14 O satisfy us in the morning with Your lovingkindness,
That we may sing for joy and be glad all our days.

153 Or *hiding place;* some ancient mss read *place of refuge*

90:4 Moses reminds us that a thousand years are like a day to the Lord. God is not limited by time. It's easy to get discouraged when years pass and the world doesn't get better. We sometimes wonder if God is able to see the future. But don't assume that God has our limitations. God is completely unrestricted by time. Because he is eternal, we can depend on him.

90:8 God knows all our sins as if they were spread out before him, even the secret ones. We don't need to cover up our sins before him because we can talk openly and honestly with him. But while he knows all that terrible information about us, God still loves us and wants to forgive us. This should encourage us to come to him rather than frighten us into covering up our sin.

90:12 Realizing that life is short helps us use the little time we have more wisely and for eternal good. Take time to number your days by asking, "What do I want to see happen in my life before I die? What small step could I take toward that purpose today?"

15 Make us glad according to the days You have afflicted us,
And the years we have seen [154]evil.
16 Let Your work appear to Your servants
And Your majesty to their children.
17 Let the favor of the Lord our God be upon us;
And [155]confirm for us the work of our hands;
Yes, [155]confirm the work of our hands.

90:15 Ps 86:4; Deut 2:14-16; Ps 31:10

90:16 Deut 32:4; Ps 44:1; 77:12; 92:4; Hab 3:2; 1 Kin 8:11; Is 6:3

90:17 Ps 27:4; Ps 37:23; Is 26:12; 1 Cor 3:7

PSALM 91

Theme: God's protection in the midst of danger. God doesn't promise a world free from danger, but he does promise his help whenever we face danger.
Author: Anonymous

1 He who dwells in the shelter of the Most High
Will abide in the shadow of the Almighty.
2 I will say to the LORD, "My refuge and my fortress,
My God, in whom I trust!"
3 For it is He who delivers you from the snare of the trapper
And from the deadly pestilence.
4 He will cover you with His pinions,
And under His wings you may seek refuge;
His faithfulness is a shield and bulwark.

5 You will not be afraid of the terror by night,
Or of the arrow that flies by day;
6 Of the pestilence that stalks in darkness,
Or of the destruction that lays waste at noon.
7 A thousand may fall at your side
And ten thousand at your right hand,
But it shall not approach you.
8 You will only look on with your eyes
And see the recompense of the wicked.
9 For you have made the LORD, my refuge,
Even the Most High, your dwelling place.
10 No evil will befall you,
Nor will any plague come near your tent.

11 For He will give His angels charge concerning you,
To guard you in all your ways.
12 They will bear you up in their hands,
That you do not strike your foot against a stone.
13 You will tread upon the lion and cobra,
The young lion and the serpent you will trample down.

14 "Because he has loved Me, therefore I will deliver him;
I will set him *securely* on high, because he has known My name.

91:1 Ps 27:5; 31:20; 32:7; Ps 17:8; 121:5; Is 25:4; 32:2

91:2 Ps 14:6; 91:9; 94:22; 142:5; Ps 18:2; 31:3; Jer 16:19; Ps 25:2; 56:4

91:3 Ps 124:7; Prov 6:5; 1 Kin 8:37; 2 Chr 20:9; Ps 91:6

91:4 Is 51:16; Ps 17:8; 36:7; 57:1; 63:7; Ps 40:11; Ps 35:2

91:5 Job 5:19-23; Ps 23:4; 27:1; Song 3:8; Ps 64:4

91:6 2 Kin 19:35; Ps 91:10; Job 5:22

91:7 Gen 7:23; Josh 14:10

91:8 Ps 37:34; 58:10

91:9 Ps 91:2; Ps 90:1

91:10 Prov 12:21

91:11 Ps 34:7; Matt 4:6; Luke 4:10, 11; Heb 1:14

91:12 Matt 4:6; Luke 4:11

91:13 Judg 14:6; Dan 6:22; Luke 10:19

91:14 Ps 145:20; Ps 59:1; Ps 9:10

154 Or *trouble* **155** Or *give permanence to*

90:17 Because our days are numbered, we want our work to count, to be effective and productive. We desire to see God's eternal plan revealed now and for our work to reflect his permanence. If we feel dissatisfied with this life and all its imperfections, remember our desire to see our work established is placed there by God (see the note on Ecclesiastes 3:11). But our desire can only be satisfied in eternity. Until then we must apply ourselves to loving and serving God.

91:1–6 God is a shelter, a refuge when we are afraid. The writer's faith in the Almighty God as Protector would carry him through all the dangers and fears of life. This should be a picture of our trust—trading all our fears for faith in him, no matter how intense our fears. To do this we must "dwell" and "abide" with him (91:1). By entrusting ourselves to his protection and pledging our daily devotion to him, we will be kept safe.

91:11 One of the functions of angels is to watch over believers (Hebrews 1:14). There are examples of guardian angels in Scripture (1 Kings 19:5; Daniel 6:22; Matthew 18:10; Luke 16:22; Acts 12:7), although there is no indication that one angel is assigned to each believer. Angels can also be God's messengers (Matthew 2:13; Acts 27:23–24). Angels are not visible, except on special occasions (Numbers 22:31; Luke 2:9). Verses 11 and 12 were quoted by Satan when he tempted Jesus (Matthew 4:6; Luke 4:10, 11). It is comforting to know that God watches over us even in times of great stress and fear.

91:15 Job 12:4; Ps 50:15; 1 Sam 2:30; John 12:26

91:16 Deut 6:2; Ps 21:4; Prov 3:1, 2; Ps 50:23

92:1 Ps 147:1; Ps 135:3

92:2 Ps 59:16; Ps 89:1

92:3 1 Sam 10:5; 1 Chr 13:8; Neh 12:27; Ps 33:2

92:4 Ps 40:5; 90:16; Ps 106:47; Ps 8:6; 111:7; 143:5

92:5 Ps 40:5; 111:2; Rev 15:3; Ps 33:11; 40:5; 139:17; Ps 36:6; Rom 11:33

92:6 Ps 49:10; 73:22; 94:8

92:7 Job 12:6; Ps 90:5; Ps 94:4; Ps 37:38

92:8 Ps 83:18; 93:4; 113:5

92:9 Ps 37:20; Ps 68:1; 89:10

92:10 Ps 75:10; 89:17; 112:9; Ps 23:5; 45:7

92:11 Ps 54:7; 91:8

92:12 Num 24:6; Ps 1:3; 52:8; 72:7; Jer 17:8; Hos 14:5, 6; Ps 104:16; Ezek 31:3

92:13 Ps 80:15; Is 60:21; Ps 100:4; 116:19

92:14 Prov 11:30; Is 37:31; John 15:2; James 3:18

92:15 Job 34:10; Ps 25:8; Deut 32:4; Ps 18:2; 94:22; Rom 9:14

15 "He will call upon Me, and I will answer him;
I will be with him in trouble;
I will rescue him and honor him.
16 "With a long life I will satisfy him
And let him see My salvation."

PSALM 92

A Psalm, a Song for the Sabbath day.

Theme: Be thankful and faithful every day.
This psalm was used in temple services on the Sabbath.
Author: Anonymous

1 It is good to give thanks to the LORD
And to sing praises to Your name, O Most High;
2 To declare Your lovingkindness in the morning
And Your faithfulness by night,
3 With the ten-stringed lute and with the harp,
With resounding music upon the lyre.
4 For You, O LORD, have made me glad by what You have done,
I will sing for joy at the works of Your hands.

5 How great are Your works, O LORD!
Your thoughts are very deep.
6 A senseless man has no knowledge,
Nor does a stupid man understand this:
7 That when the wicked sprouted up like grass
And all who did iniquity flourished,
It *was only* that they might be destroyed forevermore.
8 But You, O LORD, are on high forever.
9 For, behold, Your enemies, O LORD,
For, behold, Your enemies will perish;
All who do iniquity will be scattered.

10 But You have exalted my horn like *that of* the wild ox;
I have been anointed with fresh oil.
11 And my eye has looked *exultantly* upon my foes,
My ears hear of the evildoers who rise up against me.
12 The righteous man will flourish like the palm tree,
He will grow like a cedar in Lebanon.
13 Planted in the house of the LORD,
They will flourish in the courts of our God.
14 They will still yield fruit in old age;
They shall be [156]full of sap and very green,
15 To declare that the LORD is upright;
He is my rock, and there is no unrighteousness in Him.

156 Lit *fat and*

92:1–2 During the Thanksgiving holiday, we focus on our blessings and express our gratitude to God for them. But thanks should be on our lips every day. We can never say thank you enough to parents, friends, leaders, and especially to God. When thanksgiving becomes an integral part of your life, you will find that your attitude toward life will change. You will become more positive, gracious, loving, and humble.

92:12–13 Palm trees are known for their long life. To flourish like palm trees means to stand tall and to live long. The cedars of Lebanon grew to 120 feet in height and up to 30 feet in circumference; thus, they were solid, strong, and immovable. The psalmist saw believers as upright, strong, and unmoved by the winds of circumstance. Those who place their faith firmly in God can have this strength and vitality.

92:14 Honoring God is not limited to young people who seem to have unlimited strength and energy. Even in old age, devoted believers can produce spiritual fruit. There are many faithful older people who continue to have a fresh outlook and can teach us from a lifetime experience of serving God. Seek out an elderly friend or relative to tell you about his or her experiences with the Lord and challenge you to new heights of spiritual growth.

PSALM 93

Theme: God's unchanging and almighty nature. His creation reminds us of his great power.
Author: Anonymous

1 The LORD reigns, He is clothed with majesty;
The LORD has clothed and girded Himself with strength;
Indeed, the world is firmly established, it will not be moved.
2 Your throne is established from of old;
You are from everlasting.

3 The floods have lifted up, O LORD,
The floods have lifted up their voice,
The floods lift up their pounding waves.
4 More than the sounds of many waters,
Than the mighty breakers of the sea,
The LORD on high is mighty.
5 Your testimonies are fully confirmed;
Holiness befits Your house,
O LORD, forevermore.

93:1 Ps 96:10; 97:1; 99:1; Ps 104:1; Ps 65:6; Is 51:9; Ps 96:10
93:2 Ps 45:6; Lam 5:19; Ps 90:2
93:3 Ps 96:11; 98:7, 8
93:4 Ps 65:7; 89:6, 9; 92:8
93:5 Ps 19:7; Ps 29:2; 96:9; 1 Cor 3:17

PSALM 94

Theme: God will keep his people form the severe punishment awaiting the wicked. Since God is holy and just, we can be certain that the wicked will not prevail.
Author: Anonymous

1 O LORD, God of vengeance,
God of vengeance, shine forth!
2 Rise up, O Judge of the earth,
Render recompense to the proud.
3 How long shall the wicked, O LORD,
How long shall the wicked exult?
4 They pour forth *words,* they speak arrogantly;
All who do wickedness vaunt themselves.
5 They crush Your people, O LORD,
And afflict Your heritage.
6 They slay the widow and the stranger
And murder the orphans.
7 They have said, "The LORD does not see,
Nor does the God of Jacob pay heed."

8 Pay heed, you senseless among the people;
And when will you understand, stupid ones?
9 He who planted the ear, does He not hear?
He who formed the eye, does He not see?
10 He who chastens the nations, will He not rebuke,
Even He who teaches man knowledge?
11 The LORD knows the thoughts of man,
That they are a *mere* breath.

12 Blessed is the man whom You chasten, O LORD,
And whom You teach out of Your law;

94:1 Deut 32:35; Is 35:4; Nah 1:2; Rom 12:19; Ps 50:2; 80:1
94:2 Ps 7:6; Gen 18:25; Ps 31:23
94:3 Job 20:5
94:4 Ps 31:18; 75:5; Ps 10:3; 52:1
94:5 Is 3:15; Ps 79:1
94:6 Is 10:2
94:7 Job 22:13; Ps 10:11
94:8 Ps 92:6
94:9 Ex 4:11; Prov 20:12
94:10 Ps 44:2; Job 35:11; Is 28:26
94:11 Job 11:11; 1 Cor 3:20
94:12 Deut 8:5; Job 5:17; Ps 119:71; Prov 3:11, 12; Heb 12:5, 6; Ps 119:171

93:1ff Jewish tradition claims that the next seven psalms (93—99) anticipated some of the works of the Messiah. Psalm 93 is said to have been used in post-captivity temple services and may have been written during Sennacherib's invasion (2 Kings 18:13—19:37).

93:5 The key to God's eternal reign is his holiness. God's glory is seen not only in his strength but in his perfect moral character as well. God will never do anything that is not morally perfect. This reassures us that we can trust him; yet it places a demand on us. Our desire to be holy (dedicated to God and morally clean) is our only suitable response. We must never use unholy means to reach a holy goal because God says, "You shall be holy, for I the LORD your God am holy" (Leviticus 19:1–2).

94:12–13 At times, God must discipline us to help us. This is similar to a loving parent's disciplining his child. The discipline is not very enjoyable to the child, but it is essential to teach him right from wrong. The Bible says that "all discipline for the moment seems not to be joyful, but sorrowful; yet to those who have been

13 That You may grant him relief from the days of adversity,
Until a pit is dug for the wicked.
14 For the LORD will not abandon His people,
Nor will He forsake His inheritance.
15 For judgment will again be righteous,
And all the upright in heart will follow it.
16 Who will stand up for me against evildoers?
Who will take his stand for me against those who do wickedness?

17 If the LORD had not been my help,
My soul would soon have dwelt in *the abode of* silence.
18 If I should say, "My foot has slipped,"
Your lovingkindness, O LORD, will hold me up.
19 When my anxious thoughts multiply within me,
Your consolations delight my soul.
20 Can a throne of destruction be allied with You,
One which devises mischief by decree?
21 They band themselves together against the life of the righteous
And condemn the innocent to death.
22 But the LORD has been my stronghold,
And my God the rock of my refuge.
23 He has brought back their wickedness upon them
And will destroy them in their evil;
The LORD our God will destroy them.

94:13 Ps 49:5; Ps 9:15; 55:23
94:14 1 Sam 12:22; Lam 3:31; Rom 11:2
94:15 Ps 97:2; Is 42:3; Mic 7:9
94:16 Num 10:35; Is 28:21; 33:10; Ps 17:13; 59:2
94:17 Ps 124:1, 2
94:18 Ps 38:16; 73:2
94:19 Is 57:18; 66:13
94:20 Amos 6:3; Ps 50:16; 58:2
94:21 Ps 56:6; 59:3; Ps 106:38; Prov 17:15; Matt 27:4
94:22 Ps 9:9; 59:9; Ps 18:2; 71:7
94:23 Ps 7:16; 140:9, 11; Gen 19:15

PSALM 95

Theme: An invitation to worship God.
Author: Anonymous

1 O come, let us sing for joy to the LORD,
Let us shout joyfully to the rock of our salvation.
2 Let us come before His presence with thanksgiving,
Let us shout joyfully to Him with psalms.
3 For the LORD is a great God
And a great King above all gods,
4 In whose hand are the depths of the earth,
The peaks of the mountains are His also.
5 The sea is His, for it was He who made it,
And His hands formed the dry land.

6 Come, let us worship and bow down,
Let us kneel before the LORD our Maker.

95:1 Ps 66:1; 81:1; Ps 89:26
95:2 Mic 6:6; Ps 100:4; 147:7; Jon 2:9; Ps 81:2; Eph 5:19; James 5:13
95:3 Ps 48:1; 135:5; 145:3; Ps 96:4; 97:9
95:4 Ps 135:6
95:5 Gen 1:9, 10; Ps 146:6; Jon 1:9
95:6 Ps 96:9; 99:5, 9; Phil 2:10; Ps 100:3; 149:2

JUSTICE IN THE BOOK OF PSALMS

Justice is a major theme in Psalms. The psalmists praise God because he is just; they plead for him to intervene and bring justice where there is oppression and wickedness; they condemn the wicked who trust in their wealth; they extol the righteous who are just toward their neighbors.

Justice in Psalms is more than honesty. It is active intervention on behalf of the helpless, especially the poor. The psalmists do not merely wish the poor could be given what they need, but they plead with God to destroy those nations that are subverting justice and oppressing God's people.

Here are some examples of psalms that speak about justice. As you read them, ask yourself, "Who is my neighbor? Does my life-style—my work, my play, my buying habits, my giving—help or hurt people who have less than I do? What one thing could I do this week to help a helpless person?"

Selected psalms that emphasize this theme are Psalms 7; 9; 15; 37; 50; 72; 75; 82; 94; 145.

---

trained by it, afterwards it yields the peaceful fruit of righteousness" (Hebrews 12:11). When you feel God's hand of correction, accept it as proof of his love. Realize that God is urging you to follow his paths instead of stubbornly going your own way.

7 For He is our God,
And we are the people of His pasture and the sheep of His hand.
Today, if you would hear His voice,
8 Do not harden your hearts, as at [157]Meribah,
As in the day of [158]Massah in the wilderness,
9 "When your fathers tested Me,
They tried Me, though they had seen My work.
10 "For forty years I loathed *that* generation,
And said they are a people who err in their heart,
And they do not know My ways.
11 "Therefore I swore in My anger,
Truly they shall not enter into My rest."

95:7 Ps 79:13; Ps 74:1; Heb 3:7-11, 15; 4:7
95:8 Ex 17:2-7; Num 20:13; Ex 17:7; Deut 6:16
95:9 Num 14:22; Ps 78:18; 1 Cor 10:9
95:10 Acts 7:36; 13:18; Heb 3:10, 17
95:11 Num 14:23, 28-30; Deut 1:35; Heb 4:3, 5; Deut 12:9

PSALM 96

Theme: How to praise God. We can sing about him, tell others about him, worship him, give him glory, bring offerings to him, and live holy lives.
Author: Possibly David because this psalm closely resembles David's hymn of praise in 1 Chronicles 16:23-36

1 Sing to the LORD a new song;
Sing to the LORD, all the earth.
2 Sing to the LORD, bless His name;
Proclaim good tidings of His salvation from day to day.
3 Tell of His glory among the nations,
His wonderful deeds among all the peoples.
4 For great is the LORD and greatly to be praised;
He is to be feared above all gods.
5 For all the gods of the peoples are idols,
But the LORD made the heavens.
6 Splendor and majesty are before Him,
Strength and beauty are in His sanctuary.

7 [159]Ascribe to the LORD, O families of the peoples,
[159]Ascribe to the LORD glory and strength.
8 [159]Ascribe to the LORD the glory of His name;
Bring an offering and come into His courts.
9 Worship the LORD in [160]holy attire;
Tremble before Him, all the earth.
10 Say among the nations, "The LORD reigns;
Indeed, the world is firmly established, it will not be moved;
He will judge the peoples with [161]equity."

96:1 1 Chr 16:23-33; Ps 40:3
96:2 Ps 71:15
96:3 Ps 145:12
96:4 Ps 48:1; 145:3; Ps 18:3; Ps 89:7; Ps 95:3
96:5 1 Chr 16:26; Jer 10:11; Ps 115:15; Is 42:5
96:6 Ps 104:1
96:7 Ps 22:27; 1 Chr 16:28, 29; Ps 29:1, 2
96:8 Ps 79:9; 115:1; Ps 45:12; 72:10
96:9 1 Chr 16:29; 2 Chr 20:21; Ps 29:2; 110:3; Ps 33:8; 114:7
96:10 Ps 93:1; 97:1; Ps 9:8; 58:11; 67:4; 98:9

157 Or *place of strife* **158** Or *temptation* **159** Lit *Give* **160** Or *the splendor of holiness* **161** Or *uprightness*

95:8 A hardened heart is as useless as a hardened lump of clay or a hardened loaf of bread. Nothing can restore it and make it useful. The psalmist warns against hardening our hearts as Israel did in the wilderness by continuing to resist God's will (Exodus 17:7). They were so convinced that God couldn't deliver them that they simply lost their faith in him. When someone's heart becomes hardened, that person is so stubbornly set in his ways that he or she cannot turn to God. This does not happen all at once; it is the result of a series of choices to disregard God's will. If you resist God long enough, God may toss you aside like hardened bread, useless and worthless.

95:8 *Meribah* means "quarreling," and *Massah* means "testing." This refers to the incident at Rephidim (Exodus 17:1–7) when the Israelites complained to Moses because they had no water (see also Numbers 20:1–13).

95:11 What keeps us from God's ultimate blessings (entering his "rest")? Ungrateful hearts (95:2), not worshiping or submitting to him (95:6), hardening our hearts (95:8), testing God because of stubborn doubts (95:9). In Hebrews 4:5–11, we are warned not to harden our hearts, but to reject the glamour of sin and anything else that would lead us away from God.

96:1–4 The psalmist sings out his praises to God, overwhelmed by all that God has done. If we believe God is great, we cannot help telling others about him. The best witnessing happens when our hearts are full of appreciation for what he has done. God has chosen to use us to "tell . . . his wonderful deeds among all the peoples." Praise for our great God overflows from his creation and should overflow from our lips. How well are you doing at telling others about God's greatness?

96:11 Ps 69:34; Is 49:13; Ps 97:1; Ps 98:7

96:12 Ps 65:13; Is 35:1; 55:12, 13; Is 44:23

96:13 Ps 98:9; Rev 19:11

97:1 Ps 96:10; Ps 96:11; Is 42:10, 12

97:2 Ex 19:9; Deut 4:11; 1 Kin 8:12; Ps 18:11; Ps 89:14

97:3 Ps 18:8; 50:3; Dan 7:10; Hab 3:5; Mal 4:1; Heb 12:29

97:4 Ex 19:16; Ps 77:18; Ps 96:9; 104:32

97:5 Ps 46:6; Amos 9:5; Mic 1:4; Nah 1:5; Josh 3:11

97:6 Ps 19:1; 50:6; Ps 98:2; Is 6:3; 40:5; 66:18

97:7 Ps 78:58; Is 42:17; 44:9, 11; Jer 10:14; Ps 106:36; Jer 50:2; Hab 2:18; Heb 1:6

97:8 Ps 48:11; Zeph 3:14

97:9 Ps 83:18; Ex 18:11; Ps 95:3; 96:4; 135:5

97:10 Ps 34:14; Prov 8:13; Amos 5:15; Rom 12:9; Ps 31:23; 145:20; Prov 2:8; Ps 37:40; Jer 15:21; Dan 3:28

97:11 Job 22:28; Ps 112:4; Prov 4:18; Ps 64:10

97:12 Ps 32:11; Ps 30:4

11 Let the heavens be glad, and let the earth rejoice;
Let the sea roar, and all it contains;
12 Let the field exult, and all that is in it.
Then all the trees of the forest will sing for joy
13 Before the LORD, for He is coming,
For He is coming to judge the earth.
He will judge the world in righteousness
And the peoples in His faithfulness.

PSALM 97

Theme: God, our awesome Conqueror, is righteous and just.
Author: Anonymous

1 The LORD reigns, let the earth rejoice;
Let the many [162]islands be glad.
2 Clouds and thick darkness surround Him;
Righteousness and justice are the foundation of His throne.
3 Fire goes before Him
And burns up His adversaries round about.
4 His lightnings lit up the world;
The earth saw and trembled.
5 The mountains melted like wax at the presence of the LORD,
At the presence of the Lord of the whole earth.
6 The heavens declare His righteousness,
And all the peoples have seen His glory.

7 Let all those be ashamed who serve graven images,
Who boast themselves of idols;
Worship Him, all you gods.
8 Zion heard *this* and was glad,
And the daughters of Judah have rejoiced
Because of Your judgments, O LORD.
9 For You are the LORD Most High over all the earth;
You are exalted far above all gods.

10 Hate evil, you who love the LORD,
Who preserves the souls of His godly ones;
He delivers them from the hand of the wicked.
11 Light is sown *like seed* for the righteous
And gladness for the upright in heart.
12 Be glad in the LORD, you righteous ones,
And give thanks to His holy name.

162 Or *coastlands*

97:2 The clouds and thick darkness that surround God symbolize his unapproachable holiness and the inability of people to find him on their own. If he were uncovered, no one could stand before his blazing holiness and glory.

97:7 People worship all kinds of images and idols. Although God reveals himself and his love through nature and the Bible, there are many who decide to ignore or reject him and pursue goals they believe are more important. The Bible makes it clear that these people are idol worshipers because they give their highest loyalty to something other than God. One day we will stand before God in all his glory and power. Then we will see all our goals and accomplishments for what they really are. How foolish our earthly pursuits will seem then!

97:10 A sincere desire to please God will result in an alignment of your desires with God's desires. You will love what God loves and hate what God hates. If you love the Lord, you will hate evil. If you do not despise the actions of people who take advantage of others, if you admire people who only look out for themselves, or if you envy those who get ahead using any means to accomplish their ends, then your primary desire in life is not to please God. Learn to love God's ways and hate evil in every form—not only the obvious sins but also the socially acceptable ones.

PSALM 98

A Psalm.

Theme: A song of joy and victory. Because God is victorious over evil, all those who follow him will be victorious with him when he judges the earth.
Author: Anonymous

1 O sing to the LORD a new song,
For He has done wonderful things,
His right hand and His holy arm have [163]gained the victory for Him.
2 The LORD has made known His salvation;
He has revealed His righteousness in the sight of the nations.
3 He has remembered His lovingkindness and His faithfulness to the house of Israel;
All the ends of the earth have seen the salvation of our God.

4 Shout joyfully to the LORD, all the earth;
Break forth and sing for joy and sing praises.
5 Sing praises to the LORD with the lyre,
With the lyre and the sound of melody.
6 With trumpets and the sound of the horn
Shout joyfully before the King, the LORD.

7 Let the sea roar and all it contains,
The world and those who dwell in it.
8 Let the rivers clap their hands,
Let the mountains sing together for joy
9 Before the LORD, for He is coming to judge the earth;
He will judge the world with righteousness
And the peoples with equity.

98:1 Ps 33:3; Ps 40:5; 96:3; Ex 15:6; Is 52:10
98:2 Is 52:10; Is 62:2; Rom 3:25
98:3 Luke 1:54, 72; Ps 22:27
98:4 Ps 100:1; Is 44:23
98:5 Ps 92:3; Is 51:3
98:6 Num 10:10; 2 Chr 15:14; Ps 66:1; Ps 47:7
98:7 Ps 96:11; Ps 24:1
98:8 Ps 93:3; Is 55:12; Ps 65:12; 89:12
98:9 Ps 96:13; Ps 96:10

PSALM 99

Theme: Praise for God's fairness and holiness. Because God is perfectly just and fair, we can trust him completely.
Author: Anonymous

1 The LORD reigns, let the peoples tremble;
He is enthroned *above* the cherubim, let the earth shake!
2 The LORD is great in Zion,
And He is exalted above all the peoples.
3 Let them praise Your great and awesome name;
Holy is He.
4 The strength of the King loves [164]justice;
You have established equity;
You have executed [164]justice and righteousness in Jacob.
5 Exalt the LORD our God
And worship at His footstool;
Holy is He.

99:1 Ps 97:1; Ex 25:22; 1 Sam 4:4; Ps 80:1
99:2 Ps 48:1; Is 12:6; Ps 97:9; 113:4
99:3 Deut 28:58; Ps 76:1; Lev 19:2; Josh 24:19; 1 Sam 2:2; Ps 22:3; Is 6:3
99:4 Ps 11:7; 33:5; Ps 17:2; 98:9; Ps 103:6; 146:7; Jer 23:5
99:5 Ps 34:3; 107:32; 118:28; Ps 132:7; Ps 99:3

163 Or *accomplished salvation* **164** Or *judgment*

98:1ff This is a psalm of praise anticipating the coming of God to rule his people. Jesus fulfilled this anticipation when he came to save all people from their sins (98:2–3), and he will come again to judge the world (98:8–9). God is both perfectly loving and perfectly just. He is merciful when he punishes, and he overlooks no sin when he loves. Praise him for his promise to save you and to return again.

99:1 Cherubim are mighty angels that comprise one of several ranks of angels. (For more on angels, see the note on 91:11.)

99:3 Everyone should praise God's great and awesome name because his name symbolizes his nature, his personage, and his reputation. But the name of God is used so often in vulgar conversation that we have lost sight of its holiness. How easy it is to treat God lightly in everyday life. If you claim him as your father, live worthy of the family name. Respect God's name and give him praise by both your *words* and your *life.*

99:5 God's holiness is terribly frightening for sinners, but a wonderful comfort for believers. God is morally perfect and is set apart from people and sin. He has no weaknesses or shortcomings. For sinners, this is frightening because all their inadequacies and evil are exposed by the light of God's holiness. God cannot tolerate, ignore, or excuse sin. For believers, God's holiness gives comfort because, as we worship him, we are lifted from the mire of sin. As we believe in him, we are made holy.

99:6 Jer 15:1; Ex 24:6-8; 29:26; 40:23-27; Lev 8:1-30; 1 Sam 7:9; 12:18; Ps 22.4, 5, Ex 15:25; 32:30-34

99:7 Ex 33:9; Num 12:5; Ps 105:28

99:8 Ps 106:44; Num 14:20; Ps 78:38; Ex 32:28; Num 20:12; Ps 95:11; 107:12

6 Moses and Aaron were among His priests,
And Samuel was among those who called on His name;
They called upon the LORD and He answered them.
7 He spoke to them in the pillar of cloud;
They kept His testimonies
And the statute that He gave them.
8 O LORD our God, You answered them;
You were a forgiving God to them,
And *yet* an avenger of their *evil* deeds.
9 Exalt the LORD our God
And worship at His holy hill,
For holy is the LORD our God.

PSALM 100

A Psalm for Thanksgiving.

Theme: An invitation to enter joyfully into God's presence. His faithfulness extends to our generation and beyond.
Author: Anonymous

100:1 Ps 95:1; 98:4, 6

100:2 Deut 12:11, 12; 28:47; Ps 95:2

100:3 Deut 4:35; 1 Kin 18:39; Ps 46:10; Job 10:3, 8; Ps 95:6; 119:73; Ps 74:1, 2; 95:7; Is 40:11; Ezek 34:30, 31

100:4 Ps 95:2; 116:17; Ps 96:2

100:5 1 Chr 16:34; 2 Chr 5:13; 7:3; Ezra 3:11; Ps 25:8; 86:5; 106:1; 107:1; 118:1; Jer 33:11; Nah 1:7; Ps 136:1; Ps 119:90

1 Shout joyfully to the LORD, all the earth.
2 Serve the LORD with gladness;
Come before Him with joyful singing.
3 Know that the LORD Himself is God;
It is He who has made us, and [165]not we ourselves;
We are His people and the sheep of His pasture.

4 Enter His gates with thanksgiving
And His courts with praise.
Give thanks to Him, bless His name.
5 For the LORD is good;
His lovingkindness is everlasting
And His faithfulness to all generations.

PSALM 101

A Psalm of David.

Theme: A prayer for help to walk a blameless path. To live with integrity, both our efforts and God's help are necessary.
Author: David

101:1 Ps 51:14; 89:1; 145:7

101:2 1 Sam 18:5, 14; 1 Kin 9:4

1 I will sing of lovingkindness and justice,
To You, O LORD, I will sing praises.
2 I will give heed to the [166]blameless way.
When will You come to me?
I will walk within my house in the integrity of my heart.

165 Some mss read *His we are* **166** Or *way of integrity*

99:6 The Bible records several instances where Moses, Aaron, and Samuel cried out to God for help (Exodus 15:25; 17:4; Numbers 11:11–15; 12:13; 14:13ff; 16:44–48; 1 Samuel 7:5, 9; 15:11).

100:3 God is our Creator; we did not create ourselves. Many people live as though they are the creator and center of their own little world. This mind-set leads to a greedy possessiveness and, if everything should be taken away, a loss of hope itself. But when we realize that God created us and gives us all we have, we will want to give to others as God gave to us (2 Corinthians 9:8). Then, if all is lost, we still have God and all he gives us.

100:4 God alone is worthy of being worshiped. What is your attitude toward worship? Do you willingly and joyfully come into God's presence, or are you just going through the motions, reluctantly going to church? This psalm tells us to remember God's goodness and dependability, and then to worship with thanksgiving and praise!

101:1ff David may have written this psalm early in his reign as king as he set down the standards he wanted to follow. David knew that to lead a blameless life he would need God's help (101:2). We can lead blameless lives if we avoid (1) looking at wickedness ("set no worthless thing before my eyes," 101:3), (2) evil associates ("a perverse heart shall depart from me," 101:4), (3) slander (101:5), and (4) pride (101:5). While avoiding the wrongs listed above, we must also let God's Word show us the standards by which to live.

3 I will set no worthless thing before my eyes;
I hate the work of those who fall away;
It shall not fasten its grip on me.
4 A perverse heart shall depart from me;
I will know no evil.
5 Whoever secretly slanders his neighbor, him I will destroy;
No one who has a haughty look and an arrogant heart will I endure.

6 My eyes shall be upon the faithful of the land, that they may dwell with me;
He who walks in a [167]blameless way is the one who will minister to me.
7 He who practices deceit shall not dwell within my house;
He who speaks falsehood shall not maintain his position before me.
8 Every morning I will [168]destroy all the wicked of the land,
So as to cut off from the city of the LORD all those who do iniquity.

101:3 Deut 15:9; Josh 23:6; Ps 40:4
101:4 Prov 11:20
101:5 Ps 50:20; Jer 9:4; Ps 10:4; 18:27; Prov 6:17
101:6 Ps 119:1
101:7 Ps 43:1; 52:2; Ps 52:4, 5
101:8 Jer 21:12; Ps 75:10; Ps 118:10-12; Ps 46:4; 48:2, 8

PSALM 102

A Prayer of the Afflicted when he is faint and pours out his complaint before the LORD.

Theme: The cure for distress. Because God is living, eternal, and unchanging, we can trust him to help his people in this generation just as he helped his people in past generations.
Author: Anonymous

1 Hear my prayer, O LORD!
And let my cry for help come to You.
2 Do not hide Your face from me in the day of my distress;
Incline Your ear to me;
In the day when I call answer me quickly.
3 For my days have been consumed in smoke,
And my bones have been scorched like a hearth.
4 My heart has been smitten like grass and has withered away,
Indeed, I forget to eat my bread.
5 Because of the loudness of my groaning
My bones cling to my flesh.
6 I resemble a pelican of the wilderness;
I have become like an owl of the waste places.
7 I lie awake,
I have become like a lonely bird on a housetop.

8 My enemies have reproached me all day long;
Those who deride me have used my *name* as a curse.
9 For I have eaten ashes like bread
And mingled my drink with weeping
10 Because of Your indignation and Your wrath,
For You have lifted me up and cast me away.
11 My days are like a lengthened shadow,
And I wither away like grass.

12 But You, O LORD, abide forever,
And Your name to all generations.

102:1 Ps 39:12; 61:1; Ex 2:23; 1 Sam 9:16
102:2 Ps 69:17; Ps 31:2
102:3 Ps 37:20; James 4:14; Job 30:30; Lam 1:13
102:4 Ps 90:5, 6; Ps 37:2; Is 40:7; 1 Sam 1:7; 2 Sam 12:17; Ezra 10:6; Job 33:20
102:5 Job 19:20; Lam 4:8
102:6 Is 34:11; Zeph 2:14
102:7 Ps 77:4
102:8 Ps 31:11; Acts 26:11; 2 Sam 16:5; Is 65:15; Jer 29:22
102:9 Ps 42:3; 80:5
102:10 Ps 38:3; Job 27:21; 30:22
102:11 Job 14:2; Ps 109:23; Ps 102:4
102:12 Ps 9:7; 10:16; Lam 5:19; Ex 3:15; Ps 135:13

167 Or *way of integrity* 168 Or *silence*

101:6 David said that he would keep his eyes "upon the faithful of the land." In other words, he would choose as models and as friends those who are godly and truthful. Our friends and associates can have a profound influence on our lives. Make sure to keep your eyes on those who are faithful to God and his Word.

102:3–4 The psalmist felt so bad that he forgot to eat. When we face sickness and despair, our days pass blindly and we don't care about even our basic needs. In these times, God alone is our comfort and strength. Even when we are too weak to fight, we can lean on him. It is often when we recognize our weaknesses that God's greatest strength becomes available.

102:6–7 These birds are pictures of loneliness and desolation. At times we may need to be alone, and solitude may comfort us. But we must be careful not to spurn those who reach out to us. Don't reject help and conversation. Suffering silently is neither Christian nor particularly healthy. Instead, accept graciously the support and help from family and friends.

102:13 Ps 12:5; 44:26; Is 60:10; Zech 1:12; Ps 119:126; Ps 75:2; Dan 8:19

102:15 1 Kin 8:43; Ps 67:7; Ps 138:4

102:16 Ps 147:2; Is 60:1, 2

102:17 Neh 1:6; Ps 22:24

102:18 Deut 31:19; Rom 15:4; 1 Cor 10:11; Ps 22:30; 48:13; Ps 22:31; 78:6f

102:19 Deut 26:15; Ps 14:2; 53:2; Ps 33:13

102:20 Ps 79:11; Ps 146:7

102:21 Ps 22:22

102:22 Ps 22:27; 86:9; Is 49:22, 23; 60:3; Zech 8:20-23

102:23 Ps 39:5

102:24 Ps 39:13; Is 38:10; Job 36:26; Ps 90:2; 102:12; Hab 1:12

102:25 Gen 1:1; Neh 9:6; Heb 1:10-12; Ps 96:5

102:26 Is 34:4; 51:6; Matt 24:35; 2 Pet 3:10; Rev 20:11

102:27 Is 41:4; 43:10; Mal 3:6; James 1:17

102:28 Ps 69:36; Ps 89:4

103:1 Ps 104:1, 35; Ps 33:21; 105:3; 145:21; Ezek 36:21; 39:7

103:2 Deut 6:12; 8:11

103:3 Ex 34:7; Ps 86:5; 130:8; Is 43:25; Ex 15:26; Ps 30:2; Jer 30:17

13 You will arise *and* have compassion on Zion;
For it is time to be gracious to her,
For the appointed time has come.
14 Surely Your servants find pleasure in her stones
And feel pity for her dust.
15 So the nations will fear the name of the LORD
And all the kings of the earth Your glory.
16 For the LORD has built up Zion;
He has appeared in His glory.
17 He has regarded the prayer of the destitute
And has not despised their prayer.

18 This will be written for the generation to come,
That a people yet to be created may praise the LORD.
19 For He looked down from His holy height;
From heaven the LORD gazed upon the earth,
20 To hear the groaning of the prisoner,
To set free those who were doomed to death,
21 That *men* may tell of the name of the LORD in Zion
And His praise in Jerusalem,
22 When the peoples are gathered together,
And the kingdoms, to serve the LORD.

23 He has weakened my strength in the way;
He has shortened my days.
24 I say, "O my God, do not take me away in the midst of my days,
Your years are throughout all generations.
25 "Of old You founded the earth,
And the heavens are the work of Your hands.
26 "Even they will perish, but You endure;
And all of them will wear out like a garment;
Like clothing You will change them and they will be changed.
27 "But You are the same,
And Your years will not come to an end.
28 "The children of Your servants will continue,
And their descendants will be established before You."

PSALM 103

A Psalm of David.

Theme: God's great love for us. What God does for us tells what he is really like.
Author: David

1 Bless the LORD, O my soul,
And all that is within me, *bless* His holy name.
2 Bless the LORD, O my soul,
And forget none of His benefits;
3 Who pardons all your iniquities,

102:16–22 Christ's future reign on earth will encompass two events mentioned in these verses. Jerusalem (Zion) will be restored, and the entire world will worship God (Revelation 11:15; 21:1–27).

102:25–27 The writer of this psalm felt rejected and tossed aside because of his great troubles (102:9–10). Problems and heartaches can overwhelm us and cause us to feel that God has rejected us. But God our Creator is eternally with us and will keep all his promises, even though we may feel alone. The world will perish, but God will remain. Hebrews 1:10–12 quotes these verses to show that Jesus Christ, God's Son, was also present and active at the creation of the world.

103:1ff David's praise focused on God's glorious deeds. It is easy to complain about life, but David's list gives us plenty for which to praise God—he pardons our iniquities, heals our diseases, redeems us from death, crowns us with lovingkindness and compassion, satisfies our desires, and gives righteousness and justice. We receive all of these without deserving any of them. No matter how difficult your life's journey, you can always count your blessings—past, present, and future. When you feel as though you have nothing for which to praise God, read David's list.

Who heals all your diseases;
4 Who redeems your life from the pit,
Who crowns you with lovingkindness and compassion;
5 Who satisfies your [169]years with good things,
So that your youth is renewed like the eagle.

6 The LORD performs righteous deeds
And judgments for all who are oppressed.
7 He made known His ways to Moses,
His acts to the sons of Israel.
8 The LORD is compassionate and gracious,
Slow to anger and abounding in lovingkindness.
9 He will not always strive *with us,*
Nor will He keep *His anger* forever.
10 He has not dealt with us according to our sins,
Nor rewarded us according to our iniquities.
11 For as high as the heavens are above the earth,
So great is His lovingkindness toward those who [170]fear Him.
12 As far as the east is from the west,
So far has He removed our transgressions from us.
13 Just as a father has compassion on *his* children,
So the LORD has compassion on those who fear Him.
14 For He Himself knows [171]our frame;
He is mindful that we are *but* dust.

15 As for man, his days are like grass;
As a flower of the field, so he flourishes.
16 When the wind has passed over it, it is no more,
And its place acknowledges it no longer.
17 But the lovingkindness of the LORD is from everlasting to everlasting on those
who [170]fear Him,
And His righteousness to children's children,
18 To those who keep His covenant
And remember His precepts to do them.

19 The LORD has established His throne in the heavens,
And His [172]sovereignty rules over all.
20 Bless the LORD, you His angels,
Mighty in strength, who perform His word,
Obeying the voice of His word!
21 Bless the LORD, all you His hosts,
You who serve Him, doing His will.
22 Bless the LORD, all you works of His,
In all places of His dominion;
Bless the LORD, O my soul!

169 Or *desire* **170** Or *revere* **171** I.e. what we are made of **172** Or *kingdom*

103:4
Ps 49:15; Ps 5:12

103:5
Ps 107:9; 145:16; Is 40:31

103:6
Ps 99:4; 146:7

103:7
Ex 33:13; Ps 99:7; 147:19; Ps 78:11; 106:22

103:8
Ex 34:6; Num 14:18; Neh 9:17; Ps 86:15; Ps 145:8; Joel 2:13; Nah 1:3

103:9
Ps 30:5; Is 57:16; Jer 3:5, 12; Mic 7:18

103:10
Ezra 9:13; Lam 3:22

103:11
Ps 36:5; 57:10

103:12
2 Sam 12:13; Is 38:17; 43:25; Zech 3:9; Heb 9:26

103:13
Mal 3:17

103:14
Is 29:16; Ps 78:39; Gen 3:19; Eccl 12:7

103:15
Ps 90:5; Is 40:6; 1 Pet 1:24; Job 14:2; James 1:10, 11

103:16
Is 40:7; Job 7:10

103:17
Ps 25:6; Ex 20:6; Deut 5:10; Ps 105:8

103:18
Deut 7:9; Ps 25:10

103:19
Ps 11:4; Ps 47:2, 8; Dan 4:17, 25

103:20
Ps 148:2; Ps 29:1; 78:25; Matt 6:10; Ps 91:11; Heb 1:14

103:21
1 Kin 22:19; Neh 9:6; Ps 148:2; Luke 2:13; Ps 104:4

103:22
Ps 145:10

103:7 God's Law was given first to Moses and the people of Israel. God's Law presents a clear picture of God's nature and will. It was God's training manual to prepare his people to serve him and to follow his ways. Review the Ten Commandments (Exodus 20) and the history of how they were given, asking God to show you his will and his ways through them.

103:12 East and west can never meet. This is a symbolic portrait of God's forgiveness—when he forgives our sin, he separates it from us and doesn't even remember it. We need never wallow in the past, for God forgives and forgets. We tend to dredge up the ugly past, but God has wiped our record clean. If we are to follow God, we must model his forgiveness. When we forgive another, we must also forget the sin. Otherwise, we have not truly forgiven.

103:13–14 We are fragile, but God's care is eternal. Too often we focus on God as Judge and Lawgiver, ignoring his compassion and concern for us. When God examines our lives, he remembers our human condition. Our weakness should never be used as a justification for sin. His mercy takes everything into account. God will deal with you compassionately. Trust him.

103:20–22 Everything everywhere is to praise the Lord: all angels—mighty ones and heavenly hosts—and all his works! Praising God means remembering all he has done for us (103:2), fearing him and obeying his commands (103:17–18), and doing his will (103:21). Does your life praise the Lord?

PSALM 104

Theme: Appreciating God through his creation. He not only creates, but maintains his creation. The Lord's care is the source of our joy.
Author: Anonymous

104:1 Ps 103:22; Ps 93:1
104:2 Dan 7:9; Is 40:22
104:3 Amos 9:6; Is 19:1; Ps 18:10
104:4 Ps 148:8; Heb 1:7; 2 Kin 2:11; 6:17

1 Bless the LORD, O my soul!
O LORD my God, You are very great;
You are clothed with splendor and majesty,
2 Covering Yourself with light as with a cloak,
Stretching out heaven like a *tent* curtain.
3 [173]He lays the beams of His upper chambers in the waters;
He makes the clouds His chariot;
He walks upon the wings of the wind;
4 He makes [174]the winds His messengers,
[175]Flaming fire His ministers.

104:5 Job 38:4; Ps 24:2
104:6 Gen 1:2
104:7 Ps 18:15; 106:9; Is 50:2; Ps 29:3; 77:18
104:8 Ps 33:7
104:9 Job 38:10, 11; Jer 5:22

5 He established the earth upon its foundations,
So that it will not [176]totter forever and ever.
6 YoYou covered it with the deep as with a garment;
The waters were standing above the mountains.
7 At Your rebuke they fled,
At the sound of Your thunder they hurried away.
8 The mountains rose; the valleys sank down
To the place which You established for them.
9 You set a boundary that they may not pass over,
So that they will not return to cover the earth.

104:10 Ps 107:35; Is 41:18
104:11 Ps 104:13; Job 39:5

10 He sends forth springs in the valleys;
They flow between the mountains;
11 They give drink to every beast of the field;

173 Lit *The one who* **174** Or *His angels, spirits* **175** Or *His ministers flames of fire* **176** Or *move out of place*

HOW GOD IS DESCRIBED IN PSALMS

Most of the psalms speak to God or about God. Because they were composed in a variety of situations, various facets of God's character are mentioned. Here is a sample of God's characteristics as understood and experienced by the psalm writers. As you read these psalms, ask yourself if this is the God you know.

God is...	*References*
All-knowing and ever-present	Psalm 139
Beautiful and desirable	Psalms 27; 36; 45
Creator	Psalms 8; 104; 148
Good and generous	Psalms 34; 81; 107
Great and sovereign	Psalms 33; 89; 96
Holy	Psalms 66; 99; 145
Loving and faithful	Psalms 23; 42; 51
Merciful and forgiving	Psalms 32; 111; 130
Powerful	Psalms 76; 89; 93
Willing to reveal his will, law, and direction	Psalms 1; 19; 119
Righteous and just	Psalms 71; 97; 113
Spirit	Psalms 104; 139; 143

104:1ff This psalm is a poetic summary of God's creation of the world as found in the first chapter of Genesis. What God created each day is mentioned by the psalmist as a reason to praise God. On day one, God created light (104:1–2; Genesis 1:3); day two, the heavens and the waters (104:2–3; Genesis 1:6); day three, land and vegetation (104:6–18; Genesis 1:9–13); day four, the sun, moon, and stars (104:19–23; Genesis 1:14–16); day five, fish and birds (104:25–26; Genesis 1:20–23); and on day six, animals, man, and food to sustain them (104:21–24, 27–30; Genesis 1:24–31). God's act of creation deserves the praise of all people.

104:5 The earth is built on God's foundations. Even though one day the heavens and the earth will be destroyed (2 Peter 3:10), he will create a new heaven and a new earth that will last forever (Isaiah 65:17; Revelation 21:1). The same power that undergirds the world also provides a firm foundation for believers.

The wild donkeys quench their thirst.
12 Beside them the birds of the heavens dwell;
They lift up *their* voices among the branches.
13 He waters the mountains from His upper chambers;
The earth is satisfied with the fruit of His works.

14 He causes the grass to grow for the cattle,
And vegetation for the labor of man,
So that he may bring forth food from the earth,
15 And wine which makes man's heart glad,
So that he may make *his* face glisten with oil,
And food which sustains man's heart.
16 The trees of the LORD drink their fill,
The cedars of Lebanon which He planted,
17 Where the birds build their nests,
And the stork, whose home is the fir trees.

18 The high mountains are for the wild goats;
The cliffs are a refuge for the shephanim.
19 He made the moon for the seasons;
The sun knows the place of its setting.
20 You appoint darkness and it becomes night,
In which all the beasts of the forest prowl about.
21 The young lions roar after their prey
And seek their food from God.
22 *When* the sun rises they withdraw
And lie down in their dens.
23 Man goes forth to his work
And to his labor until evening.

24 O LORD, how many are Your works!
In wisdom You have made them all;
The earth is full of Your [177]possessions.
25 There is the sea, great and broad,
In which are swarms without number,
Animals both small and great.
26 There the ships move along,
And [178]Leviathan, which You have formed to sport in it.

27 They all wait for You
To give them their food in [179]due season.
28 You give to them, they gather *it* up;
You open YoYour hand, they are satisfied with good.
29 You hide Your face, they are dismayed;
YoYou take away their [180]spirit, they expire
And return to their dust.
30 You send forth Your [180]Spirit, they are created;
And You renew the face of the ground.

177 Or *creatures* **178** Or *a sea monster* **179** Lit *its appointed time* **180** Or *breath*

104:12 Matt 8:20
104:13 Ps 65:9; 147:8; Jer 10:13
104:14 Job 38:27; Ps 147:8; Gen 1:29; Job 28:5
104:15 Judg 9:13; Prov 31:6; Eccl 10:19; Ps 23:5; 92:10; 141:5; Luke 7:46; Gen 18:5; Judg 19:5, 8
104:17 Ps 104:12; Lev 11:19
104:18 Job 39:1; Prov 30:26; Lev 11:5
104:19 Gen 1:14; Ps 19:6
104:20 Ps 74:16; Is 45:7; Ps 50:10; Is 56:9; Mic 5:8
104:21 Job 38:39; Ps 145:15; Joel 1:20
104:22 Job 37:8
104:23 Gen 3:19
104:24 Ps 40:5; Ps 136:5; Prov 3:19; Jer 10:12; 51:15; Ps 65:9
104:25 Ps 8:8; 69:34
104:26 Ps 107:23; Ezek 27:9; Job 41:1; Ps 74:14; Is 27:1
104:27 Ps 145:15; Job 36:31; 38:41; Ps 136:25; 147:9
104:28 Ps 145:16
104:29 Deut 31:17; Ps 30:7; Job 34:14, 15; Ps 146:4; Eccl 12:7; Gen 3:19; Job 10:9; Ps 90:3
104:30 Job 33:4; Ezek 37:9

104:24 Creation is filled with stunning variety, revealing the rich creativity, goodness, and wisdom of our loving God. As you observe your natural surroundings, thank God for his creativity. Take a fresh look at people, seeing each one as God's unique creation, each with his or her own special talents, abilities, and gifts.

104:26 Here *Leviathan* simply means a large and active sea creature.

104:28–30 Psalm 105 expresses God's sovereignty in history; this psalm tells of his sovereignty over all creation. God has supreme, unlimited power over the entire universe. He creates; he preserves; he governs. As we understand God's power, we realize that he is sufficient to handle our lives.

104:29 Today many people are arrogant enough to think they don't need God. But our every breath depends on the Spirit he has breathed into us (Genesis 2:7; 3:19; Job 33:4; 34:14–15; Daniel 5:23). Not only do we depend on God for our very lives, but he wants the best for us. We should also desire to learn more of his plans for us each day.

104:31 Ps 86:12; 111:10; Gen 1:31

104:32 Judg 5:5; Ps 97:4, 5; 114:7; Hab 3:10; Ex 19:18; Ps 144:5

104:33 Ps 63:4; Ps 146:2

104:34 Ps 19:14; Ps 9:2

104:35 Ps 59:13; Ps 37:10; Ps 104:1; Ps 105:45; 106:48

31 Let the glory of the LORD endure forever;
Let the LORD be glad in His works;
32 He looks at the earth, and it trembles;
He touches the mountains, and they smoke.
33 I will sing to the LORD as long as I live;
I will sing praise to my God while I have my being.
34 Let my meditation be pleasing to Him;
As for me, I shall be glad in the LORD.
35 Let sinners be consumed from the earth
And let the wicked be no more.
Bless the LORD, O my soul.
Praise the LORD!

PSALM 105

105:1 1 Chr 16:8-22, 34; Ps 106:1; Is 12:4; Ps 99:6; Ps 145:12

105:2 Ps 96:1; 98:5; Ps 77:12; 119:27; 145:5

105:3 Ps 33:21

105:4 Ps 63:2; Ps 27:8

105:5 Ps 40:5; 77:11; Ps 119:13

105:6 Ps 105:42; Ps 135:4; 1 Chr 16:13; Ps 106:5; 135:4

105:7 Is 26:9

105:8 Ps 105:42; 106:45; Luke 1:72; Deut 7:9

105:9 Gen 12:7; 17:2, 8; 22:16-18; Gal 3:17; Gen 26:3

Theme: God's mighty deeds in bringing Israel to the promised land. Remembering his miracles encourages us to keep living close to him.
Author: David

1 Oh give thanks to the LORD, call upon His name;
Make known His deeds among the peoples.
2 Sing to Him, sing praises to Him;
[181]Speak of all His wonders.
3 Glory in His holy name;
Let the heart of those who seek the LORD be glad.
4 Seek the LORD and His strength;
Seek His face continually.
5 Remember His wonders which He has done,
His marvels and the judgments uttered by His mouth,
6 O seed of Abraham, His servant,
O sons of Jacob, His chosen ones!
7 He is the LORD our God;
His judgments are in all the earth.

8 He has remembered His covenant forever,
The word which He commanded to a thousand generations,
9 *The covenant* which He made with Abraham,
And His oath to Isaac.

181 Or *Meditate on*

HISTORY IN THE BOOK OF PSALMS

For the original hearers, the historical psalms were vivid reminders of God's past acts on behalf of Israel. These history songs were written for passing on important lessons to succeeding generations. They celebrated the many promises God had made and faithfully kept; they also recounted the faithlessness of the people.

We cannot read this ancient history without reflecting on how consistently God's people failed to learn from the past. They repeatedly turned from fresh examples of God's faithfulness and forgiveness only to plunge back into sin. God can use these psalms to remind us how often we do exactly the same thing: having every reason to live for God, we choose instead to live for everything but God. If we paid more attention to "his story" we wouldn't make so many mistakes in our own stories.

Selected historical psalms include: Psalms 68; 78; 95; 105; 106; 111; 114; 135; 136; 149.

105:1ff The first 15 verses of this psalm are also found in 1 Chronicles 16:8–22, where they are sung as part of the celebration of David's bringing the ark of the covenant to Jerusalem. Three other psalms are also hymns recounting Israel's history—78, 106, and 136.

105:4–5 If God seems far away, persist in your search for him. God rewards those who sincerely look for him (Hebrews 11:6). Jesus promised, "Seek, and you will find" (Matthew 7:7). The psalmist suggested a valuable way to find God—become familiar with the way he has helped his people in the past. The Bible records the history of God's people. In searching its pages we will discover a loving God who is waiting for us to find him.

105:6–11 The nation Israel, the people through whom God revealed his laws to mankind, is descended from Abraham. God chose Abraham and promised that his descendants would live in the land of Canaan (now called Israel), and that they would be too numerous to count (Genesis 17:6–8). Abraham's son was Isaac; Isaac's son was Jacob. These three men are considered the patriarchs or founders of Israel. God blessed them because of their faith (see Hebrews 11:8–21).

10 Then He confirmed it to Jacob for a statute,
To Israel as an everlasting covenant,
11 Saying, "To you I will give the land of Canaan
As the portion of your inheritance,"
12 When they were only a few men in number,
Very few, and strangers in it.
13 And they wandered about from nation to nation,
From *one* kingdom to another people.
14 He permitted no man to oppress them,
And He reproved kings for their sakes:
15 "Do not touch My anointed ones,
And do My prophets no harm."

16 And He called for a famine upon the land;
He broke the whole staff of bread.
17 He sent a man before them,
Joseph, *who* was sold as a slave.
18 They afflicted his feet with fetters,
He himself was laid in irons;
19 Until the time that his word came to pass,
The word of the LORD tested him.
20 The king sent and released him,
The ruler of peoples, and set him free.
21 He made him lord of his house
And ruler over all his possessions,
22 To imprison his princes at will,
That he might teach his elders wisdom.
23 Israel also came into Egypt;
Thus Jacob sojourned in the land of Ham.
24 And He caused His people to be very fruitful,
And made them stronger than their adversaries.

25 He turned their heart to hate His people,
To deal craftily with His servants.
26 He sent Moses His servant,
And Aaron, whom He had chosen.
27 They performed His wondrous acts among them,
And miracles in the land of Ham.
28 He sent darkness and made *it* dark;
And they did not rebel against His words.
29 He turned their waters into blood
And caused their fish to die.
30 Their land swarmed with frogs
Even in the chambers of their kings.
31 He spoke, and there came a swarm of flies
And gnats in all their territory.
32 He gave them hail for rain,
And flaming fire in their land.
33 He struck down their vines also and their fig trees,
And shattered the trees of their territory.
34 He spoke, and locusts came,
And young locusts, even without number,
35 And ate up all vegetation in their land,
And ate up the fruit of their ground.

105:10 Gen 28:13-15
105:11 Gen 13:15; 15:18; Josh 23:4; Ps 78:55
105:12 Gen 34:30; Deut 7:7; Gen 23:4; Heb 11:9
105:14 Gen 20:7; 35:5; Gen 12:17; 20:3, 7
105:15 Gen 26:11
105:16 Gen 41:54; Lev 26:26; Is 3:1; Ezek 4:16
105:17 Gen 45:5; Gen 37:28, 36; Acts 7:9
105:18 Gen 39:20; 40:15
105:19 Gen 40:20, 21; Ps 66:10
105:20 Gen 41:14
105:21 Gen 41:40-44
105:22 Gen 41:44
105:23 Gen 46:6; Acts 7:15; Acts 13:17
105:24 Ex 1:7, 9
105:25 Ex 1:8; 4:21; Ex 1:10; Acts 7:19
105:26 Ex 3:10; 4:12; Ex 4:14; Num 16:5; 17:5-8
105:27 Ps 78:43-51; 105:27-36
105:28 Ex 10:21, 22; Ps 99:7
105:29 Ex 7:20, 21
105:30 Ex 8:6; Ex 8:3
105:31 Ex 8:21; Ex 8:16, 17
105:32 Ex 9:23-25
105:33 Ps 78:47
105:34 Ex 10:12-15

105:23–25 Did God cause the Egyptians to hate the Israelites? God is not the author of evil, but the Bible writers don't always distinguish between God's ultimate action and the intermediate steps. Thus by God blessing the Israelites, the Egyptians came to hate them (Exodus 1:8–22). Because God caused the Israelites' blessing, he is also said to have caused the Egyptians to hate them. God used their animosity as a means to lead the Israelites out of Egypt.

105:36 Ex 12:29; 13:15; Ps 135:8; 136:10; Gen 49:3

105:37 Ex 12:35, 36

105:38 Ex 12:33; Ex 15:16

105:39 Ex 13:21; Neh 9:12; Ps 78:14; Is 4:5; Ex 40:38

105:40 Ex 16:12; Ps 78:18; Ex 16:13; Num 11:31; Ps 78:27; Ex 16:15; Neh 9:15; Ps 78:24; John 6:31

105:41 Ex 17:6; Num 20:11; Ps 78:15; 114:8; Is 48:21; 1 Cor 10:4

105:42 Gen 15:13, 14; Ps 105:8

105:43 Ex 15:1; Ps 106:12

105:44 Josh 11:16-23; 13:7; Ps 78:55; Deut 6:10, 11

105:45 Deut 4:1, 40

106:1 Ps 105:1; 107:1; 118:1; 136:1; Jer 33:11; 2 Chr 5:13; 7:3; Ezra 3:11; Ps 100:5; 1 Chr 16:34, 41

106:2 Ps 145:4, 12; 150:2

106:3 Ps 15:2

106:4 Ps 44:3; 119:132

106:5 Ps 1:3; Ps 118:15; Ps 105:3

106:6 1 Kin 8:47; Ezra 9:7; Neh 1:7; Jer 3:25; Dan 9:5; 2 Chr 30:7; Neh 9:2; Ps 78:8, 57; Zech 1:4

106:7 Judg 3:7; Ps 78:11, 42; Ex 14:11, 12; Ps 78:17

106:8 Ezek 20:9; Ex 9:16

36 He also struck down all the firstborn in their land,
The first fruits of all their vigor.

37 Then He brought them out with silver and gold,
And among His tribes there was not one who stumbled.
38 Egypt was glad when they departed,
For the dread of them had fallen upon them.
39 He spread a cloud for a [182]covering,
And fire to illumine by night.
40 They asked, and He brought quail,
And satisfied them with the bread of heaven.
41 He opened the rock and water flowed out;
It ran in the dry places *like* a river.
42 For He remembered His holy word
With Abraham His servant;
43 And He brought forth His people with joy,
His chosen ones with a joyful shout.
44 He gave them also the lands of the nations,
That they might take possession of *the fruit of* the peoples' labor,
45 So that they might keep His statutes
And observe His laws,
Praise the LORD!

PSALM 106

Theme: A song of national repentance as the people return from captivity. God patiently delivers us, in spite of our forgetfulness and self-willed rebellion.
Author: Anonymous

1 Praise the LORD!
Oh give thanks to the LORD, for He is good;
For His lovingkindness is everlasting.
2 Who can speak of the mighty deeds of the LORD,
Or can show forth all His praise?
3 How blessed are those who keep justice,
Who practice righteousness at all times!

4 Remember me, O LORD, in *Your* favor toward Your people;
Visit me with Your salvation,
5 That I may see the prosperity of Your chosen ones,
That I may rejoice in the gladness of Your nation,
That I may glory with Your [183]inheritance.

6 We have sinned like our fathers,
We have committed iniquity, we have behaved wickedly.
7 Our fathers in Egypt did not understand Your wonders;
They did not remember Your abundant kindnesses,
But rebelled by the sea, at the [184]Red Sea.
8 Nevertheless He saved them for the sake of His name,
That He might make His power known.

182 Or *curtain* **183** I.e. people **184** Lit *Sea of Reeds*

105:45 God's purpose for saving the Israelites was that they would "keep His statutes and observe His laws." Too often we use our lives and freedom to please ourselves, but we should honor God. That is God's purpose for our lives and why he gave us his Word.

106:1ff While Psalm 105 is a summary of God's faithfulness, Psalm 106 is a summary of man's sinfulness. Psalm 105 covers events up to the exodus from Egypt (Exodus 5—14), and Psalm 106 covers events from the exodus up to what appears to be the Babylonian captivity (2 Kings 25).

106:2 If we ever stopped to list all the mighty acts or miracles in the Bible, we would be astounded. They cover every aspect of life. The more we think about what God has done, the more we can appreciate the miracles he has done for us individually—birth, personality development, loving friends and family, specific guidance, healing, salvation—the list goes on and on. If you think you have never seen a miracle, look closer—you will see God's power and loving intervention on your behalf. God still performs great miracles!

9 Thus He rebuked the [185]Red Sea and it dried up,
And He led them through the deeps, as through the wilderness.
10 So He saved them from the hand of the one who hated *them,*
And redeemed them from the hand of the enemy.
11 The waters covered their adversaries;
Not one of them was left.
12 Then they believed His words;
They sang His praise.

13 They quickly forgot His works;
They did not wait for His counsel,
14 But craved intensely in the wilderness,
And tempted God in the desert.
15 So He gave them their request,
But sent a wasting disease among them.

16 When they became envious of Moses in the camp,
And of Aaron, the holy one of the LORD,
17 The earth opened and swallowed up Dathan,
And engulfed the company of Abiram.
18 And a fire blazed up in their company;
The flame consumed the wicked.

19 They made a calf in Horeb
And worshiped a molten image.
20 Thus they exchanged their glory
For the image of an ox that eats grass.
21 They forgot God their Savior,
Who had done great things in Egypt,
22 Wonders in the land of Ham
And awesome things by the [187]Red Sea.
23 Therefore He said that He would destroy them,
Had not Moses His chosen one stood in the breach before Him,
To turn away His wrath from destroying *them.*
24 Then they despised the pleasant land;
They did not believe in His word,
25 But grumbled in their tents;
They did not listen to the voice of the LORD.
26 Therefore He swore to them
That He would cast them down in the wilderness,
27 And that He would cast their seed among the nations
And scatter them in the lands.

28 They joined themselves also to Baal-peor,
And ate sacrifices offered to the dead.
29 Thus they provoked *Him* to anger with their deeds,
And the plague broke out among them.
30 Then Phinehas stood up and interposed,
And so the plague was stayed.
31 And it was reckoned to him for righteousness,
To all generations forever.

185 Lit *Sea of Reeds*

106:9 Ex 14:21; Is 51:10; Is 63:11-13
106:10 Ex 14:30; Ps 78:42
106:11 Ex 14:27, 28; 15:5; Ps 78:53
106:12 Ex 14:31; Ex 15:1-21; Ps 105:43
106:13 Ex 15:24; 16:2; 17:2; Ps 107:11
106:14 Num 11:4; Ps 78:18; 1 Cor 10:6; Ex 17:2
106:15 Num 11:31; Ps 78:29; Is 10:16
106:16 Num 16:1-3
106:17 Num 16:32
106:18 Num 16:35
106:19 Ex 32:4; Deut 9:8; Acts 7:41
106:20 Jer 2:11; Rom 1:23
106:21 Ps 78:11; 106:7, 13; Deut 10:21
106:23 Ex 32:10; Deut 9:14; Ezek 20:8, 13; Ex 32:11-14; Deut 9:25-29
106:24 Num 14:31; Deut 8:7; Jer 3:19; Ezek 20:6; Deut 1:32; 9:23; Heb 3:19
106:25 Num 14:2; Deut 1:27
106:26 Num 14:28-35; Ps 95:11; Ezek 20:15; Heb 3:11
106:27 Deut 4:27; Lev 26:33; Ps 44:11
106:28 Num 25:3; Deut 4:3
106:29 Num 25:4
106:30 Num 25:7
106:31 Gen 15:6; Num 25:11-13

106:13–15 In the wilderness, Israel was so intent on getting the food and water *they* wanted that they became blind to what God wanted. They were more concerned about immediate physical gratification than lasting spiritual satisfaction. They did not want what was best for them, and they refused to trust in God's care and provision (Numbers 11:18–33). If you complain enough, God may give you what you ask for, even if it is not the best for you. If you're not getting what you want, perhaps God knows it is not in your best interest. Trust in his care and provision.

106:22 The land of Ham is Egypt.

106:23 "Stood in the breach" means that Moses served as the people's intercessor. This refers to the time when the Lord wanted to destroy the people for worshiping the golden calf (Exodus 32:7–14).

106:32 Num 20:2-13; Ps 81:7; 95:9; Num 20:12
106:33 Num 20:3, 10; Ps 78:40; 107:11
106:34 Judg 1:21, 27-36; Deut 7:2, 16
106:35 Judg 3:5, 6
106:36 Judg 2:12; Deut 7:16
106:37 Deut 12:31; 32:17; 2 Kin 16:3; 17:17; Ezek 16:20, 21; 1 Cor 10:20; Lev 17:7
106:38 Ps 94:21; Deut 18:10; Num 35:33; Is 24:5; Jer 3:1, 2
106:39 Lev 18:24; Ezek 20:18; Lev 17:7; Num 15:39; Judg 2:17; Hos 4:12
106:40 Judg 2:14; Ps 78:59; Lev 26:30; Deut 32:19; Deut 9:29; 32:9
106:41 Judg 2:14; Neh 9:27
106:42 Judg 4:3; 10:12
106:43 Judg 2:16-18; Ps 81:12; Judg 6:6
106:44 Judg 3:9; 6:7; 10:10
106:45 Lev 26:42; Ps 105:8; Judg 2:18; Ps 69:16
106:46 1 Kin 8:50; 2 Chr 30:9; Ezra 9:9; Neh 1:11; Jer 42:12
106:47 1 Chr 16:35, 36; Ps 147:2; Ps 47:1
106:48 Ps 41:13; 72:18; 89:52

32 They also provoked *Him* to wrath at the waters of [186]Meribah,
So that it went hard with Moses on their account;
33 Because they were rebellious against His Spirit,
He spoke rashly with his lips.

34 They did not destroy the peoples,
As the LORD commanded them,
35 But they mingled with the nations
And learned their practices,
36 And served their idols,
Which became a snare to them.
37 They even sacrificed their sons and their daughters to the demons,
38 And shed innocent blood,
The blood of their sons and their daughters,
Whom they sacrificed to the idols of Canaan;
And the land was polluted with the blood.
39 Thus they became unclean in their practices,
And played the harlot in their deeds.

40 Therefore the anger of the LORD was kindled against His people
And He abhorred His inheritance.
41 Then He gave them into the hand of the nations,
And those who hated them ruled over them.
42 Their enemies also oppressed them,
And they were subdued under their power.
43 Many times He would deliver them;
They, however, were rebellious in their counsel,
And *so* sank down in their iniquity.

44 Nevertheless He looked upon their distress
When He heard their cry;
45 And He remembered His covenant for their sake,
And relented according to the greatness of His lovingkindness.
46 He also made them *objects* of compassion
In the presence of all their captors.

47 Save us, O LORD our God,
And gather us from among the nations,
To give thanks to Your holy name
And glory in Your praise.
48 Blessed be the LORD, the God of Israel,
From everlasting even to everlasting.
And let all the people say, "Amen."
Praise the LORD!

186 Lit *strife*

106:34–39 Israel constantly turned away from God. How, after the great miracles they saw, could they turn from God and worship the idols of the land? We also have seen God's great miracles, but sometimes find ourselves enticed by the world's gods—power, convenience, fame, sex, and pleasure. As Israel forgot God, so we are susceptible to forgetting him and giving in to the pressures of an evil world. Remember all that God has done for you so you won't be drawn away from him by the world's pleasures.

106:40–42 God allowed trouble to come to the Israelites in order to help them. Our troubles can be helpful because they (1) humble us, (2) wean us from the allurements of the world and drive us back to God, (3) vitalize our prayers, (4) allow us to experience more of God's faithfulness, (5) make us more dependent upon God, (6) encourage us to submit to God's purpose for our lives, and (7) make us more compassionate toward others in trouble.

106:44–46 This is a beautiful picture of God's great love for his people who deserved only judgment. Fortunately, God's compassion and mercy toward us are not limited by our faithfulness to him. God was merciful to us in sending his Son to die for our sins. If he did this while we were captive to sin, how much more merciful will he be now that we are his children?

BOOK 5
PSALMS 107:1—150:6

These psalms praise God's works, recount the blessings of righteous living, thank God for deliverance, and praise God for his wonderful Word. These psalms remind us that the best sacrifice we can offer to God is a faithful and obedient life.

PSALM 107

Theme: Thankfulness to God should constantly be on the lips of those whom he has saved. This psalm was written to celebrate the Jews' return from their exile in Babylon.
Author: Anonymous

1 Oh give thanks to the LORD, for He is good,
For His lovingkindness is everlasting.
2 Let the redeemed of the LORD say *so,*
Whom He has redeemed from the hand of the adversary
3 And gathered from the lands,
From the east and from the west,
From the north and from the south.

4 They wandered in the wilderness in a desert region;
They did not find a way to an inhabited city.
5 *They were* hungry and thirsty;
Their soul fainted within them.
6 Then they cried out to the LORD in their trouble;
He delivered them out of their distresses.
7 He led them also by a straight way,
To go to an inhabited city.
8 Let them give thanks to the LORD for His lovingkindness,
And for His wonders to the sons of men!
9 For He has satisfied the thirsty soul,
And the hungry soul He has filled with what is good.

10 There were those who dwelt in darkness and in the shadow of death,
Prisoners in misery and chains,
11 Because they had rebelled against the words of God
And spurned the counsel of the Most High.
12 Therefore He humbled their heart with labor;
They stumbled and there was none to help.
13 Then they cried out to the LORD in their trouble;
He saved them out of their distresses.
14 He brought them out of darkness and the shadow of death
And broke their bands apart.
15 Let them give thanks to the LORD for His lovingkindness,
And for His wonders to the sons of men!
16 For He has shattered gates of bronze
And cut bars of iron asunder.

17 Fools, because of their rebellious way,
And because of their iniquities, were afflicted.

107:1
1 Chr 16:34; Ps 106:1; 118:1; 136:1; Jer 33:11; 2 Chr 5:13; 7:3; Ezra 3:11; Ps 100:5

107:2
Is 35:9, 10; 62:12; 63:4; Ps 78:42; 106:10

107:3
Deut 30:3; Neh 1:9; Ps 106:47; Is 11:12; 43:5; 56:8; Ezek 11:17; 20:34

107:4
Num 14:33; 32:13; Deut 2:7; 32:10; Josh 5:6; 14:10; Ps 107:7, 36

107:5
Ps 77:3

107:6
Ps 50:15; 107:13

107:7
Ezra 8:21; Ps 5:8; Jer 31:9; Ps 107:4, 36

107:8
Ps 107:15, 21, 31

107:9
Ps 22:26; 34:10; 63:5; 103:5; Ps 146:7; Matt 5:6; Luke 1:53

107:10
Ps 143:3; Is 42:7; Mic 7:8; Luke 1:79; Job 36:8; Ps 102:20

107:11
Ps 78:40; 106:7; Lam 3:42; Num 15:31; 2 Chr 36:16; Prov 1:25; Is 5:24; Ps 73:24

107:12
Ps 22:11; 72:12

107:13
Ps 107:6

107:14
Ps 86:13; 107:10; Ps 116:16; Jer 2:20; 30:8; Nah 1:13; Luke 13:16; Acts 12:7

107:16
Is 45:1, 2

107:17
Is 65:6, 7; Jer 30:14, 15; Lam 3:39; Ezek 24:23

107:1ff This psalm speaks of four different types of people in distress and how God rescues them: wanderers (107:4–9), prisoners (107:10–16), the sick (107:17–20), and the storm-tossed (107:23–30). No matter how extreme our calamity, God is able to break through to help us. He is loving and kind to those who are distressed.

107:1–2 "Let the redeemed of the LORD say . . ." God has done so much for us, and we have so much for which to thank him (see Psalm 103). He wants us to tell everyone all that he has done. These verses are not so much a mandate to witness as a declaration that when we live in God's presence we will not be able to keep this glorious experience to ourselves (see also Acts 1:8; 2 Corinthians 5:18–20). What has God done for you? Is there someone you can tell?

107:5–9 Lost, hungry, thirsty, and exhausted, these wanderers typify the Israelites in exile. But they also typify anyone who has not found the satisfaction that comes from knowing God. Anyone who recognizes his or her own lostness can receive the offer of Jesus to satisfy these needs. Jesus is the way (John 14:6), the bread from heaven (John 6:33, 35), the living water (John 4:10–14), and the giver of rest (Matthew 11:28–30). Have you received his life-giving offer?

107:18 Job 33:20; Ps 102:4; Job 33:22; Ps 88:3; Job 38:17; Ps 9:13
107:20 Ps 147:15, 18; Matt 8:8; 2 Kin 20:5; Ps 30:2; 103:3; 147:3; Job 33:28, 30; Ps 30:3; 49:15; 56:13
107:22 Lev 7:12; Ps 50:14; 116:17; Ps 9:11; 73:28; 118:17
107:23 Is 42:10; Jon 1:3
107:25 Ps 105:31, 34; Ps 148:8; Jon 1:4
107:26 Ps 22:14; 119:28
107:27 Job 12:25; Is 24:20
107:29 Ps 65:7; 89:9; Matt 8:26; Luke 8:24
107:31 Ps 107:8, 15, 21; Ps 78:4; 111:4
107:32 Ps 34:3; 99:5; Is 25:1; Ps 22:22, 25; Ps 35:18
107:33 1 Kin 17:1, 7; Ps 74:15; Is 42:15; 50:2
107:34 Gen 13:10; 14:3; 19:24, 25; Deut 29:23; Job 39:6; Jer 17:6
107:35 Ps 105:41; 114:8; Is 35:6, 7; 41:18
107:37 2 Kin 19:29; Is 65:21; Amos 9:14
107:38 Gen 12:2; 17:20; Ex 1:7; Deut 1:10; Deut 7:14
107:39 2 Kin 10:32; Ezek 5:11; 29:15; Ps 38:6; 44:25; 57:6
107:40 Job 12:21; Job 12:24; Deut 32:10
107:41 1 Sam 2:8; Ps 59:1; 113:7, 8; Job 21:11; Ps 78:52; 113:9
107:42 Job 22:19; Ps 52:6; Job 5:16; Ps 63:11; Rom 3:19
107:43 Ps 64:9; Jer 9:12; Hos 14:9; Ps 107:1

18 Their soul abhorred all kinds of food,
And they drew near to the gates of death.
19 Then they cried out to the LORD in their trouble;
He saved them out of their distresses.
20 He sent His word and healed them,
And delivered *them* from their [187]destructions.
21 Let them give thanks to the LORD for His lovingkindness,
And for His wonders to the sons of men!
22 Let them also offer sacrifices of thanksgiving,
And tell of His works with joyful singing.

23 Those who go down to the sea in ships,
Who do business on great waters;
24 They have seen the works of the LORD,
And His wonders in the deep.
25 For He spoke and raised up a stormy wind,
Which lifted up the waves of the sea.
26 They rose up to the heavens, they went down to the depths;
Their soul melted away in *their* misery.
27 They reeled and staggered like a drunken man,
And [188]were at their wits' end.
28 Then they cried to the LORD in their trouble,
And He brought them out of their distresses.
29 He caused the storm to be still,
So that the waves of the sea were hushed.
30 Then they were glad because they were quiet,
So He guided them to their desired haven.
31 Let them give thanks to the LORD for His lovingkindness,
And for His wonders to the sons of men!
32 Let them extol Him also in the congregation of the people,
And praise Him at the seat of the elders.

33 He [189]changes rivers into a wilderness
And springs of water into a thirsty ground;
34 A fruitful land into a salt waste,
Because of the wickedness of those who dwell in it.
35 He changes a wilderness into a pool of water
And a dry land into springs of water;
36 And there He makes the hungry to dwell,
So that they may establish an inhabited city,
37 And sow fields and plant vineyards,
And gather a fruitful harvest.
38 Also He blesses them and they multiply greatly,
And He does not let their cattle decrease.

39 When they are diminished and bowed down
Through oppression, misery and sorrow,
40 He pours contempt upon princes
And makes them wander in a pathless waste.
41 But He sets the needy securely on high away from affliction,
And makes *his* families like a flock.
42 The upright see it and are glad;
But all unrighteousness shuts its mouth.
43 Who is wise? Let him give heed to these things,
And consider the lovingkindnesses of the LORD.

187 Or *pits* **188** Lit *all their wisdom was swallowed up* **189** Or *turns*

107:32 Those who have never truly suffered may not appreciate God as much as those who have matured under hardship. Those who have seen God work in times of distress have a deeper insight into his lovingkindness. If you have experienced great trials, you have the potential for great praise.

PSALM 108

A Song, a Psalm of David.

Theme: Victory in God's strength. With God's help, we can do more than we think.
Author: David

1 My heart is steadfast, O God;
I will sing, I will sing praises, even with my soul.
2 Awake, harp and lyre;
I will awaken the dawn!
3 I will give thanks to You, O LORD, among the peoples,
And I will sing praises to You among the nations.
4 For Your lovingkindness is great above the heavens,
And Your truth *reaches* to the skies.
5 Be exalted, O God, above the heavens,
And Your glory above all the earth.
6 That Your beloved may be delivered,
Save with Your right hand, and answer me!

7 God has spoken in His [190]holiness:
"I will exult, I will portion out Shechem
And measure out the valley of Succoth.
8 "Gilead is Mine, Manasseh is Mine;
Ephraim also is the helmet of My head;
Judah is My [191]scepter.
9 "Moab is My washbowl;
Over Edom I shall throw My shoe;
Over Philistia I will shout aloud."

10 Who will bring me into the besieged city?
Who will lead me to Edom?
11 Have not You Yourself, O God, rejected us?
And will You not go forth with our armies, O God?
12 Oh give us help against the adversary,
For deliverance by man is in vain.
13 Through God we will do valiantly,
And it is He who shall tread down our adversaries.

108:1 Ps 57:7-11; 108:1-5
108:4 Num 14:18; Deut 7:9; Ps 36:5; 100:5; Mic 7:18-20; Ps 113:4
108:5 Ps 57:5
108:6 Ps 60:5-12; 108:6-13
108:8 Gen 49:10
108:10 Ps 60:9
108:11 Ps 44:9
108:12 Is 30:3
108:13 Is 60:12; 63:1-4

PSALM 109

For the choir director. A Psalm of David.

Theme: Righteous indignation against liars and slanderers.
We can tell God our true feelings and desires.
Author: David

1 O God of my praise,
Do not be silent!
2 For they have opened the wicked and deceitful mouth against me;
They have spoken against me with a lying tongue.
3 They have also surrounded me with words of hatred,
And fought against me without cause.

109:1 Deut 10:21; Ps 28:1; 83:1
109:2 Ps 10:7; 52:4; Ps 120:2
109:3 Ps 35:7; 69:4; John 15:25

190 Or *sanctuary* **191** Or *lawgiver*

108:1ff The conclusions from two previous psalms have been put together to make this psalm. The first five verses are quoted from Psalm 57:7–11, and the next eight verses (108:6–13) are from Psalm 60:5–12.

108:9 Moab, Edom, and Philistia were Israel's enemies to the east, south, and west, respectively. They despised the Israelites and Israel's God.

108:13 Do our prayers end with requests for help to make it through stressful situations? David prayed not merely for rescue, but for victory. With God's help we can claim more than mere survival; we can claim victory! Look for ways God can use your distress as an opportunity to show his mighty power.

109:1ff David endured many false accusations (1 Samuel 22:7–13; 2 Samuel 15:3–4), as did Christ centuries later (Matthew 26:59–61; 27:39–44). Verse 8 is quoted in Acts 1:20 as being fulfilled in Judas's death.

4 In return for my love they act as my accusers;
But I am *in* prayer.
5 Thus they have repaid me evil for good
And hatred for my love.

6 Appoint a wicked man over him,
And let an accuser stand at his right hand.
7 When he is judged, let him come forth guilty,
And let his prayer become sin.
8 Let his days be few;
Let another take his office.
9 Let his children be fatherless
And his wife a widow.
10 Let his children wander about and beg;
And let them seek *sustenance* far from their ruined homes.
11 Let the creditor seize all that he has,
And let strangers plunder the product of his labor.
12 Let there be none to extend lovingkindness to him,
Nor any to be gracious to his fatherless children.
13 Let his posterity be cut off;
In a following generation let their name be blotted out.

14 Let the iniquity of his fathers be remembered before the LORD,
And do not let the sin of his mother be blotted out.
15 Let them be before the LORD continually,
That He may cut off their memory from the earth;
16 Because he did not remember to show lovingkindness,
But persecuted the afflicted and needy man,
And the despondent in heart, to put *them* to death.
17 He also loved cursing, so it came to him;
And he did not delight in blessing, so it was far from him.
18 But he clothed himself with cursing as with his garment,
And it entered into his body like water
And like oil into his bones.
19 Let it be to him as a garment with which he covers himself,
And for a belt with which he constantly girds himself.
20 Let this be the reward of my accusers from the LORD,
And of those who speak evil against my soul.

21 But You, O GOD, the Lord, deal *kindly* with me for Your name's sake;
Because Your lovingkindness is good, deliver me;
22 For I am afflicted and needy,
And my heart is wounded within me.
23 I am passing like a shadow when it lengthens;
I am shaken off like the locust.
24 My knees are weak from fasting,
And my flesh has grown lean, without fatness.
25 I also have become a reproach to them;
When they see me, they wag their head.

26 Help me, O LORD my God;
Save me according to Your lovingkindness.

109:4 Ps 38:20; Ps 69:13
109:5 Ps 35:12; 38:20; John 7:7; 10:32
109:7 Ps 1:5; Prov 28:9
109:8 Ps 55:23; Acts 1:20
109:9 Ex 22:24; Jer 18:21
109:10 Gen 4:12; Job 30:5-8; Ps 59:15; Ps 37:25
109:11 Neh 5:7; Job 5:5; 20:15; Is 1:7; Lam 5:2; Ezek 7:21
109:12 Ezra 7:28; 9:9; Job 5:4; Is 9:17
109:13 Job 18:19; Ps 21:10; 37:28; Ps 9:5; Prov 10:7
109:14 Is 65:6, 7; Jer 32:18; Neh 4:5; Jer 18:23
109:15 Ps 90:8; Jer 16:17; Job 18:17; Ps 34:16
109:16 Ps 37:14; Ps 34:18; Ps 37:32; 94:6
109:17 Prov 14:14; Ezek 35:9; Matt 7:2
109:18 Ps 73:6; 109:29; Ezek 7:27; Num 5:22
109:20 Ps 54:5; 94:23; Is 3:11; 2 Tim 4:14; Ps 41:5; 71:10
109:21 Ps 23:3; 25:11; 79:9
109:22 Ps 40:17; 86:1; Job 24:12; Ps 143:4; Prov 18:14
109:23 Ps 102:11; Ex 10:19
109:24 Heb 12:12; Ps 35:13
109:25 Ps 22:6; Lam 2:15; Matt 27:39; Mark 15:29
109:26 Ps 119:86

109:4 David was angry at being attacked by evil people who slandered him and lied. Yet David remained a friend and a man of prayer. While we must hate evil and work to overcome it, we must love everyone, including those who do evil, because God loves them. We are called to hate the sin, but love the person. Only through God's strength will we be able to follow David's example.

109:6–20 This is another of the imprecatory psalms, a call for God to judge the wicked. (For an explanation of imprecatory psalms, see the note on 35:1ff.) David was not taking vengeance into his own hands, but was asking that God be swift in his promised judgment of evil people. David's words depict the eventual doom of all God's enemies.

109:21 A name is more than a label; it is a representation of character and reputation. David is pleading for God to live up to his name—to his character of love and mercy. "For Your name's sake," then, means "in accordance with your character."

27 And let them know that this is Your hand;
You, LORD, have done it.
28 Let them curse, but You bless;
When they arise, they shall be ashamed,
But Your servant shall be glad.
29 Let my accusers be clothed with dishonor,
And let them cover themselves with their own shame as with a robe.

30 With my mouth I will give thanks abundantly to the LORD;
And in the midst of many I will praise Him.
31 For He stands at the right hand of the needy,
To save him from those who judge his soul.

109:27 Job 37:7

109:28 2 Sam 16:11, 12; Is 65:14

109:29 Job 8:22; Ps 132:18; Ps 35:26

109:30 Ps 22:22; 35:18; 111:1

109:31 Ps 16:8; 73:23; 110:5; 121:5; Ps 37:33

PSALM 110

A Psalm of David.

Theme: The credentials for the Messiah. Jesus is the Messiah.
Author: David

1 The LORD says to my Lord:
"Sit at My right hand
Until I make Your enemies a footstool for Your feet."
2 The LORD will stretch forth Your strong scepter from Zion, *saying,*
"Rule in the midst of Your enemies."
3 Your people will volunteer freely in the day of Your power;
In holy array, from the womb of the dawn,
Your youth are to You *as* the dew.

4 The LORD has sworn and will not change His mind,
"You are a priest forever
According to the order of Melchizedek."
5 The Lord is at Your right hand;
He will shatter kings in the day of His wrath.
6 He will judge among the nations,
He will fill *them* with corpses,
He will shatter the chief men over a broad country.
7 He will drink from the brook by the wayside;
Therefore He will lift up *His* head.

110:1 Matt 22:44; Mark 12:36; Luke 20:42, 43; Acts 2:34, 35; Heb 1:13; Matt 26:64; Eph 1:20; Col 3:1; Heb 1:3; 8:1; 10:12; 12:2; 1 Cor 15:25; Eph 1:22

110:2 Ps 45:6; Jer 48:17; Ezek 19:14; Ps 2:9; 72:8; Dan 7:13, 14

110:3 Judg 5:2; Neh 11:2; 1 Chr 16:29; Ps 96:9; 2 Sam 17:12; Mic 5:7

110:4 Heb 7:21; Num 23:19; Zech 6:13; Heb 5:6, 10; 6:20; 7:17, 21

110:5 Ps 16:8; 109:31; Ps 68:14; 76:12; Ps 2:5, 12; Rom 2:5; Rev 6:17

110:6 Is 2:4; Joel 3:12; Mic 4:3; Is 66:24; Ps 68:21

110:7 Judg 7:5, 6; Ps 27:6

PSALM 111

Theme: All that God does is good. Reverence for God is the beginning of wisdom.
Author: Anonymous

1 Praise the LORD!
I will give thanks to the LORD with all *my* heart,
In the company of the upright and in the assembly.

111:1 Ps 35:18; 138:1; Ps 89:7; 149:1

110:1 This is one of the most-quoted psalms in the New Testament because of its clear references to the Messiah. In Matthew 22:41–45, Jesus recited the words of this verse and applied them to himself. Verses 1 and 6 look forward to Christ's final and total destruction of the wicked (Revelation 6—9); 110:2 prophesies of Christ's reign on the earth (Revelation 20:1–7); 110:3–4 tell of Christ's priestly work for his people (Hebrews 5—8); and 110:5–6 look forward to the final battle on earth when Christ will overcome the forces of evil (Revelation 19:11–21).

110:1–7 Many people have a vague belief in God, but refuse to accept Jesus as anything more than a great human teacher. But the Bible does not allow that option. Both the Old and New Testaments proclaim the deity of the One who came to save and to reign. Jesus explained that this psalm spoke of the Messiah as greater than David, Israel's greatest king (Mark 12:35–37). Peter used this psalm to show that Jesus, the Messiah, sits at God's right hand and is Lord over all (Acts 2:32–35). You can't straddle the fence, calling Jesus "just a good teacher," because the Bible clearly calls him Lord.

110:4 For more about Melchizedek, see his Profile at the end of Genesis 16. As a priest like Melchizedek, Christ will never abuse his divine position, and his reign will be forever. Jesus is more fully described as our High Priest in Hebrews 5.

111—118 Psalms 111—118 are called hallelujah psalms. *Hallelujah* means "praise the LORD" and expresses the uplifting and optimistic tone of these songs.

111:2 Ps 92:5; Ps 143:5

111:3 Ps 96:6; 145:5; Ps 112:3, 9; 119:142

111:4 Ps 86:5, 15; 103:8; 145:8

111:5 Matt 6:31-33; Ps 105:8

2 Great are the works of the LORD;
They are studied by all who delight in them.
3 Splendid and majestic is His work,
And His righteousness endures forever.
4 He has made His wonders to be remembered;
The LORD is gracious and compassionate.
5 He has given food to those who [192]fear Him;
He will remember His covenant forever.
6 He has made known to His people the power of His works,
In giving them the heritage of the nations.

111:7 Rev 15:3; Ps 19:7; 93:5

111:8 Ps 119:160; Is 40:8; Matt 5:18; Ps 19:9

111:9 Luke 1:68; Ps 99:3; Luke 1:49

111:10 Job 28:28; Prov 1:7; 9:10; Eccl 12:13; Ps 119:98; Prov 3:4; Ps 145:2

7 The works of His hands are truth and justice;
All His precepts are sure.
8 They are upheld forever and ever;
They are performed in truth and uprightness.
9 He has sent redemption to His people;
He has ordained His covenant forever;
Holy and awesome is His name.
10 The [193]fear of the LORD is the beginning of wisdom;
A good understanding have all those who do *His commandments;*
His praise endures forever.

PSALM 112

Theme: The advantages of having faith in God. God guards the minds and actions of those who follow his commands.
Author: Anonymous

112:1 Ps 128:1; Ps 1:2; 119:14, 16

112:2 Ps 102:28; 127:4; Ps 128:4

112:3 Prov 3:16; 8:18; Matt 6:33

112:4 Job 11:17; Ps 97:11; Ps 37:26

112:5 Ps 37:21

112:6 Ps 15:5; 55:22; Prov 10:7

1 Praise the LORD!
How blessed is the man who fears the LORD,
Who greatly delights in His commandments.
2 His [194]descendants will be mighty on earth;
The generation of the upright will be blessed.
3 Wealth and riches are in his house,
And his righteousness endures forever.
4 Light arises in the darkness for the upright;
He is gracious and compassionate and righteous.
5 It is well with the man who is gracious and lends;
He will maintain his cause in judgment.
6 For he will never be shaken;
The righteous will be remembered forever.

112:7 Prov 1:33; Ps 57:7; 108:1; Ps 56:4

7 He will not fear evil tidings;
His heart is steadfast, trusting in the LORD.

192 Or *revere* **193** Or *reverence for* **194** Lit *seed*

111:9 The redemption here pictures the rescue by God of the Israelites from Egypt and the future return from captivity in Babylon (see Deuteronomy 7:8; Jeremiah 31:11). *Redemption* means recovery of something or someone upon payment of a ransom. All people were being held in slavery by sin, until Jesus paid the price to free us—giving his life as a perfect sacrifice. Before Jesus offered himself as a sacrifice for sin, people were not permitted into God's presence (the holy of holies); now, all believers can freely approach God's throne through prayer and have God in their lives through the Holy Spirit.

111:10 The only way to become truly wise is to fear (revere) God. This same thought is expressed in Proverbs 1:7–9. Too often people want to skip this step, thinking they can become wise by life experience and academic knowledge alone. But if we do not acknowledge God as the source of wisdom, then our foundation for making wise decisions is shaky, and we are prone to mistakes and foolish choices.

112:1 Many blessings are available to us—honor, prosperity, security, freedom from fear (112:2–9)—if we *fear* the Lord and *delight* in obeying his commands. If you expect God's blessings, you must revere him and gladly obey him.

112:5 Generosity will cure two problems that money can create. The rich man may abuse others in his desire to accumulate wealth. Generosity will eliminate that abuse. Also, the fear of losing money can be a snare. Generosity and respect for God places our trust in him, not our money, for justice and security.

112:7–8 We all want to live without fear; our heroes are fearless people who take on all dangers and overcome them. The psalmist teaches us that *fear* of God can lead to a *fearless* life. To fear God means to respect and revere him as the almighty Lord. When we trust God completely to take care of us, we will find that our other fears—even of death itself—will subside.

8 His heart is upheld, he will not fear,
Until he looks *with satisfaction* on his adversaries.
9 He has given freely to the poor,
His righteousness endures forever;
His horn will be exalted in honor.

10 The wicked will see it and be vexed,
He will gnash his teeth and melt away;
The desire of the wicked will perish.

112:8 Heb 13:9; Ps 27:1; 56:11; Prov 1:33; 3:24; Is 12:2; Ps 54:7; 59:10

112:9 2 Cor 9:9; Ps 75:10; 89:17; 92:10; 148:14

112:10 Ps 86:17; Ps 35:16; 37:12; Matt 8:12; 25:30; Luke 13:28; Ps 58:7; Job 8:13; Prov 10:28; 11:7

PSALM 113

Theme: The scope of God's care. God's great mercy is demonstrated by his concern for the poor and oppressed.
Author: Anonymous

1 Praise the LORD!
Praise, O servants of the LORD,
Praise the name of the LORD.
2 Blessed be the name of the LORD
From this time forth and forever.
3 From the rising of the sun to its setting
The name of the LORD is to be praised.
4 The LORD is high above all nations;
His glory is above the heavens.

5 Who is like the LORD our God,
Who is enthroned on high,
6 Who humbles Himself to behold
The things that are in heaven and in the earth?
7 He raises the poor from the dust
And lifts the needy from the ash heap,
8 To make *them* sit with princes,
With the princes of His people.
9 He makes the barren woman abide in the house
As a joyful mother of children.
Praise the LORD!

113:1 Ps 135:1; Ps 34:22; 69:36; 79:10; 90:13

113:2 Ps 145:21; Dan 2:20

113:3 Ps 50:1; Is 59:19; Mal 1:11; Ps 18:3; 48:1, 10

113:4 Ps 97:9; 99:2; Ps 8:1; 57:11; 148:13

113:5 Ex 15:11; Ps 35:10; 89:6; Ps 103:19

113:6 Ps 11:4; 138:6; Is 57:15

113:7 1 Sam 2:8; Ps 107:41

113:8 Job 36:7

113:9 1 Sam 2:5; Ps 68:6; Is 54:1

PSALM 114

Theme: The mighty God who delivered Israel from Egypt. We can celebrate God's great work in our lives.
Author: Anonymous

1 When Israel went forth from Egypt,
The house of Jacob from a people of strange language,
2 Judah became His sanctuary,
Israel, His dominion.

3 The sea looked and fled;
The Jordan turned back.
4 The mountains skipped like rams,
The hills, like lambs.
5 What ails you, O sea, that you flee?

114:1 Ex 12:51; 13:3; Ps 81:5

114:2 Ex 15:17; 29:45, 46; Ps 78:68, 69; Ex 19:6

114:3 Ex 14:21; Ps 77:16; Josh 3:13, 16

114:4 Ex 19:18; Judg 5:5; Ps 18:7; 29:6; Hab 3:6

114:5 Hab 3:8

112:9 "His horn will be exalted in honor" means that God's dignity will be uplifted and those faithful to God will be honored. The horn was a symbol of power and dignity just as the horns of animals represent their strength.

113:5–9 In God's eyes, a person's value has no relationship to his or her wealth or position on the social ladder. Many people who have excelled in God's work began in poverty or humble beginnings. God supersedes the social orders of this world, often choosing his future leaders and ambassadors from among social outcasts. Do you treat the unwanted in society as though they have value? Demonstrate by your actions that all people are valuable and useful in God's eyes.

O Jordan, that you turn back?
6 O mountains, that you skip like rams?
O hills, like lambs?

7 Tremble, O earth, before the Lord,
Before the God of Jacob,
8 Who turned the rock into a pool of water,
The flint into a fountain of water.

114:7 Ps 96:9
114:8 Ex 17:6; Num 20:11; Ps 78:15; 105:41; Ps 107:35; Deut 8:15

PSALM 115

Theme: God is alive. He is thinking about us and caring for us, and we should put him first in our lives.
Author: Anonymous

1 Not to us, O LORD, not to us,
But to Your name give glory
Because of Your lovingkindness, because of Your truth.
2 Why should the nations say,
"Where, now, is their God?"
3 But our God is in the heavens;
He does whatever He pleases.
4 Their idols are silver and gold,
The work of man's hands.
5 They have mouths, but they cannot speak;
They have eyes, but they cannot see;
6 They have ears, but they cannot hear;
They have noses, but they cannot smell;
7 They have hands, but they cannot feel;
They have feet, but they cannot walk;
They cannot make a sound with their throat.
8 Those who make them will become like them,
Everyone who trusts in them.

9 O Israel, trust in the LORD;
He is their help and their shield.
10 O house of Aaron, trust in the LORD;
He is their help and their shield.
11 You who [195]fear the LORD, trust in the LORD;
He is their help and their shield.
12 The LORD has been mindful of us; He will bless *us;*
He will bless the house of Israel;
He will bless the house of Aaron.

115:1 Is 48:11; Ezek 36:22; Ps 29:2; 96:8
115:2 Ps 79:10; Ps 42:3, 10
115:3 Ps 103:19; Ps 135:6; Dan 4:35
115:4 Ps 115:4-8; 135:15-18; Jer 10:4; Deut 4:28; 2 Kin 19:18; Is 37:19; 44:10, 20; Jer 10:3
115:5 Jer 10:5
115:8 Ps 135:18; Is 44:9-11
115:9 Ps 118:2; 135:19; Ps 37:3; 62:8; Ps 33:20
115:10 Ps 118:3; 135:19
115:11 Ps 22:23; 103:11; 135:20
115:12 Ps 98:3

195 Or *revere*

114:7 When God gave the Law at Mount Sinai, the mountain trembled in God's presence. Even with our great technology, the seas, rivers, and mountains still present us with formidable challenges. But to God, who controls nature, they are as nothing. When observing the power of an ocean wave or the majesty of a mountain peak, think of God's greatness and glory, which are far more awesome than the natural wonders you can see. To tremble at God's presence means to recognize God's complete power and authority and our frailty by comparison.

115—118 Psalms 115—118 were traditionally sung at the Passover meal, commemorating Israel's escape from slavery in Egypt (Exodus 11–12).

115:1 The psalmist asked that God's name, not the nation's, be glorified. Too often we ask God to glorify his name *with* ours. For example, we may pray for help to do a good job so that our work will be noticed. Or we may ask that a presentation go well so we will get applause. There is nothing wrong with looking good or impressing others; the problem comes when we want to look good no matter what happens to God's reputation in the process. Before you pray, ask yourself, "Who will get the credit if God answers my prayer?"

115:4–8 When the psalms were written, many people worshiped idols—statues of wood, stone, or metal. They took pride in what they could see and had contempt for what they couldn't see. Today, we still may value tangible objects (home, clothing, possessions) rather than intangible realities (spiritual growth, salvation, giving to those in need, spending time with loved ones). Those who spend their time obtaining tangible objects are as foolish and empty as the idols themselves. (For more on the foolishness of idols, see Isaiah 44:9–20.)

115:12 "The LORD has been mindful of us," says the psalm writer. What a fantastic truth! There are many times when we feel isolated, alone, and abandoned, even by God. In reality, he sees, understands, and thinks about us. When depressed by problems or struggling with self-worth, be encouraged that God keeps you in his thoughts. If he thinks about you, surely his help is near.

13 He will bless those who [196]fear the LORD,
The small together with the great.
14 May the LORD give you increase,
You and your children.
15 May you be blessed of the LORD,
Maker of heaven and earth.

16 The heavens are the heavens of the LORD,
But the earth He has given to the sons of men.
17 The dead do not praise the LORD,
Nor *do* any who go down into silence;
18 But as for us, we will bless the LORD
From this time forth and forever.
Praise the LORD!

115:13 Ps 103:11; 112:1; 128:1; Rev 11:18; 19:5
115:14 Deut 1:11
115:15 Gen 1:1; Neh 9:6; Ps 96:5; 102:25; 121:2; 124:8; 134:3; 146:6; Acts 14:15; Rev 14:7
115:16 Ps 89:11; Ps 8:6
115:17 Ps 6:5; 88:10-12; Is 38:18; Ps 31:17
115:18 Ps 113:2; Dan 2:20

PSALM 116

Theme: Praise for being saved from certain death. Worship is a thankful response and not a repayment for what God has done.
Author: Anonymous

1 I love the LORD, because He hears
My voice *and* my supplications.
2 Because He has inclined His ear to me,
Therefore I shall call *upon Him* as long as I live.
3 The cords of death encompassed me
And the terrors of Sheol came upon me;
I found distress and sorrow.
4 Then I called upon the name of the LORD:
"O LORD, I beseech You, save my life!"

5 Gracious is the LORD, and righteous;
Yes, our God is compassionate.
6 The LORD preserves the simple;
I was brought low, and He saved me.
7 Return to your rest, O my soul,
For the LORD has dealt bountifully with you.
8 For You have rescued my soul from death,
My eyes from tears,
My feet from stumbling.
9 I shall walk before the LORD
In the land of the living.
10 I believed when I said,
"I am greatly afflicted."
11 I said in my alarm,
"All men are liars."

12 What shall I render to the LORD
For all His benefits toward me?
13 I shall lift up the cup of salvation
And call upon the name of the LORD.
14 I shall pay my vows to the LORD,
Oh *may it be* in the presence of all His people.
15 Precious in the sight of the LORD
Is the death of His godly ones.

116:1 Ps 18:1; Ps 6:8; 66:19; Is 37:17; Dan 9:18
116:2 Ps 17:6; 31:2; 40:1
116:3 Ps 18:4, 5
116:4 Ps 18:6; 118:5; Ps 17:13; 22:20
116:5 Ps 86:15; 103:8; Ezra 9:15; Neh 9:8; Ps 119:137; 145:17; Jer 12:1; Dan 9:14; Ex 34:6
116:6 Ps 19:7; Prov 1:4; Ps 79:8; 142:6
116:7 Jer 6:16; Matt 11:29; Ps 13:6; 142:7
116:8 Ps 49:15; 56:13; 86:13
116:9 Ps 27:13
116:10 2 Cor 4:13; Ps 88:7
116:11 Ps 31:22; Ps 62:9; Rom 3:4
116:12 2 Chr 32:25; 1 Thess 3:9; Ps 103:2
116:13 Ps 16:5; Ps 80:18; 105:1
116:14 Ps 50:14; 116:18; Ps 22:25
116:15 Ps 72:14

196 Or *revere*

116:1–2 God is so responsive that you can always reach him. He bends down and listens to your voice. This writer's love for the Lord had grown because he had experienced answers to his prayers. If you are discouraged, remember that God is near, listening carefully to every prayer and answering each prayer in order to give you his best.

116:15 God stays close to us even in death. When someone we love is nearing death, we may become angry and feel abandoned.

116:16 Ps 86:16; 119:125; 143:12; Ps 86:16; Ps 107:14
116:17 Lev 7:12; Ps 50:14; Ps 116:13
116:18 Ps 116:14
116:19 Ps 92:13; 96:8; 135:2; Ps 102:21

16 O LORD, surely I am Your servant,
I am Your servant, the son of Your handmaid,
You have loosed my bonds.
17 To You I shall offer a sacrifice of thanksgiving,
And call upon the name of the LORD.
18 I shall pay my vows to the LORD,
Oh *may it be* in the presence of all His people,
19 In the courts of the LORD'S house,
In the midst of you, O Jerusalem.
Praise the LORD!

PSALM 117

Theme: Another reason for praise—God's love for the whole world. We should praise God for his unlimited love.
Author: Anonymous

117:1 Rom 15:11
117:2 Ps 103:11; Ps 100:5; 146:6

1 Praise the LORD, all nations;
Laud Him, all peoples!
2 For His lovingkindness [197]is great toward us,
And the truth of the LORD is everlasting.
Praise the LORD!

PSALM 118

Theme: Confidence in God's eternal love. God's love is unchanging in the midst of changing situations. This gives us security.
Author: Anonymous

118:1 1 Chr 16:8, 34; Ps 106:1; 107:1; Jer 33:11; 2 Chr 5:13; 7:3; Ezra 3:11; Ps 100:5; 136:1-26
118:2 Ps 115:9
118:3 Ps 115:10
118:4 Ps 115:11
118:5 Ps 18:6; 86:7; 120:1; Ps 18:19
118:6 Job 19:27; Ps 56:9; Heb 13:6; Ps 23:4; 27:1; Ps 56:4, 11
118:7 Ps 54:4; Ps 54:7; 59:10
118:8 2 Chr 32:7, 8; Ps 40:4; 108:12; Is 31:1, 3; 57:13; Jer 17:5
118:9 Ps 146:3

1 Give thanks to the LORD, for He is good;
For His lovingkindness is everlasting.
2 Oh let Israel say,
"His lovingkindness is everlasting."
3 Oh let the house of Aaron say,
"His lovingkindness is everlasting."
4 Oh let those who [198]fear the LORD say,
"His lovingkindness is everlasting."

5 From *my* distress I called upon the LORD;
The LORD answered me *and set me* in a large place.
6 The LORD is for me; I will not fear;
What can man do to me?
7 The LORD is for me among those who help me;
Therefore I will look *with satisfaction* on those who hate me.
8 It is better to take refuge in the LORD
Than to trust in man.
9 It is better to take refuge in the LORD
Than to trust in princes.

197 Lit *prevails over us* **198** Or *revere*

But believers (godly ones) are precious to God, and he carefully chooses the time when they will be called into his presence. Let this truth provide comfort when you've lost a loved one. God sees, and each life is valuable to him (see Jesus' statement in Matthew 10:29).

117:1–2 Not only is Psalm 117 the shortest chapter in the Bible, but it is also the middle chapter. Paul quotes from this psalm in Romans 15:11 to show that God's salvation is for *all* people, not just the Jews.

117:1–2 Have you ever said, "I can't think of anything God has done for me. How can I praise him?" This psalm gives two reasons for praising God: his great love toward us and his faithfulness that endures forever. If he did nothing else for us, he would still be worthy of our highest praise.

118:8 Pilots put confidence in their planes. Commuters place confidence in trains, cars, or buses. Each day we must put our confidence in something or someone. If you are willing to trust a plane or car to get you to your destination, are you willing to trust God to guide you here on earth and to your eternal destination? Do you trust him more than any human being? How futile it is to trust anything or anyone more than God.

10 All nations surrounded me;
In the name of the LORD I will surely cut them off.
11 They surrounded me, yes, they surrounded me;
In the name of the LORD I will surely cut them off.
12 They surrounded me like bees;
They were extinguished as a fire of thorns;
In the name of the LORD I will surely cut them off.
13 You pushed me violently so that I was falling,
But the LORD helped me.
14 The LORD is my strength and song,
And He has become my salvation.

15 The sound of joyful shouting and salvation is in the tents of the righteous;
The right hand of the LORD does valiantly.
16 The right hand of the LORD is exalted;
The right hand of the LORD does valiantly.
17 I will not die, but live,
And tell of the works of the LORD.
18 The LORD has disciplined me severely,
But He has not given me over to death.

19 Open to me the gates of righteousness;
I shall enter through them, I shall give thanks to the LORD.
20 This is the gate of the LORD;
The righteous will enter through it.
21 I shall give thanks to You, for You have answered me,
And You have become my salvation.

22 The stone which the builders rejected
Has become the chief corner *stone.*
23 This is [199]the LORD'S doing;
It is marvelous in our eyes.
24 This is the day which the LORD has made;
Let us rejoice and be glad in it.
25 O LORD, do save, we beseech You;
O LORD, we beseech You, do send prosperity!
26 Blessed is the one who comes in the name of the LORD;
We have blessed you from the house of the LORD.
27 The LORD is God, and He has given us light;
Bind the festival sacrifice with cords to the horns of the altar.
28 You are my God, and I give thanks to You;
You are my God, I extol You.
29 Give thanks to the LORD, for He is good;
For His lovingkindness is everlasting.

199 Lit *from the LORD*

118:10 Ps 3:6; 88:17; Ps 18:40

118:11 Ps 88:17

118:12 Deut 1:44; Ps 58:9; Nah 1:10

118:13 Ps 140:4; Ps 86:17

118:14 Ex 15:2; Ps 27:1

118:15 Ps 68:3; Ex 15:6; Ps 89:13; Luke 1:51

118:16 Ex 15:6; Ps 89:13

118:17 Ps 6:5; 116:8, 9; Hab 1:12; Ps 73:28; 107:22

118:18 Ps 73:14; Jer 31:18; 1 Cor 11:32; 2 Cor 6:9; Ps 86:13

118:19 Is 26:2

118:20 Ps 15:1, 2; 24:3-6; 140:13; Is 35:8; Rev 22:14

118:21 Ps 116:1; 118:5

118:22 Matt 21:42; Mark 12:10, 11; Luke 20:17; Acts 4:11; Eph 2:20; 1 Pet 2:7

118:24 Ps 31:7

118:25 Ps 106:47; Ps 122:6

118:26 Matt 21:9; 23:39; Mark 11:9; Luke 13:35; 19:38; John 12:13; Ps 129:8

118:27 1 Kin 18:39; Esth 8:16; Ps 18:28; 27:1; 1 Pet 2:9; Ex 27:2

118:28 Ps 63:1; 140:6; Ex 15:2; Is 25:1

118:22–23 Jesus referred to this verse when he spoke of being rejected by his own people (Matthew 21:42; Mark 12:10–11; Luke 20:17). Although he was rejected, Jesus is now the "chief corner stone," the most important part of the church (Acts 4:11; Ephesians 2:20; 1 Peter 2:6–7). The corner stone is the foundation stone, holding the structure together.

118:24 There are days when the last thing we want to do is rejoice. Our mood is down, our situation is out of hand, and our sorrow or guilt is overwhelming. We can relate to the writers of the psalms who often felt this way. But no matter how low the psalmists felt, they were always honest with God. And as they talked to God, their prayers ended in praise. When you don't feel like rejoicing, tell God how you truly feel. You will find that God will give you a reason to rejoice. God has given you this day to live and to serve him—be glad!

118:27 The "horns of the altar" were the projections from the four corners of the altar.

119:1 Ps 101:2, 6; Prov 11:20; 13:6; Ps 128:1; Ezek 11:20; 18:17; Mic 4:2

119:2 Ps 25:10; 99:7; 119:22, 168; Deut 4:29; Ps 119:10; Deut 6:5; 10:12; 11:13; 13:3; 30:2

119:3 1 John 3:9; 5:18

119:4 Deut 4:13; Neh 9:13

119:5 Ps 40:2; Prov 4:26; Deut 12:1; 2 Chr 7:17

119:6 Job 22:26; Ps 119:80

119:7 Ps 119:62

119:8 Ps 38:21; 71:9, 18

119:9 1 Kin 2:4; 8:25; 2 Chr 6:16

119:10 2 Chr 15:15; Ps 119:2, 145; Ps 119:21, 118

119:11 Ps 37:31; 40:8; Luke 2:19, 51

119:12 Ps 119:26, 64, 108, 124, 135, 171

119:13 Ps 40:9; Ps 119:72

119:14 Ps 119:111, 162

119:15 Ps 1:2; 119:23, 48, 78, 97, 148; Ps 25:4; 27:11; Is 58:2

119:16 Ps 1:2; 119:24, 35, 47, 70, 77, 92, 143, 174; Ps 119:93

119:17 Ps 13:6; 116:7

PSALM 119

Theme: God's Word is true and wonderful. Stay true to God and his Word no matter how bad the world becomes. Obedience to God's laws is the only way to achieve real happiness.
Author: Anonymous; some suggest Ezra the priest

א Aleph.

1 How blessed are those whose way is [200]blameless,
Who walk in the law of the LORD.
2 How blessed are those who observe His testimonies,
Who seek Him with all *their* heart.
3 They also do no unrighteousness;
They walk in His ways.
4 YoYou have ordained Your precepts,
That we should keep *them* diligently.
5 Oh that my ways may be established
To keep Your statutes!
6 Then I shall not be ashamed
When I look upon all Your commandments.
7 I shall give thanks to You with uprightness of heart,
When I learn Your righteous judgments.
8 I shall keep Your statutes;
Do not forsake me utterly!

ב Beth.

9 How can a young man keep his way pure?
By keeping *it* according to Your word.
10 With all my heart I have sought You;
Do not let me wander from Your commandments.
11 Your word I have treasured in my heart,
That I may not sin against You.
12 Blessed are You, O LORD;
Teach me Your statutes.
13 With my lips I have told of
All the ordinances of Your mouth.
14 I have rejoiced in the way of YoYour testimonies,
As much as in all riches.
15 I will meditate on Your precepts
And regard Your ways.
16 I shall delight in Your statutes;
I shall not forget Your word.

ג Gimel.

17 Deal bountifully with Your servant,
That I may live and keep Your word.

200 Lit *complete;* or *having integrity*

119:1ff This is both the longest psalm and the longest chapter in the Bible. It may have been written by Ezra after the temple was rebuilt (Ezra 6:14–15) as a repetitive meditation on the beauty of God's Word and how it helps us stay pure and grow in faith. Psalm 119 has 22 carefully constructed sections, each corresponding to a different letter in the Hebrew alphabet and each verse beginning with the letter of its section. Almost every verse mentions God's Word. Such repetition was common in the Hebrew culture. People did not have personal copies of the Scriptures to read as we do, so God's people memorized his Word and passed it along orally. The structure of this psalm allowed for easy memorization. Remember, God's Word, the Bible, is the only sure guide for living a pure life.

119:9 We are drowning in a sea of impurity. Everywhere we look we find temptation to lead impure lives. The psalmist asked a question that troubles us all: How do we stay pure in a filthy environment? We cannot do this on our own but must have counsel and strength more dynamic than the tempting influences around us. Where can we find that strength and wisdom? By reading God's Word and doing what it says.

119:11 Treasuring (keeping) God's Word in our hearts is a deterrent to sin. This alone should inspire us to memorize Scripture. But memorization alone will not keep us from sin; we must also put God's Word to work in our lives, making it a vital guide for everything we do.

119:12–24 Most of us chafe under rules, for we think they restrict us from doing what we want. At first glance, then, it may seem strange to hear the psalmist talk of rejoicing in following God's statutes as much as in great riches. But God's laws were given to free us to be all he wants us to be. They restrict us from doing what might cripple us and keep us from being our best. God's guidelines help us follow his path and avoid paths that lead to destruction.

18 Open my eyes, that I may behold
Wonderful things from Your law.
19 I am a stranger in the earth;
Do not hide Your commandments from me.
20 My soul is crushed with longing
After Your ordinances at all times.
21 You rebuke the arrogant, the cursed,
Who wander from Your commandments.
22 Take away reproach and contempt from me,
For I observe Your testimonies.
23 Even though princes sit *and* talk against me,
Your servant meditates on Your statutes.
24 Your testimonies also are my delight;
They are my counselors.

ד Daleth.

25 My soul cleaves to the dust;
Revive me according to Your word.
26 I have told of my ways, and You have answered me;
Teach me Your statutes.
27 Make me understand the way of Your precepts,
So I will meditate on Your wonders.
28 My soul weeps because of grief;
Strengthen me according to Your word.
29 Remove the false way from me,
And graciously grant me Your law.
30 I have chosen the faithful way;
I have placed Your ordinances *before me.*
31 I cling to Your testimonies;
O LORD, do not put me to shame!
32 I shall run the way of Your commandments,
For You will enlarge my heart.

ה He.

33 Teach me, O LORD, the way of Your statutes,
And I shall observe it to the end.
34 Give me understanding, that I may observe Your law
And keep it with all *my* heart.
35 Make me walk in the path of Your commandments,
For I delight in it.
36 Incline my heart to Your testimonies
And not to *dishonest* gain.
37 Turn away my eyes from looking at vanity,
And revive me in Your ways.
38 Establish Your word to Your servant,
As that which produces reverence for You.
39 Turn away my reproach which I dread,
For Your ordinances are good.

119:19 Gen 47:9; Lev 25:23; 1 Chr 29:15; Ps 39:12; 119:54; Heb 11:13

119:20 Ps 42:1, 2; 63:1; 84:2; 119:40, 131

119:21 Ps 68:30; Deut 27:26; Ps 37:22; Ps 119:10, 118

119:22 Ps 39:8; 119:39; Ps 119:2

119:23 Ps 119:161; Ps 119:15

119:24 Ps 119:16

119:25 Ps 44:25; Ps 119:37, 40, 88, 93, 107, 149, 154, 156, 159; 143:11; Ps 119:65

119:26 Ps 25:4; 27:11; 86:11; 119:12

119:27 Ps 105:2; 145:5

119:28 Ps 22:14; 107:26; Ps 20:2; 1 Pet 5:10

119:31 Deut 11:22

119:32 1 Kin 4:29; Is 60:5; 2 Cor 6:11, 13

119:33 Ps 119:5, 12

119:34 Ps 119:27, 73, 125, 144, 169; 1 Chr 22:12; Ezek 44:24; Ps 119:2, 69

119:35 Ps 25:4; Is 40:14; Ps 112:1; 119:16

119:36 1 Kin 8:58; Ezek 33:31; Mark 7:21, 22; Luke 12:15; Heb 13:5

119:37 Is 33:15; Ps 71:20; 119:25

119:38 2 Sam 7:25

119:19 The psalmist says that he is a "stranger in the earth," and so he needed guidance. Almost any long trip requires a map or guide. As we travel through life, the Bible should be our road map, pointing out safe routes, obstacles to avoid, and our final destination. We must recognize ourselves as pilgrims, travelers here on earth who need to study God's map to learn the way. If we ignore the map, we will wander aimlessly through life and risk missing our real destination.

119:27–28 Our lives are cluttered with rule books, but the authors never come with us to help us follow the rules. But God does. That is the uniqueness of our Bible. God not only provides the rules and guidelines, but comes with us personally each day to strengthen us so that we can live according to those rules. All we must do is invite him and respond to his direction.

119:36 In today's world, people most often covet financial gain. Money represents power, influence, and success. For many people, money is a god. They think about little else. True, money can buy certain comforts and offer some security. But far more valuable than wealth is obedience to God because it is a heavenly treasure rather than an earthly one (Luke 12:33). We should do what God wants, regardless of the financial implications. Make the psalmist's prayer your own, asking God to turn your heart toward his statutes and not toward making money; it's in your own best interest in the long run.

119:40 Ps 119:20
119:41 Ps 119:77; Ps 119:58, 76, 116, 170
119:42 Prov 27:11; Ps 102:8; 119:39
119:43 Ps 119:49, 74, 81, 114, 147
119:44 Ps 119:33
119:45 Prov 4:12; Ps 119:94, 155
119:46 Matt 10:18; Acts 26:1, 2
119:47 Ps 119:16; Ps 119:97, 127, 159
119:48 Ps 119:97, 127, 159; Ps 119:15
119:50 Job 6:10; Rom 15:4
119:51 Job 30:1; Jer 20:7; Job 23:11; Ps 44:18; 119:157
119:52 Ps 103:18
119:53 Ex 32:19; Ezra 9:3; Neh 13:25; Ps 119:158; Ps 89:30
119:54 Gen 47:9; Ps 119:19
119:55 Ps 63:6; Ps 42:8; 92:2; 119:62; Is 26:9; Acts 16:25
119:56 Ps 119:22, 69, 100
119:57 Ps 16:5; Lam 3:24; Deut 33:9
119:58 1 Kin 13:6; Ps 119:2; Ps 41:4; 56:1; 57:1; Ps 119:41
119:59 Mark 14:72; Luke 15:17
119:61 Job 36:8; Ps 140:5; Ps 119:83, 141, 153, 176
119:62 Ps 119:55; Ps 119:7
119:63 Ps 101:6

40 Behold, I long for Your precepts;
Revive me through Your righteousness.

ו Vav.

41 May Your lovingkindnesses also come to me, O LORD,
Your salvation according to Your word;
42 So I will have an answer for him who reproaches me,
For I trust in Your word.
43 And do not take the word of truth utterly out of my mouth,
For I wait for Your ordinances.
44 So I will keep Your law continually,
Forever and ever.
45 And I will walk at liberty,
For I seek Your precepts.
46 I will also speak of Your testimonies before kings
And shall not be ashamed.
47 I shall delight in Your commandments,
Which I love.
48 And I shall lift up my hands to Your commandments,
Which I love;
And I will meditate on Your statutes.

ז Zayin.

49 Remember the word to Your servant,
In which You have made me hope.
50 This is my comfort in my affliction,
That Your word has revived me.
51 The arrogant utterly deride me,
Yet I do not turn aside from Your law.
52 I have remembered Your ordinances from [201]of old, O LORD,
And comfort myself.
53 Burning indignation has seized me because of the wicked,
Who forsake Your law.
54 Your statutes are my songs
In the house of my pilgrimage.
55 O LORD, I remember Your name in the night,
And keep Your law.
56 This has become mine,
That I observe Your precepts.

ח Heth.

57 The LORD is my portion;
I have promised to keep Your words.
58 I sought Your favor with all *my* heart;
Be gracious to me according to Your word.
59 I considered my ways
And turned my feet to Your testimonies.
60 I hastened and did not delay
To keep Your commandments.
61 The cords of the wicked have encircled me,
But I have not forgotten Your law.
62 At midnight I shall rise to give thanks to You
Because of Your righteous ordinances.
63 I am a companion of all those who fear You,
And of those who keep Your precepts.

201 Or *everlasting*

119:44–46 The psalmist talks about keeping the laws and yet being free. Contrary to what we often expect, obeying God's laws does not inhibit or restrain us. Instead it frees us to be what God designed us to be. By seeking God's salvation and forgiveness, we have freedom from sin and the resulting oppressive guilt. By living God's way, we have freedom to fulfill God's plan for our lives.

64 The earth is full of Your lovingkindness, O LORD;
Teach me Your statutes.

ט Teth.

65 You have dealt well with Your servant,
O LORD, according to Your word.
66 Teach me good discernment and knowledge,
For I believe in Your commandments.
67 Before I was afflicted I went astray,
But now I keep Your word.
68 You are good and do good;
Teach me Your statutes.
69 The arrogant [202]have forged a lie against me;
With all *my* heart I will observe Your precepts.
70 Their heart is covered with fat,
But I delight in Your law.
71 It is good for me that I was afflicted,
That I may learn Your statutes.
72 The law of Your mouth is better to me
Than thousands of gold and silver *pieces.*

י Yodh.

73 Your hands made me and [203]fashioned me;
Give me understanding, that I may learn Your commandments.
74 May those who fear You see me and be glad,
Because I wait for Your word.
75 I know, O LORD, that Your judgments are righteous,
And that in faithfulness You have afflicted me.
76 O may Your lovingkindness comfort me,
According to Your word to Your servant.
77 May Your compassion come to me that I may live,
For Your law is my delight.
78 May the arrogant be ashamed, for they subvert me with a lie;
But I shall meditate on Your precepts.
79 May those who fear You turn to me,
Even those who know Your testimonies.
80 May my heart be blameless in Your statutes,
So that I will not be ashamed.

כ Kaph.

81 My soul languishes for Your salvation;
I wait for Your word.
82 My eyes fail *with longing* for Your word,
While I say, "When will You comfort me?"
83 Though I have become like a wineskin in the smoke,
I do not forget Your statutes.
84 How many are the days of Your servant?
When will You execute judgment on those who persecute me?
85 The arrogant have dug pits for me,
Men who are not in accord with Your law.
86 All Your commandments are faithful;
They have persecuted me with a lie; help me!
87 They almost destroyed me on earth,
But as for me, I did not forsake Your precepts.
88 Revive me according to Your lovingkindness,
So that I may keep the testimony of Your mouth.

ל Lamedh.

89 Forever, O LORD,
Your word [204]is settled in heaven.

202 Lit *besmear me with lies* **203** Lit *established* **204** Lit *stands firm*

119:64 Ps 33:5; Ps 119:12

119:66 Phil 1:9

119:67 Ps 119:71, 75; Jer 31:18, 19; Heb 12:5-11

119:68 Ps 86:5; 100:5; 106:1; 107:1; Matt 19:17; Deut 8:16; 28:63; 30:5; Ps 125:4; Ps 119:12

119:69 Job 13:4; Ps 109:2; Ps 119:56

119:70 Deut 32:15; Job 15:27; Ps 17:10; Is 6:10; Jer 5:28; Acts 28:27; Ps 119:16

119:71 Ps 119:67, 75

119:72 Ps 19:10; 119:127; Prov 8:10, 11, 19

119:73 Job 10:8; 31:15; Ps 100:3; 138:8; 139:15, 16; Ps 119:34

119:74 Ps 34:2; 35:27; 107:42; Ps 119:43

119:75 Ps 119:138; Heb 12:10

119:77 Ps 119:41; Ps 119:16

119:78 Jer 50:32; Ps 119:86; Ps 119:15

119:80 Ps 119:1; Ps 119:46

119:81 Ps 84:2; Ps 119:43

119:82 Ps 69:3; 119:123; Is 38:14; Lam 2:11

119:83 Job 30:30; Ps 119:61

119:84 Ps 39:4; Rev 6:10

119:85 Ps 7:15; 35:7; 57:6; Jer 18:22

119:86 Ps 119:138; Ps 35:19; 119:78, 161; Ps 109:26

119:87 Is 58:2

119:89 Ps 89:2; 119:160; Is 40:8; Matt 24:35; 1 Pet 1:25

90 Your faithfulness *continues* throughout all generations;
You established the earth, and it stands.
91 They stand this day according to Your ordinances,
For all things are Your servants.
92 If Your law had not been my delight,
Then I would have perished in my affliction.
93 I will never forget Your precepts,
For by them You have revived me.
94 I am Yours, save me;
For I have sought Your precepts.
95 The wicked wait for me to destroy me;
I shall diligently consider Your testimonies.
96 I have seen a limit to all perfection;
Your commandment is exceedingly broad.

מ Mem.

97 O how I love Your law!
It is my meditation all the day.
98 Your commandments make me wiser than my enemies,
For they are ever mine.
99 I have more insight than all my teachers,
For Your testimonies are my meditation.
100 I understand more than the aged,
Because I have observed Your precepts.
101 I have restrained my feet from every evil way,
That I may keep Your word.
102 I have not turned aside from Your ordinances,
For You Yourself have taught me.
103 How sweet are Your words to my taste!
Yes, sweeter than honey to my mouth!
104 From Your precepts I get understanding;
Therefore I hate every false way.

נ Nun.

105 Your word is a lamp to my feet
And a light to my path.
106 I have sworn and I will confirm it,
That I will keep Your righteous ordinances.
107 I am exceedingly afflicted;
Revive me, O LORD, according to Your word.
108 O accept the freewill offerings of my mouth, O LORD,
And teach me Your ordinances.
109 My life is continually [205]in my hand,
Yet I do not forget Your law.
110 The wicked have laid a snare for me,
Yet I have not gone astray from Your precepts.
111 I have inherited Your testimonies forever,
For they are the joy of my heart.
112 I have inclined my heart to perform Your statutes
Forever, *even* to the end.

205 I.e. in danger

119:90 Ps 36:5; 89:1, 2; Ps 148:6; Eccl 1:4
119:91 Jer 31:35; 33:25; Ps 104:2-4
119:92 Ps 119:16; Ps 119:50
119:93 Ps 119:16, 83; Ps 119:25
119:94 Ps 119:146; Ps 119:45
119:95 Ps 40:14; Is 32:7
119:97 Ps 119:47, 48, 127, 163, 165; Ps 1:2; 119:15
119:98 Deut 4:6; Ps 119:130
119:99 Ps 119:15
119:100 Job 32:7-9; Ps 119:22, 56
119:101 Prov 1:15
119:102 Deut 17:20; Josh 23:6; 1 Kin 15:5
119:103 Ps 19:10; Prov 8:11; 24:13, 14
119:104 Ps 119:130; Ps 119:128
119:105 Prov 6:23
119:106 Neh 10:29
119:107 Ps 119:25, 50; Ps 119:25
119:108 Hos 14:2; Heb 13:15; Ps 119:12
119:109 Judg 12:3; Job 13:14; Ps 119:16
119:110 Ps 91:3; 140:5; 141:9; Ps 119:10
119:111 Deut 33:4; Ps 119:14, 162
119:112 Ps 119:36; Ps 119:33

119:97–104 God's Word makes us wise—wiser than our enemies and wiser than any teachers who ignore it. True wisdom goes beyond amassing knowledge; it is *applying* knowledge in a life-changing way. Intelligent or experienced people are not necessarily wise. Wisdom comes from allowing what God teaches to guide us.

119:105 To walk safely in the woods at night we need a light so we don't trip over tree roots or fall into holes. In this life, we walk through a dark forest of evil. But the Bible can be our light to show us the way ahead so we won't stumble as we walk. It reveals the entangling roots of false values and philosophies. Study the Bible so you will be able to see your way clear enough to stay on the right path.

ס Samekh.

113 I hate those who are double-minded,
But I love Your law.
114 You are my hiding place and my shield;
I wait for Your word.
115 Depart from me, evildoers,
That I may observe the commandments of my God.
116 Sustain me according to Your word, that I may live;
And do not let me be ashamed of my hope.
117 Uphold me that I may be safe,
That I may have regard for Your statutes continually.
118 You have rejected all those who wander from Your statutes,
For their deceitfulness is useless.
119 You have removed all the wicked of the earth *like* dross;
Therefore I love Your testimonies.
120 My flesh trembles for fear of You,
And I am afraid of Your judgments.

ע Ayin.

121 I have done justice and righteousness;
Do not leave me to my oppressors.
122 Be surety for Your servant for good;
Do not let the arrogant oppress me.
123 My eyes fail *with longing* for Your salvation
And for Your righteous word.
124 Deal with Your servant according to Your lovingkindness
And teach me Your statutes.
125 I am Your servant; give me understanding,
That I may know Your testimonies.
126 It is time for the LORD to act,
For they have broken Your law.
127 Therefore I love Your commandments
Above gold, yes, above fine gold.
128 Therefore I esteem right all *Your* precepts concerning everything,
I hate every false way.

פ Pe.

129 Your testimonies are wonderful;
Therefore my soul observes them.
130 The unfolding of Your words gives light;
It gives understanding to the simple.
131 I opened my mouth wide and panted,
For I longed for Your commandments.
132 Turn to me and be gracious to me,
After Your manner with those who love Your name.
133 Establish my footsteps in Your word,
And do not let any iniquity have dominion over me.
134 Redeem me from the oppression of man,
That I may keep Your precepts.
135 Make Your face shine upon Your servant,
And teach me Your statutes.
136 My eyes shed streams of water,
Because they do not keep Your law.

119:113 1 Kin 18:21; James 1:8; 4:8; Ps 119:47

119:114 Ps 31:20; 32:7; 61:4; 91:1; Ps 84:9; Ps 119:74

119:115 Ps 6:8; 139:19; Matt 7:23; Ps 119:22

119:116 Ps 37:17, 24; 54:4; Ps 25:2, 20; 31:1, 17; Rom 5:5; 9:33; Phil 1:20

119:117 Ps 12:5; Prov 29:25; Ps 119:6, 15

119:119 Is 1:22, 25; Ezek 22:18, 19; Ps 119:47

119:120 Job 4:14; Hab 3:16; Ps 119:161

119:121 2 Sam 8:15; Job 29:14

119:122 Job 17:3; Heb 7:22; Ps 119:134

119:124 Ps 51:1; 106:45; 109:26; 119:88, 149, 159; Ps 119:12

119:125 Ps 116:16; Ps 119:27

119:126 Jer 18:23; Ezek 31:11

119:127 Ps 19:10; 119:47

119:128 Ps 19:8; Ps 119:104

119:130 Prov 6:23; Ps 19:7

119:131 Job 29:23; Ps 81:10; Ps 42:1; Ps 119:20

119:132 Ps 25:16; 106:4

119:133 Ps 17:5; Ps 19:13; Rom 6:12

119:134 Ps 119:84; 142:6; Luke 1:74

119:135 Num 6:25; Ps 4:6; 31:16; 67:1; 80:3, 7, 19; Ps 119:12

119:136 Jer 9:1, 18; 14:17; Lam 3:48; Ps 119:158

119:113 Double-minded people cannot make up their minds between good and evil. But when it comes to obeying God, there is no middle ground; you must take a stand. Either you are obeying him or you are not. Either you are doing what he wants or you are undecided. Choose to obey God, and say with the psalmist, "I love Your law."

119:125 The psalmist asked God for understanding. Faith comes alive when we apply Scripture to our daily tasks and concerns. We need understanding so we can discern, and we need the desire to apply Scripture where we need help. The Bible is like medicine—it goes to work only when we apply it to the affected areas. As you read the Bible, be alert for lessons, commands, or examples that you can put into practice.

119:137 Ezra 9:15; Neh 9:33; Ps 116:5; 129:4; 145:17; Jer 12:1; Lam 1:18; Dan 9:7, 14

119:138 Ps 19:7-9; 119:144, 172; Ps 119:86, 90

119:139 Ps 69:9; John 2:17

119:140 Ps 12:6; 19:8; Ps 119:47

119:141 Ps 22:6; Ps 119:61

119:142 Ps 19:9; 119:151, 160

119:144 Ps 19:9; Ps 119:27

119:145 Ps 119:10; Ps 119:22, 55

119:146 Ps 3:7

119:147 Ps 5:3; 57:8; 108:2

119:148 Ps 63:6; Ps 119:15

119:149 Ps 119:124

119:151 Ps 34:18; 145:18; Is 50:8; Ps 119:142

119:152 Ps 119:125; Ps 119:89; Luke 21:33

119:153 Lam 5:1; Ps 119:50; Ps 119:16; Prov 3:1; Hos 4:6

119:154 1 Sam 24:15; Ps 35:1; Mic 7:9; Ps 119:134

119:155 Job 5:4; Ps 119:45, 94

119:156 2 Sam 24:14

119:157 Ps 7:1; 119:86, 161; Ps 119:51

119:158 Is 21:2; 24:16; Ps 139:21

119:159 Ps 119:47; Ps 119:25

119:160 Ps 139:17; Ps 119:142; Ps 119:89, 152

צ Tsadhe.

137 Righteous are You, O LORD,
And upright are Your judgments.
138 You have commanded Your testimonies in righteousness
And exceeding faithfulness.
139 My zeal has consumed me,
Because my adversaries have forgotten Your words.
140 Your word is very pure,
Therefore Your servant loves it.
141 I am small and despised,
Yet I do not forget Your precepts.
142 Your righteousness is an everlasting righteousness,
And Your law is truth.
143 Trouble and anguish have come upon me,
Yet Your commandments are my delight.
144 Your testimonies are righteous forever;
Give me understanding that I may live.

ק Qoph.

145 I cried with all my heart; answer me, O LORD!
I will observe Your statutes.
146 I cried to You; save me
And I shall keep Your testimonies.
147 I rise before dawn and cry for help;
I wait for Your words.
148 My eyes anticipate the night watches,
That I may meditate on Your word.
149 Hear my voice according to Your lovingkindness;
Revive me, O LORD, according to Your ordinances.
150 Those who follow after wickedness draw near;
They are far from Your law.
151 You are near, O LORD,
And all Your commandments are truth.
152 Of old I have known from Your testimonies
That You have founded them forever.

ר Resh.

153 Look upon my affliction and rescue me,
For I do not forget Your law.
154 Plead my cause and redeem me;
Revive me according to Your word.
155 Salvation is far from the wicked,
For they do not seek Your statutes.
156 Great are Your mercies, O LORD;
Revive me according to Your ordinances.
157 Many are my persecutors and my adversaries,
Yet I do not turn aside from Your testimonies.
158 I behold the treacherous and loathe *them,*
Because they do not keep Your word.
159 Consider how I love Your precepts;
Revive me, O LORD, according to Your lovingkindness.
160 The sum of Your word is truth,
And every one of Your righteous ordinances is everlasting.

119:160 One of God's characteristics is truthfulness. He embodies perfect truth; therefore, his Word cannot lie. It is true and dependable for guidance and help (see John 17:14–17). The Bible is completely true and trustworthy.

ש Shin.

161 Princes persecute me without cause,
But my heart stands in awe of Your words.
162 I rejoice at Your word,
As one who finds great spoil.
163 I hate and despise falsehood,
But I love Your law.
164 Seven times a day I praise You,
Because of Your righteous ordinances.
165 Those who love Your law have great peace,
And nothing causes them to stumble.
166 I hope for Your salvation, O LORD,
And do Your commandments.
167 My soul keeps Your testimonies,
And I love them exceedingly.
168 I keep Your precepts and Your testimonies,
For all my ways are before You.

ת Tav.

169 Let my cry come before You, O LORD;
Give me understanding according to Your word.
170 Let my supplication come before You;
Deliver me according to Your word.
171 Let my lips utter praise,
For You teach me Your statutes.
172 Let my tongue sing of Your word,
For all Your commandments are righteousness.
173 Let Your hand be ready to help me,
For I have chosen Your precepts.
174 I long for Your salvation, O LORD,
And Your law is my delight.
175 Let my soul live that it may praise You,
And let Your ordinances help me.
176 I have gone astray like a lost sheep; seek Your servant,
For I do not forget Your commandments.

PSALM 120

A Song of Ascents.

Theme: A prayer for deliverance from false accusers. All believers must live with the tension of being in the world but not belonging to it.
Author: Anonymous, some suggest Hezekiah

1 In my trouble I cried to the LORD,
And He answered me.
2 Deliver my soul, O LORD, from lying lips,
From a deceitful tongue.
3 What shall be given to you, and what more shall be done to you,
You deceitful tongue?
4 Sharp arrows of the warrior,
With the *burning* coals of the broom tree.

119:161 1 Sam 24:11; 26:18; Ps 119:23; Ps 119:120
119:162 1 Sam 30:16; Is 9:3
119:163 Ps 31:6; 119:104, 128; Prov 13:5; Ps 119:47
119:165 Ps 37:11; Prov 3:2; Is 26:3; 32:17; Prov 3:23; Is 63:13; 1 John 2:10
119:166 Gen 49:18; Ps 119:81, 174
119:168 Ps 119:22; Job 24:23; Ps 139:3; Prov 5:21
119:169 Job 16:18; Ps 18:6; 102:1; Ps 119:27, 144; Ps 119:65, 154
119:170 Ps 28:2; 130:2; 140:6; 143:1; Ps 22:20; 31:2; 59:1
119:171 Ps 51:15; 63:3; Ps 94:12; 119:12; Is 2:3; Mic 4:2
119:172 Ps 51:14; Ps 119:138
119:173 Ps 37:24; 73:23; Josh 24:22; Luke 10:42
119:174 Ps 119:166; Ps 119:16, 24
119:175 Is 55:3
119:176 Is 53:6; Jer 50:6; Matt 18:12; Luke 15:4; Ps 119:16
120:1 Ps 18:6; 66:14; 102:2; Jon 2:2
120:2 Ps 109:2; Prov 12:22; Ps 52:4; Zeph 3:13
120:3 Ps 52:4; Zeph 3:13
120:4 Ps 45:5; Prov 25:18; Is 5:28; Ps 140:10

119:165 Modern society longs for peace of mind. Here is clear-cut instruction on how to attain this: If we love God and obey his laws, we will have "great peace." Trust in God, who alone stands above the pressures of daily life and gives us full assurance.

120—134 Psalms 120—134 are called "Pilgrim Psalms" or "Songs of Ascent." They were sung by those who journeyed (and thus "ascended") to the temple for the annual feasts. Each psalm is a "step" along the journey. Psalm 120 begins the journey in a distant land in hostile surroundings; Psalm 122 pictures the pilgrims arriving in Jerusalem; and the rest of the psalms move toward the temple, mentioning various characteristics of God.

120:5 Gen 10:2; 1 Chr 1:5; Ezek 27:13; 38:2, 3; 39:1; Song 1:5; Gen 25:13; Is 21:16; 60:7; Jer 2:10, 49:28; Ezek 27:21

120:6 Ps 35:20

120:7 Ps 109:4; Ps 55:21

5 Woe is me, for I sojourn in Meshech,
For I dwell among the tents of Kedar!
6 Too long has my soul had its dwelling
With those who hate peace.
7 I am *for* peace, but when I speak,
They are for war.

PSALM 121

A Song of Ascents.

Theme: We can depend upon God for help. Pilgrims must travel through lonely country to their destination; they are protected, not by anything created, but by the Creator of everything.
Author: Anonymous; some suggest Hezekiah

121:1 Ps 123:1; Is 40:26; Ps 87:1

121:2 Ps 124:8; Ps 115:15

121:3 1 Sam 2:9; Ps 66:9; Ps 41:2; 127:1; Is 27:3

121:5 Ps 91:4; Ps 16:8; 91:1; Is 25:4

121:6 Ps 91:5; Is 49:10; Jon 4:8; Rev 7:16

121:7 Ps 41:2; 91:10-12

121:8 Deut 28:6; Ps 113:2; 115:18

1 I will lift up my eyes to the mountains;
From where shall my help come?
2 My help *comes* from the LORD,
Who made heaven and earth.
3 He will not allow your foot to slip;
He who keeps you will not slumber.
4 Behold, He who keeps Israel
Will neither slumber nor sleep.

5 The LORD is your keeper;
The LORD is your shade on your right hand.
6 The sun will not smite you by day,
Nor the moon by night.
7 The LORD will [206]protect you from all evil;
He will keep your soul.
8 The LORD will [206]guard your going out and your coming in
From this time forth and forever.

PSALM 122

A Song of Ascents, of David.

Theme: Stepping into the presence of God. What Jerusalem was for the Israelites, the church is to the believer.
Author: David

122:1 Ps 42:4; Is 2:3; Mic 4:2; Zech 8:21

122:2 Ps 9:14; 87:2; 116:19; Jer 7:2

122:3 Ps 48:13; 147:2; 2 Sam 5:9; Neh 4:6

122:4 Ex 23:17; Deut 16:16; Ps 84:5

1 I was glad when they said to me,
"Let us go to the house of the LORD."
2 Our feet are standing
Within your gates, O Jerusalem,
3 Jerusalem, that is built
As a city that is compact together;
4 To which the tribes go up, even the tribes of the LORD—
An ordinance for Israel—
To give thanks to the name of the LORD.

206 Or *keep*

120:5–6 Meshech was a nation far to the north of Israel; Kedar a nation to the southeast. Both were known for being warlike and barbarian. Because the psalmist couldn't have been in two places at one time, he was lamenting that he felt far from home and surrounded by pagan people.

120:7 Peacemaking is not always popular. Some people prefer to fight for what they believe in. The glory of battle is in the hope of winning, but someone must be a loser. The glory of peacemaking is that it may actually produce two winners. Peacemaking is God's way, so we should carefully and prayerfully attempt to be peacemakers.

121:1ff This song expresses assurance and hope in God's protection day and night. He not only made the hills but heaven and earth as well. We should never trust a lesser power than God himself. But not only is he all-powerful; he also watches over us. Nothing diverts or deters him. We are safe. We never outgrow our need for God's untiring watch over our lives.

122:1 Going to God's house can be a chore or a delight. For the psalmist, it was a delight. As a pilgrim attending one of the three great religious festivals, he rejoiced to worship with God's people in God's house. We may find worship a chore if we have unconfessed sin or if our love for God has cooled. But if we are close to God and enjoy his presence, we will be eager to worship and praise him. Our attitude toward God will determine our view of worship.

5 For there thrones were set for judgment,
The thrones of the house of David.

6 Pray for the peace of Jerusalem:
"May they prosper who love you.
7 "May peace be within your walls,
And prosperity within your palaces."
8 For the sake of my brothers and my friends,
I will now say, "May peace be within you."
9 For the sake of the house of the LORD our God,
I will seek your good.

122:5 Deut 17:8; 2 Chr 19:8; Ps 89:29
122:6 Ps 29:11; Jer 29:7; Ps 102:14
122:7 Ps 51:18; Is 62:6; Ps 48:3, 13; Jer 17:27
122:8 Ps 133:1; 1 Sam 25:6; John 20:19
122:9 Neh 2:10; Esth 10:3

PSALM 123

A Song of Ascents.

Theme: Look to God for mercy. We are encouraged to be attentive to God's leading.
Author: Anonymous, some suggest Hezekiah.

1 To You I lift up my eyes,
O You who are enthroned in the heavens!
2 Behold, as the eyes of servants *look* to the hand of their master,
As the eyes of a maid to the hand of her mistress,
So our eyes *look* to the LORD our God,
Until He is gracious to us.

3 Be gracious to us, O LORD, be gracious to us,
For we are greatly filled with contempt.
4 Our soul is greatly filled
With the scoffing of those who are at ease,
And with the contempt of the proud.

123:1 Ps 121:1; 141:8; Ps 2:4; 11:4
123:2 Prov 27:18; Mal 1:6; Ps 25:15
123:3 Ps 4:1; 51:1; Neh 4:4; Ps 119:22
123:4 Neh 2:19; Ps 79:4; Job 12:5; Is 32:9, 11; Amos 6:1; Neh 4:4; Ps 119:22

PSALM 124

A Song of Ascents, of David.

Theme: God delivers us from those who seek to destroy us.
God is on the side of those who seek him.
Author: David, possibly written after his defeat of the Philistines (2 Samuel 5:17-25)

1 "Had it not been the LORD who was on our side,"
Let Israel now say,
2 "Had it not been the LORD who was on our side
When men rose up against us,
3 Then they would have swallowed us alive,
When their anger was kindled against us;
4 Then the waters would have engulfed us,
The stream would have swept over our soul;
5 Then the raging waters would have swept over our soul."

124:1 Ps 94:17; Ps 129:1
124:3 Num 16:30; Ps 35:25; 56:1; 57:3; Prov 1:12; Gen 39:19; Ps 138:7
124:4 Job 22:11; Ps 18:16; 32:6; 69:2; 144:7
124:5 Job 38:11

122:5 The "thrones . . . set for judgment" are the courts of justice by the town gate. In Bible times, the elders in a town sat to hear cases and administer justice at the gate (Ruth 4:1–2). Sometimes the king himself would sit at the gate to meet his subjects and make legal decisions (2 Samuel 19:8). Speeches and prophecies were also made at the city gate (Nehemiah 8:1; Jeremiah 17:19–20).

122:6–9 The psalmist was not praying for his own peace and prosperity, but for that of his brothers and friends in Jerusalem. This is intercessory prayer, prayer on behalf of others. Too often we are quick to pray for our own needs and desires, and omit interceding for others. Will you intercede for someone in need today?

122:6–9 The peace sought in these verses is much more than the mere absence of conflict. It suggests completeness, health, justice, prosperity, and protection. The world cannot provide this peace. Real peace comes from faith in God because he alone embodies all the characteristics of peace. To find peace of mind and peace with others, you must find peace with God.

123:1ff The psalmist lifted his eyes to God, waiting and watching for God to send his mercy. The more he waited, the more he cried out to God because he knew that the evil and proud offered no help—they had only contempt for God.

124:6
Ps 27:2; Prov 30:14

124:7
Ps 141:10; 2 Cor 11:33; Heb 11:34; Prov 6:5; Ps 91:3; Hos 9:8

124:8
Ps 121:2; Gen 1:1; Ps 134:3

6 Blessed be the LORD,
Who has not given us to be torn by their teeth.
7 Our soul has escaped as a bird out of the snare of the trapper;
The snare is broken and we have escaped.
8 Our help is in the name of the LORD,
Who made heaven and earth.

PSALM 125

A Song of Ascents.

Theme: God is our Protector. The mountains around Jerusalem symbolize God's protection for his people.
Author: Anonymous; some suggest Hezekiah

125:1
Ps 46:5; Ps 61:7; Eccl 1:4

125:2
Zech 2:5; Ps 121:8

125:3
Ps 89:22; Prov 22:8; Is 14:5; 1 Sam 24:10; Ps 55:20; Acts 12:1

125:4
Ps 119:68; Ps 7:10; 11:2; 32:11; 36:10; 94:15

125:5
Job 23:11; Ps 40:4; 101:3; Prov 2:15; Is 59:8; Ps 92:7; 94:4; Ps 128:6; Gal 6:16

1 Those who trust in the LORD
Are as Mount Zion, which cannot be moved but abides forever.
2 As the mountains surround Jerusalem,
So the LORD surrounds His people
From this time forth and forever.
3 For the scepter of wickedness shall not rest upon the land of the righteous,
So that the righteous will not put forth their hands to do wrong.

4 Do good, O LORD, to those who are good
And to those who are upright in their hearts.
5 But as for those who turn aside to their crooked ways,
The LORD will lead them away with the doers of iniquity.
Peace be upon Israel.

PSALM 126

A Song of Ascents.

Theme: God does great things. His power not only releases us from sin's captive hold, but also brings us back to him.
Author: Anonymous, possibly written to celebrate the exiles' return form captivity (Ezra 1)

126:1
Ps 85:1; Jer 29:14; Hos 6:11; Acts 12:9

126:2
Job 8:21; Ps 51:14; Is 35:6; 1 Sam 12:24; Ps 71:19; Luke 1:49

126:3
Is 25:9; Zeph 3:14

126:4
Is 35:6; 43:19

126:5
Ps 80:5; Jer 31:9, 16; Lam 1:2; Is 35:10; 51:11; 61:7; Gal 6:9

1 When the LORD brought back the captive ones of Zion,
We were like those who dream.
2 Then our mouth was filled with laughter
And our tongue with joyful shouting;
Then they said among the nations,
"The LORD has done great things for them."
3 The LORD has done great things for us;
We are glad.

4 Restore our captivity, O LORD,
As the streams in the South.
5 Those who sow in tears shall reap with joyful shouting.

124:7–8 Do you ever feel trapped by overwhelming odds? With God, there is always a way out because he is the Creator of all that exists. No problem is beyond his ability to solve; no circumstance is too difficult for him. We can turn to the Creator for help in our time of need, for he is on our side. God will provide a way out; we need only trust him and look for it. David compared this to a bird escaping the snare of a trapper.

125:1 Have you ever known people who were drawn to every new fad or idea? Such people are inconsistent and therefore unreliable. The secret to consistency is to trust in God, because he never changes. He cannot be shaken by the changes in our world, and he endures forever. The fads and ideas of our world, and our world itself, will not.

125:3 Although the psalmist wrote, "The scepter of wickedness shall not rest upon the land of the righteous," often Israel had to put up with evil rulers. The psalmist was expressing what will ultimately happen when God executes his final judgment. Human sinfulness often ruins God's ideal on earth, but that doesn't mean God has lost control. Evil prevails only as long as God allows.

126:5–6 God's ability to restore life is beyond our understanding. Forests burn down and are able to grow back. Broken bones heal. Even grief is not a permanent condition. Our tears can be seeds that will grow into a harvest of joy because God is able to bring good out of tragedy. When burdened by sorrow, know that your times of grief will end and that you will again find joy. We must be patient as we wait. God's great harvest of joy is coming!

6 He who goes to and fro weeping, carrying *his* bag of seed,
Shall indeed come again with a shout of joy, bringing his sheaves *with him.*

PSALM 127

A Song of Ascents, of Solomon.

Theme: Life without God is senseless. All of life's work—building a home, establishing a career, and raising a family—must have God as the foundation.
Author: Solomon

1 Unless the LORD builds the house,
They labor in vain who build it;
Unless the LORD guards the city,
The watchman keeps awake in vain.
2 It is vain for you to rise up early,
To retire late,
To eat the bread of painful labors;
For He gives to His beloved *even in his* sleep.

3 Behold, children are a gift of the LORD,
The fruit of the womb is a reward.
4 Like arrows in the hand of a warrior,
So are the children of one's youth.
5 How blessed is the man whose quiver is full of them;
They will not be ashamed
When they speak with their enemies in the gate.

127:1 Ps 78:69; Ps 121:4

127:2 Gen 3:17, 19; Ps 60:5; Job 11:18, 19; Prov 3:24; Eccl 5:12

127:3 Gen 33:5; 48:4; Josh 24:3, 4; Ps 113:9; Deut 7:13; 28:4; Is 13:18

127:4 Ps 112:2; 120:4

127:5 Ps 128:2, 3; Prov 27:11; Is 29:21; Amos 5:12; Gen 34:20

PSALM 128

A Song of Ascents.

Theme: God, the true head of the home. [This is called the marriage prayer because it was often sung at Israelite marriages.] God will reward your devotion to him with inner peace.
Author: Anonymous; some suggest Hezekiah

1 How blessed is everyone who fears the LORD,
Who walks in His ways.
2 When you shall eat of the [207]fruit of your hands,
You will be happy and it will be well with you.
3 Your wife shall be like a fruitful vine
Within your house,
Your children like olive plants
Around your table.
4 Behold, for thus shall the man be blessed
Who fears the LORD.

128:1 Ps 112:1; 119:1; Ps 119:3

128:2 Is 3:10; Ps 109:11; Hag 2:17; Eccl 8:12; Eph 6:3

128:3 Ezek 19:10; Ps 52:8; 144:12

207 Lit *labor*

127:1 Families establish homes and watchmen guard cities, but both these activities are futile unless God is with them. A family without God can never experience the spiritual bond God brings to relationships. A city without God will crumble from evil and corruption on the inside. Don't make the mistake of leaving God out of your life—if you do, all your accomplishments will be futile. Make God your highest priority, and let him do the building.

127:2 God is not against human effort. Hard work honors God (Proverbs 31:10–29). But working to the exclusion of rest or to the neglect of family may be a cover-up for an inability to trust God to provide for our needs. We all need adequate rest and times of spiritual refreshment. On the other hand, this verse is not an excuse to be lazy (Proverbs 18:9). Be careful to maintain a balance: Work while trusting God, and also rest while trusting him.

127:3–5 Too often children are seen as liabilities rather than assets. But the Bible calls children "a gift of the LORD," a reward. We can learn valuable lessons from their inquisitive minds and trusting spirits. Those who view children as a distraction or nuisance should instead see them as an opportunity to shape the future. We dare not treat children as an inconvenience when God values them so highly.

128:1ff The psalmist wrote that a good family life is a reward for following God. The values outlined in God's Word include love, service, honesty, integrity, and prayer. These help all relationships, and they are especially vital to home life. Is your home life heavenly or hectic? Reading and obeying God's Word is a good place to start to make your family all that it should be.

128:5
Ps 134:3; Ps 20:2; 135:21

128.6
Gen 48:11; 50:23; Job 42:16; Ps 103:17; Prov 17:6; Ps 125:5

5 The LORD bless you from Zion,
And may you see the prosperity of Jerusalem all the days of your life.
6 Indeed, may you see your children's children.
Peace be upon Israel!

PSALM 129

A Song of Ascents.

Theme: Confidence in times of persecution. God will bring us through tough times.
Author: Anonymous; some suggest Hezekiah

129:1
Ex 1:11; Judg 3:8; Ps 88:15; Is 47:12; Jer 2:2; 22:21; Ezek 16:22; Hos 2:15; 11:1; Ps 124:1

129:2
Jer 1:19; 15:20; 20:11; Matt 16:18; 2 Cor 4:8, 9

129:4
Ps 119:137; Ps 140:5

129:5
Mic 4:11; Ps 70:3; 71:13

129:6
2 Kin 19:26; Ps 37:2; Is 37:27

129:7
Ps 79:12

129:8
Ruth 2:4; Ps 118:26

1 "Many times they have persecuted me from my youth up,"
Let Israel now say,
2 "Many times they have persecuted me from my youth up;
Yet they have not prevailed against me.
3 "The plowers plowed upon my back;
They lengthened their furrows."
4 The LORD is righteous;
He has cut in two the cords of the wicked.

5 May all who hate Zion
Be put to shame and turned backward;
6 Let them be like grass upon the housetops,
Which withers before it grows up;
7 With which the reaper does not fill his hand,
Or the binder of sheaves his bosom;
8 Nor do those who pass by say,
"The blessing of the LORD be upon you;
We bless you in the name of the LORD."

PSALM 130

A Song of Ascents.

Theme: Assurance of the Lord's forgiveness.
God will surely forgive us if we confess our sins to him.
Author: Anonymous; some suggest Hezekiah

130:1
Ps 42:7; 69:2; Lam 3:55

130:2
Ps 64:1; 119:149; 2 Chr 6:40; Neh 1:6, 11; Ps 28:2; 140:6

130:3
Ps 76:7; 143:2; Nah 1:6; Mal 3:2; Rev 6:17

130:4
Ex 34:7; Neh 9:17; Ps 86:5; Is 55:7; Dan 9:9; 1 Kin 8:39, 40; Jer 33:8, 9

1 Out of the depths I have cried to You, O LORD.
2 Lord, hear my voice!
Let Your ears be attentive
To the voice of my supplications.
3 If You, LORD, should mark iniquities,
O Lord, who could stand?
4 But there is forgiveness with You,
That You may be feared.

129:2 The people of Israel were persecuted from their earliest days, but never destroyed completely. The same is true of the church. Christians have faced times of severe persecution, but the church has never been destroyed. As Jesus said to Peter, "Upon this rock I will build My church; and the gates of Hades will not overpower it" (Matthew 16:18). When you face persecution and discrimination, take courage—the church will never be destroyed.

129:3 This verse foreshadowed Jesus' unjust punishment before his death. He endured horrible lashes from the whip of his tormentors, which indeed made "furrows" on his back (John 19:1).

130:1–2 In the depths of despair, the psalmist cried out to God. Despair makes us feel isolated and distant from God, but this is precisely when we need God most. Despair over sin should not lead to self-pity, causing us to think more about ourselves than God. Instead, it should lead to confession and then to God's mercy, forgiveness, and redemption. When we feel overwhelmed by a problem, feeling sorry for ourselves will only increase feelings of hopelessness; but crying out to God will turn our attention to the only One who can really help.

130:3–4 Keeping a record of sins (or holding a grudge) is like building a wall between you and another person, and it is nearly impossible to talk openly while the wall is there. God doesn't keep a record of our sins; when he forgives, he forgives completely, tearing down any wall between us and him. Therefore, we fear (revere) God, yet we can talk to him about anything. When you pray, realize that God is holding nothing against you. His lines of communication are completely open.

5 I wait for the LORD, my soul does wait,
And in His word do I hope.
6 My soul *waits* for the Lord
More than the watchmen for the morning;
Indeed, more than the watchmen for the morning.
7 O Israel, hope in the LORD;
For with the LORD there is lovingkindness,
And with Him is abundant redemption.
8 And He will redeem Israel
From all his iniquities.

130:5 Ps 27:14; 33:20; 40:1; 62:1, 5; Is 8:17; 26:8; Ps 119:74, 81

130:6 Ps 63:6; 119:147

130:7 Ps 131:3; Ps 86:5; 103:4; Ps 111:9; Rom 3:24; Eph 1:7

130:8 Ps 103:3, 4; Luke 1:68; Titus 2:14

PSALM 131

A Song of Ascents, of David.

Theme: Trust and contentment. Quiet trust in God is the basis for our contentment.
Author: David

1 O LORD, my heart is not proud, nor my eyes haughty;
Nor do I involve myself in great matters,
Or in things too difficult for me.
2 Surely I have composed and quieted my soul;
Like a weaned child *rests* against his mother,
My soul is like a weaned child within me.
3 O Israel, hope in the LORD
From this time forth and forever.

131:1 2 Sam 22:28; Ps 101:5; Is 2:12; Zeph 3:11; Prov 30:13; Is 5:15; Jer 45:5; Rom 12:16; Job 42:3; Ps 139:6

131:2 Ps 62:1; Matt 18:3; 1 Cor 14:20

131:3 Ps 130:7; Ps 113:2

PSALM 132

A Song of Ascents.

Theme: Honor God and he will honor you. The psalmist reflects upon that great day when the ark of the covenant was brought to Jerusalem and praises God for his promise to perpetuate David's line.
Author: Anonymous

1 Remember, O LORD, on David's behalf,
All his affliction;
2 How he swore to the LORD
And vowed to the Mighty One of Jacob,
3 "Surely I will not enter my house,
Nor lie on my bed;
4 I will not give sleep to my eyes
Or slumber to my eyelids,
5 Until I find a place for the LORD,
A dwelling place for the Mighty One of Jacob."

6 Behold, we heard of it in Ephrathah,
We found it in the field of Jaar.
7 Let us go into His dwelling place;
Let us worship at His footstool.
8 Arise, O LORD, to Your resting place,
You and the ark of Your strength.

132:1 Gen 49:24; 2 Sam 16:12

132:2 Gen 49:24; Is 49:26; 60:16

132:3 Job 21:28

132:4 Prov 6:4

132:5 1 Kin 8:17; 1 Chr 22:7; Ps 26:8; Acts 7:46; Ps 132:2

132:6 Gen 35:19; 1 Sam 17:12; 1 Sam 7:1

132:7 Ps 43:3; Ps 5:7; 99:5; 1 Chr 28:2

132:8 Num 10:35; 2 Chr 6:41; Ps 68:1; Ps 132:14; Ps 78:61

131:1–2 Pride results from overvaluing ourselves and undervaluing others. It leads to restlessness because it makes us dissatisfied with what we have and concerned about what everyone else is doing. It keeps us always hungering for more attention and adoration. By contrast, humility puts others first and allows us to be content with God's leading in our lives. Such contentment gives us security so that we no longer have to prove ourselves to others. Let humility and trust affect your perspective and give you the strength and freedom to serve God and others.

132:2–5 This refers to David's desire to build the temple. When David became king, he built a beautiful palace, but he was troubled that the ark of the covenant, the symbol of God's presence among his people (Exodus 25:10–22), remained in a tent (2 Samuel 6:17; 7:1–17). This so bothered David that he couldn't sleep until he corrected the situation. He began to lay the plans for the temple to house the ark. (Eventually the temple was built by his son, Solomon.) We must live so close to God that we become restless until God's will is accomplished through us.

9 Let Your priests be clothed with righteousness,
And let Your godly ones sing for joy.

10 For the sake of David Your servant,
Do not turn away the face of Your anointed.
11 The LORD has sworn to David
A truth from which He will not turn back:
"Of the fruit of your body I will set upon your throne.
12 "If your sons will keep My covenant
And My testimony which I will teach them,
Their sons also shall sit upon your throne forever."

13 For the LORD has chosen Zion;
He has desired it for His habitation.
14 "This is My resting place forever;
Here I will dwell, for I have desired it.
15 "I will abundantly bless her provision;
I will satisfy her needy with bread.
16 "Her priests also I will clothe with salvation,
And her godly ones will sing aloud for joy.
17 "There I will cause the horn of David to spring forth;
I have prepared a lamp for Mine anointed.
18 "His enemies I will clothe with shame,
But upon himself his crown shall shine."

132:9 Job 29:14; Ps 30:4; 132:16; 149:5
132:10 Ps 2:2; 132:17
132:11 Ps 89:3, 35; 2 Sam 7:12-16; 1 Chr 17:11-14; 2 Chr 6:16; Ps 89:4; Acts 2:30
132:12 Luke 1:32; Acts 2:30
132:13 Ps 48:1, 2; 78:68; Ps 68:16
132:14 Ps 132:8; Ps 68:16; Matt 23:21
132:15 Ps 147:14; Ps 107:9
132:16 2 Chr 6:41; Ps 132:9
132:17 Ezek 29:21; Luke 1:69; 1 Kin 11:36; 15:4; 2 Kin 8:19; 2 Chr 21:7; Ps 18:28
132:18 Job 8:22; Ps 35:26; 109:29; Ps 21:3

PSALM 133

A Song of Ascents, of David.

Theme: The joy of harmonious relationships.
Author: David

1 Behold, how good and how pleasant it is
For brothers to dwell together in unity!
2 It is like the precious oil upon the head,
Coming down upon the beard,
Even Aaron's beard,
Coming down upon the edge of his robes.
3 It is like the dew of Hermon
Coming down upon the mountains of Zion;
For there the LORD commanded the blessing—life forever.

133:1 Gen 13:8; Heb 13:1
133:2 Ex 29:7; 30:25, 30; Lev 8:12; Ex 28:33; 39:24
133:3 Prov 19:12; Hos 14:5; Mic 5:7; Deut 3:9; 4:48; Ps 48:2; 74:2; 78:68; Lev 25:21; Deut 28:8; Ps 42:8; Ps 21:4

132:11–12 The promise that David's sons would sit on Israel's throne forever is found in 2 Samuel 7:8–29. This promise had two parts: (1) David's descendants would perpetually rule over Israel as long as they followed God, and (2) David's royal line would never end. The first part was conditional; as long as the kings obeyed God ("keep My covenant and My testimony which I will teach them"), their dynasty continued. The second part of the promise was unconditional. It was fulfilled in Jesus Christ, a descendant of David, who reigns forever.

132:17–18 The horn of David to "spring forth" refers to one of his mighty descendants. David's son, Solomon, was indeed a glorious king (1 Kings 3:10–14); but these verses look ahead even further to another descendant of David, Jesus the Messiah (Matthew 1:17). The power, might, and glory of the Messiah will last forever.

133:1–3 David stated that unity is pleasant and precious. Unfortunately, unity does not abound in the church as it should. People disagree and cause division over unimportant issues. Some delight in causing tension by discrediting others. Unity is important because (1) it makes the church a positive example to the world and helps draw others to us; (2) it helps us cooperate as a body of believers as God meant us to, giving us a foretaste of heaven; (3) it renews and revitalizes ministry because there is less tension to sap our energy.

Living in unity does not mean that we will agree on everything; there will be many opinions just as there are many notes in a musical chord. But we must agree on our purpose in life—to work together for God. Our outward expression of unity will reflect our inward unity of purpose.

133:2 Expensive oil was used by Moses to anoint Aaron as the first high priest of Israel (Exodus 29:7) and to dedicate all the priests to God's service. Brotherly unity, like the anointing oil, shows that we are dedicated to serving God wholeheartedly.

133:3 Mount Hermon is the tallest mountain in Palestine, located northeast of the Sea of Galilee.

PSALM 134

A Song of Ascents.

Theme: Worship God and experience the joy of his blessings.
Author: Anonymous; some suggest Hezekiah

1 Behold, bless the LORD, all servants of the LORD,
Who serve by night in the house of the LORD!
2 Lift up your hands to the sanctuary
And bless the LORD.
3 May the LORD bless you from Zion,
He who made heaven and earth.

134:1 Ps 103:21; Ps 135:1, 2; Deut 10:8; 1 Chr 23:30; 2 Chr 29:11; 1 Chr 9:33

134:2 Ps 28:2; 1 Tim 2:8; Ps 63:2

134:3 Ps 128:5; Ps 124:8

PSALM 135

Theme: A hymn of praise. This psalm contrasts the greatness of God with the powerfulness of idols. Pagans worship idols while God's people worship the living God.
Author: Anonymous

1 Praise the LORD!
Praise the name of the LORD;
Praise *Him,* O servants of the LORD,
2 You who stand in the house of the LORD,
In the courts of the house of our God!
3 Praise the LORD, for the LORD is good;
Sing praises to His name, for it is lovely.
4 For the LORD has chosen Jacob for Himself,
Israel for His own possession.

5 For I know that the LORD is great
And that our Lord is above all gods.
6 Whatever the LORD pleases, He does,
In heaven and in earth, in the seas and in all deeps.
7 He causes the vapors to ascend from the ends of the earth;
Who makes lightnings for the rain,
Who brings forth the wind from His treasuries.

8 He smote the firstborn of Egypt,
Both of man and beast.
9 He sent signs and wonders into your midst, O Egypt,
Upon Pharaoh and all his servants.
10 He smote many nations
And slew mighty kings,
11 Sihon, king of the Amorites,
And Og, king of Bashan,
And all the kingdoms of Canaan;
12 And He gave their land as a heritage,
A heritage to Israel His people.
13 Your name, O LORD, is everlasting,
Your remembrance, O LORD, throughout all generations.
14 For the LORD will judge His people
And will have compassion on His servants.
15 The idols of the nations are *but* silver and gold,

135:1 Ps 113:1; Ps 134:1

135:2 Ps 92:13; 116:19

135:3 Ps 100:5; 119:68; Ps 68:4; Ps 147:1

135:4 Deut 7:6; 10:15; Ps 105:6; Ex 19:5; Mal 3:17; Titus 2:14; 1 Pet 2:9

135:5 Ps 48:1; 95:3; 145:3; Ps 97:9

135:6 Ps 115:3

135:7 Jer 10:13; 51:16; Job 28:25, 26; 38:25, 26; Zech 10:1

135:8 Ex 12:12; Ps 78:51; 105:36

135:9 Ex 7:10; Deut 6:22; Ps 78:43; Ps 136:15

135:10 Num 21:24; Ps 135:10-12; 136:17-21; Ps 44:2

135:11 Num 21:21-26; Deut 29:7; Num 21:33-35; Josh 12:7-24

135:12 Deut 29:8; Ps 78:55; 136:21, 22

135:13 Ex 3:15; Ps 102:12

135:14 Deut 32:36; Ps 50:4; Ps 90:13; 106:46

135:15 Ps 115:4-8; 135:15-18

134:1–3 This psalm is about a very small group—the Levites who served as temple watchmen ("servants of the LORD, who serve by night"). Singing this psalm, the last of the "songs of ascent" (Psalms 120—134), the worshipers would ascend the hill where the temple sits and see the watchmen who protect it day and night. They saw the watchmen's work as an act of praise to God, done reverently and responsibly. Make your job or your responsibility in the church an act of praise by doing it with reverence to God. Honor him by the quality of your work and the attitude of service you bring to it.

134:3 Zion is another name for Jerusalem.

135:4 That the descendants of Jacob, Israel, were a chosen people reflects God's commission to the nation in Deuteronomy 7:6–8 and in Peter's sermon to the church in 1 Peter 2:9. God treasures us. He gives love and mercy to all those who believe in him.

135:15–18 Those who worshiped idols were as blind and insensitive as the idols themselves. They couldn't see or hear what God had to say. In subtle, imperceptible ways we become like the idols

The work of man's hands.
16 They have mouths, but they do not speak;
They have eyes, but they do not see;
17 They have ears, but they do not hear,
Nor is there any breath at all in their mouths.
18 Those who make them will be like them,
Yes, everyone who trusts in them.

19 O house of Israel, bless the LORD;
O house of Aaron, bless the LORD;
20 O house of Levi, bless the LORD;
You who [208]revere the LORD, bless the LORD.
21 Blessed be the LORD from Zion,
Who dwells in Jerusalem.
Praise the LORD!

135:19 Ps 115:9
135:20 Ps 118:4
135:21 Ps 128:5; 134:3; Ps 132:14
136:1 1 Chr 16:34; Ps 106:1; 107:1; 118:1; Jer 33:11; 2 Chr 5:13; 7:3; Ezra 3:11; Ps 100:5; 1 Chr 16:41; 2 Chr 20:21; Ps 118:1-4
136:2 Deut 10:17
136:3 Deut 10:17
136:4 Deut 6:22; Job 9:10; Ps 72:18
136:5 Gen 1:1; Ps 104:24; Prov 3:19; Jer 10:12; 51:15
136:6 Gen 1:2, 6, 9; Ps 24:2; Is 42:5; 44:24; Jer 10:12
136:7 Gen 1:14-18; Ps 74:16
136:8 Gen 1:16
136:9 Gen 1:16
136:10 Ex 12:29; Ps 78:51; 135:8
136:11 Ex 12:51; 13:3; Ps 105:43
136:12 Ex 6:1; 13:9; 1 Kin 8:42; Neh 1:10; Ps 44:3; Jer 32:21; Ex 6:6; Deut 4:34; 5:15; 7:19; 9:29; 11:2; 2 Kin 17:36; 2 Chr 6:32; Jer 32:17
136:13 Ex 14:21; Ps 66:6; 78:13
136:14 Ex 14:22; Ps 106:9
136:15 Ex 14:27; Ps 78:53; 106:11

PSALM 136

Theme: The never-ending story of God's love.
God deserves our praise because his endless love never fails.
Author: Anonymous

1 Give thanks to the LORD, for He is good,
For His lovingkindness is everlasting.
2 Give thanks to the God of gods,
For His lovingkindness is everlasting.
3 Give thanks to the Lord of lords,
For His lovingkindness is everlasting.
4 To Him who alone does great wonders,
For His lovingkindness is everlasting;
5 To Him who made the heavens with skill,
For His lovingkindness is everlasting;
6 To Him who spread out the earth above the waters,
For His lovingkindness is everlasting;
7 To Him who made *the* great lights,
For His lovingkindness is everlasting:
8 The sun to rule by day,
For His lovingkindness is everlasting,
9 The moon and stars to rule by night,
For His lovingkindness is everlasting.

10 To Him who smote the Egyptians in their firstborn,
For His lovingkindness is everlasting,
11 And brought Israel out from their midst,
For His lovingkindness is everlasting,
12 With a strong hand and an outstretched arm,
For His lovingkindness is everlasting.
13 To Him who divided the Red Sea asunder,
For His lovingkindness is everlasting,
14 And made Israel pass through the midst of it,
For His lovingkindness is everlasting;
15 But He overthrew Pharaoh and his army in the Red Sea,
For His lovingkindness is everlasting.

208 Lit *fear*

we worship. If the true God is your God, you will become more like him as you worship him. What are your goals? What takes priority in your life? Choose carefully because you will take on the characteristics of whatever you worship.

136:1ff Repeated throughout this psalm is the phrase, "His lovingkindness is everlasting." This psalm may have been a responsive reading, with the congregation saying these words in unison after each sentence. The repetition made this important lesson sink in. God's love includes aspects of love, kindness, mercy, and faithfulness. We never have to worry that God will run out of love because it flows from a well that will never run dry.

16 To Him who led His people through the wilderness,
For His lovingkindness is everlasting;
17 To Him who smote great kings,
For His lovingkindness is everlasting,
18 And slew mighty kings,
For His lovingkindness is everlasting:
19 Sihon, king of the Amorites,
For His lovingkindness is everlasting,
20 And Og, king of Bashan,
For His lovingkindness is everlasting,
21 And gave their land as a heritage,
For His lovingkindness is everlasting,
22 Even a heritage to Israel His servant,
For His lovingkindness is everlasting.

23 Who remembered us in our low estate,
For His lovingkindness is everlasting,
24 And has rescued us from our adversaries,
For His lovingkindness is everlasting;
25 Who gives food to all flesh,
For His lovingkindness is everlasting.
26 Give thanks to the God of heaven,
For His lovingkindness is everlasting.

136:16 Ex 13:18; 15:22; Deut 8:15; Ps 78:52

136:17 Ps 135:10-12; 136:17-22

136:18 Deut 29:7

136:19 Num 21:21-24

136:20 Num 21:33-35

136:21 Josh 12:1

136:22 Ps 105:6; Is 41:8; 44:1; 45:4

136:23 Ps 9:12; 103:14; 106:45

136:24 Judg 6:9; Neh 9:28; Ps 107:2

136:25 Ps 104:27; 145:15

136:26 Gen 24:3, 7; 2 Chr 36:23; Ezra 1:2; 5:11; Neh 1:4

PSALM 137

Theme: A person in exile weeps over the bitterness of captivity. Our sorrow can make it difficult to imagine singing joyful songs again.
Author: Anonymous

1 By the rivers of Babylon,
There we sat down and wept,
When we remembered Zion.
2 Upon the willows in the midst of it
We hung our harps.
3 For there our captors demanded of us songs,
And our tormentors mirth, *saying,*
"Sing us one of the songs of Zion."

4 How can we sing the LORD'S song
In a foreign land?
5 If I forget you, O Jerusalem,
May my right hand forget *her skill.*
6 May my tongue cling to the roof of my mouth
If I do not remember you,
If I do not exalt Jerusalem
Above my chief joy.

7 Remember, O LORD, against the sons of Edom
The day of Jerusalem,
Who said, "Raze it, raze it
To its very foundation."
8 O daughter of Babylon, you devastated one,

137:1 Ezek 1:1, 3; Neh 1:4

137:2 Lev 23:40; Is 44:4; Job 30:31; Is 24:8; Ezek 26:13

137:3 Ps 80:6; Is 49:17

137:4 2 Chr 29:27; Neh 12:46

137:5 Is 65:11

137:6 Job 29:10; Ps 22:15; Ezek 3:26; Neh 2:3

137:7 Ps 83:4-8; Is 34:5, 6; Jer 49:7-22; Lam 4:21; Ezek 25:12-14; 35:2; Amos 1:11; Obad 10-14; Ps 74:7; Hab 3:13

137:8 Is 13:1-22; 47:1-15; Jer 25:12; 50:1-46; 51:1-64; Jer 50:15; 51:24, 35, 36, 49; Rev 18:6

137:7 The Edomites were related to the Israelites, both nations having descended from Abraham through Ishmael and Isaac, respectively. Although Israel shared its southern border with Edom, there was bitter hatred between the two nations. The Edomites did not come to help when the city of Jerusalem was besieged by the Babylonian army. In fact, they rejoiced when the city was destroyed (Jeremiah 49:7–22; Joel 3:19; Obadiah 1–20).

137:8–9 God destroyed Babylon and its offspring for their proud assault against God and his kingdom. The Medes and Persians destroyed Babylon in 539 B.C. Many of those who were oppressed lived to see the victory. The phrase about the infants is harsh because the psalmist is crying out for judgment: "Treat the Babylonians the way they treated us."

How blessed will be the one who repays you
With the recompense with which you have repaid us.
9 How blessed will be the one who seizes and dashes your little ones
Against the rock.

137:9 2 Kin 8:12; Is 13:16; Hos 13:16; Nah 3:10

PSALM 138

A Psalm of David.

Theme: Thanksgiving for answered prayer. God works out his plan for our lives and will bring us through the difficulties we face.
Author: David

1 I will give You thanks with all my heart;
I will sing praises to You before the gods.
2 I will bow down toward Your holy temple
And give thanks to Your name for Your lovingkindness and Your truth;
For You have magnified Your word according to all Your name.
3 On the day I called, You answered me;
You made me bold with strength in my soul.

4 All the kings of the earth will give thanks to You, O LORD,
When they have heard the words of Your mouth.
5 And they will sing of the ways of the LORD,
For great is the glory of the LORD.
6 For though the LORD is exalted,
Yet He regards the lowly,
But the haughty He knows from afar.

7 Though I walk in the midst of trouble, You will revive me;
You will stretch forth Your hand against the wrath of my enemies,
And Your right hand will save me.
8 The LORD will accomplish what concerns me;
Your lovingkindness, O LORD, is everlasting;
Do not forsake the works of Your hands.

138:1 Ps 111:1; Ps 95:3; 96:4; 97:7

138:2 1 Kin 8:29; Ps 5:7; 28:2; Ps 140:13; Is 42:21

138:3 Ps 118:5; Ps 28:7; 46:1

138:4 Ps 72:11; 102:15

138:5 Ps 145:7; Ps 21:5

138:6 Ps 113:4-7; Prov 3:34; Is 57:15; Luke 1:48; James 4:6; 1 Pet 5:5; Ps 40:4; 101:5

138:7 Ps 23:4; 143:11; Ezra 9:8, 9; Ps 71:20; Is 57:15; Ex 7:5; 15:12; Is 5:25; Jer 51:25; Ezek 6:14; 25:13; Ps 20:6; 60:5

138:8 Ps 57:2; Phil 1:6; Ps 136:1; Job 10:8; Ps 27:9; 71:9; 119:8; Job 10:3; 14:15; Ps 100:3

PSALM 139

For the choir director. A Psalm of David.

Theme: God is all-seeing, all-knowing, all-powerful, and everywhere present. God knows us, God is with us, and his greatest gift is to allow us to know him.
Author: David

1 O LORD, You have searched me and known *me.*
2 You know when I sit down and when I rise up;
You understand my thought from afar.
3 You scrutinize my path and my lying down,
And are intimately acquainted with all my ways.
4 Even before there is a word on my tongue,

139:1 Ps 17:3; 44:21; Jer 12:3

139:2 2 Kin 19:27; Ps 94:11; Is 66:18; Matt 9:4

139:3 Job 14:16; 31:4

139:4 Heb 4:13

138:1 "Before the gods" may mean in the presence of subordinate heavenly beings (angels), or, more likely, it may be a statement ridiculing the kings or gods of the pagan nations. God is the highest in the whole earth.

138:1–3 Thanksgiving should be an integral part of our praise to God. This theme is woven throughout the psalms. As we praise and thank God for material and spiritual blessings, we should also thank him for answered prayer. Remember when you asked God for protection, strength, comfort, patience, love, or other special needs, and he supplied them? Beware of taking God's provision and answered prayer for granted.

138:8 Every person dreams and makes plans for the future. Then they work hard to see those dreams and plans come true. But to make the most of life, we must include God's plan in our plans. He alone knows what is best for us; he alone can fulfill his purpose for us. As you make plans and dream dreams, talk with God about them.

139:1–5 Sometimes we don't let people get to know us completely because we are afraid they will discover something about us that they won't like. But God already knows everything about us, even to the number of hairs on our heads (Matthew 10:30), and still he accepts and loves us. God is with us through every situation, in every trial—protecting, loving, guiding. He knows and loves us completely.

Behold, O LORD, You know it all.
5 You have enclosed me behind and before,
And laid Your hand upon me.
6 *Such* knowledge is too wonderful for me;
It is *too* high, I cannot attain to it.

7 Where can I go from Your Spirit?
Or where can I flee from Your presence?
8 If I ascend to heaven, You are there;
If I make my bed in Sheol, behold, You are there.
9 If I take the wings of the dawn,
If I dwell in the remotest part of the sea,
10 Even there Your hand will lead me,
And Your right hand will lay hold of me.
11 If I say, "Surely the darkness will overwhelm me,
And the light around me will be night,"
12 Even the darkness is not dark to You,
And the night is as bright as the day.
Darkness and light are alike *to You.*

13 For You formed my inward parts;
You wove me in my mother's womb.
14 I will give thanks to You, for [209]I am fearfully and wonderfully made;
Wonderful are Your works,
And my soul knows it very well.
15 My frame was not hidden from You,
When I was made in secret,
And skillfully wrought in the depths of the earth;
16 Your eyes have seen my unformed substance;
And in Your book were all written
The days that were ordained *for me,*
When as yet there was not one of them.

17 How precious also are Your thoughts to me, O God!
How vast is the sum of them!
18 If I should count them, they would outnumber the sand.
When I awake, I am still with You.

19 O that You would slay the wicked, O God;
Depart from me, therefore, men of bloodshed.
20 For they speak against You wickedly,
And Your enemies take *Your name* in vain.
21 Do I not hate those who hate You, O LORD?
And do I not loathe those who rise up against You?
22 I hate them with the utmost hatred;
They have become my enemies.

209 Some ancient versions read *You are fearfully wonderful*

139:5 Ps 34:7; 125:2; Job 9:33
139:6 Rom 11:33; Job 42:3
139:7 Jer 23:24
139:8 Amos 9:2-4; Job 26:6; Prov 15:11
139:10 Ps 23:2, 3
139:11 Job 22:13
139:12 Job 34:22; Dan 2:22; 1 John 1:5
139:13 Ps 119:73; Is 44:24; Job 10:11
139:14 Ps 40:5
139:15 Job 10:8-10; Eccl 11:5; Ps 63:9
139:16 Job 10:8-10; Eccl 11:5; Ps 56:8; Job 14:5
139:17 Ps 40:5; 92:5
139:18 Ps 40:5; Ps 3:5
139:19 Is 11:4; Ps 6:8; 119:115; Ps 5:6; 26:9
139:20 Jude 15; Ex 20:7; Deut 5:11
139:21 2 Chr 19:2; Ps 26:5; 31:6; Ps 119:158

139:7 God is omnipresent—he is present everywhere. Because this is so, you can never be lost to his Spirit. This is good news to those who know and love God, because no matter what we do or where we go, we can never be far from God's comforting presence (see Romans 8:35–39).

139:13–15 God's character goes into the creation of every person. When you feel worthless or even begin to hate yourself, remember that God's Spirit is ready and willing to work within you. We should have as much respect for ourselves as our Maker has for us.

139:21–24 David's hatred for his enemies came from his zeal for God. David regarded his enemies as God's enemies, so his hatred was a desire for God's righteous justice and not for personal vengeance. Is it all right to be angry at people who hate God? Yes, but we must remember that it is God who will deal with them, not us. If we truly love God, then we will be deeply hurt if someone hates him. David asked God to search his heart and mind and point out any wrong motives that may have been behind his strong words. But while we seek justice against evil, we must also pray that God's enemies will turn to him before he judges them (see Matthew 5:44).

139:23 Job 31:6; Ps 26:2; Ps 7:9; Prov 17:3; Jer 11:20; 1 Thess 2:4

139:24 Ps 146:9; Prov 15:9; 28:10; Jer 25:5; 36:3; Ps 5:8; 143:10; Ps 16:11

23 Search me, O God, and know my heart;
Try me and know my anxious thoughts;
24 And see if there be any hurtful way in me,
And lead me in the everlasting way.

PSALM 140

For the choir director. A Psalm of David.

140:1 Ps 17:13; 59:2; 71:4; Ps 18:48; 86:14; 140:11

Theme: Prayer for protection against those who slander or threaten you. Deliverance begins with concentrating on our future life with God.
Author: David

140:2 Ps 7:14; 36:4; 52:2; Prov 6:14; Is 59:4; Hos 7:15; Ps 56:6

140:3 Ps 57:4; 64:3; Ps 58:4; Rom 3:13; James 3:8

1 Rescue me, O LORD, from evil men;
Preserve me from violent men
2 Who devise evil things in *their* hearts;
They continually stir up wars.
3 They sharpen their tongues as a serpent;
Poison of a viper is under their lips. Selah.

140:4 Ps 71:4; Ps 140:1; Ps 36:11

140:5 Job 18:9; Ps 35:7; 141:9; 142:3; Ps 31:4; 57:6; Lam 1:13; Ps 141:9; Is 8:14; Amos 3:5

4 Keep me, O LORD, from the hands of the wicked;
Preserve me from violent men
Who have purposed to [210]trip up my feet.
5 The proud have hidden a trap for me, and cords;
They have spread a net by the wayside;
They have set snares for me. Selah.

210 Lit *push violently*

ANGER AND VENGEANCE IN THE BOOK OF PSALMS

Several psalms shock those familiar with New Testament teachings. The psalmists didn't hesitate to demand God's justice and make vivid suggestions on how he might carry it out. Apparently, no subject was unsuitable for discussion with God, but our tendency is to avoid the subjects of anger and vengeance in the psalms.

To understand the words of anger and vengeance, we need to understand several things:

(1) The judgments asked for are to be carried out by God, and are written out of intense personal and national suffering. The people are unable or unwilling to take revenge themselves and are asking God to intervene. Because few of us have suffered intense cruelty on a personal or national level, we find it difficult to grasp these outbursts.

(2) These writers were intimately aware of God's justice. Some of their words are efforts to vividly imagine what God might allow to happen to those who had harmed his people.

(3) If we dared to write down our thoughts while unjustly attacked or suffering cruelty, we might be shocked at our own bold desire for vengeance. We would be surprised at how much we have in common with these men of old. The psalmists did not have Jesus' command to pray for one's enemies, but they did point to the right place to start. We are challenged to pay back good for evil, but until we respond to this challenge, we will not know how much we need God's help in order to forgive others.

(4) There is a helpful parallel between the psalms of anger and the psalms of vengeance. The "angry" psalms are intense and graphic, but they are directed at God. He is boldly told how disappointing it is when he turns his back on his people or acts too slowly. But while these thoughts and feelings were sincerely expressed, we know from the psalms themselves that these passing feelings were followed by renewed confidence in God's faithfulness. It is reasonable to expect the same of the "vengeance" psalms. We read, for example, David's angry outburst against Saul's pursuit in Psalm 59, yet we know that David never took personal revenge on Saul. The psalmists freely spoke their minds to God, having confidence that he could sort out what was meant and what was felt. Pray with that same confidence—God can be trusted with your heart.

Selected psalms that emphasize these themes are Psalms 10; 23; 28; 35; 59; 69; 109; 137; 139; 140.

139:23–24 David asked God to search for sin and point it out, even to the level of testing his thoughts. This is exploratory surgery for sin. How are we to recognize sin unless God points it out? Then, when God shows us, we can repent and be forgiven. Make this verse your prayer. If you ask the Lord to search your heart and your thoughts and to reveal your sin, you will be continuing on God's "everlasting way."

6 I said to the LORD, "You are my God;
Give ear, O LORD, to the voice of my supplications.
7 "O GOD the Lord, the strength of my salvation,
You have covered my head in the day of battle.
8 "Do not grant, O LORD, the desires of the wicked;
Do not promote his *evil* device, *that* they *not* be exalted. Selah.

9 "As for the head of those who surround me,
May the mischief of their lips cover them.
10 "May burning coals fall upon them;
May they be cast into the fire,
Into deep pits from which they cannot rise.
11 "May a slanderer not be established in the earth;
May evil hunt the violent man [211]speedily."

12 I know that the LORD will maintain the cause of the afflicted
And justice for the poor.
13 Surely the righteous will give thanks to Your name;
The upright will dwell in Your presence.

140:6 Ps 16:2; 31:14; Ps 143:1; Ps 116:1; 130:2

140:7 Ps 28:8; 118:14; Ps 144:10

140:8 Ps 112:10; Esth 9:25; Ps 10:2, 3

140:9 Ps 7:16; Prov 18:7

140:10 Ps 11:6; Ps 21:9; Matt 3:10; Ps 36:12

140:11 Ps 34:21

140:12 1 Kin 8:45, 49; Ps 9:4; 18:27; 82:3; Ps 12:5; 35:10

140:13 Ps 97:12; Ps 11:7; 16:11; 17:15

PSALM 141

A Psalm of David.

Theme: A prayer for help when facing temptation. David asks God to protect him and to give him wisdom in accepting criticism. Be open to honest criticism—God may be speaking to you through others.
Author: David

1 O LORD, I call upon You; hasten to me!
Give ear to my voice when I call to You!
2 May my prayer be counted as incense before You;
The lifting up of my hands as the evening offering.
3 Set a guard, O LORD, over my mouth;
Keep watch over the door of my lips.
4 Do not incline my heart to any evil thing,
To practice deeds of wickedness
With men who do iniquity;
And do not let me eat of their delicacies.

5 Let the righteous smite me in kindness and reprove me;
It is oil upon the head;
Do not let my head refuse it,
For still my prayer is against their wicked deeds.
6 Their judges are thrown down by the sides of the rock,
And they hear my words, for they are pleasant.

141:1 Ps 22:19; 38:22; 70:5; Ps 5:1; 143:1

141:2 Ex 30:8; Luke 1:10; Rev 5:8; 8:3, 4; 1 Tim 2:8; Ex 29:39, 41; 1 Kin 18:29, 36; Dan 9:21

141:3 Ps 34:13; 39:1; Prov 13:3; 21:23; Mic 7:5

141:4 Ps 119:36; Is 32:6; Hos 6:8; Mal 3:15; Prov 23:6

141:5 Prov 9:8; 19:25; 25:12; 27:6; Eccl 7:5; Gal 6:1; Ps 23:5; 133:2; Ps 35:14

141:6 2 Chr 25:12

211 Lit *thrust upon thrust*

140:12 To whom can the poor turn when they are persecuted? They lack the money to get professional help; they may be unable to defend themselves. But there is always someone on their side—the Lord will stand by them and ultimately bring about justice. This should be a comfort for us all. No matter what our situation may be, the Lord is with us. But this truth should also call us to responsibility. As God's people, we are required to defend the rights of the powerless.

141:3 James wrote that "the tongue is a small part of the body, and yet it boasts of great things" (James 3:5). On the average, a person opens his or her mouth approximately 700 times a day to speak. David wisely asked God to help keep him from speaking evil—sometimes even as he underwent persecution. Jesus himself was silent before his accusers (Matthew 26:63). Knowing the power of the tongue, we would do well to ask God to guard what we say so that our words will bring honor to his name.

141:4 David asked God to guard his heart. Evil acts begin with evil desires. It isn't enough to ask God to keep you away from temptation, make you stronger, or change your circumstances. You must ask him to change you on the inside—at the level of your desires.

141:5 David says that being rebuked by a righteous person is a kindness. Nobody really likes criticism, but everybody can benefit from it when it is given wisely and taken humbly. David suggested how to accept criticism: (1) Don't refuse it, (2) consider it a kindness, and (3) keep quiet (Don't fight back). Putting these suggestions into practice will help you control how you react to criticism, making it productive rather than destructive, no matter how it was originally intended.

141:7 Ps 129:3; Ps 53:5; Num 16:32, 33; Ps 88:3-5

7 As when one plows and breaks open the earth,
Our bones have been scattered at the mouth of Sheol.

141:8 Ps 25:15; 123:2; Ps 2:12; 11:1; Ps 27:9

141:9 Ps 38:12; 64:5; 91:3; 119:110; Ps 140:5

141:10 Ps 7:15; 35:8; 57:6; Ps 124:7

8 For my eyes are toward You, O GOD, the Lord;
In You I take refuge; do not leave me defenseless.
9 Keep me from the jaws of the trap which they have set for me,
And from the snares of those who do iniquity.
10 Let the wicked fall into their own nets,
While I pass by safely.

PSALM 142

Maskil of David, when he was in the cave. A Prayer.

Theme: A prayer when overwhelmed and desperate.
When we feel cornered by our enemies, only God can keep us safe.
Author: David

142:1 Ps 77:1; Ps 30:8

142:2 Ps 102: title

Ps 77:2

142:3 Ps 77:3; 143:4; Ps 140:5

142:4 Ps 31:11; 88:8, 18; Job 11:20; Jer 25:35; Jer 30:17

1 I cry aloud with my voice to the LORD;
I make supplication with my voice to the LORD.
2 I pour out my complaint before Him;
I declare my trouble before Him.
3 When my spirit was overwhelmed within me,
You knew my path.
In the way where I walk
They have hidden a trap for me.
4 Look to the right and see;
For there is no one who regards me;
There is no escape for me;
No one cares for my soul.

142:5 Ps 91:2, 9; Ps 16:5; 73:26; Ps 27:13

142:6 Ps 17:1; Ps 79:8; 116:6; Ps 18:17

142:7 Ps 143:11; 146:7; Ps 13:6

5 I cried out to You, O LORD;
I said, "You are my refuge,
My portion in the land of the living.
6 "Give heed to my cry,
For I am brought very low;
Deliver me from my persecutors,
For they are too strong for me.
7 "Bring my soul out of prison,
So that I may give thanks to Your name;
The righteous will surround me,
For You will deal bountifully with me."

PSALM 143

A Psalm of David.

143:1 Ps 140:6; Ps 89:1, 2; Ps 71:2

143:2 Job 14:3; 22:4; 1 Kin 8:46; Job 4:17; 9:2; 25:4; Ps 130:3; Eccl 7:20; Rom 3:10, 20; Gal 2:16

143:3 Ps 44:25; Ps 88:6; Lam 3:6

Theme: A prayer in the midst of hopelessness and depression. Our prayers should fit into what we know is consistent with God's character and plans.
Author: David

1 Hear my prayer, O LORD,
Give ear to my supplications!
Answer me in Your faithfulness, in Your righteousness!
2 And do not enter into judgment with Your servant,
For in Your sight no man living is righteous.
3 For the enemy has persecuted my soul;

142:4–5 Have you ever felt that no one cared what happened to you? David had good reason to feel that way, and he wrote, "I cried out to You, O LORD." Through prayer we can pull out of our tailspin and be reminded that God cares for us deeply.

142:7 This psalm was written when David was hiding from Saul in caves like the ones at Adullam (1 Samuel 22) or Engedi (1 Samuel 24). These may have seemed like prisons to him because of the confinement.

He has crushed my life to the ground;
He has made me dwell in dark places, like those who have long been dead.
4 Therefore my spirit is overwhelmed within me;
My heart is [212]appalled within me.

5 I remember the days of old;
I meditate on all Your doings;
I muse on the work of Your hands.
6 I stretch out my hands to You;
My soul *longs* for You, as a parched land. Selah.

7 Answer me quickly, O LORD, my spirit fails;
Do not hide Your face from me,
Or I will become like those who go down to the pit.
8 Let me hear Your lovingkindness in the morning;
For I trust in You;
Teach me the way in which I should walk;
For to You I lift up my soul.
9 Deliver me, O LORD, from my enemies;
I take refuge in You.

10 Teach me to do Your will,
For You are my God;
Let Your good Spirit lead me on level ground.
11 For the sake of Your name, O LORD, revive me.
In Your righteousness bring my soul out of trouble.
12 And in Your lovingkindness, cut off my enemies
And destroy all those who afflict my soul,
For I am Your servant.

143:4 Ps 77:3; 142:3; Lam 3:11

143:5 Ps 77:5, 10, 11; Ps 77:12; Ps 105:2

143:6 Job 11:13; Ps 88:9; Ps 42:2; 63:1

143:7 Ps 69:17; Ps 73:26; 84:2; Jer 8:18; Lam 1:22; Ps 27:9; 69:17; 102:2; Ps 28:1; 88:4

143:8 Ps 90:14; Ps 46:5; Ps 25:2; Ps 27:11; 32:8; 86:11; Ps 25:1; 86:4

143:9 Ps 31:15; 59:1

143:10 Ps 25:4, 5; 119:12; Neh 9:20; Ps 23:3

143:11 Ps 25:11; Ps 119:25; Ps 31:1; 71:2

143:12 Ps 54:5; Ps 52:5; Ps 116:16

PSALM 144

A Psalm of David.

Theme: Rejoicing in God's care. Whether in times of prosperity or adversity, blessed are those whose God is the Lord.
Author: David

1 Blessed be the LORD, my rock,
Who trains my hands for war,
And my fingers for battle;
2 My lovingkindness and my fortress,
My stronghold and my deliverer,
My shield and He in whom I take refuge,
Who subdues my people under me.
3 O LORD, what is man, that You take knowledge of him?
Or the son of man, that You think of him?
4 Man is like a mere breath;
His days are like a passing shadow.

144:1 Ps 18:2; 2 Sam 22:35; Ps 18:34

144:2 Ps 18:2; 91:2; Ps 59:9; Ps 3:3; 28:7; 84:9; Ps 18:39

144:3 Job 7:17; Ps 8:4; Heb 2:6

144:4 Ps 39:11; Job 8:9; 14:2; Ps 102:11; 109:23

212 Or *desolate*

143:7 David was losing hope, caught in paralyzing fear and deep depression. At times, we feel caught in deepening depression, and we are unable to pull ourselves out. At those times, we can come to the Lord and, like David, express our true feelings. Then he will help us as we remember his works (143:5), reach out to him in prayer (143:6), trust him (143:8), and decide to do his will (143:10).

143:10 David's prayer was to be taught to do God's will, not his own. A prayer for guidance is self-centered if it doesn't recognize God's power to redirect our lives. Asking God to restructure our priorities awakens our minds and stirs our wills.

144:3–4 Life is short. David reminds us that it is "like a mere breath" and that our "days are like a passing shadow." James says that our lives are "a vapor that appears for a little while and then vanishes away" (James 4:14). Because life is short, we should live for God while we have the time. Don't waste your life by selecting an inferior purpose that has no lasting value. Live for God—he alone can make your life worthwhile, purposeful, and meaningful.

144:5 Ps 18:9; Is 64:1; Ps 104:32
144:6 Ps 18:14; Ps 7:13; 58:7; Hab 3:11; Zech 9:14
144:7 Ps 18:16; Ps 69:1, 14; Ps 18:44; 54:3
144:8 Ps 12:2; 41:6; Gen 14:22; Deut 32:40; Ps 106:26; Is 44:20
144:9 Ps 33:3; 40:3; Ps 33:2
144:10 Ps 18:50; 2 Sam 18:7; Ps 140:7
144:11 Ps 18:44; 54:3; Ps 12:2; 41:6; Gen 14:22; Deut 32:40; Ps 106:26; Is 44:20
144:12 Ps 92:12-14; 128:3; Song 4:4; 7:4
144:13 Prov 3:9, 10
144:14 Prov 14:4; 2 Kin 25:10, 11; Amos 5:3; Is 24:11; Jer 14:2
144:15 Ps 33:12
145:1 Ps 30:1; 66:17; Ps 5:2; Ps 34:1
145:2 Ps 71:6
145:3 Ps 48:1; 86:10; 147:5; Job 5:9; 9:10; 11:7; Is 40:28; Rom 11:33
145:4 Ps 22:30, 31; Is 38:19
145:5 Ps 145:12; Ps 119:27
145:6 Deut 10:21; Ps 66:3; 106:22; Deut 32:3

5 Bow Your heavens, O LORD, and come down;
Touch the mountains, that they may smoke.
6 Flash forth lightning and scatter them;
Send out Your arrows and confuse them.
7 Stretch forth Your hand from on high;
Rescue me and deliver me out of great waters,
Out of the hand of aliens
8 Whose mouths speak deceit,
And whose right hand is a right hand of falsehood.

9 I will sing a new song to You, O God;
Upon a harp of ten strings I will sing praises to You,
10 Who gives salvation to kings,
Who rescues David His servant from the evil sword.
11 Rescue me and deliver me out of the hand of aliens,
Whose mouth speaks deceit
And whose right hand is a right hand of falsehood.

12 Let our sons in their youth be as grown-up plants,
And our daughters as corner pillars fashioned as for a palace;
13 Let our garners be full, furnishing every kind of produce,
And our flocks bring forth thousands and ten thousands in our fields;
14 Let our cattle bear
Without mishap and without loss,
Let there be no outcry in our streets!
15 How blessed are the people who are so situated;
How blessed are the people whose God is the LORD!

PSALM 145

A Psalm of Praise, of David.

Theme: A time will come when all people will join together in recognizing and worshipping God. Because God is full of love, he satisfies all who trust in him.
Author: David

1 I will extol You, my God, O King,
And I will bless Your name forever and ever.
2 Every day I will bless You,
And I will praise Your name forever and ever.
3 Great is the LORD, and highly to be praised,
And His greatness is unsearchable.
4 One generation shall praise Your works to another,
And shall declare Your mighty acts.
5 On the glorious splendor of Your majesty
And on Your wonderful works, I will meditate.
6 Men shall speak of the power of Your awesome acts,
And I will tell of Your greatness.

PRAISE IN THE BOOK OF PSALMS

Most of the psalms are prayers, and most of the prayers include praise to God. Praise expresses admiration, appreciation, and thanks. Praise in the book of Psalms is often directed to God, and just as often the praise is shared with others. Considering all that God has done and does for us, what could be more natural than outbursts of heartfelt praise?

As you read Psalms, note the praise given to God, not only for what he does—his creation, his blessings, his forgiveness—but also for who he is—loving, just, faithful, forgiving, patient. Note also those times when the praise of God is shared with others, and they too are encouraged to praise him. In what ways have you recently praised God or told others all that he has done for you?

Selected psalms that emphasize this theme are Psalms 8; 19; 30; 65; 84; 96; 100; 136; 145; 150.

7 They shall eagerly utter the memory of Your abundant goodness
And will shout joyfully of Your righteousness.

8 The LORD is gracious and merciful;
Slow to anger and great in lovingkindness.
9 The LORD is good to all,
And His mercies are over all His works.
10 All Your works shall give thanks to You, O LORD,
And Your godly ones shall bless You.
11 They shall speak of the glory of Your kingdom
And talk of Your power;
12 To make known to the sons of men Your mighty acts
And the glory of the majesty of Your kingdom.
13 Your kingdom is an everlasting kingdom,
And Your dominion *endures* throughout all generations.

14 The LORD sustains all who fall
And raises up all who are bowed down.
15 The eyes of all look to You,
And You give them their food in due time.
16 You open Your hand
And satisfy the desire of every living thing.

17 The LORD is righteous in all His ways
And kind in all His deeds.
18 The LORD is near to all who call upon Him,
To all who call upon Him in truth.
19 He will fulfill the desire of those who fear Him;
He will also hear their cry and will save them.
20 The LORD keeps all who love Him,
But all the wicked He will destroy.
21 My mouth will speak the praise of the LORD,
And all flesh will bless His holy name forever and ever.

145:7 Ps 31:19; Is 63:7; Ps 51:14
145:8 Ex 34:6; Num 14:18; Ps 86:5, 15; 103:8
145:9 Ps 100:5; 136:1; Jer 33:11; Nah 1:7; Matt 19:17; Mark 10:18; Ps 145:15
145:10 Ps 19:1; 103:22; Ps 68:26
145:11 Jer 14:21
145:12 Ps 105:1; Ps 145:5; Is 2:10, 19, 21
145:13 Ps 10:16; 29:10; 1 Tim 1:17; 2 Pet 1:11
145:14 Ps 37:24; Ps 146:8
145:15 Ps 104:27; 136:25
145:16 Ps 104:28
145:17 Ps 116:5
145:18 Deut 4:7; Ps 34:18; 119:151; John 4:24
145:19 Ps 21:2; 37:4; Ps 10:17; Prov 15:29; 1 John 5:14
145:20 Ps 31:23; 91:14; 97:10; Ps 9:5; 37:38
145:21 Ps 71:8; Ps 65:2; 150:6; Ps 145:1, 2

PSALM 146

Theme: The help of man versus the help of God. Help from man is temporal and unstable, but help from God is lasting and complete.
Author: Anonymous

1 Praise the LORD!
Praise the LORD, O my soul!
2 I will praise the LORD while I live;
I will sing praises to my God while I have my being.
3 Do not trust in princes,
In mortal man, in whom there is no salvation.

146:1 Ps 103:1
146:2 Ps 63:4; Ps 104:33
146:3 Ps 118:9; Ps 118:8; Is 2:22; Ps 60:11; 108:12

145:14 Sometimes our burdens seem more than we can bear, and we wonder how we can go on. David stands at this bleak intersection of life's road and points toward the Lord, the great burden-bearer. God is able to lift us up because (1) his greatness is unsearchable (145:3); (2) he does mighty acts across many generations (145:4); (3) he is full of glorious splendor and majesty (145:5); (4) he does wonderful and awesome works (145:5–6); (5) he is righteous (145:7); (6) he is gracious, merciful, patient, and loving (145:8–9); (7) he rules over an everlasting kingdom (145:13); (8) he is our source of all our daily needs (145:15–16); (9) he is righteous and loving in all his dealings (145:17); (10) he remains near to those who call on him (145:18); (11) he hears our cries and saves us (145:19–20). If you are bending under a burden and feel that you are about to fall, turn to God for help. He is ready to lift you up and bear your burden.

146—150 These last five psalms overflow with praise. Each begins and ends with "Praise the LORD." They show us where, why, and how to praise God. What does praise do? (1) Praise takes our minds off our problems and shortcomings, and focuses them on God. (2) Praise leads us from individual meditation to corporate worship. (3) Praise causes us to consider and appreciate God's character. (4) Praise lifts our perspective from the earthly to the heavenly.

146:3–8 The psalmist portrays man as an inadequate savior, a false hope; even princes cannot deliver (146:3). God is the hope and the help of the needy. Jesus affirms his concern for the poor and afflicted in Luke 4:18–21; 7:21–23. He does not separate the social and spiritual needs of people, but attends to both. While God, not the government, is the hope of the needy, *we* are his instruments to help here on earth.

146:4 Ps 104:29; Eccl 12:7; Ps 33:10; 1 Cor 2:6
146:5 Ps 144:15; Jer 17:7; Ps 71:5
146:6 Ps 115:15; Rev 14:7; Acts 14:15; Ps 117:2
146:7 Ps 103:6; Ps 107:9; 145:15; Ps 68:6; Is 61:1
146:8 Matt 9:30; John 9:7; Ps 145:14; Ps 11:7
146:9 Ex 22:21; Lev 19:34; Deut 10:18; Ps 68:5; Ps 147:6
146:10 Ex 15:18; Ps 10:16

4 His spirit departs, he returns to the earth;
In that very day his thoughts perish.
5 How blessed is he whose help is the God of Jacob,
Whose hope is in the LORD his God,
6 Who made heaven and earth,
The sea and all that is in them;
Who keeps faith forever;
7 Who executes justice for the oppressed;
Who gives food to the hungry.
The LORD sets the prisoners free.

8 The LORD opens *the eyes of* the blind;
The LORD raises up those who are bowed down;
The LORD loves the righteous;
9 The LORD protects the strangers;
He supports the fatherless and the widow,
But He thwarts the way of the wicked.
10 The LORD will reign forever,
Your God, O Zion, to all generations.
Praise the LORD!

147:1 Ps 92:1; 135:3; Ps 33:1
147:2 Ps 51:18; 102:16; Deut 30:3; Ps 106:47; Is 11:12; 56:8; Ezek 39:28
147:3 Ps 34:18; 51:17; Is 61:1; Job 5:18; Is 30:26; Ezek 34:16
147:4 Gen 15:5; Is 40:26
147:5 Ps 48:1; 145:3; Is 40:28
147:6 Ps 37:24; 146:8, 9
147:7 Ps 33:2; 95:1, 2
147:8 Job 26:8; Job 5:10; 38:26; Ps 104:13; Job 38:27; Ps 104:14
147:9 Ps 104:27, 28; 145:15; Job 38:41; Matt 6:26
147:10 Ps 33:17; 1 Sam 16:7

PSALM 147

Theme: What gives God joy. Although God created everything, his greatest joy comes from our genuine worship and trust.
Author: Anonymous, possibly written when the exiles returned to Jerusalem

1 Praise the LORD!
For it is good to sing praises to our God;
For [213]it is pleasant *and* praise is becoming.
2 The LORD builds up Jerusalem;
He gathers the outcasts of Israel.
3 He heals the brokenhearted
And binds up their [214]wounds.
4 He counts the number of the stars;
He gives names to all of them.
5 Great is our Lord and abundant in strength;
His understanding is infinite.
6 The LORD [215]supports the afflicted;
He brings down the wicked to the ground.

7 Sing to the LORD with thanksgiving;
Sing praises to our God on the lyre,
8 Who covers the heavens with clouds,
Who provides rain for the earth,
Who makes grass to grow on the mountains.
9 He gives to the beast its food,
And to the young ravens which cry.
10 He does not delight in the strength of the horse;

213 Or *He is gracious* **214** Lit *sorrows* **215** Or *relieves*

146:9 God's plans frustrate the "way of the wicked" because his values are the opposite of society's. Jesus turned society's values upside down when he proclaimed that "many who are first will be last; and the last, first" (Matthew 19:30), and that "whoever wishes to save his life will lose it; but whoever loses his life for My sake will find it" (Matthew 16:25). Don't be surprised when others don't understand your Christian values, but don't give in to theirs.

147:5 Sometimes we feel as if we don't understand ourselves—what we want, how we feel, what's wrong with us, or what we should do about it. But God's understanding has no limit, and therefore he understands us fully. If you feel troubled and don't understand yourself, remember that God understands you perfectly. Take your mind off yourself and focus it on God. Strive to become more and more like him. The more you learn about God and his ways, the better you will understand yourself.

147:10–11 We spend much effort trying to sharpen our skills or increase our strength. There is nothing wrong with doing so, and, in fact, our gifts can be used to glorify God. But when we use our skills with no regard for God, they are indeed worth little. It is our *fear* (reverence) and trust that God desires. When he has those, then he will use our skills and strengths in ways far greater than we can imagine.

He does not take pleasure in the legs of a man.
11 The LORD favors those who fear Him,
Those who wait for His lovingkindness.

12 Praise the LORD, O Jerusalem!
Praise your God, O Zion!
13 For He has strengthened the bars of your gates;
He has blessed your sons within you.
14 He makes peace in your borders;
He satisfies you with the finest of the wheat.
15 He sends forth His command to the earth;
His word runs very swiftly.
16 He gives snow like wool;
He scatters the frost like ashes.
17 He casts forth His ice as fragments;
Who can stand before His cold?
18 He sends forth His word and melts them;
He causes His wind to blow and the waters to flow.
19 He declares His words to Jacob,
His statutes and His ordinances to Israel.
20 He has not dealt thus with any nation;
And as for His ordinances, they have not known them.
Praise the LORD!

147:11
Ps 149:4; Ps 33:18

147:13
Neh 3:3; 7:3; Ps 37:26

147:14
Ps 29:11; Is 54:13; 60:17, 18; Ps 132:15; Deut 32:14; Ps 81:16

147:15
Job 37:12; Ps 148:5; Ps 104:4

147:16
Job 37:6; Ps 148:8; Job 38:29

147:17
Job 37:10; Job 37:9

147:18
Ps 33:9; 107:20; 147:15; Ps 107:25

147:19
Deut 33:3, 4; Mal 4:4

147:20
Deut 4:7, 8, 32-34; Rom 3:1, 2; Ps 79:6; Jer 10:25

PSALM 148

Theme: Let all creation praise and worship the Lord.
Author: Anonymous

1 Praise the LORD!
Praise the LORD from the heavens;
Praise Him in the heights!
2 Praise Him, all His angels;
Praise Him, all His hosts!
3 Praise Him, sun and moon;
Praise Him, all stars of light!
4 Praise Him, highest heavens,
And the waters that are above the heavens!
5 Let them praise the name of the LORD,
For He commanded and they were created.
6 He has also established them forever and ever;
He has made a decree which will not pass away.

7 Praise the LORD from the earth,
Sea monsters and all deeps;
8 Fire and hail, snow and clouds;
Stormy wind, fulfilling His word;
9 Mountains and all hills;
Fruit trees and all cedars;
10 Beasts and all cattle;
Creeping things and winged fowl;
11 Kings of the earth and all peoples;
Princes and all judges of the earth;

148:1
Ps 69:34; Job 16:19; Ps 102:19; Matt 21:9

148:2
Ps 103:20; Ps 103:21

148:4
Deut 10:14; 1 Kin 8:27; Neh 9:6; Ps 68:33; Gen 1:7

148:5
Gen 1:1; Ps 33:6, 9

148:6
Ps 89:37; Jer 31:35, 36; 33:20, 25; Job 38:33

148:7
Gen 1:21; Ps 74:13; Gen 1:2; Deut 33:13; Hab 3:10

148:8
Ps 18:12; Ps 147:16; Ps 135:7; Ps 107:25; Job 37:12; Ps 103:20

148:9
Is 44:23; 49:13; Is 55:12

148:10
Is 43:20; Hos 2:18

148:11
Ps 102:15

147:19–20 The nation of Israel (the descendants of Jacob) was special to God because to its people God brought his laws, and through its people he sent his Son, Jesus Christ. Now any individual who follows God is just as special to him. In fact, the Bible says that the real nation of Israel is not a specific people or geographic place, but the community of all who believe in and obey God (see Galatians 3:28–29).

148:5–14 All creation is like a majestic symphony or a great choir composed of many harmonious parts that together offer up songs of praise. Each part (independent, yet part of the whole) is caught up and carried along in the swelling tides of praise. This is a picture of how we as believers should praise God—individually, yet as part of the great choir of believers worldwide. Are you singing your part well in the worldwide choir of praise?

12 Both young men and virgins;
Old men and children.

148:13
Is 12:4; Ps 8:1; 113:4

148:14
1 Sam 2:1; Ps 75:10; Deut 10:21; Ps 109:1; Jer 17:14; Lev 10:3; Eph 2:17

13 Let them praise the name of the LORD,
For His name alone is exalted;
His glory is above earth and heaven.
14 And He has lifted up a horn for His people,
Praise for all His godly ones;
Even for the sons of Israel, a people near to Him.
Praise the LORD!

PSALM 149

Theme: A victory celebration. We have the assurance that God truly enjoys his people.
Author: Anonymous

149:1
Ps 33:3; Ps 35:18; 89:5

149:2
Ps 95:6; Judg 8:23; Ps 47:6; Zech 9:9

149:3
2 Sam 6:14; Ps 150:4; Ex 15:20; Ps 81:2

149:4
Job 36:11; Ps 16:11; 35:27; 147:11; Ps 132:16; Is 61:3

149:5
Ps 132:16; Job 35:10; Ps 42:8

149:6
Ps 66:17; Heb 4:12; Neh 4:17

149:7
Ezek 25:17; Mic 5:15

149:8
Job 36:8; Nah 3:10

149:9
Deut 7:12; Ezek 28:26; Ps 112:9; 148:14

1 Praise the LORD!
Sing to the LORD a new song,
And His praise in the congregation of the godly ones.
2 Let Israel be glad in his Maker;
Let the sons of Zion rejoice in their King.
3 Let them praise His name with dancing;
Let them sing praises to Him with timbrel and lyre.
4 For the LORD takes pleasure in His people;
He will beautify the afflicted ones with salvation.

5 Let the godly ones exult in glory;
Let them sing for joy on their beds.
6 *Let* the high praises of God *be* in their mouth,
And a two-edged sword in their hand,
7 To execute vengeance on the nations
And punishment on the peoples,
8 To bind their kings with chains
And their nobles with fetters of iron,
9 To execute on them the judgment written;
This is an honor for all His godly ones.
Praise the LORD!

PSALM 150

Theme: A closing hymn of praise. God's creation praises him everywhere in every way. We should join this rejoicing song of praise.
Author: Anonymous

150:1
Ps 73:17; 102:19; Ps 19:1

150:2
Ps 145:12; Deut 3:24; Ps 145:3

150:3
Ps 98:6; Ps 33:2

150:4
Ps 149:3; Ps 45:8; Is 38:20; Gen 4:21; Job 21:12

1 Praise the LORD!
Praise God in His sanctuary;
Praise Him in His mighty expanse.
2 Praise Him for His mighty deeds;
Praise Him according to His excellent greatness.

3 Praise Him with trumpet sound;
Praise Him with harp and lyre.
4 Praise Him with timbrel and dancing;

149:3–5 Although the Bible invites us to praise God, we often aren't sure how to go about it. Here, several ways are suggested—in the dance, with the voice, with musical instruments. God enjoys his people, and we should enjoy praising him.

149:6–7 The two-edged sword symbolizes the completeness of judgment that will be executed by the Messiah when he returns to punish all evildoers (Revelation 1:16).

150:3–5 Music and song were an integral part of Old Testament worship. David introduced music into the tabernacle and temple services (1 Chronicles 16:4–7). The music must have been loud and joyous as evidenced by the list of instruments and the presence of choirs and songleaders. Music was also important in New Testament worship (Ephesians 5:19; Colossians 3:16).

Praise Him with stringed instruments and pipe.
5 Praise Him with loud cymbals;
Praise Him with resounding cymbals.
6 Let everything that has breath praise the LORD.
Praise the LORD!

150:5 2 Sam 6:5; 1 Chr 13:8; 15:16; Ezra 3:10; Neh 12:27

150:6 Ps 103:22; 145:21

WHERE TO GET HELP IN THE BOOK OF PSALMS

When you feel...

Afraid: 3; 4; 27; 46; 49; 56; 91; 118
Alone: 9; 10; 12; 13; 27; 40; 43
"Burned out": 6; 63
Cheated: 41
Confused: 10; 12; 73
Depressed: 27; 34; 42; 43; 88; 143
Distressed: 13; 25; 31; 40; 107
Elated: 19; 96
Guilty: 19; 32; 38; 51
Hateful: 11
Impatient: 13; 27; 37; 40
Insecure: 3; 5; 12; 91
Insulted: 41; 70
Jealous: 37
Like Quitting: 29; 43; 145
Lost: 23; 139
Overwhelmed: 25; 69; 142
Penitent/Sorry: 32; 51; 66
Proud: 14; 30; 49
Purposeless: 14; 25; 39; 49; 90
Sad: 13
Self–confident: 24
Tense: 4
Thankful: 118; 136; 138
Threatened: 3; 11; 17
Tired/Weak: 6; 13; 18; 28; 29; 40; 86
Trapped: 7; 17; 42; 88; 142
Unimportant: 8; 90; 139
Vengeful: 3; 7; 109
Worried: 37
Worshipful: 8; 19; 27; 29; 150

When you're facing...

Atheists: 10; 14; 19; 52; 53; 115
Competition: 133
Criticism: 35; 56; 120
Danger: 11
Death: 6; 71; 90
Decisions: 1; 119
Discrimination: 54
Doubts: 34; 37; 94
Evil people: 10; 35; 36; 49; 52; 109; 140
Enemies: 3; 25; 35; 41; 56; 59
Heresy: 14
Hypocrisy: 26; 28; 40; 50
Illness: 6; 139
Lies: 5; 12; 120
Old Age: 71; 92
Persecution: 1; 3; 7; 56
Poverty: 9; 10; 12
Punishment: 6; 38; 39
Slander/Insults: 7; 15; 35; 43; 120
Slaughter: 6; 46; 83
Sorrow: 23; 34
Success: 18; 112; 127; 128
Temptation: 38; 141
Troubles: 34; 55; 86; 102; 142; 145
Verbal Cruelty: 35; 120

When you want...

Acceptance: 139
Answers: 4; 17
Confidence: 46; 71
Courage: 11; 42
Fellowship with God: 5; 16; 25; 27; 37; 133
Forgiveness: 32; 38; 40; 51; 69; 86; 103; 130
Friendship: 16
Godliness: 15; 25
Guidance: 1; 5; 15; 19; 25; 32; 48
Healing: 6; 41
Hope: 16; 17; 18; 23; 27
Humility: 19; 147
Illumination: 19
Integrity: 24; 25
Joy: 9; 16; 28; 126
Justice: 2; 7; 14; 26; 37; 49; 58; 82
Knowledge: 2; 8; 18; 19; 25; 29; 97; 103
Leadership: 72
Miracles: 60; 111
Money: 15; 16; 17; 49
Peace: 3; 4
Perspective: 2; 11
Prayer: 5; 17; 27; 61
Protection: 3; 4; 7; 16; 17; 18; 23; 27; 31; 91; 121; 125
Provision: 23
Rest: 23; 27
Salvation: 26; 37; 49; 126
Stability: 11; 33; 46
Vindication: 9; 14; 28; 35; 109
Wisdom: 1; 16; 19; 64; 111

150:6 How could the message be more clear? The writer was telling the individual listeners to praise God. What a fitting way to end this book of praise—with a direct encouragement for *you* to praise God too. Remember to praise him every day!

150:6 In a way, the book of Psalms parallels our spiritual journey through life. It begins by presenting us with two roads—the way to life and the way to death. If we choose God's way to life, we still face both blessings and troubles, joy and grief, successes and obstacles. Throughout it all, God is at our side, guiding, encouraging, comforting, and caring. As the wise and faithful person's life draws to an end, he or she realizes clearly that God's road is the right road. Knowing this will cause us to praise God for leading us in the right direction and for assuring our place in the perfect world God has in store for those who have faithfully followed him.

EIGHT WORDS FOR LAW
Hebrew law served as the personal and national guide for living under God's authority. It directed the moral, spiritual, and social life. Its purpose was to produce better understanding of God and greater commitment to him.

Word	*Meaning*	*Examples*	*Significance*
Torah	Direction, Guidance, Instruction	Exodus 24:12; Isaiah 30:20	Need for law in general; a command from a higher person to a lower
Mitswah	Commandment, Command	Genesis 25:5; Exodus 15:26; 20:2-17; Deuteronomy 5:6–21	God's specific instruction to be obeyed rather than a general law; used of the Ten Commandments.
Mishpat	Judgment, Ordinance	Genesis 18:19; Deuteronomy 34:2; 16:18; 17:9	Refers to the civil, social, and sanitation laws.
Eduth	Admonition, Testimony	Exodus 25:22	Refers to God's law as he deals with his people.
Huqqim	Statutes, Oracles	Leviticus 18:4; Deuteronomy 4:1	Dealt with the royal pronouncements; mainly connected to worship and feasts.
Piqqudim	Orders, Precepts	Psalms 19:8; 103:8	Used often in the psalms to describe God's orders and assignments.
Dabar	Word	Exodus 34:28; Deuteronomy 4:13	Used to indicate divine oracles or revelations of God.
Dath	Royal Edict Public Law	Ezekiel 7:26; Daniel 2:3, 15; 6:8, 12	Refers to the divine law or Jewish religious traditions in general.

PROVERBS

VITAL STATISTICS

PURPOSE:
To teach people how to attain wisdom and discipline and a prudent life, and how to do what is right and just and fair (see 1:2–3)—in short, to apply divine wisdom to daily life and to provide moral instruction

AUTHOR:
Solomon wrote most of this book, with Agur and Lemuel contributing some of the later sections

DATE WRITTEN:
Solomon wrote and compiled most of these proverbs early in his reign

SETTING:
This is a book of wise sayings, a textbook for teaching people how to live godly lives through the repetition of wise thoughts.

KEY VERSE:
"The fear of the LORD is the beginning of knowledge; fools despise wisdom and instruction" (1:7).

SPECIAL FEATURES:
The book uses varied literary forms: poems, brief parables, pointed questions, and couplets. Other literary devices include antithesis, comparison, and personification.

ALPHABET letters, vowels, and consonants formed into words, sentences, paragraphs, and books—spoken, signed, whispered, written, and printed. From friendly advice to impassioned speeches and from dusty volumes to daily tabloids, messages are sent and received, with each sender trying to impart knowledge . . . and wisdom.

Woven into human fabric is the desire to learn and understand. Our mind sets us apart from animals, and we analyze, conceptualize, theorize, discuss, and debate everything from science to the supernatural. We build schools, institutes, and universities, where learned professors can teach us about the world and about life.

Knowledge is good, but there is a vast difference between "knowledge" (having the facts) and "wisdom" (applying those facts to life). We may amass knowledge, but without wisdom our knowledge is useless. We must learn how to *live out* what we know.

The wisest man who ever lived, Solomon, left us a legacy of written wisdom in three volumes—Proverbs, Ecclesiastes, and Song of Solomon. In these books, under the inspiration of the Holy Spirit, he gives practical insights and guidelines for life.

In the first of these three volumes, Solomon passes on his practical advice in the form of proverbs. A proverb is a short, concise sentence that conveys moral truth. The book of Proverbs is a collection of these wise statements. The main theme of Proverbs, as we might expect, is the nature of true wisdom. Solomon writes, "The fear of the LORD is the beginning of knowledge; fools despise wisdom and instruction" (1:7). He then proceeds to give hundreds of practical examples of how to live according to godly wisdom.

Proverbs covers a wide range of topics, including youth and discipline, family life, self-control and resisting temptation, business matters, words and the tongue, knowing God, marriage, seeking the truth, wealth and poverty, immorality, and, of course, wisdom. These proverbs are short poems (usually in couplet form), containing a holy mixture of common sense and timely warnings. Although they are not meant to teach doctrine, a person who follows their advice will walk closely with God. The word *proverb* comes from a Hebrew word that means "to rule or to govern," and these sayings, reminders, and admonitions provide profound advice for governing our lives.

As you read Proverbs, understand that knowing God is the key to wisdom. Listen to the thoughts and lessons from the world's wisest man, and apply these truths to your life. Don't just read these proverbs; act on them!

THE BLUEPRINT

A. WISDOM FOR YOUNG PEOPLE (1:1—9:18)	Solomon instructed the young people of his day like a father giving advice to his child. While many of these proverbs are directed toward young people, the principles supporting them are helpful to all believers, male and female, young and old. Anyone beginning his or her journey to discover more of wisdom will benefit greatly from these wise sayings.
B. WISDOM FOR ALL PEOPLE (10:1—24:34)	Solomon wanted to impart wisdom to all people, regardless of their age, sex, or position in society. These short, wise sayings give us practical wisdom for daily living. We should study them diligently and integrate them into our life.
C. WISDOM FOR THE LEADERS (25:1—31:31)	In addition to the proverbs that Solomon collected, the men of Hezekiah collected many proverbs that Solomon and others wrote. While most of these are general in nature, many are directed specifically to the king and those who dealt with the king. These are particularly useful for those who are leaders or aspire to be leaders.

MEGATHEMES

THEME	EXPLANATION	IMPORTANCE
Wisdom	God wants his people to be wise. Two kinds of people portray two contrasting paths of life. The fool is the wicked, stubborn person who hates or ignores God. The wise person seeks to know and love God.	When we choose God's way, he grants us wisdom. His Word, the Bible, leads us to live right, have right relationships, and make right decisions.
Relationships	Proverbs gives us advice for developing our personal relationships with friends, family members, and co-workers. In every relationship, we must show love, dedication, and high moral standards.	To relate to people, we need consistency, tact, and discipline to use the wisdom God gives us. If we don't treat others according to the wisdom God gives, our relationships will suffer.
Speech	What we say shows our real attitude toward others. How we talk reveals what we're really like. Our speech is a test of how wise we have become.	To be wise in our speech we need to use self-control. Our words should be honest and well chosen.
Work	God controls the final outcome of all we do. We are accountable to carry out our work with diligence and discipline, not laziness.	Because God evaluates how we live, we should work purposefully. We must never be lax or self-satisfied in using our skills.
Success	Although people work very hard for money and fame, God views success as having a good reputation, moral character, and the spiritual devotion to obey him.	A successful relationship with God counts for eternity. Everything else is perishable. All our resources, time, and talents come from God. We should strive to use them wisely.

A. WISDOM FOR YOUNG PEOPLE (1:1—9:18)

Proverbs begins with a clear statement of its purpose—to impart wisdom for godly living. The first few chapters are Solomon's fatherly advice to young people. Although most of the material in this section is directed toward young people, all who seek wisdom will greatly benefit from these wise words. This is where one can discover the source of wisdom, the value of wisdom, and the benefits of wisdom.

The Usefulness of Proverbs

1 The proverbs of Solomon the son of David, king of Israel:
2 To know wisdom and instruction,
To discern the sayings of understanding,
3 To receive instruction in wise behavior,
Righteousness, justice and equity;
4 To give prudence to the naive,
To the youth knowledge and discretion,
5 A wise man will hear and increase in learning,
And a man of understanding will acquire wise counsel,
6 To understand a proverb and a figure,
The words of the wise and their riddles.

7 The fear of the LORD is the beginning of knowledge;
Fools despise wisdom and instruction.

The Enticement of Sinners

8 Hear, my son, your father's instruction
And do not forsake your mother's teaching;
9 Indeed, they are a graceful wreath to your head
And ornaments about your neck.
10 My son, if sinners entice you,
Do not consent.
11 If they say, "Come with us,
Let us lie in wait for blood,
Let us ambush the innocent without cause;
12 Let us swallow them alive like Sheol,
Even whole, as those who go down to the pit;
13 We will find all *kinds* of precious wealth,

1:1 1 Kin 4:32; Prov 10:1; 25:1; Eccl 12:9; Eccl 1:1

1:2 Prov 15:33; Prov 4:1

1:3 Prov 2:1; 19:20; Prov 2:9

1:4 Prov 8:5, 12; Prov 2:10, 11; 3:21

1:5 Prov 9:9; Prov 14:6; Eccl 9:11

1:6 Num 12:8; Ps 49:4; 78:2; Dan 8:23

1:7 Job 28:28; Ps 111:10; Prov 9:10; 15:33; Eccl 12:13

1:8 Prov 4:1; Prov 6:20

1:9 Prov 4:9; Gen 41:42; Dan 5:29

1:10 Prov 16:29; Gen 39:7-10; Deut 13:8; Ps 50:18; Eph 5:11

1:11 Prov 12:6; Jer 5:26; Ps 10:8; Prov 1:18

1:12 Ps 124:3; Ps 28:1

1:1 What the book of Psalms is to prayer and devotional life, the book of Proverbs is to everyday life. Proverbs gives practical suggestions for effective living. This book is not just a collection of homey sayings; it contains deep spiritual insights drawn from experience. A *proverb* is a short, wise, easy-to-learn saying that calls a person to action. It doesn't argue about basic spiritual and moral beliefs; it assumes we already hold them. The book of Proverbs focuses on God—his character, works, and blessings—and it tells how we can live in close relationship to him.

1:1 Solomon, the third king of Israel, son of the great King David, reigned during Israel's golden age. When God said he would give him whatever he wanted, he asked for an understanding heart (1 Kings 3:5–14). God was pleased with this request, and he not only made Solomon wise but also gave him great riches and power and an era of peace. Solomon built the glorious temple in Jerusalem (1 Kings 6) and wrote most of the book of Proverbs. His Profile is found in 1 Kings 4.

1:6 Riddles were thought-provoking questions.

1:7 One of the most annoying types of people is a know-it-all, a person who has a dogmatic opinion about everything, is closed to anything new, resents discipline, and refuses to learn. Solomon calls this kind of person a fool. Don't be a know-it-all. Instead, be open to the advice of others, especially those who know you well and can give valuable insight and counsel. Learn how to learn from others. Remember, only God knows it all.

1:7–9 In this age of information, knowledge is plentiful, but wisdom is scarce. Wisdom means far more than simply knowing a lot. It is a basic attitude that affects every aspect of life. The foundation of knowledge is to fear the Lord—to honor and respect God, to live in awe of his power, and to obey his Word. Faith in God should be the controlling principle for your understanding of the world, your attitudes, and your actions. Trust in God—he will make you truly wise.

1:8 Our actions speak louder than our words. This is especially true in the home. Children learn values, morals, and priorities by observing how their parents act and react every day. If parents exhibit a deep reverence for and dependence on God, the children will catch these attitudes. Let them see your reverence for God. Teach them right living by giving worship an important place in your family life and by reading the Bible together.

1:10–19 Sin is enticing because it offers a quick route to prosperity and makes us feel like one of the crowd. But when we go along with others and refuse to listen to the truth, our own appetites become our masters, and we'll do anything to satisfy them. Sin, even when attractive, is deadly. We must learn to make choices, not on the basis of flashy appeal or short-range pleasure, but in view of the long-range effects. Sometimes this means steering clear of people who want to entice us into activities that we know are wrong. We can't be friendly with sin and expect our lives to remain unaffected.

We will fill our houses with spoil;
14 Throw in your lot with us,
We shall all have one purse,"
15 My son, do not walk in the way with them.
Keep your feet from their path,
16 For their feet run to evil
And they hasten to shed blood.
17 Indeed, it is useless to spread the *baited* net
In the sight of any bird;
18 But they lie in wait for their own blood;
They ambush their own lives.
19 So are the ways of everyone who gains by violence;
It takes away the life of its possessors.

1:15 Ps 1:1; Prov 4:14; Ps 119:101
1:16 Prov 6:17, 18; Is 59:7
1:18 Prov 11:19
1:19 Prov 15:27

Wisdom Warns

20 Wisdom shouts in the street,
She lifts her voice in the square;
21 At the head of the noisy *streets* she cries out;
At the entrance of the gates in the city she utters her sayings:
22 "How long, O naive ones, will you love being simple-minded?
And scoffers delight themselves in scoffing
And fools hate knowledge?
23 "Turn to my reproof,
Behold, I will pour out my spirit on you;
I will make my words known to you.
24 "Because I called and you refused,
I stretched out my hand and no one paid attention;
25 And you neglected all my counsel
And did not want my reproof;
26 I will also laugh at your calamity;
I will mock when your dread comes,
27 When your dread comes like a storm
And your calamity comes like a whirlwind,

1:20 Prov 8:1-3; 9:3
1:22 Prov 1:4, 32; 8:5; 9:4; 22:3; Ps 1:1; Prov 1:29; 5:12
1:23 Is 32:15; Joel 2:28; John 7:39
1:24 Is 65:12; 66:4; Jer 7:13; Zech 7:11; Is 65:2; Rom 10:21
1:25 Ps 107:11; Luke 7:30; Prov 15:10
1:26 Ps 2:4; Prov 6:15; Prov 10:24
1:27 Prov 10:25

UNDERSTANDING PROVERBS
Most often, proverbs are written in the form of couplets. These are constructed in three ways:

Type	*Description*	*Key Word(s)*	*Examples*
Contrasting	Meaning and application come from the differences or contrast between the two statements of the proverb	"but"	10:6; 15:25, 27
Comparing	Meaning and application come from the similarities or comparison between the two statements of the proverb	"like/so" "better/than"	10:26; 15:16–17; 25:25
Complementing	Meaning and application come from the way the second statement complements the first	"and"	10:18; 14:10; 15:23

1:19 Making "gains by violence" is one of Satan's surest traps. It begins when he plants the suggestion that we can't live without some possession or more money. Then that desire fans its own fire until it becomes an all-consuming obsession. Ask God for wisdom to recognize any greedy desire before it destroys you. God will help you overcome it.

1:20 The picture of wisdom shouting in the streets is a personification—a literary device to make wisdom come alive for us. Wisdom is not a separate being; it is the mind of God revealed. By reading about Jesus Christ's earthly ministry, we can see wisdom in action. In order to understand how to become wise, we can listen to wisdom calling and instructing us in the book of Proverbs (see the chart in chapter 14). For New Testament calls to wisdom, see 2 Timothy 1:7 and James 1:5. Make sure you don't reject God's offer of wisdom to you.

1:22 In the book of Proverbs, the "simple-minded" or a fool is not someone with a *mental* deficiency but someone with a *character* deficiency (such as rebellion, laziness, or anger). The fool is not stupid, but he or she is unable to tell right from wrong or good from bad.

1:23–28 God is more than willing to pour out his heart and make known his thoughts to us. To receive his advice, we must be willing to listen, refusing to let pride stand in our way. Pride is thinking more highly of our own wisdom and desires than of God's. If we think we know better than God or feel we have no need of God's direction, we have fallen into foolish and disastrous pride.

When distress and anguish come upon you.
28 "Then they will call on me, but I will not answer;
They will seek me diligently but they will not find me,
29 Because they hated knowledge
And did not choose the fear of the LORD.
30 "They would not accept my counsel,
They spurned all my reproof.
31 "So they shall eat of the fruit of their own way
And be satiated with their own devices.
32 "For the waywardness of the naive will kill them,
And the complacency of fools will destroy them.
33 "But he who listens to me shall live securely
And will be at ease from the dread of evil."

The Pursuit of Wisdom Brings Security

2 My son, if you will receive my words
And treasure my commandments within you,
2 Make your ear attentive to wisdom,
Incline your heart to understanding;
3 For if you cry for discernment,
Lift your voice for understanding;
4 If you seek her as silver
And search for her as for hidden treasures;
5 Then you will discern the fear of the LORD
And discover the knowledge of God.
6 For the LORD gives wisdom;
From His mouth *come* knowledge and understanding.
7 He stores up sound wisdom for the upright;
He is a shield to those who walk in integrity,
8 Guarding the paths of justice,
And He preserves the way of His godly ones.
9 Then you will discern righteousness and justice
And equity *and* every good course.
10 For wisdom will enter your heart
And knowledge will be pleasant to your soul;
11 Discretion will guard you,
Understanding will watch over you,
12 To deliver you from the way of evil,
From the man who speaks perverse things;
13 From those who leave the paths of uprightness
To walk in the ways of darkness;
14 Who delight in doing evil
And rejoice in the perversity of evil;

1:28 Ps 18:41; Is 1:15; Jer 11:11; 14:12; Ezek 8:18; Mic 3:4; Zech 7:13; James 4:3; Prov 8:17

1:29 Job 21:14; Prov 1:22

1:30 Ps 81:11; Prov 1:25

1:31 Job 4:8; Prov 5:22, 23; 22:8; Is 3:11; Jer 6:19; Prov 14:14

1:33 Ps 25:12, 13; Prov 3:24-26

2:1 Prov 4:10; Prov 3:1

2:2 Prov 22:17

2:4 Prov 3:14; Job 3:21; Matt 13:44

2:5 Prov 1:7

2:6 1 Kin 3:12; Job 32:8; James 1:5

2:7 Ps 84:11; Prov 30:5

2:8 1 Sam 2:9; Ps 66:9

2:9 Prov 8:20; Prov 4:18

2:10 Prov 14:33; Prov 22:18

2:11 Prov 4:6; 6:22

2:12 Prov 28:26; Prov 6:12

2:13 Prov 21:16; Ps 82:5; Prov 4:19; John 3:19, 20

2:14 Prov 10:23; Jer 11:15

1:31–32 Many proverbs point out that the "fruit of their own way" will be the consequences people will experience in this life. Faced with either choosing God's wisdom or persisting in rebellious independence, many decide to go it alone. The problems such people create for themselves will destroy them. Don't ignore God's advice even if it is painful for the present. It will keep you from greater pain in the future.

2:3–6 Wisdom comes in two ways: It is a God-given gift and also the result of an energetic search. Wisdom's starting point is God and his revealed Word, the source of "knowledge and understanding" (2:6). In that sense, wisdom is his gift to us. But he gives it only to those who earnestly seek it. Because God's wisdom is hidden from the rebellious and foolish, it takes effort to find it and use it. The pathway to wisdom is strenuous. When we are on the path, we discover that true wisdom is God's and that he will guide us and reward our sincere and persistent search.

2:6–7 God gives us wisdom and victory but not for drifting through life or acting irresponsibly with his gifts and resources. If we are faithful and keep our purpose in life clearly in mind, he will keep us from pride and greed.

2:9–10 We gain wisdom through a constant process of growing. First, we must trust and honor God. Second, we must realize that the Bible reveals God's wisdom to us. Third, we must make a lifelong series of right choices and avoid moral pitfalls. Fourth, when we make sinful or mistaken choices, we must learn from our errors and recover. People don't develop all aspects of wisdom at once. For example, some people have more insight than discretion; others have more knowledge than common sense. But we can pray for all aspects of wisdom and take the steps to develop them in our lives.

2:11 Discretion is the ability to tell right from wrong. It enables the believer to detect evil motives in men (2:12) and women (2:16). With practice it helps us evaluate courses of action and consequences. For some it is a gift; for most it is developed by using God's truth to make wise choices day by day. Hebrews 5:14 emphasizes that we must train ourselves in order to have discretion.

2:15 Ps 125:5; Prov 21:8
2:16 Prov 6:24; 7:5
2:17 Mal 2:14, 15; Gen 2:24
2:19 Eccl 7:26; Ps 16:11; Prov 5:6
2:20 Heb 6:12; Prov 4:18
2:21 Ps 37:9, 29; Prov 10:30; Prov 28:10
2:22 Ps 37:38; Prov 10:30; Prov 11:3; Deut 28:63; Ps 52:5
3:1 Ps 119:61; Prov 4:5; Ex 20:6; Deut 30:16
3:2 Ps 91:16; Prov 3:16; 4:10; 9:11; 10:27
3:3 Prov 1:9; 6:21; Prov 7:3; Jer 17:1

15 Whose paths are crooked,
And who are devious in their ways;
16 To deliver you from the strange woman,
From the adulteress who flatters with her words;
17 That leaves the companion of her youth
And forgets the covenant of her God;
18 For her house sinks down to death
And her tracks *lead* to the dead;
19 None who go to her return again,
Nor do they reach the paths of life.
20 So you will walk in the way of good men
And keep to the paths of the righteous.
21 For the upright will live in the land
And the blameless will remain in it;
22 But the wicked will be cut off from the land
And the treacherous will be uprooted from it.

The Rewards of Wisdom

3 My son, do not forget my teaching,
But let your heart keep my commandments;
2 For length of days and years of life
And peace they will add to you.
3 Do not let kindness and truth leave you;

PEOPLE CALLED "WISE" IN THE BIBLE
The special description "wise" is used for 12 significant people in the Bible. They can be helpful models in our own pursuit of wisdom.

The Person	*Their Role*	*Reference*	*How They Practiced Wisdom*
Joseph	Wise leader	Acts 7:10	Prepared for a major famine. Helped rule Egypt.
Moses	Wise leader	Acts 7:20–22	Learned all the Egyptian wisdom, then graduated to God's lessons in wisdom to lead Israel out of Egypt.
Bezalel	Wise artist	Exodus 31:1–5	Designed and supervised the construction of the tabernacle and its utensils in the wilderness.
Joshua	Wise leader	Deuteronomy 34:9	Learned by observing Moses, obeyed God, led the people into the promised land.
David	Wise leader	2 Samuel 14:20	Never let his failures keep him from the source of wisdom—reverence for God.
Abigail	Wise wife	1 Samuel 25:3	Managed her household well in spite of a surly and mean husband.
Solomon	Wise leader	1 Kings 3:5–14; 4:29–34	Knew what to do even though he often failed to put his own wisdom into action.
Daniel	Wise counselor	Daniel 5:11–12	Known as a man in touch with God. A solver of complex problems with God's help.
Magi	Wise learners	Matthew 2:1–12	Not only received special knowledge of God's visit to earth, but checked it out personally.
Stephen	Wise leader	Acts 6:8–10	Organized the distribution of food to the Grecian widows. Preached the gospel to the Jews.
Paul	Wise messenger	2 Peter 3:15–16	Spent his life communicating God's love to all who would listen.
Christ	Wise youth, Wise Savior, Wisdom of God	Luke 2:40, 52; 1 Corinthians 1:20–25	Not only lived a perfect life, but died on the cross to save us and make God's wise plan of eternal life available to us.

2:16–17 An *adulteress* is a seductive woman or a prostitute. Two of the most difficult sins to resist are pride and sexual immorality. Both are seductive. Pride says, "I deserve it"; sexual desire says, "I need it." In combination, their appeal is deadly. In fact, says Solomon, only by relying on God's strength can we overcome them. Pride appeals to the empty head; sexual enticement to the empty heart. By looking to God, we can fill our heads with his wisdom and our hearts with his love. Don't be fooled—remember what God says about who you are and what you were meant to be. Ask him for strength to resist these temptations.

3:3 Kindness and truth are important character qualities. Both involve actions as well as attitudes. A kind person acts with compassion and love. A truthful person not only believes the truth; he or she also works for justice for others. Thoughts and words are not enough—our lives reveal whether we are truly kind and truthful. Do your actions measure up to your attitudes?

Bind them around your neck,
Write them on the tablet of your heart.
4 So you will find favor and good repute
In the sight of God and man.
5 Trust in the LORD with all your heart
And do not lean on your own understanding.
6 In all your ways acknowledge Him,
And He will make your paths straight.
7 Do not be wise in your own eyes;
Fear the LORD and turn away from evil.
8 It will be healing to your body
And refreshment to your bones.
9 Honor the LORD from your wealth
And from the first of all your produce;
10 So your barns will be filled with plenty
And your vats will overflow with new wine.
11 My son, do not reject the discipline of the LORD
Or loathe His reproof,
12 For whom the LORD loves He reproves,
Even as a father *corrects* the son in whom he delights.

13 How blessed is the man who finds wisdom
And the man who gains understanding.
14 For her profit is better than the profit of silver
And her gain better than fine gold.
15 She is more precious than jewels;
And nothing you desire compares with her.
16 Long life is in her right hand;
In her left hand are riches and honor.
17 Her ways are pleasant ways
And all her paths are peace.

3:4 1 Sam 2:26; Prov 8:35; Luke 2:52

3:5 Ps 37:3, 5; Prov 22:19; Prov 23:4; Jer 9:23

3:6 Prov 16:3; Phil 4:6; James 1:5

3:7 Rom 12:16; Job 1:1; 28:28; Prov 8:13

3:8 Prov 4:22; Job 21:24

3:9 Is 43:23; Ex 23:19; Deut 26:2; Mal 3:10

3:10 Deut 28:8; Joel 2:24

3:11 Job 5:17; Heb 12:5

3:12 Rev 3:19; Prov 13:24

3:13 Prov 8:32, 34

3:14 Job 28:15-19; Prov 8:10, 19; 16:16

3:15 Job 28:18; Prov 8:11

3:16 Prov 8:18; 22:4

3:17 Matt 11:29; Ps 119:165; Prov 16:7

3:5–6 *Leaning* has the sense of putting your whole weight on something, resting on and trusting in that person or thing. When we have an important decision to make, we sometimes feel that we can't trust anyone—not even God. But God knows what is best for us. He is a better judge of what we want than even we are! We must trust him completely in every choice we make. We should not omit careful thinking or belittle our God-given ability to reason, but neither should we trust our own ideas to the exclusion of all others. We must not be wise in our own eyes. We should always be willing to listen to and be corrected by God's Word and wise counselors. Bring your decisions to God in prayer, use the Bible as your guide, and then follow God's leading. He will make your paths straight by both guiding and protecting you.

3:6 To receive God's guidance, said Solomon, we must acknowledge God in all our ways. This means turning every area of life over to him. About a thousand years later, Jesus emphasized this same truth (Matthew 6:33). Look at your values and priorities. What is important to you? In what areas have you not acknowledged him? What is his advice? In many areas of your life you may already acknowledge God, but it is the areas where you attempt to restrict or ignore his influence that will cause you grief. Make him a vital part of everything you do; then he will guide you because you will be working to accomplish his purposes.

3:9–10 The first of all your produce refers to the practice of giving to God's use the first and best portion of the harvest (Deuteronomy 26:9–11). Many people give God their leftovers. If they can afford to donate anything, they do so. These people may be sincere and contribute willingly, but their attitude is nonetheless backward. It is better to give God the first part of our income. This demonstrates that God, not possessions, has first place in our lives and that our resources belong to him (we are only managers of God's resources). Giving to God first helps us conquer greed, helps us properly manage God's resources, and opens us up to receive God's special blessings.

3:11–12 Since righteous people are not always prosperous, we are to regard adversity as discipline. *Discipline* means "to teach and to train." Discipline sounds negative to many people because some disciplinarians are not loving. God, however, is the source of all love. He doesn't punish us because he enjoys inflicting pain but because he is deeply concerned about our development. He knows that in order to become morally strong and good, we must learn the difference between right and wrong. His loving discipline enables us to do that.

3:11–12 It's difficult to know when God has been disciplining us until we look back on the situation later. Not every calamity comes directly from God, of course. But if we rebel against God and refuse to repent when God has identified some sin in our lives, he may use guilt, crises, or bad experiences to bring us back to him. Sometimes, however, difficult times come even when there is no flagrant sin in our lives. Then, our response should be patience, integrity, and confidence that God will show us what to do.

3:16–17 Proverbs contains many strong statements about the benefits of wisdom, including long life, wealth, honor, and peace. If you aren't experiencing them, does this mean you are short on wisdom? Not necessarily. Instead of guarantees, these statements are general principles. In a perfect world, wise behavior would always lead to these benefits. Even in our troubled world, living wisely usually results in obvious blessings—but not always. Sometimes sin intervenes, and some blessings must be delayed until Jesus returns to establish his eternal kingdom. That is why we must "walk by faith, not by sight" (2 Corinthians 5:7). We can be sure that wisdom ultimately leads to blessing.

18 She is a tree of life to those who take hold of her,
And happy are all who hold her fast.
19 The LORD by wisdom founded the earth,
By understanding He established the heavens.
20 By His knowledge the deeps were broken up
And the skies drip with dew.
21 My son, let them not vanish from your sight;
Keep sound wisdom and discretion,
22 So they will be life to your soul
And adornment to your neck.
23 Then you will walk in your way securely
And your foot will not stumble.
24 When you lie down, you will not be afraid;
When you lie down, your sleep will be sweet.
25 Do not be afraid of sudden fear
Nor of the onslaught of the wicked when it comes;
26 For the LORD will be your confidence
And will keep your foot from being caught.

27 Do not withhold good from those to whom it is due,
When it is in your power to do *it.*
28 Do not say to your neighbor, "Go, and come back,
And tomorrow I will give *it,*"
When you have it with you.
29 Do not devise harm against your neighbor,
While he lives securely beside you.
30 Do not contend with a man without cause,
If he has done you no harm.
31 Do not envy a man of violence
And do not choose any of his ways.
32 For the devious are an abomination to the LORD;
But He is intimate with the upright.
33 The curse of the LORD is on the house of the wicked,
But He blesses the dwelling of the righteous.
34 Though He scoffs at the scoffers,
Yet He gives grace to the afflicted.
35 The wise will inherit honor,
But fools display dishonor.

3:18 Gen 2:9; Prov 11:30; 13:12; 15:4; Rev 2:7
3:19 Ps 104:24; Prov 8:27; Prov 8:27, 28
3:20 Gen 7:11; Deut 33:28; Job 36:28
3:21 Prov 4:21
3:22 Deut 32:47; Prov 4:22; 8:35; 16:22; 21:21; Prov 1:9
3:23 Prov 4:12; 10:9; Ps 91:12; Is 5:27; 63:13
3:24 Job 11:19; Ps 3:5; Prov 1:33; 6:22
3:25 Ps 91:5; 1 Pet 3:14; Job 5:21
3:27 Rom 13:7; Gal 6:10
3:28 Lev 19:13; Deut 24:15
3:29 Prov 6:14; 14:22
3:30 Prov 26:17; Rom 12:18
3:31 Ps 37:1; Prov 24:1
3:32 Prov 11:20; Job 29:4; Ps 25:14
3:33 Lev 26:14, 16; Deut 11:28; Zech 5:3, 4; Mal 2:2; Job 8:6; Ps 1:3
3:34 James 4:6; 1 Pet 5:5

WISDOM: APPLIED TRUTH
The book of Proverbs tells us about people who have wisdom and enjoy its benefits.

Reference	*The Person Who Has Wisdom*	*Benefits of Wisdom*
Proverbs 3—4 A father's instructions	Is loving	Long, prosperous life
	Is faithful	Favor with God and people
	Trusts in the Lord	Reputation for good judgment
	Puts God first	Success
	Turns away from evil	Health, vitality
	Knows right from wrong	Riches, honor, pleasure, peace
	Listens and learns	Protection
	Does what is right	
Proverbs 8—9 Wisdom speaks	Possesses knowledge and discretion	Riches, honor
	Hates pride, arrogance, and evil behavior	Justice
	Respects and fears God	Righteousness
	Gives good advice and has common sense	Life
	Loves correction and is teachable	God's favor
	Knows God	Constant learning
		Understanding

3:27–28 Withholding good is inconsiderate and unfair, whether it is repaying a loan, returning a tool, or fulfilling a promise. Withholding destroys trust and creates a great inconvenience. Be as eager to do good as you are to have good done to you.

A Father's Instruction

4 Hear, *O* sons, the instruction of a father,
And give attention that you may gain understanding,
2 For I give you sound teaching;
Do not abandon my instruction.
3 When I was a son to my father,
Tender and the only son in the sight of my mother,
4 Then he taught me and said to me,
"Let your heart hold fast my words;
Keep my commandments and live;
5 Acquire wisdom! Acquire understanding!
Do not forget nor turn away from the words of my mouth.
6 "Do not forsake her, and she will guard you;
Love her, and she will watch over you.
7 "The beginning of wisdom *is:* Acquire wisdom;
And with all your acquiring, get understanding.
8 "Prize her, and she will exalt you;
She will honor you if you embrace her.
9 "She will place on your head a garland of grace;
She will present you with a crown of beauty."

10 Hear, my son, and accept my sayings
And the years of your life will be many.
11 I have directed you in the way of wisdom;
I have led you in upright paths.
12 When you walk, your steps will not be impeded;
And if you run, you will not stumble.
13 Take hold of instruction; do not let go.
Guard her, for she is your life.
14 Do not enter the path of the wicked
And do not proceed in the way of evil men.
15 Avoid it, do not pass by it;
Turn away from it and pass on.
16 For they cannot sleep unless they do evil;
And they are robbed of sleep unless they make *someone* stumble.
17 For they eat the bread of wickedness
And drink the wine of violence.
18 But the path of the righteous is like the light of dawn,
That shines brighter and brighter until the full day.
19 The way of the wicked is like darkness;
They do not know over what they stumble.

4:1 Ps 34:11; Prov 1:8; Prov 1:2; 2:2
4:2 Deut 32:2; Job 11:4; Ps 89:30; 119:87; Prov 3:1
4:3 1 Chr 22:5; 29:1; Zech 12:10
4:4 Eph 6:4; Ps 119:168; Prov 7:2
4:5 Prov 4:7; Prov 16:16
4:6 2 Thess 2:10
4:7 Prov 8:23; Prov 23:23
4:8 1 Sam 2:30
4:9 Prov 1:9
4:10 Prov 2:1; Prov 3:2
4:11 1 Sam 12:23
4:12 Job 18:7; Ps 18:36; Ps 91:11; Prov 3:23
4:13 Prov 3:18; Prov 3:22; John 6:63
4:14 Ps 1:1; Prov 1:15
4:16 Ps 36:4; Mic 2:1
4:17 Prov 13:2
4:18 Is 26:7; Matt 5:14; Phil 2:15; 2 Sam 23:4; Dan 12:3; Job 11:17
4:19 Job 18:5, 6; Prov 2:13; Is 59:9, 10; Jer 23:12; John 12:35; John 11:10

4:3–4 One of the greatest responsibilities of parents is to encourage their children to become wise. Here Solomon tells how his father, David, encouraged him to seek wisdom when he was young ("tender") (see 1 Kings 2:1–9 and 1 Chronicles 28—29 for David's charge to his son). This encouragement may have prompted Solomon to ask God for an understanding heart above everything else (1 Kings 3:9). Wisdom can be passed on from parents to children, from generation to generation. Ultimately, of course, all wisdom comes from God; parents can only urge their children to turn to him. If your parents never taught you in this way, God's Word can function as a loving and compassionate mother or father to you. You can learn from the Scriptures and then create a legacy of wisdom as you teach your own children.

4:5–7 If you want wisdom, you must decide to go after it. It takes resolve—a determination not to abandon the search once you begin no matter how difficult the road may become. This is not a once-in-a-lifetime step, but a daily process of choosing between two paths—the wicked (4:14–17, 19) and the righteous (4:18). Nothing else is more important or more valuable.

4:7 David taught Solomon as a young boy that seeking God's wisdom was the most important choice he could make. Solomon learned the lesson well. When God appeared to the new king to fulfill any request, Solomon chose wisdom above all else. We should also make God's wisdom our first choice. We don't have to wait for God to appear to us. We can boldly ask him for wisdom today through prayer. James 1:5 assures us that God will grant our request.

4:13–17 Even friends can make you fall. It is difficult for people to accept the fact that friends and acquaintances might be luring them to do wrong. Young people want to be accepted, so they would never want to confront or criticize a friend for wrong plans or actions. Many other people can't even see how their friends' actions could lead to trouble. While we should be accepting of others, we need a healthy skepticism about human behavior. When you feel yourself being heavily influenced, proceed with caution. Don't let your friends cause you to fall into sin.

4:20 Prov 5:1; Prov 2:2
4:21 Prov 3:21; Prov 7:1, 2
4:22 Prov 3:22; Prov 3:8; 12:18
4:23 Matt 12:34; 15:18, 19; Mark 7:21; Luke 6:45
4:24 Prov 6:12; 10:32; Prov 19:1
4:26 Prov 5:21; Heb 12:13; Ps 119:5
4:27 Deut 5:32; 28:14; Prov 1:15; Is 1:16

20 My son, give attention to my words;
Incline your ear to my sayings.
21 Do not let them depart from your sight;
Keep them in the midst of your heart.
22 For they are life to those who find them
And health to all their body.
23 Watch over your heart with all diligence,
For from it *flow* the springs of life.
24 Put away from you a deceitful mouth
And put devious speech far from you.
25 Let your eyes look directly ahead
And let your gaze be fixed straight in front of you.
26 Watch the path of your feet
And all your ways will be established.
27 Do not turn to the right nor to the left;
Turn your foot from evil.

Pitfalls of Immorality

5:1 Prov 4:20; Prov 22:17
5:2 Prov 3:21; Mal 2:7
5:3 Prov 2:16; 5:20; 7:5; 22:14; Song 4:11; Ps 55:21
5:4 Eccl 7:26; Ps 57:4; Heb 4:12
5:5 Prov 7:27
5:6 Prov 4:26; 5:21; 2 Pet 2:14; Prov 30:20
5:7 Prov 7:24; Ps 119:102
5:8 Prov 7:25; Prov 9:14

5 My son, give attention to my wisdom,
Incline your ear to my understanding;
2 That you may observe discretion
And your lips may reserve knowledge.
3 For the lips of an adulteress drip honey
And smoother than oil is her speech;
4 But in the end she is bitter as wormwood,
Sharp as a two-edged sword.
5 Her feet go down to death,
Her steps take hold of Sheol.
6 She does not ponder the path of life;
Her ways are unstable, she does not know *it.*

7 Now then, *my* sons, listen to me
And do not depart from the words of my mouth.
8 Keep your way far from her
And do not go near the door of her house,
9 Or you will give your vigor to others
And your years to the cruel one;
10 And strangers will be filled with your strength

STRATEGY FOR EFFECTIVE LIVING			
	Begins with	God's Wisdom	Respecting and appreciating who God is. Reverence and awe in recognizing the almighty God.
	Requires	Moral Application	Trusting in God and his Word. Allowing his Word to speak to us personally. Willing to obey.
	Requires	Practical Application	Acting on God's direction in daily devotions.
	Results in	Effective Living	Experiencing what God does with our obedience.

4:23–27 Our heart—our feelings of love and desire—dictates to a great extent how we live because we always find time to do what we enjoy. Solomon tells us to guard our heart above all else, making sure we concentrate on those desires that will keep us on the right path. Make sure your affections push you in the right direction. Put boundaries on your desires: Don't go after everything you see. Look straight ahead, keep your eyes fixed on your goal, and don't get sidetracked on detours that lead to sin.

5:3 This "adulteress" is a prostitute. Proverbs includes many warnings against illicit sex for several reasons. First, a prostitute's charm is used as an example of any temptation to do wrong or to leave the pursuit of wisdom. Second, sexual immorality of any kind was and still is extremely dangerous. It destroys family life. It erodes a person's ability to love. It degrades human beings and turns them into objects. It can lead to disease. It can result in unwanted children. Third, sexual immorality is against God's law.

5:3–8 Any person should be on guard against those who use flattery and smooth speech (lips that drip honey) that would lead him or her into sin. The best advice is to take a detour and even avoid conversation with such people.

And your hard-earned goods *will go* to the house of an alien;
11 And you groan at your final end,
When your flesh and your body are consumed;
12 And you say, "How I have hated instruction!
And my heart spurned reproof!
13 "I have not listened to the voice of my teachers,
Nor inclined my ear to my instructors!
14 "I was almost in utter ruin
In the midst of the assembly and congregation."

15 Drink water from your own cistern
And fresh water from your own well.
16 Should your springs be dispersed abroad,
Streams of water in the streets?
17 Let them be yours alone
And not for strangers with you.
18 Let your fountain be blessed,
And rejoice in the wife of your youth.
19 *As* a loving hind and a graceful doe,
Let her breasts satisfy you at all times;
Be exhilarated always with her love.
20 For why should you, my son, be exhilarated with an adulteress
And embrace the bosom of a foreigner?
21 For the ways of a man are before the eyes of the LORD,
And He watches all his paths.
22 His own iniquities will capture the wicked,
And he will be held with the cords of his sin.
23 He will die for lack of instruction,
And in the greatness of his folly he will go astray.

Parental Counsel

6 My son, if you have become surety for your neighbor,
Have given a pledge for a stranger,
2 *If* you have been snared with the words of your mouth,
Have been caught with the words of your mouth,
3 Do this then, my son, and deliver yourself;
Since you have come into the hand of your neighbor,
Go, humble yourself, and importune your neighbor.
4 Give no sleep to your eyes,
Nor slumber to your eyelids;

5:12 Prov 1:7, 22, 29; Prov 1:25; 12:1

5:13 Prov 1:8

5:16 Prov 5:18; 9:17; Song 4:12, 15

5:18 Prov 9:17; Song 4:12, 15; Eccl 9:9; Mal 2:14

5:19 Song 2:9, 17; 4:5; 7:3

5:20 Prov 5:3; Prov 2:16; 6:24; 7:5; 23:27

5:21 Job 14:16; 31:4; 34:21; Ps 119:168; Prov 15:3; Jer 16:17; 32:19; Hos 7:2; Heb 4:13; Prov 4:26

5:22 Num 32:23; Ps 7:15; 9:15; 40:12; Prov 1:31, 32

5:23 Job 4:21; 36:12

6:1 Prov 11:15; 17:18; 20:16; 22:26; 27:13

6:4 Ps 132:4

5:11–13 At the end of your life, it will be too late to ask for advice. When desire is fully activated, people don't want advice—they want satisfaction. The best time to learn the dangers and foolishness of going after forbidden sex (or anything else that is harmful) is long before the temptation comes. Resistance is easier if the decision has already been made. Don't wait to see what happens. Prepare for temptation by deciding *now* how you will act when you face it.

5:15 "Drink water from your own cistern" is a picture of faithfulness in marriage. It means to enjoy the spouse God has given you. In desert lands, water is precious, and a well is a family's most important possession. In Old Testament times, it was considered a crime to steal water from someone else's well, just as it was a crime to have intercourse with another man's wife. In both cases, the offender is endangering the health and security of family.

5:15–21 In contrast to much of what we read, see, and hear today, this passage urges couples to look to each other for lifelong satisfaction and companionship. Many temptations entice husbands and wives to desert each other for excitement and pleasures to be found elsewhere when marriage becomes dull. But God designed marriage and sanctified it, and only within this covenant relationship can we find real love and fulfillment. Don't let God's best for you be wasted on the illusion of greener pastures somewhere else. Instead, rejoice with your spouse as you give yourselves to God and to each other.

5:18–20 God does not intend faithfulness in marriage to be boring, lifeless, pleasureless, and dull. Sex is a gift God gives to married people for their mutual enjoyment. Real happiness comes when we decide to find pleasure in the relationship God has given or will give us and to commit ourselves to making it pleasurable for our spouse. The real danger is in doubting that God knows and cares for us. We then may resent his timing and carelessly pursue sexual pleasure without his blessing.

5:19 See Song of Solomon, chapter 4, for parallels to this frank expression of the joys of sexual pleasure in marriage.

6:1–5 These verses are not a plea against generosity, but against overextending one's financial resources and acting in irresponsible ways that could lead to poverty. It is important to maintain a balance between generosity and good stewardship. God wants us to help our friends and the needy, but he does not promise to cover the costs of every unwise commitment we make. We should also act responsibly so that our family does not suffer.

6:5 Ps 91:3; 124:7

6:6 Prov 30:24, 25; Prov 6:9; 10:26; 13:4; 20:4; 26:16

6:7 Prov 30:27

6:8 Prov 10:5

6:10 Prov 24:33

6:11 Prov 24:34

6:12 Prov 16:27; Prov 4:24; 10:32

6:13 Job 15:12; Ps 35:19; Prov 10:10

6:14 Prov 17:20; Prov 3:29; Mic 2:1; Prov 6:19; 16:28

6:15 Prov 24:22; Is 30:13, 14; Jer 19:11; 2 Chr 36:16

6:17 Ps 18:27; 101:5; Prov 21:4; 30:13; Ps 31:18; 120:2; Prov 12:22; 17:7; Deut 19:10; Prov 28:17; Is 1:15; 59:7

6:18 Gen 6:5; Prov 24:2; Prov 1:16; Is 59:7; Rom 3:15

6:19 Ps 27:12; Prov 12:17; 19:5, 9; 21:28; Prov 6:14

6:20 Eph 6:1

6:21 Prov 3:3

5 Deliver yourself like a gazelle from *the hunter's* hand
And like a bird from the hand of the fowler.

6 Go to the ant, O sluggard,
Observe her ways and be wise,
7 Which, having no chief,
Officer or ruler,
8 Prepares her food in the summer
And gathers her provision in the harvest.
9 How long will you lie down, O sluggard?
When will you arise from your sleep?
10 "A little sleep, a little slumber,
A little folding of the hands to rest"—
11 Your poverty will come in like a vagabond
And your need like an armed man.

12 A worthless person, a wicked man,
Is the one who walks with a perverse mouth,
13 Who winks with his eyes, who signals with his feet,
Who points with his fingers;
14 Who *with* perversity in his heart continually devises evil,
Who spreads strife.
15 Therefore his calamity will come suddenly;
Instantly he will be broken and there will be no healing.

16 There are six things which the LORD hates,
Yes, seven which are an abomination to Him:
17 Haughty eyes, a lying tongue,
And hands that shed innocent blood,
18 A heart that devises wicked plans,
Feet that run rapidly to evil,
19 A false witness *who* utters lies,
And one who spreads strife among brothers.

20 My son, observe the commandment of your father
And do not forsake the teaching of your mother;
21 Bind them continually on your heart;
Tie them around your neck.

THINGS GOD HATES
The book of Proverbs notes 14 types of people and actions that God hates. Let these be guidelines of what we are not to be and do!

Violent people	Proverbs 3:31
Haughtiness, lying, murdering, scheming, eagerness to do evil, a false witness, stirring up strife	Proverbs 6:16–19
Those who are untruthful	Proverbs 12:22
The sacrifice of the wicked	Proverbs 15:8
The way of the wicked	Proverbs 15:9
The evil plans of the wicked	Proverbs 15:26
Those who are proud	Proverbs 16:5
Those who judge unjustly	Proverbs 17:15

6:6–11 Those last few moments of sleep are delicious—we savor them as we resist beginning another workday. But Proverbs warns against giving in to the temptation of laziness, of sleeping instead of working. This does not mean we should never rest: God gave the Jews the Sabbath, a weekly day of rest and restoration. But we should not rest when we should be working. The ant is used as an example because it utilizes its energy and resources economically. If laziness turns us from our responsibilities, poverty may soon bar us from the legitimate rest we should enjoy. (See also the chart in chapter 28.)

6:20–23 It is natural and good for children, as they grow toward adulthood, to become increasingly independent of their parents. Young adults, however, should take care not to turn a deaf ear to their parents—to reject their advice just when it is needed most. If you are struggling with a decision or looking for insight, check with your parents or other older adults who know you well. Their extra years of experience may have given them the wisdom you seek.

22 When you walk about, they will guide you;
When you sleep, they will watch over you;
And when you awake, they will talk to you.
23 For the commandment is a lamp and the teaching is light;
And reproofs for discipline are the way of life
24 To keep you from the evil woman,
From the smooth tongue of the adulteress.
25 Do not desire her beauty in your heart,
Nor let her capture you with her eyelids.
26 For on account of a harlot *one is reduced* to a loaf of bread,
And an adulteress hunts for the precious life.
27 Can a man take fire in his bosom
And his clothes not be burned?
28 Or can a man walk on hot coals
And his feet not be scorched?
29 So is the one who goes in to his neighbor's wife;
Whoever touches her will not go unpunished.
30 Men do not despise a thief if he steals
To satisfy himself when he is hungry;
31 But when he is found, he must repay sevenfold;
He must give all the substance of his house.
32 The one who commits adultery with a woman is lacking sense;
He who would destroy himself does it.
33 Wounds and disgrace he will find,
And his reproach will not be blotted out.
34 For jealousy enrages a man,
And he will not spare in the day of vengeance.
35 He will not accept any ransom,
Nor will he be satisfied though you give many gifts.

6:22 Prov 3:23
6:23 Ps 19:8; 119:105
6:24 Prov 5:3; 7:5, 21
6:25 Matt 5:28; 2 Kin 9:30; Jer 4:30; Ezek 23:40
6:26 Prov 5:9, 10; 29:3; Prov 7:23; Ezek 13:18
6:29 Ezek 18:6; 33:26; Prov 16:5
6:30 Job 38:39
6:31 Ex 22:1-4
6:32 Prov 7:7; 9:4, 16; 10:13, 21; 11:12; 12:11; Prov 7:22, 23
6:34 Prov 27:4; Song 8:6; Prov 11:4

The Wiles of the Harlot

7 My son, keep my words
And treasure my commandments within you.
2 Keep my commandments and live,
And my teaching as the apple of your eye.
3 Bind them on your fingers;
Write them on the tablet of your heart.
4 Say to wisdom, "You are my sister,"
And call understanding *your* intimate friend;
5 That they may keep you from an adulteress,
From the foreigner who flatters with her words.

6 For at the window of my house
I looked out through my lattice,
7 And I saw among the naive,
And discerned among the youths
A young man lacking sense,

7:1 Prov 2:1; 6:20
7:2 Prov 4:4; Deut 32:10; Ps 17:8; Zech 2:8
7:3 Deut 6:8; 11:18; Prov 6:21; Prov 3:3
7:6 Judg 5:28; Song 2:9
7:7 Prov 1:22; Prov 6:32; 9:4

6:25 Regard lust as a warning sign of danger ahead. When you notice that you are attracted to a person of the opposite sex or preoccupied with thoughts of him or her, your desires may lead you to sin. Ask God to help you change your desires before you are drawn into sin.

6:25–35 Some people argue that it is all right to break God's law against sexual sin if nobody gets hurt. In truth, somebody always gets hurt. Spouses are devastated. Children are scarred. The partners themselves, even if they escape disease and unwanted pregnancy, lose their ability to fulfill commitments, to feel sexual desire, to trust, and to be entirely open with another person. God's laws are not arbitrary. They do not forbid good, clean fun; rather, they warn us against destroying ourselves through unwise actions or running ahead of God's timetable.

7:6–23 Although this advice is directed toward young men, young women should heed it as well. The person who has no purpose in life lacks sense (7:7). Without aim or direction, an empty life is unstable, vulnerable to many temptations. Even though the young man in this passage doesn't know where he is going, the adulteress knows where she wants him. Notice her strategies: She is dressed to allure men (7:10); her approach is bold (7:13); She invites him over to her place (7:16–18); she cunningly answers his every objection (7:19, 20); she persuades him with smooth talk (7:21); she traps him (7:23). To combat temptation, make sure your life is full of God's Word and wisdom (7:4). Recognize the strategies of temptation, and run away from them—fast.

7:8 Prov 7:12; Prov 7:27
7:9 Job 24:15
7:10 Gen 38:14, 15; 1 Tim 2:9
7:11 Prov 9:13; 1 Tim 5:13; Titus 2:5
7:12 Prov 9:14; Prov 23:28
7:13 Prov 21:29
7:14 Lev 7:11; Lev 7:16
7:16 Prov 31:22; Is 19:9; Ezek 27:7
7:17 Ps 45:8; Ex 30:23
7:20 Gen 42:35
7:21 Prov 5:3; 6:24
7:23 Eccl 9:12
7:24 Prov 5:7
7:25 Prov 5:8
7:26 Prov 9:18
7:27 Prov 2:18; 5:5; 9:18; 1 Cor 6:9, 10; Rev 22:15
8:1 Prov 1:20, 21; 8:1-3; 9:3; 1 Cor 1:24
8:2 Prov 9:3, 14
8:3 Job 29:7

8 Passing through the street near her corner;
And he takes the way to her house,
9 In the twilight, in the evening,
In the middle of the night and *in* the darkness.
10 And behold, a woman *comes* to meet him,
Dressed as a harlot and cunning of heart.
11 She is boisterous and rebellious,
Her feet do not remain at home;
12 *She is* now in the streets, now in the squares,
And lurks by every corner.
13 So she seizes him and kisses him
And with a brazen face she says to him:
14 "I was due to offer peace offerings;
Today I have paid my vows.
15 "Therefore I have come out to meet you,
To seek your presence earnestly, and I have found you.
16 "I have spread my couch with coverings,
With colored linens of Egypt.
17 "I have sprinkled my bed
With myrrh, aloes and cinnamon.
18 "Come, let us drink our fill of love until morning;
Let us delight ourselves with caresses.
19 "For my husband is not at home,
He has gone on a long journey;
20 He has taken a bag of money with him,
At the full moon he will come home."
21 With her many persuasions she entices him;
With her flattering lips she seduces him.
22 Suddenly he follows her
As an ox goes to the slaughter,
Or as *one in* fetters to the discipline of a fool,
23 Until an arrow pierces through his liver;
As a bird hastens to the snare,
So he does not know that it *will cost him* his life.

24 Now therefore, *my* sons, listen to me,
And pay attention to the words of my mouth.
25 Do not let your heart turn aside to her ways,
Do not stray into her paths.
26 For many are the victims she has cast down,
And numerous are all her slain.
27 Her house is the way to Sheol,
Descending to the chambers of death.

The Commendation of Wisdom

8 Does not wisdom call,
And understanding lift up her voice?
2 On top of the heights beside the way,
Where the paths meet, she takes her stand;
3 Beside the gates, at the opening to the city,
At the entrance of the doors, she cries out:
4 "To you, O men, I call,

7:25–27 There are definite steps you can take to avoid sexual sins. First, guard your mind. Don't read books, look at pictures, or encourage fantasies that stimulate the wrong desires. Second, keep away from settings and friends that tempt you to sin. Third, don't think only of the moment—focus on the future. Today's thrill may lead to tomorrow's ruin.

8:1ff Wisdom's call is contrasted to the call of the adulteress in chapter 7. Wisdom is portrayed as a woman who guides us (8:1–13) and makes us succeed (8:14–21). Wisdom was present at the creation and works with the Creator (8:22–31). God approves of those who listen to wisdom's counsel (8:32–35). Those who hate wisdom love death (8:36). Wisdom should affect every aspect of our entire life, from beginning to end. Be sure to open all corners of your life to God's direction and guidance.

And my voice is to the sons of men.
5 "O naive ones, understand prudence;
And, O fools, understand wisdom.
6 "Listen, for I will speak noble things;
And the opening of my lips *will reveal* right things.
7 "For my mouth will utter truth;
And wickedness is an abomination to my lips.
8 "All the utterances of my mouth are in righteousness;
There is nothing crooked or perverted in them.
9 "They are all straightforward to him who understands,
And right to those who find knowledge.
10 "Take my instruction and not silver,
And knowledge rather than choicest gold.
11 "For wisdom is better than jewels;
And all desirable things cannot compare with her.

12 "I, wisdom, dwell with prudence,
And I find knowledge *and* discretion.
13 "The fear of the LORD is to hate evil;
Pride and arrogance and the evil way
And the perverted mouth, I hate.
14 "Counsel is mine and sound wisdom;
I am understanding, power is mine.
15 "By me kings reign,
And rulers decree justice.
16 "By me princes rule, and nobles,
All who judge rightly.
17 "I love those who love me;
And those who diligently seek me will find me.
18 "Riches and honor are with me,
Enduring wealth and righteousness.
19 "My fruit is better than gold, even pure gold,
And my yield *better* than choicest silver.
20 "I walk in the way of righteousness,
In the midst of the paths of justice,
21 To endow those who love me with wealth,
That I may fill their treasuries.

22 "The LORD possessed me at the beginning of His way,
Before His works of old.
23 "From everlasting I was established,
From the beginning, from the earliest times of the earth.
24 "When there were no depths I was brought forth,
When there were no springs abounding with water.
25 "Before the mountains were settled,
Before the hills I was brought forth;
26 While He had not yet made the earth and the fields,
Nor the first dust of the world.
27 "When He established the heavens, I was there,
When He inscribed a circle on the face of the deep,
28 When He made firm the skies above,
When the springs of the deep became fixed,
29 When He set for the sea its boundary
So that the water would not transgress His command,
When He marked out the foundations of the earth;

8:5 Prov 1:4; Prov 1:22, 32; 3:35

8:6 Prov 22:20; Prov 23:16

8:7 Ps 37:30; John 8:14; Rom 15:8

8:8 Deut 32:5; Prov 2:15; Phil 2:15

8:9 Prov 14:6; Prov 3:13

8:10 Prov 3:14, 15; 8:19

8:11 Job 28:15, 18; Ps 19:10; Prov 3:15

8:12 Prov 8:5; Prov 1:4

8:13 Prov 3:7; 16:6; 1 Sam 2:3; Prov 16:18; Is 13:11; Prov 15:9; Prov 6:12

8:14 Prov 1:25; 19:20; Is 28:29; Jer 32:19; Prov 2:7; 3:21; 18:1; Eccl 7:19; 9:16

8:15 2 Chr 1:10; Prov 29:4; Dan 2:21; Matt 28:18; Rom 13:1

8:17 1 Sam 2:30; Prov 4:6; John 14:21; Prov 2:4, 5; John 7:37; James 1:5

8:18 Prov 3:16; Ps 112:3; Matt 6:33

8:19 Job 28:15; Prov 3:14; Prov 10:20

8:21 Prov 24:4

8:22 Job 28:26-28; Ps 104:24; Prov 3:19

8:23 John 1:1-3; John 17:5

8:24 Gen 1:2; Ex 15:5; Job 38:16; Prov 3:20

8:25 Job 15:7; Ps 90:2

8:27 Prov 3:19; Job 26:10

8:29 Job 38:10; Ps 104:9; Job 38:6; Ps 104:5

8:13 The more a person fears and respects God, the more he or she will hate evil. Love for God and love for sin cannot coexist. Harboring secret sins means that you are tolerating evil within yourself. Make a clean break with sin and commit yourself completely to God.

8:22–31 God says wisdom is primary and fundamental. It is the foundation on which all life is built. Paul and John may have alluded to some of Solomon's statements about wisdom to describe Christ's presence at the creation of the world (Colossians 1:15–17; 2:2–3; Revelation 3:14).

8:30
John 1:2, 3

8:31
Ps 16:3; John 13:1

8:32
Prov 5:7; 7:24; Ps 119:1, 2; 128:1; Prov 29:18; Luke 11:28

8:33
Prov 4:1

8:34
Prov 3:13, 18

8:35
Prov 4:22; John 17:3; Prov 3:4; 12:2

8:36
Prov 1:31, 32; 15:32; Prov 5:12; 12:1; Prov 21:6

9:1
1 Cor 3:9, 10; Eph 2:20-22; 1 Pet 2:5

9:2
Matt 22:4; Song 8:2; Luke 14:16, 17

9:3
Ps 68:11; Matt 22:3; Prov 8:1, 2; Prov 9:14

9:4
Prov 8:5; 9:16; Prov 6:32

9:5
Song 5:1; Is 55:1; John 6:27

9:6
Prov 8:35; 9:11; Ezek 11:20; 37:24

9:7
Prov 23:9

9:8
Prov 15:12; Matt 7:6; Ps 141:5; Prov 10:8

9:9
Prov 1:5

9:10
Job 28:28; Ps 111:10; Prov 1:7

9:11
Prov 3:16; 10:27

9:12
Job 22:2; Prov 14:14; Prov 19:29

9:13
Prov 7:11; Prov 5:6

30 Then I was beside Him, *as* a master workman;
And I was daily *His* delight,
Rejoicing always before Him,
31 Rejoicing in the world, His earth,
And *having* my delight in the sons of men.

32 "Now therefore, *O* sons, listen to me,
For blessed are they who keep my ways.
33 "Heed instruction and be wise,
And do not neglect *it.*
34 "Blessed is the man who listens to me,
Watching daily at my gates,
Waiting at my doorposts.
35 "For he who finds me finds life
And obtains favor from the LORD.
36 "But he who sins against me injures himself;
All those who hate me love death."

Wisdom's Invitation

9 Wisdom has built her house,
She has hewn out her seven pillars;
2 She has prepared her food, she has mixed her wine;
She has also set her table;
3 She has sent out her maidens, she calls
From the tops of the heights of the city:
4 "Whoever is naive, let him turn in here!"
To him who lacks understanding she says,
5 "Come, eat of my food
And drink of the wine I have mixed.
6 "Forsake *your* folly and live,
And proceed in the way of understanding."

7 He who corrects a scoffer gets dishonor for himself,
And he who reproves a wicked man *gets* insults for himself.
8 Do not reprove a scoffer, or he will hate you,
Reprove a wise man and he will love you.
9 Give *instruction* to a wise man and he will be still wiser,
Teach a righteous man and he will increase *his* learning.
10 The fear of the LORD is the beginning of wisdom,
And the knowledge of the Holy One is understanding.
11 For by me your days will be multiplied,
And years of life will be added to you.
12 If you are wise, you are wise for yourself,
And if you scoff, you alone will bear it.

13 The woman of folly is boisterous,
She is naive and knows nothing.

9:1 The seven pillars are figurative; they do not represent seven principles of wisdom. In the Bible, the number seven represents completeness and perfection. This verse poetically states that wisdom lacks nothing—it is complete and perfect.

9:1ff Wisdom and folly (foolishness) are portrayed in this chapter as rival young women, each preparing a feast and inviting people to it. But wisdom is a responsible woman of character, while folly is a prostitute serving stolen food. Wisdom appeals first to the mind; folly to the senses. It is easier to excite the senses, but the pleasures of folly are temporary. By contrast, the satisfaction that wisdom brings lasts forever.

9:1–5 The banquet described in this chapter has some interesting parallels to the banquet Jesus described in one of his parables (Luke 14:15–24). Many may intend to go, but they never make it because they get sidetracked by other activities that seem more important at the time. Don't let anything become more important than your search for God's wisdom.

9:7–10 Are you a scoffer or a wise person? You can tell by the way you respond to criticism. Instead of tossing back a quick put-down or clever retort when rebuked, listen to what is being said. Learn from your critics; this is the path to wisdom. Wisdom begins with knowing God. He gives insight into living because he created life. To know God is not just to know the facts about him, but to stand in awe of him and have a relationship with him. Do you really want to be wise? Get to know God better and better. (See James 1:5, 2 Peter 1:2–4 for more on how to become wise.)

14 She sits at the doorway of her house,
On a seat by the high places of the city,
15 Calling to those who pass by,
Who are making their paths straight:
16 "Whoever is naive, let him turn in here,"
And to him who lacks understanding she says,
17 "Stolen water is sweet;
And bread *eaten* in secret is pleasant."
18 But he does not know that the dead are there,
That her guests are in the depths of Sheol.

9:14 Prov 9:3
9:16 Prov 9:4
9:17 Prov 20:17
9:18 Prov 7:27

B. WISDOM FOR ALL PEOPLE (10:1—24:34)

These short couplets are what we commonly recognize as proverbs. They cover a wide range of topics. The first section was written by Solomon. The next two sections were written by others, but collected by Solomon. These sayings give people practical wisdom for godly living at every stage of life.

Contrast of the Righteous and the Wicked

10 The proverbs of Solomon.
A wise son makes a father glad,
But a foolish son is a grief to his mother.
2 Ill-gotten gains do not profit,
But righteousness delivers from death.
3 The LORD will not allow the righteous to hunger,
But He will reject the craving of the wicked.
4 Poor is he who works with a negligent hand,
But the hand of the diligent makes rich.
5 He who gathers in summer is a son who acts wisely,
But he who sleeps in harvest is a son who acts shamefully.
6 Blessings are on the head of the righteous,
But the mouth of the wicked conceals violence.
7 The memory of the righteous is blessed,
But the name of the wicked will rot.
8 The wise of heart will receive commands,
But a babbling fool will be ruined.
9 He who walks in integrity walks securely,
But he who perverts his ways will be found out.
10 He who winks the eye causes trouble,
And a babbling fool will be ruined.
11 The mouth of the righteous is a fountain of life,
But the mouth of the wicked conceals violence.
12 Hatred stirs up strife,
But love covers all transgressions.
13 On the lips of the discerning, wisdom is found,
But a rod is for the back of him who lacks understanding.
14 Wise men store up knowledge,
But with the mouth of the foolish, ruin is at hand.

10:1 Prov 1:1; Prov 15:20; 29:3; Prov 17:25; 29:15
10:2 Ps 49:7; Prov 11:4; 21:6; Ezek 7:19; Luke 12:19, 20
10:3 Ps 34:9, 10; 37:25; Prov 28:25; Matt 6:33; Ps 112:10; Prov 28:9
10:4 Prov 13:4; 21:5
10:6 Prov 28:20; Prov 10:11; Obad 10
10:7 Ps 112:6; Ps 9:5, 6; 109:13; Eccl 8:10
10:8 Prov 9:8; Matt 7:24
10:9 Ps 23:4; Prov 3:23; 28:18; Is 33:15, 16; Prov 26:26; Matt 10:26; 1 Tim 5:25
10:10 Ps 35:19; Prov 6:13; Prov 10:8
10:11 Ps 37:30; Prov 13:14; 18:4; Prov 10:6
10:12 Prov 17:9; 1 Cor 13:4-7; James 5:20; 1 Pet 4:8
10:13 Prov 10:31; Prov 19:29; 26:3
10:14 Prov 9:9; Prov 10:8, 10; 13:3; 18:7

9:14–17 There is something hypnotic and intoxicating about wickedness. One sin leads us to want more; sinful behavior seems more exciting than the Christian life. That is why many people put aside all thought of wisdom's sumptuous banquet (9:1–5) in order to eat the stolen food of folly. Don't be deceived—sin is dangerous. Before reaching for forbidden fruit, take a long look at what happens to those who eat it. (See the chart in chapter 22.)

10:2 Some people bring unhappiness on themselves by choosing ill-gotten treasures. For example, craving satisfaction, they may do something that destroys their chances of ever achieving happiness. God's principles for right living bring lasting happiness because they guide us into long-term right behavior in spite of our ever-changing feelings.

10:3 Proverbs is full of verses contrasting the righteous person with the wicked. These statements are not intended to apply universally to all people in every situation. For example, some good people do go hungry. Rather, they are intended to communicate the general truth that the life of the person who seeks God is better in the long run than the life of the wicked person—a life that leads to ruin. These statements are not ironclad promises, but general truths. In addition, a proverb like this assumes a just government that cares for the poor and needy—the kind of government Israel was intended to have (see Deuteronomy 24:17–22). A corrupt government often thwarts the plans of righteous men and women.

10:4–5 Every day has 24 hours filled with opportunities to grow, serve, and be productive. Yet it is so easy to waste time, letting life slip from our grasp. Refuse to be a lazy person, sleeping or frittering away the hours meant for productive work. See time as God's gift and seize your opportunities to live diligently for him.

10:15 Ps 52:7; Prov 18:11; Prov 19:7
10:17 Prov 6:23
10:18 Prov 26:24
10:19 Job 11:2; Prov 18:21; Eccl 5:3; Prov 17:27; James 1:19; 3:2
10:20 Prov 8:19
10:23 Prov 2:14; 15:21
10:24 Ps 145:19; Prov 15:8; Matt 5:6; 1 John 5:14, 15
10:25 Job 21:18; Ps 58:9; Prov 12:7; Ps 15:5; Prov 12:3; Matt 7:24
10:26 Prov 26:6
10:27 Prov 3:2; 9:11; 14:27; Job 15:32, 33; 22:16; Ps 55:23
10:28 Prov 11:23; Job 8:13; 11:20; Prov 11:7
10:29 Prov 13:6; Prov 21:15
10:30 Ps 37:29; 125:1; Prov 2:21; Prov 2:22
10:31 Ps 37:30

15 The rich man's wealth is his fortress,
The ruin of the poor is their poverty.
16 The wages of the righteous is life,
The income of the wicked, punishment.
17 He is *on* the path of life who heeds instruction,
But he who ignores reproof goes astray.
18 He who conceals hatred *has* lying lips,
And he who spreads slander is a fool.
19 When there are many words, transgression is unavoidable,
But he who restrains his lips is wise.
20 The tongue of the righteous is *as* choice silver,
The heart of the wicked is *worth* little.
21 The lips of the righteous feed many,
But fools die for lack of understanding.
22 It is the blessing of the LORD that makes rich,
And He adds no sorrow to it.
23 Doing wickedness is like sport to a fool,
And *so is* wisdom to a man of understanding.
24 What the wicked fears will come upon him,
But the desire of the righteous will be granted.
25 When the whirlwind passes, the wicked is no more,
But the righteous *has* an everlasting foundation.
26 Like vinegar to the teeth and smoke to the eyes,
So is the lazy one to those who send him.
27 The fear of the LORD prolongs life,
But the years of the wicked will be shortened.
28 The hope of the righteous is gladness,
But the expectation of the wicked perishes.
29 The way of the LORD is a stronghold to the upright,
But ruin to the workers of iniquity.
30 The righteous will never be shaken,
But the wicked will not dwell in the land.
31 The mouth of the righteous flows with wisdom,
But the perverted tongue will be cut out.

GOD'S ADVICE ABOUT MONEY

Proverbs gives some practical instruction on the use of money, although sometimes it is advice we would rather not hear. It's more comfortable to continue in our habits than to learn how to use money more wisely. The advice includes:

Be generous in giving	11:24–25; 22:9
Place people's needs ahead of profit	11:26
Be cautious of countersigning for another	17:18; 22:26–27
Don't accept bribes	17:23
Help the poor	19:17; 21:13
Store up for the future	21:20
Be careful about borrowing	22:7

Other verses to study include: 11:15; 20:16; 25:14; 27:13

10:18 By hating another person you may become a liar or a fool. If you try to conceal your hatred, you end up lying. If you slander the other person and are proven wrong, you are a fool. The only way out is to admit your hateful feelings to God. Ask him to change your heart, to help you love instead of hate.

10:20 Words from a good person are valuable ("choice silver"). A lot of poor advice is worth less than a little good advice. It is easy to get opinions from people who will tell us only what they think will please us, but such advice is not helpful. Instead we should look for those who will speak the truth, even when it hurts. Think about the people to whom you go for advice. What do you expect to hear from them?

10:22 God supplies most people with the personal and financial abilities to respond to the needs of others. If we all realized how God has blessed us, and if we all used our resources to do God's will, hunger and poverty would be wiped out. Wealth is a blessing only if we use it in the way God intended.

10:24 The wicked person dreads death. Those who do not believe in God usually fear death, and with good reason. By contrast, believers desire eternal life and God's salvation—their hopes will be rewarded. This verse offers a choice: You can have either your fears or your desires come true. You make that choice by rejecting God and living your own way, or by accepting God and following him.

32 The lips of the righteous bring forth what is acceptable,
But the mouth of the wicked what is perverted.

Contrast the Upright and the Wicked

11 A false balance is an abomination to the LORD,
But a just weight is His delight.
2 When pride comes, then comes dishonor,
But with the humble is wisdom.
3 The integrity of the upright will guide them,
But the crookedness of the treacherous will destroy them.
4 Riches do not profit in the day of wrath,
But righteousness delivers from death.
5 The righteousness of the blameless will smooth his way,
But the wicked will fall by his own wickedness.
6 The righteousness of the upright will deliver them,
But the treacherous will be caught by *their own* greed.
7 When a wicked man dies, *his* expectation will perish,
And the hope of strong men perishes.
8 The righteous is delivered from trouble,
But the wicked takes his place.
9 With *his* mouth the godless man destroys his neighbor,
But through knowledge the righteous will be delivered.
10 When it goes well with the righteous, the city rejoices,
And when the wicked perish, there is joyful shouting.
11 By the blessing of the upright a city is exalted,
But by the mouth of the wicked it is torn down.
12 He who despises his neighbor lacks sense,
But a man of understanding keeps silent.
13 He who goes about as a talebearer reveals secrets,
But he who is trustworthy conceals a matter.
14 Where there is no guidance the people fall,
But in abundance of counselors there is victory.
15 He who is guarantor for a stranger will surely suffer for it,
But he who hates being a guarantor is secure.
16 A gracious woman attains honor,
And ruthless men attain riches.
17 The merciful man does himself good,
But the cruel man does himself harm.
18 The wicked earns deceptive wages,
But he who sows righteousness *gets* a true reward.
19 He who is steadfast in righteousness *will attain* to life,
And he who pursues evil *will bring about* his own death.
20 The perverse in heart are an abomination to the LORD,
But the blameless in *their* walk are His delight.

10:32 Eccl 12:10; Prov 2:12; 6:12
11:1 Lev 19:35, 36; Deut 25:13-16; Prov 20:10, 23; Mic 6:11; Prov 16:11
11:2 Prov 16:18; 18:12; 29:23
11:3 Prov 13:6; Prov 19:3; 22:12
11:4 Prov 10:2; Ezek 7:19; Zeph 1:18
11:5 Prov 3:6; Prov 5:22
11:6 Ps 7:15, 16; 9:15; Eccl 10:8
11:7 Prov 10:28; Job 8:13, 14
11:9 Prov 16:29; Prov 11:6
11:10 Prov 28:12
11:13 Lev 19:16; Prov 20:19; 1 Tim 5:13; Prov 19:11
11:14 Prov 15:22; 20:18; 24:6
11:15 Prov 6:1; 27:13
11:16 Prov 31:28, 30
11:17 Matt 5:7; 25:34-36
11:18 Hos 10:12; Gal 6:8, 9; James 3:18
11:19 Prov 10:16; 12:28; 19:23; Prov 21:16; Rom 6:23; James 1:15
11:20 Ps 119:1; Prov 13:6; 1 Chr 29:17

11:4 "The day of wrath" refers to when we die or to the time when God settles accounts with all people. On judgment day, each of us will stand alone, accountable for all our deeds. At that time, no amount of riches will buy reconciliation with God. Only our love for God and obedience to him will count.

11:7–8 These verses, like 10:3, contrast two paths in life, but are not intended to apply universally to all people in all circumstances. God's people are not excluded from problems or struggles. If a person follows God's wisdom, however, God can rescue him or her from trouble. But a wicked person will fall into his or her own traps. Even if good people suffer, they can be sure they will ultimately be rescued from eternal death.

11:9 The mouth can be used either as a weapon or a tool, hurting relationships or building them up. Sadly, it is often easier to destroy than to build, and most people have received more destructive comments than those that build up. Every person you meet today is either a demolition site or a construction opportunity. Your words will make a difference. Will they be weapons for destruction or tools for construction?

11:14 A good leader needs and uses wise counselors. One person's perspective and understanding is severely limited; he or she may not have all the facts or may be blinded by bias, emotions, or wrong impressions. To be a wise leader at home, at church, or at work, seek the counsel of others and be open to their advice. Then, after considering all the facts, make your decision. (See the chart in chapter 29.)

11:19 Righteous people attain life because they live life more fully each day. They also attain life because people usually live longer when they live right, with proper diet, exercise, and rest. In addition, they need not fear death because eternal life is God's gift to them (John 11:25). By contrast, evil people not only find eternal death, but also miss out on real life on earth.

11:22 Gen 24:47
11:23 Prov 10:28; Rom 2:8, 9
11:25 Prov 3:9, 10; 2 Cor 9:6, 7; Matt 5:7
11:26 Prov 24:24; Job 29:13; Gen 42:6
11:27 Esth 7:10; Ps 7:15, 16; 57:6
11:28 Ps 49:6; Mark 10:25; 1 Tim 6:17; Ps 1:3; 92:12; Jer 17:8
11:29 Prov 15:27; Eccl 5:16; Prov 14:19
11:30 Prov 3:18; Prov 14:25; Dan 12:3; 1 Cor 9:19-22; James 5:20
11:31 2 Sam 22:21, 25; Prov 13:21; 1 Pet 4:18
12:2 Prov 3:4; 8:35
12:3 Prov 11:5; Prov 10:25
12:4 Prov 31:11; 1 Cor 11:7; Prov 14:30; Hab 3:16
12:6 Prov 1:11, 16; Prov 14:3

21 Assuredly, the evil man will not go unpunished,
But the descendants of the righteous will be delivered.
22 *As* a ring of gold in a swine's snout
So is a beautiful woman who lacks [1]discretion.
23 The desire of the righteous is only good,
But the expectation of the wicked is wrath.
24 There is one who scatters, and *yet* increases all the more,
And there is one who withholds what is justly due, *and yet it results* only in want.
25 The generous man will be prosperous,
And he who waters will himself be watered.
26 He who withholds grain, the people will curse him,
But blessing will be on the head of him who sells *it.*
27 He who diligently seeks good seeks favor,
But he who seeks evil, evil will come to him.
28 He who trusts in his riches will fall,
But the righteous will flourish like the *green* leaf.
29 He who troubles his own house will inherit wind,
And the foolish will be servant to the wisehearted.
30 The fruit of the righteous is a tree of life,
And he who is wise wins souls.
31 If the righteous will be rewarded in the earth,
How much more the wicked and the sinner!

Contrast the Upright and the Wicked

12 Whoever loves discipline loves knowledge,
But he who hates reproof is stupid.
2 A good man will obtain favor from the LORD,
But He will condemn a man who devises evil.
3 A man will not be established by wickedness,
But the root of the righteous will not be moved.
4 An excellent wife is the crown of her husband,
But she who shames *him* is like rottenness in his bones.
5 The thoughts of the righteous are just,
But the counsels of the wicked are deceitful.
6 The words of the wicked lie in wait for blood,

1 Lit *taste*

11:22 Physical attractiveness without discretion soon wears thin. We are to seek those character strengths that help us make wise decisions, not just those that make us look good. Not everyone who looks good is pleasant to live or work with. While taking good care of our body and appearance is not wrong, we also need to develop our ability to think.

11:24–25 These two verses present a paradox: that we become richer by being generous. The world says to hold on to as much as possible, but God blesses those who give freely of their possessions, time, and energy. When we give, God supplies us with more so that we can give more. In addition, giving helps us gain a right perspective on our possessions. We realize they were never really ours to begin with, but they were given to us by God to be used to help others. What then do we gain by giving? Freedom from enslavement to our possessions, the joy of helping others, and God's approval.

11:29 One of the greatest resources God gives us is the family. Families provide acceptance, encouragement, guidance, and counsel. Bringing trouble on your family—whether through anger or through an exaggerated desire for independence—is foolish because you cut yourself off from all they provide. In your family, strive for healing, communication, and understanding.

11:30 A wise person is a model of a meaningful life. Like a tree attracts people to its shade, his or her sense of purpose attracts others who want to know how they too can find meaning. Gaining wisdom yourself, then, can be the first step in leading people to God. Leading people to God is important because it keeps us in touch with God while offering others eternal life.

11:31 Contrary to popular opinion, no one sins and gets away with it. The faithful are rewarded for their faith. The wicked are punished for their sins. Don't think for a moment that "it won't matter" or "nobody will know" or "we won't get caught" (see also 1 Peter 4:18).

12:1 If you don't want to learn, years of schooling will teach you very little. But if you want to be taught, there is no end to what you can learn. This includes being willing to accept discipline and correction and to learn from the wisdom of others. A person who refuses constructive criticism has a problem with pride. Such a person is unlikely to learn very much.

12:3 To be established means to be successful. Real success comes only to those who do what is right. Their efforts stand the test of time. Then, what kind of success does wickedness bring? We all know people who cheated to pass the course or to get a larger tax refund—is this not success? And what about the person who ignores his family commitments and mistreats his workers but gets ahead in business? These apparent successes are only temporary. They are bought at the expense of character. Cheaters grow more and more dishonest, and those who hurt others become callous and cruel. In the long run, evil behavior does not lead to success; it leads only to more evil. Real success maintains personal integrity. If you are not a success by God's standards, you have not achieved true success. (See the chart in chapter 19.)

But the mouth of the upright will deliver them.
7 The wicked are overthrown and are no more,
But the house of the righteous will stand.
8 A man will be praised according to his insight,
But one of perverse mind will be despised.
9 Better is he who is lightly esteemed and has a servant
Than he who honors himself and lacks bread.
10 A righteous man has regard for the life of his animal,
But *even* the compassion of the wicked is cruel.
11 He who tills his land will have plenty of bread,
But he who pursues worthless *things* lacks sense.
12 The wicked man desires the booty of evil men,
But the root of the righteous yields *fruit*.
13 An evil man is ensnared by the transgression of his lips,
But the righteous will escape from trouble.
14 A man will be satisfied with good by the fruit of his words,
And the deeds of a man's hands will return to him.
15 The way of a fool is right in his own eyes,
But a wise man is he who listens to counsel.
16 A fool's anger is known at once,
But a prudent man conceals dishonor.
17 He who speaks truth tells what is right,
But a false witness, deceit.
18 There is one who speaks rashly like the thrusts of a sword,
But the tongue of the wise brings healing.
19 Truthful lips will be established forever,
But a lying tongue is only for a moment.
20 Deceit is in the heart of those who devise evil,
But counselors of peace have joy.
21 No harm befalls the righteous,
But the wicked are filled with trouble.
22 Lying lips are an abomination to the LORD,
But those who deal faithfully are His delight.
23 A prudent man conceals knowledge,
But the heart of fools proclaims folly.
24 The hand of the diligent will rule,
But the slack *hand* will be put to forced labor.
25 Anxiety in a man's heart weighs it down,
But a good word makes it glad.
26 The righteous is a guide to his neighbor,
But the way of the wicked leads them astray.
27 A lazy man does not roast his prey,
But the precious possession of a man *is* diligence.

12:7 Job 34:25; Prov 10:25; Matt 7:24-27
12:10 Deut 25:4
12:11 Prov 28:19
12:12 Prov 21:10; Prov 11:30
12:13 Prov 11:8; 21:23; 2 Pet 2:9
12:14 Prov 13:2; 15:23; 18:20; Job 34:11; Prov 1:31; 24:12; Is 3:10, 11; Hos 4:9
12:15 Prov 14:12; 16:2; 21:2
12:16 Prov 14:33; 27:3; 29:11
12:18 Ps 57:4; Prov 4:22; 15:4
12:19 Ps 52:4, 5; Prov 19:9
12:21 Ps 91:10; 121:7; Prov 1:33; 1 Pet 3:13
12:22 Rev 22:15
12:23 Prov 10:14; 11:13; 13:16; 15:2; 29:11
12:24 Gen 49:15; Judg 1:28; 1 Kin 9:21
12:25 Prov 15:13; Is 50:4
12:27 Prov 10:4; 13:4

12:13 Sinful talk is twisting the facts to support your claims. Those who do this are likely to be trapped by their own lies. But for someone who always tells the truth, the facts—plain and unvarnished—give an unshakable defense. If you find that you always have to defend yourself to others, maybe your honesty is less than it should be. (See the chart in chapter 20.)

12:16 When someone annoys or insults you, it is natural to retaliate. But this solves nothing and only encourages trouble. Instead, answer slowly and quietly. Your positive response will achieve positive results. Proverbs 15:1 says, "A gentle answer turns away wrath."

12:19 Truth is always timely; it applies today and in the future. Because it is connected with God's changeless character, it is also changeless. Think for a moment about the centuries that have passed since these proverbs were written. Consider the countless hours that have been spent carefully studying every sentence of Scripture. The Bible has withstood the test of time. Because God is truth, you can trust his Word to guide you.

12:21 This is a general, but not universal, truth. Although harm does befall the righteous, they are able to see opportunities in their problems and move ahead. The wicked, without God's wisdom, are ill-equipped to handle their problems. (See the notes on 3:16–17; 10:3; 11:7–8 for more about general truths that are not intended as universal statements.)

12:23 Prudent people have a quiet confidence. Insecure or uncertain people feel the need to prove themselves, but prudent people don't have to prove anything. They know they are capable, so they can get on with their work. Beware of showing off. If you are modest, people may not notice you at first, but they will respect you later.

12:27 The diligent make wise use of their possessions and resources; the lazy waste them. Waste has become a way of life for many who live in a land of plenty. Waste is poor stewardship. Make good use of everything God has given you, and prize it.

12:28 Deut 30:15f; 32:46f; Jer 21:8

28 In the way of righteousness is life,
And in *its* pathway there is no death.

Contrast the Upright and the Wicked

13:1 Prov 10:1; 15:20; Prov 9:7, 8; 15:12

13:2 Prov 12:14; Prov 1:31; Hos 10:13

13:3 Prov 18:21; 21:23; James 3:2; Prov 18:7; 20:19

13:5 Col 3:9; Prov 3:35

13:6 Prov 11:3

13:7 Prov 11:24; Luke 12:20, 21; Luke 12:33; 2 Cor 6:10; James 2:5

13:9 Job 29:3; Prov 4:18; Job 18:5; Prov 24:20

13 A wise son *accepts his* father's discipline,
But a scoffer does not listen to rebuke.
2 From the fruit of a man's mouth he enjoys good,
But the desire of the treacherous is violence.
3 The one who guards his mouth preserves his life;
The one who opens wide his lips comes to ruin.
4 The soul of the sluggard craves and *gets* nothing,
But the soul of the diligent is made fat.
5 A righteous man hates falsehood,
But a wicked man acts disgustingly and shamefully.
6 Righteousness guards the one whose way is blameless,
But wickedness subverts the sinner.
7 There is one who pretends to be rich, but has nothing;
Another pretends to be poor, but has great wealth.
8 The ransom of a man's life is his wealth,
But the poor hears no rebuke.
9 The light of the righteous [2]rejoices,
But the lamp of the wicked goes out.
10 Through insolence comes nothing but strife,
But wisdom is with those who receive counsel.
11 Wealth *obtained* by fraud dwindles,
But the one who gathers by labor increases *it.*

2 I.e. shines brightly

TEACHING AND LEARNING

Good teaching comes from good learning—and Proverbs has more to say to students than to teachers. Proverbs is concerned with the learning of wisdom. The book makes it clear that there are no good alternatives to learning wisdom. We are either becoming wise learners or refusing to learn and becoming foolish failures. Proverbs encourages us to make the right choice.

Wise Learners	*Proverb(s)*	*Foolish Failures*
Quietly accept instruction and criticism	10:8; 23:12; 25:12	Ignore instruction
Love discipline	12:1	Hate correction
Listen to advice	12:15; 21:11; 24:6	Think they need no advice
Accept parents' discipline	13:1	Mock parents
Lead others to life	10:17	Lead others astray
Receive honor	13:18	End in poverty and shame
Profit from constructive rebuke	15:31–32; 29:1	Self-destruct by refusing rebuke

Advice to Teachers:
Help people avoid traps (13:14), use pleasant words (16:21), and speak at the right time (15:23; 18:20).

12:28 For many, death is a darkened door at the end of life, a passageway to an unknown and feared destiny. But for God's people, death is a bright pathway to a new and better life. So why do we fear death? Is it because of the pain we expect, the separation from loved ones, its surprise? God can help us deal with those fears. He has shown us that death is not final, but is just another step in the eternal life we received when we followed him.

13:3 You have not mastered self-control if you do not control what you say. Words can cut and destroy. James recognized this truth when he stated, "The tongue is a small part of the body, and yet it boasts of great things" (James 3:5). If you want to be self-controlled, begin with your tongue. Stop and think before you react or speak. If you can control this small but powerful member, you can control the rest of your body. (See the chart in chapter 26.)

13:6 Living right is like posting a guard for your life. Every choice for good sets into motion other opportunities for good. Evil choices follow the same pattern, but in the opposite direction. Each decision you make to obey God's Word will bring a greater sense of order to your life, while each decision to disobey will bring confusion and destruction. The right choices you make reflect your integrity. Obedience brings the greatest safety and security.

13:10 "I was wrong" or "I need advice" are difficult phrases to utter because they require humility. Pride is an ingredient in every quarrel. It stirs up conflict and divides people. Humility, by contrast, heals. Guard against pride. If you find yourself constantly arguing, examine your life for pride. Be open to the advice of others, ask for help when you need it, and be willing to admit your mistakes.

12 Hope deferred makes the heart sick,
But desire fulfilled is a tree of life.
13 The one who despises the word will be in debt to it,
But the one who fears the commandment will be rewarded.
14 The teaching of the wise is a fountain of life,
To turn aside from the snares of death.
15 Good understanding produces favor,
But the way of the treacherous is hard.
16 Every prudent man acts with knowledge,
But a fool displays folly.
17 A wicked messenger falls into adversity,
But a faithful envoy *brings* healing.
18 Poverty and shame *will come* to him who neglects discipline,
But he who regards reproof will be honored.
19 Desire realized is sweet to the soul,
But it is an abomination to fools to turn away from evil.
20 He who walks with wise men will be wise,
But the companion of fools will suffer harm.
21 Adversity pursues sinners,
But the righteous will be rewarded with prosperity.
22 A good man leaves an inheritance to his children's children,
And the wealth of the sinner is stored up for the righteous.
23 Abundant food *is in* the fallow ground of the poor,
But it is swept away by injustice.
24 He who withholds his rod hates his son,
But he who loves him disciplines him diligently.
25 The righteous has enough to satisfy his appetite,
But the stomach of the wicked is in need.

Contrast the Upright and the Wicked

14 The wise woman builds her house,
But the foolish tears it down with her own hands.
2 He who walks in his uprightness fears the LORD,
But he who is devious in his ways despises Him.

13:13
Num 15:31; 2 Chr 36:16; Prov 13:21

13:14
Prov 10:11; 14:27; Ps 18:5

13:15
Ps 111:10; Prov 3:4

13:16
Prov 12:23

13:17
Prov 25:13

13:18
Prov 15:5, 32

13:20
Prov 2:20; 15:31

13:21
Ps 32:10; 54:5; Is 47:11; Prov 11:31; 13:13; Is 3:10

13:22
Ezra 9:12; Ps 37:25; Job 27:16, 17; Prov 28:8; Eccl 2:26

13:23
Prov 12:11

13:24
Prov 19:18; 22:15; 23:13, 14; 29:15, 17; Deut 8:5; Prov 3:12; Heb 12:7

13:25
Ps 34:10; 103:5; 132:15; Prov 10:3; Prov 13:18; Luke 15:14

14:1
Ruth 4:11; Prov 31:10-27

14:2
Prov 19:1; 28:6; Prov 2:15

13:13 God created us, knows us, and loves us. It only makes sense, then, to listen to his instructions and do what he says. The Bible is his unfailing Word to us. It is like an owner's manual for a car. If you obey God's instructions, you will "run right" and find his kind of power to live. If you ignore them, you will have breakdowns, accidents, and failures.

13:17 In Solomon's day, a king had to rely on messengers for information about his country. These messengers had to be trustworthy. Inaccurate information could even lead to bloodshed. Reliable communication is still vital. If the message received is different from the message sent, marriages, businesses, and diplomatic relations can all break down. It is important to choose your words well and to avoid reacting until you clearly understand what the other person means.

13:19 Whether a "desire realized" is good or bad depends on the nature of the desire. It is "sweet to the soul" to achieve worthwhile goals, but not all goals are worth pursuing. When you set your heart on something, you may lose your ability to assess it objectively. With your desire blinding your judgment, you may proceed with an unwise relationship, a wasteful purchase, or a poorly conceived plan. Faithfulness is a virtue, but stubbornness is not.

13:20 The old saying "A rotten apple spoils the barrel" is often applied to friendships, and with good reason. Our friends and associates affect us, sometimes profoundly. Be careful whom you choose as your closest friends. Spend time with people you want to be like—because you and your friends will surely grow to resemble each other.

13:20 When most people need advice, they go to their friends first because friends accept them and usually agree with them. But that is why they may not be able to help them with difficult problems. Our friends are so much like us that they may not have any answers we haven't already heard. Instead, we should seek out older and wiser people to advise us. Wise people have experienced a lot of life—and have succeeded. They are not afraid to tell the truth. Who are the wise, godly people who can warn you of the pitfalls ahead?

13:23 The poor are often victims of an unjust society. A poor man's soil may be good, but unjust laws may rob him of his own produce. This proverb does not take poverty lightly or wink at injustice; it simply describes what often occurs. We should do what we can to fight injustice of every sort. Our efforts may seem inadequate; but it is comforting to know that in the end God's justice will prevail.

13:24 It is not easy for a loving parent to discipline a child, but it is necessary. The greatest responsibility that God gives parents is the nurture and guidance of their children. Lack of discipline puts parents' love in question because it shows a lack of concern for the character development of their children. Disciplining children averts long-range disaster. Without correction, children grow up with no clear understanding of right and wrong and with little direction to their lives. Don't be afraid to discipline your children. It is an act of love. Remember, however, that your efforts cannot make your children wise; they can only encourage your children to seek God's wisdom above all else!

14:3 Prov 12:6

3 In the mouth of the foolish is a rod for *his* back,
But the lips of the wise will protect them.
4 Where no oxen are, the manger is clean,
But much revenue *comes* by the strength of the ox.

14:5 Rev 1:5; 3:14; Ex 23:1; Deut 19:16; Prov 6:19; 12:17; Prov 19:5

5 A trustworthy witness will not lie,
But a false witness utters lies.
6 A scoffer seeks wisdom and *finds* none,
But knowledge is easy to one who has understanding.

14:7 Prov 23:9

7 Leave the presence of a fool,
Or you will not discern words of knowledge.

WISDOM AND FOOLISHNESS
The wise and the foolish are often contrasted in Proverbs. The characteristics, reputation, and results of each are worth knowing if wisdom is our goal.

	The Wise	*The Foolish*	*Reference*
Characteristics	Help others with good advice	Lack understanding	10:21
	Enjoy wisdom	Enjoy wickedness	10:23
	Consider their steps	Naive	14:15
		Avoid the wise	15:12
	Seek knowledge	Feed on folly	15:14
	Value wisdom above riches		16:16
	Receive life	Receive discipline	16:22
	Respond to rebuke	Respond to punishment	17:10
	Pursue wisdom	Pursue illusive dreams	17:24
		Blame failure on God	19:3
	Profit from correction	An example to others	19:25
		Are proud and arrogant	21:24
		Despise wisdom	23:9
		Make truth useless	26:7
		Repeat their folly	26:11
	Trust in wisdom	Trust in themselves	28:26
	Control their anger	Unleash their anger	29:11
Reputation	Admired as counselors	Beaten as servants	10:13
	Crowned with knowledge	Inherit foolishness	14:18
		Cause strife and quarrels	22:10
		Receive no honor	26:1
	Keep peace	Stir up anger	29:8
Results	Stay on straight paths	Go the wrong way	15:21
		Lash out when discovered in folly	17:12
		Endangered by their words	18:6–7
	Their wisdom conquers others' strength		21:22
	Avoid wicked paths	Walk a troublesome path	22:5
	Have great strength		24:5
		Will never be chosen as counselors	24:7
		Must be guided by hardship	26:3
		Persist in foolishness	27:22

14:4 When a farmer has no oxen for plowing, the manger for the animals will be empty. The only way to keep your life free of people problems is to keep it free of other people. But if your life is empty of people, it is useless; and if you live only for yourself, your life loses its meaning. Instead of avoiding people, we should serve others, share the faith, and work for justice. Is your life clean, but empty? Or does it give evidence of your serving God wholeheartedly?

14:6 We all know scoffers, people who mock every word of instruction or advice. They never find wisdom because they don't seek it seriously. Wisdom comes easily to those who pay attention to experienced people and to God. If the wisdom you need does not come easily to you, perhaps your attitude is the barrier.

8 The wisdom of the sensible is to understand his way,
But the foolishness of fools is deceit.
9 Fools mock at sin,
But among the upright there is good will.
10 The heart knows its own bitterness,
And a stranger does not share its joy.
11 The house of the wicked will be destroyed,
But the tent of the upright will flourish.
12 There is a way *which seems* right to a man,
But its end is the way of death.
13 Even in laughter the heart may be in pain,
And the end of joy may be grief.
14 The backslider in heart will have his fill of his own ways,
But a good man will *be satisfied* with his.
15 The naive believes everything,
But the sensible man considers his steps.
16 A wise man is cautious and turns away from evil,
But a fool is arrogant and careless.
17 A quick-tempered man acts foolishly,
And a man of evil devices is hated.
18 The naive inherit foolishness,
But the sensible are crowned with knowledge.
19 The evil will bow down before the good,
And the wicked at the gates of the righteous.
20 The poor is hated even by his neighbor,
But those who love the rich are many.
21 He who despises his neighbor sins,
But happy is he who is gracious to the poor.
22 Will they not go astray who devise evil?
But kindness and truth *will be to* those who devise good.
23 In all labor there is profit,
But mere talk *leads* only to poverty.
24 The crown of the wise is their riches,
But the folly of fools is foolishness.
25 A truthful witness saves lives,
But he who utters lies is treacherous.
26 In the [3]fear of the LORD there is strong confidence,
And his children will have refuge.
27 The [3]fear of the LORD is a fountain of life,
That one may avoid the snares of death.
28 In a multitude of people is a king's glory,
But in the dearth of people is a prince's ruin.
29 He who is slow to anger has great understanding,
But he who is quick-tempered exalts folly.
30 A tranquil heart is life to the body,
But passion is rottenness to the bones.

14:8 1 Cor 3:19
14:9 Prov 3:34; 11:20
14:10 1 Sam 1:10; Job 21:25
14:11 Job 8:15
14:12 Prov 12:15; 16:25; Rom 6:21
14:13 Eccl 2:1, 2
14:14 Prov 1:31; 12:21; Prov 12:14; 18:20
14:16 Job 28:28; Ps 34:14; Prov 3:7; 22:3
14:19 1 Sam 2:36; Prov 11:29
14:20 Prov 19:7
14:21 Prov 11:12; Ps 41:1; Prov 19:17; 28:8
14:22 Ps 36:4; Prov 3:29; 12:2; Mic 2:1
14:24 Prov 10:22; 13:8; 21:20
14:25 Prov 14:5
14:26 Prov 18:10; 19:23; Is 33:6
14:29 Prov 16:32; 19:11; Eccl 7:9; James 1:19
14:30 Prov 15:13; Prov 12:4; Hab 3:16

3 Or *reverence*

14:9 How rarely we find goodwill around us today. Angry drivers scowl at each other in the streets. People fight to be first in line. Disgruntled employers and employees both demand their rights. But the common bond of God's people should be goodwill. Those with goodwill think the best of others and assume that others have good motives and intend to do what is right. When someone crosses you, and you feel your blood pressure rising, ask yourself, "How can I show goodwill to this person?"

14:12 The "way which seems right" may offer many options and require few sacrifices. Easy choices, however, should make us take a second look. Is this solution attractive because it allows me to be lazy? Because it doesn't ask me to change my life-style? Because it requires no moral restraints? The right choice often requires hard work and self-sacrifice. Don't be enticed by apparent shortcuts that seem right but end in death.

14:29 A quick temper can be like a fire out of control. It can burn us and everyone else in its path. Anger divides people. It pushes us into hasty decisions that only cause bitterness and guilt. Yet anger, in itself, is not wrong. Anger can be a legitimate reaction to injustice and sin. When you feel yourself getting angry, look for the cause. Are you reacting to an evil situation that you are going to set right? Or are you responding selfishly to a personal insult? Pray that God will help you control your quick temper, channeling your feelings into effective action and conquering selfish anger through humility and repentance.

14:31 Prov 17:5; Matt 25:40; 1 John 3:17; Job 31:15; Prov 22:2

14:32 Prov 6:15; 24:16; Gen 49:18; Ps 16:11; 17:15; 37:37; 73:24; 2 Cor 1:9; 5:8; 2 Tim 4:18

14:35 Matt 24:45, 47; 25:21, 23

31 He who oppresses the poor taunts his Maker,
But he who is gracious to the needy honors Him.
32 The wicked is thrust down by his wrongdoing,
But the righteous has a refuge when he dies.
33 Wisdom rests in the heart of one who has understanding,
But in the hearts of fools it is made known.
34 Righteousness exalts a nation,
But sin is a disgrace to *any* people.
35 The king's favor is toward a servant who acts wisely,
But his anger is toward him who acts shamefully.

Contrast the Upright and the Wicked

15:1 Judg 8:1-3; Prov 15:18; 25:15; 1 Sam 25:10-13

15:2 Prov 15:7; Prov 12:23; 13:16; 15:28

15:3 2 Chr 16:9; Job 31:4; Jer 16:17; Zech 4:10; Heb 4:13

15:6 Prov 8:21

15:8 Prov 21:27; Eccl 5:1; Is 1:11; Jer 6:20; Mic 6:7; Prov 15:29

15:9 1 Tim 6:11

15:11 Job 26:6; Ps 139:8; 1 Sam 16:7; 2 Chr 6:30; Ps 44:21; Acts 1:24

15:12 Prov 13:1; Amos 5:10

15:13 Prov 17:22; Prov 12:25; Prov 17:22; 18:14

15:14 Prov 18:15

15:16 Ps 37:16; Prov 16:8; Eccl 4:6; 1 Tim 6:6

15 A gentle answer turns away wrath,
But a harsh word stirs up anger.
2 The tongue of the wise makes knowledge acceptable,
But the mouth of fools spouts folly.
3 The eyes of the LORD are in every place,
Watching the evil and the good.
4 A soothing tongue is a tree of life,
But perversion in it crushes the spirit.
5 A fool rejects his father's discipline,
But he who regards reproof is sensible.
6 Great wealth is *in* the house of the righteous,
But trouble is in the income of the wicked.
7 The lips of the wise spread knowledge,
But the hearts of fools are not so.
8 The sacrifice of the wicked is an abomination to the LORD,
But the prayer of the upright is His delight.
9 The way of the wicked is an abomination to the LORD,
But He loves one who pursues righteousness.
10 Grievous punishment is for him who forsakes the way;
He who hates reproof will die.
11 Sheol and Abaddon *lie open* before the LORD,
How much more the hearts of men!
12 A scoffer does not love one who reproves him,
He will not go to the wise.
13 A joyful heart makes a cheerful face,
But when the heart is sad, the spirit is broken.
14 The mind of the intelligent seeks knowledge,
But the mouth of fools feeds on folly.
15 All the days of the afflicted are bad,
But a cheerful heart *has* a continual feast.
16 Better is a little with the fear of the LORD
Than great treasure and turmoil with it.

14:31 God has a special concern for the poor. He insists that people who have material goods should be generous with those who are needy. Providing for the poor is not just a suggestion in the Bible; it is a command that may require a change of attitude (see Leviticus 23:22; Deuteronomy 15:7, 8; Psalms 113:5–9; 146:5–9; Isaiah 58:7; 2 Corinthians 9:9; James 2:1–9).

15:1 Have you ever tried to argue in a whisper? It is equally hard to argue with someone who insists on answering gently. On the other hand, a rising voice and harsh words almost always trigger an angry response. To turn away wrath and seek peace, choose gentle words.

15:3 At times it seems that God has let evil run rampant in the world, and we wonder if he even notices it. But God sees everything clearly—both the evil actions and the evil intentions lying behind them (15:11). He is not an indifferent observer. He cares and is active in our world. Right now, his work may be unseen and unfelt, but don't give up. One day he will wipe out evil and punish the evildoers, just as he will establish the good and reward those who do his will.

15:14 What we feed our minds is just as important as what we feed our bodies. The kinds of books we read, the people we talk with, the music we listen to, and the films we watch are all part of our mental diet. Be discerning because what you feed your mind influences your total health and well-being. Thus, a strong desire to discover knowledge is a mark of wisdom.

15:15 Our attitudes color our whole personality. We cannot always choose what happens to us, but we can choose our attitude toward each situation. The secret to a cheerful heart is filling our minds with thoughts that are true, pure, and lovely, with thoughts that dwell on the good things in life (Philippians 4:8). This was Paul's secret as he faced imprisonment, and it can be ours as we face the struggles of daily living. Look at your attitudes and then examine what you allow to enter your mind and what you choose to dwell on. You may need to make some changes.

17 Better is a dish of vegetables where love is
Than a fattened ox *served* with hatred.
18 A hot-tempered man stirs up strife,
But the slow to anger calms a dispute.
19 The way of the lazy is as a hedge of thorns,
But the path of the upright is a highway.
20 A wise son makes a father glad,
But a foolish man despises his mother.
21 Folly is joy to him who lacks sense,
But a man of understanding walks straight.
22 Without consultation, plans are frustrated,
But with many counselors they succeed.
23 A man has joy in an apt answer,
And how delightful is a timely word!
24 The path of life *leads* upward for the wise
That he may keep away from Sheol below.
25 The LORD will tear down the house of the proud,
But He will establish the boundary of the widow.
26 Evil plans are an abomination to the LORD,
But pleasant words are pure.
27 He who profits illicitly troubles his own house,
But he who hates bribes will live.
28 The heart of the righteous ponders how to answer,
But the mouth of the wicked pours out evil things.
29 The LORD is far from the wicked,
But He hears the prayer of the righteous.
30 Bright eyes gladden the heart;
Good news puts fat on the bones.
31 He whose ear listens to the life-giving reproof
Will dwell among the wise.
32 He who neglects discipline despises himself,
But he who listens to reproof acquires understanding.
33 The fear of the LORD is the instruction for wisdom,
And before honor *comes* humility.

Contrast the Upright and the Wicked

16 The plans of the heart belong to man,
But the answer of the tongue is from the LORD.
2 All the ways of a man are clean in his own sight,
But the LORD weighs the motives.
3 Commit your works to the LORD

15:17 Prov 17:1; Matt 22:4; Luke 15:23
15:18 Prov 16:28; 26:21; 29:22; Prov 14:29; Gen 13:8; Prov 16:14; Eccl 10:4
15:20 Prov 10:1; 29:3; Prov 30:17
15:21 Prov 14:8; Eph 5:15
15:23 Prov 12:14; Prov 25:11; Is 50:4
15:24 Prov 4:18
15:25 Prov 12:7; 14:11; Deut 19:14; Prov 23:10; Ps 68:5; 146:9
15:27 Prov 1:19; 28:25; 1 Tim 6:10; Ex 23:8; Deut 16:19; 1 Sam 12:3; Is 33:15
15:28 1 Pet 3:15; Prov 10:32; 15:2
15:29 Ps 18:41; Prov 1:28; Ps 145:18, 19
15:32 Prov 1:7; 8:33; Prov 8:36; Prov 15:5
16:1 Prov 16:9; 19:21
16:2 1 Sam 16:7; Dan 5:27
16:3 Ps 37:5; 55:22; Prov 3:6; 1 Pet 5:7

15:17–19 The "path of the upright" doesn't always seem easy (15:19), but look at the alternatives. Hatred (15:17), dispute (15:18), and laziness (15:19) cause problems that the upright person does not have to face. By comparison, his or her life is a smooth, level road because it is built on a solid foundation of love for God.

15:22 People with tunnel vision, those who are locked into one way of thinking, are likely to miss the right road because they have closed their minds to any new options. We need the help of those who can enlarge our vision and broaden our perspective. Seek out the advice of those who know you and have a wealth of experience. Build a network of advisers. Then be open to new ideas and be willing to weigh their suggestions carefully. Your plans will be stronger and more likely to succeed.

15:28 The righteous weigh their answers; the wicked don't wait to speak because they don't care about the effects of their words. It is important to have something to say, but it is equally important to weigh it first. Do you carefully plan your words, or do you pour out your thoughts without concern for their impact?

16:1 "The answer of the tongue is from the LORD" means that the final outcome of the plans we make is in God's hands. If this is so, why make plans? In doing God's will, there must be partnership between our efforts and God's control. He wants us to use our minds, to seek the advice of others, and to plan. Nevertheless, the results are up to him. Planning, then, helps us act God's way. As you live for him, ask for guidance as you plan, and then act on your plan as you trust in him.

16:2 "All the ways of a man are clean in his own sight." People can rationalize anything if they have no standards for judging right and wrong. We can always prove that we are right. Before putting any plan into action, ask yourself these three questions: (1) Is this plan in harmony with God's truth? (2) Will it work under real-life conditions? (3) Is my attitude pleasing to God?

16:3 There are different ways to fail to commit whatever we do to the Lord. Some people commit their work only superficially. They say the project is being done for the Lord, but in reality they are doing it for themselves. Others give God temporary control of their interests, only to take control back the moment things stop going the way they expect. Still others commit a task fully to the Lord, but

And your plans will be established.

4 The LORD has made everything for its own purpose,
Even the wicked for the day of evil.
5 Everyone who is proud in heart is an abomination to the LORD;
Assuredly, he will not be unpunished.
6 By lovingkindness and truth iniquity is atoned for,
And by the fear of the LORD one keeps away from evil.
7 When a man's ways are pleasing to the LORD,
He makes even his enemies to be at peace with him.
8 Better is a little with righteousness
Than great income with injustice.
9 The mind of man plans his way,
But the LORD directs his steps.
10 A divine decision is in the lips of the king;
His mouth should not err in judgment.
11 A just balance and scales belong to the LORD;
All the weights of the bag are His concern.
12 It is an abomination for kings to commit wicked acts,
For a throne is established on righteousness.

16:4 Gen 1:31; Eccl 3:11; Rom 9:22

16:6 Dan 4:27; Luke 11:41; Prov 8:13; 14:16

16:7 Gen 33:4; 2 Chr 17:10

16:9 Prov 16:1; 19:21; Ps 37:23; Prov 20:24; Jer 10:23

16:10 1 Kin 3:28

16:11 Prov 11:1

16:12 Prov 25:5

HOW GOD IS DESCRIBED IN PROVERBS

Proverbs is a book about wise living. It often focuses on a person's response and attitude toward God, who is the source of wisdom. And a number of proverbs point out aspects of God's character. Knowing God helps us on the way to wisdom.

God . . .	is aware of all that happens	15:3
	knows the heart of all people	15:11; 16:2; 21:2
	controls all things	16:33; 21:30
	is a place of safety	18:10
	rescues good people from danger	11:8, 21
	condemns the wicked	11:31
	delights in our prayers	15:8, 29
	loves those who obey him	15:9; 22:12
	cares for poor and needy	15:25; 22:22–23
	purifies hearts	17:3
	hates evil	17:5; 21:27; 28:9
Our response should be . . .	to fear and reverence God	10:27; 14:26–27; 15:16; 16:6; 19:23; 28:14
	to obey God's Word	13:13; 19:16
	to please God	21:3
	to trust in God	22:17–19; 29:25

put forth no effort themselves, and then they wonder why they do not succeed. We must maintain a delicate balance: trusting God as if everything depended on him, while working as if everything depended on us. Think of a specific effort in which you are involved right now. Have you committed it to the Lord?

16:4 This verse doesn't mean that God created some people to be wicked, but rather that God uses even the activities of wicked people to fulfill his good purposes. God is infinite and we are finite. No matter how great our intellects, we will never be able to understand him completely. But we can accept by faith that he is all-powerful, all-loving, and perfectly good. We can believe that he is not the cause of evil (James 1:13, 17); and we can trust that there are no loose ends in his system of judgment. Evil is a temporary condition in the universe. One day God will destroy it. In the meantime, he uses even the evil intentions of people for his good purposes (see Genesis 50:20).

16:5 Pride is the inner voice that whispers, "My way is best." It is resisting God's leadership and believing that you are able to live without his help. Whenever you find yourself wanting to do it your way and looking down on other people, you are being pulled by pride. Only when you eliminate pride can God help you become all he meant you to be. (See the chart in chapter 18.)

16:7 We want other people to like us, and sometimes we will do almost anything to win their approval. But God tells us to put our energy into pleasing him instead. Our effort to be peacemakers will usually make us more attractive to those around us, even our enemies. But even if it doesn't, we haven't lost anything. We are still pleasing God, the only one who truly matters.

16:11 Whether we buy or sell, make a product or offer a service, we know what is honest and what is dishonest. Sometimes we feel pressure to be dishonest in order to advance ourselves or gain more profit. But if we want to obey God, there is no middle ground: God demands honesty in every business transaction. No amount of rationalizing can cover for a dishonest business practice. Honesty and fairness are not always easy, but they are what God demands. Ask him for discernment and courage to be consistently honest and fair.

13 Righteous lips are the delight of kings,
And he who speaks right is loved.
14 The fury of a king is *like* messengers of death,
But a wise man will appease it.
15 In the light of a king's face is life,
And his favor is like a cloud with the spring rain.
16 How much better it is to get wisdom than gold!
And to get understanding is to be chosen above silver.
17 The highway of the upright is to depart from evil;
He who watches his way preserves his life.
18 Pride *goes* before destruction,
And a haughty spirit before stumbling.
19 It is better to be humble in spirit with the lowly
Than to divide the spoil with the proud.
20 He who gives attention to the word will find good,
And blessed is he who trusts in the LORD.
21 The wise in heart will be called understanding,
And sweetness of speech increases persuasiveness.
22 Understanding is a fountain of life to one who has it,
But the discipline of fools is folly.
23 The heart of the wise instructs his mouth
And adds persuasiveness to his lips.
24 Pleasant words are a honeycomb,
Sweet to the soul and healing to the bones.
25 There is a way *which seems* right to a man,
But its end is the way of death.
26 A worker's appetite works for him,
For his hunger urges him *on.*
27 A worthless man digs up evil,
While his words are like scorching fire.
28 A perverse man spreads strife,
And a slanderer separates intimate friends.
29 A man of violence entices his neighbor
And leads him in a way that is not good.
30 He who winks his eyes *does so* to devise perverse things;
He who compresses his lips brings evil to pass.
31 A gray head is a crown of glory;
It is found in the way of righteousness.
32 He who is slow to anger is better than the mighty,
And he who rules his spirit, than he who captures a city.
33 The lot is cast into the lap,
But its every decision is from the LORD.

16:15 Job 29:23

16:16 Prov 8:10, 19

16:17 Is 35:8

16:18 Prov 11:2; 18:12; Jer 49:16; Obad 3, 4

16:19 Prov 3:34; 29:23; Is 57:15; Ex 15:9; Judg 5:30; Prov 1:13, 14

16:20 Prov 19:8; Ps 2:12; 34:8; Jer 17:7

16:21 Hos 14:9; Prov 16:23

16:23 Ps 37:30; Prov 15:28; Matt 12:34

16:24 Ps 19:10; Prov 15:26; 24:13, 14; Prov 4:22; 17:22

16:25 Prov 12:15; 14:12

16:27 Prov 6:12, 14, 18; James 3:6

16:29 Prov 1:10; 12:26

16:31 Prov 20:29; Prov 3:1, 2

16:33 Prov 18:18; Prov 29:26

16:18 Proud people take little account of their weaknesses and do not anticipate stumbling blocks. They think they are above the frailties of common people. In this state of mind they are easily tripped up. Ironically, proud people seldom realize that pride is their problem, although everyone around them is well aware of it. Ask someone you trust whether self-satisfaction has blinded you to warning signs. He or she may help you avoid a fall.

16:22 For centuries people sought a fountain of youth, a spring that promised to give eternal life and vitality. It was never found. But God's wisdom is a fountain of life that can make a person happy, healthy, and alive forever. How? When we live by God's Word, he washes away the deadly effects of sin (see Titus 3:4–8), and the hope of eternal life with him gives us a joyful perspective on our present life. The fountain of youth was only a dream, but the fountain of life is reality. The choice is yours. You can be enlightened by God's wisdom, or you can be dragged down by the weight of your own foolishness.

16:26 "The worker's appetite works for him" means that no matter how much difficulty or drudgery we may find in our work, our appetite is an incentive to keep going. Hunger makes us work to satisfy that hunger.

16:31 The Hebrews believed that a long life was a sign of God's blessing; therefore, gray hair and old age were good. While young people glory in their strength, old people can rejoice in their years of experience and practical wisdom. Gray hair is not a sign of disgrace to be covered over; it is a crown of splendor. As you deal with older people, treat them with respect.

16:32 Self-control is superior to conquest. Success in business, school, or home life can be ruined by a person who has lost control of his or her temper. So it is a great personal victory to control your temper. When you feel yourself ready to explode, remember that losing control may cause you to forfeit what you want the most.

16:33 The lot was almost always used in ceremonial settings and was the common method for determining God's will. Several important events occurred by lot, including the identification of Achan as the man who had sinned (Joshua 7:14), the division of the promised land among the tribes (Joshua 14:2), and the selection of the first king for the nation (1 Samuel 10:16–26).

17:1 Prov 15:17
17:3 Prov 27:21; Ps 26:2; Prov 15:11; Jer 17:10; Mal 3:3
17:4 Prov 14:15
17:5 Prov 14:31; Job 31:29; Prov 24:17
17:6 Gen 48:11; Prov 13:22; Ex 20:12; Mal 1:6
17:7 Prov 24:7; Ps 31:18; Prov 12:22
17:8 Prov 21:14; Is 1:23; Amos 5:12
17:9 Prov 10:12; James 5:20; 1 Pet 4:8; Prov 16:28
17:13 Ps 35:12; 109:5; Jer 18:20; 2 Sam 12:10; 1 Kin 21:22; Prov 13:21
17:14 Prov 20:3; 25:8; 1 Thess 4:11
17:15 Ex 23:7; Prov 18:5; 24:24; Is 5:23
17:17 Ruth 1:16; Prov 18:24
17:18 Prov 6:1; 11:15; 22:26
17:19 Prov 29:22; Prov 16:18; 29:23
17:20 Prov 24:20; James 3:8
17:21 Prov 10:1; 17:25; 19:13

Contrast the Upright and the Wicked

17 Better is a dry morsel and quietness with it
Than a house full of feasting with strife.
2 A servant who acts wisely will rule over a son who acts shamefully,
And will share in the inheritance among brothers.
3 The refining pot is for silver and the furnace for gold,
But the LORD tests hearts.
4 An evildoer listens to wicked lips;
A liar pays attention to a destructive tongue.
5 He who mocks the poor taunts his Maker;
He who rejoices at calamity will not go unpunished.
6 Grandchildren are the crown of old men,
And the glory of sons is their fathers.
7 Excellent speech is not fitting for a fool,
Much less are lying lips to a prince.
8 A bribe is a charm in the sight of its owner;
Wherever he turns, he prospers.
9 He who conceals a transgression seeks love,
But he who repeats a matter separates intimate friends.
10 A rebuke goes deeper into one who has understanding
Than a hundred blows into a fool.
11 A rebellious man seeks only evil,
So a cruel messenger will be sent against him.
12 Let a man meet a bear robbed of her cubs,
Rather than a fool in his folly.
13 He who returns evil for good,
Evil will not depart from his house.
14 The beginning of strife is *like* letting out water,
So abandon the quarrel before it breaks out.
15 He who justifies the wicked and he who condemns the righteous,
Both of them alike are an abomination to the LORD.
16 Why is there a price in the hand of a fool to buy wisdom,
When he has no sense?
17 A friend loves at all times,
And a brother is born for adversity.
18 A man lacking in sense pledges
And becomes guarantor in the presence of his neighbor.
19 He who loves transgression loves strife;
He who raises his door seeks destruction.
20 He who has a crooked mind finds no good,
And he who is perverted in his language falls into evil.
21 He who sires a fool *does so* to his sorrow,

17:3 It takes intense heat to refine gold and silver. Similarly, it often takes the heat of trials for the Christian to be purified. Through trials, God shows us what is in us and clears out anything that gets in the way of complete trust in him. Peter says that trials come "so that the proof of your faith, being more precious than gold which is perishable, even though tested by fire, may be found to result in praise and glory and honor at the revelation of Jesus Christ" (1 Peter 1:7). So when tough times come your way, realize that God wants to use them to refine your faith and purify your heart.

17:5 Few acts are as cruel as making fun of the less fortunate, but many people do this because it makes them feel good to be better off or more successful than someone else. Mocking the poor is mocking the God who made them. We also ridicule God when we mock the weak, those who are different, or anyone else. When you catch yourself putting down others just for fun, stop and think about who created them.

17:8 Solomon is not condoning bribery (see 17:15, 23), but he is making an observation about the way the world operates. Bribes may get people what they want, but the Bible clearly condemns using them (Exodus 23:8; Proverbs 17:23; Matthew 28:11–15).

17:9 This proverb is saying that we should be willing to forgive others' sins against us. Covering over offenses is necessary to any relationship. It is tempting, especially in an argument, to bring up all the mistakes the other person has ever made. Love, however, keeps its mouth shut—difficult though that may be. Try never to bring anything into an argument that is unrelated to the topic being discussed. As we grow to be like Christ, we will acquire God's ability to forget the confessed sins of the past.

17:17 What kind of friend are you? There is a vast difference between knowing someone well and being a true friend. The greatest evidence of genuine friendship is loyalty (loving "at all times") (see 1 Corinthians 13:7)—being available to help in times of distress or personal struggles. Too many people are fair-weather friends. They stick around when the friendship helps them and leave when they're not getting anything out of the relationship. Think of your friends and assess your loyalty to them. Be the kind of true friend the Bible encourages.

And the father of a fool has no joy.
22 A joyful heart is good medicine,
But a broken spirit dries up the bones.
23 A wicked man receives a bribe from the bosom
To pervert the ways of justice.
24 Wisdom is in the presence of the one who has understanding,
But the eyes of a fool are on the ends of the earth.
25 A foolish son is a grief to his father
And bitterness to her who bore him.
26 It is also not good to fine the righteous,
Nor to strike the noble for *their* uprightness.
27 He who restrains his words has knowledge,
And he who has a cool spirit is a man of understanding.
28 Even a fool, when he keeps silent, is considered wise;
When he closes his lips, he is *considered* prudent.

Contrast the Upright and the Wicked

18 He who separates himself seeks *his own* desire,
He quarrels against all sound wisdom.
2 A fool does not delight in understanding,
But only in revealing his own mind.
3 When a wicked man comes, contempt also comes,
And with dishonor *comes* scorn.
4 The words of a man's mouth are deep waters;
The fountain of wisdom is a bubbling brook.
5 To show partiality to the wicked is not good,
Nor to thrust aside the righteous in judgment.
6 A fool's lips bring strife,
And his mouth calls for blows.
7 A fool's mouth is his ruin,
And his lips are the snare of his soul.
8 The words of a whisperer are like dainty morsels,
And they go down into the innermost parts of the body.
9 He also who is slack in his work
Is brother to him who destroys.
10 The name of the LORD is a strong tower;
The righteous runs into it and is safe.
11 A rich man's wealth is his strong city,
And like a high wall in his own imagination.
12 Before destruction the heart of man is haughty,
But humility *goes* before honor.
13 He who gives an answer before he hears,

17:22 Prov 15:13; Ps 22:15
17:23 Mic 3:11; 7:3
17:24 Eccl 2:14
17:25 Prov 19:13; Prov 10:1
17:26 Prov 17:15; 18:5
17:27 Prov 10:19; James 1:19; Prov 14:29
18:1 Prov 3:21; 8:14
18:2 Prov 12:23; 13:16; Eccl 10:3
18:4 Prov 20:5
18:5 Lev 19:15; Deut 1:17; 16:19; Ps 82:2; Prov 17:15; 24:23; 28:21; Ex 23:2, 6; Prov 17:26; 31:5; Mic 3:9
18:6 Prov 19:29
18:7 Ps 64:8; 140:9; Prov 10:14; 12:13; 13:3; Eccl 10:12
18:9 Prov 10:4; Prov 28:24
18:10 Ex 3:15; 2 Sam 22:2, 3, 33; Ps 18:2; 61:3; 91:2; 144:2; Prov 29:25
18:11 Prov 10:15
18:12 Prov 11:2; 16:18; 29:23; Prov 15:33
18:13 Prov 20:25; John 7:51

17:22 To be joyful is to be ready to greet others with a welcome, a word of encouragement, an enthusiasm for the task at hand, and a positive outlook on the future. Such people are as welcome as pain-relieving medicine.

17:24 While there is something to be said for having big dreams, this proverb points out the folly of chasing fantasies (having eyes that wander to "the ends of the earth," see 12:11). How much better to align your goals with God's, being the kind of person he wants you to be! Such goals (wisdom, honesty, patience, love) may not seem exciting, but they will determine your eternal future. Take time to think about your dreams and goals, and make sure they cover the really important areas of life.

17:27–28 This proverb highlights several benefits of keeping quiet: (1) It is the best policy if you have nothing worthwhile to say; (2) it allows you the opportunity to listen and learn; (3) it gives you something in common with those who are wiser. Make sure to pause to think and to listen so that when you do speak, you will have something important to say.

18:8 It is as hard to refuse to listen to a gossip (a whisperer) as it is to turn down a delicious dessert. Taking just one morsel of either one creates a taste for more. You can resist rumors the same way a determined dieter resists candy—never even open the box. If you don't nibble on the first bite of gossip, you can't take the second and the third.

18:11 In imagining that their wealth is their strongest defense, rich people are sadly mistaken. Money cannot provide safety—there are too many ways for it to lose its power. The government may cease to back it; thieves may steal it; inflation may rob it of all value. But God never loses his power. He is always dependable. Where do you look for security and safety—uncertain wealth or God who is always faithful?

18:13, 15, 17 In these concise statements, there are three basic principles for making sound decisions: (1) Get the facts before answering; (2) be open to new ideas; (3) make sure you hear both sides of the story before judging. All three principles center around seeking additional information. This is difficult work, but the only alternative is prejudice—judging before getting the facts.

18:14 Prov 17:22; Prov 15:13

18:15 Prov 15:14; Eph 1:17; Prov 15:31

18:16 Gen 32:20; 1 Sam 25:27

18:18 Prov 16:33

18:20 Prov 12:14; Prov 14:14

18:21 Prov 12:13; 13:3; Matt 12:37; Prov 13:2; Is 3:10; Hos 10:13

18:22 Gen 2:18; Prov 12:4; 19:14; 31:10-31; Prov 8:35

18:23 Prov 19:7; James 2:3, 6; 1 Kin 12:13; 2 Chr 10:13

18:24 Prov 17:17; John 15:14, 15

19:1 Prov 28:6; Ps 26:11; Prov 14:2; 20:7

It is folly and shame to him.
14 The spirit of a man can endure his sickness,
But *as for* a broken spirit who can bear it?
15 The mind of the prudent acquires knowledge,
And the ear of the wise seeks knowledge.
16 A man's gift makes room for him
And brings him before great men.
17 The first to plead his case *seems* right,
Until another comes and examines him.
18 The *cast* lot puts an end to strife
And decides between the mighty ones.
19 A brother offended *is harder to be won* than a strong city,
And contentions are like the bars of a citadel.
20 With the fruit of a man's mouth his stomach will be satisfied;
He will be satisfied *with* the product of his lips.
21 Death and life are in the power of the tongue,
And those who love it will eat its fruit.
22 He who finds a wife finds a good thing
And obtains favor from the LORD.
23 The poor man utters supplications,
But the rich man answers roughly.
24 A man of *too many* friends *comes* to ruin,
But there is a friend who sticks closer than a brother.

On Life and Conduct

19 Better is a poor man who walks in his integrity
Than he who is perverse in speech and is a fool.

HUMILITY AND PRIDE
Proverbs is direct and forceful in rejecting pride. The proud attitude heads the list of seven things God hates (6:16–17). The harmful results of pride are constantly contrasted with humility and its benefits.

Results of . . .	*Humility*	*Pride*	
	Leads to wisdom	Leads to dishonor	11:2
	Takes counsel	Produces strife	13:10
	Leads to honor		15:33
		Leads to punishment	16:5
		Leads to destruction	16:18
	Ends in honor	Ends in downfall	18:12
	Brings one to honor	Brings one low	29:23

18:22 This verse states that it is good to be married. Today's emphasis on individual freedom is misguided. Strong individuals are important, but so are strong marriages. God created marriage for our enjoyment and he pronounced it good. This is one of many passages in the Bible that show marriage as a joyful and good creation of God (Genesis 2:21–25; Proverbs 5:15–19; John 2:1–11).

18:23 This verse does not condone insulting the poor; it is simply recording an unfortunate fact of life. It is wrong for rich people to treat the less fortunate with contempt and arrogance, and God will judge such actions severely (see 14:31).

18:24 Loneliness is everywhere—many people feel cut off and alienated from others. Being in a crowd just makes people more aware of their isolation. We all need friends who will stick close, listen, care, and offer help when it is needed—in good times and bad. It is better to have one such friend than dozens of superficial acquaintances. Instead of wishing you could find a true friend, seek to become one. There are people who need your friendship. Ask God to reveal them to you, and then take on the challenge of being a true friend.

19:1 A life of integrity is far more valuable than wealth, but most people don't act as if they believe this. Afraid of not getting everything they want, they will pay any price to increase their wealth—cheating on their taxes, stealing from stores or employers, withholding tithes, refusing to give. But when we know and love God, we realize that a lower standard of living—or even poverty—is a small price to pay for personal integrity. Do your actions show that you sacrifice your integrity to increase your wealth? What changes do you need to make in order to get your priorities straight?

2 Also it is not good for a person to be without knowledge,
And he who hurries his footsteps errs.
3 The foolishness of man ruins his way,
And his heart rages against the LORD.
4 Wealth adds many friends,
But a poor man is separated from his friend.
5 A false witness will not go unpunished,
And he who tells lies will not escape.
6 Many will seek the favor of a generous man,
And every man is a friend to him who gives gifts.
7 All the brothers of a poor man hate him;
How much more do his friends abandon him!
He pursues *them with* words, *but* they are gone.
8 He who gets wisdom loves his own soul;
He who keeps understanding will find good.
9 A false witness will not go unpunished,
And he who tells lies will perish.
10 Luxury is not fitting for a fool;
Much less for a slave to rule over princes.
11 A man's discretion makes him slow to anger,
And it is his glory to overlook a transgression.
12 The king's wrath is like the roaring of a lion,
But his favor is like dew on the grass.
13 A foolish son is destruction to his father,
And the contentions of a wife are a constant dripping.
14 House and wealth are an inheritance from fathers,
But a prudent wife is from the LORD.
15 Laziness casts into a deep sleep,
And an idle man will suffer hunger.
16 He who keeps the commandment keeps his soul,
But he who is careless of conduct will die.
17 One who is gracious to a poor man lends to the LORD,
And He will repay him for his good deed.
18 Discipline your son while there is hope,
And do not desire his death.
19 *A man of* great anger will bear the penalty,
For if you rescue *him,* you will only have to do it again.
20 Listen to counsel and accept discipline,
That you may be wise the rest of your days.
21 Many plans are in a man's heart,
But the counsel of the LORD will stand.
22 What is desirable in a man is his [4]kindness,
And *it is* better to be a poor man than a liar.
23 The fear of the LORD *leads* to life,

4 Or *loyalty*

19:2
Prov 21:5; 28:20; 29:20

19:3
Prov 11:3; Is 8:21

19:4
Prov 14:20

19:5
Ex 23:1; Deut 19:16-19; 21:28; Prov 6:19

19:6
Prov 29:26; Prov 18:16; 21:14

19:7
Ps 38:11; Prov 18:23

19:8
Prov 16:20

19:9
Prov 19:5; Dan 6:24

19:10
Prov 17:7; 26:1; Eccl 10:6, 7; Prov 30:22

19:11
Prov 14:29; 16:32; Matt 5:44; Eph 4:32; Col 3:13

19:13
Prov 17:25; Prov 21:9, 19; 27:15

19:14
2 Cor 12:14

19:15
Prov 6:9, 10; 24:33

19:16
Prov 13:13; 16:17; Luke 10:28; 11:28

19:17
Prov 14:31; 28:27; Eccl 11:1, 2; Matt 10:42; 25:40; 2 Cor 9:6-8; Heb 6:10; Luke 6:38

19:18
Prov 13:24; 23:13; 29:15, 17

19:20
Prov 4:1; 8:33; 12:15

19:21
Prov 16:1, 9; Ps 33:10, 11; Is 14:26

19:23
Prov 14:27; 1 Tim 4:8; Ps 25:13; Ps 91:10; Prov 12:21

19:2 We often move hastily through life, rushing headlong into the unknown. Many people marry without knowing what to expect of their partner or of married life. Others try illicit sex or drugs without considering the consequences. Some plunge into jobs without evaluating whether they are suitable to that line of work. Don't rush into the unknown. Be sure you understand what you're getting into and where you want to go before you take the first step. And if it still seems unknown, be sure you are following God.

19:8 Is it good to love yourself? Yes, when your soul is at stake! This proverb does not condone the self-centered person who loves and protects his or her selfish interests and will do anything to serve them. Instead it encourages those who really care about themselves to seek wisdom.

19:16 The instructions we are told to obey are those found in God's Word—both the Ten Commandments (Exodus 20) and other passages of instruction. To obey what God teaches in the Bible is self-preserving. To disobey is self-destructive.

19:17 Here God identifies with the poor as Jesus does in Matthew 25:31–46. As our Creator, God values all of us, whether we are poor or rich. When we help the poor, we honor both the Creator and his creation. God accepts our help as if we had offered it directly to him.

19:23 Those who fear the Lord are "untouched by evil" because of their healthy habits, their beneficial life-style, and sometimes through God's direct intervention. Nevertheless, the fear of the Lord does not always protect us from trouble in this life: Evil things still happen to people who love God. This verse is not a universal promise, but a general guideline. It describes what would happen if this world were sinless, and what will happen in the new earth, when faithful believers will be under God's protection forever. (See the note on 3:16–17 for more about this concept.)

19:24 Prov 26:15; Matt 26:23; Mark 14:20
19:25 Prov 21:11; Prov 9:8
19:26 Prov 28:24
19:28 Job 15:16; 20:12, 13; 34:7
19:29 Ps 1:1; Prov 9:12; Prov 10:13; 18:6; 26:3
20:1 Gen 9:21; Prov 23:29, 30; Is 28:7; Hos 4:11; Prov 31:4; Is 5:22; 56:12
20:2 Num 16:38; 1 Kin 2:23; Prov 8:36; Hab 2:10
20:3 Gen 13:7f; Prov 17:14
20:4 Prov 13:4; 21:25
20:6 Prov 25:14; Matt 6:2; Luke 18:11; Ps 12:1; Luke 18:8
20:7 Prov 19:1; Ps 37:26; 112:2

So that one may sleep satisfied, untouched by evil.
24 The sluggard buries his hand in the dish,
But will not even bring it back to his mouth.
25 Strike a scoffer and the naive may become shrewd,
But reprove one who has understanding and he will gain knowledge.
26 He who assaults *his* father *and* drives *his* mother away
Is a shameful and disgraceful son.
27 Cease listening, my son, to discipline,
And you will stray from the words of knowledge.
28 A rascally witness makes a mockery of justice,
And the mouth of the wicked spreads iniquity.
29 Judgments are prepared for scoffers,
And blows for the back of fools.

On Life and Conduct

20 Wine is a mocker, strong drink a brawler,
And whoever is intoxicated by it is not wise.
2 The terror of a king is like the growling of a lion;
He who provokes him to anger forfeits his own life.
3 Keeping away from strife is an honor for a man,
But any fool will quarrel.
4 The sluggard does not plow after the autumn,
So he begs during the harvest and has nothing.
5 A plan in the heart of a man is *like* deep water,
But a man of understanding draws it out.
6 Many a man proclaims his own loyalty,
But who can find a trustworthy man?
7 A righteous man who walks in his integrity—

HOW TO SUCCEED IN GOD'S EYES
Proverbs notes two significant by-products of wise living: success and good reputation. Several verses also point out what causes failure and poor reputation.

Qualities that promote success and a good reputation:	
Righteousness	10:7; 12:3; 28:12
Hating what is false	13:5
Committing all work to the Lord	16:3
Using words with restraint; being even-tempered	17:27–28
Loving wisdom and understanding	19:8
Humility and fear of the Lord	22:4
Willingness to confess and forsake sin	28:13
Qualities that prevent success and cause a bad reputation:	
Wickedness	10:7; 12:3; 28:12
Seeking glory	25:27
Hatred	26:24–26
Praising oneself	27:2
Concealing sin	28:13

Other verses dealing with one's reputation are: 11:10, 16; 14:3; 19:10; 22:1; 23:17–18; 24:13–14

19:24 "Buries his hand in the dish" refers to the custom of eating where a dish would be passed and people would reach in and get food for themselves. This proverb is saying that some people are so lazy that they won't even feed themselves.

19:25 There is a great difference between the person who learns from criticism and the person who refuses to accept correction. How we respond to criticism determines whether or not we grow in wisdom. The next time someone criticizes you, listen carefully to all that is said. You might learn something.

20:3 A person who is truly confident of his or her strength does not need to parade it. A truly brave person does not look for chances to prove it. A resourceful woman can find a way out of a fight. A man of endurance will avoid retaliating. Foolish people find it impossible to avoid strife. Men and women of character can. What kind of person are you?

20:4 You've heard similar warnings: If you don't study, you'll fail the test; if you don't save, you won't have money when you need it. God wants us to anticipate future needs and prepare for them. We can't expect him to come to our rescue when we cause our own problems through lack of planning and action. He provides for us, but he also expects us to be responsible.

How blessed are his sons after him.
8 A king who sits on the throne of justice
Disperses all evil with his eyes.
9 Who can say, "I have cleansed my heart,
I am pure from my sin"?
10 Differing weights and differing measures,
Both of them are abominable to the LORD.
11 It is by his deeds that a lad distinguishes himself
If his conduct is pure and right.
12 The hearing ear and the seeing eye,
The LORD has made both of them.
13 Do not love sleep, or you will become poor;
Open your eyes, *and* you will be satisfied with food.
14 "Bad, bad," says the buyer,
But when he goes his way, then he boasts.
15 There is gold, and an abundance of jewels;
But the lips of knowledge are a more precious thing.
16 Take his garment when he becomes surety for a stranger;
And for foreigners, hold him in pledge.
17 Bread obtained by falsehood is sweet to a man,
But afterward his mouth will be filled with gravel.
18 Prepare plans by consultation,
And make war by wise guidance.
19 He who goes about as a slanderer reveals secrets,
Therefore do not associate with a gossip.
20 He who curses his father or his mother,
His lamp will go out in time of darkness.
21 An inheritance gained hurriedly at the beginning
Will not be blessed in the end.
22 Do not say, "I will repay evil";
Wait for the LORD, and He will save you.
23 Differing weights are an abomination to the LORD,
And a false scale is not good.
24 Man's steps are *ordained* by the LORD,
How then can man understand his way?
25 It is a trap for a man to say rashly, "It is holy!"
And after the vows to make inquiry.
26 A wise king winnows the wicked,
And drives the *threshing* wheel over them.
27 The spirit of man is the lamp of the LORD,
Searching all the innermost parts of his being.

20:8 Prov 20:26; 25:5

20:9 1 Kin 8:46; 2 Chr 6:36; Job 14:4; Eccl 7:20; Rom 3:9; 1 John 1:8

20:10 Prov 11:1; 20:23

20:11 Matt 7:16

20:12 Ex 4:11; Ps 94:9

20:13 Prov 6:9, 10; 19:15; 24:33

20:17 Prov 9:17

20:18 Prov 11:14; 15:22; Prov 24:6; Luke 14:31

20:19 Prov 11:13; Prov 13:3

20:20 Ex 21:17; Lev 20:9; Prov 30:11; Matt 15:4; Job 18:5; Prov 13:9; 24:20

20:22 Prov 24:29; Matt 5:39; Rom 12:17, 19; 1 Thess 5:15; 1 Pet 3:9; Ps 27:14

20:23 Prov 20:10; Prov 11:1

20:24 Prov 16:9

20:25 Eccl 5:4, 5

20:26 Prov 20:8; Is 28:27

20:27 1 Cor 2:11

20:9 No one is without sin. As soon as we confess our sin and repent, sinful thoughts and actions begin to creep back into our lives. We all need ongoing cleansing, moment by moment. Thank God he provides forgiveness by his mercy when we ask for it. Make confession and repentance a regular part of your talks with God. Rely on him moment by moment for the cleansing you need.

20:23 "Differing weights" refers to the loaded scales a merchant might use in order to cheat the customers. Dishonesty is a difficult sin to avoid. It is easy to cheat if we think no one else is looking. But dishonesty affects the very core of a person. It makes him untrustworthy and untrusting. It eventually makes him unable to know himself or relate to others. Don't take dishonesty lightly. Even the smallest portion of dishonesty contains enough of the poison of deceit to kill your spiritual life. If there is any dishonesty in your life, tell God about it now.

20:24 We are often confused by the events around us. Many things we will never understand; others will fall into place in years to come as we look back and see how God was working. This proverb counsels us not to worry if we don't understand everything as it happens. Instead, we should trust that God knows what he's doing, even if his timing or design is not clear to us. See Psalm 37:23 for a reassuring promise of God's direction in your life.

20:25 To say something is holy means to dedicate it, to give it as an offering to God. *Dedicated* means set apart for religious use. This proverb points out the evil of making a vow rashly and then reconsidering it. God takes vows seriously and requires that they be carried out (Deuteronomy 23:21–23). We often have good intentions when making a vow because we want to show God that we are determined to please him. Jesus, however, says it is better not to make promises to God because he knows how difficult they are to keep (Matthew 5:33–37). If you still feel it is important to make a vow, make sure that you weigh the consequences of breaking that vow. (In Judges 11, Jephthah made a rash promise to sacrifice the first thing he saw on his return home. As it happened, he saw his daughter first.) It is better not to make promises than to make them and then later want to change them. It is better still to count the cost beforehand and then to fulfill them. (For a list of other Bible people who made rash vows, see the chart in Judges 11.)

20:28 Prov 29:14
20:29 Prov 16:31
20:30 Ps 89:32; Prov 22:15; Is 53:5; 1 Pet 2:24
21:1 Ezra 6:22
21:2 Prov 16:2; Prov 16:2; 24:12; Luke 16:15
21:3 1 Sam 15:22; Prov 15:8; Is 1:11, 16, 17; Hos 6:6; Mic 6:7, 8
21:4 Prov 24:20; Luke 11:34

28 Loyalty and truth preserve the king,
And he upholds his throne by righteousness.
29 The glory of young men is their strength,
And the honor of old men is their gray hair.
30 Stripes that wound scour away evil,
And strokes *reach* the innermost parts.

On Life and Conduct

21 The king's heart is *like* channels of water in the hand of the LORD;
He turns it wherever He wishes.
2 Every man's way is right in his own eyes,
But the LORD weighs the hearts.
3 To do righteousness and justice
Is desired by the LORD more than sacrifice.
4 Haughty eyes and a proud heart,
The lamp of the wicked, is sin.

HONESTY AND DISHONESTY
Proverbs tells us plainly that God despises all forms of dishonesty. Not only does God hate dishonesty, but we are told that it works against us—others no longer trust us, and we cannot even enjoy our dishonest gains. It is wiser to be honest because "the righteous will escape from trouble" (12:13).

Others' Opinions	
Leaders value those who speak the truth.	16:13
Most people will appreciate truth in the end more than flattery.	28:23
Quality of Life	
The righteous person's plans are just.	12:5
Truthful witnesses do not deceive; false witnesses utter lies.	14:5
Truthful witnesses save lives.	14:25
The children of the righteous are blessed.	20:7
Short-Term Results	
Ill-gotten gain is of no value.	10:2
The righteous are delivered from trouble.	11:8
The evil are trapped by sinful talk.	12:13
Fraudulent gain is sweet only for a while.	20:17
Long-Term Results	
The upright are guided by integrity.	11:3
Truthful lips endure.	12:19
Riches gained quickly don't last.	20:21
Riches gained dishonestly don't last.	21:6
The blameless are kept safe.	28:18
God's Opinion	
God delights in honesty.	11:1
God delights in those who deal truthfully.	12:22
God detests unjust measures.	20:10
God is pleased when we do what is right and just.	21:3

21:1 In Solomon's day, kings possessed absolute authority and were often considered to be like gods. This proverb shows that God, not earthly rulers, has ultimate authority over world politics. Although they may not have realized it, the earth's most powerful kings have always been under God's control. (See Isaiah 10:5–8 for an example of a king who was used for God's purposes.)

21:2 People can find an excuse for doing almost anything, but God looks behind the excuses to the motives of the heart. We often have to make choices in areas where the right action is difficult to discern. We can help ourselves make such decisions by trying to identify our motives first and then asking, "Would God be pleased with my real reasons for doing this?" God is not pleased when we do good deeds only to receive something in return.

21:3 Sacrifices and offerings are not bribes to make God overlook our character faults. If our personal and business dealings are not characterized by justice, no amount of generosity when the offering plate is passed will make up for it.

5 The plans of the diligent *lead* surely to advantage,
But everyone who is hasty *comes* surely to poverty.
6 The acquisition of treasures by a lying tongue
Is a fleeting vapor, the pursuit of death.
7 The violence of the wicked will drag them away,
Because they refuse to act with justice.
8 The way of a guilty man is crooked,
But as for the pure, his conduct is upright.
9 It is better to live in a corner of a roof
Than in a house shared with a contentious woman.
10 The soul of the wicked desires evil;
His neighbor finds no favor in his eyes.
11 When the scoffer is punished, the naive becomes wise;
But when the wise is instructed, he receives knowledge.
12 The righteous one considers the house of the wicked,
Turning the wicked to ruin.
13 He who shuts his ear to the cry of the poor
Will also cry himself and not be answered.
14 A gift in secret subdues anger,
And a bribe in the bosom, strong wrath.

21:5 Prov 10:4; 13:4; Prov 28:22

21:6 Prov 13:11; 20:21; Prov 8:36

21:7 Amos 5:7; Mic 3:9

21:8 Prov 2:15

21:10 Ps 52:3; Prov 2:14; 14:21

21:11 Prov 19:25

21:12 Prov 14:11

21:13 Matt 18:30-34; 1 John 3:17; James 2:13

21:14 Prov 18:16; 19:6

RIGHTEOUSNESS

Proverbs often compares the lifestyles of the wicked and the righteous, and makes a strong case for living by God's pattern. The advantages of righteous living and the disadvantages of wicked living are pointed out. The kind of person we decide to be will affect every area of our lives.

	Righteous	*Wicked*	*Reference*
Outlook on life	Hopeful	Fearful	10:24
	Concerned about the welfare of God's creation	Even their compassion is cruel	12:10
	Understand justice	Don't understand justice	28:5
Response to life	Covered with blessings	Covered with violence	10:6
		Bent on evil	16:30
	Give thought to their ways	Put up a bold front	21:29
	Persevere against evil	Brought down by calamity	24:15–16
		Hate those with integrity	29:10
How they are seen by others	Are seen with favor	Their way is hard	13:15
		Lead others into sin	16:29
	Conduct is upright	Conduct is crooked	21:8
	Are not to desire the company of evil people	Plot violence	24:1–2
	Others are glad when they triumph	Others hide when they rise to power	28:12
	Concerned for the poor	Unconcerned about the poor	29:7
	Detest the dishonest	Detest the upright	29:27
Quality of life	Stand firm	Swept away	10:25
	Delivered by righteousness	Caught by their own greed	11:6

21:5 Faithful completion of mundane tasks is a great accomplishment. Such work is patiently carried out according to a plan. Diligence does not come naturally to most people; it is a result of strong character. Don't look for quick and easy answers. Be a diligent servant of God.

21:11–12 It is usually better to learn from the mistakes of others than from our own. We can do this by listening to their advice. Take counsel from others instead of plunging ahead and learning the hard way.

21:13 We should work to meet the needs of the poor and protect their rights—we may be in need of such services ourselves someday.

21:15 Prov 10:29
21:17 Prov 23:21
21:18 Is 43:3; Prov 11:8
21:19 Prov 21:9
21:20 Ps 112:3; Prov 8:21; 22:4; Job 20:15, 18
21:21 Prov 15:9; Matt 5:6; 1 Cor 15:58
21:22 Prov 24:5; Eccl 7:19; 9:15, 16
21:23 Prov 12:13; 13:3; 18:21; James 3:2
21:24 Ps 1:1; Prov 1:22; 3:34; 24:9; Is 29:20

15 The exercise of justice is joy for the righteous,
But is terror to the workers of iniquity.
16 A man who wanders from the way of understanding
Will rest in the assembly of the dead.
17 He who loves pleasure *will become* a poor man;
He who loves wine and oil will not become rich.
18 The wicked is a ransom for the righteous,
And the treacherous is in the place of the upright.
19 It is better to live in a desert land
Than with a contentious and vexing woman.
20 There is precious treasure and oil in the dwelling of the wise,
But a foolish man swallows it up.
21 He who pursues righteousness and loyalty
Finds life, righteousness and honor.
22 A wise man scales the city of the mighty
And brings down the stronghold in which they trust.
23 He who guards his mouth and his tongue,
Guards his soul from troubles.
24 "Proud," "Haughty," "Scoffer," are his names,
Who acts with insolent pride.

AND WICKEDNESS

	Righteous	*Wicked*	*Reference*
Quality of life (cont.)	No real harm befalls them	Filled with trouble	12:21
	Income results in treasure	Income results in trouble	15:6
	Avoid evil		16:17
		Fall into constant trouble	17:20
	Are bold as lions	Are fearful constantly	28:1
	Will be safe	Will suddenly fall	28:18
Short-term results	Walk securely	Will be found out	10:9
	Rewarded with prosperity	Pursued by adversity	13:21
Long-term results	God protects them	God destroys them	10:29
		Will be punished for rebellion	17:11
Eternal expectations	Never be shaken	Will not remain	10:30
	Earn a true reward	Earn deceptive wages	11:18
	Attain life	Go to death	11:19
	End only in good	End only in wrath	11:23
	Will stand firm	Will be overthrown	12:7
	Have a refuge when they die	Will be brought down by calamity	14:32
God's opinion of them	Delights in the walk of the blameless	Detests the perverse in heart	11:20
	Evil people will bow to them	They will bow before the good	14:19

21:20 This proverb is about saving for the future. Easy credit has many people living on the edge of bankruptcy. The desire to keep up and to accumulate more pushes them to spend every penny they earn, and they stretch their credit to the limit. But anyone who spends all he has is spending more than he can afford. A wise person puts money aside for when he or she may have less. God approves of foresight and restraint. God's people need to examine their lifestyles to see whether their spending is God-pleasing or merely self-pleasing.

25 The desire of the sluggard puts him to death,
For his hands refuse to work;
26 All day long he is craving,
While the righteous gives and does not hold back.
27 The sacrifice of the wicked is an abomination,
How much more when he brings it with evil intent!
28 A false witness will perish,
But the man who listens *to the truth* will speak forever.
29 A wicked man displays a bold face,
But as for the upright, he makes his way sure.
30 There is no wisdom and no understanding
And no counsel against the LORD.
31 The horse is prepared for the day of battle,
But victory belongs to the LORD.

21:25 Prov 13:4
21:26 Ps 37:26; 112:5, 9; Matt 5:42; Eph 4:28
21:27 Prov 15:8; Is 66:3; Jer 6:20; Amos 5:22
21:28 Prov 19:5, 9
21:29 Eccl 8:1; Ps 119:5; Prov 11:5
21:30 Jer 9:23; Acts 5:38, 39; 1 Cor 3:19, 20
21:31 Ps 20:7; 33:17; Is 31:1; Ps 3:8; Jer 3:23; 1 Cor 15:57

On Life and Conduct

22 A *good* name is to be more desired than great wealth,
Favor is better than silver and gold.
2 The rich and the poor have a common bond,
The LORD is the maker of them all.
3 The prudent sees the evil and hides himself,
But the naive go on, and are punished for it.
4 The reward of humility *and* the fear of the LORD
Are riches, honor and life.
5 Thorns *and* snares are in the way of the perverse;
He who guards himself will be far from them.
6 Train up a child in the way he should go,
Even when he is old he will not depart from it.
7 The rich rules over the poor,
And the borrower *becomes* the lender's slave.
8 He who sows iniquity will reap vanity,
And the rod of his fury will perish.
9 He who is generous will be blessed,
For he gives some of his food to the poor.
10 Drive out the scoffer, and contention will go out,
Even strife and dishonor will cease.
11 He who loves purity of heart
And whose speech is gracious, the king is his friend.

22:1 Prov 10:7; Eccl 7:1
22:2 Job 31:15; Prov 14:31
22:3 Prov 14:16; 27:12; Is 26:20
22:5 Prov 15:19
22:6 Eph 6:4
22:7 Prov 18:23; James 2:6
22:8 Job 4:8; Ps 125:3
22:9 Prov 19:17; 2 Cor 9:6; Luke 14:13
22:10 Gen 21:9, 10; Prov 18:6; 26:20
22:11 Ps 24:4; Matt 5:8; Prov 14:35; 16:13

21:27 The kind of worship ("sacrifice") described in this proverb is no better than a bribe. How do people try to bribe God? They may go to church, tithe, or volunteer, not because of their love and devotion to God, but because they hope God will bless them in return. But God has made it very clear that he desires obedience and love more than religious ritual (see 21:3; 1 Samuel 15:22). God does not want our sacrifices of time, energy, and money alone; he wants our hearts—our complete love and devotion. We may be able to bribe people (21:14), but we cannot bribe God.

21:31 This proverb refers to preparing for battle. All our preparation for any task is useless without God. But even with God's help we still must do our part and prepare. His control of the outcome does not negate our responsibilities. God may want you to produce a great book, but you must learn to write. God may want to use you in foreign missions, but you must learn the language. God will accomplish his purposes, and he will be able to use you if you have done your part by being well prepared.

22:4 This is a general observation that would have been especially applicable to an obedient Israelite living in Solomon's God-fearing kingdom. Nevertheless, some have been martyrs at a young age, and some have given away all their wealth for the sake of God's kingdom. The book of Proverbs describes life the way it should be. It does not dwell on the exceptions. (For more on this concept, see the note on 3:16–17.)

22:6 "In the way he should go" is literally, "according to his [the child's] way." It is natural to want to bring up all our children alike or train them the same way. This verse implies that parents should discern the individuality and special strengths that God has given each one. While we should not condone or excuse self-will, each child has natural inclinations that parents can develop. By talking to teachers, other parents, and grandparents, we can better discern and develop the individual capabilities of each child.

22:6 Many parents want to make all the choices for their child, but this hurts him or her in the long run. When parents teach a child how to make decisions, they don't have to watch every step he or she takes. They know their children will remain on the right path because they have made the choice themselves. Train your children to choose the right way.

22:7 Does this mean we should never borrow? No, but it warns us never to take on a loan without carefully examining our ability to repay it. A loan we can handle is enabling; a loan we can't handle is enslaving. The borrower must realize that until the loan is repaid, he or she is a servant to the individual or institution that made it.

12 The eyes of the LORD preserve knowledge,
But He overthrows the words of the treacherous man.

22:13 Prov 26:13

13 The sluggard says, "There is a lion outside;
I will be killed in the streets!"

22:14 Prov 2:16; 5:3; 7:5; 23:27; Eccl 7:26

14 The mouth of an adulteress is a deep pit;
He who is cursed of the LORD will fall into it.

22:15 Prov 13:24; 23:14

15 Foolishness is bound up in the heart of a child;
The rod of discipline will remove it far from him.

22:16 Eccl 5:8; James 2:13; Prov 28:22

16 He who oppresses the poor to make more for himself
Or who gives to the rich, *will* only *come to* poverty.

22:17 Prov 5:1

17 Incline your ear and hear the words of the wise,
And apply your mind to my knowledge;

22:18 Prov 2:10

18 For it will be pleasant if you keep them within you,
That they may be ready on your lips.

22:19 Prov 3:5

19 So that your trust may be in the LORD,
I have taught you today, even you.

22:20 Prov 8:6

20 Have I not written to you excellent things
Of counsels and knowledge,

22:21 Luke 1:3, 4; Prov 25:13; 1 Pet 3:15

21 To make you know the certainty of the words of truth
That you may correctly answer him who sent you?

22:22 Ex 23:6; Job 31:16; Prov 22:16; Zech 7:10; Mal 3:5

22 Do not rob the poor because he is poor,
Or crush the afflicted at the gate;

22:23 1 Sam 25:39; Ps 12:5; 35:10; 140:12; Prov 23:11; Jer 51:36

23 For the LORD will plead their case
And take the life of those who rob them.

22:24 Prov 29:22

24 Do not associate with a man *given* to anger;
Or go with a hot-tempered man,

22:25 1 Cor 15:33

25 Or you will learn his ways
And find a snare for yourself.

22:26 Prov 17:18

26 Do not be among those who give pledges,
Among those who become guarantors for debts.

22:27 Ex 22:26; Prov 20:16

27 If you have nothing with which to pay,
Why should he take your bed from under you?

22:28 Deut 19:14; 27:17; Job 24:2; Prov 23:10

28 Do not move the ancient boundary
Which your fathers have set.

22:12 "Knowledge" refers to those who have knowledge, those who live right and speak the truth. It takes discipline, determination, and hard work to live God's way, but God protects and rewards those who make the commitment to follow him.

22:13 This proverb refers to an excuse a lazy person might use to avoid going to work. The excuse sounds silly to us, but that's often how our excuses sound to others. Don't rationalize laziness. Take your responsibilities seriously and get to work.

22:15 Young children often do foolish and dangerous things simply because they don't understand the consequences. Wisdom and common sense are not transferred by just being a good example. The wisdom a child learns must be taught consciously. "The rod of discipline" stands for all forms of discipline or training. Just as God trains and corrects us to make us better, so parents must discipline their children to make them learn the difference between right and wrong. To see how God corrects us, read 3:11–12.

22:22–23 This proverb is a message of hope to people who must live and work under unjust authoritarian leaders. It is also a warning to those who enjoy ruling with an iron hand. Sometimes God intervenes and directly destroys tyrants. More often, he uses other rulers to overthrow them or their own oppressed people to rebel against them. If you are in a position of authority at church, work, or home, remember what happens to tyrants. Leadership through kindness is more effective and longer lasting than leadership by force.

22:24–25 People tend to become like those with whom they spend a lot of time. Even the negative characteristics sometimes rub off. The Bible exhorts us to be cautious in our choice of companions. Choose people with characteristics you would like to develop in your own life.

22:26 This verse is saying that it is wise to be slow to countersign a note or to be liable for another person's debt.

22:28 In Joshua 13—21, the land was divided and the boundaries marked out for each tribe. Moses had already warned the people that when they reached the promised land they shouldn't cheat their neighbors by moving one of the landmarks to give themselves more land and their neighbors less (Deuteronomy 19:14; 27:17). "Gerrymandering"—changing political boundaries so that one group of voters benefits and another loses—is a modern form of moving boundary markers.

29 Do you see a man skilled in his work?
He will stand before kings;
He will not stand before obscure men.

22:29 Gen 41:46; 1 Kin 10:8

On Life and Conduct

23 When you sit down to dine with a ruler,
Consider carefully what is before you,
2 And put a knife to your throat
If you are a man of *great* appetite.
3 Do not desire his delicacies,
For it is deceptive food.

23:2 Prov 23:20
23:3 Ps 141:4; Prov 23:6; Dan 1:5, 8, 13, 15, 16

4 Do not weary yourself to gain wealth,
Cease from your consideration *of it.*
5 When you set your eyes on it, it is gone.
For *wealth* certainly makes itself wings
Like an eagle that flies *toward* the heavens.

23:4 Prov 15:27; 28:20; Matt 6:19; 1 Tim 6:9; Heb 13:5; Prov 3:5, 7
23:5 Prov 27:24; 1 Tim 6:17

6 Do not eat the bread of a selfish man,
Or desire his delicacies;
7 For as he thinks within himself, so he is.
He says to you, "Eat and drink!"
But his heart is not with you.
8 You will vomit up the morsel you have eaten,
And waste your compliments.

23:6 Ps 141:4; Deut 15:9; Prov 28:22
23:7 Prov 26:24, 25
23:8 Prov 25:16

9 Do not speak in the hearing of a fool,
For he will despise the wisdom of your words.

23:9 Matt 7:6; Prov 1:7

10 Do not move the ancient boundary
Or go into the fields of the fatherless,
11 For their Redeemer is strong;
He will plead their case against you.
12 Apply your heart to discipline
And your ears to words of knowledge.

23:10 Jer 22:3; Zech 7:10
23:11 Job 19:25; Jer 50:34; Prov 22:23

13 Do not hold back discipline from the child,
Although you strike him with the rod, he will not die.
14 You shall strike him with the rod
And rescue his soul from Sheol.

23:13 Prov 13:24; 19:18
23:14 1 Cor 5:5

15 My son, if your heart is wise,
My own heart also will be glad;
16 And my inmost being will rejoice
When your lips speak what is right.

23:15 Prov 23:24f; 27:11; 29:3
23:16 Prov 8:6

23:1–3 The point of this proverb is to be careful when eating with an important or influential person because he or she may try to bribe you. No good will come from the meal.

23:4–5 We have all heard of people who have won millions of dollars and then lost it all. Even the average person can spend an inheritance—or a paycheck—with lightning speed and have little to show for it. Don't spend your time chasing fleeting earthly treasures. Instead store up treasures in heaven, for such treasures will never be lost. (See Luke 12:33–34 for Jesus' teaching.)

23:6–8 In graphic language, the writer warns us not to envy the life-styles of those who have become rich by being stingy and miserly, and not to gain their favor by fawning over them. Their "friendship" is phony—they will just use you for their own gain.

23:10–11 The term *Redeemer* refers to someone who bought back a family member who had fallen into slavery or who accepted the obligation to marry the widow of a family member (Ruth 4:3–10). God is also called a Redeemer (Exodus 6:6; Job 19:25). (For an explanation of ancient boundary stones, see the note on 22:28.)

23:12 The people most likely to gain knowledge are those who are willing to listen. It is a sign of strength, not weakness, to pay attention to what others have to say. People who are eager to listen continue to learn and grow throughout their lives. If we refuse to become set in our ways, we can always expand the limits of our knowledge.

23:13–14 The stern tone of discipline here is offset by the affection expressed in verse 15. However, many parents are reluctant to discipline their children at all. Some fear they will forfeit their relationship, that their children will resent them, or that they will stifle their children's development. But correction won't kill children, and it may prevent them from foolish moves that will.

23:17 Ps 37:1; Prov 24:1, 19; Prov 28:14
23:18 Ps 19:11; 58:11; Prov 24:14; Ps 9:18
23:19 Prov 6:6; Prov 4:23; 9:6
23:20 Prov 20:1; 23:29, 30; Is 5:22; Matt 24:49; Luke 21:34; Rom 13:13; Eph 5:18; Deut 21:20; Prov 28:7
23:21 Prov 21:17; Prov 6:10, 11
23:22 Prov 1:8; Eph 6:1; Prov 15:20; 30:17
23:23 Prov 4:7; 18:15; Matt 13:44
23:24 Prov 10:1; 15:20; 29:3
23:25 Prov 27:11
23:26 Prov 3:1; 4:4; Ps 1:2; 119:24
23:27 Prov 22:14; Prov 5:20
23:28 Prov 6:26; 7:12; Eccl 7:26
23:29 Is 5:11, 22
23:30 1 Sam 25:36; Prov 20:1; Is 5:11; 28:7; Eph 5:18; Ps 75:8
23:31 Song 7:9
23:32 Job 20:16; Prov 20:1; Eph 5:18; Ps 91:13; Is 11:8
23:33 Prov 2:12
23:35 Prov 27:22; Jer 5:3; Prov 26:11; Is 56:12

17 Do not let your heart envy sinners,
But *live* in the fear of the LORD always.
18 Surely there is a future,
And your hope will not be cut off.
19 Listen, my son, and be wise,
And direct your heart in the way.
20 Do not be with heavy drinkers of wine,
Or with gluttonous eaters of meat;
21 For the heavy drinker and the glutton will come to poverty,
And drowsiness will clothe *one* with rags.

22 Listen to your father who begot you,
And do not despise your mother when she is old.
23 Buy truth, and do not sell *it,*
Get wisdom and instruction and understanding.

24 The father of the righteous will greatly rejoice,
And he who sires a wise son will be glad in him.
25 Let your father and your mother be glad,
And let her rejoice who gave birth to you.

26 Give me your heart, my son,
And let your eyes delight in my ways.
27 For a harlot is a deep pit
And an adulterous woman is a narrow well.
28 Surely she lurks as a robber,
And increases the faithless among men.

29 Who has woe? Who has sorrow?
Who has contentions? Who has complaining?
Who has wounds without cause?
Who has redness of eyes?
30 Those who linger long over wine,
Those who go to taste mixed wine.
31 Do not look on the wine when it is red,
When it sparkles in the cup,
When it goes down smoothly;
32 At the last it bites like a serpent
And stings like a viper.
33 Your eyes will see strange things
And your mind will utter perverse things.
34 And you will be like one who lies down in the middle of the sea,
Or like one who lies down on the top of a [5]mast.
35 "They struck me, *but* I did not become ill;
They beat me, *but* I did not know *it.*
When shall I awake?
I will seek another drink."

5 Or *lookout*

23:17–18 How easy it is to envy those who get ahead unhampered by Christian responsibility or God's laws. For a time they do seem to get ahead without paying any attention to what God wants. But to those who follow him, God promises a hope and a wonderful future even if we don't realize it in this life.

23:29–30 The soothing comfort of alcohol is only temporary. Real relief comes from dealing with the cause of the anguish and sorrow and turning to God for peace. Don't lose yourself in alcohol; find yourself in God.

23:29–35 Israel was a wine-producing country. In the Old Testament, winepresses bursting with new wine were considered a sign of blessing (3:10). Wisdom is even said to have set her table with wine (9:2, 5). But the Old Testament writers were alert to the dangers of wine. It dulls the senses; it limits clear judgment (31:1–9); it lowers the capacity for control (4:17); it destroys a person's efficiency (21:17). To make wine an end in itself, a means of self-indulgence, or as an escape from life is to misuse it and invite the consequences of the drunkard.

Precepts and Warnings

24 Do not be envious of evil men,
Nor desire to be with them;
2 For their minds devise violence,
And their lips talk of trouble.

3 By wisdom a house is built,
And by understanding it is established;
4 And by knowledge the rooms are filled
With all precious and pleasant riches.

5 A wise man is strong,
And a man of knowledge increases power.
6 For by wise guidance you will wage war,
And in abundance of counselors there is victory.

7 Wisdom is *too* exalted for a fool,
He does not open his mouth in the gate.

8 One who plans to do evil,
Men will call a schemer.
9 The devising of folly is sin,
And the scoffer is an abomination to men.

10 If you are slack in the day of distress,
Your strength is limited.

11 Deliver those who are being taken away to death,
And those who are staggering to slaughter, Oh hold *them* back.
12 If you say, "See, we did not know this,"
Does He not consider *it* who weighs the hearts?
And does He not know *it* who keeps your soul?
And will He not render to man according to his work?

13 My son, eat honey, for it is good,
Yes, the honey from the comb is sweet to your taste;
14 Know *that* wisdom is thus for your soul;
If you find *it,* then there will be a future,
And your hope will not be cut off.

15 Do not lie in wait, O wicked man, against the dwelling of the righteous;
Do not destroy his resting place;
16 For a righteous man falls seven times, and rises again,
But the wicked stumble in *time of* calamity.

24:1 Ps 37:1; Prov 3:31; 23:17; 24:19; Ps 1:1; Prov 1:15
24:2 Is 30:12; Jer 22:17; Job 15:35; Ps 10:7; 38:12
24:3 Prov 9:1; 14:1
24:4 Prov 8:21
24:5 Prov 21:22
24:6 Prov 20:18; Prov 11:14
24:7 Ps 10:5; Prov 14:6; 17:16; Job 5:4; Ps 127:5
24:8 Prov 6:14; 14:22; Rom 1:30
24:9 Matt 15:19; Acts 8:22
24:10 Deut 20:8; Job 4:5; Jer 51:46; Heb 12:3
24:11 Ps 82:4; Is 58:6, 7
24:12 Eccl 5:8; 1 Sam 16:7; Prov 21:2; Ps 94:9-11; Ps 121:3-8; Job 34:11; Prov 12:14
24:13 Ps 19:10; 119:103; Prov 25:16; Song 5:1; Prov 16:24; 27:7; Song 4:11
24:14 Prov 2:10; Prov 23:18
24:15 Ps 10:9, 10
24:16 Job 5:19; Ps 37:24; Mic 7:8; Prov 6:15; 14:32; 24:22; Jer 18:17

24:5 The athlete who thinks—who assesses the situation and plans strategies—has an advantage over a physically stronger but unthinking opponent. And wisdom, not muscle, is certainly why God has put people in charge of the animal kingdom. We exercise regularly and eat well to build our strength, but do we take equal pains to develop wisdom? Because wisdom is a vital part of strength, it pays to attain it.

24:6 In any major decision we make concerning college, marriage, career, children, etc., it is not a sign of weakness to ask for advice. Instead, it is foolish not to ask for it. Find good advisers before making any big decision. They can help you expand your alternatives and evaluate your choices.

24:8 Plotting to do evil can be as wrong as doing it because what you think determines what you will do. Left unchecked, wrong desires will lead us to sin. God wants pure lives, free from sin, and planning evil spoils the purity even if the evil action has not yet been committed. Should you say, "Then I might as well go ahead and do it because I've already planned it"? No. You have sinned in your attitude, but you have not yet damaged other people. Stop in your tracks and ask God to forgive you and put you on a different path.

24:10 Times of trouble can be useful. They can show you who you really are, what kind of character you have developed. In addition, they can help you grow stronger. When Jeremiah questioned God because of the trouble he faced, God asked how he ever expected to face big challenges if the little ones tired him out (Jeremiah 12:5). Don't complain about your problems. The trouble you face today is training you to be strong for the more difficult situations you will face in the future.

24:17 Job 31:29; Ps 35:15, 19; Prov 17:5; Obad 12

17 Do not rejoice when your enemy falls,
And do not let your heart be glad when he stumbles;
18 Or the LORD will see *it* and be displeased,
And turn His anger away from him.

24:19 Ps 37:1; Prov 23:17; 24:1

24:20 Job 15:31; Prov 23:18; Job 18:5, 6; 21:17; Prov 13:9; 20:20

19 Do not fret because of evildoers
Or be envious of the wicked;
20 For there will be no future for the evil man;
The lamp of the wicked will be put out.

24:21 Rom 13:1-7; 1 Pet 2:17

24:22 Prov 24:16

21 My son, fear the LORD and the king;
Do not associate with those who are given to change,
22 For their calamity will rise suddenly,
And who knows the ruin *that comes* from both of them?

24:23 Prov 1:6; 22:17; Prov 18:5; 28:21

24:24 Prov 17:15; Is 5:23; Prov 11:26

24:25 Prov 28:23

23 These also are sayings of the wise.
To show partiality in judgment is not good.
24 He who says to the wicked, "You are righteous,"
Peoples will curse him, nations will abhor him;
25 But to those who rebuke the *wicked* will be delight,
And a good blessing will come upon them.
26 He kisses the lips
Who gives a right answer.

24:27 Prov 27:23-27

27 Prepare your work outside
And make it ready for yourself in the field;
Afterwards, then, build your house.

24:28 Prov 25:18; Lev 6:2, 3; 19:11; Eph 4:25

24:29 Prov 20:22; Matt 5:39; Rom 12:17

28 Do not be a witness against your neighbor without cause,
And do not deceive with your lips.
29 Do not say, "Thus I shall do to him as he has done to me;
I will render to the man according to his work."

24:30 Prov 6:32

24:31 Gen 3:18; Job 30:7; Is 5:5

24:33 Prov 6:10

30 I passed by the field of the sluggard
And by the vineyard of the man lacking sense,
31 And behold, it was completely overgrown with thistles;
Its surface was covered with nettles,
And its stone wall was broken down.
32 When I saw, I reflected upon it;
I looked, *and* received instruction.
33 "A little sleep, a little slumber,
A little folding of the hands to rest,"
34 Then your poverty will come *as* a robber
And your want like an armed man.

C. WISDOM FOR THE LEADERS (25:1—31:31)

These proverbs were collected by Hezekiah's aides. The first section was written by Solomon, and the next two sections were written by others. While we all can learn from these proverbs, many were originally directed toward the king or those who dealt with the king. These are particularly helpful for those who are leaders or aspire to become leaders. The book ends with a description of a truly good wife, who is an example of godly wisdom.

24:17–18 David, Solomon's father, refused to gloat over the death of his lifelong enemy Saul (see 2 Samuel 1). On the other hand, the nation of Edom rejoiced over Israel's defeat and was punished by God for their attitude (Obadiah 12). To gloat over others' misfortune is to make yourself the avenger and to put yourself in the place of God, who alone is the real judge of all the earth (see Deuteronomy 32:35).

24:26 A kiss on the lips was a sign of true friendship. People often think that they should bend the truth to avoid hurting a friend. But one who gives an honest answer is a true friend.

24:27 We should carry out our work in its proper order. If a farmer builds his house in the spring, he will miss the planting season and go a year without food. If a businessman invests his money in a house while his business is struggling to grow, he may lose both. It is possible to work hard and still lose everything if the timing is wrong or the resources to carry it out are not in place.

24:29 Here is a reverse version of the Golden Rule (see Luke 6:31). Revenge is the way the world operates, but it is not God's way.

Similitudes, Instructions

25 These also are proverbs of Solomon which the men of Hezekiah, king of Judah, transcribed.

2 It is the glory of God to conceal a matter,
But the glory of kings is to search out a matter.
3 *As* the heavens for height and the earth for depth,
So the heart of kings is unsearchable.
4 Take away the dross from the silver,
And there comes out a vessel for the smith;
5 Take away the wicked before the king,
And his throne will be established in righteousness.
6 Do not claim honor in the presence of the king,
And do not stand in the place of great men;
7 For it is better that it be said to you, "Come up here,"
Than for you to be placed lower in the presence of the prince,
Whom your eyes have seen.

8 Do not go out hastily to argue *your case;*
Otherwise, what will you do in the end,
When your neighbor humiliates you?
9 Argue your case with your neighbor,
And do not reveal the secret of another,
10 Or he who hears *it* will reproach you,
And the evil report about you will not pass away.

11 *Like* apples of gold in settings of silver
Is a word spoken in right circumstances.
12 *Like* an earring of gold and an ornament of fine gold
Is a wise reprover to a listening ear.
13 Like the cold of snow in the time of harvest
Is a faithful messenger to those who send him,
For he refreshes the soul of his masters.
14 *Like* clouds and wind without rain
Is a man who boasts of his gifts falsely.
15 By forbearance a ruler may be persuaded,
And a soft tongue breaks the bone.
16 Have you found honey? Eat *only* what you need,
That you not have it in excess and vomit it.
17 Let your foot rarely be in your neighbor's house,
Or he will become weary of you and hate you.
18 *Like* a club and a sword and a sharp arrow
Is a man who bears false witness against his neighbor.
19 *Like* a bad tooth and an unsteady foot
Is confidence in a faithless man in time of trouble.
20 *Like* one who takes off a garment on a cold day, *or like* vinegar on soda,
Is he who sings songs to a troubled heart.

25:1 Prov 1:1
25:2 Deut 29:29; Rom 11:33; Ezra 6:1
25:4 Prov 26:23; Ezek 22:18; Mal 3:2, 3
25:5 Prov 20:8; Prov 16:12
25:7 Luke 14:7-11
25:8 Prov 17:14; Matt 5:25
25:9 Matt 18:15; Prov 11:13
25:11 Prov 15:23
25:12 Ex 32:2; 35:22; Ezek 16:12; 2 Sam 1:24; Job 28:17; Prov 15:31; 20:12
25:13 Prov 13:17
25:14 Jude 12; Jer 5:13; Mic 2:11
25:15 Gen 32:4; 1 Sam 25:24; Eccl 10:4
25:16 Judg 14:8; 1 Sam 14:25
25:18 Ps 57:4; Prov 12:18; Jer 9:8; Ex 20:16; Prov 24:28
25:19 Job 6:15; Is 36:6

25:1 Hezekiah's story is told in 2 Kings 18—20; 2 Chronicles 29—32; and Isaiah 36—39. He was one of the few kings of Judah who honored the Lord. By contrast, his father Ahaz actually nailed the temple door shut. Hezekiah restored the temple, destroyed idol worship centers, and earned the respect of surrounding nations, many of whom brought gifts to God because of him. It is not surprising that Hezekiah had these proverbs copied and read, for "every work which he began in the service of the house of God in law and in commandment, seeking his God, he did with all his heart and prospered" (2 Chronicles 31:21).

25:6–7 Jesus made this proverb into a parable (see Luke 14:7–11). We should not seek honor for ourselves. It is better to quietly and faithfully accomplish the work God has given us to do. As others notice the quality of our lives, then they will draw attention to us.

25:13 It is often difficult to find people you can really trust. A faithful employee ("messenger") is punctual, responsible, honest, and hardworking. This person is invaluable as he or she helps take some of the pressure off his or her employer. Find out what your employer needs from you to make his or her job easier, and do it.

25:14 Most churches, missions organizations, and Christian groups depend on the gifts of people to keep their ministries going. But many who promise to give fail to follow through. The Bible is very clear about the effect this has on those involved in the ministry. If you make a pledge, keep your promise.

25:18 Lying ("false witness") is vicious. Its effects can be as permanent as those of a stab wound. The next time you are tempted to pass on a bit of gossip, imagine yourself stabbing the victim of your remarks with a sword. This image may shock you into silence.

25:21 Matt 5:44; Rom 12:20
25:22 Matt 6:4, 6
25:23 Ps 101:5
25:24 Prov 21:9
25:25 Prov 15:30
25:27 Prov 27:2; Luke 14:11
25:28 Prov 16:32; 2 Chr 32:5; Neh 1:3
26:1 1 Sam 12:17; Prov 17:7
26:2 Num 23:8; Deut 23:5; 2 Sam 16:12
26:3 Ps 32:9; Prov 10:13; 19:29
26:4 Prov 23:9; 29:9; Is 36:21; Matt 7:6

21 If your enemy is hungry, give him food to eat;
And if he is thirsty, give him water to drink;
22 For you will heap burning coals on his head,
And the LORD will reward you.
23 The north wind brings forth rain,
And a backbiting tongue, an angry countenance.
24 It is better to live in a corner of the roof
Than in a house shared with a contentious woman.
25 *Like* cold water to a weary soul,
So is good news from a distant land.
26 *Like* a trampled spring and a polluted well
Is a righteous man who gives way before the wicked.
27 It is not good to eat much honey,
Nor is it glory to search out one's own glory.
28 *Like* a city that is broken into *and* without walls
Is a man who has no control over his spirit.

Similitudes, Instructions

26 Like snow in summer and like rain in harvest,
So honor is not fitting for a fool.
2 Like a sparrow in *its* flitting, like a swallow in *its* flying,
So a curse without cause does not alight.
3 A whip is for the horse, a bridle for the donkey,
And a rod for the back of fools.
4 Do not answer a fool according to his folly,

THE FOUR TONGUES
What we say probably affects more people than any other action we take. It is not surprising, then, to find that Proverbs gives special attention to words and how they are used. Four common speech patterns are described in Proverbs. The first two should be copied, while the last two should be avoided.

The Controlled Tongue	Those with this speech pattern think before speaking, know when silence is best, and give wise advice.	10:19; 11:12–13; 12:16; 13:3; 15:1, 4, 28; 16:23; 17:14, 27–28; 21:23; 24:26
The Caring Tongue	Those with this speech pattern speak truthfully while seeking to encourage.	10:32; 12:18, 25; 15:23; 16:24; 25:15; 27:9
The Conniving Tongue	Those with this speech pattern are filled with wrong motives, gossip, slander, and a desire to twist truth.	6:12–14; 8:13; 16:28; 18:8; 25:18; 26:20–28
The Careless Tongue	Those with this speech pattern are filled with lies, curses, quick-tempered words—which can lead to rebellion and destruction.	10:18, 32; 11:9; 12:16, 18; 15:4; 17:9, 14, 19; 20:19; 25:23

Other verses about our speech include: 10:11, 20, 31; 12:6, 17–19; 13:2; 14:3; 19:5, 28; 25:11; 27:2, 5, 14, 17; 29:9

25:21–22 God's form of retaliation is most effective and yet difficult to do. Paul quotes this proverb in Romans 12:19–21. In Matthew 5:44, Jesus encourages us to pray for those who hurt us. By returning good for evil, we are acknowledging God as the balancer of all accounts and trusting him to be the judge.

25:26 To give way to the wicked means setting aside your standards of right and wrong. No one is helped by someone who compromises with the wicked.

25:27 Dwelling on the honors you deserve can only be harmful. It can make you bitter, discouraged, or angry, and it will not bring you the rewards that you think should be yours. Pining for what you should have received may make you miss the satisfaction of knowing you did your best.

25:28 Even though city walls restricted the inhabitants' movements, people were happy to have them. Without walls, they would have been vulnerable to attack by any passing group of marauders. Self-control limits us, to be sure, but it is necessary. An out-of-control life is open to all sorts of enemy attack. Think of self-control as a wall for defense and protection.

26:2 "A curse without cause does not alight" means that it has no effect.

26:4–5 These two verses seem to be in contradiction. But the writer is saying that we shouldn't take a foolish person seriously and try to reason with his or her empty arguments. This will only make him or her proud and determined to win the argument. In some situations, you ought not to even try to answer a fool, for there is no way you can penetrate his or her closed mind. You may, in fact, be stooping to that person's level if you do choose to answer. Such a fool will abuse you and you will be tempted to abuse him or her in return. There are other situations where your common sense tells you to answer in order to expose the fool's pride and folly.

Or you will also be like him.
5 Answer a fool as his folly *deserves,*
That he not be wise in his own eyes.
6 He cuts off *his own* feet *and* drinks violence
Who sends a message by the hand of a fool.
7 *Like* the legs *which* are useless to the lame,
So is a proverb in the mouth of fools.
8 Like one who binds a stone in a sling,
So is he who gives honor to a fool.
9 *Like* a thorn *which* falls into the hand of a drunkard,
So is a proverb in the mouth of fools.
10 *Like* an archer who wounds everyone,
So is he who hires a fool or who hires those who pass by.
11 Like a dog that returns to its vomit
Is a fool who repeats his folly.
12 Do you see a man wise in his own eyes?
There is more hope for a fool than for him.
13 The sluggard says, "There is a lion in the road!
A lion is in the open square!"
14 *As* the door turns on its hinges,
So *does* the sluggard on his bed.
15 The sluggard buries his hand in the dish;
He is weary of bringing it to his mouth again.
16 The sluggard is wiser in his own eyes
Than seven men who can give a discreet answer.
17 *Like* one who takes a dog by the ears
Is he who passes by *and* meddles with strife not belonging to him.
18 Like a madman who throws
Firebrands, arrows and death,
19 So is the man who deceives his neighbor,
And says, "Was I not joking?"
20 For lack of wood the fire goes out,
And where there is no whisperer, contention quiets down.
21 *Like* charcoal to hot embers and wood to fire,
So is a contentious man to kindle strife.
22 The words of a whisperer are like dainty morsels,
And they go down into the innermost parts of the body.
23 *Like* an earthen vessel overlaid with silver dross
Are burning lips and a wicked heart.

26:5 Matt 16:1-4; 21:24-27; Prov 3:7; 28:11; Rom 12:16

26:11 2 Pet 2:22; Ex 8:15

26:12 Prov 3:7; 26:5; Prov 29:20

26:13 Prov 22:13

26:14 Prov 6:9

26:15 Prov 19:24

26:16 Prov 27:11

26:17 Prov 3:30

26:18 Is 50:11

26:19 Prov 24:28; Eph 5:4

26:20 Prov 16:28; Prov 22:10

26:21 Prov 15:18; 29:22

26:22 Prov 18:8

26:23 Matt 23:27; Luke 11:39; Prov 25:4

26:7 In the mouth of a fool, a proverb becomes as useless as a paralyzed leg. Some people are so blind that they won't get much wisdom from reading these proverbs. Only those who want to be wise have the receptive attitude needed to make the most of them. If we want to learn from God, he will respond and pour out his heart to us (1:23).

26:8 Sometimes when someone in a group causes discord or dissension, the leader tries to make him loyal and productive by giving him a place of privilege or responsibility. This usually doesn't work. In fact, it is like tying the stone to the sling—it won't go anywhere and will swing back and hurt you. The dissenter's new power may be just what he needs to manipulate the group.

26:9 Normally the first prick of a thorn alerts us, so we remove the thorn before it damages us. A drunk person, however, may not feel the thorn, and so it will work its way into his flesh. Similarly, a fool may not feel the sting of a proverb because he does not see where it touches his life. Instead of taking its point to heart, a fool will apply it to his church, his employer, his spouse, or whomever he is rebelling against. The next time you find yourself saying, "So-and-so should really pay attention to that," stop and ask yourself, "Is there a message in it for me?"

26:13–16 If a person is not willing to work, he or she can find endless excuses to avoid it. But laziness is more dangerous than a prowling lion. The less you do, the less you want to do, and the more useless you become. To overcome laziness, take a few small steps toward change. Set a concrete, realistic goal. Figure out the steps needed to reach it, and follow those steps. Pray for strength and persistence. To keep your excuses from making you useless, stop making useless excuses.

26:17 Seizing the ears of a dog is a good way to get bitten, and interfering in arguments is a good way to get hurt. Many times both arguers will turn on the person who interferes. It is best simply to keep out of arguments that are none of your business. If you must become involved, try to wait until the arguers have stopped fighting and cooled off a bit. Then maybe you can help them mend their differences and their relationship.

26:20 Talking about every little irritation or piece of gossip only keeps the fires of anger going. Refusing to discuss them cuts the fuel line and makes the fires die out. Does someone continually irritate you? Decide not to complain about the person, and see if your irritation dies from lack of fuel.

26:24 Ps 41:6; Prov 10:18; Prov 12:20
26:25 Ps 28:3; Prov 26:23; Jer 9:8
26:26 Matt 23:28; Luke 8:17
26:27 Esth 7:10; Prov 28:10
26:28 Prov 29:5

24 He who hates disguises *it* with his lips,
But he lays up deceit in his heart.
25 When he speaks graciously, do not believe him,
For there are seven abominations in his heart.
26 *Though his* hatred covers itself with guile,
His wickedness will be revealed before the assembly.
27 He who digs a pit will fall into it,
And he who rolls a stone, it will come back on him.
28 A lying tongue hates those it crushes,
And a flattering mouth works ruin.

Warnings and Instructions

27:1 James 4:13-16; Luke 12:19, 20; James 4:14
27:2 Prov 25:27; 2 Cor 10:12, 18; 12:11
27:4 Prov 6:34; 1 John 3:12
27:5 Prov 28:23; Gal 2:14
27:6 Ps 141:5; Prov 20:30; Matt 26:49
27:8 Prov 26:2; Is 16:2; Gen 21:14
27:9 Ps 23:5; 141:5
27:10 Prov 18:24; 1 Kin 12:6-8; 2 Chr 10:6-8
27:11 Prov 10:1; 23:15; 29:3; Ps 119:42
27:13 Prov 20:16
27:14 Ps 12:2
27:15 Prov 19:13

27 Do not boast about tomorrow,
For you do not know what a day may bring forth.
2 Let another praise you, and not your own mouth;
A stranger, and not your own lips.
3 A stone is heavy and the sand weighty,
But the provocation of a fool is heavier than both of them.
4 Wrath is fierce and anger is a flood,
But who can stand before jealousy?
5 Better is open rebuke
Than love that is concealed.
6 Faithful are the wounds of a friend,
But deceitful are the kisses of an enemy.
7 A sated man loathes honey,
But to a famished man any bitter thing is sweet.
8 Like a bird that wanders from her nest,
So is a man who wanders from his home.
9 Oil and perfume make the heart glad,
So a man's counsel is sweet to his friend.
10 Do not forsake your own friend or your father's friend,
And do not go to your brother's house in the day of your calamity;
Better is a neighbor who is near than a brother far away.
11 Be wise, my son, and make my heart glad,
That I may reply to him who reproaches me.
12 A prudent man sees evil *and* hides himself,
The naive proceed *and* pay the penalty.
13 Take his garment when he becomes surety for a stranger;
And for an adulterous woman hold him in pledge.
14 He who blesses his friend with a loud voice early in the morning,
It will be reckoned a curse to him.
15 A constant dripping on a day of steady rain
And a contentious woman are alike;
16 He who would restrain her restrains the wind,
And grasps oil with his right hand.
17 Iron sharpens iron,

26:24–26 This proverb means that people with hate in their hearts may sound pleasant enough; don't believe what they say.

27:6 Who would prefer a friend's wounds to an enemy's kisses? Anyone who considers the source. A friend who has your best interests at heart may have to give you unpleasant advice at times, but you know it is for your own good. An enemy, by contrast, may whisper sweet words and happily send you on your way to ruin. We tend to hear what we want to hear, even if an enemy is the only one who will say it. A friend's advice, no matter how painful, is much better.

27:15–16 Quarrelsome nagging, a steady stream of unwanted advice, is a form of torture. People nag because they think they're not getting through, but nagging hinders communication more than it helps. When tempted to engage in this destructive habit, stop and examine your motives. Are you more concerned about yourself—getting your way, being right—than about the person you are pretending to help? If you are truly concerned about other people, think of a more effective way to get through to them. Surprise them with words of patience and love, and see what happens.

27:17 There is a mental sharpness that comes from being around good people. And a meeting of minds can help people see their ideas with new clarity, refine them, and shape them into brilliant insights. This requires discussion partners who can challenge each other and stimulate thought—people who focus on the idea without involving their egos in the discussion; people who know how to attack the thought and not the thinker. Two friends who bring their ideas together can help each other become sharper.

So one man sharpens another.
18 He who tends the fig tree will eat its fruit,
And he who cares for his master will be honored.
19 As in water face *reflects* face,
So the heart of man *reflects* man.
20 Sheol and Abaddon are never satisfied,
Nor are the eyes of man ever satisfied.
21 The crucible is for silver and the furnace for gold,
And each *is tested* by the praise accorded him.
22 Though you pound a fool in a mortar with a pestle along with crushed grain,
Yet his foolishness will not depart from him.

23 Know well the condition of your flocks,
And pay attention to your herds;
24 For riches are not forever,
Nor does a crown *endure* to all generations.
25 *When* the grass disappears, the new growth is seen,
And the herbs of the mountains are gathered in,
26 The lambs *will be* for your clothing,
And the goats *will bring* the price of a field,
27 And *there will be* goats' milk enough for your food,
For the food of your household,
And sustenance for your maidens.

Warnings and Instructions

28 The wicked flee when no one is pursuing,
But the righteous are bold as a lion.
2 By the transgression of a land many are its princes,
But by a man of understanding *and* knowledge, so it endures.
3 A poor man who oppresses the lowly
Is *like* a driving rain which leaves no food.
4 Those who forsake the law praise the wicked,
But those who keep the law strive with them.
5 Evil men do not understand justice,
But those who seek the LORD understand all things.
6 Better is the poor who walks in his integrity
Than he who is crooked though he be rich.
7 He who keeps the law is a discerning son,
But he who is a companion of gluttons humiliates his father.
8 He who increases his wealth by interest and usury
Gathers it for him who is gracious to the poor.

27:18 2 Kin 18:31; Song 8:12; Is 36:16; 1 Cor 3:8; 9:7; 2 Tim 2:6; Luke 12:42-44; 19:17

27:20 Job 26:6; Prov 15:11; Prov 30:15, 16; Hab 2:5; Eccl 1:8; 4:8

27:21 Prov 17:3; Luke 6:26

27:22 Prov 23:35; 26:11; Jer 5:3

27:23 Jer 31:10; Ezek 34:12; John 10:3

27:24 Job 19:9; Ps 89:39; Jer 13:18; Lam 5:16; Ezek 21:26

27:25 Is 17:5; Jer 40:10, 12

28:1 Lev 26:17, 36; Ps 53:5

28:2 1 Kin 16:8-28; 2 Kin 15:8-15; Prov 11:11

28:3 Matt 18:28

28:4 Ps 49:18; Rom 1:32; 1 Kin 18:18; Neh 13:11, 15; Matt 3:7; 14:4; Eph 5:11

28:5 Ps 92:6; Is 6:9; 44:18; Ps 119:100; Prov 2:9; John 7:17; 1 Cor 2:15; 1 John 2:20, 27

28:6 Prov 19:1

28:7 Prov 23:20

28:8 Ex 22:25; Lev 25:36; Job 27:17; Prov 13:22; 14:31

27:18 With all the problems and concerns a leader has, it can be easy to overlook the very people who most deserve attention—faithful employees or volunteers (those who tend the fig trees). The people who stand behind you, who work hard and help you get the job done, deserve to share in your success. Be sure that in all your worrying, planning, and organizing, you don't forget the people who are helping you the most.

27:21 Praise tests a person, just as high temperatures test metal. How does praise affect you? Do you work to get it? Do you work harder after you've gotten it? Your attitude toward praise tells a lot about your character. People of high integrity are not swayed by praise. They are attuned to their inner convictions, and they do what they should whether or not they are praised for it.

27:23–27 Because life is short and our fortunes uncertain, we should be all the more diligent in what we do with our lives. We should act with foresight, giving responsible attention to our homes, our families, and our careers. We should be responsible stewards, like a farmer with his lands and herds. Thinking ahead is a duty, not an option, for God's people.

28:2 For a government or a society to endure, it needs wise, informed leaders—and these are hard to find. "Many are its princes" may mean that anarchy is prevailing. Each person's selfishness quickly affects others. A selfish employee who steals from his company ruins its productivity. A selfish driver who drinks before taking the wheel makes the state highways unsafe. A selfish spouse who has an adulterous affair often breaks up several families. When enough people live for themselves with little concern for how their actions affect others, the resulting moral rot contaminates the entire nation. Are you part of the problem . . . or the solution?

28:5 Because justice is part of God's character, a person who follows God treats others justly. The beginning of justice is concern for what is happening to others. A Christian cannot be indifferent to human suffering because God isn't. And we certainly must not contribute to human suffering through selfish business practices or unfair government policies. Be sure you are more concerned for justice than for the bottom line.

28:9 Ps 66:18; 109:7; Prov 15:8; 21:27

28:10 Matt 6:33; Heb 6:12; 1 Pet 3:9

28:11 Prov 3:7; 26:5, 12

28:12 Prov 11:10; 29:2; Eccl 10:5, 6

28:13 Ps 32:5; 1 John 1:9

28:14 Prov 23:17; Ps 95:8; Rom 2:5

28:15 Ex 1:14; Prov 29:2; Matt 2:16

9 He who turns away his ear from listening to the law,
Even his prayer is an abomination.
10 He who leads the upright astray in an evil way
Will himself fall into his own pit,
But the blameless will inherit good.
11 The rich man is wise in his own eyes,
But the poor who has understanding sees through him.
12 When the righteous triumph, there is great glory,
But when the wicked rise, men hide themselves.
13 He who conceals his transgressions will not prosper,
But he who confesses and forsakes *them* will find compassion.
14 How blessed is the man who fears always,
But he who hardens his heart will fall into calamity.
15 *Like* a roaring lion and a rushing bear
Is a wicked ruler over a poor people.
16 A leader who is a great oppressor lacks understanding,
But he who hates unjust gain will prolong *his* days.

DILIGENCE AND LAZINESS

Proverbs makes it clear that diligence—being willing to work hard and do one's best at any job given to him or her—is a vital part of wise living. We work hard not to become rich, famous, or admired (although those may be by-products), but to serve God with our very best during our lives.

The Diligent	*The Lazy*	*References*
Become rich	Are soon poor	10:4
Gather crops early	Sleep during harvest	10:5
	Are an annoyance	10:26
Have abundant food	Chase fantasies	12:11
Hard work returns rewards		12:14
Will rule	Will become slaves	12:24
Prize their possessions	Waste good resources	12:27
Are fully satisfied	Want much but get little	13:4
Bring profit	Experience poverty	14:23
Have an easy path	Have trouble all through life	15:19
	Are like those who destroy	18:9
	Go hungry	19:15
	Won't feed themselves	19:24
	Won't plow in season	20:4
Stay awake and have food to spare	Love sleep and grow poor	20:13
Make careful plans	Make hasty speculations	21:5
	Love pleasure and become poor	21:17
Give without sparing	Desire things but refuse to work for them	21:25–26
	Are full of excuses for not working	22:13
Will serve before kings		22:29
	Sleep too much, which leads to poverty	24:30–34
Reap abundance through hard work	Experience poverty because of laziness	28:19

28:9 God does not listen to our prayers if we intend to go back to our sin as soon as we get off our knees. If we want to forsake our sin and follow him, however, he willingly listens—no matter how bad our sin has been. What closes his ears is not the depth of our sin, but our secret intention to do it again.

28:11 Rich people often think they are wonderful; depending on no one, they take credit for all they do. But that's a hollow self-esteem. Through dependence on God in their struggles, the poor may develop a richness of spirit that no amount of wealth can provide. The rich man can lose all his material wealth, while no one can take away the poor man's character. Don't be jealous of the rich; money may be all they will ever have.

28:13 It is human nature to hide our sins or overlook our mistakes. But it is hard to learn from a mistake you don't acknowledge making. And what good is a mistake if it doesn't teach you something? To learn from an error you need to admit it, confess it, analyze it, and make adjustments so that it doesn't happen again. Everybody makes mistakes, but only fools repeat them.

28:13 Something in each of us strongly resists admitting we are wrong. That is why we admire people who openly and graciously admit their mistakes and sins. These people have a strong self-image. They do not always have to be right to feel good about themselves. Be willing to reconsider—to admit you are wrong and to change your plans when necessary. And remember, the first step toward forgiveness is confession.

28:14 To fear means to revere and honor the Lord.

17 A man who is laden with the guilt of human blood
Will be a fugitive until death; let no one support him.
18 He who walks blamelessly will be delivered,
But he who is crooked will fall all at once.
19 He who tills his land will have plenty of food,
But he who follows empty *pursuits* will have poverty in plenty.
20 A faithful man will abound with blessings,
But he who makes haste to be rich will not go unpunished.
21 To show partiality is not good,
Because for a piece of bread a man will transgress.
22 A man with an evil eye hastens after wealth
And does not know that want will come upon him.
23 He who rebukes a man will afterward find *more* favor
Than he who flatters with the tongue.
24 He who robs his father or his mother
And says, "It is not a transgression,"
Is the companion of a man who destroys.
25 An arrogant man stirs up strife,
But he who trusts in the LORD will prosper.
26 He who trusts in his own heart is a fool,
But he who walks wisely will be delivered.
27 He who gives to the poor will never want,
But he who shuts his eyes will have many curses.
28 When the wicked rise, men hide themselves;
But when they perish, the righteous increase.

Warnings and Instructions

29 A man who hardens *his* neck after much reproof
Will suddenly be broken beyond remedy.
2 When the righteous increase, the people rejoice,
But when a wicked man rules, people groan.
3 A man who loves wisdom makes his father glad,
But he who keeps company with harlots wastes *his* wealth.
4 The king gives stability to the land by justice,
But a man who takes bribes overthrows it.
5 A man who flatters his neighbor
Is spreading a net for his steps.
6 By transgression an evil man is ensnared,
But the righteous sings and rejoices.
7 The righteous is concerned for the rights of the poor,
The wicked does not understand *such* concern.
8 Scorners set a city aflame,
But wise men turn away anger.
9 When a wise man has a controversy with a foolish man,
The foolish man either rages or laughs, and there is no rest.
10 Men of bloodshed hate the blameless,
But the upright are concerned for his life.

28:17 Gen 9:6; Ex 21:14
28:18 Prov 10:27
28:19 Prov 12:11; Prov 20:13
28:20 Prov 10:6; Matt 24:45; 25:21; Prov 20:21; 28:22; 1 Tim 6:9
28:21 Prov 24:23; Ezek 13:19
28:22 Prov 23:6; Prov 21:5
28:23 Prov 27:5, 6
28:24 Prov 19:26; Prov 18:9
28:25 Prov 15:18; Prov 29:25; 1 Tim 6:6; Prov 11:25
28:26 Prov 3:5
28:27 Prov 11:24; 19:17
29:1 Prov 1:24-31; Prov 6:15
29:2 Prov 11:10; 28:12
29:3 Prov 10:1; 15:20; 27:11; 28:7; Prov 5:10; 6:26; Luke 15:30
29:4 2 Chr 9:8; Prov 8:15; 29:14
29:5 Ps 5:9
29:6 Prov 22:5; Eccl 9:12
29:7 Job 29:16; Ps 41:1; Prov 31:8, 9
29:8 Prov 11:11; Prov 16:14
29:10 Gen 4:5-8; 1 John 3:12

28:17–18 A sinner's conscience will drive him either into guilt resulting in repentance or to death itself because of a refusal to repent. It is no act of kindness to try to make him feel better; the more guilt he feels, the more likely he is to turn to God and repent. If we interfere with the natural consequences of his act, we may make it easier for him to continue in sin.

28:26 For many people, the rugged individualist is a hero. We admire the bold, self-directed men and women who know what they want and fight for it. They are self-reliant, neither giving nor asking advice. What a contrast to God's way. A person can't know the future and can't predict the consequences of his or her choices with certainty. And so the totally self-reliant person is doomed to failure. The wise person depends on God.

28:27 God wants us to identify with the needy, not ignore them. The second part of this proverb could be restated positively: "Those who open their eyes to poor people will be blessed." If we help others when they are in trouble, they will do whatever they can to return the favor (see 11:24–25). Paul promises that God will supply all our needs (Philippians 4:19); he usually does this through other people. What can you do today to help God supply someone's need?

29:1 Making the same mistake over and over is an invitation to disaster. Eventually people have to face the consequences of refusing to learn. If their mistake is refusing God's invitations or rejecting his commands, the consequences will be especially serious. In the end, God may have to turn them away. Make sure you are not stiff-necked.

29:11 Prov 12:16; 14:33; Prov 19:11
29:13 Prov 22:2; Ps 13:3
29:14 Ps 72:4; Is 11:4; Prov 16:12; 25:5
29:15 Prov 13:24; 22:15; Prov 10:1; 17:25
29:16 Ps 37:34, 36; 58:10; 91:8; 92:11
29:17 Prov 13:24; 29:15; Prov 10:1
29:18 Ex 32:25; Ps 1:1, 2; 106:3; 119:2; Prov 8:32; John 13:17
29:20 James 1:19
29:22 Prov 15:18; 26:21
29:23 Prov 11:2; 16:18; Matt 23:12; James 4:6; Prov 15:33; 18:12; 22:4; Is 66:2; Luke 14:11; 18:14; James 4:10

11 A fool always loses his temper,
But a wise man holds it back.
12 If a ruler pays attention to falsehood,
All his ministers *become* wicked.
13 The poor man and the oppressor have this in common:
The LORD gives light to the eyes of both.
14 If a king judges the poor with truth,
His throne will be established forever.
15 The rod and reproof give wisdom,
But a child who gets his own way brings shame to his mother.
16 When the wicked increase, transgression increases;
But the righteous will see their fall.
17 Correct your son, and he will give you comfort;
He will also delight your soul.
18 Where there is no vision, the people are unrestrained,
But happy is he who keeps the law.
19 A slave will not be instructed by words *alone;*
For though he understands, there will be no response.
20 Do you see a man who is hasty in his words?
There is more hope for a fool than for him.
21 He who pampers his slave from childhood
Will in the end find him to be a son.
22 An angry man stirs up strife,
And a hot-tempered man abounds in transgression.
23 A man's pride will bring him low,
But a humble spirit will obtain honor.

LEADERSHIP
Since many of the proverbs came from King Solomon, it is natural to expect some of his interest to be directed toward leadership.

Qualities of good leadership	*References*
Diligence	12:24
Trustworthy messengers	13:17
Don't penalize people for integrity	17:26
Listen before answering	18:13
Able to discern	18:15
Listen to both sides of the story	18:17
Able to stand up under adversity	24:10
Able to stand up under praise	27:21
What happens without good leadership	
Honoring the wrong people backfires	26:8
A wicked ruler is dangerous	28:15
People despair	29:2
A wicked ruler has wicked officials	29:12

Other verses to study: 24:27; 25:13; 27:18

29:13 "The LORD gives light to the eyes of both" means that everyone depends on God for sight. Both the oppressor and the poor have the gift of sight from the same God. God sees and judges both, and his judgment falls on those whose greed or power drives them to oppress the poor.

29:15 Parents of young children often weary of disciplining them. They feel like all they do is nag, scold, and punish. When you're tempted to give up and let your children do what they want, or when you wonder if you've ruined every chance for a loving relationship with them, remember—kind, firm correction helps them learn, and learning makes them wise. Consistent, loving discipline will ultimately teach them to discipline themselves.

29:16 When the wicked are in leadership, sin prevails. In any organization—whether a church, a business, a family, or a government—the climate comes from the top. The people become like their leaders. What kind of climate are you setting for the people you lead?

29:18 "Vision" refers to words from God received by prophets. Where there is ignorance of God, crime and sin run wild. Public morality depends on the knowledge of God, but it also depends on keeping God's laws. In order for both nations and individuals to function well, people must know God's ways and keep his rules.

24 He who is a partner with a thief hates his own life;
He hears the oath but tells nothing.
25 The fear of man brings a snare,
But he who trusts in the LORD will be exalted.
26 Many seek the ruler's favor,
But justice for man *comes* from the LORD.
27 An unjust man is abominable to the righteous,
And he who is upright in the way is abominable to the wicked.

The Words of Agur

30 The words of Agur the son of Jakeh, the oracle.
The man declares to Ithiel, to Ithiel and Ucal:
2 Surely I am more stupid than any man,
And I do not have the understanding of a man.
3 Neither have I learned wisdom,
Nor do I have the knowledge of the Holy One.
4 Who has ascended into heaven and descended?
Who has gathered the wind in His fists?
Who has wrapped the waters in His garment?
Who has established all the ends of the earth?
What is His name or His son's name?
Surely you know!

5 Every word of God is tested;
He is a shield to those who take refuge in Him.
6 Do not add to His words
Or He will reprove you, and you will be proved a liar.

7 Two things I asked of You,
Do not refuse me before I die:
8 Keep deception and lies far from me,
Give me neither poverty nor riches;
Feed me with the food that is my portion,
9 That I not be full and deny *You* and say, "Who is the LORD?"
Or that I not be in want and steal,
And profane the name of my God.

10 Do not slander a slave to his master,
Or he will curse you and you will be found guilty.

11 There is a [6]kind of *man* who curses his father
And does not bless his mother.
12 There is a kind who is pure in his own eyes,
Yet is not washed from his filthiness.

6 Or *generation*

29:24 Lev 5:1

29:25 Gen 12:12; 20:2; Luke 12:4; John 12:42, 43; Ps 91:1-16; Prov 18:10; 28:25

29:26 Prov 19:6; Is 49:4; 1 Cor 4:4

29:27 Ps 6:8; 139:21, 22; Prov 12:8; Ps 69:4; Prov 29:10; Matt 10:22; 24:9; John 15:18; 17:14; 1 John 3:13

30:2 Ps 49:10; 73:22; Prov 12:1

30:3 Prov 9:10

30:4 Ps 68:18; John 3:13; Eph 4:8; Ex 15:10; Ps 135:7; Job 26:8; 38:8, 9; Ps 24:2; Is 45:18; Rev 19:12

30:5 Ps 12:6; 18:30; Ps 3:3; 84:11; Prov 2:7

30:6 Deut 4:2; 12:32; Rev 22:18

30:8 Job 23:12; Matt 6:11

30:9 Deut 8:12; 31:20; Neh 9:25; Hos 13:6; Josh 24:27; Job 31:28; Prov 6:30; Ex 20:7

30:10 Eccl 7:21

30:11 Ex 21:17; Prov 20:20

30:12 Prov 16:2; Is 65:5; Luke 18:11; Titus 1:15, 16

29:24 This proverb is saying that a thief's accomplice won't tell the truth when under oath. Thus, by his perjury, he will hurt himself.

29:25 Fear of people can hamper everything you try to do. In extreme forms, it can make you afraid to leave your home. By contrast, fear of God—respect, reverence, and trust—is liberating. Why fear people who can do no eternal harm? Instead, fear God who can turn the harm intended by others into good for those who trust him.

30:1 The origin of these sayings is not clear. Nothing is known about Agur except that he was a wise teacher who may have come from Lemuel's kingdom (see the note on 31:1).

30:2–4 Because God is infinite, certain aspects of his nature will always remain a mystery. Compare these questions with the questions God asked Job (Job 38—41).

30:4 Some scholars feel that the son referred to is the Son of God, the preincarnate being of the Messiah who, before the foundation of the earth, participated in the creation. Colossians 1:16–17 teaches that through Christ the world was created.

30:7–9 Having too much money can be dangerous, but so can having too little. Being poor can, in fact, be hazardous to spiritual as well as physical health. On the other hand, being rich is not the answer. As Jesus pointed out, rich people have trouble getting into God's kingdom (Matthew 19:23–24). Like Paul, we can learn how to live whether we have little or plenty (Philippians 4:12), but our lives are more likely to be effective if we have "neither poverty nor riches."

30:13 Prov 6:17; Is 2:11; 5:15

30:14 Ps 57:4; Job 29:17; Ps 14:4; Amos 8:4

13 There is a kind—oh how lofty are his eyes!
And his eyelids are raised *in arrogance.*
14 There is a kind of *man* whose teeth are *like* swords
And his jaw teeth *like* knives,
To devour the afflicted from the earth
And the needy from among men.

15 The leech has two daughters,
"Give," "Give."
There are three things that will not be satisfied,
Four that will not say, "Enough":

30:16 Prov 27:20; Gen 30:1

16 Sheol, and the barren womb,
Earth that is never satisfied with water,
And fire that never says, "Enough."

30:17 Gen 9:22; Prov 15:20; Deut 28:26

17 The eye that mocks a father
And scorns a mother,
The ravens of the valley will pick it out,
And the young eagles will eat it.

18 There are three things which are too wonderful for me,
Four which I do not understand:

30:19 Deut 28:49; Jer 48:40; 49:22

19 The way of an eagle in the sky,
The way of a serpent on a rock,
The way of a ship in the middle of the sea,
And the way of a man with a maid.

30:20 Prov 5:6

20 This is the way of an adulterous woman:
She eats and wipes her mouth,
And says, "I have done no wrong."

21 Under three things the earth quakes,
And under four, it cannot bear up:

30:22 Prov 19:10; Eccl 10:7

22 Under a slave when he becomes king,
And a fool when he is satisfied with food,
23 Under an unloved woman when she gets a husband,
And a maidservant when she supplants her mistress.

24 Four things are small on the earth,
But they are exceedingly wise:

30:25 Prov 6:6

25 The ants are not a strong people,
But they prepare their food in the summer;

30:26 Lev 11:5; Ps 104:18

26 The shephanim are not mighty people,
Yet they make their houses in the rocks;

30:27 Joel 2:7

27 The locusts have no king,
Yet all of them go out in ranks;
28 The lizard you may grasp with the hands,
Yet it is in kings' palaces.

29 There are three things which are stately in *their* march,
Even four which are stately when they walk:

30:30 Judg 14:18; 2 Sam 1:23; Mic 5:8

30 The lion *which* is mighty among beasts
And does not retreat before any,
31 The strutting rooster, the male goat also,
And a king *when his* army is with him.

30:13 This phrase refers to prideful and haughty people who look down on others. Verses 11–14 contain a fourfold description of arrogance.

30:15ff "Three things . . . Four" is a poetic way of saying the list is not complete. The writer of these proverbs is observing the world with delighted interest. Verses 15–30 are an invitation to look at nature from the perspective of a keen observer.

30:24–28 Ants can teach us about preparation; shephanim (badgers) about wise building; locusts about cooperation and order; and lizards about fearlessness.

32 If you have been foolish in exalting yourself
Or if you have plotted *evil, put your* hand on your mouth.
33 For the churning of milk produces butter,
And pressing the nose brings forth blood;
So the churning of anger produces strife.

30:32 Job 21:5; 40:4; Mic 7:16
30:33 Prov 10:12; 29:22

The Words of Lemuel

31 The words of King Lemuel, the oracle which his mother taught him:
2 What, O my son?
And what, O son of my womb?
And what, O son of my vows?
3 Do not give your strength to women,
Or your ways to that which destroys kings.
4 It is not for kings, O Lemuel,
It is not for kings to drink wine,
Or for rulers to desire strong drink,
5 For they will drink and forget what is decreed,
And pervert the rights of all the afflicted.
6 Give strong drink to him who is perishing,
And wine to him whose life is bitter.
7 Let him drink and forget his poverty
And remember his trouble no more.
8 Open your mouth for the mute,
For the rights of all the unfortunate.
9 Open your mouth, judge righteously,
And defend the rights of the afflicted and needy.

31:2 Is 49:15; 1 Sam 1:11
31:3 Prov 5:9; Deut 17:17; 1 Kin 11:1; Neh 13:26
31:4 Eccl 10:17; Prov 20:1; Is 5:22; Hos 4:11
31:5 Ex 23:6; Deut 16:19; Prov 17:15
31:6 Job 29:13; Job 3:20; Is 38:15
31:8 Job 29:12-17; Ps 82
31:9 Lev 19:15; Deut 1:16; Is 1:17; Jer 22:16

Description of a Worthy Woman

10 An excellent wife, who can find?
For her worth is far above jewels.
11 The heart of her husband trusts in her,
And he will have no lack of gain.
12 She does him good and not evil
All the days of her life.
13 She looks for wool and flax
And works with her hands in delight.
14 She is like merchant ships;
She brings her food from afar.
15 She rises also while it is still night
And gives food to her household
And portions to her maidens.
16 She considers a field and buys it;
From her earnings she plants a vineyard.
17 She girds herself with strength
And makes her arms strong.

31:10 Ruth 3:11; Prov 12:4; 19:14; Job 28:18; Prov 8:11
31:14 Ezek 27:25
31:15 Prov 20:13; Rom 12:11; Luke 12:42
31:17 1 Kin 18:46; 2 Kin 4:29; Job 38:3

31:1 Little is known about Lemuel except that he was a king who received wise teachings from his mother. His name means "devoted to God." Some believe that Lemuel and Agur were both from the kingdom of Massa in northern Arabia.

31:4–7 Drunkenness might be understandable among dying people in great pain, but it is inexcusable for national leaders. Alcohol clouds the mind and can lead to injustice and poor decisions. Leaders have better things to do than anesthetize themselves with alcohol.

31:10–31 Proverbs has a lot to say about women. How fitting that the book ends with a picture of a woman of strong character, great wisdom, many skills, and great compassion.

Some people have the mistaken idea that the ideal woman in the Bible is retiring, servile, and entirely domestic. Not so! This woman is an excellent wife and mother. She is also a manufacturer, importer, manager, realtor, farmer, seamstress, upholsterer, and merchant. Her strength and dignity do not come from her amazing achievements, however. They are a result of her reverence for God. In our society where physical appearance counts for so much, it may surprise us to realize that her appearance is never mentioned. Her attractiveness comes entirely from her character.

The woman described in this chapter has outstanding abilities. Her family's social position is high. In fact, she may not be one woman at all—she may be a composite portrait of ideal womanhood. Do not see her as a model to imitate in every detail; your days are not long enough to do everything she does! See her instead as an inspiration to be all you can be. We can't be just like her, but we can learn from her industry, integrity, and resourcefulness.

18 She senses that her gain is good;
Her lamp does not go out at night.
19 She stretches out her hands to the distaff,
And her hands grasp the spindle.
20 She extends her hand to the poor,
And she stretches out her hands to the needy.
21 She is not afraid of the snow for her household,
For all her household are clothed with scarlet.
22 She makes coverings for herself;
Her clothing is fine linen and purple.
23 Her husband is known in the gates,
When he sits among the elders of the land.
24 She makes linen garments and sells *them,*
And supplies belts to the tradesmen.
25 Strength and dignity are her clothing,
And she smiles at the future.
26 She opens her mouth in wisdom,
And the teaching of kindness is on her tongue.
27 She looks well to the ways of her household,
And does not eat the bread of idleness.
28 Her children rise up and bless her;
Her husband *also,* and he praises her, *saying:*
29 "Many daughters have done nobly,
But you excel them all."
30 Charm is deceitful and beauty is vain,
But a woman who fears the LORD, she shall be praised.
31 Give her the product of her hands,
And let her works praise her in the gates.

31:20 Deut 15:11; Job 31:16-20; Prov 22:9; Rom 12:13; Eph 4:28

31:21 2 Sam 1:24

31:22 Prov 7:16; Gen 41:42; Rev 19:8, 14; Judg 8:26; Luke 16:19

31:23 Deut 16:18; Ruth 4:1, 11

31:24 Judg 14:12

31:25 1 Tim 2:9, 10

31:26 Prov 10:31

31:27 Prov 19:15

31:30 Ps 112:1; Prov 22:4

31:19 The distaff and spindle are two implements used in hand spinning.

31:31 The book of Proverbs begins with the command to fear the Lord (1:7) and ends with the picture of a woman who fulfills this command. Her qualities are mentioned throughout the book: hard work, fear of God, respect for spouse, foresight, encouragement, care for others, concern for the poor, wisdom in handling money. These qualities, when coupled with fear of God, lead to enjoyment, success, honor, and worth. Proverbs is very practical for our day because it shows us how to become wise, make good decisions, and live according to God's ideal.

ECCLESIASTES

VITAL STATISTICS

PURPOSE:
To spare future generations the bitterness of learning through their own experience that life is meaningless apart from God

AUTHOR:
Solomon

TO WHOM WRITTEN:
Solomon's subjects in particular, and all people in general

DATE WRITTEN:
Probably around 935 B.C., late in Solomon's life

SETTING:
Solomon was looking back on his life, much of which was lived apart from God.

KEY VERSE:
"The conclusion, when all has been heard, is: fear God and keep His commandments, because this applies to every person" (12:13).

THE MOLDED bunny lies in the basket, surrounded by green paper "grass." With Easter morning eyes wide with anticipation, the little boy carefully lifts the chocolate figure and bites into one of the long ears. But the sweet taste fades quickly, and the child looks again at the candy in his hand. It's hollow!

Empty, futile, hollow, nothing—the words have a ring of disappointment and disillusionment. Yet this is the life experience of many. Grasping the sweet things—possessions, experience, power, and pleasure—they find nothing inside. Life is empty, meaningless—and they sink into despair.

Almost 3,000 years ago, Solomon spoke of this human dilemma; but the insights and applications of his message are relevant to our time. Ecclesiastes, Solomon's written sermon, is an analysis of life's experiences and a critical essay about life's true meaning. In this profound book, Solomon takes us on a reflective journey through his life, explaining how everything he had tried, tested, or tasted had been "vanity"—useless, irrational, pointless, foolish, and empty—an exercise in futility. And remember, these words are from one who "had it all"—tremendous intellect, power, and wealth. After this biographical tour, Solomon made his triumphant conclusion: "Fear God and keep His commandments, because this applies to every person. For God will bring every act to judgment, everything which is hidden, whether it is good or evil" (12:13–14).

When Solomon became king, he asked God for wisdom (2 Chronicles 1:7–12), and he became the wisest man in the world (1 Kings 4:29–34). He studied, taught, judged, and wrote. Kings and leaders from other nations came to Jerusalem to learn from him. But with all of his practical insight on life, Solomon failed to heed his own advice, and he began a downward spiral. Near the end of his life, Solomon looked back with an attitude of humility and repentance. He took stock of his life, hoping to spare his readers the bitterness of learning through personal experience that everything apart from God is empty, hollow, and meaningless.

Although the tone of Ecclesiastes is negative and pessimistic, we must not conclude that the only chapter worth reading and applying is the last one, where he draws his conclusions. In reality, the entire book is filled with practical wisdom (how to accomplish things in the world and stay out of trouble) and spiritual wisdom (how to find and know eternal values). Solomon had a very honest approach to life. All of his remarks relating to the futility of life are there for a purpose: to lead us to seek fulfillment and happiness in God alone. He was not trying to destroy all hope, but to direct our hopes to the only one who can truly fulfill them and give our life meaning. Solomon affirms the value of knowledge, relationships, work, and pleasure, but only *in their proper place.* All of these temporal things in life must be seen in light of the eternal.

Read Ecclesiastes and learn about life. Hear the stern warnings and dire predictions, and commit yourself to remember your Creator now (12:1).

THE BLUEPRINT

1. Solomon's personal experience (1:1—2:26)
2. Solomon's general observations (3:1—5:20)
3. Solomon's practical counsel (6:1—8:17)
4. Solomon's final conclusion (9:1—12:14)

Ecclesiastes shows that certain paths in life lead to emptiness. This profound book also helps us discover true purpose in life. Such wisdom can spare us from the emptiness that results from a life without God. Solomon teaches that people will not find meaning in life through knowledge, money, pleasure, work, or popularity. True satisfaction comes from knowing that what we are doing is part of God's purpose for our life. This is a book that can help free us from our scramble for power, approval, and money, and draw us closer to God.

MEGATHEMES

THEME	EXPLANATION	IMPORTANCE
Searching	Solomon searched for satisfaction almost as though he was conducting a scientific experiment. Through this process, he discovered that life without God is a long and fruitless search for enjoyment, meaning, and fulfillment. True happiness is not in our power to attain because we always want more than we can have. In addition, there are circumstances beyond our control that can snatch away our possessions or attainments.	People are still searching. Yet the more they try to get, the more they realize how little they really have. No pleasure or happiness is possible without God. Without him, satisfaction is a lost search. Above everything we should strive to know and love God. He gives wisdom, knowledge, and joy.
Emptiness	Solomon shows how empty it is to pursue the pleasures that this life has to offer rather than seek to have a relationship with the eternal God. The search for pleasure, wealth, and success is ultimately disappointing. Nothing in the world can fill the emptiness and satisfy the deep longings in our restless hearts.	The cure for emptiness is to center on God. His love also can fill the emptiness of human experience. Fear God throughout your life, and fill your life with serving God and others rather than with selfish pleasures.
Work	Solomon tried to shake people's confidence in their own efforts, abilities, and wisdom and to direct them to faith in God as the only sound basis for living. Without God, there is no lasting reward or benefit in hard work.	Work done with the wrong attitude will leave us empty. But work accepted as an assignment from God can be seen as a gift. Examine what you expect from your efforts. God gives you abilities and opportunities to work so that you can use your time well.
Death	The certainty of death makes all human achievements futile. God has a plan for each one of us that goes beyond life and death. The reality of aging and dying reminds each individual of the end to come when God will judge each person's life.	Because life is short, we need wisdom that is greater than this world can offer. We need the words of God so we can live right. If we listen to him, his wisdom spares us the bitterness of futile human experience and gives us a hope that goes beyond death.
Wisdom	Human wisdom doesn't contain all the answers. Knowledge and education have their limits. To understand life and make right choices, we need the wisdom that can be found only in God's Word—the Bible.	When we realize that God will evaluate all that we do, we should learn to live wisely, remembering that he is present each day, and learn to obey his guidelines for living. But in order to have God's wisdom, we must first get to know and honor him.

1. Solomon's personal experience

The Futility of All Endeavor

1 The words of the Preacher, the son of David, king in Jerusalem.
2 "[1]Vanity of vanities," says the Preacher,
"[1]Vanity of vanities! All is vanity."

3 What advantage does man have in all his work
Which he does under the sun?
4 A generation goes and a generation comes,
But the earth remains forever.
5 Also, the sun rises and the sun sets;
And hastening to its place it rises there *again.*
6 Blowing toward the south,
Then turning toward the north,
The wind continues swirling along;
And on its circular courses the wind returns.
7 All the rivers flow into the sea,
Yet the sea is not full.
To the place where the rivers flow,
There they flow again.
8 All things are wearisome;
Man is not able to tell *it.*
The eye is not satisfied with seeing,
Nor is the ear filled with hearing.
9 That which has been is that which will be,
And that which has been done is that which will be done.
So there is nothing new under the sun.
10 Is there anything of which one might say,
"See this, it is new"?
Already it has existed for ages
Which were before us.
11 There is no remembrance of earlier things;
And also of the later things which will occur,
There will be for them no remembrance
Among those who will come later *still.*

1 Or *Futility of futilities*

1:1 Eccl 1:12; 7:27; 12:8-10
1:2 Ps 39:5, 6; 62:9; 144:4; Eccl 12:8; Rom 8:20
1:3 Eccl 2:11; 3:9; 5:16
1:4 Ps 104:5; 119:90
1:5 Ps 19:6
1:6 Eccl 11:5; John 3:8
1:8 Prov 27:20; Eccl 4:8
1:9 Eccl 1:10; 2:12; 3:15; 6:10
1:11 Eccl 2:16; 9:5

1:1 The author, Solomon (the "king over Israel in Jerusalem"; see 1:12), referred to himself as the Preacher, or leader of the assembly. He was both assembling people to hear a message and gathering wise sayings (proverbs). Solomon, one person in the Bible who had everything (wisdom, power, riches, honor, reputation, God's favor), is the one who discussed the ultimate emptiness of all that this world has to offer. He tried to destroy people's confidence in their own efforts, abilities, and righteousness and direct them to commitment to God as the only reason for living.

1:1–11 Solomon had a purpose for writing skeptically and pessimistically. Near the end of his life, he looked back over everything he had done, and most of it seemed meaningless. A common belief was that only good people prospered and that only the wicked suffered, but that hadn't proven true in his experience. Solomon wrote this book after he had tried everything and achieved much, only to find that nothing apart from God made him happy. He wanted his readers to avoid these same senseless pursuits. If we try to find meaning in our accomplishments rather than in God, we will never be satisfied, and everything we pursue will become wearisome.

1:2 Solomon's kingdom, Israel, was in its golden age, but Solomon wanted the people to understand that success and prosperity don't last long (Psalm 103:14–16; Isaiah 40:6–8; James 4:14). All human accomplishments will one day disappear, and we must keep this in mind in order to live wisely. If we don't, we will become either proud and self-sufficient when we succeed or sorely disappointed when we fail. Solomon's goal was to show that earthly possessions and accomplishments are ultimately meaningless. Only the pursuit of God brings real satisfaction. We should honor God in all we say, think, and do.

1:8–11 Many people feel restless and dissatisfied. They wonder: (1) If I am in God's will, why am I so tired and unfulfilled? (2) What is the meaning of life? (3) When I look back on it all, will I be happy with my accomplishments? (4) Why do I feel burned out, disillusioned, dry? (5) What is to become of me? Solomon tests our faith, challenging us to find true and lasting meaning in God alone. As you take a hard look at your life, as Solomon did his, you will see how important serving God is over all other options. Perhaps God is asking you to rethink your purpose and direction in life, just as Solomon did in Ecclesiastes.

The Futility of Wisdom

12 I, the Preacher, have been king over Israel in Jerusalem.
13 And I set my mind to seek and explore by wisdom concerning all that has been done
under heaven. *It* is a grievous task *which* God has given to the sons of men to be afflicted
with.
14 I have seen all the works which have been done under the sun, and behold, all is
vanity and striving after wind.
15 What is crooked cannot be straightened and what is lacking cannot be counted.
16 I said to myself, "Behold, I have magnified and increased wisdom more than all who
were over Jerusalem before me; and my mind has observed a wealth of wisdom and
knowledge."
17 And I set my mind to know wisdom and to know madness and folly; I realized that
this also is striving after wind.
18 Because in much wisdom there is much grief, and increasing knowledge *results in*
increasing pain.

The Futility of Pleasure and Possessions

2 I said to myself, "Come now, I will test you with pleasure. So enjoy yourself." And
behold, it too was futility.
2 I said of laughter, "It is madness," and of pleasure, "What does it accomplish?"
3 I explored with my mind *how* to stimulate my body with wine while my mind was
guiding *me* wisely, and how to take hold of folly, until I could see what good there is for
the sons of men to do under heaven the few years of their lives.
4 I enlarged my works: I built houses for myself, I planted vineyards for myself;
5 I made gardens and parks for myself and I planted in them all kinds of fruit trees;
6 I made ponds of water for myself from which to irrigate a forest of growing trees.
7 I bought male and female slaves and I had homeborn slaves. Also I possessed flocks
and herds larger than all who preceded me in Jerusalem.
8 Also, I collected for myself silver and gold and the treasure of kings and provinces.
I provided for myself male and female singers and the pleasures of men—many concubines.
9 Then I became great and increased more than all who preceded me in Jerusalem.
My wisdom also stood by me.
10 All that my eyes desired I did not refuse them. I did not withhold my heart from any
pleasure, for my heart was pleased because of all my labor and this was my reward for all
my labor.

1:12 Eccl 1:1; 7:27
1:13 Eccl 7:25; 8:17; Eccl 2:23, 26; 3:10; 4:8
1:14 Eccl 2:11, 17; 4:4; 6:9
1:15 Eccl 7:13
1:17 Eccl 1:14; 2:11, 17; 4:4, 6, 16; 6:9
1:18 Eccl 2:23; 12:12
2:1 Eccl 7:4; 8:15
2:2 Prov 14:13; Eccl 7:3, 6
2:3 Judg 9:13; Ps 104:15; Eccl 10:19; Eccl 7:25; Eccl 2:24; 3:12, 13; 5:18; 6:12; 8:15; 12:13
2:4 1 Kin 7:1-12
2:5 Song 4:16; 5:1; Neh 2:8
2:7 Gen 14:14; 15:3; 1 Kin 4:23
2:8 1 Kin 9:28; 10:10, 14, 21; 2 Sam 19:35
2:9 1 Chr 29:25; Eccl 1:16
2:10 Eccl 6:2; Eccl 3:22; 5:18; 9:9

1:12–15 "What is crooked cannot be straightened" refers to the ultimate perplexity and confusion that come to us because of all the unanswered questions in life. Solomon, writing about his own life, discovered that neither his accomplishments nor his wisdom could make him truly happy. True wisdom is found in God, and true happiness comes from pleasing him.

1:16–18 The more you understand, the more pain and difficulty you experience. For example, the more you know, the more imperfection you see around you; and the more you observe, the more evil becomes evident. As you set out with Solomon to find the meaning of life, you must be ready to feel more, think more, question more, hurt more, and do more. Are you ready to pay the price for wisdom?

1:16–18 Solomon highlights two kinds of wisdom in the book of Ecclesiastes: (1) human knowledge, reasoning, or philosophy, and (2) the wisdom that comes from God. In these verses Solomon is talking about human knowledge. When human knowledge ignores God, it only highlights our problems because it can't provide answers without God's eternal perspective and solution.

2:1ff Solomon conducted his search for life's meaning as an experiment. He first tried pursuing pleasure. He undertook great projects, bought slaves and herds and flocks, amassed wealth, acquired singers, added many women to his harem, and became the greatest person in Jerusalem. But none of these gave him satisfaction—"I considered all my activities which my hands had done and the labor which I had exerted, and behold all was vanity and striving after wind and there was no profit under the sun" (2:11). Some of the pleasures Solomon sought were wrong and some were worthy, but even the worthy pursuits were futile when he pursued them as an end in themselves. We must look beyond our activities to the reasons we do them and the purpose they fulfill. Is your goal in life to search for meaning or to search for God who gives meaning?

2:4–6 Solomon had built houses, a temple, a kingdom, a family (see 1 Kings 3—11). In the course of history, they all would be ruined. In Psalm 127:1, Solomon wrote, "Unless the LORD builds the house, they labor in vain who build it; unless the LORD guards the city, the watchman keeps awake in vain." This book is part of Solomon's testimony to what happens to a kingdom or family that forgets God. As you examine your projects or goals, what is your starting point, your motivation? Without God as your foundation, all you are living for is meaningless.

11 Thus I considered all my activities which my hands had done and the labor which I
had exerted, and behold all was [2]vanity and striving after wind and there was no profit
under the sun.

Wisdom Excels Folly

12 So I turned to consider wisdom, madness and folly; for what *will* the man *do* who
will come after the king *except* what has already been done?
13 And I saw that wisdom excels folly as light excels darkness.
14 The wise man's eyes are in his head, but the fool walks in darkness. And yet I know
that one fate befalls them both.
15 Then I said to myself, "As is the fate of the fool, it will also befall me. Why then have
I been extremely wise?" So I said to myself, "This too is vanity."
16 For there is no lasting remembrance of the wise man *as* with the fool, inasmuch as
in the coming days all will be forgotten. And how the wise man and the fool alike die!
17 So I hated life, for the work which had been done under the sun was grievous to me;
because everything is futility and striving after wind.

The Futility of Labor

18 Thus I hated all the fruit of my labor for which I had labored under the sun, for I
must leave it to the man who will come after me.
19 And who knows whether he will be a wise man or a fool? Yet he will have control
over all the fruit of my labor for which I have labored by acting wisely under the sun.
This too is vanity.
20 Therefore I completely despaired of all the fruit of my labor for which I had labored
under the sun.
21 When there is a man who has labored with wisdom, knowledge and skill, then he
gives his legacy to one who has not labored with them. This too is vanity and a great evil.
22 For what does a man get in all his labor and in his striving with which he labors under
the sun?
23 Because all his days his task is painful and grievous; even at night his mind does not
rest. This too is vanity.
24 There is nothing better for a man *than* to eat and drink and tell himself that his labor is good. This also I have seen that it is from the hand of God.
25 For who can eat and who can have enjoyment without Him?
26 For to a person who is good in His sight He has given wisdom and knowledge and
joy, while to the sinner He has given the task of gathering and collecting so that he may
give to one who is good in God's sight. This too is vanity and striving after wind.

2 Or *futility,* and so throughout the ch

2:11 Eccl 1:14; 2:22, 23; Eccl 1:3; 3:9; 5:16
2:12 Eccl 1:17; Eccl 1:9, 10; 3:15
2:13 Eccl 7:11, 12, 19; 9:18; 10:10
2:14 1 John 2:11; Ps 49:10; Eccl 3:19; 6:6; 7:2; 9:2, 3
2:15 Eccl 2:16; Eccl 6:8, 11
2:16 Eccl 1:11; 9:5; Eccl 2:14
2:17 Eccl 4:2, 3
2:18 Eccl 1:3; 2:11; Ps 39:6; 49:10
2:19 1 Kin 12:13; 1 Tim 6:10
2:21 Eccl 4:4; Eccl 2:18
2:22 Eccl 1:3; 2:11
2:23 Job 5:7; 14:1; Eccl 1:18; 5:17; Ps 127:2
2:24 Eccl 2:3; 3:12, 13, 22; 5:18; 6:12; 8:15; 9:7; Is 56:12; Luke 12:19; 1 Cor 15:32; 1 Tim 6:17; Eccl 3:13
2:26 Job 32:8; Prov 2:6; Job 27:16, 17; Prov 13:22; Eccl 1:14

2:11 Solomon summarized all his attempts at finding life's meaning as "striving after wind." We feel the wind as it passes, but we can't catch hold of it or keep it. In all our accomplishments, even the big ones, our good feelings are only temporary. Security and self-worth are not found in these accomplishments, but far beyond them in the love of God. Think about what you consider worthwhile in your life—where you place your time, energy, and money. Will you one day look back and decide that these, too, were a "striving after wind"?

2:16 Solomon realized that wisdom alone cannot guarantee eternal life. Wisdom, riches, and personal achievement matter very little after death—and everyone must die. We must not build our lives on perishable pursuits, but on the solid foundation of God. Then even if everything we have is taken away, we still will have God, who is all we really need anyway. This is the point of the book of Job (see the introduction to Job).

2:16 Is death the ultimate equalizer of all people, no matter what they have attained in life? While this appears to be true from an earthly perspective, God makes it clear (as Solomon later points out in 12:14) that what we do here has a great impact upon our eternal reward.

2:18–23 Solomon continues to show that hard work bears no lasting fruit for those who work solely to earn money and gain possessions. Not only will everything be left behind at death, but it may be left to those who have done nothing to earn it. In addition, it may not be well cared for, and all that was gained may be lost. In fact, Solomon's son, who inherited his throne, was often foolish—see 1 Kings 12. Hard work done with proper motives (caring for your family, serving God) is not wrong. We must work to survive, and, more importantly, we are responsible for the physical and spiritual well-being of those under our care. But the fruit of hard work done to glorify only ourselves will be passed on to those who may later lose or spoil it all. Such toil often leads to grief, while serving God leads to everlasting joy. Do you know the real reason you are working so hard?

2:24–26 Is Solomon recommending we make life a big, irresponsible party? No, he is encouraging us to take pleasure in what we're doing now and to enjoy life because it comes from God's hand. True enjoyment in life comes only as we follow God's guidelines for living. Without him, satisfaction is a lost search. Those who really know how to enjoy life are the ones who take life each day as a gift from God, thanking him for it and serving him in it. Those without God will have no relief from toil and no direction to guide them through life's complications.

2. Solomon's general observations

A Time for Everything

3:1 Eccl 3:17; 8:6
3:2 Job 14:5; Heb 9:27
3:3 Gen 9:6; 1 Sam 2:6; Hos 6:1, 2
3:4 Rom 12:15; Ps 126:2; Ex 15:20

3 There is an appointed time for everything. And there is a time for every event under
heaven—

2 A time to give birth and a time to die;
A time to plant and a time to uproot what is planted.
3 A time to kill and a time to heal;
A time to tear down and a time to build up.
4 A time to weep and a time to laugh;
A time to mourn and a time to dance.
5 A time to throw stones and a time to gather stones;
A time to embrace and a time to shun embracing.
6 A time to search and a time to give up as lost;
A time to keep and a time to throw away.

3:7 Amos 5:13
3:8 Ps 101:3; Prov 13:5

7 A time to tear apart and a time to sew together;
A time to be silent and a time to speak.
8 A time to love and a time to hate;
A time for war and a time for peace.

3:9 Eccl 1:3; 2:11; 5:16
3:10 Eccl 1:13; 2:26

9 What profit is there to the worker from that in which he toils?
10 I have seen the task which God has given the sons of men with which to occupy themselves.

God Set Eternity in the Heart of Man

3:11 Gen 1:31; Job 5:9; Eccl 7:23; 8:17; Rom 11:33
3:12 Eccl 2:24
3:13 Eccl 2:24; 5:19
3:14 Eccl 5:7; 7:18; 8:12, 13; 12:13
3:15 Eccl 1:9; 6:10

11 He has made everything [3]appropriate in its time. He has also set eternity in their
heart, yet so that man will not find out the work which God has done from the beginning
even to the end.
12 I know that there is nothing better for them than to rejoice and to do good in one's
lifetime;
13 moreover, that every man who eats and drinks sees good in all his labor—it is the
gift of God.
14 I know that everything God does will remain forever; there is nothing to add to it
and there is nothing to take from it, for God has *so* worked that men should fear Him.
15 That which is has been already and that which will be has already been, for God
seeks what has passed by.

3 Lit *beautiful*

3:1—5:20 Solomon's point in this section is that God has a plan for all people. Thus he provides cycles of life, each with its work for us to do. Although we may face many problems that seem to contradict God's plan, these should not be barriers to believing in him, but rather opportunities to discover that, without God, life's problems have no lasting solutions!

3:1–8 Timing is important. All the experiences listed in these verses are appropriate at certain times. The secret to peace with God is to discover, accept, and appreciate God's perfect timing. The danger is to doubt or resent God's timing. This can lead to despair, rebellion, or moving ahead without his advice.

3:8 When is there a time for hating? We shouldn't hate evil people, but we should hate what they do. We should also hate it when people are mistreated, when children are starving, and when God is being dishonored. In addition, we must hate sin in our lives—this is God's attitude (see Psalm 5:5).

3:9–13 Your ability to find satisfaction in your work depends to a large extent upon your attitude. You will become dissatisfied if you lose the sense of purpose God intended for your work. We can enjoy our work if we (1) remember that God has given us work to do (3:10), and (2) realize that the fruit of our labor is a gift from him (3:13). See your work as a way to serve God.

3:11 God has "set eternity" in people's hearts. This means that we can never be completely satisfied with earthly pleasures and pursuits. Because we are created in God's image, (1) we have a spiritual thirst, (2) we have eternal value, and (3) nothing but the eternal God can truly satisfy us. He has built in us a restless yearning for the kind of perfect world that can only be found in his perfect rule. He has given us a glimpse of the perfection of his creation. But it is only a glimpse; we cannot see into the future or comprehend everything. So we must trust him now and do his work on earth.

3:12 To rejoice and do good while we live are worthy goals for life, but we can pursue them the wrong way. God wants us to enjoy life. When we have the proper view of God, we discover that real pleasure is found in enjoying whatever we have as gifts from God, not in what we accumulate.

3:14 What is the purpose of life? It is that we should fear the all-powerful God. To *fear* God means to respect and stand in awe of him because of who he is. Purpose in life starts with *whom* we know, not what we know or how good we are. It is impossible to fulfill your God-given purpose unless you fear God and give him first place in your life.

16 Furthermore, I have seen under the sun *that* in the place of justice there is wickedness and in the place of righteousness there is wickedness.
17 I said to myself, "God will judge both the righteous man and the wicked man," for
a time for every matter and for every deed is there.
18 I said to myself concerning the sons of men, "God has surely tested them in order
for them to see that they are but beasts."
19 For the fate of the sons of men and the fate of beasts is the same. As one dies so
dies the other; indeed, they all have the same breath and there is no advantage for man
over beast, for all is vanity.
20 All go to the same place. All came from the dust and all return to the dust.
21 Who knows that the breath of man ascends upward and the breath of the beast
descends downward to the earth?
22 I have seen that nothing is better than that man should be happy in his activities, for
that is his lot. For who will bring him to see what will occur after him?

The Evils of Oppression

4 Then I looked again at all the acts of oppression which were being done under the
sun. And behold *I saw* the tears of the oppressed and *that* they had no one to comfort *them;* and on the side of their oppressors was power, but they had no one to comfort
them.
2 So I congratulated the dead who are already dead more than the living who are still
living.
3 But better *off* than both of them is the one who has never existed, who has never
seen the evil activity that is done under the sun.
4 I have seen that every labor and every skill which is done is *the result of* rivalry between a man and his neighbor. This too is vanity and striving after wind.
5 The fool folds his hands and consumes his own flesh.
6 One hand full of rest is better than two fists full of labor and striving after wind.
7 Then I looked again at vanity under the sun.
8 There was a certain man without a dependent, having neither a son nor a brother,
yet there was no end to all his labor. Indeed, his eyes were not satisfied with riches *and*
he never asked, "And for whom am I laboring and depriving myself of pleasure?" This
too is vanity and it is a grievous task.
9 Two are better than one because they have a good return for their labor.
10 For if either of them falls, the one will lift up his companion. But woe to the one
who falls when there is not another to lift him up.
11 Furthermore, if two lie down together they keep warm, but how can one be warm
alone?

3:16 Eccl 4:1; 5:8; 8:9
3:17 Gen 18:25; Ps 96:13; 98:9; Eccl 11:9; Matt 16:27; Rom 2:6-10; 2 Thess 1:6-9; Eccl 3:1; 8:6
3:18 Ps 49:12, 20; 73:22
3:19 Ps 49:12; Eccl 9:12
3:20 Gen 3:19; Ps 103:14; Eccl 12:7
3:21 Eccl 12:7
3:22 Eccl 2:24; Eccl 2:18; 6:12; 8:7; 10:14
4:1 Job 35:9; Ps 12:5; Eccl 3:16; 5:8; Is 5:7; Jer 16:7; Lam 1:9
4:2 Job 3:11-26; Eccl 2:17; 7:1
4:3 Job 3:11-22; Eccl 6:3; Luke 23:29
4:4 Eccl 2:21; Eccl 1:14
4:5 Prov 6:10; 24:33; Is 9:20
4:6 Prov 15:16, 17; 16:8
4:8 Prov 27:20; Eccl 1:8; 5:10; Eccl 2:21; Eccl 1:13
4:11 1 Kin 1:1-4

3:16 There is wickedness in the place of justice. It even affects the legal system. Solomon asked how God's plan can be perfect when there is so much injustice and oppression in the world (4:1). He concluded that God does not ignore injustice, but will bring it to an end at his appointed time (12:13–14).

3:16ff Solomon reflects on several apparent contradictions in God's control of the world: (1) There is wickedness where there should be justice (3:16–17); (2) people created in God's image die just like the animals (3:18–21); (3) no one comforts the oppressed (4:1–3); (4) many people are motivated by envy (4:4–6); (5) people are lonely (4:7–12); (6) recognition for accomplishments is temporary (4:13–16). It is easy to use such contradictions as excuses not to believe in God. But Solomon used them to show how we can honestly look at life's problems and still keep our faith. This life is not all there is, yet even in this life we should not pass judgment on God because we don't know everything. God's plan is for us to live forever with him. So live with eternal values in view, realizing that all contradictions will one day be cleared up by the Creator himself (12:14).

3:19–22 Our bodies can't live forever in their present state. In that sense, humans and animals are alike. But Solomon acknowledged that God has given people the hope of eternity (see the note on 3:11), and that we will undergo judgment in the next life (3:17; 12:7, 14)—making us different from animals. Because man has eternity set in his heart, he has a unique purpose in God's overall plan. Yet we cannot discover God's purpose for our lives by our own efforts—only through building a relationship with him and seeking his guidance. Are you now living as God wants? Do you see life as a gift from him?

4:4–6 Some people are lazy while others are workaholics. The lazy person, seeing the futility of dashing about for success, folds his hands and hurts both himself and those who depend on him. The workaholic is often driven by envy, greed, and a constant desire to stay ahead of everyone else. Both extremes are foolish and irresponsible. The answer is to work hard but with moderation. Take time to enjoy the other gifts God has given and realize that it is God who gives out the assignments and the rewards, not us.

4:9–12 There are advantages to cooperating with others. Life is designed for companionship, not isolation; for intimacy, not loneliness. Some people prefer isolation, thinking they cannot trust anyone. We are not here on earth to serve ourselves, however, but to serve God and others. Don't isolate yourself and try to go it alone. Seek companions; be a team member.

12 And if one can overpower him who is alone, two can resist him. A cord of three
strands is not quickly torn apart.

4:13
Eccl 7:19; 9:15

13 A poor yet wise lad is better than an old and foolish king who no longer knows *how*
to receive instruction.

4:14
Gen 41:14, 41-43

14 For he has come out of prison to become king, even though he was born poor in his
kingdom.
15 I have seen all the living under the sun throng to the side of the second lad who
replaces him.

4:16
Eccl 1:14

16 There is no end to all the people, to all who were before them, and even the ones
who will come later will not be happy with him, for this too is vanity and striving after
wind.

Your Attitude Toward God

5:1
Ex 3:5; 30:18-20; Is 1:12; 1 Sam 15:22; Prov 15:8; 21:27

5 Guard your steps as you go to the house of God and draw near to listen rather than
to offer the sacrifice of fools; for they do not know they are doing evil.

5:2
Prov 20:25; Prov 10:19; Matt 6:7

2 Do not be hasty in word or impulsive in thought to bring up a matter in the presence of God. For God is in heaven and you are on the earth; therefore let your words be
few.

5:3
Job 11:2; Prov 15:2; Eccl 10:14

3 For the dream comes through much effort and the voice of a fool through many
words.

5:4
Num 30:2; Ps 50:14; 76:11; Ps 66:13, 14

4 When you make a vow to God, do not be late in paying it; for *He takes* no delight in
fools. Pay what you vow!

5:5
Prov 20:25; Acts 5:4

5 It is better that you should not vow than that you should vow and not pay.

5:6
Lev 4:2, 22; Num 15:25

6 Do not let your speech cause you to sin and do not say in the presence of the messenger *of God* that it was a mistake. Why should God be angry on account of your voice
and destroy the work of your hands?

5:7
Eccl 3:14; 7:18; 8:12, 13; 12:13

7 For in many dreams and in many words there is emptiness. Rather, fear God.

5:8
Eccl 4:1; Ezek 18:18; 1 Pet 4:12

8 If you see oppression of the poor and denial of justice and righteousness in the province, do not be shocked at the sight; for one official watches over another official, and
there are higher officials over them.
9 After all, a king who cultivates the field is an advantage to the land.

The Folly of Riches

5:10
Eccl 1:8; 2:10, 11; 4:8

10 He who loves money will not be satisfied with money, nor he who loves abundance
with its income. This too is vanity.

5:11
Eccl 2:9

11 When good things increase, those who consume them increase. So what is the advantage to their owners except to look on?

5:12
Prov 3:24

12 The sleep of the working man is pleasant, whether he eats little or much; but the
full stomach of the rich man does not allow him to sleep.

5:13
Eccl 6:2

13 There is a grievous evil *which* I have seen under the sun: riches being hoarded by
their owner to his hurt.
14 When those riches were lost through a bad investment and he had fathered a son,
then there was nothing to support him.

5:15
Job 1:21; Ps 49:17; 1 Tim 6:7

15 As he had come naked from his mother's womb, so will he return as he came. He
will take nothing from the fruit of his labor that he can carry in his hand.

4:13–16 Advancement or getting to the top is meaningless. Position, popularity, and prestige are poor goals for a life's work. Although many seek them, they are shadows without substance. Many people seek recognition for their accomplishments; but people are fickle, changing quickly and easily. How much better to seek God's approval. His love never changes.

5:1 "Guard your steps" means "be careful." When we enter the house of God, we should have the attitude of being open and ready to listen to God, not to dictate to him what we think he should do.

5:4–5 Solomon warns his readers about making foolish vows (promises) to God. In Israelite culture, making vows was a serious matter. Vows were voluntary but, once made, were unbreakable (Deuteronomy 23:21–23). It is foolish to make a vow you cannot keep or to play games with God by only partially fulfilling your vow (Proverbs 20:25). It's better not to vow than to make a vow to God and break it. It's better still to make a vow and keep it. (See the note on Matthew 5:33ff.)

5:10–11 We always want more than we have. Solomon observed that those who love money and seek it obsessively never find the happiness it promises. Wealth also attracts freeloaders and thieves, causes sleeplessness and fear, and ultimately ends in loss because it must be left behind (Mark 10:23–25; Luke 12:16–21). No matter how much you earn, if you try to create happiness by accumulating wealth, you will never have enough. Money in itself is not wrong, but loving money leads to all sorts of sin. Whatever financial situation you are in, don't depend on money to make you happy. Instead, use what you have for the Lord.

16 This also is a grievous evil—exactly as a man is born, thus will he die. So what is the
advantage to him who toils for the wind?

5:16 Eccl 1:3; 2:11; 3:9; Prov 11:29

17 Throughout his life *he* also eats in darkness with great vexation, sickness and anger.

5:17 Ps 127:2; Eccl 2:23

18 Here is what I have seen to be good and fitting: to eat, to drink and enjoy oneself in
all one's labor in which he toils under the sun *during* the few years of his life which God
has given him; for this is his reward.

5:18 Eccl 2:24; Eccl 2:10

19 Furthermore, as for every man to whom God has given riches and wealth, He has
also empowered him to eat from them and to receive his reward and rejoice in his labor;
this is the gift of God.

5:19 2 Chr 1:12; Eccl 6:2; Eccl 6:2; Eccl 3:13

20 For he will not often consider the years of his life, because God keeps him occupied
with the gladness of his heart.

5:20 Ex 23:25

3. Solomon's practical counsel

The Futility of Life

6 There is an evil which I have seen under the sun and it is prevalent among
men—

6:1 Eccl 5:13

2 a man to whom God has given riches and wealth and honor so that his soul lacks
nothing of all that he desires; yet God has not empowered him to eat from them, for a
foreigner enjoys them. This is vanity and a severe affliction.

6:2 1 Kin 3:13; Ps 17:14; 73:7; Eccl 2:10

3 If a man fathers a hundred *children* and lives many years, however many they be,
but his soul is not satisfied with good things and he does not even have a *proper* burial,
then I say, "Better the miscarriage than he,
4 for it comes in futility and goes into obscurity; and its name is covered in obscurity.
5 "It never sees the sun and it never knows *anything;* it is better off than he.

6:3 Is 14:20; Jer 8:2; 22:19; Job 3:16; Eccl 4:3

6 "Even if the *other* man lives a thousand years twice and does not enjoy good things—
do not all go to one place?"

6:6 Eccl 2:14

7 All a man's labor is for his mouth and yet the appetite is not satisfied.

6:7 Prov 16:26

8 For what advantage does the wise man have over the fool? What *advantage* does
the poor man have, knowing *how* to walk before the living?

6:8 Eccl 2:15

9 What the eyes see is better than what the soul desires. This too is futility and a striving after wind.

6:9 Eccl 11:9; Eccl 1:14

10 Whatever exists has already been named, and it is known what man is; for he cannot dispute with him who is stronger than he is.
11 For there are many words which increase futility. What *then* is the advantage to a
man?

6:10 Eccl 1:9; 3:15; Job 9:32; 40:2; Prov 21:30; Is 45:9

12 For who knows what is good for a man during *his* lifetime, *during* the few years of
his futile life? He will spend them like a shadow. For who can tell a man what will be
after him under the sun?

6:12 Eccl 3:22

5:19–20 God wants us to view what we have (whether it is much or little) with the right perspective—our possessions are a gift from God. Although they are not the source of joy, they are a reason to rejoice because every good thing comes from God. We should focus more on the Giver than the gift. We can be content with what we have when we realize that with God we have everything we need.

6:1—8:15 In this section, Solomon shows that having the right attitude about God can help us deal with present injustices. Prosperity is not always good, and adversity is not always bad. But God is always good; if we live as he wants us to, we will be content.

6:1–6 "God has not empowered him to eat from them" probably means that the person has died. Even if he had lived a long life, it is ultimately meaningless in itself because all that he has accumulated is left behind. Everyone dies, and both rich and poor end up in the grave. Many people work hard to prolong life and improve their physical condition. Yet people don't spend nearly as much time or effort on their spiritual health. How shortsighted it is to work hard to extend this life and not take the steps God requires to gain eternal life.

6:6 "All go to one place" means that everyone dies.

6:9 "What the soul desires" refers to wasting time dreaming and wishing for what one doesn't have.

6:10 God knows and directs everything that happens, and he is in complete control over our lives, even though at times it may not seem like it. How foolish it is for us to contend with our Creator, who knows us completely and can see the future. (See also Jeremiah 18:6; Romans 9:19–24.)

6:12 Solomon is stating the profound truth that we cannot predict what the future holds. The only One who knows what will happen after we're gone is God. No human knows the future, so each day must be lived for its own value. Solomon is arguing against the notion that human beings can take charge of their own destiny. In all our plans we should look up to God, not just ahead to the future.

Wisdom and Folly Contrasted

7:1 Prov 22:1; Eccl 4:2; 7:8

7:2 Eccl 2:14, 16; 3:19, 20; 6:6; 9:2, 3; Ps 90:12

7:3 Eccl 2:2; 2 Cor 7:10

7:5 Ps 141:5; Prov 6:23; 13:18; 15:31, 32; 25:12; Eccl 9:17

7:6 Ps 58:9; 118:12; Eccl 2:2

7:7 Eccl 4:1; 5:8; Ex 23:8; Deut 16:19; Prov 17:8, 23

7:8 Eccl 7:1; Prov 14:29; 16:32; Gal 5:22; Eph 4:2

7:9 Prov 14:17; James 1:19

7:11 Prov 8:10, 11; Eccl 2:13

7:12 Eccl 7:19; 9:18; Prov 3:18; 8:35

7:13 Eccl 3:11; 8:17; Eccl 1:15

7:14 Deut 26:11; Eccl 3:22; 9:7; 11:9; Deut 8:5; Job 2:10; Eccl 3:22

7:15 Eccl 6:12; 9:9; Eccl 8:14; Eccl 8:12, 13

7 A good name is better than a good ointment,
And the day of *one's* death is better than the day of one's birth.
2 It is better to go to a house of mourning
Than to go to a house of feasting,
Because that is the end of every man,
And the living takes *it* to heart.
3 Sorrow is better than laughter,
For when a face is sad a heart may be happy.
4 The mind of the wise is in the house of mourning,
While the mind of fools is in the house of pleasure.
5 It is better to listen to the rebuke of a wise man
Than for one to listen to the song of fools.
6 For as the crackling of thorn bushes under a pot,
So is the laughter of the fool;
And this too is futility.
7 For oppression makes a wise man mad,
And a bribe corrupts the heart.
8 The end of a matter is better than its beginning;
Patience of spirit is better than haughtiness of spirit.
9 Do not be eager in your heart to be angry,
For anger resides in the bosom of fools.
10 Do not say, "Why is it that the former days were better than these?"
For it is not from wisdom that you ask about this.
11 Wisdom along with an inheritance is good
And an advantage to those who see the sun.
12 For wisdom is protection *just as* money is protection,
But the advantage of knowledge is that wisdom preserves the lives of its possessors.
13 Consider the work of God,
For who is able to straighten what He has bent?
14 In the day of prosperity be happy,
But in the day of adversity consider—
God has made the one as well as the other
So that man will not discover anything *that will be* after him.

15 I have seen everything during my lifetime of futility; there is a righteous man who
perishes in his righteousness and there is a wicked man who prolongs *his life* in his wickedness.

7:1–4 This seems to contradict Solomon's previous advice to eat, drink, and find satisfaction in one's work—to enjoy what God has given. We are to enjoy what we have while we can, but realize that adversity also strikes. Adversity reminds us that life is short, teaches us to live wisely, and refines our character. Christianity and Judaism see value in suffering and sorrow. The Greeks and Romans despised it; Eastern religions seek to live above it; but Christians and Jews see it as a refining fire. Most would agree that we learn more about God from difficult times than from happy times. Do you try to avoid sorrow and suffering at all costs? See your struggles as great opportunities to learn from God.

7:2, 4 Many people avoid thinking about death, refuse to face it, and are reluctant to attend funerals. Solomon is not encouraging us to think morbidly, but he knows that it is helpful to think clearly about death. It reminds us that there is still time for change, time to examine the direction of our lives, and time to confess our sins and find forgiveness from God. Because everyone will eventually die, it makes sense to plan ahead to experience God's mercy rather than his justice.

7:7 Money talks, and it can confuse those who would otherwise judge fairly. We hear about bribes given to judges, police officers, and witnesses. Bribes are given to hurt those who tell the truth and help those who oppose it. The person who is involved in extortion or takes a bribe is indeed a fool, no matter how wise he thought he was beforehand. It is said that everyone has a price, but those who are truly wise cannot be bought at any price.

7:8 To finish what we start takes hard work, wise guidance, self-discipline, and patience. Anyone with vision can start a big project. But vision without wisdom often results in unfinished projects and goals.

7:14 God allows both good times and bad times to come to everyone. He blends them in our lives in such a way that we can't predict the future or count on human wisdom and power. We usually give ourselves the credit for the good times. Then in bad times, we tend to blame God without thanking him for the good that comes out of it. When life appears certain and controllable, don't let self-satisfaction or complacency make you too comfortable, or God may allow bad times to drive you back to him. When life seems uncertain and uncontrollable, don't despair—God is in control and will bring good results out of tough times.

16 Do not be excessively righteous and do not be overly wise. Why should you ruin
yourself?
17 Do not be excessively wicked and do not be a fool. Why should you die before your
time?
18 It is good that you grasp one thing and also not let go of the other; for the one who
fears God comes forth with both of them.
19 Wisdom strengthens a wise man more than ten rulers who are in a city.
20 Indeed, there is not a righteous man on earth who *continually* does good and who
never sins.
21 Also, do not take seriously all words which are spoken, so that you will not hear
your servant cursing you.
22 For you also have realized that you likewise have many times cursed others.
23 I tested all this with wisdom, *and* I said, "I will be wise," but it was far from me.
24 What has been is remote and exceedingly mysterious. Who can discover it?
25 I directed my mind to know, to investigate and to seek wisdom and an explanation,
and to know the evil of folly and the foolishness of madness.
26 And I discovered more bitter than death the woman whose heart is snares and nets,
whose hands are chains. One who is pleasing to God will escape from her, but the sinner
will be captured by her.
27 "Behold, I have discovered this," says the Preacher, "*adding* one thing to another to
find an explanation,
28 which I am still seeking but have not found. I have found one man among a thousand, but I have not found a woman among all these.
29 "Behold, I have found only this, that God made men upright, but they have sought
out many devices."

Obey Rulers

8 Who is like the wise man and who knows the interpretation of a matter? A man's
wisdom illumines him and causes his stern face to beam.
2 I say, "Keep the command of the king because of the oath before God.
3 "Do not be in a hurry to leave him. Do not join in an evil matter, for he will do whatever he pleases."
4 Since the word of the king is authoritative, who will say to him, "What are you doing?"
5 He who keeps a *royal* command experiences no trouble, for a wise heart knows the
proper time and procedure.
6 For there is a proper time and procedure for every delight, though a man's trouble
is heavy upon him.
7 If no one knows what will happen, who can tell him when it will happen?
8 No man has authority to restrain the wind with the wind, or authority over the day
of death; and there is no discharge in the time of war, and evil will not deliver those who
practice it.

7:16 Prov 25:16; Phil 3:6; Rom 12:3
7:17 Job 22:16; Ps 55:23; Prov 10:27
7:18 Eccl 3:14; 5:7; 8:12, 13; 12:13
7:19 Eccl 7:12; 9:13-18
7:20 1 Kin 8:46; 2 Chr 6:36; Ps 143:2; Prov 20:9; Rom 3:23
7:21 Prov 30:10
7:23 Eccl 3:11; 8:17
7:24 Rom 11:33; Job 11:7; 37:23; Eccl 8:17
7:25 Eccl 1:15, 17; 10:13
7:26 Prov 5:4; Prov 7:23; Prov 6:23, 24; Prov 22:14
7:29 Gen 1:27
8:1 Ex 34:29, 30; Deut 28:50
8:2 Ex 22:11; 2 Sam 21:7; Ezek 17:18
8:3 Eccl 10:4
8:5 Eccl 12:13; Prov 12:21
8:6 Eccl 3:1, 17
8:7 Eccl 3:22; 6:12; 7:14; 9:12
8:8 Ps 49:7; Eccl 8:13

7:16–18 How can a person be too righteous or too wise? This is a warning against religious conceit—legalism or false righteousness. Solomon was saying that some people become overly righteous or wise *in their own eyes* because they are deluded by their own religious acts. They are so rigid or narrow in their views that they lose their sensitivity to the true reason for being good—to honor God. Balance is important. God created us to be whole people who seek his righteousness and goodness. Thus we should avoid both extremes of legalism and immorality.

7:23–25 Solomon, the wisest man in the world, confessed how difficult it had been to act and think wisely. He emphasized that no matter how much we know, there are always mysteries we will never understand. So thinking you have enough wisdom is a sure sign that you don't.

7:27–28 Did Solomon think women were not capable of being upright (wise and good)? No, because in the book of Proverbs he personified wisdom as a responsible woman. The point of Solomon's statement is not that women are unwise, but that hardly anyone, man or woman, is upright before God. In his search, Solomon found that goodness and wisdom were almost as scarce among men as among women, even though men were given a religious education program in his culture and women were not. In effect, the verse is saying, "I have found only one in a thousand people who is wise in God's eyes. No, I have found even fewer than that!"

7:29 God created human beings to live uprightly and do what is right. Instead, they have left God's path to follow their own downward road.

8:1 Wisdom is the ability to see life from God's perspective and then to know the best course of action to take. Most people would agree that wisdom is a valuable asset, but how can we acquire it? Proverbs 9:10 teaches that the fear of the Lord (respect and honor) is the beginning of wisdom. Wisdom comes from knowing and trusting God; it is not merely the way to find God. Knowing God will lead to understanding and then to sharing this knowledge with others.

9 All this I have seen and applied my mind to every deed that has been done under
the sun wherein a man has exercised authority over *another* man to his hurt.
10 So then, I have seen the wicked buried, those who used to go in and out from the
holy place, and they are *soon* forgotten in the city where they did thus. This too is futility.
11 Because the sentence against an evil deed is not executed quickly, therefore the hearts
of the sons of men among them are given fully to do evil.
12 Although a sinner does evil a hundred *times* and may lengthen his *life,* still I know
that it will be well for those who fear God, who fear Him openly.
13 But it will not be well for the evil man and he will not lengthen his days like a shadow, because he does not fear God.
14 There is futility which is done on the earth, that is, there are righteous men to whom
it happens according to the deeds of the wicked. On the other hand, there are evil men
to whom it happens according to the deeds of the righteous. I say that this too is futility.
15 So I commended pleasure, for there is nothing good for a man under the sun except
to eat and to drink and to be merry, and this will stand by him in his toils *throughout* the
days of his life which God has given him under the sun.
16 When I gave my heart to know wisdom and to see the task which has been done on
the earth (even though one should never sleep day or night),
17 and I saw every work of God, *I concluded* that man cannot discover the work which
has been done under the sun. Even though man should seek laboriously, he will not discover; and though the wise man should say, "I know," he cannot discover.

4. Solomon's final conclusion

Men Are in the Hand of God

9 For I have taken all this to my heart and explain it that righteous men, wise men,
and their deeds are in the hand of God. Man does not know whether *it will be* love or
hatred; anything awaits him.
2 It is the same for all. There is one fate for the righteous and for the wicked; for the
good, for the clean and for the unclean; for the man who offers a sacrifice and for the
one who does not sacrifice. As the good man is, so is the sinner; as the swearer is, so is
the one who is afraid to swear.
3 This is an evil in all that is done under the sun, that there is one fate for all men.
Furthermore, the hearts of the sons of men are full of evil and insanity is in their hearts
throughout their lives. Afterwards they *go* to the dead.
4 For whoever is joined with all the living, there is hope; surely a live dog is better
than a dead lion.
5 For the living know they will die; but the dead do not know anything, nor have they
any longer a reward, for their memory is forgotten.
6 Indeed their love, their hate and their zeal have already perished, and they will no
longer have a share in all that is done under the sun.

8:9 Eccl 4:1; 5:8; 7:7
8:10 Eccl 1:11; 2:16; 9:5, 15
8:11 Ex 34:6; Ps 86:15; Rom 2:4; 2 Pet 3:9; Eccl 9:3
8:12 Eccl 7:15; Deut 4:40; 12:25; Ps 37:11; Prov 1:33; Is 3:10
8:13 Eccl 8:8; Is 3:11; Job 14:2; Eccl 6:12
8:14 Ps 73:14; Eccl 7:15; Job 21:7; Ps 73:3, 12; Jer 12:1; Mal 3:15
8:15 Eccl 2:24; 3:12, 13; 5:18; 9:7
8:16 Eccl 1:13, 14; Eccl 2:23
8:17 Eccl 3:11; Ps 73:16; Eccl 7:23; Rom 11:33
9:1 Deut 33:3; Job 12:10; Ps 119:109; Eccl 10:14; Eccl 9:6
9:2 Job 9:22; Eccl 9:11; Eccl 2:14; 3:19; 6:6; 7:2
9:3 Eccl 9:2; Jer 17:10; Eccl 8:11; Eccl 1:17
9:5 Job 14:21; Ps 88:12; Eccl 1:11; 2:16; 8:10; Is 26:14
9:6 Eccl 2:10; 3:22

8:10 This verse probably refers to how we quickly forget the evil done by some people after they have died. Returning from the cemetery, we praise them in the very city where they did their evil deeds.

8:11 If God doesn't punish us immediately, we must not assume that he doesn't care or that sin has no consequences, even though it is easy to sin when we don't feel the consequences right away. When a young child does something wrong, and the wrong is not discovered, it will be much easier for the child to repeat the act. But God knows every wrong we commit, and one day we will have to answer for all that we have done (12:14).

8:15 Solomon recalls the remedy for life's unanswered questions. He recommends joy and contentment as encouragement for us along life's pilgrimage. We must accept each day with its daily measure of work, food, and pleasure. Let us learn to enjoy what God has given us to refresh and strengthen us to continue his work.

8:16–17 Even if he had access to all the world's wisdom, the wisest man would know very little. No one can fully comprehend God and all that he has done, and there are always more questions than answers. But the unknown should not cast a shadow over our joy, faith, or work because we know that someone greater is in control and that we can put our trust in him. Don't let what you don't know about the future destroy the joy God wants to give you today.

9:2 "There is one fate" means that all will die.

9:5, 10 When Solomon says the dead know nothing and that there is no work, planning, knowledge, or wisdom in death, he is not contrasting life with afterlife, but life with death. After you die, you can't change what you have done. Resurrection to a new life after death was a vague concept for Old Testament believers. It was only made clear after Jesus rose from the dead.

7 Go *then,* eat your bread in happiness and drink your wine with a cheerful heart; for
God has already approved your works.
8 Let your clothes be white all the time, and let not oil be lacking on your head.
9 Enjoy life with the woman whom you love all the days of your fleeting life which He
has given to you under the sun; for this is your reward in life and in your toil in which you
have labored under the sun.

Whatever Your Hand Finds to Do

10 Whatever your hand finds to do, do *it* with *all* your might; for there is no activity or
planning or knowledge or wisdom in Sheol where you are going.
11 I again saw under the sun that the race is not to the swift and the battle is not to the
warriors, and neither is bread to the wise nor wealth to the discerning nor favor to men
of ability; for time and chance overtake them all.
12 Moreover, man does not know his time: like fish caught in a treacherous net and
birds trapped in a snare, so the sons of men are ensnared at an evil time when it suddenly falls on them.
13 Also this I came to see as wisdom under the sun, and it impressed me.
14 There was a small city with few men in it and a great king came to it, surrounded it
and constructed large siegeworks against it.
15 But there was found in it a poor wise man and he delivered the city by his wisdom.
Yet no one remembered that poor man.
16 So I said, "Wisdom is better than strength." But the wisdom of the poor man is
despised and his words are not heeded.
17 The words of the wise heard in quietness are *better* than the shouting of a ruler among
fools.
18 Wisdom is better than weapons of war, but one sinner destroys much good.

A Little Foolishness

10 Dead flies make a perfumer's oil stink, so a little foolishness is weightier than wisdom *and* honor.
2 A wise man's heart *directs him* toward the right, but the foolish man's heart *directs
him* toward the left.
3 Even when the fool walks along the road, his sense is lacking and he demonstrates
to everyone *that* he is a fool.
4 If the ruler's temper rises against you, do not abandon your position, because composure allays great offenses.
5 There is an evil I have seen under the sun, like an error which goes forth from the
ruler—
6 folly is set in many exalted places while rich men sit in humble places.
7 I have seen slaves *riding* on horses and princes walking like slaves on the land.

9:7 Eccl 2:24; 8:15
9:9 Eccl 6:12; 7:15
9:10 Eccl 11:6; Rom 12:11; Col 3:23; Eccl 9:5; Gen 37:35; Job 21:13; Is 38:10
9:11 Amos 2:14, 15; 2 Chr 20:15; Ps 76:5; Zech 4:6; Deut 8:17, 18; 1 Sam 6:9
9:12 Eccl 8:7; Prov 7:23; Prov 29:6; Is 24:18; Hos 9:8; Luke 21:34, 35
9:14 2 Sam 20:16-22
9:15 Eccl 4:13; 2 Sam 20:22; Eccl 2:16; 8:10
9:16 Prov 21:22; Eccl 7:12, 19
9:17 Eccl 7:5; 10:12
9:18 Eccl 9:16; Josh 7:1-26; 2 Kin 21:2-17
10:1 Ex 30:25
10:2 Matt 6:33; Col 3:1
10:3 Prov 13:16; 18:2
10:4 Eccl 8:3; 1 Sam 25:24-33; Prov 25:15
10:6 Esth 3:1, 5f; Prov 28:12; 29:2
10:7 Prov 19:10; Esth 6:8-10

9:7–10 Considering the uncertainties of the future and the certainty of death, Solomon recommends enjoying life as God's gift. He may have been criticizing those who put off all present pleasures in order to accumulate wealth, much like those who get caught up in today's rat race. Solomon asks, "What is your wealth really worth, anyway?" Because the future is so uncertain, we should enjoy God's gifts while we are able.

9:8 Wearing white clothes and having oil on the head were signs of happiness and celebration.

9:9 Solomon also wrote a proverb about marriage. "He who finds a wife finds a good thing and obtains favor from the LORD" (Proverbs 18:22). How sad it would be to be married and not appreciate the enjoyment and companionship God has given you.

9:10–11 It isn't difficult to think of cases where the swiftest or the strongest don't win, the wise go hungry, and the intelligent are unrewarded with wealth or honor. Some people see such examples and call life unfair, and they are right. The world is finite, and sin has twisted life, making it what God did not intend. Solomon is trying to reduce our expectations. The book of Proverbs emphasizes how life would go if everyone acted fairly; Ecclesiastes explains what usually happens in our sinful and imperfect world. We must keep our perspective. Don't let the inequities of life keep you from earnest, dedicated work. We serve God, not people (see Colossians 3:23).

9:13–18 Our society honors wealth, attractiveness, and success above wisdom. Yet wisdom is a greater asset than strength, although it is often unrecognized by the masses. Even though it is more effective, wisdom is not always heard, and wise people often go unheeded. From this parable we can learn to be receptive to wisdom, no matter who it comes from.

10:4 This proverb has implications for employer/employee relationships. Employees should ride out the temper tantrums of their employer. If we quietly do our work and don't get upset, the employer will probably get over his or her anger and calm down.

10:5–7 By describing these circumstances that aren't fair or don't make sense, Solomon is saying that wisdom alone can't bring justice. Solomon continues to build to his conclusion that everything we have (from wisdom to riches) is nothing without God. But when God uses what little we have, it becomes all we could ever want or need.

10:8 Ps 7:15; Prov 26:27; Amos 5:19

10:11 Ps 58:4, 5; Jer 8:17

10:12 Prov 10:32; 22:11; Luke 4:22; Prov 10:14; 18:7; Eccl 4:5

10:13 Eccl 7:25

10:14 Prov 15:2; Eccl 5:3; Eccl 3:22; 6:12; 7:14; 8:7

10:17 Prov 31:4; Is 5:11

10:18 Prov 24:30-34

10:19 Judg 9:13; Ps 104:15; Eccl 2:3; Eccl 7:12

10:20 2 Kin 6:12; Luke 12:3; Ex 22:28; Acts 23:5

11:1 Deut 15:10; Prov 19:17; Matt 10:42; Gal 6:9; Heb 6:10

11:2 Ps 112:9; Matt 5:42; Luke 6:30; 1 Tim 6:18, 19; Eccl 11:8; 12:1

11:5 John 3:8; Ps 139:13-16; Eccl 1:13; 3:10, 11; 8:17

11:6 Eccl 9:10

11:7 Eccl 6:5; 7:11

8 He who digs a pit may fall into it, and a serpent may bite him who breaks through a
wall.
9 He who quarries stones may be hurt by them, and he who splits logs may be endangered by them.
10 If the axe is dull and he does not sharpen *its* edge, then he must exert more strength.
Wisdom has the advantage of giving success.
11 If the serpent bites before being charmed, there is no profit for the charmer.
12 Words from the mouth of a wise man are gracious, while the lips of a fool consume
him;
13 the beginning of his talking is folly and the end of it is wicked madness.
14 Yet the fool multiplies words. No man knows what will happen, and who can tell
him what will come after him?
15 The toil of a fool *so* wearies him that he does not *even* know how to go to a city.
16 Woe to you, O land, whose king is a lad and whose princes feast in the morning.
17 Blessed are you, O land, whose king is of nobility and whose princes eat at the appropriate time—for strength and not for drunkenness.
18 Through indolence the rafters sag, and through slackness the house leaks.
19 *Men* prepare a meal for enjoyment, and wine makes life merry, and money is the
answer to everything.
20 Furthermore, in your bedchamber do not curse a king, and in your sleeping rooms
do not curse a rich man, for a bird of the heavens will carry the sound and the winged
creature will make the matter known.

Cast Your Bread on the Waters

11 Cast your bread on the surface of the waters, for you will find it after many days.
2 Divide your portion to seven, or even to eight, for you do not know what misfortune may occur on the earth.
3 If the clouds are full, they pour out rain upon the earth; and whether a tree falls
toward the south or toward the north, wherever the tree falls, there it lies.
4 He who watches the wind will not sow and he who looks at the clouds will not reap.
5 Just as you do not know the path of the wind and how bones *are formed* in the womb
of the pregnant woman, so you do not know the activity of God who makes all things.
6 Sow your seed in the morning and do not be idle in the evening, for you do not know
whether morning or evening sowing will succeed, or whether both of them alike will be
good.
7 The light is pleasant, and *it is* good for the eyes to see the sun.

10:10 Trying to do anything without the necessary skills or tools is like chopping wood with a dull axe. If your tool is dull, you should sharpen it to do a better job. Similarly, if you lack skills, you should sharpen them through training and practice. In each situation, sharpening the axe means recognizing where a problem exists, acquiring or honing the skills (or tools) to do the job better, and then going out and doing it. Find the areas of your life where your "axe" is dull, and sharpen your skills so you can be more effective for God's work.

10:16–18 When the Israelites had immature and irresponsible leaders, their nation fell. The books of 1 and 2 Kings describe the decline of the kingdoms when the leaders were concerned only about themselves. These verses pinpoint the basic problems of these leaders—selfishness and laziness.

10:19 Government leaders, businesses, families, even churches get trapped into thinking money is the answer to every problem. We throw money at our problems. But just as the thrill of wine is only temporary, the soothing effect of the last purchase soon wears off and we have to buy more. Scripture recognizes that money is necessary for survival, but it warns against the love of money (see Matthew 6:24; 1 Timothy 6:10; Hebrews 13:5). Money is dangerous because it deceives us into thinking that wealth is the easiest way to get everything we want. The love of money is sinful because we trust money rather than God to solve our problems. Those who pursue its empty promises will one day discover that they have nothing because they are spiritually bankrupt.

11:1–5 In these verses Solomon summarizes that life involves both risk and opportunity. Because life has no guarantees, we must be prepared. "Cast your bread on the surface of the waters" means that life has opportunities and we must seize them, not merely play it safe. Solomon does not support a despairing attitude. Just because life is uncertain does not mean we should do nothing. We need a spirit of trust and adventure, facing life's risks and opportunities with God-directed enthusiasm and faith.

11:4 Waiting for perfect conditions will mean inactivity. This practical insight is especially applicable to our spiritual life. If we wait for the perfect time and place for personal Bible reading, we will never begin. If we wait for a perfect church, we will never join. If we wait for the perfect ministry, we will never serve. Take steps now to grow spiritually. Don't wait for conditions that may never exist.

11:7–8 Solomon is no dreary pessimist in 11:7—12:14. He encourages us to rejoice in every day but to remember that eternity is far longer than a person's life span. Psalm 90:12 says, "Teach us to number our days, that we may present to You a heart of wisdom." The wise person does not just think about the moment and its impact; he or she takes the long-range view toward eternity. Approach your decisions from God's perspective—consider their impact ten years from now and into eternity. Live with the attitude that although our lives are short, we will live with God forever.

8 Indeed, if a man should live many years, let him rejoice in them all, and let him remember the days of darkness, for they will be many. Everything that is to come *will be*
futility.
9 Rejoice, young man, during your childhood, and let your heart be pleasant during
the days of young manhood. And follow the impulses of your heart and the desires of
your eyes. Yet know that God will bring you to judgment for all these things.
10 So, remove grief and anger from your heart and put away pain from your body,
because childhood and the prime of life are fleeting.

Remember God in Your Youth

12 Remember also your Creator in the days of your youth, before the evil days come
and the years draw near when you will say, "I have no delight in them";
2 before the sun and the light, the moon and the stars are darkened, and clouds return after the rain;
3 in the day that the watchmen of the house tremble, and mighty men stoop, the grinding ones stand idle because they are few, and those who look through windows grow dim;
4 and the doors on the street are shut as the sound of the grinding mill is low, and one
will arise at the sound of the bird, and all the daughters of song will sing softly.
5 Furthermore, men are afraid of a high place and of terrors on the road; the almond
tree blossoms, the grasshopper drags himself along, and the caperberry is ineffective.
For man goes to his eternal home while mourners go about in the street.
6 *Remember Him* before the silver cord is broken and the golden bowl is crushed, the
pitcher by the well is shattered and the wheel at the cistern is crushed;
7 then the dust will return to the earth as it was, and the spirit will return to God who
gave it.
8 "Vanity of vanities," says the Preacher, "all is vanity!"

Purpose of the Preacher

9 In addition to being a wise man, the Preacher also taught the people knowledge;
and he pondered, searched out and arranged many proverbs.
10 The Preacher sought to find delightful words and to write words of truth correctly.
11 The words of wise men are like goads, and masters of *these* collections are like well-
driven nails; they are given by one Shepherd.
12 But beyond this, my son, be warned: the writing of many books is endless, and excessive devotion *to books* is wearying to the body.

11:8 Eccl 9:7; Eccl 12:1
11:9 Num 15:39; Job 31:7; Eccl 2:10; Eccl 3:17; 12:14; Rom 14:10
11:10 2 Cor 7:1; 2 Tim 2:22
12:1 Deut 8:18; Neh 4:14; Ps 63:6; 119:55
12:2 Is 5:30; 13:10; Ezek 32:7, 8; Joel 3:15; Matt 24:29
12:3 Ps 35:14; 38:6; Gen 27:1; 48:10
12:4 Jer 25:10; Rev 18:22; 2 Sam 19:35
12:5 Job 17:13; 30:23; Gen 50:10; Jer 9:17
12:6 Zech 4:2, 3
12:7 Gen 3:19; Job 34:15; Ps 104:29; Eccl 3:20; Job 34:14; Luke 23:46; Acts 7:59
12:8 Eccl 1:2
12:10 Prov 10:32; Prov 22:20, 21
12:11 Prov 1:6; 22:17; Eccl 7:5; 10:12; Acts 2:37; Ezra 9:8; Is 22:23

11:9–10 We often hear people say, "It doesn't matter." But many of your choices will be irreversible—they will stay with you for a lifetime. What you do when you're young *does* matter. Enjoy life now, but don't do anything physically, morally, or spiritually that will prevent you from enjoying life when you are old.

12:1 A life without God can produce a bitter, lonely, and hopeless old age. A life centered around God is fulfilling; it will make the "evil days"—when disabilities, sickness, and handicaps cause barriers to enjoying life—satisfying because of the hope of eternal life. Being young is exciting. But the excitement of youth can become a barrier to closeness with God if it makes young people focus on passing pleasures instead of eternal values. Make your strength available to God when it is still yours—during your youthful years. Don't waste it on evil or meaningless activities that become bad habits and make you callous. Seek God now.

12:6–8 The silver cord, golden bowl, pitcher, and wheel symbolize life's fragility. How easily death comes to us; how swiftly and unexpectedly we can return to the dust from which we came. Therefore, we should recognize life as a precious resource to be used wisely and not squandered frivolously.

12:7–8 Stripped of God's Spirit, our bodies return to dust. Stripped of God's purpose, our work is in vain. Stripped of God's love, our service is futile. We must put God first over all we do and in all we do because without him we have nothing. Knowing that life is futile without God motivates the wise person to seek God first.

12:11 A goad (also called an oxgoad) was a sharp metal tip attached to a handle and used to keep oxen or cattle moving. Like a goad, a wise word or important truth might be unpleasant when first applied, but it will keep us moving in God's direction.

12:12 There are endless opinions about life and philosophies about how we should live that could be read and studied forever. It is not wrong to study these opinions, but we should spend the majority of our time feeding on the truth of God's Word. Wisdom should lead to action. Wise students of the Bible will understand and do what they are taught. Because our time on earth is so short, we should use it to learn important truths—they affect this life and eternity.

12:13
Eccl 3:14; 5:7; 7:18; 8:12; Deut 4:2; Eccl 8:5; Deut 10:12; Mic 6:8

13 The conclusion, when all has been heard, *is:* fear God and keep His commandments,
because this *applies to* every person.
14 For God will bring every act to judgment, everything which is hidden, whether it is
good or evil.

12:13–14 In his conclusion, Solomon presents his antidotes for the two main ailments presented in this book. Those who lack purpose and direction in life should fear God and keep his commandments. Those who think life is unfair should remember that God will review every person's life to determine how he or she has responded to him, and he will bring every deed into judgment. Have you committed your life to God, both present and future? Does your life measure up to his standards?

12:13–14 The book of Ecclesiastes cannot be interpreted correctly without reading these final verses. No matter what the mysteries and apparent contradictions of life are, we must work toward the single purpose of knowing God.

In Ecclesiastes, Solomon shows us that we should enjoy life, but this does not exempt us from obeying God's commandments. We should search for purpose and meaning in life, but they cannot be found in human endeavors. We should acknowledge the evil, foolishness, and injustice in life, yet maintain a positive attitude and strong faith in God.

All people will have to stand before God and be judged for what they did in this life. We will not be able to use life's inconsistencies as an excuse for failing to live properly. To live properly, we need to (1) recognize that human effort apart from God is futile; (2) put God first—now; (3) receive everything good as a gift from God; (4) realize that God will judge both evil and good; (5) know that God will judge the quality of every person's life. How strange that people spend their lives striving for the very enjoyment that God gives freely, as a gift.

S O N G   O F   S O L O M O N

VITAL STATISTICS

PURPOSE:
To tell of the love between a bridegroom (King Solomon) and his bride, to affirm the sanctity of marriage, and to picture God's love for his people

AUTHOR:
Solomon

DATE WRITTEN:
Probably early in Solomon's reign

SETTING:
Israel—the Shulammite woman's garden and the king's palace

KEY VERSE:
"I am my beloved's and my beloved is mine, he who pastures his flock among the lilies" (6:3).

KEY PEOPLE:
King Solomon, the Shulammite woman, and friends

SATURATED with stories of sexual escapades, secret rendezvouses, and extramarital affairs, today's media teach that immorality means freedom, perversion is natural, and commitment is old-fashioned. Sex, created by God and pronounced good in Eden, has been twisted, exploited, and turned into an urgent, illicit, casual, and self-gratifying activity. Love has turned into lust, giving into getting, and lasting commitment into "no strings attached."

In reality, sexual intercourse, the physical and emotional union of male and female, should be a holy means of celebrating love, producing children, and experiencing pleasure, protected by the commitment of marriage.

God thinks sex is important, and Scripture contains numerous guidelines for its use and warnings about its misuse. And sex is always mentioned in the context of a loving relationship between husband and wife. Perhaps the highlight of this is Song of Solomon, the intimate story of a man and a woman, their love, courtship, and marriage. Solomon probably wrote this "song" in his youth, before being overtaken by his own obsession with women, sex, and pleasure.

A moving story, drama, and poem, Song of Solomon features the love dialogue between a simple Jewish maiden (the young woman) and her lover (Solomon, the king). They describe in intimate detail their feelings for each other and their longings to be together. Throughout the dialogue, sex and marriage are put in their proper, God-given perspective.

There has been much debate over the meaning of this song. Some say it is an allegory of God's love for Israel and/or for the church. Others say it is a literal story about married love. But in reality, it is both—a historical story with two layers of meaning. On one level, we learn about love, marriage, and sex; and on the other level, we see God's overwhelming love for his people. As you read Song of Solomon, remember that you are loved by God, and commit yourself to seeing life, sex, and marriage from his point of view.

THE BLUEPRINT

1. The wedding day (1:1—2:7)
2. Memories of courtship (2:8—3:5)
3. Memories of engagement (3:6—5:1)
4. A troubling dream (5:2—6:3)
5. Praising the bride's beauty (6:4—7:9)
6. The bride's tender appeal (7:10—8:4)
7. The power of love (8:5–14)

Song of Solomon is a wedding song honoring marriage. The most explicit statements on sex in the Bible can be found in this book. It has often been criticized down through the centuries because of its sensuous language. The purity and sacredness of love represented here, however, are greatly needed in our day in which distorted attitudes about love and marriage are commonplace. God created sex and intimacy, and they are holy and good when enjoyed within marriage. A husband and wife honor God when they love and enjoy each other.

MEGATHEMES

THEME	EXPLANATION	IMPORTANCE
Sex	Sex is God's gift to his creatures. He endorses sex but restricts its expression to those committed to each other in marriage.	God wants sex to be motivated by love and commitment, not lust. It is for mutual pleasure, not selfish enjoyment.
Love	As the relationship developed, the beauty and wonder of a romance unfolded between Solomon and his bride. The intense power of love affected the hearts, minds, and bodies of the two lovers.	Because love is such a powerful expression of feeling and commitment between two people, it is not to be regarded casually. We are not to manipulate others into loving us, and love should not be prematurely encouraged in a relationship.
Commitment	The power of love requires more than the language of feeling to protect it. Sexual expression is such an integral part of our selfhood that we need the boundary of marriage to safeguard our love. Marriage is the celebration of daily commitment to each other.	While romance keeps a marriage interesting, commitment keeps romance from dwindling away. The decision to commit yourself to your spouse alone *begins* at the marriage altar. It must be maintained day by day.
Beauty	The two lovers praise the beauty they see in each other. The language they use shows the spontaneity and mystery of love. Praise should not be limited to physical beauty; beautiful personality and moral purity should also be praised.	Our love for someone makes him or her appear beautiful to us. As you consider marriage, don't just look for physical attractiveness in a person. Look for the inner qualities that don't fade with time—spiritual commitment, integrity, sensitivity, and sincerity.
Problems	Over time, feelings of loneliness, indifference, and isolation came between Solomon and his bride. During those times, love grew cold, and barriers were raised.	Through careful communication, lovers can be reconciled, commitment can be renewed, and romance refreshed. Don't let walls come between you and your partner. Take care of problems while they are still small.

1. The wedding day

The Young Shulammite Bride and Jerusalem's Daughters

1 The [1]Song of Songs, which is Solomon's.
2 "[2]May he kiss me with the kisses of his mouth!
For your love is better than wine.
3 "Your oils have a pleasing fragrance,
Your name is *like* purified oil;
Therefore the maidens love you.
4 "Draw me after you *and* let us run *together!*
The king has brought me into his chambers."

"[3]We will rejoice in you and be glad;
We will extol your love more than wine.
Rightly do they love you."

5 "[2]I am black but lovely,
O daughters of Jerusalem,
Like the tents of Kedar,
Like the curtains of Solomon.
6 "Do not stare at me because I am swarthy,
For the sun has burned me.
My mother's sons were angry with me;
They made me caretaker of the vineyards,
But I have not taken care of my own vineyard.
7 "Tell me, O you whom my soul loves,
Where do you pasture *your flock,*
Where do you make *it* lie down at noon?
For why should I be like one who veils herself
Beside the flocks of your companions?"

Solomon, the Lover, Speaks

8 "[4]If you yourself do not know,
Most beautiful among women,

1 Or *Best of the Songs* 2 BRIDE 3 CHORUS 4 BRIDEGROOM

1:1 1 Kin 4:32
1:2 Song 1:4; 4:10
1:3 Song 4:10; John 12:3; Eccl 7:1; Ps 45:14
1:4 Ps 45:14, 15; Song 1:4; 4:10
1:5 Song 2:14; 4:3; 6:4; Song 2:7; 3:5, 10; 5:8, 16; 8:4; Ps 120:5; Is 60:7
1:6 Ps 69:8; Song 8:11
1:7 Song 3:1-4; Song 2:16; 6:3; Is 13:20; Jer 33:12; Song 8:13
1:8 Song 5:9; 6:1

1:1 Solomon, a son of King David, became king and was chosen by God to build the temple in Jerusalem. God gave him extraordinary wisdom. Much of his reign was characterized by wisdom and reverence for God, although toward the end of his life he became proud and turned from God. Read about Solomon in 1 Kings 1—11 and 1 Chronicles 28—2 Chronicles 9. Solomon wrote more than 3,000 proverbs (see the book of Proverbs) and over 1,000 songs, one of which is this book, Song of Solomon. His Profile is found in 1 Kings 4.

1:1ff Solomon frequently visited the various parts of his kingdom. One day, as he visited some royal vineyards in the north, his royal entourage came by surprise upon a beautiful peasant woman tending the vines. Embarrassed, she ran from them. But Solomon could not forget her. Later, disguised as a shepherd, he returned to the vineyards and won her love. Then, he revealed his true identity and asked her to return to Jerusalem with him. Solomon and his beloved are being married in the palace as this book begins.

The Song of Solomon is a series of seven poems, not necessarily in chronological order. It reflects upon the first meeting of Solomon and the peasant woman, their engagement, their wedding, their wedding night, and the growth of their marriage after the wedding.

1:1ff There are three characters or groups of characters in this book: the bride, Solomon (the lover), and "Jerusalem's daughters." The girl who caught Solomon's attention may have been from Shunem, a farming community about 60 miles north of Jerusalem. Her tanned skin indicates that she probably worked outside in the vineyards (1:6)—thus she may not have been from the upper class. The daughters of Jerusalem include either members of Solomon's harem or workers in the palace.

1:1–4 This vivid description of a love relationship begins with a picture of love itself. Love is "better than wine"; it makes the lovers rejoice. Acts 10:9–16 teaches that what God has created and cleansed we should not misuse or call common. We can enjoy love. God created it as a gift to us and a delight for all our senses.

1:5 Kedar was a nomadic community in northern Arabia. It was known for its tents that were woven from black goat hair.

1:6 The vineyard mentioned here was apparently owned by Solomon (because he came to visit it) and leased to the girl's stepbrothers (her "mother's sons"), who made her take care of the vineyards in the hot sun. Thus she could not take care of her own skin ("I have not taken care of my own vineyard"). When she was brought to Jerusalem, the young girl was embarrassed about her tanned complexion because the girls in the city had the fair, delicate skin that was considered much more beautiful. But Solomon loved her dark skin.

1:7 The girl felt insecure at being different from the women of Jerusalem (1:6) and at being alone while her lover was away (1:7). She longed for the security of his presence. The basis of true love is commitment; so in a relationship where there is genuine love, there is never any fear of deceit, manipulation, or exploitation.

Go forth on the trail of the flock
And pasture your young goats
By the tents of the shepherds.

1:9 Song 1:15; 2:2, 10, 13; 2 Chr 1:16, 17

1:10 Song 5:13; Gen 24:53; Is 61:10

9 "To me, my darling, you are like
My mare among the chariots of Pharaoh.
10 "Your cheeks are lovely with ornaments,
Your neck with strings of beads."

11 "[5]We will make for you ornaments of gold
With beads of silver."

1:12 Song 4:14; Mark 14:3; John 12:3

1:13 Ps 45:8; John 19:39

1:14 Song 4:13; 1 Sam 23:29

12 "[6]While the king was at his table,
My perfume gave forth its fragrance.
13 "My beloved is to me a pouch of myrrh
Which lies all night between my breasts.
14 "My beloved is to me a cluster of henna blossoms
In the vineyards of Engedi."

1:15 Song 1:16; 2:10, 13; 4:1, 7; 6:4, 10; Song 4:1; 5:12

15 "[7]How beautiful you are, my darling,
How beautiful you are!
Your eyes are *like* doves."

1:16 Song 2:3, 9, 17; 5:2, 5, 6, 8

1:17 1 Kin 6:9, 10; Jer 22:14; 2 Chr 3:5

16 "[6]How handsome you are, my beloved,
And so pleasant!
Indeed, our couch is luxuriant!
17 "The beams of our houses are cedars,
Our rafters, cypresses.

The Bride's Admiration

2:1 Is 35:1; Is 33:9; 35:2; Song 5:13; 7:2; Hos 14:5

2:2 Song 1:9

2 "[6]I am the rose of Sharon,
The lily of the valleys."

2 "[7]Like a lily among the thorns,
So is my darling among the maidens."

2:3 Song 8:5; Song 4:13, 16; 8:11, 12

2:4 Song 1:4; Ps 20:5

2:5 2 Sam 6:19; 1 Chr 16:3; Hos 3:1; Song 7:8; Song 5:8

2:6 Song 8:3; Prov 4:8

3 "[6]Like an apple tree among the trees of the forest,
So is my beloved among the young men.
In his shade I took great delight and sat down,
And his fruit was sweet to my taste.
4 "He has brought me to *his* banquet hall,
And his banner over me is love.
5 "Sustain me with raisin cakes,
Refresh me with apples,
Because I am lovesick.
6 "Let his left hand be under my head
And his right hand embrace me."

5 CHORUS **6** BRIDE **7** BRIDEGROOM

1:14 Engedi was an oasis hidden at the base of rugged limestone cliffs west of the Dead Sea. It was known for its fruitful palm trees and fragrant balsam oil. The terrain surrounding Engedi was some of the most desolate in Palestine, and it had an extremely hot desert climate. The henna blossoms in Engedi would have appeared all the more beautiful because of their stark surroundings; thus Solomon was complimenting his beloved's beauty and comparing her favorably with the women she feared.

1:16, 17 The lover and his beloved describe their woodland surroundings as a wedding bedroom.

2:1 The rose of Sharon and lily of the valleys were flowers commonly found in Israel. Perhaps the girl was saying, "I'm not so special; I'm just an ordinary flower," to which Solomon replied, "Oh, no, you are extraordinary—a lily among thorns." Solomon used the language of love. There is nothing more vital than encouraging and appreciating the person you love. Be sure to tell your spouse "I love you" every day, and show that love by your actions.

7 "[8]I adjure you, O daughters of Jerusalem,
By the gazelles or by the hinds of the field,
That you do not arouse or awaken *my* love
Until she pleases."

2:7 Song 3:5; 5:8, 9; 8:4; Song 1:5; Prov 6:5; Song 2:9, 17; 3:5; 8:14; Gen 49:21; Ps 18:33; Hab 3:19

2. Memories of courtship

8 "[9]Listen! My beloved!
Behold, he is coming,
Climbing on the mountains,
Leaping on the hills!
9 "My beloved is like a gazelle or a young stag.
Behold, he is standing behind our wall,
He is looking through the windows,
He is peering through the lattice.

2:8 Song 2:17; Is 52:7

2:9 Prov 6:5; Song 2:17; 3:5; 8:14; Song 2:17; 8:14; Judg 5:28

10 "My beloved responded and said to me,
'Arise, my darling, my beautiful one,
And come along.
11 'For behold, the winter is past,
The rain is over *and* gone.
12 'The flowers have *already* appeared in the land;
The time has arrived for pruning *the vines,*
And the voice of the turtledove has been heard in our land.
13 'The fig tree has ripened its figs,
And the vines in blossom have given forth *their* fragrance.
Arise, my darling, my beautiful one,
And come along!' "

2:10 Song 2:13

2:12 Gen 15:9; Ps 74:19; Jer 8:7

2:13 Matt 24:32; Song 7:12

14 "O my dove, in the clefts of the rock,
In the secret place of the steep pathway,
Let me see your form,
Let me hear your voice;
For your voice is sweet,
And your form is lovely."

2:14 Song 5:2; 6:9; Jer 48:28; Song 8:13; Song 1:5

15 "Catch the foxes for us,
The little foxes that are ruining the vineyards,
While our vineyards are in blossom."

2:15 Ezek 13:4; Luke 13:32; Song 2:13

16 "My beloved is mine, and I am his;
He pastures *his flock* among the lilies.
17 "Until the cool of the day when the shadows flee away,
Turn, my beloved, and be like a gazelle
Or a young stag on the mountains of Bether."

2:16 Song 6:3; 7:10; Song 4:5; 6:2, 3

2:17 Song 4:6; Song 2:9; Song 2:8

8 BRIDEGROOM **9** BRIDE

2:7 Feelings of love can create intimacy that overpowers reason. Young people are too often in a hurry to develop an intimate relationship based on their strong feelings. But feelings aren't enough to support a lasting relationship. This verse encourages us not to force romance lest the feelings of love grow faster than the commitment needed to make love last. Patiently wait for feelings of love and commitment to develop together.

2:8—3:5 In this section Solomon's beloved reflects on her courtship with Solomon, remembering the first day they met and recalling one of her dreams about their being together.

2:12–13 The lovers celebrated their joy in the creation and in their love. God created the world, the beauty we see, the joy of love and sex, and gave us senses to enjoy them. Never let problems, conflicts, or the ravages of time ruin your ability to enjoy God's gifts. Take time to enjoy the world God has created.

2:15 "The little foxes" are an example of the kinds of problems that can disturb or destroy a relationship. The lovers wanted anything that could potentially cause problems between them to be removed. It is often the "little foxes" that cause the biggest problems in marriage. These irritations must not be minimized or ignored, but identified so that, together, the couple can deal with them.

The Bride's Troubled Dream

3:1 Song 1:7; Song 5:6

3 "[10]On my bed night after night I sought him
Whom my soul loves;
I sought him but did not find him.

3:2 Jer 5:1

2 'I must arise now and go about the city;
In the streets and in the squares
I must seek him whom my soul loves.'
I sought him but did not find him.

3:3 Song 5:7; Is 21:6-8, 11, 12

3 "The watchmen who make the rounds in the city found me,
And I said, 'Have you seen him whom my soul loves?'

3:4 Prov 8:17; Prov 4:13; Rom 8:35, 39; Song 8:2

4 "Scarcely had I left them
When I found him whom my soul loves;
I held on to him and would not let him go
Until I had brought him to my mother's house,
And into the room of her who conceived me."

3:5 Song 2:7; 5:8; 8:4

5 "[11]I adjure you, O daughters of Jerusalem,
By the gazelles or by the hinds of the field,
That you will not arouse or awaken *my* love
Until she pleases."

3. Memories of engagement

Solomon's Wedding Day

3:6 Song 8:5; Ex 13:21; Joel 2:30; Song 1:13; 4:6, 14; Matt 2:11; Ex 30:34; Rev 18:13

6 "[12]What is this coming up from the wilderness
Like columns of smoke,
Perfumed with myrrh and frankincense,
With all scented powders of the merchant?
7 "Behold, it is the *traveling* couch of Solomon;
Sixty mighty men around it,
Of the mighty men of Israel.

3:8 Jer 50:9; Ps 45:3; Ps 91:5

8 "All of them are wielders of the sword,
Expert in war;
Each man has his sword at his side,
Guarding against the terrors of the night.
9 "King Solomon has made for himself a sedan chair
From the timber of Lebanon.

3:10 Song 1:5

10 "He made its posts of silver,
Its back of gold
And its seat of purple fabric,
With its interior lovingly fitted out
By the daughters of Jerusalem.

3:11 Is 3:16, 17; 4:4; Is 62:5

11 "Go forth, O daughters of Zion,
And gaze on King Solomon with the crown
With which his mother has crowned him
On the day of his wedding,
And on the day of his gladness of heart."

10 BRIDE **11** BRIDEGROOM **12** CHORUS

3:1-4 Many scholars agree that in these verses the girl was recalling a dream that caused her to become so concerned about her lover's whereabouts that she arose in the middle of the night to search for him. When you love someone, you will do all you can to ensure the safety of that person and care for his or her needs, even at a cost to your personal comfort. This shows up most often in small actions—walking upstairs to get your spouse a glass of water, leaving work early to attend some function your child is involved in, or sacrificing your personal comfort to tend to the needs of a friend.

3:6—5:1 Here the scene changes. Some believe that the wedding procession is described in 3:6–11, the wedding night in 4:1—5:1, and the consummation of the marriage in 4:16—5:1. Another possible explanation is that the period of Solomon's engagement to the girl is being remembered. In the previous section (2:8—3:5), Solomon and the girl fell in love. In this section, Solomon returns to the girl in all his royal splendor (3:6–11), expresses his great love for her (4:1–5), and then proposes (4:7–15). The girl accepts (4:16), and Solomon responds to her acceptance (5:1).

3:7, 9 Solomon's carriage (his traveling couch) was probably a covered and curtained couch used for carrying a single passenger on the shoulders of men.

Solomon's Love Expressed

4 "[13]How beautiful you are, my darling,
How beautiful you are!
Your eyes are *like* doves behind your veil;
Your hair is like a flock of goats
That have descended from Mount Gilead.
2 "Your teeth are like a flock of *newly* shorn ewes
Which have come up from *their* washing,
All of which bear twins,
And not one among them has lost her young.
3 "Your lips are like a scarlet thread,
And your mouth is lovely.
Your temples are like a slice of a pomegranate
Behind your veil.
4 "Your neck is like the tower of David,
Built with rows of stones
On which are hung a thousand shields,
All the round shields of the mighty men.
5 "Your two breasts are like two fawns,
Twins of a gazelle
Which feed among the lilies.
6 "Until the cool of the day
When the shadows flee away,
I will go my way to the mountain of myrrh
And to the hill of frankincense.
7 "You are altogether beautiful, my darling,
And there is no blemish in you.
8 "*Come* with me from Lebanon, *my* bride,
May you come with me from Lebanon.
Journey down from the summit of Amana,
From the summit of Senir and Hermon,
From the dens of lions,
From the mountains of leopards.
9 "You have made my heart beat faster, my sister, *my* bride;
You have made my heart beat faster with a single *glance* of your eyes,
With a single strand of your necklace.
10 "How beautiful is your love, my sister, *my* bride!
How much better is your love than wine,
And the fragrance of your oils
Than all *kinds* of spices!
11 "Your lips, *my* bride, drip honey;
Honey and milk are under your tongue,
And the fragrance of your garments is like the fragrance of Lebanon.
12 "A garden locked is my sister, *my* bride,
A rock garden locked, a spring sealed up.
13 "Your shoots are an orchard of pomegranates
With choice fruits, henna with nard plants,
14 Nard and saffron, calamus and cinnamon,
With all the trees of frankincense,
Myrrh and aloes, along with all the finest spices.

13 BRIDEGROOM

4:1
Song 1:15; Song 1:15; 5:12; Song 6:7; Song 6:5; Mic 7:14

4:2
Song 6:6

4:3
Josh 2:18; Song 5:16; Song 6:7

4:4
Song 7:4; Ezek 27:10, 11; 2 Sam 1:21

4:5
Song 7:3; Song 2:16; 6:2, 3

4:6
Song 2:17; Song 4:14

4:7
Song 1:15; Eph 5:27

4:8
1 Kin 4:33; Ps 72:16; Song 5:1; Is 62:5; 2 Kin 5:12; Deut 3:9; 1 Chr 5:23; Ezek 27:5

4:9
Song 4:10, 12; 5:1, 2; Gen 41:42; Prov 1:9; Ezek 16:11; Dan 5:7

4:10
Song 7:6; Song 1:2, 4; Song 1:3

4:11
Prov 5:3; Ps 19:10; Prov 24:13; Gen 27:27; Hos 14:6

4:12
Prov 5:15-18; Gen 29:3

4:13
Eccl 2:5; Song 6:11; 7:12; Song 2:3; 4:16; 7:13; Song 1:14

4:14
Song 1:12; Ex 30:23; Song 4:6; Ps 45:8; Song 3:6; John 19:39

4:1–7 We feel like awkward onlookers when we read this intensely private and intimate exchange. In the ecstasy of their love, the lovers praised each other using beautiful imagery. Their words may seem strange to readers from a different culture, but their intense feelings of love and admiration are universal. Communicating love and expressing admiration in both words and actions can enhance every marriage.

4:12 In comparing his bride to a locked garden, Solomon was praising her virginity. Virginity, considered old-fashioned by many in today's culture, has always been God's plan for unmarried people—and with good reason. Sex without marriage is cheap. It cannot compare with the joy of giving yourself completely to the one who is totally committed to you.

4:15 Zech 14:8; John 4:10

15 "*You are* a garden spring,
A well of fresh water,
And streams *flowing* from Lebanon."

4:16 Song 5:1; 6:2; Song 1:13; 2:3, 8; 6:2; Song 4:13

16 "[14]Awake, O north *wind,*
And come, *wind of* the south;
Make my garden breathe out *fragrance,*
Let its spices be wafted abroad.
May my beloved come into his garden
And eat its choice fruits!"

The Torment of Separation

5:1 Song 6:2; Song 4:9; Song 1:13; 4:14; Song 4:11; Prov 9:5; Is 55:1; Judg 14:11, 20; John 3:29

5 "[15]I have come into my garden, my sister, *my* bride;
I have gathered my myrrh along with my balsam.
I have eaten my honeycomb and my honey;
I have drunk my wine and my milk.
Eat, friends;
Drink and imbibe deeply, O lovers."

5:2 Song 4:9; Song 2:14; 6:9; Song 5:11

4. A troubling dream

2 "[14]I was asleep but my heart was awake.
A voice! My beloved was knocking:
'Open to me, my sister, my darling,
My dove, my perfect one!
For my head is drenched with dew,
My locks with the damp of the night.'

5:3 Luke 11:7; Gen 19:2

3 "I have taken off my dress,
How can I put it on *again?*
I have washed my feet,
How can I dirty them *again?*

5:4 Jer 31:20

4 "My beloved extended his hand through the opening,
And my feelings were aroused for him.

5:5 Song 5:13

5 "I arose to open to my beloved;
And my hands dripped with myrrh,
And my fingers with liquid myrrh,
On the handles of the bolt.

5:6 Song 6:1; Song 5:2; Song 3:1; Prov 1:28

6 "I opened to my beloved,
But my beloved had turned away *and* had gone!
My heart went out *to him* as he spoke.
I searched for him but I did not find him;
I called him but he did not answer me.

14 BRIDE **15** BRIDEGROOM

4:15 Solomon's bride was as refreshing to him as a fountain. Could your spouse say the same about you? Sometimes the familiarity that comes with marriage causes us to forget the overwhelming feelings of love and refreshment we shared at the beginning. Many marriages could use a course in "refreshing." Do you refresh your spouse, or are you a burden of complaints, sorrows, and problems? Partners in marriage should continually work at refreshing each other by an encouraging word, an unexpected gift, a change of pace, a surprise call or note, or even a withholding of a discussion of some problem until the proper time. Your spouse needs you to be a haven of refreshment because the rest of the world usually isn't.

5:2ff This new section tells how the couple's marriage grew and matured in spite of problems. Some time had passed since the wedding, and the girl felt as though some indifference had developed in their relationship. She had become cool to her husband's advances, and by the time she changed her mind and responded to him, he had left. Her self-centeredness and impatience, though brief, caused separation. But she quickly moved to correct the problem by searching for her husband (5:6–8).

5:2–8 It is inevitable that, with the passing of time and the growth of familiarity, a marriage will start to lose its initial sparkle. Glances and touches no longer produce the same emotional response. Conflicts and pressures may creep in, causing you to lose your tenderness toward your spouse. The world is not a haven for lovers; in fact, external stress often works against the marriage relationship. But spouses can learn to be havens for each other. If intimacy and passion decline, remember that they can be renewed and regenerated. Take time to remember those first thrills, the excitement of sex, your spouse's strengths, and the commitment you made. When you focus on the positives, reconciliation and renewal can result.

7 "The watchmen who make the rounds in the city found me,
They struck me *and* wounded me;
The guardsmen of the walls took away my shawl from me.
8 "I adjure you, O daughters of Jerusalem,
If you find my beloved,
As to what you will tell him:
For I am lovesick."

5:7 Song 3:3
5:8 Song 2:7; 3:5; Song 2:5

9 "[16]What kind of beloved is your beloved,
O most beautiful among women?
What kind of beloved is your beloved,
That thus you adjure us?"

5:9 Song 1:8; 6:1

Admiration by the Bride

10 "[17]My beloved is dazzling and ruddy,
Outstanding among ten thousand.
11 "His head is *like* gold, pure gold;
His locks are *like* clusters of dates
And black as a raven.
12 "His eyes are like doves
Beside streams of water,
Bathed in milk,
And reposed in *their* setting.
13 "His cheeks are like a bed of balsam,
Banks of sweet-scented herbs;
His lips are lilies
Dripping with liquid myrrh.
14 "His hands are rods of gold
Set with beryl;
His abdomen is carved ivory
Inlaid with sapphires.
15 "His legs are pillars of alabaster
Set on pedestals of pure gold;
His appearance is like Lebanon
Choice as the cedars.
16 "His mouth is *full of* sweetness.
And he is wholly desirable.
This is my beloved and this is my friend,
O daughters of Jerusalem."

5:10 1 Sam 16:12; Ps 45:2
5:11 Song 5:2
5:12 Song 1:15; 4:1; Ex 25:7
5:13 Song 6:2; Song 2:1; Song 5:5
5:14 Ex 28:20; 39:13; Ezek 1:16; Dan 10:6; Ex 24:10; 28:18; Job 28:16; Is 54:11
5:15 Song 7:4; 1 Kin 4:33; Ps 80:10; Ezek 17:23; 31:8
5:16 Song 7:9; 2 Sam 1:23

Mutual Delight in Each Other

6 "[16]Where has your beloved gone,
O most beautiful among women?
Where has your beloved turned,
That we may seek him with you?"

6:1 Song 5:6; Song 1:8

2 "[17]My beloved has gone down to his garden,
To the beds of balsam,
To pasture *his flock* in the gardens
And gather lilies.

6:2 Song 4:16; 5:1; Song 5:13; Song 1:7; Song 2:1; 5:13

16 CHORUS **17** BRIDE

5:7 The girl was alone outside during the night. In Old Testament times, she would have been looked upon as a criminal or a prostitute and treated as such. This image symbolizes the pain she felt at being separated from her lover.

5:16 The girl calls Solomon her "friend." In a healthy marriage, lovers are also good friends. Too often people are driven into marriage by the exciting feelings of love and passion before they take the time to develop a deep friendship. This involves listening, sharing, and showing understanding for the other's likes and dislikes. Friendship takes time, but it makes a love relationship much deeper and far more satisfying.

6:3 Song 2:16; 7:10; Song 2:16; 4:5

3 "I am my beloved's and my beloved is mine,
He who pastures *his flock* among the lilies."

5. Praising the bride's beauty

6:4 Song 1:15; 1 Kin 14:17; Song 1:5; Ps 48:2; 50:2; Song 6:10

6:5 Song 4:1

6:6 Song 4:2

6:7 Song 4:3

6:8 1 Kin 11:3; Song 1:3

6:9 Song 2:14; 5:2; Gen 30:13; 1 Kin 11:3

4 "[18]You are as beautiful as Tirzah, my darling,
As lovely as Jerusalem,
As awesome as an army with banners.
5 "Turn your eyes away from me,
For they have confused me;
Your hair is like a flock of goats
That have descended from Gilead.
6 "Your teeth are like a flock of ewes
Which have come up from *their* washing,
All of which bear twins,
And not one among them has lost her young.
7 "Your temples are like a slice of a pomegranate
Behind your veil.
8 "There are sixty queens and eighty concubines,
And maidens without number;
9 *But* my dove, my perfect one, is unique:
She is her mother's only *daughter;*
She is the pure *child* of the one who bore her.
The maidens saw her and called her blessed,
The queens and the concubines *also,* and they praised her, *saying,*

6:10 Job 31:26; Matt 17:2; Rev 1:16; Song 6:4

6:11 Song 7:12; Song 4:13

10 'Who is this that grows like the dawn,
As beautiful as the full moon,
As pure as the sun,
As awesome as an army with banners?'
11 "I went down to the orchard of nut trees
To see the blossoms of the valley,
To see whether the vine had budded
Or the pomegranates had bloomed.
12 "Before I was aware, my soul set me
Over the chariots of my noble people."

6:13 Judg 21:21; Gen 32:2; 2 Sam 17:24

13 "[19]Come back, come back, O Shulammite;
Come back, come back, that we may gaze at you!"

"[18]**Why** should you gaze at the Shulammite,
As at the dance of the two companies?

Admiration by the Bridegroom

7:1 Ps 45:13

7 "How beautiful are your feet in sandals,
O prince's daughter!
The curves of your hips are like jewels,
The work of the hands of an artist.
2 "Your navel is *like* a round goblet
Which never lacks mixed wine;

18 BRIDEGROOM **19** CHORUS

6:3 The girl said that she and her lover belonged to each other—they had given themselves to each other unreservedly. No matter how close we may be to our parents or our best friends, it is only in marriage that we realize complete union of mind, heart, and body.

6:4 Tirzah was a city about 35 miles northeast of Jerusalem. Its name means "pleasure" or "beauty." Jeroboam made Tirzah the first capital of the divided northern kingdom (1 Kings 14:17). "As awesome as an army with banners" means that the beloved must have had awe-inspiring beauty, like a mighty army readying for battle.

6:8–9 Solomon did indeed have many queens (wives) and concubines (1 Kings 11:3). Polygamy, though not condoned, was common in Old Testament days. Solomon says that his love for this woman has not diminished since their wedding night, even though many other women are available to him.

Your belly is like a heap of wheat
Fenced about with lilies.
3 "Your two breasts are like two fawns,
Twins of a gazelle.
4 "Your neck is like a tower of ivory,
Your eyes *like* the pools in Heshbon
By the gate of Bath-rabbim;
Your nose is like the tower of Lebanon,
Which faces toward Damascus.
5 "Your head crowns you like Carmel,
And the flowing locks of your head are like purple threads;
The king is captivated by *your* tresses.
6 "How beautiful and how delightful you are,
My love, with *all* your charms!
7 "Your stature is like a palm tree,
And your breasts are *like its* clusters.
8 "I said, 'I will climb the palm tree,
I will take hold of its fruit stalks.'
Oh, may your breasts be like clusters of the vine,
And the fragrance of your breath like apples,
9 And your mouth like the best wine!"

"[20]It goes *down* smoothly for my beloved,
Flowing gently *through* the lips of those who fall asleep.

7:3 Song 4:5

7:4 Song 4:4; Num 21:26

7:5 Is 35:2

7:6 Song 1:15, 16; 4:10

7:8 Song 2:5

7:9 Song 5:16; Prov 23:31

6. The bride's tender appeal

The Union of Love

10 "I am my beloved's,
And his desire is for me.
11 "Come, my beloved, let us go out into the country,
Let us spend the night in the villages.
12 "Let us rise early *and go* to the vineyards;
Let us see whether the vine has budded
And its blossoms have opened,
And whether the pomegranates have bloomed.
There I will give you my love.
13 "The mandrakes have given forth fragrance;
And over our doors are all choice *fruits,*
Both new and old,
Which I have saved up for you, my beloved.

7:10 Song 2:16; 6:3; Ps 45:11; Gal 2:20

7:12 Song 6:11

7:13 Gen 30:14; Song 2:3; 4:13, 16; Matt 13:52

The Lovers Speak

8 "Oh that you were like a brother to me
Who nursed at my mother's breasts.
If I found you outdoors, I would kiss you;
No one would despise me, either.

20 BRIDE

7:4–5 The phrase "your eyes like the pools in Heshbon" suggests sparkling eyes. Heshbon was the ancient capital of the Amorites. Bath-rabbim may have been a gate of Heshbon. The "tower of Lebanon" may have been a watchtower (evidently a prominent one and seen as very beautiful). Some suggest that this refers to the Lebanon mountain range. Mount Carmel overlooks the Mediterranean Sea and Palestine.

7:10–13 As a marriage matures, there should be more love and freedom between marriage partners. Here the girl takes the initiative in lovemaking. Many cultures have stereotypes of the roles men and women play in lovemaking, but the security of true love gives both marriage partners the freedom to initiate acts of love and express their true feelings.

7:13 Mandrakes were a somewhat rare plant often thought to increase fertility. Mandrakes are also mentioned in Genesis 30:14–17.

8:1 In the ancient Near East, it was improper to show public affection except between family members. The girl is wishing that she could freely show affection to her lover, even in public.

8:2 Song 3:4

2 “I would lead you *and* bring you
Into the house of my mother, who used to instruct me;
I would give you spiced wine to drink from the juice of my pomegranates.

8:3 Song 2:6

3 “Let his left hand be under my head
And his right hand embrace me.”

8:4 Song 2:7; 3:5

4 “[21]I want you to swear, O daughters of Jerusalem,
Do not arouse or awaken *my* love
Until she pleases.”

7. The power of love

8:5 Song 3:6; Song 2:3

5 “[22]Who is this coming up from the wilderness
Leaning on her beloved?”

“[23]**Beneath** the apple tree I awakened you;
There your mother was in labor with you,
There she was in labor *and* gave you birth.

8:6 Is 49:16; Jer 22:24; Hag 2:23; Prov 6:34

6 “Put me like a [24]seal over your heart,
Like a seal on your arm.
For love is as strong as death,
Jealousy is as severe as Sheol;
Its flashes are flashes of fire,
The *very* flame of the LORD.

8:7 Prov 6:35

7 “Many waters cannot quench love,
Nor will rivers overflow it;
If a man were to give all the riches of his house for love,
It would be utterly despised.”

8:8 Ezek 16:7

8 “[22]We have a little sister,
And she has no breasts;
What shall we do for our sister
On the day when she is spoken for?

8:9 1 Kin 6:15

9 “If she is a wall,
We will build on her a battlement of silver;
But if she is a door,
We will barricade her with planks of cedar.”

8:10 Ezek 16:7

10 “[23]I was a wall, and my breasts were like towers;
Then I became in his eyes as one who finds peace.

8:11 Eccl 2:4; Matt 21:33; Song 1:6; Is 7:23; Song 2:3; 8:12

11 “Solomon had a vineyard at Baal-hamon;
He entrusted the vineyard to caretakers.
Each one was to bring a thousand *shekels* of silver for its fruit.
12 “My very own vineyard is at my disposal;
The thousand *shekels* are for you, Solomon,
And two hundred are for those who take care of its fruit.”

21 BRIDEGROOM **22** CHORUS **23** BRIDE **24** Or *signet*

8:6–7 In this final description of their love, the girl includes some of its significant characteristics (see also 1 Corinthians 13). Love is as strong as death; it cannot be killed by time or disaster; and it cannot be bought for any price because it is freely given. Love is priceless, and even the richest king cannot buy it. Love must be accepted as a gift from God and then shared within the guidelines God provides. Accept the love of your spouse as God's gift, and strive to make your love a reflection of the perfect love that comes from God himself.

8:8–9 The girl was reflecting on the days when she was younger and under the care of her brothers, who wondered how to help her prepare for marriage. They decided that if she was like a wall, standing firm against sexual temptation, they would praise her. But if she was like a door, open to immorality, they would take steps to guard her from doing something foolish. In 8:10, she testifies that she has been persistent in her morality and thus has found favor in Solomon's eyes.

8:11–12 Solomon could demand rent from the tenants for his vineyard, but the girl had her own vineyard and it was her right to assign it. But she willingly gave Solomon its fruit. In a good marriage, there is no private property, for everything is shared between the partners. Baal-hamon is mentioned only here in the Bible, and its location is unknown.

13 "[25]O you who sit in the gardens,
My companions are listening for your voice—
Let me hear it!"

14 "[26]Hurry, my beloved,
And be like a gazelle or a young stag
On the mountains of spices."

25 BRIDEGROOM **26** BRIDE

8:13
Song 1:7; Song 2:14

8:14
Song 2:7, 9, 17; Song 4:6

8:14 The love between Solomon and his bride did not diminish in intensity after their wedding night. The lovers relied on each other and kept no secrets from each other. Devotion and commitment were the keys to their relationship, just as they are in our relationships to our spouses and to God. The faithfulness of our marital love should reflect God's perfect faithfulness to us.

Paul shows how marriage represents Christ's relationship to his church (Ephesians 5:22–33), and John pictures the second coming as a great marriage feast for Christ and his bride, his faithful followers (Revelation 19:7–8; 21:1–2). Many theologians have thought that Song of Solomon is an allegory showing Christ's love for his church. It makes even better sense to say that it is a love poem about a real human love relationship, and that all loving, committed marriages reflect God's love.

ISAIAH AND THE BIBLE

The book of Isaiah has been described as the Bible in miniature. It has remarkable similarities to the Bible as a whole—in both its structure and its message.

The Book of Isaiah	*The Bible*
Has 66 chapters	Has 66 books
Can be broken into two sections: chapters 1—39 (39 chapters) and chapters 40—66 (27 chapters)	Is broken into two parts: 39 books in the Old Testament and 27 books in the New Testament
The focus in the first section (chapters 1—39) is on God's righteousness, holiness, and justice	The focus in the 39 Old Testament books is on God's righteousness, holiness, and justice
The focus in the second section (chapters 40—66) is on God's glory, compassion, and grace	The focus in the 27 New Testament books is on God's glory, compassion, and grace
Chapters 1—39 depict Israel's need for restoration.	The Old Testament depicts humanity's need for salvation.
Chapters 40—66 foretell God's future provision of salvation for his people through a suffering Servant.	The New Testament describes God's provision of salvation for all people in the Messiah, who suffered and died to bring salvation and eternal life.
Isaiah begins with a description of Israel's rebellion and ends with predictions of restoration.	The Bible begins with a description of humanity's rebellion and ends with a depiction of salvation in Jesus Christ.
Message: A holy God will gain glory by judging sin and restoring his people.	Message: A holy God will gain glory by judging sin and saving those who call on the name of his Son, Jesus Christ.

ISAIAH

Amos becomes a prophet 760 B.C.	Hosea becomes a prophet 753	Micah becomes a prophet 742	Isaiah becomes a prophet 740	Ahaz becomes king of Judah 735	Hoshea becomes king of Israel 732	Israel falls to the Assyrians 722	Hezekiah becomes king of Judah 715

VITAL STATISTICS

PURPOSE:
To call the nation of Judah back to God and to tell of God's salvation through the Messiah

AUTHOR:
The prophet Isaiah son of Amoz

DATE WRITTEN:
The events of chapters 1—39 occurred during Isaiah's ministry, so they were probably written about 700 B.C. Chapters 40—66, however, may have been written near the end of his life, about 681 B.C.

SETTING:
Isaiah is speaking and writing mainly in Jerusalem

KEY VERSE:
"But He was pierced through for our transgressions, He was crushed for our iniquities; the chastening for our well-being fell upon Him, and by His scourging we are healed" (53:5).

KEY PEOPLE:
Isaiah; his two sons, Shear-jashub and Maher-shalal-hash-baz

SPECIAL FEATURES:
The book of Isaiah contains both prose and poetry and uses personification (attributing personal qualities to divine beings or inanimate objects). Also, many of the prophecies in Isaiah contain predictions that foretell a soon-to-occur event and a distant future event at the same time.

SLOWLY he rose, and the crowd fell silent. Those at the back leaned forward, straining to hear. The atmosphere was electric. He spoke, and his carefully chosen words flew like swift arrows and found their mark. The great man, a spokesman for God, was warning—and condemning. The crowd became restless—shifting positions, clenching fists, and murmuring. Some agreed with his message, nodding their heads and weeping softly. But most were angry, and they began to shout back insults and threats.

Such was the life of a prophet.

The "office" of prophet was instituted during the days of Samuel, the last of the judges. Prophets stood with the priests as God's special representatives. The prophet's role was to speak for God, confronting the people and their leaders with God's commands and promises. Because of this confrontational stance and the continuing tendency of people to disobey God, true prophets usually were not very popular. But though their message often went unheeded, they faithfully and forcefully proclaimed the truth.

The book of Isaiah is the first of the writings of the prophets in the Bible; and Isaiah, the author, is generally considered to be the greatest prophet. He was probably reared in an aristocratic home and was married to a prophet. In the beginning of his ministry he was well liked. But, like most prophets, he soon became unpopular because his messages were so difficult to hear. He called the people to turn from their lives of sin and warned them of God's judgment and punishment. Isaiah had an active ministry for 60 years before he was executed during Manasseh's reign (according to tradition). As God's special messenger to Judah, Isaiah prophesied during the reigns of several of its rulers. Many of those messages are recorded in his book: Uzziah and Jotham, chapters 1—6; Ahaz, chapters 7—14; and Hezekiah, chapters 15—39.

The first half of the book of Isaiah (chapters 1—39) contains scathing denunciations and pronouncements as he calls Judah, Israel, and the surrounding nations to repent of their sins. However, the last 27 chapters (40—66) are filled with consolation and hope as Isaiah unfolds God's promise of future blessings through his Messiah.

As you read Isaiah, imagine this strong and courageous man of God, fearlessly proclaiming God's word, and listen to his message in relation to your own life—*return, repent, and be renewed.* Then trust in God's *redemption* through Christ and *rejoice.* Your Savior has come, and he's coming again!

Sennacherib surrounds Jerusalem 701	Manasseh becomes king of Judah 697	Isaiah's ministry ends 681	Josiah becomes king of Judah 640

THE BLUEPRINT

A. WORDS OF JUDGMENT (1:1—39:8)
1. The sins of Israel and Judah
2. Judgment against heathen nations
3. God's purpose in judgment
4. Jerusalem's true and false hopes
5. Events during the reign of Hezekiah

The 39 chapters in the first half of Isaiah generally carry the message of judgment for sin. Isaiah brings the message of judgment to Judah, Israel, and the surrounding pagan nations. The people of Judah had a form of godliness, but in their hearts they were corrupt. Isaiah's warnings were intended to purify the people by helping them understand God's true nature and message. However, they ignored the repeated warnings that Isaiah brought. We need to heed the prophetic voice and not repeat their error.

B. WORDS OF COMFORT (40:1—66:24)
1. Israel's release from captivity
2. The future Redeemer
3. The future kingdom

The 27 chapters in the second half of Isaiah generally bring a message of forgiveness, comfort, and hope. This message of hope looks forward to the coming of the Messiah. Isaiah speaks more about the Messiah than does any other Old Testament prophet. He describes the Messiah as both a suffering Servant and a sovereign Lord. The fact that the Messiah was to be both a suffering Servant and a sovereign Lord could not be understood clearly until New Testament times. Based on what Jesus Christ has done, God freely offers forgiveness to all who turn to him in faith. This is God's message of comfort to us because those who heed it find eternal peace and fellowship with him.

MEGATHEMES

THEME	EXPLANATION	IMPORTANCE
Holiness	God is highly exalted above all his creatures. His moral perfection stands in contrast to evil people and nations. God is perfect and sinless in all his motives and actions, so he is in perfect control of his power, judgment, love, and mercy. His holy nature is our yardstick for morality.	Because God is without sin, he alone can help us with our sin. It is only right that we regard him as supreme in power and moral perfection. We must never treat God as common or ordinary. He alone deserves our devotion and praise. He is always truthful, fair, and just.
Punishment	Because God is holy, he requires his people to treat others justly. He promised to punish Israel, Judah, and other nations for faithless immorality and idolatry. True faith had degenerated into national pride and empty religious rituals.	We must trust in God alone and fulfill his commands. We cannot forsake justice nor give in to selfishness. If we harden our heart against his message, punishment will surely come to us.
Salvation	Because God's judgment is coming, we need a Savior. No man or nation can be saved without God's help. Christ's perfect sacrifice for our sins is foretold and portrayed in Isaiah. All who trust God can be freed from their sin and restored to him.	Christ died to save us from our sin. We cannot save ourselves. He is willing to save all those who turn from their sin and come to him. Salvation is from God alone. No amount of good works can earn it.
Messiah	God will send the Messiah to save his people. He will set up his own Kingdom as the faithful Prince of Peace, who rules with righteousness. He will come as sovereign Lord, but he will do so as a servant who will die to take away sins.	Our trust must be in the Messiah, not in ourselves or in any nation or power. There is no hope unless we believe in him. Trust Christ fully and let him rule in your life as your sovereign Lord.
Hope	God promises comfort, deliverance, and restoration in his future kingdom. The Messiah will rule over his faithful followers in the age to come. Hope is possible because Christ is coming.	We can be refreshed because there is compassion for those who repent. No matter how bleak our situation or how evil the world is, we must continue to be God's faithful people who hope for his return.

A. WORDS OF JUDGMENT (1:1—39:8)

Isaiah begins by bringing a message of divine judgment for both Israel and Judah. Although the advance of the Assyrians poses a problem for Judah, God foretells the destruction of Assyria and other evil surrounding nations through the prophet Isaiah. This section ends with the Assyrian invasion being held off, demonstrating the clear unfolding of God's plan and promises for the nation at this time.

1. The sins of Israel and Judah

Rebellion of God's People

1 The vision of Isaiah the son of Amoz concerning Judah and Jerusalem, which he saw
during the reigns of Uzziah, Jotham, Ahaz *and* Hezekiah, kings of Judah.

2 Listen, O heavens, and hear, O earth;
For the LORD speaks,
"Sons I have reared and brought up,
But they have revolted against Me.
3 "An ox knows its owner,
And a donkey its master's manger,
But Israel does not know,
My people do not understand."

4 Alas, sinful nation,
People weighed down with iniquity,
Offspring of evildoers,
Sons who act corruptly!
They have abandoned the LORD,
They have despised the Holy One of Israel,
They have turned away from Him.

5 Where will you be stricken again,
As you continue in *your* rebellion?
The whole head is sick
And the whole heart is faint.
6 From the sole of the foot even to the head
There is nothing sound in it,
Only bruises, welts and raw wounds,
Not pressed out or bandaged,
Nor softened with oil.

7 Your land is desolate,
Your cities are burned with fire,
Your fields—strangers are devouring them in your presence;
It is desolation, as overthrown by strangers.
8 The daughter of Zion is left like a shelter in a vineyard,
Like a watchman's hut in a cucumber field, like a besieged city.

1:1 Is 2:1; 40:9; 2 Kin 15:1-7, 13; 2 Chr 26:1-23; 2 Kin 15:32-38; 2 Chr 27:1-9; 2 Kin 16:1-20; 2 Chr 28:1-27; Is 7:1; 2 Kin 18:1-20:21; 2 Chr 29:1-32:33

1:2 Deut 32:1; Mic 1:2; Jer 3:22; Is 30:1, 9; 65:2

1:3 Jer 9:3, 6; Is 44:18

1:4 Is 14:20; Neh 1:7; Is 1:28; Is 5:24

1:5 Is 31:6; Is 33:24; Ezek 34:4, 16

1:6 Job 2:7; Ps 38:3; Jer 8:22

1:7 Lev 26:33; Jer 44:6

1:1 Isaiah was a prophet during the time when the original nation of Israel had been divided into two kingdoms—Israel in the north, and Judah in the south. The northern kingdom had sinned greatly against God, and the southern kingdom was headed in the same direction—perverting justice, oppressing the poor, turning from God to idols, and looking for military aid from pagan nations rather than from God. Isaiah came primarily as a prophet to Judah, but his message was also for the northern kingdom. Sometimes "Israel" refers to both kingdoms. Isaiah lived to see the destruction and captivity of the northern kingdom in 722 B.C.; thus, his ministry began with warning the northern kingdom.

1:2–4 Here "Israel" means the southern kingdom, Judah. The people of Judah were sinning greatly and refused to know and understand God. God brought charges against them through Isaiah because they had rebelled and had forsaken the Lord. By these acts, they had broken their moral and spiritual covenant with God (see Deuteronomy 28). By breaking their agreement, they were bringing God's punishment upon themselves. First God gave them prosperity, but they didn't serve him. Then God sent them warnings, but they refused to listen. Finally, he would bring the fire of his judgment (see 1:7).

1:4–9 As long as the people of Judah continued to sin, they cut themselves off from God's help and isolated themselves. When you feel lonely and separated from God, remember that God does not abandon you. Our sins cut us off from him. The only sure cure for this kind of loneliness is to restore a meaningful relationship with God by confessing your sin, obeying his instructions, and communicating regularly with him (see Psalm 140:13; Isaiah 1:16–19; 1 John 1:9).

1:7 Was this destruction taking place at that time? Judah was attacked many times during Isaiah's lifetime. To be overthrown by strangers (foreigners) was the worst kind of judgment. This verse could be a picture of the results of these invasions or a prediction of the coming invasion of Israel by Assyria. But most likely it pointed to Babylon's future invasion of Judah and the fall of Jerusalem in 586 B.C. as well.

1:9 Rom 9:29; Is 10:20-22; 11:11, 16; 37:4, 31, 32; 46:3; Gen 19:24

9 Unless the LORD of hosts
Had left us a few survivors,
We would be like Sodom,
We would be like Gomorrah.

God Has Had Enough

1:10 Is 8:20; 28:14; Is 3:9; Ezek 16:49; Rom 9:29; Rev 11:8

10 Hear the word of the LORD,
You rulers of Sodom;
Give ear to the instruction of our God,
You people of Gomorrah.

1:11 Ps 50:8; Jer 6:20; Amos 5:21, 22; Mal 1:10

11 "What are your multiplied sacrifices to Me?"
Says the LORD.
"I have had enough of burnt offerings of rams
And the fat of fed cattle;
And I take no pleasure in the blood of bulls, lambs or goats.

1:12 Ex 23:17

12 "When you come to appear before Me,
Who requires of you this trampling of My courts?

1:13 Is 66:3; 1 Chr 23:31; Ex 12:16; Jer 7:9, 10

13 "Bring your worthless offerings no longer,
Incense is an abomination to Me.
New moon and sabbath, the calling of assemblies—
I cannot endure iniquity and the solemn assembly.

1:14 Is 29:1, 2; Is 7:13; 43:24

14 "I hate your new moon *festivals* and your appointed feasts,
They have become a burden to Me;
I am weary of bearing *them.*

1:15 1 Kin 8:22; Lam 1:17; Is 8:17; 59:2; Mic 3:4; Is 59:3

15 "So when you spread out your hands *in prayer,*
I will hide My eyes from you;
Yes, even though you multiply prayers,
I will not listen.
Your hands are covered with blood.

1:16 Ps 26:6; Is 52:11; Is 55:7; Jer 25:5

16 "Wash yourselves, make yourselves clean;
Remove the evil of your deeds from My sight.
Cease to do evil,

ISAIAH Isaiah served as a prophet to Judah from 740–681 B.C		
	Climate of the times	Society was in a great upheaval. Under King Ahaz and King Manasseh the people reverted to idolatry, and there was even child sacrifice.
	Main message	Although judgment from other nations was inevitable, the people could still have a special relationship with God.
	Importance of message	Sometimes we must suffer judgment and discipline before we are restored to God.
	Contemporary prophets	Hosea (753–715 B.C.), Micah (742–687 B.C.)

1:9 Sodom and Gomorrah were two cities that God completely destroyed for their great wickedness (Genesis 19:1–25). They are mentioned elsewhere in the Bible as examples of God's judgment against sin (Jeremiah 50:40; Ezekiel 16:46–63; Matthew 11:23, 24; Jude 7). "A few survivors" from Judah were spared by God because they were faithful.

1:10 Isaiah compared the rulers and people of Judah to the rulers and people of Sodom and Gomorrah. To hear what God wanted to say, the people had to listen and be willing to obey. When we can't hear God's message, perhaps we are not listening carefully or we are not truly willing to do what he says.

1:10–14 God was unhappy with their sacrifices, but he was not revoking the system of sacrifices he had initiated with Moses. Instead, God was calling for sincere faith and devotion. The leaders were carefully making the traditional sacrifices and offerings at holy celebrations, but they were still unfaithful to God in their hearts. Sacrifices were to be an outward sign of their inward faith in God, but the outward signs became empty because no inward faith existed. Why, then, did they continue to offer sacrifices? Like many people today, they had come to place more faith in the rituals of their religion than in the God they worshiped. Examine your own religious practices: do they spring from your faith in the living God? God does not take pleasure in our outward expressions if our inward faith is missing (see Deuteronomy 10:12–16; 1 Samuel 15:22–23; Psalm 51:16–19; Hosea 6:6).

1:13 "New moon" and "sabbath" refer to monthly offerings (Numbers 28:11–14) and weekly and special annual sabbaths on the day of atonement and Feast of Booths (Leviticus 16:31, 23–34, 39). For all the feasts, see the chart in Leviticus 23. Although the people did not feel sorry for their sins, they continued to offer sacrifices for forgiveness. Gifts and sacrifices mean nothing to God when they come from someone with a corrupt heart. God wants us to love him, trust him, and turn from our sin; after that, he will be pleased with our "sacrifices" of time, money, or service.

17 Learn to do good;
Seek justice,
Reprove the ruthless,
Defend the orphan,
Plead for the widow.

1:17 Jer 22:3; Zeph 2:3; Ps 82:3

"Let Us Reason"

18 "Come now, and let us reason together,"
Says the LORD,
"Though your sins are as scarlet,
They will be as white as snow;
Though they are red like crimson,
They will be like wool.
19 "If you consent and obey,
You will eat the best of the land;
20 "But if you refuse and rebel,
You will be devoured by the sword."
Truly, the mouth of the LORD has spoken.

1:18 Is 41:1, 21; 43:26; Mic 6:2; Ps 51:7; Is 43:25; 44:22; Rev 7:14

1:19 Deut 28:1; 30:15, 16; Is 55:2

1:20 Is 3:25; 65:12; Is 40:5; 58:14; Mic 4:4; Titus 1:2

Zion Corrupted, to be Redeemed

21 How the faithful city has become a harlot,
She *who* was full of justice!
Righteousness once lodged in her,
But now murderers.
22 Your silver has become dross,
Your drink diluted with water.
23 Your rulers are rebels
And companions of thieves;
Everyone loves a bribe
And chases after rewards.
They do not defend the orphan,
Nor does the widow's plea come before them.

1:21 Is 57:3-9; Jer 2:20

1:23 Hos 5:10; Mic 7:3; Ex 23:8; Mic 7:3; Is 10:2; Jer 5:28; Ezek 22:7; Zech 7:10

24 Therefore the Lord GOD of hosts,
The Mighty One of Israel, declares,
"Ah, I will be relieved of My adversaries
And avenge Myself on My foes.
25 "I will also turn My hand against you,
And will smelt away your dross as with lye
And will remove all your alloy.
26 "Then I will restore your judges as at the first,
And your counselors as at the beginning;
After that you will be called the city of righteousness,
A faithful city."

1:24 Ps 132:2; Is 49:26; 60:16; Deut 28:63; Is 35:4; 59:18; 61:2; 63:4

1:25 Ezek 22:19-22; Mal 3:3

1:26 Is 60:17; Is 33:5; 60:14; 62:1, 2; Zech 8:3

27 Zion will be redeemed with justice
And her repentant ones with righteousness.

1:27 Is 35:9f; 62:12; 63:4

1:18 Scarlet, or crimson, was the color of a deep-red permanent dye, and its deep stain was virtually impossible to remove from clothing. The bloodstained hands of the murderers are probably in view here (see 1:15, 21). The stain of sin seems equally permanent, but God can remove sin's stain from our lives as he promised to do for the Israelites. We don't have to go through life permanently soiled. God's Word assures us that if we are willing and obedient, Christ will forgive and remove our most indelible stains (Psalm 51:1–7).

1:21–22 "The faithful city" refers to Jerusalem, representing all of Judah. God compares the actions of his people to a harlot. The people had turned from the worship of the true God to worshiping idols. Their faith was defective, impure, and diluted. Idolatry, outward or inward, is spiritual adultery, breaking our commitment to God in order to love something else. Jesus described the people of his day as adulterous, even though they were religiously strict. As the church, we are the "bride" of Christ (Revelation 19:7), and, by faith, we can be clothed in his righteousness. Has your faith become impure? Ask God to restore you. Keep your devotion to him strong and pure.

1:25 God promised to refine his people similar to the way that metal is purged with lye in a smelting pot. This process involves melting the metal and skimming off the impure dross until the worker can see his own image in the liquid metal. We must be willing to submit to God, allowing him to remove our sin so that we might reflect his image.

1:28 Ps 9:5; Is 66:24; 2 Thess 1:8, 9

1:29 Is 57:5; Is 65:3; 66:17

1:30 Is 64:6

1:31 Is 5:24; 9:19; 26:11; 33:11-14; Is 66:24; Matt 3:12; Mark 9:43

28 But transgressors and sinners will be crushed together,
And those who forsake the LORD will come to an end.
29 Surely you will be ashamed of the oaks which you have desired,
And you will be embarrassed at the gardens which you have chosen.
30 For you will be like an oak whose leaf fades away
Or as a garden that has no water.
31 The strong man will become tinder,
His work also a spark.
Thus they shall both burn together
And there will be none to quench *them.*

God's Universal Reign

2:1 Is 1:1

2:2 Mic 4:1-3; Is 27:13; 66:20; Is 56:7

2:3 Is 51:4, 5; Luke 24:47

2:4 Is 32:17, 18; Joel 3:10; Is 9:5, 7; 11:6-9; Hos 2:18; Zech 9:10

2 The word which Isaiah the son of Amoz saw concerning Judah and Jerusalem.
2 Now it will come about that
In the last days
The mountain of the house of the LORD
Will be established as the chief of the mountains,
And will be raised above the hills;
And all the nations will stream to it.
3 And many peoples will come and say,
"Come, let us go up to the mountain of the LORD,
To the house of the God of Jacob;
That He may teach us concerning His ways
And that we may walk in His paths."
For the law will go forth from Zion
And the word of the LORD from Jerusalem.
4 And He will judge between the nations,
And will render decisions for many peoples;
And they will hammer their swords into plowshares and their spears into pruning hooks.
Nation will not lift up sword against nation,
And never again will they learn war.

2:5 Is 58:1; Is 60:1, 2, 19, 20; 1 John 1:5

2:6 Deut 31:17; 2 Kin 1:2; 2 Kin 16:7, 8; Prov 6:1

2:7 Deut 17:16; Is 30:16; 31:1; Mic 5:10

5 Come, house of Jacob, and let us walk in the light of the LORD.
6 For You have abandoned Your people, the house of Jacob,
Because they are filled *with influences* from the east,
And *they are* soothsayers like the Philistines,
And they strike *bargains* with the children of foreigners.
7 Their land has also been filled with silver and gold
And there is no end to their treasures;

1:29–30 Throughout history, the oak tree has been a symbol of strength, but the people were worshiping "sacred oaks." Ezekiel mentions that groves of oak trees were used as places for idol worship (Ezekiel 6:13). Are you devoted to symbols of strength and power that rival God's place in your life? Do you have interests and commitments where your love for them borders on worship? Make God your first loyalty; everything else will fade in time and burn away under his scrutiny.

1:31 A spark set to tinder ignites a quick, devouring fire. God compares mighty people whose evil deeds devour them to a roaring fire. Our lives can be destroyed quickly by a small but deadly spark of evil. What potential "fire hazards" do you need to remove?

2:2 The temple (house of the Lord) was built on the mountain of the Lord, Mount Moriah, highly visible to all the people of Jerusalem. For more on the significance of the temple, see the note on 2 Chronicles 5:1ff. In the last days the temple will attract the nations, not because of its architecture and prominence, but because of God's presence and influence.

2:2–4 God gave Isaiah the gift of seeing the future. At this time, God showed Isaiah what would eventually happen to Jerusalem. Revelation 21 depicts the glorious fulfillment of this prophecy in the new Jerusalem, where only those whose names are written in the Lamb's book of life will be allowed to enter. God made a covenant (promise) with his people and will never break it. God's faithfulness gives us hope for the future.

2:4–5 This describes a wonderful future of peace when instruments of war will be converted to instruments of farming, when we will be taught God's laws and will obey them. Although we know that eventually God will remove all sin and thus the causes of war, conflicts, and other problems, we should not wait for him to act before we begin to obey him. Just as Judah was told in 2:5, we should walk in his light now. Though our eternal reward awaits us, we already can enjoy many benefits of obedience now as we apply God's Word to our lives.

2:6 The people were following practices of the Assyrian empire. "Soothsayers like the Philistines" meant claiming to know and control the future by the power of demons or by interpreting omens. These practices were forbidden by God (see Leviticus 19:26; Deuteronomy 18:10, 14). The Philistines worshiped Dagon, Ashtaroth, and Baal-zebub. During the more sinful periods of their history, the people of Israel worshiped these pagan gods along with Yahweh, and even gave them Hebrew names.

Their land has also been filled with horses
And there is no end to their chariots.
8 Their land has also been filled with idols;
They worship the work of their hands,
That which their fingers have made.
9 So the *common* man has been humbled
And the man *of importance* has been abased,
But do not forgive them.
10 Enter the rock and hide in the dust
From the terror of the LORD and from the splendor of His majesty.
11 The proud look of man will be abased
And the loftiness of man will be humbled,
And the LORD alone will be exalted in that day.

2:8 Is 10:11; Ps 115:4-8; Is 17:8; 37:19; 40:19; 44:17
2:9 Ps 49:2; 62:9; Is 5:15; Neh 4:5
2:10 Is 2:19, 21; Rev 6:15, 16; 2 Thess 1:9
2:11 Is 5:15; 37:23; Ps 18:27; Is 13:11; 23:9; 2 Cor 10:5

A Day of Reckoning Coming

12 For the LORD of hosts will have a day *of reckoning*
Against everyone who is proud and lofty
And against everyone who is lifted up,
That he may be abased.
13 And *it will be* against all the cedars of Lebanon that are lofty and lifted up,
Against all the oaks of Bashan,
14 Against all the lofty mountains,
Against all the hills that are lifted up,
15 Against every high tower,
Against every fortified wall,
16 Against all the ships of Tarshish
And against all the beautiful craft.
17 The pride of man will be humbled
And the loftiness of men will be abased;
And the LORD alone will be exalted in that day,
18 But the idols will completely vanish.
19 *Men* will go into caves of the rocks
And into holes of the ground
Before the terror of the LORD
And the splendor of His majesty,
When He arises to make the earth tremble.
20 In that day men will cast away to the moles and the bats
Their idols of silver and their idols of gold,
Which they made for themselves to worship,
21 In order to go into the caverns of the rocks and the clefts of the cliffs
Before the terror of the LORD and the splendor of His majesty,
When He arises to make the earth tremble.
22 Stop regarding man, whose breath *of life* is in his nostrils;
For why should he be esteemed?

2:12 Job 40:11, 12; Is 24:4, 21; Mal 4:1
2:13 Zech 11:2
2:14 Is 40:4
2:15 Is 25:12
2:16 1 Kin 10:22; Is 23:1, 14; 60:9
2:18 Is 21:9; Mic 1:7
2:19 Is 2:10; Ps 18:7; Is 2:21; 13:13; 24:1, 19, 20; Hag 2:6, 7; Heb 12:26
2:20 Is 30:22; 31:7; Lev 11:19
2:21 Is 2:19
2:22 Ps 146:3; Jer 17:5; Ps 8:4; 144:3, 4; Is 40:15, 17; James 4:14

2:8–9 Under the reign of evil kings, idol worship flourished in both Israel and Judah. A few good kings in Judah stopped it during their reigns. Though very few people worship carved or molded images today, worshiping objects that symbolize power continues. We pay homage to cars, homes, sports stars, celebrities, money, etc. Idol worship is evil because (1) it insults God when we worship something he created rather than worshiping him; (2) it keeps us from knowing and serving God when we put our confidence in anything other than him; (3) it causes us to rely on our own efforts rather than on God. (See also Deuteronomy 27:15.)

2:12 The "day of reckoning" is the day of judgment, the time when God will judge both evil and good. That day will come, and we will want a proper relationship with God when it does. God alone must be exalted (2:11, 17) as the first step toward developing that relationship with him.

2:15–17 High towers were part of a city or nation's defenses. This phrase refers to security based on military fortresses. "Ships of Tarshish" pictures economic prosperity, and a "beautiful craft" is a pleasure vessel. Nothing can compare with or rival the place God must have in our hearts and minds. To place our hope elsewhere is nothing but false pride. Place your confidence in God alone.

2:19 See Revelation 6:15–17 for a description of the terror in God's enemies on the day of his wrath.

2:22 "Whose breath of life is in his nostrils" refers to mankind's mortality. People are very limited when compared to God. They can be unreliable, selfish, and shortsighted. Yet we trust our lives and futures more readily to mortal human beings than to the all-knowing God. Beware of people who want you to trust them instead of God. Remember that only God is completely reliable. He is perfect and he loves us with an enduring love (Psalm 100:5).

God Will Remove the Leaders

3:1 Lev 26:26; Is 5:13; 9:20; Ezek 4:16

3 For behold, the Lord GOD of hosts is going to remove from Jerusalem and Judah
Both supply and support, the whole supply of bread
And the whole supply of water;

3:2 2 Kin 24:14; Is 9:14, 15; Ezek 17:12, 13

2 The mighty man and the warrior,
The judge and the prophet,
The diviner and the elder,
3 The captain of fifty and the honorable man,
The counselor and the expert artisan,
And the skillful enchanter.

3:4 Eccl 10:16

4 And I will make mere lads their princes,
And capricious children will rule over them,

3:5 Mic 7:3-6; Is 9:19; Jer 9:3-8

5 And the people will be oppressed,
Each one by another, and each one by his neighbor;
The youth will storm against the elder
And the inferior against the honorable.

3:6 Is 4:1

6 When a man lays hold of his brother in his father's house, *saying,*
"You have a cloak, you shall be our ruler,
And these ruins will be under your charge,"

3:7 Ezek 34:4; Hos 5:13

7 He will protest on that day, saying,
"I will not be *your* healer,
For in my house there is neither bread nor cloak;
You should not appoint me ruler of the people."

3:8 Is 1:7; 6:11; Ps 73:9-11; Is 9:17; 59:3; Is 65:3

8 For Jerusalem has stumbled and Judah has fallen,
Because their speech and their actions are against the LORD,
To rebel against His glorious presence.

3:9 Gen 13:13; Is 1:10-15; Prov 8:36; 15:32; Rom 6:23

9 The expression of their faces bears witness against them,
And they display their sin like Sodom;
They do not *even* conceal *it.*
Woe to them!
For they have brought evil on themselves.

3:10 Deut 28:1-14; Eccl 8:12; Is 54:17

10 Say to the righteous that *it will go* well *with them,*
For they will eat the fruit of their actions.

3:11 Deut 28:15-68; Is 65:6, 7

11 Woe to the wicked! *It will go* badly *with him,*
For what he deserves will be done to him.

3:12 Is 3:4; Is 9:16; 28:14, 15

12 O My people! Their oppressors are children,
And women rule over them.
O My people! Those who guide you lead *you* astray
And confuse the direction of your paths.

God Will Judge

3:13 Is 66:16; Hos 4:1; Mic 6:2

13 The LORD arises to contend,
And stands to judge the people.

3:1–3 Jerusalem besieged, her leaders destroyed—this unhappy picture would soon become a reality. Disobedience would bring serious affliction and great destruction, as God had warned (Deuteronomy 28).

3:2 Isaiah was not condoning the use of soothsayers (diviners) by including them on this list. He was showing how far the nation had sunk. See the note on 2:6.

3:4–9 This section describes what happens when a nation loses its leadership.

3:9–11 The people would be proud of their sins, parading them out in the open. But sin is self-destructive. In today's world, sinful living often appears glamorous, exciting, and clever. But sin is wrong regardless of how society perceives it, and, in the long run, sin will make us miserable and destroy us. God tries to protect us by warning us about the harm we will cause ourselves by sinning. Those who are proud of their sins will receive the punishment from God they deserve. Having rejected God's path to life (see Psalm 1), the only alternative is the path to destruction.

3:10–11 In the middle of this gloomy message, God gives hope—eventually the righteous will receive God's reward and the wicked will receive their punishment. It is disheartening to see the wicked prosper while we struggle to obey God and follow his plan. Yet we keep holding on to God's truth and take heart! God will bring about justice in the end, and he will reward those who have been faithful.

14 The LORD enters into judgment with the elders and princes of His people,
"It is you who have devoured the vineyard;
The plunder of the poor is in your houses.
15 "What do you mean by crushing My people
And grinding the face of the poor?"
Declares the Lord GOD of hosts.

Judah's Women Denounced

16 Moreover, the LORD said, "Because the daughters of Zion are proud
And walk with heads held high and seductive eyes,
And go along with mincing steps
And tinkle the bangles on their feet,
17 Therefore the Lord will afflict the scalp of the daughters of Zion with scabs,
And the LORD will make their foreheads bare."
18 In that day the Lord will take away the beauty of *their* anklets, headbands, crescent ornaments,
19 dangling earrings, bracelets, veils,
20 headdresses, ankle chains, sashes, perfume boxes, amulets,
21 finger rings, nose rings,
22 festal robes, outer tunics, cloaks, money purses,
23 hand mirrors, undergarments, turbans and veils.
24 Now it will come about that instead of sweet perfume there will be putrefaction;
Instead of a belt, a rope;
Instead of well-set hair, a plucked-out scalp;
Instead of fine clothes, a donning of sackcloth;
And branding instead of beauty.
25 Your men will fall by the sword
And your mighty ones in battle.
26 And her gates will lament and mourn,
And deserted she will sit on the ground.

A Remnant Prepared

4 For seven women will take hold of one man in that day, saying, "We will eat our own bread and wear our own clothes, only let us be called by your name; take away our reproach!"
2 In that day the Branch of the LORD will be beautiful and glorious, and the fruit of
the earth *will be* the pride and the adornment of the survivors of Israel.
3 It will come about that he who is left in Zion and remains in Jerusalem will be called
holy—everyone who is recorded for life in Jerusalem.
4 When the Lord has washed away the filth of the daughters of Zion and purged the
bloodshed of Jerusalem from her midst, by the spirit of judgment and the spirit of burning,

3:14 Job 22:4; Ps 143:2; Ezek 20:35, 36; Ps 14:4; Mic 3:3; Job 24:9, 14; Ps 10:9; Prov 30:14; Is 10:1, 2; Ezek 18:12; James 2:6

3:15 Ps 94:5

3:16 Song 3:11; Is 3:16-4:1, 4; 32:9-15

3:18 Judg 8:21, 26

3:20 Ex 39:28

3:21 Gen 24:47; Ezek 16:12

3:24 Esth 2:12; 1 Pet 3:3; Is 22:12; Ezek 27:31; Amos 8:10; Is 15:3; Lam 2:10

3:25 Is 1:20; 65:12

3:26 Jer 14:2; Lam 1:4; Lam 2:10

4:1 Is 13:12; Gen 30:23; Is 54:4

4:2 Is 11:1; 53:2; Jer 23:5; 33:15; Zech 3:8; 6:12; Ps 72:16; Is 10:20; 37:31, 32; Joel 2:32; Obad 17

4:3 Is 28:5; 46:3; Rom 11:4, 5; Is 52:1; 62:12; Ex 32:32; Ps 69:28; Luke 10:20

4:4 Is 3:16; Is 1:15; Is 28:6; Is 1:31; 9:19; Matt 3:11

3:14 The elders and princes were responsible to help people, but instead they stole from the poor. Because they were unjust, Isaiah said the leaders would be the first to receive God's judgment. Leaders will be held accountable. If you are in a position of leadership, you must lead according to God's just commands. Corruption will bring God's wrath, especially if others follow your example.

3:14 Why is justice so important in the Bible? (1) Justice is part of God's nature; it is the way he runs the universe. (2) It is a natural desire in every person. Even as sinners, we all want justice for ourselves. (3) When government and church leaders are unjust, the poor and powerless suffer. Thus they are hindered from worshiping God. (4) God holds the poor in high regard. They are the ones most likely to turn to him for help and comfort. Injustice, then, attacks God's children. When we do nothing to help the oppressed, we are in fact joining with the oppressor. Because we follow a just God, we must uphold justice.

3:16–26 The women of Judah had placed their emphasis on clothing and jewelry rather than on God. They dressed to be noticed, to gain approval, and to be fashionable. Yet they ignored the real purpose for their lives. Instead of being concerned about the oppression around them (3:14–15), they were self-serving and self-centered. People who abuse their possessions will end up with nothing. These verses are not an indictment against clothing and jewelry, but a judgment on those who use them lavishly while remaining blind to the needs of others. When God blesses you with money or position, don't flaunt it. Use what you have to help others, not impress them.

4:2–4 The "Branch of the LORD" probably refers to the Messiah, although some believe it refers to Judah. The point is that during the distress predicted by Isaiah, some people will be protected by God's loving grace. Those protected will be set apart to God when Messiah rules the earth (Jeremiah 23:5–6; Zechariah 6:12–13). Their distinctive mark will be their holiness, not wealth or prestige. This holiness comes from a sincere desire to obey God and from wholehearted devotion to him. Evil will not always continue as it does now. The time will come when God will put an end to all evil, and his faithful followers will share in his glorious reign.

4:5 Ex 13:21, 22; 24:16; Num 9:15-23; Is 60:1, 2

4:6 Ps 27:5; Is 25:4; 32:1, 2

5 then the LORD will create over the whole area of Mount Zion and over her assemblies a cloud by day, even smoke, and the brightness of a flaming fire by night; for over
all the glory will be a canopy.
6 There will be a shelter to *give* shade from the heat by day, and refuge and protection from the storm and the rain.

Parable of the Vineyard

5:1 Ps 80:8; Jer 12:10; Matt 21:33; Mark 12:1; Luke 20:9

5:2 Jer 2:21; Matt 21:19; Mark 11:13; Luke 13:6

5 Let me sing now for my well-beloved
A song of my beloved concerning His vineyard.
My well-beloved had a vineyard on a fertile hill.
2 He dug it all around, removed its stones,
And planted it with the choicest vine.
And He built a tower in the middle of it
And also hewed out a wine vat in it;
Then He expected *it* to produce *good* grapes,
But it produced *only* worthless ones.

5:3 Matt 21:40

5:4 2 Chr 36:16; Jer 2:5; 7:25, 26; Mic 6:3; Matt 23:37

5:5 Ps 89:40; Ps 80:12; Is 10:6; 28:18; Lam 1:15; Luke 21:24; Rev 11:2

5:6 2 Chr 36:19-21; Is 7:19-25; 24:1, 3; Jer 25:11; 1 Kin 8:35; 17:1; Jer 14:1-22

5:7 Ps 80:8-11; Is 3:14, 15; 30:12; 59:13

3 "And now, O inhabitants of Jerusalem and men of Judah,
Judge between Me and My vineyard.
4 "What more was there to do for My vineyard that I have not done in it?
Why, when I expected *it* to produce *good* grapes did it produce worthless ones?
5 "So now let Me tell you what I am going to do to My vineyard:
I will remove its hedge and it will be consumed;
I will break down its wall and it will become trampled ground.
6 "I will lay it waste;
It will not be pruned or hoed,
But briars and thorns will come up.
I will also charge the clouds to rain no rain on it."

7 For the vineyard of the LORD of hosts is the house of Israel
And the men of Judah His delightful plant.
Thus He looked for justice, but behold, bloodshed;
For righteousness, but behold, a cry of distress.

5:8 Jer 22:13-17; Mic 2:2; Hab 2:9-12

5:9 Is 6:11, 12; Matt 23:38

5:10 Lev 26:26; Is 7:23; Hag 1:6; 2:16; Ezek 45:11

5:11 Prov 23:29, 30; Eccl 10:16, 17; Is 5:22; 22:13; 28:1, 3, 7, 8

5:12 Amos 6:5, 6; Job 34:27; Ps 28:5

Woes for the Wicked

8 Woe to those who add house to house *and* join field to field,
Until there is no more room,
So that you have to live alone in the midst of the land!
9 In my ears the LORD of hosts *has sworn,* "Surely, many houses shall become
desolate,
Even great and fine ones, without occupants.
10 "For ten acres of vineyard will yield *only* one [1]bath *of wine,*
And a homer of seed will yield *but* an [2]ephah of grain."
11 Woe to those who rise early in the morning that they may pursue strong drink,
Who stay up late in the evening that wine may inflame them!
12 Their banquets are *accompanied* by lyre and harp, by tambourine and flute, and
by wine;

1 I.e. Approx 10 1/2 gal. **2** I.e. Approx one bu

5:1–7 The lesson of the song of the vineyard shows that God's chosen nation was to bear fruit—to carry out his work, to uphold justice. It did bear fruit, but the fruit was bad. This passage uses plays on words: the Hebrew words for *justice* and *bloodshed* sound very much alike, as do those for *righteousness* and *distress.* Jesus said, "You will know them by their fruits" (Matthew 7:20). Have you examined your own "fruit" lately? Is it good or bad—useful or wild?

5:8–25 In this section, God condemns six sins: (1) exploiting others (5:8–10); (2) drunkenness (5:11–12); (3) taking sarcastic pride in sin (5:18–19); (4) confusing moral standards (5:20); (5) being conceited (5:21); (6) perverting justice (5:22–24). Because of these sins, God punished Israel with destruction by Assyria (5:25–30). A similar fate was awaiting Judah if they didn't turn from these sins.

5:11–13 These people spent many hours drinking and partying, but Isaiah predicted that eventually many would die of hunger and thirst. Ironically, our pleasures—if they do not have God's blessing—may destroy us. Leaving God out of our lives allows sin to come into them. God wants us to enjoy life (1 Timothy 6:17) but to avoid those activities that could lead us away from him.

But they do not pay attention to the deeds of the LORD,
Nor do they consider the work of His hands.

13 Therefore My people go into exile for their lack of knowledge;
And their honorable men are famished,
And their multitude is parched with thirst.
14 Therefore Sheol has enlarged its throat and opened its mouth without measure;
And Jerusalem's splendor, her multitude, her din *of revelry* and the jubilant within her, descend *into it.*
15 So the *common* man will be humbled and the man of *importance* abased,
The eyes of the proud also will be abased.
16 But the LORD of hosts will be exalted in judgment,
And the holy God will show Himself holy in righteousness.
17 Then the lambs will graze as in their pasture,
And strangers will eat in the waste places of the wealthy.

18 Woe to those who drag iniquity with the cords of falsehood,
And sin as if with cart ropes;
19 Who say, "Let Him make speed, let Him hasten His work, that we may see *it;*
And let the purpose of the Holy One of Israel draw near
And come to pass, that we may know *it!*"
20 Woe to those who call evil good, and good evil;
Who substitute darkness for light and light for darkness;
Who substitute bitter for sweet and sweet for bitter!
21 Woe to those who are wise in their own eyes
And clever in their own sight!
22 Woe to those who are heroes in drinking wine
And valiant men in mixing strong drink,
23 Who justify the wicked for a bribe,
And take away the rights of the ones who are in the right!

24 Therefore, as a tongue of fire consumes stubble
And dry grass collapses into the flame,
So their root will become like rot and their blossom blow away as dust;
For they have rejected the law of the LORD of hosts
And despised the word of the Holy One of Israel.
25 On this account the anger of the LORD has burned against His people,
And He has stretched out His hand against them and struck them down.
And the mountains quaked, and their corpses lay like refuse in the middle of the streets.
For all this His anger is not spent,
But His hand is still stretched out.

5:13 Is 1:3; 27:11; Hos 4:6; Is 3:3

5:14 Prov 30:16; Hab 2:5

5:15 Is 2:11; 10:33

5:16 Is 28:17; 30:18; 61:8; Is 2:11, 17; 33:5, 10; Is 8:13; 29:23; 1 Pet 3:15

5:17 Is 7:25; Mic 2:12; Zeph 2:6

5:18 Is 59:4-8; Jer 23:10-14

5:19 Ezek 12:22; 2 Pet 3:4

5:20 Prov 17:15; Amos 5:7; Job 17:12; Matt 6:22, 23; Luke 11:34, 35

5:21 Prov 3:7; Rom 12:16; 1 Cor 3:18-20

5:22 Prov 23:20; Is 5:11; 56:12; Hab 2:15

5:23 Ex 23:8; Is 1:23; 10:1, 2; Mic 3:11; 7:3; Ps 94:21; James 5:6

5:24 Is 9:18, 19; Joel 2:5; Job 18:16; Hos 5:12; Is 8:6; 30:9, 12; Acts 13:41

5:25 2 Kin 22:13, 17; Is 66:15; Ps 18:7; Is 64:3; Jer 4:24; Nah 1:5; 2 Kin 9:37; Is 14:19; Jer 16:4; Is 9:12, 17, 19, 21; 10:4; Jer 4:8; Dan 9:16; Ex 7:19; Is 23:11

5:13 The nation's heroes—the "honorable men"—would suffer the same humiliation as the common people. Why? Because they lived by their own values rather than God's. Many of today's media and sports heroes are idolized because of their ability to live as they please. Are your heroes those who defy God, or those who defy the world in order to serve God?

5:18–19 Some people drag their sins around with them. Some do so arrogantly, but for others, their sins have become a burden that wears them out. Are you dragging around a cartload of sins that you refuse to give up? Before you find yourself worn out and useless, turn to the One who promises to take away your burden of sin and replace it with a purpose for living that is a joy to fulfill (see Matthew 11:28–30).

5:20 When people do not carefully observe the distinction between good and evil, destruction soon follows. It is easy for people to say, "No one can decide for anyone else what is really right or wrong." They may think getting drunk can't hurt them, extramarital sex isn't really wrong, or money doesn't control them. But when we make excuses for our actions, we break down the distinction between right and wrong. If we do not take God's Word, the Bible, as our standard, soon all moral choices will appear fuzzy. Without God, we are headed for a breakdown and much suffering.

5:24 The people suffered because they rejected God's Law. It is sad to see so many people today searching for meaning in life while spurning God's Word. We can avoid the error of Israel and Judah by making reading the Bible a high priority in our lives.

5:26 Is 13:2, 3; Is 7:18; Zech 10:8; Deut 28:49; Is 13:4, 5

26 He will also lift up a standard to the distant nation,
And will whistle for it from the ends of the earth;
And behold, it will come with speed swiftly.

5:27 Joel 2:7, 8; Job 12:18

27 No one in it is weary or stumbles,
None slumbers or sleeps;
Nor is the belt at its waist undone,
Nor its sandal strap broken.

5:28 Ps 7:12, 13; 45:5; Is 13:18; Is 21:1; Jer 4:13

28 Its arrows are sharp and all its bows are bent;
The hoofs of its horses seem like flint and its *chariot* wheels like a whirlwind.

5:29 Jer 51:38; Zeph 3:3; Zech 11:3; Is 10:6; 49:24, 25; Mic 5:8; Is 42:22

29 Its roaring is like a lioness, and it roars like young lions;
It growls as it seizes the prey
And carries *it* off with no one to deliver *it.*

5:30 Is 17:12; Jer 6:23; Luke 21:25; Is 8:22; Jer 4:23-28; Joel 2:10; Luke 21:25, 26

30 And it will growl over it in that day like the roaring of the sea.
If one looks to the land, behold, there is darkness *and* distress;
Even the light is darkened by its clouds.

Isaiah's Vision

6:1 2 Kin 15:7; 2 Chr 26:23; Is 1:1; John 12:41; Rev 4:2, 3; 20:11

6 In the year of King Uzziah's death I saw the Lord sitting on a throne, lofty and exalted, with the train of His robe filling the temple.

6:2 Rev 4:8

2 Seraphim stood above Him, each having six wings: with two he covered his face,
and with two he covered his feet, and with two he flew.

6:3 Rev 4:8; Num 14:21; Ps 72:19

3 And one called out to another and said,
"Holy, Holy, Holy, is the LORD of hosts,
The whole earth is full of His glory."

6:4 Rev 15:8

4 And the foundations of the thresholds trembled at the voice of him who called out,
while the temple was filling with smoke.

6:5 Ex 33:20; Luke 5:8; Ex 6:12, 30; Is 59:3; Jer 9:3-8; Jer 51:57

5 Then I said,
"Woe is me, for I am ruined!
Because I am a man of unclean lips,
And I live among a people of unclean lips;
For my eyes have seen the King, the LORD of hosts."

6:6 Rev 8:3

6 Then one of the seraphim flew to me with a burning coal in his hand, which he had
taken from the altar with tongs.

6:7 Jer 1:9; Dan 10:16; Is 40:2; 53:5, 6, 11; 1 John 1:7

7 He touched my mouth *with it* and said, "Behold, this has touched your lips; and your
iniquity is taken away and your sin is forgiven."

5:26–30 This passage describes what God would do if the people disobeyed him (Deuteronomy 28). Assyria began to torment Israel during the reign of Ahaz (735—715 B.C.). This powerful aggressor destroyed the northern kingdom in 722 B.C. and scattered the people throughout its own empire. Sin has consequences. Although this judgment was not immediate, eventually Israel was punished.

6:1 The year of King Uzziah's death was approximately 740 B.C. He remained leprous until he died because he tried to take over the high priest's duties (2 Chronicles 26:18–21). Although Uzziah was generally a good king with a long and prosperous reign, many of his people turned away from God.

6:1ff Isaiah's vision was his commission to be God's messenger to his people. Isaiah was given a difficult mission. He had to tell people who believed they were blessed by God that instead God was going to destroy them because of their disobedience.

6:1ff Isaiah's lofty view of God in 6:1–4 gives us a sense of God's greatness, mystery, and power. Isaiah's example of recognizing his sinfulness before God encourages us to confess our sin. His picture of forgiveness reminds us that we, too, are forgiven. When we recognize how great our God is, how sinful we are, and the extent of God's forgiveness, we receive power to do his work. How does your concept of the greatness of God measure up to Isaiah's?

6:1–3 The throne, the attending seraphim or angels, and the threefold *holy* all stressed God's holiness. Seraphim were a type of angel whose name is derived from the word for "burn," perhaps indicating their purity as God's ministers. In a time when moral and spiritual decay had peaked, it was important for Isaiah to see God in his holiness. Holiness means morally perfect, pure, and set apart from all sin. We also need to discover God's holiness. Our daily frustrations, society's pressures, and our shortcomings reduce and narrow our view of God. We need the Bible's view of God as high and lifted up to empower us to deal with our problems and concerns. God's moral perfection, properly seen, will purify us from sin, cleanse our minds from our problems, and enable us to worship and to serve.

6:5–8 Seeing the Lord and listening to the praise of the angels, Isaiah realized that he was unclean before God, with no hope of measuring up to God's standard of holiness. When Isaiah's lips were touched with a live burning coal, however, he was told that his sins were forgiven. It wasn't the coal that cleansed him, but God. In response Isaiah submitted himself entirely to God's service. No matter how difficult his task would be, he said, "Here am I. Send me!" The painful cleansing process was necessary before Isaiah could fulfill the task to which God was calling him. Before we accept God's call to speak for him to those around us, we must be cleansed as Isaiah was, confessing our sins and submitting to God's control. Letting God purify us may be painful, but we must be purified so that we can truly represent God, who is pure and holy.

Isaiah's Commission

8 Then I heard the voice of the Lord, saying, "Whom shall I send, and who will go for
Us?" Then I said, "Here am I. Send me!"
9 He said, "Go, and tell this people:
'Keep on listening, but do not perceive;
Keep on looking, but do not understand.'
10 "Render the hearts of this people insensitive,
Their ears dull,
And their eyes dim,
Otherwise they might see with their eyes,
Hear with their ears,
Understand with their hearts,
And return and be healed."
11 Then I said, "Lord, how long?" And He answered,
"Until cities are devastated *and* without inhabitant,
Houses are without people
And the land is utterly desolate,
12 "The LORD has removed men far away,
And the forsaken places are many in the midst of the land.
13 "Yet there will be a tenth portion in it,
And it will again be *subject* to burning,
Like a terebinth or an oak
Whose stump remains when it is felled.
The holy seed is its stump."

War against Jerusalem

7 Now it came about in the days of Ahaz, the son of Jotham, the son of Uzziah, king of
Judah, that Rezin the king of Aram and Pekah the son of Remaliah, king of Israel,
went up to Jerusalem to *wage* war against it, but could not conquer it.
2 When it was reported to the house of David, saying, "The Arameans have camped
in Ephraim," his heart and the hearts of his people shook as the trees of the forest shake
with the wind.
3 Then the LORD said to Isaiah, "Go out now to meet Ahaz, you and your son Shear-
jashub, at the end of the conduit of the upper pool, on the highway to the fuller's field,
4 and say to him, 'Take care and be calm, have no fear and do not be fainthearted

6:8 Ezek 10:5; Acts 9:4; Acts 26:19
6:9 Is 43:8; Matt 13:14; Mark 4:12; Luke 8:10; John 12:40; Acts 28:26; Rom 11:8
6:10 Matt 13:15; Deut 31:20; 32:15; Jer 5:21
6:11 Ps 79:5; Lev 26:31; Is 1:7; 3:8, 26
6:12 Deut 28:64; Jer 4:29
6:13 Job 14:7; Deut 7:6; Ezra 9:2
7:1 2 Kin 16:1; Is 1:1; 2 Kin 15:37; 2 Kin 15:25; 2 Chr 28:6; Is 7:6, 7
7:2 Is 7:13; 22:22; Is 8:12; Is 9:9
7:3 2 Kin 18:17; Is 36:2
7:4 Ex 14:13; Is 30:15; Lam 3:26; Is 10:24; Matt 24:6; Deut 20:3; 1 Sam 17:32; Is 35:4; Amos 4:11; Zech 3:2; Is 7:1, 9

6:8 The more clearly Isaiah saw God (6:5), the more aware Isaiah became of his own powerlessness and inadequacy to do anything of lasting value without God. But he was willing to be God's spokesman. When God calls, will you also say, "Here am I. Send me!"?

6:9–13 God told Isaiah that the people would listen but not learn from his message because their hearts had become insensitive (hardened) beyond repentance. God's patience with their chronic rebellion was finally exhausted. His judgment was to abandon them to their rebellion and hardness of heart. Why did God send Isaiah if he knew the people wouldn't listen? Although the nation itself would not repent and would reap judgment, some individuals would listen. In 6:13 God explains his plan for a remnant (holy seed) of faithful followers. God is merciful even when he judges. We can gain encouragement from God's promise to preserve his people. If we are faithful to him we can be sure of his mercy.

6:11–13 When would the people listen? Only after they had come to the end and had nowhere to turn but to God. This would happen when the land was destroyed by invading armies and the people taken into captivity. The "tenth" refers either to those who remained in the land after the captivity, or those who returned from Babylon to rebuild the land. Each group was about a tenth of the total population. When will we listen to God? Must we, like Judah, go through calamities before we will listen to God's words? Consider what God may be telling you, and obey him before time runs out.

7:1 The year was 734 B.C. Ahaz, king of Judah in Jerusalem, was about to be attacked by an alliance of the northern kingdom of Israel and Aram. He was frightened by the possible end of his reign and by the invading armies who killed many people or took them as captives (2 Chronicles 28:5–21). But, as Isaiah predicted, the kingdom of Judah did not come to an end at this time. The sign of Immanuel would be a sign of deliverance.

7:2 "The house of David" refers to Judah, the southern kingdom. "Ephraim," the dominant tribe in the north, is a reference to Israel, the northern kingdom.

7:3 *Shear-jashub* means "a remnant will return." God told Isaiah to give his son this name as a reminder of his plan for mercy. From the beginning of God's judgment he planned to restore a remnant of his people. Shear-jashub was a reminder to the people of God's faithfulness to them.

7:3 The "conduit of the upper pool" may have been the site of the Gihon spring, located east of Jerusalem. The Gihon spring was the main source of water for the holy city, and was also the spring that emptied into Hezekiah's famous water tunnel (2 Chronicles 32:30). The fuller's field was a well-known place where clothing or newly woven cloth was laid in the sun to dry and whiten (see 36:2).

7:4—8:15 Isaiah predicted the breakup of Israel's alliance with Aram (7:4–9). Because of this alliance, Israel would be destroyed; Assyria would be the instrument God would use to destroy them (7:8–25) and to punish Judah. But God would not let Assyria destroy Judah (8:1–15). They would be spared because God's gracious plans cannot be thwarted.

because of these two stubs of smoldering firebrands, on account of the fierce anger of
Rezin and Aram and the son of Remaliah.

7:5 Is 7:2

5 'Because Aram, *with* Ephraim and the son of Remaliah, has planned evil against you,
saying,

7:7 Is 8:10; 28:18; Acts 4:25, 26

6 "Let us go up against Judah and terrorize it, and make for ourselves a breach in its
walls and set up the son of Tabeel as king in the midst of it,"
7 thus says the Lord GOD: "It shall not stand nor shall it come to pass.

7:8 Gen 14:15; Is 17:1-3

8 "For the head of Aram is Damascus and the head of Damascus is Rezin (now within
another 65 years Ephraim will be shattered, *so that it is* no longer a people),

7:9 2 Chr 20:20; Is 5:24; 8:6-8; 30:12-14

9 and the head of Ephraim is Samaria and the head of Samaria is the son of Remaliah. If you will not believe, you surely shall not last." ' "

ISAIAH

Trees and prophets share at least one important characteristic—both are planted for the future. Yet seedlings are often overlooked and prophets often ignored. Isaiah is one of the best examples of this. The people of his time could have been rescued by his words. Instead, they refused to believe him. With the passing of centuries, however, Isaiah's words have cast a shadow on all of history.

Isaiah was active as a prophet during the reigns of five kings, but he did not set out to be a prophet. By the time King Uzziah died, Isaiah may have been established as a scribe in the royal palace in Jerusalem. It was a respectable career, but God had other plans for his servant. Isaiah's account of God's call leaves little doubt about what motivated the prophet for the next half century. His vision of God was unforgettable.

The encounter with God permanently affected Isaiah's character. He reflected the God he represented. Isaiah's messages—some comforting, some confronting—are so distinct that some have guessed they came from different authors. Isaiah's testimony is that the messages came from the only One capable of being perfect in justice as well as in mercy—God himself.

When he called Isaiah as a prophet, God did not encourage him with predictions of great success. God told Isaiah that the people would not listen. But he was to speak and write his messages anyway because eventually some *would* listen. God compared his people to a tree that would have to be cut down so that a new tree could grow from the old stump (Isaiah 6:13).

We who are part of that future can see that many of the promises God gave through Isaiah have been fulfilled in Jesus Christ. We also gain the hope of knowing that God is active in all of history, including our own.

Strengths and accomplishments:
- Considered the greatest Old Testament prophet
- Quoted at least 50 times in the New Testament
- Had powerful messages of both judgment and hope
- Carried out a consistent ministry even though there was little positive response from his listeners
- His ministry spanned the reigns of five kings of Judah

Lessons from his life:
- God's help is needed in order to effectively confront sin while comforting people
- One result of experiencing forgiveness is the desire to share that forgiveness with others
- God is purely and perfectly holy, just, and loving

Vital statistics:
- Where: Jerusalem
- Occupations: Scribe, prophet
- Relatives: Father: Amoz. Sons: Shear-jashub, Maher-shalal-hash-baz
- Contemporaries: Uzziah, Jotham, Ahaz, Hezekiah, Manasseh, Micah

Key verse:
"Then I heard the voice of the Lord, saying, 'Whom shall I send, and who will go for Us?' Then I said, 'Here am I. Send me!' " (Isaiah 6:8).

Isaiah's story is told in 2 Kings 19:2—20:19. He is also mentioned in 2 Chronicles 26:22; 32:20, 32; Matthew 3:3; 8:17; 12:17–21; John 12:38–41; Romans 10:16, 20–21.

7:8 Ahaz, one of Judah's worst kings, refused God's help and, instead, he tried to buy aid from the Assyrians with silver and gold from the temple (2 Kings 16:8). When the Assyrians came, they brought further trouble instead of help. In 722 B.C., Samaria, the capital of Ephraim (another name for Israel, the northern kingdom), fell to the Assyrian armies, thus ending the northern kingdom.

The Child Immanuel

10 Then the LORD spoke again to Ahaz, saying,
11 "Ask a sign for yourself from the LORD your God; make *it* deep as Sheol or high as
heaven."
12 But Ahaz said, "I will not ask, nor will I test the LORD!"
13 Then he said, "Listen now, O house of David! Is it too slight a thing for you to try
the patience of men, that you will try the patience of my God as well?
14 "Therefore the Lord Himself will give you a sign: Behold, a virgin will be with child
and bear a son, and she will call His name [3]Immanuel.
15 "He will eat curds and honey at the time He knows *enough* to refuse evil and choose
good.
16 "For before the boy will know *enough* to refuse evil and choose good, the land whose
two kings you dread will be forsaken.

Trials to Come for Judah

17 "The LORD will bring on you, on your people, and on your father's house such days
as have never come since the day that Ephraim separated from Judah, the king of
Assyria."
18 In that day the LORD will whistle for the fly that is in the remotest part of the rivers
of Egypt and for the bee that is in the land of Assyria.
19 They will all come and settle on the steep ravines, on the ledges of the cliffs, on all
the thorn bushes and on all the watering places.
20 In that day the Lord will shave with a razor, hired from regions beyond the Euphrates (*that is,* with the king of Assyria), the head and the hair of the legs; and it will also
remove the beard.
21 Now in that day a man may keep alive a heifer and a pair of sheep;
22 and because of the abundance of the milk produced he will eat curds, for everyone
that is left within the land will eat curds and honey.
23 And it will come about in that day, that every place where there used to be a thousand vines, *valued* at a thousand *shekels* of silver, will become briars and thorns.
24 *People* will come there with bows and arrows because all the land will be briars and
thorns.
25 As for all the hills which used to be cultivated with the hoe, you will not go there for
fear of briars and thorns; but they will become a place for pasturing oxen and for sheep
to trample.

7:11 2 Kin 19:29; Is 37:30; 38:7, 8; 55:13
7:13 Is 7:2; Is 1:14; 43:24; Is 25:1
7:14 Matt 1:23; Is 8:8, 10
7:15 Is 7:22
7:16 Is 8:4; Is 8:14; 17:3; Jer 7:15; Hos 5:3, 9, 14; Amos 1:3-5
7:17 1 Kin 12:16; 2 Chr 28:20; Is 8:7, 8; 10:5, 6
7:18 Is 5:26; Is 13:5
7:19 Is 2:19; Jer 16:16; Is 7:24, 25
7:20 2 Kin 18:13-16; Is 24:1; Ezek 5:1-4; Is 10:5, 15; Is 8:7; 11:15; Jer 2:18
7:21 Is 14:30; 27:10; Jer 39:10
7:22 Is 8:15
7:23 Is 5:10; 32:13, 14; Is 5:6
7:25 Is 5:17

3 I.e. God is with us

7:12 Ahaz appeared righteous by saying he would not test God with a sign ("I will not ask, nor will I test the LORD"). In fact, God had told him to ask, but Ahaz didn't really want to know what God would say. Often we use some excuse, such as not wanting to bother God, to keep us from communicating with him. Don't let anything keep you from hearing and obeying God.

7:14–16 *Virgin* is translated from a Hebrew word used for an unmarried woman old enough to be married, one who is sexually mature (see Genesis 24:43; Exodus 2:8; Psalm 68:25; Proverbs 30:19; Song of Solomon 1:3; 6:8). Some have compared this young woman to Isaiah's young wife and newborn son (8:1–4). This is not likely because she had a child, Shear-jashub, and her second child was not named Immanuel. Some believe that Isaiah's first wife may have died, and so this is his second wife. It is more likely that this prophecy had a double fulfillment. (1) A young woman from the house of Ahaz who was not married would marry and have a son. Before three years passed (one year for pregnancy and two for the child to be old enough to talk), the two invading kings would be destroyed. (2) Matthew 1:23 quotes Isaiah 7:14 to show a further fulfillment of this prophecy in that a virgin named Mary conceived and bore a son, Immanuel, the Christ.

7:18 Flies and bees are symbols of God's judgment (see Exodus 23:28). Egypt and Assyria did not at this time devastate Judah. Hezekiah followed Ahaz as king, and he honored God; therefore God held back his hand of judgment. Two more evil kings reigned before Josiah, of whom it was said that no other king turned so completely to the Lord (2 Kings 23:25). However, Judah's doom had been sealed by the extreme evil of Josiah's father, Amon. During Josiah's reign, Egypt marched against the Assyrians. Josiah then declared war on Egypt, though God told him not to. After Josiah was killed (2 Chronicles 35:20–27), only weak kings reigned in Judah. The Egyptians carried off Josiah's son, Jehoahaz (Joahaz), after three months. The next king, Jehoiakim, was taken by Nebuchadnezzar to Babylon. Egypt and Assyria had dealt death blows to Judah.

7:20 Hiring Assyria to save them would be Judah's downfall (2 Kings 16:7–8). To "shave" Judah's hair was symbolic of total humiliation. Numbers 6:9 explains that after being defiled, a person who had been set apart for the Lord had to shave his head as part of the cleansing process. Shaving bodily hair was an embarrassment—an exposure of nakedness. For a Hebrew man, having his beard shaved was humiliating (2 Samuel 10:4–5).

7:21–25 Judah's rich farmland would be trampled until it became pastureland fit only for grazing. No longer would it be a place of agricultural abundance, a land "flowing with milk and honey" (Exodus 3:8), but a land with only curds, briars, and thorns.

Damascus and Samaria Fall

8 Then the LORD said to me, "Take for yourself a large tablet and write on it in ordinary letters: Swift is the booty, speedy is the prey.
2 "And I will take to Myself faithful witnesses for testimony, Uriah the priest and Zechariah the son of Jeberechiah."
3 So I approached the prophetess, and she conceived and gave birth to a son. Then
the LORD said to me, "Name him [4]Maher-shalal-hash-baz;
4 for before the boy knows how to cry out 'My father' or 'My mother,' the wealth of
Damascus and the spoil of Samaria will be carried away before the king of Assyria."
5 Again the LORD spoke to me further, saying,

6 "Inasmuch as these people have rejected the gently flowing waters of Shiloah
And rejoice in Rezin and the son of Remaliah;
7 "Now therefore, behold, the Lord is about to bring on them the strong and
abundant waters of the Euphrates,
Even the king of Assyria and all his glory;
And it will rise up over all its channels and go over all its banks.
8 "Then it will sweep on into Judah, it will overflow and pass through,
It will reach even to the neck;
And the spread of its wings will fill the breadth of your land, O Immanuel.

A Believing Remnant

9 "Be broken, O peoples, and be shattered;
And give ear, all remote places of the earth.
Gird yourselves, yet be shattered;
Gird yourselves, yet be shattered.
10 "Devise a plan, but it will be thwarted;
State a proposal, but it will not stand,
For God is with us."

11 For thus the LORD spoke to me with mighty power and instructed me not to walk in
the way of this people, saying,

12 "You are not to say, '*It is* a conspiracy!'
In regard to all that this people call a conspiracy,
And you are not to fear what they fear or be in dread of *it.*
13 "It is the LORD of hosts whom you should regard as holy.
And He shall be your fear,
And He shall be your dread.
14 "Then He shall become a sanctuary;
But to both the houses of Israel, a stone to strike and a rock to stumble over,
And a snare and a trap for the inhabitants of Jerusalem.
15 "Many will stumble over them,
Then they will fall and be broken;
They will even be snared and caught."

16 Bind up the testimony, seal the law among my disciples.

4 I.e. swift is the booty, speedy is the prey

8:1 Is 30:8; Hab 2:2; Is 8:3
8:2 2 Kin 16:10, 11, 15, 16
8:3 Is 8:1
8:4 Is 7:16; Is 7:8, 9
8:6 Is 1:20; 5:24; 7:9; 30:12; Is 7:1
8:7 Is 17:12, 13; Is 7:20; 11:15; Is 7:17; 10:5; Amos 8:8; 9:5
8:8 Is 10:6; Is 30:28; Is 7:14
8:9 Is 17:12-14; Dan 2:34, 35
8:10 Job 5:12; Is 28:18; Is 7:7; Is 8:8; Rom 8:31
8:11 Ezek 3:14; Ezek 2:8
8:12 Is 7:2; 30:1; 1 Pet 3:14, 15
8:13 Is 5:16; 29:23; Num 20:12
8:14 Is 4:6; 25:4; Ezek 11:16; Luke 2:34; Rom 9:33; 1 Pet 2:8; Is 24:17, 18
8:15 Is 28:13; 59:10; Luke 20:18; Rom 9:32
8:16 Is 8:1, 2; 29:11, 12; Dan 12:4; Is 50:4

8:1–4 These verses predict the fall of Israel and Aram. Aram fell to Assyria in 732 B.C., and Israel followed in 722 B.C. Isaiah put his message on a large scroll in a public place. God was warning all his people.

8:6–8 "The gently flowing waters of Shiloah" refers to God's gentle and sustaining care. Because Judah rejected God's kindness, choosing instead to seek help from other nations, God would punish them. We see two distinct attributes of God—his love and his wrath. To ignore his love and guidance results in sin and invites his wrath. We must recognize the consequences of our choices. God wants to protect us from bad choices, but he still gives us the freedom to make them.

8:7–8 The heart of the Assyrian empire was located between the Tigris and Euphrates Rivers. This flood is a poetic way of describing the overwhelming force of the Assyrian army.

8:9 To "be shattered" means to lose courage by the pressure of sudden fear.

8:11–15 Isaiah, along with most of the prophets, was viewed as a traitor because he did not support Judah's national policies. He called the people to commit themselves first to God, and then to the king. He even predicted the overthrow of the government.

8:16 "Bind up the testimony" and "seal the law" mean that the words would be written down and preserved for future generations. Because some people faithfully passed on these words from generation to generation, we have the book of Isaiah today. Each of us needs to accept the responsibility to pass on God's Word to our children and grandchildren, encouraging them to love the Bible, read it, and learn from it. Then they will faithfully pass it on to their children and grandchildren.

17 And I will wait for the LORD who is hiding His face from the house of Jacob; I will
even look eagerly for Him.
18 Behold, I and the children whom the LORD has given me are for signs and wonders
in Israel from the LORD of hosts, who dwells on Mount Zion.
19 When they say to you, "Consult the mediums and the spiritists who whisper and
mutter," should not a people consult their God? *Should they consult* the dead on behalf
of the living?
20 To the law and to the testimony! If they do not speak according to this word, it is
because they have no dawn.
21 They will pass through the land hard-pressed and famished, and it will turn out that
when they are hungry, they will be enraged and curse their king and their God as they
face upward.
22 Then they will look to the earth, and behold, distress and darkness, the gloom of
anguish; and *they will be* driven away into darkness.

8:17 Is 25:9; 30:18; Hab 2:3; Deut 31:17; Is 1:15; 45:15; 54:8

8:18 Heb 2:13; Luke 2:34; Ps 9:11; Zech 8:3

8:19 Lev 20:6; 2 Kin 21:6; 23:24; Is 19:3; 29:4; 47:12, 13; Is 30:2; 45:11; 1 Sam 28:8-11

8:20 Is 1:10; 8:16; Luke 16:29; Is 8:22; Mic 3:6

8:21 Is 9:20, 21

8:22 Is 5:30; 59:9; Jer 13:16; Amos 5:18, 20; Zeph 1:14, 15; Is 8:20

Birth and Reign of the Prince of Peace

9 But there will be no *more* gloom for her who was in anguish; in earlier times He treated
the land of Zebulun and the land of Naphtali with contempt, but later on He shall
make *it* glorious, by the way of the sea, on the other side of Jordan, Galilee of the Gentiles.

2 The people who walk in darkness
Will see a great light;
Those who live in a dark land,
The light will shine on them.
3 You shall multiply the nation,
You shall increase their gladness;
They will be glad in Your presence
As with the gladness of harvest,
As men rejoice when they divide the spoil.
4 For You shall break the yoke of their burden and the staff on their shoulders,
The rod of their oppressor, as at the battle of Midian.
5 For every boot of the booted warrior in the *battle* tumult,
And cloak rolled in blood, will be for burning, fuel for the fire.
6 For a child will be born to us, a son will be given to us;
And the government will rest on His shoulders;
And His name will be called Wonderful Counselor, Mighty God,
Eternal Father, Prince of Peace.
7 There will be no end to the increase of *His* government or of peace,
On the throne of David and over his kingdom,
To establish it and to uphold it with justice and righteousness
From then on and forevermore.
The zeal of the LORD of hosts will accomplish this.

9:1 Is 8:22; 2 Kin 15:29; 2 Chr 16:4; Matt 4:15, 16

9:2 Matt 4:16; Luke 1:79; Eph 5:8

9:3 Is 26:15; Is 35:10; 65:14, 18, 19; 66:10; 1 Sam 30:16

9:4 Is 10:27; 14:25; Is 14:4; 49:26; 51:13; 54:14; Judg 7:25; Is 10:26

9:6 Is 7:14; 11:1, 2; 53:2; Luke 2:11; John 3:16; Matt 28:18; 1 Cor 15:25; Is 22:22; Is 28:29; Deut 10:17; Neh 9:32; Is 10:21; Is 63:16; 64:8; Is 26:3, 12; 54:10; 66:12

9:7 Dan 2:44; Luke 1:32, 33; Is 16:5; Is 11:4, 5; 32:1; 42:3, 4; 63:1; Is 37:32; 59:17

8:17 Isaiah decided to wait for the Lord, though God was "hiding His face from the house of Jacob." Many of the prophecies God gave through the prophets would not come true for 700 years; others still haven't been fulfilled. Are you willing to accept the Lord's timing, not yours?

8:19 The people would consult mediums and spiritists to seek answers from dead people instead of consulting the living God. God alone knows the future, and only he is eternal. We can trust God to guide us.

8:21 After rejecting God's plan for them, the people of Judah would blame God for their trials. People continually blame God for their self-induced problems. How do you respond to the unpleasant results of your own choices? Where do you fix the blame? Instead of blaming God, look for ways to grow through your failures.

9:1 In our gloom and despair, we fear that our sorrows and troubles will never end. But we can take comfort in this certainty: although the Lord may not always take us around our troubles, if we follow him wholeheartedly, he will lead us safely through them.

9:1–7 This child who would become their deliverer is the Messiah, Jesus. Matthew quotes these verses in describing Christ's ministry (Matthew 4:15–16). The territories of Zebulun and Naphtali represent the northern kingdom as a whole. These were also the territories where Jesus grew up and often ministered; this is why "upon them a Light dawned."

9:2 The apostle John also referred to Jesus as the "true Light" (John 1:9). Jesus referred to himself as "the Light of the world" (John 8:12).

9:2–6 In a time of great darkness, God promised to send a light who would shine on everyone living in the shadow of death. He is both "Wonderful Counselor" and "Mighty God." This message of hope was fulfilled in the birth of Christ and the establishment of his eternal kingdom. He came to deliver all people from their slavery to sin.

God's Anger with Israel's Arrogance

8 The Lord sends a message against Jacob,
And it falls on Israel.

9 And all the people know *it,*
That is, Ephraim and the inhabitants of Samaria,
Asserting in pride and in arrogance of heart:

10 "The bricks have fallen down,
But we will rebuild with smooth stones;
The sycamores have been cut down,
But we will replace *them* with cedars."

11 Therefore the LORD raises against them adversaries from Rezin
And spurs their enemies on,

12 The Arameans on the east and the Philistines on the west;
And they devour Israel with gaping jaws.
In *spite of* all this, His anger does not turn away
And His hand is still stretched out.

13 Yet the people do not turn back to Him who struck them,
Nor do they seek the LORD of hosts.

14 So the LORD cuts off head and tail from Israel,
Both palm branch and bulrush in a single day.

15 The head is the elder and honorable man,
And the prophet who teaches falsehood is the tail.

16 For those who guide this people are leading *them* astray;
And those who are guided by them are brought to confusion.

17 Therefore the Lord does not take pleasure in their young men,
Nor does He have pity on their orphans or their widows;
For every one of them is godless and an evildoer,
And every mouth is speaking foolishness.
In *spite of* all this, His anger does not turn away
And His hand is still stretched out.

18 For wickedness burns like a fire;
It consumes briars and thorns;
It even sets the thickets of the forest aflame
And they roll upward in a column of smoke.

19 By the fury of the LORD of hosts the land is burned up,
And the people are like fuel for the fire;
No man spares his brother.

20 They slice off *what is* on the right hand but *still* are hungry,
And they eat *what is* on the left hand but they are not satisfied;
Each of them eats the flesh of his own arm.

21 Manasseh *devours* Ephraim, and Ephraim Manasseh,
And together they are against Judah.

9:9 Is 7:8, 9; 28:1, 3; Is 46:12
9:10 Mal 1:4
9:11 Is 7:1, 8
9:12 2 Chr 28:18; Ps 79:7; Jer 10:25; Is 5:25
9:13 Jer 5:3; Hos 7:10; Is 31:1; Hos 3:5
9:14 Is 19:15; Rev 18:8
9:15 Is 3:2, 3; Is 28:15; 59:3, 4; Jer 23:14, 32; Matt 24:24
9:16 Is 3:12; Matt 15:14; 23:16, 24
9:17 Jer 18:21; Amos 4:10; 8:13; Is 27:11; Is 10:6; 32:6; Is 1:4; 14:20; 31:2; Matt 12:34; Is 5:25
9:18 Ps 83:14; Is 1:7; Nah 1:10; Mal 4:1
9:19 Is 10:6; 13:9, 13; 42:25; Joel 2:3; Is 1:31; 24:6; Mic 7:2, 6
9:20 Is 8:21, 22; Is 49:26
9:21 2 Chr 28:6, 8; Is 11:13; Is 5:25

NAMES FOR MESSIAH
Isaiah uses four names to describe the Messiah. These names have special meaning to us.

Wonderful Counselor	• He is exceptional, distinguished, and without peer, the one who gives the right advice.
Mighty God	• He is God himself.
Eternal Father	• He is timeless; he is God our Father.
Prince of Peace	• His government is one of justice and peace

9:8–10 Pride made Israel think it would recover and rebuild in its own strength. Even though God made Israel a nation and gave them the land they occupied, the people put their trust in themselves rather than in him. Too often we take pride in our accomplishments, forgetting that it is God who has given us our every resource and ability. We may even become proud of our unique status as Christians. God is not pleased with *any* pride or trust in ourselves because it cuts off our contact with him.

9:21 Ephraim and Manasseh were tribes in the northern kingdom descended from Joseph's two sons. They fought a civil war because of their selfishness and wickedness (see Judges 12:4).

In *spite of* all this, His anger does not turn away
And His hand is still stretched out.

Assyria Is God's Instrument

10 Woe to those who enact evil statutes
And to those who constantly record unjust decisions,
2 So as to deprive the needy of justice
And rob the poor of My people of *their* rights,
So that widows may be their spoil
And that they may plunder the orphans.
3 Now what will you do in the day of punishment,
And in the devastation which will come from afar?
To whom will you flee for help?
And where will you leave your wealth?
4 Nothing *remains* but to crouch among the captives
Or fall among the slain.
In *spite of* all this, His anger does not turn away
And His hand is still stretched out.

5 Woe to Assyria, the rod of My anger
And the staff in whose hands is My indignation,
6 I send it against a godless nation
And commission it against the people of My fury
To capture booty and to seize plunder,
And to trample them down like mud in the streets.
7 Yet it does not so intend,
Nor does it plan so in its heart,
But rather it is its purpose to destroy
And to cut off many nations.
8 For it says, "Are not my princes all kings?
9 "Is not Calno like Carchemish,
Or Hamath like Arpad,
Or Samaria like Damascus?
10 "As my hand has reached to the kingdoms of the idols,
Whose graven images *were* greater than those of Jerusalem and Samaria,
11 Shall I not do to Jerusalem and her images
Just as I have done to Samaria and her idols?"
12 So it will be that when the Lord has completed all His work on Mount Zion and on
Jerusalem, *He will say,* "I will punish the fruit of the arrogant heart of the king of Assyria
and the pomp of his haughtiness."
13 For he has said,
"By the power of my hand and by my wisdom I did *this,*
For I have understanding;
And I removed the boundaries of the peoples

10:1 Ps 94:20; Is 29:21; 59:4, 13

10:2 Is 5:23; Is 1:23; 3:14, 15

10:3 Job 31:14; Is 13:6; 26:14, 21; 29:6; Jer 9:9; Hos 9:7; Luke 19:44; Is 5:26; Is 20:6; 30:5, 7; 31:3

10:4 Is 24:22; Is 22:2; 34:3; 66:16; Is 5:25

10:5 Is 7:17; 8:7; 14:24-27; Zeph 2:13-15; Jer 51:20; Is 13:5; 30:30; 34:2; 66:14

10:6 Is 9:17; Is 9:19; Is 5:29; Is 5:25

10:7 Gen 50:20; Mic 4:11, 12; Acts 2:23, 24

10:9 Gen 10:10; Amos 6:2; 2 Chr 35:20; Num 34:8; 2 Kin 17:6; 2 Kin 16:9

10:10 2 Kin 19:17, 18

10:11 Is 2:8

10:12 2 Kin 19:31; Is 28:21, 22; 29:14; 65:7; Is 37:23

10:13 2 Kin 19:22-24; Is 37:24-27; Ezek 28:4; Dan 4:30; Hab 2:6-11

10:1 God will judge crooked judges and those who make unjust laws. Those who oppress others will be oppressed themselves. It is not enough to live in a land founded on justice; each individual must deal justly with the poor and the powerless. Don't pass your responsibility off to your nation or even your church. You are accountable to God for what you do.

10:7 Although Assyria did not know it was part of God's plan, God used this nation to judge his people. God accomplishes his plans in history despite people or nations who reject him. He did not merely set the world in motion and let it go! Because our all-powerful, sovereign God is still in control today, we have security even in a rapidly changing world.

10:9 Calno, Carchemish, Hamath, Arpad, Samaria, and Damascus were cities conquered by Assyria. Assured of great victories that would enlarge the empire, the king of Assyria gave an arrogant speech. Already Assyria had conquered several cities and thought Judah would be defeated along with the others. Little did they know that they were under the mightier hand of God.

10:10 Samaria and Jerusalem were filled with idols that were powerless against the Assyrian military machine. Only the God of the universe could and would overthrow Assyria, but not until he had used the Assyrians for his purposes.

10:12 The predicted punishment of the Assyrians soon took place. In 701 B.C., 185,000 Assyrian soldiers were slain by the angel of the Lord (37:36–37). Later, the Assyrian empire fell to Babylon, never to rise again as a world power.

10:12 The Assyrians were haughty. They thought they had accomplished everything in their own power. Our perspective can become distorted by our accomplishments if we fail to recognize God working his purposes through us. When we think we are strong enough for anything, we are bound to fail because pride has blinded us to the reality that God is ultimately in control.

And plundered their treasures,
And like a mighty man I brought down *their* inhabitants,
14 And my hand reached to the riches of the peoples like a nest,
And as one gathers abandoned eggs, I gathered all the earth;
And there was not one that flapped its wing or opened *its* beak or chirped."

15 Is the axe to boast itself over the one who chops with it?
Is the saw to exalt itself over the one who wields it?
That would be like a club wielding those who lift it,
Or like a rod lifting *him who* is not wood.
16 Therefore the Lord, the GOD of hosts, will send a wasting disease among his stout warriors;
And under his glory a fire will be kindled like a burning flame.
17 And the light of Israel will become a fire and his Holy One a flame,
And it will burn and devour his thorns and his briars in a single day.
18 And He will destroy the glory of his forest and of his fruitful garden, both soul and body,
And it will be as when a sick man wastes away.
19 And the rest of the trees of his forest will be so small in number
That a child could write them down.

A Remnant Will Return

20 Now in that day the remnant of Israel, and those of the house of Jacob who have
escaped, will never again rely on the one who struck them, but will truly rely on the LORD,
the Holy One of Israel.
21 A remnant will return, the remnant of Jacob, to the mighty God.
22 For though your people, O Israel, may be like the sand of the sea,
Only a remnant within them will return;
A destruction is determined, overflowing with righteousness.
23 For a complete destruction, one that is decreed, the Lord GOD of hosts will execute
in the midst of the whole land.
24 Therefore thus says the Lord GOD of hosts, "O My people who dwell in Zion, do
not fear the Assyrian who strikes you with the rod and lifts up his staff against you, the
way Egypt *did.*
25 "For in a very little while My indignation *against you* will be spent and My anger *will*
be directed to their destruction."
26 The LORD of hosts will arouse a scourge against him like the slaughter of Midian at
the rock of Oreb; and His staff will be over the sea and He will lift it up the way *He did*
in Egypt.
27 So it will be in that day, that his burden will be removed from your shoulders and
his yoke from your neck, and the yoke will be broken because of fatness.
28 He has come against Aiath,
He has passed through Migron;
At Michmash he deposited his baggage.
29 They have gone through the pass, *saying,*
"Geba will be our lodging place."
Ramah is terrified, and Gibeah of Saul has fled away.

10:14 Jer 49:16; Obad 4
10:15 Jer 51:20; Is 29:16; 45:9; Rom 9:20, 21; Is 10:5
10:16 Ps 106:15; Is 17:4; Is 8:7; 10:18
10:17 Is 30:33; 31:9; Is 37:23; Num 11:1-3; Is 27:4; 33:12; Jer 4:4; 7:20
10:18 Is 10:33, 34
10:19 Is 21:17
10:20 Is 1:9; 11:11, 16; 46:3; Is 4:2; 37:31, 32; 2 Chr 14:11; Is 17:7, 8; 50:10
10:21 Is 7:3; Is 9:6
10:22 Rom 9:27, 28; Is 28:22; Dan 9:27; Rom 9:28
10:23 Is 28:22; Dan 9:27; Rom 9:28
10:24 Ps 87:5, 6; Is 7:4; 12:2; 37:6; Ex 5:14-16
10:25 Is 17:14; Hag 2:6; Is 10:5; 26:20; Dan 11:36
10:26 Is 37:36-38; Judg 7:25; Is 9:4; Ex 14:16; Ex 14:27
10:27 Is 9:4; 14:25; Is 30:23; 55:2
10:28 1 Sam 14:2; 1 Sam 13:2, 5; Judg 18:21; 1 Sam 17:22
10:29 1 Sam 13:23; Josh 21:17; 1 Sam 13:16; Josh 18:25; 1 Sam 7:17; 1 Sam 10:26

10:15 No instrument or tool accomplishes its purposes without a greater power. The Assyrians were a tool in God's hands, but they failed to recognize it. When a tool boasts of greater power than the one who uses it, it is in danger of being discarded. We are useful only to the extent that we allow God to use us.

10:17 Assyria's downfall came in 612 B.C. when Nineveh, the capital city, was destroyed. Assyria had been God's instrument of judgment against Israel, but it too would be judged for its wickedness. No one escapes God's judgment against sin, not even the most powerful of nations (Psalm 2).

10:20–21 Once Assyria's army was destroyed, a small group of God's people would stop relying on Assyria and start trusting God. This remnant would be but a fraction of Israel's former population: see Ezra 2:64–65 for the small number who returned to Judah (see also 11:10–16).

10:20–21 Those who remained faithful to God despite the horrors of the invasion are called the remnant. The key to being a part of the remnant was *faith.* Being a descendant of Abraham, living in the promised land, having trusted God at one time—none of these were good enough. Are you relying on your Christian heritage, the rituals of worship, or past experience to put you in a right relationship with God? The key to being set apart by God is faith in him.

10:28–34 The way these cities are listed approximates the route the Assyrians would take in their invasion of Judah in 701 B.C. They would go from Aiath (probably Ai) at the northern border to Nob (only two miles from Jerusalem).

30 Cry aloud with your voice, O daughter of Gallim!
Pay attention, Laishah *and* wretched Anathoth!
31 Madmenah has fled.
The inhabitants of Gebim have sought refuge.
32 Yet today he will halt at Nob;
He shakes his fist at the mountain of the daughter of Zion, the hill of Jerusalem.

33 Behold, the Lord, the GOD of hosts, will lop off the boughs with a terrible crash;
Those also who are tall in stature will be cut down
And those who are lofty will be abased.
34 He will cut down the thickets of the forest with an iron *axe,*
And Lebanon will fall by the Mighty One.

10:30 1 Sam 25:44; Josh 21:18; Jer 1:1

10:32 1 Sam 21:1; 22:9; Is 19:16; Zech 2:9; Is 1:8; Jer 6:23

10:33 Is 37:24, 36-38; Ezek 31:3; Amos 2:9

10:34 Is 2:13; 33:9; 37:24

Righteous Reign of the Branch

11 Then a shoot will spring from the stem of Jesse,
And a branch from his roots will bear fruit.
2 The Spirit of the LORD will rest on Him,
The spirit of wisdom and understanding,
The spirit of counsel and strength,
The spirit of knowledge and the fear of the LORD.
3 And He will delight in the fear of the LORD,
And He will not judge by what His eyes see,
Nor make a decision by what His ears hear;
4 But with righteousness He will judge the poor,
And decide with fairness for the afflicted of the earth;
And He will strike the earth with the rod of His mouth,
And with the breath of His lips He will slay the wicked.
5 Also righteousness will be the belt about His loins,
And faithfulness the belt about His waist.

6 And the wolf will dwell with the lamb,
And the leopard will lie down with the young goat,
And the calf and the young lion [5]and the fatling together;
And a little boy will lead them.
7 Also the cow and the bear will graze,
Their young will lie down together,
And the lion will eat straw like the ox.
8 The nursing child will play by the hole of the cobra,
And the weaned child will put his hand on the viper's den.
9 They will not hurt or destroy in all My holy mountain,
For the earth will be full of the knowledge of the LORD
As the waters cover the sea.

10 Then in that day
The nations will resort to the root of Jesse,

11:1 Is 4:2; 53:2; Is 9:7; 11:10; Acts 13:23; Is 6:13; Jer 23:5; Zech 3:8; Rev 5:5; 22:16

11:2 Is 42:1; 48:16; 61:1; Matt 3:16; John 1:32; John 16:13; 1 Cor 1:30; Eph 1:17, 18; 2 Tim 1:7

11:3 John 2:25; 7:24

11:4 Is 9:7; 16:5; 32:1; Ps 72:2, 13, 14; Is 3:14; Is 29:19; 32:7; 61:1; Ps 2:9; Is 49:2; Mal 4:6; Job 4:9; Is 30:28, 33; 2 Thess 2:8

11:5 Eph 6:14; Is 25:1

11:6 Is 65:25

11:7 Is 65:25

11:9 Job 5:23; Is 65:25; Ezek 34:25; Hos 2:18; Ps 98:2, 3; Is 45:6; 52:10; 66:18-23; Hab 2:14

11:10 Luke 2:32; Acts 11:18; Is 11:1; Rom 15:12; Is 11:12; 49:22; 62:10; John 3:14, 15; 12:32; Is 14:3; 28:12; 32:17, 18

5 Some versions read *will feed together*

11:1–9 Assyria would be like a tree cut down at the height of its power (10:33–34), never to rise again. Judah (the royal line of David) would be like a tree chopped down to a stump. But from that stump a new shoot would grow—the Messiah. He would be greater than the original tree and would bear much fruit. The Messiah is the fulfillment of God's promise that a descendant of David would rule forever (2 Samuel 7:16).

11:3–5 God will judge with righteousness and justice. How we long for fair treatment from others, but do we give it? We hate those who base their judgments on appearance, false evidence, or hearsay, but are we quick to judge others using those standards? Only Christ can be the perfectly fair judge. Only as he governs our hearts can we learn to be as fair in our treatment of others as we expect others to be toward us.

11:4–5 Judah had become corrupt and was surrounded by hostile, foreign powers. The nation desperately needed a revival of righteousness, justice, and faithfulness. They needed to turn from selfishness and show justice to the poor and the oppressed. The righteousness that God values is more than refraining from sin. It is actively turning toward others and offering them the help they need.

11:6–10 A golden age is yet to come, a time of peace when children can play with formerly dangerous animals. Not all of this was fulfilled at Christ's first coming. For example, nature has not returned to its intended balance and harmony (see Romans 8:9–22). Such perfect tranquility is possible only when Christ reigns over the earth.

Who will stand as a signal for the peoples;
And His resting place will be glorious.

The Restored Remnant

11:11
Is 10:20-22; 37:4, 31, 32; 46:3; Is 19:23-25; Hos 11:11; Zech 10:10; Is 19:21, 22; Mic 7:12; Gen 10:22; 14:1; Is 24:15; 42:4, 10, 12; 49:1; 51:5; 60:9; 66:19

11:12
Is 11:10; Is 56:8; Zeph 3:10; Zech 10:6

11:13
Is 9:21; Jer 3:18; Ezek 37:16, 17, 22; Hos 1:11

11:14
Jer 48:40; 49:22; Hab 1:8; Is 9:12; Jer 49:28; Is 63:1; Dan 11:41; Joel 3:19; Amos 9:12; Is 16:14; 25:10

11:15
Is 43:16; 44:27; 50:2; 51:10, 11; Is 19:16; Is 7:20; 8:7; Rev 16:12

11:16
Is 19:23; 35:8; 40:3; 62:10; Is 11:11; Ex 14:26-29

11 Then it will happen on that day that the Lord
Will again recover the second time with His hand
The remnant of His people, who will remain,
From Assyria, Egypt, Pathros, Cush, Elam, Shinar, Hamath,
And from the islands of the sea.
12 And He will lift up a standard for the nations
And assemble the banished ones of Israel,
And will gather the dispersed of Judah
From the four corners of the earth.
13 Then the jealousy of Ephraim will depart,
And those who harass Judah will be cut off;
Ephraim will not be jealous of Judah,
And Judah will not harass Ephraim.
14 They will swoop down on the slopes of the Philistines on the west;
Together they will plunder the sons of the east;
They will possess Edom and Moab,
And the sons of Ammon will be subject to them.
15 And the LORD will utterly destroy
The tongue of the Sea of Egypt;
And He will wave His hand over the River
With His scorching wind;
And He will strike it into seven streams
And make *men* walk over dry-shod.
16 And there will be a highway from Assyria
For the remnant of His people who will be left,
Just as there was for Israel
In the day that they came up out of the land of Egypt.

Thanksgiving Expressed

12:1
Ps 9:1; Is 25:1; Ps 30:5; Is 40:1, 2; 54:7-10

12:2
Is 32:2; 45:17; 62:11; Is 26:3; Ex 15:2; Ps 118:14

12:3
John 4:10; 7:37, 38; Is 41:18; Jer 2:13

12:4
Is 24:15; 42:12; 48:20; Ps 105:1; Ps 145:4

12 Then you will say on that day,
"I will give thanks to You, O LORD;
For although You were angry with me,
Your anger is turned away,
And You comfort me.
2 "Behold, God is my salvation,
I will trust and not be afraid;
For the LORD GOD is my strength and song,
And He has become my salvation."
3 Therefore you will joyously draw water
From the springs of salvation.
4 And in that day you will say,
"Give thanks to the LORD, call on His name.
Make known His deeds among the peoples;

11:11 When will this remnant of God's people be returned to their land? Old Testament prophecy is often applied both to the near future and the distant future. Judah would soon be exiled to Babylon, and a remnant would return to Jerusalem in 537 B.C. at Cyrus's decree. In the ages to come, however, God's people would be dispersed throughout the world. These cities represent the four corners of the known world. Ultimately God's people will be regathered when Christ comes to reign over the earth.

11:13 Ephraim, the dominant tribe of the north, is used as another name for Israel, the northern kingdom.

11:14 Edom, Moab, and Ammon were three countries bordering Judah (along with Philistia). They were the nations who, when Judah was defeated, rejoiced and took their land.

11:15–16 Isaiah is talking about a new or second exodus when God will bring his scattered people back to Judah and the Messiah will come to rule the world. The Lord dried up the Red Sea so the Israelites could walk through it on their way to the promised land (Exodus 14). He dried up the Jordan River so the nation could cross into the land (Joshua 3). God will again provide the way of return for his people.

12:1ff This chapter is a hymn of praise—another graphic description of the people's joy when Jesus Christ comes to reign over the earth. Even now we need to express our gratitude to God—thanking him, praising him, and telling others about him. From the depths of our gratitude, we must praise him. And we should share the Good News with others.

Make *them* remember that His name is exalted."
5 Praise the LORD in song, for He has done excellent things;
Let this be known throughout the earth.
6 Cry aloud and shout for joy, O inhabitant of Zion,
For great in your midst is the Holy One of Israel.

Prophecies about Babylon

13 The oracle concerning Babylon which Isaiah the son of Amoz saw.
2 Lift up a standard on the [6]bare hill,
Raise your voice to them,
Wave the hand that they may enter the doors of the nobles.
3 I have commanded My consecrated ones,
I have even called My mighty warriors,
My proudly exulting ones,
To *execute* My anger.
4 A sound of tumult on the mountains,
Like that of many people!
A sound of the uproar of kingdoms,
Of nations gathered together!
The LORD of hosts is mustering the army for battle.
5 They are coming from a far country,
From the farthest horizons,
The LORD and His instruments of indignation,
To destroy the whole land.

Judgment on the Day of the LORD

6 Wail, for the day of the LORD is near!
It will come as destruction from the Almighty.
7 Therefore all hands will fall limp,
And every man's heart will melt.
8 They will be terrified,
Pains and anguish will take hold of *them;*
They will writhe like a woman in labor,
They will look at one another in astonishment,
Their faces aflame.
9 Behold, the day of the LORD is coming,
Cruel, with fury and burning anger,
To make the land a desolation;
And He will exterminate its sinners from it.
10 For the stars of heaven and their constellations
Will not flash forth their light;
The sun will be dark when it rises
And the moon will not shed its light.
11 Thus I will punish the world for its evil
And the wicked for their iniquity;
I will also put an end to the arrogance of the proud
And abase the haughtiness of the ruthless.
12 I will make mortal man scarcer than pure gold
And mankind than the gold of Ophir.
13 Therefore I will make the heavens tremble,

6 Or *wind-swept mountain*

12:5 Ex 15:1; Ps 98:1; Is 24:14; 42:10, 11; 44:23

12:6 Is 52:9; 54:1; Zeph 3:14; Is 1:24; 49:26; 60:16; Zeph 3:15-17; Zech 2:5, 10, 11

13:1 Is 14:28; 15:1; Is 13:19; 14:4; 47:1-15; Jer 24:1; 50:1-51:64; Matt 1:11; Rev 14:8; Is 1:1

13:2 Is 5:26; Jer 50:2; Jer 51:25; Is 10:32; 19:16; Is 45:1-3; Jer 51:58

13:3 Joel 3:11

13:4 Is 5:30; 17:12; Joel 3:14

13:5 Is 5:26; 7:18; Is 10:5; Is 24:1

13:6 Is 2:12; 10:3; 13:9; 34:2, 8; 61:2; Ezek 30:3; Amos 5:18; Zeph 1:7; Is 10:25; 14:23; Joel 1:15

13:7 Ezek 7:17; Is 19:1; Ezek 21:7; Nah 2:10

13:8 2 Kin 19:26; Is 21:3; Jer 46:5; Is 26:17; Jer 4:31; John 16:21

13:9 Is 13:6

13:10 Is 5:30; Ezek 32:7; Joel 2:10; Matt 24:29; Mark 13:24; Luke 21:25; Rev 6:13; 8:12; Is 24:23; 50:3; Ezek 32:7; Acts 2:20; Rev 6:12

13:11 Is 26:21; Is 3:11; 11:4; 14:5; Is 2:11; 23:9; Dan 5:22, 23; Jer 48:29; Is 25:3; 29:5, 20

13:12 Is 4:1; 6:11, 12; 1 Kin 9:28; Job 28:16; Ps 45:9

13:13 Is 34:4; 51:6; Ps 18:7; Is 2:19; 24:1, 19, 20; Hag 2:6; Lam 1:12

13:1ff Chapters 1—12 speak of judgment against the southern kingdom and, to a lesser extent, against the northern kingdom. Chapters 13—23 are about the judgment on other nations. Chapter 13 is an oracle or message from God concerning Babylon. Long before Babylon became a world power and threatened Judah, Isaiah spoke of its destruction. Babylon was the rallying point of rebellion against God after the flood (Genesis 11). Revelation 17 and 18 use Babylon as a symbol of God's enemies. At the time of this oracle, Babylon was still part of the Assyrian empire. Isaiah communicated a message of challenge and hope to God's people, telling them not to rely on other nations but to rely on God alone. And he let them know that their greatest enemies would receive from God the punishment they deserve.

13:12 Ophir was known for its rare and valuable gold. It is thought to have been located on the southwestern coast of Arabia.

13:14 1 Kin 22:17; Matt 9:36; Mark 6:34; 1 Pet 2:25

13:15 Is 14:19; Jer 50:25; 51:3, 4

13:16 Ps 137:8, 9; Is 13:18; 14:21; Hos 10:14; Nah 3:10

And the earth will be shaken from its place
At the fury of the LORD of hosts
In the day of His burning anger.
14 And it will be that like a hunted gazelle,
Or like sheep with none to gather *them,*
They will each turn to his own people,
And each one flee to his own land.
15 Anyone who is found will be thrust through,
And anyone who is captured will fall by the sword.
16 Their little ones also will be dashed to pieces
Before their eyes;
Their houses will be plundered
And their wives ravished.

Babylon Will Fall to the Medes

13:17 Jer 51:11; Dan 5:28; Prov 6:34, 35

13:18 2 Kin 8:12; 2 Chr 36:17; Ezek 9:5, 10

13:19 Is 21:9; 48:14; Dan 4:30; Rev 18:11-16, 19, 21; Gen 19:24; Deut 29:23; Jer 49:18; Amos 4:11

13:20 Is 14:23; 34:10-15; Jer 51:37-43; 2 Chr 17:11

13:21 Is 34:11-15; Zeph 2:14; Rev 18:2

13:22 Is 25:2; 32:14; 34:13

17 Behold, I am going to stir up the Medes against them,
Who will not value silver or take pleasure in gold.
18 And *their* bows will mow down the young men,
They will not even have compassion on the fruit of the womb,
Nor will their eye pity children.
19 And Babylon, the beauty of kingdoms, the glory of the Chaldeans' pride,
Will be as when God overthrew Sodom and Gomorrah.
20 It will never be inhabited or lived in from generation to generation;
Nor will the Arab pitch *his* tent there,
Nor will shepherds make *their flocks* lie down there.
21 But desert creatures will lie down there,
And their houses will be full of owls;
Ostriches also will live there, and shaggy goats will frolic there.
22 Hyenas will howl in their fortified towers
And jackals in their luxurious palaces.
Her *fateful* time also will soon come
And her days will not be prolonged.

Israel's Taunt

14:1 Ps 102:13; Is 49:13, 15; 54:7, 8; Is 41:8, 9; 44:1; 49:7; Zech 1:17; 2:12; Is 56:3, 6; Eph 2:12-19

14:2 Is 45:14; 49:23; 54:3; Is 60:10; 61:5; Dan 7:18, 27

14:3 Ezra 9:8, 9; Is 11:10; 40:2; Jer 30:10; 46:27

14:4 Hab 2:6; Is 9:4; 16:4; 49:26; 51:13; 54:14

14:6 Is 10:14; 47:6

14 When the LORD will have compassion on Jacob and again choose Israel, and settle them in their own land, then strangers will join them and attach themselves to
the house of Jacob.
2 The peoples will take them along and bring them to their place, and the house of
Israel will possess them as an inheritance in the land of the LORD as male servants and
female servants; and they will take their captors captive and will rule over their oppressors.
3 And it will be in the day when the LORD gives you rest from your pain and turmoil
and harsh service in which you have been enslaved,
4 that you will take up this taunt against the king of Babylon, and say,
"How the oppressor has ceased,
And how fury has ceased!
5 "The LORD has broken the staff of the wicked,
The scepter of rulers
6 Which used to strike the peoples in fury with unceasing strokes,

13:20 Even before Babylon became a world power, Isaiah prophesied that, though it would shine for a while, Babylon's destruction would be so complete that the land would never again be inhabited. Babylon, in present-day Iraq, still lies in utter ruin, burned under mounds of dirt and sand.

14:1 A prominent theme in Isaiah is that strangers (non-Israelites) would join the returning Israelites (56:6–7; 60:10; 61:5). God's intention was that through his faithful people all the world would be blessed (Genesis 12:3). Through the family of David, the whole world could be saved by Christ. We must not limit God's love to our own people. God loves the whole world.

14:4–11 These verses could have both present and future significance in reference to Babylon. The historical city and empire would be permanently destroyed. Babylon has also been used as a picture of all those who oppose God. Thus, in the end times, all who oppose God will be destroyed and all evil will be removed from the earth forever.

14:5–6 Power fades quickly. God permitted Babylon to have temporary power for a purpose—to punish his wayward people. When the purpose ended, so did the power. Beware of placing confidence in human power because one day it will fade, no matter how strong it appears now.

Which subdued the nations in anger with unrestrained persecution.
7 "The whole earth is at rest *and* is quiet;
They break forth into shouts of joy.
8 "Even the cypress trees rejoice over you, *and* the cedars of Lebanon, *saying,*
'Since you were laid low, no *tree* cutter comes up against us.'
9 "Sheol from beneath is excited over you to meet you when you come;
It arouses for you the spirits of the dead, all the leaders of the earth;
It raises all the kings of the nations from their thrones.
10 "They will all respond and say to you,
'Even you have been made weak as we,
You have become like us.
11 'Your pomp *and* the music of your harps
Have been brought down to Sheol;
Maggots are spread out *as your bed* beneath you
And worms are your covering.'
12 "How you have fallen from heaven,
O star of the morning, son of the dawn!
You have been cut down to the earth,
You who have weakened the nations!
13 "But you said in your heart,
'I will ascend to heaven;
I will raise my throne above the stars of God,
And I will sit on the mount of assembly
In the recesses of the north.
14 'I will ascend above the heights of the clouds;
I will make myself like the Most High.'
15 "Nevertheless you will be thrust down to Sheol,
To the recesses of the pit.
16 "Those who see you will gaze at you,
They will ponder over you, *saying,*
'Is this the man who made the earth tremble,
Who shook kingdoms,
17 Who made the world like a wilderness
And overthrew its cities,
Who did not allow his prisoners to *go* home?'
18 "All the kings of the nations lie in glory,
Each in his own tomb.
19 "But you have been cast out of your tomb
Like a rejected branch,
Clothed with the slain who are pierced with a sword,
Who go down to the stones of the pit
Like a trampled corpse.
20 "You will not be united with them in burial,
Because you have ruined your country,
You have slain your people.
May the offspring of evildoers not be mentioned forever.
21 "Prepare for his sons a place of slaughter
Because of the iniquity of their fathers.
They must not arise and take possession of the earth
And fill the face of the world with cities."

14:7 Ps 47:1-3; 98:1-9; 126:1-3

14:8 Is 55:12; Ezek 31:16

14:9 Is 5:14

14:10 Ezek 32:21

14:11 Is 5:14

14:12 Is 34:4; Luke 10:18; Rev 8:10; 9:1; 2 Pet 1:19; Rev 2:28; 22:16

14:13 Ezek 28:2; Dan 5:22, 23; 8:10; 2 Thess 2:4

14:14 Is 47:8; 2 Thess 2:4

14:15 Ezek 28:8; Matt 11:23; Luke 10:15

14:17 Joel 2:3; Is 45:13

14:19 Is 22:16-18; Jer 41:7, 9; Is 5:25

14:20 Job 18:16, 19; Ps 21:10; 37:28; Is 1:4; 31:2

14:21 Ex 20:5; Lev 26:39; Is 13:16; Matt 23:35

14:12 "Star of the morning, son of the dawn" could be names used to worship the kings of Assyria and Babylon. More likely, it means that they will fade like the morning star when the sun rises.

14:12–14 There are several interpretations for the fallen one in these verses. (1) He is Satan, because the person here is too powerful to be any human king. Although Satan may fit verses 12–14, he does not fit well with the rest of the chapter. (2) This could be Sennacherib or Nebuchadnezzar, kings with supreme power. Their people looked upon them as gods. These kings wanted to rule the world. (3) This could refer to both Satan and a great human king, possibly Nebuchadnezzar, because Babylon is pictured as the seat of evil in Revelation 17—18. Pride was Satan's sin as well as Babylon's. Common to all three viewpoints is the truth that pride willfully opposes God and will result in judgment. Israel made the mistake of being too proud to depend on God, and we are vulnerable to that same mistake.

22 "I will rise up against them," declares the LORD of hosts, "and will cut off from Babylon name and survivors, offspring and posterity," declares the LORD.
23 "I will also make it a possession for the hedgehog and swamps of water, and I will
sweep it with the broom of destruction," declares the LORD of hosts.

Judgment on Assyria

24 The LORD of hosts has sworn saying, "Surely, just as I have intended so it has happened, and just as I have planned so it will stand,
25 to break Assyria in My land, and I will trample him on My mountains. Then his yoke
will be removed from them and his burden removed from their shoulder.
26 "This is the plan devised against the whole earth; and this is the hand that is stretched
out against all the nations.
27 "For the LORD of hosts has planned, and who can frustrate *it?* And as for His
stretched-out hand, who can turn it back?"
28 In the year that King Ahaz died this oracle came:

Judgment on Philistia

29 "Do not rejoice, O Philistia, all of you,
Because the rod that struck you is broken;
For from the serpent's root a viper will come out,
And its fruit will be a flying serpent.
30 "Those who are most helpless will eat,
And the needy will lie down in security;
I will destroy your root with famine,
And it will kill off your survivors.
31 "Wail, O gate; cry, O city;
Melt away, O Philistia, all of you;
For smoke comes from the north,
And there is no straggler in his ranks.
32 "How then will one answer the messengers of the nation?
That the LORD has founded Zion,
And the afflicted of His people will seek refuge in it."

Judgment on Moab

15 The oracle concerning Moab.
Surely in a night Ar of Moab is devastated *and* ruined;
Surely in a night Kir of Moab is devastated *and* ruined.
2 They have gone up to the temple and *to* Dibon, *even* to the high places to weep.
Moab wails over Nebo and Medeba;
Everyone's head is bald *and* every beard is cut off.
3 In their streets they have girded themselves with sackcloth;
On their housetops and in their squares
Everyone is wailing, dissolved in tears.
4 Heshbon and Elealeh also cry out,
Their voice is heard all the way to Jahaz;
Therefore the armed men of Moab cry aloud;
His soul trembles within him.
5 My heart cries out for Moab;
His fugitives are as far as Zoar *and* Eglath-shelishiyah,
For they go up the ascent of Luhith weeping;
Surely on the road to Horonaim they raise a cry of distress over *their* ruin.
6 For the waters of Nimrim are desolate.

14:22 Prov 10:7; Job 18:19; Is 47:9
14:23 Is 34:11; Zeph 2:14; 1 Kin 14:10; Is 13:6
14:24 Job 23:13; Is 46:11; 55:8, 9; Acts 4:28
14:25 Is 10:12; 30:31; 31:8; Is 9:4; 10:27; Nah 1:13
14:26 Is 23:9; Zeph 3:6, 8; Ex 15:12
14:27 2 Chr 20:6; Is 43:13; Dan 4:31, 35
14:28 2 Kin 16:20; 2 Chr 28:27; Is 13:1
14:29 Is 2:6; 11:14; Jer 47:1-7; Ezek 25:15-17; Joel 3:4-8; Amos 1:6-8; Zeph 2:4-7; Zech 9:5-7; 2 Chr 26:6; Is 11:8; Is 30:6
14:30 Is 3:14, 15; 7:21, 22; 11:4; Is 8:21; 9:20; 51:19
14:31 Is 3:26; 24:12; 45:2; Is 14:29; Jer 1:14; Is 34:16
14:32 Is 37:9; Ps 87:1, 5; 102:16; Is 28:16; 44:28; 54:11; Is 4:6; 25:4; 57:13; Zeph 3:12; Heb 11:10; James 2:5
15:1 Is 11:14; 25:10; Jer 48:1; Ezek 25:8-11; Amos 2:1-3; Zeph 2:8-11; Num 21:28
15:2 Jer 48:18, 22; Lev 21:5; Jer 48:37
15:3 Jon 3:6-8; Jer 48:38; Is 22:4
15:4 Num 21:28; 32:3; Jer 48:34
15:5 Jer 48:34; Jer 48:5; Is 59:7; Jer 4:20
15:6 Is 19:5-7; Jer 48:34; Joel 1:10-12; 2:3

14:24–27 This prophecy came true as Isaiah predicted (see 2 Kings 19 and Isaiah 37:21–38).

14:28–31 Isaiah received this message from the Lord in 715 B.C., the year that King Ahaz of Judah died. "The rod that struck you" (14:29) was not Ahaz but Shalmaneser V or Sargon of Assyria. The smoke from the north (14:31) refers to the soldiers of Sargon of Assyria.

15:1 Moab was east of the Dead Sea. The Moabites were descendants of Lot through his incestuous relationship with his older daughter (Genesis 19:31–38). Moab had always been Israel's enemy. They oppressed Israel and invaded their land (Judges 3:12–14) and fought against Saul (1 Samuel 14:47) and against David (2 Samuel 8:2, 11–12). Moab would be punished for treating Israel harshly.

Surely the grass is withered, the tender grass died out,
There is no green thing.
7 Therefore the abundance *which* they have acquired and stored up
They carry off over the brook of Arabim.
8 For the cry of distress has gone around the territory of Moab,
Its wail *goes* as far as Eglaim and its wailing even to Beer-elim.
9 For the waters of Dimon are full of blood;
Surely I will bring added *woes* upon Dimon,
A lion upon the fugitives of Moab and upon the remnant of the land.

15:7 Is 30:6; Jer 48:36

15:9 2 Kin 17:25; Jer 50:17

Prophecy of Moab's Devastation

16 Send the *tribute* lamb to the ruler of the land,
From Sela by way of the wilderness to the mountain of the daughter of Zion.
2 Then, like fleeing birds *or* scattered nestlings,
The daughters of Moab will be at the fords of the Arnon.
3 "Give *us* advice, make a decision;
Cast your shadow like night at high noon;
Hide the outcasts, do not betray the fugitive.
4 "Let the outcasts of Moab stay with you;
Be a hiding place to them from the destroyer."
For the extortioner has come to an end, destruction has ceased,
Oppressors have completely *disappeared* from the land.
5 A throne will even be established in lovingkindness,
And a judge will sit on it in faithfulness in the tent of David;
Moreover, he will seek justice
And be prompt in righteousness.

16:1 2 Kin 3:4; Ezra 7:17; 2 Kin 14:7; Is 42:11; Is 10:32

16:2 Prov 27:8; Jer 48:20, 46; Num 21:13, 14

16:3 Is 25:4; 32:2; 1 Kin 18:4

16:4 Is 9:4; 14:4; 49:26; 51:13; 54:14

16:5 Is 9:6, 7; 32:1; 55:4; Dan 7:14; Mic 4:7; Luke 1:33; Is 9:7

6 We have heard of the pride of Moab, an excessive pride;
Even of his arrogance, pride, and fury;
His idle boasts are false.
7 Therefore Moab will wail; everyone of Moab will wail.
You will moan for the raisin cakes of Kir-hareseth
As those who are utterly stricken.
8 For the fields of Heshbon have withered, the vines of Sibmah *as well;*
The lords of the nations have trampled down its choice clusters
Which reached as far as Jazer *and* wandered to the deserts;
Its tendrils spread themselves out *and* passed over the sea.
9 Therefore I will weep bitterly for Jazer, for the vine of Sibmah;
I will drench you with my tears, O Heshbon and Elealeh;
For the shouting over your summer fruits and your harvest has fallen away.
10 Gladness and joy are taken away from the fruitful field;
In the vineyards also there will be no cries of joy or jubilant shouting,
No treader treads out wine in the presses,
For I have made the shouting to cease.
11 Therefore my heart intones like a harp for Moab
And my inward feelings for Kir-hareseth.
12 So it will come about when Moab presents himself,
When he wearies himself upon *his* high place
And comes to his sanctuary to pray,
That he will not prevail.

16:6 Jer 48:29; Amos 2:1; Obad 3, 4; Zeph 2:8, 10; Jer 48:30

16:7 1 Chr 16:3; 2 Kin 3:25; Jer 48:31

16:8 Is 15:4; Num 32:38; Jer 48:32

16:9 Jer 48:32; Is 15:4; Jer 40:10, 12; 48:32

16:10 Is 24:8; Jer 48:33; Judg 9:27; Is 24:7; Amos 5:11, 17; Job 24:11; Amos 9:13

16:11 Is 15:5; 63:15; Jer 48:36; Hos 11:8; Phil 2:1

16:12 Num 22:39-41; Jer 48:35; 1 Kin 18:29; Is 15:2

16:1ff Attacked by the Assyrians, Moabite refugees would flee to Sela, which lay in the country of Edom to the south. Desperate Moabites would send a tribute of lambs to Jerusalem asking for Judah's protection. Jerusalem would be a safe refuge for a while. Isaiah advised Judah to accept these refugees as a sign of compassion during the enemy's time of devastation.

16:10 The treading of grapes (squeezing the juice from grapes by mashing them with bare feet) was the climax of the harvest season, a time of great joy in the vineyards. But the joy of harvest would soon be ended because the people in their pride ignored God and rebelled against him.

16:12 When the people of Moab experienced God's wrath, they sought their own idols and gods. Nothing happened, however, because there was no one there to save them. When we seek our own ways of escape in order to get through our daily troubles, the effect is the same: no pleasure, pastime, or man-made religious idea will come to save us. Our hope lies in God, the only One who can hear and help.

13 This is the word which the LORD spoke earlier concerning Moab.
14 But now the LORD speaks, saying, "Within three years, as a hired man would count
them, the glory of Moab will be degraded along with all *his* great population, and *his*
remnant will be very small *and* impotent."

16:14 Job 7:1; 14:6; Is 21:16; Is 25:10; Jer 48:42

Prophecy about Damascus

17 The oracle concerning Damascus.
"Behold, Damascus is about to be removed from being a city
And will become a fallen ruin.
2 "The cities of Aroer are forsaken;
They will be for flocks to lie down in,
And there will be no one to frighten *them.*
3 "The fortified city will disappear from Ephraim,
And sovereignty from Damascus
And the remnant of Aram;
They will be like the glory of the sons of Israel,"
Declares the LORD of hosts.

17:1 Is 13:1; Gen 14:15; 15:2; 2 Kin 16:9; Jer 49:23; Amos 1:3-5; Zech 9:1; Acts 9:2; Is 7:16; 8:4; 10:9; Is 25:2; Jer 49:2; Mic 1:6

17:2 Num 32:34; Is 7:21, 22; Ezek 25:5; Zeph 2:6; Mic 4:4

17:3 Is 7:8, 16; 8:4; Is 17:4; Hos 9:11

4 Now in that day the glory of Jacob will fade,
And the fatness of his flesh will become lean.
5 It will be even like the reaper gathering the standing grain,
As his arm harvests the ears,
Or it will be like one gleaning ears of grain
In the valley of Rephaim.
6 Yet gleanings will be left in it like the shaking of an olive tree,
Two *or* three olives on the topmost bough,
Four *or* five on the branches of a fruitful tree,
Declares the LORD, the God of Israel.
7 In that day man will have regard for his Maker
And his eyes will look to the Holy One of Israel.
8 He will not have regard for the altars, the work of his hands,
Nor will he look to that which his fingers have made,
Even the [7]Asherim and incense stands.
9 In that day their strong cities will be like forsaken places in the forest,
Or like branches which they abandoned before the sons of Israel;
And the land will be a desolation.
10 For you have forgotten the God of your salvation
And have not remembered the rock of your refuge.
Therefore you plant delightful plants
And set them with vine slips of a strange *god.*
11 In the day that you plant *it* you carefully fence *it* in,
And in the morning you bring your seed to blossom;
But the harvest will *be* a heap
In a day of sickliness and incurable pain.

17:4 Is 10:3; Is 10:16

17:5 Is 17:11; Jer 51:33; Joel 3:13; Matt 13:30; 2 Sam 5:18, 22

17:6 Deut 4:27; Is 24:13; 27:12; Obad 5

17:7 Is 10:20; Hos 3:5; 6:1; Mic 7:7

17:8 2 Chr 34:7; Is 27:9; Is 2:8, 20; 30:22; 31:7; Ex 34:13; Deut 7:5; Mic 5:14

17:10 Is 51:13; Ps 68:19; Is 12:2; 33:2; 61:10; 62:11; Deut 32:4, 18, 31; Is 26:4; 30:29; 44:8

17:11 Ps 90:6; Job 4:8; Hos 8:7; 10:13

7 I.e. wooden symbols of a female deity

16:13–14 Tiglath-pileser III invaded Moab in 732 B.C.; Sennacherib invaded Moab the same year that he invaded Judah, 701 B.C. The earlier event occurred three years after Isaiah's prediction, marking Isaiah as a true prophet. In these events, the people of Israel saw prophecy fulfilled before their very eyes.

17:1ff The northern kingdom and Aram made an alliance to fight against Assyria. But Tiglath-pileser III captured Damascus, the capital of Aram, in 732 B.C., and annexed the northern kingdom to the Assyrian empire. Ahaz, king of Judah, paid tribute to Tiglath-pileser III (2 Kings 16:1–14).

17:7–11 God's message to Damascus is that it will be completely destroyed. The Arameans had turned from the God who could save them, depending instead on their idols and their own strength. No matter how successful they were, God's judgment was sure. Often we depend on the trappings of success (expensive cars, pastimes, clothes, homes) to give us fulfillment. But God says we will reap grief and pain if we have depended on temporal things to give us eternal security. If we don't want the same treatment Damascus received, we must turn from these false allurements and trust in God.

17:8 The Asherim were images of Asherah, a Canaanite goddess who was the female consort of Baal. Queen Jezebel may have brought the worship of Asherah into the northern kingdom. The cult encouraged immoral sexual practices and attracted many people. The Bible warns against worshiping Asherim (Exodus 34:13; Deuteronomy 12:3; 16:21), and Manasseh was condemned for putting up an image of Asherah in the temple (2 Kings 21:7). Unlike pagan gods, our God does not try to attract the greatest number of people but instead seeks the greatest good for all people.

12 Alas, the uproar of many peoples
Who roar like the roaring of the seas,
And the rumbling of nations
Who rush on like the rumbling of mighty waters!
13 The nations rumble on like the rumbling of many waters,
But He will rebuke them and they will flee far away,
And be chased like chaff in the mountains before the wind,
Or like whirling dust before a gale.
14 At evening time, behold, *there is* terror!
Before morning they are no more.
Such *will be* the portion of those who plunder us
And the lot of those who pillage us.

17:12 Is 5:30; Jer 6:23; Ezek 43:2; Luke 21:25; Ps 18:4

17:13 Is 33:3; Ps 9:5; Is 41:11; Job 21:18; Ps 1:4; 83:13; Is 29:5; 41:15, 16

17:14 2 Kin 19:35; Is 41:12

Message to Ethiopia

18 Alas, oh land of whirring wings
Which lies beyond the rivers of [8]Cush,
2 Which sends envoys by the sea,
Even in papyrus vessels on the surface of the waters.
Go, swift messengers, to a nation tall and smooth,
To a people feared far and wide,
A powerful and oppressive nation
Whose land the rivers divide.
3 All you inhabitants of the world and dwellers on earth,
As soon as a standard is raised on the mountains, you will see *it*,
And as soon as the trumpet is blown, you will hear *it*.
4 For thus the LORD has told me,
"I will look from My dwelling place quietly
Like dazzling heat in the sunshine,
Like a cloud of dew in the heat of harvest."
5 For before the harvest, as soon as the bud blossoms
And the flower becomes a ripening grape,
Then He will cut off the sprigs with pruning knives
And remove *and* cut away the spreading branches.
6 They will be left together for mountain birds of prey,
And for the beasts of the earth;
And the birds of prey will spend the summer *feeding* on them,
And all the beasts of the earth will spend harvest time on them.
7 At that time a gift of homage will be brought to the LORD of hosts
From a people tall and smooth,
Even from a people feared far and wide,
A powerful and oppressive nation,
Whose land the rivers divide—
To the place of the name of the LORD of hosts, *even* Mount Zion.

18:1 2 Kin 19:9; Is 20:3-5; Ezek 30:4, 5, 9; Zeph 2:12; 3:10

18:2 Ex 2:3; Is 18:7; Gen 10:8, 9; 2 Chr 12:2-4; 14:9; 16:8

18:3 Ps 49:1; Mic 1:2; Is 26:11

18:4 Is 26:21; Hos 5:15; 2 Sam 23:4; Prov 19:12; Is 26:19; Hos 14:5

18:5 Is 17:10, 11; Ezek 17:6-10

18:6 Is 46:11; 56:9; Jer 7:33; Ezek 32:4-6; 39:17-20

18:7 Ps 68:31; Is 45:14; Zeph 3:10; Acts 8:27-38; Zech 14:16, 17

Message to Egypt

19 The oracle concerning Egypt.
Behold, the LORD is riding on a swift cloud and is about to come to Egypt;
The idols of Egypt will tremble at His presence,
And the heart of the Egyptians will melt within them.

19:1 Is 13:1; Joel 3:19; Ps 18:9, 10; 104:3; Matt 26:64; Rev 1:7; Ex 12:12; Jer 43:12; 44:8; Josh 2:11; Is 13:7

8 Or *Ethiopia*

18:1ff This prophecy was probably given in the days of Hezekiah (2 Kings 19; 20). The "land of whirring wings" refers to locusts, and probably pictures the armies of Cush. The king of Cush had heard that Assyria's great army was marching south toward them. He sent messengers up the Nile asking the surrounding nations to form an alliance. Judah was also asked, but Isaiah told the messengers to return home because Judah needed only God's help to repel the Assyrians. Isaiah prophesied that Assyria would be destroyed at the proper time (37:21–38).

18:3 This is a signal of the doom of Cush and Assyria's victory over Cush (see 20:1–6).

19:1 Egypt, the nation where God's people were enslaved for 400 years (Exodus 1), was hated by the people of Israel. Yet Judah was considering an alliance with Egypt against Assyria (2 Kings 18:17ff). But Isaiah warned against this alliance because God would destroy Assyria in his time.

19:2 Judg 7:22; 1 Sam 14:20; 2 Chr 20:23; Matt 10:21, 36

2 "So I will incite Egyptians against Egyptians;
And they will each fight against his brother and each against his neighbor,
City against city *and* kingdom against kingdom.

19:3 1 Chr 10:13; Is 8:19; Dan 2:2

3 "Then the spirit of the Egyptians will be demoralized within them;
And I will confound their strategy,
So that they will resort to idols and ghosts of the dead
And to mediums and spiritists.

19:4 Is 20:4; Jer 46:26; Ezek 29:19

4 "Moreover, I will deliver the Egyptians into the hand of a cruel master,
And a mighty king will rule over them," declares the Lord GOD of hosts.

19:5 Is 50:2; Jer 51:36; Ezek 30:12

5 The waters from the sea will dry up,
And the river will be parched and dry.

19:6 Ex 7:18; Is 37:25; Ex 2:3; Job 8:11; Is 15:6

6 The canals will emit a stench,
The streams of Egypt will thin out and dry up;
The reeds and rushes will rot away.

19:7 Is 23:3, 10

7 The bulrushes by the Nile, by the edge of the Nile
And all the sown fields by the Nile
Will become dry, be driven away, and be no more.

19:8 Ezek 47:10; Hab 1:15

8 And the fishermen will lament,
And all those who cast a line into the Nile will mourn,
And those who spread nets on the waters will pine away.

19:9 Prov 7:16; Ezek 27:7

9 Moreover, the manufacturers of linen made from combed flax
And the weavers of white cloth will be utterly dejected.

19:10 Ps 11:3

10 And the pillars *of Egypt* will be crushed;
All the hired laborers will be grieved in soul.

19:11 Num 13:22; Ps 78:12, 43; Is 30:4; Gen 41:38, 39; 1 Kin 4:30; Acts 7:22

11 The princes of Zoan are mere fools;
The advice of Pharaoh's wisest advisers has become stupid.
How can you *men* say to Pharaoh,
"I am a son of the wise, a son of ancient kings"?

19:12 Is 14:24; Rom 9:17

12 Well then, where are your wise men?
Please let them tell you,
And let them understand what the LORD of hosts
Has purposed against Egypt.

19:13 Jer 2:16; 46:14, 19; Ezek 30:13; Zech 10:4

13 The princes of Zoan have acted foolishly,
The princes of Memphis are deluded;
Those who are the cornerstone of her tribes
Have led Egypt astray.

19:14 Prov 12:8; Matt 17:17; Is 3:12; 9:16; Is 28:7

14 The LORD has mixed within her a spirit of distortion;
They have led Egypt astray in all that it does,
As a drunken man staggers in his vomit.

ALLIANCES TODAY		
	Government	We rely on government legislation to protect the moral decisions we want made, but legislation cannot change people's hearts.
	Science	We enjoy the benefits of science and technology. We look to scientific predictions and analysis before we look to the Bible.
	Education	We act as though education and degrees can guarantee our future and success without considering what God plans for our future.
	Medical care	We regard medicine as the way to prolong life and preserve its quality—quite apart from faith and moral living.
	Financial systems	We place our faith in financial "security"—making as much money as we can for ourselves—forgetting that, while being wise with our money, we must trust God for our needs.

Isaiah warned Judah not to ally with Egypt (20:5; 30:1–2; 31:1). He knew that trust in any nation or any military might was futile. Their only hope was to trust in God. Although we don't consciously put our hope for deliverance in political alliances in quite the same way, we often put our hope in other forces.

19:11–15 Egypt was noted for its wisdom, but here its wise men and princes were deceived and foolish. True wisdom can come only from God. We must ask him for wisdom to guide our decisions, or we will also be uncertain and misdirected. Are you confused about something now? Ask God for wisdom to deal with it.

15 There will be no work for Egypt
Which *its* head or tail, *its* palm branch or bulrush, may do.
16 In that day the Egyptians will become like women, and they will tremble and be in
dread because of the waving of the hand of the LORD of hosts, which He is going to wave
over them.
17 The land of Judah will become a terror to Egypt; everyone to whom it is mentioned
will be in dread of it, because of the purpose of the LORD of hosts which He is purposing
against them.
18 In that day five cities in the land of Egypt will be speaking the language of Canaan
and swearing *allegiance* to the LORD of hosts; one will be called the City of [9]Destruction.
19 In that day there will be an altar to the LORD in the midst of the land of Egypt, and
a pillar to the LORD near its border.
20 It will become a sign and a witness to the LORD of hosts in the land of Egypt; for
they will cry to the LORD because of oppressors, and He will send them a Savior and a
Champion, and He will deliver them.
21 Thus the LORD will make Himself known to Egypt, and the Egyptians will know the
LORD in that day. They will even worship with sacrifice and offering, and will make a
vow to the LORD and perform it.
22 The LORD will strike Egypt, striking but healing; so they will return to the LORD,
and He will respond to them and will heal them.
23 In that day there will be a highway from Egypt to Assyria, and the Assyrians will
come into Egypt and the Egyptians into Assyria, and the Egyptians will worship with the
Assyrians.
24 In that day Israel will be the third *party* with Egypt and Assyria, a blessing in the
midst of the earth,
25 whom the LORD of hosts has blessed, saying, "Blessed is Egypt My people, and
Assyria the work of My hands, and Israel My inheritance."

Prophecy about Egypt and Ethiopia

20 In the year that the commander came to Ashdod, when Sargon the king of Assyria sent him and he fought against Ashdod and captured it,
2 at that time the LORD spoke through Isaiah the son of Amoz, saying, "Go and loos-
en the sackcloth from your hips and take your shoes off your feet." And he did so, going
naked and barefoot.
3 And the LORD said, "Even as My servant Isaiah has gone naked and barefoot three
years as a sign and token against Egypt and Cush,
4 so the king of Assyria will lead away the captives of Egypt and the exiles of Cush,
young and old, naked and barefoot with buttocks uncovered, to the shame of Egypt.
5 "Then they will be dismayed and ashamed because of Cush their hope and Egypt
their boast.

9 Some ancient mss and versions read *the Sun*

19:15 Is 9:14, 15
19:16 2 Cor 5:11; Heb 10:31; Is 11:15
19:17 Is 14:24; Dan 4:35
19:18 Is 45:23; 65:16
19:19 Is 56:7; 60:7; Gen 28:18; Ex 24:4; Josh 22:10, 26, 27
19:20 Is 43:3, 11; 45:15, 21; 49:26; 60:16; 63:8; Is 49:25
19:21 Is 56:7; 60:7; Zech 14:16-18
19:22 Deut 32:39; Is 30:26; 57:18; Heb 12:11; Is 27:13; 45:14; Hos 14:1
19:23 Is 11:16; 35:8; 49:11; 62:10; Is 27:13
19:25 Is 45:14; Ps 100:3; Is 29:23; 45:11; 60:21; 64:8; Eph 2:10
20:1 2 Kin 18:17; 1 Sam 5:1
20:2 Is 1:1; 13:1; Zech 13:4; Matt 3:4; Ezek 24:17, 23; 1 Sam 19:24; Mic 1:8
20:3 Is 8:18; Is 37:9; 43:3
20:4 Is 19:4; Is 47:2, 3
20:5 2 Kin 18:21; Is 30:3-5; 31:1; Ezek 29:6, 7; Jer 9:23, 24; 17:5; 1 Cor 3:21

19:19, 23 After Egypt's chastening, it would turn from idols and worship the one true God. Even more amazing is Isaiah's prophecy that the two chief oppressors of Israel, Egypt and Assyria, would unite in worship. This prophecy will come true "in that day," the future day of Christ's reign.

19:20 When Egypt calls to God for help, he will send a savior to deliver them. Our Savior, Jesus Christ, is available to all who call upon him. We too can pray and receive his saving power (John 1:12).

19:22 Egypt is but one Gentile nation who will bow before the Lord. Philippians 2:10–11 says *every* knee will bow, every tongue confess that Jesus Christ is Lord. So we shouldn't be surprised that Egyptians and Assyrians are part of the "every." Each of us is part of that "every" too. We may bow now in devotion, or later in submission.

19:23–25 In Jesus Christ, former enemies may unite in love. In Christ, people and nations that are poles apart politically will bow at his feet as brothers and sisters. Christ breaks down every barrier that threatens relationships (see Ephesians 2:13–19).

20:1ff Sargon II was king of Assyria from 722—705 B.C., and this event happened in 711 B.C. Isaiah graphically reminds Judah that they should not count on foreign alliances to protect them.

20:2 God's command to Isaiah was to walk about naked for three years, a humiliating experience. God was using Isaiah to demonstrate the humiliation that Egypt and Cush would experience at the hands of Assyria. But the message was really for Judah: Don't put your trust in foreign governments, or you will experience this kind of shame and humiliation from your captors.

20:2 God asked Isaiah to do something that seemed shameful and illogical. At times, God may ask us to do things we don't understand. We must obey God in complete faith, for he will never ask us to do something wrong.

20:6 Is 10:3; 30:7; 31:3; Jer 30:1, 7, 15-17; 31:1-3; Matt 23:33; 1 Thess 5:3; Heb 2:3

6"So the inhabitants of this coastland will say in that day, 'Behold, such is our hope, where we fled for help to be delivered from the king of Assyria; and we, how shall we escape?' "

God Commands That Babylon Be Taken

21:1 Is 13:1; Is 13:20-22; 14:23; Jer 51:42; Zech 9:14

21 The oracle concerning the [10]wilderness of the sea.
As windstorms in the Negev sweep on,
It comes from the wilderness, from a terrifying land.

21:2 Ps 60:3; Is 24:16; 33:1; Is 22:6; Jer 49:34

2 A harsh vision has been shown to me;
The treacherous one *still* deals treacherously, and the destroyer *still* destroys.
Go up, Elam, lay siege, Media;
I have made an end of all the groaning she has caused.

21:3 Is 13:8; 16:11; Ps 48:6; Is 13:8; 26:17; 1 Thess 5:3

3 For this reason my loins are full of anguish;
Pains have seized me like the pains of a woman in labor.
I am so bewildered I cannot hear, so terrified I cannot see.

21:4 Deut 28:67

4 My mind reels, horror overwhelms me;
The twilight I longed for has been turned for me into trembling.

21:5 Jer 51:39, 57; Dan 5:1-4

5 They set the table, they [11]spread out the cloth, they eat, they drink;
"Rise up, captains, oil the shields,"

21:6 2 Kin 9:17-20

6 For thus the Lord says to me,
"Go, station the lookout, let him report what he sees.

21:7 Is 21:9

7"When he sees riders, horsemen in pairs,
A train of donkeys, a train of camels,
Let him pay close attention, very close attention."

21:8 Hab 2:1

8 Then the lookout called,
"O Lord, I stand continually by day on the watchtower,
And I am stationed every night at my guard post.

21:9 Is 13:19; 47:5, 9; 48:14; Jer 51:8; Rev 14:8; 18:2; Is 46:1; Jer 50:2; 51:44

9"Now behold, here comes a troop of riders, horsemen in pairs."
And one said, "Fallen, fallen is Babylon;
And all the images of her gods are shattered on the ground."

21:10 Jer 51:33; Mic 4:13

10 O my threshed *people,* and my afflicted of the threshing floor!
What I have heard from the LORD of hosts,
The God of Israel, I make known to you.

Oracles about Edom and Arabia

21:11 Gen 25:14; Gen 32:3

11 The oracle concerning Edom.
One keeps calling to me from Seir,
"Watchman, [12]how far gone is the night?
Watchman, [12]how far gone is the night?"
12 The watchman says,
"Morning comes but also night.
If you would inquire, inquire;
Come back again."

10 Or *sandy wastes, sea country* **11** Or *spread out the rugs* or possibly *they arranged the seating* **12** Lit *what* is the time *of the night?*

21:1ff "The wilderness of the sea" is Babylon by the Persian Gulf. Some scholars say this prophecy was fulfilled at Babylon's fall in 539 B.C. (see Daniel 5). But others say this was a prophecy of Babylon's revolt against Assyria around 700 B.C.

21:5 If the prophecy refers to the fall of Babylon in 539 B.C., this may picture the feast in Daniel 5.

21:6–7 Lookouts (watchmen on the city walls) often appear in prophetic visions of destruction. They are the first to see trouble coming. The prophet Habakkuk was a watchman (Habakkuk 2:1). The vision of the riders could represent the Medes and Persians attacking Babylon in 539 B.C.

21:8–9 Babylon was not only a great and powerful city, it was also filled with horrible sin (idolatry, witchcraft, and temple prostitution). Babylon was, and remains, a symbol of all that stands against God. Despite all its glory and power, Babylon would be destroyed, along with all its idols. They would give no help in time of trouble.

21:10 Threshing and winnowing were two steps in ancient Israel's farming process. The heads of wheat (often used to symbolize Israel) were first trampled to break open the seeds and expose the valued grain inside (threshing). The seeds were then thrown into the air, and the worthless chaff blew away while the grain fell back to the ground (winnowing). Israel would experience this same kind of process—the worthless, sinful, rebellious people would be taken away, but God would keep the good "grain" to replenish Israel.

21:11 Edom had been a constant enemy of God's people. They rejoiced when Israel fell to the Assyrians, and this sealed Edom's doom (34:8ff; 63:4). Seir was another name for Edom because the hill country of Seir was given to Esau and his descendants (see Joshua 24:4). Obadiah foretells, in great detail, the destruction of Edom.

13 The oracle about Arabia.
In the thickets of Arabia you must spend the night,
O caravans of Dedanites.
14 Bring water for the thirsty,
O inhabitants of the land of Tema,
Meet the fugitive with bread.
15 For they have fled from the swords,
From the drawn sword, and from the bent bow
And from the press of battle.
16 For thus the Lord said to me, "In a year, as a hired man would count it, all the splendor of Kedar will terminate;
17 and the remainder of the number of bowmen, the mighty men of the sons of Kedar,
will be few; for the LORD God of Israel has spoken."

21:13 Jer 25:23, 24; 49:28; Gen 10:7; Ezek 27:15
21:14 Gen 25:15; Job 6:19
21:15 Is 13:14, 15; 17:13
21:16 Is 16:14; Ps 120:5; Song 1:5; Is 42:11; 60:7; Ezek 27:21
21:17 Is 10:19; Num 23:19; Zech 1:6

The Valley of Vision

22 The oracle concerning the valley of vision.
What is the matter with you now, that you have all gone up to the housetops?
2 You who were full of noise,
You boisterous town, you exultant city;
Your slain were not slain with the sword,
Nor did they die in battle.
3 All your rulers have fled together,
And have been captured without the bow;
All of you who were found were taken captive together,
Though they had fled far away.
4 Therefore I say, "Turn your eyes away from me,
Let me weep bitterly,
Do not try to comfort me concerning the destruction of the daughter of my people."
5 For the Lord GOD of hosts has a day of panic, subjugation and confusion
In the valley of vision,
A breaking down of walls
And a crying to the mountain.
6 Elam took up the quiver
With the chariots, infantry *and* horsemen;
And Kir uncovered the shield.
7 Then your choicest valleys were full of chariots,
And the horsemen took up fixed positions at the gate.
8 And He removed the defense of Judah.
In that day you depended on the weapons of the house of the forest,
9 And you saw that the breaches
In the *wall* of the city of David were many;
And you collected the waters of the lower pool.
10 Then you counted the houses of Jerusalem
And tore down houses to fortify the wall.
11 And you made a reservoir between the two walls
For the waters of the old pool.

22:1 Ps 125:2; Jer 21:13; Joel 3:12, 14; Is 15:3
22:2 Is 23:7; 32:13; Jer 14:18; Lam 2:20
22:3 Is 21:15
22:4 Is 15:3; Jer 9:1; Luke 19:41
22:5 Lam 1:5; 2:2; Is 37:3; Is 10:6; 63:3; Is 22:1
22:6 Is 21:2; Jer 49:35; 2 Kin 16:9; Amos 1:5; 9:7
22:8 1 Kin 7:2; 10:17
22:9 2 Kin 20:20; Neh 3:16
22:11 2 Kin 25:4; Jer 39:4; 2 Kin 20:20; 2 Chr 32:3, 4

21:13ff The places listed here are all in Arabia. They are border cities that controlled the trade routes through the land. This is Isaiah's prediction of disaster.

22:1–13 "The valley of vision" refers to the city of Jerusalem, where God revealed himself. Jerusalem would be attacked unless God's people returned to him. Instead they used every means of protection possible except asking God for help. They wanted to trust in their ingenuity, their weapons, and even their pagan neighbors (see 2 Chronicles 32 for the description of a siege of Jerusalem).

22:4 Isaiah had warned his people, but they did not repent; thus they would experience God's judgment. Because of his care for them, Isaiah was hurt by their punishment and mourned deeply for them. Sometimes people we care for ignore our attempts to help, so they suffer the very grief we wanted to spare them. At times like that we grieve because of our concern. God expects us to be involved with others, and this may sometimes require us to suffer with them.

22:6–7 Elam and Kir were under Assyrian rule. The entire Assyrian army, including its vassals, joined in the attack against Jerusalem.

22:8–11 The leaders did what they could to prepare for war: They got weapons, inspected the walls, and stored up water in a reservoir. But all their work was pointless because they never asked God for help. Too often we take steps that, though good in themselves, really won't give us the help we need. We must get the weapons and inspect the walls, but God must guide the work.

But you did not depend on Him who made it,
Nor did you take into consideration Him who planned it long ago.

22:12 Is 32:11; Joel 1:13; 2:17; Mic 1:16

12 Therefore in that day the Lord GOD of hosts called *you* to weeping, to wailing,
To shaving the head and to wearing sackcloth.

22:13 Is 5:11, 22; 28:7, 8; Luke 17:26-29; Is 56:12; 1 Cor 15:32

13 Instead, there is gaiety and gladness,
Killing of cattle and slaughtering of sheep,
Eating of meat and drinking of wine:
"Let us eat and drink, for tomorrow we may die."

22:14 Is 13:11; 26:21; 30:13; 65:7; 1 Sam 3:14; Ezek 24:13; Is 65:20

14 But the LORD of hosts revealed Himself to me,
"Surely this iniquity shall not be forgiven you
Until you die," says the Lord GOD of hosts.

22:15 2 Kin 18:18, 26, 37; Is 36:3, 11, 22; 37:2

15 Thus says the Lord GOD of hosts,
"Come, go to this steward,
To Shebna, who is in charge of the *royal* household,

22:16 2 Sam 18:18; 2 Chr 16:14; Matt 27:60

16 'What right do you have here,
And whom do you have here,
That you have hewn a tomb for yourself here,
You who hew a tomb on the height,
You who carve a resting place for yourself in the rock?
17 'Behold, the LORD is about to hurl you headlong, O man.
And He is about to grasp you firmly

22:18 Job 18:18; Is 17:13

18 *And* roll you tightly like a ball,
To be cast into a vast country;
There you will die
And there your splendid chariots will be,
You shame of your master's house.'

22:19 Job 40:11, 12; Ezek 17:24

19 "I will depose you from your office,
And I will pull you down from your station.

22:20 2 Kin 18:18; Is 36:3, 22; 37:2

20 "Then it will come about in that day,
That I will summon My servant Eliakim the son of Hilkiah,

22:21 Gen 45:8; Job 29:16

21 And I will clothe him with your tunic
And tie your sash securely about him.
I will entrust him with your authority,
And he will become a father to the inhabitants of Jerusalem and to the house of Judah.

22:22 Rev 3:7; Is 7:2, 13; Job 12:14

22 "Then I will set the key of the house of David on his shoulder,
When he opens no one will shut,
When he shuts no one will open.

22:23 Ezra 9:8; Zech 10:4; 1 Sam 2:8; Job 36:7

23 "I will drive him *like* a peg in a firm place,
And he will become a throne of glory to his father's house.
24 "So they will hang on him all the glory of his father's house, offspring and issue, all the least of vessels, from bowls to all the jars.

22:25 Is 22:23; Esth 9:24, 25; Is 46:11; Mic 4:4

25 "In that day," declares the LORD of hosts, "the peg driven in a firm place will give way; it will even break off and fall, and the load hanging on it will be cut off, for the LORD has spoken."

22:13–14 The people said, "Let us eat and drink," because they had given up hope. Attacked on every side (22:7), they should have repented (22:12), but they chose to feast instead. The root problem was that Judah did not trust God's power or his promises (see 56:12; 1 Corinthians 15:32). When you face difficulties, turn to God. Today we still see people giving up hope. There are two common responses to hopelessness: despair and self-indulgence. But this life is not all there is, so we are not to act as if we have no hope. Our proper response should be to trust God and his promise to include us in the perfect and just new world that he will create.

22:15–25 Shebna, a high court steward or official, was just as materialistic as the rest of the people in Jerusalem (22:13). He may have been in the group favoring an alliance with foreigners, thus ignoring Isaiah's advice. The Lord revealed that Shebna would lose his position and be replaced by Eliakim (22:20–21). Eliakim would be the "peg" driven into "a firm place" (22:23). Unfortunately, Eliakim too would fall (22:25).

The Fall of Tyre

23 The oracle concerning Tyre.
Wail, O ships of Tarshish,
For *Tyre* is destroyed, without house *or* harbor;
It is reported to them from the land of Cyprus.
2 Be silent, you inhabitants of the coastland,
You merchants of Sidon;
Your messengers crossed the sea
3 And *were* on many waters.
The grain of the Nile, the harvest of the River was her revenue;
And she was the market of nations.
4 Be ashamed, O Sidon;
For the sea speaks, the stronghold of the sea, saying,
"I have neither travailed nor given birth,
I have neither brought up young men *nor* reared virgins."
5 When the report *reaches* Egypt,
They will be in anguish at the report of Tyre.
6 Pass over to Tarshish;
Wail, O inhabitants of the coastland.
7 Is this your jubilant *city,*
Whose origin is from antiquity,
Whose feet used to carry her to colonize distant places?

8 Who has planned this against Tyre, the bestower of crowns,
Whose merchants were princes, whose traders were the honored of the earth?
9 The LORD of hosts has planned it, to defile the pride of all beauty,
To despise all the honored of the earth.
10 Overflow your land like the Nile, O daughter of Tarshish,
There is no more restraint.
11 He has stretched His hand out over the sea,
He has made the kingdoms tremble;
The LORD has given a command concerning Canaan to demolish its strongholds.

12 He has said, "You shall exult no more, O crushed virgin daughter of Sidon.
Arise, pass over to Cyprus; even there you will find no rest."
13 Behold, the land of the Chaldeans—this is the people *which* was not; Assyria appointed it for desert creatures—they erected their siege towers, they stripped its
palaces, they made it a ruin.
14 Wail, O ships of Tarshish,
For your stronghold is destroyed.
15 Now in that day Tyre will be forgotten for seventy years like the days of one king. At
the end of seventy years it will happen to Tyre as *in* the song of the harlot:
16 Take *your* harp, walk about the city,
O forgotten harlot;
Pluck the strings skillfully, sing many songs,
That you may be remembered.
17 It will come about at the end of seventy years that the LORD will visit Tyre. Then she

23:1 Josh 19:29; 1 Kin 5:1; Jer 25:22; 47:4; Ezek 26:1-27:36; Joel 3:4-8; Amos 1:9; Zech 9:2-4; Is 2:16; Gen 10:4; 1 Kin 10:22; Is 24:10; Gen 10:4; Is 23:12; Ezek 27:6

23:2 Is 47:5

23:3 Is 19:7-9; Josh 13:3; 1 Chr 13:5; Jer 2:18; Ezek 27:3-23

23:4 Gen 10:15, 19; Josh 11:8; Judg 10:6; Jer 25:22; 27:3; 47:4; Ezek 28:21, 22

23:5 Ex 15:14-16; Josh 2:9-11

23:6 Is 23:1

23:7 Is 22:2; 32:13

23:8 Ezek 28:2

23:9 Is 2:11; 13:11; Job 40:11, 12; Dan 4:37; Is 5:13; 9:15

23:11 Ex 14:21; Is 14:26; Is 19:5; 50:2; Is 13:13; Is 25:2; Zech 9:3, 4

23:12 Ezek 26:13, 14; Rev 18:22; Is 23:1

23:13 Is 10:5; Is 13:21; 18:6; Is 10:7

23:14 Is 2:16; Ezek 27:25, 26

23:15 Jer 25:11, 22

23:17 Is 23:15; Ezek 16:25-29; Nah 3:4

23:1ff Isaiah's prophecies against other nations began in the east with Babylon (chapter 13) and ended in the west with Tyre in Phoenicia. Tyre was one of the most famous cities of the ancient world. A major trading center with a large seaport, Tyre was very wealthy and very evil. Tyre was rebuked by Jeremiah (Jeremiah 25:22, 27; 47:4), Ezekiel (Ezekiel 26—28), Joel (Joel 3:4–8), Amos (Amos 1:9, 10), and Zechariah (Zechariah 9:3–4). This is another warning against political alliances with unstable neighbors.

23:5 Why would Egypt be "in anguish" when Tyre fell? Egypt depended on Tyre's shipping expertise to promote and carry their products around the world. Egypt would lose an important trading partner with the fall of Tyre.

23:9 God would destroy Tyre because he hated its people's pride. Pride separates people from God, and he will not tolerate it. We must examine our lives and remember that all true accomplishment comes from our Creator. We have no reason for pride in ourselves.

23:15–16 Some scholars believe this is a literal 70 years; some say it is symbolic of a long period of time. If it is literal, this may have occurred between 700—630 B.C. during the Assyrian captivity of Israel, or it may have been during the 70-year captivity of the Jews in Babylon (605—536 B.C.). During the 70 years, the Jews would forget about Tyre. But when they returned from captivity, they would once again trade with Tyre.

will go back to her harlot's wages and will play the harlot with all the kingdoms on the
face of the earth.
18 Her gain and her harlot's wages will be set apart to the LORD; it will not be stored
up or hoarded, but her gain will become sufficient food and choice attire for those who
dwell in the presence of the LORD.

Judgment on the Earth

24 Behold, the LORD lays the earth waste, devastates it, distorts its surface and scatters its inhabitants.
2 And the people will be like the priest, the servant like his master, the maid like her
mistress, the buyer like the seller, the lender like the borrower, the creditor like the debtor.
3 The earth will be completely laid waste and completely despoiled, for the LORD has
spoken this word.
4 The earth mourns *and* withers, the world fades *and* withers, the exalted of the people of the earth fade away.
5 The earth is also polluted by its inhabitants, for they transgressed laws, violated statutes, broke the everlasting covenant.
6 Therefore, a curse devours the earth, and those who live in it are held guilty. Therefore, the inhabitants of the earth are burned, and few men are left.
7 The new wine mourns,
The vine decays,
All the merry-hearted sigh.
8 The gaiety of tambourines ceases,
The noise of revelers stops,
The gaiety of the harp ceases.
9 They do not drink wine with song;
Strong drink is bitter to those who drink it.
10 The city of chaos is broken down;
Every house is shut up so that none may enter.
11 There is an outcry in the streets concerning the wine;
All joy turns to gloom.
The gaiety of the earth is banished.
12 Desolation is left in the city
And the gate is battered to ruins.
13 For thus it will be in the midst of the earth among the peoples,
As the shaking of an olive tree,
As the gleanings when the grape harvest is over.
14 They raise their voices, they shout for joy;
They cry out from the west concerning the majesty of the LORD.
15 Therefore glorify the LORD in the east,
The name of the LORD, the God of Israel,
In the coastlands of the sea.
16 From the ends of the earth we hear songs, "Glory to the Righteous One,"
But I say, "Woe to me! Woe to me! Alas for me!
The treacherous deal treacherously,
And the treacherous deal very treacherously."
17 Terror and pit and snare
Confront you, O inhabitant of the earth.

23:18 Ps 72:10, 11; Is 60:5-9; Mic 4:13; Ex 28:36; Zech 14:20

24:1 Is 2:19; 13:13; 24:19, 20; 30:32; 33:9

24:2 Lev 25:36, 37; Deut 23:19, 20

24:4 Is 33:9; Is 2:12; 24:21

24:5 Gen 3:17; Num 35:33; Is 9:17; 10:6; Is 33:8

24:6 Josh 23:15; Is 34:5; 43:28; Zech 5:3, 4; Is 1:31; 5:24; 9:19

24:7 Is 16:10; Joel 1:10, 12

24:8 Is 5:12, 14; Ezek 26:13; Hos 2:11; Rev 18:22

24:9 Is 5:11, 22; Is 5:20

24:10 Is 34:11; Is 23:1

24:11 Jer 14:2; 46:12; Is 16:10; 32:13

24:12 Is 14:31; 45:2

24:13 Is 17:6; 27:12

24:14 Is 12:6; 48:20; 52:8; 54:1

24:15 Is 25:3; Mal 1:11; Is 11:11; 42:4, 10, 12; 49:1; 51:5; 60:9; 66:19

24:16 Is 11:12; 42:10; Is 28:5; 60:21; Lev 26:39; Is 21:2; 33:1; Jer 3:20; 5:11

24:17 Jer 48:43; Amos 5:19

24—27 These four chapters are often called "Isaiah's Apocalypse." They discuss God's judgment on the entire world for its sin. Isaiah's prophecies were first directed to Judah, then to Israel, then to the surrounding nations, and finally to the whole world. These chapters describe the last days when God will judge the whole world. At that time he will finally and permanently remove evil.

24:4–5 Not only the people suffered from their sins; even the land suffered the effects of evil and lawbreaking. Today we see the results of sin in our own land—pollution, crime, addiction, poverty. Sin affects every aspect of society so extensively that even those faithful to God suffer. We cannot blame God for these conditions because human sin has brought them about. The more we who are believers renounce sin, speak against immoral practices, and share God's Word with others, the more we slow our society's deterioration. We must not give up: Sin is rampant, but we can make a difference.

24:14–16 The believers who are left behind after God judges Judah will sing to the glory of God's righteousness. Isaiah grieved because of his world's condition. We too can become depressed by the evil all around us. At those times we need to hold on to God's promises for the future and look forward to singing praises to him when he restores heaven and earth.

18 Then it will be that he who flees the report of disaster will fall into the pit,
And he who climbs out of the pit will be caught in the snare;
For the windows above are opened, and the foundations of the earth shake.
19 The earth is broken asunder,
The earth is split through,
The earth is shaken violently.
20 The earth reels to and fro like a drunkard
And it totters like a shack,
For its transgression is heavy upon it,
And it will fall, never to rise again.
21 So it will happen in that day,
That the LORD will punish the host of heaven on high,
And the kings of the earth on earth.
22 They will be gathered together
Like prisoners in the dungeon,
And will be confined in prison;
And after many days they *will be* punished.
23 Then the moon will be abashed and the sun ashamed,
For the LORD of hosts will reign on Mount Zion and in Jerusalem,
And *His* glory will be before His elders.

24:18 Gen 7:11; Ps 18:7; 46:2; Is 2:19, 21; 13:13
24:19 Is 24:1; Num 16:31, 32; Deut 11:6
24:20 Is 19:14; 24:1; 28:7; Is 1:28; 43:27; 66:24; Dan 11:19; Amos 8:14
24:21 Is 10:12; 13:11; Ps 76:12
24:22 Is 10:4; 42:22; Ezek 38:8; Zech 9:11, 12
24:23 Is 13:10; Is 60:19, 20; Zech 14:6, 7; Rev 21:23; 22:5; Mic 4:7; Heb 12:22

Song of Praise for God's Favor

25 O LORD, You are my God;
I will exalt You, I will give thanks to Your name;
For You have worked wonders,
Plans *formed* long ago, with perfect faithfulness.
2 For You have made a city into a heap,
A fortified city into a ruin;
A palace of strangers is a city no more,
It will never be rebuilt.
3 Therefore a strong people will glorify You;
Cities of ruthless nations will revere You.
4 For You have been a defense for the helpless,
A defense for the needy in his distress,
A refuge from the storm, a shade from the heat;
For the breath of the ruthless
Is like a *rain* storm *against* a wall.
5 Like heat in drought, You subdue the uproar of aliens;
Like heat by the shadow of a cloud, the song of the ruthless is silenced.

6 The LORD of hosts will prepare a lavish banquet for all peoples on this mountain;
A banquet of aged wine, choice pieces with marrow,
And refined, aged wine.
7 And on this mountain He will swallow up the covering which is over all peoples,
Even the veil which is stretched over all nations.
8 He will swallow up death for all time,

25:1 Ex 15:2; Ps 118:28; Is 7:13; 49:4, 5; 61:10; Ps 40:5; 98:1; Eph 1:11
25:2 Is 17:1; 26:5; 27:10; 32:19; Is 17:3; 25:12; Is 13:22; 32:14; 34:13
25:3 Is 24:15; Is 13:11
25:4 Is 14:32; 17:10; 27:5; 33:16; Is 4:6; 32:2; Is 29:5, 20; 49:25
25:5 Jer 51:54-56
25:6 Is 1:19; Is 2:2-4; 56:7
25:7 2 Cor 3:15, 16; Eph 4:18
25:8 Hos 13:14; 1 Cor 15:54; Is 30:19; 35:10; 51:11; 65:19; Rev 7:17; 21:4; Ps 69:9; 89:50, 51; Is 51:7; 54:4; Matt 5:11; 1 Pet 4:14

24:21 "The host of heaven on high" refers to spiritual forces opposed to God. Nobody, not even the fallen angels, will escape due punishment.

25:1 Isaiah exalted and praised God because he realized that God completes his plans as promised. God also fulfills his promises to you. Think of the prayers he has answered, and praise him for his goodness and faithfulness.

25:4 The poor suffered because ruthless people oppressed them. But God is concerned for the poor and is a refuge for them. When we are disadvantaged or oppressed, we can turn to God for comfort and help. Jesus states that the kingdom of God belongs to the poor (Luke 6:20).

25:6 Here is a marvelous prophecy of "all peoples"—Gentiles and Jews together—at God's Messianic feast, celebrating the overthrow of evil and the joy of eternity with God. It shows that God intended his saving message to go out to the whole world, not just to the Jews. During the feast, God will end death forever (25:7–8). The people who participate in this great feast will be those who have been living by faith. That is why they say, "Behold, this is our God for whom we have waited that He might save us" (25:9). See also chapter 55 for another presentation of this great banquet.

25:8 When the Lord speaks, he does what he says. It is comforting to know that God's plans and activities are closely tied to his Word. When we pray according to God's will (as expressed in the Bible) and claim his promises (as recorded in the Bible), he hears us and answers our requests.

And the Lord GOD will wipe tears away from all faces,
And He will remove the reproach of His people from all the earth;
For the LORD has spoken.
9 And it will be said in that day,
"Behold, this is our God for whom we have waited that He might save us.
This is the LORD for whom we have waited;
Let us rejoice and be glad in His salvation."
10 For the hand of the LORD will rest on this mountain,
And Moab will be trodden down in his place
As straw is trodden down in the water of a manure pile.
11 And he will spread out his hands in the middle of it
As a swimmer spreads out *his hands* to swim,
But *the Lord* will lay low his pride together with the trickery of his hands.
12 The unassailable fortifications of your walls He will bring down,
Lay low *and* cast to the ground, even to the dust.

Song of Trust in God's Protection

26 In that day this song will be sung in the land of Judah:
"We have a strong city;
He sets up walls and ramparts for security.
2 "Open the gates, that the righteous nation may enter,
The one that remains faithful.
3 "The steadfast of mind You will keep in perfect peace,
Because he trusts in You.
4 "Trust in the LORD forever,
For in GOD the LORD, *we have* an everlasting Rock.
5 "For He has brought low those who dwell on high, the unassailable city;
He lays it low, He lays it low to the ground, He casts it to the dust.
6 "The foot will trample it,
The feet of the afflicted, the steps of the helpless."

7 The way of the righteous is smooth;
O Upright One, make the path of the righteous level.
8 Indeed, *while following* the way of Your judgments, O LORD,
We have waited for You eagerly;
Your name, even Your memory, is the desire of *our* souls.
9 At night my soul longs for You,
Indeed, my spirit within me seeks You diligently;
For when the earth experiences Your judgments
The inhabitants of the world learn righteousness.
10 *Though* the wicked is shown favor,
He does not learn righteousness;
He deals unjustly in the land of uprightness,
And does not perceive the majesty of the LORD.

25:9 Is 35:2; 40:9; 52:10; Is 8:17; 30:18; 33:2; Is 33:22; 35:1; 49:25, 26; 60:16; Ps 20:5; Is 35:1, 2, 10; 65:18; 66:10

25:10 Is 16:14; Jer 48:1-47; Ezek 25:8-11; Amos 2:1-3; Zeph 2:9

25:11 Is 5:25; 14:26; Job 40:11; Is 2:10-12, 15-17; 16:6, 14

25:12 Is 15:1; 25:2; 26:5

26:1 Is 4:2; 12:1; Is 14:31; 31:5, 9; 33:5, 6, 20-24; Is 60:18

26:2 Is 60:11, 18; 62:10; Is 45:25; 54:14, 17; 58:8; 60:21; 61:3; 62:1, 2

26:3 Is 26:12; 27:5; 57:19; 66:12

26:4 Is 12:2; 50:10; 51:5; Is 17:10; 30:29; 44:8

26:5 Is 25:12; Job 40:11-13

26:6 Is 28:3; Is 3:14, 15; 11:4; 29:19

26:7 Is 57:2; Ps 25:4, 5; 27:11; Is 42:16; 52:12

26:8 Is 51:4; 56:1; Is 12:4; 24:15; 25:1; 26:13; Ex 3:15

26:9 Ps 63:5, 6; 77:2; 119:62; Is 50:10; Luke 6:12; Ps 63:1; 78:34; Matt 6:33; Is 55:6; Hos 5:15

26:10 Is 22:12, 13; 32:6, 7; Hos 11:7; John 5:37, 38

25:8 Part of this verse is quoted in 1 Corinthians 15:54 to describe Christ's victory over death. God's ultimate victory is seen when death, our ultimate enemy, is defeated (see also Hosea 13:14). Another part of this verse is quoted in Revelation 21:4, which describes the glorious scene of God's presence with his people.

25:10 Moab was a symbol of all who oppose God and are rebellious to the end. Moab was Israel's enemy for years (see the note on 15:1).

26:1ff People will praise God on the day of the Lord when Christ establishes his kingdom (see chapter 12). Chapter 26 is a psalm of trust, praise, and meditation. Once more, God revealed the future to Isaiah.

26:3 We can never avoid strife in the world around us, but with God we can know perfect peace even in turmoil. When we are devoted to him, our whole attitude is steady and stable. Supported by God's unchanging love and mighty power, we are not shaken by the surrounding chaos (see Philippians 4:7). Do you want peace? Keep your thoughts on and your trust in God.

26:7–8 At times the "way of the righteous" doesn't seem smooth and it isn't easy to do God's will, but we are never alone when we face tough times. God is there to help us through difficulties, to comfort us, and to lead us. God does this by giving us a purpose (keeping our mind centered on him, 26:3) and giving us provisions as we travel. God provides us with relationships of family, friends, and mentors. God gives us wisdom to make decisions and faith to trust him. Don't despair; stay on God's path.

26:10 Even wicked people receive God's benefits, but that doesn't teach them to do what is right. Sometimes God's judgment teaches us more than God's good gifts. If you have been enriched by God's goodness and grace, respond to him with your grateful devotion.

11 O LORD, Your hand is lifted up *yet* they do not see it.
They see *Your* zeal for the people and are put to shame;
Indeed, fire will devour Your enemies.
12 LORD, You will establish peace for us,
Since You have also performed for us all our works.
13 O LORD our God, other masters besides You have ruled us;
But through You alone we confess Your name.
14 The dead will not live, the departed spirits will not rise;
Therefore You have punished and destroyed them,
And You have wiped out all remembrance of them.
15 You have increased the nation, O LORD,
You have increased the nation, You are glorified;
You have extended all the borders of the land.
16 O LORD, they sought You in distress;
They could only whisper a prayer,
Your chastening was upon them.
17 As the pregnant woman approaches *the time* to give birth,
She writhes *and* cries out in her labor pains,
Thus were we before You, O LORD.
18 We were pregnant, we writhed *in labor,*
We gave birth, as it seems, *only* to wind.
We could not accomplish deliverance for the earth,
Nor were inhabitants of the world born.
19 Your dead will live;
Their corpses will rise.
You who lie in the dust, awake and shout for joy,
For your dew *is as* the dew of the dawn,
And the earth will give birth to the departed spirits.

20 Come, my people, enter into your rooms
And close your doors behind you;
Hide for a little while
Until indignation runs *its* course.
21 For behold, the LORD is about to come out from His place
To punish the inhabitants of the earth for their iniquity;
And the earth will reveal her bloodshed
And will no longer cover her slain.

The Deliverance of Israel

27 In that day the LORD will punish Leviathan the fleeing serpent,
With His fierce and great and mighty sword,
Even Leviathan the twisted serpent;
And He will kill the dragon who *lives* in the sea.

2 In that day,
"A vineyard of wine, sing of it!

26:11 Is 44:9, 18; Is 9:7; 37:32; 59:17; Is 5:24; 9:18, 19; 10:17; 66:15, 24; Heb 10:27

26:12 Is 26:3

26:13 Is 2:8; 10:11; Is 63:7

26:14 Deut 4:28; Ps 135:17; Is 8:19; Hab 2:19; Is 10:3

26:15 Is 9:3; Is 33:17; 54:2, 3

26:16 Is 37:3; Hos 5:15

26:17 Is 13:8; 21:3; John 16:21

26:18 Is 33:11; 59:4; Ps 17:14

26:19 Is 25:8; Ezek 37:1-14; Dan 12:2; Hos 13:14; Eph 5:14

26:20 Ex 12:22, 23; Ps 91:1, 4; Ps 30:5; Is 54:7, 8; 2 Cor 4:17; Is 10:5, 25; 13:5; 34:2; 66:14

26:21 Mic 1:3; Jude 14; Is 13:11; 30:12-14; 65:6, 7; Job 16:18; Luke 11:50

27:1 Is 66:16; Job 3:8; 41:1; Ps 74:14; 104:26; Is 51:9

27:2 Ps 80:8; Is 5:7; Jer 2:21

26:16–19 The people realized the pain of being away from God's presence, and yet they are assured that they will live again. God turned his back on his people when they disobeyed, but a small number never lost hope and continued to seek him. No matter how difficult times may be, we have hope when we keep our trust in him. Can you wait patiently for God to act?

26:19 Some people say there is no life after death. Others believe that there is, but it is not physical life. But Isaiah tells us that our bodies shall rise again. According to 1 Corinthians 15:50–53, all the dead believers will arise with new imperishable bodies—bodies like the one Jesus had when he was resurrected (see Philippians 3:21). Isaiah 26:19 is not the only Old Testament verse to speak about the resurrection; see also Job 19:26; Psalm 16:10; Daniel 12:2, 13.

26:20–21 When God comes to judge the earth, the guilty will find no place to hide. Jesus said that the hidden will be made known because his truth, like a light shining in a dark corner, will reveal it (Matthew 10:26). Instead of trying to hide your shameful thoughts and actions from God, confess them to him and receive his forgiveness.

27:1 "That day" is a reference to the end of the evil world as we know it. In ancient Aramean (Ugaritic) literature, Leviathan was a seven-headed monster, the enemy of God's created order. Thus Isaiah is comparing God's slaughter of the wicked to the conquering of a great enemy. Although evil is a powerful foe, God will crush it and abolish it from the earth forever.

27:2–6 The trampled vineyard of chapter 5 will be restored in God's new earth. God will protect and care for the vineyard, his

27:3
Is 58:11; 1 Sam 2:9; Is 31:5; John 10:28

27:4
2 Sam 23:6; Is 10:17; Is 33:12; Matt 3:12; Heb 6:8

27:5
Is 12:2; 25:4; Job 22:21; Is 26:3, 12; Rom 5:1; 2 Cor 5:20

27:6
Is 37:31; Is 35:1, 2; Hos 14:5, 6; Is 4:2

27:7
Is 10:12, 17; 30:31-33; 31:8, 9; 37:36-38

27:8
Is 50:1; 54:7; Jer 4:11; Ezek 19:12; Hos 13:15

27:9
Is 1:25; 48:10; Dan 11:35; Rom 11:27; Ex 34:13; Deut 12:3; 2 Kin 10:26; Is 17:8

27:10
Is 32:13, 14; Is 17:2

27:11
Is 18:5; Deut 32:28; Is 1:3; 5:13; Jer 8:7; Deut 32:18; Is 43:1, 7; 44:2, 21, 24; Is 9:17

27:12
Is 11:11; 17:6; 24:13; 56:8; Gen 15:18; Deut 30:3, 4; Neh 1:9

27:13
Lev 25:9; 1 Chr 15:24; Matt 24:31; Rev 11:15; Is 19:24, 25; Is 19:21, 23; 49:7; 66:23; Zech 14:16; Heb 12:22

28:1
Is 28:7; Hos 7:5; Is 9:9

28:2
Is 8:7; 40:10; Is 28:17; 30:30; 32:19; Ezek 13:11; Is 8:6, 7; 30:28; Nah 1:8

3 "I, the LORD, am its keeper;
I water it every moment.
So that no one will damage it,
I guard it night and day.
4 "I have no wrath.
Should someone give Me briars *and* thorns in battle,
Then I would step on them, I would burn them completely.
5 "Or let him rely on My protection,
Let him make peace with Me,
Let him make peace with Me."
6 In the days to come Jacob will take root,
Israel will blossom and sprout,
And they will fill the whole world with fruit.

7 Like the striking of Him who has struck them, has He struck them?
Or like the slaughter of His slain, have they been slain?
8 You contended with them by banishing them, by driving them away.
With His fierce wind He has expelled *them* on the day of the east wind.
9 Therefore through this Jacob's iniquity will be forgiven;
And this will be the full price of the pardoning of his sin:
When he makes all the altar stones like pulverized chalk stones;
When Asherim and incense altars will not stand.
10 For the fortified city is isolated,
A homestead forlorn and forsaken like the desert;
There the calf will graze,
And there it will lie down and feed on its branches.
11 When its limbs are dry, they are broken off;
Women come *and* make a fire with them,
For they are not a people of discernment,
Therefore their Maker will not have compassion on them.
And their Creator will not be gracious to them.
12 In that day the LORD will start *His* threshing from the flowing stream of the Euphrates to the brook of Egypt, and you will be gathered up one by one, O sons of Israel.
13 It will come about also in that day that a great trumpet will be blown, and those who
were perishing in the land of Assyria and who were scattered in the land of Egypt will
come and worship the LORD in the holy mountain at Jerusalem.

Ephraim's Captivity Predicted

28 Woe to the proud crown of the drunkards of Ephraim,
And to the fading flower of its glorious beauty,
Which is at the head of the fertile valley
Of those who are overcome with wine!
2 Behold, the Lord has a strong and mighty *agent;*
As a storm of hail, a tempest of destruction,
Like a storm of mighty overflowing waters,

---

people. It will no longer produce worthless fruit but will produce enough good fruit for the whole world. Gentiles will come to know God through Israel.

27:9 Only God can take away sin, but to be driven out of the land was considered the penalty that would purify God's people. Deuteronomy 28:49–52, 64 explains God's warning about these consequences.

27:11 Isaiah compares the state of Israel's spiritual life with dry limbs that are broken off and used to make fires. Trees in Scripture often represent spiritual life. The trunk is the channel of strength from God; the branches are the people who serve him. Tree branches sometimes waver and blow in the wind. Like Israel, they may dry up from internal rottenness and become useless for anything except building a fire. What kind of branch are you? If you are withering spiritually, check to see if you are firmly attached to God.

27:12 To "thresh" means to "judge." God's purpose in judging the earth is not vengeance, but purging. He wants to correct us and bring us back to him. God does not punish us for our sin just to make us suffer, but to make those who are faithful better equipped for fruitful service.

28:1 Ephraim represents the northern kingdom of Israel, ruled by a line of evil kings. When Israel split into two kingdoms after Solomon's reign, Jerusalem ended up in the southern kingdom. Leaders in the northern kingdom, wishing to stay entirely separate from their relatives to the south, set up idols to keep the people from going to the temple in Jerusalem to worship (see 1 Kings 12). Thus the people in the northern kingdom were led into idolatry. Isaiah gave this message to Israel to warn them, as well as to Judah to encourage them to repent before being punished as the northern kingdom would be only a few years later.

He has cast *it* down to the earth with *His* hand.
3 The proud crown of the drunkards of Ephraim is trodden under foot.
4 And the fading flower of its glorious beauty,
Which is at the head of the fertile valley,
Will be like the first-ripe fig prior to summer,
Which one sees,
And as soon as it is in his hand,
He swallows it.
5 In that day the LORD of hosts will become a beautiful crown
And a glorious diadem to the remnant of His people;
6 A spirit of justice for him who sits in judgment,
A strength to those who repel the onslaught at the gate.
7 And these also reel with wine and stagger from strong drink:
The priest and the prophet reel with strong drink,
They are confused by wine, they stagger from strong drink;
They reel while having visions,
They totter *when rendering* judgment.
8 For all the tables are full of filthy vomit, without a *single clean* place.

9 "To whom would He teach knowledge,
And to whom would He interpret the message?
Those *just* weaned from milk?
Those *just* taken from the breast?
10 "For *He says,*
'Order on order, order on order,
Line on line, line on line,
A little here, a little there.' "
11 Indeed, He will speak to this people
Through stammering lips and a foreign tongue,
12 He who said to them, "Here is rest, give rest to the weary,"
And, "Here is repose," but they would not listen.
13 So the word of the LORD to them will be,
"Order on order, order on order,
Line on line, line on line,
A little here, a little there,"
That they may go and stumble backward, be broken, snared and taken captive.

Judah Is Warned

14 Therefore, hear the word of the LORD, O scoffers,
Who rule this people who are in Jerusalem,
15 Because you have said, "We have made a covenant with death,
And with Sheol we have made a pact.
The overwhelming scourge will not reach us when it passes by,
For we have made falsehood our refuge and we have concealed ourselves with deception."
16 Therefore thus says the Lord GOD,
"Behold, I am laying in Zion a stone, a tested stone,
A costly cornerstone *for* the foundation, firmly placed.
He who believes *in it* will not be disturbed.

28:3 Is 26:6; 28:18
28:4 Hos 9:10; Mic 7:1; Nah 3:12
28:5 Is 41:16; 45:25; 60:1, 19; Is 62:3
28:6 1 Kin 3:28; Is 11:2; 32:15, 16; John 5:30; 2 Chr 32:6-8; Is 25:4
28:7 Is 5:11, 22; 22:13; 56:12; Hos 4:11; Is 24:2; Is 9:15; Hab 2:15, 16; Is 29:11
28:8 Jer 48:26
28:9 Is 2:3; 28:26; 30:20; 48:17; 50:4; 54:13; Ps 131:2
28:10 2 Chr 36:15; Neh 9:30
28:11 Is 33:19; 1 Cor 14:21
28:12 Is 11:10; 30:15; 32:17, 18; Jer 6:16; Matt 11:28, 29
28:13 Is 8:15; Matt 21:44
28:14 Is 1:10; 28:22; Is 29:20
28:15 Is 28:18; Is 8:8; 28:2; 30:28; Dan 11:22; Is 9:15; 30:9; 44:20; 59:3, 4; Ezek 13:22; Is 29:15
28:16 Rom 9:33; 10:11; 1 Pet 2:6; Ps 118:22; Is 8:14, 15; Matt 21:42; Mark 12:10; Luke 20:17; Acts 4:11; Eph 2:20

28:9–14 These verses characterize the people's reaction to Isaiah. In effect, they were saying, "He's speaking to us like a school teacher speaks to small children. We don't need to be taught. We'll make up our own minds." For this attitude, Isaiah prophesied that the Assyrians would teach them in a way they would like even less.

28:15 Judah was afraid of the Assyrians, the "overwhelming scourge." Instead of trusting God, the Judeans turned to other sources for security. God accused them of making a covenant with death. It is used to mean the grave or state of being dead. This passage may refer to Hezekiah's alliance with Pharaoh Tirhakah against Assyria (2 Kings 19:9; Isaiah 37:9). God would cancel this agreement—Egypt would be of no help when Assyria attacked. Is it worth selling out what you believe in for temporary protection against an enemy? If you want lasting protection, turn to the only one able to deliver you from *eternal* death—God.

28:16 If you're building anything, you need a firm base. Isaiah speaks of a foundation stone, a *cornerstone,* that will be laid in Zion. This cornerstone is the Messiah, the foundation on whom we build our lives. Is your life built on the flimsy base of your own successes or dreams? Or is it set on a firm foundation (see Psalm 118:22; 1 Peter 2:8)?

28:17 2 Kin 21:13; Is 5:16; 30:18; 61:8; Amos 7:7-9; Is 28:2

17 "I will make justice the measuring line
And righteousness the level;
Then hail will sweep away the refuge of lies
And the waters will overflow the secret place.

28:18 Is 28:15; Is 7:7; 8:10; Is 28:3; Dan 8:13

18 "Your covenant with death will be canceled,
And your pact with Sheol will not stand;
When the overwhelming scourge passes through,
Then you become its trampling *place.*

28:19 2 Kin 24:2; Is 50:4; Job 6:4; 18:11; 24:17; Ps 55:4; 88:15; Lam 2:22

19 "As often as it passes through, it will seize you;
For morning after morning it will pass through, *anytime* during the day or night,
And it will be sheer terror to understand what it means."

28:20 Is 59:6

20 The bed is too short on which to stretch out,
And the blanket is too small to wrap oneself in.

28:21 2 Sam 5:20; 1 Chr 14:11; Josh 10:10, 12; 2 Sam 5:25; 1 Chr 14:16; Is 10:12; 29:14; 65:7; Lam 2:15; 3:33; Luke 19:41-44

21 For the LORD will rise up as *at* Mount Perazim,
He will be stirred up as in the valley of Gibeon,
To do His task, His unusual task,
And to work His work, His extraordinary work.
22 And now do not carry on as scoffers,
Or your fetters will be made stronger;

28:22 Is 28:14; Is 10:22, 23

For I have heard from the Lord GOD of hosts
Of decisive destruction on all the earth.

23 Give ear and hear my voice,
Listen and hear my words.
24 Does the farmer plow continually to plant seed?
Does he *continually* turn and harrow the ground?

28:25 Matt 23:23; Ex 9:32

25 Does he not level its surface
And sow dill and scatter cummin
And plant wheat in rows,
Barley in its place and rye within its area?
26 For his God instructs and teaches him properly.

28:27 Amos 1:3

27 For dill is not threshed with a threshing sledge,
Nor is the cartwheel driven over cummin;
But dill is beaten out with a rod, and cummin with a club.
28 *Grain for* bread is crushed,
Indeed, he does not continue to thresh it forever.
Because the wheel of *his* cart and his horses *eventually* damage *it,*
He does not thresh it longer.

28:29 Is 9:6; Is 31:2; Rom 11:33

29 This also comes from the LORD of hosts,
Who has made *His* counsel wonderful and *His* wisdom great.

Jerusalem Is Warned

29:1 2 Sam 5:9; Is 1:14; 5:12; 22:12, 13; 29:9, 13

29 Woe, O Ariel, Ariel the city *where* David *once* camped!
Add year to year, observe *your* feasts on schedule.
2 I will bring distress to Ariel,

29:2 Is 3:26; Lam 2:5

And she will be *a city of* lamenting and mourning;
And she will be like an Ariel to me.

29:3 Luke 19:43, 44

3 I will camp against you encircling *you,*
And I will set siegeworks against you,
And I will raise up battle towers against you.

29:4 Is 8:19

4 Then you will be brought low;
From the earth you will speak,

28:21 God fought on Joshua's side at the valley of Gibeon (Joshua 10:1–14) and on David's side at Mount Perazim (2 Samuel 5:20). But here he would fight *against* Israel, his own people, in these same places.

28:23–29 The farmer uses special tools to plant and harvest tender herbs so he will not destroy them. He takes into account how fragile they are. In the same way God takes all our individual circumstances and weaknesses into account. He deals with each of us sensitively. We should follow his example when we deal with others. Different people require different treatment. Be sensitive to the needs of those around you and the special treatment they may need.

29:1 *Ariel* is a special name for Jerusalem, David's city. It may mean "lion of God" (Jerusalem is strong as a lion) or "altar hearth" (Jerusalem is the place of the altar in the temple. See 29:2; Ezekiel 43:15–16).

And from the dust *where* you are prostrate
Your words *will come.*
Your voice will also be like that of a spirit from the ground,
And your speech will whisper from the dust.

5 But the multitude of your enemies will become like fine dust,
And the multitude of the ruthless ones like the chaff which blows away;
And it will happen instantly, suddenly.
6 From the LORD of hosts you will be punished with thunder and earthquake and loud noise,
With whirlwind and tempest and the flame of a consuming fire.
7 And the multitude of all the nations who wage war against Ariel,
Even all who wage war against her and her stronghold, and who distress her,
Will be like a dream, a vision of the night.
8 It will be as when a hungry man dreams—
And behold, he is eating;
But when he awakens, his hunger is not satisfied,
Or as when a thirsty man dreams—
And behold, he is drinking,
But when he awakens, behold, he is faint
And his thirst is not quenched.
Thus the multitude of all the nations will be
Who wage war against Mount Zion.

9 Be delayed and wait,
Blind yourselves and be blind;
They become drunk, but not with wine,
They stagger, but not with strong drink.
10 For the LORD has poured over you a spirit of deep sleep,
He has shut your eyes, the prophets;
And He has covered your heads, the seers.
11 The entire vision will be to you like the words of a sealed book, which when they
give it to the one who is literate, saying, "Please read this," he will say, "I cannot, for it
is sealed."
12 Then the book will be given to the one who is illiterate, saying, "Please read this."
And he will say, "I cannot read."
13 Then the Lord said,
"Because this people draw near with their words
And honor Me with their lip service,
But they remove their hearts far from Me,
And their reverence for Me consists of tradition learned *by rote,*
14 Therefore behold, I will once again deal marvelously with this people, wondrously marvelous;
And the wisdom of their wise men will perish,
And the discernment of their discerning men will be concealed."

15 Woe to those who deeply hide their plans from the LORD,
And whose deeds are *done* in a dark place,
And they say, "Who sees us?" or "Who knows us?"
16 You turn *things* around!
Shall the potter be considered as equal with the clay,

29:5 Is 17:13; 41:15, 16; Is 13:11; 25:3; 29:20; Is 17:14; 30:13; 47:11; 1 Thess 5:3

29:6 Is 10:3; 26:14, 21; 1 Sam 2:10; Matt 24:7; Mark 13:8; Luke 21:11; Rev 11:13, 19; 16:18

29:7 Mic 4:11, 12; Zech 12:9; Job 20:8; Ps 73:20; Is 17:14

29:8 Is 54:17

29:9 Is 29:1; Is 51:17, 21, 22; 63:6

29:10 Ps 69:23; Is 6:9, 10; Mic 3:6; Rom 11:8; Is 44:18; 2 Thess 2:9-12

29:11 Is 8:16; Dan 12:4, 9; Matt 13:11

29:13 Ezek 33:31; Matt 15:8, 9; Mark 7:6, 7

29:14 Is 6:9, 10; 28:21; 65:7; Hab 1:5; Is 44:25; Jer 8:9; 49:7; 1 Cor 1:19

29:15 Ps 10:11, 13; Is 28:15; 30:1; Job 22:13; Is 57:12; Ezek 8:12; Ps 94:7; Is 47:10; Mal 2:17

29:16 Is 45:9; 64:8; Jer 18:1-6; Rom 9:19-21

29:13–14 The people claimed to be close to God, but they were disobedient and merely went through the motions; therefore, God would bring judgment upon them. Religion had become routine instead of real. Jesus quoted Isaiah's condemnation of Israel's hypocrisy when he spoke to the Pharisees, the religious leaders of his day (Matthew 15:7–9; Mark 7:6–7). We are all capable of hypocrisy. Often we slip into routine patterns when we worship and we neglect to give God our love and devotion. If we want to be called God's people, we must be obedient and worship him honestly and sincerely.

29:15 Thinking God couldn't see them and didn't know what was happening, the people of Jerusalem tried to hide their plans from him. How strange that so many people think they can hide from God. In Psalm 139 we learn that God has examined us and knows everything about us. Would you be embarrassed if your best friends knew your personal thoughts? Remember that God knows all of them.

That what is made would say to its maker, "He did not make me";
Or what is formed say to him who formed it, "He has no understanding"?

Blessing after Discipline

17 Is it not yet just a little while
Before Lebanon will be turned into a fertile field,
And the fertile field will be considered as a forest?
18 On that day the deaf will hear words of a book,
And out of *their* gloom and darkness the eyes of the blind will see.
19 The afflicted also will increase their gladness in the LORD,
And the needy of mankind will rejoice in the Holy One of Israel.
20 For the ruthless will come to an end and the scorner will be finished,
Indeed all who are intent on doing evil will be cut off;
21 Who cause a person to be indicted by a word,
And ensnare him who adjudicates at the gate,
And defraud the one in the right with meaningless arguments.
22 Therefore thus says the LORD, who redeemed Abraham, concerning the house of
Jacob:
"Jacob shall not now be ashamed, nor shall his face now turn pale;
23 But when he sees his children, the work of My hands, in his midst,
They will sanctify My name;
Indeed, they will sanctify the Holy One of Jacob
And will stand in awe of the God of Israel.
24 "Those who err in mind will know the truth,
And those who criticize will accept instruction.

Judah Warned against Egyptian Alliance

30 "Woe to the rebellious children," declares the LORD,
"Who execute a plan, but not Mine,
And make an alliance, but not of My Spirit,
In order to add sin to sin;
2 Who proceed down to Egypt
Without consulting Me,
To take refuge in the safety of Pharaoh
And to seek shelter in the shadow of Egypt!
3 "Therefore the safety of Pharaoh will be your shame
And the shelter in the shadow of Egypt, your humiliation.
4 "For their princes are at Zoan
And their ambassadors arrive at Hanes.
5 "Everyone will be ashamed because of a people who cannot profit them,
Who are not for help or profit, but for shame and also for reproach."

6 The oracle concerning the beasts of the Negev.
Through a land of distress and anguish,
From where *come* lioness and lion, viper and flying serpent,
They carry their riches on the backs of young donkeys
And their treasures on camels' humps,
To a people who cannot profit *them;*

29:17 Ps 84:6; 107:33, 35; Is 32:15
29:18 Is 35:5; 42:18, 19; 43:8; Matt 11:5; Mark 7:37; Is 29:11; Ps 119:18; Prov 20:12; Is 32:3
29:19 Ps 25:9; 37:11; Is 11:4; 61:1; Matt 5:5; 11:29; Is 3:14, 15; 11:4; 14:30, 32; 25:4; 26:6; Matt 11:5; James 1:9; 2:5
29:20 Is 29:5; Is 28:14; Is 59:4; Mic 2:1
29:21 Amos 5:10; Is 32:7; Amos 5:12
29:22 Is 41:8; 51:2; 63:16; Is 45:17; 49:23; 50:7; 54:4
29:23 Is 49:20-26; Is 26:12; 45:11; Eph 2:10; Is 5:16; 8:13
29:24 Is 30:21; Heb 5:2; Is 41:20; 60:16; Is 54:13
30:1 Is 1:2, 23; 30:9; 65:2; Is 29:15; Is 8:11, 12
30:2 Is 31:1; Jer 43:7; Is 8:19; Is 36:9
30:3 Is 20:5, 6; 36:6; Jer 42:18, 22
30:4 Is 19:11
30:5 Jer 2:36; Is 10:3; 30:7; 31:3
30:6 Is 46:1, 2; Gen 12:9; Ex 5:10, 21; Deut 4:20; 8:15; Is 5:30; 8:22; Jer 11:4; Deut 8:15; Is 14:29; Is 15:7; 46:1, 2; 1 Kin 10:2

29:17–24 The world described here, under Christ's rule, will be far different from the one we live in today. There will be no more violence or gloom. This new world will be characterized by joy, understanding, justice, and praise to God.

30:1 The rebellious children are the people of Judah (see 1:2), those who have rebelled against God. The negotiations for an alliance were underway, and Isaiah condemned their twisted plans. The people of Judah sought advice from everyone but God. When we are driven by fear, we tend to search everywhere for comfort, advice, and relief, hoping to find an easy way out of our troubles. Instead, we should consult God. Although he gives emergency help in a crisis, he prefers to be our Guide throughout our lives. By reading his Word and actively seeking to do his will, we can maintain our bond with him who provides stability no matter what the crisis.

30:2ff Hezekiah had been seeking a defensive alliance with Egypt against Sennacherib of Assyria (see 2 Kings 18:21).

30:6 This oracle is titled "concerning the beasts of the Negev," but is directed to those who carried bribes to Egypt through the wilderness in the Negev region.

7 Even Egypt, whose help is vain and empty.
Therefore, I have called her
"Rahab who has been exterminated."
8 Now go, write it on a tablet before them
And inscribe it on a scroll,
That it may serve in the time to come
As a witness forever.
9 For this is a rebellious people, false sons,
Sons who refuse to listen
To the instruction of the LORD;
10 Who say to the seers, "You must not see *visions*";
And to the prophets, "You must not prophesy to us what is right,
Speak to us pleasant words,
Prophesy illusions.
11 "Get out of the way, turn aside from the path,
Let us hear no more about the Holy One of Israel."
12 Therefore thus says the Holy One of Israel,
"Since you have rejected this word
And have put your trust in oppression and guile, and have relied on them,
13 Therefore this iniquity will be to you
Like a breach about to fall,
A bulge in a high wall,
Whose collapse comes suddenly in an instant,
14 "Whose collapse is like the smashing of a potter's jar,
So ruthlessly shattered
That a sherd will not be found among its pieces
To take fire from a hearth
Or to scoop water from a cistern."
15 For thus the Lord GOD, the Holy One of Israel, has said,
"In repentance and rest you will be saved,
In quietness and trust is your strength."
But you were not willing,
16 And you said, "No, for we will flee on horses,"
Therefore you shall flee!
"And we will ride on swift *horses*,"
Therefore those who pursue you shall be swift.
17 One thousand *will flee* at the threat of one *man*;
You will flee at the threat of five,
Until you are left as a flag on a mountain top
And as a signal on a hill.

God Is Gracious and Just

18 Therefore the LORD longs to be gracious to you,
And therefore He waits on high to have compassion on you.
For the LORD is a God of justice;
How blessed are all those who long for Him.
19 O people in Zion, inhabitant in Jerusalem, you will weep no longer. He will surely
be gracious to you at the sound of your cry; when He hears it, He will answer you.

30:7 Is 30:5; Job 9:13; Ps 87:4; 89:10; Is 51:9

30:8 Is 8:1

30:9 Is 30:1; Is 28:15; 59:3, 4; Is 1:10; 5:24; 24:5

30:10 Is 29:10; Is 5:20; Jer 11:21; Amos 2:12; 7:13; 1 Kin 22:8, 13; Jer 6:14; 23:17, 26; Ezek 13:7; Rom 16:18; 2 Tim 4:3, 4

30:11 Acts 13:8; Job 21:14

30:12 Is 5:24; 7:9; 8:6; Is 3:14, 15; 5:7; 59:13

30:13 Is 26:21; 1 Kin 20:30; Ps 62:4; Is 58:12; Is 29:5; 47:11

30:14 Ps 2:9; Jer 19:10, 11

30:15 Ps 116:7; Is 28:12; Is 7:4; 32:17

30:16 Is 2:7; 31:1, 3

30:17 Lev 26:36; Deut 28:25; 32:30; Josh 23:10; Prov 28:1

30:18 Is 42:14, 16; 48:9; Jon 3:4, 10; 2 Pet 3:9, 15; Is 2:11, 17; 33:5; Is 5:16; 28:17; 61:8; Is 8:17; 25:9; 26:8; 33:2

30:19 Is 65:9; Ezek 37:25, 28; Is 25:8; 60:20; 61:1-3; Ps 50:15; Is 58:9; 65:24; Matt 7:7-11

30:7 Rahab was a mythological female sea monster associated with Leviathan (see the note on 27:1; also Job 9:13; 26:12). It was a name associated with Egypt, where hippopotamuses, perhaps a likeness to Rahab, sat on the Nile River and did nothing.

30:10–11 Some people in Judah may have sought refuge in Egypt. In their desire to find security, they wanted to hear only good news. They did not welcome the truth from God's prophets. Often the truth makes us uncomfortable. We prefer lies and illusions when they make us feel more secure. It is much better to face reality than to live a lie. Don't settle for something that makes you feel comfortable but is not true.

30:15 God warned Judah that turning to Egypt and other nations for military might could not save them. Only God could do that. They must wait for him in "quietness and trust." No amount of fast talking or hasty activity could speed up God's grand design. We have nothing to say to God but thank you. Salvation comes from God alone. Because he has saved us, we can trust him and be peacefully confident that he will give us strength to face our difficulties. We should lay aside our busy care and endless effort and allow him to act.

20 Although the Lord has given you bread of privation and water of oppression, *He,*
your Teacher will no longer hide Himself, but your eyes will behold your Teacher.
21 Your ears will hear a word behind you, "This is the way, walk in it," whenever you
turn to the right or to the left.
22 And you will defile your graven images overlaid with silver, and your molten images plated with gold. You will scatter them as an impure thing, *and* say to them, "Be
gone!"
23 Then He will give *you* rain for the seed which you will sow in the ground, and bread
from the yield of the ground, and it will be rich and plenteous; on that day your livestock
will graze in a roomy pasture.
24 Also the oxen and the donkeys which work the ground will eat salted fodder, which
has been winnowed with shovel and fork.
25 On every lofty mountain and on every high hill there will be streams running with
water on the day of the great slaughter, when the towers fall.
26 The light of the moon will be as the light of the sun, and the light of the sun will be
seven times *brighter,* like the light of seven days, on the day the LORD binds up the fracture of His people and heals the bruise He has inflicted.

27 Behold, the name of the LORD comes from a remote place;
Burning is His anger and dense is *His* smoke;
His lips are filled with indignation
And His tongue is like a consuming fire;
28 His breath is like an overflowing torrent,
Which reaches to the neck,
To shake the nations back and forth in a sieve,
And to *put* in the jaws of the peoples the bridle which leads to ruin.
29 You will have songs as in the night when you keep the festival,
And gladness of heart as when one marches to *the sound of* the flute,
To go to the mountain of the LORD, to the Rock of Israel.
30 And the LORD will cause His voice of authority to be heard,
And the descending of His arm to be seen in fierce anger,
And *in* the flame of a consuming fire
In cloudburst, downpour and hailstones.
31 For at the voice of the LORD Assyria will be terrified,
When He strikes with the rod.
32 And every blow of the rod of punishment,
Which the LORD will lay on him,
Will be with *the music of* tamborines and lyres;
And in battles, brandishing weapons, He will fight them.
33 For [13]Topheth has long been ready,
Indeed, it has been prepared for the king.
He has made it deep and large,
A pyre of fire with plenty of wood;
The breath of the LORD, like a torrent of brimstone, sets it afire.

Help Not in Egypt but in God

31 Woe to those who go down to Egypt for help
And rely on horses,
And trust in chariots because they are many

30:20 1 Kin 22:27; Ps 80:5; Ps 74:9; Amos 8:11
30:21 Ps 25:8, 9; Prov 3:6; Is 35:8, 9; 42:16; Is 29:24
30:22 Ex 32:2, 4; Judg 17:3, 4; Is 46:6; Matt 4:10
30:23 Ps 65:9-13; 104:13, 14; Ps 144:13; Is 32:20; Hos 4:16
30:24 Matt 3:12; Luke 3:17
30:25 Is 35:6, 7; 41:18; 43:19, 20; Is 34:2
30:26 Is 24:23; 60:19, 20; Rev 21:23; 22:5; Is 61:1; Is 1:6; 30:13, 14; Deut 32:39; Job 5:18; Is 33:24; Jer 33:6; Hos 6:1, 2
30:27 Is 59:19; Is 10:17; Is 10:5; 13:5; 66:14; Is 66:15
30:28 Is 11:4; 30:33; 2 Thess 2:8; Is 8:8; Amos 9:9; 2 Kin 19:28; Is 37:29
30:31 Is 11:4; Is 10:12; 14:25; 31:8; Is 10:26; 11:4
30:32 Is 10:24; 1 Sam 18:6; Jer 31:4; Ezek 32:10
30:33 2 Kin 23:10; Jer 7:31; 19:6; Is 11:4; 30:28; Gen 19:24; Is 34:9
31:1 Is 30:2, 7; 36:6; Deut 17:16; Ps 20:7; 33:17; Is 2:7; 30:16; Is 9:13; Dan 9:13; Amos 5:4-8; Is 10:17; 43:15; Hos 11:9; Hab 1:12; 3:3

13 I.e. the place of human sacrifice to Molech

30:20 The Lord gave his people the bread of privation and the water of oppression, but he promised to be with them, teach them, and guide them during hard times. God expects a lot from us, and many times following him can be painful; but he always acts out of his love for us. Next time you go through a difficult time, try to appreciate the experience and grow from it, learning what God wants to teach you. God may be showing you his love by patiently walking with you through adversity.

30:21 When the people of Jerusalem left God's path, he would correct them. He will do the same for us. But when we hear his voice of correction, we must be willing to follow it!

31:1 It was wrong for Judah to look to other nations for military help. (1) They were trusting in human beings instead of God. Judah sought protection from those who had far less power than God. Both Egypt and Judah would fall as a result of their arrogance. (2) They were serving their own interests instead of God's, and thus they did not even consult him. They violated God's stipulation in Deuteronomy 17:16. (3) They did not want to pay the price of looking to God and repenting of their sinful ways. When we have problems, it is good to seek help, but we must never bypass God or his previous directions to us.

And in horsemen because they are very strong,
But they do not look to the Holy One of Israel, nor seek the LORD!
2 Yet He also is wise and will bring disaster
And does not retract His words,
But will arise against the house of evildoers
And against the help of the workers of iniquity.
3 Now the Egyptians are men and not God,
And their horses are flesh and not spirit;
So the LORD will stretch out His hand,
And he who helps will stumble
And he who is helped will fall,
And all of them will come to an end together.

4 For thus says the LORD to me,
"As the lion or the young lion growls over his prey,
Against which a band of shepherds is called out,
And he will not be terrified at their voice nor disturbed at their noise,
So will the LORD of hosts come down to wage war on Mount Zion and on its hill."
5 Like flying birds so the LORD of hosts will protect Jerusalem.
He will protect and deliver *it;*
He will pass over and rescue *it.*
6 Return to Him from whom you have deeply defected, O sons of Israel.
7 For in that day every man will cast away his silver idols and his gold idols, which
your sinful hands have made for you as a sin.
8 And the Assyrian will fall by a sword not of man,
And a sword not of man will devour him.
So he will not escape the sword,
And his young men will become forced laborers.
9 "His rock will pass away because of panic,
And his princes will be terrified at the standard,"
Declares the LORD, whose fire is in Zion and whose furnace is in Jerusalem.

31:2 Is 28:29; Rom 16:27; Is 45:7; Num 23:19; Jer 44:29; Is 1:4; 9:17; 14:20; Is 22:14; 32:6

31:3 Ezek 28:9; 2 Thess 2:4; Is 36:9; Is 9:17; Jer 15:6; Ezek 20:33, 34; Is 30:5, 7; Matt 15:14

31:4 Num 24:9; Hos 11:10; Amos 3:8; Is 42:13; Zech 12:8

31:5 Deut 32:11; Ps 91:4; Is 37:35; 38:6

31:6 Is 44:22; 55:7; Jer 3:10, 14, 22; Ezek 18:31, 32; Is 1:2, 5

31:7 Is 2:20; 30:22; 1 Kin 12:30

31:8 Is 10:12; 14:25; 30:31-33; 37:7, 36-38; Is 66:16; Is 21:15; Gen 49:15; Is 14:2

31:9 Deut 32:31, 37; Is 5:26; 13:2; 18:3; Is 10:16, 17; 30:33; Zech 2:5

The Glorious Future

32 Behold, a king will reign righteously
And princes will rule justly.
2 Each will be like a refuge from the wind
And a shelter from the storm,
Like streams of water in a dry country,
Like the shade of a huge rock in a parched land.
3 Then the eyes of those who see will not be blinded,
And the ears of those who hear will listen.
4 The mind of the hasty will discern the truth,
And the tongue of the stammerers will hasten to speak clearly.
5 No longer will the fool be called noble,
Or the rogue be spoken of *as* generous.
6 For a fool speaks nonsense,
And his heart inclines toward wickedness:
To practice ungodliness and to speak error against the LORD,

32:1 Ps 72:1-4; Is 9:6, 7; 11:4, 5; Jer 23:5; 33:15; Ezek 37:24; Zech 9:9

32:2 Is 4:6; 25:4; Is 35:6; 41:18; 43:19, 20

32:3 Is 29:18

32:4 Is 29:24

32:5 1 Sam 25:25

32:6 Prov 19:3; 24:7-9; Is 59:7, 13; Is 9:17; 10:6; Is 3:15; 10:2

31:7 Someday these people would throw their idols away, recognizing that they are nothing but man-made objects. Idols such as money, fame, or success are seductive. Instead of contributing to our spiritual development, they rob us of our time, energy, and devotion that ought to be directed toward God. At first our idols seem exciting and promise to take us places, but in the end we will find that we have become their slaves. We need to recognize their worthlessness now, before they rob us of our freedom.

32:1 Having suffered much injustice from evil rulers, many in Judah were hungry for a strong king who would rule with justice. This desire will be fulfilled when Christ reigns. Evil will be banished, and the King will reign in righteousness and rule with justice. In the immediate future, Judah would be destroyed and taken into captivity. But one day, God's Son, the King unlike any other king, will reign in righteousness.

32:5–6 When the righteous King comes, people's motives will become transparent. Fools will not be regarded as noble. Those who have opposed God's standards of living will be unable to maintain their deception. In the blazing light of the holy Savior, sin cannot disguise itself and appear good. Christ's revealing light shines into the darkest corners of our hearts, showing sin clearly for what it is. When King Jesus reigns in your heart, there is no place for sin, no matter how well hidden you may think it is.

32:7 Jer 5:26-28; Mic 7:3; Is 11:4; 61:1; Is 5:23
32:8 Prov 11:25
32:9 Is 47:8; Amos 6:1; Zeph 2:15; Is 28:23
32:10 Is 5:5, 6; 7:23; 24:7
32:11 Is 22:12; Is 47:2
32:12 Nah 2:7
32:13 Is 5:6, 10, 17; 27:10; Is 22:2; 23:9
32:14 Is 13:22; 25:2; 34:13; Is 6:11; 22:2; 24:10, 12; Is 13:21; 34:13; Ps 104:11; Jer 14:6
32:15 Is 11:2; 44:3; 59:21; Ezek 39:29; Joel 2:28; Ps 107:35; Is 29:17; 35:1, 2
32:16 Is 33:5; Zech 8:3
32:17 Ps 72:2, 3; 85:8; 119:165; Is 2:4; Rom 14:17; James 3:18; Is 30:15
32:18 Is 26:3, 12; Is 11:10; 14:3; 30:15; Hos 2:18-23; Zech 2:5; 3:10
32:19 Is 28:2, 17; 30:30; Is 10:18, 19, 34; Is 24:10, 12; 26:5; 27:10; 29:4
32:20 Eccl 11:1; Is 30:23, 24
33:1 Is 10:6; 21:2; Is 24:16; 48:8; Is 10:12; 14:25; 31:8; Hab 2:8; Jer 25:12-14; Matt 7:2
33:2 Is 30:18, 19; Is 25:9; Is 40:10; 51:5; 59:16; Is 37:3

To keep the hungry person unsatisfied
And to withhold drink from the thirsty.
7 As for a rogue, his weapons are evil;
He devises wicked schemes
To destroy *the* afflicted with slander,
Even though *the* needy one speaks what is right.
8 But the noble man devises noble plans;
And by noble plans he stands.

9 Rise up, you women who are at ease,
And hear my voice;
Give ear to my word,
You complacent daughters.
10 Within a year and *a few* days
You will be troubled, O complacent *daughters;*
For the vintage is ended,
And the *fruit* gathering will not come.
11 Tremble, you *women* who are at ease;
Be troubled, you complacent *daughters;*
Strip, undress and put *sackcloth* on *your* waist,
12 Beat your breasts for the pleasant fields, for the fruitful vine,
13 For the land of my people *in which* thorns *and* briars shall come up;
Yea, for all the joyful houses *and for* the jubilant city.
14 Because the palace has been abandoned, the populated city forsaken.
Hill and watch-tower have become caves forever,
A delight for wild donkeys, a pasture for flocks;
15 Until the Spirit is poured out upon us from on high,
And the wilderness becomes a fertile field,
And the fertile field is considered as a forest.
16 Then justice will dwell in the wilderness
And righteousness will abide in the fertile field.
17 And the work of righteousness will be peace,
And the service of righteousness, quietness and confidence forever.
18 Then my people will live in a peaceful habitation,
And in secure dwellings and in undisturbed resting places;
19 And it will hail when the forest comes down,
And the city will be utterly laid low.
20 How blessed will you be, you who sow beside all waters,
Who let out freely the ox and the donkey.

The Judgment of God

33 Woe to you, O destroyer,
While you were not destroyed;
And he who is treacherous, while *others* did not deal treacherously with him.
As soon as you finish destroying, you will be destroyed;
As soon as you cease to deal treacherously, *others* will deal treacherously with you.
2 O LORD, be gracious to us; we have waited for You.

32:9–13 The people turned their backs on God and concentrated on their own pleasures. This warning is not just to the women of Jerusalem (see 3:16—4:1), but to all who sit back in their thoughtless complacency, enjoying crops, clothes, land, and cities while an enemy approaches. Wealth and luxury bring false security, lulling us into thinking all is well when disaster is around the corner. By abandoning God's purpose for our lives, we also abandon his help.

32:15–17 God acts from above to change man's condition here on earth. Only when God's Spirit is among us can we achieve true peace and fruitfulness (Ezekiel 36:22–38; Galatians 5:22–23). This will happen in the end times. We can also have God's Spirit with us now, for he is available to all believers through Christ (John 15:26). But the outpouring mentioned here happens when the worldwide kingdom of God is established for all eternity (see Joel 2:28–29).

33:1 The "destroyer" is Assyria. Assyria continually broke its promises, but demanded that others keep theirs. It is easy to put ourselves in the same selfish position, demanding our rights while ignoring the rights of others. Broken promises shatter trust and destroy relationships. Determine to keep your promises; at the same time, ask forgiveness for past promises you have broken. Treat others with the same fairness that you demand for yourself.

33:2 These are the words of the righteous remnant who were waiting for God to deliver them from their oppression.

Be their strength every morning,
Our salvation also in the time of distress.
3 At the sound of the tumult peoples flee;
At the lifting up of Yourself nations disperse.
4 Your spoil is gathered *as* the caterpillar gathers;
As locusts rushing about men rush about on it.
5 The LORD is exalted, for He dwells on high;
He has filled Zion with justice and righteousness.
6 And He will be the stability of your times,
A wealth of salvation, wisdom and knowledge;
The fear of the LORD is his treasure.
7 Behold, their brave men cry in the streets,
The ambassadors of peace weep bitterly.
8 The highways are desolate, the traveler has ceased,
He has broken the covenant, he has despised the cities,
He has no regard for man.
9 The land mourns *and* pines away,
Lebanon is shamed *and* withers;
Sharon is like a desert plain,
And Bashan and Carmel lose *their foliage.*
10 "Now I will arise," says the LORD,
"Now I will be exalted, now I will be lifted up.
11 "You have conceived chaff, you will give birth to stubble;
My breath will consume you like a fire.
12 "The peoples will be burned to lime,
Like cut thorns which are burned in the fire.

13 "You who are far away, hear what I have done;
And you who are near, acknowledge My might."
14 Sinners in Zion are terrified;
Trembling has seized the godless.
"Who among us can live with the consuming fire?
Who among us can live with continual burning?"
15 He who walks righteously and speaks with sincerity,
He who rejects unjust gain
And shakes his hands so that they hold no bribe;
He who stops his ears from hearing about bloodshed
And shuts his eyes from looking upon evil;
16 He will dwell on the heights,
His refuge will be the impregnable rock;
His bread will be given *him,*
His water will be sure.

17 Your eyes will see the King in His beauty;
They will behold a far-distant land.
18 Your heart will meditate on terror:
"Where is he who counts?
Where is he who weighs?
Where is he who counts the towers?"
19 You will no longer see a fierce people,

33:3 Is 17:13; 21:15; Is 10:33; 17:13; 59:16-18; Jer 25:30, 31

33:5 Ps 97:9; Is 1:26; 28:6; 32:16

33:6 Is 33:20; Is 45:17; 51:6; Is 11:9; 2 Kin 18:7; Ps 112:1-3; Is 11:3; Matt 6:33

33:7 2 Kin 18:18, 37

33:8 Is 35:8; Is 24:5

33:9 Is 3:26; 24:4; 29:2; Is 2:13; 10:34; Is 35:2; 65:10

33:10 Ps 12:5; Is 2:19, 21

33:11 Ps 7:14; Is 26:18; 59:4; James 1:15; Is 1:31

33:12 2 Sam 23:6, 7; Is 10:17; 27:4

33:13 Ps 48:10; Is 49:1

33:14 Is 1:28; Is 32:11; Is 30:27, 30; Heb 12:29; Is 9:18, 19; 10:16; 47:14

33:15 Ps 15:2; 24:4; Is 58:6-11; Ps 119:37

33:16 Is 25:4; Is 49:10

33:17 Is 6:5; 24:23; 33:21, 22; Is 26:15

33:18 Is 17:14; 1 Cor 1:20

33:19 Deut 28:49, 50; Is 28:11; Jer 5:15

33:4 See 2 Kings 19:20–37 and Isaiah 37:21–38 for a description of the victory over Assyria described here.

33:5 When Christ's kingdom is established, Zion—Jerusalem—will be the home of justice and righteousness because the Messiah will reign there. As a light to the world, the new Jerusalem will be the Holy City (Revelation 21:2).

33:8 The Assyrians broke their peace treaty (2 Kings 18:14–17).

33:9 These fruitful, productive areas would become deserts. Lebanon was known for its huge cedars. Sharon was very fertile. Bashan was very productive in grain and cattle. Carmel was thickly forested.

33:14–16 These sinners realized that they could not live in the presence of the holy God, for he is like a fire that consumes evil. Only those who walk righteously and speak what is right can live with God. Isaiah gives examples of how to demonstrate our righteousness and uprightness: we can reject gain from extortion and bribes, refuse to listen to plots of wrong actions, and shut our eyes to evil. If we are fair and honest in our relationships, we will dwell with God, and he will supply our needs.

A people of unintelligible speech which no one comprehends,
Of a stammering tongue which no one understands.
20 Look upon Zion, the city of our appointed feasts;
Your eyes will see Jerusalem, an undisturbed habitation,
A tent which will not be folded;
Its stakes will never be pulled up,
Nor any of its cords be torn apart.
21 But there the majestic *One,* the LORD, will be for us
A place of rivers *and* wide canals
On which no boat with oars will go,
And on which no mighty ship will pass—
22 For the LORD is our judge,
The LORD is our lawgiver,
The LORD is our king;
He will save us—
23 Your tackle hangs slack;
It cannot hold the base of its mast firmly,
Nor spread out the sail.
Then the prey of an abundant spoil will be divided;
The lame will take the plunder.
24 And no resident will say, "I am sick";
The people who dwell there will be forgiven *their* iniquity.

God's Wrath against Nations

34 Draw near, O nations, to hear; and listen, O peoples!
Let the earth and all it contains hear, and the world and all that springs from it.
2 For the LORD'S indignation is against all the nations,
And *His* wrath against all their armies;
He has utterly destroyed them,
He has given them over to slaughter.
3 So their slain will be thrown out,
And their corpses will give off their stench,
And the mountains will be drenched with their blood.
4 And all the host of heaven will wear away,
And the sky will be rolled up like a scroll;
All their hosts will also wither away
As a leaf withers from the vine,
Or as *one* withers from the fig tree.
5 For My sword is satiated in heaven,
Behold it shall descend for judgment upon Edom
And upon the people whom I have devoted to destruction.
6 The sword of the LORD is filled with blood,
It is sated with fat, with the blood of lambs and goats,
With the fat of the kidneys of rams.
For the LORD has a sacrifice in Bozrah
And a great slaughter in the land of Edom.
7 Wild oxen will also fall with them
And young bulls with strong ones;
Thus their land will be soaked with blood,
And their dust become greasy with fat.
8 For the LORD has a day of vengeance,
A year of recompense for the cause of Zion.
9 Its streams will be turned into pitch,
And its loose earth into brimstone,
And its land will become burning pitch.
10 It will not be quenched night or day;

33:20 Ps 48:12; Ps 46:5, 125:1, 2; Is 32:18; Is 54:2

33:21 Is 41:18; 43:19, 20; 48:18; 66:12

33:22 Is 2:4; 11:4; 16:5; 51:5; Is 1:10; 51:4, 7; James 4:12; Ps 89:18; Is 33:17; Zech 9:9; Is 25:9; 35:4; 49:25, 26; 60:16

33:23 2 Kin 7:16; 2 Kin 7:8; Is 35:6

33:24 Is 30:26; 58:8; Jer 30:17; Is 40:2; 44:22; Jer 50:20; Mic 7:18, 19; 1 John 1:7-9

34:1 Ps 49:1; Is 41:1; 43:9; Deut 32:1; Is 1:2

34:2 Is 26:20; Is 13:5; 24:1; Is 30:25; 63:6; 65:12

34:3 Is 14:19; Joel 2:20; Amos 4:10; Ezek 14:19; 35:6; 38:22

34:4 Is 13:13; 51:6; Ezek 32:7, 8; Joel 2:31; Matt 24:29; 2 Pet 3:10; Rev 6:12-14

34:5 Deut 32:41, 42; Jer 46:10; Ezek 21:3-5; Is 63:1; Jer 49:7, 8, 20; Ezek 25:12-14; 35:1-15; Amos 1:11, 12; Obad 1-14; Mal 1:4; Is 24:6; 43:28

34:6 Is 63:1; Jer 49:13; Is 63:1

34:7 Num 23:22; Ps 22:21; Ps 68:30; Jer 50:27; Is 63:6

34:8 Is 13:6; 35:4; 47:3; 61:2; 63:4

34:9 Deut 29:23; Ps 11:6; Is 30:33

34:10 Is 1:31; 66:24; Rev 14:11; 19:3; Is 13:20-22; 24:1; 34:10-15; Mal 1:3, 4; Ezek 29:11

34:5 The Edomites shared a common ancestry with Israel. The Israelites were descended from Jacob; the Edomites from Jacob's twin brother, Esau. Edom was always Israel's bitter enemy. The destruction of Edom mentioned here is a picture of the ultimate end of all who oppose God and his people.

Its smoke will go up forever.
From generation to generation it will be desolate;
None will pass through it forever and ever.
11 But pelican and hedgehog will possess it,
And owl and raven will dwell in it;
And He will stretch over it the line of desolation
And the plumb line of emptiness.
12 Its nobles—there is no one there
Whom they may proclaim king—
And all its princes will be nothing.
13 Thorns will come up in its fortified towers,
Nettles and thistles in its fortified cities;
It will also be a haunt of jackals
And an abode of ostriches.
14 The desert creatures will meet with the wolves,
The hairy goat also will cry to its kind;
Yes, the night monster will settle there
And will find herself a resting place.
15 The tree snake will make its nest and lay *eggs* there,
And it will hatch and gather *them* under its protection.
Yes, the hawks will be gathered there,
Every one with its kind.

16 Seek from the book of the LORD, and read:
Not one of these will be missing;
None will lack its mate.
For His mouth has commanded,
And His Spirit has gathered them.
17 He has cast the lot for them,
And His hand has divided it to them by line.
They shall possess it forever;
From generation to generation they will dwell in it.

34:11 Zeph 2:14; 2 Kin 21:13; Is 24:10; Lam 2:8

34:12 Jer 27:20; 39:6; Is 41:11, 12

34:13 Is 13:22; 25:2; 32:13; Ps 44:19; Jer 9:11; 10:22

34:14 Is 13:21

34:15 Deut 14:13

34:16 Is 30:8; Is 1:20; 40:5; 58:14

34:17 Is 17:13, 14; Jer 13:25; Is 34:11; Is 34:10

Zion's Happy Future

35 The wilderness and the desert will be glad,
And the Arabah will rejoice and blossom;
Like the crocus
2 It will blossom profusely
And rejoice with rejoicing and shout of joy.
The glory of Lebanon will be given to it,
The majesty of Carmel and Sharon.
They will see the glory of the LORD,
The majesty of our God.
3 Encourage the exhausted, and strengthen the feeble.
4 Say to those with anxious heart,
"Take courage, fear not.
Behold, your God will come *with* vengeance;

35:1 Is 6:11; 7:21-25; 27:10; 41:18; 55:12, 13; Is 41:19; 51:3

35:2 Is 27:6; 32:15; Is 25:9; 35:10; 55:12, 13; 66:10, 14; Is 60:13; Song 7:5; Is 25:9

35:3 Job 4:3, 4; Heb 12:12

35:4 Is 32:4; Is 1:24; 47:3; 61:2; 63:4; Is 34:8; 59:18; Ps 145:19; Is 33:22; 35:4

34:16 Isaiah referred to the prophecies that God commanded him to write down as the "book of the LORD." Whoever lived to see the time of Edom's destruction would have only to look to these prophecies to find agreement between what happened and what was predicted. Prophecy predicts and history reveals what has been in God's mind for all time.

35:1ff In chapters 1—34, Isaiah has delivered a message of judgment on all nations, including Israel and Judah, for rejecting God. Although there have been glimpses of relief and restoration for the remnant of faithful believers, the climate of wrath, fury, judgment, and destruction has prevailed. Now Isaiah breaks through with a vision of beauty and encouragement. God is just as thorough in his mercy as he is severe in his judgment. God's complete moral perfection is revealed by his hatred of all sin, and this leads to judgment. This same moral perfection is revealed in his love for all he has created. This leads to mercy for those who have sinned but who have sincerely loved Jesus and put their trust in him.

35:1ff This chapter is a beautiful picture of the final kingdom in which God will establish his justice and destroy all evil. This is the world the redeemed can anticipate after the judgment when creation itself will rejoice in God. Chapter 34 spoke of great distress when God will judge all people for their actions. Chapter 35 pictures the days when life will be peaceful at last and everything will be made right. Carmel and Sharon were regions of thick vegetation and fertile soil. They were symbols of productivity and plenty.

The recompense of God will come,
But He will save you."

35:5 Is 29:18; 32:3, 4; 42:7, 16; 50:4; Matt 11:5; John 9:6, 7

5 Then the eyes of the blind will be opened
And the ears of the deaf will be unstopped.

35:6 Matt 15:30; John 5:8, 9; Acts 3:8; Matt 9:32; Luke 11:14; Is 35:1; 41:18; 43:19; 49:10; 51:3; John 7:38

6 Then the lame will leap like a deer,
And the tongue of the mute will shout for joy.
For waters will break forth in the wilderness
And streams in the Arabah.

35:7 Is 49:10; Is 13:22; 34:13

7 The scorched land will become a pool
And the thirsty ground springs of water;
In the haunt of jackals, its resting place,
Grass *becomes* reeds and rushes.

35:8 Is 11:16; 19:23; 40:3; 49:11; 62:10; Is 30:21; 51:10; Is 4:3; 52:1; Matt 7:13, 14; 1 Pet 1:15, 16; Is 33:8

8 A highway will be there, a roadway,
And it will be called the Highway of Holiness.
The unclean will not travel on it,
But it *will* be for him who walks *that* way,
And fools will not wander *on it.*

35:9 Is 5:29; 30:6; Is 51:10; 62:12; 63:4

9 No lion will be there,
Nor will any vicious beast go up on it;
These will not be found there.
But the redeemed will walk *there,*

35:10 Is 1:27; 51:11; Is 25:8; 30:19; 65:19; Rev 7:17; 21:4

10 And the ransomed of the LORD will return
And come with joyful shouting to Zion,
With everlasting joy upon their heads.
They will find gladness and joy,
And sorrow and sighing will flee away.

Sennacherib Invades Judah

36:1 2 Kin 18:13; 2 Chr 32:1

36:2 2 Kin 18:17-20:11; 2 Chr 32:9-24; Is 36:2-38:8; Is 7:3

36:3 Is 22:20; Is 22:15

36:4 2 Kin 18:19

36:5 2 Kin 18:7

36:6 Ezek 29:6, 7; Ps 146:3; Is 30:3, 5, 7

36:7 Deut 12:2-5; 2 Kin 18:4, 5

36 Now in the fourteenth year of King Hezekiah, Sennacherib king of Assyria came
up against all the fortified cities of Judah and seized them.
2 And the king of Assyria sent Rabshakeh from Lachish to Jerusalem to King Hezekiah with a large army. And he stood by the conduit of the upper pool on the highway of the fuller's field.
3 Then Eliakim the son of Hilkiah, who was over the household, and Shebna the scribe, and Joah the son of Asaph, the recorder, came out to him.
4 Then Rabshakeh said to them, "Say now to Hezekiah, 'Thus says the great king, the king of Assyria, "What is this confidence that you have?
5 "I say, 'Your counsel and strength for the war are only empty words.' Now on whom do you rely, that you have rebelled against me?
6 "Behold, you rely on the staff of this crushed reed, *even* on Egypt, on which if a man leans, it will go into his hand and pierce it. So is Pharaoh king of Egypt to all who rely on him.
7 "But if you say to me, 'We trust in the LORD our God,' is it not He whose high places and whose altars Hezekiah has taken away and has said to Judah and to Jerusalem, 'You shall worship before this altar'?

35:8–10 This highway, the "Highway of Holiness," is the way that righteous pilgrims will take from the desert of suffering to Zion (Jerusalem). It is found only by following God. Only the redeemed will travel God's highway; they will be protected from wicked travelers and harmful animals. God is preparing a way for his people to travel to his home, and he will walk with us. God never stops at simply pointing the way; he is always beside us as we go.

36:4–6 Chapter 19 describes Isaiah's prophecy of judgment upon Egypt, while chapters 30 and 31 pronounce woe on those from Judah who would ally themselves with Egypt in the face of Assyria's impending attack. Sennacherib of Assyria was taunting Judah for trusting in Egypt. Even the Assyrians knew that Egypt could not help Judah.

36:5 Hezekiah put great trust in Pharaoh's promise to help Israel against the Assyrians, but promises are only as good as the credibility of the person making them. It was Pharaoh's word against God's. How quickly we organize our lives around human advice while we neglect God's eternal promises. When choosing between God's word and someone else's, whose will you believe?

36:7 The field commander from Assyria claimed that Hezekiah had insulted God by tearing down his altars and making the people worship only in Jerusalem. But Hezekiah's reform sought to eliminate idol worship (which occurred mainly on high hills) so that the people worshiped only the true God. Either the Assyrians didn't know about the religion of the true God, or they wanted to deceive the people into thinking they had angered a powerful god.

In the same way, Satan tries to confuse or deceive us. People don't necessarily need to be sinful to be ineffective for God; they need only be confused about what God wants. To avoid Satan's deceit, study God's Word carefully and regularly. When you know what God says, you will not fall for Satan's lies.

8 "Now therefore, come make a bargain with my master the king of Assyria, and I will
give you two thousand horses, if you are able on your part to set riders on them.
9 "How then can you repulse one official of the least of my master's servants and rely
on Egypt for chariots and for horsemen?
10 "Have I now come up without the LORD'S approval against this land to destroy it?
The LORD said to me, 'Go up against this land and destroy it.' " ' "
11 Then Eliakim and Shebna and Joah said to Rabshakeh, "Speak now to your servants in Aramaic, for we understand *it;* and do not speak with us in Judean in the hearing of the people who are on the wall."
12 But Rabshakeh said, "Has my master sent me only to your master and to you to speak these words, *and* not to the men who sit on the wall, *doomed* to eat their own dung and drink their own urine with you?"
13 Then Rabshakeh stood and cried with a loud voice in Judean and said, "Hear the
words of the great king, the king of Assyria.
14 "Thus says the king, 'Do not let Hezekiah deceive you, for he will not be able to deliver you;
15 nor let Hezekiah make you trust in the LORD, saying, "The LORD will surely deliver
us, this city will not be given into the hand of the king of Assyria."
16 'Do not listen to Hezekiah,' for thus says the king of Assyria, 'Make your peace with
me and come out to me, and eat each of his vine and each of his fig tree and drink each
of the waters of his own cistern,
17 until I come and take you away to a land like your own land, a land of grain and new
wine, a land of bread and vineyards.

36:9 Is 20:5; 30:2-5, 7; 31:3

36:10 1 Kin 13:18; 22:6, 12

36:11 Ezra 4:7; Dan 2:4; Is 36:13

36:13 2 Chr 32:18

36:14 Is 37:10

36:15 Is 36:18, 20; 37:10, 11

36:16 1 Kin 4:25; Mic 4:4; Zech 3:10; Prov 5:15

ASSYRIA ADVANCES
As Sennacherib beautified his capital city, Nineveh, Hezekiah withheld tribute and prepared for battle. The Assyrians advanced toward their rebellious western border, attacking swiftly down the Mediterranean coast. From Lachish, Sennacherib threatened to take Jerusalem, but Isaiah knew his threats would die with him on his return to Nineveh.

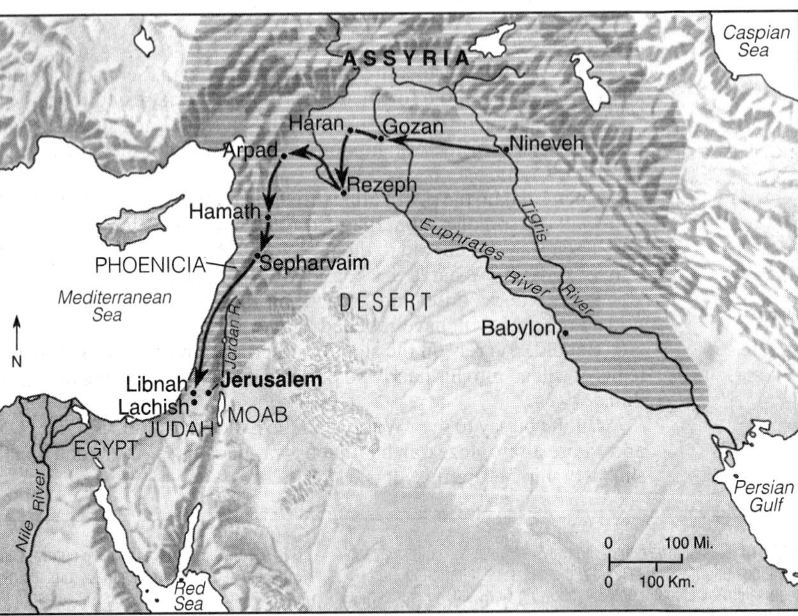

36:10 Sennacherib continued his demoralization campaign by sending the field commander to try to convince the people of Judah that God had turned against them. The Assyrians hoped to convince the people of Judah to surrender without fighting. But Isaiah had already said that the Assyrians *would not* destroy Jerusalem, so the people did not need to be afraid of them (10:24–27; 29:5–8).

36:11 Aramaic was an international language at this time. See also 22:15–25 for Isaiah's prophecies concerning Eliakim and Shebna.

36:17 Sennacherib's commander tried yet another ploy to demoralize the people. He appealed to the starving city under siege by offering to take them to a land with plenty of food if they surrendered. The Assyrian policy for dealing with conquered nations was to resettle the inhabitants and then to move other conquered peoples into the recently conquered area. This provided manpower for their armies and prevented revolts in conquered territories.

36:18 Is 36:15
36:19 Is 10:9-11; 37:11-13; Jer 49:23; 2 Kin 17:6
36:20 1 Kin 20:23, 28; Is 36:15
36:21 Prov 9:7, 8; 26:4
36:22 Is 22:20; 36:3; Is 22:15

18 '*Beware* that Hezekiah does not mislead you, saying, "The LORD will deliver us."
Has any one of the gods of the nations delivered his land from the hand of the king of
Assyria?
19 'Where are the gods of Hamath and Arpad? Where are the gods of Sepharvaim?
And when have they delivered Samaria from my hand?
20 'Who among all the gods of these lands have delivered their land from my hand, that
the LORD would deliver Jerusalem from my hand?' "
21 But they were silent and answered him not a word; for the king's commandment
was, "Do not answer him."
22 Then Eliakim the son of Hilkiah, who was over the household, and Shebna the scribe
and Joah the son of Asaph, the recorder, came to Hezekiah with their clothes torn and
told him the words of Rabshakeh.

Hezekiah Seeks Isaiah's Help

37:1 2 Kin 19:1-37; Is 37:1-38
37:2 Is 22:20; Is 22:15; Is 1:1; 20:2
37:3 Is 22:5; 26:16; 33:2; Is 26:17, 18; 66:9; Hos 13:13
37:4 Is 36:13-15, 18, 20; Is 1:9; 10:20-22; 37:31, 32; 46:3
37:6 Is 7:4; 35:4
37:7 Is 37:9; Is 37:37, 38
37:8 Num 33:20; Josh 10:29; Josh 10:31, 32
37:9 Is 37:7; Is 18:1; 20:5
37:10 Is 36:15
37:11 Is 10:9-11; 36:18-20
37:12 2 Kin 17:6; 18:11; Gen 11:31; 12:1-4; Acts 7:2

37 And when King Hezekiah heard *it,* he tore his clothes, covered himself with sack
cloth and entered the house of the LORD.
2 Then he sent Eliakim who was over the household with Shebna the scribe and the
elders of the priests, covered with sackcloth, to Isaiah the prophet, the son of Amoz.
3 They said to him, "Thus says Hezekiah, 'This day is a day of distress, rebuke and
rejection; for children have come to birth, and there is no strength to deliver.
4 'Perhaps the LORD your God will hear the words of Rabshakeh, whom his master
the king of Assyria has sent to reproach the living God, and will rebuke the words which
the LORD your God has heard. Therefore, offer a prayer for the remnant that is left.' "
5 So the servants of King Hezekiah came to Isaiah.
6 Isaiah said to them, "Thus you shall say to your master, 'Thus says the LORD, "Do
not be afraid because of the words that you have heard, with which the servants of the
king of Assyria have blasphemed Me.
7 "Behold, I will put a spirit in him so that he will hear a rumor and return to his own
land. And I will make him fall by the sword in his own land." ' "
8 Then Rabshakeh returned and found the king of Assyria fighting against Libnah,
for he had heard that the king had left Lachish.
9 When he heard *them* say concerning Tirhakah king of Cush, "He has come out to
fight against you," and when he heard *it* he sent messengers to Hezekiah, saying,
10 "Thus you shall say to Hezekiah king of Judah, 'Do not let your God in whom you
trust deceive you, saying, "Jerusalem will not be given into the hand of the king of
Assyria."
11 'Behold, you have heard what the kings of Assyria have done to all the lands, destroying them completely. So will you be spared?
12 'Did the gods of those nations which my fathers have destroyed deliver them, *even*
Gozan and Haran and Rezeph and the sons of Eden who *were* in Telassar?
13 'Where is the king of Hamath, the king of Arpad, the king of the city of Sepharvaim,
and of Hena and Ivvah?' "

Hezekiah's Prayer in the Temple

14 Then Hezekiah took the letter from the hand of the messengers and read it, and he
went up to the house of the LORD and spread it out before the LORD.
15 Hezekiah prayed to the LORD saying,

36:19–20 The field commander said that the gods of the other cities he had conquered had not been able to save their people, so how could the God of Jerusalem save them? The Lord was supposedly the God of Samaria (the northern kingdom), and it fell. But the Lord was the God of Samaria in name only because the people were not worshiping him. That is why prophets foretold the fall of Samaria. But for the Lord's own sake and for the sake of David, the Lord would rescue them from the Assyrian army (37:35).

37:3 Judah is compared to a woman who is trying to give birth to a child but is too weak to deliver. When the situation seemed hopeless, Hezekiah didn't give up. Instead, he asked the prophet Isaiah to pray that God would help his people. No matter how bad your circumstances seem, don't despair. Turn to God.

37:4 Hezekiah did exactly what Isaiah had been calling the people to do (chapters 1—35). He turned to God and watched him come to Judah's aid. Turning to God means believing that God is there and that he is able to help us.

37:8–10 Although the answer to Hezekiah's prayer was already in motion because Tirhakah was poised to attack, Hezekiah did not know it. He persisted in prayer and faith even though he could not see the answer coming. When we pray, we must have faith that God has already prepared the best answer. Our task is to ask in faith and wait in humility.

16 "O LORD of hosts, the God of Israel, who is enthroned *above* the cherubim, You are
the God, You alone, of all the kingdoms of the earth. You have made heaven and earth.
17 "Incline Your ear, O LORD, and hear; open Your eyes, O LORD, and see; and listen
to all the words of Sennacherib, who sent *them* to reproach the living God.
18 "Truly, O LORD, the kings of Assyria have devastated all the countries and their lands,
19 and have cast their gods into the fire, for they were not gods but the work of men's
hands, wood and stone. So they have destroyed them.
20 "Now, O LORD our God, deliver us from his hand that all the kingdoms of the earth
may know that You alone, LORD, are God."

God Answers through Isaiah

21 Then Isaiah the son of Amoz sent *word* to Hezekiah, saying, "Thus says the LORD,
the God of Israel, 'Because you have prayed to Me about Sennacherib king of Assyria,
22 this is the word that the LORD has spoken against him:

"She has despised you and mocked you,
The virgin daughter of Zion;
She has shaken *her* head behind you,
The daughter of Jerusalem!

23 "Whom have you reproached and blasphemed?
And against whom have you raised *your* voice
And haughtily lifted up your eyes?
Against the Holy One of Israel!

24 "Through your servants you have reproached the Lord,
And you have said, 'With my many chariots I came up to the heights of the mountains,
To the remotest parts of Lebanon;
And I cut down its tall cedars *and* its choice cypresses.
And I will go to its highest peak, its thickest forest.

25 'I dug *wells* and drank waters,
And with the sole of my feet I dried up
All the rivers of Egypt.'

26 "Have you not heard?
Long ago I did it,
From ancient times I planned it.
Now I have brought it to pass,
That you should turn fortified cities into ruinous heaps.

27 "Therefore their inhabitants were short of strength,
They were dismayed and put to shame;
They were *as* the vegetation of the field and *as* the green herb,
As grass on the housetops is scorched before it is grown up.

28 "But I know your sitting down
And your going out and your coming in
And your raging against Me.

29 "Because of your raging against Me
And because your arrogance has come up to My ears,
Therefore I will put My hook in your nose
And My bridle in your lips,
And I will turn you back by the way which you came.

30 "Then this shall be the sign for you: you will eat this year what grows of itself, in the
second year what springs from the same, and in the third year sow, reap, plant vineyards
and eat their fruit.
31 "The surviving remnant of the house of Judah will again take root downward and
bear fruit upward.

37:16 Ex 25:22; 1 Sam 4:4; Ps 80:1; 99:1; Deut 10:17; Ps 86:10; 136:2, 3; Is 42:5; 45:12; Jer 10:12

37:17 2 Chr 6:40; Ps 17:6; Dan 9:18; Ps 74:22; Is 37:4

37:18 2 Kin 15:29; 16:9; 17:6, 24; 1 Chr 5:26

37:19 Is 2:8; 17:8; 41:24, 29; Is 26:14

37:20 Is 25:9; 33:22; 35:4; 1 Kin 18:36, 37; Ps 46:10; Is 37:16; Ezek 36:23

37:21 Is 37:2

37:22 Jer 14:17; Lam 2:13; Ps 9:14; Zeph 3:14; Zech 2:10; Job 16:4

37:23 Is 37:4; Is 2:11; 5:15, 21; Ezek 39:7; Hab 1:12

37:24 Is 10:33, 34; Is 14:8; Is 10:18

37:25 Deut 11:10; 1 Kin 20:10

37:26 Is 40:21, 28; Acts 2:23; 4:27, 28; 1 Pet 2:8; Is 46:11; Is 10:6; Is 17:1; 25:2

37:27 Is 40:7; Ps 129:6

37:28 Ps 139:1

37:29 Is 10:12; Ezek 29:4; 38:4; Is 30:28; Is 37:34

37:30 Lev 25:5, 11

37:31 Is 4:2; 10:20; Is 37:4; Is 27:6

37:16 Cherubim are mighty angels. "Enthroned above the cherubim" refers to the atonement cover on the ark of the covenant in the Jerusalem temple. This is a description of God's holiness, power, and sovereignty.

37:29 This was a common torture the Assyrians used on their captives. They were often led away with hooks in their noses or bits in their mouths as signs of humiliation.

32 "For out of Jerusalem will go forth a remnant and out of Mount Zion survivors. The
zeal of the LORD of hosts will perform this." '
33 "Therefore, thus says the LORD concerning the king of Assyria, 'He will not come to
this city or shoot an arrow there; and he will not come before it with a shield, or throw
up a siege ramp against it.
34 'By the way that he came, by the same he will return, and he will not come to this
city,' declares the LORD.
35 'For I will defend this city to save it for My own sake and for My servant David's
sake.' "

Assyrians Destroyed

36 Then the angel of the LORD went out and struck 185,000 in the camp of the Assyrians; and when men arose early in the morning, behold, all of these were dead.
37 So Sennacherib king of Assyria departed and returned *home* and lived at Nineveh.
38 It came about as he was worshiping in the house of Nisroch his god, that Adrammelech and Sharezer his sons killed him with the sword; and they escaped into the land of
Ararat. And Esarhaddon his son became king in his place.

Hezekiah Healed

38 In those days Hezekiah became mortally ill. And Isaiah the prophet the son of
Amoz came to him and said to him, "Thus says the LORD, 'Set your house in order, for you shall die and not live.' "
2 Then Hezekiah turned his face to the wall and prayed to the LORD,
3 and said, "Remember now, O LORD, I beseech You, how I have walked before You
in truth and with a whole heart, and have done what is good in Your sight." And Hezekiah wept bitterly.
4 Then the word of the LORD came to Isaiah, saying,
5 "Go and say to Hezekiah, 'Thus says the LORD, the God of your father David, "I
have heard your prayer, I have seen your tears; behold, I will add fifteen years to your
life.
6 "I will deliver you and this city from the hand of the king of Assyria; and I will defend
this city." '
7 "This shall be the sign to you from the LORD, that the LORD will do this thing that
He has spoken:
8 "Behold, I will cause the shadow on the stairway, which has gone down with the sun
on the stairway of Ahaz, to go back ten steps." So the sun's *shadow* went back ten steps
on the stairway on which it had gone down.
9 A writing of Hezekiah king of Judah after his illness and recovery:

10 I said, "In the middle of my life
I am to enter the gates of Sheol;
I am to be deprived of the rest of my years."
11 I said, "I will not see the LORD,
The LORD in the land of the living;
I will look on man no more among the inhabitants of the world.
12 "Like a shepherd's tent my dwelling is pulled up and removed from me;
As a weaver I rolled up my life.
He cuts me off from the loom;
From day until night You make an end of me.
13 "I composed *my soul* until morning.

37:32 Is 37:4; 2 Kin 19:31; Is 9:7; 59:17; Joel 2:18; Zech 1:14
37:33 Jer 6:6; 32:24
37:34 Is 37:29
37:35 2 Kin 20:6; Is 31:5; 38:6; Is 43:25; 48:9, 11
37:36 2 Kin 19:35; Is 10:12, 33, 34
37:37 Gen 10:11; Jon 1:2; 3:3; 4:11; Zeph 2:13
37:38 Gen 8:4; Jer 51:27; Ezra 4:2
38:1 2 Kin 20:1-6, 9-11; 2 Chr 32:24; Is 38:1-8; Is 1:1; 37:2; 2 Sam 17:23
38:3 Neh 13:14; 2 Kin 18:5, 6; Ps 26:3; 1 Chr 28:9; 29:19; Deut 6:18; Ps 6:6-8
38:5 2 Kin 18:2, 13
38:6 Is 31:5; 37:35
38:7 Judg 6:17, 21, 36-40; Is 7:11, 14; 37:30
38:8 2 Kin 20:9-11; Josh 10:12-14
38:10 Ps 102:24; Ps 107:18; Job 17:11, 15; 2 Cor 1:9
38:11 Ps 27:13; 116:9
38:12 2 Cor 5:1, 4; 2 Pet 1:13, 14; Job 7:6; Heb 1:12; Job 6:9; Job 4:20; Ps 73:14
38:13 Job 10:16; Ps 51:8; Dan 6:24; Ps 32:4

37:35 God would defend Jerusalem for the sake of his honor and for David's sake in remembrance of his promise to David. Assyria had insulted God. They would not be his instrument to punish Jerusalem. What Jerusalem could not possibly do, God would do for them. God is prepared to do the impossible if we trust him enough to ask.

37:38 The death of Sennacherib was prophesied by Isaiah in 10:12, 33–34 and in 37:7. His death is also recorded in 2 Kings 19.

38:1ff The events of chapters 38 and 39 happened before those of chapters 36 and 37.

38:1–5 When Isaiah went to Hezekiah, who was extremely ill, and told him of his impending death, Hezekiah immediately turned to God. God responded to his prayer, allowing Hezekiah to live another 15 years. In response to fervent prayer, God may change the course of our lives too. Never hesitate to ask God for radical changes if you will honor him with those changes.

38:1–6 According to 2 Chronicles 32:24–26, Hezekiah had a problem with pride even after this double miracle of healing and deliverance. Eventually he and his subjects humbled themselves, so God's judgment was put off for several more generations.

Like a lion—so He breaks all my bones,
From day until night You make an end of me.
14 "Like a swallow, *like* a crane, so I twitter;
I moan like a dove;
My eyes look wistfully to the heights;
O Lord, I am oppressed, be my security.

15 "What shall I say?
For He has spoken to me, and He Himself has done it;
I will wander about all my years because of the bitterness of my soul.
16 "O Lord, by *these* things *men* live,
And in all these is the life of my spirit;
O restore me to health and let me live!
17 "Lo, for *my own* welfare I had great bitterness;
It is You who has kept my soul from the pit of nothingness,
For You have cast all my sins behind Your back.
18 "For Sheol cannot thank You,
Death cannot praise You;
Those who go down to the pit cannot hope for Your faithfulness.
19 "It is the living who give thanks to You, as I do today;
A father tells his sons about Your faithfulness.
20 "The LORD will surely save me;
So we will play my songs on stringed instruments
All *the* days of our life at the house of the LORD."
21 Now Isaiah had said, "Let them take a cake of figs and apply it to the boil, that he
may recover."
22 Then Hezekiah had said, "What is the sign that I shall go up to the house of the
LORD?"

38:14
Job 30:29; Ps 102:6; Is 59:11; Ezek 7:16; Nah 2:7; Ps 119:123; Job 17:3; Ps 119:122

38:15
Ps 39:9; 1 Kin 21:27; Job 7:11; 10:1; Is 38:17

38:16
Ps 119:71, 75; Ps 39:13; Ps 119:25

38:17
Ps 30:3; 86:13; Jon 2:6; Is 43:25; Jer 31:34; Mic 7:19

38:18
Ps 6:5; 30:9; 88:11; Eccl 9:10; Num 16:33; Ps 28:1

38:19
Ps 118:17; 119:175; Deut 6:7; 11:19; Ps 78:5-7

38:20
Ps 33:1-3; 68:24-26; Ps 104:33; 116:2; 146:2; Ps 116:17-19

38:21
2 Kin 20:7, 8

38:22
Is 38:7

Hezekiah Shows His Treasures

39 At that time Merodach-baladan son of Baladan, king of Babylon, sent letters and
a present to Hezekiah, for he heard that he had been sick and had recovered.
2 Hezekiah was pleased, and showed them *all* his treasure house, the silver and the
gold and the spices and the precious oil and his whole armory and all that was found in
his treasuries. There was nothing in his house nor in all his dominion that Hezekiah did
not show them.
3 Then Isaiah the prophet came to King Hezekiah and said to him, "What did these
men say, and from where have they come to you?" And Hezekiah said, "They have come
to me from a far country, from Babylon."
4 He said, "What have they seen in your house?" So Hezekiah answered, "They have
seen all that is in my house; there is nothing among my treasuries that I have not shown
them."
5 Then Isaiah said to Hezekiah, "Hear the word of the LORD of hosts,
6 'Behold, the days are coming when all that is in your house and all that your fathers

39:1
2 Kin 20:12-19; 2 Chr 32:31; Is 39:1-8

39:2
2 Chr 32:25, 31; Job 31:25; 2 Kin 18:15, 16

39:3
2 Sam 12:1; 2 Chr 16:7; Deut 28:49; Jer 5:15

39:5
1 Sam 13:13, 14; 15:16

39:6
2 Kin 24:13; 25:13-15; Jer 20:5

38:16–18 Hezekiah realized that his prayer brought deliverance and forgiveness. His words "death cannot praise You" may reveal that he was unaware of the blessedness of the future life for those who trust in God (57:1–2), or he may have meant that dead bodies cannot praise God. In either case, Hezekiah knew that God had spared his life, so in his poem Hezekiah praises God. Hezekiah recognized the good that came from his bitter experience. The next time you have difficult struggles, pray for God's help to gain something beneficial from them.

38:19 Hezekiah spoke of the significance of passing the joy of the Lord from father to child, from generation to generation. The heritage of our faith has come to us because of faithful men and women who have carried God's message to us across the centuries. Do you share with your children or other young people the excitement of your relationship with God?

39:1ff Merodach-baladan, a Babylonian prince, was planning a revolt against Assyria and was forming an alliance. He probably hoped to convince Hezekiah to join this alliance against Assyria. Hezekiah, feeling honored by this attention and perhaps feeling some sympathy for their proposal, showed the Babylonian envoys his treasures. But Isaiah warned the king not to trust Babylon. Someday they would turn on Judah and devour Jerusalem's wealth.

39:4–7 What was so wrong about showing these Babylonians around? Hezekiah failed to see that the Babylonians would become his next threat, and that they, not the Assyrians, would conquer his city. When Isaiah told him that Babylon would someday carry it all away, this was an amazing prophecy because Babylon was struggling for independence under Assyria. Hezekiah's self-satisfied display of his earthly treasures brought its own consequences (2 Kings 25; Daniel 1:1–2). His response (39:8) may seem a bit shortsighted, but he simply was expressing gratitude for the blessing from God that peace would reign during his lifetime and that God's judgment would not be more severe.

have laid up in store to this day will be carried to Babylon; nothing will be left,' says the
LORD.
7 'And *some* of your sons who will issue from you, whom you will beget, will be taken
away, and they will become officials in the palace of the king of Babylon.' "
8 Then Hezekiah said to Isaiah, "The word of the LORD which you have spoken is
good." For he thought, "For there will be peace and truth in my days."

39:7 2 Kin 24:10-16; 2 Chr 36:10; Dan 1:1-7
39:8 2 Chr 32:26; 2 Chr 34:28

B. WORDS OF COMFORT (40:1—66:24)

Isaiah now speaks of events that will occur after the captivity. This includes the decree by Cyrus to release the remnant captives and allow them to return to Jerusalem after he conquered Babylon. But Isaiah also foretells the coming of the suffering Servant, Jesus Christ, and describes his life and death with incredible detail. Isaiah also speaks about the coming of the new heavens and earth, when God's people will be completely restored. Because all believers will participate in this new world to come, we can have confident hope in the future.

1. Israel's release from captivity

The Greatness of God

40 "Comfort, O comfort My people," says your God.
2 "Speak kindly to Jerusalem;
And call out to her, that her warfare has ended,
That her iniquity has been removed,
That she has received of the LORD'S hand
Double for all her sins."

3 A voice is calling,
"Clear the way for the LORD in the wilderness;
Make smooth in the desert a highway for our God.
4 "Let every valley be lifted up,
And every mountain and hill be made low;
And let the rough ground become a plain,
And the rugged terrain a broad valley;
5 Then the glory of the LORD will be revealed,
And all flesh will see *it* together;
For the mouth of the LORD has spoken."
6 A voice says, "Call out."
Then he answered, "What shall I call out?"
All flesh is grass, and all its loveliness is like the flower of the field.
7 The grass withers, the flower fades,
When the breath of the LORD blows upon it;
Surely the people are grass.

40:1 Is 12:1; 49:13; 51:3, 12; 52:9; 61:2; 66:13; Jer 31:10-14; Zeph 3:14-17; 2 Cor 1:4
40:2 Is 35:4; Zech 1:13; Is 41:11-13; 49:25; 54:15, 17; Is 33:24; 53:5, 6, 11; Jer 16:18; Zech 9:12; Rev 18:6
40:3 Matt 3:3; Mark 1:3; Luke 3:4-6; John 1:23; Mal 3:1; 4:5, 6
40:5 Is 6:3; Hab 2:14; Is 52:10; Joel 2:28; Is 1:20; 34:16; 58:14
40:6 Job 14:2; Ps 102:11; 103:15; 1 Pet 1:24, 25
40:7 Ps 90:5, 6; James 1:10, 11; Job 4:9; 41:21; Is 11:4; 40:24

39:8 Hezekiah, one of Judah's most faithful kings, worked hard throughout his reign to stamp out idol worship and to purify the worship of the true God at the Jerusalem temple. Nevertheless, he knew his kingdom was not pure. Powerful undercurrents of evil invited destruction, and only God's miraculous interventions preserved Judah from its enemies. Here Hezekiah was grateful that God would preserve peace during his reign. As soon as Hezekiah died, the nation rushed back to its sinful ways under the leadership of Manasseh, Hezekiah's son. He actually rebuilt the centers of idolatry his father had destroyed.

40:1ff The book of Isaiah makes a dramatic shift at this point. The following chapters discuss the majesty of God, who is coming to rule the earth and judge all people. God will reunite Israel and Judah and restore them to glory. Instead of warning the people of impending judgment, Isaiah here comforts them. Chapter 40 refers to the restoration after the exile. Cyrus is the instrument of their deliverance from Babylon. Secondarily, it looks to the end of time when "Babylon"—the future evil world system—will be destroyed and the persecution of God's people will end.

40:1–2 Judah still had 100 years of trouble before Jerusalem would fall, then 70 years of exile. So God tells Isaiah to speak tenderly and to comfort Jerusalem.

The seeds of comfort may take root in the soil of adversity. When your life seems to be falling apart, ask God to comfort you. You may not escape adversity, but you may find God's comfort as you face it. Sometimes, however, the only comfort we have is in the knowledge that someday we will be with God. Appreciate the comfort and encouragement found in his Word, his presence, and his people.

40:3–5 Preparing a smooth highway means removing obstacles and rolling out the red carpet for the coming of the Lord. The wilderness is a picture of life's trials and sufferings. We are not immune to these, but our faith need not be hindered by them. Isaiah told people to prepare to see God work. John the Baptist used these words as he challenged the people to prepare for the coming Messiah (Matthew 3:3).

40:6–8 People are compared here to grass and flowers that wither away. We are mortal, but God's Word is eternal and unfailing. Public opinion changes and is unreliable, but God's Word is constant. Only in God's eternal Word will we find lasting solutions to our problems and needs.

8 The grass withers, the flower fades,
But the word of our God stands forever.

9 Get yourself up on a high mountain,
O Zion, bearer of good news,
Lift up your voice mightily,
O Jerusalem, bearer of good news;
Lift *it* up, do not fear.
Say to the cities of Judah,
"Here is your God!"
10 Behold, the Lord GOD will come with might,
With His arm ruling for Him.
Behold, His reward is with Him
And His recompense before Him.
11 Like a shepherd He will tend His flock,
In His arm He will gather the lambs
And carry *them* in His bosom;
He will gently lead the nursing *ewes*.

12 Who has measured the waters in the hollow of His hand,
And marked off the heavens by the span,
And calculated the dust of the earth by the measure,
And weighed the mountains in a balance
And the hills in a pair of scales?
13 Who has directed the Spirit of the LORD,
Or as His counselor has informed Him?
14 With whom did He consult and *who* gave Him understanding?
And *who* taught Him in the path of justice and taught Him knowledge
And informed Him of the way of understanding?
15 Behold, the nations are like a drop from a bucket,
And are regarded as a speck of dust on the scales;
Behold, He lifts up the islands like fine dust.
16 Even Lebanon is not enough to burn,
Nor its beasts enough for a burnt offering.
17 All the nations are as nothing before Him,
They are regarded by Him as less than nothing and meaningless.

18 To whom then will you liken God?
Or what likeness will you compare with Him?
19 *As for* the idol, a craftsman casts it,
A goldsmith plates it with gold,
And a silversmith *fashions* chains of silver.
20 He who is too impoverished for *such* an offering
Selects a tree that does not rot;
He seeks out for himself a skillful craftsman
To prepare an idol that will not totter.

21 Do you not know? Have you not heard?
Has it not been declared to you from the beginning?
Have you not understood from the foundations of the earth?

40:8 Is 55:11; 59:21; Matt 5:18
40:9 Is 52:7; Is 61:1; Is 44:26; Is 25:9; 35:2
40:10 Is 9:6, 7; Is 59:16, 18; Is 62:11; Rev 22:12
40:11 Jer 31:10; Ezek 34:12-14, 23, 31; Mic 5:4; John 10:11, 14-16
40:12 Job 38:8-11; Ps 102:25, 26; Is 48:13; Heb 1:10-12
40:13 Rom 11:34; 1 Cor 2:16; Is 41:28
40:14 Job 38:4; Job 21:22; Col 2:3
40:15 Jer 10:10; Is 17:13; 29:5
40:16 Ps 50:9-11; Mic 6:6, 7; Heb 10:5-9
40:17 Is 29:7
40:18 Ex 8:10; 15:11; 1 Sam 2:2; Is 40:25; 46:5; Mic 7:18; Acts 17:29
40:19 Ps 115:4-8; Is 41:7; 44:10; Hab 2:18, 19; Is 2:20; 30:22
40:20 Is 44:14; 1 Sam 5:3, 4; Is 41:7; 46:7
40:21 Ps 19:1; 50:6; Is 37:26; Acts 14:17; Rom 1:19; Is 48:13; 51:13

40:11 God is often pictured as a shepherd, gently caring for and guiding his flock. He is powerful (40:10), yet careful and gentle. He is called a shepherd (Psalm 23); the good shepherd (John 10:11, 14); the great Shepherd (Hebrews 13:20); and the Chief Shepherd (1 Peter 5:4). Note that the shepherd is caring for the most defenseless members of his society: children and those caring for them. This reinforces the prophetic theme that the truly powerful nation is not the one with a strong military, but rather the one that relies on God's caring strength.

40:12–31 Isaiah describes God's power to create, his provision to sustain, and his presence to help. God is almighty and all-powerful; but even so, he cares for each of us personally. No person or thing can be compared to God (40:25). We describe God as best we can with our limited knowledge and language, but we only limit our understanding of him and his power when we compare him to what we experience on earth. What is your concept of God, especially as revealed in his Son, Jesus Christ? Don't limit his work in your life by underestimating him.

40:22
Job 22:14; Prov 8:27; Num 13:33; Job 9:8; Is 37:16; 42:5; 44:24; Ps 104:2; Job 36:29; Ps 18:11; 19:4

40:23
Job 12:21; Ps 107:40; Is 34:12; Is 5:21; Jer 25:18-27

40:24
Is 17:13; 41:16

40:25
Is 40:18

40:26
Is 51:6; Is 42:5; 48:12, 13; Ps 147:4; Ps 89:11-13; Is 34:16; 48:13

22 It is He who [14]sits above the [15]circle of the earth,
And its inhabitants are like grasshoppers,
Who stretches out the heavens like a curtain
And spreads them out like a tent to dwell in.
23 He *it is* who reduces rulers to nothing,
Who makes the judges of the earth meaningless.
24 [16]Scarcely have they been planted,
[16]Scarcely have they been sown,
[16]Scarcely has their stock taken root in the earth,
But He merely blows on them, and they wither,
And the storm carries them away like stubble.
25 "To whom then will you liken Me
That I would be *his* equal?" says the Holy One.
26 Lift up your eyes on high
And see who has created these *stars,*
The One who leads forth their host by number,
He calls them all by name;
Because of the greatness of His might and the strength of *His* power,
Not one *of them* is missing.

40:27
Is 49:4, 14; Is 54:8; Job 27:2; 34:5; Luke 18:7, 8; Is 25:1

40:28
Is 40:21; Gen 21:33; Ps 90:2; Ps 147:5; Rom 11:33

40:29
Is 50:4; Jer 31:25; Is 41:10

40:30
Jer 6:11; 9:21; Is 9:17

40:31
Job 17:9; Ps 103:5; 2 Cor 4:8-10, 16; Ex 19:4; Deut 32:11; Luke 18:1; 2 Cor 4:1, 16; Gal 6:9; Heb 12:3

27 Why do you say, O Jacob, and assert, O Israel,
"My way is hidden from the LORD,
And the justice due me escapes the notice of my God"?
28 Do you not know? Have you not heard?
The Everlasting God, the LORD, the Creator of the ends of the earth
Does not become weary or tired.
His understanding is inscrutable.
29 He gives strength to the weary,
And to *him who* lacks might He increases power.
30 Though youths grow weary and tired,
And vigorous young men stumble badly,
31 Yet those who wait for the LORD
Will gain new strength;
They will mount up *with* wings like eagles,
They will run and not get tired,
They will walk and not become weary.

Israel Encouraged

41:1
Is 11:11; Hab 2:20; Zech 2:13; Is 40:31; Is 34:1; 48:16; Is 1:18; 43:26; 50:8

41:2
Is 41:25; 45:1-3; 46:11; Is 42:6; 2 Chr 36:23; Ezra 1:2; 2 Sam 22:43; Is 40:24

41 "Coastlands, listen to Me in silence,
And let the peoples gain new strength;
Let them come forward, then let them speak;
Let us come together for judgment.
2 "Who has aroused one from the east
Whom He calls in righteousness to His feet?
He delivers up nations before him
And subdues kings.
He makes them like dust with his sword,
As the wind-driven chaff with his bow.
3 "He pursues them, passing on in safety,
By a way he had not been traversing with his feet.

14 Or *is enthroned* **15** Or *vault* **16** Or *Not even*

40:29–31 Even the strongest people get tired at times, but God's power and strength never diminish. He is never too tired or too busy to help and listen. His strength is our source of strength. When you feel all of life crushing you and cannot go another step, remember that you can call upon God to renew your strength.

40:31 Hoping in the Lord is expecting that his promise of strength will help us to rise above life's distractions and difficulties. It also means trusting in God. Trusting helps us to be prepared when he speaks to us. Then we will be patient when he asks us to wait and expect him to fulfill the promises found in his Word.

41:1ff The "one from the east" is Cyrus II of Persia, who would be king within a century and a half (he is also mentioned by name in 44:28). He conquered Babylon in 539 B.C. and was responsible for the decree releasing the exiled Jews to return to Jerusalem. God could even use a pagan ruler to protect and care for Israel, because God is in control of all world empires and politics.

4 "Who has performed and accomplished *it,*
Calling forth the generations from the beginning?
'I, the LORD, am the first, and with the last. I am He.' "

5 The coastlands have seen and are afraid;
The ends of the earth tremble;
They have drawn near and have come.
6 Each one helps his neighbor
And says to his brother, "Be strong!"
7 So the craftsman encourages the smelter,
And he who smooths *metal* with the hammer *encourages* him who beats the anvil,
Saying of the soldering, "It is good";
And he fastens it with nails,
So that it will not totter.
8 "But you, Israel, My servant,
Jacob whom I have chosen,
Descendant of Abraham My friend,
9 You whom I have taken from the ends of the earth,
And called from its remotest parts
And said to you, 'You are My servant,
I have chosen you and not rejected you.
10 'Do not fear, for I am with you;
Do not anxiously look about you, for I am your God.
I will strengthen you, surely I will help you,
Surely I will uphold you with My righteous right hand.'
11 "Behold, all those who are angered at you will be shamed and dishonored;
Those who contend with you will be as nothing and will perish.
12 "You will seek those who quarrel with you, but will not find them,
Those who war with you will be as nothing and non-existent.
13 "For I am the LORD your God, who upholds your right hand,
Who says to you, 'Do not fear, I will help you.'
14 "Do not fear, you worm Jacob, you men of Israel;
I will help you," declares the LORD, "and your Redeemer is the Holy One of Israel.
15 "Behold, I have made you a new, sharp threshing sledge with double edges;
You will thresh the mountains and pulverize *them,*
And will make the hills like chaff.
16 "You will winnow them, and the wind will carry them away,
And the storm will scatter them;
But you will rejoice in the LORD,
You will glory in the Holy One of Israel.

17 "The afflicted and needy are seeking water, but there is none,
And their tongue is parched with thirst;
I, the LORD, will answer them Myself,
As the God of Israel I will not forsake them.
18 "I will open rivers on the bare heights
And springs in the midst of the valleys;
I will make the wilderness a pool of water
And the dry land fountains of water.
19 "I will put the cedar in the wilderness,

41:4 Is 41:26; 44:7; 46:10; Is 43:10; 44:6; Rev 1:8, 17; 22:13; Is 43:13; 46:4; 48:12

41:5 Is 41:1; Ezek 26:15, 16; Josh 5:1; Ps 67:7

41:7 Is 44:12, 13; Is 40:19; Is 40:20; 46:7

41:8 Is 42:19; 43:10; 44:1, 2, 21; Is 29:22; 51:2; 63:16; 2 Chr 20:7; James 2:23

41:9 Is 11:11; Is 43:5-7; Is 42:1; 44:1; Deut 7:6; 14:2; Ps 135:4

41:10 Deut 20:1; 31:6; Josh 1:9; Ps 27:1; Is 41:13, 14; 43:2, 5; Rom 8:31; Is 41:14; 44:2; 49:8; Ps 89:13, 14

41:11 Is 45:24; Is 17:13; 29:5, 7, 8

41:12 Job 20:7-9; Ps 37:35, 36; Is 17:14

41:13 Is 42:6; 45:1; Is 41:10

41:14 Job 25:6; Ps 22:6; Is 35:10; 43:14; 44:6, 22-24

41:15 Mic 4:13; Hab 3:12; Is 42:15; 64:1; Jer 9:10; Ezek 33:28

41:16 Jer 51:2; Is 25:9; 35:10; 51:3; 61:10

41:17 Is 43:20; 44:3; 49:10; 55:1; Is 30:19; 65:24; Is 42:16; 62:12

41:18 Is 30:25; 43:19; Ps 107:35; Is 35:6, 7

41:19 Is 35:1; 55:13; 60:13

41:4 Each generation gets caught up in its own problems, but God's plan embraces all generations. When your great-grandparents lived, God worked personally in the lives of his people. When your great-grandchildren live, God will still work personally in the lives of his people. He is the only one who sees 100 years from now as clearly as 100 years ago. When you are concerned about the future, talk with God, who knows the generations of the future as well as he knows the generations of the past.

41:8–10 God chose Israel through Abraham because he wanted to, not because the people deserved it (Deuteronomy 7:6–8; 9:4–6). Although God chose the Israelites to represent him to the world, they failed to do this; so God punished them and sent them into captivity. Now all believers are God's chosen people, and all share the responsibility of representing him to the world. One day God will bring all his faithful people together. We need not fear because (1) God is with us ("I am with you"), (2) God has established a relationship with us ("I am your God"), and (3) God gives us assurance of his strength, help, and victory over sin and death. Have you realized all the ways God has helped you?

The acacia and the myrtle and the olive tree;
I will place the juniper in the desert
Together with the box tree and the cypress,
20 That they may see and recognize,
And consider and gain insight as well,
That the hand of the LORD has done this,
And the Holy One of Israel has created it.

21 "Present your case," the LORD says.
"Bring forward your strong *arguments,*"
The King of Jacob says.
22 Let them bring forth and declare to us what is going to take place;
As for the former *events,* declare what they *were,*
That we may consider them and know their outcome.
Or announce to us what is coming;
23 Declare the things that are going to come afterward,
That we may know that you are gods;
Indeed, do good or evil, that we may anxiously look about us and fear together.
24 Behold, you are of no account,
And your work amounts to nothing;
He who chooses you is an abomination.

25 "I have aroused one from the north, and he has come;
From the rising of the sun he will call on My name;
And he will come upon rulers as *upon* mortar,
Even as the potter treads clay."
26 Who has declared *this* from the beginning, that we might know?
Or from former times, that we may say, "*He is* right!"?
Surely there was no one who declared,
Surely there was no one who proclaimed,
Surely there was no one who heard your words.
27 "Formerly *I said* to Zion, 'Behold, here they are.'
And to Jerusalem, 'I will give a messenger of good news.'
28 "But when I look, there is no one,
And there is no counselor among them
Who, if I ask, can give an answer.
29 "Behold, all of them are [17]false;
Their works are worthless,
Their molten images are wind and emptiness.

41:20 Is 40:5; 43:10; Job 12:9; Is 66:14
41:21 Is 44:6
41:22 Is 44:7; 45:21; 46:10; Is 43:9
41:23 Is 42:9; 44:7, 8; 45:3; John 13:19; Jer 10:5
41:24 Ps 115:8; Is 44:9; 1 Cor 8:4; Is 37:19; 41:29; Prov 3:32; 28:9
41:25 Is 41:2; Jer 50:3; 2 Sam 22:43; Is 10:6; Mic 7:10; Zech 10:5
41:26 Is 41:22; 44:7; 45:21; Hab 2:18, 19
41:27 Is 48:3-8; Is 40:9; 44:28; 52:7; Nah 1:15
41:28 Is 50:2; 59:16; 63:5; Is 40:13, 14; Is 46:7
41:29 Is 2:8; 17:8; 41:24; Is 44:9; Jer 5:13

God's Promise concerning His Servant

42 "Behold, My Servant, whom I uphold;
My chosen one *in whom* My soul delights.
I have put My Spirit upon Him;
He will bring forth justice to the nations.
2 "He will not cry out or raise *His voice,*
Nor make His voice heard in the street.

42:1 Matt 12:18-21; Is 41:8; 43:10; 49:3-6; 52:13; 53:11; Matt 12:18-21; Phil 2:7; Luke 9:35; 1 Pet 2:4, 6; Matt 3:17; 17:5; Mark 1:11; Luke 3:22; Is 11:2; 59:21; 61:1; Matt 3:16; Luke 4:18, 19, 21; Is 2:4

17 Another reading is *nothing*

41:21–24 Israel was surrounded by many nations whose gods supposedly had special powers, such as raising crops and providing victories in war. These gods, however, failed to deliver. A god with limited or no power at all is not really a god. When we are tempted to put our trust in something other than the living God—money, career, family, or even military power—we should stop and ask some serious questions. Will it come through? Will it unfailingly provide what I am looking for? God delivers. When he makes a promise, he keeps it. He is the only completely trustworthy God.

42:1–4 These verses are quoted in Matthew 12:18–21 with reference to Christ. The chosen Servant reveals a character of gentleness, encouragement, justice, and truth. When you feel broken and bruised or burned out in your spiritual life, God won't step on you or toss you aside as useless, but will gently pick you up. God's loving attributes are desperately needed in the world today. Through God's Spirit, we can show such sensitivity to people around us, reflecting God's goodness and honesty to them.

42:1–9 Sometimes called the Servant Song, these verses are about the Servant-Messiah, not the servant Cyrus (described in chapter 41). Israel and the Messiah are both often called *servant.* Israel, as God's servant, was to help bring the world to a knowledge of God. The Messiah, Jesus, would fulfill this task and show God himself to the world.

3 "A bruised reed He will not break
And a dimly burning wick He will not extinguish;
He will faithfully bring forth justice.
4 "He will not be disheartened or crushed
Until He has established justice in the earth;
And the coastlands will wait expectantly for His law."

42:3 Ps 72:2, 4; 96:13
42:4 Is 40:28; Is 11:11; 24:15; 42:10, 12; 49:1; 51:5; 60:9; 66:19

5 Thus says God the LORD,
Who created the heavens and stretched them out,
Who spread out the earth and its offspring,
Who gives breath to the people on it
And spirit to those who walk in it,
6 "I am the LORD, I have called you in righteousness,
I will also hold you by the hand and watch over you,
And I will appoint you as a covenant to the people,
As a light to the nations,
7 To open blind eyes,
To bring out prisoners from the dungeon
And those who dwell in darkness from the prison.
8 "I am the LORD, that is My name;
I will not give My glory to another,
Nor My praise to graven images.
9 "Behold, the former things have come to pass,
Now I declare new things;
Before they spring forth I proclaim *them* to you."

42:5 Ps 102:25, 26; Is 45:18; Ps 104:2; Is 40:22; Ps 24:1, 2; 136:6; Job 12:10; 33:4; Is 57:16; Dan 5:23; Acts 17:25
42:6 Is 41:2; Jer 23:5, 6; Is 41:13; 45:1; Is 26:3; 27:3; Is 49:8; Is 49:6; 51:4; 60:1, 3; Luke 2:32; Acts 13:47; 26:23
42:7 Is 29:18; 35:5; Is 49:9; 61:1
42:8 Is 43:3, 11, 15; Ex 3:15; Ps 83:18; Ex 20:3-5; Is 48:11
42:9 Is 48:3; Is 43:19; 48:6

10 Sing to the LORD a new song,
Sing His praise from the end of the earth!
You who go down to the sea, and all that is in it.
You islands, and those who dwell on them.
11 Let the wilderness and its cities lift up *their voices,*
The settlements where Kedar inhabits.
Let the inhabitants of Sela sing aloud,
Let them shout for joy from the tops of the mountains.
12 Let them give glory to the LORD
And declare His praise in the coastlands.
13 The LORD will go forth like a warrior,
He will arouse *His* zeal like a man of war.
He will utter a shout, yes, He will raise a war cry.
He will prevail against His enemies.

42:10 Ps 33:3; 40:3; 98:1; Is 49:6; 62:11; Ps 65:5; 107:23; Ex 20:11; 1 Chr 16:32; Ps 96:11; Is 42:4
42:11 Is 32:16; 35:1, 6; Is 21:16; 60:7; Is 16:1; Is 52:7; Nah 1:15
42:12 Is 24:15; Is 42:4
42:13 Ex 15:3; Is 9:7; 26:11; 37:32; 59:17; Is 66:14-16

The Blindness of the People

14 "I have kept silent for a long time,
I have kept still and restrained Myself.
Now like a woman in labor I will groan,
I will both gasp and pant.
15 "I will lay waste the mountains and hills
And wither all their vegetation;
I will make the rivers into coastlands
And dry up the ponds.
16 "I will lead the blind by a way they do not know,
In paths they do not know I will guide them.
I will make darkness into light before them

42:14 Ps 50:21; Is 57:11
42:15 Is 2:12-16; Ezek 38:19, 20; Is 44:27; 50:2; Nah 1:4-6
42:16 Is 29:18; 30:21; 32:3; Jer 31:8, 9; Luke 1:78, 79; Is 29:18; Eph 5:8; Is 40:4; Luke 3:5; Josh 1:5; Ps 94:14; Is 41:17; Heb 13:5

42:6–7 Part of Christ's mission on earth was to demonstrate God's righteousness and to be a light for the Gentiles (to the nations). Through Christ, all people have the opportunity to share in his mission. God calls us to be servants of his Son, demonstrating God's righteousness and bringing his light. What a rare privilege it is to help the Messiah fulfill his mission! But we must seek his righteousness (Matthew 6:33) before we demonstrate it to others, and let his light shine in us before we can be lights ourselves (Matthew 5:16; 2 Corinthians 4:6).

42:10 Look at all the Lord will do for us and through us (42:6–9)! Majestic works prompt majestic responses. Do you really appreciate the good that God does for you and through you? If so, let your praise to him reflect how you really feel.

And rugged places into plains.
These are the things I will do,
And I will not leave them undone."

42:17 Ps 97:7; Is 1:29; 44:9, 11; 45:16

17 They will be turned back *and* be utterly put to shame,
Who trust in idols,
Who say to molten images,
"You are our gods."

42:18 Is 29:18; 35:5

18 Hear, you deaf!
And look, you blind, that you may see.

42:19 Is 41:8; Is 44:26; Is 26:3; 27:5

19 Who is blind but My servant,
Or so deaf as My messenger whom I send?
Who is so blind as he that is at peace *with Me,*
Or so blind as the servant of the LORD?

42:20 Rom 2:21

20 You have seen many things, but you do not observe *them;*
Your ears are open, but none hears.

42:21 Is 42:4; 51:4

21 The LORD was pleased for His righteousness' sake
To make the law great and glorious.

42:22 Is 24:18; Is 24:22

22 But this is a people plundered and despoiled;
All of them are trapped in caves,
Or are hidden away in prisons;
They have become a prey with none to deliver *them,*
And a spoil, with none to say, "Give *them* back!"

23 Who among you will give ear to this?
Who will give heed and listen hereafter?

42:24 Is 30:15; Is 48:18; 57:17

24 Who gave Jacob up for spoil, and Israel to plunderers?
Was it not the LORD, against whom we have sinned,
And in whose ways they were not willing to walk,
And whose law they did not obey?

42:25 Is 5:25; 9:19; Is 29:13; 47:7; 57:1; Hos 7:9

25 So He poured out on him the heat of His anger
And the fierceness of battle;
And it set him aflame all around,
Yet he did not recognize *it;*
And it burned him, but he paid no attention.

THE SERVANT IN ISAIAH

The nation Israel is called the servant:	41:8 42:19 43:10 44:1–2, 21 45:4 48:20
The Messiah is called the Servant:	42:1–17 49:3, 5–7 50:10 52:13 53:11

The nation was given a mission to serve God, to be custodian of his word, and to be a light to the Gentile nations. Because of sin and rebellion, they failed. God sent his Son, Christ, as Messiah to fulfill his mission on earth.

42:19–20 How could Israel and Judah be God's servants and yet be so blind? How could they be so close to God and see so little? Jesus condemned the religious leaders of his day for the same disregard of God (John 9:39–41). Yet do we not fail in the same way? Sometimes partial blindness—seeing but not understanding, or knowing what is right but not doing it—can be worse than not seeing at all.

42:23 We may condemn our predecessors for their failures, but we are twice as guilty if we repeat the same mistakes that we recognize as failures. Often we are so ready to direct God's message at others that we can't see how it touches our own lives. Make sure you are willing to take your own advice as you teach or lead.

Israel Redeemed

43 But now, thus says the LORD, your Creator, O Jacob,
And He who formed you, O Israel,
"Do not fear, for I have redeemed you;
I have called you by name; you are Mine!
2 "When you pass through the waters, I will be with you;
And through the rivers, they will not overflow you.
When you walk through the fire, you will not be scorched,
Nor will the flame burn you.
3 "For I am the LORD your God,
The Holy One of Israel, your Savior;
I have given Egypt as your ransom,
Cush and Seba in your place.
4 "Since you are precious in My sight,
Since you are honored and I love you,
I will give *other* men in your place and *other* peoples in exchange for your life.
5 "Do not fear, for I am with you;
I will bring your offspring from the east,
And gather you from the west.
6 "I will say to the north, 'Give *them* up!'
And to the south, 'Do not hold *them* back.'
Bring My sons from afar
And My daughters from the ends of the earth,
7 Everyone who is called by My name,
And whom I have created for My glory,
Whom I have formed, even whom I have made."

43:1 Is 43:15; Is 43:7, 21; 44:2, 21, 24; Is 43:5; Is 44:22, 23; 48:20; Gen 32:28; Is 43:7; 45:3, 4; Is 43:21

43:2 Ps 66:12; Is 8:7, 8; Deut 31:6, 8; Is 29:6; 30:27-29; Dan 3:25, 27

43:3 Ex 20:2; Is 19:20; 43:11; 45:15, 21; 49:26; 60:16; 63:8; Is 20:3-5

43:4 Ex 19:5, 6; Is 49:5; Is 63:9

43:5 Is 8:10; 43:2; Is 41:8; 49:12; 61:9; Is 49:12

43:6 Ps 107:3; 2 Cor 6:18; Is 45:22

43:7 Is 56:5; 62:2; James 2:7; Ps 100:3; Is 29:23; Eph 2:10; Is 44:23; 46:13; Is 43:1

Israel Is God's Witness

8 Bring out the people who are blind, even though they have eyes,
And the deaf, even though they have ears.
9 All the nations have gathered together
So that the peoples may be assembled.
Who among them can declare this
And proclaim to us the former things?
Let them present their witnesses that they may be justified,
Or let them hear and say, "It is true."
10 "You are My witnesses," declares the LORD,
"And My servant whom I have chosen,
So that you may know and believe Me
And understand that I am He.
Before Me there was no God formed,
And there will be none after Me.
11 "I, even I, am the LORD,
And there is no savior besides Me.
12 "It is I who have declared and saved and proclaimed,
And there was no strange *god* among you;

43:8 Is 6:9; 42:19; Ezek 12:2

43:9 Is 34:1; 41:1; Is 41:22, 23, 26; Is 44:9; Is 43:26

43:10 Is 44:8; Is 41:8; Is 41:4; Is 45:5, 6

43:11 Is 43:3; 45:21; Hos 13:4; Is 44:6, 8

43:12 Deut 32:16; Ps 81:9

43:1ff Chapter 42 ends with God's sorrow over the spiritual decay of his people. In chapter 43, God says that despite the people's spiritual failure, he will show them mercy, bring them back from captivity, and restore them. He would give them an outpouring of love, not wrath. Then the world would know that God alone had done this.

43:1–4 God created Israel and made it special to him. God redeemed Israel and summoned them by name to be those who belong to him. God protected Israel in times of trouble. We are important to God, and he also summons us by name and gives us his name (43:7)! When we bear God's wonderful name, we must never do anything that would bring shame to it.

43:2 Going through rivers of difficulty will either cause you to drown or force you to grow stronger. If you go in your own strength, you are more likely to drown. If you invite the Lord to go with you, he will protect you.

43:3 God gave other nations to Persia in exchange for returning the Jews to their homeland. Egypt, Cush, and parts of Arabia (Seba) had attacked Persia, and the Persians defeated them.

43:5–6 Isaiah was speaking primarily of Israel's return from Babylon. But there is a broader meaning: All God's people will be regathered when Christ comes to rule in peace over the earth.

43:10–11 Israel's task was to be a witness (44:8), telling the world who God is and what he has done. Believers today share the responsibility of being God's witnesses. Do people know what God is like through your words and example? They cannot see God directly, but they can see him reflected in you.

So you are My witnesses," declares the LORD,
"And I am God.
13 "Even from eternity I am He,
And there is none who can deliver out of My hand;
I act and who can reverse it?"

43:13 Ps 90:2; Is 48:16; Is 41:4; Ps 50:22; Job 9:12; Is 14:27

Babylon to Be Destroyed

14 Thus says the LORD your Redeemer, the Holy One of Israel,
"For your sake I have sent to Babylon,
And will bring them all down as fugitives,
Even the Chaldeans, into the ships [18]in which they rejoice.
15 "I am the LORD, your Holy One,
The Creator of Israel, your King."
16 Thus says the LORD,
Who makes a way through the sea
And a path through the mighty waters,
17 Who brings forth the chariot and the horse,
The army and the mighty man
(They will lie down together *and* not rise again;
They have been quenched *and* extinguished like a wick):
18 "Do not call to mind the former things,
Or ponder things of the past.
19 "Behold, I will do something new,
Now it will spring forth;
Will you not be aware of it?
I will even make a roadway in the wilderness,
Rivers in the desert.
20 "The beasts of the field will glorify Me,
The jackals and the ostriches,
Because I have given waters in the wilderness
And rivers in the desert,
To give drink to My chosen people.
21 "The people whom I formed for Myself
Will declare My praise.

43:14 Is 41:14; Is 23:13; Jer 51:13

43:15 Is 43:1; Is 41:20; 44:6

43:16 Ex 14:21, 22; Ps 77:19; Is 11:15; 44:27; 50:2; 51:10; 63:11, 12

43:17 Ex 15:19; Ps 118:12; Is 1:31

43:18 Is 65:17; Jer 23:7

43:19 Is 42:9; 48:6; 2 Cor 5:17; Ex 17:6; Num 20:11; Deut 8:15; Ps 78:16; Is 35:1, 6; 41:18, 19; 49:10; 51:3

43:20 Is 13:22; 35:7; Is 41:17, 18; 48:21

43:21 Is 43:1; Ps 102:18; Is 42:12; Luke 1:74, 75; 1 Pet 2:9

The Shortcomings of Israel

22 "Yet you have not called on Me, O Jacob;
But you have become weary of Me, O Israel.
23 "You have not brought to Me the sheep of your burnt offerings,
Nor have you honored Me with your sacrifices.
I have not burdened you with offerings,
Nor wearied you with incense.
24 "You have bought Me not sweet cane with money,
Nor have you filled Me with the fat of your sacrifices;
Rather you have burdened Me with your sins,
You have wearied Me with your iniquities.

25 "I, even I, am the one who wipes out your transgressions for My own sake,
And I will not remember your sins.
26 "Put Me in remembrance, let us argue our case together;

43:22 Mic 6:3; Mal 1:13; 3:14

43:23 Amos 5:25; Zech 7:5, 6; Mal 1:6-8; Jer 7:21-26; Ex 30:34; Lev 2:1; 24:7

43:24 Ex 30:23; Jer 6:20; Ps 95:10; Is 1:14; 7:13; Ezek 6:9; Mal 2:17

43:25 Is 44:22; 55:7; Jer 50:20; Is 37:35; 48:9, 11; Ezek 36:22; Is 38:17; Jer 31:34

43:26 Is 1:18; 41:1; 50:8; Is 43:9

18 Lit *of their rejoicing*

43:15–21 This section pictures a new exodus for a people once again oppressed, as the Israelites had been as slaves in Egypt before the exodus. They would cry to God, and again he would hear and deliver them. A new exodus would take place through a new wilderness. The past miracles were nothing compared to what God would do for his people in the future.

43:22–24 Sweet cane may have been an ingredient in the incense used in worship. A sacrifice required both giving up a valuable animal and pleading with God for forgiveness. But the people presented God with sins instead of sacrifices. Can you imagine bringing the best of your sins to God's altar? This ironic picture shows the depths to which Israel had sunk. What do you present to God—your sins, or a plea for his forgiveness?

43:25 How tempting it is to remind someone of a past offense! But when God forgives our sins he totally forgets them. We never have to fear that he will remind us of them later. Because God forgives our sin, we need to forgive others.

State your *cause,* that you may be proved right.
27 "Your first forefather sinned,
And your spokesmen have transgressed against Me.
28 "So I will pollute the princes of the sanctuary,
And I will consign Jacob to the ban and Israel to revilement.

43:27 Is 51:2; Ezek 16:3; Is 9:15; 28:7; 29:10; Jer 5:31

43:28 Is 24:6; 34:5; Jer 24:9; Dan 9:11; Zech 8:13; Ps 79:4; Ezek 5:15

The Blessings of Israel

44 "But now listen, O Jacob, My servant,
And Israel, whom I have chosen:
2 Thus says the LORD who made you
And formed you from the womb, who will help you,
'Do not fear, O Jacob My servant;
And you Jeshurun whom I have chosen.
3 'For I will pour out water on the thirsty *land*
And streams on the dry ground;
I will pour out My Spirit on your offspring
And My blessing on your descendants;
4 And they will spring up among the grass
Like poplars by streams of water.'
5 "This one will say, 'I am the LORD'S';
And that one will call on the name of Jacob;
And another will write *on* his hand, 'Belonging to the LORD,'
And will name Israel's name with honor.

44:1 Is 41:8; Jer 30:10; 46:27, 28

44:2 Is 44:21, 24; Is 41:10; Is 43:5; Deut 32:15; 33:5, 26

44:3 Is 41:17; Ezek 34:26; Joel 3:18; Is 32:15; Joel 2:28; Is 61:9; 65:23

44:4 Lev 23:40; Job 40:22

44:5 Ex 13:9; Neh 9:38

6 "Thus says the LORD, the King of Israel and his Redeemer, the LORD of hosts:
'I am the first and I am the last,
And there is no God besides Me.
7 'Who is like Me? Let him proclaim and declare it;
Yes, let him recount it to Me in order,
From the time that I established the ancient nation.
And let them declare to them the things that are coming
And the events that are going to take place.
8 'Do not tremble and do not be afraid;
Have I not long since announced *it* to you and declared *it?*
And you are My witnesses.
Is there any God besides Me,
Or is there any *other* Rock?
I know of none.' "

44:6 Is 41:21; 43:15; Is 41:14; 43:1, 14; Is 41:4; 43:10; 48:12; Rev 1:8, 17; 22:13; Is 43:11; 44:8; 45:5, 6, 21

44:7 Is 41:22, 26

44:8 Is 42:9; 48:5; Is 43:10; Deut 4:35, 39; 1 Sam 2:2; Is 45:5; Joel 2:27; Is 17:10; 26:4; 30:29

The Folly of Idolatry

9 Those who fashion a graven image are all of them futile, and their precious things
are of no profit; even their own witnesses fail to see or know, so that they will be put to
shame.
10 Who has fashioned a god or cast an idol to no profit?
11 Behold, all his companions will be put to shame, for the craftsmen themselves are
mere men. Let them all assemble themselves, let them stand up, let them tremble, let
them together be put to shame.
12 The man shapes iron into a cutting tool and does his work over the coals, fashion-
ing it with hammers and working it with his strong arm. He also gets hungry and his
strength fails; he drinks no water and becomes weary.
13 *Another* shapes wood, he extends a measuring line; he outlines it with red chalk. He

44:9 Ps 97:7; Is 42:17; 44:11; 45:16

44:10 Is 41:29; Jer 10:5; Hab 2:18; Acts 19:26

44:11 Ps 97:7; Is 42:17; 44:9; 45:16

44:12 Is 40:19, 20; 41:6, 7; 46:6, 7; Jer 10:3-5; Hab 2:18

44:13 Is 41:7; Ps 115:5-7; Judg 17:4, 5; Ezek 8:10, 11

44:2 Jeshurun ("the upright one") is a poetic name for Israel (Deuteronomy 32:15; 33:5, 26).

44:5 The time will come when Israel will be proud of belonging to God. If we are truly God's, we should be unashamed and delighted to let everyone know about our relationship with him (44:8).

44:9–20 Here Isaiah describes how people make their own gods. How absurd to make a god from the same tree that gives firewood. Do we make our own gods—money, fame, or power? If we make a god of our own choosing, we deceive ourselves. We cannot expect it to empower our lives.

works it with planes and outlines it with a compass, and makes it like the form of a man, like the beauty of man, so that it may sit in a house.

14 Surely he cuts cedars for himself, and takes a cypress or an oak and raises *it* for himself among the trees of the forest. He plants a fir, and the rain makes it grow.

15 Then it becomes *something* for a man to burn, so he takes one of them and warms himself; he also makes a fire to bake bread. He also makes a god and worships it; he makes it a graven image and falls down before it.

16 Half of it he burns in the fire; over *this* half he eats meat as he roasts a roast and is satisfied. He also warms himself and says, "Aha! I am warm, I have seen the fire."

17 But the rest of it he makes into a god, his graven image. He falls down before it and worships; he also prays to it and says, "Deliver me, for you are my god."

18 They do not know, nor do they understand, for He has smeared over their eyes so that they cannot see and their hearts so that they cannot comprehend.

19 No one recalls, nor is there knowledge or understanding to say, "I have burned half of it in the fire and also have baked bread over its coals. I roast meat and eat *it.* Then I make the rest of it into an abomination, I fall down before a block of wood!"

20 He feeds on ashes; a deceived heart has turned him aside. And he cannot deliver himself, nor say, "Is there not a lie in my right hand?"

God Forgives and Redeems

21 "Remember these things, O Jacob,
And Israel, for you are My servant;
I have formed you, you are My servant,
O Israel, you will not be forgotten by Me.
22 "I have wiped out your transgressions like a thick cloud
And your sins like a heavy mist.
Return to Me, for I have redeemed you."
23 Shout for joy, O heavens, for the LORD has done *it!*
Shout joyfully, you lower parts of the earth;
Break forth into a shout of joy, you mountains,
O forest, and every tree in it;
For the LORD has redeemed Jacob
And in Israel He shows forth His glory.

24 Thus says the LORD, your Redeemer, and the one who formed you from the womb,
"I, the LORD, am the maker of all things,
Stretching out the heavens by Myself
And spreading out the earth all alone,
25 Causing the omens of boasters to fail,
Making fools out of diviners,
Causing wise men to draw back
And turning their knowledge into foolishness,
26 Confirming the word of His servant
And performing the purpose of His messengers.

44:15 Is 44:17; 2 Chr 25:14

44:17 Is 44:15; 1 Kin 18:26, 28; Is 45:20

44:18 Is 1:3; Jer 10:8, 14; Ps 81:12; Is 6:9, 10; 29:10

44:19 Is 5:13; 44:18, 19; 45:20; Deut 27:15; 1 Kin 11:5, 7; 2 Kin 23:13, 14

44:20 Ps 102:9; Job 15:31; Hos 4:12; Rom 1:21, 22; 2 Thess 2:11; 2 Tim 3:13; Is 57:11; 59:3, 4, 13; Rom 1:25

44:21 Is 46:8; Zech 10:9; Is 44:1, 2; Is 49:15

44:22 Ps 51:1, 9; Is 43:25; Acts 3:19; Is 31:6; 55:7; Is 43:1; 48:20; 1 Cor 6:20; 1 Pet 1:18, 19

44:23 Ps 69:34; 96:11, 12; Is 42:10; 49:13; Ps 98:7, 8; 148:7, 9; Is 55:12; Is 43:1; Is 49:3; 61:3

44:24 Is 41:14; 43:14; Is 44:2; Is 40:22; 42:5; 45:12, 18; 51:13

44:25 Is 47:13; 2 Sam 15:31; Job 5:12-14; Ps 33:10; Is 29:14; Jer 51:57; 1 Cor 1:20, 27

44:26 Zech 1:6; Matt 5:18; Is 40:9; Jer 32:15, 44

TODAY'S IDOLATRY

Isaiah tells us, "Who but a fool would make his own god—an idol that cannot help him one bit!" We think of idols as statues of wood or stone, but in reality an idol is anything natural that is given sacred value and power. If your answer to any of the following questions is anything or anyone other than God, you may need to check out who or what you are worshiping.

- Who created me?
- Whom do I ultimately trust?
- Whom do I look to for ultimate truth?
- Whom do I look to for security and happiness?
- Who is in charge of my future?

44:21 God said that we should serve our Creator (17:7; 40:28; 43:15; 45:9). Idolaters do the opposite—serving or worshiping what they have made rather than the One who made them. Our Creator paid the price to set us free from our sins against him. By contrast, no idol ever created anybody, and no idol can redeem us from our sins.

44:25–26 False prophets were people who claimed to bring messages from the gods. Diviners were people who would fake omens for their own benefit. Because God is truth, he is the standard for all teachings. We can always trust his Word as absolute truth. His Word is completely accurate, and against it we can measure all other teachings. If you are unsure about a teaching, test it against God's Word. God condemned the false prophets because they gave advice opposite to his.

It is I who says of Jerusalem, 'She shall be inhabited!'
And of the cities of Judah, 'They shall be built.'
And I will raise up her ruins *again.*
27 "*It is I* who says to the depth of the sea, 'Be dried up!'
And I will make your rivers dry.
28 "*It is I* who says of Cyrus, '*He is* My shepherd!
And he will perform all My desire.'
And he declares of Jerusalem, 'She will be built,'
And of the temple, 'Your foundation will be laid.' "

44:27 Is 42:15; 50:2; Jer 50:38; 51:36

44:28 Is 45:1; 2 Chr 36:22, 23; Ezra 1:1; Is 14:32; 45:13; 54:11

God Uses Cyrus

45 Thus says the LORD to Cyrus His anointed,
Whom I have taken by the right hand,
To subdue nations before him
And to loose the loins of kings;
To open doors before him so that gates will not be shut:
2 "I will go before you and make the rough places smooth;
I will shatter the doors of bronze and cut through their iron bars.
3 "I will give you the treasures of darkness
And hidden wealth of secret places,
So that you may know that it is I,
The LORD, the God of Israel, who calls you by your name.
4 "For the sake of Jacob My servant,
And Israel My chosen *one,*
I have also called you by your name;
I have given you a title of honor
Though you have not known Me.
5 "I am the LORD, and there is no other;
Besides Me there is no God.
I will gird you, though you have not known Me;
6 That men may know from the rising to the setting of the sun
That there is no one besides Me.
I am the LORD, and there is no other,
7 The One forming light and creating darkness,
Causing well-being and creating calamity;
I am the LORD who does all these.

45:1 Is 44:28; Ps 73:23; Is 41:13; 42:6; Is 41:2, 25; Jer 50:3, 35; 51:11, 20, 24; Job 12:21; Is 45:5

45:2 Is 40:4; Ps 107:16; Jer 51:30

45:3 Jer 41:8; 50:37; Ex 33:12, 17; Is 43:1; 49:1

45:4 Is 41:8, 9; 44:1; Is 43:1; Acts 17:23

45:5 Is 45:6, 14, 18, 21; 46:9; Is 44:6, 8; Ps 18:39

45:6 Ps 102:15; Mal 1:11; Is 45:5

45:7 Is 42:16; Ps 104:20; 105:28; Is 31:2; 47:11; Amos 3:6

God's Supreme Power

8 "Drip down, O heavens, from above,
And let the clouds pour down righteousness;
Let the earth open up and salvation bear fruit,
And righteousness spring up with it.
I, the LORD, have created it.

9 "Woe to *the one* who quarrels with his Maker—
An earthenware vessel among the vessels of earth!
Will the clay say to the potter, 'What are you doing?'
Or the thing you are making *say,* 'He has no hands'?

45:8 Ps 72:6; Hos 10:12; 14:5; Joel 3:18; Ps 85:11; Is 60:21; 61:11

45:9 Job 15:25; 40:8, 9; Ps 2:2, 3; Prov 21:30; Jer 50:24; Is 29:16; 64:8; Jer 18:6; Rom 9:20, 21

44:28 Isaiah, who prophesied from about 740—681 B.C., called Cyrus by name almost 150 years before he ruled (559—530 B.C.)! Later historians said that Cyrus read this prophecy and was so moved that he carried it out. Isaiah also predicted that Jerusalem would fall more than 100 years before it happened (586 B.C.) and that the temple would be rebuilt about 200 years before it happened. It is clear these prophecies came from a God who knows the future.

45:1–8 This is the only place in the Bible where a Gentile ruler is said to be "anointed." God is the power over all powers, and he anoints whom he chooses for his special tasks. Cyrus's kingdom spread across 2,000 miles (the largest of any empire then known), including the territories of both the Assyrian and the Babylonian empires. Why did God anoint Cyrus? Because God had a special task for him to do for Israel. Cyrus would allow God's city, Jerusalem, to be rebuilt, and he would set the exiles free without expecting anything in return. Few kings of Israel or Judah had done as much for God's people as Cyrus would.

45:7 God is ruler over light and darkness, over prosperity and disaster. Our lives are sprinkled with both types of experiences, and both are needed for us to grow spiritually. When good times come, thank God and use your prosperity for him. When bad times come, don't resent them, but ask what you can learn from this refining experience to make you a better servant of God.

10 "Woe to him who says to a father, 'What are you begetting?'
Or to a woman, 'To what are you giving birth?' "

45:11 Is 43:15; 48:17; Ezek 39:7; Is 44:2; 54:5; Is 8:19; Jer 31:9; Is 19:25; 29:23; 60:21; 64:8

45:12 Is 42:5; 45:18; Jer 27:5; Ps 104:2; Is 42:5; 44:24; Gen 2:1; Neh 9:6

45:13 Is 41:2; Is 45:2; 2 Chr 36:22, 23; Is 44:28; Is 52:3

11 Thus says the LORD, the Holy One of Israel, and his Maker:
"Ask Me about the things to come concerning My sons,
And you shall commit to Me the work of My hands.
12 "It is I who made the earth, and created man upon it.
I stretched out the heavens with My hands
And I ordained all their host.
13 "I have aroused him in righteousness
And I will make all his ways smooth;
He will build My city and will let My exiles go free,
Without any payment or reward," says the LORD of hosts.

45:14 Ps 68:31; Is 19:21; Is 18:1; 43:3; Is 14:1, 2; 49:23; 54:3; Ps 149:8; Is 49:23; 60:14; Jer 16:19; Zech 8:20-23; 1 Cor 14:25; Is 45:5

45:15 Ps 44:24; Is 1:15; 8:17; 57:17; Is 43:3

45:16 Is 42:17; 44:9; Is 44:11

45:17 Is 26:4; 51:6; Rom 11:26; Is 49:23; 50:7; 54:4

14 Thus says the LORD,
"The products of Egypt and the merchandise of Cush
And the Sabeans, men of stature,
Will come over to you and will be yours;
They will walk behind you, they will come over in chains
And will bow down to you;
They will make supplication to you:
'Surely, God is with you, and there is none else,
No other God.' "
15 Truly, You are a God who hides Himself,
O God of Israel, Savior!
16 They will be put to shame and even humiliated, all of them;
The manufacturers of idols will go away together in humiliation.
17 Israel has been saved by the LORD
With an everlasting salvation;
You will not be put to shame or humiliated
To all eternity.

45:18 Is 42:5; Is 45:12; Gen 1:2; Gen 1:26; Ps 115:16; Is 45:5

45:19 Is 48:16; Is 45:25; 65:9; 2 Chr 15:2; Ps 78:34; Jer 29:13, 14; Ps 19:8; Is 45:23; 63:1; Is 43:12; 44:8

18 For thus says the LORD, who created the heavens (He is the God who formed the
earth and made it, He established it *and* did not create it a waste place, *but* formed it to
be inhabited),
"I am the LORD, and there is none else.
19 "I have not spoken in secret,
In some dark land;
I did not say to the offspring of Jacob,
'Seek Me in a waste place';
I, the LORD, speak righteousness,
Declaring things that are upright.

45:20 Is 43:9; Is 44:18, 19; 48:5-7; Is 46:1, 7; Jer 10:5; Is 44:17; 46:6, 7

45:21 Is 41:23; 43:9; Is 41:26; 44:7; 48:14; Is 45:5; Is 43:3, 11

20 "Gather yourselves and come;
Draw near together, you fugitives of the nations;
They have no knowledge,
Who carry about their wooden idol
And pray to a god who cannot save.
21 "Declare and set forth *your case;*
Indeed, let them consult together.
Who has announced this from of old?
Who has long since declared it?
Is it not I, the LORD?
And there is no other God besides Me,

45:14 The Sabeans were people from Seba in southern Arabia.

45:17 Until this time, Israel had anticipated temporal salvation—God would save them from their enemies. Here Isaiah tells of everlasting salvation with God.

45:18–19 God's promises are public, and their fulfillment is sure. So why do we ever doubt him? We never have to be uncertain when we have a God of truth and righteousness.

A righteous God and a Savior;
There is none except Me.
22 "Turn to Me and be saved, all the ends of the earth;
For I am God, and there is no other.
23 "I have sworn by Myself,
The word has gone forth from My mouth in righteousness
And will not turn back,
That to Me every knee will bow, every tongue will swear *allegiance*.
24 "They will say of Me, 'Only in the LORD are righteousness and strength.'
Men will come to Him,
And all who were angry at Him will be put to shame.
25 "In the LORD all the offspring of Israel
Will be justified and will glory."

45:22 Num 21:8, 9; 2 Chr 20:12; Mic 7:7; Zech 12:10; Is 30:15; 49:6, 12; 52:10

45:23 Gen 22:16; Is 62:8; Heb 6:13; Is 55:11; Rom 14:11; Phil 2:10; Deut 6:13; Ps 63:11; Is 19:18; 65:16

45:24 Jer 33:16; Is 41:11

45:25 1 Kin 8:32; Is 53:11; Is 41:16; 60:19

Babylon's Idols and the True God

46 Bel has bowed down, Nebo stoops over;
Their images are *consigned* to the beasts and the cattle.
The things that you carry are burdensome,
A load for the weary *beast*.
2 They stooped over, they have bowed down together;
They could not rescue the burden,
But have themselves gone into captivity.
3 "Listen to Me, O house of Jacob,
And all the remnant of the house of Israel,
You who have been borne by Me from birth
And have been carried from the womb;
4 Even to *your* old age I will be the same,
And even to *your* graying years I will bear *you*!
I have done *it*, and I will carry *you*;
And I will bear *you* and I will deliver *you*.

5 "To whom would you liken Me
And make Me equal and compare Me,
That we would be alike?
6 "Those who lavish gold from the purse
And weigh silver on the scale
Hire a goldsmith, and he makes it *into* a god;
They bow down, indeed they worship it.
7 "They lift it upon the shoulder *and* carry it;
They set it in its place and it stands *there*.
It does not move from its place.
Though one may cry to it, it cannot answer;
It cannot deliver him from his distress.

8 "Remember this, and be assured;
Recall it to mind, you transgressors.
9 "Remember the former things long past,
For I am God, and there is no other;
I am God, and there is no one like Me,

46:1 Is 2:18; 21:9; Jer 50:2-4; 51:44

46:2 Judg 18:17, 18, 24; 2 Sam 5:21; Jer 43:12, 13; 48:7; Hos 10:5, 6

46:3 Is 46:12; Is 10:21, 22; Ps 71:6; Is 49:1

46:4 Is 41:4; 43:13; 48:12; Ps 71:18

46:5 Is 40:18, 25

46:6 Is 40:19; 41:7; 44:12-17; Jer 10:4; Is 44:15, 17

46:7 Is 45:20; 46:1; Jer 10:5; Is 40:20; 41:7; Is 41:28; Is 45:20

46:8 Is 44:21; Is 44:19; Is 50:1

46:9 Deut 32:7; Is 42:9; 65:17; Is 45:5, 21; Is 41:26, 27

45:22 Salvation is for all nations, not just the Israelites. Many times it seems as though Israel had an inside track on salvation. But God makes it clear that his people include *all* those who follow him. Israel was to be the means through which the whole world would come to know God. Jesus, the Messiah, fulfilled Israel's role and gave all people the opportunity to follow God. (See also Romans 11:11; Galatians 3:28; Ephesians 3:6; Philippians 2:10.)

46:1–4 Cyrus would carry out God's judgment against Babylon. Bel was the chief deity of the Babylonians; Nebo was the god of science and learning. These "gods," however, needed animals and people to carry them around and could not even save themselves from being taken into captivity. They had no power at all. In contrast to gods who must be hauled around by people, our God created us and cares for us. His love is so enduring that he will care for us throughout our lifetime and even through death.

46:8–11 Israel was tempted to waver between the Lord God and pagan gods. Isaiah affirms the sole lordship of God. God is unique in his knowledge and in his control of the future. His consistent purpose is to carry out what he has planned. When we are tempted to pursue anything that promises pleasure, comfort, peace, or security apart from God, we must remember our commitment to God.

46:10 Ps 33:11; Prov 19:21; Is 14:24; 25:1; 40:8; Acts 5:39

46:11 Is 18:6; Is 41:2; Num 23:19; Is 14:24; 37:26

46:12 Is 46:3; Ps 76:5; Is 48:4; Zech 7:11, 12; Mal 3:13; Ps 119:150; Is 48:1; Jer 2:5

46:13 Is 51:5; 61:11; Rom 3:21; Is 61:3; 62:11; Joel 3:17; 1 Pet 2:6; Is 43:7; 44:23

47:1 Is 3:26; Jer 48:18; Is 23:12; 37:22; Jer 46:11; Ps 137:8; Jer 50:42; 51:33; Zech 2:7; Deut 28:56

47:2 Ex 11:5; Jer 25:10; Job 31:10; Eccl 12:4; Matt 24:41; Gen 24:65; Is 3:23; 1 Cor 11:5; Is 32:11

47:3 Ezek 16:37; Nah 3:5; Is 34:8; 63:4

47:4 Is 41:14

47:5 Is 23:2; Jer 8:14; Lam 2:10; Is 13:10; Is 47:7; Is 13:19; Dan 2:37

47:6 Deut 28:50

10 Declaring the end from the beginning,
And from ancient times things which have not been done,
Saying, 'My purpose will be established,
And I will accomplish all My good pleasure';
11 Calling a bird of prey from the east,
The man of My purpose from a far country.
Truly I have spoken; truly I will bring it to pass.
I have planned *it, surely* I will do it.

12 "Listen to Me, you stubborn-minded,
Who are far from righteousness.
13 "I bring near My righteousness, it is not far off;
And My salvation will not delay.
And I will grant salvation in Zion,
And My glory for Israel.

Lament for Babylon

47 "Come down and sit in the dust,
O virgin daughter of Babylon;
Sit on the ground without a throne,
O daughter of the Chaldeans!
For you shall no longer be called tender and delicate.
2 "Take the millstones and grind meal.
Remove your veil, strip off the skirt,
Uncover the leg, cross the rivers.
3 "Your nakedness will be uncovered,
Your shame also will be exposed;
I will take vengeance and will not spare a man."
4 Our Redeemer, the LORD of hosts is His name,
The Holy One of Israel.
5 "Sit silently, and go into darkness,
O daughter of the Chaldeans,
For you will no longer be called
The queen of kingdoms.
6 "I was angry with My people,

MAJOR IDOLS MENTIONED IN THE BIBLE

Name	Where they were worshiped	What they stood for	What the worship included
Bel (Marduk)	Babylon	Weather, war, sun god	Prostitution, child sacrifice
Nebo (son of Marduk)	Babylon	Learning, astronomy, science	
Ashtoreth (Asherah)	Canaan	Goddess of love, childbirth, and fertility	Prostitution
Chemosh	Moab		Child sacrifice
Molech (Milcom)	Ammon	National god	Child sacrifice
Baal	Canaan	Rain, harvest, symbolized strength and fertility	Prostitution
Dagon	Philistia	Harvest, grain, success in farming	Child sacrifice

46:13 Much of the book of Isaiah speaks of a future deliverance when we will all live with God in perfect peace. God offers not only this future hope but also help for our present needs. His righteousness is near us, and we do not have to wait for his salvation.

47:1ff Here Isaiah predicted the fall of Babylon more than 150 years before it happened. At this time, Babylon had not yet emerged as the mightiest force on earth, the proud empire that would destroy Judah and Jerusalem. But the Babylonians, Judah's captors, would become captives themselves in 539 B.C. God, not Babylon, has the ultimate power. He used Babylon to punish his sinful people; he would use Medo-Persia to destroy Babylon and free his people.

I profaned My heritage
And gave them into your hand.
You did not show mercy to them,
On the aged you made your yoke very heavy.
7 "Yet you said, 'I will be a queen forever.'
These things you did not consider
Nor remember the outcome of them.

8 "Now, then, hear this, you sensual one,
Who dwells securely,
Who says in your heart,
'I am, and there is no one besides me.
I will not sit as a widow,
Nor know loss of children.'
9 "But these two things will come on you suddenly in one day:
Loss of children and widowhood.
They will come on you in full measure
In spite of your many sorceries,
In spite of the great power of your spells.
10 "You felt secure in your wickedness and said,
'No one sees me,'
Your wisdom and your knowledge, they have deluded you;
For you have said in your heart,
'I am, and there is no one besides me.'
11 "But evil will come on you
Which you will not know how to charm away;
And disaster will fall on you
For which you cannot atone;
And destruction about which you do not know
Will come on you suddenly.

12 "Stand *fast* now in your spells
And in your many sorceries
With which you have labored from your youth;
Perhaps you will be able to profit,
Perhaps you may cause trembling.
13 "You are wearied with your many counsels;
Let now the astrologers,
Those who prophesy by the stars,
Those who predict by the new moons,
Stand up and save you from what will come upon you.
14 "Behold, they have become like stubble,
Fire burns them;
They cannot deliver themselves from the power of the flame;
There will be no coal to warm by
Nor a fire to sit before!
15 "So have those become to you with whom you have labored,
Who have trafficked with you from your youth;
Each has wandered in his own way;
There is none to save you.

47:7 Is 47:5; Is 42:25; 57:11; Deut 32:29; Jer 5:31; Ezek 7:2, 3

47:8 Is 22:13; 32:9; Jer 50:11; Is 32:9, 11; Zeph 2:15; Is 45:5, 6, 18; 47:10; Zeph 2:15; Rev 18:7

47:9 Is 13:16, 18; 14:22; Ps 73:19; 1 Thess 5:3; Rev 18:8, 10; Is 47:13; Nah 3:4; Rev 18:23

47:10 Ps 52:7; 62:10; Is 59:4; Is 29:15; Ezek 8:12; 9:9; Is 5:21; 44:20; Is 47:8

47:11 Is 57:1; Is 13:6; Jer 51:8, 43; Luke 17:27; 1 Thess 5:3; Is 47:9

47:12 Is 47:9

47:13 Jer 51:58, 64; Is 8:19; 44:25; 47:9; Dan 2:2, 10; Is 47:15

47:14 Is 5:24; Nah 1:10; Mal 4:1; Is 10:17; Jer 51:30, 32, 58; Is 44:16

47:15 Rev 18:11; Is 5:29; 43:13; 46:7

47:8–9 Caught up in the pursuit of power and pleasure, Babylon believed in its own greatness and claimed to be the *only* power on earth. Babylon felt completely secure, and Nebuchadnezzar, its king, exalted himself as a "god." But the true God taught Nebuchadnezzar a powerful lesson by taking everything away from him (Daniel 4:28–37). Our society is addicted to pleasure and power, but these can quickly pass away. Look at your own life and ask yourself how you can be more responsible with the talents and possessions God has given you. How can you use your life for God's honor rather than your own?

47:12–15 The people of Babylon sought advice and help from astrologers and stargazers. But like the idols of wood or gold, astrologers could not even deliver themselves from what was to come from the hand of God. Why rely on those who are powerless? The helpless cannot help us. Alternatives to God are destined to fail. If you want help, find it in God, who has proven his power in creation and in history.

Israel's Obstinacy

48 "Hear this, O house of Jacob, who are named Israel
And who came forth from the loins of Judah,
Who swear by the name of the LORD
And invoke the God of Israel,
But not in truth nor in righteousness.
2 "For they call themselves after the holy city
And lean on the God of Israel;
The LORD of hosts is His name.
3 "I declared the former things long ago
And they went forth from My mouth, and I proclaimed them.
Suddenly I acted, and they came to pass.
4 "Because I know that you are obstinate,
And your neck is an iron sinew
And your forehead bronze,
5 Therefore I declared *them* to you long ago,
Before they took place I proclaimed *them* to you,
So that you would not say, 'My idol has done them,
And my graven image and my molten image have commanded them.'
6 "You have heard; look at all this.
And you, will you not declare it?
I proclaim to you new things from this time,
Even hidden things which you have not known.
7 "They are created now and not long ago;
And before today you have not heard them,
So that you will not say, 'Behold, I knew them.'
8 "You have not heard, you have not known.
Even from long ago your ear has not been open,
Because I knew that you would deal very treacherously;
And you have been called a rebel from birth.
9 "For the sake of My name I delay My wrath,
And *for* My praise I restrain *it* for you,
In order not to cut you off.
10 "Behold, I have refined you, but not as silver;
I have tested you in the furnace of affliction.
11 "For My own sake, for My own sake, I will act;
For how can *My name* be profaned?
And My glory I will not give to another.

Deliverance Promised

12 "Listen to Me, O Jacob, even Israel whom I called;
I am He, I am the first, I am also the last.
13 "Surely My hand founded the earth,
And My right hand spread out the heavens;
When I call to them, they stand together.

48:1 Is 46:12; Num 24:7; Deut 33:28; Ps 68:26; Deut 6:13; Is 45:23; 65:16; Is 58:2; Jer 4:2

48:2 Is 52:1; 64:10; Is 10:20; Jer 7:4; 21:2; Mic 3:11; Rom 2:17

48:3 Is 41:22; 42:9; 43:9; 44:7, 8; 45:21; 46:10; Is 29:5; 30:13; Josh 21:45; Is 42:9

48:4 Ex 32:9; Deut 31:27; Ezek 2:4; 3:7; 2 Chr 36:13; Prov 29:1; Acts 7:51; Ezek 3:7-9

48:5 Jer 44:15-18

48:6 Is 42:9; 43:19

48:8 Is 42:25; 47:11; Hos 7:9; Deut 9:7, 24; Ps 58:3; Is 46:8

48:9 Is 48:11; Neh 9:30, 31; Ps 78:38; 103:8-10; Is 30:18; 65:8

48:10 Jer 9:7; Ezek 22:18-22; Deut 4:20; 1 Kin 8:51; Jer 11:4

48:11 1 Sam 12:22; Ps 25:11; 106:8; Is 37:35; 43:25; Jer 14:7; Ezek 20:9, 14, 22, 44; Dan 9:17-19; Deut 32:26, 27; Is 42:8

48:12 Is 41:4; 43:10-13; 46:4; Is 44:6; Rev 1:17; 22:13

48:13 Ex 20:11; Ps 102:25; Is 42:5; 45:12, 18; Heb 1:10-12; Is 40:26

48:1 The people of Judah felt confident because they lived in Jerusalem, the city with God's temple. They depended on their heritage, their city, and their temple—but this was false security because they did not depend on God. Do you feel secure because you go to church or live in a Christian country? Heritage, buildings, or nations cannot give us a relationship with God; we must truly depend on him personally, with all our hearts and minds.

48:9–11 There was nothing in Israel's actions, attitudes, or accomplishments to compel God to love and to save them. But for his own sake, to show who he is and what he can do, he saved them. God does not save us because we are good but because he loves us and because of his forgiving nature.

48:10 Do you find it easy to complain when your life becomes complicated or difficult? Why would a loving God allow all kinds of unpleasant experiences to come to his children? This verse shows us plainly that God tests us in the "furnace of affliction." Rather than complain, our response should be to turn to God in faith for the strength to endure, and rejoice in our sufferings (see Romans 5:3; James 1:2–4). For without the testing, we would never know what we are capable of doing, nor would we grow. And without the refining, we will not become more pure and more like Christ. What kinds of adversity are you currently facing?

14 "Assemble, all of you, and listen!
Who among them has declared these things?
The LORD loves him; he will carry out His good pleasure on Babylon,
And His arm *will be against* the Chaldeans.
15 "I, even I, have spoken; indeed I have called him,
I have brought him, and He will make his ways successful.
16 "Come near to Me, listen to this:
From the first I have not spoken in secret,
From the time it took place, I was there.
And now the Lord GOD has sent Me, and His Spirit."

17 Thus says the LORD, your Redeemer, the Holy One of Israel,
"I am the LORD your God, who teaches you to profit,
Who leads you in the way you should go.
18 "If only you had paid attention to My commandments!
Then your well-being would have been like a river,
And your righteousness like the waves of the sea.
19 "Your descendants would have been like the sand,
And your offspring like its grains;
Their name would never be cut off or destroyed from My presence."

20 Go forth from Babylon! Flee from the Chaldeans!
Declare with the sound of joyful shouting, proclaim this,
Send it out to the end of the earth;
Say, "The LORD has redeemed His servant Jacob."
21 They did not thirst when He led them through the deserts.
He made the water flow out of the rock for them;
He split the rock and the water gushed forth.
22 "There is no peace for the wicked," says the LORD.

2. The future redeemer

Salvation Reaches to the End of the Earth

49 Listen to Me, O islands,
And pay attention, you peoples from afar.
The LORD called Me from the womb;
From the body of My mother He named Me.
2 He has made My mouth like a sharp sword,
In the shadow of His hand He has concealed Me;
And He has also made Me a select arrow,
He has hidden Me in His quiver.
3 He said to Me, "You are My Servant, Israel,
In Whom I will show My glory."
4 But I said, "I have toiled in vain,
I have spent My strength for nothing and vanity;
Yet surely the justice *due* to Me is with the LORD,
And My reward with My God."

48:14
Is 43:9; 45:20; Is 45:21; Is 46:10, 11; Is 13:4, 5, 17-19; Jer 50:21-29; 51:24

48:15
Is 41:2; 45:1, 2

48:16
Is 34:1; 41:1; 57:3; Is 45:19; Is 43:13; Zech 2:9, 11

48:17
Is 41:14; 43:14; 49:7, 26; 54:5, 8; Ps 32:8; Is 30:21; 49:9, 10

48:18
Deut 5:29; 32:29; Ps 81:13-16; Ps 119:165; Is 32:16-18; 66:12; Is 45:8; 61:10, 11; 62:1; Hos 10:12; Amos 5:24

48:19
Gen 22:17; Is 10:22; 44:3, 4; 54:3; Jer 33:22; Is 56:5; 66:22

48:20
Jer 50:8; 51:6, 45; Zech 2:6, 7; Rev 18:4; Is 42:10; 49:13; 52:9; Is 62:11; Jer 31:10; 50:2; Is 43:1; 52:9; 63:9

48:21
Is 30:25; 35:6, 7; 41:17, 18; 43:19, 20; 49:10; Ex 17:6; Ps 78:15, 16; Ps 78:20; 105:41

48:22
Is 57:21

49:1
Is 42:4; Is 44:2, 24; 46:3; Jer 1:5

49:2
Is 11:4; Heb 4:12; Rev 1:16; 2:12, 16; Is 51:16; Hab 3:11

49:3
Zech 3:8; Is 44:23

49:4
Is 65:23; Is 35:4; 59:18

48:14–15 "The LORD loves him" refers to Cyrus—and this must have shocked his audience. How could the Lord choose a pagan king, an enemy? But it was Cyrus whom God would use to free his people from their captivity in Babylon. Cyrus's mission was to set Israel free by conquering Babylon, then to decree that all Jews could return to their homeland. Who but a prophet of God could tell such an inconceivable but true story almost 200 years before it happened?

48:17–18 Like a loving parent, God teaches and directs us. We should listen to him because peace and righteousness come to us as we obey his Word. Refusing to pay attention to God's commands invites punishment and threatens that peace and righteousness.

48:20 Do you see the captives leaving Babylon many years later? No wonder they are shouting with joy, as their ancestors shouted joyfully after they crossed the Red Sea, free from slavery at last! What is holding you captive? Be free! The Lord has redeemed his servants from the slavery of sin. When you let him free you from your captivity, you will feel like shouting with joy.

48:22 Many people cry out for comfort, security, and relief, but they haven't taken the first steps to turn away from sin and open the channels to God. They have not repented and trusted in him. If you want true peace, seek God first. Then he will give you his peace.

49:1–7 Before the servant, the Messiah, was born, God had chosen him to bring the light of the gospel (the message of salvation) to the world (see Acts 13:47). Christ offered salvation to all nations, and his apostles began the missionary movement to take this gospel to the ends of the earth. Missionary work today continues Jesus' Great Commission (Matthew 28:18–20), taking the light of the gospel to all nations.

49:5 Is 44:2; Is 11:12; 27:12; Is 43:4; Is 12:2

5 And now says the LORD, who formed Me from the womb to be His Servant,
To bring Jacob back to Him, so that Israel might be gathered to Him
(For I am honored in the sight of the LORD,
And My God is My strength),

49:6 Ps 37:28; 97:10; Is 42:6; 51:4; Luke 2:32; Acts 13:47; 26:23; Is 48:20

6 He says, "It is too small a thing that You should be My Servant
To raise up the tribes of Jacob and to restore the preserved ones of Israel;
I will also make You a light of the nations
So that My salvation may reach to the end of the earth."

49:7 Is 48:17; Ps 22:6-8; 69:7-9; Is 53:3; Is 52:15; Is 19:21, 23; 27:13; 66:23

7 Thus says the LORD, the Redeemer of Israel *and* its Holy One,
To the despised One,
To the One abhorred by the nation,
To the Servant of rulers,
"Kings will see and arise,
Princes will also bow down,
Because of the LORD who is faithful, the Holy One of Israel who has chosen You."

49:8 Ps 69:13; 2 Cor 6:2; Is 26:3; 27:3; 42:6; Is 42:6; Is 44:26

8 Thus says the LORD,
"In a favorable time I have answered You,
And in a day of salvation I have helped You;
And I will keep You and give You for a covenant of the people,
To restore the land, to make *them* inherit the desolate heritages;

49:9 Is 42:7; 61:1; Luke 4:18; Is 41:18

9 Saying to those who are bound, 'Go forth,'
To those who are in darkness, 'Show yourselves.'
Along the roads they will feed,
And their pasture *will be* on all bare heights.

49:10 Is 33:16; 48:21; Rev 7:16; Ps 121:6; Is 14:1; Ps 23:2; Is 40:11; Is 35:7; 41:17

10 "They will not hunger or thirst,
Nor will the scorching heat or sun strike them down;
For He who has compassion on them will lead them
And will guide them to springs of water.

49:11 Is 40:4; Is 11:16; 19:23; 35:8; 62:10

11 "I will make all My mountains a road,
And My highways will be raised up.

49:12 Is 49:1; 60:4; Is 43:5, 6

12 "Behold, these will come from afar;
And lo, these *will come* from the north and from the west,
And these from the land of Sinim."

49:13 Is 44:23; Is 40:1; 51:3, 12; Is 54:7, 8, 10

13 Shout for joy, O heavens! And rejoice, O earth!
Break forth into joyful shouting, O mountains!
For the LORD has comforted His people
And will have compassion on His afflicted.

Promise to Zion

14 But Zion said, "The LORD has forsaken me,
And the Lord has forgotten me."

49:15 Is 44:21

15 "Can a woman forget her nursing child
And have no compassion on the son of her womb?
Even these may forget, but I will not forget you.

49:16 Song 8:6; Hag 2:23; Ps 48:12, 13; Is 62:6, 7

16 "Behold, I have inscribed you on the palms *of My hands;*
Your walls are continually before Me.

49:17 Is 10:6; 37:18

17 "Your builders hurry;
Your destroyers and devastators
Will depart from you.

49:18 Is 60:4; John 4:35; Is 43:5; 54:7; 60:4; Is 49:12; Is 45:23; 54:9; Is 52:1; 61:10

18 "Lift up your eyes and look around;
All of them gather together, they come to you.
As I live," declares the LORD,
"You will surely put on all of them as jewels and bind them on as a bride.

49:19 Is 1:7; 3:8; 5:6; 51:3; Is 54:1, 2; Zech 10:10; Ps 56:1, 2

19 "For your waste and desolate places and your destroyed land—

49:12 The land of Sinim is in southern Egypt (see Ezekiel 29:10).

49:14–15 The people of Israel felt that God had forsaken them in Babylon; but Isaiah pointed out that God would never forget them, as a loving mother would not forget her little child. When we feel that God has forsaken us, we must ask if we have forsaken and forgotten God (see Deuteronomy 31:6).

Surely now you will be too cramped for the inhabitants,
And those who swallowed you will be far away.
20 "The children of whom you were bereaved will yet say in your ears,
'The place is too cramped for me;
Make room for me that I may live *here.*'
21 "Then you will say in your heart,
'Who has begotten these for me,
Since I have been bereaved of my children
And am barren, an exile and a wanderer?
And who has reared these?
Behold, I was left alone;
From where did these come?' "

49:20 Is 54:1-3

49:21 Is 29:23; 54:6, 7; Is 27:10; Lam 1:1; Is 5:13; Is 1:8; Is 60:8

22 Thus says the Lord GOD,
"Behold, I will lift up My hand to the nations
And set up My standard to the peoples;
And they will bring your sons in *their* bosom,
And your daughters will be carried on *their* shoulders.
23 "Kings will be your guardians,
And their princesses your nurses.
They will bow down to you with their faces to the earth
And lick the dust of your feet;
And *you* will know that I am the LORD;
Those who hopefully wait for Me will not be put to shame.

49:22 Is 11:10, 12; 18:3; 62:10; Is 14:2; 43:6; 60:4

49:23 Is 14:1, 2; 60:3, 10, 11; Is 45:14; 60:14; Ps 72:9; Mic 7:17; Is 41:20; 43:10; 60:16; Ps 37:9; Is 25:9; 26:8; Ps 25:3; Is 45:17; Joel 2:27

24 "Can the prey be taken from the mighty man,
Or the captives of a tyrant be rescued?"
25 Surely, thus says the LORD,
"Even the captives of the mighty man will be taken away,
And the prey of the tyrant will be rescued;
For I will contend with the one who contends with you,
And I will save your sons.
26 "I will feed your oppressors with their own flesh,
And they will become drunk with their own blood as with sweet wine;
And all flesh will know that I, the LORD, am your Savior
And your Redeemer, the Mighty One of Jacob."

49:24 Matt 12:29; Luke 11:21

49:25 Is 10:6; 14:1, 2; Jer 50:33, 34; Is 25:9; 33:22; 35:4

49:26 Is 9:4; 14:4; 16:4; 51:13; 54:14; Is 9:20; Is 45:6; Ezek 39:7; Is 43:3; Is 49:7

God Helps His Servant

50 Thus says the LORD,
"Where is the certificate of divorce
By which I have sent your mother away?
Or to whom of My creditors did I sell you?
Behold, you were sold for your iniquities,
And for your transgressions your mother was sent away.
2 "Why was there no man when I came?
When I called, *why* was there none to answer?
Is My hand so short that it cannot ransom?
Or have I no power to deliver?
Behold, I dry up the sea with My rebuke,
I make the rivers a wilderness;
Their fish stink for lack of water
And die of thirst.

50:1 Deut 24:1, 3; Jer 3:8; Is 54:6, 7; Deut 32:30; 2 Kin 4:1; Neh 5:5; Is 52:3; 59:2; Is 1:28; 43:27; Jer 3:8

50:2 Is 41:28; 59:16; 66:4; Gen 18:14; Num 11:23; Is 59:1; Ex 14:21; Is 19:5; 43:16; 44:27; Josh 3:16; Is 42:15

49:24–25 God would prove to the world that he is God by doing the impossible—causing warriors to set their captives free; and these warriors would even return the plunder they had taken from the captives! God had done this before at the exodus and would do it again when the exiles returned to Israel. Never should we doubt that God will fulfill his promises. He will even do the impossible to make them come true.

50:1–2 God promised to fight for Israel, but Israel sold itself into sin. Israel had caused its own problems. "Is My hand so short?" means "Am I powerless to help?" The people of Israel forgot God and trusted in other countries to help them. God did not reject Israel, but Israel rejected God.

50:3
Is 13:10; Rev 6:12

3"I clothe the heavens with blackness
And make sackcloth their covering."

50:4
Is 8:16; 54:13; Is 57:19; Jer 31:25; Ps 5:3; 88:13; 119:147; 143:8

4 The Lord GOD has given Me the tongue of disciples,
That I may know how to sustain the weary one with a word.
He awakens *Me* morning by morning,
He awakens My ear to listen as a disciple.

50:5
Ps 40:6; Is 35:5; Matt 26:39; John 8:29; 14:31; 15:10; Acts 26:19; Phil 2:8; Heb 5:8; 10:7

5 The Lord GOD has opened My ear;
And I was not disobedient
Nor did I turn back.

50:6
Matt 26:67; 27:30; Mark 14:65; 15:19; Luke 22:63

6 I gave My back to those who strike *Me,*
And My cheeks to those who pluck out the beard;
I did not cover My face from humiliation and spitting.

50:7
Is 42:1; 49:8; Is 45:17; 54:4; Ezek 3:8, 9

7 For the Lord GOD helps Me,
Therefore, I am not disgraced;
Therefore, I have set My face like flint,
And I know that I will not be ashamed.

50:8
Is 45:25; Rom 8:33, 34; Is 1:18; 41:1; 43:26

8 He who vindicates Me is near;
Who will contend with Me?
Let us stand up to each other;
Who has a case against Me?
Let him draw near to Me.

50:9
Is 41:10; Is 54:17; Job 13:28; Is 51:8

9 Behold, the Lord GOD helps Me;
Who is he who condemns Me?
Behold, they will all wear out like a garment;
The moth will eat them.

50:10
Is 49:2, 3; 50:4; Is 9:2; 26:9; Eph 5:8; Is 12:2; 26:4

10 Who is among you that fears the LORD,
That obeys the voice of His servant,
That walks in darkness and has no light?
Let him trust in the name of the LORD and rely on his God.

50:11
Prov 26:18; Is 9:18; James 3:6; Is 8:22; 65:13-15; Amos 4:9, 10

11 Behold, all you who kindle a fire,
Who encircle yourselves with firebrands,
Walk in the light of your fire
And among the brands you have set ablaze.
This you will have from My hand:
You will lie down in torment.

Israel Exhorted

51:1
Is 46:3; 48:12; 51:7; Ps 94:15; Prov 15:9; Gen 17:15-17

51 "Listen to me, you who pursue righteousness,
Who seek the LORD:
Look to the rock from which you were hewn
And to the quarry from which you were dug.

51:2
Is 29:22; 41:8; 63:16; Gen 12:1; 15:5; Deut 1:10; Ezek 33:24

2"Look to Abraham your father
And to Sarah who gave birth to you in pain;
When *he was but* one I called him,
Then I blessed him and multiplied him."

51:3
Is 40:1; 49:13; Is 52:9; Is 35:1; 41:19; Gen 2:8; Joel 2:3; Gen 13:10; Is 25:9; 41:16; 65:18; 66:10

3 Indeed, the LORD will comfort Zion;
He will comfort all her waste places.
And her wilderness He will make like Eden,
And her desert like the garden of the LORD;
Joy and gladness will be found in her,
Thanksgiving and sound of a melody.

50:10–11 If we walk by our own light and reject God's, we become self-sufficient, and the result of self-sufficiency is torment. When we place confidence in our own intelligence, appearance, or accomplishments instead of in God, we risk torment later when these strengths fade.

51:1–2 The faithful remnant may have felt alone because they were few. But God reminded them of their ancestors, the source of their spiritual heritage—Abraham and Sarah. Abraham was only one person, but much came from his faithfulness. If the faithful few would remain faithful, even more could come from them. If we Christians, even a faithful few, remain faithful, think what God can do through us!

4 "Pay attention to Me, O My people,
And give ear to Me, O My nation;
For a law will go forth from Me,
And I will set My justice for a light of the peoples.
5 "My righteousness is near, My salvation has gone forth,
And My arms will judge the peoples;
The coastlands will wait for Me,
And for My arm they will wait expectantly.
6 "Lift up your eyes to the sky,
Then look to the earth beneath;
For the sky will vanish like smoke,
And the earth will wear out like a garment
And its inhabitants will die in like manner;
But My salvation will be forever,
And My righteousness will not wane.
7 "Listen to Me, you who know righteousness,
A people in whose heart is My law;
Do not fear the reproach of man,
Nor be dismayed at their revilings.
8 "For the moth will eat them like a garment,
And the grub will eat them like wool.
But My righteousness will be forever,
And My salvation to all generations."

9 Awake, awake, put on strength, O arm of the LORD;
Awake as in the days of old, the generations of long ago.
Was it not You who cut Rahab in pieces,
Who pierced the dragon?
10 Was it not You who dried up the sea,
The waters of the great deep;
Who made the depths of the sea a pathway
For the redeemed to cross over?
11 So the ransomed of the LORD will return
And come with joyful shouting to Zion,
And everlasting joy *will be* on their heads.
They will obtain gladness and joy,
And sorrow and sighing will flee away.

12 "I, even I, am He who comforts you.
Who are you that you are afraid of man who dies
And of the son of man who is made like grass,
13 That you have forgotten the LORD your Maker,
Who stretched out the heavens
And laid the foundations of the earth,
That you fear continually all day long because of the fury of the oppressor,
As he makes ready to destroy?
But where is the fury of the oppressor?
14 "The exile will soon be set free, and will not die in the dungeon, nor will his bread be lacking.

51:4 Ps 50:7; 78:1; Deut 18:18; Is 2:3; Mic 4:2; Is 1:27; 42:4; Is 42:6; 49:6

51:5 Is 46:13; 54:17; Is 40:10; Is 42:4; 60:9; Is 59:16; 63:5

51:6 Is 40:26; Ps 102:25, 26; Is 13:13; 34:4; Matt 24:35; Heb 1:10-12; 2 Pet 3:10; Is 45:17; 51:8

51:7 Is 51:1; Ps 37:31; Is 25:8; 54:4; Matt 5:11; Acts 5:41

51:8 Is 50:9; Is 14:11; 66:24; Is 51:6

51:9 Is 51:17; 52:1; Ex 6:6; Deut 4:34; Job 26:12; Ps 89:10; Is 30:7; Ps 74:13; Is 27:1

51:10 Is 11:15, 16; 50:2; 63:11, 12; Ex 15:13; Ps 106:10; Is 63:9

51:11 Is 35:10; Jer 31:11, 12; Is 60:19; 61:7; Is 25:8; 60:20; 65:19; Rev 7:17; 21:1, 4; 22:3

51:12 Is 51:3; Ps 118:6; Is 2:22; Is 40:6, 7; 1 Pet 1:24

51:13 Deut 6:12; 8:11; Is 17:10; Job 9:8; Ps 104:2; Is 40:22; 45:12, 18; 48:13; Is 7:4; 10:24; Is 49:26; 54:14

51:14 Is 48:20; 52:2; Is 33:6; 49:10

51:7 Isaiah encouraged those who follow God's laws. He gave them hope when they faced people's reproach or insults because of their faith. We need not fear when people insult us for our faith because God is with us and truth will prevail. If people make fun of you or dislike you because you believe in God, remember that they are not against you personally but against God. God will deal with them; you should concentrate on loving and obeying him.

51:9–10 "Rahab" was a derogatory term used for Egypt (see the note on 30:7). God had performed many powerful miracles in founding Israel, perhaps none more exciting than the drying up of the sea (the Red Sea, see Exodus 14). Our God is the same God who made a road in the depths of the sea. His methods may change, but his love and care do not.

51:12–16 God's people feared Babylon, but not God. They had reason to fear Babylon for the harm it wanted to do, but they should also have realized that God's power is much greater than Babylon's. Babylon was interested in making the people captives; God was interested in setting them free. The people had misplaced their fear and their love. Jerusalem should have feared God's power and loved his mercy.

51:15 Ps 107:25; Jer 31:35

15 "For I am the LORD your God, who stirs up the sea and its waves roar (the LORD of
hosts is His name).

51:16 Deut 18:18; Is 59:21; Ex 33:22; Is 49:2; Is 66:22

16 "I have put My words in your mouth and have covered you with the shadow of My
hand, to establish the heavens, to found the earth, and to say to Zion, 'You are My
people.' "

51:17 Is 51:9; 52:1; Job 21:20; Is 29:9; 63:6; Jer 25:15; Rev 14:10; 16:19

51:18 Ps 88:18; 142:4; Is 49:21

51:19 Is 8:21; 9:20; 14:30

51:20 Is 5:25; Jer 14:16; Deut 14:5; Is 66:15

17 Rouse yourself! Rouse yourself! Arise, O Jerusalem,
You who have drunk from the LORD'S hand the cup of His anger;
The chalice of reeling you have drained to the dregs.
18 There is none to guide her among all the sons she has borne,
Nor is there one to take her by the hand among all the sons she has reared.
19 These two things have befallen you;
Who will mourn for you?
The devastation and destruction, famine and sword;
How shall I comfort you?
20 Your sons have fainted,
They lie *helpless* at the head of every street,
Like an antelope in a net,
Full of the wrath of the LORD,
The rebuke of your God.

51:21 Is 54:11; Is 29:9; 51:17; 63:6

51:22 Is 3:12, 13; 49:25; Jer 50:34; Is 51:17

51:23 Is 49:26; Jer 25:15-17, 26, 28; Zech 12:2; Josh 10:24

21 Therefore, please hear this, you afflicted,
Who are drunk, but not with wine:
22 Thus says your Lord, the LORD, even your God
Who contends for His people,
"Behold, I have taken out of your hand the cup of reeling,
The chalice of My anger;
You will never drink it again.
23 "I will put it into the hand of your tormentors,
Who have said to you, 'Lie down that we may walk over *you.*'
You have even made your back like the ground
And like the street for those who walk over *it.*"

52:1 Is 51:9, 17; Ex 28:2, 40; 1 Chr 16:29; Ps 110:3; Is 49:18; 61:3, 10; Zech 3:4; Neh 11:1; Is 48:2; 64:10; Zech 14:20, 21; Matt 4:5; Rev 21:2-27; Is 35:8

52:2 Is 29:4; Is 60:1; Is 9:4; 10:27; 14:25; Zech 2:7

52:3 Ps 44:12; Jer 15:13; Is 1:27; 62:12; 63:4; Is 45:13

52:4 Gen 46:6

52:5 Ezek 36:20, 23; Rom 2:24

52:6 Is 49:23

52:7 Is 40:9; 61:1; Nah 1:15; Rom 10:15; Eph 6:15; Ps 93:1; Is 24:23

Cheer for Prostrate Zion

52 Awake, awake,
Clothe yourself in your strength, O Zion;
Clothe yourself in your beautiful garments,
O Jerusalem, the holy city;
For the uncircumcised and the unclean
Will no longer come into you.
2 Shake yourself from the dust, rise up,
O captive Jerusalem;
Loose yourself from the chains around your neck,
O captive daughter of Zion.
3 For thus says the LORD, "You were sold for nothing and you will be redeemed without money."
4 For thus says the Lord GOD, "My people went down at the first into Egypt to reside
there; then the Assyrian oppressed them without cause.
5 "Now therefore, what do I have here," declares the LORD, "seeing that My people
have been taken away without cause?" *Again* the LORD declares, "Those who rule over
them howl, and My name is continually blasphemed all day long.
6 "Therefore My people shall know My name; therefore in that day I am the one who
is speaking, 'Here I am.' "
7 How lovely on the mountains
Are the feet of him who brings good news,

51:17—52:10 Jerusalem was God's holy city, the city with God's temple. But the people of Judah experienced ruin instead of prosperity, destruction instead of liberty. Because of their sins, the people suffered. But God promised to restore Jerusalem as a holy city where sinners cannot enter. "Bared His holy arm" (52:10) means that God has revealed his holy power and justice. God reigns. He is in control.

52:7 God says that the feet of those who bring good news are "lovely." It is a wonderful privilege to be able to share God's Good News with others, his news of redemption, salvation, and peace. To whom do you need to give the Good News?

Who announces peace
And brings good news of happiness,
Who announces salvation,
And says to Zion, "Your God reigns!"
8 Listen! Your watchmen lift up *their* voices,
They shout joyfully together;
For they will see with their own eyes
When the LORD restores Zion.
9 Break forth, shout joyfully together,
You waste places of Jerusalem;
For the LORD has comforted His people,
He has redeemed Jerusalem.
10 The LORD has bared His holy arm
In the sight of all the nations,
That all the ends of the earth may see
The salvation of our God.

52:8 Is 62:6

52:9 Ps 98:4; Is 44:23; Is 44:26; 51:3; 61:4; Is 43:1; 48:20

52:10 Ps 98:1-3; Is 51:9; 66:18, 19; Is 45:22; 48:20

11 Depart, depart, go out from there,
Touch nothing unclean;
Go out of the midst of her, purify yourselves,
You who carry the vessels of the LORD.
12 But you will not go out in haste,
Nor will you go as fugitives;
For the LORD will go before you,
And the God of Israel *will be* your rear guard.

52:11 Is 48:20; Jer 50:8; Zech 2:6, 7; 2 Cor 6:17; Num 19:11, 16; Lev 22:2; Is 1:16

52:12 Ex 12:11, 33; Deut 16:3; Is 26:7; 42:16; 49:10, 11; Ex 14:19, 20; Is 58:8

The Exalted Servant

13 Behold, My servant will prosper,
He will be high and lifted up and greatly exalted.
14 Just as many were astonished at you, *My people,*
So His appearance was marred more than any man
And His form more than the sons of men.
15 Thus He will sprinkle many nations,
Kings will shut their mouths on account of Him;
For what had not been told them they will see,
And what they had not heard they will understand.

52:13 Is 42:1; 49:1-7; 53:11; Is 57:15; Phil 2:9

52:14 Is 53:2, 3

52:15 Num 19:18-21; Ezek 36:25; Job 21:5; Rom 15:21; Eph 3:5

The Suffering Servant

53 Who has believed our message?
And to whom has the arm of the LORD been revealed?
2 For He grew up before Him like a tender shoot,
And like a root out of parched ground;
He has no *stately* form or majesty
That we should look upon Him,
Nor appearance that we should [19]be attracted to Him.

53:1 John 12:38; Rom 10:16

53:2 Is 11:1; Is 52:14

19 Lit *desire*

52:12 The people did not have to leave in fearful haste because Cyrus, God's anointed (45:1), decreed that the Jewish exiles could return safely to Jerusalem (Ezra 1:1–4). They had the king's approval, his guaranteed protection. More important, the Lord would go ahead to point the way and be behind to protect them.

52:13 The "servant," as the term is used here, is the Messiah, our Lord Jesus. He would be highly exalted because of his sacrifice, described in chapter 53.

52:14–15 This servant, Christ, would be "marred more than any man"; but through his suffering, he would cleanse the nations (Hebrews 10:14; 1 Peter 1:2).

53:1ff This chapter continues to speak of the Messiah, Jesus, who would suffer for the sins of all people. Such a prophecy is astounding! Who would believe that God would choose to save the world through a humble, suffering servant rather than a glorious king? The idea is contrary to human pride and worldly ways. But God often works in ways we don't expect. The Messiah's strength is shown by humility, suffering, and mercy.

53:2 There was nothing beautiful or majestic in the physical appearance of this servant. Israel would miscalculate the servant's importance—they would consider him an ordinary man. But even though Jesus would not attract a large following based on his physical appearance, he would bring salvation and healing. Many people miscalculate the importance of Jesus' life and work, and they need faithful Christians to point out his extraordinary nature.

53:3 Ps 22:6; Is 49:7; Luke 18:31-33; Is 53:10; Mark 10:33, 34; John 1:10, 11

3 He was despised and forsaken of men,
A man of sorrows and acquainted with grief;
And like one from whom men hide their face
He was despised, and we did not esteem Him.

53:4 Matt 8:17; John 19:7

4 Surely our [20]griefs He Himself bore,
And our sorrows He carried;
Yet we ourselves esteemed Him stricken,
Smitten of God, and afflicted.

53:5 Is 53:8; Heb 9:28; Is 53:10; Rom 4:25; 1 Cor 15:3; Deut 11:2; Heb 5:8; 1 Pet 2:24, 25

5 But He was [21]pierced through for our transgressions,
He was crushed for our iniquities;
The chastening for our well-being *fell* upon Him,
And by His scourging we are healed.
6 All of us like sheep have gone astray,
Each of us has turned to his own way;
But the LORD has caused the iniquity of us all
To fall on Him.

53:7 Matt 26:63; 27:12-14; Mark 14:61; 15:5; Luke 23:9; John 19:9; Acts 8:32, 33; Rev 5:6

7 He was oppressed and He was afflicted,
Yet He did not open His mouth;
Like a lamb that is led to slaughter,
And like a sheep that is silent before its shearers,
So He did not open His mouth.

53:8 Is 53:5, 12

8 By oppression and judgment He was taken away;
And as for His generation, who considered
That He was cut off out of the land of the living
For the transgression of my people, to whom the stroke *was due?*

53:9 Matt 27:57-60; Is 42:1-3; 1 Pet 2:22

9 His grave was assigned with wicked men,
Yet He was with a rich man in His death,
Because He had done no violence,
Nor was there any deceit in His mouth.

53:10 Is 53:5; Is 53:3, 4; Is 53:6, 12; John 1:29; Ps 22:30; Is 54:3; 61:9; 66:22; Is 46:10

10 But the LORD was pleased
To crush Him, putting *Him* to grief;
If He would render Himself *as* a guilt offering,
He will see *His* offspring,
He will prolong *His* days,
And the good pleasure of the LORD will prosper in His hand.

53:11 John 10:14-18; Is 45:25; Rom 5:18, 19; Is 53:5, 6

11 As a result of the anguish of His soul,
He will see *it and* be satisfied;
By His knowledge the Righteous One,
My Servant, will justify the many,

20 Or *sickness* **21** Or *wounded*

53:3 This man of sorrows was despised and rejected by those around him, and he is still despised and rejected by many today. Some reject Christ by standing against him. Others despise Christ and his great gift of forgiveness. Do you despise him, reject him, or accept him?

53:4–5 How could an Old Testament person understand the idea of Christ dying for our sins (our transgressions and iniquities)—actually bearing the punishment that we deserved? The sacrifices suggested this idea, but it is one thing to kill a lamb and something quite different to think of God's chosen servant as that Lamb. But God was pulling aside the curtain of time to let the people of Isaiah's day look ahead to the suffering of the future Messiah and the resulting forgiveness made available to all mankind.

53:6 Isaiah speaks of Israel straying from God and compares them to wandering sheep. Yet God would send the Messiah to bring them back into the fold. We have the hindsight to see and know the identity of the promised Messiah who has come and died for our sins. But if we can see all that Jesus did and still reject him, our sin is much greater than that of the ancient Israelites who could not see what we have seen. Have you given your life to Jesus Christ, the "good shepherd" (John 10:11–16), or are you still like a wandering sheep?

53:7–12 In the Old Testament, people offered animals as sacrifices for their sins. Here, the sinless servant of the Lord offers himself for our sins. He is the lamb (53:7) offered for the sins of all people (John 1:29; Revelation 5:6–14). The Messiah suffered for our sakes, bearing our sins to make us acceptable to God. What can we say to such love? How will we respond to him?

53:11 "My Servant, will justify the many" tells of the enormous family of believers who will become righteous, not by their own works, but by the Messiah's great work on the cross. They are justified because they have claimed Christ, the righteous servant, as their Savior and Lord (see Romans 10:9; 2 Corinthians 5:21). Their life of sin is stripped away, and they are clothed with Christ's goodness (Ephesians 4:22–24).

As He will bear their iniquities.
12 Therefore, I will allot Him a portion with the great,
And He will divide the booty with the strong;
Because He poured out Himself to death,
And was numbered with the transgressors;
Yet He Himself bore the sin of many,
And interceded for the transgressors.

53:12 Is 52:13; Phil 2:9-11; Matt 26:38, 39, 42; Mark 15:28; Luke 22:37; Is 53:6, 11; 2 Cor 5:21

The Fertility of Zion

54 "Shout for joy, O barren one, you who have borne no *child;*
Break forth into joyful shouting and cry aloud, you who have not travailed;
For the sons of the desolate one *will be* more numerous
Than the sons of the married woman," says the LORD.
2 "Enlarge the place of your tent;
Stretch out the curtains of your dwellings, spare not;
Lengthen your cords
And strengthen your pegs.
3 "For you will spread abroad to the right and to the left.
And your descendants will possess nations
And will resettle the desolate cities.

54:1 Gal 4:27; Is 62:4; 1 Sam 2:5; Is 49:20

54:2 Is 33:20; 49:19, 20; Ex 35:18; 39:40

54:3 Gen 28:14; Is 43:5, 6; 60:3; Is 14:1, 2; Is 49:19

4 "Fear not, for you will not be put to shame;
And do not feel humiliated, for you will not be disgraced;
But you will forget the shame of your youth,
And the reproach of your widowhood you will remember no more.
5 "For your husband is your Maker,
Whose name is the LORD of hosts;
And your Redeemer is the Holy One of Israel,
Who is called the God of all the earth.
6 "For the LORD has called you,
Like a wife forsaken and grieved in spirit,
Even like a wife of *one's* youth when she is rejected,"
Says your God.
7 "For a brief moment I forsook you,
But with great compassion I will gather you.
8 "In an outburst of anger
I hid My face from you for a moment,
But with everlasting lovingkindness I will have compassion on you,"
Says the LORD your Redeemer.

54:4 Is 45:17; Jer 31:19; Is 4:1; 25:8; 51:7

54:5 Jer 3:14; Hos 2:19; Is 43:14; 48:17; Is 6:3; 11:9; 65:16

54:6 Is 49:14-21; 50:1, 2; 62:4

54:7 Is 26:20; Is 11:12; 43:5; 49:18

54:8 Is 60:10; Is 54:10; 63:7; Is 49:10, 13; Is 54:5

9 "For this is like the days of Noah to Me,
When I swore that the waters of Noah
Would not flood the earth again;
So I have sworn that I will not be angry with you
Nor will I rebuke you.
10 "For the mountains may be removed and the hills may shake,
But My lovingkindness will not be removed from you,
And My covenant of peace will not be shaken,"
Says the LORD who has compassion on you.

54:9 Gen 9:11; Is 12:1; Ezek 39:29

54:10 Ps 102:26; Is 51:6; 2 Sam 23:5; Ps 89:34; Is 55:3; 59:21; 61:8; Is 54:8

54:1 To be childless ("barren") at that time was a woman's great shame, a disgrace. Families depended on children for survival, especially when the parents became elderly. Israel (Zion) was unfruitful, like a childless woman, but God would permit her to have many children and would change her mourning into singing.

54:6–8 God said that he had abandoned Israel for a brief moment, so the nation was like a young wife rejected by her husband. But God still called Israel his own. The God we serve is holy, and he cannot tolerate sin. When his people blatantly sinned, God in his anger chose to punish them. Sin separates us from God and brings us pain and suffering. But if we confess our sin and repent, then God will forgive us. Have you ever been separated from a loved one and then experienced joy when that person returned? That is like the joy God experiences when you repent and return to him.

54:9–13 God made a covenant with Noah that he has never broken (Genesis 9:8–17). Likewise, God made a covenant of peace with the people of Israel that the time would come when he would stop rebuking them, would restore their wealth, and would personally teach their children.

54:11 Is 51:21; Is 51:18, 19; Is 14:32; 28:16; 44:28; Job 28:16; Rev 21:19

11 "O afflicted one, storm-tossed, *and* not comforted,
Behold, I will set your stones in antimony,
And your foundations I will lay in sapphires.
12 "Moreover, I will make your battlements of rubies,
And your gates of crystal,
And your entire wall of precious stones.

54:13 John 6:45; Is 48:18; 66:12

13 "All your sons will be taught of the LORD;
And the well-being of your sons will be great.

54:14 Is 1:26, 27; 9:7; 62:1; Is 9:4; 14:4; Is 54:4; Is 33:18

14 "In righteousness you will be established;
You will be far from oppression, for you will not fear;
And from terror, for it will not come near you.

54:15 Is 41:11-16

15 "If anyone fiercely assails *you* it will not be from Me.
Whoever assails you will fall because of you.
16 "Behold, I Myself have created the smith who blows the fire of coals
And brings out a weapon for its work;
And I have created the destroyer to ruin.

54:17 Is 17:12-14; 29:8; Is 50:8, 9; Is 45:24; 46:13

17 "No weapon that is formed against you will prosper;
And every tongue that accuses you in judgment you will condemn.
This is the heritage of the servants of the LORD,
And their vindication is from Me," declares the LORD.

The Free Offer of Mercy

55:1 Ps 42:1, 2; 63:1; 143:6; Is 41:17; 44:3; John 4:14; 7:37; Rev 21:6; Lam 5:4; Song 5:1; Joel 3:18; Hos 14:4; Matt 10:8

55 "Ho! Every one who thirsts, come to the waters;
And you who have no money come, buy and eat.
Come, buy wine and milk
Without money and without cost.

55:2 Eccl 6:2; Hos 8:7; Ps 22:26; Is 1:19; 62:8, 9; Is 25:6; Jer 31:14

2 "Why do you spend money for what is not bread,
And your wages for what does not satisfy?
Listen carefully to Me, and eat what is good,
And delight yourself in abundance.

55:3 Is 51:4; Lev 18:5; Rom 10:5; Is 61:8; Acts 13:34

3 "Incline your ear and come to Me.
Listen, that you may live;
And I will make an everlasting covenant with you,
According to the faithful mercies shown to David.

55:4 Ps 18:43; Jer 30:9; Hos 3:5; Ezek 34:24; 37:24, 25; Dan 9:25; Mic 5:2

4 "Behold, I have made him a witness to the peoples,
A leader and commander for the peoples.

55:5 Is 45:14, 22-24; 49:6, 12, 23; Zech 8:22; Is 60:9

5 "Behold, you will call a nation you do not know,
And a nation which knows you not will run to you,
Because of the LORD your God, even the Holy One of Israel;
For He has glorified you."

55:6 Ps 32:6; Is 45:19, 22; 49:8; Amos 5:6; Is 58:9; 65:24

6 Seek the LORD while He may be found;
Call upon Him while He is near.

55:7 Is 1:16, 19; 58:6; Is 32:7; 59:7; Is 31:6; 44:22; Is 14:1; 54:8, 10; Is 1:18; 40:2; 43:25; 44:22

7 Let the wicked forsake his way
And the unrighteous man his thoughts;
And let him return to the LORD,
And He will have compassion on him,
And to our God,
For He will abundantly pardon.

55:1–6 Food costs money, lasts only a short time, and meets only physical needs. But God offers us *free* nourishment that feeds our soul. How do we get it? We come (55:1), listen (55:2), seek, and call on God (55:6). God's salvation is freely offered, but to nourish our souls we must eagerly receive it. We will starve spiritually without this food as surely as we will starve physically without our daily bread.

55:3 God's covenant with David promised a permanent homeland for the Israelites, no threat from pagan nations, and no wars (2 Samuel 7:10–11). But Israel did not fulfill its part of the covenant by obeying God and staying away from idols. Even so, God was ready to renew his covenant again. He is a forgiving God!

55:6 Isaiah tells us to call on the Lord while he is near. God is not planning to move away from us, but we often move far from him or erect a barrier between ourselves and him. Don't wait until you have drifted far away from God to seek him. Later in life turning to him may be far more difficult. Or God may come to judge the earth before you decide to turn to him. Seek God now, while you can, before it is too late.

8 "For My thoughts are not your thoughts,
Nor are your ways My ways," declares the LORD.
9 "For *as* the heavens are higher than the earth,
So are My ways higher than your ways
And My thoughts than your thoughts.
10 "For as the rain and the snow come down from heaven,
And do not return there without watering the earth
And making it bear and sprout,
And furnishing seed to the sower and bread to the eater;
11 So will My word be which goes forth from My mouth;
It will not return to Me empty,
Without accomplishing what I desire,
And without succeeding *in the matter* for which I sent it.
12 "For you will go out with joy
And be led forth with peace;
The mountains and the hills will break forth into shouts of joy before you,
And all the trees of the field will clap *their* hands.
13 "Instead of the thorn bush the cypress will come up,
And instead of the nettle the myrtle will come up,
And it will be a memorial to the LORD,
For an everlasting sign which will not be cut off."

55:8 Is 65:2; 66:18; Is 53:6

55:9 Ps 103:11

55:10 Is 30:23; 2 Cor 9:10

55:11 Is 45:23; Matt 24:35; Is 44:26; 59:21; Is 46:10; 53:10

55:12 Ps 105:43; Is 51:11; 52:9; Is 54:10, 13; Jer 29:11; Is 44:23; 49:13; 1 Chr 16:33

55:13 Is 7:19; Is 60:13; Is 5:6; 7:24; 32:13; Is 63:12, 14; Jer 33:9; Is 19:20; Is 56:5

Rewards for Obedience to God

56 Thus says the LORD,
"Preserve justice and do righteousness,
For My salvation is about to come
And My righteousness to be revealed.
2 "How blessed is the man who does this,
And the son of man who takes hold of it;
Who keeps from profaning the sabbath,
And keeps his hand from doing any evil."
3 Let not the foreigner who has joined himself to the LORD say,
"The LORD will surely separate me from His people."
Nor let the eunuch say, "Behold, I am a dry tree."
4 For thus says the LORD,
"To the eunuchs who keep My sabbaths,
And choose what pleases Me,
And hold fast My covenant,
5 To them I will give in My house and within My walls a memorial,
And a name better than that of sons and daughters;
I will give them an everlasting name which will not be cut off.

6 "Also the foreigners who join themselves to the LORD,
To minister to Him, and to love the name of the LORD,
To be His servants, every one who keeps from profaning the sabbath
And holds fast My covenant;
7 Even those I will bring to My holy mountain
And make them joyful in My house of prayer.
Their burnt offerings and their sacrifices will be acceptable on My altar;

56:1 Is 1:17; 33:5; 61:8; Ps 85:9; Is 46:13; 51:5

56:2 Ps 112:1; 119:1, 2; Is 56:4, 6; Ex 20:8-11; 31:13-17; Is 56:6; 58:13; Jer 17:21, 22; Ezek 20:12, 20

56:3 Is 14:1; 56:6; Deut 23:1; Jer 38:7; Acts 8:27

56:4 Is 56:2, 6; Is 56:6

56:5 Is 2:2, 3; 56:7; 66:20; Is 26:1; 60:18; Is 62:2; Is 48:19; 55:13

56:6 Is 56:3; 60:10; 61:5; Is 56:2, 4

56:7 Is 2:2, 3; 60:11; Mic 4:1, 2; Is 11:9; 65:25; Is 61:10; Is 60:7; Matt 21:13; Mark 11:17; Luke 19:46

55:8–9 The people of Israel were foolish to act as if they knew what God was thinking and planning. His knowledge and wisdom are far greater than man's. We are foolish to try to fit God into our mold—to make his plans and purposes conform to ours. Instead, we must strive to fit into *his* plans.

56:2 God commanded his people to rest and honor him on the Sabbath (Exodus 20:8–11). He wants us to serve him every day, but he wants us to make one day special when we rest and focus our thoughts on him. For the Israelites, this special day was the Sabbath (Saturday). Some Christians set Saturday aside as this special day, but many accept Sunday (the day of the week that Jesus rose from the dead) as the "Lord's Day," a day of rest and honor to God.

56:3 Isaiah clearly proclaims the radical message that God's blessings are for *all* people, even foreigners and eunuchs, who were often excluded from worship and not even considered citizens in Israel. Whatever your race, social position, work, or financial situation, God's blessings are as much for you as for anyone else. No one must exclude in any way those God chooses to include.

56:7 Jesus quoted from this verse when he threw the moneychangers out of the temple (Mark 11:17). See the second note on Mark 11:15–17.

For My house will be called a house of prayer for all the peoples."

56:8 Is 11:12; Is 60:3-11; 66:18-21; John 10:16

8 The Lord GOD, who gathers the dispersed of Israel, declares,
"Yet *others* I will gather to them, to those *already* gathered."

56:9 Is 18:6; 46:11

9 All you beasts of the field,
All you beasts in the forest,
Come to eat.

56:10 Ezek 3:17; Is 29:9-14; Jer 14:13, 14

10 His watchmen are blind,
All of them know nothing.
All of them are mute dogs unable to bark,
Dreamers lying down, who love to slumber;

56:11 Is 28:7; Ezek 13:19; Mic 3:5, 11; Is 1:3; Is 57:17; Jer 22:17

11 And the dogs are greedy, they are not satisfied.
And they are shepherds who have no understanding;
They have all turned to their own way,
Each one to his unjust gain, to the last one.

56:12 Is 5:11, 12, 22; Ps 10:6; Luke 12:19, 20

12 "Come," *they say,* "let us get wine, and let us drink heavily of strong drink;
And tomorrow will be like today, only more so."

Evil Leaders Rebuked

57:1 Is 42:25; 47:7; 2 Kin 22:20; Is 47:11; Jer 18:11

57 The righteous man perishes, and no man takes it to heart;
And devout men are taken away, while no one understands.
For the righteous man is taken away from evil,

57:2 Is 26:7

2 He enters into peace;
They rest in their beds,
Each one who walked in his upright way.

57:3 Mal 3:5; Is 1:4; Matt 16:4; Is 1:21; 57:7-9

3 "But come here, you sons of a sorceress,
Offspring of an adulterer and a prostitute.

57:4 Is 48:8

4 "Against whom do you jest?
Against whom do you open wide your mouth
And stick out your tongue?
Are you not children of rebellion,
Offspring of deceit,

57:5 Is 1:29; 2 Kin 16:4; Jer 2:20; 3:13; 2 Kin 23:10; Ps 106:37, 38; Jer 7:31

5 *Who* inflame yourselves among the oaks,
Under every luxuriant tree,
Who slaughter the children in the ravines,
Under the clefts of the crags?

57:6 Jer 3:9; Hab 2:19; Jer 7:18; Jer 5:9, 29; 9:9

6 "Among the smooth *stones* of the ravine
Is your portion, they are your lot;
Even to them you have poured out a drink offering,
You have made a grain offering.
Shall I relent concerning these things?

57:7 Jer 3:6; Ezek 16:16; Ezek 23:41

7 "Upon a high and lofty mountain
You have made your bed.
You also went up there to offer sacrifice.

57:8 Ezek 23:18

8 "Behind the door and the doorpost
You have set up your sign;
Indeed, far removed from Me, you have uncovered yourself,
And have gone up and made your bed wide.
And you have made an agreement for yourself with them,
You have loved their bed,
You have looked on *their* manhood.

57:9 Ezek 23:16, 40

9 "You have journeyed to the king with oil
And increased your perfumes;

56:9–11 The "watchmen" were the nation's leaders. The leaders of Israel were blind to every danger. Apathetic about their people's needs, they were more concerned about satisfying their own greed. Leadership's special privileges can cause leaders either to sacrifice for the good of their people or to sacrifice their people for their own greed. If you are in a leadership position, use it for the good of your people.

57:7–8 Marriage is an exclusive relationship where a man and a woman become one. Adultery breaks this beautiful bond of unity. When the people turned from God and gave their love to idols, God said they were committing adultery—breaking their exclusive commitment to God. How could people give their love to worthless wood and stone instead of to the God who made them and loved them so very much?

You have sent your envoys a great distance
And made *them* go down to Sheol.
10 "You were tired out by the length of your road,
Yet you did not say, 'It is hopeless.'
You found renewed strength,
Therefore you did not faint.

11 "Of whom were you worried and fearful
When you lied, and did not remember Me
Nor give *Me* a thought?
Was I not silent even for a long time
So you do not fear Me?
12 "I will declare your righteousness and your deeds,
But they will not profit you.
13 "When you cry out, let your collection *of idols* deliver you.
But the wind will carry all of them up,
And a breath will take *them away.*
But he who takes refuge in Me will inherit the land
And will possess My holy mountain."

14 And it will be said,
"Build up, build up, prepare the way,
Remove *every* obstacle out of the way of My people."
15 For thus says the high and exalted One
Who lives forever, whose name is Holy,
"I dwell *on* a high and holy place,
And *also* with the contrite and lowly of spirit
In order to revive the spirit of the lowly
And to revive the heart of the contrite.
16 "For I will not contend forever,
Nor will I always be angry;
For the spirit would grow faint before Me,
And the breath *of those whom* I have made.
17 "Because of the iniquity of his unjust gain I was angry and struck him;
I hid *My face* and was angry,
And he went on turning away, in the way of his heart.
18 "I have seen his ways, but I will heal him;
I will lead him and restore comfort to him and to his mourners,
19 Creating the praise of the lips.
Peace, peace to him who is far and to him who is near,"
Says the LORD, "and I will heal him."
20 But the wicked are like the tossing sea,
For it cannot be quiet,
And its waters toss up refuse and mud.
21 "There is no peace," says my God, "for the wicked."

57:10 Jer 2:25; 18:12

57:11 Prov 29:25; Is 51:12, 13; Jer 2:32; 3:21; Ps 50:21; Is 42:14

57:12 Is 58:1, 2; Is 29:15; 59:6; 65:7; 66:18; Mic 3:2-4

57:13 Jer 22:20; 30:14; Ps 37:3, 9; Is 25:4; Is 49:8; 60:21; Is 65:9

57:14 Is 62:10; Jer 18:15

57:15 Is 52:13; Deut 33:27; Is 40:28; Is 33:5; 66:1; Ps 34:18; 51:17; Is 66:2; Ps 147:3; Is 61:1-3

57:16 Gen 6:3; Ps 85:5; 103:9; Mic 7:18; Is 42:5

57:17 Is 2:7; 56:11; Jer 6:13; Is 1:4; Jer 3:14, 22

57:18 Is 19:22; 30:26; 53:5; Is 52:12; Is 61:1-3

57:19 Is 6:7; 51:16; 59:21; Heb 13:15; Is 26:12; 32:17; Acts 2:39; Eph 2:17

57:20 Job 18:5-14; Is 3:9, 11

57:21 Is 48:22; 59:8; Is 49:4

Observances of Fasts

58 "Cry loudly, do not hold back;
Raise your voice like a trumpet,
And declare to My people their transgression

58:1 Is 40:6; Is 43:27; 50:1; 59:12

57:12 God says that he will expose their righteousness and works for what they really were—mere pretentions of doing good. Isaiah warned these people that their righteousness and works would not save them any more than their weak, worthless idols. We cannot gain our salvation through good deeds because our best deeds are not good enough to outweigh our sins. Salvation is a gift from God, received only through faith in Christ, not good deeds (Ephesians 2:8, 9).

57:14–21 Verses 1–13 speak of pride and lust; verses 14–21 tell how God relates to those who are humble and repentant ("contrite"). The high and holy God came down to our level to save us because it is impossible for us to go up to his level to save ourselves (see 2 Chronicles 6:18; Psalm 51:1–7; Philippians 2).

58:1ff True worship was more than religious ritual, going to the temple every day, fasting, and listening to Scripture readings. These people missed the point of a living, vital relationship with God. He doesn't want us acting pious when we have unforgiven sin in our hearts and perform sinful practices with our hands. More important even than correct worship and doctrine is genuine compassion for the poor, the helpless, and the oppressed.

And to the house of Jacob their sins.
2 "Yet they seek Me day by day and delight to know My ways,
As a nation that has done righteousness
And has not forsaken the ordinance of their God.
They ask Me *for* just decisions,
They delight in the nearness of God.
3 'Why have we fasted and You do not see?
Why have we humbled ourselves and You do not notice?'
Behold, on the day of your fast you find *your* desire,
And drive hard all your workers.
4 "Behold, you fast for contention and strife and to strike with a wicked fist.
You do not fast like *you do* today to make your voice heard on high.
5 "Is it a fast like this which I choose, a day for a man to humble himself?
Is it for bowing one's head like a reed
And for spreading out sackcloth and ashes as a bed?
Will you call this a fast, even an acceptable day to the LORD?
6 "Is this not the fast which I choose,
To loosen the bonds of wickedness,
To undo the bands of the yoke,
And to let the oppressed go free
And break every yoke?
7 "Is it not to divide your bread with the hungry
And bring the homeless poor into the house;
When you see the naked, to cover him;
And not to hide yourself from your own flesh?
8 "Then your light will break out like the dawn,
And your recovery will speedily spring forth;
And your righteousness will go before you;
The glory of the LORD will be your rear guard.
9 "Then you will call, and the LORD will answer;
You will cry, and He will say, 'Here I am.'
If you remove the yoke from your midst,
The pointing of the finger and speaking wickedness,
10 And if you give yourself to the hungry
And satisfy the desire of the afflicted,
Then your light will rise in darkness
And your gloom *will become* like midday.
11 "And the LORD will continually guide you,
And satisfy your desire in scorched places,
And give strength to your bones;
And you will be like a watered garden,
And like a spring of water whose waters do not fail.
12 "Those from among you will rebuild the ancient ruins;
You will raise up the age-old foundations;
And you will be called the repairer of the breach,
The restorer of the streets in which to dwell.

Keeping the Sabbath

13 "If because of the sabbath, you turn your foot
From doing your *own* pleasure on My holy day,
And call the sabbath a delight, the holy *day* of the LORD honorable,
And honor it, desisting from your *own* ways,

58:2 Is 1:11; Titus 1:16; Is 48:1; Jer 7:9, 10; Is 1:4, 28; 59:13; Ps 119:151; Is 29:13; 57:3; James 4:8

58:3 Mal 3:14; Luke 18:12; Is 22:12, 13; Zech 7:5, 6

58:4 Is 3:14, 15; 59:6; Is 1:15; 59:2; Joel 2:12-14

58:5 1 Kin 21:27; Is 49:8; 61:2

58:6 Neh 5:10-12; Jer 34:8; Is 1:17; Is 58:9

58:7 Job 31:19, 20; Is 58:10; Ezek 18:7, 16; Is 16:3, 4; Heb 13:2; Matt 25:35, 36; Luke 3:11; Deut 22:1-4; Luke 10:31, 32

58:8 Is 58:10; Is 30:26; 33:24; Jer 30:17; 33:6; Ps 85:13; Is 62:1; Ex 14:19; Is 52:12

58:9 Ps 50:15; Is 55:6; 65:24; Is 58:6; Prov 6:13; Ps 12:2; Is 59:13

58:10 Deut 15:7; Is 58:7; Job 11:17; Ps 37:6; Is 42:16; 58:8

58:11 Is 49:10; 57:18; Ps 107:9; Is 41:17; Is 66:14; Song 4:15; Is 27:3; Jer 31:12; John 4:14; 7:38

58:12 Is 49:8; 61:4; Ezek 36:10; Is 44:28; Is 30:13; Amos 9:11

58:13 Ex 31:16, 17; 35:2, 3; Is 56:2, 4, 6; Jer 17:21-27; Ps 27:4; 42:4; 84:2, 10; Is 55:8; Is 59:13

58:6–12 We cannot be saved by deeds of service without faith in Christ, but our faith lacks sincerity if it doesn't reach out to others. Fasting can be beneficial spiritually and physically, but at its best fasting helps only the person doing it. God says he wants our service to go beyond our own personal growth to acts of kindness, charity, justice, and generosity. True fasting is more than what we don't eat; it is pleasing God by applying his Word to our society.

58:13–14 The day of rest should also be honored not only because Sabbath-keeping is a commandment but also because it is best for us and because it honors God. Keeping the Sabbath honors God, our Creator, who also rested on the seventh day (Genesis 2:3). It also unifies our family and sets priorities for them. Our day of rest refreshes us spiritually and physically—providing time when we can gather together for worship and when we can reflect on God without the stress of our everyday activities.

From seeking your *own* pleasure
And speaking *your own* word,
14 Then you will take delight in the LORD,
And I will make you ride on the heights of the earth;
And I will feed you *with* the heritage of Jacob your father,
For the mouth of the LORD has spoken."

58:14 Job 22:26; Is 61:10; Deut 32:13; 33:29; Is 33:16; Hab 3:19; Is 1:20; 40:5

Separation from God

59 Behold, the LORD'S hand is not so short
That it cannot save;
Nor is His ear so dull
That it cannot hear.
2 But your iniquities have made a separation between you and your God,
And your sins have hidden *His* face from you so that He does not hear.
3 For your hands are defiled with blood
And your fingers with iniquity;
Your lips have spoken falsehood,
Your tongue mutters wickedness.
4 No one sues righteously and no one pleads honestly.
They trust in confusion and speak lies;
They conceive mischief and bring forth iniquity.
5 They hatch adders' eggs and weave the spider's web;
He who eats of their eggs dies,
And *from* that which is crushed a snake breaks forth.
6 Their webs will not become clothing,
Nor will they cover themselves with their works;
Their works are works of iniquity,
And an act of violence is in their hands.
7 Their feet run to evil,
And they hasten to shed innocent blood;
Their thoughts are thoughts of iniquity,
Devastation and destruction are in their highways.
8 They do not know the way of peace,
And there is no justice in their tracks;
They have made their paths crooked,
Whoever treads on them does not know peace.

59:1 Num 11:23; Is 50:2; Jer 32:17; Is 58:9; 65:24; Ezek 8:18

59:2 Is 1:15; 50:1; Is 58:4

59:3 Is 1:15, 21; Jer 2:30, 34; Ezek 7:23; Hos 4:2; Is 28:15; 30:9; 59:13

59:4 Is 5:7; 59:14; Is 59:14, 15; Is 30:12; Jer 7:4, 8; Job 15:35; Ps 7:14; Is 33:11

59:5 Job 8:14

59:6 Is 28:20; Is 57:12; Jer 6:7; Is 58:4; Ezek 7:11

59:7 Prov 1:16; 6:17; Rom 3:15-17; Is 65:2; 66:18; Mark 7:21, 22

59:8 Luke 1:79; Is 59:9, 11; Hos 4:1; Is 57:20, 21

A Confession of Wickedness

9 Therefore justice is far from us,
And righteousness does not overtake us;
We hope for light, but behold, darkness,
For brightness, but we walk in gloom.
10 We grope along the wall like blind men,
We grope like those who have no eyes;
We stumble at midday as in the twilight,
Among those who are vigorous *we are* like dead men.
11 All of us growl like bears,
And moan sadly like doves;
We hope for justice, but there is none,
For salvation, *but* it is far from us.
12 For our transgressions are multiplied before You,
And our sins testify against us;
For our transgressions are with us,
And we know our iniquities:

59:9 Is 59:14; Is 5:30; 8:21, 22

59:10 Deut 28:29; Job 5:14; Is 8:14, 15; 28:13; Lam 3:6

59:11 Is 38:14; Ezek 7:16; Is 59:9, 14

59:12 Ezra 9:6; Is 58:1; Is 3:9; Jer 14:7; Hos 5:5

59:1–14 Sin offends our holy God and separates us from him. Because God is holy, he cannot ignore, excuse, or tolerate sin as though it didn't matter. Sin cuts people off from him, forming a wall to isolate God from the people he loves. No wonder this long list of wretched sins makes God angry and forces him to look the other way. People who die with their life of sin unforgiven separate themselves eternally from God. God wants them to live with him forever, but he cannot take them into his holy presence unless their sin is removed. Have you confessed your sin to God, allowing him to remove it? The Lord can save you if you turn to him.

59:13 Josh 24:27; Prov 30:9; Matt 10:33; Titus 1:16; Is 5:7; 30:12; Jer 9:3, 4; Is 59:3, 4; Mark 7:21, 22

13 Transgressing and denying the LORD,
And turning away from our God,
Speaking oppression and revolt,
Conceiving *in* and uttering from the heart lying words.

59:14 Is 1:21; 5:7; Is 46:12; Hab 1:4

14 Justice is turned back,
And righteousness stands far away;
For truth has stumbled in the street,
And uprightness cannot enter.

59:15 Is 5:23; 10:2; 29:21; 32:7; Is 1:21-23

15 Yes, truth is lacking;
And he who turns aside from evil makes himself a prey.

Now the LORD saw,
And it was displeasing in His sight that there was no justice.

59:16 Is 41:28; 63:5; Ezek 22:30; Ps 98:1; Is 52:10; 63:5

16 And He saw that there was no man,
And was astonished that there was no one to intercede;
Then His own arm brought salvation to Him,
And His righteousness upheld Him.

59:17 Eph 6:14; Eph 6:17; 1 Thess 5:8; Is 63:2, 3; Is 9:7; 37:32; Zech 1:14

17 He put on righteousness like a breastplate,
And a helmet of salvation on His head;
And He put on garments of vengeance for clothing
And wrapped Himself with zeal as a mantle.

59:18 Job 34:11; Is 65:6, 7; 66:6; Jer 17:10

18 According to *their* deeds, so He will repay,
Wrath to His adversaries, recompense to His enemies;
To the coastlands He will make recompense.

59:19 Is 49:12; Ps 113:3; Is 30:28; 66:12

19 So they will fear the name of the LORD from the west
And His glory from the rising of the sun,
For He will come like a rushing stream
Which the wind of the LORD drives.

59:20 Rom 11:26; Ezek 18:30, 31; Acts 2:38, 39

20 "A Redeemer will come to Zion,
And to those who turn from transgression in Jacob," declares the LORD.

59:21 Jer 31:31-34; Rom 11:27; Is 11:2; 32:15; 44:3; Is 55:11

21 "As for Me, this is My covenant with them," says the LORD: "My Spirit which is upon
you, and My words which I have put in your mouth shall not depart from your mouth,
nor from the mouth of your offspring, nor from the mouth of your offspring's offspring,"
says the LORD, "from now and forever."

3. The future kingdom

A Glorified Zion

60:1 Is 52:2; Is 60:19, 20; Is 24:23; 35:2; 58:8

60 "Arise, shine; for your light has come,
And the glory of the LORD has risen upon you.

60:2 Is 58:10; Jer 13:16; Col 1:13; Is 4:5

2 "For behold, darkness will cover the earth
And deep darkness the peoples;
But the LORD will rise upon you
And His glory will appear upon you.

60:3 Is 2:3; 45:14, 22-25; 49:23

3 "Nations will come to your light,
And kings to the brightness of your rising.

60:4 Is 11:12; 49:18; Is 49:20-22; Is 43:6; 49:22

4 "Lift up your eyes round about and see;
They all gather together, they come to you.

59:15 Because of Israel's willful, persistent rebellion (chapters 56—59), the nation became unable to take action against its sins. Sin fills the vacuum left when God's truth no longer fills our lives. Only God can defeat sin.

59:16–17 God would, in fact, act to rescue the nation from enemy armies (Assyria and Babylon) and to punish wicked Israelites as well. He would also rescue his people from sin. Because this is an impossible task for any human, God himself, as the Messiah, would personally step in to help (Romans 11:26–27). Whether we sin once or many times, out of rebellion or out of ignorance, our sin separates us from God and will continue to separate us until God forgives us and removes it.

59:21 When the Holy Spirit dwells within his people, they change. Their former desires no longer entice them; now their chief aim is to please God. We who are Christians today are the heirs of this prophecy; we are able to respond to God's will and distinguish between good and evil because the Holy Spirit dwells within us (John 14:26; Philippians 2:13; Hebrews 5:14).

60:1ff As we read these promises, we long for their fulfillment. But we must patiently wait for God's timing. He is in control of history, and he weaves together all our lives into his plan.

Your sons will come from afar,
And your daughters will be carried in the arms.
5 "Then you will see and be radiant,
And your heart will thrill and rejoice;
Because the abundance of the sea will be turned to you,
The wealth of the nations will come to you.
6 "A multitude of camels will cover you,
The young camels of Midian and Ephah;
All those from Sheba will come;
They will bring gold and frankincense,
And will bear good news of the praises of the LORD.
7 "All the flocks of Kedar will be gathered together to you,
The rams of Nebaioth will minister to you;
They will go up with acceptance on My altar,
And I shall glorify My glorious house.
8 "Who are these who fly like a cloud
And like the doves to their lattices?
9 "Surely the coastlands will wait for Me;
And the ships of Tarshish *will come* first,
To bring your sons from afar,
Their silver and their gold with them,
For the name of the LORD your God,
And for the Holy One of Israel because He has glorified you.

10 "Foreigners will build up your walls,
And their kings will minister to you;
For in My wrath I struck you,
And in My favor I have had compassion on you.
11 "Your gates will be open continually;
They will not be closed day or night,
So that *men* may bring to you the wealth of the nations,
With their kings led in procession.
12 "For the nation and the kingdom which will not serve you will perish,
And the nations will be utterly ruined.
13 "The glory of Lebanon will come to you,
The juniper, the box tree and the cypress together,
To beautify the place of My sanctuary;
And I shall make the place of My feet glorious.
14 "The sons of those who afflicted you will come bowing to you,
And all those who despised you will bow themselves at the soles of your feet;
And they will call you the city of the LORD,
The Zion of the Holy One of Israel.

15 "Whereas you have been forsaken and hated
With no one passing through,
I will make you an everlasting pride,
A joy from generation to generation.
16 "You will also suck the milk of nations
And suck the breast of kings;
Then you will know that I, the LORD, am your Savior
And your Redeemer, the Mighty One of Jacob.
17 "Instead of bronze I will bring gold,
And instead of iron I will bring silver,
And instead of wood, bronze,
And instead of stones, iron.
And I will make peace your administrators

60:5 Ps 34:5; Is 23:18; 24:14; Is 61:6

60:6 Gen 25:4; Gen 25:3; Ps 72:10; Is 60:9; Matt 2:11; Is 42:10

60:7 Gen 25:13; Is 19:19; 56:7; Is 60:13; Hag 2:7, 9

60:8 Is 49:21

60:9 Is 11:11; 24:15; 42:4, 10, 12; 49:1; 51:5; 66:19; Ps 48:7; Is 2:16; Is 14:2; 43:6; 49:22; Is 55:5

60:10 Is 14:1, 2; 61:5; Zech 6:15; Is 49:23; Rev 21:24; Is 54:8

60:11 Is 26:2; 60:18; 62:10; Rev 21:25, 26; Is 60:5; Ps 149:8; Is 24:21

60:12 Is 14:2; Zech 14:17

60:13 Is 35:2; Is 41:19; 1 Chr 28:2; Ps 99:5; 132:7

60:14 Is 14:1, 2; 45:14, 23; 49:23; Rev 3:9; Is 1:26; Heb 12:22

60:15 Is 1:7-9; 6:11-13; Jer 30:17; Is 66:5; Is 4:2; 65:18

60:16 Is 66:11; Is 19:20; 43:3, 11; 45:15, 21; 63:8; Is 59:20; 63:16

60:6–7 The places mentioned belonged to obscure tribes in the Arabian desert hundreds of miles from Israel. All people would come to Jerusalem because God would be living there and they would be attracted to his light. Don't be discouraged when you look around and see so few people turning to God; one day people throughout the earth will recognize him as the one true God.

And righteousness your overseers.

60:18 Is 54:14; Is 51:19; Is 26:1; Is 60:11

18 "Violence will not be heard again in your land,
Nor devastation or destruction within your borders;
But you will call your walls salvation, and your gates praise.

60:19 Rev 21:23; 22:5; Is 2:5; 9:2; Is 41:16; 45:25; Zech 2:5

19 "No longer will you have the sun for light by day,
Nor for brightness will the moon give you light;
But you will have the LORD for an everlasting light,
And your God for your glory.

60:20 Is 30:26; Is 35:10; 65:19; Rev 21:4

20 "Your sun will no longer set,
Nor will your moon wane;
For you will have the LORD for an everlasting light,
And the days of your mourning will be over.

60:21 Is 45:24, 25; 52:1; Ps 37:11, 22; Is 57:13; 61:7; Is 19:25; 29:23; 45:11; 64:8; Is 61:3

21 "Then all your people *will be* righteous;
They will possess the land forever,
The branch of My planting,
The work of My hands,
That I may be glorified.

60:22 Is 10:22; 51:2

22 "The smallest one will become a clan,
And the least one a mighty nation.
I, the LORD, will hasten it in its time."

Exaltation of the Afflicted

61:1 Is 11:2; 48:16; Luke 4:18; Matt 11:5; Luke 7:22; Is 11:4; 29:19; 32:7; Is 57:15; Is 42:7; 49:9

61 The Spirit of the Lord GOD is upon me,
Because the LORD has anointed me
To bring good news to the afflicted;
He has sent me to bind up the brokenhearted,
To proclaim liberty to captives
And freedom to prisoners;

61:2 Is 49:8; 60:10; Is 2:12; 13:6; 34:2, 8; Is 57:18; Jer 31:13; Matt 5:4

2 To proclaim the favorable year of the LORD
And the day of vengeance of our God;
To comfort all who mourn,

61:3 Is 60:20; Ps 23:5; 45:7; 104:15; Is 60:21; Jer 17:7, 8

3 To grant those who mourn *in* Zion,
Giving them a garland instead of ashes,
The oil of gladness instead of mourning,
The mantle of praise instead of a spirit of fainting.
So they will be called oaks of righteousness,
The planting of the LORD, that He may be glorified.

61:4 Is 49:8; 58:12; Ezek 36:33; Amos 9:14

4 Then they will rebuild the ancient ruins,
They will raise up the former devastations;
And they will repair the ruined cities,
The desolations of many generations.

61:5 Is 14:2; 60:10

5 Strangers will stand and pasture your flocks,
And foreigners will be your farmers and your vinedressers.

61:6 Is 66:21; Is 56:6; Is 60:5, 11

6 But you will be called the priests of the LORD;
You will be spoken of *as* ministers of our God.
You will eat the wealth of nations,
And in their riches you will boast.

61:7 Is 54:4; Is 40:2; Zech 9:12; Ps 16:11

7 Instead of your shame *you will have a* double *portion,*
And *instead of* humiliation they will shout for joy over their portion.
Therefore they will possess a double *portion* in their land,
Everlasting joy will be theirs.

60:19–20 See Revelation 21:23–24 and 22:5, where this beautiful reality is also promised.

61:1–2 Jesus quoted these words in Luke 4:18–19. As he read to the people in the synagogue, he stopped in the middle of 61:2 after the words, "to proclaim the favorable year of the LORD." Rolling up the scroll, he said, "Today this Scripture has been fulfilled in your hearing" (Luke 4:21). The next phrase in 61:2, "and the day of vengeance of our God," will come true when Jesus returns to earth again. We are now under God's favor; his wrath is yet to come.

61:6 Under the old covenant, God ordained the priests of Israel to stand between him and his people. They brought God's word to the people and the people's needs and sins to God. Under the new covenant, all believers are priests of the Lord, reading God's Word and seeking to understand it, confessing their sins directly to God, and ministering to others.

8 For I, the LORD, love justice,
I hate robbery in the burnt offering;
And I will faithfully give them their recompense
And make an everlasting covenant with them.
9 Then their offspring will be known among the nations,
And their descendants in the midst of the peoples.
All who see them will recognize them
Because they are the offspring *whom* the LORD has blessed.

10 I will rejoice greatly in the LORD,
My soul will exult in my God;
For He has clothed me with garments of salvation,
He has wrapped me with a robe of righteousness,
As a bridegroom decks himself with a garland,
And as a bride adorns herself with her jewels.
11 For as the earth brings forth its sprouts,
And as a garden causes the things sown in it to spring up,
So the Lord GOD will cause righteousness and praise
To spring up before all the nations.

61:8 Is 5:16; 28:17; 30:18; Gen 17:7; Ps 105:10; Is 55:3; Jer 32:40

61:9 Is 44:3

61:10 Is 12:1, 2; 25:9; 41:16; 51:3; Is 49:4; Is 49:18; 52:1; Rev 21:2

61:11 Is 4:2; 55:10; Is 45:23, 24; 60:18, 21; Ps 72:3; 85:11

Zion's Glory and New Name

62 For Zion's sake I will not keep silent,
And for Jerusalem's sake I will not keep quiet,
Until her righteousness goes forth like brightness,
And her salvation like a torch that is burning.
2 The nations will see your righteousness,
And all kings your glory;
And you will be called by a new name
Which the mouth of the LORD will designate.
3 You will also be a crown of beauty in the hand of the LORD,
And a royal diadem in the hand of your God.
4 It will no longer be said to you, "Forsaken,"
Nor to your land will it any longer be said, "Desolate";
But you will be called, "My delight is in her,"
And your land, "Married";
For the LORD delights in you,
And *to Him* your land will be married.
5 For *as* a young man marries a virgin,
So your sons will marry you;
And *as* the bridegroom rejoices over the bride,
So your God will rejoice over you.

6 On your walls, O Jerusalem, I have appointed watchmen;
All day and all night they will never keep silent.
You who remind the LORD, take no rest for yourselves;
7 And give Him no rest until He establishes
And makes Jerusalem a praise in the earth.
8 The LORD has sworn by His right hand and by His strong arm,
"I will never again give your grain *as* food for your enemies;
Nor will foreigners drink your new wine for which you have labored."

62:1 Is 1:26; 58:8; 61:11; Is 46:13; 52:10

62:2 Is 60:3; Is 56:5; 62:4, 12; 65:15

62:3 Is 28:5; Zech 9:16; 1 Thess 2:19

62:4 Is 54:6, 7; 60:15, 18; Hos 2:19, 20; Jer 32:41; Zeph 3:17

62:5 Is 65:19

62:6 Is 52:8; Jer 6:17; Ezek 3:17; 33:7; Ps 74:2; Jer 14:21; Lam 5:1, 20

62:7 Luke 18:1-8; Is 60:18; Jer 33:9; Zeph 3:19, 20

62:8 Is 45:23; 54:9; Lev 26:16; Deut 28:31, 33; Judg 6:3-6; Is 1:7; Jer 5:17

61:8 We suffer for many reasons—our own mistakes, someone else's mistakes, injustice. When we suffer for our own mistakes, we get what we deserve. When we suffer because of others or because of injustice, God is angry. God in his mercy says that his people have suffered enough. God will reward those who suffer because of injustice. He will settle all accounts.

61:10 "Me" could refer to the Messiah, the person anointed with the Spirit of the Lord (61:1), or to Zion (62:1), which symbolizes God's people. The imagery of the bridegroom is often used in Scripture to depict the Messiah (see Matthew 9:15), while the imagery of the bride is used to depict God's people (see Revelation 19:6–8). We too can be clothed with the righteousness of Christ when we believe in him (2 Corinthians 5:21).

62:1–7 Many commentators believe Isaiah is speaking in verse 1. If so, Isaiah's zeal for his people and his desire to see the work of salvation completed caused him to pray without resting, hoping that Israel would be saved. We should have Isaiah's zeal to see God's will done. This is what we mean when we pray, "Your kingdom come. Your will be done, on earth as it is in heaven." It is good to keep praying persistently for others.

62:9
Is 65:13, 21-23

9 But those who garner it will eat it and praise the LORD;
And those who gather it will drink it in the courts of My sanctuary.

62:10
Is 26:1; 60:11, 18; Is 57:14; Is 11:16; 19:23; 35:8; 49:11; Is 11:10, 12; 49:22

62:11
Is 42:10; 49:6; Matt 21:5; Zech 9:9; Is 51:5; Is 40:10; Rev 22:12

62:12
Deut 7:6; Is 4:3; 1 Pet 2:9; Is 35:9; 51:10; Is 41:17; 42:16; 62:4

10 Go through, go through the gates,
Clear the way for the people;
Build up, build up the highway,
Remove the stones, lift up a standard over the peoples.
11 Behold, the LORD has proclaimed to the end of the earth,
Say to the daughter of Zion, "Lo, your salvation comes;
Behold His reward is with Him, and His recompense before Him."
12 And they will call them, "The holy people,
The redeemed of the LORD";
And you will be called, "Sought out, a city not forsaken."

God's Vengeance on the Nations

63:1
Ps 137:7; Is 34:5, 6; Ezek 25:12-14; 35:1-15; Obad 1-14; Mal 1:2-5; Is 63:2; Is 34:6; Jer 49:13; Amos 1:12; Zeph 3:17

63:2
Rev 19:13, 15

63:3
Rev 14:20; 19:15; Is 22:5; 28:3; Mic 7:10; Rev 19:13

63:4
Is 34:8; 35:4; 61:2; Jer 51:6

63:5
Is 59:16; Ps 44:3; Is 40:10; 52:10

63:6
Is 22:5; 34:2; 65:12; Is 29:9; 51:17, 21

63 Who is this who comes from Edom,
With garments of glowing colors from Bozrah,
This One who is majestic in His apparel,
Marching in the greatness of His strength?
"It is I who speak in righteousness, mighty to save."
2 Why is Your apparel red,
And Your garments like the one who treads in the wine press?
3 "I have trodden the wine trough alone,
And from the peoples there was no man with Me.
I also trod them in My anger
And trampled them in My wrath;
And their lifeblood is sprinkled on My garments,
And I stained all My raiment.
4 "For the day of vengeance was in My heart,
And My year of redemption has come.
5 "I looked, and there was no one to help,
And I was astonished and there was no one to uphold;
So My own arm brought salvation to Me,
And My wrath upheld Me.
6 "I trod down the peoples in My anger

THE SPIRIT IN ISAIAH

Reference	*Main Teaching*
11:2	The Spirit of the Lord brings wisdom, understanding, knowledge, and the fear of the Lord.
32:15	The Spirit of the Lord brings abundance.
34:16	The Spirit of the Lord carries out God's word.
40:13	The Spirit of the Lord is the Master Counselor.
42:1	The Messiah, God's Servant, will be given the Spirit.
44:3–5	Through the Spirit, God's true children will thrive.
48:16	The Spirit of the Lord sent Isaiah to prophesy.
61:1	God's servants (Isaiah and then Jesus) were anointed by the Spirit to proclaim the Good News.
63:10–11	The Spirit of the Lord was grieved because of God's people.
63:14	The Spirit of the Lord gives rest.

62:12 The people of Jerusalem (Zion) will have new names—"the holy people" and "the redeemed of the LORD." Believers today also have new names—Christians. In 1 Peter 2:5, we are called "a holy priesthood."

63:1–4 Edom was a constant enemy of Israel despite its common ancestry in Isaac (Genesis 25:23). Edom rejoiced at any trouble Israel faced. The imagery in this passage is of a watchman on the wall of Jerusalem, seeing Edom approaching and fearing that the Edomite king in his red garment is leading an attack. But it turns out to be the Lord, in bloodstained clothes, who has trampled and destroyed Edom. Bozrah is a city in Edom. (For other prophecies against Edom, see Amos 1:11–12; Obadiah 10–11; Malachi 1:2–4.)

And made them drunk in My wrath,
And I poured out their lifeblood on the earth."

God's Ancient Mercies Recalled

7 I shall make mention of the lovingkindnesses of the LORD, the praises of the LORD,
According to all that the LORD has granted us,
And the great goodness toward the house of Israel,
Which He has granted them according to His compassion
And according to the abundance of His lovingkindnesses.
8 For He said, "Surely, they are My people,
Sons who will not deal falsely."
So He became their Savior.
9 In all their affliction He was afflicted,
And the angel of His presence saved them;
In His love and in His mercy He redeemed them,
And He lifted them and carried them all the days of old.
10 But they rebelled
And grieved His Holy Spirit;
Therefore He turned Himself to become their enemy,
He fought against them.
11 Then His people remembered the days of old, of Moses.
Where is He who brought them up out of the sea with the shepherds of His flock?
Where is He who put His Holy Spirit in the midst of them,
12 Who caused His glorious arm to go at the right hand of Moses,
Who divided the waters before them to make for Himself an everlasting name,
13 Who led them through the depths?
Like the horse in the wilderness, they did not stumble;
14 As the cattle which go down into the valley,
The Spirit of the LORD gave them rest.
So You led Your people,
To make for Yourself a glorious name.

63:7 Ps 25:6; 92:2; Is 54:8, 10; 1 Kin 8:66; Neh 9:25, 35; Ps 51:1; 86:5, 15; Is 54:7, 8; Eph 2:4

63:8 Ex 6:7; Is 3:15; 51:4; Is 60:16

63:9 Judg 10:16; Ex 23:20-23; 33:14, 15; Deut 7:7, 8; Is 43:1; 52:9; Deut 1:31; 32:10-12; Is 46:3

63:10 Ps 78:40; 106:33; Acts 7:51; Eph 4:30; Ps 51:11; Is 63:11

63:11 Ps 106:44, 45; Is 51:10; Num 11:17, 25, 29; Hag 2:5

63:12 Ex 6:6; 15:16; Ex 14:21, 22; Is 11:15; 51:10

63:13 Jer 31:9

63:14 Josh 21:44; 23:1; Deut 32:12

"You Are Our Father"

15 Look down from heaven and see from Your holy and glorious habitation;
Where are Your zeal and Your mighty deeds?
The stirrings of Your heart and Your compassion are restrained toward me.
16 For You are our Father, though Abraham does not know us
And Israel does not recognize us.
You, O LORD, are our Father,
Our Redeemer from of old is Your name.
17 Why, O LORD, do You cause us to stray from Your ways
And harden our heart from fearing You?
Return for the sake of Your servants, the tribes of Your heritage.
18 Your holy people possessed Your sanctuary for a little while,
Our adversaries have trodden *it* down.
19 We have become *like* those over whom You have never ruled,
Like those who were not called by Your name.

63:15 Deut 26:15; Ps 80:14; Ps 68:5; 123:1; Is 9:7; 26:11; 37:32; 42:13; 59:17; Jer 31:20; Hos 11:8

63:16 Is 1:2; 64:8; Is 29:22; 41:8; 51:2; Is 41:14; 44:6; 60:16

63:17 Is 30:28; Ezek 14:7-9; Is 29:13, 14; Num 10:36

63:18 Ps 74:3-7; Is 64:11

Prayer for Mercy and Help

64 Oh, that You would rend the heavens *and* come down,
That the mountains might quake at Your presence—

64:1 Ex 19:18; Ps 18:9; 144:5; Mic 1:3, 4; Hab 3:13; Judg 5:5; Ps 68:8; Nah 1:5

63:10 Grieving the Holy Spirit is willfully thwarting his leading by disobedience or rebellion. Isaiah mentions the work of the Holy Spirit more than any other Old Testament writer. See the note on Ephesians 4:28–32 for more on grieving the Holy Spirit.

63:15—64:7 On behalf of the faithful remnant, Isaiah asks God for two favors: to show tenderness and compassion to them and to punish their enemies. Before making these requests, Isaiah recited the Lord's past favors, reminding him of his compassion in former days (63:7–14).

64:1–6 God's appearance is so intense that it is like a consuming fire that burns everything in its path. If we are so impure, how can we be saved? Only by God's mercy. The Israelites had experienced God's appearance at Mount Sinai (Exodus 19:16–19). When God met with Moses there was a thunderstorm, smoke, and an earthquake. If God were to meet us today, his glory would overwhelm us, especially when we look at our "filthy" garments (64:6).

64:2 Ps 99:1; Jer 5:22; 33:9
64:3 Ps 65:5; 66:3, 5; 106:22
64:4 1 Cor 2:9; Is 25:9; 30:18; 40:31
64:5 Ex 20:24; Is 56:1; Is 26:13; 63:7; Is 12:1
64:6 Is 6:5; Is 46:12; 48:1; Ps 90:5, 6; Is 1:30; Is 50:1
64:7 Is 59:4; Ezek 22:30; Deut 31:18; Is 1:15; 54:8

2 As fire kindles the brushwood, *as* fire causes water to boil—
To make Your name known to Your adversaries,
That the nations may tremble at Your presence!
3 When You did awesome things which we did not expect,
You came down, the mountains quaked at Your presence.
4 For from days of old they have not heard or perceived by ear,
Nor has the eye seen a God besides You,
Who acts in behalf of the one who waits for Him.
5 You meet him who rejoices in doing righteousness,
Who remembers You in Your ways.
Behold, You were angry, for we sinned,
We continued in them a long time;
And shall we be saved?
6 For all of us have become like one who is unclean,
And all our righteous deeds are like a filthy garment;
And all of us wither like a leaf,
And our iniquities, like the wind, take us away.
7 There is no one who calls on Your name,
Who arouses himself to take hold of You;
For You have hidden Your face from us
And have delivered us into the power of our iniquities.

64:8 Is 63:16; Is 29:16; 45:9; Ps 100:3; Is 60:21
64:9 Is 57:17; 60:10; Is 43:25; Mic 7:18; Ps 79:13; Is 63:8
64:10 Is 48:2; 52:1; Is 1:7; 6:11
64:11 2 Kin 25:9; Ps 74:5-7; Is 63:18; Lam 1:7, 10, 11
64:12 Ps 74:10, 11, 18, 19; Is 42:14; 63:15

8 But now, O LORD, You are our Father,
We are the clay, and You our potter;
And all of us are the work of Your hand.
9 Do not be angry beyond measure, O LORD,
Nor remember iniquity forever;
Behold, look now, all of us are Your people.
10 Your holy cities have become a wilderness,
Zion has become a wilderness,
Jerusalem a desolation.
11 Our holy and beautiful house,
Where our fathers praised You,
Has been burned *by* fire;
And all our precious things have become a ruin.
12 Will You restrain Yourself at these things, O LORD?
Will You keep silent and afflict us beyond measure?

65:1 Rom 9:24-26; 10:20; Is 63:19; Hos 1:10
65:2 Rom 10:21; Is 1:2, 23; 30:1, 9; Ps 81:11, 12; Is 59:7; 66:18
65:3 Job 1:11; 2:5; Is 3:8; Is 1:29; 66:17; Is 66:3

A Rebellious People

65 "I permitted Myself to be sought by those who did not ask *for Me;*
I permitted Myself to be found by those who did not seek Me.
I said, 'Here am I, here am I,'
To a nation which did not call on My name.
2 "I have spread out My hands all day long to a rebellious people,
Who walk *in* the way which is not good, following their own thoughts,
3 A people who continually provoke Me to My face,
Offering sacrifices in gardens and burning incense on bricks;

64:6 Sin makes us unclean so that we cannot approach God (6:5; Romans 3:23) any more than a beggar in rotten rags could dine at a king's table. Our best efforts are still infected with sin. Our only hope, therefore, is faith in Jesus Christ, who can cleanse us and bring us into God's presence (read Romans 3).

This passage can easily be misunderstood. It doesn't mean that God will reject us if we come to him in faith, nor that he despises our efforts to please him. It means that if we come to him demanding acceptance on the basis of our "good" conduct, God will point out that our righteousness is nothing compared to his infinite righteousness. This message is primarily for the unrepentant person, not the true follower of God.

65:1 Israel considered itself to be the only people of God, but the time would come when other nations would seek him. Paul mentions Isaiah's statement in Romans 10:20 and points out that these other nations were the Gentiles. God's people today are those who accept Jesus as Savior and Lord, whether they are Jews or Gentiles. The gospel is for every person. Do not ignore or reject anyone when you share the gospel. You may be surprised at how many are sincerely searching for God.

65:3–5 God said these people directly disobeyed his laws when they worshiped and sacrificed to idols (Exodus 20:1–6), consulted mediums and spiritists (Leviticus 19:31), and ate forbidden foods (Leviticus 11). But they were so perverse that they still thought they were more sacred than others. Jesus called such people hypocrites (Matthew 23:13–36).

4 Who sit among graves and spend the night in secret places;
Who eat swine's flesh,
And the broth of unclean meat is *in* their pots.
5 "Who say, 'Keep to yourself, do not come near me,
For I am holier than you!'
These are smoke in My nostrils,
A fire that burns all the day.
6 "Behold, it is written before Me,
I will not keep silent, but I will repay;
I will even repay into their bosom,
7 Both their own iniquities and the iniquities of their fathers together," says the LORD.
"Because they have burned incense on the mountains
And scorned Me on the hills,
Therefore I will measure their former work into their bosom."

8 Thus says the LORD,
"As the new wine is found in the cluster,
And one says, 'Do not destroy it, for there is benefit in it,'
So I will act on behalf of My servants
In order not to destroy all of them.
9 "I will bring forth offspring from Jacob,
And an heir of My mountains from Judah;
Even My chosen ones shall inherit it,
And My servants will dwell there.
10 "Sharon will be a pasture land for flocks,
And the valley of Achor a resting place for herds,
For My people who seek Me.
11 "But you who forsake the LORD,
Who forget My holy mountain,
Who set a table for Fortune,
And who fill *cups* with mixed wine for Destiny,
12 I will destine you for the sword,
And all of you will bow down to the slaughter.
Because I called, but you did not answer;
I spoke, but you did not hear.
And you did evil in My sight
And chose that in which I did not delight."

13 Therefore, thus says the Lord GOD,
"Behold, My servants will eat, but you will be hungry.
Behold, My servants will drink, but you will be thirsty.
Behold, My servants will rejoice, but you will be put to shame.
14 "Behold, My servants will shout joyfully with a glad heart,
But you will cry out with a heavy heart,
And you will wail with a broken spirit.
15 "You will leave your name for a curse to My chosen ones,
And the Lord GOD will slay you.
But My servants will be called by another name.
16 "Because he who is blessed in the earth
Will be blessed by the God of truth;
And he who swears in the earth
Will swear by the God of truth;
Because the former troubles are forgotten,
And because they are hidden from My sight!

65:4 Lev 11:7; Is 66:3, 17

65:5 Matt 9:11; Luke 7:39; 18:9-12

65:6 Ps 50:3, 21; Is 42:14; 64:12; Jer 16:18

65:7 Is 13:11; 22:14; 26:21; 30:13, 14; Is 57:7; Hos 2:13; Ezek 20:27, 28; Jer 5:29; 13:25

65:8 Is 1:9; 10:21, 22; 48:9

65:9 Is 45:19, 25; Jer 31:36, 37; Is 49:8; 60:21; Amos 9:11-15; Is 57:13; Is 32:18

65:10 Is 33:9; 35:2; Josh 7:24, 26; Hos 2:15; Is 51:1; 55:6

65:11 Deut 29:24, 25; Is 1:4, 28; Is 2:2, 3; 66:20

65:12 Is 27:1; 34:5, 6; 66:16; Is 63:6; 2 Chr 36:15, 16; Prov 1:24; Is 41:28; 50:2; 66:4; Jer 7:13

65:13 Is 1:19; Is 8:21; Is 41:17, 18; 49:10; Is 5:13; Is 61:7; 66:14; Is 42:17; 44:9, 11; 66:5

65:14 Ps 66:4; Is 51:11; James 5:13; Is 13:6; Matt 8:12

65:15 Jer 24:9; 25:18; Zech 8:13; Is 62:2

65:16 Ex 34:6; Ps 31:5; Is 19:18; 45:23

65:6 God said he would pay back the people for their sins. Judgment is not our job but his because he alone is just. Who else knows our hearts and minds? Who else knows what is a completely fair reward or punishment?

65:8–9 God will always preserve a faithful remnant of his people. No matter how bad the world is, there are always a few who remain loyal to him. Jesus made this point in Matthew 13:36–43.

65:10 Sharon is a plain in the western part of Israel. The valley of Achor is in the east, near Jericho. Achan was executed there for hiding the devoted goods of battle (Joshua 7:10–26). Even in this valley there will be peace: The coming restoration will be complete.

New Heavens and a New Earth

17 "For behold, I create new heavens and a new earth;
And the former things will not be remembered or come to mind.
18 "But be glad and rejoice forever in what I create;
For behold, I create Jerusalem *for* rejoicing
And her people *for* gladness.
19 "I will also rejoice in Jerusalem and be glad in My people;
And there will no longer be heard in her
The voice of weeping and the sound of crying.
20 "No longer will there be in it an infant *who lives but a few* days,
Or an old man who does not live out his days;
For the youth will die at the age of one hundred
And the one who does not reach the age of one hundred
Will be *thought* accursed.
21 "They will build houses and inhabit *them;*
They will also plant vineyards and eat their fruit.
22 "They will not build and another inhabit,
They will not plant and another eat;
For as the lifetime of a tree, *so will be* the days of My people,
And My chosen ones will wear out the work of their hands.
23 "They will not labor in vain,
Or bear *children* for calamity;
For they are the offspring of those blessed by the LORD,
And their descendants with them.
24 "It will also come to pass that before they call, I will answer; and while they are still
speaking, I will hear.
25 "The wolf and the lamb will graze together, and the lion will eat straw like the ox;
and dust will be the serpent's food. They will do no evil or harm in all My holy mountain," says the LORD.

Heaven Is God's Throne

66 Thus says the LORD,
"Heaven is My throne and the earth is My footstool.
Where then is a house you could build for Me?
And where is a place that I may rest?
2 "For My hand made all these things,
Thus all these things came into being," declares the LORD.
"But to this one I will look,
To him who is humble and contrite of spirit, and who trembles at My word.

Hypocrisy Rebuked

3 "*But* he who kills an ox is *like* one who slays a man;
He who sacrifices a lamb is *like* the one who breaks a dog's neck;
He who offers a grain offering *is like one who offers* swine's blood;
He who burns incense is *like* the one who blesses an idol.
As they have chosen their *own* ways,
And their soul delights in their abominations,
4 So I will choose their punishments

65:17 Is 66:22; 2 Pet 3:13; Rev 21:1; Is 43:18; Jer 3:16

65:18 Ps 98; Is 12:1, 2; 25:9; 35:10; 41:16; 51:3; 61:10

65:19 Is 62:4, 5; Jer 32:41; Is 25:8; 30:19; 35:10; 51:11; Rev 7:17; 21:4

65:20 Deut 4:40; Job 5:26; Ps 34:12; Eccl 8:12, 13; Is 3:11; 22:14

65:21 Is 32:18; Amos 9:14; Is 30:23; 37:30; Jer 31:5

65:22 Is 62:8, 9; Ps 92:12-14; Ps 21:4; 91:16

65:23 Deut 28:3-12; Is 55:2; Is 61:9; Jer 32:38, 39; Acts 2:39

65:24 Ps 91:15; Is 55:6; 58:9; Dan 9:20-23; 10:12

65:25 Is 11:6; Is 11:7; Gen 3:14; Mic 7:17; Is 11:9; Mic 4:3; Is 65:11

66:1 1 Kin 8:27; Ps 11:4; Matt 5:34, 35; 23:22; 2 Sam 7:5-7; Jer 7:4; John 4:20, 21; Acts 7:48-50

66:2 Is 40:26; Ps 34:18; Is 57:15; Matt 5:3, 4; Luke 18:13, 14; Ps 119:120; Is 66:5

66:3 Is 65:4; Lev 2:2; Is 1:13; Is 57:17; 65:2; Is 44:19

66:4 Prov 1:31, 32; Is 65:7; Prov 10:24; Prov 1:24; Is 65:12; Jer 7:13; 2 Kin 21:2, 6; Is 59:7; 65:12; Jer 7:30

65:17–25 In 65:17–19 we have a pictorial description of the new heavens and the new earth. They are eternal, and in them safety, peace, and plenty will be available to all (see also 66:22–23; 2 Peter 3:13; Revelation 21:1). Verses 20–25 may refer to the reign of Christ on earth because sin and death have not yet been finally destroyed.

66:1 Even the beautiful temple in Jerusalem was woefully inadequate for a God who is present everywhere. God cannot be confined to any human structure (see 2 Chronicles 6:18; Acts 7:49, 50). This chapter is a fitting climax to the book. God will lift up the humble, judge all people, destroy the wicked, bring all believers together, and establish the new heavens and the new earth. Let this hope encourage you each day.

66:2–3 These key verses summarize Isaiah's message. He contrasted two ways of living: that of humble persons who have a profound reverence for God's messages and their application to life, and that of those who choose their own way. The sacrifices of the arrogant were only external compliance. In their hearts they were murderers, perverts, and idolaters. God shows mercy to the humble, but he curses the proud and self-sufficient (see Luke 1:51–53). Our society urges us to be assertive and to affirm ourselves. Don't let your freedom and right to choose lead you away from God's pathway to eternal life.

And will bring on them what they dread.
Because I called, but no one answered;
I spoke, but they did not listen.
And they did evil in My sight
And chose that in which I did not delight."
5 Hear the word of the LORD, you who tremble at His word:
"Your brothers who hate you, who exclude you for My name's sake,
Have said, 'Let the LORD be glorified, that we may see your joy.'
But they will be put to shame.
6 "A voice of uproar from the city, a voice from the temple,
The voice of the LORD who is rendering recompense to His enemies.

7 "Before she travailed, she brought forth;
Before her pain came, she gave birth to a boy.
8 "Who has heard such a thing? Who has seen such things?
Can a land be born in one day?
Can a nation be brought forth all at once?
As soon as Zion travailed, she also brought forth her sons.
9 "Shall I bring to the point of birth and not give delivery?" says the LORD.
"Or shall I who gives delivery shut *the womb?*" says your God.

Joy in Jerusalem's Future

10 "Be joyful with Jerusalem and rejoice for her, all you who love her;
Be exceedingly glad with her, all you who mourn over her,
11 That you may nurse and be satisfied with her comforting breasts,
That you may suck and be delighted with her bountiful bosom."
12 For thus says the LORD, "Behold, I extend peace to her like a river,
And the glory of the nations like an overflowing stream;
And you will be nursed, you will be carried on the hip and fondled on the knees.
13 "As one whom his mother comforts, so I will comfort you;
And you will be comforted in Jerusalem."
14 Then you will see *this,* and your heart will be glad,
And your bones will flourish like the new grass;
And the hand of the LORD will be made known to His servants,
But He will be indignant toward His enemies.
15 For behold, the LORD will come in fire
And His chariots like the whirlwind,
To render His anger with fury,
And His rebuke with flames of fire.
16 For the LORD will execute judgment by fire
And by His sword on all flesh,
And those slain by the LORD will be many.
17 "Those who sanctify and purify themselves *to go* to the gardens,
Following one in the center,
Who eat swine's flesh, detestable things and mice,
Will come to an end altogether," declares the LORD.
18 "For I know their works and their thoughts; the time is coming to gather all nations
and tongues. And they shall come and see My glory.
19 "I will set a sign among them and will send survivors from them to the nations: Tarshish, Put, Lud, Meshech, Rosh, Tubal and Javan, to the distant coastlands that have
neither heard My fame nor seen My glory. And they will declare My glory among the
nations.
20 "Then they shall bring all your brethren from all the nations as a grain offering to the
LORD, on horses, in chariots, in litters, on mules and on camels, to My holy mountain

66:5 Is 66:2; Ps 38:20; Is 60:15; Matt 5:10-12; 10:22; John 9:34; 15:18-20; Luke 13:17

66:6 Is 59:18; 65:6; Joel 3:7

66:7 Is 37:3; 54:1; Rev 12:5

66:8 Is 64:4

66:9 Is 37:3

66:10 Deut 32:43; Is 65:18; Rom 15:10; Ps 26:8; 122:6; Ps 137:6

66:11 Is 49:23; 60:16; Joel 3:18; Is 60:1, 2; 62:2

66:12 Ps 72:3, 7; Is 48:18; Is 60:5; 61:6; Is 60:4

66:13 Is 12:1; 40:1, 2; 49:13; 51:3; 2 Cor 1:3, 4

66:14 Is 33:20; Zech 10:7; Prov 3:8; Is 58:11; Ezra 7:9; 8:31; Is 10:5; 13:5; 34:2

66:15 Is 10:17; 30:27, 33; 31:9; Ps 68:17; Is 5:28; Hab 3:8

66:16 Is 30:30; Ezek 38:22; Is 65:12; Ezek 38:21

66:17 Is 1:29; 65:3; Lev 11:7; Is 65:4; Is 1:28, 31

66:18 Is 59:7; 65:2; Is 45:22-25; Jer 3:17

66:19 Is 11:10, 12; 49:22; 62:10; Is 2:16; 60:9; Ezek 27:10; Gen 10:2; Is 11:11; 24:15; 60:9; 1 Chr 16:24; Is 42:12

66:20 Is 43:6; 49:22; 60:4; Is 2:2, 3; 11:9; 56:7; 65:11, 25; Is 52:11

66:7–9 God will not leave his work of national restoration unfinished. In this image of birth, God shows that he will accomplish what he has promised. It is as unstoppable as the birth of a baby. When all the pain is over, the joy begins.

66:15–17 This is a vivid picture of the great judgment that will occur at Christ's second coming (2 Thessalonians 1:7–9).

66:19 God's people will go out as missionaries to all parts of the earth—to Tarshish (Spain), to the Libyans in northern Africa, to the Lydians in western Asia Minor, to northeastern Asia Minor (Tubal), and to Greece.

66:21 Ex 19:6; Is 61:6; 1 Pet 2:5, 9

66:22 Is 65:17; Heb 12:26, 27; 2 Pet 3:13; Rev 21:1; Is 61:8, 9; 65:22, 23; John 10:27-29; 1 Pet 1:4, 5; Is 56:5

66:23 Is 1:13, 14; Ezek 46:1, 6; Is 19:21, 23; 27:13; 49:7

66:24 Is 5:25; 34:3; Is 1:28; 24:20; Is 14:11; Mark 9:48; Is 1:31; Matt 3:12; Dan 12:2

Jerusalem," says the LORD, "just as the sons of Israel bring their grain offering in a clean vessel to the house of the LORD.
21 "I will also take some of them for priests *and* for Levites," says the LORD.
22 "For just as the new heavens and the new earth
Which I make will endure before Me," declares the LORD,
"So your offspring and your name will endure.
23 "And it shall be from new moon to new moon
And from sabbath to sabbath,
All mankind will come to bow down before Me," says the LORD.
24 "Then they will go forth and look
On the corpses of the men
Who have transgressed against Me.
For their worm will not die
And their fire will not be quenched;
And they will be an abhorrence to all mankind."

66:22–24 Isaiah brings his book to a close with great drama. For the faithless there is a sobering portrayal of judgment. For the faithful, there is a glorious picture of rich reward—"so your offspring and your name will endure." The contrast is so striking that it would seem that everyone would want to be God's follower. But we are often just as rebellious, foolish, and reluctant to change as the Israelites. We are just as negligent in feeding the hungry, working for justice, and obeying God's Word. Make sure you are among those who will be richly blessed.

JEREMIAH

Zephaniah becomes a prophet 640 B.C.

Jeremiah becomes a prophet 627

King Josiah killed in battle 609

VITAL STATISTICS

PURPOSE:
To urge God's people to turn from their sins and back to God

AUTHOR:
Jeremiah

TO WHOM WRITTEN:
Judah (the southern kingdom) and its capital city, Jerusalem

DATE WRITTEN:
During Jeremiah's ministry, approximately 627–586 B.C.

SETTING:
Jeremiah ministered under Judah's last five kings—Josiah, Jehoahaz, Jehoiakim, Jehoiachin, and Zedekiah. The nation was sliding quickly toward destruction and was eventually conquered by Babylon in 586 B.C. (see 2 Kings 21—25). The prophet Zephaniah preceded Jeremiah, and Habakkuk was Jeremiah's contemporary.

KEY VERSE:
" 'Your own wickedness will correct you, and your apostasies will reprove you; know therefore and see that it is evil and bitter for you to forsake the LORD your God, and the dread of Me is not in you' " (2:19).

KEY PEOPLE:
Judah's kings (listed above), Baruch, Ebed-melech, King Nebuchadnezzar, the Rechabites

KEY PLACES:
Anathoth, Jerusalem, Ramah, Egypt

SPECIAL FEATURES:
This book is a combination of history, poetry, and biography. Jeremiah often used symbolism to communicate his message.

WHAT is success? Most definitions include references to achieving goals and acquiring wealth, prestige, favor, and power. "Successful" people enjoy the good life—being financially and emotionally secure, being surrounded by admirers, and enjoying the fruits of their labors. They are leaders, opinion makers, and trendsetters. Their example is emulated; their accomplishments are noticed. They know who they are and where they are going, and they stride confidently to meet their goals.

By these standards, Jeremiah was a miserable failure. For 40 years he served as God's spokesman to Judah; but when Jeremiah spoke, nobody listened. Consistently and passionately he urged them to act, but nobody moved. And he certainly did not attain material success. He was poor and underwent severe deprivation to deliver his prophecies. He was thrown into prison (chapter 37) and into a cistern (chapter 38), and he was taken to Egypt against his will (chapter 43). He was rejected by his neighbors (11:19–21), his family (12:6), the false priests and prophets (20:1–2; 28:1–17), friends (20:10), his audience (26:8), and the kings (36:23). Throughout his life, Jeremiah stood alone, declaring God's messages of doom, announcing the new covenant, and weeping over the fate of his beloved country. In the eyes of the world, Jeremiah was not a success.

But in God's eyes, Jeremiah was one of the most successful people in all of history. Success, as measured by God, involves obedience and faithfulness. Regardless of opposition and personal cost, Jeremiah courageously and faithfully proclaimed the word of God. He was obedient to his calling. Jeremiah's book begins with his call to be a prophet. The next 38 chapters are prophecies about Israel (the nation united) and Judah (the southern kingdom). Chapters 2—20 are general and undated, and chapters 21—39 are particular and dated. The basic theme of Jeremiah's message is simple: "Repent and turn to God, or he will punish." Because the people rejected this warning, Jeremiah then began predicting the destruction of Jerusalem. This terrible event is described in chapter 39. Chapters 40—45 describe events following Jerusalem's fall. The book concludes with prophecies concerning a variety of nations (chapters 46—52).

As you read Jeremiah, feel with him as he agonizes over the message he must deliver, pray with him for those who refuse to respond to the truth, and watch his example of faith and courage. Then commit yourself to being successful in God's eyes.

Daniel taken captive 605	*Ezekiel begins to prophesy in Babylonia 593*	*Judah falls: Jerusalem destroyed; Jeremiah's ministry ends 586*	*First exiles return to Judah 538*

THE BLUEPRINT

A. GOD'S JUDGMENT ON JUDAH (1:1—45:5)
1. The call of Jeremiah
2. Jeremiah condemns Judah for its sins
3. Jeremiah prophesies destruction
4. Jeremiah accuses Judah's leaders
5. Restoration is promised
6. God's promised judgment arrives

Jeremiah confronts many people with their sins: kings, false prophets, those at the temples, and those at the gates. A lack of response made Jeremiah wonder if he was doing any good at all. He often felt discouraged and sometimes bitter. To bring such gloomy messages to these people was a hard task. We, too, have a responsibility to bring this news to a fallen world: Those who continue in their sinful ways are eternally doomed. Although we may feel discouraged at the lack of response, we must press on to tell others about the consequences of sin and the hope that God offers. Those who tell people only what they want to hear are being unfaithful to God's message.

B. GOD'S JUDGMENT ON THE NATIONS (46:1—52:34)
1. Prophecies about foreign nations
2. The fall of Jerusalem

Jeremiah lived to see many of his prophecies come true—most notably the fall of Jerusalem. The fulfillment of this and other prophecies against the foreign nations came as a result of sin. Those who refuse to confess their sin bring judgment upon themselves.

MEGATHEMES

THEME	EXPLANATION	IMPORTANCE
Sin	King Josiah's reformation failed because the people's repentance was shallow. They continued in their selfishness and worship of idols. All the leaders rejected God's law and will for the people. Jeremiah lists all their sins, predicts God's judgment, and begs for repentance.	Judah's deterioration and disaster came from a callous disregard and disobedience of God. When we ignore sin and refuse to listen to God's warning, we invite disaster. Don't settle for half measures in removing sin.
Punishment	Because of sin, Jerusalem was destroyed, the temple was ruined, and the people were captured and carried off to Babylon. The people were responsible for their destruction and captivity because they refused to listen to God's message.	Unconfessed sin brings God's full punishment. It is useless to blame anyone else for our sin; we are accountable to God before anyone else. We must answer to him for how we live.
God Is Lord of All	God is the righteous Creator. He is accountable to no one but himself. He wisely and lovingly directs all creation to fulfill his plans, and he brings events to pass according to his timetable. He is Lord over all the world.	Because of God's majestic power and love, our only duty is to submit to his authority. By following his plans, not our own, we can have a loving relationship with him and serve him with our whole heart.
New Hearts	Jeremiah predicted that after the destruction of the nation, God would send a new shepherd, the Messiah. He would lead them into a new future, a new covenant, and a new day of hope. He would accomplish this by changing their sinful hearts into hearts of love for God.	God still transforms people by changing their hearts. His love can eliminate the problems created by sin. We can have assurance of a new heart by loving God, trusting Christ to save us, and repenting of our sin.
Faithful Service	Jeremiah served God faithfully for 40 years. During that time the people ignored, rejected, and persecuted him. Jeremiah's preaching was unsuccessful by human standards, yet he did not fail in his task. He remained faithful to God.	People's acceptance or rejection of us is not the measure of our success. God's approval alone should be our standard for service. We must bring God's message to others even when we are rejected. We must do God's work even if it means suffering for it.

A. GOD'S JUDGMENT ON JUDAH (1:1—45:5)

Jeremiah was called by God to be a prophet to Judah (the southern kingdom). He faithfully confronted the leaders and the people with their sin, prophesying both their 70-year captivity in Babylon and their eventual return from exile. After surviving the fall of Jerusalem, Jeremiah was forcefully taken to Egypt. Yet Jeremiah remained faithful in spite of Jerusalem's destruction. Years of obedience had made him strong and courageous. May we be able to stand through difficult times as did Jeremiah.

1. The call of Jeremiah

Jeremiah's Call and Commission

1 The words of Jeremiah the son of Hilkiah, of the priests who were in Anathoth in
the land of Benjamin,
2 to whom the word of the LORD came in the days of Josiah the son of Amon, king of
Judah, in the thirteenth year of his reign.
3 It came also in the days of Jehoiakim the son of Josiah, king of Judah, until the end
of the eleventh year of Zedekiah the son of Josiah, king of Judah, until the exile of Jerusalem in the fifth month.
4 Now the word of the LORD came to me saying,
5 "Before I formed you in the womb I knew you,
And before you were born I consecrated you;
I have appointed you a prophet to the nations."
6 Then I said, "Alas, Lord GOD!
Behold, I do not know how to speak,
Because I am a youth."
7 But the LORD said to me,
"Do not say, 'I am a youth,'
Because everywhere I send you, you shall go,
And all that I command you, you shall speak.
8 "Do not be afraid of them,
For I am with you to deliver you," declares the LORD.
9 Then the LORD stretched out His hand and touched my mouth, and the LORD said
to me,
"Behold, I have put My words in your mouth.
10 "See, I have appointed you this day over the nations and over the kingdoms,
To pluck up and to break down,
To destroy and to overthrow,
To build and to plant."

1:1 2 Chr 35:25; 36:12, 21, 22; Ezra 1:1; Dan 9:2; Matt 2:17; 16:14; 27:9; Josh 21:18; 1 Kin 2:26; 1 Chr 6:60; Is 10:30; Jer 11:21; 32:7

1:2 1 Kin 13:2; 2 Kin 21:24; 22:3; 2 Chr 34:1; Jer 3:6; 36:2; 2 Kin 21:18, 24; Jer 25:3

1:3 2 Kin 23:34; 1 Chr 3:15; 2 Chr 36:5-8; Jer 25:1; 2 Kin 24:17; 1 Chr 3:15; 2 Chr 36:11-13; Jer 39:2

1:5 Ps 139:15, 16; Is 49:1, 5; Luke 1:15; Jer 1:10; 25:15-26

1:6 Ex 4:10; 1 Kin 3:7

1:7 Ezek 2:3, 4; Num 22:20; Jer 1:17

1:8 Ex 3:12; Deut 31:6; Josh 1:5; Jer 15:20; Ezek 2:6

1:9 Is 6:7; Mark 7:33-35; Ex 4:11-16; Deut 18:18; Is 51:16

1:10 Rev 11:3-6; Jer 18:7-10; Ezek 32:18; 2 Cor 10:4; Is 44:26-28; Jer 24:6; 31:28, 40

1:1–2 After King Solomon's death, the united kingdom of Israel had split into rival northern and southern kingdoms. The northern kingdom was called Israel; the southern, Judah. Jeremiah was from Anathoth, four miles north of Jerusalem in the southern kingdom. He lived and prophesied during the reigns of the last five kings of Judah. This was a chaotic time politically, morally, and spiritually. As Babylon, Egypt, and Assyria battled for world supremacy, Judah found itself caught in the middle of the triangle. Although Jeremiah prophesied for 40 years, he never saw his people heed his words and turn from their sins.

1:5 God knew you, as he knew Jeremiah, long before you were born or even conceived. He thought about you and planned for you. When you feel discouraged or inadequate, remember that God has always thought of you as valuable and that he has a purpose in mind for you.

1:5 Jeremiah was "appointed" by God as "a prophet to the nations." God has a purpose for each Christian, but some people are appointed by God for specific kinds of work. Samson (Judges 13:3–5), David (1 Samuel 16:12–13), John the Baptist (Luke 1:13–17), and Paul (Galatians 1:15–16) were also called to do particular jobs for God. Whatever work you do should be done for the glory of God (Philippians 1:11). If God gives you a specific task, accept it cheerfully and do it with diligence. If God has not given you a specific call or assignment, then seek to fulfill the mission common to all believers—to love, obey, and serve God—until his guidance becomes more clear.

1:6–8 Often people struggle with new challenges because they lack self-confidence, feeling that they have inadequate ability, training, or experience. Jeremiah thought he was only "a youth"—too young and inexperienced to be God's spokesman to the world. But God promised to be with him. We should not allow feelings of inadequacy to keep us from obeying God's call. He will *always* be with us. When you find yourself avoiding something you know you should do, be careful not to use lack of self-confidence as an excuse. If God gives you a job to do, he will provide all you need to do it.

1:8 God promised to "deliver" Jeremiah from trouble, not to keep trouble from coming. God did not insulate him from jailings, deportation, or insults. God does not keep us from encountering life's storms, but he will see us through them. In fact, God walks through these storms with us and rescues us.

1:10 God appointed Jeremiah to bring his word to nations and kingdoms. Jeremiah's work was to warn not only the Jews but all the nations of the world about God's judgment on sin. Don't forget in reading the Old Testament that, while God was consistently working through the people of Judah and Israel, his plan was to communicate to every nation and person. We are included in Jeremiah's message of judgment and hope, and as believers we are to share God's desire to reach the whole world for him.

The Almond Rod and Boiling Pot

11 The word of the LORD came to me saying, "What do you see, Jeremiah?" And I
said, "I see a rod of an almond tree."
12 Then the LORD said to me, "You have seen well, for I am watching over My word to
perform it."
13 The word of the LORD came to me a second time saying, "What do you see?" And
I said, "I see a boiling pot, facing away from the north."
14 Then the LORD said to me, "Out of the north the evil will break forth on all the
inhabitants of the land.
15 "For, behold, I am calling all the families of the kingdoms of the north," declares the
LORD; "and they will come and they will set each one his throne at the entrance of the
gates of Jerusalem, and against all its walls round about and against all the cities of
Judah.
16 "I will pronounce My judgments on them concerning all their wickedness, whereby
they have forsaken Me and have offered sacrifices to other gods, and worshiped the works
of their own hands.
17 "Now, gird up your loins and arise, and speak to them all which I command you. Do
not be dismayed before them, or I will dismay you before them.
18 "Now behold, I have made you today as a fortified city and as a pillar of iron and as
walls of bronze against the whole land, to the kings of Judah, to its princes, to its priests
and to the people of the land.
19 "They will fight against you, but they will not overcome you, for I am with you to
deliver you," declares the LORD.

1:11 Jer 24:3; Amos 7:8
1:12 Jer 31:28
1:13 Zech 4:2; Ezek 11:3, 7
1:14 Is 41:25; Jer 4:6; 10:22
1:15 Jer 25:9; Is 22:7; Jer 39:3; Jer 4:16; 9:11
1:16 Deut 28:20; Jer 7:9; 19:4; 44:17; Is 2:8; 37:19; Jer 10:3-5
1:17 1 Kin 18:46; Job 38:3; Ezek 2:6; 3:16-18
1:19 Num 14:9; Jer 1:8; 20:11

2. Jeremiah condemns Judah for her sins

Judah's Apostasy

2 Now the word of the LORD came to me saying,
2 "Go and proclaim in the ears of Jerusalem, saying, 'Thus says the LORD,
"I remember concerning you the devotion of your youth,
The love of your betrothals,
Your following after Me in the wilderness,

2:2 Is 58:1; Jer 7:2; 11:6; Ezek 16:8; Hos 2:15; Deut 2:7; Jer 2:6

JEREMIAH
Jeremiah served as a prophet to Judah from 627 B.C. until the exile in 586 B.C.

Climate of the times	• Society was deteriorating economically, politically, spiritually. • Wars and captivity. • God's word was deemed offensive.
Main message	Repentance from sin would postpone Judah's coming judgment at the hands of Babylon.
Importance of message	Repentance is one of the greatest needs in our immoral world. God's promises to the faithful shine brightly by bringing hope for tomorrow and strength for today.
Contemporary prophets	Habakkuk (612–588 B.C.), Zephaniah (640–621 B.C.)

1:11–14 The vision of the branch (rod) of an almond tree revealed the beginning of God's judgment because the almond tree is among the first to blossom in the spring. God saw the sins of Judah and the nations, and he would carry out swift and certain judgment. The boiling pot tilting away from the north and spilling over Judah pictured Babylon delivering God's scalding judgment against Jeremiah's people.

1:14–19 The problems we face may not seem as ominous as Jeremiah's, but they are critical to us and may overwhelm us! God's promise to Jeremiah and to us is that nothing will defeat us completely; he will help us through the most agonizing problems. Face each day with the assurance that God will be with you and see you through.

1:16 The people of Judah sinned greatly by continuing to burn incense to and worship other gods. God had commanded them specifically against this (Exodus 20:3–6) because idolatry places trust in created things rather than the Creator. Although these people belonged to God, they chose to follow false gods. Many "gods" entice us to turn away from God. Material possessions, dreams for the future, approval of others, and vocational goals compete for our total commitment. Striving after these at the expense of our commitment to God puts our heart where Judah's was—and God severely punished Judah.

2:1—3:5 In this section, the marriage analogy sharply contrasts God's love for his people with their love for other gods and reveals Judah's faithlessness. Jeremiah condemned Judah (he sometimes called Judah "Jerusalem," the name of its capital city) for seeking security in worthless, changeable things rather than the unchangeable God. We may be tempted to seek security from possessions, people, or our own abilities, but these will fail us. There is no lasting security apart from the eternal God.

2:2 We appreciate a friend who remains true to his or her commitment, and we are disappointed with someone who fails to keep a promise. God was pleased when his people obeyed initially, but he became angry with them when they refused to keep their commitment. Temptations distract us from God. Think about your original commitment to obey God, and ask yourself if you are remaining truly devoted.

Through a land not sown.
3 "Israel was holy to the LORD,
The first of His harvest.
All who ate of it became guilty;
Evil came upon them," declares the LORD.' "
4 Hear the word of the LORD, O house of Jacob, and all the families of the house of
Israel.
5 Thus says the LORD,
"What injustice did your fathers find in Me,
That they went far from Me
And walked after emptiness and became empty?
6 "They did not say, 'Where is the LORD
Who brought us up out of the land of Egypt,
Who led us through the wilderness,
Through a land of deserts and of pits,
Through a land of drought and of deep darkness,
Through a land that no one crossed
And where no man dwelt?'
7 "I brought you into the fruitful land
To eat its fruit and its good things.
But you came and defiled My land,
And My inheritance you made an abomination.
8 "The priests did not say, 'Where is the LORD?'
And those who handle the law did not know Me;
The rulers also transgressed against Me,
And the prophets prophesied by Baal
And walked after things that did not profit.

9 "Therefore I will yet contend with you," declares the LORD,
"And with your sons' sons I will contend.
10 "For cross to the coastlands of Kittim and see,
And send to Kedar and observe closely
And see if there has been such *a thing* as this!
11 "Has a nation changed gods
When they were not gods?
But My people have changed their glory
For that which does not profit.
12 "Be appalled, O heavens, at this,
And shudder, be very desolate," declares the LORD.
13 "For My people have committed two evils:
They have forsaken Me,
The fountain of living waters,

2:3 Ex 19:5, 6; Deut 7:6; 14:2; James 1:18; Rev 14:4; Is 41:11; Jer 30:16; 50:7

2:5 Is 5:4; Mic 6:3; 2 Kin 17:15; Jer 8:19; Rom 1:21

2:6 Ex 20:2; Is 63:11; Deut 8:15; 32:10

2:7 Deut 8:7-9; 11:10-12; Ps 106:38; Jer 3:2; 16:18

2:8 Jer 10:21; Jer 4:22; Mal 2:7, 8; Jer 23:13; Jer 16:19; Hab 2:18

2:9 Jer 2:35; Ezek 20:35, 36

2:10 Is 23:12; Ps 120:5; Is 21:16; Jer 49:28

2:11 Is 37:19; Jer 5:7; 16:20; Ps 106:20; Rom 1:23

2:12 Is 1:2; Jer 4:23

2:13 Ps 36:9; Jer 17:13; John 4:14; Jer 14:3

2:3 The first part of the harvest was set aside for God (Deuteronomy 26:1–11). That's how Israel was dedicated to him in years gone by. Israel had been as eager to please God as if she were his young bride, a holy, devoted people. This contrasted greatly with the situation in Jeremiah's time.

2:4–8 The united nation of Israel included both the "house of Israel" and the "house of Jacob" (Judah). Jeremiah knew Israel's history well. The prophets recited history to the people for several reasons: (1) to remind them of God's faithfulness; (2) to make sure the people wouldn't forget (they didn't have Bibles to read); (3) to emphasize God's love for them; (4) to remind the people that there had been a time when they *were* close to God. We should learn from history so we can build on the successes and avoid repeating the failures of others.

2:8 Baal was the chief male god of the Canaanite religion. "Baals" (2:23) refers to the fact that Baal was worshiped in many centers in Canaanite practice. Baal was the god of fertility. Worship of Baal included animal sacrifice and sacred prostitution (male and female) in the high places. Jezebel, the wife of King Ahab, introduced Baal worship into the northern kingdom, and eventually it spread to Judah. The sexual orientation of this worship was a constant temptation to the Israelites, who were called to be holy.

2:10 God was saying that even pagan nations like Kittim (Cyprus, in the west) and Kedar (the home of Arab tribes living in the desert east of Palestine) remained loyal to their national gods. But Israel had abandoned the one and only God for a completely worthless object of worship.

2:13 Who would set aside a sparkling fountain of water for a cistern, a pit that collected rainwater? God told the Israelites they were doing that very thing when they turned from him, the fountain of living water, to the worship of idols. Not only that, but the cisterns they chose were broken and empty. The people had built religious systems in which to store truth, but those systems were worthless. Why should we cling to the broken promises of unstable "cisterns" (money, power, religious systems, or whatever transitory thing we are putting in place of God) when God promises to constantly refresh us with himself, the living water (John 4:10)?

To hew for themselves cisterns,
Broken cisterns
That can hold no water.

2:14 Jer 5:19; 17:4
2:15 Jer 50:17; Jer 4:7
2:16 Is 19:13; Jer 44:1; Hos 9:6; Deut 33:20; Jer 48:45

14 "Is Israel a slave? Or is he a homeborn servant?
Why has he become a prey?
15 "The young lions have roared at him,
They have roared loudly.
And they have made his land a waste;
His cities have been destroyed, without inhabitant.
16 "Also the men of Memphis and Tahpanhes
Have shaved the crown of your head.

JEREMIAH

Endurance is not a common quality. Many people lack the long-term commitment, caring, and willingness that are vital to sticking with a task against all odds. But Jeremiah was a prophet who endured.

Jeremiah's call by God teaches how intimately God knows us. He valued us before anyone else knew we would exist. He cared for us while we were in our mother's womb. He planned our lives while our bodies were still being formed. He values us more highly than we value ourselves.

Jeremiah had to depend on God's love as he developed endurance. His audiences were usually antagonistic or apathetic to his messages. He was ignored; his life was often threatened. He saw both the excitement of a spiritual awakening and the sorrow of a national return to idolatry. With the exception of the good King Josiah, Jeremiah watched king after king ignore his warnings and lead the people away from God. He saw fellow prophets murdered. He himself was severely persecuted. Finally, he watched Judah's defeat at the hands of the Babylonians.

Jeremiah responded to all this with God's message and human tears. He felt firsthand God's love for his people and the people's rejection of that love. But even when he was angry with God and tempted to give up, Jeremiah knew he had to keep going. God had called him to endure. He expressed intense feelings, but he also saw beyond the feelings to the God who was soon to execute justice, but who afterward would administer mercy.

It may be easy for us to identify with Jeremiah's frustrations and discouragement, but we need to realize that this prophet's life is also an encouragement to faithfulness.

Strengths and accomplishments:
- Wrote two Old Testament books, Jeremiah and Lamentations
- Ministered during the reigns of the last five kings of Judah
- Was a catalyst for the great spiritual reformation under King Josiah
- Acted as God's faithful messenger in spite of many attempts on his life
- Was so deeply sorrowful for the fallen condition of Judah that he earned the title "weeping prophet"

Lessons from his life:
- The majority opinion is not necessarily God's will
- Although punishment for sin is severe, there is hope in God's mercy
- God will not accept empty or insincere worship
- Serving God does not guarantee earthly security

Vital statistics:
- Where: Anathoth
- Occupation: Prophet
- Relative: Father: Hilkiah
- Contemporaries: Josiah, Jehoahaz, Jehoiakim, Jehoiachin, Zedekiah, Baruch

Key verses:
" 'Alas, Lord GOD! Behold, I do not know how to speak, because I am a youth.' But the LORD said to me, 'Do not say, "I am a youth," because everywhere I send you, you shall go, and all that I command you, you shall speak. Do not be afraid of them, for I am with you to deliver you,' declares the LORD" (Jeremiah 1:6–8).

Jeremiah's story is told in the book of Jeremiah. He is also mentioned in Ezra 1:1; Daniel 9:2; Matthew 2:17; 16:14; 27:9. See also 2 Chronicles 34, 35 for the story of the spiritual revival under Josiah.

2:16–17 Memphis was near modern Cairo's present location in lower Egypt, and Tahpanhes was in northeastern Egypt. Jeremiah could be speaking of Pharaoh Shishak's previous invasion of Judah in 926 B.C. (1 Kings 14:25), or he may have been predicting Pharaoh Neco's invasion in 609 B.C. when King Josiah of Judah would be killed (2 Kings 23:29–30). Jeremiah's point is that the people brought this on themselves by rebelling against God.

17 "Have you not done this to yourself
By your forsaking the LORD your God
When He led you in the way?
18 "But now what are you doing on the road to Egypt,
To drink the waters of the Nile?
Or what are you doing on the road to Assyria,
To drink the waters of the Euphrates?
19 "Your own wickedness will correct you,
And your apostasies will reprove you;
Know therefore and see that it is evil and bitter
For you to forsake the LORD your God,
And the dread of Me is not in you," declares the Lord GOD of hosts.

20 "For long ago I broke your yoke
And tore off your bonds;
But you said, 'I will not serve!'
For on every high hill
And under every green tree
You have lain down as a harlot.
21 "Yet I planted you a choice vine,
A completely faithful seed.
How then have you turned yourself before Me
Into the degenerate shoots of a foreign vine?
22 "Although you wash yourself with lye
And use much soap,
The stain of your iniquity is before Me," declares the Lord GOD.
23 "How can you say, 'I am not defiled,
I have not gone after the Baals'?
Look at your way in the valley!
Know what you have done!
You are a swift young camel entangling her ways,
24 A wild donkey accustomed to the wilderness,
That sniffs the wind in her passion.
In *the time of* her heat who can turn her away?
All who seek her will not become weary;
In her month they will find her.
25 "Keep your feet from being unshod
And your throat from thirst;
But you said, 'It is hopeless!
No! For I have loved strangers,
And after them I will walk.'

26 "As the thief is shamed when he is discovered,
So the house of Israel is shamed;
They, their kings, their princes
And their priests and their prophets,
27 Who say to a tree, 'You are my father,'
And to a stone, 'You gave me birth.'
For they have turned *their* back to Me,
And not *their* face;
But in the time of their trouble they will say,

2:17 Deut 32:10; Jer 4:18

2:18 Is 30:2; Josh 13:3

2:19 Is 3:9; Jer 4:18; Hos 5:5; Jer 3:6, 8, 11, 14; Hos 11:7; Job 20:12-16; Amos 8:10; Ps 36:1; Jer 5:24

2:20 Lev 26:13; Deut 12:2; Is 57:5, 7; Jer 3:2, 6; 17:2

2:21 Ex 15:17; Ps 44:2; 80:8; Is 5:2; Is 5:4

2:22 Jer 4:14; Job 14:17; Hos 13:12

2:23 Prov 30:12; Jer 9:14; Jer 7:31; Jer 2:33, 36; 31:22

2:24 Jer 14:6

2:25 Jer 18:12; Deut 32:16; Jer 14:10

2:26 Jer 48:27

2:27 Jer 18:17; 32:33; Judg 10:10; Is 26:16

2:22 The stain of sin is more than skin-deep. Israel had stains that could not be washed out, even with the strongest cleansers. Spiritual cleansing must reach deep into the heart—and this is a job that God alone can do. We cannot ignore the effects of sin and hope they will go away. Your sin has caused a deep stain that God can and will remove if you are willing to let him cleanse you (Isaiah 1:18; Ezekiel 36:25).

2:23–27 The people are compared to animals who search for mates in mating season. Unrestrained, they rush for power, money, alliances with foreign powers, and other gods. The idols did not seek the people; the people sought the idols and then ran wildly after them. Then they became so comfortable in their sin that they could not think of giving it up. Their only shame was in getting caught. If we desire something so much that we'll do anything to get it, this is a sign that we are addicted to it and out of tune with God.

'Arise and save us.'

2:28 Deut 32:37; Judg 10:14; Is 45:20; Jer 1:16; Jer 11:12; 2 Kin 17:30, 31; Jer 11:13

28 "But where are your gods
Which you made for yourself?
Let them arise, if they can save you
In the time of your trouble;
For *according to* the number of your cities
Are your gods, O Judah.

2:29 Jer 5:1; 6:13; Dan 9:11

2:30 Is 1:5; Jer 5:3; 7:28; Neh 9:26; Jer 26:20-24; Acts 7:52; 1 Thess 2:15

2:31 Is 45:19; Deut 32:15; Jer 2:20, 25

29 "Why do you contend with Me?
You have all transgressed against Me," declares the LORD.
30 "In vain I have struck your sons;
They accepted no chastening.
Your sword has devoured your prophets
Like a destroying lion.
31 "O generation, heed the word of the LORD.
Have I been a wilderness to Israel,
Or a land of thick darkness?
Why do My people say, 'We *are free to* roam;
We will no longer come to You'?

2:32 Ps 106:21; Is 17:10; Jer 3:21; 13:25; Hos 8:14

32 "Can a virgin forget her ornaments,
Or a bride her attire?
Yet My people have forgotten Me
Days without number.
33 "How well you prepare your way
To seek love!
Therefore even the wicked women
You have taught your ways.

2:34 2 Kin 21:16; 24:4; Ps 106:38; Jer 7:6; 19:4; Ex 22:2

34 "Also on your skirts is found
The lifeblood of the innocent poor;
You did not find them breaking in.
But in spite of all these things,

2:35 Jer 25:31; Prov 28:13; 1 John 1:8, 10

35 Yet you said, 'I am innocent;
Surely His anger is turned away from me.'
Behold, I will enter into judgment with you
Because you say, 'I have not sinned.'

2:36 Jer 2:23; 31:22; Hos 12:1; Is 30:3; 2 Chr 28:16, 20, 21

36 "Why do you go around so much
Changing your way?
Also, you will be put to shame by Egypt
As you were put to shame by Assyria.

2:37 2 Sam 13:19; Jer 14:3, 4; Jer 37:7-10

37 "From this *place* also you will go out
With your hands on your head;
For the LORD has rejected those in whom you trust,
And you will not prosper with them."

3:1 Deut 24:1-4; Jer 2:20; Ezek 16:26, 28, 29; Jer 4:1; Zech 1:3

The Polluted Land

3 *God* says, "If a husband divorces his wife
And she goes from him

2:30 Being a prophet in Jeremiah's day was risky business. Prophets had to criticize the policies of evil kings, and this made them appear to be traitors. The kings hated the prophets for standing against their policies, and the people often hated the prophets for preaching against their idolatrous life-styles. (See Acts 7:52.)

2:31–32 Forgetting can be dangerous, whether it is intentional or an oversight. Israel forgot God by focusing its affections on the allurements of the world. The more we focus on the pleasures of the world, the easier it becomes to forget God's care, his love, his dependability, his guidance, and most of all, God himself. What pleases you most? Have you been forgetting God lately?

2:36 God is not against alliances or working partnerships, but he is against people trusting others for the help that should come from him. This was the problem in Jeremiah's time. After the days of David and Solomon, Israel fell apart because the leaders turned to other nations and gods instead of the true God. They played power politics, thinking that their strong neighbors could protect them. But Judah would soon learn that its alliance with Egypt would be just as disappointing as its former alliance with Assyria (2 Kings 16:8, 9; Isaiah 7:13–25).

3:1 This law, found in Deuteronomy 24:1–4, says that a divorced woman who remarries can never be reunited with her first husband. Judah "divorced" God and "married" other gods. God had every right to permanently disown his wayward people, but in his mercy he was willing to take them back again.

And belongs to another man,
Will he still return to her?
Will not that land be completely polluted?
But you are a harlot *with* many lovers;
Yet you turn to Me," declares the LORD.
2 "Lift up your eyes to the bare heights and see;
Where have you not been violated?
By the roads you have sat for them
Like an Arab in the desert,
And you have polluted a land
With your harlotry and with your wickedness.
3 "Therefore the showers have been withheld,
And there has been no spring rain.
Yet you had a harlot's forehead;
You refused to be ashamed.
4 "Have you not just now called to Me,
'My Father, You are the friend of my youth?
5 'Will He be angry forever?
Will He be indignant to the end?'
Behold, you have spoken
And have done evil things,
And you have had your way."

3:2 Deut 12:2; Jer 2:20; 3:21; 7:29; Gen 38:14; Ezek 16:25; Jer 2:7
3:3 Lev 26:19; Jer 14:3-6; Jer 6:15; 8:12
3:4 Jer 3:19; 31:9; Ps 71:17; Prov 2:17; Jer 2:2; Hos 2:15
3:5 Ps 103:9; Is 57:16; Jer 3:12

Faithless Israel

6 Then the LORD said to me in the days of Josiah the king, "Have you seen what faithless Israel did? She went up on every high hill and under every green tree, and she was
a harlot there.
7 "I thought, 'After she has done all these things she will return to Me'; but she did not
return, and her treacherous sister Judah saw it.
8 "And I saw that for all the adulteries of faithless Israel, I had sent her away and given
her a writ of divorce, yet her treacherous sister Judah did not fear; but she went and was
a harlot also.
9 "Because of the lightness of her harlotry, she polluted the land and committed adultery with stones and trees.
10 "Yet in spite of all this her treacherous sister Judah did not return to Me with all her
heart, but rather in deception," declares the LORD.

God Invites Repentance

11 And the LORD said to me, "Faithless Israel has proved herself more righteous than
treacherous Judah.
12 "Go and proclaim these words toward the north and say,
'Return, faithless Israel,' declares the LORD;

3:6 Jer 17:2; Ezek 23:4-10
3:7 2 Kin 17:13; Jer 3:11; Ezek 16:47
3:8 Deut 24:1, 3; Is 50:1; Ezek 16:46, 47; 23:11
3:9 Jer 2:7; 3:2; Is 57:6; Jer 2:27; 10:8
3:10 Jer 12:2; Hos 7:14
3:11 Ezek 16:51, 52; 23:11
3:12 Jer 3:14, 22; Ezek 33:11; Jer 3:5; Ps 86:15; Jer 12:15; 31:20; 33:26

3:2 "Like an Arab in the desert" means that, just as an Arab thief might hide and wait to plunder a passing caravan, so Judah ran to idolatry. It was a national preoccupation.

3:4–5 In spite of their great sin, the people of Israel continued to talk like they were God's children. The only way they could do this was to minimize their sin. When we know we've done something wrong, we want to downplay the error and relieve some of the guilt we feel. As we minimize our sinfulness, we naturally shy away from making changes, and so we keep on sinning. But if we view every wrong attitude and action as a serious offense against God, we will begin to understand what living for God is all about. Is there any sin in your life that you've written off as too small to worry about? God says that we must confess and turn away from *every* sin.

3:6—6:30 The northern kingdom, Israel, had fallen to Assyria, and its people had been taken into captivity. The tragic lesson of their fall should have caused the southern kingdom, Judah, to return to God, but Judah paid no attention. Jeremiah urged Judah to return to God to avoid certain disaster. This message came between 627 and 621 B.C., during Josiah's reign. Although Josiah obeyed God's commands, his example apparently did not penetrate the hearts of the people. If the people refused to repent, God said he would destroy the nation because of the evils of Josiah's grandfather, King Manasseh (2 Kings 23:25–27).

3:11–13 Israel was not even trying to look as if it were obeying God, but Judah maintained the appearance of right faith without a true heart. Believing the right doctrines without heartfelt commitment is like offering sacrifices without true repentance. Judah's false repentance brought Jeremiah's words of condemnation. To live without faith is hopeless; to express sorrow without change is treacherous and unfaithful. Being sorry for sin is not enough. Repentance demands a change of mind and heart that results in changed behavior.

3:12–18 The northern kingdom, Israel, was in captivity, being punished for its sins. The people of Judah undoubtedly looked down on these northern neighbors for their blatant heresy and degraded morals. Even so, Jeremiah promised the remnant of Israel God's blessings if they would turn to him. Judah, still secure in its own mind, should have turned to God after seeing the destruction

'I will not look upon you in anger.
For I am gracious,' declares the LORD;
'I will not be angry forever.
13 'Only acknowledge your iniquity,
That you have transgressed against the LORD your God
And have scattered your favors to the strangers under every green tree,
And you have not obeyed My voice,' declares the LORD.
14 'Return, O faithless sons,' declares the LORD;
'For I am a master to you,
And I will take you one from a city and two from a family,
And I will bring you to Zion.'
15 "Then I will give you shepherds after My own heart, who will feed you on knowledge
and understanding.
16 "It shall be in those days when you are multiplied and increased in the land," declares the LORD, "they will no longer say, 'The ark of the covenant of the LORD.' And it
will not come to mind, nor will they remember it, nor will they miss *it,* nor will it be made
again.
17 "At that time they will call Jerusalem 'The Throne of the LORD,' and all the nations
will be gathered to it, to Jerusalem, for the name of the LORD; nor will they walk anymore after the stubbornness of their evil heart.
18 "In those days the house of Judah will walk with the house of Israel, and they will
come together from the land of the north to the land that I gave your fathers as an inheritance.
19 "Then I said,
'How I would set you among My sons
And give you a pleasant land,
The most beautiful inheritance of the nations!'
And I said, 'You shall call Me, My Father,
And not turn away from following Me.'
20 "Surely, as a woman treacherously departs from her lover,
So you have dealt treacherously with Me,
O house of Israel," declares the LORD.

21 A voice is heard on the bare heights,
The weeping *and* the supplications of the sons of Israel;
Because they have perverted their way,
They have forgotten the LORD their God.

3:13 Deut 30:1-3; Jer 3:25; 14:20; 1 John 1:9; Jer 2:20, 25; 3:2, 6; Deut 12:2

3:14 Jer 31:32; Hos 2:19; Jer 31:6, 12

3:15 Jer 23:4; 31:10; Ezek 34:23; Eph 4:11; Acts 20:28

3:16 Is 65:17

3:17 Jer 17:12; Ezek 43:7; Jer 3:19; 4:2; 12:15, 16; 16:19; Is 60:9; Jer 11:8

3:18 Is 11:13; Jer 50:4, 5; Hos 1:11; Jer 16:15; 31:8; Amos 9:15

3:19 Ps 16:6; Is 63:16; Jer 3:4

3:20 Is 48:8

3:21 Is 15:2; Jer 3:2; 7:29; Is 17:10; Jer 2:32; 13:25

THE KINGS OF JEREMIAH'S LIFETIME

King	*Story of his reign*	*Dates of his reign*	*Character of reign*	*Jeremiah's message to the king*
Josiah	2 Kings 22:1—23:30	640–609 B.C.	Mostly good	3:6–25
Jehoahaz	2 Kings 23:31–33	609 B.C.	Evil	22:11–17
Jehoiakim	2 Kings 23:34—24:7	609–598 B.C.	Evil	22:18–23; 25:1–38; 26:1–24; 27:1–11; 35:1–19; 36:1–32
Jehoiachin	2 Kings 24:8–17	598–597 B.C.	Evil	13:18–27; 22:24–30
Zedekiah	2 Kings 24:18—25:26	597–586 B.C.	Evil	21:1–14; 24:8–10; 27:12–22; 32:1–5; 34:1–22; 37:1–21; 38:1–28; 51:59–64

of Israel. But the people of Judah refused, so Jeremiah startled them by telling about God's promise to Israel's remnant if they would repent.

3:15 God promised to give his people leaders ("shepherds" after his own heart) who would follow him, filled with knowledge (wisdom) and understanding. God saw Israel's lack of direction, so he promised to provide the right kind of leadership. We look to and trust our leaders for guidance and direction. But if they do not follow God, they will lead us astray. Pray for God-honoring leaders in our nations, communities, and churches—those who will be good examples and bring us God's wisdom.

3:16–17 In the days of Solomon's reign over a united Israel, the people had a beautiful temple where they worshiped God. The temple housed the ark of the covenant, the symbol of God's presence with the people. The ark held the tablets of the Ten Commandments (see Exodus 25:10–22). Those days with the ark wouldn't be missed in the future kingdom because God's presence by the Holy Spirit would be there personally among his people.

22 "Return, O faithless sons,
I will heal your faithlessness."
"Behold, we come to You;
For You are the LORD our God.
23 "Surely, the hills are a deception,
A tumult *on* the mountains.
Surely in the LORD our God
Is the salvation of Israel.
24 "But the shameful thing has consumed the labor of our fathers since our youth, their
flocks and their herds, their sons and their daughters.
25 "Let us lie down in our shame, and let our humiliation cover us; for we have sinned
against the LORD our God, we and our fathers, from our youth even to this day. And we
have not obeyed the voice of the LORD our God."

3:22 Jer 30:17; 33:6; Hos 6:1; 14:4
3:23 Jer 17:2; Ps 3:8; Jer 17:14; 31:7
3:24 Hos 9:10
3:25 Ezra 9:6, 7; Jer 22:21

Judah Threatened with Invasion

4 "If you will return, O Israel," declares the LORD,
"*Then* you should return to Me.
And if you will put away your detested things from My presence,
And will not waver,
2 And you will swear, 'As the LORD lives,'
In truth, in justice and in righteousness;
Then the nations will bless themselves in Him,
And in Him they will glory."

3 For thus says the LORD to the men of Judah and to Jerusalem,
"Break up your fallow ground,
And do not sow among thorns.
4 "Circumcise yourselves to the LORD
And remove the foreskins of your heart,
Men of Judah and inhabitants of Jerusalem,
Or else My wrath will go forth like fire
And burn with none to quench it,
Because of the evil of your deeds."

5 Declare in Judah and proclaim in Jerusalem, and say,
"Blow the trumpet in the land;
Cry aloud and say,
'Assemble yourselves, and let us go
Into the fortified cities.'
6 "Lift up a standard toward Zion!
Seek refuge, do not stand *still,*
For I am bringing evil from the north,
And great destruction.
7 "A lion has gone up from his thicket,
And a destroyer of nations has set out;
He has gone out from his place
To make your land a waste.
Your cities will be ruins
Without inhabitant.

4:1 Jer 3:22; 15:19; Joel 2:12; Jer 7:3, 7; 35:15
4:2 Deut 10:20; Is 45:23; 65:16; Jer 12:16; Is 48:1; Gen 22:18; Jer 3:17; 12:15, 16; Gal 3:8; Is 45:25; Jer 9:24; 1 Cor 1:31
4:3 Hos 10:12; Matt 13:7
4:4 Deut 10:16; 30:6; Jer 9:25, 26; Rom 2:28, 29; Col 2:11; Is 30:27, 33; Jer 21:12; Zeph 2:2; Amos 5:6; Mark 9:43, 48
4:5 Jer 6:1; Hos 8:1; Josh 10:20; Jer 8:14
4:6 Is 62:10; Jer 4:21; 50:2; Jer 1:14, 15; 6:1, 22
4:7 Jer 5:6; 25:38; 50:17; Jer 25:9; Ezek 26:7-10; Is 1:7; 6:11; Jer 2:15

3:22–25 Jeremiah predicted a day when the nation would be reunited, true worship would be reinstated, and sin would be seen for what it is. Our world glorifies the thrill that comes from wealth, competition, and sexual pleasure, and it ignores the sin that is so often associated with these thrills. It is sad that so few see sin as it really is—a deception. Most people can't see this until they are destroyed by the sin they pursue. The advantage of believing God's Word is that we don't have to learn by hard experience the destructive results of sin.

4:3 Jeremiah told the people to break up the hardness of their hearts as a plow breaks up unplowed ground—soil that has not been tilled for a season. Good kings like Josiah had tried to turn the people back to God, but the people had continued to worship their idols in secret. Their hearts had become hardened to God's will. Jeremiah said the people needed to remove the sin that hardened their hearts before the good seed of God's commands could take root. Likewise we must remove our heart-hardening sin if we expect God's Word to take root and grow in our lives.

4:6–7 The evil from the north would come from Babylon when Nabopolassar and Nebuchadnezzar II would attack (see 2 Chronicles 36).

4:8 Is 22:12; Jer 6:26; Is 5:25; 10:4; Jer 30:24

8 "For this, put on sackcloth,
Lament and wail;
For the fierce anger of the LORD
Has not turned back from us."

4:9 Is 22:3-5; Jer 48:41; Is 29:9, 10; Ezek 13:9-16

9 "It shall come about in that day," declares the LORD, "that the heart of the king and
the heart of the princes will fail; and the priests will be appalled and the prophets will be
astounded."

4:10 Ezek 14:9; 2 Thess 2:11; Jer 5:12; 14:13

10 Then I said, "Ah, Lord GOD! Surely You have utterly deceived this people and Jerusalem, saying, 'You will have peace'; whereas a sword touches the throat."

4:11 Jer 13:24; 51:1; Ezek 17:10; Hos 13:15

11 In that time it will be said to this people and to Jerusalem, "A scorching wind from
the bare heights in the wilderness in the direction of the daughter of My people—not to
winnow and not to cleanse,
12 a wind too strong for this—will come at My command; now I will also pronounce
judgments against them.

4:13 Is 19:1; Nah 1:3; Is 5:28; 66:15; Lam 4:19; Hab 1:8; Is 3:8

13 "Behold, he goes up like clouds,
And his chariots like the whirlwind;
His horses are swifter than eagles.
Woe to us, for we are ruined!"

4:14 Prov 1:22; Jer 6:19; 13:27; James 4:8

14 Wash your heart from evil, O Jerusalem,
That you may be saved.
How long will your wicked thoughts
Lodge within you?

4:15 Jer 8:16

15 For a voice declares from Dan,
And proclaims wickedness from Mount Ephraim.

4:16 Is 39:3; Jer 5:15; Ezek 21:22

16 "Report *it* to the nations, now!
Proclaim over Jerusalem,
'Besiegers come from a far country,
And lift their voices against the cities of Judah.

4:17 2 Kin 25:1, 4; Is 1:20, 23; Jer 5:23

17 'Like watchmen of a field they are against her round about,
Because she has rebelled against Me,' declares the LORD.

4:18 Ps 107:17; Is 50:1; Jer 2:17, 19; Jer 2:19

18 "Your ways and your deeds
Have brought these things to you.
This is your evil. How bitter!
How it has touched your heart!"

Lament over Judah's Devastation

4:19 Is 15:5; 16:11; 21:3; 22:4; Jer 9:1, 10; 20:9; Hab 3:16; Num 10:9

19 My soul, my soul! I am in anguish! Oh, my heart!
My heart is pounding in me;
I cannot be silent,
Because you have heard, O my soul,
The sound of the trumpet,
The alarm of war.

4:20 Ps 42:7; Ezek 7:26; Jer 4:27; Jer 10:20

20 Disaster on disaster is proclaimed,
For the whole land is devastated;
Suddenly my tents are devastated,
My curtains in an instant.
21 How long must I see the standard
And hear the sound of the trumpet?

4:10 Jeremiah, deeply moved by God's words, expressed his sorrow and confusion to God. Jeremiah was intercessor for the people. These people had false expectations because of the past promises of blessings, their blindness to their own sin, and the false prophets who kept telling them that all was well.

4:15 Disaster was announced first from Dan and then on to the hills of Ephraim because Dan was located at the northern border of Israel. Thus the Danites would be the first to see the approaching armies as they invaded from the north. No one would be able to stop the armies because they would be coming as punishment for the people's sin.

4:19–31 Jeremiah was anguished by the sure devastation of the coming judgment. This judgment would continue until the people turned from their sin and listened to God. Although this prophecy refers to the future destruction by Babylon, it could also describe the judgment of all sinners at the end of the world.

22 "For My people are foolish,
They know Me not;
They are stupid children
And have no understanding.
They are shrewd to do evil,
But to do good they do not know."

4:22 Jer 5:4, 21; 10:8; Rom 1:22; Jer 9:3; 13:23; Rom 16:19; 1 Cor 14:20

23 I looked on the earth, and behold, *it was* formless and void;
And to the heavens, and they had no light.
24 I looked on the mountains, and behold, they were quaking,
And all the hills moved to and fro.
25 I looked, and behold, there was no man,
And all the birds of the heavens had fled.
26 I looked, and behold, the fruitful land was a wilderness,
And all its cities were pulled down
Before the LORD, before His fierce anger.

4:23 Gen 1:2; Is 24:19

4:24 Is 5:25; Jer 10:10; Ezek 38:20

4:25 Jer 9:10; 12:4; Zeph 1:3

4:26 Jer 9:10

27 For thus says the LORD,
"The whole land shall be a desolation,
Yet I will not execute a complete destruction.
28 "For this the earth shall mourn
And the heavens above be dark,
Because I have spoken, I have purposed,
And I will not change My mind, nor will I turn from it."
29 At the sound of the horseman and bowman every city flees;
They go into the thickets and climb among the rocks;
Every city is forsaken,
And no man dwells in them.
30 And you, O desolate one, what will you do?
Although you dress in scarlet,
Although you decorate *yourself with* ornaments of gold,
Although you enlarge your eyes with paint,
In vain you make yourself beautiful.
Your lovers despise you;
They seek your life.
31 For I heard a cry as of a woman in labor,
The anguish as of one giving birth to her first child,
The cry of the daughter of Zion gasping for breath,
Stretching out her hands, *saying,*
"Ah, woe is me, for I faint before murderers."

4:27 Jer 12:11, 12; 25:11; Jer 5:10, 18; 30:11; 46:28

4:28 Jer 12:4, 11; 14:2; Hos 4:3; Is 5:30; 50:3; Joel 2:30, 31; Num 23:19; Jer 23:20; 30:24

4:29 2 Kin 25:4; Is 2:19-21; Jer 16:16; Jer 4:7

4:30 Is 10:3; 20:6; Jer 13:21; 2 Kin 9:30; Ezek 23:40; Jer 22:20, 22; Lam 1:2, 19; Ezek 23:9, 10, 22

4:31 Is 42:14; Is 1:15; Lam 1:17

Jerusalem's Godlessness

5 "Roam to and fro through the streets of Jerusalem,
And look now and take note.
And seek in her open squares,
If you can find a man,
If there is one who does justice, who seeks truth,
Then I will pardon her.
2 "And although they say, 'As the LORD lives,'
Surely they swear falsely."

5:1 2 Chr 16:9; Dan 12:4; Ezek 22:30; Gen 18:26, 32

5:2 Is 48:1; Titus 1:16

4:22 Judah was skilled in doing evil and did not know how to do good. Right living is more than simply avoiding sin. It requires decision and discipline. We must develop skills in right living because our behavior attracts attention to our God. We should pursue excellence in Christian living with as much effort as we pursue excellence at work.

4:27 God warned that destruction was certain, but he promised that the faithful remnant would be spared. God is committed to preserving those who are faithful to him.

5:1 Jerusalem was the capital city and center of worship for Judah, but God challenged anyone to find *one* honest and truthful person in the entire city. God was willing to spare the city if one upright person could be found (he made a similar statement about Sodom; see Genesis 18:32). Think how significant your testimony may be in your city or community. You may represent the only witness for God to many people. Are you faithful to that opportunity?

5:3 2 Chr 16:9; Is 1:5; 9:13; Jer 2:30; Jer 7:28; 8:5; Zeph 3:2; Jer 7:26; 19:15; Ezek 3:8

3 O LORD, do not Your eyes *look* for truth?
You have smitten them,
But they did not weaken;
You have consumed them,
But they refused to take correction.
They have made their faces harder than rock;
They have refused to repent.

5:4 Is 27:11; Jer 8:7; Hos 4:6

4 Then I said, "They are only the poor,
They are foolish;
For they do not know the way of the LORD
Or the ordinance of their God.

5:5 Mic 3:1; Ex 32:25; Ps 2:3; Jer 2:20

5 "I will go to the great
And will speak to them,
For they know the way of the LORD
And the ordinance of their God."
But they too, with one accord, have broken the yoke
And burst the bonds.

5:6 Jer 4:7; Ezek 22:27; Hab 1:8; Zeph 3:3; Hos 13:7; Jer 30:14, 15

6 Therefore a lion from the forest will slay them,
A wolf of the deserts will destroy them,
A leopard is watching their cities.
Everyone who goes out of them will be torn in pieces,
Because their transgressions are many,
Their apostasies are numerous.

5:7 Josh 23:7; Jer 12:16; Zeph 1:5; Deut 32:21; Jer 2:11; Gal 4:8; Jer 7:9

7 "Why should I pardon you?
Your sons have forsaken Me
And sworn by those who are not gods.
When I had fed them to the full,
They committed adultery
And trooped to the harlot's house.

5:8 Jer 13:27; 29:23; Ezek 22:11

8 "They were well-fed lusty horses,
Each one neighing after his neighbor's wife.

5:9 Jer 9:9

9 "Shall I not punish these *people,*" declares the LORD,
"And on a nation such as this
Shall I not avenge Myself?

10 "Go up through her vine rows and destroy,
But do not execute a complete destruction;
Strip away her branches,
For they are not the LORD'S.

5:11 Jer 3:6, 7, 20

11 "For the house of Israel and the house of Judah
Have dealt very treacherously with Me," declares the LORD.

5:12 2 Chr 36:16; Prov 30:9; Jer 14:22; 43:1-4; Jer 23:17; Jer 14:13

12 They have lied about the LORD
And said, "[1]Not He;
Misfortune will not come on us,
And we will not see sword or famine.

5:13 Job 8:2; Jer 14:13, 15; 22:22

13 "The prophets are *as* wind,
And the word is not in them.
Thus it will be done to them!"

1 Lit *He is not*

5:3 Nothing but truth is acceptable to God. When we pray, sing, speak, or serve, nothing closes the door of God's acceptance more than hypocrisy, lying, or pretense. God sees through us and refuses to listen. To be close to God, be honest with him.

5:4–5 Even the leaders who knew God's laws and understood his words of judgment had rejected him. They were supposed to teach and guide the people, but instead they led them into sin. Jeremiah observed the poor and foolish (ignorant)—those who were uninformed of God's ways—and realized they were not learning God's laws from their leaders. Thus God's search in Jerusalem was complete. There were no true followers in any level of society.

5:7 God held these people responsible for the sins of their children because the children had followed their parents' example. The sin of leading others, especially our children, astray by our example is one for which God will hold us accountable.

Judgment Proclaimed

14 Therefore, thus says the LORD, the God of hosts,
"Because you have spoken this word,
Behold, I am making My words in your mouth fire
And this people wood, and it will consume them.
15 "Behold, I am bringing a nation against you from afar, O house of Israel," declares
the LORD.
"It is an enduring nation,
It is an ancient nation,
A nation whose language you do not know,
Nor can you understand what they say.
16 "Their quiver is like an open grave,
All of them are mighty men.
17 "They will devour your harvest and your food;
They will devour your sons and your daughters;
They will devour your flocks and your herds;
They will devour your vines and your fig trees;
They will demolish with the sword your fortified cities in which you trust.
18 "Yet even in those days," declares the LORD, "I will not make you a complete de-
struction.
19 "It shall come about when they say, 'Why has the LORD our God done all these things
to us?' then you shall say to them, 'As you have forsaken Me and served foreign gods in
your land, so you will serve strangers in a land that is not yours.'
20 "Declare this in the house of Jacob
And proclaim it in Judah, saying,
21 'Now hear this, O foolish and senseless people,
Who have eyes but do not see;
Who have ears but do not hear.
22 'Do you not fear Me?' declares the LORD.
'Do you not tremble in My presence?
For I have placed the sand as a boundary for the sea,
An eternal decree, so it cannot cross over it.
Though the waves toss, yet they cannot prevail;
Though they roar, yet they cannot cross over it.
23 'But this people has a stubborn and rebellious heart;
They have turned aside and departed.
24 'They do not say in their heart,
"Let us now fear the LORD our God,
Who gives rain in its season,
Both the autumn rain and the spring rain,
Who keeps for us
The appointed weeks of the harvest."
25 'Your iniquities have turned these away,
And your sins have withheld good from you.
26 'For wicked men are found among My people,
They watch like fowlers lying in wait;
They set a trap,
They catch men.
27 'Like a cage full of birds,

5:14 Is 24:6; Jer 1:9; 23:29; Hos 6:5; Zech 1:6

5:15 Deut 28:49; Is 5:26; Jer 4:16; Is 28:11

5:16 Is 5:28; 13:18; Ps 5:9

5:17 Lev 26:16; Deut 28:31, 33; Jer 8:16; 50:7, 17; Jer 8:13; Hos 8:14

5:19 Deut 29:24-26; 1 Kin 9:8, 9; Jer 13:22; 16:10-13; Deut 28:48; Jer 16:13

5:21 Is 6:9; 43:8; Ezek 12:2; Matt 13:14; Mark 8:18; John 12:40; Acts 28:26; Rom 11:8

5:22 Deut 28:58; Ps 119:120; Jer 2:19; 10:7; Rev 15:4; Job 38:8-11; Ps 104:9; Prov 8:29

5:23 Deut 21:18; Ps 78:8; Jer 4:17; 6:28

5:24 Ps 147:8; Jer 3:3; Matt 5:45; Acts 14:17; Joel 2:23; Gen 8:22

5:25 Jer 2:17; 4:18

5:26 Ps 10:9; Prov 1:11; Jer 18:22; Hab 1:15

5:27 Jer 9:6

5:15 Babylon was indeed an ancient nation. The old Babylonian empire had lasted from about 1900 B.C. to 1550 B.C., and earlier kingdoms had been on her soil as early as 3000 B.C. Babylon in Jeremiah's day would shortly rebel against Assyrian domination, form its own army, conquer Assyria, and become the next dominant world power.

5:21 Have you spoken to someone, only to realize that the person hasn't heard a word you were saying? Jeremiah told the people that their eyes and ears did them no good because they refused to see or hear God's message. The people of Judah and Israel were foolishly deaf when God promised blessings for obedience and destruction for disobedience. When God speaks through his Word or his messengers, we harm ourselves if we fail to listen. God's message will never change us unless we listen to it.

5:22–24 What is your attitude when you come into God's presence? We should come with fear and trembling (that is, awe and respect) because God sets the boundaries of the roaring seas and establishes the rains and harvests. God had to strip away all the benefits that Judah and Israel had grown to respect more than him, with the hope that the people would turn back to God. Don't wait until God removes your cherished resources before committing yourself to him as you should.

So their houses are full of deceit;
Therefore they have become great and rich.

5:28 Deut 32:15; Is 1:23; Jer 7:6; 22:3; Zech 7:10

28 "They are fat, they are sleek,
They also [2]excel in deeds of wickedness;
They do not plead the cause,
The cause of the orphan, that they may prosper;
And they do not defend the rights of the poor.

5:29 Jer 5:9; Mal 3:5

29 'Shall I not punish these *people?*' declares the LORD,
'On a nation such as this
Shall I not avenge Myself?'

5:30 Jer 23:14; Hos 6:10

30 "An appalling and horrible thing
Has happened in the land:

5:31 Ezek 13:6; Mic 2:11

31 The prophets prophesy falsely,
And the priests rule on their *own* authority;
And My people love it so!
But what will you do at the end of it?

Destruction of Jerusalem Impending

6:1 Josh 18:28; Neh 3:14; Jer 1:14; 4:6; 6:22

6 "Flee for safety, O sons of Benjamin,
From the midst of Jerusalem!
Now blow a trumpet in Tekoa
And raise a signal over [3]Beth-haccerem;
For evil looks down from the north,
And a great destruction.

6:2 Deut 28:56; Is 1:8; Jer 4:31

2 "The comely and dainty one, the daughter of Zion, I will cut off.

6:3 Jer 12:10; 2 Kin 25:1; Jer 4:17; Luke 19:43

3 "Shepherds and their flocks will come to her,
They will pitch *their* tents around her,
They will pasture each in his place.

6:4 Jer 6:23; Joel 3:9; Jer 15:8; Zeph 2:4

4 "Prepare war against her;
Arise, and let us attack at noon.
Woe to us, for the day declines,
For the shadows of the evening lengthen!

6:5 Is 32:14; Jer 52:13

5 "Arise, and let us attack by night
And destroy her palaces!"

6:6 Deut 20:19, 20; Jer 32:24; 33:4; Jer 22:17

6 For thus says the LORD of hosts,
"Cut down her trees
And cast up a siege against Jerusalem.
This is the city to be punished,
In whose midst there is only oppression.

6:7 James 3:11f; Jer 20:8; Ezek 7:11, 23; Jer 30:12, 13

7 "As a well keeps its waters fresh,
So she keeps fresh her wickedness.
Violence and destruction are heard in her;
Sickness and wounds are ever before Me.

6:8 Jer 7:28; 17:23; Ezek 23:18; Hos 9:12

8 "Be warned, O Jerusalem,
Or I shall be alienated from you,
And make you a desolation,
A land not inhabited."

2 Lit *pass over,* or, *overlook deeds* **3** I.e. house of the vineyard

---

5:28–29 People and nations who please God treat the fatherless (orphans) justly and care for the poor. Wicked men in Israel treated the defenseless unjustly, which displeased God greatly. Some defenseless people—orphans, the poor, the homeless, and the lonely—are within your reach. What action can you take to help at least one of them?

6:1 The Lord warned Jeremiah's own tribe of Benjamin to flee, not to the security of the great walled city of Jerusalem because it would be under siege, but toward Tekoa, a town about 12 miles south of Jerusalem. The warning smoke signal was lit at Beth-haccerem, halfway between Jerusalem and Bethlehem.

6:3 The shepherds were the leaders of Babylon's armies, and their flocks were their troops.

9 Thus says the LORD of hosts,
"They will thoroughly glean as the vine the remnant of Israel;
Pass your hand again like a grape gatherer
Over the branches."
10 To whom shall I speak and give warning
That they may hear?
Behold, their ears are closed
And they cannot listen.
Behold, the word of the LORD has become a reproach to them;
They have no delight in it.
11 But I am full of the wrath of the LORD;
I am weary with holding *it* in.
"Pour *it* out on the children in the street
And on the gathering of young men together;
For both husband and wife shall be taken,
The aged and the very old.
12 "Their houses shall be turned over to others,
Their fields and their wives together;
For I will stretch out My hand
Against the inhabitants of the land," declares the LORD.
13 "For from the least of them even to the greatest of them,
Everyone is greedy for gain,
And from the prophet even to the priest
Everyone deals falsely.
14 "They have healed the brokenness of My people superficially,
Saying, 'Peace, peace,'
But there is no peace.
15 "Were they ashamed because of the abomination they have done?
They were not even ashamed at all;
They did not even know how to blush.
Therefore they shall fall among those who fall;
At the time that I punish them,
They shall be cast down," says the LORD.

16 Thus says the LORD,
"Stand by the ways and see and ask for the ancient paths,
Where the good way is, and walk in it;
And you will find rest for your souls.
But they said, 'We will not walk *in it.*'
17 "And I set watchmen over you, *saying,*
'Listen to the sound of the trumpet!'
But they said, 'We will not listen.'
18 "Therefore hear, O nations,
And know, O congregation, what is among them.
19 "Hear, O earth: behold, I am bringing disaster on this people,
The fruit of their plans,
Because they have not listened to My words,
And as for My law, they have rejected it also.

6:9 Jer 16:16; 49:9; Obad 5, 6; Jer 8:3; 11:23

6:10 Jer 5:21; 7:26; Acts 7:51; Jer 20:8

6:11 Job 32:18, 19; Mic 3:8; Jer 15:6; 20:9; Jer 7:20; 9:21

6:12 Deut 28:30; Jer 8:10; 38:22, 23; Jer 15:6

6:13 Jer 8:10; Is 56:11; 57:17; Jer 8:10; 22:17

6:14 Jer 8:11; Ezek 13:10

6:15 Jer 3:3; 8:12

6:16 Is 8:20; Jer 12:16; 18:15; 31:21; Mal 4:4; Luke 16:29; Matt 11:29

6:17 Is 21:11; 58:1; Jer 25:4; Ezek 3:17; Hab 2:1

6:19 Is 1:2; Jer 19:3, 15; 22:29; Prov 1:31; Jer 8:9

6:9 The remnant mentioned here is not to be confused with the righteous remnant. This remnant is those left after the first wave of destruction. Like a grape-gatherer, Babylon wouldn't be satisfied until every person was taken. Babylonians invaded Judah three times until they destroyed the nation and its temple completely (2 Kings 24; 25).

6:10 The people became angry and closed their ears. They wanted no part of God's commands because living for God did not appear very exciting. As in Jeremiah's day, people today dislike God's demand for disciplined living. As unsettling as people's responses might be, we must continue to share God's Word. Our responsibility is to present God's Word; their responsibility is to accept it. We must not let what people want to hear determine what we say.

6:14 "Ignore it and maybe it will go away!" Sound familiar? This was Israel's response to Jeremiah's warnings. They kept listening to predictions of peace because they did not like Jeremiah's condemnation of their sin. But denying the truth never changes it; what God says always happens. Sin is never removed by denying its existence. We must confess to God that we have sinned and ask him to forgive us.

6:16 The right path for living is ancient and has been marked out by God. But the people refused to take God's path, going their own way instead. We face the same decision today, going God's old but true way, or following a new path of our own choosing. Don't be misled. The only way to find peace and "rest for your souls" is to walk on God's path.

6:20 Ps 50:7-9; Is 1:11; 66:3; Mic 6:6; Is 60:6; Ex 30:23; Ps 40:6; Amos 5:22

20 "For what purpose does frankincense come to Me from Sheba
And the sweet cane from a distant land?
Your burnt offerings are not acceptable
And your sacrifices are not pleasing to Me."

6:21 Is 8:14; Jer 13:16; Is 9:14-17; Jer 9:21, 22

21 Therefore, thus says the LORD,
"Behold, I am laying stumbling blocks before this people.
And they will stumble against them,
Fathers and sons together;
Neighbor and friend will perish."

The Enemy from the North

6:22 Jer 1:15; 10:22; 50:41-43; Neh 1:9

22 Thus says the LORD,
"Behold, a people is coming from the north land,
And a great nation will be aroused from the remote parts of the earth.

6:23 Is 13:18; Jer 4:29; Jer 50:42; Is 5:30

23 "They seize bow and spear;
They are cruel and have no mercy;
Their voice roars like the sea,
And they ride on horses,
Arrayed as a man for the battle
Against you, O daughter of Zion!"

6:24 Is 28:19; Jer 4:19-21; Is 21:3; Jer 4:31; 13:21; 30:6; 49:24; 50:43

24 We have heard the report of it;
Our hands are limp.
Anguish has seized us,
Pain as of a woman in childbirth.

6:25 Jer 14:18; Judg 5:6; Jer 20:10; 46:5; 49:29

25 Do not go out into the field
And do not walk on the road,
For the enemy has a sword,
Terror is on every side.

6:26 Jer 4:8; Jer 25:34; Mic 1:10; Amos 8:10; Zech 12:10

26 O daughter of my people, put on sackcloth
And roll in ashes;
Mourn as for an only son,
A lamentation most bitter.
For suddenly the destroyer
Will come upon us.

6:27 Jer 1:18; 15:20

27 "I have made you an assayer *and* a tester among My people,
That you may know and assay their way."

6:28 Jer 9:4; Ezek 22:18

28 All of them are stubbornly rebellious,
Going about as a talebearer.
They are bronze and iron;
They, all of them, are corrupt.

6:29 Jer 15:19

29 The bellows blow fiercely,
The lead is consumed by the fire;
In vain the refining goes on,
But the wicked are not separated.

6:30 Ps 119:119; Is 1:22; Jer 7:29; Hos 9:17; Zech 11:8

30 They call them rejected silver,
Because the LORD has rejected them.

Message at the Temple Gate

7:2 Jer 17:19; 26:2

7 The word that came to Jeremiah from the LORD, saying,
2 "Stand in the gate of the LORD'S house and proclaim there this word and say,
'Hear the word of the LORD, all you of Judah, who enter by these gates to worship the
LORD!' "

6:20 Sheba, located in southwest Arabia, was a center of trade in incense and spices used in pagan religious rituals.

6:29–30 Metal is purified by fire. As it is heated, impurities are burned away and only the pure metal remains. As God tested the people of Judah, however, he could find no purity in their lives. They continued in their sinful ways. Do you see impurities in your life that should be burned away? Confess these to God and allow him to purify you as he sees fit. Take time right now to reflect on the areas of your life that he has already refined; then thank him for what he is doing.

7:1—10:25 As this section opens, God sends Jeremiah to the temple gates to confront the false belief that God will not let harm

3 Thus says the LORD of hosts, the God of Israel, "Amend your ways and your deeds,
and I will let you dwell in this place.
4 "Do not trust in deceptive words, saying, 'This is the temple of the LORD, the temple
of the LORD, the temple of the LORD.'
5 "For if you truly amend your ways and your deeds, if you truly practice justice between a man and his neighbor,
6 *if* you do not oppress the alien, the orphan, or the widow, and do not shed innocent
blood in this place, nor walk after other gods to your own ruin,
7 then I will let you dwell in this place, in the land that I gave to your fathers forever
and ever.
8 "Behold, you are trusting in deceptive words to no avail.
9 "Will you steal, murder, and commit adultery and swear falsely, and offer sacrifices
to Baal and walk after other gods that you have not known,
10 then come and stand before Me in this house, which is called by My name, and say,
'We are delivered!'—that you may do all these abominations?
11 "Has this house, which is called by My name, become a den of robbers in your sight?
Behold, I, even I, have seen *it,*" declares the LORD.
12 "But go now to My place which was in Shiloh, where I made My name dwell at the
first, and see what I did to it because of the wickedness of My people Israel.
13 "And now, because you have done all these things," declares the LORD, "and I spoke
to you, rising up early and speaking, but you did not hear, and I called you but you did
not answer,
14 therefore, I will do to the house which is called by My name, in which you trust, and
to the place which I gave you and your fathers, as I did to Shiloh.
15 "I will cast you out of My sight, as I have cast out all your brothers, all the offspring
of Ephraim.
16 "As for you, do not pray for this people, and do not lift up cry or prayer for them, and
do not intercede with Me; for I do not hear you.
17 "Do you not see what they are doing in the cities of Judah and in the streets of Jerusalem?
18 "The children gather wood, and the fathers kindle the fire, and the women knead
dough to make cakes for the queen of heaven; and *they* pour out drink offerings to other
gods in order to spite Me.
19 "Do they spite Me?" declares the LORD. "Is it not themselves *they spite,* to their own
shame?"
20 Therefore thus says the Lord GOD, "Behold, My anger and My wrath will be poured
out on this place, on man and on beast and on the trees of the field and on the fruit of
the ground; and it will burn and not be quenched."

7:4 Jer 7:8; Mic 3:11
7:5 Is 1:19; Jer 4:1, 2; 1 Kin 6:12; Jer 21:12; 22:3
7:6 Ex 22:21-24; Jer 5:28; Jer 2:34; 19:4; Deut 6:14, 15; 8:19; 11:28; Jer 13:10
7:7 Deut 4:40; Jer 3:18
7:9 Jer 11:13, 17; Ex 20:3; Jer 7:6; 19:4
7:10 Ezek 23:39
7:11 Matt 21:13; Mark 11:17; Luke 19:46
7:12 Ps 78:60-64
7:13 Jer 7:25; Jer 35:17; Prov 1:24; Is 65:12; 66:4
7:14 Deut 12:5; 1 Kin 9:7
7:15 Jer 15:1; 52:3; Ps 78:67; Hos 7:13; 9:13; 12:1
7:16 Ex 32:10; Deut 9:14
7:18 Deut 32:16, 21; 1 Kin 14:9; 16:2
7:19 Job 35:6; 1 Cor 10:22; Jer 9:19; 15:9; 22:22
7:20 Is 42:25; Jer 6:11, 12; 42:18; Lam 2:3-5; 4:11; Jer 8:13

---

come to the temple and those who live near it. Jeremiah rebukes the people for their false and worthless religion, their idolatry, and the shameless behavior of the people and their leaders. Judah, he says, is ripe for judgment and exile. This happened during the reign of Jehoiakim, a puppet of Egypt. The nation, in shock over the death of Josiah, was going through a spiritual reversal that removed much of the good Josiah had done. The themes of this section are false religion, idolatry, and hypocrisy. Jeremiah was almost put to death for this sermon, but he was saved by the officials of Judah (see chapter 26).

7:2–3 The people followed a worship ritual but maintained a sinful life-style. It was religion without personal commitment to God. We can easily do the same. Attending church, taking communion, teaching church school, singing in the choir—all are empty exercises unless we are truly doing them for God. It is good to do these activities, not because we ought to do them for the church, but because we want to do them for God.

7:9–11 There are several parallels between how the people of Judah viewed their temple and how many today view their churches. (1) *They didn't make the temple part of their daily living.* We go to beautiful churches well-prepared for worship, but often we don't take the presence of God with us through the week. (2) *The image of the temple became more important than the substance of faith.* The image of going to church and belonging to a group can become more important than a life changed for God. (3) *The people used their temple as a sanctuary.* Many use religious affiliation as a hideout, thinking it will protect them from evil and problems.

7:11–12 Jesus used these words from 7:11 in clearing the temple (Mark 11:17; Luke 19:46). This passage applied to the evil in the temple in Jesus' day as well as in Jeremiah's. God's tabernacle had been at Shiloh, but Shiloh had been abandoned (Psalm 78:60; Jeremiah 26:6). If God did not preserve Shiloh because the tabernacle was there, why would he preserve Jerusalem because of the temple?

7:15 Ephraim is another name for Israel, the northern kingdom, which had been taken into captivity by Assyria in 722 B.C.

7:18 The queen of heaven was a name for Ishtar, the Mesopotamian goddess of love and fertility. After the fall of Jerusalem, the refugees from Judah who fled to Egypt continued to worship her (44:17). A papyrus dating from the 5th century B.C., found at Hermopolis in Egypt, mentions the queen of heaven among the gods honored by the Jewish community living there.

7:19 This verse answers the question, "Who gets hurt when we turn away from God?" We do! Separating ourselves from God is like keeping a green plant away from sunlight or water. God is our only source of spiritual strength. Cut yourself off from him, and you cut off life itself.

21 Thus says the LORD of hosts, the God of Israel, "Add your burnt offerings to your
sacrifices and eat flesh.
22 "For I did not speak to your fathers, or command them in the day that I brought them
out of the land of Egypt, concerning burnt offerings and sacrifices.
23 "But this is what I commanded them, saying, 'Obey My voice, and I will be your God,
and you will be My people; and you will walk in all the way which I command you, that
it may be well with you.'
24 "Yet they did not obey or incline their ear, but walked in *their own* counsels *and* in
the stubbornness of their evil heart, and went backward and not forward.
25 "Since the day that your fathers came out of the land of Egypt until this day, I have
sent you all My servants the prophets, daily rising early and sending *them.*
26 "Yet they did not listen to Me or incline their ear, but stiffened their neck; they did
more evil than their fathers.
27 "You shall speak all these words to them, but they will not listen to you; and you shall
call to them, but they will not answer you.
28 "You shall say to them, 'This is the nation that did not obey the voice of the LORD
their God or accept correction; truth has perished and has been cut off from their mouth.
29 'Cut off your hair and cast *it* away,
And take up a lamentation on the bare heights;
For the LORD has rejected and forsaken
The generation of His wrath.'
30 "For the sons of Judah have done that which is evil in My sight," declares the LORD,
"they have set their detestable things in the house which is called by My name, to defile it.
31 "They have built the high places of Topheth, which is in the valley of the son of Hinnom, to burn their sons and their daughters in the fire, which I did not command, and it
did not come into My mind.
32 "Therefore, behold, days are coming," declares the LORD, "when it will no longer be
called Topheth, or the valley of the son of Hinnom, but the valley of the Slaughter; for
they will bury in Topheth because there is no *other* place.
33 "The dead bodies of this people will be food for the birds of the sky and for the beasts
of the earth; and no one will frighten *them away.*
34 "Then I will make to cease from the cities of Judah and from the streets of Jerusalem
the voice of joy and the voice of gladness, the voice of the bridegroom and the voice of
the bride; for the land will become a ruin.

The Sin and Treachery of Judah

8 "At that time," declares the LORD, "they will bring out the bones of the kings of Judah and the bones of its princes, and the bones of the priests and the bones of the
prophets, and the bones of the inhabitants of Jerusalem from their graves.
2 "They will spread them out to the sun, the moon and to all the host of heaven, which
they have loved and which they have served, and which they have gone after and which
they have sought, and which they have worshiped. They will not be gathered or buried;
they will be as dung on the face of the ground.
3 "And death will be chosen rather than life by all the remnant that remains of this evil
family, that remains in all the places to which I have driven them," declares the LORD of
hosts.

7:21 Is 1:11; Jer 6:20; 14:12; Amos 5:22; Ezek 33:25
7:22 1 Sam 15:22; Ps 51:16; Hos 6:6
7:23 Ex 15:26; 16:32; Deut 6:3; Ex 19:5, 6; Lev 26:12; Jer 11:4; 13:11; Is 3:10
7:24 Deut 29:19; Ps 81:11; Jer 11:8; Ezek 20:8, 13, 16
7:25 2 Chr 36:15; Luke 11:49
7:26 Neh 9:16; Jer 17:23; 19:15; Matt 23:32
7:27 Ezek 2:7; Is 50:2; 65:12; Zech 7:13
7:28 Is 59:14, 15; Jer 9:5
7:29 Job 1:20; Is 15:2; 22:12; Jer 16:6; Mic 1:16; Jer 3:21; 9:17
7:30 2 Kin 21:3f; 2 Chr 33:3-5, 7; Jer 32:34, 35; Ezek 7:20
7:31 2 Kin 23:10; Ps 106:38; Deut 17:3
7:33 Deut 28:26; Ps 79:2;
7:34 Is 24:7, 8; Jer 16:9; 25:10; Ezek 26:13; Hos 2:11
8:1 Ezek 6:5
8:2 2 Kin 23:5; Jer 19:13; Zeph 1:5; Acts 7:42; Jer 22:19; 36:30; 2 Kin 9:37; Ps 83:10; Jer 9:22
8:3 Job 3:21, 22; 7:15, 16; Jon 4:3; Rev 9:6; Deut 30:1, 4; Jer 23:3, 8; 29:14

7:21–23 God had set up a system of sacrifices to encourage the people to joyfully obey him (see the book of Leviticus). He required the people to make these sacrifices, not because the sacrifices themselves pleased him, but because they caused the people to recognize their sin and refocus on living for God. They faithfully made the sacrifices but forgot the reason they were offering them, and thus they disobeyed God. Jeremiah reminded the people that acting out religious rituals was meaningless unless they were prepared to obey God in all areas of life. (See the chart in Hosea 7.)

7:25 From the time of Moses to the end of the Old Testament period, God sent many prophets to Israel and Judah. No matter how bad the circumstances were, God always raised up a prophet to speak against their stubborn spiritual attitudes.

7:31–32 The high places (or altars) of Topheth (meaning "fire-place") were set up in the valley of the son of Hinnom, where debris and rubbish from the city were thrown away. This altar was used to worship Molech—a god who required child sacrifice (2 Kings 23:10). Their valley of sacrifice would become their valley of slaughter by the Babylonians. At the place where the people had killed their children in sinful idol worship, they themselves would be slaughtered.

8:1–2 The threat that the graves of Judah's people would be opened was horrible to a people who highly honored the dead and believed that it was the highest desecration to open graves. This would be an ironic punishment for idol worshipers: Their bones would be laid out before the sun, moon, and stars—the gods they thought could save them.

4 "You shall say to them, 'Thus says the LORD,
"Do *men* fall and not get up again?
Does one turn away and not repent?
5 "Why then has this people, Jerusalem,
Turned away in continual apostasy?
They hold fast to deceit,
They refuse to return.
6 "I have listened and heard,
They have spoken what is not right;
No man repented of his wickedness,
Saying, 'What have I done?'
Everyone turned to his course,
Like a horse charging into the battle.
7 "Even the stork in the sky
Knows her seasons;
And the turtledove and the swift and the thrush
Observe the time of their migration;
But My people do not know
The ordinance of the LORD.

8 "How can you say, 'We are wise,
And the law of the LORD is with us'?
But behold, the lying pen of the scribes
Has made *it* into a lie.
9 "The wise men are put to shame,
They are dismayed and caught;
Behold, they have rejected the word of the LORD,
And what kind of wisdom do they have?
10 "Therefore I will give their wives to others,
Their fields to new owners;
Because from the least even to the greatest
Everyone is greedy for gain;
From the prophet even to the priest
Everyone practices deceit.
11 "They heal the brokenness of the daughter of My people superficially,
Saying, 'Peace, peace,'
But there is no peace.
12 "Were they ashamed because of the abomination they had done?
They certainly were not ashamed,
And they did not know how to blush;
Therefore they shall fall among those who fall;
At the time of their punishment they shall be brought down,"
Says the LORD.

13 "I will surely snatch them away," declares the LORD;
"There will be no grapes on the vine
And no figs on the fig tree,
And the leaf will wither;
And what I have given them will pass away." ' "
14 Why are we sitting still?
Assemble yourselves, and let us go into the fortified cities
And let us perish there,
Because the LORD our God has doomed us
And given us poisoned water to drink,
For we have sinned against the LORD.

8:4
Prov 24:16; Amos 5:2; Mic 7:8

8:5
Jer 5:6; 7:24; Jer 5:27; 9:6; Jer 5:3

8:6
Ps 14:2; Mal 3:16; Ezek 22:30; Mic 7:2; Rev 9:20; Job 39:21-25

8:7
Prov 6:6-8; Is 1:3; Song 2:12; Jer 5:4

8:8
Job 5:12, 13; Jer 4:22; Rom 1:22

8:9
Is 19:11; Jer 6:15; 1 Cor 1:27; Jer 6:19

8:10
Deut 28:30; Jer 6:12, 13; 38:22f; Is 56:11; 57:17; Jer 6:13

8:11
Jer 6:14; 14:13, 14; Lam 2:14; Ezek 13:10

8:12
Ps 52:1, 7; Is 3:9; Jer 3:3; 6:15; Zeph 3:5; Is 9:14; Jer 6:21; Hos 4:5; Deut 32:35; Jer 10:15

8:13
Jer 14:12; Ezek 22:20, 21; Jer 5:17; 7:20; Joel 1:7; Matt 21:19; Luke 13:6

8:14
Jer 4:5; 2 Sam 20:6; Jer 35:11; Deut 29:18; Ps 69:21; Jer 9:15; 23:15; Lam 3:19; Matt 27:34; Jer 3:25; 14:20

8:4–6 When people fall down or realize that they are headed in the wrong direction, it only makes sense for them to get up or change directions. But as God watched the nation, he saw people living sinful lives by choice, deceiving themselves that there would be no consequences. They had lost perspective concerning God's will for their lives and were trying to minimize their sin. Are there some indicators that you have fallen down or are heading the wrong way? What are you doing to get back on the right path?

8:15 Jer 8:11; 14:19

15 *We* waited for peace, but no good *came;*
For a time of healing, but behold, terror!

8:16 Judg 18:29; Jer 4:15; Judg 5:22; Jer 3:24; 10:25

16 From Dan is heard the snorting of his horses,
At the sound of the neighing of his stallions
The whole land quakes;
For they come and devour the land and its fullness,
The city and its inhabitants.

8:17 Num 21:6; Deut 32:24; Ps 58:4, 5

17 "For behold, I am sending serpents against you,
Adders, for which there is no charm,
And they will bite you," declares the LORD.

8:18 Is 22:4; Lam 1:16, 17; Jer 23:9; Lam 5:17

18 My sorrow is beyond healing,
My heart is faint *within me!*

8:19 Is 13:5; 39:3; Jer 4:16; 9:16; Deut 32:21; Jer 7:19; Ps 31:6

19 Behold, listen! The cry of the daughter of my people from a distant land:
"Is the LORD not in Zion? Is her King not within her?"
"Why have they provoked Me with their graven images, with foreign idols?"
20 "Harvest is past, summer is ended,
And we are not saved."

8:21 Jer 4:19; 9:1; 14:17; Jer 14:2; Joel 2:6; Nah 2:10

21 For the brokenness of the daughter of my people I am broken;
I mourn, dismay has taken hold of me.

8:22 Gen 37:25; Jer 46:11; Jer 14:19; 30:13

22 Is there no balm in Gilead?
Is there no physician there?
Why then has not the health of the daughter of my people been restored?

A Lament over Zion

9:1 Is 22:4; Jer 8:18; 13:17; Lam 2:18; Jer 6:26; 8:21, 22

9 Oh that my head were waters
And my eyes a fountain of tears,
That I might weep day and night
For the slain of the daughter of my people!

9:2 Ps 55:6, 7; 120:5, 6; Jer 5:7, 8; 23:10; Hos 4:2; Jer 5:11; 12:1, 6

2 Oh that I had in the desert
A wayfarers' lodging place;
That I might leave my people
And go from them!
For all of them are adulterers,
An assembly of treacherous men.

9:3 Ps 64:3; Is 59:4; Jer 9:8; Jer 4:22; Judg 2:10; 1 Sam 2:12; Jer 4:22; 5:4, 5; Hos 4:1; 1 Cor 15:34

3 "They bend their tongue *like* their bow;
Lies and not truth prevail in the land;
For they proceed from evil to evil,
And they do not know Me," declares the LORD.

9:4 Ps 12:2; Prov 26:24, 25; Jer 9:8; Mic 7:5, 6; Jer 12:6; Gen 27:35; Ps 15:3; Prov 10:18; Jer 6:28

4 "Let everyone be on guard against his neighbor,
And do not trust any brother;
Because every brother deals craftily,
And every neighbor goes about as a slanderer.

9:5 Mic 6:12; Jer 12:13; 51:58, 64

5 "Everyone deceives his neighbor
And does not speak the truth,
They have taught their tongue to speak lies;
They weary themselves committing iniquity.

9:6 Ps 120:5, 6; Jer 5:27; 8:5; Job 21:14, 15; Prov 1:24; Jer 11:10; 13:10; John 3:19, 20

6 "Your dwelling is in the midst of deceit;
Through deceit they refuse to know Me," declares the LORD.

8:16 Dan was the northernmost tribe in Israel.

8:18 Jeremiah was pleading with God to save his people.

8:20–22 These words vividly portray Jeremiah's emotion as he watched his people reject God. He responded with anguish to a world dying in sin. We watch that same world still dying in sin, still rejecting God. But how often is our heart broken for our lost friends and neighbors, our lost world? Only when we have Jeremiah's kind of passionate concern will we be moved to help. We must begin by asking God to break our hearts for the world he loves.

8:22 Gilead was famous for its healing balm (medicine). This is a rhetorical question. The obvious answer is, "Yes—God," but Israel was not applying the "balm"; they were not obeying the Lord. Although the people's spiritual sickness was still very deep, it could be healed. But the people refused the medicine. God could heal their self-inflicted wounds, but he would not force his healing on them.

9:1–6 Jeremiah felt conflicting emotions concerning his people. Lying, deceit, treachery, adultery, and idolatry had become common sins. He was angered by their sin, but he had compassion too. He was set apart from them by his mission for God, but he was also one of them. Jesus had similar feelings when he stood before Jerusalem, the city that would reject him (Matthew 23:37).

7 Therefore thus says the LORD of hosts,
"Behold, I will refine them and assay them;
For what *else* can I do, because of the daughter of My people?
8 "Their tongue is a deadly arrow;
It speaks deceit;
With his mouth one speaks peace to his neighbor,
But inwardly he sets an ambush for him.
9 "Shall I not punish them for these things?" declares the LORD.
"On a nation such as this
Shall I not avenge Myself?

10 "For the mountains I will take up a weeping and wailing,
And for the pastures of the wilderness a dirge,
Because they are laid waste so that no one passes through,
And the lowing of the cattle is not heard;
Both the birds of the sky and the beasts have fled; they are gone.
11 "I will make Jerusalem a heap of ruins,
A haunt of jackals;
And I will make the cities of Judah a desolation, without inhabitant."
12 Who is the wise man that may understand this? And *who is* he to whom the mouth
of the LORD has spoken, that he may declare it? Why is the land ruined, laid waste like
a desert, so that no one passes through?
13 The LORD said, "Because they have forsaken My law which I set before them, and
have not obeyed My voice nor walked according to it,
14 but have walked after the stubbornness of their heart and after the Baals, as their
fathers taught them,"
15 therefore thus says the LORD of hosts, the God of Israel, "behold, I will feed them,
this people, with wormwood and give them poisoned water to drink.
16 "I will scatter them among the nations, whom neither they nor their fathers have
known; and I will send the sword after them until I have annihilated them."
17 Thus says the LORD of hosts,
"Consider and call for the mourning women, that they may come;
And send for the wailing women, that they may come!
18 "Let them make haste and take up a wailing for us,
That our eyes may shed tears
And our eyelids flow with water.
19 "For a voice of wailing is heard from Zion,
'How are we ruined!
We are put to great shame,
For we have left the land,
Because they have cast down our dwellings.' "
20 Now hear the word of the LORD, O you women,
And let your ear receive the word of His mouth;
Teach your daughters wailing,
And everyone her neighbor a dirge.
21 For death has come up through our windows;
It has entered our palaces
To cut off the children from the streets,
The young men from the town squares.
22 Speak, "Thus says the LORD,
'The corpses of men will fall like dung on the open field,
And like the sheaf after the reaper,
But no one will gather *them*.' "
23 Thus says the LORD, "Let not a wise man boast of his wisdom, and let not the mighty
man boast of his might, let not a rich man boast of his riches;
24 but let him who boasts boast of this, that he understands and knows Me, that I am

9:7 Is 1:25; Jer 6:27; Mal 3:3; Hos 11:8
9:8 Jer 9:3; Ps 28:3; Jer 5:26
9:9 Is 1:24; Jer 5:9, 29
9:10 Jer 4:24; 7:29; Jer 4:26; Hos 4:3; Jer 12:4, 10; Ezek 14:15; 29:11; 33:28; Jer 4:25; 12:4; Hos 4:3
9:11 Is 25:2; Jer 51:37; Is 13:22; 34:13; Jer 4:27; 26:9
9:12 Ps 107:43; Is 42:23; Hos 14:9; Jer 9:20; 23:16; Ps 107:34; Jer 23:10
9:13 2 Chr 7:19; Ps 89:30; Jer 5:19; 22:9
9:14 Jer 7:24; 11:8; Rom 1:21-24; Jer 2:8, 23; 23:27; Gal 1:14; 1 Pet 1:18
9:15 Ps 80:5; Deut 29:18; Jer 8:14; 23:15; Lam 3:15
9:16 Lev 26:33; Deut 28:64; Jer 13:24; Jer 44:27; Ezek 5:2, 12
9:17 2 Chr 35:25; Eccl 12:5; Amos 5:16
9:18 Is 22:4; Jer 9:1; 14:17
9:19 Jer 7:29; Ezek 7:16-18; Deut 28:29; Jer 4:13; Jer 7:15; 15:1
9:20 Is 32:9
9:21 2 Chr 36:17; Jer 15:7; 18:21; Ezek 9:5, 6; Amos 6:9, 10; Jer 6:11
9:22 Ps 83:10; Is 5:25; Jer 8:2; 16:4; 25:33
9:23 Eccl 9:11; Is 47:10; Ezek 28:3-7; 1 Kin 20:10, 11; Is 10:8-12; Job 31:24, 25; Ps 49:6-9
9:24 Ps 20:7; 44:8; Is 41:16; Jer 4:2; 1 Cor 1:31; 2 Cor 10:17; Gal 6:14; Ex 34:6, 7; Ps 36:5, 7; 51:1; Is 61:8; Mic 7:18

9:23–24 People tend to admire four qualities in others: human wisdom, power (strength), kindness, and riches. But God puts a higher priority on knowing him personally and living a life that reflects his justice and righteousness. What do you want people to admire most about you?

the LORD who exercises lovingkindness, justice and righteousness on earth; for I delight
in these things," declares the LORD.
25 "Behold, the days are coming," declares the LORD,
"that I will punish all who are circumcised and yet uncircumcised—
26 Egypt and Judah, and Edom and the sons of Ammon, and Moab and all those inhabiting the desert who clip the hair on their temples; for all the nations are uncircumcised, and all the house of Israel are uncircumcised of heart."

9:25 Jer 4:4; Rom 2:28, 29

9:26 Jer 25:23; Lev 26:41; Jer 4:4; 6:10; Ezek 44:7; Rom 2:28

A Satire on Idolatry

10 Hear the word which the LORD speaks to you, O house of Israel.
2 Thus says the LORD,
"Do not learn the way of the nations,
And do not be terrified by the signs of the heavens
Although the nations are terrified by them;
3 For the customs of the peoples are delusion;
Because it is wood cut from the forest,
The work of the hands of a craftsman with a cutting tool.
4 "They decorate *it* with silver and with gold;
They fasten it with nails and with hammers
So that it will not totter.
5 "Like a scarecrow in a cucumber field are they,
And they cannot speak;
They must be carried,
Because they cannot walk!
Do not fear them,
For they can do no harm,
Nor can they do any good."

6 There is none like You, O LORD;
You are great, and great is Your name in might.
7 Who would not fear You, O King of the nations?
Indeed it is Your due!
For among all the wise men of the nations
And in all their kingdoms,
There is none like You.
8 But they are altogether stupid and foolish
In their discipline of delusion—their idol is wood!
9 Beaten silver is brought from Tarshish,
And gold from Uphaz,
The work of a craftsman and of the hands of a goldsmith;
Violet and purple are their clothing;
They are all the work of skilled men.
10 But the LORD is the true God;
He is the living God and the everlasting King.
At His wrath the earth quakes,
And the nations cannot endure His indignation.

10:2 Lev 18:3; 20:23; Deut 12:30

10:3 Jer 14:22; Is 44:9-20

10:4 Is 40:19; Is 40:20; 41:7

10:5 Ps 115:5; Is 46:7; Jer 10:14; 1 Cor 12:2; Ps 115:7; Is 46:1, 7; Is 41:23, 24

10:6 Ex 15:11; Deut 33:26; Ps 86:8, 10; Jer 10:16; Ps 48:1; 96:4; Is 12:6; Jer 32:18

10:7 Rev 15:4; Ps 22:28; Dan 2:27, 28; 1 Cor 1:19, 20

10:8 Jer 4:22; 5:4; 10:14

10:9 Is 40:19; Ps 72:10; Is 23:6; Dan 10:5; Ps 115:4

10:10 Is 65:16; Jer 4:2; Ps 10:16; 29:10; Jer 4:24; 50:46; Ps 76:7

9:25–26 Circumcision went back to the time of Abraham. For the people of Israel it was a symbol of their covenant relationship to God (Genesis 17:9–14). Circumcision was also practiced by pagan nations, but not as the sign of a covenant with God. By Jeremiah's time, the Israelites had forgotten the spiritual significance of circumcision even though they continued to do the physical ritual.

10:2–3 Most people would like to know the future. Decisions would be easier, certain failures avoided, and some successes assured. The people of Judah wanted to know the future too, and they tried to discern it through reading the signs in the sky. Jeremiah's response applies today: God made the earth and the heavens, including stars that people consult and worship (10:12). No one will discover the future in made-up charts of God's stars. But God, who promises to guide you, knows your future and will be with you all the way. He may not reveal your future to you, but he will walk with you as the future unfolds. Don't trust the stars; trust the One who made the stars.

10:8 Those who put their trust in a chunk of wood, even though it is carved well and clothed beautifully, are foolish. The simplest person who worships God is wiser than the wisest person who worships a worthless substitute, because this person has discerned who God really is. In what or whom do you place your trust?

10:9 Tarshish was located at the westward limit of the ancient world, perhaps in what is now Spain (see Jonah 1:3). It was a source of silver, tin, lead, and iron for Tyre (Ezekiel 27:12). The location of Uphaz is unknown. Instead, it may be a metallurgical term for "refined gold." No matter how well made or how beautiful idols are, they can never have the power and life of the true and living God.

11 Thus you shall say to them, "The gods that did not make the heavens and the earth
will perish from the earth and from under the heavens."
12 *It is* He who made the earth by His power,
Who established the world by His wisdom;
And by His understanding He has stretched out the heavens.
13 When He utters His voice, *there is* a tumult of waters in the heavens,
And He causes the clouds to ascend from the end of the earth;
He makes lightning for the rain,
And brings out the wind from His storehouses.
14 Every man is stupid, devoid of knowledge;
Every goldsmith is put to shame by his idols;
For his molten images are deceitful,
And there is no breath in them.
15 They are worthless, a work of mockery;
In the time of their punishment they will perish.
16 The portion of Jacob is not like these;
For the Maker of all is He,
And Israel is the tribe of His inheritance;
The LORD of hosts is His name.

17 Pick up your bundle from the ground,
You who dwell under siege!
18 For thus says the LORD,
"Behold, I am slinging out the inhabitants of the land
At this time,
And will cause them distress,
That they may be found."

19 Woe is me, because of my injury!
My wound is incurable.
But I said, "Truly this is a sickness,
And I must bear it."
20 My tent is destroyed,
And all my ropes are broken;
My sons have gone from me and are no more.
There is no one to stretch out my tent again
Or to set up my curtains.
21 For the shepherds have become stupid
And have not sought the LORD;
Therefore they have not prospered,
And all their flock is scattered.
22 The sound of a report! Behold, it comes—
A great commotion out of the land of the north—
To make the cities of Judah
A desolation, a haunt of jackals.

23 I know, O LORD, that a man's way is not in himself,
Nor is it in a man who walks to direct his steps.
24 Correct me, O LORD, but with justice;
Not with Your anger, or You will bring me to nothing.
25 Pour out Your wrath on the nations that do not know You
And on the families that do not call Your name;
For they have devoured Jacob;
They have devoured him and consumed him
And have laid waste his habitation.

10:11 Ps 96:5; Is 2:18; Zeph 2:11

10:12 Gen 1:1, 6; Job 38:4-7; Ps 136:5; 148:4, 5; Jer 51:15, 19; Ps 78:69; Is 45:18; Job 9:8; Is 40:22

10:13 Ps 29:3-9; Job 36:27-29; Ps 135:7

10:14 Jer 10:8; 51:17, 18

10:15 Is 41:24; Jer 8:19; 14:22; Jer 8:12; 51:18

10:16 Ps 16:5; 73:26; 119:57; Jer 51:19; Lam 3:24; Is 45:7; Jer 10:12; Deut 32:9; Ps 74:2; Jer 31:35; 32:18

10:17 Ezek 12:3-12

10:18 1 Sam 25.29

10:19 Jer 4:31; Jer 14:17; Mic 7:9

10:20 Jer 4:20; Lam 2:4; Jer 31:15; Lam 1:5; Is 51:18

10:21 Jer 2:8; Jer 23:2

10:22 Jer 4:15; Jer 1:14; 25:9; Jer 9:11; 49:33

10:23 Prov 16:1; 20:24; Is 26:7

10:24 Ps 6:1; 38:1

10:25 Ps 79:6, 7; Zeph 3:8; Job 18:21; 1 Thess 4:5; 2 Thess 1:8; Zeph 1:6; Jer 8:16; 50:7, 17

10:19–21 In this section, Jeremiah uses the picture of nomads wandering in the wilderness trying to pitch their tents. The shepherds of the nation are the evil leaders responsible for the distress. The flock is the people of Judah. Instead of guiding the people to God, the leaders were leading them astray.

10:23–24 God's ability to direct our lives well is infinitely beyond our ability. Sometimes we are afraid of God's power and God's plans because we know his power would easily crush us if he used it against us. Don't be afraid to let God correct your plans. He will give you wisdom if you are willing.

3. Jeremiah prophesies destruction

The Broken Covenant

11 The word which came to Jeremiah from the LORD, saying,
2 "Hear the words of this covenant, and speak to the men of Judah and to the
inhabitants of Jerusalem;
3 and say to them, 'Thus says the LORD, the God of Israel, "Cursed is the man who
does not heed the words of this covenant
4 which I commanded your forefathers in the day that I brought them out of the land
of Egypt, from the iron furnace, saying, 'Listen to My voice, and do according to all which
I command you; so you shall be My people, and I will be your God,'
5 in order to confirm the oath which I swore to your forefathers, to give them a land
flowing with milk and honey, as *it is* this day." ' " Then I said, "Amen, O LORD."
6 And the LORD said to me, "Proclaim all these words in the cities of Judah and in
the streets of Jerusalem, saying, 'Hear the words of this covenant and do them.
7 'For I solemnly warned your fathers in the day that I brought them up from the land
of Egypt, even to this day, warning persistently, saying, "Listen to My voice."
8 'Yet they did not obey or incline their ear, but walked, each one, in the stubbornness
of his evil heart; therefore I brought on them all the words of this covenant, which I
commanded *them* to do, but they did not.' "
9 Then the LORD said to me, "A conspiracy has been found among the men of Judah
and among the inhabitants of Jerusalem.
10 "They have turned back to the iniquities of their ancestors who refused to hear My
words, and they have gone after other gods to serve them; the house of Israel and the
house of Judah have broken My covenant which I made with their fathers."
11 Therefore thus says the LORD, "Behold I am bringing disaster on them which they
will not be able to escape; though they will cry to Me, yet I will not listen to them.
12 "Then the cities of Judah and the inhabitants of Jerusalem will go and cry to the gods
to whom they burn incense, but they surely will not save them in the time of their
disaster.
13 "For your gods are as many as your cities, O Judah; and as many as the streets of
Jerusalem are the altars you have set up to the shameful thing, altars to burn incense to
Baal.
14 "Therefore do not pray for this people, nor lift up a cry or prayer for them; for I will
not listen when they call to Me because of their disaster.
15 "What right has My beloved in My house
When she has done many vile deeds?
Can the sacrificial flesh take away from you your disaster,
So *that* you can rejoice?"
16 The LORD called your name,
"A green olive tree, beautiful in fruit and form";
With the noise of a great tumult
He has kindled fire on it,
And its branches are worthless.
17 The LORD of hosts, who planted you, has pronounced evil against you because of
the evil of the house of Israel and of the house of Judah, which they have done to pro-
voke Me by offering up sacrifices to Baal.

11:3 Deut 27:26; Jer 17:5; Gal 3:10
11:4 Ex 24:3-8; Jer 31:32; Deut 4:20; 1 Kin 8:51; Lev 26:3; Deut 11:27; Jer 7:23; 26:13; Jer 24:7; Zech 8:8
11:5 Ex 13:5; Deut 7:12; Ps 105:9; Jer 32:22; Jer 28:6
11:6 Jer 3:12; 7:2; John 13:17; Rom 2:13; James 1:22
11:7 1 Sam 8:9; Ex 15:26; 2 Chr 36:15
11:8 Ezek 20:8; Lev 26:14-43
11:9 Ezek 22:25; Hos 6:9
11:10 1 Sam 15:11; Jer 3:10, 11; Ezek 20:18; Deut 9:7; Ps 78:8-10; Jer 13:10; Judg 2:11-13; Jer 3:6-11; Ezek 16:59
11:11 2 Kin 22:16; Jer 6:19; 11:17; Is 24:17; Jer 25:35; Ps 18:41; Prov 1:28; Is 1:15; Ezek 8:18; Mic 3:4; Zech 7:13
11:12 Deut 32:37; Jer 44:17
11:13 2 Kin 23:13; Jer 2:28; Jer 3:24; Jer 7:9
11:14 Ex 32:10; Jer 7:16; 14:11; 1 John 5:16; Ps 66:18; Hos 5:6
11:15 Jer 13:27; Ezek 16:25
11:16 Ps 52:8; Rom 11:17; Ps 83:2; Ps 80:16; Is 27:11; Jer 21:14
11:17 Is 5:2; Jer 2:21; 12:2; Jer 1:14

11:1—13:27 This section concerns the broken covenant, and a rebuke for those who returned to idols after Josiah's reform. Jeremiah's rebuke prompted a threat against his life by his own countrymen. As Jeremiah suffered, he pondered the prosperity of the wicked. As he brought these words to a close, he used a ruined linen waistband and filled wineskins as object lessons of God's coming judgment (see the note on 13:1–11).

11:14 At first glance this command is shocking—God tells Jeremiah not to pray and says he won't listen to the people if they pray. A time comes when God must dispense justice. Sin brings its own bitter reward. If the people were unrepentant and continued in their sin, neither their prayers nor Jeremiah's would prevent God's judgment. Their only hope was repentance—sorrow for sin, turning from it, and turning to God. How can we keep praying for God's help if we haven't committed our lives to him? God's blessings come when we are committed to him, not when we selfishly hang on to our sinful ways.

Plots against Jeremiah

18 Moreover, the LORD made it known to me and I knew it;
Then You showed me their deeds.
19 But I was like a gentle lamb led to the slaughter;
And I did not know that they had devised plots against me, *saying,*
"Let us destroy the tree with its fruit,
And let us cut him off from the land of the living,
That his name be remembered no more."
20 But, O LORD of hosts, who judges righteously,
Who tries the feelings and the heart,
Let me see Your vengeance on them,
For to You have I committed my cause.
21 Therefore thus says the LORD concerning the men of Anathoth, who seek your life,
saying, "Do not prophesy in the name of the LORD, so that you will not die at our hand";
22 therefore, thus says the LORD of hosts, "Behold, I am about to punish them! The
young men will die by the sword, their sons and daughters will die by famine;
23 and a remnant will not be left to them, for I will bring disaster on the men of Anathoth—the year of their punishment."

Jeremiah's Prayer

12 Righteous are You, O LORD, that I would plead *my* case with You;
Indeed I would discuss matters of justice with You:
Why has the way of the wicked prospered?
Why are all those who deal in treachery at ease?
2 You have planted them, they have also taken root;
They grow, they have even produced fruit.
You are near to their lips
But far from their mind.
3 But You know me, O LORD;
You see me;
And You examine my heart's *attitude* toward You.
Drag them off like sheep for the slaughter
And set them apart for a day of carnage!
4 How long is the land to mourn
And the vegetation of the countryside to wither?
For the wickedness of those who dwell in it,
Animals and birds have been snatched away,
Because *men* have said, "He will not see our latter ending."

5 "If you have run with footmen and they have tired you out,
Then how can you compete with horses?
If you fall down in a land of peace,
How will you do in the thicket of the Jordan?
6 "For even your brothers and the household of your father,
Even they have dealt treacherously with you,

11:18 1 Sam 23:11, 12; 2 Kin 6:9, 10; Ezek 8:6

11:19 Is 53:7; Jer 18:18; 20:10; Ps 83:4; Is 53:8; Job 28:13; Ps 52:5; Ps 109:13

11:20 Gen 18:25; Ps 7:8; Jer 20:12; 1 Sam 16:7; Ps 7:9; Jer 17:10

11:21 Jer 1:1; Jer 12:5, 6; 20:10; Amos 2:12; Jer 26:8; 38:4

11:22 Jer 21:14; 2 Chr 36:17; Jer 18:21

11:23 Jer 6:9; Jer 23:12; Hos 9:7; Mic 7:4; Luke 19:44

12:1 Ezra 9:15; Ps 51:4; 129:4; Jer 11:20; Job 13:3; Job 12:6; Jer 5:27, 28; Hab 1:4; Mal 3:15; Jer 3:7, 20; 5:11

12:2 Jer 11:17; 45:4; Ezek 17:5-10; Is 29:13; Jer 3:10; Ezek 33:31; Titus 1:16

12:3 Ps 139:1-4; Ps 7:9; 11:5; Jer 11:20; Jer 17:18; 50:27; James 5:5

12:4 Jer 4:28; 9:10; 23:10; Joel 1:10-17; Ps 107:34; Jer 4:25; 7:20; 9:10; Hos 4:3; Hab 3:17; Jer 5:31; Ezek 7:2

12:5 Jer 49:19; 50:44

12:6 Gen 37:4-11; Job 6:15; Ps 69:8; Jer 9:4, 5; Ps 12:2; Prov 26:25

11:18–23 To Jeremiah's surprise, the people of Anathoth, his hometown, were plotting to kill him. They wanted to silence Jeremiah's message for several reasons: (1) economic—his condemnation of idol worship would hurt the business of the idol-makers; (2) religious—the message of doom and gloom made the people feel depressed and guilty; (3) political—he openly rebuked their hypocritical politics; and (4) personal—the people hated him for showing them that they were wrong. Jeremiah had two options: run and hide, or call on God. Jeremiah called, and God answered. Like Jeremiah, we can either run and hide when we face threats because of our faithfulness to God, or we can call on God for help. Hiding compromises our message; calling on God lets him reinforce it.

12:1–6 Many people have asked, "Why has the way of the wicked prospered?" (See, for example, Job 21:4–21 and Habakkuk 1:1–4.) Jeremiah knew that God's justice would ultimately come, but he was impatient because he wanted justice to come quickly. God didn't give a doctrinal answer; instead he gave a challenge—if Jeremiah couldn't handle this, how would he handle the injustices ahead? It is natural for us to demand fair play and cry for justice against those who take advantage of others. But when we call for justice, we must realize that we ourselves would be in big trouble if God gave each of us what we truly deserve.

12:5–6 Life was extremely difficult for Jeremiah despite his love for and obedience to God. When he called to God for relief, God's reply in effect was, "If you think this is bad, how are you going to cope when it gets really tough?" Not all of God's answers to prayer are nice or easy to handle. Any Christian who has experienced war, bereavement, or a serious illness knows this. But we are to be committed to God even when the going gets tough and when his answers to our prayers don't bring immediate relief.

Even they have cried aloud after you.
Do not believe them, although they may say nice things to you."

God's Answer

12:7 Is 2:6; Jer 7:29; 23:39; Jer 11:15; Hos 11:1-8

7 "I have forsaken My house,
I have abandoned My inheritance;
I have given the beloved of My soul
Into the hand of her enemies.

12:8 Is 59:13; Hos 9:15; Amos 6:8

8 "My inheritance has become to Me
Like a lion in the forest;
She has roared against Me;
Therefore I have come to hate her.

12:9 2 Kin 24:2; Ezek 23:22-25; Is 56:9; Jer 7:33; 15:3; 34:20

9 "Is My inheritance like a speckled bird of prey to Me?
Are the birds of prey against her on every side?
Go, gather all the beasts of the field,
Bring them to devour!

12:10 Jer 6:3; 23:1; Ps 80:8-16; Is 5:1-7; Is 63:18; Jer 3:19

10 "Many shepherds have ruined My vineyard,
They have trampled down My field;
They have made My pleasant field
A desolate wilderness.

12:11 Jer 12:4; 14:2; 23:10; Jer 4:20, 27; 25:11; Is 42:25

11 "It has been made a desolation,
Desolate, it mourns before Me;
The whole land has been made desolate,
Because no man lays it to heart.

12:12 Jer 3:2, 21; Is 34:6; Jer 47:6; Amos 9:4; Jer 16:5; 30:5

12 "On all the bare heights in the wilderness
Destroyers have come,
For a sword of the LORD is devouring
From one end of the land even to the other;
There is no peace for anyone.

12:13 Lev 26:16; Deut 28:38; Mic 6:15; Hag 1:6; Is 55:2; Jer 9:5; Jer 17:10; Jer 4:26; 25:37, 38

13 "They have sown wheat and have reaped thorns,
They have strained themselves to no profit.
But be ashamed of your harvest
Because of the fierce anger of the LORD."

12:14 Jer 49:1, 7; Zeph 2:8-10; Jer 2:3; 50:11, 12; Zech 2:8; Deut 30:3; Ps 106:47; Is 11:11-16

14 Thus says the LORD concerning all My wicked neighbors who strike at the inheritance with which I have endowed My people Israel, "Behold I am about to uproot them
from their land and will uproot the house of Judah from among them.

12:15 Jer 48:47; 49:6, 39; Amos 9:14

15 "And it will come about that after I have uprooted them, I will again have compassion on them; and I will bring them back, each one to his inheritance and each one to his
land.

12:16 Is 42:6; 49:6; Jer 4:2; Zeph 1:5; Josh 23:7; Jer 5:7; Jer 3:17; 4:2; 16:19

16 "Then if they will really learn the ways of My people, to swear by My name, 'As the
LORD lives,' even as they taught My people to swear by Baal, they will be built up in the
midst of My people.

12:17 Ps 2:8-12; Is 60:12

17 "But if they will not listen, then I will uproot that nation, uproot and destroy it,"
declares the LORD.

The Ruined Waistband

13:1 Jer 13:11

13 Thus the LORD said to me, "Go and buy yourself a linen waistband and put it around
your waist, but do not put it in water."

13:2 Is 20:2; Ezek 2:8

2 So I bought the waistband in accordance with the word of the LORD and put it around
my waist.
3 Then the word of the LORD came to me a second time, saying,

13:4 Jer 51:63

4 "Take the waistband that you have bought, which is around your waist, and arise, go
to the Euphrates and hide it there in a crevice of the rock."

13:1 A linen waistband was one of the more intimate pieces of clothing, clinging close to the body. It was like underwear. Jeremiah's action showed how God would ruin Judah just as Jeremiah had ruined the linen belt.

13:1–11 Actions speak louder than words. Jeremiah often used vivid object lessons to arouse the people's curiosity and get his point across. This lesson of the linen waistband illustrated Judah's destiny. Although the people had once been close to God, their pride had made them useless. Proud people may look important, but God says their pride makes them good for nothing, completely useless. Pride rots our hearts until we lose our usefulness to God.

5 So I went and hid it by the Euphrates, as the LORD had commanded me.
6 After many days the LORD said to me, "Arise, go to the Euphrates and take from
there the waistband which I commanded you to hide there."
7 Then I went to the Euphrates and dug, and I took the waistband from the place
where I had hidden it; and lo, the waistband was ruined, it was totally worthless.
8 Then the word of the LORD came to me, saying,
9 "Thus says the LORD, 'Just so will I destroy the pride of Judah and the great pride of
Jerusalem.
10 'This wicked people, who refuse to listen to My words, who walk in the stubbornness of their hearts and have gone after other gods to serve them and to bow down to
them, let them be just like this waistband which is totally worthless.
11 'For as the waistband clings to the waist of a man, so I made the whole household of
Israel and the whole household of Judah cling to Me,' declares the LORD, 'that they might
be for Me a people, for renown, for praise and for glory; but they did not listen.'

13:5 Ex 39:42, 43; 40:16
13:9 Lev 26:19; Is 2:10-17; 23:9; Jer 13:15-17; Zeph 3:11
13:10 Num 14:11; 2 Chr 36:15, 16; Jer 11:10; Jer 9:14; 11:8; 16:12
13:11 Ex 19:5, 6; Deut 32:10, 11; Jer 32:20; Is 43:21; Jer 33:9; Ps 81:11; Jer 7:13, 24, 26

Captivity Threatened

12 "Therefore you are to speak this word to them, 'Thus says the LORD, the God of Israel,
"Every jug is to be filled with wine." ' And when they say to you, 'Do we not very well
know that every jug is to be filled with wine?'
13 then say to them, 'Thus says the LORD, "Behold I am about to fill all the inhabitants
of this land—the kings that sit for David on his throne, the priests, the prophets and all
the inhabitants of Jerusalem—with drunkenness!
14 "I will dash them against each other, both the fathers and the sons together," declares the LORD. "I will not show pity nor be sorry nor have compassion so as not to
destroy them." ' "

13:13 Ps 60:3; 75:8; Is 51:17; 63:6; Jer 25:27; 51:7, 57
13:14 Is 9:20, 21; Jer 19:9-11; Jer 6:21; Ezek 5:10; Deut 29:20; Is 27:11; Jer 16:5; 21:7

15 Listen and give heed, do not be haughty,
For the LORD has spoken.
16 Give glory to the LORD your God,
Before He brings darkness
And before your feet stumble
On the dusky mountains,
And while you are hoping for light
He makes it into deep darkness,
And turns *it* into gloom.
17 But if you will not listen to it,
My soul will sob in secret for *such* pride;
And my eyes will bitterly weep
And flow down with tears,
Because the flock of the LORD has been taken captive.
18 Say to the king and the queen mother,
"Take a lowly seat,
For your beautiful crown
Has come down from your head."
19 The cities of the Negev have been locked up,
And there is no one to open *them;*
All Judah has been carried into exile,
Wholly carried into exile.

13:15 Prov 16:5; Is 28:14-22
13:16 Josh 7:19; Ps 96:8; Is 5:30; 8:22; 59:9; Amos 5:18; 8:9; Prov 4:19; Jer 23:12; Ps 44:19; 107:10, 14; Jer 2:6
13:17 Mal 2:2; Ps 119:136; Jer 9:1; 14:17; Luke 19:41, 42; Ps 80:1; Jer 23:1, 2
13:18 2 Kin 24:12, 15; Jer 22:26; 2 Chr 33:12, 19; Ex 39:28; Is 3:20; Ezek 24:17, 23; 44:18
13:19 Jer 32:44; Jer 20:4; 52:27-30

20 "Lift up your eyes and see
Those coming from the north.
Where is the flock that was given you,
Your beautiful sheep?

13:20 Jer 1:15; 6:22; Hab 1:6; Jer 13:17; 23:2

13:15 While it is good to respect our country and our church, our loyalties always carry a hidden danger—arrogance. When is pride harmful? When it causes us to (1) look down on others; (2) be selfish with our resources; (3) force our solutions on others' problems; (4) think God is blessing us because of our own merits; (5) be content with our plans rather than seeking God's plans.

13:18 The king was Jehoiachin, and the queen mother was Nehushta. The king's father, Jehoiakim, had surrendered to Nebuchadnezzar but later rebelled. During Jehoiachin's reign, Nebuchadnezzar's armies besieged Jerusalem, and both Jehoiachin and Nehushta surrendered. Jehoiachin was sent to Babylon and imprisoned (2 Kings 24:1–12). Jeremiah's prophecy came true.

13:19 The Negev region is the dry wasteland stretching south from Beersheba. The towns in this area would be closed to any refugees fleeing the invading army.

13:21 Jer 2:25; 38:22; Is 13:8; Jer 4:31

21 "What will you say when He appoints over you—
And you yourself had taught them—
Former companions to be head over you?
Will not pangs take hold of you
Like a woman in childbirth?

13:22 Deut 7:17; Jer 5:19; 16:10; Jer 2:17-19; 9:2-9; Is 47:2; Ezek 16:37; Nah 3:5

22 "If you say in your heart,
'Why have these things happened to me?'
Because of the magnitude of your iniquity
Your skirts have been removed
And your heels have been exposed.

13:23 Prov 27:22; Is 1:5; Jer 4:22; 9:5

23 "Can the Ethiopian change his skin
Or the leopard his spots?
Then you also can do good
Who are accustomed to doing evil.

13:24 Lev 26:33; Jer 9:16; Ezek 5:2, 12; Jer 4:11; 18:17

24 "Therefore I will scatter them like drifting straw
To the desert wind.

13:25 Job 20:29; Ps 11:6; Matt 24:51; Ps 9:17; Jer 2:32; 3:21

25 "This is your lot, the portion measured to you
From Me," declares the LORD,
"Because you have forgotten Me
And trusted in falsehood.

13:26 Lam 1:8; Ezek 23:29; Hos 2:10

26 "So I Myself have also stripped your skirts off over your face,
That your shame may be seen.

13:27 Jer 5:7, 8; Jer 11:15; Is 65:7; Jer 2:20; Ezek 6:13; Prov 1:22; Hos 8:5

27 "As for your adulteries and your *lustful* neighings,
The lewdness of your prostitution
On the hills in the field,
I have seen your abominations.
Woe to you, O Jerusalem!
How long will you remain unclean?"

Drought and a Prayer for Mercy

14:1 Jer 17:8

14 That which came as the word of the LORD to Jeremiah in regard to the drought:

14:2 Is 3:26; Jer 8:21; 1 Sam 5:12; Jer 11:11; 46:12; Zech 7:13

2 "Judah mourns
And her gates languish;
They sit on the ground in mourning,
And the cry of Jerusalem has ascended.

14:3 1 Kin 18:5; 2 Kin 18:31; Jer 2:13; Job 6:20; Ps 40:14; 2 Sam 15:30

3 "Their nobles have sent their servants for water;
They have come to the cisterns and found no water.
They have returned with their vessels empty;
They have been put to shame and humiliated,
And they cover their heads.

14:4 Joel 1:19, 20; Jer 3:3; Joel 1:11

4 "Because the ground is cracked,
For there has been no rain on the land;
The farmers have been put to shame,
They have covered their heads.

14:5 Is 15:6

5 "For even the doe in the field has given birth only to abandon *her young,*
Because there is no grass.

14:6 Job 39:5, 6; Jer 2:24; Joel 1:18

6 "The wild donkeys stand on the bare heights;
They pant for air like jackals,
Their eyes fail
For there is no vegetation.

14:7 Is 59:12; Hos 5:5; Ps 25:11; Jer 14:21; Jer 5:6; 8:5; Jer 3:25; 8:14; 14:20

7 "Although our iniquities testify against us,

13:23 Not even the threat of captivity could move the people to repent. The people had become so accustomed to doing evil that they had lost their ability to change. God never rejects those who sincerely turn to him. God is warning them to repent before it becomes impossible to change. We must never put off until tomorrow those changes God wants us to make. Our attitudes and patterns for living can become so set that we will lose all desire to change and will no longer fear the consequences.

14:1—15:21 This section opens with God sending a drought on Judah and refusing to answer their prayers for rain. It continues with Jeremiah's description of judgment to come.

14:1ff Drought was a judgment with devastating consequences. As usual, when their backs were to the wall, the people cried out to God. But God rejected their plea because they did not repent; they merely wanted his rescue. Not even Jeremiah's prayers would help. Their only hope was to turn to God.

O LORD, act for Your name's sake!
Truly our apostasies have been many,
We have sinned against You.
8 "O Hope of Israel,
Its Savior in time of distress,
Why are You like a stranger in the land
Or like a traveler who has pitched his *tent* for the night?
9 "Why are You like a man dismayed,
Like a mighty man who cannot save?
Yet You are in our midst, O LORD,
And we are called by Your name;
Do not forsake us!"

10 Thus says the LORD to this people, "Even so they have loved to wander; they have
not kept their feet in check. Therefore the LORD does not accept them; now He will
remember their iniquity and call their sins to account."
11 So the LORD said to me, "Do not pray for the welfare of this people.
12 "When they fast, I am not going to listen to their cry; and when they offer burnt offering and grain offering, I am not going to accept them. Rather I am going to make an
end of them by the sword, famine and pestilence."

False Prophets

13 But, "Ah, Lord GOD!" I said, "Look, the prophets are telling them, 'You will not see
the sword nor will you have famine, but I will give you lasting peace in this place.' "
14 Then the LORD said to me, "The prophets are prophesying falsehood in My name.
I have neither sent them nor commanded them nor spoken to them; they are prophesying to you a false vision, divination, futility and the deception of their own minds.
15 "Therefore thus says the LORD concerning the prophets who are prophesying in My
name, although it was not I who sent them—yet they keep saying, 'There will be no sword
or famine in this land'—by sword and famine those prophets shall meet their end!
16 "The people also to whom they are prophesying will be thrown out into the streets of
Jerusalem because of the famine and the sword; and there will be no one to bury them—
neither them, *nor* their wives, nor their sons, nor their daughters—for I will pour out their
own wickedness on them.
17 "You will say this word to them,
'Let my eyes flow down with tears night and day,
And let them not cease;
For the virgin daughter of my people has been crushed with a mighty blow,
With a sorely infected wound.
18 'If I go out to the country,
Behold, those slain with the sword!
Or if I enter the city,
Behold, diseases of famine!
For both prophet and priest
Have gone roving about in the land that they do not know.' "

19 Have You completely rejected Judah?
Or have You loathed Zion?
Why have You stricken us so that we are beyond healing?
We waited for peace, but nothing good *came;*
And for a time of healing, but behold, terror!
20 We know our wickedness, O LORD,

14:8 Jer 17:13; Is 43:3; 63:8; Ps 9:9; 50:15

14:9 Num 11:23; Is 50:2; 59:1; Ex 29:45; Ps 46:5; Jer 8:19; Is 63:19; Jer 15:16

14:10 Jer 2:25; 3:13; Ps 119:101; Jer 6:20; Amos 5:22; Jer 44:21-23; Hos 8:13; 9:9

14:11 Ex 32:10; Jer 7:16; 11:14

14:12 Prov 1:28; Is 1:15; Jer 11:11; Ezek 8:18; Mic 3:4; Zech 7:13; Jer 6:20; 7:21; Jer 8:13; Jer 21:9

14:13 Jer 5:12; 23:17; Jer 6:14; 8:11

14:14 Jer 5:31; 23:25; Jer 23:21; Jer 23:16, 26; 27:9, 10; Ezek 12:24

14:15 Jer 23:15; Ezek 14:10

14:16 Ps 79:2, 3; Jer 7:33; 15:2, 3; Jer 8:1, 2; Prov 1:31; Jer 13:22-25

14:17 Jer 9:1; 13:17; Lam 1:16; Is 37:22; Jer 8:21; Lam 1:15; 2:13; Jer 10:19; 30:14

14:18 Jer 6:25; Lam 1:20; Ezek 7:15; Jer 6:13; 8:10

14:19 Jer 6:30; 7:29; 12:7; Lam 5:22; Jer 30:13; Job 30:26; Jer 8:15; 1 Thess 5:3

14:20 Neh 9:2; Ps 32:5; Jer 3:25; Jer 8:14; 14:7; Dan 9:8

14:14 What made the people listen to and support the false prophets? These "prophets" said what the people wanted to hear. False teachers earn fame and money by telling people what they want to hear, but they lead people away from God. If we encourage false teachers, we are as guilty as they are.

14:19–22 Interceding for the people, Jeremiah asked God if Judah's repentance would bring his help. But God refused to come to their aid (15:1) because the people were insincere, wicked, and stubborn. They knew he wanted to bless them, and they knew what they needed to do to receive that blessing. They wanted God to do his part, but they did not want to do theirs. It's easy to express sorrow for wrong actions, especially when we want something, but we must be willing to stop doing what is wrong. God will forgive those who are truly repentant, but hypocrites will be severely punished.

14:21
Ps 25:11; Jer 14:7; Jer 3:17; 17:12

14:22
Is 41:29; Jer 10:3; 1 Kin 17:1; Jer 5:24; Lam 3:26

15:1
Ps 99:6; Ezek 14:14, 20; Ex 32:11-14; Num 14:13-20; Ps 99:6; 106:23; 1 Sam 7:9; 12:23; Jer 15:19; 18:20; 35:19; 2 Kin 17:20; Jer 7:15; 10:18; 52:3

15:2
Jer 14:12; 24:10; 43:11; Ezek 5:2, 12; Zech 11:9; Rev 13:10

15:3
Lev 26:16, 22, 25; Ezek 14:21; 1 Kin 21:23, 24; Deut 28:26; Is 18:6; Jer 7:33

15:4
Lev 26:33; Jer 24:9; 29:18; Ezek 23:46; 2 Kin 21:1-18; 23:26, 27; 24:3, 4; 2 Chr 33:1-9

15:5
Ps 69:20; Is 51:19; Jer 13:14; 21:7; Nah 3:7

15:6
Jer 6:19; 8:9; Is 1:4; Jer 7:24; Jer 6:12; Zeph 1:4; Jer 6:11; 7:16

15:7
Ps 1:4; Jer 51:2; Jer 18:21; Hos 9:12-16; Is 9:13

15:8
Is 3:25, 26; 4:1; Jer 22:7

15:9
1 Sam 2:5; Is 47:9; Jer 6:4; Amos 8:9; Jer 50:12; Jer 21:7

15:10
Job 3:1, 3; Jer 20:14; Jer 1:18, 19; 15:20; 20:7, 8; Ex 22:25; Lev 25:36, 37; Deut 23:19

The iniquity of our fathers, for we have sinned against You.
21 Do not despise *us,* for Your own name's sake;
Do not disgrace the throne of Your glory;
Remember *and* do not annul Your covenant with us.
22 Are there any among the idols of the nations who give rain?
Or can the heavens grant showers?
Is it not You, O LORD our God?
Therefore we hope in You,
For You are the one who has done all these things.

Judgment Must Come

15 Then the LORD said to me, "Even though Moses and Samuel were to stand before
Me, My heart would not be with this people; send them away from My presence
and let them go!
2 "And it shall be that when they say to you, 'Where should we go?' then you are to tell
them, 'Thus says the LORD:
"Those *destined* for death, to death;
And those *destined* for the sword, to the sword;
And those *destined* for famine, to famine;
And those *destined* for captivity, to captivity." '
3 "I will appoint over them four kinds *of doom,*" declares the LORD: "the sword to slay,
the dogs to drag off, and the birds of the sky and the beasts of the earth to devour and
destroy.
4 "I will make them an object of horror among all the kingdoms of the earth because
of Manasseh, the son of Hezekiah, the king of Judah, for what he did in Jerusalem.
5 "Indeed, who will have pity on you, O Jerusalem,
Or who will mourn for you,
Or who will turn aside to ask about your welfare?
6 "You who have forsaken Me," declares the LORD,
"You keep going backward.
So I will stretch out My hand against you and destroy you;
I am tired of relenting!
7 "I will winnow them with a winnowing fork
At the gates of the land;
I will bereave *them* of children, I will destroy My people;
They did not repent of their ways.
8 "Their widows will be more numerous before Me
Than the sand of the seas;
I will bring against them, against the mother of a young man,
A destroyer at noonday;
I will suddenly bring down on her
Anguish and dismay.
9 "She who bore seven *sons* pines away;
Her breathing is labored.
Her sun has set while it was yet day;
She has been shamed and humiliated.
So I will give over their survivors to the sword
Before their enemies," declares the LORD.

10 Woe to me, my mother, that you have borne me
As a man of strife and a man of contention to all the land!

15:1 Moses and Samuel were two of God's greatest prophets. Like Jeremiah, both interceded between God and the people (Exodus 32:11; Numbers 14:11–20; 1 Samuel 7:9; 12:17; Psalm 99:6). Intercession is often effective. In this case, however, the people were so wicked and stubborn that God knew they would not turn to him.

15:3–4 The goal of these destroyers was to destroy the living and devour the dead. This would happen because of Manasseh's evil reign and the people's sin (2 Kings 21:1–16; 23:26; 24:3), and the destruction would be complete. The people may have argued that they should not be responsible for Manasseh's sins, but they continued what Manasseh began. If we follow corrupt leaders knowingly, we can't excuse ourselves by blaming their bad example.

I have not lent, nor have men lent money to me,
Yet everyone curses me.
11 The LORD said, "Surely I will set you free for *purposes of* good;
Surely I will cause the enemy to make supplication to you
In a time of disaster and a time of distress.

15:11 Ps 138:3; Is 41:10; Jer 21:2; 37:3; 38:14; 42:2

12 "Can anyone smash iron,
Iron from the north, or bronze?
13 "Your wealth and your treasures
I will give for booty without cost,
Even for all your sins
And within all your borders.
14 "Then I will cause your enemies to bring *it*
Into a land you do not know;
For a fire has been kindled in My anger,
It will burn upon you."

15:12 Jer 28:14

15:13 Jer 17:3; 20:5; Ps 44:12; Is 52:3

15:14 Deut 28:36, 64; Jer 16:13; Deut 32:22; Ps 21:9; Jer 17:4

Jeremiah's Prayer and God's Answer

15 You who know, O LORD,
Remember me, take notice of me,
And take vengeance for me on my persecutors.
Do not, in view of Your patience, take me away;
Know that for Your sake I endure reproach.
16 Your words were found and I ate them,
And Your words became for me a joy and the delight of my heart;
For I have been called by Your name,
O LORD God of hosts.
17 I did not sit in the circle of merrymakers,
Nor did I exult.
Because of Your hand *upon me* I sat alone,
For You filled me with indignation.
18 Why has my pain been perpetual
And my wound incurable, refusing to be healed?
Will You indeed be to me like a deceptive *stream*
With water that is unreliable?

15:15 Jer 12:3; Jer 11:20; Ps 44:22; 69:7-9; Jer 20:8

15:16 Ezek 3:3; Job 23:12; Ps 119:103; Jer 14:9

15:17 Ps 1:1; Jer 16:8; 2 Cor 6:17; Ps 102:7; Jer 13:17; Lam 3:28; Ezek 3:24, 25; Jer 6:11

15:18 Job 34:6; Jer 30:12, 15; Mic 1:9; Job 6:15, 20; Jer 14:3

19 Therefore, thus says the LORD,
"If you return, then I will restore you—
Before Me you will stand;
And if you extract the precious from the worthless,
You will become My spokesman.
They for their part may turn to you,
But as for you, you must not turn to them.
20 "Then I will make you to this people
A fortified wall of bronze;
And though they fight against you,
They will not prevail over you;
For I am with you to save you
And deliver you," declares the LORD.
21 "So I will deliver you from the hand of the wicked,
And I will redeem you from the grasp of the violent."

15:19 Jer 4:1; Zech 3:7; 1 Kin 17:1; Jer 15:1; 35:19; Jer 6:29; Ezek 22:26; 44:23

15:20 Jer 1:18, 19; Ezek 3:9; Ps 46:7; Is 41:10; Jer 1:8, 19; 15:15; 20:11

15:21 Ps 37:40; Is 49:25; Jer 20:13; 39:11, 12; Gen 48:16; Is 49:26; 60:16; Jer 31:11; 50:34

15:17–21 Jeremiah accused God of not helping him when he really needed it. Jeremiah had taken his eyes off God's purposes and was feeling sorry for himself. He was angry, hurt, and afraid. In response, God didn't get angry at Jeremiah; he answered by rearranging Jeremiah's priorities. As God's mouthpiece, he was to influence the people, not let them influence him. There are three important lessons in this passage: (1) In prayer we can reveal our deepest thoughts to God; (2) God expects us to trust him, no matter what; (3) we are here to influence others for God.

Distresses Foretold

16 The word of the LORD also came to me saying,
2 "You shall not take a wife for yourself nor have sons or daughters in this place."
3 For thus says the LORD concerning the sons and daughters born in this place, and
concerning their mothers who bear them, and their fathers who beget them in this land:
4 "They will die of deadly diseases, they will not be lamented or buried; they will be as
dung on the surface of the ground and come to an end by sword and famine, and their
carcasses will become food for the birds of the sky and for the beasts of the earth."
5 For thus says the LORD, "Do not enter a house of mourning, or go to lament or to
console them; for I have withdrawn My peace from this people," declares the LORD,
"*My* lovingkindness and compassion.
6 "Both great men and small will die in this land; they will not be buried, they will not
be lamented, nor will anyone gash himself or shave his head for them.
7 "Men will not break *bread* in mourning for them, to comfort anyone for the dead,
nor give them a cup of consolation to drink for anyone's father or mother.
8 "Moreover you shall not go into a house of feasting to sit with them to eat and drink."
9 For thus says the LORD of hosts, the God of Israel: "Behold, I am going to eliminate from this place, before your eyes and in your time, the voice of rejoicing and the
voice of gladness, the voice of the groom and the voice of the bride.
10 "Now when you tell this people all these words, they will say to you, 'For what reason
has the LORD declared all this great calamity against us? And what is our iniquity, or
what is our sin which we have committed against the LORD our God?'
11 "Then you are to say to them, '*It is* because your forefathers have forsaken Me,' declares the LORD, 'and have followed other gods and served them and bowed down to
them; but Me they have forsaken and have not kept My law.
12 'You too have done evil, *even* more than your forefathers; for behold, you are each
one walking according to the stubbornness of his own evil heart, without listening to Me.
13 'So I will hurl you out of this land into the land which you have not known, neither
you nor your fathers; and there you will serve other gods day and night, for I will grant
you no favor.'

God Will Restore Them

14 "Therefore behold, days are coming," declares the LORD, "when it will no longer be
said, 'As the LORD lives, who brought up the sons of Israel out of the land of Egypt,'
15 but, 'As the LORD lives, who brought up the sons of Israel from the land of the north
and from all the countries where He had banished them.' For I will restore them to their
own land which I gave to their fathers.
16 "Behold, I am going to send for many fishermen," declares the LORD, "and they will
fish for them; and afterwards I will send for many hunters, and they will hunt them from
every mountain and every hill and from the clefts of the rocks.
17 "For My eyes are on all their ways; they are not hidden from My face, nor is their
iniquity concealed from My eyes.

16:4 Ps 83:10; Jer 9:22; 25:33; Ps 79:2; Is 18:6; Jer 15:3; 34:20

16:5 Ezek 24:16-23; Jer 12:12; 15:1-4; Ps 25:6; Is 27:11; Jer 13:14

16:6 2 Chr 36:17; Ezek 9:6; Deut 14:1; Jer 41:5; 47:5; Is 22:12

16:7 Deut 26:14; Ezek 24:17; Hos 9:4

16:8 Eccl 7:2-4; Is 22:12-14; Jer 15:17; Amos 6:4-6

16:9 Jer 7:34; 25:10; Ezek 26:13; Hos 2:11; Rev 18:23

16:10 Deut 29:24; 1 Kin 9:8; Jer 5:19; 13:22

16:11 Deut 29:25; 1 Kin 9:9; 2 Chr 7:22

16:12 Eccl 9:3; Mark 7:21

16:13 Deut 4:26, 27; 2 Chr 7:20; Jer 15:1; Deut 4:28; 28:36; Jer 5:19

16:14 Is 43:18; Jer 23:7; Ex 20:2; Deut 15:15

16:15 Ps 106:47; Is 11:11-16; 14:1; Jer 3:18; 23:8; 24:6

16:16 Amos 4:2; Hab 1:14, 15; 1 Sam 26:20; Mic 7:2; Is 2:21

16:17 2 Chr 16:9; Job 34:21; Ps 90:8; Prov 5:21; 15:3; Jer 23:24; 32:19; Zech 4:10; Luke 12:2; 1 Cor 4:5; Heb 4:13; Jer 2:22

16:1—17:18 This section portrays the coming day of disaster. It begins by showing Jeremiah's loneliness. He is a social outcast because of his harsh messages and his celibate life-style. He must not marry, have children, or take part in funerals or festivals. The section concludes with another appeal to avoid judgment by turning to God. The people did not heed Jeremiah's words, however, and the first wave of destruction came almost immediately, in 605 B.C. (2 Kings 24:8–12). The second wave came in 597 B.C., and Judah was completely destroyed in 586 B.C.

16:5–7 In Jeremiah's culture, it was unthinkable not to show grief publicly. The absence of mourning showed the people how complete their devastation would be. So many people would die that it would be impossible to carry out mourning rituals for all of them.

16:8–13 Jeremiah was also told not to participate in parties or other joyful events to show how seriously God took the nation's sins. In both cases (no public grief or joy), Jeremiah's life was to be an attention-getter and an illustration of God's truth. Sometimes we think that the only way to communicate is through speaking or teaching, but God can use a wide variety of means to bring his message. Use your creativity.

16:14–15 The book of Exodus records God's miraculous rescue of his people from Egyptian slavery (Exodus 1—15). The people's return from exile would be so momentous that it would overshadow even the exodus from Egypt. Even though his people had been so stubborn, God would once again show his great mercy.

16:17 Small children think that if they can't see you, then you can't see them. The people of Israel may have wished that hiding from God were as simple as closing their eyes. Although they closed their eyes to their sinful ways, their sins certainly weren't hidden from God. He who sees everything cannot be deceived. Do you have a sinful attitude or action that you hope God won't notice? He knows about it. The first step of repentance is to acknowledge that God knows about your sins.

18 "I will first doubly repay their iniquity and their sin, because they have polluted My
land; they have filled My inheritance with the carcasses of their detestable idols and with
their abominations."

19 O LORD, my strength and my stronghold,
And my refuge in the day of distress,
To You the nations will come
From the ends of the earth and say,
"Our fathers have inherited nothing but falsehood,
Futility and things of no profit."
20 Can man make gods for himself?
Yet they are not gods!

21 "Therefore behold, I am going to make them know—
This time I will make them know
My power and My might;
And they shall know that My name is the LORD."

The Deceitful Heart

17 The sin of Judah is written down with an iron stylus;
With a diamond point it is engraved upon the tablet of their heart
And on the horns of their altars,
2 As they remember their children,
So they *remember* their altars and their Asherim
By green trees on the high hills.
3 O mountain of Mine in the countryside,
I will give over your wealth and all your treasures for booty,
Your high places for sin throughout your borders.
4 And you will, even of yourself, let go of your inheritance
That I gave you;
And I will make you serve your enemies
In the land which you do not know;
For you have kindled a fire in My anger
Which will burn forever.

5 Thus says the LORD,
"Cursed is the man who trusts in mankind
And makes flesh his strength,
And whose heart turns away from the LORD.
6 "For he will be like a bush in the desert
And will not see when prosperity comes,
But will live in stony wastes in the wilderness,
A land of salt without inhabitant.
7 "Blessed is the man who trusts in the LORD
And whose trust is the LORD.
8 "For he will be like a tree planted by the water,
That extends its roots by a stream
And will not fear when the heat comes;

16:18 Jer 17:18; Rev 18:6; Num 35:33, 34; Jer 2:7; 3:9; Jer 7:30; Ezek 11:18, 21

16:19 Ps 18:1, 2; Is 25:4; Nah 1:7; Ps 22:27; Is 2:2; Jer 3:17; 4:2; Is 44:20; Hab 2:18; Is 44:10

16:20 Ps 115:4-8; Is 37:19; Jer 2:11; 5:7; Hos 8:4-6; Gal 4:8

16:21 Ps 9:16; Ps 83:18; Is 43:3; Jer 33:2; Amos 5:8

17:1 Jer 2:22; 4:14; Job 19:24; Prov 3:3; 7:3; Is 49:16; 2 Cor 3:3

17:2 Jer 7:18; Ex 34:13; 2 Chr 24:18; 33:3; Is 17:8; Jer 3:6

17:3 Jer 26:18; Mic 3:12; 2 Kin 24:13; Is 39:4-6; Jer 15:13; 20:5

17:4 Jer 12:7; Lam 5:2; Deut 28:48; Is 14:3; Jer 15:14; 27:12, 13; Jer 16:13; Is 5:25; Jer 7:20; 15:14

17:5 Ps 146:3; Is 2:22; 30:1; Ezek 29:7; 2 Chr 32:8; Is 31:3

17:6 Jer 48:6; Deut 29:23; Job 39:6

17:7 Ps 2:12; 34:8; 84:12; Prov 16:20; Ps 40:4

17:8 Ps 1:3; 92:12-14; Ezek 31:3-9; Jer 14:1-6

16:19 In this prayer, Jeremiah approached God with three descriptive names: strength, stronghold, and refuge. Each name gives a slightly different glimpse of how Jeremiah experienced God's presence, and each is a picture of security and protection. Let God be your strength when you feel weak, your stronghold when enemies come against you, and your refuge when you need to retreat from life's pressures.

17:1 God's people continued to sin even though they had the law, the prophets of God, and history filled with God's miracles. How could they do that? Why do we continue to cherish sin even though we understand the eternal consequences? Jeremiah says the heart is deceitful (17:9), and "the sin of Judah is written down . . . upon the tablet of their heart." The Hebrews symbolized the various aspects of a person by locating them in certain physical organs. The heart was the organ of reason, intelligence, and will. So deep is our tendency to sin that only God's redemption can deliver us.

17:5–8 Two kinds of people are contrasted here: those who trust in human beings and those who trust in the Lord. The people of Judah were trusting in false gods and military alliances instead of God, and thus they were barren and unfruitful. In contrast, those who trust in the Lord flourish like trees planted by water (see Psalm 1). In times of trouble, those who trust in human beings will be impoverished and spiritually weak, so they will have no strength to draw on. But those who trust in the Lord will have abundant strength, not only for their own needs, but even for the needs of others. Are you satisfied with being unfruitful, or do you, like a well-watered tree, have strength for the time of crisis and even some to share as you bear fruit for the Lord?

And they have stumbled from their ways,
From the ancient paths,
To walk in bypaths,
Not on a highway,

18:16 Jer 25:9; 49:13; 50:13; Ezek 33:28, 29; 1 Kin 9:8; Lam 2:15; Mic 6:16; Ps 22:7; Is 37:22; Jer 48:27

16 To make their land a desolation,
An object of perpetual hissing;
Everyone who passes by it will be astonished
And shake his head.

18:17 Ps 48:7; Job 27:21; Jer 13:24; Jer 2:27; 32:33; Jer 46:21

17 'Like an east wind I will scatter them
Before the enemy;
I will show them My back and not *My* face
In the day of their calamity.' "

18:18 Jer 11:19; 18:11; Jer 2:8; Mal 2:7; Job 5:13; Jer 8:8; Jer 5:13; Ps 52:2; Jer 20:10; Jer 43:2

18 Then they said, "Come and let us devise plans against Jeremiah. Surely the law is
not going to be lost to the priest, nor counsel to the sage, nor the *divine* word to the prophet! Come on and let us strike at him with *our* tongue, and let us give no heed to any of his
words."

19 Do give heed to me, O LORD,
And listen to what my opponents are saying!

18:20 Ps 109:4; Ps 35:7; 57:6; Jer 5:26; 18:22; Ps 106:23

20 Should good be repaid with evil?
For they have dug a pit for me.
Remember how I stood before You
To speak good on their behalf,
So as to turn away Your wrath from them.

18:21 Ps 109:9-20; Jer 11:22; 14:16; 1 Sam 15:33; Is 13:18; Jer 15:8; Ezek 22:25; Jer 9:21; 11:22

21 Therefore, give their children over to famine
And deliver them up to the power of the sword;
And let their wives become childless and widowed.
Let their men also be smitten to death,
Their young men struck down by the sword in battle.

18:22 Jer 6:26; 25:34, 36; Jer 18:20; Ps 140:5

22 May an outcry be heard from their houses,
When You suddenly bring raiders upon them;
For they have dug a pit to capture me

GOD'S OBJECT LESSONS IN JEREMIAH

Reference	Object Lesson	Significance
1:11–12	Branch (rod) of an almond tree	God will carry out his threats of punishment.
1:13	Boiling pot, tilting away from the north	God will punish Judah.
13:1–11	A ruined linen waistband	Because the people refused to listen to God, they had become useless, good for nothing, like a ruined belt.
18:1–17	Potter's clay	God could destroy his sinful people if he so desired. This is a warning to them to repent before he is forced to bring judgment.
19:1–12	Broken clay jars	God would smash Judah just as Jeremiah smashed the clay jars.
24:1–10	Two baskets of figs	Good figs represent God's remnant. Bad figs are the people left behind.
27:2–11	Yoke	Any nation who refused to submit to Babylon's yoke of control would be punished.
43:8–13	Large stones	The stones marked the place where Nebuchadnezzar would set his throne when God allowed him to conquer Egypt.
51:59–64	Scroll sunk in the river	Babylon would sink to rise no more.

10:10 Jeremiah's words and actions challenged the people's social and moral behavior. He had openly spoken against the king, the officials, the priests and prophets, the scribes, and the wise (4:9; 8:8–9). He wasn't afraid to give unpopular criticism. The people could either obey him or silence him. They chose the latter. They did not think they needed Jeremiah; their false prophets told them what they wanted to hear. How do you respond to criticism? Listen carefully—God may be trying to tell you something.

And hidden snares for my feet.
23 Yet You, O LORD, know
All their deadly designs against me;
Do not forgive their iniquity
Or blot out their sin from Your sight.
But may they be overthrown before You;
Deal with them in the time of Your anger!

The Broken Jar

19 Thus says the LORD, "Go and buy a potter's earthenware jar, and *take* some of the
elders of the people and some of the senior priests.
2 "Then go out to the valley of Ben-hinnom, which is by the entrance of the potsherd
gate, and proclaim there the words that I tell you,
3 and say, 'Hear the word of the LORD, O kings of Judah and inhabitants of Jerusalem: thus says the LORD of hosts, the God of Israel, "Behold I am about to bring a calamity upon this place, at which the ears of everyone that hears of it will tingle.
4 "Because they have forsaken Me and have made this an alien place and have burned
sacrifices in it to other gods, that neither they nor their forefathers nor the kings of Judah
had *ever* known, and *because* they have filled this place with the blood of the innocent
5 and have built the high places of Baal to burn their sons in the fire as burnt offerings to Baal, a thing which I never commanded or spoke of, nor did it *ever* enter My mind;
6 therefore, behold, days are coming," declares the LORD, "when this place will no
longer be called Topheth or the valley of Ben-hinnom, but rather the valley of Slaughter.
7 "I will make void the counsel of Judah and Jerusalem in this place, and I will cause
them to fall by the sword before their enemies and by the hand of those who seek their
life; and I will give over their carcasses as food for the birds of the sky and the beasts of
the earth.
8 "I will also make this city a desolation and an *object of* hissing; everyone who passes
by it will be astonished and hiss because of all its disasters.
9 "I will make them eat the flesh of their sons and the flesh of their daughters, and
they will eat one another's flesh in the siege and in the distress with which their enemies
and those who seek their life will distress them." '
10 "Then you are to break the jar in the sight of the men who accompany you
11 and say to them, 'Thus says the LORD of hosts, "Just so will I break this people and
this city, even as one breaks a potter's vessel, which cannot again be repaired; and they
will bury in Topheth because there is no *other* place for burial.
12 "This is how I will treat this place and its inhabitants," declares the LORD, "so as to
make this city like Topheth.
13 "The houses of Jerusalem and the houses of the kings of Judah will be defiled like
the place Topheth, because of all the houses on whose rooftops they burned sacrifices to
all the heavenly host and poured out drink offerings to other gods." ' "
14 Then Jeremiah came from Topheth, where the LORD had sent him to prophesy; and
he stood in the court of the LORD'S house and said to all the people:
15 "Thus says the LORD of hosts, the God of Israel, 'Behold, I am about to bring on this
city and all its towns the entire calamity that I have declared against it, because they have
stiffened their necks so as not to heed My words.' "

Pashhur Persecutes Jeremiah

20 When Pashhur the priest, the son of Immer, who was chief officer in the house of
the LORD, heard Jeremiah prophesying these things,

18:23 Neh 4:5; Ps 109:14; Is 2:9; Jer 6:15, 21; Jer 7:20; 17:4
19:1 Jer 18:2; Jer 19:10; Num 11:16; 2 Kin 19:2; Ezek 8:11
19:2 Josh 15:8; 2 Kin 23:10; Jer 7:31, 32; 32:35; Prov 1:20
19:3 Jer 17:20; Jer 6:19; 19:15; 1 Sam 3:11
19:4 Deut 28:20; Is 65:11; Jer 2:13, 17, 19; 17:13; Ezek 7:22; Dan 11:31; Jer 7:9; 11:13; 2 Kin 21:6, 16; Jer 2:34; 7:6
19:5 Num 22:41; Jer 32:35; Lev 18:21; 2 Kin 17:17; Ps 106:37, 38
19:6 Jer 7:32; Is 30:33; Josh 15:8
19:7 Ps 33:10, 11; Is 28:17, 18; Jer 8:8, 9; Lev 26:17; Deut 28:25; Jer 15:2, 9; Ps 79:2; Jer 16:4
19:8 Jer 18:16; 49:13; 50:13; 1 Kin 9:8; 2 Chr 7:21
19:9 Lev 26:29; Deut 28:53, 55; Is 9:20; Lam 4:10; Ezek 5:10
19:11 Ps 2:9; Is 30:14; Lam 4:2; Rev 2:27; Jer 7:32
19:13 Jer 52:13; 2 Kin 23:10; Ps 74:7; 79:1; Ezek 7:21, 22; Jer 32:29; Zeph 1:5; Deut 4:19; 2 Kin 17:16; Jer 8:2; Jer 7:18; 44:18; Ezek 20:28
19:14 2 Chr 20:5; Jer 26:2
19:15 Neh 9:17, 29; Jer 7:26; 17:23; Ps 58:4
20:1 1 Chr 24:14; Ezra 2:37, 38; 2 Kin 25:18

19:6 The valley of Ben-hinnom was the garbage dump of Jerusalem and the place where children were sacrificed to the god Molech. It is also mentioned in 7:31–32. Topheth was located in the valley and means "fireplace," and it was probably the place where children were burned as sacrifices.

19:7–13 The horrible carnage that Jeremiah predicted happened twice, in 586 B.C. during the Babylonian invasion under Nebuchadnezzar, and in A.D. 70 when Titus destroyed Jerusalem. During the Babylonian siege, food became so scarce that people became cannibals, even eating their own children. (See Leviticus 26:29 and Deuteronomy 28:53–57 for prophecies concerning this; and see 2 Kings 6:28–29; Lamentations 2:20; 4:10 for accounts of actual occurrences.)

20:1ff This event took place during the reign of Jehoiakim of Judah. Jeremiah preached at the valley of Ben-hinnom, the center of idolatry in the city. He also preached in the temple, which should have been the center of true worship. Both places attracted many people; both were places of false worship.

2 Pashhur had Jeremiah the prophet beaten and put him in the stocks that were at
the upper Benjamin Gate, which was by the house of the LORD.
3 On the next day, when Pashhur released Jeremiah from the stocks, Jeremiah said
to him, "Pashhur is not the name the LORD has called you, but rather [6]Magor-missabib.
4 "For thus says the LORD, 'Behold, I am going to make you a terror to yourself and to
all your friends; and while your eyes look on, they will fall by the sword of their enemies.
So I will give over all Judah to the hand of the king of Babylon, and he will carry them
away as exiles to Babylon and will slay them with the sword.
5 'I will also give over all the wealth of this city, all its produce and all its costly things;
even all the treasures of the kings of Judah I will give over to the hand of their enemies,
and they will plunder them, take them away and bring them to Babylon.
6 'And you, Pashhur, and all who live in your house will go into captivity; and you will
enter Babylon, and there you will die and there you will be buried, you and all your friends
to whom you have falsely prophesied.' "

Jeremiah's Complaint

7 O LORD, You have deceived me and I was deceived;
You have overcome me and prevailed.
I have become a laughingstock all day long;
Everyone mocks me.
8 For each time I speak, I cry aloud;
I proclaim violence and destruction,
Because for me the word of the LORD has resulted
In reproach and derision all day long.
9 But if I say, "I will not remember Him
Or speak anymore in His name,"
Then in my heart it becomes like a burning fire
Shut up in my bones;
And I am weary of holding *it* in,
And I cannot endure *it.*
10 For I have heard the whispering of many,
"Terror on every side!
Denounce *him;* yes, let us denounce him!"
All my trusted friends,
Watching for my fall, say:
"Perhaps he will be deceived, so that we may prevail against him
And take our revenge on him."
11 But the LORD is with me like a dread champion;
Therefore my persecutors will stumble and not prevail.
They will be utterly ashamed, because they have failed,
With an everlasting disgrace that will not be forgotten.
12 Yet, O LORD of hosts, You who test the righteous,
Who see the mind and the heart;
Let me see Your vengeance on them;
For to You I have set forth my cause.
13 Sing to the LORD, praise the LORD!

6 I.e. terror on every side

20:2 1 Kin 22:27; 2 Chr 16:10; 24:21; Jer 1:19; Amos 7:10-13; Job 13:27; 33:11; Jer 37:13; 38:7; Zech 14:10

20:3 Is 8:3; Hos 1:4, 9; Jer 6:25; 20:10

20:4 Job 18:11-21; Jer 6:25; 46:5; Ezek 26:21; Jer 29:21; 39:6, 7; Jer 21:4-10; 25:9; Jer 13:10; 52:27

20:5 Jer 15:13; 17:3; 2 Kin 20:17, 18; 2 Chr 36:10; Jer 27:21, 22

20:6 Jer 20:1; Jer 20:4; 29:21; Jer 14:14, 15; Lam 2:14

20:7 Ezek 3:14; Job 12:4; Lam 3:14; Ps 22:7; Jer 38:19

20:8 Jer 6:7; 2 Chr 36:16; Jer 6:10

20:9 1 Kin 19:3, 4; Jon 1:2, 3; Job 32:18-20; Ps 39:3; Jer 4:19; 23:9; Ezek 3:14; Acts 4:20; Job 32:18-20

20:10 Ps 31:13; Jer 6:25; Neh 6:6-13; Is 29:21; Jer 18:18; Ps 41:9; 1 Kin 19:2

20:11 Jer 1:8; 15:20; Rom 8:31; Deut 32:35, 36; Jer 15:15, 20; 17:18; Jer 23:40

20:12 Ps 7:9; 11:5; 17:3; 139:23; Jer 11:20; 17:10; Ps 54:7; 59:10; Jer 11:20; Ps 62:8

20:13 Jer 31:7; Ps 34:6; 69:33; Jer 15:21

20:1–3 Pashhur was the official in charge of maintaining order in the temple (see 29:26 for a description of the responsibility). He was also a priest and had pretended to be a prophet. After hearing Jeremiah's words, Pashhur had him beaten and put in the stocks (locked up) instead of taking his message to heart and acting on it. The truth sometimes stings, but our reaction to the truth shows what we are made of. We can deny the charges and destroy evidence of our misdeeds, or we can take the truth humbly to heart and let it change us. Pashhur may have thought he was a strong leader, but he was really a coward.

20:4–6 This prophecy of destruction came true in three waves of invasion by Babylon. The first wave happened within the year (605 B.C.). Pashhur was probably exiled to Babylon during the second wave in 597 B.C. when Jehoiachin was taken captive. The third invasion occurred in 586 B.C.

20:7–18 Jeremiah cried out in despair mixed with praise, unburdening his heart to God. He had faithfully proclaimed God's word and had received nothing in return but persecution and sorrow. Yet when he withheld God's word for a while, it became fire in his bones until he could hold it back no longer. When God's living message of forgiveness becomes fire in your bones, you also will feel compelled to share it with others, regardless of the results.

For He has delivered the soul of the needy one
From the hand of evildoers.

14 Cursed be the day when I was born;
Let the day not be blessed when my mother bore me!
15 Cursed be the man who brought the news
To my father, saying,
"A baby boy has been born to you!"
And made him very happy.
16 But let that man be like the cities
Which the LORD overthrew without [7]relenting,
And let him hear an outcry in the morning
And a shout of alarm at noon;
17 Because he did not kill me before birth,
So that my mother would have been my grave,
And her womb ever pregnant.
18 Why did I ever come forth from the womb
To look on trouble and sorrow,
So that my days have been spent in shame?

4. Jeremiah accuses Judah's leaders

Jeremiah's Message for Zedekiah

21 The word which came to Jeremiah from the LORD when King Zedekiah sent to
him Pashhur the son of Malchijah, and Zephaniah the priest, the son of Maaseiah, saying,
2 "Please inquire of the LORD on our behalf, for Nebuchadnezzar king of Babylon is
warring against us; perhaps the LORD will deal with us according to all His wonderful
acts, so that *the enemy* will withdraw from us."
3 Then Jeremiah said to them, "You shall say to Zedekiah as follows:
4 'Thus says the LORD God of Israel, "Behold, I am about to turn back the weapons
of war which are in your hands, with which you are warring against the king of Babylon
and the Chaldeans who are besieging you outside the wall; and I will gather them into
the center of this city.
5 "I Myself will war against you with an outstretched hand and a mighty arm, even in
anger and wrath and great indignation.
6 "I will also strike down the inhabitants of this city, both man and beast; they will die
of a great pestilence.
7 "Then afterwards," declares the LORD, "I will give over Zedekiah king of Judah and
his servants and the people, even those who survive in this city from the pestilence, the
sword and the famine, into the hand of Nebuchadnezzar king of Babylon, and into the
hand of their foes and into the hand of those who seek their lives; and he will strike them
down with the edge of the sword. He will not spare them nor have pity nor compassion." '
8 "You shall also say to this people, 'Thus says the LORD, "Behold, I set before you the
way of life and the way of death.
9 "He who dwells in this city will die by the sword and by famine and by pestilence; but

7 Lit *being sorry*

20:14 Job 3:3-6; Jer 15:10

20:15 Gen 21:6, 7

20:16 Gen 19:25; Jer 18:22; 48:3, 4

20:17 Job 3:10, 11, 16; 10:18, 19

20:18 Job 3:20; 5:7; 14:1; Jer 15:10; Lam 3:1; Ps 90:9; 102:3; Ps 69:19; Jer 3:25; 1 Cor 4:9-13

21:1 2 Kin 24:17, 18; Jer 32:1-3; 37:1; 52:1-3; 1 Chr 9:12; Jer 38:1; 2 Kin 25:18; Jer 29:25, 29; 37:3; 52:24

21:2 Ex 9:28; Jer 37:3, 17; Ezek 14:7; 20:1-3; 2 Kin 25:1; Gen 10:10; 2 Kin 17:24; Ps 44:1-3; Jer 32:17

21:4 Jer 32:5; 33:5; 37:8-10; 38:2, 3, 17, 18; Is 5:5; 13:4; Jer 39:3; Lam 2:5, 7; Zech 14:2

21:5 Is 63:10; Ex 6:6; Deut 4:34; Jer 6:12; Is 5:25; Jer 32:37

21:6 Jer 14:12; 32:24

21:7 2 Kin 25:5-7, 18-21; Jer 37:17; 39:5-9; 52:9; 2 Chr 36:17; Jer 13:14; Ezek 7:9; Hab 1:6-10

21:8 Deut 30:15, 19; Is 1:19, 20

21:9 Jer 38:2, 17-23; 39:18; 45:5; Jer 14:12; 24:10

21:1 Chapters 21—28 are Jeremiah's messages concerning Nebuchadnezzar's attacks on Jerusalem between 588 and 586 B.C. (see also 2 Kings 25). King Zedekiah decided to rebel against Nebuchadnezzar (2 Kings 24:20), and the nobles advised allying with Egypt. Jeremiah pronounced judgment on the kings (21:1—23:8) and false prophets (23:9–40) for leading the people astray.

21:1–2 King Zedekiah probably was referring to God's deliverance of Jerusalem from Sennacherib, king of Assyria, in the days of Hezekiah (Isaiah 36; 37). But Zedekiah's hopes were dashed. He was Judah's last ruler during the time of the exile of 586 B.C.

21:1–2 Pashhur came to the prophet for help. (This is not the same Pashhur as in 20:1.) God still had work for Jeremiah to do. In living out our faith, we may find that rejection, disappointment, or hard work has brought us to the point of despondency. But we are still needed. God has important work for us as well.

21:1–14 Jeremiah had foretold Jerusalem's destruction. The city's leaders had denied his word and mocked his announcements. In desperation, King Zedekiah turned to God for help, but without acknowledging God's warnings or admitting his sin. Too often we expect God to help us in our time of trouble even though we have ignored him in our time of prosperity. But God wants a lasting relationship. Are you trying to build a lasting friendship with God, or are you merely using him occasionally to escape trouble? What would you think of your family or friends if they thought of you only as a temporary resource?

he who goes out and falls away to the Chaldeans who are besieging you will live, and he
will have his own life as booty.
10 "For I have set My face against this city for harm and not for good," declares the
LORD. "It will be given into the hand of the king of Babylon and he will burn it with
fire." '
11 "Then *say* to the household of the king of Judah, 'Hear the word of the LORD,
12 O house of David, thus says the LORD:
"Administer justice every morning;
And deliver the *person* who has been robbed from the power of *his* oppressor,
That My wrath may not go forth like fire
And burn with none to extinguish *it,*
Because of the evil of their deeds.

13 "Behold, I am against you, O valley dweller,
O rocky plain," declares the LORD,
"You men who say, 'Who will come down against us?
Or who will enter into our habitations?'
14 "But I will punish you according to the results of your deeds," declares the LORD,
"And I will kindle a fire in its forest
That it may devour all its environs." ' "

Warning of Jerusalem's Fall

22 Thus says the LORD, "Go down to the house of the king of Judah, and there speak
this word
2 and say, 'Hear the word of the LORD, O king of Judah, who sits on David's throne,
you and your servants and your people who enter these gates.
3 'Thus says the LORD, "Do justice and righteousness, and deliver the one who has
been robbed from the power of *his* oppressor. Also do not mistreat *or* do violence to the
stranger, the orphan, or the widow; and do not shed innocent blood in this place.
4 "For if you men will indeed perform this thing, then kings will enter the gates of this
house, sitting in David's place on his throne, riding in chariots and on horses, *even the
king* himself and his servants and his people.
5 "But if you will not obey these words, I swear by Myself," declares the LORD, "that
this house will become a desolation." ' "
6 For thus says the LORD concerning the house of the king of Judah:
"You are *like* Gilead to Me,
Like the summit of Lebanon;
Yet most assuredly I will make you like a wilderness,
Like cities which are not inhabited.
7 "For I will set apart destroyers against you,
Each with his weapons;
And they will cut down your choicest cedars
And throw *them* on the fire.
8 "Many nations will pass by this city; and they will say to one another, 'Why has the
LORD done thus to this great city?'
9 "Then they will answer, 'Because they forsook the covenant of the LORD their God
and bowed down to other gods and served them.' "
10 Do not weep for the dead or mourn for him,
But weep continually for the one who goes away;
For he will never return
Or see his native land.

21:10 Lev 17:10; Jer 44:11, 27; Amos 9:4; Jer 32:28, 29; 38:3; 2 Chr 36:19; Jer 34:2; 37:10; 38:18; 39:8; 52:13

21:11 Jer 17:20

21:12 Is 7:2, 13; Ps 72:1; Is 1:17; Jer 7:5; 22:3; Zech 7:9, 10; Ps 101:8; Zeph 3:5; Jer 4:4; 17:4; Ezek 20:47, 48; Nah 1:6; Is 1:31; Jer 7:20

21:13 Jer 23:30-32; Ezek 13:8; Ps 125:2; Is 22:1; 2 Sam 5:6, 7; Jer 49:4; Lam 4:12; Obad 3, 4

21:14 Is 3:10, 11; Jer 17:10; 32:19; 2 Chr 36:19; Is 10:16, 18; Jer 11:16; 17:27; 52:13; Ezek 20:47, 48

22:2 Is 9:7; Jer 17:25; 22:4, 30; Luke 1:32

22:3 Is 58:6, 7; Jer 7:5, 23; 21:12; Mic 6:8; Zech 7:9; 8:16; Matt 23:23; Ps 72:4; Ex 22:21-24; Jer 7:6; 19:4; 22:17

22:4 Jer 17:25

22:5 Jer 17:27; 26:4; Gen 22:16; Amos 6:8; Heb 6:13

22:6 Gen 37:25; Num 32:1; Song 4:1; Ps 107:34; Is 6:11; Jer 7:34; Mic 3:12

22:7 Is 10:3-6; Jer 4:6, 7; Is 10:33, 34; 37:24; Jer 21:14

22:8 Deut 29:24-26; 1 Kin 9:8, 9; 2 Chr 7:20-22; Jer 16:10

22:9 2 Kin 22:17; 2 Chr 34:25; Jer 11:3

22:10 Eccl 4:2; Is 57:1; Jer 16:7; 22:18; Jer 25:27; 44:14

21:13 Jerusalem was built on a plateau with valleys on three sides. Because of its strategic location, the inhabitants thought they were safe.

22:1ff Chapters 22—25 may not be in chronological order. In 21:8–10 God implied that it was too late for repentance. In 22:4, however, God said that there was still time to change. The events to which this chapter refer occurred before those of chapter 21.

22:3 God gave the king the basis for rebuilding the nation—turn from evil and do right. Doing what is right is more than simply believing all the right doctrines about God. It means living obediently to God. Good deeds do not save us, but they display our faith (James 2:17–26).

22:10–12 Good King Josiah had died at the battle of Megiddo (2 Kings 23:29); his son Shallum (Jehoahaz) reigned for only three months in 609 B.C. before being taken away to Egypt by Pharaoh Neco. He would be the first ruler to die in exile. The people were told not to waste their tears on the death of Josiah, but to cry for the king who was taken into exile and would never return.

11 For thus says the LORD in regard to Shallum the son of Josiah, king of Judah, who
became king in the place of Josiah his father, who went forth from this place, "He will
never return there;
12 but in the place where they led him captive, there he will die and not see this land
again.

22:11 2 Kin 23:30-34; 1 Chr 3:15; 2 Chr 36:1-4

22:12 2 Kin 23:34; Jer 22:18

Messages about the Kings

13 "Woe to him who builds his house without righteousness
And his upper rooms without justice,
Who uses his neighbor's services without pay
And does not give him his wages,
14 Who says, 'I will build myself a roomy house
With spacious upper rooms,
And cut out its windows,
Paneling *it* with cedar and painting *it* bright red.'
15 "Do you become a king because you are competing in cedar?
Did not your father eat and drink
And do justice and righteousness?
Then it was well with him.
16 "He pled the cause of the afflicted and needy;
Then it was well.
Is not that what it means to know Me?"
Declares the LORD.
17 "But your eyes and your heart
Are *intent* only upon your own dishonest gain,
And on shedding innocent blood
And on practicing oppression and extortion."
18 Therefore thus says the LORD in regard to Jehoiakim the son of Josiah, king of Judah,
"They will not lament for him:
'Alas, my brother!' or, 'Alas, sister!'
They will not lament for him:
'Alas for the master!' or, 'Alas for his splendor!'
19 "He will be buried with a donkey's burial,
Dragged off and thrown out beyond the gates of Jerusalem.
20 "Go up to Lebanon and cry out,
And lift up your voice in Bashan;
Cry out also from Abarim,
For all your lovers have been crushed.
21 "I spoke to you in your prosperity;
But you said, 'I will not listen!'
This has been your practice from your youth,
That you have not obeyed My voice.
22 "The wind will sweep away all your shepherds,
And your lovers will go into captivity;
Then you will surely be ashamed and humiliated
Because of all your wickedness.
23 "You who dwell in Lebanon,
Nested in the cedars,
How you will groan when pangs come upon you,
Pain like a woman in childbirth!

22:13 Jer 17:11; Mic 3:10; Hab 2:9; Lev 19:13; James 5:4

22:14 Is 5:8; 2 Sam 7:2; Hag 1:4

22:15 2 Kin 23:25; Jer 7:5; 21:12; Ps 128:2; Is 3:10; Jer 42:6

22:16 Ps 72:1-4, 12, 13; 1 Chr 28:9; Jer 9:24

22:17 Jer 6:13; 8:10; Luke 12:15-20; 2 Kin 24:4; Jer 22:3

22:18 2 Kin 23:36-24:6; 2 Chr 36:5; Jer 22:10; 34:5; 1 Kin 13:30

22:19 1 Kin 21:23, 24; Jer 36:30

22:20 Num 27:12; Deut 32:49; Jer 2:25; 3:1

22:21 Jer 13:10; 19:15; Jer 3:25; Jer 3:24; 32:30

22:22 Jer 23:1; Jer 30:14; Is 65:13; Jer 20:11

22:23 Jer 4:31; 6:24

22:15–16 God passed judgment on King Jehoiakim. His father, Josiah, had been one of Judah's great kings, but Jehoiakim was evil. Josiah had been faithful to his responsibility to be a model of right living, but Jehoiakim had been unfaithful to his responsibility to imitate his father. God's judgment was on unfaithful Jehoiakim. He could not claim his father's blessings when he had not followed his father's God. We may inherit our parents' money, but we cannot inherit their faith. A great heritage, a good education, or a beautiful home doesn't guarantee strong character. We must have our own relationship with God.

22:21 Jehoiakim had been hardheaded and hardhearted since childhood. God warned him, but he refused to listen. His prosperity always took a higher priority than his relationship with God. If you ever find yourself so comfortable that you don't have time for God, stop and ask which is more important—the comforts of this life or a close relationship with God.

24 "As I live," declares the LORD, "even though [8]Coniah the son of Jehoiakim king of
Judah were a signet *ring* on My right hand, yet I would pull you off;
25 and I will give you over into the hand of those who are seeking your life, yes, into
the hand of those whom you dread, even into the hand of Nebuchadnezzar king of Babylon and into the hand of the Chaldeans.
26 "I will hurl you and your mother who bore you into another country where you were
not born, and there you will die.
27 "But as for the land to which they desire to return, they will not return to it.
28 "Is this man Coniah a despised, shattered jar?
Or is he an undesirable vessel?
Why have he and his descendants been hurled out
And cast into a land that they had not known?
29 "O land, land, land,
Hear the word of the LORD!
30 "Thus says the LORD,
'Write this man down childless,
A man who will not prosper in his days;
For no man of his descendants will prosper
Sitting on the throne of David
Or ruling again in Judah.' "

The Coming Messiah: the Righteous Branch

23 "Woe to the shepherds who are destroying and scattering the sheep of My pasture!" declares the LORD.
2 Therefore thus says the LORD God of Israel concerning the shepherds who are tending My people: "You have scattered My flock and driven them away, and have not attended to them; behold, I am about to attend to you for the evil of your deeds," declares
the LORD.
3 "Then I Myself will gather the remnant of My flock out of all the countries where I
have driven them and bring them back to their pasture, and they will be fruitful and
multiply.
4 "I will also raise up shepherds over them and they will tend them; and they will not
be afraid any longer, nor be terrified, nor will any be missing," declares the LORD.
5 "Behold, *the* days are coming," declares the LORD,
"When I will raise up for David a righteous Branch;
And He will reign as king and act wisely
And do justice and righteousness in the land.
6 "In His days Judah will be saved,
And Israel will dwell securely;
And this is His name by which He will be called,
'The LORD our righteousness.'
7 "Therefore behold, *the* days are coming," declares the LORD, "when they will no longer
say, 'As the LORD lives, who brought up the sons of Israel from the land of Egypt,'
8 but, 'As the LORD lives, who brought up and led back the descendants of the house-
hold of Israel from *the* north land and from all the countries where I had driven them.'
Then they will live on their own soil."

8 I.e. Jehoiachin

22:24 2 Kin 24:6; 1 Chr 3:16; 2 Chr 36:9

22:25 2 Kin 24:15, 16; Jer 21:7; 34:20, 21

22:26 2 Kin 24:15; Jer 10:18; 16:13; 2 Kin 24:8

22:28 Ps 31:12; Jer 48:38; Hos 8:8; Jer 15:1; Jer 17:4

22:29 Deut 4:26; Jer 6:19; Mic 1:2

22:30 1 Chr 3:17; Matt 1:12; Jer 2:37; 10:21; Ps 94:20; Jer 36:30

23:1 Ezek 13:3; 34:2; Zech 11:17; Is 56:9-12; Jer 10:21; 50:6; Ezek 34:31

23:2 Ex 32:34; Jer 21:12; 44:22

23:3 Is 11:11, 12, 16; Jer 31:7, 8; 32:37

23:4 Jer 3:15; 31:10; Ezek 34:23; Jer 30:10; 46:27, 28; John 6:39; 10:28; 1 Pet 1:5

23:5 Jer 33:14; Is 4:2; 11:1-5; 53:2; Jer 30:9; 33:15, 16; Zech 3:8; 6:12, 13; Is 9:7; 52:13; Luke 1:32, 33; Ps 72:2; Is 9:7; 32:1; Dan 9:24

23:6 Deut 33:28; Jer 30:10; Zech 14:11; Is 7:14; 9:6; Matt 1:21-23; Is 45:24; Jer 33:16; Dan 9:24; Rom 3:22; 1 Cor 1:30

23:7 Is 43:18, 19; Jer 16:14, 15

23:8 Jer 16:15; Is 43:5, 6; Ezek 34:13; Amos 9:14, 15

22:24–25 A signet ring was extremely valuable because a king used it to authenticate important documents. Jehoiachin's sins spoiled his usefulness to God. Even if he were God's own signet ring, God would depose him because of his sins (see 24:1).

22:30 Zedekiah reigned after Jehoiachin but died before him (52:10–11). Jehoiachin was the last king of David's line to sit on the throne in Judah (1 Chronicles 3:15–20). He had seven sons, but not one served as king. Jehoiachin's grandson Zerubbabel ruled after the return from exile (Ezra 2:2). He was only a governor, not a king.

23:1–4 Those responsible to lead Israel in God's path were the very ones responsible for Israel's present plight, and so God had decreed harsh judgment against them. Leaders are held responsible for those entrusted to their care. Whom has God placed in your care? Remember that you are accountable to God for those you influence and lead.

23:5–6 Jeremiah contrasted the present corrupt leaders with the coming Messiah, the perfect King who would come from David's line to reign over Israel. The King is called a righteous Branch because he will sprout up from the stump of David's fallen dynasty (Isaiah 11:1). This new growth will have God's own characteristics. Like the Creator, the Branch will be righteous.

False Prophets Denounced

9 As for the prophets:
My heart is broken within me,
All my bones tremble;
I have become like a drunken man,
Even like a man overcome with wine,
Because of the LORD
And because of His holy words.
10 For the land is full of adulterers;
For the land mourns because of the curse.
The pastures of the wilderness have dried up.
Their course also is evil
And their might is not right.
11 "For both prophet and priest are polluted;
Even in My house I have found their wickedness," declares the LORD.
12 "Therefore their way will be like slippery paths to them,
They will be driven away into the gloom and fall down in it;
For I will bring calamity upon them,
The year of their punishment," declares the LORD.

13 "Moreover, among the prophets of Samaria I saw an offensive thing:
They prophesied by Baal and led My people Israel astray.
14 "Also among the prophets of Jerusalem I have seen a horrible thing:
The committing of adultery and walking in falsehood;
And they strengthen the hands of evildoers,
So that no one has turned back from his wickedness.
All of them have become to Me like Sodom,
And her inhabitants like Gomorrah.
15 "Therefore thus says the LORD of hosts concerning the prophets,
'Behold, I am going to feed them wormwood
And make them drink poisonous water,
For from the prophets of Jerusalem
Pollution has gone forth into all the land.' "

16 Thus says the LORD of hosts,
"Do not listen to the words of the prophets who are prophesying to you.
They are leading you into futility;
They speak a vision of their own imagination,
Not from the mouth of the LORD.
17 "They keep saying to those who despise Me,
'The LORD has said, "You will have peace" ';
And as for everyone who walks in the stubbornness of his own heart,
They say, 'Calamity will not come upon you.'
18 "But who has stood in the council of the LORD,
That he should see and hear His word?
Who has given heed to His word and listened?
19 "Behold, the storm of the LORD has gone forth in wrath,
Even a whirling tempest;
It will swirl down on the head of the wicked.
20 "The anger of the LORD will not turn back
Until He has performed and carried out the purposes of His heart;

23:9 Jer 8:18; Hab 3:16

23:10 Jer 9:2; Hos 4:2, 3; Mal 3:5; Jer 12:4; Ps 107:34; Jer 9:10

23:11 Jer 6:13; Zeph 3:4

23:12 Ps 35:6; Prov 4:19; Jer 13:16; Is 8:22; John 12:35; Jer 11:23

23:13 Hos 9:7, 8; 1 Kin 18:18-21; Jer 2:8; 23:32; Is 9:16

23:14 Jer 5:30; Jer 29:23; Jer 23:22; Ezek 13:22, 23; Gen 18:20; Deut 32:32; Is 1:9, 10; Jer 20:16; 49:18; Matt 11:24

23:15 Deut 29:18; Jer 8:14; 9:15

23:16 Jer 27:9, 10, 14-17; 1 John 4:1; Matt 7:15; 2 Cor 11:13-15; Gal 1:8, 9; Jer 14:14; Ezek 13:3, 6; Jer 9:12, 20

23:17 Mic 2:11; Jer 8:11; Ezek 13:10; Jer 13:10; 18:12; Jer 5:12; Amos 9:10; Mic 3:11

23:18 Job 15:8, 9; Jer 23:22; 1 Cor 2:16; Job 33:31

23:19 Jer 25:32; 30:23; Amos 1:14

23:20 2 Kin 23:26, 27; Jer 30:24; Is 55:11; Zech 1:6; Gen 49:1

23:9–14 How did the nation become so corrupt? A major factor was false prophecy. The false prophets had a large, enthusiastic audience and were very popular because they made the people believe that all was well. By contrast, Jeremiah's message from God was unpopular because it showed the people how bad they were.

There are four warning signs of false prophets—characteristics we need to watch for even today. (1) They may appear to speak God's message, but they do not live according to his principles. (2) They water down God's message in order to make it more palatable. (3) They encourage their listeners, often subtly, to disobey God. (4) They tend to be arrogant and self-serving, appealing to the desires of their audience instead of being true to God's Word.

23:14 Sodom and Gomorrah were sinful cities destroyed by God (Genesis 19:23–24). In the Bible they typify the ultimate in degrading, sinful behavior and rebellion against God.

23:20 "In the last days you will clearly understand it" means that the people would see the truth of this prophecy when Jerusalem fell.

In the last days you will clearly understand it.
21 "I did not send *these* prophets,
But they ran.
I did not speak to them,
But they prophesied.
22 "But if they had stood in My council,
Then they would have announced My words to My people,
And would have turned them back from their evil way
And from the evil of their deeds.

23 "Am I a God who is near," declares the LORD,
"And not a God far off?
24 "Can a man hide himself in hiding places
So I do not see him?" declares the LORD.
"Do I not fill the heavens and the earth?" declares the LORD.
25 "I have heard what the prophets have said who prophesy falsely in My name, saying,
'I had a dream, I had a dream!'
26 "How long? Is there *anything* in the hearts of the prophets who prophesy falsehood,
even *these* prophets of the deception of their own heart,
27 who intend to make My people forget My name by their dreams which they relate
to one another, just as their fathers forgot My name because of Baal?
28 "The prophet who has a dream may relate *his* dream, but let him who has My word
speak My word in truth. What does straw have *in common* with grain?" declares the LORD.
29 "Is not My word like fire?" declares the LORD, "and like a hammer which shatters a
rock?
30 "Therefore behold, I am against the prophets," declares the LORD, "who steal My
words from each other.
31 "Behold, I am against the prophets," declares the LORD, "who use their tongues and
declare, '*The Lord* declares.'
32 "Behold, I am against those who have prophesied false dreams," declares the LORD,
"and related them and led My people astray by their falsehoods and reckless boasting;
yet I did not send them or command them, nor do they furnish this people the slightest
benefit," declares the LORD.
33 "Now when this people or the prophet or a priest asks you saying, 'What is the [9]ora-
cle of the LORD?' then you shall say to them, 'What oracle?' The LORD declares, 'I will
abandon you.'
34 "Then as for the prophet or the priest or the people who say, 'The oracle of the LORD,'
I will bring punishment upon that man and his household.
35 "Thus will each of you say to his neighbor and to his brother, 'What has the LORD
answered?' or, 'What has the LORD spoken?'
36 "For you will no longer remember the oracle of the LORD, because every man's own
word will become the oracle, and you have perverted the words of the living God, the
LORD of hosts, our God.
37 "Thus you will say to *that* prophet, 'What has the LORD answered you?' and, 'What
has the LORD spoken?'
38 "For if you say, 'The oracle of the LORD!' surely thus says the LORD, 'Because you
said this word, "The oracle of the LORD!" I have also sent to you, saying, "You shall not
say, 'The oracle of the LORD!' " '

9 Or *burden,* and so throughout the ch

23:21 Jer 14:14; 23:32; 27:15
23:22 Jer 9:12; 23:18; Jer 35:15; Zech 1:4
23:23 Ps 139:1-10
23:24 Job 22:13, 14; 34:21, 22; Ps 139:7-12; Is 29:15; Jer 49:10; Heb 4:13; 1 Kin 8:27; 2 Chr 2:6; Is 66:1
23:25 Jer 8:6; 1 Cor 4:5; Jer 14:14; Num 12:6; Jer 23:28, 32; 29:8; Joel 2:28
23:26 1 Tim 4:1, 2
23:27 Deut 13:1-3; Jer 29:8; Judg 3:7; 8:33, 34
23:28 Jer 9:12, 20; 1 Cor 3:12, 13
23:29 Jer 5:14; 20:9; 2 Cor 10:4, 5
23:30 Deut 18:20; Ps 34:16; Jer 14:14, 15; Ezek 13:8
23:32 Deut 13:1, 2; Jer 23:25; Zeph 3:4; Jer 23:21; Lam 3:37; Jer 7:8; Lam 2:14
23:33 Is 13:1; Nah 1:1; Hab 1:1; Zech 9:1; Mal 1:1; Jer 12:7; 23:39
23:34 Lam 2:14; Zech 13:3
23:35 Jer 33:3; 42:4
23:36 Gal 1:7, 8; 2 Pet 3:16; 2 Kin 19:4; Jer 10:10

23:28 True prophets and false prophets are as different as straw and grain. Straw is useless for food and cannot compare to nourishing grain. To share the gospel is a great responsibility because the way we present it and live it will encourage people either to accept it or reject it. Whether we speak from a pulpit, teach in a class, or share with friends, we are entrusted with accurately communicating and living out God's Word. As you share God's Word with friends and neighbors, they will look for its effectiveness in your life. Unless it has changed you, why should they let it change them? If you preach it, make sure you live it!

23:33–40 People mocked Jeremiah by saying sarcastically, "What is the oracle of the LORD?" (*oracle* meaning "utterance" or "burden"). The people mocked Jeremiah and God because it seemed that Jeremiah brought nothing but God's sad news of condemnation. But this sad news was the truth. If they had accepted it, they would have had to repent and turn to God. Because they did not want to do this, they rejected Jeremiah's message. Have you ever rejected a message or made fun of it because it would require you to change your ways? Before dismissing someone who brings sad news, look carefully at your motives.

39 "Therefore behold, I will surely forget you and cast you away from My presence, along
with the city which I gave you and your fathers.
40 "I will put an everlasting reproach on you and an everlasting humiliation which will
not be forgotten."

Baskets of Figs and the Returnees

24 After Nebuchadnezzar king of Babylon had carried away captive Jeconiah the son
of Jehoiakim, king of Judah, and the officials of Judah with the craftsmen and
smiths from Jerusalem and had brought them to Babylon, the LORD showed me: behold,
two baskets of figs set before the temple of the LORD!
2 One basket had very good figs, like first-ripe figs, and the other basket had very bad
figs which could not be eaten due to rottenness.
3 Then the LORD said to me, "What do you see, Jeremiah?" And I said, "Figs, the
good figs, very good; and the bad *figs,* very bad, which cannot be eaten due to rottenness."
4 Then the word of the LORD came to me, saying,
5 "Thus says the LORD God of Israel, 'Like these good figs, so I will regard as good the
captives of Judah, whom I have sent out of this place *into* the land of the Chaldeans.
6 'For I will set My eyes on them for good, and I will bring them again to this land; and
I will build them up and not overthrow them, and I will plant them and not pluck them
up.
7 'I will give them a heart to know Me, for I am the LORD; and they will be My people,
and I will be their God, for they will return to Me with their whole heart.
8 'But like the bad figs which cannot be eaten due to rottenness—indeed, thus says
the LORD—so I will abandon Zedekiah king of Judah and his officials, and the remnant
of Jerusalem who remain in this land and the ones who dwell in the land of Egypt.
9 'I will make them a terror *and an* evil for all the kingdoms of the earth, as a reproach
and a proverb, a taunt and a curse in all places where I will scatter them.
10 'I will send the sword, the famine and the pestilence upon them until they are destroyed from the land which I gave to them and their forefathers.' "

Prophecy of the Captivity

25 The word that came to Jeremiah concerning all the people of Judah, in the fourth
year of Jehoiakim the son of Josiah, king of Judah (that was the first year of Nebuchadnezzar king of Babylon),
2 which Jeremiah the prophet spoke to all the people of Judah and to all the inhabitants of Jerusalem, saying,
3 "From the thirteenth year of Josiah the son of Amon, king of Judah, even to this day,
these twenty-three years the word of the LORD has come to me, and I have spoken to
you again and again, but you have not listened.
4 "And the LORD has sent to you all His servants the prophets again and again, but
you have not listened nor inclined your ear to hear,

23:39 Jer 7:14, 15; 23:33; Ezek 8:18

23:40 Jer 20:11; 42:18; Ezek 5:14, 15

24:1 2 Kin 24:10-16; 2 Chr 36:10; Jer 27:20; 29:1, 2; Amos 8:1

24:2 Mic 7:1; Nah 3:12; Is 5:4, 7; Jer 29:17

24:5 Nah 1:7; Zech 13:9

24:6 Jer 12:15; 29:10; 32:37; Ezek 11:17; Jer 31:4; 32:41; 33:7; 42:10

24:7 Deut 30:6; Jer 31:33; 32:40; Ezek 11:19; 36:26; Is 51:16; Jer 7:23; 30:22; 31:33; 32:38; Ezek 14:11; Zech 8:8; Heb 8:10; 1 Sam 7:3; Ps 119:2; Jer 29:13

24:8 Jer 29:17; Jer 39:5; Ezek 12:12, 13; Jer 39:9; Jer 44:1, 26-30

24:9 Jer 15:4; 29:18; 34:17; 1 Kin 9:7; Ps 44:13, 14; Is 65:15

24:10 Is 51:19; Jer 21:9; 27:8; Ezek 5:12-17

25:1 Jer 36:1; 46:2; 2 Kin 24:1, 2; 2 Chr 36:4-6; Dan 1:1, 2

25:2 Jer 18:11

25:3 Jer 1:2; 2 Chr 34:1-3, 8; Jer 36:2; Jer 7:25; 11:7; 26:5

25:4 2 Chr 36:15

24:1 This happened in 597 B.C. Jehoiachin was taken to Babylon, and Zedekiah became king. Often royal officials were exiled to keep them from exerting power and starting a rebellion. Skilled craftsmen and artisans were taken because they were valuable for Babylon's building program. Jeremiah foretold this event in 22:24–28.

24:2–10 The good figs represented the exiles to Babylon—not because they themselves were good, but because their hearts would respond to God. He would preserve them and bring them back to the land. The bad figs represented those who remained in Judah or ran away to Egypt. Those people may have arrogantly believed they would be blessed if they remained in the land or escaped to Egypt, but the opposite was true because God would use the captivity to refine the exiles. We may assume we are blessed when life goes well and cursed when it does not. But trouble is a blessing when it makes us stronger, and prosperity is a curse if it entices us away from God. If you are facing trouble, ask God to help you grow stronger for him. If things are going your way, ask God to help you use your prosperity for him.

24:6 The exiles in Babylon were cared for by the Lord. Although they were moved to a foreign land, their captivity was not enslavement. The people could function in business and own homes. Some, like Daniel, even held high positions in the government (see Daniel 2:48).

25:1ff Jeremiah gave this message in 605 B.C., the year Nebuchadnezzar came to power. From verse 3 we learn that the beginning of Jeremiah's ministry was in 627 B.C. He predicted the 70 years of captivity a full 20 years before it began.

25:2–6 Imagine preaching the same message for 23 years and continually being rejected! Jeremiah faced this, but because he had committed his life to God, he continued to proclaim the message—"Turn now everyone from his evil way and from the evil of your deeds." Regardless of the people's response, Jeremiah did not give up. God never stops loving us, even when we reject him. We can thank God that he won't give up on us, and, like Jeremiah, we can commit ourselves to never forsaking him. No matter how people respond when you tell them about God, remain faithful to God's high call and continue to witness for him.

5 saying, 'Turn now everyone from his evil way and from the evil of your deeds, and
dwell on the land which the LORD has given to you and your forefathers forever and
ever;
6 and do not go after other gods to serve them and to worship them, and do not provoke Me to anger with the work of your hands, and I will do you no harm.'
7 "Yet you have not listened to Me," declares the LORD, "in order that you might provoke Me to anger with the work of your hands to your own harm.
8 "Therefore thus says the LORD of hosts, 'Because you have not obeyed My words,
9 behold, I will send and take all the families of the north,' declares the LORD, 'and *I*
will send to Nebuchadnezzar king of Babylon, My servant, and will bring them against
this land and against its inhabitants and against all these nations round about; and I will
utterly destroy them and make them a horror and a hissing, and an everlasting desolation.
10 'Moreover, I will take from them the voice of joy and the voice of gladness, the voice
of the bridegroom and the voice of the bride, the sound of the millstones and the light of
the lamp.
11 'This whole land will be a desolation and a horror, and these nations will serve the
king of Babylon seventy years.

Babylon Will Be Judged

12 'Then it will be when seventy years are completed I will punish the king of Babylon
and that nation,' declares the LORD, 'for their iniquity, and the land of the Chaldeans;
and I will make it an everlasting desolation.
13 'I will bring upon that land all My words which I have pronounced against it, all that
is written in this book which Jeremiah has prophesied against all the nations.
14 '(For many nations and great kings will make slaves of them, even them; and I will
recompense them according to their deeds and according to the work of their hands.)' "
15 For thus the LORD, the God of Israel, says to me, "Take this cup of the wine of wrath
from My hand and cause all the nations to whom I send you to drink it.
16 "They will drink and stagger and go mad because of the sword that I will send among
them."
17 Then I took the cup from the LORD'S hand and made all the nations to whom the
LORD sent me drink it:
18 Jerusalem and the cities of Judah and its kings *and* its princes, to make them a ruin,
a horror, a hissing and a curse, as it is this day;
19 Pharaoh king of Egypt, his servants, his princes and all his people;
20 and all the foreign people, all the kings of the land of Uz, all the kings of the land of
the Philistines (even Ashkelon, Gaza, Ekron and the remnant of Ashdod);
21 Edom, Moab and the sons of Ammon;
22 and all the kings of Tyre, all the kings of Sidon and the kings of the coastlands which
are beyond the sea;
23 and Dedan, Tema, Buz and all who cut the corners *of their hair;*
24 and all the kings of Arabia and all the kings of the foreign people who dwell in the
desert;
25 and all the kings of Zimri, all the kings of Elam and all the kings of Media;
26 and all the kings of the north, near and far, one with another; and all the kingdoms
of the earth which are upon the face of the ground, and the king of Sheshach shall drink
after them.
27 "You shall say to them, 'Thus says the LORD of hosts, the God of Israel, "Drink, be
drunk, vomit, fall and rise no more because of the sword which I will send among you." '
28 "And it will be, if they refuse to take the cup from your hand to drink, then you will
say to them, 'Thus says the LORD of hosts: "You shall surely drink!
29 "For behold, I am beginning to work calamity in *this* city which is called by My name,
and shall you be completely free from punishment? You will not be free from punish-

25:5 2 Kin 17:13; Is 55:6, 7; Jer 4:1; 35:15; Ezek 18:30; Jon 3:8-10; Gen 17:8

25:6 Deut 6:14; 8:19; 2 Kin 17:35; Jer 35:15

25:7 2 Kin 17:17; 21:15; Jer 7:19; 32:30-33

25:9 Jer 1:15; 6:22, 23; Is 13:3; Jer 27:6; 43:10; 1 Kin 9:7, 8

25:10 Is 24:8-11; Jer 7:34; 16:9; Ezek 26:13; Rev 18:23; Is 47:2

25:11 Jer 4:27; 12:11, 12; 2 Chr 36:21; Jer 29:10; Dan 9:2; Zech 7:5

25:12 Ezra 1:1; Jer 29:10; Dan 9:2; Is 13:14; Jer ch 50, 51; Is 13:19

25:13 Jer 36:4, 29, 32

25:14 Jer 27:7; 50:9, 41; 51:27, 28; Jer 51:6, 24, 56

25:15 Job 21:20; Ps 75:8; Is 51:17, 22; Jer 51:7

25:16 Nah 3:11

25:18 Ps 60:3; Is 51:17

25:19 Jer 46:2-28; Nah 3:8-10

25:20 Ezek 30:5; Job 1:1; Lam 4:21; Jer 47:1-7; Is 20:1

25:23 Is 21:13; Jer 49:7, 8; Gen 22:21; Jer 9:26

25:24 2 Chr 9:14; Ezek 30:5

25:27 Hab 2:16; Ezek 21:4, 5

25:29 Prov 11:31; Is 10:12; Jer 13:13; Ezek 9:6; 1 Pet 4:17; 1 Kin 8:43; Ezek 38:21

25:12 This event is further described in Daniel 5. The troops of Cyrus the Great entered Babylon in 539 B.C. and killed Belshazzar, the last Babylonian ruler.

25:15–38 Judah would not be the only nation to drink the cup of God's wrath. Here Jeremiah listed other wicked nations who would experience God's wrath at the hand of Babylon. Finally, Babylon itself (called Sheshach in 25:26) would be destroyed because of its sin.

ment; for I am summoning a sword against all the inhabitants of the earth," declares the
LORD of hosts.'
30 "Therefore you shall prophesy against them all these words, and you shall say to them,
'The LORD will roar from on high
And utter His voice from His holy habitation;
He will roar mightily against His fold.
He will shout like those who tread *the grapes,*
Against all the inhabitants of the earth.
31 'A clamor has come to the end of the earth,
Because the LORD has a controversy with the nations.
He is entering into judgment with all flesh;
As for the wicked, He has given them to the sword,' declares the LORD."

32 Thus says the LORD of hosts,
"Behold, evil is going forth
From nation to nation,
And a great storm is being stirred up
From the remotest parts of the earth.
33 "Those slain by the LORD on that day will be from one end of the earth to the other.
They will not be lamented, gathered or buried; they will be like dung on the face of the
ground.
34 "Wail, you shepherds, and cry;
And wallow *in ashes,* you masters of the flock;
For the days of your slaughter and your dispersions have come,
And you will fall like a choice vessel.
35 "Flight will perish from the shepherds,
And escape from the masters of the flock.
36 "*Hear* the sound of the cry of the shepherds,
And the wailing of the masters of the flock!
For the LORD is destroying their pasture,
37 "And the peaceful folds are made silent
Because of the fierce anger of the LORD.
38 "He has left His hiding place like the lion;
For their land has become a horror
Because of the fierceness of the oppressing *sword*
And because of His fierce anger."

Cities of Judah Warned

26 In the beginning of the reign of Jehoiakim the son of Josiah, king of Judah, this
word came from the LORD, saying,
2 "Thus says the LORD, 'Stand in the court of the LORD'S house, and speak to all the
cities of Judah who have come to worship *in* the LORD'S house all the words that I have
commanded you to speak to them. Do not omit a word!
3 'Perhaps they will listen and everyone will turn from his evil way, that I may repent
of the calamity which I am planning to do to them because of the evil of their deeds.'
4 "And you will say to them, 'Thus says the LORD, "If you will not listen to Me, to walk
in My law which I have set before you,

25:30 Is 42:13; Jer 25:38; Joel 2:11; 3:16; Amos 1:2

25:31 Hos 4:1; Mic 6:2; Is 66:16; Ezek 20:35, 36; Joel 3:2

25:32 2 Chr 15:6; Is 34:2; Is 30:30; Jer 23:19

25:33 Is 34:2, 3; 66:16; Ps 79:3; Jer 16:4; Ezek 39:4, 17; Is 5:25

25:34 Jer 6:26; Ezek 27:30; Is 34:6, 7; Jer 50:27

25:35 Job 11:20; Jer 11:11; Amos 2:14

25:37 Is 27:10, 11; Jer 5:17; 13:20; Ps 97:1-3; Is 66:15; Heb 12:29

25:38 Jer 4:7; 5:6; Hos 5:14; 13:7, 8

26:1 2 Kin 23:36; 2 Chr 36:4, 5

26:2 2 Chr 24:20, 21; Jer 7:2; 19:14; Deut 12:5; Jer 1:17; 42:4; Matt 28:20; Acts 20:20, 27; Deut 4:2

26:3 Is 1:16-19; Jer 36:3-7; Jer 18:8; Jon 3:8

26:4 Lev 26:14; 1 Kin 9:6; Is 1:20; Jer 17:27; 22:5; Jer 32:23; 44:10, 23

26:1ff The events described in this chapter took place in 609—608 B.C., before the events described in chapter 25. Jehoiakim was a materialistic and self-centered king who persecuted and murdered innocent people (36:22–32; 2 Kings 23:36—24:6). Chapter 26 describes how and why Jeremiah was on trial for his life.

26:2 God reminded Jeremiah that he wanted his entire message given—"Do not omit a word!" Jeremiah may have been tempted to leave out the parts that would turn his audience against him, would sound too harsh, or would make him sound like a traitor. But by God's command, he was not to delete parts of God's message to suit himself, his audience, or the circumstances in which he found himself. Like Jeremiah, we must never ignore or repress important parts of God's Word to please anyone.

26:2–9 Shiloh was where the tabernacle had been set up after the conquest of Canaan (Joshua 18:1). It was destroyed in 1050 B.C. by the Philistines. "I will make this house like Shiloh" means that Jerusalem and the temple would be destroyed. When Jeremiah said that Jerusalem, the city of God, would become an object of cursing and the temple would be destroyed (26:6), the priests and false prophets were infuriated. The temple was important to them because the people's reverence for it brought them power. By saying that the temple would be destroyed, Jeremiah undermined their authority. Jesus also infuriated the religious leaders of his time by foretelling the destruction of Jerusalem and the temple (Matthew 24:2).

5 to listen to the words of My servants the prophets, whom I have been sending to
you again and again, but you have not listened;
6 then I will make this house like Shiloh, and this city I will make a curse to all the
nations of the earth." ' "

A Plot to Murder Jeremiah

7 The priests and the prophets and all the people heard Jeremiah speaking these words
in the house of the LORD.
8 When Jeremiah finished speaking all that the LORD had commanded *him* to speak
to all the people, the priests and the prophets and all the people seized him, saying, "You
must die!
9 "Why have you prophesied in the name of the LORD saying, 'This house will be like
Shiloh and this city will be desolate, without inhabitant'?" And all the people gathered
about Jeremiah in the house of the LORD.
10 When the officials of Judah heard these things, they came up from the king's house
to the house of the LORD and sat in the entrance of the New Gate of the LORD'S *house.*
11 Then the priests and the prophets spoke to the officials and to all the people, saying, "A death sentence for this man! For he has prophesied against this city as you have
heard in your hearing."
12 Then Jeremiah spoke to all the officials and to all the people, saying, "The LORD
sent me to prophesy against this house and against this city all the words that you have
heard.
13 "Now therefore amend your ways and your deeds and obey the voice of the LORD
your God; and the LORD will change His mind about the misfortune which He has pronounced against you.
14 "But as for me, behold, I am in your hands; do with me as is good and right in your
sight.
15 "Only know for certain that if you put me to death, you will bring innocent blood on
yourselves, and on this city and on its inhabitants; for truly the LORD has sent me to you
to speak all these words in your hearing."

Jeremiah Is Spared

16 Then the officials and all the people said to the priests and to the prophets, "No
death sentence for this man! For he has spoken to us in the name of the LORD our God."
17 Then some of the elders of the land rose up and spoke to all the assembly of the
people, saying,
18 "Micah of Moresheth prophesied in the days of Hezekiah king of Judah; and he spoke
to all the people of Judah, saying, 'Thus the LORD of hosts has said,
"Zion will be plowed *as* a field,
And Jerusalem will become ruins,
And the mountain of the house as the high places of a forest." '
19 "Did Hezekiah king of Judah and all Judah put him to death? Did he not fear the
LORD and entreat the favor of the LORD, and the LORD changed His mind about the
misfortune which He had pronounced against them? But we are committing a great evil
against ourselves."
20 Indeed, there was also a man who prophesied in the name of the LORD, Uriah the
son of Shemaiah from Kiriath-jearim; and he prophesied against this city and against
this land words similar to all those of Jeremiah.
21 When King Jehoiakim and all his mighty men and all the officials heard his words,
then the king sought to put him to death; but Uriah heard *it,* and he was afraid and fled
and went to Egypt.

26:5 2 Kin 9:7; Ezra 9:11; Jer 7:13; 25:3, 4

26:6 Josh 18:1; 1 Sam 4:12; Ps 78:60, 61; Jer 7:12, 14; 2 Kin 22:19; Is 65:15; Jer 24:9; 25:18

26:7 Jer 5:31; Mic 3:11

26:8 Jer 11:19; 18:23; Lam 4:13, 14; Matt 21:35, 36; 23:34, 35; 27:20

26:9 Jer 9:11; 33:10; Acts 3:11; 5:12

26:10 Jer 26:21; Jer 36:10

26:11 Jer 18:23; Deut 18:20; Matt 26:66; Jer 38:4; Acts 6:11-14

26:12 Jer 1:17, 18; 26:15; Amos 7:15; Acts 4:19; 5:29

26:13 Jer 7:3, 5; 18:8, 11; 26:3; 35:15; Joel 2:14; Jon 3:9; 4:2

26:14 Jer 38:5

26:15 Num 35:33; Prov 6:16, 17; Jer 7:6

26:16 Jer 26:11; 36:19, 25; 38:7, 13; Acts 5:34-39; 23:9, 29; 25:25; 26:31

26:17 Acts 5:34

26:18 Mic 1:1; Neh 4:2; Ps 79:1; Jer 9:11; Mic 3:12; Is 2:2, 3; Jer 17:3; Mic 4:1; Zech 8:3

26:19 2 Chr 29:6-11; 32:26; Is 37:1, 4, 15-20; Ex 32:14; 2 Sam 24:16; Jer 44:7; Hab 2:10

26:20 Josh 9:17; 1 Sam 6:21; 7:2

26:21 2 Chr 16:10; 24:21; Jer 36:26; Matt 14:5; 1 Kin 19:2-4; Matt 10:23

26:11 Jeremiah was branded a traitor because he prophesied the destruction of the city and the temple. But the "courageous" people advocated a foreign alliance to fight Babylon and retain their independence.

26:17–19 The elders remembered the words of the prophet Micah (Micah 3:12), which were similar to the words Jeremiah spoke. When Micah called the people to repent, they turned from their wickedness. Although these people did not kill Jeremiah, they missed the main point—that the application of the story was for them. They spared Jeremiah, but they did not spare themselves by repenting of their sins. As you recall a great story of the Bible, ask how it can be applied to *your* life.

26:20–23 Uriah is an otherwise unknown prophet who was executed for faithfully proclaiming God's words. This shows us that God has had other prophets whose words are not included in the Bible.

22 Then King Jehoiakim sent men to Egypt: Elnathan the son of Achbor and *certain*
men with him *went* into Egypt.
23 And they brought Uriah from Egypt and led him to King Jehoiakim, who slew him
with a sword and cast his dead body into the burial place of the common people.
24 But the hand of Ahikam the son of Shaphan was with Jeremiah, so that he was not
given into the hands of the people to put him to death.

The Nations to Submit to Nebuchadnezzar

27 In the beginning of the reign of Zedekiah the son of Josiah, king of Judah, this
word came to Jeremiah from the LORD, saying—
2 thus says the LORD to me—"Make for yourself bonds and yokes and put them on
your neck,
3 and send word to the king of Edom, to the king of Moab, to the king of the sons of
Ammon, to the king of Tyre and to the king of Sidon by the messengers who come to
Jerusalem to Zedekiah king of Judah.
4 "Command them *to go* to their masters, saying, 'Thus says the LORD of hosts, the
God of Israel, thus you shall say to your masters,
5 "I have made the earth, the men and the beasts which are on the face of the earth by
My great power and by My outstretched arm, and I will give it to the one who is pleasing
in My sight.
6 "Now I have given all these lands into the hand of Nebuchadnezzar king of Babylon,
My servant, and I have given him also the wild animals of the field to serve him.
7 "All the nations shall serve him and his son and his grandson until the time of his
own land comes; then many nations and great kings will make him their servant.
8 "It will be, *that* the nation or the kingdom which will not serve him, Nebuchadnezzar
king of Babylon, and which will not put its neck under the yoke of the king of Babylon,
I will punish that nation with the sword, with famine and with pestilence," declares the
LORD, "until I have destroyed it by his hand.
9 "But as for you, do not listen to your prophets, your diviners, your dreamers, your
soothsayers or your sorcerers who speak to you, saying, 'You will not serve the king of
Babylon.'
10 "For they prophesy a lie to you in order to remove you far from your land; and I will
drive you out and you will perish.
11 "But the nation which will bring its neck under the yoke of the king of Babylon and
serve him, I will let remain on its land," declares the LORD, "and they will till it and dwell
in it."' ' "
12 I spoke words like all these to Zedekiah king of Judah, saying, "Bring your necks
under the yoke of the king of Babylon and serve him and his people, and live!
13 "Why will you die, you and your people, by the sword, famine and pestilence, as the
LORD has spoken to that nation which will not serve the king of Babylon?
14 "So do not listen to the words of the prophets who speak to you, saying, 'You will not
serve the king of Babylon,' for they prophesy a lie to you;
15 for I have not sent them," declares the LORD, "but they prophesy falsely in My name,
in order that I may drive you out and that you may perish, you and the prophets who
prophesy to you."
16 *Then* I spoke to the priests and to all this people, saying, "Thus says the LORD: Do
not listen to the words of your prophets who prophesy to you, saying, 'Behold, the vessels of the LORD'S house will now shortly be brought again from Babylon'; for they are
prophesying a lie to you.

26:22 Jer 36:12
26:23 Jer 2:30
26:24 2 Kin 22:12-14; Jer 39:14; 40:5-7; 1 Kin 18:4; Jer 1:18, 19
27:1 2 Kin 24:18-20; 2 Chr 36:11-13
27:2 Jer 30:8; Jer 28:10, 13
27:5 Ps 96:5; 146:5, 6; Is 42:5; 45:12; Jer 10:12; 51:15; Deut 9:29; Jer 32:17; Dan 4:17; Ps 115:15, 16; Acts 17:26
27:6 Jer 21:7; 22:25; Ezek 29:18-20; Is 44:28; Jer 25:9; 43:10; Jer 28:14; Dan 2:38
27:7 2 Chr 36:20; Jer 44:30; 46:13; Dan 5:26; Zech 2:8, 9; Is 14:4-6; Jer 25:12
27:8 Jer 38:17-19; 42:15, 16; Ezek 17:19-21; Jer 24:10; 27:13; 29:17, 18; Ezek 14:21
27:9 Ex 22:18; Deut 18:10; Is 8:19; Mal 3:5; Eph 5:6
27:10 Jer 23:25; Jer 8:19; 32:31
27:12 Jer 27:3; 28:1; 38:17
27:13 Prov 8:36; Jer 27:8; 38:23; Ezek 18:31
27:14 2 Cor 11:13-15; Jer 14:14; 23:21; 27:10; 29:8, 9; Ezek 13:22
27:15 Jer 23:21; 29:9; 2 Chr 25:16; Jer 6:13-15; 14:15, 16
27:16 2 Kin 24:13; 2 Chr 36:7, 10; Dan 1:2

27:1ff The year was 593 B.C., and Nebuchadnezzar had already invaded Judah once and had taken many captives. Jeremiah wore a yoke (a wooden frame used to fasten a team of animals to a plow) as a symbol of bondage. This was an object lesson, telling the people they must put themselves under Babylon's yoke or be destroyed.

27:5–6 God punished the people of Judah in an unusual way, by appointing a foreign ruler to be his "servant." Nebuchadnezzar was not employed to proclaim God's message, but to fulfill God's promise of judgment on sin. Because God is in control of all events, he uses whomever he wants. God may use unlikely people or circumstances to correct you. Be ready to accept God's improvement, even if it comes from unexpected sources.

27:12–18 Zedekiah was in a tough spot. Jeremiah called on him to surrender to Nebuchadnezzar at a time when many of the other leaders wanted him to form an alliance and fight. It would be disgraceful for a king to surrender, and he would look like a coward. This was a great opportunity for the false prophets, who kept saying that the Babylonians would not defeat the great city of Jerusalem and that God would never allow the magnificent, holy temple to be destroyed.

17 "Do not listen to them; serve the king of Babylon, and live! Why should this city
become a ruin?
18 "But if they are prophets, and if the word of the LORD is with them, let them now
entreat the LORD of hosts that the vessels which are left in the house of the LORD, in the
house of the king of Judah and in Jerusalem may not go to Babylon.
19 "For thus says the LORD of hosts concerning the pillars, concerning the sea, concerning
the stands and concerning the rest of the vessels that are left in this city,
20 which Nebuchadnezzar king of Babylon did not take when he carried into exile Jeconiah the son of Jehoiakim, king of Judah, from Jerusalem to Babylon, and all the nobles of Judah and Jerusalem.
21 "Yes, thus says the LORD of hosts, the God of Israel, concerning the vessels that are
left in the house of the LORD and in the house of the king of Judah and in Jerusalem,
22 'They will be carried to Babylon and they will be there until the day I visit them,'
declares the LORD. 'Then I will bring them back and restore them to this place.' "

Hananiah's False Prophecy

28 Now in the same year, in the beginning of the reign of Zedekiah king of Judah, in
the fourth year, in the fifth month, Hananiah the son of Azzur, the prophet, who
was from Gibeon, spoke to me in the house of the LORD in the presence of the priests
and all the people, saying,
2 "Thus says the LORD of hosts, the God of Israel, 'I have broken the yoke of the king
of Babylon.
3 'Within two years I am going to bring back to this place all the vessels of the LORD'S
house, which Nebuchadnezzar king of Babylon took away from this place and carried to
Babylon.
4 'I am also going to bring back to this place Jeconiah the son of Jehoiakim, king of
Judah, and all the exiles of Judah who went to Babylon,' declares the LORD, 'for I will
break the yoke of the king of Babylon.' "
5 Then the prophet Jeremiah spoke to the prophet Hananiah in the presence of the
priests and in the presence of all the people who were standing in the house of the LORD,
6 and the prophet Jeremiah said, "Amen! May the LORD do so; may the LORD confirm your words which you have prophesied to bring back the vessels of the LORD'S house
and all the exiles, from Babylon to this place.
7 "Yet hear now this word which I am about to speak in your hearing and in the hearing of all the people!
8 "The prophets who were before me and before you from ancient times prophesied
against many lands and against great kingdoms, of war and of calamity and of pestilence.
9 "The prophet who prophesies of peace, when the word of the prophet comes to pass,
then that prophet will be known *as* one whom the LORD has truly sent."
10 Then Hananiah the prophet took the yoke from the neck of Jeremiah the prophet
and broke it.
11 Hananiah spoke in the presence of all the people, saying, "Thus says the LORD, 'Even
so will I break within two full years the yoke of Nebuchadnezzar king of Babylon from
the neck of all the nations.' " Then the prophet Jeremiah went his way.
12 The word of the LORD came to Jeremiah after Hananiah the prophet had broken
the yoke from off the neck of the prophet Jeremiah, saying,
13 "Go and speak to Hananiah, saying, 'Thus says the LORD, "You have broken the yokes
of wood, but you have made instead of them yokes of iron."
14 "For thus says the LORD of hosts, the God of Israel, "I have put a yoke of iron on the
neck of all these nations, that they may serve Nebuchadnezzar king of Babylon; and they
will serve him. And I have also given him the beasts of the field." ' "

27:17 Jer 7:34

27:18 1 Kin 18:24; 1 Sam 7:8; 12:19, 23; Jer 18:20

27:19 1 Kin 7:15; 2 Kin 25:13, 17; Jer 52:17-23

27:20 2 Kin 24:12, 14-16; 2 Chr 36:10, 18; Jer 22:28; 24:1

27:22 Jer 34:2, 3; Jer 25:11, 12; 27:7; 29:10; 32:5; Ezra 1:7-11; 5:13-15; 7:19

28:1 Jer 27:1; 49:34; 2 Kin 24:18-20; 2 Chr 36:11-13; Jer 27:3, 12; Jer 28:17; Josh 9:3; 10:12; 1 Kin 3:4

28:2 Jer 27:12; 28:11

28:3 2 Kin 24:13; 2 Chr 36:10; Jer 27:16; Dan 1:2

28:4 Jer 22:26, 27; 2 Kin 25:27; Jer 22:24; 24:1; Jer 22:10; Jer 27:8

28:5 Jer 28:1

28:6 1 Kin 1:36; Ps 41:13; Jer 11:5

28:7 1 Kin 22:28

28:8 Lev 26:14-39; 1 Kin 14:15; 17:1; 22:17; Is 5:5-7; Joel 1:20; Amos 1:2; Nah 1:2

28:9 Deut 18:22

28:10 Jer 27:2

28:11 Jer 14:14; 27:10; 28:15

28:12 Jer 1:2

28:13 Ps 107:16; Is 45:2

28:14 Deut 28:48; Jer 27:8; Jer 25:11

27:19–22 When Nebuchadnezzar invaded Judah, first in 605 and then in 597 B.C., he took away many important people living in Jerusalem—including Daniel and Ezekiel. Although these men were captives, they had a profound impact on the exiles and leaders in Babylon. Jeremiah predicted that more people and even the precious objects in the temple would be taken. This happened in 586 B.C. during Babylon's third and last invasion.

28:8–17 Jeremiah spoke the truth, but it was unpopular; Hananiah spoke lies, but his deceitful words brought false hope and comfort to the people. God had already outlined the marks of a true prophet (Deuteronomy 13; 18:20–22): A true prophet's predictions always come true and his words never contradict previous revelation. Jeremiah's predictions were already coming true, from Hananiah's death to the Babylonian invasions. But the people still preferred to listen to comforting lies rather than painful truth.

15 Then Jeremiah the prophet said to Hananiah the prophet, "Listen now, Hananiah,
the LORD has not sent you, and you have made this people trust in a lie.
16 "Therefore thus says the LORD, 'Behold, I am about to remove you from the face of
the earth. This year you are going to die, because you have counseled rebellion against
the LORD.' "
17 So Hananiah the prophet died in the same year in the seventh month.

Message to the Exiles

29 Now these are the words of the letter which Jeremiah the prophet sent from Jerusalem to the rest of the elders of the exile, the priests, the prophets and all the
people whom Nebuchadnezzar had taken into exile from Jerusalem to Babylon.
2 (This was after King Jeconiah and the queen mother, the court officials, the princes
of Judah and Jerusalem, the craftsmen and the smiths had departed from Jerusalem.)
3 *The letter was sent* by the hand of Elasah the son of Shaphan, and Gemariah the son
of Hilkiah, whom Zedekiah king of Judah sent to Babylon to Nebuchadnezzar king of
Babylon, saying,
4 "Thus says the LORD of hosts, the God of Israel, to all the exiles whom I have sent
into exile from Jerusalem to Babylon,
5 'Build houses and live *in them;* and plant gardens and eat their produce.
6 'Take wives and become the fathers of sons and daughters, and take wives for your
sons and give your daughters to husbands, that they may bear sons and daughters; and
multiply there and do not decrease.
7 'Seek the welfare of the city where I have sent you into exile, and pray to the LORD
on its behalf; for in its welfare you will have welfare.'
8 "For thus says the LORD of hosts, the God of Israel, 'Do not let your prophets who
are in your midst and your diviners deceive you, and do not listen to the dreams which
they dream.
9 'For they prophesy falsely to you in My name; I have not sent them,' declares the
LORD.
10 "For thus says the LORD, 'When seventy years have been completed for Babylon, I
will visit you and fulfill My good word to you, to bring you back to this place.
11 'For I know the plans that I have for you,' declares the LORD, 'plans for welfare and
not for calamity to give you a future and a hope.
12 'Then you will call upon Me and come and pray to Me, and I will listen to you.
13 'You will seek Me and find *Me* when you search for Me with all your heart.
14 'I will be found by you,' declares the LORD, 'and I will restore your fortunes and will
gather you from all the nations and from all the places where I have driven you,' declares the LORD, 'and I will bring you back to the place from where I sent you into exile.'
15 "Because you have said, 'The LORD has raised up prophets for us in Babylon'—
16 for thus says the LORD concerning the king who sits on the throne of David, and

28:15 Jer 20:6; 29:31; Lam 2:14; Ezek 13:2, 3, 22; 22:28; Zech 13:3

28:16 Gen 7:4; Ex 32:12; Deut 6:15; 1 Kin 13:34; Jer 20:6;

29:1 2 Chr 30:1, 6; Esth 9:20; Jer 29:25, 29

29:2 2 Kin 24:12-16; 2 Chr 36:9, 10; Jer 22:24-28; 24:1; 27:20; Jer 13:18; 22:26

29:3 1 Chr 6:13

29:7 Dan 4:27; 6:4, 5; Ezra 6:10; 7:23; Dan 4:19; 1 Tim 2:1, 2

29:8 Jer 27:9; 29:1; Jer 14:14; 23:21; 27:14, 15; 28:15; Eph 5:6

29:9 Jer 27:15; 29:21

29:10 2 Chr 36:21-23; Jer 25:12; 27:22; Dan 9:2; Zech 7:5; Jer 24:6, 7; Zeph 2:7

29:11 Ps 40:5; Jer 23:5, 6; 30:9, 10; Is 40:9-11; Jer 30:18-22; Jer 31:17; Hos 2:15

29:12 Ps 50:15; Jer 33:3; Dan 9:3; Ps 145:19

29:13 Deut 4:29; Ps 32:6; Matt 7:7; 1 Chr 22:19; 2 Chr 22:9; Jer 24:7

29:14 Deut 30:1-10; Ps 32:6; Is 55:6; Jer 30:3; 32:37-41; Is 43:5, 6; Jer 23:8

29:4–7 Jeremiah wrote to the captives in Babylon (29:4–23 is the letter) instructing them to move ahead with their lives and to pray for the pagan nation that enslaved them. Life cannot grind to a halt during troubled times. In an unpleasant or distressing situation, we must adjust and keep moving. You may find it difficult to pray for those in authority if they are evil, but that is when your prayers are most needed (1 Timothy 2:1–2). When you enter times of trouble or sudden change, pray diligently and move ahead, doing whatever you can rather than giving up because of fear and uncertainty.

29:10 Scholars differ on the exact dates of this 70-year period in Babylon. Some say it refers to the years 605—538 B.C., from the first deportation to Babylon to the arrival of the first exiles back in Jerusalem after Cyrus's freedom decree. Others point to the years 586—516 B.C., from the last deportation to Babylon and the destruction of the temple until its rebuilding. A third possibility is that 70 years is an approximate number meaning a lifetime. All agree that God sent his people to Babylon for a long time, not the short captivity predicted by the false prophets.

29:11 We're all encouraged by a leader who stirs us to move ahead, someone who believes we can do the task he has given and who will be with us all the way. God is that kind of leader. He knows the future, and his plans for us are good and full of hope. As long as God, who knows the future, provides our agenda and goes with us as we fulfill his mission, we can have boundless hope. This does not mean that we will be spared pain, suffering, or hardship, but that God will see us through to a glorious conclusion.

29:12–14 God did not forget his people, even though they were captive in Babylon. He planned to give them a new beginning with a new purpose—to turn them into new people. In times of deep trouble, it may appear as though God has forgotten you. But God may be preparing you, as he did the people of Judah, for a new beginning with him at the center.

29:13 According to God's wise plan, his people were to have hope and a future; consequently they could call upon him in confidence. Although the exiles were in a difficult place and time, they should not despair because they had God's presence, the privilege of prayer, and God's grace. God can be sought and found when we seek him wholeheartedly. Neither strange lands, sorrows, frustration, nor physical problems can break that communion.

concerning all the people who dwell in this city, your brothers who did not go with you
into exile—
17 thus says the LORD of hosts, 'Behold, I am sending upon them the sword, famine
and pestilence, and I will make them like split-open figs that cannot be eaten due to rottenness.
18 'I will pursue them with the sword, with famine and with pestilence; and I will make
them a terror to all the kingdoms of the earth, to be a curse and a horror and a hissing,
and a reproach among all the nations where I have driven them,
19 because they have not listened to My words,' declares the LORD, 'which I sent to
them again and again by My servants the prophets; but you did not listen,' declares the
LORD.
20 "You, therefore, hear the word of the LORD, all you exiles, whom I have sent away
from Jerusalem to Babylon.
21 "Thus says the LORD of hosts, the God of Israel, concerning Ahab the son of Kolaiah and concerning Zedekiah the son of Maaseiah, who are prophesying to you falsely
in My name, 'Behold, I will deliver them into the hand of Nebuchadnezzar king of Babylon, and he will slay them before your eyes.
22 'Because of them a curse will be used by all the exiles from Judah who are in Babylon, saying, "May the LORD make you like Zedekiah and like Ahab, whom the king of
Babylon roasted in the fire,
23 because they have acted foolishly in Israel, and have committed adultery with their
neighbors' wives and have spoken words in My name falsely, which I did not command
them; and I am He who knows and am a witness," declares the LORD.' "
24 To Shemaiah the Nehelamite you shall speak, saying,
25 "Thus says the LORD of hosts, the God of Israel, 'Because you have sent letters in
your own name to all the people who are in Jerusalem, and to Zephaniah the son of
Maaseiah, the priest, and to all the priests, saying,
26 "The LORD has made you priest instead of Jehoiada the priest, to be the overseer in
the house of the LORD over every madman who prophesies, to put him in the stocks and
in the iron collar,
27 now then, why have you not rebuked Jeremiah of Anathoth who prophesies to you?
28 "For he has sent to us in Babylon, saying, '*The exile* will be long; build houses and live
in them and plant gardens and eat their produce.' " ' "
29 Zephaniah the priest read this letter to Jeremiah the prophet.
30 Then came the word of the LORD to Jeremiah, saying,
31 "Send to all the exiles, saying, 'Thus says the LORD concerning Shemaiah the Nehelamite, "Because Shemaiah has prophesied to you, although I did not send him, and he
has made you trust in a lie,"
32 therefore thus says the LORD, "Behold, I am about to punish Shemaiah the Nehelamite and his descendants; he will not have anyone living among this people, and he will
not see the good that I am about to do to My people," declares the LORD, "because he
has preached rebellion against the LORD." ' "

5. Restoration is promised

Deliverance from Captivity Promised

30 The word which came to Jeremiah from the LORD, saying,
2 "Thus says the LORD, the God of Israel, 'Write all the words which I have spoken to you in a book.
3 'For behold, days are coming,' declares the LORD, 'when I will restore the fortunes
of My people Israel and Judah.' The LORD says, 'I will also bring them back to the land
that I gave to their forefathers and they shall possess it.' "

29:17 Jer 27:8; 29:18; 32:24; Jer 24:3, 8-10

29:18 Deut 28:25; 2 Chr 29:8; Jer 15:4; 24:9; 34:17; Ezek 12:15; Is 65:15; Jer 42:18; Jer 25:9; Lam 2:15, 16

29:19 Jer 6:19; Jer 25:4; 26:5; 35:15

29:20 Jer 24:5; Ezek 11:9; Mic 4:10

29:21 Jer 14:14, 15; 29:8, 9; Lam 2:14; 2 Pet 2:1

29:22 Is 65:15; Dan 3:6, 21

29:23 Gen 34:7; 2 Sam 13:12; Jer 5:8; 23:14; Jer 29:8, 9, 21; Prov 5:21; Jer 7:11; 16:17; Mal 3:5; Heb 4:13

29:25 Jer 29:1; 2 Kin 25:18; Jer 21:1; 29:29; 37:3; 52:24

29:26 Jer 20:1; 2 Kin 9:11; Hos 9:7; Mark 3:21; John 10:20; Acts 26:24, 25; 2 Cor 5:13; Deut 13:1-5; Zech 13:1-5; Jer 20:1, 2; Acts 16:24

29:27 Jer 1:1

29:31 Jer 14:14, 15; 29:9, 23; Ezek 13:8-16, 22, 23; Jer 28:15

29:32 Jer 36:31; 1 Sam 2:30-34; Jer 22:30; 2 Kin 7:2, 19, 20; Jer 17:6; 29:10; Deut 13:5; Jer 28:16

30:2 Is 30:8; Jer 25:13; 36:4, 28, 32; Hab 2:2

30:3 Jer 29:10; Ps 53:6; Jer 29:14; 30:18; 32:44; Ezek 39:25; Amos 9:14; Zeph 3:20; Jer 3:18; Jer 16:15; 23:7, 8; Ezek 20:42; 36:24

29:21 These false prophets, Ahab and Zedekiah, should not be confused with the kings who had the same names. Their family connections clearly identify them.

29:24–28 These verses describe the reaction of Shemaiah, a false prophet exiled in 597 B.C. who had protested about Jeremiah's letter. To discredit Jeremiah, Shemaiah accused him of false prophecy. Although Jeremiah's message was true and his words were from God, the people hated him because he told them to make the most of the exile. But Jeremiah's truth from God offered temporary correction and long-range benefit, while the false teachers' lies offered only temporary comfort and long-range punishment.

30:1ff Chapters 30 and 31 show that Jeremiah spoke of hope and consolation as well as trouble and gloom. The people would one day be restored to their land, and God would make a new covenant with them to replace the one they broke. Where once they sinned and disobeyed, eventually they would repent and obey.

4 Now these are the words which the LORD spoke concerning Israel and concerning
Judah:
5 "For thus says the LORD,
'I have heard a sound of terror,
Of dread, and there is no peace.
6 'Ask now, and see
If a male can give birth.
Why do I see every man
With his hands on his loins, as a woman in childbirth?
And *why* have all faces turned pale?
7 'Alas! for that day is great,
There is none like it;
And it is the time of Jacob's distress,
But he will be saved from it.
8 'It shall come about on that day,' declares the LORD of hosts, 'that I will break his
yoke from off their neck and will tear off their bonds; and strangers will no longer make
them their slaves.
9 'But they shall serve the LORD their God and David their king, whom I will raise up
for them.
10 'Fear not, O Jacob My servant,' declares the LORD,
'And do not be dismayed, O Israel;
For behold, I will save you from afar
And your offspring from the land of their captivity.
And Jacob will return and will be quiet and at ease,
And no one will make him afraid.
11 'For I am with you,' declares the LORD, 'to save you;
For I will destroy completely all the nations where I have scattered you,
Only I will not destroy you completely.
But I will chasten you justly
And will by no means leave you unpunished.'

12 "For thus says the LORD,
'Your wound is incurable
And your injury is serious.
13 'There is no one to plead your cause;
No healing for *your* sore,
No recovery for you.
14 'All your lovers have forgotten you,
They do not seek you;
For I have wounded you with the wound of an enemy,
With the punishment of a cruel one,
Because your iniquity is great
And your sins are numerous.
15 'Why do you cry out over your injury?
Your pain is incurable.
Because your iniquity is great
And your sins are numerous,
I have done these things to you.
16 'Therefore all who devour you will be devoured;
And all your adversaries, every one of them, will go into captivity;

30:5 Is 5:30; Jer 6:25; 8:16; Amos 5:16-18

30:6 Jer 4:31; 6:24; 22:23

30:7 Is 2:12; Hos 1:11; Joel 2:11; Amos 5:18; Zeph 1:14; Lam 1:12; Dan 9:12; 12:1; Jer 2:27, 28; 14:8; Jer 30:10; 50:19

30:8 Is 9:4; Jer 2:20; Ezek 34:27; Jer 27:2; Ezek 34:27

30:9 Is 55:3-5; Ezek 34:23, 24; 37:24, 25; Hos 3:5; Luke 1:69; Acts 2:30; 13:23, 34

30:10 Is 41:13; 43:5; 44:2; Jer 46:27, 28; Is 60:4; Jer 23:3, 8; 29:14; Is 35:9; Jer 33:16; Hos 2:18; Mic 4:4

30:11 Jer 1:8, 19; Jer 46:28; Amos 9:8; Jer 4:27; 5:10, 18; Ps 6:1; Jer 10:24

30:12 2 Chr 36:16; Jer 15:18; 30:15

30:13 Jer 14:19; 46:11

30:14 Jer 22:20, 22; Lam 1:2; Lam 2:4, 5; Job 30:21; Jer 6:23; 50:42; Jer 32:30-35; 44:22; Jer 5:6

30:16 Jer 2:3; 8:16; 10:25; Is 14:2; Joel 3:8

30:8–9 Like Isaiah, Jeremiah associated events of the near future and those of the distant future. Reading these prophecies is like looking at several mountain peaks in a range. From a distance they look as though they are next to each other, when actually they are miles apart. Jeremiah presents near and distant events as if they will all happen soon. He sees the exile, but he sees also the future day when Christ will reign forever. The reference to David is not to King David, but to his famous descendant, the Messiah (Luke 1:69).

30:12, 13, 17 The medical language here conveys the idea that sin is terminal. Sinful people cannot be cured by being good or being religious. Beware of putting your confidence in useless cures while your sin spreads and causes you pain. God alone can cure the disease of sin, but you must be willing to let him do it.

30:15 Judah protested its punishment, even though the sin that caused the pain was scandalous. But punishment is an opportunity for growth because it makes us aware of sin's consequences. The people should have asked how they could profit from their mistakes. Remember this the next time you are corrected.

And those who plunder you will be for plunder,
And all who prey upon you I will give for prey.
17 'For I will restore you to health
And I will heal you of your wounds,' declares the LORD,
'Because they have called you an outcast, saying:
"It is Zion; no one cares for her." '

30:17 Ex 15:26; Ps 107:20; Is 30:26; Jer 8:22; 33:6; Is 11:12; 56:8; Jer 33:24

Restoration of Jacob

18 "Thus says the LORD,
'Behold, I will restore the fortunes of the tents of Jacob
And have compassion on his dwelling places;
And the city will be rebuilt on its ruin,
And the palace will stand on its rightful place.
19 'From them will proceed thanksgiving
And the voice of those who celebrate;
And I will multiply them and they will not be diminished;
I will also honor them and they will not be insignificant.
20 'Their children also will be as formerly,
And their congregation shall be established before Me;
And I will punish all their oppressors.
21 'Their leader shall be one of them,
And their ruler shall come forth from their midst;
And I will bring him near and he shall approach Me;
For who would dare to risk his life to approach Me?' declares the LORD.
22 'You shall be My people,
And I will be your God.' "

30:18 Jer 30:3; 31:23; Ps 102:13; Jer 31:4, 38-40; 1 Chr 29:1, 19; Ps 48:3, 13; 122:7
30:19 Is 12:1; 35:10; 51:3; Jer 17:26; 33:11; Ps 126:1, 2; Is 51:11; Jer 31:4; Zeph 3:14; Jer 33:22; Is 55:5; 60:9
30:20 Is 54:14
30:21 Jer 30:9; Ezek 34:23, 24; 37:24; Num 16:5; Ps 65:4; Ex 3:5; Jer 50:44
30:22 Ex 6:7; Jer 32:38; Ezek 36:28; Hos 2:23; Zech 13:9

23 Behold, the tempest of the LORD!
Wrath has gone forth,
A sweeping tempest;
It will burst on the head of the wicked.
24 The fierce anger of the LORD will not turn back
Until He has performed and until He has accomplished
The intent of His heart;
In the latter days you will understand this.

30:23 Jer 23:19
30:24 Jer 4:8; Jer 23:20

Israel's Mourning Turned to Joy

31 "At that time," declares the LORD, "I will be the God of all the families of Israel,
and they shall be My people."
2 Thus says the LORD,
"The people who survived the sword
Found grace in the wilderness—
Israel, when it went to find its rest."
3 The LORD appeared to him from afar, *saying,*
"I have loved you with an everlasting love;
Therefore I have drawn you with lovingkindness.
4 "Again I will build you and you will be rebuilt,
O virgin of Israel!
Again you will take up your tambourines,
And go forth to the dances of the merrymakers.

31:1 Jer 30:22; Gen 17:7, 8; Is 41:10; Rom 11:26-28
31:2 Num 14:20; Ex 33:14; Num 10:33; Deut 1:33; Josh 1:13
31:3 Deut 4:37; 7:8; Mal 1:2; Ps 25:6
31:4 Jer 24:6; 33:7; Is 30:32; Jer 30:19

30:18 This prophecy that Jerusalem would be rebuilt was not completely fulfilled by the work of Ezra, Nehemiah, and Zerubbabel. The city was indeed rebuilt after the captivity, but the final restoration will occur when all believers are gathered in Christ's kingdom. This restoration will include buildings (30:18), people (30:19), and rulers (30:21).

30:21 This verse refers to the restoration after the Babylonian captivity, as well as to the final restoration under Christ.

31:1 This promise is to all the families (tribes) of Israel, not only to the tribe of Judah. The restoration will include all people who trust God.

31:3 God reaches toward his people with kindness motivated by deep and everlasting love. He is eager to do the best for them if they will only let him. After many words of warning about sin, this reminder of God's magnificent love is a breath of fresh air. Rather than thinking of God with dread, look carefully and see him lovingly drawing us toward himself.

5 "Again you will plant vineyards
On the hills of Samaria;
The planters will plant
And will enjoy *them.*
6 "For there will be a day when watchmen
On the hills of Ephraim call out,
'Arise, and let us go up *to* Zion,
To the LORD our God.' "

7 For thus says the LORD,
"Sing aloud with gladness for Jacob,
And shout among the chief of the nations;
Proclaim, give praise and say,
'O LORD, save Your people,
The remnant of Israel.'
8 "Behold, I am bringing them from the north country,
And I will gather them from the remote parts of the earth,
Among them the blind and the lame,
The woman with child and she who is in labor with child, together;
A great company, they will return here.
9 "With weeping they will come,
And by supplication I will lead them;
I will make them walk by streams of waters,
On a straight path in which they will not stumble;
For I am a father to Israel,
And Ephraim is My firstborn."

10 Hear the word of the LORD, O nations,
And declare in the coastlands afar off,
And say, "He who scattered Israel will gather him
And keep him as a shepherd keeps his flock."
11 For the LORD has ransomed Jacob
And redeemed him from the hand of him who was stronger than he.
12 "They will come and shout for joy on the height of Zion,
And they will be radiant over the bounty of the LORD—
Over the grain and the new wine and the oil,
And over the young of the flock and the herd;
And their life will be like a watered garden,
And they will never languish again.
13 "Then the virgin will rejoice in the dance,
And the young men and the old, together,
For I will turn their mourning into joy
And will comfort them and give them joy for their sorrow.
14 "I will fill the soul of the priests with abundance,
And My people will be satisfied with My goodness," declares the LORD.

15 Thus says the LORD,
"A voice is heard in Ramah,
Lamentation *and* bitter weeping.
Rachel is weeping for her children;
She refuses to be comforted for her children,
Because they are no more."
16 Thus says the LORD,
"Restrain your voice from weeping
And your eyes from tears;

31:5 Ps 107:37; Is 65:21; Ezek 28:26; Amos 9:14

31:6 Is 2:3; Jer 31:12; 50:4, 5; Mic 4:2

31:7 Ps 14:7; Jer 20:13; Deut 28:13; Is 61:9; Ps 28:9; Is 37:31; Jer 23:3

31:8 Jer 3:18; 23:8; Deut 30:4; Is 43:6; Ezek 34:13; Is 42:16; Is 40:11; Ezek 34:16; Mic 4:6

31:9 Ps 126:5; Jer 50:4; Is 43:20; 49:10; Is 63:13; Is 64:8; Jer 3:4, 19; Ex 4:22

31:10 Is 66:19; Jer 25:22; Jer 50:19; Is 40:11; Ezek 34:12

31:11 Is 44:23; 48:20; Jer 15:21; 50:34; Ps 142:6

31:12 Jer 31:6, 7; Ezek 17:23; Is 2:2; Mic 4:1; Hos 2:22; Joel 3:18; Jer 31:24; 33:12, 13; Is 58:11; Is 35:10; 60:20; 65:19; John 16:22; Rev 21:4

31:13 Judg 21:21; Ps 30:11; Zech 8:4, 5; Is 61:3; Is 51:11

31:14 Jer 50:19

31:15 Matt 2:18; Josh 18:25; Judg 4:5; Is 10:29; Jer 40:1; Gen 37:35; Ps 77:2; Gen 5:24; 42:13, 36; Jer 10:20

31:16 Is 25:8; 30:19; Ruth 2:12; Heb 6:10; Jer 30:3; Ezek 11:17

31:14 This means that many sacrifices will be made at the temple so that the priests will have a feast with their portion. It is also a symbol of life and prosperity (Psalms 36:8; 63:5; Isaiah 55:2)

31:15 Rachel, Jacob's favorite wife, was the symbolic mother of the northern tribes, who were taken away by the Assyrians as slaves. Rachel is pictured crying for the exiles at Ramah, a staging point of deportation. This verse is quoted in Matthew 2:18 to describe the sadness of the mothers of Bethlehem as the male children were killed. The weeping was great in both cases.

For your work will be rewarded," declares the LORD,
"And they will return from the land of the enemy.
17 "There is hope for your future," declares the LORD,
"And *your* children will return to their own territory.
18 "I have surely heard Ephraim grieving,
'You have chastised me, and I was chastised,
Like an untrained calf;
Bring me back that I may be restored,
For You are the LORD my God.
19 'For after I turned back, I repented;
And after I was instructed, I smote on *my* thigh;
I was ashamed and also humiliated
Because I bore the reproach of my youth.'
20 "Is Ephraim My dear son?
Is he a delightful child?
Indeed, as often as I have spoken against him,
I certainly *still* remember him;
Therefore My heart yearns for him;
I will surely have mercy on him," declares the LORD.

21 "Set up for yourself roadmarks,
Place for yourself guideposts;
Direct your mind to the highway,
The way by which you went.
Return, O virgin of Israel,
Return to these your cities.
22 "How long will you go here and there,
O faithless daughter?
For the LORD has created a new thing in the earth—
A woman will encompass a man."
23 Thus says the LORD of hosts, the God of Israel, "Once again they will speak this
word in the land of Judah and in its cities when I restore their fortunes,
'The LORD bless you, O abode of righteousness,
O holy hill!'
24 "Judah and all its cities will dwell together in it, the farmer and they who go about
with flocks.
25 "For I satisfy the weary ones and refresh everyone who languishes."
26 At this I awoke and looked, and my sleep was pleasant to me.

A New Covenant

27 "Behold, days are coming," declares the LORD, "when I will sow the house of Israel
and the house of Judah with the seed of man and with the seed of beast.
28 "As I have watched over them to pluck up, to break down, to overthrow, to destroy
and to bring disaster, so I will watch over them to build and to plant," declares the LORD.
29 "In those days they will not say again,
'The fathers have eaten sour grapes,
And the children's teeth are set on edge.'
30 "But everyone will die for his own iniquity; each man who eats the sour grapes, his
teeth will be set on edge.
31 "Behold, days are coming," declares the LORD, "when I will make a new covenant
with the house of Israel and with the house of Judah,
32 not like the covenant which I made with their fathers in the day I took them by the

31:17 Jer 29:11
31:18 Jer 3:21; Job 5:17; Ps 94:12; Hos 4:16; Ps 80:3, 7, 19; Jer 17:14; Lam 5:21; Acts 3:26
31:19 Ezek 36:31; Zech 12:10; Ezek 21:12; Luke 18:13; Jer 3:25
31:20 Hos 11:8; Gen 43:30; Judg 10:16; Is 63:15; Hos 11:8; Is 55:7; 57:18; Hos 14:4; Mic 7:18
31:21 Jer 50:5; Is 48:20; 52:11
31:22 Jer 3:6; 49:4
31:23 Jer 30:18; 32:44; Is 1:26; Jer 50:7; Ps 48:1; 87:1; Zech 8:3
31:24 Jer 31:12; Ezek 36:10; Zech 8:4-8
31:25 Ps 107:9; Jer 31:12, 14; Matt 5:6; John 4:14
31:26 Zech 4:1; Prov 3:24
31:27 Ezek 36:9, 11; Hos 2:23
31:28 Jer 44:27; Dan 9:14; Jer 1:10; 18:7; Jer 24:6
31:29 Lam 5:7; Ezek 18:2
31:30 Deut 24:16; Is 3:11; Ezek 18:4, 20
31:31 Jer 31:31-34; Heb 8:8-12; Jer 32:40; 33:14; Ezek 37:26; Luke 22:20; 1 Cor 11:25; 2 Cor 3:6; Heb 8:8-12; 10:16, 17
31:32 Ex 19:5; 24:6-8; Deut 5:2, 3; Deut 1:31; Is 63:12; Jer 11:7, 8

31:18–20 "I smote on my thigh" was an expression picturing grief and mourning. Ephraim was one of the major tribes of the northern kingdom. Although the northern kingdom had sunk into the most degrading sins, God still loved the people. A remnant would turn to God, repenting of their sins, and God would forgive. God still loves you, despite anything you may have done. He will forgive you if you turn back to him.

31:29–30 The people tried to blame God's judgment on the sins of their fathers. One person's sin does indeed affect other people, but all people are still held personally accountable for the sin in their own lives (Deuteronomy 24:16; Ezekiel 18:2). What excuses do you use for your sins?

hand to bring them out of the land of Egypt, My covenant which they broke, although I
was a husband to them," declares the LORD.
33 "But this is the covenant which I will make with the house of Israel after those days,"
declares the LORD, "I will put My law within them and on their heart I will write it; and
I will be their God, and they shall be My people.
34 "They will not teach again, each man his neighbor and each man his brother, saying,
'Know the LORD,' for they will all know Me, from the least of them to the greatest of
them," declares the LORD, "for I will forgive their iniquity, and their sin I will remember
no more."
35 Thus says the LORD,
Who gives the sun for light by day
And the fixed order of the moon and the stars for light by night,
Who stirs up the sea so that its waves roar;
The LORD of hosts is His name:
36 "If this fixed order departs
From before Me," declares the LORD,
"Then the offspring of Israel also will cease
From being a nation before Me forever."
37 Thus says the LORD,
"If the heavens above can be measured
And the foundations of the earth searched out below,
Then I will also cast off all the offspring of Israel
For all that they have done," declares the LORD.
38 "Behold, days are coming," declares the LORD, "when the city will be rebuilt for the
LORD from the Tower of Hananel to the Corner Gate.
39 "The measuring line will go out farther straight ahead to the hill Gareb; then it will
turn to Goah.
40 "And the whole valley of the dead bodies and of the ashes, and all the fields as far as
the brook Kidron, to the corner of the Horse Gate toward the east, shall be holy to the
LORD; it will not be plucked up or overthrown anymore forever."

Jeremiah Imprisoned

32 The word that came to Jeremiah from the LORD in the tenth year of Zedekiah
king of Judah, which was the eighteenth year of Nebuchadnezzar.
2 Now at that time the army of the king of Babylon was besieging Jerusalem, and
Jeremiah the prophet was shut up in the court of the guard, which *was in* the house of
the king of Judah,
3 because Zedekiah king of Judah had shut him up, saying, "Why do you prophesy,
saying, 'Thus says the LORD, "Behold, I am about to give this city into the hand of the
king of Babylon, and he will take it;
4 and Zedekiah king of Judah will not escape out of the hand of the Chaldeans, but
he will surely be given into the hand of the king of Babylon, and he will speak with him
face to face and see him eye to eye;

31:33 Jer 32:40; Heb 10:16; Ps 40:8; 2 Cor 3:3; Jer 24:7; 30:22; 32:38

31:34 1 Thess 4:9; 1 John 2:27; Is 11:9; 54:13; Jer 24:7; Hab 2:14; John 6:45; 1 John 2:20; Jer 33:8; 50:20; Mic 7:18; Rom 11:27; Is 43:25; Heb 10:17

31:35 Gen 1:14-18; Deut 4:19; Ps 19:1-6; 136:7-9; Is 51:15; Jer 10:16; 32:18; 50:34

31:36 Ps 89:36, 37; 148:6; Is 54:9, 10; Jer 33:20-26; Amos 9:8, 9

31:37 Is 40:12; Jer 33:22; Jer 33:24-26; Rom 11:2-5, 26, 27

31:38 Jer 30:18; 31:4; Neh 3:1; 12:39; Zech 14:10; 2 Kin 14:13; 2 Chr 26:9

31:39 Zech 2:1

31:40 Jer 7:32; 8:2; 2 Sam 15:23; 2 Kin 23:6, 12; John 18:1; 2 Kin 11:16; 2 Chr 23:15; Neh 3:28; Joel 3:17; Zech 14:20

32:1 2 Kin 25:1, 2; Jer 39:1, 2

32:2 Neh 3:25; Jer 33:1; 37:21; 38:6; 39:14

32:3 2 Kin 6:32; Jer 26:8, 9; Jer 21:3-7; 34:2, 3; Jer 21:4-7; 32:28, 29; 34:2, 3

32:4 2 Kin 25:4-7; Jer 37:17; 38:18, 23; 39:4-7; Jer 39:5

31:33 God would write his law on their hearts rather than on tablets of stone, as he did the Ten Commandments. In 17:1 their sin was engraved on their hearts so that they wanted above all to disobey. This change seems to describe an experience very much like the new birth, with God taking the initiative. When we turn our lives over to God, he, by his Holy Spirit, builds into us the desire to obey him.

31:33 The old covenant, broken by the people, would be replaced by a new covenant. The foundation of this new covenant is Christ (Hebrews 8:6). It is revolutionary, involving not only Israel and Judah, but even the Gentiles. It offers a unique personal relationship with God himself, with his laws written on individuals' hearts instead of on stone. Jeremiah looked forward to the day when Jesus would come to establish this covenant. But for us today, this covenant is here. We have the wonderful opportunity to make a fresh start and establish a permanent, personal relationship with God (see 29:11; 32:38–40).

31:35–37 God has the power to do away with the decrees of nature or even to do away with his people. But he will do neither. This is not a prediction; it is a promise. This is God's way of saying that he will not reject Israel any more than he will do away with nature's laws. Neither will happen!

31:38–40 These points mark the boundaries of restored Jerusalem in the days of Nehemiah. Gareb and Goah are unknown. The valley of the dead bodies and ashes is probably the valley of Ben-hinnom where children were sacrified in pagan worship.

32:1–12 God told Jeremiah to buy a field outside Jerusalem. The city had been under siege for a year, and Jeremiah bought land that the soldiers occupied—certainly a poor investment. In addition, Jeremiah was a prisoner in the palace. But Jeremiah was demonstrating his faith in God's promises to bring his people back and to rebuild Jerusalem.

32:5 Jer 27:22; 39:7; Ezek 12:12, 13; Ezek 17:9, 10, 15

32:10 Is 44:5; Deut 32:34; Job 14:17; Ruth 4:1, 9; Is 8:2

32:11 Luke 2:27

32:15 Jer 30:18; 31:5, 12, 24; Amos 9:14, 15; Zech 3:10

32:17 Jer 1:6; 4:10; 2 Kin 19:15; Ps 102:25; Is 40:26-29; Jer 27:5; Gen 18:14; Zech 8:6; Matt 19:26; Mark 10:27; Luke 1:37; 18:27

32:18 Ex 20:6; 34:6, 7; Deut 5:9, 10; 7:9, 10; 1 Kin 14:9, 10; 16:1-3; Matt 23:32-36; Ps 145:3; Ps 50:1; Is 9:6; Jer 20:11; Jer 10:16; 31:35

32:19 Is 9:6; 28:29; Job 34:21; Jer 23:24; Ps 62:12; Jer 17:10; 21:14; Matt 16:27; John 5:29

32:20 Ps 78:43; 105:27; Ex 9:16; Is 63:12, 14; Dan 9:15

32:21 Ex 6:6; Deut 4:34; 7:19; 26:8; 2 Sam 7:23; 1 Chr 17:21; Ps 136:11

32:22 Ex 3:8, 17; 13:5; Deut 1:8; Ps 105:9-11; Jer 11:5

32:23 Ps 44:2, 3; 78:54, 55; Jer 2:7; Neh 9:26; Jer 11:8; Dan 9:10-14; Ezra 9:7; Jer 26:4; 44:10; Lam 1:18; Dan 9:11, 12

32:24 Jer 33:4; Ezek 21:22; Ezek 14:21; Deut 4:26; Josh 23:15, 16; Zech 1:6

5 and he will take Zedekiah to Babylon, and he will be there until I visit him," declares the LORD. "If you fight against the Chaldeans, you will not succeed" '?"
6 And Jeremiah said, "The word of the LORD came to me, saying,
7 'Behold, Hanamel the son of Shallum your uncle is coming to you, saying, "Buy for
yourself my field which is at Anathoth, for you have the right of redemption to buy *it*." '
8 "Then Hanamel my uncle's son came to me in the court of the guard according to
the word of the LORD and said to me, 'Buy my field, please, that is at Anathoth, which is
in the land of Benjamin; for you have the right of possession and the redemption is yours;
buy *it* for yourself.' Then I knew that this was the word of the LORD.
9 "I bought the field which was at Anathoth from Hanamel my uncle's son, and I
weighed out the silver for him, seventeen shekels of silver.
10 "I signed and sealed the deed, and called in witnesses, and weighed out the silver on
the scales.
11 "Then I took the deeds of purchase, both the sealed *copy containing* the terms and
conditions and the open *copy;*
12 and I gave the deed of purchase to Baruch the son of Neriah, the son of Mahseiah,
in the sight of Hanamel my uncle's *son* and in the sight of the witnesses who signed the
deed of purchase, before all the Jews who were sitting in the court of the guard.
13 "And I commanded Baruch in their presence, saying,
14 'Thus says the LORD of hosts, the God of Israel, "Take these deeds, this sealed deed
of purchase and this open deed, and put them in an earthenware jar, that they may last
a long time."
15 'For thus says the LORD of hosts, the God of Israel, "Houses and fields and vineyards will again be bought in this land." '

Jeremiah Prays and God Explains

16 "After I had given the deed of purchase to Baruch the son of Neriah, then I prayed
to the LORD, saying,
17 'Ah Lord GOD! Behold, You have made the heavens and the earth by Your great
power and by Your outstretched arm! Nothing is too difficult for You,
18 who shows lovingkindness to thousands, but repays the iniquity of fathers into the
bosom of their children after them, O great and mighty God. The LORD of hosts is His
name;
19 great in counsel and mighty in deed, whose eyes are open to all the ways of the sons
of men, giving to everyone according to his ways and according to the fruit of his deeds;
20 who has set signs and wonders in the land of Egypt, *and* even to this day both in
Israel and among mankind; and You have made a name for Yourself, as at this day.
21 'You brought Your people Israel out of the land of Egypt with signs and with wonders, and with a strong hand and with an outstretched arm and with great terror;
22 and gave them this land, which You swore to their forefathers to give them, a land
flowing with milk and honey.
23 'They came in and took possession of it, but they did not obey Your voice or walk in
Your law; they have done nothing of all that You commanded them to do; therefore
You have made all this calamity come upon them.
24 'Behold, the siege ramps have reached the city to take it; and the city is given into
the hand of the Chaldeans who fight against it, because of the sword, the famine and the
pestilence; and what You have spoken has come to pass; and behold, You see *it*.
25 'You have said to me, O Lord GOD, "Buy for yourself the field with money and call
in witnesses"—although the city is given into the hand of the Chaldeans.' "
26 Then the word of the LORD came to Jeremiah, saying,

32:6–17 Trust doesn't come easily. It wasn't easy for Jeremiah to publicly buy land already captured by the enemy. But he trusted God. It wasn't easy for David to believe that he would become king, even after he was anointed. But he trusted God (1 Samuel 16—31). It wasn't easy for Moses to believe that he and his people would escape Egypt, even after God spoke to him from a burning bush. But he trusted God (Exodus 3:1—4:20). It isn't easy for us to believe that God can fulfill his "impossible" promises either, but we must trust him. God, who worked in the lives of Biblical heroes, will work in our lives too, if we will let him.

32:17–25 After Jeremiah bought the field, he began to wonder if such a move was wise. He sought relief in prayer from his nagging doubts. In this prayer, Jeremiah affirmed that God is the Creator (32:17), the wise Judge of all the ways of people (32:19), and the Redeemer (32:21). God loves us and sees our situation. Whenever we doubt God's wisdom or wonder if it is practical to obey him, we can review what we already know about him. Such thoughts and prayers will quiet our doubts and calm our fears.

27 "Behold, I am the LORD, the God of all flesh; is anything too difficult for Me?"
28 Therefore thus says the LORD, "Behold, I am about to give this city into the hand of
the Chaldeans and into the hand of Nebuchadnezzar king of Babylon, and he will take it.
29 "The Chaldeans who are fighting against this city will enter and set this city on fire
and burn it, with the houses where *people* have offered incense to Baal on their roofs
and poured out drink offerings to other gods to provoke Me to anger.
30 "Indeed the sons of Israel and the sons of Judah have been doing only evil in My
sight from their youth; for the sons of Israel have been only provoking Me to anger by
the work of their hands," declares the LORD.
31 "Indeed this city has been to Me *a provocation of* My anger and My wrath from the
day that they built it, even to this day, so that it should be removed from before My face,
32 because of all the evil of the sons of Israel and the sons of Judah which they have
done to provoke Me to anger—they, their kings, their leaders, their priests, their prophets, the men of Judah and the inhabitants of Jerusalem.
33 "They have turned *their* back to Me and not *their* face; though *I* taught them, teaching again and again, they would not listen and receive instruction.
34 "But they put their detestable things in the house which is called by My name, to
defile it.
35 "They built the high places of Baal that are in the valley of Ben-hinnom to cause their
sons and their daughters to pass through *the fire* to Molech, which I had not commanded
them nor had it entered My mind that they should do this abomination, to cause Judah
to sin.
36 "Now therefore thus says the LORD God of Israel concerning this city of which you
say, 'It is given into the hand of the king of Babylon by sword, by famine and by pestilence.'
37 "Behold, I will gather them out of all the lands to which I have driven them in My
anger, in My wrath and in great indignation; and I will bring them back to this place and
make them dwell in safety.
38 "They shall be My people, and I will be their God;
39 and I will give them one heart and one way, that they may fear Me always, for their
own good and for *the good of* their children after them.
40 "I will make an everlasting covenant with them that I will not turn away from them,
to do them good; and I will put the fear of Me in their hearts so that they will not turn
away from Me.
41 "I will rejoice over them to do them good and will faithfully plant them in this land
with all My heart and with all My soul.
42 "For thus says the LORD, 'Just as I brought all this great disaster on this people, so I
am going to bring on them all the good that I am promising them.
43 'Fields will be bought in this land of which you say, "It is a desolation, without man
or beast; it is given into the hand of the Chaldeans."
44 'Men will buy fields for money, sign and seal deeds, and call in witnesses in the land
of Benjamin, in the environs of Jerusalem, in the cities of Judah, in the cities of the hill
country, in the cities of the lowland and in the cities of the [10]Negev; for I will restore
their fortunes,' declares the LORD."

Restoration Promised

33 Then the word of the LORD came to Jeremiah the second time, while he was still
confined in the court of the guard, saying,
2 "Thus says the LORD who made *the earth,* the LORD who formed it to establish it, the
LORD is His name,

10 I.e. South country

32:27 Num 16:22; 27:16; Jer 32:17; Matt 19:26

32:28 2 Kin 25:11; 2 Chr 36:17-21

32:29 Jer 19:13; 44:17-19, 25; 52:13

32:30 Deut 9:7-12; Is 63:10; Jer 2:7

32:31 1 Kin 11:7, 8; Matt 23:37; 2 Kin 23:27; 24:3, 4; Jer 27:10

32:32 Ezra 9:7; Is 1:4-6, 23; Jer 2:26; 44:17, 21; Dan 9:8

32:33 2 Chr 36:15, 16; Jer 7:13; 25:3; 26:5; 35:15; John 8:2

32:34 2 Kin 21:1-7; Jer 7:30; 19:4-6; Ezek 8:5

32:35 2 Chr 28:2, 3; 33:6; Lev 18:21; 20:2-5; 1 Kin 11:7; 2 Kin 23:10; Acts 7:43

32:37 Deut 30:3; Ps 106:47; Is 11:11-16; Hos 1:11; Amos 9:14, 15; Jer 23:6; Ezek 34:25, 28; Zech 14:11

32:38 Jer 24:7

32:39 2 Chr 30:12; Jer 31:33; Ezek 11:19; John 17:21; Acts 4:32; Deut 11:18-21; Ezek 37:25

32:40 Is 55:3; Jer 31:33, 34; 50:5; Ezek 37:26; Deut 31:6, 8

32:41 Deut 30:9; Is 62:5; 65:19; Jer 24:6; 31:28; Amos 9:15; Hos 2:19, 20

32:42 Jer 31:28; Zech 8:14, 15; Jer 33:14

32:43 Ezek 37:11-14

32:44 Jer 31:23; 33:7

32:35 These high places were where the most important and grotesque part of Molech worship took place. Children were offered in sacrifice to this pagan god.

32:36–42 God uses his power to accomplish *his* purposes through *his* people. God doesn't give you power to be all you want to be, but he gives you power to be all *he* wants you to be. The people of Israel had to learn that trusting God meant radically realigning their purposes and desires toward him. God gave them "one heart" toward him (32:39). We must develop that singleness of heart and action to love God above anything else.

32:44 The hill country is in western Palestine. The Negev is the southern part of Judah.

33:1ff God would restore Jerusalem, not because the people cried, but because it was part of his ultimate plan. The Babylonian disaster did not change God's purposes for his people. Although Jerusalem would be destroyed, it would be restored (after the 70-year captivity and in the end times when the Messiah will rule). God's justice is always tempered by his mercy.

33:3 Ps 50:15; 91:15; Is 55:6, 7; Jer 29:12; Jer 32:17, 27; Is 48:6

33:4 Is 32:13, 14; Jer 32:24; Ezek 4:2; 21:22; Hab 1:10

33:5 Jer 21:4-7; 32:5; Is 8:17; Mic 3:4

33:6 Jer 17:14; 30:17; Hos 6:1; Is 66:12; Gal 5:22, 23

33:7 Ps 85:1; Jer 30:18; 32:44; 33:26; Amos 9:14; Is 1:26; Amos 9:14, 15

33:8 Ps 51:2; Is 44:22; Jer 50:20; Ezek 36:25, 33; Mic 7:18, 19; Zech 13:1; Heb 9:11-14

33:9 Is 62:2, 4, 7; Jer 13:11; Jer 3:17, 19; 4:2; 16:19; Jer 24:6; 32:42; Neh 6:16; Ps 40:3; Is 60:5; Hos 3:5

33:11 Is 35:10; 51:3, 11; 1 Chr 16:8, 34; 2 Chr 5:13; 7:3; Ezra 3:11; Ps 100:4, 5; 106:1; 107:1; 118:1; 136:1; Heb 13:15

33:12 Jer 32:43; 36:29; 51:62; Is 65:10; Jer 31:12; Ezek 34:12-15; Zeph 2:6, 7

33:13 Jer 17:26; Lev 27:32; Luke 15:4

33:14 Jer 23:5; Is 32:1, 2; Jer 33:9; Ezek 34:23-25; Hag 2:6-9

3 'Call to Me and I will answer you, and I will tell you great and mighty things, which you do not know.'
4 "For thus says the LORD God of Israel concerning the houses of this city, and concerning the houses of the kings of Judah which are broken down *to make a defense* against the siege ramps and against the sword,
5 'While *they* are coming to fight with the Chaldeans and to fill them with the corpses of men whom I have slain in My anger and in My wrath, and I have hidden My face from this city because of all their wickedness:
6 'Behold, I will bring to it health and healing, and I will heal them; and I will reveal to them an abundance of peace and truth.
7 'I will restore the fortunes of Judah and the fortunes of Israel and will rebuild them as they were at first.
8 'I will cleanse them from all their iniquity by which they have sinned against Me, and I will pardon all their iniquities by which they have sinned against Me and by which they have transgressed against Me.
9 '[11]It will be to Me a name of joy, praise and glory before all the nations of the earth which will hear of all the good that I do for them, and they will fear and tremble because of all the good and all the peace that I make for it.'
10 "Thus says the LORD, 'Yet again there will be heard in this place, of which you say, "It is a waste, without man and without beast," *that is,* in the cities of Judah and in the streets of Jerusalem that are desolate, without man and without inhabitant and without beast,
11 the voice of joy and the voice of gladness, the voice of the bridegroom and the voice of the bride, the voice of those who say,

"Give thanks to the LORD of hosts,
For the LORD is good,
For His lovingkindness is everlasting";

and of those who bring a thank offering into the house of the LORD. For I will restore the fortunes of the land as they were at first,' says the LORD.
12 "Thus says the LORD of hosts, 'There will again be in this place which is waste, without man or beast, and in all its cities, a habitation of shepherds who rest their flocks.
13 'In the cities of the hill country, in the cities of the lowland, in the cities of the Negev, in the land of Benjamin, in the environs of Jerusalem and in the cities of Judah, the flocks will again pass under the hands of the one who numbers them,' says the LORD.

The Davidic Kingdom

14 'Behold, days are coming,' declares the LORD, 'when I will fulfill the good word which I have spoken concerning the house of Israel and the house of Judah.

11 I.e. This city

BABYLON ATTACKS JUDAH
Zedekiah incurred Babylon's wrath in allying with Egypt (37:5) and not surrendering as God told him through Jeremiah (38:17). Nebuchadnezzar attacked Judah for the third and final time, moving systematically until all its cities fell. Jerusalem withstood siege for several months but was burned, as Jeremiah predicted (chapter 39).

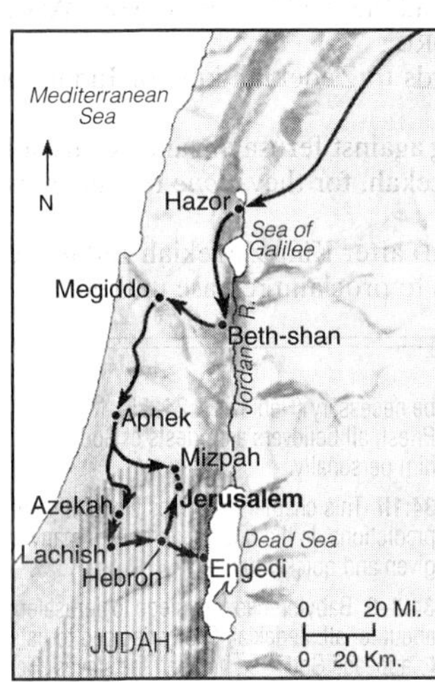

33:3 God assured Jeremiah that he had only to call to God and God would answer (see also Psalm 145:18; Isaiah 58:9; Matthew 7:7). God is ready to answer our prayers, but we must ask for his assistance. Surely God could take care of our needs without our asking. But when we ask, we are acknowledging that he alone is God and that we cannot accomplish in our own strength all that is his domain to do. When we ask, we must humble ourselves, lay aside our willfulness and worry, and determine to obey him.

15 'In those days and at that time I will cause a righteous Branch of David to spring
forth; and He shall execute justice and righteousness on the earth.
16 'In those days Judah will be saved and Jerusalem will dwell in safety; and this is *the*
name by which she will be called: the LORD is our righteousness.'
17 "For thus says the LORD, 'David shall never lack a man to sit on the throne of the
house of Israel;
18 and the Levitical priests shall never lack a man before Me to offer burnt offerings,
to burn grain offerings and to prepare sacrifices continually.' "
19 The word of the LORD came to Jeremiah, saying,
20 "Thus says the LORD, 'If you can break My covenant for the day and My covenant
for the night, so that day and night will not be at their appointed time,
21 then My covenant may also be broken with David My servant so that he will not
have a son to reign on his throne, and with the Levitical priests, My ministers.
22 'As the host of heaven cannot be counted and the sand of the sea cannot be measured, so I will multiply the descendants of David My servant and the Levites who minister to Me.' "
23 And the word of the LORD came to Jeremiah, saying,
24 "Have you not observed what this people have spoken, saying, 'The two families which
the LORD chose, He has rejected them'? Thus they despise My people, no longer are
they as a nation in their sight.
25 "Thus says the LORD, 'If My covenant *for* day and night *stand* not, *and* the fixed patterns of heaven and earth I have not established,
26 then I would reject the descendants of Jacob and David My servant, not taking from
his descendants rulers over the descendants of Abraham, Isaac and Jacob. But I will
restore their fortunes and will have mercy on them.' "

6. God's promised judgment arrives

A Prophecy against Zedekiah

34 The word which came to Jeremiah from the LORD, when Nebuchadnezzar king
of Babylon and all his army, with all the kingdoms of the earth that were under
his dominion and all the peoples, were fighting against Jerusalem and against all its cities, saying,
2 "Thus says the LORD God of Israel, 'Go and speak to Zedekiah king of Judah and
say to him: "Thus says the LORD, 'Behold, I am giving this city into the hand of the king
of Babylon, and he will burn it with fire.
3 'You will not escape from his hand, for you will surely be captured and delivered
into his hand; and you will see the king of Babylon eye to eye, and he will speak with you
face to face, and you will go to Babylon.' " '
4 "Yet hear the word of the LORD, O Zedekiah king of Judah! Thus says the LORD
concerning you, 'You will not die by the sword.
5 'You will die in peace; and as *spices* were burned for your fathers, the former kings
who were before you, so they will burn *spices* for you; and they will lament for you, "Alas,
lord!" ' For I have spoken the word," declares the LORD.
6 Then Jeremiah the prophet spoke all these words to Zedekiah king of Judah in
Jerusalem
7 when the army of the king of Babylon was fighting against Jerusalem and against all
the remaining cities of Judah, *that is,* Lachish and Azekah, for they *alone* remained as
fortified cities among the cities of Judah.
8 The word which came to Jeremiah from the LORD after King Zedekiah had made
a covenant with all the people who were in Jerusalem to proclaim release to them:

33:15 Is 4:2; 11:1-5; Jer 23:5, 6; 30:9; Zech 3:8; 6:12, 13; Ps 72:1-5

33:16 Is 45:17, 22; Jer 23:6; 1 Cor 1:30; 2 Cor 5:21; Phil 3:9

33:17 2 Sam 7:16; 1 Kin 2:4; 8:25; 1 Chr 17:11-14; Ps 89:29-37

33:18 Num 3:5-10; Deut 18:1; 24:8; Josh 3:3; Ezek 44:15; Ezra 3:5; Heb 13:15

33:20 Ps 89:37; 104:19-23; Is 54:9, 10

33:21 2 Sam 23:5; 2 Chr 7:18; 21:7

33:22 Gen 15:5; Jer 31:37; Gen 22:17; Ezek 37:24-27; Is 66:21

33:24 Is 7:17; 11:13; Ezek 37:22; Jer 30:17; Neh 4:2-4; Ps 44:13, 14; 83:4

33:25 Gen 8:22; Jer 31:35, 36; Ps 74:16, 17

33:26 Jer 31:37; Gen 49:10; Is 14:1; 54:8; Ezek 39:25; Hos 1:7; 2:23

34:2 2 Chr 36:11, 12

34:3 2 Kin 25:4, 5; Jer 21:7; 32:4; 34:21; 2 Kin 25:6, 7; Jer 39:6

34:5 2 Chr 16:14; 21:19; Jer 22:18

34:6 1 Sam 3:18; 15:16-24

34:7 Josh 10:3, 5; 2 Kin 14:19; 18:14; Is 36:2; 2 Chr 11:5-10

34:8 2 Kin 11:17; 23:2, 3; Ex 21:2; Lev 25:10, 39-46; Neh 5:1-13; Is 58:6; Jer 34:14, 17

33:15–16 These verses refer to both the first and second comings of Christ. At his first coming he would set up his reign in the hearts of believers; at his second coming he would execute justice and righteousness throughout the whole earth. Christ is the "Branch" sprouting from David, the man after God's own heart.

33:18 As Christ fulfills the role of King, he also fulfills the role of Priest, maintaining constant fellowship with God and mediating for the people (see the note on 22:30). This verse does not mean that actual priests will perform sacrifices, for sacrifices will no longer be necessary (Hebrews 7:24–25). Now that Christ is our High Priest, all believers are priests of God, and we can come before him personally.

34:1ff This chapter describes the fulfillment of many of Jeremiah's predictions. In the book of Jeremiah, many prophecies were both given and quickly fulfilled.

34:8–9 Babylon had laid siege to Jerusalem, and the city was about to fall. Zedekiah finally decided to listen to Jeremiah and try to appease God—so he freed the slaves. He thought he could win

34:9 Gen 14:13; Ex 2:6; Lev 25:39

34:13 Ex 24:3, 7, 8; Deut 5:2, 3, 27; Jer 31:32; Ex 20:2

34:14 Ex 21:2; Deut 15:12; 1 Kin 9:22; 1 Sam 8:7, 8; 2 Kin 17:13, 14

34:15 Jer 34:8; 2 Kin 23:3; Neh 10:29; Jer 7:10f; 32:34

34:16 1 Sam 15:11; Jer 34:11; Ezek 3:20; 18:24; Ex 20:7; Lev 19:12

34:17 Lev 26:34, 35; Esth 7:10; Dan 6:24; Matt 7:2; Jer 32:24; 38:2; Deut 28:25; Jer 29:18

34:18 Deut 17:2; Hos 6:7; 8:1; Rom 2:8; Gen 15:10

34:19 Jer 34:10; Ezek 22:27; Zeph 3:3, 4

34:20 Jer 11:21; 21:7; 22:25; Deut 28:26; 1 Sam 17:44, 46; 1 Kin 14:11; 16:4; Ps 79:2; Jer 7:33; 16:4; 19:7

34:21 2 Kin 25:18-21; Jer 32:3, 4; 39:6; 52:10, 24-27; Ezek 17:16; Jer 37:5-11

34:22 Jer 34:2; 39:1, 2, 8; 52:7, 13; Jer 4:7; 9:11; Jer 33:10; 44:22

35:1 2 Kin 23:34-36; 24:1; 2 Chr 36:5-7; Jer 1:3; 27:20; Dan 1:1

35:2 2 Kin 10:15; 1 Chr 2:55; 1 Kin 6:5, 8; 1 Chr 9:26, 33

9 that each man should set free his male servant and each man his female servant, a Hebrew man or a Hebrew woman; so that no one should keep them, a Jew his brother, in bondage.

10 And all the officials and all the people obeyed who had entered into the covenant that each man should set free his male servant and each man his female servant, so that no one should keep them any longer in bondage; they obeyed, and set *them free.*

11 But afterward they turned around and took back the male servants and the female servants whom they had set free, and brought them into subjection for male servants and for female servants.

12 Then the word of the LORD came to Jeremiah from the LORD, saying,

13 "Thus says the LORD God of Israel, 'I made a covenant with your forefathers in the day that I brought them out of the land of Egypt, from the house of bondage, saying,

14 "At the end of seven years each of you shall set free his Hebrew brother who has been sold to you and has served you six years, you shall send him out free from you; but your forefathers did not obey Me or incline their ear to Me.

15 "Although recently you *had* turned and done what is right in My sight, each man proclaiming release to his neighbor, and you had made a covenant before Me in the house which is called by My name.

16 "Yet you turned and profaned My name, and each man took back his male servant and each man his female servant whom you had set free according to their desire, and you brought them into subjection to be your male servants and female servants." '

17 "Therefore thus says the LORD, 'You have not obeyed Me in proclaiming release each man to his brother and each man to his neighbor. Behold, I am proclaiming a release to you,' declares the LORD, 'to the sword, to the pestilence and to the famine; and I will make you a terror to all the kingdoms of the earth.

18 'I will give the men who have transgressed My covenant, who have not fulfilled the words of the covenant which they made before Me, *when* they cut the calf in two and passed between its parts—

19 the officials of Judah and the officials of Jerusalem, the court officers and the priests and all the people of the land who passed between the parts of the calf—

20 I will give them into the hand of their enemies and into the hand of those who seek their life. And their dead bodies will be food for the birds of the sky and the beasts of the earth.

21 'Zedekiah king of Judah and his officials I will give into the hand of their enemies and into the hand of those who seek their life, and into the hand of the army of the king of Babylon which has gone away from you.

22 'Behold, I am going to command,' declares the LORD, 'and I will bring them back to this city; and they will fight against it and take it and burn it with fire; and I will make the cities of Judah a desolation without inhabitant.' "

The Rechabites' Obedience

35 The word which came to Jeremiah from the LORD in the days of Jehoiakim the son of Josiah, king of Judah, saying,

2 "Go to the house of the Rechabites and speak to them, and bring them into the house of the LORD, into one of the chambers, and give them wine to drink."

3 Then I took Jaazaniah the son of Jeremiah, son of Habazziniah, and his brothers and all his sons and the whole house of the Rechabites,

---

God's favor with a kind act, but what he needed was a change of heart. The people had been disobeying God's Law from the beginning (Exodus 21:2–11; Leviticus 25:39–55; Deuteronomy 15:12–18). When the siege was temporarily lifted, the people became bold and returned to their sins (34:11–17; 37:5, 11).

34:15–16 The people of Israel had a hard time keeping their promises to God. In the temple, they would solemnly promise to obey God, but back in their homes and at work they wouldn't do it. God expressed his great displeasure. If you want to please God, make sure you keep your promises. God wants promises lived out, not just piously made.

34:18–20 Cutting a calf in two and walking between the halves was a customary way to ratify a contract (Genesis 15:9–10). This action symbolized the judgment on anyone who broke the contract. God was saying, "You have broken the contract you made with me, so you know the judgment awaiting you!"

35:1ff The Rechabites' code of conduct resembled that of the Nazirites, who took a special vow of dedication to God (Numbers 6). For 200 years, they had obeyed their ancestors' vow to abstain from wine. While the rest of the nation was breaking its covenant with God, these people were steadfast in their commitment. God wanted the rest of his people to remain as committed to their covenant with him as the Rechabites were to their vow. God had Jeremiah tempt the Rechabites with wine to demonstrate their commitment and dedication. God knew they wouldn't break their vow.

4 and I brought them into the house of the LORD, into the chamber of the sons of
Hanan the son of Igdaliah, the man of God, which was near the chamber of the officials,
which was above the chamber of Maaseiah the son of Shallum, the doorkeeper.
5 Then I set before the men of the house of the Rechabites pitchers full of wine and
cups; and I said to them, "Drink wine!"
6 But they said, "We will not drink wine, for Jonadab the son of Rechab, our father,
commanded us, saying, 'You shall not drink wine, you or your sons, forever.
7 'You shall not build a house, and you shall not sow seed and you shall not plant a
vineyard or own one; but in tents you shall dwell all your days, that you may live many
days in the land where you sojourn.'
8 "We have obeyed the voice of Jonadab the son of Rechab, our father, in all that he
commanded us, not to drink wine all our days, we, our wives, our sons or our daughters,
9 nor to build ourselves houses to dwell in; and we do not have vineyard or field or
seed.
10 "We have only dwelt in tents, and have obeyed and have done according to all that
Jonadab our father commanded us.
11 "But when Nebuchadnezzar king of Babylon came up against the land, we said, 'Come
and let us go to Jerusalem before the army of the Chaldeans and before the army of the
Arameans.' So we have dwelt in Jerusalem."

Judah Rebuked

12 Then the word of the LORD came to Jeremiah, saying,
13 "Thus says the LORD of hosts, the God of Israel, 'Go and say to the men of Judah
and the inhabitants of Jerusalem, "Will you not receive instruction by listening to My
words?" declares the LORD.
14 "The words of Jonadab the son of Rechab, which he commanded his sons not to drink
wine, are observed. So they do not drink *wine* to this day, for they have obeyed their
father's command. But I have spoken to you again and again; yet you have not listened
to Me.
15 "Also I have sent to you all My servants the prophets, sending *them* again and again,
saying: 'Turn now every man from his evil way and amend your deeds, and do not go
after other gods to worship them. Then you will dwell in the land which I have given to
you and to your forefathers; but you have not inclined your ear or listened to Me.
16 'Indeed, the sons of Jonadab the son of Rechab have observed the command of their
father which he commanded them, but this people has not listened to Me.' " '
17 "Therefore thus says the LORD, the God of hosts, the God of Israel, 'Behold, I am
bringing on Judah and on all the inhabitants of Jerusalem all the disaster that I have
pronounced against them; because I spoke to them but they did not listen, and I have
called them but they did not answer.' "
18 Then Jeremiah said to the house of the Rechabites, "Thus says the LORD of hosts,
the God of Israel, 'Because you have obeyed the command of Jonadab your father, kept
all his commands and done according to all that he commanded you;
19 therefore thus says the LORD of hosts, the God of Israel, "Jonadab the son of Rechab
shall not lack a man to stand before Me always." ' "

Jeremiah's Scroll Read in the Temple

36 In the fourth year of Jehoiakim the son of Josiah, king of Judah, this word came
to Jeremiah from the LORD, saying,
2 "Take a scroll and write on it all the words which I have spoken to you concerning

35:4 Deut 33:1; Josh 14:6; 1 Kin 12:22; 2 Kin 1:9-13
35:5 Amos 2:12
35:6 2 Kin 10:15, 23; 1 Chr 2:55; Lev 10:9; Num 6:2-4; Judg 13:7, 14; Luke 1:15
35:7 Gen 25:27; Heb 11:9; Ex 20:12; Eph 6:2, 3; Gen 36:7
35:8 Prov 1:8, 9; 4:1, 2, 10; 6:20; Eph 6:1; Col 3:20
35:9 Ps 37:16; Jer 35:7; 1 Tim 6:6
35:11 2 Kin 24:1, 2; Dan 1:1, 2; Jer 4:5-7
35:13 Is 28:9-12; Jer 5:3; 6:8-10; 32:33
35:14 Jer 35:6-10; 2 Chr 36:15; Jer 7:13, 25; 11:7; 25:3, 4; Is 30:9; 50:2
35:15 Ezek 18:30-32; Acts 26:20; Deut 6:14; Jer 7:6; 13:10; 25:6
35:16 Jer 35:14; Mal 1:6
35:17 Josh 23:15; Mic 3:12; Prov 1:24, 25; Is 65:12; 66:4; Luke 13:34, 35; Rom 10:21
35:18 Ex 20:12; Eph 6:1-3
35:19 1 Chr 2:55; Jer 33:17; Jer 15:19; Luke 21:36
36:1 2 Kin 24:1; 2 Chr 36:5-7; Jer 25:1, 3; 45:1; 46:2; Dan 1:1
36:2 Ex 17:14; Is 8:1; Zech 5:1, 2; Jer 1:9, 10; 30:2; Hab 2:2; Jer 3:3-10; 23:13, 14; 32:30-32; Jer 25:9-29; chs 47-51

35:6 Jonadab son of Recab had joined Jehu in purging the northern kingdom of Baal worship (2 Kings 10:15–28).

35:13–17 There is a vivid contrast between the Rechabites and the other Israelites. (1) The Rechabites kept their vows to a fallible human leader; the people of Israel broke their covenant with their infallible divine Leader. (2) Jonadab told his family one time not to drink, and they obeyed; God commanded Israel constantly to turn from sin, and they refused. (3) The Rechabites obeyed laws that dealt with temporal issues; Israel refused to obey God's laws that dealt with eternal issues. (4) The Rechabites had obeyed for hundreds of years; Israel had disobeyed for hundreds of years. (5) The Rechabites would be rewarded; Israel would be punished. We often are willing to observe customs merely for the sake of tradition; how much more should we obey God's Word because it is eternal.

36:1ff This happened in the summer of 605 B.C., shortly after Nebuchadnezzar's victory over the Egyptian army at Carchemish, before the events recorded in chapters 34 and 35.

36:2–4 Most people in ancient times could neither read nor write, so those who could were extremely valuable. These scribes held positions of great importance and were very respected for their knowledge. Baruch was Jeremiah's scribe. Writing was often done on vellum or papyrus sheets that were sewn or glued together and

Israel and concerning Judah, and concerning all the nations, from the day I *first* spoke to
you, from the days of Josiah, even to this day.
3 "Perhaps the house of Judah will hear all the calamity which I plan to bring on them,
in order that every man will turn from his evil way; then I will forgive their iniquity and
their sin."
4 Then Jeremiah called Baruch the son of Neriah, and Baruch wrote on a scroll at the
dictation of Jeremiah all the words of the LORD which He had spoken to him.
5 Jeremiah commanded Baruch, saying, "I am restricted; I cannot go into the house
of the LORD.
6 "So you go and read from the scroll which you have written at my dictation the words
of the LORD to the people in the LORD'S house on a fast day. And also you shall read
them to all *the people of* Judah who come from their cities.
7 "Perhaps their supplication will come before the LORD, and everyone will turn from
his evil way, for great is the anger and the wrath that the LORD has pronounced against
this people."
8 Baruch the son of Neriah did according to all that Jeremiah the prophet commanded him, reading from the book the words of the LORD in the LORD'S house.
9 Now in the fifth year of Jehoiakim the son of Josiah, king of Judah, in the ninth
month, all the people in Jerusalem and all the people who came from the cities of Judah
to Jerusalem proclaimed a fast before the LORD.
10 Then Baruch read from the book the words of Jeremiah in the house of the LORD
in the chamber of Gemariah the son of Shaphan the scribe, in the upper court, at the
entry of the New Gate of the LORD'S house, to all the people.
11 Now when Micaiah the son of Gemariah, the son of Shaphan, had heard all the words
of the LORD from the book,
12 he went down to the king's house, into the scribe's chamber. And behold, all the
officials were sitting there—Elishama the scribe, and Delaiah the son of Shemaiah, and
Elnathan the son of Achbor, and Gemariah the son of Shaphan, and Zedekiah the son
of Hananiah, and all the *other* officials.
13 Micaiah declared to them all the words that he had heard when Baruch read from
the book to the people.
14 Then all the officials sent Jehudi the son of Nethaniah, the son of Shelemiah, the
son of Cushi, to Baruch, saying, "Take in your hand the scroll from which you have read
to the people and come." So Baruch the son of Neriah took the scroll in his hand and
went to them.
15 They said to him, "Sit down, please, and read it to us." So Baruch read it to them.
16 When they had heard all the words, they turned in fear one to another and said to
Baruch, "We will surely report all these words to the king."
17 And they asked Baruch, saying, "Tell us, please, how did you write all these words?
Was it at his dictation?"
18 Then Baruch said to them, "He dictated all these words to me, and I wrote them
with ink on the book."
19 Then the officials said to Baruch, "Go, hide yourself, you and Jeremiah, and do not
let anyone know where you are."

The Scroll Is Burned

20 So they went to the king in the court, but they had deposited the scroll in the chamber of Elishama the scribe, and they reported all the words to the king.
21 Then the king sent Jehudi to get the scroll, and he took it out of the chamber of
Elishama the scribe. And Jehudi read it to the king as well as to all the officials who stood
beside the king.

36:3 Jer 26:3; 36:7; Ezek 12:3; Deut 30:2, 8; 1 Sam 7:3; Is 55:7; Jer 18:8, 11; 35:15; Jon 3:8; Jon 3:10; Mark 4:12; Acts 3:19

36:4 Jer 32:12; 36:18; 43:3; 45:1; Jer 36:14; Ezek 2:9

36:5 Jer 32:2; 33:1; 2 Cor 11:23

36:6 Jer 36:8; Jer 36:4; Jer 36:9; Zech 8:19

36:7 1 Kin 8:33; 2 Chr 33:12, 13; Jer 26:3; 36:3; Deut 28:15; 31:16, 17; 2 Kin 22:13, 17; Jer 4:4; 21:5; Lam 4:11

36:8 Jer 1:17; 36:6

36:9 Jer 36:1; Jer 36:22; Jer 36:6; Judg 20:26; 1 Sam 7:6; 2 Chr 20:3; Esth 4:16; Joel 1:14; 2:15; Jon 3:5

36:10 Jer 35:4; Jer 36:11, 25; 2 Sam 8:17; Jer 52:25; Jer 26:10

36:11 Jer 36:13

36:12 Jer 36:20; Jer 36:25; Jer 26:22

36:13 2 Kin 22:10

36:14 Jer 36:21; Jer 36:2; Ezek 2:7-10

36:15 Jer 36:21

36:16 Jer 36:24; Acts 24:25; Jer 13:18; Amos 7:10, 11

36:17 John 9:10, 15, 26

36:19 1 Kin 17:3; 18:4, 10; Jer 26:20-24; 36:26

36:20 Jer 36:12

36:21 2 Kin 22:10; 2 Chr 34:18; Ezek 2:4, 5

---

stored in long rolls called scrolls. After the exile, scribes became teachers of the law. In New Testament times, the scribes formed a powerful political party.

36:9 A time of fasting (when people abstained from eating food to show their humility and repentance) was often called during times of national emergency. Babylon was destroying city after city and closing in on Jerusalem. As the people came to the temple, Baruch told them how to avert the coming tragedy. But they refused to listen.

36:10–32 God told Jeremiah to write his words on a scroll. Because he was not allowed to go to the temple, Jeremiah asked his scribe, Baruch, to whom he had dictated the scroll to read it to the people gathered there. Baruch then read it to the officials, and finally Jehudi read it to the king himself. Although the king burned the scroll, he could not destroy the word of God. Today many people try to put God's Word aside or say that it contains errors and therefore cannot be trusted. People may reject God's Word, but they cannot destroy it. God's Word will stand forever (Psalm 119:89).

22 Now the king was sitting in the winter house in the ninth month, with *a fire* burning in the brazier before him.

23 When Jehudi had read three or four columns, *the king* cut it with a scribe's knife and threw *it* into the fire that was in the brazier, until all the scroll was consumed in the fire that was in the brazier.

24 Yet the king and all his servants who heard all these words were not afraid, nor did they rend their garments.

25 Even though Elnathan and Delaiah and Gemariah pleaded with the king not to burn the scroll, he would not listen to them.

26 And the king commanded Jerahmeel the king's son, Seraiah the son of Azriel, and Shelemiah the son of Abdeel to seize Baruch the scribe and Jeremiah the prophet, but the LORD hid them.

The Scroll Is Replaced

27 Then the word of the LORD came to Jeremiah after the king had burned the scroll and the words which Baruch had written at the dictation of Jeremiah, saying,

28 "Take again another scroll and write on it all the former words that were on the first scroll which Jehoiakim the king of Judah burned.

29 "And concerning Jehoiakim king of Judah you shall say,
'Thus says the LORD, "You have burned this scroll, saying, 'Why have you written on it that the king of Babylon will certainly come and destroy this land, and will make man and beast to cease from it?' "

30 'Therefore thus says the LORD concerning Jehoiakim king of Judah, "He shall have no one to sit on the throne of David, and his dead body shall be cast out to the heat of the day and the frost of the night.

31 "I will also punish him and his descendants and his servants for their iniquity, and I will bring on them and the inhabitants of Jerusalem and the men of Judah all the calamity that I have declared to them—but they did not listen." ' "

32 Then Jeremiah took another scroll and gave it to Baruch the son of Neriah, the scribe, and he wrote on it at the dictation of Jeremiah all the words of the book which Jehoiakim king of Judah had burned in the fire; and many similar words were added to them.

Jeremiah Warns against Trust in Pharaoh

37 Now Zedekiah the son of Josiah whom Nebuchadnezzar king of Babylon had made king in the land of Judah, reigned as king in place of Coniah the son of Jehoiakim.

2 But neither he nor his servants nor the people of the land listened to the words of the LORD which He spoke through Jeremiah the prophet.

3 Yet King Zedekiah sent Jehucal the son of Shelemiah, and Zephaniah the son of Maaseiah, the priest, to Jeremiah the prophet, saying, "Please pray to the LORD our God on our behalf."

4 Now Jeremiah was *still* coming in and going out among the people, for they had not *yet* put him in the prison.

5 Meanwhile, Pharaoh's army had set out from Egypt; and when the Chaldeans who

36:22 Judg 3:20; Amos 3:15; Jer 36:9

36:23 1 Kin 22:8, 27; Prov 1:30; Is 5:18, 19; 28:14, 22; Jer 36:29

36:24 Ps 36:1; 64:5; Jer 36:16; Gen 37:29, 34; 2 Sam 1:11; 1 Kin 21:27; 2 Kin 19:1, 2; 22:11, 19; Is 36:22; 37:1; Jon 3:6

36:25 Gen 37:22, 26, 27; Acts 5:34-39

36:26 1 Kin 19:1-3, 10, 14; Matt 23:34, 37; Ps 91:1

36:28 Zech 1:5, 6; Jer 36:4, 23

36:29 Deut 29:19; Job 15:24, 25; Is 45:9; Is 29:21; 30:10; Jer 26:9; 32:3; Jer 25:9-11

36:30 2 Kin 24:12-15; Jer 22:30; Jer 22:19

36:31 Jer 23:34; Deut 28:15; Prov 29:1; Jer 19:15; 35:17

36:32 Ex 4:15, 16; 34:1

37:1 2 Kin 24:17; 1 Chr 3:15; 2 Chr 36:10; Ezek 17:12-21; 2 Kin 24:12; 1 Chr 3:16; 2 Chr 36:9, 10; Jer 22:24, 28; 24:1; 52:31

37:2 2 Kin 24:19, 20; 2 Chr 36:12-16; Prov 29:12

37:3 Jer 29:25; 52:24; 1 Kin 13:6; Jer 2:27; 15:11; 21:1, 2; 42:1-4, 20; Acts 8:24

37:5 2 Kin 24:7; Ezek 17:15; Jer 37:11

36:22 A brazier is a pan for holding burning coals, used to heat a room.

36:25 Only three leaders protested this evil act of burning the scroll containing God's word. This shows how complacent and insensitive to God the people had become.

36:30 Jehoiakim's son, Jehoiachin, was king for three months before he was taken into captivity, but this did not qualify as sitting "on the throne of David"—an expression that implied permanence. Jehoiakim did not secure a dynasty. Zedekiah, the next ruler, was Jehoiachin's uncle. Thus the line of mortal human kings descended from David's son Solomon was finished, but in less than 600 years the eternal King would come through the descendants of Solomon's brother Nathan (see also the note on 22:30).

37:1ff King Jehoiakim died on the way to Babylon (2 Chronicles 36:6), and his son Jehoiachin was appointed king, but Jehoiachin was taken captive to Babylon three months later. Nebuchadnezzar then appointed Zedekiah as his vassal in Judah.

37:2–3 King Zedekiah and his officials did not want to listen to Jeremiah's words, but they wanted the blessings of his prayers. They wanted a superficial religion that wouldn't cost anything. But God is not pleased with those who come to him only for what they can get rather than seeking to establish or deepen a relationship with him. We would not accept that kind of relationship with someone else, and we shouldn't expect God to accept it from us.

37:5 When Nebuchadnezzar besieged Jerusalem in 589 B.C., Pharaoh Hophra marched against him at Zedekiah's invitation. Jerusalem looked to Egypt for help in spite of Jeremiah's warnings. But the Egyptians were no help, for as soon as the Babylonians turned on them, they retreated. Jeremiah's warnings had been correct.

37:7 2 Kin 22:18; Jer 21:1, 2; 37:3; Is 30:1-3; 31:1-3; Jer 2:18, 36; Lam 4:17; Ezek 17:17

37:8 Jer 34:22; 38:23; 39:2-8

37:9 Jer 29:8; Obad 3; Matt 24:4, 5; Eph 5:6

37:10 Lev 26:36-38; Is 30:17; Jer 21:4, 5; Jer 37:8

37:13 Jer 38:7; Zech 14:10; Jer 18:18; 20:10; Luke 23:2; Acts 6:11; 24:5-9, 13

37:14 Ps 27:12; 52:1, 2; Jer 40:4-6; Matt 5:11, 12

37:15 Jer 18:23; 20:1-3; 26:16; Matt 21:35; Gen 39:20; 2 Chr 16:10; 18:26; Jer 38:26; Acts 5:18

37:17 1 Kin 14:1-4; Jer 38:5, 14-16, 24-27; 1 Kin 22:15, 16; 2 Kin 3:11, 12; Jer 15:11; 21:1, 2; 37:3; Jer 21:7; 24:8; Ezek 12:12, 13; 17:19, 20

37:18 1 Sam 24:9; 26:18; Dan 6:22; John 10:32; Acts 25:8, 11, 25

37:19 Deut 32:37, 38; 2 Kin 3:13; Jer 2:28

37:21 Jer 32:2; 38:13, 28; 1 Kin 17:6; Job 5:20; Ps 33:18, 19; Is 33:16; 2 Kin 25:3; Jer 38:9; 52:6

38:1 Jer 37:3; Jer 21:1

38:2 Jer 21:9; Jer 34:17; 42:17; Jer 21:9; 39:18; 45:5

38:3 Jer 21:10; 32:3-5

38:4 Jer 18:23; 26:11, 21; 36:12; Ex 5:4; 1 Kin 18:17, 18; 21:20; Neh 6:9; Amos 7:10; Acts 16:20; Jer 29:7

had been besieging Jerusalem heard the report about them, they lifted the *siege* from
Jerusalem.
6 Then the word of the LORD came to Jeremiah the prophet, saying,
7 "Thus says the LORD God of Israel, 'Thus you are to say to the king of Judah, who
sent you to Me to inquire of Me: "Behold, Pharaoh's army which has come out for your
assistance is going to return to its own land of Egypt.
8 "The Chaldeans will also return and fight against this city, and they will capture it
and burn it with fire." '
9 "Thus says the LORD, 'Do not deceive yourselves, saying, "The Chaldeans will surely
go away from us," for they will not go.
10 'For even if you had defeated the entire army of Chaldeans who were fighting against
you, and there were *only* wounded men left among them, each man in his tent, they would
rise up and burn this city with fire.' "

Jeremiah Imprisoned

11 Now it happened when the army of the Chaldeans had lifted *the siege* from Jerusalem because of Pharaoh's army,
12 that Jeremiah went out from Jerusalem to go to the land of Benjamin in order to
take possession of *some* property there among the people.
13 While he was at the Gate of Benjamin, a captain of the guard whose name was Irijah, the son of Shelemiah the son of Hananiah was there; and he arrested Jeremiah the
prophet, saying, "You are going over to the Chaldeans!"
14 But Jeremiah said, "A lie! I am not going over to the Chaldeans"; yet he would not
listen to him. So Irijah arrested Jeremiah and brought him to the officials.
15 Then the officials were angry at Jeremiah and beat him, and they put him in jail in
the house of Jonathan the scribe, which they had made into the prison.
16 For Jeremiah had come into the dungeon, that is, the vaulted cell; and Jeremiah
stayed there many days.
17 Now King Zedekiah sent and took him *out;* and in his palace the king secretly asked
him and said, "Is there a word from the LORD?" And Jeremiah said, "There is!" Then
he said, "You will be given into the hand of the king of Babylon!"
18 Moreover Jeremiah said to King Zedekiah, "*In* what *way* have I sinned against you,
or against your servants, or against this people, that you have put me in prison?
19 "Where then are your prophets who prophesied to you, saying, 'The king of Babylon
will not come against you or against this land'?
20 "But now, please listen, O my lord the king; please let my petition come before you
and do not make me return to the house of Jonathan the scribe, that I may not die there."
21 Then King Zedekiah gave commandment, and they committed Jeremiah to the court
of the guardhouse and gave him a loaf of bread daily from the bakers' street, until all the
bread in the city was gone. So Jeremiah remained in the court of the guardhouse.

Jeremiah Thrown into the Cistern

38 Now Shephatiah the son of Mattan, and Gedaliah the son of Pashhur, and Jucal
the son of Shelemiah, and Pashhur the son of Malchijah heard the words that
Jeremiah was speaking to all the people, saying,
2 "Thus says the LORD, 'He who stays in this city will die by the sword and by famine
and by pestilence, but he who goes out to the Chaldeans will live and have his *own* life as
booty and stay alive.'
3 "Thus says the LORD, 'This city will certainly be given into the hand of the army of
the king of Babylon and he will capture it.' "
4 Then the officials said to the king, "Now let this man be put to death, inasmuch as

37:17 Zedekiah teetered between surrender and resistance. Too frightened and weak to exercise authority, he asked Jeremiah to come secretly to the palace, perhaps hoping for some better news from God. Zedekiah was desperate; he wanted to hear a word from the Lord, but he feared the political ramifications of being caught talking to Jeremiah.

38:4–5 No wonder Judah was in turmoil: The king agreed with everybody. He listened to Jeremiah (37:21), then he agreed Jeremiah should be killed (38:5), and finally he rescued Jeremiah (38:10). Jeremiah was not popular; his words undermined the morale of the army and the people. Zedekiah couldn't decide between public opinion and God's will. What is most influential in your life—what others say and think or what God wants?

he is discouraging the men of war who are left in this city and all the people, by speaking
such words to them; for this man is not seeking the well-being of this people but rather
their harm."
5 So King Zedekiah said, "Behold, he is in your hands; for the king can *do* nothing
against you."
6 Then they took Jeremiah and cast him into the cistern *of* Malchijah the king's son,
which was in the court of the guardhouse; and they let Jeremiah down with ropes. Now
in the cistern there was no water but only mud, and Jeremiah sank into the mud.
7 But Ebed-melech the Ethiopian, a eunuch, while he was in the king's palace, heard
that they had put Jeremiah into the cistern. Now the king was sitting in the Gate of Benjamin;
8 and Ebed-melech went out from the king's palace and spoke to the king, saying,
9 "My lord the king, these men have acted wickedly in all that they have done to Jeremiah the prophet whom they have cast into the cistern; and he will die right where he
is because of the famine, for there is no more bread in the city."
10 Then the king commanded Ebed-melech the Ethiopian, saying, "Take thirty men
from here under your authority and bring up Jeremiah the prophet from the cistern before
he dies."
11 So Ebed-melech took the men under his authority and went into the king's palace
to *a place* beneath the storeroom and took from there worn-out clothes and worn-out
rags and let them down by ropes into the cistern to Jeremiah.
12 Then Ebed-melech the Ethiopian said to Jeremiah, "Now put these worn-out clothes
and rags under your armpits under the ropes"; and Jeremiah did so.
13 So they pulled Jeremiah up with the ropes and lifted him out of the cistern, and
Jeremiah stayed in the court of the guardhouse.
14 Then King Zedekiah sent and had Jeremiah the prophet brought to him at the third
entrance that is in the house of the LORD; and the king said to Jeremiah, "I am going to
ask you something; do not hide anything from me."
15 Then Jeremiah said to Zedekiah, "If I tell you, will you not certainly put me to death?
Besides, if I give you advice, you will not listen to me."
16 But King Zedekiah swore to Jeremiah in secret saying, "As the LORD lives, who made
this life for us, surely I will not put you to death nor will I give you over to the hand of
these men who are seeking your life."

Interview with Zedekiah

17 Then Jeremiah said to Zedekiah, "Thus says the LORD God of hosts, the God of
Israel, 'If you will indeed go out to the officers of the king of Babylon, then you will live,
this city will not be burned with fire, and you and your household will survive.
18 'But if you will not go out to the officers of the king of Babylon, then this city will be
given over to the hand of the Chaldeans; and they will burn it with fire, and you yourself
will not escape from their hand.' "
19 Then King Zedekiah said to Jeremiah, "I dread the Jews who have gone over to the
Chaldeans, for they may give me over into their hand and they will abuse me."
20 But Jeremiah said, "They will not give you over. Please obey the LORD in what I am
saying to you, that it may go well with you and you may live.

38:5 2 Sam 3:39

38:6 Jer 37:16, 21; Acts 16:24; Ps 40:2; 69:2, 14, 15; Jer 38:22; Zech 9:11

38:7 Jer 39:16; Jer 29:2; Acts 8:27; Deut 21:19; Job 29:7; Jer 37:13; Amos 5:10

38:9 Jer 37:21; 52:6

38:13 Neh 3:25; Jer 32:2; 37:21; 38:6; 39:14, 15; Acts 23:35; 24:27; 28:16, 30

38:14 Jer 21:1, 2; 37:17; 1 Sam 3:17, 18; 1 Kin 22:16; Jer 15:11; 42:2-5, 20

38:15 Luke 22:67, 68

38:16 Jer 37:17; John 3:2; Num 16:22; 27:16; Is 42:5; 57:16; Zech 12:1; Acts 17:25, 28; Jer 34:20; 38:4-6

38:17 Ps 80:7, 14; Amos 5:27; 1 Chr 17:24; Ezek 8:4; 2 Kin 24:12; 25:27-30; Jer 21:8-10; 27:12, 17; 38:2; 39:3

38:18 Jer 27:8; 2 Kin 25:4-10; Jer 24:8-10; 32:3-5; 37:8; 38:3; Jer 32:4; 34:3

38:19 Is 51:12, 13; 57:11; John 12:42; 19:12, 13; Jer 39:9; 2 Chr 30:10; Neh 4:1; Jer 38:22

38:20 2 Chr 20:20; Jer 11:4, 8; 26:13; Dan 4:27; Acts 26:29; Jer 7:23; Gen 19:20; Is 55:3

38:6 Officials put Jeremiah in a cistern to kill him. A cistern was a large hole in the ground lined with rocks to collect rainwater. The bottom would have been dark, damp, and, in this case, full of mud. Jeremiah could drown, die of exposure, or starve to death in the cistern.

38:6 Judah's leaders persecuted Jeremiah repeatedly for faithfully proclaiming God's messages. For 40 years of faithful ministry, he received no acclaim, no love, no popular following. He was beaten, jailed, threatened, and even forced to leave his homeland. Only the pagan Babylonians showed him any respect (39:11–12). God does not guarantee that his servants will escape persecution, even when they are faithful. But God does promise that he will be with them and will give them strength to endure (2 Corinthians 1:3–7). As you minister to others, recognize that your service is for God and not just for human approval. God rewards our faithfulness, but not always during our stay on earth.

38:7–8 The Gate of Benjamin was one of Jerusalem's city gates where legal matters were handled. A palace official, Ebed-melech, had access to the king. When Ebed-melech heard of Jeremiah's plight, he went immediately to deal with the injustice.

38:9–13 Ebed-melech feared God more than man. He alone among the palace officials stood up against the murder plot. His obedience could have cost him his life. Because he obeyed, however, he was spared when Jerusalem fell (39:15–18). You can either go along with the crowd or speak up for God. When someone is treated unkindly or unjustly, for example, reach out to that person with God's love. You may be the only one who does. And, when you are being treated unkindly yourself, be sure to thank God when he sends an "Ebed-melech" your way.

21 "But if you keep refusing to go out, this is the word which the LORD has shown me:
22 'Then behold, all of the women who have been left in the palace of the king of Judah are going to be brought out to the officers of the king of Babylon; and those women
will say,

"Your close friends
Have misled and overpowered you;
While your feet were sunk in the mire,
They turned back."

23 'They will also bring out all your wives and your sons to the Chaldeans, and you yourself will not escape from their hand, but will be seized by the hand of the king of Babylon, and this city will be burned with fire.' "
24 Then Zedekiah said to Jeremiah, "Let no man know about these words and you
will not die.
25 "But if the officials hear that I have talked with you and come to you and say to you,
'Tell us now what you said to the king and what the king said to you; do not hide *it* from
us and we will not put you to death,'
26 then you are to say to them, 'I was presenting my petition before the king, not to
make me return to the house of Jonathan to die there.' "
27 Then all the officials came to Jeremiah and questioned him. So he reported to them
in accordance with all these words which the king had commanded; and they ceased
speaking with him, since the conversation had not been overheard.
28 So Jeremiah stayed in the court of the guardhouse until the day that Jerusalem was
captured.

Jerusalem Captured

39 Now when Jerusalem was captured in the ninth year of Zedekiah king of Judah,
in the tenth month, Nebuchadnezzar king of Babylon and all his army came to
Jerusalem and laid siege to it;
2 in the eleventh year of Zedekiah, in the fourth month, in the ninth *day* of the month,
the city *wall* was breached.
3 Then all the officials of the king of Babylon came in and sat down at the Middle
Gate: Nergal-sar-ezer, Samgar-nebu, Sar-sekim the Rab-saris, Nergal-sar-ezer *the* Rab-
mag, and all the rest of the officials of the king of Babylon.
4 When Zedekiah the king of Judah and all the men of war saw them, they fled and
went out of the city at night by way of the king's garden through the gate between the
two walls; and he went out toward the [12]Arabah.
5 But the army of the Chaldeans pursued them and overtook Zedekiah in the plains
of Jericho; and they seized him and brought him up to Nebuchadnezzar king of Babylon
at Riblah in the land of Hamath, and he passed sentence on him.
6 Then the king of Babylon slew the sons of Zedekiah before his eyes at Riblah; the
king of Babylon also slew all the nobles of Judah.
7 He then blinded Zedekiah's eyes and bound him in fetters of bronze to bring him to
Babylon.
8 The Chaldeans also burned with fire the king's palace and the houses of the people,
and they broke down the walls of Jerusalem.
9 As for the rest of the people who were left in the city, the deserters who had gone
over to him and the rest of the people who remained, Nebuzaradan the captain of the
bodyguard carried *them* into exile in Babylon.

12 I.e. Jordan valley

38:22 Jer 6:12; 8:10; 43:6
38:23 2 Kin 25:7; Jer 39:6; 41:10; Jer 38:18
38:25 Jer 38:4-6, 27
38:26 Jer 37:20
38:28 Ps 23:4; Jer 15:20, 21; 37:20, 21; 38:13; 39:13, 14
39:1 2 Kin 25:1-12; Jer 52:4; Ezek 24:1, 2
39:2 2 Kin 25:4; Jer 52:7
39:3 Jer 38:17; Jer 21:4
39:4 2 Kin 25:4; Is 30:16; Jer 52:7; Amos 2:14; 2 Chr 32:5
39:5 Jer 32:4, 5; 38:18, 23; 52:8; Josh 4:13; 5:10; 2 Kin 23:33; Jer 52:9, 26, 27
39:6 2 Kin 25:7; Jer 52:10; Deut 28:34; Jer 21:7; 24:8-10; 34:19-21
39:7 2 Kin 25:7; Jer 52:11; Ezek 12:13; Judg 16:21; Jer 32:5
39:8 2 Kin 25:9; Jer 21:10; 38:18; 52:13; 2 Kin 25:10; Neh 1:3; Jer 52:14
39:9 Jer 38:19; 52:15; Jer 24:8; 2 Kin 25:11, 20; Jer 39:13; 40:1; 52:12-16, 26; Gen 37:36

38:27 The officials wanted accurate information, but not God's truth. They wanted to use this information against God, his prophet, and the king. But Jeremiah told the officials only what the king ordered him to say. We must not withhold God's truth from others, but we should withhold information that will be used to bring evil to God's people.

39:1ff Zedekiah, son of Josiah and last king of Judah, ruled 11 years, from 597 to 586 B.C. Zedekiah's two older brothers, Jehoahaz and Jehoiakim, and his nephew Jehoiachin ruled before him. When Jehoiachin was exiled to Babylon, Nebuchadnezzar made 21-year-old Mattaniah the king, changing his name to Zedekiah. Zedekiah rebelled against Nebuchadnezzar, who captured him, killed his sons in front of him, and then blinded him and took him back to Babylon where he later died (see 2 Kings 24; 25; 2 Chronicles 36; and Jeremiah 52).

39:5 Riblah was 200 miles north of Jerusalem. This was the Babylonian headquarters for ruling the region.

10 But some of the poorest people who had nothing, Nebuzaradan the captain of the
bodyguard left behind in the land of Judah, and gave them vineyards and fields at that
time.

Jeremiah Spared

11 Now Nebuchadnezzar king of Babylon gave orders about Jeremiah through Nebuzaradan the captain of the bodyguard, saying,
12 "Take him and look after him, and do nothing harmful to him, but rather deal with
him just as he tells you."
13 So Nebuzaradan the captain of the bodyguard sent *word,* along with Nebushazban
the Rab-saris, and Nergal-sar-ezer the Rab-mag, and all the leading officers of the king
of Babylon;
14 they even sent and took Jeremiah out of the court of the guardhouse and entrusted
him to Gedaliah, the son of Ahikam, the son of Shaphan, to take him home. So he stayed
among the people.
15 Now the word of the LORD had come to Jeremiah while he was confined in the court
of the guardhouse, saying,
16 "Go and speak to Ebed-melech the Ethiopian, saying, 'Thus says the LORD of hosts,
the God of Israel, "Behold, I am about to bring My words on this city for disaster and
not for prosperity; and they will take place before you on that day.
17 "But I will deliver you on that day," declares the LORD, "and you will not be given
into the hand of the men whom you dread.
18 "For I will certainly rescue you, and you will not fall by the sword; but you will have
your *own* life as booty, because you have trusted in Me," declares the LORD.' "

Jeremiah Remains in Judah

40 The word which came to Jeremiah from the LORD after Nebuzaradan captain of
the bodyguard had released him from Ramah, when he had taken him bound in
chains among all the exiles of Jerusalem and Judah who were being exiled to Babylon.
2 Now the captain of the bodyguard had taken Jeremiah and said to him, "The LORD
your God promised this calamity against this place;
3 and the LORD has brought *it* on and done just as He promised. Because you *people*
sinned against the LORD and did not listen to His voice, therefore this thing has happened to you.
4 "But now, behold, I am freeing you today from the chains which are on your hands.
If you would prefer to come with me to Babylon, come *along,* and I will look after you;
but if you would prefer not to come with me to Babylon, never mind. Look, the whole
land is before you; go wherever it seems good and right for you to go."
5 As Jeremiah was still not going back, *he said,* "Go on back then to Gedaliah the son
of Ahikam, the son of Shaphan, whom the king of Babylon has appointed over the cities
of Judah, and stay with him among the people; or else go anywhere it seems right for
you to go." So the captain of the bodyguard gave him a ration and a gift and let him go.

39:10 2 Kin 25:12; Jer 52:16

39:11 Job 5:15, 16; Jer 1:8; 15:20, 21; Acts 24:23

39:12 Ps 105:14, 15; Prov 16:7; 21:1; 1 Pet 3:13

39:14 Jer 38:28; 40:1-6; Jer 40:5; 2 Kin 22:12, 14; 2 Chr 34:20; Jer 26:24

39:15 Jer 38:28

39:16 Jer 38:7; Jer 21:10; Dan 9:12; Zech 1:6; Ps 91:8

39:17 Ps 41:1, 2; 50:15

39:18 Jer 21:9; 38:2; 45:5; Ps 34:22; Jer 17:7, 8

40:1 Jer 39:9, 11; Jer 31:15; Acts 12:6, 7; 21:13; 28:20; Eph 6:20

40:2 Lev 26:14-38; Deut 28:15-68; 29:24-28; 31:17; 32:19-25; Jer 22:8, 9

40:3 Jer 50:7; Dan 9:11; Rom 2:5

40:4 Jer 39:11, 12; Gen 13:9; 20:15; 47:6

40:5 Jer 39:14; 2 Kin 25:23; Jer 52:34; 2 Kin 8:7-9

39:10 Babylon had a shrewd foreign policy toward conquered lands. They deported the rich and powerful, leaving only the very poor in charge, thus making them grateful to their conquerors. This policy assured that conquered populations would be too loyal and too weak to revolt.

39:11–12 God had promised to rescue Jeremiah from his trouble (1:8). The superstitious Babylonians, who highly respected magicians and fortune-tellers, treated Jeremiah as a seer. Because he had been imprisoned by his own people, they assumed he was a traitor and on their side. They undoubtedly knew he had counseled cooperation with Babylon and predicted a Babylonian victory. So the Babylonians freed Jeremiah and protected him.

39:13–14 What a difference there is between Jeremiah's fate and Zedekiah's! Jeremiah was freed; Zedekiah was imprisoned. Jeremiah was saved because of his faith; Zedekiah was destroyed because of his fear. Jeremiah was treated with respect; Zedekiah was treated with contempt. Jeremiah was concerned for the people; Zedekiah was concerned for himself.

39:17–18 Ebed-melech had risked his life to save God's prophet Jeremiah (38:7–13). When Babylon conquered Jerusalem, God protected Ebed-melech from the Babylonians. God has special rewards for his faithful people, but not everyone will receive them in this life (see the note on 38:6).

40—45 These six chapters cover events following Jerusalem's fall to Babylon.

40:2–3 The Babylonian commander, who did not know God, acknowledged that God had given the Babylonians victory. It is strange when people recognize that God exists and does miracles, but still they do not personally accept him. Knowing God is more than knowing about him. Be sure you know him personally.

40:4 Jeremiah was free to go anywhere. In Babylon he would have had great comfort and power. In Judah he would continue to face hardship. In Babylon Jeremiah would have been favored by the Babylonians, but hated by the Judean exiles. In Judah he would remain poor and unwanted, but the Judean remnant would know he was not a traitor. Jeremiah returned to Judah.

6 Then Jeremiah went to Mizpah to Gedaliah the son of Ahikam and stayed with him
among the people who were left in the land.
7 Now all the commanders of the forces that were in the field, they and their men,
heard that the king of Babylon had appointed Gedaliah the son of Ahikam over the land
and that he had put him in charge of the men, women and children, those of the poorest
of the land who had not been exiled to Babylon.
8 So they came to Gedaliah at Mizpah, along with Ishmael the son of Nethaniah, and
Johanan and Jonathan the sons of Kareah, and Seraiah the son of Tanhumeth, and the
sons of Ephai the Netophathite, and Jezaniah the son of the Maacathite, *both* they and
their men.
9 Then Gedaliah the son of Ahikam, the son of Shaphan, swore to them and to their
men, saying, "Do not be afraid of serving the Chaldeans; stay in the land and serve the
king of Babylon, that it may go well with you.
10 "Now as for me, behold, I am going to stay at Mizpah to stand *for you* before the
Chaldeans who come to us; but as for you, gather in wine and summer fruit and oil and
put *them* in your *storage* vessels, and live in your cities that you have taken over."
11 Likewise, also all the Jews who were in Moab and among the sons of Ammon and
in Edom and who were in all the other countries, heard that the king of Babylon had left
a remnant for Judah, and that he had appointed over them Gedaliah the son of Ahikam,
the son of Shaphan.
12 Then all the Jews returned from all the places to which they had been driven away
and came to the land of Judah, to Gedaliah at Mizpah, and gathered in wine and summer fruit in great abundance.
13 Now Johanan the son of Kareah and all the commanders of the forces that were in
the field came to Gedaliah at Mizpah
14 and said to him, "Are you well aware that Baalis the king of the sons of Ammon has
sent Ishmael the son of Nethaniah to take your life?" But Gedaliah the son of Ahikam
did not believe them.
15 Then Johanan the son of Kareah spoke secretly to Gedaliah in Mizpah, saying, "Let
me go and kill Ishmael the son of Nethaniah, and not a man will know! Why should he
take your life, so that all the Jews who are gathered to you would be scattered and the
remnant of Judah would perish?"
16 But Gedaliah the son of Ahikam said to Johanan the son of Kareah, "Do not do
this thing, for you are telling a lie about Ishmael."

Gedaliah Is Murdered

41 In the seventh month Ishmael the son of Nethaniah, the son of Elishama, of the
royal family and *one* of the chief officers of the king, along with ten men, came to
Mizpah to Gedaliah the son of Ahikam. While they were eating bread together there in
Mizpah,
2 Ishmael the son of Nethaniah and the ten men who were with him arose and struck
down Gedaliah the son of Ahikam, the son of Shaphan, with the sword and put to death
the one whom the king of Babylon had appointed over the land.
3 Ishmael also struck down all the Jews who were with him, *that is* with Gedaliah at
Mizpah, and the Chaldeans who were found there, the men of war.
4 Now it happened on the next day after the killing of Gedaliah, when no one knew
about *it,*
5 that eighty men came from Shechem, from Shiloh, and from Samaria with their
beards shaved off and their clothes torn and their bodies gashed, having grain offerings
and incense in their hands to bring to the house of the LORD.
6 Then Ishmael the son of Nethaniah went out from Mizpah to meet them, weeping
as he went; and as he met them, he said to them, "Come to Gedaliah the son of Ahikam!"

40:6 Judg 20:1; 21:1; 1 Sam 7:5; 2 Chr 16:6; Jer 39:14

40:7 2 Kin 25:23; Jer 39:10; 52:16

40:8 Jer 40:14; 41:2; Jer 40:13, 15; 42:1; 43:2; 2 Sam 23:28, 29; Ezra 2:22; Neh 7:26; Jer 42:1; Deut 3:14; Josh 12:5; 2 Sam 10:6, 8

40:9 1 Sam 20:16, 17; 2 Kin 25:24; Jer 27:11; 38:17-20

40:10 Deut 1:38; 1 Kin 10:8; Jer 35:19; Deut 16:13; Jer 39:10; Is 16:9; Jer 40:12; 48:32

40:11 Num 22:1; 25:1, 2; Is 16:4; Jer 9:26; 1 Sam 11:1; 12:12; Gen 36:8; Is 11:14

40:12 Jer 43:5

40:14 1 Sam 11:1-3; 2 Sam 10:1-6; Jer 25:21; 41:10

40:15 1 Sam 26:8; 2 Sam 21:17; Jer 42:2

40:16 Matt 10:16; 1 Cor 13:5

41:1 2 Kin 25:25; Jer 40:8, 14; Jer 39:14; 40:5, 6; Ps 41:9; Jer 40:13, 14

41:2 2 Sam 3:27; 20:9, 10; 2 Kin 25:25; Ps 41:9; 109:5; John 13:18; 2 Kin 25:25; Jer 40:5

41:5 2 Kin 10:13, 14; Gen 33:18; 37:12; Judg 9:1; 1 Kin 12:1, 25; Josh 18:1; Judg 18:31; 1 Sam 3:21; Ps 78:60; 1 Kin 16:24, 29; Lev 19:27; Deut 14:1; Deut 14:1; Jer 16:6; 1 Sam 1:7; 2 Kin 25:9

41:6 2 Sam 3:16; Jer 50:4

40:6 Mizpah was a few miles north of Jerusalem. Not thoroughly destroyed by the Babylonians, Mizpah served as a refuge after the destruction of Jerusalem.

40:13—41:3 Gedaliah, appointed governor of Judah, foolishly ignored the warnings of assassination. Ishmael, in the line of David, may have been angry that he had been passed over for leadership. This is similar to the chaotic political situation that Ezra and Nehemiah faced when they returned to rebuild the temple and the city.

41:4–9 The 80 men came from three cities of the northern kingdom to worship in Jerusalem. Ishmael probably killed them for the money and food they were carrying. Without a king, with no law and no loyalty to God, Judah was subjected to complete anarchy.

7 Yet it turned out that as soon as they came inside the city, Ishmael the son of Nethaniah and the men that were with him slaughtered them *and cast them* into the cistern.
8 But ten men who were found among them said to Ishmael, "Do not put us to death;
for we have stores of wheat, barley, oil and honey hidden in the field." So he refrained
and did not put them to death along with their companions.
9 Now as for the cistern where Ishmael had cast all the corpses of the men whom he
had struck down because of Gedaliah, it was the one that King Asa had made on account of Baasha, king of Israel; Ishmael the son of Nethaniah filled it with the slain.
10 Then Ishmael took captive all the remnant of the people who were in Mizpah, the
king's daughters and all the people who were left in Mizpah, whom Nebuzaradan the
captain of the bodyguard had put under the charge of Gedaliah the son of Ahikam; thus
Ishmael the son of Nethaniah took them captive and proceeded to cross over to the sons
of Ammon.

Johanan Rescues the People

11 But Johanan the son of Kareah and all the commanders of the forces that were with
him heard of all the evil that Ishmael the son of Nethaniah had done.
12 So they took all the men and went to fight with Ishmael the son of Nethaniah and
they found him by the great pool that is in Gibeon.
13 Now as soon as all the people who were with Ishmael saw Johanan the son of Kareah and the commanders of the forces that were with him, they were glad.
14 So all the people whom Ishmael had taken captive from Mizpah turned around and
came back, and went to Johanan the son of Kareah.
15 But Ishmael the son of Nethaniah escaped from Johanan with eight men and went
to the sons of Ammon.
16 Then Johanan the son of Kareah and all the commanders of the forces that were
with him took from Mizpah all the remnant of the people whom he had recovered from
Ishmael the son of Nethaniah, after he had struck down Gedaliah the son of Ahikam,
that is, the men who were soldiers, *the* women, *the* children, and *the* eunuchs, whom he
had brought back from Gibeon.
17 And they went and stayed in Geruth Chimham, which is beside Bethlehem, in order to proceed into Egypt
18 because of the Chaldeans; for they were afraid of them, since Ishmael the son of
Nethaniah had struck down Gedaliah the son of Ahikam, whom the king of Babylon had
appointed over the land.

Warning against Going to Egypt

42 Then all the commanders of the forces, Johanan the son of Kareah, Jezaniah the
son of Hoshaiah, and all the people both small and great approached
2 and said to Jeremiah the prophet, "Please let our petition come before you, and
pray for us to the LORD your God, *that is* for all this remnant; because we are left *but* a
few out of many, as your own eyes *now* see us,
3 that the LORD your God may tell us the way in which we should walk and the thing
that we should do."
4 Then Jeremiah the prophet said to them, "I have heard *you.* Behold, I am going to
pray to the LORD your God in accordance with your words; and I will tell you the whole
message which the LORD will answer you. I will not keep back a word from you."
5 Then they said to Jeremiah, "May the LORD be a true and faithful witness against
us if we do not act in accordance with the whole message with which the LORD your God
will send you to us.
6 "Whether *it* is pleasant or unpleasant, we will listen to the voice of the LORD our
God to whom we are sending you, so that it may go well with us when we listen to the
voice of the LORD our God."
7 Now at the end of ten days the word of the LORD came to Jeremiah.

41:7 Ps 55:23; Is 59:7; Ezek 22:27; 33:24, 26
41:8 Is 45:3
41:9 1 Kin 15:17-22; 2 Chr 16:1-6; Judg 6:2; 1 Sam 13:6; 2 Sam 17:9; Heb 11:38
41:10 Jer 40:11, 12; Jer 43:6; Neh 2:10, 19; 4:7; Jer 40:14
41:11 Jer 40:7, 8, 13-16
41:12 Gen 14:14-16; 1 Sam 30:1-8, 18, 20; 2 Sam 2:13
41:15 1 Sam 30:17; 1 Kin 20:20; Job 21:30; Prov 28:17
41:16 Jer 42:8; 43:4-7
41:17 2 Sam 19:37, 38, 40; Jer 42:14
41:18 Is 51:12, 13; 57:11; Jer 42:11, 16; 43:2, 3; Luke 12:4, 5; Jer 40:5
42:1 Jer 40:8, 13; 41:11, 18; Jer 6:13; 8:10; 42:8; 44:12; Acts 8:10
42:2 Jer 36:7; 37:20; Ex 8:28; 1 Sam 7:8; 12:19; 1 Kin 13:6; Is 37:4; Jer 37:3; 42:20; Acts 8:24; James 5:16; Lev 26:22; Deut 28:62; Is 1:9; Lam 1:1
42:3 Ps 86:11; Prov 3:6; Jer 6:16; Mic 4:2
42:4 Ex 8:29; 1 Sam 12:23; 1 Kin 22:14; Jer 23:28; 1 Sam 3:17, 18; Ps 40:10; Acts 20:20
42:5 Gen 31:50; Judg 11:10; Jer 43:2; Mic 1:2; Mal 2:14; 3:5
42:6 Ex 24:7; Deut 5:27; Josh 24:24; Deut 5:29, 33; 6:3; Jer 7:23
42:7 Ps 27:14; Is 30:18

41:16–17 Johanan and his group were already on their way to Egypt, headed south from Gibeon, stopping first at Geruth Chimham, near Bethlehem. Their visit to Jeremiah (42:1–6) was hypocritical, as Jeremiah later told them (42:20).

42:5–6 Johanan and his associates spoke their own curse; Jeremiah merely elaborated on it. It was a tragic mistake to ask for God's guidance with no intention of following it. Be sure never to ask God for something that you know in your heart you really do not want. It is better not to pray than to pray hypocritically. God cannot be deceived.

8 Then he called for Johanan the son of Kareah and all the commanders of the forces that were with him, and for all the people both small and great,

9 and said to them, "Thus says the LORD the God of Israel, to whom you sent me to present your petition before Him:

10 'If you will indeed stay in this land, then I will build you up and not tear you down, and I will plant you and not uproot you; for I will relent concerning the calamity that I have inflicted on you.

11 'Do not be afraid of the king of Babylon, whom you are *now* fearing; do not be afraid of him,' declares the LORD, 'for I am with you to save you and deliver you from his hand.

12 'I will also show you compassion, so that he will have compassion on you and restore you to your own soil.

13 'But if you are going to say, "We will not stay in this land," so as not to listen to the voice of the LORD your God,

14 saying, "No, but we will go to the land of Egypt, where we will not see war or hear the sound of a trumpet or hunger for bread, and we will stay there";

15 then in that case listen to the word of the LORD, O remnant of Judah. Thus says the LORD of hosts, the God of Israel, "If you really set your mind to enter Egypt and go in to reside there,

16 then the sword, which you are afraid of, will overtake you there in the land of Egypt; and the famine, about which you are anxious, will follow closely after you there *in* Egypt, and you will die there.

17 "So all the men who set their mind to go to Egypt to reside there will die by the sword, by famine and by pestilence; and they will have no survivors or refugees from the calamity that I am going to bring on them." ' "

18 For thus says the LORD of hosts, the God of Israel, "As My anger and wrath have been poured out on the inhabitants of Jerusalem, so My wrath will be poured out on you when you enter Egypt. And you will become a curse, an object of horror, an imprecation and a reproach; and you will see this place no more."

19 The LORD has spoken to you, O remnant of Judah, "Do not go into Egypt!" You should clearly understand that today I have testified against you.

20 For you have *only* deceived yourselves; for it is you who sent me to the LORD your God, saying, "Pray for us to the LORD our God; and whatever the LORD our God says, tell us so, and we will do it."

21 So I have told you today, but you have not obeyed the LORD your God, even in whatever He has sent me to *tell* you.

22 Therefore you should now clearly understand that you will die by the sword, by famine and by pestilence, in the place where you wish to go to reside.

In Egypt Jeremiah Warns of Judgment

43 But as soon as Jeremiah, whom the LORD their God had sent, had finished telling all the people all the words of the LORD their God—that is, all these words—

2 Azariah the son of Hoshaiah, and Johanan the son of Kareah, and all the arrogant men said to Jeremiah, "You are telling a lie! The LORD our God has not sent you to say, 'You are not to enter Egypt to reside there';

3 but Baruch the son of Neriah is inciting you against us to give us over into the hand of the Chaldeans, so they will put us to death or exile us to Babylon."

4 So Johanan the son of Kareah and all the commanders of the forces, and all the people, did not obey the voice of the LORD to stay in the land of Judah.

5 But Johanan the son of Kareah and all the commanders of the forces took the entire remnant of Judah who had returned from all the nations to which they had been driven away, in order to reside in the land of Judah—

6 the men, the women, the children, the king's daughters and every person that

42:10 Jer 24:6; 31:28; 33:7; Ezek 36:36; Jer 18:7, 8; Hos 11:8; Joel 2:13; Amos 7:3, 6; Jon 3:10; 4:2

42:11 Jer 1:8; 27:12, 17; 41:18; Num 14:9; 2 Chr 32:7, 8; Ps 46:7, 11; 118:6; Is 8:9, 10; 43:2, 5; Jer 1:19; 15:20; Rom 8:31

42:12 Neh 1:11; Ps 106:46; Prov 16:7

42:14 Is 31:1; Jer 41:17; Ex 16:3; Num 11:4; Jer 4:19, 21

42:15 Deut 17:16

42:16 Jer 44:13, 27; Ezek 11:8; Amos 9:1-4

42:17 Jer 42:22; 44:13

42:18 2 Chr 36:16-19; Jer 7:20; 33:5; 39:1-9; Deut 29:21; Is 65:15; Jer 18:16; 24:9; 29:18; 44:12; Jer 22:10, 27

42:19 Deut 17:16; Is 30:1-7; Ezek 2:5; Neh 9:26, 29, 30

42:20 Jer 43:2; Ezek 14:3

42:21 Deut 11:26; Jer 43:1; Ezek 2:7; Zech 7:11; Acts 20:26, 27; Jer 43:4

42:22 Jer 43:11; Ezek 6:11; Hos 9:6

43:2 Jer 42:1; 2 Chr 36:13; Is 7:9; Jer 5:12, 13; 42:5

43:3 Jer 36:4, 10, 26, 32; 43:6; 45:1-3

43:4 Jer 42:8; 2 Chr 25:16; Jer 42:5, 6; 44:5; Ps 37:3

43:5 Jer 40:11

43:6 Jer 41:10; Jer 39:10; 40:7; Eccl 9:1, 2; Lam 3:1

43:1–3 Johanan and his tiny band had come to Jeremiah for God's approval of their plan, not for God's direction. This is a recurring problem for most of us—seeking God's approval of our desires rather than asking him for guidance. It's not good to make plans unless we are willing to have God change them, and it is not good to pray unless we are willing to accept God's answer.

43:4–7 Afraid to obey the Lord, the people headed for Egypt, even forcing Jeremiah to go with them. (They thought that perhaps God would spare them if Jeremiah was with them.) Jeremiah had served as a prophet for 40 years. Many of his words had already come true, and he had turned down an offer to live comfortably in Babylon, returning instead to his beloved people. But the people still rejected Jeremiah's advice. The response of our audience is not necessarily a measure of our success. Jeremiah was doing all God asked, but he had been called to minister to a very stubborn group of people.

Nebuzaradan the captain of the bodyguard had left with Gedaliah the son of Ahikam
and grandson of Shaphan, together with Jeremiah the prophet and Baruch the son of
Neriah—
7 and they entered the land of Egypt (for they did not obey the voice of the LORD)
and went in as far as Tahpanhes.
8 Then the word of the LORD came to Jeremiah in Tahpanhes, saying,
9 "Take *some* large stones in your hands and hide them in the mortar in the brick *ter-*
race which is at the entrance of Pharaoh's palace in Tahpanhes, in the sight of some *of*
the Jews;
10 and say to them, 'Thus says the LORD of hosts, the God of Israel, "Behold, I am
going to send and get Nebuchadnezzar the king of Babylon, My servant, and I am going
to set his throne *right* over these stones that I have hidden; and he will spread his canopy
over them.
11 "He will also come and strike the land of Egypt; those who are *meant* for death *will*
be given over to death, and those for captivity to captivity, and those for the sword to the
sword.
12 "And I shall set fire to the temples of the gods of Egypt, and he will burn them and
take them captive. So he will wrap himself with the land of Egypt as a shepherd wraps
himself with his garment, and he will depart from there safely.
13 "He will also shatter the obelisks of Heliopolis, which is in the land of Egypt; and the
temples of the gods of Egypt he will burn with fire." ' "

Conquest of Egypt Predicted

44 The word that came to Jeremiah for all the Jews living in the land of Egypt, those
who were living in Migdol, Tahpanhes, Memphis, and the land of Pathros, saying,
2 "Thus says the LORD of hosts, the God of Israel, 'You yourselves have seen all the
calamity that I have brought on Jerusalem and all the cities of Judah; and behold, this
day they are in ruins and no one lives in them,
3 because of their wickedness which they committed so as to provoke Me to anger by
continuing to burn sacrifices *and* to serve other gods whom they had not known, *neither*
they, you, nor your fathers.
4 'Yet I sent you all My servants the prophets, again and again, saying, "Oh, do not do
this abominable thing which I hate."
5 'But they did not listen or incline their ears to turn from their wickedness, so as not
to burn sacrifices to other gods.
6 'Therefore My wrath and My anger were poured out and burned in the cities of Judah and in the streets of Jerusalem, so they have become a ruin and a desolation as it is
this day.
7 'Now then thus says the LORD God of hosts, the God of Israel, "Why are you doing

43:10 Jer 25:9, 11; Is 44:28; 45:1; Jer 25:9; 27:6; Ps 18:11; 27:5; 31:20

43:11 Is 19:1-25; Jer 25:15-19; 44:13; 46:1, 2, 13-26; Ezek 29:19, 20; Jer 15:2

43:12 Ex 12:12; Is 19:1; Jer 46:25; Ezek 30:13; Ps 104:2; 109:18, 19; Is 49:18

44:1 Ex 14:2; Jer 46:14; Jer 43:7; Ezek 30:18; Is 19:13; Jer 2:16; 46:14; Ezek 30:13, 16; Hos 9:6; Is 11:11; Ezek 29:14; 30:14

44:2 Is 6:11; Jer 4:7; 9:11; 34:22; Mic 3:12

44:3 Neh 9:33; Jer 2:17-19; 44:23; Ezek 8:17, 18; Dan 9:5; Is 3:8; Jer 7:19; 32:30-32; 44:8; Jer 19:4; Deut 13:6; 29:26; 32:17

44:4 Jer 7:13, 25; 25:4; 26:5; 29:19; 35:15; Zech 7:7; Jer 16:18; 32:34, 35; Ezek 8:10

44:5 Jer 11:8, 10; 13:10

44:6 Is 51:17-20; Jer 42:18; Ezek 8:18; Jer 7:17, 34; Jer 4:27; 34:22

44:7 Num 16:38; Jer 26:19; Ezek 33:11; Hab 2:10; Jer 3:24; 9:21; 51:22

43:10–13 Nebuchadnezzar invaded Egypt in 568—567 B.C. Like Judah, Egypt rebelled against him and was quickly crushed. So much for the great empire on which Judah had constantly placed its hopes!

44:1ff This message, given in 580 B.C. while Jeremiah was in Egypt against his will, reminded the people that their following other gods had brought destruction on their land. Jeremiah told them that they would never return to Judah because the escape to Egypt had been against God's advice (42:9ff). But the people refused to learn any lessons from all the destruction their sins had caused.

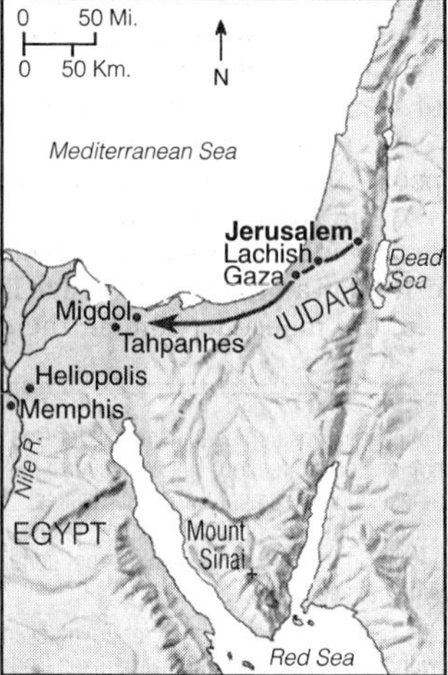

ESCAPE TO EGYPT
With Judah in turmoil after the murder of Gedaliah, the people turned to Jeremiah for guidance. Jeremiah had God's answer, "Stay in this land." But the leaders disobeyed and went to Egypt, taking Jeremiah with them. In Egypt, Jeremiah told them they were in grave danger.

great harm to yourselves, so as to cut off from you man and woman, child and infant,
from among Judah, leaving yourselves without remnant,
8 provoking Me to anger with the works of your hands, burning sacrifices to other
gods in the land of Egypt, where you are entering to reside, so that you might be cut off
and become a curse and a reproach among all the nations of the earth?
9 "Have you forgotten the wickedness of your fathers, the wickedness of the kings of
Judah, and the wickedness of their wives, your own wickedness, and the wickedness of
your wives, which they committed in the land of Judah and in the streets of Jerusalem?
10 "But they have not become contrite even to this day, nor have they feared nor walked
in My law or My statutes, which I have set before you and before your fathers." '
11 "Therefore thus says the LORD of hosts, the God of Israel, 'Behold, I am going to set
My face against you for woe, even to cut off all Judah.
12 'And I will take away the remnant of Judah who have set their mind on entering the
land of Egypt to reside there, and they will all meet their end in the land of Egypt; they
will fall by the sword *and* meet their end by famine. Both small and great will die by the
sword and famine; and they will become a curse, an object of horror, an imprecation
and a reproach.
13 'And I will punish those who live in the land of Egypt, as I have punished Jerusalem,
with the sword, with famine and with pestilence.
14 'So there will be no refugees or survivors for the remnant of Judah who have entered the land of Egypt to reside there and then to return to the land of Judah, to which
they are longing to return and live; for none will return except *a few* refugees.' "
15 Then all the men who were aware that their wives were burning sacrifices to other
gods, along with all the women who were standing by, *as* a large assembly, including all
the people who were living in Pathros in the land of Egypt, responded to Jeremiah, saying,
16 "As for the message that you have spoken to us in the name of the LORD, we are not
going to listen to you!
17 "But rather we will certainly carry out every word that has proceeded from our mouths,
by burning sacrifices to the queen of heaven and pouring out drink offerings to her, just
as we ourselves, our forefathers, our kings and our princes did in the cities of Judah and
in the streets of Jerusalem; for *then* we had plenty of food and were well off and saw no
misfortune.
18 "But since we stopped burning sacrifices to the queen of heaven and pouring out drink
offerings to her, we have lacked everything and have met our end by the sword and by
famine."
19 "And," *said the women,* "when we were burning sacrifices to the queen of heaven
and were pouring out drink offerings to her, was it without our husbands that we made
for her *sacrificial* cakes in her image and poured out drink offerings to her?"

Calamity for the Jews

20 Then Jeremiah said to all the people, to the men and women—even to all the people who were giving him *such* an answer—saying,
21 "As for the smoking sacrifices that you burned in the cities of Judah and in the streets
of Jerusalem, you and your forefathers, your kings and your princes, and the people of
the land, did not the LORD remember them and did not *all this* come into His mind?
22 "So the LORD was no longer able to endure *it,* because of the evil of your deeds,
because of the abominations which you have committed; thus your land has become a
ruin, an object of horror and a curse, without an inhabitant, as *it is* this day.
23 "Because you have burned sacrifices and have sinned against the LORD and not
obeyed the voice of the LORD or walked in His law, His statutes or His testimonies, therefore this calamity has befallen you, as *it has* this day."

44:8 2 Kin 17:15-17; Jer 25:6, 7; 44:3; 1 Cor 10:21, 22; Jer 7:9; 11:12, 17; 44:3; Hos 4:13; Hab 1:16; 1 Kin 9:7, 8; 2 Chr 7:20; Jer 42:18

44:9 Jer 7:9, 10, 17, 18; 44:17, 21

44:10 Jer 6:15; 8:12

44:11 Lev 17:10; 20:5, 6; 26:17; Jer 21:10; Amos 9:4

44:12 Jer 42:15-18, 22; Is 1:28; Jer 16:4; 44:7; Is 65:15; Jer 18:16; 24:9; 26:6; 29:18; 42:18; Zech 8:13

44:13 Jer 11:22; 44:27, 28

44:14 Jer 22:10; 44:27; Jer 22:26, 27; Is 4:2; 10:20; Rom 9:27

44:15 Prov 11:21; Is 1:5; Jer 5:1-5

44:16 Jer 43:2; Prov 1:24-27; Jer 11:8, 10; 13:10

44:17 Num 30:12; Deut 23:23; 2 Kin 17:16; Jer 7:18; Neh 9:34; Jer 32:32; 44:21; Ex 16:3; Hos 2:5-9; Phil 3:19

44:18 Num 11:5, 6; Jer 40:12; Mal 3:13-15

44:19 Jer 7:18; Num 30:6

44:21 Ezek 8:10, 11; Ps 79:8; Is 64:9; Jer 14:10; Hos 7:2; Amos 8:7

44:22 Is 7:13; 43:24; Mal 2:17; Jer 4:4; 21:12; 30:14; Gen 19:13; Ps 107:33, 34; Jer 25:11, 18, 38; 29:18; 42:18; 44:12

44:23 Jer 7:13-15; 40:3; Jer 44:10; Ps 119:136, 150; 1 Kin 9:9; Neh 13:18; Jer 44:2; Dan 9:11, 12

44:9–10 When we forget a lesson or refuse to learn it, we risk repeating our mistakes. The people of Judah struggled with this; to forget their former sins was to repeat them. To fail to learn from failure is to assure future failure. Your past is your school of experience. Let your past mistakes point you to God's way.

44:15–18 The farther we drift from God, the more confused our thinking becomes. Whatever spiritual life was left in the Israelites when they went to Egypt was lost as they sank into the depths of idolatry. (For more information on the "queen of heaven," see the note on 7:18.) The escape to Egypt had brought a change in their pagan worship habits, and they blamed their troubles on their neglect of their idols. But idol worship had started all their problems in the first place. The people refused to recognize the true source of their problems—departure from God's leading. When calamity forces you to examine your life, take a close look at God's instructions for you.

24 Then Jeremiah said to all the people, including all the women, "Hear the word of
the LORD, all Judah who are in the land of Egypt,
25 thus says the LORD of hosts, the God of Israel, as follows: 'As for you and your wives,
you have spoken with your mouths and fulfilled *it* with your hands, saying, "We will certainly perform our vows that we have vowed, to burn sacrifices to the queen of heaven
and pour out drink offerings to her." Go ahead and confirm your vows, and certainly
perform your vows!'
26 "Nevertheless hear the word of the LORD, all Judah who are living in the land of Egypt,
'Behold, I have sworn by My great name,' says the LORD, 'never shall My name be invoked again by the mouth of any man of Judah in all the land of Egypt, saying, "As the
Lord GOD lives."
27 'Behold, I am watching over them for harm and not for good, and all the men of
Judah who are in the land of Egypt will meet their end by the sword and by famine until
they are completely gone.
28 'Those who escape the sword will return out of the land of Egypt to the land of Judah few in number. Then all the remnant of Judah who have gone to the land of Egypt
to reside there will know whose word will stand, Mine or theirs.
29 'This will be the sign to you,' declares the LORD, 'that I am going to punish you in
this place, so that you may know that My words will surely stand against you for harm.'
30 "Thus says the LORD, 'Behold, I am going to give over Pharaoh Hophra king of Egypt
to the hand of his enemies, to the hand of those who seek his life, just as I gave over
Zedekiah king of Judah to the hand of Nebuchadnezzar king of Babylon, *who was* his
enemy and was seeking his life.' "

44:24 Jer 42:15; 44:16; Jer 43:7; 44:15, 26

44:25 Jer 44:17; Matt 14:9; Acts 23:12; Ezek 20:39

44:26 Gen 22:16; Deut 32:40, 41; Jer 22:5; Amos 6:8; Heb 6:13; Ps 50:16; Ezek 20:39; Is 48:1, 2; Jer 5:2

44:27 Jer 1:10; 31:28; 39:16; 2 Kin 21:14; Jer 44:14

44:28 Jer 44:14; Is 10:19; 27:12, 13; Ps 33:11; Is 14:27; 46:10, 11; Zech 1:6

44:29 Is 7:11, 14; 8:18; Jer 44:30; Matt 24:15, 16, 32; Prov 19:21; Is 40:8

44:30 Jer 43:9-13; 46:25; Ezek 29:3; 30:21; 2 Kin 25:4-7; Jer 34:21; 39:5-7

Message to Baruch

45 *This is* the message which Jeremiah the prophet spoke to Baruch the son of Neriah, when he had written down these words in a book at Jeremiah's dictation, in
the fourth year of Jehoiakim the son of Josiah, king of Judah, saying:
2 "Thus says the LORD the God of Israel to you, O Baruch:
3 'You said, "Ah, woe is me! For the LORD has added sorrow to my pain; I am weary
with my groaning and have found no rest." '
4 "Thus you are to say to him, 'Thus says the LORD, "Behold, what I have built I am
about to tear down, and what I have planted I am about to uproot, that is, the whole
land."
5 'But you, are you seeking great things for yourself? Do not seek *them;* for behold, I
am going to bring disaster on all flesh,' declares the LORD, 'but I will give your life to
you as booty in all the places where you may go.' "

45:1 Jer 32:12, 16; 43:3, 6; Jer 36:4, 18, 32; 2 Kin 24:1; 2 Chr 36:5-7; Jer 25:1; 36:1; 46:2; Dan 1:1

45:3 Ps 6:6; 69:3; 2 Cor 4:1, 16; Gal 6:9

45:4 Is 5:5; Jer 1:10; 11:17; 18:7-10; 31:28

45:5 1 Kin 3:9, 11; 2 Kin 5:26; Matt 6:25, 32; Rom 12:16; Is 66:16; Jer 25:31; Jer 21:9; 38:2; 39:18

B. GOD'S JUDGMENT ON THE NATIONS (46:1—52:34)

All of Jeremiah's prophecies against foreign nations have been grouped together. Many of the people in these nations assumed that they were free from judgment and punishment for their sin. Following these prophecies is a historical appendix recounting the fall of Jerusalem. Just as Jerusalem received its punishment, these nations were certain to receive theirs as well. Those today who think that judgment will never touch them are forewarned.

1. Prophecies about foreign nations

Defeat of Pharaoh Foretold

46 That which came as the word of the LORD to Jeremiah the prophet concerning
the nations.

46:1 Jer 1:10; 25:15-38

44:28 After Jeremiah's forced move to Egypt, there is no word in the Bible about the events in the rest of his life.

44:30 Pharaoh Hophra ruled Egypt from 588 to 569 B.C. and was killed by Ahmose, one of his generals, who was then crowned in his place.

45:1ff The event relating to this chapter is recorded in 36:1–8. The chapter was written in 605—604 B.C. Baruch was the scribe who recorded Jeremiah's words on a scroll.

45:5 Baruch had long been serving this unpopular prophet, writing his book of struggles and judgments, and now he was upset. God told Baruch to take his eyes off himself and whatever rewards he thought he deserved. If Baruch did this, God would protect him. It is easy to lose the joy of serving our God when we take our eyes off him. The more we look away from God's purposes toward our own sacrifices, the more frustrated we will become. As you serve God, beware of focusing on what you are giving up. When this happens, ask God's forgiveness; then look at him rather than at yourself.

46:1ff In this chapter, we gain several insights about God and his plan for this world. (1) Although God chose Israel for a special purpose, he loves all people and wants all to come to him. (2) God is holy and will not tolerate sin. (3) God's judgments are not based on prejudice and a desire for revenge, but on fairness and justice. (4) God does not delight in judgment, but in salvation. (5) God is impartial—he judges everyone by the same standard.

2 To Egypt, concerning the army of Pharaoh Neco king of Egypt, which was by the
Euphrates River at Carchemish, which Nebuchadnezzar king of Babylon defeated in the
fourth year of Jehoiakim the son of Josiah, king of Judah:
3 "Line up the shield and buckler,
And draw near for the battle!
4 "Harness the horses,
And mount the steeds,
And take your stand with helmets *on!*
Polish the spears,
Put on the scale-armor!
5 "Why have I seen *it?*
They are terrified,
They are drawing back,
And their mighty men are defeated
And have taken refuge in flight,
Without facing back;
Terror is on every side!"
Declares the LORD.
6 Let not the swift man flee,
Nor the mighty man escape;
In the north beside the river Euphrates
They have stumbled and fallen.
7 Who is this that rises like the Nile,
Like the rivers whose waters surge about?
8 Egypt rises like the Nile,
Even like the rivers whose waters surge about;
And He has said, "I will rise and cover *that* land;
I will surely destroy the city and its inhabitants."
9 Go up, you horses, and drive madly, you chariots,
That the mighty men may march forward:
Ethiopia and Put, that handle the shield,
And the Lydians, that handle *and* bend the bow.
10 For that day belongs to the Lord GOD of hosts,
A day of vengeance, so as to avenge Himself on His foes;
And the sword will devour and be satiated
And drink its fill of their blood;
For there will be a slaughter for the Lord GOD of hosts,
In the land of the north by the river Euphrates.
11 Go up to Gilead and obtain balm,
O virgin daughter of Egypt!
In vain have you multiplied remedies;
There is no healing for you.
12 The nations have heard of your shame,
And the earth is full of your cry *of distress;*
For one warrior has stumbled over another,
And both of them have fallen down together.
13 *This is* the message which the LORD spoke to Jeremiah the prophet about the com-
ing of Nebuchadnezzar king of Babylon to smite the land of Egypt:
14 "Declare in Egypt and proclaim in Migdol,
Proclaim also in Memphis and Tahpanhes;
Say, 'Take your stand and get yourself ready,
For the sword has devoured those around you.'
15 "Why have your mighty ones become prostrate?
They do not stand because the LORD has thrust them down.

46:2 Jer 46:14; Ezek chs 29-32; 2 Kin 18:21; 23:29, 33-35; Jer 25:19; 2 Chr 35:20; Is 10:9; Jer 45:1

46:3 Is 21:5; Jer 51:11; Joel 3:9; Nah 2:1; 3:14

46:4 Ezek 21:9-11; 1 Sam 17:5, 38; 2 Chr 26:14; Neh 4:16; Jer 51:3

46:5 Is 42:17; Jer 46:21; Is 5:25; Ezek 39:18; Jer 6:25; 20:3; 49:29

46:6 Is 30:16; Jer 46:12, 16; Dan 11:19

46:7 Jer 47:2

46:8 Is 37:24; Is 10:13

46:9 Jer 47:3; Nah 2:4; Nah 3:9; Is 66:19

46:10 Joel 1:15; Jer 50:15, 18; Deut 32:42; Is 31:8; Jer 12:12; Is 34:6; Zeph 1:7

46:11 Jer 8:22; Is 47:1; Jer 31:4, 21; Jer 30:13; Mic 1:9; Nah 3:19

46:12 Jer 2:36; Nah 3:8-10; Jer 14:2; Is 19:2

46:13 Jer 43:10-13; Is 19:1

46:14 Jer 44:1; Jer 43:8; Is 1:20; Jer 2:30; 46:10; Nah 2:13

46:15 Is 66:15, 16; Jer 46:5; Ps 18:14, 39; 68:1, 2

46:2 At the battle of Carchemish in 605 B.C., Babylon and Egypt, the two major world powers after Assyria's fall, clashed. The Babylonians entered Carchemish by surprise and defeated Egypt. This battle, which passed world leadership to Babylon, was Nebuchadnezzar's first victory, establishing him in his new position as king of the Babylonian empire. With Egypt's power declining, it was both poor strategy and disobedience to God for Judah to form an alliance with Egypt.

46:9 The soldiers from Ethiopia and Put were from eastern and northern Africa. The men of Lydia may have been from Greece.

16"They have repeatedly stumbled;
Indeed, they have fallen one against another.
Then they said, 'Get up! And let us go back
To our own people and our native land
Away from the sword of the oppressor.'
17"They cried there, 'Pharaoh king of Egypt *is but* a big noise;
He has let the appointed time pass by!'
18"As I live," declares the King
Whose name is the LORD of hosts,
"Surely one shall come *who looms up* like Tabor among the mountains,
Or like Carmel by the sea.
19"Make your baggage ready for exile,
O daughter dwelling in Egypt,
For Memphis will become a desolation;
It will even be burned down *and* bereft of inhabitants.
20"Egypt is a pretty heifer,
But a horsefly is coming from the north—it is coming!
21"Also her mercenaries in her midst
Are like fattened calves,
For even they too have turned back *and* have fled away together;
They did not stand *their ground.*
For the day of their calamity has come upon them,
The time of their punishment.
22"Its sound moves along like a serpent;
For they move on like an army
And come to her as woodcutters with axes.
23"They have cut down her forest," declares the LORD;
"Surely it will no *more* be found,
Even though they are *now* more numerous than locusts
And are without number.
24"The daughter of Egypt has been put to shame,
Given over to the power of the people of the north."
25 The LORD of hosts, the God of Israel, says, "Behold, I am going to punish Amon of
Thebes, and Pharaoh, and Egypt along with her gods and her kings, even Pharaoh and
those who trust in him.
26"I shall give them over to the power of those who are seeking their lives, even into
the hand of Nebuchadnezzar king of Babylon and into the hand of his officers. Afterwards, however, it will be inhabited as in the days of old," declares the LORD.
27"But as for you, O Jacob My servant, do not fear,
Nor be dismayed, O Israel!
For, see, I am going to save you from afar,
And your descendants from the land of their captivity;
And Jacob will return and be undisturbed
And secure, with no one making *him* tremble.
28"O Jacob My servant, do not fear," declares the LORD,
"For I am with you.
For I will make a full end of all the nations
Where I have driven you,
Yet I will not make a full end of you;
But I will correct you properly
And by no means leave you unpunished."

46:16 Lev 26:36, 37; Jer 46:6; Jer 51:9; Jer 50:16

46:17 Ex 15:9, 10; 1 Kin 20:10, 11; Is 19:11-16

46:18 Jer 48:15; Mal 1:14; Josh 19:22; Judg 4:6; Ps 89:12; Josh 12:22; 1 Kin 18:42

46:19 Is 20:4; Jer 48:18; Jer 46:14; Ezek 30:13

46:20 Hos 10:11; Jer 1:14; 47:2

46:21 2 Sam 10:6; 2 Kin 7:6; Jer 46:5; Is 34:7; Jer 48:44; Hos 9:7; Obad 13; Mic 7:4

46:23 Jer 21:14; Judg 6:5; 7:12; Joel 2:25

46:24 Jer 1:15

46:25 Ezek 30:14-16; Nah 3:8; Jer 44:30; Ex 12:12; Jer 43:12, 13; Ezek 30:13; Zeph 2:11; Is 20:5

46:26 Jer 44:30; Ezek 32:11; Ezek 29:8-14

46:27 Is 41:13, 14; Jer 30:10, 11; Is 11:11; Jer 23:3, 4; 29:14; Mic 7:12; Jer 23:6; 50:19

46:28 Ps 46:7, 11; Is 8:10; 43:2; Jer 1:19; Jer 4:27; Amos 9:8, 9; Jer 10:24; Hab 3:2

46:17 In 589 B.C. when Nebuchadnezzar besieged Jerusalem, Pharaoh Hophra marched against him at Zedekiah's invitation. But when the Babylonians stood up to the Egyptians, Pharaoh Hophra and his troops retreated. Jeremiah had prophesied that Pharaoh Hophra would be killed by his enemies (44:30). This was fulfilled nearly 20 years later when his co-regent Ahmose led a revolt.

46:28 God punished his people in order to bring them back to himself, and he punishes us to correct and purify us. No one welcomes punishment, but we should all welcome its results: correction and purity.

Prophecy against Philistia

47:1 Jer 25:20; Zech 9:6; Gen 10:19; 1 Kin 4:24; Jer 25:20; Amos 1:6; Zeph 2:4

47 That which came as the word of the LORD to Jeremiah the prophet concerning the Philistines, before Pharaoh conquered Gaza.

47:2 Is 14:31; Jer 1:14; 6:22; 46:20, 24; Is 8:7, 8; Is 15:2-5; Jer 46:12

2 Thus says the LORD:
"Behold, waters are going to rise from the north
And become an overflowing torrent,
And overflow the land and all its fullness,
The city and those who live in it;
And the men will cry out,
And every inhabitant of the land will wail.

47:3 Judg 5:22; Jer 8:16; Nah 3:2

3 "Because of the noise of the galloping hoofs of his stallions,
The tumult of his chariots, *and* the rumbling of his wheels,
The fathers have not turned back for *their* children,
Because of the limpness of *their* hands,

47:4 Is 14:31; Is 23:5; Jer 25:22; Joel 3:4; Amos 1:9, 10; Zech 9:2-4; Gen 10:14; Deut 2:23; Amos 9:7

4 On account of the day that is coming
To destroy all the Philistines,
To cut off from Tyre and Sidon
Every ally that is left;
For the LORD is going to destroy the Philistines,
The remnant of the coastland of Caphtor.

47:5 Jer 48:37; Mic 1:16; Judg 1:18; Jer 25:20; Amos 1:7, 8; Zeph 2:4, 7; Zech 9:5; Jer 16:6; 41:5

5 "Baldness has come upon Gaza;
Ashkelon has been ruined.
O remnant of their valley,
How long will you gash yourself?

47:6 Judg 7:20; Jer 12:12; Ezek 21:3-5

6 "Ah, sword of the LORD,
How long will you not be quiet?
Withdraw into your sheath;
Be at rest and stay still.

47:7 Is 10:6; Ezek 14:17; Mic 6:9

7 "How can it be quiet,
When the LORD has given it an order?
Against Ashkelon and against the seacoast—
There He has assigned it."

Prophecy against Moab

48:1 Is 15:1; Ezek 25:9; Num 32:3, 38; Jer 48:22; Num 32:37; Jer 48:23; Ezek 25:9

48 Concerning Moab. Thus says the LORD of hosts, the God of Israel,
"Woe to Nebo, for it has been destroyed;
Kiriathaim has been put to shame, it has been captured;
The lofty stronghold has been put to shame and shattered.

48:2 Num 21:25; Jer 48:34, 45; 49:3

2 "There is praise for Moab no longer;
In Heshbon they have devised calamity against her:
'Come and let us cut her off from *being* a nation!'
You too, [13]Madmen, will be silenced;
The sword will follow after you.

48:3 Is 15:5; Jer 48:5, 34

3 "The sound of an outcry from Horonaim,
'Devastation and great destruction!'
4 "Moab is broken,
Her little ones have sounded out a cry *of distress.*

48:5 Is 15:5

5 "For by the ascent of Luhith
They will ascend with continual weeping;
For at the descent of Horonaim
They have heard the anguished cry of destruction.

48:6 Jer 51:6

6 "Flee, save your lives,

13 I.e. a city of Moab

47:1 Located on the coastal plain next to Judah, Philistia had always been a thorn in Israel's side. The two nations battled constantly. Other prophets who spoke against Philistia include Isaiah (14:28–32), Ezekiel (25:15–17), Amos (1:6–8), and Zephaniah (2:4–7).

48:1 The Moabites were descendants of Lot through an incestuous relationship with one of his daughters (Genesis 19:30–37). They led the Israelites into idolatry (Numbers 25:1–3) and joined the bands of raiders Nebuchadnezzar sent into Judah in 602 B.C. They were later conquered by Babylon and disappeared as a nation.

That you may be like a juniper in the wilderness.
7 "For because of your trust in your own achievements and treasures,
Even you yourself will be captured;
And Chemosh will go off into exile
Together with his priests and his princes.
8 "A destroyer will come to every city,
So that no city will escape;
The valley also will be ruined
And the plateau will be destroyed,
As the LORD has said.
9 "Give wings to Moab,
For she will flee away;
And her cities will become a desolation,
Without inhabitants in them.
10 "Cursed be the one who does the LORD'S work negligently,
And cursed be the one who restrains his sword from blood.

11 "Moab has been at ease since his youth;
He has also been undisturbed, *like wine* on its dregs,
And he has not been emptied from vessel to vessel,
Nor has he gone into exile.
Therefore he retains his flavor,
And his aroma has not changed.
12 "Therefore behold, the days are coming," declares the LORD, "when I will send to
him those who tip *vessels,* and they will tip him over, and they will empty his vessels and
shatter his jars.
13 "And Moab will be ashamed of Chemosh, as the house of Israel was ashamed of
Bethel, their confidence.
14 "How can you say, 'We are mighty warriors,
And men valiant for battle'?
15 "Moab has been destroyed and men have gone up to his cities;
His choicest young men have also gone down to the slaughter,"
Declares the King, whose name is the LORD of hosts.
16 "The disaster of Moab will soon come,
And his calamity has swiftly hastened.
17 "Mourn for him, all you who *live* around him,
Even all of you who know his name;
Say, 'How has the mighty scepter been broken,
A staff of splendor!'
18 "Come down from your glory
And sit on the parched ground,
O daughter dwelling in Dibon,
For the destroyer of Moab has come up against you,
He has ruined your strongholds.
19 "Stand by the road and keep watch,
O inhabitant of Aroer;
Ask him who flees and her who escapes
And say, 'What has happened?'
20 "Moab has been put to shame, for it has been shattered.
Wail and cry out;
Declare by the Arnon
That Moab has been destroyed.
21 "Judgment has also come upon the plain, upon Holon, Jahzah and against Mepha-
ath,

48:7 Ps 52:7; Is 59:4; Jer 9:23; Num 21:29; 1 Kin 11:33; Jer 48:13, 46

48:8 Josh 13:9, 17, 21

48:9 Ps 11:1; Is 16:2; Jer 48:28; Jer 44:22

48:10 Jer 11:3; 1 Kin 20:39, 40, 42; 2 Kin 13:19; Jer 47:6, 7

48:11 Jer 22:21; Ezek 16:49; Zech 1:15; Zeph 1:12; Nah 2:2

48:13 Is 45:16; Jer 48:39; Judg 11:24; 1 Kin 12:29; Hos 8:5, 6

48:14 Ps 33:16; Is 10:13-16

48:15 Is 40:30, 31; Jer 50:27; Jer 46:18; 51:57; Mal 1:14

48:16 Is 13:22

48:17 Is 9:4; 14:5

48:18 Is 47:1; Jer 46:19; Num 21:30; Josh 13:9, 17; Is 15:2; Jer 48:22

48:19 Deut 2:36; Josh 12:2; 1 Sam 4:13, 14, 16

48:20 Num 21:13

48:21 Num 21:23; Is 15:4; Jer 48:34; Josh 13:18

48:7 Chemosh was the main god of the nation of Moab (Numbers 21:29), and child sacrifice was an important part of his worship (2 Kings 3:26–27).

48:11–12 When making wine, the grapes were crushed. After 40 days, the wine was poured off from the dregs in the bottom of the jar. If this was not done, the wine would be inferior. The prophet was saying that because of Moab's complacency and refusal to do God's work, Moab would be totally destroyed.

48:13 After Israel divided into northern and southern kingdoms, the northern kingdom set up golden calf-idols in Bethel and Dan to keep people from going to worship in Jerusalem, capital of the southern kingdom (1 Kings 12:25–29).

48:23 Josh 13:17
48:24 Jer 48:41; Amos 2:2
48:25 Ps 75:10; Zech 1:19-21; Job 22:9; Ps 10:15
48:26 Jer 25:15; Dan 5:23
48:27 Lam 2:15-17; Mic 7:8-10; Jer 2:26; Job 16:4; Jer 18:16
48:28 Judg 6:2; Is 2:19; Jer 49:16; Obad 3; Ps 55:6; Song 2:14
48:29 Is 16:6; Zeph 2:8; Job 40:11, 12; Ps 138:6
48:30 Is 37:28
48:31 Is 15:5; 16:7, 11; 2 Kin 3:25; Is 16:7, 11; Jer 48:36
48:32 Is 16:8, 9; Num 21:32
48:33 Is 16:10; Jer 25:10; Joel 1:12; Is 5:10; Hag 2:16
48:34 Is 15:4-6; Num 32:3, 37; Gen 13:10; 14:2; Is 15:5, 6
48:35 Is 15:2; 16:12; Jer 7:9; 11:13
48:36 Is 15:5; 16:11; Is 15:7
48:37 Is 15:2; Jer 16:6; 41:5; 47:5; Gen 37:34; Is 15:3; 20:2
48:38 Is 22:1; Jer 19:10, 11; 22:28; 25:34
48:39 Ezek 26:16
48:40 Deut 28:49; Jer 49:22; Hos 8:1; Hab 1:8; Is 8:8
48:41 Jer 49:22; Is 13:8; 21:3; Jer 30:6; Mic 4:9, 10
48:42 Ps 83:4; Is 37:23
48:43 Is 24:17, 18; Lam 3:47

22 against Dibon, Nebo and Beth-diblathaim,
23 against Kiriathaim, Beth-gamul and Beth-meon,
24 against Kerioth, Bozrah and all the cities of the land of Moab, far and near.
25 "The horn of Moab has been cut off and his arm broken," declares the LORD.
26 "Make him drunk, for he has become arrogant toward the LORD; so Moab will wallow in his vomit, and he also will become a laughingstock.
27 "Now was not Israel a laughingstock to you? Or was he caught among thieves? For
each time you speak about him you shake *your head in scorn.*
28 "Leave the cities and dwell among the crags,
O inhabitants of Moab,
And be like a dove that nests
Beyond the mouth of the chasm.
29 "We have heard of the pride of Moab—he *is* very proud—
Of his haughtiness, his pride, his arrogance and his self-exaltation.
30 "I know his fury," declares the LORD,
"But it is futile;
His idle boasts have accomplished nothing.
31 "Therefore I will wail for Moab,
Even for all Moab will I cry out;
I will moan for the men of Kir-heres.
32 "More than the weeping for Jazer
I will weep for you, O vine of Sibmah!
Your tendrils stretched across the sea,
They reached to the sea of Jazer;
Upon your summer fruits and your grape harvest
The destroyer has fallen.
33 "So gladness and joy are taken away
From the fruitful field, even from the land of Moab.
And I have made the wine to cease from the wine presses;
No one will tread *them* with shouting,
The shouting will not be shouts *of joy.*
34 "From the outcry at Heshbon even to Elealeh, even to Jahaz they have raised their
voice, from Zoar even to Horonaim *and to* Eglath-shelishiyah; for even the waters of
Nimrim will become desolate.
35 "I will make an end of Moab," declares the LORD, "the one who offers *sacrifice* on
the high place and the one who burns incense to his gods.
36 "Therefore My heart wails for Moab like flutes; My heart also wails like flutes for
the men of Kir-heres. Therefore they have lost the abundance it produced.
37 "For every head is bald and every beard cut short; there are gashes on all the hands
and sackcloth on the loins.
38 "On all the housetops of Moab and in its streets there is lamentation everywhere; for
I have broken Moab like an undesirable vessel," declares the LORD.
39 "How shattered it is! *How* they have wailed! How Moab has turned his back—he is
ashamed! So Moab will become a laughingstock and an object of terror to all around
him."
40 For thus says the LORD:
"Behold, one will fly swiftly like an eagle
And spread out his wings against Moab.
41 "Kerioth has been captured
And the strongholds have been seized,
So the hearts of the mighty men of Moab in that day
Will be like the heart of a woman in labor.
42 "Moab will be destroyed from *being* a people
Because he has become arrogant toward the LORD.
43 "Terror, pit and snare are *coming* upon you,

48:29 Moab was condemned for its pride. God cannot tolerate pride because pride is taking personal credit for what God has done or looking down on others. God does not condemn our taking satisfaction in what we do (Ecclesiastes 3:22), but he stands against overestimates of our own importance. Romans 12:3 teaches us to have an honest estimate of ourselves.

48:31 Kir-heres was a stronghold city in Moab. God's compassion reaches to all creation, even to his enemies.

O inhabitant of Moab," declares the LORD.
44 "The one who flees from the terror
Will fall into the pit,
And the one who climbs up out of the pit
Will be caught in the snare;
For I shall bring upon her, *even* upon Moab,
The year of their punishment," declares the LORD.

48:44 1 Kin 19:17; Is 24:18; Amos 5:19; Jer 46:21

45 "In the shadow of Heshbon
The fugitives stand without strength;
For a fire has gone forth from Heshbon
And a flame from the midst of Sihon,
And it has devoured the forehead of Moab
And the scalps of the riotous revelers.
46 "Woe to you, Moab!
The people of Chemosh have perished;
For your sons have been taken away captive
And your daughters into captivity.
47 "Yet I will restore the fortunes of Moab
In the latter days," declares the LORD.
Thus far the judgment on Moab.

48:45 Num 21:28, 29; Num 21:21, 26; Ps 135:11; Num 24:17

48:46 Num 21:29; Judg 11:24; 1 Kin 11:7; Jer 48:7

48:47 Jer 12:14-17; 49:6, 39

Prophecy against Ammon

49 Concerning the sons of Ammon. Thus says the LORD:
"Does Israel have no sons?
Or has he no heirs?
Why then has Malcam taken possession of Gad
And his people settled in its cities?
2 "Therefore behold, the days are coming," declares the LORD,
"That I will cause a trumpet blast of war to be heard
Against Rabbah of the sons of Ammon;
And it will become a desolate heap,
And her towns will be set on fire.
Then Israel will take possession of his possessors,"
Says the LORD.
3 "Wail, O Heshbon, for Ai has been destroyed!
Cry out, O daughters of Rabbah,
Gird yourselves with sackcloth and lament,
And rush back and forth inside the walls;
For Malcam will go into exile
Together with his priests and his princes.
4 "How boastful you are about the valleys!
Your valley is flowing *away,*
O backsliding daughter
Who trusts in her treasures, *saying,*
'Who will come against me?'
5 "Behold, I am going to bring terror upon you,"
Declares the Lord GOD of hosts,
"From all *directions* around you;
And each of you will be driven out headlong,
With no one to gather the fugitives together.
6 "But afterward I will restore
The fortunes of the sons of Ammon,"
Declares the LORD.

49:1 Deut 23:3, 4; 2 Chr 20:1; Ezek 21:28-32; 25:2-10; Amos 1:13-15; Zeph 2:8-11

49:2 Num 10:9; Jer 4:19; Deut 3:11; 2 Sam 11:1; Ezek 21:20; Josh 17:11, 16; Is 14:2

49:3 Jer 48:2; Josh 7:2-5; 8:1-29; Ezra 2:28; Is 32:11; Jer 48:37; Jer 46:25; 48:7

49:4 Jer 9:23; Jer 31:22; Ps 62:10; Ezek 28:4, 5; 1 Tim 6:17; Jer 21:13

49:5 Jer 48:43f; 49:29; Jer 16:16; 46:5; Lam 4:15

49:6 Jer 48:47; 49:39

49:1 The Ammonites were descendants of Lot through an incestuous relationship with one of his daughters (as were the Moabites; see Genesis 19:30–38). They were condemned for stealing land from God's people and for worshiping the idol Molech, to whom they made child sacrifices.

49:7
Gen 25:30; 32:3; Is 34:5, 6; Jer 25:21; Ezek 25:12; Amos 1:11; Obad 1-21; Job 2:11; Jer 8:9; Gen 36:11, 15, 34; Jer 49:20

49:8
Is 21:13; Jer 25:23; Jer 46:21; Mal 1:3, 4

49:9
Obad 5

49:10
Jer 13:26; Is 17:14

49:11
Ps 68:5; Hos 14:3; Ps 68:5; Zech 7:10

49:12
Jer 25:15; Jer 25:28, 29; 1 Pet 4:17

49:13
Gen 22:16; Is 45:23; Jer 44:26; Amos 6:8; Gen 36:33; 1 Chr 1:44; Is 34:6; 63:1; Amos 1:12; Is 34:9-15; Jer 18:16

49:14
Obad 1-4; Is 18:2; 30:4; Jer 50:14

49:16
2 Kin 14:7; Jer 48:28; Job 39:27; Is 14:13-15; Amos 9:2

49:17
Jer 18:16; 49:13; 50:13; Ezek 35:7; 1 Kin 9:8; Jer 51:37

49:18
Gen 19:24, 25; Deut 29:23; Jer 50:40; Amos 4:11; Zeph 2:9; Job 18:15-18; Jer 49:33

49:19
Jer 50:44; Josh 3:15; Jer 12:5; Num 16:5; Ex 15:11; Is 46:9; Job 41:10

49:20
Is 14:24, 27; Jer 50:45; Mal 1:3, 4

Prophecy against Edom

7 Concerning Edom.
Thus says the LORD of hosts,
"Is there no longer any wisdom in Teman?
Has good counsel been lost to the prudent?
Has their wisdom decayed?
8 "Flee away, turn back, dwell in the depths,
O inhabitants of Dedan,
For I will bring the disaster of Esau upon him
At the time I punish him.
9 "If grape gatherers came to you,
Would they not leave gleanings?
If thieves *came* by night,
They would destroy *only* until they had enough.
10 "But I have stripped Esau bare,
I have uncovered his hiding places
So that he will not be able to conceal himself;
His offspring has been destroyed along with his relatives
And his neighbors, and he is no more.
11 "Leave your orphans behind, I will keep *them* alive;
And let your widows trust in Me."
12 For thus says the LORD, "Behold, those who were not sentenced to drink the cup
will certainly drink *it,* and are you the one who will be completely acquitted? You will
not be acquitted, but you will certainly drink *it.*
13 "For I have sworn by Myself," declares the LORD, "that Bozrah will become an ob-
ject of horror, a reproach, a ruin and a curse; and all its cities will become perpetual ruins."
14 I have heard a message from the LORD,
And an envoy is sent among the nations, *saying,*
"Gather yourselves together and come against her,
And rise up for battle!"
15 "For behold, I have made you small among the nations,
Despised among men.
16 "As for the terror of you,
The arrogance of your heart has deceived you,
O you who live in the clefts of the rock,
Who occupy the height of the hill.
Though you make your nest as high as an eagle's,
I will bring you down from there," declares the LORD.
17 "Edom will become an object of horror; everyone who passes by it will be horrified
and will hiss at all its wounds.
18 "Like the overthrow of Sodom and Gomorrah with its neighbors," says the LORD,
"no one will live there, nor will a son of man reside in it.
19 "Behold, one will come up like a lion from the thickets of the Jordan against a perennially watered pasture; for in an instant I will make him run away from it, and whoever is chosen I shall appoint over it. For who is like Me, and who will summon Me *into
court?* And who then is the shepherd who can stand against Me?"
20 Therefore hear the plan of the LORD which He has planned against Edom, and His
purposes which He has purposed against the inhabitants of Teman: surely they will drag

---

49:7 Because the Israelites descended from Jacob and the Edomites from his twin brother, Esau, both nations descended from their father, Isaac. There was constant conflict between these nations, and Edom rejoiced at the fall of Jerusalem (see the book of Obadiah). Teman, a town in the northern part of Edom, was known for its wisdom and was the hometown of Eliphaz, one of Job's friends (Job 2:11). But even the wisdom of Teman could not save Edom from God's wrath.

49:8 Dedan was a flourishing city that supported caravan travel. God told its inhabitants to flee to the caves or they would also be destroyed. Teman and Dedan were at opposite ends of the country, so this shows the completeness of God's destruction of Edom. Bozrah (49:13) is a town in northern Edom.

49:16 Edom was located in a rock fortress that today is known as Petra, in southern Jordan. Edom thought she was invincible because of her location. Edom was destroyed because of her pride. Pride destroys individuals as well as nations. It makes us think we can take care of ourselves without God's help. Even serving God and others can lead us into pride. Take inventory of your life and service for God; ask God to point out and remove any pride you may be harboring.

them off, *even* the little ones of the flock; surely He will make their pasture desolate
because of them.
21 The earth has quaked at the noise of their downfall. There is an outcry! The noise
of it has been heard at the Red Sea.
22 Behold, He will mount up and swoop like an eagle and spread out His wings against
Bozrah; and the hearts of the mighty men of Edom in that day will be like the heart of a
woman in labor.

49:21 Jer 50:46; Ezek 26:15, 18

49:22 Jer 4:13; 48:40; Hos 8:1; Is 13:8; Jer 30:6; 48:41

Prophecy against Damascus

23 Concerning Damascus.
"Hamath and Arpad are put to shame,
For they have heard bad news;
They are disheartened.
There is anxiety by the sea,
It cannot be calmed.
24 "Damascus has become helpless;
She has turned away to flee,
And panic has gripped her;
Distress and pangs have taken hold of her
Like a woman in childbirth.
25 "How the city of praise has not been deserted,
The town of My joy!
26 "Therefore, her young men will fall in her streets,
And all the men of war will be silenced in that day," declares the LORD of hosts.
27 "I will set fire to the wall of Damascus,
And it will devour the fortified towers of Ben-hadad."

49:23 Gen 14:15; 15:2; 2 Kin 5:12; 2 Chr 16:2; Is 7:8; 17:1; Amos 1:3; Acts 9:2; Num 13:21; Is 10:9; Jer 39:5; Amos 6:2; 2 Kin 18:34; 19:13; Is 10:9; Ex 15:15; Nah 2:10; Is 57:20

49:24 Is 13:8

49:25 Jer 33:9; 51:41

49:26 Jer 11:22; 50:30; Amos 4:10

49:27 Jer 43:12; Amos 1:3-5; 1 Kin 15:18-20; 2 Kin 13:3

Prophecy against Kedar and Hazor

28 Concerning Kedar and the kingdoms of Hazor, which Nebuchadnezzar king of
Babylon defeated. Thus says the LORD,
"Arise, go up to Kedar
And devastate the men of the east.
29 "They will take away their tents and their flocks;
They will carry off for themselves
Their tent curtains, all their goods and their camels,
And they will call out to one another, 'Terror on every side!'
30 "Run away, flee! Dwell in the depths,
O inhabitants of Hazor," declares the LORD;
"For Nebuchadnezzar king of Babylon has formed a plan against you
And devised a scheme against you.
31 "Arise, go up against a nation which is at ease,
Which lives securely," declares the LORD.
"It has no gates or bars;
They dwell alone.
32 "Their camels will become plunder,
And their many cattle for booty,
And I will scatter to all the winds those who cut the corners *of their hair;*
And I will bring their disaster from every side," declares the LORD.
33 "Hazor will become a haunt of jackals,
A desolation forever;
No one will live there,
Nor will a son of man reside in it."

49:28 Gen 25:13; Ps 120:5; Is 21:16, 17; Jer 2:10; Ezek 27:21; Job 1:3; Is 11:14

49:29 Hab 3:7; 1 Chr 5:21; Jer 46:5

49:30 Jer 25:9; 27:6

49:31 Judg 18:7; Is 47:8; Is 42:11; Num 23:9; Deut 33:28; Mic 7:14

49:32 Ezek 5:10; 12:14, 15; Jer 9:26; 25:23

49:33 Is 13:20-22; Jer 9:11; 10:22; 51:37; Zeph 2:9, 13-15; Mal 1:3

49:23–26 Damascus was the capital of Aram, north of Israel. This city was defeated by both Assyria and Babylon. Nebuchadnezzar attacked and defeated Damascus in 605 B.C. (Amos 1:4–5). It is difficult to attribute the defeat of the army to a particular event, but God utterly destroyed Aram.

49:28 Kedar and Hazor were nomadic tribes east of Israel and south of Aram, in the desert. In 599 B.C. Nebuchadnezzar destroyed them.

Prophecy against Elam

34 That which came as the word of the LORD to Jeremiah the prophet concerning Elam,
at the beginning of the reign of Zedekiah king of Judah, saying:
35 "Thus says the LORD of hosts,
'Behold, I am going to break the bow of Elam,
The finest of their might.
36 'I will bring upon Elam the four winds
From the four ends of heaven,
And will scatter them to all these winds;
And there will be no nation
To which the outcasts of Elam will not go.
37 'So I will shatter Elam before their enemies
And before those who seek their lives;
And I will bring calamity upon them,
Even My fierce anger,' declares the LORD,
'And I will send out the sword after them
Until I have consumed them.
38 'Then I will set My throne in Elam
And destroy out of it king and princes,'
Declares the LORD.
39 'But it will come about in the last days
That I will restore the fortunes of Elam,' "
Declares the LORD.

Prophecy against Babylon

50 The word which the LORD spoke concerning Babylon, the land of the Chaldeans,
through Jeremiah the prophet:
2 "Declare and proclaim among the nations.
Proclaim it and lift up a standard.
Do not conceal *it but* say,
'Babylon has been captured,
Bel has been put to shame, Marduk has been shattered;
Her images have been put to shame, her idols have been shattered.'
3 "For a nation has come up against her out of the north; it will make her land an object of horror, and there will be no inhabitant in it. Both man and beast have wandered
off, they have gone away!
4 "In those days and at that time," declares the LORD, "the sons of Israel will come,
both they and the sons of Judah as well; they will go along weeping as they go, and it will
be the LORD their God they will seek.
5 "They will ask for the way to Zion, *turning* their faces in its direction; they will come
that they may join themselves to the LORD *in* an everlasting covenant that will not be
forgotten.
6 "My people have become lost sheep;
Their shepherds have led them astray.
They have made them turn aside *on* the mountains;
They have gone along from mountain to hill
And have forgotten their resting place.
7 "All who came upon them have devoured them;
And their adversaries have said, 'We are not guilty,

49:34 Gen 10:22; 14:1, 9; Is 11:11; Jer 25:25; Ezek 32:24; Dan 8:2; 2 Kin 24:17, 18; Jer 28:1

49:35 Ps 46:9; Is 22:6; Jer 51:56

49:36 Dan 7:2; 8:8; Rev 7:1; Jer 49:32; Ezek 5:10; Amos 9:9

49:37 Jer 6:19; Jer 30:24; Jer 9:16; 48:2

49:39 Jer 48:47

50:1 Gen 10:10; 11:9; 2 Kin 17:24; Is 13:1; 47:1; Dan 1:1; Rev 14:8

50:2 Jer 4:16; Jer 51:27; Jer 51:31; Is 46:1; Jer 51:47

50:3 Is 13:17; Jer 50:9; 51:11, 27; Is 14:22, 23; Jer 50:13; Jer 9:10, 11; Zeph 1:3

50:4 Is 11:12, 13; Jer 3:18; 31:31; 33:7; Hos 1:11; Ezra 3:12, 13; Ps 126:5; Jer 31:9; Hos 3:5

50:5 Is 35:8; Jer 6:16; Is 55:3; Jer 32:40; Heb 8:6-10

50:6 Is 53:6; Ezek 34:15, 16; Matt 9:36; 10:6; Jer 23:11-14; Jer 13:16; Ezek 34:6; Jer 33:12; 50:19

50:7 Jer 2:3; Zech 11:5; Jer 31:23; 40:2, 3; Ps 22:4; Jer 14:8; 17:13

49:34 Elam lay east of Babylon and was attacked by Nebuchadnezzar in 597 B.C. Later Elam became the nucleus of the Persian empire (Daniel 8:2) and the residence of Darius.

49:38 The throne represents God's judgment and sovereignty. God would preside over Elam's destruction. He is the King over all kings, including Elam's.

50:1ff At the height of its power, the Babylonian empire seemed immovable. But when Babylon had finished serving God's purpose of punishing Judah for her sins, it would be punished and crushed for its own. Babylon was destroyed in 539 B.C. by the Medo-Persians (Daniel 5:30–31). Babylon is also used in Scripture as a symbol of all evil. This message can thus apply to the end times when God wipes out all evil, once and for all.

50:3 The nation from the north was Medo-Persia, an alliance of Media and Persia that would become the next world power. Cyrus took the city of Babylon by surprise and brought the nation to its knees in 539 B.C. (Daniel 5:30–31). The complete destruction of the city was accomplished by later Persian kings.

Inasmuch as they have sinned against the LORD *who is* the habitation of righteousness,
Even the LORD, the hope of their fathers.'

8 "Wander away from the midst of Babylon
And go forth from the land of the Chaldeans;
Be also like male goats at the head of the flock.
9 "For behold, I am going to arouse and bring up against Babylon
A horde of great nations from the land of the north,
And they will draw up *their* battle lines against her;
From there she will be taken captive.
Their arrows will be like an expert warrior
Who does not return empty-handed.
10 "Chaldea will become plunder;
All who plunder her will have enough," declares the LORD.

11 "Because you are glad, because you are jubilant,
O you who pillage My heritage,
Because you skip about like a threshing heifer
And neigh like stallions,
12 Your mother will be greatly ashamed,
She who gave you birth will be humiliated.
Behold, *she will be* the least of the nations,
A wilderness, a parched land and a desert.
13 "Because of the indignation of the LORD she will not be inhabited,
But she will be completely desolate;
Everyone who passes by Babylon will be horrified
And will hiss because of all her wounds.
14 "Draw up your battle lines against Babylon on every side,
All you who bend the bow;
Shoot at her, do not be sparing with *your* arrows,
For she has sinned against the LORD.
15 "Raise your battle cry against her on every side!
She has given herself up, her pillars have fallen,
Her walls have been torn down.
For this is the vengeance of the LORD:
Take vengeance on her;
As she has done *to others, so* do to her.
16 "Cut off the sower from Babylon
And the one who wields the sickle at the time of harvest;
From before the sword of the oppressor
They will each turn back to his own people
And they will each flee to his own land.

17 "Israel is a scattered flock, the lions have driven *them* away. The first one *who* devoured him was the king of Assyria, and this last one *who* has broken his bones is Nebuchadnezzar king of Babylon.
18 "Therefore thus says the LORD of hosts, the God of Israel: 'Behold, I am going to
punish the king of Babylon and his land, just as I punished the king of Assyria.
19 'And I will bring Israel back to his pasture and he will graze on Carmel and Bashan,
and his desire will be satisfied in the hill country of Ephraim and Gilead.
20 'In those days and at that time,' declares the LORD, 'search will be made for the iniquity of Israel, but there will be none; and for the sins of Judah, but they will not be
found; for I will pardon those whom I leave as a remnant.'

21 "Against the land of [14]Merathaim, go up against it,

50:8 Is 48:20; Jer 51:6; Rev 18:4
50:9 Jer 51:1
50:10 Jer 51:24, 35; Ezek 11:24
50:11 Jer 12:14; Jer 46:20
50:12 Jer 15:9; Jer 22:6; 51:43
50:13 Jer 34:22; Jer 51:26; Jer 18:16; 49:17
50:14 Hab 2:8, 17
50:15 1 Chr 29:24; 2 Chr 30:8; Lam 5:6; Jer 50:44; 51:58; Jer 46:10; Ps 137:8; Rev 18:6
50:16 Joel 1:11; Jer 25:38; 46:16; Is 13:14
50:17 Joel 3:2; Jer 2:15; 4:7; 2 Kin 15:19; 17:6; 18:9-13; 2 Kin 24:1, 10-12; 25:1-7
50:18 Is 10:12; Ezek 31:3, 11, 12; Nah 3:7, 18, 19
50:19 Is 65:10; Jer 31:10; 33:12; Ezek 34:13; Jer 31:6
50:20 Is 43:25; Jer 31:34; Mic 7:19; Is 1:9
50:21 Ezek 23:23

14 Or *Double Rebellion*

50:17–20 God would punish wicked Babylon as he punished Assyria for what they had done to Israel. Assyria was crushed by Babylon, over which it had once ruled. Babylon in turn would be crushed by Medo-Persia, formerly under its authority. These verses also look to the time when the Messiah will rule and Israel will be fully restored. No sin will then be found in Israel because those who sought God will be forgiven.

50:21 Merathaim was located in southern Babylonia; Pekod was in eastern Babylonia.

And against the inhabitants of [15]Pekod.
Slay and utterly destroy them," declares the LORD,
"And do according to all that I have commanded you.
22 "The noise of battle is in the land,
And great destruction.
23 "How the hammer of the whole earth
Has been cut off and broken!
How Babylon has become
An object of horror among the nations!
24 "I set a snare for you and you were also caught, O Babylon,
While you yourself were not aware;
You have been found and also seized
Because you have engaged in conflict with the LORD."
25 The LORD has opened His armory
And has brought forth the weapons of His indignation,
For it is a work of the Lord GOD of hosts
In the land of the Chaldeans.
26 Come to her from the farthest border;
Open up her barns,
Pile her up like heaps
And utterly destroy her,
Let nothing be left to her.
27 Put all her young bulls to the sword;
Let them go down to the slaughter!
Woe be upon them, for their day has come,
The time of their punishment.

28 There is a sound of fugitives and refugees from the land of Babylon,
To declare in Zion the vengeance of the LORD our God,
Vengeance for His temple.

29 "Summon [16]many against Babylon,
All those who bend the bow:
Encamp against her on every side,
Let there be no escape.
Repay her according to her work;
According to all that she has done, *so* do to her;
For she has become arrogant against the LORD,
Against the Holy One of Israel.
30 "Therefore her young men will fall in her streets,
And all her men of war will be silenced in that day," declares the LORD.
31 "Behold, I am against you, O arrogant one,"
Declares the Lord GOD of hosts,
"For your day has come,
The time when I will punish you.
32 "The arrogant one will stumble and fall
With no one to raise him up;
And I will set fire to his cities
And it will devour all his environs."

33 Thus says the LORD of hosts,
"The sons of Israel are oppressed,
And the sons of Judah as well;
And all who took them captive have held them fast,
They have refused to let them go.

50:22 Jer 4:19-21; 51:54-56
50:23 Jer 51:20-24
50:24 Jer 48:43, 44; Jer 51:31; Dan 5:30, 31; Job 9:4; 40:2, 9
50:25 Is 13:5; Jer 50:15; 51:12, 25, 55
50:26 Is 45:3; Jer 50:10; Is 14:23
50:27 Is 34:7; Jer 48:10; Ps 37:13; Jer 46:21; 48:44; Ezek 7:7
50:28 Is 48:20; Ps 149:6-9; Jer 50:15; 51:10; Lam 1:10; 2:6, 7
50:29 Ps 137:8; Jer 50:15; 51:56; 2 Thess 1:6; Ex 10:3; Jer 49:16; Dan 4:37
50:30 Is 13:17, 18; Jer 9:21; 18:21; 49:26; 51:4; Jer 51:57
50:31 Jer 21:13; Nah 2:13
50:32 Is 10:12-15; Jer 21:14; 49:27
50:33 Is 14:17; 58:6

15 Or *Punishment* **16** Another reading is *archers*

50:32 Arrogance (pride) was Babylon's characteristic sin. Pride comes from feeling self-sufficient or believing that we don't need God. Proud nations or persons, however, will eventually fail because they refuse to recognize God as the ultimate power. Getting rid of pride is not easy, but we can admit that it often rules us and ask God to forgive us and help us overcome it. The best antidote to pride is to focus our attention on the greatness and goodness of God.

34 "Their Redeemer is strong, the LORD of hosts is His name;
He will vigorously plead their case
So that He may bring rest to the earth,
But turmoil to the inhabitants of Babylon.
35 "A sword against the Chaldeans," declares the LORD,
"And against the inhabitants of Babylon
And against her officials and her wise men!
36 "A sword against the oracle priests, and they will become fools!
A sword against her mighty men, and they will be shattered!
37 "A sword against their horses and against their chariots
And against all the foreigners who are in the midst of her,
And they will become women!
A sword against her treasures, and they will be plundered!
38 "A drought on her waters, and they will be dried up!
For it is a land of idols,
And they are mad over fearsome idols.

39 "Therefore the desert creatures will live *there* along with the jackals;
The ostriches also will live in it,
And it will never again be inhabited
Or dwelt in from generation to generation.
40 "As when God overthrew Sodom
And Gomorrah with its neighbors," declares the LORD,
"No man will live there,
Nor will *any* son of man reside in it.

41 "Behold, a people is coming from the north,
And a great nation and many kings
Will be aroused from the remote parts of the earth.
42 "They seize *their* bow and javelin;
They are cruel and have no mercy.
Their voice roars like the sea;
And they ride on horses,
Marshalled like a man for the battle
Against you, O daughter of Babylon.
43 "The king of Babylon has heard the report about them,
And his hands hang limp;
Distress has gripped him,
Agony like a woman in childbirth.
44 "Behold, one will come up like a lion from the thicket of the Jordan to a perennially watered pasture; for in an instant I will make them run away from it, and whoever is chosen I will appoint over it. For who is like Me, and who will summon Me *into court?* And who then is the shepherd who can stand before Me?"
45 Therefore hear the plan of the LORD which He has planned against Babylon, and His purposes which He has purposed against the land of the Chaldeans: surely they will drag them off, *even* the little ones of the flock; surely He will make their pasture desolate because of them.
46 At the shout, "Babylon has been seized!" the earth is shaken, and an outcry is heard among the nations.

Babylon Judged for Sins against Israel

51 Thus says the LORD:
"Behold, I am going to arouse against Babylon
And against the inhabitants of [17]Leb-kamai
The spirit of a destroyer.

17 Cryptic name for Chaldea; or *the heart of those who rise up against Me*

50:34 Prov 23:11; Is 43:14; Jer 15:21; 31:11; Rev 18:8; Is 47:4; Jer 32:18; 51:19; Jer 51:36; Mic 7:9; Is 14:3-7

50:35 Jer 47:6; Hos 11:6; Dan 5:1, 2; Dan 5:7, 8

50:36 Is 44:25; Jer 49:22; Nah 3:13

50:37 Ps 20:7, 8; Jer 51:21, 22; Jer 25:20; Ezek 30:5; Jer 48:41; 51:30; Nah 3:13

50:38 Is 44:27; Jer 51:32, 36; Rev 16:12; Is 46:1, 6, 7

50:39 Is 13:21; 34:14; Rev 18:2; Is 13:20; Jer 25:12

50:40 Gen 19:24, 25; Is 13:19; Jer 49:18; Luke 17:28-30; 2 Pet 2:6; Jude 7

50:41 Is 13:2-5; Jer 6:22; 50:3, 9; 51:27, 28

50:42 Jer 6:23; Is 13:17, 18; 47:6; Is 5:30; Jer 8:16; 47:3; Hab 1:8; Jer 50:9, 14; Joel 2:5

50:43 Jer 51:31; Jer 30:6; 49:24

50:44 Jer 49:19-21; Num 16:5; Is 46:9; Job 41:10; Jer 30:21

50:45 Ps 33:11; Is 14:24; Jer 51:10, 11; Jer 49:20

50:46 Jer 10:10; 49:21; Ezek 26:18; 31:16; Is 5:7; 15:5; Jer 46:12; 51:54; Ezek 27:28

51:1 Jer 4:11, 12; 23:19; Hos 13:15

50:39 Babylon remains a wasteland to this day. See also Isaiah 13:19–22.

50:44–46 This invader was Cyrus, who attacked Babylon by surprise and overthrew it. The world was shocked that its greatest empire was overthrown so quickly. No earthly power, no matter how great, can last forever.

51:2
Is 41:16; Jer 15:7; Matt 3:12

2 "I will dispatch foreigners to Babylon that they may winnow her
And may devastate her land;
For on every side they will be opposed to her
In the day of *her* calamity.

51:3
Jer 50:14, 29; Jer 46:4

3 "Let not him who bends his bow bend *it,*
Nor let him rise up in his scale-armor;
So do not spare her young men;
Devote all her army to destruction.

51:4
Is 13:15; 14:19; Jer 49:26; 50:30, 37

4 "They will fall down slain in the land of the Chaldeans,
And pierced through in their streets."

51:5
Is 54:7, 8; Jer 33:24-26; Hos 4:1, 2

5 For neither Israel nor Judah has been forsaken
By his God, the LORD of hosts,
Although their land is full of guilt
Before the Holy One of Israel.

51:6
Jer 50:8, 28; Rev 18:4; Num 16:26; Jer 50:15; Jer 25:14

6 Flee from the midst of Babylon,
And each of you save his life!
Do not be destroyed in her punishment,
For this is the LORD'S time of vengeance;
He is going to render recompense to her.

51:7
Jer 25:15; Hab 2:16; Rev 14:8; 17:4; Rev 14:8; 18:3; Jer 25:16

7 Babylon has been a golden cup in the hand of the LORD,
Intoxicating all the earth.
The nations have drunk of her wine;
Therefore the nations are going mad.

51:8
Is 21:9; Jer 50:2; Rev 14:8; 18:2; Is 13:6; Rev 18:9; Jer 46:11

8 Suddenly Babylon has fallen and been broken;
Wail over her!
Bring balm for her pain;
Perhaps she may be healed.

51:9
Is 13:14; Jer 46:16; 50:16; Ezra 9:6; Rev 18:5

9 We applied healing to Babylon, but she was not healed;
Forsake her and let us each go to his own country,
For her judgment has reached to heaven
And towers up to the very skies.

51:10
Ps 37:6; Mic 7:9; Is 40:2; Jer 50:28

10 The LORD has brought about our vindication;
Come and let us recount in Zion
The work of the LORD our God!

51:11
Jer 46:4, 9; Joel 3:9, 10; Jer 50:28

11 Sharpen the arrows, fill the quivers!
The LORD has aroused the spirit of the kings of the Medes,
Because His purpose is against Babylon to destroy it;
For it is the vengeance of the LORD, vengeance for His temple.

51:12
Is 13:2; Jer 50:2; 51:27; Jer 4:28; 23:20; 51:29

12 Lift up a signal against the walls of Babylon;
Post a strong guard,
Station sentries,
Place men in ambush!
For the LORD has both purposed and performed
What He spoke concerning the inhabitants of Babylon.

51:13
Rev 17:1; Is 45:3; Is 57:17; Hab 2:9-11

13 O you who dwell by many waters,
Abundant in treasures,
Your end has come,
The measure of your end.

51:14
Jer 49:13; Jer 51:27; Nah 3:15

14 The LORD of hosts has sworn by Himself:
"Surely I will fill you with a population like locusts,
And they will cry out with shouts of victory over you."

51:2 Winnowers worked to separate the wheat from the chaff. When they threw the mixture into the air, the wind blew away the worthless chaff while the wheat settled to the floor. Babylon would be blown away like chaff in the wind. (See also Matthew 3:12 where John the Baptist says Jesus will separate the wheat from the chaff.)

51:11 Cyrus, king of Persia, had allied with Babylon to defeat Nineveh (capital of the Assyrian empire) in 612 B.C. Then the Medes joined Persia to defeat Babylon (539 B.C.).

15 *It is* He who made the earth by His power,
Who established the world by His wisdom,
And by His understanding He stretched out the heavens.
16 When He utters His voice, *there is* a tumult of waters in the heavens,
And He causes the clouds to ascend from the end of the earth;
He makes lightning for the rain
And brings forth the wind from His storehouses.
17 All mankind is stupid, devoid of knowledge;
Every goldsmith is put to shame by his idols,
For his molten images are deceitful,
And there is no breath in them.
18 They are worthless, a work of mockery;
In the time of their punishment they will perish.
19 The portion of Jacob is not like these;
For the Maker of all is He,
And of the tribe of His inheritance;
The LORD of hosts is His name.
20 *He says,* "You are My war-club, *My* weapon of war;
And with you I shatter nations,
And with you I destroy kingdoms.
21 "With you I shatter the horse and his rider,
And with you I shatter the chariot and its rider,
22 And with you I shatter man and woman,
And with you I shatter old man and youth,
And with you I shatter young man and virgin,
23 And with you I shatter the shepherd and his flock,
And with you I shatter the farmer and his team,
And with you I shatter governors and prefects.
24 "But I will repay Babylon and all the inhabitants of Chaldea for all their evil that
they have done in Zion before your eyes," declares the LORD.
25 "Behold, I am against you, O destroying mountain,
Who destroys the whole earth," declares the LORD,
"And I will stretch out My hand against you,
And roll you down from the crags,
And I will make you a burnt out mountain.
26 "They will not take from you *even* a stone for a corner
Nor a stone for foundations,
But you will be desolate forever," declares the LORD.
27 Lift up a signal in the land,
Blow a trumpet among the nations!
Consecrate the nations against her,
Summon against her the kingdoms of Ararat, Minni and Ashkenaz;
Appoint a marshal against her,
Bring up the horses like bristly locusts.
28 Consecrate the nations against her,
The kings of the Medes,
Their governors and all their prefects,
And every land of their dominion.
29 So the land quakes and writhes,
For the purposes of the LORD against Babylon stand,
To make the land of Babylon
A desolation without inhabitants.
30 The mighty men of Babylon have ceased fighting,
They stay in the strongholds;
Their strength is exhausted,
They are becoming *like* women;

51:15 Gen 1:1; Jer 10:12-16; 51:15-19; Job 9:8; Ps 146:5, 6; Jer 32:17; Acts 14:15; Rom 1:20

51:16 Job 37:2-6; Ps 18:13; Ps 135:7; Jer 10:13; Jon 1:4

51:17 Is 44:18-20; Jer 10:14; Hab 2:18, 19

51:18 Jer 18:15

51:19 Ps 73:26; Jer 10:16; Jer 50:34

51:20 Is 10:5; 41:15, 16; Jer 50:23; Is 8:9; 41:15, 16; Mic 4:12, 13

51:21 Ex 15:1

51:22 Ex 15:4; Is 43:17; 2 Chr 36:17; Is 13:15, 16; Is 13:18

51:24 Jer 50:10; Jer 50:15, 29

51:25 Jer 50:31; Is 13:2; Zech 4:7; Rev 8:8

51:26 Is 13:19-22; Jer 50:13; 51:29

51:27 Is 13:2-5; 18:3; Jer 50:2; 51:12; Jer 50:3, 9; Gen 8:4; 2 Kin 19:37; Is 37:38; Gen 10:3; Jer 50:42

51:29 Jer 8:16; 10:10; 50:46; Amos 8:8; Is 13:19, 20; 47:11; Jer 50:13; 51:26, 43

51:30 Ps 76:5; Jer 50:15, 36, 37; Is 13:7, 8; Nah 3:13; Is 45:1, 2; Lam 2:9; Amos 1:5; Nah 3:13

51:17–19 It is foolish to trust in man-made images rather than in God. It is easy to think that the things we see and touch will bring us more security than God. But things rust, rot, and decay. God is eternal. Why put your trust in something that will disappear within a few years?

51:31 2 Chr 30:6; 2 Sam 18:19-31

Their dwelling places are set on fire,
The bars of her *gates* are broken.
31 One courier runs to meet another,
And one messenger to meet another,
To tell the king of Babylon
That his city has been captured from end *to end;*
32 The fords also have been seized,
And they have burned the marshes with fire,
And the men of war are terrified.

51:33 Is 21:10; 41:15, 16; Mic 4:13; Is 17:5; Hos 6:11; Joel 3:13; Rev 14:15

33 For thus says the LORD of hosts, the God of Israel:
"The daughter of Babylon is like a threshing floor
At the time it is stamped firm;
Yet in a little while the time of harvest will come for her."

51:34 Jer 50:17; Is 24:1-3; Job 20:15; Jer 51:44

34 "Nebuchadnezzar king of Babylon has devoured me *and* crushed me,
He has set me down *like* an empty vessel;
He has swallowed me like a monster,
He has filled his stomach with my delicacies;
He has washed me away.

51:35 Ps 137:8

35 "May the violence *done* to me and to my flesh be upon Babylon,"
The inhabitant of Zion will say;
And, "May my blood be upon the inhabitants of Chaldea,"
Jerusalem will say.

51:36 Ps 140:12; Jer 51:6, 11; Rom 12:19; Jer 50:38

36 Therefore thus says the LORD,
"Behold, I am going to plead your case
And exact full vengeance for you;
And I will dry up her sea
And make her fountain dry.

51:37 Rev 18:2; Jer 25:9

37 "Babylon will become a heap *of ruins,* a haunt of jackals,
An object of horror and hissing, without inhabitants.

51:38 Jer 2:15

38 "They will roar together like young lions,
They will growl like lions' cubs.

51:39 Jer 25:27; 48:26; 51:57; Ps 76:5

39 "When they become heated up, I will serve *them* their banquet
And make them drunk, that they may become jubilant
And may sleep a perpetual sleep
And not wake up," declares the LORD.

51:40 Jer 48:15; 50:27

40 "I will bring them down like lambs to the slaughter,
Like rams together with male goats.

51:41 Jer 25:26; Jer 49:25

41 "How [18]Sheshak has been captured,
And the praise of the whole earth been seized!
How Babylon has become an object of horror among the nations!

51:42 Is 8:7, 8; Jer 51:55; Dan 9:26

42 "The sea has come up over Babylon;
She has been engulfed with its tumultuous waves.

51:43 Jer 50:12; Is 13:20; Jer 2:6

43 "Her cities have become an object of horror,
A parched land and a desert,
A land in which no man lives
And through which no son of man passes.

51:44 Is 46:1; Jer 50:2; Ezra 1:7, 8; Is 2:2; Jer 50:15; 51:58

44 "I will punish Bel in Babylon,
And I will make what he has swallowed come out of his mouth;

18 Cryptic name for Babylon

51:33 Grain was threshed on a threshing floor, where sheaves were brought from the field. The stalks of grain were distributed on the floor, a large level section of hard ground. There the grain was crushed to separate the kernels from the stalk; then the kernels were beaten with a wooden tool. Sometimes a wooden sledge was pulled over the grain by animals to break the kernels loose. Babylon would soon be "threshed" as God judged it for its sins.

51:36 This verse may refer to an event accomplished by Cyrus, who took Babylon by surprise by diverting the river that ran through the city far upstream and walking in on the dry riverbed. More likely it is saying that Babylon will be deprived of life-giving water. Unlike Jerusalem, Babylon will not be restored.

51:44 Bel is one of the names of Marduk, the chief god of the city of Babylon.

And the nations will no longer stream to him.
Even the wall of Babylon has fallen down!

45 "Come forth from her midst, My people,
And each of you save yourselves
From the fierce anger of the LORD.
46 "Now so that your heart does not grow faint,
And you are not afraid at the report that *will be* heard in the land—
For the report will come one year,
And after that another report in another year,
And violence *will be* in the land
With ruler against ruler—
47 Therefore behold, days are coming
When I will punish the idols of Babylon;
And her whole land will be put to shame
And all her slain will fall in her midst.
48 "Then heaven and earth and all that is in them
Will shout for joy over Babylon,
For the destroyers will come to her from the north,"
Declares the LORD.

49 Indeed Babylon is to fall *for* the slain of Israel,
As also for Babylon the slain of all the earth have fallen.
50 You who have escaped the sword,
Depart! Do not stay!
Remember the LORD from afar,
And let Jerusalem come to your mind.
51 We are ashamed because we have heard reproach;
Disgrace has covered our faces,
For aliens have entered
The holy places of the LORD'S house.

52 "Therefore behold, the days are coming," declares the LORD,
"When I will punish her idols,
And the mortally wounded will groan throughout her land.
53 "Though Babylon should ascend to the heavens,
And though she should fortify her lofty stronghold,
From Me destroyers will come to her," declares the LORD.

54 The sound of an outcry from Babylon,
And of great destruction from the land of the Chaldeans!
55 For the LORD is going to destroy Babylon,
And He will make her loud noise vanish from her.
And their waves will roar like many waters;
The tumult of their voices sounds forth.
56 For the destroyer is coming against her, against Babylon,
And her mighty men will be captured,
Their bows are shattered;
For the LORD is a God of recompense,
He will fully repay.
57 "I will make her princes and her wise men drunk,
Her governors, her prefects and her mighty men,
That they may sleep a perpetual sleep and not wake up,"
Declares the King, whose name is the LORD of hosts.
58 Thus says the LORD of hosts,
"The broad wall of Babylon will be completely razed
And her high gates will be set on fire;

51:45 Is 48:20; Jer 50:8, 28; 51:6; Rev 18:4; Gen 19:12-16; Acts 2:40

51:46 Is 43:5; Jer 46:27, 28; 2 Kin 19:7; Is 13:3-5; Is 19:2

51:47 Is 21:9; 46:1, 2; Jer 50:2; 51:52; Jer 50:12, 35-37

51:48 Is 44:23; 48:20; 49:13; Rev 18:20; Jer 50:3

51:49 Ps 137:8; Jer 50:29; Rev 18:24

51:50 Jer 44:28; Deut 4:29-31; Ps 137:6

51:51 Ps 44:15; Ps 74:3-8; Lam 1:10

51:52 Jer 50:38

51:53 Gen 11:4; Job 20:6; Ps 139:8-10; Is 14:12-14; Jer 49:16; Amos 9:2; Obad 4; Is 13:3

51:54 Jer 48:3-5; 50:22, 46

51:55 Ps 18:4; 69:2; 124:2, 4, 5; Jer 51:42

51:56 Jer 51:48, 53; Hab 2:8; Ps 46:9; 76:3; Deut 32:35; Ps 94:1, 2; Jer 51:6, 24

51:57 Jer 25:27; Ps 76:5, 6; Jer 46:18; 48:15

51:58 Jer 50:15; Is 45:1, 2; Hab 2:13; Jer 9:5; 51:64; Lam 5:5

51:51 The people were paralyzed with guilt over their past. The Babylonian armies had desecrated the temple, and the people were ashamed to return to Jerusalem. But God told them to return to the city because he would destroy Babylon for its sins.

So the peoples will toil for nothing,
And the nations become exhausted *only* for fire."
59 The message which Jeremiah the prophet commanded Seraiah the son of Neriah,
the grandson of Mahseiah, when he went with Zedekiah the king of Judah to Babylon in
the fourth year of his reign. (Now Seraiah was quartermaster.)
60 So Jeremiah wrote in a single scroll all the calamity which would come upon Babylon, *that is,* all these words which have been written concerning Babylon.
61 Then Jeremiah said to Seraiah, "As soon as you come to Babylon, then see that you
read all these words aloud,
62 and say, 'You, O LORD, have promised concerning this place to cut it off, so that
there will be nothing dwelling in it, whether man or beast, but it will be a perpetual desolation.'
63 "And as soon as you finish reading this scroll, you will tie a stone to it and throw it
into the middle of the Euphrates,
64 and say, 'Just so shall Babylon sink down and not rise again because of the calamity
that I am going to bring upon her; and they will become exhausted.' " Thus far are the
words of Jeremiah.

2. The fall of Jerusalem

52 Zedekiah was twenty-one years old when he became king, and he reigned eleven
years in Jerusalem; and his mother's name was Hamutal the daughter of Jeremiah of Libnah.
2 He did evil in the sight of the LORD like all that Jehoiakim had done.
3 For through the anger of the LORD *this* came about in Jerusalem and Judah until
He cast them out from His presence. And Zedekiah rebelled against the king of Babylon.
4 Now it came about in the ninth year of his reign, on the tenth *day* of the tenth month,
that Nebuchadnezzar king of Babylon came, he and all his army, against Jerusalem,
camped against it and built a siege wall all around it.
5 So the city was under siege until the eleventh year of King Zedekiah.
6 On the ninth *day* of the fourth month the famine was so severe in the city that there
was no food for the people of the land.
7 Then the city was broken into, and all the men of war fled and went forth from the
city at night by way of the gate between the two walls which *was* by the king's garden,
though the Chaldeans were all around the city. And they went by way of the Arabah.
8 But the army of the Chaldeans pursued the king and overtook Zedekiah in the plains
of Jericho, and all his army was scattered from him.
9 Then they captured the king and brought him up to the king of Babylon at Riblah in
the land of Hamath, and he passed sentence on him.
10 The king of Babylon slaughtered the sons of Zedekiah before his eyes, and he also
slaughtered all the princes of Judah in Riblah.
11 Then he blinded the eyes of Zedekiah; and the king of Babylon bound him with
bronze fetters and brought him to Babylon and put him in prison until the day of his
death.
12 Now on the tenth *day* of the fifth month, which was the nineteenth year of King
Nebuchadnezzar, king of Babylon, Nebuzaradan the captain of the bodyguard, who was
in the service of the king of Babylon, came to Jerusalem.
13 He burned the house of the LORD, the king's house and all the houses of Jerusalem; even every large house he burned with fire.

51:59 Jer 32:12; 36:4; 45:1; Jer 28:1; 52:1

51:60 Is 30:8; Jer 30:2, 3; 36:2, 4, 32

51:62 Is 13:19-22; 14:22, 23; Jer 50:3, 13, 39, 40; Ezek 35:9

51:63 Jer 19:10, 11; Rev 18:21

51:64 Nah 1:8, 9; Jer 51:58; Job 31:40; Ps 72:20

52:1 2 Kin 24:18; 2 Chr 36:11; 2 Kin 23:31; 24:18; Josh 10:29; 2 Kin 8:22; Is 37:8

52:2 1 Kin 14:22; 2 Kin 24:19; 2 Chr 36:12; Jer 36:30, 31

52:3 2 Kin 24:20; Is 3:1, 4, 5; 2 Chr 36:13; Ezek 17:12-16

52:4 2 Kin 25:1; Jer 39:1; Ezek 24:1, 2; Zech 8:19; Jer 32:24

52:5 2 Kin 25:2

52:6 Jer 39:2; 2 Kin 25:3; Is 3:1; Jer 38:9; Ezek 4:16; 5:16; 14:13

52:7 2 Kin 25:4; Jer 39:2; Ezek 33:21

52:9 2 Kin 25:6; Jer 32:4; 39:5; Num 34:11; Jer 39:5; Num 13:21; Josh 13:5

52:10 2 Kin 25:7; Jer 22:30; 39:6

52:11 Jer 39:7; Ezek 12:13

52:12 2 Kin 25:8-21; Zech 7:5; 8:19; 2 Kin 24:12; 25:8

52:13 1 Kin 9:8; 2 Kin 25:9; 2 Chr 36:19; Ps 74:6-8; 79:1; Is 64:10, 11; Lam 2:7; Mic 3:12; Jer 39:8

51:59 Jeremiah could not visit Babylon, so he sent the message with Seraiah, the officer who cared for the comforts of the army. Seriah was probably Baruch's brother (32:12).

51:60–64 In this last of Jeremiah's messages, we find again the twin themes of God's sovereignty and his judgment. Babylon had been allowed to oppress the people of Israel, but Babylon itself would be judged. Although God brings good out of evil, he does not allow evil to remain unpunished. The wicked may succeed for a while, but resist the temptation to follow them or you may share in their judgment.

52:1ff This chapter provides more detail about the destruction of Jerusalem recorded in chapter 39 (similar material is found in 2 Kings 24:18—25:21). This appendix shows that Jeremiah's prophecies concerning the destruction of Jerusalem and the Babylonian captivity happened just as he predicted. For more information on Zedekiah, see the note on 39:1ff.

52:8–9 Riblah was 200 miles north of Jerusalem. This was the Babylonian headquarters for ruling the region. Hamath was the district of Aram containing the nation's capital.

14 So all the army of the Chaldeans who *were* with the captain of the guard broke down
all the walls around Jerusalem.
15 Then Nebuzaradan the captain of the guard carried away into exile some of the
poorest of the people, the rest of the people who were left in the city, the deserters who
had deserted to the king of Babylon and the rest of the artisans.
16 But Nebuzaradan the captain of the guard left some of the poorest of the land to be
vinedressers and plowmen.
17 Now the bronze pillars which belonged to the house of the LORD and the stands
and the bronze sea, which were in the house of the LORD, the Chaldeans broke in pieces
and carried all their bronze to Babylon.
18 They also took away the pots, the shovels, the snuffers, the basins, the pans and all
the bronze vessels which were used in *temple* service.
19 The captain of the guard also took away the bowls, the firepans, the basins, the pots,
the lampstands, the pans and the drink offering bowls, what was fine gold and what was
fine silver.
20 The two pillars, the one sea, and the twelve bronze bulls that were under the sea,
and the stands, which King Solomon had made for the house of the LORD—the bronze
of all these vessels was beyond weight.
21 As for the pillars, the height of each pillar *was* eighteen cubits, and it *was* twelve
cubits in circumference and four fingers in thickness, *and* hollow.
22 Now a capital of bronze was on it; and the height of each capital was five cubits,
with network and pomegranates upon the capital all around, all of bronze. And the second pillar was like these, including pomegranates.
23 There were ninety-six exposed pomegranates; all the pomegranates *numbered* a
hundred on the network all around.
24 Then the captain of the guard took Seraiah the chief priest and Zephaniah the second priest, with the three officers of the temple.
25 He also took from the city one official who was overseer of the men of war, and
seven of the king's advisers who were found in the city, and the scribe of the commander
of the army who mustered the people of the land, and sixty men of the people of the
land who were found in the midst of the city.
26 Nebuzaradan the captain of the guard took them and brought them to the king of
Babylon at Riblah.
27 Then the king of Babylon struck them down and put them to death at Riblah in the
land of Hamath. So Judah was led away into exile from its land.
28 These are the people whom Nebuchadnezzar carried away into exile: in the seventh
year 3,023 Jews;
29 in the eighteenth year of Nebuchadnezzar 832 persons from Jerusalem;
30 in the twenty-third year of Nebuchadnezzar, Nebuzaradan the captain of the guard
carried into exile 745 Jewish people; there were 4,600 persons in all.
31 Now it came about in the thirty-seventh year of the exile of Jehoiachin king of Judah, in the twelfth month, on the twenty-fifth of the month, that Evil-merodach king of
Babylon, in the *first* year of his reign, showed favor to Jehoiachin king of Judah and
brought him out of prison.
32 Then he spoke kindly to him and set his throne above the thrones of the kings who
were with him in Babylon.
33 So Jehoiachin changed his prison clothes, and had his meals in the king's presence
regularly all the days of his life.
34 For his allowance, a regular allowance was given him by the king of Babylon, a daily
portion all the days of his life until the day of his death.

52:14 2 Kin 25:10; Neh 1:3
52:15 2 Kin 25:11; Jer 39:9
52:16 2 Kin 25:12; Jer 39:10; 40:2-6
52:17 1 Kin 7:15-22; 2 Kin 25:13; Jer 27:19-22
52:18 Ex 27:3; 1 Kin 7:40, 45; 2 Kin 25:14
52:19 1 Kin 7:49, 50; 2 Kin 25:15
52:20 1 Kin 7:47; 2 Kin 25:16
52:21 1 Kin 7:15; 2 Kin 25:17; 2 Chr 3:15
52:22 1 Kin 7:16; 2 Kin 25:17; 1 Kin 7:20, 42
52:23 1 Kin 7:20
52:24 2 Kin 25:18; 1 Chr 6:14; Ezra 7:1; 2 Kin 25:18; 1 Chr 9:19
52:27 2 Kin 25:21; Ezek 8:11-18; Is 6:11, 12; 27:10; 32:13, 14; Jer 13:19; 20:4; 25:9-11; 39:9; Ezek 33:28; Mic 4:10
52:28 2 Kin 24:2, 3, 12-16; 2 Chr 36:20; Ezra 2:1; Neh 7:6; Dan 1:1-3
52:30 2 Kin 25:11; Jer 39:9
52:31 2 Kin 25:27; Gen 40:13, 20; Ps 3:3; 27:6
52:32 2 Kin 25:28
52:33 Gen 41:14, 42; 2 Kin 25:29; 2 Sam 9:7, 13; 1 Kin 2:7
52:34 2 Sam 9:10; 2 Kin 25:30

52:21 A cubit was a standard of measure about 17 to 20 inches long.

52:31 Babylon's king showed kindness to Jehoiachin. In 561 B.C. Jehoiachin was released from prison and allowed to eat with the king. God continued to show kindness to the descendants of King David, even in exile.

52:34 In the world's eyes, Jeremiah looked totally unsuccessful. He had no money, family, or friends. He prophesied the destruction of the nation, the capital city, and the temple, but the political and religious leaders would not accept or follow his advice. No group of people liked him or listened to him. Yet as we look back, we see that he successfully completed the work God gave him to do. Success must never be measured by popularity, fame, or fortune, for these are temporal measures. King Zedekiah, for example, lost everything by pursuing selfish goals. God measures our success with the yardsticks of obedience, faithfulness, and righteousness. If you are faithfully doing the work God gives you, you are successful in his eyes.

LAMENTATIONS

TEARS are defined simply as "drops of salty fluid flowing from the eyes." They can be caused by irritation or laughter but are usually associated with weeping, sorrow, and grief. When we cry, friends wonder what's wrong and try to console us. Babies cry for food; children cry at the loss of a pet; adults cry when confronted with trauma and death.

Jeremiah's grief ran deep. He is remembered as the "weeping prophet," and his tears flowed from a broken heart. As God's spokesman, he knew what lay ahead for Judah, his country, and for Jerusalem, the capital and "the city of God." God's judgment would fall and destruction would come. And so Jeremiah wept. His tears were not self-centered, mourning over personal suffering or loss. He wept because the people had rejected their God—the God who had made them, loved them, and sought repeatedly to bless them. Jeremiah's heart was broken because he knew that the selfishness and sinfulness of the people would bring them much suffering and an extended exile. Jeremiah's tears were tears of empathy and sympathy. His heart was broken with those things that break God's heart.

Jeremiah's two books focus on one event—the destruction of Jerusalem. The book of Jeremiah predicts it, and Lamentations looks back on it. Known as the book of tears, Lamentations is a dirge, a funeral song written for the fallen city of Jerusalem.

What makes a person cry says a lot about that person—whether he or she is self-centered or God-centered. The book of Lamentations allows us to see what made Jeremiah sorrowful. As one of God's choice servants, he stands alone in the depth of his emotions, broken by his care for the people, his love for the nation, and his devotion to God.

What causes your tears? Do you weep because your selfish pride has been wounded or because the people around you lead sinful lives and reject the God who loves them dearly? Do you weep because you have lost something of value or because people all around you will suffer for their sinfulness? Our world is filled with injustice, poverty, war, and rebellion against God, all of which should move us to tears and to action. Read Lamentations and learn what it means to grieve with God.

VITAL STATISTICS

PURPOSE:
To teach people that to disobey God is to invite disaster, and to show that God suffers when his people suffer

AUTHOR:
Jeremiah

DATE WRITTEN:
Soon after the fall of Jerusalem in 586 B.C.

SETTING:
Jerusalem had been destroyed by Babylon and her people killed, tortured, or taken captive.

KEY VERSE:
"My eyes fail because of tears, my spirit is greatly troubled; my heart is poured out on the earth because of the destruction of the daughter of my people, when little ones and infants faint in the streets of the city" (2:11).

KEY PEOPLE:
Jeremiah, the people of Jerusalem

KEY PLACE:
Jerusalem

SPECIAL FEATURES:
Three strands of Hebrew thought meet in Lamentations—prophecy, ritual, and wisdom. Lamentations is written in the rhythm and style of ancient Jewish funeral songs or chants. It contains five poems corresponding to the five chapters (see the second note on 3:1ff).

THE BLUEPRINT

1. Jeremiah mourns for Jerusalem (1:1–22)
2. God's anger at sin (2:1–22)
3. Hope in the midst of affliction (3:1–66)
4. God's anger is satisfied (4:1–22)
5. Jeremiah pleads for restoration (5:1–22)

Jeremiah grieves deeply because of the destruction of Jerusalem and the devastation of his nation. But in the middle of the book, in the depths of his grief, there shines a ray of hope. God's compassion is ever present. His faithfulness is great. Jeremiah realizes that it is only the Lord's mercy that has prevented total annihilation. This book shows us the serious consequences of sin and how we can still have hope in the midst of tragedy because God is able to turn it around for good. We see the timeless importance of prayer and confession of sin. We will all face tragedy in our life. But in the midst of our afflictions, there is hope in God.

MEGATHEMES

THEME	EXPLANATION	IMPORTANCE
Destruction of Jerusalem	Lamentations is a sad funeral song for the great capital city of the Jews. The temple has been destroyed, the king is gone, and the people are in exile. God had warned that he would destroy them if they abandoned him. Now, afterward, the people realize their condition and confess their sin.	God's warnings are justified. He does what he says he will do. His punishment for sin is certain. Only by confessing and renouncing our sin can we turn to him for deliverance. How much better to do so before his warnings are fulfilled.
God's Mercy	God's compassion was at work even when the Israelites were experiencing the affliction of their Babylonian conquerors. Although the people had been unfaithful, God's faithfulness was great. He used this affliction to bring his people back to him.	God will always be faithful to his people. His merciful, refining work is evident even in affliction. At those times, we must pray for forgiveness and then turn to him for deliverance.
Sin's Consequences	God was angry at the prolonged rebellion by his people. Sin was the cause of their misery, and destruction was the result of their sin. The destruction of the nation shows the vanity of human glory and pride.	To continue in rebellion against God is to invite disaster. We must never trust our own leadership, resources, intelligence, or power more than God. If we do, we will experience consequences similar to Jerusalem's.
Hope	God's mercy in sparing some of the people offers hope for better days. One day, the people will be restored to a true and fervent relationship with God.	Only God can deliver us from sin. Without him there is no comfort or hope for the future. Because of Christ's death for us and his promise to return, we have a bright hope for tomorrow.

1. Jeremiah mourns for Jerusalem

The Sorrows of Zion

1 How lonely sits the city
That was full of people!
She has become like a widow
Who was *once* great among the nations!
She who was a princess among the provinces
Has become a forced laborer!

1:1 Is 3:26; Is 22:2; Is 54:4; 1 Kin 4:21; Ezra 4:20; Jer 31:7; 2 Kin 23:35; Jer 40:9

2 She weeps bitterly in the night
And her tears are on her cheeks;
She has none to comfort her
Among all her lovers.
All her friends have dealt treacherously with her;
They have become her enemies.

1:2 Ps 6:6; 77:2-6; Lam 1:16; Jer 2:25; 3:1; 22:20-22; Job 19:13, 14; Ps 31:11; Mic 7:5

3 Judah has gone into exile under affliction
And under harsh servitude;
She dwells among the nations,
But she has found no rest;
All her pursuers have overtaken her
In the midst of distress.

1:3 Jer 13:19; Lev 26:39; Deut 28:64-67; 2 Kin 25:4, 5

4 The roads of Zion are in mourning
Because no one comes to the appointed feasts.
All her gates are desolate;
Her priests are groaning,
Her virgins are afflicted,

1:4 Is 24:4-6; Lam 2:6, 7; Jer 9:11; 10:22; Lam 2:10, 21; Joel 1:8-13

1:1 This is the prophet Jeremiah's song of sorrow for Jerusalem's destruction. The nation of Judah had been utterly defeated, the temple destroyed, and captives taken away to Babylon. Jeremiah's tears were for the suffering and humiliation of the people, but those tears penetrated even deeper into his heart. He wept because God had rejected the people for their rebellious ways. Each year this book was read aloud to remind all the Jews that their great city fell because of their stubborn sinfulness.

1:2 The term *lovers* refers to nations such as Egypt, to whom Judah kept turning for help. As the Babylonians closed in on Jerusalem, the nation of Judah turned away from God and sought help and protection from other nations instead.

And she herself is bitter.
1:5 Ps 90:7, 8; Ezek 8:17, 18; 9:9, 10
5 Her adversaries have become her masters,
Her enemies prosper;
For the LORD has caused her grief
Because of the multitude of her transgressions;
Her little ones have gone away
As captives before the adversary.
1:6 Jer 13:18; 2 Kin 25:4, 5
6 All her majesty
Has departed from the daughter of Zion;
Her princes have become like deer
That have found no pasture;
And they have fled without strength
Before the pursuer.
1:7 Ps 42:4; 77:5-9; Jer 37:7; Lam 4:17; Ps 79:4; Jer 48:27
7 In the days of her affliction and homelessness
Jerusalem remembers all her precious things
That were from the days of old,
When her people fell into the hand of the adversary
And no one helped her.
The adversaries saw her,
They mocked at her ruin.
1:8 Is 59:2-13; Lam 1:5, 20; Lam 1:17; Lam 1:11, 21, 22
8 Jerusalem sinned greatly,
Therefore she has become an unclean thing.
All who honored her despise her
Because they have seen her nakedness;
Even she herself groans and turns away.
1:9 Jer 2:34; Ezek 24:13; Deut 32:29; Is 47:7; Is 3:8; Jer 13:17, 18; Eccl 4:1; Jer 16:7; Ps 25:18; 119:153; Ps 74:23; Zeph 2:10
9 Her uncleanness was in her skirts;
She did not consider her future.
Therefore she has fallen astonishingly;
She has no comforter.
"See, O LORD, my affliction,
For the enemy has magnified himself!"
1:10 Ps 74:4-8; Is 64:10, 11; Jer 51:51; Deut 23:3
10 The adversary has stretched out his hand
Over all her precious things,
For she has seen the nations enter her sanctuary,
The ones whom You commanded
That they should not enter into Your congregation.
1:11 Jer 38:9; 52:6; 1 Sam 30:12; Jer 15:19
11 All her people groan seeking bread;
They have given their precious things for food
To restore their lives themselves.
"See, O LORD, and look,
For I am despised."
1:12 Jer 18:16; 48:27; Jer 30:23, 24; Is 13:13; Jer 4:8
12 "Is it nothing to all you who pass this way?
Look and see if there is any pain like my pain
Which was severely dealt out to me,
Which the LORD inflicted on the day of His fierce anger.
1:13 Job 30:30; Ps 22:14; Hab 3:16; Job 19:6; Ps 66:11; Jer 44:6
13 "From on high He sent fire into my bones,
And it prevailed *over them*.
He has spread a net for my feet;
He has turned me back;
He has made me desolate,
Faint all day long.
1:14 Prov 5:22; Is 47:6; Jer 28:13, 14; Jer 32:3, 5; Ezek 25:4, 7
14 "The yoke of my transgressions is bound;

1:9 The warning was loud and clear: If Judah played with fire, its people would get burned. Jerusalem foolishly took a chance and lost, refusing to believe that immoral living brings God's punishment. The ultimate consequence of sin is punishment (Romans 6:23). We can choose to ignore God's warnings, but as surely as judgment came upon Jerusalem, so will it come upon those who defy God. Are you listening to God's Word? Are you obeying it? Obedience is a sure sign of your love for God.

1:14 At first, sin seems to offer freedom. But the liberty to do anything we want gradually becomes a desire to do everything. Then we become captive to sin, bound by its "yoke." Freedom from sin's captivity comes only from God. He gives us freedom, not to do anything we want, but to do what he knows is best for us. Strange as it may seem, true freedom comes in obeying God—following his guidance so that we can receive his best.

By His hand they are knit together.
They have come upon my neck;
He has made my strength fail.
The Lord has given me into the hands
Of *those against whom* I am not able to stand.
15 "The Lord has rejected all my strong men
In my midst;
He has called an appointed time against me
To crush my young men;
The Lord has trodden *as in* a wine press
The virgin daughter of Judah.
16 "For these things I weep;
My eyes run down with water;
Because far from me is a comforter,
One who restores my soul.
My children are desolate
Because the enemy has prevailed."
17 Zion stretches out her hands;
There is no one to comfort her;
The LORD has commanded concerning Jacob
That the ones round about him should be his adversaries;
Jerusalem has become an unclean thing among them.
18 "The LORD is righteous;
For I have rebelled against His command;
Hear now, all peoples,
And behold my pain;
My virgins and my young men
Have gone into captivity.
19 "I called to my lovers, *but* they deceived me;
My priests and my elders perished in the city
While they sought food to restore their strength themselves.
20 "See, O LORD, for I am in distress;
My spirit is greatly troubled;
My heart is overturned within me,
For I have been very rebellious.
In the street the sword slays;
In the house it is like death.
21 "They have heard that I groan;
There is no one to comfort me;
All my enemies have heard of my calamity;
They are glad that You have done *it*.
Oh, that You would bring the day which You have proclaimed,
That they may become like me.
22 "Let all their wickedness come before You;
And deal with them as You have dealt with me
For all my transgressions;
For my groans are many and my heart is faint."

1:15 Is 41:2; Jer 13:24; 37:10; Jer 6:11; 18:21; Mal 4:3

1:16 Jer 14:17; Lam 2:11, 18; 3:48, 49; Ps 69:20; Eccl 4:1; Lam 1:2

1:17 Is 1:15; Jer 4:31; 2 Kin 24:2-4; Jer 12:9; Lam 1:8

1:18 Ps 119:75; Jer 12:1; 1 Sam 12:14, 15; Jer 4:17; Lam 1:12; Deut 28:32, 41

1:19 Job 19:13-19; Lam 1:2; Jer 14:15; Lam 2:20; Lam 1:11

1:20 Is 16:11; Lam 2:11; Jer 14:20

1:21 Lam 1:4, 8, 22; Ps 35:15; Jer 50:11; Lam 2:15; Is 14:5, 6; 47:6, 11; Jer 30:16

1:22 Neh 4:4, 5; Ps 137:7, 8

2. God's anger at sin

God's Anger over Israel

2 How the Lord has covered the daughter of Zion
With a cloud in His anger!

2:1 Ezek 30:18; Is 14:12-15; Ezek 28:14-16; Is 64:11; Ps 99:5; 132:7

1:16 God is the comforter, but because of the people's sins, he had to turn away from them and become their judge.

1:19 Jerusalem's allies could not come to help because, like Jerusalem, they failed to seek God. Though these allies appeared strong, they were actually weak because God was not with them. Dependable assistance can come only from an ally whose power is from God. When you seek wise counsel, go to Christians who get their wisdom from the all-knowing God.

1:22 Babylon, although sinful, was God's instrument for punishing Judah and its capital, Jerusalem. The people of Jerusalem were pleading for God to punish sinful Babylon as he had punished them ("deal with them as You have dealt with me"). God would do this, for he had already passed judgment on Babylon (see Jeremiah 50:1–27).

He has cast from heaven to earth
The glory of Israel,
And has not remembered His footstool
In the day of His anger.

2:2 Ps 21:9; Lam 3:43; Lam 2:5; Mic 5:11, 14; Is 25:12; 26:5; Ps 89:39, 40; Is 43:28

2 The Lord has swallowed up; He has not spared
All the habitations of Jacob.
In His wrath He has thrown down
The strongholds of the daughter of Judah;
He has brought *them* down to the ground;
He has profaned the kingdom and its princes.

2:3 Ps 75:5, 10; Jer 48:25; Ps 74:11; Jer 21:4, 5; Is 42:25; Jer 21:14

3 In fierce anger He has cut off
All the strength of Israel;
He has drawn back His right hand
From before the enemy.
And He has burned in Jacob like a flaming fire
Consuming round about.

2:4 Job 6:4; 16:13; Lam 3:12, 13; Ezek 24:25; Is 42:25; Jer 7:20

4 He has bent His bow like an enemy;
He has set His right hand like an adversary
And slain all that were pleasant to the eye;
In the tent of the daughter of Zion
He has poured out His wrath like fire.

2:5 Jer 30:14; Lam 2:2; Jer 52:13; Jer 9:17-20

5 The Lord has become like an enemy.
He has swallowed up Israel;
He has swallowed up all its palaces,
He has destroyed its strongholds
And multiplied in the daughter of Judah
Mourning and moaning.

2:6 Jer 52:13; Jer 17:27; Lam 1:4; Zeph 3:18; Lam 4:16

6 And He has violently treated His tabernacle like a garden *booth;*
He has destroyed His appointed meeting place.
The LORD has caused to be forgotten
The appointed feast and sabbath in Zion,
And He has despised king and priest
In the indignation of His anger.

2:7 Ps 78:59-61; Is 64:11; Ezek 7:20-22; Jer 33:4, 5; 52:13; Ps 74:3-8

7 The Lord has rejected His altar,
He has abandoned His sanctuary;
He has delivered into the hand of the enemy
The walls of her palaces.
They have made a noise in the house of the LORD
As in the day of an appointed feast.

2:8 2 Kin 21:13; Is 34:11; Amos 7:7-9; Is 3:26; Jer 14:2

8 The LORD determined to destroy
The wall of the daughter of Zion.
He has stretched out a line,
He has not restrained His hand from destroying,
And He has caused rampart and wall to lament;
They have languished together.

2:9 Neh 1:3; Hos 3:4; Jer 14:14; 23:16; Ezek 7:26

9 Her gates have sunk into the ground,
He has destroyed and broken her bars.
Her king and her princes are among the nations;

2:6 King Solomon's temple (here called God's "tabernacle" and "meeting place") in Jerusalem represented God's presence with the people (1 Kings 8:1–11). The temple was the central place of worship. Its destruction symbolized God's rejection of his people—that he no longer lived among them.

2:7 Our place of worship is not as important to God as our pattern of worship. A church building may be beautiful, but if its people don't sincerely follow God, the church will decay from within. The people of Judah, despite their beautiful temple, had rejected in their daily lives what they proclaimed in their worship rituals. Thus their worship had turned into a mocking lie. When you worship, are you saying words you don't really mean? Do you pray for help you don't really believe will come? Do you express love for God you don't really have? Earnestly seek God and catch a fresh vision of his love and care. Then worship him wholeheartedly.

2:9 Four powerful symbols and sources of security were lost: the protection of the *gates,* the leadership of the *king and princes,* the guidance of the *law,* and the vision of the *prophets.* With those four factors present, the people were lulled into a false sense of security and felt comfortable with their sins. But after each was removed, the people were confronted with the choice of repenting and returning to God or continuing on this path of suffering. Don't substitute symbols, even good ones, for the reality of a living, personal relationship with God himself.

The law is no more.
Also, her prophets find
No vision from the LORD.
10 The elders of the daughter of Zion
Sit on the ground, they are silent.
They have thrown dust on their heads;
They have girded themselves with sackcloth.
The virgins of Jerusalem
Have bowed their heads to the ground.
11 My eyes fail because of tears,
My spirit is greatly troubled;
My heart is poured out on the earth
Because of the destruction of the daughter of my people,
When little ones and infants faint
In the streets of the city.
12 They say to their mothers,
"Where is grain and wine?"
As they faint like a wounded man
In the streets of the city,
As their life is poured out
On their mothers' bosom.
13 How shall I admonish you?
To what shall I compare you,
O daughter of Jerusalem?
To what shall I liken you as I comfort you,
O virgin daughter of Zion?
For your ruin is as vast as the sea;
Who can heal you?
14 Your prophets have seen for you
False and foolish *visions;*
And they have not exposed your iniquity
So as to restore you from captivity,
But they have seen for you false and misleading oracles.
15 All who pass along the way
Clap their hands *in derision* at you;
They hiss and shake their heads
At the daughter of Jerusalem,
"Is this the city of which they said,
'The perfection of beauty,
A joy to all the earth'?"
16 All your enemies
Have opened their mouths wide against you;
They hiss and gnash *their* teeth.
They say, "We have swallowed *her* up!
Surely this is the day for which we waited;
We have reached *it,* we have seen *it.*"
17 The LORD has done what He purposed;
He has accomplished His word
Which He commanded from days of old.
He has thrown down without sparing,
And He has caused the enemy to rejoice over you;
He has exalted the might of your adversaries.

2:10
Job 2:13; Is 3:26; 47:1; Amos 8:3; Job 2:12; Ezek 27:30; Is 15:3; Jon 3:6-8; Lam 1:4

2:11
Lam 1:16; 3:48, 51; Jer 4:19; Job 16:13; Is 22:4; Lam 4:10; Jer 44:7; Lam 2:19

2:12
Jer 5:17; Job 30:16; Ps 42:4; 62:8

2:13
Lam 1:12; Is 37:22; Jer 8:22; 30:12-15

2:14
Jer 23:25-29; 29:8, 9; Is 58:1; Ezek 23:36; Mic 3:8; Jer 23:36; Ezek 22:25, 28

2:15
Job 27:23; Ezek 25:6; Ps 22:7; Is 37:22; Jer 18:16; 19:8; Zeph 2:15; Ps 50:2; Ps 48:2

2:16
Job 16:10; Ps 22:13; Lam 3:46; Job 16:9; Ps 35:16; 37:12; Ps 56:2; 124:3; Jer 51:34; Obad 12-15

2:17
Jer 4:28; Lam 2:1, 2; Ezek 5:11; 7:8, 9; 8:18; Ps 35:24, 26; 89:42; Is 14:29; Deut 28:43, 44; Lam 1:5

2:11 Jeremiah's tears were sincere and full of compassion. Sorrow does not mean that we lack faith or strength. There is nothing wrong with crying—Jesus himself felt sorrow and even wept (John 11:35). How do we react to the tearing down of our society and to moral degradation? This may not be as obvious as an invading enemy army, but the destruction is just as certain. We too should be deeply moved when we see the moral decay that surrounds us.

2:14 False prophets were everywhere in Jeremiah's day. They gave false and misleading "oracles" (messages to people from God). While Jeremiah warned the people of coming destruction and lengthy captivity, the false prophets said that all was well and so the people need not fear. All of Jeremiah's words came true because he was a true prophet of God (Jeremiah 14:14–16).

2:15 Clapping hands, hissing, and shaking heads were all signs of derision and mockery. They were contemptuous gestures.

2:18 Ps 119:145; Hos 7:14; Lam 2:8; Hab 2:11; Ps 119:136; Jer 9:1; Lam 1:2, 16; 3:48, 49

18 Their heart cried out to the Lord,
"O wall of the daughter of Zion,
Let *your* tears run down like a river day and night;
Give yourself no relief,
Let your eyes have no rest.

2:19 Ps 42:3; Is 26:9; 1 Sam 1:15; Ps 42:4; 62:8; Lam 2:11; Is 51:20

19 "Arise, cry aloud in the night
At the beginning of the night watches;
Pour out your heart like water
Before the presence of the Lord;
Lift up your hands to Him
For the life of your little ones
Who are faint because of hunger
At the head of every street."

2:20 Ex 32:11; Deut 9:26; Jer 19:9; Lam 4:10; Ps 78:64; Jer 14:15; 23:11, 12

20 See, O LORD, and look!
With whom have You dealt thus?
Should women eat their offspring,
The little ones who were born healthy?
Should priest and prophet be slain
In the sanctuary of the Lord?

2:21 2 Chr 36:17; Jer 6:11; Ps 78:62, 63; Jer 13:14; Zech 11:6

21 On the ground in the streets
Lie young and old;
My virgins and my young men
Have fallen by the sword.
You have slain *them* in the day of Your anger,
You have slaughtered, not sparing.

2:22 Ps 31:13; Is 24:17; Jer 6:25; Jer 11:11; Jer 16:2-4; 44:7

22 You called as in the day of an appointed feast
My terrors on every side;
And there was no one who escaped or survived
In the day of the LORD'S anger.
Those whom I bore and reared,
My enemy annihilated them.

3. Hope in the midst of affliction

Jeremiah Shares Israel's Affliction

3:1 Ps 88:7, 15, 16

3:2 Job 30:26; Is 59:9; Jer 4:23

3:3 Ps 38:2; Is 5:25

3:4 Ps 31:9, 10; 38:2-8; 102:3-5; Ps 51:8; Is 38:13

3 I am the man who has seen affliction
Because of the rod of His wrath.
2 He has driven me and made me walk
In darkness and not in light.
3 Surely against me He has turned His hand
Repeatedly all the day.
4 He has caused my flesh and my skin to waste away,
He has broken my bones.

2:19 Chapter 1 describes Jerusalem's desolation and calls for God's revenge on his enemies. Chapter 2 includes a call for God's people to pour out their hearts in the Lord's presence. The people must turn from their sins; they must sincerely mourn over their wrongs against God (3:40–42). The people had much to cry about. Because of their stubborn rebellion against God, they had brought great suffering to all, especially to the innocent. Was this suffering God's fault? No, it was the fault of the wayward people. Sinful people brought destruction on themselves, but tragically, sin's consequences affected everyone—good and evil alike.

2:19 The people's suffering and sin should have brought them to the Lord, weeping for forgiveness. Only when sin breaks our hearts can God come to our rescue. Just feeling sorry about experiencing sin's consequences does not bring forgiveness. But if we cry out to God, he will forgive us.

2:21–22 This horrible scene could have been avoided. Jeremiah had warned the people for years that this day of destruction would come, and it broke his heart to see it fulfilled. We are always shocked when we hear of tragedy striking the innocent. But often innocent bystanders are victims of judgment on a nation. Sin has a way of causing great sorrow and devastation to many.

3:1ff In Jeremiah's darkest moment, his hope was strengthened with this assurance: God had been faithful and would continue to be faithful. Jeremiah saw both God's judgment and God's steadfast love. In the time of judgment, Jeremiah could still cling to God's love just as in times of prosperity he had warned of God's judgment.

3:1ff In the original Hebrew, the first four chapters in Lamentations are acrostic poems. Each verse in each chapter begins with a successive letter of the Hebrew alphabet. Chapter 3 has 66 verses rather than 22 because it is a triple acrostic: the first three verses begin with the equivalent of *A,* the next three with *B,* and so on. This was a typical form of Hebrew poetry. Other examples of acrostics are Psalms 37, 119, and 145, and Proverbs 31:10–31.

5 He has besieged and encompassed me with bitterness and hardship.
6 In dark places He has made me dwell,
Like those who have long been dead.
7 He has walled me in so that I cannot go out;
He has made my chain heavy.
8 Even when I cry out and call for help,
He shuts out my prayer.
9 He has blocked my ways with hewn stone;
He has made my paths crooked.
10 He is to me like a bear lying in wait,
Like a lion in secret places.
11 He has turned aside my ways and torn me to pieces;
He has made me desolate.
12 He bent His bow
And set me as a target for the arrow.
13 He made the arrows of His quiver
To enter into my inward parts.
14 I have become a laughingstock to all my people,
Their *mocking* song all the day.
15 He has filled me with bitterness,
He has made me drunk with wormwood.
16 He has broken my teeth with gravel;
He has made me cower in the dust.
17 My soul has been rejected from peace;
I have forgotten happiness.
18 So I say, "My strength has perished,
And *so has* my hope from the LORD."

Hope of Relief in God's Mercy

19 Remember my affliction and my wandering, the wormwood and bitterness.
20 Surely my soul remembers
And is bowed down within me.
21 This I recall to my mind,
Therefore I have hope.
22 The LORD'S lovingkindnesses indeed never cease,
For His compassions never fail.
23 *They* are new every morning;
Great is Your faithfulness.
24 "The LORD is my portion," says my soul,
"Therefore I have hope in Him."
25 The LORD is good to those who wait for Him,
To the person who seeks Him.
26 *It is* good that he waits silently
For the salvation of the LORD.
27 *It is* good for a man that he should bear
The yoke in his youth.
28 Let him sit alone and be silent
Since He has laid *it* on him.
29 Let him put his mouth in the dust,
Perhaps there is hope.

3:5 Job 19:8; Jer 23:15
3:6 Ps 88:5, 6; 143:3
3:7 Job 3:23; 19:8; Jer 40:4
3:8 Job 30:20; Ps 22:2
3:9 Is 63:17; Hos 2:6
3:11 Job 16:12, 13; Jer 15:3; Hos 6:1
3:12 Ps 7:12; Job 6:4; 7:20; Ps 38:2
3:14 Ps 22:6, 7; 123:4; Jer 20:7; Job 30:9; Lam 3:63
3:15 Jer 9:15
3:16 Ps 3:7; 58:6; Prov 20:17; Jer 6:26
3:17 Is 59:11; Jer 12:12
3:18 Job 17:15; Ezek 37:11
3:19 Jer 9:15; Lam 3:5
3:20 Job 21:6; Ps 42:5, 6, 11; 43:5; 44:25
3:21 Ps 130:7
3:22 Ps 78:38; Jer 3:12; 30:11; Mal 3:6
3:23 Is 33:2; Zeph 3:5; Heb 10:23
3:24 Ps 16:5; 73:26; Ps 33:18
3:25 Ps 27:14; Is 25:9; Is 26:9
3:26 Ps 37:7
3:28 Jer 15:17
3:29 Job 16:15; 40:4; Jer 31:17

3:21–22 Jeremiah saw one ray of hope in all the sin and sorrow surrounding him: "The LORD's lovingkindnesses indeed never cease, for His compassions never fail." God willingly responds with help when we ask. Perhaps there is some sin in your life that you thought God would not forgive. God's steadfast love and mercy are greater than any sin, and he promises forgiveness.

3:23 Jeremiah knew from personal experience about God's faithfulness. God had promised that punishment would follow disobedience, and it did. But God also had promised future restoration and blessing, and Jeremiah knew that God would keep that promise also. Trusting in God's faithfulness day by day makes us confident in his great promises for the future.

3:27–33 To "bear the yoke" means to willingly come under God's discipline and learn what he wants to teach. This involves several important factors: (1) silent reflection on what God wants, (2) repentant humility, (3) self-control in the face of adversity, and (4) confident patience, depending on the divine Teacher to bring about loving lessons in our lives. God has several long-term and short-term lessons for you right now. Are you doing your homework?

3:30 Job 16:10; Is 50:6
3:31 Ps 77:7; 94:14; Is 54:7-10
3:32 Ps 78:38; 106:43-45; Hos 11:8
3:33 Ps 119:67, 71, 75; Ezek 33:11; Heb 12:10
3:35 Ps 140:12; Prov 17:15
3:36 Jer 22:3; Hab 1:13
3:37 Ps 33:9-11
3:38 Job 2:10; Is 45:7; Jer 32:42
3:39 Jer 30:15; Mic 7:9; Heb 12:5, 6
3:40 Ps 119:59; 139:23, 24; 2 Cor 13:5
3:41 Ps 25:1; 28:2; 141:2
3:42 Neh 9:26; Jer 14:20; Dan 9:5; 2 Kin 24:4
3:43 Lam 2:21; Ps 83:15
3:44 Ps 97:2; Lam 3:8; Zech 7:13
3:46 Job 30:9, 10; Ps 22:6-8; Lam 2:16
3:47 Is 24:17, 18; Jer 48:43, 44
3:48 Ps 119:136; Jer 9:1, 18; Lam 1:16; 2:11
3:49 Ps 77:2; Jer 14:17
3:50 Ps 80:14; Is 63:15; Lam 5:1
3:52 Ps 35:7, 19; 1 Sam 26:20; Ps 11:1
3:53 Jer 37:16; 38:6, 9
3:54 Ps 69:2; Jon 2:3-5
3:55 Ps 130:1; Jon 2:2

30 Let him give his cheek to the smiter,
Let him be filled with reproach.
31 For the Lord will not reject forever,
32 For if He causes grief,
Then He will have compassion
According to His abundant lovingkindness.
33 For He does not afflict willingly
Or grieve the sons of men.
34 To crush under His feet
All the prisoners of the land,
35 To deprive a man of justice
In the presence of the Most High,
36 To defraud a man in his lawsuit—
Of these things the Lord does not approve.
37 Who is there who speaks and it comes to pass,
Unless the Lord has commanded *it?*
38 *Is it* not from the mouth of the Most High
That both good and ill go forth?

39 Why should *any* living mortal, or *any* man,
Offer complaint in view of his sins?
40 Let us examine and probe our ways,
And let us return to the LORD.
41 We lift up our heart and hands
Toward God in heaven;
42 We have transgressed and rebelled,
You have not pardoned.
43 You have covered *Yourself* with anger
And pursued us;
You have slain *and* have not spared.
44 You have covered Yourself with a cloud
So that no prayer can pass through.
45 *You have made us mere* offscouring and refuse
In the midst of the peoples.
46 All our enemies have opened their mouths against us.
47 Panic and pitfall have befallen us,
Devastation and destruction;
48 My eyes run down with streams of water
Because of the destruction of the daughter of my people.
49 My eyes pour down unceasingly,
Without stopping,
50 Until the LORD looks down
And sees from heaven.
51 My eyes bring pain to my soul
Because of all the daughters of my city.
52 My enemies without cause
Hunted me down like a bird;
53 They have silenced me in the pit
And have placed a stone on me.
54 Waters flowed over my head;
I said, "I am cut off!"
55 I called on Your name, O LORD,

3:30 To "give [your] cheek to the smiter" means to submit to physical abuse without defending yourself or fighting back. Jesus taught his followers to turn the other cheek (Matthew 5:39), and he exemplified this at the highest level just before his crucifixion (Matthew 27:27–31; Luke 22:64; John 18:22; 19:3).

3:39–42 Parents discipline children to produce right behavior. God disciplined Judah to produce right living and genuine worship. We must not complain about discipline but learn from it, trusting God and being willing to change. We must allow God's correction to bring about the kind of behavior in our lives that pleases him.

3:52–57 At one point in his ministry, Jeremiah was thrown into an empty cistern, and he was left to die in the mire at the bottom (Jeremiah 38:6–13). But God rescued him. Jeremiah used this experience as a picture of the nation sinking into sin. If they turned to God, he would rescue them.

Out of the lowest pit.
56 You have heard my voice,
"Do not hide Your ear from my *prayer for* relief,
From my cry for help."
57 You drew near when I called on You;
You said, "Do not fear!"
58 O Lord, You have pleaded my soul's cause;
You have redeemed my life.
59 O LORD, You have seen my oppression;
Judge my case.
60 You have seen all their vengeance,
All their schemes against me.
61 You have heard their reproach, O LORD,
All their schemes against me.
62 The lips of my assailants and their whispering
Are against me all day long.
63 Look on their sitting and their rising;
I am their mocking song.
64 You will recompense them, O LORD,
According to the work of their hands.
65 You will give them hardness of heart,
Your curse will be on them.
66 You will pursue them in anger and destroy them
From under the heavens of the LORD!

3:56 Job 34:28; Ps 55:1
3:57 Ps 145:18; Is 41:10, 14
3:58 Jer 50:34; Ps 34:22
3:59 Jer 18:19, 20; Ps 26:1; 43:1
3:60 Jer 11:19
3:61 Ps 74:18; 89:50; Lam 5:1; Zeph 2:8
3:62 Ps 59:7, 12; 140:3; Ezek 36:3
3:63 Ps 139:2; Job 30:9; Lam 3:14
3:64 Ps 28:4; Jer 51:6, 24, 56
3:65 Ex 14:8; Deut 2:30; Is 6:10
3:66 Lam 3:43; Ps 8:3

4. God's anger is satisfied

Distress of the Siege Described

4 How dark the gold has become,
How the pure gold has changed!
The sacred stones are poured out
At the corner of every street.
2 The precious sons of Zion,
Weighed against fine gold,
How they are regarded as earthen jars,
The work of a potter's hands!
3 Even jackals offer the breast,
They nurse their young;
But the daughter of my people has become cruel
Like ostriches in the wilderness.
4 The tongue of the infant cleaves
To the roof of its mouth because of thirst;
The little ones ask for bread,
But no one breaks *it* for them.
5 Those who ate delicacies
Are desolate in the streets;
Those reared in purple
Embrace ash pits.
6 For the iniquity of the daughter of my people
Is greater than the sin of Sodom,

4:1 Ezek 7:19-22
4:2 Is 30:14; Jer 19:1, 11
4:3 Is 13:22; 34:13; Is 49:15; Ezek 5:10; Job 39:14-17
4:4 Ps 22:15; Jer 14:3; Lam 2:12
4:5 Jer 6:2; Amos 6:3-7
4:6 Gen 19:24; Gen 19:25; Jer 20:16

4:1ff This chapter contrasts the situation before the siege of Jerusalem with the situation after the siege. The sights and sounds of prosperity were gone because of the people's sin. This chapter warns us not to assume that when life is going well, it will always stay that way. We must be careful not to glory in our prosperity and fall into spiritual bankruptcy.

4:1–10 When a city was under siege, the city wall—built for protection—sealed the people inside. They could not get out to the fields to get food and water because the enemy was camped around the city. As food in the city ran out, the people watched their enemies harvest and eat the food in the fields. The siege was a test of wills to see which army could outlast the other. Jerusalem was under siege for two years. Life became so harsh that people even ate their own children, and dead bodies were left to rot in the streets. All hope was gone.

4:6 Sodom, destroyed by brimstone and fire from heaven because of its wickedness (Genesis 18:20—19:29), became a symbol of God's ultimate judgment. Yet the sin of Jerusalem was even greater than the sin of Sodom!

Which was overthrown as in a moment,
And no hands were turned toward her.

4:7 Ps 51:7; Ex 24:10; Job 28:16

7 Her consecrated ones were purer than snow,
They were whiter than milk;
They were more ruddy *in* body than corals,
Their polishing *was like* lapis lazuli.

4:8 Job 30:30; Lam 5:10; Job 19:20; Ps 102:3-5

8 Their appearance is blacker than soot,
They are not recognized in the streets;
Their skin is shriveled on their bones,
It is withered, it has become like wood.

4:9 Jer 16:4; Lev 26:39; Ezek 24:23

9 Better are those slain with the sword
Than those slain with hunger;
For they pine away, being stricken
For lack of the fruits of the field.

4:10 Lev 26:29; Deut 28:57; 2 Kin 6:29; Jer 19:9; Lam 2:20; Ezek 5:10; Deut 28:53-55

10 The hands of compassionate women
Boiled their own children;
They became food for them
Because of the destruction of the daughter of my people.

4:11 Jer 7:20; Lam 2:17; Ezek 22:31; Deut 32:22; Jer 17:27

11 The LORD has accomplished His wrath,
He has poured out His fierce anger;
And He has kindled a fire in Zion
Which has consumed its foundations.

4:12 Deut 29:24; Jer 21:13

12 The kings of the earth did not believe,
Nor *did* any of the inhabitants of the world,
That the adversary and the enemy
Could enter the gates of Jerusalem.

4:13 Jer 5:31; 6:13; Lam 2:14; Ezek 22:26-28; Jer 2:30; 26:8, 9; Matt 23:31

13 Because of the sins of her prophets
And the iniquities of her priests,
Who have shed in her midst
The blood of the righteous;

4:14 Deut 28:28, 29; Is 29:10; 56:10; 59:9, 10; Is 1:15; Jer 2:34

14 They wandered, blind, in the streets;
They were defiled with blood
So that no one could touch their garments.

4:15 Lev 13:45, 46; Jer 49:5

15 "Depart! Unclean!" they cried of themselves.
"Depart, depart, do not touch!"
So they fled and wandered;
Men among the nations said,
"They shall not continue to dwell *with us.*"

4:16 Is 9:14-16; Jer 52:24-27

16 The presence of the LORD has scattered them,
He will not continue to regard them;
They did not honor the priests,
They did not favor the elders.

4:17 Jer 37:7; Lam 1:7; Ezek 29:6, 7, 16

17 Yet our eyes failed,
Looking for help was useless;
In our watching we have watched
For a nation that could not save.

4:18 Jer 16:16; Jer 5:31; Ezek 7:2-12; Amos 8:2

18 They hunted our steps
So that we could not walk in our streets;
Our end drew near,
Our days were finished
For our end had come.

4:19 Is 5:26-28; 30:16, 17; Jer 4:13; Hab 1:8

19 Our pursuers were swifter
Than the eagles of the sky;
They chased us on the mountains,

4:13–15 To be defiled or unclean meant to be unfit to enter the temple or to worship before God. The priests and prophets should have been the most careful to maintain ceremonial purity so that they could continue to perform their duties before God. But many priests and prophets did evil and were defiled. As the nation's leaders, their example led the people into sin and caused the ultimate downfall of the nation and its capital city, Jerusalem.

4:17 Judah asked Egypt to help them fight the Babylonian army. Egypt gave Judah false hope—they started to help, but then retreated (Jeremiah 37:5–7). Jeremiah warned Judah not to ally itself with Egypt. He told the leaders to rely on God, but they refused to listen.

They waited in ambush for us in the wilderness.
20 The breath of our nostrils, the LORD'S anointed,
Was captured in their pits,
Of whom we had said, "Under his shadow
We shall live among the nations."
21 Rejoice and be glad, O daughter of Edom,
Who dwells in the land of Uz;
But the cup will come around to you as well,
You will become drunk and make yourself naked.
22 *The punishment* of your iniquity has been completed, O daughter of Zion;
He will exile you no longer.
But He will punish your iniquity, O daughter of Edom;
He will expose your sins!

4:20 Gen 2:7; 2 Sam 1:14; 19:21; Jer 39:5; 52:9; Dan 4:12

4:21 Ps 137:7; Jer 25:21; Obad 16

4:22 Is 40:2; Jer 33:7, 8; Jer 49:10; Mal 1:3, 4

5. Jeremiah pleads for restoration

A Prayer for Mercy

5 Remember, O LORD, what has befallen us;
Look, and see our reproach!
2 Our inheritance has been turned over to strangers,
Our houses to aliens.
3 We have become orphans without a father,
Our mothers are like widows.
4 We have to pay for our drinking water,
Our wood comes *to us* at a price.
5 Our pursuers are at our necks;
We are worn out, there is no rest for us.
6 We have submitted to Egypt *and* Assyria to get enough bread.
7 Our fathers sinned, *and* are no more;
It is we who have borne their iniquities.
8 Slaves rule over us;
There is no one to deliver us from their hand.
9 We get our bread at the risk of our lives
Because of the sword in the wilderness.
10 Our skin has become as hot as an oven,
Because of the burning heat of famine.
11 They ravished the women in Zion,
The virgins in the cities of Judah.
12 Princes were hung by their hands;
Elders were not respected.
13 Young men worked at the grinding mill,
And youths stumbled under *loads* of wood.
14 Elders are gone from the gate,
Young men from their music.
15 The joy of our hearts has ceased;
Our dancing has been turned into mourning.
16 The crown has fallen from our head;
Woe to us, for we have sinned!

5:1 Ps 44:13-16

5:2 Is 1:7; Hos 8:7, 8; Zeph 1:13

5:3 Ex 22:24; Jer 15:8; 18:21

5:4 Is 3:1

5:5 Neh 9:36, 37

5:6 Hos 9:3; 12:1

5:7 Jer 14:20; 16:12

5:8 Neh 5:15; Ps 7:2; Zech 11:6

5:9 Jer 40:9-12

5:10 Job 30:30; Lam 4:8

5:11 Is 13:16; Zech 14:2

5:12 Is 47:6; Lam 4:16

5:13 Judg 16:21; Jer 7:18

5:14 Is 24:8; Jer 7:34

5:15 Jer 25:10; Amos 8:10

5:16 Job 19:9; Ps 89:39; Jer 13:18; Is 3:9-11

4:20 King Zedekiah, although called "the LORD's anointed," had little spiritual depth and leadership power. Instead of putting his faith in God and listening to God's true prophet, Jeremiah, he listened to the false prophets. To make matters worse, the people chose to follow and trust in their king (2 Chronicles 36:11–23). They chose the path of false confidence and complacency, wanting to feel secure rather than to follow the directives God was giving his people through Jeremiah. But the object of their confidence—King Zedekiah—was captured.

4:21–22 Edom was Judah's archenemy, even though they had a common ancestor, Isaac (see Genesis 25:19–26; 36:1). Edom had actively aided Babylon in the siege of Jerusalem. As a reward, Nebuchadnezzar gave the outlying lands of Judah to Edom. Jeremiah said that Edom would be judged for her treachery against her brothers. (See also Jeremiah 49:7–22; Ezekiel 25:12–14; Amos 9:12; Obadiah 1–21.)

5:1ff After expressing the full extent of his or her grief, the true believer should turn to God in prayer. Here Jeremiah prayed for mercy for his people. At the end of his prayer he wondered if God was "exceedingly angry." But God would not stay angry with them forever—as it says in Micah 7:18, "He does not retain His anger forever, because He delights in unchanging love."

5:14 During peace and prosperity, the leaders and elders of the city would sit at the city gate and talk over politics, theology, and philosophy, as well as conduct business.

5:17 Is 1:5; Job 17:7; Lam 2:11

5:18 Mic 3:12; Neh 4:3

5:19 Ps 102:12, 25-27; Ps 45:6

5:20 Ps 13:1; 44:24

5:21 Ps 80:3; Jer 31:18; Is 60:20-22

5:22 Ps 60:1, 2; Jer 7:29; Is 64:9

17 Because of this our heart is faint,
Because of these things our eyes are dim;
18 Because of Mount Zion which lies desolate,
Foxes prowl in it.

19 You, O LORD, rule forever;
Your throne is from generation to generation.
20 Why do You forget us forever?
Why do You forsake us so long?
21 Restore us to You, O LORD, that we may be restored;
Renew our days as of old,
22 Unless You have utterly rejected us
And are exceedingly angry with us.

5:22 A high calling flouted by low living results in deep suffering. Lamentations gives us a portrait of the bitter suffering the people of Jerusalem experienced when sin caught up with them and God turned his back on them. Every material goal they had lived for collapsed. But although God turned away from them because of their sin, he did not abandon them—that was their great hope. Despite their sinful past, God would restore them if they returned to him. Hope is found only in the Lord. Thus our grief should turn us toward him, not away from him.

EZEKIEL

Jeremiah becomes a prophet to Judah 627 B.C.	*Daniel taken captive to Babylon 605*	*Ezekiel taken captive to Babylon 597*	*Ezekiel becomes a prophet to exiles 593*

VITAL STATISTICS

PURPOSE:
To announce God's judgment on Israel and other nations and to foretell the eventual salvation of God's people

AUTHOR:
Ezekiel son of Buzi, a Zadokite priest

TO WHOM WRITTEN:
The Jews in captivity in Babylonia and God's people everywhere

DATE WRITTEN:
Approximately 571 B.C.

SETTING:
Ezekiel was a younger contemporary of Jeremiah. While Jeremiah ministered to the people still in Judah, Ezekiel prophesied to those already exiled in Babylonia after the defeat of Jehoiachin. He was taken there in 597 B.C.

KEY VERSES:
"For I will take you from the nations, gather you from all the lands and bring you into your own land. Then I will sprinkle clean water on you, and you will be clean; I will cleanse you from all your filthiness and from all your idols. Moreover, I will give you a new heart and put a new spirit within you; and I will remove the heart of stone from your flesh and give you a heart of flesh" (36:24–26).

KEY PEOPLE:
Ezekiel, Israel's leaders, Ezekiel's wife, Nebuchadnezzar, "the prince"

KEY PLACES:
Jerusalem, Babylon, and Egypt

A COMPUTER can be programmed to respond at your command. And by conditioning a dog with rewards and punishments, you can teach it to obey. But as every parent knows, children are not so easily taught. People have wills and must choose to submit, to follow the instructions of those who have authority over them. Surely discipline is part of the process—boys and girls should know that they will reap the consequences of disobedience.

God's children must learn to obey their heavenly Father. Created in his image, they have a choice, and God allows them to choose.

Ezekiel was a man who chose to obey God. Although he was a priest (1:3), he served as a Jewish "street preacher" in Babylon for 22 years, telling everyone about God's judgment and salvation, and calling them to repent and obey. And Ezekiel *lived* what he preached. During his ministry God told him to illustrate his messages with dramatic object lessons. Some of these acts included (1) lying on his side for 390 days during which he could eat only one eight-ounce meal a day cooked over manure, (2) shaving his head and beard, and (3) showing no sorrow when his wife died. He obeyed and faithfully proclaimed God's word.

God may not ask you to do anything quite so dramatic or difficult; but if he did, would you do it?

The book of Ezekiel chronicles the prophet's life and ministry. Beginning with his call as a prophet and commissioning as a "watchman for Israel" (chapters 1—3), Ezekiel immediately began to preach and demonstrate God's truth, as he predicted the approaching siege and destruction of Jerusalem (chapters 4—24). This devastation would be God's judgment for the people's idolatry. Ezekiel challenged them to turn from their wicked ways. In the next section, he spoke to the surrounding nations, prophesying that God would judge them for their sins as well (chapters 25—32). The book concludes with a message of hope, as Ezekiel proclaimed the faithfulness of God and foretold the future blessings for God's people (chapters 33— 48).

As you read this exciting record, observe how Ezekiel fearlessly preached the word of God to the exiled Jews in the streets of Babylon, and hear the timeless truth of God's love and power. Think about each person's responsibility to trust God and about the inevitability of God's judgment against idolatry, rebellion, and indifference. Then commit yourself to obey God, whatever, wherever, and whenever he asks.

THE BLUEPRINT

A. MESSAGES OF DOOM (1:1—24:27)
1. Ezekiel's call and commission
2. Visions of sin and judgment
3. Punishment is certain

While Jeremiah was prophesying in Jerusalem that the city would soon fall to the Babylonians, Ezekiel was giving the same message to the captives who were already in Babylon. Like those in Jerusalem, the captives stubbornly believed that Jerusalem would not fall and that they would soon return to their land. Ezekiel warned them that punishment was certain because of their sins and that God was purifying his people. God will always punish sin, whether we believe it or not.

Judah falls; Jerusalem destroyed 586	*Ezekiel's ministry ends 571*	*Babylon overthrown by Cyrus 539*	*First exiles return to Judah 538*

B. MESSAGES AGAINST FOREIGN NATIONS (25:1—32:32)

Ezekiel condemns the sinful actions of seven nations. The people in these nations were saying that God was obviously too weak to defend his people and the city of Jerusalem. But God was allowing his people to be defeated in order to punish them for their sins. These pagan nations, however, would face a similar fate, and then they would know that God is all-powerful. Those who dare to mock God today will also face a terrible fate.

C. MESSAGES OF HOPE (33:1—48:35)
1. Restoring the people of God
2. Restoring the worship of God

After the fall of Jerusalem, Ezekiel delivered messages of future restoration and hope for the people. God is holy, but Jerusalem and the temple had become defiled. The nation had to be cleansed through 70 years of captivity. Ezekiel gives a vivid picture of the unchangeable holiness of God. We, too, must gain a vision of the glory of God, a fresh sense of his greatness, as we face the struggles of daily life.

MEGATHEMES

THEME	EXPLANATION	IMPORTANCE
God's Holiness	Ezekiel saw a vision that revealed God's absolute moral perfection. God was spiritually and morally superior to members of Israel's corrupt and compromising society. Ezekiel wrote to let the people know that God in his holiness was also present in Babylon, not just in Jerusalem.	Because God is morally perfect, he can help us live above our tendency to compromise with this world. When we focus on his greatness, he gives us the power to overcome sin and to reflect his holiness.
Sin	Israel had sinned, and God's punishment came. The fall of Jerusalem and the Babylonian exile were used by God to correct the rebels and draw them back from their sinful way of life. Ezekiel warned them that not only was the nation responsible for sin but each individual was also accountable to God.	We cannot excuse ourselves from our responsibilities before God. We are accountable to God for our choices. Rather than neglect him, we must recognize sin for what it is—rebellion against God—and choose to follow him instead.
Restoration	Ezekiel consoles the people by telling them that the day will come when God will restore those who turn from sin. God will be their King and shepherd. He will give his people a new heart to worship him, and he will establish a new government and a new temple.	The certainty of future restoration encourages believers in times of trial. But we must be faithful to God because we love him, not merely for what he can do for us. Is our faith in *him* or merely in our future benefits?
Leaders	Ezekiel condemned the shepherds (unfaithful priests and leaders), who led the people astray. By contrast, he served as a caring shepherd and a faithful watchman to warn the people about their sin. One day God's perfect shepherd, the Messiah, will lead his people.	Jesus is our perfect leader. If we truly want him to lead us, our devotion must be more than talk. If we are given the responsibility of leading others, we must take care of them even if it means sacrificing personal pleasure, happiness, time, or money. We are responsible for those we lead.
Worship	An angel gave Ezekiel a vision of the temple in great detail. God's holy presence had departed from Israel and the temple because of sin. The building of a future temple portrays the return of God's glory and presence. God will cleanse his people and restore true worship.	All of God's promises will be fulfilled under the rule of the Messiah. The faithful followers will be restored to perfect fellowship with God and with one another. To be prepared for this time, we must focus on God. We do this through regular worship. Through worship we learn about God's holiness and the changes we must make in how we live.

A. MESSAGES OF DOOM (1:1—24:27)

Ezekiel prophesied to the exiles in Babylon. He had to dispel the false hope that Israel's captivity would be short, explain the reasons for the severe judgments on their nation, and bring a message of future hope. Although the people did not respond positively, they heard the messages and knew the truth. God's people were not without explanation and direction, and neither are we.

1. Ezekiel's call and commission

The Vision of Four Figures

1 Now it came about in the thirtieth year, on the fifth *day* of the fourth month, while
I was by the river Chebar among the exiles, the heavens were opened and I saw visions of God.
2 (On the fifth of the month in the fifth year of King Jehoiachin's exile,
3 the word of the LORD came expressly to Ezekiel the priest, son of Buzi, in the land
of the Chaldeans by the river Chebar; and there the hand of the LORD came upon him.)
4 As I looked, behold, a storm wind was coming from the north, a great cloud with
fire flashing forth continually and a bright light around it, and in its midst something like
glowing metal in the midst of the fire.
5 Within it there were figures resembling four living beings. And this was their appearance: they had human form.
6 Each of them had four faces and four wings.
7 Their legs were straight and their feet were like a calf's hoof, and they gleamed like
burnished bronze.
8 Under their wings on their four sides *were* human hands. As for the faces and wings
of the four of them,
9 their wings touched one another; *their faces* did not turn when they moved, each
went straight forward.
10 As for the form of their faces, *each* had the face of a man; all four had the face of a
lion on the right and the face of a bull on the left, and all four had the face of an eagle.
11 Such were their faces. Their wings were spread out above; each had two touching
another *being*, and two covering their bodies.
12 And each went straight forward; wherever the spirit was about to go, they would go,
without turning as they went.

1:1 Ezek 3:23; 10:15, 20; Matt 3:16; Mark 1:10; Luke 3:21; Acts 7:56; 10:11; Rev 4:1; 19:11; Ex 24:10; Num 12:6; Is 1:1; 6:1; Ezek 8:3; 11:24; 40:2; Dan 8:1, 2

1:2 2 Kin 24:12-15; Ezek 8:1; 20:1

1:3 2 Pet 1:21; Ezek 12:13; 1 Kin 18:46; 2 Kin 3:15; Ezek 3:14, 22

1:4 Is 21:1; Jer 23:19; Ezek 13:11, 13; Ezek 1:27; 8:2

1:5 Ezek 10:15, 17, 20; Rev 4:6-8; Ezek 1:26

1:6 Ezek 1:10; 10:14, 21; Ezek 1:23

1:7 Dan 10:6; Rev 1:15

1:8 Ezek 1:17; 10:11; Ezek 10:8, 21

1:9 Ezek 1:17; Ezek 1:12; 10:22

1:10 Rev 4:7; Ezek 10:14

1:11 Is 6:2; Ezek 1:23

1:1 Ezekiel, born and raised in the land of Judah, was preparing to become a priest in God's temple when the Babylonians attacked in 597 B.C. and carried him away along with 10,000 other captives (2 Kings 24:10–14). The nation was on the brink of complete destruction. Four to five years later, when Ezekiel was 30 (the normal age for becoming a priest), God called him to be a prophet. During the first six years when Ezekiel ministered in Babylonia (1:3), Jeremiah was preaching to the Jews still in Judah, and Daniel was serving in Nebuchadnezzar's court. The Chebar River connected to the Euphrates in Babylonia and was the location of a Jewish settlement of exiles.

1:1 Why did the Jewish exiles in Babylonia need a prophet? God wanted Ezekiel to (1) help the exiles understand why they had been taken captive, (2) dispel the false hope that the captivity was going to be short, (3) bring a new message of hope, and (4) call the people to a new awareness of their dependence upon God.

1:1ff Ezekiel's latest dated message from God (29:17) was given in 571 B.C. He was taken captive during the second Babylonian invasion of Judah in 597 B.C. The Babylonians invaded Judah a third and final time in 586 B.C., completely destroying Jerusalem, burning the temple, and deporting the rest of the people (see 2 Kings 25). Ezekiel dates all his messages from the year he was taken captive (597). His first prophecy to the exiles occurred four to five years after he arrived in the land of Babylon (593 B.C.).

1:1 God communicated to Ezekiel in visions. A vision is a miraculous revelation of God's truth. These visions seem strange to us because they are *apocalyptic.* This means that Ezekiel saw symbolic pictures that vividly conveyed an idea. Daniel and John were other Bible writers who used apocalyptic imagery. The people in exile had lost their perspective of God's purpose and presence, and Ezekiel came to them with a vision from God to show God's awesome glory and holiness and to warn the exiles of sin's consequences before it was too late.

1:3 The name *Ezekiel* means "God is strong" or "God strengthens." In a very real sense, this sums up the basic message of the book—that in spite of the captivity, God's sovereign strength prevails, and he will judge his enemies and restore his true people.

1:4ff In this first vision, God called Ezekiel to be a prophet (see 2:5). Nothing in Ezekiel's previous experience had prepared him for such a display of God's glorious presence and power. The great cloud flashed with lightning and was surrounded by a bright light. From the fire in the cloud came four living beings. They showed Ezekiel that Jerusalem's coming destruction was God's punishment of Judah for its sins. (These living beings are also seen in Revelation 4:6–7.)

When Ezekiel received this vision, he was far away from the temple in Jerusalem, the physical symbol of God's presence. Through this vision, he learned that God is present everywhere and that God's activities in heaven are shaping the events on earth.

1:5 Each of the four living beings had four faces, symbolizing God's perfect nature. Some believe that the lion represented strength; the bull, diligent service; the man, intelligence; and the eagle, divinity. Others see these as the most majestic of God's creatures and say that they therefore represent God's whole creation. The early church fathers saw a connection between these beings and the four Gospels: the lion with Matthew, presenting Christ as the Lion of Judah; the bull with Mark, portraying Christ as the Servant; the human with Luke, portraying Christ as the perfect human; the eagle with John, portraying Christ as the Son of God, exalted and divine. The vision of John in Revelation 4 parallels Ezekiel's vision.

1:13 Ps 104:4; Rev 4:5
1:14 Zech 4:10; Matt 24:27; Luke 17:24
1:15 Ezek 1:19-21; 10:9
1:16 Ezek 10:9-11; Ezek 10:9; Dan 10:6
1:17 Ezek 1:9, 12; 10:11
1:18 Ezek 10:12; Rev 4:6, 8
1:19 Ezek 10:16; Ezek 10:19
1:20 Ezek 1:12
1:21 Ezek 10:17

13 In the midst of the living beings there was something that looked like burning coals
of fire, like torches darting back and forth among the living beings. The fire was bright,
and lightning was flashing from the fire.
14 And the living beings ran to and fro like bolts of lightning.
15 Now as I looked at the living beings, behold, there was one wheel on the earth beside the living beings, for *each of* the four of them.
16 The appearance of the wheels and their workmanship *was* like sparkling beryl, and
all four of them had the same form, their appearance and workmanship *being* as if one
wheel were within another.
17 Whenever they moved, they moved in any of their four directions without turning
as they moved.
18 As for their rims they were lofty and awesome, and the rims of all four of them were
full of eyes round about.
19 Whenever the living beings moved, the wheels moved with them. And whenever the
living beings rose from the earth, the wheels rose *also.*
20 Wherever the spirit was about to go, they would go in that direction. And the wheels
rose close beside them; for the spirit of the living beings *was* in the wheels.
21 Whenever those went, these went; and whenever those stood still, these stood still.
And whenever those rose from the earth, the wheels rose close beside them; for the spirit
of the living beings *was* in the wheels.

Vision of Divine Glory

1:22 Ezek 10:1
1:23 Ezek 1:6, 11
1:24 Ezek 43:2; Rev 1:15; 19:6; Ezek 10:5; 2 Kin 7:6; Dan 10:6

22 Now over the heads of the living beings *there was* something like an expanse, like
the awesome gleam of crystal, spread out over their heads.
23 Under the expanse their wings *were stretched out* straight, one toward the other; each
one also had two wings covering its body on the one side and on the other.
24 I also heard the sound of their wings like the sound of abundant waters as they went,
like the voice of the Almighty, a sound of tumult like the sound of an army camp; whenever they stood still, they dropped their wings.

EZEKIEL
Ezekiel served as a prophet to the exiles in Babylon from 593–571 B.C.

Climate of the times	• Ezekiel and his people are taken to Babylon as captives. • The Jews become foreigners in a strange land ruled by an authoritarian government.
Main message	Because of the people's sins, God allowed the nation of Judah to be destroyed. But there was still hope—God promised to restore the land to those who remained faithful to him.
Importance of message	God never forgets those who faithfully seek to obey him. They have a glorious future ahead.
Contemporary prophets	Daniel (605–536 B.C.) Habakkuk (612–588 B.C.) Jeremiah (627–586 B.C.)

EXILE IN BABYLON Ezekiel worked for God right where he was—among the exiles in various colonies near the Chebar River in Babylonia. Jerusalem and its temple lay over 500 miles away, but Ezekiel helped the people understand that, although they were far from home, they did not need to be far from God.

1:16–18 The "wheel . . . within another" was probably two wheels at right angles to each other, one on a north-south and the other on an east-west axis. Able to move anywhere, these wheels show that God is present everywhere and is able to see all things (1:18). God is not restricted to Jerusalem, but rules all of life and history. Though the exiles had experienced great change, God was still in control.

25 And there came a voice from above the expanse that was over their heads; whenever they stood still, they dropped their wings.
26 Now above the expanse that was over their heads there was something resembling
a throne, like lapis lazuli in appearance; and on that which resembled a throne, high up,
was a figure with the appearance of a man.
27 Then I noticed from the appearance of His loins and upward something like glowing metal that looked like fire all around within it, and from the appearance of His loins
and downward I saw something like fire; and *there was* a radiance around Him.
28 As the appearance of the rainbow in the clouds on a rainy day, so *was* the appearance of the surrounding radiance. Such *was* the appearance of the likeness of the glory
of the LORD. And when I saw *it,* I fell on my face and heard a voice speaking.

The Prophet's Call

2 Then He said to me, "Son of man, stand on your feet that I may speak with you!"
2 As He spoke to me the Spirit entered me and set me on my feet; and I heard *Him*
speaking to me.
3 Then He said to me, "Son of man, I am sending you to the sons of Israel, to a rebellious people who have rebelled against Me; they and their fathers have transgressed
against Me to this very day.
4 "I am sending you to them who are stubborn and obstinate children, and you shall
say to them, 'Thus says the Lord GOD.'
5 "As for them, whether they listen or not—for they are a rebellious house—they will
know that a prophet has been among them.
6 "And you, son of man, neither fear them nor fear their words, though thistles and
thorns are with you and you sit on scorpions; neither fear their words nor be dismayed at
their presence, for they are a rebellious house.
7 "But you shall speak My words to them whether they listen or not, for they are rebellious.
8 "Now you, son of man, listen to what I am speaking to you; do not be rebellious like
that rebellious house. Open your mouth and eat what I am giving you."
9 Then I looked, and behold, a hand was extended to me; and lo, a scroll *was* in it.

1:26 Ezek 1:22; 10:1; Is 6:1; Dan 7:9; Ex 24:10; Is 54:11; Ezek 43:6, 7; Rev 1:13

1:27 Ezek 1:4; 8:2

1:28 Ex 24:16; Ezek 8:4; 11:22, 23; 43:4, 5; Gen 17:3; Ezek 3:23; Dan 8:17; Rev 1:17

2:3 1 Sam 8:7, 8; Jer 3:25; Ezek 20:18, 30

2:4 Ps 95:8; Is 48:4; Jer 5:3; 6:15; Ezek 3:7

2:5 Ezek 2:7; 3:11, 27; Matt 10:12-15; Acts 13:46; Ezek 33:33; Luke 10:10, 11; John 15:22

2:6 Is 51:12; Jer 1:8, 17; Ezek 3:9; 2 Sam 23:6, 7; Ezek 28:24; Mic 7:4

2:7 Jer 1:7, 17; Ezek 3:10, 17; Ezek 2:5

2:8 Jer 15:16; Ezek 3:3; Rev 10:9

2:9 Ezek 8:3; Jer 36:2; Ezek 3:1; Rev 5:1-5; 10:8-11

1:26 This "figure with the appearance of a man" revealed God's holiness and prepared Ezekiel for what God was about to tell him. The figure represented God himself on the throne. In a similar way, Christ revealed God in human form and prepared us for his message of salvation. Christ came into history in a real, human body.

1:27–28 The glory of the Lord appeared like fire and brilliant light to Ezekiel. Ezekiel fell facedown, overwhelmed by the contrast between God's holiness and his own sinfulness and insignificance. Eventually every person will fall before God, either out of reverence and awe for his mercy or out of fear of his judgment. Based on the way you are living today, how will you respond to God's holiness?

1:27–28 The four living beings and the four wheels are powerful pictures of judgment, yet the rainbow over the throne symbolizes God's never-ending faithfulness to his people. Just as God sent a rainbow to Noah to symbolize his promise never again to destroy the earth by a flood (Genesis 9:8–17), so this rainbow symbolizes God's promise to preserve those who remain faithful to him. The purpose of God's judgment is to correct us and, ultimately, to allow perfect peace and righteousness to reign on the earth forever.

2:1 The immortal God addressed Ezekiel by calling him *son of man,* emphasizing the distance between them. It is amazing that God chooses to work his divine will on earth through finite, imperfect beings. We are made from the dust of the ground, yet God chooses to place within us his life and breath and to ask us to serve him.

2:2 We can only imagine what it was like for Ezekiel to experience this vision. Certainly there was much he did not understand, but Ezekiel knew that each part had significance because it came from God. When God saw Ezekiel's open and obedient attitude, he filled him with his Spirit and gave him power for the job ahead. God doesn't expect us to understand everything about him, but to be willing and obedient servants, faithful to what we know is true and right.

2:3–5 The world of business defines success in terms of giving customers what they want. Ezekiel, however, was called to give God's message to the people, whether they would listen or not. The measure of Ezekiel's success would not be how well the people responded, but how well he obeyed God and thus fulfilled God's purpose for him. Isaiah and Jeremiah also prophesied with little positive response (see Isaiah 6:9–12; Jeremiah 1:17–19). God's truth does not depend on how people respond. God will not judge us for how well others respond to our faith, but for how faithful we have been. God always gives us the strength to accomplish what he asks us to do.

2:4–5 God called the people "stubborn and obstinate" because they refused to admit their sin. Rebelliousness was the nation's primary characteristic at this time. Even when God pointed out their wrongdoing, the people ignored the truth. Is God pointing at some sin in your life? Don't be stubborn—confess your sin and begin to live for God. By obeying him now you will be ready for God's final review of your life (Matthew 25:31–46).

2:6–8 God gave Ezekiel the difficult responsibility of presenting his message to ungrateful and abusive people. Sometimes we must be an example to or share our faith with unkind people. The Lord told Ezekiel not to be afraid and rebel, but to speak his words, whether or not the people would listen. He also wants us to tell the Good News, whether it's convenient or not (2 Timothy 4:2).

2:6–10 Three times God told Ezekiel not to be afraid. When God's Spirit is within us, we can lay aside our fears of rejection or ridicule. God's strength is powerful enough to help us live for him even under the heaviest criticism.

2:9–10 Ancient books were usually scrolls, one page (up to 30

2:10 Is 3:11; Rev 8:13

10 When He spread it out before me, it was written on the front and back, and written
on it were lamentations, mourning and woe.

Ezekiel's Commission

3:1 Ezek 2:9

3:2 Jer 25:17

3:3 Jer 6:11; 20:9; Jer 15:16; Ps 19:10; 119:103; Rev 10:9, 10

3 Then He said to me, "Son of man, eat what you find; eat this scroll, and go, speak to
the house of Israel."
2 So I opened my mouth, and He fed me this scroll.
3 He said to me, "Son of man, feed your stomach and fill your body with this scroll
which I am giving you." Then I ate it, and it was sweet as honey in my mouth.
4 Then He said to me, "Son of man, go to the house of Israel and speak with My words
to them.

Although Ezekiel's visions and prophecies were clear and vivid, very little is known about the prophet's personal life. He was among the thousands of young men deported from Judah to Babylon when King Jehoiakim surrendered. Until those tragic days, Ezekiel was being trained for the priesthood. But during the exile in Babylon, God called Ezekiel to be his prophet during one of Israel's darkest times.

Ezekiel experienced the same kind of shocking encounter with God that Isaiah had reported 150 years earlier. Like Isaiah, Ezekiel was never the same after his personal encounter with God. Although God's messages through both these prophets had many points in common, the conditions in which they lived were very different. Isaiah warned of the coming storm; Ezekiel spoke in the midst of the storm of national defeat that devastated his people. He announced that even Jerusalem would not escape destruction. In addition, during this time Ezekiel had to endure the pain of his wife's death.

God's description of Ezekiel as a watchman on the walls of the city captures the personal nature of his ministry. A watchman's job was dangerous. If he failed at his post, he and the entire city might be destroyed. His own safety depended on the quality of his work. The importance of each person's accountability before God was a central part of Ezekiel's message. He taught the exiles that God expected personal obedience and worship from each of them.

As in Ezekiel's day, it is easy for us today to forget that God has a personal interest in each one of us. We may feel insignificant or out of control when we look at world events. But knowing that God is ultimately in control, that he cares, and that he is willing to be known by us can bring a new sense of purpose to our lives. How do you measure your worth? Are you valuable because of your achievements and potential, or because God, your Creator and Designer, declares you valuable?

Strengths and accomplishments:
- Was a priest by training, a prophet by God's call
- Received vivid visions and delivered powerful messages
- Served as God's messenger during Israel's captivity in Babylon
- God shaped his character to fit his mission—a tough and courageous man to reach a hard and stubborn people (Ezekiel 3:8)

Lessons from his life:
- Even the repeated failures of his people will not prevent God's plan for the world from being fulfilled
- Each person's response to God determines his or her eternal destiny
- In seemingly hopeless situations God still has people through whom he can work

Vital statistics:
- Where: Babylon
- Occupation: Prophet to the captives in Babylon
- Relatives: Father: Buzi. Wife: Unknown
- Contemporaries: Jehoiachin, Jeremiah, Jehoiakim, Nebuchadnezzar

Key verses:
"Moreover, He said to me, 'Son of man, take into your heart all My words which I will speak to you and listen closely. Go to the exiles, to the sons of your people, and speak to them and tell them, whether they listen or not, "Thus says the LORD GOD" ' " (Ezekiel 3:10–11).

Ezekiel's story is told in the book of Ezekiel and 2 Kings 24:10–17.

feet long) rolled up simultaneously from both ends. Normally, scrolls had writing on only one side. But in this case, the warnings overflowed to the scroll's other side, showing the full measure of judgment about to descend on Judah.

3:1–3 In his vision, Ezekiel ate God's message and found this spiritual food not only good for him, but also sweet as honey (see Revelation 10:8–10 for a similar use of this image). If you "digest" God's Word, you will find that not only does it make you stronger in your faith, but its wisdom also sweetens your life. You need to feed yourself spiritually just as you do physically. This means doing more than simply giving God's message a casual glance. You must make digesting God's Word a regular part of your life.

5 "For you are not being sent to a people of unintelligible speech or difficult language,
but to the house of Israel,
6 nor to many peoples of unintelligible speech or difficult language, whose words you
cannot understand. But I have sent you to them who should listen to you;
7 yet the house of Israel will not be willing to listen to you, since they are not willing
to listen to Me. Surely the whole house of Israel is stubborn and obstinate.
8 "Behold, I have made your face as hard as their faces and your forehead as hard as
their foreheads.
9 "Like emery harder than flint I have made your forehead. Do not be afraid of them
or be dismayed before them, though they are a rebellious house."
10 Moreover, He said to me, "Son of man, take into your heart all My words which I
will speak to you and listen closely.
11 "Go to the exiles, to the sons of your people, and speak to them and tell them, whether
they listen or not, 'Thus says the Lord GOD.' "
12 Then the Spirit lifted me up, and I heard a great rumbling sound behind me, "Blessed
be the glory of the LORD in His place."
13 And I *heard* the sound of the wings of the living beings touching one another and
the sound of the wheels beside them, even a great rumbling sound.
14 So the Spirit lifted me up and took me away; and I went embittered in the rage of
my spirit, and the hand of the LORD was strong on me.
15 Then I came to the exiles who lived beside the river Chebar at Tel-abib, and I sat
there seven days where they were living, causing consternation among them.
16 At the end of seven days the word of the LORD came to me, saying,
17 "Son of man, I have appointed you a watchman to the house of Israel; whenever you
hear a word from My mouth, warn them from Me.
18 "When I say to the wicked, 'You will surely die,' and you do not warn him or speak
out to warn the wicked from his wicked way that he may live, that wicked man shall die
in his iniquity, but his blood I will require at your hand.
19 "Yet if you have warned the wicked and he does not turn from his wickedness or from
his wicked way, he shall die in his iniquity; but you have delivered yourself.
20 "Again, when a righteous man turns away from his righteousness and commits iniquity, and I place an obstacle before him, he will die; since you have not warned him, he
shall die in his sin, and his righteous deeds which he has done shall not be remembered;
but his blood I will require at your hand.
21 "However, if you have warned the righteous man that the righteous should not sin
and he does not sin, he shall surely live because he took warning; and you have delivered
yourself."
22 The hand of the LORD was on me there, and He said to me, "Get up, go out to the
plain, and there I will speak to you."

3:5 Jon 1:2; Acts 14:11; 26:17; Is 28:11; 33:19

3:7 1 Sam 8:7

3:10 Job 22:22; Ezek 2:8; 3:1-3

3:12 Ezek 3:14; 8:3; Acts 8:39; Acts 2:2

3:13 Ezek 1:15; 10:16, 17

3:14 2 Kin 3:15

3:15 Job 2:13

3:16 Jer 42:7

3:17 Is 52:8; 56:10; 62:6; Jer 6:17; Ezek 33:7-9; 2 Chr 19:10; Is 58:1; Hab 2:1

3:18 Ezek 3:20; 33:6, 8

3:19 2 Kin 17:13, 14; Ezek 33:3, 9; Ezek 14:14, 20; Acts 18:6; 1 Tim 4:16

3:20 Ps 125:5; Ezek 18:24; 33:18; Zeph 1:6; Is 8:14; Jer 6:21; Ezek 14:3, 7-9

3:21 Acts 20:31

3:22 Acts 9:6

3:10–11 Ezekiel needed to take God's words to heart before preaching them to others. God's message must sink deep into your heart and show in your actions before you can effectively help others understand and apply the gospel.

3:14–15 Ezekiel was bitter and angry, not at God, but at the sins and attitudes of the people. Ezekiel's extraordinary vision had ended, and he had to begin the tedious job of prophesying among his people, who cared little about God's messages. Before the exile, the people had heard Jeremiah, but they would not listen. Here Ezekiel had to give a similar message, and he expected to be rejected as well. But Ezekiel had the vision of the living creatures and the rumbling wheels on his side. He had nothing to fear because God was with him. Despite knowing the probable outcome, Ezekiel obeyed God.

As we grow, we will have times of great joy when we feel close to God, and times when sins, struggles, or everyday tasks overwhelm us. Like Ezekiel, we should obey God even when we don't feel like it. Don't let feelings hinder your obedience.

3:15 Ezekiel sat quietly among the people for seven days. This was the customary period of mourning for the dead (Genesis 50:10; 1 Samuel 31:13; Job 2:13). Ezekiel was mourning for those who were spiritually dead. Tel-abib was the location of the settlement of Jews who were exiled from Jerusalem.

3:17–18 A watchman's job was to stand on the city wall and warn the people of approaching danger. Ezekiel's role was to be a spiritual watchman, warning the people of the judgment to come. Some think that "his blood I will require at your hand" means that, just as a watchman on the wall would pay with his life if he failed to warn the city of approaching enemies, so Ezekiel would have been held accountable if he had refused to warn the people of coming judgment. Others believe this phrase simply means that God would hold Ezekiel responsible.

3:18–21 In these verses, God is not talking about loss of salvation but rather about physical death. If the people back in Judah continued in their sins, they and their land and cities would be destroyed by Nebuchadnezzar's armies. If, on the other hand, the people would turn to God, God would spare them. God would hold Ezekiel responsible for his fellow Jews if he failed to warn them of the consequences of their sins. All people are individually responsible to God, but believers have a special responsibility to warn unbelievers of the consequences of rejecting God. If we fail to do this, God will hold us responsible for what happens to them. This should motivate us to begin sharing our faith with others—by both word and deed—and to avoid becoming callous or unconcerned in our attitude.

3:23 Ezek 1:28; Acts 7:55; Ezek 1:1
3:24 Ezek 2:2
3:25 Ezek 4:8
3:26 Luke 1:20, 22
3:27 Ezek 24:27; 33:22; Ezek 12:2, 3

23 So I got up and went out to the plain; and behold, the glory of the LORD was standing there, like the glory which I saw by the river Chebar, and I fell on my face.
24 The Spirit then entered me and made me stand on my feet, and He spoke with me
and said to me, "Go, shut yourself up in your house.
25 "As for you, son of man, they will put ropes on you and bind you with them so that
you cannot go out among them.
26 "Moreover, I will make your tongue stick to the roof of your mouth so that you will
be mute and cannot be a man who rebukes them, for they are a rebellious house.
27 "But when I speak to you, I will open your mouth and you will say to them, 'Thus
says the Lord GOD.' He who hears, let him hear; and he who refuses, let him refuse; for
they are a rebellious house.

2. Visions of sin and judgment

Siege of Jerusalem Predicted

4:1 Is 20:2; Jer 13:1; 18:2; 19:1
4:2 Jer 6:6; Ezek 21:22
4:3 Jer 39:1, 2; Ezek 5:2; Is 8:18; 20:3; Ezek 12:6, 11; 24:24-27
4:4 Lev 10:17; 16:22; Num 18:1
4:5 Num 14:34

4 "Now you son of man, get yourself a brick, place it before you and inscribe a city on
it, Jerusalem.
2 "Then lay siege against it, build a siege wall, raise up a ramp, pitch camps and place
battering rams against it all around.
3 "Then get yourself an iron plate and set it up as an iron wall between you and the
city, and set your face toward it so that it is under siege, and besiege it. This is a sign to
the house of Israel.
4 "As for you, lie down on your left side and lay the iniquity of the house of Israel on
it; you shall bear their iniquity for the number of days that you lie on it.
5 "For I have assigned you a number of days corresponding to the years of their iniquity,
three hundred and ninety days; thus you shall bear the iniquity of the house of Israel.

EZEKIEL'S ACTS OF OBEDIENCE

2:1	Stood and received God's message
3:24–27	Shut himself inside his house
3:27	Faithfully proclaimed God's message
4:1–3	Drew the city of Jerusalem on a clay tablet
4:4–5	Lay on his left side for 390 days
4:6	Lay on his right side for 40 days
4:9–17	Followed specific cooking instructions
5:1–4	Shaved his head and beard
12:3–7	Left home to demonstrate exile
13:1–23	Spoke against false prophets
19:1–14	Sang a lament concerning the leaders
21:2	Prophesied against Israel and the temple
21:19–23	Marked out two roads for Babylon's king
24:16–17	Did not mourn his wife's death

3:23 Ezekiel recognized his helplessness before God and fell facedown in his presence. Sometimes our prosperity, popularity, or physical strength blind us to our spiritual helplessness. But nothing we do on our own can accomplish much for God. Only when God is in control of our wills can we accomplish great tasks for him. The first step to being God's person is to admit that you need his help; then you can begin to see what God can really do in your life.

3:24–27 Ezekiel was allowed to speak only when God had a message for the people. Thus the people knew that whatever Ezekiel said was God's message. They did not have to wonder whether Ezekiel was speaking by God's authority or his own.

4:1ff Ezekiel acted out the coming siege and fall of Jerusalem before it actually happened. God gave Ezekiel specific instructions about what to do and say and how to do and say it. Each detail had a specific meaning. Often we ignore or disregard the smaller details of God's Word, thinking God probably doesn't care. Like Ezekiel, we should want to obey God completely, even in the details.

4:4–17 Ezekiel's unusual actions symbolically portrayed the fate of Jerusalem. He lay on his left side for 390 days to show that Israel would be punished for 390 years; then he lay on his right side for 40 days to show that Judah would be punished for 40 years. Ezekiel was not allowed to move, symbolizing the fact that the people of Jerusalem would be imprisoned within the walls of the city. We know that Ezekiel did not have to lie on his side all day because these verses tell of other tasks God asked him to do during this time. The small amount of food he was allowed to eat represented the normal ration provided to those living in a city under siege by enemy armies. The food that was to be cooked over human excrement was a symbol of Judah's spiritual uncleanness.

Certainly many people saw these spectacles and, in the process, heard Ezekiel's occasional speeches (3:27). How many of us would be willing to so dramatically portray the sins of our nation? We need to pray for greater boldness in our witness.

6 "When you have completed these, you shall lie down a second time, *but* on your right
side and bear the iniquity of the house of Judah; I have assigned it to you for forty days,
a day for each year.
7 "Then you shall set your face toward the siege of Jerusalem with your arm bared and
prophesy against it.
8 "Now behold, I will put ropes on you so that you cannot turn from one side to the
other until you have completed the days of your siege.

Defiled Bread

9 "But as for you, take wheat, barley, beans, lentils, millet and spelt, put them in one
vessel and make them into bread for yourself; you shall eat it according to the number of
the days that you lie on your side, three hundred and ninety days.
10 "Your food which you eat *shall be* twenty shekels a day by weight; you shall eat it
from time to time.
11 "The water you drink shall be the sixth part of a hin by measure; you shall drink it
from time to time.
12 "You shall eat it as a barley cake, having baked *it* in their sight over human dung."
13 Then the LORD said, "Thus will the sons of Israel eat their bread unclean among
the nations where I will banish them."
14 But I said, "Ah, Lord GOD! Behold, I have never been defiled; for from my youth
until now I have never eaten what died of itself or was torn by beasts, nor has any unclean meat ever entered my mouth."
15 Then He said to me, "See, I will give you cow's dung in place of human dung over
which you will prepare your bread."
16 Moreover, He said to me, "Son of man, behold, I am going to break the staff of
bread in Jerusalem, and they will eat bread by weight and with anxiety, and drink water
by measure and in horror,
17 because bread and water will be scarce; and they will be appalled with one another
and waste away in their iniquity.

Jerusalem's Desolation Foretold

5 "As for you, son of man, take a sharp sword; take and use it *as* a barber's razor on
your head and beard. Then take scales for weighing and divide the hair.
2 "One third you shall burn in the fire at the center of the city, when the days of the
siege are completed. Then you shall take one third and strike *it* with the sword all around
the city, and one third you shall scatter to the wind; and I will unsheathe a sword behind
them.
3 "Take also a few in number from them and bind them in the edges of your *robes.*
4 "Take again some of them and throw them into the fire and burn them in the fire;
from it a fire will spread to all the house of Israel.
5 "Thus says the Lord GOD, 'This is Jerusalem; I have set her at the center of the nations, with lands around her.
6 'But she has rebelled against My ordinances more wickedly than the nations and
against My statutes more than the lands which surround her; for they have rejected My
ordinances and have not walked in My statutes.'
7 "Therefore, thus says the Lord GOD, 'Because you have more turmoil than the na-

4:6 Num 14:34; Dan 9:24-26; 12:11, 12; Rev 11:2, 3
4:7 Ezek 21:2
4:8 Ezek 3:25
4:9 Ex 9:32; Is 28:25
4:10 Ezek 45:12
4:12 Is 36:12
4:13 Dan 1:8; Hos 9:3
4:14 Jer 1:6; Ezek 9:8; 20:49; Acts 10:14; Lev 17:15; 22:8; Ezek 44:31; Deut 14:3; Is 65:4; 66:17
4:16 Lev 26:26; Is 3:1; Ezek 5:16; 14:13; Ezek 4:10, 11; 12:19; Lam 5:4; Ezek 12:18, 19
4:17 Lev 26:39; Ezek 24:23; 33:10
5:1 Lev 21:5; Is 7:20; Ezek 44:20; Dan 5:27
5:2 Jer 39:1, 2; Ezek 4:2-8; Lev 26:33
5:5 Jer 6:6; Ezek 4:1; Deut 4:6; Lam 1:1; Ezek 16:14
5:6 2 Kin 17:8-20; Ezek 16:47, 48, 51; Neh 9:16, 17; Ps 78:10; Jer 11:10; Zech 7:11
5:7 2 Kin 21:9-11; 2 Chr 33:9; Jer 2:10, 11

4:12–14 Ezekiel asked God not to make him use human dung for fuel because it violated the laws for purity (Leviticus 21; 22; Deuteronomy 23:12–14). As a priest, Ezekiel would have been careful to keep all these laws. To use human dung for fuel would paint a dramatic picture of ruin. If nothing was left in the city that could be burned, it would be impossible to continue to follow God's laws for sacrifices.

5:1–10 Shaving one's head and beard signified mourning, humiliation, and repentance. God told Ezekiel to shave his head and beard and then to divide the hair into three parts, symbolizing what was going to happen to the people in Jerusalem (see 5:12). Along with verbal prophecies, God asked Ezekiel to use dramatic visual images to command the people's attention and to burn an indelible impression on their minds. Just as God gave Ezekiel creative ways to communicate his message to the exiles, so we can creatively communicate the Good News about God to a lost generation.

5:3–4 The few strands of hair Ezekiel put in his garment symbolized the small remnant of faithful people whom God would preserve. But even some from this remnant would be judged and destroyed because their faith was not genuine. Where will you stand in the coming judgment? Matthew 7:22–23 warns that many who believe they are safe are not. Make sure your commitment is vital and heartfelt.

5:7 The people's wickedness was so great that they couldn't even keep the laws of the pagan nations around them, not to mention God's laws.

tions which surround you *and* have not walked in My statutes, nor observed My ordinances, nor observed the ordinances of the nations which surround you,'
8 therefore, thus says the Lord GOD, 'Behold, I, even I, am against you, and I will
execute judgments among you in the sight of the nations.
9 'And because of all your abominations, I will do among you what I have not done,
and the like of which I will never do again.
10 'Therefore, fathers will eat *their* sons among you, and sons will eat their fathers; for
I will execute judgments on you and scatter all your remnant to every wind.
11 'So as I live,' declares the Lord GOD, 'surely, because you have defiled My sanctuary
with all your detestable idols and with all your abominations, therefore I will also withdraw, and My eye will have no pity and I will not spare.
12 'One third of you will die by plague or be consumed by famine among you, one third
will fall by the sword around you, and one third I will scatter to every wind, and I will
unsheathe a sword behind them.
13 'Thus My anger will be spent and I will satisfy My wrath on them, and I will be appeased; then they will know that I, the LORD, have spoken in My zeal when I have spent
My wrath upon them.
14 'Moreover, I will make you a desolation and a reproach among the nations which
surround you, in the sight of all who pass by.
15 'So it will be a reproach, a reviling, a warning and an object of horror to the nations
who surround you when I execute judgments against you in anger, wrath and raging rebukes. I, the LORD, have spoken.
16 'When I send against them the deadly arrows of famine which were for the destruction of those whom I will send to destroy you, then I will also intensify the famine upon
you and break the staff of bread.
17 'Moreover, I will send on you famine and wild beasts, and they will bereave you of
children; plague and bloodshed also will pass through you, and I will bring the sword on
you. I, the LORD, have spoken.' "

Idolatrous Worship Denounced

6 And the word of the LORD came to me saying,
2 "Son of man, set your face toward the mountains of Israel, and prophesy against
them
3 and say, 'Mountains of Israel, listen to the word of the Lord GOD! Thus says the
Lord GOD to the mountains, the hills, the ravines and the valleys: "Behold, I Myself am
going to bring a sword on you, and I will destroy your high places.
4 "So your altars will become desolate and your incense altars will be smashed; and I
will make your slain fall in front of your idols.
5 "I will also lay the dead bodies of the sons of Israel in front of their idols; and I will
scatter your bones around your altars.
6 "In all your dwellings, cities will become waste and the high places will be desolate,
that your altars may become waste and desolate, your idols may be broken and brought
to an end, your incense altars may be cut down, and your works may be blotted out.
7 "The slain will fall among you, and you will know that I am the LORD.

5:8 Jer 21:5, 13; Ezek 15:7; 21:3; Zech 14:2; Jer 24:9; Ezek 5:15; 11:9

5:9 Dan 9:12; Amos 3:2; Matt 24:21

5:10 Lev 26:29; Jer 19:9; Lam 4:10; Ps 44:11; Ezek 5:2, 12; 6:8; 12:14; Amos 9:9; Zech 2:6; 7:14

5:11 Jer 7:9-11; Ezek 8:5, 6, 16; Jer 16:18; Ezek 7:20

5:12 Jer 15:2; 21:9; Ezek 5:17; 6:11, 12; Ezek 5:2, 10; Amos 9:9; Zech 2:6; Jer 43:10, 11; 44:27; Ezek 5:2; 12:14

5:13 Is 1:24; Is 59:17; Ezek 36:5, 6; 38:19

5:14 Ps 74:3-10; 79:1-4; Ezek 22:4

5:15 Is 26:9; Jer 22:8, 9; 1 Cor 10:11; Is 66:15, 16; Ezek 5:8; 25:17

5:17 Lev 26:22; Rev 6:8; Ezek 38:22

6:2 Ezek 36:1

6:3 Lev 26:30

6:4 Lev 26:30; 2 Chr 14:5; Is 27:9; Ezek 6:6

6:5 2 Kin 23:14, 16, 20; Jer 8:1, 2

6:6 Lev 26:31; Is 6:11; Ezek 5:14; Ezek 6:4; Mic 1:7; Zech 13:2

5:11 It was a serious sin to defile the temple, God's sanctuary, by worshiping idols and practicing evil within its very walls. In the New Testament, we learn that God now makes his home *within* those who are his. Our bodies are God's temple (see 1 Corinthians 6:19). We defile God's temple today by allowing gossiping, bitterness, love of money, lying, or any other wrong actions or attitudes to be a part of our lives. By asking the Holy Spirit's help, we can keep from defiling his temple, our bodies.

5:13 Have you ever seen someone try to discipline a child by saying, "If you do that one more time . . ."? If the parent doesn't follow through, the child learns not to listen. Empty threats backfire. God was going to punish the Israelites for their blatant sins, and he wanted them to know that he would do what he said. The people learned the hard way that God always follows through on his word. Too many people ignore God's warnings, treating them as empty threats. But what God threatens, he does. Don't make the mistake of thinking God doesn't really mean what he says.

6:1ff This is the beginning of a two-part message. Remember that Ezekiel could speak only when giving messages from God. The message in chapter 6 is that Judah's idolatry will surely call down God's judgment. The message in chapter 7 describes the nature of that judgment—utter destruction of the nation. Nevertheless, God in his mercy saved a remnant. Ezekiel prophesies against the mountains of Israel because mountains were sites of the "high places" used to worship idols.

8 "However, I will leave a remnant, for you will have those who escaped the sword
among the nations when you are scattered among the countries.
9 "Then those of you who escape will remember Me among the nations to which they
will be carried captive, how I have been hurt by their adulterous hearts which turned
away from Me, and by their eyes which played the harlot after their idols; and they will
loathe themselves in their own sight for the evils which they have committed, for all their
abominations.
10 "Then they will know that I am the LORD; I have not said in vain that I would inflict
this disaster on them." '
11 "Thus says the Lord GOD, 'Clap your hand, stamp your foot and say, "Alas, because
of all the evil abominations of the house of Israel, which will fall by sword, famine and
plague!
12 "He who is far off will die by the plague, and he who is near will fall by the sword, and
he who remains and is besieged will die by the famine. Thus will I spend My wrath on
them.
13 "Then you will know that I am the LORD, when their slain are among their idols around
their altars, on every high hill, on all the tops of the mountains, under every green tree
and under every leafy oak—the places where they offered soothing aroma to all their
idols.
14 "So throughout all their habitations I will stretch out My hand against them and make
the land more desolate and waste than the wilderness toward Diblah; thus they will know
that I am the LORD." ' "

Punishment for Wickedness Foretold

7 Moreover, the word of the LORD came to me saying,
2 "And you, son of man, thus says the Lord GOD to the land of Israel, 'An end! The
end is coming on the four corners of the land.
3 'Now the end is upon you, and I will send My anger against you; I will judge you
according to your ways and bring all your abominations upon you.
4 'For My eye will have no pity on you, nor will I spare *you,* but I will bring your ways
upon you, and your abominations will be among you; then you will know that I am the
LORD!'
5 "Thus says the Lord GOD, 'A disaster, unique disaster, behold it is coming!
6 'An end is coming; the end has come! It has awakened against you; behold, it has come!
7 'Your doom has come to you, O inhabitant of the land. The time has come, the day
is near—tumult rather than joyful shouting on the mountains.
8 'Now I will shortly pour out My wrath on you and spend My anger against you; judge
you according to your ways and bring on you all your abominations.
9 'My eye will show no pity nor will I spare. I will repay you according to your ways,
while your abominations are in your midst; then you will know that I, the LORD, do the
smiting.
10 'Behold, the day! Behold, it is coming! *Your* doom has gone forth; the rod has budded, arrogance has blossomed.
11 'Violence has grown into a rod of wickedness. None of them *shall remain,* none of
their people, none of their wealth, nor anything eminent among them.
12 'The time has come, the day has arrived. Let not the buyer rejoice nor the seller
mourn; for wrath is against all their multitude.

6:8 Is 6:13; Jer 30:11; Jer 44:14, 28; Ezek 7:16; 14:22
6:9 Deut 4:29; 30:2; Jer 51:50; Ps 78:40; Is 7:13; 43:24; Hos 11:8; Job 42:6; Ezek 20:43; 36:31
6:11 Ezek 25:6; Ezek 9:4; Ezek 5:12; 7:15
6:12 Dan 9:7; Lam 4:11, 22; Ezek 5:13
6:13 Ezek 6:4-7; 1 Kin 14:23; 2 Kin 16:4; Is 57:5-7; Ezek 20:28; Hos 4:13
6:14 Is 5:25; 9:12; Ezek 14:13; 20:33, 34
7:2 Ezek 7:3, 5, 6; 11:13; Amos 8:2, 10
7:4 Ezek 11:21; 22:31; Hos 9:7; Ezek 6:7, 14; 7:27
7:5 2 Kin 21:12, 13; Nah 1:9
7:6 Zech 13:7
7:7 Ezek 7:12; 12:23-25, 28; Is 22:5
7:8 Is 42:25; Ezek 9:8; 14:19; Nah 1:6; Ezek 7:3; 33:20; 36:19
7:10 Ps 89:32; Is 10:5
7:11 Ps 73:8; 125:3; Is 59:6-8; Zeph 1:18
7:12 Ezek 7:5-7, 10; 1 Cor 7:29-31; James 5:8, 9; Prov 20:14; 1 Cor 7:30; Is 5:13, 14; Ezek 6:11, 12; 7:14

6:8–10 A ray of light appears in this prophecy of darkness—God would spare a remnant of people, but only after they had learned some hard lessons. God sometimes has to break a person in order to bring him or her to true repentance. The people needed new attitudes, but they wouldn't change until God broke their hearts with humiliation, pain, suffering, and defeat. Does your heart long for God enough to change those areas displeasing him? Or will God have to break your heart?

6:11 Prophets often used this threefold description of judgment upon Jerusalem—sword, famine, and plague—as a way of saying that the destruction would be complete. The sword meant death in battle; famine came when enemies besieged a city; plague was always a danger during famine. Don't make the mistake of underestimating the extent of God's judgment. If you ignore the Biblical warnings and turn away from God, God's punishment awaits you.

6:14 The phrase "they will know that I am the LORD" (or a variation on this phrase) occurs 65 times in the book of Ezekiel. The purpose of all God's punishment was not to take revenge, but to impress upon the people the truth that the Lord is the only true and living God. People in Ezekiel's day were worshiping man-made idols and calling them gods. Today money, sex, and power have become idols for many. Punishment will come upon all who put other things ahead of God. It is easy to forget that the Lord alone is God, the supreme authority and the only source of eternal love and life. Remember that God may use the difficulties of your life to teach you that he alone is God.

7:10–11 In chapter 7, Ezekiel predicts the complete destruction of Judah. The wicked and proud will finally get what they deserve. If it

13 'Indeed, the seller will not regain what he sold as long as they *both* live; for the vision
regarding all their multitude will not be averted, nor will any of them maintain his life by
his iniquity.
14 'They have blown the trumpet and made everything ready, but no one is going to the
battle, for My wrath is against all their multitude.
15 'The sword is outside and the plague and the famine are within. He who is in the
field will die by the sword; famine and the plague will also consume those in the city.
16 'Even when their survivors escape, they will be on the mountains like doves of the
valleys, all of them mourning, each over his own iniquity.
17 'All hands will hang limp and all knees will become *like* water.
18 'They will gird themselves with sackcloth and shuddering will overwhelm them; and
shame *will be* on all faces and baldness on all their heads.
19 'They will fling their silver into the streets and their gold will become an abhorrent
thing; their silver and their gold will not be able to deliver them in the day of the wrath
of the LORD. They cannot satisfy their appetite nor can they fill their stomachs, for their
iniquity has become an occasion of stumbling.

The Temple Profaned

20 'They transformed the beauty of His ornaments into pride, and they made the images of their abominations *and* their detestable things with it; therefore I will make it an
abhorrent thing to them.
21 'I will give it into the hands of the foreigners as plunder and to the wicked of the
earth as spoil, and they will profane it.
22 'I will also turn My face from them, and they will profane My secret place; then robbers will enter and profane it.
23 'Make the chain, for the land is full of bloody crimes and the city is full of violence.
24 'Therefore, I will bring the worst of the nations, and they will possess their houses. I
will also make the pride of the strong ones cease, and their holy places will be profaned.
25 'When anguish comes, they will seek peace, but there will be none.
26 'Disaster will come upon disaster and rumor will be *added* to rumor; then they will
seek a vision from a prophet, but the law will be lost from the priest and counsel from
the elders.
27 'The king will mourn, the prince will be clothed with horror, and the hands of the
people of the land will tremble. According to their conduct I will deal with them, and by
their judgments I will judge them. And they will know that I am the LORD.' "

Vision of Abominations in Jerusalem

8 It came about in the sixth year, on the fifth *day* of the sixth month, as I was sitting in
my house with the elders of Judah sitting before me, that the hand of the Lord GOD
fell on me there.

7:13 Lev 25:24-28, 31
7:14 Num 10:9; Jer 4:5
7:15 Jer 14:18; Ezek 5:12; 6:11, 12; 12:16
7:16 Ezra 9:15; Is 37:31; Ezek 6:8; 14:22; Is 38:14; Is 59:11; Nah 2:7
7:17 Is 13:7; Ezek 21:7; 22:14; Heb 12:12
7:18 Is 15:3; Ezek 27:31; Amos 8:10; Job 21:6; Ps 55:5; Ezek 27:31
7:19 Is 2:20; 30:22; Prov 11:4; Zeph 1:18
7:20 Jer 7:30
7:21 2 Kin 24:13; Ps 74:2-8; Jer 52:13
7:22 Jer 18:17; Ezek 39:23, 24
7:23 Jer 27:2; Ezek 9:9; Hos 4:2; Ezek 8:17
7:24 Ezek 21:31; 28:7; Ezek 33:28; 2 Chr 7:20; Ezek 24:21
7:25 Ezek 13:10, 16
7:26 Is 47:11; Jer 4:20; Ezek 21:7; Jer 21:2; 37:17; Ps 74:9; Ezek 22:26; Mic 3:6; Jer 18:18; Ezek 11:2
7:27 Job 8:22; Ps 35:26; 109:18, 29; Ezek 26:16

---

seems as though God ignores the evil and proud people of our day, be assured that a day of judgment will come, just as it came for the people of Judah. God is waiting patiently for sinners to repent (see 2 Peter 3:9), but when his judgment comes, "none of them shall remain." What you decide about God now will determine your fate then.

7:12–13 The nation of Judah trusted in its prosperity and possessions instead of in God. So God planned to destroy the basis of its prosperity. Whenever we begin to trust in jobs, the economy, a political system, or military might for our security, we put God in the back seat.

7:19 God's people had allowed their love of money to lead them into sin. And for this, God would destroy them. Money has a strange power to lead people into sin. Paul said that "the love of money is a root of all sorts of evil" (1 Timothy 6:10). It is ironic that we use money—a gift of God—to buy things that separate us from him. It is tragic that we spend so much money seeking to satisfy ourselves, and so little time seeking God, the true source of satisfaction.

7:20 God gave the people silver and gold, but they used that silver and gold to make idols. The resources God gives us should be used to do his work and carry out his will, but too often we use them to satisfy our own desires. When we abuse God's gifts or use resources selfishly, we miss the real purpose God had in mind. This is as shortsighted as idolatry.

7:24 The people of Jerusalem took great pride in their buildings. The temple itself was a source of pride (see 24:20–21). This pride would be crushed when the evil and godless Babylonians destroyed Jerusalem's houses and holy places. If you are going through a humiliating experience, God may be using that experience to weed out pride in your life.

8:1ff This prophecy's date corresponds to 592 B.C. The message of chapters 8—11 is directed specifically toward Jerusalem and its leaders. Chapter 8 records Ezekiel being taken in a vision from Babylon to the temple in Jerusalem to see the great wickedness being practiced there. The people and their religious leaders were thoroughly corrupt. While Ezekiel's first vision (chapters 1—3) showed that judgment was from God, this vision showed that their sin was the reason for judgment.

2 Then I looked, and behold, a likeness as the appearance of a man; from His loins
and downward *there was* the appearance of fire, and from His loins and upward the appearance of brightness, like the appearance of glowing metal.
3 He stretched out the form of a hand and caught me by a lock of my head; and the
Spirit lifted me up between earth and heaven and brought me in the visions of God to
Jerusalem, to the entrance of the north gate of the inner *court,* where the seat of the idol
of jealousy, which provokes to jealousy, was *located.*
4 And behold, the glory of the God of Israel *was* there, like the appearance which I
saw in the plain.
5 Then He said to me, "Son of man, raise your eyes now toward the north." So I raised
my eyes toward the north, and behold, to the north of the altar gate *was* this idol of jealousy at the entrance.
6 And He said to me, "Son of man, do you see what they are doing, the great abominations which the house of Israel are committing here, so that I would be far from My
sanctuary? But yet you will see still greater abominations."
7 Then He brought me to the entrance of the court, and when I looked, behold, a
hole in the wall.
8 He said to me, "Son of man, now dig through the wall." So I dug through the wall,
and behold, an entrance.
9 And He said to me, "Go in and see the wicked abominations that they are committing here."
10 So I entered and looked, and behold, every form of creeping things and beasts *and*
detestable things, with all the idols of the house of Israel, were carved on the wall all
around.
11 Standing in front of them were seventy elders of the house of Israel, with Jaazaniah
the son of Shaphan standing among them, each man with his censer in his hand and the
fragrance of the cloud of incense rising.
12 Then He said to me, "Son of man, do you see what the elders of the house of Israel
are committing in the dark, each man in the room of his carved images? For they say,
'The LORD does not see us; the LORD has forsaken the land.' "
13 And He said to me, "Yet you will see still greater abominations which they are committing."
14 Then He brought me to the entrance of the gate of the LORD'S house which *was*
toward the north; and behold, women were sitting there weeping for Tammuz.
15 He said to me, "Do you see *this,* son of man? Yet you will see still greater abominations than these."
16 Then He brought me into the inner court of the LORD'S house. And behold, at the
entrance to the temple of the LORD, between the porch and the altar, *were* about twenty-five men with their backs to the temple of the LORD and their faces toward the east;
and they were prostrating themselves eastward toward the sun.
17 He said to me, "Do you see *this,* son of man? Is it too light a thing for the house of
Judah to commit the abominations which they have committed here, that they have filled
the land with violence and provoked Me repeatedly? For behold, they are putting the
twig to their nose.
18 "Therefore, I indeed will deal in wrath. My eye will have no pity nor will I spare; and
though they cry in My ears with a loud voice, yet I will not listen to them."

8:2 Ezek 1:27; Ezek 14:27

8:3 Ezek 3:12; 11:1; Ex 20:4; Deut 32:16

8:4 Ezek 1:28; 3:22, 23

8:5 Jer 3:2; Zech 5:5; Ps 78:58; Jer 7:30; 32:34; Ezek 8:3

8:6 2 Kin 23:4, 5; Ezek 5:11; 8:9, 17

8:8 Is 29:15

8:11 Num 11:16, 25; Luke 10:1; Jer 19:1; Num 16:17, 35

8:12 Ps 14:1; Is 29:15; Ezek 9:9; Ps 10:11

8:14 Ezek 44:4; 46:9

8:16 2 Chr 29:6; Jer 2:27; Ezek 23:39; Deut 4:19; 17:3; Job 31:26-28; Jer 44:17

8:17 Ezek 7:11, 23; 9:9; Amos 3:10; Mic 2:2; Jer 7:18, 19; Ezek 16:26

8:18 Is 1:15; Jer 11:11; Mic 3:4; Zech 7:13

8:2 This person could have been an angel or a manifestation of God himself. In Ezekiel's previous vision, a man with a similar appearance was pictured as God on his throne (1:26–28).

8:3–5 This "idol of jealousy" could be an image of Asherah, the Canaanite goddess of fertility, whose character encouraged sexual immorality and self-gratification. King Manasseh had placed such an idol in the temple (2 Kings 21:7). King Josiah had burned the Asherah pole (2 Kings 23:6), but there were certainly many other idols around.

8:6ff In scene after scene, God revealed to Ezekiel the extent to which the people had embraced idolatry and wickedness. God's Spirit works within us in a similar way, revealing sin that lurks in our lives. How comfortable would you feel if God held an open house in your life today?

8:14 Tammuz was the Babylonian god of spring. He was the husband or lover of the goddess Ishtar. The followers of this cult believed that the green vegetation shriveled and died in the hot summer because Tammuz had died and descended into the underworld. Thus, the worshipers wept and mourned his death. In the springtime, when the new vegetation appeared, they rejoiced, believing that Tammuz had come back to life. God was showing Ezekiel that many people were no longer worshiping the *true* God of life and vegetation. We must also be careful not to spend so much time thinking about the benefits of creation that we lose sight of the Creator.

8:17 The twig to the nose could refer either to a cultic worship practice or to the fact that Judah's sins had become a stench to God.

The Vision of Slaughter

9 Then He cried out in my hearing with a loud voice saying, "Draw near, O execution-
ers of the city, each with his destroying weapon in his hand."
2 Behold, six men came from the direction of the upper gate which faces north, each
with his shattering weapon in his hand; and among them was a certain man clothed in
linen with a writing case at his loins. And they went in and stood beside the bronze altar.
3 Then the glory of the God of Israel went up from the cherub on which it had been,
to the threshold of the temple. And He called to the man clothed in linen at whose loins
was the writing case.
4 The LORD said to him, "Go through the midst of the city, *even* through the midst of
Jerusalem, and put a mark on the foreheads of the men who sigh and groan over all the
abominations which are being committed in its midst."
5 But to the others He said in my hearing, "Go through the city after him and strike;
do not let your eye have pity and do not spare.
6 "Utterly slay old men, young men, maidens, little children, and women, but do not
touch any man on whom is the mark; and you shall start from My sanctuary." So they
started with the elders who *were* before the temple.
7 And He said to them, "Defile the temple and fill the courts with the slain. Go out!"
Thus they went out and struck down *the people* in the city.
8 As they were striking *the people* and I *alone* was left, I fell on my face and cried out
saying, "Alas, Lord GOD! Are You destroying the whole remnant of Israel by pouring
out Your wrath on Jerusalem?"
9 Then He said to me, "The iniquity of the house of Israel and Judah is very, very
great, and the land is filled with blood and the city is full of perversion; for they say, 'The
LORD has forsaken the land, and the LORD does not see!'
10 "But as for Me, My eye will have no pity nor will I spare, but I will bring their conduct upon their heads."
11 Then behold, the man clothed in linen at whose loins was the writing case reported,
saying, "I have done just as You have commanded me."

Vision of God's Glory Departing from the Temple

10 Then I looked, and behold, in the expanse that was over the heads of the cherubim something like a sapphire stone, in appearance resembling a throne, appeared
above them.

9:1 Is 6:8
9:2 Lev 16:4
9:3 Ezek 10:4; 11:22, 23
9:4 Ex 12:7, 13; Ezek 9:6; 2 Cor 1:22; 2 Tim 2:19; Rev 7:2, 3; 9:4; 14:1; Ps 119:53, 136; Jer 13:17; Ezek 6:11; 21:6
9:6 2 Chr 36:17; Ex 12:23; Rev 9:4; Jer 25:29; Amos 3:2; Luke 12:47
9:7 2 Chr 36:17; Ezek 7:20-22
9:8 1 Chr 21:16; Ezek 11:13; Amos 7:2-6
9:9 2 Kin 21:16; Jer 2:34; Ezek 7:23; 22:2, 3; Ezek 22:29; Mic 3:1-3; 7:3; Job 22:13; Ps 10:11; 94:7; Is 29:15; Ezek 8:12
9:10 Is 65:6; Ezek 8:18; 24:14; Ezek 7:4; 11:21; Hos 9:7
10:1 Ezek 1:22, 26; Ex 24:10; Rev 4:2, 3

9:1ff This chapter presents a picture of coming judgment. After Ezekiel had seen how corrupt Jerusalem had become, God called one man to spare the small minority who had been faithful. Then he called six men to slaughter the wicked people in the city. This judgment was ordered by God himself (9:5–7).

9:2 The writing case was a common object in Ezekiel's day. It included a long narrow board with a groove to hold the reed brush that was used to write on parchment, papyrus, or dried clay. The board had hollowed out areas for holding cakes of black and red ink that had to be moistened before use.

9:3 What is God's glory? It is the manifestation of God's character—his ultimate power, transcendence, and moral perfection. God is completely above man and his limitations. Yet God reveals himself to us so that we can worship and follow him.

9:3 Cherubim ("cherub" is singular) are an order of powerful angelic beings created to glorify God. They are associated with God's absolute holiness and moral perfection. God placed cherubim at the entrance of Eden to keep Adam and Eve out after they sinned (Genesis 3:24). Representations of cherubim were used to decorate the tabernacle and temple. The lid of the ark of the covenant, called the atonement cover, was adorned with two gold cherubim (Exodus 37:6–9). It was a symbol of the very presence of God. The cherubim seen by Ezekiel left the temple along with the glory of God (chapter 10). Ezekiel then recognized them as the living creatures he had seen in his first vision (see chapter 1).

9:4–5 God told the man with the writing case to put a mark on those who were faithful to God. Their faithfulness was determined by their sensitivity to and sorrow over their nation's sin. Those with the mark were spared when the six men began to destroy the wicked people. During the exodus, the Israelites put a mark of blood on their doorposts to save them from death. In the final days, God will mark the foreheads of those destined for salvation (Revelation 7:3), and Satan will mark his followers (Revelation 13:16–17), who, like him, are destined for destruction. When God punishes sin, he won't forget his promise to preserve his people.

9:6 The spiritual leaders ("elders") of Israel blatantly promoted their idolatrous beliefs, and the people abandoned God and followed them. Spiritual leaders are especially accountable to God because they are entrusted with the task of teaching the truth (see James 3:1). When they pervert the truth, they can lead countless people away from God and even cause a nation to fall. It is not surprising, then, that when God began to judge the nation, he started at the temple and worked outward (see 1 Peter 4:17). How sad it is that in the temple, the one place where they should have been teaching God's truth, they were teaching lies.

9:9–10 The people said that the Lord had forsaken the land and wouldn't see their sin. People have many convenient explanations to make it easier to sin: "It doesn't matter," "Everybody's doing it," or "Nobody will ever know." Do you find yourself making excuses for sin? Rationalizing sin makes it easier to commit, but rationalization does not convince God or cancel the punishment.

10:1ff Chapters 8—11 depict God's glory departing from the temple. In 8:3–4, his glory was over the north gate. It then moved to the door (the "threshold," 9:3), the south side of the temple (10:3–4), the eastern gate (10:18–19; 11:1), and finally the mountain east of the temple (11:23), probably the Mount of Olives. Because of the nation's sins, God's glory had departed.

2 And He spoke to the man clothed in linen and said, "Enter between the whirling
wheels under the cherubim and fill your hands with coals of fire from between the cherubim and scatter *them* over the city." And he entered in my sight.

10:2 Ezek 1:15-21; 10:13; Ps 18:10-13; Is 6:6; Ezek 1:13; Rev 8:5

3 Now the cherubim were standing on the right side of the temple when the man
entered, and the cloud filled the inner court.

10:3 Ezek 8:3, 16

4 Then the glory of the LORD went up from the cherub to the threshold of the temple, and the temple was filled with the cloud and the court was filled with the brightness
of the glory of the LORD.

10:4 Ezek 9:3; 11:22, 23; Ex 40:34, 35; Is 6:1-4; Ezek 1:28

5 Moreover, the sound of the wings of the cherubim was heard as far as the outer court,
like the voice of God Almighty when He speaks.

10:5 Job 40:9; Ezek 1:24; Rev 10:3

6 It came about when He commanded the man clothed in linen, saying, "Take fire
from between the whirling wheels, from between the cherubim," he entered and stood
beside a wheel.

7 Then the cherub stretched out his hand from between the cherubim to the fire which
was between the cherubim, took *some* and put *it* into the hands of the one clothed in
linen, who took *it* and went out.

8 The cherubim appeared to have the form of a man's hand under their wings.

9 Then I looked, and behold, four wheels beside the cherubim, one wheel beside each
cherub; and the appearance of the wheels *was* like the gleam of a Tarshish stone.

10:9 Ezek 1:15-17; Dan 10:6; Rev 21:20

10 As for their appearance, all four of them had the same likeness, as if one wheel were
within another wheel.

11 When they moved, they went in *any of* their four directions without turning as they
went; but they followed in the direction which they faced, without turning as they went.

10:11 Ezek 1:17

12 Their whole body, their backs, their hands, their wings and the wheels were full of
eyes all around, the wheels belonging to all four of them.

10:12 Rev 4:6, 8; Ezek 1:18

13 The wheels were called in my hearing, the whirling wheels.

14 And each one had four faces. The first face *was* the face of a cherub, the second
face *was* the face of a man, the third the face of a lion, and the fourth the face of an
eagle.

10:14 1 Kin 7:29, 36; Ezek 1:6, 10; 10:21; Rev 4:7

15 Then the cherubim rose up. They are the living beings that I saw by the river Chebar.

10:15 Ezek 1:3, 5

16 Now when the cherubim moved, the wheels would go beside them; also when the
cherubim lifted up their wings to rise from the ground, the wheels would not turn from
beside them.

17 When the cherubim stood still, the wheels would stand still; and when they rose up,
the wheels would rise with them, for the spirit of the living beings *was* in them.

10:17 Ezek 1:21

18 Then the glory of the LORD departed from the threshold of the temple and stood
over the cherubim.

10:18 Ps 18:10

19 When the cherubim departed, they lifted their wings and rose up from the earth in
my sight with the wheels beside them; and they stood still at the entrance of the east gate
of the LORD'S house, and the glory of the God of Israel hovered over them.

10:19 Ezek 11:22

20 These are the living beings that I saw beneath the God of Israel by the river Chebar;
so I knew that they *were* cherubim.

10:20 Ezek 1:5, 22, 26; 10:15; Ezek 1:1

21 Each one had four faces and each one four wings, and beneath their wings *was* the
form of human hands.

10:21 Ezek 1:6, 8; 10:14; 41:18, 19

22 As for the likeness of their faces, they were the same faces whose appearance I had
seen by the river Chebar. Each one went straight ahead.

Evil Rulers to Be Judged

11 Moreover, the Spirit lifted me up and brought me to the east gate of the LORD'S
house which faced eastward. And behold, *there were* twenty-five men at the entrance of the gate, and among them I saw Jaazaniah son of Azzur and Pelatiah son of
Benaiah, leaders of the people.

11:1 Ezek 3:12, 14; 8:3; 11:24; 43:5; Ezek 11:13

10:2 God's perfect holiness demands judgment for sin. The cherubim are mighty angels. The coals of fire scattered over the city represent the purging of sin. For Jerusalem, this meant the destruction of all the people who blatantly sinned and refused to repent. Shortly after this prophecy, the Babylonians destroyed Jerusalem by fire (2 Kings 25:9; 2 Chronicles 36:19).

10:18 God's glory departed from the temple and was never completely present again until Christ himself visited it in New Testament times. God's holiness required that he leave the temple because the people had so defiled it. God had to completely destroy what people had perverted in order for true worship to be revived. We must commit ourselves, our families, our churches, and our nation to follow God faithfully so that we never have to experience God's abandoning us.

11:1-4 God had abandoned his altar and temple (chapters 9—11); here his judgment was complete as his glory stopped above

11:2 Ps 2:1, 2; 52:2; Is 30:1; Jer 5:5; Mic 2:1
11:3 Jer 1:13; Ezek 11:7, 11; 24:3, 6
11:5 Jer 11:20; 17:10; Ezek 38:10
11:6 Is 1:15; Ezek 7:23; 22:2-6, 9, 12, 27
11:7 Ezek 24:3-13; Mic 3:2, 3; 2 Kin 25:18-22; Jer 52:24-27
11:8 Prov 10:24; Is 66:4; Job 3:25; Is 24:17
11:9 Deut 28:36, 49, 50; Ps 106:41; Ezek 5:8; 16:41
11:10 Jer 52:9, 10; 2 Kin 14:25
11:11 Ezek 11:3, 7; 24:3, 6
11:12 Ezek 18:8, 9; Ezek 8:10, 14, 16
11:13 Ezek 11:1; Ezek 9:8
11:15 Ezek 33:24
11:16 Ps 31:20; 90:1; 91:9; Is 8:14; Jer 29:7, 11
11:17 Is 11:11-16; Jer 3:12, 18; 24:5; Ezek 20:41, 42; 28:25

2 He said to me, "Son of man, these are the men who devise iniquity and give evil
advice in this city,
3 who say, 'Is not *the time* near to build houses? This *city* is the pot and we are the
flesh.'
4 "Therefore, prophesy against them, son of man, prophesy!"
5 Then the Spirit of the LORD fell upon me, and He said to me, "Say, 'Thus says the
LORD, "So you think, house of Israel, for I know your thoughts.
6 "You have multiplied your slain in this city, filling its streets with them."
7 'Therefore, thus says the Lord GOD, "Your slain whom you have laid in the midst of
the city are the flesh and this *city* is the pot; but I will bring you out of it.
8 "You have feared a sword; so I will bring a sword upon you," the Lord GOD declares.
9 "And I will bring you out of the midst of the city and deliver you into the hands of
strangers and execute judgments against you.
10 "You will fall by the sword. I will judge you to the border of Israel; so you shall know
that I am the LORD.
11 "This *city* will not be a pot for you, nor will you be flesh in the midst of it, *but* I will
judge you to the border of Israel.
12 "Thus you will know that I am the LORD; for you have not walked in My statutes nor
have you executed My ordinances, but have acted according to the ordinances of the
nations around you." ' "
13 Now it came about as I prophesied, that Pelatiah son of Benaiah died. Then I fell
on my face and cried out with a loud voice and said, "Alas, Lord GOD! Will You bring
the remnant of Israel to a complete end?"

Promise of Restoration

14 Then the word of the LORD came to me, saying,
15 "Son of man, your brothers, your relatives, your fellow exiles and the whole house of
Israel, all of them, *are those* to whom the inhabitants of Jerusalem have said, 'Go far
from the LORD; this land has been given us as a possession.'
16 "Therefore say, 'Thus says the Lord GOD, "Though I had removed them far away
among the nations and though I had scattered them among the countries, yet I was a
sanctuary for them a little while in the countries where they had gone." '
17 "Therefore say, 'Thus says the Lord GOD, "I will gather you from the peoples and
assemble you out of the countries among which you have been scattered, and I will give
you the land of Israel." '

---

the mountain east of the city (11:23). The city gate was where merchants and politicians conducted business, so the 25 men may have represented the nation's rulers. Because of their leadership positions, they were responsible for leading the people astray. They had wrongly said that they were secure from another attack by the Babylonians. "This city is the pot and we are the flesh" means they believed that they were the elite, the influential, the ones who would be protected from all harm. Without God our situation is always precarious.

11:5 God knew everything about the Israelites, even their thoughts. He also knows everything about us, even the sins we try to hide. Instead of worrying about people noticing how we look or what we do, we should care about what God thinks, for he sees everything. Trying to hide our thoughts and actions from God is futile. "Secret" sins are never secret from God. The only effective way to deal with sin is to confess it and ask God to help us overcome it.

11:12 From the time they entered the promised land, the Israelites were warned not to copy the customs and religious practices of other nations. Disobeying this command and following pagan customs instead of God's laws always got them into trouble. Today, believers are still tempted to conform to the ways of the world. But we must get our standards of right and wrong from God, not from the popular trends of society.

11:14ff God promised the exiles in Babylonia that he would continue to be with them even though they were not in Jerusalem. This was a major concern to the Jews because they believed that God was present primarily in the temple. But God assured them that he would continue to be their God regardless of where they were. In the midst of Ezekiel's burning message of judgment stands a cool oasis—God's promise to restore the faithful few to their homeland. God's arms are now open to receive those who will repent of their sins.

11:15–21 God's messages through Ezekiel are full of irony. Here God says that the Jews in captivity are the faithful ones, and those in Jerusalem are the sinful and wicked ones. This was the opposite of the people's perception. Appearances can be deceiving. God will evaluate your life by your faith and obedience, not by your apparent earthly success. Furthermore, we should not judge others by outward appearances.

11:16 God was a sanctuary for the righteous remnant. Idolatrous people, even though they worshiped in the Jerusalem temple (11:15), would find no true sanctuary; but the faithful exiles, even though they were far from home, would be protected by God. Likewise, our external circumstances do not truly indicate our standing with God. Those who appear safe and secure may be far from him, while those going through difficult times may be safely under God's spiritual protection. We can depend on God to keep us safe if we pledge ourselves to his care.

18 "When they come there, they will remove all its detestable things and all its abominations from it.
19 "And I will give them one heart, and put a new spirit within them. And I will take the heart of stone out of their flesh and give them a heart of flesh,
20 that they may walk in My statutes and keep My ordinances and do them. Then they will be My people, and I shall be their God.
21 "But as for those whose hearts go after their detestable things and abominations, I will bring their conduct down on their heads," declares the Lord GOD.
22 Then the cherubim lifted up their wings with the wheels beside them, and the glory of the God of Israel hovered over them.
23 The glory of the LORD went up from the midst of the city and stood over the mountain which is east of the city.
24 And the Spirit lifted me up and brought me in a vision by the Spirit of God to the exiles in Chaldea. So the vision that I had seen left me.
25 Then I told the exiles all the things that the LORD had shown me.

11:18 Ezek 37:23; Ezek 5:11; 7:20
11:19 Jer 24:7; 32:39; Ezek 18:31; 36:26; Zech 7:12; Rom 2:4, 5; 2 Cor 3:3
11:20 Ps 105:45; Ezek 36:27; Ezek 14:11
11:21 Jer 16:18; Ezek 11:18; Ezek 9:10; 16:43
11:22 Ezek 10:19; Ezek 43:2
11:23 Ezek 8:4; Zech 14:4
11:24 Ezek 8:3; 11:1; 37:1; 2 Cor 12:2-4; Acts 10:16

3. Punishment is certain

Ezekiel Prepares for Exile

12 Then the word of the LORD came to me, saying,
2 "Son of man, you live in the midst of the rebellious house, who have eyes to see but do not see, ears to hear but do not hear; for they are a rebellious house.
3 "Therefore, son of man, prepare for yourself baggage for exile and go into exile by day in their sight; even go into exile from your place to another place in their sight. Perhaps they will understand though they are a rebellious house.
4 "Bring your baggage out by day in their sight, as baggage for exile. Then you will go out at evening in their sight, as those going into exile.
5 "Dig a hole through the wall in their sight and go out through it.
6 "Load *the baggage* on *your* shoulder in their sight *and* carry *it* out in the dark. You shall cover your face so that you cannot see the land, for I have set you as a sign to the house of Israel."
7 I did so, as I had been commanded. By day I brought out my baggage like the baggage of an exile. Then in the evening I dug through the wall with my hands; I went out in the dark *and* carried *the baggage* on *my* shoulder in their sight.
8 In the morning the word of the LORD came to me, saying,
9 "Son of man, has not the house of Israel, the rebellious house, said to you, 'What are you doing?'
10 "Say to them, 'Thus says the Lord GOD, "This burden *concerns* the prince in Jerusalem as well as all the house of Israel who are in it." '
11 "Say, 'I am a sign to you. As I have done, so it will be done to them; they will go into exile, into captivity.'
12 "The prince who is among them will load *his baggage* on *his* shoulder in the dark and go out. They will dig a hole through the wall to bring *it* out. He will cover his face so that he can not see the land with *his* eyes.
13 "I will also spread My net over him, and he will be caught in My snare. And I will

12:2 Is 6:5; Ps 78:40; Is 1:23; Ezek 2:7, 8; Is 6:9f; 43:8; Jer 5:21; Matt 13:13, 14; Mark 4:12; 8:18; Luke 8:10; John 9:39-41; 12:40; Acts 28:26f; Rom 11:8
12:3 Jer 26:3; 36:3, 7; Luke 20:13; 2 Tim 2:25
12:4 2 Kin 25:4; Jer 39:4
12:6 Is 8:18; 20:3; Ezek 4:3; 12:11; 24:24
12:7 Ezek 24:18; 37:7, 10; Ezek 12:3-6
12:10 2 Kin 9:25; Is 13:1
12:11 Jer 15:2; 52:15, 28-30; Ezek 12:3
12:12 2 Kin 25:4; Jer 39:4; 52:7; Ezek 12:6
12:13 Is 24:17, 18; Ezek 17:20; 19:8; Hos 7:12; Jer 39:7; 52:11

11:18–19 "One heart" indicates a unanimous singleness of purpose. No longer will God's people seek many gods; they will be content with God. The hard, deaf, immovable heart of stone will be radically transplanted with a tender, receptive, and responsive heart of flesh (see Jeremiah 32:39; Ezekiel 18:31; 36:26). This new life can only be the work of the Holy Spirit. It is God's work, but we must recognize and turn from our sin. When we do, God will give us new motives, new guidelines, and new purpose. Have you received your new heart?

11:23 God's glory left Jerusalem and stood above a mountain on the east side of the city—almost certainly the Mount of Olives. Ezekiel 43:1–4 implies that God will return the same way he left, when he comes back to earth to set up his perfect kingdom.

12:1ff Ezekiel played the role of a captive being led away to exile, portraying what was about to happen to King Zedekiah and the people remaining in Jerusalem. The exiles knew exactly what Ezekiel was doing because only six years earlier they had made similar preparations as they left Jerusalem for Babylonia. This was to show the people that they should not trust the king or the capital city to save them from the Babylonian army—only God could do that. And the exiles who hoped for an early return from exile would be disappointed. Ezekiel's graphic demonstration was proven correct to the last detail. But when he warned them, many refused to listen.

12:10–12 Zedekiah, Judah's last king (597–586 B.C.), was reigning in Jerusalem when Ezekiel gave these oracles or messages from God. Ezekiel showed the people what would happen to Zedekiah. Jerusalem would be attacked again, and Zedekiah would join the exiles already in Babylon. Zedekiah would be unable to see because Nebuchadnezzar would have his eyes gouged out (2 Kings 25:3–7; Jeremiah 52:10–11).

bring him to Babylon in the land of the Chaldeans; yet he will not see it, though he will
die there.
14 "I will scatter to every wind all who are around him, his helpers and all his troops;
and I will draw out a sword after them.
15 "So they will know that I am the LORD when I scatter them among the nations and
spread them among the countries.
16 "But I will spare a few of them from the sword, the famine and the pestilence that
they may tell all their abominations among the nations where they go, and may know
that I am the LORD."
17 Moreover, the word of the LORD came to me saying,
18 "Son of man, eat your bread with trembling and drink your water with quivering and
anxiety.
19 "Then say to the people of the land, 'Thus says the Lord GOD concerning the inhabitants of Jerusalem in the land of Israel, "They will eat their bread with anxiety and drink
their water with horror, because their land will be stripped of its fullness on account of
the violence of all who live in it.
20 "The inhabited cities will be laid waste and the land will be a desolation. So you will
know that I am the LORD." ' "
21 Then the word of the LORD came to me, saying,
22 "Son of man, what is this proverb you *people* have concerning the land of Israel, saying, 'The days are long and every vision fails'?
23 "Therefore say to them, 'Thus says the Lord GOD, "I will make this proverb cease so
that they will no longer use it as a proverb in Israel." But tell them, "The days draw near
as well as the fulfillment of every vision.
24 "For there will no longer be any false vision or flattering divination within the house
of Israel.
25 "For I the LORD will speak, and whatever word I speak will be performed. It will no
longer be delayed, for in your days, O rebellious house, I will speak the word and perform it," declares the Lord GOD.' "
26 Furthermore, the word of the LORD came to me, saying,
27 "Son of man, behold, the house of Israel is saying, 'The vision that he sees is for many
years *from now,* and he prophesies of times far off.'
28 "Therefore say to them, 'Thus says the Lord GOD, "None of My words will be delayed any longer. Whatever word I speak will be performed," ' " declares the Lord GOD.

False Prophets Condemned

13 Then the word of the LORD came to me saying,
2 "Son of man, prophesy against the prophets of Israel who prophesy, and say to
those who prophesy from their own inspiration, 'Listen to the word of the LORD!
3 'Thus says the Lord GOD, "Woe to the foolish prophets who are following their own
spirit and have seen nothing.
4 "O Israel, your prophets have been like foxes among ruins.
5 "You have not gone up into the breaches, nor did you build the wall around the house
of Israel to stand in the battle on the day of the LORD.
6 "They see falsehood and lying divination who are saying, 'The LORD declares,' when
the LORD has not sent them; yet they hope for the fulfillment of *their* word.
7 "Did you not see a false vision and speak a lying divination when you said, 'The LORD
declares,' but it is not I who have spoken?" ' "
8 Therefore, thus says the Lord GOD, "Because you have spoken falsehood and seen
a lie, therefore behold, I am against you," declares the Lord GOD.
9 "So My hand will be against the prophets who see false visions and utter lying divina-

12:14 2 Kin 25:4, 5; Ezek 5:2; 17:21
12:15 Ezek 6:7, 14; 12:16
12:16 Ezek 7:15; 14:21; Jer 22:8, 9
12:18 Lam 5:9; Ezek 4:16
12:19 Jer 10:22; Ezek 6:6, 7, 14; Mic 7:13; Zech 7:14
12:20 Is 3:26; Jer 4:7; Ezek 5:14; Is 7:23, 24; Jer 25:9
12:22 Ezek 16:44; 18:2, 3; Jer 5:12; Ezek 11:3; 12:27; Amos 6:3; 2 Pet 3:4; Ezek 7:26
12:23 Ps 37:13; Joel 2:1; Zeph 1:14
12:24 Jer 14:13-16; Ezek 13:6, 23; Zech 13:2-4
12:25 Num 14:28-34; Is 14:24; Ezek 6:10; Jer 16:9; Hab 1:5
12:27 Dan 10:14
13:2 Is 9:15; Jer 37:19; Ezek 22:25, 28; Is 1:10; Amos 7:16
13:3 Lam 2:14; Hos 9:7; Zech 11:15; Jer 23:28-32
13:5 Ps 106:23; Jer 23:22; Ezek 22:30; Is 58:12; Is 13:6, 9; Ezek 7:19
13:6 Jer 29:8; Ezek 22:28; Jer 28:15; 37:19
13:7 Ezek 22:28
13:8 Ezek 5:8; 21:3; Nah 2:13
13:9 Jer 20:3-6; 28:15-17; Ps 69:28; 87:6; Jer 17:13; Dan 12:1

12:21–28 These two short messages were warnings that God's words would come true—*soon!* Less than six years later, Jerusalem would be destroyed. Yet the people were skeptical. Unbelief and false security led them to believe it would never happen. The apostle Peter dealt with this problem in the church (2 Peter 3:9). It is dangerous to say Christ will never return or to regard his coming as so far in the future as to be irrelevant today. All that God says is sure to happen. Don't dare assume that you have plenty of time to get right with God.

13:1ff This warning was directed against false prophets whose messages were not from God, but were lies intended to win popularity by saying whatever made the people happy. False prophets did not care about the truth as Ezekiel did. They lulled people into a false sense of security, making Ezekiel's job even more difficult. Beware of people who bend the truth in their quest for popularity and power.

tions. They will have no place in the council of My people, nor will they be written down
in the register of the house of Israel, nor will they enter the land of Israel, that you may
know that I am the Lord GOD.
10 "It is definitely because they have misled My people by saying, 'Peace!' when there is
no peace. And when anyone builds a wall, behold, they plaster it over with whitewash;
11 *so* tell those who plaster *it* over with whitewash, that it will fall. A flooding rain will
come, and you, O hailstones, will fall; and a violent wind will break out.
12 "Behold, when the wall has fallen, will you not be asked, 'Where is the plaster with
which you plastered *it?*' "
13 Therefore, thus says the Lord GOD, "I will make a violent wind break out in My
wrath. There will also be in My anger a flooding rain and hailstones to consume *it* in
wrath.
14 "So I will tear down the wall which you plastered over with whitewash and bring it
down to the ground, so that its foundation is laid bare; and when it falls, you will be consumed in its midst. And you will know that I am the LORD.
15 "Thus I will spend My wrath on the wall and on those who have plastered it over with
whitewash; and I will say to you, 'The wall is gone and its plasterers are gone,
16 *along with* the prophets of Israel who prophesy to Jerusalem, and who see visions of
peace for her when there is no peace,' declares the Lord GOD.
17 "Now you, son of man, set your face against the daughters of your people who are
prophesying from their own inspiration. Prophesy against them
18 and say, 'Thus says the Lord GOD, "Woe to the women who sew *magic* bands on all
wrists and make veils for the heads of *persons* of every stature to hunt down lives! Will
you hunt down the lives of My people, but preserve the lives *of others* for yourselves?
19 "For handfuls of barley and fragments of bread, you have profaned Me to My people to put to death some who should not die and to keep others alive who should not
live, by your lying to My people who listen to lies." ' "
20 Therefore, thus says the Lord GOD, "Behold, I am against your *magic* bands by which
you hunt lives there as birds and I will tear them from your arms; and I will let them go,
even those lives whom you hunt as birds.
21 "I will also tear off your veils and deliver My people from your hands, and they will
no longer be in your hands to be hunted; and you will know that I am the LORD.
22 "Because you disheartened the righteous with falsehood when I did not cause him
grief, but have encouraged the wicked not to turn from his wicked way *and* preserve his
life,
23 therefore, you women will no longer see false visions or practice divination, and I
will deliver My people out of your hand. Thus you will know that I am the LORD."

Idolatrous Elders Condemned

14 Then some elders of Israel came to me and sat down before me.
2 And the word of the LORD came to me, saying,
3 "Son of man, these men have set up their idols in their hearts and have put right before
their faces the stumbling block of their iniquity. Should I be consulted by them at all?
4 "Therefore speak to them and tell them, 'Thus says the Lord GOD, "Any man of the
house of Israel who sets up his idols in his heart, puts right before his face the stumbling
block of his iniquity, and *then* comes to the prophet, I the LORD will be brought to give
him an answer in the matter in view of the multitude of his idols,

13:10 Jer 23:32; 50:6; Jer 6:14; 8:11; 14:13; Ezek 7:25; 13:16

13:11 Ezek 38:22

13:13 Ex 9:24, 25; Ps 18:12, 13; Is 30:30; Rev 11:19; 16:21

13:14 Mic 1:6; Hab 3:13; Jer 6:15; 14:15; Ezek 13:9

13:16 Jer 6:14; 8:11; Ezek 13:10; Is 57:21

13:17 Judg 4:4; 2 Kin 22:14; Luke 2:36; Acts 21:9; Ezek 13:2; Rev 2:20

13:18 2 Pet 2:14

13:19 Prov 28:21; Mic 3:5; Jer 23:14, 17

13:21 Ps 91:3; 124:7

13:22 Amos 5:12; Jer 23:14; 34:16, 22; Ezek 18:21, 27, 30-32; 33:14-16

13:23 Ezek 12:24; 13:6; Mic 3:6; Zech 13:3; Ezek 13:21; 34:10; Ezek 13:9, 21

14:1 2 Kin 6:32; Ezek 8:1; 20:1; Is 29:13; Ezek 33:31, 32

14:3 Ezek 20:16; Ezek 7:19; 14:4, 7; Zeph 1:3; Is 1:15; Jer 11:11; Ezek 20:3, 31

14:4 1 Kin 21:20-24; 2 Kin 1:16; Is 66:4

13:10–12 These false prophets covered their lies with "white-wash"—a pleasing front. Such superficiality can't hold up under God's scrutiny.

13:17 In the Bible, the gift of prophecy was given to women as well as men. Miriam (Exodus 15:20), Deborah (Judges 4:4), and Huldah (2 Kings 22:14) were prophetesses. But the women mentioned here are more like the medium of 1 Samuel 28:7, and they are condemned for disheartening the righteous (13:22).

13:18 These magic charms and veils were used in witchcraft practices. They were advertised as good luck charms, but were used to ensnare the people in idolatry.

14:3 God condemned the elders for worshiping idols in their hearts and then daring to come to God's prophet for advice. On the outside, they appeared to worship God, making regular visits to the temple to offer sacrifices. But they were not sincere. It is easy for us to criticize the Israelites for worshiping idols when they so clearly needed God instead. But we have idols in our hearts when we pursue reputation, acceptance, wealth, or sensual pleasure with the intensity and commitment that should be reserved for serving God.

14:3–5 For Hebrew writers, important functions of life were assigned to different physical organs. The heart was considered the core of a person's intellectual and spiritual function. Because all people have someone or something as the object of their heart's devotion, they have the potential for idolatry within them. God wants to recapture the hearts of his people. We must never let anything captivate our allegiance or imagination in such a way to replace or weaken our devotion to God.

5 in order to lay hold of the hearts of the house of Israel who are estranged from Me
through all their idols." '
6"Therefore say to the house of Israel, 'Thus says the Lord GOD, "Repent and turn
away from your idols and turn your faces away from all your abominations.
7"For anyone of the house of Israel or of the immigrants who stay in Israel who separates himself from Me, sets up his idols in his heart, puts right before his face the stumbling block of his iniquity, and *then* comes to the prophet to inquire of Me for himself, I
the LORD will be brought to answer him in My own person.
8"I will set My face against that man and make him a sign and a proverb, and I will cut
him off from among My people. So you will know that I am the LORD.
9"But if the prophet is prevailed upon to speak a word, it is I, the LORD, who have
prevailed upon that prophet, and I will stretch out My hand against him and destroy him
from among My people Israel.
10"They will bear *the punishment of* their iniquity; as the iniquity of the inquirer is, so
the iniquity of the prophet will be,
11 in order that the house of Israel may no longer stray from Me and no longer defile
themselves with all their transgressions. Thus they will be My people, and I shall be their
God," ' declares the Lord GOD."

The City Will Not Be Spared

12 Then the word of the LORD came to me saying,
13"Son of man, if a country sins against Me by committing unfaithfulness, and I stretch
out My hand against it, destroy its supply of bread, send famine against it and cut off
from it both man and beast,
14 even *though* these three men, Noah, Daniel and Job were in its midst, by their *own*
righteousness they could *only* deliver themselves," declares the Lord GOD.
15"If I were to cause wild beasts to pass through the land and they depopulated it, and
it became desolate so that no one would pass through it because of the beasts,
16 *though* these three men were in its midst, as I live," declares the Lord GOD, "they
could not deliver either *their* sons or *their* daughters. They alone would be delivered, but
the country would be desolate.
17"Or *if* I should bring a sword on that country and say, 'Let the sword pass through
the country and cut off man and beast from it,'
18 even *though* these three men were in its midst, as I live," declares the Lord GOD,
"they could not deliver either *their* sons or *their* daughters, but they alone would be delivered.
19"Or *if* I should send a plague against that country and pour out My wrath in blood on
it to cut off man and beast from it,
20 even *though* Noah, Daniel and Job were in its midst, as I live," declares the Lord
GOD, "they could not deliver either *their* son or *their* daughter. They would deliver only
themselves by their righteousness."
21 For thus says the Lord GOD, "How much more when I send My four severe judgments against Jerusalem: sword, famine, wild beasts and plague to cut off man and beast
from it!
22"Yet, behold, survivors will be left in it who will be brought out, *both* sons and daughters. Behold, they are going to come forth to you and you will see their conduct and actions; then you will be comforted for the calamity which I have brought against Jerusalem
for everything which I have brought upon it.
23"Then they will comfort you when you see their conduct and actions, for you will know
that I have not done in vain whatever I did to it," declares the Lord GOD.

14:5 Jer 17:10; Zech 7:12; Is 1:4; Jer 2:11; Zech 11:8

14:6 1 Sam 7:3; Neh 1:9; Is 2:20; 30:22; 55:6, 7; Ezek 18:30; Ezek 8:6; 14:4

14:7 Ex 12:48; 20:10; Ezek 14:4

14:8 Jer 44:11; Ezek 15:7; Is 65:15; Ezek 5:15

14:9 Jer 6:14, 15; 14:15

14:11 Ezek 44:10, 15; 48:11; Ezek 11:18; 37:23; Ezek 11:20; 34:30; 36:28

14:13 Ezek 15:8; 20:27; Lev 26:26; Is 3:1; Ezek 4:16

14:14 Jer 15:1; Gen 6:8; 7:1; Heb 11:7; Ezek 28:3; Dan 1:6; 9:21; 10:11; Job 1:1, 5; 42:8, 9; Ezek 16:18, 20; 18:20

14:15 Lev 26:22; Num 21:6; Ezek 5:17; 14:21

14:16 Gen 19:29; Ezek 18:20

14:17 Lev 26:25; Ezek 5:12; 21:3, 4; Ezek 25:13; Zeph 1:3

14:19 Jer 14:12; Ezek 5:12; 14:21

14:21 Ezek 5:17; 33:27; Amos 4:6-10; Rev 6:8

14:22 Ezek 12:16; 36:20; Ezek 16:54; 31:16; 32:31

14:23 Jer 22:8, 9

14:6–11 The people of Judah, though eager to accept the messages of false prophets, considered the presence of a few God-fearing men in the nation an insurance policy against disaster. In a pinch, they could always ask God's prophets for advice. But merely having God's people around doesn't help. We must remember that the relationship our pastor, family, or friends have with God will not protect us from the consequences of our own sins. Each person is responsible for his or her own relationship with God. Is your faith personal and real, or are you resting in what others have done?

14:14 Noah, Daniel, and Job were great men in Israel's history, renowned for their relationships with God and for their wisdom (see Genesis 6:8, 9; Daniel 2:47, 48; Job 1:1). Daniel had been taken into captivity during Babylon's first invasion of Judah in 605 B.C., eight years before Ezekiel was taken captive. At the time of Ezekiel's message, Daniel occupied a high government position in Babylon. But even these great men of God could not have saved the people of Judah because God had already passed judgment on the nation's pervasive evil.

Jerusalem like a Useless Vine

15 Then the word of the LORD came to me, saying,
2 "Son of man, how is the wood of the vine *better* than any wood of a branch which
is among the trees of the forest?

15:2 Ps 80:8-16; Is 5:1-7; Hos 10:1

3 "Can wood be taken from it to make anything, or can *men* take a peg from it on which
to hang any vessel?
4 "If it has been put into the fire for fuel, *and* the fire has consumed both of its ends
and its middle part has been charred, is it *then* useful for anything?

15:4 Is 27:11; Ezek 15:6; 19:14

5 "Behold, while it is intact, it is not made into anything. How much less, when the fire
has consumed it and it is charred, can it still be made into anything!
6 "Therefore, thus says the Lord GOD, 'As the wood of the vine among the trees of the
forest, which I have given to the fire for fuel, so have I given up the inhabitants of Jerusalem;
7 and I set My face against them. *Though* they have come out of the fire, yet the fire
will consume them. Then you will know that I am the LORD, when I set My face against
them.

15:7 Lev 26:17; Ps 34:16; Jer 21:10; Ezek 14:8; 1 Kin 19:17; Is 24:18; Amos 9:1-4

8 'Thus I will make the land desolate, because they have acted unfaithfully,' " declares
the Lord GOD.

15:8 Ezek 14:13; 17:20

God's Grace to Unfaithful Jerusalem

16 Then the word of the LORD came to me, saying,
2 "Son of man, make known to Jerusalem her abominations

16:2 Is 58:1; Ezek 20:4; 22:2

3 and say, 'Thus says the Lord GOD to Jerusalem, "Your origin and your birth are
from the land of the Canaanite, your father was an Amorite and your mother a Hittite.
4 "As for your birth, on the day you were born your navel cord was not cut, nor were
you washed with water for cleansing; you were not rubbed with salt or even wrapped in
cloths.

16:4 Hos 2:3

5 "No eye looked with pity on you to do any of these things for you, to have compassion on you. Rather you were thrown out into the open field, for you were abhorred on
the day you were born.

16:5 Deut 32:10

6 "When I passed by you and saw you squirming in your blood, I said to you *while you*
were in your blood, 'Live!' Yes, I said to you *while you were* in your blood, 'Live!'
7 "I made you numerous like plants of the field. Then you grew up, became tall and
reached the age for fine ornaments; *your* breasts were formed and your hair had grown.
Yet you were naked and bare.

16:7 Ex 1:7; Deut 1:10

8 "Then I passed by you and saw you, and behold, you were at the time for love; so I
spread My skirt over you and covered your nakedness. I also swore to you and entered
into a covenant with you so that you became Mine," declares the Lord GOD.

16:8 Ruth 3:9; Jer 2:2; Gen 22:16-18; Ex 24:7, 8; Ex 19:5; Ezek 20:5; Hos 2:19, 20

9 "Then I bathed you with water, washed off your blood from you and anointed you
with oil.

16:9 Ruth 3:3

10 "I also clothed you with embroidered cloth and put sandals of porpoise skin on your
feet; and I wrapped you with fine linen and covered you with silk.

16:10 Ex 26:36; Ezek 16:13, 18; 26:16; 27:7, 16

11 "I adorned you with ornaments, put bracelets on your hands and a necklace around
your neck.

16:11 Gen 24:22, 47; Is 3:19; Ezek 23:42; Gen 41:42; Prov 1:9

12 "I also put a ring in your nostril, earrings in your ears and a beautiful crown on your
head.

16:12 Gen 24:47; Is 3:21; Is 26:5; Jer 13:18; Ezek 16:14

13 "Thus you were adorned with gold and silver, and your dress was of fine linen, silk
and embroidered cloth. You ate fine flour, honey and oil; so you were exceedingly beautiful and advanced to royalty.

16:13 Ps 45:13, 14; Ezek 16:17; 1 Sam 10:1; 1 Kin 4:21

15:1ff The messages given to Ezekiel in chapters 15—17 provided further evidence that God was going to destroy Jerusalem. The first message was about a vine, useless at first and even more useless after being burned. The people of Jerusalem were useless to God because of their idol worship, and so they would be destroyed and their cities burned. Isaiah also compared the nation of Israel to a vineyard (see Isaiah 5:1–8). Have you also become dormant and unfruitful to God? How can you begin fulfilling his plan for you?

16:1ff This message reminded Jerusalem of its former despised status among the Canaanite nations. Using the imagery of a young baby growing to mature womanhood, God reminded Jerusalem that he raised her from a lowly state to great glory as his bride. However, she betrayed God's trust and prostituted herself by seeking alliances with pagan nations and adopting their customs. If we push God aside for anything, even education, family, career, or pleasure, we are abandoning him in the same way.

16:3 *Canaan* was the ancient name of the territory taken over by the children of Israel. The Bible often uses this name to refer to all the corrupt pagan nations of the region. The Amorites and Hittites, two Canaanite peoples, were known for their wickedness. But here God implies that his people are no better than the Canaanites.

16:14 1 Kin 10:1, 24; Ps 50:2; Lam 2:15
16:15 Ezek 16:25; 27:3; Is 57:8; Jer 2:20
16:17 Ezek 16:11, 12
16:19 Hos 2:8
16:20 Ex 13:2, 12; Deut 29:11, 12; Ps 106:37, 38; Jer 7:31; Ezek 20:31; 23:37
16:21 Ex 13:2; 2 Kin 17:17; Jer 19:5
16:22 Jer 2:2
16:24 Jer 11:13; Ezek 16:31, 39; 20:28, 29; Ps 78:58; Is 57:7
16:25 Prov 9:14
16:26 Jer 7:18, 19; Ezek 8:17
16:27 Is 9:12; Ezek 16:57
16:28 2 Kin 16:7, 10-18; 2 Chr 28:16, 20-23; Jer 2:18, 36; Ezek 23:12; Hos 10:6
16:30 Prov 9:13; Is 1:3; Jer 4:22; Is 3:9; Jer 3:3
16:31 Is 52:3
16:33 Is 57:9; Ezek 16:41; Hos 8:9, 10
16:36 Jer 19:5; Ezek 20:31; 23:37
16:37 Jer 13:22, 26; Ezek 23:9, 22; Hos 2:3, 10; Nah 3:5, 6; Ezek 23:17, 28; Is 47:3

14 "Then your fame went forth among the nations on account of your beauty, for it was perfect because of My splendor which I bestowed on you," declares the Lord GOD.
15 "But you trusted in your beauty and played the harlot because of your fame, and you poured out your harlotries on every passer-by who might be *willing.*
16 "You took some of your clothes, made for yourself high places of various colors and played the harlot on them, which should never come about nor happen.
17 "You also took your beautiful jewels *made* of My gold and of My silver, which I had given you, and made for yourself male images that you might play the harlot with them.
18 "Then you took your embroidered cloth and covered them, and offered My oil and My incense before them.
19 "Also My bread which I gave you, fine flour, oil and honey with which I fed you, you would offer before them for a soothing aroma; so it happened," declares the Lord GOD.
20 "Moreover, you took your sons and daughters whom you had borne to Me and sacrificed them to idols to be devoured. Were your harlotries so small a matter?
21 "You slaughtered My children and offered them up to idols by causing them to pass through *the fire.*
22 "Besides all your abominations and harlotries you did not remember the days of your youth, when you were naked and bare and squirming in your blood.
23 "Then it came about after all your wickedness ('Woe, woe to you!' declares the Lord GOD),
24 that you built yourself a shrine and made yourself a high place in every square.
25 "You built yourself a high place at the top of every street and made your beauty abominable, and you spread your legs to every passer-by to multiply your harlotry.
26 "You also played the harlot with the Egyptians, your lustful neighbors, and multiplied your harlotry to make Me angry.
27 "Behold now, I have stretched out My hand against you and diminished your rations. And I delivered you up to the desire of those who hate you, the daughters of the Philistines, who are ashamed of your lewd conduct.
28 "Moreover, you played the harlot with the Assyrians because you were not satisfied; you played the harlot with them and still were not satisfied.
29 "You also multiplied your harlotry with the land of merchants, Chaldea, yet even with this you were not satisfied." ' "
30 "How languishing is your heart," declares the Lord GOD, "while you do all these things, the actions of a bold-faced harlot.
31 "When you built your shrine at the beginning of every street and made your high place in every square, in disdaining money, you were not like a harlot.
32 "You adulteress wife, who takes strangers instead of her husband!
33 "Men give gifts to all harlots, but you give your gifts to all your lovers to bribe them to come to you from every direction for your harlotries.
34 "Thus you are different from those women in your harlotries, in that no one plays the harlot as you do, because you give money and no money is given you; thus you are different."
35 Therefore, O harlot, hear the word of the LORD.
36 Thus says the Lord GOD, "Because your lewdness was poured out and your nakedness uncovered through your harlotries with your lovers and with all your detestable idols, and because of the blood of your sons which you gave to idols,
37 therefore, behold, I will gather all your lovers with whom you took pleasure, even all those whom you loved *and* all those whom you hated. So I will gather them against you from every direction and expose your nakedness to them that they may see all your nakedness.

16:15 God cared for and loved Judah, only to have it turn away to other nations and their false gods. The nation had grown to maturity and become famous, but they forgot who had given them their life (16:22). This is a picture of spiritual adultery (called harlotry—turning from the one true God). As you become wise and more mature, don't turn away from the One who truly loves you.

16:20–21 Child sacrifice had been practiced by the Canaanites long before Israel invaded their land. But it was strictly forbidden by God (Leviticus 20:1–3). By Ezekiel's time, however, the people were openly sacrificing their own children (2 Kings 16:3; 21:6). Jeremiah confirmed that this was a common practice (Jeremiah 7:31; 32:35). Because of such vile acts among the people and priesthood, the temple became unfit for God to inhabit. When God left the temple, he was no longer Judah's guide and protector.

16:27 The conduct of the Jews was so lewd that even those who worshiped other gods, including their great enemy the Philistines, would have been ashamed to behave that way. The Jews outdid them in doing evil.

38 "Thus I will judge you like women who commit adultery or shed blood are judged;
and I will bring on you the blood of wrath and jealousy.
39 "I will also give you into the hands of your lovers, and they will tear down your shrines,
demolish your high places, strip you of your clothing, take away your jewels, and will
leave you naked and bare.
40 "They will incite a crowd against you and they will stone you and cut you to pieces
with their swords.
41 "They will burn your houses with fire and execute judgments on you in the sight of
many women. Then I will stop you from playing the harlot, and you will also no longer
pay your lovers.
42 "So I will calm My fury against you and My jealousy will depart from you, and I will
be pacified and angry no more.
43 "Because you have not remembered the days of your youth but have enraged Me by
all these things, behold, I in turn will bring your conduct down on your own head," declares the Lord GOD, "so that you will not commit this lewdness on top of all your *other*
abominations.
44 "Behold, everyone who quotes proverbs will quote *this* proverb concerning you, saying, 'Like mother, like daughter.'
45 "You are the daughter of your mother, who loathed her husband and children. You
are also the sister of your sisters, who loathed their husbands and children. Your mother
was a Hittite and your father an Amorite.
46 "Now your older sister is Samaria, who lives north of you with her daughters; and
your younger sister, who lives south of you, is Sodom with her daughters.
47 "Yet you have not merely walked in their ways or done according to their abominations; but, as if that were too little, you acted more corruptly in all your conduct than
they.
48 "As I live," declares the Lord GOD, "Sodom, your sister and her daughters have not
done as you and your daughters have done.
49 "Behold, this was the guilt of your sister Sodom: she and her daughters had arrogance, abundant food and careless ease, but she did not help the poor and needy.
50 "Thus they were haughty and committed abominations before Me. Therefore I removed them when I saw *it.*
51 "Furthermore, Samaria did not commit half of your sins, for you have multiplied your
abominations more than they. Thus you have made your sisters appear righteous by all
your abominations which you have committed.
52 "Also bear your disgrace in that you have made judgment favorable for your sisters.
Because of your sins in which you acted more abominably than they, they are more in
the right than you. Yes, be also ashamed and bear your disgrace, in that you made your
sisters appear righteous.
53 "Nevertheless, I will restore their captivity, the captivity of Sodom and her daughters, the captivity of Samaria and her daughters, and along with them your own captivity,
54 in order that you may bear your humiliation and feel ashamed for all that you have
done when you become a consolation to them.
55 "Your sisters, Sodom with her daughters and Samaria with her daughters, will return to their former state, and you with your daughters will *also* return to your former
state.
56 "As *the name of* your sister Sodom was not heard from your lips in your day of pride,

16:38 Ezek 23:45; Ps 79:3, 5; Jer 18:21; Ezek 23:25; Zeph 1:17

16:39 Ezek 23:26; Hos 2:3

16:40 Ezek 23:47; Hab 1:6-10

16:41 2 Kin 25:9; Jer 39:8; 52:13; Ezek 23:48

16:42 2 Sam 24:25; Ezek 5:13; 21:17; Zech 6:8; Is 40:1, 2; 54:9, 10; Ezek 39:29

16:43 Ps 78:42; 106:13; Ezek 16:22; Is 63:10; Ezek 6:9; Ezek 11:21; 22:31

16:44 1 Sam 24:13; Ezek 12:22, 23; 18:2, 3

16:45 Ezek 23:2; Is 1:4; Ezek 23:37-39; Zech 11:8

16:46 Jer 3:8-11; Ezek 23:4; Gen 13:10-13; 18:20; Ezek 16:48, 49, 53-56, 61

16:47 1 Kin 16:31; 2 Kin 21:9; Ezek 5:6; 16:48, 51

16:48 Matt 10:15; 11:23, 24

16:49 Gen 19:9; Ps 138:6; Is 3:9; Ezek 28:2, 9, 17; Gen 13:10; Is 22:13; Amos 6:4-6; Luke 12:16-20; 16:19; Ezek 18:7, 12, 16

16:50 Gen 13:13; 18:20; 19:5; Gen 19:24, 25

16:51 Jer 3:8-11

16:52 Ezek 16:47, 48, 51

16:54 Jer 2:26; Ezek 14:22, 23

16:44–52 The city of Sodom, a symbol of total corruption, was completely destroyed by God for its wickedness (Genesis 19:24–25). Samaria, the capital of what had been the northern kingdom (Israel), was despised and rejected by the Jews in Judah. To be called a sister of Samaria and Sodom was bad enough, but to be called *more depraved* than that meant that Judah's sins were an unspeakable abomination and that its doom was inevitable. The reason it was considered worse was not necessarily that Judah's sins were worse, but that Judah knew better. In that light, we who live in an age when God's message is made clear to us through the Bible are worse than Judah if we continue in sin! (See also Matthew 11:20–24.)

16:49 It is easy to judge and condemn Sodom, especially for its terrible sexual sins. Ezekiel reminded Judah, however, that Sodom was destroyed because its people were arrogant, overfed, and unconcerned about the needy people within their reach. It is easy to be selective in what we consider gross sin. If we do not commit such horrible sins as adultery, homosexuality, stealing, and murder, we may think we are living good enough lives. But what about sins like arrogance, gluttony, and indifference to the needy? These sins may not be as shocking to you as the others, but they are also forbidden by God.

57 before your wickedness was uncovered, so now you have become the reproach of
the daughters of Edom and of all who are around her, of the daughters of the Philistines—those surrounding *you* who despise you.
58 "You have borne *the penalty of* your lewdness and abominations," the LORD declares.
59 For thus says the Lord GOD, "I will also do with you as you have done, you who
have despised the oath by breaking the covenant.

The Covenant Remembered

60 "Nevertheless, I will remember My covenant with you in the days of your youth, and
I will establish an everlasting covenant with you.
61 "Then you will remember your ways and be ashamed when you receive your sisters,
both your older and your younger; and I will give them to you as daughters, but not because of your covenant.
62 "Thus I will establish My covenant with you, and you shall know that I am the LORD,
63 so that you may remember and be ashamed and never open your mouth anymore
because of your humiliation, when I have forgiven you for all that you have done," the
Lord GOD declares.

Parable of Two Eagles and a Vine

17 Now the word of the LORD came to me saying,
2 "Son of man, propound a riddle and speak a parable to the house of Israel,
3 saying, 'Thus says the Lord GOD, "A great eagle with great wings, long pinions and
a full plumage of many colors came to Lebanon and took away the top of the cedar.
4 "He plucked off the topmost of its young twigs and brought it to a land of merchants;
he set it in a city of traders.
5 "He also took some of the seed of the land and planted it in fertile soil. He placed *it*
beside abundant waters; he set it *like* a willow.
6 "Then it sprouted and became a low, spreading vine with its branches turned toward
him, but its roots remained under it. So it became a vine and yielded shoots and sent out
branches.
7 "But there was another great eagle with great wings and much plumage; and behold,
this vine bent its roots toward him and sent out its branches toward him from the beds
where it was planted, that he might water it.
8 "It was planted in good soil beside abundant waters, that it might yield branches and
bear fruit *and* become a splendid vine." '
9 "Say, 'Thus says the Lord GOD, "Will it thrive? Will he not pull up its roots and cut
off its fruit, so that it withers—so that all its sprouting leaves wither? And neither by
great strength nor by many people can it be raised from its roots *again*.
10 "Behold, though it is planted, will it thrive? Will it not completely wither as soon as
the east wind strikes it—wither on the beds where it grew?" ' "

Zedekiah's Rebellion

11 Moreover, the word of the LORD came to me, saying,
12 "Say now to the rebellious house, 'Do you not know what these things *mean?*' Say,
'Behold, the king of Babylon came to Jerusalem, took its king and princes and brought
them to him in Babylon.
13 'He took one of the royal family and made a covenant with him, putting him under
oath. He also took away the mighty of the land,

16:57 Ezek 16:36, 37; 2 Kin 10:5-7; 2 Chr 28:5, 6, 18-23; Ezek 5:14, 15; 22:4
16:58 Ezek 23:49
16:59 Is 24:5; Ezek 17:19
16:60 Is 55:3; Jer 32:38-41; Ezek 37:26
16:61 Jer 50:4, 5; Ezek 6:9
16:62 Ezek 20:37; 34:25; 37:26; Jer 24:7; Ezek 20:43, 44
16:63 Ezek 36:31, 32; Dan 9:7, 8; Ps 39:9; Rom 3:19; Ps 65:3; 78:38; 79:9
17:2 Ezek 20:49; 24:3
17:3 Jer 48:40; Ezek 17:12; Hos 8:1; Dan 4:22; Jer 22:23
17:5 Deut 8:7-9; Is 44:4
17:7 Ezek 31:4
17:10 Ezek 19:14; Hos 13:15
17:12 Ezek 2:3-5; Ezek 12:9-11; 24:19; 2 Kin 24:11, 12, 15; Ezek 1:2; 17:3
17:13 2 Kin 24:17; Ezek 17:5; 2 Chr 36:13; 2 Kin 24:15, 16

16:59–63 Although the people had broken their promises and did not deserve anything but punishment, God would not break his promises. If the people turned back to him, he would again forgive them and renew his covenant. This covenant was put into effect when Jesus paid for the sins of all mankind by his death on the cross (Hebrews 10:8–10). No one is beyond the reach of God's forgiveness. Although we don't deserve anything but punishment for our sins, God's arms are still outstretched. He will not break his promise to give us salvation and forgiveness if we repent and turn to him.

17:1ff The first eagle in this chapter represents King Nebuchadnezzar of Babylon (see 17:12), who appointed or "planted" Zedekiah as king in Jerusalem. Zedekiah rebelled against this arrangement and tried to ally with Egypt, the second eagle, to battle against Babylon. This took place while Ezekiel, miles away in Babylon, was describing these events. Jeremiah, a prophet in Judah, was also warning Zedekiah not to form this alliance (Jeremiah 2:36–37). Although many miles apart, the prophets had the same message because both spoke for God. God still directs his chosen spokesmen to speak his truth all around the world.

17:10 This east wind was the hot, dry wind blowing off the desert, a wind that could wither a flourishing crop. The hot wind of Nebuchadnezzar's armies was about to overcome the nation of Judah.

14 that the kingdom might be in subjection, not exalting itself, *but* keeping his covenant
that it might continue.
15 'But he rebelled against him by sending his envoys to Egypt that they might give him
horses and many troops. Will he succeed? Will he who does such things escape? Can he
indeed break the covenant and escape?
16 'As I live,' declares the Lord GOD, 'Surely in the country of the king who put him on
the throne, whose oath he despised and whose covenant he broke, in Babylon he shall
die.
17 'Pharaoh with *his* mighty army and great company will not help him in the war, when
they cast up ramps and build siege walls to cut off many lives.
18 'Now he despised the oath by breaking the covenant, and behold, he pledged his
allegiance, yet did all these things; he shall not escape.' "
19 Therefore, thus says the Lord GOD, "As I live, surely My oath which he despised
and My covenant which he broke, I will inflict on his head.
20 "I will spread My net over him, and he will be caught in My snare. Then I will bring
him to Babylon and enter into judgment with him there *regarding* the unfaithful act which
he has committed against Me.
21 "All the choice men in all his troops will fall by the sword, and the survivors will be
scattered to every wind; and you will know that I, the LORD, have spoken."
22 Thus says the Lord GOD, "I will also take *a sprig* from the lofty top of the cedar and
set *it* out; I will pluck from the topmost of its young twigs a tender one and I will plant *it*
on a high and lofty mountain.
23 "On the high mountain of Israel I will plant it, that it may bring forth boughs and
bear fruit and become a stately cedar. And birds of every kind will nest under it; they will
nest in the shade of its branches.
24 "All the trees of the field will know that I am the LORD; I bring down the high tree,
exalt the low tree, dry up the green tree and make the dry tree flourish. I am the LORD;
I have spoken, and I will perform *it*."

God Deals Justly with Individuals

18 Then the word of the LORD came to me, saying,
2 "What do you mean by using this proverb concerning the land of Israel, saying,
'The fathers eat the sour grapes,
But the children's teeth are set on edge'?
3 "As I live," declares the Lord GOD, "you are surely not going to use this proverb in
Israel anymore.
4 "Behold, all souls are Mine; the soul of the father as well as the soul of the son is
Mine. The soul who sins will die.
5 "But if a man is righteous and practices justice and righteousness,
6 and does not eat at the mountain *shrines* or lift up his eyes to the idols of the house
of Israel, or defile his neighbor's wife or approach a woman during her menstrual
period—
7 if a man does not oppress anyone, but restores to the debtor his pledge, does not
commit robbery, *but* gives his bread to the hungry and covers the naked with clothing,
8 if he does not lend *money* on interest or take increase, *if* he keeps his hand from
iniquity *and* executes true justice between man and man,

17:14 Ezek 29:14

17:15 2 Kin 24:20; 2 Chr 36:13; Jer 52:3; Ezek 17:7; Jer 34:3; 38:18, 23; Ezek 17:18

17:16 2 Kin 24:17, 20; Ezek 16:59; 17:13, 18, 19; Jer 52:11; Ezek 12:13

17:17 Is 36:6; Jer 37:5, 7; Ezek 29:6, 7

17:18 1 Chr 29:24

17:20 Ezek 12:13; 32:3; Jer 39:5-7; Jer 2:35; Ezek 20:35, 36

17:21 2 Kin 25:5, 11; Ezek 5:2, 10, 12-14

17:22 Ps 72:16; Ezek 20:40; 37:22

17:23 Ps 92:12

17:24 Ps 96:12; Is 55:12; Amos 9:11

18:2 Is 3:15; Jer 31:29; Lam 5:7

18:4 Num 16:22; 27:16; Is 42:5; 57:16; Ezek 18:20; Rom 6:23

18:6 Ezek 6:13; 18:15; 22:9; Deut 4:19; Ezek 18:12, 15; 20:24; 33:25; Ezek 18:15; 22:11

18:7 Deut 24:13; Ezek 33:15; Amos 2:8; Lev 19:13; Amos 3:10; Deut 15:11; Ezek 18:16; Matt 25:35-40; Luke 3:11

18:8 Ex 22:25; Deut 23:19, 20; Lev 25:36; Zech 7:9; 8:16

17:22–23 Ezekiel's prophecy of judgment ends in hope. When the people put their hope in foreign alliances, they were disappointed. Only God could give them true hope. God said he would plant a tender sprig, the Messiah, whose kingdom would grow and become a shelter for all who come to him (see Isaiah 11:1–5). This prophecy was fulfilled at the coming of Jesus Christ.

18:1ff The people of Judah believed they were being punished for the sins of their ancestors, not their own. They thought this way because this was the teaching of the Ten Commandments (Exodus 20:5). Ezekiel taught that the destruction of Jerusalem was due to the spiritual decay in previous generations. But this belief in the corporate life of Israel led to fatalism and irresponsibility. So Ezekiel gave God's new policy for this new land because the people had misconstrued the old one. God judges each person individually. Although we often suffer from the effects of sins committed by those who came before us, God does not punish us for someone else's sins, and we can't use their mistakes as an excuse for our sins. Each person is accountable to God for his or her actions.

In addition, some people of Judah used the corporate umbrella of God's blessing as an excuse for disobeying God. They thought that because of their righteous ancestors (18:5–9) they would live. God told them that they would not; they were the evil sons of righteous parents and, as such, would die (18:10–13). If, however, anyone returned to God, he or she would live (18:14–18).

18:8 The Law of Moses had rules about charging interest (Exodus 22:25; Leviticus 25:36; Deuteronomy 23:19–20) to prevent God's people from taking advantage of the poor or of fellow Israelites.

9 *if* he walks in My statutes and My ordinances so as to deal faithfully—he is righteous *and* will surely live," declares the Lord GOD.
10 "Then he may have a violent son who sheds blood and who does any of these things
to a brother
11 (though he himself did not do any of these things), that is, he even eats at the mountain *shrines,* and defiles his neighbor's wife,
12 oppresses the poor and needy, commits robbery, does not restore a pledge, but lifts
up his eyes to the idols *and* commits abomination,
13 he lends *money* on interest and takes increase; will he live? He will not live! He has
committed all these abominations, he will surely be put to death; his blood will be on his
own head.
14 "Now behold, he has a son who has observed all his father's sins which he committed, and observing does not do likewise.
15 "He does not eat at the mountain *shrines* or lift up his eyes to the idols of the house
of Israel, or defile his neighbor's wife,
16 or oppress anyone, or retain a pledge, or commit robbery, *but* he gives his bread to
the hungry and covers the naked with clothing,
17 he keeps his hand from the poor, does not take interest or increase, *but* executes
My ordinances, and walks in My statutes; he will not die for his father's iniquity, he will
surely live.
18 "As for his father, because he practiced extortion, robbed *his* brother and did what
was not good among his people, behold, he will die for his iniquity.
19 "Yet you say, 'Why should the son not bear the punishment for the father's iniquity?'
When the son has practiced justice and righteousness and has observed all My statutes
and done them, he shall surely live.
20 "The person who sins will die. The son will not bear the punishment for the father's
iniquity, nor will the father bear the punishment for the son's iniquity; the righteousness
of the righteous will be upon himself, and the wickedness of the wicked will be upon
himself.
21 "But if the wicked man turns from all his sins which he has committed and observes
all My statutes and practices justice and righteousness, he shall surely live; he shall not die.
22 "All his transgressions which he has committed will not be remembered against him;
because of his righteousness which he has practiced, he will live.
23 "Do I have any pleasure in the death of the wicked," declares the Lord GOD, "rather
than that he should turn from his ways and live?
24 "But when a righteous man turns away from his righteousness, commits iniquity and
does according to all the abominations that a wicked man does, will he live? All his righteous deeds which he has done will not be remembered for his treachery which he has
committed and his sin which he has committed; for them he will die.
25 "Yet you say, 'The way of the Lord is not right.' Hear now, O house of Israel! Is My
way not right? Is it not your ways that are not right?
26 "When a righteous man turns away from his righteousness, commits iniquity and dies
because of it, for his iniquity which he has committed he will die.
27 "Again, when a wicked man turns away from his wickedness which he has committed
and practices justice and righteousness, he will save his life.
28 "Because he considered and turned away from all his transgressions which he had
committed, he shall surely live; he shall not die.
29 "But the house of Israel says, 'The way of the Lord is not right.' Are My ways not
right, O house of Israel? Is it not your ways that are not right?
30 "Therefore I will judge you, O house of Israel, each according to his conduct," declares

18:9 Lev 18:5; Rom 8:1; Amos 5:4; Hab 2:4; Rom 1:17

18:11 1 Cor 6:9

18:12 Amos 4:1; Zech 7:10; Is 59:6, 7; Jer 22:3, 17; Ezek 7:23; 18:7, 16, 18; 2 Kin 21:11; Ezek 8:6, 17

18:13 Ex 22:25; Ezek 33:4, 5

18:14 2 Chr 29:6-10; 34:21

18:16 Job 31:16, 20; Ps 41:1; Is 58:7, 10; Ezek 18:7

18:17 Rom 2:7

18:19 Ex 20:5; Jer 15:4; Ezek 18:2; Ezek 18:9; 20:18-20; Zech 1:3-6

18:20 2 Kin 14:6; 22:18-20; Ezek 18:4; Deut 24:16; Jer 31:30; 1 Kin 8:32; Is 3:10, 11; Matt 16:27; Rom 2:6-9

18:21 Ezek 18:27, 28; 33:12, 19

18:22 Is 43:25; Jer 50:20; Ezek 18:24; 33:16; Mic 7:19; Ps 18:20-24

18:23 Ezek 18:32; 33:11; Ps 147:11; Mic 7:18

18:24 1 Sam 15:11; 2 Chr 24:2, 17-22; Ezek 3:20; 18:26; 33:18; Ezek 18:22; Gal 3:3, 4; Prov 21:16; Ezek 17:20; 20:27

18:25 Ezek 18:29; 33:17, 20; Mal 2:17; 3:13-15; Gen 18:25; Jer 12:1; Zeph 3:5

18:27 Is 1:18; 55:7

18:30 Ezek 14:6; 33:11; Hos 12:6

18:12 Returning what one took in pledge referred to the lender letting the debtor use the cloak each night that he has placed as security on his loan. Without the cloak, the debtor would be cold at night. (See Exodus 22:26 and Deuteronomy 24:10–13 for the giving of this law.)

18:23 God is a God of love, but he is also a God of perfect justice. His perfect love causes him to be merciful to those who recognize their sin and turn back to him, but he cannot wink at those who willfully sin. Wicked people die both physically and spiritually. God takes no joy in their deaths; he would prefer that they turn to him and have eternal life. Likewise, we should not rejoice in the misfortunes of nonbelievers. Instead, we should do all in our power to bring them to faith.

18:25 A typical childish response to punishment is to say, "That isn't fair!" In reality, God is fair, but *we* have broken the rules. It is not God who must live up to our ideas of fairness; instead, we must live up to his. Don't spend your time looking for the loopholes in God's law. Instead, live up to God's standards.

the Lord GOD. "Repent and turn away from all your transgressions, so that iniquity may
not become a stumbling block to you.
31 "Cast away from you all your transgressions which you have committed and make
yourselves a new heart and a new spirit! For why will you die, O house of Israel?
32 "For I have no pleasure in the death of anyone who dies," declares the Lord GOD.
"Therefore, repent and live."

18:31 Is 1:16, 17; 55:7; Ps 51:10; Ezek 11:19; 36:26

18:32 Ezek 18:23; 33:11

Lament for the Princes of Israel

19 "As for you, take up a lamentation for the princes of Israel
2 and say,
'What was your mother?
A lioness among lions!
She lay down among young lions,
She reared her cubs.
3 'When she brought up one of her cubs,
He became a lion,
And he learned to tear *his* prey;
He devoured men.
4 'Then nations heard about him;
He was captured in their pit,
And they brought him with hooks
To the land of Egypt.
5 'When she saw, as she waited,
That her hope was lost,
She took another of her cubs
And made him a young lion.
6 'And he walked about among the lions;
He became a young lion,
He learned to tear *his* prey;
He devoured men.
7 'He destroyed their fortified towers
And laid waste their cities;
And the land and its fullness were appalled
Because of the sound of his roaring.
8 'Then nations set against him
On every side from *their* provinces,
And they spread their net over him;
He was captured in their pit.
9 'They put him in a cage with hooks
And brought him to the king of Babylon;
They brought him in hunting nets
So that his voice would be heard no more
On the mountains of Israel.
10 'Your mother was like a vine in your vineyard,
Planted by the waters;
It was fruitful and full of branches
Because of abundant waters.
11 'And it had strong branches *fit* for scepters of rulers,

19:1 Ezek 2:10; 19:14; 2 Kin 23:29, 30, 34; 24:6, 12; 25:5-7

19:4 2 Kin 23:34; 2 Chr 36:4, 6

19:6 2 Kin 24:9; 2 Chr 36:9

19:8 2 Kin 24:11

19:9 2 Chr 36:6; 2 Kin 24:15

19:10 Ps 80:8-11

19:11 Ps 80:15; Ezek 31:3

18:30–32 Ezekiel's solution to the problem of inherited guilt is for each person to have a changed life. This is God's work in us and not something we can do for ourselves. The Holy Spirit does it (Psalm 51:10–12). If we renounce our life's direction of sin and rebellion and turn to God, he will give us a new direction, a new love, and a new power to change. You can begin by faith, trusting in God's power to change your heart and mind. Then determine to live each day with him in control (Ephesians 4:22–24).

19:1ff Ezekiel used illustrations to communicate many of his messages. With the picture of the lioness and her cubs, he raised the curiosity of his listeners. The lioness symbolized the nation of Judah, and the two cubs were two of its kings. The first cub was King Jehoahaz, who was taken captive to Egypt in 609 B.C. by Pharaoh Neco (2 Kings 23:31–33). The second cub was either King Jehoiachin, who had already been taken into captivity in Babylon (2 Kings 24:8ff), or King Zedekiah, who soon would be (2 Kings 25:7). This illustration showed that for Judah, there was no hope for a quick return from exile, and no escape from the approaching Babylonian armies.

19:11–12 Not even the political and military might of Judah's kings could save the nation. Like branches of a vine, they would be cut off and uprooted by "the east wind"—the powerful Babylonian army.

And its height was raised above the clouds
So that it was seen in its height with the mass of its branches.

19:12 Jer 31:28; Lam 2:1; Ezek 28:17; Ezek 17:10; Hos 13:15; Is 27:11; Ezek 19:11

12 'But it was plucked up in fury;
It was cast down to the ground;
And the east wind dried up its fruit.
Its strong branch was torn off
So that it withered;
The fire consumed it.

19:13 2 Kin 24:12-16; Ezek 19:10; 20:35; Hos 2:3

13 'And now it is planted in the wilderness,
In a dry and thirsty land.

19:14 Ezek 15:4; 20:47, 48

14 'And fire has gone out from *its* branch;
It has consumed its shoots *and* fruit,
So that there is not in it a strong branch,
A scepter to rule.' "
This is a lamentation, and has become a lamentation.

God's Dealings with Israel Rehearsed

20:1 Ezek 8:1, 11, 12

20 Now in the seventh year, in the fifth *month,* on the tenth of the month, certain of
the elders of Israel came to inquire of the LORD, and sat before me.
2 And the word of the LORD came to me saying,

20:3 Ezek 14:3

3 "Son of man, speak to the elders of Israel and say to them, 'Thus says the Lord GOD,
"Do you come to inquire of Me? As I live," declares the Lord GOD, "I will not be inquired of by you." '

20:4 Ezek 16:2; 22:2; Matt 23:32

4 "Will you judge them, will you judge them, son of man? Make them know the abominations of their fathers;

20:5 Ex 6:6-8; Ex 6:2, 3

5 and say to them, 'Thus says the Lord GOD, "On the day when I chose Israel and
swore to the descendants of the house of Jacob and made Myself known to them in the
land of Egypt, when I swore to them, saying, I am the LORD your God,

20:6 Jer 32:22; Ex 13:5; 33:3; Ps 48:2

6 on that day I swore to them, to bring them out from the land of Egypt into a land
that I had selected for them, flowing with milk and honey, which is the glory of all lands.

20:7 Ex 20:4, 5; 22:20; Lev 18:3; Deut 29:16-18; Ex 20:2

7 "I said to them, 'Cast away, each of you, the detestable things of his eyes, and do not
defile yourselves with the idols of Egypt; I am the LORD your God.'

20:8 Deut 9:7; Is 63:10; Ex 32:1-9; Ezek 5:13; 7:8; 20:13, 21

8 "But they rebelled against Me and were not willing to listen to Me; they did not cast
away the detestable things of their eyes, nor did they forsake the idols of Egypt.
Then I resolved to pour out My wrath on them, to accomplish My anger against them
in the midst of the land of Egypt.

20:9 Ex 32:11-14; Ezek 20:14, 22; 36:21, 22; Ezek 39:7

9 "But I acted for the sake of My name, that it should not be profaned in the sight of
the nations among whom they *lived,* in whose sight I made Myself known to them by
bringing them out of the land of Egypt.

20:10 Ex 19:1

10 "So I took them out of the land of Egypt and brought them into the wilderness.

20:11 Ex 20:1-23:33; Lev 18:5; Ezek 20:13

11 "I gave them My statutes and informed them of My ordinances, by which, if a man
observes them, he will live.

20:12 Ex 31:13, 17; Ezek 20:20

12 "Also I gave them My sabbaths to be a sign between Me and them, that they might
know that I am the LORD who sanctifies them.

20:13 Num 14:11, 12, 22; Ezek 20:8; Lev 18:5; Is 56:6; Ezek 20:21; Ex 32:10; Deut 9:8; Ezek 20:8, 21

13 "But the house of Israel rebelled against Me in the wilderness. They did not walk in
My statutes and they rejected My ordinances, by which, if a man observes them, he will
live; and My sabbaths they greatly profaned. Then I resolved to pour out My wrath on
them in the wilderness, to annihilate them.
14 "But I acted for the sake of My name, that it should not be profaned in the sight of
the nations, before whose sight I had brought them out.

20:1ff Here Ezekiel gives a panoramic view of Israel's history of rebellion. The emphasis is on God's attempts to bring the nation back to himself and on God's mercy for his constantly rebellious and disobedient people. Ezekiel gives the message that the people alone are responsible for the troubles and judgments they have experienced. Those who persist in rebellion God will "purge" (20:38), while he will bring the faithful "into the land of Israel, into the land which I swore to give to your forefathers." The reason: that "you will know that I am the LORD" (20:42).

20:12–13 The Sabbath, instituted by God at creation, was entrusted to Israel as a sign that God had created and redeemed them (Exodus 20:8–11; Deuteronomy 5:12–15). This day of rest was a gift from a loving God, not a difficult obligation. But the people repeatedly desecrated the Sabbath and ignored their God (see also 20:20–21). It was meant to be a memory device but they ignored it. Today, many Christians celebrate the Lord's Day, Sunday, as their Sabbath. Whatever the day, we must be careful to fulfill God's purpose for the Sabbath. He wants us to rest, to refocus, and to remember him.

15 "Also I swore to them in the wilderness that I would not bring them into the land
which I had given them, flowing with milk and honey, which is the glory of all lands,
16 because they rejected My ordinances, and as for My statutes, they did not walk in
them; they even profaned My sabbaths, for their heart continually went after their idols.
17 "Yet My eye spared them rather than destroying them, and I did not cause their annihilation in the wilderness.
18 "I said to their children in the wilderness, 'Do not walk in the statutes of your fathers
or keep their ordinances or defile yourselves with their idols.
19 'I am the LORD your God; walk in My statutes and keep My ordinances and observe
them.
20 'Sanctify My sabbaths; and they shall be a sign between Me and you, that you may
know that I am the LORD your God.'
21 "But the children rebelled against Me; they did not walk in My statutes, nor were
they careful to observe My ordinances, by which, *if* a man observes them, he will live;
they profaned My sabbaths. So I resolved to pour out My wrath on them, to accomplish
My anger against them in the wilderness.
22 "But I withdrew My hand and acted for the sake of My name, that it should not be
profaned in the sight of the nations in whose sight I had brought them out.
23 "Also I swore to them in the wilderness that I would scatter them among the nations
and disperse them among the lands,
24 because they had not observed My ordinances, but had rejected My statutes and
had profaned My sabbaths, and their eyes were on the idols of their fathers.
25 "I also gave them statutes that were not good and ordinances by which they could
not live;
26 and I pronounced them unclean because of their gifts, in that they caused all their
firstborn to pass through *the fire* so that I might make them desolate, in order that they
might know that I am the LORD." '
27 "Therefore, son of man, speak to the house of Israel and say to them, 'Thus says
the Lord GOD, "Yet in this your fathers have blasphemed Me by acting treacherously
against Me.
28 "When I had brought them into the land which I swore to give to them, then they
saw every high hill and every leafy tree, and they offered there their sacrifices and there
they presented the provocation of their offering. There also they made their soothing
aroma and there they poured out their drink offerings.
29 "Then I said to them, 'What is the high place to which you go?' So its name is called
[1]Bamah to this day." '
30 "Therefore, say to the house of Israel, 'Thus says the Lord GOD, "Will you defile
yourselves after the manner of your fathers and play the harlot after their detestable
things?
31 "When you offer your gifts, when you cause your sons to pass through the fire, you are
defiling yourselves with all your idols to this day. And shall I be inquired of by you,
O house of Israel? As I live," declares the Lord GOD, "I will not be inquired of by you.
32 "What comes into your mind will not come about, when you say: 'We will be like the
nations, like the tribes of the lands, serving wood and stone.'

God Will Restore Israel to Her Land

33 "As I live," declares the Lord GOD, "surely with a mighty hand and with an outstretched arm and with wrath poured out, I shall be king over you.
34 "I will bring you out from the peoples and gather you from the lands where you are
scattered, with a mighty hand and with an outstretched arm and with wrath poured out;

20:15 Num 14:30; Ps 95:11; 106:26
20:16 Ezek 11:21; 14:3-7
20:17 Jer 4:27; 5:18; Ezek 11:13
20:18 Num 14:31; Deut 4:3-6; Zech 1:4
20:19 Ex 6:7; 20:2; Deut 5:32, 33; 6:1, 2; 8:1, 2; 11:1; 12:1
20:20 Jer 17:22
20:21 Num 21:5; 25:1-3
20:22 Job 13:21; Ps 78:38; Ezek 20:17; Is 48:9-11; Jer 14:7, 21
20:23 Lev 26:33; Deut 4:27; 28:64
20:24 Ezek 6:9
20:25 Ps 81:12; Is 66:4; Rom 1:21-25, 28
20:26 Lev 18:21; 20:2-5; Is 63:17; Ezek 20:30; Rom 11:8; Jer 7:31; 19:4-9; Ezek 6:7
20:27 Ezek 2:7; 3:4, 11, 27; Num 15:30; Rom 2:24; Ezek 18:24; 39:23, 26
20:28 Josh 23:3, 14; Neh 9:22-26; Ps 78:55; Jer 2:7; 1 Kin 14:23; Ps 78:58; Is 57:5-7; Jer 3:6; Ezek 6:13
20:30 Judg 2:19; Jer 7:26; 16:12
20:31 Ps 106:37-39; Jer 7:31; Ezek 16:20
20:32 Ezek 11:5; Jer 2:25; 44:17
20:33 Jer 21:5; Jer 51:57
20:34 Is 27:12, 13; Ezek 20:38; 34:16; Jer 42:18; 44:6; Lam 2:4

1 Or *High Place*

20:23–24 At the very beginning of Israel's history, God clearly warned the people about the consequences of disobedience (Deuteronomy 28:15ff). When the people disobeyed, God let them experience those devastating consequences to remind them of the seriousness of their sins. If you choose to live for yourself, apart from God, you may experience similar destructive consequences. However, even through such consequences, God may be drawing you to himself. Let your misfortunes bring you to your senses and to the merciful God before it is too late.

20:25 Why would God give them laws that weren't good? This isn't talking about any aspect of the Mosaic Law—Ezekiel reinforces that Law (20:11, 13, 21). Evidently the Jews had taken Exodus 13:12 and 22:29, the dedication of firstborn animals and children, as a justification for child sacrifice to the Canaanite god Molech. God was giving them over to this delusion to get them to acknowledge him, to jar their consciences, and to revitalize their faith (20:26).

35 and I will bring you into the wilderness of the peoples, and there I will enter into
judgment with you face to face.
36 "As I entered into judgment with your fathers in the wilderness of the land of Egypt,
so I will enter into judgment with you," declares the Lord GOD.
37 "I will make you pass under the rod, and I will bring you into the bond of the covenant;
38 and I will purge from you the rebels and those who transgress against Me; I will bring
them out of the land where they sojourn, but they will not enter the land of Israel. Thus
you will know that I am the LORD.
39 "As for you, O house of Israel," thus says the Lord GOD, "Go, serve everyone his
idols; but later you will surely listen to Me, and My holy name you will profane no longer
with your gifts and with your idols.
40 "For on My holy mountain, on the high mountain of Israel," declares the Lord GOD,
"there the whole house of Israel, all of them, will serve Me in the land; there I will accept them and there I will seek your contributions and the choicest of your gifts, with all
your holy things.
41 "As a soothing aroma I will accept you when I bring you out from the peoples and
gather you from the lands where you are scattered; and I will prove Myself holy among
you in the sight of the nations.
42 "And you will know that I am the LORD, when I bring you into the land of Israel, into
the land which I swore to give to your forefathers.
43 "There you will remember your ways and all your deeds with which you have defiled
yourselves; and you will loathe yourselves in your own sight for all the evil things that
you have done.
44 "Then you will know that I am the LORD when I have dealt with you for My name's
sake, not according to your evil ways or according to your corrupt deeds, O house of
Israel," declares the Lord GOD.' "
45 Now the word of the LORD came to me, saying,
46 "Son of man, set your face toward Teman, and speak out against the south and prophesy against the forest land of the Negev,
47 and say to the forest of the Negev, 'Hear the word of the LORD: thus says the Lord
GOD, "Behold, I am about to kindle a fire in you, and it will consume every green tree in
you, as well as every dry tree; the blazing flame will not be quenched and the whole surface from south to north will be burned by it.
48 "All flesh will see that I, the LORD, have kindled it; it shall not be quenched." ' "
49 Then I said, "Ah Lord GOD! They are saying of me, 'Is he not *just* speaking parables?' "

Parable of the Sword of the LORD

21 And the word of the LORD came to me saying,
2 "Son of man, set your face toward Jerusalem, and speak against the sanctuaries and prophesy against the land of Israel;

20:35 Hos 2:14
20:36 Num 11:1-35; Ps 106:15; 1 Cor 10:5-10; Deut 32:10
20:37 Lev 27:32; Jer 33:13
20:38 Ezek 34:17-22; Amos 9:9, 10; Zech 13:8, 9; Mal 3:3; 4:1-3; Num 14:29, 30; Ps 95:11; Ezek 13:9; 20:15, 16; Heb 4:3
20:39 Jer 44:25, 26; Is 1:13-15; Ezek 23:38, 39; 43:7
20:40 Is 66:23; Ezek 37:22, 24; Is 56:7; 60:7; Ezek 43:12, 27
20:41 Is 27:12, 13; Is 5:16; Ezek 28:25; 36:23
20:43 Ezek 6:9; 16:61, 63; Hos 5:15; Jer 31:18; Ezek 36:31; Zech 12:10
20:44 Ezek 24:24; Ezek 36:22
20:46 Jer 13:19; Ezek 21:4; Ezek 21:2; Amos 7:16; Is 30:6-11
20:47 Is 9:18, 19; Jer 21:14; Is 13:8
20:48 Jer 7:20; 17:27
20:49 Ezek 17:2; Matt 13:13; John 16:25
21:2 Ezek 20:46; 25:2; 28:21; Job 29:22; Ezek 20:46

20:35–36 When the Israelites disobeyed God by refusing to enter the promised land the first time, God chose to purify his people by forcing them to wander in the wilderness until that entire generation died (Numbers 14:26–35). Here he promised to purge the nation of its rebellious people again as they cross the vast wilderness from their captivity in Babylon. Only those who faithfully followed God would be able to return to their land. The purpose of this wilderness judgment would be to purge all those who worship idols and to restore all those faithful to God.

20:39 The Israelites were worshiping idols and giving gifts to God at the same time! They did not believe in their God as the one true God; instead, they worshiped him along with the other gods of the land. Perhaps they enjoyed the immoral pleasures of idol worship; or perhaps they didn't want to miss out on the benefits the idols might give them. Often people believe in God and give him gifts of church attendance or service, while still holding on to their idols of money, power, or pleasure. They don't want to miss out on any possible benefits. But God wants all of our lives and all of our devotion; he will not share it because devotion to anything else is idol worship. Beware of trying to keep God pleased while you also pursue the pleasures of sin. You must choose one or the other.

20:45–47 "The south" refers to Jerusalem and Judah. The Negev region is compared to a forest about to be destroyed by fire.

20:49 Ezekiel was exasperated and discouraged. Many Israelites were complaining that he spoke only in riddles ("parables"), so they refused to listen. No matter how important our work or how significant our ministry, we will have moments of discouragement. Apparently God did not answer Ezekiel's plea; instead, he gave Ezekiel another message to proclaim. What has been discouraging you? Have you felt like giving up? Instead, continue doing what God has told you to do. He promises to reward the faithful (Mark 13:13). God's cure for discouragement may be another assignment. In serving others, we may find the renewal we need.

21:1ff The short message in 20:45–48 introduces the first of three messages about the judgments that would come upon Jerusalem: (1) the sword of the Lord (21:1–7); (2) the sharpened sword (21:8–17); (3) the sword of Nebuchadnezzar (21:18–22). The city would be destroyed because it was defiled. According to Jewish law, defiled objects were to be passed through fire in order to purify them (see Numbers 31:22–23; Psalm 66:10–12; Proverbs 17:3). God's judgment is designed to purify; destruction is often a necessary part of that process.

3 and say to the land of Israel, 'Thus says the LORD, "Behold, I am against you; and
I will draw My sword out of its sheath and cut off from you the righteous and the wicked.
4 "Because I will cut off from you the righteous and the wicked, therefore My sword
will go forth from its sheath against all flesh from south *to* north.
5 "Thus all flesh will know that I, the LORD, have drawn My sword out of its sheath. It
will not return *to its sheath* again." '
6 "As for you, son of man, groan with breaking heart and bitter grief, groan in their
sight.
7 "And when they say to you, 'Why do you groan?' you shall say, 'Because of the news
that is coming; and every heart will melt, all hands will be feeble, every spirit will faint
and all knees will be weak as water. Behold, it comes and it will happen,' declares the
Lord GOD."
8 Again the word of the LORD came to me, saying,
9 "Son of man, prophesy and say, 'Thus says the LORD.' Say,
'A sword, a sword sharpened
And also polished!
10 'Sharpened to make a slaughter,
Polished to flash like lightning!'
Or shall we rejoice, the rod of My son despising every tree?
11 "It is given to be polished, that it may be handled; the sword is sharpened and polished, to give it into the hand of the slayer.
12 "Cry out and wail, son of man; for it is against My people, it is against all the officials
of Israel. They are delivered over to the sword with My people, therefore strike *your*
thigh.
13 "For *there is* a testing; and what if even the rod which despises will be no more?"
declares the Lord GOD.
14 "You therefore, son of man, prophesy and clap *your* hands together; and let the sword
be doubled the third time, the sword for the slain. It is the sword for the great one slain,
which surrounds them,
15 that *their* hearts may melt, and many fall at all their gates. I have given the glittering
sword. Ah! It is made *for striking* like lightning, it is wrapped up *in readiness* for slaughter.
16 "Show yourself sharp, go to the right; set yourself; go to the left, wherever your edge
is appointed.
17 "I will also clap My hands together, and I will appease My wrath; I, the LORD, have
spoken."

The Instrument of God's Judgment

18 The word of the LORD came to me saying,
19 "As for you, son of man, make two ways for the sword of the king of Babylon to come;
both of them will go out of one land. And make a signpost; make it at the head of the
way to the city.
20 "You shall mark a way for the sword to come to Rabbah of the sons of Ammon, and
to Judah into fortified Jerusalem.
21 "For the king of Babylon stands at the parting of the way, at the head of the two ways,
to use divination; he shakes the arrows, he consults the household idols, he looks at the
liver.
22 "Into his right hand came the divination, 'Jerusalem,' to set battering rams, to open
the mouth for slaughter, to lift up the voice with a battle cry, to set battering rams against
the gates, to cast up ramps, to build a siege wall.

21:3 Jer 21:13; Ezek 5:8; Nah 2:13; 3:5; Is 57:1
21:4 Jer 12:12; Ezek 7:2; 20:47
21:5 1 Sam 3:12; Jer 23:20; Ezek 21:30; Nah 1:9
21:7 Ezek 7:26; Is 13:7; Nah 2:10
21:9 Deut 32:41
21:10 Is 34:5, 6; Ps 110:5, 6; Ezek 20:47
21:12 Ezek 21:6; Joel 1:13; Ezek 21:25; 22:6
21:14 Lev 26:21, 24; 2 Kin 24:1, 10-16; 25:1
21:15 Josh 2:11; 2 Sam 17:10; Ps 22:14; Ezek 21:7; Is 59:10; Jer 13:16; 18:15; Jer 17:27; Ezek 21:19
21:17 Ezek 5:13
21:19 Jer 1:10; Ezek 4:1-3
21:20 Deut 3:11; Jer 49:2; Ezek 25:5; Amos 1:14; Ps 48:12, 13; 125:1, 2
21:21 Num 22:7; 23:23; Prov 16:33; Gen 31:19, 30; Judg 17:5; 18:17, 20
21:22 Ezek 4:2; 26:9

21:12 Striking the thigh was a gesture of grief.

21:18–23 Ammon evidently rebelled against Babylon about the same time as King Zedekiah of Judah. In 589 B.C. the nations of Judah and Ammon were among those who conspired against Babylon (Jeremiah 27:3). Ezekiel gave this message to the exiles who had heard the news and were again filled with hope of returning to their homeland. Ezekiel said that Babylon's king would march his armies into the region to stop the rebellion. Traveling from the north, he would stop at a fork in the road, one leading to Rabbah, the capital of Ammon, and the other leading to Jerusalem, the capital of Judah. He had to decide which city to destroy. Just as Ezekiel predicted, King Nebuchadnezzar went to Jerusalem and besieged it.

21:21 Nebuchadnezzar had three ways to get advice on the future. One was shaking the arrows, much like drawing straws, to see which course of action was right; the second was consulting an idol to see if some spirit might direct him; the third was having priests inspect the liver of a sacrificed animal to see if its shape and size would indicate a decision.

21:23 Ezek 17:16, 18; Num 5:15
21:25 Ps 37:13; Ezek 7:2
21:26 Jer 13:18; Ezek 16:12; Ps 75:7
21:27 Hag 2:21, 22; Ps 2:6; 72:7, 10; Jer 23:5, 6; Ezek 34:24
21:28 Ezek 36:15; Zeph 2:8-10; Is 31:8; Jer 12:12; 46:10, 14
21:29 Jer 27:9; Ezek 13:6-9; 22:28
21:30 Jer 47:6, 7; Ezek 25:5
21:31 Ezek 14:19; 25:7; Nah 1:6; Ps 18:15; Is 30:33; Ezek 22:20, 21; Hag 1:9; Jer 4:7; 6:22, 23; 51:20-23; Hab 1:6
21:32 Ezek 20:47, 48; Mal 4:1; Ezek 25:10
22:4 2 Kin 21:16; Ezek 24:7, 8; Ps 44:13, 14; Ezek 5:14, 15; 16:57
22:6 Is 1:23; Ezek 22:27
22:7 Ex 20:12; Lev 20:9; Deut 5:16; 27:16; Ex 22:21f; 23:9; Deut 24:17; Jer 7:6; Zech 7:10; Ex 22:22; Ezek 22:25; Mal 3:5
22:8 Ezek 20:13, 21, 24; 23:38, 39
22:9 Ezek 23:29; Hos 4:2, 10, 14
22:10 Lev 18:8; Lev 18:19; Ezek 18:6
22:11 Ezek 18:11; 33:26; Lev 18:15; 2 Sam 13:11-14
22:12 Ex 23:8; Deut 16:19; 27:25; Mic 7:2, 3; Lev 25:36; Deut 23:19; Lev 19:13; Ps 106:21; Ezek 23:35

23 "And it will be to them like a false divination in their eyes; they have *sworn* solemn
oaths. But he brings iniquity to remembrance, that they may be seized.
24 "Therefore, thus says the Lord GOD, 'Because you have made your iniquity to be
remembered, in that your transgressions are uncovered, so that in all your deeds your
sins appear—because you have come to remembrance, you will be seized with the hand.
25 'And you, O slain, wicked one, the prince of Israel, whose day has come, in the time
of the punishment of the end,'
26 thus says the Lord GOD, 'Remove the turban and take off the crown; this *will* no
longer *be* the same. Exalt that which is low and abase that which is high.
27 'A ruin, a ruin, a ruin, I will make it. This also will be no more until He comes whose
right it is, and I will give it *to Him.*'
28 "And you, son of man, prophesy and say, 'Thus says the Lord GOD concerning the
sons of Ammon and concerning their reproach,' and say: 'A sword, a sword is drawn,
polished for the slaughter, to cause it to consume, that it may be like lightning—
29 while they see for you false visions, while they divine lies for you—to place you on
the necks of the wicked who are slain, whose day has come, in the time of the punishment of the end.
30 'Return *it* to its sheath. In the place where you were created, in the land of your
origin, I will judge you.
31 'I will pour out My indignation on you; I will blow on you with the fire of My wrath,
and I will give you into the hand of brutal men, skilled in destruction.
32 'You will be fuel for the fire; your blood will be in the midst of the land. You will not
be remembered, for I, the LORD, have spoken.' "

The Sins of Israel

22 Then the word of the LORD came to me, saying,
2 "And you, son of man, will you judge, will you judge the bloody city? Then cause
her to know all her abominations.
3 "You shall say, 'Thus says the Lord GOD, "A city shedding blood in her midst, so that
her time will come, and that makes idols, contrary to her *interest,* for defilement!
4 "You have become guilty by the blood which you have shed, and defiled by your idols
which you have made. Thus you have brought your day near and have come to your years;
therefore I have made you a reproach to the nations and a mocking to all the lands.
5 "Those who are near and those who are far from you will mock you, you of ill repute,
full of turmoil.
6 "Behold, the rulers of Israel, each according to his power, have been in you for the
purpose of shedding blood.
7 "They have treated father and mother lightly within you. The alien they have oppressed in your midst; the fatherless and the widow they have wronged in you.
8 "You have despised My holy things and profaned My sabbaths.
9 "Slanderous men have been in you for the purpose of shedding blood, and in you
they have eaten at the mountain *shrines.* In your midst they have committed acts of lewdness.
10 "In you they have uncovered *their* fathers' nakedness; in you they have humbled her
who was unclean in her menstrual impurity.
11 "One has committed abomination with his neighbor's wife and another has
lewdly defiled his daughter-in-law. And another in you has humbled his sister, his father's
daughter.
12 "In you they have taken bribes to shed blood; you have taken interest and profits,
and you have injured your neighbors for gain by oppression, and you have forgotten Me,"
declares the Lord GOD.

21:28 The Ammonites and Israelites were usually fighting with each other. God told the Israelites not to ally with foreign nations, but Judah and Ammon united against Babylon in 589 B.C. (Jeremiah 27:3). God first judged Judah when Nebuchadnezzar first went to Jerusalem (21:22); but Ammon will also be judged, not for allying with Judah, but for watching Jerusalem's destruction with insulting delight.

22:1ff Chapter 22 explains why Jerusalem's judgment would come (22:2–16), how it would come (22:17–22), and who would be judged by it (22:23–31).

22:6–13 The leaders were especially responsible for the moral climate of the nation because God chose them to lead. The same is true today (see James 3:1). Unfortunately, many of the sins mentioned here have been committed in recent years by Christian leaders. We are living in a time of unprecedented attacks by Satan. We must uphold our leaders in prayer, and leaders must seek accountability to help them keep their moral and spiritual integrity.

13 "Behold, then, I smite My hand at your dishonest gain which you have acquired and
at the bloodshed which is among you.
14 "Can your heart endure, or can your hands be strong in the days that I will deal with
you? I, the LORD, have spoken and will act.
15 "I will scatter you among the nations and I will disperse you through the lands, and
I will consume your uncleanness from you.
16 "You will profane yourself in the sight of the nations, and you will know that I am the
LORD." ' "
17 And the word of the LORD came to me, saying,
18 "Son of man, the house of Israel has become dross to Me; all of them are bronze and
tin and iron and lead in the furnace; they are the dross of silver.
19 "Therefore, thus says the Lord GOD, 'Because all of you have become dross, therefore, behold, I am going to gather you into the midst of Jerusalem.
20 'As they gather silver and bronze and iron and lead and tin into the furnace to blow
fire on it in order to melt *it,* so I will gather *you* in My anger and in My wrath and I will
lay you *there* and melt you.
21 'I will gather you and blow on you with the fire of My wrath, and you will be melted
in the midst of it.
22 'As silver is melted in the furnace, so you will be melted in the midst of it; and you
will know that I, the LORD, have poured out My wrath on you.' "
23 And the word of the LORD came to me, saying,
24 "Son of man, say to her, 'You are a land that is not cleansed or rained on in the day
of indignation.'
25 "There is a conspiracy of her prophets in her midst like a roaring lion tearing the
prey. They have devoured lives; they have taken treasure and precious things; they have
made many widows in the midst of her.
26 "Her priests have done violence to My law and have profaned My holy things; they
have made no distinction between the holy and the profane, and they have not taught
the difference between the unclean and the clean; and they hide their eyes from My sabbaths, and I am profaned among them.
27 "Her princes within her are like wolves tearing the prey, by shedding blood *and* destroying lives in order to get dishonest gain.
28 "Her prophets have smeared whitewash for them, seeing false visions and divining
lies for them, saying, 'Thus says the Lord GOD,' when the LORD has not spoken.
29 "The people of the land have practiced oppression and committed robbery, and they
have wronged the poor and needy and have oppressed the sojourner without justice.
30 "I searched for a man among them who would build up the wall and stand in the gap
before Me for the land, so that I would not destroy it; but I found no one.
31 "Thus I have poured out My indignation on them; I have consumed them with the
fire of My wrath; their way I have brought upon their heads," declares the Lord GOD.

Oholah and Oholibah's Sin and Its Consequences

23 The word of the LORD came to me again, saying,
2 "Son of man, there were two women, the daughters of one mother;

22:13 Is 33:15; Amos 2:6-8; Mic 2:2
22:14 Ezek 21:7; Ezek 17:24
22:15 Deut 4:27; Neh 1:8; Ezek 20:23; Zech 7:14; Ezek 23:27, 48
22:16 Ps 83:18; Ezek 6:7
22:18 Ps 119:119; Is 1:22; Lam 4:1; Jer 6:28-30; Prov 17:3; Is 48:10
22:20 Is 1:25
22:22 Ezek 20:8, 33; Hos 5:10
22:24 Is 9:13; Jer 2:30; Ezek 24:13; Zeph 3:2
22:25 Jer 11:9; Hos 6:9; Jer 2:34; Ezek 13:19; 22:27; Jer 15:8; Ezek 22:7
22:26 Jer 2:8, 26; Ezek 7:26; 1 Sam 2:12-17, 22; Ezek 22:8; Lev 10:10; Ezek 44:23; Hag 2:11-14
22:28 Jer 23:25-32; Ezek 13:6
22:29 Is 5:7; Ezek 9:9; 22:7; Amos 3:10; Ex 23:9
22:30 Is 59:16; 63:5; Jer 5:1; Ezek 13:5; Ps 106:23; Jer 15:1
22:31 Is 10:5; 13:5; 30:27; Ezek 22:20; Ezek 7:3, 8, 9; 9:10; 16:43; Rom 2:8, 9
23:2 Ezek 16:46

22:17–22 Precious metals are refined with intense heat to remove the impurities. When heated, the dross (impurities) rises to the top of the molten metal and is skimmed off and thrown away. The purpose of the invasion of Jerusalem was to refine the people, but the refining process showed that the people, like worthless dross, had nothing good in them.

22:26 The priests were supposed to keep God's worship pure and teach the people right living. But the worship of God had become commonplace to them; they ignored the Sabbath, and they refused to teach the people. They no longer carried out their God-given duties (Leviticus 10:10–11; Ezekiel 44:23). When doing God's work becomes no more important than any mundane task, we are no longer giving God the reverence he deserves. Instead of bringing God down to our level, we should live up to his level.

22:30 The wall spoken of here is not made of stones, but of faithful people united in their efforts to resist evil. This wall was in disrepair because there was no one who could lead the people back to God. The feeble attempts to repair the gap—through religious rituals or messages based on opinion rather than God's will—were as worthless as whitewash, only covering over the real problems. What the people really needed was total spiritual reconstruction! When we give the appearance of loving God without living his way, we are covering up sins that could eventually damage us beyond repair. Don't use religion as a whitewash; repair your life by applying the principles of God's Word. Then you can join with others to stand "in the gap" and make a difference for God in the world.

23:1ff Ezekiel continued his discussion of the reasons for God's judgment by telling a further allegory. He compared the northern and southern kingdoms to two sisters who became prostitutes. The proud citizens of Jerusalem had long scorned their sister city of Samaria, thinking that they of Jerusalem were superior. But God called both of these cities prostitutes—a shock to the people of Jerusalem who thought that they were righteous. Just as the imagery of this message was shocking and distasteful to the people, so our sins are repugnant to God.

3 and they played the harlot in Egypt. They played the harlot in their youth; there
their breasts were pressed and there their virgin bosom was handled.
4 "Their names were Oholah the elder and Oholibah her sister. And they became Mine,
and they bore sons and daughters. And *as for* their names, Samaria is Oholah and Jerusalem is Oholibah.
5 "Oholah played the harlot while she was Mine; and she lusted after her lovers, after
the Assyrians, *her* neighbors,
6 who were clothed in purple, governors and officials, all of them desirable young men,
horsemen riding on horses.
7 "She bestowed her harlotries on them, all of whom *were* the choicest men of Assyria;
and with all whom she lusted after, with all their idols she defiled herself.
8 "She did not forsake her harlotries from *the time in* Egypt; for in her youth men had
lain with her, and they handled her virgin bosom and poured out their lust on her.
9 "Therefore, I gave her into the hand of her lovers, into the hand of the Assyrians,
after whom she lusted.
10 "They uncovered her nakedness; they took her sons and her daughters, but they slew
her with the sword. Thus she became a byword among women, and they executed judgments on her.
11 "Now her sister Oholibah saw *this,* yet she was more corrupt in her lust than she, and
her harlotries were more than the harlotries of her sister.
12 "She lusted after the Assyrians, governors and officials, the ones near, magnificently
dressed, horsemen riding on horses, all of them desirable young men.
13 "I saw that she had defiled herself; they both took the same way.
14 "So she increased her harlotries. And she saw men portrayed on the wall, images of
the Chaldeans portrayed with vermilion,
15 girded with belts on their loins, with flowing turbans on their heads, all of them looking like officers, like the Babylonians *in* Chaldea, the land of their birth.
16 "When she saw them she lusted after them and sent messengers to them in Chaldea.
17 "The Babylonians came to her to the bed of love and defiled her with their harlotry.
And when she had been defiled by them, she became disgusted with them.
18 "She uncovered her harlotries and uncovered her nakedness; then I became disgusted with her, as I had become disgusted with her sister.
19 "Yet she multiplied her harlotries, remembering the days of her youth, when she
played the harlot in the land of Egypt.
20 "She lusted after their paramours, whose flesh is *like* the flesh of donkeys and whose
issue is *like* the issue of horses.
21 "Thus you longed for the lewdness of your youth, when the Egyptians handled your
bosom because of the breasts of your youth.
22 "Therefore, O Oholibah, thus says the Lord GOD, 'Behold I will arouse your lovers
against you, from whom you were alienated, and I will bring them against you from every
side:
23 the Babylonians and all the Chaldeans, Pekod and Shoa and Koa, *and* all the Assyrians with them; desirable young men, governors and officials all of them, officers and
men of renown, all of them riding on horses.

23:3 Lev 17:7; Jer 3:9
23:5 2 Kin 15:19; 16:7; 17:3; Ezek 16:28; Hos 5:13; 8:9, 10
23:6 Ezek 23:12, 13
23:7 Ezek 20:7; 22:3, 4; Hos 5:3; 6:10
23:8 Ex 32:4; 1 Kin 12:28; 2 Kin 10:29; 17:16; Ezek 23:3, 19
23:9 Ezek 16:37; 23:22
23:10 Ezek 16:37, 41
23:11 Jer 3:8-11; Ezek 16:51
23:12 2 Kin 16:7
23:14 Ezek 8:10; Ezek 16:29
23:16 Ezek 23:20; Matt 5:28
23:17 2 Kin 24:17
23:18 Jer 8:12; Ezek 21:24; 23:10; Ps 78:59; 106:40; Jer 12:8; Ezek 23:9; Amos 5:21
23:20 Ezek 16:26; 17:15
23:21 Jer 3:9; Ezek 23:3
23:23 2 Kin 20:14-17; Ezek 21:19; 23:14-17; 2 Kin 24:2; Job 1:17; Is 23:13; Jer 50:21; Gen 2:14; 25:18; Ezra 6:22

23:4–6 Oholah (meaning, "her tent"), the northern kingdom of Israel, was lured away from God by the dashing Assyrians—their fashionable clothes and powerful positions. The people coveted youth, strength, power, wealth, and pleasure—the same qualities people think will bring happiness today. But the charming Assyrians drew Israel away from God.

23:11ff Oholibah (meaning, "my tent is in her") was shown to be worse because she did not learn from the judgment upon her sister, but continued in her lust for the Assyrians and Babylonians. Therefore, her judgment was equally certain. Just as Oholibah was privileged and should have known better, so we are privileged because we know about Christ. We need to be doubly sure that we follow him.

23:12 "She lusted after the Assyrians" may mean excessively trying to please and probably refers to Ahaz paying protection money to Tiglath-pileser III (2 Kings 16:7–8).

23:16 An invitation to Chaldea (Babylon) was given by Hezekiah to the envoys from Babylon (2 Kings 20:12ff; Isaiah 38; 39).

23:17 At first, Judah made an alliance with Babylonia (Chaldea), but then changed its mind. During the reigns of the last two Judean kings, Jehoiakim and Zedekiah, Judah looked to Egypt for help. Judah's unfaithfulness (its alliances with godless nations) cost it the only real protection it ever had—God.

23:21 "Lewdness" is promiscuity (see also 23:27, 49)—giving sexual favors instead of being faithful to a spouse or to God. We don't think of ourselves as being spiritually promiscuous, but we often spend more time seeking advice from magazines, television commercials, and non-Christian experts than we do from God and his Word.

23:22–26 This predicts the last attack on Jerusalem that would destroy the city and bring to Babylonia the third wave of captives in 586 B.C. (2 Kings 25; Jeremiah 52). The first attack came in 605 B.C., the second in 597 B.C. Pekod, Shoa, and Koa were Babylonian allies.

24 'They will come against you with weapons, chariots and wagons, and with a company of peoples. They will set themselves against you on every side with buckler and shield
and helmet; and I will commit the judgment to them, and they will judge you according
to their customs.
25 'I will set My jealousy against you, that they may deal with you in wrath. They will
remove your nose and your ears; and your survivors will fall by the sword. They will take
your sons and your daughters; and your survivors will be consumed by the fire.
26 'They will also strip you of your clothes and take away your beautiful jewels.
27 'Thus I will make your lewdness and your harlotry *brought* from the land of Egypt to
cease from you, so that you will not lift up your eyes to them or remember Egypt anymore.'
28 "For thus says the Lord GOD, 'Behold, I will give you into the hand of those whom
you hate, into the hand of those from whom you were alienated.
29 'They will deal with you in hatred, take all your property, and leave you naked and
bare. And the nakedness of your harlotries will be uncovered, both your lewdness and
your harlotries.
30 'These things will be done to you because you have played the harlot with the nations, because you have defiled yourself with their idols.
31 'You have walked in the way of your sister; therefore I will give her cup into your
hand.'
32 "Thus says the Lord GOD,
'You will drink your sister's cup,
Which is deep and wide.
You will be laughed at and held in derision;
It contains much.
33 'You will be filled with drunkenness and sorrow,
The cup of horror and desolation,
The cup of your sister Samaria.
34 'You will drink it and drain it.
Then you will gnaw its fragments
And tear your breasts;
for I have spoken,' declares the Lord GOD.
35 "Therefore, thus says the Lord GOD, 'Because you have forgotten Me and cast Me
behind your back, bear now the *punishment* of your lewdness and your harlotries.' "
36 Moreover, the LORD said to me, "Son of man, will you judge Oholah and Oholibah? Then declare to them their abominations.
37 "For they have committed adultery, and blood is on their hands. Thus they have committed adultery with their idols and even caused their sons, whom they bore to Me, to
pass through *the fire* to them as food.
38 "Again, they have done this to Me: they have defiled My sanctuary on the same day
and have profaned My sabbaths.
39 "For when they had slaughtered their children for their idols, they entered My sanctuary on the same day to profane it; and lo, thus they did within My house.
40 "Furthermore, they have even sent for men who come from afar, to whom a messenger was sent; and lo, they came—for whom you bathed, painted your eyes and decorated yourselves with ornaments;
41 and you sat on a splendid couch with a table arranged before it on which you had
set My incense and My oil.
42 "The sound of a carefree multitude was with her; and drunkards were brought from
the wilderness with men of the common sort. And they put bracelets on the hands of the
women and beautiful crowns on their heads.
43 "Then I said concerning her who was worn out by adulteries, 'Will they now commit
adultery with her when she is *thus?*'
44 "But they went in to her as they would go in to a harlot. Thus they went in to Oholah
and to Oholibah, the lewd women.
45 "But they, righteous men, will judge them with the judgment of adulteresses and with

23:24 Jer 47:3; Ezek 26:10; Nah 2:3, 4; Jer 39:5, 6; Ezek 16:38; 23:45

23:25 Ex 34:14; Ezek 5:13; 8:17, 18; Zeph 1:18; Ezek 23:47; Hos 2:4

23:26 Jer 13:22; Ezek 16:39; 23:29; Is 3:18-23

23:27 Ezek 16:41

23:28 Jer 21:7-10; 34:20

23:29 Deut 28:48; Ezek 23:25, 26, 45-47

23:30 Ezek 6:9

23:31 2 Kin 21:13; Jer 7:14, 15; Ezek 23:33

23:32 Ps 60:3; Is 51:17; Jer 25:15; Ezek 5:14, 15; 16:57; 22:4, 5

23:33 Jer 25:15, 16, 27; Hab 2:16

23:34 Ps 75:8; Is 51:17

23:35 Is 17:10; Jer 3:21; Ezek 22:12; Hos 8:14; 13:6; 1 Kin 14:9; Jer 2:27; 32:33

23:36 Jer 1:10; Ezek 20:4; 22:2; Is 58:1; Ezek 16:2; Mic 3:8

23:37 Ezek 16:20; 20:26

23:38 2 Kin 21:4, 7; Ezek 5:11; 7:20; Jer 17:27; Ezek 20:13

23:39 Jer 7:9-11

23:40 2 Kin 9:30; Jer 4:30; Is 3:18-23; Ezek 16:13-16

23:41 Esth 1:6; Is 57:7; Amos 6:4; Is 65:11; Ezek 44:16; Jer 44:17; Hos 2:8

23:42 Ezek 16:49; Amos 6:3-6; Jer 51:7; Gen 24:30; Ezek 16:11, 12

23:45 Ezek 16:38

23:39 The Israelites went so far as to sacrifice their own children to idols and then to sacrifice to the Lord the same day. This made a mockery of worship. We cannot praise God and willfully sin at the same time. That would be like celebrating one's wedding anniversary and then going to bed with a neighbor.

the judgment of women who shed blood, because they are adulteresses and blood is on their hands.

23:46 Jer 15:4; 24:9; 29:18

46 "For thus says the Lord GOD, 'Bring up a company against them and give them over to terror and plunder.

23:47 Lev 20:10; Ezek 16:40; Jer 39:8

47 'The company will stone them with stones and cut them down with their swords; they will slay their sons and their daughters and burn their houses with fire.

48 'Thus I will make lewdness cease from the land, that all women may be admonished and not commit lewdness as you have done.

23:49 Is 59:18; Ezek 7:4, 9; 9:10; 23:35

49 'Your lewdness will be requited upon you, and you will bear the penalty of *worshiping* your idols; thus you will know that I am the Lord GOD.' "

Parable of the Boiling Pot

24 And the word of the LORD came to me in the ninth year, in the tenth month, on the tenth of the month, saying,

24:2 2 Kin 25:1; Jer 39:1; 52:4

2 "Son of man, write the name of the day, this very day. The king of Babylon has laid siege to Jerusalem this very day.

24:3 Ps 78:2; Ezek 17:2; 20:49; Is 1:2; 30:1, 9; Ezek 2:3, 6, 8; Jer 1:13, 14; Ezek 11:3, 7, 11; 24:6

3 "Speak a parable to the rebellious house and say to them, 'Thus says the Lord GOD,
"Put on the pot, put *it* on and also pour water in it;
4 Put in it the pieces,
Every good piece, the thigh and the shoulder;
Fill *it* with choice bones.

24:4 Mic 3:2, 3

5 "Take the choicest of the flock,
And also pile wood under the pot.
Make it boil vigorously.
Also seethe its bones in it."

24:5 Jer 39:6; 52:10, 24-27

24:6 2 Kin 24:3, 4; Ezek 22:2, 3, 27; Mic 7:2; Nah 3:1

6 'Therefore, thus says the Lord GOD,
"Woe to the bloody city,
To the pot in which there is rust
And whose rust has not gone out of it!
Take out of it piece after piece,
Without making a choice.

24:7 Lev 17:13; Deut 12:16

7 "For her blood is in her midst;
She placed it on the bare rock;
She did not pour it on the ground
To cover it with dust.

24:8 Is 26:21

8 "That it may cause wrath to come up to take vengeance,
I have put her blood on the bare rock,
That it may not be covered."

24:9 Ezek 24:6; Hab 2:12

9 'Therefore, thus says the Lord GOD,
"Woe to the bloody city!
I also will make the pile great.
10 "Heap on the wood, kindle the fire,
Boil the flesh well
And mix in the spices,
And let the bones be burned.

24:11 Jer 21:10; Mal 4:1; Ezek 22:15; 23:27

11 "Then set it empty on its coals
So that it may be hot
And its bronze may glow

24:1–14 Ezekiel gave this illustration in 588 B.C., three years after the first of the previous messages (see 20:1–2). The people in Judah thought they were the choice meat because they hadn't been taken into captivity in 597 when the Babylonians last invaded the land. Ezekiel used this illustration before (chapter 11) to show that though the people thought they were safe and secure inside the cooking pot, this pot would actually be the place of their destruction. This message was given to the exiles in Babylonia the very day that the Babylonians attacked Jerusalem (24:2), beginning a siege that lasted over two years and resulted in the city's destruction. When God's punishment comes, it is relentless.

24:6–13 The city of Jerusalem was like a pot so encrusted with sin that it would not come clean. God wanted to cleanse the lives of those who lived in Jerusalem, and he wants to cleanse our lives today. Sometimes he tries to purify us through difficulties and troublesome circumstances. When you face tough times, allow the sin to be burned from your life. Look at your problems as an opportunity for your faith to grow. When these times come, unnecessary priorities and diversions are purged away. We can reexamine our lives so that we will do what really counts.

And its filthiness may be melted in it,
Its rust consumed.
12 "She has wearied *Me* with toil,
Yet her great rust has not gone from her;
Let her rust *be* in the fire!
13 "In your filthiness is lewdness.
Because I *would* have cleansed you,
Yet you are not clean,
You will not be cleansed from your filthiness again
Until I have spent My wrath on you.
14 "I, the LORD, have spoken; it is coming and I will act. I will not relent, and I will not
pity and I will not be sorry; according to your ways and according to your deeds I will
judge you," declares the Lord GOD.' "

24:12 Jer 9:5

24:13 Jer 6:28-30; Ezek 22:24; Ezek 5:13; 8:18

24:14 Ps 33:9; Is 55:11; Jer 13:14; Ezek 9:10; Is 3:11; Ezek 18:30; 36:19

Death of Ezekiel's Wife Is a Sign

15 And the word of the LORD came to me saying,
16 "Son of man, behold, I am about to take from you the desire of your eyes with a blow;
but you shall not mourn and you shall not weep, and your tears shall not come.
17 "Groan silently; make no mourning for the dead. Bind on your turban and put your
shoes on your feet, and do not cover *your* mustache and do not eat the bread of men."
18 So I spoke to the people in the morning, and in the evening my wife died. And in
the morning I did as I was commanded.
19 The people said to me, "Will you not tell us what these things that you are doing
mean for us?"
20 Then I said to them, "The word of the LORD came to me saying,
21 'Speak to the house of Israel, "Thus says the Lord GOD, 'Behold, I am about to profane My sanctuary, the pride of your power, the desire of your eyes and the delight of
your soul; and your sons and your daughters whom you have left behind will fall by the
sword.
22 'You will do as I have done; you will not cover *your* mustache and you will not eat
the bread of men.
23 'Your turbans will be on your heads and your shoes on your feet. You will not mourn
and you will not weep, but you will rot away in your iniquities and you will groan to one
another.
24 'Thus Ezekiel will be a sign to you; according to all that he has done you will do;
when it comes, then you will know that I am the Lord GOD.' "
25 'As for you, son of man, will *it* not be on the day when I take from them their stronghold, the joy of their pride, the desire of their eyes and their heart's delight, their sons
and their daughters,
26 that on that day he who escapes will come to you with information for *your* ears?
27 'On that day your mouth will be opened to him who escaped, and you will speak and
be mute no longer. Thus you will be a sign to them, and they will know that I am the
LORD.' "

24:16 Song 7:10; Ezek 24:18; Job 23:2; Jer 16:5; 22:10; Jer 13:17

24:17 Lev 21:10-12; Jer 16:7; Hos 9:4

24:21 Ps 27:4; 84:1; Ezek 24:16; Jer 6:11; 16:3, 4; Ezek 23:25, 47

24:23 Job 27:15; Ps 78:64; Lev 26:39; Ezek 33:10

24:24 Ezek 4:3; Luke 11:29, 30

24:25 Ps 48:2; 50:2; Ezek 24:21

24:26 1 Sam 4:12; Job 1:15-19

24:27 Ezek 3:26; 33:22

B. MESSAGES AGAINST FOREIGN NATIONS (25:1—32:32)

These messages were given concerning seven nations which surrounded Judah. The Ammonites were judged because of their joy over the desecration of the temple, the

---

24:15–18 God told Ezekiel that his wife would die and that he should not grieve for her. Ezekiel obeyed God fully, even as Hosea did when he was told to marry an unfaithful woman (Hosea 1:2–3). In both cases, these unusual events were intended as symbolic acts to picture God's relationship with his people. Obeying God can carry a high cost. The only grief more excruciating than losing your spouse and not being allowed to grieve would be to lose eternal life because you did not obey God. Ezekiel always obeyed God wholeheartedly. We should be wholehearted in our obedience. We can begin by doing all that God commands us to do, even when we don't feel like it. Are you willing to serve God as completely as Ezekiel did?

24:20–24 Ezekiel was not allowed to mourn for his dead wife in order to show his fellow exiles that they were not to mourn over Jerusalem when it was destroyed. Any personal sorrow felt would soon be eclipsed by national sorrow over the horror of the city's total destruction. The individuals would waste away because of their sins, which caused the city's destruction.

24:27 For some time Ezekiel had not been allowed to speak except when God gave him a message to deliver to the people (3:25–27). This restriction would soon end when Jerusalem was destroyed and all Ezekiel's prophecies about Judah and Jerusalem had come true (33:21–22).

Moabites because they scorned Judah as special people, the Edomites because of their special hatred of the Jews, and the Philistines because of their vengeance. All these nations, and others specifically addressed, would soon realize that God is supreme. Nations today are also under limits imposed by God.

Judgment on Gentile Nations—Ammon

25 And the word of the LORD came to me saying,
2 "Son of man, set your face toward the sons of Ammon and prophesy against
them,
3 and say to the sons of Ammon, 'Hear the word of the Lord GOD! Thus says the Lord
GOD, "Because you said, 'Aha!' against My sanctuary when it was profaned, and against
the land of Israel when it was made desolate, and against the house of Judah when they
went into exile,
4 therefore, behold, I am going to give you to the sons of the east for a possession,
and they will set their encampments among you and make their dwellings among you;
they will eat your fruit and drink your milk.
5 "I will make Rabbah a pasture for camels and the sons of Ammon a resting place for
flocks. Thus you will know that I am the LORD."
6 'For thus says the Lord GOD, "Because you have clapped your hands and stamped
your feet and rejoiced with all the scorn of your soul against the land of Israel,
7 therefore, behold, I have stretched out My hand against you and I will give you for
spoil to the nations. And I will cut you off from the peoples and make you perish from
the lands; I will destroy you. Thus you will know that I am the LORD."

Moab

8 'Thus says the Lord GOD, "Because Moab and Seir say, 'Behold, the house of Judah
is like all the nations,'
9 therefore, behold, I am going to deprive the flank of Moab of *its* cities, of its cities
which are on its frontiers, the glory of the land, Beth-jeshimoth, Baal-meon and Kiriathaim,
10 and I will give it for a possession along with the sons of Ammon to the sons of the
east, so that the sons of Ammon will not be remembered among the nations.
11 "Thus I will execute judgments on Moab, and they will know that I am the LORD."

Edom

12 'Thus says the Lord GOD, "Because Edom has acted against the house of Judah by
taking vengeance, and has incurred grievous guilt, and avenged themselves upon them,"
13 therefore thus says the Lord GOD, "I will also stretch out My hand against Edom
and cut off man and beast from it. And I will lay it waste; from Teman even to Dedan
they will fall by the sword.
14 "I will lay My vengeance on Edom by the hand of My people Israel. Therefore, they

25:2 Jer 49:1-6; Amos 1:13-15; Zeph 2:9

25:3 Ps 70:2, 3; Ezek 21:28; 25:6; 26:2; 36:2

25:4 Judg 6:3, 33; 1 Kin 4:30; Deut 28:33, 51; Is 1:7

25:5 Deut 3:11; 2 Sam 12:26; Jer 49:2; Ezek 21:20

25:6 Job 27:23; Nah 3:19; Obad 12; Zeph 2:8, 10

25:7 Ezek 25:13, 16; Zeph 1:4; Is 33:4; Ezek 26:5; Ezek 21:32; Amos 1:14, 15; Ezek 6:14

25:8 Is 15:1; Jer 48:1; Amos 2:1, 2

25:9 Num 33:49; Josh 12:3; 13:20; Num 32:3, 38; Josh 13:17; 1 Chr 5:8; Jer 48:23; Num 32:37; Josh 13:19; Jer 48:1, 23

25:10 Ezek 25:4

25:12 2 Chr 28:17; Ps 137:7; Jer 49:7-22

25:13 Jer 49:8, 13; Ezek 29:8; Mal 1:3, 4; Gen 36:34; Jer 49:7; Amos 1:12; Jer 25:23; 49:8

25:14 Is 11:14; Ezek 35:11

25:1ff Chapters 25—32 are God's word concerning the seven nations surrounding Judah. The judgments in these chapters are not simply the vengeful statements of Jews against their enemies; they are God's judgments on nations that failed to acknowledge the one true God and fulfill the good purposes God intended for them. The Ammonites were judged because of their joy over the desecration of the temple (25:1–7), the Moabites because they found pleasure in Judah's wickedness (25:8–11), the Edomites because of their racial hatred for the Jews (25:12–14), and the Philistines because they sought revenge against Judah for defeating them in battle (25:15–17).

25:5 Rabbah was the capital city of the Ammonites.

25:9 These towns were on the northern border of Moab.

25:13–14 The Edomites were blood brothers of the Jews, both nations having descended from Isaac (Genesis 25:19–26). Edom shared its northern border with Israel, and the two nations were always in conflict. The Edomites hated Israel so much that they rejoiced when Jerusalem, Israel's capital, was destroyed. Teman was in the northern part of Edom; Dedan was in the southern part. Thus, Ezekiel was saying that the entire country would be destroyed.

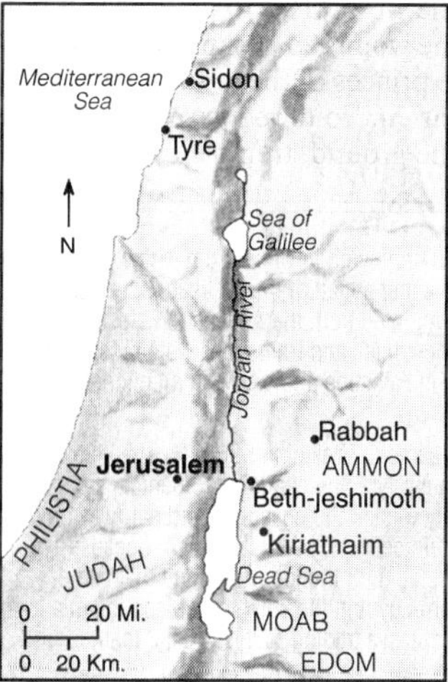

JUDAH'S ENEMIES Ammon, Moab, Edom, and Philistia, although once united with Judah against Babylon, had abandoned Judah and rejoiced to see its ruin. But these nations were as sinful as Judah and would also feel the sting of God's judgment.

will act in Edom according to My anger and according to My wrath; thus they will know
My vengeance," declares the Lord GOD.

Philistia

15 'Thus says the Lord GOD, "Because the Philistines have acted in revenge and have
taken vengeance with scorn of soul to destroy with everlasting enmity,"
16 therefore thus says the Lord GOD, "Behold, I will stretch out My hand against the
Philistines, even cut off the Cherethites and destroy the remnant of the seacoast.
17 "I will execute great vengeance on them with wrathful rebukes; and they will know
that I am the LORD when I lay My vengeance on them." ' "

Judgment on Tyre

26 Now in the eleventh year, on the first of the month, the word of the LORD came
to me saying,
2 "Son of man, because Tyre has said concerning Jerusalem, 'Aha, the gateway of the
peoples is broken; it has opened to me. I shall be filled, *now that* she is laid waste,'
3 therefore thus says the Lord GOD, 'Behold, I am against you, O Tyre, and I will bring
up many nations against you, as the sea brings up its waves.
4 'They will destroy the walls of Tyre and break down her towers; and I will scrape her
debris from her and make her a bare rock.
5 'She will be a place for the spreading of nets in the midst of the sea, for I have spoken,' declares the Lord GOD, 'and she will become spoil for the nations.
6 'Also her daughters who are on the mainland will be slain by the sword, and they will
know that I am the LORD.' "
7 For thus says the Lord GOD, "Behold, I will bring upon Tyre from the north Nebuchadnezzar king of Babylon, king of kings, with horses, chariots, cavalry and a great army.
8 "He will slay your daughters on the mainland with the sword; and he will make siege
walls against you, cast up a ramp against you and raise up a large shield against you.
9 "The blow of his battering rams he will direct against your walls, and with his axes he
will break down your towers.
10 "Because of the multitude of his horses, the dust *raised by* them will cover you; your
walls will shake at the noise of cavalry and wagons and chariots when he enters your gates
as men enter a city that is breached.
11 "With the hoofs of his horses he will trample all your streets. He will slay your people
with the sword; and your strong pillars will come down to the ground.
12 "Also they will make a spoil of your riches and a prey of your merchandise, break
down your walls and destroy your pleasant houses, and throw your stones and your timbers and your debris into the water.
13 "So I will silence the sound of your songs, and the sound of your harps will be heard
no more.
14 "I will make you a bare rock; you will be a place for the spreading of nets. You will be
built no more, for I the LORD have spoken," declares the Lord GOD.
15 Thus says the Lord GOD to Tyre, "Shall not the coastlands shake at the sound of
your fall when the wounded groan, when the slaughter occurs in your midst?
16 "Then all the princes of the sea will go down from their thrones, remove their robes
and strip off their embroidered garments. They will clothe themselves with trembling;
they will sit on the ground, tremble every moment and be appalled at you.

25:15 Is 14:29-31; Ezek 25:6, 12; Joel 3:4
25:16 Jer 25:20; 47:1-7; 1 Sam 30:14; Zeph 2:5
25:17 Ps 9:16
26:2 2 Sam 5:11; Is 23:1; Jer 25:22; Is 62:10
26:3 Mic 4:11; Is 5:30; Jer 50:42; 51:42
26:4 Is 23:11; Ezek 26:9; Amos 1:10
26:5 Ezek 25:7; 29:19
26:6 Ezek 16:46, 53; 26:8
26:7 Ezra 7:12; Is 10:8; Jer 52:32; Dan 2:37, 47; Ezek 23:24; Nah 2:3, 4
26:8 Jer 52:4; Ezek 21:22; Jer 32:24
26:10 Jer 4:13; 47:3; Jer 39:3
26:11 Is 5:28; Hab 1:8; Is 26:5; Jer 43:13
26:12 Is 23:8, 18; Ezek 27:3-27; Zech 9:3; Jer 52:14; 2 Chr 32:27; Amos 5:11
26:13 Is 23:16; 24:8, 9; Amos 6:5; Is 5:12; Rev 18:22
26:14 Deut 13:16; Job 12:14; Mal 1:4; Is 14:27
26:15 Jer 49:21; Ezek 31:16
26:16 Jon 3:6; Job 8:22; Ps 35:26; Ezek 7:27; 1 Pet 5:5; Ezek 32:10; Hos 11:10

25:16 The Cherethites originated in Crete, from which they take their name. They were either a clan of the Philistines, or possibly a separate people who migrated from the Aegean to Palestine about the same time. The Cherethites and Philistines were closely intermixed once they were in Palestine and are often mentioned together.

26:1ff This message came to Ezekiel in 586 B.C. Chapters 26 and 27 are a prophecy against Tyre, the capital of Phoenicia just north of Israel. Part of the city was on the coastline, and part was on a beautiful island. Tyre rejoiced when Jerusalem fell, because Tyre and Judah always competed for the lucrative trade that came through their lands from Egypt in the south and Mesopotamia to the north. Tyre dominated the sea trading routes while Judah dominated the land caravan routes. After Judah was defeated, Tyre thought it had all the trade routes to itself. But this gloating didn't last long. In 586 B.C., Nebuchadnezzar attacked the city. It took him 15 years to capture Tyre (586–571) because the city's back side lay on the sea so fresh supplies could be shipped in daily.

26:14 After a 15-year siege, Nebuchadnezzar could not conquer the part of Tyre located on the island; thus certain aspects of the description in 26:12, 14 exceed the actual damage done to Tyre by Nebuchadnezzar. But the prophecy predicted what would happen to the island settlement later during the conquests of Alexander the Great. Alexander threw the rubble of the mainland city into the sea until it made a bridge to the island. Then he marched across the bridge and destroyed the island (332 B.C.). Today the island city is still a pile of rubble, a testimony to God's judgment.

17 "They will take up a lamentation over you and say to you,
'How you have perished, O inhabited one,
From the seas, O renowned city,
Which was mighty on the sea,
She and her inhabitants,
Who imposed her terror
On all her inhabitants!
18 'Now the coastlands will tremble
On the day of your fall;
Yes, the coastlands which are by the sea
Will be terrified at your passing.' "
19 For thus says the Lord GOD, "When I make you a desolate city, like the cities which
are not inhabited, when I bring up the deep over you and the great waters cover you,
20 then I will bring you down with those who go down to the pit, to the people of old,
and I will make you dwell in the lower parts of the earth, like the ancient waste places,
with those who go down to the pit, so that you will not be inhabited; but I will set glory
in the land of the living.
21 "I will bring terrors on you and you will be no more; though you will be sought, you
will never be found again," declares the Lord GOD.

Lament over Tyre

27 Moreover, the word of the LORD came to me saying,
2 "And you, son of man, take up a lamentation over Tyre;
3 and say to Tyre, who dwells at the entrance to the sea, merchant of the peoples to
many coastlands, 'Thus says the Lord GOD,
"O Tyre, you have said, 'I am perfect in beauty.'
4 "Your borders are in the heart of the seas;
Your builders have perfected your beauty.
5 "They have made all *your* planks of fir trees from Senir;
They have taken a cedar from Lebanon to make a mast for you.
6 "Of oaks from Bashan they have made your oars;
With ivory they have inlaid your deck of boxwood from the coastlands of Cyprus.
7 "Your sail was of fine embroidered linen from Egypt
So that it became your distinguishing mark;
Your awning was blue and purple from the coastlands of Elishah.
8 "The inhabitants of Sidon and Arvad were your rowers;
Your wise men, O Tyre, were aboard; they were your pilots.
9 "The elders of Gebal and her wise men were with you repairing your seams;
All the ships of the sea and their sailors were with you in order to deal in your merchandise.
10 "Persia and Lud and Put were in your army, your men of war. They hung shield and
helmet in you; they set forth your splendor.
11 "The sons of Arvad and your army were on your walls, *all* around, and the Gammadim
were in your towers. They hung their shields on your walls *all* around; they perfected
your beauty.
12 "Tarshish was your customer because of the abundance of all *kinds* of wealth; with
silver, iron, tin and lead they paid for your wares.
13 "Javan, Tubal and Meshech, they were your traders; with the lives of men and vessels of bronze they paid for your merchandise.
14 "Those from Beth-togarmah gave horses and war horses and mules for your wares.
15 "The sons of Dedan were your traders. Many coastlands were your market; ivory tusks
and ebony they brought as your payment.

26:17 Ezek 19:1, 14; 27:2, 32; 32:2, 16; Is 14:12; Jer 48:39; 50:23; Ezek 27:3, 10, 11; 28:2

26:18 Is 41:5; Ezek 26:15; 27:35; Is 23:5-7, 10, 11

26:19 Is 8:7, 8; Ezek 26:3

26:20 Is 14:9, 10; Ezek 32:30; Ps 88:6; Amos 9:2; Jon 2:2, 6; Jer 33:9; Zech 2:8

26:21 Ezek 26:15, 16; 27:36; Rev 18:21

27:2 Jer 9:10, 17-20; Ezek 28:12

27:3 Ezek 28:2; Is 23:3

27:5 Deut 3:9; 1 Chr 5:23; Song 4:8

27:6 Is 2:13; Zech 11:2; Num 21:33; Is 2:13; Jer 22:20; Gen 10:4; Is 23:1, 12; Jer 2:10

27:7 Ex 25:4; Jer 10:9; Gen 10:4

27:8 Gen 10:18; 1 Chr 1:16; Ezek 27:11; 1 Kin 9:27

27:9 Josh 13:5; 1 Kin 5:18

27:10 Ezek 30:5; 38:5

27:13 Gen 10:2; Is 66:19; Ezek 27:19; Gen 10:2; Ezek 38:2; 39:1; Joel 3:3; Rev 18:13

27:14 Gen 10:3; Ezek 38:6

27:15 Jer 25:23; Ezek 25:13; 27:20; 1 Kin 10:22; Rev 18:12

27:1ff Chapter 27 is a funeral lament over Tyre's fall. It compares the city to a ship (27:1–9), mentions many of its trading partners (27:10–25), and then describes how the ship sank (27:26–36). Jesus spoke of Tyre in Matthew 11:22 as a city worthy of God's judgment.

27:3–4 The beauty of Tyre was the source of its pride, and Tyre's pride guaranteed its judgment. Unwarranted conceit or pride in our own accomplishments should be a danger signal to us (see James 4:13–17). God is not against our finding pleasure or satisfaction in what we do; he is against arrogant, inflated self-esteem that looks down on others. We must acknowledge God as the basis and source of our lives.

16 "Aram was your customer because of the abundance of your goods; they paid for
your wares with emeralds, purple, embroidered work, fine linen, coral and rubies.
17 "Judah and the land of Israel, they were your traders; with the wheat of Minnith,
cakes, honey, oil and balm they paid for your merchandise.
18 "Damascus was your customer because of the abundance of your goods, because of
the abundance of all *kinds* of wealth, because of the wine of Helbon and white wool.
19 "Vedan and Javan paid for your wares from Uzal; wrought iron, cassia and sweet cane
were among your merchandise.
20 "Dedan traded with you in saddlecloths for riding.
21 "Arabia and all the princes of Kedar, they were your customers for lambs, rams and
goats; for these they were your customers.
22 "The traders of Sheba and Raamah, they traded with you; they paid for your wares
with the best of all *kinds* of spices, and with all *kinds* of precious stones and gold.
23 "Haran, Canneh, Eden, the traders of Sheba, Asshur *and* Chilmad traded with you.
24 "They traded with you in choice garments, in clothes of blue and embroidered work,
and in carpets of many colors *and* tightly wound cords, *which were* among your merchandise.
25 "The ships of Tarshish were the carriers for your merchandise.
And you were filled and were very glorious
In the heart of the seas.

26 "Your rowers have brought you
Into great waters;
The east wind has broken you
In the heart of the seas.
27 "Your wealth, your wares, your merchandise,
Your sailors and your pilots,
Your repairers of seams, your dealers in merchandise
And all your men of war who are in you,
With all your company that is in your midst,
Will fall into the heart of the seas
On the day of your overthrow.
28 "At the sound of the cry of your pilots
The pasture lands will shake.
29 "All who handle the oar,
The sailors *and* all the pilots of the sea
Will come down from their ships;
They will stand on the land,
30 And they will make their voice heard over you
And will cry bitterly.
They will cast dust on their heads,
They will wallow in ashes.
31 "Also they will make themselves bald for you
And gird themselves with sackcloth;
And they will weep for you in bitterness of soul
With bitter mourning.
32 "Moreover, in their wailing they will take up a lamentation for you
And lament over you:
'Who is like Tyre,
Like her who is silent in the midst of the sea?
33 'When your wares went out from the seas,
You satisfied many peoples;
With the abundance of your wealth and your merchandise
You enriched the kings of earth.
34 'Now that you are broken by the seas
In the depths of the waters,
Your merchandise and all your company
Have fallen in the midst of you.
35 'All the inhabitants of the coastlands
Are appalled at you,
And their kings are horribly afraid;

27:16 Judg 10:6; Is 7:1-8; Ezek 16:57; Ezek 28:13; Ezek 16:13, 18

27:17 Judg 11:33

27:18 Gen 14:15; Is 7:8; Jer 49:23; Ezek 47:16-18

27:20 Gen 25:3

27:21 Is 21:13; Is 60:7

27:22 Gen 10:7; Is 60:6; Ezek 38:13; Gen 43:11; 1 Kin 10:2

27:23 2 Kin 19:12; Is 37:12; Amos 1:5

27:25 Is 2:16

27:26 Ezek 26:19; Ps 48:7; Jer 18:17; Acts 27:14

27:28 Ezek 26:10, 15, 18

27:29 Rev 18:17-19

27:30 Is 23:1-6; Ezek 26:17; 1 Sam 4:12; 2 Sam 1:2; Lam 2:10; Rev 18:19; Jer 6:26; Jon 3:6

27:31 Is 15:2; Ezek 29:18; Is 22:12; Ezek 7:18; Is 16:9; 22:4

27:32 Ezek 26:17; 27:2; 28:12

27:33 Ezek 27:12, 18; 28:4, 5

27:34 Ezek 26:12; 27:26, 27; Zech 9:3, 4

27:35 Is 23:6; Ezek 26:16

27:36 Jer 18:16; 19:8; 49:17; 50:13; Zeph 2:15; Ps 37:10, 36

They are troubled in countenance.
36 'The merchants among the peoples hiss at you;
You have become terrified
And you will cease to be forever.' " ' "

Tyre's King Overthrown

28:2 Is 14:14; 47:8; Ezek 28:9; 2 Thess 2:4; Ps 9:20; 82:6, 7; Is 31:3; Ezek 28:9

28 The word of the LORD came again to me, saying,
2 "Son of man, say to the leader of Tyre, 'Thus says the Lord GOD,
"Because your heart is lifted up
And you have said, 'I am a god,
I sit in the seat of gods
In the heart of the seas';
Yet you are a man and not God,
Although you make your heart like the heart of God—

28:3 Dan 1:20; 2:20-23, 28; 5:11, 12

3 Behold, you are wiser than Daniel;
There is no secret that is a match for you.

28:4 Ezek 27:33; Zech 9:2, 3

4 "By your wisdom and understanding
You have acquired riches for yourself
And have acquired gold and silver for your treasuries.

28:5 Ezek 27:12; Hos 12:7, 8; Job 31:24, 25; Ps 52:7; Ezek 28:2; Hos 13:6

5 "By your great wisdom, by your trade
You have increased your riches
And your heart is lifted up because of your riches—

28:6 Ex 9:17; Ezek 28:2

6 Therefore thus says the Lord GOD,
'Because you have made your heart
Like the heart of God,

28:7 Ezek 26:7; Ezek 30:11; 31:12; 32:12; Hab 1:6-8

7 Therefore, behold, I will bring strangers upon you,
The most ruthless of the nations.
And they will draw their swords
Against the beauty of your wisdom
And defile your splendor.

28:8 Ezek 27:26, 27, 34

8 'They will bring you down to the pit,
And you will die the death of those who are slain
In the heart of the seas.
9 'Will you still say, "I am a god,"
In the presence of your slayer,
Though you are a man and not God,
In the hands of those who wound you?

28:10 1 Sam 17:26, 36; Ezek 31:18; 32:30

10 'You will die the death of the uncircumcised
By the hand of strangers,
For I have spoken!' declares the Lord GOD!" ' "
11 Again the word of the LORD came to me saying,

28:12 Ezek 19:1; 26:17; 27:2

12 "Son of man, take up a lamentation over the king of Tyre and say to him, 'Thus says
the Lord GOD,
"You had the seal of perfection,
Full of wisdom and perfect in beauty.

28:13 Gen 2:8; Is 51:3; Ezek 31:8, 9, 16; 36:35; Ezek 27:16, 22; Ex 28:17-20; Is 24:8; 30:32

13 "You were in Eden, the garden of God;
Every precious stone was your covering:
The ruby, the topaz and the diamond;

28:1ff Previously Ezekiel had prophesied against the city of Tyre (chapters 26; 27). Here he focused his prophecy on Tyre's leader. The chief sin of Tyre's king was pride—believing himself to be a god. But Ezekiel also may have made a broader spiritual application, speaking about the spiritual king of Tyre, Satan, whom the people were really following (see the note on 28:12–19).

28:2–3 Daniel, an important official in Nebuchadnezzar's kingdom (14:14), was already renowned for his wisdom. Daniel proclaimed that all his wisdom came from God (Daniel 2:20–23). By contrast, the king of Tyre thought that he himself *was* a god. When truly wise people get closer to God, they recognize their need to depend on him for guidance.

28:6–10 The enemy army ("strangers") that attacked Tyre was the Babylonian army under Nebuchadnezzar. This attack occurred in 573/572 B.C.

28:12–19 Some of the phrases in this passage describing the human king of Tyre may describe Satan. Great care must be taken to interpret these verses with discernment. It is clear that, at times, Ezekiel describes this king in terms that could not apply to a mere man. This king had been in the Garden of Eden (28:13), had been an "anointed cherub" (28:14), and had access to the holy mountain of God (28:14), but was driven from there (28:16–17). Ezekiel, therefore, may have been condemning not only the king of Tyre, but also Satan, who had motivated the king to sin.

The beryl, the onyx and the jasper;
The lapis lazuli, the turquoise and the emerald;
And the gold, the workmanship of your settings and sockets,
Was in you.
On the day that you were created
They were prepared.
14 "You were the anointed cherub who covers,
And I placed you *there.*
You were on the holy mountain of God;
You walked in the midst of the stones of fire.
15 "You were blameless in your ways
From the day you were created
Until unrighteousness was found in you.
16 "By the abundance of your trade
You were internally filled with violence,
And you sinned;
Therefore I have cast you as profane
From the mountain of God.
And I have destroyed you, O covering cherub,
From the midst of the stones of fire.
17 "Your heart was lifted up because of your beauty;
You corrupted your wisdom by reason of your splendor.
I cast you to the ground;
I put you before kings,
That they may see you.
18 "By the multitude of your iniquities,
In the unrighteousness of your trade
You profaned your sanctuaries.
Therefore I have brought fire from the midst of you;
It has consumed you,
And I have turned you to ashes on the earth
In the eyes of all who see you.
19 "All who know you among the peoples
Are appalled at you;
You have become terrified
And you will cease to be forever." ' "

28:14 Ex 25:17-20; 30:26; 40:9; Ezek 28:16; Ezek 20:40; 28:16; Ezek 28:13, 16; Rev 18:16

28:15 Ezek 27:3, 4; 28:3-6, 12; Ezek 28:17, 18

28:16 Ezek 27:12; Ezek 8:17; Hab 2:8, 17

28:17 Ezek 27:3, 4; 28:7; Is 19:11; Ezek 26:16

28:18 Amos 1:9, 10; Mal 4:3

28:19 Ezek 26:21; 27:36; Jer 51:64

Judgment of Sidon

20 And the word of the LORD came to me saying,
21 "Son of man, set your face toward Sidon, prophesy against her
22 and say, 'Thus says the Lord GOD,
"Behold, I am against you, O Sidon,
And I will be glorified in your midst.
Then they will know that I am the LORD when I execute judgments in her,
And I will manifest My holiness in her.
23 "For I will send pestilence to her
And blood to her streets,
And the wounded will fall in her midst
By the sword upon her on every side;
Then they will know that I am the LORD.
24 "And there will be no more for the house of Israel a prickling brier or a painful thorn
from any round about them who scorned them; then they will know that I am the Lord
GOD."

28:21 Ezek 6:2; 25:2; Gen 10:15, 19; Is 23:2, 4; Ezek 27:8

28:22 Ezek 28:26; 30:19

28:23 Ezek 38:22; Jer 51:52

28:24 Num 33:55; Josh 23:13; Is 55:13; Ezek 2:6

28:20–21 Sidon was another famous seaport, located about 25 miles north of Tyre. God charged this city with contempt for his people. Sidon's economy was bound to Tyre's, so when Tyre fell to Nebuchadnezzar, Sidon was doomed to follow.

28:24–26 This promise that God's people will live in complete safety has yet to be fulfilled. While many were allowed to return from exile under Zerubbabel, Ezra, and Nehemiah, and although the political nation is restored today, the inhabitants do not yet live in complete safety (28:26). Therefore, this promise will have its ultimate fulfillment when Christ sets up his eternal kingdom. Then all people who have been faithful to God will dwell together in harmony and complete safety.

Israel Regathered

25 'Thus says the Lord GOD, "When I gather the house of Israel from the peoples among
whom they are scattered, and will manifest My holiness in them in the sight of the nations, then they will live in their land which I gave to My servant Jacob.
26 "They will live in it securely; and they will build houses, plant vineyards and live securely when I execute judgments upon all who scorn them round about them. Then they
will know that I am the LORD their God." ' "

Judgment of Egypt

29 In the tenth year, in the tenth *month,* on the twelfth of the month, the word of the
LORD came to me saying,
2 "Son of man, set your face against Pharaoh king of Egypt and prophesy against him
and against all Egypt.
3 "Speak and say, 'Thus says the Lord GOD,
"Behold, I am against you, Pharaoh king of Egypt,
The great monster that lies in the midst of his rivers,
That has said, 'My Nile is mine, and I myself have made *it.*'
4 "I will put hooks in your jaws
And make the fish of your rivers cling to your scales.
And I will bring you up out of the midst of your rivers,
And all the fish of your rivers will cling to your scales.
5 "I will abandon you to the wilderness, you and all the fish of your rivers;
You will fall on the open field; you will not be brought together or gathered.
I have given you for food to the beasts of the earth and to the birds of the sky.
6 "Then all the inhabitants of Egypt will know that I am the LORD,
Because they have been *only* a staff *made* of reed to the house of Israel.
7 "When they took hold of you with the hand,
You broke and tore all their hands;
And when they leaned on you,
You broke and made all their loins quake."
8 'Therefore thus says the Lord GOD, "Behold, I will bring upon you a sword and I
will cut off from you man and beast.
9 "The land of Egypt will become a desolation and waste. Then they will know that I
am the LORD.
Because you said, 'The Nile is mine, and I have made *it,*'
10 therefore, behold, I am against you and against your rivers, and I will make the land
of Egypt an utter waste and desolation, from Migdol *to* Syene and even to the border of
Ethiopia.
11 "A man's foot will not pass through it, and the foot of a beast will not pass through it,
and it will not be inhabited for forty years.
12 "So I will make the land of Egypt a desolation in the midst of desolated lands. And
her cities, in the midst of cities that are laid waste, will be desolate forty years; and I will
scatter the Egyptians among the nations and disperse them among the lands."

28:25 Ps 106:47; Is 11:12, 13; Jer 32:37; Ezek 20:41; 34:13, 27; Jer 23:8; 27:11

28:26 Jer 23:6; Ezek 34:25-28; 38:8; Jer 32:15, 43, 44; Amos 9:13, 14; Ezek 25:11; 28:22

29:1 Ezek 26:1; 29:17; 30:20

29:2 Jer 44:30; Is 19:1-17; Jer 46:2-26; Ezek 30:1-32:32

29:3 Is 27:1; Ezek 32:2; Ezek 29:9; 30:12

29:4 2 Kin 19:28; Ezek 38:4

29:5 Ezek 32:4-6; Jer 8:2; 25:33; Jer 7:33; 34:20; Ezek 39:4

29:6 2 Kin 18:21; Is 36:6

29:7 2 Kin 18:21; Is 36:6; Ezek 17:15-17

29:8 Jer 46:13; Ezek 14:17

29:9 Ezek 29:10-12; 30:7, 8, 13-19; Prov 16:18; 18:12; Ezek 29:3

29:10 Ezek 13:8; 21:3; 26:3; 29:3

29:11 Jer 43:11, 12; 46:19; Ezek 32:13

29:12 Jer 25:15-19; 27:6-11; Ezek 30:7; Jer 46:19; Ezek 30:23, 26

29:1ff There are seven prophecies in chapters 29—32, all dealing with judgment on Egypt. This is probably the first prophecy that was given by Ezekiel in 587 B.C. Hezekiah, Jehoiakim, and Zedekiah (kings of Judah) had all sought help from Egypt despite God's warnings.

There are three key reasons for this prophecy: (1) Egypt was an ancient enemy of the Jews, having once enslaved them for 400 years; (2) Egypt worshiped many gods; (3) Egypt's wealth and power made it seem like a good ally. Egypt offered to help Judah only because of the benefits it hoped to receive from such an alliance. When the Egyptians didn't get what they hoped for, they bailed out of their agreement without regard to any promises they had made.

29:2ff Egypt had great artistic treasures, a flourishing civilization, and world-renowned military power. Unfortunately, it was also evil, egotistical, idolatrous, and it treated slaves cruelly. For those sins God condemned Egypt. At the battle of Carchemish in 605 B.C., Babylon crushed Egypt along with Assyria, its rivals for the position of world ruler.

29:9–10 The Nile was Egypt's pride and joy, a life-giving river cutting through the middle of the desert. Rather than thanking God, however, Egypt declared, "The Nile is mine, and I have made it." We do the same when we say "This house is mine; I built it," or "I have brought myself to the place where I am today," or "I have built this church, business, or reputation, from the ground up." These statements reveal our pride. Sometimes we take for granted what God has given us, thinking we have made it ourselves. Of course, we have put forth a lot of hard effort, but God supplied the resources, gave us the abilities, and provided us with the opportunities to make it happen. Instead of claiming our own greatness, as the Egyptians did, we should proclaim God's greatness and give him the credit. (Migdol is in the north of Egypt, and Syene in the south. Thus, this meant all of Egypt.)

13 'For thus says the Lord GOD, "At the end of forty years I will gather the Egyptians
from the peoples among whom they were scattered.
14 "I will turn the fortunes of Egypt and make them return to the land of Pathros, to the
land of their origin, and there they will be a lowly kingdom.
15 "It will be the lowest of the kingdoms, and it will never again lift itself up above the
nations. And I will make them so small that they will not rule over the nations.
16 "And it will never again be the confidence of the house of Israel, bringing to mind
the iniquity of their having turned to Egypt. Then they will know that I am the Lord
GOD." ' "
17 Now in the twenty-seventh year, in the first *month,* on the first of the month, the
word of the LORD came to me saying,
18 "Son of man, Nebuchadnezzar king of Babylon made his army labor hard against Tyre;
every head was made bald and every shoulder was rubbed bare. But he and his army had
no wages from Tyre for the labor that he had performed against it."
19 Therefore thus says the Lord GOD, "Behold, I will give the land of Egypt to Nebuchadnezzar king of Babylon. And he will carry off her wealth and capture her spoil and
seize her plunder; and it will be wages for his army.
20 "I have given him the land of Egypt *for* his labor which he performed, because they
acted for Me," declares the Lord GOD.
21 "On that day I will make a horn sprout for the house of Israel, and I will open your
mouth in their midst. Then they will know that I am the LORD."

29:13 Is 19:22; Jer 46:26
29:14 Is 11:11; Jer 44:1, 15; Ezek 30:14
29:15 Ezek 17:6, 14; 30:13; Zech 10:11; Ezek 31:2; 32:2; Nah 3:8-10
29:16 Is 20:5; 30:1-3; 31:1; 36:6; Ezek 17:15; 29:6, 7; Is 64:9; Jer 14:10; Ezek 21:23; Hos 8:13
29:17 Ezek 24:1; 26:1; 29:1; 30:20;40:1
29:18 Jer 25:9; 27:6; Ezek 26:7-12; Jer 48:37; Ezek 27:31
29:19 Ezek 30:10, 24, 25; 32:11; Jer 43:10-13; Ezek 30:14
29:20 Is 10:6, 7; 45:1-3; Jer 25:9
29:21 1 Sam 2:10; Ps 92:10; 132:17; Ezek 3:27; 24:27; 33:22; Amos 3:7, 8; Luke 21:15

Lament over Egypt

30 The word of the LORD came again to me saying,
2 "Son of man, prophesy and say, 'Thus says the Lord GOD,
"Wail, 'Alas for the day!'
3 "For the day is near,
Even the day of the LORD is near;
It will be a day of clouds,
A time *of doom* for the nations.
4 "A sword will come upon Egypt,
And anguish will be in Ethiopia;
When the slain fall in Egypt,
They take away her wealth,
And her foundations are torn down.
5 "Ethiopia, Put, Lud, all Arabia, Libya and the people of the land that is in league
will fall with them by the sword."
6 'Thus says the LORD,
"Indeed, those who support Egypt will fall
And the pride of her power will come down;
From Migdol *to* Syene
They will fall within her by the sword,"
Declares the Lord GOD.
7 "They will be desolate
In the midst of the desolated lands;
And her cities will be
In the midst of the devastated cities.
8 "And they will know that I am the LORD,
When I set a fire in Egypt

30:2 Is 13:6; 15:2; Ezek 21:12; Joel 1:5, 11, 13
30:3 Ezek 7:19; 13:5; Joel 1:15; 2:1; Obad 15; Ezek 30:18; 32:7; 34:12
30:4 Ezek 29:19
30:5 Jer 25:20, 24
30:6 Is 20:3-6
30:7 Jer 25:18-26; Ezek 29:12
30:8 Ps 58:11; Ezek 29:6, 9, 16; Ezek 22:31; 30:14, 16; Amos 1:4, 7, 10, 12, 14

29:13–16 This 40-year period of desolation in Egypt is hard to pinpoint. Nebuchadnezzar attacked Egypt around 572 B.C. and carried many people off to Babylon, while others fled for safety to surrounding nations. Approximately 33 years later, Cyrus, king of the Persian empire, conquered Babylon and allowed the nations which Babylon had conquered to return to their homelands. Adding a possible seven-year regrouping and travel period, this could then make up that 40-year time period. Since that time, Egypt has never returned to its previous dominance as a world power.

29:17–18 This prophecy was given in 571 B.C. and is actually the latest prophecy in Ezekiel. Nebuchadnezzar had finally conquered Tyre after a long and costly 15-year siege (586–571 B.C.). He had not counted on such an expense, so he went south and conquered Egypt to make up for all he had lost in taking Tyre. Ezekiel placed this prophecy here to describe *who* would bring this punishment to Egypt. God was using Nebuchadnezzar, an evil man, as an instrument of his judgment on Tyre, Judah, and Egypt—evil nations themselves. When Babylon didn't recognize God's favor, he judged it too.

30:1–19 This is a lament for Egypt and its allies. Because of the Egyptians' pride and idolatry, they would be brought down.

And all her helpers are broken.

30:9 Is 18:1, 2; Is 47:8; Ezek 38:11; 39:6; Is 19:17; 23:5; Ezek 32:9, 10

9 "On that day messengers will go forth from Me in ships to frighten secure Ethiopia;
and anguish will be on them as on the day of Egypt; for behold, it comes!"

30:10 Ezek 29:19

10 'Thus says the Lord GOD,
"I will also make the hordes of Egypt cease
By the hand of Nebuchadnezzar king of Babylon.

30:11 Ezek 28:7

11 "He and his people with him,
The most ruthless of the nations,
Will be brought in to destroy the land;
And they will draw their swords against Egypt
And fill the land with the slain.

30:12 Ezek 29:3, 9; Is 19:4

12 "Moreover, I will make the Nile canals dry
And sell the land into the hands of evil men.
And I will make the land desolate
And all that is in it,
By the hand of strangers; I the LORD have spoken."

30:13 Is 2:18; Is 19:13; Jer 2:16; 44:1; 46:14; Ezek 30:16

13 'Thus says the Lord GOD,
"I will also destroy the idols
And make the images cease from Memphis.
And there will no longer be a prince in the land of Egypt;
And I will put fear in the land of Egypt.

30:14 Is 11:11; Jer 44:1, 15; Ezek 29:14; Ps 78:12, 43; Is 19:11, 13; Jer 46:25; Ezek 30:15, 16; Nah 3:8

14 "I will make Pathros desolate,
Set a fire in Zoan
And execute judgments on [2]Thebes.
15 "I will pour out My wrath on [3]Sin,
The stronghold of Egypt;
I will also cut off the hordes of Thebes.
16 "I will set a fire in Egypt;
Sin will writhe in anguish,
Thebes will be breached
And [4]Memphis *will have* distresses daily.

30:17 Gen 41:45; 46:20

17 "The young men of [5]On and of Pi-beseth
Will fall by the sword,
And the women will go into captivity.

30:18 Jer 43:8-13; Ezek 30:3; Lev 26:13; Is 10:27; Jer 27:2; 28:10, 13; 30:8; Ezek 34:27

18 "In Tehaphnehes the day will be dark
When I break there the yoke bars of Egypt.
Then the pride of her power will cease in her;
A cloud will cover her,
And her daughters will go into captivity.

30:19 Ps 9:16; Ezek 5:8, 15; 25:11; 30:14

19 "Thus I will execute judgments on Egypt,
And they will know that I am the LORD." ' "

30:20 Ezek 26:1; 29:1, 17; 31:1

Victory for Babylon

30:21 Ps 10:15; 37:17; Ezek 30:24; Jer 30:13; 46:11

20 In the eleventh year, in the first *month,* on the seventh of the month, the word of
the LORD came to me saying,
21 "Son of man, I have broken the arm of Pharaoh king of Egypt; and, behold, it has not

2 Or *No* **3** Or *Pelusium* **4** Or *Noph* **5** Or *Aven*

30:12 Egypt's pharaohs claimed that they had made the Nile—the river on which the entire nation depended. If God dried up the Nile, the nation would be doomed.

30:13–19 The list of cities to be destroyed shows the breadth of the destruction; the drying up of the Nile (30:12) shows its depth. Egypt would be completely incapacitated. This was a clear message to Judah not to trust Egypt for help against the Babylonians.

30:20–21 This message came in 587 B.C. while Jerusalem was under attack from Babylon. Judah had rebelled against Babylon and made an alliance with Egypt in spite of God's warnings (Jeremiah 2:36–37). Pharaoh Hophra made a halfhearted attempt to help Jerusalem, but when Nebuchadnezzar's army turned on him, he fled back to Egypt (Jeremiah 37:5–7). This defeat is what Ezekiel meant when he said that God had broken the arm of Pharaoh.

30:21–26 This prophecy was given to Ezekiel in 587 B.C. God destroyed Egypt's military superiority and gave it to Babylon. God allows nations to rise to power to accomplish a particular purpose, often beyond our immediate understanding. When you read about armies and wars, don't despair. Remember that God is sovereign and in charge of everything, even military might. Besides praying for your military and government leaders, pray that God's greater purposes would be carried out and that his will would be done "on earth as it is in heaven" (see Matthew 6:10).

been bound up for healing or wrapped with a bandage, that it may be strong to hold the
sword.
22 "Therefore thus says the Lord GOD, 'Behold, I am against Pharaoh king of Egypt
and will break his arms, both the strong and the broken; and I will make the sword fall
from his hand.
23 'I will scatter the Egyptians among the nations and disperse them among the lands.
24 'For I will strengthen the arms of the king of Babylon and put My sword in his hand;
and I will break the arms of Pharaoh, so that he will groan before him with the groanings
of a wounded man.
25 'Thus I will strengthen the arms of the king of Babylon, but the arms of Pharaoh will
fall. Then they will know that I am the LORD, when I put My sword into the hand of the
king of Babylon and he stretches it out against the land of Egypt.
26 'When I scatter the Egyptians among the nations and disperse them among the lands,
then they will know that I am the LORD.' "

Pharaoh Warned of Assyria's Fate

31 In the eleventh year, in the third *month,* on the first of the month, the word of the
LORD came to me saying,

2 "Son of man, say to Pharaoh king of Egypt and to his hordes,
'Whom are you like in your greatness?
3 'Behold, Assyria *was* a cedar in Lebanon
With beautiful branches and forest shade,
And very high,
And its top was among the clouds.
4 'The waters made it grow, the deep made it high.
With its rivers it continually extended all around its planting place,
And sent out its channels to all the trees of the field.
5 'Therefore its height was loftier than all the trees of the field
And its boughs became many and its branches long
Because of many waters as it spread them out.
6 'All the birds of the heavens nested in its boughs,
And under its branches all the beasts of the field gave birth,
And all great nations lived under its shade.
7 'So it was beautiful in its greatness, in the length of its branches;
For its roots extended to many waters.
8 'The cedars in God's garden could not match it;
The cypresses could not compare with its boughs,
And the plane trees could not match its branches.
No tree in God's garden could compare with it in its beauty.
9 'I made it beautiful with the multitude of its branches,
And all the trees of Eden, which were in the garden of God, were jealous of it.

10 'Therefore thus says the Lord GOD, "Because it is high in stature and has set its top
among the clouds, and its heart is haughty in its loftiness,
11 therefore I will give it into the hand of a despot of the nations; he will thoroughly
deal with it. According to its wickedness I have driven it away.
12 "Alien tyrants of the nations have cut it down and left it; on the mountains and in all
the valleys its branches have fallen and its boughs have been broken in all the ravines of
the land. And all the peoples of the earth have gone down from its shade and left it.
13 "On its ruin all the birds of the heavens will dwell, and all the beasts of the field will
be on its *fallen* branches
14 so that all the trees by the waters may not be exalted in their stature, nor set their
top among the clouds, nor their well-watered mighty ones stand *erect* in their height. For

30:22 Jer 46:25; Ezek 29:3; 2 Kin 24:7; Jer 37:7; Jer 46:21

30:24 Neh 6:9; Is 45:1, 5; Ezek 30:10, 25; Zech 10:12; Ezek 30:11, 25; Zeph 2:12

30:25 Josh 8:18; 1 Chr 21:16; Is 5:25

31:1 Jer 52:5, 6; Ezek 30:20; 32:1

31:2 Ezek 29:19; 30:10; Nah 3:9

31:3 Is 10:33, 34; Ezek 17:3, 4, 22; 31:16; Dan 4:10, 20-23; Is 10:33; Ezek 31:5, 10

31:4 Ezek 17:5, 8; Rev 17:1, 15

31:5 Dan 4:11; Ps 1:3; Ezek 17:5

31:6 Ezek 17:23; 31:13; Dan 4:12, 21; Matt 13:32

31:8 Ps 80:10; Ezek 31:3; Gen 2:8, 9; 13:10; Is 51:3; Ezek 28:13

31:9 Gen 2:8, 9; 13:10; Is 51:3; Ezek 28:13

31:10 2 Chr 32:25; Is 10:12; 14:13, 14; Ezek 28:17; Dan 5:20

31:11 Ezek 30:10, 11; 32:11, 12; Dan 5:18, 19; Deut 18:12; Nah 3:18

31:12 Ezek 7:21; 28:7; 30:12; Hab 1:6; Ezek 28:7; 30:11; 32:12; Ezek 32:5; 35:8; Ezek 31:17; Dan 4:14; Nah 3:17, 18

31:13 Is 18:6; Ezek 29:5; 31:6; 32:4

31:14 Num 16:30, 33; Ps 63:9; Ezek 26:20; 31:18; 32:24; Amos 9:2; Jon 2:2, 6; Eph 4:9

31:1ff This message was given in 587 B.C. Ezekiel compared Egypt to Assyria, calling Assyria a great cedar tree. The Egyptians were to look at the fall of the mighty nation of Assyria (whose demise they had seen) as an example of what would happen to them. Just like Assyria, Egypt took pride in her strength and beauty; this would be her downfall. She would crash like a mighty tree and be sent to the place of the dead. There is no permanence apart from God, even for a great society with magnificent culture and military power.

31:9 "All the trees of Eden" may refer to all the other nations of the world who were jealous of Assyria's power and grandeur.

31:11 The "despot of the nations" may be Nebuchadnezzar (see Daniel 2:37–38).

they have all been given over to death, to the earth beneath, among the sons of men,
with those who go down to the pit."
15 'Thus says the Lord GOD, "On the day when it went down to Sheol I caused lamentations; I closed the deep over it and held back its rivers. And *its* many waters were stopped
up, and I made Lebanon mourn for it, and all the trees of the field wilted away on account of it.
16"I made the nations quake at the sound of its fall when I made it go down to Sheol
with those who go down to the pit; and all the well-watered trees of Eden, the choicest
and best of Lebanon, were comforted in the earth beneath.
17"They also went down with it to Sheol to those who were slain by the sword; and those
who were its strength lived under its shade among the nations.
18"To which among the trees of Eden are you thus equal in glory and greatness? Yet
you will be brought down with the trees of Eden to the earth beneath; you will lie in the
midst of the uncircumcised, with those who were slain by the sword. So is Pharaoh and
all his hordes!" ' declares the Lord GOD."

Lament over Pharaoh and Egypt

32 In the twelfth year, in the twelfth *month,* on the first of the month, the word of the
LORD came to me saying,
2"Son of man, take up a lamentation over Pharaoh king of Egypt and say to him,
'You compared yourself to a young lion of the nations,
Yet you are like the monster in the seas;
And you burst forth in your rivers
And muddied the waters with your feet
And fouled their rivers.' "
3 Thus says the Lord GOD,
"Now I will spread My net over you
With a company of many peoples,
And they shall lift you up in My net.
4"I will leave you on the land;
I will cast you on the open field.
And I will cause all the birds of the heavens to dwell on you,
And I will satisfy the beasts of the whole earth with you.
5"I will lay your flesh on the mountains
And fill the valleys with your refuse.
6"I will also make the land drink the discharge of your blood
As far as the mountains,
And the ravines will be full of you.
7"And when *I* extinguish you,
I will cover the heavens and darken their stars;
I will cover the sun with a cloud
And the moon will not give its light.
8"All the shining lights in the heavens
I will darken over you
And will set darkness on your land,"
Declares the Lord GOD.
9"I will also trouble the hearts of many peoples when I bring your destruction among
the nations, into lands which you have not known.
10"I will make many peoples appalled at you, and their kings will be horribly afraid of
you when I brandish My sword before them; and they will tremble every moment, every
man for his own life, on the day of your fall."
11 For thus says the Lord GOD, "The sword of the king of Babylon will come
upon you.

31:15 Ezek 32:7; Nah 2:10

31:16 Ezek 26:15; 27:28; Hag 2:7; Is 14:15; Ezek 32:18; Is 14:8; Hab 2:17; Ezek 14:22, 23; 32:31

31:17 Ps 9:17; Ezek 32:20f

Ezek 31:3, 6; Dan 4:12

31:18 Jer 9:25, 26; Ezek 28:10; 32:19, 21; Ps 52:7; Matt 13:19

32:1 Ezek 30:20; 31:1; 32:17; 33:21

32:2 Ezek 19:1; 27:2; 28:12; 32:16; Jer 4:7; Ezek 19:2-6; Nah 2:11-13; Is 27:1; Ezek 29:3; Jer 46:7, 8

32:3 Ezek 12:13

32:4 Is 18:6

32:5 Ezek 31:12

32:6 Ex 7:17; Is 34:3, 7; Ezek 35:6; Rev 14:20

32:7 Job 18:5, 6; Prov 13:9; Ex 10:21-23; Is 34:4; Ezek 30:3, 18; 34:12; Is 13:10; Joel 2:2, 31; 3:15; Amos 8:9; Matt 24:29; Mark 13:24f; Luke 21:25; Rev 6:12; 8:12

32:8 Gen 1:14

32:9 Ezek 27:29-32; 28:19; Rev 18:10-15; Ex 15:14-16

32:10 Ezek 27:35; Ezek 26:16

32:11 Jer 46:26

32:1ff This prophecy was given in 585 B.C., two months after the news of Jerusalem's fall had reached the exiles in Babylon. Ezekiel prophesied numerous judgments upon many wicked nations. These judgments served a positive purpose: They showed that evil forces are continually being overcome and that one day God will overthrow all evil, making the world the perfect place he intended. They also serve as warnings that God alone is sovereign. Even the mightiest rulers, like Pharaoh, will fall before God. All are accountable to him.

32:2 Although Pharaoh thought of himself as a strong lion, in God's eyes he was nothing but a crocodile ("monster") muddying the water. God's judgment would reduce Pharaoh to his true size. Anyone who defies God will face his judgment.

12 "By the swords of the mighty ones I will cause your hordes to fall; all of them are
tyrants of the nations,
And they will devastate the pride of Egypt,
And all its hordes will be destroyed.
13 "I will also destroy all its cattle from beside many waters;
And the foot of man will not muddy them anymore
And the hoofs of beasts will not muddy them.
14 "Then I will make their waters settle
And will cause their rivers to run like oil,"
Declares the Lord GOD.
15 "When I make the land of Egypt a desolation,
And the land is destitute of that which filled it,
When I smite all those who live in it,
Then they shall know that I am the LORD.
16 "This is a lamentation and they shall chant it. The daughters of the nations shall chant
it. Over Egypt and over all her hordes they shall chant it," declares the Lord GOD.
17 In the twelfth year, on the fifteenth of the month, the word of the LORD came to me
saying,
18 "Son of man, wail for the hordes of Egypt and bring it down, her and the daughters
of the powerful nations, to the nether world, with those who go down to the pit;
19 'Whom do you surpass in beauty?
Go down and make your bed with the uncircumcised.'
20 "They shall fall in the midst of those who are slain by the sword. She is given over to
the sword; they have drawn her and all her hordes away.
21 "The strong among the mighty ones shall speak of him *and* his helpers from the midst
of Sheol, 'They have gone down, they lie still, the uncircumcised, slain by the sword.'
22 "Assyria is there and all her company; her graves are round about her. All of them
are slain, fallen by the sword,
23 whose graves are set in the remotest parts of the pit and her company is round about
her grave. All of them are slain, fallen by the sword, who spread terror in the land of the
living.
24 "Elam is there and all her hordes around her grave; all of them slain, fallen by
the sword, who went down uncircumcised to the lower parts of the earth, who instilled
their terror in the land of the living and bore their disgrace with those who went down to
the pit.
25 "They have made a bed for her among the slain with all her hordes. Her graves are
around it, they are all uncircumcised, slain by the sword (although their terror was instilled in the land of the living), and they bore their disgrace with those who go down to
the pit; they were put in the midst of the slain.
26 "Meshech, Tubal and all their hordes are there; their graves surround them. All of
them were slain by the sword uncircumcised, though they instilled their terror in the land
of the living.
27 "Nor do they lie beside the fallen heroes of the uncircumcised, who went down to
Sheol with their weapons of war and whose swords were laid under their heads; but the
punishment for their iniquity rested on their bones, though the terror of *these* heroes
was once in the land of the living.

32:12 Ezek 28:7; Ezek 28:19

32:13 Ezek 29:11

32:15 Ps 107:33, 34; Ezek 29:12, 19, 20; Ex 7:5; 14:4, 18; Ps 9:16; 83:17, 18; Ezek 6:7; 30:19, 26

32:16 2 Sam 1:17; 3:33, 34; 2 Chr 35:25; Jer 9:17; Ezek 26:17; 32:2

32:17 Ezek 31:1; 32:1; 33:21

32:18 Is 16:9; Ezek 21:6; 32:2, 16; Mic 1:8; Jer 1:10; Ezek 43:3; Hos 6:5; Ezek 31:14, 16, 18; 32:24

32:19 Jer 9:25, 26; Ezek 31:18; 32:21, 24, 29, 30

32:20 Ps 28:3

32:21 Is 14:9-12; Ezek 32:27

32:22 Ezek 27:23; 31:3, 16

32:23 Is 14:15

32:24 Gen 10:22; 14:1; Is 11:11; Jer 25:25; 49:34-39; Ezek 26:20; 31:14, 18; 32:18; Job 28:13; Ps 27:13; 52:5; 142:5; Is 38:11; Jer 11:19; Ezek 16:52, 54; 32:25, 30

32:25 Ps 139:8

32:26 Gen 10:2; Ezek 27:13; 38:2, 3; 39:1; Gen 10:2; Is 66:19; Ezek 27:13; 38:2, 3; 39:1; Ezek 32:19

32:27 Is 14:18, 19; Job 3:13-15; Ezek 32:21; Job 20:11; Ps 109:18

32:18 The Hebrews believed in an afterlife for all people, good and bad. Ezekiel's message assumed that the evil nations had already been sent there (to the "pit") and that Egypt would share their fate. The words here are more poetic than doctrinal (see Job 24:19; Psalm 16:10; Isaiah 38:10, and the note on Matthew 25:46). The Egyptians had a preoccupation with the afterlife (the pyramids were built solely to ensure the pharaohs' comfort in the next life). This message should remind us that any attempt to control our afterlife and ignore God is foolish. God alone controls the future and life after death.

32:21–32 In these verses, Ezekiel conducts a guided tour of the grave, the region of the afterlife. In the grave, all of God's enemies are condemned in judgment; many of them experience the fate they so quickly imposed on others. Though Babylon is not mentioned, Ezekiel's readers would have concluded that if all the other nations would be judged for their rebellion against God, Babylon would be judged as well. These words would comfort the captives.

32:24–26 Elam was a nation of fierce warriors from the region east of Assyria. They were conquered by Nebuchadnezzar (Jeremiah 49:34–39) and eventually rebuilt themselves and became part of Persia. Meshech and Tubal were territories located in the eastern region of Asia Minor, now eastern and central Turkey. In chapters 38 and 39 they are described as allies of Gog, the chief prince of a confederacy. They are included with the evil nations who will be judged for fighting against God's people.

28 "But in the midst of the uncircumcised you will be broken and lie with those slain by
the sword.

32:29 Is 34:5-15; Jer 49:7-22; Ezek 25:13; 35:9, 15

29 "There also is Edom, its kings and all its princes, who for *all* their might are laid with
those slain by the sword; they will lie with the uncircumcised and with those who go down
to the pit.

32:30 Jer 1:15; 25:26; Ezek 38:6, 15; 39:2; Jer 25:22; Ezek 28:21-23

30 "There also are the chiefs of the north, all of them, and all the Sidonians, who in
spite of the terror resulting from their might, in shame went down with the slain. So they
lay down uncircumcised with those slain by the sword and bore their disgrace with those
who go down to the pit.

32:31 Ezek 14:22; 31:16

31 "These Pharaoh will see, and he will be comforted for all his hordes slain by the sword,
even Pharaoh and all his army," declares the Lord GOD.
32 "Though I instilled a terror of him in the land of the living, yet he will be made to lie
down among *the* uncircumcised *along* with those slain by the sword, *even* Pharaoh and
all his hordes," declares the Lord GOD.

C. MESSAGES OF HOPE (33:1—48:35)

This section begins a new direction in Ezekiel's prophecies. Ezekiel is reminded that he is the nation's watchman. Before Jerusalem's fall, he told the people of their punishment and dispersion. Now he is to proclaim the hope of restoration, but even this message does not improve the people's response. They listen to him with curiosity and then live as they please. Today we have the good news of forgiveness, but how easy it is to ignore the message and continue to live sinful lives.

1. Restoring the people of God

The Watchman's Duty

33:2 Ezek 3:11; 33:12, 17, 30; 37:18

33:3 Neh 4:18-20; Is 58:1; Ezek 33:9; Hos 8:1; Joel 2:1

33 And the word of the LORD came to me, saying,
2 "Son of man, speak to the sons of your people and say to them, 'If I bring a
sword upon a land, and the people of the land take one man from among them and make
him their watchman,

33:4 2 Chr 25:16; Jer 6:17; Zech 1:4; Ezek 18:13; 33:5, 9; Acts 18:6

3 and he sees the sword coming upon the land and blows on the trumpet and warns
the people,

33:5 Ex 9:19-21; Heb 11:7

4 then he who hears the sound of the trumpet and does not take warning, and a sword
comes and takes him away, his blood will be on his *own* head.

33:6 Ezek 18:20, 24; 33:8, 9; Ezek 3:18, 20

5 'He heard the sound of the trumpet but did not take warning; his blood will be on
himself. But had he taken warning, he would have delivered his life.
6 'But if the watchman sees the sword coming and does not blow the trumpet and the
people are not warned, and a sword comes and takes a person from them, he is taken
away in his iniquity; but his blood I will require from the watchman's hand.'

33:7 Is 62:6; Ezek 3:17-21; Jer 1:17; 26:2; Ezek 2:7, 8; Acts 5:20

7 "Now as for you, son of man, I have appointed you a watchman for the house of Israel; so you will hear a message from My mouth and give them warning from Me.

33:8 Is 3:11; Ezek 18:4, 13, 18, 20; 33:14

8 "When I say to the wicked, 'O wicked man, you will surely die,' and you do not speak
to warn the wicked from his way, that wicked man shall die in his iniquity, but his blood
I will require from your hand.

33:9 Acts 13:40, 41, 46; Ezek 3:19, 21; Acts 20:26

9 "But if you on your part warn a wicked man to turn from his way and he does not
turn from his way, he will die in his iniquity, but you have delivered your life.

32:30 The chiefs of the north were probably the princes of the Phoenician city-states.

32:32 After reading Ezekiel's prophecies against all these foreign nations, we may wonder if he was blindly loyal to his own nation. But Ezekiel spoke only when God gave him a message (3:27). Besides, God's prophets pronounced judgment on God's sinful people just as much as on God's enemies. But if Babylon was God's enemy, why isn't it mentioned in Ezekiel's judgments? Perhaps because (1) God wanted to foster a spirit of cooperation between the exiles and Babylon in order to preserve his people; (2) God was still using Babylon to refine his own people; (3) God wanted to use Daniel, a powerful official in Babylon, to draw the Babylonians to him.

33:1ff This chapter sets forth a new direction for Ezekiel's prophecies. Up to this point, Ezekiel has pronounced judgment upon Judah (chapters 1—24) and the surrounding evil nations (chapters 25—32) for their sins. After Jerusalem fell, he turned from messages of doom and judgment to messages of comfort, hope, and future restoration for God's people (chapters 33—48). God previously appointed Ezekiel to be a watchman warning the nation of coming judgment (see 3:17–21). Here God appointed him to be a watchman again, but this time to preach a message of hope. There are still sections full of warnings (33:23—34:10; 36:1–7), but these are part of the larger picture of hope. God will remember to bless those who are faithful to him. We must pay attention to both aspects of Ezekiel's message: warning and promise. Those who persist in rebelling against God should take warning. Those faithful to God should find encouragement and hope.

10 "Now as for you, son of man, say to the house of Israel, 'Thus you have spoken, saying, "Surely our transgressions and our sins are upon us, and we are rotting away in them;
how then can we survive?"'
11 "Say to them, 'As I live!' declares the Lord GOD, 'I take no pleasure in the death of
the wicked, but rather that the wicked turn from his way and live. Turn back, turn back
from your evil ways! Why then will you die, O house of Israel?'
12 "And you, son of man, say to your fellow citizens, 'The righteousness of a righteous
man will not deliver him in the day of his transgression, and as for the wickedness of the
wicked, he will not stumble because of it in the day when he turns from his wickedness;
whereas a righteous man will not be able to live by his righteousness on the day when he
commits sin.'
13 "When I say to the righteous he will surely live, and he *so* trusts in his righteousness
that he commits iniquity, none of his righteous deeds will be remembered; but in that
same iniquity of his which he has committed he will die.
14 "But when I say to the wicked, 'You will surely die,' and he turns from his sin and
practices justice and righteousness,
15 *if a* wicked man restores a pledge, pays back what he has taken by robbery, walks by
the statutes which ensure life without committing iniquity, he shall surely live; he shall
not die.
16 "None of his sins that he has committed will be remembered against him. He has
practiced justice and righteousness; he shall surely live.
17 "Yet your fellow citizens say, 'The way of the Lord is not right,' when it is their own
way that is not right.
18 "When the righteous turns from his righteousness and commits iniquity, then he shall
die in it.
19 "But when the wicked turns from his wickedness and practices justice and righteousness, he will live by them.
20 "Yet you say, 'The way of the Lord is not right.' O house of Israel, I will judge each
of you according to his ways."

Word of Jerusalem's Capture

21 Now in the twelfth year of our exile, on the fifth of the tenth month, the refugees
from Jerusalem came to me, saying, "The city has been taken."
22 Now the hand of the LORD had been upon me in the evening, before the refugees
came. And He opened my mouth at the time *they* came to me in the morning; so my
mouth was opened and I was no longer speechless.
23 Then the word of the LORD came to me saying,
24 "Son of man, they who live in these waste places in the land of Israel are saying, 'Abraham was *only* one, yet he possessed the land; so to us who are many the land has been
given as a possession.'
25 "Therefore say to them, 'Thus says the Lord GOD, "You eat *meat* with the blood *in
it,* lift up your eyes to your idols as you shed blood. Should you then possess the land?
26 "You rely on your sword, you commit abominations and each of you defiles his
neighbor's wife. Should you then possess the land?"'
27 "Thus you shall say to them, 'Thus says the Lord GOD, "As I live, surely those who
are in the waste places will fall by the sword, and whoever is in the open field I will give
to the beasts to be devoured, and those who are in the strongholds and in the caves will
die of pestilence.

33:10 Lev 26:39; Ezek 4:17; 24:23; Is 49:14; Ezek 37:11

33:11 Is 49:18; Ezek 5:11; Ezek 18:23, 32; Hos 11:8; Jer 31:20; 1 Tim 2:4; 2 Pet 3:9; Is 55:6, 7; Jer 3:22; Ezek 18:30, 31; Hos 14:1; Acts 3:19

33:12 Ezek 3:18; 18:24; 33:20; 2 Chr 7:14; Ezek 18:21; 33:19

33:13 Ezek 18:26; Heb 10:38; 2 Pet 2:20, 21

33:14 Is 55:7; Jer 18:7, 8; Ezek 18:27; 33:8, 19; Hos 14:1, 4; Mic 6:8

33:15 Ex 22:1-4; Lev 6:4, 5; Luke 19:8; Ps 119:59; 143:8; Ezek 20:11

33:16 Is 1:18; 43:25; Ezek 18:22

33:18 Ezek 3:20; 18:24; 33:12, 13

33:20 Ezek 18:25

33:21 Ezek 31:1; 32:1, 17; Jer 39:1, 2; 40:1; 52:4-7; Ezek 24:1, 2; 2 Kin 25:10; Jer 39:8

33:22 Ezek 1:3; 8:1; 37:1; Ezek 3:26, 27; 24:27; Luke 1:64

33:24 Jer 39:10; 40:7; Ezek 33:27; Is 51:2; Luke 3:8; Acts 7:5; Rom 4:12; Ezek 11:15

33:25 Lev 17:10, 12, 14; Deut 12:16, 23; 15:23; Jer 7:9, 10

33:26 Mic 2:1, 2; Zeph 3:3

33:27 Jer 15:2, 3; 42:22; Ezek 5:12; 1 Sam 13:6; Is 2:19

33:10–12 The exiles were discouraged by their past sins. This is an important turning point in this book—elsewhere in Ezekiel the people had refused to face their sins. Here, they felt heavy guilt for rebelling against God for so many years. Therefore, God assured them of forgiveness if they repented. God *wants* everyone to turn to him. He looks at what we are and will become, not what we have been. God gives you the opportunity to turn to him, if you will take it. Sincerely follow God, and ask him to forgive you when you fail.

33:13 Past good deeds will not save a person who decides to turn to a life of sin. Some people think they have done enough good deeds to overshadow the sins they don't want to give up. But it's useless to try to be good in some areas so you can be deliberately bad in others. God wants wholehearted love and obedience.

33:15 While good deeds will not save us, our salvation must lead to righteous actions (see Ephesians 2:10; James 2:14–17). This includes restitution for past sins (as exemplified in the story of Zacchaeus, see Luke 19:1–10). God expects us to make restitution, whenever necessary, for the wrongs we have committed.

33:21–22 Near the beginning of his ministry, Ezekiel was unable to speak except to give specific messages from God (3:26–27). After Ezekiel's prophecies came true and the false prophets were exposed, Ezekiel was again able to talk freely. No longer needing to prove himself, he was free to offer God's message of restoration and hope.

33:28 Ezek 5:14; 6:14; Mic 7:13; Ezek 7:24; 24:21; 30:6

33:30 Is 29:13; 58:2; Ezek 14:3; 20:3, 31

33:31 Ps 78:36, 37; Is 29:13; 1 John 3:18; Ezek 22:13, 27; Luke 12:15

33:32 Mark 6:20

33:33 Jer 28:9; Ezek 33:29

34:2 Jer 2:8; 3:15; 10:21; 12:10; Jer 23:1; Ezek 22:25; 34:8-10; Mic 3:1-3, 11; Ps 78:71, 72; Is 40:11; Ezek 34:14, 15; John 10:11; 21:15-17

34:3 Zech 11:16; Ezek 22:25, 27

34:4 Zech 11:16; Matt 9:36; 10:6; 18:12, 13; Luke 15:4

34:5 Num 27:17; 2 Chr 18:16; Jer 10:21; 23:2; 50:6, 7; Matt 9:36; Mark 6:34; Ezek 34:8, 28

34:6 Jer 40:11, 12; Ezek 7:16; 1 Pet 2:25; John 10:16; Ps 142:4

34:8 Acts 20:29

34:10 Jer 21:13; Ezek 5:8; 13:8; 34:2; Zech 10:3; 1 Sam 2:29, 30; Jer 52:24-27; Ps 72:12-14

28 "I will make the land a desolation and a waste, and the pride of her power will cease;
and the mountains of Israel will be desolate so that no one will pass through.
29 "Then they will know that I am the LORD, when I make the land a desolation and a
waste because of all their abominations which they have committed." '
30 "But as for you, son of man, your fellow citizens who talk about you by the walls and
in the doorways of the houses, speak to one another, each to his brother, saying, 'Come
now and hear what the message is which comes forth from the LORD.'
31 "They come to you as people come, and sit before you *as* My people and hear your
words, but they do not do them, for they do the lustful desires *expressed* by their mouth,
and their heart goes after their gain.
32 "Behold, you are to them like a sensual song by one who has a beautiful voice and
plays well on an instrument; for they hear your words but they do not practice them.
33 "So when it comes to pass—as surely it will—then they will know that a prophet has
been in their midst."

Prophecy against the Shepherds of Israel

34 Then the word of the LORD came to me saying,
2 "Son of man, prophesy against the shepherds of Israel. Prophesy and say to
those shepherds, 'Thus says the Lord GOD, "Woe, shepherds of Israel who have been
feeding themselves! Should not the shepherds feed the flock?
3 "You eat the fat and clothe yourselves with the wool, you slaughter the fat *sheep* without feeding the flock.
4 "Those who are sickly you have not strengthened, the diseased you have not healed,
the broken you have not bound up, the scattered you have not brought back, nor have
you sought for the lost; but with force and with severity you have dominated them.
5 "They were scattered for lack of a shepherd, and they became food for every beast of
the field and were scattered.
6 "My flock wandered through all the mountains and on every high hill; My flock was
scattered over all the surface of the earth, and there was no one to search or seek *for
them.*" ' "
7 Therefore, you shepherds, hear the word of the LORD:
8 "As I live," declares the Lord GOD, "surely because My flock has become a prey, My
flock has even become food for all the beasts of the field for lack of a shepherd, and My
shepherds did not search for My flock, but *rather* the shepherds fed themselves and did
not feed My flock;
9 therefore, you shepherds, hear the word of the LORD:
10 'Thus says the Lord GOD, "Behold, I am against the shepherds, and I will demand
My sheep from them and make them cease from feeding sheep. So the shepherds will

---

33:30–32 The people refused to act upon Ezekiel's message. When people mock your witness for Christ or fail to act upon your advice, don't give up. You are not witnessing for them alone, but out of faithfulness to God. You cannot make them accept your message; you can only be faithful in delivering it.

33:31 In your heart, do you really love God? These people gave the appearance of following God, but they loved their money more. Many today also give the outward impression of being religious while remaining inwardly greedy. Jesus warned that we cannot love God and Money at the same time (Matthew 6:24). It's easy to say "I surrender all" when we don't have much. It's when we start gaining some money that it becomes difficult to avoid loving it.

33:32 The people were coming to listen to Ezekiel in order to be entertained. They weren't interested in hearing a message from the Lord and then putting it into practice. Many people see church as entertainment. They enjoy the music, the people, and the activities, but they don't take the messages to heart. They don't seek to be challenged or to serve. Have you reduced church services to the level of entertainment, or does your worship truly have an impact on your life? Listen to God's words and then obey—apply his words and put them into practice in your life.

34:1ff Ezekiel called the exiles "Israel," referring to all Jews in captivity from both the northern and southern kingdoms. Ezekiel criticized Israel's leaders for taking care of themselves rather than taking care of their people. He outlined their sins (34:1–6) and pronounced judgment upon them (34:7–10). Then he promised that a true shepherd (the Messiah) would come who would take care of the people as the other leaders were supposed to do (34:11–31). This beautiful message portrays the fate of the present shepherds, the work of the new shepherd, and the future of the sheep.

34:4–6 God would judge the religious leaders because they were selfishly caught up in their own concerns and were neglecting their service to others. Spiritual leaders must be careful not to pursue self-development at the expense of broken, scattered people. When we give too much attention to our own needs and ideas, we may push God aside and abandon those who depend on us.

34:9–10 Those shepherds who failed their flock would be removed from office and held responsible for what happened to the people they were supposed to lead. Christian leaders must heed this warning and care for their flock, or total failure and judgment will be the result (see 1 Corinthians 9:24–27). True leadership focuses on helping others, not just on getting ahead.

not feed themselves anymore, but I will deliver My flock from their mouth, so that they
will not be food for them." ' "

The Restoration of Israel

11 For thus says the Lord GOD, "Behold, I Myself will search for My sheep and seek
them out.
12 "As a shepherd cares for his herd in the day when he is among his scattered sheep, so
I will care for My sheep and will deliver them from all the places to which they were
scattered on a cloudy and gloomy day.
13 "I will bring them out from the peoples and gather them from the countries and bring
them to their own land; and I will feed them on the mountains of Israel, by the streams,
and in all the inhabited places of the land.
14 "I will feed them in a good pasture, and their grazing ground will be on the mountain
heights of Israel. There they will lie down on good grazing ground and feed in rich pasture on the mountains of Israel.
15 "I will feed My flock and I will lead them to rest," declares the Lord GOD.
16 "I will seek the lost, bring back the scattered, bind up the broken and strengthen the
sick; but the fat and the strong I will destroy. I will feed them with judgment.
17 "As for you, My flock, thus says the Lord GOD, 'Behold, I will judge between one
sheep and another, between the rams and the male goats.
18 'Is it too slight a thing for you that you should feed in the good pasture, that you
must tread down with your feet the rest of your pastures? Or that you should drink of
the clear waters, that you must foul the rest with your feet?
19 'As for My flock, they must eat what you tread down with your feet and drink what
you foul with your feet!' "
20 Therefore, thus says the Lord GOD to them, "Behold, I, even I, will judge between
the fat sheep and the lean sheep.
21 "Because you push with side and with shoulder, and thrust at all the weak with your
horns until you have scattered them abroad,
22 therefore, I will deliver My flock, and they will no longer be a prey; and I will judge
between one sheep and another.
23 "Then I will set over them one shepherd, My servant David, and he will feed them;
he will feed them himself and be their shepherd.
24 "And I, the LORD, will be their God, and My servant David will be prince among
them; I the LORD have spoken.
25 "I will make a covenant of peace with them and eliminate harmful beasts from the
land so that they may live securely in the wilderness and sleep in the woods.
26 "I will make them and the places around My hill a blessing. And I will cause showers
to come down in their season; they will be showers of blessing.
27 "Also the tree of the field will yield its fruit and the earth will yield its increase, and
they will be secure on their land. Then they will know that I am the LORD, when I have
broken the bars of their yoke and have delivered them from the hand of those who enslaved them.
28 "They will no longer be a prey to the nations, and the beasts of the earth will not
devour them; but they will live securely, and no one will make *them* afraid.
29 "I will establish for them a renowned planting place, and they will not again be victims of famine in the land, and they will not endure the insults of the nations anymore.
30 "Then they will know that I, the LORD their God, am with them, and that they, the
house of Israel, are My people," declares the Lord GOD.
31 "As for you, My sheep, the sheep of My pasture, you are men, and I am your God,"
declares the Lord GOD.

34:12 Jer 31:10; Is 40:11; 56:8; Jer 23:3; 31:8; Luke 19:10; John 10:16; Jer 13:16; Ezek 30:3; Joel 2:2

34:13 Ezek 34:23; 36:29, 30; Mic 7:14; Is 30:25

34:14 Ps 23:2; Jer 31:12-14, 25; John 10:9; Ezek 28:25, 26; 36:29, 30

34:15 Ps 23:1, 2

34:16 Is 10:16; Is 49:26

34:17 Ezek 20:38; 34:20-22; Mal 4:1; Matt 25:32

34:18 Num 16:9, 13; 2 Sam 7:19; Is 7:13

34:21 Deut 33:17; Dan 8:4; Luke 13:14-16

34:22 Ps 72:12-14; Jer 23:3; Ezek 34:10

34:23 Rev 7:17; Is 40:11; John 10:11; Jer 30:9; Ezek 37:24

34:24 Is 55:3; Jer 30:9; Ezek 37:24, 25; Hos 3:5

34:25 Ezek 16:60; 20:37; 37:26; Job 5:22, 23; Is 11:6-9; Jer 33:16; Ezek 28:26; 34:27, 28

34:26 Gen 12:2; Deut 11:13-15; 28:12; Lev 25:21; Is 44:3

34:27 Ezek 38:8, 11; Lev 26:13; Is 52:2, 3; Jer 30:8

34:28 Jer 30:10

34:29 Is 4:2; 60:21; 61:3; Ezek 36:6, 15

34:30 Ps 46:7, 11

34:31 Ps 78:52; 80:1; Ezek 36:38; Ps 100:3; Jer 23:1

34:11–16 God promises to take over as shepherd of his scattered flock. When our leaders fail us, we must not despair but remember that God is in control and that he promises to return and care for his flock. Thus we know that we can turn to God for help. He is still in control and can transform any tragic situation to produce good for his kingdom (see Genesis 50:20; Romans 8:28).

34:18–20 A bad shepherd is not only selfish but destructive. A minister who muddies the waters for others by raising unnecessary doubts, teaching false ideas, and acting sinfully is destroying his flock's spiritual nourishment.

34:23–25 In contrast to the present evil shepherds (leaders) of God's people (34:1–6), God will send a perfect shepherd, the Messiah ("My servant David"), who will take care of every need his people have and set up a kingdom of perfect peace and justice (see Psalm 23; Jeremiah 23:5–6; John 10:11; Hebrews 13:20–21; Revelation 21). "Peace" here means more than the absence of conflict. It is contentment, fulfillment, and security.

Prophecy against Mount Seir

35 Moreover, the word of the LORD came to me saying,
2 "Son of man, set your face against Mount Seir, and prophesy against it
3 and say to it, 'Thus says the Lord GOD,
"Behold, I am against you, Mount Seir,
And I will stretch out My hand against you
And make you a desolation and a waste.
4 "I will lay waste your cities
And you will become a desolation.
Then you will know that I am the LORD.
5 "Because you have had everlasting enmity and have delivered the sons of Israel
to the power of the sword at the time of their calamity, at the time of the punishment of
the end,
6 therefore as I live," declares the Lord GOD, "I will give you over to bloodshed, and
bloodshed will pursue you; since you have not hated bloodshed, therefore bloodshed will
pursue you.
7 "I will make Mount Seir a waste and a desolation and I will cut off from it the one
who passes through and returns.
8 "I will fill its mountains with its slain; on your hills and in your valleys and in all your
ravines those slain by the sword will fall.
9 "I will make you an everlasting desolation and your cities will not be inhabited. Then
you will know that I am the LORD.
10 "Because you have said, 'These two nations and these two lands will be mine, and we
will possess them,' although the LORD was there,
11 therefore as I live," declares the Lord GOD, "I will deal *with you* according to your
anger and according to your envy which you showed because of your hatred against them;
so I will make Myself known among them when I judge you.
12 "Then you will know that I, the LORD, have heard all your revilings which you have
spoken against the mountains of Israel saying, 'They are laid desolate; they are given to
us for food.'
13 "And you have spoken arrogantly against Me and have multiplied your words against
Me; I have heard *it*."
14 'Thus says the Lord GOD, "As all the earth rejoices, I will make you a desolation.
15 "As you rejoiced over the inheritance of the house of Israel because it was desolate,
so I will do to you. You will be a desolation, O Mount Seir, and all Edom, all of it. Then
they will know that I am the LORD." '

The Mountains of Israel to Be Blessed

36 "And you, son of man, prophesy to the mountains of Israel and say, 'O mountains
of Israel, hear the word of the LORD.

35:2 Gen 36:8; Ezek 25:12; 36:5
35:3 Jer 6:12; 15:6; Ezek 25:13; Jer 49:13, 17
35:4 Ezek 6:6; 35:9; Mal 1:3, 4
35:5 Ps 137:7; Ezek 25:12, 15; 36:5; Amos 1:11; Obad 10; Ezek 7:2; 21:25
35:6 Is 63:2-6; Ezek 16:38; 32:6
35:8 Is 34:5, 6; Ezek 31:12; 32:4, 5; 39:4
35:9 Jer 49:13; Ezek 25:13
35:10 Ps 83:4-12; Ezek 36:2, 5; Ps 48:1-3; 132:13, 14; Is 12:6; Ezek 48:35; Zeph 3:15
35:11 Ps 137:7; Ezek 25:14; Amos 1:11; Ps 9:16; 73:17, 18
35:12 Jer 50:7; Ezek 36:2
35:13 Is 10:13, 14; 36:20; Jer 48:26, 42; Dan 11:36; Jer 7:11; 29:23
35:14 Is 44:23; 49:13; Jer 51:48
35:15 Jer 50:11; Lam 4:21; Obad 15; Is 34:5, 6

BAD SHEPHERDS VERSUS GOOD SHEPHERDS

Bad Shepherds	*Good Shepherds*
Take care of themselves	Take care of their flock
Worry about their own health	Strengthen the weak and sick, search for the lost
Rule harshly and brutally	Rule lovingly and gently
Abandon and scatter the sheep	Gather and protect the sheep
Keep the best for themselves	Give their best to the sheep

35:1ff Ezekiel gave another prophecy against Edom (also called Seir); his first prophecy against Edom is found in 25:12–14. In this prophecy, Ezekiel is probably using Edom to represent *all* the nations opposed to God's people. Chapter 36 says that Israel will be restored, while this chapter says that Edom (God's enemies) will be made "a desolation and a waste."

35:2 Edom offered to help destroy Jerusalem and rejoiced when the city fell. Edom's long-standing hostility against God's people resulted in God's judgment.

35:6–8 Ezekiel prophesied not only against the people of Edom, but also against their mountains and land. Their home territory was Mount Seir. Mountains, symbols of strength and power, represented the pride of these people who thought they could get away with evil. Edom's desire for revenge turned against them. Edom received the punishment they were so hasty to give out. God has a way of turning our treatment of others into a boomerang. So we must be careful in our judgment of others (Matthew 7:1–2).

36:1ff In this prophecy, Ezekiel said that Israel would be restored as a nation and would return to its own land. The mountains were symbolic of Israel's strength (see the note on 35:6–8). To the exiles in Babylon, this seemed impossible. This message again emphasizes God's sovereignty and trustworthiness. He would first judge the nations used to punish Israel (36:1–7) and then restore his people (36:8–15).

2 'Thus says the Lord GOD, "Because the enemy has spoken against you, 'Aha!' and,
'The everlasting heights have become our possession,'
3 therefore prophesy and say, 'Thus says the Lord GOD, "For good reason they have
made you desolate and crushed you from every side, that you would become a possession of the rest of the nations and you have been taken up in the talk and the whispering
of the people." ' "
4 'Therefore, O mountains of Israel, hear the word of the Lord GOD. Thus says the
Lord GOD to the mountains and to the hills, to the ravines and to the valleys, to the
desolate wastes and to the forsaken cities which have become a prey and a derision to
the rest of the nations which are round about,
5 therefore thus says the Lord GOD, "Surely in the fire of My jealousy I have spoken
against the rest of the nations, and against all Edom, who appropriated My land for themselves as a possession with wholehearted joy *and* with scorn of soul, to drive it out for a
prey."
6 'Therefore prophesy concerning the land of Israel and say to the mountains and to
the hills, to the ravines and to the valleys, "Thus says the Lord GOD, 'Behold, I have
spoken in My jealousy and in My wrath because you have endured the insults of the
nations.'
7 "Therefore thus says the Lord GOD, 'I have sworn that surely the nations which are
around you will themselves endure their insults.
8 'But you, O mountains of Israel, you will put forth your branches and bear your fruit
for My people Israel; for they will soon come.
9 'For, behold, I am for you, and I will turn to you, and you will be cultivated and sown.
10 'I will multiply men on you, all the house of Israel, all of it; and the cities will be
inhabited and the waste places will be rebuilt.
11 'I will multiply on you man and beast; and they will increase and be fruitful; and I
will cause you to be inhabited as you were formerly and will treat you better than at the
first. Thus you will know that I am the LORD.
12 'Yes, I will cause men—My people Israel—to walk on you and possess you, so that
you will become their inheritance and never again bereave them of children.'
13 "Thus says the Lord GOD, 'Because they say to you, "You are a devourer of men and
have bereaved your nation of children,"
14 therefore you will no longer devour men and no longer bereave your nation of children,' declares the Lord GOD.
15 "I will not let you hear insults from the nations anymore, nor will you bear disgrace
from the peoples any longer, nor will you cause your nation to stumble any longer,"
declares the Lord GOD.' "
16 Then the word of the LORD came to me saying,
17 "Son of man, when the house of Israel was living in their own land, they defiled it by
their ways and their deeds; their way before Me was like the uncleanness of a woman in
her impurity.
18 "Therefore I poured out My wrath on them for the blood which they had shed on the
land, because they had defiled it with their idols.
19 "Also I scattered them among the nations and they were dispersed throughout the
lands. According to their ways and their deeds I judged them.
20 "When they came to the nations where they went, they profaned My holy name,
because it was said of them, 'These are the people of the LORD; yet they have come out
of His land.'
21 "But I had concern for My holy name, which the house of Israel had profaned among
the nations where they went.

36:2 Deut 32:13; Ps 78:69; Is 58:14; Hab 3:19

36:3 Jer 2:15; Ps 44:13, 14; Jer 18:16; Ezek 35:13

36:4 Deut 11:11; Ezek 36:1, 6, 8; Ezek 34:8, 28

36:5 Ezek 5:13; 36:6; 38:19; Jer 25:9, 15-29; Ezek 36:3; Jer 50:11; Ezek 35:15; Mic 7:8

36:6 Ps 74:10; 123:3, 4; Ezek 34:29

36:8 Is 4:2; 27:6; Ezek 17:23; 34:26-29

36:9 Lev 26:9; Ezek 28:26; 34:14; 36:34

36:10 Is 27:6; 49:17-23; Ezek 37:21, 22; Jer 31:27, 28; 33:12; Ezek 36:33

36:11 Jer 30:18; Ezek 16:55; Mic 7:14; Job 42:12; Is 51:3

36:12 Ezek 34:13, 14; Ezek 47:14; Jer 15:7; Ezek 22:12, 27

36:13 Num 13:32

36:15 Is 60:14; Ezek 34:29; 36:7; Ps 89:50; Is 54:4; Ezek 22:4; Is 63:13; Jer 13:16; 18:15

36:17 Jer 2:7; Lev 15:19

36:18 2 Chr 34:21, 25; Lam 2:4; 4:11; Ezek 22:20, 22

36:19 Deut 28:64; Ezek 5:12; 22:15; Amos 9:9; Ezek 24:14; 39:24; Rom 2:6

36:20 Is 52:5; Ezek 12:16; Rom 2:24; Jer 33:24

36:21 Ps 74:18; Is 48:9; Ezek 20:44

36:2 "The everlasting heights" refers to the promised land—the land of Israel. Israel's enemies challenged not only their boundaries but also God's promises to Israel.

36:21-23 Why did God want to protect his holy name—his reputation—among the nations of the world? God was concerned about the salvation not only of his people, but also of the whole world. To allow his people to remain in sin and be permanently destroyed by their enemies would lead other nations to conclude that their pagan gods were more powerful than Israel's God (Isaiah 48:11). Thus, to protect his holy name, God would return a remnant of his people to their land. God will not share his glory with false gods—he alone is the one true God. The people had the responsibility to represent God properly to the rest of the world. Believers today have that same responsibility. How do you represent God to the world?

36:22 Deut 7:7, 8; 9:5, 6
36:23 Is 5:16; Ezek 20:41; 38:23; 39:7, 25; Ps 102:15; 126:2
36:24 Is 43:5, 6
36:25 Num 19:17-19; Ps 51:7; Titus 3:5, 6; Heb 9:13, 19; 10:22; Is 4:4; Zech 13:1; Is 2:18, 20; Hos 14:3
36:26 Ps 51:10; Ezek 11:19; 18:31; John 3:3, 5; 2 Cor 5:17; Zech 7:12
36:27 Is 44:3; 59:21; Ezek 37:14; 39:29; Joel 2:28, 29
36:29 Ezek 34:27, 29; Hos 2:21-23
36:30 Lev 26:4; Ezek 34:27
36:31 Ezek 16:61-63; 20:43
36:32 Deut 9:5
36:33 Ezek 36:10; Zech 8:7, 8; Is 58:12
36:35 Is 51:3; Ezek 31:9; Joel 2:3
36:36 Ezek 17:24; 22:14; 37:14; Hos 14:4-9
36:38 1 Kin 8:63; 2 Chr 35:7-9; John 2:14; Ps 74:1; 100:3; Jer 23:1; John 10:7, 9, 16

Israel to Be Renewed for His Name's Sake

22 "Therefore say to the house of Israel, 'Thus says the Lord GOD, "It is not for your
sake, O house of Israel, that I am about to act, but for My holy name, which you have
profaned among the nations where you went.
23 "I will vindicate the holiness of My great name which has been profaned among the
nations, which you have profaned in their midst. Then the nations will know that I am
the LORD," declares the Lord GOD, "when I prove Myself holy among you in their sight.
24 "For I will take you from the nations, gather you from all the lands and bring you
into your own land.
25 "Then I will sprinkle clean water on you, and you will be clean; I will cleanse you
from all your filthiness and from all your idols.
26 "Moreover, I will give you a new heart and put a new spirit within you; and I will
remove the heart of stone from your flesh and give you a heart of flesh.
27 "I will put My Spirit within you and cause you to walk in My statutes, and you will be
careful to observe My ordinances.
28 "You will live in the land that I gave to your forefathers; so you will be My people,
and I will be your God.
29 "Moreover, I will save you from all your uncleanness; and I will call for the grain and
multiply it, and I will not bring a famine on you.
30 "I will multiply the fruit of the tree and the produce of the field, so that you will not
receive again the disgrace of famine among the nations.
31 "Then you will remember your evil ways and your deeds that were not good, and you
will loathe yourselves in your own sight for your iniquities and your abominations.
32 "I am not doing *this* for your sake," declares the Lord GOD, "let it be known to you.
Be ashamed and confounded for your ways, O house of Israel!"
33 'Thus says the Lord GOD, "On the day that I cleanse you from all your iniquities, I
will cause the cities to be inhabited, and the waste places will be rebuilt.
34 "The desolate land will be cultivated instead of being a desolation in the sight of
everyone who passes by.
35 "They will say, 'This desolate land has become like the garden of Eden; and the waste,
desolate and ruined cities are fortified *and* inhabited.'
36 "Then the nations that are left round about you will know that I, the LORD, have
rebuilt the ruined places *and* planted that which was desolate; I, the LORD, have spoken
and will do it."
37 'Thus says the Lord GOD, "This also I will let the house of Israel ask Me to do for
them: I will increase their men like a flock.
38 "Like the flock for sacrifices, like the flock at Jerusalem during her appointed feasts,
so will the waste cities be filled with flocks of men. Then they will know that I am the
LORD." ' "

OLD AND NEW COVENANTS

Old Covenant	*New Covenant*
Placed upon stone	Placed upon people's hearts
Based on the Law	Based on desire to love and serve God
Must be taught	Known by all
Legal relationship with God	Personal relationship with God

36:25–27 God promised to restore Israel not only physically, but spiritually. To accomplish this, God would give them a new heart for following him and put his Spirit within them (see 11:19–20; Psalm 51:7–11) to transform them and empower them to do his will. Again the new covenant was promised (16:61–63; 34:23–25), ultimately to be fulfilled in Christ. No matter how impure your life is right now, God offers you a fresh start. You can have your sins washed away, receive a new heart for God, and have his Spirit within you—if you accept God's promise. Why try to patch up your old life when you can have a new one?

36:32 God said his people should be ashamed of their sins. The people had become so callous that they had lost all sensitivity to sin. First they had to "remember" (36:31) their sins, then despise them, and finally repent of them (see James 4:8–9). As we examine our lives, we may find that we too have lost our sensitivity to certain sins. But if we measure ourselves against God's standards of right living, we will be ashamed. To regain sensitivity we must recognize our sin for what it is, feel sorry for displeasing God, and ask his forgiveness. The Holy Spirit will guide us, making us responsive and receptive to God's truth (John 14:26; 16:8, 13).

36:37–38 God said that if the people asked, he would come to their aid. We cannot expect his mercy, however, until we have sought new hearts from him (36:26). We can be thankful that his invitation is open to all.

Vision of the Valley of Dry Bones

37 The hand of the LORD was upon me, and He brought me out by the Spirit of the
LORD and set me down in the middle of the valley; and it was full of bones.
2 He caused me to pass among them round about, and behold, *there were* very many
on the surface of the valley; and lo, *they were* very dry.
3 He said to me, "Son of man, can these bones live?" And I answered, "O Lord GOD,
You know."
4 Again He said to me, "Prophesy over these bones and say to them, 'O dry bones,
hear the word of the LORD.'
5 "Thus says the Lord GOD to these bones, 'Behold, I will cause [6]breath to enter you
that you may come to life.
6 'I will put sinews on you, make flesh grow back on you, cover you with skin and put
breath in you that you may come alive; and you will know that I am the LORD.' "
7 So I prophesied as I was commanded; and as I prophesied, there was a noise, and
behold, a rattling; and the bones came together, bone to its bone.
8 And I looked, and behold, sinews were on them, and flesh grew and skin covered
them; but there was no breath in them.
9 Then He said to me, "Prophesy to the breath, prophesy, son of man, and say to the
breath, 'Thus says the Lord GOD, "Come from the four winds, O breath, and breathe on
these slain, that they come to life." ' "
10 So I prophesied as He commanded me, and the breath came into them, and they
came to life and stood on their feet, an exceedingly great army.

The Vision Explained

11 Then He said to me, "Son of man, these bones are the whole house of Israel; behold, they say, 'Our bones are dried up and our hope has perished. We are completely
cut off.'
12 "Therefore prophesy and say to them, 'Thus says the Lord GOD, "Behold, I will open
your graves and cause you to come up out of your graves, My people; and I will bring
you into the land of Israel.
13 "Then you will know that I am the LORD, when I have opened your graves and caused
you to come up out of your graves, My people.
14 "I will put My [7]Spirit within you and you will come to life, and I will place you on
your own land. Then you will know that I, the LORD, have spoken and done it," declares
the LORD.' "

Reunion of Judah and Israel

15 The word of the LORD came again to me saying,
16 "And you, son of man, take for yourself one stick and write on it, 'For Judah and for
the sons of Israel, his companions'; then take another stick and write on it, 'For Joseph,
the stick of Ephraim and all the house of Israel, his companions.'
17 "Then join them for yourself one to another into one stick, that they may become
one in your hand.
18 "When the sons of your people speak to you saying, 'Will you not declare to us what
you mean by these?'
19 say to them, 'Thus says the Lord GOD, "Behold, I will take the stick of Joseph, which
is in the hand of Ephraim, and the tribes of Israel, his companions; and I will put them

37:1 Ezek 1:3; 33:22; 40:1; Ezek 8:3; 11:24; 43:5; Acts 8:39; Jer 7:32-8:2
37:3 Ezek 26:19; Deut 32:39; 1 Sam 2:6
37:4 Ezek 37:9, 12; Jer 22:29; Ezek 36:1
37:5 Gen 2:7; Ps 104:29, 30; Ezek 37:9, 10, 14
37:6 Is 49:23; Ezek 35:9; 38:23; 39:6; Joel 2:27; 3:17
37:7 Jer 13:5-7
37:9 Ps 104:30; Hos 13:14
37:10 Rev 11:11; Jer 30:19; 33:22
37:11 Jer 33:24; Ezek 36:10; 39:25; Ps 141:7; Ps 88:5; Lam 3:54
37:12 Deut 32:39; 1 Sam 2:6; Is 26:19; 66:14; Hos 13:14
37:14 Is 32:15; Ezek 11:19; 36:27; 37:6, 9; 39:29; Joel 2:28, 29; Zech 12:10
37:16 Num 17:2, 3; 2 Chr 10:17; 11:11-17; 15:9; 1 Kin 12:16-20; 2 Chr 10:19
37:17 Is 11:13; Jer 50:4; Ezek 37:22-24; Hos 1:11; Zeph 3:9
37:18 Ezek 12:9; 17:12; 20:49; 24:19

6 Or *spirit,* and so throughout the ch **7** Or *breath*

37:1ff This vision illustrates the promise of chapter 36—new life and a nation restored, both physically and spiritually. The dry bones are a picture of the Jews in captivity—scattered and dead. The two sticks (37:15–17) represent the reunion of the entire nation of Israel that had divided into northern and southern kingdoms after Solomon. The scattered exiles of both Israel and Judah would be released from the "graves" of captivity and one day regathered in their homeland, with the Messiah as their leader. This vision has yet to be fulfilled. Ezekiel felt he was speaking to the dead as he preached to the exiles because they rarely responded to his message. But these bones responded! And just as God brought life to the dead bones, he would bring life again to his spiritually dead people.

37:4–5 The dry bones represented the people's spiritually dead condition. Your church may seem like a heap of dry bones to you, spiritually dead with no hope of vitality. But just as God promised to restore his nation, he can restore any church, no matter how dry or dead it may be. Rather than give up, pray for renewal, for God can restore it to life. The hope and prayer of every church should be that God will put his Spirit into it (37:14). In fact, God is at work calling his people back to himself, bringing new life into dead churches.

37:16 The first stick was for Judah, being the leading tribe in the southern kingdom. The other was for Joseph, because he was the father of Ephraim, the leading tribe in the northern kingdom.

37:21 Is 43:5, 6; Jer 29:14; Ezek 36:24; 39:27; Amos 9:14, 15

37:22 Jer 3:18; 50:4, 5; Ezek 36:10; Ezek 34:23, 24; 37:24

37:23 Ezek 36:25; Ezek 36:28, 29

37:24 Jer 30:9; Ezek 34:24; 37:25; Hos 3:5; Ps 78:71; Is 40:11; Ezek 34:23

37:25 Is 11:1; Ezek 37:24; Zech 6:12

37:26 Ezek 16:62; 20:37; 34:25; Ps 89:3, 4; Is 55:3; 59:21; Ezek 16:60; Jer 30:19; Ezek 36:10, 11, 37; Ezek 20:40; 43:7

37:27 John 1:14; Rev 21:3; Ezek 37:23; 2 Cor 6:16

37:28 Ex 31:13; Ezek 20:12

38:2 Ezek 38:3, 14, 16, 18; 39:1, 11; Rev 20:8; Gen 10:2; Ezek 39:6; Rev 20:8; Ezek 38:3; 39:1; Ezek 27:13; 38:3; 39:1

38:4 Is 43:17; Ezek 38:15; Dan 11:40

38:5 2 Chr 36:20; Ezra 1:1; Ezek 27:10; Dan 8:20; Gen 10:6-8; Ezek 30:4, 5; Ezek 27:10; 30:5

38:6 Gen 10:2, 3; Gen 10:3; Ezek 27:14

38:7 Is 8:9

38:8 Is 24:22; Is 11:11; Ezek 36:24; 37:21; 38:12; 39:27, 28; Ezek 34:13; 36:1-8; Ezek 38:11, 14; 39:26

with it, with the stick of Judah, and make them one stick, and they will be one in My
hand." '
20 "The sticks on which you write will be in your hand before their eyes.
21 "Say to them, 'Thus says the Lord GOD, "Behold, I will take the sons of Israel from
among the nations where they have gone, and I will gather them from every side and
bring them into their own land;
22 and I will make them one nation in the land, on the mountains of Israel; and one
king will be king for all of them; and they will no longer be two nations and no longer be
divided into two kingdoms.
23 "They will no longer defile themselves with their idols, or with their detestable things,
or with any of their transgressions; but I will deliver them from all their [8]dwelling places
in which they have sinned, and will cleanse them. And they will be My people, and I will
be their God.

The Davidic Kingdom

24 "My servant David will be king over them, and they will all have one shepherd; and
they will walk in My ordinances and keep My statutes and observe them.
25 "They will live on the land that I gave to Jacob My servant, in which your fathers
lived; and they will live on it, they, and their sons and their sons' sons, forever; and David My servant will be their prince forever.
26 "I will make a covenant of peace with them; it will be an everlasting covenant with
them. And I will place them and multiply them, and will set My sanctuary in their midst
forever.
27 "My dwelling place also will be with them; and I will be their God, and they will be
My people.
28 "And the nations will know that I am the LORD who sanctifies Israel, when My sanctuary is in their midst forever." ' "

Prophecy about Gog and Future Invasion of Israel

38 And the word of the LORD came to me saying,
2 "Son of man, set your face toward Gog of the land of Magog, the prince of
Rosh, Meshech and Tubal, and prophesy against him
3 and say, 'Thus says the Lord GOD, "Behold, I am against you, O Gog, prince of Rosh,
Meshech and Tubal.
4 "I will turn you about and put hooks into your jaws, and I will bring you out, and all
your army, horses and horsemen, all of them splendidly attired, a great company *with*
buckler and shield, all of them wielding swords;
5 Persia, Ethiopia and Put with them, all of them *with* shield and helmet;
6 Gomer with all its troops; Beth-togarmah *from* the remote parts of the north with
all its troops—many peoples with you.
7 "Be prepared, and prepare yourself, you and all your companies that are assembled
about you, and be a guard for them.
8 "After many days you will be summoned; in the latter years you will come into the
land that is restored from the sword, *whose inhabitants* have been gathered from many
nations to the mountains of Israel which had been a continual waste; but its people were
brought out from the nations, and they are living securely, all of them.

8 Another reading is *backslidings*

37:24–25 The Messiah was often called David because he is David's descendant. David was a good king, but the Messiah would be the perfect King (Revelation 17:14; 19:16; 21:1ff).

37:26–27 God's promise here goes beyond the physical and geographical restoration of Israel. He promises to breathe new spiritual life into his people so that their hearts and attitudes will be right with him and united with one another. This same process is described throughout God's Word as the cleansing and renewing of our hearts by God's Spirit (Titus 3:4–6).

38:1ff In chapter 37, Ezekiel revealed how Israel (God's people) would be restored to their land from many parts of the world. Once Israel became strong, a confederacy of nations from the north would attack, led by Gog (see also Revelation 20:8). Their purpose would be to destroy God's people. Gog's allies would come from the mountainous area southeast of the Black Sea and southwest of the Caspian Sea (central Turkey), as well as from the area that is present-day Iran, Ethiopia, Libya, and possibly the Soviet Union. Gog could be a person (he sometimes is identified with Gyges, king of Lydia in 660 B.C.), or Gog could also be a symbol of all the evil in the world. Whether symbolic or literal, Gog represents the aggregate military might of all the forces opposed to God.

Many say that the battle Ezekiel described will occur at the end of human history, but there are many differences between the events described here and those in Revelation 20. Regardless of when this battle will occur, the message is clear: God will deliver his people—no enemy can stand before his mighty power.

9 "You will go up, you will come like a storm; you will be like a cloud covering the land,
you and all your troops, and many peoples with you."
10 'Thus says the Lord GOD, "It will come about on that day, that thoughts will come
into your mind and you will devise an evil plan,
11 and you will say, 'I will go up against the land of [9]unwalled villages. I will go against
those who are at rest, that live securely, all of them living without walls and having no
bars or gates,
12 to capture spoil and to seize plunder, to turn your hand against the waste places
which are *now* inhabited, and against the people who are gathered from the nations, who
have acquired cattle and goods, who live at the center of the world.'
13 "Sheba and Dedan and the merchants of Tarshish with all its villages will say to you,
'Have you come to capture spoil? Have you assembled your company to seize plunder,
to carry away silver and gold, to take away cattle and goods, to capture great spoil?' " '
14 "Therefore prophesy, son of man, and say to Gog, 'Thus says the Lord GOD, "On
that day when My people Israel are living securely, will you not know *it?*
15 "You will come from your place out of the remote parts of the north, you and many
peoples with you, all of them riding on horses, a great assembly and a mighty army;
16 and you will come up against My people Israel like a cloud to cover the land. It shall
come about in the last days that I will bring you against My land, so that the nations may
know Me when I am sanctified through you before their eyes, O Gog."
17 'Thus says the Lord GOD, "Are you the one of whom I spoke in former days through
My servants the prophets of Israel, who prophesied in those days for *many* years that I
would bring you against them?
18 "It will come about on that day, when Gog comes against the land of Israel," declares
the Lord GOD, "that My fury will mount up in My anger.
19 "In My zeal and in My blazing wrath I declare *that* on that day there will surely be a
great earthquake in the land of Israel.
20 "The fish of the sea, the birds of the heavens, the beasts of the field, all the creeping
things that creep on the earth, and all the men who are on the face of the earth will shake
at My presence; the mountains also will be thrown down, the steep pathways will collapse and every wall will fall to the ground.
21 "I will call for a sword against him on all My mountains," declares the Lord GOD.
"Every man's sword will be against his brother.
22 "With pestilence and with blood I will enter into judgment with him; and I will rain
on him and on his troops, and on the many peoples who are with him, a torrential rain,
with hailstones, fire and brimstone.
23 "I will magnify Myself, sanctify Myself, and make Myself known in the sight of many
nations; and they will know that I am the LORD." '

Prophecy against Gog—Invaders Destroyed

39 "And you, son of man, prophesy against Gog and say, 'Thus says the Lord GOD,
"Behold, I am against you, O Gog, prince of Rosh, Meshech and Tubal;
2 and I will turn you around, drive you on, take you up from the remotest parts of the
north and bring you against the mountains of Israel.
3 "I will strike your bow from your left hand and dash down your arrows from your
right hand.
4 "You will fall on the mountains of Israel, you and all your troops and the peoples
who are with you; I will give you as food to every kind of predatory bird and beast of the
field.
5 "You will fall on the open field; for it is I who have spoken," declares the Lord GOD.

9 Or *open country*

38:9 Is 5:28; 21:1; 25:4; 28:2; Jer 4:13; Ezek 30:18; 38:16; Joel 2:2
38:10 Ps 36:4; Mic 2:1
38:11 Zech 2:4; Jer 49:31
38:12 Is 10:6; Ezek 29:19
38:13 Ezek 25:13; 27:15, 20; Ezek 27:12; Is 10:6; 33:23; Jer 15:13
38:14 Jer 23:6;Zech 2:5, 8
38:15 Ezek 39:2
38:16 Ps 83:18; Is 5:16; 8:13; 29:23; Ezek 28:22
38:17 Is 5:26-29; 34:1-6; 63:1-6; 66:15, 16; Joel 3:9-14
38:18 Ps 18:8, 15
38:19 Deut 32:22; Ps 18:7, 8; Ezek 5:13; 36:5, 6; Nah 1:2; Heb 12:29; Joel 3:16; Hag 2:6, 7, 21
38:20 Jer 4:24, 25; Hos 4:3; Nah 1:4-6; Zech 14:4
38:21 Ezek 14:17; Judg 7:22; 1 Sam 14:20; 2 Chr 20:23; Hag 2:22
38:22 Is 66:16; Jer 25:31; Ps 11:6; 18:12-14; Is 28:17
38:23 Ps 9:16; Ezek 37:28; 38:16
39:3 Ps 76:3; Jer 21:4, 5; Ezek 30:21-24; Hos 1:5
39:4 Is 14:24, 25; Ezek 39:17-20; Ezek 29:5; 32:4, 5; 33:27

38:13 Sheba and Dedan, great trading centers in Arabia, would in effect say to Gog, "Who are you to usurp our position as the world's trade leaders?" Sheba and Dedan would then join this confederacy. Tarshish was the leading trade center in the west; many believe it was in Spain.

38:21 God will directly intervene in the defense of Israel, unleashing severe natural disasters on the invaders from the north. In the end, the stricken pagan nations will turn on themselves in confusion and panic. All those who set themselves against God will be destroyed.

39:1ff The story of the battle continues. The defeat of the evil forces will be final and complete; they will be destroyed by divine intervention. Because of this victory, God's name will be known throughout the world. His glory will be evident, and the nations will understand that he alone is in charge of human history. God will clearly show his love for his people by restoring them to their homeland.

6 "And I will send fire upon Magog and those who inhabit the coastlands in safety;
and they will know that I am the LORD.
7 "My holy name I will make known in the midst of My people Israel; and I will not let
My holy name be profaned anymore. And the nations will know that I am the LORD, the
Holy One in Israel.
8 "Behold, it is coming and it shall be done," declares the Lord GOD. "That is the day
of which I have spoken.
9 "Then those who inhabit the cities of Israel will go out and make fires with the weapons and burn *them,* both shields and bucklers, bows and arrows, war clubs and spears,
and for seven years they will make fires of them.
10 "They will not take wood from the field or gather firewood from the forests, for they
will make fires with the weapons; and they will take the spoil of those who despoiled
them and seize the plunder of those who plundered them," declares the Lord GOD.
11 "On that day I will give Gog a burial ground there in Israel, the valley of those who
pass by east of the sea, and it will block off those who would pass by. So they will bury
Gog there with all his horde, and they will call *it* the valley of Hamon-gog.
12 "For seven months the house of Israel will be burying them in order to cleanse the
land.
13 "Even all the people of the land will bury *them;* and it will be to their renown *on* the
day that I glorify Myself," declares the Lord GOD.
14 "They will set apart men who will constantly pass through the land, burying those
who were passing through, even those left on the surface of the ground, in order to cleanse
it. At the end of seven months they will make a search.
15 "As those who pass through the land pass through and anyone sees a man's
bone, then he will set up a marker by it until the buriers have buried it in the valley of
Hamon-gog.
16 "And even *the* name of *the* city will be Hamonah. So they will cleanse the land." '
17 "As for you, son of man, thus says the Lord GOD, 'Speak to every kind of bird and to
every beast of the field, "Assemble and come, gather from every side to My sacrifice which
I am going to sacrifice for you, as a great sacrifice on the mountains of Israel, that you
may eat flesh and drink blood.
18 "You will eat the flesh of mighty men and drink the blood of the princes of the earth,
as *though they were* rams, lambs, goats and bulls, all of them fatlings of Bashan.
19 "So you will eat fat until you are glutted, and drink blood until you are drunk, from
My sacrifice which I have sacrificed for you.
20 "You will be glutted at My table with horses and charioteers, with mighty men and
all the men of war," declares the Lord GOD.
21 "And I will set My glory among the nations; and all the nations will see My judgment
which I have executed and My hand which I have laid on them.
22 "And the house of Israel will know that I am the LORD their God from that day onward.
23 "The nations will know that the house of Israel went into exile for their iniquity because they acted treacherously against Me, and I hid My face from them; so I gave them
into the hand of their adversaries, and all of them fell by the sword.
24 "According to their uncleanness and according to their transgressions I dealt with
them, and I hid My face from them." ' "

Israel Restored

25 Therefore thus says the Lord GOD, "Now I will restore the fortunes of Jacob and
have mercy on the whole house of Israel; and I will be jealous for My holy name.
26 "They will [10]forget their disgrace and all their treachery which they [11]perpetrated
against Me, when they live securely on their *own* land with no one to make *them* afraid.

10 Another reading is *bear* **11** Lit *did treacherously*

39:7 Ezek 36:20-22; 39:25; Ex 20:7; Ezek 20:9, 14, 39; Ezek 38:16, 23; Is 12:6; 43:3, 14; 55:5; 60:9, 14

39:9 Is 66:24; Mal 1:5; Josh 11:6; Ps 46:9

39:10 Is 14:2; 33:1; Mic 5:8; Hab 2:8

39:12 Deut 21:23; Ezek 39:14, 16

39:13 Jer 33:9; Zeph 3:19, 20; Ezek 28:22

39:14 Jer 14:16

39:17 Is 56:9; Jer 12:9; Ezek 39:4; Rev 19:17, 18; Is 34:6, 7; Jer 46:10; Zeph 1:7

39:18 Ezek 29:5; Rev 19:18; Jer 51:40; Jer 50:27; Ps 22:12; Amos 4:1

39:20 Ps 76:5, 6; Ezek 38:4; Hag 2:22; Rev 19:18

39:21 Ex 9:16; Is 37:20; Ezek 36:23; 38:16, 23; 39:13

39:22 Jer 24:7

39:23 Jer 22:8, 9; 44:22; Ezek 36:18, 19; Is 1:15; 59:2; Ezek 39:29

39:24 2 Kin 17:7; Jer 2:17, 19; 4:18; Ezek 36:19

39:25 Is 27:12, 13; Jer 33:7; Ezek 34:13; Jer 31:1; Ezek 36:10; 37:21, 22; Hos 1:11; Ex 20:5; Nah 1:2

39:26 Ezek 16:63; 20:43; 36:31; 1 Kin 4:25; Ezek 34:25-28; Is 17:2; Mic 4:4

39:12–16 Two themes are intertwined: God's total victory over his enemies and the need to cleanse the land to make it holy. After the final battle, teams will be used to give proper burial to the bodies of the dead enemies in order for the land to be cleansed. The land would have been defiled by unburied corpses. Those who would come in contact with the corpses out in the open would become ceremonially unclean (according to Numbers 19:14–16). Yet there will be so many that all kinds of birds will be called in order to help dispose of the corpses (39:17–20). The message for us is an exciting one: With God on our side, we are assured of ultimate victory over his foes because God will fight on our behalf (see also Zephaniah 3:14–17; Romans 8:38–39).

27 "When I bring them back from the peoples and gather them from the lands of their
enemies, then I shall be sanctified through them in the sight of the many nations.
28 "Then they will know that I am the LORD their God because I made them go into
exile among the nations, and then gathered them *again* to their own land; and I will leave
none of them there any longer.
29 "I will not hide My face from them any longer, for I will have poured out My Spirit
on the house of Israel," declares the Lord GOD.

1. Restoring the worship of God

Vision of the Man with a Measuring Rod

40 In the twenty-fifth year of our exile, at the beginning of the year, on the tenth of
the month, in the fourteenth year after the city was taken, on that same day the
hand of the LORD was upon me and He brought me there.
2 In the visions of God He brought me into the land of Israel and set me on a very
high mountain, and on it to the south *there was* a structure like a city.
3 So He brought me there; and behold, there was a man whose appearance was like
the appearance of bronze, with a line of flax and a measuring rod in his hand; and he was
standing in the gateway.
4 The man said to me, "Son of man, see with your eyes, hear with your ears, and give
attention to all that I am going to show you; for you have been brought here in order to
show *it* to you. Declare to the house of Israel all that you see."

Measurements Relating to the Temple

5 And behold, there was a wall on the outside of the temple all around, and in the
man's hand was a measuring rod of six cubits, *each of which was* a cubit and a handbreadth.
So he measured the thickness of the wall, one rod; and the height, one rod.
6 Then he went to the gate which faced east, went up its steps and measured the threshold of the gate, one rod in width; and the other threshold *was* one rod in width.
7 The guardroom *was* one rod long and one rod wide; and *there were* five cubits between the guardrooms. And the threshold of the gate by the porch of the gate facing
inward *was* one rod.

39:27 Ezek 36:24; 37:21; Ezek 36:23; 38:16, 23

39:29 Is 32:15; Ezek 36:27; 37:14; Joel 2:28

40:1 Ezek 32:1, 17; 33:21; 2 Kin 25:1-7; Jer 39:1-9; 52:4-11; Ezek 33:21; Ezek 1:3; 3:14, 22; 37:1

40:2 Ezek 1:1; 8:3; Dan 7:1, 7; Is 2:2, 3; Ezek 17:23; 20:40; 37:22; Mic 4:1; Rev 21:10; Ps 48:2; Is 14:13; 1 Chr 28:12, 19

40:3 Ezek 1:7; Dan 10:6; Rev 1:15; Ezek 47:3; Zech 2:1, 2; Rev 11:1; 21:15

40:4 Ezek 2:1, 3, 6, 8; 44:5; Ezek 2:7, 8; 44:5; Is 21:10; Jer 26:2; Acts 20:27

40:5 Is 26:1; Ezek 42:20

40:6 Ezek 8:16; 11:1; 40:20; 43:1

40:7 Ezek 40:10-16, 21, 29, 33, 36

39:29 Both in this prophecy and in Joel 2:28–29, God promises to pour out his Spirit on mankind. The early church believed this began to be fulfilled at Pentecost, when God's Holy Spirit came to live in all believers (Acts 2:1–18).

40:1ff The building of the temple envisioned a time of complete restoration to the exiles, a time when God would return to his people. The temple was built in 520–515 B.C. (see Ezra 5; 6), but fell short of Ezekiel's plan (Haggai 2:3; Zechariah 4:10). This vision of the temple has been interpreted in four main ways: (1) This is the temple Zerubbabel should have built in 520–515 B.C. and is the actual blueprint Ezekiel intended. But due to disobedience (43:2–10), it was never followed. (2) This is a literal temple to be rebuilt during the millennial reign of Christ. (3) This temple is symbolic of the true worship of God by the Christian church right now. (4) This temple is symbolic of the future and eternal reign of God when his presence and blessing fill the earth.

Whether the temple is literal or symbolic, it seems clear that this is a vision of God's final perfect kingdom. This gave hope to the people of Ezekiel's time who had just seen their nation and its temple destroyed with no hope of rebuilding it in the near future. The details given in this vision gave the people even more hope that what Ezekiel saw had come from God and would surely happen in the future.

40:1ff One argument against the view that Ezekiel's temple is a literal building of the future is that sacrifices are mentioned (40:38–43). If the sacrifices were to be reinstituted in the last days, then Christ's final sacrifice would not have been final. The New Testament makes it clear that Christ died once and for all (Romans 6:10; Hebrews 9:12; 10:10, 18). Our sins have been removed; no further sacrifice is needed.

In Ezekiel's day, however, the only kind of worship the people knew was the kind that revolved around the sacrifices and ceremonies described in Exodus through Deuteronomy. Ezekiel had to explain the new order of worship in terms the people would understand. The next nine chapters tell how the temple is the focal point of everything, showing that the ideal relationship with God is when all of life centers on him.

40:1ff Ezekiel explained God's dwelling place in words and images the people could understand. God wanted them to see the great splendor he had planned for those who lived faithfully. This kind of temple was never built, but it was a vision intended to typify God's perfect plan for his people—the centrality of worship, the presence of the Lord, the blessings flowing from it, and the orderliness of worship and worship duties. Don't let the details obscure the point of this vision—one day all those who have been faithful to God will enjoy eternal life with him. Let the majesty of this vision lift you and teach you about the God you worship and serve.

40:1—43:27 This vision came to Ezekiel in 573 B.C. Chapters 40—43 give the temple's measurements and then describe how it would be filled with God's glory. Because Ezekiel was a priest, he would have been familiar with the furnishings and ceremonies of Solomon's temple. As in Revelation 11:1–2, the command to "measure" defines the areas God has marked out for special use. As you read all these details, remember that God is sovereign over all our worship and over the timetable for restoring the faithful to himself.

40:3–4 Who was this man? He was obviously not a human being, so he may have been the angel in 9:1–11 or one like him. Some say he may have been Christ himself because he speaks as God had been speaking to Ezekiel, calling him "Son of man."

40:5 The cubit and a handbreadth was about 21 inches, compared with the ordinary cubit of about 18 inches.

8 Then he measured the porch of the gate facing inward, one rod.

9 He measured the porch of the gate, eight cubits; and its side pillars, two cubits. And
the porch of the gate was faced inward.

10 The guardrooms of the gate toward the east *numbered* three on each side; the three
of them had the same measurement. The side pillars also had the same measurement on
each side.

11 And he measured the width of the gateway, ten cubits, and the length of the gate,
thirteen cubits.

12 *There was* a barrier *wall* one cubit *wide* in front of the guardrooms on each side; and
the guardrooms *were* six cubits *square* on each side.

13 He measured the gate from the roof of the one guardroom to the roof of the other,
a width of twenty-five cubits from *one* door to *the* door opposite.

14 He made the side pillars sixty cubits *high;* the gate *extended* round about to the side
pillar of the courtyard.

15 *From* the front of the entrance gate to the front of the inner porch of the gate *was*
fifty cubits.

16 *There were* shuttered windows *looking* toward the guardrooms, and toward their side
pillars within the gate all around, and likewise for the porches. And *there were* windows
all around inside; and on *each* side pillar *were* palm tree ornaments.

17 Then he brought me into the outer court, and behold, *there were* chambers and a
pavement made for the court all around; thirty chambers faced the pavement.

18 The pavement (*that is,* the lower pavement) *was* by the side of the gates, corresponding to the length of the gates.

19 Then he measured the width from the front of the lower gate to the front of the
exterior of the inner court, a hundred cubits on the east and on the north.

20 *As for* the gate of the outer court which faced the north, he measured its length and
its width.

21 It had three guardrooms on each side; and its side pillars and its porches had the same
measurement as the first gate. Its length *was* fifty cubits and the width twenty-five cubits.

22 Its windows and its porches and its palm tree ornaments *had* the same measurements as the gate which faced toward the east; and it was reached by seven steps, and its
porch *was* in front of them.

23 The inner court had a gate opposite the gate on the north as well as *the gate* on the
east; and he measured a hundred cubits from gate to gate.

24 Then he led me toward the south, and behold, there was a gate toward the south;
and he measured its side pillars and its porches according to those same measurements.

25 The gate and its porches had windows all around like those other windows; the length
was fifty cubits and the width twenty-five cubits.

26 *There were* seven steps going up to it, and its porches *were* in front of them; and it
had palm tree ornaments on its side pillars, one on each side.

27 The inner court had a gate toward the south; and he measured from gate to gate
toward the south, a hundred cubits.

28 Then he brought me to the inner court by the south gate; and he measured the south
gate according to those same measurements.

29 Its guardrooms also, its side pillars and its porches *were* according to those same
measurements. And the gate and its porches had windows all around; it *was* fifty cubits
long and twenty-five cubits wide.

30 *There were* porches all around, twenty-five cubits long and five cubits wide.

31 Its porches *were* toward the outer court; and palm tree ornaments *were* on its side
pillars, and its stairway *had* eight steps.

32 He brought me into the inner court toward the east. And he measured the gate
according to those same measurements.

33 Its guardrooms also, its side pillars and its porches *were* according to those same
measurements. And the gate and its porches had windows all around; it *was* fifty cubits
long and twenty-five cubits wide.

34 Its porches *were* toward the outer court; and palm tree ornaments *were* on its side
pillars, on each side, and its stairway *had* eight steps.

35 Then he brought me to the north gate; and he measured *it* according to those same
measurements,

36 *with* its guardrooms, its side pillars and its porches. And the gate had windows all
around; the length *was* fifty cubits and the width twenty-five cubits.

40:14 Ex 27:9; 1 Chr 28:6; Ps 100:4; Is 62:9; Ezek 8:7; 42:1

40:16 1 Kin 6:4; Ezek 41:16, 26; 1 Kin 6:29, 32, 35; 2 Chr 3:5; Ezek 40:22, 26, 31, 34, 37; 41:18-20, 25, 26

40:17 Ezek 10:5; 42:1; 46:21; Rev 11:2; 2 Kin 23:11; 1 Chr 9:26; 23:28; 2 Chr 31:11; Ezek 40:38

40:19 Ezek 40:23, 27; 46:1, 2; Ezek 40:23, 27

40:20 Ezek 40:6

40:21 Ezek 40:7; Ezek 40:16, 30; Ezek 40:15; Ezek 40:13

40:22 Ezek 40:16; Ezek 40:6; Ezek 40:26, 31, 34, 37, 49

40:23 Ezek 40:19, 27

40:24 Ezek 40:6, 20, 35; 46:9; Ezek 40:21

40:25 Ezek 40:16, 22, 29; Ezek 40:21, 33

40:26 Ezek 40:6, 22; Ezek 40:16

40:27 Ezek 40:23, 32; Ezek 40:19

40:28 Ezek 40:32, 35

40:29 Ezek 40:7, 10, 21; Ezek 40:16, 22, 25; Ezek 40:21

40:30 Ezek 40:16, 21

40:31 Ezek 40:16; Ezek 40:22, 26, 34, 37

40:32 Ezek 40:28-31, 35; Ezek 40:28

40:33 Ezek 40:29; Ezek 40:16; Ezek 40:21

40:34 Ezek 40:16; Ezek 40:22, 37

40:35 Ezek 40:27, 32; 44:4; 47:2

40:36 Ezek 40:7, 29; Ezek 40:16; Ezek 40:21

37 Its side pillars *were* toward the outer court; and palm tree ornaments *were* on its
side pillars on each side, and its stairway had eight steps.
38 A chamber with its doorway was by the side pillars at the gates; there they rinse the
burnt offering.
39 In the porch of the gate *were* two tables on each side, on which to slaughter the burnt
offering, the sin offering and the guilt offering.
40 On the outer side, as one went up to the gateway toward the north, *were* two tables;
and on the other side of the porch of the gate *were* two tables.
41 Four tables *were* on each side next to the gate; *or,* eight tables on which they slaughter *sacrifices.*
42 For the burnt offering *there were* four tables of hewn stone, a cubit and a half long,
a cubit and a half wide and one cubit high, on which they lay the instruments with which
they slaughter the burnt offering and the sacrifice.
43 The double hooks, one handbreadth in length, were installed in the house all around;
and on the tables *was* the flesh of the offering.
44 From the outside to the inner gate were chambers for the singers in the inner court,
one of which was at the side of the north gate, with its front toward the south, and one at
the side of the south gate facing toward the north.
45 He said to me, "This is the chamber which faces toward the south, *intended* for the
priests who keep charge of the temple;
46 but the chamber which faces toward the north is for the priests who keep charge of
the altar. These are the sons of Zadok, who from the sons of Levi come near to the LORD
to minister to Him."
47 He measured the court, a *perfect* square, a hundred cubits long and a hundred cubits wide; and the altar was in front of the temple.
48 Then he brought me to the porch of the temple and measured *each* side pillar of the
porch, five cubits on each side; and the width of the gate was three cubits on each side.
49 The length of the porch *was* twenty cubits and the width eleven cubits; and at the
stairway by which it was ascended *were* columns belonging to the side pillars, one on each
side.

The Inner Temple

41 Then he brought me to the nave and measured the side pillars; six cubits wide on
each side *was* the width of the side pillar.
2 The width of the entrance *was* ten cubits and the sides of the entrance *were* five cubits
on each side. And he measured the length of the nave, forty cubits, and the width, twenty cubits.
3 Then he went inside and measured each side pillar of the doorway, two cubits, and
the doorway, six cubits *high;* and the width of the doorway, seven cubits.
4 He measured its length, twenty cubits, and the width, twenty cubits, before the nave;
and he said to me, "This is the most holy *place.*"
5 Then he measured the wall of the temple, six cubits; and the width of the side chambers, four cubits, all around about the house on every side.
6 The side chambers were in three stories, one above another, and thirty in each story; and the side chambers extended to the wall which *stood* on their inward side all around,
that they might be fastened, and not be fastened into the wall of the temple *itself.*
7 The side chambers surrounding the temple were wider at each successive story.
Because the structure surrounding the temple went upward by stages on all sides of the
temple, therefore the width of the temple *increased* as it went higher; and thus one went
up from the lowest *story* to the highest by way of the second *story.*
8 I saw also that the house had a raised platform all around; the foundations of the
side chambers were a full rod of six long cubits *in height.*
9 The thickness of the outer wall of the side chambers *was* five cubits. But the free
space between the side chambers belonging to the temple

40:37 Ezek 40:16; Ezek 40:34

40:38 1 Chr 28:12; Neh 13:5, 9; Jer 35:4; 36:10; Ezek 40:17; 41:10; 42:13; 2 Chr 4:6

40:39 Ezek 40:42; Lev 1:3-17; Ezek 46:2

40:41 Ezek 40:39, 40

40:42 Ezek 40:39; Ex 20:25

40:44 Ezek 40:23, 27; Ezek 40:17, 38; 1 Chr 6:31, 32; 16:41-43; 25:1-7

40:45 Ezek 40:17, 38; 1 Chr 9:23; Ps 134:1

40:46 Ezek 40:17, 38; Lev 6:12, 13; Ezek 44:15; 1 Kin 2:35; Ezek 43:19; 48:11; Lev 10:3; Num 16:5, 40; Ezek 42:13; 45:4

40:47 Ezek 40:19, 23, 27

40:48 1 Kin 6:3; 2 Chr 3:4

40:49 Ezek 40:31, 34, 37; 1 Kin 7:15-22; 2 Chr 3:17; Jer 52:17-23; Rev 3:12

41:1 Ezek 40:2, 3, 17; Ezek 41:21, 23; Ezek 40:9; 41:3

41:2 1 Kin 6:2, 17; 2 Chr 3:3

41:3 Ezek 40:16; Ezek 41:1

41:4 1 Kin 6:20; 1 Kin 6:5; Ex 26:33, 34; 1 Kin 6:16; 7:50; 8:6; 2 Chr 5:7; Heb 9:3-8

41:5 1 Kin 6:5; Ezek 41:6-11

41:6 1 Kin 6:5-10; 1 Kin 6:6, 10

41:7 1 Kin 6:8

41:8 Ezek 40:5

40:38–39 The washing of the sacrifices was done according to the standards of preparation established in Leviticus 1:6–9. This washing was part of the process of presenting an acceptable sacrifice to God.

41:4 God's holiness is a central theme throughout both the Old and New Testaments. The most holy place (holy of holies) was the innermost room in the temple (Exodus 26:33–34). This was where the ark of the covenant was kept and where God's glory was said to dwell. This room was entered only once a year by the high priest, who performed a ceremony to atone for the nation's sins.

41:10 Ezek 40:17
41:12 Ezek 41:13, 15; 42:1; Ezek 41:14; 42:10, 13
41:13 Ezek 40:47; Ezek 41:13-15; 42:1, 10, 13; Ezek 41:12
41:15 Ezek 41:12, 13; 42:1; Ezek 41:14; 42:1, 10, 13; Ezek 41:16; 42:3, 5
41:16 Is 6:4; Ezek 10:18; 40:6; 41:25; 1 Kin 6:4; Ezek 40:16, 25; 41:26; Ezek 41:15; Ezek 42:3; 1 Kin 6:15
41:18 1 Kin 6:29, 32, 35; 7:36; Ezek 41:20, 25; 2 Chr 3:5; Ezek 40:16
41:19 Ezek 1:10; 10:14
41:20 Ezek 41:18
41:21 1 Kin 6:33; Ezek 40:9, 14, 16; 41:1; Ezek 41:1
41:22 Ex 30:1-3; 1 Kin 6:20; Rev 8:3; Ex 25:23, 30; Lev 24:6; Ezek 23:41; 44:16; Mal 1:7, 12
41:23 Ezek 41:1; Ezek 41:4; 1 Kin 6:31-35
41:24 1 Kin 6:34
41:25 Ezek 41:18; Ezek 41:16
41:26 Ezek 41:16; Ezek 40:16; Ezek 40:9, 48; Ezek 41:5
42:1 Ezek 40:17, 28, 48; 41:1; Ezek 40:17, 20; Ezek 40:20; Ezek 40:17; 42:4; Ezek 41:12; 42:10, 13; Ezek 41:12
42:2 Ezek 41:13
42:3 Ezek 41:10; Ezek 40:17; Ezek 41:15, 16; 42:5
42:4 Ezek 46:19
42:6 Ezek 41:6

10 and the *outer* chambers *was* twenty cubits in width all around the temple on every side.

11 The doorways of the side chambers toward the free space *consisted of* one doorway toward the north and another doorway toward the south; and the width of the free space *was* five cubits all around.

12 The building that *was* in front of the separate area at the side toward the west *was* seventy cubits wide; and the wall of the building *was* five cubits thick all around, and its length *was* ninety cubits.

13 Then he measured the temple, a hundred cubits long; the separate area with the building and its walls *were* also a hundred cubits long.

14 Also the width of the front of the temple and *that of* the separate areas along the east *side totaled* a hundred cubits.

15 He measured the length of the building along the front of the separate area behind it, with a gallery on each side, a hundred cubits; *he* also *measured* the inner nave and the porches of the court.

16 The thresholds, the latticed windows and the galleries round about their three stories, opposite the threshold, were paneled with wood all around, and *from* the ground to the windows (but the windows were covered),

17 over the entrance, and to the inner house, and on the outside, and on all the wall all around inside and outside, by measurement.

18 It was carved with cherubim and palm trees; and a palm tree was between cherub and cherub, and every cherub had two faces,

19 a man's face toward the palm tree on one side and a young lion's face toward the palm tree on the other side; they were carved on all the house all around.

20 From the ground to above the entrance cherubim and palm trees were carved, as well as *on* the wall of the nave.

21 The doorposts of the nave were square; as for the front of the sanctuary, the appearance of one doorpost was like that of the other.

22 The altar *was* of wood, three cubits high and its length two cubits; its corners, its base and its sides *were* of wood. And he said to me, "This is the table that is before the LORD."

23 The nave and the sanctuary each had a double door.

24 Each of the doors had two leaves, two swinging leaves; two *leaves* for one door and two leaves for the other.

25 Also there were carved on them, on the doors of the nave, cherubim and palm trees like those carved on the walls; and *there was* a threshold of wood on the front of the porch outside.

26 *There were* latticed windows and palm trees on one side and on the other, on the sides of the porch; thus *were* the side chambers of the house and the thresholds.

Chambers of the Temple

42 Then he brought me out into the outer court, the way toward the north; and he brought me to the chamber which *was* opposite the separate area and opposite the building toward the north.

2 Along the length, *which was* a hundred cubits, *was* the north door; the width *was* fifty cubits.

3 Opposite the twenty *cubits* which belonged to the inner court, and opposite the pavement which belonged to the outer court, *was* gallery corresponding to gallery in three stories.

4 Before the chambers *was* an inner walk ten cubits wide, a way of one *hundred* cubits; and their openings *were* on the north.

5 Now the upper chambers *were* smaller because the galleries took more *space* away from them than from the lower and middle ones in the building.

6 For they *were* in three stories and had no pillars like the pillars of the courts; therefore *the upper chambers* were set back from the ground upward, more than the lower and middle ones.

41:18 Cherubim are mighty angels.

41:22 The dimensions given would fit either the table of the bread of the Presence (Exodus 25:30) or the altar of incense (Exodus 30:1–3).

7 As for the outer wall by the side of the chambers, toward the outer court facing the
chambers, its length *was* fifty cubits.
8 For the length of the chambers which *were* in the outer court *was* fifty cubits; and
behold, *the length of those* facing the temple *was* a hundred cubits.
9 Below these chambers *was* the entrance on the east side, as one enters them from
the outer court.
10 In the thickness of the wall of the court toward the east, facing the separate area
and facing the building, *there were* chambers.
11 The way in front of them *was* like the appearance of the chambers which *were* on
the north, according to their length so was their width, and all their exits *were* both according to their arrangements and openings.
12 Corresponding to the openings of the chambers which were toward the south was
an opening at the head of the way, the way in front of the wall toward the east, as one
enters them.
13 Then he said to me, "The north chambers *and* the south chambers, which are opposite the separate area, they are the holy chambers where the priests who are near to the
LORD shall eat the most holy things. There they shall lay the most holy things, the grain
offering, the sin offering and the guilt offering; for the place is holy.
14 "When the priests enter, then they shall not go out into the outer court from the
sanctuary without laying there their garments in which they minister, for they are
holy. They shall put on other garments; then they shall approach that which is for the
people."
15 Now when he had finished measuring the inner house, he brought me out by the
way of the gate which faced toward the east and measured it all around.
16 He measured on the east side with the measuring reed five hundred reeds by the
measuring reed.
17 He measured on the north side five hundred reeds by the measuring reed.
18 On the south side he measured five hundred reeds with the measuring reed.
19 He turned to the west side *and* measured five hundred reeds with the measuring
reed.
20 He measured it on the four sides; it had a wall all around, the length five hundred
and the width five hundred, to divide between the holy and the profane.

Vision of the Glory of God Filling the Temple

43 Then he led me to the gate, the gate facing toward the east;
2 and behold, the glory of the God of Israel was coming from the way of the east.
And His voice was like the sound of many waters; and the earth shone with His glory.
3 And *it was* like the appearance of the vision which I saw, like the vision which I saw
when He came to destroy the city. And the visions *were* like the vision which I saw by the
river Chebar; and I fell on my face.
4 And the glory of the LORD came into the house by the way of the gate facing toward
the east.
5 And the Spirit lifted me up and brought me into the inner court; and behold, the
glory of the LORD filled the house.
6 Then I heard one speaking to me from the house, while a man was standing beside me.
7 He said to me, "Son of man, *this is* the place of My throne and the place of the soles
of My feet, where I will dwell among the sons of Israel forever. And the house of Israel

42:8 Ezek 41:13, 14
42:9 Ezek 44:5; 46:19
42:10 Ezek 42:7; Ezek 42:1, 13; Ezek 40:17
42:12 Ezek 42:7
42:13 Ezek 42:1, 10; Ex 29:31; Lev 7:6; 10:13, 14, 17; Lev 10:3; Deut 21:5; Ezek 40:46; Lev 6:25, 29; 14:13; Num 18:9, 10
42:14 Ezek 44:19; Ex 29:4-9; Lev 8:7, 13; Is 61:10; Zech 3:4, 5
42:15 Ezek 40:6; 43:1
42:16 Ezek 40:3
42:20 Is 60:18; Ezek 40:5; Zech 2:5; Ezek 45:2; Rev 21:16; Ezek 22:26; 44:23; 48:15
43:1 Ezek 10:19; 40:6; 42:15; 43:4; 44:1; 46:1
43:2 Is 6:3; Ezek 1:28; 3:23; 10:18, 19; Ezek 11:23; Ezek 1:24; Rev 1:15; 14:2; Ezek 1:28; 10:4; Rev 18:1
43:3 Ezek 1:4-28; Jer 1:10; Ezek 9:1, 5; 32:18; Ezek 1:3; 10:20; Ezek 1:28; 3:23
43:4 Ezek 10:19; 11:23; 43:2
43:5 Ezek 3:14; 8:3; 11:1, 24; 2 Cor 12:2-4; Ezek 10:4
43:6 Ezek 1:26; 40:3
43:7 Ps 47:8; Ezek 1:26; Ezek 37:26, 28; Lev 26:30; Ezek 6:5, 13

42:14 Approaching our holy God must not be taken lightly. The holy garments the priests were required to wear may symbolize the importance of having a holy heart when approaching God. The priests had to wear these special clothes in order to minister in the inner rooms of the temple. Because the garments were holy, the priests had to change their clothes before going back out to the public.

42:16–20 The perfect symmetry of Ezekiel's temple may represent the order and harmony in God's future kingdom.

43:1ff This is the culmination of chapters 40—42 because God's glory returns to the temple. It reverses the negative cast of the book and serves as a fitting end for all the passages dealing with the blessings reserved for the restored remnant. All true believers should long for that moment when God's name will finally be glorified and he will live among his people forever.

43:2 In 11:23, God's glory stopped over the Mount of Olives, to the east of Jerusalem, before leaving the city. This prophecy states that his glory would also return from the east.

43:2–4 Just as it was completely devastating when God's glory departed (11:23) from his temple, so it was overwhelming awe and joy beyond expression when Ezekiel saw God's glory return.

43:3 The river Chebar connected with the Euphrates River and was the location of a Jewish settlement of exiles in Babylonia.

will not again defile My holy name, neither they nor their kings, by their harlotry and by
the [12]corpses of their kings [13]when they die,
8 by setting their threshold by My threshold and their door post beside My door post,
with *only* the wall between Me and them. And they have defiled My holy name by their
abominations which they have committed. So I have consumed them in My anger.
9 "Now let them put away their harlotry and the [12]corpses of their kings far from Me;
and I will dwell among them forever.
10 "As for you, son of man, describe the temple to the house of Israel, that they may be
ashamed of their iniquities; and let them measure the plan.
11 "If they are ashamed of all that they have done, make known to them the design of
the house, its structure, its exits, its entrances, all its designs, all its statutes, and all its
laws. And write *it* in their sight, so that they may observe its whole design and all its statutes and do them.
12 "This is the law of the house: its entire area on the top of the mountain all around
shall be most holy. Behold, this is the law of the house.

The Altar of Sacrifice

13 "And these are the measurements of the altar by cubits (the cubit being a cubit and
a handbreadth): the base *shall be* a cubit and the width a cubit, and its border on its edge
round about one span; and this *shall be* the *height* of the base of the altar.
14 "From the base on the ground to the lower ledge *shall be* two cubits and the width
one cubit; and from the smaller ledge to the larger ledge *shall be* four cubits and the width
one cubit.
15 "The altar hearth *shall be* four cubits; and from the altar hearth shall extend upwards
four horns.
16 "Now the altar hearth *shall be* twelve *cubits* long by twelve wide, square in its four
sides.
17 "The ledge *shall be* fourteen *cubits* long by fourteen wide in its four sides, the border
around it *shall be* half a cubit and its base *shall be* a cubit round about; and its steps shall
face the east."

The Offerings

18 And He said to me, "Son of man, thus says the Lord GOD, 'These are the statutes
for the altar on the day it is built, to offer burnt offerings on it and to sprinkle blood
on it.
19 'You shall give to the Levitical priests who are from the offspring of Zadok, who
draw near to Me to minister to Me,' declares the Lord GOD, 'a young bull for a sin offering.
20 'You shall take some of its blood and put it on its four horns and on the four corners
of the ledge and on the border round about; thus you shall cleanse it and make atonement for it.
21 'You shall also take the bull for the sin offering, and it *shall be* burned in the appointed place of the house, outside the sanctuary.
22 'On the second day you shall offer a male goat without blemish for a sin offering,
and they shall cleanse the altar as they cleansed *it* with the bull.
23 'When you have finished cleansing *it,* you shall present a young bull without blemish
and a ram without blemish from the flock.

43:8 Ezek 8:3, 16
43:9 Ezek 18:30, 31; Ezek 37:26-28; 43:7
43:10 Ezek 40:4; Ezek 16:61, 63; 43:11; Ezek 28:12
43:11 Ezek 44:5; Ezek 12:3; Ezek 11:20; 36:27
43:12 Ezek 40:2
43:13 Ex 27:1-8; 2 Chr 4:1; Ezek 40:5; 41:8
43:14 Ezek 43:17, 20; 45:19
43:15 Ex 27:2; Lev 9:9; 1 Kin 1:50; Ps 118:27
43:16 Ex 27:1
43:17 Ex 20:26; Ezek 40:6
43:18 Ezek 2:1; Ex 40:29; Lev 1:5, 11; Heb 9:21, 22
43:19 1 Kin 2:35; Ezek 40:46; 44:15; Num 16:5, 40; Lev 4:3; Ezek 43:23; 45:18; Ezek 45:19; Heb 7:27
43:20 Lev 8:15; 9:9; Ezek 43:15; Ezek 43:14, 17; Lev 16:19; Ezek 43:22, 26
43:21 Ex 29:14; Lev 4:12; Heb 13:11
43:22 Ezek 43:25; Ezek 43:20, 26
43:23 Ex 29:1, 10; Ezek 45:18; Ex 29:1

12 Or *monuments* as in Ugaritic **13** Or *in their high places*

43:9–11 God's departure from the city had been a signal for the destruction of the city and the temple. Now for God to return, his conditions had to be met: Idolatry had to be removed. Some commentators feel these verses indicate that Ezekiel was commanding the people of his day to build this temple according to the designs and regulations that the angelic architect had given. But the people never repented, the conditions were not met, so the fulfillment was postponed.

43:12 The basic law of God's temple was holiness. In all he does, God is holy, perfect, and blameless. There is no trace of evil or sin in him. Just as God is holy, so we are to be holy (Leviticus 19:1; 1 Peter 1:15–16). People are holy when they are devoted to God and separated from sin. If we do not understand the basic concept of holiness, we will never progress very far in our Christian growth.

43:18–27 This vision was simultaneously flashing back to Mount Sinai and forward to Mount Calvary. When the people returned from exile, they would seek forgiveness through the sacrificial system instituted in Moses' day. Today, Christ's death has made the forgiveness of our sins possible, making us acceptable to God (Hebrews 9:9–15). God stands ready to forgive those who come to him in faith.

24 'You shall present them before the LORD, and the priests shall throw salt on them,
and they shall offer them up as a burnt offering to the LORD.
25 'For seven days you shall prepare daily a goat for a sin offering; also a young bull
and a ram from the flock, without blemish, shall be prepared.
26 'For seven days they shall make atonement for the altar and purify it; so shall they
consecrate it.
27 'When they have completed the days, it shall be that on the eighth day and onward,
the priests shall offer your burnt offerings on the altar, and your peace offerings; and I
will accept you,' declares the Lord GOD."

Gate for the Prince

44 Then He brought me back by the way of the outer gate of the sanctuary, which
faces the east; and it was shut.
2 The LORD said to me, "This gate shall be shut; it shall not be opened, and no one
shall enter by it, for the LORD God of Israel has entered by it; therefore it shall be
shut.
3 "As for the prince, he shall sit in it as prince to eat bread before the LORD; he shall
enter by way of the porch of the gate and shall go out by the same way."
4 Then He brought me by way of the north gate to the front of the house; and I
looked, and behold, the glory of the LORD filled the house of the LORD, and I fell
on my face.
5 The LORD said to me, "Son of man, mark well, see with your eyes and hear
with your ears all that I say to you concerning all the statutes of the house of the
LORD and concerning all its laws; and mark well the entrance of the house, with all
exits of the sanctuary.
6 "You shall say to the rebellious ones, to the house of Israel, 'Thus says the Lord
GOD, "Enough of all your abominations, O house of Israel,
7 when you brought in foreigners, uncircumcised in heart and uncircumcised in
flesh, to be in My sanctuary to profane it, *even* My house, when you offered My
food, the fat and the blood; for they made My covenant void—*this* in addition to
all your abominations.
8 "And you have not kept charge of My holy things yourselves, but you have set
foreigners to keep charge of My sanctuary."
9 'Thus says the Lord GOD, "No foreigner uncircumcised in heart and uncircumcised in flesh, of all the foreigners who are among the sons of Israel, shall enter My sanctuary.
10 "But the Levites who went far from Me when Israel went astray, who went astray
from Me after their idols, shall bear the punishment for their iniquity.
11 "Yet they shall be ministers in My sanctuary, having oversight at the gates of the house
and ministering in the house; they shall slaughter the burnt offering and the sacrifice for
the people, and they shall stand before them to minister to them.
12 "Because they ministered to them before their idols and became a stumbling block
of iniquity to the house of Israel, therefore I have sworn against them," declares the Lord
GOD, "that they shall bear *the punishment for* their iniquity.
13 "And they shall not come near to Me to serve as a priest to Me, nor come near to any
of My holy things, to the things that are most holy; but they will bear their shame and
their abominations which they have committed.

43:24 Lev 2:13; Num 18:19; Mark 9:49, 50; Col 4:6

43:25 Ex 29:35-37; Lev 8:33, 35

43:27 Lev 9:1; Lev 3:1; 17:5; Ezek 20:40

44:1 Ezek 40:6, 17; 42:14

44:2 Ezek 43:2-4

44:3 Ezek 34:24; 37:25; Gen 31:54; Ex 24:9-11; Ezek 46:2, 8-10; Ezek 40:9

44:4 Ezek 40:20, 40; Is 6:3, 4; Ezek 1:28; 3:23; 43:4, 5; Hag 2:7; Ezek 1:28; 43:3

44:5 Deut 32:46; Ezek 40:4; Deut 12:32; Ezek 43:10, 11

44:6 Ezek 2:5-7; 3:9; Ezek 45:9; 1 Pet 4:3

44:7 Ex 12:43-49; Lev 26:41; Deut 10:16; Jer 4:4; 9:26; Lev 22:25; Gen 17:14

44:8 Lev 22:2; Num 18:7

44:9 Ezek 44:7; Joel 3:17; Zech 14:21

44:10 2 Kin 23:8, 9; Ezek 22:26; 44:12; Num 18:23

44:11 Num 3:5-37; 4:1-33; 18:2-7; 1 Chr 26:1-19; Ezek 40:45; 44:14; 2 Chr 29:34; 30:17; Num 16:9

44:12 2 Kin 16:10-16; Ezek 14:3, 4; Ezek 20:15, 23; Ezek 44:10

44:13 Num 18:3; Ezek 16:61, 63; 39:26

44:2 Why was this east gate to remain closed? Several reasons have been suggested. (1) This was the gate through which God entered the temple, and no one else could walk where God had (43:2); (2) the closed gate indicated that God would never again leave the temple (10:19; 11:23); (3) it would prevent people from worshiping the sun as it rises in the east from within the temple grounds (8:16).

44:3 Although Christ is called a prince (37:25), this prince is probably not Christ because he offers a sacrifice to God (46:4) and he can enter only by the "porch of the gate." He is a princely ruler of the city, but he is distinguished from other princes because he will be just and fair (see 45:8). Another view is that this picture anticipates Christ offering a sacrifice of his own life to God.

44:9 Unbelievers would not be allowed to enter the temple. Ezekiel's vision was for a restored, purified worship where only those who prepared themselves physically and spiritually could participate. In 47:22–23, we find that people from other nations are allowed to join in worship by accepting the standards of faith and practice declared in the law (see Leviticus 24:22; Numbers 15:29).

14 "Yet I will appoint them to keep charge of the house, of all its service and of all that
shall be done in it.

Ordinances for the Levites

15 "But the Levitical priests, the sons of Zadok, who kept charge of My sanctuary when
the sons of Israel went astray from Me, shall come near to Me to minister to Me;
and they shall stand before Me to offer Me the fat and the blood," declares the Lord
GOD.
16 "They shall enter My sanctuary; they shall come near to My table to minister to Me
and keep My charge.
17 "It shall be that when they enter at the gates of the inner court, they shall be clothed
with linen garments; and wool shall not be on them while they are ministering in the
gates of the inner court and in the house.
18 "Linen turbans shall be on their heads and linen undergarments shall be on their loins;
they shall not gird themselves with *anything which makes them* sweat.
19 "When they go out into the outer court, into the outer court to the people, they shall
put off their garments in which they have been ministering and lay them in the holy chambers; then they shall put on other garments so that they will not transmit holiness to the
people with their garments.
20 "Also they shall not shave their heads, yet they shall not let their locks grow long;
they shall only trim *the hair of* their heads.
21 "Nor shall any of the priests drink wine when they enter the inner court.
22 "And they shall not marry a widow or a divorced woman but shall take virgins from
the offspring of the house of Israel, or a widow who is the widow of a priest.
23 "Moreover, they shall teach My people *the difference* between the holy and the profane, and cause them to discern between the unclean and the clean.
24 "In a dispute they shall take their stand to judge; they shall judge it according to My
ordinances. They shall also keep My laws and My statutes in all My appointed feasts
and sanctify My sabbaths.
25 "They shall not go to a dead person to defile *themselves;* however, for father, for
mother, for son, for daughter, for brother, or for a sister who has not had a husband,
they may defile themselves.
26 "After he is cleansed, seven days shall [14]elapse for him.
27 "On the day that he goes into the sanctuary, into the inner court to minister in the
sanctuary, he shall offer his sin offering," declares the Lord GOD.
28 "And it shall be with regard to an inheritance for them, *that* I am their inheritance;
and you shall give them no possession in Israel—I am their possession.
29 "They shall eat the grain offering, the sin offering and the guilt offering; and every
devoted thing in Israel shall be theirs.
30 "The first of all the first fruits of every kind and every contribution of every kind,
from all your contributions, shall be for the priests; you shall also give to the priest the
first of your dough to cause a blessing to rest on your house.
31 "The priests shall not eat any bird or beast that has died a natural death or has been
torn to pieces.

The LORD's Portion of the Land

45 "And when you divide by lot the land for inheritance, you shall offer an allotment
to the LORD, a holy portion of the land; the length shall be the length of 25,000
cubits, and the width shall be 20,000. It shall be holy within all its boundary round about.
2 "Out of this there shall be for the holy place a square round about five hundred by
five hundred *cubits,* and fifty cubits for its open space round about.

14 Lit *be counted*

44:14 Num 18:4; 1 Chr 23:28-32
44:15 Jer 33:18-22; Num 18:7; Zech 3:1, 7; Lev 3:16, 17; 17:5
44:16 Num 18:5, 7, 8; Ezek 41:22; Mal 1:7
44:17 Ex 28:42, 43; 39:27-29; Rev 19:8
44:18 Ex 28:40; Is 3:20; Ezek 24:17, 23; Ex 28:42; Lev 16:4
44:19 Lev 6:10; 16:4, 23, 24; Ezek 42:14; Lev 6:27; Ezek 46:20
44:20 Lev 21:5; Num 6:5
44:21 Lev 10:9
44:22 Lev 21:7, 14; Lev 21:13
44:23 Lev 10:10; Ezek 22:26; Hos 4:6; Mic 3:9-11; Zeph 3:4; Hag 2:11-13; Mal 2:6-8
44:24 Deut 17:8, 9; 19:17; 21:5; 1 Chr 23:4; 2 Chr 19:8-10; Lev 23:2, 4, 44; Ezek 20:12, 20
44:25 Lev 21:1-4
44:26 Num 19:13-19
44:27 Ezek 44:17; Lev 5:3, 6; Num 6:9-11
44:28 Num 18:20; Deut 10:9; 18:1, 2; Josh 13:33
44:29 Num 18:9, 14; Josh 13:14; Lev 27:21
44:30 Num 18:12, 13; 2 Chr 31:4-6, 10; Neh 10:35-37; Num 15:20, 21; Mal 3:10
44:31 Lev 22:8; Deut 14:21; Ezek 4:14
45:1 Num 34:13; Josh 13:7; 14:3; Zech 14:20, 21

44:15 Zadok's descendants are mentioned because many of the priests in Zadok's line had remained faithful to God, while others had become corrupt. Zadok supported God's choice of Solomon to succeed David, and was therefore appointed high priest during his reign (1 Kings 1:32–35; 2:27, 35). Zadok's descendants were considered the true priestly line throughout the time between the Old and New Testaments.

44:20–31 These laws were originally given to God's people in the wilderness. They are recorded in the books of Exodus and Leviticus. They reveal the importance of approaching God respectfully, and they give guidelines for the priests to live above reproach so they could carry out their responsibility to teach the people to distinguish "between the holy and the profane" (44:23).

45:1–7 The land allotted to the temple was in the center of the nation. God is central to life. He must be our first priority.

3 "From this area you shall measure a length of 25,000 *cubits* and a width of 10,000
cubits; and in it shall be the sanctuary, the most holy place.
4 "It shall be the holy portion of the land; it shall be for the priests, the ministers of the
sanctuary, who come near to minister to the LORD, and it shall be a place for their houses
and a holy place for the sanctuary.
5 "*An area* 25,000 *cubits* in length and 10,000 in width shall be for the Levites, the ministers of the house, *and* for their possession cities to dwell in.
6 "You shall give the city possession of *an area* 5,000 *cubits* wide and 25,000 *cubits* long,
alongside the [15]allotment of the holy portion; it shall be for the whole house of Israel.

Portion for the Prince

7 "The prince shall have *land* on either side of the holy [15]allotment and the property of
the city, adjacent to the holy [15]allotment and the property of the city, on the west side
toward the west and on the east side toward the east, and in length comparable to one of
the portions, from the west border to the east border.
8 "This shall be his land for a possession in Israel; so My princes shall no longer oppress My people, but they shall give *the rest of* the land to the house of Israel according
to their tribes."
9 'Thus says the Lord GOD, "Enough, you princes of Israel; put away violence and
destruction, and practice justice and righteousness. Stop your expropriations from My
people," declares the Lord GOD.
10 "You shall have just balances, a just ephah and a just bath.
11 "The ephah and the bath shall be the same quantity, so that the bath will contain a
tenth of a homer and the ephah a tenth of a homer; their standard shall be according to
the homer.
12 "The shekel shall be twenty gerahs; twenty shekels, twenty-five shekels, *and* fifteen
shekels shall be your maneh.
13 "This is the offering that you shall offer: a sixth of an ephah from a homer of wheat;
a sixth of an ephah from a homer of barley;
14 and the prescribed portion of oil (*namely,* the bath of oil), a tenth of a bath from
each kor (*which is* ten baths *or* a homer, for ten baths are a homer);
15 and one sheep from *each* flock of two hundred from the watering places of Israel—
for a grain offering, for a burnt offering and for peace offerings, to make atonement for
them," declares the Lord GOD.
16 "All the people of the land shall give to this offering for the prince in Israel.
17 "It shall be the prince's part *to provide* the burnt offerings, the grain offerings and
the drink offerings, at the feasts, on the new moons and on the sabbaths, at all the appointed feasts of the house of Israel; he shall provide the sin offering, the grain offering,
the burnt offering and the peace offerings, to make atonement for the house of Israel."
18 'Thus says the Lord GOD, "In the first *month,* on the first of the month, you shall
take a young bull without blemish and cleanse the sanctuary.
19 "The priest shall take some of the blood from the sin offering and put *it* on the door
posts of the house, on the four corners of the ledge of the altar and on the posts of the
gate of the inner court.
20 "Thus you shall do on the seventh *day* of the month for everyone who goes astray or
is naive; so you shall make atonement for the house.
21 "In the first *month,* on the fourteenth day of the month, you shall have the Passover,
a feast of seven days; unleavened bread shall be eaten.
22 "On that day the prince shall provide for himself and all the people of the land a bull
for a sin offering.

15 Or *contribution*

45:4 Ezek 48:10, 11; Num 16:5; Ezek 40:45; 43:19
45:5 Ezek 48:13
45:6 Ezek 48:15-18, 30-35
45:7 Ezek 34:24; 37:24; 46:16-18; 48:21
45:8 Is 11:3-5; Jer 23:5; Ezek 19:7; 22:27; 46:18; Josh 11:23
45:9 Ezek 44:6; Jer 6:7; Ezek 7:11, 23; 8:17; Jer 22:3; Zech 8:16; Neh 5:1-5
45:10 Lev 19:36; Deut 25:15; Prov 16:11; Amos 8:4-6; Mic 6:10, 11; Is 5:10
45:11 Is 5:10
45:12 Ex 30:13; Lev 27:25; Num 3:47
45:15 Ezek 45:17; Lev 1:4; 6:30
45:16 Ex 30:14, 15; Is 16:1
45:17 Ezek 46:4-12; 1 Kin 8:64; 1 Chr 16:2; 2 Chr 31:3; Lev 23:1-44; Num 28:1-29:39; Is 66:23; 1 Kin 8:63; Ezek 43:27
45:18 Ex 12:2; Lev 22:20; Heb 9:14; Lev 16:16, 33; Ezek 43:22, 26
45:19 Lev 16:18-20; Ezek 43:20; Ezek 43:14, 17, 20
45:20 Lev 4:27; Ps 19:12; Lev 16:20; Ezek 45:15, 18
45:21 Num 28:16f
Ex 12:1-24; Lev 23:5-8
45:22 Lev 4:14

45:8–12 Greed and extortion were two of the major social sins of the nation during this time (see Amos 5:10–13). In the new economy there would be plenty of land for the "princes" (45:7–8) and no longer any basis for greed. Therefore, God commanded the princes and the people to be just and do right, especially in their business dealings. Consider the ways that you measure goods, money, or services. If you are paid for an hour of work, be sure you work for a full hour. If you sell a bushel of apples, make sure it is a full bushel. God is completely trustworthy, and his followers should be too.

45:17 The conditions and regulations for these offerings are described in detail in Leviticus 1—7.

45:21 The Passover was an annual seven-day feast instituted by God so that his people would remember when he brought them out of slavery in Egypt. On that first Passover night, the destroyer passed over the homes marked by lamb's blood; he struck only the unmarked homes (see Exodus 11; 12).

45:23 Lev 23:8; Num 28:16-25; Num 23:1, 2; Job 42:8
45:24 Num 28:12-15; Ezek 46:5-7
45:25 Lev 23:33-43; Num 29:12-38; 2 Chr 5:3; 7:8, 10
46:1 Ezek 45:19; Ezek 8:16; 10:3; Ezek 44:1, 2; Ex 20:9; Is 66:23; Ezek 45:17; Ezek 45:18; 46:3, 6
46:2 Ezek 44:3; 46:8; Ezek 45:19; Ezek 46:12
46:3 Luke 1:10; Ezek 46:1
46:4 Ezek 45:17; Num 28:9
46:5 Num 28:12; Ezek 45:24; 46:7, 11; Ezek 46:7
46:6 Ezek 46:1
46:7 Ezek 46:5; Lev 14:21; Deut 16:17; Ezek 46:5
46:8 Ezek 44:3; 46:2
46:9 Ex 34:23; Ps 84:7; Mic 6:6
46:10 2 Sam 6:14, 15; 1 Chr 29:20, 22; 2 Chr 6:3; 7:4; Ps 42:4
46:11 Ezek 45:17; Ezek 46:5, 7
46:12 Lev 23:38; 2 Chr 29:31; Ezek 44:3; 46:1, 2, 8; Ezek 45:17
46:13 Num 28:3-5; Is 50:4
46:14 Num 28:5
46:15 Ex 29:42; Num 28:6
46:16 2 Chr 21:3
46:17 Lev 25:10
46:18 Ezek 45:8; 1 Kin 21:19; Ezek 22:27; Mic 2:1, 2

23 "*During* the seven days of the feast he shall provide as a burnt offering to the LORD seven bulls and seven rams without blemish on every day of the seven days, and a male goat daily for a sin offering.

24 "He shall provide as a grain offering an ephah with a bull, an ephah with a ram and a hin of oil with an ephah.

25 "In the seventh *month,* on the fifteenth day of the month, at the feast, he shall provide like this, seven days for the sin offering, the burnt offering, the grain offering and the oil."

The Prince's Offerings

46 'Thus says the Lord GOD, "The gate of the inner court facing east shall be shut the six working days; but it shall be opened on the sabbath day and opened on the day of the new moon.

2 "The prince shall enter by way of the porch of the gate from outside and stand by the post of the gate. Then the priests shall provide his burnt offering and his peace offerings, and he shall worship at the threshold of the gate and then go out; but the gate shall not be shut until the evening.

3 "The people of the land shall also worship at the doorway of that gate before the LORD on the sabbaths and on the new moons.

4 "The burnt offering which the prince shall offer to the LORD on the sabbath day shall be six lambs without blemish and a ram without blemish;

5 and the grain offering shall be an ephah with the ram, and the grain offering with the lambs as much as he is able to give, and a hin of oil with an ephah.

6 "On the day of the new moon *he shall offer* a young bull without blemish, also six lambs and a ram, *which* shall be without blemish.

7 "And he shall provide a grain offering, an ephah with the bull and an ephah with the ram, and with the lambs as much as he is able, and a hin of oil with an ephah.

8 "When the prince enters, he shall go in by way of the porch of the gate and go out by the same way.

9 "But when the people of the land come before the LORD at the appointed feasts, he who enters by way of the north gate to worship shall go out by way of the south gate. And he who enters by way of the south gate shall go out by way of the north gate. No one shall return by way of the gate by which he entered but shall go straight out.

10 "When they go in, the prince shall go in among them; and when they go out, he shall go out.

11 "At the festivals and the appointed feasts the grain offering shall be an ephah with a bull and an ephah with a ram, and with the lambs as much as one is able to give, and a hin of oil with an ephah.

12 "When the prince provides a freewill offering, a burnt offering, or peace offerings *as* a freewill offering to the LORD, the gate facing east shall be opened for him. And he shall provide his burnt offering and his peace offerings as he does on the sabbath day. Then he shall go out, and the gate shall be shut after he goes out.

13 "And you shall provide a lamb a year old without blemish for a burnt offering to the LORD daily; morning by morning you shall provide it.

14 "Also you shall provide a grain offering with it morning by morning, a sixth of an ephah and a third of a hin of oil to moisten the fine flour, a grain offering to the LORD continually by a perpetual ordinance.

15 "Thus they shall provide the lamb, the grain offering and the oil, morning by morning, for a continual burnt offering."

16 'Thus says the Lord GOD, "If the prince gives a gift *out of* his inheritance to any of his sons, it shall belong to his sons; it is their possession by inheritance.

17 "But if he gives a gift from his inheritance to one of his servants, it shall be his until the year of liberty; then it shall return to the prince. His inheritance *shall be* only his sons'; it shall belong to them.

18 "The prince shall not take from the people's inheritance, thrusting them out of their

---

45:25 This annual feast celebrated in October is called the Feast of Booths. It commemorates God's protection of his people as they traveled through the wilderness from Egypt to the promised land (see Leviticus 23:33–43; Deuteronomy 16:13–17).

46:1–15 Ezekiel continued to describe various aspects of daily worship. While allowing for diversity in worship, God prescribed order and continuity. This continuity gave a healthy rhythm to the spiritual life of his people.

possession; he shall give his sons inheritance from his own possession so that My people
will not be scattered, anyone from his possession." ' "

The Boiling Places

19 Then he brought me through the entrance, which *was* at the side of the gate, into
the holy chambers for the priests, which faced north; and behold, there *was* a place at
the extreme rear toward the west.
20 He said to me, "This is the place where the priests shall boil the guilt offering and
the sin offering *and* where they shall bake the grain offering, in order that they may not
bring *them* out into the outer court to transmit holiness to the people."
21 Then he brought me out into the outer court and led me across to the four corners
of the court; and behold, in every corner of the court *there was* a *small* court.
22 In the four corners of the court *there were* enclosed courts, forty *cubits* long and thirty
wide; these four in the corners *were* the same size.
23 *There was* a row *of masonry* round about in them, around the four of them, and boiling
places were made under the rows round about.
24 Then he said to me, "These are the boiling places where the ministers of the house
shall boil the sacrifices of the people."

46:19 Ezek 42:9; 44:5

46:20 2 Chr 35:13; Ezek 44:29; Lev 2:4-7

Water from the Temple

47 Then he brought me back to the door of the house; and behold, water was flowing
from under the threshold of the house toward the east, for the house faced east.
And the water was flowing down from under, from the right side of the house, from south
of the altar.
2 He brought me out by way of the north gate and led me around on the outside to
the outer gate by way of *the gate* that faces east. And behold, water was trickling from
the south side.
3 When the man went out toward the east with a line in his hand, he measured a thousand cubits, and he led me through the water, water *reaching* the ankles.
4 Again he measured a thousand and led me through the water, water *reaching* the
knees. Again he measured a thousand and led me through *the water,* water *reaching* the
loins.
5 Again he measured a thousand; *and it was* a river that I could not ford, for the water
had risen, *enough* water to swim in, a river that could not be forded.
6 He said to me, "Son of man, have you seen *this?*" Then he brought me back to the
bank of the river.
7 Now when I had returned, behold, on the bank of the river there *were* very many
trees on the one side and on the other.
8 Then he said to me, "These waters go out toward the eastern region and go down
into the Arabah; then they go toward the sea, being made to flow into the sea, and the
waters *of the sea* become fresh.
9 "It will come about that every living creature which swarms in every place where the
river goes, will live. And there will be very many fish, for these waters go there and *the
others* become fresh; so everything will live where the river goes.
10 "And it will come about that fishermen will stand beside it; from Engedi to Eneglaim
there will be a place for the spreading of nets. Their fish will be according to their kinds,
like the fish of the Great Sea, very many.
11 "But its swamps and marshes will not become fresh; they will be left for salt.
12 "By the river on its bank, on one side and on the other, will grow all *kinds of* trees for
food. Their leaves will not wither and their fruit will not fail. They will bear every month
because their water flows from the sanctuary, and their fruit will be for food and their
leaves for healing."

47:1 Ezek 41:2, 23-25; Ps 46:4; Is 30:25; 55:1; Jer 2:13; Joel 3:18; Zech 13:1; 14:8; Rev 22:1, 17

47:5 Is 11:9; Hab 2:14

47:6 Ezek 8:6; 40:4; 44:5

47:7 Is 60:13, 21; 61:3; Ezek 47:12

47:8 Deut 3:17; Is 35:6, 7; 41:17-19; 44:3; Josh 3:16

47:9 Is 12:3; 55:1; John 4:14; 7:37, 38

47:10 Matt 4:19; 13:47; Luke 5:10; Gen 14:7; Josh 15:62; 1 Sam 23:29; 24:1; 2 Chr 20:2; Ezek 26:5, 14; Num 34:6; Ps 104:25; Ezek 47:15; 48:28; Luke 5:5-9; John 21:6

47:11 Deut 29:23

47:12 Ezek 47:7; Rev 22:2; Gen 2:9; Ps 1:3; Jer 17:8; Rev 22:2

47:1–12 This river is similar to the river mentioned in Revelation 22:1–2. Both rivers are associated with the river in the Garden of Eden (see Genesis 2:10). The river symbolizes life from God and the blessings that flow from his throne. It is a gentle, safe, deep river, expanding as it flows.

47:8–9 The Arabah is the geological depression in which the Dead Sea lies. The sea that will become fresh refers to the Dead Sea, a body of water so salty that nothing can live in it. The river will freshen the Dead Sea's water so it can support life. This is another picture of the life-giving nature of the water that flows from God's temple. God's power can transform us no matter how lifeless or corrupt we may be. Even when we feel messed up and beyond hope, his power can heal us.

47:10 Engedi and Eneglaim were on the western shore of the Dead Sea.

Boundaries and Division of the Land

13 Thus says the Lord GOD, "This *shall be* the boundary by which you shall divide the
land for an inheritance among the twelve tribes of Israel; Joseph *shall have* two portions.
14 "You shall divide it for an inheritance, each one equally with the other; for I swore to
give it to your forefathers, and this land shall fall to you as an inheritance.
15 "This *shall be* the boundary of the land: on the north side, from the Great Sea *by* the
way of Hethlon, to the entrance of Zedad;
16 Hamath, Berothah, Sibraim, which is between the border of Damascus and the
border of Hamath; Hazer-hatticon, which is by the border of Hauran.
17 "The boundary shall extend from the sea *to* Hazar-enan *at* the border of Damascus,
and on the north toward the north is the border of Hamath. This is the north side.
18 "The east side, from between Hauran, Damascus, Gilead and the land of Israel, *shall
be* the Jordan; from the *north* border to the eastern sea you shall measure. This is the
east side.
19 "The south side toward the south *shall extend* from Tamar as far as the waters of
Meribath-kadesh, to the brook *of Egypt and* to the Great Sea. This is the south side toward the south.
20 "The west side *shall be* the Great Sea, from the *south* border to a point opposite Lebo-
hamath. This is the west side.
21 "So you shall divide this land among yourselves according to the tribes of Israel.
22 "You shall divide it by lot for an inheritance among yourselves and among the aliens
who stay in your midst, who bring forth sons in your midst. And they shall be to you as
the native-born among the sons of Israel; they shall be allotted an inheritance with you
among the tribes of Israel.
23 "And in the tribe with which the alien stays, there you shall give *him* his inheritance,"
declares the Lord GOD.

Division of the Land

48 "Now these are the names of the tribes: from the northern extremity, beside the
way of Hethlon to Lebo-hamath, *as far as* Hazar-enan *at* the border of Damascus,
toward the north beside Hamath, running from east to west, Dan, one *portion.*
2 "Beside the border of Dan, from the east side to the west side, Asher, one *portion.*
3 "Beside the border of Asher, from the east side to the west side, Naphtali, one *portion.*
4 "Beside the border of Naphtali, from the east side to the west side, Manasseh, one
portion.
5 "Beside the border of Manasseh, from the east side to the west side, Ephraim, one
portion.
6 "Beside the border of Ephraim, from the east side to the west side, Reuben, one
portion.
7 "Beside the border of Reuben, from the east side to the west side, Judah, one *portion.*
8 "And beside the border of Judah, from the east side to the west side, shall be the
[16]allotment which you shall set apart, 25,000 *cubits* in width, and in length like one of the
portions, from the east side to the west side; and the sanctuary shall be in the middle of
it.
9 "The allotment that you shall set apart to the LORD *shall be* 25,000 *cubits* in length
and 10,000 in width.

Portion for the Priests

10 "The holy allotment shall be for these, *namely* for the priests, toward the north 25,000
cubits in length, toward the west 10,000 in width, toward the east 10,000 in width, and
toward the south 25,000 in length; and the sanctuary of the LORD shall be in its midst.

47:13 Num 34:2-12; Gen 48:5; Ezek 48:4, 5
47:14 Deut 1:8; Ezek 20:6
47:15 Num 34:7-9; Num 34:8
47:16 Num 13:21; Is 10:9; Ezek 47:17, 20; 48:1; Zech 9:2; Gen 14:15; Ezek 47:17, 18; 48:1
47:17 Num 34:9
47:18 Num 34:10-12; Gen 37:25; Jer 50:19; Gen 13:10, 11
47:19 Num 34:3-5; Ezek 48:28; Deut 32:51; Num 34:5; 1 Kin 8:65; Is 27:12; Ezek 47:10, 15
47:20 Num 34:6; Judg 3:3; 2 Chr 7:8; Ezek 48:1; Amos 6:14
47:22 Num 26:55, 56; Is 14:1; 56:6, 7; Acts 11:18; 15:9; Eph 2:12-14; 3:6; Col 3:11
48:1 Ex 1:1; Josh 19:40-48
48:2 Josh 19:24-31
48:3 Josh 19:32-39
48:4 Josh 13:29-31; 17:1-11
48:5 Josh 16:5-9; 17:8-10, 14-18
48:6 Josh 13:15-21
48:7 Josh 15:1-63; 19:9
48:8 Is 12:6; 33:20-22; Ezek 45:3, 4
48:10 Ezek 44:28; 45:4

16 Or *contribution,* and so throughout the ch

47:22–23 In the restoration there will be room for foreigners ("aliens"). The regulations of Leviticus 24:22 and Numbers 15:29 provided for this. Isaiah also taught it (Isaiah 56:3–8). The children of foreigners will even inherit property like Israelites. Anyone who accepts the standards and is willing to obey may enjoy the blessings of God's rule.

48:1ff The land would be divided into 13 parallel portions (one for each tribe plus a sacred district) that would stretch from the Jordan River or Dead Sea to the Mediterranean Sea. The division of the land shows that in God's kingdom there is a place for all who believe in and obey the one true God (see John 14:1–6).

11 "*It shall be* for the priests who are sanctified of the sons of Zadok, who have kept My
charge, who did not go astray when the sons of Israel went astray as the Levites went
astray.
12 "It shall be an allotment to them from the allotment of the land, a most holy place,
by the border of the Levites.
13 "Alongside the border of the priests the Levites *shall have* 25,000 *cubits* in length and
10,000 in width. The whole length *shall be* 25,000 *cubits* and the width 10,000.
14 "Moreover, they shall not sell or exchange any of it, or alienate this choice *portion* of
land; for it is holy to the LORD.
15 "The remainder, 5,000 *cubits* in width and 25,000 in length, shall be for common use
for the city, for dwellings and for open spaces; and the city shall be in its midst.
16 "These *shall be* its measurements: the north side 4,500 *cubits,* the south side 4,500
cubits, the east side 4,500 *cubits,* and the west side 4,500 *cubits.*
17 "The city shall have open spaces: on the north 250 *cubits,* on the south 250 *cubits,* on
the east 250 *cubits,* and on the west 250 *cubits.*
18 "The remainder of the length alongside the holy allotment shall be 10,000 *cubits* toward the east and 10,000 toward the west; and it shall be alongside the holy allotment.
And its produce shall be food for the workers of the city.
19 "The workers of the city, out of all the tribes of Israel, shall cultivate it.
20 "The whole allotment *shall be* 25,000 by 25,000 *cubits;* you shall set apart the holy
allotment, a square, with the property of the city.

48:11 Ezek 40:46; 44:15; Ezek 44:10, 12
48:14 Lev 25:32-34; 27:10, 28, 33
48:15 Ezek 42:20; 45:6
48:16 Rev 21:16

Portion for the Prince

21 "The remainder *shall be* for the prince, on the one side and on the other of the holy
allotment and of the property of the city; in front of the 25,000 *cubits* of the allotment
toward the east border and westward in front of the 25,000 toward the west border, alongside the portions, *it shall be* for the prince. And the holy allotment and the sanctuary of
the house shall be in the middle of it.
22 "Exclusive of the property of the Levites and the property of the city, *which* are in
the middle of that which belongs to the prince, *everything* between the border of Judah
and the border of Benjamin shall be for the prince.

48:21 Ezek 34:24; 45:7; 48:22

Portion for Other Tribes

23 "As for the rest of the tribes: from the east side to the west side, Benjamin, one *portion.*
24 "Beside the border of Benjamin, from the east side to the west side, Simeon, one
portion.
25 "Beside the border of Simeon, from the east side to the west side, Issachar, one *portion.*
26 "Beside the border of Issachar, from the east side to the west side, Zebulun, one
portion.
27 "Beside the border of Zebulun, from the east side to the west side, Gad, one *portion.*
28 "And beside the border of Gad, at the south side toward the south, the border
shall be from Tamar to the waters of Meribath-kadesh, to the brook *of Egypt,* to the
Great Sea.
29 "This is the land which you shall divide by lot to the tribes of Israel for an inheritance, and these are their *several* portions," declares the Lord GOD.

48:23 Josh 18:21-28
48:24 Josh 19:1-9
48:25 Josh 19:17-23
48:26 Josh 19:10-16
48:27 Josh 13:24-28
48:28 Gen 14:7; 2 Chr 20:2; Ezek 47:19; Ezek 47:10, 15, 19, 20
48:29 Ezek 47:13-20

The City Gates

30 "These are the exits of the city: on the north side, 4,500 *cubits* by measurement,
31 shall be the gates of the city, named for the tribes of Israel, three gates toward the
north: the gate of Reuben, one; the gate of Judah, one; the gate of Levi, one.
32 "On the east side, 4,500 *cubits,* shall be three gates: the gate of Joseph, one; the gate
of Benjamin, one; the gate of Dan, one.
33 "On the south side, 4,500 *cubits* by measurement, shall be three gates: the gate of
Simeon, one; the gate of Issachar, one; the gate of Zebulun, one.

48:30 Ezek 48:32-34
48:31 Rev 21:12, 13

48:28 The Great Sea is the Mediterranean.

48:35 Jer 23:6; 33:16; Is 12:6; 14:32; 24:23; Jer 3:17; 8:19; 14:9; Ezek 35:10; Joel 3:21; Zech 2:10; Rev 21:3; 22:3

34 "On the west side, 4,500 *cubits, shall be* three gates: the gate of Gad, one; the gate of
Asher, one; the gate of Naphtali, one.
35 "*The city shall be* 18,000 *cubits* round about; and the name of the city from *that* day
shall be, 'The LORD is there.' "

48:35 The book of Ezekiel begins by describing the holiness of God that Israel had despised and ignored. As a result, God's presence departed from the temple, the city, and the people. The book ends with a detailed vision of the new temple, the new city, and the new people—all demonstrating God's holiness. The pressures of everyday life may persuade us to focus on the here and now and thus forget God. That is why worship is so important; it takes our eyes off our current worries, gives us a glimpse of God's holiness, and allows us to look toward his future kingdom. God's presence makes everything glorious, and worship brings us into his presence.

DANIEL

Daniel taken captive to Babylon 605 B.C.

Ezekiel becomes a prophet to exiles 593

Judah falls; Jerusalem is destroyed; Jeremiah's ministry ends 586

VITAL STATISTICS

PURPOSE:
To give a historical account of the faithful Jews who lived in captivity and to show how God is in control of heaven and earth, directing the forces of nature, the destiny of nations, and the care of his people

AUTHOR:
Daniel

TO WHOM WRITTEN:
The other captives in Babylon and God's people everywhere

DATE WRITTEN:
Approximately 535 B.C., recording events that occurred from about 605–535 B.C.

SETTING:
Daniel had been taken captive and deported to Babylon by Nebuchadnezzar in 605 B.C. There he served in the government for about 70 years during the reigns of Nebuchadnezzar, Belshazzar, Darius, and Cyrus.

KEY VERSE:
"It is He [God] who reveals the profound and hidden things; He knows what is in the darkness, and the light dwells with Him" (2:22).

KEY PEOPLE:
Daniel, Nebuchadnezzar, Shadrach, Meshach, Abednego, Belshazzar, Darius

KEY PLACES:
Nebuchadnezzar's palace, the blazing furnace, Belshazzar's feast, the den of lions

SPECIAL FEATURES:
Daniel's apocalyptic visions (chapters 7—12) give a glimpse of God's plan for the ages, including a direct prediction of the Messiah.

AN EARTHQUAKE shakes the foundation of our security; a tornado blows away a lifetime of treasures; an assassin's bullet changes national history; a drunk driver claims an innocent victim; a divorce shatters a home. International and personal tragedies make our world seem a fearful place, overflowing with evil and seemingly out of control. And the litany of bombings, coups, murders, and natural disasters could cause us to think that God is absent or impotent. "Where is God?" we cry, engulfed by sorrow and despair.

Twenty-five centuries ago, Daniel could have despaired. He and thousands of his countrymen had been deported to a foreign land after Judah was conquered. Daniel found himself facing an egocentric despot and surrounded by idolaters. Instead of giving in or giving up, this courageous young man held fast to his faith in his God. Daniel knew that despite the circumstances, God was sovereign and was working out his plan for nations and individuals. The book of Daniel centers around this profound truth—the sovereignty of God.

After a brief account of Nebuchadnezzar's siege and defeat of Jerusalem, the scene quickly shifts to Daniel and his three friends, Hananiah, Mishael, and Azariah (Shadrach, Meshach, and Abednego). These men held prominent positions within the Babylonian government. Daniel, in particular, held such a position because of his ability to interpret the king's dreams that tell of God's unfolding plan (chapters 2 and 4). Sandwiched between the dreams is the fascinating account of Daniel's three friends and the furnace (chapter 3). Because they refused to bow down to an image of gold, they were condemned to a fiery death. But God intervened and spared their lives.

Belshazzar ruled Babylon after Nebuchadnezzar, and chapter 5 tells of his encounter with God's message written on a wall. Daniel, who was summoned to interpret the message, predicted Babylon's fall to the Medes and Persians. This prediction came true that very night, and Darius the Mede conquered the Babylonian kingdom.

Daniel became one of Darius's most trusted advisers. His privileged position angered other administrators, who plotted his death by convincing the king to outlaw prayer. In spite of the law, Daniel continued to pray to his sovereign Lord. As a result, he was condemned to die in a den of hungry lions. Again, God intervened and saved him, shutting the mouths of the lions (chapter 6).

The book concludes with a series of visions that Daniel had during the reigns of Belshazzar (chapters 7—8), Darius (chapter 9), and Cyrus (chapters 10—12). These dreams dramatically outline God's future plans, beginning with Babylon and continuing to the end of the age. They give a preview of God's redemption and have been called the key to all Biblical prophecy.

God is sovereign. He was in control in Babylon, and he has been moving in history, controlling the destinies of people ever since. And he is here now! Despite news reports or personal stress, we can be confident that God is in control. As you read Daniel, watch God work and find your security in his sovereignty.

Daniel's first vision 553	*Babylon overthrown; Daniel thrown to lions*	*First exiles return to Judah 538*	*Daniel's ministry ends 535*

THE BLUEPRINT

A. DANIEL'S LIFE (1:1—6:28)

Daniel and his three friends chose not to eat the king's food. They did not bow down to the king's image, even under penalty of death. Daniel continued to pray even though he knew he might be noticed and sentenced to death. These men are inspiring examples for us of how to live a godly life in a sinful world. When we face trials, we can expect God to also be with us through them. May God grant us similar courage to remain faithful under pressure.

B. DANIEL'S VISIONS (7:1—12:13)

These visions gave the captives added confidence that God is in control of history. They were to wait patiently in faith and not worship the gods of Babylon or accept that society's way of life. God still rules over human activities. Evil will be overcome, so we should wait patiently and not give in to the temptations and pressures of the sinful way of life around us.

MEGATHEMES

THEME	EXPLANATION	IMPORTANCE
God is in Control	God is all-knowing, and he is in charge of world events. God overrules and removes rebellious leaders who defy him. God will overcome evil; no one is exempt. But he will deliver the faithful who follow him.	Although nations vie for world control now, one day Christ's kingdom will replace and surpass the kingdoms of this world. Our faith is sure because our future is secure in Christ. We must have courage and put our faith in God, who controls everything.
Purpose in Life	Daniel and his three friends are examples of dedication and commitment. They determined to serve God regardless of the consequences. They did not give in to pressures from an ungodly society because they had a clear purpose in life.	It is wise to make trusting and obeying God alone our true purpose in life. This will give us direction and peace in spite of the circumstances or consequences. We should disobey anyone who asks us to disobey God. Our first allegiance must be to God.
Perseverance	Daniel served for 70 years in a foreign land that was hostile to God, yet he did not compromise his faith in God. He was truthful, persistent in prayer, and disinterested in power for personal glory.	In order to fulfill your life's purpose, you need staying power. Don't let your Christian distinctness become blurred. Be relentless in your prayers, maintain your integrity, and be content to serve God wherever he puts you.
God's Faithfulness	God was faithful in Daniel's life. He delivered him from prison, from a den of lions, and from enemies who hated him. God cares for his people and deals patiently with them.	We can trust God to be with us through any trial. Because he has been faithful to us, we should remain faithful to him.

A. DANIEL'S LIFE (1:1—6:28)

While Ezekiel was ministering to the captives in Babylon, Daniel was drafted as a counselor to King Nebuchadnezzar. With God's help, Daniel interpreted two of the king's dreams, Daniel's three friends were rescued from certain death in the fiery furnace, and Daniel was rescued from a lions' den. Daniel's life is a picture of the triumph of faith. May God grant us this type of faith so that we may also live courageously each day.

The Choice Young Men

1 In the third year of the reign of Jehoiakim king of Judah, Nebuchadnezzar king of
Babylon came to Jerusalem and besieged it.
2 The Lord gave Jehoiakim king of Judah into his hand, along with some of the vessels of the house of God; and he brought them to the land of Shinar, to the house of his
[1]god, and he brought the vessels into the treasury of his [1]god.
3 Then the king ordered Ashpenaz, the chief of his [2]officials, to bring in some of the
sons of Israel, including some of the royal family and of the nobles,
4 youths in whom was no defect, who were good-looking, showing intelligence in every
branch of wisdom, endowed with understanding and discerning knowledge, and who had
ability for serving in the king's court; and *he ordered him* to teach them the [3]literature
and language of the Chaldeans.
5 The king appointed for them a daily ration from the king's choice food and from
the wine which he drank, and *appointed* that they should be educated three years, at the
end of which they were to enter the king's personal service.
6 Now among them from the sons of Judah were Daniel, Hananiah, Mishael and
Azariah.
7 Then the commander of the officials assigned *new* names to them; and to Daniel he
assigned *the name* Belteshazzar, to Hananiah Shadrach, to Mishael Meshach and to
Azariah Abed-nego.

Daniel's Resolve

8 But Daniel made up his mind that he would not defile himself with the king's choice
food or with the wine which he drank; so he sought *permission* from the commander of
the officials that he might not defile himself.

1:1 2 Kin 24:1; 2 Chr 36:5, 6; Jer 25:1; 52:12, 28-30
1:2 Is 42:24; Dan 2:37, 38; 2 Chr 36:7; Jer 27:19, 20; Dan 5:2; Gen 10:10; 11:2; Is 11:11; Zech 5:11; Jer 50:2; 51:44
1:3 2 Kin 24:15; Is 39:7
1:4 2 Sam 14:25; Dan 1:17; Is 36:11; Jer 5:15; Dan 2:4; Dan 2:2, 4, 5, 10; 3:8; 4:7; 5:7, 11, 30; 9:1
1:5 Dan 1:8; 1 Sam 16:22; Dan 1:19
1:6 Ezek 14:14, 20; 28:3; Matt 24:15
1:7 Dan 2:26; 4:8; 5:12; Dan 2:49; 3:12
1:8 Lev 11:47; Ezek 4:13, 14; Hos 9:3, 4; Ps 141:4; Dan 1:5; Deut 32:38; Dan 5:4

1 Or *gods* 2 Or *eunuchs,* and so throughout the ch 3 Or *writing*

1:1–2 Born during the middle of Josiah's reign (2 Kings 22; 23), Daniel grew up during the king's reforms. During this time, Daniel probably heard Jeremiah, a prophet he quoted in 9:2. In 609 B.C., Josiah was killed in a battle against Egypt, and within four years the southern kingdom of Judah had returned to its evil ways.

In 605 B.C. Nebuchadnezzar became king of Babylonia. In September of that year, he swept into Palestine and surrounded Jerusalem, making Judah his vassal state. To demonstrate his dominance, Nebuchadnezzar took many of Jerusalem's wisest men and most beautiful women to Babylon as captives. Daniel was among this group.

1:1–2 Nebuchadnezzar, the supreme leader of Babylonia, was feared throughout the world. When he invaded a country, defeat was certain. After a victory, the Babylonians usually took the most talented and useful people back to Babylon and left only the poor behind to take whatever land they wanted and to live peacefully there (2 Kings 24:14). This system fostered great loyalty from conquered lands and ensured a steady supply of wise and talented people for civil service.

1:2 At certain times God allows his work to suffer. In this instance, the Babylonians raided the temple of God and took the worship articles to the temple of a god in Babylon. This god may have been Bel, also called Marduk, the chief god of the Babylonians. Those who loved the Lord must have felt disheartened and discouraged. We feel greatly disappointed when our churches suffer physical damage, split, close down for financial reasons, or are wracked by scandals. We do not know why God allows his church to experience these calamities. But like the people who witnessed the plundering of the temple by the Babylonians, we must trust that God is in control and that he is watching over all who trust in him.

1:4 The common language of Babylonia was Aramaic, while the language of scholarship included the ancient and complicated Babylonian language. The academic program would have included mathematics, astronomy, history, science, and magic. These young men demonstrated not only aptitude, but also discipline. This character trait, combined with integrity, served them well in their new culture.

1:7 Nebuchadnezzar changed the names of Daniel and his friends because he wanted to make them Babylonian—in their own eyes and in the eyes of the Babylonian people. New names would help them assimilate into the culture. Daniel means "God is my Judge" in Hebrew; his name was changed to Belteshazzar meaning "Bel, protect his life!" (Bel, also called Marduk, was the chief Babylonian god). Hananiah means "the LORD shows grace"; his new name, Shadrach, probably means "under the command of Aku" (the moon god). Mishael means "who is like God?"; his new name, Meshach, probably means "who is like Aku?" Azariah means "the LORD helps"; his new name, Abed-nego, means "servant of Nego/Nebo" (or Nabu, the god of learning and writing). This was how the king attempted to change the religious loyalty of these young men from Judah's God to Babylonia's gods.

1:8 Daniel resolved not to eat this food, either because the meat was some food forbidden by Jewish law, like pork (see Leviticus 11), or because accepting the king's food and drink was the first step toward depending on his gifts and favors. Although Daniel was in a culture that did not honor God, he still obeyed God's laws.

1:8 Daniel made up his mind to be devoted to principle and to be committed to a course of action. When Daniel resolved not to defile himself, he was being true to a lifelong determination to do what was right and not to give in to the pressures around him. We too are often assaulted by pressures to compromise our standards and live more like the world around us. Merely wanting or preferring God's

1:9 Gen 39:21; 1 Kin 8:50; Job 5:15, 16; Ps 106:46; Prov 16:7

9 Now God granted Daniel favor and compassion in the sight of the commander of
the officials,
10 and the commander of the officials said to Daniel, "I am afraid of my lord the king,
who has appointed your food and your drink; for why should he see your faces looking
more haggard than the youths who are your own age? Then you would make me forfeit
my head to the king."
11 But Daniel said to the overseer whom the commander of the officials had appointed over Daniel, Hananiah, Mishael and Azariah,

1:12 Dan 1:16

12 "Please test your servants for ten days, and let us be given some vegetables to eat
and water to drink.
13 "Then let our appearance be observed in your presence and the appearance of the
youths who are eating the king's choice food; and deal with your servants according to
what you see."
14 So he listened to them in this matter and tested them for ten days.

1:15 Ex 23:25; Prov 10:22

15 At the end of ten days their appearance seemed better and they were fatter than all
the youths who had been eating the king's choice food.

1:16 Dan 1:12

16 So the overseer continued to withhold their choice food and the wine they were to
drink, and kept giving them vegetables.

1:17 1 Kin 3:12, 28; Job 32:8; Dan 1:20; 2:21, 23; Acts 7:22; Dan 2:19; 7:1; 8:1

17 As for these four youths, God gave them knowledge and intelligence in every *branch*
of literature and wisdom; Daniel even understood all *kinds of* visions and dreams.
18 Then at the end of the days which the king had specified for presenting them, the
commander of the officials presented them before Nebuchadnezzar.

1:19 Dan 1:6, 7; Gen 41:46; Dan 1:5

19 The king talked with them, and out of them all not one was found like Daniel, Hananiah, Mishael and Azariah; so they entered the king's personal service.

DANIEL
Daniel served as a prophet to the exiles in Babylon from 605–536 B.C.

Climate of the times	The people of Judah were captives in a strange land, feeling hopeless.
Main message	God is sovereign over all of human history, past, present, and future.
Importance of message	We should spend less time wondering when future events will happen and more time learning how we should live now.
Contemporary prophets	Jeremiah (627–586 B.C.) Habakkuk (612–588 B.C.) Ezekiel (593–571 B.C.)

---

will and way is not enough to stand against the onslaught of temptation. Like Daniel, we must resolve to obey God.

1:8 It is easier to resist temptation if you have thought through your convictions well before the temptation arrives. Daniel and his friends made their decision to be faithful to the laws of God before they were faced with the king's delicacies, so they did not hesitate to stick with their convictions. We will get into trouble if we have not previously decided where to draw the line. Before such situations arise, decide on your commitments. Then when temptation comes, you will be ready to say no.

1:9 God moved with an unseen hand to change the heart of this Babylonian official. The strong moral conviction of these four young men made an impact. God promises to be with his people in times of trial and temptation (Psalm 106:46; Isaiah 43:2–5; 1 Corinthians 10:13). His active intervention often comes just when we take a stand for him. Stand for God and trust him to protect you in ways you may not be able to see.

1:10 Anything short of complete obedience meant execution for the officials who served Nebuchadnezzar. Even in such a small matter as this, the official feared for his life.

1:12 The Babylonians were trying to change the *thinking* of these Jews by giving them a Babylonian education, their *loyalty* by changing their names, and their *life-style* by changing their diet. Without compromising, Daniel found a way to live by God's standards in a culture that did not honor God. Wisely choosing to negotiate rather than to rebel, Daniel suggested an experimental ten-day diet of vegetables and water, instead of the royal foods and wine the king offered. Without compromising, Daniel quickly thought of a practical, creative solution that saved his life and the lives of his companions. As God's people, we may adjust to our culture as long as we do not compromise God's laws.

1:17 Daniel and his friends learned all they could about their new culture so they could do their work with excellence. But while they learned, they maintained steadfast allegiance to God, and God gave them skill and wisdom. Culture need not be God's enemy. If it does not violate his commands, it can aid in accomplishing his purpose. We who follow God are free to be competent leaders in our culture, but we are required to pledge our allegiance to God first.

20 As for every matter of wisdom and understanding about which the king consulted
them, he found them ten times better than all the magicians *and* conjurers who *were* in
all his realm.
21 And Daniel continued until the first year of Cyrus the king.

The King's Forgotten Dream

2 Now in the second year of the reign of Nebuchadnezzar, Nebuchadnezzar had dreams;
and his spirit was troubled and his sleep left him.
2 Then the king gave orders to call in the [4]magicians, the conjurers, the sorcerers and
the [5]Chaldeans to tell the king his dreams. So they came in and stood before the king.
3 The king said to them, "I had a dream and my spirit is anxious to understand the
dream."
4 Then the Chaldeans spoke to the king in Aramaic: "O king, live forever! Tell the
dream to your servants, and we will declare the interpretation."
5 The king replied to the Chaldeans, "The command from me is firm: if you do not
make known to me the dream and its interpretation, you will be torn limb from limb and
your houses will be made a rubbish heap.
6 "But if you declare the dream and its interpretation, you will receive from me gifts
and a reward and great honor; therefore declare to me the dream and its interpretation."
7 They answered a second time and said, "Let the king tell the dream to his servants,
and we will declare the interpretation."
8 The king replied, "I know for certain that you are bargaining for time, inasmuch as
you have seen that the command from me is firm,
9 that if you do not make the dream known to me, there is only one decree for you.
For you have agreed together to speak lying and corrupt words before me until the situation is changed; therefore tell me the dream, that I may know that you can declare to
me its interpretation."
10 The Chaldeans answered the king and said, "There is not a man on earth who could
declare the matter for the king, inasmuch as no great king or ruler has *ever* asked anything like this of any magician, conjurer or Chaldean.

4 Or *soothsayer priests* 5 Or *master astrologers,* and so throughout the ch

1:20 1 Kin 4:30, 31; Dan 1:17; Gen 31:7; Num 14:22; Neh 4:12; Job 19:3; Dan 2:27, 28, 46, 48; Is 19:3; Dan 2:2; 4:18; 5:7

1:21 Dan 6:28; 10:1

2:1 Gen 40:5-8; 41:1, 8; Job 33:15-17; Dan 2:3; 4:5; Esth 6:1; Dan 6:18

2:2 Gen 41:8; Ex 7:11; Is 47:12, 13; Dan 1:20; 2:10, 27; 4:6; 5:7

2:3 Gen 40:8; 41:15; Dan 4:5

2:4 Ezra 4:7; Is 36:11; Dan 3:9; 5:10; Dan 2:7

2:5 Ezra 6:11; Dan 2:12; 3:29

2:6 Dan 2:48; 5:7, 16, 29

2:7 Dan 2:4

2:9 Esth 4:11; Dan 3:15; Is 41:23

2:10 Dan 2:2, 27

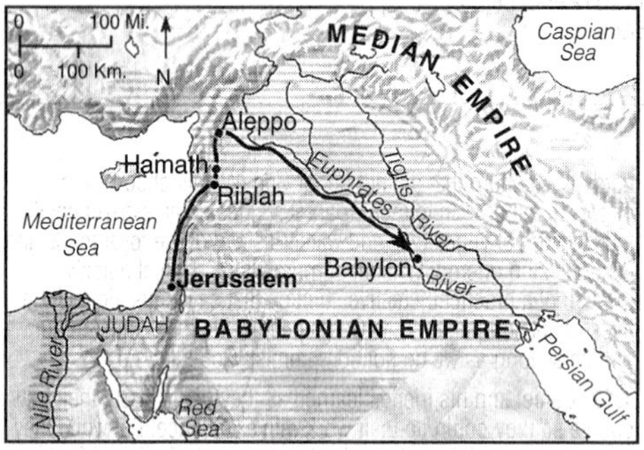

TAKEN TO BABYLON Daniel, as a captive of Babylonian soldiers, faced a long and difficult march to a new land. The 500-mile trek, under harsh conditions, certainly tested his faith in God.

1:20 Nebuchadnezzar put Daniel and his friends on his staff of advisers. This staff included many "magicians and conjurers." These were astrologers who claimed to be able to tell the future through occult practices. They were masters at communicating their message so that it sounded authoritative—as though it came directly from their gods. In addition to knowledge, Daniel and his three friends had wisdom and understanding, given to them by God. Thus the king was far more pleased with them than with his magicians. As we serve others, we must not merely pretend to have God's wisdom. Our wisdom will be genuine when we are rightly related to God.

1:20 How did the captives survive in a foreign culture? They learned about the culture, achieved excellence in their work, served the people, prayed for God's help, and maintained their integrity. We may feel like foreigners whenever we experience change. Alien cultures come in many forms: a new job, a new school, a new neighborhood. We can use the same principles to help us adapt to our new surroundings without abandoning God.

1:21 Daniel was one of the first captives taken to Babylon, and he lived to see the first exiles return to Jerusalem in 538 B.C. Throughout this time Daniel honored God, and God honored him. While serving as an adviser to the kings of Babylon, Daniel was God's spokesman to the Babylonian empire. Babylon was a wicked nation, but it would have been much worse without Daniel's influence.

2:1–11 Dreams were considered to be messages from the gods, and the wise men were expected to interpret them. Usually the wise men could give some sort of interpretation as long as they knew what the dream was about. This time, however, Nebuchadnezzar demanded to be told the dream also. God sent a series of dreams to Nebuchadnezzar with prophetic messages that could be revealed and understood only by a servant of God. People from other time periods who received dreams from God include Jacob (Genesis 28:10–15), Joseph (Genesis 37:5–11), Pharaoh's cupbearer and his baker (Genesis 40), Pharaoh (Genesis 41), Solomon (1 Kings 3:5–15), and Joseph (Matthew 1:20–24).

2:10–11 The Chaldeans (astrologers) told the king that "not a man on earth" could know the dreams of another person. What the king asked was humanly impossible. But Daniel could tell what the king had dreamed, and he could also give the interpretation because God was working through him. In daily life, we face many appar-

2:11 Gen 41:39; Dan 5:11; Ex 29:45; Is 57:15

11 "Moreover, the thing which the king demands is difficult, and there is no one else
who could declare it to the king except gods, whose dwelling place is not with *mortal*
flesh."

2:12 Ps 76:10; Dan 2:5; 3:13, 19

12 Because of this the king became indignant and very furious and gave orders to destroy all the wise men of Babylon.

2:13 Dan 1:19, 20

13 So the decree went forth that the wise men should be slain; and they looked for
Daniel and his friends to kill *them.*

2:14 Dan 2:24

14 Then Daniel replied with discretion and discernment to Arioch, the captain of the
king's bodyguard, who had gone forth to slay the wise men of Babylon;
15 he said to Arioch, the king's commander, "For what reason is the decree from the
king *so* urgent?" Then Arioch informed Daniel about the matter.
16 So Daniel went in and requested of the king that he would give him time, in order
that he might declare the interpretation to the king.

2:17 Dan 1:6

17 Then Daniel went to his house and informed his friends, Hananiah, Mishael and
Azariah, about the matter,

2:18 Esth 4:15, 16; Is 37:4; Jer 33:3; Ezek 36:37; Dan 2:23; Gen 18:28; Mal 3:18

18 so that they might request compassion from the God of heaven concerning this mystery, so that Daniel and his friends would not be destroyed with the rest of the wise men
of Babylon.

THE FULFILLMENT OF DANIEL'S INTERPRETATION

The large statue in Nebuchadnezzar's dream (2:24–45) represented the four kingdoms that would dominate as world powers. We recognize these as the Babylonian empire, the Medo-Persian empire, the Grecian empire, and the Roman empire. All of these will be crushed and brought to an end by the kingdom of God, which will continue forever.

Part	*Material*	*Empire*	*Period of Domination*
Head	Gold	Babylonian	606-539 B.C.
Chest and Arms	Silver	Medo-Persian	539-331 B.C.
Belly and Thighs	Bronze	Grecian	331-146 B.C.
Legs and Feet	Iron and Clay	Roman	146 B.C.–A.D. 476

ently impossible situations that would be hopeless if we had to handle them with our limited strength. But God specializes in working through us to achieve the impossible.

2:10–11 The astrologers were unable to persuade the king with any amount of logic or rational argument. The king asked for something impossible and didn't want anyone to change his mind. When power goes to a leader's head, whether at work, at home, or in the church, that leader can sometimes begin demanding the impossible from subordinates. At times, this may be the challenge needed to motivate workers to achieve more than they thought they could. At other times, it may be the rantings and ravings of someone deluded with power. Just as Daniel dealt wisely in the situation, so we can ask God to give us wisdom to know how to deal with unreasonable bosses.

2:11 The wise men said that the gods' "dwelling place is not with mortal flesh." Of course their gods didn't live among people—they didn't even exist! This exposed the limitations of these wise men. They could invent interpretations of dreams but could not tell Nebuchadnezzar *what* he had dreamed. Although his request was unreasonable, Nebuchadnezzar was furious when his advisers couldn't fulfill it. It was not unusual in these times for wise men to be in conflict with the king. They sometimes used their craft to gain political power.

2:11 By answering that the gods do not live "with mortal flesh," the wise men betrayed their concept of the gods. Theirs was a hollow religion, a religion of convenience. They believed in the gods, but that belief made no difference in their conduct. Today, many people profess to believe in God, but it is also a hollow belief. In essence, they are practical atheists because they don't listen to him or do what he says. Do you believe in God? He *does* live among people, and he wants to change your life.

2:16–18 Daniel was at a crisis point. Imagine going to see the powerful, temperamental king who had just angrily ordered your death! Daniel did not shrink back in fear, however, but confidently believed God would tell him all the king wanted to know. When the king gave Daniel time to find the answer, Daniel found his three friends and they prayed. When you find yourself in a tight spot, share your needs with trusted friends who also believe in God's power. Prayer is more effective than panic. Panic confirms your hopelessness; prayer confirms your hope in God. Daniel's trust in God saved himself, his three friends, and all the other wise men of Babylon.

The Secret Is Revealed to Daniel

19 Then the mystery was revealed to Daniel in a night vision. Then Daniel blessed the
God of heaven;
20 Daniel said,
"Let the name of God be blessed forever and ever,
For wisdom and power belong to Him.
21 "It is He who changes the times and the epochs;
He removes kings and establishes kings;
He gives wisdom to wise men
And knowledge to men of understanding.
22 "It is He who reveals the profound and hidden things;
He knows what is in the darkness,
And the light dwells with Him.
23 "To You, O God of my fathers, I give thanks and praise,
For You have given me wisdom and power;
Even now You have made known to me what we requested of You,
For You have made known to us the king's matter."
24 Therefore, Daniel went in to Arioch, whom the king had appointed to destroy the
wise men of Babylon; he went and spoke to him as follows: "Do not destroy the wise
men of Babylon! Take me into the king's presence, and I will declare the interpretation
to the king."
25 Then Arioch hurriedly brought Daniel into the king's presence and spoke to him as
follows: "I have found a man among the exiles from Judah who can make the interpretation known to the king!"
26 The king said to Daniel, whose name was Belteshazzar, "Are you able to make known
to me the dream which I have seen and its interpretation?"
27 Daniel answered before the king and said, "As for the mystery about which the king
has inquired, neither wise men, conjurers, magicians *nor* diviners are able to declare *it*
to the king.
28 "However, there is a God in heaven who reveals mysteries, and He has made known
to King Nebuchadnezzar what will take place in the latter days. This was your dream
and the visions in your mind *while* on your bed.
29 "As for you, O king, *while* on your bed your thoughts turned to what would take place
in the future; and He who reveals mysteries has made known to you what will take place.
30 "But as for me, this mystery has not been revealed to me for any wisdom residing in
me more than *in* any *other* living man, but for the purpose of making the interpretation
known to the king, and that you may understand the thoughts of your mind.

The King's Dream

31 "You, O king, were looking and behold, there was a single great statue; that statue,
which was large and of extraordinary splendor, was standing in front of you, and its appearance was awesome.

2:19 Num 12:6; Job 33:15, 16; Dan 1:17; 7:2, 7, 13

2:20 Ps 103:1, 2; 113:1, 2; 115:18; 145:1, 2, 21; 1 Chr 29:11, 12; Job 12:13, 16-22; Dan 2:21-23

2:21 Ps 31:15; Dan 2:9; 7:25; Job 12:18; Ps 75:6, 7; Dan 4:17, 32; 1 Kin 3:9, 10; 4:29; James 1:5

2:22 Job 12:22; Ps 25:14; Dan 2:19, 28; Job 26:6; Ps 139:12; Is 45:7; Jer 23:24; Heb 4:13; Ps 36:9; Dan 5:11, 14; James 1:17; 1 John 1:5

2:23 Gen 31:42; Ex 3:15; Dan 1:17; 2:21; Ps 21:2, 4; Dan 2:18, 29, 30

2:24 Dan 2:12, 13; Acts 27:24

2:25 Gen 41:14; Dan 1:6; 5:13; 6:13

2:26 Dan 1:7; 4:8; 5:12

2:27 Dan 2:2, 10, 11; 5:7, 8

2:28 Gen 40:8; 41:16; Dan 2:22, 45; Gen 49:1; Is 2:2; Dan 10:14; Mic 4:1; Dan 4:5

2:29 Dan 2:23, 47

2:30 Gen 41:16; Dan 1:17; Ps 139:2; Amos 4:13

2:31 Hab 1:7

2:19–23 After Daniel asked God to reveal Nebuchadnezzar's dream to him, he saw a vision of the dream. Daniel's prayer was answered. Before rushing to Arioch with the news, Daniel took time to give God credit for all wisdom and power, thanking God for answering his request. How do you feel when your prayers are answered? Excited, surprised, relieved? There are times when we seek God in prayer and, after having been answered, dash off in our excitement, forgetting to give God credit for the answer. Match your persistence in prayer with gratitude when your requests are answered.

2:21 If you ever think that you have much to learn in life, and if you ever wish that you knew more about how to handle people, then look to God for wisdom. While educational institutions provide diplomas at great expense, God gives wisdom freely to all who ask. (See James 1:5 for more on asking God for wisdom.)

2:21 When we see evil leaders who live long and good leaders who die young, we may wonder if God controls world events. Daniel saw evil rulers with almost limitless power, but Daniel knew and proclaimed that God "removes kings and establishes kings," that he controls everything that happens. God governs the world according to his purposes. You may be dismayed when you see evil people prosper, but God is in control. Let this knowledge give you confidence and peace no matter what happens.

2:24 Daniel did not use his success to promote his own self-interest. He thought of others. When striving to succeed or survive, remember the needs of others.

2:27–30 Before Daniel told the king anything else, he gave credit to God, explaining that he did not know the dream through his own wisdom but only because God revealed it. How easily we take credit for what God does through us! This robs God of the honor that he alone deserves. Instead we should be like Daniel and point people to God so that we give him the glory.

2:31ff The head of gold on the statue in the dream represented Nebuchadnezzar, ruler of the Babylonian empire. The silver chest and two arms represented the Medo-Persian empire, which conquered Babylon in 539 B.C. The belly and thighs of bronze were Greece and Macedonia under Alexander the Great, who conquered the Medo-Persian empire in 334–330 B.C. The legs of iron repre-

2:32 Dan 2:38

2:34 Dan 2:45; Dan 8:25; Zech 4:6; Ps 2:9; Is 60:12

2:35 Ps 1:4; Is 17:13; 41:15, 16; Hos 13:3; Ps 37:10, 36; Is 2:2; Mic 4:1

2:36 Dan 2:24

2:37 Is 47:5; Jer 27:6, 7; Ezek 26:7; Ps 62:11

32 "The head of that statue *was made* of fine gold, its breast and its arms of silver, its
belly and its thighs of bronze,
33 its legs of iron, its feet partly of iron and partly of clay.
34 "You continued looking until a stone was cut out without hands, and it struck the
statue on its feet of iron and clay and crushed them.
35 "Then the iron, the clay, the bronze, the silver and the gold were crushed all at the
same time and became like chaff from the summer threshing floors; and the wind carried them away so that not a trace of them was found. But the stone that struck the statue became a great mountain and filled the whole earth.

The Interpretation—Babylon the First Kingdom

36 "This *was* the dream; now we will tell its interpretation before the king.
37 "You, O king, are the king of kings, to whom the God of heaven has given the kingdom, the power, the strength and the glory;

DANIEL

Daniel's early life demonstrates that there is more to being young than making mistakes. No characteristic wins the hearts of adults more quickly than wisdom in the words and actions of a young person. Daniel and his friends had been taken from their homes in Judah and exiled. Their futures were in doubt, but they all had personal traits that qualified them for jobs as servants in the king's palace. They took advantage of the opportunity without letting the opportunity take advantage of them.

Our first hint of Daniel's greatness comes in his quiet refusal to give up his convictions. He had applied God's will to his own life, and he resisted changing the good habits he had formed. Both his physical and spiritual diets were an important part of his relationship with God. He ate carefully and lived prayerfully. One of the benefits of being in training for royal service was eating food from the king's table. Daniel tactfully chose a simpler menu and proved it was a healthy choice. As with Daniel, mealtimes are obvious and regular tests of our efforts to control our appetites.

While Daniel limited his food intake, he indulged in prayer. He was able to communicate with God because he made it a habit. He put into practice his convictions, even when that meant being thrown into a den of hungry lions. His life proved he made the right choice.

Do you hold so strongly to your faith in God that whatever happens you will do what God says? Such conviction keeps you a step ahead of temptation; such conviction gives you wisdom and stability in changing circumstances. Prayerfully live out your convictions in everyday life and trust God for the results.

Strengths and accomplishments:
- Although young when deported, remained true to his faith
- Served as an adviser to two Babylonian kings and two Medo-Persian kings
- Was a man of prayer and a statesman with the gift of prophecy
- Survived the lions' den

Lessons from his life:
- Quiet convictions often earn long-term respect
- Don't wait until you are in a tough situation to learn about prayer
- God can use people wherever they are

Vital statistics:
- Where: Judah and the courts of both Babylon and Persia
- Occupation: A captive from Israel who became an adviser of kings
- Contemporaries: Hananiah, Mishael, Azariah, Nebuchadnezzar, Belshazzar, Darius, Cyrus

Key verse:
"This was because an extraordinary spirit, knowledge and insight, interpretation of dreams, explanation of enigmas and solving of difficult problems were found in this Daniel, whom the king named Belteshazzar. Let Daniel now be summoned and he will declare the interpretation" (Daniel 5:12).

Daniel's story is told in the book of Daniel. He is also mentioned in Matthew 24:15.

sented Rome, which conquered the Greeks in 63 B.C. The feet of clay and iron represented the breakup of the Roman empire, when the territory Rome ruled divided into a mixture of strong and weak nations. The type of metal in each part depicted the strength of the political power it represented. The stone cut out of the mountain depicted God's kingdom, which would be ruled eternally by the Messiah, the King of kings. The dream revealed Daniel's God as the power behind all earthly kingdoms.

2:36 When Daniel says "we," he is referring to himself and his three friends. Just as Daniel involved them in praying for God's help, he gave them credit when he presented the interpretation. Because they helped Daniel in the prayer, he was careful to share the credit with them.

38 and wherever the sons of men dwell, *or* the beasts of the field, or the birds of the
sky, He has given *them* into your hand and has caused you to rule over them all. You are
the head of gold.

2:38 Ps 50:10, 11; Dan 4:21, 22

Medo-Persia and Greece

39 "After you there will arise another kingdom inferior to you, then another third kingdom of bronze, which will rule over all the earth.

Rome

40 "Then there will be a fourth kingdom as strong as iron; inasmuch as iron crushes and
shatters all things, so, like iron that breaks in pieces, it will crush and break all these in
pieces.
41 "In that you saw the feet and toes, partly of potter's clay and partly of iron, it will be
a divided kingdom; but it will have in it the toughness of iron, inasmuch as you saw the
iron mixed with common clay.
42 "*As* the toes of the feet *were* partly of iron and partly of pottery, *so* some of the kingdom will be strong and part of it will be brittle.
43 "And in that you saw the iron mixed with common clay, they will combine with one
another in the seed of men; but they will not adhere to one another, even as iron does
not combine with pottery.

2:40 Dan 7:23

The Divine Kingdom

44 "In the days of those kings the God of heaven will set up a kingdom which will never
be destroyed, and *that* kingdom will not be left for another people; it will crush and put
an end to all these kingdoms, but it will itself endure forever.
45 "Inasmuch as you saw that a stone was cut out of the mountain without hands and
that it crushed the iron, the bronze, the clay, the silver and the gold, the great God has
made known to the king what will take place in the future; so the dream is true and its
interpretation is trustworthy."

2:44 Dan 2:28, 37; Is 9:6, 7; Ps 145:13; Ezek 37:25; Dan 4:3, 34; 6:26; 7:14, 27; Mic 4:7; Luke 1:32, 33; Ps 2:9; Is 60:12; Dan 2:34, 35

2:45 Dan 2:34; Deut 10:17; 2 Sam 7:22; Ps 48:1; Jer 32:18, 19; Dan 2:29; Mal 1:11; Gen 41:28, 32

Daniel Promoted

46 Then King Nebuchadnezzar fell on his face and did homage to Daniel, and gave
orders to present to him an offering and fragrant incense.
47 The king answered Daniel and said, "Surely your God is a God of gods and a Lord
of kings and a revealer of mysteries, since you have been able to reveal this mystery."
48 Then the king promoted Daniel and gave him many great gifts, and he made him
ruler over the whole province of Babylon and chief prefect over all the wise men of Babylon.
49 And Daniel made request of the king, and he appointed Shadrach, Meshach and
Abed-nego over the administration of the province of Babylon, while Daniel *was* at the
king's court.

2:46 Dan 3:5, 7; Acts 10:25; 14:13; Rev 19:10; 22:8; Lev 26:31; Ezra 6:10

2:47 Dan 3:15; 4:25; Deut 10:17; Ps 136:2, 3; Dan 11:36; Dan 2:22, 30; Amos 3:7

2:48 Gen 41:39-43; Dan 2:6; 5:16, 29; Dan 3:1, 12, 30

2:49 Dan 3:12; Dan 1:7; Esth 2:19, 21; Amos 5:15

The King's Golden Image

3 Nebuchadnezzar the king made an image of gold, the height of which *was* sixty
cubits *and* its width six cubits; he set it up on the plain of Dura in the province of
Babylon.

3:1 1 Kin 12:28; Is 46:6; Jer 16:20; Dan 2:31; Hos 2:8; 8:4; Hab 2:19; Dan 2:48; 3:30

2:44 God's kingdom will never be destroyed. If you are upset by threats of war and the prosperity of evil leaders, remember that God, not world leaders, decides the outcome of history. Under God's protection, God's kingdom is indestructible. Those who believe in God are members of his kingdom and are secure in him.

2:47 Nebuchadnezzar honored Daniel and Daniel's God. If Daniel had taken the credit himself, the king would have honored only Daniel. Because Daniel gave God the credit, the king honored both of them. Part of our mission in this world is to show unbelievers what God is like. We can do that by giving God credit for what he does in our lives. Our acts of love and compassion may impress people, and if we give God credit for our actions, they will want to know more about him. Give thanks to God for what he is doing in and through you.

2:49 After being named ruler over the whole province of Babylon and placed in charge of the wise men, Daniel requested that his companions, Shadrach, Meshach, and Abed-nego, be appointed as his assistants. Daniel knew that he could not handle such an enormous responsibility without capable assistants, so he chose the best men he knew—his three Hebrew companions. A competent leader never does all the work alone; he or she knows how to delegate and supervise. Moses, Israel's greatest leader, shared the burden of administration with dozens of assistants. (This story is in Exodus 18:13–27.)

3:1 In Babylon's religious culture, statues were frequently worshiped. Nebuchadnezzar hoped to use this huge image (ninety feet high by nine feet wide) as a strategy to unite the nation and solidify his power by centralizing worship. This gold image may have been

3:2 Dan 3:3, 27; 6:1-7

2 Then Nebuchadnezzar the king sent *word* to assemble the satraps, the prefects and
the governors, the counselors, the treasurers, the judges, the magistrates and all the rulers of the provinces to come to the dedication of the image that Nebuchadnezzar the
king had set up.
3 Then the satraps, the prefects and the governors, the counselors, the treasurers, the
judges, the magistrates and all the rulers of the provinces were assembled for the dedication of the image that Nebuchadnezzar the king had set up; and they stood before the
image that Nebuchadnezzar had set up.

3:4 Dan 3:7; 4:1; 6:25

4 Then the herald loudly proclaimed: "To you the command is given, O peoples, nations and *men of every* language,

3:5 Dan 3:7, 10, 15

5 that at the moment you hear the sound of the horn, flute, lyre, trigon, psaltery,
bagpipe and all kinds of music, you are to fall down and worship the golden image that
Nebuchadnezzar the king has set up.

3:6 Dan 3:11, 15, 21; 6:7; Jer 29:22; Ezek 22:18-22; Matt 13:42, 50; Rev 9:2; 14:11

6 "But whoever does not fall down and worship shall immediately be cast into the midst
of a furnace of blazing fire."
7 Therefore at that time, when all the peoples heard the sound of the horn, flute, lyre,
trigon, psaltery, bagpipe and all kinds of music, all the peoples, nations and *men of every*
language fell down *and* worshiped the golden image that Nebuchadnezzar the king had
set up.

Worship of the Image Refused

3:8 Dan 2:2, 10; 4:7; Ezra 4:12-16; Esth 3:8, 9; Dan 6:12, 13

8 For this reason at that time certain Chaldeans came forward and brought charges
against the Jews.
9 They responded and said to Nebuchadnezzar the king: "O king, live forever!

3:9 Dan 2:4; 5:10; 6:6, 21

10 "You, O king, have made a decree that every man who hears the sound of the horn,
flute, lyre, trigon, psaltery, and bagpipe and all kinds of music, is to fall down and worship the golden image.

3:10 Esth 3:12-14; Dan 3:4-6; 6:12; Dan 3:5, 7, 15

11 "But whoever does not fall down and worship shall be cast into the midst of a furnace of blazing fire.
12 "There are certain Jews whom you have appointed over the administration of the

3:12 Dan 2:49

province of Babylon, *namely* Shadrach, Meshach and Abed-nego. These men, O king,
have disregarded you; they do not serve your gods or worship the golden image which
you have set up."

3:13 Dan 2:12; 3:19

13 Then Nebuchadnezzar in rage and anger gave orders to bring Shadrach, Meshach
and Abed-nego; then these men were brought before the king.

3:14 Is 46:1; Jer 50:2; Dan 3:1; 4:8

14 Nebuchadnezzar responded and said to them, "Is it true, Shadrach, Meshach and
Abed-nego, that you do not serve my gods or worship the golden image that I have
set up?

---

inspired by his dream. Instead of having only a head of gold, however, it was gold from head to toe. Nebuchadnezzar wanted his kingdom to last forever. When he made the statue, Nebuchadnezzar showed that his devotion to Daniel's God was short-lived. He neither feared nor obeyed the God who was behind the dream.

3:2 Satraps were governors over major divisions of the empire, serving as the chief representatives of the king. Prefects were the governors over conquered cities. Governors were civil administrators over provinces.

3:6 This blazing furnace was not a small oven for cooking dinner or heating a house; it was a huge industrial furnace that could have been used for baking bricks or smelting metals. The temperatures were hot enough to assure that no one could survive. The roaring flames could be seen leaping from its top opening, and a fiery blast killed the soldiers who went up to the large opening (3:22).

3:12 We don't know if other Jews refused to fall down and worship the image, but these three were singled out as public examples. Why didn't the three men just bow to the image and tell God that they didn't mean it? They had determined never to worship another god, and they courageously took their stand. As a result, they were condemned and led away to be executed. The men did not know whether they would be delivered from the fire; all they knew was that they would not fall down and worship an idol. Are you ready to take a stand for God no matter what? When you stand for God, you will stand out. It may be painful, and it may not always have a happy ending. Be prepared to say, "If he rescues me, or if he doesn't, I will serve only God."

3:13 Nebuchadnezzar had lost control. How could anyone dare to disobey his commands? As the supreme ruler of Babylonia, he expected absolute obedience. But his pride had caused him to go beyond his own authority. His demands were unjust and his reactions extreme. If you find yourself angered when people don't follow your directions, ask yourself, "Why am I reacting?" Your ego may be overly involved with your authority.

15 "Now if you are ready, at the moment you hear the sound of the horn, flute, lyre,
trigon, psaltery and bagpipe and all kinds of music, to fall down and worship the image
that I have made, *very well.* But if you do not worship, you will immediately be cast into
the midst of a furnace of blazing fire; and what god is there who can deliver you out of
my hands?"
16 Shadrach, Meshach and Abed-nego replied to the king, "O Nebuchadnezzar, we
do not need to give you an answer concerning this matter.
17 "If it be *so,* our God whom we serve is able to deliver us from the furnace of blazing
fire; and He will deliver us out of your hand, O king.
18 "But *even* if *He does* not, let it be known to you, O king, that we are not going to serve
your gods or worship the golden image that you have set up."

Daniel's Friends Protected

19 Then Nebuchadnezzar was filled with wrath, and his facial expression was altered
toward Shadrach, Meshach and Abed-nego. He answered by giving orders to heat the
furnace seven times more than it was usually heated.
20 He commanded certain valiant warriors who *were* in his army to tie up Shadrach,
Meshach and Abed-nego in order to cast *them* into the furnace of blazing fire.
21 Then these men were tied up in their trousers, their coats, their caps and their *other*
clothes, and were cast into the midst of the furnace of blazing fire.
22 For this reason, because the king's command *was* urgent and the furnace had been
made extremely hot, the flame of the fire slew those men who carried up Shadrach,
Meshach and Abed-nego.
23 But these three men, Shadrach, Meshach and Abed-nego, fell into the midst of the
furnace of blazing fire *still* tied up.
24 Then Nebuchadnezzar the king was astounded and stood up in haste; he said to his
high officials, "Was it not three men we cast bound into the midst of the fire?" They
replied to the king, "Certainly, O king."
25 He said, "Look! I see four men loosed *and* walking *about* in the midst of the fire
without harm, and the appearance of the fourth is like a son of *the* gods!"
26 Then Nebuchadnezzar came near to the door of the furnace of blazing fire; he responded and said, "Shadrach, Meshach and Abed-nego, come out, you servants of the
Most High God, and come here!" Then Shadrach, Meshach and Abed-nego came out
of the midst of the fire.
27 The satraps, the prefects, the governors and the king's high officials gathered around
and saw in regard to these men that the fire had no effect on the bodies of these men nor

3:15 Dan 3:5; Dan 3:6; Ex 5:2; Is 36:18-20; Dan 2:47

3:16 Dan 1:7; 3:12

3:17 Job 5:19; Ps 27:1, 2; Is 26:3, 4; Jer 1:8; 15:20, 21; 1 Sam 17:37; Mic 7:7; 2 Cor 1:10

3:18 Josh 24:15; 1 Kin 19:14, 18; Is 51:12, 13; Dan 3:28; Heb 11:25

3:19 Esth 7:7; Dan 3:13

3:21 Dan 3:27

3:22 Ex 12:33; Dan 2:15

3:23 Is 43:2

3:25 Ps 91:3-9; Is 43:2; Jer 1:8, 19; 15:21

3:26 Dan 3:17; 4:2; Deut 4:20; 1 Kin 8:51; Jer 11:4

3:27 Dan 3:2, 3; Is 43:2; Heb 11:34; Dan 3:21

3:15 The three men were given one more chance. Here are eight excuses they could have used to bow to the image and save their lives: (1) We will fall down but not actually *worship* the idol. (2) We won't become idol worshipers, but will worship it this one time, and then ask God for forgiveness. (3) The king has absolute power, and we must obey him. God will understand. (4) The king appointed us—we owe this to him. (5) This is a foreign land, so God will excuse us for following the customs of the land. (6) Our ancestors set up idols in God's temple! This isn't half as bad! (7) We're not hurting anybody. (8) If we get ourselves killed and some pagans take our high positions, they won't help our people in exile!

Although all these excuses sound sensible at first, they are dangerous rationalizations. To fall down and worship the image would violate God's command in Exodus 20:3, "You shall have no other gods before Me." It would also erase their testimony for God forever. Never again could they talk about the power of their God above all other gods. What excuses do you use for not standing up for him?

3:16–18 Shadrach, Meshach, and Abed-nego were pressured to deny God, but they chose to be faithful to him no matter what happened! They trusted God to deliver them, but they were determined to be faithful regardless of the consequences. If God always rescued those who were true to him, Christians would not need faith. Their religion would be a great insurance policy, and there would be lines of selfish people ready to sign up. We should be faithful to serve God whether he intervenes on our behalf or not. Our eternal reward is worth any suffering we may have to endure first.

3:19 "His facial expression was altered." When we do something that offends non-Christians, their attitude toward us often changes because they are basically selfish. Christians should be different; they should still love those who offend them.

3:25 It was obvious to those watching that this fourth person was supernatural. We cannot be certain who the fourth man was. It could have been an angel or a pre-incarnate appearance of Christ. In either case, God sent a heavenly visitor to accompany these faithful men during their time of great trial.

3:25–30 God's deliverance of Shadrach, Meshach, and Abed-nego was a great victory of faith for the Jews in captivity. They were protected from harm, they were comforted in trial, God was glorified, and they were rewarded. Let us determine to be true to God no matter how difficult the pressure or punishment. God's protection transcends anything we could imagine.

3:27 These young men had been completely untouched by the fire and heat. Only the rope that bound them had been burned. No human can bind us if God wants us to be free. The power available to us is the same that delivered Shadrach, Meshach, and Abed-nego and raised Christ from the dead (Ephesians 1:18–20). Trust God in every situation. There are eternal reasons for temporary trials; so be thankful that your destiny is in God's hands, not in human hands.

was the hair of their head singed, nor were their trousers damaged, nor had the smell of
fire *even* come upon them.
28 Nebuchadnezzar responded and said, "Blessed be the God of Shadrach, Meshach
and Abed-nego, who has sent His angel and delivered His servants who put their trust in
Him, violating the king's command, and yielded up their bodies so as not to serve or
worship any god except their own God.
29 "Therefore I make a decree that any people, nation or tongue that speaks anything
offensive against the God of Shadrach, Meshach and Abed-nego shall be torn limb from
limb and their houses reduced to a rubbish heap, inasmuch as there is no other god who
is able to deliver in this way."
30 Then the king caused Shadrach, Meshach and Abed-nego to prosper in the province of Babylon.

The King Acknowledges God

4 Nebuchadnezzar the king to all the peoples, nations, and *men of every* language that
live in all the earth: "May your peace abound!
2 "It has seemed good to me to declare the signs and wonders which the Most High
God has done for me.
3 "How great are His signs
And how mighty are His wonders!
His kingdom is an everlasting kingdom
And His dominion is from generation to generation.

The Vision of a Great Tree

4 "I, Nebuchadnezzar, was at ease in my house and flourishing in my palace.
5 "I saw a dream and it made me fearful; and *these* fantasies *as I lay* on my bed and the
visions in my mind kept alarming me.
6 "So I gave orders to bring into my presence all the wise men of Babylon, that they
might make known to me the interpretation of the dream.
7 "Then the magicians, the conjurers, the Chaldeans and the diviners came in and I
related the dream to them, but they could not make its interpretation known to me.
8 "But finally Daniel came in before me, whose name is Belteshazzar according to the
name of my god, and in whom is [6]a spirit of the holy gods; and I related the dream to
him, *saying,*
9 'O Belteshazzar, chief of the magicians, since I know that a spirit of the holy gods is
in you and no mystery baffles you, tell *me* the visions of my dream which I have seen,
along with its interpretation.
10 'Now *these were* the visions in my mind *as I lay* on my bed: I was looking, and behold,
there was a tree in the midst of the earth and its height *was* great.
11 'The tree grew large and became strong
And its height reached to the sky,
And it *was* visible to the end of the whole earth.
12 'Its foliage *was* beautiful and its fruit abundant,
And in it *was* food for all.
The beasts of the field found shade under it,
And the birds of the sky dwelt in its branches,
And all living creatures fed themselves from it.
13 'I was looking in the visions in my mind *as I lay* on my bed, and behold, an *angelic*
watcher, a holy one, descended from heaven.

6 Or possibly *the Spirit of the holy God,* and so throughout the ch

3:28 Dan 2:47; 3:15-17; Ps 34:7, 8; Is 37:36; Dan 3:25; 6:22; Acts 5:19; 12:7; Ps 22:4, 5; 40:4; 84:12; Is 12:2; 26:3, 4; 50:10; Jer 17:7; Dan 3:16-18

3:29 Dan 6:26; Dan 1:7, 19; 2:17, 49; 3:12; Ezra 6:11; Dan 2:5; Dan 2:47; 3:15

3:30 Dan 2:49; 3:12

4:1 Ezra 4:17; Dan 6:25

4:2 Dan 3:26; 4:17, 24, 25, 32, 34

4:3 Ps 77:19; 105:27; Is 25:1; Dan 6:27; Dan 2:44; 4:34; 6:26

4:4 Ps 30:6; Is 47:7, 8

4:5 Dan 2:3; Dan 2:1, 28; 4:10, 13

4:6 Gen 41:8; Dan 2:2

4:7 Gen 41:8; Dan 2:10, 27; 5:7; Is 44:25; Jer 27:9, 10; Dan 2:7

4:8 Dan 1:7; 2:26; 5:12; Dan 4:9, 18; 5:11, 14

4:9 Dan 1:20; 2:48; 5:11; Gen 41:38; Dan 4:8; Ezek 28:3; Dan 2:47; Gen 41:15; Dan 2:4, 5

4:10 Dan 4:5; Ezek 31:3, 6

4:11 Deut 9:1; Dan 4:21, 22

4:12 Ezek 31:7; Jer 27:6; Ezek 31:6; Lam 4:20; Ezek 17:23; Matt 13:32; Luke 13:19

4:13 Dan 7:1; Dan 4:17, 23; Deut 33:2; Ps 89:7; Dan 8:13

3:28–29 Nebuchadnezzar was not making a commitment here to serve the Hebrews' God alone. Instead, he was acknowledging that God is powerful, and he commanded his people not to speak against God. Nebuchadnezzar didn't tell the people to throw away all the other gods, but to add this one to the list.

3:30 Where was Daniel in this story? The Bible doesn't say, but there are several possibilities. (1) He may have been on official business in another part of the kingdom. (2) He may have been present, but because he was a ruler, the officials didn't accuse him of not falling down and worshiping the image. (3) He may have been in the capital city handling the administration while Nebuchadnezzar was away. (4) He may have been considered exempt from bowing down to the image because of his reputation for interpreting dreams through his God. Whether Daniel was there or not, we can be sure that he would not have worshiped the image.

4:2–3 Although Nebuchadnezzar praised Daniel's God, he still did not believe in him completely or submit to him alone (4:8). Many people attend church and use spiritual language, but they really don't believe in God or obey him. Profession doesn't always mean possession. How do your beliefs match with your obedience?

14 'He shouted out and spoke as follows:
"Chop down the tree and cut off its branches,
Strip off its foliage and scatter its fruit;
Let the beasts flee from under it
And the birds from its branches.

4:14 Ezek 31:10-14; Dan 4:23; Matt 3:10; 7:19; Luke 13:7-9; Ezek 31:12, 13; Dan 4:12

15 "Yet leave the stump with its roots in the ground,
But with a band of iron and bronze *around it*
In the new grass of the field;
And let him be drenched with the dew of heaven,
And let him share with the beasts in the grass of the earth.

4:15 Job 14:7-9

16 "Let his mind be changed from *that of* a man
And let a beast's mind be given to him,
And let seven periods of time pass over him.

4:16 Dan 4:23, 25, 32

17 "This sentence is by the decree of the *angelic* watchers
And the decision is a command of the holy ones,
In order that the living may know
That the Most High is ruler over the realm of mankind,
And bestows it on whom He wishes
And sets over it the lowliest of men."

4:17 Ps 9:16; 83:18; Dan 2:21; 5:21; Jer 27:5-7; Dan 4:25; 5:18, 19; 1 Sam 2:8; Dan 11:21

18 'This is the dream *which* I, King Nebuchadnezzar, have seen. Now you, Belteshazzar,
tell *me* its interpretation, inasmuch as none of the wise men of my kingdom is able to make
known to me the interpretation; but you are able, for a spirit of the holy gods is in you.'

4:18 Gen 41:8, 15; Dan 4:7; 5:8, 15; Dan 4:8, 9

Daniel Interprets the Vision

19 "Then Daniel, whose name is Belteshazzar, was appalled for a while as his thoughts
alarmed him. The king responded and said, 'Belteshazzar, do not let the dream or its
interpretation alarm you.' Belteshazzar replied, 'My lord, *if only* the dream applied to
those who hate you and its interpretation to your adversaries!
20 'The tree that you saw, which became large and grew strong, whose height reached
to the sky and was visible to all the earth
21 and whose foliage *was* beautiful and its fruit abundant, and in which *was* food for
all, under which the beasts of the field dwelt and in whose branches the birds of the sky
lodged—
22 it is you, O king; for you have become great and grown strong, and your majesty has
become great and reached to the sky and your dominion to the end of the earth.
23 'In that the king saw an *angelic* watcher, a holy one, descending from heaven and
saying, "Chop down the tree and destroy it; yet leave the stump with its roots in the ground,
but with a band of iron and bronze *around it* in the new grass of the field, and let him be
drenched with the dew of heaven, and let him share with the beasts of the field until
seven periods of time pass over him,"
24 this is the interpretation, O king, and this is the decree of the Most High, which has
come upon my lord the king:
25 that you be driven away from mankind and your dwelling place be with the beasts of
the field, and you be given grass to eat like cattle and be drenched with the dew of heav-
en; and seven periods of time will pass over you, until you recognize that the Most High
is ruler over the realm of mankind and bestows it on whomever He wishes.

4:19 Jer 4:19; Dan 7:15, 28; 8:27; 10:16, 17; 1 Sam 3:17; Dan 4:4, 5; 2 Sam 18:31; Dan 4:24; 10:16; 2 Sam 18:32

4:20 Dan 4:10-12

4:22 2 Sam 12:7; Dan 2:37, 38; Jer 27:6, 7

4:23 Dan 4:14, 15; Dan 4:16

4:24 Job 40:11, 12; Ps 107:40

4:25 Dan 4:33; 5:21; Ps 83:18; Jer 27:5; Dan 4:2, 17; Dan 2:37; 4:17; 5:21

4:17 One of the most difficult lessons to learn is that God is sovereign. He is above all of those who are above us. He limits the power and authority of all the government, business, and religious leaders in the world. Those who live in freedom and with a relatively high degree of autonomy find this difficult to understand. While we may feel as though we are free to do what we please, God is sovereign over all of our plans and desires.

4:19 When Daniel understood Nebuchadnezzar's dream, he was stunned, and he wondered how to break the news. He told the king he wished what the dream foreshadowed would happen to the king's enemies and not to Nebuchadnezzar. How could Daniel be so deeply grieved at the fate of Nebuchadnezzar—the king who was responsible for the destruction of Daniel's home and nation? Daniel had forgiven Nebuchadnezzar, and so God was able to use Daniel. Very often when we have been wronged by someone, we find it difficult to forget the past. We may even be glad when that person suffers. Forgiveness means putting the past behind us. Can you love someone who has hurt you? Can you serve someone who mistreated you? Ask God to help you forgive, forget, and love. God may use you in an extraordinary way in that person's life!

4:23ff Although much of the world thought that Nebuchadnezzar was a mighty (even divine) king, God demonstrated that Nebuchadnezzar was an ordinary man. The king would go insane and become like an animal for a set period of time ("seven periods of time"). God humiliated Nebuchadnezzar to show that almighty God, not Nebuchadnezzar, was Lord of the nations. No matter how powerful a person may become, self-centered pride will push God from his or her life. Pride may be one of the most dangerous temptations you will face. Don't let your accomplishments cause you to forget God.

26 'And in that it was commanded to leave the stump with the roots of the tree, your
kingdom will be assured to you after you recognize that *it is* Heaven *that* rules.
27 'Therefore, O king, may my advice be pleasing to you: break away now from your
sins by *doing* righteousness and from your iniquities by showing mercy to *the* poor, in
case there may be a prolonging of your prosperity.'

The Vision Fulfilled

28 "All *this* happened to Nebuchadnezzar the king.
29 "Twelve months later he was walking on the *roof of* the royal palace of Babylon.
30 "The king reflected and said, 'Is this not Babylon the great, which I myself have built
as a royal residence by the might of my power and for the glory of my majesty?'
31 "While the word *was* in the king's mouth, a voice came from heaven, *saying,* 'King
Nebuchadnezzar, to you it is declared: sovereignty has been removed from you,
32 and you will be driven away from mankind, and your dwelling place *will be* with the
beasts of the field. You will be given grass to eat like cattle, and seven periods of time
will pass over you until you recognize that the Most High is ruler over the realm of mankind and bestows it on whomever He wishes.'

4:26 Dan 4:15, 23; Dan 2:18, 19, 28, 37, 44; 4:31

4:27 Gen 41:33-37; Prov 28:13; Is 55:6, 7; Ezek 18:7, 21, 22; Acts 8:22; Ps 41:1-3; Is 58:6, 7, 10; 1 Kin 21:29; Jon 3:9

4:28 Num 23:19; Zech 1:6

4:29 2 Pet 3:9

4:30 Hab 2:4

4:32 Dan 4:25; Dan 4:16; Dan 4:17

SHADRACH, MESHACH, ABED-NEGO

Friendships make life enjoyable and difficult times bearable. Friendships are tested and strengthened by hardships. Such was the relationship between three young Jewish men deported to Babylon along with Daniel. Shadrach, Meshach, and Abed-nego help us think about the real meaning of friendship. As much as these friends meant to each other, they never allowed their friendship to usurp God's place in their lives—not even in the face of death.

Together they silently defied King Nebuchadnezzar's order to fall down and worship the image of gold. They shared a courageous act, while others, eager to get rid of them, told the king that the three Jews were being disloyal. While this was not true, Nebuchadnezzar could not spare them without shaming himself.

This was the moment of truth. Death was about to end their friendship. A small compromise would have allowed them to live and go on enjoying each other, serving God, and serving their people while in this foreign land. But they were wise enough to see that compromise would have poisoned the very conviction that bound them so closely—each had a higher allegiance to God. So they did not hesitate to place their lives in the hands of God. The rest was victory!

When we leave God out of our most important relationships, we tend to expect those relationships to meet needs in us that only God can meet. Friends are helpful, but they cannot meet our deepest spiritual needs. Leaving God out of our relationships indicates how unimportant he really is in our own lives. Our relationship with God should be important enough to touch our other relationships—especially our closest friendships.

Strengths and accomplishments:
- Stood with Daniel against eating food from the king's table
- Shared a friendship that stood the tests of hardship, success, wealth, and possible death
- Unwilling to compromise their convictions even in the face of death
- Survived the fiery furnace

Lessons from their lives:
- There is great strength in real friendship
- It is important to stand with others with whom we share convictions
- God can be trusted even when we can't predict the outcome

Vital statistics:
- Where: Babylon
- Occupations: King's servants and advisers
- Contemporaries: Daniel, Nebuchadnezzar

Key verses:
"Shadrach, Meshach and Abed-nego replied to the king, 'O Nebuchadnezzar, we do not need to give you an answer concerning this matter. If it be so, our God whom we serve is able to deliver us from the furnace of blazing fire; and He will deliver us out of your hand, O king. But even if He does not, let it be known to you, O king, that we are not going to serve your gods or worship the golden image that you have set up' " (Daniel 3:16–18).

The story of Shadrach (Hananiah), Meshach (Mishael), and Abed-nego (Azariah) is told in the book of Daniel.

4:27–33 Daniel pleaded with Nebuchadnezzar to change his ways, and God gave Nebuchadnezzar 12 months to do it. Unfortunately, there was no repentance in the heart of this proud king, and so the dream was fulfilled.

33 "Immediately the word concerning Nebuchadnezzar was fulfilled; and he was driven
away from mankind and began eating grass like cattle, and his body was drenched with the
dew of heaven until his hair had grown like eagles' *feathers* and his nails like birds' *claws*.
34 "But at the end of that period, I, Nebuchadnezzar, raised my eyes toward heaven
and my reason returned to me, and I blessed the Most High and praised and honored
Him who lives forever;
For His dominion is an everlasting dominion,
And His kingdom *endures* from generation to generation.
35 "All the inhabitants of the earth are accounted as nothing,
But He does according to His will in the host of heaven
And *among* the inhabitants of earth;
And no one can ward off His hand
Or say to Him, 'What have You done?'
36 "At that time my reason returned to me. And my majesty and splendor were restored
to me for the glory of my kingdom, and my counselors and my nobles began seeking me
out; so I was reestablished in my sovereignty, and surpassing greatness was added to me.
37 "Now I, Nebuchadnezzar, praise, exalt and honor the King of heaven, for all His works
are true and His ways just, and He is able to humble those who walk in pride."

Belshazzar's Feast

5 Belshazzar the king held a great feast for a thousand of his nobles, and he was drinking wine in the presence of the thousand.
2 When Belshazzar tasted the wine, he gave orders to bring the gold and silver vessels
which Nebuchadnezzar his father had taken out of the temple which *was* in Jerusalem,
so that the king and his nobles, his wives and his concubines might drink from them.
3 Then they brought the gold vessels that had been taken out of the temple, the house
of God which *was* in Jerusalem; and the king and his nobles, his wives and his concubines drank from them.
4 They drank the wine and praised the gods of gold and silver, of bronze, iron, wood
and stone.
5 Suddenly the fingers of a man's hand emerged and began writing opposite the lampstand on the plaster of the wall of the king's palace, and the king saw the back of the
hand that did the writing.
6 Then the king's face grew pale and his thoughts alarmed him, and his hip joints went
slack and his knees began knocking together.
7 The king called aloud to bring in the conjurers, the Chaldeans and the diviners. The
king spoke and said to the wise men of Babylon, "Any man who can read this inscription
and explain its interpretation to me shall be clothed with purple and *have* a necklace of
gold around his neck, and have authority as third *ruler* in the kingdom."
8 Then all the king's wise men came in, but they could not read the inscription or make
known its interpretation to the king.

4:33 Dan 4:25; 5:21
4:34 Dan 4:2; 5:18, 21; Ps 102:24-27; Dan 6:26; 12:7; Rev 4:10; Ps 145:13; Jer 10:10; Dan 4:3; Mic 4:7; Luke 1:33
4:35 Ps 39:5; Is 40:15, 17; Ps 33:11; 115:3; 135:6; Dan 6:27; Job 42:2; Is 43:13; Job 9:12; Is 45:9; Rom 9:20
4:36 2 Chr 33:12, 13; Dan 4:34; Dan 2:31; Prov 22:4; Dan 4:22
4:37 Dan 4:26; 5:23; Deut 32:4; Ps 33:4, 5; Is 5:16; Ex 18:11; Job 40:11, 12; Dan 5:20
5:1 Esth 1:3; Is 22:12-14
5:2 2 Kin 24:13; 25:15; Ezra 1:7-11; Dan 1:2
5:4 Is 42:8; Dan 5:23; Rev 9:20; Ps 115:4; 135:15; Is 40:19, 20; Dan 3:1; Hab 2:19
5:6 Dan 5:9, 10; 7:28; Ps 69:23; Ezek 7:17; 21:7; Nah 2:10
5:7 Is 44:25; 47:13; Dan 4:6, 7; 5:11, 15; Gen 41:42-44; Dan 5:16, 29; Ezek 16:11; Dan 2:48; 5:16, 29; 6:2, 3
5:8 Gen 41:8; Dan 2:27; 4:7; 5:15

4:34 Ancient kings tried to avoid mentioning their weaknesses or defeats in their monuments and official records. From Nebuchadnezzar's records, however, we can infer that for a time during his 43-year reign he did not rule. The Bible, however, explains Nebuchadnezzar's pride and punishment.

4:36 Nebuchadnezzar's pilgrimage with God is one of the themes of this book. In 2:47, he acknowledged that God revealed mysteries to Daniel. In 3:28–29 he praised the God who rescued the three Hebrews. Despite Nebuchadnezzar's recognition that God exists and works great miracles, in 4:30 we see that he still did not acknowledge God as his Lord. We may recognize that God exists and does wonderful miracles, but God is not going to change us until we acknowledge him as Lord.

5:1 Sixty-six years have elapsed since chapter 1, which tells of Nebuchadnezzar's strike against Jerusalem in 605 B.C. Nebuchadnezzar died in 562 B.C. after a reign of 43 years. His son, Evil-merodach, ruled from 562–560 B.C.; his brother-in-law Neriglissar reigned four years from 560–556 B.C. After a two-month reign by Labashi-marduk in 556 B.C., the Babylonian empire continued from 556–539 B.C. under the command of Nabonidus. Belshazzar was the son of Nabonidus. He co-reigned with his father from 553–539 B.C. Nebuchadnezzar is called Belshazzar's "father." The term could also mean "ancestor."

5:1 Archaeologists have recently discovered Belshazzar's name on several documents. He ruled with his father, Nabonidus, staying home to administer the affairs of the kingdom while his father tried to reopen trade routes taken over by Cyrus and the Persians. Belshazzar was in charge of the city of Babylon when it was captured.

5:7 Belshazzar served as co-regent with his father Nabonidus. Thus, Nabonidus was the first ruler and his son Belshazzar, the second. The person who could read the writing would be given third place, which was the highest position and honor that Belshazzar could offer.

5:8 Although the writing on the wall contained only three words in Aramaic, a language understood by Babylonians (see 2:4), the people could not determine its prophetic significance. God gave Daniel alone the ability to interpret the message of doom to Babylon. The wise men of the kingdom were ignorant of God's wisdom, no matter how great the reward. Daniel did not rush into the banquet hall with the others. His loyalty was to God, not money.

5:9 Job 18:11; Is 21:2-4; Jer 6:24; Dan 2:1; 5:6; Is 13:6-8
5:10 Dan 3:9; 6:6
5:11 Gen 41:11-15; Dan 2:47; Dan 4:8, 9, 18; 5:14; Dan 2:48
5:12 Dan 5:14; 6:3; Dan 1:7; 4:8

9 Then King Belshazzar was greatly alarmed, his face grew *even* paler, and his nobles
were perplexed.
10 The queen entered the banquet hall because of the words of the king and his nobles; the queen spoke and said, "O king, live forever! Do not let your thoughts alarm
you or your face be pale.
11 "There is a man in your kingdom in whom is a spirit of the holy gods; and in the days
of your father, illumination, insight and wisdom like the wisdom of the gods were found
in him. And King Nebuchadnezzar, your father, your father the king, appointed him chief
of the magicians, conjurers, Chaldeans *and* diviners.
12 "*This was* because an extraordinary spirit, knowledge and insight, interpretation of
dreams, explanation of enigmas and solving of difficult problems were found in this

NEBUCHADNEZZAR

Nebuchadnezzar was one world leader who decided he could get more cooperation from the people he conquered by letting them keep their gods. Their lands he took, their riches he robbed, their lives he controlled, but their idols he allowed them to worship, sometimes even worshiping them himself. Nebuchadnezzar's plan worked well, with one glaring exception. When he conquered the little nation of Judah, he met a God who demanded *exclusive* worship—not just his share among many gods. In a sense, Nebuchadnezzar had always been able to rule the gods. This new God was different; this God dared to claim that he had made Nebuchadnezzar all that he was. One of the great conquerors in history was himself conquered by his Creator.

The Bible allows us to note the ways in which God worked on Nebuchadnezzar. God allowed him victories, but he was accomplishing God's purposes. God allowed him to deport the best young Jewish leaders as his palace servants, while placing close to him a young man named Daniel, who would change the king's life. God allowed Nebuchadnezzar to attempt to kill three of his servants to teach the king that he did not really have power over life and death. God warned him of the dangers in his pride, and then allowed Nebuchadnezzar to live through seven years of insanity before restoring him to the throne. God showed the king who was really in control!

These lessons are clear to us today because of our place in history. When our attention shifts to our own lives, we find ourselves unable to see how God is working. But we do have the advantage of God's Word as our guide for today's challenges. We are commanded to obey God; we are also commanded to trust him. Trusting him covers those times when we are not sure about the outcome. God has entrusted us with this day; have we trusted him with our lives?

Strengths and accomplishments:
- Greatest of the Babylonian kings
- Known as a builder of cities
- Described in the Bible as one of the foreign rulers God used for his purposes

Weaknesses and mistakes:
- Thought of himself as a god and was persuaded to build an image of gold that all were to worship
- Became extremely proud, which led to a bout of insanity
- Tended to forget the demonstrations of God's power he had witnessed

Lessons from his life:
- History records the actions of God's willing servants and those who were his unwitting tools
- A leader's greatness is affected by the quality of his advisers
- Uncontrolled pride is self-destructive

Vital statistics:
- Where: Babylon
- Occupation: King
- Relatives: Father: Nabopolassar. Son: Evil-merodach. Grandson: Belshazzar
- Contemporaries: Jeremiah, Ezekiel, Daniel, Jehoiakim, Jehoiachin

Key verse:
"Now I, Nebuchadnezzar, praise, exalt and honor the King of heaven, for all His works are true and His ways just, and He is able to humble those who walk in pride" (Daniel 4:37).

Nebuchadnezzar's story is told in 2 Kings 24; 25; 2 Chronicles 36; Jeremiah 21—52; Daniel 1—4.

5:10 This queen was either Nabonidus's wife or the wife of one of his predecessors, possibly even of Nebuchadnezzar. She was not Belshazzar's wife, because his wives were with him in the banquet hall.

Daniel, whom the king named Belteshazzar. Let Daniel now be summoned and he will
declare the interpretation."

Daniel Interprets Handwriting on the Wall

13 Then Daniel was brought in before the king. The king spoke and said to Daniel,
"Are you that Daniel who is one of the exiles from Judah, whom my father the king brought
from Judah?
14 "Now I have heard about you that a spirit of the gods is in you, and that illumination,
insight and extraordinary wisdom have been found in you.
15 "Just now the wise men *and* the conjurers were brought in before me that they might
read this inscription and make its interpretation known to me, but they could not declare the interpretation of the message.
16 "But I personally have heard about you, that you are able to give interpretations and
solve difficult problems. Now if you are able to read the inscription and make its interpretation known to me, you will be clothed with purple and *wear* a necklace of gold around
your neck, and you will have authority as the third *ruler* in the kingdom."
17 Then Daniel answered and said before the king, "Keep your gifts for yourself or
give your rewards to someone else; however, I will read the inscription to the king and
make the interpretation known to him.
18 "O king, the Most High God granted sovereignty, grandeur, glory and majesty to
Nebuchadnezzar your father.
19 "Because of the grandeur which He bestowed on him, all the peoples, nations and
men of every language feared and trembled before him; whomever he wished he killed
and whomever he wished he spared alive; and whomever he wished he elevated and
whomever he wished he humbled.
20 "But when his heart was lifted up and his spirit became so proud that he behaved
arrogantly, he was deposed from his royal throne and *his* glory was taken away from him.
21 "He was also driven away from mankind, and his heart was made like *that of* beasts,
and his dwelling place *was* with the wild donkeys. He was given grass to eat like cattle,
and his body was drenched with the dew of heaven until he recognized that the Most
High God is ruler over the realm of mankind and *that* He sets over it whomever He wishes.
22 "Yet you, his son, Belshazzar, have not humbled your heart, even though you knew
all this,
23 but you have exalted yourself against the Lord of heaven; and they have brought
the vessels of His house before you, and you and your nobles, your wives and your concubines have been drinking wine from them; and you have praised the gods of silver and
gold, of bronze, iron, wood and stone, which do not see, hear or understand. But the
God in whose hand are your life-breath and your ways, you have not glorified.
24 "Then the hand was sent from Him and this inscription was written out.
25 "Now this is the inscription that was written out: 'MENĒ, MENĒ, TEKĒL,
UPHARSIN.'
26 "This is the interpretation of the message: 'MENĒ'—God has numbered your kingdom and put an end to it.
27 " 'TEKĒL'—you have been weighed on the scales and found deficient.

5:13 Ezra 4:1; 6:16, 19, 20; Dan 2:25; 6:13; Dan 1:1, 2

5:15 Dan 5:7; Is 47:12f; Dan 5:8

5:16 Gen 40:8; Dan 5:7, 29

5:17 2 Kin 5:16

5:18 Dan 4:2; 5:21; Dan 2:37, 38; 4:17; Jer 25:9; 27:5-7

5:19 Dan 2:12, 13; 3:6; 11:3, 16, 36

5:20 Ex 9:17; Job 15:25; Is 14:13-15; Dan 4:30, 31; 2 Kin 17:14; 2 Chr 36:13; Job 40:11, 12; Jer 13:18

5:21 Job 30:3-7; Dan 4:32, 33; Job 39:5-8; Ex 9:14-16; Ps 83:17, 18; Ezek 17:24; Dan 4:17, 34, 35

5:22 Ex 10:3; 2 Chr 33:23; 36:12

5:23 2 Kin 14:10; Is 2:12; 37:23; Jer 50:29; Dan 5:3, 4; Dan 4:37; Ps 115:4-8; Is 37:19; Hab 2:18, 19; Job 12:10; Job 31:4; Ps 139:3; Prov 20:24; Jer 10:23

5:24 Dan 5:5

5:26 Is 13:6, 17-19; Jer 50:41-43

5:27 Job 31:6; Ps 62:9

5:17 The king offered Daniel beautiful gifts and great power if he would explain the writing, but Daniel turned him down. Daniel was not motivated by material rewards. His entire life had been characterized by doing right. Daniel was not showing disrespect in refusing the gifts, but he was growing older himself and knew the gifts would do him little good. Daniel wanted to show that he was giving an unbiased interpretation to the king. Doing right should be our first priority, not gaining power or rewards. Do you love God enough to do what is right, even if it means giving up personal rewards?

5:21–23 Belshazzar knew Babylonian history, and so he knew how God had humbled Nebuchadnezzar. Nevertheless, Belshazzar's banquet was a rebellious challenge to God's authority as he took the sacred goblets from God's temple and drank from them. No one who understands that God is the Creator of the universe should be foolish enough to challenge him.

5:22 Often kings would kill the bearer of bad news. But Daniel was not afraid to tell the truth to the king even though it was not what he wanted to hear. We should be just as courageous in telling the truth under pressure.

5:24 Belshazzar used the goblets from the temple for his party, and God condemned him for this act. We must not use for sinful purposes what has been dedicated to God. Today this would include church buildings, financial donations, and anything else that has been set apart for serving God. Be careful how you use what is God's.

5:27 The writing on the wall was a message for all those who defy God. Although Belshazzar had power and wealth, his kingdom was totally corrupt, and he could not withstand the judgment of God. God's time of judgment comes for all people. If you have forgotten God and slipped into a sinful way of life, turn away from your sin now before he removes any opportunities to repent. Ask God to forgive you, and begin to live by his standards of justice.

28 " 'PERĒS'—your kingdom has been divided and given over to the Medes and Persians."
29 Then Belshazzar gave orders, and they clothed Daniel with purple and *put* a necklace of gold around his neck, and issued a proclamation concerning him that he *now* had
authority as the third *ruler* in the kingdom.
30 That same night Belshazzar the Chaldean king was slain.
31 So Darius the Mede received the kingdom at about the age of sixty-two.

Daniel Serves Darius

6 It seemed good to Darius to appoint 120 satraps over the kingdom, that they would
be in charge of the whole kingdom,
2 and over them three commissioners (of whom Daniel was one), that these satraps
might be accountable to them, and that the king might not suffer loss.
3 Then this Daniel began distinguishing himself among the commissioners and satraps because he possessed an extraordinary spirit, and the king planned to appoint him
over the entire kingdom.
4 Then the commissioners and satraps began trying to find a ground of accusation
against Daniel in regard to government affairs; but they could find no ground of accusation or *evidence of* corruption, inasmuch as he was faithful, and no negligence or corruption was *to be* found in him.
5 Then these men said, "We will not find any ground of accusation against this Daniel unless we find *it* against him with regard to the law of his God."
6 Then these commissioners and satraps came by agreement to the king and spoke to
him as follows: "King Darius, live forever!
7 "All the commissioners of the kingdom, the prefects and the satraps, the high officials and the governors have consulted together that the king should establish a statute
and enforce an injunction that anyone who makes a petition to any god or man besides
you, O king, for thirty days, shall be cast into the lions' den.

5:28 Is 13:17; 21:2; 45:1, 2; Dan 5:31; 6:8, 28; Acts 2:9
5:29 Dan 5:7, 16
5:30 Dan 5:1, 2; Is 21:4-9; 47:9; Jer 51:11, 31, 39, 57
6:2 Dan 2:48, 49; 5:16, 29; Ezra 4:22; Esth 7:4
6:3 Dan 5:12, 14; 9:23; Gen 41:40; Esth 10:3
6:4 Gen 43:18; Judg 14:4; Jer 20:10; Dan 3:8; Luke 20:20; Dan 6:22; Luke 20:26; 23:14, 15; Phil 2:15; 1 Pet 2:12; 3:16
6:5 Acts 24:13-16, 20
6:6 Neh 2:3; Dan 2:4; 5:10; 6:21
6:7 Dan 3:2, 27; Ps 59:3; 62:4; 64:2-6; 83:1-3; Ps 10:9; Dan 3:6; 6:16

KINGS DANIEL SERVED

Name	*Empire*	*Story told in*	*Memorable event*
Nebuchadnezzar	Babylonia	Daniel 1—4	Shadrach, Meshach, and Abed-nego thrown into fiery furnace; Nebuchadnezzar went mad for 7 years
Belshazzar	Babylonia	Daniel 5; 7; 8	Daniel read the writing on the wall, which signaled the end of the Babylonian empire
Darius	Medo-Persia	Daniel 6; 9	Daniel thrown into a lions' den
Cyrus	Medo-Persia	Daniel 10—12	The exiles return to their homeland in Judah and their capital city, Jerusalem

5:28 The Medes and Persians joined forces to overthrow Babylon. This event was predicted in the second phase of Nebuchadnezzar's dream in chapter 2—the silver chest and arms.

5:31 Darius and his soldiers entered Babylon by diverting the river that ran through the city, then walking in on the dry riverbed.

5:31 This Darius is not to be confused with Darius I, mentioned in Ezra, Haggai, and Zechariah, or Darius II (the Persian), mentioned in Nehemiah. Darius the Mede is named only in the book of Daniel. Other records name no king between Belshazzar and Cyrus. Thus, Darius may have been (1) appointed by Cyrus to rule over Babylon as a province of Persia, (2) another name for Cyrus himself or for his son, Cambyses, or (3) a descendant of Ahasuerus.

6:1–3 At this time, Daniel was over 80 years old and one of Darius's top three administrators. Daniel was working with those who did not believe in his God, but he worked more efficiently and capably than all the rest. Thus, he attracted the attention of the pagan king and earned a place of respect. One of the best ways to influence non-Christian employers is to work diligently and responsibly. How well do you represent God to your employer?

6:3–4 Daniel made enemies at work by doing a good job. Perhaps you have had a similar experience. When you begin to excel, you will find that coworkers may look for ways to hold you back and tear you down. How should you deal with those who would cheer at your downfall and even try to hasten it? Conduct your whole life above reproach. Then you will have nothing to hide, and your enemies will have a difficult time finding legitimate charges against you. Of course, this will not always save you from attacks, and, like Daniel, you will have to rely on God for protection.

6:4–5 The jealous officials couldn't find anything about Daniel's life to criticize, so they attacked his religion. If you face jealous critics because of your faith, be glad they're criticizing that part of your life—perhaps they had to focus on your religion as a last resort! Respond by continuing to believe and live as you should. Then remember that God is in control, fighting this battle for you.

8 "Now, O king, establish the injunction and sign the document so that it may not be
changed, according to the law of the Medes and Persians, which may not be revoked."
9 Therefore King Darius signed the document, that is, the injunction.
10 Now when Daniel knew that the document was signed, he entered his house (now
in his roof chamber he had windows open toward Jerusalem); and he continued kneeling on his knees three times a day, praying and giving thanks before his God, as he had
been doing previously.
11 Then these men came by agreement and found Daniel making petition and supplication before his God.
12 Then they approached and spoke before the king about the king's injunction, "Did
you not sign an injunction that any man who makes a petition to any god or man besides
you, O king, for thirty days, is to be cast into the lions' den?" The king replied, "The
statement is true, according to the law of the Medes and Persians, which may not be
revoked."
13 Then they answered and spoke before the king, "Daniel, who is one of the exiles
from Judah, pays no attention to you, O king, or to the injunction which you signed, but
keeps making his petition three times a day."
14 Then, as soon as the king heard this statement, he was deeply distressed and set *his*
mind on delivering Daniel; and even until sunset he kept exerting himself to rescue him.
15 Then these men came by agreement to the king and said to the king, "Recognize, O
king, that it is a law of the Medes and Persians that no injunction or statute which the
king establishes may be changed."

Daniel in the Lions' Den

16 Then the king gave orders, and Daniel was brought in and cast into the lions' den.
The king spoke and said to Daniel, "Your God whom you constantly serve will Himself
deliver you."
17 A stone was brought and laid over the mouth of the den; and the king sealed it with
his own signet ring and with the signet rings of his nobles, so that nothing would be
changed in regard to Daniel.
18 Then the king went off to his palace and spent the night fasting, and no entertainment was brought before him; and his sleep fled from him.
19 Then the king arose at dawn, at the break of day, and went in haste to the
lions' den.
20 When he had come near the den to Daniel, he cried out with a troubled voice. The
king spoke and said to Daniel, "Daniel, servant of the living God, has your God, whom
you constantly serve, been able to deliver you from the lions?"
21 Then Daniel spoke to the king, "O king, live forever!
22 "My God sent His angel and shut the lions' mouths and they have not harmed me,
inasmuch as I was found innocent before Him; and also toward you, O king, I have committed no crime."

6:8 Esth 3:12; 8:10; Is 10:1; Esth 1:19; 8:8; Dan 6:12, 15

6:10 1 Kin 8:44, 48, 49; Ps 5:7; Jon 2:4; Ps 55:17; 95:6; Dan 9:4-19; Ps 34:1; Phil 4:6; 1 Thess 5:17, 18

6:11 Ps 37:32, 33

6:12 Dan 3:8-12; Acts 16:19-21; Esth 1:19; Dan 6:8, 15

6:13 Dan 2:25; 5:13; Esth 3:8; Dan 3:12; Acts 5:29

6:14 Mark 6:26

6:15 Esth 8:8; Ps 94:20, 21; Dan 6:8, 12

6:16 2 Sam 3:39; Jer 38:5; Dan 6:7; Job 5:19; Ps 37:39, 40; Is 41:10; Dan 3:17, 28; 6:20; 2 Cor 1:10

6:17 Lam 3:53; Matt 27:66

6:18 2 Sam 12:16, 17; Esth 6:1; Ps 77:4; Dan 2:1

6:20 Dan 6:16, 27; Gen 18:14; Num 11:23; Jer 32:17; Dan 3:17

6:21 Dan 2:4; 6:6

6:22 Num 20:16; Is 63:9; Dan 3:28; Acts 12:11; Heb 1:14; Ps 91:11-13; 2 Tim 4:17; Heb 11:33

6:8–9 In Babylon, the king's word *was* the law. In the Medo-Persian empire, however, when a law was made, even the king couldn't change it. Darius was an effective government administrator, but he had a fatal flaw—pride. By appealing to his vanity, the men talked Darius into signing a law effectively making himself a god for 30 days. This law could not be broken—not even by an important official like Daniel. Another example of the irrevocable nature of the laws of the Medes and Persians appears in Esther 8:8.

6:10 Daniel stood alone. Although he knew about the law against praying to anyone except the king, he continued to pray three times a day as he always had. Daniel had a disciplined prayer life. Our prayers are usually interrupted not by threats, but simply by the pressure of our schedules. Don't let threats or pressures cut into your prayer time. Pray regularly, no matter what, for prayer is your lifeline to God.

6:10 Daniel made no attempt to hide his daily prayer routine from his enemies in government, even though he knew he would be disobeying the new law. Hiding his daily prayers would have been futile because surely the conspirators would have caught him at something else during the month. Also, hiding would have demonstrated that he was afraid of the other government officials. Daniel continued to pray because he could not look to the king for the guidance and strength that he needed during this difficult time. Only God could provide what he really needed.

6:16 Lions roamed the countryside and forests in Mesopotamia, and the people feared them and greatly respected their power. Some kings hunted lions for sport. The Persians captured lions, keeping them in large parks where they were fed and attended. Lions were also used for executing people. But God has ways of delivering his people (6:22) that none of us can imagine. It is always premature to give up and give in to the pressure of unbelievers, because God has power they know nothing about. God can even shut the lions' mouths.

6:16 Even unbelievers witnessed to Daniel's consistency. By his continual service, Daniel had demonstrated his faithful devotion to God. What can unbelievers determine about your life?

6:21–23 The man or woman who trusts in God and obeys his will is untouchable until God takes him or her. To trust God is to have immeasurable peace. God, who delivered Daniel, will deliver you. Do you trust him with your life?

6:23
Dan 3:25, 27; 1 Chr 5:20; 2 Chr 20:20; Ps 118:8, 9; Is 26:3; Dan 3:17, 28

6:24
Deut 19:18, 19; Esth 7:10; Deut 24:16; 2 Kin 14:6; Esth 9:10

6:25
Ezra 1:1, 2; Esth 3:12; 8:9; Dan 4:1; Ezra 4:17; 1 Pet 1:2

6:26
Ezra 6:8-12; 7:13, 21; Dan 3:29; Dan 4:34; 6:20; Hos 1:10; Rom 9:26; Ps 93:1, 2; Mal 3:6; Dan 2:44; 4:3; 7:14, 27; Luke 1:33

6:27
Dan 4:2, 3

6:28
Dan 1:21; 2 Chr 36:22, 23; Dan 10:1

23 Then the king was very pleased and gave orders for Daniel to be taken up out of the
den. So Daniel was taken up out of the den and no injury whatever was found on him,
because he had trusted in his God.
24 The king then gave orders, and they brought those men who had maliciously accused Daniel, and they cast them, their children and their wives into the lions' den; and
they had not reached the bottom of the den before the lions overpowered them and
crushed all their bones.
25 Then Darius the king wrote to all the peoples, nations and *men of every* language
who were living in all the land: "May your peace abound!
26 "I make a decree that in all the dominion of my kingdom men are to fear and tremble before the God of Daniel;

For He is the living God and enduring forever,
And His kingdom is one which will not be destroyed,
And His dominion *will be* forever.
27 "He delivers and rescues and performs signs and wonders
In heaven and on earth,
Who has *also* delivered Daniel from the power of the lions."

28 So this Daniel enjoyed success in the reign of Darius and in the reign of Cyrus the
Persian.

B. DANIEL'S VISIONS (7:1—12:13)

Daniel had many dreams and visions he did not understand. He dreamed of four beasts, which represented four kingdoms of the world, and of a ram and goat, which depicted two of those kingdoms in greater detail. Daniel's visions reveal that the Messiah will be the ruler of a spiritual kingdom that will overpower and overshadow all other earthly kingdoms. These visions help us see that we should interpret all of history in light of God's eternal kingdom.

Vision of the Four Beasts

7:1
Job 33:14-16; Dan 1:17; 2:1, 26-28; 4:5-9; Joel 2:28; Jer 36:4, 32

7:2
Dan 7:7, 13; Rev 7:1

7:3
Dan 7:17; Rev 13:1; 17:8

7:4
Jer 4:7

7 In the first year of Belshazzar king of Babylon Daniel saw a dream and visions in his
mind *as he lay* on his bed; then he wrote the dream down *and* related the *following*
summary of it.
2 Daniel said, "I was looking in my vision by night, and behold, the four winds of heaven
were stirring up the great sea.
3 "And four great beasts were coming up from the sea, different from one another.
4 "The first *was* like a lion and had *the* wings of an eagle. I kept looking until its wings
were plucked, and it was lifted up from the ground and made to stand on two feet like a
man; a human mind also was given to it.
5 "And behold, another beast, a second one, resembling a bear. And it was raised up
on one side, and three ribs *were* in its mouth between its teeth; and thus they said to it,
'Arise, devour much meat!'

6:24 In accordance with Persian custom, this cruel punishment was transferred to those who had conspired against the king by provoking him into an unjust action (see also Esther 7:9–10). The king's great anger resulted in the execution of the evil officials and their families. Evil deeds often backfire on those who plan cruelty.

6:25–27 Nebuchadnezzar had come to believe that Israel's God was real because of the faithfulness of Daniel and his friends. Here Darius was also convinced of God's power because Daniel was faithful and God rescued him. Although Daniel was captive in a strange land, his devotion to God was a testimony to powerful rulers. If you find yourself in new surroundings, take the opportunity to testify about God's power in your life. Be faithful to God so he can use you to make an impact on others.

7:1 Chronologically, this chapter takes place before chapter five. At this time, Belshazzar had just been given a position of authority (553 B.C.), and Daniel was probably in his late sixties. The first six chapters of Daniel present history; the last six chapters are visions relating mainly to the future.

7:1ff Daniel had a vision of four great beasts, each representing a world empire. This was similar to Nebuchadnezzar's dream in chapter two. Nebuchadnezzar's dream covered the political aspects of the empires; Daniel's dream depicted their moral characteristics. These nations, which would reign over Israel, were evil and cruel; but Daniel also saw God's everlasting, indestructible kingdom arrive and conquer them all.

7:4–8 The lion with an eagle's wings represents Babylon with her swift conquests (statues of winged lions have been recovered from Babylon's ruins). The bear that ravaged the lion is Medo-Persia. The three ribs in its mouth represent the conquests of three major enemies. The leopard is Greece. Its wings show the swiftness of Alexander the Great's campaign as he conquered much of the civilized world in four years (334–330 B.C.). The leopard's four heads are the four divisions of the Greek empire after Alexander's death.

The fourth beast points to both Rome and the end times. Many Bible scholars believe that the horns correspond to ten kings who will reign shortly before God sets up his everlasting kingdom. These ten kings had still not come to power at the time of John's vision recorded in the book of Revelation (Revelation 17:12). The little horn is a future human ruler or the antichrist (see also 2 Thessalonians 2:3–4). God is illustrating the final end of all worldly kingdoms in contrast to his eternal kingdom.

6 "After this I kept looking, and behold, another one, like a leopard, which had on its
back four wings of a bird; the beast also had four heads, and dominion was given to it.
7 "After this I kept looking in the night visions, and behold, a fourth beast, dreadful
and terrifying and extremely strong; and it had large iron teeth. It devoured and crushed
and trampled down the remainder with its feet; and it was different from all the beasts
that were before it, and it had ten horns.
8 "While I was contemplating the horns, behold, another horn, a little one, came up
among them, and three of the first horns were pulled out by the roots before it; and behold,
this horn possessed eyes like the eyes of a man and a mouth uttering great *boasts*.

7:6 Rev 13:2; Dan 8:22

7:7 Dan 7:19, 20, 23; Rev 12:3; 13:1

7:8 Dan 8:9; Rev 13:5, 6

The Ancient of Days Reigns

9 "I kept looking
Until thrones were set up,
And the Ancient of Days took *His* seat;
His vesture *was* like white snow
And the hair of His head like pure wool.
His throne *was* ablaze with flames,
Its wheels *were* a burning fire.
10 "A river of fire was flowing
And coming out from before Him;
Thousands upon thousands were attending Him,
And myriads upon myriads were standing before Him;
The court sat,
And the books were opened.
11 "Then I kept looking because of the sound of the boastful words which the horn was
speaking; I kept looking until the beast was slain, and its body was destroyed and given
to the burning fire.
12 "As for the rest of the beasts, their dominion was taken away, but an extension of life
was granted to them for an appointed period of time.

7:9 Rev 20:4; Mark 9:3; Rev 1:14; Ezek 1:13, 26; Ezek 10:2, 6

7:10 Ps 18:8; 50:3; 97:3; Is 30:27, 33; Deut 33:2; 1 Kin 22:19; Rev 5:11; Ps 96:11-13; Dan 7:22, 26; Dan 12:1; Rev 20:11-15

7:11 Rev 19:20; 20:10

The Son of Man Presented

13 "I kept looking in the night visions,
And behold, with the clouds of heaven
One like a Son of Man was coming,
And He came up to the Ancient of Days
And was presented before Him.
14 "And to Him was given dominion,
Glory and a kingdom,
That all the peoples, nations and *men of every* language
Might serve Him.
His dominion is an everlasting dominion
Which will not pass away;
And His kingdom is one
Which will not be destroyed.

7:13 Matt 24:30; 26:64; Mark 13:26; 14:62; Luke 21:27; Rev 1:7, 13; 14:14

7:14 Dan 7:27; John 3:35; 1 Cor 15:27; Eph 1:20-22; Phil 2:9-11; Rev 1:6; 11:15; Dan 2:37; Ps 72:11; 102:22; Mic 4:7; Luke 1:33; Heb 12:28

The Vision Interpreted

15 "As for me, Daniel, my spirit was distressed within me, and the visions in my mind
kept alarming me.

7:15 Dan 7:1; Dan 4:19; 7:28

7:9 Here the prophecy shifts to the end times. This judgment scene is similar to one that was seen by the apostle John (Revelation 1:14–15). The Ancient of Days is almighty God, who assigns power to kingdoms and who will himself judge those kingdoms in the end.

7:10 Daniel saw God judging millions of people as they stood before him. We all must stand before almighty God and give an account of our lives. If your life were judged by God today, what would he say about it? How would he measure it against his will for us? We should live each day with the full awareness that we must appear before God to give account for how we used our lives. How will your life measure up?

7:11–12 The slaying of the beast represents the fall of Rome. While this beast was destroyed, the other beasts were allowed to live for a period of time. The kingdoms (or their cultures) continued to be recognizable in some form; history did not end when God intervened with his judgment.

7:13–14 This "one like a Son of Man" is the Messiah. Jesus used this verse to refer to himself (Matthew 26:64; Luke 21:27; John 1:51). The clouds of heaven portray the Son of Man as divine; throughout the Bible clouds represent his majesty and awesome presence. God's glory appeared in a cloud in Exodus 16:10 and 19:9 at the giving of the law at Sinai.

7:16 Zech 1:9, 19; Rev 5:5; 7:13, 14; Dan 8:16, 17; 9:22

7:18 Dan 7:22, 25, 27; Ps 149:5-9; Is 60:12-14; Dan 7:14; Rev 2:26, 27; 20:4; 22:5

7:19 Dan 7:7, 8

7:21 Rev 11:7; 13:7

7:22 Dan 7:10; 1 Cor 6:2, 3

7:24 Dan 7:7; Rev 17:12

7:25 Dan 11:36; Rev 13:6; Dan 3:26; 4:2, 17, 34; Rev 13:7; 18:24; Dan 2:21; Dan 12:7; Rev 12:14

7:26 Rev 17:14; 19:2

7:27 Is 54:3; Dan 7:14, 18, 22; Rev 20:4; Ps 145:13; Is 9:7; Dan 2:44; 4:34; 7:14; Luke 1:33; Rev 11:15; 22:5; Ps 2:6-12; 22:27; 72:11; 86:9; Is 60:12; Rev 11:1

7:28 Dan 4:19; Luke 2:19, 51

16 "I approached one of those who were standing by and began asking him the exact
meaning of all this. So he told me and made known to me the interpretation of these
things:
17 'These great beasts, which are four *in number,* are four kings *who* will arise from the
earth.
18 'But the saints of the Highest One will receive the kingdom and possess the kingdom forever, for all ages to come.'
19 "Then I desired to know the exact meaning of the fourth beast, which was different
from all the others, exceedingly dreadful, with its teeth of iron and its claws of bronze,
and which devoured, crushed and trampled down the remainder with its feet,
20 and *the meaning* of the ten horns that *were* on its head and the other *horn* which
came up, and before which three *of them* fell, namely, that horn which had eyes and a
mouth uttering great *boasts* and which was larger in appearance than its associates.
21 "I kept looking, and that horn was waging war with the saints and overpowering them
22 until the Ancient of Days came and judgment was passed in favor of the saints of
the Highest One, and the time arrived when the saints took possession of the kingdom.
23 "Thus he said: 'The fourth beast will be a fourth kingdom on the earth, which will be
different from all the *other* kingdoms and will devour the whole earth and tread it down
and crush it.
24 'As for the ten horns, out of this kingdom ten kings will arise; and another will arise
after them, and he will be different from the previous ones and will subdue three kings.
25 'He will speak out against the Most High and wear down the saints of the Highest
One, and he will intend to make alterations in times and in law; and they will be given
into his hand for a time, times, and half a time.
26 'But the court will sit *for judgment,* and his dominion will be taken away, annihilated
and destroyed forever.
27 'Then the sovereignty, the dominion and the greatness of *all* the kingdoms under
the whole heaven will be given to the people of the saints of the Highest One; His kingdom *will be* an everlasting kingdom, and all the dominions will serve and obey Him.'
28 "At this point the revelation ended. As for me, Daniel, my thoughts were greatly
alarming me and my face grew pale, but I kept the matter to myself."

Vision of the Ram and Goat

8:2 Num 12:6; Dan 7:2, 15; 8:3; Neh 1:1; Esth 1:2; 2:8; Gen 10:22; 14:1; Is 11:11; Jer 25:25; Ezek 32:24

8:3 Dan 8:20

8:4 Deut 33:17; 1 Kin 22:11; Ezek 34:21; Dan 11:3

8 In the third year of the reign of Belshazzar the king a vision appeared to me, Daniel,
subsequent to the one which appeared to me previously.
2 I looked in the vision, and while I was looking I was in the citadel of Susa, which is
in the province of Elam; and I looked in the vision and I myself was beside the Ulai Canal.
3 Then I lifted my eyes and looked, and behold, a ram which had two horns was standing in front of the canal. Now the two horns *were* long, but one *was* longer than the other,
with the longer one coming up last.
4 I saw the ram butting westward, northward, and southward, and no *other* beasts could
stand before him nor was there anyone to rescue from his power, but he did as he pleased
and magnified *himself.*

7:18 The "saints of the Highest One" are the true Israel, the people ruled by the Messiah. Jesus Christ gave the kingdom to the new Israel, his church, made up of all faithful believers. His coming ushered in the kingdom of God, and all believers are its citizens (see also 7:22, 27). Although God may allow persecution to continue for a while, the destiny of his followers is to possess the kingdom and be with him forever.

7:24 The ten horns, or ten kings, are also mentioned in Revelation 17:12. There were also ten toes in Nebuchadnezzar's vision (2:41–42). While all do not agree concerning the identity of these ten kings, we are reminded in Revelation 17:12–14 that these kings will make war against Christ, but, as the King of kings, he will conquer them. The other king mentioned here in verse 24 is the future antichrist of 2 Thessalonians 2:3–4.

7:25 While the exact meaning of this "time, times, and half a time" is debated, we do know that God told Daniel that persecution would continue only a relatively short time. God has promised to give his kingdom to his saints.

8:1 As with chapter 7, this chapter precedes chapter 5 chronologically; the dream probably occurred in 551 B.C. when Daniel was about 70 years old. Chapters 7 and 8 correspond to the first and third years of Belshazzar and belong chronologically between chapters 4 and 5. Chapter 9 took place at approximately the same time as chapter 6. It gives us more details about the Medo-Persian and Greek empires, the two world powers that ruled after Babylonia.

8:2 Susa was one of the capitals of the Babylonian empire. Located in what is now Iran, Susa was a well-developed city. It was the winter capital of the Persian empire and a mighty fortress (citadel). In his vision, Daniel saw himself in this important location. The earliest known code of law, the Code of Hammurapi, was found there. Susa rivaled Babylon itself in cultural sophistication.

8:3 The two horns were the kings of Media and Persia (8:20). The longer horn represented the growing dominance of Persia in the Medo-Persian empire.

5 While I was observing, behold, a male goat was coming from the west over the surface of the whole earth without touching the ground; and the goat *had* a conspicuous
horn between his eyes.
6 He came up to the ram that had the two horns, which I had seen standing in front of
the canal, and rushed at him in his mighty wrath.
7 I saw him come beside the ram, and he was enraged at him; and he struck the ram
and shattered his two horns, and the ram had no strength to withstand him. So he hurled
him to the ground and trampled on him, and there was none to rescue the ram from his
power.
8 Then the male goat magnified *himself* exceedingly. But as soon as he was mighty,
the large horn was broken; and in its place there came up four conspicuous *horns* toward the four winds of heaven.

The Little Horn

9 Out of one of them came forth a rather small horn which grew exceedingly great
toward the south, toward the east, and toward the [7]Beautiful *Land*.
10 It grew up to the host of heaven and caused some of the host and some of the stars
to fall to the earth, and it trampled them down.
11 It even magnified *itself* to be equal with the Commander of the host; and it removed
the regular sacrifice from Him, and the place of His sanctuary was thrown down.
12 And on account of transgression the host will be given over *to the horn* along with
the regular sacrifice; and it will fling truth to the ground and perform *its will* and prosper.
13 Then I heard a holy one speaking, and another holy one said to that particular one
who was speaking, "How long will the vision *about* the regular sacrifice apply, while the
transgression causes horror, so as to allow both the holy place and the host to be trampled?"
14 He said to me, "For 2,300 evenings *and* mornings; then the holy place will be properly restored."

Interpretation of the Vision

15 When I, Daniel, had seen the vision, I sought to understand it; and behold, standing before me was one who looked like a man.
16 And I heard the voice of a man between *the banks of* Ulai, and he called out and
said, "Gabriel, give this *man* an understanding of the vision."
17 So he came near to where I was standing, and when he came I was frightened and
fell on my face; but he said to me, "Son of man, understand that the vision pertains to
the time of the end."
18 Now while he was talking with me, I sank into a deep sleep with my face to the ground;
but he touched me and made me stand upright.
19 He said, "Behold, I am going to let you know what will occur at the final period of
the indignation, for *it* pertains to the appointed time of the end.

7 I.e. Palestine

8:5 Dan 8:8, 21; 11:3

8:8 2 Chr 26:16; Dan 5:20; Dan 8:22; Dan 7:2; Rev 7:1

8:9 Dan 8:23; Ps 48:2; Dan 11:16, 41

8:10 Is 14:13; Jer 48:26; Rev 12:4; Dan 7:7; 8:7

8:11 2 Kin 19:22, 23; 2 Chr 32:15-17; Is 37:23; Dan 8:25; 11:36, 37; Ezek 46:14; Dan 11:31; 12:11

8:12 Is 59:14

8:13 Dan 4:13, 23; 1 Pet 1:12; Ps 74:10; 79:5; Is 6:11; Dan 12:6, 8; Rev 6:10; Is 63:18; Jer 12:10; Luke 21:24; Heb 10:29; Rev 11:2

8:14 Dan 7:25; 12:7, 11; Rev 11:2, 3; 12:14; 13:5

8:15 Dan 8:1; Dan 7:13; 10:16, 18

8:16 Dan 9:21; Luke 1:19, 26

8:17 Ezek 1:28; 44:4; Dan 2:46; Rev 1:17; Dan 8:19; 11:35, 40

8:18 Dan 10:9; Luke 9:32; Ezek 2:2; Dan 10:10, 16, 18

8:19 Dan 8:15-17

8:5–7 The goat represented Greece, and its large horn, Alexander the Great (8:21). This is an amazing prediction because Greece was not yet considered a world power when this prophecy was given. Alexander the Great conquered the world with great speed and military strategy, indicated by the goat's rapid movement. Shattering both horns symbolized Alexander breaking both parts of the Medo-Persian empire.

8:8 Alexander the Great died in his thirties at the height of his power. His kingdom was split into four parts under four generals: Ptolemy I of Egypt and Palestine; Seleucus of Babylonia and Syria; Lysimachus of Asia Minor; and Antipater of Macedon and Greece.

8:9 Israel ("the Beautiful Land") was attacked by Antiochus IV Epiphanes (the small horn) in the second century B.C. He was the eighth ruler of the Seleucid empire (Babylonia and Syria). He overthrew the high priest, looted the temple, and replaced worship of God with a Greek form of worship. A further fulfillment of this prophecy of a powerful horn will occur in the future with the coming of the antichrist (see 8:17, 19, 23; 11:36; 2 Thessalonians 2:4).

8:11 The "Commander of the host" here refers to a heavenly authority, perhaps an angel or even God himself. (See also Joshua 5:13–15.)

8:14 The phrase "evenings and mornings" means evening and morning sacrifices, and refers to the time from the desecration of the altar in the temple by Antiochus IV Epiphanes to the restoration of temple worship under Judas Maccabeus in 165 B.C.

8:16 Gabriel is an angel, the heavenly messenger God used to explain Daniel's visions (9:21). He also announced the birth of John the Baptist (Luke 1:11) and the Messiah (Luke 1:26).

8:17 The "time of the end," in this case, refers to the whole period from the end of the exile until the second coming of Christ. Many of the events that would happen under Antiochus IV Epiphanes will be repeated on a broader scale just before Christ's second coming. During these times, God deals with Israel in a radically different way, with divine discipline coming through Gentile nations. This period is sometimes referred to as the "times of the Gentiles" (Luke 21:24).

The Ram's Identity

8:20 Dan 8:3

20 "The ram which you saw with the two horns represents the kings of Media and Persia.

The Goat

21 "The shaggy goat *represents* the kingdom of Greece, and the large horn that is between his eyes is the first king.

8:22 Dan 8:8

22 "The broken *horn* and the four *horns that* arose in its place *represent* four kingdoms *which* will arise from *his* nation, although not with his power.

23 "In the latter period of their rule,
When the transgressors have run *their course,*
A king will arise,
Insolent and skilled in intrigue.

8:24 Dan 8:11-13; 11:36; 12:7

24 "His power will be mighty, but not by his *own* power,
And he will destroy to an extraordinary degree
And prosper and perform *his will;*
He will destroy mighty men and the holy people.

8:25 Dan 8:11; Job 34:20; Dan 2:34, 45

25 "And through his shrewdness
He will cause deceit to succeed by his influence;
And he will magnify *himself* in his heart,
And he will destroy many while *they are* at ease.
He will even oppose the Prince of princes,
But he will be broken without human agency.

8:26 Dan 10:1; Ezek 12:27; Dan 12:4, 9; Rev 22:10; Dan 10:14

26 "The vision of the evenings and mornings
Which has been told is true;
But keep the vision secret,
For *it* pertains to many days *in the future.*"

8:27 Dan 7:28; 8:17; Hab 3:16; Dan 2:48

27 Then I, Daniel, was exhausted and sick for days. Then I got up *again* and carried on the king's business; but I was astounded at the vision, and there was none to explain *it.*

Daniel's Prayer for His People

9:1 Dan 5:31; 11:1

9 In the first year of Darius the son of Ahasuerus, of Median descent, who was made king over the kingdom of the Chaldeans—

9:2 2 Chr 36:21; Ezra 1:1; Jer 25:11, 12; 29:10; Zech 7:5

2 in the first year of his reign, I, Daniel, observed in the books the number of the years which was *revealed as* the word of the LORD to Jeremiah the prophet for the completion of the desolations of Jerusalem, *namely,* seventy years.

3 So I gave my attention to the Lord God to seek *Him by* prayer and supplications, with fasting, sackcloth and ashes.

9:4 Deut 7:21; Neh 9:32; Deut 7:9

4 I prayed to the LORD my God and confessed and said, "Alas, O Lord, the great and awesome God, who keeps His covenant and lovingkindness for those who love Him and keep His commandments,

---

8:23 This insolent king describes both Antiochus IV Epiphanes and the antichrist at the end of human history.

8:25 This Prince of princes is God himself. No human power could defeat the king whom Daniel saw in his vision, but God would bring him down. Antiochus IV Epiphanes reportedly went insane and died in Persia in 164 B.C. God's power and justice will prevail, so we should never give up our faith or lose hope, no matter how powerful God's enemies may seem.

9:1 The vision in chapter 9 was given to Daniel during the same time period of chapter 6. This Darius is the person mentioned in chapter 6. The Ahasuerus mentioned here is not Esther's husband. The events described in the book of Esther happened about 50 years later.

9:2–3 Daniel pleaded with God to bring about the promised return of his people to their land. The prophet Jeremiah had written that God would not allow the captives to return to their land for 70 years (Jeremiah 25:11–12; 29:10). Daniel knew of this prophecy and realized that this 70-year period was coming to an end.

9:3ff In Daniel's prayer for the nation he confessed his own sin, using the pronoun *we* throughout. In times of adversity, it's easy to blame others and excuse our own actions. If any Israelite was righteous, it was Daniel; and yet he confessed his sinfulness and need for God's forgiveness. Instead of looking for others to blame, first look inside and confess your own sins to God.

9:3–19 Daniel knew how to pray. As he prayed, he fasted, confessed his sins, and pleaded that God would reveal his will. He prayed with complete surrender to God and with complete openness to what God was saying to him. When you pray, do you speak openly to God? Examine your attitude. Talk to God with openness, vulnerability, and honesty, and be ready for God's reply.

9:4–6 The captives from Judah had rebelled against God. Their sins had led to their captivity. But God is merciful even to rebels, if they confess their sins and return to him. Don't let your past disobedience keep you from returning to God. He is waiting for you and wants you to return to him.

5 we have sinned, committed iniquity, acted wickedly and rebelled, even turning aside
from Your commandments and ordinances.
6 "Moreover, we have not listened to Your servants the prophets, who spoke in Your
name to our kings, our princes, our fathers and all the people of the land.
7 "Righteousness belongs to You, O Lord, but to us open shame, as it is this day—to
the men of Judah, the inhabitants of Jerusalem and all Israel, those who are nearby and
those who are far away in all the countries to which You have driven them, because of
their unfaithful deeds which they have committed against You.
8 "Open shame belongs to us, O Lord, to our kings, our princes and our fathers, because we have sinned against You.
9 "To the Lord our God *belong* compassion and forgiveness, for we have rebelled
against Him;
10 nor have we obeyed the voice of the LORD our God, to walk in His teachings which
He set before us through His servants the prophets.
11 "Indeed all Israel has transgressed Your law and turned aside, not obeying Your voice;
so the curse has been poured out on us, along with the oath which is written in the law of
Moses the servant of God, for we have sinned against Him.
12 "Thus He has confirmed His words which He had spoken against us and against our
rulers who ruled us, to bring on us great calamity; for under the whole heaven there has
not been done *anything* like what was done to Jerusalem.
13 "As it is written in the law of Moses, all this calamity has come on us; yet we have not
sought the favor of the LORD our God by turning from our iniquity and giving attention
to Your truth.
14 "Therefore the LORD has kept the calamity in store and brought it on us; for the LORD
our God is righteous with respect to all His deeds which He has done, but we have not
obeyed His voice.
15 "And now, O Lord our God, who have brought Your people out of the land of Egypt
with a mighty hand and have made a name for Yourself, as it is this day—we have sinned,
we have been wicked.
16 "O Lord, in accordance with all Your righteous acts, let now Your anger and Your
wrath turn away from Your city Jerusalem, Your holy mountain; for because of our sins
and the iniquities of our fathers, Jerusalem and Your people *have become* a reproach to
all those around us.
17 "So now, our God, listen to the prayer of Your servant and to his supplications, and
for Your sake, O Lord, let Your face shine on Your desolate sanctuary.
18 "O my God, incline Your ear and hear! Open Your eyes and see our desolations and
the city which is called by Your name; for we are not presenting our supplications before
You on account of any merits of our own, but on account of Your great compassion.
19 "O Lord, hear! O Lord, forgive! O Lord, listen and take action! For Your own sake,
O my God, do not delay, because Your city and Your people are called by Your name."

9:5 1 Kin 8:48; Neh 9:33; Ps 106:6; Is 64:5-7; Jer 14:7; Lam 1:18, 20; Ps 119:176; Is 53:6

9:6 2 Chr 36:16; Jer 44:4, 5

9:7 Ps 44:15; Jer 2:26, 27; 3:25; Deut 4:27

9:9 Neh 9:17; Ps 130:4; Ps 106:43; Jer 14:7; Dan 9:5, 6

9:10 2 Kin 17:13-15

9:11 Is 1:3, 4; Jer 8:5-10; Deut 27:15-26

9:12 Is 44:26; Jer 44:2-6; Lam 2:17; Zech 1:6; Job 12:17; Ps 82:2-7; 148:11; Lam 1:12; 2:13; Ezek 5:9

9:13 Lev 26:14-45; Deut 28:15-68; Dan 9:11; Job 36:13; Is 9:13; Jer 2:30; 5:3; 31:18

9:14 Jer 31:28; 44:27; Ps 51:14; Dan 9:7

9:15 Deut 5:15; Neh 9:10; Jer 32:20

9:16 Jer 32:31, 32; Ps 87:1-3; Dan 9:20; Joel 3:17; Zech 8:3; Ezek 5:14

9:17 Num 6:24-26; Ps 80:3, 7, 19; Lam 5:18

9:18 Is 37:17; Ps 80:14; Jer 7:10-12; Jer 36:7

9:19 Ps 44:23; 74:10, 11

9:6 God had sent many prophets to speak to his people through the years, but their messages had been ignored. The truth was too painful to hear. God still speaks clearly and accurately through the Bible, and he also speaks through preachers, teachers, and concerned friends. Sometimes the truth hurts, and we would rather hear words that soothe, even if they are false. If you are unwilling to accept God's message, maybe you are trying to avoid making a painful change. Don't settle for a soothing lie that will bring harsh judgment. Accepting the truth even if it is painful can only help you.

9:11–13 Daniel mentioned the curses outlined in Deuteronomy 28. God had given the people of Israel a choice: Obey me and receive blessings, or disobey me and face curses. The affliction was meant to turn the people to God. When we face difficult circumstances, we should ask ourselves if God has reason to send judgment. If we think so, we must urgently seek his forgiveness. Then we can ask him to help us through our troubles.

9:14 Daniel spoke about how God continually tried to bring Israel back to himself. Yet even after disaster struck them, they refused to obey him. God still uses circumstances, other people, and, most important, his Word to bring his people back to him. What would it take for God to get your attention?

9:17–19 It would be a mistake to read the Bible as dry history and miss the deep personal feelings. In this section, Daniel was crying out to the Lord. He had a deep concern for his nation and his people. So often our prayers are without passion and true compassion for others. Are you willing to pray by pouring out your deep feelings to God?

9:18 Daniel begged for mercy, not for help, because he knew that his people deserved God's wrath and punishment. God sends his help, not because we deserve it, but because he wants to show great mercy. If God would refuse to help us because of our sin, how could we complain? But when he sends mercy when we deserve punishment, how can we withhold our praise and thanksgiving?

Gabriel Brings an Answer

20 Now while I was speaking and praying, and confessing my sin and the sin of my people
Israel, and presenting my supplication before the LORD my God in behalf of the holy
mountain of my God,
21 while I was still speaking in prayer, then the man Gabriel, whom I had seen in the
vision previously, came to me in *my* extreme weariness about the time of the evening
offering.
22 He gave *me* instruction and talked with me and said, "O Daniel, I have now come
forth to give you insight with understanding.
23 "At the beginning of your supplications the command was issued, and I have come
to tell *you,* for you are highly esteemed; so give heed to the message and gain understanding of the vision.

Seventy Weeks and the Messiah

24 "Seventy weeks have been decreed for your people and your holy city, to finish the
transgression, to make an end of sin, to make atonement for iniquity, to bring in everlasting righteousness, to seal up vision and prophecy and to anoint the most holy *place.*
25 "So you are to know and discern *that* from the issuing of a decree to restore and rebuild Jerusalem until Messiah the Prince *there will be* seven weeks and sixty-two weeks;
it will be built again, with plaza and moat, even in times of distress.
26 "Then after the sixty-two weeks the Messiah will be cut off and have nothing, and
the people of the prince who is to come will destroy the city and the sanctuary. And its
end *will come* with a flood; even to the end there will be war; desolations are determined.
27 "And he will make a firm covenant with the many for one week, but in the middle of
the week he will put a stop to sacrifice and grain offering; and on the wing of abominations *will come* one who makes desolate, even until a complete destruction, one that is
decreed, is poured out on the one who makes desolate."

Daniel Is Terrified by a Vision

10 In the third year of Cyrus king of Persia a message was revealed to Daniel, who
was named Belteshazzar; and the message was true and *one of* great conflict, but
he understood the message and had an understanding of the vision.
2 In those days, I, Daniel, had been mourning for three entire weeks.
3 I did not eat any tasty food, nor did meat or wine enter my mouth, nor did I use any
ointment at all until the entire three weeks were completed.
4 On the twenty-fourth day of the first month, while I was by the bank of the great
river, that is, the Tigris,

9:20 Ps 145:18; Is 58:9; Dan 9:3; 10:12; Is 6:5

9:21 Dan 8:16; Luke 1:19, 26; Ex 29:39; 1 Kin 18:36; Ezra 9:4

9:22 Dan 8:16; 10:21; Zech 1:9

9:23 Dan 10:12; Dan 10:11, 19; Matt 24:15

9:24 Lev 25:8; Num 14:34; Ezek 4:5, 6; 2 Chr 29:24; Is 53:10; Rom 5:10; Is 51:6, 8; 56:1; Jer 23:5, 6; Rom 3:21, 22

9:25 Ezra 4:24; 6:1-15; Neh 2:1-8; 3:1; John 1:41; 4:25; Is 9:6; Dan 8:11, 25

9:26 Is 53:8; Mark 9:12; Luke 24:26; Matt 24:2; Mark 13:2; Luke 19:43, 44; Nah 1:8

9:27 Dan 11:31; Matt 24:15; Mark 13:14; Luke 21:20; Is 10:23; 28:22

10:1 Dan 1:21; 6:28; Dan 1:7; Dan 8:26; Dan 1:17; 2:21

10:2 Ezra 9:4, 5; Neh 1:4

10:3 Dan 6:18

10:4 Ezek 1:3; Dan 8:2

9:23 Just as God answered Daniel's prayer, so we can have confidence that God hears and answers our prayers.

9:24–25 Each day of these 70 weeks may represent one year. The Bible often uses round numbers to make a point, not to give an exact count. For example, Jesus said we are to forgive others "seventy times seven" times (Matthew 18:22). He did not mean a literal number, but that we should be abundantly forgiving. Similarly, some scholars see this figure of 70 weeks as a figurative time period. Others, however, interpret this time period as a literal 70 weeks or 490 years, observing that Christ's death came at the end of the 69 weeks (i.e., 483 years later). One interpretation places the 70th week as the seven years of the great tribulation, still in the future. Consequently the number would symbolize both the first and second comings of Christ.

9:25 A moat is a conduit for water. This shows that Jerusalem will be rebuilt as a complete, fully functioning city.

9:26 The Messiah, the Anointed One, will be rejected and killed by his own people. His perfect eternal kingdom will come later.

9:26–27 There has been much discussion on the numbers, times, and events in these verses, and there are three basic views: (1) the prophecy was fulfilled in the past at the desecration of the temple by Antiochus IV Epiphanes in 168–167 B.C. (see 11:31); (2) it was fulfilled in the past at the destruction of the temple by the Roman general Titus in A.D. 70 when one million Jews were killed; or (3) it is still to be fulfilled in the future under the antichrist (see Matthew 24:15).

10:1ff This is Daniel's final vision (536 B.C.). In it, he was given further insight into the great spiritual battle between God's people and those who want to destroy them. There is also more detailed information on the future, specifically the struggles between the Ptolemies (kings of the South) and the Seleucids (kings of the North).

10:1ff Prior to this vision, Cyrus allowed the Jews to return to Jerusalem, but Daniel stayed in Babylonia. Why didn't Daniel return to Jerusalem? He may have been too old to make the long, hazardous journey (he was over 80); his government duties could have prevented him; or God may have told him to stay behind to complete the work he was called to do.

10:3 Daniel refrained from eating choice foods and using lotions because these were signs of feasting and rejoicing.

5 I lifted my eyes and looked, and behold, there was a certain man dressed in linen,
whose waist was girded with *a belt of* pure gold of Uphaz.
6 His body also *was* like beryl, his face had the appearance of lightning, his eyes were
like flaming torches, his arms and feet like the gleam of polished bronze, and the sound
of his words like the sound of a tumult.
7 Now I, Daniel, alone saw the vision, while the men who were with me did not see
the vision; nevertheless, a great dread fell on them, and they ran away to hide themselves.
8 So I was left alone and saw this great vision; yet no strength was left in me, for my
natural color turned to a deathly pallor, and I retained no strength.
9 But I heard the sound of his words; and as soon as I heard the sound of his words,
I fell into a deep sleep on my face, with my face to the ground.

10:5 Ezek 9:2; Dan 12:6, 7; Rev 1:13; 15:6; Jer 10:9
10:6 Rev 1:14; 2:18; 19:12
10:7 2 Kin 6:17-20; Acts 9:7; Ezek 12:18
10:8 Gen 32:24; Dan 7:28; 8:27; Hab 3:16
10:9 Gen 15:12; Job 4:13; Dan 8:18

Daniel Comforted

10 Then behold, a hand touched me and set me trembling on my hands and knees.
11 He said to me, "O Daniel, man of high esteem, understand the words that I am about
to tell you and stand upright, for I have now been sent to you." And when he had spoken
this word to me, I stood up trembling.
12 Then he said to me, "Do not be afraid, Daniel, for from the first day that you set
your heart on understanding *this* and on humbling yourself before your God, your words
were heard, and I have come in response to your words.
13 "But the prince of the kingdom of Persia was withstanding me for twenty-one days;
then behold, Michael, one of the chief princes, came to help me, for I had been left there
with the kings of Persia.
14 "Now I have come to give you an understanding of what will happen to your people
in the latter days, for the vision pertains to the days yet *future.*"
15 When he had spoken to me according to these words, I turned my face toward the
ground and became speechless.
16 And behold, one who resembled a human being was touching my lips; then I opened
my mouth and spoke and said to him who was standing before me, "O my lord, as a result of the vision anguish has come upon me, and I have retained no strength.
17 "For how can such a servant of my lord talk with such as my lord? As for me, there
remains just now no strength in me, nor has any breath been left in me."
18 Then *this* one with human appearance touched me again and strengthened me.
19 He said, "O man of high esteem, do not be afraid. Peace be with you; take courage
and be courageous!" Now as soon as he spoke to me, I received strength and said, "May
my lord speak, for you have strengthened me."
20 Then he said, "Do you understand why I came to you? But I shall now return to
fight against the prince of Persia; so I am going forth, and behold, the prince of Greece
is about to come.
21 "However, I will tell you what is inscribed in the writing of truth. Yet there is no one
who stands firmly with me against these *forces* except Michael your prince.

10:10 Jer 1:9; Dan 8:18
10:11 Dan 10:19; Dan 8:16, 17; Ezek 2:1; Job 4:14, 15
10:12 Is 41:10, 14; Dan 10:19; Dan 9:20-23; 10:2, 3; Acts 10:30, 31
10:13 Dan 10:21; 12:1; Jude 9; Rev 12:7
10:14 Dan 8:16; 9:22; Deut 31:29; Dan 2:28; Dan 8:26; 12:4, 9
10:15 Ezek 3:26; 24:27; Luke 1:20
10:16 Dan 8:15; Is 6:7; Jer 1:9; Dan 7:15, 28; 8:17, 27; 10:8, 9
10:17 Ex 24:10, 11; Is 6:1-5; Dan 10:8
10:18 Is 35:3, 4
10:19 Judg 6:23; Is 43:1; Dan 10:12; Josh 1:6, 7, 9; Is 35:4; Ps 138:3; 2 Cor 12:9
10:21 Dan 12:4; Dan 10:13; Rev 12:7

Conflicts to Come

11 "In the first year of Darius the Mede, I arose to be an encouragement and a protection for him.
2 "And now I will tell you the truth. Behold, three more kings are going to arise in Persia.

11:2 Dan 8:26; 10:1, 21; Dan 8:21; 10:20

10:5–6 The man seen by Daniel was a heavenly being. Some commentators believe that this was an appearance of Christ (see Revelation 1:13–15), while others think it was an angel (because he required Michael's help—10:13). In either case, Daniel caught a glimpse of the battle between good and evil supernatural powers.

10:6 Beryl is a translucent, semi-precious stone.

10:10–18 Daniel was frightened by this vision, but the messenger reassured him. Daniel lost his speech, but the messenger's touch restored it. Daniel felt weak and helpless, but the messenger's words strengthened him. God can bring us healing when we are hurt, peace when we are troubled, and strength when we are weak. Trust God to minister to you as he did to Daniel.

10:12–13 Although God sent a messenger to Daniel, a powerful spiritual being ("prince of the kingdom of Persia") detained the messenger for three weeks. Daniel faithfully continued praying and fasting, and God's messenger eventually arrived, assisted by Michael, the archangel. Answers to our prayers may be hindered by unseen obstacles. Don't expect God's answers to come too easily or too quickly. Prayer may be challenged by evil forces, so pray fervently and pray earnestly. Then expect God to answer at the right time.

10:20–21 The heavenly warfare was to be directed against Persia, and then Greece. Each of these nations was to have power over God's people. Both Persia and Greece were represented by evil angelic "princes," or demons. But God is in control of the past, present, and future.

11:2 The angelic messenger was revealing Israel's future (see

Then a fourth will gain far more riches than all *of them;* as soon as he becomes strong
through his riches, he will arouse the whole *empire* against the realm of Greece.
3"And a mighty king will arise, and he will rule with great authority and do as he pleases.
4"But as soon as he has arisen, his kingdom will be broken up and parceled out toward the four points of the compass, though not to his *own* descendants, nor according
to his authority which he wielded, for his sovereignty will be uprooted and *given* to others besides them.
5"Then the king of the South will grow strong, along with *one* of his princes who will
gain ascendancy over him and obtain dominion; his domain *will be* a great dominion
indeed.
6"After some years they will form an alliance, and the daughter of the king of the South
will come to the king of the North to carry out a peaceful arrangement. But she will not
retain her position of power, nor will he remain with his power, but she will be given up,
along with those who brought her in and the one who sired her as well as he who supported her in *those* times.
7"But one of the descendants of her line will arise in his place, and he will come against
their army and enter the fortress of the king of the North, and he will deal with them and
display *great* strength.
8"Also their gods with their metal images *and* their precious vessels of silver and gold
he will take into captivity to Egypt, and he on his part will refrain from *attacking* the king
of the North for *some* years.
9"Then the latter will enter the realm of the king of the South, but will return to his
own land.
10"His sons will mobilize and assemble a multitude of great forces; and one of them
will keep on coming and overflow and pass through, that he may again wage war up to
his *very* fortress.
11"The king of the South will be enraged and go forth and fight with the king of the
North. Then the latter will raise a great multitude, but *that* multitude will be given into
the hand of the *former.*
12"When the multitude is carried away, his heart will be lifted up, and he will cause
tens of thousands to fall; yet he will not prevail.
13"For the king of the North will again raise a greater multitude than the former, and
after an interval of some years he will press on with a great army and much equipment.
14"Now in those times many will rise up against the king of the South; the violent ones
among your people will also lift themselves up in order to fulfill the vision, but they will
fall down.
15"Then the king of the North will come, cast up a siege ramp and capture a well-fortified city; and the forces of the South will not stand *their ground,* not even their choicest
troops, for there will be no strength to make a stand.
16"But he who comes against him will do as he pleases, and no one will *be able to* withstand him; he will also stay *for a time* in the Beautiful Land, with destruction in his hand.

11:3 Dan 8:5, 21; Dan 5:19; 8:4; 11:16, 36
11:4 Dan 8:8, 22; Jer 49:36; Ezek 37:9; Dan 7:2; 8:8; Zech 2:6; Rev 7:1; Jer 12:15, 17; 18:7
11:5 Dan 11:9, 11, 14, 25, 40
11:6 Dan 11:7, 13, 15, 40
11:7 Dan 11:19, 38, 39
11:8 Is 37:19; 46:1, 2; Jer 43:12, 13
11:10 Is 8:8; Jer 46:7, 8; 51:42; Dan 11:26, 40
11:11 Dan 11:5
11:13 Dan 4:16; 12:7
11:15 Jer 6:6; Ezek 4:2; 17:17
11:16 Dan 5:19; 11:3, 36; Josh 1:5; Dan 8:9; 11:41

10:20–21). Only God can reveal future events so clearly. God's work not only deals with the sweeping panorama of history, but also focuses on the intricate details of people's lives. And his plans—whether for nations or individuals—are unshakable.

11:2 The fourth Persian king may have been Ahasuerus (486–465 B.C.), who launched an all-out effort against Greece in 480 (Esther 1:1).

11:2ff Babylonia was defeated by Medo-Persia. Medo-Persia was defeated by Greece under Alexander the Great, who conquered most of the Mediterranean and Middle Eastern lands. After Alexander's death, the empire was divided into four parts. The Ptolemies gained control of the southern section of Palestine, and the Seleucids took the northern part. Verses 1–20 show the conflict between the Ptolemies and Seleucids over control of Palestine in 300–200 B.C. Verses 21–35 describe the persecution of Israel under Antiochus IV Epiphanes. In verses 36–45 the prophecy shifts to the end times. Antiochus IV fades from view and the antichrist of the last days becomes the center of attention.

11:3 This mighty king of Greece was Alexander the Great, who conquered Medo-Persia and built a huge empire in only four years.

11:4–5 Eventually Alexander the Great's empire was divided into four nations. These four weaker nations were comprised of the following regions: (1) Egypt, (2) Babylonia and Syria, (3) Asia Minor, and (4) Macedon and Greece. The king of Egypt ("the king of the South") was Ptolemy I or perhaps a reference to the Ptolemaic dynasty in general.

11:6–7 These prophecies seem to have been fulfilled many years later in the Seleucid wars between Egypt and Syria. In 252 B.C., Ptolemy II of Egypt ("the South") gave his daughter Berenice in marriage to Antiochus II of Syria ("the North") to finalize a peace treaty between their two lands. But Berenice was murdered in Antioch by Antiochus II's former wife, Laodice. Berenice's brother, Ptolemy III, ascended the Egyptian throne and declared war against the Seleucids to avenge his sister's murder.

11:9–11 The king of Syria ("the North") was Seleucus II, and the king of Egypt ("the South") was Ptolemy IV.

11:13 This king of the North may have been Antiochus III (the Great). He defeated many Egyptian cities (11:15) and established himself in Israel ("the Beautiful Land," 11:16). He was later defeated by the Romans at Magnesia (11:18).

17 "He will set his face to come with the power of his whole kingdom, bringing with him
a proposal of peace which he will put into effect; he will also give him the daughter of
women to ruin it. But she will not take a stand *for him* or be on his side.
18 "Then he will turn his face to the coastlands and capture many. But a commander
will put a stop to his scorn against him; moreover, he will repay him for his scorn.
19 "So he will turn his face toward the fortresses of his own land, but he will stumble
and fall and be found no more.
20 "Then in his place one will arise who will send an oppressor through the [8]Jewel of *his*
kingdom; yet within a few days he will be shattered, though not in anger nor in battle.
21 "In his place a despicable person will arise, on whom the honor of kingship has not
been conferred, but he will come in a time of tranquility and seize the kingdom by intrigue.
22 "The overflowing forces will be flooded away before him and shattered, and also the
prince of the covenant.
23 "After an alliance is made with him he will practice deception, and he will go up and
gain power with a small *force of* people.
24 "In a time of tranquility he will enter the richest *parts* of the realm, and he will accomplish what his fathers never did, nor his ancestors; he will distribute plunder, booty
and possessions among them, and he will devise his schemes against strongholds, but
only for a time.
25 "He will stir up his strength and courage against the king of the South with a large
army; so the king of the South will mobilize an extremely large and mighty army for war;
but he will not stand, for schemes will be devised against him.
26 "Those who eat his choice food will destroy him, and his army will overflow, but many
will fall down slain.
27 "As for both kings, their hearts will be *intent* on evil, and they will speak lies *to each
other* at the same table; but it will not succeed, for the end is still *to come* at the appointed time.
28 "Then he will return to his land with much plunder; but his heart will be *set* against
the holy covenant, and he will take action and *then* return to his *own* land.
29 "At the appointed time he will return and come into the South, but this last time it
will not turn out the way it did before.
30 "For ships of Kittim will come against him; therefore he will be disheartened and
will return and become enraged at the holy covenant and take action; so he will come
back and show regard for those who forsake the holy covenant.
31 "Forces from him will arise, desecrate the sanctuary fortress, and do away with the
regular sacrifice. And they will set up the abomination of desolation.
32 "By smooth *words* he will turn to godlessness those who act wickedly toward the covenant, but the people who know their God will display strength and take action.
33 "Those who have insight among the people will give understanding to the many; yet
they will fall by sword and by flame, by captivity and by plunder for *many* days.

11:17 2 Kin 12:17; Ezek 4:3, 7
11:18 Gen 10:5; Is 66:19; Jer 2:10; 31:10; Zeph 2:11; Hos 12:14
11:19 Ps 27:2; Jer 46:6; Job 20:8; Ps 37:36; Ezek 26:21
11:20 Is 60:17
11:21 2 Sam 15:6
11:22 Dan 9:26; 11:10
11:24 Num 13:20; Neh 9:25; Ezek 34:14
11:25 Dan 11:5
11:26 Dan 11:10, 40
11:27 Ps 52:1; 64:6; Ps 12:2; Jer 9:3-5; 41:1-3; Dan 8:19; 11:35, 40; Hab 2:3
11:30 Gen 10:4; Num 24:24; Is 23:1, 12; Jer 2:10
11:31 Dan 8:11-13; 12:11; Dan 9:27; Matt 24:15; Mark 13:14
11:32 Dan 11:21, 34; Mic 5:7-9; Zech 9:13-16; 10:3-6
11:33 Mal 2:7; Matt 24:9; John 16:2; Heb 11:36-38

8 Lit *adornment;* i.e. probably Jerusalem and its temple

11:17 The invader, Antiochus III, tried to bring peace between Egypt and Syria by having his daughter marry Ptolemy V Epiphanes of Egypt, but the plan failed.

11:20 The successor to Antiochus III was Seleucus IV. He sent Heliodorus to collect money from the temple treasury in Jerusalem.

11:21 Seleucus IV was succeeded by his brother, Antiochus IV Epiphanes, who found favor with the Romans.

11:22 The "overflowing forces" refers to the way all opposition against Antiochus IV will be broken. The prince of the covenant may be the high priest Onias III, who was assassinated by Menelaus in 170 B.C.

11:27 These two treacherous kings were probably Antiochus IV of Syria and Ptolemy VI of Egypt. Treachery and deceit are a power broker's way to position himself over someone else. When two power brokers try to gain the upper hand, it is a mutually weakening and self-destructive process. It is also futile because God ultimately holds all power in his hands.

11:29–31 Antiochus IV would again invade "the South," but enemy ships would cause him to retreat. On his way back, he plundered Jerusalem, desecrated the temple, and stopped the Jews' daily sacrifices. The temple was desecrated when he sacrificed pigs on an altar erected in honor of Zeus. According to Jewish Law, pigs were unclean and were not to be touched or eaten. To sacrifice a pig in the temple was the worst kind of insult an enemy could level against the Jews. This happened in 168–167 B.C.

11:32 This reference to those who have violated the covenant may include Menelaus, the high priest, who was won over by Antiochus and who conspired with him against the Jews who were loyal to God. The "people who know their God" may refer to the Maccabees and their sympathizers, but a further fulfillment may lie in the future.

11:33–34 Those who are wise will teach many, but they will also face great persecution. Difficult times remind us of our weaknesses and our inability to cope. We want answers, leadership, and clear direction. During these times, God's Word begins to interest even those who would never look at it. We should be ready to use our

11:34 Matt 7:15; Acts 20:29, 30; Rom 16:18

11:35 Deut 8:16; Prov 17:3; Dan 12:10; Zech 13:9; Mal 3:2, 3; John 15:2; Rev 7:14; Dan 11:27

11:36 Dan 5:19; 11:3, 16; Is 14:13; Dan 5:20; 8:11, 25; 2 Thess 2:4; Rev 13:5, 6; Deut 10:17; Ps 136:2; Dan 2:47; Is 10:25; 26:20; Dan 8:19; Dan 9:27

11:40 Dan 11:27, 35; 12:4, 9; Dan 11:11, 25; Dan 11:7, 13, 15; Is 5:28; Jer 4:13

11:41 Dan 8:9; 11:16; Jer 48:47; Jer 49:6

11:43 2 Chr 12:3; Nah 3:9; 2 Chr 12:3; Ezek 30:4, 5; Nah 3:9

11:45 Is 11:9; 27:13; 65:25; 66:20; Dan 9:16, 20

12:1 Dan 10:13, 21; Rev 12:7; Rev 7:14; 16:18; Jer 30:7; Ezek 5:9; Dan 9:12; Matt 24:21; Mark 13:19; Dan 7:10

12:2 Is 26:19; Ezek 37:12-14; Matt 25:46; John 5:28, 29

12:3 Dan 11:33, 35; 12:10; John 5:35; Is 53:11; Dan 11:33

34 "Now when they fall they will be granted a little help, and many will join with them in
hypocrisy.
35 "Some of those who have insight will fall, in order to refine, purge and make them
pure until the end time; because *it is* still *to come* at the appointed time.
36 "Then the king will do as he pleases, and he will exalt and magnify himself above
every god and will speak monstrous things against the God of gods; and he will prosper
until the indignation is finished, for that which is decreed will be done.
37 "He will show no regard for the gods of his fathers or for the desire of women, nor
will he show regard for any *other* god; for he will magnify himself above *them* all.
38 "But instead he will honor a god of fortresses, a god whom his fathers did not know;
he will honor *him* with gold, silver, costly stones and treasures.
39 "He will take action against the strongest of fortresses with *the help of* a foreign god;
he will give great honor to those who acknowledge *him* and will cause them to rule over
the many, and will parcel out land for a price.
40 "At the end time the king of the South will collide with him, and the king of the North
will storm against him with chariots, with horsemen and with many ships; and he will
enter countries, overflow *them* and pass through.
41 "He will also enter the Beautiful Land, and many *countries* will fall; but these will be
rescued out of his hand: Edom, Moab and the foremost of the sons of Ammon.
42 "Then he will stretch out his hand against *other* countries, and the land of Egypt will
not escape.
43 "But he will gain control over the hidden treasures of gold and silver and over all the
precious things of Egypt; and Libyans and Ethiopians *will follow* at his heels.
44 "But rumors from the East and from the North will disturb him, and he will go forth
with great wrath to destroy and annihilate many.
45 "He will pitch the tents of his royal pavilion between the seas and the beautiful Holy
Mountain; yet he will come to his end, and no one will help him.

The Time of the End

12 "Now at that time Michael, the great prince who stands *guard* over the sons of your
people, will arise. And there will be a time of distress such as never occurred since
there was a nation until that time; and at that time your people, everyone who is found
written in the book, will be rescued.
2 "Many of those who sleep in the dust of the ground will awake, these to everlasting
life, but the others to disgrace *and* everlasting contempt.
3 "Those who have insight will shine brightly like the brightness of the expanse of heav-
en, and those who lead the many to righteousness, like the stars forever and ever.

---

opportunities to share God's Word in needy times. We must also be prepared to face persecution and rejection as we teach and preach.

11:35 God's messenger described a time of trial when even wise believers may stumble. This could mean (1) falling into sin, (2) being fearful and losing faith, (3) mistakenly following wrong teaching, or (4) experiencing severe suffering and martyrdom. If we persevere in our faith, any such experience will only refine us and make us stronger. Are you facing trials? Recognize them as opportunities to strengthen your faith. If we remain steadfast in these experiences, we will be stronger in our faith and closer to God.

11:36–39 These verses could refer to Antiochus IV Epiphanes, Titus (the Roman general), or the antichrist. Some of these events may have been fulfilled in the past, and some have yet to be fulfilled.

11:37 The "desire of women" may refer to Tammuz, a Babylonian fertility god. Tammuz is also mentioned in Ezekiel 8:14. In other words, this person won't recognize any deity or religions at all, not even pagan ones. Instead, he will proclaim himself to be divine and the ultimate power.

11:38 The "god of fortresses" is believed by some to be Jupiter or Zeus. The implication is that this king will make *war* his god. More than all his predecessors, he will wage war and glorify its horrors.

11:40 The antichrist of the last days becomes the center of attention from this point through the rest of the book of Daniel.

11:45 "The beautiful Holy Mountain" is Mount Zion or the city of Jerusalem.

12:1 Great suffering is in store for God's people throughout the years ahead. This way of describing the future is also used by Jeremiah (Jeremiah 30:7) and Jesus (Matthew 24:21ff). Yet the great suffering is tempered by a great promise of hope for true believers.

12:2 This is a clear reference to the resurrection of both the righteous and the wicked, although the eternal fates of each will be quite different. Up to this point in time, teaching about the resurrection was not common, although every Israelite believed that one day he or she would be included in the restoration of the new kingdom. This reference to a bodily resurrection of both the saved and the lost was a sharp departure from common belief. (See also Job 19:25, 26; Psalm 16:10; and Isaiah 26:19 for other Old Testament references to the resurrection.)

12:3 Many people try to be stars in the world of entertainment, only to find their stardom temporary. God tells us how we can be eternal "stars"—by being wise and leading many to God's righteousness. If we share our Lord with others, we can be true stars—radiantly beautiful in God's sight!

4 "But as for you, Daniel, conceal these words and seal up the book until the end of
time; many will go back and forth, and knowledge will increase."
5 Then I, Daniel, looked and behold, two others were standing, one on this bank of
the river and the other on that bank of the river.
6 And one said to the man dressed in linen, who was above the waters of the river,
"How long *will it be* until the end of *these* wonders?"
7 I heard the man dressed in linen, who was above the waters of the river, as he raised
his right hand and his left toward heaven, and swore by Him who lives forever that it
would be for a time, times, and half *a time;* and as soon as they finish shattering the power
of the holy people, all these *events* will be completed.
8 As for me, I heard but could not understand; so I said, "My lord, what *will be* the
outcome of these *events?*"
9 He said, "Go *your way,* Daniel, for *these* words are concealed and sealed up until
the end time.
10 "Many will be purged, purified and refined, but the wicked will act wickedly; and none
of the wicked will understand, but those who have insight will understand.
11 "From the time that the regular sacrifice is abolished and the abomination of desolation is set up, *there will be* 1,290 days.
12 "How blessed is he who keeps waiting and attains to the 1,335 days!
13 "But as for you, go *your way* to the end; then you will enter into rest and rise *again* for
your allotted portion at the end of the age."

12:4
Is 8:16; Rev 22:10; Is 11:9; 29:18, 19

12:6
Dan 8:16; Zech 1:12, 13; Ezek 9:2; Dan 10:5; Dan 8:13; 12:8; Matt 24:3; Mark 13:4

12:7
Ezek 20:5; Rev 10:5, 6; Dan 4:34; Rev 12:14; Dan 8:24; Luke 21:24

12:10
Zech 13:9; Is 32:6, 7; Rev 22:11; Dan 12:3; Hos 14:9; John 7:17; 8:47

12:11
Dan 9:27; 11:31; Matt 24:15; Mark 13:14

12:12
Is 30:18; Dan 8:14; Rev 11:2; 12:6; 13:5

12:13
Is 57:2; Rev 14:13; Ps 16:5

12:4 Concealing and sealing up the words of the book meant that it was to be kept safe and preserved. This was to be done so that believers of all times could look back on God's work in history and find hope. Daniel did not understand the exact meaning of the times and events in his vision. We can see events as they unfold, for we are in the end times. The whole book will not be understood until the climax of earth's history.

12:7 "Time, times, and half a time" may add up to 3 1/2 years, and may be taken as either literal or figurative.

12:7 "The power of the holy people" seems to be crushed again and again throughout history. God's recurring purpose in this is to break the pride and self-sufficiency of his rebellious people and to bring them to accept him as their Lord.

12:10 Trials and persecutions make very little sense to us when we experience them. But they can purify us if we are willing to learn from them. After you survive a difficult time, seek to learn from it so that it can help you in the future. See Romans 5:3–5 for more on God's purpose in our sufferings.

12:11 "The abomination of desolation" set up in the temple refers to the altar of Zeus, where Antiochus IV Epiphanes sacrificed a pig. Some think it will have another fulfillment in the antichrist and one of his horrible acts of evil (Matthew 24:15). However, this and the predictions at the early part of the chapter may refer specifically to Antiochus IV Epiphanes, and the rest of the prophecy may refer to the end times.

12:11–12 Either these are further calculations relating to the persecution of the Jews under Antiochus IV Epiphanes, or they refer to the end times. The abolishing of the daily sacrifices means the removal of worship of the true God, as well as oppression of believers. There is much speculation about these numbers in verses 11 and 12. The point is that this time of persecution has an end; God is in control of it, and he will be victorious over evil.

12:13 The promise of resurrection was reaffirmed to Daniel. He would one day see the fulfillment of his words, but he was not to spend the rest of his life wondering what his visions might mean. Instead, he was to rest in the comfort of God's sovereignty and look forward to the time when he would rise to receive and share eternal life with God. God does not reveal everything to us in this life. We must be content with the partial picture until he wants us to see more. He will tell us all we need to know.

12:13 Daniel stands tall in the gallery of God's remarkable servants. Born of royal heritage, yet taken into captivity when only a teenager, Daniel determined to remain faithful to God in the land of his captivity. Even at great personal cost, Daniel spent his entire lifetime advising his captors with unusual wisdom. God chose him as his servant to record some of the events of the captivity and some significant events concerning the future. As an old man, having been faithful to God throughout his years, Daniel was assured by God that he would rise from the dead and receive his portion in God's eternal kingdom. Faithfulness to God has a rich reward, not necessarily in this life, but most certainly in the life to come.

THE MESSAGE OF THE MINOR PROPHETS

The twelve books from Hosea to Malachi are called the books of the Minor Prophets. They are called "minor" because they are shorter in length—not because they have any less value or authority. Their prophecies were directed to the northern kingdom of Israel, the southern kingdom of Judah, as well as other surrounding nations. The minor prophets made a major contribution to the Bible.

Prophet	*Contemporary Kings*	*Historical Setting*	*Main Message*
Hosea	Jereboam II, Zechariah, Shallum, Menahem, Pekahiah, Pekah, Hoshea	2 Kings 14:23—18:23	The people of Israel had sinned against God. Judgment was sure to come for living in total disregard for God and fellow man.
Joel	Joash (Jehoash), Amaziah, Uzziah (Azariah)	2 Kings 11:1—15:7; 2 Chronicles 22:11—26:23	A plague of locusts had come to discipline the nation of Judah. Joel called the people to turn back to God before an even greater judgment occurred.
Amos	Uzziah (Azariah), Jeroboam II	2 Kings 14:23—15:7	Amos spoke against those who exploited or ignored the needy.
Obadiah	possibly Jehoram (Joram)	2 Kings 8:16-24; 2 Chronicles 21:1-20	God would judge Edom for its evil actions toward God's people.
Jonah	Jeroboam II	2 Kings 14:23-29	Jonah was called by God to warn those living in Nineveh that they would receive judgment if they did not repent.
Micah	Jotham, Ahaz, Hezekiah	2 Kings 15:1—20:21; 2 Chronicles 27:1—32:33	Micah predicted the fall of both Israel and Judah. This was to warn of judgment and to offer pardon to all who would repent. Israel's destruction was swift, but Hezekiah's good reign helped postpone Judah's punishment.
Nahum	Manasseh	2 Kings 21:1-18; 2 Chronicles 33:1-20	The nation of Assyria made Judah one of its vassal states. Nahum predicted that Assyria would soon tumble.
Habakkuk	Jehoiakim	2 Kings 23:36—24:7; 2 Chronicles 36:5-8	Habakkuk couldn't understand why God seemed to do nothing about the wickedness in society. He soon learned that God is still in control of the world despite the apparent triumph of evil.
Zephaniah	Josiah	2 Kings 22:1—23:30; 2 Chronicles 34:1—36:1	A day will come when God, as Judge, will severely punish all nations. But after judgment, he will show mercy to the faithful.
Haggai	Darius	Ezra 5:1—6:22	The people returned to Jerusalem to begin rebuilding the temple, but the work was halted. Haggai's message encouraged the people to finish the work.
Zechariah	Darius	Ezra 5:1—6:22	Zechariah encouraged the people to finish building the temple. He told them of a future king who would one day establish an eternal kingdom.
Malachi	Artaxerxes I	Nehemiah 13:1-31	The people had become complacent in their worship of God. They would soon be punished for their sin, but those who repented would receive God's blessing.

HOSEA

Jeroboam II becomes king of Israel 793 B.C.

Amos becomes a prophet 760

VITAL STATISTICS

PURPOSE:
To illustrate God's love for his sinful people

AUTHOR:
Hosea son of Beeri ("Hosea" means "salvation")

TO WHOM WRITTEN:
Israel (the northern kingdom) and God's people everywhere

DATE WRITTEN:
Approximately 715 B.C., recording events from about 753–715 B.C.

SETTING:
Hosea began his ministry during the end of the prosperous but morally declining reign of Jeroboam II of Israel (the upper classes were doing well, but they were oppressing the poor). He prophesied until shortly after the fall of Samaria in 722 B.C.

KEY VERSE:
"Then the LORD said to me,'Go again, love a woman who is loved by her husband, yet an adulteress, even as the LORD loves the sons of Israel, though they turn to other gods and love raisin cakes' " (3:1).

KEY PEOPLE:
Hosea, Gomer, their children

KEY PLACES:
The northern kingdom (Israel), Samaria, Ephraim

SPECIAL FEATURES:
Hosea employs many images from daily life: God is depicted as husband, father, lion, leopard, bear, dew, rain, moth, and others; Israel is pictured as wife, sick person, vine, grapes, early fruit, olive tree, woman in childbirth, oven, morning mist, chaff, and smoke, to name a few.

GROOMSMEN stand at attention as the music swells and the bride begins her long walk down the aisle, arm in arm with her father. The smiling, but nervous, husband-to-be follows every step, his eyes brimming with love. Then happy tears are shed, vows stated, and families merged. A wedding is a joyous celebration of love. It is the holy mystery of two becoming one, of beginning life together, and of commitment. Marriage is ordained by God and illustrates his relationship with his people. Thus, there is perhaps no greater tragedy than the violation of those sacred vows.

God told Hosea to find a wife and revealed to him ahead of time that she would be unfaithful to him. Although she would bear many children, some of these offspring would be fathered by others. In obedience to God, Hosea married Gomer. His relationship with her, her adultery, and their children became living, prophetic examples to Israel.

The book of Hosea is a love story—real, tragic, and true. Transcending the tale of young man and wife, it tells of God's love for his people and the response of his "bride." A covenant had been made, and God had been faithful. His love was steadfast, and his commitment unbroken. But Israel, like Gomer, was adulterous and unfaithful, spurning God's love and turning instead to false gods. Then after warning of judgment, God reaffirmed his love and offered reconciliation. His love and mercy were overflowing, but justice would be served.

The book begins with God's marriage instructions to Hosea. After Hosea's marriage, children were born, and each given a name signifying a divine message (chapter 1). Then, as predicted, Gomer left Hosea to pursue her lusts (chapter 2). But Hosea (whose name means "salvation") found her, redeemed her, and brought her home again, fully reconciled (chapter 3). Images of God's love, judgment, grace, and mercy were woven into their relationship. Next, God outlined his case against the people of Israel: Their sins would ultimately cause their destruction (chapters 4; 6; 7; 12) and would rouse his anger, resulting in punishment (chapters 5; 8—10; 12—13). But even in the midst of Israel's immorality, God was merciful and offered hope, expressing his infinite love for his people (chapter 11) and the fact that their repentance would bring about blessing (chapter 14).

The book of Hosea dramatically portrays our God's constant and persistent love. As you read this book, watch the prophet submit himself willingly to his Lord's direction; grieve with him over the unfaithfulness of his wife and his people; and hear the clear warning of judgment. Then reaffirm your commitment to being God's person, faithful in your love and true to your vows.

Hosea becomes a prophet; King Zechariah of Israel is killed 753	King Shallum of Israel is killed 752	Tiglath-pileser III invades Israel 743	Micah becomes a prophet to Judah 742	Isaiah becomes a prophet to Judah 740	Israel (northern kingdom) falls 722	Hosea's ministry ends 715

THE BLUEPRINT

A. HOSEA'S WAYWARD WIFE (1:1—3:5)

Hosea was commanded by God to marry a woman who would be unfaithful to him and would cause him many heartaches. Just as Gomer lost interest in Hosea and ran after other lovers, we, too, can easily lose appreciation for our special relationship with God and pursue dreams and goals that do not include him. When we compromise our Christian life-styles and adopt the ways of the world, we are being unfaithful.

B. GOD'S WAYWARD PEOPLE (4:1—14:9)
1. Israel's sinfulness
2. Israel's punishment
3. God's love for Israel

God wanted the people in the northern kingdom to turn from their sin and return to worshiping him alone, but they persisted in their wickedness. Throughout the book, Israel is described as ignorant of God, with no desire to please him. Israel did not understand God at all, just as Gomer did not understand Hosea. Like a loving husband or patient father, God wants people to know him and to turn to him daily.

MEGATHEMES

THEME	EXPLANATION	IMPORTANCE
The Nation's Sin	Just as Hosea's wife, Gomer, was unfaithful to him, so the nation of Israel had been unfaithful to God. Israel's idolatry was like adultery. They sought illicit relationships with Assyria and Egypt in pursuit of military might, and they mixed Baal worship with the worship of God.	Like Gomer, we can chase after other loves—love of power, pleasure, money, or recognition. The temptations in this world can be very seductive. Are we loyal to God, remaining completely faithful, or have other loves taken his rightful place?
God's Judgment	Hosea solemnly warned Judah against following Israel's example. Because Judah broke the covenant, turned away from God, and forgot her Maker, she experienced a devastating invasion and exile. Sin has terrible consequences.	Disaster surely follows ingratitude toward God and rebellion. The Lord is our only true refuge. If we harden our heart against him, there is no safety or security anywhere else. We cannot escape God's judgment.
God's Love	Just as Hosea went after his unfaithful wife to bring her back, so the Lord pursues us with his love. His love is tender, loyal, unchanging, and undying. No matter what, God still loves us.	Have you forgotten God and become disloyal to him? Don't let prosperity diminish your love for him or let success blind you to your need for his love.
Restoration	Although God will discipline his people for sin, he encourages and restores those who have repented. True repentance opens the way to a new beginning. God forgives and restores.	There is still hope for those who turn back to God. No loyalty, achievement, or honor can be compared to loving him. Turn to the Lord while the offer is still good. No matter how far you have strayed, God is willing to forgive you.

A. HOSEA'S WAYWARD WIFE (1:1—3:5)

Hosea highlights the parallels between his relationship with Gomer and God's relationship with the nation of Israel. Although Israel made a covenant with the one true God, she went after other false gods. In the same way, Hosea married Gomer, knowing ahead of time that she would leave him. Hosea tenderly dealt with his wife in spite of her sin. And God was merciful toward the people of Israel despite their sins. God has not changed; he is still merciful and forgiving.

Hosea's Wife and Children

1 The word of the LORD which came to Hosea the son of Beeri, during the days of
Uzziah, Jotham, Ahaz *and* Hezekiah, kings of Judah, and during the days of Jeroboam the son of Joash, king of Israel.
2 When the LORD first spoke through Hosea, the LORD said to Hosea, "Go, take to
yourself a wife of harlotry and *have* children of harlotry; for the land commits flagrant
harlotry, forsaking the LORD."
3 So he went and took Gomer the daughter of Diblaim, and she conceived and bore
him a son.
4 And the LORD said to him, "Name him Jezreel; for yet a little while, and I will punish the house of Jehu for the bloodshed of Jezreel, and I will put an end to the kingdom
of the house of Israel.
5 "On that day I will break the bow of Israel in the valley of Jezreel."
6 Then she conceived again and gave birth to a daughter. And the LORD said to him,
"Name her [1]Lo-ruhamah, for I will no longer have compassion on the house of Israel,
that I would ever forgive them.
7 "But I will have compassion on the house of Judah and deliver them by the LORD
their God, and will not deliver them by bow, sword, battle, horses or horsemen."
8 When she had weaned Lo-ruhamah, she conceived and gave birth to a son.
9 And the LORD said, "Name him [2]Lo-ammi, for you are not My people and I am not
your God."

1 I.e. she has not obtained compassion 2 I.e. not my people

1:1 Rom 9:25; 2 Chr 26:1-23; Is 1:1; Amos 1:1; 2 Kin 15:5, 7, 32-38; 2 Chr 27:1-9; 2 Kin 16:1-20; 2 Chr 28:1-27; Is 1:1; 7:1-17; Mic 1:1; 2 Kin 18:1-20:21; 2 Chr 29:1-32:33; Mic 1:1; 2 Kin 13:13; 14:23-29; Amos 1:1

1:2 Hos 3:1; Deut 31:16; Jer 3:1; Ezek 23:3-21; Hos 2:5; 5:3

1:3 Ezek 23:4

1:4 Hos 2:22; 2 Kin 10:11; 2 Kin 15:8-10

1:5 Jer 49:35; Ezek 39:3; Josh 17:16; Judg 6:33

1:6 Hos 2:4

1:7 2 Kin 19:29-35; Is 30:18; Jer 25:5, 6; Zech 9:9, 10; Ps 44:3-7; Zech 4:6

1:1 Hosea was a prophet to the northern kingdom of Israel. He served from 753 to 715 B.C. Under the reign of Jeroboam II, the northern kingdom had prospered materially but had decayed spiritually. The people were greedy and had adopted the moral behavior and idolatrous religion of the surrounding Canaanites.

Hosea's role was to show how the northern kingdom had been unfaithful to God, their "husband" and provider, and had married themselves to Baal and the gods of Canaan. He warned that unless they repented of their sin and turned back to God, they were headed for destruction. Hosea spoke of God's characteristics—his powerful love and fierce justice—and how their practical experience of these should affect their lives and make them return to God. Unfortunately, the people had broken their covenant with God, and they would receive the punishments God had promised (Deuteronomy 27; 28).

1:2–3 Did God really order his prophet to marry a woman who would commit adultery? Some who find it difficult to believe God could make such a request view this story as an illustration, not an historical event. Many, however, think the story is historical and give one of these explanations: (1) According to God's law, a priest could not marry a prostitute or a divorced woman (Leviticus 21:7). However, Hosea was not a priest. (2) It is possible that Gomer was not an adulterous woman when Hosea married her, and that God was letting Hosea know that Gomer would later turn to adultery and prostitution. In any case, Hosea knew ahead of time that his wife would be unfaithful and that their married life would become a living object lesson to the adulterous northern kingdom. Hosea's marriage to an unfaithful woman would illustrate God's relationship to the unfaithful nation of Israel.

1:2–3 It is difficult to imagine Hosea's feelings when God told him to marry a woman who would be unfaithful to him. He may not have wanted to do it, but he obeyed. God often required extraordinary obedience from his prophets who were facing extraordinary times. God may ask you to do something difficult and extraordinary, too. If he does, how will you respond? Will you obey him, trusting that he who knows everything has a special purpose for his request? Will you be able to accept the fact that the pain involved in obedience may benefit those you serve, and not you personally?

1:4–5 Elijah had predicted that the family of Israel's King Ahab would be destroyed because of their wickedness (1 Kings 21:20–22), but Jehu went too far in carrying out God's command (2 Kings 10:1–11). Therefore, Jehu's dynasty would also be punished—in the valley of Jezreel, the very place where he carried out the massacre of Ahab's family. God's promise to put an end to Israel as an independent kingdom ("break the bow of Israel") came true 25 years later when the Assyrians conquered the northern kingdom and carried the people into captivity.

1:6–8 In 1:3, we read that Gomer "bore him [Hosea] a son." In 1:6 and 1:8, we learn that Gomer gave birth to two more children, but there is no indication that Hosea was their natural father, and some translations imply that he was not. Whether or not the children were Hosea's, the key to this part of the story is found in the names God chose for the children, showing his reaction to Israel's unfaithfulness. God's reaction to unfaithfulness is no different today. He wants our complete devotion.

1:7 God said he would personally rescue the people of Judah from their enemies with no help from their armies or weapons. Although God asks us to do our part, we should remember that he is not limited to human effort. God often chooses to work through people, but only because it is good for *them.* He can accomplish all his purposes without any help from us if he so chooses. You are very important to God, but on your own you have neither the ability to fulfill nor the power to disrupt God's plans.

1:9 Here God was in essence dissolving the covenant (Jeremiah 7:23). The name of the third child conveys the finality of God's judgment. God's warnings recorded in Deuteronomy 28:15–68 were beginning to come true: Israel was abandoning God, and in turn, he was leaving them alone and without his blessings.

1:10 Gen 22:17; 32:12; Jer 33:22; Rom 9:26; Is 65:1; Hos 1:9; Is 63:16; 64:8; John 1:12; 1 Pet 2:10

1:11 Is 11:12; Jer 23:5, 6; 50:4, 5; Ezek 37:21-24; Jer 30:21; Hos 3:5

10 Yet the number of the sons of Israel
Will be like the sand of the sea,
Which cannot be measured or numbered;
And in the place
Where it is said to them,
"You are not My people,"
It will be said to them,
"*You are* the sons of the living God."
11 And the sons of Judah and the sons of Israel will be gathered together,
And they will appoint for themselves one leader,
And they will go up from the land,
For great will be the day of Jezreel.

Israel's Unfaithfulness Condemned

2:2 Ezek 23:45; Hos 2:5; 4:5; Is 50:1; Jer 3:1, 9, 13

2:3 Jer 13:22; Ezek 16:7, 22, 39; Ezek 16:4; Is 32:13, 14; Hos 13:15; Jer 14:3; Amos 8:11-13

2:4 Jer 13:14

2 Say to your brothers, "[3]Ammi," and to your sisters, "[4]Ruhamah."
2 "Contend with your mother, contend,
For she is not my wife, and I am not her husband;
And let her put away her harlotry from her face
And her adultery from between her breasts,
3 Or I will strip her naked
And expose her as on the day when she was born.
I will also make her like a wilderness,
Make her like desert land
And slay her with thirst.
4 "Also, I will have no compassion on her children,
Because they are children of harlotry.

3 I.e. my people **4** I.e. she has obtained compassion

HOSEA
Hosea served as a prophet to Israel (the northern kingdom) from 753–715 B.C.

Climate of the times	Israel's last six kings were especially wicked; they promoted heavy taxes, oppression of the poor, idol worship, and total disregard for God. Israel was subjected to Assyria and was forced to pay tribute, which depleted its few remaining resources.
Main message	The people of Israel had sinned against God, as an adulterous woman sins against her husband. Judgment was sure to come for living in total disregard for God and fellow humans. Israel fell to Assyria in 722 B.C.
Importance of message	When we sin, we sever our relationship with God, breaking our commitment to him. While all must answer to God for their sins, those who seek God's forgiveness are spared eternal judgment.
Contemporary prophets	Jonah (793–753 B.C.) Amos (760–750 B.C.) Micah (742–687 B.C.) Isaiah (740–681 B.C.)

1:10 The Old Testament prophetic books sometimes use the word *Israel* to refer to the people of the united kingdom (north and south) and sometimes just to the northern kingdom. In talking about past events, Hosea usually thought of Israel as the northern kingdom with its capital in Samaria. But when Hosea spoke about future events relating to God's promises of restoration, it is difficult to understand his words as applying only to the northern kingdom because the exiled northerners would become hopelessly intermingled with their conquerors. Thus most scholars see the promises of return as either: (1) conditional—the Israelites chose not to return to God, and therefore they were not entitled to the blessings included in the promises of restoration, or (2) unconditional—God's promises of restoration have been fulfilled in Jesus Christ, and therefore the church (the new Israel) receives his blessings (Romans 9:25–26; 1 Peter 2:10).

1:10–11 Although Israel was unfaithful, God's commitment remained unchanged. This promise of a future reuniting reiterated the covenant made with Moses (Deuteronomy 30:1–10) and foreshadowed the prophecies of Jeremiah (Jeremiah 29:11–14; 31:31–40) and Ezekiel (Ezekiel 11:16–21). It was a prediction of the day when all the people of God will be united under Christ. Today all believers everywhere are God's chosen people, a royal priesthood (see 1 Peter 2:9).

1:11 Just as the other children's names carried significance, so did Jezreel. In verse 4, the name depicts divine judgment; here it represents the scattering. The name means "God scatters." Here it represents the scattering a farmer does when he plants seeds. This was a sign of a new day and a new relationship between God and Israel.

2:2ff Israel's punishment and restoration are the themes of this chapter. As in a court case, the adulteress is brought to trial and found guilty. But after her punishment, she is joyfully and tenderly restored to God.

5 "For their mother has played the harlot;
She who conceived them has acted shamefully.
For she said, 'I will go after my lovers,
Who give *me* my bread and my water,
My wool and my flax, my oil and my drink.'
6 "Therefore, behold, I will hedge up her way with thorns,
And I will build a wall against her so that she cannot find her paths.
7 "She will pursue her lovers, but she will not overtake them;
And she will seek them, but will not find *them*.
Then she will say, 'I will go back to my first husband,
For it was better for me then than now!'

2:5 Is 1:21; Jer 2:25; 3:1, 2; Hos 3:1; Jer 44:17, 18; Hos 2:12; Hos 2:8

2:6 Job 19:8; Lam 3:7, 9; Hos 9:6; 10:8; Jer 18:15

2:7 Hos 5:13; Luke 15:17, 18; Jer 2:2; 3:1; Ezek 16:8; 23:4; Jer 14:22; Hos 13:6

8 "For she does not know that it was I who gave her the grain, the new wine and the oil,
And lavished on her silver and gold,
Which they used for Baal.
9 "Therefore, I will take back My grain at harvest time
And My new wine in its season.
I will also take away My wool and My flax
Given to cover her nakedness.
10 "And then I will uncover her lewdness
In the sight of her lovers,
And no one will rescue her out of My hand.
11 "I will also put an end to all her gaiety,
Her feasts, her new moons, her sabbaths
And all her festal assemblies.
12 "I will destroy her vines and fig trees,
Of which she said, 'These are my wages
Which my lovers have given me.'
And I will make them a forest,
And the beasts of the field will devour them.
13 "I will punish her for the days of the Baals
When she used to offer sacrifices to them
And adorn herself with her earrings and jewelry,
And follow her lovers, so that she forgot Me," declares the LORD.

2:8 Is 1:3; Ezek 16:19

2:9 Hos 8:7; 9:2

2:10 Ezek 16:37

2:11 Jer 7:34; 16:9; Hos 3:4; Amos 5:21; 8:10; Is 1:13, 14

2:12 Jer 5:17; 8:13; Is 5:5; 7:23; Hos 13:8

2:13 Hos 4:13; 11:2; Jer 7:9; Ezek 16:12, 17; 23:40; Hos 4:6; 8:14; 13:6

Restoration of Israel

14 "Therefore, behold, I will allure her,
Bring her into the wilderness

2:14 Ezek 20:33-38

2:5–7 The Israelites were thanking false gods (specifically Baal, the god whom they believed controlled weather and thus farming) for their food, shelter, and clothing, instead of the true God who gave those blessings. Therefore, God would block Israel's path with thorns and "build a wall against her" by making the rewards of idol worship so disappointing that the people would be persuaded to turn back to God. Despite Israel's unfaithfulness, God was still faithful and merciful. He would continue to hold his arms out to his people, even to the point of placing obstacles in their wayward path to turn them back to him.

2:7 Just as Gomer would return to her husband if she thought she would be better off with him, so people often return to God when they find life's struggle too difficult to handle. Returning to God out of desperation is better than rebelling against him, but it is better yet to turn to God out of gratitude for his care.

2:8 Material possessions are success symbols in most societies. Israel was a wealthy nation at this time, and Gomer may have accumulated silver and gold. But Gomer didn't realize that Hosea had given her all she owned, just as Israel did not recognize God as the Giver of blessings. Both Gomer and Israel used their possessions irresponsibly as they ran after other lovers and other gods. How do you use your possessions? Use what God has given you to honor him.

2:12 The Israelites were so immersed in idolatry that they actually believed pagan gods gave them their vineyards and orchards ("her vines and fig trees"). They had forgotten that the entire land was a gift from God (Deuteronomy 32:49). Today many people give credit to everything and everyone but God for their prosperity—luck, hard work, quick thinking, the right contacts. When *you* succeed, who gets the credit?

2:13 Baal was the most important of the Canaanite gods, and his name came to be used to describe all the local deities worshiped throughout the land occupied by Israel. Unfortunately, Israel did not get rid of the idols and pagan worship centers as they had been commanded. Instead, they tolerated and frequently joined Baal worshipers, often through the influence of corrupt kings. One Israelite king especially noted for his Baal worship was Ahab. The prophet Elijah, in a dramatic showdown with Ahab's hired prophets, proved God's power far superior to Baal's (1 Kings 18).

2:14–15 God was promising (1) to bring the people to the wilderness, a place free from distractions, so he could clearly communicate with them, and (2) to change what had been a time of difficulty into a day of hope. The valley of Achor ("trouble") is the

And speak kindly to her.
15 "Then I will give her her vineyards from there,
And the valley of Achor as a door of hope.
And she will sing there as in the days of her youth,
As in the day when she came up from the land of Egypt.
16 "It will come about in that day," declares the LORD,
"That you will call Me [5]Ishi
And will no longer call Me [6]Baali.
17 "For I will remove the names of the Baals from her mouth,
So that they will be mentioned by their names no more.
18 "In that day I will also make a covenant for them
With the beasts of the field,
The birds of the sky
And the creeping things of the ground.
And I will abolish the bow, the sword and war from the land,
And will make them lie down in safety.
19 "I will betroth you to Me forever;
Yes, I will betroth you to Me in righteousness and in justice,
In lovingkindness and in compassion,
20 And I will betroth you to Me in faithfulness.
Then you will know the LORD.

21 "It will come about in that day that I will respond," declares the LORD.
"I will respond to the heavens, and they will respond to the earth,

2:15 Ezek 28:25, 26; Josh 7:26; Jer 2:1-3; Ezek 16:8-14; Hos 11:1; 12:9, 13; 13:4
2:16 Is 54:5; Hos 2:7
2:17 Ex 23:13; Josh 23:7; Ps 16:4
2:18 Job 5:23; Is 11:6-9; Ezek 34:25; Is 2:4; Ezek 39:1-10; Lev 26:5; Jer 23:6; Ezek 34:25
2:19 Is 62:4, 5; Is 1:27; 54:6-8
2:20 Jer 31:33, 34; Hos 6:6; 13:4
2:21 Is 55:10; Zech 8:12; Mal 3:10, 11

5 I.e. my husband **6** I.e. my master, or my Baal

SPIRITUAL UNFAITHFULNESS
Spiritual adultery and physical adultery are alike in many ways, and both are dangerous. God was disappointed with his people because they had committed spiritual adultery against him, as Gomer had committed physical adultery against Hosea.

Parallels	*The danger*
Both spiritual and physical adultery are against God's Law.	When we break God's Law in full awareness of what we're doing, our hearts become hardened to the sin and our relationship with God is broken.
Both spiritual and physical adultery begin with disappointment and dissatisfaction—either real or imagined—with an already existing relationship.	The feeling that God disappoints can lead you away from him. Feelings of disappointment and dissatisfaction are normal and, when endured, will pass.
Both spiritual and physical adultery begin with diverting affection from one object of devotion to another.	The diverting of our affection is the first step in the blinding process that leads into sin.
Both spiritual and physical adultery involve a process of deterioration; it is not usually an impulsive decision.	The process is dangerous because you don't always realize it is happening until it is too late.
Both spiritual and physical adultery involve the creation of a fantasy about what a new object of love can do for you.	Such fantasy creates unrealistic expectations of what a new relationship can do and only leads to disappointment in all existing and future relationships.

site where Achan had sinned by keeping forbidden war plunder (see Joshua 7). He had brought great disaster to Joshua's troops when they were attempting to conquer the land. God uses even our negative experiences to create opportunities to turn back to him. As you face problems and trials, remember that God speaks to you in the wilderness, and not just in times of prosperity.

2:16 Not until Judah's exile would the entire nation begin to come to its senses, give up its idols, and turn back to God; and not until that day when God rules through Jesus the Messiah will the relationship between God and his people be restored. In that day, God will no longer be like a master to them; he will be like a husband (Isaiah 54:4–8). The relationship will be deep and personal, the kind of relationship we can know, though imperfectly, in marriage.

2:19–20 The time will come when unfaithfulness will be impossible—God will bind us to himself in his perfect righteousness, justice, love, compassion, and faithfulness. Betrothal in Hosea's time was more than a simple agreement to marry. It was a binding engagement, a deep commitment between two families for a future, permanent relationship. God was promising a fresh new beginning, not just a temporary rewriting of a tired old agreement. (See Jeremiah 31:31–34.)

2:19–20 God's wedding gift to his people, both in Hosea's day and in our own, is his compassion. Through no merit of our own, God forgives us and makes us right with him. There is no way for us by our own efforts to reach God's high standard for moral and spiritual life, but he graciously accepts us, forgives us, and draws us into a relationship with himself. In that relationship we have personal and intimate communion with him.

22 And the earth will respond to the grain, to the new wine and to the oil,
And they will respond to [7]Jezreel.
23 "I will sow her for Myself in the land.
I will also have compassion on her who had not obtained compassion,
And I will say to those who were not My people,
'You are My people!'
And they will say, '*You are* my God!' "

2:22 Jer 31:12; Joel 2:19

2:23 Jer 31:27; Hos 1:6; Rom 9:25; 1 Pet 2:10; Hos 1:9

Hosea's Second Symbolic Marriage

3 Then the LORD said to me, "Go again, love a woman *who* is loved by *her* husband,
yet an adulteress, even as the LORD loves the sons of Israel, though they turn to other
gods and love raisin cakes."
2 So I bought her for myself for fifteen *shekels* of silver and a homer and a half of
barley.
3 Then I said to her, "You shall stay with me for many days. You shall not play the
harlot, nor shall you have a man; so I will also be toward you."
4 For the sons of Israel will remain for many days without king or prince, without
sacrifice or *sacred* pillar and without ephod or household idols.
5 Afterward the sons of Israel will return and seek the LORD their God and David
their king; and they will come trembling to the LORD and to His goodness in the last
days.

3:1 Jer 3:20; 2 Sam 6:19; 1 Chr 16:3; Song 2:5

3:2 Ruth 4:10

3:3 Deut 21:13

3:4 Hos 10:3; 13:10, 11; Dan 9:27; 11:31; 12:11; Hos 2:11; Hos 10:1, 2; Ex 28:4-12; 1 Sam 23:9-12; Gen 31:19, 34; Judg 17:5; 18:14, 17; 1 Sam 15:23

3:5 Jer 50:4, 5; Jer 30:9; Ezek 34:24; Is 2:2, 3; Jer 31:9

B. GOD'S WAYWARD PEOPLE (4:1—14:9)

The rest of the book deals with Israel's sin and her impending judgment. Hosea points out the moral and spiritual decay of the nation. He describes the punishment awaiting the people and pleads with them to return to God. Although judgment and condemnation of sin are prevalent in the book, a strand of love and restoration runs throughout. Even in the midst of judgment, God is merciful and will restore those who repent and turn to him.

1. Israel's sinfulness

God's Controversy with Israel

4 Listen to the word of the LORD, O sons of Israel,
For the LORD has a case against the inhabitants of the land,
Because there is no faithfulness or kindness
Or knowledge of God in the land.

4:1 Hos 5:1; Hos 12:2; Mic 6:2; Is 59:4; Jer 7:28; Jer 4:22

7 I.e. God sows

3:1 This short chapter pictures the nation's exile and return. Israel would experience a time of purification in a foreign land, but God would still love the people and would be willing to accept them back. God commanded Hosea to show the same forgiving spirit to Gomer. Although Hosea had good reason to divorce Gomer, he was told to buy her back and love her.

3:2 Apparently Gomer was on her own for a while. Needing to support herself, she must have either sold herself into slavery or become the mistress of another man. In either case, Hosea had to pay to get her back—although the required amount was pitifully small. Gomer was no longer worth much to anyone except Hosea, but he loved her just as God loved Israel. No matter how low we sink, God is willing to buy us back—to redeem us—and to lift us up again.

3:3 After this, Gomer is no longer mentioned by Hosea. This is explained in 3:4. Gomer's isolation showed how God would deal with the northern kingdom (5:6, 15). It is dangerous to rebel against God. If he were ever to withdraw his love and mercy, we would be without hope.

3:4 God would separate the Israelites from their treasured idolatrous practices. Sacrifices and sacred pillars were elements of idol worship. Here the ephod is not the official vest of the priest, but an image used in idol worship; household idols were strictly forbidden for God's people.

3:4–5 The northern kingdom had rebelled against David's dynasty and had taken Jeroboam as their king (1 Kings 12; 13). Their rebellion was both political and religious. At that time, they reverted back to the worship of golden idols. "David their king" refers to the time of Messiah's rule when all people will bow before him in humility and submission. Those who won't accept Christ's blessings now will face his power and judgment later. How much better it is to love and follow Christ now than face his angry judgment later.

4:1ff In this chapter, God brings a charge of disobedience against Israel. The religious leaders had failed to turn the people to God, and ritual prostitution had replaced right worship. The nation had declined spiritually and morally, breaking the laws that God had given them. The people found it easy to condemn Hosea's wife for her adultery. They were not so quick to see that *they* had been unfaithful to God.

4:1–3 God explained the reasons for Israel's suffering. Their lawless behavior had brought the twin judgments of increased violence and ecological crisis. There is not always a direct cause-and-effect relationship between our actions and the problems we face. Nevertheless, when we are surrounded with difficulties, we should seriously ask, "Have I done anything sinful or irresponsible that has caused my suffering?" If we discover that we are at fault, even partially, we must change our ways before God will help us.

4:2
Deut 5:11; Hos 10:4; Hos 7:3; 10:13; 11:12; Gen 4:8; Hos 6:9; Deut 5:19; Hos 7:1; Deut 5:18; Hos 7:4; Hos 6:8; 12:14

4:3
Is 24:4; 33:9; Amos 5:16; Zeph 1:3

4:4
Ezek 3:26; Amos 5:10, 13; Deut 17:12

4:5
Ezek 14:3, 7; Hos 5:5; Jer 15:8; Hos 2:2, 5

4:6
Is 5:13; Hos 4:14; Mal 2:7, 8; Zech 11:8, 9, 15-17; Hos 2:13; 8:14; 13:6; Hos 8:1, 12

4:7
Hos 10:1; 13:6; Hab 2:16

4:8
Hos 10:13; Is 56:11; Mic 3:11

4:9
Is 24:2; Jer 5:31; Hos 8:13; 9:9

4:10
Lev 26:26; Is 65:13; Mic 6:14; Hos 7:4; Hos 9:17

4:11
Prov 20:1; Is 5:12; 28:7

4:12
Is 44:19; Jer 2:27

4:13
Jer 3:6; Hos 2:13; 11:2; Is 1:29; Jer 2:20

2 *There is* swearing, deception, murder, stealing and adultery.
They employ violence, so that bloodshed follows bloodshed.
3 Therefore the land mourns,
And everyone who lives in it languishes
Along with the beasts of the field and the birds of the sky,
And also the fish of the sea disappear.

4 Yet let no one find fault, and let none offer reproof;
For your people are like those who contend with the priest.
5 So you will stumble by day,
And the prophet also will stumble with you by night;
And I will destroy your mother.
6 My people are destroyed for lack of knowledge.
Because you have rejected knowledge,
I also will reject you from being My priest.
Since you have forgotten the law of your God,
I also will forget your children.

7 The more they multiplied, the more they sinned against Me;
I will change their glory into shame.
8 They feed on the sin of My people
And direct their desire toward their iniquity.
9 And it will be, like people, like priest;
So I will punish them for their ways
And repay them for their deeds.
10 They will eat, but not have enough;
They will play the harlot, but not increase,
Because they have stopped giving heed to the LORD.

11 Harlotry, wine and new wine take away the understanding.
12 My people consult their wooden idol, and their *diviner's* wand informs them;
For a spirit of harlotry has led *them* astray,
And they have played the harlot, *departing* from their God.
13 They offer sacrifices on the tops of the mountains
And burn incense on the hills,
Under oak, poplar and terebinth,
Because their shade is pleasant.
Therefore your daughters play the harlot

4:2 This verse may allude to the assassinations of kings during Hosea's lifetime. Shallum killed Zechariah (the king, not the prophet) and took the throne. Then Menahem killed Shallum and destroyed an entire city because it refused to accept him as king (2 Kings 15:8–16). God pointed out that even murder was being taken casually in Israel.

4:4–9 Hosea leveled his charges against the religious leaders. Who were these religious leaders? When Jeroboam I rebelled against Solomon's son Rehoboam and set up a rival kingdom in the north, he also set up his own religious system (see 1 Kings 12:25–33). In violation of God's Law, he made two golden calves and told the people to worship them. He also appointed his own priests, who were not descendants of Aaron. At first the residents of the northern kingdom continued to worship God, even though they were doing it in the wrong way, but very soon they also began to worship Canaanite gods. Before long they had substituted Baal for God and no longer worshiped God at all. It is not surprising that Jeroboam's false priests were unable to preserve the true worship of God.

4:6–9 God accused the religious leaders of keeping the people from knowing him ("destroyed for lack of knowledge"). They were supposed to be spiritual leaders, but they had become leaders in wrongdoing. The people may have said to one another, "It must be OK if the priests do it." Spiritual leadership is a heavy responsibility. Whether you teach a church school class, hold a church office, or lead a Bible study, don't take your leadership responsibilities lightly. Be a leader who leads others to God.

4:8 The priests relished the people's sins. Every time a person brought a sin offering, the priest received a portion of it. The more the people sinned, the more the priests received. Because they couldn't eat all of the offerings themselves, they sold some and gave some to their relatives. The priests profited from the continuation of sin; it gave them power and position in the community. So instead of trying to lead the people out of sin, they encouraged sin to increase their profits.

4:10–12 The chief Canaanite gods, Baal and Asherah, represented the power of fertility and sexual reproduction. Not surprisingly, their worship included rituals with vile sexual practices. Male worshipers had sex with female temple prostitutes, or priestesses, and young women wishing to bear children had sex with male priests. But God said their efforts to increase fertility would not succeed.

4:12 The "diviner's wand" was a way of attempting to tell the future. By divorcing themselves from God's authoritative religion centered in Jerusalem, inhabitants of the northern kingdom had effectively cut themselves off from God's word and from his way of forgiveness. The drive to be free from all restrictions can move us completely out of God's will.

And your brides commit adultery.
14 I will not punish your daughters when they play the harlot
Or your brides when they commit adultery,
For *the men* themselves go apart with harlots
And offer sacrifices with temple prostitutes;
So the people without understanding are ruined.

4:14 Deut 23:17

15 Though you, Israel, play the harlot,
Do not let Judah become guilty;
Also do not go to Gilgal,
Or go up to Beth-aven
And take the oath:
"As the LORD lives!"
16 Since Israel is stubborn
Like a stubborn heifer,
Can the LORD now pasture them
Like a lamb in a large field?
17 Ephraim is joined to idols;
Let him alone.
18 Their liquor gone,
They play the harlot continually;
Their rulers dearly love shame.
19 The wind wraps them in its wings,
And they will be ashamed because of their sacrifices.

4:15 Hos 9:15; 12:11; Jer 5:2; 44:26; Amos 8:14

4:16 Ps 78:8; Is 5:17; 7:25

4:17 Hos 13:2; Ps 81:12; Hos 4:4

4:18 Mic 3:11

4:19 Hos 12:1; 13:15

The People's Apostasy Rebuked

5 Hear this, O priests!
Give heed, O house of Israel!
Listen, O house of the king!
For the judgment applies to you,
For you have been a snare at Mizpah
And a net spread out on Tabor.
2 The revolters have gone deep in depravity,
But I will chastise all of them.
3 I know Ephraim, and Israel is not hidden from Me;
For now, O Ephraim, you have played the harlot,
Israel has defiled itself.
4 Their deeds will not allow them
To return to their God.
For a spirit of harlotry is within them,
And they do not know the LORD.
5 Moreover, the pride of Israel testifies against him,
And Israel and Ephraim stumble in their iniquity;
Judah also has stumbled with them.
6 They will go with their flocks and herds
To seek the LORD, but they will not find *Him;*
He has withdrawn from them.

5:1 Hos 9:8

5:2 Hos 9:15; Is 29:15; Hos 4:2; 6:9

5:3 Amos 3:2; 5:12

5:4 Hos 4:12; Hos 4:6, 14

5:5 Hos 7:10; Ezek 23:31-35

5:6 Hos 8:13; Mic 6:6, 7; Prov 1:28; Is 1:15; Jer 14:12; Ezek 8:6

4:15 God sent a warning to the southern kingdom of Judah that its priests should not become like those in Israel. Israel's priests who remained in the north had forgotten their spiritual heritage and had sold out to Baal. They were promoting idol worship and ritual prostitution. Israel would not escape punishment, but Judah could if it refused to follow Israel's example.

4:17 Ephraim is another name for Israel, the northern kingdom, because Ephraim was the most powerful of the ten tribes in the north. In the same way, the southern kingdom was called Judah after its most powerful tribe.

4:19 The wind that would sweep Israel away referred to the Assyrian invasion that would destroy the nation about 20 years later.

5:1–2 Mizpah and Tabor may have been sites prominent in the false worship of Baal. The leaders likely even encouraged the people to sin at these places. With both their civil and religious leaders hopelessly corrupt, the people of Israel did not have much of a chance. They looked to their leaders for guidance, and they should have found it. Today we can often choose our own leaders, but we still need to be aware of whether they are taking us toward or away from God. God held the people responsible for what they did. Similarly, God holds us responsible for our actions and choices.

5:4 Persistent sin hardens a person's heart, making it difficult to repent. Deliberately choosing to disobey God can sear the conscience; each sin makes the next one easier to commit. Don't allow sin to groove a hard path deep within you. Steer as far away from sinful practices as possible.

7 They have dealt treacherously against the LORD,
For they have borne illegitimate children.
Now the new moon will devour them with their land.

8 Blow the horn in Gibeah,
The trumpet in Ramah.
Sound an alarm at Beth-aven:
"Behind you, Benjamin!"
9 Ephraim will become a desolation in the day of rebuke;
Among the tribes of Israel I declare what is sure.
10 The princes of Judah have become like those who move a boundary;
On them I will pour out My wrath like water.
11 Ephraim is oppressed, crushed in judgment,
Because he was determined to follow *man's* command.
12 Therefore I am like a moth to Ephraim
And like rottenness to the house of Judah.
13 When Ephraim saw his sickness,
And Judah his wound,
Then Ephraim went to Assyria
And sent to King Jareb.
But he is unable to heal you,
Or to cure you of your wound.
14 For I *will be* like a lion to Ephraim
And like a young lion to the house of Judah.
I, even I, will tear to pieces and go away,
I will carry away, and there will be none to deliver.
15 I will go away *and* return to My place
Until they acknowledge their guilt and seek My face;
In their affliction they will earnestly seek Me.

2. Israel's punishment

The Response to God's Rebuke

6 "Come, let us return to the LORD.
For He has torn *us,* but He will heal us;
He has wounded *us,* but He will bandage us.
2 "He will revive us after two days;
He will raise us up on the third day,
That we may live before Him.
3 "So let us know, let us press on to know the LORD.
His going forth is as certain as the dawn;
And He will come to us like the rain,
Like the spring rain watering the earth."

4 What shall I do with you, O Ephraim?
What shall I do with you, O Judah?

5:7 Is 48:8; Jer 3:20; Hos 6:7; Hos 2:4; Is 1:14; Hos 2:11
5:8 Joel 2:1; Hos 9:9; 10:9; Judg 5:14
5:9 Is 28:1-4; Hos 9:11-17; Is 37:3; Is 46:10; Zech 1:6
5:10 Deut 19:14; 27:17; Ezek 7:8; Ps 32:6; 93:3, 4
5:11 Deut 28:33; Mic 6:16
5:12 Ps 39:11; Is 51:8
5:13 Hos 7:11; 8:9; 12:1; Hos 10:6; Jer 30:12-15
5:14 Ps 7:2; Hos 13:7, 8; Amos 3:4; Ps 50:22; Mic 5:8
5:15 Is 64:7-9; Jer 3:13, 14; Ps 50:15; 78:34; Jer 2:27; Hos 3:5
6:1 Jer 50:4, 5; Deut 32:39; Hos 5:14; Jer 30:17; Hos 14:4; Is 30:26
6:2 Ps 30:5; 1 Cor 15:4
6:3 Is 2:3; Mic 4:2; Ps 19:6; Mic 5:2; Job 29:23; Ps 72:6; Joel 2:23
6:4 Hos 7:1; 11:8; Ps 78:34-37; Hos 13:3

5:8 Gibeah and Ramah were Israelite cities near Jerusalem. Hosea prophesied that these cities would sound the alarm of the coming judgment.

5:10 Those who "move a boundary" are guilty of a serious crime (Deuteronomy 27:17). Hosea was saying that the leaders of Judah were like those who cheat people by moving the boundary stones on their land (see Deuteronomy 19:14).

5:13 During the reigns of Menahem and Hoshea, Israel turned to Assyria for help (2 Kings 15:19–20; 17:3–4). But even the great world powers of that time could not help Israel, for God himself had determined to judge the nation. If we neglect God's call to repentance, how can we escape? (See Hebrews 2:3.)

6:1–3 This is presumption, not genuine repentance. The people did not understand the depth of their sins. They did not turn from idols, regret their sins, or pledge to make changes. They thought that God's wrath would last only a few days; little did they know that their nation would soon be taken into exile. Israel was interested in God only for the material benefits he provided; they did not value the eternal benefits that come from worshiping him. Before judging Israel, however, consider your attitude. What do you hope to gain from your religion? Do you "repent" easily, without seriously considering what changes need to take place in your life?

6:4 God answered his people, pointing out that their profession of loyalty, like clouds and dew, evaporated easily and had no substance. Many find it easy and comfortable to maintain the appearance of being committed without deep and sincere loyalty. If you profess loyalty to God, back it up with your actions.

For your loyalty is like a morning cloud
And like the dew which goes away early.
5 Therefore I have hewn *them* in pieces by the prophets;
I have slain them by the words of My mouth;
And the judgments on you are *like* the light that goes forth.
6 For I delight in loyalty rather than sacrifice,
And in the knowledge of God rather than burnt offerings.
7 But like Adam they have transgressed the covenant;
There they have dealt treacherously against Me.
8 Gilead is a city of wrongdoers,
Tracked with bloody *footprints.*
9 And as raiders wait for a man,
So a band of priests murder on the way to Shechem;
Surely they have committed crime.
10 In the house of Israel I have seen a horrible thing;
Ephraim's harlotry is there, Israel has defiled itself.
11 Also, O Judah, there is a harvest appointed for you,
When I restore the fortunes of My people.

6:5 1 Sam 15:32, 33; Jer 1:10; 5:14; Jer 23:29

6:6 Matt 9:13; 12:7; Is 1:11

6:7 Job 31:33; Hos 8:1; Hos 5:7

6:8 Hos 12:11; Hos 4:2

6:9 Hos 7:1; Jer 7:9, 10; Hos 4:2; Ezek 22:9; 23:27; Hos 2:10

6:10 Jer 5:30, 31; 23:14; Hos 5:3

6:11 Jer 51:33; Joel 3:13; Zeph 2:7

Ephraim's Iniquity

7 When I would heal Israel,
The iniquity of Ephraim is uncovered,
And the evil deeds of Samaria,
For they deal falsely;
The thief enters in,
Bandits raid outside,
2 And they do not consider in their hearts
That I remember all their wickedness.
Now their deeds are all around them;
They are before My face.
3 With their wickedness they make the king glad,
And the princes with their lies.
4 They are all adulterers,
Like an oven heated by the baker
Who ceases to stir up *the fire*
From the kneading of the dough until it is leavened.
5 On the day of our king, the princes became sick with the heat of wine;
He stretched out his hand with scoffers,
6 For their hearts are like an oven
As they approach their plotting;
Their anger smolders all night,
In the morning it burns like a flaming fire.

7:1 Ezek 24:13; Hos 6:4; 7:13; 11:8; Hos 4:2; Hos 6:9

7:2 Ps 25:7; Jer 14:10; 17:1; Hos 8:13; 9:9; Amos 8:7; Jer 2:19; 4:18; Hos 4:9

7:3 Rom 1:32; Jer 28:1-4; Hos 7:5; Mic 7:3; Hos 4:2; 11:12

7:4 Jer 9:2; 23:10

7:5 Is 28:1, 7; Is 28:14

7:6 Ps 21:9

6:6 Religious rituals can help people understand God and nourish their relationship with him. That is why God instituted circumcision and the sacrificial system in the Old Testament and baptism and the Lord's Supper in the New Testament. But a religious ritual is helpful only if it is carried out with an attitude of love for and obedience to God. If a person's heart is far from God, ritual will become empty mockery. God didn't want the Israelites' rituals; he wanted their hearts. Why do you worship? What is the motive behind your "offerings" and "sacrifices"?

6:7 One of Hosea's key themes is that Israel had broken the covenant God had made with them at Mount Sinai (Exodus 19; 20). God wanted to make Israel a blessing and a light to all the nations (Genesis 12:2, 3; Isaiah 49:6), and if God's chosen people obeyed him and proclaimed him to the world he would give them special blessings. If they broke the covenant, however, they would suffer severe penalties, as they should have known (see Deuteronomy 28:15–68). Sadly, the people broke the agreement and proved themselves unfaithful to God. How about you? Have you also broken faith with God? What about your forgotten promises to serve him?

6:8–9 Gilead was once a sacred place, but here it was corrupt. Shechem was once a city of refuge designated by Joshua (Joshua 20:1–2, 7–8); Gilead was a region that included Ramoth, also a city of refuge. At this time these areas were associated with murder and crime, with bands of evil priests lying in wait to murder travelers passing through the territory.

6:11 So that Judah would not become proud as they saw the northern kingdom's destruction, Hosea interjected a solemn warning about God's "harvest." God's temple was in Judah (Jerusalem), and the people thought that what happened in Israel could never happen to them. But when they had become utterly corrupt, they too were led off into captivity (see 2 Kings 25).

7:1–2 God sees and knows everything. Like Israel, we often forget this. Thoughts like "No one will ever know," or "No one is watching" may tempt us to try to get away with sin. If you are facing difficult temptations, you will be less likely to give in if you remind yourself that God is watching. When faced with the opportunity to sin, remember that God sees everything.

7:7 Hos 13:10; Is 64:7

7:8 Ps 106:35

7:9 Is 1:7; Hos 8:7; Hos 4:6

7:10 Hos 5:5; Is 9:13

7:11 Hos 11:11; Hos 4:6, 11, 14; 5:4; Hos 8:13; 9:3, 6; Hos 5:13; 8:9; 12:1

7:12 Ezek 12:13; Lev 26:14-39; Deut 28:15

7:13 Hos 9:12; Jer 14:10; Ezek 34:6; Hos 9:17; Jer 51:9; Hos 7:1; Matt 23:37

7:14 Job 35:9-11; Hos 8:2; Zech 7:5; Judg 9:27; Amos 2:8; Mic 2:11; Hos 13:16

7:15 Nah 1:9

7:16 Ps 78:57; Ps 12:3, 4; 17:10; 73:9; Dan 7:25; Mal 3:13, 14; Ezek 23:32; Hos 9:3, 6

7 All of them are hot like an oven,
And they consume their rulers;
All their kings have fallen.
None of them calls on Me.

8 Ephraim mixes himself with the nations;
Ephraim has become a cake not turned.
9 Strangers devour his strength,
Yet he does not know *it;*
Gray hairs also are sprinkled on him,
Yet he does not know *it.*
10 Though the pride of Israel testifies against him,
Yet they have not returned to the LORD their God,
Nor have they sought Him, for all this.
11 So Ephraim has become like a silly dove, without sense;
They call to Egypt, they go to Assyria.
12 When they go, I will spread My net over them;
I will bring them down like the birds of the sky.
I will chastise them in accordance with the proclamation to their assembly.
13 Woe to them, for they have strayed from Me!
Destruction is theirs, for they have rebelled against Me!
I would redeem them, but they speak lies against Me.
14 And they do not cry to Me from their heart
When they wail on their beds;
For the sake of grain and new wine they assemble themselves,
They turn away from Me.
15 Although I trained *and* strengthened their arms,
Yet they devise evil against Me.
16 They turn, *but* not upward,
They are like a deceitful bow;
Their princes will fall by the sword

OBEDIENCE VERSUS SACRIFICES
God says many times that he doesn't want our gifts and sacrifices when we give them out of ritual or hypocrisy. God wants us first to love and obey him.

1 Samuel 15:22–23	Obedience is far better than sacrifice.
Psalm 40:6–8	God doesn't want burnt offerings; he wants our lifelong service.
Psalm 51:16–19	God isn't interested in penance; he wants a broken and contrite heart.
Jeremiah 7:21–23	It isn't sacrifices God wants; he desires our obedience and promises that he will be our God and we will be his people.
Hosea 6:6	God doesn't want sacrifices; he wants our loving loyalty. He doesn't want offerings; he wants us to acknowledge him.
Amos 5:21–24	God hates pretense and hypocrisy; he wants to see justice roll on like a river.
Micah 6:6–8	God is not satisfied with offerings; he wants us to be fair and just and merciful, and to walk humbly with him.
Matthew 9:13	God doesn't want sacrifices; he wants us to be merciful.

7:7 "Hot like an oven" refers to the lust for power and intrigue that was burning in these leaders' hearts. Three Israelite kings were assassinated during Hosea's lifetime—Zechariah, Shallum, and Pekahiah (2 Kings 15:8–26). The kings' foreign relations and domestic lives were ruined because they ignored God and his word.

7:8 The people of Israel had intermarried with foreign people and had picked up their evil ways. When we spend a lot of time with people, we can easily pick up their attitudes and begin to imitate their actions. When you work, live, or play with unbelievers, beware of the influence they may have on you. Instead of drifting into bad habits, see if you can have a positive influence and point these people to God.

7:10 Pride keeps a person from returning to God because arrogance acknowledges no need of help from anyone, human or divine. Pride intensifies all our other sins because we cannot repent of any of them without first giving up our pride.

7:11 Israel's King Menahem had paid Assyria to support him in power (2 Kings 15:19–20); King Hoshea turned against Assyria and went to Egypt for help (2 Kings 17:4). Israel's kings went back and forth, allying themselves with different nations when they should have allied themselves with God.

7:16 A deceitful bow is unreliable. Its arrows miss the target, and its owner would be quite vulnerable in battle. Life without God is as unreliable as a faulty bow. Without God's direction, our thoughts are filled with lust, cheating, selfishness, and deceit. As long as we are warped by sin, we will never reach our true potential.

Because of the insolence of their tongue.
This *will be* their derision in the land of Egypt.

Israel Reaps the Whirlwind

8 *Put* the trumpet to your lips!
Like an eagle *the enemy comes* against the house of the LORD,
Because they have transgressed My covenant
And rebelled against My law.
2 They cry out to Me,
"My God, we of Israel know You!"
3 Israel has rejected the good;
The enemy will pursue him.
4 They have set up kings, but not by Me;
They have appointed princes, but I did not know *it.*
With their silver and gold they have made idols for themselves,
That they might be cut off.
5 He has rejected your calf, O Samaria, *saying,*
"My anger burns against them!"
How long will they be incapable of innocence?
6 For from Israel is even this!
A craftsman made it, so it is not God;
Surely the calf of Samaria will be broken to pieces.
7 For they sow the wind
And they reap the whirlwind.
The standing grain has no heads;
It yields no grain.
Should it yield, strangers would swallow it up.

8 Israel is swallowed up;
They are now among the nations
Like a vessel in which no one delights.
9 For they have gone up to Assyria,
Like a wild donkey all alone;
Ephraim has hired lovers.
10 Even though they hire *allies* among the nations,
Now I will gather them up;
And they will begin to diminish
Because of the burden of the king of princes.

11 Since Ephraim has multiplied altars for sin,
They have become altars of sinning for him.
12 Though I wrote for him ten thousand *precepts* of My law,

8:1 Jer 4:13; Hos 5:8; Hab 1:8; Deut 28:49; Hos 6:7; Hos 4:6

8:2 Ps 78:34; Hos 7:14; Titus 1:16

8:4 2 Kin 15:13, 17, 25; Hos 13:10, 11; Hos 2:8; 13:1, 2

8:5 Hos 10:5; 13:2; Ps 19:13; Jer 13:27

8:6 Hos 13:2

8:7 Prov 22:8; Is 66:15; Nah 1:3; Hos 2:9

8:8 2 Kin 17:6; Jer 51:34; Jer 22:28; 25:34

8:9 Hos 7:11; Jer 2:24; Ezek 16:33, 34

8:10 Ezek 16:37; 22:20; Jer 42:2; Is 10:8

8:11 Hos 10:1

8:12 Deut 4:6, 8; Hos 4:6

7:16 People look everywhere except to God for happiness and fulfillment, pursuing possessions, activities, and relationships. In reality, only God can truly satisfy the deep longings of the soul. Look first to heaven, to the Most High God. He will meet your *spiritual* needs, not all your materialistic wants.

8:1–4 "An eagle . . . against the house of the LORD" referred to Assyria coming to attack Israel and take the people into captivity (2 Kings 15:28–29). The people would call to God, but it would be too late because they had stubbornly refused to give up their idols. We, like Israel, often call on God to ease our pain without wanting him to change our behavior. And we, like Israel, may repent after it is too late to avoid the painful consequences of sin.

8:5 Samaria was the capital of the northern kingdom, and sometimes it stands for the whole kingdom of Israel. Jeroboam I had set up worship of calf-idols at Bethel and Dan and had encouraged the people to worship them (1 Kings 12:25–33). Thus the people were worshiping the image of a created animal rather than the Creator.

8:7 Crop yield is the result of good seed planted in good soil, and, given the proper proportions of sunlight, moisture, and fertilizer, a single seed can produce multiple fruit in good conditions. Israel, however, had sown its spiritual seed to the wind—it had invested itself in activities without substance. Like the wind that comes and goes, its idolatry and foreign alliances offered no protection. In seeking self-preservation apart from God, it had brought about its own destruction. Like a forceful whirlwind, God's judgment would come upon Israel by means of the Assyrians. When we seek security in anything except God, we expose ourselves to great danger. Without God there is no lasting security.

8:11 The altars that were supposed to remove sin were actually increasing sin through their misuse in worshiping Baal.

8:12 Though the laws were written for *them,* Israel considered them as "strange." It is easy to listen to a sermon and think of all the people we know who should be listening, or to read the Bible and think of those who should do what the passage teaches. The Israelites did this constantly, applying God's laws to others but not to themselves. This is just another way to deflect God's will and avoid making needed changes. As you think of others who need to

They are regarded as a strange thing.
13 As for My sacrificial gifts,
They sacrifice the flesh and eat *it,*
But the LORD has taken no delight in them.
Now He will remember their iniquity,
And punish *them* for their sins;
They will return to Egypt.
14 For Israel has forgotten his Maker and built palaces;
And Judah has multiplied fortified cities,
But I will send a fire on its cities that it may consume its palatial dwellings.

8:13 Hos 5:6; Jer 6:20; 7:21; Jer 14:10; Hos 7:2; Luke 12:2; 1 Cor 4:5; Hos 4:9; 9:7; Hos 9:3, 6

8:14 Deut 32:18; Hos 2:13; 4:6; 13:6; Is 9:9, 10; Jer 17:27

Ephraim Punished

9 Do not rejoice, O Israel, with exultation like the nations!
For you have played the harlot, forsaking your God.
You have loved *harlots'* earnings on every threshing floor.
2 Threshing floor and wine press will not feed them,
And the new wine will fail them.
3 They will not remain in the LORD'S land,
But Ephraim will return to Egypt,
And in Assyria they will eat unclean *food.*
4 They will not pour out drink offerings of wine to the LORD,
Their sacrifices will not please Him.
Their bread will be like mourners' bread;
All who eat of it will be defiled,
For their bread will be for themselves *alone;*
It will not enter the house of the LORD.
5 What will you do on the day of the appointed festival
And on the day of the feast of the LORD?
6 For behold, they will go because of destruction;
Egypt will gather them up, Memphis will bury them.
Weeds will take over their treasures of silver;
Thorns *will be* in their tents.

7 The days of punishment have come,
The days of retribution have come;
Let Israel know *this!*
The prophet is a fool,

9:1 Is 22:12, 13; Hos 10:5; Hos 4:12

9:2 Hos 2:9

9:3 Lev 25:23; Jer 2:7; Hos 7:16; 8:13; Hos 7:11; Ezek 4:13

9:4 Ex 29:40; Jer 6:20; Hos 8:13; Hag 2:13, 14

9:5 Is 10:3; Jer 5:31; Hos 2:11; Joel 1:13

9:6 Is 19:13; Jer 2:16; 44:1; 46:14, 19; Ezek 30:13, 16; Is 5:6; 7:23; Hos 10:8

9:7 Is 10:3; Jer 10:15; Mic 7:4; Luke 21:22; Is 34:8; Jer 16:18; 25:14; Lam 2:14; Ezek 13:3, 10; Is 44:25; Ezek 14:9, 10

---

apply what you are hearing or reading, check to see if the same application could fit you. Apply the lessons to your own life first because often our own faults are the very first ones we see in others.

8:13 The people's sacrifices had become mere ritual, and God refused to accept them. We have rituals too—attending church, observing a regular quiet time, celebrating Christian holidays, praying before meals. Rituals give us security in a changing world. Because they are repeated often, they can drive God's lessons deep within us. But rituals can be abused. Beware if you find yourself observing a religious ritual for any of the following reasons: (1) to gain community approval, (2) to avoid the risks of doing something different, (3) to make thought unnecessary, (4) to substitute for personal relationships, (5) to make up for bad behavior, (6) to earn God's favor. We should not reject the rituals of our worship, but we must be careful with them. Think about why you do them. Focus on God, and perform every act with sincere devotion.

8:13 In Egypt, the Israelites had been slaves (Exodus 1:11). The people would not literally return to Egypt, but they would return to slavery—this time scattered throughout the Assyrian empire.

8:14 Israel had placed its confidence in military strength, strong defenses, and economic stability, just as nations do today. But because of the people's inner moral decay, their apparent sources of strength were inadequate. There is a tendency in many nations toward removing all traces of God from daily life. But if a nation forgets its Maker, its strengths may prove worthless when put to the test.

9:1 A threshing floor was a flat area, often built on a hilltop, where harvesters beat the wheat and separated it from the chaff. Often men would stay overnight at the threshing floor to protect their grain, and prostitutes would visit there. Because of the location of threshing floors in the hilltops, they began to be used as places to sacrifice to false gods.

9:6 Israel's leaders vacillated between alliances with Egypt and alliances with Assyria. Hosea was saying that both were wrong. Breaking an alliance with untrustworthy Assyria and fleeing for help to the equally untrustworthy Egypt would not forestall Israel's destruction. Their only hope was to return to God.

9:7 By the time Israel began to experience the consequences of its sins, it was no longer listening to God's messengers. Refusing to hear the truth from prophets who spoke out so clearly about its sins, the nation did not hear God's warnings about what was soon to happen. We all listen and read selectively—focusing on what seems to support our present life-style, ignoring what demands a radical reordering of our priorities. In doing this, we are likely to miss the warnings we need most. Listen to people who think your approach is all wrong. Read articles that present viewpoints you would be unlikely to take. Ask yourself, "Is God speaking to me through these speakers and writers? Is there something I need to change?"

The inspired man is demented,
Because of the grossness of your iniquity,
And *because* your hostility is *so* great.
8 Ephraim *was* a watchman with my God, a prophet;
Yet the snare of a bird catcher is in all his ways,
And there is *only* hostility in the house of his God.
9 They have gone deep in depravity
As in the days of Gibeah;
He will remember their iniquity,
He will punish their sins.

9:9 Is 31:6; Judg 19:12, 16-30; Hos 10:9; Hos 7:2; 8:13

10 I found Israel like grapes in the wilderness;
I saw your forefathers as the earliest fruit on the fig tree in its first *season.*
But they came to Baal-peor and devoted themselves to [8]shame,
And they became as detestable as that which they loved.
11 As for Ephraim, their glory will fly away like a bird—
No birth, no pregnancy and no conception!
12 Though they bring up their children,
Yet I will bereave them until not a man is left.
Yes, woe to them indeed when I depart from them!
13 Ephraim, as I have seen,
Is planted in a pleasant meadow like Tyre;
But Ephraim will bring out his children for slaughter.
14 Give them, O LORD—what will You give?
Give them a miscarrying womb and dry breasts.

9:10 Mic 7:1; Jer 24:2; Num 25:1-5; Ps 106:28, 29; Jer 11:13; Hos 4:18; Ps 115:8; Ezek 20:8

9:11 Hos 4:7; 10:5

9:12 Deut 31:17; Hos 7:13

9:13 Ezek 26:1-21

9:14 Hos 9:11

15 All their evil is at Gilgal;
Indeed, I came to hate them there!
Because of the wickedness of their deeds
I will drive them out of My house!
I will love them no more;
All their princes are rebels.
16 Ephraim is stricken, their root is dried up,
They will bear no fruit.
Even though they bear children,
I will slay the precious ones of their womb.
17 My God will cast them away
Because they have not listened to Him;
And they will be wanderers among the nations.

9:15 Hos 4:15; 12:11; Hos 4:9; 7:2; 12:2; Is 1:23; Hos 5:2

9:16 Hos 5:11; Hos 8:7; Ezek 24:21

9:17 Hos 4:10; Hos 7:13

Retribution for Israel's Sin

10 Israel is a luxuriant vine;
He produces fruit for himself.

10:1 Is 5:1-7; Ezek 15:1-6; Jer 2:28; Hos 8:11; 12:11; 1 Kin 14:23; Hos 3:4

8 I.e. Baal

9:9 A couple had stopped to stay overnight in Gibeah when some wicked men gathered around the house and demanded that the man come out so they could have sex with him. Instead, the traveler gave them his concubine. They raped and abused her all night and then left her dead on the doorstep (Judges 19:14–30). That horrible act revealed the depths to which the people had sunk. Gibeah was destroyed for its evil (Judges 20:8–48), but Hosea said that the whole nation was now as evil as that city. Just as the city didn't escape punishment, neither would the nation.

9:10 Baal-peor was the god of Peor, a mountain in Moab. In Numbers 22, Balaam, a prophet, was hired by King Balak of Moab to curse the Israelites as they were coming through his land. The Moabites enticed the Israelites into sexual sin and Baal worship. Before long, the Israelites became as corrupt as the gods they worshiped. People can take on the characteristics of what or whom they love. What do you worship? Are you becoming more like God, or are you becoming more like someone or something else?

9:14 Hosea prayed this prayer when he foresaw the destruction that Israel's sins would bring (2 Kings 17:7–23). This vision of Israel's terrible fate moved him to pray that women would not get pregnant and that children would die as infants so they would not have to experience the tremendous suffering and pain that lay ahead.

9:15 At Gilgal, both the political and the religious failure of the nation began. Here idols and kings were substituted for God. Saul, the united nation's first king, was crowned at Gilgal (1 Samuel 11:15), but by Hosea's time, Baal worship flourished there (4:15; 12:11).

10:1 Israel prospered under Jeroboam II, gaining military and economic strength. But the more prosperous the nation became, the more love it lavished on idols. It seems as though the more God gives, the more we spend. We want bigger houses, better cars, and finer clothes. But the finest things the world offers line the pathway to destruction. As you prosper, consider where your money is going. Is it being used for God's purposes, or are you consuming it all on yourself?

The more his fruit,
The more altars he made;
The richer his land,
The better he made the *sacred* pillars.

2 Their heart is faithless;
Now they must bear their guilt.
The LORD will break down their altars
And destroy their *sacred* pillars.

10:2 1 Kin 18:21; Zeph 1:5; Hos 13:16; Hos 10:8; Mic 5:13

3 Surely now they will say, "We have no king,
For we do not revere the LORD.
As for the king, what can he do for us?"

10:3 Ps 12:4; Is 5:19

4 They speak *mere* words,
With worthless oaths they make covenants;
And judgment sprouts like poisonous weeds in the furrows of the field.

10:4 Ezek 17:13-19; Hos 4:2; Deut 31:16, 17; 2 Kin 17:3, 4; Amos 5:7

5 The inhabitants of Samaria will fear
For the calf of Beth-aven.
Indeed, its people will mourn for it,
And its idolatrous priests will cry out over it,
Over its glory, since it has departed from it.

10:5 Hos 8:5, 6; Hos 4:15; 5:8; 2 Kin 23:5; Hos 9:11

6 The thing itself will be carried to Assyria
As tribute to King Jareb;
Ephraim will be seized with shame
And Israel will be ashamed of its own counsel.

10:6 Hos 11:5; Hos 5:13; Hos 4:7; Is 30:3; Jer 7:24

7 Samaria will be cut off *with* her king
Like a stick on the surface of the water.

10:7 Hos 13:11

8 Also the high places of Aven, the sin of Israel, will be destroyed;
Thorn and thistle will grow on their altars;
Then they will say to the mountains,
"Cover us!" And to the hills, "Fall on us!"

10:8 Hos 4:13; 1 Kin 12:28-30; 13:34; Is 32:13; Hos 9:6; 10:2; Is 2:19; Luke 23:30; Rev 6:16

9 From the days of Gibeah you have sinned, O Israel;
There they stand!
Will not the battle against the sons of iniquity overtake them in Gibeah?

10 When it is My desire, I will chastise them;
And the peoples will be gathered against them
When they are bound for their double guilt.

10:10 Ezek 5:13; Hos 4:9; Jer 16:16

11 Ephraim is a trained heifer that loves to thresh,
But I will come over her fair neck *with a yoke;*
I will harness Ephraim,
Judah will plow, Jacob will harrow for himself.

10:11 Jer 50:11; Hos 4:16; Mic 4:13; Jer 28:14

12 Sow with a view to righteousness,
Reap in accordance with kindness;
Break up your fallow ground,
For it is time to seek the LORD
Until He comes to rain righteousness on you.

10:12 Prov 11:18; Jer 4:3; Hos 12:6; Hos 6:3; Is 44:3; 45:8

10:4 God was angry with the people of Israel for their insincere promises. Because the people did not keep their word, there were many lawsuits. People break their promises, but God always keeps his. Are you remaining true to your promises, both to other people and to God? If not, ask God for forgiveness and help to get back on track. Then be careful about the promises you make. Never make a promise unless you are sure you can keep it.

10:5 Beth-aven means "house of wickedness," and it refers to Bethel ("house of God") where false worship took place. If the Israelites' idols were really gods, they should have been able to protect the people. How ironic that the people were fearing for their gods' safety! For more information on this calf-idol, see the notes on 3:4–5 and 8:5.

10:9–10 For information on "the days of Gibeah," see the note on 9:9 or read Judges 19 and 20. Gibeah stands for cruelty and sensuality as in Judges, and for rebellion as in Saul's day (Gibeah was Saul's hometown; see 1 Samuel 10:5; 11:4).

10:12 Hosea repeatedly uses illustrations about fields and crops. Here he envisions a plowed field, earth that is ready to receive seeds. It is no longer stony and hard; it has been carefully prepared, and it is available. Is your life ready for God to work in it? You can break up the unplowed ground of your heart by acknowledging your sins and receiving God's forgiveness and guidance.

13 You have plowed wickedness, you have reaped injustice,
You have eaten the fruit of lies.
Because you have trusted in your way, in your numerous warriors,
14 Therefore a tumult will arise among your people,
And all your fortresses will be destroyed,
As Shalman destroyed Beth-arbel on the day of battle,
When mothers were dashed in pieces with *their* children.
15 Thus it will be done to you at Bethel because of your great wickedness.
At dawn the king of Israel will be completely cut off.

10:13 Job 4:8; Prov 22:8; Gal 6:7, 8; Hos 4:2; 7:3; 11:12; Ps 33:16

10:14 Is 17:3; Hos 13:16

3. God's love for Israel

God Yearns over His People

11 When Israel *was* a youth I loved him,
And out of Egypt I called My son.
2 The more they called them,
The more they went from them;
They kept sacrificing to the Baals
And burning incense to idols.
3 Yet it is I who taught Ephraim to walk,
I took them in My arms;
But they did not know that I healed them.
4 I led them with cords of a man, with bonds of love,
And I became to them as one who lifts the yoke from their jaws;
And I bent down *and* fed them.

5 They will not return to the land of Egypt;
But Assyria—he will be their king
Because they refused to return *to Me.*
6 The sword will whirl against their cities,
And will demolish their gate bars
And consume *them* because of their counsels.
7 So My people are bent on turning from Me.
Though they call them to *the One* on high,
None at all exalts *Him.*

11:1 Hos 2:15; 12:9, 13; 13:4; Ex 4:22, 23; Matt 2:15

11:2 2 Kin 17:13-15; Hos 2:13; 4:13; Is 65:7; Jer 18:15

11:3 Deut 1:31; 32:10, 11; Ps 107:20; Jer 30:17

11:4 Jer 31:2, 3; Lev 26:13; Ex 16:32; Ps 78:25

11:5 Hos 7:16

11:6 Hos 13:16; Lam 2:9; Hos 4:16, 17

11:7 Jer 3:6, 7; 8:5

10:13 The Israelites trusted in the lie that military power could keep them safe. Believers today are also capable of falling for lies. Those who want to lead others astray often follow these rules for effective lying: Make it big; keep it simple; repeat it often. Believers can avoid falling for lies by asking: (1) Am I believing this because there is personal gain in it for me? (2) Am I discounting important facts? (3) Does this conflict with a direct command of Scripture? (4) Are there any Biblical parallels to the situation I'm facing that would help me know what to believe?

10:14 Some say Shalman was Shalmaneser, king of Assyria; others say Shalman was Salmanu, a Moabite king mentioned in the inscriptions of Tiglath-pileser. Shalman had invaded Gilead around 740 B.C. and destroyed the city of Beth-arbel, killing many people, including women and children. This kind of cruelty was not uncommon in ancient warfare. Hosea was saying such would be Israel's fate.

10:15 Because Israel had put its confidence in military might rather than in God, it would be destroyed by military power. Israel's king, who had led the people into idol worship, would be the first to fall. Divine judgment is *sometimes* swift, but it is *always* sure.

11:1ff In the final four chapters, Hosea shifts to the theme of God's intense love for Israel. God had always loved Israel as a parent loves a stubborn child, and that is why he would not release Israel from the consequences of its behavior. The Israelites were sinful, and they would be punished like a rebellious son brought by his parents before the elders (Deuteronomy 21:18–21). All through Israel's sad history, God repeatedly offered to restore the nation if it would only turn to him. By stubbornly refusing God's invitation, the northern kingdom had sealed its doom. It would be destroyed, never to rise again. Even so, Israel as a nation was not finished. A remnant of faithful Israelites would return to Jerusalem, where one day the Messiah would come, offering pardon and reconciliation to all who would faithfully follow him.

11:3 God had consistently provided for his people, but they refused to see what he had done, and they showed no interest in thanking him. Ungratefulness is a common human fault. For example, when was the last time you thanked your parents for caring for you? Your pastor for the service he gives your church? Your child's teacher for the care taken with each day's activities? Your heavenly Father for his guidance? Many of the benefits and privileges we enjoy are the result of loving actions done long ago. Look for hidden acts of nurturing, and thank those who make the world better through their love. But begin by thanking God for all his blessings.

11:4 God's discipline requires times of leading and times of feeding. Sometimes the rope is taut; sometimes it is slack. God's discipline is always loving, and its object is always the well-being of the beloved. When you are called to discipline others—children, students, employees, or church members—do not be rigid. Vary your approach according to the goals you are seeking to accomplish. In each case, ask yourself, "does this person need guidance, or does he or she need to be nurtured?"

11:5 The northern kingdom survived for only two centuries after its break with Jerusalem. Its spiritual and political leaders did not help the people learn the way to God, so as a nation they would never repent. Hosea prophesied its downfall, which happened when Shalmaneser of Assyria conquered Israel in 722 B.C. Judah also would go into captivity, but a remnant would return to their homeland.

11:8 Hos 6:4; 7:1; Gen 14:8; Deut 29:23

8 How can I give you up, O Ephraim?
How can I surrender you, O Israel?
How can I make you like Admah?
How can I treat you like Zeboiim?
My heart is turned over within Me,
All My compassions are kindled.

11:9 Deut 13:17; Jer 26:3; 30:11; Num 23:19; Is 5:24; 12:6; 41:14, 16

9 I will not execute My fierce anger;
I will not destroy Ephraim again.
For I am God and not man, the Holy One in your midst,
And I will not come in wrath.

11:10 Hos 3:5; 6:1-3; Is 31:4; Joel 3:16; Amos 1:2; Is 66:2, 5

10 They will walk after the LORD,
He will roar like a lion;
Indeed He will roar
And *His* sons will come trembling from the west.

11:11 Is 11:11; Is 60:8; Hos 7:11; Ezek 28:25, 26; 34:27, 28

11 They will come trembling like birds from Egypt
And like doves from the land of Assyria;
And I will settle them in their houses, declares the LORD.

11:12 Hos 4:2; 7:3

12 Ephraim surrounds Me with lies
And the house of Israel with deceit;
Judah is also unruly against God,
Even against the Holy One who is faithful.

Ephraim Reminded

12:1 Jer 22:22; Gen 41:6; Ezek 17:10

12 Ephraim feeds on wind,
And pursues the east wind continually;
He multiplies lies and violence.
Moreover, he makes a covenant with Assyria,
And oil is carried to Egypt.

12:2 Hos 4:1; Mic 6:2; Hos 4:9; 7:2

2 The LORD also has a dispute with Judah,
And will punish Jacob according to his ways;
He will repay him according to his deeds.

12:3 Gen 25:26; Gen 32:28

3 In the womb he took his brother by the heel,
And in his maturity he contended with God.

12:4 Gen 32:26; Gen 28:13-19; 35:10-15

4 Yes, he wrestled with the angel and prevailed;
He wept and sought His favor.
He found Him at Bethel
And there He spoke with us,

12:5 Ex 3:15

5 Even the LORD, the God of hosts,
The LORD is His name.

12:6 Hos 6:1-3; 10:12; Mic 6:8; Mic 7:7

6 Therefore, return to your God,

11:8 Admah and Zeboiim were cities of the plain that perished with Sodom and Gomorrah (Genesis 14:8; Deuteronomy 29:23).

11:9 "I am God and not man." It is easy for us to define God in terms of our own expectations and behavior. In so doing, we make him just slightly larger than ourselves. In reality, God is infinitely greater than we are. We should seek to become like him rather than attempting to remake him in our image.

11:12 Unlike Israel, Judah had some fairly good kings—Asa, Jehoshaphat, Joash, Amaziah, Azariah (Uzziah), Jotham, and especially Hezekiah and Josiah. Under some of these kings, God's law was dusted off and taught to the people. The priests continued to serve in God's appointed temple in Jerusalem, and the festivals were celebrated at least some of the time. Unfortunately, the political or religious leaders were unable to completely wipe out idol worship and pagan rites (although Hezekiah and Josiah came close), which continued to fester until they eventually erupted and infected the whole country. Still, the influence of the good kings enabled Judah to survive more than 150 years longer than Israel, and that memory of their positive influence fortified a small group—a remnant—of faithful people who would one day return and restore their land and temple.

12:2–5 Jacob, whose name was later changed to Israel, was the common ancestor of all 12 tribes of Israel (both northern and southern kingdoms). Like the nations that descended from him, Jacob practiced deceit. Unlike Israel and Judah, however, he constantly searched for God. Jacob wrestled with the angel in order to be blessed, but his descendants thought their blessings came from their own successes. Jacob purged his house of idols (Genesis 35:2), but his descendants could not quit their idol worship.

12:6 The two principles that Hosea called his nation to live by, kindness and justice, are at the very foundation of God's character. They are essential to his followers, but they are not easy to keep in balance. Some people are kind and loving to the point that they excuse wrongdoing. Others are just to the extent that they forget love. Love without justice, because it is not aiming at a higher standard, leaves people in their sins. Justice without love, because it has no heart, drives people away from God. To specialize in one at the expense of the other is to distort our witness. Today's church, just like Hosea's nation, must live by both principles.

Observe kindness and justice,
And wait for your God continually.
7 A merchant, in whose hands are false balances,
He loves to oppress.
8 And Ephraim said, "Surely I have become rich,
I have found wealth for myself;
In all my labors they will find in me
No iniquity, which *would be* sin."
9 But I *have been* the LORD your God since the land of Egypt;
I will make you live in tents again,
As in the days of the appointed festival.
10 I have also spoken to the prophets,
And I gave numerous visions,
And through the prophets I gave parables.
11 Is there iniquity *in* Gilead?
Surely they are worthless.
In Gilgal they sacrifice bulls,
Yes, their altars are like the stone heaps
Beside the furrows of the field.

12 Now Jacob fled to the land of Aram,
And Israel worked for a wife,
And for a wife he kept *sheep.*
13 But by a prophet the LORD brought Israel from Egypt,
And by a prophet he was kept.
14 Ephraim has provoked to bitter anger;
So his Lord will leave his bloodguilt on him
And bring back his reproach to him.

12:7 Prov 11:1; Amos 8:5; Mic 6:11
12:8 Ps 62:10; Hos 13:6; Rev 3:17; Hos 4:8; 14:1
12:9 Lev 23:42
12:10 2 Kin 17:13; Jer 7:25; Ezek 17:2; 20:49
12:11 Hos 8:11; 10:1, 2
12:12 Gen 28:5; Gen 29:20
12:13 Ex 14:19-22; Is 63:11-14
12:14 2 Kin 17:7-18; Ezek 18:10-13; Dan 11:18; Mic 6:16

Ephraim's Idolatry

13 When Ephraim spoke, *there was* trembling.
He exalted himself in Israel,
But through Baal he did wrong and died.
2 And now they sin more and more,
And make for themselves molten images,
Idols skillfully made from their silver,
All of them the work of craftsmen.
They say of them, "Let the men who sacrifice kiss the calves!"
3 Therefore they will be like the morning cloud
And like dew which soon disappears,
Like chaff which is blown away from the threshing floor
And like smoke from a chimney.

13:1 Job 29:21, 22; Judg 8:1; 12:1; Hos 2:8-17; 11:2
13:2 Is 46:6; Jer 10:4; Hos 2:8; Is 44:17-20; Hos 8:6; Hos 8:5, 6; 10:5
13:3 Hos 6:4; Ps 1:4; Is 17:13; Dan 2:35; Ps 68:2

12:7–8 In Israel, dishonesty had become an accepted means of attaining wealth. Israelites who were financially successful could not imagine that God would consider them sinful. They thought that their wealth was a sign of God's approval, and they didn't bother to consider how they had gotten it. But God said that Israel's riches would not make up for its sin. Remember that God's measure of success is different from ours. He calls us to faithfulness, not to affluence. Character is more important to him than our pocketbooks.

12:8 Rich people and nations often claim that their material success is due to their own hard work, initiative, and intelligence. Because they have every possession they want, they don't feel the need for God. They believe that their riches are their own, and they think that they have the right to use them any way they please. If you find yourself feeling proud of your accomplishments, remember that all your opportunities, abilities, and resources come from God, and that you hold them in sacred trust for him.

12:9 Once a year the Israelites spent a week living in tents during the Feast of Booths, which commemorated God's protection as they wandered in the wilderness for 40 years (see Deuteronomy 1:19—2:1). Here, because of their sin, God would cause them to live in tents again—this time not as part of a festival, but in actual bondage.

12:12 Hosea was using this reference to Jacob to say, "Don't forget your humble beginnings. What you have is not a result of your own efforts, but it is yours because God has been gracious to you."

12:13 The prophet who brought Israel up from Egypt was Moses (Exodus 13:17–19).

13:1 Israel, represented here by the northern tribe of Ephraim, had been great, but by Hosea's time the people had rebelled against God and had lost their authority among the nations. Greatness in the past is no guarantee of greatness in the future. It is good to remember what God has done for you and through you, but it is equally important to keep your relationship with him vital and up-to-date. Commit yourself to God moment by moment.

13:4 Hos 12:9; Ex 20:3; 2 Kin 18:35; Is 43:11; 45:21, 22

4 Yet I *have been* the LORD your God
Since the land of Egypt;
And you were not to know any god except Me,
For there is no savior besides Me.

13:5 Deut 2:7; 32:10; Deut 8:15

5 I cared for you in the wilderness,
In the land of drought.

13:6 Deut 8:12, 14; 32:13-15; Jer 5:7; Hos 7:14; Hos 2:13; 4:6; 8:14

6 As *they had* their pasture, they became satisfied,
And being satisfied, their heart became proud;
Therefore they forgot Me.

13:7 Lam 3:10; Hos 5:14; Jer 5:6

7 So I will be like a lion to them;
Like a leopard I will lie in wait by the wayside.

13:8 2 Sam 17:8; Ps 50:22

8 I will encounter them like a bear robbed of her cubs,
And I will tear open their chests;
There I will also devour them like a lioness,
As a wild beast would tear them.

13:9 Jer 2:17, 19; Mal 1:12, 13; Deut 33:26, 29

9 *It is* your destruction, O Israel,
That *you are* against Me, against your help.

13:10 2 Kin 17:4; Hos 8:4; 1 Sam 8:5, 6

10 Where now is your king
That he may save you in all your cities,
And your judges of whom you requested,
"Give me a king and princes"?

13:11 1 Sam 8:7; 10:17-24; 1 Sam 15:26; 1 Kin 14:7-10; Hos 10:7

11 I gave you a king in My anger
And took him away in My wrath.

13:12 Deut 32:34, 35; Job 14:17; Rom 2:5

12 The iniquity of Ephraim is bound up;
His sin is stored up.

13:13 Is 13:8; Mic 4:9, 10; Deut 32:6; Hos 5:4; Is 37:3; 66:9

13 The pains of childbirth come upon him;
He is not a wise son,
For it is not the time that he should delay at the opening of the womb.

13:14 Ps 49:15; Ezek 37:12, 13; 1 Cor 15:55; Jer 20:16; 31:35-37

14 Shall I ransom them from the power of Sheol?
Shall I redeem them from death?
O Death, where are your thorns?
O Sheol, where is your sting?
Compassion will be hidden from My sight.

13:15 Gen 49:22; Hos 10:1; Gen 41:6; Jer 4:11, 12; Ezek 17:10; 19:12; Jer 51:36; Jer 20:5

15 Though he flourishes among the reeds,
An east wind will come,
The wind of the LORD coming up from the wilderness;
And his fountain will become dry
And his spring will be dried up;

CYCLES OF JUDGMENT/ SALVATION IN HOSEA

Judgment	1:2–9; 2:2–13; 4:1—5:14; 6:4—11:7; 11:12—13:16
Salvation	1:10—2:1; 2:14—3:5; 5:15—6:3; 11:8–11; 14:1–9

God promises to judge, but he also promises mercy. Here you can see the cycles of judgment and salvation in Hosea. Prophecies of judgment are consistently followed by prophecies of forgiveness.

13:4–6 When abundant possessions made Israel feel self-sufficient, it turned its back on God and forgot him. Self-sufficiency is as destructive today as it was in Hosea's time. Do you see your constant need of God's presence and help? Learn to rely on God both in good times and bad. If you are traveling along a smooth and easy path right now, beware of forgetting who gave you your good fortune. Don't depend on your gifts; depend on the Giver. See Deuteronomy 6:10–12 and 8:7–20 for God's warning.

13:11 God had warned Israel that kings would cause more problems than they would solve, and he reluctantly gave them Saul as their first king (1 Samuel 8:4–22). The second king, David, was a good king, and Solomon, David's son, had his strengths. But after the nation divided in two, the northern kingdom never had another good ruler. Evil kings led the nation deeper into idolatry and unwise political alliances. Eventually the evil kings destroyed the nation; with Hoshea, the northern kingdom's kings were cut off (2 Kings 17:1–6).

13:12 Ephraim's (Israel's) sins were recorded for later punishment. All our sins are known and will be revealed at the day of judgment (2 Corinthians 5:10; Revelation 20:11–15).

13:14 The apostle Paul used this passage to teach the resurrection of our bodies from death (1 Corinthians 15:55). For those who have trusted in Christ for deliverance from sin, death holds no threat of annihilation.

It will plunder *his* treasury of every precious article.
16 Samaria will be held guilty,
For she has rebelled against her God.
They will fall by the sword,
Their little ones will be dashed in pieces,
And their pregnant women will be ripped open.

13:16 Hos 10:2; Hos 7:14; 2 Kin 8:12; Hos 11:6; Hos 10:14; 2 Kin 15:16

Israel's Future Blessing

14 Return, O Israel, to the LORD your God,
For you have stumbled because of your iniquity.
2 Take words with you and return to the LORD.
Say to Him, "Take away all iniquity
And receive *us* graciously,
That we may present the fruit of our lips.
3 "Assyria will not save us,
We will not ride on horses;
Nor will we say again, 'Our god,'
To the work of our hands;
For in You the orphan finds mercy."

4 I will heal their apostasy,
I will love them freely,
For My anger has turned away from them.
5 I will be like the dew to Israel;
He will blossom like the lily,
And he will take root like *the cedars of* Lebanon.
6 His shoots will sprout,
And his beauty will be like the olive tree
And his fragrance like *the cedars of* Lebanon.
7 Those who live in his shadow
Will again raise grain,
And they will blossom like the vine.
His renown *will be* like the wine of Lebanon.

8 O Ephraim, what more have I to do with idols?
It is I who answer and look after you.
I am like a luxuriant cypress;
From Me comes your fruit.

9 Whoever is wise, let him understand these things;
Whoever is discerning, let him know them.

14:1 Hos 6:1; 10:12; 12:6; Joel 2:13; Hos 4:8; 5:5; 9:7

14:2 Mic 7:18, 19; Ps 51:16, 17; Hos 6:6; Heb 13:15

14:3 Ps 33:17; Is 31:1; Hos 8:6; 13:2; Hos 4:12; Ps 10:14; 68:5

14:4 Is 57:18; Hos 6:1; Zeph 3:17; Is 12:1

14:5 Prov 19:12; Is 26:19; Song 2:1; Matt 6:28; Is 35:2

14:6 Jer 11:16; Song 4:11

14:7 Ezek 17:23; Hos 2:21, 22

14:8 Job 34:32; Hos 14:3; Is 41:19; Ezek 17:23

14:9 Ps 107:43; Jer 9:12; Ps 111:7, 8; Prov 10:29; Zeph 3:5; Is 26:7; Is 1:28

14:1ff Verses 1–3 are Hosea's call to repent. Verses 4–8 are God's promise of restoration. God had to punish Israel for its gross and repeated violations of his law, but he would do so with a heavy heart. What God really wanted to do was restore the nation and make it prosper.

14:1–2 The people could return to God by asking him to forgive their sins. The same is true for us: We can pray Hosea's prayer and know our sins are forgiven because Christ died for them on the cross (John 3:16).

Forgiveness begins when we see the destructiveness of sin and the futility of life without God. Then we must admit we cannot save ourselves; our only hope is in God's mercy. When we request forgiveness, we must recognize that we do not deserve it and therefore cannot demand it. Our appeal must be for God's love and mercy, not for his justice. Although we cannot demand forgiveness, we can be confident that we have received it because God is gracious and loving and wants to restore us to himself, just as he wanted to restore Israel.

14:2 "The fruit of our lips" refers to thank offerings to God. God desired real, heartfelt repentance, not merely annual sacrifices.

14:3–8 When our will is weak, when our thinking is confused, and when our conscience is burdened with a load of guilt, we must remember that God cares for us continually; his compassion never fails. When friends and family desert us, when coworkers don't understand us, and when we are tired of being good, God's compassion never fails. When we can't see the way or seem to hear God's voice, and when we lack courage to go on, God's compassion never fails. When our shortcomings and our awareness of our sins overcome us, God's compassion never fails.

14:9 Hosea closes with an appeal to listen, learn, and benefit from God's word. To those receiving the Lord's message through Hosea, this meant the difference between life and death. For you, the reader of the book of Hosea, the choice is similar: either listen to the book's message and follow God's ways, or refuse to walk along the Lord's path. But people who insist on following their own direction without God's guidance are "like darkness; they do not know over what they stumble" (Proverbs 4:19). If you are lost, you can find the way by turning from your sin and following God.

For the ways of the LORD are right,
And the righteous will walk in them,
But transgressors will stumble in them.

14:9 God's concern for *justice* that requires faithfulness and *love* that offers forgiveness can be seen in his dealings with Hosea. We can err by forgetting God's love and feeling that our sins are hopeless, but we can also err by forgetting his wrath against our sins and thinking he will continue to accept us no matter how we act. *Forgiveness* is a key word: when God forgives us, he judges the sin but shows mercy to the sinner. We should never be afraid to come to God for a clean slate and a renewed life.

JOEL

King Ahab dies in battle 853 B.C.	Elisha becomes a prophet 848	Jehu becomes king of Israel; Athaliah seizes Judah's throne 841	Joel becomes a prophet? Joash becomes king of Judah 835

VITAL STATISTICS

PURPOSE:
To warn Judah of God's impending judgment because of its sins and to urge the people to turn back to God

AUTHOR:
Joel son of Pethuel

TO WHOM WRITTEN:
The people of Judah, the southern kingdom, and God's people everywhere

DATE WRITTEN:
Probably during the time Joel may have prophesied, from approximately 835–796 B.C.

SETTING:
The people of Judah had become prosperous and complacent. Taking God for granted, they had turned to self-centeredness, idolatry, and sin. Joel warned them that this kind of life-style would inevitably bring down God's judgment.

KEY VERSES:
" 'Yet even now,' declares the LORD, 'Return to Me with all your heart, and with fasting, weeping and mourning; and rend your heart and not your garments.' Now return to the LORD your God, for He is gracious and compassionate, slow to anger, abounding in lovingkindness and relenting of evil" (2:12–13).

KEY PEOPLE:
Joel, the people of Judah

KEY PLACE:
Jerusalem

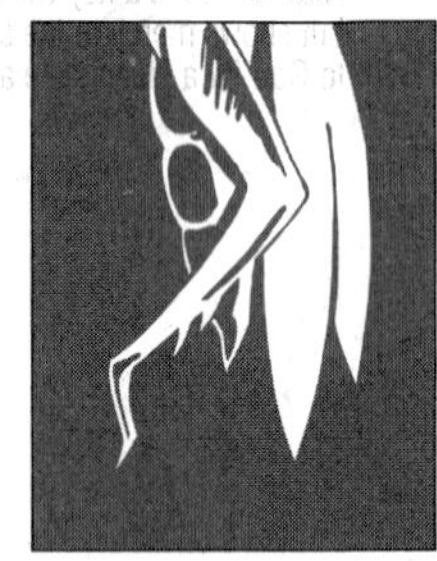

A SINGLE bomb devastates a city, and the world is ushered into the nuclear age. A split atom—power and force such as we had never seen.

At a launch site, rockets roar and a payload is thrust into space. Discoveries dreamed of for centuries are ours as we begin to explore the edge of the universe.

Volcanos, earthquakes, tidal waves, hurricanes, and tornados unleash uncontrollable and unstoppable force. And we can only avoid them and then pick up the pieces.

Power, strength, might—we stand in awe at the natural and man-made display. But these forces cannot touch the power of omnipotent God. Creator of galaxies, atoms, and natural laws, the Sovereign Lord rules all there is and ever will be. How silly to live without him; how foolish to run and hide from him; how ridiculous to disobey him. But we do. Since Eden, we have sought independence from his control, as though we were gods and could control our destiny. And he has allowed our rebellion. But soon *the day of the Lord* will come.

It is about this day that the prophet Joel speaks, and it is the theme of his book. On this day God will judge all unrighteousness and disobedience—all accounts will be settled and the crooked made straight.

We know very little about Joel—only that he was a prophet and the son of Pethuel. He may have lived in Jerusalem because his audience was Judah, the southern kingdom. Whoever he was, Joel speaks forthrightly and forcefully in this short and powerful book. His message is one of foreboding and warning, but it is also filled with hope. Joel states that our Creator, the omnipotent Judge, is also merciful, and he wants to bless all those who trust him.

Joel begins by describing a terrible plague of locusts that covers the land and devours the crops. The devastation wrought by these creatures is but a foretaste of the coming judgment of God, the "day of the LORD." Joel, therefore, urges the people to turn from their sin and turn back to God. Woven into this message of judgment and the need for repentance is an affirmation of God's kindness and the blessings he promises for all who follow him. In fact, "whoever calls on the name of the LORD will be delivered" (2:32).

As you read Joel, catch his vision of the power and might of God and of God's ultimate judgment of sin. Choose to follow, obey, and worship God alone as your sovereign Lord.

Jehoahaz becomes king of Israel 814	Jehoash becomes king of Israel 798	Joel's ministry ends 796?

THE BLUEPRINT

1. The day of the locusts (1:1—2:27)
2. The day of the LORD (2:28—3:21)

The locust plague was only a foretaste of the judgment to come in the day of the Lord. This is a timeless call to repentance with the promise of blessing. Just as the people faced the tragedy of their crops being destroyed, we, too, will face tragic judgment if we live in sin. But God's grace is available to us both now and in that coming day.

MEGATHEMES

THEME	EXPLANATION	IMPORTANCE
Punishment	Like a destroying army of locusts, God's punishment for sin is overwhelming, dreadful, and unavoidable. When it comes, there will be no food, no water, no protection, and no escape. The day for settling accounts with God for how we have lived is fast approaching.	God is the one with whom we all must reckon—not nature, the economy, or a foreign invader. We can't ignore or offend God forever. We must pay attention to his message now, or we will face his anger later.
Forgiveness	God stood ready to forgive and restore all those who would come to him and turn away from sin. God wanted to shower his people with his love and restore them to a proper relationship with him.	Forgiveness comes by turning from sin and turning toward God. It is not too late to receive God's forgiveness. God's greatest desire is for you to come to him.
Promise of the Holy Spirit	Joel predicts the time when God will pour out his Holy Spirit on all people. It will be the beginning of new and fresh worship of God by those who believe in him, as well as the beginning of judgment on all who reject him.	God is in control. Justice and restoration are in his hands. The Holy Spirit confirms God's love for us just as he did for the first Christians (Acts 2). We must be faithful to God and place our life under the guidance and power of his Holy Spirit.

1. The day of the locusts

The Devastation of Locusts

1:1 Jer 1:2; Ezek 1:3; Hos 1:1; Acts 2:16

1:2 Hos 4:1; 5:1; Job 8:8; Joel 1:14; Jer 30:7; Joel 2:2

1:3 Ex 10:2; Ps 78:4

1 The word of the LORD that came to Joel, the son of Pethuel:
2 Hear this, O elders,
And listen, all inhabitants of the land.
Has *anything like* this happened in your days
Or in your fathers' days?
3 Tell your sons about it,
And *let* your sons *tell* their sons,
And their sons the next generation.

1:1 Joel was a prophet to the nation of Judah, also known as the southern kingdom. The book does not mention when Joel lived, but many believe that he prophesied during the reign of King Joash (835–796 B.C.). But the date of Joel's book is not nearly so important as its timeless message: Sin brings God's judgment; yet with God's justice there is also great mercy.

1:3 God urged parents to pass their history down to their children, telling over and over the important lessons they learned. One of the greatest gifts you can give younger people is your life's story to help them repeat your successes and avoid your mistakes.

4 What the gnawing locust has left, the swarming locust has eaten;
And what the swarming locust has left, the creeping locust has eaten;
And what the creeping locust has left, the stripping locust has eaten.
5 Awake, drunkards, and weep;
And wail, all you wine drinkers,
On account of the sweet wine
That is cut off from your mouth.
6 For a nation has invaded my land,
Mighty and without number;
Its teeth are the teeth of a lion,
And it has the fangs of a lioness.
7 It has made my vine a waste
And my fig tree splinters.
It has stripped them bare and cast *them* away;
Their branches have become white.

8 Wail like a virgin girded with sackcloth
For the bridegroom of her youth.
9 The grain offering and the drink offering are cut off
From the house of the LORD.
The priests mourn,
The ministers of the LORD.
10 The field is ruined,
The land mourns;
For the grain is ruined,
The new wine dries up,
Fresh oil fails.
11 Be ashamed, O farmers,
Wail, O vinedressers,
For the wheat and the barley;
Because the harvest of the field is destroyed.
12 The vine dries up
And the fig tree fails;
The pomegranate, the palm also, and the apple tree,
All the trees of the field dry up.
Indeed, rejoicing dries up
From the sons of men.

13 Gird yourselves *with sackcloth*
And lament, O priests;
Wail, O ministers of the altar!
Come, spend the night in sackcloth
O ministers of my God,
For the grain offering and the drink offering
Are withheld from the house of your God.

1:4
Deut 28:38; Joel 2:25; Amos 4:9; Nah 3:15, 16; Is 33:4

1:5
Joel 3:3; Is 32:10

1:6
Joel 2:2, 11, 25; Rev 9:8

1:7
Is 5:6; Amos 4:9

1:8
Is 22:12; Joel 1:13; Amos 8:10

1:9
Hos 9:4; Joel 1:13; 2:14; Joel 2:17

1:10
Is 24:4, 7; Jer 12:11

1:11
Jer 14:4; Amos 5:16; Is 17:11; Jer 9:12

1:12
Joel 1:10; Hab 3:17; Hag 2:19; Song 7:8; Song 2:3; Is 16:10; 24:11; Jer 48:33

1:13
Jer 4:8; Ezek 7:18; Jer 9:10; 1 Kin 21:27

1:4 A locust plague can be as devastating as an invading army. Locusts gather in swarms too great to number (1:6) and fly several feet above the ground, seeming to darken the sun as they pass by (2:2). When they land, they devour almost every piece of vegetation (1:7–12), covering and entering everything in their path (2:9).

1:4 Joel's detailed description has caused many to believe that he was referring to an actual locust plague that had come or was about to come upon the land. Another view is that the locusts symbolize an invading enemy army. Both may be foreseen. The locusts represent devastation, and Joel's point was that God would punish the people because of their sin. Joel calls this judgment the "day of the LORD" (see the note on 1:15).

1:5 The people's physical and moral senses were dulled, making them oblivious to sin. Joel called them to awaken from their complacency and admit their sins before it was too late. Otherwise, everything would be destroyed, even the grapes that caused their drunkenness. Our times of peace and prosperity can lull us to sleep. We must never let material abundance hinder our spiritual readiness.

1:9 Because of the devastation, there was no fine flour or wine for the grain or drink offerings (see Leviticus 1 and 2 for a detailed explanation of these offerings).

1:13 Sackcloth is the clothing put on by mourners at a funeral. Used here, it would be a sign of repentance.

Starvation and Drought

1:14 Joel 2:15, 16; Lev 23:36; Jon 3:8

14 Consecrate a fast,
Proclaim a solemn assembly;
Gather the elders
And all the inhabitants of the land
To the house of the LORD your God,
And cry out to the LORD.

1:15 Is 13:9; Jer 30:7; Amos 5:16; Joel 2:1, 11, 31; Is 13:6; Ezek 7:2-12

15 Alas for the day!
For the day of the LORD is near,
And it will come as destruction from the Almighty.

1:16 Is 3:7; Amos 4:6; Deut 12:7; Ps 43:4

16 Has not food been cut off before our eyes,
Gladness and joy from the house of our God?

1:17 Is 17:10, 11

17 The seeds shrivel under their clods;
The storehouses are desolate,
The barns are torn down,
For the grain is dried up.

1:18 1 Kin 8:5; Jer 12:4; 14:5, 6; Hos 4:3

18 How the beasts groan!
The herds of cattle wander aimlessly
Because there is no pasture for them;
Even the flocks of sheep suffer.

1:19 Ps 50:15; Mic 7:7; Jer 9:10; Amos 7:4

19 To You, O LORD, I cry;
For fire has devoured the pastures of the wilderness
And the flame has burned up all the trees of the field.

1:20 Ps 104:21; 147:9; Joel 1:18; 1 Kin 17:7; 18:5

20 Even the beasts of the field pant for You;
For the water brooks are dried up
And fire has devoured the pastures of the wilderness.

The Terrible Visitation

2:1 Jer 4:5; Joel 2:15; Zeph 1:16; Joel 1:15; 2:11, 31; 3:14; Obad 15; Zeph 1:14

2 Blow a trumpet in Zion,
And sound an alarm on My holy mountain!
Let all the inhabitants of the land tremble,
For the day of the LORD is coming;

JOEL
Joel served as a prophet to Judah, possibly from 835–796 B.C.

Climate of the times	Wicked Queen Athaliah seized power in a bloody coup, but was overthrown after a few years. Joash was crowned king, but he was only seven years old and in great need of spiritual guidance. Joash followed God in his early years, but then turned away from him.
Main message	A plague of locusts had come to discipline the nation. Joel called the people to turn back to God before an even greater judgment occurred.
Importance of message	God judges all people for their sins, but he is merciful to those who turn to him and offers them eternal salvation.
Contemporary prophets	Elisha (848–797 B.C.) Jonah (793–753 B.C.)

1:14 A fast was a period of time when no food was eaten and people approached God with humility, sorrow for sin, and urgent prayer. In the Old Testament, people often would fast during times of calamity in order to focus their attention on God and to demonstrate their change of heart and their true devotion (see, for example, Judges 20:26; 1 Kings 21:27; Ezra 8:21; Jonah 3:5). The sacred assembly was a public religious gathering called so that everyone could repent and pray to God for mercy.

1:15 The "day of the LORD" is a common phrase in the Old Testament and in the book of Joel (see 2:1, 11, 31; 3:14). It always refers to some extraordinary happening, whether a present event (like a locust plague), an event in the near future (like the destruction of Jerusalem or the defeat of enemy nations), or the final period of history when God will defeat all the forces of evil.

Even when the day of the Lord refers to a present event, it also foreshadows the *final* day of the Lord. This final event of history has two aspects to it: (1) the last judgment on all evil and sin and (2) the final reward for faithful believers. Righteousness and truth will prevail, but not before much suffering (Zechariah 14:1–3). If you trust the Lord, looking toward this final day should give you hope, because then all who are faithful will be united forever with God.

1:15–19 Without God, destruction is sure. Those who have not personally accepted God's love and forgiveness will stand before him with no appeal. Be sure to call on God's love and mercy while you have the opportunity (2:32).

2:1ff Joel was still describing the devastating effects of the locust plague (see 2:25). The alarm showed that the crisis was at hand. However, Joel implied that the locust plague would be only the forerunner of an even greater crisis if the people didn't turn from their sins.

Surely it is near,
2 A day of darkness and gloom,
A day of clouds and thick darkness.
As the dawn is spread over the mountains,
So there is a great and mighty people;
There has never been *anything* like it,
Nor will there be again after it
To the years of many generations.
3 A fire consumes before them
And behind them a flame burns.
The land is like the garden of Eden before them
But a desolate wilderness behind them,
And nothing at all escapes them.
4 Their appearance is like the appearance of horses;
And like war horses, so they run.
5 With a noise as of chariots
They leap on the tops of the mountains,
Like the crackling of a flame of fire consuming the stubble,
Like a mighty people arranged for battle.
6 Before them the people are in anguish;
All faces turn pale.
7 They run like mighty men,
They climb the wall like soldiers;
And they each march in line,
Nor do they deviate from their paths.
8 They do not crowd each other,
They march everyone in his path;
When they burst through the defenses,
They do not break ranks.
9 They rush on the city,
They run on the wall;
They climb into the houses,
They enter through the windows like a thief.
10 Before them the earth quakes,
The heavens tremble,
The sun and the moon grow dark
And the stars lose their brightness.
11 The LORD utters His voice before His army;
Surely His camp is very great,
For strong is he who carries out His word.
The day of the LORD is indeed great and very awesome,
And who can endure it?
12 "Yet even now," declares the LORD,
"Return to Me with all your heart,
And with fasting, weeping and mourning;
13 And rend your heart and not your garments."
Now return to the LORD your God,
For He is gracious and compassionate,
Slow to anger, abounding in lovingkindness
And relenting of evil.
14 Who knows whether He will *not* turn and relent
And leave a blessing behind Him,
Even a grain offering and a drink offering

2:2 Joel 2:10, 31; Amos 5:18; Zeph 1:15; Joel 1:6; 2:11, 25; Lam 1:12; Dan 9:12; 12:1; Joel 1:2

2:3 Ps 97:3; Is 9:18, 19; Is 51:3; Ezek 36:35; Ex 10:5, 15; Ps 105:34, 35; Zech 7:14

2:4 Rev 9:7

2:5 Rev 9:9; Is 5:24; 30:30

2:6 Is 13:8; Nah 2:10; Jer 30:6

2:7 Prov 30:27

2:9 Ex 10:6; Jer 9:21; John 10:1

2:10 Ps 18:7; Joel 3:16; Nah 1:5; Is 13:10; 34:4; Jer 4:23; Ezek 32:7, 8; Joel 2:31; 3:15; Matt 24:29; Rev 8:12

2:11 Ps 46:6; Is 13:4; Jer 25:30; Joel 3:16; Joel 2:25; Jer 50:34; Rev 18:8; Jer 30:7; Joel 1:15; 2:1, 31; 3:14; Zeph 1:14, 15; Rev 6:17; Ezek 22:14; Mal 3:2

2:12 Deut 4:29; Jer 4:1, 2; Ezek 33:11; Hos 12:6; Dan 9:3

2:13 Ps 34:18; 51:17; Is 57:15; Gen 37:34; 2 Sam 1:11; Job 1:20; Jer 41:5; Ex 34:6; Jer 18:8; 42:10; Amos 7:3, 6

2:14 Jer 26:3; Jon 3:9; Hag 2:19; Joel 1:9, 13

2:3 The garden of Eden was Adam and Eve's first home (Genesis 2:8). Known for its beauty, here it is used to describe the beauty of the land prior to the devastation.

2:12–13 God told the people to turn to him while there was still time. Destruction would soon be upon them. Time is also running out for us. Because we don't know when our lives will end, we should trust and obey God now, while we can. Don't let anything hold you back from turning to him.

2:13 Deep remorse was often shown by tearing (rending) one's clothes. But God didn't want an outward display of penitence without true inward repentance (1 Samuel 16:7; Matthew 23:1–36). Be sure your attitude toward God is correct, not just your outward actions.

For the LORD your God?
15 Blow a trumpet in Zion,
Consecrate a fast, proclaim a solemn assembly,
16 Gather the people, sanctify the congregation,
Assemble the elders,
Gather the children and the nursing infants.
Let the bridegroom come out of his room
And the bride out of her *bridal* chamber.
17 Let the priests, the LORD'S ministers,
Weep between the porch and the altar,
And let them say, "Spare Your people, O LORD,
And do not make Your inheritance a reproach,
A byword among the nations.
Why should they among the peoples say,
'Where is their God?' "

2:15 Num 10:3; 2 Kin 10:20; Joel 1:14
2:16 1 Sam 16:5; 2 Chr 29:5; Ps 19:5
2:17 2 Chr 8:12; Ezek 8:16; Ex 32:11, 12; Is 37:20; Amos 7:2, 5; Ps 44:13; 74:10; Ps 42:10; 79:10; 115:2

Deliverance Promised

18 Then the LORD will be zealous for His land
And will have pity on His people.
19 The LORD will answer and say to His people,
"Behold, I am going to send you grain, new wine and oil,
And you will be satisfied *in full* with them;
And I will never again make you a reproach among the nations.
20 "But I will remove the northern *army* far from you,
And I will drive it into a parched and desolate land,
And its vanguard into the eastern sea,
And its rear guard into the western sea.
And its stench will arise and its foul smell will come up,
For it has done great things."

2:18 Zech 1:14; 8:2; Is 60:10; 63:9, 15
2:19 Jer 31:12; Hos 2:21, 22; Joel 1:10; Mal 3:10; Ezek 34:29; 36:15
2:20 Jer 1:14, 15; Zech 14:8; Deut 11:24; Is 34:3; Amos 4:10

21 Do not fear, O land, rejoice and be glad,
For the LORD has done great things.
22 Do not fear, beasts of the field,
For the pastures of the wilderness have turned green,
For the tree has borne its fruit,
The fig tree and the vine have yielded in full.
23 So rejoice, O sons of Zion,
And be glad in the LORD your God;
For He has given you [1]the early rain for *your* vindication.
And He has poured down for you the rain,
The [2]early and [3]latter rain as before.
24 The threshing floors will be full of grain,
And the vats will overflow with the new wine and oil.
25 "Then I will make up to you for the years
That the swarming locust has eaten,
The creeping locust, the stripping locust and the gnawing locust,

2:21 Is 54:4; Jer 30:10; Zeph 3:16, 17; Ps 126:3; Joel 2:26
2:22 Ps 65:12, 13
2:23 Ps 149:2; Is 12:2-6; Deut 11:14; Is 41:16; Jer 5:24; Hab 3:18; Zech 10:7; Lev 26:4; Hos 6:3; Zech 10:1
2:24 Lev 26:10; Amos 9:13; Mal 3:10
2:25 Joel 1:4-7; 2:2-11

1 I.e. autumn; or possibly *the teacher for righteousness* **2** I.e. autumn **3** I.e. spring

---

2:18 Joel reached a turning point in his prophecy, moving from prophesying about an outpouring of God's judgment to prophesying about an outpouring of God's forgiveness and blessing. But this would come only if the people began to live as God wanted them to, giving up their sins. Where there is repentance, there is hope. This section of the book feeds that hope. Without it, Joel's prophecy could bring only despair. This promise of forgiveness should have encouraged the people to repent.

2:20 Joel foresaw the invasion from the north by the armies of Assyria and Babylon, typified by the locusts.

2:21 Joel contrasts the fear of God's judgment (2:1) with the joy of God's intervention (2:21). On the day of the Lord, sin will bring judgment, and only God's forgiveness will bring rejoicing. Unless you repent, your sin will result in punishment. Let God intervene in your life. Then you will be able to rejoice in that day because you will have nothing to fear. Before, there were fasting, plagues, and funeral dirges; then, there will be feasting, harvesting, and songs of praise. When God rules, his restoration will be complete. In the meantime, we must remember that God does not promise that all his followers will be prosperous now. When God pardons, he restores our relationship with him, but this does not guarantee individual wealth. Instead, God promises to meet the deepest needs of those who love him—by loving us, forgiving us, giving us purpose in life, and giving us a caring Christian community.

My great army which I sent among you.
26 "You will have plenty to eat and be satisfied
And praise the name of the LORD your God,
Who has dealt wondrously with you;
Then My people will never be put to shame.
27 "Thus you will know that I am in the midst of Israel,
And that I am the LORD your God,
And there is no other;
And My people will never be put to shame.

2:26 Lev 26:5; Deut 11:15; Is 62:9; Deut 12:7; Ps 67:5-7; Ps 126:2, 3; Is 25:1; Is 45:17

2:27 Lev 26:11, 12; Joel 3:17, 21; Is 45:5, 6; Is 49:23

2. The day of the LORD

The Promise of the Spirit

28 "It will come about after this
That I will pour out My Spirit on all mankind;
And your sons and daughters will prophesy,
Your old men will dream dreams,
Your young men will see visions.
29 "Even on the male and female servants
I will pour out My Spirit in those days.
30 "I will display wonders in the sky and on the earth,
Blood, fire and columns of smoke.
31 "The sun will be turned into darkness
And the moon into blood
Before the great and awesome day of the LORD comes.
32 "And it will come about that whoever calls on the name of the LORD
Will be delivered;
For on Mount Zion and in Jerusalem
There will be those who escape,
As the LORD has said,
Even among the survivors whom the LORD calls.

2:28 Acts 2:17-21; Is 32:15; 44:3; Ezek 39:29; Zech 12:10; Is 40:5; 49:26

2:29 1 Cor 12:13; Gal 3:28

2:30 Matt 24:29; Mark 13:24, 25; Luke 21:11, 25, 26; Acts 2:19

2:31 Is 13:10; 34:4; Joel 2:10; 3:15; Matt 24:29; Mark 13:24; Luke 21:25; Acts 2:20; Rev 6:12, 13; Is 13:9; Zeph 1:14-16; Mal 4:1, 5

2:32 Jer 33:3; Acts 2:21; Rom 10:13; Is 46:13; Rom 11:26; Is 4:2; Obad 17; Is 11:11; Jer 31:7; Mic 4:7; Rom 9:27

The Nations Will Be Judged

3 "For behold, in those days and at that time,
When I restore the fortunes of Judah and Jerusalem,
2 I will gather all the nations
And bring them down to the valley of Jehoshaphat.

3:1 Jer 30:3; Ezek 38:14; Jer 16:15

3:2 Is 66:18; Mic 4:12; Zech 14:2; Joel 3:12, 14; Is 66:16; Jer 25:31; Ezek 38:22; Jer 50:17; Ezek 34:6; Ezek 35:10; 36:1-5

2:26–27 If the Jews would never again experience a disaster like this locust plague ("never be put to shame"), how do we explain the captivity in Babylon, the Jews' slavery under the Greeks and Romans, and their persecution under Hitler? It is important not to take these verses out of context. This is still part of the "blessings" section of Joel's prophecy. Only if the people truly repented would they avoid a disaster like the one Joel had described. God's blessings are promised only to those who sincerely and consistently follow him. God does promise that after the final day of judgment, his people will never again experience this kind of disaster (Zechariah 14:9–11; Revelation 21).

2:28–32 Peter quoted this passage (see Acts 2:16–21)—the outpouring of the Spirit predicted by Joel occurred on Pentecost. While in the past God's Spirit seemed available to kings, prophets, and judges, Joel envisioned a time when the Spirit would be available to every believer. Ezekiel also spoke of an outpouring of the Spirit (Ezekiel 39:28–29). God's Spirit is available now to anyone who calls on the Lord (2:32).

2:30 These "wonders" would give a hint or a picture of a coming event.

2:31–32 The "day of the LORD" is used here as God's appointed time to judge the nations (see the note on 1:15). Judgment and mercy go hand in hand. Joel had said that if the people repented, the Lord would save them from judgment (2:12–14). In this day of judgment and catastrophe, therefore, some will be saved. God's intention is not to destroy but to heal and to save. However, we must accept his salvation or we will certainly perish with the unrepentant.

3:1–2 The phrase "in those days and at that time" refers to the time when those who call on the Lord will be saved (2:32). God will not only bless believers with everything they need; he will also bless them by destroying all evil and ending the pain and suffering on earth. This prophecy had three fulfillments: immediate, ongoing, and final. Its immediate interpretation could apply to King Jehoshaphat's recent battle against several enemy nations, including Moab and Ammon (2 Chronicles 20). Its ongoing fulfillment could be the partial restoration of the people to their land after the exile to Babylon. The final fulfillment will come in the great battle that precedes the Messiah's reign over the earth (Revelation 20:7–9).

3:2 The geographic location of the valley of Jehoshaphat is not known, and some suggest it is being used as a symbol for the place where the Lord is to judge. Some think it may be a future valley created by the splitting of the Mount of Olives when the Messiah returns (Zechariah 14:4). The most important fact for us is that the name means "the LORD judges."

3:3 Obad 11; Nah 3:10; Amos 2:6
3:4 Is 23:1-18; Amos 1:9, 10; Zech 9:2-4; Matt 11:21, 22; Luke 10:13, 14; Is 14:29-31; Jer 47:1-7; Ezek 25:15-17; Amos 1:6-8; Is 34:8; 59:18
3:5 2 Kin 12:18; 2 Chr 21:16, 17
3:6 Ezek 27:13
3:7 Is 43:5, 6; Jer 23:8; Zech 9:13
3:8 Is 14:2; 60:14; Job 1:15; Ps 72:10; Ezek 38:13
3:9 Jer 51:27; Jer 6:4; Ezek 38:7; Mic 3:5; Is 8:9, 10; Jer 46:3, 4; Zech 14:2, 3
3:10 Is 2:4; Mic 4:3; Zech 12:8
3:11 Ezek 38:15, 16; Is 13:3
3:12 Ps 7:6; 96:13; 98:9; Is 2:4; 3:13
3:13 Rev 14:14-19; Jer 51:33; Hos 6:11; 19:15; Is 63:3; Lam 1:15; Gen 18:20
3:14 Is 34:2-8; Joel 3:2, 12; 2:1, 11, 31
3:15 Joel 2:10, 31
3:16 Hos 11:10; Amos 1:2; Hag 2:6; Ps 61:3; Is 33:16; Jer 17:17; Jer 16:19; Nah 1:7
3:17 Joel 2:27; Is 11:9; 56:7; Ezek 20:40; Is 4:3; Obad 17; Is 52:1; Nah 1:15

Then I will enter into judgment with them there
On behalf of My people and My inheritance, Israel,
Whom they have scattered among the nations;
And they have divided up My land.
3 "They have also cast lots for My people,
Traded a boy for a harlot
And sold a girl for wine that they may drink.
4 "Moreover, what are you to Me, O Tyre, Sidon and all the regions of Philistia? Are
you rendering Me a recompense? But if you do recompense Me, swiftly and speedily I
will return your recompense on your head.
5 "Since you have taken My silver and My gold, brought My precious treasures to your
temples,
6 and sold the sons of Judah and Jerusalem to the Greeks in order to remove them
far from their territory,
7 behold, I am going to arouse them from the place where you have sold them, and
return your recompense on your head.
8 "Also I will sell your sons and your daughters into the hand of the sons of Judah, and
they will sell them to the Sabeans, to a distant nation," for the LORD has spoken.
9 Proclaim this among the nations:
Prepare a war; rouse the mighty men!
Let all the soldiers draw near, let them come up!
10 Beat your plowshares into swords
And your pruning hooks into spears;
Let the weak say, "I am a mighty man."
11 Hasten and come, all you surrounding nations,
And gather yourselves there.
Bring down, O LORD, Your mighty ones.
12 Let the nations be aroused
And come up to the valley of Jehoshaphat,
For there I will sit to judge
All the surrounding nations.
13 Put in the sickle, for the harvest is ripe.
Come, tread, for the wine press is full;
The vats overflow, for their wickedness is great.
14 Multitudes, multitudes in the valley of decision!
For the day of the LORD is near in the valley of decision.
15 The sun and moon grow dark
And the stars lose their brightness.
16 The LORD roars from Zion
And utters His voice from Jerusalem,
And the heavens and the earth tremble.
But the LORD is a refuge for His people
And a stronghold to the sons of Israel.
17 Then you will know that I am the LORD your God,
Dwelling in Zion, My holy mountain.

3:4 Tyre and Sidon were major cities in Phoenicia to the northwest of Israel; Philistia was the nation southwest of Judah. Phoenicia and Philistia were small countries who rejoiced at the fall of Judah and Israel because they would benefit from the increased trade. God would judge them for their wrong attitude.

3:6 Jews were sold to Greeks, a pagan and unclean people. Some think this verse and 3:1 indicate that Joel lived after the captivity in Babylon (586 B.C.), when the Greek culture began to flourish. But archaeological studies have shown that the Greeks were trading with Phoenicia as early as 800 B.C. Also 3:4 mentions Tyre, Sidon, and Philistia. These places were contemporary with Judah before their captivity.

3:8 The Sabeans came from Sheba, a nation in southwestern Arabia. One of Sheba's queens had visited Solomon over a century earlier (1 Kings 10:1–13). The Sabeans controlled the eastern trade routes.

3:14 Joel described multitudes waiting in the "valley of decision" (the valley of judgment of verses 2 and 12). Billions of people have lived on earth, and every one of them—dead, living, and yet to be born—will face judgment. Look around you. See your friends, those with whom you work and live. Have they received God's forgiveness? Have they been warned about sin's consequences? If we understand the severity of God's final judgment, we will want to take God's offer of hope to those we know.

3:17 The last word will be God's; his ultimate sovereignty will be revealed in the end. We cannot predict when that end will come, but we can have confidence in his control over the world's events. The world's history, as well as our own pilgrimage, is in God's hands. We can be secure in his love and trust him to guide our decisions.

So Jerusalem will be holy,
And strangers will pass through it no more.

Judah Will Be Blessed

18 And in that day
The mountains will drip with sweet wine,
And the hills will flow with milk,
And all the brooks of Judah will flow with water;
And a spring will go out from the house of the LORD
To water the valley of Shittim.
19 Egypt will become a waste,
And Edom will become a desolate wilderness,
Because of the violence done to the sons of Judah,
In whose land they have shed innocent blood.
20 But Judah will be inhabited forever
And Jerusalem for all generations.
21 And I will avenge their blood which I have not avenged,
For the LORD dwells in Zion.

3:18 Amos 9:13; Ex 3:8; Is 30:25; 35:6; Ezek 47:1-12

3:19 Obad 10

3:20 Ezek 37:25; Amos 9:15

3:21 Is 4:4

3:18 The picture of this restored land is one of perfect beauty, similar to the garden of Eden. The life-giving fountain flowing from the Lord's house illustrates the blessings that come from God. Those who attach themselves to him will be forever fruitful. (See also Ezekiel 47:1–12; Revelation 22:1–2.)

3:19 Egypt and Edom were two of Israel's most persistent enemies. They represent all the nations hostile to God's people. God's promise that they would be destroyed is also a promise that all evil in the world will one day be destroyed.

3:20–21 The word *Judah* is used here to refer to all God's people—anyone who has called on the name of the Lord. There is full assurance of victory and peace for those who trust in God (2:32).

3:21 Joel began with a prophecy about the destruction of the land and ended with a prophecy about its restoration. He began by stressing the need for repentance and ended with the promise of forgiveness that repentance brings. Joel was trying to convince the people to wake up (1:5), get rid of their complacency, and realize the danger of living apart from God. His message to us is that there is still time; anyone who calls on God's name can be saved (2:12–14, 32). Those who turn to God will enjoy the blessings mentioned in Joel's prophecy; those who refuse will face destruction.

PROPHECIES AGAINST THE NATIONS
The Old Testament prophets usually targeted Israel and Judah in their messages. But other surrounding nations also received warnings of impending judgment.

AMMON	The nation of Ammon was located east of the Jordan River. They were related to the Israelites because they were descendants of Lot. They would become slaves of the Babylonians because they rejoiced at Israel's fall.	Prophets who spoke against Ammon included Ezekiel (25:1-7), Jeremiah (49:1-6), Amos (1:13-15), and Zephaniah (2:8-11).
EDOM	The nation of Edom was located south of the Dead Sea. They were related to the Israelites as descendants of Esau, but had acted revengefully against Israel.	Prophets who spoke against Edom included Ezekiel (25:12-14), Jeremiah (49:7-22), Joel (3:19), Amos (9:11-12), and Obadiah (10-21).
EGYPT	The Egyptians lived along the Nile River. The Israelites had lived in Egypt for over 400 years and were delivered from slavery there by Moses. The Babylonians would plunder Egypt because the Egyptians did not respect the Lord.	Prophets who spoke against Egypt included Moses (Exodus 5:1—12:42), Isaiah (19:1—20:6), Jeremiah (46:1-28), Ezekiel (29:1—32:32), Daniel (11:42-43), Joel (3:19), and Zechariah (10:11; 14:18-19).
MOAB	The nation of Moab was located to the south of Ammon and east of the Dead Sea. They were related to the Israelites as they were descended from Lot. Because Moab said that Judah is just like any other nation, God would sell them with Ammon into the Babylonians' hands.	Prophets who spoke against Moab included Isaiah (15:1—16:14), Jeremiah (9:26; 25:21; 27:3; 48:1-47), Ezekiel (25:8-11), Amos (2:1-3), and Zephaniah (2:8-11).
PHILISTIA	The Philistines lived in southwestern Palestine, along the Mediterranean coast. They were constant enemies of the Israelites from the time of Joshua to Solomon. They would be destroyed because of their unending hostilities toward God's people.	Prophets who spoke against Philistia included Jeremiah (47:5-7), Ezekiel (25:15-17), Amos (1:6-8; 6:2), Obadiah (19), Zephaniah (2:4-5), and Zechariah (9:5-7).
PHOENICIA (TYRE AND SIDON)	The Phoenicians lived on the Mediterranean coast, north of Palestine. They had always been good (though often competing) trading partners with the Israelites. They would be destroyed because they rejoiced at Israel's demise.	Prophets who spoke against Tyre and Sidon included Jeremiah (25:22; 27:1-11), Ezekiel (26:1—28:24), Amos (1:9-10), and Zechariah (9:2-4).

AMOS

Jeroboam II becomes king of Israel 793 B.C.

VITAL STATISTICS

PURPOSE:
To pronounce God's judgment upon Israel, the northern kingdom, for its complacency, idolatry, and oppression of the poor

AUTHOR:
Amos

TO WHOM WRITTEN:
Israel, the northern kingdom, and God's people everywhere

DATE WRITTEN:
Probably during the reigns of Jeroboam II of Israel and Uzziah (Azariah) of Judah (approximately 760–750 B.C.)

SETTING:
The wealthy people of Israel were enjoying peace and prosperity. They were quite complacent and were oppressing the poor, even selling them into slavery. Soon, however, Israel would be conquered by Assyria, and the rich would themselves become slaves.

KEY VERSE:
"But let justice roll down like waters and righteousness like an ever-flowing stream" (5:24).

KEY PEOPLE:
Amos, Amaziah, Jeroboam II

KEY PLACES:
Bethel, Samaria

SPECIAL FEATURES:
Amos uses striking metaphors from his shepherding and farming experience—a loaded wagon (2:13), a roaring lion (3:8), a mutilated sheep (3:12), fat cows (4:1), and a basket of ripe fruit (8:1–2).

WHEN we hear, "He's a man of God," the images that most often come to mind are some famous evangelist, a "Reverend," a missionary, or the campus minister—professionals, Christian workers, those who preach and teach the Word as a vocation.

Surely Amos was a man of God, a person whose life was devoted to serving the Lord and whose life-style reflected this devotion—but he was a layperson. Herding sheep and tending sycamore-fig trees in the Judean countryside, Amos was not the son of a prophet; he was not the son of a priest. As a humble shepherd, he could have stayed in Tekoa, doing his job, providing for his family, and worshiping his God. But God gave Amos a vision of the future (1:1) and told him to take his message to Israel, the northern kingdom (7:15). Amos obeyed and thus proved he was a man of God.

Amos's message has had an impact on God's people throughout the centuries, and it needs to be heard today by individuals and nations. Although they were divided from their southern brothers and sisters in Judah, the northern Israelites were still God's people. But they were living beneath a pious veneer of religion, worshiping idols and oppressing the poor. Amos, a fiery, fearless, and honest shepherd from the south, confronted them with their sin and warned them of the impending judgment.

The book of Amos opens with this humble shepherd watching his sheep. God then gave him a vision of what was about to happen to the nation of Israel. God condemned all the nations who had sinned against him and harmed his people. Beginning with Aram, he moved quickly through Philistia, Tyre, Edom, Ammon, and Moab. All were condemned, and we can almost hear the Israelites shouting, "Amen!" And then, even Judah, Amos's homeland, was included in God's scathing denunciation (2:4–5). How Amos's listeners must have enjoyed hearing those words! Suddenly, however, Amos turned to the people of Israel and pronounced God's judgment on *them.* The next four chapters enumerate and describe their sins. It is no wonder that Amaziah the priest intervened and tried to stop the preaching (7:10–13). Fearlessly, Amos continued to relate the visions of future judgment that God gave to him (chapters 8—9). After all the chapters on judgment, the book concludes with a message of hope. Eventually God will restore his people and make them great again (9:8–15).

As you read Amos's book, put yourself in the place of those Israelites and listen to God's message. Have you grown complacent? Have other concerns taken God's place in your life? Do you ignore those in need or oppress the poor? Picture yourself as Amos, faithfully doing what God calls you to do. You, too, can be God's person. Listen for his clear call and do what he says, wherever it leads.

Amos becomes a prophet to Israel 760	*Hosea becomes a prophet to Israel 753*	*King Shallum of Israel is assassinated 752*	*Amos's ministry ends 750*	*Isaiah becomes a prophet to Judah 740*

THE BLUEPRINT

1. Announcement of judgment (1:1—2:16)
2. Reasons for judgment (3:1—6:14)
3. Visions of judgment (7:1—9:15)

Amos speaks with brutal frankness in denouncing sin. He collided with the false religious leaders of his day and was not intimidated by priest or king. He continued to speak his message boldly. God requires truth and goodness, justice and righteousness, from all people and nations today as well. Many of the conditions in Israel during Amos's time are evident in today's society. We need Amos's courage to ignore danger and stand against sin.

MEGATHEMES

THEME	EXPLANATION	IMPORTANCE
Everyone Answers to God	Amos pronounced judgment from God on all the surrounding nations. Then he included Judah and Israel. God is in supreme control of all the nations. Everyone is accountable to him.	All people will have to account for their sin. When those who reject God seem to get ahead, don't envy their prosperity or feel sorry for yourself. Remember that we all must answer to God for how we live.
Complacency	Everyone was optimistic, business was booming, and people were happy (except for the poor and oppressed). With all the comfort and luxury came self-sufficiency and a false sense of security. But prosperity brought corruption and destruction.	A complacent present leads to a disastrous future. Don't congratulate yourself for the blessings and benefits you now enjoy. They are from God. If you are more satisfied with yourself than with God, remember that everything is meaningless without him. A self-sufficient attitude may be your downfall.
Oppressing the Poor	The wealthy and powerful people of Samaria, the capital of Israel, had become prosperous, greedy, and unjust. Illegal and immoral slavery came as the result of over-taxation and land-grabbing. There was also cruelty and indifference toward the poor. God is weary of greed and will not tolerate injustice.	God made all people; therefore, to ignore the poor is to ignore those whom God loves and whom Christ came to save. We must go beyond feeling bad for the poor and oppressed. We must act compassionately to stop injustice and to help care for those in need.
Superficial Religion	Although many people had abandoned real faith in God, they still pretended to be religious. They were carrying on superficial religious exercises instead of having spiritual integrity and practicing heartfelt obedience toward God.	Merely participating in ceremony or ritual falls short of true religion. God wants simple trust in him, not showy external actions. Don't settle for impressing others with external rituals when God wants heartfelt obedience and commitment.

1. Announcement of judgment

Judgment on Neighbor Nations

1 The words of Amos, who was among the sheepherders from Tekoa, which he envi-
sioned in visions concerning Israel in the days of Uzziah king of Judah, and in the
days of Jeroboam son of Joash, king of Israel, two years before the earthquake.
2 He said,
"The LORD roars from Zion
And from Jerusalem He utters His voice;
And the shepherds' pasture grounds mourn,
And the summit of Carmel dries up."

3 Thus says the LORD,
"For three transgressions of Damascus and for four
I will not revoke its *punishment,*
Because they threshed Gilead with *implements* of sharp iron.
4 "So I will send fire upon the house of Hazael
And it will consume the citadels of Ben-hadad.
5 "I will also break the *gate* bar of Damascus,
And cut off the inhabitant from the valley of Aven,
And him who holds the scepter, from Beth-eden;
So the people of Aram will go exiled to Kir,"
Says the LORD.

6 Thus says the LORD,
"For three transgressions of Gaza and for four
I will not revoke its *punishment,*
Because they deported an entire population
To deliver *it* up to Edom.
7 "So I will send fire upon the wall of Gaza
And it will consume her citadels.
8 "I will also cut off the inhabitant from Ashdod,
And him who holds the scepter, from Ashkelon;

1:1 Amos 7:14; 2 Sam 14:2; Jer 6:1; 2 Chr 26:1-23; Is 1:1; 2 Kin 14:23-29; Hos 1:1; Amos 7:10, 11; Zech 14:5

1:2 Is 42:13; Jer 25:30; Joel 3:16; Jer 12:4; Joel 1:18, 19; Amos 9:3

1:3 Amos 2:1, 4, 6; Is 8:4; 17:1-3; Jer 49:23-27; Zech 9:1

1:4 1 Kin 20:1; 2 Kin 6:24

1:5 Jer 51:30; Lam 2:9; 2 Kin 16:9; Amos 9:7

1:6 1 Sam 6:17; Jer 47:1, 5; Zeph 2:4; Ezek 35:5; Obad 11

1:8 2 Chr 26:6; Amos 3:9; Zech 9:6; Jer 47:5; Zeph 2:4; Is 14:29-31; Jer 47:1-7; Ezek 25:16; Joel 3:4-8; Zeph 2:4-7; Zech 9:5-7

1:1 Amos was a shepherd and fig grower from the southern kingdom (Judah), but he prophesied to the northern kingdom (Israel). Israel was politically at the height of its power with a prosperous economy, but the nation was spiritually corrupt. Idols were worshiped throughout the land, and especially at Bethel, which was supposed to be the nation's religious center. Like Hosea, Amos was sent by God to denounce this social and religious corruption. About 30 or 40 years after Amos prophesied, Assyria destroyed the capital city, Samaria, and conquered Israel (722 B.C.). Uzziah reigned in Judah from 792–740; Jeroboam II reigned in Israel from 793–753.

1:1 Tekoa, Amos's hometown, was located in the rugged sheep country of Judah, about ten miles south of Jerusalem. Long before Amos was born, a woman of Tekoa had helped reconcile David and his rebellious son, Absalom (2 Samuel 14:1–23).

1:1 Amos raised sheep—not a particularly "spiritual" job—yet he became a channel of God's message to others. Your job may not cause you to feel spiritual or successful, but it is a vital work if you are in the place God wants you to be. God can work through you to do extraordinary things, no matter how ordinary your occupation.

1:1 The prophet Zechariah and other historical records from this period mention an earthquake that occurred at this time (Zechariah 14:5).

1:2 In the Bible, God is often pictured as a shepherd and his people as sheep. As a shepherd, God leads and protects his flock. But here God is depicted as a ferocious lion ready to devour those who are evil or unfaithful. (See also Hosea 11:10.)

1:2 Carmel means "fertile field." It was a very fertile area. A drought capable of drying up this area would have to be quite severe.

1:3 Damascus was the capital of Aram. In the past, Aram had been one of Israel's most formidable enemies. After the defeat of Aram by Assyria in 732 B.C. (2 Kings 16:9), Damascus was no longer a real threat.

1:3—2:6 Amos pronounced God's judgment on nation after nation around Israel's borders—even Judah. Perhaps the people of Israel cheered when they heard the rebukes leveled against those nations. But then Amos proclaimed God's judgment on Israel. They could not excuse their own sin just because the sins of their neighbors seemed worse. God is no respecter of persons. He judges all people fairly and impartially.

1:3—2:6 The accusation "For three transgressions . . . and for four" means that these nations had sinned again and again. This phrase echoes through these verses as God evaluates nation after nation. Each nation had persistently refused to follow God's commands. A sinful practice can become a way of life. Ignoring or denying the problem will not help us. We must begin the process of correction by confessing our sins to God and asking him to forgive us. Otherwise, we have no hope but to continue our pattern of sin.

1:4 The "house of Hazael" refers to the king of Aram. Ben-hadad was Hazael's son (2 Kings 13:24).

1:5 The Arameans had been slaves in Kir, but here they were free (9:7). Decreeing that the Arameans should go back to Kir was like saying the Israelites should go back to Egypt as slaves (Exodus 1).

1:7–8 Gaza, Ashdod, Ashkelon, and Ekron were four of the five major cities of Philistia, an enemy who often threatened Israel. The fifth city, Gath, had probably already been destroyed. Therefore, Amos was saying that the entire nation of Philistia would be destroyed for its sins.

I will even unleash My power upon Ekron,
And the remnant of the Philistines will perish,"
Says the Lord GOD.

1:9 Is 23:1-18; Jer 25:22; Ezek 26:2-4; Joel 3:4-8; Zech 9:1-4; Matt 11:21, 22; Luke 10:13, 14; 1 Kin 9:11-14

1:10 Zech 9:4

9 Thus says the LORD,
"For three transgressions of Tyre and for four
I will not revoke its *punishment*,
Because they delivered up an entire population to Edom
And did not remember *the* covenant of brotherhood.
10 "So I will send fire upon the wall of Tyre
And it will consume her citadels."

1:11 Is 34:5, 6; 63:1-6; Jer 49:7-22; Ezek 25:12-14; 35:1-15; Obad 1-14; Mal 1:2-5; Num 20:14-21; 2 Chr 28:17; Obad 10-12; Is 57:16; Mic 7:18

1:12 Jer 49:7, 20; Obad 9

11 Thus says the LORD,
"For three transgressions of Edom and for four
I will not revoke its *punishment*,
Because he pursued his brother with the sword,
While he stifled his compassion;
His anger also tore continually,
And he maintained his fury forever.
12 "So I will send fire upon Teman
And it will consume the citadels of Bozrah."

1:13 Jer 49:1-6; Ezek 21:28-32; 25:2-7; Zeph 2:8, 9; 2 Kin 15:16; Hos 13:16; Is 5:8; Ezek 35:10

1:14 Deut 3:11; 1 Chr 20:1; Jer 49:2; Ezek 21:22; Amos 2:2; Is 29:6; 30:30

1:15 Jer 49:3

13 Thus says the LORD,
"For three transgressions of the sons of Ammon and for four
I will not revoke its *punishment*,
Because they ripped open the pregnant women of Gilead
In order to enlarge their borders.
14 "So I will kindle a fire on the wall of Rabbah
And it will consume her citadels
Amid war cries on the day of battle,
And a storm on the day of tempest.
15 "Their king will go into exile,
He and his princes together," says the LORD.

AMOS
Amos served as a prophet to Israel (the northern kingdom) from 760–750 B.C.

Climate of the times	Israel was enjoying peace and economic prosperity. But this blessing had caused her to become a selfish, materialistic society. Those who were well-off ignored the needs of those less fortunate. The people were self-centered and indifferent toward God.
Main message	Amos spoke against those who exploited or ignored the needy.
Importance of message	Believing in God is more than a matter of individual faith. God calls all believers to work against injustices in society and to aid those less fortunate.
Contemporary prophets	Jonah (793–753 B.C.) Hosea (753–715 B.C.)

1:9 Tyre was one of two major cities in Phoenicia. Several treaties had been made with this city, which supplied the cedar used to build David's palace and God's temple (2 Samuel 5:11; 1 Kings 5).

1:11–12 Both Edom and Israel had descended from Isaac: Edom from Isaac's son Esau, and Israel from Esau's twin brother, Jacob (Genesis 25:19–28; 27). But these two nations, like the two brothers, were always fighting. Edom had rejoiced at Israel's misfortunes. As a result, God promised to destroy Edom completely, from Teman in the south to Bozrah in the north.

1:13–15 The Ammonites had descended from an incestuous relationship between Lot and his younger daughter (Genesis 19:30–38). The Ammonites were hostile to Israel; although Israel began to worship their idols, the Ammonites still attacked (Judges 10:6–8). After Saul had been anointed Israel's king, his first victory in battle was against the Ammonites (1 Samuel 11). Rabbah was Ammon's capital city. Amos's prophecy of Ammon's destruction was fulfilled through the Assyrian invasion.

Judgment on Judah and Israel

2 Thus says the LORD,
"For three transgressions of Moab and for four
I will not revoke its *punishment,*
Because he burned the bones of the king of Edom to lime.
2 "So I will send fire upon Moab
And it will consume the citadels of Kerioth;
And Moab will die amid tumult,
With war cries and the sound of a trumpet.
3 "I will also cut off the judge from her midst
And slay all her princes with him," says the LORD.

4 Thus says the LORD,
"For three transgressions of Judah and for four
I will not revoke its *punishment,*
Because they rejected the law of the LORD
And have not kept His statutes;
Their lies also have led them astray,
Those after which their fathers walked.
5 "So I will send fire upon Judah
And it will consume the citadels of Jerusalem."

6 Thus says the LORD,
"For three transgressions of Israel and for four
I will not revoke its *punishment,*
Because they sell the righteous for money
And the needy for a pair of sandals.
7 "These who pant after the *very* dust of the earth on the head of the helpless
Also turn aside the way of the humble;
And a man and his father resort to the same girl
In order to profane My holy name.
8 "On garments taken as pledges they stretch out beside every altar,
And in the house of their God they drink the wine of those who have been fined.

9 "Yet it was I who destroyed the Amorite before them,
Though his height *was* like the height of cedars
And he *was* strong as the oaks;
I even destroyed his fruit above and his root below.

2:1 Is 15:1-16:14; 25:10-12; Jer 48:1-47; Ezek 25:8-11; Zeph 2:8, 9; 2 Kin 3:26, 27

2:2 Jer 48:24, 41; Jer 48:45

2:3 Ps 2:10; 141:6; Amos 5:7, 12; 6:12; Job 12:21; Is 40:23

2:4 2 Kin 17:19; Hos 12:2; Amos 3:2; Judg 2:17-20; 2 Kin 22:11-17; Jer 6:19; 8:9; Is 9:15, 16; 28:15; Jer 16:19; Hab 2:18; Jer 9:14; 16:11, 12; Ezek 20:18, 24, 30

2:5 Jer 17:27; 21:10; Hos 8:14

2:6 2 Kin 18:11, 12; Joel 3:3; Amos 5:11, 12; 8:6

2:7 Amos 8:4; Mic 2:2, 9; Amos 5:12; Hos 4:14

2:8 Ex 22:26; Amos 3:14; Amos 4:1; 6:6

2:9 Num 21:23-25; Josh 10:12; Num 13:32; Ezek 17:9; Mal 4:1

2:1–3 The Moabites had descended from an incestuous relationship between Lot and his older daughter (Genesis 19:30–38). Balak, king of Moab, had tried to hire the prophet Balaam to curse the Israelites so they could be defeated (Numbers 22—24). Balaam spoke instead the Lord's word of blessing, but some of the Moabites had succeeded in getting Israel to worship Baal (Numbers 25:1–3). The Moabites were known for their atrocities (2 Kings 3:26–27). An archaeological artifact, the Moabite Stone, reveals that Moab was always ready to profit from the downfall of others.

2:4–6 After Solomon died, the kingdom divided, and the tribes of Judah and Benjamin became the southern kingdom (Judah) under Solomon's son, Rehoboam. The other ten tribes became the northern kingdom (Israel) and followed Jeroboam, who had rebelled against Rehoboam.

God had punished other nations harshly for their evil actions and atrocities. But God also promised to judge both Israel and Judah because they ignored the revealed law of God. The other nations were ignorant, but Judah and Israel, God's people, knew what God wanted. Still they ignored him and joined pagan nations in worshiping idols. If we know God's Word and refuse to obey it, like Israel we will carry a greater guilt.

2:4–6 Amos must have won over his audience as he proclaimed God's judgment against the evil nations surrounding Israel. But then he even spoke against his own nation, Judah, before focusing on God's indictment of Israel.

2:6ff God condemned Israel for five specific sins: (1) selling the poor as slaves (see Deuteronomy 15:7–11; Amos 8:6), (2) exploiting the poor (see Exodus 23:6; Deuteronomy 16:19), (3) engaging in perverse sexual sins (see Leviticus 20:11–12), (4) taking illegal collateral for loans (see Exodus 22:26–27; Deuteronomy 24:6, 12–13), and (5) worshiping false gods (see Exodus 20:3–5).

2:6–7 Amos was speaking to the upper class. There was no middle class in the country—only the very rich and the very poor. The rich kept religious rituals. They gave extra tithes, went to places of worship, and offered sacrifices. But they were greedy and unjust, and they took advantage of the helpless. Be sure that you do not neglect the needs of the poor while you faithfully attend church and fulfill religious rituals. God expects us to live out our faith—this means responding to those in need.

2:9–11 The prophets were constantly challenging people to remember what God had done! When we read a list like this one, we are amazed at Israel's forgetfulness. But what would the prophets say about us? God's past faithfulness should have reminded the Israelites to obey him; likewise, what he has done for us should remind us to live for him.

2:10 Ex 12:51; 20:2; Amos 3:1; 9:7; Deut 2:7; Ex 3:8
2:11 Deut 18:18; Jer 7:25; Num 6:2, 3; Judg 13:5
2:12 Is 30:10; Jer 11:21; Amos 7:13, 16; Mic 2:6
2:13 Is 1:14
2:14 Is 30:16, 17; Ps 33:16; Jer 9:23
2:15 Jer 51:56; Ezek 39:3; Is 31:3
2:16 Judg 4:17
3:1 Jer 8:3; 13:11
3:2 Gen 18:19; Ex 19:5, 6; Deut 4:32-37; 7:6; Jer 14:10; Ezek 20:36; Dan 9:12; Rom 2:9
3:4 Ps 104:21; Hos 5:14; 11:10
3:6 Jer 4:5, 19, 21; 6:1; Hos 5:8; Zeph 1:16; Is 14:24-27; 45:7
3:7 Gen 6:13; 18:17; Jer 23:22; Dan 9:22; John 15:15
3:8 Amos 1:2; Jon 1:1-3; 3:1-3; Jer 20:9; Acts 4:20
3:9 1 Sam 5:1; Amos 4:1; 6:1; Amos 5:11; 8:6

10 "It was I who brought you up from the land of Egypt,
And I led you in the wilderness forty years
That you might take possession of the land of the Amorite.
11 "Then I raised up some of your sons to be prophets
And some of your young men to be Nazirites.
Is this not so, O sons of Israel?" declares the LORD.
12 "But you made the Nazirites drink wine,
And you commanded the prophets saying, 'You shall not prophesy!'
13 "Behold, I am weighted down beneath you
As a wagon is weighted down when filled with sheaves.
14 "Flight will perish from the swift,
And the stalwart will not strengthen his power,
Nor the mighty man save his life.
15 "He who grasps the bow will not stand *his ground,*
The swift of foot will not escape,
Nor will he who rides the horse save his life.
16 "Even the bravest among the warriors will flee naked in that day," declares the LORD.

2. Reasons for judgment

All the Tribes Are Guilty

3 Hear this word which the LORD has spoken against you, sons of Israel, against the
entire family which He brought up from the land of Egypt:
2 "You only have I chosen among all the families of the earth;
Therefore I will punish you for all your iniquities."
3 Do two men walk together unless they have made an appointment?
4 Does a lion roar in the forest when he has no prey?
Does a young lion growl from his den unless he has captured *something?*
5 Does a bird fall into a trap on the ground when there is no bait in it?
Does a trap spring up from the earth when it captures nothing at all?
6 If a trumpet is blown in a city will not the people tremble?
If a calamity occurs in a city has not the LORD done it?
7 Surely the Lord GOD does nothing
Unless He reveals His secret counsel
To His servants the prophets.
8 A lion has roared! Who will not fear?
The Lord GOD has spoken! Who can but prophesy?
9 Proclaim on the citadels in Ashdod and on the citadels in the land of Egypt and say,
"Assemble yourselves on the mountains of Samaria and see *the* great tumults within her
and *the* oppressions in her midst.

2:11 The Nazirites took a vow of service to God. The vow included abstaining from wine and never cutting their hair. But instead of being respected for their disciplined and temperate lives, they were being urged to break their vows. If the Nazirites were corrupted, there would remain little influence for good among the Israelites.

2:16 "That day" refers to when Assyria would attack Israel, destroy Samaria, and take the people captive (722 B.C.). This military defeat came only a few decades after this pronouncement.

2:16 Television and movies are filled with images of people who seem to have no fear. Many today have modeled their lives after these images—they want to be tough. But God is not impressed with bravado. He says that even the toughest people will run in fear when God's judgment comes. Do you know people who think they can make it through life without God? Don't be swayed by their self-assured rhetoric. Recognize that God fears no one, and one day all people will fear him.

3:2 God chose Israel to be the people through whom all other nations of the world could know him. He made this promise to Abraham, father of the Israelites (Genesis 12:1–3). Israel didn't have to do anything to be chosen; God had given them this special privilege because he wanted to, not because they deserved special treatment (Deuteronomy 9:4–6). Pride in their privileged position, however, ruined Israel's sensitivity to the will of God and to the plight of others.

3:3–6 With a series of seven rhetorical questions, Amos shows how two events can be linked together. Once one event takes place, the second will surely follow. Amos was showing that God's revelation to him was the sure sign that judgment would follow.

3:6 This verse means that God himself would be sending disaster to Israel.

3:7 Even in anger, God is merciful: He always warned his people through prophets before punishing them. Warnings about sin and judgment apply to people today just as they did to Israel. Because we have been warned about our sin, we have no excuse when punishment comes. God had warned his people through his prophets, so they could not rationalize or complain when God punished them for refusing to repent. Do not take lightly the warnings in God's Word about judgment. His warnings are a way of showing mercy to you.

3:9 Ashdod was a Philistine city and the site of the temple of Dagon, a pagan god. Amos pictured Philistia and Egypt summoned to witness Israel's great sins. Even Israel's most wicked and idolatrous neighbors would see God judge Israel.

10 "But they do not know how to do what is right," declares the LORD, "these who hoard
up violence and devastation in their citadels."
11 Therefore, thus says the Lord GOD,
"An enemy, even one surrounding the land,
Will pull down your strength from you
And your citadels will be looted."
12 Thus says the LORD,
"Just as the shepherd snatches from the lion's mouth a couple of legs
or a piece of an ear,
So will the sons of Israel dwelling in Samaria be snatched away—
With *the* corner of a bed and *the* cover of a couch!
13 "Hear and testify against the house of Jacob,"
Declares the Lord GOD, the God of hosts.
14 "For on the day that I punish Israel's transgressions,
I will also punish the altars of Bethel;
The horns of the altar will be cut off
And they will fall to the ground.
15 "I will also smite the winter house together with the summer house;
The houses of ivory will also perish
And the great houses will come to an end,"
Declares the LORD.

3:10 Ps 14:4; Jer 4:22; Amos 5:7; 6:12; Hab 2:8-10; Zeph 1:9; Zech 5:3, 4

3:11 Amos 6:14; Amos 2:5

3:12 1 Sam 17:34-37; Ps 132:3; Esth 1:6; 7:8; Amos 6:4

3:13 Ezek 2:7

3:14 2 Kin 23:15; Hos 10:5-8, 14, 15; Amos 4:4; 5:5, 6; 7:10, 13

3:15 Jer 36:22; Judg 3:20; 1 Kin 22:39; Ps 45:8; Amos 2:5; 6:11

"Yet You Have Not Returned to Me"

4 Hear this word, you cows of Bashan who are on the mountain of Samaria,
Who oppress the poor, who crush the needy,
Who say to your husbands, "Bring now, that we may drink!"
2 The Lord GOD has sworn by His holiness,
"Behold, the days are coming upon you
When they will take you away with meat hooks,
And the last of you with fish hooks.
3 "You will go out *through* breaches *in the walls,*
Each one straight before her,
And you will be cast to Harmon," declares the LORD.

4 "Enter Bethel and transgress;
In Gilgal multiply transgression!
Bring your sacrifices every morning,
Your tithes every three days.
5 "Offer a thank offering also from that which is leavened,
And proclaim freewill offerings, make them known.
For so you love *to do,* you sons of Israel,"
Declares the Lord GOD.

4:1 Ps 22:12; Ezek 39:18; Amos 3:9; 6:1; Amos 5:11; 8:6; Amos 2:8; 6:6

4:2 Amos 6:8; 8:7; Ps 89:35; Is 37:29; Ezek 38:4; Jer 16:16; Ezek 29:4; Hab 1:15

4:3 Jer 52:7

4:4 Num 28:3; Amos 5:21, 22

4:5 Lev 7:13; Lev 22:18-21; Jer 7:9, 10; Hos 9:1, 10

3:10 Israel no longer knew how to do what was right. The more they sinned, the harder it was to remember what God wanted. The same is true for us. The longer we wait to deal with sin, the greater it holds onto us. Finally, we forget what it means to do right. Are you on the verge of forgetting?

3:11–12 The enemy mentioned here was Assyria, who conquered Israel and did just as Amos predicted. The people were scattered to foreign lands, and foreigners were placed in the land to keep the peace. Israel's leaders had robbed their defenseless countrymen, and here they would be rendered defenseless by the Assyrians. Amos added that even if the Israelites tried to repent, it would be too late. The destruction would be so complete that nothing of value would be left.

3:14 God's judgment against Israel's altars shows that he was rejecting Israel's entire religious system because it was so polluted. The horns of the altar stood for protection (1 Kings 1:49–53), and the false altars would soon be gone. Then the people would have no sanctuary, protection, or refuge (see 4:4) when judgment came.

4:1 Israel's wealthy women were called "cows of Bashan"—pampered, sleek, and well-fed (see Psalm 22:12). These women selfishly pushed their husbands to oppress the helpless in order to support their lavish life-styles. Be careful not to desire material possessions so much that you are willing to oppress others and displease God to get them.

4:4 Amos sarcastically invited the people to sin in Bethel and Gilgal where they worshiped idols instead of God. Bethel was where God had renewed his covenant to Abraham with Jacob (Genesis 28:10–22). At this time, Bethel was the religious center of the northern kingdom, and Jeroboam had placed an idol there to discourage the people from traveling to Jerusalem in the southern kingdom to worship (1 Kings 12:26–29). Gilgal was Israel's first campground after entering the promised land (Joshua 4:19). Here Joshua had renewed the covenant and the rite of circumcision, and the people had celebrated the Passover (Joshua 5:2–11). Saul was crowned Israel's first king in Gilgal (1 Samuel 11:15).

6 "But I gave you also cleanness of teeth in all your cities
And lack of bread in all your places,
Yet you have not returned to Me," declares the LORD.
7 "Furthermore, I withheld the rain from you
While *there were* still three months until harvest.
Then I would send rain on one city
And on another city I would not send rain;
One part would be rained on,
While the part not rained on would dry up.
8 "So two or three cities would stagger to another city to drink water,
But would not be satisfied;
Yet you have not returned to Me," declares the LORD.
9 "I smote you with scorching *wind* and mildew;
And the caterpillar was devouring
Your many gardens and vineyards, fig trees and olive trees;
Yet you have not returned to Me," declares the LORD.
10 "I sent a plague among you after the manner of Egypt;
I slew your young men by the sword along with your captured horses,
And I made the stench of your camp rise up in your nostrils;
Yet you have not returned to Me," declares the LORD.
11 "I overthrew you, as God overthrew Sodom and Gomorrah,
And you were like a firebrand snatched from a blaze;
Yet you have not returned to Me," declares the LORD.
12 "Therefore thus I will do to you, O Israel;
Because I will do this to you,
Prepare to meet your God, O Israel."
13 For behold, He who forms mountains and creates the wind
And declares to man what are His thoughts,
He who makes dawn into darkness
And treads on the high places of the earth,
The LORD God of hosts is His name.

"Seek Me that You May Live"

5 Hear this word which I take up for you as a dirge, O house of Israel:
2 She has fallen, she will not rise again—
The virgin Israel.
She *lies* neglected on her land;
There is none to raise her up.
3 For thus says the Lord GOD,
"The city which goes forth a thousand *strong*
Will have a hundred left,
And the one which goes forth a hundred *strong*
Will have ten left to the house of Israel."
4 For thus says the LORD to the house of Israel,
"Seek Me that you may live.
5 "But do not resort to Bethel
And do not come to Gilgal,
Nor cross over to Beersheba;
For Gilgal will certainly go into captivity
And Bethel will come to trouble.

4:6 Is 3:1; Jer 14:18; Is 9:13; Jer 5:3; Hag 2:17

4:7 Deut 11:17; 2 Chr 7:13; Is 5:6; Ex 9:4, 26; 10:22, 23

4:8 1 Kin 18:5; Jer 14:4; Ezek 4:16, 17; Hag 1:6; Jer 3:7

4:9 Deut 28:22; Hag 2:17; Joel 1:4, 7; Amos 7:1, 2; Jer 3:10

4:10 Ex 9:3; Lev 26:25; Deut 28:27, 60; Ps 78:50; Jer 11:22; 18:21; 48:15; 2 Kin 13:3, 7; Joel 2:20; Is 9:13

4:11 Gen 19:24, 25; Deut 29:23; Is 13:19; Zech 3:2; Jer 23:14

4:12 Is 32:11; 64:2; Jer 5:22

4:13 Job 38:4-7; Ps 65:6; Is 40:12; Ps 135:7; Jer 10:13; Dan 2:28, 30; Jer 13:16; Joel 2:2; Amos 5:8; Mic 1:3; Is 47:4; Jer 10:16; Amos 5:8, 27; 9:6

5:1 Jer 7:29; 9:10, 17; Ezek 19:1

5:2 Amos 8:14; Jer 14:17; Is 51:18; Jer 50:32

5:3 Is 6:13; Amos 6:9

5:4 Deut 4:29; 32:46, 47; Jer 29:13; Is 55:3

5:5 1 Kin 12:28, 29; Amos 3:14; 4:4; 7:10, 13; 1 Sam 7:16; 11:14; Gen 21:31-33; Amos 8:14

4:6–13 No matter how God warned the people—through famine, drought, blight, locusts, plagues, or war—they still ignored him. Because the Israelites didn't get the message, they would have to meet God face to face in judgment. No longer would they ignore God; they would have to face the One they had rejected, the One they had refused to obey when he commanded them to care for the poor. One day each of us will meet God face-to-face to account for what we have done or refused to do. Are you prepared to meet him?

5:1 Amos shocked his listeners by singing a lament or song of grief for them as though they had already been destroyed. The Israelites believed that their wealth and religious ritual made them secure, but Amos lamented their sure destruction.

6 "Seek the LORD that you may live,
Or He will break forth like a fire, O house of Joseph,
And it will consume with none to quench *it* for Bethel,
7 *For* those who turn justice into wormwood
And cast righteousness down to the earth."

8 He who made the Pleiades and Orion
And changes deep darkness into morning,
Who also darkens day *into* night,
Who calls for the waters of the sea
And pours them out on the surface of the earth,
The LORD is His name.
9 It is He who flashes forth *with* destruction upon the strong,
So that destruction comes upon the fortress.

10 They hate him who reproves in the gate,
And they abhor him who speaks *with* integrity.
11 Therefore because you impose heavy rent on the poor
And exact a tribute of grain from them,
Though you have built houses of well-hewn stone,
Yet you will not live in them;
You have planted pleasant vineyards, yet you will not drink their wine.
12 For I know your transgressions are many and your sins are great,
You who distress the righteous *and* accept bribes
And turn aside the poor in the gate.
13 Therefore at such a time the prudent person keeps silent, for it is an evil time.

14 Seek good and not evil, that you may live;
And thus may the LORD God of hosts be with you,
Just as you have said!
15 Hate evil, love good,
And establish justice in the gate!
Perhaps the LORD God of hosts
May be gracious to the remnant of Joseph.

16 Therefore thus says the LORD God of hosts, the Lord,
"There is wailing in all the plazas,

5:6 Is 55:3, 6, 7; Amos 5:14; Deut 4:24

5:7 Amos 2:3; 5:12; 6:12

5:8 Job 9:9; 38:31; Job 12:22; 38:12; Is 42:16; Ps 104:20; Ps 104:6-9; Amos 9:6; Amos 4:13

5:9 Is 29:5; Amos 2:14; Mic 5:11

5:10 Is 29:21; Amos 5:15; 1 Kin 22:8; Is 59:15; Jer 17:16-18

5:11 Amos 3:15; 6:11; Mic 6:15

5:12 Is 1:23; 5:23; Amos 2:6

5:13 Eccl 3:7; Hos 4:4

5:14 Mic 3:11

5:15 Ps 97:10; Rom 12:9; Joel 2:14; Mic 5:3, 7, 8

5:16 Jer 9:10, 18-20; Amos 8:3; Joel 1:11; 2 Chr 35:25; Jer 9:17

5:6 There is one sure remedy for a world that is sick and dying in sin—"seek the LORD that you may live." Sin seeks to destroy, but hope is found in seeking God. In times of difficulty, seek God. In personal discomfort and struggle, seek God. When others are struggling, encourage them to seek God too.

5:7 The law courts should have been places of justice where the poor and oppressed could find relief. Instead, they had become places of greed and injustice.

5:8 Pleiades and Orion are star constellations. For thousands of years, navigators have staked lives and fortunes on the reliability of the stars. The constancy and orderliness of the heavens challenge us to look beyond them to their Creator.

5:10–12 "Him who reproves in the gate" refers to an honest judge, a champion of justice. A society is in trouble when those who try to do right are hated for their commitment to justice. Any society that exploits the poor and defenseless or hates the truth is bent on destroying itself.

5:12 Why does God put so much emphasis on the way we treat the poor and needy? How we treat the rich, or those of equal standing, often reflects what we hope to get from them. But because the poor can give us nothing, how we treat them reflects our true character. Do we, like Christ, give without thought of gain? We should treat the poor as we would like God to treat us.

5:12 Here are eight common excuses for not helping the poor and needy: (1) They don't deserve help. They got themselves into poverty; let them get themselves out. (2) God's call to help the poor applies to another time. (3) We don't know any people like this. (4) I have my own needs. (5) Any money I give will be wasted, stolen, or spent. The poor will never see it. (6) I may become a victim myself. (7) I don't know where to start, and I don't have time. (8) My little bit won't make any difference.

Instead of making lame excuses, ask what can be done to help. Does your church have programs to help the needy? Could you volunteer to work with a community group that fights poverty? As one individual, you may not be able to accomplish much, but join up with similarly motivated people and watch mountains begin to move.

5:15 If Israel were to sweep away the corrupt system of false accusations, bribery, and corruption, and were to insist that only just decisions be given, this would show their change of heart. We dare not read this passage lightly or write it off simply as encouragement to be good. It is a command to reform our own legal and social system.

5:16 Failure to honor the dead was considered horrible in Israel, so loud weeping was common at funerals. Paid mourners, usually women, cried and mourned loudly with dirges and eulogies. Amos said there would be so many funerals that there would be a shortage of professional mourners, so farmers would be called from the fields to help. (See also Jeremiah 9:17–20.)

And in all the streets they say, 'Alas! Alas!'
They also call the farmer to mourning
And professional mourners to lamentation.
17 "And in all the vineyards *there is* wailing,
Because I will pass through the midst of you," says the LORD.

5:17 Is 16:10; Jer 48:33

18 Alas, you who are longing for the day of the LORD,
For what purpose *will* the day of the LORD *be* to you?
It *will be* darkness and not light;
19 As when a man flees from a lion
And a bear meets him,
Or goes home, leans his hand against the wall
And a snake bites him.
20 *Will* not the day of the LORD *be* darkness instead of light,
Even gloom with no brightness in it?

5:18 Is 5:19; Jer 30:7; Joel 1:15; 2:1, 11, 31; Is 5:30; Joel 2:2
5:19 Job 20:24; Is 24:17, 18; Jer 15:2, 3; 48:44
5:20 Is 13:10; Zeph 1:15

21 "I hate, I reject your festivals,
Nor do I delight in your solemn assemblies.
22 "Even though you offer up to Me burnt offerings and your grain offerings,
I will not accept *them;*
And I will not *even* look at the peace offerings of your fatlings.
23 "Take away from Me the noise of your songs;
I will not even listen to the sound of your harps.
24 "But let justice roll down like waters
And righteousness like an ever-flowing stream.
25 "Did you present Me with sacrifices and grain offerings in the wilderness for forty
years, O house of Israel?
26 "You also carried along Sikkuth your king and Kiyyun, your images, the star of your
gods which you made for yourselves.
27 "Therefore, I will make you go into exile beyond Damascus," says the LORD, whose
name is the God of hosts.

5:21 Is 1:11-16; 66:3; Amos 4:4, 5; 8:10; Lev 26:31; Jer 14:12; Hos 5:6
5:22 Is 66:3; Mic 6:6, 7; Lev 7:11-15; Amos 4:5
5:24 Jer 22:3; Ezek 45:9; Mic 6:8
5:25 Deut 32:17; Josh 24:14; Neh 9:18-21; Acts 7:42, 43
5:26 Acts 7:43

"Those at Ease in Zion"

6 Woe to those who are at ease in Zion
And to those who *feel* secure in the mountain of Samaria,
The distinguished men of the foremost of nations,
To whom the house of Israel comes.
2 Go over to Calneh and look,
And go from there to Hamath the great,
Then go down to Gath of the Philistines.
Are they better than these kingdoms,
Or is their territory greater than yours?

6:1 Is 32:9-11; Zeph 1:12; Luke 6:24; Ex 19:5; Amos 3:2
6:2 Gen 10:10; Is 10:9; 1 Kin 8:65; 2 Kin 18:34; Is 10:9; 1 Sam 5:8; 2 Chr 26:6

5:18 Here "the day of the LORD" means the imminent destruction by the Assyrian army, as well as the future day of God's judgment. For the faithful, "the day of the LORD" will be glorious, but for the unfaithful it will be a day of darkness and doom. (See Joel 1:15 for more discussion of the day of the Lord.)

5:18–24 These people were calling for the day of the Lord, thinking it would bring an end to their troubles. But God said, "You don't know what you are asking for." This "day of the LORD" would bring justice, and justice would bring the punishment the people deserved for their sins.

5:21–23 God hates false worship ("festivals" and "solemn assemblies") by people who go through the motions out of pretense or for show. If we are living sinful lives and using religious ritual and traditions to make ourselves look good, God will despise our worship and will not accept what we offer. He wants sincere hearts, not the songs of hypocrites. When you worship at church, are you more concerned about your image or your attitude toward God?

5:26 In days past, Israel had turned to worshiping stars and planets, preferring nature over nature's God (2 Kings 23:4–5). Pagan religion allowed them to indulge in sexual immorality and to become wealthy through any means possible. Because they refused to worship and obey the one true God, they would cause their own destruction.

5:27 Israel's captivity was indeed beyond Damascus—the people were taken to Assyria. God's punishment was more than defeat; it was complete exile from their homeland.

6:1–6 Amos leveled his attack at those living in complacency and luxury in both Israel and Judah. Great wealth and comfortable lifestyles may make people think they are secure, but God is not pleased if we isolate ourselves from others' needs. God wants us to care for others as he cares for us. His kingdom has no place for selfishness or indifference. We must learn to put the needs of others before our wants. Using our wealth to help others is one way to guard against pride and complacency.

6:2 Great cities to the east, north, and west had been destroyed because of their pride. What happened to them would happen to Israel because Israel's sin was just as great as theirs.

3 Do you put off the day of calamity,
And would you bring near the seat of violence?

4 Those who recline on beds of ivory
And sprawl on their couches,
And eat lambs from the flock
And calves from the midst of the stall,
5 Who improvise to the sound of the harp,
And like David have composed songs for themselves,
6 Who drink wine from sacrificial bowls
While they anoint themselves with the finest of oils,
Yet they have not grieved over the ruin of Joseph.
7 Therefore, they will now go into exile at the head of the exiles,
And the sprawlers' banqueting will pass away.

8 The Lord GOD has sworn by Himself, the LORD God of hosts has declared:
"I loathe the arrogance of Jacob,
And detest his citadels;
Therefore I will deliver up *the* city and all it contains."
9 And it will be, if ten men are left in one house, they will die.
10 Then one's uncle, or his undertaker, will lift him up to carry out *his* bones from the
house, and he will say to the one who is in the innermost part of the house, "Is anyone
else with you?" And that one will say, "No one." Then he will answer, "Keep quiet. For
the name of the LORD is not to be mentioned."
11 For behold, the LORD is going to command that the great house be smashed to pieces
and the small house to fragments.
12 Do horses run on rocks?
Or does one plow them with oxen?
Yet you have turned justice into poison
And the fruit of righteousness into [1]wormwood,
13 You who rejoice in [2]Lodebar,
And say, "Have we not by our *own* strength taken [3]Karnaim for ourselves?"
14 "For behold, I am going to raise up a nation against you,
O house of Israel," declares the LORD God of hosts,
"And they will afflict you from the entrance of Hamath
To the brook of the Arabah."

6:3 Is 56:12; Amos 9:10; Amos 3:10

6:4 Amos 3:12; Ezek 34:2, 3

6:5 1 Chr 15:16; 23:5; Is 5:12

6:6 Amos 2:8; 4:1; Ezek 9:4

6:7 Amos 7:11, 17; 1 Kin 20:16-21; Dan 5:4-6, 30

6:8 Gen 22:16; Jer 22:5; 51:14; Amos 4:2; 8:7; Lev 26:30; Deut 32:19; Ps 106:40; Amos 5:21; Amos 3:10, 11; Hos 11:6

6:9 Amos 5:3

6:10 1 Sam 31:12; Amos 5:13; 8:3; Jer 44:26; Ezek 20:39

6:11 Is 55:11; 2 Kin 25:9; Amos 3:15; 5:11

6:12 1 Kin 21:7-13; Is 59:13, 14; Hos 10:4; Amos 5:7, 11, 12

6:13 Job 8:14, 15; Ps 2:2-4; Luke 12:19, 20; Ps 75:4, 5; Is 28:14, 15

6:14 Jer 5:15; Num 34:7, 8; 1 Kin 8:65; 2 Kin 14:25

3. Visions of judgment

Warning Through Visions

7 Thus the Lord GOD showed me, and behold, He was forming a locust-swarm when
the spring crop began to sprout. And behold, the spring crop *was* after the king's
mowing.
2 And it came about, when it had finished eating the vegetation of the land, that I said,
"Lord GOD, please pardon!
How can Jacob stand,
For he is small?"

7:1 Joel 1:4; Amos 4:9; Nah 3:15

7:2 Ex 10:15; Jer 14:7, 20, 21; Ezek 9:8; 11:13; Is 37:4; Jer 42:2

1 I.e. bitterness 2 Lit *a thing of nothing* 3 Lit *a pair of horns*

6:4 Ivory was an imported luxury, rare and extremely expensive. Even a small amount of ivory symbolized wealth. Something as extravagant as a bed of ivory shows the gross waste of resources that should have been used to help the poor.

6:8–11 The people had built luxurious homes to flaunt their achievements. While it is not wrong to live in comfortable houses, we must not let them become sources of inflated pride and self-glorification. God gave our homes to us, and they are to be used for service, not just for show.

6:10 Amos gives us a picture of God's fearful judgment: The people hesitated to speak God's name, even during a time of grief, for fear that they would attract his attention and be judged also.

6:13–14 Karnaim was a city northeast of Israel, an insignificant border town compared to the nation they were about to face, Assyria. Hamath was to the north, and the brook of the Arabah to the south. The entire nation would be destroyed by Assyria (2 Kings 17).

7:1ff The following series of visions conveyed God's message to the people using images that were familiar to them—locusts, fire, and a plumb line.

7:1–6 Twice Amos was shown a vision of Israel's impending punishment, and his immediate response was to pray that God would spare Israel. Prayer is a powerful privilege. Amos's prayers should remind us to pray for our nation.

7:3 Deut 32:36; Jer 26:19; Hos 11:8; Amos 5:15; Jon 3:10

7:4 Deut 32:22; Is 66:15, 16; Amos 2:5

7:5 Ps 85:4; Joel 2:17; Amos 7:2

7:6 Ps 106:45; Amos 7:3; Jon 3:10

7:8 Jer 1:11; Amos 8:2; 2 Kin 21:13; Is 28:17; 34:11; Lam 2:8; Jer 15:6; Ezek 7:4-9; Amos 8:2

7:9 Gen 46:1; Hos 10:8; Mic 1:5; Lev 26:31; Is 63:18; Jer 51:51; Amos 7:13; 2 Kin 15:8-10; Amos 7:11

7:10 1 Kin 12:31, 32; 13:33; 2 Kin 14:23, 24; Jer 26:8-11; 38:4

7:12 Matt 8:34

7:13 Amos 2:12; Acts 4:18; 1 Kin 12:29, 32; Amos 7:9

7:14 1 Kin 20:35; 2 Kin 2:3, 5; 4:38; 2 Chr 19:2

3 The LORD changed His mind about this.
"It shall not be," said the LORD.
4 Thus the Lord GOD showed me, and behold, the Lord GOD was calling to contend
with them by fire, and it consumed the great deep and began to consume the farm land.
5 Then I said,
"Lord GOD, please stop!
How can Jacob stand, for he is small?"
6 The LORD changed His mind about this.
"This too shall not be," said the Lord GOD.
7 Thus He showed me, and behold, the Lord was standing by a vertical wall with a
plumb line in His hand.
8 The LORD said to me, "What do you see, Amos?" And I said, "A plumb line." Then
the Lord said,
"Behold I am about to put a plumb line
In the midst of My people Israel.
I will spare them no longer.
9 "The high places of Isaac will be desolated
And the sanctuaries of Israel laid waste.
Then I will rise up against the house of Jeroboam with the sword."

Amos Accused, Answers

10 Then Amaziah, the priest of Bethel, sent *word* to Jeroboam king of Israel, saying,
"Amos has conspired against you in the midst of the house of Israel; the land is unable to
endure all his words.
11 "For thus Amos says, 'Jeroboam will die by the sword and Israel will certainly go from
its land into exile.' "
12 Then Amaziah said to Amos, "Go, you seer, flee away to the land of Judah and there
eat bread and there do your prophesying!
13 "But no longer prophesy at Bethel, for it is a sanctuary of the king and a royal residence."
14 Then Amos replied to Amaziah, "I am not a prophet, nor am I the son of a prophet;
for I am a herdsman and a grower of sycamore figs.

AMOS'S VISIONS

Vision	*Reference*	*Significance*
Swarm of locusts	7:1–3	God was preparing punishment, which he delayed only because of Amos's intervention.
Fire	7:4–6	God was preparing to devour the land, but Amos intervened on behalf of the people.
Wall and plumb line	7:7–9	God would see if the people were crooked, and, if they were, he would punish them.
Basket of ripe fruit	8:1–14	The people were ripe for punishment; though once beautiful, they were now rotten.
God standing by the altar	9:1–15	Punishment was executed.

Amos had a series of visions concerning God's judgment on Israel. God was planning to judge Israel by sending a swarm of locusts or by sending fire. In spite of Amos's intercession on Israel's behalf, God would still carry out his judgment because Israel persisted in her disobedience.

7:7–9 A plumb line is a device used to ensure the straightness of a wall. A wall that is not straight will eventually collapse. God wants people to be right with him; he wants the sin that makes us crooked removed immediately. God's Word is the plumb line that helps us be aware of our sin. How do you measure up to God's plumb line?

7:10 Prophets like Amos were often seen as traitors and conspirators because they spoke out against the king and his advisers, questioning their authority and exposing their sin. The kings often saw the prophets as enemies rather than as God's spokesmen who were really trying to help them and the nation.

7:10ff Amaziah was the chief priest in Bethel, representing Israel's official religion. He was not concerned about hearing God's message; he was only worried about his own position. Maintaining his position was more important than listening to the truth. Don't let your desire for prestige, authority, or money keep you tied to a job or position you should leave. Don't let anything come between you and obeying God.

7:14–15 Without any special preparation, education, or upbringing, Amos obeyed God's call to "Go prophesy to My people Israel." Obedience is the test of a faithful servant of God. Are you obeying God's call to you?

15 "But the LORD took me from following the flock and the LORD said to me, 'Go prophesy to My people Israel.'
16 "Now hear the word of the LORD: you are saying, 'You shall not prophesy against
Israel nor shall you speak against the house of Isaac.'
17 "Therefore, thus says the LORD, 'Your wife will become a harlot in the city, your sons
and your daughters will fall by the sword, your land will be parceled up by a *measuring*
line and you yourself will die upon unclean soil. Moreover, Israel will certainly go from
its land into exile.' "

7:15 Jer 1:7; Ezek 2:3, 4
7:16 Amos 2:12; 7:13; Deut 32:2; Ezek 20:46; 21:2
7:17 Hos 4:13, 14; Jer 14:16; 2 Kin 17:6; Ezek 4:13; Hos 9:3

Basket of Fruit and Israel's Captivity

8 Thus the Lord GOD showed me, and behold, *there was* a basket of summer fruit.
2 He said, "What do you see, Amos?" And I said, "A basket of summer fruit." Then
the LORD said to me, "The end has come for My people Israel. I will spare them no longer.
3 "The songs of the palace will turn to wailing in that day," declares the Lord GOD.
"Many *will be* the corpses; in every place they will cast them forth in silence."
4 Hear this, you who trample the needy, to do away with the humble of the land,
5 saying,
"When will the new moon be over,
So that we may sell grain,
And the sabbath, that we may open the wheat *market*,
To make the bushel smaller and the shekel bigger,
And to cheat with dishonest scales,
6 So as to buy the helpless for money
And the needy for a pair of sandals,
And *that* we may sell the refuse of the wheat?"

7 The LORD has sworn by the pride of Jacob,
"Indeed, I will never forget any of their deeds.
8 "Because of this will not the land quake
And everyone who dwells in it mourn?
Indeed, all of it will rise up like the Nile,
And it will be tossed about
And subside like the Nile of Egypt.
9 "It will come about in that day," declares the Lord GOD,
"That I will make the sun go down at noon
And make the earth dark in broad daylight.
10 "Then I will turn your festivals into mourning
And all your songs into lamentation;
And I will bring sackcloth on everyone's loins
And baldness on every head.
And I will make it like *a time of* mourning for an only son,
And the end of it will be like a bitter day.

11 "Behold, days are coming," declares the Lord GOD,
"When I will send a famine on the land,
Not a famine for bread or a thirst for water,
But rather for hearing the words of the LORD.
12 "People will stagger from sea to sea
And from the north even to the east;
They will go to and fro to seek the word of the LORD,
But they will not find *it*.

8:2 Jer 24:3; Ezek 7:2, 3, 6; Amos 7:8
8:3 Amos 5:23; 6:4, 5; 8:10; Amos 5:16; Amos 6:8-10
8:4 Ps 14:4; Prov 30:14; Amos 2:7; 5:11, 12
8:5 Num 28:11; 2 Kin 4:23; Ex 31:13-17; Neh 13:15; Hos 12:7; Mic 6:11
8:6 Amos 2:6
8:7 Amos 4:2; Deut 33:26, 29; Ps 68:34; Amos 6:8; Ps 10:11; Hos 7:2; 8:13
8:8 Ps 18:7; 60:2; Is 5:25; Hos 4:3; Jer 46:7, 8; Amos 9:5
8:9 Job 5:14; Is 13:10; Jer 15:9; Mic 3:6; Is 59:9, 10; Amos 4:13; 5:8
8:10 Job 20:23; Amos 5:21; Is 15:2, 3; Jer 48:37; Ezek 7:18; 27:31; Jer 6:26; Zech 12:10
8:11 1 Sam 3:1; 2 Chr 15:3; Ps 74:9; Ezek 7:26; Mic 3:6
8:12 Ezek 20:3, 31

8:5–6 These merchants were keeping the religious festivals, but not in spirit. They couldn't wait for the holy days and Sabbaths to be over so they could go back to making money. Their real interest was in enriching themselves, even if that meant cheating (short-changing the quantity while boosting the price, or even selling chaff as wheat). Do you take a day to rest and worship God at least once a week, or is making money more important to you than anything else? When you give time to God, is your heart in your worship? Or is your religion only a front for unethical practices?

8:11–13 The people had no appetite for God's word when prophets like Amos brought it. Because of their apathy, God said he would take away even the opportunity to hear his word. We have God's Word, the Bible. But many still look everywhere for answers to life's problems *except* in Scripture. You can help them by directing them to the Bible, showing them the parts that speak to their special needs and questions. God's Word is available to us. Let us help people know it before a time comes when they cannot find it.

8:13 Lam 1:18; 2:21; Is 41:17; Hos 2:3

8:14 Hos 8:5; 1 Kin 12:28, 29; Amos 5:5; Amos 5:2

13 "In that day the beautiful virgins
And the young men will faint from thirst.
14 "*As for* those who swear by the guilt of Samaria,
Who say, 'As your god lives, O Dan,'
And, 'As the way of Beersheba lives,'
They will fall and not rise again."

God's Judgment Unavoidable

9:1 Amos 3:14; Zeph 2:14; Ps 68:21; Hab 3:13; Amos 7:17; Jer 11:11

9 I saw the Lord standing beside the altar, and He said,
"Smite the capitals so that the thresholds will shake,
And break them on the heads of them all!
Then I will slay the rest of them with the sword;
They will not have a fugitive who will flee,
Or a refugee who will escape.

9:2 Ps 139:8; Jer 51:53; Obad 4

2 "Though they dig into Sheol,
From there will My hand take them;
And though they ascend to heaven,
From there will I bring them down.

9:3 Jer 16:16; Job 34:22; Ps 139:9, 10; Is 27:1

3 "Though they hide on the summit of Carmel,
I will search them out and take them from there;
And though they conceal themselves from My sight on the floor of the sea,
From there I will command the serpent and it will bite them.

9:4 Lev 26:33; Lev 17:10; Jer 21:10; 39:16; 44:11

4 "And though they go into captivity before their enemies,
From there I will command the sword that it slay them,
And I will set My eyes against them for evil and not for good."

9:5 Ps 104:32; 144:5; Is 64:1; Mic 1:4; Amos 8:8

5 The Lord GOD of hosts,
The One who touches the land so that it melts,
And all those who dwell in it mourn,
And all of it rises up like the Nile
And subsides like the Nile of Egypt;

9:6 Ps 104:3, 13; Amos 5:8; Ps 104:6; Amos 4:13

6 The One who builds His upper chambers in the heavens
And has founded His vaulted dome over the earth,
He who calls for the waters of the sea
And pours them out on the face of the earth,
The LORD is His name.

9:7 2 Chr 14:9, 12; Is 20:4; 43:3; Deut 2:23; Jer 47:4; Amos 1:5; 2 Kin 16:9; Is 22:6

7 "Are you not as the sons of Ethiopia to Me,
O sons of Israel?" declares the LORD.
"Have I not brought up Israel from the land of Egypt,
And the Philistines from Caphtor and the Arameans from Kir?

9:8 Jer 44:27; Amos 9:4; Amos 7:17; 9:10; Jer 5:10; 30:11; 31:35, 36; Joel 2:32; Amos 3:12; Obad 17

8 "Behold, the eyes of the Lord GOD are on the sinful kingdom,
And I will destroy it from the face of the earth;
Nevertheless, I will not totally destroy the house of Jacob,"

9:1 Judgment would begin at the altar, the center of the nation's life, the place where the people expected protection and blessing. This judgment would cover all 12 tribes. Commentators disagree concerning this altar—some think it was the altar at Bethel; more likely it was the altar in the temple in Jerusalem. God would destroy their base of security in order to bring them to himself. But in 9:11 he promises to restore his renewed people and their broken world.

9:2–4 Sheol was the place of the dead, and Carmel is a mountain. Both were symbols of inaccessibility. No one can escape God's judgment. This was good news for the faithful but bad news for the unfaithful. Whether we go to the mountaintops or the bottom of the sea, God will find us and judge us for our deeds. Amos pictured the judgment of the wicked as a monster of the sea, relentlessly pursuing the condemned. For God's faithful followers, however, the judgment brings a new earth of peace and prosperity. Does God's judgment sound like good news or bad news to you?

9:7 Ethiopia, south of Egypt, was a remote and exotic land to the Israelites. Caphtor is the island of Crete, where the Philistines lived as they migrated to Palestine. God would judge Israel no differently than he judges foreign nations. He is not the God of Israel only; he is God of the universe, and he controls all nations.

9:8 Amos assured the Israelites that God would not "totally destroy" Israel—in other words, the punishment would not be permanent or total. God wants to redeem, not punish. But when punishment is necessary, he doesn't withhold it. Like a loving father, God disciplines those he loves in order to correct them. If God disciplines you, accept it as a sign of his love.

9:8–9 Although Assyria would destroy Israel and take the people into exile, some would be preserved. This exile had been predicted hundreds of years earlier (Deuteronomy 28:63–68). Although the nation would be purified through this invasion and captivity, not one true believer would be eternally lost. Our system of justice is not always perfect, but God is. Sinners will not get away, and the faithful will not be forgotten. True believers will not be lost.

Declares the LORD.
9 "For behold, I am commanding,
And I will shake the house of Israel among all nations
As *grain* is shaken in a sieve,
But not a kernel will fall to the ground.
10 "All the sinners of My people will die by the sword,
Those who say, 'The calamity will not overtake or confront us.'

9:9 Is 30:28; Luke 22:31

9:10 Is 33:14; Zech 13:8; Amos 6:3

The Restoration of Israel

11 "In that day I will raise up the fallen booth of David,
And wall up its breaches;
I will also raise up its ruins
And rebuild it as in the days of old;
12 That they may possess the remnant of Edom
And all the nations who are called by My name,"
Declares the LORD who does this.

9:11 Acts 15:16-18; Is 16:5; Ps 80:12; Is 63:11; Jer 46:26

9:12 Obad 19; Num 24:18; Is 11:14; Is 43:7

13 "Behold, days are coming," declares the LORD,
"When the plowman will overtake the reaper
And the treader of grapes him who sows seed;
When the mountains will drip sweet wine
And all the hills will be dissolved.
14 "Also I will restore the captivity of My people Israel,
And they will rebuild the ruined cities and live *in them;*
They will also plant vineyards and drink their wine,
And make gardens and eat their fruit.
15 "I will also plant them on their land,
And they will not again be rooted out from their land
Which I have given them,"
Says the LORD your God.

9:13 Lev 26:5; Joel 3:18; Gen 49:11

9:14 Ps 53:6; Is 60:4; Jer 30:3, 18; Is 61:4; 65:21; Jer 24:6; 31:28

9:15 Is 60:21; Ezek 34:28; 37:25

9:11–12 In the punishment, the house of David was reduced to a "fallen booth' (tent).' God's covenant with David stated that one of David's descendants would always sit on his throne (2 Samuel 7:12–16). The exile made this promise seem impossible. But "in that day" God would raise up and restore the kingdom to its promised glory. This was a promise to both Israel and Judah, not to be fulfilled by an earthly, political ruler, but by the Messiah, who would renew the spiritual kingdom and rule forever.

James quoted these verses (Acts 15:16–17), finding the promise fulfilled in Christ's resurrection and in the presence of both Jews and Gentiles in the church. "Possess the remnant of Edom" envisions the Messianic kingdom, which will be universal and include Gentiles. When God brings in the Gentiles, he is restoring the ruins. After the Gentiles are called together, God will renew and restore the fortunes of the new Israel. All the land that was once under David's rule will again be part of God's nation.

9:13 This verse describes a time of such an abundance of crops that the people won't be able to harvest them all.

9:13–15 The Jews of Amos's day had lost sight of God's care and love for them. The rich were carefree and comfortable, refusing to help others in need. They observed their religious rituals in hopes of appeasing God, but they did not truly love him. Amos announced God's warnings of destruction for their evil ways.

We must not assume that going to church and being good is enough. God expects our belief in him to penetrate all areas of our conduct and to extend to all people and circumstances. We should let Amos's words inspire us to live faithfully according to God's desires.

OBADIAH

WRINKLED face, tiny hands with fingernail chips, folds of new skin, and miniature eyes, nose, and mouth—she's a newborn. After months of formation, she burst forth into the world and into her family. "She has her mother's eyes." "I can sure tell who her parents are." "Now that's your nose." Relatives and friends gaze into the little face and see her mom and dad. Mother and Father rejoice in their daughter, a miracle, a new member of the family. As loving parents, they will feed, protect, nurture, guide, and discipline her. This is their duty and joy.

God, too, has children—men and women whom he has chosen as his very own. There have always been individuals marked as his, but with Abraham he promised to build a nation. Israel was to be God's country, and her people, the Jews, his very own sons and daughters. Down through the centuries, God meted out discipline and punishment, but always with love and mercy. God, the eternal Father, protected and cared for his children.

Obadiah, the shortest book in the Old Testament, is a dramatic example of God's response to anyone who would harm his children. Edom was a mountainous nation, occupying the region southeast of the Dead Sea including Petra, the spectacular city discovered by archaeologists a few decades ago. As descendants of Esau (Genesis 25:19—27:45), the Edomites were blood relatives of Israel, and like their father, they were rugged, fierce, and proud warriors with a seemingly invincible mountain home. Of all people, they should have rushed to the aid of their northern brothers. Instead, however, they gloated over Israel's problems, captured and delivered fugitives to the enemy, and even looted Israel's countryside.

Obadiah gave God's message to the Edomites. Because of their indifference to and defiance of God, their cowardice and pride, and their treachery toward their brothers in Judah, they stood condemned and would be destroyed. The book begins with the announcement that disaster was coming to Edom (1:1–9). Despite their "impregnable" cliffs and mountains, they would not be able to escape God's judgment. Obadiah then gave the reasons for their destruction (1: 10–14)—their blatant arrogance toward God and their persecution of God's children. This concise prophecy ends with a description of the "day of the LORD," when judgment will fall on all who have harmed God's people (1:15–21).

Today, God's holy nation is his church—all who have trusted Christ for their salvation and have given their lives to him. These men and women are God's born-again and adopted children. As you read Obadiah, catch a glimpse of what it means to be God's child, under his love and protection. See how the heavenly Father responds to all who would attack those whom he loves.

VITAL STATISTICS

PURPOSE:
To show that God judges those who have harmed his people

AUTHOR:
Obadiah. Very little is known about this man, whose name means "servant (or worshiper) of the LORD"

TO WHOM WRITTEN:
The Edomites, the Jews in Judah, and God's people everywhere

DATE WRITTEN:
Possibly during the reign of Jehoram in Judah, 853–841 B.C., or possibly during Jeremiah's ministry, 627–586 B.C.

SETTING:
Historically, Edom had constantly harassed the Jews. Prior to the time this book was written, they had participated in attacks against Judah. Given the dates above, this prophecy came after the division of Israel into the northern and southern kingdoms and before the conquering of Judah by Nebuchadnezzar in 586 B.C.

KEY VERSE:
"For the day of the LORD draws near on all the nations. As you have done, it will be done to you. Your dealings will return on your own head" (1:15).

KEY PEOPLE:
The Edomites

KEY PLACES:
Edom, Jerusalem

SPECIAL FEATURES:
The book of Obadiah uses vigorous poetic language and is written in the form of a dirge of doom.

THE BLUEPRINT

1. Edom's destruction (1–16)
2. Israel's restoration (17–21)

The book of Obadiah shows the outcome of the ancient feud between Edom and Israel. Edom was proud of its high position, but God would bring her down. Those who are high and powerful today should not be overconfident in themselves, whether they are a nation, a corporation, a church, or a family. Just as Edom was destroyed for its pride, so will anyone be who lives in defiance of God.

MEGATHEMES

THEME	EXPLANATION	IMPORTANCE
Justice	Obadiah predicted that God would destroy Edom as punishment for standing by when Babylon invaded Judah. Because of their treachery, Edom's land would be given to Judah in the day when God rights the wrongs against his people.	God will judge and fiercely punish all who harm his people. We can be confident in God's final victory. He is our champion, and we can trust him to bring about true justice.
Pride	Because of their seemingly invincible rock fortress, the Edomites were proud and self-confident. But God humbled them and their nation disappeared from the face of the earth.	All those who defy God will meet their doom as Edom did. Any nation who trusts in its power, wealth, technology, or wisdom more than in God will be brought low. All who are proud will one day be shocked to discover that no one is exempt from God's justice.

1. Edom's destruction

Edom Will Be Humbled

1 The vision of Obadiah.
Thus says the Lord GOD concerning Edom—
We have heard a report from the LORD,
And an envoy has been sent among the nations *saying,*
"Arise and let us go against her for battle"—
2 "Behold, I will make you small among the nations;
You are greatly despised.
3 "The arrogance of your heart has deceived you,
You who live in the clefts of the rock,
In the loftiness of your dwelling place,
Who say in your heart,
'Who will bring me down to earth?'

1:1 Ps 137:7; Is 21:11, 12; 34:1-17; 63:1-6; Jer 49:7-22; Ezek 25:12-14; 35:15; Joel 3:19; Amos 1:11, 12; Mal 1:4; Jer 49:14-16; Obad 1-4; Is 18:2; 30:4; Jer 6:4, 5

1:2 Num 24:18; Is 23:9

1:3 Is 16:6; Jer 49:16; 2 Kin 14:7; 2 Chr 25:11f; Is 14:13-15; Rev 18:7

1 Obadiah was a prophet from Judah who told of God's judgment against the nation of Edom. Two commonly accepted dates for this prophecy are (1) between 853 and 841 B.C., when King Jehoram and Jerusalem were attacked by a Philistine/Arab coalition (2 Chronicles 21:16ff), or (2) 586 B.C., when Jerusalem was completely destroyed by the Babylonians (2 Kings 25; 2 Chronicles 36). Edom had rejoiced over the misfortunes of both Israel and Judah, and yet the Edomites and Jews descended from two brothers—Esau and Jacob (Genesis 25:19–26). But just as these two brothers were constantly fighting, so were Israel and Edom. God pronounced judgment on Edom for their callous and malicious actions toward his people.

3 Edom was Judah's southern neighbor, sharing a common boundary. But neighbors are not always friends, and Edom liked nothing about Judah. Edom's capital at this time was Sela (perhaps the later city of Petra), a city considered impregnable because it was cut into rock cliffs and set in a canyon that could be entered only through a narrow gap. What Edom perceived as its strengths would be its downfall: (1) safety in their city (verses 3–4)—God would send them plummeting from the heights; (2) pride in their self-sufficiency (verse 4)—God would humble them; (3) wealth (verses 5–6)—thieves would steal all they had; (4) allies (verse 7)—God would cause them to turn against Edom; (5) wisdom (verses 8–9)—the wise would be destroyed.

3 The Edomites felt secure, and they were proud of their self-sufficiency. But they were fooling themselves because there is no lasting security apart from God. Is your security in objects or people? Ask yourself how much lasting security they really offer. Possessions and people can disappear in a moment, but God does not change. Only he can supply true security.

4 The Edomites were proud of their city carved right into the rock. Today Sela, or Petra, is considered one of the marvels of the ancient world, but only as a tourist attraction. The Bible warns that pride is the surest route to self-destruction (Proverbs 16:18). Just

1:4 Job 20:6, 7; Hab 2:9; Is 14:12-15

1:5 Jer 49:9; Deut 24:21

1:6 Jer 49:10

1:7 Jer 30:14; Ps 41:9; Is 19:11; Jer 49:7

1:8 Job 5:12-14; Is 29:14

1:9 Jer 49:22; Gen 36:11; 1 Chr 1:45; Job 2:11; Jer 49:7; Ezek 25:13; Amos 1:12; Hab 3:3; Is 34:5-8; 63:1-3; Obad 5

1:10 Gen 27:41; Ezek 25:12; Joel 3:19; Amos 1:11; Ezek 35:9

1:11 Ps 83:5, 6; 137:7; Amos 1:6, 9; Joel 3:3; Nah 3:10; Ezek 35:10

4 "Though you build high like the eagle,
Though you set your nest among the stars,
From there I will bring you down," declares the LORD.
5 "If thieves came to you,
If robbers by night—
O how you will be ruined!—
Would they not steal *only* until they had enough?
If grape gatherers came to you,
Would they not leave *some* gleanings?
6 "O how Esau will be ransacked,
And his hidden treasures searched out!
7 "All the men allied with you
Will send you forth to the border,
And the men at peace with you
Will deceive you and overpower you.
They who eat your bread
Will set an ambush for you.
(There is no understanding in him.)
8 "Will I not on that day," declares the LORD,
"Destroy wise men from Edom
And understanding from the mountain of Esau?
9 "Then your mighty men will be dismayed, O Teman,
So that everyone may be cut off from the mountain of Esau by slaughter.

10 "Because of violence to your brother Jacob,
You will be covered *with* shame,
And you will be cut off forever.
11 "On the day that you stood aloof,
On the day that strangers carried off his wealth,

HISTORY OF THE CONFLICT BETWEEN ISRAEL AND EDOM

The nation of Israel descended from Jacob; the nation of Edom descended from Esau	Genesis 25:23
Jacob and Esau struggled in their mother's womb	Genesis 25:19–26
Esau sold his birthright and blessing to Jacob	Genesis 25:29–34
Edom refused to let the Israelites pass through its land	Numbers 20:14–22
Israel's kings had constant conflict with Edom	
• Saul	1 Samuel 14:47
• David	2 Samuel 8:13–14
• Solomon	1 Kings 11:14–22
• Jehoram	2 Kings 8:20–22; 2 Chronicles 21:8ff
• Ahaz	2 Chronicles 28:16
Edom urged Babylon to destroy Jerusalem	Psalm 137:7

as Petra and Edom fell, so will proud people fall. A humble person is more secure than a proud person because humility gives a more accurate perspective of oneself and the world.

4–9 Esau was named here (verse 6) because he was the father of the nation of Edom. God did not pronounce these harsh judgments against Edom out of vengeance but in order to bring about justice. God is morally perfect and demands complete justice and fairness. The Edomites were simply getting what they deserved. Because they murdered, they would be murdered. Because they robbed, they would be robbed. Because they took advantage of others, they would be used. Don't talk yourself into sin, thinking that "nobody will know" or "I won't get caught." God knows all our sins, and he will be just.

8 Edom was noted for its wise men. There is a difference, however, between human wisdom and God's wisdom. The Edomites may have been wise in the ways of the world, but they were foolish because they ignored and even mocked God.

9 Eliphaz, one of Job's three friends (Job 2:11), was from Teman, about five miles east of Petra. Teman was named after Esau's grandson (Genesis 36:11).

10–11 The Israelites had descended from Jacob, and the Edomites from his brother, Esau (Genesis 25:19–26). Instead of helping Israel and Judah when they were in need, Edom allowed them to be destroyed and even plundered what was left behind. Edom, therefore, acted like a stranger, and it would be punished. Anyone who does not help God's people is God's enemy. If you have withheld your help from someone in a time of need, this is sin (James 4:17). Sin includes not only what we do, but also what we refuse to do. Don't ignore or refuse to help those in need.

And foreigners entered his gate
And cast lots for Jerusalem—
You too were as one of them.
12 "Do not gloat over your brother's day,
The day of his misfortune.
And do not rejoice over the sons of Judah
In the day of their destruction;
Yes, do not boast
In the day of *their* distress.
13 "Do not enter the gate of My people
In the day of their disaster.
Yes, you, do not gloat over their calamity
In the day of their disaster.
And do not loot their wealth
In the day of their disaster.
14 "Do not stand at the fork of the road
To cut down their fugitives;
And do not imprison their survivors
In the day of their distress.

1:12 Mic 4:11; 7:10; Prov 17:5; Ezek 35:15; 36:5; Ps 31:18; Ezek 35:12

1:13 Ezek 35:5; Ezek 35:10; 36:2, 3

1:14 Is 16:3, 4

The Day of the LORD and the Future

15 "For the day of the LORD draws near on all the nations.
As you have done, it will be done to you.
Your dealings will return on your own head.
16 "Because just as you drank on My holy mountain,
All the nations will drink continually.
They will drink and swallow
And become as if they had never existed.

1:15 Ezek 30:3; Joel 1:15; 2:1, 11, 31; Amos 5:18, 20; Jer 50:29; 51:56; Hab 2:8; Ezek 35:11

1:16 Jer 49:12; Joel 3:17; Is 51:22, 23; Jer 25:15, 16

2. Israel's restoration

17 "But on Mount Zion there will be those who escape,
And it will be holy.
And the house of Jacob will possess their possessions.
18 "Then the house of Jacob will be a fire
And the house of Joseph a flame;
But the house of Esau *will be* as stubble.
And they will set them on fire and consume them,
So that there will be no survivor of the house of Esau,"
For the LORD has spoken.
19 Then *those of* the [1]Negev will possess the mountain of Esau,
And *those of* the [2]Shephelah the Philistine *plain;*
Also, possess the territory of Ephraim and the territory of Samaria,
And Benjamin *will possess* Gilead.

1:17 Is 4:2, 3; Is 14:1, 2; Amos 9:11-15

1:18 Is 5:24; 9:18, 19; Zech 12:6; Jer 11:23; Amos 1:8

1:19 Is 11:14; Amos 9:12; Is 11:14; Jer 31:5; 32:44

1 I.e. South country **2** I.e. the foothills

---

12 Edom was glad to see Judah in trouble. Their hatred made them want the nation destroyed. For their wrong attitudes and actions, God wiped out Edom. How often do you find yourself rejoicing at the misfortunes of others? Because God alone is the judge, we must never be happy about others' misfortunes, even if we think they deserve them (see Proverbs 24:17).

12–14 Of all Israel and Judah's neighbors, Edom was the only one not promised any mercy from God. This was because they looted Jerusalem and rejoiced at the misfortunes of Israel and Judah. They betrayed their blood brothers in times of crisis and aided their brothers' enemies. (See also Psalm 137:7; Jeremiah 49:7–22; Ezekiel 25:12–14; Amos 1:11–12.)

15 Why will God's judgment fall on all the nations? Edom was not the only nation to rejoice at Judah's fall. All nations and individuals will be judged for the way they have treated God's people. Some nations today treat God's people favorably, while others are hostile toward them. God will judge all people according to the way they treat others, especially believers (Revelation 20:12–13). Jesus talked about this in Matthew 25:31–46.

17–21 The Edomites were routed by Judas Maccabeus in 164 B.C. The nation no longer existed by the first century A.D. At the time of Obadiah's prophecy, Edom may have seemed more likely to survive than Judah. Yet Edom has vanished, and Judah still exists. This demonstrates the absolute certainty of God's Word and of the punishment awaiting all who have mistreated God's people.

19 The Negev was the southern part of Judah, a dry, hot region. The Shephelah refers to the foothills in the western part of Judah.

1:20
1 Kin 17:9; Luke 4:26; Jer 32:44; 33:13

20 And the exiles of this host of the sons of Israel,
Who are *among* the Canaanites as far as Zarephath,
And the exiles of Jerusalem who are in Sepharad
Will possess the cities of the Negev.

1:21
Neh 9:27; Ps 22:28; 47:7-9; 67:4; Zech 14:9; Rev 11:15

21 The deliverers will ascend Mount Zion
To judge the mountain of Esau,
And the kingdom will be the LORD'S.

OBADIAH Obadiah served as a prophet to Judah possibly around 853 B.C.		
	Climate of the times	Edom was a constant thorn in Judah's side. The Edomites often participated in attacks initiated by other enemies.
	Main message	God will judge Edom for its evil actions toward God's people.
	Importance of message	Just as Edom was destroyed and disappeared as a nation, so God will destroy proud and wicked people.
	Contemporary prophets	Elijah (875–848 B.C.) Micaiah (865–853 B.C.) Jehu (855–840? B.C.)

---

20 The boundaries of the kingdom would be extended to include the Canaanites (Phoenicians) as far south as Zarephath, located between Tyre and Sidon on the Mediterranean coast. Sepharad was most likely the city of Sardis.

21 Obadiah brought God's message of judgment on Edom. God was displeased with both their inward and their outward rebellion. People today are much the same as people in Obadiah's time, filled with arrogance, envy, and dishonesty. We may wonder where it will all end. Regardless of sin's effects, however, God is in control. Don't despair or give up hope. Know that when all is said and done, the Lord will still be King, and the confidence you place in him will not be in vain.

21 Edom is an example to all the nations that are hostile to God. Nothing can break God's promise to protect his people from complete destruction. In the book of Obadiah we see four aspects of God's message of judgment: (1) Evil will certainly be punished; (2) those faithful to God have hope for a new future; (3) God is sovereign in human history; (4) God's ultimate purpose is to establish his eternal kingdom. The Edomites had been cruel to God's people. They were arrogant and proud, and they took advantage of others' misfortunes. Any nation that mistreats people who obey God will be punished, regardless of how invincible they appear. Similarly we, as individuals, cannot allow ourselves to feel so comfortable with our wealth or security that we fail to help God's people. This is sin. And because God is just, sin will be punished.

JONAH

Jeroboam II becomes king; Jonah becomes a prophet 793 B.C.	*Uzziah (Azariah) becomes king of Judah 792*	*Jonah preaches to Nineveh 785?*	*Shalmaneser IV becomes king of Assyria 783*	*Ashur-dan III becomes king of Assyria 772*

VITAL STATISTICS

PURPOSE:
To show the extent of God's grace—the message of salvation is for *all* people

AUTHOR:
Jonah son of Amittai

TO WHOM WRITTEN:
Israel and God's people everywhere

DATE WRITTEN:
Approximately 785–760 B.C.

SETTING:
Jonah preceded Amos and ministered under Jeroboam II, Israel's most powerful king (793–753 B.C.; see 2 Kings 14:23–25). Assyria was Israel's great enemy; it conquered Israel in 722 B.C. Nineveh's repentance must have been short-lived, for it was destroyed in 612 B.C.

KEY VERSE:
"Should I not have compassion on Nineveh, the great city in which there are more than 120,000 persons who do not know the difference between their right and left hand, as well as many animals?" (4:11).

KEY PEOPLE:
Jonah, the ship's captain and crew

KEY PLACES:
Joppa, Nineveh

SPECIAL FEATURES:
This book is different from the other prophetic books because it tells the story of the prophet and does not center on his prophecies. In fact, only one verse summarizes his message to the people of Nineveh (3:4). Jonah is a historical narrative. It is also mentioned by Jesus as a picture of his death and resurrection (Matthew 12:38–42).

SIN runs rampant in society—daily headlines and overflowing prisons bear dramatic witness to that fact. With child abuse, pornography, serial killings, terrorism, anarchy, and ruthless dictatorships, the world seems to be filled to overflowing with violence, hatred, and corruption. Reading and hearing about these tragedies—and perhaps even experiencing them—we begin to understand the necessity of God's judgment. We may even find ourselves wishing for vengeance by any means upon the violent perpetrators. Surely they are beyond redemption! But suppose that in the midst of such thoughts, God told you to take the gospel to the worst of the offenders—how would you respond?

Jonah was given such a task. Assyria—a great but evil empire—was Israel's most dreaded enemy. The Assyrians flaunted their power before God and the world through numerous acts of heartless cruelty. So when Jonah heard God tell him to go to Assyria and call the people to repentance, he ran in the opposite direction.

The book of Jonah tells the story of this prophet's flight and how God stopped him and turned him around. But it is much more than a story of a man and a great fish. Jonah's story is a profound illustration of God's mercy and grace. No one deserved God's favor less than the people of Nineveh, Assyria's capital. Jonah knew this. But he knew that God would forgive and bless them if they would turn from their sin and worship him. Jonah also knew the power of God's message, that even through his own weak preaching, they would respond and be spared God's judgment. But Jonah hated the Assyrians, and he wanted vengeance, not mercy. So he ran. Eventually, Jonah obeyed and preached in the streets of Nineveh, and the people repented and were delivered from judgment. Then Jonah sulked and complained to God, "I knew that You are a gracious and compassionate God, slow to anger and abundant in lovingkindness, and one who relents concerning calamity" (4:2). In the end, God confronted Jonah about his self-centered values and lack of compassion, saying, "Should I not have compassion on Nineveh, the great city in which there are more than 120,000 persons who do not know the difference between their right and left hand, as well as many animals?" (4:11).

As you read Jonah, see the full picture of God's love and compassion and realize that no one is beyond redemption. The gospel is for all who will repent and believe. Begin to pray for those who seem to be farthest from the kingdom, and look for ways to tell them about God. Learn from the story of this reluctant prophet and determine to obey God, doing whatever he asks and going wherever he leads.

Amos becomes a prophet 760	Ashur-nirari V becomes king of Assyria 754	Jonah's ministry ends 753	Israel falls to Assyria 722

THE BLUEPRINT

1. Jonah forsakes his mission (1:1—2:10)
2. Jonah fulfills his mission (3:1—4:11)

Jonah was a reluctant prophet given a mission he found distasteful. He chose to run away from God rather than obey him. Like Jonah, we may have to do things in life that we don't want to do. Sometimes we find ourselves wanting to turn and run. But it is better to obey God than to defy him or run away. Often, in spite of our defiance, God in his mercy will give us another chance to serve him when we return to him.

MEGATHEMES

THEME	EXPLANATION	IMPORTANCE
God's Sovereignty	Although the prophet Jonah tried to run away from God, God was in control. By controlling the stormy seas and a great fish, God displayed his absolute, yet loving guidance.	Rather than running from God, trust him with your past, present, and future. Saying no to God quickly leads to disaster. Saying yes brings new understanding of God and his purpose in the world.
God's Message to All the World	God had given Jonah a purpose—to preach to the great Assyrian city of Nineveh. Jonah hated Nineveh, and so he responded with anger and indifference. Jonah had yet to learn that God loves all people. Through Jonah, God reminded Israel of its missionary purpose.	We must not limit our focus to our own people. God wants his people to proclaim his love in words and actions to the whole world. He wants us to be his missionaries wherever we are, wherever he sends us.
Repentance	When the reluctant preacher went to Nineveh, there was a great response. The people repented and turned to God. This was a powerful rebuke to the people of Israel, who thought they were better but refused to respond to God's message. God will forgive all those who turn from their sin.	God doesn't honor sham or pretense. He wants the sincere devotion of each person. It is not enough to share the privileges of Christianity; we must ask God to forgive us and to remove our sin. Refusing to repent shows that we still love our sin.
God's Compassion	God's message of love and forgiveness was not for the Jews alone. God loves all the people of the world. The Assyrians didn't deserve it, but God spared them when they repented. In his mercy, God did not reject Jonah for aborting his mission. God has great love, patience, and forgiveness.	God loves each of us, even when we fail him. But he also loves other people, including those not of our group, background, race, or denomination. When we accept his love, we must also learn to accept all those whom he loves. We will find it much easier to love others when we truly love God.

1. Jonah forsakes his mission

Jonah's Disobedience

1 The word of the LORD came to Jonah the son of Amittai saying,
2 "Arise, go to Nineveh the great city and cry against it, for their wickedness has
come up before Me."
3 But Jonah rose up to flee to Tarshish from the presence of the LORD. So he went
down to Joppa, found a ship which was going to Tarshish, paid the fare and went down
into it to go with them to Tarshish from the presence of the LORD.
4 The LORD hurled a great wind on the sea and there was a great storm on the sea so
that the ship was about to break up.
5 Then the sailors became afraid and every man cried to his god, and they threw the
cargo which was in the ship into the sea to lighten *it* for them. But Jonah had gone below
into the hold of the ship, lain down and fallen sound asleep.
6 So the captain approached him and said, "How is it that you are sleeping? Get up,
call on your god. Perhaps *your* god will be concerned about us so that we will not perish."
7 Each man said to his mate, "Come, let us cast lots so we may learn on whose account this calamity *has struck* us." So they cast lots and the lot fell on Jonah.
8 Then they said to him, "Tell us, now! On whose account *has* this calamity *struck* us?
What is your occupation? And where do you come from? What is your country? From
what people are you?"
9 He said to them, "I am a Hebrew, and I fear the LORD God of heaven who made
the sea and the dry land."
10 Then the men became extremely frightened and they said to him, "How could you
do this?" For the men knew that he was fleeing from the presence of the LORD, because
he had told them.
11 So they said to him, "What should we do to you that the sea may become calm for
us?"—for the sea was becoming increasingly stormy.
12 He said to them, "Pick me up and throw me into the sea. Then the sea will become
calm for you, for I know that on account of me this great storm *has come* upon you."

1:2 2 Kin 19:36; Is 37:37; Nah 1:1; Zeph 2:13; Is 58:1; Gen 18:20; Hos 7:2

1:3 Is 23:1, 6, 10; Jer 10:9; Gen 4:16; Ps 139:7, 9, 10; Josh 19:46; 2 Chr 2:16; Ezra 3:7; Acts 9:36, 43

1:4 Ps 107:23-28; 135:6

1:5 1 Kin 18:26; Acts 27:18, 19, 38

1:6 Ps 107:28; 2 Sam 12:22; Amos 5:15; Jon 3:9

1:7 Josh 7:14-18; 1 Sam 10:20, 21; 14:41, 42; Acts 1:23-26; Num 32:23; Prov 16:33

1:9 Gen 14:13; Ex 1:15; 2:13; 2 Kin 17:25, 28, 32, 33; Ezra 1:2; Neh 1:4; Ps 136:26; Dan 2:18; Neh 9:6; Ps 95:5; 146:6

1:10 Job 27:22; Jon 1:3

1:12 2 Sam 24:17; 1 Chr 21:17

1:1–2 Jonah is mentioned in 2 Kings 14:25. He prophesied during the reign of Jeroboam II, the king of Israel from 793–753 B.C. He may have been a member of the company of prophets mentioned in connection with Elisha's ministry (2 Kings 2:3).

God told Jonah to preach to Nineveh, the most important city in Assyria, the rising world power of Jonah's day. Within 50 years, Nineveh would become the capital of the vast Assyrian empire. Jonah doesn't say much about Nineveh's wickedness, but the prophet Nahum gives us more insight. Nahum says that Nineveh was guilty of (1) evil plots against God (Nahum 1:9), (2) exploitation of the helpless (Nahum 2:12), (3) cruelty in war (Nahum 2:12–13), (4) idolatry, prostitution, and witchcraft (Nahum 3:4). God told Jonah to go to Nineveh, about 500 miles northeast of Israel, to warn of judgment and to declare that the people could receive mercy and forgiveness if they repented.

1:3 Nineveh was a powerful and wicked city. Jonah had grown up hating the Assyrians and fearing their atrocities. His hatred was so strong that he didn't want them to receive God's mercy. Jonah was actually afraid the people would repent (4:2–3). Jonah's attitude is representative of Israel's reluctance to share God's love and mercy with others, even though this was their God-given mission (Genesis 12:3). They, like Jonah, did not want non-Jews (Gentiles) to obtain God's favor.

1:3 Jonah knew that God had a specific job for him, but he didn't want to do it. Tarshish could be one of any number of Phoenicia's western ports. Nineveh was toward the east. Jonah decided to go as far west as he could. When God gives us directions through his Word, sometimes we run in fear or in stubbornness, claiming that God is asking too much. It may have been fear, or anger at the wideness of God's mercy, that made Jonah run. But running got him into worse trouble. In the end, Jonah understood that it is best to do what God asks in the first place. But by then he had paid a costly price for running. It is far better to obey from the start.

1:4 Before settling in the promised land, the Israelites had been nomads, wandering from place to place, seeking good pastureland for their flocks. Although they were not a seafaring people, their location along the Mediterranean Sea and near the neighboring maritime powers of Phoenicia and Philistia allowed much contact with ships and sailors. The ship Jonah sailed on was probably a large trading vessel with a deck.

1:4 Jonah's disobedience to God endangered the lives of the ship's crew. We have a great responsibility to obey God's Word because our sin and disobedience can hurt others around us.

1:4–5 While the storm raged, Jonah was sound asleep below deck. Even as he ran from God, Jonah's actions apparently didn't bother his conscience. But the absence of guilt isn't always a barometer of whether we are doing right. Because we can deny reality, we cannot measure obedience by our feelings. Instead, we must compare what we do with God's standards for living.

1:7 The crew cast lots to find the guilty person, relying on their superstition to give them the answer. Their system worked, but only because God intervened to let Jonah know that he couldn't run away.

1:9–12 You cannot seek God's love and run from him at the same time. Jonah soon realized that no matter where he went, he couldn't get away from God. But before Jonah could return to God, he first had to stop going in the opposite direction. What has God told you to do? If you want more of God's love and power, you must be willing to carry out the responsibilities he gives you. You cannot say that you truly believe in God if you don't do what he says (1 John 2:3–6).

1:12 Jonah knew that he had disobeyed and that the storm was his fault, but he didn't say anything until the crew cast lots and the lot fell on him (1:7). Then Jonah was willing to give his life to save the sailors, although he had refused to do the same for the people of Nineveh. Jonah's hatred for the Assyrians had affected his perspective.

13 However, the men rowed *desperately* to return to land but they could not, for the
sea was becoming *even* stormier against them.
14 Then they called on the LORD and said, "We earnestly pray, O LORD, do not let
us perish on account of this man's life and do not put innocent blood on us; for You,
O LORD, have done as You have pleased."
15 So they picked up Jonah, threw him into the sea, and the sea stopped its raging.
16 Then the men feared the LORD greatly, and they offered a sacrifice to the LORD
and made vows.
17 And the LORD appointed a great fish to swallow Jonah, and Jonah was in the stomach of the fish three days and three nights.

Jonah's Prayer

2 Then Jonah prayed to the LORD his God from the stomach of the fish,
2 and he said,

"I called out of my distress to the LORD,
And He answered me.
I cried for help from the depth of Sheol;

1:14 Ps 107:28; Jon 1:16; Ps 115:3; 135:6; Dan 4:34, 35
1:15 Ps 65:7; 93:3, 4; 107:29
1:16 Ps 50:14; 66:13, 14
1:17 Matt 12:40; 16:4
2:1 Job 13:15; Ps 130:1, 2; Lam 3:53-56
2:2 1 Sam 30:6; Ps 18:4-6; 22:24; 120:1; Ps 18:5, 6; 86:13; 88:1-7

JONAH
Jonah served as a prophet to Israel and Assyria from 793–753 B.C.

Climate of the times	Nineveh was the most important city in Assyria and would soon become the capital of the huge Assyrian empire. But Nineveh was also a very wicked city.
Main message	Jonah, who hated the powerful and wicked Assyrians, was called by God to warn the Assyrians that they would receive judgment if they did not repent.
Importance of message	Jonah didn't want to go to Nineveh, so he tried to run from God. But God has ways of teaching us to obey and follow him. When Jonah preached, the city repented and God withheld his judgment. Even the most wicked will be saved if they truly repent of their sins and turn to God.
Contemporary prophets	Joel (853–796? B.C.) Amos (760–750 B.C.)

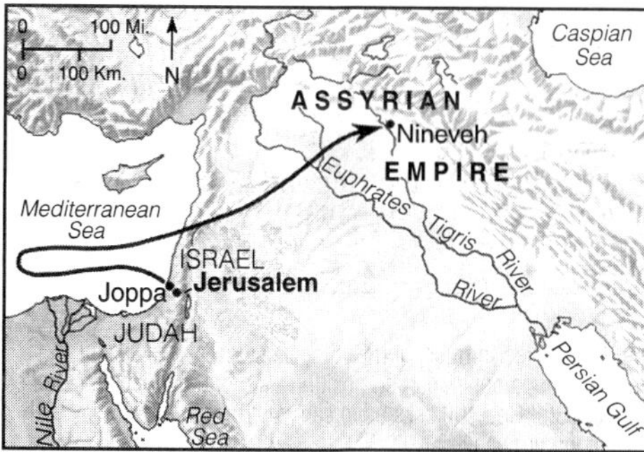

JONAH'S ROUNDABOUT JOURNEY God told Jonah to go to Nineveh, the capital of the Assyrian empire. Many of Jonah's countrymen had experienced the atrocities of these fierce people. The last place Jonah wanted to go was on a missionary trip to Nineveh! So he went in the opposite direction. He boarded a ship in Joppa that was headed for Tarshish. But Jonah could not run from God.

1:13 By trying to save Jonah's life, the pagan sailors showed more compassion than Jonah, because Jonah did not want to warn the Ninevites of the coming judgment of God. Believers should be ashamed when unbelievers show more concern and compassion than they do. God wants us to be concerned for all of his people, lost and saved.

1:14–16 Jonah had disobeyed God. While he was running away, he stopped and submitted to God. Then the ship's crew began to worship God because they saw the storm quiet down. God is able to use even our mistakes to help others come to know him. It may be painful, but admitting our sins can be a powerful example to those who don't know God. Ironically, the pagan sailors did what the entire nation of Israel would not do—prayed to God and vowed to serve him.

1:17 Many have tried to dismiss this miraculous event as fiction, but the Bible does not describe it as a dream or a legend. We should not explain away this miracle as if we could pick and choose which of the miracles in the Bible we believe and which ones we don't. That kind of attitude would allow us to question any part of the Bible and cause us to lose our trust in the Bible as God's true and reliable Word. Jonah's experience was used by Christ himself as an illustration of Christ's death and resurrection (Matthew 12:39–40).

2:1ff This is a prayer of thanksgiving, not a prayer for deliverance. Jonah was simply thankful that he had not drowned. He was delivered in a most spectacular way and was overwhelmed that he had escaped certain death. Even from inside the fish, Jonah's prayer was heard by God. We can pray anywhere and at any time, and God will hear us. Your sin is never too great, your predicament never too difficult, for God.

2:1–7 Jonah said, "While I was fainting away, I remembered the LORD" (2:7). Often we act the same way. When life is going well, we tend to take God for granted; but when we lose hope, we cry out to him. This kind of relationship with God can result only in an inconsistent, up-and-down spiritual life. A consistent, daily commitment to God promotes a solid relationship with him. Look to God during both the good and bad times, and you will have a stronger spiritual life.

2:2 Jonah pictured his predicament in the belly of the fish as though he had been buried alive.

You heard my voice.
3 "For You had cast me into the deep,
Into the heart of the seas,
And the current engulfed me.
All Your breakers and billows passed over me.
4 "So I said, 'I have been expelled from Your sight.
Nevertheless I will look again toward Your holy temple.'
5 "Water encompassed me to the point of death.
The great deep engulfed me,
Weeds were wrapped around my head.
6 "I descended to the roots of the mountains.
The earth with its bars *was* around me forever,
But You have brought up my life from the pit, O LORD my God.
7 "While I was fainting away,
I remembered the LORD,
And my prayer came to You,
Into Your holy temple.
8 "Those who regard vain idols
Forsake their faithfulness,
9 But I will sacrifice to You
With the voice of thanksgiving.
That which I have vowed I will pay.
Salvation is from the LORD."
10 Then the LORD commanded the fish, and it vomited Jonah up onto the dry land.

2:3 Ps 69:1, 2, 14, 15; Lam 3:54; Ps 42:7
2:4 Ps 31:22; Jer 7:15; 1 Kin 8:38; 2 Chr 6:38; Ps 5:7
2:5 Lam 3:54; Ps 69:1, 2
2:6 Ps 18:5; 116:3; Is 38:10; Matt 16:18; Job 33:28; Ps 16:10; 30:3; Is 38:17
2:7 Ps 142:3; Ps 77:10, 11; 143:5; 2 Chr 30:27; Ps 18:6; Ps 11:4; 65:4; Jon 2:4; Mic 1:2; Hab 2:20
2:8 2 Kin 17:15; Ps 31:6; Jer 10:8
2:9 Ps 50:14, 23; Jer 33:11; Hos 14:2; Job 22:27; Eccl 5:4, 5; Ps 3:8; Is 45:17
2:10 Jon 1:17

2. Jonah fulfills his mission

Nineveh Repents

3 Now the word of the LORD came to Jonah the second time, saying,
2 "Arise, go to Nineveh the great city and proclaim to it the proclamation which I
am going to tell you."
3 So Jonah arose and went to Nineveh according to the word of the LORD. Now Nineveh was [1]an exceedingly great city, a three days' walk.
4 Then Jonah began to go through the city one day's walk; and he cried out and said,
"Yet forty days and Nineveh will be overthrown."
5 Then the people of Nineveh believed in God; and they called a fast and put on sackcloth from the greatest to the least of them.
6 When the word reached the king of Nineveh, he arose from his throne, laid aside
his robe from him, covered *himself* with sackcloth and sat on the ashes.
7 He issued a proclamation and it said, "In Nineveh by the decree of the king and his

3:2 Zeph 2:13; Jer 1:17; Ezek 2:7
3:3 Jon 1:2; 4:11
3:4 Matt 12:41; Luke 11:32
3:5 Dan 9:3; Joel 1:14
3:6 Esth 4:1-4; Jer 6:26; Ezek 27:30, 31
3:7 2 Chr 20:3; Ezra 8:21; Jon 3:5

1 Lit *a great city to God*

2:8 Those who worship worthless idols forfeit God's grace and abandon any hope for mercy from the Lord. Any object of our devotion that replaces God is a lying vanity. We deceive ourselves with something that is ultimately empty and foolish. Make sure that nothing takes God's rightful place in your life.

2:9 Obviously Jonah was not in a position to bargain with God. Instead, he simply thanked God for saving his life. Our troubles should cause us to cling tightly to God, not attempt to bargain our way out of the pain. We can thank and praise God for what he has already done for us, and for his love and mercy.

2:9 It took a miracle of deliverance to get Jonah to do as God had commanded. As a prophet, Jonah was obligated to obey God's word, but he had tried to escape his responsibilities. At this time, he pledged to keep his vows. Jonah's story began with a tragedy, but a greater tragedy would have happened if God had allowed him to keep running. When you know God wants you to do something, don't run. God may not stop you as he did Jonah.

3:1–2 Jonah had run away from God, but was given a second chance to participate in God's work. You may feel as though you are disqualified from serving God because of past mistakes. But serving God is not an earned position—no one qualifies for God's service. Still God still asks us to carry out his work. You may yet have another chance.

3:1–2 Jonah was to preach only what God told him—a message of doom to one of the most powerful cities in the world. This was not the most desirable assignment, but those who bring God's word to others should not let social pressures or fear of people dictate their words. They are called to preach God's message and his truth, no matter how unpopular it may be.

3:3 The Hebrew text makes no distinction between the city proper (the walls of which were only about eight miles in circumference, accommodating a population of about 175,000 persons) and the administrative district of Nineveh that was about 30 to 60 miles across. An "exceedingly great city," Nineveh took three days just to visit.

3:4–9 God's Word is for everyone. Despite the wickedness of the Ninevite people, they were open to God's message and repented immediately. If we simply proclaim what we know about God, we may be surprised at how many people will listen.

nobles: Do not let man, beast, herd, or flock taste a thing. Do not let them eat or drink
water.
8 "But both man and beast must be covered with sackcloth; and let men call on God
earnestly that each may turn from his wicked way and from the violence which is in his
hands.
9 "Who knows, God may turn and relent and withdraw His burning anger so that we
will not perish."
10 When God saw their deeds, that they turned from their wicked way, then God relented concerning the calamity which He had declared He would bring upon them. And
He did not do *it.*

Jonah's Displeasure Rebuked

4 But it greatly displeased Jonah and he became angry.
2 He prayed to the LORD and said, "Please LORD, was not this what I said while I
was still in my *own* country? Therefore in order to forestall this I fled to Tarshish, for I
knew that You are a gracious and compassionate God, slow to anger and abundant in
lovingkindness, and one who relents concerning calamity.
3 "Therefore now, O LORD, please take my life from me, for death is better to me than
life."
4 The LORD said, "Do you have good reason to be angry?"
5 Then Jonah went out from the city and sat east of it. There he made a shelter for
himself and sat under it in the shade until he could see what would happen in the city.
6 So the LORD God appointed a plant and it grew up over Jonah to be a shade over
his head to deliver him from his discomfort. And Jonah was extremely happy about the
plant.
7 But God appointed a worm when dawn came the next day and it attacked the plant
and it withered.
8 When the sun came up God appointed a scorching east wind, and the sun beat down

3:8 Ps 130:1; Jon 1:6, 14; Is 1:16-19; 55:6, 7; Jer 18:11

3:9 2 Sam 12:22; Joel 2:14

3:10 1 Kin 21:27-29; Jer 31:18; Ex 32:14; Jer 18:8; Amos 7:3, 6

4:1 Jon 4:4, 9; Matt 20:15; Luke 15:28

4:2 Jer 20:7; Jon 1:3; Ex 34:6; Num 14:18; Ps 86:5, 15; Joel 2:13

4:3 1 Kin 19:4; Job 6:8, 9; Job 7:15, 16; Eccl 7:1

4:5 1 Kin 19:9, 13

4:7 Joel 1:12

4:8 Ezek 19:12; Hos 13:15; Ps 121:6; Is 49:10; Jon 4:3

MIRACLES IN THE BOOK OF JONAH

God sent a violent storm	1:4
God provided a great fish to swallow Jonah	1:17
God ordered the fish to vomit Jonah	2:10
God made a plant to shade Jonah	4:6
God provided a worm to eat the vine	4:7
God provided a scorching wind to blow on Jonah	4:8

3:10 The pagan people of Nineveh believed Jonah's message and repented. What a miraculous effect God's words had on those evil people! Their repentance stood in stark contrast to Israel's stubbornness. The people of Israel had heard many messages from the prophets, but they had refused to repent. The people of Nineveh only needed to hear God's message once. Jesus said that at the judgment, the men of Nineveh will stand up to condemn the Israelites for their failure to repent (Matthew 12:39–41). It is not our hearing God's Word that pleases him, but our responding obediently to it.

3:10 God responded in mercy by canceling his threatened punishment. God had said that any nation on which he had pronounced judgment would be saved if they repented (Jeremiah 18:7–8). God forgave Nineveh, just as he had forgiven Jonah. The purpose of God's judgment is correction, not revenge. He is always ready to show compassion to anyone willing to seek him.

4:1 Why did Jonah become angry when God spared Nineveh? The Jews did not want to share God's message with Gentile nations in Jonah's day, just as they resisted that role in Paul's day (1 Thessalonians 2:14–16). They had forgotten their original purpose as a nation—to be a blessing to the rest of the world by sharing God's message with other nations (Genesis 22:18). Jonah thought that God should not freely give his salvation to a wicked pagan nation. Yet this is exactly what God does for all who come to him today in faith.

4:1–2 Jonah revealed the reason for his reluctance to go to Nineveh (1:3). He didn't want the Ninevites forgiven; he wanted them destroyed. Jonah did not understand that the God of Israel was also the God of the whole world. Are you surprised when some unlikely person turns to God? Is it possible that your view is as narrow as Jonah's? We must not forget that, in reality, *we* do not deserve to be forgiven by God.

4:3 Jonah had run from the job of delivering God's message of destruction to Nineveh (1:2–3); then he wanted to die because the destruction wouldn't happen. How quickly Jonah had forgotten God's mercy for him when he was in the fish (2:9–10). Jonah was happy when God saved him, but angry when Nineveh was saved. But Jonah was learning a valuable lesson about God's mercy and forgiveness. God's forgiveness was not only for Jonah or for Israel alone; it extends to all who repent and believe.

4:3 Jonah may have been more concerned about his own reputation than God's. He knew that if the people repented, none of his warnings to Nineveh would come true. This would embarrass him, although it would give glory to God. Are you more interested in getting glory for God or for yourself?

4:5–11 God ministered tenderly to Jonah just as he had done to Nineveh and to Israel, and just as he does to us. God could have destroyed Jonah for his defiant anger, but instead he gently taught him a lesson. If we will obey God's will, he will lead us. His harsh judgment is reserved for those who persist in rebellion.

on Jonah's head so that he became faint and begged with *all* his soul to die, saying, "Death
is better to me than life."
9 Then God said to Jonah, "Do you have good reason to be angry about the plant?"
And he said, "I have good reason to be angry, even to death."
10 Then the LORD said, "You had compassion on the plant for which you did not work
and *which* you did not cause to grow, which came up overnight and perished overnight.
11 "Should I not have compassion on Nineveh, the great city in which there are more
than 120,000 persons who do not know *the difference* between their right and left hand,
as well as many animals?"

4:11
Jon 3:10; Deut 1:39; Is 7:16; Ps 36:6

4:9 Jonah was angry at the withering of the plant, but not over what could have happened to Nineveh. Most of us have cried at the death of a pet or when an object with sentimental value was broken, but have we cried over the fact that a friend does not know God? How easy it is to be more sensitive to our own interests than to the spiritual needs of people around us.

4:10–11 Sometimes people wish that judgment and destruction would come upon sinful people whose wickedness seems to demand immediate punishment. But God is more merciful than we can imagine. God feels compassion for the sinners we want judged, and he devises plans to bring them to himself. What is your attitude toward those who are especially wicked? Do you want them destroyed? Or do you wish that they could experience God's mercy and forgiveness?

4:11 God spared the sailors when they pleaded for mercy. God saved Jonah when he prayed from inside the fish. God saved the people of Nineveh when they responded to Jonah's preaching. God answers the prayers of those who call upon him. God will always work his will, and he desires that all come to him, trust in him, and be saved. We can be saved if we heed God's warnings to us through his Word. If we respond in obedience, God will be gracious, and we will receive his mercy, not his punishment.

GOD'S PATIENCE	Exodus 34:6	"Then the LORD passed by in front of him and proclaimed, 'The LORD, the LORD God, compassionate and gracious, slow to anger, and abounding in lovingkindness and truth.'"
	Numbers 14:18	"The LORD is slow to anger and abundant in lovingkindness, forgiving iniquity and transgression; but He will by no means clear the guilty, visiting the iniquity of the fathers on the children to the third and the fourth generations."
	Psalm 86:15	"But You, O Lord, are a God merciful and gracious, slow to anger and abundant in lovingkindness and truth."
	Jeremiah 15:15	"You who know, O LORD, remember me, take notice of me, and take vengeance for me on my persecutors. Do not, in view of Your patience, take me away; know that for Your sake I endure reproach."
	Ezekiel 18:23	"'Do I have any pleasure in the death of the wicked,' declares the Lord GOD, 'rather than that he should turn from his ways and live?'"
	Jonah 4:2	"I knew that You are a gracious and compassionate God, slow to anger and abundant in lovingkindness, and one who relents concerning calamity."
	Romans 2:4	"Or do you think lightly of the riches of His kindness and tolerance and patience, not knowing that the kindness of God leads you to repentance?"
	Romans 9:22	"What if God, although willing to demonstrate His wrath and to make His power known, endured with much patience vessels of wrath prepared for destruction?"
	Romans 11:32	"For God has shut up all in disobedience so that He may show mercy to all."
	1 Timothy 2:4	"[God] desires all men to be saved and to come to the knowledge of the truth."

MICAH

Hosea becomes a prophet 753 B.C.	Jotham becomes king of Judah 750	Tiglath-pileser III invades Israel 743	Micah becomes a prophet; Pekahiah becomes king 742	Isaiah becomes a prophet 740	Ahaz becomes king of Judah 735

VITAL STATISTICS

PURPOSE:
To warn God's people that judgment is coming and to offer pardon to all who repent

AUTHOR:
Micah, a native of Moresheth, near Gath, about 20 miles southwest of Jerusalem

TO WHOM WRITTEN:
The people of Israel (the northern kingdom) and of Judah (the southern kingdom)

DATE WRITTEN:
Possibly during the reigns of Jotham, Ahaz, and Hezekiah (742–687 B.C.)

SETTING:
The political situation is described in 2 Kings 15—20 and 2 Chronicles 26—30. Micah was a contemporary of Isaiah and Hosea.

KEY VERSE:
"He has told you, O man, what is good; and what does the LORD require of you but to do justice, to love kindness, and to walk humbly with your God?" (6:8).

KEY PEOPLE:
The people of Samaria and Jerusalem

KEY PLACES:
Samaria, Jerusalem, Bethlehem

SPECIAL FEATURES:
This is a beautiful example of classical Hebrew poetry. There are three parts, each beginning with "Hear" (1:2; 3:1; 6:1) and closing with a promise.

"I HATE YOU!" she screams and runs from the room. Words from a child thrown as emotional darts. Perhaps she learned the phrase from Mom and Dad, or maybe it just burst forth from that inner well of "sinful nature." Whatever the case, hate and love have become society's bywords, almost tired clichés, tossed carelessly at objects, situations, and even people.

The casual use of such words as *love* and *hate* has emptied them of their meaning. We no longer understand statements that describe a loving God who hates sin. So we picture God as gentle and kind—a cosmic "pushover"; and our concept of what he hates is tempered by our misconceptions and wishful thinking.

The words of the prophets stand in stark contrast to such misconceptions. God's hatred is real—burning, consuming, and destroying. He hates sin, and he stands as the righteous Judge, ready to mete out just punishment to all who defy his rule. God's love is also real. So real that he sent his Son, the Messiah, to save and accept judgment in the sinner's place. Love and hate are together—both unending, irresistible, and unfathomable.

In seven short chapters, Micah presents this true picture of God—the almighty Lord who hates sin and loves the sinner. Much of the book is devoted to describing God's judgment on Israel (the northern kingdom), on Judah (the southern kingdom), and on all the earth. This judgment will come "for the rebellion of Jacob and for the sins of the house of Israel" (1:5). And the prophet lists their despicable sins, including fraud (2:2), theft (2:8), greed (2:9), debauchery (2:11), oppression (3:3), hypocrisy (3:4), heresy (3:5), injustice (3:9), extortion and lying (6:12), murder (7:2), and other offenses. God's judgment will come.

In the midst of this overwhelming prediction of destruction, Micah gives hope and consolation because he also describes God's love. The truth is that judgment comes only after countless opportunities to repent, to turn back to true worship and obedience—"to do justice, to love kindness, and to walk humbly with your God" (6:8). But even in the midst of judgment, God promises to deliver the small minority who have continued to follow him. He states, "Their king goes on before them, and the LORD at their head" (2:13). The king, of course, is Jesus; and we read in 5:2 that he will be born as a baby in Bethlehem, an obscure Judean village.

As you read Micah, catch a glimpse of God's anger in action as he judges and punishes sin. See God's love in action as he offers eternal life to all who repent and believe. And then determine to join the faithful remnant of God's people, who live according to his will.

Israel (the northern kingdom) falls 722 | *Hosea's ministry ends; Hezekiah becomes king of Judah 715* | *Sennacherib surrounds Jerusalem 701* | *Micah's ministry ends 687*

THE BLUEPRINT

1. The trial of the capitals (1:1—2:13)
2. The trial of the leaders (3:1—5:15)
3. The trial of the people (6:1—7:20)

Micah emphasized the need for justice and peace. Like a lawyer, he set forth God's case against Israel and Judah, their leaders, and their people. Throughout the book are prophecies about Jesus, the Messiah, who will gather the people into one nation. He will be their king and ruler, acting mercifully toward them. Micah makes it clear that God hates unkindness, idolatry, injustice, and empty ritual—and he still hates these today. But God is very willing to pardon the sins of any who repent.

MEGATHEMES

THEME	EXPLANATION	IMPORTANCE
Perverting Faith	God will judge the false prophets, dishonest leaders, and selfish priests in Israel and Judah. While they publicly carried out religious ceremonies, they were privately seeking to gain money and influence. To mix selfish motives with an empty display of religion is to pervert faith.	Don't try to mix your own selfish desires with true faith in God. One day God will reveal how foolish it is to substitute anything for loyalty to him. Coming up with your own private blend of religion will pervert your faith.
Oppression	Micah predicted ruin for all nations and leaders who were oppressive toward others. The upper classes oppressed and exploited the poor. Yet no one was speaking against them or doing anything to stop them. God will not put up with such injustice.	We dare not ask God to help us while we ignore those who are needy and oppressed, or while we silently condone the actions of those who oppress them.
The Messiah—King of Peace	God promised to provide a new king to bring strength and peace to his people. Hundreds of years before Christ's birth, God promised that the eternal king would be born in Bethlehem. It was God's great plan to restore his people through the Messiah.	Christ our king leads us just as God promised. But until his final judgment, his leadership is only visible among those who welcome his authority. We can have God's peace now by giving up our sins and welcoming him as king.
Pleasing God	Micah preached that God's greatest desire was not the offering of sacrifices at the temple. God delights in faith that produces justice, love for others, and obedience to him.	True faith in God generates kindness, compassion, justice, and humility. We can please God by seeking these attributes in our work, our family, our church, and our neighborhood.

1:1 2 Pet 1:21; Jer 26:18; 2 Kin 15:5, 32-38; 2 Chr 27:1-9; Is 1:1; Hos 1:1; 2 Kin 16:1-20; 2 Chr 28:1-27; Is 7:1-12; 2 Kin 18:1-20; 2 Chr 29:1-31

1:2 Jer 6:19; 22:29; Is 50:7

1. The trial of the capitals

Destruction in Israel and Judah

1 The word of the LORD which came *to* Micah of Moresheth in the days of Jotham,
Ahaz *and* Hezekiah, kings of Judah, which he saw concerning Samaria and Jerusalem.

2 Hear, O peoples, all of you;
Listen, O earth and all it contains,

1:1 Micah and Isaiah lived at the same time, about 750–680 B.C., and undoubtedly knew of each other. Micah directed his message mainly to Judah, the southern kingdom, but he also had some words for Israel, the northern kingdom. Judah was enjoying great prosperity at this time. Of the three kings mentioned, Jotham (750–732) and Hezekiah (715–686) had tried to follow God (2 Kings 15:32-38; 18—20), but Ahaz (735–715) was one of the most evil kings ever to reign in Judah (2 Kings 16). Moresheth was a Judean village, near Gath on the border with Philistia.

And let the Lord GOD be a witness against you,
The Lord from His holy temple.
3 For behold, the LORD is coming forth from His place.
He will come down and tread on the high places of the earth.
4 The mountains will melt under Him
And the valleys will be split,
Like wax before the fire,
Like water poured down a steep place.
5 All this is for the rebellion of Jacob
And for the sins of the house of Israel.
What is the rebellion of Jacob?
Is it not Samaria?
What is the high place of Judah?
Is it not Jerusalem?
6 For I will make Samaria a heap of ruins in the open country,
Planting places for a vineyard.
I will pour her stones down into the valley
And will lay bare her foundations.
7 All of her idols will be smashed,
All of her earnings will be burned with fire
And all of her images I will make desolate,
For she collected *them* from a harlot's earnings,
And to the earnings of a harlot they will return.

8 Because of this I must lament and wail,
I must go barefoot and naked;
I must make a lament like the jackals
And a mourning like the ostriches.
9 For her wound is incurable,
For it has come to Judah;
It has reached the gate of my people,
Even to Jerusalem.
10 Tell it not in Gath,
Weep not at all.
At [1]Beth-le-aphrah roll yourself in the dust.
11 Go on your way, inhabitant of [2]Shaphir, in shameful nakedness.
The inhabitant of [3]Zaanan does not escape.
The lamentation of [4]Beth-ezel: "He will take from you its support."
12 For the inhabitant of [5]Maroth
Becomes weak waiting for good,
Because a calamity has come down from the LORD
To the gate of Jerusalem.

1:3 Is 26:21; Amos 4:13
1:4 Ps 97:5; Is 64:1, 2; Nah 1:5
1:5 Jer 2:19; Is 7:9; Amos 8:14; 2 Chr 34:3, 4
1:6 2 Kin 19:25; Mic 3:12; Jer 31:5; Amos 5:11; Lam 4:1; Ezek 13:14
1:7 Deut 9:21; 2 Chr 34:7; Deut 23:18; Is 23:17
1:8 Is 32:11; Is 13:21, 22
1:9 Is 3:26; Jer 30:12, 15; 2 Kin 18:13; Is 8:7, 8; Mic 1:12
1:10 2 Sam 1:20
1:11 Ezek 23:29; Josh 15:37
1:12 Is 59:9-11; Jer 14:19; Mic 1:9

1 I.e. house of dust **2** I.e. pleasantness **3** I.e. going out **4** I.e. house of removal **5** I.e. bitterness

1:3 "High places" could simply mean "mountaintops" or may refer to the altars dedicated to various idols, usually placed in such elevated areas (see also 1:5).

1:3–7 Jerusalem was the capital city of Judah (the southern kingdom); Samaria was the capital city of Israel (the northern kingdom). The destruction of Samaria was literally fulfilled during Micah's lifetime, in 722 B.C. (2 Kings 17:1–18), just as he had predicted.

1:5 There are two sins identified in Micah's message—the perversion of worship (1:7; 3:5–7, 11; 5:12–13) and injustice toward others (2:1, 2, 8–9; 3:2, 3, 9–11; 7:2–6). Rampant in the capital cities, these sins infiltrated and infected the entire country.

1:9 Samaria's sins were incurable, and God's judgment on the city had already begun. This sin was not like a gash in the skin, but more like a stab wound in a vital organ, causing an injury that would soon prove fatal (Samaria was, in fact, destroyed early in Micah's ministry). Tragically, Samaria's sin had influenced Jerusalem, and judgment would come to its very gates. This probably refers to Sennacherib's siege in 701 B.C. (see 2 Kings 18–19).

1:10–16 Micah declared God's judgment on city after city because of the people's sins. There is a clever wordplay in the Hebrew of 1:10–13. Micah bitterly denounced each town by using puns. *Shaphir* sounds like the Hebrew word for "pleasant"; *Zaanan* sounds like the verb meaning "come out"; and *Maroth* sounds like a word for "bitter." Read 1:11 aloud, substituting the meaning for each city's name, and you will realize the effect of Micah's word choice. Not all these cities can be identified now, but Lachish was on the border with Philistia and took the brunt of the Assyrian invasion.

1:13 Josh 10:3; 2 Kin 14:19; Is 36:2; Mic 1:5

13 Harness the chariot to the team of horses,
O inhabitant of Lachish—
She was the beginning of sin
To the daughter of Zion—
Because in you were found
The rebellious acts of Israel.

1:14 2 Kin 16:8; Josh 15:44; Jer 15:18

14 Therefore you will give parting gifts
On behalf of Moresheth-gath;
The houses of Achzib *will* become a deception
To the kings of Israel.

1:15 Josh 15:44; Josh 12:15; 15:35; 2 Sam 23:13

15 Moreover, I will bring on you
The one who takes possession,
O inhabitant of [6]Mareshah.
The glory of Israel will enter Adullam.

1:16 Is 22:12; 2 Kin 17:6; Amos 7:11, 17

16 Make yourself bald and cut off your hair,
Because of the children of your delight;
Extend your baldness like the eagle,
For they will go from you into exile.

Woe to Oppressors

2:1 Ps 36:4; Is 32:7; Nah 1:11; Hos 7:6, 7; Gen 31:29; Deut 28:32; Prov 3:27

2 Woe to those who scheme iniquity,
Who work out evil on their beds!
When morning comes, they do it,
For it is in the power of their hands.

2:2 Jer 22:17; Amos 8:4; Is 5:8; 1 Kin 21:1-15

2 They covet fields and then seize *them,*
And houses, and take *them* away.
They rob a man and his house,
A man and his inheritance.

2:3 Deut 28:48; Jer 18:11; Jer 8:3; Amos 3:1, 2; Lam 1:14; 5:5; Is 2:11, 12; Amos 5:13

3 Therefore thus says the LORD,
"Behold, I am planning against this family a calamity
From which you cannot remove your necks;
And you will not walk haughtily,
For it will be an evil time.

6 I.e. possession

MICAH
Micah served as a prophet to Judah from 742–687 B.C.

Climate of the times	King Ahaz set up pagan idols in the temple and finally nailed the temple door shut. Four different nations harassed Judah. When Hezekiah became king, the nation began a slow road to recovery and economic strength. Hezekiah probably heeded much of Micah's advice.
Main message	Prediction of the fall of both the northern kingdom of Israel and the southern kingdom of Judah. This was God's discipline upon the people, actually showing how much he cared for them. Hezekiah's good reign helped postpone Judah's punishment.
Importance of message	Choosing to live a life apart from God is making a commitment to sin. Sin leads to judgment and death. God alone shows us the way to eternal peace. His discipline often keeps us on the right path.
Contemporary prophets	Hosea (753–715 B.C.) Isaiah (740–681 B.C.)

1:13 The people of Lachish had influenced many to follow their evil example. They were "the beginning of sin." We often do the same when we sin. Regardless of whether you consider yourself a leader, your daily actions and words are observed by others who may choose to follow your example, whether you know it or not.

1:14 Moresheth-gath was Micah's hometown (1:1).

1:15 The terrain surrounding Adullam had numerous caves. Micah was warning that when the enemy approached, Judah's proud princes would be forced to flee and hide in these caves.

1:16 Micah pictured the devastating sorrow of parents seeing their children taken away to be slaves in a distant land. This happened frequently in both Israel and Judah, most horribly when each nation was completely conquered—Israel in 722 B.C. and Judah in 586 B.C.

2:1–2 Micah spoke out against those who planned evil deeds at night and rose at dawn to do them. A person's thoughts and plans reflect his or her character. What do you think about as you lie down to sleep? Do your desires involve greed or stepping on others to achieve your goals? Evil thoughts lead to evil deeds.

4 "On that day they will take up against you a taunt
And utter a bitter lamentation *and* say,
'We are completely destroyed!
He exchanges the portion of my people;
How He removes it from me!
To the apostate He apportions our fields.'
5 "Therefore you will have no one stretching a measuring line
For you by lot in the assembly of the LORD.

2:4 Hab 2:6; Jer 9:10, 17-21; Mic 1:8; Is 6:11; 24:3; Jer 4:13; Jer 6:12; 8:10

2:5 Num 34:13, 16-29; Deut 32:8; Josh 18:4, 10

6 'Do not speak out,' *so* they speak out.
But if they do not speak out concerning these things,
Reproaches will not be turned back.
7 "Is it being said, O house of Jacob:
'Is the Spirit of the LORD impatient?
Are these His doings?'
Do not My words do good
To the one walking uprightly?
8 "Recently My people have arisen as an enemy—
You strip the robe off the garment
From unsuspecting passers-by,
From those returned from war.
9 "The women of My people you evict,
Each *one* from her pleasant house.
From her children you take My splendor forever.
10 "Arise and go,
For this is no place of rest
Because of the uncleanness that brings on destruction,
A painful destruction.
11 "If a man walking after wind and falsehood
Had told lies *and said,*
'I will speak out to you concerning wine and liquor,'
He would be spokesman to this people.

2:6 Is 30:10; Amos 2:12; 7:16; Is 29:10; Mic 3:6; Mic 6:16

2:7 Is 50:2; 59:1; Ps 119:65, 68, 116; Jer 15:16; Ps 15:2; 84:11

2:8 Jer 12:8; Mic 3:2, 3; 7:2, 3; Ps 120:6, 7

2:9 Jer 10:20; Ezek 39:21; Hab 2:14

2:10 Deut 12:9; Ps 106:38

2:11 Jer 5:31; Is 28:7; Is 30:10, 11

12 "I will surely assemble all of you, Jacob,
I will surely gather the remnant of Israel.
I will put them together like sheep in the fold;
Like a flock in the midst of its pasture
They will be noisy with men.
13 "The breaker goes up before them;
They break out, pass through the gate and go out by it.
So their king goes on before them,
And the LORD at their head."

2:12 Mic 4:6, 7; Mic 5:7, 8; 7:18

2:5 Those who have been oppressing others will find the tables turned. They will end up not having any share in the decisions to divide the land because they won't have any surviving relatives.

2:6–7 If these messages seem harsh, remember that God did not want to take revenge on Israel; he wanted to get them back on the right path. The people had rejected what was true and right, and they needed stern discipline. Children may think discipline is harsh, but it helps keep them going in the right direction. If we only want God's comforting messages, we may miss what he has for us. Listen whenever God speaks, even when the message is hard to take.

2:11 The people liked the false prophets who told them only what they wanted to hear. Micah spoke against prophets who encouraged the people to feel comfortable in their sin. Preachers are popular when they don't ask too much of us and when they tell us our greed or lust might even be good for us. But a true teacher of God speaks the truth, regardless of what the listeners want to hear.

2:12–13 Micah's prophecy telescopes two great events—Judah's return from captivity in Babylon, and the great gathering of all believers when the Messiah returns. God gave his prophets visions of various future events, but not necessarily the ability to discern when these events would happen. For example, they could not see the long period of time between the Babylonian captivity and the coming of the Messiah, but they could clearly see that the Messiah was coming. The purpose of this prophecy was not to predict exactly *how* this would occur, but *that* it would. This gave the people hope and helped them turn from sin.

2. The trial of the leaders

Rulers Denounced

3:1 Is 1:10; Mic 3:9; Ps 82:1-5; Jer 5:5

3 And I said,
"Hear now, heads of Jacob
And rulers of the house of Israel.
Is it not for you to know justice?

3:2 Ps 53:4; Ezek 22:27; Mic 2:8; 7:2, 3

2 "You who hate good and love evil,
Who tear off their skin from them
And their flesh from their bones,

3:3 Ps 14:4; 27:2; Zeph 3:3; Ezek 11:3, 6, 7

3 Who eat the flesh of my people,
Strip off their skin from them,
Break their bones
And chop *them* up as for the pot
And as meat in a kettle."

3:4 Ps 18:41; Prov 1:28; Is 1:15; Jer 11:11; Deut 31:17; Is 59:2; Is 3:11; Mic 7:13

4 Then they will cry out to the LORD,
But He will not answer them.
Instead, He will hide His face from them at that time
Because they have practiced evil deeds.

3:5 Is 3:12; 9:15, 16; Jer 14:14, 15; Jer 6:14

5 Thus says the LORD concerning the prophets who lead my people astray;
When they have *something* to bite with their teeth,
They cry, "Peace,"
But against him who puts nothing in their mouths
They declare holy war.

3:6 Is 8:20-22; 29:10-12; Is 59:10

6 Therefore *it will be* night for you—without vision,
And darkness for you—without divination.
The sun will go down on the prophets,
And the day will become dark over them.

3:7 Zech 13:4; Is 44:25; 47:12-14; Mic 7:16; 1 Sam 28:6; Mic 3:4

7 The seers will be ashamed
And the diviners will be embarrassed.
Indeed, they will all cover *their* mouths
Because there is no answer from God.

3:8 Is 61:1, 2; Jer 1:18; Is 58:1

8 On the other hand I am filled with power—
With the Spirit of the LORD—
And with justice and courage

MICAH'S CHARGES OF INJUSTICE
Micah charged the people with injustice of many kinds.

Plotting evil	2:1
Fraud, coveting, violence	2:2
Stealing, dishonesty	2:8
Driving widows from their homes	2:9
Hating good, loving evil	3:1–2
Despising justice, distorting what is right	3:9
Murder	3:10
Taking bribes	3:11

3:1ff Micah denounced the sins of the leaders, priests, and prophets ("heads" and "rulers")—those responsible for teaching the people right from wrong. The leaders, who should have known the law and taught it to the people, had set the law aside and had become the worst of sinners. They were taking advantage of the very people they were supposed to serve. All sin is bad, but the sin that leads others astray is the worst of all.

3:2–4 The leaders had no compassion or respect for those they were supposed to serve. They were treating the people miserably in order to satisfy their own desires, and then they had the gall to ask for God's help when they found themselves in trouble. We, like the leaders, should not treat God like a light switch to be turned on only as needed. Instead, we should always rely on him.

3:5–7 Micah remained true to his calling and proclaimed God's words. In contrast, the false prophets' messages were geared to the favors they received. Not all those who claim to have messages from God really do. Micah prophesied that one day the false prophets would be shamed by their actions.

3:8 Micah attributed the power of his ministry to the Spirit of the Lord. Our power comes from the same source. Jesus told his followers they would receive power to witness about him when the Holy Spirit came on them (Acts 1:8). You can't witness effectively by relying on your own strength, because fear will keep you from speaking out for God. Only by relying on the power of the Holy Spirit can you live and witness for him.

To make known to Jacob his rebellious act,
Even to Israel his sin.
9 Now hear this, heads of the house of Jacob
And rulers of the house of Israel,
Who abhor justice
And twist everything that is straight,
10 Who build Zion with bloodshed
And Jerusalem with violent injustice.
11 Her leaders pronounce judgment for a bribe,
Her priests instruct for a price
And her prophets divine for money.
Yet they lean on the LORD saying,
"Is not the LORD in our midst?
Calamity will not come upon us."
12 Therefore, on account of you
Zion will be plowed as a field,
Jerusalem will become a heap of ruins,
And the mountain of the temple *will become* high places of a forest.

3:9 Mic 1:1; Ps 58:1, 2; Is 1:23

3:10 Jer 22:13, 17; Hab 2:12

3:11 Is 1:23; Mic 7:3; Jer 6:13; Is 48:2

3:12 Jer 26:18; Ps 79:1; Jer 9:11; Mic 4:1

Peaceful Latter Days

4 And it will come about in the last days
That the mountain of the house of the LORD
Will be established as the chief of the mountains.
It will be raised above the hills,
And the peoples will stream to it.
2 Many nations will come and say,
"Come and let us go up to the mountain of the LORD
And to the house of the God of Jacob,
That He may teach us about His ways
And that we may walk in His paths."
For from Zion will go forth the law,
Even the word of the LORD from Jerusalem.
3 And He will judge between many peoples
And render decisions for mighty, distant nations.
Then they will hammer their swords into plowshares
And their spears into pruning hooks;
Nation will not lift up sword against nation,
And never again will they train for war.
4 Each of them will sit under his vine
And under his fig tree,
With no one to make *them* afraid,
For the mouth of the LORD of hosts has spoken.
5 Though all the peoples walk
Each in the name of his god,
As for us, we will walk
In the name of the LORD our God forever and ever.

4:1 Is 2:2-4; Dan 2:28; 10:14; Hos 3:5; Ezek 43:12; Mic 3:12; Zech 8:3; Ps 22:27; 86:9; Jer 3:17

4:2 Zech 2:11; 14:16; Is 2:3; Jer 31:6; Ps 25:8, 9, 12; Is 54:13; Is 42:1-4; Zech 14:8, 9

4:3 Is 2:4; 11:3-5; Joel 3:10

4:4 1 Kin 4:25; Zech 3:10; Lev 26:6; Jer 30:10; Is 1:20; 40:5

4:5 2 Kin 17:29; Zech 10:12; Josh 24:15; Is 26:8, 13

3:11 Micah warned the leaders, priests, and prophets of his day to avoid bribes. Pastors today accept bribes when they allow those who contribute much to control the church. When fear of losing money or members influences pastors to remain silent when they should speak up for what is right, their churches are in danger. We should remember that Judah was finally destroyed because of the behavior of its religious leaders. A similar warning must be directed at those who have money—*never* use your resources to influence or manipulate God's ministers—that is bribery.

3:12 Jerusalem would be destroyed just as Samaria was (1:6). This happened in 586 B.C. when Nebuchadnezzar and the Babylonian army attacked the city (2 Kings 25). Although Micah blamed the corrupt leaders, the people were not without fault. They allowed the corruption to continue without turning to God or calling for justice.

4:1ff The phrase "in the last days" describes the days when God will reign over his perfect kingdom (see 4:1–8). The "mountain of the house of the LORD" is Mount Zion. This will be an era of peace and blessing, a time when war will be forever ended. We cannot pinpoint its date, but God has promised that it *will* arrive (see also Isaiah 2:2; Jeremiah 16:15; Joel 3:1ff; Zechariah 14:9–11; Malachi 3:17, 18; Revelation 19—22).

Verses 9–13 predicted the Babylonian captivity in 586 B.C., even before Babylon became a powerful empire. Just as God promises a time of peace and prosperity, he also promises judgment and punishment for all who refuse to follow him. Both results are certain.

4:6 Zeph 3:19; Ps 147:2; Ezek 34:13, 16; 37:21

6 "In that day," declares the LORD,
"I will assemble the lame
And gather the outcasts,
Even those whom I have afflicted.

4:7 Mic 5:7, 8; 7:18; Is 24:23

7 "I will make the lame a remnant
And the outcasts a strong nation,
And the LORD will reign over them in Mount Zion
From now on and forever.

4:8 Ps 48:3, 12; 61:3; Mic 2:12; Is 1:26; Zech 9:10

8 "As for you, tower of the flock,
Hill of the daughter of Zion,
To you it will come—
Even the former dominion will come,
The kingdom of the daughter of Jerusalem.

4:9 Jer 8:19; Is 3:1-3

9 "Now, why do you cry out loudly?
Is there no king among you,
Or has your counselor perished,
That agony has gripped you like a woman in childbirth?

4:10 Mic 5:3; 2 Kin 20:18; Hos 2:14; Is 43:14; 45:13; Mic 7:8-12; Is 48:20; 52:9-12

10 "Writhe and labor to give birth,
Daughter of Zion,
Like a woman in childbirth;
For now you will go out of the city,
Dwell in the field,
And go to Babylon.
There you will be rescued;
There the LORD will redeem you
From the hand of your enemies.

4:11 Is 5:25-30; 17:12-14

11 "And now many nations have been assembled against you
Who say, 'Let her be polluted,
And let our eyes gloat over Zion.'

4:12 Ps 147:19, 20

12 "But they do not know the thoughts of the LORD,
And they do not understand His purpose;
For He has gathered them like sheaves to the threshing floor.

4:13 Is 41:15; Jer 51:20-23; Is 60:9

13 "Arise and thresh, daughter of Zion,
For your horn I will make iron
And your hoofs I will make bronze,
That you may pulverize many peoples,
That you may devote to the LORD their unjust gain
And their wealth to the Lord of all the earth.

5:1 1 Kin 22:24; Job 16:10; Lam 3:30

5:2 Gen 35:19; 48:7; Ruth 4:11; Matt 2:6; Is 11:1; Luke 2:4; John 7:42; Jer 30:21; Zech 9:9; Ps 102:25; Prov 8:22, 23

Birth of the King in Bethlehem

5 "Now muster yourselves in troops, daughter of troops;
They have laid siege against us;
With a rod they will smite the judge of Israel on the cheek.
2 "But as for you, Bethlehem Ephrathah,

4:9–13 Micah predicted the end of the kings. This was a drastic statement to the people of Judah, who thought that their kingdom would last forever. Micah also said that Babylon would destroy the land of Judah and carry away its king, but that after a while God would help his people return to their land. This all happened just as Micah prophesied, and these events are recorded in 2 Chronicles 36:9–23 and Ezra 1; 2.

4:12 When God reveals the future, his purpose goes beyond satisfying our curiosity. He wants us to change our present behavior because of what we know about the future. Forever begins now; and a glimpse of God's plan for his followers should motivate us to serve him, no matter what the rest of the world may do.

5:1 This judge was probably King Zedekiah, who was reigning in Jerusalem when Nebuchadnezzar conquered the city (2 Kings 25:1–2). Zedekiah was the last of the kings in David's line to sit on the throne in Jerusalem. Micah said that the next king in David's line would be the Messiah, who would establish a kingdom that would never end.

5:1ff Jerusalem's leaders were obsessed with wealth and position, but Micah prophesied that mighty Jerusalem, with all its wealth and power, would be besieged and destroyed. Its king could not save it. In contrast, Bethlehem, a tiny town, would be the birthplace of the only king who could save his people. This deliverer, the Messiah, would be born as a baby in Bethlehem (Luke 2:4–7), and eventually would reign as the eternal King (Revelation 19—22).

5:2 Ephrathah was the district in which Bethlehem was located.

5:2 This ruler is Jesus, the Messiah. Micah accurately predicted Christ's birthplace hundreds of years before Jesus was born. The promised eternal King in David's line, who would come to live as a man, had been alive forever—"from the days of eternity." Although eternal, Christ entered human history as the man, Jesus of Nazareth.

Too little to be among the clans of Judah,
From you One will go forth for Me to be ruler in Israel.
His goings forth are from long ago,
From the days of eternity."
3 Therefore He will give them *up* until the time
When she who is in labor has borne a child.
Then the remainder of His brethren
Will return to the sons of Israel.
4 And He will arise and shepherd *His flock*
In the strength of the LORD,
In the majesty of the name of the LORD His God.
And they will remain,
Because at that time He will be great
To the ends of the earth.
5 This One will be *our* peace.

When the Assyrian invades our land,
When he tramples on our citadels,
Then we will raise against him
Seven shepherds and eight leaders of men.
6 They will shepherd the land of Assyria with the sword,
The land of Nimrod at its entrances;
And He will deliver *us* from the Assyrian
When he attacks our land
And when he tramples our territory.

7 Then the remnant of Jacob
Will be among many peoples
Like dew from the LORD,
Like showers on vegetation
Which do not wait for man
Or delay for the sons of men.
8 The remnant of Jacob
Will be among the nations,
Among many peoples
Like a lion among the beasts of the forest,
Like a young lion among flocks of sheep,
Which, if he passes through,
Tramples down and tears,
And there is none to rescue.
9 Your hand will be lifted up against your adversaries,
And all your enemies will be cut off.

10 "It will be in that day," declares the LORD,
"That I will cut off your horses from among you
And destroy your chariots.
11 "I will also cut off the cities of your land

5:3 Hos 11:8; Mic 4:10; 7:13; Mic 4:9, 10; Is 10:20-22; Mic 5:7, 8

5:4 Is 40:11; 49:9; Ezek 34:13-15, 23, 24; Mic 7:14; Is 45:22; 52:10

5:5 Is 9:6; Luke 2:14; Eph 2:14; Col 1:20; Is 8:7, 8; 10:24-27

5:6 Nah 2:11-13; Zeph 2:13; Gen 10:8-11; Is 14:25; 37:36, 37

5:7 Mic 2:12; 4:7; 5:3; 7:18; Deut 32:2; Ps 110:3; Hos 14:5; Ps 72:6; Is 44:3

5:8 Gen 49:9; Num 24:9; Ps 44:5; Is 41:15, 16; Mic 4:13; Zech 10:5; Hos 5:14; Ps 50:22

5:9 Ps 10:12; 21:8; Is 26:11

5:10 Zech 9:10; Deut 17:16; Is 2:7; Hos 14:3

5:11 Is 1:7; 6:11; Is 2:12-17; Hos 10:14; Amos 5:9

5:5 This chapter provides one of the clearest Old Testament prophecies of Christ's coming. The key descriptive phrase is "this One will be our peace." In one of Christ's final talks he said, "Peace I leave with you; My peace I give to you; not as the world gives do I give to you. Do not let your heart be troubled, nor let it be fearful" (John 14:27). Because of Christ's first coming, we have the opportunity to experience peace with God with no more fear of judgment and no more conflict and guilt. Christ's peace gives us assurance even though wars continue. At Christ's second coming, all wars and weapons will be destroyed (4:3–5).

5:5 Micah's prophecy of seven shepherds and eight leaders is a figurative way of saying that the Messiah will raise up many good leaders when he returns to reign. This contrasts with Micah's words in chapter three about Judah's corrupt leaders. "The Assyrian" symbolically refers to all nations in every age that oppose God's people. These good leaders will help Christ defeat all evil in the world.

5:6 The land of Nimrod is another name for Assyria, which, in this case, is a symbol of all the evil nations in the world.

5:10 When God rules in his eternal kingdom, our strength and deliverance will not be found in military might but in God's almighty power. God will destroy all the weapons that people use for security. There will be no need for armies because God will rule in the heart of every person. Instead of being overwhelmed by fear of invasion or nuclear attack, we should have confidence in God.

And tear down all your fortifications.
12 "I will cut off sorceries from your hand,
And you will have fortune-tellers no more.
13 "I will cut off your carved images
And your *sacred* pillars from among you,
So that you will no longer bow down
To the work of your hands.
14 "I will root out your Asherim from among you
And destroy your cities.
15 "And I will execute vengeance in anger and wrath
On the nations which have not obeyed."

5:12 Deut 18:10-12; Is 2:6; 8:19
5:13 Is 2:18; 17:8; Ezek 6:9
5:14 Ex 34:13; Is 17:8; 27:9
5:15 Is 1:24; 65:12

3. The trial of the people

God's Indictment of His People

6 Hear now what the LORD is saying,
"Arise, plead your case before the mountains,
And let the hills hear your voice.
2 "Listen, you mountains, to the indictment of the LORD,
And you enduring foundations of the earth,
Because the LORD has a case against His people;
Even with Israel He will dispute.
3 "My people, what have I done to you,
And how have I wearied you? Answer Me.
4 "Indeed, I brought you up from the land of Egypt
And ransomed you from the house of slavery,
And I sent before you Moses, Aaron and Miriam.
5 "My people, remember now
What Balak king of Moab counseled
And what Balaam son of Beor answered him,
And from Shittim to Gilgal,
So that you might know the righteous acts of the LORD."

6:2 2 Sam 22:16; Ps 104:5; Is 1:18; Hos 4:1; 12:2
6:3 Ps 50:7; Jer 2:5; Is 43:22, 23
6:4 Ex 12:51; 20:2; Deut 7:8; Ex 4:10-16; Ps 77:20; Ex 15:20
6:5 Num 22:5, 6; Num 25:1; Josh 2:1; 3:1; Josh 4:19; 5:9, 10; 1 Sam 12:7; Is 1:27

What God Requires of Man

6 With what shall I come to the LORD
And bow myself before the God on high?
Shall I come to Him with burnt offerings,
With yearling calves?
7 Does the LORD take delight in thousands of rams,
In ten thousand rivers of oil?
Shall I present my firstborn *for* my rebellious acts,
The fruit of my body for the sin of my soul?

6:6 Ps 40:6-8; Ps 51:16, 17
6:7 Ps 50:9; Is 1:1; 40:16; Lev 18:21; 20:1-5; 2 Kin 16:3; Jer 7:31

5:12–14 Carved images, sacred pillars, and Asherim were all part of pagan worship.

6:1ff Here Micah pictures a courtroom. God, the judge, tells his people what he requires of them and recites all the ways they have wronged both him and others. Chapters 4 and 5 are full of hope; chapters 6 and 7 proclaim judgment and appeal to the people to repent.

6:1–2 God called to the mountains to confirm the people's guilt. The mountains would serve as excellent witnesses, for it was in the high places that the people had built pagan altars and had sacrificed to false gods (1 Kings 14:23; Jeremiah 17:2–3; Ezekiel 20:28).

6:3 The people would never be able to answer this question because God had done nothing wrong. In fact, God had been exceedingly patient with them, had always lovingly guided them, and had given them every opportunity to return to him. If God asked you, "What have I done to you?" how would you reply?

6:5 The story of Balak and Balaam is found in Numbers 22—24. Shittim was the Israelites' campsite east of the Jordan River just before they entered the promised land (Joshua 2:1). There the people received many of God's instructions about how to live. Gilgal, their first campsite after crossing the Jordan (Joshua 4:19), was where the people renewed their covenant with God (Joshua 5:3–9). These two places represent God's loving care for his people: his willingness both to protect them and to warn them about potential troubles. In Micah's day, the people had forgotten this covenant and its benefits and had turned away from God.

6:5 God continued to be kind to his forgetful people, but their short memory and lack of thankfulness condemned them. When people refuse to see how fortunate they are and begin to take God's gifts for granted, they become self-centered. Regularly remember God's goodness and thank him. Remembering God's past protection will help you see his present provision.

8 He has told you, O man, what is good;
And what does the LORD require of you
But to do justice, to love kindness,
And to walk humbly with your God?

6:8
Deut 30:15; Deut 10:12; Is 56:1; Jer 22:3; Hos 6:6; Is 57:15; 66:2

9 The voice of the LORD will call to the city—
And it is sound wisdom to fear Your name:
"Hear, O tribe. Who has appointed its time?
10 "Is there yet a man in the wicked house,
Along with treasures of wickedness
And a short measure *that is* cursed?
11 "Can I justify wicked scales
And a bag of deceptive weights?
12 "For the rich men of *the* city are full of violence,
Her residents speak lies,
And their tongue is deceitful in their mouth.
13 "So also I will make *you* sick, striking you down,
Desolating *you* because of your sins.
14 "You will eat, but you will not be satisfied,
And your [7]vileness will be in your midst.
You will *try to* remove *for safekeeping,*
But you will not preserve *anything,*
And what you do preserve I will give to the sword.
15 "You will sow but you will not reap.
You will tread the olive but will not anoint yourself with oil;
And the grapes, but you will not drink wine.
16 "The statutes of Omri
And all the works of the house of Ahab are observed;
And in their devices you walk.
Therefore I will give you up for destruction
And your inhabitants for derision,
And you will bear the reproach of My people."

6:10
Jer 5:26, 27; Amos 3:10; Ezek 45:9, 10; Amos 8:5

6:11
Lev 19:36; Hos 12:7

6:12
Is 1:23; 5:7; Amos 6:3, 4; Mic 2:1, 2; Jer 9:2-6, 8; Hos 7:13; Amos 2:4; Is 3:8

6:13
Mic 1:9; Is 1:7; 6:11

6:14
Is 9:20; Is 30:6

6:15
Deut 28:38-40; Jer 12:13; Amos 5:11; Zeph 1:13

6:16
1 Kin 16:25, 26; 1 Kin 16:29-33; Jer 7:24; Jer 18:16; Mic 6:13; Jer 19:8; 25:9, 18; 29:18; Ps 44:13; Jer 51:51; Hos 12:14

The Prophet Acknowledges

7 Woe is me! For I am
Like the fruit pickers, like the grape gatherers.
There is not a cluster of grapes to eat,
Or a first-ripe fig *which* I crave.
2 The godly person has perished from the land,
And there is no upright *person* among men.
All of them lie in wait for bloodshed;
Each of them hunts the other with a net.
3 Concerning evil, both hands do it well.
The prince asks, also the judge, for a bribe,
And a great man speaks the desire of his soul;
So they weave it together.

7:1
Is 24:13; Is 28:4; Hos 9:10

7:2
Is 57:1; Is 59:7; Mic 3:10; Jer 5:26; Hos 5:1

7:3
Prov 4:16, 17; Amos 5:12; Mic 3:11

7 Or possibly *garbage* or *excreta*

6:8 People have tried all kinds of ways to please God (6:6–7), but God has made his wishes clear: He wants his people to be just, love kindness, and walk humbly with him. In your efforts to please God, examine these areas on a regular basis. Are you fair in your dealings with people? Do you show kindness to those who wrong you? Are you learning humility?

6:16 Omri reigned over Israel and led the people into idol worship (1 Kings 16:21–26). Ahab, his son, was Israel's most wicked king (1 Kings 16:29–33). If the people were following the commands and practices of these kings, they were in bad shape. Such pervasive evil was ripe for punishment.

7:1ff This chapter begins in gloom (7:1–6) and ends in hope (7:8–20). Micah watched as society rotted around him. Rulers demanded gifts; judges accepted bribes; corruption was universal. But God promised to lead the people out of the darkness of sin and into his light. Then the people would praise him for his faithfulness. God alone is perfectly faithful.

7:1–4 Micah could not find an upright person anywhere in the land. Even today, uprightness (honesty, integrity) is difficult to find. Society rationalizes sin, and even Christians sometimes compromise Christian principles in order to do what they want. It is easy to convince ourselves that we deserve a few breaks, especially when "everyone else" is doing it. But the standards for honesty come from God, not society. We are honest because God is truth, and we are to be like him.

7:4 Ezek 2:6; 28:24; Nah 1:10; Is 10:3; Hos 9:7; Is 22:5

4 The best of them is like a briar,
The most upright like a thorn hedge.
The day when you post your watchmen,
Your punishment will come.
Then their confusion will occur.

7:5 Jer 9:4

5 Do not trust in a neighbor;
Do not have confidence in a friend.
From her who lies in your bosom
Guard your lips.

7:6 Matt 10:21, 35; Luke 12:53; Matt 10:36

6 For son treats father contemptuously,
Daughter rises up against her mother,
Daughter-in-law against her mother-in-law;
A man's enemies are the men of his own household.

God Is the Source of Salvation and Light

7:7 Hab 2:1; Ps 130:5; Is 25:9; Ps 4:3

7 But as for me, I will watch expectantly for the LORD;
I will wait for the God of my salvation.
My God will hear me.

7:8 Prov 24:17; Obad 12; Mic 7:10; Amos 9:11; Is 9:2

8 Do not rejoice over me, O my enemy.
Though I fall I will rise;
Though I dwell in darkness, the LORD is a light for me.

7:9 Jer 50:34; Ps 37:6; Is 42:7, 16; Is 46:13; 56:1

9 I will bear the indignation of the LORD
Because I have sinned against Him,
Until He pleads my case and executes justice for me.
He will bring me out to the light,
And I will see His righteousness.

7:10 Joel 2:17; Is 51:23; Zech 10:5

10 Then my enemy will see,
And shame will cover her who said to me,
"Where is the LORD your God?"
My eyes will look on her;
At that time she will be trampled down
Like mire of the streets.

7:11 Is 54:11; Amos 9:11

11 *It will be* a day for building your walls.
On that day will your boundary be extended.

7:12 Is 19:23-25; 60:4, 9

12 It *will be* a day when they will come to you
From Assyria and the cities of Egypt,
From Egypt even to the Euphrates,
Even from sea to sea and mountain to mountain.

7:13 Jer 25:11; Mic 6:13; Is 3:10, 11; Mic 3:4

13 And the earth will become desolate because of her inhabitants,
On account of the fruit of their deeds.

7:14 Ps 95:7; Is 40:11; 49:10; Mic 5:4; Lev 27:32; Ps 23:4; Jer 50:19; Amos 9:11

14 Shepherd Your people with Your scepter,
The flock of Your possession
Which dwells by itself in the woodland,
In the midst of a fruitful field.
Let them feed in Bashan and Gilead
As in the days of old.

7:15 Ex 3:20; 34:10; Ps 78:12

15 "As in the days when you came out from the land of Egypt,
I will show you miracles."

7:16 Is 26:11; Mic 3:7

16 Nations will see and be ashamed

7:5–6 Sin had affected the government leaders and society in general. Deceit and dishonesty had even ruined the family, the core of society. As a result, the only way left to purify the people was God's judgment. This would draw the nation back to God and restore them from the inside out.

7:7–10 Micah showed great faith in God both personally (7:7) and on Israel's behalf (7:8–10) as he proclaimed that (1) he would wait upon God, because God hears and saves when help is needed, (2) God would bring his people through when times were tough, (3) Israel must be patient in punishment because God would bring them out of the darkness, and (4) their enemies would be punished. We too can have a relationship with God that can allow us to have confidence like Micah's. It doesn't take unusual talent; it simply takes faith in God and a willingness to act on that faith.

7:14 Bashan and Gilead were fertile areas east of the Jordan, previously the territory of Reuben, Gad, and the half tribe of Manasseh.

Of all their might.
They will put *their* hand on *their* mouth,
Their ears will be deaf.
17 They will lick the dust like a serpent,
Like reptiles of the earth.
They will come trembling out of their fortresses;
To the LORD our God they will come in dread
And they will be afraid before You.
18 Who is a God like You, who pardons iniquity
And passes over the rebellious act of the remnant of His possession?
He does not retain His anger forever,
Because He delights in unchanging love.
19 He will again have compassion on us;
He will tread our iniquities under foot.
Yes, You will cast all their sins
Into the depths of the sea.
20 You will give truth to Jacob
And unchanging love to Abraham,
Which You swore to our forefathers
From the days of old.

7:17
Ps 72:9; Is 49:23; Deut 32:24; Ps 18:45; Is 25:3; 59:19

7:18
Ex 34:7, 9; Is 43:25; Mic 2:12; 4:7; 5:7, 8; Ps 103:8, 9, 13; Jer 32:41

7:19
Jer 50:20; Is 38:17; 43:25; Jer 31:34

7:20
Gen 24:27; 32:10; Deut 7:8, 12

7:18 God delights to show mercy! He does not forgive grudgingly, but is glad when we repent and offers forgiveness to all who come back to him. Today you can confess your sins and receive his loving forgiveness. Don't be too proud to accept God's free offer.

7:20 In an age when religion was making little difference in people's lives, Micah said that God expected his people to be just, kind, and humble (6:8). He requires the same of Christians today. In a world that is unjust, we must act justly. In a world of tough breaks, we must be kind and merciful. In a world of pride and self-sufficiency, we must walk humbly with God. Only when we live according to God's way will we begin to affect our homes, our society, and our world.

OLD TESTAMENT TESTS FOR FALSE PROPHETS
In the Old Testament, various signs or works pointed to a true or false prophet. Many of these can be applied today.

1. *Does the prophet use fortune-telling?*
   Divination was expressly forbidden by God (Deuteronomy 18:9-14). No true teacher or prophet would use fortune-telling or have any dealings with spirits of the dead (Jeremiah 14:14; Ezekiel 12:24; Micah 3:7).

2. *Have the prophet's short-term prophecies been fulfilled?*
   Deuteronomy 18:22 used this as a test. Do the prophet's predictions come to pass?

3. *Is the prophet marked by a desire to say only what pleases people?*
   Many false prophets told people what they wanted to hear. A true prophet serves God, not people (Jeremiah 8:11; 14:13; 23:17; Ezekiel 13:10; Micah 3:5).

4. *Does the prophet draw people away from God?*
   Many teachers draw people to themselves or to the system or organization they have built (Deuteronomy 13:1-3).

5. *Does the prophet's prophecy confirm the Bible's main teaching?*
   If a prophecy is inconsistent with or contradictory to Scripture, it is not to be believed.

6. *What is the prophet's moral character?*
   False prophets were charged with lying (Jeremiah 8:10; 14:14), drunkenness (Isaiah 28:7), and immorality (Jeremiah 23:14).

7. *Do other Spirit-led people discern authenticity in this prophet?*
   Discernment by others who are led of the Spirit is a key test (1 Kings 22:7). The New Testament speaks of this a great deal (John 10:4-15; 1 Corinthians 2:14; 14:29, 32; 1 John 4:1).

NAHUM

Manasseh becomes king of Judah 697 B.C.

Ashurbanipal becomes king of Assyria 669

The fall of Thebes; Nahum becomes a prophet 663

VITAL STATISTICS

PURPOSE:
To pronounce God's judgment on Assyria and to comfort Judah with this truth

AUTHOR:
Nahum

TO WHOM WRITTEN:
The people of Nineveh and Judah

DATE WRITTEN:
Sometime during Nahum's prophetic ministry (probably between 663 and 612 B.C.)

SETTING:
This particular prophecy took place after the fall of Thebes in 663 B.C. (see 3:8–10).

KEY VERSES:
"The LORD is good, a stronghold in the day of trouble, and He knows those who take refuge in Him. But with an overflowing flood He will make a complete end of its site, and will pursue His enemies into darkness. Whatever you devise against the LORD, He will make a complete end of it. Distress will not rise up twice" (1:7–9).

KEY PLACE:
Nineveh

THE SHRILL whistle pierces the air, and all the action on the court abruptly stops. Pointing to the offending player, the referee shouts, "Foul!"

Rules, fouls, and penalties are part of any game and are regulated and enforced vigorously by referees, umpires, judges, and other officials. Every participant knows that boundaries must be set and behavior monitored, or the game will degenerate into chaos.

There are laws in the world as well—boundaries and rules for living established by God. But men and women regularly flaunt these regulations, hiding their infractions or overpowering others and declaring that might makes right. God calls this sin—willful disobedience, rebellion against his control, or apathy. And at times it seems as though the violators succeed—no whistles blow, no fouls are called, and individual dictators rule. The truth is, however, that ultimately justice will be served in the world. God will settle all accounts.

Assyria was the most powerful nation on earth. Proud in their self-sufficiency and military might, they plundered, oppressed, and slaughtered their victims. One hundred years earlier, Jonah had preached in the streets of the great city Nineveh; the people had heard God's message and had turned from their evil. But generations later, evil was again reigning, and the prophet Nahum pronounced judgment on this wicked nation. Nineveh is called "the bloody city" (3:1), an evil city (3:19), and the Assyrians are judged for their arrogance (1:11), idolatry (1:14), murder, lies, treachery, and social injustice (3:1–19). Nahum predicted that this proud and powerful nation would be utterly destroyed because of its sins. The end came within 50 years.

In this judgment of Assyria and its capital city, Nineveh, God is judging a sinful world. And the message is clear: Disobedience, rebellion, and injustice will not prevail but will be punished severely by a righteous and holy God, who rules over all the earth.

As you read Nahum, sense God's wrath as he avenges sin and brings about justice. Then decide to live under his guidance and within his rules, commands, and guidelines for life.

THE BLUEPRINT

1. Nineveh's judge (1:1–15)
2. Nineveh's judgment (2:1—3:19)

Nineveh, the capital of the Assyrian empire, is the subject of Nahum's prophecy. The news of its coming destruction was a relief for Judah, who was subject to Assyrian domination. No longer would Judah be forced to pay tribute as insurance against invasions. Judah was comforted to know that God was still in control. Nineveh is an example to all rulers and nations of the world today. God is sovereign over even those who are seemingly invincible. We can be confident that God's power and justice will one day conquer all evil.

Josiah becomes king of Judah; Zephaniah becomes a prophet 640	Jeremiah becomes a prophet 627	Nineveh falls 612	Assyria completely conquered 609	Babylonians win battle of Carchemish 605	Judah falls to Babylon 586

MEGATHEMES

THEME	EXPLANATION	IMPORTANCE
God Judges	God would judge the city of Nineveh for its idolatry, arrogance, and oppression. Although Assyria was the leading military power in the world, God would completely destroy this "invincible" nation. God allows no person or power to usurp or scoff at his authority.	Anyone who remains arrogant and resists God's authority will face his anger. No ruler or nation will get away with rejecting him. No individual will be able to hide from his judgment. Yet those who keep trusting God will be kept safe forever.
God Rules	God rules over all the earth, even over those who don't acknowledge him. God is all-powerful, and no one can thwart his plans. God will overcome any who attempt to defy him. Human power is futile against God.	If you are impressed by or afraid of any weapons, armies, or powerful people, remember that God alone can truly rescue you from fear or oppression. We must place our confidence in God because he alone rules all of history, all the earth, and our life.

1:1
Is 13:1; 19:1; Jer 23:33, 34; Hab 1:1; Zech 9:1; Mal 1:1; 2 Kin 19:36; Jon 1:2; Nah 2:8; Zeph 2:13

1:2
Ex 20:5; Josh 24:19; Deut 32:35, 41; Ps 94:1

1. Nineveh's judge

God Is Awesome

1 The [1]oracle of Nineveh. The book of the vision of Nahum the Elkoshite.
2 A jealous and avenging God is the LORD;
The LORD is avenging and wrathful.
The LORD takes vengeance on His adversaries,
And He reserves wrath for His enemies.

1 Or *burden*

NAHUM
Nahum served as a prophet to Judah and Assyria from 663–612 B.C.

Climate of the times	Manasseh, one of Judah's most wicked kings, ruled the land. He openly defied God and persecuted God's people. Assyria, the world power at that time, made Judah one of its vassal states. The people of Judah wanted to be like the Assyrians, who seemed to have all the power and possessions they wanted.
Main message	The mighty empire of Assyria that oppressed God's people would soon tumble.
Importance of message	Those who do evil and oppress others will one day meet a bitter end.
Contemporary prophet	Zephaniah (640–621 B.C.)

1:1 Nahum, like Jonah, was a prophet to Nineveh, the capital of the Assyrian empire, and he prophesied between 663 and 612 B.C. Jonah had seen Nineveh repent a century earlier (see the book of Jonah), but the city had fallen back into wickedness. Assyria, the world power controlling the Fertile Crescent, seemed unstoppable. Its ruthless and savage warriors had already conquered Israel, the northern kingdom, and were causing great suffering in Judah. So Nahum proclaimed God's anger against Assyria's evil. Within a few decades, the mighty Assyrian empire would be toppled by Babylon.

1:1 An oracle is a message from God. Elkosh was a village thought by some to be in southwest Judah.

1:2 God alone has the right to be jealous and to carry out vengeance. Jealousy and vengeance may be surprising terms to associate with God. When humans are jealous and take vengeance, they are usually acting in a spirit of selfishness. But it is appropriate for God to insist on our complete allegiance, and it is just for him to punish unrepentant evildoers. His jealousy and vengeance are unmixed with selfishness. Their purpose is to remove sin and restore peace to the world (Deuteronomy 4:24; 5:9).

3 The LORD is slow to anger and great in power,
And the LORD will by no means leave *the guilty* unpunished.
In whirlwind and storm is His way,
And clouds are the dust beneath His feet.
4 He rebukes the sea and makes it dry;
He dries up all the rivers.
Bashan and Carmel wither;
The blossoms of Lebanon wither.
5 Mountains quake because of Him
And the hills dissolve;
Indeed the earth is upheaved by His presence,
The world and all the inhabitants in it.
6 Who can stand before His indignation?
Who can endure the burning of His anger?
His wrath is poured out like fire
And the rocks are broken up by Him.
7 The LORD is good,
A stronghold in the day of trouble,
And He knows those who take refuge in Him.
8 But with an overflowing flood
He will make a complete end of its site,
And will pursue His enemies into darkness.

9 Whatever you devise against the LORD,
He will make a complete end of it.
Distress will not rise up twice.
10 Like tangled thorns,
And like those who are drunken with their drink,
They are consumed
As stubble completely withered.
11 From you has gone forth
One who plotted evil against the LORD,
A wicked counselor.
12 Thus says the LORD,
"Though they are at full *strength* and likewise many,
Even so, they will be cut off and pass away.
Though I have afflicted you,
I will afflict you no longer.
13 "So now, I will break his yoke bar from upon you,
And I will tear off your shackles."

1:3
Ex 34:6, 7; Neh 9:17; Ps 103:8; Ex 19:16; Is 29:6; Ps 104:3; Is 19:1

1:4
Josh 3:15, 16; Ps 106:9; Is 50:2; Matt 8:26; Is 33:9

1:5
Ex 19:18; 2 Sam 22:8; Ps 18:7; Mic 1:4; Is 24:1, 20; Ps 98:7

1:6
Jer 10:10; Mal 3:2; Is 13:13; Is 66:15; 1 Kin 19:11

1:7
Ps 25:8; 37:39, 40; Jer 33:11; Ps 1:6; John 10:14; 2 Tim 2:19

1:8
Is 28:2, 17f; Amos 8:8; Is 13:9, 10

1:9
Ps 2:1; Nah 1:11; Is 28:22

1:10
2 Sam 23:6; Mic 7:4; Is 56:12; Nah 3:11; Is 5:24; 10:17; Mal 4:1

1:11
Is 10:7-11; Nah 1:9; Ezek 11:2

1:12
Is 10:16-19, 33, 34; Lam 3:31, 32

1:13
Is 9:4; 10:27; Jer 2:20

1:3 God is slow to get angry, but when he is ready to punish, even the earth trembles. Often people avoid God because they see evildoers in the world and hypocrites in the church. They don't realize that because God is slow to anger, he gives his true followers time to share his love and truth with evildoers. But judgment *will* come; God will not allow sin to go unchecked forever. When people wonder why God doesn't punish evil immediately, help them remember that if he did, none of us would be here. We can all be thankful that God gives people time to turn to him.

1:4 Bashan and Carmel were very fertile areas.

1:6 No person on earth can safely defy God, the Almighty, the Creator of all the universe. God, who controls the sun, the galaxies, and the vast stretches beyond, also controls the rise and fall of nations. How could a small temporal kingdom like Assyria, no matter how powerful, challenge God's awesome power? If only Assyria could have looked ahead to see the desolate mound of rubble that it would become—and yet God would still be alive and well! Don't defy God; he will be here forever with greater power than that of all armies and nations combined.

1:6–8 To people who refuse to believe, God's punishment is like an angry fire. To those who love him, his mercy is a refuge, supplying all their needs without diminishing his supply. But to God's enemies he is an overwhelming flood that will sweep them away. The relationship we have with God is up to us. What kind of relationship will you choose?

1:11 The one "who plotted evil against the LORD, a wicked counselor" could have been (1) Ashurbanipal (669–627 B.C.), king of Assyria during much of Nahum's life and the one who brought Assyria to the zenith of its power; (2) Sennacherib (705–681), who openly defied God (2 Kings 18:13–35), epitomizing rebellion against God; (3) no one king in particular, but the entire evil monarchy. The point is that Nineveh would be destroyed for rebelling against God.

1:12–15 The good news for Judah, whom Assyria afflicted, was that its conquerors and tormentors would be destroyed and would never rise to torment it again. Nineveh was so completely wiped out that its ruins were not identified until 1845.

1:14 Job 18:17; Ps 109:13; Is 14:22; Is 46:1, 2; Mic 5:13, 14; Ezek 32:22, 23

14 The LORD has issued a command concerning you:
"Your name will no longer be perpetuated.
I will cut off idol and image
From the house of your gods.
I will prepare your grave,
For you are contemptible."

1:15 Is 40:9; 52:7; Rom 10:15; Lev 23:2, 4; Is 52:1; Joel 3:17; Is 29:7, 8

15 Behold, on the mountains the feet of him who brings good news,
Who announces peace!
Celebrate your feasts, O Judah;
Pay your vows.
For never again will the wicked one pass through you;
He is cut off completely.

2. Nineveh's judgment

The Overthrow of Nineveh

2:1 Jer 51:20-23

2 The one who scatters has come up against you.
Man the fortress, watch the road;
Strengthen your back, summon all *your* strength.

2:2 Is 60:15; Ezek 37:21-23; Ps 80:12, 13

2 For the LORD will restore the splendor of Jacob
Like the splendor of Israel,
Even though devastators have devastated them
And destroyed their vine branches.

2:3 Ezek 23:14, 15; Job 39:23

3 The shields of his mighty men are *colored* red,
The warriors are dressed in scarlet,
The chariots are *enveloped* in flashing steel
When he is prepared *to march,*
And the cypress *spears* are brandished.

2:4 Is 66:15; Jer 4:13; Ezek 26:10; Nah 3:2, 3

4 The chariots race madly in the streets,
They rush wildly in the squares,
Their appearance is like torches,
They dash to and fro like lightning flashes.

2:5 Nah 3:18; Jer 46:12

5 He remembers his nobles;
They stumble in their march,
They hurry to her wall,
And the mantelet is set up.
6 The gates of the rivers are opened
And the palace is dissolved.

2:7 Is 38:14; 59:11; Is 32:12

7 It is fixed:
She is stripped, she is carried away,
And her handmaids are moaning like the sound of doves,
Beating on their breasts.

2:8 Jer 46:5; 47:3

8 Though Nineveh *was* like a pool of water throughout her days,
Now they are fleeing;
"Stop, stop,"
But no one turns back.

2:9 Rev 18:12, 16

9 Plunder the silver!
Plunder the gold!
For there is no limit to the treasure—
Wealth from every kind of desirable object.

2:1ff This chapter predicts the events of 612 B.C., when the combined armies of the Babylonians and the Medes sacked the seemingly impregnable Nineveh.

2:2 Assyria had plundered and crushed the northern kingdom (Israel) and had deported its people in 722 B.C. (2 Kings 17:3–6; 18:9–11). Assyria had also attacked the southern kingdom (here called Jacob) and had forced it to pay tribute.

2:6 This reference to the opening of river gates could refer either to the enemy flowing into Nineveh like a flood (1:8) or to an actual flood of water. Some scholars suggest that dam gates, which were found in archaeological excavations, were closed to dam up the river. When an enormous amount of water had been accumulated, the gates were opened, allowing the water to flood Nineveh.

10 She is emptied! Yes, she is desolate and waste!
Hearts are melting and knees knocking!
Also anguish is in the whole body
And all their faces are grown pale!
11 Where is the den of the lions
And the feeding place of the young lions,
Where the lion, lioness and lion's cub prowled,
With nothing to disturb *them?*
12 The lion tore enough for his cubs,
Killed *enough* for his lionesses,
And filled his lairs with prey
And his dens with torn flesh.
13 "Behold, I am against you," declares the LORD of hosts. "I will burn up her chariots
in smoke, a sword will devour your young lions; I will cut off your prey from the land,
and no longer will the voice of your messengers be heard."

2:10 Is 24:1; 34:10-13; Nah 2:2; Ps 22:14; Is 13:7, 8; Ezek 21:7; Joel 2:6

2:11 Is 5:29

2:13 Jer 21:13; Ezek 5:8; Nah 3:5; Josh 11:6, 9; Ps 46:9; Is 49:24, 25; Nah 3:1

Nineveh's Complete Ruin

3 Woe to the bloody city, completely full of lies *and* pillage;
Her prey never departs.
2 The noise of the whip,
The noise of the rattling of the wheel,
Galloping horses
And bounding chariots!
3 Horsemen charging,
Swords flashing, spears gleaming,
Many slain, a mass of corpses,
And countless dead bodies—
They stumble over the dead bodies!
4 *All* because of the many harlotries of the harlot,
The charming one, the mistress of sorceries,
Who sells nations by her harlotries
And families by her sorceries.
5 "Behold, I am against you," declares the LORD of hosts;
"And I will lift up your skirts over your face,
And show to the nations your nakedness
And to the kingdoms your disgrace.
6 "I will throw filth on you
And make you vile,
And set you up as a spectacle.
7 "And it will come about that all who see you
Will shrink from you and say,
'Nineveh is devastated!
Who will grieve for her?'
Where will I seek comforters for you?"

3:1 Ezek 24:6, 9

3:2 Job 39:22-25; Jer 47:3; Nah 2:3, 4

3:3 Hab 3:11; Is 34:3; 66:16; Is 37:36; Ezek 39:4

3:4 Is 23:17; Ezek 16:25-29; Rev 17:1, 2; Is 47:9, 12, 13; Rev 18:3

3:5 Jer 50:31; Ezek 26:3; Nah 2:13; Is 47:2, 3; Jer 13:26; Ezek 16:37

3:6 Job 9:31; Job 30:8; Mal 2:9; Is 14:16; Jer 51:37

3:7 Is 51:19; Jer 15:5

2:12—3:1 The major source of wealth for the Assyrian economy was the plunder taken from other nations. The Assyrians had taken the food of innocent people to maintain their luxurious standard of living, depriving others to supply their excesses. Depriving innocent people to support the luxury of a few is a sin that angers God. As Christians we must stand firm against this common but evil practice.

2:13 God had given the people of Nineveh a chance to repent, which they did after hearing Jonah (see the book of Jonah). But they had returned to their sin, and its consequences were destroying them. There is a point for people, cities, and nations after which there is no turning back; Assyria had passed that point. We must warn others to repent while there is still time.

3:4 Nineveh had used its beauty, prestige, and power to seduce other nations. Like a harlot, she had enticed them into false friendships. Then when the other nations relaxed, thinking Assyria was a friend, Assyria destroyed and plundered them. Beautiful and impressive on the outside, Nineveh was vicious and deceitful on the inside. Beneath beautiful facades sometimes lie seduction and death. Don't let an attractive institution, company, movement, or person seduce you into lowering your standards or compromising your moral principles.

3:8
Jer 46:25; Ezek 30:14-16; Is 19:6-8

3:9
Is 20:5; Jer 46:9; Ezek 27:10; 30:5; 38:5; 2 Chr 12:3; 16:8

3:10
Is 19:4; 20:4; Ps 137:9; Is 13:16; Hos 13:16; Lam 2:19; Joel 3:3; Obad 11

3:11
Is 49:26; Jer 25:27; Nah 1:10; Is 2:10, 19; Hos 10:8

3:12
Rev 6:13; Is 28:4

3:13
Is 19:16; Jer 50:37; 51:30; Is 45:1, 2; Nah 2:6

3:14
2 Chr 32:3, 4; Nah 2:1

3:15
Is 66:15, 16; Nah 2:13; 3:13; Joel 1:4

3:16
Is 23:8

3:17
Rev 9:7; Jer 51:27

3:18
Ps 76:5, 6; Is 56:10; Jer 51:57; Jer 50:18; Nah 2:5; 1 Kin 22:17; Is 13:14

3:19
Jer 46:11; Mic 1:9; Jer 30:12; Job 27:23; Lam 2:15

8 Are you better than [2]No-amon,
Which was situated by the waters of the Nile,
With water surrounding her,
Whose rampart *was* the sea,
Whose wall *consisted* of the sea?
9 Ethiopia was *her* might,
And Egypt too, without limits.
Put and Lubim were among her helpers.
10 Yet she became an exile,
She went into captivity;
Also her small children were dashed to pieces
At the head of every street;
They cast lots for her honorable men,
And all her great men were bound with fetters.
11 You too will become drunk,
You will be hidden.
You too will search for a refuge from the enemy.
12 All your fortifications are fig trees with ripe fruit—
When shaken, they fall into the eater's mouth.
13 Behold, your people are women in your midst!
The gates of your land are opened wide to your enemies;
Fire consumes your gate bars.
14 Draw for yourself water for the siege!
Strengthen your fortifications!
Go into the clay and tread the mortar!
Take hold of the brick mold!
15 There fire will consume you,
The sword will cut you down;
It will consume you as the locust *does.*

Multiply yourself like the creeping locust,
Multiply yourself like the swarming locust.
16 You have increased your traders more than the stars of heaven—
The creeping locust strips and flies away.
17 Your guardsmen are like the swarming locust.
Your marshals are like hordes of grasshoppers
Settling in the stone walls on a cold day.
The sun rises and they flee,
And the place where they are is not known.
18 Your shepherds are sleeping, O king of Assyria;
Your nobles are lying down.
Your people are scattered on the mountains
And there is no one to regather *them.*
19 There is no relief for your breakdown,
Your wound is incurable.
All who hear about you
Will clap *their* hands over you,
For on whom has not your evil passed continually?

2 I.e. the city of Amon: Thebes

3:8–10 No-amon is Thebes, a city in Egypt, the previous world power, which stood in the path of Assyria's expansion in the south. The Assyrians conquered Thebes 51 years before this prophecy was given. To Judah, surrounded to the north and south by Assyria, the situation appeared hopeless. But God said that the same atrocities done in Thebes would happen in Nineveh.

3:8–10 No power on earth can protect us from God's judgment or be a suitable substitute for his power in our lives. Thebes and Assyria put their trust in alliances and military power, but history would show that these were inadequate. Don't insist on learning through personal experience; instead, learn the lessons history has already taught. Put your trust in God above all else.

3:19 All the nations hated to be ruled by the merciless Assyrians, but the nations wanted to be like Assyria—powerful, wealthy, prestigious—and they courted Assyria's friendship. In the same way, we don't like the idea of being ruled harshly, so we do what we can to stay on good terms with a powerful leader. And deep down, we would like to have that kind of power. The thought of being on top can be captivating. But power is seductive, so we should not scheme to get it or hold on to it. Those who lust after power will be powerfully destroyed, as was the mighty Assyrian empire.

HABAKKUK

Jeremiah becomes a prophet 627 B.C.	Habakkuk becomes a prophet 612	King Josiah dies in battle 609	Daniel taken captive to Babylon 605

VITAL STATISTICS

PURPOSE:
To show that God is still in control of the world despite the apparent triumph of evil

AUTHOR:
Habakkuk

TO WHOM WRITTEN:
Judah (the southern kingdom), and God's people everywhere

DATE WRITTEN:
Between 612 and 588 B.C.

SETTING:
Babylon was becoming the dominant world power, and Judah would soon feel Babylon's destructive force.

KEY VERSE:
"I have heard the report about You and I fear. O LORD, revive Your work in the midst of the years, in the midst of the years make it known; in wrath remember mercy" (3:2).

KEY PEOPLE:
Habakkuk, the Babylonians

KEY PLACE:
Judah

FROM innocent childhood queries to complex university discussions, life is filled with questions. Asking how and why and when, we probe beneath the surface to find satisfying answers. But not all questions have answers wrapped and neatly tied. These unanswered interrogations create more questions and nagging, spirit-destroying doubt. Some choose to live with their doubts, ignoring them and moving on with life. Others become cynical and hardened. But there are those who reject those options and continue to ask, looking for answers.

Habakkuk was a man who sought answers. Troubled by what he observed, he asked difficult questions. These questions were not merely intellectual exercises or bitter complaints. Habakkuk saw a dying world, and it broke his heart. Why is there evil in the world? Why do the wicked seem to be winning? He boldly and confidently took his complaints directly to God. And God answered with an avalanche of proof and prediction.

The prophet's questions and God's answers are recorded in this book. As we turn the pages, we are immediately confronted with his urgent cries, "How long, O LORD, will I call for help, and You will not hear? I cry out to You, 'Violence!' Yet You do not save" (1:2). In fact, most of the first chapter is devoted to his questions. As chapter two begins, Habakkuk declares that he will wait to hear God's answers to his complaints. Then God begins to speak, telling the prophet to write his answer plainly so that all will see and understand. It may seem, God says, as though the wicked triumph, but eventually they will be judged, and righteousness will prevail. Judgment may not come quickly, but it *will* come. God's answers fill chapter two. Then Habakkuk concludes his book with a prayer of triumph. With questions answered and a new understanding of God's power and love, Habakkuk rejoices in who God is and in what he will do. "Yet I will exult in the LORD, I will rejoice in the God of my salvation. The Lord GOD is my strength, and He has made my feet like hinds' feet, and makes me walk on my high places" (3:18–19).

Listen to the profound questions that Habakkuk boldly brings to God, and realize that you can also bring your complaints and inquiries to him. Listen to God's answers and rejoice that he is at work in the world and in your life.

THE BLUEPRINT

1. Habakkuk's complaints (1:1—2:20)
2. Habakkuk's prayer (3:1–19)

When Habakkuk was troubled, he brought his concerns directly to God. After receiving God's answers, he responded with a prayer of faith. Habakkuk's example is one that should encourage us as we struggle to move from doubt to faith. We don't have to be afraid to ask questions of God. The problem is not with God and his ways but with our limited understanding of him.

Ezekiel a captive in Babylon; Zedekiah becomes king 597	*Habakkuk's ministry ends 588*	*Fall of Judah; Jerusalem destroyed 586*

MEGATHEMES

THEME	EXPLANATION	IMPORTANCE
Struggle and Doubt	Habakkuk asked God why the wicked in Judah were not being punished for their sin. He couldn't understand why a just God would allow such evil to exist. God promised to use the Babylonians to punish Judah. When Habakkuk cried out for answers in his time of struggle, God answered him with words of hope.	God wants us to come to him with our struggles and doubts. But his answers may not be what we expect. God sustains us by revealing himself to us. Trusting him leads to quiet hope, not bitter resignation.
God's Sovereignty	Habakkuk asked God why he would use the wicked Babylonians to punish his people. God said that he would also punish the Babylonians after they had fulfilled his purpose.	God is still in control of this world in spite of the apparent triumph of evil. God doesn't overlook sin. One day he will rule the whole earth with perfect justice.
Hope	God is the Creator; he is all-powerful. He has a plan, and he will carry it out. He will punish sin. He is our strength and our place of safety. We can have confidence that he will love us and guard our relationship with him forever.	Hope means going beyond our unpleasant daily experiences to the joy of knowing God. We live by trusting in him, not by the benefits, happiness, or success we may experience in this life. Our hope comes from God.

1. Habakkuk's complaints

Chaldeans Used to Punish Judah

1:1 Is 13:1; Nah 1:1

1:2 Ps 13:1, 2; 22:1, 2; Jer 14:9

1 The [1]oracle which Habakkuk the prophet saw.
2 How long, O LORD, will I call for help,
And You will not hear?

1 Or *burden*

HABAKKUK
Habakkuk served as a prophet to Judah from 612–588 B.C.

Climate of the times	Judah's last four kings were wicked men who rejected God and oppressed their own people. Babylon invaded Judah twice before finally destroying it in 586. It was a time of fear, oppression, persecution, lawlessness, and immorality.
Main message	Habakkuk couldn't understand why God seemed to do nothing about the wickedness in society. Then he realized that faith in God alone would supply the answers to his questions.
Importance of message	Instead of questioning the ways of God, we should realize that he is totally just, and we should have faith that he is in control and that one day evil will be utterly destroyed.
Contemporary prophets	Jeremiah (627–586 B.C.) Daniel (605–536 B.C.) Ezekiel (593–571 B.C.)

1:1 Habakkuk lived in Judah during the reign of Jehoiakim (2 Kings 23:36—24:5). He prophesied between the fall of Nineveh (the capital of Assyria) in 612 B.C. and the Babylonian invasion of Judah in 588 B.C. With Assyria in disarray, Babylon was becoming the dominant world power. This book records the prophet's dialogue with God concerning the questions, "Why does God often seem indifferent in the face of evil? Why do evil people seem to go unpunished?" While other prophetic books brought God's Word to people, this brought people's questions to God. An "oracle" is a message from God.

1:2–4 Saddened by the violence and corruption he saw around him, Habakkuk poured out his heart to God. Today injustice is still rampant, but don't let your concern cause you to doubt God or rebel against him. Instead, consider the message that God gave Habakkuk and recognize God's long-range plans and purposes. Realize that God is doing right, even when you do not understand why he works as he does.

I cry out to You, "Violence!"
Yet You do not save.
3 Why do You make me see iniquity,
And cause *me* to look on wickedness?
Yes, destruction and violence are before me;
Strife exists and contention arises.
4 Therefore the law is ignored
And justice is never upheld.
For the wicked surround the righteous;
Therefore justice comes out perverted.

5 "Look among the nations! Observe!
Be astonished! Wonder!
Because *I am* doing something in your days—
You would not believe if you were told.
6 "For behold, I am raising up the Chaldeans,
That fierce and impetuous people
Who march throughout the earth
To seize dwelling places which are not theirs.
7 "They are dreaded and feared;
Their justice and authority originate with themselves.
8 "Their horses are swifter than leopards
And keener than wolves in the evening.
Their horsemen come galloping,
Their horsemen come from afar;
They fly like an eagle swooping *down* to devour.
9 "All of them come for violence.
Their horde of faces *moves* forward.
They collect captives like sand.
10 "They mock at kings
And rulers are a laughing matter to them.
They laugh at every fortress
And heap up rubble to capture it.
11 "Then they will sweep through *like* the wind and pass on.
But they will be held guilty,
They whose strength is their god."

12 Are You not from everlasting,
O LORD, my God, my Holy One?
We will not die.
You, O LORD, have appointed them to judge;
And You, O Rock, have established them to correct.

1:3 Ps 55:9-11; Jer 20:18; Jer 20:8; Jer 15:10

1:4 Ps 58:1, 2; 119:126; Is 59:12-14; Ps 22:12; Is 1:21-23; Is 5:20; Ezek 9:9

1:5 Acts 13:41; Is 29:9; Is 29:14; Ezek 12:22-28

1:6 2 Kin 24:2; Jer 4:11-13; Jer 8:10

1:7 Is 18:2, 7; Jer 39:5-9

1:8 Jer 4:13; Zeph 3:3; Ezek 17:3; Hos 8:1

1:9 2 Kin 12:17; Dan 11:17

1:10 2 Chr 36:6, 10; Is 37:13; Is 10:9; 14:16; Jer 32:24; Ezek 26:8

1:11 Jer 4:11, 12; Jer 2:3; Dan 4:30; Hab 1:16

1:12 Deut 33:27; Ps 90:2; Mal 3:6; Is 10:5, 6; Mal 3:5; Deut 32:4

1:5 God responded to Habakkuk's questions and concerns by stating that he would do amazing acts that would astound Habakkuk. When circumstances around us become almost unbearable, we wonder if God has forgotten us. But remember, he is in control. God has a plan and will judge evildoers in his time. If we are truly humble, we will be willing to accept God's answers and await his timing.

1:5ff God told the inhabitants of Jerusalem that they would be utterly amazed at what he was about to do. The people would, in fact, see a series of unbelievable events: (1) Their own independent and prosperous kingdom, Judah, would suddenly become a vassal nation; (2) Egypt, a world power for centuries, would be crushed almost overnight; (3) Nineveh, the capital of the Assyrian empire, would be so completely ransacked that people would forget where it had been; and (4) the Babylonians would rise to power. Though these words were indeed amazing, the people saw them fulfilled during their lifetime.

1:6 The Babylonians, who lived northwest of the Persian Gulf, made a rapid rise to power around 630 B.C. They began to assert themselves against the Assyrian empire, and by 605 B.C. had conquered Assyria and Egypt to become the strongest world power. But they were as wicked as the Assyrians, for they loved to collect prisoners (1:9), were proud of their warfare tactics (1:10), and trusted in their military strength (1:11).

1:10 Armies were able to take fortress (walled) cities by building earthen ramps—heaping mounds of earth against the walls.

1:11 Babylon was proud of its military might, strategies, armies, and weapons. With no regard for humanity, the armies brought home riches, plunder, prisoners, and tribute from the nations they conquered. Such is the essence of idolatry—asking the gods we make to help us get all we want. The essence of Christianity is asking the God *who made us* to help us give all we can in service to him. The goal of idolatry is self-glory; the aim of Christianity is God's glory.

1:13 Ps 11:4-6; 34:15, 16; Jer 12:1, 2; Is 24:16; Ps 50:21; Ps 35:25

13 *Your* eyes are too pure to approve evil,
And You can not look on wickedness *with favor.*
Why do You look with favor
On those who deal treacherously?
Why are You silent when the wicked swallow up
Those more righteous than they?
14 *Why* have You made men like the fish of the sea,
Like creeping things without a ruler over them?

1:15 Jer 16:16; Amos 4:2; Ps 10:9

15 *The Chaldeans* bring all of them up with a hook,
Drag them away with their net,
And gather them together in their fishing net.
Therefore they rejoice and are glad.

1:16 Jer 44:17

16 Therefore they offer a sacrifice to their net
And burn incense to their fishing net;
Because through these things their catch is large,
And their food is plentiful.

1:17 Is 19:8; Is 14:5, 6

17 Will they therefore empty their net
And continually slay nations without sparing?

God Answers the Prophet

2:1 Is 21:8; Ps 5:3; Ps 85:8

2 I will stand on my guard post
And station myself on the rampart;
And I will keep watch to see what He will speak to me,
And how I may reply when I am reproved.

2:2 Deut 27:8; Rom 15:4; Rev 1:19

2 Then the LORD answered me and said,
"Record the vision
And inscribe *it* on tablets,
That the one who reads it may run.

2:3 Dan 8:17, 19; 10:14; Ps 27:14; Ezek 12:25; Heb 10:37

3 "For the vision is yet for the appointed time;
It hastens toward the goal and it will not fail.
Though it tarries, wait for it;
For it will certainly come, it will not delay.

2:4 Ps 49:18; Is 13:11; Rom 1:17; Gal 3:11; Heb 10:38

4 "Behold, as for the proud one,
His soul is not right within him;
But the righteous will live by his faith.

2:5 Prov 20:1; Prov 21:24; 2 Kin 14:10; Prov 27:20; 30:16; Is 5:11-15

5 "Furthermore, wine betrays the haughty man,
So that he does not stay at home.
He enlarges his appetite like Sheol,
And he is like death, never satisfied.

1:13 Judah's forthcoming punishment would be at the hands of the Babylonians. Habakkuk was appalled that God would use a nation more wicked than Judah to punish Judah. But the Babylonians did not know they were being used by God to help Judah return to him, and Babylon's pride in its victories would be its downfall. Evil is self-destructive, and it is never beyond God's control. God may use whatever unusual instrument he chooses to correct or punish us. When we deserve punishment or correction, how can we complain about the kind of "rod" God uses on us?

2:1 The watchman and guard post, often used by the prophets to show an attitude of expectation (Isaiah 21:8, 11; Jeremiah 6:17; Ezekiel 3:17), are pictures of Habakkuk's attitude of patient waiting and watching for God's response. Stone guard posts were built on city walls or ramparts so that watchmen could see people (enemies or messengers) approaching their city while still at a distance. Watchtowers were also erected in vineyards to help guard the ripening grapes (Isaiah 5:2). Habakkuk wanted to be in the best position to receive God's message.

2:2ff This chapter records God's answers to Habakkuk's questions: (1) How long would evil prevail (1:2–3)? (2) Why was Babylon chosen to punish Judah (1:13)? God said that the judgment, though slow to come, was certain. Although God used Babylon against Judah, he knew Babylon's sins and would punish it in due time.

2:3 Evil and injustice seem to have the upper hand in the world. Like Habakkuk, Christians often feel angry and discouraged as they see what goes on. Habakkuk complained vigorously to God about the situation. God's answer to Habakkuk is the same answer he would give us, "Be patient! I will work out my plans in my perfect timing." It isn't easy to be patient, but it helps to remember that God hates sin even more than we do. Punishment of sin will certainly come. As God told Habakkuk, "Wait for it." To trust God fully means to trust him even when we don't understand why events occur as they do.

2:4 The wicked Babylonians trusted in themselves and would fall; but the righteous live by their faith and trust in God. This verse has inspired countless Christians. Paul quotes it in Romans 1:17 and Galatians 3:11. The writer of Hebrews quotes it in 10:38, just before the famous chapter on faith. And it is helpful to all Christians who must live through difficult times without seeing signs of hope. Christians must trust that God is directing all things according to his purposes.

He also gathers to himself all nations
And collects to himself all peoples.

6 "Will not all of these take up a taunt-song against him,
Even mockery *and* insinuations against him
And say, 'Woe to him who increases what is not his—
For how long—
And makes himself rich with loans?'
7 "Will not your creditors rise up suddenly,
And those who collect from you awaken?
Indeed, you will become plunder for them.
8 "Because you have looted many nations,
All the remainder of the peoples will loot you—
Because of human bloodshed and violence done to the land,
To the town and all its inhabitants.

9 "Woe to him who gets evil gain for his house
To put his nest on high,
To be delivered from the hand of calamity!
10 "You have devised a shameful thing for your house
By cutting off many peoples;
So you are sinning against yourself.
11 "Surely the stone will cry out from the wall,
And the rafter will answer it from the framework.

12 "Woe to him who builds a city with bloodshed
And founds a town with violence!
13 "Is it not indeed from the LORD of hosts
That peoples toil for fire,
And nations grow weary for nothing?
14 "For the earth will be filled
With the knowledge of the glory of the LORD,
As the waters cover the sea.

15 "Woe to you who make your neighbors drink,
Who mix in your venom even to make *them* drunk
So as to look on their nakedness!
16 "You will be filled with disgrace rather than honor.
Now you yourself drink and expose your *own* nakedness.
The cup in the LORD'S right hand will come around to you,
And utter disgrace *will come* upon your glory.
17 "For the violence done to Lebanon will overwhelm you,
And the devastation of *its* beasts by which you terrified them,
Because of human bloodshed and violence done to the land,
To the town and all its inhabitants.

18 "What profit is the idol when its maker has carved it,
Or an image, a teacher of falsehood?
For *its* maker trusts in his *own* handiwork
When he fashions speechless idols.
19 "Woe to him who says to a *piece of* wood, 'Awake!'
To a mute stone, 'Arise!'
And that is *your* teacher?

2:6 Is 14:4-10; Jer 50:13; Job 20:15-29; Hab 2:12

2:7 Prov 29:1

2:8 Is 33:1; Jer 27:7; Zech 2:8

2:9 Jer 22:13; Ezek 22:27; Jer 49:16

2:10 2 Kin 9:26; Nah 1:14; Hab 2:16; Jer 26:19

2:11 Josh 24:27; Luke 19:40

2:12 Mic 3:10; Nah 3:1

2:13 Is 50:11; Jer 51:58

2:14 Ps 22:27; Is 11:9; Zech 14:9

2:16 Lam 4:21; Jer 25:15, 17; Nah 3:6

2:17 Joel 3:19; Zech 11:1; Ps 55:23; Hab 2:8; Jer 51:35; Hab 2:8

2:18 Is 42:17; 44:9; Jer 2:27, 28; Jer 10:8, 14; Zech 10:2; Ps 115:4, 8

2:19 Jer 2:27, 28; 10:3; 1 Kin 18:26-29; Ps 135:15-18; Jer 10:4, 9, 14; Ps 135:17

2:9–13 Babylon's riches had come from the misfortunes of others, but these riches would only be fuel for the fire. The victims and their cities would cry out against Babylon. Money is not evil, but God condemns the love of riches and the evil means of acquiring it (1 Timothy 6:10). Be careful not to hunger for wealth so much that you lose your appetite for God. Do not allow money to take the place of family, friends, or God.

2:18 Idolatry may seem like a sin that modern people need not fear. But idolatry is not just bowing down to idols; it is trusting in what one has made, and therefore, in one's own power as creator and sustainer. If we say we worship God but put our trust in bank accounts, homes, businesses, and organizations, then we are idolaters. Do you trust God more than you trust what your hands have made?

Behold, it is overlaid with gold and silver,
And there is no breath at all inside it.
20 "But the LORD is in His holy temple.
Let all the earth be silent before Him."

2:20 Mic 1:2; Zeph 1:7; Zech 2:13

2. Habakkuk's prayer

God's Deliverance of His People

3 A prayer of Habakkuk the prophet, according to [2]Shigionoth.
2 LORD, I have heard the report about You *and* I fear.
O LORD, revive Your work in the midst of the years,
In the midst of the years make it known;
In wrath remember mercy.

3 God comes from Teman,
And the Holy One from Mount Paran. Selah.
His splendor covers the heavens,
And the earth is full of His praise.
4 *His* radiance is like the sunlight;
He has rays *flashing* from His hand,
And there is the hiding of His power.
5 Before Him goes pestilence,
And plague comes after Him.
6 He stood and surveyed the earth;
He looked and startled the nations.
Yes, the perpetual mountains were shattered,
The ancient hills collapsed.
His ways are everlasting.
7 I saw the tents of Cushan under distress,
The tent curtains of the land of Midian were trembling.

8 Did the LORD rage against the rivers,
Or *was* Your anger against the rivers,
Or *was* Your wrath against the sea,
That You rode on Your horses,
On Your chariots of salvation?
9 Your bow was made bare,
The rods of chastisement were sworn. Selah.
You cleaved the earth with rivers.
10 The mountains saw You *and* quaked;
The downpour of waters swept by.
The deep uttered forth its voice,
It lifted high its hands.
11 Sun *and* moon stood in their places;
They went away at the light of Your arrows,
At the radiance of Your gleaming spear.

3:2 Job 42:5; Ps 119:120; Jer 10:7; Ps 71:20; 85:6; Ps 44:1-8; Hab 1:5; Num 14:19; 2 Sam 24:15-17; Is 54:8

3:3 Jer 49:7; Amos 1:12; Obad 9; Gen 21:21; Deut 33:2; Ps 113:4; 148:13; Ps 48:10

3:4 Ps 18:12; Job 26:14

3:5 Ex 12:29, 30; Num 16:46-49; Num 11:1-3; Ps 18:12, 13

3:6 Job 21:18; Ps 35:5; Hab 1:12

3:7 Ex 15:14-16; Num 31:7, 8; Judg 7:24, 25; 8:12

3:8 Ex 7:19, 20; Josh 3:16; Is 50:2; Ex 14:16, 21; Ps 114:3, 5; Deut 33:26; Ps 18:10; Hab 3:15; Ps 68:17

3:9 Ps 7:12, 13; Hab 3:11; Ps 78:16; 105:41

3:10 Ps 93:3; 98:7, 8

3:11 Josh 10:12-14; Ps 18:14

2 I.e. a highly emotional poetic form

2:20 Idols have no life, no personhood, no power; they are empty chunks of wood or stone. Temples built to idols are equally empty; no one lives there. But the Lord *is* in his temple. He is real, alive, and powerful. He is truly and fully God. Idolaters command their idols to save them, but we who worship the living God come to him in silent awe, great respect, and reverence. We acknowledge that God is in control and knows what he is doing. Idols remain silent, because they cannot answer. The living God, by contrast, speaks through his Word. Approach God reverently and wait silently to hear what he has to say.

3:1ff Habakkuk praised God for answering his questions. Evil will not triumph forever; God is in control, and he can be completely trusted to vindicate those who are faithful to him. We must patiently wait for him to act (3:16).

3:2 Habakkuk knew that God was going to discipline the people of Judah and that it wasn't going to be a pleasant experience. But Habakkuk accepted God's will, asking for help and mercy. Habakkuk did not ask to escape the discipline, but he accepted the truth that Judah needed to learn a lesson. God still disciplines in love to bring his children back to him (Hebrews 12:5–6). Accept God's discipline gladly, and ask him to help you change.

3:3 The word *Selah* occurs 71 times in Psalms and three times in Habakkuk. Although its precise meaning is unknown, it most likely was a musical term. It could be a signal to lift up the hands or voice in worship, or it could be an exclamation like "Amen!" or "Hallelujah!" affirming the truth of the passage.

12 In indignation You marched through the earth;
In anger You trampled the nations.
13 You went forth for the salvation of Your people,
For the salvation of Your anointed.
You struck the head of the house of the evil
To lay him open from thigh to neck. Selah.
14 You pierced with his own spears
The head of his throngs.
They stormed in to scatter us;
Their exultation *was* like those
Who devour the oppressed in secret.
15 You trampled on the sea with Your horses,
On the surge of many waters.

16 I heard and my inward parts trembled,
At the sound my lips quivered.
Decay enters my bones,
And in my place I tremble.
Because I must wait quietly for the day of distress,
For the people to arise *who* will invade us.
17 Though the fig tree should not blossom
And there be no fruit on the vines,
Though the yield of the olive should fail
And the fields produce no food,
Though the flock should be cut off from the fold
And there be no cattle in the stalls,
18 Yet I will exult in the LORD,
I will rejoice in the God of my salvation.
19 The Lord GOD is my strength,
And He has made my feet like hinds' *feet,*
And makes me walk on my high places.

For the choir director, on my stringed instruments.

3:12 Ps 68:7; Is 41:15; Jer 51:33; Mic 4:13

3:13 Ex 15:2; 2 Sam 5:20; Ps 68:19, 20; Ps 20:6; 28:8; Ps 68:21; 110:6

3:14 Judg 7:22; Dan 11:40; Zech 9:14; Ps 10:8; 64:2-5

3:15 Ps 77:19; Hab 3:8; Ex 15:8

3:16 Dan 10:8; Hab 3:2; Job 30:17, 30; Jer 23:9; Luke 21:19; Jer 5:15

3:17 Joel 1:10-12; Amos 4:9; 2 Cor 4:8, 9; Mic 6:15; Joel 1:18; Jer 5:17

3:18 Ex 15:1, 2; Job 13:15; Is 61:10; Rom 5:2, 3; Ps 46:1-5; Phil 4:4; Ps 25:5; 27:1; Is 12:2

3:19 Ps 18:32, 33; 27:1; 46:1; Is 45:24; 2 Sam 22:34; Deut 33:29

3:17–19 Crop failure and the death of animals would devastate Judah. But Habakkuk affirmed that even in the times of starvation and loss, he would still rejoice in the Lord. Habakkuk's feelings were not controlled by the events around him but by faith in God's ability to give him strength. When nothing makes sense, and when troubles seem more than you can bear, remember that God gives strength. Take your eyes off your difficulties and look to God.

3:19 God will give his followers surefooted confidence through difficult times. They will run like deer across rough and dangerous terrain. At the proper time, God will bring about his justice and completely rid the world of evil. In the meantime, God's people need to live in the strength of his Spirit, confident in his ultimate victory over evil.

3:19 The note to the choir director was to be used when this passage was sung as a psalm in temple worship.

3:19 Habakkuk had asked God why evil people prosper while the righteous suffer. God's answer: They don't, not in the long run. Habakkuk saw his own limitations in contrast to God's unlimited control of all the world's events. God is alive and in control of the world and its events. We cannot see all that God is doing, and we cannot see all that God will do. But we can be assured that he is God and will do what is right. Knowing this can give us confidence and hope in a confusing world.

BIBLE "WAITERS"
In the Bible we find many people who had to "wait on the Lord," just as believers today must patiently wait for Christ's return. We can learn a lesson in patience from these Bible waiters.

Noah waited for God's timing before leaving the ark	Genesis 8:10, 12
Moses waited on God on the mountain	Exodus 24:12
Job waited for God's answers	Job 14:14
Isaiah waited for God to work in Israel	Isaiah 8:17; 25:9; 26:8; 30:18; 33:2; 40:31; 49:23; 59:9, 11; 64:4
Jeremiah understood the need to wait quietly for God's salvation	Lamentations 3:25
Hosea warned the people to return to God and wait for him to work	Hosea 12:6
Micah waited for the God of his salvation	Micah 7:7
Habakkuk warned the people to hold on to their hope and to wait because it would surely come	Habakkuk 2:3
Zephaniah explained that the Lord wanted his people to wait for him	Zephaniah 3:8
Joseph of Arimathea was waiting for God's kingdom	Luke 23:51
The disciples were ordered by Jesus to wait in Jerusalem for the coming of the Holy Spirit	Acts 1:4
Believers are called to wait for heaven, for the promise is sure	Romans 8:23, 25; Galatians 5:5; 1 Thessalonians 1:10; Titus 2:13; 2 Peter 3:12-14

ZEPHANIAH

Zephaniah becomes a prophet; Josiah becomes king of Judah 640 B.C.

Jeremiah becomes a prophet 627

Book of the Law found in the temple 622

Zephaniah's ministry ends 621

Habakkuk becomes a prophet 612

VITAL STATISTICS

PURPOSE:
To shake the people of Judah out of their complacency and urge them to return to God

AUTHOR:
Zephaniah

TO WHOM WRITTEN:
Judah and all nations

DATE WRITTEN:
Probably near the end of Zephaniah's ministry (640–621 B.C.), when King Josiah's great reforms began

SETTING:
King Josiah of Judah was attempting to reverse the evil trends set by the two previous kings of Judah—Manasseh and Amon. Josiah was able to extend his influence because there wasn't a strong superpower dominating the world at that time (Assyria was declining rapidly). Zephaniah's prophecy may have been the motivating factor in Josiah's reform. Zephaniah was a contemporary of Jeremiah.

KEY VERSE:
"Seek the LORD, all you humble of the earth who have carried out His ordinances; seek righteousness, seek humility. Perhaps you will be hidden in the day of the LORD's anger" (2:3).

KEY PLACE:
Jerusalem

OVERWHELMING grief, prolonged distress, incessant abuse, continual persecution, and imminent punishment breed hopelessness and despair. "If only," we cry, as we search our mind for a way out and look to the skies for rescue. With just a glimmer of hope, we would take courage and carry on, enduring until the end.

Hope is the silver shaft of sun breaking through the storm-darkened sky, words of comfort in the intensive care unit, a letter from across the sea, the first spring bird perched on a snow-covered twig, and the finish line in sight. It is a rainbow, a song, a loving touch. Hope is knowing God and resting in his love.

As God's prophet, Zephaniah was bound to speak the truth. This he did clearly, thundering certain judgment and horrible punishment for all who would defy the Lord. God's awful wrath would sweep away everything in the land and destroy it. " 'I will remove man and beast; I will remove the birds of the sky and the fish of the sea, and the ruins along with the wicked; and I will cut off man from the face of the earth,' declares the LORD" (1:3). No living thing in the land would escape. And that terrible day was coming soon: "Near is the great day of the LORD, near and coming very quickly; listen, the day of the LORD! In it the warrior cries out bitterly. A day of wrath is that day, a day of trouble and distress, a day of destruction and desolation, a day of darkness and gloom, a day of clouds and thick darkness" (1:14–15). We can sense the oppression and depression his listeners must have felt. They were judged guilty, and they were doomed.

But in the midst of this terrible pronouncement, there is hope. The first chapter of Zephaniah's prophecy is filled with terror. In chapter two, however, a whispered promise appears. "Seek the LORD, all you humble of the earth who have carried out His ordinances; seek righteousness, seek humility. Perhaps you will be hidden in the day of the LORD's anger" (2:3). And a few verses later we read of "the remnant of the house of Judah" (2:7) who will be restored.

Finally in chapter three, the quiet refrain grows to a crescendo as God's salvation and deliverance for those who are faithful to him is declared. "Shout for joy, O daughter of Zion! Shout in triumph, O Israel! Rejoice and exult with all your heart, O daughter of Jerusalem! The LORD has taken away His judgments against you, He has cleared away your enemies. The King of Israel, the LORD, is in your midst; you will fear disaster no more" (3:14–15). This is true hope, grounded in the knowledge of God's justice and in his love for his people.

As you read Zephaniah, listen carefully to the words of judgment. God does not take sin lightly, and it will be punished. But be encouraged by the words of hope—our God reigns, and he will rescue his own. Decide to be part of that faithful remnant of souls who humbly worship and obey the living Lord.

Josiah dies in battle 609	*First captives taken to Babylon 605*	*Babylon's second attack on Judah 597*	*Judah (the southern kingdom) falls 586*

THE BLUEPRINT

1. The day of judgment (1:1—3:8)
2. The day of hope (3:9–20)

Zephaniah warned the people of Judah that if they refused to repent, the entire nation, including the beloved city of Jerusalem, would be lost. The people knew that God would eventually bless them, but Zephaniah made it clear that there would be judgment first, then blessing. This judgment would not be merely punishment for sin, but it would also be a means of purifying the people. Though we live in a fallen world surrounded by evil, we can hope in the perfect kingdom of God to come, and we can allow any punishment that touches us now to purify us from sin.

MEGATHEMES

THEME	EXPLANATION	IMPORTANCE
Day of Judgment	Destruction was coming because Judah had forsaken the Lord. The people worshiped Baal, Molech, and the starry hosts. Even the priests mixed pagan practices with faith in God. God's punishment for sin was on the way.	To escape God's judgment we must listen to him, accept his correction, trust him, and seek his guidance. If we accept him as our Lord, we can escape his condemnation.
Indifference to God	Although there had been occasional attempts at renewal, Judah had no sorrow for its sins. The people were prosperous, and they no longer cared about God. God's demands for righteous living seemed irrelevant to the people, whose security and wealth made them complacent.	Don't let material comfort be a barrier to your commitment to God. Prosperity can lead to an attitude of proud self-sufficiency. We need to admit that money won't save us and that we cannot save ourselves. Only God can save us.
Day of Cheer	The day of judgment will also be a day of cheer. God will judge all those who mistreat his people. He will purify his people, purging away all sin and evil. God will restore his people and give them hope.	When people are purged of sin, there is great relief and hope. No matter how difficult our experience now, we can look forward to the day of celebration when God will completely restore us. It will truly be a day to rejoice!

1:1 2 Kin 22:1, 2; 2 Chr 34:1-33; Jer 1:2; 22:11; 2 Kin 21:18-26; 2 Chr 33:20-25

1:2 Gen 6:7; Jer 7:20; Ezek 33:27, 28

1:3 Is 6:11, 12; Jer 4:25; 9:10; Ezek 7:19; 14:3, 4, 8

1. The day of wrath

Day of Judgment on Judah

1 The word of the LORD which came to Zephaniah son of Cushi, son of Gedaliah, son of Amariah, son of Hezekiah, in the days of Josiah son of Amon, king of Judah:

2 "I will completely remove all *things*
From the face of the earth," declares the LORD.
3 "I will remove man and beast;
I will remove the birds of the sky

1:1 Zephaniah prophesied in the days of Josiah king of Judah (640–609 B.C.). Josiah followed God, and during his reign the book of the law was discovered in the temple. After reading it, Josiah began a great religious revival in Judah (2 Kings 22:1—23:25). Zephaniah helped fan the revival by warning the people that judgment would come if they did not turn from their sins. Although this great revival turned the nation back to God, it did not fully eliminate idolatry and lasted only a short time. Twelve years after Josiah's death, Judah was invaded by Babylon, and a number of people were sent into exile.

1:2ff The people of Judah were clearly warned by the highest authority of all—God. They refused to listen, either because they doubted God's prophet and thus did not believe that the message was from God, or because they doubted God himself and thus did not believe that he would do what he said. If we refuse to listen to God's Word, the Bible, we are as shortsighted as the people of Judah, and like them, we will be punished.

And the fish of the sea,
And the ruins along with the wicked;
And I will cut off man from the face of the earth," declares the LORD.
4 "So I will stretch out My hand against Judah
And against all the inhabitants of Jerusalem.
And I will cut off the remnant of Baal from this place,
And the names of the idolatrous priests along with the priests.
5 "And those who bow down on the housetops to the host of heaven,
And those who bow down *and* swear to the LORD and *yet* swear by Milcom,
6 And those who have turned back from following the LORD,
And those who have not sought the LORD or inquired of Him."

7 Be silent before the Lord GOD!
For the day of the LORD is near,
For the LORD has prepared a sacrifice,
He has consecrated His guests.
8 "Then it will come about on the day of the LORD'S sacrifice
That I will punish the princes, the king's sons
And all who clothe themselves with foreign garments.
9 "And I will punish on that day all who leap on the *temple* threshold,
Who fill the house of their lord with violence and deceit.
10 "On that day," declares the LORD,
"There will be the sound of a cry from the Fish Gate,
A wail from the [1]Second Quarter,
And a loud crash from the hills.
11 "Wail, O inhabitants of the [1]Mortar,
For all the people of Canaan will be silenced;
All who weigh out silver will be cut off.
12 "It will come about at that time
That I will search Jerusalem with lamps,
And I will punish the men
Who are stagnant in spirit,
Who say in their hearts,

1:4 Jer 6:12; Ezek 6:14; Mic 5:13; 2 Kin 23:5; Hos 10:5

1:5 2 Kin 23:12; Jer 19:13; Jer 5:2, 7; 7:9, 10; 1 Kin 11:5, 33; Jer 49:1

1:6 Is 1:4; Hos 7:10; Is 9:13

1:7 Hab 2:20; Zech 2:13; Zeph 1:14; Is 34:6; Jer 46:10; 1 Sam 16:5; Is 13:3

1:8 Is 24:21; Hab 1:10; Is 2:6

1:9 Jer 5:27; Amos 3:10

1:10 2 Chr 33:14; Neh 3:3; 12:39; 2 Chr 34:22; Ezek 6:13

1:11 Zeph 2:5; Zech 14:21; Job 27:16, 17; Hos 9:6

1:12 Jer 16:16, 17; Ezek 9:4-11; Amos 9:1-3; Jer 48:11; Amos 6:1; Ezek 8:12; 9:9

1 I.e. a district of Jerusalem

1:4 When the Israelites arrived in the promised land, God had commanded that they completely rid the land of its pagan inhabitants, who worshiped idols. But the Israelites failed to do so, and gradually they began to worship the Canaanites' gods. The Canaanites believed in many gods that represented many aspects of life, and the chief god was Baal, symbolizing strength and fertility. God was extremely angry when his people turned from him to Baal.

1:4–6 The terrain of history is littered with idols and their worship. More than just a stone statue, an idol can be anything reverenced more than God. Thus idol worship is prevalent even today as people trust in themselves, money, or power and not in God. But ultimately all idols will prove worthless, and the true God will prevail. Seek God first (Matthew 6:33), and have no other gods before him (Exodus 20:3).

1:5 The people had become polytheistic, worshiping the Lord [and] all the other gods of the land. They added the "best" of pagan worship to true faith in God. But God commands that he alone be worshiped (Exodus 20:1–5); thus the people committed a horrible sin. One of these other gods was Milcom (also called Molech), the national god of the Ammonites. Molech worship included child sacrifice, an abominable sin. From the time of Moses, the Israelites had been warned about worshiping this false god (Leviticus 18:21; 20:5), but they refused to take heed. Because of their sins, God would destroy them.

1:7 A day of judgment and great slaughter occurred during the lifetime of these people when Babylon invaded the land. The prophet saw these prophecies as future events, but he could not see when or in what order these events would take place. Many think that these prophecies have a double fulfillment—one for the near future (soon after the prophecy was made) and another for the distant future (possibly during the end times). Some scholars believe that these prophecies of judgment refer to events entirely in the future.

1:8–9 Wearing "foreign" (pagan) clothes showed a desire for foreign gods and foreign ways. Leaders who should have been good examples to the people were adopting foreign practices and thus showing their contempt for the Lord by ignoring his commands against adopting pagan culture. To "leap on the temple threshold" was a pagan observance (see 1 Samuel 5:5).

1:12 God would search the city with lamps and punish those who deserve punishment. Because they did not search their own hearts, and because they were content with the moral chaos around them and indifferent to God, God would use the Babylonians to judge them. Within 20 years, the Babylonians would enter Jerusalem, drag people out of hiding, and take them captive or kill them. No one would escape God's judgment; there would be no place to hide.

1:12–14 Some people think of God as an indulgent heavenly grandfather, nice to have around, but not a real force in shaping modern life. They don't believe in his power or his coming judgment. But God is holy, and therefore he will actively judge and justly punish everyone who is content to live in sin, indifferent to him, or unconcerned about justice. When people are indifferent to God, they tend to think that he is indifferent to them and their sin. They will be surprised to find that "near is the great day of the LORD."

'The LORD will not do good or evil!'

1:13 Jer 15:13; 17:3; Amos 5:11; Mic 6:15

13 "Moreover, their wealth will become plunder
And their houses desolate;
Yes, they will build houses but not inhabit *them,*
And plant vineyards but not drink their wine."

1:14 Jer 30:7; Joel 2:11; Mal 4:5; Ezek 7:7, 12; 30:3; Joel 1:15; 3:14; Zeph 1:7; Ezek 7:16-18

14 Near is the great day of the LORD,
Near and coming very quickly;
Listen, the day of the LORD!
In it the warrior cries out bitterly.

1:15 Is 22:5; Joel 2:2, 31; Amos 5:18-20

15 A day of wrath is that day,
A day of trouble and distress,
A day of destruction and desolation,
A day of darkness and gloom,
A day of clouds and thick darkness,

1:16 Is 27:13; Jer 4:19; Is 2:12-15

16 A day of trumpet and battle cry
Against the fortified cities
And the high corner towers.

1:17 Jer 10:18; Deut 28:29; Ezek 24:7, 8; Jer 8:2; 9:22

17 I will bring distress on men
So that they will walk like the blind,
Because they have sinned against the LORD;
And their blood will be poured out like dust
And their flesh like dung.

1:18 Ezek 7:19; Zeph 3:8; Gen 6:7; Ezek 7:5-7

18 Neither their silver nor their gold
Will be able to deliver them
On the day of the LORD'S wrath;
And all the earth will be devoured
In the fire of His jealousy,
For He will make a complete end,
Indeed a terrifying one,
Of all the inhabitants of the earth.

Judgments on Judah's Enemies

2:1 2 Chr 20:4; Joel 1:14; Jer 3:3; 6:15

2 Gather yourselves together, yes, gather,
O nation without shame,

2:2 Is 17:13; Hos 13:3; Lam 4:11; Nah 1:6; Zeph 1:18

2 Before the decree takes effect—
The day passes like the chaff—
Before the burning anger of the LORD comes upon you,

ZEPHANIAH Zephaniah served as a prophet to Judah from 640–621 B.C.

Climate of the times	Josiah was the last good king in Judah. His bold attempts to reform the nation and turn it back to God were probably influenced by Zephaniah.
Main message	A day will come when God, as Judge, will severely punish all nations. But after judgment, he will show mercy to all who have been faithful to him.
Importance of message	We will all be judged for our disobedience to God; but if we remain faithful to him, he will show us mercy.
Contemporary prophet	Jeremiah (627–586 B.C.)

1:14–18 The great day of the Lord was near; the Babylonians would soon come and destroy Jerusalem. The day of the Lord is also near for us. God promises a final judgment, a day of worldwide destruction (Revelation 20:12–15). The Babylonian conquest occurred just as surely and horribly as Zephaniah had predicted. And God's final day of judgment is also sure—but so is his ability to save. To be spared from judgment, recognize that you have sinned, that your sin will bring judgment, that you cannot save yourself, and that God alone can save you.

1:18 Money is not evil in itself, but it is useless to save us. In this life, money can warp our perspective, giving us feelings of security and power. Just as the Israelites' wealth could not save them from the Babylonian invasion, so at the final judgment, our riches will be worthless. Only Christ's redemptive work on our behalf matters for eternity. Christ alone will ransom us if we believe in him. Don't trust money; trust Christ.

2:1–3 There was still time for the people to avert God's judgment. They simply had to turn from their sins, humble themselves, and obey God. The Old Testament prophets announced news of destruction, but they also offered the only means of escape and protection—turning from sin and walking with God (see also Micah 6:8).

Before the day of the LORD'S anger comes upon you.
3 Seek the LORD,
All you humble of the earth
Who have carried out His ordinances;
Seek righteousness, seek humility.
Perhaps you will be hidden
In the day of the LORD'S anger.

4 For Gaza will be abandoned
And Ashkelon a desolation;
Ashdod will be driven out at noon
And Ekron will be uprooted.
5 Woe to the inhabitants of the seacoast,
The nation of the [2]Cherethites!
The word of the LORD is against you,
O Canaan, land of the Philistines;
And I will destroy you
So that there will be no inhabitant.
6 So the seacoast will be pastures,
With caves for shepherds and folds for flocks.
7 And the coast will be
For the remnant of the house of Judah,
They will pasture on it.
In the houses of Ashkelon they will lie down at evening;
For the LORD their God will care for them
And restore their fortune.

8 "I have heard the taunting of Moab
And the revilings of the sons of Ammon,
With which they have taunted My people
And become arrogant against their territory.
9 "Therefore, as I live," declares the LORD of hosts,
The God of Israel,
"Surely Moab will be like Sodom
And the sons of Ammon like Gomorrah—
A place possessed by nettles and salt pits,
And a perpetual desolation.
The remnant of My people will plunder them
And the remainder of My nation will inherit them."

2:3 Ps 105:4; Amos 5:6; Ps 22:26; Is 11:4; Amos 5:14, 15; Ps 57:1; Is 26:20

2:4 Amos 1:7, 8; Zech 9:5-7

2:5 Ezek 25:16; Amos 3:1; Zeph 1:11; Is 14:29, 30; Zeph 3:6

2:6 Is 5:17; 7:25

2:7 Is 11:16; Is 32:14; Ex 4:31; Ps 80:14; Jer 32:44; Zeph 3:20

2:8 Ezek 25:8; Ezek 25:3; Amos 1:13

2:9 Is 15:1-9; Jer 48:1-47; Amos 2:1-3; Gen 19:24; Jer 49:1-6; Ezek 25:1-10; Deut 29:23; Is 11:14

2 I.e. a segment of the Philistines with roots in Crete

2:4 The four cities mentioned here are in Philistia, the nation southwest of Judah on the coast of the Mediterranean Sea. Age-old enemies of Israel from the days of Joshua, the Philistines were known for their cruelty. God judged these cities for their idolatry and their constant taunting of Israel. These four cities were four of the five capitals. The fifth (Gath) had probably already been destroyed.

2:5 The Cherethites were a clan of the Philistines located near southern Judah. They migrated to Palestine along with other Philistine people. Their name may have been derived from "Crete," the island where they lived before they moved to Palestine.

2:7 All the prophets, even while prophesying doom and destruction, speak of a "remnant"—a small group of God's people who remain faithful to him and whom God will restore to the land. Although God said he would destroy Judah, he also promised to save a remnant, thus keeping his original covenant to preserve Abraham's descendants (Genesis 17:4–8). Because God is holy, he cannot allow sin to continue. But God is also faithful to his promises. He cannot stay angry forever with Israel, or with you, if you are his child, because he loves his children and always seeks their good.

2:8 The Moabites and Ammonites lived to the east of Judah, and they often ridiculed and attacked Judah. These nations worshiped Chemosh and Molech (1 Kings 11:7). Moab's king once sacrificed his son on the city wall to stop an invasion (2 Kings 3:26–27). God would judge these nations for their wickedness and for their treatment of his people.

2:8–11 Judah had been taunted and mocked by the neighboring nations, Moab and Ammon, but God reminded them that he had "heard the taunting . . . and the revilings" (2:8), and that the taunters would be punished for their pride (2:10). At times the whole world seems to mock God and those who have faith in him. When you are ridiculed, remember that God hears and will answer. Eventually, in God's timing, justice will be carried out.

2:9 The nations of Moab and Ammon trace their roots to Lot's incest with his daughters after escaping the destruction of evil Sodom and Gomorrah (Genesis 19). Ironically, Moab and Ammon would be the same kind of perpetual wasteland that God had made those evil cities. Sodom and Gomorrah were so completely destroyed that their exact location is still unknown.

2:10 Is 16:6; Zeph 2:8

10 This they will have in return for their pride, because they have taunted and become
arrogant against the people of the LORD of hosts.

2:11 Joel 2:11; Zeph 1:4; Is 24:15; Ps 72:8-11; Zeph 3:9

11 The LORD will be terrifying to them, for He will starve all the gods of the earth; and
all the coastlands of the nations will bow down to Him, everyone from his *own* place.

2:12 Is 18:1-7; 20:4, 5; Ezek 30:4-9

12 "You also, O Ethiopians, will be slain by My sword."

2:13 Is 14:26; Zeph 1:4; Is 10:16; Mic 5:6; Nah 3:7

13 And He will stretch out His hand against the north
And destroy Assyria,
And He will make Nineveh a desolation,
Parched like the wilderness.

2:14 Is 14:23; 34:11

14 Flocks will lie down in her midst,
All beasts which range in herds;
Both the pelican and the hedgehog
Will lodge in the tops of her pillars;
Birds will sing in the window,
Desolation *will be* on the threshold;
For He has laid bare the cedar work.

2:15 Is 22:2; Is 32:9, 11; 47:8; Is 47:8; Ezek 28:2, 9; Is 32:14; Jer 18:16; 19:8

15 This is the exultant city
Which dwells securely,
Who says in her heart,
"I am, and there is no one besides me."
How she has become a desolation,
A resting place for beasts!
Everyone who passes by her will hiss
And wave his hand *in contempt.*

Woe to Jerusalem and the Nations

3:1 Jer 5:23; Ezek 23:30; Jer 6:6

3 Woe to her who is rebellious and defiled,
The tyrannical city!

3:2 Jer 7:23-28; Jer 2:30; 5:3; 2 Tim 3:16; Ps 78:22; Jer 13:25; Ps 73:28

2 She heeded no voice,
She accepted no instruction.
She did not trust in the LORD,
She did not draw near to her God.

3:3 Ezek 22:27; Jer 5:6; Hab 1:8

3 Her princes within her are roaring lions,
Her judges are wolves at evening;
They leave nothing for the morning.

3:4 Judg 9:4; Ezek 22:26; Mal 2:7, 8

4 Her prophets are reckless, treacherous men;
Her priests have profaned the sanctuary.
They have done violence to the law.

2:12 Ethiopia, at the southern end of the Red Sea, controlled Egypt at this time. No one can escape deserved judgment. The Ethiopians were "slain by [God's] sword" when the Babylonians invaded Egypt in 605 B.C. (See Isaiah 18 and Ezekiel 30:9 for other prophecies concerning Ethiopia, also called Cush.)

2:13 Zephaniah mentioned the large nation to the south and then moved to the nation that invaded from the north, Assyria. Though declining, Assyria was still the strongest military power of the day, dominating the world for three centuries and destroying anyone in its path. Nineveh, the large capital city, was considered impregnable. However, just as Zephaniah predicted, Nineveh was wiped out in 612 B.C. by the Babylonians, who would become the next world power.

2:13–15 To predict the destruction of Nineveh ten years before it happened would be equivalent to predicting the destruction of Tokyo, Moscow, or New York. Nineveh was the ancient Near Eastern center for culture, technology, and beauty. It had great libraries, buildings, and a vast irrigation system that created lush gardens in the city. The city wall was 60 miles long, 100 feet high, over 30 feet wide, and fortified with 1,500 towers. Yet the entire city was destroyed so completely that its very existence was questioned until it was discovered, with great difficulty, by 19th century archaeologists. Nineveh had indeed become as desolate and dry as the desert.

3:1ff After predicting the destruction of the surrounding nations, Zephaniah returned to the problem at hand—sin in Jerusalem. The city of God, and God's people themselves, had become "defiled"—as sinful as their pagan neighbors. The people pretended to worship and serve God, but in their hearts they had rejected him and continued to be complacent about their sins. They no longer cared about the consequences of turning away from God.

3:2 Do you know people who refuse to listen when someone disagrees with their opinions? Their root problem is pride—inflated self-esteem. God's people had become so proud that they would not hear or accept God's correction. Do you find it difficult to listen to the spiritual counsel of others or God's words from the Bible? Don't let pride make you unable or unwilling to let God work in your life. You will be more willing to listen when you consider how weak and sinful you really are compared to God.

3:3–4 Leading God's people is a privilege and a responsibility. Through Zephaniah, God rebuked all types of leadership in Jerusalem—princes, judges, prophets, and priests—because of their callous disobedience, irresponsibility, and sin. If you are a leader in the church, consider yourself in a privileged position, but be careful. God holds you responsible for the purity of your actions, the quality of your example, and the truth of your words.

5 The LORD is righteous within her;
He will do no injustice.
Every morning He brings His justice to light;
He does not fail.
But the unjust knows no shame.
6 "I have cut off nations;
Their corner towers are in ruins.
I have made their streets desolate,
With no one passing by;
Their cities are laid waste,
Without a man, without an inhabitant.
7 "I said, 'Surely you will revere Me,
Accept instruction.'
So her dwelling will not be cut off
According to all that I have appointed concerning her.
But they were eager to corrupt all their deeds.

3:5 Deut 32:4; Zeph 3:15, 17; Ps 92:15; Job 7:18; Zeph 2:1

3:6 Jer 9:12; Zech 7:14; Matt 23:38; Lev 26:31; Is 6:11; Zeph 2:5

3:7 Job 36:10; Ps 32:8; 1 Tim 1:5; Jer 7:7; Hos 9:9

2. The day of hope

8 "Therefore wait for Me," declares the LORD,
"For the day when I rise up as a witness.
Indeed, My decision is to gather nations,
To assemble kingdoms,
To pour out on them My indignation,
All My burning anger;
For all the earth will be devoured
By the fire of My zeal.
9 "For then I will give to the peoples purified lips,
That all of them may call on the name of the LORD,
To serve Him shoulder to shoulder.
10 "From beyond the rivers of Ethiopia
My worshipers, My dispersed ones,
Will bring My offerings.
11 "In that day you will feel no shame
Because of all your deeds
By which you have rebelled against Me;
For then I will remove from your midst
Your proud, exulting ones,
And you will never again be haughty
On My holy mountain.

3:8 Ps 27:14; Is 30:18; Hab 2:3; Ezek 38:14-23; Joel 3:2; Zeph 1:18

3:9 Is 19:18; 57:19; Ps 22:27; 86:9; Hab 2:14; Zeph 2:11

3:10 Ps 68:31; Is 18:1; Is 60:6, 7

3:11 Is 45:17; 54:4; Joel 2:26, 27; Is 2:12; 5:15; Is 11:9; 56:7; Ezek 20:40

A Remnant of Israel

12 "But I will leave among you
A humble and lowly people,

3:12 Is 14:30; Is 14:32; 50:10; Nah 1:7; Zech 13:8, 9

3:5 Jerusalem's citizens, of all people, had no excuse for their sins. Jerusalem, where the temple was located, was the religious center of the nation. But even though the people didn't follow God, God was "within" the city, present in the midst of corruption, persecution, and unbelief. No matter how spiritually desolate the world seems, God is here, and he is at work. Ask yourself, "What is he doing now, and how can I be part of his work?"

3:7 We may wonder how the Israelites could have had such clear warnings and still not turn to God. The problem was that they had allowed sin to so harden them that they no longer cared to follow God. They refused to heed God's warnings and to repent. The more God punished them, the more they sinned. In fact, they were "eager" to sin. If you disobey God now, your heart may grow hard, and you may lose your desire for God.

3:8 In the last days, God will judge all people according to what they have done (Revelation 20:12). Justice will prevail; evildoers will be punished; and the obedient will be blessed. Don't try to avenge yourself. Be patient, and God's justice will come.

3:9 God will purify lips and unify language so that all his people from all nations will be able to worship him in unison. In the new earth, all believers will speak the same language; the confusion of languages at the tower of Babel will be reversed (Genesis 11). God will purify our hearts, so that the words coming from our lips will be pure as well.

3:10 The "dispersed ones" refers to Jews dispersed beyond the rivers of Ethiopia. It symbolizes that all Jews, no matter how far they have been scattered, will return to worship God.

3:11–12 God will remove the proud people and leave the meek and humble. God is opposed to the proud and haughty of every generation. But those who are meek and humble, both physically and spiritually, will be rewarded because they trust in God. Self-reliance and arrogance have no place among God's people or in his kingdom.

And they will take refuge in the name of the LORD.

3:13 Is 10:20-22; Mic 4:7; Zeph 2:7; Ps 119:3; Jer 31:33; Zeph 3:5; Zech 8:3, 16; Rev 14:5; Ezek 34:13-15

13 "The remnant of Israel will do no wrong
And tell no lies,
Nor will a deceitful tongue
Be found in their mouths;
For they will feed and lie down
With no one to make them tremble."

3:14 Zech 9:9

14 Shout for joy, O daughter of Zion!
Shout *in triumph,* O Israel!
Rejoice and exult with all *your* heart,
O daughter of Jerusalem!

3:15 Ps 19:9; John 5:30; Rev 18:20; Ezek 37:26-28; Zeph 3:5; Is 54:14

15 The LORD has taken away *His* judgments against you,
He has cleared away your enemies.
The King of Israel, the LORD, is in your midst;
You will fear disaster no more.

3:16 Is 25:9; Is 35:3, 4; Job 4:3; Heb 12:12

16 In that day it will be said to Jerusalem:
"Do not be afraid, O Zion;
Do not let your hands fall limp.

3:17 Zeph 3:5, 15; Is 63:1; Is 62:5

17 "The LORD your God is in your midst,
A victorious warrior.
He will exult over you with joy,
He will be quiet in His love,
He will rejoice over you with shouts of joy.

3:18 Ps 42:2-4; Ezek 9:4

18 "I will gather those who grieve about the appointed feasts—
They came from you, *O Zion;*
The reproach *of exile* is a burden on them.

3:19 Is 60:14; Ezek 34:16; Mic 4:6; Ezek 16:27, 57; Is 60:18; 62:7; Zech 8:23

19 "Behold, I am going to deal at that time
With all your oppressors,
I will save the lame
And gather the outcast,
And I will turn their shame into praise and renown
In all the earth.

3:20 Ezek 37:12, 21; Deut 26:18, 19; Is 56:5; 66:22; Jer 29:14; Joel 3:1; Zeph 2:7

20 "At that time I will bring you in,
Even at the time when I gather you together;
Indeed, I will give you renown and praise
Among all the peoples of the earth,
When I restore your fortunes before your eyes,"
Says the LORD.

3:14–18 The Lord himself will remove his hand of judgment, disperse Israel's enemies, and come to live among his people. He will give them gladness. We sin when we pursue happiness by cutting ourselves off from fellowship with God—the only person who can make us truly happy. Zephaniah points out that gladness results when we allow God to be with us. We do that by faithfully following him and obeying his commands. Then God rejoices over us with singing. If you want to be happy, draw close to the source of happiness by obeying God.

3:20 "Before your eyes" does not necessarily mean that this promise would be fulfilled during Zephaniah's generation. Rather, it means that the restoration will be an obvious work of the Lord.

3:20 The message of doom in the beginning of the book becomes a message of hope by the end. There will be a new day when God will bless his people. If the leaders in the church today were to hear a message from a prophet of God, the message would probably resemble the book of Zephaniah. Under Josiah's religious reforms, the people did return to God [outwardly], but their hearts were far from him. Zephaniah encouraged the nation to gather together and pray for salvation. We must also ask ourselves: Is our reform merely an outward show, or is it changing our hearts and lives? We need to gather together and pray, to walk humbly with God, to do what is right, and to hear the message of hope regarding the new world to come.

HAGGAI

Babylon overthrown by Cyrus 539 B.C.

Cyrus's decree allowing the exiles to return 538

Temple construction begins 536

VITAL STATISTICS

PURPOSE:
To call the people to complete the rebuilding of the temple

AUTHOR:
Haggai

TO WHOM WRITTEN:
The people living in Jerusalem and those who had returned from exile

DATE WRITTEN:
520 B.C.

SETTING:
The temple in Jerusalem had been destroyed in 586 B.C. Cyrus allowed the Jews to return to their homeland and rebuild their temple in 538 B.C. They began the work but were unable to complete it. Through the ministry of Haggai and Zechariah, the temple was completed (520–515 B.C.).

KEY VERSE:
"Is it time for you yourselves to dwell in your paneled houses while this house lies desolate?" (1:4).

KEY PEOPLE:
Haggai, Zerubbabel, Joshua

KEY PLACE:
Jerusalem

SPECIAL FEATURES:
Haggai was the first of the postexilic prophets. The other two were Zechariah and Malachi. The literary style of this book is simple and direct.

PRESSURES, demands, expectations, and tasks push in from all sides and assault our schedules. Do this! Be there! Finish that! Call them! It seems as though everyone wants something from us—family, friends, employer, school, church, clubs. Soon there is little left to give, as we run out of energy and time. We find ourselves rushing through life, attending to the necessary, the immediate, and the urgent. The important is all too often left in the dust. Our problem is not the volume of demands or lack of scheduling skills, but values—what is *truly* important to us.

Our values and priorities are reflected in how we use our resources—time, money, strength, and talent. Often our actions belie our words. We say God is number one, but then we relegate him to a lesser number on our "to do" lists.

Twenty-five centuries ago, a voice was heard, calling men and women to the right priorities. Haggai knew what was important and what had to be done, and he challenged God's people to respond.

In 586 B.C., the armies of Babylon had destroyed the temple in Jerusalem—God's house, the symbol of his presence. In 538 B.C. King Cyrus decreed that Jews could return to their beloved city and rebuild the temple. So they traveled to Jerusalem and began the work. But then they forgot their purpose and lost their priorities, as opposition and apathy brought the work to a standstill (Ezra 4:4–5). Then Haggai spoke, calling them back to God's values. "Is it time for you yourselves to dwell in your paneled houses while this house lies desolate?" (1:4). The people were more concerned with their own needs than with doing God's will, and, as a result, they suffered. Then Haggai called them to action: "Thus says the LORD of hosts, 'Consider your ways! Go up to the mountains, bring wood and rebuild the temple, that I may be pleased with it and be glorified' says the LORD" (1:7–8). And God's message through his servant Haggai became the catalyst for finishing the work.

Although Haggai is a small book, it is filled with challenge and promise, reminding us of God's claim on our life and our priorities. As you read Haggai, imagine him walking the streets and alleys of Jerusalem, urging the people to get back to doing God's work. And listen to Haggai speaking to you, urging you to reorder your priorities in accordance with God's will. What has God told you to do? Put all else aside and obey him.

Temple work halted 530	*Haggai, Zechariah become prophets; temple work resumed 520*	*Temple completed 515*

THE BLUEPRINT

1. The call to rebuild the temple (1:1–15)
2. Encouragement to complete the temple (2:1–23)

When the exiles first returned from Babylon, they set about rebuilding the temple right away. Although they began with the right attitudes, they slipped back into wrong behavior, and the work came to a standstill. In this regard, we need to be on guard to keep our priorities straight. Remain active in your service to God and continue to put first things first.

MEGATHEMES

THEME	EXPLANATION	IMPORTANCE
Right Priorities	God had given the Jews the assignment to finish the temple in Jerusalem when they returned from captivity. After 15 years, they still had not completed it. They were more concerned about building their own homes than finishing God's work. Haggai told them to get their priorities straight.	It is easy to make other priorities more important than doing God's work. But God wants us to follow through and build up his kingdom. Don't stop and don't make excuses. Set your heart on what is right and do it. Get your priorities straight.
God's Encouragement	Haggai encouraged the people as they worked. He assured them of the divine presence of the Holy Spirit and of final victory, and instilled in them the hope that the Messiah would reign.	If God gives you a task, don't be afraid to get started. His resources are infinite. God will help you complete it by giving you encouragement from others along the way.

1. The call to rebuild the temple

Haggai Begins Temple Building

1:1 Ezra 4:24; Ezra 5:1; 6:14; Hag 1:3, 12, 13; 2:1, 10, 20; Ezra 2:2; Neh 7:7; Hag 1:12, 14; Zech 4:6; Matt 1:12, 13; 1 Kin 10:15; Ezra 5:3; Zech 6:11

1:4 Jer 33:10, 12; Hag 1:9

1 In the second year of Darius the king, on the first day of the sixth month, the word of
the LORD came by the prophet Haggai to Zerubbabel the son of Shealtiel, governor
of Judah, and to Joshua the son of Jehozadak, the high priest, saying,
2 "Thus says the LORD of hosts, 'This people says, "The time has not come, *even* the
time for the house of the LORD to be rebuilt." ' "
3 Then the word of the LORD came by Haggai the prophet, saying,
4 "Is it time for you yourselves to dwell in your paneled houses while this house *lies*
desolate?"

1:1 Zerubbabel, governor of Judah, and Joshua, the high priest, were key leaders in rebuilding the temple. They had already reestablished the altar, but work on the temple had slowed. Haggai gave a message to these outstanding leaders and to the exiles who had returned from Babylon, encouraging them to complete the rebuilding of the temple in Jerusalem.

1:1ff The Jews who had returned from Babylon in 538 B.C. to rebuild the temple in Jerusalem were not able to finish their work because they were hindered by their enemies. After opposition put a halt to progress, no further work had been done on the temple for over 15 years. In August, 520 B.C., Haggai delivered a message to encourage the people to rebuild the temple! Haggai was probably born in captivity in Babylon and returned to Jerusalem with Zerubbabel in 538 B.C. (Ezra 1; 2). Haggai and Zechariah, two prophets who encouraged the temple rebuilding, are mentioned in Ezra 5:1.

1:2–15 Haggai encouraged the people to finish rebuilding the temple. Opposition from hostile neighbors had caused them to feel discouraged and to neglect the temple, and thus neglect God. But Haggai's message turned them around and motivated them to pick up their tools and continue the work they had begun.

1:3–6 God asked his people how they could live in luxury when his house was lying in ruins. The temple was the focal point of Judah's relationship with God, but it was still demolished. Instead of rebuilding the temple, the people put their energies into beautifying their own homes. However, the harder the people worked for themselves, the less they had, because they ignored their spiritual lives. The same happens to us. If we put God first, he will provide for our deepest needs. If we put him in any other place, all our efforts will be futile. Caring only for your physical needs while ignoring your relationship with God will lead to ruin.

5 Now therefore, thus says the LORD of hosts, "Consider your ways!
6 "You have sown much, but harvest little; *you* eat, but *there is* not *enough* to be satisfied; *you* drink, but *there is* not *enough* to become drunk; *you* put on clothing, but no one
is warm *enough;* and he who earns, earns wages *to put* into a purse with holes."
7 Thus says the LORD of hosts, "Consider your ways!
8 "Go up to the mountains, bring wood and rebuild the temple, that I may be pleased
with it and be glorified," says the LORD.
9 "*You* look for much, but behold, *it comes* to little; when you bring *it* home, I blow it
away. Why?" declares the LORD of hosts, "Because of My house which *lies* desolate, while
each of you runs to his own house.
10 "Therefore, because of you the sky has withheld its dew and the earth has withheld
its produce.
11 "I called for a drought on the land, on the mountains, on the grain, on the new wine,
on the oil, on what the ground produces, on men, on cattle, and on all the labor of your
hands."
12 Then Zerubbabel the son of Shealtiel, and Joshua the son of Jehozadak, the high
priest, with all the remnant of the people, obeyed the voice of the LORD their God and
the words of Haggai the prophet, as the LORD their God had sent him. And the people
showed reverence for the LORD.
13 Then Haggai, the messenger of the LORD, spoke by the commission of the LORD to
the people saying, " 'I am with you,' declares the LORD."
14 So the LORD stirred up the spirit of Zerubbabel the son of Shealtiel, governor of
Judah, and the spirit of Joshua the son of Jehozadak, the high priest, and the spirit of all
the remnant of the people; and they came and worked on the house of the LORD of hosts,
their God,
15 on the twenty-fourth day of the sixth month in the second year of Darius the king.

1:6 Deut 28:38-40; Hos 8:7; Hag 1:9, 10; 2:16, 17

1:8 1 Kin 6:1; Ps 132:13, 14; Hag 2:7, 9

1:9 Prov 27:20; Eccl 1:8; Is 40:7; Hag 1:4

1:10 Deut 28:23, 24; 1 Kin 17:1; Joel 1:18-20

1:11 Jer 14:2-6; Mal 3:9, 11; Deut 28:22; Hag 2:17

1:12 Hag 1:1; Hag 1:14; 2:2; Is 1:19; 1 Thess 2:13; Deut 31:12, 13; Ps 112:1; Is 50:10

1:13 Is 44:26; Ezek 3:17; Mal 2:7; 3:1; Ps 46:11; Is 41:10; 43:2

1:14 Hag 1:1; 2:2, 21; Hag 1:12; Ezra 5:2; Neh 4:6

2. Encouragement to complete the temple

The Builders Encouraged

2 On the twenty-first of the seventh month, the word of the LORD came by Haggai the
prophet saying,
2 "Speak now to Zerubbabel the son of Shealtiel, governor of Judah, and to Joshua
the son of Jehozadak, the high priest, and to the remnant of the people saying,
3 'Who is left among you who saw this temple in its former glory? And how do you see
it now? Does it not seem to you like nothing in comparison?
4 'But now take courage, Zerubbabel,' declares the LORD, 'take courage also, Joshua
son of Jehozadak, the high priest, and all you people of the land take courage,' declares
the LORD, 'and work; for I am with you,' declares the LORD of hosts.

2:1 Hag 1:1

2:2 Hag 1:1; Hag 1:12

2:3 Ezra 3:12; Hag 2:9

2:4 Deut 31:23; 1 Chr 22:13; 28:20; Zech 8:9; Eph 6:10; 2 Sam 5:10; Acts 7:9

1:6 Because the people had not given God first place in their lives, their work was not fruitful or productive, and their material possessions did not satisfy. While they concentrated on building and beautifying their own homes, God's blessing was withheld because they no longer put him in first place. Moses had predicted that this would be the result if the people neglected God (Deuteronomy 28:38–45).

1:9 Judah's problem was confused priorities. Like Judah, our priorities involving occupation, family, and God's work are often confused. Jobs, homes, vacations, and leisure activities may rank higher on our list of importance than God. What is most important to you? Where is God on your list of priorities?

1:11 Grain, grapes for wine, and olives for oil were Israel's major crops. The people depended on these for security while neglecting the worship of God. As a result, God would send a drought to destroy their livelihood and call them back to himself.

1:14–15 The people began rebuilding the temple just 23 days after Haggai's first message. Rarely did a prophet's message produce such a quick response. How often we hear a sermon and respond, "That was an excellent point—I ought to do that," only to leave church and forget to act. These people put their words into action. When you hear a good sermon or lesson, ask what you should *do* about it, and then make plans to put it into practice.

2:1–9 This is Haggai's second message. It was given during the Feast of Booths in October, 520 B.C. The older people could remember the incredible beauty of Solomon's temple, destroyed 66 years earlier. Many were discouraged because the rebuilt temple was inferior to Solomon's. But Haggai encouraged them with God's message that the glory of this temple would surpass that of its predecessor. The most important part of the temple is God's presence. Some 500 years later, Jesus Christ would walk in the temple courts.

2:4 "Take courage . . . and work; for I am with you." Judah's people had returned to worshiping God, and God had promised to bless their efforts. But it was time for them to *work.* We must be people of prayer, Bible study, and worship—but eventually we must get out and *do* what God has in mind for us. He wants to change the world through us. God has given you a job to do in the church, at your place of employment, and at home. The time has come to be strong and work because God is with you!

2:5 Ex 19:4-6; 29:45, 46; 33:12-14; 34:8-10; Neh 9:20; Is 63:11, 14; Is 41:10, 13; Zech 8:13
2:6 Heb 12:26; Is 10:25
2:7 Dan 2:44; Joel 3:9, 16; Is 60:4-9; 1 Kin 8:11; Is 60:7
2:9 Zech 2:5; Hag 2:3; Is 9:6, 7; 66:12
2:11 Deut 17:8-11; Mal 2:7
2:12 Ex 29:37; Lev 6:27, 29; 7:6; Ezek 44:19; Matt 23:19
2:13 Lev 22:4-6; Num 19:22
2:14 Prov 15:8; Is 1:11-15
2:15 Hag 1:5, 7; 2:18; Ezra 3:10; 4:24
2:17 Deut 28:22; 1 Kin 8:37; Amos 4:9

5 'As for the promise which I made you when you came out of Egypt, My Spirit is abiding in your midst; do not fear!'
6 "For thus says the LORD of hosts, 'Once more in a little while, I am going to shake
the heavens and the earth, the sea also and the dry land.
7 'I will shake all the nations; and they will come with the wealth of all nations, and I
will fill this house with glory,' says the LORD of hosts.
8 'The silver is Mine and the gold is Mine,' declares the LORD of hosts.
9 'The latter glory of this house will be greater than the former,' says the LORD of hosts,
'and in this place I will give peace,' declares the LORD of hosts."
10 On the twenty-fourth of the ninth *month,* in the second year of Darius, the word of
the LORD came to Haggai the prophet, saying,
11 "Thus says the LORD of hosts, 'Ask now the priests *for* a ruling:
12 'If a man carries holy meat in the fold of his garment, and touches bread with this
fold, or cooked food, wine, oil, or any *other* food, will it become holy?' " And the priests
answered, "No."
13 Then Haggai said, "If one who is unclean from a corpse touches any of these, will
the latter become unclean?" And the priests answered, "It will become unclean."
14 Then Haggai said, " 'So is this people. And so is this nation before Me,' declares
the LORD, 'and so is every work of their hands; and what they offer there is unclean.
15 'But now, do consider from this day onward: before one stone was placed on another in the temple of the LORD,
16 from that time *when* one came to a *grain* heap of twenty *measures,* there would be
only ten; and *when* one came to the wine vat to draw fifty measures, there would be *only*
twenty.
17 'I smote you *and* every work of your hands with blasting wind, mildew and hail; yet
you *did* not *come back* to Me,' declares the LORD.

HAGGAI
Haggai served as a prophet to Judah about 520 B.C., after the return from exile.

Climate of the times	The people of Judah had been exiled to Babylon in 586 B.C., and Jerusalem and the temple had been destroyed. Under Cyrus king of Persia, the Jews were allowed to return to Judah and rebuild their temple.
Main message	The people returned to Jerusalem to begin rebuilding the temple, but they hadn't finished. Haggai's message encouraged the people to finish rebuilding God's temple.
Importance of message	The temple lay half-finished while the people lived in beautiful homes. Haggai warned them against putting their possessions and jobs ahead of God. We must put God first in our lives.
Contemporary prophet	Zechariah (520–480 B.C.)

2:5 The Israelites had been led from captivity in Egypt to their promised land. They were God's chosen people, guided and cared for by his Holy Spirit. Although God had punished them for their sins, he kept his promise and never left them (Exodus 29:45–46). No matter what difficulties we face or how frustrating our work may be, God's Spirit is with us.

2:6–9 The focus shifts from the local temple being rebuilt in Jerusalem to the worldwide reign of the Messiah on earth. The words "in a little while" are not limited to the immediate historical context; they refer to God's control of history—he can act any time he chooses. God will act *in his time* (see also Hebrews 12:26–27).

2:7 When God promised to shake all the nations with his judgment, he was speaking of both his present judgment on evil nations and future judgment during the last days.

2:7–9 The "latter glory of this house" has two possible meanings: (1) It could refer to the Messiah, Jesus, who, some 500 years later, would enter the temple and fill it with his glory and his peace (Luke 2:27, 32). (2) It could also refer to the riches that would flow into the temple, given as offerings to God's people.

2:8–9 God wanted the temple to be rebuilt, and he had the gold and silver to do it, but he needed willing hands. God has chosen to do his work through people. He provides the resources, but willing hands must do the work. Are your hands available for God's work in the world?

2:10–19 The example given in this message (delivered in December, 520 B.C.) makes it clear that holiness will not rub off on others, but contamination will. ("Holy meat" is meat made holy for the sacrifice.) As the people began to obey God, God promised to encourage and prosper them. But they needed to understand that activities in the temple would not clean up their sin; only repentance and obedience could do that. If we insist on harboring wrong attitudes and sins or on maintaining close relationships with sinful people, we will be defiled. Holy living will come only when we are empowered by God's Holy Spirit.

2:14 When a child eats spaghetti sauce, very soon his or her face, hands, and clothes become red. Sin and selfish attitudes produce the same result: They stain everything they touch. Even good deeds done for God can be tainted by sinful attitudes. The only remedy is God's cleansing.

2:16 A "heap" refers to a stack of grain at the harvest. For many years, the grain had only given 50 percent of the expected yield, and wine had done even worse.

18 'Do consider from this day onward, from the twenty-fourth day of the ninth *month;*
from the day when the temple of the LORD was founded, consider:
19 'Is the seed still in the barn? Even including the vine, the fig tree, the pomegranate
and the olive tree, it has not borne *fruit.* Yet from this day on I will bless *you.*' "
20 Then the word of the LORD came a second time to Haggai on the twenty-fourth *day*
of the month, saying,
21 "Speak to Zerubbabel governor of Judah, saying, 'I am going to shake the heavens
and the earth.
22 'I will overthrow the thrones of kingdoms and destroy the power of the kingdoms of
the nations; and I will overthrow the chariots and their riders, and the horses and their
riders will go down, everyone by the sword of another.'
23 'On that day,' declares the LORD of hosts, 'I will take you, Zerubbabel, son of Shealtiel, My servant,' declares the LORD, 'and I will make you like a signet *ring,* for I have
chosen you,' " declares the LORD of hosts.

2:18 Deut 32:29; Ezra 5:1, 2; Zech 8:9, 12

2:19 Ps 128:1-6; Jer 31:12, 14; Mal 3:10

2:21 Ezra 5:2; Hag 1:1; Zech 4:6-10; Hag 2:6; Heb 12:26, 27

2:22 Ezek 26:16; Zeph 3:8; Mic 7:16; Ps 46:9; Ezek 39:20; Mic 5:10; Amos 2:15; Judg 7:22; 2 Chr 20:23

2:23 Song 8:6; Jer 22:24; Is 42:1; 43:10

2:18–19 The people relaid the temple foundation, and immediately God blessed them. He did not wait for the project to be completed. God often sends his encouragement and approval with our first few obedient steps. He is eager to bless us!

2:20–23 Haggai's final message acknowledged that he was merely the messenger who brings the word of the Lord. It is addressed to Zerubbabel, the governor of Judah.

2:23 A signet ring was used to guarantee the authority and authenticity of a letter. It served as a signature when pressed in soft wax on a written document. God was reaffirming and guaranteeing his promise of a Messiah through David's line (Matthew 1:12).

2:23 God closed his message to Zerubbabel with this tremendous affirmation: "I have chosen you." Such a proclamation is ours as well—each of us has been chosen by God (Ephesians 1:4). This truth should make us see our value in God's eyes and motivate us to work for him. When you feel down, remind yourself, "God has chosen me!"

2:23 Haggai's message to the people sought to get their priorities straight, help them quit worrying, and motivate them to rebuild the temple. Like them, we often place a higher priority on our personal comfort than on God's work and true worship. But God is pleased and promises strength and guidance when we give him first place in our lives.

HOW GOD USED FOREIGN KINGS TO REBUILD THE TEMPLE
Despite the suffering of God's people in the exile, God's promises of restoration would come true. Under the rule of the seemingly invincible Babylonians, the rebuilding of the temple and the city of Jerusalem appeared impossible. God's people had little hope. Through the decrees of these pagan kings, God fulfilled his promises of restoration.

King	*Date (B.C.)*	*Event*	*Reference*
Cyrus the Great	539-530	Persia conquers Babylon. Jewish captives are allowed to return under Zerubbabel.	Daniel 5; Ezra 1—6
Smerdis	522-520	When political leaders send letters objecting to the work on the temple, he stops the work.	Ezra 4:1-23
Darius	520-486	Darius allows the work on the temple to continue. Haggai and Zechariah deliver their messages to continue rebuilding the temple.	Ezra 4:24; 6:1-22 Haggai 1:1—2:23; Zechariah 1:1—8:23
Ahasuerus (Xerxes)	486-465	He makes Esther his queen. The Jews are protected from their enemies.	Esther 1:1—10:3
Artaxerxes	465-424	He allows Ezra to return with a large group of Jewish exiles. Nehemiah is allowed to take a leave of absence as his royal cupbearer to rebuild the walls of Jerusalem.	Ezra 7:1—10:44 Nehemiah 1:1—13:31

ZECHARIAH

Daniel taken to Babylon 605 B.C. | *Ezekiel taken to Babylon 597* | *Jerusalem falls 586* | *Babylon overthrown by Cyrus 539* | *Cyrus's decree allowing the exiles to return 538*

VITAL STATISTICS

PURPOSE:
To give hope to God's people by revealing God's future deliverance through the Messiah

AUTHOR:
Zechariah

TO WHOM WRITTEN:
The Jews in Jerusalem who had returned from their captivity in Babylon and to God's people everywhere

DATE WRITTEN:
Chapters 1—8 were written approximately 520–518 B.C. Chapters 9—14 were written around 480 B.C.

SETTING:
The exiles had returned from Babylon to rebuild the temple, but the work had been thwarted and stalled. Haggai and Zechariah confronted the people with their task and encouraged them to complete it.

KEY VERSES:
"Rejoice greatly, O daughter of Zion! Shout in triumph, O daughter of Jerusalem! Behold, your king is coming to you; He is just and endowed with salvation, humble, and mounted on a donkey, even on a colt . . . He will speak peace to the nations; and His dominion will be from sea to sea and from the River to the ends of the earth" (9:9–10).

KEY PEOPLE:
Zerubbabel, Joshua

KEY PLACE:
Jerusalem

SPECIAL FEATURES:
This book is the most apocalyptic and messianic of all the minor prophets.

THE FUTURE—that vast uncharted sea of the unknown, holding joy or terror, comfort or pain, love or loneliness. Some people fear the days to come, wondering what evils lurk in the shadows; others consult seers and future-telling charlatans, trying desperately to discover its secrets. But tomorrow's story is known only to God and to those special messengers called prophets, to whom God has revealed a chapter or two.

A prophet's primary task was to proclaim the word of the Lord, pointing out sin, explaining its consequences, and calling men and women to repentance and obedience. Elijah, Elisha, Isaiah, Jeremiah, Ezekiel, Hosea, and Amos stand with scores of others who faithfully delivered God's message despite rejection, ridicule, and persecution. And at times they were given prophetic visions foretelling coming events.

Nestled near the end of the Old Testament, among what are known as "minor prophets," is the book of Zechariah. As one of three postexilic prophets, along with Haggai and Malachi, Zechariah ministered to the small remnant of Jews who had returned to Judah to rebuild the temple and their nation. Like Haggai, he encouraged the people to finish rebuilding the temple, but his message went far beyond those physical walls and contemporary issues. With spectacular apocalyptic imagery and graphic detail, Zechariah told of the Messiah, the one whom God would send to rescue his people and to reign over all the earth. Zechariah is one of our most important prophetic books, giving detailed messianic references that were clearly fulfilled in the life of Jesus Christ. The rebuilding of the temple, he says, was just the first act in the drama of the end and the ushering in of the messianic age. Zechariah proclaimed a stirring message of hope to these ex-captives and exiles—their King was coming!

Jesus is Messiah, the promised "great deliverer" of Israel. Unlike Zechariah's listeners, we can look back at Christ's ministry and mission. As you study Zechariah's prophecy, you will see details of Christ's life that were written 500 years before their fulfillment. Read and stand in awe of our God, who keeps his promises. But there is also a future message that has not yet been fulfilled—the return of Christ at the end of the age. As you read Zechariah, think through the implications of this promised event. *Your King is coming,* and he will reign forever and ever.

God knows and controls the future. We may never see more than a moment ahead, but we can be secure if we trust in him. Read Zechariah and strengthen your faith in God—he alone is your hope and security.

Temple construction begins 536	Temple work halted 530	Haggai, Zechariah become prophets; temple work resumed 520	Temple completed 515	Ezra comes to Jerusalem 458	Nehemiah comes to Jerusalem 445

THE BLUEPRINT

A. MESSAGES WHILE REBUILDING THE TEMPLE (1:1—8:23)
1. Zechariah's night visions
2. Zechariah's words of encouragement

Zechariah encouraged the people to put away the sin in their lives and to continue rebuilding the temple. His visions described the judgment of Israel's enemies, the blessings to Jerusalem, and the need for God's people to remain pure—avoiding hypocrisy, superficiality, and sin. Zechariah's visions provided hope for the people. We also need to carefully follow the instruction to remain pure until Christ returns.

B. MESSAGES AFTER COMPLETING THE TEMPLE (9:1—14:21)

Besides encouragement and hope, Zechariah's messages were also a warning that God's messianic kingdom would not begin as soon as the temple was complete. Israel's enemies would be judged and the King would come, but God's people would themselves face many difficult circumstances before experiencing the blessing of the messianic kingdom. We, too, may face much sorrow, disappointment, and distress before coming into Christ's eternal kingdom.

MEGATHEMES

THEME	EXPLANATION	IMPORTANCE
God's Jealousy	God was angry at his people for ignoring his prophets through the years, and he was concerned that they not follow the careless and false leaders who exploited them. Disobedience was the root of their problems and the cause of their misery. God was jealous for their devotion to him.	God is jealous for our devotion. To avoid Israel's ruin, don't walk in their steps. Don't reject God, follow false teachers, or lead others astray. Turn to God, faithfully obey his commands, and make sure you are leading others correctly.
Rebuild the Temple	The Jews were discouraged. They were free from exile, yet the temple was not completed. Zechariah encouraged them to rebuild it. God would both protect his workmen and empower them by his Holy Spirit to carry out his work.	More than the rebuilding of the temple was at stake—the people were staging the first act in God's wonderful drama of the end times. Those of us who love God must complete his work. To do so we must have the Holy Spirit's help. God will empower us with his Spirit.
The King Is Coming	The Messiah will come both to rescue people from sin and to reign as king. He will establish his kingdom, conquer all his enemies, and rule over all the earth. Everything will one day be under his loving and powerful control.	The Messiah came as a servant to die for us. He will return as a victorious king. At that time, he will usher in peace throughout the world. Submit to his leadership now to be ready for the King's triumphant return.
God's Protection	There was opposition to God's plan in Zechariah's day, and he prophesied future times of trouble. But God's Word endures. God remembers the agreements he makes with his people. He cares for his people and will deliver them from all the world powers that oppress them.	Although evil is still present, God's infinite love and personal care have been demonstrated through the centuries. God keeps his promises. Although our bodies may be destroyed, we need never fear our ultimate destiny if we love and obey him.

A. MESSAGES WHILE REBUILDING THE TEMPLE (1:1—8:23)

Zechariah begins by describing eight visions that came to him at night. Then he gives a collection of messages about the crowning of Joshua, answers to questions of feasting and fasting, and encouragement to continue rebuilding the temple. We, too, can be inspired to continue following God in faithfulness throughout our lives.

1. Zechariah's night visions

A Call to Repentance

1 In the eighth month of the second year of Darius, the word of the LORD came to
Zechariah the prophet, the son of Berechiah, the son of Iddo saying,
2 "The LORD was very angry with your fathers.
3 "Therefore say to them, 'Thus says the LORD of hosts, "Return to Me," declares the
LORD of hosts, "that I may return to you," says the LORD of hosts.
4 "Do not be like your fathers, to whom the former prophets proclaimed, saying, 'Thus
says the LORD of hosts, "Return now from your evil ways and from your evil deeds." '
But they did not listen or give heed to Me," declares the LORD.
5 "Your fathers, where are they? And the prophets, do they live forever?
6 "But did not My words and My statutes, which I commanded My servants the prophets, overtake your fathers? Then they repented and said, 'As the LORD of hosts purposed
to do to us in accordance with our ways and our deeds, so He has dealt with us.' " ' "

Patrol of the Earth

7 On the twenty-fourth day of the eleventh month, which is the month Shebat, in the
second year of Darius, the word of the LORD came to Zechariah the prophet, the son of
Berechiah, the son of Iddo, as follows:
8 I saw at night, and behold, a man was riding on a red horse, and he was standing
among the myrtle trees which were in the ravine, with red, sorrel and white horses behind him.
9 Then I said, "My lord, what are these?" And the angel who was speaking with me
said to me, "I will show you what these are."
10 And the man who was standing among the myrtle trees answered and said, "These
are those whom the LORD has sent to patrol the earth."
11 So they answered the angel of the LORD who was standing among the myrtle trees
and said, "We have patrolled the earth, and behold, all the earth is peaceful and quiet."
12 Then the angel of the LORD said, "O LORD of hosts, how long will You have no
compassion for Jerusalem and the cities of Judah, with which You have been indignant
these seventy years?"
13 The LORD answered the angel who was speaking with me with gracious words, comforting words.

1:1 Ezra 4:24; 6:15; Hag 1:15; 2:10; Zech 1:7; 7:1; Ezra 5:1; 6:14; Zech 7:1; Matt 23:35; Luke 11:51; Neh 12:4, 16

1:2 2 Chr 36:16; Jer 44:6; Ezek 8:18; Zech 1:15

1:3 Is 31:6; 44:22; Mal 3:7

1:4 Ps 78:8; 106:6, 7; 2 Chr 24:19; 36:15; Is 1:16-19; Jer 4:1; Ezek 33:11; Jer 6:17; 11:7, 8

1:5 Lam 5:7; John 8:52

1:6 Jer 12:16, 17; 44:28, 29; Amos 9:10; Lam 2:17

1:8 Zech 6:2; Rev 6:4; Neh 8:15; Is 41:19; 55:13; Zech 1:10, 11; Zech 6:3; Rev 6:2

1:9 Zech 1:19; 4:4, 5, 13; 6:4; Zech 2:3; 5:5

1:10 Job 1:7; Zech 1:11; 4:10; 6:5-8

1:11 Zech 1:8, 10; Is 14:7

1:12 Ps 74:10; Jer 12:4; Hab 1:2; Ps 102:13; Jer 30:18; Ps 102:10; Jer 15:17; Jer 25:11; 29:10; Dan 9:2; Zech 7:5

1:13 Zech 1:9; 4:1; Is 40:1, 2; 57:18

1:1 Born in Babylon during the exile, Zechariah was a fairly young man when he returned to Jerusalem in 538 B.C. King Cyrus of Persia had defeated Babylon in 539 and had decreed that captives in exile could return to their homelands. Zechariah and Haggai were among the first to leave. Zechariah, a prophet and a priest, began ministering at the same time as the prophet Haggai (520–518 B.C.). His first prophecy was delivered two months after Haggai's first prophecy.

Like Haggai, Zechariah encouraged the people to continue rebuilding the temple, whose reconstruction had been halted for nearly 15 years. Zechariah combated the people's spiritual apathy, despair over pressures from their enemies, and discouragement about the smaller scale of the new temple foundation. Neglect of our spiritual priorities can be just as devastating today to fulfilling God's purpose.

1:2–6 The familiar phrase "Like father, like son," implies that children turn out like their parents. But here, God warned Israel *not* to be like their forefathers, who disobeyed him and reaped the consequences—his punishment. We are responsible before God for our actions. We aren't trapped by our heredity or environment, and we can't use these as excuses for our sins. We are free to choose, and individually we must return to God and follow him.

1:5–6 The words God had spoken through his prophets a century earlier, before the captivity, also applied to Zechariah's generation, and they are still relevant for us. Because God's Word endures, we must read, study, and apply what is preserved for us in Scripture. Learn the lessons of God's Word so you will not have to repeat the mistakes of others.

1:7–17 The man among the myrtle trees was the angel of the Lord (1:11). The horses and their colors were symbols of God's involvement in world governments. The full meaning of the colors is unknown, although the red horse is often associated with war and the white horse with final victory.

1:11 The angel of the Lord saw that all the nations were secure and at peace while Israel was still oppressed and despised. But God was planning a change. He had released his people, and he would allow them to return and rebuild his temple.

1:12 Seventy years was the time that God had decreed for Israel to remain in captivity (Jeremiah 25:11; 29:10). This time was over, and the angel asked God to act swiftly to complete the promised return of his people to Jerusalem.

1:13 God's people had lived under his judgment for 70 years during their captivity in Babylon. But here God spoke words of comfort and assurance. God promises that when we return to him, he will heal us (Hosea 6:1). If you feel wounded and torn by the events of your life, turn to God so he can heal and comfort you.

14 So the angel who was speaking with me said to me, "Proclaim, saying, 'Thus says
the LORD of hosts, "I am exceedingly jealous for Jerusalem and Zion.
15 "But I am very angry with the nations who are at ease; for while I was only a little
angry, they furthered the disaster."
16 'Therefore thus says the LORD, "I will return to Jerusalem with compassion; My house
will be built in it," declares the LORD of hosts, "and a measuring line will be stretched
over Jerusalem." '
17 "Again, proclaim, saying, 'Thus says the LORD of hosts, "My cities will again overflow with prosperity, and the LORD will again comfort Zion and again choose Jerusalem." ' "
18 Then I lifted up my eyes and looked, and behold, *there were* four horns.
19 So I said to the angel who was speaking with me, "What are these?" And he answered me, "These are the horns which have scattered Judah, Israel and Jerusalem."
20 Then the LORD showed me four craftsmen.
21 I said, "What are these coming to do?" And he said, "These are the horns which
have scattered Judah so that no man lifts up his head; but these *craftsmen* have come to
terrify them, to throw down the horns of the nations who have lifted up *their* horns against
the land of Judah in order to scatter it."

God's Favor to Zion

2 Then I lifted up my eyes and looked, and behold, *there was* a man with a measuring
line in his hand.
2 So I said, "Where are you going?" And he said to me, "To measure Jerusalem, to
see how wide it is and how long it is."
3 And behold, the angel who was speaking with me was going out, and another angel
was coming out to meet him,
4 and said to him, "Run, speak to that young man, saying, 'Jerusalem will be inhabited without walls because of the multitude of men and cattle within it.
5 'For I,' declares the LORD, 'will be a wall of fire around her, and I will be the glory in
her midst.' "
6 "Ho there! Flee from the land of the north," declares the LORD, "for I have dispersed
you as the four winds of the heavens," declares the LORD.
7 "Ho, Zion! Escape, you who are living with the daughter of Babylon."
8 For thus says the LORD of hosts, "After glory He has sent me against the nations
which plunder you, for he who touches you, touches the apple of His eye.

1:14 Is 40:2, 6
1:15 Zech 1:2; Ps 123:4; Jer 48:11; Amos 1:11
1:16 Is 54:8-10; Zech 2:10, 11; Ezra 6:14, 15; Zech 4:9; Jer 31:39; Zech 2:2, 4
1:17 Is 44:26; 61:4; Is 51:3; Zech 2:12
1:19 1 Kin 22:11; Ps 75:4, 5; Amos 6:13
1:20 Is 44:12; 54:16
1:21 Zech 1:19; Ps 75:10
2:1 Jer 31:39; Ezek 40:3; 47:3
2:2 Jer 31:39; Ezek 40:3; Rev 21:15-17
2:4 Jer 1:6; Dan 1:4; 1 Tim 4:12; Zech 1:17; 8:4; Ezek 38:11; Is 49:20; Jer 30:19; 33:22
2:5 Is 4:5; 26:1; 60:18; Hag 2:9; Zech 2:10
2:6 Jer 3:18; Jer 31:10
2:7 Is 48:20; Jer 51:6
2:8 Is 60:7-9; Deut 32:10; Ps 17:8

ZECHARIAH
Zechariah served as a prophet to Judah about 520 B.C., after the return from exile.

Climate of the times	The exiles had returned from captivity to rebuild their temple. But work on the temple had stalled and the people were ignoring their service to God.
Main message	Zechariah, like Haggai, encouraged the people to finish rebuilding the temple. His visions gave the people hope. He told the people of a future king who would one day establish an eternal kingdom.
Importance of message	Even in times of discouragement and despair, God is working out his plan. God protects and guides us; we must trust and follow him.
Contemporary prophet	Haggai (approximately 520 B.C.)

1:15 Although the pagan nations afflicted God's people beyond his intentions, God was not powerless to stop them. God used these nations to punish his sinful people. When the nations went beyond his plans by trying to destroy Israel as a nation, he intervened.

1:18–21 The horns were the four world powers that oppressed Israel—Egypt, Assyria, Babylon, and Medo-Persia. The four craftsmen (1:20) were the nations used to overthrow Israel's enemies. God raised them up to judge the oppressors of his people.

2:1 The man with the measuring line symbolizes the hope of a rebuilt Jerusalem and a restored people. The man would be measuring to mark out the boundaries for a foundation (see 1:16; and Jeremiah 31:38–40).

2:6–7 Many of the captive Israelites did not return to Jerusalem because they preferred to stay with the security and wealth they had experienced in Babylon. But Zechariah instructed them to leave Babylon quickly. This was an urgent request because Babylon would be destroyed and because its decadent culture would cause God's people to forget their spiritual priorities. A vast majority of the Israelites rejected these warnings and remained in Babylon.

2:8 Believers are precious to God (Psalm 116:15); they are his very own children (Psalm 103:13). Treating any believer unkindly is the same as treating God that way. As Jesus told his disciples, when we help others we are helping him; when we neglect or abuse them, we are neglecting or abusing him (Matthew 25:34–46). Be careful, therefore, how you treat fellow believers—that is the way you are treating God.

9 "For behold, I will wave My hand over them so that they will be plunder for their
slaves. Then you will know that the LORD of hosts has sent Me.
10 "Sing for joy and be glad, O daughter of Zion; for behold I am coming and I will
dwell in your midst," declares the LORD.
11 "Many nations will join themselves to the LORD in that day and will become My
people. Then I will dwell in your midst, and you will know that the LORD of hosts has
sent Me to you.
12 "The LORD will possess Judah as His portion in the holy land, and will again choose
Jerusalem.
13 "Be silent, all flesh, before the LORD; for He is aroused from His holy habitation."

Joshua, the High Priest

3 Then he showed me Joshua the high priest standing before the angel of the LORD,
and Satan standing at his right hand to accuse him.
2 The LORD said to Satan, "The LORD rebuke you, Satan! Indeed, the LORD who has
chosen Jerusalem rebuke you! Is this not a brand plucked from the fire?"
3 Now Joshua was clothed with filthy garments and standing before the angel.
4 He spoke and said to those who were standing before him, saying, "Remove the
filthy garments from him." Again he said to him, "See, I have taken your iniquity away
from you and will clothe you with festal robes."
5 Then I said, "Let them put a clean turban on his head." So they put a clean turban
on his head and clothed him with garments, while the angel of the LORD was standing
by.
6 And the angel of the LORD admonished Joshua, saying,
7 "Thus says the LORD of hosts, 'If you will walk in My ways and if you will perform
My service, then you will also govern My house and also have charge of My courts, and
I will grant you free access among these who are standing *here*.

The Branch

8 'Now listen, Joshua the high priest, you and your friends who are sitting in front of
you—indeed they are men who are a symbol, for behold, I am going to bring in My servant the Branch.

2:9 Is 19:16; Is 14:2
2:10 Is 65:18, 19
2:11 Mic 4:2; Zech 2:5
2:12 Deut 32:9; Ps 33:12; Jer 10:16; 2 Chr 6:6; Ps 132:13, 14; Zech 1:17
2:13 Hab 2:20; Zeph 1:7; Ps 78:65; Is 51:9
3:1 Job 1:6; Ps 109:6; Rev 12:10
3:2 Mark 9:25; Jude 9; Zech 2:12; Amos 4:11; Jude 23
3:3 Ezra 9:15; Is 4:4; 64:6
3:4 Is 43:25; Ezek 36:25; Mic 7:18, 19; Is 52:1; 61:10
3:5 Job 29:14; Is 3:23
3:7 1 Kin 3:14; Deut 17:9, 12; Is 62:9
3:8 Is 8:18; 20:3; Ezek 12:11; Is 11:1; 53:2; Jer 23:5; 33:15; Zech 6:12

2:9–12 *Me* (2:9) may refer to the Messiah who, in the end, will judge all who have oppressed God's people. God promises to live among his people, and he says that many nations will come to know him (John 1:14; Revelation 21:3).

2:11–12 God did not forget his words to Abraham, "In you all the families of the earth will be blessed" (Genesis 12:3). Abraham, the father of the nation of Israel, was promised that his descendants would bless the whole world. Since the coming of Jesus, the Messiah, this promise is being fulfilled—people from all nations are coming to God through him.

3:1 Joshua was Israel's high priest when the remnant returned to Jerusalem and began rebuilding the walls (Haggai 1:1, 12; 2:4).

3:1–3 Satan accused Joshua, who here represents the nation of Israel. The accusations were accurate—Joshua stood in "filthy garments" (sins). Yet God revealed his mercy, stating that he chose to save his people in spite of their sin. Satan is always accusing people of their sins before God (Job 1:6). But he greatly misunderstands the breadth of God's mercy and forgiveness toward those who believe in him. Satan the accuser will ultimately be destroyed (Revelation 12:10), while everyone who is a believer will be saved (John 3:16). To be prepared, we can ask God to remove our clothing of sin and dress us with his goodness.

3:2 God punished Judah through the fire of great trials, but he rescued the nation before it was completely destroyed, like "a brand plucked from the fire."

3:2–4 Zechariah's vision graphically portrays how we receive God's mercy. We do nothing ourselves. God removes our filthy clothes (sins), then provides us with new, clean, rich garments (the righteousness and holiness of God—2 Corinthians 5:21; Ephesians 4:24; Revelation 19:8). All we need to do is repent and ask God to forgive us. When Satan tries to make you feel dirty and unworthy, remember that the clean clothes of Christ's righteousness make you worthy to draw near to God.

3:5–7 The Greek name for Joshua is Jesus, meaning "the LORD saves." This Joshua should not be confused with the warrior of the book of Joshua. Both the warrior Joshua and the high priest Joshua, however, have been seen as symbols of Jesus, the Messiah.

3:7–10 There was no priesthood during the exile, so it had to be reinstated upon the return to the land. In this vision, Joshua is installed as high priest. One of the high priest's duties was to offer a sacrifice on the day of atonement to make amends for all the sins of the people. The priest was the mediator between God and the nation. Thus, he represented the coming Messiah (Isaiah 11:1), who would change the entire order of God's dealing with people's sin (Hebrews 10:8–14 explains this in detail). Jesus, the Messiah, was the high priest who offered, once for all, the sacrifice of himself to take away our sins. In the new order, every Christian is a priest offering a holy, cleansed life to God (1 Peter 2:9; Revelation 5:10).

3:8–9 The "Branch" refers to the Messiah. The meaning of the stone with seven eyes is unclear. It could mean (1) the Branch himself as the foundation stone of the temple, (2) the rock struck by Moses that produced water for the Israelites (Numbers 20:7–11), or (3) the renewed spiritual priesthood of the church (1 Peter 2:5). These verses were fulfilled hundreds of years later by Jesus Christ. God said, "I will remove the iniquity of that land in one day," and this was fulfilled in Christ who "died for sins once for all, the just for the unjust, so that He might bring us to God" (1 Peter 3:18). You cannot remove your sins by your own effort. You must allow God to remove them through Christ.

ZECHARIAH'S VISIONS

Vision	Reference	Significance
Zechariah sees messengers reporting to God that the surrounding nations that have oppressed Judah are living in careless and sinful ease.	1:7–17	Israel was asking, "Why isn't God punishing the wicked?" Wicked nations may prosper, but not forever. God will bring upon them the judgment they deserve.
Zechariah sees four horns, representing the four world powers that oppressed and scattered the people of Judah and Israel. Then he sees four craftsmen who will throw down the horns.	1:18–21	God will do what he promised. After the evil nations have carried out his will in punishing his people, God will destroy those nations for their sin.
Zechariah sees a man measuring the city of Jerusalem. The city will one day be full of people, and God himself will be a wall around the city.	2:1–13	The city will be restored in God's future kingdom. God will keep his promise to protect his people.
Zechariah sees Joshua the high priest standing before God. Joshua's filthy clothes are exchanged for clean garments; Satan's accusations against him are rejected by God.	3:1–10	The story of Joshua the high priest pictures how the filthy clothes of sin are replaced with the pure linen of God's righteousness. Christ has taken our clothes of sin and replaced them with God's righteousness. (See Ephesians 4:24; 1 John 1:9.)
Zechariah sees a lampstand that is continually kept burning by an unlimited reservoir of oil. This picture reminds the people that it is only through God's Spirit that they will succeed, not by their own might and resources.	4:1–14	The Spirit of God is given without measure. Human effort does not make a difference. The work of God is not accomplished in human strength.
Zechariah sees a flying scroll, which represents God's curse.	5:1–4	By God's Word and spirit every person will be judged. The individual's sin is the focus here, not the sins of the nation. Each person is responsible for his or her deeds; no one has an excuse. God's curse is a symbol of destruction; all sin will be judged and removed.
Zechariah sees a vision of a woman in an ephah (a basket). She represents the wickedness of the nations. The angel packed the woman back into the basket and sent her back to Babylon.	5:5–11	Sins of the individual were judged in the last vision (5:1–4); now sin is being removed from society. Sin has to be eradicated in order to clean up the nation and the individual.
Zechariah sees a vision of four horses and chariots. The horses represent God's judgment on the world—one is sent north, the direction from which most of Judah's enemies came. The other horses are patrolling the world, ready to execute judgment at God's command.	6:1–8	Judgment will come upon those who oppress God's people—it will come in God's time and at his command.

9 'For behold, the stone that I have set before Joshua; on one stone are seven eyes.
Behold, I will engrave an inscription on it,' declares the LORD of hosts, 'and I will remove the iniquity of that land in one day.
10 'In that day,' declares the LORD of hosts, 'every one of you will invite his neighbor to
sit under *his* vine and under *his* fig tree.' "

The Golden Lampstand and Olive Trees

4 Then the angel who was speaking with me returned and roused me, as a man who is
awakened from his sleep.
2 He said to me, "What do you see?" And I said, "I see, and behold, a lampstand all
of gold with its bowl on the top of it, and its seven lamps on it with seven spouts belonging to each of the lamps which are on the top of it;
3 also two olive trees by it, one on the right side of the bowl and the other on its left
side."
4 Then I said to the angel who was speaking with me saying, "What are these, my lord?"
5 So the angel who was speaking with me answered and said to me, "Do you not know
what these are?" And I said, "No, my lord."
6 Then he said to me, "This is the word of the LORD to Zerubbabel saying, 'Not by
might nor by power, but by My Spirit,' says the LORD of hosts.
7 'What are you, O great mountain? Before Zerubbabel *you will become* a plain; and
he will bring forth the top stone with shouts of "Grace, grace to it!" ' "
8 Also the word of the LORD came to me, saying,
9 "The hands of Zerubbabel have laid the foundation of this house, and his hands will
finish *it.* Then you will know that the LORD of hosts has sent me to you.
10 "For who has despised the day of small things? But these seven will be glad when
they see the plumb line in the hand of Zerubbabel—*these are* the eyes of the LORD which
range to and fro throughout the earth."
11 Then I said to him, "What are these two olive trees on the right of the lampstand
and on its left?"
12 And I answered the second time and said to him, "What are the two olive branches
which are beside the two golden pipes, which empty the golden *oil* from themselves?"
13 So he answered me, saying, "Do you not know what these are?" And I said, "No,
my lord."
14 Then he said, "These are the two anointed ones who are standing by the Lord of
the whole earth."

The Flying Scroll

5 Then I lifted up my eyes again and looked, and behold, *there was* a flying scroll.
2 And he said to me, "What do you see?" And I answered, "I see a flying scroll; its
length is twenty cubits and its width ten cubits."

3:9 Zech 4:10; Jer 31:34; 50:20; Zech 3:4
3:10 1 Kin 4:25; Is 36:16; Mic 4:4
4:1 Zech 1:9; 1 Kin 19:5-7; Jer 31:26
4:2 Jer 1:13; Zech 5:2; Ex 25:31, 37; Jer 52:19; Rev 4:5
4:3 Zech 4:11; Rev 11:4
4:6 Ezra 5:2; Hag 2:4, 5; Is 11:2-4; 30:1; Hos 1:7; 2 Chr 32:7, 8; Eph 6:17
4:7 Ps 114:4, 6; Is 40:4; Jer 51:25; Nah 1:5; Zech 14:4, 5; Ezra 3:10, 11; Ps 84:11
4:9 Ezra 3:8-10; 5:16; Hag 2:18; Ezra 6:14, 15; Zech 6:12, 13
4:10 Neh 4:2-4; Amos 7:2, 5; Hag 2:3; Zech 3:9; Rev 8:2; Amos 7:7, 8; 2 Chr 16:9; Prov 15:3; Jer 16:17; Zech 1:10; Rev 5:6
4:11 Zech 4:3; Rev 11:4
4:14 Ex 29:7; 40:15; 1 Sam 16:1, 12, 13; Is 61:1-3; Dan 9:24-26; Zech 3:1-7; Mic 4:13
5:1 Jer 36:2; Ezek 2:9; Rev 5:1

3:10 God promises that each person will have his or her own place of security during Christ's reign (see also Micah 4:4). Sitting under the vine and fig tree was a symbol of peace and prosperity.

4:1 The gold lampstand with a bowl and seven lights on it represents a steady supply of oil, signifying that God's power would be reflected in the light. Oil was obtained from crushed olives and used in bowls with wicks to produce light. The two olive trees stood for the priestly and royal offices.

4:6 Zerubbabel was given the responsibility of rebuilding the temple in Jerusalem (Ezra 3:2, 8; Haggai 1:1; 2:23). While the prophets Haggai and Zechariah gave the moral and spiritual encouragement to resume work on the temple, Zerubbabel saw that the task was carried out. As the work was being completed, the prophets encouraged Zerubbabel and told him of a time when spiritual apathy and foreign oppression would forever be abolished.

4:6 Many people believe that to survive in this world a person must be tough, strong, unbending, and harsh. But God says, "Not by might nor by power, but by My Spirit." The key words are "by My Spirit." It is *only* through God's Spirit that anything of lasting value is accomplished. The returned exiles were indeed weak—harassed by their enemies, tired, discouraged, and poor. But actually they had God on their side! As you live for God, determine not to trust in your own strength or abilities. Instead, depend on God and work in the power of his Spirit! (See also Hosea 1:7.)

4:9 The temple was completed in 516 B.C. (Ezra 6:14–15).

4:10 Many of the older Jews were disheartened when they realized this new temple would not match the size and splendor of the previous temple built during King Solomon's reign. But bigger and more beautiful is not always better. What you do for God may seem small and insignificant at the time, but God rejoices in what is right, not necessarily in what is big. Be faithful in the small opportunities. Begin where you are and do what you can, and leave the results to God.

4:14 The two anointed ones may be Joshua and Zerubbabel, dedicated for this special task. Also note that in Revelation 11:3, two witnesses arise to prophesy to the nations during the time of tribulation. These witnesses will be killed but will rise again.

5:1–9 The judgment of the flying scroll was leveled against those who violated God's law, specifically by stealing and lying (5:1–4). The woman sitting in the ephah (basket) personified wickedness,

3 Then he said to me, "This is the curse that is going forth over the face of the whole
land; surely everyone who steals will be purged away according to the writing on one
side, and everyone who swears will be purged away according to the writing on the other
side.
4 "I will make it go forth," declares the LORD of hosts, "and it will enter the house of
the thief and the house of the one who swears falsely by My name; and it will spend the
night within that house and consume it with its timber and stones."
5 Then the angel who was speaking with me went out and said to me, "Lift up now
your eyes and see what this is going forth."
6 I said, "What is it?" And he said, "This is the ephah going forth." Again he said,
"This is their appearance in all the land
7 (and behold, a lead cover was lifted up); and this is a woman sitting inside the ephah."
8 Then he said, "This is Wickedness!" And he threw her down into the middle of the
ephah and cast the lead weight on its opening.
9 Then I lifted up my eyes and looked, and there two women were coming out with
the wind in their wings; and they had wings like the wings of a stork, and they lifted up
the ephah between the earth and the heavens.
10 I said to the angel who was speaking with me, "Where are they taking the ephah?"
11 Then he said to me, "To build a temple for her in the land of Shinar; and when it is
prepared, she will be set there on her own pedestal."

The Four Chariots

6 Now I lifted up my eyes again and looked, and behold, four chariots were coming
forth from between the two mountains; and the mountains *were* bronze mountains.
2 With the first chariot *were* red horses, with the second chariot black horses,
3 with the third chariot white horses, and with the fourth chariot strong dappled horses.
4 Then I spoke and said to the angel who was speaking with me, "What are these, my
lord?"
5 The angel replied to me, "These are the four spirits of heaven, going forth after
standing before the Lord of all the earth,
6 with one of which the black horses are going forth to the north country; and the
white ones go forth after them, while the dappled ones go forth to the south country.
7 "When the strong ones went out, they were eager to go to patrol the earth." And He
said, "Go, patrol the earth." So they patrolled the earth.
8 Then He cried out to me and spoke to me saying, "See, those who are going to the
land of the north have appeased My wrath in the land of the north."

2. Zechariah's words of encouragement

9 The word of the LORD also came to me, saying,
10 "Take *an offering* from the exiles, from Heldai, Tobijah and Jedaiah; and you go the
same day and enter the house of Josiah the son of Zephaniah, where they have arrived
from Babylon.

5:3 Is 24:6; 43:28; Jer 26:6; Ex 20:15; Lev 19:11; Mal 3:8, 9; Lev 19:12; Is 48:1; Jer 5:2; Zech 5:4
5:4 Mal 3:5; Hos 4:2, 3; Jer 2:26; Lev 14:34, 35; Job 18:15
5:5 Zech 1:9
5:6 Lev 19:36; Amos 8:5
5:8 Hos 12:7; Amos 8:5; Mic 6:11
5:9 Lev 11:13, 19; Ps 104:17; Jer 8:7
5:11 Gen 10:10; 11:2; 14:1; Is 11:11; Dan 1:2
6:1 Dan 7:3; 8:22; Zech 1:18; 6:5
6:2 Zech 1:8; Rev 6:4; Rev 6:5
6:3 Rev 6:2; Rev 6:8
6:4 Zech 1:9
6:5 Jer 49:36; Ezek 37:9; Dan 7:2; 11:4; Matt 24:31; Rev 7:1
6:6 Jer 1:14, 15; 4:6; 6:1; 25:9; 46:10; Ezek 1:4; Is 43:6; Dan 11:5
6:7 Zech 1:10
6:8 Ezek 5:13; 24:13; Zech 1:15
6:9 Zech 1:1; 7:1; 8:1
6:10 Ezra 7:14-16; 8:26-30; Jer 28:6

---

and so this vision showed that wickedness would be not only severely punished (the vision of the flying scroll), but also banished (the vision of the woman in a basket, 5:6–9).

5:9–11 The woman in the ephah (basket) was carried away to "the land of Shinar" (Babylon), which had become a symbol for the center of world idolatry and wickedness. This woman was a picture to Zechariah that wickedness and sin would be taken away from Israel, and one day sin would be removed from the entire earth. When Christ died, he removed sin's power and penalty. When we trust Christ to forgive us, he removes the penalty of sin and gives us the power to overcome sin in our lives. When Christ returns, he will remove all sin from the earth, allowing people to live in eternal safety and security.

6:1–8 The four chariots were similar to the four horsemen in the first vision. These chariots represent the four angels of God's judgment on the earth.

6:8 The black horse that went north executed God's judgment in the north country. God is angry with sin and with the wicked (Psalm 7:11), and his anger is expressed in judgment. As much as we like to concentrate on God's love and mercy, anger and judgment are also part of his righteous character. If you have unconfessed or habitual sin in your life, confess it and turn away from it. Confession releases God's mercy, but refusing to repent invites his judgment.

6:9–15 This vision is about the Messiah, the King-Priest. In the days of the kings and after the exile, Judah's government was to be ruled by two distinct persons—the king, ruling the nation's political life, and the high priest, ruling its religious life. Kings and priests had often been corrupt. God was telling Zechariah that someone worthy of the crown would come to rule as both king ("rule on His throne") and priest ("a priest on His throne"). This was an unlikely combination for that day.

The Symbolic Crowns

11 "Take silver and gold, make an *ornate* crown and set *it* on the head of Joshua the son of Jehozadak, the high priest.

12 "Then say to him, 'Thus says the LORD of hosts, "Behold, a man whose name is Branch, for He will branch out from where He is; and He will build the temple of the LORD.

13 "Yes, it is He who will build the temple of the LORD, and He who will bear the honor and sit and rule on His throne. Thus, He will be a priest on His throne, and the counsel of peace will be between the two offices." '

14 "Now the crown will become a reminder in the temple of the LORD to Helem, Tobijah, Jedaiah and Hen the son of Zephaniah.

15 "Those who are far off will come and build the temple of the LORD." Then you will know that the LORD of hosts has sent me to you. And it will take place if you completely obey the LORD your God.

Hearts like Flint

7 In the fourth year of King Darius, the word of the LORD came to Zechariah on the fourth *day* of the ninth month, *which is* Chislev.

2 Now *the town of* Bethel had sent Sharezer and Regemmelech and their men to seek the favor of the LORD,

3 speaking to the priests who belong to the house of the LORD of hosts, and to the prophets, saying, "Shall I weep in the fifth month and abstain, as I have done these many years?"

4 Then the word of the LORD of hosts came to me, saying,

5 "Say to all the people of the land and to the priests, 'When you fasted and mourned in the fifth and seventh months these seventy years, was it actually for Me that you fasted?

6 'When you eat and drink, do you not eat for yourselves and do you not drink for yourselves?

7 'Are not *these* the words which the LORD proclaimed by the former prophets, when Jerusalem was inhabited and prosperous along with its cities around it, and the Negev and the foothills were inhabited?' "

8 Then the word of the LORD came to Zechariah saying,

9 "Thus has the LORD of hosts said, 'Dispense true justice and practice kindness and compassion each to his brother;

10 and do not oppress the widow or the orphan, the stranger or the poor; and do not devise evil in your hearts against one another.'

11 "But they refused to pay attention and turned a stubborn shoulder and stopped their ears from hearing.

12 "They made their hearts *like* flint so that they could not hear the law and the words which the LORD of hosts had sent by His Spirit through the former prophets; therefore great wrath came from the LORD of hosts.

13 "And just as He called and they would not listen, so they called and I would not listen," says the LORD of hosts;

6:11 2 Sam 12:30; Ps 21:3; Song 3:11; Ezra 3:2; Hag 1:1

6:12 Is 4:2; 11:1; Jer 23:5; 33:15; Zech 3:8; Is 53:2; Ezra 3:8, 10; Amos 9:11; Zech 4:6-9

6:13 Is 9:6; 11:10; 22:24; 49:5, 6; Is 9:7; Ps 110:1, 4

6:15 Is 56:6-8; 60:10; Zech 2:9-11; 4:9; Is 58:10-14; Jer 7:23; Zech 3:7

7:1 Neh 1:1

7:2 1 Kin 13:6; Jer 26:19; Zech 8:21

7:3 Ezra 3:10-12; Zech 8:19

7:5 Zech 1:12; Is 1:11, 12; 58:5

7:7 Is 1:16-20; Jer 7:5, 23; Zech 1:4; Jer 22:21; Jer 13:19; 32:44

7:9 Ezek 18:8; 45:9; Zech 8:16; 2 Sam 9:7; Job 6:14; Mic 6:8

7:10 Ex 22:22; Ps 72:4; Jer 7:6; Ps 21:11; Mic 2:1; Zech 8:17

7:11 Jer 5:3; 8:5; 11:10; Jer 7:26; 17:23; Ps 58:4; Jer 5:21

7:12 2 Chr 36:13; Ezek 2:4; 3:7-9; Jer 17:1; Ezek 3:9; Zech 7:7; Neh 9:30; 2 Chr 36:16; Dan 9:11, 12

7:13 Jer 11:10, 14; 14:12; Prov 1:24-28; Is 1:15

6:15 Some of God's promises are conditional—we must obey him to receive them. The rebuilding of the temple required careful obedience. God would protect the people as long as they obeyed. Casual or occasional obedience, the result of a halfhearted or divided commitment, would not lead to blessing. Many of God's blessings come to us as a result of diligent obedience. Inconsistent obedience can't produce consistent blessing.

7:1ff The fourth year of King Darius's reign was 518 B.C. For the previous 70 years, the people had been holding a fast in August to remember the destruction of Jerusalem. Because Jerusalem was being rebuilt, they came to the temple to ask if they had to continue this annual fast. God did not answer their question directly. Instead, he told them that their acts of justice and mercy were more important than their fasting. What he wanted from his people was true justice in their dealings and mercy and compassion for the weak.

7:5–7 The Israelites had lost their sincere desire for a loving relationship with God. Zechariah told them that they had been fasting without a proper attitude of repentance or worship. They fasted and mourned during their exile with no thought of God or their sins that had caused the exile in the first place. When you go to church, pray, or have fellowship with other believers, are you doing these from habit or for what you get out of it? God says that an attitude of worship without a sincere desire to know and love him will lead to ruin.

7:7 The Negev was the southern part of Judah.

7:11–12 Zechariah explained to the people that their ancestors brought God's great wrath on themselves by hardening their hearts. Any sin seems more natural the second time—as we become hardened, each repetition is easier. Ignoring or refusing God's warning hardens you each time you do wrong. Read God's Word and apply it to your life. Sensitivity and submission to God's Word can soften your heart and allow you to live as you should.

14“but I scattered them with a storm wind among all the nations whom they have not
known. Thus the land is desolated behind them so that no one went back and forth, for
they made the pleasant land desolate.”

The Coming Peace and Prosperity of Zion

8 Then the word of the LORD of hosts came, saying,
2 “Thus says the LORD of hosts, ‘I am exceedingly jealous for Zion, yes, with great
wrath I am jealous for her.’
3“Thus says the LORD, ‘I will return to Zion and will dwell in the midst of Jerusalem.
Then Jerusalem will be called the City of Truth, and the mountain of the LORD of hosts
will be called the Holy Mountain.’
4“Thus says the LORD of hosts, ‘Old men and old women will again sit in the [1]streets
of Jerusalem, each man with his staff in his hand because of age.
5 ‘And the [1]streets of the city will be filled with boys and girls playing in its [1]streets.’
6“Thus says the LORD of hosts, ‘If it is too difficult in the sight of the remnant of this
people in those days, will it also be too difficult in My sight?’ declares the LORD of hosts.
7“Thus says the LORD of hosts, ‘Behold, I am going to save My people from the land
of the east and from the land of the west;
8 and I will bring them *back* and they will live in the midst of Jerusalem; and they shall
be My people, and I will be their God in truth and righteousness.’
9“Thus says the LORD of hosts, ‘Let your hands be strong, you who are listening in
these days to these words from the mouth of the prophets, *those* who *spoke* in the day
that the foundation of the house of the LORD of hosts was laid, to the end that the temple might be built.
10 ‘For before those days there was no wage for man or any wage for animal; and for
him who went out or came in there was no peace because of his enemies, and I set all
men one against another.
11 ‘But now I will not treat the remnant of this people as in the former days,’ declares
the LORD of hosts.
12 ‘For *there will be* peace for the seed: the vine will yield its fruit, the land will yield its
produce and the heavens will give their dew; and I will cause the remnant of this people
to inherit all these *things*.
13 ‘It will come about that just as you were a curse among the nations, O house of Judah and house of Israel, so I will save you that you may become a blessing. Do not fear;
let your hands be strong.’
14“For thus says the LORD of hosts, ‘Just as I purposed to do harm to you when your
fathers provoked Me to wrath,’ says the LORD of hosts, ‘and I have not relented,

1 Or *squares*

7:14 Deut 4:27; 28:64; Jer 23:19; Jer 44:6; Is 60:15; Jer 12:10
8:2 Zech 1:14
8:3 Zech 2:10, 11
8:4 Is 65:20
8:5 Jer 30:19, 20; 31:12, 13
8:6 Ps 118:23; 126:1-3; Jer 32:17, 27
8:7 Ps 107:3; Is 11:11; 27:12, 13; 43:5
8:8 Zeph 3:20; Zech 10:10; Jer 3:17; Ezek 37:25; Ezek 11:20; 36:28; Zech 2:11
8:9 1 Chr 22:13; Is 35:4; Hag 2:4; Ezra 5:1; 6:14
8:10 Hag 2:15-19; 2 Chr 15:5; Is 19:2; Amos 3:6; 9:4
8:11 Ps 103:9; Is 12:1; Hag 2:19
8:12 Lev 26:3-6; Gen 27:28; Deut 33:13, 28; Hos 13:3; Is 61:7; Obad 17
8:13 Jer 29:18; Dan 9:11; Ps 72:17; Is 19:24, 25; Ezek 34:26
8:14 Jer 31:28; Jer 4:28; Ezek 24:14

8:3 One day Christ will reign in his kingdom on earth. There all his people will live with him. This truth should encourage us to look forward to the Messiah's reign.

8:4–5 In troubled times, the very old and very young are the first to suffer and die. But both groups are plentiful in this vision, filling the streets with their normal everyday activities. This is a sign of the complete peace and prosperity of God's new earth.

8:6 The remnant was the small group of exiles who had returned from Babylon to rebuild Jerusalem and the temple. Struggling to survive in the land, they became discouraged over the opposition they often faced from hostile neighbors. It was hard to believe that one day God himself would reign from this city and that their land would enjoy great peace and prosperity. Our God is all-powerful; he can do anything! When confronting seemingly impossible tasks or situations, remember that “with God all things are possible” (Matthew 19:26).

8:8 The covenant relationship will be renewed, and the whole community will be filled with the presence of God. This promise of forgiveness and restoration extends to all God's people wherever they may be found. (For other references to this promise, see Exodus 6:6–7; 19:5–6; 29:45; Leviticus 26:12; Deuteronomy 7:6; Jeremiah 31:1, 33.)

8:9 God had to give the temple workers a little push to get them moving. They had heard the prophets' words of encouragement; at this time they needed to stop just listening and get to work. We need to listen to what God says, but after he has made our course of action plain, we need to “be strong” and do what he wants.

8:13–15 For more than 15 years, God and his prophets had been urging the people to finish building the temple. Here again, God encouraged them with visions of the future. We may be tempted to slow down for many reasons: People aren't responding; we feel physically or emotionally drained; the workers are uncooperative; the work is distasteful, too difficult, or not worth the effort. God's promises about the future should encourage us *now*. He knows what the results of our labors will be, and thus he can give us a perspective that will help us continue in our work for him.

8:14–17 God promised to give his people rich rewards, reassuring them that despite the punishments they had endured, he would not change his mind to bless them. But he also said they had a job to do: “These are the things which you should do.” God will be faithful, but we also have responsibilities: to tell the truth, exercise justice, and live peacefully. If you expect God to do his part, be sure to do yours.

15 so I have again purposed in these days to do good to Jerusalem and to the house of
Judah. Do not fear!
16 'These are the things which you should do: speak the truth to one another; judge
with truth and judgment for peace in your [2]gates.
17 'Also let none of you devise evil in your heart against another, and do not love perjury; for all these are what I hate,' declares the LORD."
18 Then the word of the LORD of hosts came to me, saying,
19 "Thus says the LORD of hosts, 'The fast of the fourth, the fast of the fifth, the fast of
the seventh and the fast of the tenth *months* will become joy, gladness, and cheerful feasts
for the house of Judah; so love truth and peace.'
20 "Thus says the LORD of hosts, '*It will* yet *be* that peoples will come, even the inhabitants of many cities.
21 'The inhabitants of one will go to another, saying, "Let us go at once to entreat the
favor of the LORD, and to seek the LORD of hosts; I will also go."
22 'So many peoples and mighty nations will come to seek the LORD of hosts in Jerusalem and to entreat the favor of the LORD.'
23 "Thus says the LORD of hosts, 'In those days ten men from all the nations will grasp
the garment of a Jew, saying, "Let us go with you, for we have heard that God is with
you." ' "

8:15 Jer 29:11; Mic 7:18-20; Zech 8:13

8:16 Ps 15:2; Prov 12:17-19; Zech 8:3; Eph 4:25; Is 9:7; 11:4, 5; Zech 7:9

8:17 Prov 3:29; Jer 4:14; Zech 7:10; Zech 5:4; Mal 3:5; Prov 6:16-19; Hab 1:13

8:19 2 Kin 25:3, 4; Jer 39:2; Zech 7:3, 5; 2 Kin 25:25; Zech 7:5; Jer 52:4; Ps 30:11; Is 12:1; Zech 8:16; Luke 1:74, 75

8:20 Ps 117:1; Jer 16:19; Mic 4:2, 3; Zech 2:11; 14:16

8:21 Zech 7:2

8:22 Is 2:2, 3; 25:7; 49:6, 22, 23; 60:3-12; Zech 8:21

8:23 Is 45:14, 24; 60:14

B. MESSAGES AFTER COMPLETING THE TEMPLE (9:1—14:21)

After the temple was completed, Zechariah gave several prophecies about Israel's future, which describe the first and second comings of Jesus Christ. This book contains more about the person, work, and glory of Christ than the other minor prophets combined. Israel's King would come, but he would be rejected by his people. They would later repent and be restored to God. The King who is coming is our king. May we be found faithful and pure in his sight when we meet him face to face.

Prophecies against Neighboring Nations

9 The burden of the word of the LORD is against the land of Hadrach, with Damascus
as its resting place (for the eyes of men, especially of all the tribes of Israel, are
toward the LORD),

2 And Hamath also, which borders on it;
Tyre and Sidon, though they are very wise.
3 For Tyre built herself a fortress
And piled up silver like dust,
And gold like the mire of the streets.
4 Behold, the Lord will dispossess her
And cast her wealth into the sea;
And she will be consumed with fire.
5 Ashkelon will see *it* and be afraid.
Gaza too will writhe in great pain;
Also Ekron, for her expectation has been confounded.
Moreover, the king will perish from Gaza,
And Ashkelon will not be inhabited.
6 And a mongrel race will dwell in Ashdod,
And I will cut off the pride of the Philistines.

9:1 Is 17:1; Jer 49:23-27; Amos 1:3-5

9:2 Jer 49:23; Ezek 28:2-5, 12; Ezek 28:21

9:3 Josh 19:29; 2 Sam 24:7; Job 27:16; Ezek 27:33; 28:4, 5; 1 Kin 10:21, 27

9:4 Ezek 26:3-5; Ezek 28:18

9:6 Amos 1:8; Zeph 2:4

2 I.e. the place where court was held

8:19–22 There will come a time when fasting for sins will be replaced by feasting and joy. People from all nations will "seek the LORD of hosts." This was also promised in 2:11.

8:23 In the past, Jerusalem had often borne the brunt of cruel jokes from other nations (8:13). The city was not respected; its citizens had sinned so much that God let them be kicked around by their enemies. But eventually, says Zechariah, Jerusalem will be a holy place—respected highly throughout the world because its people will have a change of heart toward God. People from other nations will see how God has rewarded his people for their faithfulness and will want to be included in their great blessings.

9:1–17 A burden is a message from God. Hadrach was probably a city in northern Aram. The last six chapters of the book are two messages delivered late in Zechariah's life. These messages point to the Messiah and his second coming. Some of these prophecies were fulfilled before the Messiah came, perhaps by Alexander the Great; others were fulfilled during the Messiah's time on earth; and others will be fulfilled when he returns. Those who oppressed Jerusalem—Aram, Philistia, Phoenicia—would be crushed. Zion's promised King would come—first as a servant on a donkey's colt, later as a powerful ruler and judge.

9:5–7 Zechariah mentions four key cities in Philistia: Ashkelon, Gaza, and Ekron would be destroyed, and Ashdod would be overtaken by foreigners. This would happen because of their great evil and idolatry. But those left in the land would be adopted into Israel as a new clan, as the Jebusites were (when David conquered Jerusalem, he did not wipe out the Jebusites, but absorbed them into Judah).

7 And I will remove their blood from their mouth
And their detestable things from between their teeth.
Then they also will be a remnant for our God,
And be like a clan in Judah,
And Ekron like a Jebusite.
8 But I will camp around My house because of an army,
Because of him who passes by and returns;
And no oppressor will pass over them anymore,
For now I have seen with My eyes.
9 Rejoice greatly, O daughter of Zion!
Shout *in triumph,* O daughter of Jerusalem!
Behold, your king is coming to you;
He is just and endowed with salvation,
Humble, and mounted on a donkey,
Even on a colt, the foal of a donkey.
10 I will cut off the chariot from Ephraim
And the horse from Jerusalem;
And the bow of war will be cut off.
And He will speak peace to the nations;
And His dominion will be from sea to sea,
And from the [3]River to the ends of the earth.

9:8 Is 52:1; Is 54:14; 60:18

9:9 Zeph 3:14, 15; Zech 2:10; Ps 110:1; Is 9:6, 7; Jer 23:5, 6; Matt 21:5; John 12:15; Zeph 3:5; Is 43:3, 11; Is 57:15; Judg 10:4; Is 30:6

9:10 Hos 1:7; Mic 5:10; Hos 2:18; Is 57:19; Mic 4:2-4; Ps 72:8; Is 60:12

Deliverance of Judah and Ephraim

11 As for you also, because of the blood of *My* covenant with you,
I have set your prisoners free from the waterless pit.
12 Return to the stronghold, O prisoners who have the hope;
This very day I am declaring that I will restore double to you.
13 For I will bend Judah as My bow,
I will fill the bow with Ephraim.
And I will stir up your sons, O Zion, against your sons, O Greece;
And I will make you like a warrior's sword.
14 Then the LORD will appear over them,
And His arrow will go forth like lightning;
And the Lord GOD will blow the trumpet,
And will march in the storm winds of the south.
15 The LORD of hosts will defend them.
And they will devour and trample on the sling stones;
And they will drink *and* be boisterous as with wine;
And they will be filled like a *sacrificial* basin,
Drenched like the corners of the altar.
16 And the LORD their God will save them in that day

9:11 Ex 24:8; Heb 10:2; Is 24:22; 51:14

9:12 Jer 16:19; Joel 3:16; Jer 14:8; 17:13; Heb 6:18, 19; Is 61:7

9:13 Jer 51:20; Joel 3:6; Ps 45:3

9:14 Is 31:5; Zech 2:5; Ps 18:14; Hab 3:11; Is 27:13; Is 21:1; 66:15

9:15 Is 37:35; Zech 12:8; Zech 12:6; Job 41:28; Ps 78:65; Ex 27:2

9:16 Jer 31:10, 11; Is 62:3

3 I.e. Euphrates

9:8 Several centuries after Zechariah's day, Antiochus IV Epiphanes would invade Israel, and in A.D. 70 Titus, a Roman general, would completely destroy the temple. This promise, therefore, may have been conditional upon the people's obedience. The day will come, however, when God's people will never again have to worry about invading enemies (Joel 3:17).

9:9 The Triumphal Entry of Jesus riding into Jerusalem (Matthew 21:1–11) was predicted here more than 500 years before it happened. Just as this prophecy was fulfilled when Jesus came to earth, so the prophecies of his second coming are just as certain to come true. We are to be ready for his return, for he is coming!

9:10 Ephraim is another name for the northern kingdom of Israel. When we view two distant mountains, they appear to be close together, perhaps even to touch each other. But as we approach them, we can see that they are in fact far apart, even separated by a huge valley. This is the situation with many Old Testament prophecies. Verse 9 was clearly fulfilled in Christ's first coming, but verse 10 can now be seen to refer to his second coming. At that time all nations will be subject to Christ, and his rule will extend over the whole earth. In Philippians 2:9–10, we are told that at that time every knee will bow to Christ and every tongue will confess him as Lord.

9:11 Covenants in Old Testament times were sealed or confirmed with blood, much as we would sign our name to a contract. The old covenant was sealed by the blood of sacrifices, pointing ahead to the blood Christ would shed at Calvary, his "signature" that confirmed God's new covenant with his people. Because God had made a covenant with these people, he delivered them from the "waterless pit," the cistern-like prison of exile.

9:14–17 After Solomon's reign, the kingdom was divided into the northern kingdom (called Israel or Ephraim) and the southern kingdom (called Judah). This prophecy says that all Israel, north and south, will someday be reunited. The first part of this chapter tells how God will help his people avoid war; here God explains that he will appear to help his people when war is inevitable. Verses 14–16 explain how the Jews will win over the Greeks, but it is also a figurative picture of the ultimate future victory over evil by God's people.

As the flock of His people;
For *they are as* the stones of a crown,
Sparkling in His land.
17 For what comeliness and beauty *will be* theirs!
Grain will make the young men flourish, and new wine the virgins.

9:17 Jer 31:12, 14; Ps 27:4; Is 33:17

God Will Bless Judah and Ephraim

10 Ask rain from the LORD at the time of the spring rain—
The LORD who makes the storm clouds;
And He will give them showers of rain, vegetation in the field to *each* man.
2 For the teraphim speak iniquity,
And the diviners see lying visions
And tell false dreams;
They comfort in vain.
Therefore *the people* wander like sheep,
They are afflicted, because there is no shepherd.
3 "My anger is kindled against the shepherds,
And I will punish the male goats;
For the LORD of hosts has visited His flock, the house of Judah,
And will make them like His majestic horse in battle.
4 "From them will come the cornerstone,
From them the tent peg,
From them the bow of battle,
From them every ruler, *all* of them together.
5 "They will be as mighty men,
Treading down *the enemy* in the mire of the streets in battle;
And they will fight, for the LORD *will be* with them;
And the riders on horses will be put to shame.
6 "I will strengthen the house of Judah,
And I will save the house of Joseph,
And I will bring them back,
Because I have had compassion on them;
And they will be as though I had not rejected them,
For I am the LORD their God and I will answer them.
7 "Ephraim will be like a mighty man,
And their heart will be glad as if *from* wine;
Indeed, their children will see *it* and be glad,
Their heart will rejoice in the LORD.
8 "I will whistle for them to gather them together,
For I have redeemed them;
And they will be as numerous as they were before.
9 "When I scatter them among the peoples,
They will remember Me in far countries,
And they with their children will live and come back.
10 "I will bring them back from the land of Egypt

10:1 Joel 2:23; Jer 10:13; Is 30:23

10:2 Ezek 21:21; Hos 3:4; Jer 27:9; Jer 23:32; Ezek 34:5, 8; Matt 9:36; Mark 6:34

10:3 Jer 25:34-36; Ezek 34:12

10:4 Luke 20:17; Eph 2:20; 1 Pet 2:6; Jer 51:20; Zech 9:10

10:5 2 Sam 22:43; Amos 2:15; Hag 2:22

10:6 Zech 10:12; Zech 8:7; 9:16; Zech 8:8; Is 54:8; Zech 1:16; Is 54:4; Zech 13:9

10:7 Is 54:13; Ezek 37:25

10:8 Is 5:26; 7:18, 19; Jer 33:22; Rev 7:9; Jer 30:20; Ezek 36:11

10:9 1 Kin 8:47, 48; Ezek 6:9

10:10 Is 11:11; Jer 50:19; Is 49:19, 20

10:2 We often create idols of money, power, fame, or success, and then we expect them to give us happiness and security. But these idols can't supply what we need any more than a stone image can make it rain. How foolish it is to trust in idols. Instead, trust God's promises for your future.

10:4 Zechariah's prophecy, more than 500 years before Christ's first coming, called Christ a "cornerstone" (see also Isaiah 28:16), a "tent peg" (Isaiah 22:23), a "bow" that wins the battle, and a "ruler" who was a man of action (see also Genesis 49:10; Micah 5:2). This Messiah would be strong, stable, victorious, and trustworthy—all in all, the answer to Israel's problems. Only in the Messiah will all the promises to God's people be fulfilled.

10:6 The "house of Judah" refers to the southern kingdom, and the "house of Joseph" refers to the northern kingdom. Ephraim, the leading tribe of the northern kingdom, was the son of Joseph. One day God will unite all his people. This verse tells about God's reuniting of the Jews (see also Jeremiah 31:10). This was a startling idea: The people of the northern kingdom of Israel were so completely absorbed into other cultures after their captivity in 722 B.C. that a regathering could not be done by human means, but only by God.

10:6, 12 God promises to strengthen his people. When we stay closely connected to God, his Spirit will enable us to do his will, despite the obstacles. When we stray away from God, we will be cut off from our power source.

10:10 This pictured return from Egypt and Assyria was a symbolic way of saying that the people would be returned from all the countries where they had been dispersed. Egypt and Assyria evoked memories of slavery and separation.

And gather them from Assyria;
And I will bring them into the land of Gilead and Lebanon
Until no *room* can be found for them.
11 "And they will pass through the sea *of* distress
And He will strike the waves in the sea,
So that all the depths of the Nile will dry up;
And the pride of Assyria will be brought down
And the scepter of Egypt will depart.
12 "And I will strengthen them in the LORD,
And in His name they will walk," declares the LORD.

The Doomed Flock

11 Open your doors, O Lebanon,
That a fire may feed on your cedars.
2 Wail, O cypress, for the cedar has fallen,
Because the glorious *trees* have been destroyed;
Wail, O oaks of Bashan,
For the impenetrable forest has come down.
3 There is a sound of the shepherds' wail,
For their glory is ruined;
There is a sound of the young lions' roar,
For the pride of the Jordan is ruined.
4 Thus says the LORD my God, "Pasture the flock *doomed* to slaughter.
5 "Those who buy them slay them and go unpunished, and *each of* those who sell them
says, 'Blessed be the LORD, for I have become rich!' And their own shepherds have no
pity on them.
6 "For I will no longer have pity on the inhabitants of the land," declares the LORD;
"but behold, I will cause the men to fall, each into another's power and into the power of
his king; and they will strike the land, and I will not deliver *them* from their power."
7 So I pastured the flock *doomed* to slaughter, hence the afflicted of the flock. And I
took for myself two staffs: the one I called Favor and the other I called Union; so I pastured the flock.
8 Then I annihilated the three shepherds in one month, for my soul was impatient
with them, and their soul also was weary of me.
9 Then I said, "I will not pasture you. What is to die, let it die, and what is to be annihilated, let it be annihilated; and let those who are left eat one another's flesh."
10 I took my staff Favor and cut it in pieces, to break my covenant which I had made
with all the peoples.
11 So it was broken on that day, and [4]thus the afflicted of the flock who were watching
me realized that it was the word of the LORD.
12 I said to them, "If it is good in your sight, give *me* my wages; but if not, never mind!"
So they weighed out thirty *shekels* of silver as my wages.

10:11 Is 51:9, 10; Is 19:5-7; Zeph 2:13; Ezek 30:13
10:12 Zech 10:6; Mic 4:5
11:1 Jer 22:6, 7; Ezek 31:3
11:3 Jer 25:34-36; Jer 2:15; 50:44
11:4 Ps 44:22; Zech 11:7
11:5 Jer 50:7; Hos 12:8; 1 Tim 6:9; Ezek 34:2, 3
11:6 Jer 13:14; Is 9:19-21; Mic 7:2-6; Zech 14:13; Ps 50:22; Mic 5:8
11:7 Zech 11:4; Jer 39:10; Zeph 3:12; Ezek 37:16; Ps 27:4; 90:17; Zech 11:10; Ps 133:1; Ezek 37:16-23; Zech 11:14
11:8 Hos 5:7
11:9 Jer 15:2
11:10 Zech 11:7; Ps 89:39; Jer 14:21
11:11 Zeph 3:12
11:12 1 Kin 5:6; Mal 3:5; Gen 37:28; Ex 21:32; Matt 26:15; 27:9, 10

4 Another reading is *the sheep dealers who*

10:11 The "sea of distress" refers to the Red Sea, through which the Israelites were miraculously delivered from Egypt. Just as the Israelites returned once again from Egypt and other lands, they would continue to be protected by God's miraculous power.

11:4–17 In this message, God told Zechariah to act out the roles of two different kinds of shepherds. The first type of shepherd demonstrated how God would reject his people (the sheep) because they rejected him (11:4–14). The second type of shepherd demonstrated how God would give over his people to evil shepherds (11:15–17). (See Ezekiel 34 for a detailed portrayal of the evil shepherds of Israel.)

11:4 God told Zechariah to take a job as shepherd of a flock of sheep being fattened for slaughter. The Messiah would shepherd God's people during a time of spiritual and political confusion. The flock represented the people feeding on their own greed and evil desires until they were ripe for God's judgment.

11:7 Zechariah took two shepherd's staffs and named them "Favor" and "Union." He broke the first one ("Favor") to show that God's gracious covenant with his people was broken. He broke the second one ("Union") to show that "the brotherhood between Judah and Israel" was broken (11:14).

11:8 The identity of the three evil shepherds is not known. But God knew they were unfit to shepherd his people, and so he removed them.

11:12 To pay this shepherd 30 shekels of silver was an insult—this was the price paid to an owner for a slave gored by an ox (Exodus 21:32). This is also the amount Judas received for betraying Jesus (Matthew 27:3–10). The priceless Messiah was sold for the price of a slave.

13 Then the LORD said to me, "Throw it to the potter, *that* magnificent price at which
I was valued by them." So I took the thirty *shekels* of silver and threw them to the potter
in the house of the LORD.
14 Then I cut in pieces my second staff Union, to break the brotherhood between Judah and Israel.
15 The LORD said to me, "Take again for yourself the equipment of a foolish
shepherd.
16 "For behold, I am going to raise up a shepherd in the land who will not care for the
perishing, seek the scattered, heal the broken, or sustain the one standing, but will devour the flesh of the fat *sheep* and tear off their hoofs.
17 "Woe to the worthless shepherd
Who leaves the flock!
A sword will be on his arm
And on his right eye!
His arm will be totally withered
And his right eye will be blind."

11:13 Matt 27:3-10; Acts 1:18, 19
11:14 Zech 11:7; Is 9:21; Zech 11:6
11:15 Is 6:10-12; Zech 11:17
11:16 Jer 23:2; Ezek 34:2-6
11:17 Jer 23:1; Zech 10:2; 11:15; Jer 50:35-37; Ezek 30:21, 22

Jerusalem to Be Attacked

12 The [5]burden of the word of the LORD concerning Israel.
Thus declares the LORD who stretches out the heavens, lays the foundation of the
earth, and forms the spirit of man within him,
2 "Behold, I am going to make Jerusalem a cup that causes reeling to all the peoples
around; and when the siege is against Jerusalem, it will also be against Judah.
3 "It will come about in that day that I will make Jerusalem a heavy stone for all the
peoples; all who lift it will be severely injured. And all the nations of the earth will be
gathered against it.
4 "In that day," declares the LORD, "I will strike every horse with bewilderment and
his rider with madness. But I will watch over the house of Judah, while I strike every
horse of the peoples with blindness.
5 "Then the clans of Judah will say in their hearts, 'A strong support for us are the inhabitants of Jerusalem through the LORD of hosts, their God.'
6 "In that day I will make the clans of Judah like a firepot among pieces of wood and
a flaming torch among sheaves, so they will consume on the right hand and on the left all
the surrounding peoples, while the inhabitants of Jerusalem again dwell on their own
sites in Jerusalem.
7 "The LORD also will save the tents of Judah first, so that the glory of the house of
David and the glory of the inhabitants of Jerusalem will not be magnified above Judah.
8 "In that day the LORD will defend the inhabitants of Jerusalem, and the one who is
feeble among them in that day will be like David, and the house of David *will be* like
God, like the angel of the LORD before them.

12:1 Is 42:5; 44:24; Jer 51:15; Job 26:7; Ps 102:25, 26; Heb 1:10-12; Is 57:16; Heb 12:9
12:2 Ps 75:8; Is 51:22, 23; Zech 14:14
12:3 Dan 2:34, 35, 44, 45; Matt 21:44; Zech 14:2
12:6 Is 10:17, 18; Obad 18; Zech 11:1; Zech 2:4; 8:3-5
12:7 Jer 30:18; Amos 9:11
12:8 Joel 3:16; Zech 9:14, 15; Lev 26:8; Josh 23:10; Mic 7:8; Ps 8:5; 82:6; Ex 14:19; 33:2

5 Or *oracle*

11:13 Potters were in the lowest social class. The "magnificent price" (a sarcastic comment) was so little that it could be thrown to the potter. It is significant that the 30 pieces of silver paid to Judas for betraying Jesus were returned to the temple and used to buy a potter's field (Matthew 27:3–10).

11:14 Because the people had rejected the Messiah, God would reject them—symbolized by Zechariah breaking the staff called "Union." Not long after Zechariah's time, the Jews began to divide into numerous factions—Pharisees, Sadducees, Essenes, Herodians, and Zealots. The discord among these groups was a key factor leading to the destruction of Jerusalem in A.D. 70.

11:15–17 Israel would not only reject the true shepherd; it would accept instead a worthless shepherd. This shepherd would serve his own concerns rather than the concerns of his flock and would destroy rather than defend them. Condemnation is his rightful fate because he trusted his arm (military might) and his eye (intellect). God would destroy both areas.

11:17 It is a great tragedy for God's people when their leaders fail to care for them adequately. God holds leaders particularly accountable for the condition of his people. The New Testament tells church leaders, "Let not many of you become teachers, . . . knowing that as such we will incur a stricter judgment" (James 3:1). If God puts you in a position of leadership, remember that it is also a place of great responsibility.

12:1–14 This chapter pictures the final siege against the people of Jerusalem.

12:3–4 This speaks of a great future battle against Jerusalem. Some say it is Armaggedon, the last great battle on earth. Those who oppose God's people will not prevail forever. Eventually, evil, pain, and oppression will be abolished once and for all.

12:7 As water flows downhill, so a city's influence usually flows to its surrounding countryside. But this time, the countryside of Judah (the "tents") would have priority over Jerusalem so that the people of Jerusalem would not become proud. Don't think you have to witness first to the "important" people—professional athletes, movie stars, and prominent businessmen. Christ came to seek and save the lost (Luke 19:10), even the "down-and-out" lost. We must be careful to avoid spiritual pride or we, like Jerusalem, may be the last to know what God is doing.

12:9 Zech 14:2, 3

12:10 Is 44:3; Ezek 39:29; Joel 2:28, 29; John 19:37; Rev 1:7; Jer 6:26; Amos 8:10

12:11 Matt 24:30; Rev 1:7

13:1 Jer 2:13; 17:13; Ps 51:2, 7; Is 1:16-18; John 1:29; Num 19:17; Is 4:4; Ezek 36:25

13:2 Ex 23:13; Hos 2:17; Jer 23:14, 15; 1 Kin 22:22; Ezek 36:25, 29

13:3 Jer 23:34; Deut 18:20; Ezek 14:9; Jer 23:25; Deut 13:6-11; Matt 10:37

13:4 Jer 6:15; 8:9; Mic 3:7; 2 Kin 1:8; Is 20:2; Matt 3:4

13:5 Amos 7:14

13:6 2 Kin 9:24

13:7 Jer 47:6; Ezek 21:3-5; Is 40:11; Ezek 34:23, 24; 37:24; Mic 5:2, 4; Ps 2:2; Jer 23:5, 6; Is 53:4, 5, 10; Matt 26:31; Mark 14:27; Is 1:25

13:8 Is 6:13; Ezek 5:2-4, 12

9 "And in that day I will set about to destroy all the nations that come against Jerusalem.
10 "I will pour out on the house of David and on the inhabitants of Jerusalem, the Spirit
of grace and of supplication, so that they will look on Me whom they have pierced; and
they will mourn for Him, as one mourns for an only son, and they will weep bitterly over
Him like the bitter weeping over a firstborn.
11 "In that day there will be great mourning in Jerusalem, like the mourning of
Hadadrimmon in the plain of Megiddo.
12 "The land will mourn, every family by itself; the family of the house of David by itself
and their wives by themselves; the family of the house of Nathan by itself and their wives
by themselves;
13 the family of the house of Levi by itself and their wives by themselves; the family of
the Shimeites by itself and their wives by themselves;
14 all the families that remain, every family by itself and their wives by themselves.

False Prophets Ashamed

13 "In that day a fountain will be opened for the house of David and for the inhabitants of Jerusalem, for sin and for impurity.
2 "It will come about in that day," declares the LORD of hosts, "that I will cut off the
names of the idols from the land, and they will no longer be remembered; and I will also
remove the prophets and the unclean spirit from the land.
3 "And if anyone still prophesies, then his father and mother who gave birth to him
will say to him, 'You shall not live, for you have spoken falsely in the name of the LORD';
and his father and mother who gave birth to him will pierce him through when he prophesies.
4 "Also it will come about in that day that the prophets will each be ashamed of his
vision when he prophesies, and they will not put on a hairy robe in order to deceive;
5 but he will say, 'I am not a prophet; I am a tiller of the ground, for a man sold me as
a slave in my youth.'
6 "And one will say to him, 'What are these wounds between your arms?' Then he will
say, '*Those* with which I was wounded in the house of my friends.'
7 "Awake, O sword, against My Shepherd,
And against the man, My Associate,"
Declares the LORD of hosts.
"Strike the Shepherd that the sheep may be scattered;
And I will turn My hand against the little ones.
8 "It will come about in all the land,"
Declares the LORD,
"That two parts in it will be cut off *and* perish;
But the third will be left in it.

12:10 The Holy Spirit was poured out at Pentecost, 50 days after Christ's resurrection (see Acts 2). Zechariah calls the Spirit "the Spirit of grace and of supplication." It is this Spirit who convicts us of sin, reveals to us God's righteousness and judgment, and helps us as we pray. "In the same way the Spirit also helps our weakness; for we do not know how to pray as we should, but the Spirit Himself intercedes for us with groanings too deep for words" (Romans 8:26). Ask God to fill you with his Spirit.

12:10–14 Eventually *all* people will realize that Jesus, the man who was pierced and killed, is indeed the Messiah. There will be an awakening, with sorrow for sin and genuine revival. The crucified Messiah will be clearly revealed (Philippians 2:10; Revelation 5:13).

12:11 Hadadrimmon could refer to the place near the plain of Megiddo where King Josiah was killed. Josiah's death was greatly mourned by his people (see 2 Chronicles 35:22–25).

12:12–14 These verses are saying that all Israel will mourn—king, prophet, priest, and people. Each family will go into private mourning, husbands and wives by themselves, to face their sorrow.

13:1ff There will be a never-ending supply of God's mercy, forgiveness, and cleansing power. This picture of a fountain is similar to the never-ending stream flowing out from the temple (Ezekiel 47:1). The fountain is used in Scripture to symbolize God's forgiveness. In John 4, Jesus tells of his "living water" that satisfies completely. Are you spiritually thirsty? Do you need to experience God's forgiveness? Drink from the fountain—ask Jesus to forgive you and give you his salvation.

13:2–6 This chapter pictures the final days of the earth as we know it. For God's new era to begin, there must be a cleansing—all evil must be abolished. Therefore, idols will be banished, and false prophets will be ashamed of themselves and will no longer try to deceive God's people.

13:7 Just before his arrest, Jesus quoted from this verse, referring to himself and his disciples (Matthew 26:31–32). He knew beforehand that his disciples would scatter when he was arrested. The Roman "sword" was the military power that put Christ to death.

9 "And I will bring the third part through the fire,
Refine them as silver is refined,
And test them as gold is tested.
They will call on My name,
And I will answer them;
I will say, 'They are My people,'
And they will say, 'The LORD is my God.' "

God Will Battle Jerusalem's Foes

14 Behold, a day is coming for the LORD when the spoil taken from you will be divided among you.
2 For I will gather all the nations against Jerusalem to battle, and the city will be captured, the houses plundered, the women ravished and half of the city exiled, but the rest
of the people will not be cut off from the city.
3 Then the LORD will go forth and fight against those nations, as when He fights on
a day of battle.
4 In that day His feet will stand on the Mount of Olives, which is in front of Jerusalem
on the east; and the Mount of Olives will be split in its middle from east to west by a very
large valley, so that half of the mountain will move toward the north and the other half
toward the south.
5 You will flee by the valley of My mountains, for the valley of the mountains will reach
to Azel; yes, you will flee just as you fled before the earthquake in the days of Uzziah
king of Judah. Then the LORD, my God, will come, *and* all the holy ones with Him!
6 In that day there will be no light; the luminaries will dwindle.
7 For it will be a unique day which is known to the LORD, neither day nor night, but
it will come about that at evening time there will be light.
8 And in that day living waters will flow out of Jerusalem, half of them toward the
eastern sea and the other half toward the western sea; it will be in summer as well as in
winter.

God Will Be King over All

9 And the LORD will be king over all the earth; in that day the LORD will be *the only*
one, and His name *the only* one.
10 All the land will be changed into a plain from Geba to Rimmon south of Jerusalem;
but Jerusalem will rise and remain on its site from Benjamin's Gate as far as the place of
the First Gate to the Corner Gate, and from the Tower of Hananel to the king's wine
presses.
11 People will live in it, and there will no longer be a curse, for Jerusalem will dwell in
security.
12 Now this will be the plague with which the LORD will strike all the peoples who have
gone to war against Jerusalem; their flesh will rot while they stand on their feet, and their
eyes will rot in their sockets, and their tongue will rot in their mouth.

13:9 Is 48:10; Mal 3:3; Ps 34:15-17; 50:15; Zech 12:10; Is 58:9; 65:24; Jer 29:11-13; Zech 10:6; Hos 2:23

14:1 Is 13:6, 9; Joel 2:1; Mal 4:1; Zech 14:14

14:2 Zech 12:2, 3; Is 13:16

14:3 Zech 9:14, 15

14:4 Ezek 11:23; Is 64:1, 2; Ezek 47:1-10; Mic 1:3, 4; Hab 3:6; Zech 4:7; 14:8

14:5 Is 29:6; Amos 1:1; Ps 96:13; Is 66:15, 16; Matt 16:27; 25:31

14:6 Is 13:10; Jer 4:23; Ezek 32:7, 8; Joel 2:30, 31; Acts 2:16, 19

14:7 Jer 30:7; Amos 8:9; Is 45:21; Acts 15:18; Is 58:10; Rev 22:5

14:8 Ezek 47:1-12; Joel 3:18; John 7:38; Rev 22:1, 2

14:9 Is 2:2-4; 45:23; Zech 9:9; 14:16, 17; Deut 6:4; Is 45:21-24

14:10 1 Kin 15:22; Josh 15:32; Judg 20:45, 47; Is 2:2; Amos 9:11; Jer 30:18; Zech 12:6; Jer 37:13; 38:7; 2 Kin 14:13; Jer 31:38

14:11 Zech 8:13; Rev 22:3; Jer 23:5, 6; Ezek 34:25-28

14:12 Lev 26:16; Deut 28:21, 22

13:9 This "third" was a remnant, a small part of the whole. Throughout the history of Israel, whenever the whole nation seemed to turn against God, God said that a righteous remnant still trusted and followed him. These believers were refined like silver and gold through the fire of their difficult circumstances. Determine to be part of God's remnant, that small part of the whole that is obedient to him. Obey God no matter what the rest of the world does. This may mean trials and troubles at times; but just as fire purifies gold and silver, so you will be purified and made more like Christ.

14:1 Many times in the Bible we are encouraged to watch for the day of the Lord. What if you knew exactly when this would happen? Would you live differently? Christ could return at any moment. Be ready for him by studying the Scriptures carefully and by making sure that you live as he intends—in obedience and spiritual readiness.

14:1–21 This chapter portrays the eventual triumph of the Messiah over all the earth and his reign over God's people. But the chronological order of these future events is not clear. They show that God has various ways of dealing with his people. Now we are to watch as the events unfold and God provides an escape for his people.

14:4 On the Mount of Olives, Jesus spoke with his disciples about the end times (Matthew 24). Near this mountain, an angel promised that Jesus would return in the same manner as he had left (Acts 1:11; see also Ezekiel 11:23).

14:5 Only God's people will escape God's punishment (Matthew 24:16–20). In this time of confusion, God will clearly know who his people are. (See the fourth note on Amos 1:1 concerning the earthquake in King Uzziah's day.)

14:8 The eastern sea and the western sea refer to the Dead Sea and the Mediterranean Sea, respectively.

14:10 Jerusalem is honored as the city of God and the focal point of all the world's worship. Jerusalem's elevation is a dramatic way of showing God's supremacy.

14:13 Zech 11:6

14:14 Zech 12:2, 5; Is 23:18; Zech 14:1

14:15 Zech 14:12

14:16 Is 60:6-9; 66:18-21, 23; Lev 23:34-44

14:17 Zech 14:9, 16; Jer 14:3-6; Amos 4:7

14:18 Zech 14:12, 15

14:20 Ex 28:36-38; Ezek 46:20

14:21 Neh 8:10; Rom 14:6, 7; 1 Cor 10:31; Zeph 1:11

13 It will come about in that day that a great panic from the LORD will fall on them;
and they will seize one another's hand, and the hand of one will be lifted against the
hand of another.
14 Judah also will fight at Jerusalem; and the wealth of all the surrounding nations will
be gathered, gold and silver and garments in great abundance.
15 So also like this plague will be the plague on the horse, the mule, the camel, the
donkey and all the cattle that will be in those camps.
16 Then it will come about that any who are left of all the nations that went against
Jerusalem will go up from year to year to worship the King, the LORD of hosts, and to
celebrate the Feast of Booths.
17 And it will be that whichever of the families of the earth does not go up to Jerusalem to worship the King, the LORD of hosts, there will be no rain on them.
18 If the family of Egypt does not go up or enter, then no *rain will fall* on them; it will
be the plague with which the LORD smites the nations who do not go up to celebrate the
Feast of Booths.
19 This will be the punishment of Egypt, and the punishment of all the nations who do
not go up to celebrate the Feast of Booths.
20 In that day there will *be inscribed* on the bells of the horses, "HOLY TO THE
LORD." And the cooking pots in the LORD'S house will be like the bowls before the
altar.
21 Every cooking pot in Jerusalem and in Judah will be holy to the LORD of hosts; and
all who sacrifice will come and take of them and boil in them. And there will no longer
be a Canaanite in the house of the LORD of hosts in that day.

14:16 This Feast of Booths is the only feast still appropriate during the Messiah's reign. The Passover was fulfilled in Christ's death; the day of atonement, in acceptance of Christ's salvation; the Feast of Firstfruits, in his resurrection; and Pentecost, with the arrival of the Holy Spirit. But the Feast of Booths, a festival of thanksgiving, celebrates the harvest of human souls for the Lord. Jesus may have alluded to it in John 4:35.

14:20–21 In the future, even such common objects as horses' bells and cooking pots will be holy. This vision of a restored, holy Jerusalem stands in contrast to its broken walls and unpleasant living conditions. One day God would fulfill the people's dreams for Jerusalem beyond what they could imagine. God still wants to do much more for us than we can imagine (Ephesians 3:20). When we walk with him, we will discover this more deeply each day.

14:21 Zechariah was speaking to a people who were enduring hardships—they were being harassed by neighbors; they were discouraged over their small numbers and seemingly inadequate temple; and their worship was apathetic. But God said, "I am exceedingly jealous for Jerusalem" (1:14). He promised to restore their land, their city, and their temple. Like other prophets, Zechariah blended prophecies of the present, near future, and final days into one sweeping panorama. Through his message we learn that our hope is found in God and his Messiah, who are in complete control of the world.

MALACHI

First exiles return to Jerusalem 538 B.C.	Temple reconstruction begins 536	Haggai, Zechariah become prophets 520	Temple completed 515

VITAL STATISTICS

PURPOSE:
To confront the people with their sins and to restore their relationship with God

AUTHOR:
Malachi

TO WHOM WRITTEN:
The Jews in Jerusalem and God's people everywhere

DATE WRITTEN:
Approximately 430 B.C.

SETTING:
Malachi, Haggai, and Zechariah were postexilic prophets to Judah (the southern kingdom). Haggai and Zechariah rebuked the people for their failure to rebuild the temple. Malachi confronted them with their neglect of the temple and their false and profane worship.

KEY VERSES:
"For behold, the day is coming, burning like a furnace . . . But for you who fear My name, the sun of righteousness will rise with healing in its wings; and you will go forth and skip about like calves from the stall" (4:1–2).

KEY PEOPLE:
Malachi, the priests

KEY PLACES:
Jerusalem, the temple

SPECIAL FEATURES:
Malachi's literary style employs a dramatic use of questions asked by God and his people (for example, see 3:7–8).

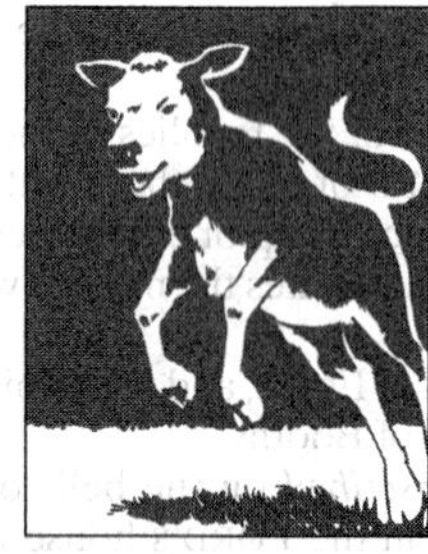

A VASE shatters, brushed by a careless elbow; a toy breaks, handled roughly by young fingers; and fabric rips, pulled by strong and angry hands. Spills and rips take time to clean up, effort to repair, and money to replace, but far more costly are shattered relationships. Unfaithfulness, untruths, hateful words, and forsaken vows tear delicate personal bonds and inflict wounds not easily healed. Most tragic, however, is a broken relationship with God.

God loves perfectly and completely. And his love is a love of action—giving, guiding, and guarding. He is altogether faithful, true to his promises to his chosen people. But consistently they spurn their loving God, breaking the covenant, following other gods, and living for themselves. So their relationship with him is shattered.

But the breach is not irreparable; all hope is not lost. God can heal and mend and reweave the fabric. Forgiveness is available. And that is grace.

This is the message of Malachi, God's prophet in Jerusalem. His words reminded the Jews, God's chosen nation, of their willful disobedience, beginning with the priests (1:1—2:9) and then including every person (2:10—3:15). They had shown contempt for God's name (1:6), offered defiled sacrifices (1:7–14), led others into sin (2:7–9), broken God's laws (2:11–16), called evil "good" (2:17), kept God's tithes and offerings for themselves (3:8–9), and become arrogant (3:13–15). The relationship was broken, and judgment and punishment would be theirs. In the midst of this wickedness, however, there were a faithful few—the remnant—who loved and honored God. God would shower his blessings upon these men and women (3:16–18).

Malachi paints a stunning picture of Israel's unfaithfulness that clearly shows the people to be worthy of punishment, but woven throughout this message is hope—the possibility of forgiveness. This is beautifully expressed in 4:2: "But for you who fear My name, the sun of righteousness will rise with healing in its wings; and you will go forth and skip about like calves from the stall."

Malachi concludes with a promise of the coming of "Elijah the prophet," who will offer God's forgiveness to all people through repentance and faith (4:5–6).

The book of Malachi forms a bridge between the Old Testament and the New Testament. As you read Malachi, see yourself as the recipient of this word of God to his people. Evaluate the depth of your commitment, the sincerity of your worship, and the direction of your life. Then allow God to restore your relationship with him through his love and forgiveness.

Ezra comes to Jerusalem 458	*Nehemiah comes to Jerusalem 445*	*Malachi becomes a prophet 430*

THE BLUEPRINT

1. The sinful priests (1:1—2:9)
2. The sinful people (2:10—3:15)
3. The faithful few (3:16—4:6)

Malachi rebuked the people and the priests for neglecting the worship of God and failing to live according to his will. The priests were corrupt; how could they lead the people? They had become stumbling blocks instead of spiritual leaders. The men were divorcing their wives and marrying pagan women; how could they have godly children? Their relationship to God had become inconsequential. If our relationship with God is unimportant, we need to take stock of ourselves by setting aside our sinful habits, putting the Lord first, and giving God our best each day.

MEGATHEMES

THEME	EXPLANATION	IMPORTANCE
God's Love	God loves his people even when they ignore or disobey him. He has great blessings to bestow on those who are faithful to him. His love never ends.	Because God loves us so much, he hates hypocrisy and careless living. This kind of living denies him the relationship he wants to have with us. What we give and how we live reflects the sincerity of our love for God.
The Sin of the Priests	Malachi singled out the priests for condemnation. They knew what God required, yet their sacrifices were unworthy and their service was insincere; they were lazy, arrogant, and insensitive. They had a casual attitude toward the worship of God and observance of God's standards.	If religious leaders go wrong, how will the people be led? We are all leaders in some capacity. Don't neglect your responsibilities or be ruled by what is convenient. Neglect and insensitivity are acts of disobedience. God wants leaders who are faithful and sincere.
The Sin of the People	The people had not learned the lesson of the exile, nor had they listened to the prophets. Men were callously divorcing their faithful wives to marry younger pagan women. This was against God's Law because it disobeyed his commands about marriage and threatened the religious training of the children. But pride had hardened the hearts of the people.	God deserves our very best honor, respect, and faithfulness. But sin hardens our heart to our true condition. Pride is unwarranted self-esteem; it is setting your own judgment above God's and looking down on others. Don't let pride keep you from giving God your devotion, money, marriage, and family.
The Lord's Coming	God's love for his faithful people is demonstrated by the Messiah's coming. The Messiah will lead the people to the realization of all their fondest hopes. The day of the Lord's coming will be a day of comfort and healing for a faithful few, and a day of judgment for those who reject him.	At Christ's first coming, he refined and purified all those who believed in him. Upon his return, he will expose and condemn those who are proud, insensitive, or unprepared. Yet God is able to heal and forgive. Forgiveness is available to all who come to him.

1. The sinful priests

God's Love for Jacob

1 The oracle of the word of the LORD to Israel through Malachi.
2 "I have loved you," says the LORD. But you say, "How have You loved us?" "*Was*
not Esau Jacob's brother?" declares the LORD. "Yet I have loved Jacob;
3 but I have hated Esau, and I have made his mountains a desolation and *appointed*
his inheritance for the jackals of the wilderness."
4 Though Edom says, "We have been beaten down, but we will return and build up
the ruins"; thus says the LORD of hosts, "They may build, but I will tear down; and *men*
will call them the wicked territory, and the people toward whom the LORD is indignant
forever."
5 Your eyes will see this and you will say, "The LORD be magnified beyond the border of Israel!"

Sin of the Priests

6 " 'A son honors *his* father, and a servant his master. Then if I am a father, where is
My honor? And if I am a master, where is My respect?' says the LORD of hosts to you,
O priests who despise My name. But you say, 'How have we despised Your name?'
7 "*You* are presenting defiled food upon My altar. But you say, 'How have we defiled
You?' In that you say, 'The table of the LORD is to be despised.'
8 "But when you present the blind for sacrifice, is it not evil? And when you present
the lame and sick, is it not evil? Why not offer it to your governor? Would he be pleased
with you? Or would he receive you kindly?" says the LORD of hosts.
9 "But now will you not entreat God's favor, that He may be gracious to us? With such
an offering on your part, will He receive any of you kindly?" says the LORD of hosts.
10 "Oh that there were one among you who would shut the gates, that you might not
uselessly kindle *fire on* My altar! I am not pleased with you," says the LORD of hosts,
"nor will I accept an offering from you.

1:1 Is 13:1; Nah 1:1; Hab 1:1; Zech 9:1
1:2 Deut 4:37; 7:8; 23:5; Is 41:8, 9; Jer 31:3; John 15:12; Rom 9:13
1:3 Jer 49:10, 16-18; Ezek 35:3, 4, 7, 8, 15
1:4 Jer 5:17; Is 9:9, 10; Amos 3:15; 5:11; 6:11; Ezek 35:9; Obad 10
1:5 Ps 35:27; Mic 5:4
1:6 Ex 20:12; Prov 30:11, 17; Deut 1:31; Is 1:2; Jer 3:4; Mal 2:10; Zeph 3:4; Mal 2:1-9
1:7 Mal 1:8, 13; Lev 3:11; 21:6, 8; Mal 1:12
1:8 Lev 22:22; Deut 15:21; Hag 1:1
1:9 Jer 27:18; Joel 2:12-14; Amos 5:22
1:10 Is 1:13; Jer 14:10, 12; Hos 5:6

1:1 An oracle is a message from God. Malachi, the last Old Testament prophet, preached after Haggai, Zechariah, and Nehemiah—about 430 B.C. The temple had been rebuilt for almost a century, and the people were losing their enthusiasm for worship. Apathy and disillusionment had set in because the exciting Messianic prophecies of Isaiah, Jeremiah, and Micah had not been fulfilled. Many of the sins that had brought the downfall of Jerusalem in 586 B.C. were still being practiced in Judah. Malachi confronted the hypocrites with their sin by portraying a graphic dialogue between a righteous God and his hardened people.

1:2 God's first message through Malachi was "I have loved you." Although this message applied specifically to Israel, it is a message of hope for all people in all times. Unfortunately, many people are cynical about God's love, using political and economic progress as a measure of success. Because the government was corrupt and the economy poor, the Israelites assumed that God didn't love them. They were wrong. God loves all people because he made them; however, his *eternal* rewards go only to those who are faithful to him.

1:2–5 The phrase "I have hated Esau" does not refer to Esau's eternal destiny. It simply means that God chose Jacob, not his brother Esau, to be the one through whom the nation of Israel and the Messiah would come (see Romans 9:10–13). God allowed Esau to father a nation, but this nation, Edom, later became one of Israel's chief enemies. The story of Jacob and Esau is found in Genesis 25:19–26. Because God chose Jacob and his descendants as the nation through whom the world would be blessed, God cared for them in a special way. Ironically, they rejected God after he chose them.

1:6ff God charged the priests with failing to honor him (to the point of showing contempt for his name) and failing to be good spiritual examples to the people. The temple had been rebuilt in 516 B.C., and worship was being conducted there, but the priests did not worship God properly—they were not following his laws for the sacrifices. Ezra, the priest, had sparked a great revival around 458 B.C. However, by Malachi's time, the nation's leaders had once again fallen away from God, and the people right along with them. The worship of God was no longer from heartfelt adoration; instead it was simply a burdensome job for the priests.

1:6–8 God's Law required that only perfect animals be offered to God (see for example, Leviticus 1:3). But these priests were allowing the people to offer blind, crippled, and diseased animals to God. God accused them of dishonoring him by offering imperfect sacrifices, and he was greatly displeased. The New Testament says that our lives should be living sacrifices to God (Romans 12:1). If we give God only our leftover time, money, and energy, we repeat the same sin as these worshipers who didn't want to bring anything valuable to God. What we give God reflects our true attitude toward him.

1:7–8 The people sacrificed to God wrongly through (1) expedience—being as cheap as possible, (2) neglect—not caring how they offered the sacrifice, and (3) outright disobedience—sacrificing their own way and not as God had commanded. Their methods of giving showed their real attitudes toward God. How about your attitude? Do expedience, neglect, or disobedience characterize your giving?

1:10 As intermediaries between God and the people, priests were responsible for reflecting God's attitudes and character. By accepting imperfect sacrifices, they were leading the people to believe that God accepted those sacrifices as well. But God says, "I am not pleased with you." As Christians, we are often in the same position as these priests because we reflect God to our friends and family. What image of God's character and attitudes do they see in you? If you casually accept sin, you are like these priests in Malachi's day, and God will not be pleased with you.

1:11 Is 45:6; Ps 111:9; Is 66:18, 19; Is 60:6; Is 12:4, 5; 54:5; Jer 10:6, 7

1:12 Mal 1:7

1:13 Is 43:22; Lev 6:4; Is 61:8; Mal 1:8; Mal 1:10

1:14 Acts 5:1-4; Lev 22:18-20; Zech 14:9; Zeph 2:11

2:2 Lev 26:14, 15; Deut 28:15; Deut 28:16-20; Mal 3:9

2:3 Lev 26:16; Deut 28:38; Nah 3:6; Ex 29:14

2:4 Num 3:11-13, 45; 18:21; Neh 13:29; Mal 3:1

2:5 Num 25:12; Num 25:7, 8, 13

2:6 Ps 119:142, 151, 160; Deut 33:8, 9; Ps 37:37; Jer 23:22

11 "For from the rising of the sun even to its setting, My name *will be* great among the
nations, and in every place incense is going to be offered to My name, and a grain offering *that is* pure; for My name *will be* great among the nations," says the LORD of hosts.
12 "But you are profaning it, in that you say, 'The table of the Lord is defiled, and as for
its fruit, its food is to be despised.'
13 "You also say, 'My, how tiresome it is!' And you disdainfully sniff at it," says the LORD
of hosts, "and you bring what was taken by robbery and *what is* lame or sick; so you bring
the offering! Should I receive that from your hand?" says the LORD.
14 "But cursed be the swindler who has a male in his flock and vows it, but sacrifices a
blemished animal to the Lord, for I am a great King," says the LORD of hosts, "and My
name is feared among the nations."

Priests to Be Disciplined

2 "And now this commandment is for you, O priests.
2 "If you do not listen, and if you do not take it to heart to give honor to My name,"
says the LORD of hosts, "then I will send the curse upon you and I will curse your blessings; and indeed, I have cursed them *already,* because you are not taking *it* to heart.
3 "Behold, I am going to rebuke your offspring, and I will spread refuse on your faces,
the refuse of your feasts; and you will be taken away with it.
4 "Then you will know that I have sent this commandment to you, that My covenant
may continue with Levi," says the LORD of hosts.
5 "My covenant with him was *one of* life and peace, and I gave them to him *as an object
of* reverence; so he revered Me and stood in awe of My name.
6 "True instruction was in his mouth and unrighteousness was not found on his lips; he
walked with Me in peace and uprightness, and he turned many back from iniquity.

MALACHI Malachi served as a prophet to Judah about 430 B.C. He was the last of the Old Testament prophets.	*Climate of the times*	The city of Jerusalem and the temple had been rebuilt for almost a century, but the people had become complacent in their worship of God.
	Main message	The people's relationship with God was broken because of their sin, and they would soon be punished. But the few who repented would receive God's blessing, highlighted in his promise to send a Messiah.
	Importance of message	Hypocrisy, neglecting God, and careless living have devastating consequences. Serving and worshiping God must be the primary focus of our lives, both now and in eternity.
	Contemporary prophets	None

1:11 A theme that can be heard throughout the Old Testament is affirmed in this book—"My name will be great among the nations." God had a chosen people, the Jews, through whom he planned to save and bless the entire world. Today God still wants to save and bless the world through all who believe in him—Jews and Gentiles. Christians are now his chosen people, and our pure offering to the Lord is our new life in Christ. Are you available to God to be used in making his name great to the nations? This mission begins in our homes and in our neighborhoods, but it doesn't stop there. We must work and pray for God's worldwide mission.

1:13 Worship was a burden to these priests. Too many think that following God is supposed to make life easy and more comfortable. They are looking for a God of convenience. The truth is that it often takes hard work to live by God's high standards. He may call us to face poverty or suffering. But if serving God is more important to us than anything else, what we must give up is of little importance compared to what we gain—eternal life with God.

2:1–2 God warned the priests that if they did not honor his name, he would punish them. Like these priests, we too are called to honor God's name—to worship him. This means acknowledging God for who he is—the almighty Creator of the universe who alone is perfect and who reaches down to sinful mankind with perfect love. According to this definition, are you honoring God's name?

2:1–2 The priests didn't take seriously (take to heart) God's priority, even though he had reminded them through his word many times. How do you find out what is most important to God? Begin by loving him with all your heart, soul, and strength (Deuteronomy 6:5). This means listening to what God says in his Word and then setting your heart, mind, and will on doing what he says. When we love God, his Word becomes a shining light that guides our daily activities. The priests in Malachi's day had stopped loving God, and thus they did not know nor care what he wanted.

2:4–6 Levi "walked with God . . . and he turned many back from iniquity" (2:6). Levi was the ancestor of the tribe of Levites, the tribe set apart for service to God (Numbers 1:47–54). The Levites became God's ministers, first in the tabernacle, then in the temple. In these verses, God was addressing the priests who were from this tribe, saying that they should listen to the laws he gave their ancestor Levi, and follow his example.

7 "For the lips of a priest should preserve knowledge, and men should seek instruction
from his mouth; for he is the messenger of the LORD of hosts.
8 "But as for you, you have turned aside from the way; you have caused many to stumble by the instruction; you have corrupted the covenant of Levi," says the LORD of hosts.
9 "So I also have made you despised and abased before all the people, just as you are
not keeping My ways but are showing partiality in the instruction.

2. The sinful people

Sin in the Family

10 "Do we not all have one father? Has not one God created us? Why do we deal treacherously each against his brother so as to profane the covenant of our fathers?
11 "Judah has dealt treacherously, and an abomination has been committed in Israel
and in Jerusalem; for Judah has profaned the sanctuary of the LORD which He loves
and has married the daughter of a foreign god.
12 "*As* for the man who does this, may the LORD cut off from the tents of Jacob *everyone* who awakes and answers, or who presents an offering to the LORD of hosts.
13 "This is another thing you do: you cover the altar of the LORD with tears, with weeping and with groaning, because He no longer regards the offering or accepts *it with* favor
from your hand.
14 "Yet you say, 'For what reason?' Because the LORD has been a witness between you
and the wife of your youth, against whom you have dealt treacherously, though she is
your companion and your wife by covenant.
15 "But not one has done *so* who has a remnant of the Spirit. And what did *that* one *do*
while he was seeking a godly offspring? Take heed then to your spirit, and let no one
deal treacherously against the wife of your youth.
16 "For I hate divorce," says the LORD, the God of Israel, "and him who covers his garment with wrong," says the LORD of hosts. "So take heed to your spirit, that you do not
deal treacherously."
17 You have wearied the LORD with your words. Yet you say, "How have we wearied
Him?" In that you say, "Everyone who does evil is good in the sight of the LORD, and He
delights in them," or, "Where is the God of justice?"

2:7 Lev 10:11; Neh 8:7; Num 27:21; Deut 17:8-11; Jer 18:18; Ezek 7:26; Hag 1:13

2:8 Jer 18:15; Num 25:12, 13; Neh 13:29; Ezek 44:10

2:9 Nah 3:6; Ezek 7:26; Deut 1:17; Mic 3:11

2:10 Is 63:16; 64:8; Jer 31:9; 1 Cor 8:6; Eph 4:6; Acts 17:24f; Jer 9:4, 5; Ex 19:4-6; 24:3, 7, 8

2:11 Jer 3:7-9; Ezra 9:1, 2

2:12 Ezek 24:21; Hos 9:12; Mal 1:10, 13

2:13 Jer 11:14; 14:12

2:14 Is 54:6; Jer 9:2; Mal 3:5

2:15 Gen 2:24; Matt 19:4, 5; Ruth 4:12; 1 Sam 2:20; Ex 20:14; Lev 20:10

2:16 Deut 24:1; Matt 5:31; 19:6-8; Ps 73:6; Is 59:6

2:17 Is 43:22, 24; Is 5:20; Zeph 1:12; Job 9:24; 2 Pet 3:4; Is 5:19; Jer 17:15

2:7–8 Malachi was angry at the priests because, though they were to be God's messengers, they did not know God's will. And this lack of knowledge caused them to lead God's people astray. Their ignorance was willful and inexcusable. Pastors and leaders of God's people *must* know God's Word—what it says, what it means, and how it applies to daily life. How much time do you spend in God's Word?

2:9 The priests had allowed influential and favored people to break the law. The priests were so dependent on these people for support that they could not afford to confront them when they did wrong. In your church, are certain people allowed to do wrong without criticism? There should be no double standard based on wealth or position. Let your standards be those presented in God's Word. Playing favorites is contemptible in God's sight (see James 2:1–9).

2:10–16 The people were being unfaithful. Though not openly saying they rejected God, they were living as if he did not exist. Men were marrying pagan women who worshiped idols. Divorce was common, occurring for no reason other than a desire for change. People acted as if they could do anything without being punished. And they wondered why God refused to accept their offerings and bless them (2:13)! We cannot successfully separate our dealings with God from the rest of our lives. He must be Lord of all.

2:11–12 After the temple had been rebuilt and the walls completed, the people were excited to see past prophecies coming true. But as time passed, the prophecies about the destruction of God's enemies and a coming Messiah were not immediately fulfilled. The people became discouraged, and they grew complacent about obeying all of God's laws. This complacency gradually led to blatant sin, such as marriage to those who worshiped idols. Ezra and Nehemiah also had confronted this problem years earlier (Ezra 9–10; Nehemiah 13:23–31).

2:14 The people were complaining about their adverse circumstances when they had only themselves to blame. People often try to avoid guilt feelings by shifting the blame. But this doesn't solve the problem. When you face problems, look first at yourself. If you changed your attitude or behavior, would the problem be solved?

2:14–15 Divorce in these times was practiced exclusively by men. They broke faith with their wives and ignored the bonding between a husband and a wife that God instills (the two become one person), as well as his purpose for them (raising children who love the Lord, "godly offspring"). Not only were men breaking faith with their wives, but they also were ignoring the bonding relationship and spiritual purpose of being united with God.

2:15–16 "Take heed then to your spirit, and let no one deal treacherously" means to have the same commitment to marriage that God has to his promises with his people. We need passion in the marriage relationship to keep the commitment and intimacy satisfying, but this passion should be focused exclusively on our spouse.

2:17—3:6 God was tired of the way the people had cynically twisted his truths. He would punish those who insisted that because God was silent, he approved of their actions or at least would never punish them. God would also punish those who professed a counterfeit faith while acting sinfully (see 3:5).

3:1
Matt 11:10, 14; Mark 1:2; Luke 1:76; 7:27; Hag 1:13; John 1:6, 7; Is 40:3; Is 63:9

3:2
Is 33:14; Ezek 22:14; Rev 6:17; Zech 13:9; Matt 3:10-12; 1 Cor 3:13-15

3:3
Is 1:25; Dan 12:10; Ps 4:5; 51:19

3:4
Ps 51:17-19; 2 Chr 7:1-3, 12

3:5
Deut 18:10; Jer 27:9, 10; Ezek 22:9-11; Jer 5:2; 7:9; Zech 5:4; Lev 19:13; Ex 22:22-24; Deut 27:19

3:6
Num 23:19; James 1:17

3:7
Jer 7:25, 26; 16:11, 12; Zech 1:3

3:8
Neh 13:11, 12

3:9
Mal 2:2

3:10
Lev 27:30; Num 18:21-24; Deut 12:6; 14:22-29; Neh 13:12; Ps 78:23-29; Ezek 34:26; Lev 26:3-5

3:11
Joel 1:4; 2:25

3:12
Is 61:9; Is 62:4

The Purifier

3 "Behold, I am going to send My messenger, and he will clear the way before
Me. And the Lord, whom you seek, will suddenly come to His temple; and the messenger of the covenant, in whom you delight, behold, He is coming," says the LORD of
hosts.
2 "But who can endure the day of His coming? And who can stand when He appears?
For He is like a refiner's fire and like fullers' soap.
3 "He will sit as a smelter and purifier of silver, and He will purify the sons of Levi and
refine them like gold and silver, so that they may present to the LORD offerings in righteousness.
4 "Then the offering of Judah and Jerusalem will be pleasing to the LORD as in the
days of old and as in former years.
5 "Then I will draw near to you for judgment; and I will be a swift witness against the
sorcerers and against the adulterers and against those who swear falsely, and against those
who oppress the wage earner in his wages, the widow and the orphan, and those who
turn aside the alien and do not fear Me," says the LORD of hosts.
6 "For I, the LORD, do not change; therefore you, O sons of Jacob, are not consumed.
7 "From the days of your fathers you have turned aside from My statutes and have not
kept *them*. Return to Me, and I will return to you," says the LORD of hosts. "But you say,
'How shall we return?'

You Have Robbed God

8 "Will a man [1]rob God? Yet you are robbing Me! But you say, 'How have we robbed
You?' In tithes and offerings.
9 "You are cursed with a curse, for you are [2]robbing Me, the whole nation *of you!*
10 "Bring the whole tithe into the storehouse, so that there may be food in My house,
and test Me now in this," says the LORD of hosts, "if I will not open for you the windows
of heaven and pour out for you a blessing until [3]it overflows.
11 "Then I will rebuke the devourer for you, so that it will not destroy the fruits of the
ground; nor will your vine in the field cast *its grapes*," says the LORD of hosts.
12 "All the nations will call you blessed, for you shall be a delightful land," says the LORD
of hosts.
13 "Your words have been arrogant against Me," says the LORD. "Yet you say, 'What
have we spoken against You?'

1 Or *defraud* **2** Or *defrauding* **3** Or *there is not* room *enough*

3:1 There are two messengers in this verse. The first is usually understood to be John the Baptist (Matthew 11:10; Luke 7:27). The second messenger is Jesus, the Messiah, for whom both Malachi and John the Baptist prepared the way.

3:2–3 In the process of refining metals, the raw metal is heated with fire until it melts. The impurities separate from it and rise to the surface. They are skimmed off, leaving the pure metal. Without this heating and melting, there could be no purifying. As the impurities are skimmed off the top, the reflection of the worker appears in the smooth, pure surface. As we are purified by God, his reflection in our lives will become more and more clear to those around us. God says that leaders (here the Levites) should be especially open to his purification process in their lives. Fullers' soap was alkali used to whiten cloth. It is also used here as a symbol of the purifying process.

3:7 God's patience seems endless! Throughout history, his people have disobeyed, even scorned, his laws, but he has always been willing to accept them back. Here, however, the people have the nerve to imply that they never disobeyed ("How shall we return?")! Many people have turned their backs on forgiveness and restoration because they have refused to admit their sin. Don't follow their example. God is ready to return to us if we are willing to return to him.

3:8–12 Malachi urged the people to stop holding back their tithes, to stop keeping from God what he deserved. The tithing system began during the time of Moses (Leviticus 27:30–34; Deuteronomy 14:22). The Levites received some of the tithe because they could not possess land of their own (Numbers 18:20–21). During Malachi's day, the people were not giving tithes, so the Levites went to work to earn a living, thereby neglecting their God-given responsibilities to care for the temple and for the service of worship. Everything we have is from God; so when we refuse to return to him a part of what he has given, we rob him. Do you selfishly want to keep 100 percent of what God gives, or are you willing to return at least 10 percent for helping to advance God's kingdom?

3:8–12 The people of Malachi's day ignored God's command to give a tithe of their income to his temple. They may have feared losing what they had worked so hard to get, but in this they misjudged God. "Give, and it will be given to you," Jesus says (Luke 6:38). When we give, we must remember that the blessings God promises are not always material and may not be experienced completely here on earth, but we will certainly receive them in our future life with him.

3:10 The "storehouse" was a place in the temple for storing grain and other food given as tithes. The priests lived off these gifts.

3:13–15 These verses describe the people's arrogant attitude toward God. When we ask, "What good does it do to serve God?" we are really asking, "What good does it do for *me?*" Our focus is selfish. Our real question should be, "What good does it do for God?" We must serve God just because he is God and deserves to be served.

14"You have said, 'It is vain to serve God; and what profit is it that we have kept His
charge, and that we have walked in mourning before the LORD of hosts?
15 'So now we call the arrogant blessed; not only are the doers of wickedness built up
but they also test God and escape.' "

3:14 Jer 2:25; 18:12; Is 58:3

3:15 Is 2:22; Mal 4:1; Jer 7:10

3. The faithful few

The Book of Remembrance

16 Then those who [4]feared the LORD spoke to one another, and the LORD gave attention and heard *it,* and a book of remembrance was written before Him for those who
[4]fear the LORD and who esteem His name.
17"They will be Mine," says the LORD of hosts, "on the day that I prepare *My* own
possession, and I will spare them as a man spares his own son who serves him."
18 So you will again distinguish between the righteous and the wicked, between one
who serves God and one who does not serve Him.

3:16 Ps 34:15; Jer 31:18-20; Is 4:3; Dan 12:1

3:17 Is 43:1; Is 4:2; Ex 19:5; Deut 7:6; Is 43:21; 1 Pet 2:9; Ps 103:13

3:18 Gen 18:25; Amos 5:15

Final Admonition

4 "For behold, the day is coming, burning like a furnace; and all the arrogant
and every evildoer will be chaff; and the day that is coming will set them ablaze,"
says the LORD of hosts, "so that it will leave them neither root nor branch."
2"But for you who [5]fear My name, the sun of righteousness will rise with healing in its
wings; and you will go forth and skip about like calves from the stall.
3"You will tread down the wicked, for they will be ashes under the soles of your feet
on the day which I am preparing," says the LORD of hosts.
4"Remember the law of Moses My servant, *even the* statutes and ordinances which I
commanded him in Horeb for all Israel.
5"Behold, I am going to send you Elijah the prophet before the coming of the great
and terrible day of the LORD.
6"He will restore the hearts of the fathers to *their* children and the hearts of the children to their fathers, so that I will not come and smite the land with a curse."

4 Or *revere(d)* **5** Or *revere*

3:16 The "book of remembrance" may or may not be an actual book. The point is that God will remember those who remain faithful to him, and who love, fear, honor, and respect him.

3:17 God's treasured possession are those faithful to him. This fulfills the promise he made in the covenant to his people (Exodus 19:5). According to 1 Peter 2:9, believers are God's treasured possession. Have you committed your life to God for safekeeping?

4:2 In the day of the Lord, God's wrath toward the wicked will burn like a furnace (4:1). But he will be like the healing warmth of the sun to those who love and obey him. John the Baptist prophesied that with the coming of Jesus, the dawn was about to break with light for those in sin's darkness (Luke 1:76–79). In Isaiah 60:20 and Revelation 21:23–24 we learn that no light will be needed in God's holy city, because God himself will be the light.

4:2ff These last verses of the Old Testament are filled with hope. Regardless of how life looks now, God controls the future, and everything will be made right. We who have loved and served God look forward to a joyful celebration. This hope for the future becomes ours when we trust God with our lives.

4:4 These laws, given to Moses at Horeb (Mount Sinai), were the foundation of the nation's civil, moral, and ceremonial life (Exodus 20; Deuteronomy 4:5–6). We still must obey these moral laws because they apply to all generations.

4:5–6 Elijah was one of the greatest prophets who ever lived (his story is recorded in 1 Kings 17—2 Kings 2). With Malachi's death, the voice of God's prophets would be silent for 400 years. Then a prophet would come, like Elijah, to herald Christ's coming (Matthew 17:10–13; Luke 1:17). This prophet was John the Baptist. John prepared people's hearts for Jesus by urging people to repent of their sins. Christ's coming would bring unity and peace, but also judgment on those who refused to turn from their sins.

4:6 Malachi gives us practical guidelines about commitment to God. God deserves the best we have to offer (1:7–10). We must be willing to change our wrong ways of living (2:1–2). We should make family a lifelong priority (2:13–16). We should welcome God's refining process in our lives (3:3). We should tithe our income (3:8–12). There is no room for pride (3:13–15).

Malachi closes his messages by pointing to that great final day of judgment. For those who are committed to God, judgment day will be a day of joy because it will usher in eternity in God's presence. Those who have ignored God will be "chaff," to be burned up (4:1). To help the people prepare for that day of judgment, God would send a prophet like Elijah (John the Baptist), who would prepare the way for Jesus, the Messiah. The New Testament begins with this prophet calling the people to turn from their sins and to turn toward God. Such a commitment to God demands great sacrifice on our part, but we can be sure it will be worth it all in the end.

THE NEW TESTAMENT

MATTHEW

Herod the Great begins to rule 37 B.C.	Jesus is born 6/5 B.C.	Escape to Egypt 5/4 B.C.	Herod the Great dies 4 B.C.	Return to Nazareth 4/3 B.C.	Judea becomes a Roman province A.D. 6	Jesus visits temple as a boy 6/7

VITAL STATISTICS

PURPOSE:
To prove that Jesus is the Messiah, the eternal King

AUTHOR:
Matthew (Levi)

TO WHOM WRITTEN:
Matthew wrote especially to the Jews

DATE WRITTEN:
Approximately A.D. 60–65

SETTING:
Matthew was a Jewish tax collector who became one of Jesus' disciples. This Gospel forms the connecting link between the Old and New Testaments because of its emphasis on the fulfillment of prophecy.

KEY VERSE:
"Do not think that I came to abolish the Law or the Prophets; I did not come to abolish but to fulfill" (5:17).

KEY PEOPLE:
Jesus, Mary, Joseph, John the Baptist, the disciples, the religious leaders, Caiaphas, Pilate, Mary Magdalene

KEY PLACES:
Bethlehem, Jerusalem, Capernaum, Galilee, Judea

SPECIAL FEATURES:
Matthew is filled with messianic language ("Son of David" is used throughout) and Old Testament references (53 quotes and 76 other references). This Gospel was not written as a chronological account; its purpose was to present the clear evidence that Jesus is the Messiah, the Savior.

AS the motorcade slowly winds through the city, thousands pack the sidewalks hoping to catch a glimpse. Marching bands with great fanfare announce the arrival, and protective agents scan the crowd and run alongside the limousine. Pomp, ceremony, protocol—modern symbols of position and evidences of importance—herald the arrival of a head of state. Whether they are leaders by birth or election, we honor and respect them.

The Jews waited for a leader who had been promised centuries before by prophets. They believed that this leader—the Messiah ("anointed one")—would rescue them from their Roman oppressors and establish a new kingdom. As their king, he would rule the world with justice. However, many Jews overlooked prophecies that also spoke of this king as a suffering servant who would be rejected and killed. It is no wonder, then, that few recognized Jesus as the Messiah. How could this humble carpenter's son from Nazareth be their king? But Jesus was and is the King of all the earth!

Matthew (Levi) was one of Jesus' 12 disciples. Once he was a despised tax collector, but his life was changed by this man from Galilee. Matthew wrote this Gospel to his fellow Jews to prove that Jesus is the Messiah and to explain God's kingdom.

Matthew begins his account by giving Jesus' genealogy. He then tells of Jesus' birth and early years, including the family's escape to Egypt from the murderous Herod and their return to Nazareth. Following Jesus' baptism by John (3:16–17) and his defeat of Satan in the wilderness, Jesus begins his public ministry by calling his first disciples and giving the Sermon on the Mount (chapters 5—7). Matthew shows Christ's authority by reporting his miracles of healing the sick and the demon-possessed, and even raising the dead.

Despite opposition from the Pharisees and others in the religious establishment (chapters 12—15), Jesus continued to teach concerning the kingdom of heaven (chapters 16—20). During this time, Jesus spoke with his disciples about his imminent death and resurrection (16:21) and revealed his true identity to Peter, James, and John (17:1–5). Near the end of his ministry, Jesus entered Jerusalem in a triumphant procession (21:1–11). But soon opposition mounted, and Jesus knew that his death was near. So he taught his disciples about the future—what they could expect before his return (chapter 24) and how to live until then (chapter 25).

In Matthew's finale (chapters 26—28), he focuses on Jesus' final days on earth—the Last Supper, his prayer in Gethsemane, the betrayal by Judas, the flight of the disciples, Peter's denial, the trials before Caiaphas and Pilate, Jesus' final words on the cross, and his burial in a borrowed tomb. But the story does not end there, for the Messiah rose from the dead—conquering death and then telling his followers to continue his work by making disciples in all nations.

As you read this Gospel, listen to Matthew's clear message: Jesus is the Christ, the King of kings and Lord of lords. Celebrate his victory over evil and death, and make Jesus the Lord of your life.

Tiberius Caesar becomes emperor 14	*Pontius Pilate appointed governor 26*	*Jesus begins his ministry 26/27*	*Jesus chooses twelve disciples 28*	*Jesus feeds 5,000 29*	*Jesus is crucified, rises again, and ascends 30*

THE BLUEPRINT

A. BIRTH AND PREPARATION OF JESUS, THE KING (1:1—4:11)

The people of Israel were waiting for the Messiah, their king. Matthew begins his book by showing how Jesus Christ was a descendant of David. But Matthew goes on to show that God did not send Jesus to be an earthly king but a heavenly King. His kingdom would be much greater than David's because it would never end. Even at Jesus' birth, many recognized him as a King. Herod, the ruler, as well as Satan, was afraid of Jesus' kingship and tried to stop him, but others worshiped him and brought royal gifts. We must be willing to recognize Jesus for who he really is and worship him as King of our life.

B. MESSAGE AND MINISTRY OF JESUS, THE KING (4:12—25:46)

1. Jesus begins his ministry
2. Jesus gives the Sermon on the Mount
3. Jesus performs many miracles
4. Jesus teaches about the kingdom
5. Jesus encounters differing reactions to his ministry
6. Jesus faces conflict with the religious leaders
7. Jesus teaches on the Mount of Olives

Jesus gave the Sermon on the Mount, directions for living in his kingdom. He also told many parables about the difference between his kingdom and the kingdoms of earth. Forgiveness, peace, and putting others first are some of the characteristics that make one great in the kingdom of God. And to be great in God's kingdom, we must live by God's standards right now. Jesus came to show us how to live as faithful subjects in his kingdom.

C. DEATH AND RESURRECTION OF JESUS, THE KING (26:1—28:20)

Jesus was formally presented to the nation of Israel but was rejected. How strange for the King to be accused, arrested, and crucified. But Jesus demonstrated his power, even over death, through his resurrection and gained access for us into his kingdom. With all this evidence that Jesus is God's Son, we, too, should accept him as our Lord.

MEGATHEMES

THEME	EXPLANATION	IMPORTANCE
Jesus Christ, the King	Jesus is revealed as the King of kings. His miraculous birth, his life and teaching, his miracles, and his triumph over death show his true identity.	Jesus cannot be equated with any person or power. He is the supreme ruler of time and eternity, heaven and earth, humans and angels. We should give him his rightful place as King of our life.
The Messiah	Jesus was the Messiah, the one for whom the Jews had waited to deliver them from Roman oppression. Yet, tragically, they didn't recognize him when he came because his kingship was not what they expected. The true purpose of God's anointed deliverer was to die for all people to free them from sin's oppression.	Because Jesus was sent by God, we can trust him with our life. It is worth everything we have to acknowledge him and give ourselves to him, because he came to be our Messiah, our Savior.
Kingdom of God	Jesus came to earth to begin his kingdom. His full kingdom will be realized at his return and will be made up of anyone who has faithfully followed him.	The way to enter God's kingdom is by faith—believing in Christ to save us from sin and change our life. We must do the work of his kingdom now to be prepared for his return.
Teachings	Jesus taught the people through sermons, illustrations, and parables. Through his teachings, he showed the true ingredients of faith and how to guard against a fruitless and hypocritical life.	Jesus' teachings show us how to prepare for life in his eternal kingdom by living properly right now. He lived what he taught, and we, too, must practice what we preach.

Resurrection	When Jesus rose from the dead, he rose in power as the true King. In his victory over death, he established his credentials as King and his power and authority over evil.	The Resurrection shows Jesus' all-powerful life for us—not even death could stop his plan of offering eternal life. Those who believe in Jesus can hope for a resurrection like his. Our role is to tell his story to all the earth so that everyone may share in his victory.

KEY PLACES IN MATTHEW

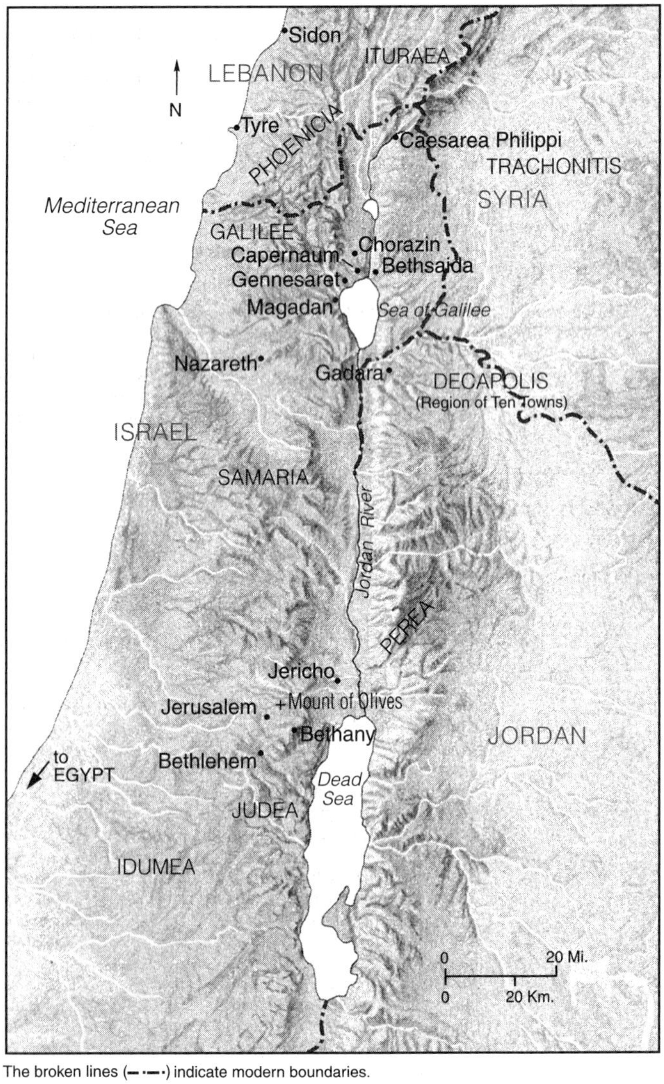

Jesus' earthly story begins in the town of Bethlehem in the Roman province of Judea (2:1). A threat to kill the infant king led Joseph to take his family to Egypt (2:14). When they returned, God led them to settle in Nazareth in Galilee (2:22–23). At about age 30, Jesus was baptized in the Jordan River and was tempted by Satan in the Judean wilderness (3:13; 4:1). Jesus set up his base of operations in Capernaum (4:12–13) and from there ministered throughout Israel, telling parables, teaching about the kingdom, and healing the sick. He traveled to Gadara and healed two demon-possessed men (8:28ff); fed over 5,000 people with five loaves and two fish on the shores of Galilee near Bethsaida (14:15ff); healed the sick in Gennesaret (14:34ff); ministered to the Gentiles in Tyre and Sidon (15:21ff); visited Caesarea Philippi, where Peter declared him to be the Messiah (16:13ff); and taught in Perea, across the Jordan (19:1). As he set out on his last visit to Jerusalem, he told the disciples what would happen to him there (20:17ff). He spent some time in Jericho (20:29) and then stayed in Bethany at night as he went back and forth to Jerusalem during his last week (21:17ff). In Jerusalem he would be crucified, but he would rise again.

The broken lines (—·—·) indicate modern boundaries.

A. BIRTH AND PREPARATION OF JESUS, THE KING (1:1—4:11)

Matthew opens his Gospel with a genealogy to prove that Jesus is the descendant of both King David and Abraham, just as the Old Testament had predicted. Jesus' birth didn't go unnoticed, for both shepherds and magi came to worship him. The Jewish people were waiting for the Messiah to appear. Finally, he was born, but the Jews didn't recognize him because they were looking for a different kind of king.

The Ancestors of Jesus
(3/Luke 3:23-38)

1:1 2 Sam 7:12-16; Ps 89:3f; 132:11; Is 9:6f; 11:1; Matt 9:27; Luke 1:32, 69; John 7:42; Acts 13:23; Rom 1:3; Rev 22:16; Matt 1:1-6: Luke 3:32-34; Gen 22:18; Gal 3:16

1:3 Ruth 4:18-22; 1 Chr 2:1-15; Matt 1:3-6

1:6 2 Sam 11:27; 12:24

1:7 1 Chr 3:10ff

1:10 1 Chr 3:14

1:11 2 Kin 24:14f; Jer 27:20; Matt 1:17

1:12 2 Kin 24:14f; Jer 27:20; Matt 1:17

1 The record of the genealogy of Jesus the Messiah, the son of David, the son of
Abraham:
2 Abraham was the father of Isaac, Isaac the father of Jacob, and Jacob the father of
[1]Judah and his brothers.
3 Judah was the father of Perez and Zerah by Tamar, Perez was the father of Hezron,
and Hezron the father of Ram.
4 Ram was the father of Amminadab, Amminadab the father of Nahshon, and Nahshon the father of Salmon.
5 Salmon was the father of Boaz by Rahab, Boaz was the father of Obed by Ruth, and
Obed the father of Jesse.
6 Jesse was the father of David the king.
David was the father of Solomon by [2]Bathsheba who had been the wife of Uriah.
7 Solomon was the father of Rehoboam, Rehoboam the father of Abijah, and Abijah
the father of Asa.
8 Asa was the father of Jehoshaphat, Jehoshaphat the father of Joram, and Joram
the father of Uzziah.
9 Uzziah was the father of Jotham, Jotham the father of Ahaz, and Ahaz the father
of Hezekiah.
10 Hezekiah was the father of Manasseh, Manasseh the father of Amon, and Amon
the father of Josiah.
11 Josiah became the father of Jeconiah and his brothers, at the time of the deportation to Babylon.
12 After the deportation to Babylon: Jeconiah became the father of Shealtiel, and
Shealtiel the father of Zerubbabel.
13 Zerubbabel was the father of Abihud, Abihud the father of Eliakim, and Eliakim
the father of Azor.
14 Azor was the father of Zadok, Zadok the father of Achim, and Achim the father of
Eliud.
15 Eliud was the father of Eleazar, Eleazar the father of Matthan, and Matthan the
father of Jacob.

1 Gr *Judas;* names of people in the Old Testament are given in their Old Testament form **2** Lit *her of Uriah*

1:1 Presenting this genealogy was one of the most interesting ways that Matthew could begin a book for a Jewish audience. Because a person's family line proved his or her standing as one of God's chosen people, Matthew began by showing that Jesus was a descendant of Abraham, the father of all Jews, and a direct descendant of David, fulfilling Old Testament prophecies about the Messiah's line. The facts of this ancestry were carefully preserved. This is the first of many proofs recorded by Matthew to show that Jesus is the true Messiah.

1:1ff More than 400 years had passed since the last Old Testament prophecies, and faithful Jews all over the world were still waiting for the Messiah (Luke 3:15). Matthew wrote this book to Jews to present Jesus as King and Messiah, the promised descendant of David who would reign forever (Isaiah 11:1–5). The Gospel of Matthew links the Old and New Testaments and contains many references that show how Jesus fulfilled Old Testament prophecy.

1:1ff Jesus entered human history when the land of Palestine was controlled by Rome and considered an insignificant outpost of the vast and mighty Roman empire. The presence of Roman soldiers in Israel gave the Jews military peace, but at the price of oppression, slavery, injustice, and immorality. Into this kind of world came the promised Messiah.

1:1–17 In the first 17 verses we meet 46 people whose lifetimes span 2,000 years. All were ancestors of Jesus, but they varied considerably in personality, spirituality, and experience. Some were heroes of faith—like Abraham, Isaac, Ruth, and David. Some had shady reputations—like Rahab and Tamar. Many were very ordinary—like Hezron, Ram, Nahshon, and Achim. And others were evil—like Manasseh and Abijah. God's work in history is not limited by human failures or sins, and he works through ordinary people. Just as God used all kinds of people to bring his Son into the world, so he uses all kinds today to accomplish his will. And God wants to use you.

1:11 The deportation, or exile, occurred in 586 B.C. when Nebuchadnezzar, king of Babylonia, conquered Judah, destroyed Jerusalem, and took thousands of captives to Babylonia.

16 Jacob was the father of Joseph the husband of Mary, by whom Jesus was born, who
is called the Messiah.
17 So all the generations from Abraham to David are fourteen generations; from David to the deportation to Babylon, fourteen generations; and from the deportation to Babylon to the Messiah, fourteen generations.

An Angel Appears to Joseph
(8)

18 Now the birth of Jesus Christ was as follows: when His mother Mary had been betrothed to Joseph, before they came together she was found to be with child by the Holy Spirit.
19 And Joseph her husband, being a righteous man and not wanting to disgrace her,
planned [3]to send her away secretly.
20 But when he had considered this, behold, an angel of the Lord appeared to him in
a dream, saying, "Joseph, son of David, do not be afraid to take Mary as your wife; for the Child who has been [4]conceived in her is of the Holy Spirit.
21 "She will bear a Son; and you shall call His name Jesus, for He will save His people
from their sins."
22 Now all this took place to fulfill what was spoken by the Lord through the prophet:
23 "BEHOLD, THE VIRGIN SHALL BE WITH CHILD AND SHALL BEAR A SON, AND THEY SHALL CALL HIS NAME IMMANUEL," which translated means, "GOD WITH US."

3 Or *to divorce her* **4** Lit *begotten*

1:16 Matt 27:17, 22; Luke 2:11; John 4:25

1:17 2 Kin 24:14f; Jer 27:20; Matt 1:11, 12

1:18 Matt 12:46; Luke 1:27; Luke 1:35

1:19 Deut 22:20-24; 24:1-4; John 8:4, 5

1:20 Luke 2:4

1:21 Luke 1:31; 2:21; Luke 2:11; John 1:29; Acts 4:12; 5:31; 13:23, 38, 39; Col 1:20-23

1:22 Luke 24:44; Rom 1:2-4

1:23 Is 7:14; Is 9:6, 7; Is 8:10

1:16 Because Mary was a virgin when she became pregnant, Matthew lists Joseph only as the husband of Mary, not the father of Jesus. Matthew's genealogy gives Jesus' legal (or royal) lineage through Joseph. Mary's ancestral line is recorded in Luke 3:23–38. Both Mary and Joseph were direct descendants of David.

Matthew traced the genealogy back to Abraham, while Luke traced it back to Adam. Matthew wrote to the Jews, so Jesus was shown as a descendant of their father, Abraham. Luke wrote to the Gentiles, so he emphasized Jesus as the Savior of all people.

1:17 Matthew breaks Israel's history into three sets of 14 generations, but there were probably more generations than those listed here. Genealogies often compressed history, meaning that not every generation of ancestors was specifically listed. Thus the phrase *the father of* can also be translated "the ancestor of."

1:18 There were three steps in a Jewish marriage. First, the two families agreed to the union. Second, a public announcement was made. At this point, the couple was "betrothed." This was similar to engagement today except that their relationship could be broken only through death or divorce (even though sexual relations were not yet permitted). Third, the couple was married and began living together. Because Mary and Joseph were engaged, Mary's apparent unfaithfulness carried a severe social stigma. According to Jewish civil law, Joseph had a right to divorce her, and the Jewish authorities could have had her stoned to death (Deuteronomy 22:23–24).

1:18 Why is the virgin birth important to the Christian faith? Jesus Christ, God's Son, had to be free from the sinful nature passed on to all other human beings by Adam. Because Jesus was born of a woman, he was a human being; but as the Son of God, Jesus was born without any trace of human sin. Jesus is both fully human and fully divine.

Because Jesus lived as a man, we know that he fully understands our experiences and struggles (Hebrews 4:15–16). Because he is God, he has the power and authority to deliver us from sin (Colossians 2:13–15). We can tell Jesus all our thoughts, feelings, and needs. He has been where we are now, and he has the ability to help.

1:18–25 Joseph was faced with a difficult choice after discovering that Mary was pregnant. Although he knew that taking Mary as his wife could be humiliating, Joseph chose to obey the angel's command to marry her. His action revealed four admirable qualities: (1) righteousness (1:19), (2) discretion and sensitivity (1:19), (3) responsiveness to God (1:24), and (4) self-discipline (1:25).

1:19 Perhaps Joseph thought he had only two options: divorce Mary quietly, or have her stoned. But God had a third option—marry her (1:20–23). In view of the circumstances, this had not occurred to Joseph. But God often shows us that there are more options available than we think. Although Joseph seemed to be doing the right thing by breaking the engagement, only God's guidance helped him make the best decision. When our decisions affect the lives of others, we must always seek God's wisdom.

1:20 The conception and birth of Jesus Christ are supernatural events beyond human logic or reasoning. Because of this, God sent angels to help certain people understand the significance of what was happening (see 2:13, 19; Luke 1:11, 26; 2:9).

Angels are spiritual beings created by God who help carry out his work on earth. They bring God's messages to people (Luke 1:26), protect God's people (Daniel 6:22), offer encouragement (Genesis 16:7ff), give guidance (Exodus 14:19), carry out punishment (2 Samuel 24:16), patrol the earth (Zechariah 1:9–14), and fight the forces of evil (2 Kings 6:16–18; Revelation 20:1–2). There are both good and bad angels (Revelation 12:7), but because bad angels are allied with the devil, or Satan, they have considerably less power and authority than good angels. Eventually the main role of angels will be to offer continuous praise to God (Revelation 7:11–12).

1:20–23 The angel declared to Joseph that Mary's child was conceived by the Holy Spirit and would be a son. This reveals an important truth about Jesus—he is both God and human. The infinite, unlimited God took on the limitations of humanity so he could live and die for the salvation of all who would believe in him.

1:21 *Jesus* means "the LORD saves." Jesus came to earth to save us because we can't save ourselves from sin and its consequences. No matter how good we are, we can't eliminate the sinful nature present in all of us. Only Jesus can do that. Jesus didn't come to help people save themselves; he came to be their Savior from the power and penalty of sin. Thank Christ for his death on the cross for your sin, and then ask him to take control of your life. Your new life begins at that moment.

1:23 Jesus was to be called *Immanuel* ("God with us"), as predicted by Isaiah the prophet (Isaiah 7:14). Jesus was God in the flesh; thus God was literally among us, "with us." Through the Holy Spirit, Christ is present today in the life of every believer. Perhaps not even Isaiah understood how far-reaching the meaning of "Immanuel" would be.

1:25 Luke 2:7; Matt 1:21; Luke 2:21

2:1 Mic 5:2; Luke 2:4-7; Luke 1:5

2:2 Jer 23:5; 30:9; Zech 9:9; Matt 27:11; Luke 19:38; 23:38; John 1:49; Num 24:17

24 And Joseph awoke from his sleep and did as the angel of the Lord commanded him,
and took *Mary* as his wife,
25 [5]but kept her a virgin until she gave birth to a Son; and he called His name Jesus.

Visitors Arrive from Eastern Lands (12)

2 Now after Jesus was born in Bethlehem of Judea in the days of Herod the king, [6]magi
from the east arrived in Jerusalem, saying,
2 "Where is He who has been born King of the Jews? For we saw His star in the east
and have come to worship Him."

5 Lit *and was not knowing her* **6** A caste of wise men specializing in astronomy, astrology, and natural science

GOSPEL ACCOUNTS FOUND ONLY IN MATTHEW

Passage	*Subject*
1:20–24	Joseph's dream*
2:1–12	The visit of the magi
2:13–15	Escape to Egypt*
2:16–18	Slaughter of the children*
27:3–10	The death of Judas*
27:19	The dream of Pilate's wife
27:52	The other resurrections
28:11–15	The bribery of the guards
28:19–20	The baptism emphasis in the Great Commission*

Matthew records nine special events that are not mentioned in any of the other Gospels. In each case, the most apparent reason for Matthew's choice has to do with his purpose in communicating the gospel to Jewish people. Five cases are fulfillments of Old Testament prophecies (marked with asterisks above). The other four would have been of particular interest to the Jews of Matthew's day.

1:24 Joseph changed his plans quickly after learning that Mary had not been unfaithful to him (1:19). He obeyed God and proceeded with the marriage plans. Although others may have disapproved of his decision, Joseph went ahead with what he knew was right. Sometimes we avoid doing what is right because of what others might think. Like Joseph, we must choose to obey God rather than seek the approval of others.

2:1 Bethlehem is a small town five miles south of Jerusalem. It sits on a high ridge over 2,000 feet above sea level. It is mentioned in more detail in the Gospel of Luke. Luke also explains why Joseph and Mary were in Bethlehem when Jesus was born, rather than in Nazareth, their hometown.

2:1 The land of Israel was divided into four political districts and several lesser territories. Judea was to the south, Samaria in the middle, Galilee to the north, and Idumea to the southeast. Bethlehem of Judea (also called Judah, 2:6) had been prophesied as the Messiah's birthplace (Micah 5:2). Jerusalem was also in Judea and was the seat of government for Herod the Great, king over all four political districts. After Herod's death, the districts were divided among three separate rulers (see the note on 2:19–22). Although he was a ruthless, evil man who murdered many in his own family, Herod the Great supervised the renovation of the temple, making it much larger and more beautiful. This made him popular with many Jews. Jesus would visit Jerusalem many times because the great Jewish festivals were held there.

2:1–2 Not much is known about these magi (traditionally called wise men). We don't know where they came from or how many there were. Tradition says they were men of high position from Parthia, near the site of ancient Babylon. How did they know that the star represented the Messiah? (1) They could have been Jews who remained in Babylon after the exile and knew the Old Testament predictions of the Messiah's coming. (2) They may have been eastern astrologers who studied ancient manuscripts from around the world. Because of the Jewish exile centuries earlier, they would have had copies of the Old Testament in their land. (3) They may have had a special message from God directing them to the Messiah. Some scholars say these magi were each from a different land, representing the entire world bowing before Jesus. These men from faraway lands recognized Jesus as the Messiah when most of God's chosen people in Israel did not. Matthew pictures Jesus as King over the whole world, not just Judea.

2:1–2 The magi traveled thousands of miles to see the king of the Jews. When they finally found him, they responded with joy, worship, and gifts. This is so different from the approach people often take today. We expect God to come looking for us, to explain himself, prove who he is, and give *us* gifts. But those who are wise still seek and worship Jesus today, not for what they can get, but for who he is.

2:2 The magi said they saw Jesus' star. Balaam referred to a coming "star . . . from Jacob" (Numbers 24:17). Some say this star may have been a conjunction of Jupiter, Saturn, and Mars in 6 B.C., and others offer other explanations. But couldn't God, who created the heavens, have created a special star to signal the arrival of his Son? Whatever the nature of the star, these magi traveled thousands of miles searching for a king, and they found him.

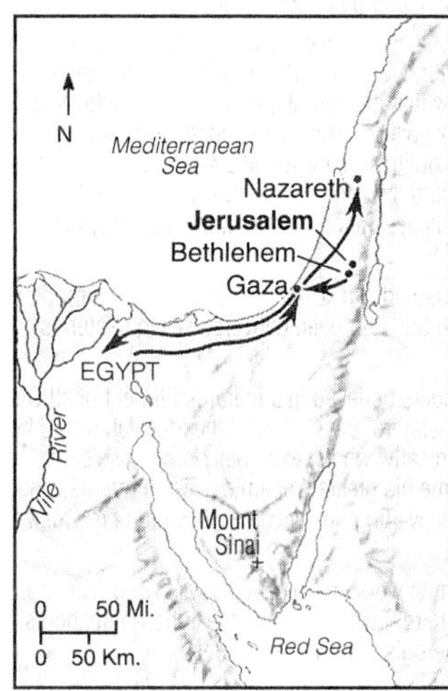

THE FLIGHT TO EGYPT
Herod planned to kill the baby Jesus, whom he perceived to be a future threat to his position. Warned of this treachery in a dream, Joseph took his family to Egypt until Herod's death, which occurred a year or two later. They then planned to return to Judea, but God led them instead to Nazareth in Galilee.

3 When Herod the king heard *this*, he was troubled, and all Jerusalem with him.
4 Gathering together all the chief priests and scribes of the people, he inquired of
them where the Messiah was to be born.
5 They said to him, "In Bethlehem of Judea; for this is what has been written by the
prophet:
6 'AND YOU, BETHLEHEM, LAND OF JUDAH,
ARE BY NO MEANS LEAST AMONG THE LEADERS OF JUDAH;
FOR OUT OF YOU SHALL COME FORTH A RULER
WHO WILL SHEPHERD MY PEOPLE ISRAEL.' "
7 Then Herod secretly called the magi and determined from them the exact time the
star appeared.
8 And he sent them to Bethlehem and said, "Go and search carefully for the Child;
and when you have found *Him,* report to me, so that I too may come and worship Him."
9 After hearing the king, they went their way; and the star, which they had seen in the
east, went on before them until it came and stood over *the place* where the Child was.
10 When they saw the star, they rejoiced exceedingly with great joy.
11 After coming into the house they saw the Child with Mary His mother; and they fell
to the ground and worshiped Him. Then, opening their treasures, they presented to Him
gifts of gold, frankincense, and myrrh.
12 And having been warned *by God* in a dream not to return to Herod, the magi left
for their own country by another way.

2:5 John 7:42

2:6 Mic 5:2; John 7:42; John 21:16

2:7 Num 24:17

2:11 Matt 1:18; 12:46; Matt 14:33

2:12 Matt 2:13, 19, 22; Luke 2:26; Acts 10:22; Heb 8:5; 11:7; Job 33:15, 16; Matt 1:20

The Escape to Egypt
(13)

13 Now when they had gone, behold, an angel of the Lord ☆appeared to Joseph in a
dream and said, "Get up! Take the Child and His mother and flee to Egypt, and remain
there until I tell you; for Herod is going to search for the Child to destroy Him."
14 So Joseph got up and took the Child and His mother while it was still night, and left
for Egypt.

2:13 Acts 5:19; 10:7; 12:7-11; Matt 2:12, 19

2:3 Herod the Great was quite disturbed when the magi asked about a newborn king of the Jews because: (1) Herod was not the rightful heir to the throne of David; therefore many Jews hated him as a usurper. If Jesus really was an heir, trouble would arise. (2) Herod was ruthless and, because of his many enemies, he was suspicious that someone would try to overthrow him. (3) Herod didn't want the Jews, a religious people, to unite around a religious figure. (4) If these magi were of Jewish descent and from Parthia (the most powerful region next to Rome), they would have welcomed a Jewish king who could swing the balance of power away from Rome. The land of Israel, far from Rome, would have been easy prey for a nation trying to gain more control.

2:4 The chief priests and scribes were aware of Micah 5:2 and other prophecies about the Messiah. The magi's news troubled Herod because he knew that the Jewish people expected the Messiah to come soon (Luke 3:15). Most Jews expected the Messiah to be a great military and political deliverer, like Alexander the Great. Herod's counselors would have told Herod this. No wonder this ruthless man took no chances and ordered all the baby boys in Bethlehem killed (2:16)!

2:5–6 Matthew often quoted Old Testament prophets. This prophecy, paraphrasing Micah 5:2, had been delivered seven centuries earlier.

2:6 Most religious leaders believed in a literal fulfillment of all Old Testament prophecy; therefore, they believed the Messiah would be born in Bethlehem. Ironically, when Jesus was born, these same religious leaders became his greatest enemies. When the Messiah for whom they had been waiting finally came, they didn't recognize him.

2:8 Herod did not want to worship Christ—he was lying. This was a trick to get the magi to return to him and reveal the whereabouts of the newborn king. Herod's plan was to kill Jesus.

2:11 Jesus was probably one or two years old when the magi found him. By this time, Mary and Joseph were married, living in a house, and intending to stay in Bethlehem for a while. For more on why Joseph and Mary stayed, see the note on Luke 2:39.

2:11 The magi gave these expensive gifts because they were worthy presents for a future king. Bible students have seen in the gifts symbols of Christ's identity and what he would accomplish. Gold was a gift for a king; frankincense, a gift for deity; myrrh, a spice for a person who was going to die. These gifts may have provided the financial resources for the trip to Egypt and back.

2:11 The magi brought gifts and worshiped Jesus for who he was. This is the essence of true worship—honoring Christ for who he is and being willing to give him what is valuable to you. Worship God because he is the perfect, just, and almighty Creator of the universe, worthy of the best you have to give.

2:12 After finding Jesus and worshiping him, the magi were warned by God not to return through Jerusalem as they had intended. Finding Jesus may mean that your life must take a different direction, one that is responsive and obedient to God's Word. Are you willing to be led a different way?

2:13 This was the second dream or vision that Joseph received from God. Joseph's first dream revealed that Mary's child would be the Messiah (1:20–21). His second dream told him how to protect the child's life. Although Joseph was not Jesus' natural father, he was Jesus' legal father and was responsible for his safety and well-being. Divine guidance comes only to prepared hearts. Joseph remained receptive to God's guidance.

2:14–15 Going to Egypt was not unusual because there were colonies of Jews in several major Egyptian cities. These colonies had developed during the time of the great captivity (see Jeremiah 43; 44). There is an interesting parallel between this flight to Egypt and Israel's history. As an infant nation, Israel went to Egypt, just as Jesus did as a child. God led Israel out (Hosea 11:1); God brought Jesus back. Both events show God working to save his people.

2:15 Hos 11:1; Num 24:8; Ex 4:22f

2:16 Matt 2:1; Is 59:7

15 He remained there until the death of Herod. *This was* to fulfill what had been spoken by the Lord through the prophet: "OUT OF EGYPT I CALLED MY SON."
16 Then when Herod saw that he had been tricked by the magi, he became very enraged, and sent and slew all the male children who were in Bethlehem and all its vicinity,
from two years old and under, according to the time which he had determined from the
magi.
17 Then what had been spoken through Jeremiah the prophet was fulfilled:

JOSEPH

The strength of what we believe is measured by how much we are willing to suffer for those beliefs. Joseph was a man with strong beliefs. He was prepared to do what was right, despite the pain he knew it would cause. But Joseph had another trait—he not only tried to do what was right, he also tried to do it in the right way.

When Mary told Joseph about her pregnancy, Joseph knew the child was not his. His respect for Mary's character and the explanation she gave him, as well as her attitude toward the expected child, must have made it hard to think his bride had done something wrong. Still, someone else was the child's father—and it was mind-boggling to accept that the "someone else" was God.

Joseph decided he had to break the engagement, but he was determined to do it in a way that would not cause public shame to Mary. He intended to act with justice and love.

At this point, God sent a messenger to Joseph to confirm Mary's story and open another way of obedience for Joseph—to take Mary as his wife. Joseph obeyed God, married Mary, and honored her virginity until the baby was born.

We do not know how long Joseph lived his role as Jesus' earthly father—he is last mentioned when Jesus was 12 years old. But Joseph trained his son in the trade of carpentry, made sure he had good spiritual training in Nazareth, and took the whole family on the yearly trip to Jerusalem for the Passover, which Jesus continued to observe during his adult years.

Joseph knew Jesus was someone special from the moment he heard the angel's words. His strong belief in that fact, and his willingness to follow God's leading, empowered him to be Jesus' chosen earthly father.

Strengths and accomplishments:
- A man of integrity
- A descendant of King David
- Jesus' legal and earthly father
- A person sensitive to God's guidance and willing to do God's will no matter what the consequence

Lessons from his life:
- God honors integrity
- Social position is of little importance when God chooses to use us
- Being obedient to the guidance we have from God leads to more guidance from him
- Feelings are not accurate measures of the rightness or wrongness of an action

Vital statistics:
- Where: Nazareth, Bethlehem
- Occupation: Carpenter
- Relatives: Wife: Mary. Children: Jesus, James, Joses, Judas, Simon, and daughters
- Contemporaries: Herod the Great, John the Baptist, Simeon, Anna

Key verses:
"And Joseph her husband, being a righteous man and not wanting to disgrace her, planned to send her away secretly. But when he had considered this, behold, an angel of the Lord appeared to him in a dream, saying, 'Joseph, son of David, do not be afraid to take Mary as your wife; for the Child who has been conceived in her is of the Holy Spirit' " (Matthew 1:19–20).

Joseph's story is told in Matthew 1:16—2:23; Luke 1:26—2:52.

2:16 Herod, the king of the Jews, killed all the boys under two years of age in an obsessive attempt to kill Jesus, the newborn King. He stained his hands with blood, but he did not harm Jesus. Herod was king by a human appointment; Jesus was King by a divine appointment. No one can thwart God's plans.

2:16 Herod was afraid that this newborn king would one day take his throne. He completely misunderstood the reason for Christ's coming. Jesus didn't want Herod's throne; he wanted to be king of Herod's life. Jesus wanted to give Herod eternal life, not take away his present life. Today people are often afraid that Christ wants to take things away when, in reality, he wants to give them real freedom, peace, and joy. Don't fear Christ—give him the throne of your life.

2:17–18 Rachel was the wife of Jacob, one of the great men of God in the Old Testament. From Jacob's 12 sons had come the 12 tribes of Israel. Rachel was buried near Bethlehem (Genesis 35:19). For more about the significance of this verse, see the note on Jeremiah 31:15, from which this verse was quoted.

18 "A VOICE WAS HEARD IN RAMAH,
WEEPING AND GREAT MOURNING,
RACHEL WEEPING FOR HER CHILDREN;
AND SHE REFUSED TO BE COMFORTED,
BECAUSE THEY WERE NO MORE."

2:18 Jer 31:15

The Return to Nazareth
(14)

19 But when Herod died, behold, an angel of the Lord ☆appeared in a dream to
Joseph in Egypt, and said,
20 "Get up, take the Child and His mother, and go into the land of Israel; for those who
sought the Child's life are dead."
21 So Joseph got up, took the Child and His mother, and came into the land of Israel.
22 But when he heard that Archelaus was reigning over Judea in place of his father
Herod, he was afraid to go there. Then after being warned *by God* in a dream, he left for
the regions of Galilee,
23 and came and lived in a city called Nazareth. *This was* to fulfill what was spoken
through the prophets: "He shall be called a Nazarene."

2:19 Matt 1:20; 2:12, 13, 22

2:22 Matt 2:12, 13, 19

2:23 Luke 1:26; 2:39; John 1:45, 46; Mark 1:24; John 18:5, 7; 19:19

John the Baptist Prepares the Way for Jesus
(16/Mark 1:1-8; Luke 3:1-18)

3 Now in those days John the Baptist ☆came, preaching in the wilderness of Judea,
saying,
2 "Repent, for the kingdom of heaven is at hand."
3 For this is the one referred to by Isaiah the prophet when he said,
"THE VOICE OF ONE CRYING IN THE WILDERNESS,
'MAKE READY THE WAY OF THE LORD,
MAKE HIS PATHS STRAIGHT!' "
4 Now John himself had a garment of camel's hair and a leather belt around his waist;
and his food was locusts and wild honey.

3:1 John 1:6-8, 19-28; Matt 11:11-14; 16:14; Josh 15:61; Judg 1:16

3:2 Matt 4:17; Dan 2:44; Matt 4:17, 23; 6:10; 10:7; Mark 1:15; Luke 10:9f; 11:20; 21:31

3:3 Luke 1:17, 76; Is 40:3; John 1:23

3:4 2 Kin 1:8; Zech 13:4; Matt 11:8; Mark 1:6; Lev 11:22

2:19–22 Herod the Great died in 4 B.C. of an incurable disease. Rome trusted him but didn't trust his sons. Herod knew that Rome wouldn't give his successor as much power, so he divided his kingdom into three parts, one for each son. Archelaus received Judea, Samaria, and Idumea; Herod Antipas received Galilee and Perea; Herod Philip II received Trachonitis and Ituraea. Archelaus, a violent man, began his reign by slaughtering 3,000 influential people. Nine years later, he was banished. God didn't want Joseph's family to go into the region of this evil ruler.

2:23 Nazareth sat in the hilly area of southern Galilee near the crossroads of great caravan trade routes. The town itself was rather small. The Roman garrison in charge of Galilee was housed there. The people of Nazareth had constant contact with people from all over the world, so world news reached them quickly. The people of Nazareth had an attitude of independence that many of the Jews despised. This may have been why Nathanael commented, "Can any good thing come out of Nazareth?" (see John 1:46).

2:23 The Old Testament does not record this specific statement, "He shall be called a Nazarene." Many scholars believe, however, that Matthew is referring to Isaiah 11:1 where the Hebrew word for "branch" is similar to the word for Nazarene. Or he may be referring to a prophecy unrecorded in the Bible. In any case, Matthew paints the picture of Jesus as the true Messiah announced by God through the prophets, and he makes the point that Jesus, the Messiah, had unexpectedly humble beginnings, just as the Old Testament had predicted (see Micah 5:2).

3:1–2 Almost 30 years had passed since the events of chapter 2. Here John the Baptist burst onto the scene. His theme was "Repent!" Repentance means doing an about-face—a 180-degree turn—from the kind of self-centeredness that leads to wrong actions such as lying, cheating, stealing, gossiping, taking revenge, abusing, and indulging in sexual immorality. A person who repents stops rebelling and begins following God's way of living prescribed in his Word. The first step in turning to God is to admit your sin, as John urged. Then God will receive you and help you live the way he wants. Remember that only God can get rid of sin. He doesn't expect us to clean up our lives *before* we come to him.

3:1–2 John the Baptist's Profile is found in John 1.

3:2 The kingdom of heaven began when God himself entered human history as a man. Today Jesus Christ reigns in the hearts of believers, but the kingdom of heaven will not be fully realized until all evil in the world is judged and removed. Christ came to earth first as a suffering servant; he will come again as King and Judge to rule victoriously over all the earth.

3:3 The prophet quoted is Isaiah (40:3), one of the greatest prophets of the Old Testament and one of the most quoted in the New. Like Isaiah, John was a prophet who urged the people to confess their sins and live for God. Both prophets taught that the message of repentance is good news to those who listen and seek the healing forgiveness of God's love, but terrible news to those who refuse to listen and thus cut off their only hope.

3:3 John the Baptist *made ready* the way for Jesus. People who do not know Jesus need to be made ready to meet him. We can prepare them by explaining their need for forgiveness, demonstrating Christ's teachings by our conduct, and telling them how Christ can give their lives meaning. We can "make His paths straight" by correcting misconceptions that might be hindering people from approaching Christ. Someone you know may be open to a relationship with Christ. What can you do to prepare the way for this person?

3:4 John was markedly different from other religious leaders of his day. While many were greedy, selfish, and preoccupied with winning the praise of the people, John was concerned only with the praise of God. Having separated himself from the evil and hypocri-

3:5 Mark 1:5; Luke 3:3
3:6 Mark 1:5; John 1:25, 26; 3:23; Acts 1:5
3:7 Matt 16:1ff; 23:13
3:8 Luke 3:8; Eph 5:8, 9

5 Then Jerusalem was going out to him, and all Judea and all the district around the
Jordan;
6 and they were being baptized by him in the Jordan River, as they confessed their
sins.
7 But when he saw many of the Pharisees and Sadducees coming for baptism, he said
to them, "You brood of vipers, who warned you to flee from the wrath to come?
8 "Therefore bear fruit in keeping with repentance;

PHARISEES AND SADDUCEES
The Pharisees and Sadducees were the two major religious groups in Israel at the time of Christ. The Pharisees were more religiously minded, while the Sadducees were more politically minded. Although the groups disliked and distrusted each other, they became allies in their common hatred for Jesus.

Name	*Positive Characteristics*	*Negative Characteristics*
PHARISEES	• Were committed to obeying all of God's commands • Were admired by the common people for their apparent piety • Believed in a bodily resurrection and eternal life • Believed in angels and demons	• Behaved as though their own religious rules were just as important as God's rules for living • Their piety was often hypocritical and their efforts often forced others to try to live up to standards they themselves could not live up to • Believed that salvation came from perfect obedience to the Law and was not based on forgiveness of sins • Became so obsessed with obeying their legal interpretations in every detail that they completely ignored God's message of mercy and grace • Were more concerned with appearing to be good than obeying God
SADDUCEES	• Believed strongly in the Mosaic law and in Levitical purity • Were more practically minded than the Pharisees	• Relied on logic while placing little importance on faith • Did not believe all the Old Testament was God's Word • Did not believe in a bodily resurrection or eternal life • Did not believe in angels or demons • Were often willing to compromise their values with the Romans and others in order to maintain their status and influential positions

sy of his day, John lived differently from other people to show that his message was new. John not only preached God's law, he *lived* it. Do you practice what you preach? Could people discover what you believe by observing the way you live?

3:4–6 John must have presented a strange image! Many people came to hear this preacher who wore odd clothes and ate unusual food. Some probably came simply out of curiosity and ended up repenting of their sins as they listened to his powerful message. People may be curious about your Christian life-style and values. You can use their simple curiosity as an opener to share how Christ makes a difference in you.

3:5 Why did John attract so many people? He was the first true prophet in 400 years. He blasted both Herod and the religious leaders, daring acts that fascinated the common people. But John also had strong words for his audience—they too were sinners and needed to repent. His message was powerful and true. The people were expecting a prophet like Elijah (Malachi 4:5; Luke 1:17), and John seemed to be the one!

3:6 When you wash dirty hands, the results are immediately visible. But repentance happens inside with a cleansing that isn't seen right away. So John used a symbolic action that people could see: baptism. The Jews used baptism to initiate converts, so John's audience was familiar with the rite. Here, baptism was used as a sign of repentance and forgiveness. *Repent* means "turn," implying a change in behavior. It is turning from sin toward God. Have you repented of sin in your life? Can others see the difference it makes in you? A changed life with new and different behavior makes your repentance real and visible.

3:6 The Jordan River is about 70 miles long, its main section stretching between the Sea of Galilee and the Dead Sea. Jerusalem lies about 20 miles west of the Jordan. This river was Israel's eastern border, and many significant events in the nation's history took place there. It was by the Jordan River that the Israelites renewed their covenant with God before entering the promised land (Joshua 1; 2). Here John the Baptist calls them to renew their covenant with God again, this time through baptism.

3:7 The Jewish religious leaders were divided into several groups. Two of the most prominent groups were the Pharisees and the Sadducees. The Pharisees separated themselves from anything non-Jewish and carefully followed both the Old Testament laws and the oral traditions handed down through the centuries. The Sadducees believed the Pentateuch alone (Genesis—Deuteronomy) to be God's Word. They were descended mainly from priestly nobility, while the Pharisees came from all classes of people. The two groups disliked each other greatly, and both opposed Jesus. John the Baptist criticized the Pharisees for being legalistic and hypocritical, following the letter of the Law while ignoring its true intent. He criticized the Sadducees for using religion to advance their political position. For more information on these two groups, see the chart in Mark 2.

3:8 John the Baptist called people to more than words or ritual; he told them to change their behavior. "Bear fruit in keeping with repentance" means that God looks beyond our words and religious activities to see if our conduct backs up what we say, and he judges our words by the actions that accompany them. Do your actions match your words?

9 and do not suppose that you can say to yourselves, 'We have Abraham for our
father'; for I say to you that from these stones God is able to raise up children to
Abraham.
10 "The axe is already laid at the root of the trees; therefore every tree that does not
bear good fruit is cut down and thrown into the fire.
11 "As for me, I baptize you [7]with water for repentance, but He who is coming after me
is mightier than I, and I am not fit to remove His sandals; He will baptize you with the
Holy Spirit and fire.
12 "His winnowing fork is in His hand, and He will thoroughly clear His threshing floor;
and He will gather His wheat into the barn, but He will burn up the chaff with unquenchable fire."

John Baptizes Jesus
(17/Mark 1:9-11; Luke 3:21–22)

13 Then Jesus ☆arrived from Galilee at the Jordan *coming* to John, to be baptized
by him.
14 But John tried to prevent Him, saying, "I have need to be baptized by You, and do
You come to me?"
15 But Jesus answering said to him, "Permit *it* at this time; for in this way it is fitting for
us to fulfill all righteousness." Then he ☆permitted Him.
16 After being baptized, Jesus came up immediately from the water; and behold, the

3:9 Luke 3:8; 16:24; John 8:33, 39, 53; Acts 13:26

3:10 Luke 3:9; Ps 92:12-14; Matt 7:19; John 15:2

3:11 Mark 1:4, 8; Luke 3:16; John 1:26f; Acts 1:5; 8:36, 38; 11:16; John 1:33; Acts 2:3, 4; Titus 3:5

3:12 Luke 3:17; Matt 13:30; Matt 13:41, 42; Mark 9:43, 48

3:13 John 1:31-34; Matt 2:22

3:15 Ps 40:7, 8; John 4:34; 8:29

3:16 Mark 1:10; Luke 3:22; John 1:32; Acts 7:56

7 The Gr here can be translated *in*, *with* or *by*

JESUS BEGINS HIS MINISTRY
From his childhood home, Nazareth, Jesus set out to begin his earthly ministry. He was baptized by John the Baptist in the Jordan River, tempted by Satan in the wilderness, and then returned to Galilee. Between the temptation and his move to Capernaum (4:12–13), he ministered in Judea, Samaria, and Galilee (see John 1—4).

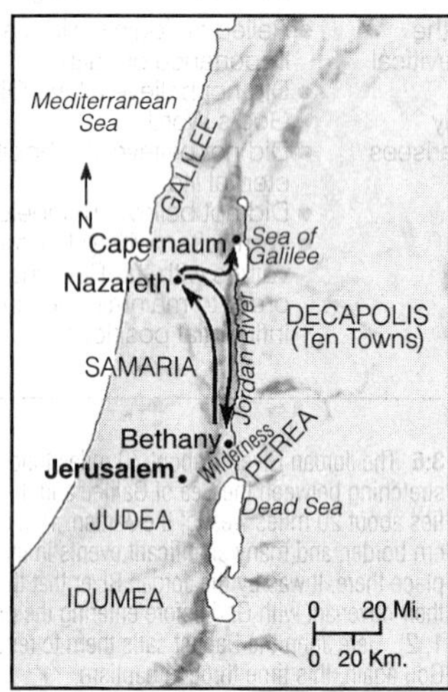

3:9–10 Just as a fruit tree is expected to bear fruit, God's people should produce a crop of good deeds. God has no use for people who call themselves Christians but do nothing about it. Like many people in John's day who were God's people in name only, we are of no value if we are Christians in name only. If others can't see our faith in the way we treat them, we may not be God's people at all.

3:10 God's message hasn't changed since the Old Testament—people will be judged for their unproductive lives. God calls us to be *active* in our obedience. John compared people who claim they believe God but don't live for God to unproductive trees that will be cut down. To be productive for God, we must obey his teachings, resist temptation, actively serve and help others, and share our faith. How productive are you for God?

3:11 John baptized people as a sign that they had asked God to forgive their sins and had decided to live as he wanted them to live. Baptism was an *outward* sign of commitment. To be effective, it had to be accompanied by an *inward* change of attitude leading to a changed life—the work of the Holy Spirit. John said that Jesus would baptize with the Holy Spirit and fire. This looked ahead to Pentecost (Acts 2), when the Holy Spirit would be sent by Jesus in the form of tongues of fire, empowering his followers to preach the gospel. John's statement also symbolizes the work of the Holy Spirit in bringing God's judgment on those who refuse to repent. Everyone will one day be baptized—either now by God's Holy Spirit, or later by the fire of his judgment.

3:12 A winnowing fork is a pitchfork used to toss wheat in the air to separate wheat from chaff. The wheat is the part of the plant that is useful; chaff is the worthless outer shell. Because it is useless, chaff is burned; wheat, however, is gathered. "Winnowing" is often used as a picture of God's judgment. Unrepentant people will be judged and discarded because they are worthless in doing God's work; those who repent and believe will be saved and used by God.

3:13–15 John had been explaining that Jesus' baptism would be much greater than his, when suddenly Jesus came to him and asked to be baptized! John felt unqualified. He wanted Jesus to baptize him. Why did Jesus ask to be baptized? It was not for repentance for sin because Jesus never sinned. "To fulfill all righteousness" means to accomplish God's mission. Jesus saw his baptism as advancing God's work. Jesus was baptized because (1) he was confessing sin on behalf of the nation, as Nehemiah, Ezra, Moses, and Daniel had done; (2) he was showing support for what John was doing; (3) he was inaugurating his public ministry; (4) he was identifying with the penitent people of God, not with the critical Pharisees who were only watching. Jesus, the perfect man, didn't need baptism for sin, but he accepted baptism in obedient service to the Father, and God showed his approval.

3:15 Put yourself in John's shoes. Your work is going well, people are taking notice, everything is growing. But you know that the purpose of your work is to prepare the people for Jesus (John 1:35–37). Then Jesus arrives, and his coming tests your integrity. Will you be able to turn your followers over to him? John passed the test by publicly baptizing Jesus. Soon he would say, "He must increase, but I must decrease" (John 3:30). Can we, like John, put our egos and profitable work aside in order to point others to Jesus? Are we willing to lose some of our status so that everyone will benefit?

3:16–17 The doctrine of the Trinity means that God is three persons and yet one in essence. In this passage, all three persons of the Trinity are present and active. God the Father speaks; God the Son is baptized; God the Holy Spirit descends on Jesus. God is one, yet in three persons at the same time. This is one of God's

3:17 Ps 2:7; Is 42:1; Matt 12:18; 17:5; Mark 9:7; Luke 9:35; John 12:28

4:1 Heb 4:15; James 1:14

4:2 Ex 34:28; 1 Kin 19:8

heavens were opened, and he saw the Spirit of God descending as a dove *and* lighting
on Him,
17 and behold, a voice out of the heavens said, "This is [8]My beloved Son, in whom I
am well-pleased."

Satan Tempts Jesus in the Wilderness
(18/Mark 1:12-13; Luke 4:1-13)

4 Then Jesus was led up by the Spirit into the wilderness to be tempted by the devil.
2 And after He had fasted forty days and forty nights, He [9]then became hungry.

8 Or *My Son, the Beloved* **9** Lit *later became;* or *afterward became*

THE TEMPTATIONS

Temptation	*Real needs used as basis for temptation*	*Possible doubts that made the temptations real*	*Potential weaknesses Satan sought to exploit*	*Jesus' answer*
Make bread	Physical need: Hunger	Would God provide food?	Hunger, impatience, need to "prove his Sonship"	Deuteronomy 8:3 "Depend on God" Focus: God's purpose
Dare God to rescue you (based on misapplied Scripture, Psalm 91:11–12)	Emotional need: Security	Would God protect?	Pride, insecurity, need to test God	Deuteronomy 6:16 "Don't test God" Focus: God's plan
Worship me! (Satan)	Psychological need: Significance, power, achievement	Would God rule?	Desire for quick power, easy solutions, need to prove equality with God	Deuteronomy 6:13 "No compromise with evil" Focus: God's person

As if going through a final test of preparation, Jesus was tempted by Satan in the wilderness. Three specific parts of the temptation are listed by Matthew. They are familiar because we face the same kinds of temptations. As the chart shows, temptation is often the combination of a real need and a possible doubt that create an inappropriate desire. Jesus demonstrates both the importance and effectiveness of knowing and applying Scripture to combat temptation.

incomprehensible mysteries. Other Bible references that speak of the Father, Son, and Holy Spirit are Matthew 28:19; John 15:26; 1 Corinthians 12:4–13; 2 Corinthians 13:14; Ephesians 2:18; 1 Thessalonians 1:2–5; and 1 Peter 1:2.

4:1 This time of testing showed that Jesus really was the Son of God, able to overcome the devil and his temptations. A person has not shown true obedience if he or she has never had an opportunity to disobey. We read in Deuteronomy 8:2 that God led Israel into the wilderness to humble and test them. God wanted to see whether or not his people would really obey him. We too will be tested. Because we know that testing will come, we should be alert and ready for it. Remember, your convictions are strong only if they hold up under pressure!

4:1 The devil, also called Satan, tempted Eve in the Garden of Eden, and here he tempted Jesus in the wilderness. Satan is a fallen angel. He is *real,* not symbolic, and is constantly fighting against those who follow and obey God. Satan's temptations are real, and he is always trying to get us to live his way or our way rather than God's way. Jesus will one day reign over all creation, but Satan tried to force his hand and get him to declare his kingship prematurely. If Jesus had given in, his mission on earth—to die for our sins and give us the opportunity to have eternal life—would have been lost. When temptations seem especially strong, or when you think you can rationalize giving in, consider whether Satan may be trying to block God's purposes for your life or for someone else's life.

4:1ff This temptation by the devil shows us that Jesus was human, and it gave Jesus the opportunity to reaffirm God's plan for his ministry. It also gives us an example to follow when we are tempted. Jesus' temptation was an important demonstration of his sinlessness. He would face temptation and not give in.

4:1ff Jesus was tempted by the devil, but he never sinned! Although we may feel dirty after being tempted, we should remember that temptation itself is not sin. We sin when we give in and disobey God. Remembering this will help us turn away from the temptation.

4:1ff Jesus wasn't tempted inside the temple or at his baptism but in the wilderness where he was tired, alone, and hungry, and thus most vulnerable. The devil often tempts us when we are vulnerable—when we are under physical or emotional stress (for example, lonely, tired, weighing big decisions, or faced with uncertainty). But he also likes to tempt us through our strengths, where we are most susceptible to pride (see the note on Luke 4:3ff). We must guard at all times against his attacks.

4:1–10 The devil's temptations focused on three crucial areas: (1) physical needs and desires, (2) possessions and power, and (3) pride (see 1 John 2:15–16 for a similar list). But Jesus did not give in. Hebrews 4:15 says that Jesus "has been tempted in all things as we are, yet without sin." He knows firsthand what we are experiencing, and he is willing and able to help us in our struggles. When you are tempted, turn to him for strength.

3 And the tempter came and said to Him, "If You are the Son of God, command that
these stones become bread."
4 But He answered and said, "It is written, 'MAN SHALL NOT LIVE ON BREAD ALONE,
BUT ON EVERY WORD THAT PROCEEDS OUT OF THE MOUTH OF GOD.' "
5 Then the devil ☆took Him into the holy city and had Him stand on the pinnacle of
the temple,
6 and ☆said to Him, "If You are the Son of God, throw Yourself down; for it is written,
'HE WILL COMMAND HIS ANGELS CONCERNING YOU';
and
'ON *their* HANDS THEY WILL BEAR YOU UP,
SO THAT YOU WILL NOT STRIKE YOUR FOOT AGAINST A STONE.' "
7 Jesus said to him, "On the other hand, it is written, 'YOU SHALL NOT PUT THE LORD
YOUR GOD TO THE TEST.' "
8 Again, the devil ☆took Him to a very high mountain and ☆showed Him all the kingdoms of the world and their glory;
9 and he said to Him, "All these things I will give You, if You fall down and worship me."
10 Then Jesus ☆said to him, "Go, Satan! For it is written, 'YOU SHALL WORSHIP THE
LORD YOUR GOD, AND SERVE HIM ONLY.' "
11 Then the devil ☆left Him; and behold, angels came and *began* to minister to Him.

4:3 1 Thess 3:5; Matt 14:33; 26:63; Mark 3:11; 5:7; Luke 1:35; 4:41; John 1:34, 49; Acts 9:20
4:4 Deut 8:3
4:5 Neh 11:1, 18; Dan 9:24; Matt 27:53
4:6 Ps 91:11, 12
4:7 Deut 6:16
4:8 Matt 16:26; 1 John 2:15-17
4:9 1 Cor 10:20f
4:10 Deut 6:13; 10:20
4:11 Matt 26:53; Luke 22:43; Heb 1:14

B. MESSAGE AND MINISTRY OF JESUS, THE KING (4:12—25:46)

Matthew features Jesus' sermons. The record of Jesus' actions is woven around great passages of his teaching. This section of Matthew, then, is topical rather than chronological. Matthew records for us the Sermon on the Mount, the parables of the kingdom, Jesus' teachings on forgiveness, and parables about the end of the age.

1. Jesus begins his ministry

Jesus Preaches in Galilee

(30/Mark 1:14-15; Luke 4:14-15; John 4:43-45)

12 Now when Jesus heard that John had been taken into custody, He withdrew into
Galilee;

4:12 Matt 14:3; Mark 1:14; Luke 3:20; John 3:24; Mark 1:14; Luke 4:14; John 1:43; 2:11

4:3–4 Jesus was hungry and weak after fasting for 40 days, but he chose not to use his divine power to satisfy his natural desire for food. Food, hunger, and eating are good, but the timing was wrong. Jesus was in the wilderness to fast, not to eat. And because Jesus had given up the unlimited, independent use of his divine power in order to experience humanity fully, he wouldn't use his power to change the stones to bread. We also may be tempted to satisfy a perfectly normal desire in a wrong way or at the wrong time. If we indulge in sex before marriage or if we steal to get food, we are trying to satisfy God-given desires in wrong ways. Remember, many of your desires are normal and good, but God wants you to satisfy them in the right way and at the right time.

4:3–4 Jesus was able to resist all of the devil's temptations because he not only knew Scripture, but he also obeyed it. Ephesians 6:17 says that God's Word is a sword to use in spiritual combat. Knowing Bible verses is an important step in helping us resist the devil's attacks, but we must also obey the Bible. Note that Satan had memorized Scripture, but he failed to obey it. Knowing and obeying the Bible helps us follow God's desires rather than the devil's.

4:5 The temple was the religious center of the Jewish nation and the place where the people expected the Messiah to arrive (Malachi 3:1). Herod the Great had renovated the temple in hopes of gaining the Jews' confidence. The temple was the tallest building in the area, and this "pinnacle" was probably the corner wall that jutted out of the hillside, overlooking the valley below. From this spot, Jesus could see all of Jerusalem behind him and the country for miles in front of him.

4:5–7 God is not our magician in the sky ready to perform on request. In response to Satan's temptations, Jesus said not to put God to a test (Deuteronomy 6:16). You may want to ask God to do something to prove his existence or his love for you. Jesus once taught through a parable that people who don't believe what is written in the Bible wouldn't believe even if someone were to come back from the dead to warn them (Luke 16:31)! God wants us to live by faith, not by magic. Don't try to manipulate God by asking for signs.

4:6 The devil used Scripture to try to convince Jesus to sin! Sometimes friends or associates will present attractive and convincing reasons why you should try something you know is wrong. They may even find Bible verses that *seem* to support their viewpoint. Study the Bible carefully, especially the broader contexts of specific verses, so that you understand God's principles for living and what he wants for your life. Only if you really understand what the *whole* Bible says will you be able to recognize errors of interpretation when people take verses out of context and twist them to say what they want them to say.

4:8–9 Did the devil have the power to give Jesus the kingdoms of the world? Didn't God, the Creator of the world, have control over these kingdoms? The devil may have been lying about his implied power, or he may have based his offer on his temporary control and free rein over the earth because of humanity's sinfulness. Jesus' temptation was to take the world as a political ruler right then, without carrying out his plan to save the world from sin. Satan was trying to distort Jesus' perspective by making him focus on worldly power and not on God's plans.

4:8–10 The devil offered the whole world to Jesus if Jesus would only fall down and worship him. Today the devil offers us the world by trying to entice us with materialism and power. We can resist temptations the same way Jesus did. If you find yourself craving something that the world offers, quote Jesus' words to the devil: "Worship the Lord your God, and serve Him only."

4:11 Angels, like these who waited on Jesus, have a significant role as God's messengers. These spiritual beings were involved in Jesus' life on earth by (1) announcing Jesus' birth to Mary, (2) re-

4:13 Matt 11:23; Mark 1:21; 2:1; Luke 4:23, 31; John 2:12; 4:46f
4:15 Is 9:1
4:16 Is 9:2; 60:1-3; Luke 2:32

13 and leaving Nazareth, He came and settled in Capernaum, which is by the sea, in
the region of Zebulun and Naphtali.
14 *This was* to fulfill what was spoken through Isaiah the prophet:
15 "THE LAND OF ZEBULUN AND THE LAND OF NAPHTALI,
BY THE WAY OF THE SEA, BEYOND THE JORDAN, GALILEE OF THE [10]GENTILES—
16 "THE PEOPLE WHO WERE SITTING IN DARKNESS SAW A GREAT LIGHT,
AND THOSE WHO WERE SITTING IN THE LAND AND SHADOW OF DEATH,
UPON THEM A LIGHT DAWNED."

10 Lit *nations*, usually non-Jewish

HEROD (THE GREAT)

The Bible records history. It has proven itself an accurate and reliable record of people, events, and places. Independent historical accounts verify the Bible's descriptions and details of many famous lives. One of these was the father of the Herodian family, Herod the Great.

Herod is remembered as a builder of cities and the lavish rebuilder of the temple in Jerusalem. But he also destroyed people. He showed little greatness in either his personal actions or his character. He was ruthless in ruling his territory. His suspicions and jealousy led to the murder of several of his children and the death of his wife Mariamne.

Herod's title, king of the Jews, was granted by Rome but never accepted by the Jewish people. He was not part of the Davidic family line, and he was only partly Jewish. Although Israel benefited from Herod's lavish efforts to repair the temple in Jerusalem, he won little admiration because he also rebuilt various pagan temples. Herod's costly attempt to gain the loyalty of the people failed because it was superficial. His only loyalty was to himself.

Because his royal title was not genuine, Herod was constantly worried about losing his position. His actions when hearing from the magi about their search for the new king are consistent with all that we know about Herod. He planned to locate and kill the child before he could become a threat. The murder of innocent children that followed is a tragic lesson in what can happen when actions are motivated by selfishness. Herod's suspicions did not spare even his own family. His life was self-destructive.

Strengths and accomplishments:
- Was given the title king of the Jews by the Romans
- Held on to his power for more than 30 years
- Was an effective, though ruthless, ruler
- Sponsored a great variety of large building projects

Weaknesses and mistakes:
- Tended to treat those around him with fear, suspicion, and jealousy
- Had several of his own children and at least one wife killed
- Ordered the killing of the infants in Bethlehem
- Although claiming to be a God-worshiper, he was still involved in many forms of pagan religion

Lessons from his life:
- Great power brings neither peace nor security
- No one can prevent God's plans from being carried out
- Superficial loyalty does not impress people or God

Vital statistics:
- Occupation: King of Judea from 37 to 4 B.C.
- Relatives: Father: Antipater. Sons: Archelaus, Antipater, Antipas, Philip, and others. Wives: Doris, Mariamne, and others
- Contemporaries: Zacharias, Elizabeth, Mary, Joseph, Mark Antony, Augustus

Notes about Herod the Great are found in Matthew 2:1–22 and Luke 1:5.

assuring Joseph, (3) naming Jesus, (4) announcing Jesus' birth to the shepherds, (5) protecting Jesus by sending his family to Egypt, (6) ministering to Jesus in Gethsemane. For more on angels, see the note on 1:20.

4:12–13 Jesus moved from Nazareth, his hometown, to Capernaum, about 20 miles farther north. Capernaum became Jesus' home base during his ministry in Galilee. Jesus probably moved (1) to get away from intense opposition in Nazareth, (2) to have an impact on the greatest number of people (Capernaum was a busy city and Jesus' message could reach more people and spread more quickly), and (3) to utilize extra resources and support for his ministry.

Jesus' move fulfilled the prophecy of Isaiah 9:1–2, which states that the Messiah will be a light to the land of Zebulun and Naphtali, the region of Galilee where Capernaum was located. Zebulun and Naphtali were two of the original 12 tribes of Israel.

4:14–16 By quoting from the book of Isaiah, Matthew continues to tie Jesus' ministry to the Old Testament. This was helpful for his Jewish readers, who were familiar with these Scriptures. In addition, it shows the unity of God's purposes as he works with his people throughout all ages.

17 From that time Jesus began to preach and say, "Repent, for the kingdom of heaven
is at hand."

Four Fishermen Follow Jesus
(33/Mark 1:16-20)

18 Now as Jesus was walking by the Sea of Galilee, He saw two brothers, Simon who
was called Peter, and Andrew his brother, casting a net into the sea; for they were fishermen.
19 And He ☆said to them, "Follow Me, and I will make you fishers of men."
20 Immediately they left their nets and followed Him.
21 Going on from there He saw two other brothers, James the *son* of Zebedee, and
John his brother, in the boat with Zebedee their father, mending their nets; and He called
them.
22 Immediately they left the boat and their father, and followed Him.

Jesus Preaches throughout Galilee
(36/Mark 1:35-39; Luke 4:42-44)

23 Jesus was going throughout all Galilee, teaching in their synagogues and proclaiming the gospel of the kingdom, and healing every kind of disease and every kind of sickness among the people.
24 The news about Him spread throughout all Syria; and they brought to Him all who
were ill, those suffering with various diseases and pains, demoniacs, epileptics, paralyt-
ics; and He healed them.
25 Large crowds followed Him from Galilee and *the* Decapolis and Jerusalem and Judea
and *from* beyond the Jordan.

2. Jesus gives the Sermon on the Mount

Jesus Gives the Beatitudes
(49/Luke 6:17-26)

5 When Jesus saw the crowds, He went up on the mountain; and after He sat down,
His disciples came to Him.

4:17 Mark 1:14, 15; Matt 3:2

4:18 Luke 5:2-11; John 1:40-42; Matt 15:29; Mark 7:31; Luke 5:1; John 6:1; Matt 10:2; 16:18; John 1:40-42

4:21 Matt 10:2; 20:20

4:23 Matt 9:35; 13:54; Mark 1:21; 6:2; 10:1; Luke 4:15; 6:6; 13:10; John 6:59; 18:20; Matt 3:2; 9:35; 24:14; Mark 1:14; Acts 20:25; 28:31; Matt 8:16; 9:35; 14:14; 15:30; 19:2; 21:14; Luke 4:40; 7:21; Acts 10:38

4:24 Mark 7:26; Luke 2:2; Acts 15:23; 18:18; 20:3; 21:3; Gal 1:21; Matt 8:16, 28, 33; 9:32; 12:22; 15:22; Mark 1:32; 5:15, 16, 18; Luke 8:36; John 10:21; Matt 17:15; Matt 8:6; 9:2, 6; Mark 2:3-5, 9; Luke 5:24

4:25 Mark 3:7, 8; Luke 6:17; Mark 5:20; 7:31; Matt 4:15

5:1 Matt ch 5-7; Luke 6:20-49; Mark 3:13; Luke 6:17; 9:28; John 6:3, 15

4:17 The "kingdom of heaven" has the same meaning as the "kingdom of God" in Mark and Luke. Matthew uses this phrase because the Jews, out of their intense reverence and respect, did not pronounce God's name. The kingdom of heaven is still near because it has arrived in our hearts. See the note on 3:2 for more on the kingdom of heaven.

4:17 Jesus started his ministry with the very word people had heard John the Baptist say: *Repent*. The message is the same today as when Jesus and John gave it. Becoming a follower of Christ means turning away from our self-centeredness and "self" control and turning our lives over to Christ's direction and control.

4:18 The Sea of Galilee is really a large lake. About 30 fishing towns surrounded it during Jesus' day, and Capernaum was the largest.

4:18–20 Jesus told Peter and Andrew to leave their fishing business and become "fishers of men," to help others find God. Jesus was calling them away from their productive trades to be productive spiritually. We all need to fish for souls. If we practice Christ's teachings and share the gospel with others, we will be able to draw those around us to Christ like a fisherman who pulls fish into his boat with nets.

4:19–20 These men already knew Jesus. He had talked to Peter and Andrew previously (John 1:35–42) and had been preaching in the area. When Jesus called them, they knew what kind of man he was and were willing to follow him. They were not in a hypnotic trance when they followed but had been thoroughly convinced that following him would change their lives forever.

4:21–22 James and his brother, John, along with Peter and Andrew, were the first disciples that Jesus called to work with him. Jesus' call motivated these men to get up and leave their jobs—immediately. They didn't make excuses about why it wasn't a good time. They left at once and followed. Jesus calls each of us to follow him. When Jesus asks us to serve him, we must be like the disciples and do it at once.

4:23 Jesus was teaching, preaching (proclaiming the gospel), and healing. These were the three main aspects of his ministry. *Teaching* shows Jesus' concern for understanding, *preaching* shows his concern for commitment, and *healing* shows his concern for wholeness. His miracles of healing authenticated his teaching and preaching, proving that he truly was from God.

4:23 Jesus soon developed a powerful preaching ministry and often spoke in the synagogues. Most towns that had ten or more Jewish families had a synagogue. The building served as a religious gathering place on the Sabbath and as a school during the week. The leader (or official) of the synagogue was not a preacher as much as an administrator. His job was to find and invite rabbis to teach and preach. It was customary to invite visiting rabbis like Jesus to speak.

4:23–24 Jesus preached the gospel—the Good News—to everyone who wanted to hear it. The gospel is that the kingdom of heaven has come, that God is with us, and that he cares for us. Christ can heal us, not just of physical sickness, but of spiritual sickness as well. There's no sin or problem too great or too small for him to handle. Jesus' words were good news because they offered freedom, hope, peace of heart, and eternal life with God.

4:25 Decapolis was a league of ten Gentile cities east of the Sea of Galilee, joined together for better trade and mutual defense. The word about Jesus was out, and Jews and Gentiles were coming long distances to hear him.

5:1ff Matthew 5—7 is called the Sermon on the Mount because

5:3 Matt 5:3-12; 19:14; 25:34; Mark 10:14

5:4 Is 61:2; John 16:20

5:6 Is 55:1, 2; John 4:14; 6:48ff; 7:37

2 He opened His mouth and *began* to teach them, saying,
3 "Blessed are the poor in spirit, for theirs is the kingdom of heaven.
4 "Blessed are those who mourn, for they shall be comforted.
5 "Blessed are the [11]gentle, for they shall inherit the earth.
6 "Blessed are those who hunger and thirst for righteousness, for they shall be satisfied.

11 Or *humble, meek*

KEY LESSONS FROM THE SERMON ON THE MOUNT

Beatitude	*Old Testament anticipation*	*Clashing worldly values*	*God's reward*	*How to develop this attitude*
Poor in spirit (5:3)	Isaiah 57:15	Pride and personal independence	Kingdom of heaven	James 4:7–10
Mourn (5:4)	Isaiah 61:1–2	Happiness at any cost	Comfort (2 Corinthians 1:4)	Psalm 51 James 4:7–10
Gentle (5:5)	Psalm 37:5–11	Power	Inherit the earth	Matthew 11:27–30
Hunger and thirst for righteousness (5:6)	Isaiah 11:4–5; 42:1–4	Pursuing personal needs	Filled (satisfied)	John 16:5–11; Philippians 3:7–11
Merciful (5:7)	Psalm 41:1	Strength without feeling	Shall receive mercy	Ephesians 5:1–2
Pure in heart (5:8)	Psalm 24:3–4; 51:10	Deception is acceptable	See God	1 John 3:1–3
Peacemaker (5:9)	Isaiah 57:18–19; 60:17	Personal peace is pursued without concern for the world's chaos	Be called sons of God	Romans 12:9–21 Hebrews 12:10–11
Persecuted (5:10)	Isaiah 52:13; 53:12	Weak commitments	Inherit the kingdom of heaven	2 Timothy 3:12

In his longest recorded sermon, Jesus began by describing the traits he was looking for in his followers. He called those who lived out those traits blessed because God had something special in store for them. Each beatitude is an almost direct contradiction of society's typical way of life. In the last beatitude, Jesus even points out that a serious effort to develop these traits is bound to create opposition. The best example of each trait is found in Jesus himself. If our goal is to become like him, the Beatitudes will challenge the way we live each day.

Jesus gave it on a hillside near Capernaum. This "sermon" probably covered several days of preaching. In it, Jesus proclaimed his attitude toward the law. Position, authority, and money are not important in his kingdom—what matters is faithful obedience from the heart. The Sermon on the Mount challenged the proud and legalistic religious leaders of the day. It called them back to the messages of the Old Testament prophets who, like Jesus, taught that heartfelt obedience is more important than legalistic observance.

5:1–2 Enormous crowds were following Jesus—he was the talk of the town, and everyone wanted to see him. The disciples, who were the closest associates of this popular man, were certainly tempted to feel important, proud, and possessive. Being with Jesus gave them not only prestige, but also opportunity for receiving money and power.

The crowds were gathering once again. But before speaking to them, Jesus pulled his disciples aside and warned them about the temptations they would face as his associates. Don't expect fame and fortune, Jesus was saying, but mourning, hunger, and persecution. Nevertheless, Jesus assured his disciples, they would be rewarded—but perhaps not in this life. There may be times when following Jesus will bring us great popularity. If we don't live by Jesus' words in this sermon, we will find ourselves using God's message only to promote our personal interests.

5:3–5 Jesus began his sermon with words that seem to contradict each other. But God's way of living usually contradicts the world's. If you want to live for God you must be ready to say and do what seems strange to the world. You must be willing to give when others take, to love when others hate, to help when others abuse. By giving up your own rights in order to serve others, you will one day receive everything God has in store for you.

5:3–12 There are at least four ways to understand the Beatitudes. (1) They are a code of ethics for the disciples and a standard of conduct for all believers. (2) They contrast kingdom values (what is eternal) with worldly values (what is temporary). (3) They contrast the superficial "faith" of the Pharisees with the real faith Christ wants. (4) They show how the Old Testament expectations will be fulfilled in the new kingdom. These beatitudes are not multiple choice—pick what you like and leave the rest. They must be taken as a whole. They describe what we should be like as Christ's followers.

5:3–12 Each beatitude tells how to be *blessed.* "Blessedness" means more than happiness. It implies the fortunate or enviable state of those who are in God's kingdom. The Beatitudes don't promise laughter, pleasure, or earthly prosperity. To Jesus, "blessed" means the experience of hope and joy, independent of outward circumstances. To find hope and joy, the deepest form of happiness, follow Jesus no matter what the cost.

7 "Blessed are the merciful, for they shall receive mercy.
8 "Blessed are the pure in heart, for they shall see God.
9 "Blessed are the peacemakers, for they shall be called sons of God.
10 "Blessed are those who have been persecuted for the sake of righteousness, for theirs
is the kingdom of heaven.
11 "Blessed are you when *people* insult you and persecute you, and falsely say all kinds
of evil against you because of Me.
12 "Rejoice and be glad, for your reward in heaven is great; for in the same way they
persecuted the prophets who were before you.

Jesus Teaches about Salt and Light (50)

13 "You are the salt of the earth; but if the salt has become tasteless, how can it be made
salty *again?* It is no longer good for anything, except to be thrown out and trampled under
foot by men.
14 "You are the light of the world. A city set on a hill cannot be hidden;
15 nor does *anyone* light a lamp and put it under a basket, but on the lampstand, and it
gives light to all who are in the house.
16 "Let your light shine before men in such a way that they may see your good works,
and glorify your Father who is in heaven.

Jesus Teaches about the Law (51)

17 "Do not think that I came to abolish the Law or the Prophets; I did not come to abolish but to fulfill.
18 "For truly I say to you, until heaven and earth pass away, not the smallest letter or
stroke shall pass from the Law until all is accomplished.
19 "Whoever then annuls one of the least of these commandments, and teaches others

5:7 Prov 11:17; Matt 6:14, 15; 18:33-35

5:8 Ps 24:4; Heb 12:14; 1 John 3:2; Rev 22:4

5:9 Rom 8:14

5:10 1 Pet 3:14; Matt 5:3; 19:14; 25:34; Mark 10:14

5:11 1 Pet 4:14

5:12 2 Chr 36:16; Matt 23:37; Acts 7:52; 1 Thess 2:15; Heb 11:33ff; James 5:10

5:13 Mark 9:50; Luke 14:34f

5:14 Prov 4:18; John 8:12; 9:5; 12:36

5:15 Mark 4:21; Luke 8:16; 11:33

5:16 1 Pet 2:12; Matt 9:8

5:17 Matt 7:12

5:18 Matt 24:35; Luke 16:17

5:3–12 With Jesus' announcement that the kingdom was at hand (4:17), people were naturally asking, "How do I qualify to be in God's kingdom?" Jesus said that God's kingdom is organized differently from worldly kingdoms. In the kingdom of heaven, wealth and power and authority are unimportant. Kingdom people seek different blessings and benefits, and they have different attitudes. Are your attitudes a carbon copy of the world's selfishness, pride, and lust for power, or do they reflect the humility and self-sacrifice of Jesus, your King?

5:11–12 Jesus said to rejoice when we're persecuted. Persecution can be good because (1) it takes our eyes off earthly rewards, (2) it strips away superficial belief, (3) it strengthens the faith of those who endure, and (4) our attitude through it serves as an example to others who follow. We can be comforted to know that God's greatest prophets were persecuted (Elijah, Jeremiah, Daniel). The fact that we are being persecuted proves that we have been faithful; faithless people would be unnoticed. In the future God will reward the faithful by receiving them into his eternal kingdom where there is no more persecution.

5:13 If a seasoning has no flavor, it has no value. If Christians make no effort to affect the world around them, they are of little value to God. If we are too much like the world, we are worthless. Christians should not blend in with everyone else. Instead, we should affect others positively, just as seasoning brings out the best flavor in food.

5:14–16 Can you hide a city that is sitting on top of a hill? Its light at night can be seen for miles. If we live for Christ, we will glow like lights, showing others what Christ is like. We hide our light by (1) being quiet when we should speak, (2) going along with the crowd, (3) denying the light, (4) letting sin dim our light, (5) not explaining our light to others, or (6) ignoring the needs of others. Be a beacon of truth—don't shut your light off from the rest of the world.

5:17 God's moral and ceremonial laws were given to help people love God with all their hearts and minds. Throughout Israel's history, however, these laws had been often misquoted and misapplied. By Jesus' time, religious leaders had turned the laws into a confusing mass of rules. When Jesus talked about a new way to understand God's law, he was actually trying to bring people back to its *original* purpose. Jesus did not speak against the law itself, but against the abuses and excesses to which it had been subjected. (See John 1:17.)

5:17–20 If Jesus did not come to abolish the law, does that mean all the Old Testament laws still apply to us today? In the Old Testament, there were three categories of law: ceremonial, civil, and moral.

(1) The *ceremonial law* related specifically to Israel's worship (see Leviticus 1:2–3, for example). Its primary purpose was to point forward to Jesus Christ; these laws, therefore, were no longer necessary after Jesus' death and resurrection. While we are no longer bound by ceremonial laws, the principles behind them—to worship and love a holy God—still apply. Jesus was often accused by the Pharisees of violating ceremonial law.

(2) The *civil law* applied to daily living in Israel (see Deuteronomy 24:10–11, for example). Because modern society and culture are so radically different from that time and setting, not all of these guidelines can be followed specifically. But the principles behind the commands are timeless and should guide our conduct. Jesus demonstrated these principles by example.

(3) The *moral law* (such as the Ten Commandments) is the direct command of God, and it requires strict obedience (see Exodus 20:13, for example). The moral law reveals the nature and will of God, and it still applies today. Jesus obeyed the moral law completely.

5:19 Some of those in the crowd were experts at telling others what to do, but they missed the central point of God's laws themselves. Jesus made it clear, however, that obeying God's law is more important than explaining it. It's much easier to study God's laws and tell others to obey them than to put them into practice. How are you doing at obeying God *yourself?*

5:20 Luke 18:11, 12
5:21 Matt 5:27, 33, 38, 43; Ex 20:13; Deut 5:17; Deut 16:18; 2 Chr 19:5f
5:22 Deut 16:18; 2 Chr 19:5f; Matt 10:17; 26:59; Mark 13:9; 14:55; 15:1; Luke 22:66; John 11:47; Acts 4:15; 5:21; 6:12; 22:30; 23:1; 24:20; Matt 5:29f; 10:28; 18:9; 23:15, 33; Mark 9:43ff; Luke 12:5; James 3:6
5:23 Matt 5:24
5:24 Rom 12:17, 18

to do the same, shall be called least in the kingdom of heaven; but whoever keeps and
teaches *them,* he shall be called great in the kingdom of heaven.
20 "For I say to you that unless your righteousness surpasses *that* of the scribes and
Pharisees, you will not enter the kingdom of heaven.

Jesus Teaches about Anger (52)

21 "You have heard that the ancients were told, 'YOU SHALL NOT COMMIT MURDER'
and 'Whoever commits murder shall be [12]liable to the court.'
22 "But I say to you that everyone who is angry with his brother shall be guilty before
the court; and whoever says to his brother, '[13]You good-for-nothing,' shall be guilty before [14]the supreme court; and whoever says, 'You fool,' shall be guilty *enough to go* into
the [15]fiery hell.
23 "Therefore if you are presenting your offering at the altar, and there remember that
your brother has something against you,
24 leave your offering there before the altar and go; first be reconciled to your brother, and then come and present your offering.

12 Or *guilty before* **13** Or *empty-head;* Gr *Raka (Raca)* fr Aram *reqa* **14** Lit *the Sanhedrin* **15** Lit *Gehenna of fire*

SIX WAYS TO THINK LIKE CHRIST

Reference	*Example*	*It's not enough to*	*We must also*
5:21–22	Murder	Avoid killing	Avoid anger and hatred
5:23–26	Offerings	Offer regular gifts	Have right relationships with God and others
5:27–30	Adultery	Avoid adultery	Keep our hearts from lusting and be faithful
5:31–32	Divorce	Be legally married	Live out our marriage commitments
5:33–37	Vows	Keep a vow	Avoid casual and irresponsible commitments to God
5:38–47	Revenge	Seek justice for ourselves	Show mercy and love to others

We are, more often than not, guilty of avoiding the extreme sins while regularly committing the types of sins with which Jesus was most concerned. In these six examples, our real struggle with sin is exposed. Jesus pointed out what kind of lives would be required of his followers. Are you living as Jesus taught?

5:20 The Pharisees were exacting and scrupulous in their attempts to follow their laws. So how could Jesus reasonably call us to a greater righteousness than theirs? The Pharisees' weakness was that they were content to obey the laws outwardly without allowing God to change their hearts (or attitudes). Jesus was saying, therefore, that the *quality* of our goodness should be greater than that of the Pharisees. They looked pious, but they were far from the kingdom of God. God judges our hearts as well as our deeds, for it is in the heart that our real allegiance lies. Be just as concerned about your attitudes that people don't see as about your actions that are seen by all.

5:20 Jesus was saying that his listeners needed a different kind of righteousness altogether (love and obedience), not just a more intense version of the Pharisees' righteousness (legal compliance). Our righteousness must (1) come from what God does in us, not what we can do by ourselves, (2) be God-centered, not self-centered, (3) be based on reverence for God, not approval from people, and (4) go beyond keeping the law to living by the principles behind the law.

5:21–22 When Jesus said, "But I say to you," he was not doing away with the law or adding his own beliefs. Rather, he was giving a fuller understanding of why God made that law in the first place. For example, Moses said, "You shall not murder" (Exodus 20:13); Jesus taught that we should not even become angry enough to murder, for then we have already committed murder in our heart. The Pharisees read this law and, not having literally murdered anyone, felt righteous. Yet they were angry enough with Jesus that they would soon plot his death, though they would not do the dirty work themselves. We miss the intent of God's Word when we read his rules for living without trying to understand why he made them. When do you keep God's rules but close your eyes to his intent?

5:21–22 Killing is a terrible sin, but *anger* is a great sin too because it also violates God's command to love. Anger in this case refers to a seething, brooding bitterness against someone. It is a dangerous emotion that always threatens to leap out of control, leading to violence, emotional hurt, increased mental stress, and spiritual damage. Anger keeps us from developing a spirit pleasing to God. Have you ever been proud that you didn't strike out and say what was really on your mind? Self-control is good, but Christ wants us to practice thought-control as well. Jesus said that we will be held accountable even for our attitudes.

5:23–24 Broken relationships can hinder our relationship with God. If we have a problem or grievance with a friend, we should resolve the problem as soon as possible. We are hypocrites if we claim to love God while we hate others. Our attitudes toward others reflect our relationship with God (1 John 4:20).

25 "Make friends quickly with your opponent at law while you are with him on the way,
so that your opponent may not hand you over to the judge, and the judge to the officer,
and you be thrown into prison.
26 "Truly I say to you, you will not come out of there until you have paid up the last
[16]cent.

Jesus Teaches about Lust

(53)

27 "You have heard that it was said, 'YOU SHALL NOT COMMIT ADULTERY';
28 but I say to you that everyone who looks at a woman with lust for her has already
committed adultery with her in his heart.
29 "If your right eye makes you stumble, tear it out and throw it from you; for it is better
for you to lose one of the parts of your body, than for your whole body to be thrown into
hell.
30 "If your right hand makes you stumble, cut it off and throw it from you; for it is better for you to lose one of the parts of your body, than for your whole body to go into hell.

Jesus Teaches about Divorce

(54)

31 "It was said, 'WHOEVER SENDS HIS WIFE AWAY, LET HIM GIVE HER A CERTIFICATE
OF DIVORCE';
32 but I say to you that everyone who divorces his wife, except for *the* reason of unchastity, makes her commit adultery; and whoever marries a divorced woman commits
adultery.

Jesus Teaches about Vows

(55)

33 "Again, you have heard that the ancients were told, 'YOU SHALL NOT MAKE FALSE
VOWS, BUT SHALL FULFILL YOUR VOWS TO THE LORD.'

5:25 Prov 25:8f; Luke 12:58
5:26 Luke 12:59
5:27 Matt 5:21, 33, 38, 43; Ex 20:14; Deut 5:18
5:28 2 Sam 11:2-5; Job 31:1; Matt 15:19; James 1:14, 15
5:29 Matt 18:9; Mark 9:47; Matt 5:22
5:30 Matt 18:8; Mark 9:43; Matt 5:22
5:31 Deut 24:1, 3; Jer 3:1; Matt 19:7; Mark 10:4
5:32 Matt 19:9; Mark 10:11f; Luke 16:18; 1 Cor 7:11f
5:33 Matt 5:21, 27, 38, 43; 23:16ff; Lev 19:12; Num 30:2; Deut 23:21, 23

16 Lit *quadrans* (equaling two mites); i.e. 1/64 of a daily wage

5:25–26 In Jesus' day, someone who couldn't pay a debt was thrown into prison until the debt was paid. Unless someone came to pay the debt for the prisoner, he or she would probably die there. It is practical advice to resolve our differences with our enemies before their anger causes more trouble (Proverbs 25:8–10). You may not get into a disagreement that takes you to court, but even small conflicts mend more easily if you try to make peace right away. In a broader sense, these verses advise us to get things right with our brothers and sisters before we have to stand before God.

5:27–28 The Old Testament law said that it is wrong for a person to have sex with someone other than his or her spouse (Exodus 20:14). But Jesus said that the *desire* to have sex with someone other than your spouse is mental adultery and thus sin. Jesus emphasized that if the *act* is wrong, then so is the *intention.* To be faithful to your spouse with your body but not your mind is to break the trust so vital to a strong marriage. Jesus is not condemning natural interest in the opposite sex or even healthy sexual desire, but the deliberate and repeated filling of one's mind with fantasies that would be evil if acted out.

5:27–28 Some think that if lustful thoughts are sin, why shouldn't a person go ahead and do the lustful actions too? Acting out sinful desires is harmful in several ways: (1) It causes people to excuse sin rather than to stop sinning; (2) it destroys marriages; (3) it is deliberate rebellion against God's Word; (4) it always hurts someone else in addition to the sinner. Sinful action is more dangerous than sinful desire, and that is why desires should not be acted out. Nevertheless, sinful desire is just as damaging to righteousness. Left unchecked, wrong desires will result in wrong actions and turn people away from God.

5:29–30 When Jesus said to get rid of your hand or your eye, he was speaking figuratively. He didn't mean literally to gouge out your eye, because even a blind person can lust. But if that were the only choice, it would be better to go into heaven with one eye or hand than to go to hell with two. We sometimes tolerate sins in our lives that, left unchecked, could eventually destroy us. It is better to experience the pain of removal (getting rid of a bad habit or something we treasure, for instance) than to allow the sin to bring judgment and condemnation. Examine your life for anything that causes you to sin, and take every necessary action to remove it.

5:31–32 Divorce is as hurtful and destructive today as in Jesus' day. God intends marriage to be a lifetime commitment (Genesis 2:24). When entering into marriage, people should never consider divorce an option for solving problems or a way out of a relationship that seems dead. In these verses, Jesus is also attacking those who purposefully abuse the marriage contract, using divorce to satisfy their lustful desire to marry someone else. Are your actions today helping your marriage grow stronger, or are you tearing it apart?

5:32 Jesus said that divorce is not permissible except for unfaithfulness. This does not mean that divorce should automatically occur when a spouse commits adultery. The word translated "unchastity" implies a sexually immoral life-style, not a confessed and repented act of adultery. Those who discover that their partner has been unfaithful should first make every effort to forgive, reconcile, and restore their relationship. We are always to look for reasons to restore the marriage relationship rather than for excuses to leave it.

5:33ff Here, Jesus was emphasizing the importance of telling the truth. People were breaking promises and using sacred language casually and carelessly. Keeping oaths and promises is important; it builds trust and makes committed human relationships possible. The Bible condemns making vows or taking oaths casually, giving your word while knowing that you won't keep it, or swearing falsely in God's name (Exodus 20:7; Leviticus 19:12; Numbers 30:1–2; Deuteronomy 19:16–20). Oaths are needed in certain situations only because we live in a sinful society that breeds distrust.

5:34 James 5:12; Is 66:1; Matt 23:22

5:35 Is 66:1; Acts 7:49; Ps 48:2

5:37 Matt 6:13; 13:19, 38; John 17:15; 2 Thess 3:3; 1 John 2:13f; 3:12; 5:18f

5:38 Matt 5:21, 27, 33, 43; Ex 21:24; Lev 24:20; Deut 19:21

5:39 Luke 6:29, 30; 1 Cor 6:7

5:42 Deut 15:7-11; Luke 6:34f; 1 Tim 6:18

5:43 Matt 5:21, 27, 33, 38; Lev 19:18; Deut 23:3-6

34 "But I say to you, make no oath at all, either by heaven, for it is the throne of God,
35 or by the earth, for it is the footstool of His feet, or by Jerusalem, for it is THE CITY
OF THE GREAT KING.
36 "Nor shall you make an oath by your head, for you cannot make one hair white or
black.
37 "But let your statement be, 'Yes, yes' *or* 'No, no'; anything beyond these is of evil.

Jesus Teaches about Retaliation
(56)

38 "You have heard that it was said, 'AN EYE FOR AN EYE, AND A TOOTH FOR A TOOTH.'
39 "But I say to you, do not resist an evil person; but whoever slaps you on your right
cheek, turn the other to him also.
40 "If anyone wants to sue you and take your [17]shirt, let him have your [18]coat also.
41 "Whoever forces you to go one mile, go with him two.
42 "Give to him who asks of you, and do not turn away from him who wants to borrow
from you.

Jesus Teaches about Loving Enemies
(57/Luke 6:27-36)

43 "You have heard that it was said, 'YOU SHALL LOVE YOUR NEIGHBOR and hate your
enemy.'

17 Lit *tunic;* i.e. a garment worn next to the body **18** Lit *cloak;* i.e. an outer garment

JESUS AND THE OLD TESTAMENT LAW

Reference	*Examples of Old Testament mercy in justice:*
Leviticus 19:18	"You shall not take vengeance, nor bear any grudge against the sons of your people, but you shall love your neighbor as yourself; I am the LORD."
Proverbs 24:28–29	"Do not be a witness against your neighbor without cause, and do not deceive with your lips. Do not say, 'Thus I shall do to him as he has done to me; I will render to the man according to his work.'"
Proverbs 25:21–22	"If your enemy is hungry, give him food to eat; and if he is thirsty, give him water to drink; for you will heap burning coals on his head, and the LORD will reward you."
Lamentations 3:27–31	"It is good for a man that he . . . give his cheek to the smiter, let him be filled with reproach. For the Lord will not reject forever."

What seems to be a case of Jesus contradicting the laws of the Old Testament deserves a careful look. It is too easy to overlook how much mercy was written into the Old Testament laws. Above are several examples. What God designed as a system of justice with mercy had been distorted over the years into a license for revenge. It was this misapplication of the law that Jesus attacked.

5:33–37 Oaths, or vows, were common, but Jesus told his followers not to use them—their word alone should be enough (see James 5:12). Are you known as a person of your word? Truthfulness seems so rare that we feel we must end our statements with "I promise." If we tell the truth all the time, we will have less pressure to back up our words with an oath or promise.

5:38 God's purpose behind this law was an expression of mercy. The law was given to judges and said, in effect, "Make the punishment fit the crime." It was not a guide for personal revenge (Exodus 21:23–25; Leviticus 24:19–20; Deuteronomy 19:21). These laws were given to *limit* vengeance and help the court administer punishment that was neither too strict nor too lenient. Some people, however, were using this phrase to justify their vendettas against others. People still try to excuse their acts of revenge by saying, "I was just doing to him what he did to me."

5:38–42 When we are wronged, often our first reaction is to get even. Instead Jesus said we should do *good* to those who wrong us! Our desire should not be to keep score, but to love and forgive. This is not natural—it is supernatural. Only God can give us the strength to love as he does. Instead of planning vengeance, pray for those who hurt you.

5:39–44 To many Jews of Jesus' day, these statements were offensive. Any Messiah who would turn the other cheek was not the military leader they wanted to lead a revolt against Rome. Since they were under Roman oppression, they wanted retaliation against their enemies, whom they hated. But Jesus suggested a new, radical response to injustice: Instead of demanding rights, give them up freely! According to Jesus, it is more important to *give* justice and mercy than to receive it.

5:43–44 By telling us not to retaliate, Jesus keeps us from taking the law into our own hands. By loving and praying for our enemies, we can overcome evil with good.

The Pharisees interpreted Leviticus 19:18 as teaching that they should love only those who love in return, and Psalm 139:19–22 and 140:9–11 as meaning that they should hate their enemies. But Jesus says we are to love our enemies. If you love your enemies and treat them well, you will truly show that Jesus is Lord of your life. This is possible only for those who give themselves fully to God, because only he can deliver people from natural selfishness. We must trust the Holy Spirit to help us *show* love to those for whom we may not *feel* love.

44 "But I say to you, love your enemies and pray for those who persecute you,
45 so that you may be sons of your Father who is in heaven; for He causes His sun to
rise on *the* evil and *the* good, and sends rain on *the* righteous and *the* unrighteous.
46 "For if you love those who love you, what reward do you have? Do not even the tax
collectors do the same?
47 "If you greet only your brothers, what more are you doing *than others?* Do not even
the Gentiles do the same?
48 "Therefore you are to be perfect, as your heavenly Father is perfect.

Jesus Teaches about Giving to the Needy
(58)

6 "Beware of practicing your righteousness before men to be noticed by them; otherwise you have no reward with your Father who is in heaven.
2 "So when you give to the poor, do not sound a trumpet before you, as the hypocrites
do in the synagogues and in the streets, so that they may be honored by men. Truly I say
to you, they have their reward in full.
3 "But when you give to the poor, do not let your left hand know what your right hand
is doing,
4 so that your giving will be in secret; and your Father who sees *what is done* in secret
will reward you.

Jesus Teaches about Prayer
(58)

5 "When you pray, you are not to be like the hypocrites; for they love to stand and pray
in the synagogues and on the street corners so that they may be seen by men. Truly I say
to you, they have their reward in full.
6 "But you, when you pray, go into your inner room, close your door and pray to your
Father who is in secret, and your Father who sees *what is done* in secret will reward you.
7 "And when you are praying, do not use meaningless repetition as the Gentiles do,
for they suppose that they will be heard for their many words.
8 "So do not be like them; for your Father knows what you need before you ask Him.
9 "Pray, then, in this way:

5:44 Luke 6:27f; 23:34; Acts 7:60; Rom 12:20

5:45 Matt 5:9; Luke 6:35; Acts 14:17

5:46 Luke 6:32

5:48 Lev 19:2; Deut 18:13; 2 Cor 7:1; Phil 3:12-15

6:1 Matt 6:5, 16; 23:5

6:2 Matt 6:5, 16; 23:5; Luke 6:24

6:4 Jer 17:10; Matt 6:6, 18; Heb 4:13

6:5 Mark 11:25; Luke 18:11, 13; Matt 6:1, 16; Matt 6:2, 16; Luke 6:24

6:6 Is 26:20; Matt 26:36-39; Acts 9:40; Matt 6:4, 18

6:7 1 Kin 18:26f

6:8 Ps 38:9; 69:17-19; Matt 6:32; Luke 12:30

6:9 Luke 11:2-4

5:48 How can we be perfect? (1) *In character.* In this life we cannot be flawless, but we can aspire to be as much like Christ as possible. (2) *In holiness.* Like the Pharisees, we are to separate ourselves from the world's sinful values. But unlike the Pharisees, we are to be devoted to God's desires rather than our own, and carry his love and mercy into the world. (3) *In maturity.* We can't achieve Christlike character and holy living all at once, but we must grow toward maturity and wholeness. Just as we expect different behavior from a baby, a child, a teenager, and an adult, so God expects different behavior from us, depending on our stage of spiritual development. (4) *In love.* We can seek to love others as completely as God loves us.

We can be perfect if our behavior is appropriate for our maturity level—perfect, yet with much room to grow. Our tendency to sin must never deter us from striving to be more like Christ. Christ calls all of his disciples to excel, to rise above mediocrity, and to mature in every area, becoming like him. Those who strive to become perfect will one day be perfect, even as Christ is perfect (1 John 3:2–3).

6:2 The term *hypocrites,* as used here, describes people who do good acts for appearances only—not out of compassion or other good motives. Their actions may be good, but their motives are hollow. These empty acts are their only reward, but God will reward those who are sincere in their faith.

6:3 When Jesus says not to let your left hand know what your right hand is doing, he is teaching that our motives for giving to God and to others must be pure. It is easy to give with mixed motives, to do something for someone if it will benefit us in return. But believers should avoid all scheming and give for the pleasure of giving and as a response to God's love. Why do *you* give?

6:3–4 It's easier to do what's right when we gain recognition and praise. To be sure our motives are not selfish, we should do our good deeds quietly or in secret, with no thought of reward. Jesus says we should check our motives in three areas: generosity (6:4), prayer (6:6), and fasting (6:18). Those acts should not be self-centered, but God-centered, done not to make us look good but to make God look good. The reward God promises is not material, and it is never given to those who seek it. Doing something only for ourselves is not a loving sacrifice. With your next good deed, ask, "Would I still do this if no one would ever know I did it?"

6:5–6 Some people, especially the religious leaders, wanted to be seen as "holy," and public prayer was one way to get attention. Jesus saw through their self-righteous acts, however, and taught that the essence of prayer is not public style but private communication with God. There is a place for public prayer, but to pray only where others will notice you indicates that your real audience is not God.

6:7–8 Repeating the same words over and over like a magic incantation is no way to ensure that God will hear your prayer. It's not wrong to come to God many times with the same requests—Jesus encourages *persistent* prayer. But he condemns the shallow repetition of words that are not offered with a sincere heart. We can never pray too much if our prayers are honest and sincere. Before you start to pray, make sure you mean what you say.

6:9 This is often called the Lord's Prayer because Jesus gave it to the disciples. It can be a pattern for our prayers. We should praise God, pray for his work in the world, pray for our daily needs, and pray for help in our daily struggles.

6:9 The phrase "Our Father who is in heaven" indicates that God is not only majestic and holy, but also personal and loving. The first

6:10 Matt 3:2; 4:17; Matt 26:42; Luke 22:42; Acts 21:14

6:11 Prov 30:8; Is 33:16; Luke 11:3

6:12 Ex 34:7; Ps 32:1; 130:4; Matt 9:2; 26:28; Eph 1:7; 1 John 1:7-9

6:13 John 17:15; 1 Cor 10:13; 2 Thess 3:3; 2 Tim 4:18; 2 Pet 2:9; 1 John 5:18; Matt 5:37

6:14 Matt 7:2; Mark 11:25f; Eph 4:32; Col 3:13

6:15 Matt 18:35

6:16 Is 58:5; Matt 6:2

6:19 Prov 23:4; Matt 19:21; Luke 12:21, 33; 18:22; 1 Tim 6:9, 10; Heb 13:5; James 5:2

'Our Father who is in heaven,
Hallowed be Your name.
10 'Your kingdom come.
Your will be done,
On earth as it is in heaven.
11 'Give us this day our daily bread.
12 'And forgive us our debts, as we also have forgiven our debtors.
13 'And do not lead us into temptation, but deliver us from evil. [For Yours is the kingdom and the power and the glory forever. Amen.]'
14 "For if you forgive others for their transgressions, your heavenly Father will also forgive you.
15 "But if you do not forgive others, then your Father will not forgive your transgressions.

Jesus Teaches about Fasting (60)

16 "Whenever you fast, do not put on a gloomy face as the hypocrites *do,* for they neglect their appearance so that they will be noticed by men when they are fasting. Truly I
say to you, they have their reward in full.
17 "But you, when you fast, anoint your head and wash your face
18 so that your fasting will not be noticed by men, but by your Father who is in secret;
and your Father who sees *what is done* in secret will reward you.

Jesus Teaches about Money (61)

19 "Do not store up for yourselves treasures on earth, where moth and rust destroy, and
where thieves break in and steal.

SEVEN REASONS NOT TO WORRY

6:25	The same God who created life in you can be trusted with the details of your life.
6:26	Worrying about the future hampers your efforts for today.
6:27	Worrying is more harmful than helpful.
6:28–30	God does not ignore those who depend on him.
6:31–32	Worry shows a lack of faith in and understanding of God.
6:33	There are real challenges God wants us to pursue, and worrying keeps us from them.
6:34	Living one day at a time keeps us from being consumed with worry.

line of this model prayer is a statement of praise and a commitment to hallow, or honor, God's holy name. We can honor God's name by being careful to use it respectfully. If we use God's name lightly, we aren't remembering God's holiness.

6:10 The phrase "Your kingdom come" is a reference to God's spiritual reign, not Israel's freedom from Rome. God's kingdom was announced in the covenant with Abraham (8:11; Luke 13:28), is present in Christ's reign in believers' hearts (Luke 17:21), and will be complete when all evil is destroyed and God establishes the new heaven and earth (Revelation 21:1).

6:10 When we pray "Your will be done," we are not resigning ourselves to fate, but praying that God's perfect purpose will be accomplished in this world as well as in the next.

6:11 When we pray "Give us this day our daily bread," we are acknowledging that God is our sustainer and provider. It is a misconception to think that we provide for our needs ourselves. We must trust God *daily* to provide what he knows we need.

6:13 God doesn't lead us into temptations, but sometimes he allows us to be tested by them. As disciples, we should pray to be delivered from these trying times and for deliverance from evil (Satan and his deceit). All Christians struggle with temptation. Sometimes it is so subtle that we don't even realize what is happening to us. God has promised that he won't allow us to be tempted beyond what we can bear (1 Corinthians 10:13). Ask God to help you recognize temptation and to give you strength to overcome it and choose God's way instead. For more on temptation, see the notes on 4:1.

6:14–15 Jesus gives a startling warning about forgiveness: If we refuse to forgive others, God will also refuse to forgive us. Why? Because when we don't forgive others, we are denying our common ground as sinners in need of God's forgiveness. God's forgiveness of sin is not the direct result of our forgiving others, but it is based on our realizing what forgiveness means (see Ephesians 4:32). It is easy to ask God for forgiveness, but difficult to grant it to others. Whenever we ask God to forgive us for sin, we should ask ourselves, "Have I forgiven the people who have wronged me?"

6:16 Fasting—going without food in order to spend time in prayer—is noble *and* difficult. It gives us time to pray, teaches self-discipline, reminds us that we can live with a lot less, and helps us appreciate God's gifts. Jesus was not condemning fasting, but hypocrisy—fasting in order to gain public approval. Fasting was mandatory for the Jewish people once a year, on the day of atonement (Leviticus 23:32). The Pharisees voluntarily fasted twice a week to impress the people with their "holiness." Jesus commended acts of self-sacrifice done quietly and sincerely. He wanted people to adopt spiritual disciplines for the right reasons, not from a selfish desire for praise.

6:17 A person would anoint his or her head with olive oil, used as a common cosmetic like a lotion. Jesus was saying, "Go about your normal daily routine when you fast. Don't make a show of it."

20 "But store up for yourselves treasures in heaven, where neither moth nor rust destroys, and where thieves do not break in or steal;
21 for where your treasure is, there your heart will be also.
22 "The eye is the lamp of the body; so then if your eye is clear, your whole body will be
full of light.
23 "But if your eye is bad, your whole body will be full of darkness. If then the light that
is in you is darkness, how great is the darkness!
24 "No one can serve two masters; for either he will hate the one and love the other, or
he will be devoted to one and despise the other. You cannot serve God and [19]wealth.

Jesus Teaches about Worry
(62)

25 "For this reason I say to you, do not be worried about your life, *as to* what you will eat
or what you will drink; nor for your body, *as to* what you will put on. Is not life more than
food, and the body more than clothing?
26 "Look at the birds of the air, that they do not sow, nor reap nor gather into barns,
and *yet* your heavenly Father feeds them. Are you not worth much more than they?
27 "And who of you by being worried can add a *single* hour to his life?
28 "And why are you worried about clothing? Observe how the lilies of the field grow;
they do not toil nor do they spin,
29 yet I say to you that not even Solomon in all his glory clothed himself like one of
these.
30 "But if God so clothes the grass of the field, which is *alive* today and tomorrow is
thrown into the furnace, *will He* not much more *clothe* you? You of little faith!
31 "Do not worry then, saying, 'What will we eat?' or 'What will we drink?' or 'What
will we wear for clothing?'
32 "For the Gentiles eagerly seek all these things; for your heavenly Father knows that
you need all these things.
33 "But seek first His kingdom and His righteousness, and all these things will be added
to you.
34 "So do not worry about tomorrow; for tomorrow will care for itself. Each day has
enough trouble of its own.

6:20 Matt 19:21; 1 Tim 6:19
6:22 Luke 11:34, 35
6:23 Matt 20:15; Mark 7:22
6:24 Gal 1:10; James 4:4; Luke 16:9, 11, 13
6:25 Luke 12:22-31; Matt 6:27, 28, 31, 34; Luke 10:41; 12:11, 22; Phil 4:6; 1 Pet 5:7
6:26 Ps 104:27, 28; Matt 10:29ff; Luke 12:24
6:27 Luke 10:41; Phil 4:6; 1 Pet 5:7
6:28 Phil 4:6; 1 Pet 5:7
6:30 James 1:10, 11; 1 Pet 1:24
6:31 Luke 10:41; 12:11, 22; Phil 4:6
6:32 Matt 6:8; Phil 4:19
6:33 Matt 19:28; Mark 10:29f; Luke 18:29f; 1 Tim 4:8
6:34 Luke 12:11, 22; Phil 4:6; 1 Pet 5:7

19 *mamona,* Gr for Ara *mammon;* i.e. wealth, etc, personified as an object of worship

---

6:20 Storing up treasures in heaven is not limited to tithing but is accomplished by all acts of obedience to God. There is a sense in which giving our money to God's work is like investing in heaven. But our intention should be to seek the fulfillment of God's purposes in all we do, not merely what we do with our money.

6:22–23 Spiritual vision is our capacity to see clearly what God wants us to do and to see the world from his point of view. But this spiritual insight can be easily clouded. Self-serving desires, interests, and goals block that vision. Serving God is the best way to restore it. A "clear" eye is one that is fixed on God.

6:24 Jesus says we can have only one master. We live in a materialistic society where many people serve money. They spend all their lives collecting and storing it, only to die and leave it behind. Their desire for money and what it can buy far outweighs their commitment to God and spiritual matters. Whatever you store up, you will spend much of your time and energy thinking about. Don't fall into the materialistic trap, because "the love of money is a root of all sorts of evil" (1 Timothy 6:10). Can you honestly say that God, and not money, is your master? One test is to ask which one occupies more of your thoughts, time, and efforts.

6:24 Jesus contrasted heavenly values with earthly values when he explained that our first loyalty should be to those things that do not fade, cannot be stolen or used up, and never wear out. We should not be fascinated with our possessions, lest *they* possess *us.* This means we may have to do some cutting back if our possessions are becoming too important to us. Jesus is calling for a decision that allows us to live contentedly with whatever we have because we have chosen what is eternal and lasting.

6:25 Because of the ill effects of worry, Jesus tells us not to worry about those needs that God promises to supply. Worry may (1) damage your health, (2) cause the object of your worry to consume your thoughts, (3) disrupt your productivity, (4) negatively affect the way you treat others, and (5) reduce your ability to trust in God. How many ill effects of worry are you experiencing? Here is the difference between worry and genuine concern—worry immobilizes, but concern moves you to action.

6:33 To "seek first His kingdom and His righteousness" means to turn to God first for help, to fill your thoughts with his desires, to take his character for your pattern, and to serve and obey him in everything. What is really important to you? People, objects, goals, and other desires all compete for priority. Any of these can quickly bump God out of first place if you don't actively choose to give him first place in every area of your life.

6:34 Planning for tomorrow is time well spent; worrying about tomorrow is time wasted. Sometimes it's difficult to tell the difference. Careful planning is thinking ahead about goals, steps, and schedules, and trusting in God's guidance. When done well, planning can help alleviate worry. Worriers, by contrast, are consumed by fear and find it difficult to trust God. They let their plans interfere with their relationship with God. Don't let worries about tomorrow affect your relationship with God today.

Jesus Teaches about Criticizing Others
(63/Luke 6:37-42)

7 "Do not judge so that you will not be judged.
2 "For in the way you judge, you will be judged; and by your standard of measure,
it will be measured to you.
3 "Why do you look at the speck that is in your brother's eye, but do not notice the log
that is in your own eye?
4 "Or how can you say to your brother, 'Let me take the speck out of your eye,' and
behold, the log is in your own eye?
5 "You hypocrite, first take the log out of your own eye, and then you will see clearly to
take the speck out of your brother's eye.
6 "Do not give what is holy to dogs, and do not throw your pearls before swine, or they
will trample them under their feet, and turn and tear you to pieces.

7:1 Rom 14:10, 13
7:2 Mark 4:24; Luke 6:38
7:3 Rom 2:1
7:4 Luke 6:42
7:6 Matt 15:26

Jesus Teaches about Asking, Seeking, Knocking
(64)

7 "Ask, and it will be given to you; seek, and you will find; knock, and it will be opened
to you.
8 "For everyone who asks receives, and he who seeks finds, and to him who knocks it
will be opened.
9 "Or what man is there among you who, when his son asks for a loaf, will give him a
stone?
10 "Or if he asks for a fish, he will not give him a snake, will he?
11 "If you then, being evil, know how to give good gifts to your children, how much more
will your Father who is in heaven give what is good to those who ask Him!
12 "In everything, therefore, treat people the same way you want them to treat you, for
this is the Law and the Prophets.

7:7 Luke 11:9-13; Matt 18:19; 21:22; Mark 11:24; John 14:13; 15:7, 16; 16:23f; James 1:5f; 1 John 3:22; 5:14f
7:11 Ps 84:11; Is 63:7; Rom 8:32; James 1:17
7:12 Luke 6:31; Matt 22:40; Rom 13:8ff; Gal 5:14

Jesus Teaches about the Way to Heaven
(65)

13 "Enter through the narrow gate; for the gate is wide and the way is broad that leads
to destruction, and there are many who enter through it.

7:13 Luke 13:24

7:1–2 Jesus tells us to examine our own motives and conduct instead of judging others. The traits that bother us in others are often the habits we dislike in ourselves. Our untamed bad habits and behavior patterns are the very ones that we most want to change in others. Do you find it easy to magnify others' faults while excusing your own? If you are ready to criticize someone, check to see if you deserve the same criticism. Judge yourself first, and then lovingly forgive and help your neighbor.

7:1–5 Jesus' statement, "Do not judge," is against the kind of hypocritical, judgmental attitude that tears others down in order to build oneself up. It is not a blanket statement against all critical thinking, but a call to be *discerning* rather than negative. Jesus said to expose false teachers (7:15–23), and Paul taught that we should exercise church discipline (1 Corinthians 5:1–2) and trust God to be the final Judge (1 Corinthians 4:3–5).

7:6 Swine (pigs) were unclean animals according to God's Law (Deuteronomy 14:8). Anyone who touched an unclean animal became "ceremonially unclean" and could not go to the temple to worship until the uncleanness was removed. Jesus says that we should not entrust holy teachings to unholy or unclean people. It is futile to try to teach holy concepts to people who don't want to listen and will only tear apart what we say. We should not stop giving God's Word to unbelievers, but we should be wise and discerning in what we teach to whom, so that we will not be wasting our time.

7:7–8 Jesus tells us to persist in pursuing God. People often give up after a few halfhearted efforts and conclude that God cannot be found. But knowing God takes faith, focus, and follow-through, and Jesus assures us that we will be rewarded. Don't give up in your efforts to seek God. Continue to ask him for more knowledge, patience, wisdom, love, and understanding. He will give them to you.

7:9–10 The child in Jesus' example asked his father for bread and fish—good and necessary items. If the child had asked for a poisonous snake, would the wise father have granted his request? Sometimes God knows we are praying for "snakes" and does not give us what we ask for, even though we persist in our prayers. As we learn to know God better as a loving Father, we learn to ask for what is good for us, and then he grants it.

7:11 Christ is showing us the heart of God the Father. God is not selfish, begrudging, or stingy, and we don't have to beg or grovel as we come with our requests. He is a loving Father who understands, cares, and comforts. If humans can be kind, imagine how kind God, the Creator of kindness, can be.

7:11 Jesus used the expression "If you then, being evil" to contrast sinful and fallible human beings with the holy and perfect God.

7:12 This is commonly known as the Golden Rule. In many religions it is stated negatively: "Don't do to others what you don't want done to you." By stating it positively, Jesus made it more significant. It is not very hard to refrain from harming others; it is much more difficult to take the initiative in doing something good for them. The Golden Rule as Jesus formulated it is the foundation of active goodness and mercy—the kind of love God shows to us every day. Think of a good and merciful action you can take today.

7:13–14 The gate that leads to eternal life (John 10:7–9) is called "narrow." This does not mean that it is difficult to become a Christian, but that there is only *one* way to live eternally with God and only a few that decide to walk that road. Believing in Jesus is the only way to heaven, because he alone died for our sins and made us right before God. Living his way may not be popular, but it is true and right. Thank God there is one way!

14 "For the gate is small and the way is narrow that leads to life, and there are few who
find it.

Jesus Teaches about Fruit in People's Lives
(66/Luke 6:43-45)

15 "Beware of the false prophets, who come to you in sheep's clothing, but inwardly are
ravenous wolves.
16 "You will know them by their fruits. Grapes are not gathered from thorn *bushes* nor
figs from thistles, are they?
17 "So every good tree bears good fruit, but the bad tree bears bad fruit.
18 "A good tree cannot produce bad fruit, nor can a bad tree produce good fruit.
19 "Every tree that does not bear good fruit is cut down and thrown into the fire.
20 "So then, you will know them by their fruits.

Jesus Teaches about Those Who Build Houses on Rock and Sand
(67/Luke 6:46-49)

21 "Not everyone who says to Me, 'Lord, Lord,' will enter the kingdom of heaven, but
he who does the will of My Father who is in heaven *will enter.*
22 "Many will say to Me on that day, 'Lord, Lord, did we not prophesy in Your name,
and in Your name cast out demons, and in Your name perform many miracles?'
23 "And then I will declare to them, 'I never knew you; DEPART FROM ME, YOU WHO
PRACTICE LAWLESSNESS.'
24 "Therefore everyone who hears these words of Mine and acts on them, may be compared to a wise man who built his house on the rock.
25 "And the rain fell, and the floods came, and the winds blew and slammed against
that house; and *yet* it did not fall, for it had been founded on the rock.
26 "Everyone who hears these words of Mine and does not act on them, will be like a
foolish man who built his house on the sand.
27 "The rain fell, and the floods came, and the winds blew and slammed against that
house; and it fell—and great was its fall."
28 When Jesus had finished these words, the crowds were amazed at His teaching;
29 for He was teaching them as *one* having authority, and not as their scribes.

7:15 Matt 24:11, 24; Mark 13:22; Luke 6:26; Acts 13:6; 2 Pet 2:1; 1 John 4:1; Rev 16:13; 19:20; 20:10; Ezek 22:27; John 10:12; Acts 20:29

7:16 Matt 7:20; 12:33; Luke 6:44; James 3:12

7:17 Matt 12:33, 35

7:19 Matt 3:10; Luke 3:9; 13:7; John 15:2, 6

7:20 Matt 7:16; 12:33; Luke 6:44; James 3:12

7:21 Luke 6:46

7:22 Matt 25:11f; Luke 13:25ff

Matt 10:15

7:23 Ps 6:8; Matt 25:41; Luke 13:27

7:24 Matt 16:18; James 1:22-25

7:28 Matt 11:1; 13:53; 19:1; 26:1; Matt 13:54; 22:33; Mark 1:22; 6:2; 11:18; Luke 4:32; John 7:46

7:15 False prophets were common in Old Testament times. They prophesied only what the king and the people wanted to hear, claiming it was God's message. False teachers are just as common today. Jesus says to beware of those whose words sound religious but who are motivated by money, fame, or power. You can tell who they are because in their teaching they minimize Christ and glorify themselves.

7:20 We should evaluate teachers' words by examining their lives. Just as trees are consistent in the kind of fruit they produce, so good teachers consistently exhibit good behavior and high moral character as they attempt to live out the truths of Scripture. This does not mean we should have witch hunts, throwing out church school teachers, pastors, and others who are less than perfect. Every one of us is subject to sin, and we must show the same mercy to others that we need for ourselves. When Jesus talks about bad trees, he means teachers who deliberately teach false doctrine. We must examine the teachers' motives, the direction they are taking, and the results they are seeking.

7:21 Some self-professed athletes can "talk" a great game, but that tells you nothing about their athletic skills. And not everyone who talks about heaven belongs to God's kingdom. Jesus is more concerned about our *walk* than our *talk.* He wants us to *do* right, not just *say* the right words. Your house (which represents your life, 7:24) will withstand the storms of life only if you do what is right instead of just talking about it. What you do cannot be separated from what you believe.

7:21–23 Jesus exposed those people who sounded religious but had no personal relationship with him. On "that day" (the day of judgment), only our relationship with Christ—our acceptance of him as Savior and our obedience to him—will matter. Many people think that if they are "good" people and say religious things, they will be rewarded with eternal life. In reality, faith in Christ is what will count at the judgment.

7:22 "That day" is the final day of reckoning when God will settle all accounts, judging sin and rewarding faith.

7:24 To build "on the rock" means to be a hearing, responding disciple, not a phony, superficial one. Practicing obedience becomes the solid foundation to weather the storms of life. See James 1:22–27 for more on putting into practice what we hear.

7:26 Like a house of cards, the fool's life crumbles. Most people do not deliberately seek to build on a false or inferior foundation; instead, they just don't think about their life's purpose. Many people are headed for destruction, not out of stubbornness but out of thoughtlessness. Part of our responsibility as believers is to help others stop and think about where their lives are headed and to point out the consequences of ignoring Christ's message.

7:29 The scribes (religious scholars) often cited traditions and quoted authorities to support their arguments and interpretations. But Jesus spoke with a new authority—his own. He didn't need to quote anyone because he was the original Word (John 1:1).

3. Jesus performs many miracles

Jesus Heals a Man with Leprosy
(38/Mark 1:40-45; Luke 5:12-16)

8 When Jesus came down from the mountain, large crowds followed Him.
8:2 Matt 9:18; 15:25; 18:26; 20:20; John 9:38; Acts 10:25
2 And a leper came to Him and bowed down before Him, and said, "Lord, if You
are willing, You can make me clean."
3 Jesus stretched out His hand and touched him, saying, "I am willing; be cleansed."
8:3 Matt 11:5; Luke 4:27
And immediately his leprosy was cleansed.
4 And Jesus ☆said to him, "See that you tell no one; but go, show yourself to the priest
8:4 Matt 9:30; 12:16; 17:9; Mark 1:44; 3:12; 5:43; 7:36; 8:30; 9:9; Luke 4:41; 8:56; 9:21; Mark 1:44; Luke 5:14; 17:14; Lev 13:49; 14:2ff
and present the offering that Moses commanded, as a testimony to them."

A Roman Centurion Demonstrates Faith
(68/Luke 7:1-10)

5 And when Jesus entered Capernaum, a centurion came to Him, imploring Him,
6 and saying, "Lord, my servant is lying paralyzed at home, fearfully tormented."
8:6 Matt 4:24
7 Jesus ☆said to him, "I will come and heal him."
8 But the centurion said, "Lord, I am not worthy for You to come under my roof, but
just say the word, and my servant will be healed.
8:9 Mark 1:27; Luke 9:1
9 "For I also am a man under authority, with soldiers under me; and I say to this one,
'Go!' and he goes, and to another, 'Come!' and he comes, and to my slave, 'Do this!' and
he does *it*."
10 Now when Jesus heard *this*, He marveled and said to those who were following, "Truly
I say to you, I have not found such great faith with anyone in Israel.
8:11 Is 49:12; 59:19; Mal 1:11; Luke 13:29
11 "I say to you that many will come from east and west, and [20]recline *at the table* with
Abraham, Isaac and Jacob in the kingdom of heaven;

20 Or *dine*

JESUS' MIRACULOUS POWER DISPLAYED
Jesus finished the sermon he had given on a hillside near Galilee and returned to Capernaum. As he and his disciples crossed the Sea of Galilee, Jesus calmed a fierce storm. Then, in the Gentile Gadarene region, Jesus commanded demons to come out of two men.

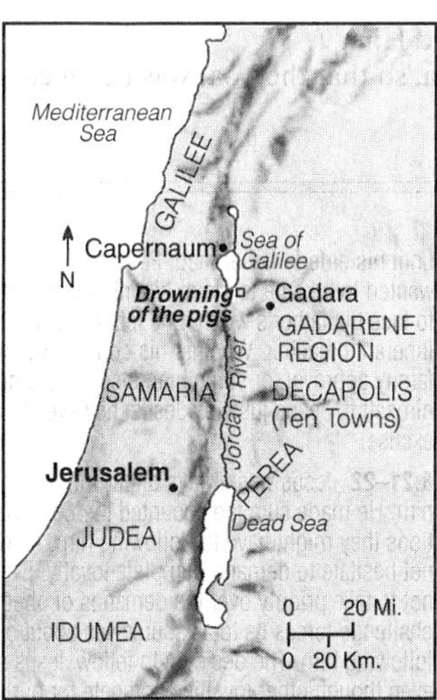

8:2–3 Leprosy, like AIDS today, was a terrifying disease because there was no known cure. In Jesus' day, the Greek word for *leprosy* was used for a variety of similar diseases, and some forms were contagious. If a person contracted the contagious type, a priest declared him a leper and banished him from his home and city. The leper was sent to live in a community with other lepers until he either got better or died. Yet when the leper begged Jesus to heal him, Jesus reached out and touched him, even though his skin was covered with the dread disease.

Sin is also an incurable disease—and we all have it. Only Christ's healing touch can miraculously take away our sins and restore us to real living. But first, just like the leper, we must realize our inability to cure ourselves and ask for Christ's saving help.

8:4 The law required a healed leper to be examined by the priest (Leviticus 14). Jesus wanted this man to give his story firsthand to the priest to prove that his leprosy was completely gone so that he could be restored to his community.

8:5–6 The centurion could have let many obstacles stand between him and Jesus—pride, doubt, money, language, distance, time, self-sufficiency, power, race. But he didn't. If he did not let these barriers block his approach to Jesus, we don't need to either. What keeps you from Christ?

8:8–12 A centurion was a career military officer in the Roman army with control over 100 soldiers. Roman soldiers, of all people, were hated by the Jews for their oppression, control, and ridicule. Yet this man's genuine faith amazed Jesus! This hated Gentile's faith put to shame the stagnant piety of many of the Jewish religious leaders.

8:10–12 Jesus told the crowd that many religious Jews who should be in the kingdom would be excluded because of their lack of faith. Entrenched in their religious traditions, they could not accept Christ and his new message. We must be careful not to become so set in our religious habits that we expect God to work only in specified ways. Don't limit God by your mind-set and lack of faith.

8:11–12 "From east and west" stands for the four corners of the earth. All the faithful people of God will be gathered to feast with the Messiah (Isaiah 6; 55). The Jews should have known that when the Messiah came, his blessings would be for Gentiles too (see Isaiah 66:12, 19). But this message came as a shock because they were too wrapped up in their own affairs and destiny. In claiming God's promises, we must not apply them so personally that we forget to see what God wants to do to reach *all* the people he loves.

8:11–12 Matthew emphasizes this universal theme—Jesus' message is for everyone. The Old Testament prophets knew this (see Isaiah 56:3, 6–8; 66:12, 19; Malachi 1:11), but many New Testament Jewish leaders chose to ignore it. Each individual has to choose to accept or reject the gospel, and no one can become part of God's kingdom on the basis of heritage or connections. Having a Christian family is a wonderful blessing, but it won't guarantee you eternal life. *You* must believe in and follow Christ.

12 but the sons of the kingdom will be cast out into the outer darkness; in that place
there will be weeping and gnashing of teeth."
13 And Jesus said to the centurion, "Go; it shall be done for you as you have believed."
And the servant was healed that *very* moment.

Jesus Heals Peter's Mother-in-law and Many Others
(35/Mark 1:29-34; Luke 4:38-41)

14 When Jesus came into Peter's home, He saw his mother-in-law lying sick in bed with
a fever.
15 He touched her hand, and the fever left her; and she got up and waited on Him.
16 When evening came, they brought to Him many who were demon-possessed; and
He cast out the spirits with a word, and healed all who were ill.
17 *This was* to fulfill what was spoken through Isaiah the prophet: "HE HIMSELF TOOK
OUR INFIRMITIES AND CARRIED AWAY OUR DISEASES."

Jesus Teaches about the Cost of Following Him
(122/Luke 9:51-62)

18 Now when Jesus saw a crowd around Him, He gave orders to depart to the other
side *of the sea*.
19 Then a scribe came and said to Him, "Teacher, I will follow You wherever You go."
20 Jesus ☆said to him, "The foxes have holes and the birds of the air *have* nests, but the
Son of Man has nowhere to lay His head."
21 Another of the disciples said to Him, "Lord, permit me first to go and bury my father."
22 But Jesus ☆said to him, "Follow Me, and allow the dead to bury their own dead."

Jesus Calms the Storm
(87/Mark 4:35-41; Luke 8:22-25)

23 When He got into the boat, His disciples followed Him.
24 And behold, there arose a great storm on the sea, so that the boat was being covered with the waves; but Jesus Himself was asleep.

8:12 Matt 13:38; Matt 22:13; 25:30; Matt 13:42, 50; 22:13; 24:51; 25:30; Luke 13:28

8:13 Matt 9:22, 29

8:16 Matt 4:24; Matt 4:23; 8:33

8:17 Is 53:4

8:18 Mark 4:35; Luke 8:22

8:20 Dan 7:13; Matt 9:6; 12:8, 32, 40; 13:41; 16:13, 27f; 17:9; 19:28; 26:64; Mark 8:38; Luke 12:8; 18:8; 21:36; John 1:51; 3:13f; 6:27; 12:34; Acts 7:56

8:22 Matt 9:9; Mark 2:14; Luke 9:59, 60; John 1:43; 21:19

8:14 Peter was one of Jesus' 12 disciples. His Profile is found in chapter 26.

8:14–15 Peter's mother-in-law gives us a beautiful example to follow. Her response to Jesus' touch was to wait on Jesus and his disciples—immediately. Has God ever helped you through a dangerous or difficult situation? If so, you should ask, "How can I express my gratitude to him?" Because God has promised us all the rewards of his kingdom, we should look for ways to serve him and his followers now.

8:16–17 Matthew continues to show Jesus' kingly nature. Through a single touch, Jesus healed (8:3, 15); when he spoke a single word, evil spirits fled his presence (8:16). Jesus has authority over all evil powers and all earthly disease. He also has power and authority to conquer sin. Sickness and evil are consequences of living in a fallen world. But in the future, when God removes all sin, there will be no more sickness and death. Jesus' healing miracles were a taste of what the whole world will one day experience in God's kingdom.

8:19–20 Following Jesus is not always easy or comfortable. Often it means great cost and sacrifice, with no earthly rewards or security. Jesus didn't have a place to call home. You may find that following Christ costs you popularity, friendships, leisure time, or treasured habits. But while the cost of following Christ is high, the value of being Christ's disciple is even higher. Discipleship is an investment that lasts for eternity and yields incredible rewards.

8:21–22 It is possible that this disciple was not asking permission to go to his father's funeral, but rather to put off following Jesus until his elderly father died. Perhaps he was the firstborn son and wanted to be sure to claim his inheritance. Perhaps he didn't want to face his father's wrath if he left the family business to follow an itinerant preacher. Whether his concern was financial security, family approval, or something else, he did not want to commit himself to Jesus just yet. Jesus, however, would not accept his excuse.

8:21–22 Jesus was always direct with those who wanted to follow him. He made sure they counted the cost and set aside any conditions they might have for following him. As God's Son, Jesus did not hesitate to demand complete loyalty. Even family loyalty was not to take priority over the demands of obedience. His direct challenge forces us to ask ourselves about our own priorities in following him. The decision to follow Jesus should not be put off, even though other loyalties compete for our attention. Nothing should be placed above a total commitment to living for him.

8:23 This would have been a fishing boat because many of Jesus' disciples were fishermen. Josephus, an ancient historian, wrote that there were usually more than 300 fishing boats on the Sea of Galilee at one time. This boat was large enough to hold Jesus and his 12 disciples and was powered both by oars and sails. During a storm, however, the sails were taken down to keep them from ripping and to make the boat easier to control.

8:24 The Sea of Galilee is an unusual body of water. It is relatively small (13 miles long, 7 miles wide), but it is 150 feet deep, and the shoreline is 680 feet below sea level. Sudden storms can appear over the surrounding mountains with little warning, stirring the water into violent 20-foot waves. The disciples had not foolishly set out in a storm. They had been caught without warning, and their danger was great.

8:25 Matt 8:2; 9:18
8:26 Matt 6:30; 14:31; 16:8; 17:20

25 And they came to *Him* and woke Him, saying, "Save *us,* Lord; we are perishing!"
26 He ☆said to them, "Why are you afraid, you men of little faith?" Then He got up
and rebuked the winds and the sea, and it became perfectly calm.
27 The men were amazed, and said, "What kind of a man is this, that even the winds
and the sea obey Him?"

Jesus Sends the Demons into a Herd of Swine
(88/Mark 5:1-20; Luke 8:26-39)

8:28 Matt 4:24
8:29 Judg 11:12; 2 Sam 16:10; 19:22; 1 Kin 17:18; 2 Kin 3:13; 2 Chr 35:21; Mark 1:24; 5:7; Luke 4:34; 8:28; John 2:4

28 When He came to the other side into the country of the Gadarenes, two men who
were demon-possessed met Him as they were coming out of the tombs. *They were* so
extremely violent that no one could pass by that way.
29 And they cried out, saying, "What business do we have with each other, Son of God?
Have You come here to torment us before the time?"
30 Now there was a herd of many swine feeding at a distance from them.
31 The demons *began* to entreat Him, saying, "If You *are going to* cast us out, send us
into the herd of swine."
32 And He said to them, "Go!" And they came out and went into the swine, and the
whole herd rushed down the steep bank into the sea and perished in the waters.

8:33 Matt 4:24
8:34 Amos 7:12; Acts 16:39

33 The herdsmen ran away, and went to the city and reported everything, including
what had happened to the demoniacs.
34 And behold, the whole city came out to meet Jesus; and when they saw Him, they
implored Him to leave their region.

8:25 Although the disciples had witnessed many miracles, they panicked in this storm. As experienced sailors, they knew its danger; what they did not know was that Christ could control the forces of nature. There is often a stormy area of our human nature where we feel God can't or won't work. When we truly understand who God is, however, we will realize that he controls both the storms of nature and the storms of the troubled heart. Jesus' power that calmed this storm can also help us deal with the problems we face. Jesus is willing to help if we only ask him. We should never discount his power even in terrible trials.

8:28 The region of the Gadarenes is located southeast of the Sea of Galilee, near the town of Gadara, one of the most important cities of the region (see map). Gadara was a member of the Decapolis (see the note on Mark 5:20). These ten cities with independent governments were largely inhabited by Gentiles, which explains the herd of swine (8:30). The Jews did not raise pigs because pigs were considered unclean and thus unfit to eat.

8:28 Demon-possessed people are under the control of one or more demons. Demons are fallen angels who joined Satan in his rebellion against God and are now evil spirits under Satan's control. They help Satan tempt people to sin and have great destructive powers. But whenever they are confronted by Jesus, they lose their power. These demons recognized Jesus as God's Son (8:29), but they didn't think they had to obey him. Just believing is not enough (see James 2:19 for a discussion of belief and devils). Faith is more than belief. By faith, you accept what Jesus has done for you, receive him as the only One who can save you from sin, and live out your faith by obeying his commands.

8:28 Matthew says there were two demon-possessed men, while Mark and Luke refer only to one. Apparently Mark and Luke mention only the man who did the talking.

8:28 According to Jewish ceremonial laws, the men Jesus encountered were unclean in three ways: they were Gentiles (non-Jews), they were demon-possessed, and they lived in a graveyard (the tombs). Jesus helped them anyway. We should not turn our backs on people who are "unclean" or repulsive to us, or who violate our moral standards and religious beliefs. Instead, we must realize that every human individual is a unique creation of God, needing to be touched by his love.

8:29 The Bible tells us that at the end of the world the devil and his angels will be thrown into the lake of fire and brimstone (Revelation 20:10). When the demons asked if Jesus had come to torment them "before the time," they showed they knew their ultimate fate.

8:32 When the demons entered the swine, they drove the animals into the sea. The demons' action proves their destructive intent—if they could not destroy the men, they would destroy the swine. Jesus' action, by contrast, shows the value he places on each human life.

8:34 Why did the people ask Jesus to leave? Unlike their own pagan gods, Jesus could not be contained, controlled, or appeased. They feared Jesus' supernatural power, a power that they had never before witnessed. And they were upset about losing a herd of swine more than they were glad about the deliverance of the demon-possessed men. Are you more concerned about property and programs than people? Human beings are created in God's image and have eternal value. How foolish and yet how easy it is to value possessions, investments, and even animals above human life. Would you rather have Jesus leave you than finish his work in you?

Jesus Heals a Paralytic
(39/Mark 2:1-12; Luke 5:17-26)

9 Getting into a boat, Jesus crossed over *the sea* and came to His own city.
2 And they brought to Him a paralytic lying on a bed. Seeing their faith, Jesus said
to the paralytic, "Take courage, son; your sins are forgiven."
3 And some of the scribes said to themselves, "This *fellow* blasphemes."
4 And Jesus knowing their thoughts said, "Why are you thinking evil in your hearts?
5 "Which is easier, to say, 'Your sins are forgiven,' or to say, 'Get up, and walk'?
6 "But so that you may know that the Son of Man has authority on earth to forgive
sins"—then He ☆said to the paralytic, "Get up, pick up your bed and go home."
7 And he got up and went home.
8 But when the crowds saw *this,* they were awestruck, and glorified God, who had given
such authority to men.

Jesus Eats with Sinners at Matthew's House
(40/Mark 2:13-17; Luke 5:27-32)

9 As Jesus went on from there, He saw a man called Matthew, sitting in the tax
collector's booth; and He ☆said to him, "Follow Me!" And he got up and followed Him.
10 Then it happened that as Jesus was reclining *at the table* in the house, behold, many
tax collectors and sinners came and were dining with Jesus and His disciples.
11 When the Pharisees saw *this,* they said to His disciples, "Why is your Teacher eating
with the tax collectors and sinners?"
12 But when Jesus heard *this*, He said, "*It is* not those who are healthy who need a
physician, but those who are sick.
13 "But go and learn what this means: 'I DESIRE COMPASSION, [21]AND NOT SACRIFICE,'
for I did not come to call the righteous, but sinners."

9:1 Matt 4:13; Mark 5:21
9:2 Matt 4:24; 9:6; 9:22; 14:27; Mark 6:50; 10:49; John 16:33; Acts 23:11
9:3 Mark 3:28, 29
9:4 Matt 12:25; Luke 6:8; 9:47
9:5 Matt 9:2, 6
9:6 Matt 8:20; John 5:27; Matt 4:24; 9:2
9:8 Matt 5:16; 15:31; Luke 2:20; 7:16; 13:13; 17:15; 23:47; John 15:8; Acts 4:21; 11:18; 21:20; 2 Cor 9:13; Gal 1:24
9:9 Matt 10:3; Mark 2:14; 3:18; Luke 6:15; Acts 1:13; Matt 8:22
9:11 Matt 11:19; Luke 5:30; 15:2
9:13 Matt 12:7; Hos 6:6; 1 Tim 1:15

21 I.e. more than

9:1 "His own city" was Capernaum, a good choice for Jesus' base of operations. It was a wealthy city due to fishing and trade. Situated on the Sea of Galilee in a densely populated area, Capernaum housed the Roman garrison that kept peace in the region. The city was a cultural melting pot, greatly influenced by Greek and Roman manners, dress, architecture, and politics.

9:2 Among the first words Jesus said to the paralyzed man were "Your sins are forgiven." Then he healed the man. We must be careful not to concentrate on God's power to heal physical sickness more than on his power to forgive spiritual sickness in the form of sin. Jesus saw that even more than physical health, this man needed spiritual health. Spiritual health comes only from Jesus' healing touch.

9:2 Both the man's body and his spirit were paralyzed—he could not walk, and he did not know Jesus. But the man's spiritual state was Jesus' first concern. If God does not heal us or someone we love, we need to remember that physical healing is not Christ's only concern. We will all be completely healed in Christ's coming kingdom; but first we have to come to know Jesus.

9:3 Blaspheming is claiming to be God and applying his characteristics to yourself. The religious leaders rightly saw that Jesus was claiming to be God. What they did not understand was that he *is* God and thus has the authority to heal and to forgive sins.

9:5–6 It's easy to tell someone his sins are forgiven; it's a lot more difficult to reverse a case of paralysis! Jesus backed up his words by healing the man's legs. Jesus' action showed that his words were true; he had the power to forgive as well as to heal. Talk is cheap, but our words lack meaning if our actions do not back them up. We can say we love God or others, but if we are not taking practical steps to demonstrate that love, our words are empty and meaningless. How well do your actions back up what you say?

9:9 Matthew was a Jew who was appointed by the Romans to be the area's tax collector. He collected taxes from the citizens as well as from merchants passing through town. Tax collectors were expected to take a commission on the taxes they collected, but most of them overcharged and kept the profits. Thus, tax collectors were hated by the Jews because of their reputation for cheating and because of their support of Rome.

9:9 When Jesus called Matthew to be one of his disciples, Matthew got up and followed, leaving a lucrative career. When God calls you to follow or obey him, do you do it with as much abandon as Matthew? Sometimes the decision to follow Christ requires difficult or painful choices. Like Matthew, we must decide to leave behind those things that would keep us from following Christ.

9:10–13 When he visited Matthew, Jesus hurt his own reputation. Matthew was cheating the people, but Jesus found and changed him. We should not be afraid to reach out to people who are living in sin—God's message can change anyone.

9:11–12 The Pharisees constantly tried to trap Jesus, and they thought his association with these "lowlifes" was the perfect opportunity. They were more concerned with their own appearance of holiness than with helping people, with criticism than encouragement, with outward respectability than practical help. But God is concerned for all people, including the sinful and hurting ones. The Christian life is not a popularity contest! Following Jesus' example, we should share the gospel with the poor, immoral, lonely, and outcast, not just the rich, moral, popular, and powerful.

9:13 Those who are sure that they are righteous can't be saved because the first step in following Jesus is acknowledging our need and admitting that we don't have all the answers. For more on "I desire compassion, and not sacrifice," see the chart in Hosea 7.

Religious Leaders Ask Jesus about Fasting
(41/Mark 2:18-22; Luke 5:33-39)

9:14 Luke 18:12

14 Then the disciples of John ☆came to Him, asking, "Why do we and the Pharisees
fast, but Your disciples do not fast?"
15 And Jesus said to them, "The attendants of the bridegroom cannot mourn as long
as the bridegroom is with them, can they? But the days will come when the bridegroom
is taken away from them, and then they will fast.
16 "But no one puts a patch of unshrunk cloth on an old garment; for the patch pulls
away from the garment, and a worse tear results.

MATTHEW

More than any other disciple, Matthew had a clear idea of how much it would cost to follow Jesus, yet he did not hesitate a moment. When he left his tax–collecting booth, he guaranteed himself unemployment. For several of the other disciples, there was always fishing to return to, but for Matthew, there was no turning back.

Two changes happened to Matthew when he decided to follow Jesus. First, Jesus gave him a new life. He not only belonged to a new group; he belonged to the Son of God. He was not just accepting a different way of life; he was now an accepted person. For a despised tax collector, that change must have been wonderful! Second, Jesus gave Matthew a new purpose for his skills. When he followed Jesus, the only tool from his past job that he carried with him was his pen. From the beginning, God had made him a record-keeper. Jesus' call eventually allowed him to put his skills to their finest work. Matthew was a keen observer, and he undoubtedly recorded what he saw going on around him. The Gospel that bears his name came as a result.

Matthew's experience points out that each of us, from the beginning, is one of God's works in progress. Much of what God has for us he gives long before we are able to consciously respond to him. He trusts us with skills and abilities ahead of schedule. He has made us each capable of being his servant. When we trust him with what he has given us, we begin a life of real adventure. Matthew couldn't have known that God would use the very skills he had sharpened as a tax collector to record the greatest story ever lived. And God has no less meaningful a purpose for each one of us. Have you recognized Jesus saying to you, "Follow me"? What has been your response?

Strengths and accomplishments:
- Was one of Jesus' 12 disciples
- Responded immediately to Jesus' call
- Invited many friends to his home to meet Jesus
- Compiled the Gospel of Matthew
- Clarified for his Jewish audience Jesus' fulfillment of Old Testament prophecies

Lessons from his life:
- Jesus consistently accepted people from every level of society
- Matthew was given a new life, and his God-given skills of record-keeping and attention to detail were given new purpose
- Having been accepted by Jesus, Matthew immediately tried to bring others into contact with Jesus

Vital statistics:
- Where: Capernaum
- Occupations: Tax collector, disciple of Jesus
- Relative: Father: Alphaeus
- Contemporaries: Jesus, Pilate, Herod, other disciples

Key verse:
"As He passed by, He saw Levi the son of Alphaeus sitting in the tax booth, and He said to him, 'Follow Me!' And he got up and followed Him" (Mark 2:14).

Matthew's story is told in the Gospels. He is also mentioned in Acts 1:13.

9:14 John's disciples fasted (went without food) as a sign of mourning for sin and to prepare for the Messiah's coming. Jesus' disciples did not need to fast because he is the Messiah and was with them! Jesus did not condemn fasting—he himself fasted (4:2). He emphasized that fasting must be done for the right reasons.

9:14 John the Baptist's message was harsh, and it focused on law. When people look at God's law and compare themselves to it, they realize how far they fall short and how badly they need to repent. Jesus' message focused on life, the result of turning from sin and turning to him. John's disciples had the right start, but they needed to take the next step and trust in Jesus. Where is your focus—on law or on Christ?

9:15 The arrival of the kingdom of heaven was like a wedding feast with Jesus as the bridegroom. His disciples, therefore, were filled with joy. It would not be right to mourn or fast when the bridegroom was present.

17 "Nor do *people* put new wine into old wineskins; otherwise the wineskins burst, and
the wine pours out and the wineskins are ruined; but they put new wine into fresh wineskins, and both are preserved."

Jesus Heals a Bleeding Woman and Restores a Girl to Life
(89/Mark 5:21-43; Luke 8:40-56)

18 While He was saying these things to them, a *synagogue* official came and bowed down
before Him, and said, "My daughter has just died; but come and lay Your hand on her,
and she will live."
19 Jesus got up and *began* to follow him, and *so did* His disciples.
20 And a woman who had been suffering from a hemorrhage for twelve years, came
up behind Him and touched the fringe of His cloak;
21 for she was saying to herself, "If I only touch His garment, I will get well."
22 But Jesus turning and seeing her said, "Daughter, take courage; your faith has made
you well." At once the woman was made well.
23 When Jesus came into the official's house, and saw the flute-players and the crowd
in noisy disorder,
24 He said, "Leave; for the girl has not died, but is asleep." And they *began* laughing at
Him.
25 But when the crowd had been sent out, He entered and took her by the hand, and
the girl got up.
26 This news spread throughout all that land.

Jesus Heals the Blind and Mute
(90)

27 As Jesus went on from there, two blind men followed Him, crying out, "Have mercy
on us, Son of David!"
28 When He entered the house, the blind men came up to Him, and Jesus ☆said to
them, "Do you believe that I am able to do this?" They ☆said to Him, "Yes, Lord."
29 Then He touched their eyes, saying, "It shall be done to you according to your faith."

9:18 Matt 8:2

9:20 Num 15:38; Deut 22:12; Matt 14:36; 23:5

9:21 Matt 14:36; Mark 3:10; Luke 6:19

9:22 Matt 9:2; Matt 9:29; 15:28; Mark 5:34; 10:52; Luke 7:50; 8:48; 17:19; 18:42

9:23 2 Chr 35:25; Jer 9:17; 16:6; Ezek 24:17

9:24 John 11:13; Acts 20:10

9:25 Acts 9:40; Mark 9:27

9:26 Matt 4:24; 9:31; 14:1; Mark 1:28, 45; Luke 4:14, 37; 5:15; 7:17

9:27 Matt 1:1; 12:23; 15:22; 20:30, 31; 21:9, 15; 22:42; Mark 10:47, 48; 12:35; Luke 18:38, 39; 20:41f

9:29 Matt 8:13; 9:22

9:17 In Bible times, wine was not kept in glass bottles but in goatskins sewn around the edges to form watertight bags. New wine expanded as it fermented, stretching its wineskin. After the wine had aged, the stretched skin would burst if more new wine was poured into it. New wine, therefore, was always put into fresh wineskins.

9:17 Jesus did not come to patch up the old religious system of Judaism with its rules and traditions. If he had, his message would have damaged it. His purpose was to bring in something new, though it had been prophesied for centuries. This new message, the gospel, said that Jesus Christ, God's Son, came to earth to offer all people forgiveness of sins and reconciliation with God. The gospel did not fit into the old rigid legalistic system of religion. It needed a fresh start. The message will always remain "new" because it must be accepted and applied in every generation. When we follow Christ, we must be prepared for new ways to live, new ways to look at people, and new ways to serve.

9:18 Mark and Luke say this man's name was Jairus (Mark 5:22; Luke 8:41). As an official of the synagogue, Jairus was responsible for administration—looking after the building, supervising worship, running the school on weekdays, and finding rabbis to teach on the Sabbath. For more information on synagogues, read the first note on Mark 1:21.

9:20–22 This woman had suffered for 12 years with bleeding (perhaps a menstrual disorder). In our times of desperation, we don't have to worry about the correct way to reach out to God. Like this woman, we can simply reach out in faith. He will respond.

9:22 God changed a situation that had been a problem for years. Like the leper and the demon-possessed men (see the notes on 8:2–3 and the second note on 8:28), this diseased woman was considered unclean. For 12 years, she too had been one of the "untouchables" and had not been able to lead a normal life. But Jesus changed that and restored her. Sometimes we are tempted to give up on people or situations that have not changed for many years. God can change what seems unchangeable, giving new purpose and hope.

9:23–26 The synagogue official didn't come to Jesus until his daughter was dead—it was too late for anyone else to help. But Jesus simply went to the girl and raised her! In our lives, Christ can make a difference when it seems too late for anyone else to help. He can bring healing to broken relationships, release from addicting habits, and forgiveness and healing to emotional scars. If your situation looks hopeless, remember that Christ can do the impossible.

9:27 "Son of David" was a popular way of addressing Jesus as the Messiah because it was known that the Messiah would be a descendant of David (Isaiah 9:7). This is the first time the title is used in Matthew. Jesus' ability to give sight to the blind was prophesied in Isaiah 29:18; 35:5; 42:7.

9:27–30 Jesus didn't respond immediately to the blind men's pleas. He waited to see if they had faith. Not everyone who says he wants help really believes God can help him. Jesus may have waited and questioned these men to emphasize and increase their faith. When you think that God is too slow in answering your prayers, consider that he might be testing you as he did the blind men. Do you believe that God can help you? Do you *really* want his help?

9:28 These blind men were persistent. They went right into the house where Jesus was staying. They knew Jesus could heal them, and they would let nothing stop them from finding him. That's real faith in action. If you believe Jesus is the answer to your every need, don't let anything or anyone stop you from reaching him.

9:30 Matt 8:4
9:31 Matt 4:24; 9:26; 14:1; Mark 1:28, 45; Luke 4:14, 37; 5:15; 7:17
9:32 Matt 12:22, 24; Matt 4:24
9:33 Mark 2:12
9:34 Matt 12:24; Mark 3:22; Luke 11:15; John 7:20f
9:35 Matt 4:23; Mark 1:14
9:36 Matt 14:14; 15:32; Mark 6:34; 8:2; Num 27:17; Ezek 34:5; Zech 10:2; Mark 6:34
9:37 Luke 10:2
10:1 Mark 3:13-15; 6:7; Matt 9:35; Luke 9:1

30 And their eyes were opened. And Jesus sternly warned them: "See that no one knows
about this!"
31 But they went out and spread the news about Him throughout all that land.
32 As they were going out, a mute, demon-possessed man was brought to Him.
33 After the demon was cast out, the mute man spoke; and the crowds were amazed,
and were saying, "Nothing like this has ever been seen in Israel."
34 But the Pharisees were saying, "He casts out the demons by the ruler of the demons."

Jesus Urges the Disciples to Pray for Workers
(92)

35 Jesus was going through all the cities and villages, teaching in their synagogues and
proclaiming the gospel of the kingdom, and healing every kind of disease and every kind
of sickness.
36 Seeing the people, He felt compassion for them, because they were distressed and
dispirited like sheep without a shepherd.
37 Then He ☆said to His disciples, "The harvest is plentiful, but the workers are few.
38 "Therefore beseech the Lord of the harvest to send out workers into His harvest."

Jesus Sends Out the Twelve Disciples
(93/Mark 6:7-13; Luke 9:1-6)

10 Jesus summoned His twelve disciples and gave them authority over unclean
spirits, to cast them out, and to heal every kind of disease and every kind of
sickness.

COUNTING THE COST OF FOLLOWING CHRIST
Jesus helped his disciples prepare for the rejection many of them would experience by being Christians. Being God's person will usually create reactions from others who are resisting him.

Who may oppose us?	*Natural response*	*Possible pressures*		*Needed truth*
GOVERNMENT 10:18–19	Fear and worry	Threats 10:26	→	The truth will be revealed (10:26)
		Physical harm 10:28	→	Our soul cannot be harmed (10:28)
RELIGIOUS PEOPLE 10:17		Public ridicule 10:22	→	God himself will acknowledge us if we acknowledge him (10:32)
FAMILY 10:21		Rejection by loved ones 10:34–37	→	God's love can sustain us (10:31)

9:30 Jesus told the people to keep quiet about his healings because he did not want to be known only as a miracle worker. He healed because he had compassion on people, but he also wanted to bring *spiritual* healing to a sin-sick world.

9:32 While Jesus was on earth, demonic forces seemed especially active. Although we cannot always be sure why or how demon-possession occurs, it causes both physical and mental problems. In this case, the demon made the man unable to talk. For more on demons and demon-possession, read the notes on 8:28 and Mark 1:23.

9:34 In chapter 9, the Pharisees accuse Jesus of four different sins: blasphemy, befriending outcasts, impiety, and serving Satan. Matthew shows how Jesus was maligned by those who should have received him most gladly. Why did the Pharisees do this? (1) Jesus bypassed their religious authority. (2) He weakened their control over the people. (3) He challenged their cherished beliefs. (4) He exposed their insincere motives.

9:34 While the Pharisees questioned, debated, and dissected Jesus, people were being healed and lives changed right in front of them. Their skepticism was based not on insufficient evidence but on jealousy of Jesus' popularity.

9:35 The gospel of the kingdom was that the promised and long-awaited Messiah had finally come. His healing miracles were a sign that his teaching was true.

9:35–38 Jesus needs workers who know how to deal with people's problems. We can comfort others and show them the way to live because we have been helped with our problems by God and his laborers (2 Corinthians 1:3–7).

9:36 Ezekiel also compared Israel to sheep without a shepherd (Ezekiel 34:5–6). Jesus came to be the Shepherd, the One who could show people how to avoid life's pitfalls (see John 10:14).

9:37–38 Jesus looked at the crowds following him and referred to them as a field ripe for harvest. Many people are ready to give their lives to Christ if someone would show them how. Jesus commands us to pray that people will respond to this need for workers. Often, when we pray for something, God answers our prayers by using *us.* Be prepared for God to use you to show another person the way to him.

10:1 Jesus *summoned* or called his 12 disciples. He didn't draft them, force them, or ask them to volunteer; he chose them to serve him in a special way. Christ calls us today. He doesn't twist our arms and make us do something we don't want to do. We can choose to join him or remain behind. When Christ calls you to follow him, how do you respond?

2 Now the names of the twelve apostles are these: The first, Simon, who is called Peter,
and Andrew his brother; and James the son of Zebedee, and John his brother;
3 Philip and Bartholomew; Thomas and Matthew the tax collector; James the son of
Alphaeus, and Thaddaeus;
4 Simon the Zealot, and Judas Iscariot, the one who betrayed Him.
5 These twelve Jesus sent out after instructing them: "Do not go in *the* way of *the*
Gentiles, and do not enter *any* city of the Samaritans;
6 but rather go to the lost sheep of the house of Israel.
7 "And as you go, preach, saying, 'The kingdom of heaven is at hand.'
8 "Heal *the* sick, raise *the* dead, cleanse *the* lepers, cast out demons. Freely you received,
freely give.
9 "Do not acquire gold, or silver, or copper for your money belts,
10 or a bag for *your* journey, or even two coats, or sandals, or a staff; for the worker is
worthy of his support.
11 "And whatever city or village you enter, inquire who is worthy in it, and stay at his
house until you leave *that city*.
12 "As you enter the house, give it your greeting.
13 "If the house is worthy, give it your *blessing of* peace. But if it is not worthy, take back
your *blessing of* peace.
14 "Whoever does not receive you, nor heed your words, as you go out of that house or
that city, shake the dust off your feet.
15 "Truly I say to you, it will be more tolerable for *the* land of Sodom and Gomorrah in
the day of judgment than for that city.
16 "Behold, I send you out as sheep in the midst of wolves; so be shrewd as serpents and
innocent as doves.

10:2 Mark 3:16-19; Luke 6:14-16; Acts 1:13
10:3 John 1:43ff 11:16; 14:5; 20:24ff; 21:2; Matt 9:9; Mark 15:40; Mark 3:18; Luke 6:16; Acts 1:13
10:4 Matt 26:14; Luke 22:3; John 6:71
10:5 Luke 9:52; 10:33; 17:16; John 4:9, 39f; 8:48; Acts 8:25
10:6 Matt 15:24
10:9 Luke 22:35
10:14 Acts 13:51
10:16 Luke 10:3; Gen 3:1; Matt 24:25; Rom 16:19; Hos 7:11

10:2–4 The list of Jesus' 12 disciples doesn't give us many details—probably because there weren't many impressive details to tell. Jesus called people from all walks of life—fishermen, political activists, tax collectors. He called common people and uncommon leaders, rich and poor, educated and uneducated. Today, many people think only certain people are fit to follow Christ, but this was not the attitude of the Master himself. God can use anyone, no matter how insignificant he or she appears. When you feel small and useless, remember that God uses ordinary people to do his extraordinary work.

10:3 Bartholomew is probably another name for Nathanael, whom we meet in John 1:45–51. Thaddaeus is also known as Judas son of James. The disciples are also listed in Mark 3:16–19; Luke 6:14–16; and Acts 1:13.

10:4 Simon the Zealot may have been a member of the Zealots, a radical political party working for the violent overthrow of Roman rule in Israel.

10:5–6 Why didn't Jesus send the disciples to the Gentiles or the Samaritans? A Gentile is anyone who is not a Jew. The Samaritans were a race that resulted from intermarriage between Jews and Gentiles after the Old Testament captivities (see 2 Kings 17:24). Jesus asked his disciples to go only to the Jews because he came *first* to the Jews (Romans 1:16). God chose them to tell the rest of the world about him. Jewish disciples and apostles preached the gospel of the risen Christ all around the Roman empire, and soon Gentiles were pouring into the church. The Bible clearly teaches that God's message of salvation is for *all* people, regardless of race, sex, or national origin (Genesis 12:3; Isaiah 25:6; 56:3–7; Malachi 1:11; Acts 10:34, 35; Romans 3:29, 30; Galatians 3:28).

10:7 The Jews were waiting for the Messiah to usher in his kingdom. They hoped for a political and military kingdom that would free them from Roman rule and bring back the days of glory under David and Solomon. But Jesus was talking about a spiritual kingdom. The gospel today is that the kingdom is still *at hand*. Jesus, the Messiah, has already begun his kingdom on earth in the hearts of his followers. One day the kingdom will be fully realized. Then evil will be destroyed and all people will live in peace with one another.

10:8 Jesus gave the disciples a principle to guide their actions as they ministered to others: "Freely you received, freely give." Because God has showered us with his blessings, we should give generously to others of our time, love, and possessions.

10:10 Jesus said that those who minister are to be cared for. The disciples could expect food and shelter in return for the spiritual service they provided. Who ministers to you? Make sure you take care of the pastors, missionaries, and teachers who serve God by serving you (see 1 Corinthians 9:9–10; 1 Timothy 5:17).

10:10 Mark's account (6:8) says to take a staff (walking stick), and Matthew and Luke (9:3) say not to. Jesus may have meant that they were not to take an *extra* pair of sandals, staff, and bag. In any case, the principle was that they were to go out ready for duty and travel, unencumbered by excess material goods.

10:14 Why did Jesus tell his disciples to shake the dust off their feet if a city or home didn't welcome them? When leaving Gentile cities, pious Jews often shook the dust from their feet to show their separation from Gentile practices. If the disciples shook the dust of a *Jewish* town from their feet, it would show their separation from Jews who rejected their Messiah. This gesture was to show the people that they were making a wrong choice—that the opportunity to choose Christ might not present itself again. Are you receptive to teaching from God? If you ignore the Spirit's prompting, you may not get another chance.

10:15 The cities of Sodom and Gomorrah were destroyed by fire from heaven because of their wickedness (Genesis 19:24–25). Those who reject the gospel when they hear it will be worse off than the wicked people of these destroyed cities, who never heard the gospel at all.

10:16 The opposition of the Pharisees would be like ravaging wolves. The disciples' only hope would be to look to their Shepherd for protection. We may face similar hostility. Like the disciples, we are not to be sheeplike in our attitude but sensible and prudent. We are not to be gullible pawns but neither are we to be deceitful connivers. We must find a balance between wisdom and vulnerability to accomplish God's work.

10:17 Luke 12:11; Acts 5:40; 22:19; 26:11

10:19 Mark 13:11-13; Luke 21:12-17; Matt 6:25

10:20 Luke 12:12; Acts 4:8; 13:9; 2 Cor 13:3

10:21 Mark 13:12; Mic 7:6

10:22 Luke 21:17; John 15:18ff; Matt 24:13

10:23 Matt 23:34

10:24 Luke 6:40; John 13:16; 15:20

10:25 Matt 12:24, 27; Mark 3:22; Luke 11:15

10:26 Mark 4:22; Luke 8:17; 12:2; 1 Cor 4:5

10:27 Luke 12:3; Matt 24:17; Acts 5:20

10:28 Heb 10:31

10:30 Luke 21:18; Acts 27:34

10:31 Matt 12:12

10:32 Luke 12:8; Rev 3:5

10:33 Mark 8:38; Luke 9:26; 2 Tim 2:12

Jesus Prepares the Disciples for Persecution
(94)

17"But beware of men, for they will hand you over to *the* courts and scourge you in
their synagogues;
18 and you will even be brought before governors and kings for My sake, as a testimony to them and to the Gentiles.
19"But when they hand you over, do not worry about how or what you are to say; for it
will be given you in that hour what you are to say.
20"For it is not you who speak, but *it is* the Spirit of your Father who speaks in you.
21"Brother will betray brother to death, and a father *his* child; and children will rise up
against parents and cause them to be put to death.
22"You will be hated by all because of My name, but it is the one who has endured to
the end who will be saved.
23"But whenever they persecute you in one city, flee to the next; for truly I say to you,
you will not finish *going through* the cities of Israel until the Son of Man comes.
24"A disciple is not above his teacher, nor a slave above his master.
25"It is enough for the disciple that he become like his teacher, and the slave like his
master. If they have called the head of the house Beelzebul, how much more *will they*
malign the members of his household!
26"Therefore do not fear them, for there is nothing concealed that will not be revealed,
or hidden that will not be known.
27"What I tell you in the darkness, speak in the light; and what you hear *whispered* in
your ear, proclaim upon the housetops.
28"Do not fear those who kill the body but are unable to kill the soul; but rather fear
Him who is able to destroy both soul and body in hell.
29"Are not two sparrows sold for a [22]cent? And *yet* not one of them will fall to the ground
apart from your Father.
30"But the very hairs of your head are all numbered.
31"So do not fear; you are more valuable than many sparrows.
32"Therefore everyone who confesses Me before men, I will also confess him before
My Father who is in heaven.
33"But whoever denies Me before men, I will also deny him before My Father who is in
heaven.

22 Gr *assarion*, the smallest copper coin

10:17–18 Later the disciples experienced these hardships (Acts 5:40; 12:1–3), not only from without (governments, courts), but also from within (friends, family; 10:21). Living for God often brings on persecution, but with it comes the opportunity to tell the Good News of salvation. In times of persecution, we can be confident because Jesus has "overcome the world" (John 16:33). And those who endure to the end will be saved (10:22).

10:19–20 Jesus told the disciples that when arrested for preaching the gospel, they should not worry about what to say in their defense—God's Spirit would speak through them. This promise was fulfilled in Acts 4:8–14 and elsewhere. Some mistakenly think this means we don't have to prepare to present the gospel because God will take care of everything. Scripture teaches, however, that we are to make carefully prepared, thoughtful statements (Colossians 4:6). Jesus is not telling us to stop preparing but to stop worrying.

10:22 Enduring to the end is not a way to be saved but the evidence that a person is really committed to Jesus. Persistence is not a means to earn salvation; it is the by-product of a truly devoted life.

10:23 Christ warned the disciples against premature martyrdom. They were to leave before the persecution got too great. We have plenty of work to do and many people to reach. Our work won't be finished until Christ returns. And only after he returns will the whole world realize his true identity (see 24:14; Romans 14:9–12).

10:25 Beelzebul was also known as the lord of flies and the prince of demons. The Pharisees accused Jesus of using Beelzebul's power to drive out demons (see 12:24). Good is sometimes labeled evil. If Jesus, who is perfect, was called evil, his followers should expect that similar accusations will be directed at them. But those who endure will be vindicated (10:22).

10:29–31 Jesus said that God is aware of everything that happens even to sparrows, and you are far more valuable to him than they are. You are so valuable that God sent his only Son to die for you (John 3:16). Because God places such value on you, you need never fear personal threats or difficult trials. These can't shake God's love or dislodge his Spirit from within you.

But this doesn't mean that God will take away all your troubles (see 10:16). The real test of value is how well something holds up under the wear, tear, and abuse of everyday life. Those who stand up for Christ in spite of their troubles truly have lasting value and will receive great rewards (see 5:11–12).

34 "Do not think that I came to bring peace on the earth; I did not come to bring peace,
but a sword.
35 "For I came to SET A MAN AGAINST HIS FATHER, AND A DAUGHTER AGAINST HER
MOTHER, AND A DAUGHTER-IN-LAW AGAINST HER MOTHER-IN-LAW;
36 and A MAN'S ENEMIES WILL BE THE MEMBERS OF HIS HOUSEHOLD.
37 "He who loves father or mother more than Me is not worthy of Me; and he who loves
son or daughter more than Me is not worthy of Me.
38 "And he who does not take his cross and follow after Me is not worthy of Me.
39 "He who has found his life will lose it, and he who has lost his life for My sake will
find it.
40 "He who receives you receives Me, and he who receives Me receives Him who
sent Me.
41 "He who receives a prophet in *the* name of a prophet shall receive a prophet's reward; and he who receives a righteous man in the name of a righteous man shall receive
a righteous man's reward.
42 "And whoever in the name of a disciple gives to one of these little ones even a cup of
cold water to drink, truly I say to you, he shall not lose his reward."

4. Jesus teaches about the kingdom

Jesus Eases John's Doubt
(70/Luke 7:18-35)

11 When Jesus had finished giving instructions to His twelve disciples, He departed
from there to teach and preach in their cities.
2 Now when John, while imprisoned, heard of the works of Christ, he sent *word* by his
disciples
3 and said to Him, "Are You the Expected One, or shall we look for someone else?"
4 Jesus answered and said to them, "Go and report to John what you hear and see:
5 *the* BLIND RECEIVE SIGHT and *the* lame walk, *the* lepers are cleansed and *the* deaf
hear, *the* dead are raised up, and *the* POOR HAVE THE GOSPEL PREACHED TO THEM.
6 "And blessed is he who does not take offense at Me."
7 As these men were going *away,* Jesus began to speak to the crowds about John, "What
did you go out into the wilderness to see? A reed shaken by the wind?
8 "But what did you go out to see? A man dressed in soft *clothing?* Those who wear
soft *clothing* are in kings' palaces!

10:35 Mic 7:6; Luke 12:53
10:36 Mic 7:6; Matt 10:21
10:37 Deut 33:9; Luke 14:26
10:38 Luke 9:23; 14:27
10:39 Matt 16:25; Mark 8:35; Luke 9:24; 17:33; John 12:25
10:40 Matt 18:5; Luke 10:16; Mark 9:37; Luke 9:48; John 12:44
10:41 Matt 25:44, 45
10:42 Mark 9:41
11:1 Matt 7:28; Matt 9:35; Luke 23:5
11:2 Mark 6:17; Luke 9:7ff
11:3 Ps 118:26; John 6:14; 11:27; Heb 10:37
11:5 Is 35:5f; Matt 8:3; 12:13; Is 61:1; Luke 4:18
11:6 Matt 5:29; 13:57; 24:10; 26:31; Mark 6:3; John 6:61; 16:1
11:7 Matt 3:1

10:34 Jesus did not come to bring the kind of peace that glosses over deep differences just for the sake of superficial harmony. Conflict and disagreement will arise between those who choose to follow Christ and those who don't. Yet we can look forward to the day when all conflict will be resolved. For more on Jesus as peacemaker, see Isaiah 9:6; Matthew 5:9; John 14:27.

10:34–39 Christian commitment may separate friends and loved ones. In saying this, Jesus was not encouraging disobedience to parents or conflict at home. Rather, he was showing that his presence demands a decision. Because some will follow Christ and some won't, conflict will inevitably arise. As we take our cross and follow him, our different values, morals, goals, and purposes will set us apart from others. Don't neglect your family, but remember that your commitment to God is even more important than they are. God should be your first priority.

10:37 Christ calls us to a higher mission than to find comfort and tranquility in this life. Love of family is a law of God, but even this love can be self-serving and used as an excuse not to serve God or do his work.

10:38 To take our cross and follow Jesus means to be willing to publicly identify with him, to experience almost certain opposition, and to be committed to face even suffering and death for his sake.

10:39 This verse is a positive and negative statement of the same truth: Clinging to this life may cause us to forfeit the best from Christ in this world *and* in the next. The more we love this life's rewards (leisure, power, popularity, financial security), the more we will discover how empty they really are. The best way to enjoy life, therefore, is to loosen our greedy grasp on earthly rewards so that we can be free to follow Christ. In doing so, we will inherit eternal life and begin at once to experience the benefits of following Christ.

10:42 How much we love God can be measured by how well we treat others. Jesus' example of giving a cup of cold water to a thirsty child is a good model of unselfish service. A child usually can't or won't return a favor. God notices every good deed we do or don't do as if he were the one receiving it. Is there something unselfish you can do for someone else today? Although no one else may see you, God will notice.

11:2–3 John the Baptist had been put in prison by Herod. Herod had married his own sister-in-law, and John publicly rebuked Herod's flagrant sin (14:3–5). John's Profile is found in John 1. Herod's Profile is found in Mark 6.

11:4–6 As John sat in prison, he began to have some doubts about whether Jesus really was the Messiah. If John's purpose was to prepare people for the coming Messiah (3:3), and if Jesus really was that Messiah, then why was John in prison when he could have been preaching to the crowds, preparing their hearts?

Jesus answered John's doubts by pointing to Jesus' acts of healing the blind, lame, and deaf, curing the lepers, raising the dead, and preaching the gospel to the poor. With so much evidence, Jesus' identity was obvious. If you sometimes doubt your salvation, the forgiveness of your sins, or God's work in your life, look at the evidence in Scripture and the changes in your life. When you doubt, don't turn away from Christ; turn *to* him.

11:9 Matt 14:5; 21:26; Luke 1:76; 20:6

11:10 Mal 3:1; Mark 1:2

11:12 Luke 16:16

11:14 Mal 4:5; Matt 17:10-13; Mark 9:11-13; Luke 1:17; John 1:21

11:18 Matt 3:4; Luke 1:15; Matt 9:34; John 7:20; 8:48f, 52

11:19 Matt 9:11; Luke 5:29-32; 15:2

11:20 Luke 10:13-15

11:21 Luke 10:13-15 Mark 6:45; 8:22; Luke 9:10; John 1:44; 12:21; Matt 11:22; 15:21; Mark 3:8; 7:24, 31; Luke 4:26; 6:17; Acts 12:20; 27:3; Rev 11:3

11:22 Matt 10:15; 12:36; Rev 20:11, 12

11:23 Matt 4:13; Is 14:13, 15; Ezek 26:20; 31:14; 32:18, 24; Matt 16:18; Luke 10:15; 16:23; Acts 2:27, 31; Rev 1:18; 6:8; 20:13f; Matt 10:15

11:24 Matt 10:15; 11:22

11:25 Luke 10:21, 22 Luke 22:42; 23:34; John 11:41; 12:27, 28; Ps 8:2; 1 Cor 1:26ff

9 "But what did you go out to see? A prophet? Yes, I tell you, and one who is more
than a prophet.
10 "This is the onc about whom it is written,
'BEHOLD, I SEND MY MESSENGER AHEAD OF YOU,
WHO WILL PREPARE YOUR WAY BEFORE YOU.'
11 "Truly I say to you, among those born of women there has not arisen *anyone* greater
than John the Baptist! Yet the one who is least in the kingdom of heaven is greater than
he.
12 "From the days of John the Baptist until now the kingdom of heaven suffers violence,
and violent men take it by force.
13 "For all the prophets and the Law prophesied until John.
14 "And if you are willing to accept *it,* John himself is Elijah who was to come.
15 "He who has ears to hear, let him hear.
16 "But to what shall I compare this generation? It is like children sitting in the market
places, who call out to the other *children,*
17 and say, 'We played the flute for you, and you did not dance; we sang a dirge, and
you did not mourn.'
18 "For John came neither eating nor drinking, and they say, 'He has a demon!'
19 "The Son of Man came eating and drinking, and they say, 'Behold, a gluttonous man
and a drunkard, a friend of tax collectors and sinners!' Yet wisdom is vindicated by her
deeds."

Jesus Promises Rest for the Soul
(71)

20 Then He began to denounce the cities in which most of His miracles were done,
because they did not repent.
21 "Woe to you, Chorazin! Woe to you, Bethsaida! For if the miracles had occurred in
Tyre and Sidon which occurred in you, they would have repented long ago in sackcloth
and ashes.
22 "Nevertheless I say to you, it will be more tolerable for Tyre and Sidon in *the* day of
judgment than for you.
23 "And you, Capernaum, will not be exalted to heaven, will you? You will descend to
Hades; for if the miracles had occurred in Sodom which occurred in you, it would have
remained to this day.
24 "Nevertheless I say to you that it will be more tolerable for the land of Sodom in *the*
day of judgment, than for you."
25 At that time Jesus said, "I praise You, Father, Lord of heaven and earth, that You
have hidden these things from *the* wise and intelligent and have revealed them to infants.
26 "Yes, Father, for this way was well-pleasing in Your sight.

11:11 No man ever fulfilled his God-given purpose better than John. Yet in God's coming kingdom all members will have a greater spiritual heritage than John because they will have seen and known Christ and his finished work on the cross.

11:12 There are three common views about the meaning of this verse. (1) Jesus may have been referring to a vast movement toward God, the momentum that began with John's preaching. (2) He may have been reflecting the Jewish activists' expectation that God's kingdom would come through a violent overthrow of Rome. (3) Or he may have meant that entering God's kingdom takes courage, unwavering faith, determination, and endurance because of the growing opposition leveled at Jesus' followers.

11:14 John was not a resurrected Elijah, but he took on Elijah's prophetic role—boldly confronting sin and pointing people to God (Malachi 3:1). See Elijah's Profile in 1 Kings 18.

11:16–19 Jesus condemned the attitude of his generation. No matter what he said or did, they took the opposite view. They were cynical and skeptical because he challenged their comfortable, secure, and self-centered lives. Too often we justify our inconsistencies because listening to God may require us to change the way we live.

11:21–24 Tyre, Sidon, and Sodom were ancient cities with a long-standing reputation for wickedness (Genesis 18; 19; Ezekiel 27; 28). Each was destroyed by God for its evil. The people of Bethsaida, Chorazin, and Capernaum saw Jesus firsthand, and yet they stubbornly refused to repent of their sins and believe in him. Jesus said that if some of the wickedest cities in the world had seen him, they would have repented. Because Bethsaida, Chorazin, and Capernaum saw Jesus and didn't believe, they would suffer even greater punishment than that of the wicked cities who didn't see Jesus. Similarly, nations and cities with churches on every corner and Bibles in every home will have no excuse on judgment day if they do not repent and believe.

11:25 Jesus mentioned two kinds of people in his prayer: the "wise"—arrogant in their own knowledge—and the "infants"—humbly open to receive the truth of God's Word. Are you wise in your own eyes, or do you seek the truth in childlike faith, realizing that only God holds all the answers?

27 "All things have been handed over to Me by My Father; and no one knows the Son
except the Father; nor does anyone know the Father except the Son, and anyone to whom
the Son wills to reveal *Him*.
28 "Come to Me, all who are weary and heavy-laden, and I will give you rest.
29 "Take My yoke upon you and learn from Me, for I am gentle and humble in heart,
and YOU WILL FIND REST FOR YOUR SOULS.
30 "For My yoke is easy and My burden is light."

11:27 Matt 28:18; John 3:35; 13:3; 17:2; John 7:29; 10:15; 17:25

11:28 Jer 31:25; John 7:37

11:29 John 13:15; Eph 4:20; Phil 2:5; 1 Pet 2:21; 1 John 2:6; Jer 6:16

11:30 1 John 5:3

The Disciples Pick Grain on the Sabbath
(45/Mark 2:23-28; Luke 6:1-5)

12 At that time Jesus went through the grainfields on the Sabbath, and His disciples
became hungry and began to pick the heads *of grain* and eat.
2 But when the Pharisees saw *this*, they said to Him, "Look, Your disciples do what is
not lawful to do on a Sabbath."
3 But He said to them, "Have you not read what David did when he became hungry,
he and his companions,
4 how he entered the house of God, and they ate the consecrated bread, which was
not lawful for him to eat nor for those with him, but for the priests alone?
5 "Or have you not read in the Law, that on the Sabbath the priests in the temple break
the Sabbath and are innocent?
6 "But I say to you that something greater than the temple is here.
7 "But if you had known what this means, 'I DESIRE COMPASSION, AND NOT A SACRI-
FICE,' you would not have condemned the innocent.
8 "For the Son of Man is Lord of the Sabbath."

12:1 Deut 23:25

12:2 Matt 12:10; Luke 13:14; 14:3; John 5:10; 7:23; 9:16

12:4 1 Sam 21:6

12:6 2 Chr 6:18; Is 66:1, 2; Matt 12:41, 42

12:7 Hos 6:6; Matt 9:13

12:8 Matt 8:20; 12:32, 40

Jesus Heals a Man's Hand on the Sabbath
(46/Mark 3:1-6; Luke 6:6-11)

9 Departing from there, He went into their synagogue.

11:27 In the Old Testament, "know" means more than knowledge. It implies an intimate relationship. The communion between God the Father and God the Son is the core of their relationship. For anyone else to know God, God must reveal himself to that person, by the Son's choice. How fortunate we are that Jesus has clearly revealed to us God, his truth, and how we can know him.

11:28–30 A yoke is a heavy wooden harness that fits over the shoulders of an ox or oxen. It is attached to a piece of equipment the oxen are to pull. A person may be carrying heavy burdens of (1) sin, (2) excessive demands of religious leaders (23:4; Acts 15:10), (3) oppression and persecution, or (4) weariness in the search for God.

Jesus frees people from all these burdens. The rest that Jesus promises is love, healing, and peace with God, not the end of all labor. A relationship with God changes meaningless, wearisome toil into spiritual productivity and purpose.

12:1–2 The Pharisees had established 39 categories of actions forbidden on the Sabbath, based on interpretations of God's law and on Jewish custom. Harvesting was one of those forbidden actions. By picking wheat and rubbing it in their hands, the disciples were technically harvesting, according to the religious leaders. Jesus and the disciples were picking grain because they were hungry, not because they wanted to harvest the grain for a profit. They were not working on the Sabbath. The Pharisees, however, could not (and did not want to) see beyond their law's technicalities. They had no room for compassion, and they were determined to accuse Jesus of wrongdoing.

12:4 This story is recorded in 1 Samuel 21:1–6. The consecrated bread was the bread of the Presence that was replaced every week; the old loaves were eaten by the priests. The loaves given to David were the old loaves that had just been replaced with fresh ones. Although the priests were the only ones allowed to eat this bread, God did not punish David because his need for food was more important than the priestly regulations. Jesus was saying, "If you condemn me, you must also condemn David," something the religious leaders could never do without causing a great uproar among the people. Jesus was not condoning disobedience to God's laws. Instead he was emphasizing discernment and compassion in enforcing the laws.

12:5 The Ten Commandments prohibit work on the Sabbath (Exodus 20:8–11). That was the *letter* of the law. But because the *purpose* of the Sabbath is to rest and to worship God, the priests were allowed to work by performing sacrifices and conducting worship services. This "Sabbath work" was serving and worshiping God. Jesus always emphasized the intent of the law, the meaning behind the letter. The Pharisees had lost the spirit of the law and were rigidly demanding that the letter (and their interpretation of it) be obeyed.

12:6 The Pharisees were so concerned about religious rituals that they missed the whole purpose of the temple—to bring people to God. And because Jesus Christ is even greater than the temple, how much better can he bring people to God. God is far more important than the created instruments of worship. If we become more concerned with the means of worship than with the One we worship, we will miss God even as we think we are worshiping him.

12:7 Jesus repeated to the Pharisees words the Jewish people had heard time and again throughout their history (1 Samuel 15:22–23; Psalm 40:6–8; Isaiah 1:11–17; Jeremiah 7:21–23; Hosea 6:6). Our heart attitude toward God comes first. Only then can we properly obey and observe religious regulations and rituals.

12:8 When Jesus said he was Lord of the Sabbath, he claimed to be greater than the law and above the law. To the Pharisees, this was heresy. They did not realize that Jesus, the divine Son of God, had created the Sabbath. The Creator is always greater than the creation; thus Jesus had the authority to overrule their traditions and regulations.

12:9 For more information on synagogues, read the notes on Mark 1:21 and 5:22.

12:10 Matt 12:2; Luke 13:14; 14:3; John 5:10; 7:23; 9:16
12:11 Luke 14:5
12:12 Matt 10:31; Luke 14:1-6
12:13 Matt 8:3; Acts 28:8
12:14 Matt 26:4; Mark 14:1; Luke 22:2; John 7:30, 44; 8:59; 10:31, 39; 11:53

10 And a man *was there* whose hand was withered. And they questioned Jesus, asking,
"Is it lawful to heal on the Sabbath?"—so that they might accuse Him.
11 And He said to them, "What man is there among you who has a sheep, and if it falls
into a pit on the Sabbath, will he not take hold of it and lift it out?
12 "How much more valuable then is a man than a sheep! So then, it is lawful to do
good on the Sabbath."
13 Then He ☆said to the man, "Stretch out your hand!" He stretched it out, and it was
restored to normal, like the other.
14 But the Pharisees went out and conspired against Him, *as to* how they might destroy Him.

Large Crowds Follow Jesus
(47/Mark 3:7-12)

12:15 Matt 4:23
12:16 Matt 8:4; 9:30; 17:9
12:18 Is 42:1; Matt 3:17; 17:5; Luke 4:18; John 3:34
12:19 Is 42:2
12:20 Is 42:3
12:21 Rom 15:12

15 But Jesus, aware of *this,* withdrew from there. Many followed Him, and He healed
them all,
16 and warned them not to tell who He was.
17 *This was* to fulfill what was spoken through Isaiah the prophet:
18 "BEHOLD, MY SERVANT WHOM I HAVE CHOSEN;
MY BELOVED IN WHOM MY SOUL is WELL-PLEASED;
I WILL PUT MY SPIRIT UPON HIM,
AND HE SHALL PROCLAIM JUSTICE TO THE GENTILES.
19 "HE WILL NOT QUARREL, NOR CRY OUT;
NOR WILL ANYONE HEAR HIS VOICE IN THE STREETS.
20 "A BATTERED REED HE WILL NOT BREAK OFF,
AND A SMOLDERING WICK HE WILL NOT PUT OUT,
UNTIL HE LEADS JUSTICE TO VICTORY.
21 "AND IN HIS NAME THE GENTILES WILL HOPE."

Religious Leaders Accuse Jesus of Being under Satan's Power
(74/Mark 3:20-30)

12:22 Luke 11:14, 15; Matt 9:32, 34; Matt 4:24; 2 Thess 2:9
12:23 Matt 9:27
12:24 Matt 9:34

22 Then a demon-possessed man *who was* blind and mute was brought to Jesus, and
He healed him, so that the mute man spoke and saw.
23 All the crowds were amazed, and were saying, "This man cannot be the Son of David,
can he?"
24 But when the Pharisees heard *this*, they said, "This man casts out demons only by
Beelzebul the ruler of the demons."

12:10 As they pointed to the man with the withered hand, the Pharisees tried to trick Jesus by asking him if it was legal to heal on the Sabbath. Their Sabbath rules said that people could be helped on the Sabbath only if their lives were in danger. Jesus healed on the Sabbath several times, and none of those healings were in response to emergencies. If Jesus had waited until another day, he would have been submitting to the Pharisees' authority, showing that their petty rules were equal to God's law. If he healed the man on the Sabbath, the Pharisees could claim that because Jesus broke their rules, his power was not from God. But Jesus made it clear how ridiculous and petty their rules were. God is a God of people, not rules. The best time to reach out to someone is when he or she needs help.

12:10–12 The Pharisees placed their laws above human need. They were so concerned about Jesus' breaking one of their rules that they did not care about the man's withered hand. What is your attitude toward others? If your convictions don't allow you to help certain people, your convictions may not be in tune with God's Word. Don't allow dogma to blind you to human need.

12:14 The Pharisees plotted Jesus' death because they were outraged. Jesus had overruled their authority (Luke 6:11) and had exposed their evil attitudes in front of the entire crowd in the synagogue. Jesus had showed that the Pharisees were more loyal to their religious system than to God.

12:15 Up to this point, Jesus had been aggressively confronting the Pharisees' hypocrisy. Here he decided to withdraw from the synagogue before a major confrontation developed because it was not time for him to die. Jesus had many lessons still to teach his disciples and the people.

12:16 Jesus did not want those he healed to tell others about his miracles because he didn't want the people coming to him for the wrong reasons. That would hinder his teaching ministry and arouse false hopes about an earthly kingdom. But the news of Jesus' miracles spread, and many came to see for themselves (see Mark 3:7–8).

12:17–21 The people expected the Messiah to be a king. This quotation from Isaiah's prophecy (Isaiah 42:1–4) showed that the Messiah was indeed a king, but it illustrated what *kind* of king—a quiet, gentle ruler who brings justice to the nations. Like the crowd in Jesus' day, we may want Christ to rule as a king and bring great and visible victories in our lives. But often Christ's work is quiet, and it happens according to *his* perfect timing, not ours.

12:24 The Pharisees had already accused Jesus of being in league with the ruler of the demons (9:34). They were trying to discredit him by using an emotional argument. Refusing to believe that Jesus came from God, they said he was in league with Satan. Jesus easily exposed the foolishness of their argument.

25 And knowing their thoughts Jesus said to them, "Any kingdom divided against itself
is laid waste; and any city or house divided against itself will not stand.
26 "If Satan casts out Satan, he is divided against himself; how then will his kingdom
stand?
27 "If I by Beelzebul cast out demons, by whom do your sons cast *them* out? For this
reason they will be your judges.
28 "But if I cast out demons by the Spirit of God, then the kingdom of God has come
upon you.
29 "Or how can anyone enter the strong man's house and carry off his property, unless
he first binds the strong *man?* And then he will plunder his house.
30 "He who is not with Me is against Me; and he who does not gather with Me scatters.
31 "Therefore I say to you, any sin and blasphemy shall be forgiven people, but blasphemy against the Spirit shall not be forgiven.
32 "Whoever speaks a word against the Son of Man, it shall be forgiven him; but whoever speaks against the Holy Spirit, it shall not be forgiven him, either in this age or in
the *age* to come.
33 "Either make the tree good and its fruit good, or make the tree bad and its fruit bad;
for the tree is known by its fruit.
34 "You brood of vipers, how can you, being evil, speak what is good? For the mouth
speaks out of that which fills the heart.
35 "The good man brings out of *his* good treasure what is good; and the evil man brings
out of *his* evil treasure what is evil.
36 "But I tell you that every careless word that people speak, they shall give an accounting for it in the day of judgment.
37 "For by your words you will be justified, and by your words you will be condemned."

Religious Leaders Ask Jesus for a Miracle
(75)

38 Then some of the scribes and Pharisees said to Him, "Teacher, we want to see a
sign from You."
39 But He answered and said to them, "An evil and adulterous generation craves for a
sign; and *yet* no sign will be given to it but the sign of Jonah the prophet;

12:25 Luke 11:17-22; Matt 9:4
12:26 Matt 4:10; 13:19
12:27 Matt 9:34; Acts 19:13
12:28 1 John 3:8
12:30 Mark 9:40; Luke 9:50; 11:23
12:31 Luke 12:10
12:32 Luke 12:10; Matt 13:22, 39; Mark 10:30; Luke 16:8; 18:30; 20:34, 35
12:33 Matt 7:16-18; Luke 6:43, 44; John 15:4-7
12:34 Matt 3:7; 23:33; Luke 3:7; Luke 6:45; Eph 4:29
12:35 Matt 13:52; Col 4:6
12:36 Matt 10:15
12:38 Matt 16:1; Mark 8:11, 12; Luke 11:16; John 2:18; 6:30; 1 Cor 1:22
12:39 Luke 11:29-32; Matt 16:4

12:25 In the incarnation, Jesus gave up the complete and unlimited use of his supernatural abilities. But he still had profound insight into human nature. His discernment stopped the religious leaders' attempts to trick him. The resurrected Christ knows all our thoughts. This can be comforting because he knows what we really mean when we speak to him. It can be threatening because we cannot hide from him, and he knows our selfish motives.

12:29 At Jesus' birth, Satan's power and control were disrupted. In the wilderness Jesus overcame the devil's temptations, and at the resurrection he defeated Satan's ultimate weapon, death. Eventually Satan will be constrained forever (Revelation 20:10), and evil will no longer pervade the earth. Jesus has complete power and authority over Satan and all his forces.

12:30 It is impossible to be neutral about Christ. Anyone who is not actively following him has chosen to reject him. Any person who tries to remain neutral in the struggle of good against evil is choosing to be separated from God, who alone is good. To refuse to follow Christ is to choose to be on Satan's team.

12:31–32 The Pharisees had blasphemed against the Spirit by attributing the power by which Christ did miracles to Satan (12:24) instead of the Holy Spirit. The unpardonable sin is the deliberate refusal to acknowledge God's power in Christ. It indicates a deliberate and irreversible hardness of heart. Sometimes believers worry that they have accidently committed this unforgivable sin. But only those who have turned their backs on God and rejected all faith have any need to worry. Jesus said they can't be forgiven—not because their sin is worse than any other, but because they will never ask for forgiveness. Whoever rejects the prompting of the Holy Spirit removes himself or herself from the only force that can lead him or her to repentance and restoration to God.

12:34–36 Jesus reminds us that what we say reveals what is in our hearts. What kinds of words come from your mouth? That is an indication of what your heart is really like. You can't solve your heart problem, however, just by cleaning up your speech. You must allow the Holy Spirit to fill you with new attitudes and motives; then your speech will be cleansed at its source.

12:38–40 The Pharisees were asking for another miraculous sign, but they were not sincerely seeking to know Jesus. Jesus knew they had already seen enough miraculous proof to convince them that he was the Messiah if they would just open their hearts. But they had already decided not to believe in him, and more miracles would not change that.

Many people have said, "If I could just see a real miracle, then I could really believe in God." But Jesus' response to the Pharisees applies to us. We have plenty of evidence—Jesus' birth, death, resurrection, and ascension, and centuries of his work in believers around the world. Instead of looking for additional evidence or miracles, accept what God has already given and move forward. He may use your life as evidence to reach another person.

12:39–41 Jonah was a prophet sent to the Assyrian city of Nineveh (see the book of Jonah). Because Assyria was such a cruel and warlike nation, Jonah tried to run from his assignment and ended up spending three days in the belly of a huge fish. When Jonah got out, he grudgingly went to Nineveh, preached God's message, and saw the city repent. By contrast, when Jesus came to his people, they refused to repent. Here Jesus is clearly saying that his resurrection will prove he is the Messiah. Three days after his death Jesus will come back to life, just as Jonah was given a new chance at life after three days in the fish.

12:40 Jon 1:17; Matt 8:20; Matt 16:21

12:41 Jon 1:2; Jon 3:5; Matt 12:6, 42

12:42 1 Kin 10:1; 2 Chr 9:1; Matt 12:6, 41

12:43 Luke 11:24-26

12:45 Mark 5:9; Luke 11:26; Heb 6:4-8; 2 Pet 2:20

40 for just as JONAH WAS THREE DAYS AND THREE NIGHTS IN THE BELLY OF THE SEA
MONSTER, so will the Son of Man be three days and three nights in the heart of the earth.
41 "The men of Nineveh will stand up with this generation at the judgment, and will
condemn it because they repented at the preaching of Jonah; and behold, something
greater than Jonah is here.
42 "*The* Queen of *the* South will rise up with this generation at the judgment and will
condemn it, because she came from the ends of the earth to hear the wisdom of Solomon; and behold, something greater than Solomon is here.
43 "Now when the unclean spirit goes out of a man, it passes through waterless places
seeking rest, and does not find *it.*
44 "Then it says, 'I will return to my house from which I came'; and when it comes, it
finds *it* unoccupied, swept, and put in order.
45 "Then it goes and takes along with it seven other spirits more wicked than itself, and
they go in and live there; and the last state of that man becomes worse than the first.
That is the way it will also be with this evil generation."

Jesus Describes His True Family
(76/Mark 3:31-35; Luke 8:19-21)

12:46 Matt 1:18; 2:11ff; 13:55; Luke 1:43; 2:33f, 48, 51; John 2:1, 5, 12; 19:25f; Acts 1:14; Matt 13:55; Mark 6:3; John 2:12; 7:3, 5, 10; Acts 1:14; 1 Cor 9:5; Gal 1:19

46 While He was still speaking to the crowds, behold, His mother and brothers were
standing outside, seeking to speak to Him.
47 Someone said to Him, "Behold, Your mother and Your brothers are standing outside seeking to speak to You."
48 But Jesus answered the one who was telling Him and said, "Who is My mother and
who are My brothers?"
49 And stretching out His hand toward His disciples, He said, "Behold My mother and
My brothers!
50 "For whoever does the will of My Father who is in heaven, he is My brother and sister and mother."

Jesus Tells the Parable of the Four Soils
(77/Mark 4:1-9; Luke 8:4-8)

13:1 Matt 9:28; 13:36; Mark 2:13

13:2 Luke 5:3

13:3 Matt 13:10ff; Mark 4:2ff

13 That day Jesus went out of the house and was sitting by the sea.
2 And large crowds gathered to Him, so He got into a boat and sat down, and the
whole crowd was standing on the beach.
3 And He spoke many things to them in parables, saying, "Behold, the sower went
out to sow;
4 and as he sowed, some *seeds* fell beside the road, and the birds came and ate
them up.
5 "Others fell on the rocky places, where they did not have much soil; and immediately they sprang up, because they had no depth of soil.
6 "But when the sun had risen, they were scorched; and because they had no root, they
withered away.
7 "Others fell among the thorns, and the thorns came up and choked them out.

12:41–42 In Jonah's day, Nineveh was the capital of the Assyrian empire, and it was as powerful as it was evil (Jonah 1:2). But the entire city repented at Jonah's preaching. The Queen of the South (also called the Queen of Sheba) traveled far to see Solomon, king of Israel, and learn about his great wisdom (1 Kings 10:1–10; also see the note on Luke 11:31–32 for more on the Queen of Sheba). These Gentiles recognized the truth about God when it was presented to them, unlike the religious leaders who ignored the truth even though it stared them in the face. How have you responded to the evidence and truth that you have?

12:43–45 Jesus was describing the attitude of the nation of Israel and the religious leaders in particular. Just cleaning up one's life without filling it with God leaves plenty of room for Satan to enter. The book of Ezra records how the people rid themselves of idolatry, but failed to replace it with love for God and obedience to him. Ridding our lives of sin is the first step. We must also take the second step: filling our lives with God's Word and the Holy Spirit. Unfilled and complacent people are easy targets for Satan.

12:46–50 Jesus was not denying his responsibility to his earthly family. On the contrary, he criticized the religious leaders for not following the Old Testament command to honor their parents (15:1–9). He provided for his mother's security as he hung on the cross (John 19:25–27). His mother and brothers were present in the upper room at Pentecost (Acts 1:14). Instead Jesus was pointing out that spiritual relationships are as binding as physical ones, and he was paving the way for a new community of believers (the universal church), our spiritual family.

13:2–3 Jesus used many *parables* when speaking to the crowds. A parable compares something familiar to something unfamiliar. It helps us understand spiritual truth by using everyday objects and relationships. Parables compel listeners to discover truth, while at the same time concealing the truth from those too lazy or too stubborn to see it. To those who are honestly searching, the truth becomes clear. We must be careful not to read too much into parables, forcing them to say what they don't mean. All parables have one meaning unless otherwise specified by Jesus.

8 "And others fell on the good soil and ☆yielded a crop, some a hundredfold, some
sixty, and some thirty.
9 "He who has ears, let him hear."

Jesus Explains the Parable of the Four Soils
(78/Mark 4:10-25; Luke 8:9-18)

10 And the disciples came and said to Him, "Why do You speak to them in parables?"
11 Jesus answered them, "To you it has been granted to know the mysteries of the kingdom of heaven, but to them it has not been granted.
12 "For whoever has, to him *more* shall be given, and he will have an abundance; but
whoever does not have, even what he has shall be taken away from him.
13 "Therefore I speak to them in parables; because while seeing they do not see, and
while hearing they do not hear, nor do they understand.
14 "In their case the prophecy of Isaiah is being fulfilled, which says,
'YOU WILL KEEP ON HEARING, BUT WILL NOT UNDERSTAND;
YOU WILL KEEP ON SEEING, BUT WILL NOT PERCEIVE;
15 FOR THE HEART OF THIS PEOPLE HAS BECOME DULL,
WITH THEIR EARS THEY SCARCELY HEAR,
AND THEY HAVE CLOSED THEIR EYES,
OTHERWISE THEY WOULD SEE WITH THEIR EYES,
HEAR WITH THEIR EARS,
AND UNDERSTAND WITH THEIR HEART AND RETURN,
AND I WOULD HEAL THEM.'
16 "But blessed are your eyes, because they see; and your ears, because they hear.
17 "For truly I say to you that many prophets and righteous men desired to see what
you see, and did not see *it*, and to hear what you hear, and did not hear *it*.
18 "Hear then the parable of the sower.
19 "When anyone hears the word of the kingdom and does not understand it, the evil
one comes and snatches away what has been sown in his heart. This is the one on whom
seed was sown beside the road.
20 "The one on whom seed was sown on the rocky places, this is the man who hears the
word and immediately receives it with joy;
21 yet he has no *firm* root in himself, but is *only* temporary, and when affliction or persecution arises because of the word, immediately he falls away.
22 "And the one on whom seed was sown among the thorns, this is the man who hears
the word, and the worry of the world and the deceitfulness of wealth choke the word,
and it becomes unfruitful.
23 "And the one on whom seed was sown on the good soil, this is the man who hears the
word and understands it; who indeed bears fruit and brings forth, some a hundredfold,
some sixty, and some thirty."

13:8 Gen 26:12; Matt 13:23
13:9 Matt 11:15; Rev 2:7, 11, 17, 29; 3:6, 13, 22
13:11 Matt 19:11; 20:23; John 6:65; 1 Cor 2:10; Col 1:27; 1 John 2:20, 27
13:12 Matt 25:29; Mark 4:25; Luke 8:18; 19:26
13:13 Deut 29:4; Is 42:19, 20; Jer 5:21; Ezek 12:2
13:14 Is 6:9; Mark 4:12; Luke 8:10; John 12:40; Acts 28:26, 27; Rom 10:16; 11:8
13:15 Is 6:10; Ps 119:70; Zech 7:11; Luke 19:42; John 8:43, 44; 2 Tim 4:4; Heb 5:11
13:16 Luke 10:23, 24; Matt 16:17; John 20:29
13:17 John 8:56; Heb 11:13; 1 Pet 1:10-12
13:18 Mark 4:13-20; Luke 8:11-15
13:19 Matt 4:23; Matt 5:37
13:21 Matt 11:6
13:22 Matt 12:32; 13:39; Mark 4:19; Rom 12:2; 1 Cor 1:20; 2:6, 8; 3:18; 2 Cor 4:4; Gal 1:4; Eph 2:2; Matt 19:23; 1 Tim 6:9, 10, 17

13:8 This parable should encourage spiritual "sowers"—those who teach, preach, and lead others. The farmer sowed good seed, but not all the seed sprouted, and even the plants that grew had varying yields. Don't be discouraged if you do not always see results as you faithfully teach the Word. Belief cannot be forced to follow a mathematical formula (i.e., a 4:1 ratio of seeds planted to seeds sprouted). Rather, it is a miracle of God's Holy Spirit as he uses your words to lead others to him.

13:9 Human ears hear many sounds, but there is a deeper kind of listening that results in spiritual understanding. If you honestly seek God's will, you have spiritual hearing, and these parables will give you new perspectives.

13:10 When speaking in parables, Jesus was not hiding truth from sincere seekers, because those who were receptive to spiritual truth understood the illustrations. To others they were only stories without meaning. This allowed Jesus to give spiritual food to those who hungered for it while preventing his enemies from trapping him sooner than they might otherwise have done.

13:12 This phrase means that we are responsible to use well what we have. When people reject Jesus, their hardness of heart drives away or renders useless even the little understanding they had.

13:22 How easy it is to agree with Christ with no intention of obeying. It is easy to denounce worries of this life and the deceitfulness of wealth, and still do nothing to change our ways. In light of eternal life with God, are your present worries justified? If you had everything you could want but forfeited eternal life with God, would those things be so desirable?

13:23 The four types of soil represent different responses to God's message. People respond differently because they are in different states of readiness. Some are hardened, others are shallow, others are contaminated by distracting worries, and some are receptive. How has God's Word taken root in your life? What kind of soil are you?

Jesus Tells the Parable of the Weeds
(80)

13:24 Matt 13:31, 33, 45, 47; 18:23; 20:1; 22:2; 25:1; Mark 4:26-30; Luke 13:18, 20

24 Jesus presented another parable to them, saying, "The kingdom of heaven may be
compared to a man who sowed good seed in his field.
25 "But while his men were sleeping, his enemy came and sowed [23]tares among the wheat,
and went away.
26 "But when the wheat sprouted and bore grain, then the tares became evident also.
27 "The slaves of the landowner came and said to him, 'Sir, did you not sow good seed
in your field? How then does it have tares?'
28 "And he said to them, 'An enemy has done this!' The slaves ☆said to him, 'Do you
want us, then, to go and gather them up?'
29 "But he ☆said, 'No; for while you are gathering up the tares, you may uproot the wheat
with them.

13:30 Matt 3:12

30 'Allow both to grow together until the harvest; and in the time of the harvest I will
say to the reapers, "First gather up the tares and bind them in bundles to burn them up;
but gather the wheat into my barn." ' "

Jesus Tells the Parable of the Mustard Seed
(81/Mark 4:30-34)

13:31 Luke 13:18, 19; Matt 13:24; Matt 17:20; Luke 17:6

13:32 Ezek 17:23; Ps 104:12; Ezek 31:6; Dan 4:12

31 He presented another parable to them, saying, "The kingdom of heaven is like a
mustard seed, which a man took and sowed in his field;
32 and this is smaller than all *other* seeds, but when it is full grown, it is larger than the
garden plants and becomes a tree, so that THE BIRDS OF THE AIR come and NEST IN ITS
BRANCHES."

Jesus Tells the Parable of the Yeast
(82)

13:33 Luke 13:21; Matt 13:24; Gen 18:6; Judg 6:19; 1 Sam 1:24

13:34 Mark 4:34; John 10:6; 16:25

13:35 Ps 78:2

33 He spoke another parable to them, "The kingdom of heaven is like leaven, which a
woman took and hid in three pecks of flour until it was all leavened."
34 All these things Jesus spoke to the crowds in parables, and He did not speak to them
without a parable.
35 *This was* to fulfill what was spoken through the prophet:
"I WILL OPEN MY MOUTH IN PARABLES;
I WILL UTTER THINGS HIDDEN SINCE THE FOUNDATION OF THE WORLD."

Jesus Explains the Parable of the Weeds
(83)

13:36 Matt 13:1; Matt 15:15

13:37 Matt 8:20

13:38 Matt 8:12; John 8:44; Acts 13:10; 1 John 3:10; Matt 5:37

13:39 Matt 12:32; 13:22, 40, 49; 24:3; 28:20; 1 Cor 10:11; Heb 9:26

36 Then He left the crowds and went into the house. And His disciples came to Him
and said, "Explain to us the parable of the tares of the field."
37 And He said, "The one who sows the good seed is the Son of Man,
38 and the field is the world; and *as for* the good seed, these are the sons of the kingdom; and the tares are the sons of the evil *one;*
39 and the enemy who sowed them is the devil, and the harvest is the end of the age;
and the reapers are angels.

23 Or *darnel*, a weed resembling wheat

13:24ff Jesus gives the meaning of this parable in verses 36–43. All the parables in this chapter teach us about God and his kingdom. They explain what the kingdom is really like as opposed to our expectations of it. The kingdom of heaven is not a geographic location, but a spiritual realm where God rules and where we share in his eternal life. We join that kingdom when we trust in Christ as Savior.

13:30 The young tares (weeds) and the young blades of wheat look the same and can't be distinguished until they are grown and ready for harvest. Weeds (unbelievers) and wheat (believers) must live side by side in this world. God allows unbelievers to remain for a while, just as a farmer allows weeds to remain in his field so the surrounding wheat isn't uprooted with them. At the harvest, however, the weeds will be uprooted and thrown away. God's harvest (judgment) of all people is coming. We are to make ourselves ready by making sure that our faith is sincere.

13:31–32 The mustard seed was the smallest seed a farmer used. Jesus used this parable to show that the kingdom has small beginnings but will grow and produce great results.

13:33 In other Bible passages, leaven (yeast) is used as a symbol of evil or uncleanness. Here it is a positive symbol of growth. Although yeast looks like a minor ingredient, it permeates the whole loaf. Although the kingdom began small and was nearly invisible, it would soon grow and have a great impact on the world.

40 "So just as the tares are gathered up and burned with fire, so shall it be at the end of
the age.
41 "The Son of Man will send forth His angels, and they will gather out of His kingdom
all stumbling blocks, and those who commit lawlessness,
42 and will throw them into the furnace of fire; in that place there will be weeping and
gnashing of teeth.
43 "Then THE RIGHTEOUS WILL SHINE FORTH AS THE SUN in the kingdom of their Father. He who has ears, let him hear.

13:40 Matt 12:32; 13:22, 39, 49; 24:3; 28:20; 1 Cor 10:11; Heb 9:26

13:41 Matt 8:20; Matt 24:31; Zeph 1:3

13:42 Matt 13:50; Matt 8:12

13:43 Dan 12:3; Matt 11:15

Jesus Tells the Parable of Hidden Treasure
(84)

44 "The kingdom of heaven is like a treasure hidden in the field, which a man found
and hid *again;* and from joy over it he goes and sells all that he has and buys that field.

13:44 Matt 13:24; Matt 13:46

Jesus Tells the Parable of the Pearl Merchant
(85)

45 "Again, the kingdom of heaven is like a merchant seeking fine pearls,
46 and upon finding one pearl of great value, he went and sold all that he had and
bought it.

13:45 Matt 13:24

Jesus Tells the Parable of the Fishing Net
(86)

47 "Again, the kingdom of heaven is like a dragnet cast into the sea, and gathering *fish*
of every kind;
48 and when it was filled, they drew it up on the beach; and they sat down and gathered the good *fish* into containers, but the bad they threw away.
49 "So it will be at the end of the age; the angels will come forth and take out the wicked
from among the righteous,
50 and will throw them into the furnace of fire; in that place there will be weeping and
gnashing of teeth.
51 "Have you understood all these things?" They *said to Him, "Yes."
52 And Jesus said to them, "Therefore every scribe who has become a disciple of the
kingdom of heaven is like a head of a household, who brings out of his treasure things
new and old."

13:47 Matt 13:44

13:49 Matt 13:39, 40

13:50 Matt 13:42; Matt 8:12

5. Jesus encounters differing reactions to his ministry

The People of Nazareth Refuse to Believe
(91/Mark 6:1-6)

53 When Jesus had finished these parables, He departed from there.
54 He came to His hometown and *began* teaching them in their synagogue, so that they

13:53 Matt 7:28

13:54 Matt 4:23; Matt 7:28

13:40–43 At the end of the world, angels will separate the evil from the good. There are true and false believers in churches today, but we should be cautious in our judgments because only Christ is qualified to make the final separation. If you start judging, you may damage some of the good "plants." It's more important to judge our own response to God than to analyze others' responses.

13:42 Jesus often uses these terms to refer to the coming judgment. The weeping indicates sorrow or remorse, and gnashing of teeth shows extreme anxiety or pain. Those who say they don't care what happens to them after they die don't realize what they are saying. They will be punished for living in selfishness and indifference to God.

13:43 Those who receive God's favor stand in bright contrast to those who receive his judgment. A similiar illustration is used in Daniel 12:3.

13:44–46 The kingdom of heaven is more valuable than anything else we can have, and a person must be willing to give up everything to obtain it. The man who discovered the treasure in the field stumbled upon it by accident but knew its value when he found it. The merchant was earnestly searching for the pearl of great value, and, when he found it, he sold everything he had to purchase it.

13:47–49 The parable of the dragnet (fishing net) has the same meaning as the parable of the wheat and tares. We are to obey God and tell others about his grace and goodness, but we cannot dictate who is part of the kingdom of heaven and who is not. This sorting will be done at the last judgment by those infinitely more qualified than we.

13:52 Anyone who understands God's real purpose in the law as revealed in the Old Testament has a real treasure. The Old Testament points the way to Jesus, the Messiah. Jesus always upheld its authority and relevance. But there is a double benefit to those who understand Jesus' teaching about the kingdom of heaven. This was a new treasure that Jesus was revealing. Both the old and new teaching give practical guidelines for faith and for living in the world. The religious leaders, however, were trapped in the old and blind to the new. They were looking for a future kingdom *preceded* by judgment. Jesus, however, taught that the kingdom was *now* and the judgment was future. The religious leaders were looking for a physical and temporal kingdom (via military rebellion and physical rule), but they were blind to the spiritual significance of the kingdom that Christ brought.

were astonished, and said, "Where *did* this man *get* this wisdom and *these* miraculous
powers?
55 "Is not this the carpenter's son? Is not His mother called Mary, and His brothers,
James and Joseph and Simon and Judas?
56 "And His sisters, are they not all with us? Where then *did* this man *get* all these things?"
57 And they took offense at Him. But Jesus said to them, "A prophet is not without
honor except in his hometown and in his *own* household."
58 And He did not do many miracles there because of their unbelief.

13:55 Matt 12:46
13:56 Mark 6:3
13:57 Matt 11:6; Mark 6:4; Luke 4:24; John 4:44

Herod Kills John the Baptist
(95/Mark 6:14-29; Luke 9:7-9)

14 At that time Herod the tetrarch heard the news about Jesus,
2 and said to his servants, "This is John the Baptist; he has risen from the dead,
and that is why miraculous powers are at work in him."
3 For when Herod had John arrested, he bound him and put him in prison because of
Herodias, the wife of his brother Philip.
4 For John had been saying to him, "It is not lawful for you to have her."
5 Although Herod wanted to put him to death, he feared the crowd, because they
regarded John as a prophet.
6 But when Herod's birthday came, the daughter of Herodias danced before *them* and
pleased Herod,
7 so *much* that he promised with an oath to give her whatever she asked.
8 Having been prompted by her mother, she ☆said, "Give me here on a platter the
head of John the Baptist."
9 Although he was grieved, the king commanded *it* to be given because of his oaths,
and because of his dinner guests.
10 He sent and had John beheaded in the prison.
11 And his head was brought on a platter and given to the girl, and she brought it to
her mother.
12 His disciples came and took away the body and buried it; and they went and reported to Jesus.

14:1 Mark 8:15; Luke 3:1, 19; 8:3; 13:31; 23:7f, 11f, 15; Acts 4:27; 12:1
14:2 Matt 16:14; Mark 6:14; Luke 9:7
14:3 Mark 8:15; Luke 3:1, 19; 8:3; 13:31; 23:7f, 11f, 15; Acts 4:27; 12:1; Matt 4:12; 11:2; Matt 14:6; Mark 6:17, 19, 22; Luke 3:19f
14:4 Lev 18:16; 20:21
14:5 Matt 11:9
14:6 Matt 14:3; Mark 6:17, 19, 22; Luke 3:19; Mark 8:15; Luke 3:1, 19; 8:3; 13:31; 23:7f, 11f, 15; Acts 4:27; 12:1

13:55 The residents of Jesus' hometown had known Jesus since he was a young child and were acquainted with his family; they could not bring themselves to believe in his message. They were too close to the situation. Jesus had come to them as a prophet, one who challenged them to respond to unpopular spiritual truth. They did not listen to the timeless message because they could not see beyond the man.

13:57 Jesus was not the first prophet to be rejected in his own country. Jeremiah experienced rejection in his hometown, even by members of his own family (Jeremiah 12:5–6).

13:58 Jesus did few miracles in his hometown "because of their unbelief." Lack of faith blinds people to the truth and robs them of hope. These people missed the Messiah. How does your faith measure up? If you can't see God's work, perhaps it is because of your unbelief. Believe, ask God for a mighty work in your life, and expect him to act. Look with the eyes of faith.

14:1 Herod was a tetrarch—one of four rulers over the four districts of Palestine. His territory included the regions of Galilee and Perea. He was the son of Herod the Great, who ordered the killing of the babies in Bethlehem (2:16). Also known as Herod Antipas, he heard Jesus' case before Jesus' crucifixion (Luke 23:6–12). His Profile is found in Mark 6.

14:2 For more information on John the Baptist, see his Profile in John 1.

14:3 Philip, Herod's half brother, was another of Palestine's four rulers. His territories were Ituraea and Trachonitis, northeast of the Sea of Galilee (Luke 3:1). Philip's wife, Herodias, left Philip to live with Herod Antipas. John the Baptist condemned the two for living immorally (see Mark 6:17–18).

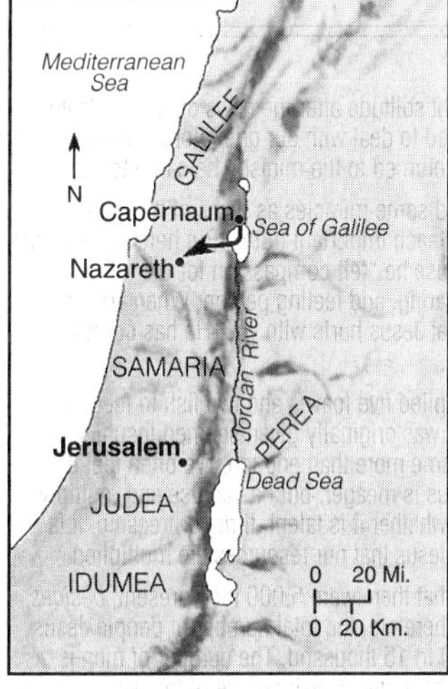

NAZARETH REJECTS JESUS Chronologically, this return to Nazareth occurred after Jesus was in the Gadarene region and healed the demon-possessed men (8:28–34), then recrossed the sea to Capernaum. From there he traveled to Nazareth, where he had grown up, only to discover that the people refused to believe he was the Christ.

14:9 Herod did not want to kill John the Baptist, but he gave the order so that he wouldn't be embarrassed in front of his guests. How easy it is to give in to the crowd and to let ourselves be pressured into doing wrong. Don't get in a situation where it will be too embarrassing to do what is right. Determine to do what is right, no matter how embarrassing or painful it may be.

Jesus Feeds Five Thousand
(96/Mark 6:30-44; Luke 9:10-17; John 6:1-15)

13 Now when Jesus heard *about John,* He withdrew from there in a boat to a secluded
place by Himself; and when the people heard *of this,* they followed Him on foot from
the cities.
14 When He went ashore, He saw a large crowd, and felt compassion for them and
healed their sick.
15 When it was evening, the disciples came to Him and said, "This place is desolate
and the hour is already late; so send the crowds away, that they may go into the villages
and buy food for themselves."
16 But Jesus said to them, "They do not need to go away; you give them *some-*
thing to eat!"
17 They ☆said to Him, "We have here only five loaves and two fish."
18 And He said, "Bring them here to Me."
19 Ordering the people to sit down on the grass, He took the five loaves and the two
fish, and looking up toward heaven, He blessed *the food,* and breaking the loaves He
gave them to the disciples, and the disciples *gave them* to the crowds,
20 and they all ate and were satisfied. They picked up what was left over of the broken
pieces, twelve full baskets.
21 There were about five thousand men who ate, besides women and children.

Jesus Walks on Water
(97/Mark 6:45-52; John 6:16-21)

22 Immediately He made the disciples get into the boat and go ahead of Him to the
other side, while He sent the crowds away.
23 After He had sent the crowds away, He went up on the mountain by Himself to pray;
and when it was evening, He was there alone.
24 But the boat was already [24]a long distance from the land, battered by the waves; for
the wind was contrary.
25 And in the [25]fourth watch of the night He came to them, walking on the sea.
26 When the disciples saw Him walking on the sea, they were terrified, and said, "It is
a ghost!" And they cried out in fear.
27 But immediately Jesus spoke to them, saying, "Take courage, it is I; do not be afraid."

14:13 Matt 15:32-38
14:14 Matt 9:36; Matt 4:23
14:17 Matt 16:9
14:19 1 Sam 9:13; Matt 15:36; 26:26; Mark 6:41; 8:7; 14:22; Luke 24:30; Acts 27:35; Rom 14:6
14:20 Matt 16:9; Mark 6:43; 8:19; Luke 9:17; John 6:13
14:23 Mark 6:46; Luke 6:12; 9:28; John 6:15
14:24 Acts 27:4
14:25 Matt 24:43; Mark 13:35
14:26 Luke 24:37
14:27 Matt 9:2; Matt 17:7; 28:5, 10; Mark 6:50; Luke 1:13, 30; 2:10; 5:10; 12:32; John 6:20; Rev 1:17

24 Lit *many stadia from;* a stadion was about 600 feet or about 182 meters **25** I.e. 3-6 a.m.

14:13–14 Jesus sought solitude after the news of John's death. Sometimes we may need to deal with our grief alone. Jesus did not dwell on his grief, but returned to the ministry he came to do.

14:14 Jesus performed some miracles as signs of his identity. He used other miracles to teach important truths. But here we read that he healed people because he "felt compassion for them." Jesus was, and is, a loving, caring, and feeling person. When you are suffering, remember that Jesus hurts with you. He has compassion for you.

14:19–21 Jesus multiplied five loaves and two fish to feed over 5,000 people. What he was originally given seemed insufficient, but in his hands it became more than enough. We often feel that our contribution to Jesus is meager, but he can use and multiply whatever we give him, whether it is talent, time, or treasure. It is when we give them to Jesus that our resources are multiplied.

14:21 The text states that there were 5,000 men present, *besides* women and children. Therefore, the total number of people Jesus fed could have been 10 to 15 thousand. The number of men is listed separately because in the Jewish culture of the day, men and women usually ate separately when in public. The children ate with the women.

14:23 Seeking solitude was an important priority for Jesus (see also 14:13). He made room in his busy schedule to be alone with the Father. Spending time with God in prayer nurtures a vital relationship and equips us to meet life's challenges and struggles. Develop the discipline of spending time alone with God—it will help you grow spiritually and become more and more like Christ.

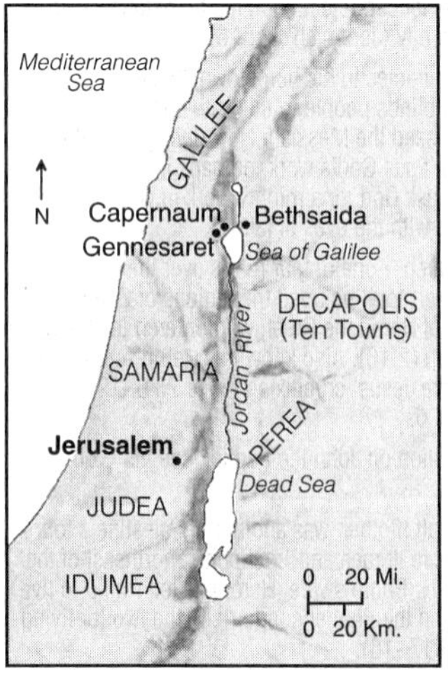

JESUS WALKS ON THE SEA
The miraculous feeding of the 5,000 occurred on the shores of the Sea of Galilee near Bethsaida. Jesus then sent his disciples across the lake. Several hours later they encountered a storm, and Jesus came to them—walking on the water. The boat then landed at Gennesaret.

28 Peter said to Him, "Lord, if it is You, command me to come to You on the water."
29 And He said, "Come!" And Peter got out of the boat, and walked on the water and
came toward Jesus.
30 But seeing the wind, he became frightened, and beginning to sink, he cried out,
"Lord, save me!"
14:31 Matt 6:30; 8:26; 16:8
31 Immediately Jesus stretched out His hand and took hold of him, and ☆said to him,
"You of little faith, why did you doubt?"
32 When they got into the boat, the wind stopped.
14:33 Matt 4:3
33 And those who were in the boat worshiped Him, saying, "You are certainly God's
Son!"

Jesus Heals All Who Touch Him
(98/Mark 6:53-56)

14:34 John 6:24, 25; Mark 6:53; Luke 5:1
14:36 Matt 9:20; Matt 9:21; Mark 3:10; 6:56; 8:22; Luke 6:19

34 When they had crossed over, they came to land at Gennesaret.
35 And when the men of that place recognized Him, they sent *word* into all that surrounding district and brought to Him all who were sick;
36 and they implored Him that they might just touch the fringe of His cloak; and as
many as touched *it* were cured.

Jesus Teaches about Inner Purity
(102/Mark 7:1-23)

15:1 Mark 3:22; 7:1; John 1:19; Acts 25:7
15:2 Luke 11:38
15:4 Ex 20:12; Deut 5:16; Ex 21:17; Lev 20:9

15 Then some Pharisees and scribes ☆came to Jesus from Jerusalem and said,
2 "Why do Your disciples break the tradition of the elders? For they do not wash
their hands when they eat bread."
3 And He answered and said to them, "Why do you yourselves transgress the commandment of God for the sake of your tradition?
4 "For God said, 'HONOR YOUR FATHER AND MOTHER,' and, 'HE WHO SPEAKS EVIL
OF FATHER OR MOTHER IS TO BE PUT TO DEATH.'
5 "But you say, 'Whoever says to *his* father or mother, "Whatever I have that would
help you has been given *to God*,"
6 he is not to honor his father or his mother[26].' And *by this* you invalidated the word
of God for the sake of your tradition.

26 I.e. by supporting them with it

14:28 Peter was not putting Jesus to the test, something we are told not to do (4:7). Instead he was the only one in the boat to react in faith. His impulsive request led him to experience a rather unusual demonstration of God's power. Peter started to sink because he took his eyes off Jesus and focused on the high waves around him. His faith wavered when he realized what he was doing. We may not walk on water, but we do walk through tough situations. If we focus on the waves of difficult circumstances around us without looking to Jesus for help, we too may despair and sink. To maintain your faith when situations are difficult, keep your eyes on Jesus' power rather than on your inadequacies.

14:30–31 Although we start out with good intentions, sometimes our faith falters. This doesn't necessarily mean we have failed. When Peter's faith faltered, he reached out to Christ, the only one who could help. He was afraid, but he still looked to Christ. When you are apprehensive about the troubles around you and doubt Christ's presence or ability to help, you must remember that he is the *only* One who can really help.

14:34 Gennesaret was located on the west side of the Sea of Galilee in a fertile, well-watered area.

14:35–36 The people recognized Jesus as a great healer, but how many understood who he truly was? They came to Jesus for physical healing, but did they come for spiritual healing? They came to prolong their lives on earth, but did they come to secure their eternal lives? People may seek Jesus to learn valuable lessons from his life or in hopes of finding relief from pain. But we miss Jesus' whole message if we seek him only to heal our bodies but not our souls, if we look to him for help only in this life, rather than for his eternal plan for us. Only when we understand the real Jesus Christ can we appreciate how he can truly change our lives.

14:36 Jewish men wore tassels (fringe) on the lower edges of their robes according to God's command (Deuteronomy 22:12). By Jesus' day, these tassels were seen as signs of holiness (23:5). It was natural that people seeking healing should reach out and touch the fringe. But as one sick woman learned, healing came from faith and not from Jesus' cloak (9:19–22).

15:1–2 The Pharisees and scribes came from Jerusalem, the center of Jewish authority, to scrutinize Jesus' activities. Over the centuries since the Jews' return from Babylonian captivity, hundreds of religious traditions had been added to God's laws. The Pharisees and scribes considered them all equally important. Many traditions are not bad in themselves. Certain religious traditions can add richness and meaning to life. But we must not assume that because our traditions have been practiced for years they should be elevated to a sacred standing. God's principles never change, and his law doesn't need additions. Traditions should help us understand God's laws better, not become laws themselves.

15:5–6 This was the practice of *Corban* (literally, "offering"; see Mark 7:11). Anyone who made a Corban vow was required to dedicate money to God's temple that otherwise would have gone to support his parents. Corban had become a religiously acceptable way to neglect parents, circumventing the child's responsibility to them. Although the action—giving money to God—seemed worthy and no doubt conferred prestige on the giver, many people who took the Corban vow were disregarding God's command to care for needy parents. These religious leaders were ignoring God's clear command to honor their parents.

7 "You hypocrites, rightly did Isaiah prophesy of you:
8 'THIS PEOPLE HONORS ME WITH THEIR LIPS,
BUT THEIR HEART IS FAR AWAY FROM ME. 15:8 Is 29:13
9 'BUT IN VAIN DO THEY WORSHIP ME,
TEACHING AS DOCTRINES THE PRECEPTS OF MEN.' " 15:9 Col 2:22
10 After Jesus called the crowd to Him, He said to them, "Hear and understand.
11 "*It is* not what enters into the mouth *that* defiles the man, but what proceeds out of 15:11 Matt 15:18; Acts 10:14, 15; 1 Tim 4:3
the mouth, this defiles the man."
12 Then the disciples *came and *said to Him, "Do You know that the Pharisees were
offended when they heard this statement?"
13 But He answered and said, "Every plant which My heavenly Father did not plant 15:13 Is 60:21; 61:3; John 15:2; 1 Cor 3:9
shall be uprooted.
14 "Let them alone; they are blind guides [27]of the blind. And if a blind man guides a
blind man, both will fall into a pit." 15:14 Matt 23:16, 24; Luke 6:39
15 Peter said to Him, "Explain the parable to us." 15:15 Matt 13:36
16 Jesus said, "Are you still lacking in understanding also?
17 "Do you not understand that everything that goes into the mouth passes into the
stomach, and is eliminated?
18 "But the things that proceed out of the mouth come from the heart, and those defile 15:18 Matt 12:34; Mark 7:20
the man.
19 "For out of the heart come evil thoughts, murders, adulteries, fornications, thefts,
false witness, slanders. 15:19 Gal 5:19ff
20 "These are the things which defile the man; but to eat with unwashed hands does not
defile the man."

Jesus Sends a Demon Out of a Girl
(103/Mark 7:24-30)

21 Jesus went away from there, and withdrew into the district of Tyre and Sidon. 15:21 Matt 11:21
22 And a Canaanite woman from that region came out and *began* to cry out, saying,
"Have mercy on me, Lord, Son of David; my daughter is cruelly demon-possessed." 15:22 Matt 9:27; Matt 4:24

27 Later mss add *of the blind*

MINISTRY IN PHOENICIA
After preaching again in Capernaum, Jesus left Galilee for Phoenicia, where he preached in Tyre and Sidon. On his return, he traveled through the region of the Decapolis (Ten Towns), fed the 4,000 beside the sea, then crossed to Magadan.

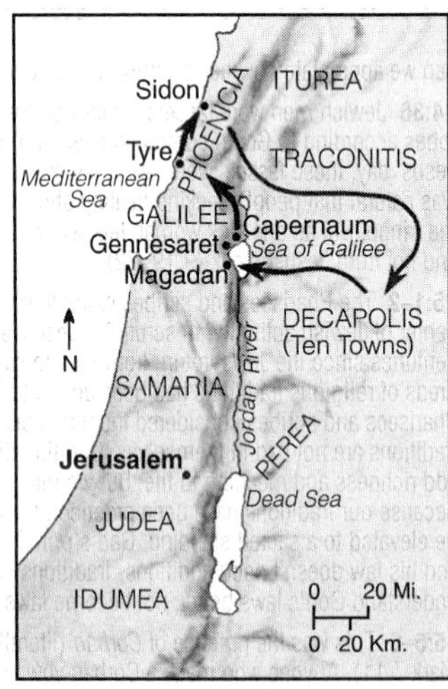

15:8–9 The prophet Isaiah also criticized hypocrites (Isaiah 29:13), and Jesus applied Isaiah's words to these religious leaders. When we claim to honor God while our hearts are far from him, our worship means nothing. It is not enough to act religious. Our actions and our attitudes must be sincere. If they are not, Isaiah's words also describe us.

15:9 The Pharisees knew a lot about God, but they didn't know God. It is not enough to study about religion or even to study the Bible. We must respond to God himself.

15:11 Jesus was referring to the Jewish regulations concerning food and drink. This verse could be paraphrased: "You aren't made unclean by eating nonkosher food! It is what you *say* and *think* that makes you unclean!" This statement offended the Pharisees who were very concerned about what people ate and drank.

15:13–14 Jesus told his disciples to leave the Pharisees alone because the Pharisees were blind to God's truth. Anyone who listened to their teaching would risk spiritual blindness as well. Not all religious leaders clearly see God's truth. Make sure that those you listen to and learn from are those with good spiritual eyesight— they teach and follow the principles of Scripture.

15:15 Later Peter would be faced with the issue of clean and unclean food (see the notes on 15:11 and Acts 10:12). Then he would learn that nothing should be a barrier to proclaiming the gospel to the Gentiles (non-Jews).

15:16–20 We work hard to keep our outward appearance attractive, but what is in our hearts is even more important. The way we are deep down (where others can't see) matters much to God. What are you like inside? When people become Christians, God makes them different on the inside. He will continue the process of change inside them if they only ask. God wants us to seek healthy thoughts and motives, not just healthy food and exercise.

15:22 This woman is called a "Gentile, of the Syrophoenician race" in Mark's Gospel (7:26), indicating that she was from the territory northwest of Galilee where the cities of Tyre and Sidon were located. Matthew calls her a Canaanite, naming her ancient ancestors who were enemies of Israel. Matthew's Jewish audience would have immediately understood the significance of Jesus helping this woman.

23 But He did not answer her a word. And His disciples came and implored Him, saying, "Send her away, because she keeps shouting at us."
15:24 Matt 10:6
24 But He answered and said, "I was sent only to the lost sheep of the house of Israel."
25 But she came and *began* to bow down before Him, saying, "Lord, help me!"
15:25 Matt 8:2
26 And He answered and said, "It is not good to take the children's bread and throw it
to the dogs."
27 But she said, "Yes, Lord; but even the dogs feed on the crumbs which fall from their
masters' table."
15:28 Matt 9:22
28 Then Jesus said to her, "O woman, your faith is great; it shall be done for you as you
wish." And her daughter was healed at once.

The Crowd Marvels at Jesus' Healings
(104/Mark 7:31-37)

15:29 Matt 4:18
29 Departing from there, Jesus went along by the Sea of Galilee, and having gone up
on the mountain, He was sitting there.
15:30 Matt 4:23
30 And large crowds came to Him, bringing with them *those who were* lame, crippled,
blind, mute, and many others, and they laid them down at His feet; and He healed them.
15:31 Matt 9:8
31 So the crowd marveled as they saw the mute speaking, the crippled restored, and
the lame walking, and the blind seeing; and they glorified the God of Israel.

Jesus Feeds Four Thousand
(105/Mark 8:1-10)

15:32 Matt 14:13-21; Matt 9:36
32 And Jesus called His disciples to Him, and said, "I feel compassion for the people,
because they have remained with Me now three days and have nothing to eat; and I do
not want to send them away hungry, for they might faint on the way."
33 The disciples ☆said to Him, "Where would we get so many loaves in *this* desolate
place to satisfy such a large crowd?"
34 And Jesus ☆said to them, "How many loaves do you have?" And they said, "Seven,
and a few small fish."
15:36 Matt 14:19; 26:27; Luke 22:17, 19; John 6:11, 23; Acts 27:35; Rom 14:6
35 And He directed the people to sit down on the ground;
36 and He took the seven loaves and the fish; and giving thanks, He broke them and
started giving them to the disciples, and the disciples *gave them* to the people.
15:37 Matt 16:10; Mark 8:8, 20; Acts 9:25
37 And they all ate and were satisfied, and they picked up what was left over of the
broken pieces, seven large baskets full.
38 And those who ate were four thousand men, besides women and children.
15:39 Mark 3:9; Mark 8:10
39 And sending away the crowds, Jesus got into the boat and came to the region of
Magadan.

15:23 The disciples asked Jesus to get rid of the woman because she was bothering them with her nagging persistence. They showed no compassion for her or sensitivity to her needs. It is possible to become so occupied with spiritual matters that we miss real needs right around us. This is especially likely if we are prejudiced against needy people or if they cause us inconvenience. Instead of being bothered, be aware of the opportunities that surround you. Be open to the beauty of God's message for *all* people, and make an effort not to shut out those who are different from you.

15:24 Jesus' words do not contradict the truth that God's message is for all people (Psalm 22:27; Isaiah 56:7; Matthew 28:19; Romans 15:9–12). After all, when Jesus said these words, he was in Gentile territory on a mission to Gentile people. He ministered to Gentiles on many other occasions also. Jesus was simply telling the woman that Jews were to have the first opportunity to accept him as the Messiah because God wanted them to present the message of salvation to the rest of the world (see Genesis 12:3). Jesus was not rejecting the Canaanite woman. He may have wanted to test her faith, or he may have wanted to use the situation as another opportunity to teach that faith is available to all people.

15:26–28 *Dog* was a term the Jews commonly applied to Gentiles because the Jews considered these pagan people no more likely than dogs to receive God's blessing. Jesus was not degrading the woman by using this term; he was reflecting the Jews' attitude so as to contrast it with his own. The woman did not argue. Instead, using Jesus' choice of words, she agreed to be considered a dog as long as she could receive God's blessing for her daughter. Ironically, many Jews would lose God's blessing and salvation because they rejected Jesus, and many Gentiles would find salvation because they recognized and accepted him.

15:29–31 A large crowd was brought to Jesus to be healed, and he healed them all. Jesus is still able to heal broken lives, and we can be the ones who bring suffering people to him. Who do you know that needs Christ's healing touch? You can bring them to Jesus through prayer or through explaining to them the reason for the hope that you have (1 Peter 3:15). Then let Christ do the healing.

15:32ff This feeding of 4,000 is a separate event from the feeding of the 5,000 (14:13–21), confirmed by Mark 8:19–20. This was the beginning of Jesus' expanded ministry to the Gentiles.

15:33 Jesus had already fed more than 5,000 people with five loaves and two fish. Here, in a similar situation, the disciples were again perplexed. How easily we throw up our hands in despair when faced with difficult situations. Like the disciples, we often forget that if God has cared for us in the past, he will do the same now. When facing a difficult situation, remember how God cared for you and trust him to work faithfully again.

15:39 Magadan was located on the west shore of the Sea of Galilee. Also known as Dalmanutha (Mark 8:10), this was Mary Magdalene's hometown.

Religious Leaders Ask for a Sign in the Sky
(106/Mark 8:11-13)

16 The Pharisees and Sadducees came up, and testing Jesus, they asked Him to show them a sign from heaven.
2 But He replied to them, "When it is evening, you say, '*It will be* fair weather, for the sky is red.'
3 "And in the morning, '*There will be* a storm today, for the sky is red and threatening.' Do you know how to discern the appearance of the sky, but cannot *discern* the signs of the times?
4 "An evil and adulterous generation seeks after a sign; and a sign will not be given it, except the sign of Jonah." And He left them and went away.

16:1 Mark 8:11-21; Matt 3:7; 16:6, 11, 12; Matt 12:38; Luke 11:16
16:2 Luke 12:54f
16:3 Luke 12:56
16:4 Matt 12:39; Luke 11:29

Jesus Warns against Wrong Teaching
(107/Mark 8:14-21)

5 And the disciples came to the other side *of the sea*, but they had forgotten to bring *any* bread.
6 And Jesus said to them, "Watch out and beware of the leaven of the Pharisees and Sadducees."
7 They began to discuss *this* among themselves, saying, "*He said that* because we did not bring *any* bread."
8 But Jesus, aware of this, said, "You men of little faith, why do you discuss among yourselves that you have no bread?
9 "Do you not yet understand or remember the five loaves of the five thousand, and how many baskets *full* you picked up?
10 "Or the seven loaves of the four thousand, and how many large baskets *full* you picked up?
11 "How is it that you do not understand that I did not speak to you concerning bread? But beware of the leaven of the Pharisees and Sadducees."
12 Then they understood that He did not say to beware of the leaven of bread, but of the teaching of the Pharisees and Sadducees.

16:6 Mark 8:15; Luke 12:1; Matt 3:7
16:8 Matt 6:30; 8:26; 14:31
16:9 Matt 14:17-21
16:10 Matt 15:34-38
16:11 Matt 16:6; Mark 8:15; Luke 12:1; Matt 3:7; 16:6, 12
16:12 Matt 3:7; 5:20

Peter Says Jesus is the Messiah
(109/Mark 8:27–30; Luke 9:18–20)

13 Now when Jesus came into the district of Caesarea Philippi, He was asking His disciples, "Who do people say that the Son of Man is?"

16:13 Mark 8:27; Matt 8:20; 16:27, 28

16:1 The Pharisees and Sadducees were Jewish religious leaders of two different parties, and their views were diametrically opposed on many issues. The Pharisees carefully followed their religious rules and traditions, believing that this was the way to God. They also believed in the authority of all Scripture and in the resurrection of the dead. The Sadducees accepted only the books of Moses as Scripture and did not believe in life after death. In Jesus, however, these two groups had a common enemy, and they joined forces to try to kill him. For more information on the Pharisees and Sadducees, see the charts in chapter 3 and Mark 2.

16:1 The Pharisees and Sadducees demanded a sign *from heaven*. They tried to explain away Jesus' other miracles as sleight of hand, coincidence, or use of evil power, but they believed that only God could do a sign in the sky. This, they were sure, would be a feat beyond Jesus' power. Although Jesus could have easily impressed them, he refused. He knew that even a miracle in the sky would not convince them he was the Messiah because they had already decided not to believe in him.

16:4 By using the sign of Jonah, who was inside a great fish for three days, Jesus was predicting his death and resurrection (see also 12:38–42).

16:4 Many people, like these Jewish leaders, say they want to see a miracle so that they can believe. But Jesus knew that miracles never convince the skeptical. Jesus had been healing, raising people from the dead, and feeding thousands, and still people wanted him to prove himself. Do you doubt Christ because you haven't *seen* a miracle? Do you expect God to prove himself to you personally before you believe? Jesus says, "Blessed are they who did not see, and yet believed" (John 20:29). We have all the miracles recorded in the Old and New Testaments, 2,000 years of church history, and the witness of thousands. With all this evidence, those who won't believe are either too proud or too stubborn. If you simply step forward in faith and believe, then you will begin to see the miracles that God can do with your life!

16:12 Leaven (yeast) is put into bread to make it rise, and it takes only a little to affect a whole batch of dough. Jesus used yeast as an example of how a small amount of evil can affect a large group of people. The wrong teachings of the Pharisees and Sadducees were leading many people astray. Beware of the tendency to say, "How can this little wrong possibly affect anyone?"

16:13 Caesarea Philippi was located several miles north of the Sea of Galilee, in the territory ruled by Philip. The influence of Greek and Roman culture was everywhere, and pagan temples and idols abounded. When Philip became ruler, he rebuilt and renamed the city after the emperor (Caesar) and himself. The city was originally called Caesarea, the same name as the capital city of Philip's brother Herod's territory.

16:13–17 The disciples answered Jesus' question with the common view—that Jesus was one of the great prophets come back to life. This belief may have stemmed from Deuteronomy 18:18, where God said he would raise up a prophet from among the people. (John the Baptist's Profile is in John 1; Elijah's Profile is in 1

16:14
Matt 14:2; 17:10; Mark 6:15; John 1:21

16:16
Matt 1:16; 16:20; John 11:27; Matt 4:3; Ps 42:2; Matt 26:63; Acts 14:15; Rom 9:26; 2 Cor 3:3; 6:16; 1 Thess 1:9; 1 Tim 3:15; 4:10; Heb 3:12; 9:14; 10:31; 12:22; Rev 7:2

16:17
John 1:42; 21:15-17

16:18
Matt 4:18; 11:23

16:19
Is 22:22; Rev 1:18; 3:7; Matt 18:18; John 20:23

16:20
Matt 8:4; John 11:27

14 And they said, "Some *say* John the Baptist; and others, Elijah; but still others, Jeremiah, or one of the prophets."
15 He ☆said to them, "But who do you say that I am?"
16 Simon Peter answered, "You are the Christ, the Son of the living God."
17 And Jesus said to him, "Blessed are you, Simon Barjona, because flesh and blood
did not reveal *this* to you, but My Father who is in heaven.
18 "I also say to you that you are Peter, and upon this rock I will build My church; and
the gates of Hades will not overpower it.
19 "I will give you the keys of the kingdom of heaven; and whatever you bind on earth
shall have been bound in heaven, and whatever you loose on earth shall have been loosed
in heaven."
20 Then He warned the disciples that they should tell no one that He was the Christ.

Jesus Predicts His Death the First Time
(110/Mark 8:31–9:1; Luke 9:21–27)

21 From that time Jesus began to show His disciples that He must go to Jerusalem,
and suffer many things from the elders and chief priests and scribes, and be killed, and
be raised up on the third day.
22 Peter took Him aside and began to rebuke Him, saying, "God forbid *it,* Lord! This
shall never happen to You."

Kings 18; and Jeremiah's Profile is in Jeremiah 2.) Peter, however, confessed Jesus as divine and as the promised and long-awaited Messiah. If Jesus were to ask you this question, how would you answer? Is he your Lord and Messiah?

16:18 The rock on which Jesus would build his church has been identified as: (1) Jesus himself (his work of salvation by dying for us on the cross); (2) Peter (the first great leader in the church at Jerusalem); (3) the confession of faith that Peter gave and that all subsequent true believers would give. It seems most likely that the rock refers to Peter as the leader of the church (for his function, not necessarily his character). Just as Peter had revealed the true identity of Christ, so Jesus revealed Peter's identity and role.

Later, Peter reminds Christians that they are the church built on the foundation of the apostles and prophets, with Jesus Christ as the cornerstone (1 Peter 2:4–6). All believers are joined into this church by faith in Jesus Christ as Savior, the same faith that Peter expressed here (see also Ephesians 2:20–21). Jesus praised Peter for his confession of faith. It is faith like Peter's that is the foundation of Christ's kingdom.

16:19 The meaning of this verse has been a subject of debate for centuries. Some say the keys represent the authority to carry out church discipline, legislation, and administration (18:15–18); while others say the keys give the authority to announce the forgiveness of sins (John 20:23). Still others say the keys may be the opportunity to bring people to the kingdom of heaven by presenting them with the message of salvation found in God's Word (Acts 15:7–9). The religious leaders thought they held the keys of the kingdom, and they tried to shut some people out. We cannot decide to open or close the kingdom of heaven for others, but God uses us to help others find the way inside. To all who believe in Christ and obey his words, the kingdom doors are swung wide open.

16:20 Jesus warned the disciples not to publicize Peter's confession because they did not yet fully understand the kind of Messiah he had come to be—not a military commander but a suffering servant. They needed to come to a full understanding of Jesus and their mission as disciples before they could proclaim it to others in a way that would not cause a rebellion. They would have a difficult time understanding what Jesus came to do until his earthly mission was complete.

16:21 The phrase "From that time" marks a turning point. In 4:17 it signaled Jesus' announcement of the kingdom of heaven. Here it points to his new emphasis on his death and resurrection. The disciples still didn't grasp Jesus' true purpose because of their preconceived notions about what the Messiah should be. This is the first of three times that Jesus predicted his death (see 17:22–23; 20:18 for others).

16:21–28 This passage corresponds to Daniel's prophecies: The Messiah would be cut off (Daniel 9:26), there would be a period of trouble (9:27), and the king would come in glory (7:13–14). The disciples would endure the same suffering as their King and, like him, would be rewarded in the end.

16:22 Peter, Jesus' friend and devoted follower who had just eloquently proclaimed Jesus' true identity, sought to protect him from the suffering he prophesied. But if Jesus hadn't suffered and died, Peter (and we) would have died in his sins. Great temptations can come from those who love us and seek to protect us. Be cautious of advice from a friend who says, "Surely God doesn't want you to face this." Often our most difficult temptations come from those who are only trying to protect us from discomfort.

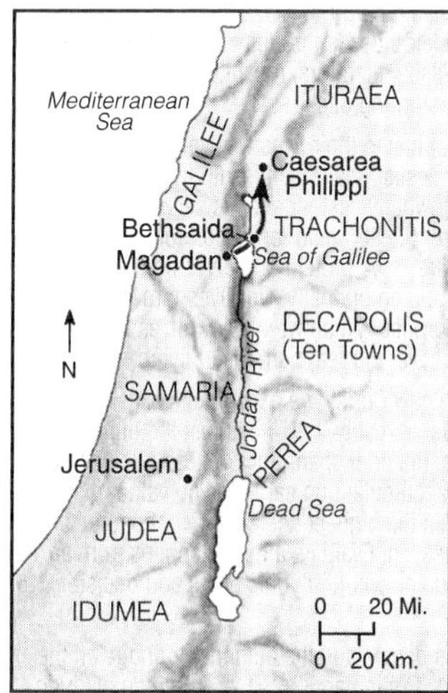

JOURNEY TO CAESAREA PHILIPPI
Jesus left Magadan, crossed the lake, and landed in Bethsaida. There he healed a man who had been born blind. From there, he and his disciples went to Caesarea Philippi, where Peter confessed Jesus as the Messiah and Son of God.

23 But He turned and said to Peter, "Get behind Me, Satan! You are a stumbling block
to Me; for you are not setting your mind on God's interests, but man's."
24 Then Jesus said to His disciples, "If anyone wishes to come after Me, he must deny
himself, and take up his cross and follow Me.
25 "For whoever wishes to save his life will lose it; but whoever loses his life for My sake
will find it.
26 "For what will it profit a man if he gains the whole world and forfeits his soul? Or
what will a man give in exchange for his soul?
27 "For the Son of Man is going to come in the glory of His Father with His angels, and
WILL THEN REPAY EVERY MAN ACCORDING TO HIS DEEDS.
28 "Truly I say to you, there are some of those who are standing here who will not taste
death until they see the Son of Man coming in His kingdom."

Jesus is Transfigured on the Mountain
(111/Mark 9:2-13; Luke 9:28-36)

17 Six days later Jesus ☆took with Him Peter and James and John his brother, and
☆led them up on a high mountain by themselves.
2 And He was transfigured before them; and His face shone like the sun, and His
garments became as white as light.
3 And behold, Moses and Elijah appeared to them, talking with Him.
4 Peter said to Jesus, "Lord, it is good for us to be here; if You wish, I will make three
tabernacles here, one for You, and one for Moses, and one for Elijah."
5 While he was still speaking, a bright cloud overshadowed them, and behold, a voice
out of the cloud said, "This is My beloved Son, with whom I am well-pleased; listen to
Him!"
6 When the disciples heard *this,* they fell face down to the ground and were terrified.
7 And Jesus came to *them* and touched them and said, "Get up, and do not be afraid."

16:23 Matt 4:10

16:24 Matt 10:38; Luke 14:27

16:25 Matt 10:39

16:27 Matt 8:20; 10:23; 24:3, 27, 37, 39; 26:64; Mark 13:26; Luke 21:27; John 21:22; Acts 1:11; 1 Cor 15:23; 1 Thess 1:10; 4:16; 2 Thess 1:7, 10; 2:1, 8; James 5:7f; 2 Pet 1:16; 3:4, 12; 1 John 2:28; Rev 1:7; Ps 62:12; Prov 24:12; Rom 2:6; 14:12; 1 Cor 3:13; 2 Cor 5:10; Eph 6:8; Col 3:25; Rev 2:23; 20:12; 22:12

17:1 Matt 26:37; Mark 5:37; 13:3

17:5 Mark 1:11; Luke 3:22; 2 Pet 1:17f; Is 42:1; Matt 3:17; 12:18

17:7 Matt 14:27

16:23 In his wilderness temptations, Jesus heard the message that he could achieve greatness without dying (4:6). Here he heard the same message from Peter. Peter had just recognized Jesus as Messiah; here, however, he forsook God's perspective and evaluated the situation from a human one. Satan is always trying to get us to leave God out of the picture. Jesus rebuked Peter for this attitude.

16:24 When Jesus used this picture of his followers taking up their crosses to follow him, the disciples knew what he meant. Crucifixion was a common Roman method of execution, and condemned criminals had to carry their crosses through the streets to the execution site. Following Jesus, therefore, meant a true commitment, the risk of death, and no turning back (see 10:39).

16:25 The possibility of losing their lives was very real for the disciples as well as for Jesus. Real discipleship implies real commitment—pledging our whole existence to his service. If we try to save our physical life from death, pain, or discomfort, we may risk losing our true eternal life. If we protect ourselves from pain, we begin to die spiritually and emotionally. Our lives turn inward, and we lose our intended purpose. When we give our lives in service to Christ, however, we discover the real purpose of living.

16:26 When we don't know Christ, we make choices as though this life were all we have. In reality, this life is just the introduction to eternity. How we live this brief span, however, determines our eternal state. What we accumulate on earth has no value in purchasing eternal life. Even the highest social or civic honors cannot earn us entrance into heaven. Evaluate all that happens from an eternal perspective, and you will find your values and decisions changing.

16:27 Jesus Christ has been given the authority to judge all the earth (Romans 14:9–11; Philippians 2:9–11). Although his judgment is already working in our lives, there is a future, final judgment when Christ returns (25:31–46) and everyone's life is reviewed and evaluated. This will not be confined to unbelievers; Christians too will face a judgment. Their eternal destiny is secure, but Jesus will look at how they handled gifts, opportunities, and responsibilities in order to determine their heavenly rewards. At the time of judgment, God will deliver the righteous and condemn the wicked. We should not judge others' salvation; that is God's work.

16:28 Because all the disciples died *before* Christ's return, many believe that Jesus' words were fulfilled at the transfiguration when Peter, James, and John saw his glory (17:1–3). Others say this statement refers to Pentecost (Acts 2) and the beginning of Christ's church. In either case, certain disciples were eyewitnesses to the power and glory of Christ's kingdom.

17:1ff The transfiguration was a vision, a brief glimpse of the true glory of the King (16:27–28). This was a special revelation of Jesus' divinity to three of the disciples, and it was God's divine affirmation of everything Jesus had done and was about to do.

17:3–5 Moses and Elijah were the two greatest prophets in the Old Testament. Moses represents the law, or the old covenant. He wrote the Pentateuch, and he predicted the coming of a great prophet (Deuteronomy 18:15–19). Elijah represents the prophets who foretold the coming of the Messiah (Malachi 4:5–6). Moses' and Elijah's presence with Jesus confirmed Jesus' Messianic mission—to fulfill God's law and the words of God's prophets. Just as God's voice in the cloud over Mount Sinai gave authority to his law (Exodus 19:9), so God's voice at the transfiguration gave authority to Jesus' words.

17:4 Peter wanted to build three tabernacles (shelters) for these three great men to stay to show how the Feast of Booths (also called the Feast of Tabernacles) was fulfilled in the coming of God's kingdom. Peter had the right idea about Christ, but his timing was wrong. Peter wanted to act, but this was a time for worship and adoration. He wanted to capture the moment, but he was supposed to learn and move on.

17:5 Jesus is more than just a great leader, a good example, a good influence, or a great prophet. He is the Son of God. When you understand this profound truth, the only adequate response is worship. When you have a correct understanding of Christ, you will obey him.

8 And lifting up their eyes, they saw no one except Jesus Himself alone.
9 As they were coming down from the mountain, Jesus commanded them, saying, "Tell
the vision to no one until the Son of Man has risen from the dead."
10 And His disciples asked Him, "Why then do the scribes say that Elijah must come
first?"
11 And He answered and said, "Elijah is coming and will restore all things;
12 but I say to you that Elijah already came, and they did not recognize him, but did to
him whatever they wished. So also the Son of Man is going to suffer at their hands."
13 Then the disciples understood that He had spoken to them about John the Baptist.

17:9 Mark 9:9-13; Matt 8:4; Matt 8:20; 17:12, 22; Matt 16:21

17:10 Mal 4:5; Matt 11:14; 16:14

17:12 Matt 8:20; 17:9, 22

Jesus Heals a Demon-Possessed Boy

(112/Mark 9:14-29; Luke 9:37-43)

14 When they came to the crowd, a man came up to Jesus, falling on his knees before
Him and saying,
15 "Lord, have mercy on my son, for he is a lunatic and is very ill; for he often falls into
the fire and often into the water.
16 "I brought him to Your disciples, and they could not cure him."
17 And Jesus answered and said, "You unbelieving and perverted generation, how long
shall I be with you? How long shall I put up with you? Bring him here to Me."
18 And Jesus rebuked him, and the demon came out of him, and the boy was cured at
once.
19 Then the disciples came to Jesus privately and said, "Why could we not drive it out?"
20 And He ☆said to them, "Because of the littleness of your faith; for truly I say to you,
if you have faith the size of a mustard seed, you will say to this mountain, 'Move from
here to there,' and it will move; and nothing will be impossible to you.
21 ["[28]But this kind does not go out except by prayer and fasting."]

17:15 Matt 4:24

17:20 Matt 21:21f; Mark 11:23f; Luke 17:6; Matt 13:31; Luke 17:6; Matt 17:9; 1 Cor 13:2; Mark 9:23; John 11:40

17:21 Mark 9:29

Jesus Predicts his Death the Second Time

(113/Mark 9:30-32; Luke 9:44-45)

22 And while they were gathering together in Galilee, Jesus said to them, "The Son of
Man is going to be delivered into the hands of men;
23 and they will kill Him, and He will be raised on the third day." And they were deeply grieved.

17:23 Matt 16:21; 17:9

28 Early mss do not contain this v

17:9 Jesus told Peter, James, and John not to tell anyone what they had seen until after his resurrection because Jesus knew that they didn't fully understand it and could not explain what they didn't understand. Their question (17:10ff) revealed their misunderstandings. They knew that Jesus was the Messiah, but they had much more to learn about the significance of his death and resurrection.

17:10–12 Based on Malachi 4:5–6, the scribes believed that Elijah must appear before the Messiah would appear. Jesus referred to John the Baptist, not to the Old Testament prophet Elijah. John the Baptist took on Elijah's prophetic role—boldly confronting sin and pointing people to God. Malachi had prophesied that a prophet like Elijah would come (Malachi 4:5).

17:17 The disciples had been given the authority to do the healing, but they had not yet learned how to appropriate the power of God. Jesus' frustration is with the unbelieving and unresponsive generation. His disciples were merely a reflection of that attitude in this instance. Jesus' purpose was not to criticize the disciples, but to encourage them to greater faith.

17:17–20 The disciples were unable to drive out this demon, and they asked Jesus why. He pointed to their lack of faith. It is the power of God, not our faith, that moves mountains, but faith must be present to do so. The mustard seed was the smallest particle imaginable. Even small or undeveloped faith would have been sufficient. Perhaps the disciples had tried to drive out the demon with their own ability rather than God's. There is great power in even a little faith when God is with us. If we feel weak or powerless as Christians, we should examine our faith, making sure we are trusting not in our own abilities to produce results, but in God's.

17:20 Jesus wasn't condemning the disciples for substandard faith; he was trying to show how important faith would be in their future ministry. If you are facing a problem that seems as big and immovable as a mountain, turn your eyes from the mountain and look to Christ for more faith. Only then will your work for him become useful and vibrant.

17:22–23 Once again Jesus predicted his death (see also 16:21); but more important, he told of his resurrection. Unfortunately, the disciples heard only the first part of Jesus' words and became discouraged. They couldn't understand why Jesus wanted to go back to Jerusalem where he would walk right into trouble.

The disciples didn't fully comprehend the purpose of Jesus' death and resurrection until Pentecost (Acts 2). We shouldn't get upset at ourselves for being slow to understand everything about Jesus. After all, the disciples were with him, saw his miracles, heard his words, and still had difficulty understanding. Despite their questions and doubts, however, they believed. We should do no less.

17:22–23 The disciples didn't understand why Jesus kept talking about his death because they expected him to set up a political kingdom. His death, they thought, would dash their hopes. They didn't know that Jesus' death and resurrection would make his kingdom possible.

Peter Finds the Coin in the Fish's Mouth
(114)

24 When they came to Capernaum, those who collected the [29]two-drachma *tax* came
to Peter and said, "Does your teacher not pay the [29]two-drachma *tax?*"
25 He ☆said, "Yes." And when he came into the house, Jesus spoke to him first, saying,
"What do you think, Simon? From whom do the kings of the earth collect customs or
poll-tax, from their sons or from strangers?"
26 When Peter said, "From strangers," Jesus said to him, "Then the sons are exempt.
27 "However, so that we do not offend them, go to the sea and throw in a hook, and
take the first fish that comes up; and when you open its mouth, you will find [30]a shekel.
Take that and give it to them for you and Me."

17:24 Ex 30:13; 38:26
17:25 Rom 13:7; Matt 22:17, 19
17:27 Matt 5:29, 30; 18:6, 8, 9; Mark 9:42, 43, 45, 47; Luke 17:2; John 6:61; 1 Cor 8:13

The Disciples Argue about Who Would Be the Greatest
(115/Mark 9:33-37; Luke 9:46-48)

18 At that time the disciples came to Jesus and said, "Who then is greatest in the kingdom of heaven?"
2 And He called a child to Himself and set him before them,
3 and said, "Truly I say to you, unless you are converted and become like children,
you will not enter the kingdom of heaven.
4 "Whoever then humbles himself as this child, he is the greatest in the kingdom of
heaven.
5 "And whoever receives one such child in My name receives Me;
6 but whoever causes one of these little ones who believe in Me to stumble, it would
be better for him to have a heavy millstone hung around his neck, and to be drowned in
the depth of the sea.

18:1 Luke 22:24
18:3 Matt 19:14; Mark 10:15; Luke 18:17; 1 Cor 14:20; 1 Pet 2:2
18:6 Mark 9:42; Luke 17:2; 1 Cor 8:12; Matt 17:27

Jesus Warns against Temptation
(117/Mark 9:42-50)

7 "Woe to the world because of *its* stumbling blocks! For it is inevitable that stumbling
blocks come; but woe to that man through whom the stumbling block comes!
8 "If your hand or your foot causes you to stumble, cut it off and throw it from you; it

18:7 Luke 17:1; 1 Cor 11:19; 1 Tim 4:1
18:8 Matt 5:30; Mark 9:43

29 Equivalent to two denarii or two days' wages, paid as a temple tax **30** Lit *standard coin,* which was a shekel

---

17:24 All Jewish males had to pay a temple tax to support temple upkeep (Exodus 30:11–16), called here the two-drachma tax. A drachma was a day's wage for a laborer. Tax collectors set up booths to collect these taxes. Only Matthew records this incident—perhaps because he had been a tax collector himself.

17:24–27 As usual, Peter answered a question without really knowing the answer, putting Jesus and the disciples in an awkward position. Jesus used this situation, however, to emphasize his kingly role. Just as kings pay no taxes and collect none from their family, Jesus, the King, owed no taxes. But Jesus supplied the tax payment for both himself and Peter rather than offend those who didn't understand his kingship. Although Jesus supplied the tax money, Peter had to go and get it. Ultimately all that we have comes to us from God's supply, but he may want us to be active in the process.

17:24–27 As God's people, we are foreigners on earth because our loyalty is always to our real King—Jesus. Still we have to cooperate with the authorities and be responsible citizens. An ambassador to another country keeps the local laws in order to represent well the one who sent him. We are Christ's ambassadors (2 Corinthians 5:20). Are you being a good foreign ambassador for him to this world?

18:1 From Mark's Gospel we learn that Jesus precipitated this conversation by asking the disciples what they had been discussing among themselves earlier (Mark 9:33–34).

18:1–4 Jesus used a child to help his self-centered disciples get the point. We are not to be *childish* (like the disciples, arguing over petty issues), but rather *childlike,* with humble and sincere hearts. Are you being childlike or childish?

18:3–4 The disciples had become so preoccupied with the organization of Jesus' earthly kingdom that they had lost sight of its divine purpose. Instead of seeking a place of service, they sought positions of advantage. It is easy to lose our eternal perspective and compete for promotions or status in the church. It is difficult to identify with "children"—weak and dependent people with no status or influence.

18:6 Children are trusting by nature. They trust adults, and through that trust their capacity to trust God grows. God holds parents and other adults who influence young children accountable for how they affect these little ones' ability to trust. Jesus warned that anyone who turns little children away from faith will receive severe punishment.

18:7ff Jesus warned the disciples about two ways to cause "little ones" to sin: tempting them (18:7–9) and neglecting or demeaning them (18:10–14). As leaders, we are to help young people or new believers avoid anything or anyone that could cause them to stumble in their faith and lead them to sin. We must never take lightly the spiritual education and protection of the young in age and in the faith.

18:8–9 We must remove stumbling blocks that cause us to sin. This does not mean to cut off a part of the body; it means that any person, program, or teaching in the church that threatens the spiritual growth of the body must be removed. For the individual, any relationship, practice, or activity that leads to sin should be stopped. Jesus says it would be better to go to heaven with one hand than to hell with both. Sin, of course, affects more than our hands; it affects our minds and hearts.

is better for you to enter life crippled or lame, than to have two hands or two feet and be
cast into the eternal fire.
9 "If your eye causes you to stumble, pluck it out and throw it from you. It is better for
you to enter life with one eye, than to have two eyes and be cast into the fiery hell.

Jesus Warns against Looking Down on Others
(118)

10 "See that you do not despise one of these little ones, for I say to you that their angels
in heaven continually see the face of My Father who is in heaven.
11 ["[31]For the Son of Man has come to save that which was lost.]
12 "What do you think? If any man has a hundred sheep, and one of them has gone
astray, does he not leave the ninety-nine on the mountains and go and search for the
one that is straying?
13 "If it turns out that he finds it, truly I say to you, he rejoices over it more than over
the ninety-nine which have not gone astray.
14 "So it is not *the* will of your Father who is in heaven that one of these little ones
perish.

Jesus Teaches How to Treat a Believer Who Sins
(119)

15 "If your brother sins[32], go and show him his fault in private; if he listens to you, you
have won your brother.
16 "But if he does not listen *to you,* take one or two more with you, so that BY THE MOUTH
OF TWO OR THREE WITNESSES EVERY FACT MAY BE CONFIRMED.
17 "If he refuses to listen to them, tell it to the church; and if he refuses to listen even to
the church, let him be to you as a Gentile and a tax collector.
18 "Truly I say to you, whatever you bind on earth shall have been bound in heaven; and
whatever you loose on earth shall have been loosed in heaven.
19 "Again I say to you, that if two of you agree on earth about anything that they may
ask, it shall be done for them by My Father who is in heaven.
20 "For where two or three have gathered together in My name, I am there in their
midst."

Jesus Tells the Parable of the Unforgiving Debtor
(120)

21 Then Peter came and said to Him, "Lord, how often shall my brother sin against me
and I forgive him? Up to seven times?"

31 Early mss do not contain this v **32** Late mss add *against you*

18:9 Matt 5:29; Mark 9:47; Matt 5:22
18:10 Luke 1:19; Acts 12:15; Rev 8:2
18:11 Luke 19:10
18:12 Luke 15:4-7
18:15 Lev 19:17; Luke 17:3; Gal 6:1; 2 Thess 3:15; James 5:19
18:16 Deut 19:15; John 8:17; 2 Cor 13:1; 1 Tim 5:19; Heb 10:28
18:17 1 Cor 6:1ff; 2 Thess 3:6, 14f
18:18 Matt 16:19; John 20:23
18:19 Matt 7:7
18:20 Matt 28:20
18:21 Matt 18:15; Luke 17:4

18:10 Our concern for children must match God's treatment of them. Certain angels are assigned to watch over children, and they have direct access to God. These words ring out sharply in cultures where children are taken lightly, ignored, or aborted. If their angels have constant access to God, the least we can do is to allow children to approach us easily in spite of our far too busy schedules.

18:14 Just as a shepherd is concerned enough about one lost sheep to go search the hills for it, so God is concerned about every human being he has created (he is "not wishing for any to perish," 2 Peter 3:9). You come in contact with children who need Christ at home, at school, in church, and in the neighborhood. Steer them toward Christ by your example, your words, and your acts of kindness.

18:15–17 These are Jesus' guidelines for dealing with those who sin against us. They were meant for (1) Christians, not unbelievers, (2) sins committed against *you* and not others, and (3) conflict resolution in the context of the church, not the community at large. Jesus' words are not a license for a frontal attack on every person who hurts or slights us. They are not a license to start a destructive gossip campaign or to call for a church trial. They are designed to reconcile those who disagree so that all Christians can live in harmony.

When someone wrongs us, we often do the opposite of what Jesus recommends. We turn away in hatred or resentment, seek revenge, or engage in gossip. By contrast, we should go to that person *first,* as difficult as that may be. Then we should forgive that person as often as he or she needs it (18:21–22). This will create a much better chance of restoring the relationship.

18:18 This *binding* and *loosing* refers to the decisions of the church in conflicts. Among believers, there is no court of appeals beyond the church. Ideally, the church's decisions should be God-guided and based on discernment of his Word. Believers have the responsibility, therefore, to bring their problems to the church, and the church has the responsibility to use God's guidance in seeking to resolve conflicts. Handling problems God's way will have an impact now and for eternity.

18:19–20 Jesus looked ahead to a new day when he would be present with his followers not in body, but through his Holy Spirit. In the body of believers (the church), the sincere agreement of two people is more powerful than the superficial agreement of thousands, because Christ's Holy Spirit is with them. Two or more believers, *filled with the Holy Spirit,* will pray according to God's will, not their own; thus their requests will be granted.

22 Jesus ☆said to him, "I do not say to you, up to seven times, but up to seventy times seven.
23 "For this reason the kingdom of heaven may be compared to a king who wished to settle accounts with his slaves.
24 "When he had begun to settle *them,* one who owed him [33]ten thousand talents was brought to him.
25 "But since he did not have *the means* to repay, his lord commanded him to be sold, along with his wife and children and all that he had, and repayment to be made.
26 "So the slave fell *to the ground* and prostrated himself before him, saying, 'Have patience with me and I will repay you everything.'
27 "And the lord of that slave felt compassion and released him and forgave him the debt.
28 "But that slave went out and found one of his fellow slaves who owed him a hundred [34]denarii; and he seized him and *began* to choke *him,* saying, 'Pay back what you owe.'
29 "So his fellow slave fell *to the ground* and *began* to plead with him, saying, 'Have patience with me and I will repay you.'
30 "But he was unwilling and went and threw him in prison until he should pay back what was owed.
31 "So when his fellow slaves saw what had happened, they were deeply grieved and came and reported to their lord all that had happened.
32 "Then summoning him, his lord ☆said to him, 'You wicked slave, I forgave you all that debt because you pleaded with me.
33 'Should you not also have had mercy on your fellow slave, in the same way that I had mercy on you?'
34 "And his lord, moved with anger, handed him over to the torturers until he should repay all that was owed him.
35 "My heavenly Father will also do the same to you, if each of you does not forgive his brother from your heart."

18:22 Gen 4:24
18:23 Matt 13:24; Matt 25:19
18:25 Luke 7:42; Ex 21:2; Lev 25:39; 2 Kin 4:1; Neh 5:5
18:26 Matt 8:2
18:27 Luke 7:42
18:33 Matt 6:12; Eph 4:32
18:35 Matt 6:14

6. Jesus faces conflict with the religious leaders

Jesus Teaches about Marriage and Divorce
(173/Mark 10:1-12)

19 When Jesus had finished these words, He departed from Galilee and came into the region of Judea beyond the Jordan;
2 and large crowds followed Him, and He healed them there.
3 *Some* Pharisees came to Jesus, testing Him and asking, "Is it lawful *for a man* to divorce his wife for any reason at all?"
4 And He answered and said, "Have you not read that He who created *them* from the beginning MADE THEM MALE AND FEMALE,
5 and said, 'FOR THIS REASON A MAN SHALL LEAVE HIS FATHER AND MOTHER AND BE JOINED TO HIS WIFE, AND THE TWO SHALL BECOME ONE FLESH'?
6 "So they are no longer two, but one flesh. What therefore God has joined together, let no man separate."

19:1 Matt 7:28
19:2 Matt 4:23
19:3 Matt 5:31
19:4 Gen 1:27; 5:2
19:5 Gen 2:24; Eph 5:31; 1 Cor 6:16

33 A talent was worth more than fifteen years' wages of a laborer **34** The denarius was a day's wages

18:22 The rabbis taught that people should forgive those who offend them—but only three times. Peter, trying to be especially generous, asked Jesus if seven (the "perfect" number) was enough times to forgive someone. But Jesus answered, "Seventy times seven," meaning that we shouldn't even keep track of how many times we forgive someone. We should always forgive those who are truly repentant, no matter how many times they ask.

18:30 In Bible times, serious consequences awaited those who could not pay their debts. A person lending money could seize the borrower who couldn't pay and force him or his family to work until the debt was paid. The debtor could also be thrown into prison, or his family could be sold into slavery to help pay off the debt. It was hoped that the debtor, while in prison, would sell off his landholdings or that relatives would pay the debt. If not, the debtor could remain in prison for life.

18:35 Because God has forgiven all our sins, we should not withhold forgiveness from others. Realizing how completely Christ has forgiven us should produce a free and generous attitude of forgiveness toward others. When we don't forgive others, we are setting ourselves outside and above Christ's law of love.

19:3–12 John was put in prison and killed, at least in part, for his public opinions on marriage and divorce, so the Pharisees hoped to trap Jesus too. They were trying to trick Jesus by having him choose sides in a theological controversy. Two schools of thought represented two opposing views of divorce. One group supported divorce for almost any reason. The other believed that divorce could be allowed only for marital unfaithfulness. This conflict hinged on how each group interpreted Deuteronomy 24:1–4. In his answer, however, Jesus focused on marriage rather than divorce. He pointed out that God intended marriage to be permanent and gave four reasons for the importance of marriage (19:4–6).

19:7 Deut 24:1-4; Matt 5:31

7 They ☆said to Him, "Why then did Moses command to GIVE HER A CERTIFICATE OF DIVORCE AND SEND *her* AWAY?"
8 He ☆said to them, "Because of your hardness of heart Moses permitted you to divorce your wives; but from the beginning it has not been this way.

19:9 Matt 5:32

9 "And I say to you, whoever divorces his wife, except for immorality, and marries another woman commits adultery."
10 The disciples ☆said to Him, "If the relationship of the man with his wife is like this, it is better not to marry."

19:11 1 Cor 7:7ff; Matt 13:11

11 But He said to them, "Not all men *can* accept this statement, but *only* those to whom it has been given.
12 "For there are eunuchs who were born that way from their mother's womb; and there are eunuchs who were made eunuchs by men; and there are *also* eunuchs who made themselves eunuchs for the sake of the kingdom of heaven. He who is able to accept *this*, let him accept *it*."

Jesus Blesses Little Children
(174/Mark 10:13-16, Luke 18:15-17)

13 Then *some* children were brought to Him so that He might lay His hands on them and pray; and the disciples rebuked them.

JESUS AND FORGIVENESS

Jesus forgave	*Reference*
the paralytic lowered on a mat through the roof.	Matthew 9:2–8
the woman caught in adultery.	John 8:3–11
the woman who anointed his feet with oil.	Luke 7:47–50
Peter, for denying he knew Jesus.	John 18:15–18, 25–27; 21:15–19
the criminal on the cross.	Luke 23:39–43
the people who crucified him.	Luke 23:34

Jesus not only taught frequently about forgiveness, he also demonstrated his own willingness to forgive. Here are several examples that should be an encouragement to recognize his willingness to forgive us also.

19:7–8 This law is found in Deuteronomy 24:1–4. In Moses' day, as well as in Jesus' day, the practice of marriage fell far short of God's intention. The same is true today. Jesus said that Moses gave this law only because of the people's hard hearts—permanent marriage was God's intention. But because sinful human nature made divorce inevitable, Moses instituted some laws to help its victims. These were civil laws designed especially to protect the women who, in that culture, were quite vulnerable when living alone. Because of Moses' law, a man could no longer just throw his wife out—he had to write a formal certificate of divorce. This was a radical step toward civil rights, for it made men think twice about divorce. God designed marriage to be indissoluble. Instead of looking for reasons to leave each other, married couples should concentrate on how to stay together (19:3–9).

19:10–12 Although divorce was relatively easy in Old Testament times (19:7), it is not what God originally intended. Couples should decide against divorce from the start and build their marriage on mutual commitment. There are also many good reasons for not marrying, one being to have more time to work for God's kingdom. Don't assume that God wants everyone to marry. For many it may be better if they don't. Be sure that you prayerfully seek God's will before you plunge into the lifelong commitment of marriage.

19:12 A "eunuch" is an emasculated male—a man with no testicles.

19:12 Some have physical limitations that prevent their marrying, while others choose not to marry because, in their particular situation, they can serve God better as single people. Jesus was not teaching us to avoid marriage because it is inconvenient or takes away our freedom. That would be selfishness. A good reason to remain single is to use the time and freedom to serve God. Paul elaborates on this in 1 Corinthians 7.

19:13–15 The disciples must have forgotten what Jesus had said about children (18:4–6). Jesus wanted little children to come because he loves them and because they have the kind of attitude needed to approach God. He didn't mean that heaven is only for children, but that people need childlike attitudes of trust in God. The receptiveness of little children was a great contrast to the stubbornness of the religious leaders who let their education and sophistication stand in the way of the simple faith needed to believe in Jesus.

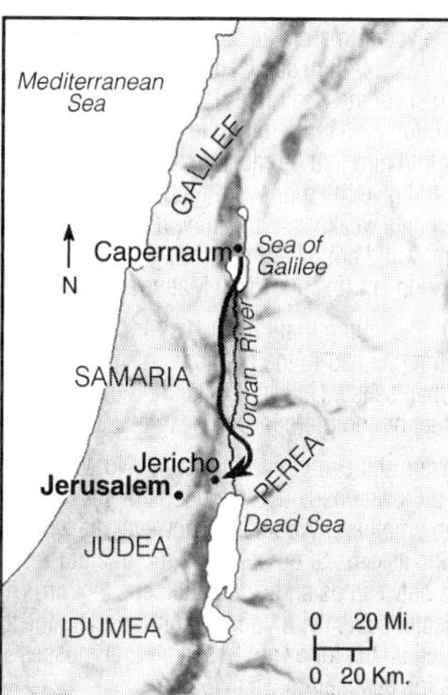

JESUS TRAVELS TOWARD JERUSALEM
Jesus left Galilee for the last time—heading toward Jerusalem and death. He again crossed the Jordan, spending some time in Perea before going on to Jericho.

14 But Jesus said, "Let the children alone, and do not hinder them from coming to
Me; for the kingdom of heaven belongs to such as these."
15 After laying His hands on them, He departed from there.

19:14 Matt 18:3; Mark 10:15; Luke 18:17; 1 Cor 14:20; 1 Pet 2:2; Matt 5:3

Jesus Speaks to the Rich Young Man
(175/Mark 10:17-31; Luke 18:18-30)

16 And someone came to Him and said, "Teacher, what good thing shall I do that I
may obtain eternal life?"
17 And He said to him, "Why are you asking Me about what is good? There is *only*
One who is good; but if you wish to enter into life, keep the commandments."
18 *Then* he ☆said to Him, "Which ones?" And Jesus said, "YOU SHALL NOT COMMIT
MURDER; YOU SHALL NOT COMMIT ADULTERY; YOU SHALL NOT STEAL; YOU SHALL
NOT BEAR FALSE WITNESS;
19 HONOR YOUR FATHER AND MOTHER; and YOU SHALL LOVE YOUR NEIGHBOR AS
YOURSELF."
20 The young man ☆said to Him, "All these things I have kept; what am I still lacking?"
21 Jesus said to him, "If you wish to be complete, go *and* sell your possessions and give
to *the* poor, and you will have treasure in heaven; and come, follow Me."
22 But when the young man heard this statement, he went away grieving; for he was
one who owned much property.
23 And Jesus said to His disciples, "Truly I say to you, it is hard for a rich man to enter
the kingdom of heaven.
24 "Again I say to you, it is easier for a camel to go through the eye of a needle, than for
a rich man to enter the kingdom of God."
25 When the disciples heard *this,* they were very astonished and said, "Then who can
be saved?"
26 And looking at *them* Jesus said to them, "With people this is impossible, but with
God all things are possible."
27 Then Peter said to Him, "Behold, we have left everything and followed You; what
then will there be for us?"
28 And Jesus said to them, "Truly I say to you, that you who have followed Me, in the
regeneration when the Son of Man will sit on His glorious throne, you also shall sit upon
twelve thrones, judging the twelve tribes of Israel.
29 "And everyone who has left houses or brothers or sisters or father or mother [35]or

19:16 Luke 10:25-28; Matt 25:46

19:17 Lev 18:5; Neh 9:29; Ezek 20:21

19:18 Ex 20:13-16; Deut 5:17-20

19:19 Ex 20:12; Deut 5:16; Lev 19:18

19:21 Luke 12:33; 16:9; Acts 2:45; 4:34f; Matt 6:20

19:23 Matt 13:22; Mark 10:23f; Luke 18:24

19:24 Mark 10:25; Luke 18:25

19:26 Gen 18:14; Job 42:2; Jer 32:17; Zech 8:6; Mark 10:27; Luke 1:37; 18:27

19:28 Matt 25:31; Luke 22:30; Rev 3:21; 4:4; 11:16; 20:4

19:29 Matt 6:33; Mark 10:29f; Luke 18:29f

35 One early ms adds *or wife*

19:16 To this man seeking assurance of eternal life, Jesus pointed out that salvation does not come from good deeds unaccompanied by love for God. The man needed a whole new starting point. Instead of adding another commandment to keep or good deed to perform, the young man needed to submit humbly to the lordship of Christ.

19:17 In response to the young man's question about how to obtain eternal life, Jesus told him to keep God's Ten Commandments. Jesus then listed six of them, all referring to relationships with others. When the young man replied that he had kept the commandments, Jesus told him that he must do something more—sell everything and give the money to the poor. Jesus' statement exposed the man's weakness. In reality, his wealth was his god, his idol, and he would not give it up. Thus he violated the first and greatest commandment (Exodus 20:3; Matthew 22:36–40).

19:21 When Jesus told this young man that he would "be complete" if he gave everything he had to the poor, Jesus wasn't speaking in the temporal, human sense. He was explaining how to be justified and made perfect or complete in God's sight.

19:21 Should all believers sell everything they own? No. We are responsible to care for our own needs and the needs of our families so as not to be a burden on others. We should, however, be willing to give up anything if God asks us to do so. This kind of attitude allows nothing to come between us and God and keeps us from using our God-given wealth selfishly. If you are comforted by the fact that Christ did not tell all his followers to sell all their possessions, then you may be too attached to what you have.

19:22 We cannot love God with all our hearts and yet keep our money to ourselves. Loving him totally means using our money in ways that please him.

19:24 Because it is impossible for a camel to go through the eye of a needle, it appears impossible for a rich person to get into the kingdom of God. Jesus explained, however, that "with God all things are possible" (19:26). Even rich people can enter the kingdom if God brings them in. Faith in Christ, not in self or riches, is what counts. On what are you counting for salvation?

19:25–26 The disciples were astonished. They thought that if anyone could be saved, it would be the rich, whom their culture considered especially blessed by God.

19:27 In the Bible, God gives rewards to his people according to his justice. In the Old Testament, obedience often brought reward in this life (Deuteronomy 28), but obedience and immediate reward are not always linked. If they were, good people would always be rich, and suffering would always be a sign of sin. As believers, our true reward is God's presence and power through the Holy Spirit. Later, in eternity, we will be rewarded for our faith and service. If material rewards in this life came to us for every faithful deed, we would be tempted to boast about our achievements and act out of wrong motivations.

19:29 Jesus assured the disciples that anyone who gives up something valuable for his sake will be repaid many times over in this life, although not necessarily in the same form. For example, a person may be rejected by his or her family for accepting Christ, but he or she will gain the larger family of believers.

children or farms for My name's sake, will receive many times as much, and will inherit
eternal life.

19:30 Matt 20:16; Mark 10:31; Luke 13:30

30 "But many *who are* first will be last; and *the* last, first.

Jesus Tells the Parable of the Workers Paid Equally
(176)

20:1 Matt 13:24; Matt 21:28, 33

20 "For the kingdom of heaven is like a landowner who went out early in the morning to hire laborers for his vineyard.
2 "When he had agreed with the laborers for a [36]denarius for the day, he sent them
into his vineyard.
3 "And he went out about the [37]third hour and saw others standing idle in the market
place;
4 and to those he said, 'You also go into the vineyard, and whatever is right I will give
you.' And *so* they went.
5 "Again he went out about the [38]sixth and the ninth hour, and did the same thing.
6 "And about the [39]eleventh *hour* he went out and found others standing *around;* and
he ☆said to them, 'Why have you been standing here idle all day long?'
7 "They ☆said to him, 'Because no one hired us.' He ☆said to them, 'You go into the
vineyard too.'

20:8 Lev 19:13; Deut 24:15; Luke 8:3

8 "When evening came, the owner of the vineyard ☆said to his foreman, 'Call the laborers and pay them their wages, beginning with the last *group* to the first.'
9 "When those *hired* about the eleventh hour came, each one received a [36]denarius.
10 "When those *hired* first came, they thought that they would receive more; but each
of them also received a denarius.
11 "When they received it, they grumbled at the landowner,

20:12 Jon 4:8; Luke 12:55; James 1:11

12 saying, 'These last men have worked *only* one hour, and you have made them equal
to us who have borne the burden and the scorching heat of the day.'

20:13 Matt 22:12; 26:50

13 "But he answered and said to one of them, 'Friend, I am doing you no wrong; did
you not agree with me for a denarius?
14 'Take what is yours and go, but I wish to give to this last man the same as to you.

20:15 Deut 15:9; Matt 6:23; Mark 7:22

15 'Is it not lawful for me to do what I wish with what is my own? Or is your eye envious
because I am generous?'
16 "So the last shall be first, and the first last."

20:16 Matt 19:30; Mark 10:31; Luke 13:30

Jesus Predicts His Death the Third Time
(177/Mark 10:32-34; Luke 18:31-34)

17 As Jesus was about to go up to Jerusalem, He took the twelve *disciples* aside by themselves, and on the way He said to them,

20:18 Matt 16:21

18 "Behold, we are going up to Jerusalem; and the Son of Man will be delivered to the
chief priests and scribes, and they will condemn Him to death,

20:19 Matt 27:2; Acts 2:23; 3:13; 4:27; 21:11; Matt 16:21; 17:23; Luke 18:32f

19 and will hand Him over to the Gentiles to mock and scourge and crucify *Him,* and
on the third day He will be raised up."

36 The denarius was a day's wages **37** I.e. 9 a.m. **38** I.e. noon and 3 p.m. **39** I.e. 5 p.m.

19:30 Jesus turned the world's values upside down. Consider the most powerful or well-known people in our world—how many got where they are by being humble, self-effacing, and gentle? Not many! But in the life to come, the last will be first—if they got in last place by choosing to follow Jesus. Don't forfeit eternal rewards for temporary benefits. Be willing to make sacrifices now for greater rewards later. Be willing to accept human disapproval, while knowing that you have God's approval.

20:1ff Jesus further clarified the membership rules of the kingdom of heaven—entrance is by God's grace alone. In this parable, God is the landowner, and believers are the laborers. This parable speaks especially to those who feel superior because of heritage or favored position, to those who feel superior because they have spent so much time with Christ, and to new believers as reassurance of God's grace.

20:15 This parable is not about rewards but about salvation. It is a strong teaching about *grace,* God's generosity. We shouldn't begrudge those who turn to God in the last moments of life, because, in reality, *no one* deserves eternal life.

Many people we don't expect to see in the kingdom will be there. The criminal who repented as he was dying (Luke 23:40–43) will be there along with people who have believed and served God for many years. Do you resent God's gracious acceptance of the despised, the outcast, and the sinners who have turned to him for forgiveness? Are you ever jealous of what God has given to another person? Instead, focus on God's gracious benefits to you, and be thankful for what you have.

20:17–19 Jesus predicted his death and resurrection for the third time (see 16:21 and 17:22–23 for the first two times). But the disciples still didn't understand what he meant. They continued to argue greedily over their positions in Christ's kingdom (20:20–28).

Jesus Teaches about Serving Others
(178/Mark 10:35-45)

20 Then the mother of the sons of Zebedee came to Jesus with her sons, bowing down
and making a request of Him.
21 And He said to her, "What do you wish?" She ☆said to Him, "Command that in
Your kingdom these two sons of mine may sit one on Your right and one on Your left."
22 But Jesus answered, "You do not know what you are asking. Are you able to drink
the cup that I am about to drink?" They ☆said to Him, "We are able."
23 He ☆said to them, "My cup you shall drink; but to sit on My right and on *My* left,
this is not Mine to give, but it is for those for whom it has been prepared by My Father."
24 And hearing *this,* the ten became indignant with the two brothers.
25 But Jesus called them to Himself and said, "You know that the rulers of the Gentiles lord it over them, and *their* great men exercise authority over them.
26 "It is not this way among you, but whoever wishes to become great among you shall
be your servant,
27 and whoever wishes to be first among you shall be your slave;
28 just as the Son of Man did not come to be served, but to serve, and to give His life
a ransom for many."

Jesus Heals a Blind Beggar
(179/Mark 10:46-52; Luke 18:35-43)

29 As they were leaving Jericho, a large crowd followed Him.
30 And two blind men sitting by the road, hearing that Jesus was passing by, cried out,
"Lord, have mercy on us, Son of David!"
31 The crowd sternly told them to be quiet, but they cried out all the more, "Lord, Son
of David, have mercy on us!"
32 And Jesus stopped and called them, and said, "What do you want Me to do for you?"
33 They ☆said to Him, "Lord, *we want* our eyes to be opened."
34 Moved with compassion, Jesus touched their eyes; and immediately they regained
their sight and followed Him.

20:20 Matt 4:21; 10:2; Matt 8:2
20:21 Matt 19:28
20:22 Is 51:17, 22; Jer 49:12; Matt 26:39, 42; Luke 22:42; John 18:11
20:23 Acts 12:2; Rev 1:9; Matt 13:11; Matt 25:34
20:25 Luke 22:25-27
20:26 Matt 23:11; Mark 9:35; 10:43; Luke 22:26
20:28 Matt 8:20; Matt 26:28; John 13:13ff; 2 Cor 8:9; Phil 2:7; 1 Tim 2:6; Titus 2:14; Heb 9:28; Rev 1:5
20:29 Matt 9:27-31
20:30 Matt 9:27; Matt 20:31
20:31 Matt 9:27

20:20 The mother of the sons of Zebedee (the disciples James and John) came to Jesus and, "bowing down," made a request of him. She gave Jesus worship, but her real motive was to get something from him. Too often this happens in our churches and in our lives. We play religious games, expecting God to give us something in return. True worship, however, adores and praises Christ for who he is and for what he has done.

20:20 The mother of James and John asked Jesus to give her sons special positions in his kingdom. Parents naturally want to see their children promoted and honored, but this desire is dangerous if it causes them to lose sight of God's specific will for their children. God may have different work in mind—not as glamorous, but just as important. Thus parents' desires for their children's advancement must be held in check as they pray that God's will be done in their children's lives.

20:20 According to 27:56, the mother of James and John was at the cross when Jesus was crucified. Some have suggested that she was the sister of Mary, the mother of Jesus. A close family relationship could have prompted her to make this request for her sons.

20:22 James, John, and their mother failed to grasp Jesus' previous teachings on rewards (19:16–30) and eternal life (20:1–16). They failed to understand the suffering they must face before living in the glory of God's kingdom. The "cup" was the suffering and crucifixion that Christ faced. Both James and John would also face great suffering. James would be put to death for his faith, and John would be exiled.

20:23 Jesus was showing that he was under the authority of the Father, who alone makes the decisions about leadership in heaven. Such rewards are not granted as favors. They are for those who have maintained their commitment to Jesus in spite of severe trials.

20:24 The other disciples were upset with James and John for trying to grab the top positions. *All* the disciples wanted to be the greatest (18:1), but Jesus taught them that the greatest person in God's kingdom is the servant of all. Authority is given not for self-importance, ambition, or respect, but for useful service to God and his creation.

20:27 Jesus described leadership from a new perspective. Instead of using people, we are to serve them. Jesus' mission was to serve others and to give his life away. A real leader has a servant's heart. Servant leaders appreciate others' worth and realize that they're not above any job. If you see something that needs to be done, don't wait to be asked. Take the initiative and do it like a faithful servant.

20:28 A ransom was the price paid to release a slave from bondage. Jesus often told his disciples that he must die, but here he told them why—to redeem all people from the bondage of sin and death. The disciples thought that as long as Jesus was alive, he could save them. But Jesus revealed that only his death would save them and the world.

20:29–34 Matthew records that there were two blind men, while Mark and Luke mention only one. This is probably the same event, but Mark and Luke singled out the more vocal of the two men.

20:30 The blind men called Jesus "Son of David" because the Jews knew that the Messiah would be a descendant of David (see Isaiah 9:6–7; 11:1; Jeremiah 23:5–6). These blind beggars could *see* that Jesus was the long-awaited Messiah, while the religious leaders who witnessed Jesus' miracles were blind to his identity, refusing to open their eyes to the truth. Seeing with your eyes doesn't guarantee seeing with your heart.

20:32–33 Although Jesus was concerned about the coming events in Jerusalem, he demonstrated what he had just told the disciples about service (20:28) by stopping to care for the blind men.

Jesus Rides into Jerusalem on a Donkey
(183/Mark 11:1-11; Luke 19:28-44; John 12:12-19)

21:1 Matt 24:3; 26:30; Mark 11:1; 13:3; 14:26; Luke 19:29, 37; 21:37; 22:39; John 8:1; Acts 1:12
21:4 Mark 11:7-10; Luke 19:35-38; John 12:12-15
21:5 Is 62:11; Zech 9:9
21:8 2 Kin 9:13
21:9 Matt 9:27; Ps 118:26; Luke 2:14
21:11 Matt 21:26; Mark 6:15; Luke 7:16, 39; 13:33; 24:19; John 1:21, 25; 4:19; 6:14; 7:40; 9:17; Acts 3:22f; 7:37; Matt 2:23
21:12 Matt 21:12, 13; John 2:13-16; Ex 30:13; Lev 1:14; 5:7; 12:8
21:13 Is 56:7; Jer 7:11
21:14 Matt 4:23
21:15 Matt 9:27
21:16 Ps 8:2; Matt 11:25

21 When they had approached Jerusalem and had come to Bethphage, at the Mount
of Olives, then Jesus sent two disciples,
2 saying to them, "Go into the village opposite you, and immediately you will find a
donkey tied *there* and a colt with her; untie them and bring them to Me.
3 "If anyone says anything to you, you shall say, 'The Lord has need of them,' and
immediately he will send them."
4 This took place to fulfill what was spoken through the prophet:
5 "SAY TO THE DAUGHTER OF ZION,
'BEHOLD YOUR KING IS COMING TO YOU,
GENTLE, AND MOUNTED ON A DONKEY,
EVEN ON A COLT, THE FOAL OF A BEAST OF BURDEN.' "
6 The disciples went and did just as Jesus had instructed them,
7 and brought the donkey and the colt, and laid their coats on them; and He sat on
the coats.
8 Most of the crowd spread their coats in the road, and others were cutting branches
from the trees and spreading them in the road.
9 The crowds going ahead of Him, and those who followed, were shouting,
"Hosanna to the Son of David;
BLESSED IS HE WHO COMES IN THE NAME OF THE LORD;
Hosanna in the highest!"
10 When He had entered Jerusalem, all the city was stirred, saying, "Who is this?"
11 And the crowds were saying, "This is the prophet Jesus, from Nazareth in Galilee."

Jesus Clears the Temple Again
(184/Mark 11:12-19; Luke 19:45-48)

12 And Jesus entered the temple and drove out all those who were buying and selling
in the temple, and overturned the tables of the money changers and the seats of those
who were selling doves.
13 And He ☆said to them, "It is written, 'MY HOUSE SHALL BE CALLED A HOUSE OF
PRAYER'; but you are making it a ROBBERS' DEN."
14 And *the* blind and *the* lame came to Him in the temple, and He healed them.
15 But when the chief priests and the scribes saw the wonderful things that He had
done, and the children who were shouting in the temple, "Hosanna to the Son of David," they became indignant
16 and said to Him, "Do You hear what these *children* are saying?" And Jesus ☆said to

---

21:2–5 Matthew mentions a donkey and a colt, while the other Gospels mention only the colt. This was the same event, but Matthew focuses on the prophecy in Zechariah 9:9, where a donkey and a colt are mentioned. He shows how Jesus' actions fulfilled the prophet's words, thus giving another indication that Jesus was indeed the Messiah. When Jesus entered Jerusalem on a donkey's colt, he affirmed his Messianic royalty as well as his humility.

21:8 This verse is one of the few places where the Gospels record that Jesus' glory is recognized on earth. Jesus boldly declared himself King, and the crowd gladly joined him. But these same people would bow to political pressure and desert him in just a few days. Today we celebrate this event on Palm Sunday. That day should remind us to guard against superficial acclaim for Christ.

21:12 This is the second time Jesus cleared the temple (see John 2:13–17). Merchants and moneychangers set up their booths in the court of the Gentiles in the temple, crowding out the Gentiles who had come from all over the civilized world to worship God. The merchants sold sacrificial animals at high prices, taking advantage of those who had come long distances. The moneychangers exchanged all international currency for the special temple coins—the only money the merchants would accept. They often deceived foreigners who didn't know the exchange rates. Their commercialism in God's house frustrated people's attempts at worship. This, of course, greatly angered Jesus. Any practice that interferes with worshiping God should be stopped.

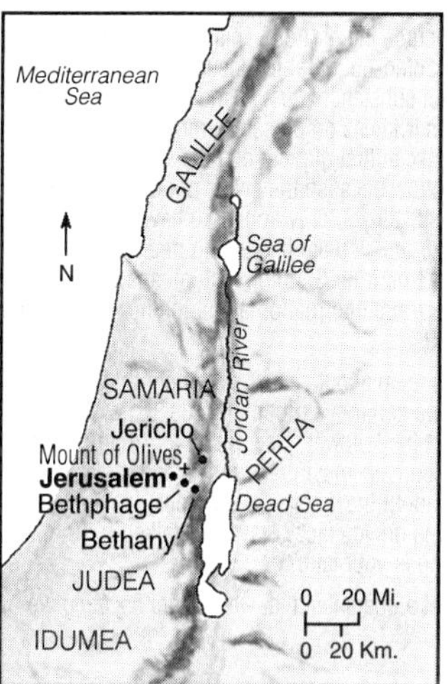

PREPARATION FOR THE TRIUMPHAL ENTRY
On their way from Jericho, Jesus and the disciples neared Bethphage, on the slope of the Mount of Olives, just outside Jerusalem. Two disciples went into the village, as Jesus told them, to bring back a donkey and its colt. Jesus rode into Jerusalem on the colt, an unmistakable sign of his kingship.

them, "Yes; have you never read, 'OUT OF THE MOUTH OF INFANTS AND NURSING BABIES YOU HAVE PREPARED PRAISE FOR YOURSELF'?"
17 And He left them and went out of the city to Bethany, and spent the night there.

21:17 Matt 26:6; Mark 11:1, 11, 12; 14:3; Luke 19:29; 24:50; John 11:1, 18; 12:1

Jesus Says the Disciples Can Pray for Anything
(188) Mark 11:20-26)

18 Now in the morning, when He was returning to the city, He became hungry.
19 Seeing a lone fig tree by the road, He came to it and found nothing on it except
leaves only; and He *said to it, "No longer shall there ever be *any* fruit from you." And
at once the fig tree withered.
20 Seeing *this,* the disciples were amazed and asked, "How did the fig tree wither *all* at
once?"
21 And Jesus answered and said to them, "Truly I say to you, if you have faith and do
not doubt, you will not only do what was done to the fig tree, but even if you say to this
mountain, 'Be taken up and cast into the sea,' it will happen.
22 "And all things you ask in prayer, believing, you will receive."

21:19 Luke 13:6-9

21:21 Matt 17:20; Mark 11:23; Luke 17:6; James 1:6

21:22 Matt 7:7

Religious Leaders Challenge Jesus' Authority
(189/Mark 11:27-33; Luke 20:1-8)

23 When He entered the temple, the chief priests and the elders of the people came to
Him while He was teaching, and said, "BY what authority are You doing these things,
and who gave You this authority?"
24 Jesus said to them, "I will also ask you one thing, which if you tell Me, I will also tell
you by what authority I do these things.
25 "The baptism of John was from what *source,* from heaven or from men?" And they
began reasoning among themselves, saying, "If we say, 'From heaven,' He will say to us,
'Then why did you not believe him?'
26 "But if we say, 'From men,' we fear the people; for they all regard John as a prophet."
27 And answering Jesus, they said, "We do not know." He also said to them, "Neither
will I tell you by what authority I do these things.

21:23 Matt 26:55

21:26 Matt 11:9; Mark 6:20

Jesus Tells the Parable of the Two Sons
(190)

28 "But what do you think? A man had two sons, and he came to the first and said, 'Son,
go work today in the vineyard.'
29 "And he answered, 'I will not'; but afterward he regretted it and went.

21:28 Matt 20:1; 21:33

21:19 Why did Jesus curse the fig tree? This was not a thoughtless, angry act, but an acted-out parable. Jesus was showing his anger at religion without substance. Just as the fig tree looked good from a distance but was fruitless on close examination, so the temple looked impressive at first glance, but its sacrifices and other activities were hollow because they were not done to worship God sincerely (see 21:43). If you only appear to have faith without putting it to work in your life, you are like the fig tree that withered and died because it bore no fruit. Genuine faith means bearing fruit for God's kingdom. For more information about the fig tree, see the note on Mark 11:13–26.

21:21 Many have wondered about Jesus' statement that if we have faith and don't doubt, we can move mountains. Jesus, of course, was not suggesting that his followers use prayer as "magic" and perform capricious "mountain-moving" acts. Instead, he was making a strong point about the disciples' (and our) lack of faith. What kinds of mountains do you face? Have you talked to God about them? How strong is your faith?

21:22 This verse is not a guarantee that we can get *anything* we want simply by asking Jesus and believing. God does not grant requests that would hurt us or others or that would violate his own nature or will. Jesus' statement is not a blank check. To be fulfilled, our requests must be in harmony with the principles of God's kingdom. The stronger our belief, the more likely our prayers will be in line with God's will, and then God will be happy to grant them.

21:23–25 In Jesus' world, as in ours, people looked for the outward sign of authority—education, title, position, connections. But Jesus' authority came from who he was, not from any outward and superficial trappings. As followers of Christ, God has given us authority—we can confidently speak and act on his behalf because he has authorized us. Are you exercising your authority?

21:23–27 The Pharisees demanded to know where Jesus got his authority. If Jesus said his authority came from God, they would accuse him of blasphemy. If he said that he was acting on his own authority, the crowds would be convinced that the Pharisees had the greater authority. But Jesus answered them with a seemingly unrelated question that exposed their real motives. They didn't really want an answer to their question; they only wanted to trap him. Jesus showed that the Pharisees wanted the truth only if it supported their own views and causes.

21:25 For more information on John the Baptist, see Matthew 3 and his Profile in John 1.

30 “The man came to the second and said the same thing; and he answered, ‘I *will*, sir’;
but he did not go.

21:31 Luke 7:29, 37-50

31 “Which of the two did the will of his father?” They ☆said, “The first.” Jesus ☆said to
them, “Truly I say to you that the tax collectors and prostitutes will get into the kingdom
of God before you.

21:32 Luke 3:12; 7:29f

32 “For John came to you in the way of righteousness and you did not believe him; but
the tax collectors and prostitutes did believe him; and you, seeing *this*, did not even feel
remorse afterward so as to believe him.

Jesus Tells the Parable of the Wicked Vine-Growers
(191/Mark 12:1-12; Luke 20:9-19)

21:33 Is 5:1, 2; Matt 20:1; 21:28; Matt 25:14

33 “Listen to another parable. There was a landowner who PLANTED A VINEYARD AND
PUT A WALL AROUND IT AND DUG A WINE PRESS IN IT, AND BUILT A TOWER, and rented
it out to vine-growers and went on a journey.

21:34 Matt 22:3

34 “When the harvest time approached, he sent his slaves to the vine-growers to receive
his produce.
35 “The vine-growers took his slaves and beat one, and killed another, and stoned a third.

21:36 Matt 22:4

36 “Again he sent another group of slaves larger than the first; and they did the same
thing to them.
37 “But afterward he sent his son to them, saying, ‘They will respect my son.’
38 “But when the vine-growers saw the son, they said among themselves, ‘This is the
heir; come, let us kill him and seize his inheritance.’
39 “They took him, and threw him out of the vineyard and killed him.
40 “Therefore when the owner of the vineyard comes, what will he do to those vine-
growers?”

21:41 Matt 8:11f; Acts 13:46; 18:6; 28:28

41 They ☆said to Him, “He will bring those wretches to a wretched end, and will rent
out the vineyard to other vine-growers who will pay him the proceeds at the *proper* seasons.”

21:42 Ps 118:22f; Acts 4:11; Rom 9:33; 1 Pet 2:7

42 Jesus ☆said to them, “Did you never read in the Scriptures,
‘THE STONE WHICH THE BUILDERS REJECTED,
THIS BECAME THE CHIEF CORNER *stone;*
THIS CAME ABOUT FROM THE LORD,
AND IT IS MARVELOUS IN OUR EYES’?
43 “Therefore I say to you, the kingdom of God will be taken away from you and given
to a people, producing the fruit of it.

21:44 Is 8:14, 15

44 “And he who falls on this stone will be broken to pieces; but on whomever it falls, it
will scatter him like dust.”
45 When the chief priests and the Pharisees heard His parables, they understood that
He was speaking about them.

21:46 Matt 21:26; Matt 21:11

46 When they sought to seize Him, they feared the people, because they considered
Him to be a prophet.

21:30 The son who said he would obey and then didn't represented the nation of Israel in Jesus' day. They said they wanted to do God's will, but they constantly disobeyed. They were phony, just going through the motions. It is dangerous to pretend to obey God when our hearts are far from him because God knows our true intentions. Our actions must match our words.

21:33ff The main elements in this parable are (1) the landowner—God, (2) the vineyard—Israel, (3) the vine-growers—the Jewish religious leaders, (4) the landowner's slaves—the prophets and priests who remained faithful to God and preached to Israel, (5) the son—Jesus (21:38), and (6) the other vine-growers—the Gentiles. Jesus was exposing the religious leaders' murderous plot (21:45).

21:37 In trying to reach us with his love, God finally sent his own Son. Jesus' perfect life, his words of truth, and his sacrifice of love are meant to cause us to listen to him and to follow him as Lord. If we ignore God's gracious gift of his Son, we reject God himself.

21:42 Jesus refers to himself as "the stone which the builders rejected." Although Jesus was rejected by many of his people, he will become the cornerstone, of his new building, the church (see Acts 4:11; 1 Peter 2:7).

21:44 Jesus used this metaphor to show that one stone can affect people different ways, depending on how they relate to it (see Isaiah 8:14–15; 28:16; Daniel 2:34, 44–45). Ideally they will build on it; many, however, will trip over it. And at the last judgment God's enemies will be crushed by it. In the end, Christ, the "corner stone," will become the "crushing stone." He offers mercy and forgiveness *now* and promises judgment later. We should choose him now!

Jesus Tells the Parable of the Wedding Feast
(192)

22 Jesus spoke to them again in parables, saying,
2 "The kingdom of heaven may be compared to a king who gave a wedding feast
for his son.
3 "And he sent out his slaves to call those who had been invited to the wedding feast,
and they were unwilling to come.
4 "Again he sent out other slaves saying, 'Tell those who have been invited, "Behold, I
have prepared my dinner; my oxen and my fattened livestock are *all* butchered and everything is ready; come to the wedding feast." '
5 "But they paid no attention and went their way, one to his own farm, another to his
business,
6 and the rest seized his slaves and mistreated them and killed them.
7 "But the king was enraged, and he sent his armies and destroyed those murderers
and set their city on fire.
8 "Then he ☆said to his slaves, 'The wedding is ready, but those who were invited were
not worthy.
9 'Go therefore to the main highways, and as many as you find *there,* invite to the
wedding feast.'
10 "Those slaves went out into the streets and gathered together all they found, both
evil and good; and the wedding hall was filled with dinner guests.
11 "But when the king came in to look over the dinner guests, he saw a man there who
was not dressed in wedding clothes,
12 and he ☆said to him, 'Friend, how did you come in here without wedding clothes?'
And the man was speechless.
13 "Then the king said to the servants, 'Bind him hand and foot, and throw him into the
outer darkness; in that place there will be weeping and gnashing of teeth.'
14 "For many are called, but few *are* chosen."

22:2 Matt 13:24; 22:2-14; Luke 14:16-24; Luke 12:36; John 2:2
22:3 Matt 21:34
22:4 Matt 21:36
22:9 Ezek 21:21; Obad 14
22:11 2 Kin 10:22; Zech 3:3, 4
22:12 Matt 20:13; 26:50
22:13 Matt 8:12; 25:30; Luke 13:28
22:14 Matt 24:22; 2 Pet 1:10; Rev 17:14

Religious Leaders Question Jesus about Paying Taxes
(193/Mark 12:13-17; Luke 20:20-26)

15 Then the Pharisees went and plotted together how they might trap Him in what He
said.
16 And they ☆sent their disciples to Him, along with the Herodians, saying, "Teacher,
we know that You are truthful and teach the way of God in truth, and defer to no one;
for You are not partial to any.
17 "Tell us then, what do You think? Is it lawful to give a poll-tax to Caesar, or not?"
18 But Jesus perceived their malice, and said, "Why are you testing Me, you hypocrites?
19 "Show Me the coin *used* for the poll-tax." And they brought Him a denarius.
20 And He ☆said to them, "Whose likeness and inscription is this?"

22:16 Mark 3:6; 8:15; 12:13
22:17 Matt 17:25; Luke 2:1; 3:1
22:19 Matt 17:25

22:1–14 In this culture, two invitations were expected when banquets were given. The first asked the guests to attend; the second announced that all was ready. In this story the king invited his guests three times—and each time they rejected his invitation. God wants us to join him at his banquet, which will last for eternity. That's why he sends us invitations again and again. Have you accepted his invitation?

22:11–12 It was customary for wedding guests to be given garments to wear to the banquet. It was unthinkable to refuse to wear these garments. That would insult the host, who could only assume that the guest was arrogant and thought he didn't need these garments, or that he did not want to take part in the wedding celebration. The wedding clothes picture the righteousness needed to enter God's kingdom—the total acceptance in God's eyes that Christ gives every believer. Christ has provided this garment of righteousness for everyone, but each person must choose to put it on in order to enter the King's banquet (eternal life). There is an open invitation, but we must be ready. For more on the imagery of clothes of righteousness and salvation, see Psalm 132:16; Isaiah 61:10; Zechariah 3:3–5; Revelation 3:4–5; 19:7–8.

22:15–17 The Pharisees, a religious group, opposed the Roman occupation of Palestine. The Herodians, a political party, supported Herod Antipas and the policies instituted by Rome. Normally these two groups were bitter enemies, but here they united against Jesus. Thinking they had a foolproof plan to corner him, together their representatives asked Jesus about paying Roman taxes. If Jesus agreed that it was right to pay taxes to Caesar, the Pharisees would say he was opposed to God, the only King they recognized. If Jesus said the taxes should not be paid, the Herodians would hand him over to Herod on the charge of rebellion. In this case the Pharisees were not motivated by love for God's laws, and the Herodians were not motivated by love for Roman justice. Jesus' answer exposed their evil motives and embarrassed them both.

22:17 The Jews were required to pay taxes to support the Roman government. They hated this taxation because the money went directly into Caesar's treasury, where some of it went to support the pagan temples and decadent life-style of the Roman aristocracy. Caesar's image on the coins was a constant reminder of Israel's subjection to Rome.

22:19 The denarius was the usual day's wage for a laborer.

22:21 Mark 12:17; Luke 20:25; Rom 13:7

21 They ☆said to Him, "Caesar's." Then He ☆said to them, "Then render to Caesar the
things that are Caesar's; and to God the things that are God's."

22:22 Mark 12:12

22 And hearing *this,* they were amazed, and leaving Him, they went away.

Religious Leaders Question Jesus about the Resurrection
(194/Mark 12:18-27; Luke 20:27-40)

22:23 Matt 3:7; Acts 23:8

23 On that day *some* Sadducees (who say there is no resurrection) came to Jesus and
questioned Him,

22:24 Deut 25:5

24 asking, "Teacher, Moses said, 'IF A MAN DIES HAVING NO CHILDREN, HIS BROTHER
AS NEXT OF KIN SHALL MARRY HIS WIFE, AND RAISE UP CHILDREN FOR HIS BROTHER.'
25 "Now there were seven brothers with us; and the first married and died, and having
no children left his wife to his brother;
26 so also the second, and the third, down to the seventh.
27 "Last of all, the woman died.
28 "In the resurrection, therefore, whose wife of the seven will she be? For they all had
married her."

22:29 John 20:9

29 But Jesus answered and said to them, "You are mistaken, not understanding the
Scriptures nor the power of God.

22:30 Matt 24:38; Luke 17:27

30 "For in the resurrection they neither marry nor are given in marriage, but are like
angels in heaven.
31 "But regarding the resurrection of the dead, have you not read what was spoken to
you by God:

22:32 Ex 3:6

32 'I AM THE GOD OF ABRAHAM, AND THE GOD OF ISAAC, AND THE GOD OF JACOB'?
He is not the God of the dead but of the living."

22:33 Matt 7:28

33 When the crowds heard *this,* they were astonished at His teaching.

Religious Leaders Question Jesus about the Greatest Commandment
(195/Mark 12:28-34)

22:34 Luke 10:25-37; Matt 3:7

34 But when the Pharisees heard that Jesus had silenced the Sadducees, they gathered
themselves together.

22:35 Luke 7:30; 10:25; 11:45, 46, 52; 14:3; Titus 3:13

35 One of them, [40]a lawyer, asked Him *a question,* testing Him,
36 "Teacher, which is the great commandment in the Law?"

22:37 Deut 6:5

37 And He said to him, " 'YOU SHALL LOVE THE LORD YOUR GOD WITH ALL YOUR
HEART, AND WITH ALL YOUR SOUL, AND WITH ALL YOUR MIND.'

40 I.e. an expert in the Mosaic Law

22:21 Jesus avoided this trap by showing that we have dual citizenship (1 Peter 2:17). Our citizenship in the nation requires that we pay money for the services and benefits we receive. Our citizenship in the kingdom of heaven requires that we pledge to God our primary obedience and commitment.

22:23ff After the Pharisees and Herodians had failed to trap Jesus, the Sadducees smugly stepped in to try. They did not believe in the resurrection because the Pentateuch (Genesis—Deuteronomy) has no direct teaching on it. The Pharisees had never been able to come up with a convincing argument from the Pentateuch for the resurrection, and the Sadducees thought they had trapped Jesus for sure. But Jesus was about to show them otherwise (see 22:31–32 for Jesus' answer).

22:24 For more information on Moses, see his Profile in Exodus 14.

22:24 The law said that when a woman's husband died without having a son, the man's brother had a responsibility to marry and care for the widow (Deuteronomy 25:5–6). This law protected women who were left alone, because in that culture they usually had no other means to support themselves.

22:29–30 The Sadducees asked Jesus what marriage would be like in heaven. Jesus said it was more important to understand God's power than know what heaven will be like. In every generation and culture, ideas of eternal life tend to be based on images and experiences of present life. Jesus answered that these faulty ideas are caused by ignorance of God's Word. We must not make up our own ideas about eternity and heaven by thinking of it and God in human terms. We should concentrate more on our relationship with God than about what heaven will look like. Eventually we will find out, and it will be far beyond our greatest expectations.

22:31–32 Because the Sadducees accepted only the Pentateuch as God's divine Word, Jesus answered them from the book of Exodus (3:6). God would not have said, "I am the God of Abraham, and the God of Isaac, and the God of Jacob" if God thought of Abraham, Isaac, and Jacob as dead. From God's perspective, they are alive. Jesus' use of the present tense pointed to the resurrection and the eternal life that all believers enjoy in him.

22:34 We might think the Pharisees would have been glad to see the Sadducees silenced. The question that the Sadducees had always used to trap them was finally answered by Jesus. But the Pharisees were too proud to be impressed. Jesus' answer gave them a theological victory over the Sadducees, but they were more interested in defeating Jesus than in learning the truth.

22:35–40 The Pharisees, who had classified over 600 laws, often tried to distinguish the more important from the less important. So one of them, a lawyer, asked Jesus to identify the most important law. Jesus quoted from Deuteronomy 6:5 and Leviticus 19:18. By fulfilling these two commands, a person keeps all the others. They summarize the Ten Commandments and the other Old Testament moral laws.

22:37–40 Jesus says that if we truly love God and our neighbor, we will naturally keep the commandments. This is looking at God's law positively. Rather than worrying about all we should *not* do, we should concentrate on all we *can* do to show our love for God and others.

38 "This is the great and foremost commandment.
39 "The second is like it, 'YOU SHALL LOVE YOUR NEIGHBOR AS YOURSELF.'
40 "On these two commandments depend the whole Law and the Prophets."

Religious Leaders Cannot Answer Jesus' Question
(196/Mark 12:35-37; Luke 20:41-44)

41 Now while the Pharisees were gathered together, Jesus asked them a question:
42 "What do you think about the Christ, whose son is He?" They ☆said to Him, "*The son* of David."
43 He ☆said to them, "Then how does David in the Spirit call Him 'Lord,' saying,
44 'THE LORD SAID TO MY LORD,
"SIT AT MY RIGHT HAND,
UNTIL I PUT YOUR ENEMIES BENEATH YOUR FEET" '?
45 "If David then calls Him 'Lord,' how is He his son?"
46 No one was able to answer Him a word, nor did anyone dare from that day on to
ask Him another question.

Jesus Warns against the Religious Leaders
(197/Mark 12:38-40; Luke 20:45-47)

23 Then Jesus spoke to the crowds and to His disciples,
2 saying: "The scribes and the Pharisees have seated themselves in the chair of
Moses;
3 therefore all that they tell you, do and observe, but do not do according to their
deeds; for they say *things* and do not do *them.*
4 "They tie up heavy burdens and lay them on men's shoulders, but they themselves
are unwilling to move them with *so much as* a finger.
5 "But they do all their deeds to be noticed by men; for they broaden their [41]phylacter-
ies and lengthen the tassels *of their garments.*
6 "They love the place of honor at banquets and the chief seats in the synagogues,
7 and respectful greetings in the market places, and being called Rabbi by men.
8 "But do not be called Rabbi; for One is your Teacher, and you are all brothers.
9 "Do not call *anyone* on earth your father; for One is your Father, He who is in
heaven.
10 "Do not be called leaders; for One is your Leader, *that is,* Christ.
11 "But the greatest among you shall be your servant.
12 "Whoever exalts himself shall be humbled; and whoever humbles himself shall be
exalted.

41 I.e. small cases containing Scripture texts worn on the left arm and forehead for religious purposes

22:39 Lev 19:18; Matt 19:19; Gal 5:14
22:40 Matt 7:12
22:41 Luke 20:41-44
22:42 Matt 9:27
22:43 2 Sam 23:2; Rev 1:10; 4:2
22:44 Ps 110:1; Matt 26:64; Mark 16:19; Acts 2:34f; 1 Cor 15:25; Heb 1:13; 10:13
22:46 Mark 12:34; Luke 14:6; 20:40
23:2 Deut 33:3f; Ezra 7:6, 25; Neh 8:4
23:4 Luke 11:46; Acts 15:10
23:5 Matt 6:1, 5, 16; 9:20
23:6 Luke 11:43; 14:7; 20:46
23:7 Mark 9:5; 10:51; 11:21; John 1:38, 49; 3:2, 26; 4:31; 6:25; 9:2; 11:8; 20:16
23:8 James 3:1
23:9 Matt 6:9; 7:11
23:11 Matt 20:26
23:12 Luke 14:11; 18:14

22:41–45 The Pharisees, Herodians, and Sadducees had asked their questions. Then Jesus turned the tables and asked them a penetrating question—who they thought Christ, the Messiah, was. The Pharisees knew that the Messiah would be a descendant of David, but they did not understand that he would be God himself. Jesus quoted from Psalm 110:1 to show that the Messiah would be greater than David. (Hebrews 1:13 uses the same text as proof of Christ's deity.) The most important question we will ever answer is what we believe about Christ. Other theological questions are irrelevant until we believe that Jesus is who he said he is.

23:2–3 The Pharisees' traditions and their interpretations and applications of the laws had become as important to them as God's law itself. Their laws were not all bad—some were beneficial. The problem arose when the religious leaders (1) took man-made rules as seriously as God's laws, (2) told the people to obey these rules but did not do so themselves, or (3) obeyed the rules not to honor God but to make themselves look good. Usually Jesus did not condemn what the Pharisees taught, but what they *were*—hypocrites.

23:5 Phylacteries were little leather boxes containing Scripture verses. Very religious people wore these boxes on their forehead and arms in order to obey Deuteronomy 6:8 and Exodus 13:9, 16. But the phylacteries had become more important for the status they gave than for the truth they contained.

23:5–7 Jesus again exposed the hypocritical attitudes of the religious leaders. They knew the Scriptures but did not live by them. They didn't care about *being* holy—just *looking* holy in order to receive the people's admiration and praise. Today, like the Pharisees, many people who know the Bible do not let it change their lives. They say they follow Jesus, but they don't live by his standards of love. People who live this way are hypocrites. We must make sure that our actions match our beliefs.

23:5–7 People desire positions of leadership not only in business but also in the church. It is dangerous when love for the position grows stronger than loyalty to God. This is what happened to the Pharisees and scribes. Jesus is not against all leadership—we need Christian leaders—but against leadership that serves itself rather than others.

23:11–12 Jesus challenged society's norms. To him, greatness comes from serving—giving of yourself to help God and others. Service keeps us aware of others' needs, and it stops us from focusing only on ourselves. Jesus came as a servant. What kind of greatness do you seek?

Jesus Condemns the Religious Leaders (198)

23:13 Matt 23:15, 16, 23, 25, 27, 29; Luke 11:52

13"But woe to you, scribes and Pharisees, hypocrites, because you shut off the kingdom of heaven from people; for you do not enter in yourselves, nor do you allow those
who are entering to go in.

23:14 Mark 12:40; Luke 20:47

14 ["[42]Woe to you, scribes and Pharisees, hypocrites, because you devour widows' houses,
and for a pretense you make long prayers; therefore you will receive greater condemnation.]

23:15 Acts 2:10; 6:5; 13:43; Matt 5:22

15"Woe to you, scribes and Pharisees, hypocrites, because you travel around on sea and
land to make one proselyte; and when he becomes one, you make him twice as much a
son of hell as yourselves.

23:16 Matt 15:14; 23:24; Matt 5:33-35

16"Woe to you, blind guides, who say, 'Whoever swears by the temple, *that* is nothing;
but whoever swears by the gold of the temple is obligated.'

23:17 Ex 30:29

17"You fools and blind men! Which is more important, the gold or the temple that
sanctified the gold?

18"And, 'Whoever swears by the altar, *that* is nothing, but whoever swears by the offering on it, he is obligated.'

23:19 Ex 29:37

19"You blind men, which is more important, the offering, or the altar that sanctifies
the offering?

20"Therefore, whoever swears by the altar, swears *both* by the altar and by everything
on it.

23:21 1 Kin 8:13; Ps 26:8; 132:14

21"And whoever swears by the temple, swears *both* by the temple and by Him who dwells
within it.

23:22 Is 66:1; Matt 5:34

22"And whoever swears by heaven, swears *both* by the throne of God and by Him who
sits upon it.

23:23 Matt 23:13; Luke 11:42

23"Woe to you, scribes and Pharisees, hypocrites! For you tithe mint and dill and cummin, and have neglected the weightier provisions of the law: justice and mercy and faithfulness; but these are the things you should have done without neglecting the others.

23:24 Matt 23:16

24"You blind guides, who strain out a gnat and swallow a camel!

23:25 Mark 7:4; Luke 11:39f

25"Woe to you, scribes and Pharisees, hypocrites! For you clean the outside of the cup
and of the dish, but inside they are full of robbery and self-indulgence.

23:26 Mark 7:4; Luke 11:39f

26"You blind Pharisee, first clean the inside of the cup and of the dish, so that the outside of it may become clean also.

23:27 Luke 11:44; Acts 23:3

27"Woe to you, scribes and Pharisees, hypocrites! For you are like whitewashed tombs
which on the outside appear beautiful, but inside they are full of dead men's bones and
all uncleanness.

28"So you, too, outwardly appear righteous to men, but inwardly you are full of hypocrisy and lawlessness.

23:29 Luke 11:47f

29"Woe to you, scribes and Pharisees, hypocrites! For you build the tombs of the prophets and adorn the monuments of the righteous,

30 and say, 'If we had been *living* in the days of our fathers, we would not have been
partners with them in *shedding* the blood of the prophets.'

42 This v not found in early mss

23:13–14 Being a religious leader in Jerusalem was very different from being a pastor in a secular society today. Israel's history, culture, and daily life centered around its relationship with God. The religious leaders were the best known, most powerful, and most respected of all leaders. Jesus made these stinging accusations because the leaders' hunger for more power, money, and status had made them lose sight of God, and their blindness was spreading to the whole nation.

23:15 The Pharisees' converts were attracted to Pharisaism, not to God. By getting caught up in the details of their additional laws and regulations, they completely missed God, to whom the laws pointed. A religion of deeds puts pressure on people to surpass others in what they know and do. Thus, a hypocritical teacher was likely to have students who were even more hypocritical. We must make sure we are not creating Pharisees by emphasizing outward obedience at the expense of inner renewal.

23:23–24 It's possible to obey the details of the laws but still be disobedient in our general behavior. For example, we could be very precise and faithful about giving 10 percent of our money to God, but refuse to give one minute of our time in helping others. Tithing is important, but giving a tithe does not exempt us from fulfilling God's other directives.

23:24 The Pharisees strained their water so they wouldn't accidentally swallow a gnat—an unclean insect according to the law. Meticulous about the details of ceremonial cleanliness, they nevertheless had lost their perspective on inner purity. Ceremonially clean on the outside, they had corrupt hearts.

23:25–28 Jesus condemned the Pharisees and religious leaders for outwardly appearing saintly and holy but inwardly remaining full of corruption and greed. Living our Christianity merely as a show for others is like washing a cup on the outside only. When we are clean on the inside, our cleanliness on the outside won't be a sham.

31 "So you testify against yourselves, that you are sons of those who murdered the
prophets.
32 "Fill up, then, the measure *of the guilt* of your fathers.
33 "You serpents, you brood of vipers, how will you escape the sentence of hell?
34 "Therefore, behold, I am sending you prophets and wise men and scribes; some of
them you will kill and crucify, and some of them you will scourge in your synagogues,
and persecute from city to city,
35 so that upon you may fall *the guilt of* all the righteous blood shed on earth, from the
blood of righteous Abel to the blood of Zechariah, the son of Berechiah, whom you
murdered between the temple and the altar.
36 "Truly I say to you, all these things will come upon this generation.

23:31 Matt 23:34, 37; Acts 7:51f
23:33 Matt 3:7; Luke 3:7; Matt 5:22
23:34 Luke 11:49-51; 2 Chr 36:15, 16; Matt 10:17; Matt 10:23
23:35 Gen 4:8ff; Heb 11:4; Zech 1:1; 2 Chr 24:21
23:36 Matt 10:23; 24:34

Jesus Grieves over Jerusalem Again
(199)

37 "Jerusalem, Jerusalem, who kills the prophets and stones those who are sent to her!
How often I wanted to gather your children together, the way a hen gathers her chicks
under her wings, and you were unwilling.
38 "Behold, your house is being left to you desolate!
39 "For I say to you, from now on you will not see Me until you say, 'BLESSED IS HE
WHO COMES IN THE NAME OF THE LORD!' "

23:37 Luke 13:34, 35; Matt 5:12; Ruth 2:12
23:38 1 Kin 9:7f; Jer 22:5
23:39 Ps 118:26; Matt 21:9

7. Jesus teaches on the Mount of Olives

Jesus Tells about the Future
(201/Mark 13:1-23; Luke 21:5-24)

24 Jesus came out from the temple and was going away when His disciples came up
to point out the temple buildings to Him.
2 And He said to them, "Do you not see all these things? Truly I say to you, not one
stone here will be left upon another, which will not be torn down."
3 As He was sitting on the Mount of Olives, the disciples came to Him privately, saying, "Tell us, when will these things happen, and what *will be* the sign of Your coming,
and of the end of the age?"
4 And Jesus answered and said to them, "See to it that no one misleads you.

24:1 Matt 21:23
24:2 Luke 19:44
24:3 Matt 21:1; Matt 16:27f; 24:27, 37, 39
24:4 Jer 29:8

23:34–36 These prophets, wise men, and scribes were probably leaders in the early church who were persecuted, scourged, and killed, as Jesus predicted. The people of Jesus' generation said they would not act as their fathers did in killing the prophets whom God had sent to them (23:30), but they were about to kill the Messiah himself and his faithful followers. Thus they would become guilty of all the righteous blood shed through the centuries.

23:35 Jesus was giving a brief history of Old Testament martyrdom. Abel was the first martyr (Genesis 4); Zechariah was the last mentioned in the Hebrew Bible, which ended with 2 Chronicles. Zechariah is a classic example of a man of God who was killed by those who claimed to be God's people (see 2 Chronicles 24:20–21).

23:37 Jesus wanted to gather his people together as a hen protects her chicks under her wings, but they wouldn't let him. Jesus also wants to protect us if we will just come to him. Many times we hurt and don't know where to turn. We reject Christ's help because we don't think he can give us what we need. But who knows our needs better than our Creator? Those who turn to Jesus will find that he helps and comforts as no one else can.

23:37 Jerusalem was the capital city of God's chosen people, the ancestral home of David, Israel's greatest king, and the location of the temple, the earthly dwelling place of God. It was intended to be the center of worship of the true God and a symbol of justice to all people. But Jerusalem had become blind to God and insensitive to human need. Here we see the depth of Jesus' feelings for lost people and for his beloved city, which would soon be destroyed.

24:1–2 Although no one knows exactly what this temple looked like, it must have been beautiful. Herod had helped the Jews remodel and beautify it, no doubt to stay on friendly terms with his subjects. Next to the inner temple, where the sacred objects were kept and the sacrifices offered, there was a large area called the court of the Gentiles (this was where the moneychangers and merchants had their booths). Outside these courts were long porches. Solomon's porch was 1,562 feet long; the royal portico was decorated with 160 columns stretching along its 921-foot length. Gazing at this glorious and massive structure, the disciples found Jesus' words about its destruction difficult to believe. But the temple was indeed destroyed only 40 years later when the Romans sacked Jerusalem in A.D. 70.

24:3ff Jesus was sitting on the Mount of Olives, the very place where the prophet Zechariah had predicted that the Messiah would stand when he came to establish his kingdom (Zechariah 14:4). It was a fitting place for the disciples to ask Jesus when he would come in power and what they could expect then. Jesus' reply emphasized the events that would take place before the end of the age. He pointed out that his disciples should be less concerned with knowing the exact date and more concerned with being prepared—living God's way consistently so that no matter when Jesus came in glory, he would claim them as his own.

24:4 The disciples asked Jesus for the sign of his coming and of the end of the age. Jesus' first response was "See to it that no one misleads you." The fact is that whenever we look for signs, we become very susceptible to being deceived. There are many "false prophets" (24:11, 24) around with counterfeit signs of spiritual power and authority. The only sure way to keep from being deceived is to focus on Christ and his words. Don't look for special signs, and don't spend time looking at other people. Look at Christ.

24:5 Acts 5:36f; 1 John 2:18; 4:3

24:7 Rev 6:8, 12; Acts 11:28; Rev 6:5, 6

24:9 Matt 10:17; John 15:18ff

24:10 Matt 11:6

24:11 Matt 7:15; 24:24

24:14 Matt 4:23; Rom 10:18; Col 1:6, 23; Luke 2:1; 4:5; Acts 11:28; 17:6, 31; 19:27; Rom 10:18; Heb 1:6; 2:5; Rev 3:10; 16:14

24:15 Dan 9:27; 11:31; 12:11

24:17 Matt 10:27; Luke 5:19; 12:3; 17:31; Acts 10:9

5 "For many will come in My name, saying, 'I am the Christ,' and will mislead many.
6 "You will be hearing of wars and rumors of wars. See that you are not frightened, for
those things must take place, but *that* is not yet the end.
7 "For nation will rise against nation, and kingdom against kingdom, and in various
places there will be famines and earthquakes.
8 "But all these things are *merely* the beginning of birth pangs.
9 "Then they will deliver you to tribulation, and will kill you, and you will be hated by
all nations because of My name.
10 "At that time many will fall away and will betray one another and hate one another.
11 "Many false prophets will arise and will mislead many.
12 "Because lawlessness is increased, most people's love will grow cold.
13 "But the one who endures to the end, he will be saved.
14 "This gospel of the kingdom shall be preached in the whole world as a testimony to
all the nations, and then the end will come.
15 "Therefore when you see the ABOMINATION OF DESOLATION which was spoken of
through Daniel the prophet, standing in the holy place (let the reader understand),
16 then those who are in Judea must flee to the mountains.
17 "Whoever is on the housetop must not go down to get the things out that are in his
house.
18 "Whoever is in the field must not turn back to get his cloak.
19 "But woe to those who are pregnant and to those who are nursing babies in those
days!
20 "But pray that your flight will not be in the winter, or on a Sabbath.

THE SEVEN WOES

23:14	Not letting others enter the kingdom of heaven and not entering yourselves
23:15	Converting people away from God to be like yourselves
23:16–22	Blindly leading God's people to follow man-made traditions instead of God's Word
23:23–24	Involving yourself in every last detail and ignoring what is really important: justice, mercy, and faith
23:25–26	Keeping up appearances while your private world is corrupt
23:27–28	Acting spiritual to cover up sin
23:29–36	Pretending to have learned from past history, but your present behavior shows you have learned nothing

Jesus mentioned seven ways to guarantee God's anger, often called the "seven woes." These seven statements about the religious leaders must have been spoken with a mixed tone of judgment and sorrow. They were strong and unforgettable. They are still applicable any time we become so involved in perfecting the practice of religion that we forget that God is also concerned with mercy, real love, and forgiveness.

24:9–13 You may not be facing intense persecution now, but Christians in other parts of the world are. As you hear about Christians suffering for their faith, remember that they are your brothers and sisters in Christ. Pray for them. Ask God what you can do to help them in their troubles. When one part suffers, the *whole* body suffers. But when all the parts join together to ease the suffering, the whole body benefits (1 Corinthians 12:26).

24:11 The Old Testament frequently mentions false prophets (see 2 Kings 3:13; Isaiah 44:25; Jeremiah 23:16; Ezekiel 13:2–3; Micah 3:5; Zechariah 13:2). False prophets claimed to receive messages from God, but they preached a "health and wealth" message. They said what the people wanted to hear, even when the nation was not following God as it should. There were false prophets in Jesus' day, and we have them today. They are the popular leaders who tell people what they want to hear—such as "God wants you to be rich," "Do whatever your desires tell you," or "There is no such thing as sin or hell." Jesus said false teachers would come, and he warned his disciples, as he warns us, not to listen to their dangerous words.

24:12 With false teaching and loose morals comes a particularly destructive disease—the loss of true love for God and others. Sin cools your love for God and others by turning your focus on yourself. You cannot truly love if you think only of yourself.

24:13 Jesus predicted that his followers would be severely persecuted by those who hated what he stood for. In the midst of terrible persecutions, however, they could have hope, knowing that salvation was theirs. Times of trial serve to sift true Christians from false or fair-weather Christians. When you are pressured to give up and turn your back on Christ, don't do it. Remember the benefits of standing firm, and continue to live for Christ.

24:14 Jesus said that before he returns, the gospel of the kingdom (the message of salvation) would be preached throughout the world. This was the disciples' mission—and it is ours today. Jesus talked about the end times and final judgment to show his followers the urgency of spreading the Good News of salvation to everyone.

24:15–16 What was this "abomination of desolation" mentioned by both Daniel and Jesus? Rather than one specific object, event, or person, it could be seen as any deliberate attempt to mock and deny the reality of God's presence. Daniel's prediction came true in 168 B.C. when Antiochus Epiphanes sacrificed a pig to Zeus on the sacred temple altar (Daniel 9:27; 11:30–31). Jesus' words were remembered in A.D. 70 when Titus placed an idol on the site of the burned temple after destroying Jerusalem. In the end times the antichrist will set up an image of himself and order everyone to worship it (2 Thessalonians 2:4; Revelation 13:14–15). These are all "abominations" that mock God.

21 "For then there will be a great tribulation, such as has not occurred since the beginning of the world until now, nor ever will.
22 "Unless those days had been cut short, no life would have been saved; but for the
sake of the elect those days will be cut short.
23 "Then if anyone says to you, 'Behold, here is the Christ,' or 'There *He is,*' do not believe
him.
24 "For false Christs and false prophets will arise and will show great signs and wonders, so as to mislead, if possible, even the elect.
25 "Behold, I have told you in advance.

Jesus Tells about His Return
(202/Mark 13:24-31; Luke 21:25-33)

26 "So if they say to you, 'Behold, He is in the wilderness,' do not go out, *or,* 'Behold, He
is in the inner rooms,' do not believe *them.*
27 "For just as the lightning comes from the east and flashes even to the west, so will the
coming of the Son of Man be.
28 "Wherever the corpse is, there the vultures will gather.
29 "But immediately after the tribulation of those days THE SUN WILL BE DARKENED,
AND THE MOON WILL NOT GIVE ITS LIGHT, AND THE STARS WILL FALL from the sky, and
the powers of the heavens will be shaken.
30 "And then the sign of the Son of Man will appear in the sky, and then all the tribes of
the earth will mourn, and they will see the SON OF MAN COMING ON THE CLOUDS OF
THE SKY with power and great glory.
31 "And He will send forth His angels with A GREAT TRUMPET and THEY WILL GATHER
TOGETHER His elect from the four winds, from one end of the sky to the other.
32 "Now learn the parable from the fig tree: when its branch has already become tender and puts forth its leaves, you know that summer is near;
33 so, you too, when you see all these things, recognize that He is near, *right* at the
door.
34 "Truly I say to you, this generation will not pass away until all these things take place.
35 "Heaven and earth will pass away, but My words will not pass away.

Jesus Tells about Remaining Watchful
(203/Mark 13:32-37; Luke 21:34-38)

36 "But of that day and hour no one knows, not even the angels of heaven, nor the Son,
but the Father alone.
37 "For the coming of the Son of Man will be just like the days of Noah.
38 "For as in those days before the flood they were eating and drinking, marrying and
giving in marriage, until the day that Noah entered the ark,
39 and they did not understand until the flood came and took them all away; so will
the coming of the Son of Man be.
40 "Then there will be two men in the field; one will be taken and one will be left.
41 "Two women *will be* grinding at the mill; one will be taken and one will be left.

24:21 Dan 12:1; Joel 2:2
24:22 Matt 22:14; 24:24, 31; Luke 18:7
24:23 Luke 17:23f
24:24 Matt 7:15; John 4:48; 2 Thess 2:9; Matt 22:14; Luke 18:7
24:27 Luke 17:24
24:28 Job 39:30; Ezek 39:17; Hab 1:8; Luke 17:37
24:29 Acts 2:20; Rev 6:12-17; 8:12; Is 34:4; Rev 6:13
24:30 Rev 1:7; Dan 7:13; Matt 16:27
24:31 1 Cor 15:52; 1 Thess 4:16; Heb 12:19; Rev 8:2; 11:15; Matt 24:22; Dan 7:2; Zech 2:6; Rev 7:1
24:33 James 5:9; Rev 3:20
24:34 Matt 10:23; 16:28; 23:36
24:35 Matt 5:18; Mark 13:31; Luke 21:33
24:36 Mark 13:32; Acts 1:7
24:37 Matt 16:27; 24:3, 30, 39; Gen 6:5; 7:6-23; Luke 17:26f
24:38 Matt 22:30; Gen 7:7
24:39 Matt 16:27; 24:3, 30, 37
24:41 Luke 17:35; Ex 11:5; Deut 24:6; Is 47:2

24:21–22 Jesus, talking about the end times, telescoped near future and far future events, as did the Old Testament prophets. Many of these persecutions have already occurred; more are yet to come. But God is in control of even the length of persecutions. He will not forget his people. This is all we need to know about the future to motivate us to live rightly now.

24:23–24 Jesus' warnings about false teachers still hold true. Upon close examination it becomes clear that many nice-sounding messages don't agree with God's message in the Bible. Only a solid foundation in God's Word can equip us to perceive the errors and distortions in false teaching.

24:24–28 In times of persecution even strong believers will find it difficult to be loyal. To keep from being deceived by false messiahs, we must understand that Jesus' return will be unmistakable (Mark 13:26); no one will doubt that it is he. If you have to be told that the Messiah has come, then he hasn't (24:27). Christ's coming will be obvious to everyone.

24:30 The nations of the earth will mourn because unbelievers will suddenly realize they have chosen the wrong side. Everything they have scoffed about will be happening, and it will be too late for them.

24:36 It is good that we don't know exactly when Christ will return. If we knew the precise date, we might be tempted to be lazy in our work for Christ. Worse yet, we might plan to keep sinning and then turn to God right at the end. Heaven is not our only goal; we have work to do here. And we must keep on doing it until death or until we see the unmistakable return of our Savior.

24:40–42 Christ's second coming will be swift and sudden. There will be no opportunity for last-minute repentance or bargaining. The choice we have already made will determine our eternal destiny.

42"Therefore be on the alert, for you do not know which day your Lord is coming.
43"But be sure of this, that if the head of the house had known at what time of the night
the thief was coming, he would have been on the alert and would not have allowed his
house to be broken into.
44"For this reason you also must be ready; for the Son of Man is coming at an hour
when you do not think *He will.*
45"Who then is the faithful and sensible slave whom his master put in charge of his
household to give them their food at the proper time?
46"Blessed is that slave whom his master finds so doing when he comes.
47"Truly I say to you that he will put him in charge of all his possessions.
48"But if that evil slave says in his heart, 'My master is not coming for a long time,'
49 and begins to beat his fellow slaves and eat and drink with drunkards;
50 the master of that slave will come on a day when he does not expect *him* and at an
hour which he does not know,
51 and will cut him in pieces and assign him a place with the hypocrites; in that place
there will be weeping and gnashing of teeth.

Jesus Tells the Parable of the Ten Virgins
(204)

25 "Then the kingdom of heaven will be comparable to ten virgins, who took their
lamps and went out to meet the bridegroom.
2"Five of them were foolish, and five were prudent.
3"For when the foolish took their lamps, they took no oil with them,
4 but the prudent took oil in flasks along with their lamps.
5"Now while the bridegroom was delaying, they all got drowsy and *began* to sleep.
6"But at midnight there was a shout, 'Behold, the bridegroom! Come out to meet *him.*'
7"Then all those virgins rose and trimmed their lamps.
8"The foolish said to the prudent, 'Give us some of your oil, for our lamps are going
out.'
9"But the prudent answered, 'No, there will not be enough for us and you *too;* go instead to the dealers and buy *some* for yourselves.'
10"And while they were going away to make the purchase, the bridegroom came, and
those who were ready went in with him to the wedding feast; and the door was shut.
11"Later the other virgins also came, saying, 'Lord, lord, open up for us.'
12"But he answered, 'Truly I say to you, I do not know you.'
13"Be on the alert then, for you do not know the day nor the hour.

Jesus Tells the Parable of the Loaned Money
(205)

14"For *it is* just like a man *about* to go on a journey, who called his own slaves and entrusted his possessions to them.

24:42 Matt 24:43, 44; 25:10, 13; Luke 12:39f; 21:36
24:43 Matt 14:25; Mark 6:48; 13:35; Luke 12:38
24:44 Matt 24:27
24:45 Luke 12:42-46; Matt 25:21, 23; Luke 16:10; Matt 7:24; 10:16; 25:2ff; Matt 25:21, 23
24:47 Matt 25:21, 23
24:51 Matt 8:12
25:1 Matt 13:24; John 18:3; Acts 20:8; Rev 4:5; 8:10
25:2 Matt 7:24; 10:16; 25:2ff
25:4 Matt 7:24; 10:16; 25:2ff
25:9 Matt 7:24; 10:16; 25:2ff
25:10 Matt 24:42ff; Luke 12:35f; Matt 7:21ff; Luke 13:25
25:11 Matt 7:21ff; Luke 13:25
25:13 Matt 24:42ff
25:14 Luke 19:12-27; Matt 21:33

24:44 Jesus' purpose in telling about his return is not to stimulate predictions and calculations about the date, but to warn us to be prepared. Will you be ready? The only safe choice is to obey him *today* (24:46).

24:45–47 Jesus asks us to spend the time of waiting taking care of his people and doing his work here on earth, both within the church and outside it. This is the best way to prepare for Christ's return.

24:50 Knowing that Christ's return will be sudden and unexpected should motivate us always to be prepared. We are not to live irresponsibly—sitting and waiting, doing nothing; seeking self-serving pleasure; using his tarrying as an excuse not to do God's work of building his kingdom; developing a false security based on precise calculations of events; or letting our curiosity about the end times divert us from doing God's work.

24:51 "Weeping and gnashing of teeth" is a phrase used to describe despair. God's coming judgment is as certain as Jesus' return to earth.

25:1ff Jesus told the following parables to clarify further what it means to be ready for his return and how to live until he comes. In the story of the ten virgins (25:1–13), we are taught that every person is responsible for his or her own spiritual condition. The story of the talents (25:14–30) shows the necessity of using well what God has entrusted to us. The parable of the sheep and goats (25:31–46) stresses the importance of serving others in need. No parable by itself *completely* describes our preparation. Instead, each paints one part of the whole picture.

25:1ff This parable is about a wedding. On the wedding day the bridegroom went to the bride's house for the ceremony; then the bride and groom, along with a great procession, returned to the groom's house where a feast took place, often lasting a full week.

These ten virgins were waiting to join the procession, and they hoped to take part in the wedding banquet. But when the groom didn't come at the expected time, five of them were out of lamp oil. By the time they had purchased extra oil, it was too late to join the feast.

When Jesus returns to take his people to heaven, we must be ready. Spiritual preparation cannot be bought or borrowed at the last minute. Our relationship with God must be our own.

15 "To one he gave five talents, to another, two, and to another, one, each according to
his own ability; and he went on his journey.
16 "Immediately the one who had received the five talents went and traded with them,
and gained five more talents.
17 "In the same manner the one who *had received* the two *talents* gained two more.
18 "But he who received the one *talent* went away, and dug *a hole* in the ground and hid
his master's money.
19 "Now after a long time the master of those slaves ☆came and ☆settled accounts with
them.
20 "The one who had received the five talents came up and brought five more talents,
saying, 'Master, you entrusted five talents to me. See, I have gained five more talents.'
21 "His master said to him, 'Well done, good and faithful slave. You were faithful with
a few things, I will put you in charge of many things; enter into the joy of your master.'
22 "Also the one who *had received* the two talents came up and said, 'Master, you entrusted two talents to me. See, I have gained two more talents.'
23 "His master said to him, 'Well done, good and faithful slave. You were faithful with
a few things, I will put you in charge of many things; enter into the joy of your master.'
24 "And the one also who had received the one talent came up and said, 'Master, I knew
you to be a hard man, reaping where you did not sow and gathering where you scattered
no *seed.*
25 'And I was afraid, and went away and hid your talent in the ground. See, you have
what is yours.'
26 "But his master answered and said to him, 'You wicked, lazy slave, you knew that I
reap where I did not sow and gather where I scattered no *seed.*
27 'Then you ought to have put my money in the bank, and on my arrival I would have
received my *money* back with interest.
28 'Therefore take away the talent from him, and give it to the one who has the ten
talents.'
29 "For to everyone who has, *more* shall be given, and he will have an abundance; but
from the one who does not have, even what he does have shall be taken away.
30 "Throw out the worthless slave into the outer darkness; in that place there will be
weeping and gnashing of teeth.

Jesus Tells about the Final Judgment (206)

31 "But when the Son of Man comes in His glory, and all the angels with Him, then He
will sit on His glorious throne.
32 "All the nations will be gathered before Him; and He will separate them from one
another, as the shepherd separates the sheep from the goats;

25:15 Matt 18:24; Luke 19:13; Matt 21:33
25:16 Matt 18:24; Luke 19:13
25:19 Matt 18:23
25:20 Matt 18:24; Luke 19:13
25:21 Matt 24:45, 47; 25:23; Luke 12:44; 22:29; Rev 3:21; 21:7
25:22 Matt 18:24; Luke 19:13
25:23 Matt 24:45, 47; 25:21
25:24 Matt 18:24; Luke 19:13
25:29 Matt 13:12; Mark 4:25; Luke 8:18; John 15:2
25:30 Matt 8:12; 22:13; Luke 13:28
25:31 Matt 16:27f; 1 Thess 4:16; 2 Thess 1:7; Heb 9:28; Jude 14; Rev 1:7; Matt 19:28
25:32 Matt 13:49; 2 Cor 5:10; Ezek 34:17, 20

25:15 The master divided the money (talents) among his servants according to their abilities. No one received more or less than he could handle. If he failed in his assignment, his excuse could not be that he was overwhelmed. Failure could come only from laziness or hatred toward the master. The talents represent any kind of resource we are given. God gives us time, gifts, and other resources according to our abilities, and he expects us to invest them wisely until he returns. We are responsible to use well what God has given us. The issue is not how much we have, but how well we use what we have.

25:21 Jesus is coming back—we know this is true. Does this mean we must quit our jobs in order to serve God? No, it means we are to use our time, talents, and treasures diligently in order to serve God completely in whatever we do. For a few people, this may mean changing professions. For most of us, it means doing our daily work out of love for God.

25:24–30 This last man was thinking only of himself. He hoped to play it safe and protect himself from his hard master, but he was judged for his self-centeredness. We must not make excuses to avoid doing what God calls us to do. If God truly is our Master, we must obey willingly. Our time, abilities, and money aren't ours in the first place—we are caretakers, not owners. When we ignore, squander, or abuse what we are given, we are rebellious and deserve to be punished.

25:29–30 This parable describes the consequences of two attitudes to Christ's return. The person who diligently prepares for it by investing his or her time and talent to serve God will be rewarded. The person who has no heart for the work of the kingdom will be punished. God rewards faithfulness. Those who bear no fruit for God's kingdom cannot expect to be treated the same as those who are faithful.

25:31–46 God will separate his obedient followers from pretenders and unbelievers. The real evidence of our belief is the way we act. To treat all persons we encounter as if they are Jesus is no easy task. What we do for others demonstrates what we really think about Jesus' words to us—feed the hungry, give the homeless a place to stay, look after the sick. How well do your actions separate you from pretenders and unbelievers?

25:32 Jesus used sheep and goats to picture the division between believers and unbelievers. Sheep and goats often grazed together but were separated when it came time to shear the sheep. Ezekiel 34:17–24 also refers to the separation of sheep and goats.

25:34 Gal 5:21; James 2:5; Matt 13:35; Luke 11:50; John 17:24; Eph 1:4; Heb 4:3; 9:26; 1 Pet 1:20; Rev 13:8; 17:8

25:35 James 2:15, 16; Job 31:32; Heb 13:2

25:36 James 2:15, 16; James 1:27; 2 Tim 1:16f

25:40 Prov 19:17; Matt 10:42; Heb 6:10

25:41 Matt 7:23; Mark 9:48; Luke 16:24; Jude 7; Matt 4:10; Rev 12:9

33 and He will put the sheep on His right, and the goats on the left.
34 "Then the King will say to those on His right, 'Come, you who are blessed of My
Father, inherit the kingdom prepared for you from the foundation of the world.
35 'For I was hungry, and you gave Me *something* to eat; I was thirsty, and you gave Me
something to drink; I was a stranger, and you invited Me in;
36 naked, and you clothed Me; I was sick, and you visited Me; I was in prison, and you
came to Me.'
37 "Then the righteous will answer Him, 'Lord, when did we see You hungry, and feed
You, or thirsty, and give You *something* to drink?
38 'And when did we see You a stranger, and invite You in, or naked, and clothe You?
39 'When did we see You sick, or in prison, and come to You?'
40 "The King will answer and say to them, 'Truly I say to you, to the extent that you did
it to one of these brothers of Mine, *even* the least *of them,* you did it to Me.'
41 "Then He will also say to those on His left, 'Depart from Me, accursed ones, into the
eternal fire which has been prepared for the devil and his angels;
42 for I was hungry, and you gave Me *nothing* to eat; I was thirsty, and you gave Me
nothing to drink;

MARY

LAZARUS'S SISTER

Hospitality is an art. Making sure a guest is welcomed, warmed, and well fed requires creativity, organization, and teamwork. Their ability to accomplish these goals makes Mary and her sister Martha one of the best hospitality teams in the Bible. Their frequent guest was Jesus Christ.

For Mary, hospitality meant giving more attention to the guest himself than to the needs he might have. She would rather talk than cook. She was more interested in her guest's words than in the cleanliness of her home or the timeliness of her meals. She let her older sister Martha take care of those details. Mary's approach to events shows her to be mainly a "responder." She did little preparation—her role was participation. Unlike her sister, who had to learn to stop and listen, Mary needed to learn that action is often appropriate and necessary.

We first meet Mary during a visit Jesus paid to her home. She simply sat at his feet and listened. When Martha became irritated at her sister's lack of help, Jesus stated that Mary's choice to enjoy his company was the most appropriate response at the time. Our last glimpse of Mary shows her to have become a woman of thoughtful and worshipful action. Again she was at Jesus' feet, washing them with perfume and wiping them with her hair. She seemed to understand, better even than the disciples, why Jesus was going to die. Jesus said her act of worship would be told everywhere, along with the gospel, as an example of costly service.

What kind of hospitality does Jesus receive in your life? Are you so busy planning and running your life that you neglect precious time with him? Or do you respond to him by listening to his Word, then finding ways to worship him with your life? It is that kind of hospitality he longs for from each of us.

Strengths and accomplishments:
- Perhaps the only person who understood and accepted Jesus' coming death, taking time to anoint his body while he was still living
- Learned when to listen and when to act

Lessons from her life:
- The busyness of serving God can become a barrier to knowing him personally
- Small acts of obedience and service have widespread effects

Vital statistics:
- Where: Bethany
- Relatives: Sister: Martha. Brother: Lazarus

Key verses:
"When she poured this perfume on My body, she did it to prepare Me for burial. Truly I say to you, wherever this gospel is preached in the whole world, what this woman has done will also be spoken of in memory of her" (Matthew 26:12–13).

Mary's story is told in Matthew 26:6–13; Mark 14:3–9; Luke 10:38–42; John 11:17–45; 12:1–11.

25:34–40 This parable describes acts of mercy we all can do every day. These acts do not depend on wealth, ability, or intelligence; they are simple acts freely given and freely received. We have no excuse to neglect those who have deep needs, and we cannot hand over this responsibility to the church or government. Jesus demands our personal involvement in caring for others' needs (Isaiah 58:7).

25:40 There has been much discussion about the identity of the "brothers." Some have said they are the Jews; others say they are all Christians; still others say they are suffering people everywhere. Such a debate is much like the lawyer's earlier question to Jesus, "Who is my neighbor?" (Luke 10:29). The point of this parable is not the *who,* but the *what*—the importance of serving where service is needed. The focus of this parable is that we should love every person and serve anyone we can. Such love for others glorifies God by reflecting our love for him.

43 I was a stranger, and you did not invite Me in; naked, and you did not clothe Me; sick, and in prison, and you did not visit Me.'

44 "Then they themselves also will answer, 'Lord, when did we see You hungry, or thirsty, or a stranger, or naked, or sick, or in prison, and did not take care of You?'

45 "Then He will answer them, 'Truly I say to you, to the extent that you did not do it to one of the least of these, you did not do it to Me.'

46 "These will go away into eternal punishment, but the righteous into eternal life."

C. DEATH AND RESURRECTION OF JESUS, THE KING (26:1—28:20)

After facing much opposition for his teaching, Jesus is betrayed by Judas, disowned by the disciples, crucified, and buried. Three days later he rises from the dead and appears to the disciples, confirming that he is indeed King over life and death. The long-awaited King has brought in his kingdom, but it is different than expected, for he reigns in our hearts until the day he comes again to establish a new and perfect world.

Religious Leaders Plot to Kill Jesus

(207/Mark 14:1-2; Luke 22:1-2)

26 When Jesus had finished all these words, He said to His disciples,

2 "You know that after two days the Passover is coming, and the Son of Man is *to be* handed over for crucifixion."

3 Then the chief priests and the elders of the people were gathered together in the court of the high priest, named Caiaphas;

4 and they plotted together to seize Jesus by stealth and kill Him.

5 But they were saying, "Not during the festival, otherwise a riot might occur among the people."

A Woman Anoints Jesus with Perfume

(182/Mark 14:3-9; John 12:1-11)

6 Now when Jesus was in Bethany, at the home of Simon the leper,

7 a woman came to Him with an alabaster vial of very costly perfume, and she poured it on His head as He reclined *at the table.*

8 But the disciples were indignant when they saw *this,* and said, "Why this waste?

9 "For this *perfume* might have been sold for a high price and *the money* given to the poor."

10 But Jesus, aware of this, said to them, "Why do you bother the woman? For she has done a good deed to Me.

11 "For you always have the poor with you; but you do not always have Me.

12 "For when she poured this perfume on My body, she did it to prepare Me for burial.

25:46 Dan 12:2; John 5:29; Acts 24:15; Matt 19:29; John 3:15f, 36; 5:24; 6:27, 40, 47, 54; 17:2f; Acts 13:46, 48; Rom 2:7; 5:21; 6:23; Gal 6:8; 1 John 5:11

26:1 Matt 7:28

26:2 John 11:55; 13:1; Matt 10:4

26:3 John 11:47; Matt 26:58, 69; 27:27; Mark 14:54, 66; 15:16; Luke 22:55; John 18:15; Matt 26:57; Luke 3:2; John 11:49; 18:13, 14, 24, 28; Acts 4:6

26:4 Matt 12:14

26:5 Matt 27:24

26:6 Luke 7:37-39; John 12:1-8; Matt 21:17

26:7 Luke 7:37f

26:11 Deut 15:11; Mark 14:7; John 12:8

26:12 John 19:40

25:46 Eternal punishment takes place in hell (the lake of fire, or Gehenna), the place of punishment after death for all those who refuse to repent. In the Bible, three words are used in connection with eternal punishment.

(1) *Sheol*, or "the grave," is used in the Old Testament to mean the place of the dead, generally thought to be under the earth. (See Job 24:19; Psalm 16:10; Isaiah 38:10.)

(2) *Hades* is the Greek word for the underworld, the realm of the dead. It is the word used in the New Testament for Sheol. (See Matthew 16:18; Revelation 1:18; 20:13–14.)

(3) *Gehenna,* or hell, was named after the valley of Hinnom near Jerusalem where children were sacrificed by fire to the pagan gods (see 2 Kings 23:10; 2 Chronicles 28:3). This is the place of eternal fire (Matthew 5:22; 10:28; Mark 9:43; Luke 12:5; James 3:6; Revelation 19:20) prepared for the devil, his angels, and all those who do not believe in God (25:46; Revelation 20:9–10). This is the final and eternal state of the wicked after the resurrection and the last judgment.

When Jesus warns against unbelief, he is trying to save us from agonizing punishment.

26:3 Caiaphas was the ruling high priest during Jesus' ministry. He was the son-in-law of Annas, the previous high priest. The Roman government had taken over the process of appointing all political and religious leaders. Caiaphas served for 18 years, longer than most high priests, suggesting that he was gifted at cooperating with the Romans. He was the first to recommend Jesus' death in order to "save" the nation (John 11:49–50).

26:3–5 This was a deliberate plot to kill Jesus. Without this plot, there would have been no groundswell of popular opinion against him. In fact, because of Jesus' popularity, the religious leaders were afraid to arrest him during the Passover. They did not want their actions to incite a riot.

26:6–13 Matthew and Mark put this event just before the Last Supper, while John has it just before the Triumphal Entry. Of the three, John places this event in the most likely chronological order. We must remember that the main purpose of the Gospel writers was to give an accurate record of Jesus' message, not to present an exact chronological account of his life. Matthew and Mark may have chosen to place this event here to contrast the complete devotion of Mary with the betrayal of Judas, the next event they record in their Gospels.

26:7 This woman was Mary, the sister of Martha and Lazarus, who lived in Bethany (John 12:1–3). Alabaster vials were carved from a translucent gypsum. These jars were used to hold perfumed oil.

26:8 All the disciples were indignant, but John's Gospel singles out Judas Iscariot as especially so (John 12:4).

26:11 Here Jesus brought back to mind Deuteronomy 15:11: "The poor will never cease to be in the land." This statement does not justify ignoring the needs of the poor. Scripture continually calls us to care for the needy. The passage in Deuteronomy continues: "You shall freely open your hand to your brother, to your needy and poor in your land."' Rather, by saying this, Jesus highlighted the special sacrifice Mary made for him.

13"Truly I say to you, wherever this gospel is preached in the whole world, what this woman has done will also be spoken of in memory of her."

Judas Agrees to Betray Jesus
(208/Mark 14:10–11; Luke 22:3-6)

26:14 Matt 10:4; 26:25, 47; 27:3; John 6:71; 12:4; 13:26; Acts 1:16

26:15 Matt 10:4; Ex 21:32; Zech 11:12

14 Then one of the twelve, named Judas Iscariot, went to the chief priests
15 and said, "What are you willing to give me to betray Him to you?" And they weighed out thirty pieces of silver to him.
16 From then on he *began* looking for a good opportunity to betray Jesus.

Disciples Prepare for the Passover
(209/Mark 14:12-16; Luke 22:7-13)

26:17 Ex 12:18-20

26:18 Mark 14:13; Luke 22:10; John 7:6, 8

17 Now on the first *day* of Unleavened Bread the disciples came to Jesus and asked, "Where do You want us to prepare for You to eat the Passover?"
18 And He said, "Go into the city to a certain man, and say to him, 'The Teacher says, "My time is near; I *am to* keep the Passover at your house with My disciples." ' "
19 The disciples did as Jesus had directed them; and they prepared the Passover.

Jesus and the Disciples Have the Last Supper
(211/Mark 14:17-26; Luke 22:14-30; John 13:21-30)

26:23 Ps 41:9; John 13:18, 26

26:24 Mark 9:12; Luke 24:25-27, 46; Acts 17:2f; 26:22f; 1 Cor 15:3; 1 Pet 1:10f; Matt 18:7

26:25 Matt 23:7; 26:49; Matt 26:64; 27:11; Luke 22:70

26:26 Luke 22:17-20; 1 Cor 11:23-25; 1 Cor 10:16; Matt 14:19

20 Now when evening came, Jesus was reclining *at the table* with the twelve disciples.
21 As they were eating, He said, "Truly I say to you that one of you will betray Me."
22 Being deeply grieved, they each one began to say to Him, "Surely not I, Lord?"
23 And He answered, "He who dipped his hand with Me in the bowl is the one who will betray Me.
24"The Son of Man *is to* go, just as it is written of Him; but woe to that man by whom the Son of Man is betrayed! It would have been good for that man if he had not been born."
25 And Judas, who was betraying Him, said, "Surely it is not I, Rabbi?" Jesus ☆said to him, "You have said *it* yourself."
26 While they were eating, Jesus took *some* bread, and after a blessing, He broke *it* and gave *it* to the disciples, and said, "Take, eat; this is My body."

26:14–15 Why would Judas want to betray Jesus? Judas, like the other disciples, expected Jesus to start a political rebellion and overthrow Rome. As treasurer, Judas certainly assumed (as did the other disciples—see Mark 10:35–37) that he would be given an important position in Jesus' new government. But when Jesus praised Mary for pouring out perfume worth a year's salary, Judas may have realized that Jesus' kingdom was not physical or political, but spiritual. Judas's greedy desire for money and status could not be realized if he followed Jesus, so he betrayed Jesus in exchange for money and favor from the religious leaders.

26:15 Matthew alone records the exact amount of money Judas accepted to betray Jesus—30 silver coins, the price of a slave (Exodus 21:32). The religious leaders had planned to wait until after the Passover to take Jesus, but with Judas's unexpected offer, they accelerated their plans.

26:17 The Passover took place on one night and at one meal, but the Feast of Unleavened Bread, which was celebrated with it, continued for a week. The people removed all yeast from their homes in commemoration of their ancestors' exodus from Egypt, when they did not have time to let the bread dough rise. Thousands of people poured into Jerusalem from all over the Roman empire for this feast. For more information on how the Passover was celebrated, see the notes on Mark 14:1 and in Exodus 12.

26:23 In Jesus' time, some food was eaten from a common bowl into which everyone dipped their hand.

26:26 Each name we use for this sacrament brings out a different dimension to it. It is the *Lord's Supper* because it commemorates the Passover meal Jesus ate with his disciples; it is the *Eucharist* (thanksgiving) because in it we thank God for Christ's work for us; it is *Communion* because through it we commune with God and with other believers. As we eat the bread and drink the wine, we should be quietly reflective as we recall Jesus' death and his promise to come again, grateful for God's wonderful gift to us, and joyful as we meet with Christ and the body of believers.

VISIT IN BETHANY
Chronologically, the events of Matthew 26:6–13 precede the events of 21:1ff. In 20:29, Jesus left Jericho, heading toward Jerusalem. Then he arrived in Bethany, where a woman anointed him. From there he went toward Bethphage, where two of his disciples got the colt that he would ride into Jerusalem.

27 And when He had taken a cup and given thanks, He gave *it* to them, saying, "Drink
from it, all of you;
28 for this is My blood of the covenant, which is poured out for many for forgiveness **26:28** Ex 24:8; Heb 9:20; Matt 20:28
of sins.
29 "But I say to you, I will not drink of this fruit of the vine from now on until that day
when I drink it new with you in My Father's kingdom."
30 After singing a hymn, they went out to the Mount of Olives. **26:30** Mark 14:26-31; Luke 22:31-34; Matt 21:1

Jesus Again Predicts Peter's Denial
(222/Mark 14:27-31)

31 Then Jesus ☆said to them, "You will all fall away because of Me this night, for it is **26:31** Matt 11:6; Zech 13:7; John 16:32
written, 'I WILL STRIKE DOWN THE SHEPHERD, AND THE SHEEP OF THE FLOCK SHALL
BE SCATTERED.'
32 "But after I have been raised, I will go ahead of you to Galilee." **26:32** Matt 28:7, 10, 16; Mark 16:7
33 But Peter said to Him, "*Even* though all may fall away because of You, I will never
fall away."
34 Jesus said to him, "Truly I say to you that this *very* night, before a rooster crows, you
will deny Me three times." **26:34** Matt 26:75; John 13:38; Mark 14:30
35 Peter ☆said to Him, "Even if I have to die with You, I will not deny You." All the
disciples said the same thing too. **26:35** John 13:37

Jesus Agonizes in the Garden
(223/Mark 14:32-42; Luke 22:39-46)

36 Then Jesus ☆came with them to a place called Gethsemane, and ☆said to His disci- **26:36** Mark 14:32; Luke 22:39; John 18:1
ples, "Sit here while I go over there and pray."
37 And He took with Him Peter and the two sons of Zebedee, and began to be grieved **26:37** Matt 4:21; 17:1; Mark 5:37
and distressed.
38 Then He ☆said to them, "My soul is deeply grieved, to the point of death; remain **26:38** John 12:27; Matt 26:40, 41
here and keep watch with Me."

26:28 How does Jesus' blood relate to the new covenant? People under the old covenant (those who lived before Jesus) could approach God only through a priest and an animal sacrifice. Now all people can come directly to God through faith because Jesus' death has made us acceptable in God's eyes (Romans 3:21–24).

The old covenant was a shadow of the new (Jeremiah 31:31; Hebrews 8:1ff), pointing forward to the day when Jesus himself would be the final and ultimate sacrifice for sin. Rather than an unblemished lamb slain on the altar, the perfect Lamb of God was slain on the cross, a sinless sacrifice so that our sins could be forgiven once and for all. All those who believe in Christ receive that forgiveness.

26:29 Again Jesus assured his disciples of victory over death and of their future with him. The next few hours would bring apparent defeat, but soon they would experience the power of the Holy Spirit and witness the great spread of the gospel message. And one day, they would all be together again in God's new kingdom.

26:30 It is possible that the hymn the disciples sang was from Psalms 115—118, the traditional psalms sung as part of the Passover meal.

26:35 All the disciples declared that they would die before denying Jesus. A few hours later, however, they all scattered. Talk is cheap. It is easy to say we are devoted to Christ, but our claims are meaningful only when they are tested in the crucible of persecution. How strong is your faith? Is it strong enough to stand up under intense trial?

26:37–38 Jesus was in great anguish over his approaching physical pain, separation from the Father, and death for the sins of the world. The divine course was set, but he, in his human nature, still struggled (Hebrews 5:7–9). Because of the anguish Jesus experienced, he can relate to our suffering. Jesus' strength to obey came from his relationship with God the Father, who is also the source of our strength (John 17:11, 15–16, 21, 26).

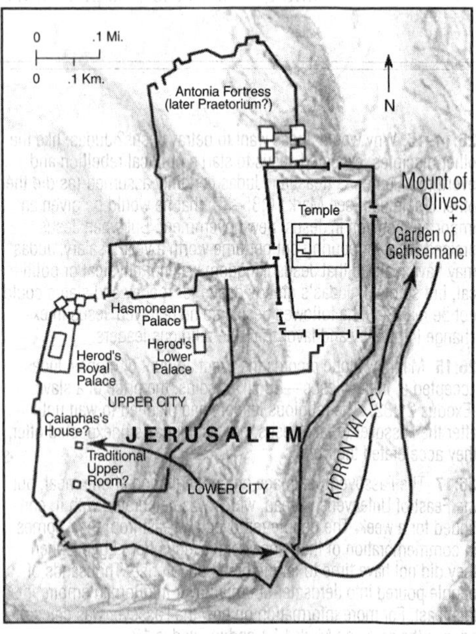

THE PASSOVER MEAL AND GETHSEMANE Jesus, who would soon be the final Passover Lamb, ate the traditional Passover meal with his disciples in the upper room of a house in Jerusalem. During the meal they partook of the bread and wine, which would be the elements of future Communion celebrations, and then went out to the Garden of Gethsemane on the Mount of Olives.

26:39 Matt 20:22; Matt 26:42; Mark 14:36; Luke 22:42; John 6:38
26:40 Matt 26:38
26:41 Matt 26:38; Mark 14:38
26:42 Matt 20:22; Matt 26:39; Mark 14:36; Luke 22:42; John 6:38
26:45 Mark 14:41; John 12:27; 13:1

39 And He went a little beyond *them,* and fell on His face and prayed, saying, "My
Father, if it is possible, let this cup pass from Me; yet not as I will, but as You will."
40 And He ☆came to the disciples and ☆found them sleeping, and ☆said to Peter, "So,
you *men* could not keep watch with Me for one hour?
41 "Keep watching and praying that you may not enter into temptation; the spirit is
willing, but the flesh is weak."
42 He went away again a second time and prayed, saying, "My Father, if this cannot
pass away unless I drink it, Your will be done."
43 Again He came and found them sleeping, for their eyes were heavy.
44 And He left them again, and went away and prayed a third time, saying the same
thing once more.
45 Then He ☆came to the disciples and ☆said to them, "Are you still sleeping and resting? Behold, the hour is at hand and the Son of Man is being betrayed into the hands of
sinners.
46 "Get up, let us be going; behold, the one who betrays Me is at hand!"

Jesus is Betrayed and Arrested
(224/Mark 14:43-52; Luke 22:47-53; John 18:1-11)

26:47 Matt 26:14
26:49 Matt 23:7; 26:25
26:50 Matt 20:13; 22:12
26:51 Mark 14:47; Luke 22:50; John 18:10; Luke 22:38
26:52 Gen 9:6; Rev 13:10
26:53 Mark 5:9, 15; Luke 8:30; Matt 4:11
26:54 Matt 26:24

47 While He was still speaking, behold, Judas, one of the twelve, came up accompanied by a large crowd with swords and clubs, *who came* from the chief priests and elders
of the people.
48 Now he who was betraying Him gave them a sign, saying, "Whomever I kiss, He is
the one; seize Him."
49 Immediately Judas went to Jesus and said, "Hail, Rabbi!" and kissed Him.
50 And Jesus said to him, "Friend, *do* what you have come for." Then they came and
laid hands on Jesus and seized Him.
51 And behold, one of those who were with Jesus reached and drew out his sword, and
struck the slave of the high priest and cut off his ear.
52 Then Jesus ☆said to him, "Put your sword back into its place; for all those who take
up the sword shall perish by the sword.
53 "Or do you think that I cannot appeal to My Father, and He will at once put at My
disposal more than twelve [43]legions of angels?
54 "How then will the Scriptures be fulfilled, *which say* that it must happen this way?"

43 A legion equaled 6,000 troops

BETRAYED!

Delilah betrayed Samson to the Philistines.	Judges 16:16–21
Absalom betrayed David, his father.	2 Samuel 15:10–17
Jehu betrayed Joram and killed him.	2 Kings 9:14–27
Officials betrayed Joash and killed him.	2 Kings 12:20–21
Judas betrayed Jesus.	Matthew 26:46–56

Scripture records a number of occasions in which a person or group was betrayed. The tragedies caused by these violations of trust are a strong lesson about the importance of keeping our commitments.

26:39 Jesus was not rebelling against his Father's will when he asked that the cup of suffering and separation be taken away. In fact, he reaffirmed his desire to do God's will by saying, "Yet not as I will, but as You will." His prayer reveals to us his terrible suffering. His agony was worse than death because he paid for *all* sin by being separated from God. The sinless Son of God took our sins upon himself to save us from suffering and separation.

26:39 In times of suffering people sometimes wish they knew the future, or they wish they could understand the reason for their anguish. Jesus knew what lay ahead of him, and he knew the reason. Even so, his struggle was intense—more wrenching than any struggle we will ever have to face. What does it take to be able to say "as You will"? It takes firm trust in God's plans; it takes prayer and obedience each step of the way.

26:40–41 Jesus used Peter's drowsiness to warn him about the kinds of temptation he would soon face. The way to overcome temptation is to keep watch and pray. Watching means being aware of the possibilities of temptation, sensitive to the subtleties, and spiritually equipped to fight it. Because temptation strikes where we are most vulnerable, we can't resist it alone. Prayer is essential because God's strength can shore up our defenses and defeat Satan's power.

26:48 Judas had told the crowd to arrest the man he kissed. This was not an arrest by Roman soldiers under Roman law, but an arrest by the religious leaders. Judas pointed Jesus out not because Jesus was hard to recognize, but because Judas had agreed to be the formal accuser in case a trial was called. Judas was able to lead the group to one of Jesus' retreats where no onlookers would interfere with the arrest.

26:51–53 The man who cut off the slave's ear was Peter (John 18:10). Peter was trying to prevent what he saw as *defeat.* He didn't realize that Jesus had to die in order to gain *victory.* But Jesus demonstrated perfect commitment to his Father's will. His kingdom would not be advanced with swords, but with faith and obedience.

55 At that time Jesus said to the crowds, "Have you come out with swords and clubs to
arrest Me as *you would* against a robber? Every day I used to sit in the temple teaching
and you did not seize Me.
56 "But all this has taken place to fulfill the Scriptures of the prophets." Then all the
disciples left Him and fled.

26:55 Mark 12:35; 14:49; Luke 4:20; 19:47; 20:1; 21:37; John 7:14, 28; 8:2, 20; 18:20

26:56 Matt 26:24

Caiaphas Questions Jesus
(226/Mark 14:53-65)

57 Those who had seized Jesus led Him away to Caiaphas, the high priest, where the
scribes and the elders were gathered together.
58 But Peter was following Him at a distance as far as the courtyard of the high priest,
and entered in, and sat down with the officers to see the outcome.
59 Now the chief priests and the whole Council kept trying to obtain false testimony
against Jesus, so that they might put Him to death.
60 They did not find *any,* even though many false witnesses came forward. But later on
two came forward,
61 and said, "This man stated, 'I am able to destroy the temple of God and to rebuild
it in three days.' "
62 The high priest stood up and said to Him, "Do You not answer? What is it that these
men are testifying against You?"
63 But Jesus kept silent. And the high priest said to Him, "I adjure You by the living
God, that You tell us whether You are the Christ, the Son of God."
64 Jesus ☆said to him, "You have said it *yourself;* nevertheless I tell you, hereafter you
will see THE SON OF MAN SITTING AT THE RIGHT HAND OF POWER, and COMING ON
THE CLOUDS OF HEAVEN."
65 Then the high priest tore his robes and said, "He has blasphemed! What further
need do we have of witnesses? Behold, you have now heard the blasphemy;
66 what do you think?" They answered, "He deserves death!"

26:57 John 18:12f, 19-24; Matt 26:3

26:58 John 18:15; Matt 26:3; Matt 5:25; John 7:32, 45f; 19:6; Acts 5:22, 26

26:59 Matt 5:22

26:60 Deut 19:15

26:61 Matt 27:40; John 2:19; Acts 6:14

26:63 Matt 27:12, 14; John 19:9; Luke 22:67-71; Lev 5:1; Matt 16:16; Matt 4:3

26:64 Matt 26:25; Ps 110:1; Dan 7:13; Matt 16:27f

26:65 Num 14:6; Acts 14:14

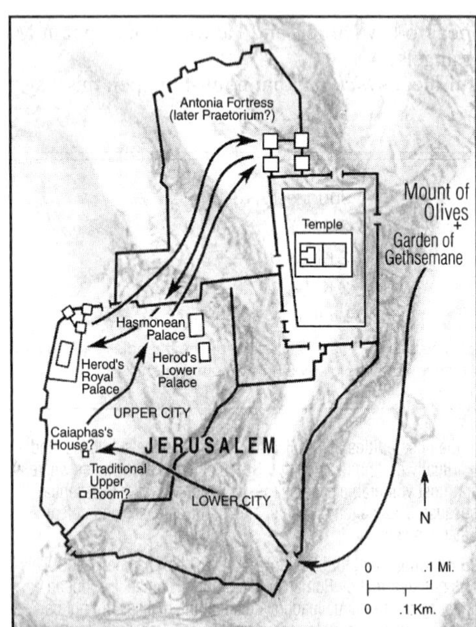

JESUS' TRIAL After Judas singled Jesus out for arrest, the mob took Jesus first to Caiaphas, the high priest. This trial, a mockery of justice, ended at daybreak with their decision to kill him; but the Jews needed Rome's permission for the death sentence. Jesus was taken to Pilate (who was probably in the Praetorium), then to Herod (Luke 23:5–12), and back to Pilate, who sentenced him to die.

26:55 Although the religious leaders could have arrested Jesus at any time, they came at night because they were afraid of the crowds that followed him each day (see 26:5).

26:56 A few hours earlier, this band of men had said they would rather die than desert their Lord (see the note on 26:35).

26:57 Earlier in the evening, Jesus had been questioned by Annas (the former high priest and father-in-law of Caiaphas). Annas then sent Jesus to Caiaphas's home to be questioned (John 18:12–24). Because of their haste to complete the trial and see Jesus die before the Sabbath, less than 24 hours away, the religious leaders met in Caiaphas's home at night instead of waiting for daylight and meeting in the temple.

26:59 The Council (also called the Sanhedrin) was the most powerful religious and political body of the Jewish people. Although the Romans controlled Israel's government, they gave the people power to handle religious disputes and some civil disputes, so the Council made many of the local decisions affecting daily life. But a death sentence had to be approved by the Romans (John 18:31).

26:60–61 The Council tried to find witnesses who would distort some of Jesus' teachings. Finally they found two witnesses who distorted Jesus' words about the temple (see John 2:19). They claimed that Jesus had said he could destroy the temple—a blasphemous boast. Actually Jesus had said, "Destroy this temple, and in three days I will raise it up." Jesus, of course, was talking about his body, not the building. Ironically, the religious leaders were about to destroy Jesus' body just as he had said, and three days later he would rise from the dead.

26:64 Jesus declared his royalty in no uncertain terms. In saying he was the Son of Man, Jesus was claiming to be the Messiah, as his listeners well knew. He knew this declaration would be his undoing, but he did not panic. He was calm, courageous, and determined.

26:65–66 The high priest accused Jesus of blasphemy—calling himself God. To the Jews, this was a great crime, punishable by

26:66 Lev 24:16; John 19:7

26:67 Is 50:6; Luke 22:63-65; John 18:22; Matt 27:30; Mark 10:34

26:69 Matt 26:3

26:73 Mark 14:70; Luke 22:59; John 18:26

67 Then they spat in His face and beat Him with their fists; and others slapped Him,
68 and said, "Prophesy to us, You Christ; who is the one who hit You?"

Peter Denies Knowing Jesus
(227/Mark 14:66-72; Luke 22:54-65; John 18:25-27)

69 Now Peter was sitting outside in the courtyard, and a servant-girl came to him and
said, "You too were with Jesus the Galilean."
70 But he denied *it* before them all, saying, "I do not know what you are talking about."
71 When he had gone out to the gateway, another *servant-girl* saw him and ☆said to
those who were there, "This man was with Jesus of Nazareth."
72 And again he denied *it* with an oath, "I do not know the man."
73 A little later the bystanders came up and said to Peter, "Surely you too are *one* of
them; for even the way you talk gives you away."

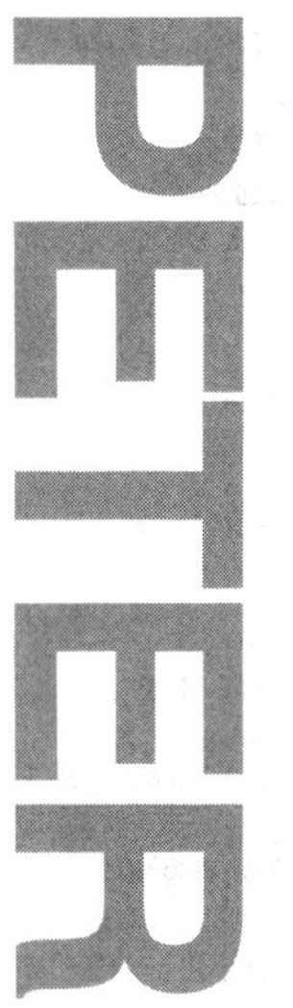

Jesus' first words to Simon Peter were "Follow Me" (Mark 1:17). His last words to him were "You follow Me" (John 21:22). Every step of the way between those two challenges, Peter never failed to follow—even though he often stumbled.

When Jesus entered Peter's life, this plain fisherman became a new person with new goals and new priorities. He did not become a perfect person, however, and he never stopped being Simon Peter. We may wonder what Jesus saw in Simon that made him greet this potential disciple with a new name, Peter—the "rock." Impulsive Peter certainly didn't act like a rock much of the time. But when Jesus chose his followers, he wasn't looking for models; he was looking for real people. He chose people who could be changed by his love, and then he sent them out to communicate that his acceptance was available to anyone—even to those who often fail.

We may wonder what Jesus sees in us when he calls us to follow him. But we know Jesus accepted Peter, and, in spite of his failures, Peter went on to do great things for God. Are you willing to keep following Jesus, even when you fail?

Strengths and accomplishments:
- Became the recognized leader among Jesus' disciples—one of the inner group of three
- Was the first great voice of the gospel during and after Pentecost
- Probably knew Mark and gave him information for the Gospel of Mark
- Wrote 1 and 2 Peter

Weaknesses and mistakes:
- Often spoke without thinking; was brash and impulsive
- During Jesus' trial, denied three times that he even knew Jesus
- Later found it hard to treat Gentile Christians as equals

Lessons from his life:
- Enthusiasm has to be backed up by faith and understanding, or it fails
- God's faithfulness can compensate for our greatest unfaithfulness
- It is better to be a follower who fails than one who fails to follow

Vital statistics:
- Occupations: Fisherman, disciple
- Relatives: Father: John. Brother: Andrew
- Contemporaries: Jesus, Pilate, Herod

Key verse:
"I also say to you that you are Peter, and upon this rock I will build My church; and the gates of Hades will not overpower it" (Matthew 16:18).

Peter's story is told in the Gospels and the book of Acts. He is mentioned in Galatians 1:18 and 2:7–14; and he wrote the books of 1 and 2 Peter.

death (Leviticus 24:16). The religious leaders refused even to consider that Jesus' words might be true. They had decided against Jesus, and in so doing, they sealed their own fate as well as his. Like the members of the Council, you must decide whether Jesus' words are blasphemy or truth. Your decision has eternal implications.

26:69ff There were three stages to Peter's denial. First he acted confused and tried to divert attention from himself by changing the subject. Second, using an oath he denied that he knew Jesus. Third, he began to curse and swear. Believers who deny Christ often begin doing so subtly by pretending not to know him. When opportunities to discuss religious issues come up, they walk away or pretend they don't know the answers. With only a little more pressure, they can be induced to deny flatly their relationship with Christ. If you find yourself subtly diverting conversation so you don't have to talk about Christ, watch out. You may be on the road to denying him.

26:72–74 That Peter denied that he knew Jesus, using an oath, curses, and swearing, does not mean he used foul language. This was the kind of swearing that a person does in a court of law. Peter was swearing that he did not know Jesus and was invoking a curse on himself if his words were untrue. In effect he was saying, "May God strike me dead if I am lying."

74 Then he began to curse and swear, "I do not know the man!" And immediately a
rooster crowed.
75 And Peter remembered the word which Jesus had said, "Before a rooster crows,
you will deny Me three times." And he went out and wept bitterly.

The Council of Religious Leaders Condemns Jesus
(228/Mark 15:1; Luke 22:66-71)

27 Now when morning came, all the chief priests and the elders of the people conferred together against Jesus to put Him to death;
2 and they bound Him, and led Him away and delivered Him to Pilate the governor.

Judas Kills Himself
(229)

3 Then when Judas, who had betrayed Him, saw that He had been condemned, he
felt remorse and returned the thirty pieces of silver to the chief priests and elders,
4 saying, "I have sinned by betraying innocent blood." But they said, "What is that to
us? See *to that* yourself!"
5 And he threw the pieces of silver into the temple sanctuary and departed; and he
went away and hanged himself.
6 The chief priests took the pieces of silver and said, "It is not lawful to put them into
the temple treasury, since it is the price of blood."
7 And they conferred together and with the money bought the Potter's Field as a burial
place for strangers.
8 For this reason that field has been called the Field of Blood to this day.
9 Then that which was spoken through Jeremiah the prophet was fulfilled: "AND THEY
TOOK THE THIRTY PIECES OF SILVER, THE PRICE OF THE ONE WHOSE PRICE HAD BEEN
SET by the sons of Israel;
10 AND THEY GAVE THEM FOR THE POTTER'S FIELD, AS THE LORD DIRECTED ME."

Jesus Stands Trial before Pilate
(230/Mark15:2-5; Luke 23:1-5; John 18:28-37)

11 Now Jesus stood before the governor, and the governor questioned Him, saying,
"Are You the King of the Jews?" And Jesus said to him, "*It is as* you say."
12 And while He was being accused by the chief priests and elders, He did not answer.

26:75 Matt 26:34
27:1 Mark 15:1; Luke 22:66; John 18:28
27:2 Matt 20:19; Luke 3:1; 13:1; 23:12; Acts 3:13; 4:27; 1 Tim 6:13
27:3 Matt 26:14; Matt 26:15
27:4 Matt 27:24
27:5 Matt 26:61; Luke 1:9, 21; Acts 1:18
27:8 Acts 1:19
27:9 Zech 11:12
27:10 Zech 11:13
27:11 Matt 2:2; Matt 26:25
27:12 Matt 26:63; John 19:9

27:1–2 The religious leaders had to persuade the Roman government to sentence Jesus to death because they did not have the authority to do it themselves. The Romans had taken away the religious leaders' authority to inflict capital punishment. Politically, it looked better for the religious leaders anyway if someone else was responsible for killing Jesus. They wanted the death to appear Roman-sponsored so the crowds couldn't blame them. The Jewish leaders had arrested Jesus on theological grounds—blasphemy. But because this charge would be thrown out of a Roman court, they had to come up with a political reason for Jesus' death. Their strategy was to show Jesus as a rebel who claimed to be a king and thus a threat to Caesar.

27:2 Pilate was the Roman governor for the regions of Samaria and Judea from A.D. 26–36. Jerusalem was located in Judea. Pilate took special pleasure in demonstrating his authority over the Jews; for example, he impounded money from the temple treasuries to build an aqueduct. Pilate was not popular, but the religious leaders had no other way to get rid of Jesus than to go to him. Ironically, when Jesus, a Jew, came before him for trial, Pilate found him innocent. He could not find a single fault in Jesus, nor could he contrive one.

27:3–4 Jesus' formal accuser (see 26:48 note) wanted to drop his charges, but the religious leaders refused to halt the trial. When he betrayed Jesus, perhaps Judas was trying to force Jesus' hand to get him to lead a revolt against Rome. This did not work, of course. Whatever his reason, Judas changed his mind, but it was too late. Many of the plans we set into motion cannot be reversed. It is best to think of the potential consequences before we launch into an action we may later regret.

27:4 The priests' job was to teach people about God and act as intercessors for them, helping administer the sacrifices to cover their sins. Judas returned to the priests, exclaiming that he had sinned. Rather than helping him find forgiveness, however, the priests said, "What is that to us? See to that yourself!" Not only had they rejected the Messiah, they had rejected their role as priests.

27:5 According to Matthew, Judas hanged himself. Acts 1:18, however, says that he fell and burst open. The best explanation is that the limb from which he was hanging broke, and the resulting fall split open his body.

27:6 These chief priests felt no guilt in giving Judas money to betray an innocent man, but when Judas returned the money, the priests couldn't accept it because it was wrong to accept blood money—payment for murder! Their hatred for Jesus had caused them to lose all sense of justice.

27:9–10 This prophecy is found specifically in Zechariah 11:12-13, but may also have been taken from Jeremiah 17:2–3; 18:1–4; 19:1–11; or 32:6–15. In Old Testament times, Jeremiah was considered the collector of some of the prophets' writings, so perhaps his name is cited rather than Zechariah.

27:12 Standing before Pilate, the religious leaders accused Jesus of a different crime than the ones for which they had arrested him. They arrested him for blasphemy (claiming to be God), but that charge would mean nothing to the Romans. So the religious leaders had to accuse Jesus of crimes that would have concerned the Roman government, such as encouraging the people not to pay

13 Then Pilate ☆said to Him, "Do You not hear how many things they testify against
You?"

27:14 Matt 27:12; Mark 15:5; Luke 23:9; John 19:9

14 And He did not answer him with regard to even a *single* charge, so the governor was
quite amazed.

Pilate Hands Jesus Over to be Crucified
(232/Mark 15:6-15; Luke 23:13-25; John 18:38—19:16)

15 Now at *the* feast the governor was accustomed to release for the people *any* one
prisoner whom they wanted.
16 At that time they were holding a notorious prisoner, called Barabbas.

27:17 Matt 1:16; 27:22

17 So when the people gathered together, Pilate said to them, "Whom do you want me
to release for you? Barabbas, or Jesus who is called Christ?"

27:19 John 19:13; Acts 12:21; 18:12, 16f; 25:6, 10, 17; Matt 27:24; Gen 20:6; 31:11; Num 12:6; Job 33:15; Matt 1:20; 2:12f, 19, 22

18 For he knew that because of envy they had handed Him over.
19 While he was sitting on the judgment seat, his wife sent him *a message*, saying, "Have
nothing to do with that righteous Man; for last night I suffered greatly in a dream because of Him."
20 But the chief priests and the elders persuaded the crowds to ask for Barabbas and
to put Jesus to death.

27:20 Acts 3:14

21 But the governor said to them, "Which of the two do you want me to release for
you?" And they said, "Barabbas."

27:22 Matt 1:16

22 Pilate ☆said to them, "Then what shall I do with Jesus who is called Christ?" They all
☆said, "Crucify Him!"
23 And he said, "Why, what evil has He done?" But they kept shouting all the more,
saying, "Crucify Him!"

---

taxes, claiming to be a king, and causing riots. These accusations were not true, but the religious leaders were determined to kill Jesus, and they broke several commandments in order to do so.

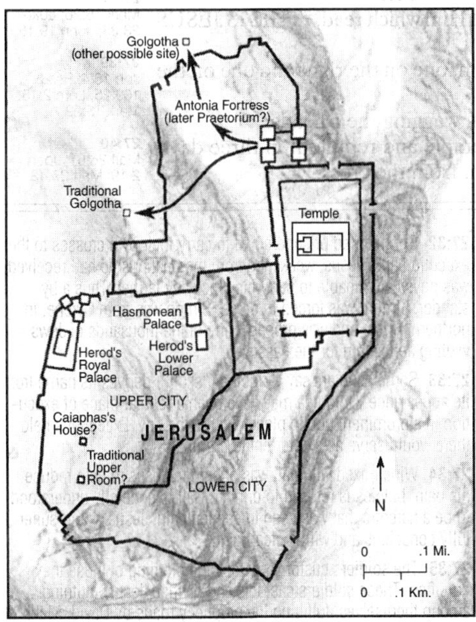

THE WAY OF THE CROSS The Roman soldiers took Jesus into the Praetorium and mocked him, dressing him in a scarlet robe and a crown of thorns. They then led him to the crucifixion site outside the city. He was so weakened by his beatings that he could not carry his cross, and a man from Cyrene was forced to carry it to Golgotha.

27:14 Jesus' silence fulfilled the words of the prophet (Isaiah 53:7). Pilate was amazed that Jesus didn't try to defend himself. He recognized the obvious plot against Jesus and wanted to let him go, but Pilate was already under pressure from Rome to keep peace in his territory. The last thing he needed was a rebellion over this quiet and seemingly insignificant man.

27:15–16 Barabbas had taken part in a rebellion against the Roman government (Mark 15:7). Although an enemy to Rome, he may have been a hero to the Jews. Ironically, Barabbas was guilty of the crime for which Jesus was accused. *Barabbas* means "son of the father," which was actually Jesus' position with God.

27:19 For a leader who was supposed to administer justice, Pilate proved to be more concerned about political expediency than about doing what was right. He had several opportunities to make the right decision. His conscience told him Jesus was innocent; Roman law said an innocent man should not be put to death; and his wife had a troubling dream. Pilate had no good excuse to condemn Jesus, but he was afraid of the crowd.

27:21 Crowds are fickle. They loved Jesus on Sunday because they thought he was going to inaugurate his kingdom. Then they hated him on Friday when his power appeared broken. In the face of the mass uprising against Jesus, his friends were afraid to speak up.

27:21 Faced with a clear choice, the people chose Barabbas, a revolutionary and murderer, over the Son of God. Faced with the same choice today, people are still choosing "Barabbas." They would rather have the tangible force of human power than the salvation offered by the Son of God.

24 When Pilate saw that he was accomplishing nothing, but rather that a riot was starting, he took water and washed his hands in front of the crowd, saying, "I am innocent of
this Man's blood; see *to that* yourselves."
25 And all the people said, "His blood shall be on us and on our children!"
26 Then he released Barabbas for them; but after having Jesus scourged, he handed
Him over to be crucified.

27:24 Matt 26:5; Deut 21:6-8; Matt 27:19; Matt 27:4
27:25 Josh 2:19; Acts 5:28
27:26 Mark 15:15; Luke 23:16; John 19:1

Roman Soldiers Mock Jesus
(223/Mark 15:16-20)

27 Then the soldiers of the governor took Jesus into the Praetorium and gathered the
whole *Roman* cohort around Him.
28 They stripped Him and put a scarlet robe on Him.
29 And after twisting together a crown of thorns, they put it on His head, and a reed in
His right hand; and they knelt down before Him and mocked Him, saying, "Hail, King
of the Jews!"
30 They spat on Him, and took the reed and *began* to beat Him on the head.
31 After they had mocked Him, they took the *scarlet* robe off Him and put His *own*
garments back on Him, and led Him away to crucify Him.

27:27 Matt 26:3; John 18:28, 33; 19:9; Acts 10:1
27:28 John 19:2
27:29 John 19:3
27:30 Matt 26:67; Mark 10:34; 14:65; 15:19

Jesus is Led Away to Be Crucified
(234/Mark 15:21-24; Luke 23:26-31; John 19:17)

Jesus is Placed on the Cross
(235/Mark 15:25-32; Luke 23:32-43; John 19:18-27)

32 As they were coming out, they found a man of Cyrene named Simon, whom they
pressed into service to bear His cross.
33 And when they came to a place called Golgotha, which means Place of a Skull,
34 they gave Him wine to drink mixed with gall; and after tasting *it,* He was unwilling
to drink.
35 And when they had crucified Him, they divided up His garments among themselves
by casting lots.
36 And sitting down, they *began* to keep watch over Him there.
37 And above His head they put up the charge against Him which read, "THIS IS JESUS
THE KING OF THE JEWS."
38 At that time two robbers ☆were crucified with Him, one on the right and one on the
left.
39 And those passing by were hurling abuse at Him, wagging their heads
40 and saying, "You who *are going to* destroy the temple and rebuild it in three days,
save Yourself! If You are the Son of God, come down from the cross."

27:32 Acts 2:10; 6:9; 11:20; 13:1
27:34 Ps 69:21; Mark 15:23
27:35 Ps 22:18
27:36 Matt 27:54
27:37 Mark 15:26; Luke 23:38; John 19:19
27:39 Job 16:4; Ps 22:7; 109:25; Lam 2:15; Mark 15:29
27:40 Matt 26:61; John 2:19; Matt 27:42

27:24 At first Pilate hesitated to give the religious leaders permission to crucify Jesus. He thought they were simply jealous of a teacher who was more popular with the people than they were. But when the Jews threatened to report Pilate to Caesar (John 19:12), Pilate became afraid. Historical records indicate that the Jews had already threatened to lodge a formal complaint against Pilate for his stubborn flouting of their traditions—and such a complaint would most likely have led to his recall by Rome. His job was in jeopardy. The Roman government could not afford to put large numbers of troops in all the regions under their control, so one of Pilate's main duties was to do whatever was necessary to maintain peace.

27:24 In making no decision, Pilate made the decision to let the crowds crucify Jesus. Although he washed his hands, the guilt remained. Washing your hands of a tough situation doesn't cancel your guilt. It merely gives you a false sense of peace. Don't make excuses—take responsibility for the decisions you make.

27:27 A cohort of soldiers was a division of the Roman legion, containing about 200 men.

27:29 People often make fun of Christians for their faith, but believers can take courage from the fact that Jesus himself was mocked as greatly as anyone. Taunting may hurt our feelings, but we should never let it change our faith (see 5:11–12).

27:32 Condemned prisoners had to carry their own crosses to the execution site. Jesus, weakened from the beatings he had received, was physically unable to carry his cross any farther. Thus a bystander, Simon, was forced to do so. Simon was from Cyrene, in northern Africa, and was probably one of the thousands of Jews visiting Jerusalem for the Passover.

27:33 Some scholars say Golgotha ("skull") derives its name from its appearance. Golgotha may have been a regular place of execution in a prominent public place outside the city. Executions held there would serve as a deterrent to criminals.

27:34 Wine mixed with gall was offered to Jesus to help reduce his pain, but Jesus refused to drink it. Gall is generally understood to be a narcotic that was used to deaden pain. Jesus would suffer fully conscious and with a clear mind.

27:35 The soldiers customarily took the clothing of those they crucified. These soldiers cast lots and divided Jesus' clothing among themselves, fulfilling the prophecy made by David. Much of Psalm 22 parallels Jesus' crucifixion.

27:40 This accusation was used against Jesus in his trial by the Council (26:61). It is ironic that Jesus was in the very process of fulfilling his own prophecy. Because Jesus is the Son of God, who always obeys the will of the Father, he did not come down from the cross.

27:42 Mark 15:31; Luke 23:35; Matt 27:37; Luke 23:37; John 1:49; 12:13
27:43 Ps 22:8
27:44 Luke 23:39-43

41 In the same way the chief priests also, along with the scribes and elders, were mocking *Him* and saying,
42 "He saved others; He cannot save Himself. He is the King of Israel; let Him now
come down from the cross, and we will believe in Him.
43 "HE TRUSTS IN GOD; LET GOD RESCUE *Him* now, IF HE DELIGHTS IN HIM; for He
said, 'I am the Son of God.' "
44 The robbers who had been crucified with Him were also insulting Him with the same
words.

Jesus Dies on the Cross
(236/Mark 15:33-41; Luke 23:44-49; John 19:28-37)

27:46 Ps 22:1
27:48 Ps 69:21; Mark 15:36; Luke 23:36; John 19:29
27:50 Mark 15:37; Luke 23:46; John 19:30
27:51 Ex 26:31ff; Mark 15:38; Luke 23:45; Heb 9:3; Matt 27:54
27:52 Acts 7:60
27:53 Matt 4:5
27:54 Mark 15:39; Luke 23:47; Matt 27:36; Matt 27:51; Matt 4:3; 27:43

45 Now from the [44]sixth hour darkness fell upon all the land until the [45]ninth hour.
46 About the ninth hour Jesus cried out with a loud voice, saying, "ELI, ELI, LAMA SA-
BACHTHANI?" that is, "MY GOD, MY GOD, WHY HAVE YOU FORSAKEN ME?"
47 And some of those who were standing there, when they heard it, *began* saying, "This
man is calling for Elijah."
48 Immediately one of them ran, and taking a sponge, he filled it with sour wine and
put it on a reed, and gave Him a drink.
49 But the rest *of them* said, "Let us see whether Elijah will come to save Him[46]."
50 And Jesus cried out again with a loud voice, and yielded up His spirit.
51 And behold, the veil of the temple was torn in two from top to bottom; and the earth
shook and the rocks were split.
52 The tombs were opened, and many bodies of the saints who had fallen asleep were
raised;
53 and coming out of the tombs after His resurrection they entered the holy city and
appeared to many.
54 Now the centurion, and those who were with him keeping guard over Jesus, when
they saw the earthquake and the things that were happening, became very frightened
and said, "Truly this was the Son of God!"

44 I.e. noon **45** I.e. 3 p.m. **46** Some early mss read *And another took a spear and pierced His side, and there came out water and blood* (cf John 19:34)

THE SEVEN LAST WORDS OF JESUS ON THE CROSS

"Father, forgive them; for they do not know what they are doing."	Luke 23:34
"Truly I say to you, today you shall be with Me in Paradise."	Luke 23:43
Speaking to Mary and John, "Woman, behold, your son! . . . Behold, your mother!"	John 19:26–27
"MY GOD, MY GOD, WHY HAVE YOU FORSAKEN ME?"	Matthew 27:46; Mark 15:34
"I am thirsty."	John 19:28
"It is finished."	John 19:30
"Father, INTO YOUR HANDS I COMMIT MY SPIRIT."	Luke 23:46

The statements that Jesus made from the cross have been treasured by all who have followed him as Lord. They demonstrate both his humanity and his divinity. They also capture the last moments of all that Jesus went through to gain our forgiveness.

27:44 Later one of these robbers repented. Jesus promised that the repentant robber would join him in Paradise (Luke 23:39–43).

27:45 We do not know how this darkness occurred, but it is clear that God caused it. Nature testified to the gravity of Jesus' death, while Jesus' friends and enemies alike fell silent in the encircling gloom. The darkness on that Friday afternoon was both physical and spiritual.

27:46 Jesus was not questioning God; he was quoting the first line of Psalm 22—a deep expression of the anguish he felt when he took on the sins of the world, which caused him to be separated from his Father. *This* was what Jesus dreaded as he prayed to God in the garden to take the cup from him (26:39). The physical agony was horrible, but even worse was the period of spiritual separation from God. Jesus suffered this double death so that we would never have to experience eternal separation from God.

27:47 The bystanders misinterpreted Jesus' words and thought he was calling for Elijah. Because Elijah ascended into heaven without dying (2 Kings 2:11), they thought he would return again to rescue them from great trouble (Malachi 4:5). At the annual Passover feast, each family set an extra place for Elijah in expectation of his return.

27:51 The temple had three main parts—the courts, the holy place (where only the priests could enter), and the holy of holies (where only the high priest could enter, and only once a year, to atone for the sins of the nation—Leviticus 16:1–35). The veil separating the holy place from the holy of holies was torn in two at Christ's death, symbolizing that the barrier between God and humanity was removed. Now all people are free to approach God because of Christ's sacrifice for our sins (see Hebrews 9:1–14; 10:19–22).

27:52–53 Christ's death was accompanied by at least four miraculous events: darkness, the tearing in two of the veil in the temple, an earthquake, and dead people rising from their tombs. Jesus' death, therefore, could not have gone unnoticed. Everyone knew something significant had happened.

55 Many women were there looking on from a distance, who had followed Jesus from
Galilee while ministering to Him.
56 Among them was Mary Magdalene, and Mary the mother of James and Joseph, and
the mother of the sons of Zebedee.

Jesus Is Laid in the Tomb

(237/Mark 15:42-47; Luke 23:50-56; John 19:38-42)

57 When it was evening, there came a rich man from Arimathea, named Joseph, who
himself had also become a disciple of Jesus.
58 This man went to Pilate and asked for the body of Jesus. Then Pilate ordered it to
be given *to him.*
59 And Joseph took the body and wrapped it in a clean linen cloth,
60 and laid it in his own new tomb, which he had hewn out in the rock; and he rolled a
large stone against the entrance of the tomb and went away.
61 And Mary Magdalene was there, and the other Mary, sitting opposite the grave.

Guards Are Posted at the Tomb

(238)

62 Now on the next day, the day after the preparation, the chief priests and the Pharisees gathered together with Pilate,
63 and said, "Sir, we remember that when He was still alive that deceiver said, 'After
three days I *am to* rise again.'
64 "Therefore, give orders for the grave to be made secure until the third day, otherwise His disciples may come and steal Him away and say to the people, 'He has risen
from the dead,' and the last deception will be worse than the first."
65 Pilate said to them, "You have a guard; go, make it *as* secure as you know how."
66 And they went and made the grave secure, and along with the guard they set a seal
on the stone.

27:55 Luke 8:2, 3
27:56 Matt 28:1; Mark 15:40, 47; 16:9; Luke 8:2; John 19:25; 20:1, 18; Matt 20:20
27:60 Matt 27:66; 28:2; Mark 16:4
27:61 Matt 27:56; 28:1
27:62 Mark 15:42; Luke 23:54; John 19:14, 31, 42
27:63 Matt 16:21; 17:23; 20:19; Mark 8:31; 9:31; 10:34; Luke 9:22; 18:31-33
27:65 Matt 27:66; 28:11
27:66 Matt 27:65; 28:11; Dan 6:17; Matt 27:60; 28:2; Mark 16:4

HOW JESUS' TRIAL WAS ILLEGAL

1. Even before the trial began, it had been determined that Jesus must die (John 11:50; Mark 14:1). There was no "innocent until proven guilty" approach.
2. False witnesses were sought to testify against Jesus (Matthew 26:59). Usually the religious leaders went through an elaborate system of screening witnesses to ensure justice.
3. No defense for Jesus was sought or allowed (Luke 22:67–71).
4. The trial was conducted at night (Mark 14:53–65; 15:1), which was illegal according to the religious leaders' own laws.
5. The high priest put Jesus under oath, but then incriminated him for what he said (Matthew 26:63–66).
6. Cases involving such serious charges were to be tried only in the Council's regular meeting place, not in the high priest's palace (Mark 14:53–65).

The religious leaders were not interested in giving Jesus a fair trial. In their minds, Jesus had to die. This blind obsession led them to pervert the justice they were appointed to protect. Here are many examples of the actions taken by the religious leaders that were illegal according to their own laws.

27:57–58 Joseph of Arimathea was a secret disciple of Jesus. He was a religious leader, an honored member of the Council (Mark 15:43). In the past, Joseph had been afraid to speak against the religious leaders who opposed Jesus; now he was bold, courageously asking to take Jesus' body from the cross and to bury it. The disciples who publicly followed Jesus had fled, but this Jewish leader, who followed Jesus in secret, came forward and did what was right.

27:60 The tomb where Jesus was laid was probably a man-made cave cut out of one of the many limestone hills in the area. These caves were often large enough to walk into.

27:64 The religious leaders took Jesus' resurrection claims more seriously than the disciples did. The disciples didn't remember Jesus' teaching about his resurrection (20:17–19); but the religious leaders did. Because of his claims, they were almost as afraid of Jesus after his death as when he was alive. They tried to take every precaution that his body would remain in the tomb.

27:66 The Pharisees were so afraid of Jesus' predictions about his resurrection that they made sure the tomb was thoroughly sealed and guarded. Because the tomb was hewn out of rock in the side of a hill, there was only one entrance. The tomb was sealed by stringing a cord across the stone that was rolled over the entrance. The cord was sealed at each end with clay. But the religious leaders took a further precaution, asking that guards be placed at the tomb's entrance. With such precautions, the only way the tomb could be empty would be for Jesus to rise from the dead. The Pharisees failed to understand that no rock, seal, guard, or army could prevent the Son of God from rising again.

Jesus Rises from the Dead
(239/Mark 16:1-8; Luke 24:1-12; John 20:1-9)

28 Now after the Sabbath, as it began to dawn toward the first *day* of the week, Mary
Magdalene and the other Mary came to look at the grave.
2 And behold, a severe earthquake had occurred, for an angel of the Lord descended
from heaven and came and rolled away the stone and sat upon it.
3 And his appearance was like lightning, and his clothing as white as snow.
4 The guards shook for fear of him and became like dead men.
5 The angel said to the women, "Do not be afraid; for I know that you are looking for
Jesus who has been crucified.
6 "He is not here, for He has risen, just as He said. Come, see the place where He was
lying.
7 "Go quickly and tell His disciples that He has risen from the dead; and behold, He is
going ahead of you into Galilee, there you will see Him; behold, I have told you."

Jesus Appears to the Women
(241)

8 And they left the tomb quickly with fear and great joy and ran to report it to His
disciples.
9 And behold, Jesus met them and greeted them. And they came up and took hold of
His feet and worshiped Him.
10 Then Jesus *said to them, "Do not be afraid; go and take word to My brethren to
leave for Galilee, and there they will see Me."

Religious Leaders Bribe the Guards
(242)

11 Now while they were on their way, some of the guard came into the city and reported to the chief priests all that had happened.
12 And when they had assembled with the elders and consulted together, they gave a
large sum of money to the soldiers,
13 and said, "You are to say, 'His disciples came by night and stole Him away while we
were asleep.'
14 "And if this should come to the governor's ears, we will win him over and keep you
out of trouble."
15 And they took the money and did as they had been instructed; and this story was
widely spread among the Jews, *and is* to this day.

28:1 Matt 27:56, 61
28:2 Luke 24:4; John 20:12; Matt 27:66; Mark 16:4
28:3 Dan 7:9; 10:6; Mark 9:3; John 20:12; Acts 1:10
28:5 Matt 14:27; 28:10; Rev 1:17
28:6 Matt 12:40; 16:21; 27:63
28:7 Matt 26:32; 28:10, 16; Mark 16:7
28:10 Matt 14:27; 28:5; John 20:17; Rom 8:29; Heb 2:11f, 17; Matt 26:32; 28:7, 16
28:11 Matt 27:65, 66
28:14 Matt 27:2
28:15 Matt 9:31; Mark 1:45; Matt 27:8

28:1 The other Mary was not Jesus' mother. She could have been the wife of Clopas (John 19:25). Or, if she was the mother of James and John (Matthew 27:56), she may have been Jesus' aunt.

28:2 The stone was not rolled away so Jesus could get out, but so others could get in and see that Jesus had indeed risen from the dead, just as he had promised.

28:5–7 The angel who announced the good news of the resurrection to the women gave them four messages: (1) *Do not be afraid.* The reality of the resurrection brings joy, not fear. When you are afraid, remember the empty tomb. (2) *He is not here.* Jesus is not dead and is not to be looked for among the dead. He is alive, with his people. (3) *Come, see.* The women could check the evidence themselves. The tomb was empty then, and it is empty today. The resurrection is a historical fact. (4) *Go quickly and tell.* They were to spread the joy of the resurrection. We too are to spread the great news about Jesus' resurrection.

28:6 Jesus' resurrection is the key to the Christian faith. Why? (1) Just as he promised, Jesus rose from the dead. We can be confident, therefore, that he will accomplish all he has promised. (2) Jesus' bodily resurrection shows us that the living Christ is ruler of God's eternal kingdom, not a false prophet or imposter. (3) We can be certain of our resurrection because he was resurrected. Death is not the end—there is future life. (4) The power that brought Jesus back to life is available to us to bring our spiritually dead selves back to life. (5) The resurrection is the basis for the church's witness to the world. Jesus is more than just a human leader; he is the Son of God.

28:10 By "brethren," Jesus probably meant his disciples. This showed that he had forgiven them, even after they had denied and deserted him. Their relationship would now be even stronger than before.

28:10 Jesus told the women to pass a message on to the disciples—that he would meet them in Galilee, as he had previously told them (Mark 14:28). But the disciples, afraid of the religious leaders, stayed hidden behind locked doors in Jerusalem (John 20:19). So Jesus met them first there (Luke 24:36) and then later in Galilee (John 21).

28:11–15 Jesus' resurrection was already causing a great stir in Jerusalem. A group of women was moving quickly through the streets, looking for the disciples to tell them the amazing news that Jesus was alive. At the same time, a group of religious leaders was plotting how to cover up the resurrection.

Today there is still a great stir over the resurrection, and there are still only two choices—to believe that Jesus rose from the dead, or to be closed to the truth—denying it, ignoring it, or trying to explain it away.

Jesus Gives the Great Commission (248/Mark 16:15-18)

16 But the eleven disciples proceeded to Galilee, to the mountain which Jesus had designated.
17 When they saw Him, they worshiped *Him;* but some were doubtful.
18 And Jesus came up and spoke to them, saying, "All authority has been given to Me in heaven and on earth.
19 "Go therefore and make disciples of all the nations, baptizing them in the name of the Father and the Son and the Holy Spirit,
20 teaching them to observe all that I commanded you; and lo, I am with you always, even to the end of the age."

28:16 Matt 26:32; 28:7, 10; Mark 15:41; 16:7

28:17 Mark 16:11

28:18 Dan 7:13f; Matt 11:27; 26:64; Rom 14:9; Eph 1:20-22; Phil 2:9f; Col 2:10; 1 Pet 3:22

28:18 God gave Jesus authority over heaven and earth. On the basis of that authority, Jesus told his disciples to make more disciples as they preached, baptized, and taught. With this same authority, Jesus still commands us to tell others the Good News and make them disciples for the kingdom.

28:18–20 When someone is dying or leaving us, his or her last words are very important. Jesus left the disciples with these last words of instruction: They were under his authority; they were to make more disciples; They were to baptize and teach these new disciples to obey Christ; Christ would be with them always. Whereas in previous missions Jesus had sent his disciples only to the Jews (10:5–6), their mission from now on would be worldwide. Jesus is Lord of the earth, and he died for the sins of people from all nations.

We are to go—whether it is next door or to another country—and make disciples. It is not an option, but a command to all who call Jesus "Lord." We are not all evangelists in the formal sense, but we have all received gifts that we can use to help fulfill the Great Commission. As we obey, we have comfort in the knowledge that Jesus is always with us.

28:19 Jesus' words affirm the reality of the Trinity. Some people accuse theologians of making up the concept of the Trinity and reading it into Scripture. As we see here, the concept comes directly from Jesus himself. He did not say baptize them into the *names,* but into the *name* of the Father, Son, and Holy Spirit. The word *Trinity* does not occur in Scripture, but it well describes the three-in-one nature of the Father, Son, and Holy Spirit.

28:19 The disciples were to baptize people because baptism unites a believer with Jesus Christ in his or her death to sin and resurrection to new life. Baptism symbolizes submission to Christ, a willingness to live God's way, and identification with God's covenant people.

28:20 How is Jesus *with* us? Jesus was with the disciples physically until he ascended into heaven, and then spiritually through the Holy Spirit (Acts 1:4). The Holy Spirit would be Jesus' presence that would never leave them (John 14:26). Jesus continues to be with us today through his Spirit.

28:20 The Old Testament prophecies and genealogies in the book of Matthew present Jesus' credentials for being King of the world—not a military or political leader, as the disciples had originally hoped, but a spiritual King who can overcome all evil and rule in the heart of every person. If we refuse to serve the King faithfully, we are disloyal subjects, fit only to be banished from the kingdom. We must make Jesus King of our lives and worship him as our Savior, King, and Lord.

OLD TESTAMENT PASSAGES QUOTED BY CHRIST

New Testament	*Old Testament*	*Occasion*
Matthew 4:4	Deuteronomy 8:3	Temptation
Matthew 4:7	Deuteronomy 6:16	
Matthew 4:10	Deuteronomy 6:13	
Matthew 5:21	Exodus 20:13	Sermon on the Mount
Matthew 5:27	Exodus 20:14	
Luke 4:18-19	Isaiah 61:1-2	Hometown sermon
Matthew 9:13	Hosea 6:6	Confrontations with Jewish rulers
Mark 10:7-8	Genesis 2:24	
Mark 12:29-30	Deuteronomy 6:4-5	
Matthew 15:7-9	Isaiah 29:13	
John 8:17	Deuteronomy 17:6	
Luke 7:27	Malachi 3:1	Tribute to John
Matthew 21:16	Psalm 8:2	Triumphal entry
Luke 19:46	Isaiah 56:7	Temple cleansing
Matthew 21:42, 44	Psalm 118:22-23	Parable about Israel
Mark 12:36	Psalm 110:1	Temple question session
John 15:25	Psalm 35:19; 69:4	Last Passover
Matthew 27:46	Psalm 22:1	On the cross
Luke 23:46	Psalm 31:5	

MARK

Herod the Great begins to rule 37 B.C.	Jesus is born 6/5 B.C.	Escape to Egypt 5/4 B.C.	Herod the Great dies 4 B.C.	Return to Nazareth 4/3 B.C.	Jesus visits temple as a boy A.D. 6/7

VITAL STATISTICS

PURPOSE:
To present the person, work, and teachings of Jesus

AUTHOR:
John Mark. He was not one of the 12 disciples, but he accompanied Paul on his first missionary journey (Acts 13:13).

TO WHOM WRITTEN:
The Christians in Rome, where he wrote the Gospel

DATE WRITTEN:
Between A.D. 55 and 65

SETTING:
The Roman empire under Tiberius Caesar. The empire, with its common language and excellent transportation and communication systems, was ripe to hear Jesus' message, which spread quickly from nation to nation.

KEY VERSE:
"For even the Son of Man did not come to be served, but to serve, and to give His life a ransom for many" (10:45).

KEY PEOPLE:
Jesus, the 12 disciples, Pilate, the Jewish religious leaders

KEY PLACES:
Capernaum, Nazareth, Caesarea Philippi, Jericho, Bethany, Mount of Olives, Jerusalem, Golgotha

SPECIAL FEATURES:
Mark was probably the first Gospel written. The other Gospels quote all but 31 verses of Mark. Mark records more miracles than does any other Gospel.

WE'RE number one! . . . The greatest, strongest, prettiest . . . champions! Daily such proclamations boldly assert claims of supremacy. Everyone wants to be associated with a winner. Losers are those who finish less than first. In direct contrast are the words of Jesus: "And whoever wishes to be first among you shall be slave of all. For even the Son of Man did not come to be served, but to serve, and to give His life a ransom for many" (10:44–45). Jesus *is* the greatest—God incarnate, our Messiah—but he entered history as a servant.

This is the message of Mark. Written to encourage Roman Christians and to prove beyond a doubt that Jesus is the Messiah, Mark presents a rapid succession of vivid pictures of Jesus in action—his true identity revealed by what he does, not necessarily by what he says. It is Jesus on the move.

Omitting the birth of Jesus, Mark begins with John the Baptist's preaching. Then, moving quickly past Jesus' baptism, temptation in the wilderness, and call of the disciples, Mark takes us directly into Jesus' public ministry. We see Jesus confronting a demon, healing a man with leprosy, and forgiving and healing the paralyzed man lowered into Jesus' presence by friends.

Next, Jesus calls Matthew (Levi) and has dinner with him and his questionable associates. This initiates the conflict with the Pharisees and other religious leaders, who condemn Jesus for eating with sinners and breaking the Sabbath.

In chapter 4, Mark pauses to give a sample of Jesus' teaching—the parable of the farmer and the illustration of the mustard seed—and then plunges back into the action. Jesus calms the waves, drives out demons, and heals Jairus's daughter.

After returning to Nazareth for a few days and experiencing rejection in his hometown, Jesus commissions the disciples to spread the Good News everywhere. Opposition from Herod and the Pharisees increases, and John the Baptist is beheaded. But Jesus continues to move, feeding 5,000, reaching out to the woman from Syrian Phoenicia, healing the deaf man, and feeding 4,000.

Finally, it is time to reveal his true identity to the disciples. Do they really know who Jesus is? Peter proclaims him Messiah but then promptly shows that he does not understand Jesus' mission. After the transfiguration, Jesus continues to teach and heal, confronting the Pharisees about divorce and the rich young man about eternal life. Blind Bartimaeus is healed.

Events move rapidly toward a climax. The Last Supper, the betrayal, the crucifixion, and the resurrection are dramatically portrayed, along with more examples of Jesus' teachings. Mark shows us Jesus—moving, serving, sacrificing, and saving! As you read Mark, be ready for action, be open for God's move in your life, and be challenged to move into your world to serve.

Tiberius Caesar becomes emperor 14	John's ministry begins 26	Jesus begins his ministry 26/27	Jesus chooses twelve disciples 28	Jesus feeds 5,000 29	Jesus is crucified, rises again, and ascends 30

THE BLUEPRINT

A. BIRTH AND PREPARATION OF JESUS, THE SERVANT (1:1–13)

Jesus did not arrive unannounced or unexpected. The Old Testament prophets had clearly predicted the coming of a great one, sent by God himself, who would offer salvation and eternal peace to Israel and the entire world. Then came John the Baptist, who announced that the long-awaited Messiah had finally come and would soon be among the people. In God's work in the world today, Jesus does not come unannounced or unexpected. Yet many still reject him. We have the witness of the Bible, but some choose to ignore it, just as many ignored John the Baptist in his day.

B. MESSAGE AND MINISTRY OF JESUS, THE SERVANT (1:14—13:37)

1. Jesus' ministry in Galilee
2. Jesus' ministry beyond Galilee
3. Jesus' ministry in Jerusalem

Jesus had all the power of almighty God: He raised the dead, gave sight to the blind, restored deformed bodies, and quieted stormy seas. But with all this power, Jesus came to mankind as a servant. We can use his life as a pattern for how to live today. As Jesus served God and others, so should we.

C. DEATH AND RESURRECTION OF JESUS, THE SERVANT (14:1—16:20)

Jesus came as a servant, so many did not recognize or acknowledge him as the Messiah. We must be careful that we also don't reject God or his will because he doesn't quite fit our image of what God should be.

MEGATHEMES

THEME	EXPLANATION	IMPORTANCE
Jesus Christ	Jesus Christ alone is the Son of God. In Mark, Jesus demonstrates his divinity by overcoming disease, demons, and death. Although he had the power to be king of the earth, Jesus chose to obey the Father and die for us.	When Jesus rose from the dead, he proved that he was God, that he could forgive sin, and that he has the power to change our lives. By trusting in him for forgiveness, we can begin a new life with him as our guide.
Servant	As the Messiah, Jesus fulfilled the prophecies of the Old Testament by coming to earth. He did not come as a conquering king; he came as a servant. He helped people by telling them about God and healing them. Even more, by giving his life as a sacrifice for sin, he performed the ultimate act of service.	Because of Jesus' example, we should be willing to serve God and others. Real greatness in Christ's kingdom is shown by service and sacrifice. Ambition or love of power or position should not be our motive; instead, we should do God's work because we love him.
Miracles	Mark records more of Jesus' miracles than sermons. Jesus is clearly a man of power and action, not just words. Jesus did miracles to convince the people who he was and to confirm to the disciples his true identity—God.	The more convinced we become that Jesus is God, the more we will see his power and his love. His mighty works show us he is able to save anyone regardless of his or her past. His miracles of forgiveness bring healing, wholeness, and changed lives to those who trust him.
Spreading the Gospel	Jesus directed his public ministry to the Jews first. When the Jewish leaders opposed him, Jesus also went to the non-Jewish world, healing and preaching. Roman soldiers, Syrians, and other Gentiles heard the Good News. Many believed and followed him. Jesus' final message to his disciples challenged them to go into all the world and preach the gospel of salvation.	Jesus crossed national, racial, and economic barriers to spread his Good News. Jesus' message of faith and forgiveness is for the whole world—not just our church, neighborhood, or nation. We must reach out beyond our own people and needs to fulfill the worldwide vision of Jesus Christ so that people everywhere may hear this great message and be saved from sin and death.

KEY PLACES IN MARK

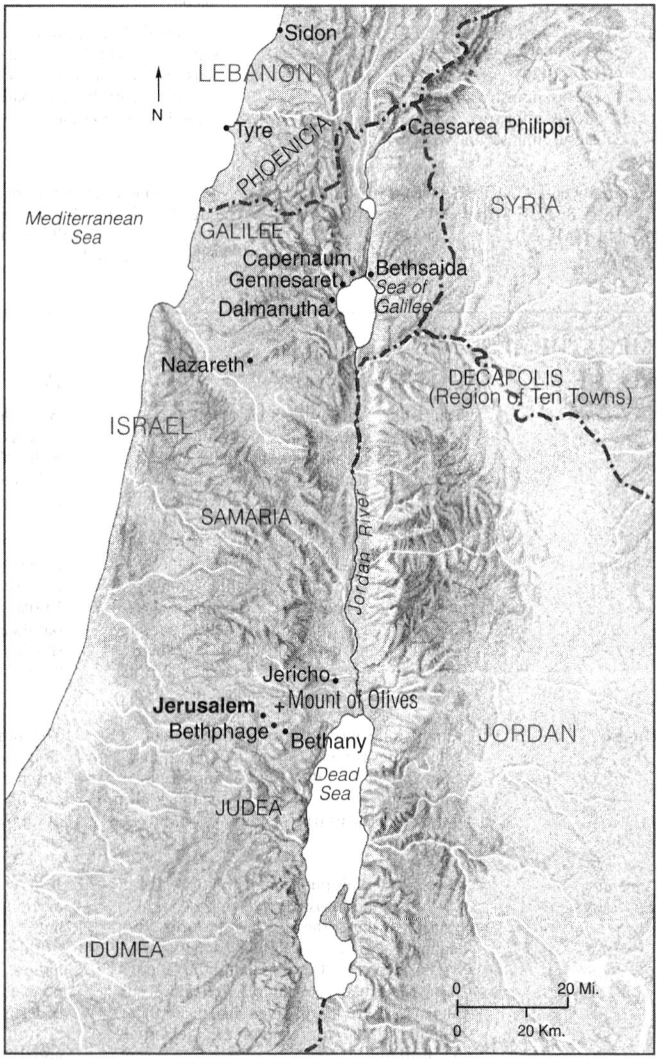

Of the four Gospels, Mark's narrative is the most chronological—that is, most of the stories are positioned in the order they actually occurred. Though the shortest of the four, the Gospel of Mark contains the most events; it is action-packed. Most of this action centers in Galilee, where Jesus began his ministry. Capernaum served as his base of operation (1:21; 2:1; 9:33), from which he would go out to cities like Bethsaida, where he healed a blind man (8:22ff); Gennesaret, where he performed many healings (6:53ff); Tyre and Sidon (to the far north), where he healed many, drove out demons, and met the woman from Syrian Phoenicia (3:8; 7:24ff); and Caesarea Philippi, where Peter declared him to be the Messiah (8:27ff). After his ministry in Galilee and the surrounding regions, Jesus headed for Jerusalem (10:1). Before going there, Jesus told his disciples three times that he would be crucified there and then come back to life (8:31; 9:31; 10:33–34).

The broken lines (—·—·) indicate modern boundaries.

A. BIRTH AND PREPARATION OF JESUS, THE SERVANT (1:1-13)

Mark, the shortest of the four Gospels, opens with Jesus' baptism and temptation. Moving right into action, Mark quickly prepares us for Christ's ministry. The Gospel of Mark is concise, straightforward, and chronological.

John the Baptist Prepares the Way for Jesus

(16/Matthew 3:1-12; Luke 3:1-18)

1:1 Matt 4:3
1:2 Mal 3:1; Matt 11:10; Luke 7:27
1:3 Is 40:3; Matt 3:3; Luke 3:4; John 1:23
1:4 Acts 13:24; Luke 1:77
1:6 2 Kin 1:8

1 The beginning of the gospel of Jesus Christ, the Son of God.
2 As it is written in Isaiah the prophet:
"BEHOLD, I SEND MY MESSENGER AHEAD OF YOU,
WHO WILL PREPARE YOUR WAY;
3 THE VOICE OF ONE CRYING IN THE WILDERNESS,
'MAKE READY THE WAY OF THE LORD,
MAKE HIS PATHS STRAIGHT.' "
4 John the Baptist appeared in the wilderness [1]preaching a baptism of repentance for
the forgiveness of sins.
5 And all the country of Judea was going out to him, and all the people of Jerusalem;
and they were being baptized by him in the Jordan River, confessing their sins.
6 John was clothed with camel's hair and *wore* a leather belt around his waist, and his
diet was locusts and wild honey.

1 Or *proclaiming*

1:1 When you experience the excitement of a big event, you naturally want to tell someone. Telling the story can bring back that original thrill as you relive the experience. Reading Mark's first words, you can sense his excitement. Picture yourself in the crowd as Jesus heals and teaches. Imagine yourself as one of the disciples. Respond to his words of love and encouragement. And remember that Jesus came for us who live today as well as for those who lived 2,000 years ago.

1:1 Mark was not one of the 12 disciples of Jesus, but he probably knew Jesus personally. Mark wrote his Gospel in the form of a fast-paced story, like a popular novel. The book portrays Jesus as a man who backed up his words with action that constantly proved who he is—the Son of God. Because Mark wrote the Gospel for Christians in Rome, where many gods were worshiped, he wanted his readers to know that Jesus is *the one true* Son of God.

1:2 Jesus came at a time in history when the entire civilized world was relatively peaceful under Roman rule, travel was easy, and there was a common language. The news about Jesus' life, death, and resurrection could spread quickly throughout the vast Roman empire.

In Israel, common men and women were ready for Jesus too. There had been no God-sent prophets for 400 years, since the days of Malachi (who wrote the last book of the Old Testament). There was growing anticipation that a great prophet, or the Messiah mentioned in the Old Testament, would soon come (see Luke 3:15).

1:2–3 Isaiah was one of the greatest prophets of the Old Testament. The second half of the book of Isaiah is devoted to the promise of salvation. Isaiah wrote about the coming of the Messiah, Jesus Christ, and the man who would announce his coming, John the Baptist. John's call to "make His paths straight" meant that people should give up their selfish way of living, renounce their sins, seek God's forgiveness, and establish a relationship with the almighty God by believing and obeying his words as found in Scripture (Isaiah 1:18–20; 57:15).

1:2–3 Mark 1:2–3 is a composite quotation, taken first from Malachi 3:1 and then from Isaiah 40:3.

1:2–3 Hundreds of years earlier, the prophet Isaiah had predicted that John the Baptist and Jesus would come. How did he know? God promised Isaiah that a Redeemer would come to Israel, and that a messenger calling in the wilderness would prepare the way for him. Isaiah's words comforted many people as they looked forward to the Messiah, and knowing that God keeps his promises can comfort you too. As you read the book of Mark, realize that it is more than just a story; it is part of God's Word. In it God is revealing to you his plans for human history.

1:4 Why does the Gospel of Mark begin with the story of John the Baptist and not mention the story of Jesus' birth? Important Roman officials of this day were always preceded by an announcer or herald. When the herald arrived in town, the people knew that someone of prominence would soon arrive. Because Mark's audience was primarily Roman Christians, he began his book with John the Baptist, whose mission it was to announce the coming of Jesus, the most important man who ever lived. Roman Christians would have been less interested in Jesus' birth than in this messenger who prepared the way.

1:4 John chose to live in the wilderness (1) to get away from distractions so he could hear God's instructions; (2) to capture the undivided attention of the people; (3) to symbolize a sharp break with the hypocrisy of the religious leaders who preferred their luxurious homes and positions of authority over doing God's work; (4) to fulfill Old Testament prophecies that said John would be "a voice . . . calling, "Clear the way for the LORD in the wilderness"" (Isaiah 40:3).

1:4 In John's ministry, baptism was a visible sign that a person had decided to change his or her life, giving up a sinful and selfish way of living and turning to God. John took a known custom and gave it new meaning. The Jews often baptized non-Jews who had converted to Judaism. But to baptize a Jew as a sign of repentance was a radical departure from Jewish custom. The early church took baptism a step further, associating it with Jesus' death and resurrection (see, for example, Romans 6:3–4; 1 Peter 3:21).

1:5 The purpose of John's preaching was to prepare people to accept Jesus as God's Son. When John challenged the people to confess sin individually, he signaled the start of a new way to relate to God.

Is change needed in your life before you can hear and understand Jesus' message? You have to admit that you need forgiveness before you can accept it. To prepare to receive Christ, repent. Denounce the world's dead-end attractions, sinful temptations, and harmful attitudes.

1:6 John's clothes were not the latest style of his day. He dressed much like the prophet Elijah (2 Kings 1:8) in order to distinguish himself from the religious leaders, whose flowing robes reflected their great pride in their position (12:38). John's striking appearance reinforced his striking message.

7 And he was preaching, and saying, "After me One is coming who is mightier than I,
and I am not fit to stoop down and untie the thong of His sandals.
8 "I baptized you [2]with water; but He will baptize you [2]with the Holy Spirit."

John Baptizes Jesus
(17/Matthew 3:13-17; Luke 3:21-22)

9 In those days Jesus came from Nazareth in Galilee and was baptized by John in the **1:9**
Jordan. Matt 2:23; Luke 2:51
10 Immediately coming up out of the water, He saw the heavens opening, and the Spirit
like a dove descending upon Him;
11 and a voice came out of the heavens: "You are My beloved Son, in You I am well- **1:11**
pleased." Ps 2:7; Is 42:1; Matt 3:17; 12:18; Mark 9:7; Luke 3:22

Satan Tempts Jesus in the Wilderness
(18/Matthew 4:1-11; Luke 4:1-13)

12 Immediately the Spirit ☆impelled Him *to go* out into the wilderness.
13 And He was in the wilderness forty days being tempted by Satan; and He was with **1:13**
the wild beasts, and the angels were ministering to Him. Matt 4:10

2 The Gr here can be translated *in, with* or *by*

1:7–8 Although John was the first genuine prophet in 400 years, Jesus the Messiah would be infinitely greater than he. John was pointing out how insignificant he was compared to the one who was coming. John was not even worthy of doing the most menial tasks for him, like untying his sandals. What John began, Jesus finished. What John prepared, Jesus fulfilled.

1:8 John said Jesus would baptize them with the Holy Spirit, sending the Holy Spirit to live within each believer. John's baptism with water prepared a person to receive Christ's message. This baptism demonstrated repentance, humility, and willingness to turn from sin. This was the *beginning* of the spiritual process.

When Jesus baptizes with the Holy Spirit, however, the entire person is transformed by the Spirit's power. Jesus offers to us both forgiveness of sin and the power to live for him.

1:9 If John's baptism was for repentance from sin, why was Jesus baptized? While even the greatest prophets (Isaiah, Jeremiah, Ezekiel) had to confess their sinfulness and need for repentance, Jesus didn't need to admit sin—he was sinless. Although Jesus didn't need forgiveness, he was baptized for the following reasons: (1) to begin his mission to bring the message of salvation to all people; (2) to show support for John's ministry; (3) to identify with our humanness and sin; (4) to give us an example to follow. We know that John's baptism was different from Christian baptism in the church because Paul had John's followers baptized again (see Acts 19:2–5).

1:9 Jesus grew up in Nazareth, where he had lived since he was a young boy (Matthew 2:22–23). Nazareth was a small town in Galilee, located about halfway between the Sea of Galilee and the Mediterranean Sea. The city was despised and avoided by many Jews because it had a reputation for independence. Nazareth was a crossroads for trade routes and had contact with other cultures. (See also John 1:46.)

1:10–11 The Spirit descended like a dove on Jesus, and the voice from heaven proclaimed the Father's approval of Jesus as his divine Son. That Jesus is God's divine Son is the foundation for all we read about Jesus in the Gospels. Here we see all three members of the Trinity together—God the Father, God the Son, and God the Holy Spirit.

1:12–13 Jesus left the crowds and went into the wilderness where he was tempted by Satan. Temptation is bad for us only when we give in. We should not hate or resent times of inner testing, because through them God can strengthen our character and teach us valuable lessons. When you face Satan and must deal with his temptations and the turmoil he brings, remember Jesus. He used God's Word against Satan and won. You can do the same.

1:12–13 Satan is an angel who rebelled against God. He is real, not symbolic, and is constantly working against God and those who obey him. Satan tempted Eve in the garden and persuaded her to sin; he tempted Jesus in the wilderness and did not persuade him to fall. To be tempted is not a sin. Tempting others or giving in to temptation *is* sin. For a more detailed account of Jesus' temptation, read Matthew 4:1–11.

1:12–13 To identify fully with human beings, Jesus had to endure Satan's temptations. Although Jesus is God, he is also man. And as fully human, he was not exempt from Satan's attacks. Because Jesus faced temptations and overcame them, he can assist us in two important ways: (1) as an example of how to face temptation without sinning, and (2) as a helper who knows just what we need because he went through the same experience. (See Hebrews 4:16 for more on Jesus and temptation.)

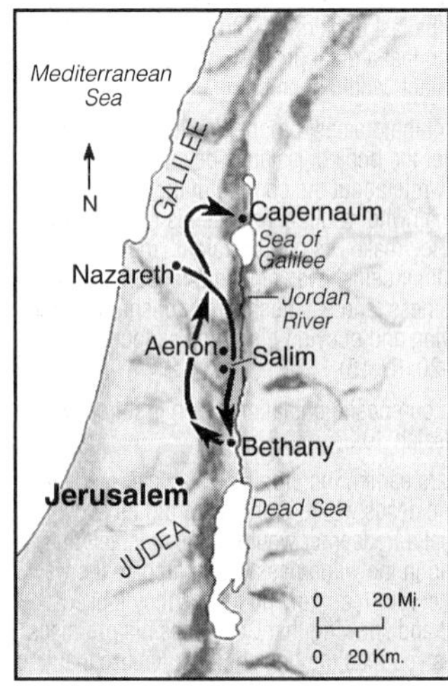

JESUS BEGINS HIS MINISTRY
When Jesus came from his home in Nazareth to begin his ministry, he first took two steps in preparation—baptism by John in the Jordan River and temptation by Satan in the rough Judean wilderness. After the temptations, Jesus returned to Galilee and later set up his home base in Capernaum.

B. MESSAGE AND MINISTRY OF JESUS, THE SERVANT (1:14—13:37)

Mark tells us dramatic, action-packed stories. He gives us the most vivid account of Christ's activities. He features facts and actions rather than teachings. The way Jesus lived his life is the perfect example of how we should live our lives today.

1. Jesus' ministry in Galilee

Jesus Preaches in Galilee
(30/Matthew 4:12-17; Luke 4:14-15; John 4:43-45)

1:14 Matt 4:12; Matt 4:23

1:15 Gal 4:4; Eph 1:10; 1 Tim 2:6; Titus 1:3; Matt 3:2; Acts 20:21

14 Now after John had been taken into custody, Jesus came into Galilee, preaching
the gospel of God,
15 and saying, "The time is fulfilled, and the kingdom of God is at hand; repent and
believe in the gospel."

Four Fishermen Follow Jesus
(33/Matthew 4:18-22)

1:16 Luke 5:2-11; John 1:40-42

16 As He was going along by the Sea of Galilee, He saw Simon and Andrew, the brother of Simon, casting a net in the sea; for they were fishermen.
17 And Jesus said to them, "Follow Me, and I will make you become fishers of men."
18 Immediately they left their nets and followed Him.
19 Going on a little farther, He saw James the son of Zebedee, and John his brother,
who were also in the boat mending the nets.
20 Immediately He called them; and they left their father Zebedee in the boat with
the hired servants, and went away to follow Him.

Jesus Teaches with Great Authority
(34/Luke 4:31-37)

1:21 Matt 4:23; Mark 1:39; 10:1

1:22 Matt 7:28

21 They ☆went into Capernaum; and immediately on the Sabbath He entered the synagogue and *began* to teach.
22 They were amazed at His teaching; for He was teaching them as *one* having authority, and not as the scribes.
23 Just then there was a man in their synagogue with an unclean spirit; and he cried out,

---

1:14–15 What is the gospel of God? These first words spoken by Jesus in Mark give the core of his teaching: that the long-awaited Messiah has come to break the power of sin and begin God's personal reign on earth. Most of the people who heard this message were oppressed, poor, and without hope. Jesus' words were good news because they offered freedom, justice, and hope.

1:16 Fishing was a major industry around the Sea of Galilee. Fishing with nets was the most common method. Capernaum, the largest of the more than 30 fishing towns around the lake at that time, became Jesus' new home (Matthew 4:12–13).

1:16–20 We often assume that Jesus' disciples were great men of faith from the first time they met Jesus. But they had to grow in their faith just as all believers do (14:48–50, 66–72; John 14:1–9; 20:26–29). This is apparently not the only time Jesus called Peter (Simon), James, and John to follow him (see Luke 5:1–11 and John 1:35–42 for two other times). Although it took time for Jesus' call and his message to get through, the disciples *followed.* In the same way, we may question and falter, but we must never stop following Jesus.

1:21 Because the temple in Jerusalem was too far for many Jews to travel to regularly for worship, many towns had synagogues serving both as places of worship and as schools. Beginning in the days of Ezra, about 450 B.C., a group of ten Jewish families could start a synagogue. There, during the week, Jewish boys were taught the Old Testament law and Jewish religion. Girls could not attend. Each Saturday, the Sabbath, the Jewish men would gather to listen to a rabbi teach from the Scriptures. Because there was no permanent rabbi or teacher, it was customary for the synagogue leader to ask visiting teachers to speak. This is why Jesus often spoke in the synagogues in the towns he visited.

1:21 Jesus had recently moved to Capernaum from Nazareth (Matthew 4:12–13). Capernaum was a thriving town with great wealth as well as great sin and decadence. Because it was the headquarters for many Roman troops, pagan influences from all over the Roman empire were pervasive. This was an ideal place for Jesus to challenge both Jews and non-Jews with the gospel of God's kingdom.

1:22 The Jewish teachers often quoted from well-known rabbis to give their words more authority. But Jesus didn't have that need. Because Jesus is God, he knew exactly what the Scriptures said and meant. He was the ultimate authority.

1:23 Unclean spirits, or demons, are ruled by Satan. They work to tempt people to sin. They were not created by Satan—because God is the Creator of all. Rather they are fallen angels who joined Satan in his rebellion. Though not all disease comes from Satan, demons can cause a person to become mute, deaf, blind, or insane. But in every case where demons confronted Jesus, they lost their power. Thus God limits what unclean spirits can do; they can do nothing without his permission. During Jesus' life on earth, demons were allowed to be very active to demonstrate once and for all Christ's power and authority over them.

1:23ff Many psychologists dismiss all accounts of demon-possession as a primitive way to describe mental illness. Although throughout history mental illness has often been wrongly diagnosed as demon-possession, clearly a hostile outside force controlled the man described here. Mark emphasized Jesus' conflict with evil powers to show his superiority over them, so he recorded many stories about Jesus driving out unclean spirits. Jesus didn't have to conduct an elaborate exorcism ritual. His word was enough to send out the demons.

1:23–24 The unclean spirit knew at once that Jesus was the Holy One of God. By including this event in his Gospel, Mark was establishing Jesus' credentials, showing that even the spiritual underworld recognized Jesus as the Messiah.

24 saying, "What business do we have with each other, Jesus [3]of Nazareth? Have You
come to destroy us? I know who You are—the Holy One of God!"
25 And Jesus rebuked him, saying, "Be quiet, and come out of him!"
26 Throwing him into convulsions, the unclean spirit cried out with a loud voice and
came out of him.
27 They were all amazed, so that they debated among themselves, saying, "What is this?
A new teaching with authority! He commands even the unclean spirits, and they obey
Him."
28 Immediately the news about Him spread everywhere into all the surrounding district of Galilee.

1:24 Matt 8:29; Matt 2:23; Mark 10:47; 14:67; 16:6; Luke 4:34; 24:19; Acts 24:5; Luke 1:35; 4:34; John 6:69; Acts 3:14

1:27 Mark 10:24, 32; 16:5, 6

Jesus Heals Peter's Mother-in-law and Many Others
(35/Matthew 8:14-17; Luke 4:38-41)

29 And immediately after they came out of the synagogue, they came into the house of
Simon and Andrew, with James and John.
30 Now Simon's mother-in-law was lying sick with a fever; and immediately they ☆spoke
to Jesus about her.
31 And He came to her and raised her up, taking her by the hand, and the fever left
her, and she [4]waited on them.
32 When evening came, after the sun had set, they *began* bringing to Him all who were
ill and those who were demon-possessed.
33 And the whole city had gathered at the door.
34 And He healed many who were ill with various diseases, and cast out many demons;
and He was not permitting the demons to speak, because they knew who He was.

1:29 Mark 1:21, 23

1:32 Matt 8:16, 17; Luke 4:40, 41; Matt 8:16; Luke 4:40; Matt 4:24

1:33 Mark 1:21

1:34 Matt 4:23

Jesus Preaches throughout Galilee
(36/Matthew 4:23-25; Luke 4:42-44)

35 In the early morning, while it was still dark, Jesus got up, left *the house*, and went
away to a secluded place, and was praying there.
36 Simon and his companions searched for Him;
37 they found Him, and ☆said to Him, "Everyone is looking for You."
38 He ☆said to them, "Let us go somewhere else to the towns nearby, so that I may
preach there also; for that is what I came for."
39 And He went into their synagogues throughout all Galilee, preaching and casting
out the demons.

1:35 Matt 14:23; Luke 5:16

1:39 Matt 4:23; 9:35; Mark 1:23; 3:1

3 Lit *the Nazarene* 4 Or *served*

1:29–31 Each Gospel writer had a slightly different perspective as he wrote; thus the comparable stories in the Gospels often highlight different details. In Matthew, Jesus touched the woman's hand. In Mark, he helped her up. In Luke, he spoke to the fever, and it left her. The accounts do not conflict. Each writer chose to emphasize different details of the story in order to emphasize a certain characteristic of Jesus.

1:32–33 The people came to Jesus in the evening after sunset. This was the Sabbath (1:21), their day of rest, lasting from sunset Friday to sunset Saturday. The Jewish leaders had proclaimed that it was against the law to be healed on the Sabbath (Matthew 12:10; Luke 13:14). The people didn't want to break this law or the Jewish law that prohibited traveling on the Sabbath, so they waited until sunset. After the sun went down, the crowds were free to find Jesus so he could heal them.

1:34 Why didn't Jesus want the demons to reveal who he was? (1) By commanding the demons to remain silent, Jesus proved his authority and power over them. (2) Jesus wanted the people to believe he was the Messiah because of what he said and did, not because of the demons' words. (3) Jesus wanted to reveal his identity as the Messiah according to his timetable, not according to Satan's timetable. Satan wanted the people to follow Jesus around for what they could get out of him, not because he was the Son of God who could truly set them free from sin's guilt and power.

1:35 Jesus took time to pray. Finding time to pray is not easy, but prayer is the vital link between us and God. Like Jesus, we must break away from others to talk with God, even if we have to get up very early in the morning to do it!

1:39 The Romans divided the land of Israel into three separate regions: Galilee, Samaria, and Judea. Galilee was the northernmost region, an area about 60 miles long and 30 miles wide. Jesus did much of his ministry in this area, an ideal place for him to teach because there were over 250 towns concentrated there, with many synagogues.

Jesus Heals a Man with Leprosy
(38/Matthew 8:1-4; Luke 5:12-16)

1:40 Matt 8:2; Mark 10:17; Luke 5:12

40 And a leper ☆came to Jesus, beseeching Him and falling on his knees before Him,
and saying, "If You are willing, You can make me clean."
41 Moved with compassion, Jesus stretched out His hand and touched him, and ☆said
to him, "I am willing; be cleansed."
42 Immediately the leprosy left him and he was cleansed.
43 And He sternly warned him and immediately sent him away,

1:44 Matt 8:4; Lev 14:1-32

44 and He ☆said to him, "See that you say nothing to anyone; but go, show yourself to
the priest and offer for your cleansing what Moses commanded, as a testimony to them."

1:45 Matt 28:15; Luke 5:15; Mark 2:2, 13; 3:7; Luke 5:17; John 6:2

45 But he went out and began to proclaim it freely and to spread the news around, to
such an extent that Jesus could no longer publicly enter a city, but [5]stayed out in
unpopulated areas; and they were coming to Him from everywhere.

Jesus Heals a Paralytic
(39/Matthew 9:1-8; Luke 5:17-26)

2 When He had come back to Capernaum several days afterward, it was heard that
He was at home.

2:2 Mark 1:45; 2:13

2 And many were gathered together, so that there was no longer room, not even near
the door; and He was speaking the word to them.

2:3 Matt 4:24

3 And they ☆came, bringing to Him a paralytic, carried by four men.

2:4 Luke 5:19; Matt 4:24

4 Being unable to get to Him because of the crowd, they removed the roof above Him;
and when they had dug an opening, they let down the pallet on which the paralytic was
lying.

2:5 Matt 9:2

5 And Jesus seeing their faith ☆said to the paralytic, "[6]Son, your sins are forgiven."
6 But some of the scribes were sitting there and reasoning in their hearts,

2:7 Is 43:25

7 "Why does this man speak that way? He is blaspheming; who can forgive sins but
God alone?"
8 Immediately Jesus, aware in His spirit that they were reasoning that way within themselves, ☆said to them, "Why are you reasoning about these things in your hearts?

2:9 Matt 4:24

9 "Which is easier, to say to the paralytic, 'Your sins are forgiven'; or to say, 'Get up,
and pick up your pallet and walk'?
10 "But so that you may know that the Son of Man has authority on earth to forgive
sins"—He ☆said to the paralytic,

5 Lit *was* **6** Lit *child*

1:40–41 In keeping with the law in Leviticus 13 and 14, Jewish leaders declared people with leprosy unclean. This meant that lepers were unfit to participate in any religious or social activity. Because the law said that contact with any unclean person made a person unclean too, some people even threw rocks at lepers to keep them at a safe distance. Even the mention of the name of this disabling disease terrified people. But Jesus touched this man who had leprosy.

The real value of a person is inside, not outside. Although a person's body may be diseased or deformed, the person inside is no less valuable to God. No person is too disgusting for God's touch. In a sense, we are all people with leprosy because we have all been deformed by the ugliness of sin. But God, by sending his Son Jesus, has touched us, giving us the opportunity to be healed. When you feel repulsed by someone, stop and remember how God feels about that person—and about you.

1:43–44 Although leprosy was incurable, many different types of skin diseases were classified together as "leprosy." According to the Old Testament laws about leprosy (Leviticus 13; 14), when a leper was cured, he or she had to go to a priest to be examined. Then the leper was to give a thank offering at the temple. Jesus adhered to these laws by sending the man to the priest, demonstrating Jesus' complete regard for God's law. Sending a healed leper to a priest was also a way to verify Jesus' great miracle to the community.

2:3 The paralytic's need moved his friends to action, and they brought him to Jesus. When you recognize someone's need, do you act? Many people have physical and spiritual needs you can meet, either by yourself or with others who are also concerned. Human need moved these four men; let it also move you to compassionate action.

2:4 Houses in Bible times were built of stone. They had flat roofs made of mud mixed with straw. Outside stairways led to the roofs. These friends may have carried the lame man up the outside stairs to the roof. They then could easily have taken apart the mud and straw mixture to make a hole through which to lower their friend to Jesus.

2:5–7 Before saying to the paralytic, "Get up," Jesus said, "Son, your sins are forgiven." To the Jewish leaders this statement was blasphemous, claiming to do something only God could do. According to the law, the punishment for this sin was death (Leviticus 24:15–16).

The religious leaders understood correctly that Jesus was claiming divine prerogatives, but their judgment of him was wrong. Jesus was not blaspheming because his claim was true. Jesus is God, and he proved his claim by healing the paralytic (2:9–12).

2:10 This is the first time in Mark that Jesus is referred to as the "Son of Man." The title *Son of Man* emphasizes that Jesus is fully human, while *Son of God* (see, for example, John 20:31) emphasizes that he is fully God. As God's Son, Jesus has the authority to forgive sin. As a man, he can identify with our deepest needs and sufferings and help us overcome sin (see the note on 8:29–31).

11 "I say to you, get up, pick up your pallet and go home."
12 And he got up and immediately picked up the pallet and went out in the sight of everyone, so that they were all amazed and were glorifying God, saying, "We have never seen anything like this."

2:12 Matt 9:8; Matt 9:33

Jesus Eats with Sinners at Matthew's House
(40/Matthew 9:9-13; Luke 5:27-32)

13 And He went out again by the seashore; and all the people were coming to Him,
and He was teaching them.
14 As He passed by, He saw Levi the *son* of Alphaeus sitting in the tax booth, and He
*said to him, "Follow Me!" And he got up and followed Him.
15 And it *happened that He was reclining *at the table* in his house, and many tax collectors and sinners were dining with Jesus and His disciples; for there were many of them, and they were following Him.
16 When the scribes of the Pharisees saw that He was eating with the sinners and tax collectors, they said to His disciples, "Why is He eating and drinking with tax collectors and sinners?"
17 And hearing *this*, Jesus *said to them, "*It is* not those who are healthy who need a physician, but those who are sick; I did not come to call the righteous, but sinners."

2:13 Mark 1:45

2:14 Matt 9:9; Matt 8:22

2:16 Luke 5:30; Acts 23:9; Matt 9:11

2:17 Matt 9:12, 13; Luke 5:31, 32

Religious Leaders Ask Jesus about Fasting
(41/Matthew 9:14-17; Luke 5:33-39)

18 John's disciples and the Pharisees were fasting; and they *came and *said to Him, "Why do John's disciples and the disciples of the Pharisees fast, but Your disciples do not fast?"
19 And Jesus said to them, "While the bridegroom is with them, the attendants of the bridegroom cannot fast, can they? So long as they have the bridegroom with them, they cannot fast.
20 "But the days will come when the bridegroom is taken away from them, and then they will fast in that day.
21 "No one sews a patch of unshrunk cloth on an old garment; otherwise the patch pulls away from it, the new from the old, and a worse tear results.
22 "No one puts new wine into old wineskins; otherwise the wine will burst the skins, and the wine is lost and the skins *as well;* but *one puts* new wine into fresh wineskins."

2:20 Matt 9:15; Luke 17:22

2:14 Levi is another name for Matthew, the disciple who wrote the Gospel of Matthew. See Matthew's Profile in Matthew 9 for more information.

2:14 Capernaum was a key military center for Roman troops, as well as a thriving business community. Several major highways intersected in Capernaum, with merchants passing through from as far away as Egypt to the south and Mesopotamia to the north.

Levi (Matthew), a Jew, was appointed by the Romans to be the area's tax collector. He collected taxes from citizens as well as from merchants passing through town. Tax collectors were expected to take a commission on the taxes they collected. Most of them overcharged and vastly enriched themselves. Tax collectors were despised by the Jews because of their reputation for cheating and their support of Rome. The Jews must also have hated to think that some of the money collected went to support pagan religions and temples.

2:14–15 The day that Levi met Jesus, Levi held a meeting at his house to introduce others to Jesus. Levi didn't waste any time starting to witness! Some people feel that new believers should wait for maturity or training before they begin to tell others about Christ. But like Levi, new believers can share their faith right away with whatever knowledge, skill, or experience they already have.

2:16–17 The self-righteous Pharisees were indignant that Jesus would eat a meal with such sinners. But Jesus gladly associated with sinners because he loved them and because he knew that they needed to hear what he had to say. Jesus spent time with whoever needed or wanted to hear his message—poor, rich, bad, good. We, too, must befriend those who need Christ, even if they do not seem to be ideal companions. Are there people you have been neglecting because of their reputation? They may be the ones who most need to see and hear the message of Christ's love in and from you.

2:18ff John had two goals: to lead people to repent of their sin, and to prepare them for Christ's coming. John's message was sobering, so he and his followers fasted. Fasting is both an outward sign of humility and regret for sin, and an inner discipline that clears the mind and keeps the spirit alert. Fasting empties the body of food; repentance empties the life of sin. Jesus' disciples did not need to fast to prepare for his coming because he was with them. Jesus did not condemn fasting, however. He himself fasted for 40 days (Matthew 4:2). Nevertheless, Jesus emphasized fasting with the right motives. The Pharisees fasted twice a week to show others how holy they were. Jesus explained that if people fast only to impress others, they will be twisting the purpose of fasting.

2:19 Jesus compared himself to a bridegroom. In the Bible, the image of a bride is often used for God's people, and the image of a bridegroom for the God who loves them (Isaiah 62:5; Matthew 25:1–14; Revelation 21:2).

2:22 A wineskin was a goatskin sewed together at the edges to form a watertight bag. New wine, expanding as it aged, stretched the wineskin. New wine, therefore, could not be put into a wineskin that had already been stretched, or the taut skin would burst.

The Pharisees had become rigid like old wineskins. They could not accept faith in Jesus that would not be contained or limited by man-made ideas or rules. Your heart, like a wineskin, can become rigid and prevent you from accepting the new life that Christ offers. Keep your heart pliable and open to accepting the life-changing truths of Christ.

The Disciples Pick Grain on the Sabbath
(45/Matthew 12:1-8; Luke 6:1-5)

2:23 Deut 23:25
2:24 Matt 12:2

23 And it happened that He was passing through the grainfields on the Sabbath, and
His disciples began to make their way along while picking the heads *of grain.*
24 The Pharisees were saying to Him, "Look, why are they doing what is not lawful on
the Sabbath?"

PROMINENT JEWISH RELIGIOUS AND POLITICAL GROUPS

Name and Selected References	*Description*	*Agreement with Jesus*	*Disagreement with Jesus*
PHARISEES Matthew 5:20 Matthew 23:1–36 Luke 6:2 Luke 7:36–47	Strict group of religious Jews who advocated minute obedience to the Jewish law and traditions. Very influential in the synagogues.	Respect for the Law, belief in the resurrection of the dead, committed to obeying God's will.	Rejected Jesus' claim to be Messiah because he did not follow all their traditions and associated with notoriously wicked people.
SADDUCEES Matthew 3:7 Matthew 16:11–12 Mark 12:18	Wealthy, upper class, Jewish priestly party. Rejected the authority of the Bible beyond the five books of Moses. Profited from business in the temple. They, along with the Pharisees, were one of the two major parties of the Jewish Council.	Showed great respect for the five books of Moses, as well as the sanctity of the temple.	Denied the resurrection of the dead. Thought the temple could also be used as a place to transact business.
SCRIBES Matthew 7:29 Mark 2:6 Mark 2:16	Professional interpreters of the Law—who especially emphasized the traditions. Many scribes were Pharisees.	Respect for the Law. Committed to obeying God.	Denied Jesus' authority to reinterpret the Law. Rejected Jesus as Messiah because he did not obey all of their traditions.
HERODIANS Matthew 22:16 Mark 3:6 Mark 12:13	A Jewish political party of King Herod's supporters.	Unknown. In the Gospels they tried to trap Jesus with questions and plotted to kill him.	Afraid of Jesus causing political instability. They saw Jesus as a threat to their political future at a time when they were trying to regain from Rome some of their lost political power.
ZEALOTS Luke 6:15 Acts 1:14	A fiercely dedicated group of Jewish patriots determined to end Roman rule in Israel.	Concerned about the future of Israel. Believed in the Messiah but did not recognize Jesus as the One sent by God.	Believed that the Messiah must be a political leader who would deliver Israel from Roman occupation.
ESSENES none	Jewish monastic group practicing ritual purity and personal holiness.	Emphasized justice, honesty, commitment.	Believed ceremonial rituals made them righteous.

2:23 Jesus and his disciples were not stealing when they picked the grain. Leviticus 19:9–10 and Deuteronomy 23:25 say that farmers were to leave the edges of their fields unharvested so that some of their crops could be picked by travelers and by the poor. Just as walking on a sidewalk is not trespassing on private property, picking heads of grain at the edge of a field was not stealing.

2:24 God's law said that crops should not be harvested on the Sabbath (Exodus 34:21). This law prevented farmers from becoming greedy and ignoring God on the Sabbath. It also protected laborers from being overworked.

The Pharisees interpreted the action of Jesus and his disciples—picking the grain and eating it as they walked through the fields—as harvesting; and so they judged Jesus a lawbreaker. But Jesus and the disciples clearly were not harvesting the grain for personal gain; they were simply looking for something to eat. The Pharisees were so focused on the words of the rule that they missed its intent.

2:24 Many of the Pharisees were so caught up in their man-made laws and traditions that they lost sight of what was good and right. Jesus implied in Mark 3:4 that the Sabbath is a day to do good. God provided the Sabbath as a day of rest and worship, but he didn't mean that concern for rest should keep us from lifting a finger to help others. Don't allow your Sabbath to become a time of selfish indulgence.

25 And He ☆said to them, "Have you never read what David did when he was in need
and he and his companions became hungry;
26 how he entered the house of God in the time of Abiathar *the* high priest, and ate
the consecrated bread, which is not lawful for *anyone* to eat except the priests, and he
also gave it to those who were with him?"
27 Jesus said to them, "The Sabbath was made for man, and not man for the Sabbath.
28 "So the Son of Man is Lord even of the Sabbath."

2:26 1 Sam 21:1; 2 Sam 8:17; 1 Chr 24:6; Lev 24:9

2:27 Ex 23:12; Deut 5:14; Col 2:16

Jesus Heals a Man's Hand on the Sabbath
(46/Matthew 12:9-14; Luke 6:6-11)

3 He entered again into a synagogue; and a man was there whose hand was withered.
2 They were watching Him *to see* if He would heal him on the Sabbath, so that they
might accuse Him.
3 He ☆said to the man with the withered hand, "Get up and come forward!"
4 And He ☆said to them, "Is it lawful to do good or to do harm on the Sabbath, to
save a life or to kill?" But they kept silent.
5 After looking around at them with anger, grieved at their hardness of heart, He ☆said
to the man, "Stretch out your hand." And he stretched it out, and his hand was restored.
6 The Pharisees went out and immediately *began* conspiring with the Herodians against
Him, *as to* how they might destroy Him.

3:1 Mark 1:21, 39

3:2 Luke 6:7; 14:1; 20:20; Matt 12:10; Luke 6:7; 11:54

3:5 Luke 6:10

3:6 Matt 22:16; Mark 12:13

Large Crowds Follow Jesus
(47/Matthew 12:15-21)

7 Jesus withdrew to the sea with His disciples; and a great multitude from Galilee
followed; and *also* from Judea,
8 and from Jerusalem, and from Idumea, and beyond the Jordan, and the vicinity of
Tyre and Sidon, a great number of people heard of all that He was doing and came to
Him.
9 And He told His disciples that a boat should stand ready for Him because of the
crowd, so that they would not crowd Him;
10 for He had healed many, with the result that all those who had afflictions pressed
around Him in order to touch Him.

3:7 Luke 6:17-19; Matt 4:25; Luke 6:17

3:8 Josh 15:1, 21; Ezek 35:15; 36:5; Matt 11:21

3:9 Mark 4:1; Luke 5:1-3

3:10 Matt 4:23; Mark 5:29, 34; Luke 7:21; Matt 9:21; 14:36; Mark 6:56; 8:22

2:25–28 Jesus used the example of David to point out how ridiculous the Pharisees' accusations were (this incident occurred in 1 Samuel 21:1–6). God created the Sabbath for our benefit, not his own. God derives no benefit from having us rest on the Sabbath, but we are restored both physically and spiritually when we take time to rest and to focus on God. For the Pharisees, Sabbath laws had become more important than Sabbath rest. Both David and Jesus understood that the intent of God's law is to promote love for God and others. When we apply a law to other people, we should make sure that we understand its purpose and intent so we don't make harmful or inappropriate judgments.

2:26 The "consecrated bread" was the bread set before God in the tabernacle. Every Sabbath, 12 baked loaves of bread were placed on the table in the holy place. Then the priests ate the old ones. See Exodus 25:30 and Leviticus 24:5–9 for more about the consecrated bread, also called the bread of the Presence.

3:2 Already the Pharisees had turned against Jesus. They were jealous of his popularity, his miracles, and the authority in his teaching and actions. They valued their status in the community and their opportunity for personal gain so much that they lost sight of their goal as religious leaders—to point people toward God. Of all people, the Pharisees should have recognized the Messiah, but they refused to acknowledge him because they were not willing to give up their treasured position and power. When Jesus exposed their attitudes, he became their enemy instead of their Messiah, and they began looking for ways to turn the people against him.

3:5 Jesus was angry about the Pharisees' uncaring attitudes. Anger itself is not wrong. It depends on what makes us angry and what we do with our anger. Too often we express our anger in selfish and harmful ways. By contrast, Jesus expressed his anger by correcting a problem—healing the man's hand. Use your anger to find constructive solutions rather than to tear people down.

3:6 The Pharisees were a Jewish religious group that zealously followed the Old Testament laws, as well as their own religious traditions. They were highly respected in the community, but they hated Jesus because he challenged their proud attitudes and dishonorable motives.

The Herodians were a Jewish political party that hoped to restore Herod the Great's line to the throne. Jesus was a threat to them as well because he challenged their political ambitions. The Pharisees and Herodians, normally enemies, joined forces against Jesus because he exposed them for what they were.

3:6 The Pharisees accused Jesus of breaking their law that said medical attention could be given to no one on the Sabbath except in matters of life and death. Ironically, the Pharisees themselves were breaking God's law by plotting murder.

3:7–8 While Jesus was drawing fire from the religious leaders, he was gaining great popularity among the people. Some were curious, some sought healing, some wanted evidence to use against him, and others wanted to know if Jesus truly was the Messiah. Most of them could only dimly guess at the real meaning of what was happening among them. Today crowds still follow Jesus, and they come for the same variety of reasons. What is your primary reason for following Jesus?

3:11 Matt 4:3
11 Whenever the unclean spirits saw Him, they would fall down before Him and shout,
"You are the Son of God!"
3:12 Matt 8:4
12 And He earnestly warned them not to tell who He was.

Jesus Selects the Twelve Disciples
(48/Luke 6:12-16)

3:13 Matt 5:1; Luke 6:12; Matt 10:1; Mark 6:7; Luke 9:1
13 And He ☆went up on the mountain and ☆summoned those whom He Himself wanted, and they came to Him.
14 And He appointed twelve, so that they would be with Him and that He *could* send
them out to preach,
15 and to have authority to cast out the demons.
3:16 Matt 10:2-4; Luke 6:14-16; Acts 1:13
16 And He appointed the twelve: Simon (to whom He gave the name Peter),
17 and James, the *son* of Zebedee, and John the brother of James (to them He gave
the name Boanerges, which means, "Sons of Thunder");
18 and Andrew, and Philip, and Bartholomew, and Matthew, and Thomas, and James
the son of Alphaeus, and Thaddaeus, and Simon the Zealot;
19 and Judas Iscariot, who betrayed Him.

Religious Leaders Accuse Jesus of Being under Satan's Power
(74/Matthew 12:22-37)

3:20 Mark 2:1; 7:17; 9:28; Mark 1:45; 3:7; Mark 6:31
20 And He ☆came [7]home, and the crowd ☆gathered again, to such an extent that they
could not even eat a meal.
3:21 Mark 3:31f; John 10:20; Acts 26:24
21 When His own [8]people heard *of this,* they went out to take custody of Him; for they
were saying, "He has lost His senses."
3:22 Matt 15:1; Matt 10:25; 11:18; Matt 9:34
22 The scribes who came down from Jerusalem were saying, "He is possessed by
Beelzebul," and "He casts out the demons by the ruler of the demons."
3:23 Matt 12:25-29; Luke 11:17-22; Matt 13:3ff; Mark 4:2ff; Matt 4:10
23 And He called them to Himself and began speaking to them in parables, "How can
Satan cast out Satan?
24 "If a kingdom is divided against itself, that kingdom cannot stand.
25 "If a house is divided against itself, that house will not be able to stand.
3:26 Matt 4:10
26 "If Satan has risen up against himself and is divided, he cannot stand, but he is finished!

7 Lit *into a house* 8 Or *kinsmen*

3:11 The unclean spirits knew that Jesus was the Son of God, but they refused to turn from their evil purposes. Knowing about Jesus, or even believing that he is God's Son, does not guarantee salvation. You must also want to follow and obey him (see also James 2:17).

3:12 Jesus warned the unclean spirits not to reveal his identity because he did not want them to reinforce a popular misconception. The huge crowds were looking for a political and military leader who would free them from Rome's control, and they thought that the Messiah predicted by the Old Testament prophets would be this kind of man. Jesus wanted to teach the people about the kind of Messiah he really was—one who was far different from their expectations. Christ's kingdom is spiritual. It begins not with the overthrow of governments, but with the overthrow of sin in people's hearts.

3:14 From the hundreds of people who followed him from place to place, Jesus chose 12 to be his *apostles. Apostle* means messenger or authorized representative. He did not choose these 12 to be his associates and companions because of their faith; their faith often faltered. He didn't choose them because of their talent and ability; no one stood out with unusual ability. The disciples represented a wide range of backgrounds and life experiences, but apparently they had no more leadership potential than those who were not chosen. The one characteristic they all shared was their willingness to obey Jesus. After Jesus' ascension, they were filled with the Holy Spirit and empowered to carry out special roles in the growth of the early church. We should not disqualify ourselves from service to Christ because we do not have the expected credentials. Being a good disciple is simply a matter of following Jesus with a willing heart.

3:14–15 Why did Jesus choose 12 men? The number 12 corresponds to the 12 tribes of Israel (Matthew 19:28), showing the continuity between the old religious system and the new one based on Jesus' message. Many people followed Jesus, but these 12 received the most intense training. We see the impact of these men throughout the rest of the New Testament.

3:18 The Zealots were Jewish nationalists who opposed the Roman occupation of Palestine.

3:21 With the crowds pressing in on him, Jesus didn't even take time to eat. Because of this, his friends and family came to take charge of him (3:31–32), thinking he had gone "over the edge" as a religious fanatic. They were concerned for him, but they missed the point of his ministry. Even those who were closest to Jesus were slow to understand who he was and what he had come to do.

3:22–27 The Pharisees and scribes could not deny the reality of Jesus' miracles and supernatural power. They refused to believe that his power was from God, however, because then they would have had to accept him as the Messiah. Their pride would not let them do that. So in an attempt to destroy Jesus' popularity among the people, the scribes accused him of having power from Satan. Jesus' reply showed that their argument didn't make sense. (*Beelzebul* refers to Satan.)

THE TWELVE

Name	*Occupation*	*Outstanding Characteristics*	*Major Events in His Life*
SIMON PETER (son of John)	Fisherman	Impulsive; later—bold in preaching about Jesus	One of three in core group of disciples; recognized Jesus as the Messiah; denied Christ and repented; preached Pentecost sermon; a leader of the Jerusalem church; baptized Gentiles; wrote 1 Peter and 2 Peter.
JAMES (son of Zebedee), who with his brother John were called the "Sons of Thunder"	Fisherman	Ambitious, short-tempered, judgmental, deeply committed to Jesus	Also in core group; he and his brother John asked Jesus for places of honor in his kingdom; wanted to call fire down to destroy a Samaritan village; first disciple to be martyred.
JOHN (son of Zebedee), James's brother, and the disciple "whom Jesus loved"	Fisherman	Ambitious, judgmental, later—very loving	Third disciple in core group; asked Jesus for a place of honor in his kingdom; wanted to call down fire on a Samaritan village; a leader of the Jerusalem church; wrote the Gospel of John and 1 John, 2 John, 3 John and Revelation.
ANDREW (Peter's brother)	Fisherman	Eager to bring others to Jesus	Accepted John the Baptist's testimony about Jesus; told Peter about Jesus; he and Philip told Jesus that Greeks wanted to see him.
PHILIP	Fisherman	Questioning attitude	Told Nathanael about Jesus; wondered how Jesus could feed the 5,000; asked Jesus to show his followers God the Father; he and Andrew told Jesus that Greeks wanted to see him.
BARTHOLOMEW (Nathanael)	Unknown	Honesty and straightforwardness	Initially rejected Jesus because Jesus was from Nazareth but acknowledged him as the "Son of God" and "King of Israel" when they met.
MATTHEW (Levi)	Tax collector	Despised outcast because of his dishonest career	Abandoned his corrupt (and financially profitable) way of life to follow Jesus; invited Jesus to a party with his notorious friends; wrote the Gospel of Matthew.
THOMAS (the Twin)	Unknown	Courage and doubt	Suggested the disciples go with Jesus to Bethany—even if it meant death; asked Jesus about where he was going; refused to believe Jesus was risen until he could see Jesus alive and touch his wounds.
JAMES (son of Alphaeus)	Unknown	Unknown	Became one of Jesus' disciples.
THADDAEUS (Judas son of James)	Unknown	Unknown	Asked Jesus why he would reveal himself to his followers and not to the world.
SIMON THE ZEALOT	Unknown	Fierce patriotism	Became a disciple of Jesus.
JUDAS ISCARIOT	Unknown	Treacherous and greedy	Became one of Jesus' disciples; betrayed Jesus; killed himself.

Jesus' faithful disciples were ordinary men who became extraordinary because of Jesus Christ. Despite their confusion and lack of understanding during his lifetime, they became powerful witnesses to his resurrection. Their lives were transformed by God's power. The story of Jesus' disciples does not end with the Gospels. It continues in the book of Acts and many of the letters.

DISCIPLES

What Jesus Said about Him	*A Key Lesson from His Life*	*Selected References*
Named him Peter, "rock"; called him "Satan" when he urged Jesus to reject the cross; said he would become a fisher of men; he received revelation from God; he would deny Jesus; he would later be crucified for his faith.	Christians falter at times, but when they return to Jesus, he forgives them and strengthens their faith.	Matthew 4:18–20 Mark 8:29–33 Luke 22:31–34 John 21:15–19 Acts 2:14–41 Acts 10:1—11:18
Called James and John "Sons of Thunder"; said he would be a fisher of men; would drink the cup Jesus drank.	Christians must be willing to die for Jesus.	Mark 3:17 Mark 10:35–40 Luke 9:52–56 Acts 12:1–2
Called James and John "Sons of Thunder"; said he would be a fisher of men; would drink the cup Jesus drank; would take care of Jesus' mother after Jesus' death.	The transforming power of the love of Christ is available to all.	Mark 1:19 Mark 10:35–40 Luke 9:52–56 John 19:26–27 John 21:20–24
Said he would become a fisher of men.	Christians are to tell other people about Jesus.	Matthew 4:18–20 John 1:35–42; 6:8–9 John 12:20–22
Asked if Philip realized that to know and see him was to know and see the Father.	God uses our questions to teach us.	Matthew 10:3 John 1:43–46; 6:2–7 John 12:20–22 John 14:8–11
Called him "an Israelite indeed, in whom there is no deceit."	Jesus respects honesty in people—even if they challenge him because of it.	Mark 3:18 John 1:45–51 John 21:1–13
Called him to be a disciple.	Christianity is not for people who think they're already good; it is for people who know they've failed and want help.	Matthew 9:9–13 Mark 2:15–17 Luke 5:27–32
Said Thomas believed because he actually saw Jesus after the resurrection.	Even when Christians experience serious doubts, Jesus reaches out to them to restore their faith.	Matthew 10:3 John 14:5; 20:24–29 John 21:1–13
Unknown	Unknown	Matthew 10:3 Mark 3:18 Luke 6:15
Unknown	Christians follow Jesus because they believe in him; they do not always understand the details of God's plan.	Matthew 10:3 Mark 3:18 John 14:22
Unknown	If we are willing to give up our plans for the future, we can participate in Jesus' plans.	Matthew 10:4 Mark 3:18 Luke 6:15
Called him "a devil"; said Judas would betray Jesus.	It is not enough to be familiar with Jesus' teachings. Jesus' true followers love and obey him.	Matthew 26:20–25 Luke 22:47–48 John 12:4–8

27 "But no one can enter the strong man's house and plunder his property unless he
first binds the strong man, and then he will plunder his house.
28 "Truly I say to you, all sins shall be forgiven the sons of men, and whatever blasphemies they utter;
29 but whoever blasphemes against the Holy Spirit never has forgiveness, but is guilty
of an eternal sin"—
30 because they were saying, "He has an unclean spirit."

3:27 Is 49:24, 25
3:28 Matt 12:31, 32; Luke 12:10
3:29 Luke 12:10

Jesus Describes His True Family
(76/Matthew 12:46-50; Luke 8:19-21)

31 Then His mother and His brothers *arrived, and standing outside they sent *word* to
Him and called Him.
32 A crowd was sitting around Him, and they *said to Him, "Behold, Your mother and
Your brothers are outside looking for You."
33 Answering them, He *said, "Who are My mother and My brothers?"
34 Looking about at those who were sitting around Him, He *said, "Behold My mother and My brothers!
35 "For whoever does the will of God, he is My brother and sister and mother."

3:34 Matt 12:49
3:35 Eph 6:6; Heb 10:36; 1 Pet 4:2; 1 John 2:17

Jesus Tells the Parable of the Four Soils
(77/Matthew 13:1-9; Luke 8:4-8)

4 He began to teach again by the sea. And such a very large crowd gathered to Him
that He got into a boat in the sea and sat down; and the whole crowd was by the sea
on the land.
2 And He was teaching them many things in parables, and was saying to them in His
teaching,
3 "Listen *to this!* Behold, the sower went out to sow;
4 as he was sowing, some *seed* fell beside the road, and the birds came and ate it up.
5 "Other *seed* fell on the rocky *ground* where it did not have much soil; and immediately it sprang up because it had no depth of soil.
6 "And after the sun had risen, it was scorched; and because it had no root, it withered
away.
7 "Other *seed* fell among the thorns, and the thorns came up and choked it, and it yielded
no crop.

4:1 Mark 2:13; 3:7; Luke 5:1-3
4:2 Matt 13:3ff; Mark 3:23

3:27 Although God permits Satan to work in our world, God is still in control. Jesus, because he is God, has power over Satan; Jesus is able to drive out demons and end their terrible work in people's lives. One day Satan will be bound forever (Revelation 20:10).

3:28–29 Christians sometimes wonder if they have committed this sin of blasphemy against the Holy Spirit. Christians need not worry about this sin because this sin is attributing to the devil what is the work of the Holy Spirit. It reveals a heart-attitude of unbelief and unrepentance. Deliberate, ongoing rejection of the work of the Holy Spirit is blasphemy because it is rejecting God himself. The religious leaders accused Jesus of blasphemy, but ironically they were the guilty ones when they looked Jesus in the face and accused him of being possessed by Satan.

3:31–35 Jesus' mother was Mary (Luke 1:30–31), and his brothers were probably the other children Mary and Joseph had after Jesus (see also 6:3). Some Christians believe the ancient tradition that Jesus was Mary's only child. If this is true, the "brothers" were possibly cousins (cousins were often called brothers in those days). Some have offered yet another suggestion: When Joseph married Mary, he was a widower, and these were his children by his first marriage. Most likely, these were Jesus' half brothers (see Mark 6:3–4).

Jesus' family did not yet fully understand his ministry, as can be seen in verse 21. Jesus explained that in our spiritual family, the relationships are ultimately more important and longer lasting than those formed in our physical families.

3:33–35 God's family is accepting and doesn't exclude anyone. Although Jesus cared for his mother and brothers, he also cared for all those who loved him. Jesus did not show partiality; he allowed everyone the privilege of obeying God and becoming part of his family. In our increasingly computerized, impersonal world, warm relationships among members of God's family take on major importance. The church can give the loving, personalized care that many people find nowhere else.

4:2 Jesus taught the people by telling parables, short stories using familiar scenes to explain spiritual truth. This method of teaching compels the listener to think. It conceals the truth from those who are too stubborn or prejudiced to hear what is being taught. Most parables have one main point, so we must be careful not to go beyond what Jesus intended to teach.

4:3 Seed was sown by hand. As the farmer walked across the field, he threw handfuls of seed onto the ground from a large bag slung across his shoulders. The plants did not grow in neat rows as accomplished by today's machine planting. No matter how skillful, no farmer could keep some of his seed from falling by the side of the road, from being scattered among rocks and thorns, or from being carried off by the wind. So the farmer would throw the seed liberally, and enough would fall on good ground to ensure the harvest.

8 "Other *seeds* fell into the good soil, and as they grew up and increased, they yielded
a crop and produced thirty, sixty, and a hundredfold."

9 And He was saying, "He who has ears to hear, let him hear."

Jesus Explains the Parable of the Four Soils
(78/Matthew 13:10-23; Luke 8:9-18)

10 As soon as He was alone, His followers, along with the twelve, *began* asking Him
about the parables.

11 And He was saying to them, "To you has been given the mystery of the kingdom of
God, but those who are outside get everything in parables,

12 so that WHILE SEEING, THEY MAY SEE AND NOT PERCEIVE, AND WHILE HEARING,
THEY MAY HEAR AND NOT UNDERSTAND, OTHERWISE THEY MIGHT RETURN AND BE
FORGIVEN."

13 And He ☆said to them, "Do you not understand this parable? How will you understand all the parables?

14 "The sower sows the word.

15 "These are the ones who are beside the road where the word is sown; and when they
hear, immediately Satan comes and takes away the word which has been sown in them.

16 "In a similar way these are the ones on whom seed was sown on the rocky *places,*
who, when they hear the word, immediately receive it with joy;

17 and they have no *firm* root in themselves, but are *only* temporary; then, when affliction or persecution arises because of the word, immediately they fall away.

18 "And others are the ones on whom seed was sown among the thorns; these are the
ones who have heard the word,

19 but the worries of the [9]world, and the deceitfulness of riches, and the desires for
other things enter in and choke the word, and it becomes unfruitful.

20 "And those are the ones on whom seed was sown on the good soil; and they hear the
word and accept it and bear fruit, thirty, sixty, and a hundredfold."

21 And He was saying to them, "A lamp is not brought to be put under a basket, is it, or
under a bed? Is it not *brought* to be put on the lampstand?

22 "For nothing is hidden, except to be revealed; nor has *anything* been secret, but that
it would come to light.

23 "If anyone has ears to hear, let him hear."

24 And He was saying to them, "Take care what you listen to. By your standard of
measure it will be measured to you; and more will be given you besides.

25 "For whoever has, to him *more* shall be given; and whoever does not have, even what
he has shall be taken away from him."

9 *Or age*

4:9 Matt 11:15; Mark 4:23; Rev 2:7, 11, 17, 29
4:11 1 Cor 5:12f; Col 4:5; 1 Thess 4:12; 1 Tim 3:7; Mark 3:23; 4:2
4:12 Is 6:9f; 43:8; Jer 5:21; Ezek 12:2; Matt 13:14; Luke 8:10; John 12:40; Rom 11:8
4:13 Matt 13:18-23; Luke 8:11-15
4:15 Matt 4:10f; 1 Pet 5:8; Rev 20:2, 3, 7-10
4:19 Matt 13:22; Rom 12:2; Eph 2:2; 6:12; Prov 23:4; 1 Tim 6:9, 10, 17
4:20 John 15:2ff; Rom 7:4
4:21 Matt 5:15; Luke 8:16; 11:33
4:22 Matt 10:26; Luke 8:17; 12:2
4:23 Matt 11:15; 13:9, 43; Mark 4:9; Luke 8:8; 14:35; Rev 3:6, 13, 22; 13:9
4:24 Matt 7:2; Luke 6:38
4:25 Matt 13:12; 25:29; Luke 8:18; 19:26

4:9 We hear with our ears, but there is a deeper kind of listening with the mind and heart that is necessary in order to gain spiritual understanding from Jesus' words. Some people in the crowd were looking for evidence to use against Jesus; others truly wanted to learn and grow. Jesus' words were for the honest seekers.

4:11–12 Some people do not understand God's truth because they are not ready for it. God reveals truth to people who will act on it, who will make it visible in their lives. When you talk with people about God, be aware that they will not understand if they are not yet ready. Be patient, taking every chance to tell them more of the truth about God, and praying that the Holy Spirit will open their minds and hearts to receive the truth and act on it.

4:14–20 The four soils represent four different ways people respond to God's message. Usually we think that Jesus was talking about four different kinds of people. But he may also have been talking about (1) different times or phases in a person's life, or (2) how we willingly receive God's message in some areas of our lives and resist it in others. For example, you may be open to God about your future, but closed concerning how you spend your money. You may respond like good soil to God's demand for worship, but like rocky soil to his demand to give to people in need. We must strive to be like good soil in every area of our lives at all times.

4:19 Worldly worries, the false sense of security brought on by prosperity, and the desire for things plagued first-century disciples as they do us today. How easy it is for our daily routines to become overcrowded. A life packed with materialistic pursuits deafens us to God's Word. Stay free so you can hear God when he speaks.

4:21 If a lamp doesn't help people see, it is useless. Does your life show other people how to find God and how to live for him? If not, ask what "baskets" have extinguished your light. Complacency, resentment, stubbornness of heart, or disobedience could keep God's light from shining through you to others.

4:24–25 The light of Jesus' truth is revealed to us, not hidden. But we may not be able to see or to use all of that truth right now. Only as we put God's teachings into practice will we understand and see more of the truth. The truth is clear, but our ability to understand is imperfect. As we obey, we will sharpen our vision and increase our understanding (see James 1:22–25).

4:25 This verse simply means that we are responsible to use well what we have. How much we have is not nearly as important as what we do with it.

Jesus Tells the Parable of the Growing Seed
(79)

26 And He was saying, "The kingdom of God is like a man who casts seed upon the soil;
27 and he goes to bed at night and gets up by day, and the seed sprouts and grows—how, he himself does not know.
28 "The soil produces crops by itself; first the blade, then the head, then the mature grain in the head.
29 "But when the crop permits, he immediately puts in the sickle, because the harvest has come."

4:29 Joel 3:13

Jesus Tells the Parable of the Mustard Seed
(81/Matthew 13:31-32)

30 And He said, "How shall we [10]picture the kingdom of God, or by what parable shall we present it?
31 "*It is* like a mustard seed, which, when sown upon the soil, though it is smaller than all the seeds that are upon the soil,
32 yet when it is sown, it grows up and becomes larger than all the garden plants and forms large branches; so that THE BIRDS OF THE [11]AIR can NEST UNDER ITS SHADE."
33 With many such parables He was speaking the word to them, so far as they were able to hear it;
34 and He did not speak to them without a parable; but He was explaining everything privately to His own disciples.

4:30 Luke 13:18, 19; Matt 13:24

4:32 Ezek 17:23; Ps 104:12; Ezek 31:6; Dan 4:12

4:34 Matt 13:34; John 10:6; 16:25; Luke 24:27

Jesus Calms the Storm
(87/Matthew 8:23-27; Luke 8:22-25)

35 On that day, when evening came, He ☆said to them, "Let us go over to the other side."
36 Leaving the crowd, they ☆took Him along with them in the boat, just as He was; and other boats were with Him.
37 And there ☆arose a fierce gale of wind, and the waves were breaking over the boat so much that the boat was already filling up.
38 Jesus Himself was in the stern, asleep on the cushion; and they ☆woke Him and ☆said to Him, "Teacher, do You not care that we are perishing?"

4:36 Mark 3:9; 4:1; 5:2, 21

10 Lit *compare* **11** Or *sky*

4:26–29 This parable about the kingdom of God, recorded only by Mark, reveals that spiritual growth is a continual, gradual process that is finally consummated in a harvest of spiritual maturity. We can understand the process of spiritual growth by comparing it to the slow but certain growth of a plant.

4:30–32 Jesus used this parable to explain that although Christianity had very small beginnings, it would grow into a worldwide community of believers. When you feel alone in your stand for Christ, realize that God is building a worldwide kingdom. He has faithful followers in every part of the world, and your faith, no matter how small, can join with that of others to accomplish great things.

4:33–34 Jesus adapted his methods to his audience's ability and desire to understand. He didn't speak in parables to confuse people, but to challenge sincere seekers to discover the meaning of his words. Much of Jesus' teaching was against hypocrisy and impure motives—characteristics of the religious leaders. Had Jesus spoken against the leaders directly, his public ministry would have been hampered. Those who listened carefully to Jesus knew what he was talking about.

4:37–38 The Sea of Galilee is 680 feet below sea level and is surrounded by hills. Winds blowing across the land intensify close to the sea, often causing violent and unexpected storms. The disciples were seasoned fishermen who had spent their lives fishing on this huge lake, but during this squall they panicked.

4:38–40 The disciples panicked because the storm threatened to destroy them all, and Jesus seemed unaware and unconcerned. Theirs was a physical storm, but storms come in other forms. Think about the storms in your life—the situations that cause you great anxiety. Whatever your difficulty, you have two options: You can worry and assume that Jesus no longer cares, or you can resist fear, putting your trust in him. When you feel like panicking, confess your need for God and then trust him to care for you.

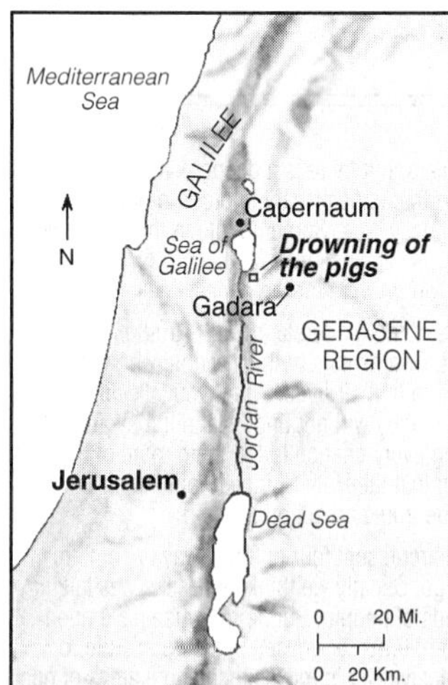

HEALING A DEMON-POSSESSED MAN
From Capernaum, Jesus and his disciples crossed the Sea of Galilee. A storm blew up unexpectedly, but Jesus calmed it. Landing in the region of the Gerasenes, Jesus sent demons out of a man and into a herd of swine that plunged over the steep bank into the lake.

4:39 Ps 65:7; 89:9; 107:29; Matt 8:26; Luke 8:24

4:40 Matt 14:31; Luke 8:25

39 And He got up and rebuked the wind and said to the sea, "Hush, be still." And the
wind died down and it became perfectly calm.
40 And He said to them, "Why are you afraid? Do you still have no faith?"
41 They became very much afraid and said to one another, "Who then is this, that even
the wind and the sea obey Him?"

Jesus Sends the Demons into a Herd of Swine
(88/Matthew 8:28-34; Luke 8:26-39)

5:2 Mark 3:9; 4:1, 36; 5:21; Mark 1:23

5:7 Matt 8:29; Matt 4:3; Luke 8:28; Acts 16:17; Heb 7:1

5 They came to the other side of the sea, into the country of the Gerasenes.
2 When He got out of the boat, immediately a man from the tombs with an unclean
spirit met Him,
3 and he had his dwelling among the tombs. And no one was able to bind him anymore, even with a chain;
4 because he had often been bound with shackles and chains, and the chains had been
torn apart by him and the shackles broken in pieces, and no one was strong enough to
subdue him.
5 Constantly, night and day, he was screaming among the tombs and in the mountains, and gashing himself with stones.
6 Seeing Jesus from a distance, he ran up and bowed down before Him;
7 and shouting with a loud voice, he ☆said, "What business do we have with each other,
Jesus, Son of the Most High God? I implore You by God, do not torment me!"

THE TOUCH OF JESUS

What kind of people did Jesus associate with? Whom did he consider important enough to touch? Here we see many of the people Jesus came to know. Some reached out to him; he reached out to them all. Regardless of how great or unknown, rich or poor, young or old, sinner or saint—Jesus cares equally for all. No person is beyond the loving touch of Jesus.

Jesus Talked with...	*Reference*
A despised tax collector	Matthew 9:9
An insane hermit	Mark 5:1–15
The Roman governor	Mark 15:1–15
A young boy	Mark 9:17–27
A prominent religious leader	John 3:1–21
A homemaker	Luke 10:38–42
A lawyer	Matthew 22:35
A criminal	Luke 23:40–43
A synagogue official	Mark 5:22
Fishermen	Matthew 4:18–20
A king	Luke 23:7–11
A poor widow	Luke 7:11–17; 21:1–4
A Roman centurion	Luke 7:1–10
A group of children	Mark 10:13–16
A prophet	Matthew 3
An adulterous woman	John 8:1–11
The Jewish Council	Luke 22:66–71
A sick woman	Mark 5:25–34
A rich man	Mark 10:17–23
A blind beggar	Mark 10:46
Jewish political leaders	Mark 12:13
A group of women	Luke 8:2–3
The high priest	Matthew 26:62–68
An outcast with leprosy	Luke 17:11–19
A royal official	John 4:46–53
A young girl	Mark 5:41–42
A traitor	John 13:1–3, 27
A helpless and paralyzed man	Mark 2:1–12
An angry mob of soldiers and police	John 18:3–9
A woman from a foreign land	Mark 7:25–30
A doubting follower	John 20:24–29
An enemy who hated him	Acts 9:1–9
A Samaritan woman	John 4:1–26

4:41 The disciples lived with Jesus, but they underestimated him. They did not see that his power applied to their very own situation. Jesus has been with his people for 20 centuries, and yet we, like the disciples, underestimate his power to handle crises in our lives. The disciples did not yet know enough about Jesus. We cannot make the same excuse.

5:1–2 Although we cannot be sure why demon-possession occurs, we know that unclean (evil) spirits can use the human body to distort and destroy people's relationship with God and likeness to him. Even today, demons are dangerous, powerful, and destructive. While it is important to recognize their evil activity so that we can stay away from demons, we should avoid any curiosity about or involvement with demonic forces or the occult (Deuteronomy 18:10–12). If we resist the devil and his influences, he will flee from us (James 4:7).

8 For He had been saying to him, "Come out of the man, you unclean spirit!"
9 And He was asking him, "What is your name?" And he ☆said to Him, "My name is
Legion; for we are many."
10 And he *began* to implore Him earnestly not to send them out of the country.
11 Now there was a large herd of swine feeding nearby on the mountain.
12 *The demons* implored Him, saying, "Send us into the swine so that we may enter
them."
13 Jesus gave them permission. And coming out, the unclean spirits entered the swine;
and the herd rushed down the steep bank into the sea, about two thousand *of them;* and
they were drowned in the sea.
14 Their herdsmen ran away and reported it in the city and in the country. And *the
people* came to see what it was that had happened.
15 They ☆came to Jesus and ☆observed the man who had been demon-possessed sitting down, clothed and in his right mind, the very man who had had the "legion"; and
they became frightened.
16 Those who had seen it described to them how it had happened to the demon-
possessed man, and *all* about the swine.
17 And they began to implore Him to leave their region.
18 As He was getting into the boat, the man who had been demon-possessed was imploring Him that he might accompany Him.
19 And He did not let him, but He ☆said to him, "Go home to your people and report
to them [12]what great things the Lord has done for you, and *how* He had mercy on you."
20 And he went away and began to proclaim in Decapolis what great things Jesus had
done for him; and everyone was amazed.

Jesus Heals a Bleeding Woman and Restores a Girl to Life
(89/Matthew 9:18-26; Luke 8:40-56)

21 When Jesus had crossed over again in the boat to the other side, a large crowd gathered around Him; and so He stayed by the seashore.
22 One of the synagogue officials named Jairus ☆came up, and on seeing Him, ☆fell at
His feet

5:9 Matt 26:53; Mark 5:15; Luke 8:30
5:15 Matt 4:24; Mark 5:16, 18; Luke 8:27; Luke 8:35; Mark 5:9
5:16 Matt 4:24; Mark 5:15
5:17 Matt 8:34; Acts 16:39
5:18 Luke 8:38, 39; Matt 4:24; Mark 5:15, 16
5:19 Luke 8:39
5:20 Ps 66:16; Matt 4:25; Mark 7:31
5:21 Matt 9:1; Luke 8:40; Mark 4:36; Mark 4:1
5:22 Matt 9:18; Mark 5:35, 36, 38; Luke 8:49; 13:14; Acts 13:15; 18:8, 17

12 Or *everything that*

5:9 The unclean spirit said its name was Legion. A legion was the largest unit of the Roman army, consisting of 3,000 to 6,000 soldiers. Obviously this man was possessed by many demons.

5:10 Mark often highlights the supernatural struggle between Jesus and Satan. The demons' goal was to control the humans they inhabited; Jesus' goal was to give people freedom from sin and Satan's control. The demons knew they had no power over Jesus; so when they saw Jesus, they begged not to be sent out of the country ("into the abyss" in Luke 8:31). Jesus granted their request to enter into the herd of swine (5:13) but ended their destructive work in people. Perhaps Jesus let the demons destroy the pigs to demonstrate his own superiority over a very powerful yet destructive force. He could have sent them to hell, but he did not, because the time for judgment had not yet come. In the end, the devil and all his angels will be sent into eternal fire (Matthew 25:41).

5:11 According to Old Testament law (Leviticus 11:7), pigs were "unclean" animals. This meant that they could not be eaten or even touched by a Jew. This incident took place southeast of the Sea of Galilee in the region of the Gerasenes, a Gentile region, which explains how a herd of pigs could be involved.

5:17 After such a wonderful miracle of saving a man's life, why did the people want Jesus to leave? They were undoubtedly afraid of his supernatural power. They may have also feared that Jesus would continue destroying their pigs. They would rather give up Jesus than lose their source of income and security.

5:19 Jesus told this man to tell his friends about the miraculous healing. Most of the time, Jesus urged those he healed to keep quiet. Why the difference? Here are possible answers: (1) The demon-possessed man had been alone and unable to speak. Telling others what Jesus did for him would prove that he was healed. (2) This was mainly a Gentile and pagan area, so Jesus was not expecting great crowds to follow him or religious leaders to hinder him. (3) By sending the man away with this good news, Jesus was expanding his ministry to people who were not Jews.

5:19–20 This man had been demon-possessed but became a living example of Jesus' power. He wanted to go with Jesus, but Jesus told him to go home and share his story with his friends. If you have experienced Jesus' power, you too are a living example. Are you, like this man, enthusiastic about sharing the Good News with those around you? Just as we would tell others about a doctor who cured a physical disease, we should tell about Christ who cures our sin.

5:20 Decapolis, or the Ten Cities, was located southeast of the Sea of Galilee. Ten cities, each with its own independent government, formed an alliance for protection and for increased trade opportunities. These cities had been settled several centuries earlier by Greek traders and immigrants. Although Jews also lived in the area, they were not in the majority. Many people from the Decapolis followed Jesus (Matthew 4:25).

5:22 Jesus recrossed the Sea of Galilee, probably landing at Capernaum. Jairus was the elected official of the local synagogue. He was responsible for supervising worship, running the weekly school, and caring for the building. Many synagogue officials had close ties to the Pharisees. It is likely, therefore, that some synagogue officials had been pressured not to support Jesus. For Jairus to bow before Jesus was a significant and perhaps daring act of respect and worship.

5:23 Mark 6:5; 7:32; 8:23; 16:18; Luke 4:40; 13:13; Acts 6:6; 9:17; 28:8

23 and ☆implored Him earnestly, saying, "My little daughter is at the point of death;
please come and lay Your hands on her, so that she will get well and live."
24 And He went off with him; and a large crowd was following Him and pressing in
on Him.
25 A woman who had had a hemorrhage for twelve years,
26 and had endured much at the hands of many physicians, and had spent all that she
had and was not helped at all, but rather had grown worse—
27 after hearing about Jesus, she came up in the crowd behind *Him* and touched His
cloak.
28 For she thought, "If I just touch His garments, I will get well."

5:29 Mark 3:10; 5:34

29 Immediately the flow of her blood was dried up; and she felt in her body that she
was healed of her affliction.

5:30 Luke 5:17

30 Immediately Jesus, perceiving in Himself that the power *proceeding* from Him had
gone forth, turned around in the crowd and said, "Who touched My garments?"
31 And His disciples said to Him, "You see the crowd pressing in on You, and You
say, 'Who touched Me?' "
32 And He looked around to see the woman who had done this.
33 But the woman fearing and trembling, aware of what had happened to her, came
and fell down before Him and told Him the whole truth.

5:34 Matt 9:22; Luke 7:50; 8:48; Acts 16:36; James 2:16; Mark 3:10; 5:29

34 And He said to her, "Daughter, your faith has made you well; go in peace and be
healed of your affliction."

5:35 Mark 5:22

35 While He was still speaking, they ☆came from the *house of* the synagogue official,
saying, "Your daughter has died; why trouble the Teacher anymore?"

5:36 Mark 5:22; Luke 8:50

36 But Jesus, overhearing what was being spoken, ☆said to the synagogue official, "Do
not be afraid *any longer,* only believe."

5:37 Matt 17:1; 26:37

37 And He allowed no one to accompany Him, except Peter and James and John the
brother of James.

5:38 Mark 5:22

38 They ☆came to the house of the synagogue official; and He ☆saw a commotion, and
people loudly weeping and wailing.
39 And entering in, He ☆said to them, "Why make a commotion and weep? The child
has not died, but is asleep."
40 They *began* laughing at Him. But putting them all out, He ☆took along the child's
father and mother and His own companions, and ☆entered *the room* where the child was.

5:41 Luke 7:14; Acts 9:40

41 Taking the child by the hand, He ☆said to her, "Talitha kum!" (which translated
means, "Little girl, I say to you, get up!").
42 Immediately the girl got up and *began* to walk, for she was twelve years old. And
immediately they were completely astounded.

5:25–34 This woman had a seemingly incurable condition causing her to bleed constantly. This may have been a menstrual or uterine disorder that would have made her ritually unclean (Leviticus 15:25–27) and would have excluded her from most social contact. She desperately wanted Jesus to heal her, but she knew that her bleeding would cause Jesus to be unclean under Jewish law if she touched him. Still, the woman reached out by faith and was healed. Sometimes we feel that our problems will keep us from God. But he is always ready to help. We should never allow our fear to keep us from approaching him.

5:32–34 Jesus was not angry with this woman for touching him. He knew she had touched him, but he stopped and asked who did it in order to teach her something about faith. Although the woman was healed when she touched him, Jesus said her faith caused the cure. Genuine faith involves action. Faith that isn't put into action is not faith at all.

5:35–36 Jairus's crisis made him feel confused, afraid, and without hope. Jesus' words to Jairus in the midst of crisis speak to us as well: "Do not be afraid any longer, only believe." In Jesus' mind, there was both hope and promise. The next time you feel hopeless and afraid, look at your problem from Jesus' point of view. He is the source of all hope and promise.

5:38 Loud weeping and wailing was customary at a person's death. Lack of it was the ultimate disgrace and disrespect. There were some people, usually women, who made mourning a profession and were paid by the dead person's family to weep over the body. On the day of death, the body was carried through the streets, followed by mourners, family members, and friends.

5:39–40 The mourners began to laugh at Jesus when he said, "The child has not died, but is asleep." The girl was dead, but Jesus used the image of sleep to indicate that her condition was temporary and that she would be restored.

Jesus tolerated the crowd's abuse in order to teach an important lesson about maintaining hope and trust in him. Today, most of the world laughs at Christ's claims, which seem ridiculous to them. When you are belittled for expressing faith in Jesus and hope for eternal life, remember that unbelievers don't see from God's perspective. For a clear statement about life after death, see 1 Thessalonians 4:13–14.

5:41 *Talitha kum* is Aramaic, one of the original languages of Palestine. Jesus' disciples spoke not only Aramaic, but probably Greek and Hebrew also.

5:41–42 Jesus not only demonstrated great power; he also showed tremendous compassion. Jesus' power over nature, unclean spirits, and death was motivated by compassion—for a demon-possessed man who lived among tombs, for a diseased woman, and for the family of a dead girl. The rabbis of the day considered such people unclean. Polite society avoided them. But Jesus reached out and helped anyone in need.

43 And He gave them strict orders that no one should know about this, and He said
that *something* should be given her to eat.

The People of Nazareth Refuse to Believe
(91/Matthew 13:53-58)

6 Jesus went out from there and ☆came into His hometown; and His disciples ☆follow-
ed Him.
2 When the Sabbath came, He began to teach in the synagogue; and the many listeners were astonished, saying, "Where did this man *get* these things, and what is *this* wisdom given to Him, and such miracles as these performed by His hands?
3 "Is not this the carpenter, the son of Mary, and brother of James and Joses and Judas
and Simon? Are not His sisters here with us?" And they took offense at Him.
4 Jesus said to them, "A prophet is not without honor except in his hometown and
among his *own* relatives and in his *own* household."
5 And He could do no miracle there except that He laid His hands on a few sick people and healed them.
6 And He wondered at their unbelief.
And He was going around the villages teaching.

Jesus Sends Out the Twelve Disciples
(93/Matthew 10:1-16; Luke 9:1-6)

7 And He ☆summoned the twelve and began to send them out in pairs, and gave them
authority over the unclean spirits;
8 and He instructed them that they should take nothing for *their* journey, except a
mere staff—no bread, no bag, no money in their belt—
9 but *to* wear sandals; and *He added*, "Do not put on two [13]tunics."
10 And He said to them, "Wherever you enter a house, stay there until you leave town.

5:43 Matt 8:4
6:1 Matt 13:54, 57; Luke 4:16, 23
6:2 Matt 4:23; Mark 10:1; Matt 7:28
6:3 Matt 13:55; Matt 12:46; Matt 13:56; Matt 11:6
6:4 Matt 13:57; John 4:44; Mark 6:1
6:5 Mark 5:23
6:6 Matt 9:35; Mark 1:39; 10:1; Luke 13:22
6:7 Luke 10:4-11; Matt 10:1, 5; Mark 3:13; Luke 9:1; Luke 10:1
6:8 Matt 10:10

13 Or *inner garments*

5:43 Jesus told the girl's parents not to spread the news of the miracle. He wanted the facts to speak for themselves, and the time was not yet right for a major confrontation with the religious leaders. Jesus still had much to accomplish, and he didn't want people following him just to see his miracles.

6:2–3 Jesus was teaching effectively and wisely, but the people of his hometown saw him as only a carpenter. "He's no better than we are—he's just a common laborer," they said. They were offended that others could be impressed by Jesus and follow him. They rejected his authority because he was one of their peers. They thought they knew him, but their preconceived notions about who he was made it impossible for them to accept his message. Don't let prejudice blind you to truth. As you learn more about Jesus, try to see him for who he really is.

PREACHING IN GALILEE
After returning to his hometown, Nazareth, from Capernaum, Jesus preached in the villages of Galilee and sent his disciples out to preach as well. After meeting back in Capernaum, they left by boat to rest, only to be met by the crowds who followed the boat along the shore.

6:4 Jesus said that a prophet (in other words, a worker for God) is never honored in his hometown. But that doesn't make his work any less important. A person doesn't need to be respected or honored to be useful to God. If friends, neighbors, or family don't respect your Christian work, don't let their rejection keep you from serving God.

6:5 Jesus could have done greater miracles in Nazareth, but he chose not to because of the people's pride and unbelief. The miracles he did had little effect on the people because they did not accept his message or believe that he was from God. Therefore, Jesus looked elsewhere, seeking those who would respond to his miracles and message.

6:7 The disciples were sent out in pairs. Individually they could have reached more areas of the country, but this was not Christ's plan. One advantage in going out by twos was that they could strengthen and encourage each other, especially when they faced rejection. Our strength comes from God, but he meets many of our needs through our teamwork with others. As you serve Christ, don't try to go it alone.

6:8–9 Mark records that the disciples were instructed to take nothing with them *except* staffs, while in the Matthew and Luke accounts Jesus told them *not* to take staffs. One explanation is that Matthew and Luke were referring to a club used for protection, whereas Mark was talking about a shepherd's crook. In any case, the point in all three accounts is the same—the disciples were to leave at once, without extensive preparation, trusting in God's care rather than in their own resources.

6:11 Matt 10:14; Acts 13:51
6:12 Matt 11:1; Luke 9:6
6:13 James 5:14

11 "Any place that does not receive you or listen to you, as you go out from there, shake the dust off the soles of your feet for a testimony against them."
12 They went out and preached that *men* should repent.
13 And they were casting out many demons and were anointing with oil many sick people and healing them.

HEROD ANTIPAS

Most people dislike having their sins pointed out, especially in public. The shame of being exposed is often stronger than the guilt brought on by the wrongdoing. Herod Antipas was a man experiencing both guilt and shame.

Herod's ruthless ambition was public knowledge, as was his illegal marriage to his brother's wife, Herodias. One man made Herod's sin a public issue. That man was John the Baptist. John had been preaching in the wilderness, and thousands flocked to hear him. Apparently it was no secret that John had rebuked Herod for his adulterous marriage. Herodias was particularly anxious to have John silenced. As a solution, Herod imprisoned John.

Herod liked John. John was probably one of the few people he met who spoke only the truth to him. But the truth about his sin was a bitter pill to swallow, and Herod wavered at the point of conflict: he couldn't afford to have John constantly reminding the people of their leader's sinfulness, but he was afraid to have John killed. He put off the choice. Eventually Herodias forced his hand, and John was executed. Of course, this only served to increase Herod's guilt.

Upon hearing about Jesus, Herod immediately identified him with John. He couldn't decide what to do about Jesus. He didn't want to repeat the mistake he had made with John, so he tried to threaten Jesus just before Jesus' final journey to Jerusalem. When the two met briefly during Jesus' trial, Jesus would not speak to Herod. Herod had proved himself a poor listener to John, and Jesus had nothing to add to John's words. Herod responded with spite and mocking. Having rejected the messenger, he found it easy to reject the Messiah.

For each person, God chooses the best possible ways to reveal himself. He uses his Word, various circumstances, our minds, or other people to get our attention. He is persuasive and persistent, but never forces himself on us. To miss or resist God's message, as did Herod, is tragedy. How aware are you of God's attempts to enter your life? Have you welcomed him?

Strengths and accomplishments:
- Built the city of Tiberias and oversaw other architectural projects
- Ruled the region of Galilee for the Romans

Weaknesses and mistakes:
- Consumed with his quest for power
- Put off decisions or made wrong ones under pressure
- Divorced his wife to marry the wife of his half brother, Philip
- Imprisoned John the Baptist and later ordered his execution
- Had a minor part in the execution of Jesus

Lessons from his life:
- A life motivated by ambition is usually characterized by self-destruction
- Opportunities to do good usually come to us in the form of choices to be made

Vital statistics:
- Where: Jerusalem
- Occupation: Roman tetrarch of the region of Galilee and Perea
- Relatives: Father: Herod the Great. Mother: Malthace. First wife: daughter of Aretas IV. Second wife: Herodias
- Contemporaries: John the Baptist, Jesus, Pilate

Key verse:
"When he heard [John], he was very perplexed; but he used to enjoy listening to him" (Mark 6:20).

Herod Antipas's story is told in the Gospels. He is also mentioned in Acts 4:27; 13:1.

6:11 Pious Jews shook the dust from their feet after passing through Gentile cities or territory to show their separation from Gentile influences and practices. When the disciples shook the dust from their feet after leaving a *Jewish* town, it was a vivid sign that they wished to remain separate from people who had rejected Jesus and his message. Jesus made it clear that the listeners were responsible for what they did with the gospel. The disciples were not to blame if the message was rejected, as long as they had faithfully and carefully presented it. We are not responsible when others reject Christ's message of salvation, but we do have the responsibility to share the gospel clearly and faithfully.

Herod Kills John the Baptist
(95/Matthew 14:1-12; Luke 9:7-9)

14 And King Herod heard *of it,* for His name had become well known; and *people* were **6:14** Matt 14:2; Luke 9:19
saying, "John the Baptist has risen from the dead, and that is why these miraculous pow-
ers are at work in Him."
15 But others were saying, "He is Elijah." And others were saying, "*He is* a prophet, **6:15** Matt 16:14; Mark 8:28; Matt 21:11
like one of the prophets *of old.*"
16 But when Herod heard *of it,* he kept saying, "John, whom I beheaded, has risen!"
17 For Herod himself had sent and had John arrested and bound in prison on account **6:17** Matt 14:3; Luke 3:19
of Herodias, the wife of his brother Philip, because he had married her.
18 For John had been saying to Herod, "It is not lawful for you to have your brother's **6:18** Matt 14:4
wife."
19 Herodias had a grudge against him and wanted to put him to death and could not **6:19** Matt 14:3
do so;
20 for Herod was afraid of John, knowing that he was a righteous and holy man, and **6:20** Matt 21:26
he kept him safe. And when he heard him, he was very perplexed; but he used to enjoy
listening to him.
21 A strategic day came when Herod on his birthday gave a banquet for his lords and **6:21** Esth 1:3; 2:18; Luke 3:1
military commanders and the leading men of Galilee;
22 and when the daughter of Herodias herself came in and danced, she pleased Herod
and his dinner guests; and the king said to the girl, "Ask me for whatever you want and **6:22** Matt 14:3
I will give it to you."
23 And he swore to her, "Whatever you ask of me, I will give it to you; up to half of my **6:23** Esth 5:3, 6; 7:2
kingdom."
24 And she went out and said to her mother, "What shall I ask for?" And she said,
"The head of John the Baptist."
25 Immediately she came in a hurry to the king and asked, saying, "I want you to give
me at once the head of John the Baptist on a platter."
26 And although the king was very sorry, *yet* because of his oaths and because of his
dinner guests, he was unwilling to refuse her.
27 Immediately the king sent an executioner and commanded *him* to bring *back* his
head. And he went and had him beheaded in the prison,
28 and brought his head on a platter, and gave it to the girl; and the girl gave it to her
mother.
29 When his disciples heard *about this,* they came and took away his body and laid it in
a tomb.

Jesus Feeds Five Thousand
(96/Matthew 14:13-21, Luke 9:10-17; John 6:1-15)

30 The apostles ☆gathered together with Jesus; and they reported to Him all that they **6:30** Luke 9:10; Matt 10:2; Mark 3:14; Luke 6:13; 9:10; 17:5; 22:14; 24:10; Acts 1:2, 26
had done and taught.

6:14–15 Herod, along with many others, wondered who Jesus really was. Unable to accept Jesus' claim to be God's Son, many people made up their own explanations for his power and authority. Herod thought that Jesus was John the Baptist come back to life, while those who were familiar with the Old Testament thought he was Elijah (Malachi 4:5). Still others believed that Jesus was a teaching prophet in the tradition of Moses, Isaiah, or Jeremiah. Today people still have to make up their minds about Jesus. Some think that if they can name what he is—prophet, teacher, good man—they can weaken the power of his claim on their lives. But what they *think* does not change who Jesus *is.*

6:17–19 Palestine was divided into four territories, each with a different ruler. Herod Antipas, called Herod in the Gospels, was ruler over Galilee; his brother Philip ruled over Trachonitis and Idumea. Philip's wife was Herodias, but she left him to marry Herod Antipas. When John confronted the two for committing adultery, Herodias formulated a plot to kill him. Instead of trying to get rid of her sin, Herodias tried to get rid of the one who brought it to public attention. This is exactly what the religious leaders were trying to do to Jesus.

6:20 Herod arrested John the Baptist under pressure from his wife and advisers. Though Herod respected John's integrity, in the end Herod had John killed because of pressure from his peers and family. What you do under pressure often shows what you are really like.

6:22–23 As a ruler under Roman authority, Herod had no kingdom to give. The offer of half his kingdom was Herod's way to say that he would give Herodias's daughter almost anything she wanted. When Herodias asked for John's head, Herod would have been greatly embarrassed in front of his guests if he had denied her request. Words are powerful. Because they can lead to great sin, we should use them with great care.

6:30 Mark uses the word *apostles* here and in 3:14. *Apostle* means "one sent" as messenger, authorized agent, or missionary. The word became an official title for Jesus' 12 disciples after his death and resurrection (Acts 1:25–26; Ephesians 2:20).

6:31 Mark 3:20
6:32 Matt 14:13-21; Luke 9:10-17; John 6:5-13; Mark 8:2-9; Mark 3:9; 4:36; 6:45
6:34 Matt 9:36; Num 27:17; 1 Kin 22:17; 2 Chr 18:16; Zech 10:2
6:37 John 6:7; Matt 18:28; Luke 7:41
6:41 Matt 14:19
6:43 Matt 14:20
6:44 Matt 14:21

31 And He ☆said to them, "Come away by yourselves to a secluded place and rest a while."
(For there were many *people* coming and going, and they did not even have time to eat.)
32 They went away in the boat to a secluded place by themselves.
33 *The people* saw them going, and many recognized *them* and ran there together on
foot from all the cities, and got there ahead of them.
34 When Jesus went ashore, He saw a large crowd, and He felt compassion for them
because they were like sheep without a shepherd; and He began to teach them many
things.
35 When it was already quite late, His disciples came to Him and said, "This place is
desolate and it is already quite late;
36 send them away so that they may go into the surrounding countryside and villages
and buy themselves something to eat."
37 But He answered them, "You give them *something* to eat!" And they ☆said to Him,
"Shall we go and spend two hundred [14]denarii on bread and give them *something* to eat?"
38 And He ☆said to them, "How many loaves do you have? Go look!" And when they
found out, they ☆said, "Five, and two fish."
39 And He commanded them all to sit down by groups on the green grass.
40 They sat down in groups of hundreds and of fifties.
41 And He took the five loaves and the two fish, and looking up toward heaven, He
blessed *the food* and broke the loaves and He kept giving *them* to the disciples to set
before them; and He divided up the two fish among them all.
42 They all ate and were satisfied,
43 and they picked up twelve full baskets of the broken pieces, and also of the fish.
44 There were five thousand men who ate the loaves.

Jesus Walks on Water

(97/Matthew 14:22-33; John 6:16-21)

6:45 Mark 6:32; Matt 11:21; Mark 8:22
6:46 Acts 18:18, 21; 2 Cor 2:13; Matt 14:23
6:48 Matt 24:43; Mark 13:35

45 Immediately Jesus made His disciples get into the boat and go ahead of *Him* to the
other side to Bethsaida, while He Himself was sending the crowd away.
46 After bidding them farewell, He left for the mountain to pray.
47 When it was evening, the boat was in the middle of the sea, and He was alone on
the land.
48 Seeing them straining at the oars, for the wind was against them, at about the fourth
watch of the night He ☆came to them, walking on the sea; and He intended to pass by
them.

14 The denarius was equivalent to one day's wage

REAL LEADERSHIP
Mark gives us some of the best insights into Jesus' character.

Herod as a leader	*Jesus as a leader*
Selfish	Compassionate
Murderer	Healer
Immoral	Just and good
Political opportunist	Servant
King over small territory	King over all creation

6:31 When the disciples had returned from their mission, Jesus took them away to rest. Doing God's work is very important, but Jesus recognized that to do it effectively we need periodic rest and renewal. Jesus and his disciples, however, did not always find it easy to get the rest they needed!

6:34 This crowd was as pitiful as a flock of sheep without a shepherd. Sheep are easily scattered; without a shepherd they are in grave danger. Jesus was the Shepherd who could teach them what they needed to know and keep them from straying from God. See Psalm 23; Isaiah 40:11; and Ezekiel 34:5ff for descriptions of the Good Shepherd.

6:37 In this chapter different people have examined Jesus' life and ministry: his neighbors and family, Herod the king, and the disciples. Yet none of these appreciated Jesus for who he was. The disciples were still pondering, still confused, still unbelieving. They did not realize that Jesus could provide for them. They were so preoccupied with the immensity of the task that they could not see what was possible with God. Do you let what seems impossible about Christianity keep you from believing?

6:37–42 When Jesus asked the disciples to provide food for over 5,000 people, they asked in astonishment if they should go and spend two hundred denarii (about eight months' wages) on bread. How do you react when you are given an impossible task? A situation that seems impossible with human resources is simply an opportunity for God. The disciples did everything they could by gathering the available food and organizing the people into groups. Then, in answer to prayer, God did the impossible. When facing a seemingly impossible task, do what you can and ask God to do the rest. He may see fit to make the impossible happen.

49 But when they saw Him walking on the sea, they supposed that it was a ghost, and
cried out;
50 for they all saw Him and were terrified. But immediately He spoke with them and 6:50 Matt 9:2; Matt 14:27
☆said to them, "Take courage; it is I, do not be afraid."
51 Then He got into the boat with them, and the wind stopped; and they were utterly 6:51 Mark 6:32
astonished,
52 for they had not gained any insight from the *incident of* the loaves, but their heart 6:52 Mark 8:17ff; Rom 11:7
was hardened.

Jesus Heals All Who Touch Him
(98/Matthew 14:34-36)

53 When they had crossed over they came to land at Gennesaret, and moored to the 6:53 John 6:24, 25
shore.
54 When they got out of the boat, immediately *the people* recognized Him,
55 and ran about that whole country and began to carry here and there on their pallets
those who were sick, to the place they heard He was.
56 Wherever He entered villages, or cities, or countryside, they were laying the sick in 6:56 Mark 3:10; Matt 9:20; Num 15:37-40
the market places, and imploring Him that they might just touch the fringe of His cloak;
and as many as touched it were being cured.

Jesus Teaches about Inner Purity 7:1 Matt 15:1
(102/Matthew 15:1-20)

7 The Pharisees and some of the scribes gathered around Him when they had come 7:2 Matt 15:2; Mark 7:5; Luke 11:38; Acts 10:14, 28; 11:8; Rom 14:14; Heb 10:29; Rev 21:27
from Jerusalem,
2 and had seen that some of His disciples were eating their bread with impure hands,
that is, unwashed.
3 (For the Pharisees and all the Jews do not eat unless they carefully wash their hands, 7:3 Mark 7:5, 8, 9, 13; Gal 1:14
thus observing the traditions of the elders;

6:49 The disciples were surprised to see Jesus walking beside them on the water. But they should have realized that Jesus would help them when they were in trouble. Though they had lost sight of Jesus, he had not lost sight of them. His concern for them overcame their lack of faith. The next time you are in "deep water," remember that Christ knows your struggle and cares for you.

6:49–50 The disciples were afraid, but Jesus' presence calmed their fears. We all experience fear. Do we try to deal with it ourselves, or do we let Jesus deal with it? In times of fear and uncertainty, it is calming to know that Christ is always with us (Matthew 28:20). To recognize Christ's presence is the antidote for fear.

JESUS WALKS ON THE WATER
After feeding the people who had followed to hear him at Bethsaida, Jesus sent the people home, sent his disciples by boat toward Bethsaida, and went to pray. The disciples encountered a storm, and Jesus walked to them on the water. They landed at Gennesaret.

6:52 The disciples' hearts were *hardened*; they didn't want to believe, perhaps because (1) they couldn't accept the fact that this human named Jesus was really the Son of God; (2) they dared not believe that the Messiah would choose them as his followers—it was too good to be true; (3) they still did not understand the real purpose for Jesus' coming to earth. Their disbelief took the form of misunderstanding.

Even after watching Jesus miraculously feed 5,000 people, they still could not take the final step of faith and believe that he was God's Son. If they had, they would not have been amazed that Jesus could walk on water. The disciples did not transfer the truth they already knew about Jesus to their own lives. We read that Jesus walked on the water, and yet we often marvel that he is able to work in our lives. We must not only believe that these miracles really occurred; we must also transfer the truth to our own life situations.

6:53 Gennesaret was a small fertile plain located on the west side of the Sea of Galilee. Capernaum, Jesus' home, sat at the northern edge of this plain.

7:1ff The religious leaders sent some investigators from their headquarters in Jerusalem to check up on Jesus. The delegation didn't like what they found, however, because Jesus scolded them for keeping the law and the traditions in order to look holy instead of to honor God. The prophet Isaiah accused the religious leaders of his day of doing the same thing (Isaiah 29:13). Jesus used Isaiah's words to accuse these men.

7:3–4 Mark explained these Jewish rituals because he was writing to a non-Jewish audience. Before each meal, devout Jews performed a short ceremony, washing their hands and arms in a specific way. The disciples did not have dirty hands, but they were simply not carrying out this traditional cleansing. The Pharisees thought this ceremony cleansed them from any contact they might have had with anything considered unclean. Jesus said they were wrong in thinking they were acceptable to God just because they were clean on the outside.

7:4 Matt 23:25
7:5 Mark 7:3, 8, 9, 13; Gal 1:14; Mark 7:2
7:6 Is 29:13
7:7 Is 29:13
7:8 Mark 7:3, 5, 9, 13; Gal 1:14
7:9 Mark 7:3, 5, 8, 13; Gal 1:14
7:10 Ex 20:12; Deut 5:16; Ex 21:17; Lev 20:9
7:11 Lev 1:2; Matt 27:6
7:13 Mark 7:3, 5, 8, 9; Gal 1:14
7:17 Mark 2:1; 3:20; 9:28; Matt 15:15
7:19 Rom 14:1-12; Col 2:16; Luke 11:41; Acts 10:15; 11:9

4 and *when they come* from the market place, they do not eat unless they cleanse themselves; and there are many other things which they have received in order to observe,
such as the washing of cups and pitchers and copper pots.)
5 The Pharisees and the scribes ☆asked Him, “Why do Your disciples not walk according to the tradition of the elders, but eat their bread with impure hands?”
6 And He said to them, “Rightly did Isaiah prophesy of you hypocrites, as it is written:
‘THIS PEOPLE HONORS ME WITH THEIR LIPS,
BUT THEIR HEART IS FAR AWAY FROM ME.
7 ‘BUT IN VAIN DO THEY WORSHIP ME,
TEACHING AS DOCTRINES THE PRECEPTS OF MEN.’
8 “Neglecting the commandment of God, you hold to the tradition of men.”
9 He was also saying to them, “You are experts at setting aside the commandment of
God in order to keep your tradition.
10 “For Moses said, ‘HONOR YOUR FATHER AND YOUR MOTHER’; and, ‘HE WHO SPEAKS
EVIL OF FATHER OR MOTHER, IS TO BE PUT TO DEATH’;
11 but you say, ‘If a man says to *his* father or *his* mother, whatever I have that would
help you is Corban (that is to say, [15]given *to God),*’
12 you no longer permit him to do anything for *his* father or *his* mother;
13 *thus* invalidating the word of God by your tradition which you have handed down;
and you do many things such as that.”
14 After He called the crowd to Him again, He *began* saying to them, “Listen to Me,
all of you, and understand:
15 there is nothing outside the man which can defile him if it goes into him; but the
things which proceed out of the man are what defile the man.
16 [“[16]If anyone has ears to hear, let him hear.”]
17 When he had left the crowd *and* entered the house, His disciples questioned Him
about the parable.
18 And He ☆said to them, “Are you so lacking in understanding also? Do you not understand that whatever goes into the man from outside cannot defile him,

15 Or *a gift,* i.e. *an offering* **16** Early mss do not contain this verse

GOSPEL ACCOUNTS FOUND ONLY IN MARK

Section	Topic	Significance
4:26–29	Story of the growing seed	We must share the Good News of Jesus with other people, but only God makes it grow in their lives.
7:31–37	Jesus heals a deaf man who could hardly talk	Jesus cares about our physical as well as spiritual needs.
8:22–26	Jesus heals the blind man at Bethsaida	Jesus is considerate because he makes sure this man's sight is fully restored.

7:6–7 Hypocrisy is pretending to be something you are not and have no intention of being. Jesus called the Pharisees hypocrites because they worshiped God for the wrong reasons. Their worship was not motivated by love, but by a desire to attain profit, to appear holy, and to increase their status. We become hypocrites when we (1) pay more attention to reputation than to character, (2) carefully follow certain religious practices while allowing our hearts to remain distant from God, and (3) emphasize our virtues but others' sins.

7:8–9 The Pharisees added hundreds of their own petty rules and regulations to God's holy laws, and then they tried to force people to follow these rules. These men claimed to know God's will in every detail of life. There are still religious leaders today who add rules and regulations to God's Word, causing much confusion among believers. It is idolatry to claim that your interpretation of God's Word is as important as God's Word itself. It is especially dangerous to set up unbiblical standards for *others* to follow. Instead, look to Christ for guidance about your own behavior, and let him lead others in the details of their lives.

7:10–11 The Pharisees used God as an excuse to avoid helping their families. They thought it was more important to put money in the temple treasury than to help their needy parents, although God's law specifically says to honor fathers and mothers (Exodus 20:12) and to care for those in need (Leviticus 25:35–43). (For an explanation of *Corban,* see the note on Matthew 15:5–6.) We should give money and time to God, but we must never use God as an excuse to neglect our responsibilities. Helping those in need is one of the most important ways to honor God.

7:18–19 Do we worry more about what is in our diets than what is in our hearts and minds? As they interpreted the dietary laws (Leviticus 11), the Jews believed they could be clean before God because of what they refused to eat. But Jesus pointed out that sin actually begins in the attitudes and intentions of the inner person. Jesus did not degrade the law, but he paved the way for the change made clear in Acts 10:9–29 when God removed the cultural restrictions regarding food. We are not pure because of outward acts—we become pure on the inside as Christ renews our minds and transforms us into his image.

19 because it does not go into his heart, but into his stomach, and is eliminated?" (*Thus He* declared all foods clean.)
20 And He was saying, "That which proceeds out of the man, that is what defiles the man. **7:20** Matt 15:18; Mark 7:23
21 "For from within, out of the heart of men, proceed the evil thoughts, fornications, thefts, murders, adulteries,
22 deeds of coveting *and* wickedness, *as well as* deceit, sensuality, envy, slander, pride *and* foolishness. **7:22** Matt 6:23; 20:15
23 "All these evil things proceed from within and defile the man."

2. Jesus' ministry beyond Galilee

Jesus Sends a Demon Out of a Girl
(103/Matthew 15:21-28)

24 Jesus got up and went away from there to the region of Tyre[17]. And when He had entered a house, He wanted no one to know *of it;* yet He could not escape notice. **7:24** Matt 11:21; Mark 7:31
25 But after hearing of Him, a woman whose little daughter had an unclean spirit immediately came and fell at His feet.
26 Now the woman was a [18]Gentile, of the Syrophoenician race. And she kept asking Him to cast the demon out of her daughter.
27 And He was saying to her, "Let the children be satisfied first, for it is not good to take the children's bread and throw it to the dogs."
28 But she answered and ☆said to Him, "Yes, Lord, *but* even the dogs under the table feed on the children's crumbs."
29 And He said to her, "Because of this answer go; the demon has gone out of your daughter."
30 And going back to her home, she found the child lying on the bed, the demon having left.

17 Two early mss add *and Sidon* **18** Lit *Greek*

7:20–23 An evil action begins with a single thought. Allowing our minds to dwell on lust, envy, hatred, or revenge will lead to sin. Don't defile yourself by focusing on evil. Instead, follow Paul's advice in Philippians 4:8 and think about what is true, honorable, right, pure, lovely, and of good repute.

MINISTRY IN PHOENICIA
Jesus' ministry was to all people—first to Jews but also to Gentiles. Jesus took his disciples from Galilee to Tyre and Sidon, large cities in Phoenicia, where he healed a Gentile woman's daughter.

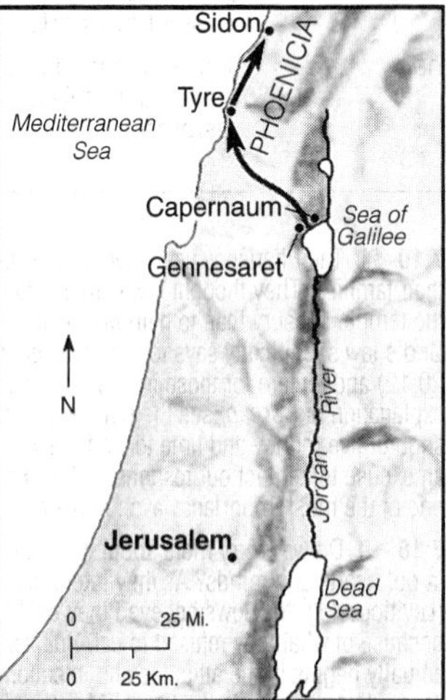

7:24 Jesus traveled about 30 miles to Tyre and then went to Sidon. These were port cities on the Mediterranean Sea north of Israel. Both cities had flourishing trade and were very wealthy. They were proud, historic Canaanite cities.

In David's day, Tyre was on friendly terms with Israel (2 Samuel 5:11), but soon afterward the city became known for its wickedness. Its king even claimed to be God (Ezekiel 28:1ff). Tyre rejoiced when Jerusalem was destroyed in 586 B.C., because without Israel's competition, Tyre's trade and profits would increase. It was into this evil and materialistic culture that Jesus brought his message. It is interesting that Jesus stressed the importance of inner purity just before visiting Tyre.

7:26 This woman is called a Gentile of the Syrophoenician race in Mark and a Canaanite in Matthew. Mark's designation refers to her political background. His Roman audience would easily identify her by the part of the empire that was her home. Matthew's description was designed for his Jewish audience, who remembered the Canaanites as bitter enemies when Israel was settling the promised land.

7:27–28 *Dog* refers to little dogs or house pets, not outdoor scavengers. Jesus was saying that his first priority was to provide food for the children (teach his disciples), not to allow pets to interrupt the family meal.

The woman did not try to argue. Using Jesus' choice of imagery, she pointed out that she was willing to be considered an interruption as long as she could receive God's healing for her daughter. Ironically, many Jews would lose God's spiritual healing because they rejected Jesus, while many Gentiles, whom the Jews rejected, would find salvation because they recognized Jesus.

7:29 This miracle shows that Jesus' power over demons is so great that he doesn't need to be present physically in order to free someone. His power transcends any distance.

The Crowd Marvels at Jesus' Healings
(104/Matthew 15:29-31)

31 Again He went out from the region of Tyre, and came through Sidon to the Sea of
Galilee, within the region of Decapolis.
32 They ☆brought to Him one who was deaf and spoke with difficulty, and they
☆implored Him to lay His hand on him.
33 Jesus took him aside from the crowd, by himself, and put His fingers into his ears,
and after spitting, He touched his tongue *with the saliva;*
34 and looking up to heaven with a deep sigh, He ☆said to him, "Ephphatha!" that is,
"Be opened!"
35 And his ears were opened, and the impediment of his tongue was removed, and he
began speaking plainly.
36 And He gave them orders not to tell anyone; but the more He ordered them, the
more widely they continued to proclaim it.
37 They were utterly astonished, saying, "He has done all things well; He makes even
the deaf to hear and the mute to speak."

7:31 Matt 11:21; Mark 7:24; Matt 4:18; Matt 4:25; Mark 5:20
7:32 Mark 5:23
7:33 Mark 8:23
7:34 Mark 8:12
7:36 Matt 8:4; Mark 1:45

Jesus Feeds Four Thousand
(105/Matthew 15:32-39)

8 In those days, when there was again a large crowd and they had nothing to eat, Jesus
called His disciples and ☆said to them,
2 "I feel compassion for the people because they have remained with Me now three
days and have nothing to eat.
3 "If I send them away hungry to their homes, they will faint on the way; and some of
them have come from a great distance."
4 And His disciples answered Him, "Where will anyone be able *to find enough* bread
here in *this* desolate place to satisfy these people?"
5 And He was asking them, "How many loaves do you have?" And they said,
"Seven."
6 And He ☆directed the people to sit down on the ground; and taking the seven loaves,
He gave thanks and broke them, and started giving them to His disciples to serve to them,
and they served them to the people.
7 They also had a few small fish; and after He had blessed them, He ordered these to
be served as well.
8 And they ate and were satisfied; and they picked up seven large baskets full of what
was left over of the broken pieces.
9 About four thousand were *there;* and He sent them away.
10 And immediately He entered the boat with His disciples and came to the district of
Dalmanutha.

8:1 Mark 6:34-44
8:2 Matt 9:36; Mark 6:34
8:7 Matt 14:19
8:8 Matt 15:37; Mark 8:20
8:10 Matt 15:39

7:36 Jesus asked the people not to talk about this healing, because he didn't want to be seen simply as a miracle worker. He didn't want the people to miss his real message. We must not be so concerned about what Jesus can do for us that we forget to listen to his message.

8:1ff This is a different miracle from the feeding of the 5,000 described in chapter 6. At that time, those fed were mostly Jews. This time Jesus was ministering to a non-Jewish crowd in the Gentile region of the Decapolis. Jesus' actions and message were beginning to have an impact on large numbers of Gentiles. That Jesus would compassionately minister to non-Jews was very reassuring to Mark's primarily Roman audience.

8:1–3 Do you ever feel that God is so busy with important concerns that he can't possibly be aware of your needs? Just as Jesus was concerned about these people's need for food, so he is concerned about our daily needs. At another time Jesus said, "Do not worry then, saying, 'What will we eat?' or 'What will we drink?' or 'What will we wear for clothing?' . . . your heavenly Father knows that you need all these things" (Matthew 6:31–32). Do you have concerns that you think would not interest God? There is nothing too large for him to handle and no need too small to escape his interest.

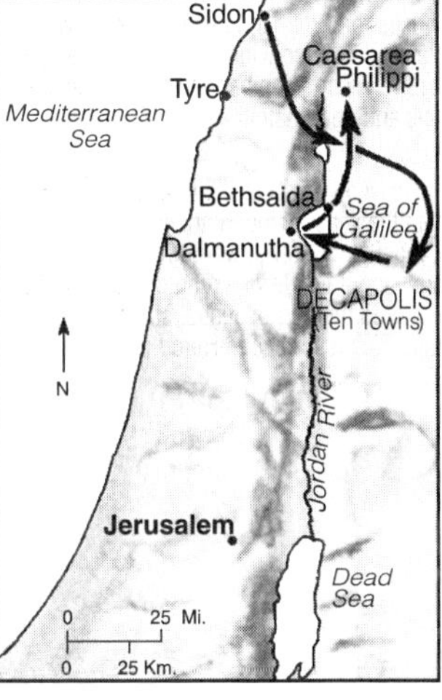

CONTINUED MINISTRY
After taking a roundabout way back to Galilee through Decapolis (the Ten Towns), Jesus returned to Dalmanutha where Jewish leaders questioned his authority. From there he went to Bethsaida and on to Caesarea Philippi. Here he talked with his disciples about his authority and coming events.

Religious Leaders Ask for a Sign in the Sky
(106/Matthew 16:1-4)

11 The Pharisees came out and began to argue with Him, seeking from Him a sign from
heaven, to test Him.
12 Sighing deeply in His spirit, He ☆said, "Why does this generation seek for a sign?
Truly I say to you, no sign will be given to this generation."
13 Leaving them, He again embarked and went away to the other side.

Jesus Warns against Wrong Teaching
(107/Matthew 16:5-12)

14 And they had forgotten to take bread, and did not have more than one loaf in the
boat with them.
15 And He was giving orders to them, saying, "Watch out! Beware of the leaven of the
Pharisees and the leaven of Herod."
16 They *began* to discuss with one another *the fact* that they had no bread.
17 And Jesus, aware of this, ☆said to them, "Why do you discuss *the fact* that you have
no bread? Do you not yet see or understand? Do you have a hardened heart?
18 "HAVING EYES, DO YOU NOT SEE? AND HAVING EARS, DO YOU NOT HEAR? And do
you not remember,
19 when I broke the five loaves for the five thousand, how many baskets full of broken
pieces you picked up?" They ☆said to Him, "Twelve."
20 "When *I broke* the seven for the four thousand, how many large baskets full of broken pieces did you pick up?" And they ☆said to Him, "Seven."
21 And He was saying to them, "Do you not yet understand?"

Jesus Restores Sight to a Blind Man
(108)

22 And they ☆came to Bethsaida. And they ☆brought a blind man to Jesus and ☆implored
Him to touch him.
23 Taking the blind man by the hand, He brought him out of the village; and after spitting on his eyes and laying His hands on him, He asked him, "Do you see anything?"
24 And he looked up and said, "I see men, for I see *them* like trees, walking around."
25 Then again He laid His hands on his eyes; and he looked intently and was restored,
and *began* to see everything clearly.
26 And He sent him to his home, saying, "Do not even enter the village."

8:11 Matt 12:38
8:12 Mark 7:34; Matt 12:39
8:15 Matt 16:6; Luke 12:1; Matt 14:1; 22:16
8:17 Mark 6:52
8:18 Jer 5:21; Ezek 12:2; Mark 4:12
8:19 Mark 6:41-44; Matt 14:20
8:20 Mark 8:6-9
8:21 Mark 6:52
8:22 Matt 11:21; Mark 6:45; Mark 3:10
8:23 Mark 7:33; Mark 5:23
8:26 Mark 8:23

8:11 The Pharisees had tried to explain away Jesus' previous miracles by claiming they were done by luck, coincidence, or evil power. Here they demanded a sign from heaven—something only God could do. Jesus refused their demand because he knew that even this kind of miracle would not convince them. They had already decided not to believe. Hearts can become so hard that even the most convincing facts and demonstrations will not change them.

8:15 Mark mentions the leaven (yeast) of the Pharisees and Herod, while Matthew talks about the yeast of the Pharisees and Sadducees. Mark's audience, mostly non-Jews, would have known about Herod, but not necessarily about the Jewish religious sect of the Sadducees. Thus Mark quoted the part of Jesus' statement that his readers would understand. This reference to Herod may mean the Herodians, a group of Jews who supported the king. Many Herodians were also Sadducees.

8:15ff Leaven (yeast) in this passage symbolizes evil. Just as only a small amount of yeast is needed to make a batch of bread rise, so the hardheartedness of the religious and political leaders could permeate and contaminate the entire society and make it rise up against Jesus.

8:17–18 How could the disciples experience so many of Jesus' miracles and yet be so slow to comprehend who he was? They had already seen Jesus feed over 5,000 people with five loaves and two fish (6:35–44), yet here they doubted whether he could feed another large group.

Sometimes we are also slow to catch on. Although Christ has brought us through trials and temptations in the past, we don't believe that he will do it in the future. Is your heart too closed to take in all that God can do for you? Don't be like the disciples. Remember what Christ has done, and have faith that he will do it again.

8:25 Why did Jesus touch the man a second time before he could see? This miracle was not too difficult for Jesus, but he chose to do it in stages, possibly to show the disciples that some healing would be gradual rather than instantaneous or to demonstrate that spiritual truth is not always perceived clearly at first. Before Jesus left, however, the man was healed completely.

Peter Says Jesus Is the Messiah
(109/Matthew 16:13–20; Luke 9:18–20)

27 Jesus went out, along with His disciples, to the villages of Caesarea Philippi; and on
the way He questioned His disciples, saying to them, "Who do people say that I am?"
28 They told Him, saying, "John the Baptist; and others *say* Elijah; but others, one of
the prophets."
29 And He *continued* by questioning them, "But who do you say that I am?" Peter
☆answered and ☆said to Him, "You are the Christ."
30 And He warned them to tell no one about Him.

Jesus Predicts His Death the First Time
(110/Matthew 16:21–28; Luke 9:21–27)

31 And He began to teach them that the Son of Man must suffer many things and be
rejected by the elders and the chief priests and the scribes, and be killed, and after three
days rise again.
32 And He was stating the matter plainly. And Peter took Him aside and began to rebuke Him.
33 But turning around and seeing His disciples, He rebuked Peter and ☆said, "Get behind Me, Satan; for you are not setting your mind on [19]God's interests, but man's."
34 And He summoned the crowd with His disciples, and said to them, "If anyone wishes
to come after Me, he must deny himself, and take up his cross and follow Me.
35 "For whoever wishes to save his life will lose it, but whoever loses his life for My sake
and the gospel's will save it.

8:27 Matt 16:13
8:28 Mark 6:14; Luke 9:7, 8
8:29 John 6:68, 69
8:30 Matt 8:4; 16:20; Luke 9:21
8:31 Matt 16:21
8:32 John 10:24; 11:14; 16:25, 29; 18:20
8:33 Matt 4:10
8:34 Matt 10:38; Luke 14:27
8:35 Matt 10:39; Luke 17:33; John 12:25

19 Lit *the things of God*

8:27 Caesarea Philippi was an especially pagan city known for its worship of Greek gods and its temples devoted to the ancient god Pan. The ruler Philip, referred to in Mark 6:17, changed the city's name from Caesarea to Caesarea Philippi so that it would not be confused with the coastal city of Caesarea (Acts 8:40), the capital of the territory ruled by his brother Herod Antipas. This pagan city where many gods were recognized was a fitting place for Jesus to ask the disciples to recognize him as the Son of God.

8:28 For the story of John the Baptist, see Mark 1:1–11 and 6:14–29. For the story of Elijah, see 1 Kings 17—20 and 2 Kings 1; 2.

8:29 Jesus asked the disciples who other people thought he was; then he asked them the same question. It is not enough to know what others say about Jesus: You must know, understand, and accept for yourself that he is the Messiah. You must move from curiosity to commitment, from admiration to adoration.

8:29–31 The name for Jesus, *Son of Man,* is Jesus' most common title for himself. It comes from Daniel 7:13, where the Son of Man is a heavenly figure who, in the end times, has authority and power. The name refers to Jesus as the Messiah, the representative man, the human agent of God who is vindicated by God. In this passage, *Son of Man* is linked closely with Peter's confession of Jesus as the Christ and confirms its Messianic significance.

From this point on, Jesus spoke plainly and directly to his disciples about his death and resurrection. He began to prepare them for what was going to happen to him by telling them three times that he would soon die (8:31; 9:31; 10:33–34).

8:30 Why did Jesus warn his own disciples not to tell anyone the truth about him? Jesus knew they needed more instruction about the work he would accomplish through his death and resurrection. Without more teaching, the disciples would have only half the picture. When they confessed Jesus as the Christ, they still didn't know all that it meant.

8:32–33 In this moment, Peter was not considering God's purposes, but only his own natural human desires and feelings. Peter wanted Christ to be king, but not the suffering servant prophesied in Isaiah 53. He was ready to receive the glory of following the Messiah, but not the persecution.

The Christian life is not a paved road to wealth and ease. It often involves hard work, persecution, deprivation, and deep suffering. Peter saw only part of the picture. Don't repeat his mistake. Instead, focus on the good that God can bring out of apparent evil, and the resurrection that follows crucifixion.

8:33 Peter was often the spokesman for all the disciples. In singling him out, Jesus may have been addressing all of them indirectly. Unknowingly, the disciples were trying to prevent Jesus from going to the cross and thus fulfilling his mission on earth. Satan also tempted Jesus to avoid the way of the cross (Matthew 4). Whereas Satan's motives were evil, the disciples were motivated by love and admiration for Jesus. Nevertheless, the disciples' job was not to guide and protect Jesus, but to follow him. Only after Jesus' death and resurrection would they fully understand why he had to die.

8:34 The Romans, Mark's original audience, knew what taking up the cross meant. Death on a cross was a form of execution used by Rome for dangerous criminals. A prisoner carried his own cross to the place of execution, signifying submission to Rome's power.

Jesus used the image of carrying a cross to illustrate the ultimate submission required of his followers. He is not against pleasure, nor was he saying that we should seek pain needlessly. Jesus was talking about the heroic effort needed to follow him moment by moment, to do his will even when the work is difficult and the future looks bleak.

8:35 We should be willing to lose our lives for the sake of the gospel, not because our lives are useless but because nothing—not even life itself—can compare to what we gain with Christ. Jesus wants us to *choose* to follow him rather than to lead a life of sin and self-satisfaction. He wants us to stop trying to control our own destiny and to let him direct us. This makes good sense because, as the Creator, Christ knows better than we do what real life is about. He asks for submission, not self-hatred; he asks us only to lose our self-centered determination to be in charge.

36 "For what does it profit a man to gain the whole world, and forfeit his soul?
37 "For what will a man give in exchange for his soul?
38 "For whoever is ashamed of Me and My words in this adulterous and sinful genera- **8:38** Matt 10:33; Luke 9:26; Heb 11:16; Matt 8:20; Matt 16:27; Mark 13:26; Luke 9:26
tion, the Son of Man will also be ashamed of him when He comes in the glory of His
Father with the holy angels."
9 And Jesus was saying to them, "Truly I say to you, there are some of those who are
standing here who will not taste death until they see the kingdom of God after it has **9:1** Matt 16:28; Mark 13:26; Luke 9:27
come with power."

Jesus Is Transfigured on the Mountain
(111/Matthew 17:1-13; Luke 9:28-36)

2 Six days later, Jesus *took with Him Peter and James and John, and *brought them **9:2** Mark 5:37
up on a high mountain by themselves. And He was transfigured before them;
3 and His garments became radiant and exceedingly white, as no launderer on earth **9:3** Matt 28:3
can whiten them.
4 Elijah appeared to them along with Moses; and they were talking with Jesus. **9:5** Matt 23:7; Matt 17:4; Luke 9:33
5 Peter *said to Jesus, "Rabbi, it is good for us to be here; let us make three taberna-
cles, one for You, and one for Moses, and one for Elijah."
6 For he did not know what to answer; for they became terrified.
7 Then a cloud formed, overshadowing them, and a voice came out of the cloud, "This **9:7** 2 Pet 1:17f; Matt 3:17; Mark 1:11; Luke 3:22
is My beloved Son, listen to Him!"
8 All at once they looked around and saw no one with them anymore, except Jesus
alone.
9 As they were coming down from the mountain, He gave them orders not to relate **9:9** Matt 17:9-13; Matt 8:4; Mark 5:43; 7:36; 8:30
to anyone what they had seen, until the Son of Man rose from the dead.
10 They seized upon that statement, discussing with one another what rising from the
dead meant.
11 They asked Him, saying, "*Why is it* that the scribes say that Elijah must come first?" **9:11** Mal 4:5; Matt 11:14
12 And He said to them, "Elijah does first come and restore all things. And *yet* how is **9:12** Mark 9:31; Matt 16:21; 26:24
it written of the Son of Man that He will suffer many things and be treated with con-
tempt?

8:36–37 Many people spend all their energy seeking pleasure. Jesus said, however, that a world of pleasure centered on possessions, position, or power is ultimately worthless. Whatever you have on earth is only temporary; it cannot be exchanged for your soul. If you work hard at getting what you want, you might eventually have a "pleasurable" life, but in the end you will find it hollow and empty. Are you willing to make the pursuit of God more important than the selfish pursuit of pleasure? Follow Jesus, and you will know what it means to live abundantly now and to have eternal life as well.

8:38 Jesus constantly turns the world's perspective upside down with talk of first and last, saving and losing. Here he gives us a choice. We can reject Jesus now and be rejected by him at his second coming, or we can accept him now and be accepted by him then. Rejecting Christ may help us escape shame for the time being, but it will guarantee an eternity of shame later.

9:1 What did Jesus mean when he said that some of the disciples would see the kingdom of God after it has come with power? There are several possibilities. He could have been foretelling his transfiguration, resurrection and ascension, the coming of the Holy Spirit at Pentecost, or his second coming. The transfiguration is a strong possibility because Mark immediately tells that story. In the transfiguration (9:2–8), Peter, James, and John saw Jesus' glory, identity, and power as the Son of God (2 Peter 1:16).

9:2 We don't know why Jesus singled out Peter, James, and John for this special revelation of his glory and purity. Perhaps they were the ones most ready to understand and accept this great truth. These three disciples were the inner circle of the group of 12. They were among the first to hear Jesus' call (1:16–19). They headed the Gospel lists of disciples (3:16). And they were present at certain healings where others were excluded (Luke 8:51).

9:2 Jesus took the disciples to either Mount Hermon or Mount Tabor. A mountain was often associated with closeness to God and readiness to receive his words. God had appeared to both Moses (Exodus 24:12–18) and Elijah (1 Kings 19:8–18) on mountains.

9:3ff The transfiguration revealed Christ's divine nature. God's voice exalted Jesus above Moses and Elijah as the long-awaited Messiah with full divine authority. Moses represented the law and Elijah the prophets. Their appearance showed Jesus as the fulfillment of both the Old Testament Law and the prophetic promises.

Jesus was not a reincarnation of Elijah or Moses. He was not merely one of the prophets. As God's only Son, he far surpasses them in authority and power. Many voices try to tell us how to live and how to know God personally. Some of these are helpful; many are not. We must first listen to the Bible, and then evaluate all other authorities in light of God's revelation.

9:9–10 Jesus told Peter, James, and John not to speak about what they had seen because they would not fully understand it until Jesus had risen from the dead. Then they would realize that only through dying could Jesus show his power over death and his authority to be King of all. The disciples could not be powerful witnesses for God until they had grasped this truth.

It was natural for the disciples to be confused about Jesus' death and resurrection because they could not see into the future. We, on the other hand, have God's revealed Word, the Bible, to give us the full meaning of Jesus' death and resurrection. We have no excuse for our unbelief.

9:11–13 When Jesus said that Elijah had indeed come, he was speaking of John the Baptist (Matthew 17:11–13), who had fulfilled the role prophesied for Elijah.

9:12–13 It was difficult for the disciples to grasp the idea that their Messiah would have to suffer. The Jews who studied the Old Testament prophecies expected the Messiah to be a great king like

13 "But I say to you that Elijah has indeed come, and they did to him whatever they
wished, just as it is written of him."

Jesus Heals a Demon-Possessed Boy
(112/Matthew 17:14-21; Luke 9:37-43)

14 When they came *back* to the disciples, they saw a large crowd around them, and
some scribes arguing with them.

9:15 Mark 14:33; 16:5, 6

15 Immediately, when the entire crowd saw Him, they were amazed and *began* running up to greet Him.
16 And He asked them, "What are you discussing with them?"
17 And one of the crowd answered Him, "Teacher, I brought You my son, possessed
with a spirit which makes him mute;
18 and whenever it seizes him, it slams him *to the ground* and he foams *at the mouth,*
and grinds his teeth and stiffens out. I told Your disciples to cast it out, and they could
not *do it.*"
19 And He ☆answered them and ☆said, "O unbelieving generation, how long shall I be
with you? How long shall I put up with you? Bring him to Me!"
20 They brought the boy to Him. When he saw Him, immediately the spirit threw him
into a convulsion, and falling to the ground, he *began* rolling around and foaming *at the*
mouth.
21 And He asked his father, "How long has this been happening to him?" And he said,
"From childhood.
22 "It has often thrown him both into the fire and into the water to destroy him. But if
You can do anything, take pity on us and help us!"

9:23 Matt 17:20; John 11:40

9:25 Mark 9:15

23 And Jesus said to him, " 'If You can?' All things are possible to him who believes."
24 Immediately the boy's father cried out and said, "I do believe; help my unbelief."
25 When Jesus saw that a crowd was rapidly gathering, He rebuked the unclean spirit,
saying to it, "You deaf and mute spirit, I command you, come out of him and do not
enter him again."
26 After crying out and throwing him into terrible convulsions, it came out; and *the*
boy became so much like a corpse that most *of them* said, "He is dead!"
27 But Jesus took him by the hand and raised him; and he got up.

9:28 Mark 2:1; 7:17

28 When He came into *the* house, His disciples *began* questioning Him privately, "Why
could we not drive it out?"
29 And He said to them, "This kind cannot come out by anything but prayer."

Jesus Predicts His Death the Second Time
(113/Matthew 17:22-23; John 9:44-45)

9:30 Luke 9:43-45

30 From there they went out and *began* to go through Galilee, and He did not want
anyone to know *about it.*

David, who would overthrow the enemy, Rome. Their vision was limited to their own time and experience.

They could not understand that the values of God's eternal kingdom were different from the values of the world. They wanted relief from their present problems. But deliverance from sin is far more important than deliverance from physical suffering or political oppression. Our understanding of and appreciation for Jesus must go beyond what he can do for us here and now.

9:18 Why couldn't the disciples drive out the unclean spirit? In 6:13 we read that they drove out demons while on their mission to the villages. Perhaps they had special authority only for that trip, or perhaps their faith was faltering. Mark tells this story to show that the battle with Satan is a difficult, ongoing struggle. Victory over sin and temptation comes through faith in Jesus Christ, not through our own efforts.

9:23 Jesus' words do not mean that we can automatically obtain anything we want if we just think positively. Jesus meant that anything is *possible* if we believe, because nothing is too difficult for God. We cannot have everything we pray for as if by magic; but with faith, we can have everything we need to serve him.

9:24 The attitude of trust and confidence that the Bible calls *belief* or *faith* (Hebrews 11:1, 6) is not something we can obtain without help. Faith is a gift from God (Ephesians 2:8–9). No matter how much faith we have, we never reach the point of being self-sufficient. Faith is not stored away like money in the bank. Growing in faith is a constant process of daily renewing our trust in Jesus.

9:29 The disciples would often face difficult situations that could be resolved only through prayer. Prayer is the key that unlocks faith in our lives. Effective prayer needs both an attitude—complete dependence—and an action—asking. Prayer demonstrates our reliance on God as we humbly invite him to fill us with faith and power. There is no substitute for prayer, especially in circumstances that seem impossible.

9:30–31 At times, Jesus limited his public ministry in order to train his disciples in depth. He knew the importance of equipping them to carry on when he returned to heaven. It takes time to learn. Deep spiritual growth isn't instant, regardless of the quality of experience or teaching. If even the disciples needed to lay aside their work periodically in order to learn from the Master, how much more do we need to alternate working and learning.

9:30–31 Leaving Caesarea Philippi, Jesus began his last tour through the region of Galilee.

31 For He was teaching His disciples and telling them, "The Son of Man is to be [20]de-
livered into the hands of men, and they will kill Him; and when He has been killed, He
will rise three days later."
32 But they did not understand *this* statement, and they were afraid to ask Him.

9:31 Matt 16:21; Mark 8:31; 9:12
9:32 Luke 2:50; 9:45; 18:34; John 12:16

The Disciples Argue about Who Would Be the Greatest
(115/Matthew 18:1-6; Luke 9:46-48)

33 They came to Capernaum; and when He was in the house, He *began* to question
them, "What were you discussing on the way?"
34 But they kept silent, for on the way they had discussed with one another which *of*
them was the greatest.
35 Sitting down, He called the twelve and ☆said to them, "If anyone wants to be first,
he shall be last of all and servant of all."
36 Taking a child, He set him before them, and taking him in His arms, He said to them,
37 "Whoever receives one child like this in My name receives Me; and whoever receives
Me does not receive Me, but Him who sent Me."

9:33 Mark 3:19
9:34 Matt 18:4; Mark 9:50; Luke 22:24
9:35 Matt 20:26; 23:11; Mark 10:43, 44; Luke 22:26
9:37 Matt 10:40; Luke 10:16; John 13:20

The Disciples Forbid Another to Use Jesus' Name
(116/Matthew 9:49-50)

38 John said to Him, "Teacher, we saw someone casting out demons in Your name,
and we tried to prevent him because he was not following us."
39 But Jesus said, "Do not hinder him, for there is no one who will perform a miracle
in My name, and be able soon afterward to speak evil of Me.
40 "For he who is not against us is [21]for us.
41 "For whoever gives you a cup of water to drink because of your name as *followers* of
Christ, truly I say to you, he will not lose his reward.

9:38 Luke 9:49, 50; Num 11:27-29
9:40 Matt 12:30; Luke 11:23
9:41 Matt 10:42

Jesus Warns against Temptation
(117/Matthew 18:7-9)

42 "Whoever causes one of these little ones who believe to stumble, it would be better
for him if, with a heavy millstone hung around his neck, he had been cast into the sea.

9:42 Matt 18:6; Luke 17:2; 1 Cor 8:12

20 Or *betrayed* **21** Or *on our side*

9:32 Why were the disciples afraid to ask Jesus about his prediction of his death? Perhaps it was because the last time they reacted to Jesus' sobering words they were scolded (8:32–33). In their minds, Jesus seemed morbidly preoccupied with death. Actually it was the disciples who were wrongly preoccupied—constantly thinking about the kingdom they hoped Jesus would bring and their positions in it. If Jesus died, the kingdom as they imagined it could not come. Consequently they preferred not to ask him about his predictions.

9:34 The disciples, caught up in their constant struggle for personal success, were embarrassed to answer Jesus' question. It is always painful to compare our motives with Christ's. It is not wrong for believers to be industrious or ambitious. But when ambition pushes obedience and service to one side, it becomes sin. Pride or insecurity can cause us to overvalue position and prestige. In God's kingdom, such motives are destructive. The only safe ambition is directed toward Christ's kingdom, not our own advancement.

9:36–37 Jesus taught the disciples to welcome children. This was a new approach in a society where children were usually treated as second-class citizens. It is important not only to treat children well, but also to teach them about Jesus. Children's ministries should never be regarded as less important than those for adults.

9:38 The disciples were jealous of a man who healed in Jesus' name because they were more concerned about their own group's position than in helping to free those troubled by demons. We do the same today when we refuse to participate in worthy causes because (1) other people or groups are not affiliated with our denomination, (2) these projects do not involve the kind of people with whom we feel most comfortable, (3) others don't do things the way we are used to doing things, (4) our efforts won't receive enough recognition. Correct theology is important but should never be an excuse to avoid helping people in need.

9:40 Jesus was not saying that being indifferent or neutral toward him is as good as being committed. As he explained in Matthew 12:30, "He who is not with Me is against Me." In both cases, Jesus was pointing out that neutrality toward him is not possible. Nevertheless, his followers will not all resemble each other or belong to the same groups. People who are on Jesus' side have the same goal of building up the kingdom of God, and they should not let their differences interfere with this goal. Those who share a common faith in Christ should cooperate. People don't have to be just like us to be following Jesus with us.

9:41–42 Luke 9:48 states, "the one who is least among all of you, this is the one who is great." In Jesus' eyes, whoever welcomes a child welcomes Jesus; giving a cup of cold water to a person in need is the same as giving an offering to God. By contrast, harming others or failing to care for them is a sin, even if they are unimportant people in the world's eyes. It is possible for thoughtless, selfish people to gain a measure of worldly greatness, but lasting greatness is measured by God's standards. What do you use as your measure—personal achievement or unselfish service?

9:42 This caution against harming little ones in the faith applies both to what we do individually as teachers and examples and to what we allow to fester in our Christian fellowship. Our thoughts and actions must be motivated by love (1 Corinthians 13), and we must be careful about judging others (Matthew 7:1–5; Romans 14:1—15:4). However, we also have a responsibility to confront flagrant sin within the church (1 Corinthians 5:12–13).

9:43 Matt 5:30; 18:8; Matt 5:22; Matt 3:12; 25:41

9:45 Matt 5:22

9:47 Matt 5:29; 18:9; Matt 5:22

9:48 Is 66:24; Matt 3:12; 25:41

9:50 Matt 5:13; Luke 14:34f; Col 4:6; Mark 9:34; Rom 12:18; 2 Cor 13:11; 1 Thess 5:13

43 "If your hand causes you to stumble, cut it off; it is better for you to enter life crippled, than, having your two hands, to go into hell, into the unquenchable fire,
44 [[22]where THEIR WORM DOES NOT DIE, AND THE FIRE IS NOT QUENCHED.]
45 "If your foot causes you to stumble, cut it off; it is better for you to enter life lame,
than, having your two feet, to be cast into hell,
46 [[23]where THEIR WORM DOES NOT DIE, AND THE FIRE IS NOT QUENCHED.]
47 "If your eye causes you to stumble, throw it out; it is better for you to enter the kingdom of God with one eye, than, having two eyes, to be cast into hell,
48 where THEIR WORM DOES NOT DIE, AND THE FIRE IS NOT QUENCHED.
49 "For everyone will be salted with fire.
50 "Salt is good; but if the salt becomes unsalty, with what will you make it salty *again?*
Have salt in yourselves, and be at peace with one another."

Jesus Teaches about Marriage and Divorce
(173/Matthew 19:1-12)

10:1 Matt 4:23; 26:55; Mark 1:21; 2:13; 4:2; 6:2, 6, 34; 12:35; 14:49

10:4 Deut 24:1, 3; Matt 5:31

10:5 Matt 19:8

10 Getting up, He ☆went from there to the region of Judea and beyond the Jordan;
crowds ☆gathered around Him again, and, according to His custom, He once more
began to teach them.
2 *Some* Pharisees came up to Jesus, testing Him, and *began* to question Him whether
it was lawful for a man to divorce a wife.
3 And He answered and said to them, "What did Moses command you?"
4 They said, "Moses permitted *a man* TO WRITE A CERTIFICATE OF DIVORCE AND SEND
her AWAY."
5 But Jesus said to them, "Because of your hardness of heart he wrote you this commandment.

22 Vv 44 and 46, which are identical to v 48, are not found in the early mss **23** See v 44 note

9:43ff Jesus used startling language to stress the importance of cutting sin out of our lives. Painful discipline is required of his true followers. Giving up a relationship, job, or habit that is against God's will may seem just as painful as cutting off a hand. Our high goal, however, is worth any sacrifice; Christ is worth any possible loss. Nothing should stand in the way of faith. We must be ruthless in removing sins from our lives now in order to avoid being stuck with them for eternity. Make your choices from an eternal perspective.

9:48–49 With these strange words, Jesus pictured the serious and eternal consequences of sin. To the Jews, worms and fire represented both internal and external pain. What could be worse?

9:50 Jesus used salt to illustrate three qualities that should be found in his people: (1) *We should remember God's faithfulness,* just as salt when used with a sacrifice recalled God's covenant with his people (Leviticus 2:13). (2) *We should make a difference in the "flavor" of the world we live in,* just as salt changes meat's flavor (see Matthew 5:13). (3) *We should counteract the moral decay in society,* just as salt preserves food from decay. When we lose this desire to "salt" the earth with the love and message of God, we become useless to him.

10:2 The Pharisees were trying to trap Jesus with their question. If he supported divorce, he would be upholding the Pharisees' procedures, and they doubted that he would do that. If Jesus spoke against divorce, however, some members of the crowd would dislike his position—some may have used the law to their advantage to divorce their wives. More important, he might incur the wrath of Herod, who had already killed John the Baptist for speaking out against divorce and adultery (6:17–28). This is what the Pharisees wanted.

The Pharisees saw divorce as a legal issue rather than a spiritual one. Jesus used this test as an opportunity to review God's intended purpose for marriage and to expose the Pharisees' selfish motives. They were not thinking about what God intended for marriage, but had settled for marriages of convenience. In addition, they were quoting Moses unfairly and out of context. Jesus showed these legal experts how superficial their knowledge really was.

10:5–9 God allowed divorce as a concession to people's sinfulness. Divorce was not approved, but it was instituted to protect the injured party in a bad situation. Unfortunately, the Pharisees used Deuteronomy 24:1 as a proof text for divorce. Jesus explained that this was not God's intent; instead, God wants married people to consider their marriage permanent. Don't enter marriage with the option of getting out. Your marriage is more likely to be happy if from the outset you are committed to permanence. Don't be hardhearted like these Pharisees, but be hardheaded in your determination, with God's help, to stay together.

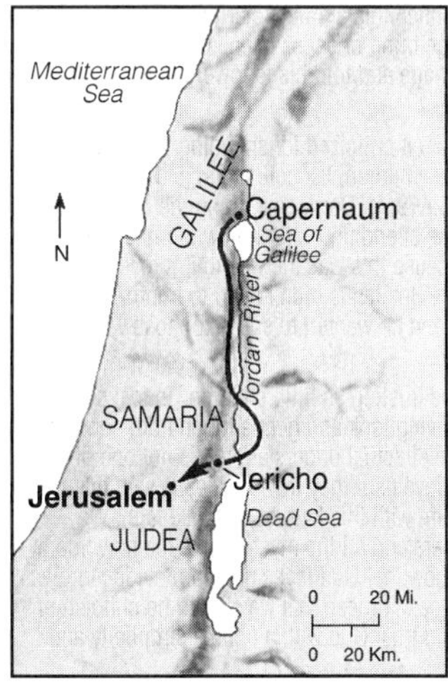

FINAL TRIP TO JUDEA
Jesus quietly left Capernaum, heading toward the borders of Judea before crossing the Jordan River. He preached there before going to Jericho. This trip from Galilee was his last; he would not return before his death.

6 "But from the beginning of creation, *God* MADE THEM MALE AND FEMALE.
7 "FOR THIS REASON A MAN SHALL LEAVE HIS FATHER AND MOTHER[24],
8 AND THE TWO SHALL BECOME ONE FLESH; so they are no longer two, but one flesh.
9 "What therefore God has joined together, let no man separate."
10 In the house the disciples *began* questioning Him about this again.
11 And He ☆said to them, "Whoever divorces his wife and marries another woman commits adultery against her;
12 and if she herself divorces her husband and marries another man, she is committing adultery."

10:6 Mark 13:19; 2 Pet 3:4; Gen 1:27; 5:2
10:7 Gen 2:24
10:8 Gen 2:24
10:11 Matt 5:32
10:12 1 Cor 7:11, 13

Jesus Blesses Little Children
(174/Matthew 19:13-15; Luke 18:15-17)

13 And they were bringing children to Him so that He might touch them; but the disciples rebuked them.
14 But when Jesus saw this, He was indignant and said to them, "Permit the children to come to Me; do not hinder them; for the kingdom of God belongs to such as these.
15 "Truly I say to you, whoever does not receive the kingdom of God like a child will not enter it *at all.*"
16 And He took them in His arms and *began* blessing them, laying His hands on them.

10:14 Matt 5:3
10:15 Matt 18:3; 19:14; Luke 18:17; 1 Cor 14:20; 1 Pet 2:2
10:16 Mark 9:36

Jesus Speaks to the Rich Young Man
(175/Matthew 19:16-30; Luke 18:18-30)

17 As He was setting out on a journey, a man ran up to Him and knelt before Him, and asked Him, "Good Teacher, what shall I do to inherit eternal life?"
18 And Jesus said to him, "Why do you call Me good? No one is good except God alone.
19 "You know the commandments, 'DO NOT MURDER, DO NOT COMMIT ADULTERY, DO NOT STEAL, DO NOT BEAR FALSE WITNESS, Do not defraud, HONOR YOUR FATHER AND MOTHER.' "
20 And he said to Him, "Teacher, I have kept all these things from my youth up."
21 Looking at him, Jesus felt a love for him and said to him, "One thing you lack: go

10:17 Mark 1:40; Matt 25:34; Luke 10:25; 18:18; Acts 20:32; Eph 1:18; 1 Pet 1:4
10:19 Ex 20:12-16; Deut 5:16-20
10:20 Matt 19:20
10:21 Matt 6:20

24 Many late mss add *and shall cling to his wife*

10:6–9 Women were often treated as property. Marriage and divorce were regarded as transactions similar to buying and selling land. But Jesus condemned this attitude, clarifying God's original intention—that marriage bring oneness (Genesis 2:24). Jesus held up God's ideal for marriage and told his followers to live by that ideal.

10:13–16 Jesus was often criticized for spending too much time with the wrong people—children, tax collectors, and sinners (Matthew 9:11; Luke 15:1–2; 19:7). Some, including the disciples, thought Jesus should be spending more time with important leaders and the devout, because this was the way to improve his position and avoid criticism. But Jesus didn't need to improve his position. He was God, and he wanted to speak to those who needed him most.

10:14 Adults are not as trusting as little children. To feel secure, all children need is a loving look and gentle touch from someone who cares. Complete intellectual understanding is not one of their requirements. They believe us if they trust us. Jesus said that people should believe in him with this kind of childlike faith. We should not have to understand all the mysteries of the universe; it should be enough to know that God loves us and provides forgiveness for our sin. This doesn't mean that we should be childish or immature, but we should trust God with a child's simplicity and receptivity.

10:17–23 This young man wanted to be sure he would get eternal life, so he asked what he could *do.* He said he'd never once broken any of the laws Jesus mentioned (10:19), and perhaps he had even kept the Pharisees' loophole-filled version of them. But Jesus lovingly broke through the young man's pride with a challenge that brought out his true motives: "Go and sell all you possess and give to the poor." This challenge exposed the barrier that could keep this young man out of the kingdom: his love of money. Money represented his pride of accomplishment and self-effort. Ironically, his attitude made him unable to keep the first commandment, to let nothing be more important than God (Exodus 20:3). He could not meet the one requirement Jesus gave—to turn his whole heart and life over to God. The man came to Jesus wondering what he could do; he left seeing what he was unable to do. What barriers are keeping you from turning your life over to Christ?

10:18 When Jesus asked this question, he was saying, "Do you really know the One to whom you are talking?" Because only God is truly good, the man was calling Jesus "God," whether or not he realized it.

10:21 What does your money mean to you? Although Jesus wanted this man to sell everything and give his money to the poor, this does not mean that all believers should sell all their possessions. Most of his followers did not sell everything, although they used their possessions to serve others. Instead, this story shows us that we must not let anything we have or desire keep us from following Jesus. We must remove all barriers to serving him fully. If Jesus asked, could you give up your house? your car? your level of income? your position on the ladder of promotion? Your reaction may show your attitude toward money—whether it is your servant or your master.

10:21 Jesus showed genuine love for this man, even though he knew that the man might not follow him. Love is able to give tough advice; it doesn't hedge around the truth. Christ loved us enough to die for us, and he also loves us enough to talk straight to us. If his love were superficial, he would give us only his approval; but because his love is complete, he gives us life-changing challenges.

and sell all you possess and give to the poor, and you will have treasure in heaven; and
come, follow Me."
22 But at these words he was saddened, and he went away grieving, for he was one who
owned much property.
23 And Jesus, looking around, ☆said to His disciples, "How hard it will be for those
who are wealthy to enter the kingdom of God!"
24 The disciples were amazed at His words. But Jesus ☆answered again and ☆said to
them, "Children, how hard it is to enter the kingdom of God!
25 "It is easier for a camel to go through the eye of a needle than for a rich man to enter
the kingdom of God."
26 They were even more astonished and said to Him, "Then who can be saved?"
27 Looking at them, Jesus ☆said, "With people it is impossible, but not with God; for
all things are possible with God."
28 Peter began to say to Him, "Behold, we have left everything and followed You."
29 Jesus said, "Truly I say to you, there is no one who has left house or brothers or
sisters or mother or father or children or farms, for My sake and for the gospel's sake,
30 but that he will receive a hundred times as much now in the present age, houses and
brothers and sisters and mothers and children and farms, along with persecutions; and
in the age to come, eternal life.
31 "But many *who are* first will be last, and the last, first."

10:23 Matt 19:23
10:24 Mark 1:27
10:25 Matt 19:24
10:27 Matt 19:26
10:28 Matt 4:20-22
10:29 Matt 6:33; 19:29; Luke 18:29f
10:30 Matt 12:32
10:31 Matt 19:30; 20:16; Luke 13:30

Jesus Predicts His Death the Third Time
(177/Matthew 20:17-19; Luke 18:31-34)

32 They were on the road going up to Jerusalem, and Jesus was walking on ahead of
them; and they were amazed, and those who followed were fearful. And again He took
the twelve aside and began to tell them what was going to happen to Him,
33 *saying,* "Behold, we are going up to Jerusalem, and the Son of Man will be [25]deliv-
ered to the chief priests and the scribes; and they will condemn Him to death and will
hand Him over to the Gentiles.
34 "They will mock Him and spit on Him, and scourge Him and kill *Him,* and three days
later He will rise again."

10:32 Mark 1:27
10:33 Mark 8:31; 9:12
10:34 Matt 16:21; 26:67; 27:30; Mark 9:31; 14:65

Jesus Teaches about Serving Others
(178/Matthew 20:20-28)

35 James and John, the two sons of Zebedee, ☆came up to Jesus, saying, "Teacher, we
want You to do for us whatever we ask of You."
36 And He said to them, "What do you want Me to do for you?"

25 Or *betrayed*

10:23 Jesus said it was very difficult for the wealthy to enter the kingdom of God. This is true because the wealthy, with most of their basic physical needs met, often become self-reliant. When they feel empty, they can buy something new to dull the pain that was meant to drive them toward God. Their abundance and self-sufficiency become their deficiency. The person who has everything on earth can still lack what is most important—eternal life.

10:26 The disciples were amazed. Was not wealth a blessing from God, a reward for being good? This misconception is still common today. Although many believers enjoy material prosperity, many others live in hardship. Wealth is not a sign of faith or of partiality on God's part.

10:29–30 Jesus assured the disciples that anyone who gives up something valuable for his sake will be repaid a hundred times over in this life, although not necessarily in the same form. For example, someone may be rejected by his family for accepting Christ, but he or she will gain the larger family of believers. Along with these rewards, however, we experience persecution because the world hates God. Jesus emphasized persecution to make sure that we do not selfishly follow him only for the rewards.

10:31 Jesus explained that in the world to come, the values of this world will be reversed. Those who seek status and importance here will have none in heaven. Those who are humble here will be great in heaven. The corrupt condition of our society encourages confusion in values. We are bombarded by messages that tell us how to be important and how to feel good, and Jesus' teaching about service to others seems alien. But those who have humbly served others are most qualified to be great in heaven.

10:32 Because Jesus had just spoken to them about facing persecution, the disciples were astonished as they thought about what awaited them in Jerusalem.

10:33–34 Jesus' death and resurrection should have come as no surprise to the disciples. Here he clearly explained to them what would happen to him. Unfortunately, they didn't really hear what he was saying. Jesus said he was the Messiah, but they thought the Messiah would be a conquering king. He spoke to them of resurrection, but they heard only his words about death. Because Jesus often spoke in parables, the disciples may have thought that his words on death and resurrection were another parable they weren't astute enough to understand. The Gospels include Jesus' predictions of his death and resurrection to show that these events were God's plan from the beginning and not accidents.

10:35 Mark records that John and James went to Jesus with their request; in Matthew, their mother also made the request. There is no contradiction in the accounts—mother and sons were in agreement in requesting honored places in Christ's kingdom.

37 They said to Him, "Grant that we may sit, one on Your right and one on *Your* left,
in Your glory."
38 But Jesus said to them, "You do not know what you are asking. Are you able to drink
the cup that I drink, or to be baptized with the baptism with which I am baptized?"
39 They said to Him, "We are able." And Jesus said to them, "The cup that I drink you
shall drink; and you shall be baptized with the baptism with which I am baptized.
40 "But to sit on My right or on *My* left, this is not Mine to give; but it is for those for
whom it has been prepared."
41 Hearing *this*, the ten began to feel indignant with James and John.
42 Calling them to Himself, Jesus ☆said to them, "You know that those who are recognized as rulers of the Gentiles lord it over them; and their great men exercise authority
over them.
43 "But it is not this way among you, but whoever wishes to become great among you
shall be your servant;
44 and whoever wishes to be first among you shall be slave of all.
45 "For even the Son of Man did not come to be served, but to serve, and to give His life
a ransom for many."

10:37 Matt 19:28
10:38 Matt 20:22; Luke 12:50
10:39 Acts 12:2; Rev 1:9
10:40 Matt 13:11
10:43 Matt 20:26; 23:11; Mark 9:35; Luke 22:26
10:45 Matt 20:28

Jesus Heals a Blind Beggar
(179/Matthew 20:29-34; Luke 18:35-43)

46 Then they ☆came to Jericho. And as He was leaving Jericho with His disciples and a
large crowd, a blind beggar *named* Bartimaeus, the son of Timaeus, was sitting by the road.
47 When he heard that it was Jesus the Nazarene, he began to cry out and say, "Jesus,
Son of David, have mercy on me!"
48 Many were sternly telling him to be quiet, but he kept crying out all the more, "Son
of David, have mercy on me!"
49 And Jesus stopped and said, "Call him *here.*" So they ☆called the blind man, saying
to him, "Take courage, stand up! He is calling for you."
50 Throwing aside his cloak, he jumped up and came to Jesus.
51 And answering him, Jesus said, "What do you want Me to do for you?" And the
blind man said to Him, "[26]Rabboni, *I want* to regain my sight!"
52 And Jesus said to him, "Go; your faith has made you well." Immediately he regained
his sight and *began* following Him on the road.

10:47 Mark 1:24; Matt 9:27
10:48 Matt 9:27
10:49 Matt 9:2
10:51 Matt 23:7; John 20:16
10:52 Matt 9:22

26 I.e. My Master

10:37 The disciples, like most Jews of that day, had the wrong idea of the Messiah's kingdom as predicted by the Old Testament prophets. They thought Jesus would establish an earthly kingdom that would free Israel from Rome's oppression, and James and John wanted honored places in it. But Jesus' kingdom is not of this world; it is not centered in palaces and thrones, but in the hearts and lives of his followers. The disciples did not understand this until after Jesus' resurrection.

10:38–39 James and John said they were willing to face any trial for Christ. Both did suffer: James died as a martyr (Acts 12:2), and John was forced to live in exile (Revelation 1:9). It is easy to say we will endure anything for Christ, and yet most of us complain over the most minor problems. If we say we are willing to suffer on a large scale for Christ, we must also be willing to suffer the irritations that come with serving others.

10:38–40 Jesus didn't ridicule James and John for asking, but he denied their request. We can feel free to ask God for anything, but our request may be denied. God wants to give us what is best for us, not merely what we want. He denies some requests for our own good.

10:42–45 James and John wanted the highest positions in Jesus' kingdom. But Jesus told them that true greatness comes in serving others. Peter, one of the disciples who had heard this message, expands the thought in 1 Peter 5:1–4.

Most businesses, organizations, and institutions measure greatness by high personal achievement. In Christ's kingdom, however, service is the way to get ahead. The desire to be on top will hinder, not help. Rather than seeking to have your needs met, look for ways that you can minister to the needs of others.

10:45 This verse reveals not only the motive for Jesus' ministry, but also the basis for our salvation. A ransom was the price paid to release a slave. Jesus paid a ransom for us because we could not pay it ourselves. His death released all of us from our slavery to sin. The disciples thought Jesus' life and power would save them from Rome; Jesus said his *death* would save them from sin, an even greater slavery than Rome's. More about the ransom Jesus paid for us is found in 1 Peter 1:18–19.

10:46 Jericho was a popular resort city rebuilt by Herod the Great in the Judean wilderness, not far from the Jordan River crossing. Jesus was on his way to Jerusalem (10:32), and, after crossing over from Perea, he would naturally enter Jericho.

10:46 Beggars were a common sight in most towns. Because most occupations of that day required physical labor, anyone with a crippling disease or disability was at a severe disadvantage and was usually forced to beg, even though God's laws commanded care for such needy people (Leviticus 25:35–38). Blindness was considered a curse from God for sin (John 9:2), but Jesus refuted this idea when he reached out to heal the blind.

10:47 "Son of David" was a popular way of addressing Jesus as the Messiah, because it was known that the Messiah would be a descendant of King David (Isaiah 9:7). The fact that Bartimaeus called Jesus the Son of David shows that he recognized Jesus as the Messiah. His faith in Jesus as the Messiah brought about his healing.

3. Jesus' ministry in Jerusalem

Jesus Rides into Jerusalem on a Donkey
(183/Matthew 21:1-11; Luke 19:28-44; John 12:12-19)

11:1 Matt 21:17; Matt 21:1

11 As they ☆approached Jerusalem, at Bethphage and Bethany, near the Mount of
Olives, He ☆sent two of His disciples,
2 and ☆said to them, "Go into the village opposite you, and immediately as you enter
it, you will find a colt tied *there,* on which no one yet has ever sat; untie it and bring it
here.
3 "If anyone says to you, 'Why are you doing this?' you say, 'The Lord has need of it';
and immediately he will send it back here."
4 They went away and found a colt tied at the door, outside in the street; and they
☆untied it.
5 Some of the bystanders were saying to them, "What are you doing, untying the colt?"
6 They spoke to them just as Jesus had told *them,* and they gave them permission.
7 They ☆brought the colt to Jesus and put their coats on it; and He sat on it.
8 And many spread their coats in the road, and others *spread* leafy branches which
they had cut from the fields.
9 Those who went in front and those who followed were shouting:
"Hosanna!

11:7 Matt 21:4-9; Luke 19:35-38; John 12:12-15

11:9 Ps 118:26; Matt 21:9

KEY CHARACTERISTICS OF CHRIST IN THE GOSPELS

Characteristic	*References*
Jesus is the Son of God	Matthew 16:15–16; Mark 1:1; Luke 22:70–71; John 8:24
Jesus is God who became human	John 1:1–2, 14; 20:28
Jesus is the Christ, the Messiah	Matthew 26:63–64; Mark 14:61–62; Luke 9:20; John 4:25–26
Jesus came to help sinners	Matthew 9:13; Luke 5:32
Jesus has power to forgive sins	Mark 2:9–12; Luke 24:47
Jesus has authority over death	Matthew 28:5–6; Mark 5:22–24, 35–42 Luke 24:5–6; John 11:1–44
Jesus has power to give eternal life	John 10:28; 17:2
Jesus healed the sick	Matthew 8:5–13; Mark 1:32–34 Luke 5:12–15; John 9:1–7
Jesus taught with authority	Matthew 7:29; Mark 1:21–22
Jesus was compassionate	Matthew 9:36; Mark 1:41; 8:2
Jesus experienced sorrow	Matthew 26:38; John 11:35
Jesus never disobeyed God	Matthew 3:15; John 8:46

JESUS NEARS JERUSALEM
Leaving Jericho, Jesus headed toward acclaim, then crucifixion, in Jerusalem. During his last week, he stayed outside the city in Bethany, a village on the eastern slope of the Mount of Olives, entering Jerusalem to teach, eat the Passover, and finally be crucified.

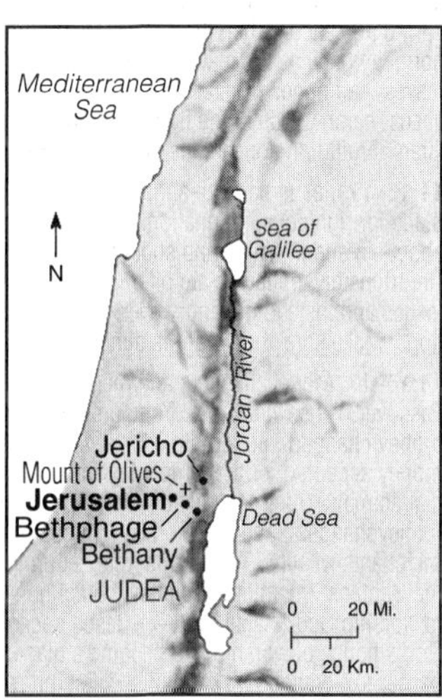

11:1–2 This was Sunday of the week that Jesus would be crucified, and the great Passover festival was about to begin. Jews came to Jerusalem from all over the Roman world during this week-long celebration to remember the great exodus from Egypt (see Exodus 12:37–51). Many in the crowds had heard of or seen Jesus and were hoping he would come to the temple (John 11:55–57).

Jesus did come, not as a warring king on a horse or in a chariot, but as a gentle and peaceable king on a donkey's colt, just as Zechariah 9:9 had predicted. Jesus knew that those who would hear him teach at the temple would return to their homes throughout the world and announce the coming of the Messiah.

11:9–10 The people exclaimed "Hosanna" (meaning, "Save!"), because they recognized that Jesus was fulfilling the prophecy in Zechariah 9:9. (See also Psalm 24:7–10; 118:26.) They spoke of David's kingdom because of God's words to David in 2 Samuel 7:12–14. The crowd correctly saw Jesus as the fulfillment of these prophecies, but they did not understand where Jesus' kingship would lead him. This same crowd cried out "Crucify him!" when Jesus stood on trial only a few days later.

BLESSED IS HE WHO COMES IN THE NAME OF THE LORD;
10 Blessed *is* the coming kingdom of our father David; 11:10 Matt 21:9
Hosanna in the highest!"
11 Jesus entered Jerusalem *and came* into the temple; and after looking around at 11:11 Matt 21:12; Matt 21:17
everything, He left for Bethany with the twelve, since it was already late.

Jesus Clears the Temple Again
(184/Matthew 21:12-17; Luke 19:45-48)

12 On the next day, when they had left Bethany, He became hungry. 11:12 Matt 21:18-22
13 Seeing at a distance a fig tree in leaf, He went *to see* if perhaps He would find anything on it; and when He came to it, He found nothing but leaves, for it was not the season for figs.
14 He said to it, "May no one ever eat fruit from you again!" And His disciples were
listening.
15 Then they ☆came to Jerusalem. And He entered the temple and began to drive out 11:15 Matt 21:12-16; Luke 19:45-47; John 2:13-16
those who were buying and selling in the temple, and overturned the tables of the mon-
ey changers and the seats of those who were selling doves;
16 and He would not permit anyone to carry merchandise through the temple.
17 And He *began* to teach and say to them, "Is it not written, 'MY HOUSE SHALL BE 11:17 Is 56:7; Jer 7:11
CALLED A HOUSE OF PRAYER FOR ALL THE NATIONS'? But you have made it a ROBBERS'
DEN."
18 The chief priests and the scribes heard *this*, and *began* seeking how to destroy Him; 11:18 Matt 21:46; Mark 12:12; Luke 20:19; John 7:1; Matt 7:28
for they were afraid of Him, for the whole crowd was astonished at His teaching.
19 When evening came, they would go out of the city. 11:19 Matt 21:17; Mark 11:11; Luke 21:37

Jesus Says the Disciples Can Pray for Anything
(188/Matthew 21:18-22)

20 As they were passing by in the morning, they saw the fig tree withered from the 11:20 Matt 21:19-22
roots *up*.

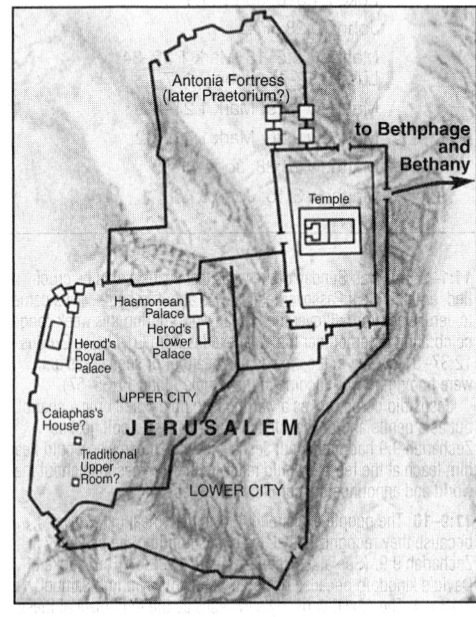

CLEARING THE TEMPLE On Monday morning of his last week, Jesus left Bethany, entered Jerusalem, and cleared the temple of money changers and merchants.

11:11–21 In this passage, two unusual incidents are related: the cursing of the fig tree and the clearing of the temple. The cursing of the fig tree was an acted-out parable related to the clearing of the temple. The temple was supposed to be a place of worship, but true worship had disappeared. The fig tree showed promise of fruit, but it produced none. Jesus was showing his anger at religious life without substance. If you claim to have faith without putting it to work in your life, you are like the barren fig tree. Genuine faith has great potential; ask God to help you bear fruit for his kingdom.

11:13–26 Fig trees, a popular source of inexpensive food in Israel, require three years from the time they are planted until they can bear fruit. Each tree yields a great amount of fruit twice a year, in late spring and in early autumn. This incident occurred early in the spring fig season when the leaves were beginning to bud. The figs normally grow as the leaves fill out, but this tree, though full of leaves, had none. The tree looked promising but offered no fruit. Jesus' harsh words to the fig tree could be applied to the nation of Israel. Fruitful in appearance only, Israel was spiritually barren.

11:15–17 Jesus became angry, but he did not sin. There is a place for righteous indignation. Christians are right to be upset about sin and injustice and should take a stand against them. Unfortunately, believers are often passive about these important issues and instead get angry over personal insults and petty irritations. Make sure your anger is directed toward the right issues.

11:15–17 Moneychangers and merchants did big business during Passover. Those who came from foreign countries had to have their money changed into temple currency because this was the only money accepted for the temple tax and for the purchase of sacrificial animals. Often the inflated exchange rate enriched the moneychangers, and the exorbitant prices of animals made the merchants wealthy. Their stalls were set up in the temple's court of the Gentiles, frustrating the intentions of non-Jews who had come to worship God (Isaiah 56:6–7). Jesus became angry because God's house of worship had become a place of extortion and a barrier to Gentiles who wanted to worship.

11:21 Matt 23:7 — 21 Being reminded, Peter ☆said to Him, “Rabbi, look, the fig tree which You cursed
has withered.”
11:22 Matt 17:20; 21:21f — 22 And Jesus ☆answered saying to them, “Have faith in God.
23 “Truly I say to you, whoever says to this mountain, ‘Be taken up and cast into the
11:23 Matt 17:20; 1 Cor 13:2 — sea,’ and does not doubt in his heart, but believes that what he says is going to happen,
it will be *granted* him.
11:24 Matt 7:7f — 24 “Therefore I say to you, all things for which you pray and ask, believe that you have
received them, and they will be *granted* you.
11:25 Matt 6:5; Matt 6:14 — 25 “Whenever you stand praying, forgive, if you have anything against anyone, so that
your Father who is in heaven will also forgive you your transgressions.
11:26 Matt 6:15; 18:35 — 26 [“[27]But if you do not forgive, neither will your Father who is in heaven forgive your
transgressions.”]

Religious Leaders Challenge Jesus' Authority
(189/Matthew 21:23-27; Luke 20:1-8)

27 They ☆came again to Jerusalem. And as He was walking in the temple, the chief
priests and the scribes and the elders ☆came to Him,
28 and *began* saying to Him, “By what authority are You doing these things, or who
gave You this authority to do these things?”
29 And Jesus said to them, “I will ask you one question, and you answer Me, and *then*
I will tell you by what authority I do these things.
30 “Was the baptism of John from heaven, or from men? Answer Me.”
31 They *began* reasoning among themselves, saying, “If we say, ‘From heaven,’ He will
say, ‘Then why did you not believe him?’
32 “But shall we say, ‘From men’?”—they were afraid of the people, for everyone considered John to have been a real prophet.
33 Answering Jesus, they ☆said, “We do not know.” And Jesus ☆said to them, “Nor will
I tell you by what authority I do these things.”

Jesus Tells the Parable of the Wicked Vine-growers
(191/Matthew 21:33-46; Luke 20:9-19)

12:1 Mark 3:23; 4:2ff; Is 5:1, 2 — **12** And He began to speak to them in parables: “A man PLANTED A VINEYARD AND
PUT A WALL AROUND IT, AND DUG A VAT UNDER THE WINE PRESS AND BUILT A
TOWER, and rented it out to [28]vine-growers and went on a journey.
2 “At the *harvest* time he sent a slave to the vine-growers, in order to receive *some* of
the produce of the vineyard from the vine-growers.

27 Early mss do not contain this v **28** Or *tenant farmers,* also vv 2, 7, 9

11:22–23 The kind of prayer that moves mountains is prayer for the fruitfulness of God's kingdom. It would seem impossible to move a mountain into the sea, so Jesus used that picture to say that God can do anything. God will answer your prayers, but not as a result of your positive mental attitude. Other conditions must be met: (1) You must be a believer; (2) you must not hold a grudge against another person; (3) you must not pray with selfish motives; (4) your request must be for the good of God's kingdom. To pray effectively, you need faith in God, not faith in the object of your request. If you focus only on your request, you will be left with nothing if your request is refused.

11:24 Jesus, our example for prayer, prayed, “All things are possible for You . . . yet not what I will, but what You will” (14:36). Our prayers are often motivated by our own interests and desires. We like to hear that we can have anything. But Jesus prayed with *God's* interests in mind. When we pray, we should express our desires, but want his will above ours. Check yourself to see if your prayers focus on your interests or God's.

11:27ff The religious leaders asked Jesus who gave him the authority to chase away the merchants and moneychangers. Their question was a trap. If Jesus said his authority was from God, they would accuse him of blasphemy; if he said his authority was his own, they would dismiss him as a fanatic. To expose their real motives, Jesus countered their question with a question about John the Baptist. The leaders' silence proved that they were not interested in the truth. They simply wanted to get rid of Jesus because he was undermining their authority.

11:30 For more information, see John the Baptist's Profile in John 1.

12:1 Parables are story illustrations that use something familiar to help us understand something new. This method of teaching compels listeners to discover truth for themselves. The message gets through only to those who are willing to listen and learn.

12:1 Israel, pictured as a vineyard, was the nation that God had cultivated to bring salvation to the world. The religious leaders not only frustrated their nation's purpose; they also killed those who were trying to fulfill it. They were so jealous and possessive that they ignored the welfare of the very people they were supposed to be bringing to God.

12:1ff In this parable, the man who planted the vineyard is God; the vineyard is the nation Israel; the vine-growers are Israel's religious leaders; the slaves are the prophets and priests who remained faithful to God; the son is Jesus; and the others are the Gentiles. By telling this story, Jesus exposed the religious leaders' plot to kill him and warned that their sins would be punished.

3 "They took him, and beat him and sent him away empty-handed.
4 "Again he sent them another slave, and they wounded him in the head, and treated
him shamefully.
5 "And he sent another, and that one they killed; and *so with* many others, beating some
and killing others.
6 "He had one more *to send,* a beloved son; he sent him last *of all* to them, saying, 'They
will respect my son.'
7 "But those vine-growers said to one another, 'This is the heir; come, let us kill him,
and the inheritance will be ours!'
8 "They took him, and killed him and threw him out of the vineyard.
9 "What will the owner of the vineyard do? He will come and destroy the vine-
growers, and will give the vineyard to others.
10 "Have you not even read this Scripture: **12:10** Ps 118:22
'THE STONE WHICH THE BUILDERS REJECTED,
THIS BECAME THE CHIEF CORNER *stone;*
11 THIS CAME ABOUT FROM THE LORD, **12:11** Ps 118:23
AND IT IS MARVELOUS IN OUR EYES'?"
12 And they were seeking to seize Him, and *yet* they feared the people, for they under- **12:12** Mark 11:18; Matt 22:22
stood that He spoke the parable against them. And *so* they left Him and went away.

Religious Leaders Question Jesus about Paying Taxes
(193/Matthew 22:15-22; Luke 20:20-26)

13 Then they ☆sent some of the Pharisees and Herodians to Him in order to trap Him **12:13** Matt 22:16; Luke 11:54
in a statement.
14 They ☆came and ☆said to Him, "Teacher, we know that You are truthful and defer
to no one; for You are not partial to any, but teach the way of God in truth. Is it lawful
to pay a poll-tax to Caesar, or not?
15 "Shall we pay or shall we not pay?" But He, knowing their hypocrisy, said to them,
"Why are you testing Me? Bring Me a [29]denarius to look at."
16 They brought *one.* And He ☆said to them, "Whose likeness and inscription is this?"
And they said to Him, "Caesar's."
17 And Jesus said to them, "Render to Caesar the things that are Caesar's, and to God **12:17** Matt 22:21
the things that are God's." And they were amazed at Him.

Religious Leaders Question Jesus about the Resurrection **12:18** Acts 23:8
(194/Matthew 22:23-33; Luke 20:27-40)

18 *Some* Sadducees (who say that there is no resurrection) ☆came to Jesus, and *began*
questioning Him, saying,

29 The denarius was a day's wages

12:10–11 Jesus referred to himself as the stone rejected by the builders. Although he would be rejected by most of the Jewish leaders, he would become the corner stone of a new "building," the church (Acts 4:11–12). The corner stone was used as a base to make sure the other stones of the building were straight and level. Likewise, Jesus' life and teaching would be the church's foundation.

12:13 The Pharisees were primarily a religious group concerned for ritual purity; the Herodians were a Jewish political group that approved of Herod's compromises with Rome. Normally the two groups had nothing to do with each other.

The Pharisees did not like Jesus because he exposed their hypocrisy. The Herodians also saw Jesus as a threat. Supporters of the dynasty of Herod the Great, they had lost political control when, as a result of reported unrest, Rome deposed Archelaus (Herod's son with authority over Judea), and replaced him with a Roman governor. The Herodians feared that Jesus would cause still more instability in Judea, and that Rome might react by never allowing the Roman leaders to step down and be replaced by a descendant of Herod.

12:14 Anyone who avoided paying taxes faced harsh penalties. The Jews hated to pay taxes to Rome because the money supported their oppressors and symbolized their subjection. Much of the tax money also went to maintain the pagan temples and luxurious life-styles of Rome's upper class. The Pharisees and Herodians hoped to trap Jesus with this tax question. Either a yes or a no could lead him into trouble. A yes would mean he supported Rome, which would turn the people against him. A no would bring accusations of treason and rebellion against Rome and could lead to civil penalties.

12:15 A denarius was the usual day's wage for a laborer.

12:17 The Pharisees and Herodians thought they had the perfect question to trap Jesus. But Jesus answered wisely, once again exposing their self-interest and wrong motives. Jesus said that the coin bearing the emperor's image should be given to the emperor. But our lives, which bear God's image, belong to God. Are you giving God all that is rightfully his? Give your life to God—you bear his image.

12:18–23 After the Pharisees and Herodians failed to trap Jesus with their tax question, the Sadducees stepped in with a question they were sure would stump him. This was a question that they had successfully used against the Pharisees, who could not come up with an answer. The Sadducees did not believe in life after death because the Pentateuch (Genesis—Deuteronomy) had no direct

12:19 Deut 25:5

19 "Teacher, Moses wrote for us that IF A MAN'S BROTHER DIES and leaves behind a wife AND LEAVES NO CHILD, HIS BROTHER SHOULD MARRY THE WIFE AND RAISE UP CHILDREN TO HIS BROTHER.
20 "There were seven brothers; and the first took a wife, and died leaving no children.
21 "The second one married her, and died leaving behind no children; and the third likewise;
22 and *so* all seven left no children. Last of all the woman died also.
23 "In the resurrection, [30]when they rise again, which one's wife will she be? For all seven had married her."
24 Jesus said to them, "Is this not the reason you are mistaken, that you do not understand the Scriptures or the power of God?
25 "For when they rise from the dead, they neither marry nor are given in marriage, but are like angels in heaven.

30 Early mss do not contain *when they rise again*

WHAT JESUS SAID ABOUT LOVE

In Mark 12:28 a scribe asked Jesus which of all the commandments was the most important to follow. Jesus mentioned two commandments, one from Deuteronomy 6:5, the other from Leviticus 19:18. Both had to do with love. Why is love so important? Jesus said that all of the commandments were given for two simple reasons—to help us love God and love others as we should.

What else did Jesus say about love?	*Reference*
God loves us.	John 3:16
We are to love God.	Matthew 22:37
Because God loves us, he cares for us.	Matthew 6:25–34
God wants people to know how much he loves them.	John 17:23
God loves even those who hate him; we are to do the same.	Matthew 5:43–47 Luke 6:35
God seeks out even those most alienated from him.	Luke 15
God must be your first love.	Matthew 6:24; 10:37
You love God when you obey him.	John 14:21; 15:10
God loves Jesus his Son.	John 5:20; 10:17
Jesus loves God.	John 14:31
Those who refuse Jesus don't have God's love.	John 5:41–44
Jesus loves us just as God loves Jesus.	John 15:9
Jesus proved his love for us by dying on the cross so that we could live eternally with him.	John 3:14–15; 15:13–14
The love between God and Jesus is the perfect example of how we are to love others.	John 17:21–26
We are to love one another (John 13:34–35) and demonstrate that love.	Matthew 5:40–42; 10:42
We are not to love the praise of men (John 12:43), selfish recognition (Matthew 23:6), earthly belongings (Luke 16:19–31), or anything more than God.	Luke 16:13
Jesus' love extends to each individual.	Mark 10:21; John 10:11–15
Jesus wants us to love him through the good and through the difficult times.	Matthew 26:31–35
Jesus wants our love to be genuine.	John 21:15–17

teaching about it, and the writings of Moses were the only Scriptures they followed. But Jesus was about to point out that Moses' books support the idea of eternal life (12:26).

12:19 According to Old Testament law, when a man died without a son, his brother had to marry the widow and produce children to care for her and allow the family line to continue. The first son of this marriage was considered the heir of the dead man (Deuteronomy 25:5–6).

12:24 What life will be like after the resurrection is far beyond our ability to understand or imagine (Isaiah 64:4; 1 Corinthians 2:9). We need not be afraid of eternal life because of the unknowns, however. Instead of wondering what God's coming kingdom will be like, we should concentrate on our relationship with Christ right now because in the new kingdom we will be with him. If we learn to love and trust Christ *now,* we will not be afraid of what he has in store for us then.

12:25–27 Jesus' statement does not mean that people won't recognize their partners in the coming kingdom. It simply means that God's new order will not be an extension of this life and that the same physical and natural rules won't apply. Jesus' comment in verse 25 was not intended to be the final word on marriage in heaven. Instead, this response was Jesus' refusal to answer the Sadducees' riddle and fall into their trap. Sidestepping their question about the much-married woman, he gave a definitive answer to their question about the resurrection.

26 "But regarding the fact that the dead rise again, have you not read in the book of Moses, in the *passage* about *the burning* bush, how God spoke to him, saying, 'I AM THE GOD OF ABRAHAM, AND THE GOD OF ISAAC, and the God of Jacob'?
27 "He is not the God of the dead, but of the living; you are greatly mistaken."

12:26 Luke 20:37; Rom 11:2; Ex 3:6

12:27 Matt 22:32; Luke 20:38

Religious Leaders Question Jesus about the Greatest Commandment
(195/Matthew 22:34-40)

28 One of the scribes came and heard them arguing, and recognizing that He had answered them well, asked Him, "What commandment is the foremost of all?"
29 Jesus answered, "The foremost is, 'HEAR, O ISRAEL! THE LORD OUR GOD IS ONE LORD;
30 AND YOU SHALL LOVE THE LORD YOUR GOD WITH ALL YOUR HEART, AND WITH ALL YOUR SOUL, AND WITH ALL YOUR MIND, AND WITH ALL YOUR STRENGTH.'
31 "The second is this, 'YOU SHALL LOVE YOUR NEIGHBOR AS YOURSELF.' There is no other commandment greater than these."
32 The scribe said to Him, "Right, Teacher; You have truly stated that HE IS ONE, AND THERE IS NO ONE ELSE BESIDES HIM;
33 AND TO LOVE HIM WITH ALL THE HEART AND WITH ALL THE UNDERSTANDING AND WITH ALL THE STRENGTH, AND TO LOVE ONE'S NEIGHBOR AS HIMSELF, is much more than all burnt offerings and sacrifices."
34 When Jesus saw that he had answered intelligently, He said to him, "You are not far from the kingdom of God." After that, no one would venture to ask Him any more questions.

12:28 Luke 10:25-28; 20:39f; Matt 22:34; Luke 20:39

12:29 Deut 6:4

12:30 Deut 6:5

12:31 Lev 19:18

12:32 Deut 4:35

12:33 Deut 6:5; 1 Sam 15:22; Hos 6:6; Mic 6:6-8; Matt 9:13; 12:7

12:34 Matt 22:46

Religious Leaders Cannot Answer Jesus' Question
(196/Matthew 22:41-46; Luke 20:41-44)

35 And Jesus *began* to say, as He taught in the temple, "How *is it that* the scribes say that the Christ is the son of David?
36 "David himself said in the Holy Spirit,
'THE LORD SAID TO MY LORD,
"SIT AT MY RIGHT HAND,
UNTIL I PUT YOUR ENEMIES BENEATH YOUR FEET." '
37 "David himself calls Him 'Lord'; so in what sense is He his son?" And the large crowd enjoyed listening to Him.

12:35 Matt 26:55; Mark 10:1; Matt 9:27

12:36 Ps 110:1

12:37 John 12:9

Jesus Warns Against the Religious Leaders
(197/Matthew 23:1-12; Luke 20:45-47)

38 In His teaching He was saying: "Beware of the scribes who like to walk around in long robes, and *like* respectful greetings in the market places,

12:38 Matt 23:7; Luke 11:43

12:26 The Sadducees' real question was not about marriage but about the doctrine of resurrection. Because the Sadducees believed only in the Pentateuch (Genesis through Deuteronomy), Jesus quoted from Exodus 3:6 to prove that there is life after death. The Pharisees had overlooked this verse in their debates with the Sadducees. God spoke of Abraham, Isaac, and Jacob years after their deaths as if they *still lived.* God's covenant with all people exists beyond death.

12:28 By Jesus' time, the Jews had accumulated hundreds of laws—613 by one historian's count. Some religious leaders tried to distinguish between major and minor laws, and some taught that all laws were equally binding and that it was dangerous to make any distinctions. This scribe's question could have provoked controversy among these groups, but Jesus' answer summarized all of God's laws.

12:29–31 God's laws are not burdensome. They can be reduced to two simple principles: Love God and love others. These commands are from the Old Testament (Deuteronomy 6:5; Leviticus 19:18). When you love God completely and care for others as you care for yourself, then you have fulfilled the intent of the Ten Commandments and the other Old Testament laws. According to Jesus, these two commandments summarize all God's laws. Let them rule your thoughts, decisions, and actions. When you are uncertain about what to do, ask yourself which course of action best demonstrates love for God and love for others.

12:32–34 This man had caught the intent of God's law as it is so often stressed in the Old Testament—that true obedience comes from the heart. Because all the Old Testament commands lead to Christ, his next step was faith in Jesus himself. This, however, was the most difficult step to take.

12:35–37 Jesus quoted Psalm 110:1 to show that David considered the Messiah to be his Lord, not just his son. The religious leaders did not understand that the Messiah would be far more than a human descendant of David; he would be God himself in human form.

12:38–40 Jesus again exposed the religious leaders' impure motives. The scribes received no pay, so they depended on the hospitality extended by devout Jews. Some of them used this custom to exploit people, cheating the poor out of everything they had and taking advantage of the rich. Through their pious actions they hoped to gain status, recognition, and respect.

12:38–40 Jesus warned against trying to make a good impression.

12:40 Luke 20:47

39 and chief seats in the synagogues and places of honor at banquets,
40 who devour widows' houses, and for appearance's sake offer long prayers; these will
receive greater condemnation."

A Poor Widow Gives All She Has
(200/Luke 21:1-4)

12:41 John 8:20; 2 Kin 12:9

41 And He sat down opposite the treasury, and *began* observing how the people were
putting money into the treasury; and many rich people were putting in large sums.
42 A poor widow came and put in two small copper coins, which amount to a cent.
43 Calling His disciples to Him, He said to them, "Truly I say to you, this poor widow
put in more than all the contributors to the treasury;

12:44 Luke 8:43; 15:12, 30; 21:4

44 for they all put in out of their surplus, but she, out of her poverty, put in all she owned,
all she had to live on."

Jesus Tells about the Future
(201/Matthew 24:1-25; Luke 21:5-24)

13 As He was going out of the temple, one of His disciples *said to Him, "Teacher,
behold [31]what wonderful stones and what wonderful buildings!"

13:2 Luke 19:44

2 And Jesus said to him, "Do you see these great buildings? Not one stone will be left
upon another which will not be torn down."

13:3 Matt 21:1; Matt 17:1

3 As He was sitting on the Mount of Olives opposite the temple, Peter and James and
John and Andrew were questioning Him privately,

31 Lit *how great*

JESUS' PROPHECIES IN THE OLIVET DISCOURSE

Type of Prophecy	*Old Testament References*	*Other New Testament References*
The Last Days Mark 13:1–23 Matthew 24:1–28 Luke 21:5–24	Daniel 9:26–27 Daniel 11:31 Joel 2:2	John 15:21 Revelation 11:2 1 Timothy 4:1–2
The Second Coming of Christ Mark 13:24–27 Luke 21:25–28 Matthew 24:29–31	Isaiah 13:6–10 Ezekiel 32:7 Daniel 7:13–14	Revelation 6:12 Mark 14:62 1 Thessalonians 4:16

In Mark 13, often called the Olivet Discourse, Jesus talked a lot about two things: the end times and his second coming. Jesus was not trying to encourage his disciples to speculate about exactly when he would return by sharing these prophecies with them. Instead, he urges all his followers to be watchful and prepared for his coming. If we serve Jesus faithfully now, we will be ready when he returns.

These scribes were religious hypocrites who had no love for God. True followers of Christ are not distinguished by showy spirituality. Reading the Bible, praying in public, or following church rituals can be phony if the motive for doing them is to be noticed or honored. Let your actions be consistent with your beliefs. Live for Christ, even when no one is looking.

12:40 The punishment for these scribes would be especially severe because as teachers they were responsible for shaping the faith of the people. But they saddled people with petty rules while they lived greedily and deceitfully. Their behavior oppressed and misled the very people they were supposed to lead.

12:41 There were several boxes in the temple where money could be placed. Some were for collecting the temple tax from Jewish males; the others were for freewill offerings. These particular collection boxes were probably in the court of the women.

12:41–44 In the Lord's eyes, this poor widow gave more than all the others put together, though her gift was by far the smallest. The value of a gift is not determined by its amount, but by the spirit in which it is given. A gift given grudgingly or for recognition loses its value. When you give, remember—gifts of any size are pleasing to God when they are given out of gratitude and a spirit of generosity.

13:1–2 About 15 years before Jesus was born (20 B.C.), Herod the Great began to remodel and rebuild the temple, which had stood for nearly 500 years since the days of Ezra (Ezra 6:14–15). Herod made the temple one of the most beautiful buildings in Jerusalem—not to honor God, but to appease the Jews whom he ruled. The magnificent building project was not completely finished until A.D. 64. Jesus' prophecy that not one stone would be left on another was fulfilled in A.D. 70, when the Romans completely destroyed the temple and the entire city of Jerusalem.

13:3ff The disciples wanted to know when the temple would be destroyed. Jesus gave them a prophetic picture of that time, including events leading up to it. He also talked about future events connected with his return to earth to judge all people. Jesus predicted both near and distant events without putting them in chronological order. Some of the disciples lived to see the destruction of Jerusalem in A.D. 70. This event would assure them that everything else Jesus predicted would also happen.

Jesus warned his followers about the future so that they could learn how to live in the present. Many predictions Jesus made in this passage have not yet been fulfilled. He did not make them so that we would guess when they might be fulfilled, but to help us remain spiritually alert and prepared at all times as we wait for his return.

13:3–4 The Mount of Olives rises above Jerusalem to the east. From its slopes a person can look down into the city and see the temple. Zechariah 14:1–4 predicts that the Messiah will stand on this very mountain when he returns to set up his eternal kingdom.

4 "Tell us, when will these things be, and what *will be* the sign when all these things are
going to be fulfilled?"
5 And Jesus began to say to them, "See to it that no one misleads you.
6 "Many will come in My name, saying, 'I am *He!*' and will mislead many. **13:6**
7 "When you hear of wars and rumors of wars, do not be frightened; *those things* must John 8:24
take place; but *that is* not yet the end.
8 "For nation will rise up against nation, and kingdom against kingdom; there will be
earthquakes in various places; there will *also* be famines. These things are *merely* the
beginning of birth pangs.
9 "But be on your guard; for they will deliver you to *the* courts, and you will be flogged **13:9**
in *the* synagogues, and you will stand before governors and kings for My sake, as a testi- Matt 10:17
mony to them.
10 "The gospel must first be preached to all the nations. **13:10**
11 "When they arrest you and hand you over, do not worry beforehand about what you Matt 24:14
are to say, but say whatever is given you in that hour; for it is not you who speak, but *it is* **13:11**
the Holy Spirit. Matt 10:19-22; Luke 21:12-17
12 "Brother will betray brother to death, and a father *his* child; and children will rise up
against parents and have them put to death.
13 "You will be hated by all because of My name, but the one who endures to the end, **13:13**
he will be saved. Matt 10:22; John 15:21
14 "But when you see the ABOMINATION OF DESOLATION standing where it should not
be (let the reader understand), then those who are in Judea must flee to the mountains. **13:14** Matt 24:15f; Dan
15 "The one who is on the housetop must not go down, or go in to get anything out of 9:27; 11:31; 12:11
his house; **13:15**
16 and the one who is in the field must not turn back to get his coat. Luke 17:31
17 "But woe to those who are pregnant and to those who are nursing babies in those days!
18 "But pray that it may not happen in the winter.
19 "For those days will be a *time of* tribulation such as has not occurred since the begin- **13:19**
ning of the creation which God created until now, and never will. Dan 12:1; Mark 10:6
20 "Unless the Lord had shortened *those* days, no life would have been saved; but for
the sake of the elect, whom He chose, He shortened the days.
21 "And then if anyone says to you, 'Behold, here is the Christ'; or, 'Behold, *He is* there';
do not believe *him;*

13:5–7 What are the signs of the end times? There have been people in every generation since Christ's resurrection claiming to know exactly when Jesus would return. No one has been right yet, however, because Christ will return on God's timetable, not ours. Jesus predicted that, before his return, many believers would be misled by false teachers claiming to have revelations from God.

According to Scripture, the one clear sign of Christ's return will be his unmistakable appearance in the clouds, which will be seen by all people (13:26; Revelation 1:7). In other words, you do not have to wonder whether a certain person is the Messiah or whether these are the "end times." When Jesus returns, *you will know* beyond a doubt, because it will be evident to all true believers. Beware of groups who claim special knowledge of the last days, because no one knows when that time will be (13:32). Be cautious about saying, "This is it!" but be bold in your total commitment to have your heart and life ready for Christ's return.

13:9–10 As the early church began to grow, most of the disciples experienced the kind of persecution Jesus was talking about. Since the time of Christ, Christians have been persecuted in their own lands and on foreign mission fields. Though you may be safe from persecution now, your vision of God's kingdom must not be limited by what happens only to you. A glance at a newspaper will reveal that many Christians in other parts of the world daily face hardships and persecution. Persecutions are an opportunity for Christians to witness for Christ to those opposed to him. These persecutions serve God's desire that the gospel be proclaimed to everyone.

13:11 Jesus did not imply that studying the Bible and gaining knowledge is useless or wrong. Before and after his resurrection Jesus himself taught his disciples what to say and how to say it. But Jesus was teaching the kind of attitude we should have when we must take a stand for the gospel. We don't have to be fearful or defensive about our faith because the Holy Spirit will be present to give us the right words to say.

13:13 To believe in Jesus and endure to the end will take perseverance because our faith will be challenged and opposed. Severe trials will sift true Christians from fair-weather believers. Enduring to the end does not earn salvation for us, but marks us as already saved. The assurance of our salvation will keep us going through the times of persecution.

13:14 The "abomination of desolation" is the desecration of the temple by God's enemies. This happened repeatedly in Israel's history: in 597 B.C. when Nebuchadnezzar looted the temple and took Judean captives to Babylon (2 Chronicles 36); in 168 B.C. when Antiochus Epiphanes sacrificed a pig to Zeus on the sacred temple altar (Daniel 9:27; 11:30–31); in A.D. 70 when the Roman general Titus placed an idol on the site of the burned-out temple after the destruction of Jerusalem. Just a few years after Jesus gave this warning, in A.D. 38, the emperor Caligula made plans to put his own statue in the temple, but he died before this could be carried out.

13:20 The *elect* are God's chosen people, those who are saved. See Romans 8:29–30 and Ephesians 1:4–5 for more on God's choice.

13:22 Matt 7:15; Matt 24:24; John 4:48
13:24 Is 13:10; Ezek 32:7; Joel 2:10, 31; 3:15; Rev 6:12
13:25 Is 34:4; Rev 6:13
13:26 Dan 7:13; Rev 1:7; Matt 16:27; Mark 8:38
13:27 Deut 30:4; Zech 2:6
13:32 Matt 24:36; Acts 1:7
13:33 Eph 6:18; Col 4:2
13:34 Luke 12:36-38
13:35 Matt 24:42; Mark 13:37; Mark 14:30; Matt 14:25; Mark 6:48
13:36 Rom 13:11
13:37 Matt 24:42; Mark 13:35

22 for false Christs and false prophets will arise, and will show signs and wonders, in
order to lead astray, if possible, the elect.
23 "But take heed; behold, I have told you everything in advance.

Jesus Tells about His Return
(202/Matthew 24:26-35; Luke 21:25-33)

24 "But in those days, after that tribulation, THE SUN WILL BE DARKENED AND THE MOON
WILL NOT GIVE ITS LIGHT,
25 AND THE STARS WILL BE FALLING from heaven, and the powers that are in the heavens will be shaken.
26 "Then they will see THE SON OF MAN COMING IN CLOUDS with great power and
glory.
27 "And then He will send forth the angels, and will gather together His elect from the
four winds, from the farthest end of the earth to the farthest end of heaven.
28 "Now learn the parable from the fig tree: when its branch has already become tender and puts forth its leaves, you know that summer is near.
29 "Even so, you too, when you see these things happening, recognize that He is near,
right at the door.
30 "Truly I say to you, this [32]generation will not pass away until all these things take place.
31 "Heaven and earth will pass away, but My words will not pass away.

Jesus Tells about Remaining Watchful
(203/Matthew 24:36-51; Luke 21:34-38)

32 "But of that day or hour no one knows, not even the angels in heaven, nor the Son,
but the Father *alone.*
33 "Take heed, keep on the alert; for you do not know when the *appointed* time will come.
34 "*It is* like a man away on a journey, *who* upon leaving his house and putting his slaves
in charge, *assigning* to each one his task, also commanded the doorkeeper to stay on the
alert.
35 "Therefore, be on the alert—for you do not know when the master of the house is coming, whether in the evening, at midnight, or when the rooster crows, or in the morning—
36 in case he should come suddenly and find you asleep.
37 "What I say to you I say to all, 'Be on the alert!' "

32 Or *race*

13:22–23 Is it possible for Christians to be deceived? Yes. So convincing will be the arguments and proofs from deceivers in the end times that it will be difficult *not* to fall away from Christ. If we are prepared, Jesus says, we can remain faithful. But if we are not prepared, we will turn away. To penetrate the disguises of false teachers we can ask: (1) Have their predictions come true, or do they have to revise them to fit what's already happened? (2) Does any teaching utilize a small section of the Bible to the neglect of the whole? (3) Does the teaching contradict what the Bible says about God? (4) Are the practices meant to glorify the teacher or Christ? (5) Do the teachings promote hostility toward other Christians?

13:31 In Jesus' day the world seemed concrete, dependable, and permanent. These days many people fear its destruction by nuclear war. Jesus tells us, however, that even if the earth passes away, the truth of his words will never be changed or abolished. God and his Word provide the only stability in our unstable world. How short-sighted people are who spend their time learning about this temporary world and accumulating its possessions, while neglecting the Bible and its eternal truths!

13:32 When Jesus said that even he did not know the time of the end, he was affirming his humanity. Of course God the Father knows the time, and Jesus and the Father are one. But when Jesus became a man, he voluntarily gave up the unlimited use of his divine attributes.

The emphasis of this verse is not on Jesus' lack of knowledge, but rather on the fact that no one knows. It is God the Father's secret to be revealed when he wills. No one can predict by Scripture or science the exact day of Jesus' return. Jesus is teaching that preparation, not calculation, is needed.

13:33–34 Months of planning go into a wedding, the birth of a baby, a career change, a speaking engagement, the purchase of a home. Do you place the same importance on preparing for Christ's return, the most important event in your life? Its results will last for eternity. You dare not postpone your preparations because you do not know when his return will occur. The way to prepare is to study God's Word and live by its instructions each day. Only then will you be ready.

13:35–37 The entire thirteenth chapter of Mark tells us how to live while we wait for Christ's return: (1) We are not to be misled by confusing claims or speculative interpretations of what will happen (13:5–6). (2) We should not be afraid to tell people about Christ, despite what they might say or do to us (13:9–11). (3) We must stand firm by faith and not be surprised by persecutions (13:13). (4) We must be morally alert, obedient to the commands for living found in God's Word. This chapter was not given to promote discussions on prophetic timetables, but to stimulate right living for God in a world where he is largely ignored.

C. DEATH AND RESURRECTION OF JESUS, THE SERVANT (14:1—16:20)

Mark tells us about Jesus' ultimate deed of servanthood—dying for us on the cross. Jesus died for our sin so we wouldn't have to. Now we can have eternal fellowship with God instead of eternal suffering and death. When first written in Rome, this Gospel was encouraging to Roman Christians during times of persecution. Christ's victory through suffering can encourage us during difficult times too.

Religious Leaders Plot to Kill Jesus
(207/Matthew 26:1-5; Luke 22:1-2)

14 Now the Passover and Unleavened Bread were two days away; and the chief priests
and the scribes were seeking how to seize Him by stealth and kill *Him;*
2 for they were saying, "Not during the festival, otherwise there might be a riot of the
people."

14:1 Ex 12:1-27; Mark 14:12; John 11:55; 13:1; Matt 12:14

A Woman Anoints Jesus with Perfume
(182/Matthew 26:6-13; John 12:1-11)

3 While He was in Bethany at the home of Simon the leper, and reclining *at the table,*
there came a woman with an alabaster vial of very costly perfume of pure nard; *and* she
broke the vial and poured it over His head.
4 But some were indignantly *remarking* to one another, "Why has this perfume been
wasted?
5 "For this perfume might have been sold for over three hundred [33]denarii, and *the*
money given to the poor." And they were scolding her.
6 But Jesus said, "Let her alone; why do you bother her? She has done a good deed
to Me.
7 "For you always have the poor with you, and whenever you wish you can do good to
them; but you do not always have Me.
8 "She has done what she could; she has anointed My body beforehand for the burial.
9 "Truly I say to you, wherever the gospel is preached in the whole world, what this
woman has done will also be spoken of in memory of her."

14:3 Luke 7:37-39; Matt 21:17; Matt 26:6f; John 12:3
14:7 Deut 15:11; Matt 26:11; John 12:8
14:8 John 19:40
14:9 Matt 26:13

Judas Agrees to Betray Jesus
(208/Matthew 26:14-16; Luke 22:3-6)

10 Then Judas Iscariot, who was one of the twelve, went off to the chief priests in order to betray Him to them.
11 They were glad when they heard *this,* and promised to give him money. And he *began*
seeking how to betray Him at an opportune time.

14:10 John 6:71

33 The denarius was equivalent to a day's wages

14:1 The Passover commemorated the night the Israelites were freed from Egypt (Exodus 12), when God "passed over" homes marked by the blood of a lamb while killing firstborn sons in unmarked homes. The day of Passover was followed by a seven-day festival called the Feast of Unleavened Bread. This, too, recalled the Israelites' quick escape from Egypt when they didn't have time to let their bread rise, so they baked it without yeast. This holiday found people gathering for a special meal that included lamb, wine, bitter herbs, and unleavened bread. Eventually the whole week came to be called Passover.

14:1 The Jewish leaders plotted secretly to kill Jesus—his murder was carefully planned. The murder plot was not being planned because popular opinion had turned against Jesus. In fact, the leaders were afraid of Jesus' popularity.

14:3 Bethany is located on the eastern slope of the Mount of Olives (Jerusalem is on the western side). This town was the home of Jesus' friends Lazarus, Mary, and Martha, who were also present at this dinner (John 11:2). The woman who anointed Jesus' feet was Mary, Lazarus and Martha's sister (John 12:1–3). An alabaster vial was a beautiful and expensive carved vase. Nard was expensive perfume.

14:3–9 Matthew and Mark placed this event just before the Last Supper, while John placed it a week earlier, just before the Triumphal Entry. It must be remembered that the main purpose of the Gospel writers was not to present an exact chronological account of Christ's life, but to give an accurate record of his message. Matthew and Mark may have chosen to place this event here to contrast the complete devotion of Mary with the betrayal of Judas, the next event in both Gospels.

14:4–5 Where Mark says "some," John specifically mentions Judas (John 12:4–5). Judas's indignation over Mary's act of worship was based not on concern for the poor but on greed. Because Judas was the treasurer of Jesus' ministry and had embezzled funds (John 12:6), he no doubt wanted the perfume sold so that the proceeds could be put into his care.

14:6–7 Jesus was not saying that we should neglect the poor, nor was he justifying indifference to them. (For Jesus' teaching about the poor, see Matthew 6:2–4; Luke 6:20–21; 14:13, 21; 18:22.) Jesus was praising Mary for her unselfish act of worship. The essence of worshiping Christ is to regard him with utmost love, respect, and devotion and to be willing to sacrifice to him what is most precious.

14:10 Why would Judas want to betray Jesus? Very likely, Judas expected Jesus to start a political rebellion and overthrow Rome. As treasurer, Judas certainly assumed (as did the other disciples—see 10:35–37) that he would be given an important position in Jesus' new government. But when Jesus praised Mary for pouring out the perfume, thought to be worth a year's salary, Judas finally began to realize that Jesus' kingdom was not physical or political, but spiritual. Judas's greedy desire for money and status could not be fulfilled if he followed Jesus, so he betrayed him in exchange for money and favor from the religious leaders.

Disciples Prepare for the Passover
(209/Matthew 26:17-19; Luke 22:7-13)

14.12 Matt 26:17; Deut 16:5; Mark 14:1; Luke 22:7; 1 Cor 5:7

12 On the first day of Unleavened Bread, when the Passover *lamb* was being sacrificed,
His disciples ☆said to Him, "Where do You want us to go and prepare for You to eat the
Passover?"

JUDAS ISCARIOT

It is easy to overlook the fact that Jesus chose Judas to be his disciple. We may also forget that while Judas betrayed Jesus, *all* the disciples abandoned him. With the other disciples, Judas shared a persistent misunderstanding of Jesus' mission. They all expected Jesus to make the right political moves. When he kept talking about dying, they all felt varying degrees of anger, fear, and disappointment. They didn't understand why they had been chosen if Jesus' mission was doomed to fail.

We do not know the exact motivation behind Judas's betrayal. What is clear is that Judas allowed his desires to place him in a position where Satan could manipulate him. Judas accepted payment to set Jesus up for the religious leaders. He identified Jesus for the guards in the dimly lit Garden of Gethsemane. It is possible that he was trying to force Jesus' hand—would Jesus or would Jesus not rebel against Rome and set up a new political government?

Whatever his plan, though, at some point Judas realized he didn't like the way things were turning out. He tried to undo the evil he had done by returning the money to the priests, but it was too late. The wheels of God's sovereign plan had been set into motion. How sad that Judas ended his life in despair without ever experiencing the gift of reconciliation God could give even to him through Jesus Christ.

Human feelings toward Judas have always been mixed. Some have fervently hated him for his betrayal. Others have pitied him for not realizing what he was doing. A few have tried to make him a hero for his part in ending Jesus' earthly mission. Some have questioned God's fairness in allowing one man to bear such guilt. While there are many feelings about Judas, there are some facts to consider as well. He, by his own choice, betrayed God's Son into the hands of soldiers (Luke 22:48). He was a thief (John 12:6). Jesus knew that Judas's life of evil would not change (John 6:70). Judas's betrayal of Jesus was part of God's sovereign plan (Psalm 41:9; Zechariah 11:12–13; Matthew 20:18; 26:20–25; Acts 1:16, 20).

In betraying Jesus, Judas made the greatest mistake in history. But the fact that Jesus knew Judas would betray him doesn't mean that Judas was a puppet of God's will. Judas made the choice. God knew what that choice would be and confirmed it. Judas didn't lose his relationship with Jesus; rather, he never found Jesus in the first place. He is called "the son of perdition" (John 17:12) because he was never saved.

Judas does us a favor if he makes us think a second time about our commitment to God and the presence of God's Spirit within us. Are we true disciples and followers, or uncommitted pretenders? We can choose despair and death, or we can choose repentance, forgiveness, hope, and eternal life. Judas's betrayal sent Jesus to the cross to guarantee that second choice, our only chance. Will we accept Jesus' free gift, or, like Judas, betray him?

Strengths and accomplishments:
- He was chosen as one of the 12 disciples; the only non-Galilean
- He kept the money bag for the expenses of the group
- He was able to recognize the evil in his betrayal of Jesus

Weaknesses and mistakes:
- He was greedy (John 12:6)
- He betrayed Jesus
- He committed suicide instead of seeking forgiveness

Lessons from his life:
- Evil plans and motives leave us open to being used by Satan for even greater evil
- The consequences of evil are so devastating that even small lies and little wrongdoings have serious results
- God's plan and his purposes are worked out even in the worst possible events

Vital statistics:
- Where: Possibly from the town of Kerioth
- Occupation: Disciple of Jesus
- Relative: Father: Simon
- Contemporaries: Jesus, Pilate, Herod, the other 11 disciples

Key verses:
"And Satan entered into Judas who was called Iscariot, belonging to the number of the twelve. And he went away and discussed with the chief priests and officers how he might betray Him to them" (Luke 22:3–4).

Judas's story is told in the Gospels. He is also mentioned in Acts 1:18–19.

13 And He ☆sent two of His disciples and ☆said to them, "Go into the city, and a man
will meet you carrying a pitcher of water; follow him;
14 and wherever he enters, say to the owner of the house, 'The Teacher says, "Where
is My guest room in which I may eat the Passover with My disciples?" '
15 "And he himself will show you a large upper room furnished *and* ready; prepare for
us there."
16 The disciples went out and came to the city, and found *it* just as He had told them;
and they prepared the Passover.

14:14
Luke 22:11

MAJOR EVENTS OF PASSION WEEK

Sunday through Wednesday Jesus spent each night in Bethany, just two miles east of Jerusalem on the opposite slope of the Mount of Olives. He probably stayed at the home of Mary, Martha, and Lazarus. Jesus spent Thursday night praying in the Garden of Gethsemane. Friday and Saturday nights Jesus' body lay in the garden tomb.

Day	*Event*	*References*
Sunday	Triumphal Entry into Jerusalem	Matthew 21:1–11 Mark 11:1–10 Luke 19:29–40 John 12:12–19
Monday	Jesus clears the temple	Matthew 21:12–13 Mark 11:15–17 Luke 19:45–46
Tuesday	Jesus' authority challenged in the temple	Matthew 21:23–27 Mark 11:27–33 Luke 20:1–8
	Jesus teaches in stories and confronts the Jewish leaders	Matthew 21:28—23:36 Mark 12:1–40 Luke 20:9–47
	Greeks ask to see Jesus	John 12:20–26
	The Olivet Discourse	Matthew 24 Mark 13 Luke 21:5–38
	Judas agrees to betray Jesus	Matthew 26:14–16 Mark 14:10–11 Luke 22:3–6
Wednesday	The Bible does not say what Jesus did on this day. He probably remained in Bethany with his disciples	
Thursday	The Last Supper	Matthew 26:26–29 Mark 14:22–25 Luke 22:14–20
	Jesus speaks to the disciples in the upper room	John 13—17
	Jesus struggles in Gethsemane	Matthew 26:36–46 Mark 14:32–42 Luke 22:39–46 John 18:1
	Jesus is betrayed and arrested	Matthew 26:47–56 Mark 14:43–52 Luke 22:47–53 John 18:2–12
Friday	Jesus is tried by Jewish and Roman authorities and denied by Peter	Matthew 26:57—27:2, 11–31 Mark 14:53—15:20 Luke 22:54—23:25 John 18:13—19:16
	Jesus is crucified	Matthew 27:31–56 Mark 15:20–41 Luke 23:26–49 John 19:17–30
Sunday	The resurrection	Matthew 28:1–10 Mark 16:1–11 Luke 24:1–12 John 20:1–18

14:13 The two men Jesus sent were Peter and John (Luke 22:8).

14:14–15 Many homes had large upstairs rooms, sometimes with stairways both inside and outside the house. The preparations for the Passover would have included setting the table and buying and preparing the Passover lamb, unleavened bread, sauces, and other ceremonial food and drink.

Jesus and the Disciples Have the Last Supper
(211/Matthew 26:20-30; Luke 22:14-30; John 13:21-30)

17 When it was evening He ☆came with the twelve.
18 As they were reclining *at the table* and eating, Jesus said, "Truly I say to you that one
of you will betray Me—one who is eating with Me."
19 They began to be grieved and to say to Him one by one, "Surely not I?"
20 And He said to them, "*It is* one of the twelve, one who dips with Me in the bowl.
21 "For the Son of Man *is to* go just as it is written of Him; but woe to that man by whom
the Son of Man is betrayed! *It would have been* good for that man if he had not been
born."

14:22 1 Cor 11:23-25; Mark 10:16; Matt 14:19

22 While they were eating, He took *some* bread, and after a blessing He broke *it*, and
gave *it* to them, and said, "Take *it;* this is My body."
23 And when He had taken a cup *and* given thanks, He gave *it* to them, and they all
drank from it.

14:24 Ex 24:8; Jer 31:31-34

24 And He said to them, "This is My blood of the covenant, which is poured out for
many.
25 "Truly I say to you, I will never again drink of the fruit of the vine until that day when
I drink it new in the kingdom of God."

14:26 Matt 26:30; Matt 21:1

26 After singing a hymn, they went out to the Mount of Olives.

Jesus Again Predicts Peter's Denial
(222/Matthew 26:31-35)

14:27 Zech 13:7

27 And Jesus ☆said to them, "You will all fall away, because it is written, 'I WILL STRIKE
DOWN THE SHEPHERD, AND THE SHEEP SHALL BE SCATTERED.'

14:28 Matt 28:16

28 "But after I have been raised, I will go ahead of you to Galilee."
29 But Peter said to Him, "*Even* though all may fall away, yet I will not."

14:19 Judas, the very man who would betray Jesus, was at the table with the others. Judas had already determined to betray Jesus, but in cold-blooded hypocrisy he shared the fellowship of this meal. It is easy to become enraged or shocked by what Judas did; yet professing commitment to Christ and then denying him with one's life is also betraying him. It is denying Christ's love to disobey him; it is denying his truth to distrust him; it is denying his deity to reject his authority. Do your words and actions match? If not, consider a change of mind and heart that will protect you from making a terrible mistake.

14:20 It was often the practice to eat from a common bowl. Meat or bread was dipped into a bowl filled with sauce often made from fruit.

14:22–25 Mark records the origin of the Lord's Supper, also called Communion or Eucharist (thanksgiving), which is still celebrated in worship services today. Jesus and his disciples ate a meal, sang psalms, read Scripture, and prayed. Then Jesus took two traditional parts of the Passover meal, the passing of bread and the drinking of wine, and gave them new meaning as representations of his body and blood. He used the bread and wine to explain the significance of what he was about to do on the cross. For more on the significance of the Last Supper, see 1 Corinthians 11:23–29.

14:24 Jesus' death for us on the cross seals a new covenant between God and people. The old covenant involved forgiveness of sins through the blood of an animal sacrifice (Exodus 24:6–8). But instead of a spotless lamb on the altar, Jesus offered himself, the spotless Lamb of God, as a sacrifice that would forgive sin once and for all. Jesus was the final sacrifice for sins, and his blood sealed the new agreement between God and us. Now all of us can come to God through Jesus, in full confidence that God will hear us and save us from our sins.

14:26 The hymn they sang was most likely taken from Psalms 115—118, traditionally sung at the Passover meal.

14:27 It's easy to think that Satan temporarily gained the upper hand in this drama about Jesus' death. But we see later that God was in control, even in the death of his Son. Satan gained no victory—everything occurred exactly as God had planned.

14:27–31 This was the second time in the same evening that Jesus predicted the disciples' denial and desertion, which probably explains their strong reaction (14:31). For Jesus' earlier prediction, see Luke 22:31–34 and John 13:36–38.

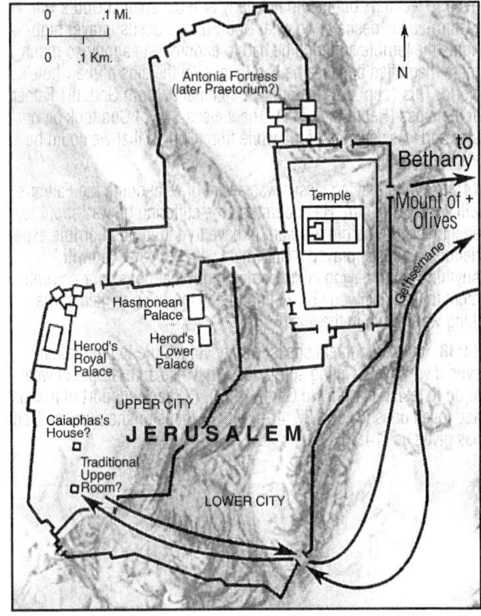

UPPER ROOM AND GETHSEMANE Jesus and the disciples ate the traditional Passover meal in an upper room in the city and then went to the Mount of Olives into a garden called Gethsemane. In the cool of the evening, Jesus prayed for strength to face the trial and suffering ahead.

30 And Jesus ☆said to him, "Truly I say to you, that this very night, before a rooster
crows twice, you yourself will deny Me three times."
31 But *Peter* kept saying insistently, "*Even* if I have to die with You, I will not deny You!"
And they all were saying the same thing also.

14:30 Matt 26:34; Mark 14:68, 72; John 13:38

Jesus Agonizes in the Garden
(223/Matthew 26:36-46; Luke 22:39-46)

32 They ☆came to a place named Gethsemane; and He ☆said to His disciples, "Sit here
until I have prayed."
33 And He ☆took with Him Peter and James and John, and began to be very distressed
and troubled.
34 And He ☆said to them, "My soul is deeply grieved to the point of death; remain
here and keep watch."
35 And He went a little beyond *them,* and fell to the ground and *began* to pray that if it
were possible, the hour might pass Him by.
36 And He was saying, "Abba! Father! All things are possible for You; remove this cup
from Me; yet not what I will, but what You will."
37 And He ☆came and ☆found them sleeping, and ☆said to Peter, "Simon, are you
asleep? Could you not keep watch for one hour?
38 "Keep watching and praying that you may not come into temptation; the spirit is
willing, but the flesh is weak."
39 Again He went away and prayed, saying the same words.
40 And again He came and found them sleeping, for their eyes were very heavy; and
they did not know what to answer Him.
41 And He ☆came the third time, and ☆said to them, "Are you still sleeping and resting? It is enough; the hour has come; behold, the Son of Man is being betrayed into the
hands of sinners.
42 "Get up, let us be going; behold, the one who betrays Me is at hand!"

14:33 Mark 9:15; 16:5, 6

14:34 Matt 26:38; John 12:27

14:35 Matt 26:45; Mark 14:41

14:36 Rom 8:15; Gal 4:6; Matt 26:39

14:38 Matt 26:41

14:41 Mark 14:35

14:35–36 Was Jesus trying to get out of his task? Jesus expressed his true feelings, but he did not deny or rebel against God's will. He reaffirmed his desire to do what God wanted. Jesus' prayer highlights the terrible suffering he had to endure—an agony so much more magnified because he had to take on the sins of the whole world. This "cup" was the agony of alienation from God, his Father, at the cross (Hebrews 5:7–9). The sinless Son of God took on our sins and was separated for a while from God so that we could be eternally saved.

14:36 While praying, Jesus was aware of what doing the Father's will would cost him. He understood the suffering he was about to encounter, and he did not want to have to endure the horrible experience. But Jesus prayed, "Not what I will, but what You will." Anything worth having costs something. What does your commitment to God cost you? Be willing to pay the price to gain something worthwhile in the end.

14:38 In times of great stress, we are vulnerable to temptation, even if we have a willing spirit. Jesus gave us an example of what to do to resist: (1) pray to God (14:35); (2) seek support of friends and loved ones (14:33, 37, 40–41); (3) focus on the purpose God has given us (14:36).

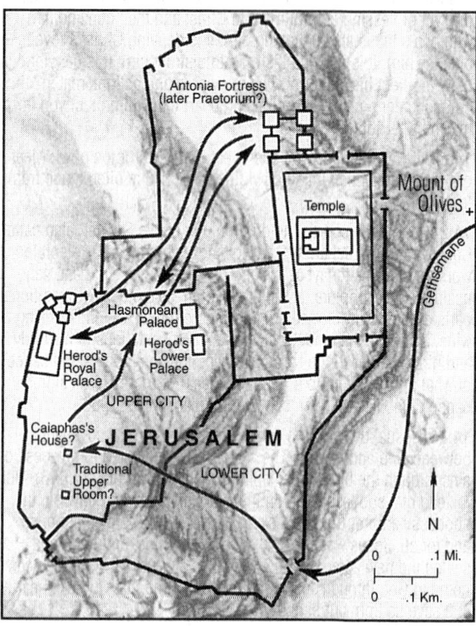

JESUS' TRIAL From Gethsemane, Jesus' trial began at the home of Caiaphas, the high priest. Jesus was then taken to Pilate, the Roman governor. Luke records that Pilate sent him to Herod, who was in Jerusalem—presumably in one of his two palaces (Luke 23:5–12). Herod sent him back to Pilate, who handed Jesus over to be crucified.

Jesus Is Betrayed and Arrested
(224/Matthew 26:47-56; Luke 22:47-53; John 18:1-11)

43 Immediately while He was still speaking, Judas, one of the twelve, ☆came up accompanied by a crowd with swords and clubs, *who were* from the chief priests and the scribes
and the elders.
44 Now he who was betraying Him had given them a signal, saying, "Whomever I kiss,
He is the one; seize Him and lead Him away under guard."

14:45 Matt 23:7

45 After coming, Judas immediately went to Him, saying, "Rabbi!" and kissed Him.
46 They laid hands on Him and seized Him.
47 But one of those who stood by drew his sword, and struck the slave of the high priest
and cut off his ear.
48 And Jesus said to them, "Have you come out with swords and clubs to arrest Me, as
you would against a robber?

14:49 Mark 12:35; Luke 19:47; 21:37

49 "Every day I was with you in the temple teaching, and you did not seize Me; but *this*
has taken place to fulfill the Scriptures."
50 And they all left Him and fled.
51 A young man was following Him, wearing *nothing but* a linen sheet over *his* naked
body; and they ☆seized him.
52 But he pulled free of the linen sheet and escaped naked.

Caiaphas Questions Jesus
(226/Matthew 26:57-68)

14:53 John 18:12f, 19-24

53 They led Jesus away to the high priest; and all the chief priests and the elders and
the scribes ☆gathered together.

14:54 Mark 14:68; Matt 26:3; Mark 14:67; John 18:18

54 Peter had followed Him at a distance, right into the courtyard of the high priest;
and he was sitting with the officers and warming himself at the fire.

14:55 Matt 5:22

55 Now the chief priests and the whole [34]Council kept trying to obtain testimony against
Jesus to put Him to death, and they were not finding any.
56 For many were giving false testimony against Him, but their testimony was not consistent.
57 Some stood up and *began* to give false testimony against Him, saying,

14:58 Matt 26:61; Mark 15:29; John 2:19

58 "We heard Him say, 'I will destroy this temple made with hands, and in three days I
will build another made without hands.' "
59 Not even in this respect was their testimony consistent.
60 The high priest stood up *and came* forward and questioned Jesus, saying, "Do You
not answer? What is it that these men are testifying against You?"

14:61 Matt 26:63; Matt 26:63ff; Luke 22:67-71

61 But He kept silent and did not answer. Again the high priest was questioning Him,
and saying to Him, "Are You the Christ, the Son of the Blessed *One?*"

14:62 Ps 110:1; Mark 13:26; Dan 7:13

62 And Jesus said, "I am; and you shall see THE SON OF MAN SITTING AT THE RIGHT
HAND OF POWER, and COMING WITH THE CLOUDS OF HEAVEN."

34 Or *Sanhedrin*

14:43–45 Judas was given a contingent of police and soldiers (John 18:3) in order to seize Jesus and bring him before the religious court for trial. The religious leaders had issued the warrant for Jesus' arrest, and Judas was acting as Jesus' official accuser.

14:47 According to John 18:10, the person who pulled the sword was Peter. Luke 22:51 records that Jesus immediately healed the man's ear and prevented any further bloodshed.

14:50 Just hours earlier, these disciples had vowed never to desert Jesus (14:31).

14:51–52 Tradition says that this young man may have been John Mark, the writer of this Gospel. The incident is not mentioned in any of the other accounts.

14:53ff This trial by the Council had two phases. A small group met at night (John 18:12–24), and then the full Council met at daybreak (Luke 22:66–71). They tried Jesus for religious offenses such as calling himself the Son of God, which, according to law, was blasphemy. The trial was fixed: These religious leaders had already decided to kill Jesus (Luke 22:2).

14:55 The Romans controlled Israel, but the Jews were given some authority over religious and minor civil disputes. The Jewish ruling body, the Council (Sanhedrin), was made up of 71 of Israel's religious leaders. It was assumed that these men would be just. Instead, they showed great injustice in the trial of Jesus, even to the point of making up lies to use against him (14:57).

14:58 The statement that the false witnesses finally agreed to use as an accusation twisted Jesus' actual words. Jesus did not say, "I will destroy this temple made with hands;" he said, "Destroy this temple, and in three days I will raise it up" (John 2:19). Jesus was not talking about Herod's temple, but about his own body.

14:60–64 To the first question, Jesus made no reply because it was based on confusing and erroneous evidence. Not answering was wiser than trying to clarify the fabricated accusations. But if Jesus had refused to answer the second question, it could have been taken as a denial of his mission. Instead, his answer predicted a powerful role reversal. Sitting on the right hand of power, he would come to judge his accusers, and they would have to answer *his* questions (Psalm 110:1; Revelation 20:11–13).

63 Tearing his clothes, the high priest ☆said, "What further need do we have of witnesses?
64 "You have heard the blasphemy; how does it seem to you?" And they all condemned
Him to be deserving of death.
65 Some began to spit at Him, and to blindfold Him, and to beat Him with their fists,
and to say to Him, "Prophesy!" And the officers received Him with slaps *in the face.*

14:63 Num 14:6; Matt 26:65; Acts 14:14
14:64 Lev 24:16
14:65 Matt 26:67; Mark 10:34; Esth 7:8; Matt 26:68; Luke 22:64

Peter Denies Knowing Jesus
(227/Matthew 26:69-75; Luke 22:54-65; John 18:25-27)

66 As Peter was below in the courtyard, one of the servant-girls of the high priest ☆came,
67 and seeing Peter warming himself, she looked at him and ☆said, "You also were with
Jesus the Nazarene."
68 But he denied *it,* saying, "I neither know nor understand what you are talking about."
And he went out onto the porch, and a rooster crowed.[35]
69 The servant-girl saw him, and began once more to say to the bystanders, "This is
one of them!"
70 But again he denied it. And after a little while the bystanders were again saying to
Peter, "Surely you are *one* of them, for you are a Galilean too."
71 But he began to curse and swear, "I do not know this man you are talking about!"
72 Immediately a rooster crowed a second time. And Peter remembered how Jesus had
made the remark to him, "Before a rooster crows twice, you will deny Me three times."
And he began to weep.

14:66 Mark 14:54
14:67 Mark 14:54; Mark 1:24
14:68 Mark 14:54
14:70 Mark 14:68; Matt 26:73; Luke 22:59
14:72 Mark 14:30, 68

The Council of Religious Leaders Condemns Jesus
(228/Matthew 27:1-2; Luke 22:66-71)

15 Early in the morning the chief priests with the elders and scribes and the whole
[36]Council, immediately held a consultation; and binding Jesus, they led Him away
and delivered Him to Pilate.

15:1 Matt 27:1; Matt 5:22

35 Later mss add *and a rooster crowed* 36 Or *Sanhedrin*

WHY DID JESUS HAVE TO DIE?

The Problem	We have all done things that are wrong, and we have failed to obey God's laws. Because of this, we have been separated from God our Creator. Separation from God is death; but, by ourselves, we can do nothing to become united with God.
Why Jesus Could Help	Jesus was not only a man; he was God's unique Son. Because Jesus never disobeyed God and never sinned, only he can bridge the gap between the sinless God and sinful mankind.
The Solution	Jesus freely offered his life for us, dying on the cross in our place, taking all our wrongdoing upon himself, and saving us from the consequences of sin—including God's judgment and death.
The Results	Jesus took our past, present, and future sins upon himself so that we could have new life. Because all our wrongdoing is forgiven, we are reconciled to God. Furthermore, Jesus' resurrection from the dead is the proof that his substitutionary sacrifice on the cross was acceptable to God, and his resurrection has become the source of new life for whoever believes that Jesus is the Son of God. All who believe in him may have this new life and live it in union with him.

14:63–64 Of all people, the high priest and members of the Council should have recognized the Messiah because they knew the Scriptures thoroughly. Their job was to point people to God, but they were more concerned about preserving their reputations and holding on to their authority. They valued human security more than eternal security.

14:66–67 Caiaphas's house, where Jesus was tried (14:53), was part of a huge palace with several courtyards. John was apparently acquainted with the high priest, and he was let into the courtyard along with Peter (John 18:15–16).

14:71 Peter's curse was more than just a common swear word. He was making the strongest denial he could think of by denying with an oath that he knew Jesus. He was saying, in effect, "May God strike me dead if I'm lying."

14:71 It is easy to get angry at the Council and the Roman governor for their injustice in condemning Jesus, but Peter and the rest of the disciples also contributed to Jesus' pain by deserting him (14:50). While most of us may not be like the Jewish and Roman leaders, we are like the disciples because all of us have been guilty of denying Christ as Lord in vital areas of our lives. We may pride ourselves that we have not committed certain sins, but we are all guilty of sin. Don't try to excuse yourself by pointing at others whose sins seem worse than yours.

15:1 Why did the Jewish leaders send Jesus to Pilate, the Roman governor? The Romans had taken away the Jews' right to inflict capital punishment; so in order for Jesus to be condemned to death, he had to be sentenced by a Roman leader. The Jewish leaders wanted Jesus executed on a cross, a method of death that they believed brought a curse from God (see Deuteronomy 21:23). They hoped to persuade the people that Jesus was cursed, not blessed, by God.

Jesus Stands Trial before Pilate
(230/Matthew 27:11-14; Luke 23:1-5; John 18:28-37)

2 Pilate questioned Him, "Are You the King of the Jews?" And He ☆answered him,
"*It is as* you say."
3 The chief priests *began* to accuse Him harshly.
4 Then Pilate questioned Him again, saying, "Do You not answer? See how many
charges they bring against You!"
15:5 Matt 27:12
5 But Jesus made no further answer; so Pilate was amazed.

PILATE

In Jesus' day, any death sentence had to be approved by the Roman official in charge of the administrative district. Pontius Pilate was governor of the province of Judea, where Jerusalem was located. When the Jewish leaders had Jesus in their power and wanted to kill him, they had to obtain Pilate's permission. So it happened that early one morning Pilate found a crowd at his door demanding a man's death.

Pilate's relationship with the Jews had always been stormy. His Roman toughness and fairness had been weakened by cynicism, compromises, and mistakes. On several occasions his actions had deeply offended the religious leaders. The resulting riots and chaos must have made Pilate wonder what he had gotten himself into. He was trying to control people who treated their Roman conquerors without respect. Jesus' trial was another episode in Pilate's ongoing problems.

For Pilate, there was never a doubt about Jesus' innocence. Three separate times he declared Jesus not guilty. He couldn't understand what made these people want to kill Jesus, but his fear of the pressure the Jews would place on him made him decide to allow Jesus' crucifixion. Because of the people's threat to inform the emperor that Pilate hadn't eliminated a rebel against Rome, Pilate went against what he knew was right. In desperation, he chose to do wrong.

We share a common humanity with Pilate. At times we know the right and choose the wrong. He had his moment in history and now we have ours. What have we done with our opportunities and responsibilities? What judgment have we passed on Jesus?

Strength and accomplishment:
- Roman governor of Judea

Weaknesses and mistakes:
- He failed in his attempt to rule a people who were defeated militarily but never dominated by Rome
- His constant political struggles made him a cynical and uncaring compromiser, susceptible to pressure
- Although he realized Jesus was innocent, he bowed to the public demand for his execution

Lessons from his life:
- Great evil can happen when truth is at the mercy of political pressures
- Resisting the truth leaves a person without purpose or direction

Vital statistics:
- Where: Judea
- Occupation: Roman governor of Judea
- Relative: Wife: unnamed
- Contemporaries: Jesus, Caiaphas, Herod

Key verses:
"Pilate said to Him, 'What is truth?' And when he had said this, he went out again to the Jews and said to them, 'I find no guilt in Him. But you have a custom that I release someone for you at the Passover; do you wish then that I release for you the King of the Jews?' " (John 18:38–39).

Pilate's story is told in the Gospels. He is also mentioned in Acts 3:13; 4:27; 13:28; 1 Timothy 6:13.

15:3–4 The Jewish leaders had to fabricate new accusations against Jesus when they brought him before Pilate. The charge of blasphemy would mean nothing to the Roman governor, so they accused Jesus of three other crimes: (1) encouraging the people not to pay their taxes to Rome, (2) claiming he was a king—"the king of the Jews," and (3) causing riots all over the countryside. Tax evasion, treason, and terrorism—all these would be cause for Pilate's concern (see also Luke 23:2).

15:5 Why didn't Jesus answer Pilate's questions? It would have been futile to answer, and the time had come to give his life to save the world. Jesus had no reason to try to prolong the trial or save himself. His was the ultimate example of self-assurance and peace, which no ordinary criminal could imitate. Nothing would stop him from completing the work he had come to earth to do (Isaiah 53:7).

Pilate Hands Jesus Over to Be Crucified
(232/Matthew 27:15-26; Luke 23:13-25; John 18:38—19:16)

6 Now at *the* feast he used to release for them *any* one prisoner whom they requested.
7 The man named Barabbas had been imprisoned with the insurrectionists who had
committed murder in the insurrection.
8 The crowd went up and began asking him *to do* as he had been accustomed to do
for them.
9 Pilate answered them, saying, "Do you want me to release for you the King of the
Jews?"
10 For he was aware that the chief priests had handed Him over because of envy.
11 But the chief priests stirred up the crowd *to ask* him to release Barabbas for them **15:11**
instead. Acts 3:14
12 Answering again, Pilate said to them, "Then what shall I do with Him whom you
call the King of the Jews?"
13 They shouted back, "Crucify Him!"
14 But Pilate said to them, "Why, what evil has He done?" But they shouted all the
more, "Crucify Him!"
15 Wishing to satisfy the crowd, Pilate released Barabbas for them, and after having **15:15**
Jesus scourged, he handed Him over to be crucified. Matt 27:26

15:7 Barabbas was arrested for his part in a rebellion against the Roman government, and, although he had committed a murder, he may have been a hero among the Jews. The fiercely independent Jews hated to be ruled by pagan Romans. They hated paying taxes to support the despised government and its gods. Most of the Roman authorities who had to settle Jewish disputes hated the Jews in return. The time was ripe for rebellion.

15:8 This crowd was most likely a group of people loyal to the Jewish leaders. But where were the disciples and the crowds who days earlier had shouted, "Hosanna in the highest" (11:10)? Jesus' sympathizers were afraid of the Jewish leaders, so they went into hiding. Another possibility is that the multitude included many people who were in the Palm Sunday parade, but who turned against Jesus when they saw that he was not going to be an earthly conqueror and their deliverer from Rome.

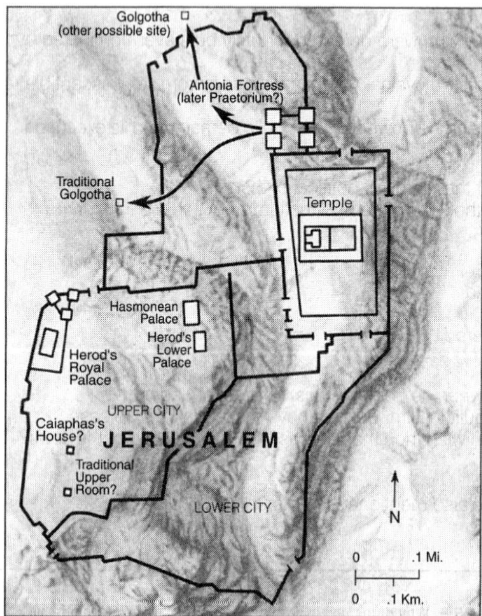

JESUS' ROUTE TO GOLGOTHA After being sentenced by Pilate, Jesus was taken from the Praetorium to Golgotha, a place outside the city, for crucifixion.

15:10 The Jews hated Pilate, but they went to him for the favor of condemning Jesus to crucifixion. Pilate could see that this was a frame-up. Why else would these people, who hated him and the Roman empire he represented, ask him to convict of treason and give the death penalty to one of their fellow Jews?

15:13 Crucifixion was the Roman penalty for rebellion. Only slaves or those who were not Roman citizens could be crucified. If Jesus died by crucifixion, he would die the death of a rebel and slave, not of the king he claimed to be. This is just what the Jewish religious leaders wanted, and the reason they whipped the mob into a frenzy. In addition, crucifixion would put the responsibility for killing Jesus on the Romans, and thus the crowds could not blame the religious leaders.

15:14–15 Who was guilty of Jesus' death? In reality, everyone was at fault. The disciples deserted him in terror. Peter denied that he ever knew Jesus. Judas betrayed him. The crowds who had followed him stood by and did nothing. Pilate tried to blame the crowds. The religious leaders actively promoted Jesus' death. The Roman soldiers tortured him. If you had been there, watching these trials, what would your response have been?

15:15 The region of Judea where Pilate ruled as governor was little more than a hot and dusty outpost of the Roman empire. Because Judea was so far from Rome, Pilate was given just a small army. His primary job was to keep peace. We know from historical records that Pilate had already been warned about other uprisings in his region. Although he may have seen no guilt in Jesus and no reason to condemn him to death, Pilate wavered when the Jews in the crowd threatened to report him to Caesar (John 19:12). Such a report, accompanied by a riot, could cost him his position and hopes for advancement.

15:15 Although Jesus was innocent according to Roman law, Pilate caved in to political pressure. He abandoned what he knew was right. Trying to second-guess the Jewish leaders, Pilate gave a decision that would please everyone while keeping himself safe. When we lay aside God's clear statements of right and wrong and make decisions based on the preferences of our audience, we fall into compromise and lawlessness. God promises to honor those who do right, not those who make everyone happy.

15:16 Matt 26:3; 27:27; Acts 10:1

Roman Soldiers Mock Jesus
(233/Matthew 27:27-31)

16 The soldiers took Him away into the palace (that is, the Praetorium), and they ☆called
together the whole *Roman* [37]cohort.
17 They ☆dressed Him up in purple, and after twisting a crown of thorns, they put it
on Him;
18 and they began to acclaim Him, "Hail, King of the Jews!"
19 They kept beating His head with a [38]reed, and spitting on Him, and kneeling and
bowing before Him.
20 After they had mocked Him, they took the purple robe off Him and put His *own*
garments on Him. And they ☆led Him out to crucify Him.

15:21 Rom 16:13

15:22 Luke 23:33; John 19:17

15:23 Matt 27:34

15:24 Ps 22:18; John 19:24

Jesus Is Led Away to Be Crucified
(234/Matthew 27:32-34; Luke 23:26-31; John 19:17)

21 They ☆pressed into service a passer-by coming from the country, Simon of Cyrene
(the father of Alexander and Rufus), to bear His cross.
22 Then they ☆brought Him to the place Golgotha, which is translated, Place of a Skull.
23 They tried to give Him wine mixed with myrrh; but He did not take it.
24 And they ☆crucified Him, and ☆divided up His garments among themselves, casting
lots for them *to decide* what each man should take.

15:25 Mark 15:33

15:26 Matt 27:37

15:29 Ps 22:7; 109:25; Matt 27:39; Mark 14:58; John 2:19

15:31 Matt 27:42; Luke 23:35

15:32 Matt 27:42; Mark 15:26; Matt 27:44; Mark 15:27; Luke 23:39-43

Jesus Is Placed on the Cross
(235/Matthew 27:35-44; Luke 23:32-43; John 19:18-27)

25 It was the [39]third hour when they crucified Him.
26 The inscription of the charge against Him read, "THE KING OF THE JEWS."
27 They ☆crucified two robbers with Him, one on His right and one on His left.
28 [[40]And the Scripture was fulfilled which says, "And He was numbered with transgressors."]
29 Those passing by were hurling abuse at Him, wagging their heads, and saying, "Ha!
You who *are going to* destroy the temple and rebuild it in three days,
30 save Yourself, and come down from the cross!"
31 In the same way the chief priests also, along with the scribes, were mocking *Him*
among themselves and saying, "He saved others; He cannot save Himself.
32 "Let *this* Christ, the King of Israel, now come down from the cross, so that we may
see and believe!" Those who were crucified with Him were also insulting Him.

37 Or *battalion* **38** Or *staff* (made of a reed) **39** I.e. 9 a.m. **40** Early mss do not contain this v

---

15:19 The soldiers were "kneeling and bowing before Him"; in other words, they mocked Jesus by pretending to worship him.

15:21 Colonies of Jews existed outside Judea. Simon had made a Passover pilgrimage to Jerusalem all the way from Cyrene in North Africa. His sons, Alexander and Rufus, are mentioned here probably because they became well known later in the early church (Romans 16:13).

15:24 Casting lots was a way of making a decision by chance, like throwing dice or drawing straws. The soldiers cast lots to decide who would receive Jesus' clothing. Roman soldiers had the right to take for themselves the clothing of those crucified. This act fulfilled the prophecy of Psalm 22:18.

15:25 Crucifixion was a feared and shameful form of execution. The victim was forced to carry his cross along the longest possible route to the crucifixion site as a warning to bystanders. There were several shapes for crosses and several different methods of crucifixion. Jesus was nailed to the cross; condemned men were sometimes tied to their crosses with ropes. In either case, death came by suffocation as the person lost strength and the weight of the body made breathing more and more difficult.

15:26 A sign stating the condemned man's crime was often placed on a cross as a warning. Because Jesus was never found guilty, the only accusation placed on his sign was the "crime" of being King of the Jews.

15:27 Luke records that one of these robbers repented before his death, and Jesus promised that criminal that he would be with him in Paradise (Luke 23:39–43).

15:31 Jesus could have saved himself, but he endured this suffering because of his love for us. He could have chosen not to take the pain and humiliation; he could have killed those who mocked him—but he suffered through it all because he loved even his enemies. We had a significant part in the drama that afternoon because our sins were on the cross too. Jesus died on that cross for us, and the penalty for our sins was paid by his death. The only adequate response we can make is to confess our sin and freely accept the fact that Jesus paid for it so we wouldn't have to. Don't insult God with indifference toward the greatest act of genuine love in history.

15:32 When James and John had asked Jesus for the places of honor next to him in his kingdom, Jesus had told them that they didn't know what they were asking (10:35–39). Here, as Jesus was preparing to inaugurate his kingdom through his death, the places on his right and on his left were taken by dying men—criminals. As Jesus explained to his two power-hungry disciples, a person who wants to be close to Jesus must be prepared to suffer and die as he himself was doing. The way to the kingdom is the way of the cross. If we want the glory of the kingdom, we must be willing to be united with the crucified Christ.

Jesus Dies on the Cross

(236/Matthew 27:45-56; Luke 23:44-49; John 19:28-37)

33 When the [41]sixth hour came, darkness fell over the whole land until the [42]ninth hour.
34 At the ninth hour Jesus cried out with a loud voice, "ELOI, ELOI, LAMA SABACH-
THANI?" which is translated, "MY GOD, MY GOD, WHY HAVE YOU FORSAKEN ME?"
35 When some of the bystanders heard it, they *began* saying, "Behold, He is calling for
Elijah."
36 Someone ran and filled a sponge with sour wine, put it on a reed, and gave Him a
drink, saying, "Let us see whether Elijah will come to take Him down."
37 And Jesus uttered a loud cry, and breathed His last.
38 And the veil of the temple was torn in two from top to bottom.
39 When the centurion, who was standing right in front of Him, saw the way He breathed
His last, he said, "Truly this man was the Son of God!"
40 There were also *some* women looking on from a distance, among whom *were* Mary
Magdalene, and Mary the mother of James the Less and Joses, and Salome.
41 When He was in Galilee, they used to follow Him and minister to Him; and *there
were* many other women who came up with Him to Jerusalem.

Jesus Is Laid in the Tomb

(237/Matthew 27:57-61; Luke 23:50-56; John 19:38-42)

42 When evening had already come, because it was the preparation day, that is, the
day before the Sabbath,
43 Joseph of Arimathea came, a prominent member of the Council, who himself was
waiting for the kingdom of God; and he gathered up courage and went in before Pilate,
and asked for the body of Jesus.
44 Pilate wondered if He was dead by this time, and summoning the centurion, he
questioned him as to whether He was already dead.
45 And ascertaining this from the centurion, he granted the body to Joseph.
46 Joseph bought a linen cloth, took Him down, wrapped Him in the linen cloth and
laid Him in a tomb which had been hewn out in the rock; and he rolled a stone against
the entrance of the tomb.

15:33 Matt 27:45f; Mark 15:25; Luke 23:44
15:34 Matt 27:45f; Mark 15:25; Luke 23:44; Ps 22:1; Matt 27:46
15:37 Matt 27:50; Luke 23:46; John 19:30
15:38 Ex 26:31-33; Matt 27:51; Luke 23:45
15:39 Matt 27:54; Mark 15:45; Luke 23:47
15:40 Matt 27:55f; Luke 23:49; John 19:25; Luke 19:3; Mark 16:1
15:41 Matt 27:55f
15:42 Matt 27:62
15:43 Matt 27:57; Luke 23:50, 51; Acts 13:50; 17:12; Matt 27:57; Luke 2:25, 38; 23:51; John 19:38; John 19:38
15:45 Mark 15:39

41 I.e. noon **42** I.e. 3 p.m.

15:34 Jesus did not ask this question in surprise or despair. He was quoting the first line of Psalm 22. The whole psalm is a prophecy expressing the deep agony of the Messiah's death for the world's sin. Jesus knew that he would be temporarily separated from God the moment he took upon himself the sins of the world. This separation was what he had dreaded as he prayed in Gethsemane. The physical agony was horrible, but the spiritual alienation from God was the ultimate torture.

15:37 Jesus' loud cry may have been his last words, "It is finished" (John 19:30).

15:38 A heavy veil hung in front of the temple room called the holy of holies, a place reserved by God for himself. Symbolically, the veil separated the holy God from sinful people. The room was entered only once a year, on the day of atonement, by the high priest as he made a sacrifice to gain forgiveness for the sins of all the people. When Jesus died, the veil was torn in two, showing that his death for our sins had opened up the way for us to approach our holy God. And it was torn from top to bottom, showing that *God* had opened the way. Read Hebrews 9 for a more complete explanation.

15:42ff The Sabbath began at sundown on Friday and ended at sundown on Saturday. Jesus died just a few hours before sundown on Friday. It was against Jewish law to do physical work or to travel on the Sabbath. It was also against Jewish law to let a dead body remain exposed overnight (Deuteronomy 21:23). Joseph came to bury Jesus' body before the Sabbath began. If Jesus had died on the Sabbath when Joseph was unavailable, his body would have been taken down by the Romans. Had the Romans taken Jesus' body, no Jews could have confirmed his death, and opponents could have disputed his resurrection.

15:42–43 After Jesus died on the cross, Joseph of Arimathea asked for his body and then sealed it in a new tomb. Although an honored member of the Jewish Council, Joseph was a secret disciple of Jesus. Not all the Jewish leaders hated Jesus. Joseph risked his reputation to give a proper burial to his Lord. It is frightening to risk one's reputation even for what is right. If your Christian witness endangers your reputation, remember Joseph. Today he is remembered with admiration in the Christian church. How many other members of the Jewish Council can you name?

15:44 Pilate was surprised that Jesus had died so quickly, so he asked an official to verify the report. Today, in an effort to deny the resurrection, there are those who say that Jesus didn't really die. His death, however, was confirmed by the centurion, Pilate, Joseph of Arimathea, the religious leaders, and the women who witnessed his burial. Jesus suffered actual physical death on the cross.

15:46 This tomb was probably a man-made cave hewn from a hill. It was large enough to walk into. Joseph wrapped Jesus' body, placed it in the tomb, and rolled a heavy stone across the entrance. The religious leaders also watched where Jesus was buried. They stationed guards by the tomb and sealed the stone to make sure that no one would steal Jesus' body and claim he had risen from the dead (Matthew 27:62–66).

15:47 Matt 27:56; Mark 15:40; 16:1

47 Mary Magdalene and Mary the *mother* of Joses were looking on *to see* where He
was laid.

Jesus Rises from the Dead

(239/Matthew 28:1-7; Luke 24:1-12; John 20:1-9)

16:1 Mark 15:47; Luke 23:56; John 19:39f

16 When the Sabbath was over, Mary Magdalene, and Mary the *mother* of James, and
Salome, bought spices, so that they might come and anoint Him.
2 Very early on the first day of the week, they ☆came to the tomb when the sun had
risen.
3 They were saying to one another, "Who will roll away the stone for us from the
entrance of the tomb?"

16:3 Matt 27:60; Mark 15:46; 16:4

4 Looking up, they ☆saw that the stone had been rolled away, although it was extremely
large.

16:5 John 20:11, 12; Mark 9:15

5 Entering the tomb, they saw a young man sitting at the right, wearing a white robe;
and they were amazed.

EVIDENCE THAT JESUS ACTUALLY DIED AND AROSE
This evidence demonstrates Jesus' uniqueness in history and proves that he is God's Son. No one else was able to predict his own resurrection and then accomplish it.

Proposed Explanations for Empty Tomb	*Evidence against These Explanations*	*References*
Jesus was only unconscious and later revived.	A Roman soldier told Pilate that Jesus was dead.	Mark 15:44–45
	The Roman soldiers did not break Jesus' legs, because he had already died, and one of them pierced Jesus' side with a spear.	John 19:32–34
	Joseph of Arimathea and Nicodemus wrapped Jesus' body and placed it in the tomb.	John 19:38–40
The women made a mistake and went to the wrong tomb.	Mary Magdalene and Mary the mother of Joses saw Jesus placed in the tomb.	Matthew 27:59–61 Mark 15:47 Luke 23:55
	On Sunday morning Peter and John also went to the same tomb.	John 20:3–9
Unknown thieves stole Jesus' body.	The tomb was sealed and guarded by Roman soldiers.	Matthew 27:65–66
The disciples stole Jesus' body.	The disciples were ready to die for their faith. Stealing Jesus' body would have been admitting that their faith was meaningless.	Acts 12:2
	The tomb was guarded and sealed	Matthew 27:66
The religious leaders stole Jesus' body to produce it later.	If the religious leaders had taken Jesus' body, they would have produced it to stop the rumors of his resurrection.	None

---

15:47 These women could do very little. They couldn't speak before the Council in Jesus' defense; they couldn't appeal to Pilate; they couldn't stand against the crowds; they couldn't overpower the Roman guards. But they did what they could. They stayed at the cross when the disciples had fled; they followed Jesus' body to its tomb; and they prepared spices for his body. Because these women used the opportunities they had, they were the first to witness the resurrection. God blessed their devotion and diligence. As believers, we should take advantage of the opportunities we have and do what we *can* for Christ, instead of worrying about what we *cannot* do.

16:1–2 The women purchased the spices on Saturday evening after the Sabbath had ended so they could go to the tomb early the next morning and anoint Jesus' body as a sign of love, devotion, and respect. Bringing spices to the tomb was like bringing flowers to a grave today.

16:4 The angels did not roll away the stone so Jesus could get out, but so others could get in and see for themselves that Jesus had indeed risen from the dead, just as he said.

16:5 Mark says that one angel met the women at the tomb, while Luke mentions two angels. These accounts are not contradictory. Each Gospel writer chose to highlight different details as he explained the same story, just as eyewitnesses to a news story each may highlight a different aspect of that event. Mark probably emphasized only the angel who spoke. The unique emphasis of each Gospel shows that the four accounts were written independently. This should give us confidence that all four are true and reliable.

6 And he ☆said to them, "Do not be amazed; you are looking for Jesus the Nazarene,
who has been crucified. He has risen; He is not here; behold, *here is* the place where they
laid Him.
7 "But go, tell His disciples and Peter, 'He is going ahead of you to Galilee; there you
will see Him, just as He told you.' "
8 They went out and fled from the tomb, for trembling and astonishment had gripped
them; and they said nothing to anyone, for they were afraid.

Jesus Appears to Mary Magdalene
(240/John 20:10-18)

9 [[43]Now after He had risen early on the first day of the week, He first appeared to
Mary Magdalene, from whom He had cast out seven demons.
10 She went and reported to those who had been with Him, while they were mourning
and weeping.
11 When they heard that He was alive and had been seen by her, they refused to believe it.

Jesus Appears to Two Believers Traveling on the Road
(243/Luke 24:13-35)

12 After that, He appeared in a different form to two of them while they were walking
along on their way to the country.
13 They went away and reported it to the others, but they did not believe them either.

Jesus Appears to the Disciples Including Thomas
(245/John 20:24-31)

14 Afterward He appeared to the eleven themselves as they were reclining *at the table;*
and He reproached them for their unbelief and hardness of heart, because they had not
believed those who had seen Him after He had risen.

Jesus Gives the Great Commission
(248/Matthew 28:16-20)

15 And He said to them, "Go into all the world and preach the gospel to all creation.
16 He who has believed and has been baptized shall be saved; but he who has disbelieved shall be condemned.

43 Later mss add vv 9-20

16:6 Mark 9:15; Mark 1:24; Matt 28:6; Luke 24:6

16:7 Matt 26:32; Mark 14:28

16:9 Matt 27:56; John 20:14

16:10 John 20:18

16:11 Matt 28:17; Mark 16:13, 14; Luke 24:11, 41; John 20:25

16:12 Mark 16:14; John 21:1, 14; Luke 24:13-35

16:13 Matt 28:17; Mark 16:11, 14; Luke 24:11, 41; John 20:25

16:14 Mark 16:12; John 21:1, 14; Luke 24:36; John 20:19, 26; 1 Cor 15:5; Matt 28:17; Mark 16:11, 13; Luke 24:11, 41; John 20:25

16:15 Matt 28:19; Acts 1:8

16:16 John 3:18, 36; Acts 16:31

16:6 The resurrection is vitally important for many reasons: (1) Jesus kept his promise to rise from the dead, so we can believe he will keep all his other promises. (2) The resurrection ensures that the ruler of God's eternal kingdom will be the living Christ, not just an idea, hope, or dream. (3) Christ's resurrection gives us the assurance that we also will be resurrected. (4) The power of God that brought Christ's body back from the dead is available to us to bring our morally and spiritually dead selves back to life so that we can change and grow (1 Corinthians 15:12–19). (5) The resurrection provides the substance of the church's witness to the world. We do not merely tell lessons from the life of a good teacher; we proclaim the reality of the resurrection of Jesus Christ.

16:7 The angel made special mention of Peter to show that, in spite of Peter's denials, Jesus had not denied and deserted him. Jesus had great responsibilities for Peter to fulfill in the church that was not yet born.

16:7 The angel told the disciples to meet Jesus in Galilee "as He told you" (see 14:28). This is where Jesus had called most of them and had said they would become "fishers of men" (Matthew 4:19), and it would be where this mission would be restated (John 21). But the disciples, filled with fear, remained behind locked doors in Jerusalem (John 20:19). Jesus met them first in Jerusalem (Luke 24:36) and later in Galilee (John 21). Then he returned to Jerusalem where he ascended into heaven from the Mount of Olives (Acts 1:12).

16:13 When the two finally realized who Jesus was, they rushed back to Jerusalem. It's not enough to read about Christ as a personality or to study his teachings. You must also believe he is God, trust him to save you, and accept him as Lord of your life. This is the difference between knowing Jesus and knowing about him. Only when you know Christ will you be motivated to share with others what he has done for you.

16:15 Jesus told his disciples to go into all the world, telling everyone that he had paid the penalty for sin and that those who believe in him can be forgiven and live eternally with God. Christian disciples today in all parts of the world are preaching this gospel to people who haven't heard about Christ. The driving power that carries missionaries around the world and sets Christ's church in motion is the faith that comes from the resurrection. Do you ever feel as though you don't have the skill or determination to be a witness for Christ? You must personally realize that Jesus rose from the dead and lives for you today. As you grow in your relationship with Christ, he will give you both the opportunities and the inner strength to tell his message.

16:16 It is not the water of baptism that saves, but God's grace accepted through faith in Christ. Because of Jesus' response to the criminal on the cross who died with him, we know it is possible to be saved without being baptized (Luke 23:43). Baptism alone, without faith, does not automatically bring a person to heaven. Those who refuse to believe will be condemned, regardless of whether or not they have been baptized.

16:17 Mark 9:38; Luke 10:17; Acts 5:16; 8:7; 16:18; 19:12; Acts 2:4; 10:46; 19:6; 1 Cor 12:10, 28, 30; 13:1; 14:2

16:18 Luke 10:19; Acts 28:3-5; Mark 5:23

16:19 Acts 1:3; Luke 9:51; 24:51; John 6:62; 20:17; Acts 1:2, 9-11; 1 Tim 3:16; Ps 110:1; Luke 22:69; Acts 7:55f; Rom 8:34; Eph 1:20; Col 3:1; Heb 1:3; 8:1; 10:12; 12:2; 1 Pet 3:22

17 "These signs will accompany those who have believed: in My name they will cast out
demons, they will speak with new tongues;
18 they will pick up serpents, and if they drink any deadly *poison*, it will not hurt them;
they will lay hands on the sick, and they will recover."

Jesus Ascends into Heaven
(250/Luke 4:50-53)

19 So then, when the Lord Jesus had spoken to them, He was received up into heaven
and sat down at the right hand of God.
20 And they went out and preached everywhere, while the Lord worked with them,
and confirmed the word by the signs that followed.]

[[44]*And they promptly reported all these instructions to Peter and his companions. And after that, Jesus Himself sent out through them from east to west the sacred and imperishable proclamation of eternal salvation.*]

44 A few late mss and versions contain this paragraph, usually after v 8; a few have it at the end of ch

16:18 There are times when God intervenes miraculously to protect his followers. Occasionally he gives them special powers. Paul handled a snake safely (Acts 28:5), and the disciples healed the sick (Matthew 10:1; Acts 3:7–8). This does not mean, however, that we should test God by putting ourselves in dangerous situations.

16:19 When Jesus ascended into heaven, his physical presence left the disciples (Acts 1:9). Jesus' sitting at God's right hand signifies the completion of his work, his authority as God, and his coronation as King.

16:20 Mark's Gospel emphasizes Christ's power as well as his servanthood. Jesus' life and teaching turn the world upside down. The world sees power as a way to gain control over others. But Jesus, with all authority and power in heaven and earth, chose to serve others. He held children in his arms, healed the sick, washed the disciples' feet, and died for the sins of the world. Following Jesus means receiving this same power to serve. As believers, we are called to be servants of Christ. As Christ served, so we are to serve.

L U K E

Herod the Great begins to rule 37 B.C. | Jesus is born 6/5 B.C. | Escape to Egypt 5/4 B.C. | Herod the Great dies 4 B.C. | Return to Nazareth 4/3 B.C. | Jesus visits temple as a boy A.D. 6/7

VITAL STATISTICS

PURPOSE:
To present an accurate account of the life of Christ and to present Christ as the perfect human and Savior

AUTHOR:
Luke—a doctor (Colossians 4:14), a Greek, and Gentile Christian. He is the only known Gentile author in the New Testament. Luke was a close friend and companion of Paul. He also wrote Acts, and the two books go together.

TO WHOM WRITTEN:
Theophilus ("one who loves God"), Gentiles, and people everywhere

DATE WRITTEN:
About A.D. 60

SETTING:
Luke wrote from Rome or possibly from Caesarea.

KEY VERSES:
"And Jesus said to him, 'Today salvation has come to this house, because he, too, is a son of Abraham. For the Son of Man has come to seek and to save that which was lost' " (19:9–10).

KEY PEOPLE:
Jesus, Elizabeth, Zacharias, John the Baptist, Mary, the disciples, Herod the Great, Pilate, Mary Magdalene

KEY PLACES:
Bethlehem, Galilee, Judea, Jerusalem

SPECIAL FEATURES:
This is the most comprehensive Gospel. The general vocabulary and diction show that the author was educated. He makes frequent references to illnesses and diagnoses. Luke stresses Jesus' relationships with people; emphasizes prayer, miracles, and angels; records inspired hymns of praise; and gives a prominent place to women. Most of 9:51—18:35 is not found in any other Gospel.

EVERY birth is a miracle, and every child is a gift from God. But nearly 20 centuries ago, there was the miracle of miracles. A baby was born, but he was the Son of God. The Gospels tell of this birth, but Dr. Luke, as though he were the attending physician, provides most of the details surrounding this awesome occasion. With a divine Father and human mother, Jesus entered history—God in the flesh.

Luke affirms Jesus' divinity, but the real emphasis of his book is on Jesus' humanity—Jesus, the Son of God, is also the Son of Man. As a doctor, Luke was a man of science, and as a Greek, he was a man of detail. It is not surprising, then, that he begins by outlining his extensive research and explaining that he is reporting the facts (1:1–4). Luke also was a close friend and traveling companion of Paul, so he could interview the other disciples, had access to other historical accounts, and was an eyewitness to the birth and growth of the early church. His Gospel and book of Acts are reliable, historical documents.

Luke's story begins with angels appearing to Zacharias and then to Mary, telling them of the upcoming births of their sons. From Zacharias and Elizabeth would come John the Baptist, who would prepare the way for Christ. And Mary would conceive a child by the Holy Spirit and bear Jesus, the Son of God. Soon after John's birth, Caesar Augustus declared a census, and so Mary and Joseph traveled to Bethlehem, the town of David, their ancient ancestor. There the child was born. Angels announced the joyous event to shepherds, who rushed to the manger. When the shepherds left, they were praising God and spreading the news. Eight days later, Jesus was circumcised and then dedicated to God in the temple, where Simeon and Anna confirmed Jesus' identity as the Savior, their Messiah.

Luke gives us a glimpse of Jesus at age 12—discussing theology with the Jewish teachers at the temple (2:41–52). Eighteen years later Jesus went out in the wilderness to be baptized by John the Baptist before beginning his public ministry (3:1–23). At this point, Luke traces Jesus' genealogy on his stepfather Joseph's side, through David and Abraham back to Adam, underscoring Jesus' identity as the Son of Man (3:23–38).

After the temptation (4:1–13), Jesus returned to Galilee to preach, teach, and heal (4:14ff). During this time, he began gathering his group of 12 disciples (5:1–11, 27–29). Later Jesus commissioned the disciples and sent them out to proclaim the kingdom of God. When they returned, Jesus revealed to them his mission, his true identity, and what it means to be his disciple (9:18–62). His mission would take him to Jerusalem (9:51–53), where he would be rejected, tried, and crucified.

While Jesus carried his own cross to Golgotha, some women in Jerusalem wept for him, but Jesus told them to weep for themselves and for their children (23:28). Luke's Gospel does not end in sadness, however. It concludes with the thrilling account of Jesus' resurrection from the dead, his appearances to the disciples, and his promise to send the Holy Spirit (24:1–53). Read Luke's beautifully written and accurate account of the life of Jesus, Son of Man and Son of God. Then praise God for sending the Savior—our risen and triumphant Lord—for all people.

Tiberius Caesar becomes emperor 14	John's ministry begins 26	Jesus begins his ministry 26/27	Jesus chooses twelve disciples 28	Jesus feeds 5,000 29	Jesus is crucified, rises again, and ascends 30

THE BLUEPRINT

A. BIRTH AND PREPARATION OF JESUS, THE SAVIOR (1:1—4:13)	From an infant who could do nothing on his own, Jesus grew to become completely able to fulfill his mission on earth. He was fully human, developing in all ways like us. Yet he remained fully God. He took no shortcuts and was not isolated from the pressures and temptations of life. There are no shortcuts for us either as we prepare for a life of service to God.
B. MESSAGE AND MINISTRY OF JESUS, THE SAVIOR (4:14—21:38) 1. Jesus' ministry in Galilee 2. Jesus' ministry on the way to Jerusalem 3. Jesus' ministry in Jerusalem	Jesus taught great crowds of people, especially through parables, which are stories that illustrate great truths. But only those with ears to hear will understand. We should pray that God's Spirit would help us understand the implications of these truths for our life so we can become more and more like Jesus.
C. DEATH AND RESURRECTION OF JESUS, THE SAVIOR (22:1—24:53)	The Savior of the world was arrested and executed. But death could not destroy him, and Jesus came back to life and ascended to heaven. In Luke's careful, historical account, we receive the facts about Jesus' resurrection. We must not only believe that these facts are true, but we must also trust Christ as our Savior. It is shortsighted to neglect the facts, but how sad it is to accept the facts and neglect the forgiveness that Jesus offers to each of us.

MEGATHEMES

THEME	EXPLANATION	IMPORTANCE
Jesus Christ, the Savior	Luke describes how God's Son entered human history. Jesus lived as the perfect example of a human. After a perfect ministry, he provided a perfect sacrifice for our sin so we could be saved.	Jesus is our perfect leader and Savior. He offers forgiveness to all who will accept him as Lord of their lives and believe that what he says is true.
History	Luke was a medical doctor and historian. He put great emphasis on dates and details, connecting Jesus to events and people in history.	Luke gives details so we can believe in the reliability of the history of Jesus' life. Even more important, we can believe with certainty that Jesus is God.
People	Jesus was deeply interested in people and relationships. He showed warm concern for his followers and friends—men, women, and children.	Jesus' love for people is good news for everyone. His message is for all people in every nation. Each one of us has an opportunity to respond to him in faith.
Compassion	As a perfect human, Jesus showed tender sympathy to the poor, the despised, the hurt, and the sinful. No one was rejected or ignored by him.	Jesus is more than a good teacher—he cares for you. Because of his deep love for you, he can satisfy your needs.
Holy Spirit	The Holy Spirit was present at Jesus' birth, baptism, ministry, and resurrection. As a perfect example for us, Jesus lived in dependence on the Holy Spirit.	The Holy Spirit was sent by God as confirmation of Jesus' authority. The Holy Spirit is given to enable people to live for Christ. By faith we can have the indwelling Holy Spirit's presence and power to witness and to serve.

KEY PLACES IN LUKE

The broken lines (—·—·) indicate modern boundaries.

Luke begins his account in the temple in Jerusalem, giving us the background for the birth of John the Baptist, then moves on to the town of Nazareth and the story of Mary, chosen to be Jesus' mother (1:26ff). As a result of Caesar's call for a census, Mary and Joseph had to travel to Bethlehem, where Jesus was born in fulfillment of prophecy (2:1ff). Jesus grew up in Nazareth and began his earthly ministry by being baptized by John (3:21–22) and tempted by Satan (4:1ff). Much of his ministry focused on Galilee: He set up his "home" in Capernaum (4:31ff), and from there he taught throughout the region (8:1ff). Later he visited Gerasa (also called Gadara), where he healed a demon-possessed man (8:36ff). He fed more than 5,000 people with one lunch on the shores of the Sea of Galilee near Bethsaida (9:10ff). Jesus always traveled to Jerusalem for the major festivals, and he enjoyed visiting friends in nearby Bethany (10:38ff). He healed 10 men with leprosy on the border between Galilee and Samaria (17:11) and helped a dishonest tax collector in Jericho turn his life around (19:1ff). The little villages of Bethphage and Bethany on the Mount of Olives were Jesus' resting places during his last days on earth. He was crucified outside Jerusalem's walls, but he would rise again. Two of Jesus' followers walking on the road leading to Emmaus were among the first to see the resurrected Christ (24:13ff).

A. BIRTH AND PREPARATION OF JESUS, THE SAVIOR (1:1—4:13)

Luke gives us the most detailed account of Jesus' birth. In describing Jesus' birth, childhood, and development, Luke lifts up the humanity of Jesus. Our Savior was the ideal human. Fully prepared, the ideal human was now ready to live the perfect life.

Luke's Purpose in Writing

(1)

1 Inasmuch as many have undertaken to compile an account of the things accomplished
among us,
2 just as they were handed down to us by those who from the beginning were eyewitnesses and servants of the [1]word,
3 it seemed fitting for me as well, having investigated everything carefully from the
beginning, to write *it* out for you in consecutive order, most excellent Theophilus;
4 so that you may know the exact truth about the things you have been taught.

An Angel Promises the Birth of John to Zacharias

(4)

5 In the days of Herod, king of Judea, there was a priest named Zacharias, of the division of [2]Abijah; and he had a wife [3]from the daughters of Aaron, and her name was
Elizabeth.
6 They were both righteous in the sight of God, walking blamelessly in all the commandments and requirements of the Lord.
7 But they had no child, because Elizabeth was barren, and they were both advanced
in years.
8 Now it happened *that* while he was performing his priestly service before God in
the *appointed* order of his division,
9 according to the custom of the priestly office, he was chosen by lot to enter the temple of the Lord and burn incense.

1 I.e. gospel **2** Gr *Abia* **3** I.e. of priestly descent

1:1 Rom 4:21; 14:5; Col 2:2; 4:12; 1 Thess 1:5; 2 Tim 4:17; Heb 6:11; 10:22

1:2 John 15:27; Acts 1:21f; 2 Pet 1:16; 1 John 1:1; Acts 26:16; 1 Cor 4:1; Heb 2:3; Mark 4:14; 16:20; Acts 8:4; 14:25; 16:6; 17:11

1:3 1 Tim 4:6; Acts 11:4; 18:23; Acts 23:26; 24:3; 26:25; Acts 1:1

1:4 Acts 18:25; Rom 2:18; 1 Cor 14:19; Gal 6:6

1:5 Matt 2:1; 1 Chr 24:10

1:6 Gen 7:1; Acts 2:25; 8:21; Phil 2:15; 3:6; 1 Thess 3:13

1:8 1 Chr 24:19; 2 Chr 8:14; 31:2

1:9 Ex 30:7f

1:1–2 Luke tells Jesus' story from Luke's unique perspective of a Gentile, a physician, and the first historian of the early church. Though not an eyewitness of Jesus' ministry, Luke nevertheless is concerned that eyewitness accounts be preserved accurately and that the foundations of Christian belief be transmitted intact to the next generation. In Luke's Gospel are many of Jesus' parables. In addition, more than any other Gospel, it gives specific instances of Jesus' concern for women.

1:1–4 There was a lot of interest in Jesus, and many people had written firsthand accounts about him. Luke may have used these accounts and all other available resources as material for an accurate and complete account of Jesus' life, teachings, and ministry. Because truth was important to Luke, he relied heavily on eyewitness accounts. Christianity doesn't say, "Close your eyes and believe," but rather, "Check it out for yourself." The Bible encourages you to investigate its claims thoroughly (John 1:46; 21:24; Acts 17:11–12), because your conclusion about Jesus is a life-and-death matter.

1:3 *Theophilus* means "one who loves God." The book of Acts, also written by Luke, is likewise addressed to Theophilus. This preface may be a general dedication to all Christian readers. Theophilus may have been Luke's patron who helped to finance the book's writing. More likely, Theophilus was a Roman acquaintance of Luke's with a strong interest in the new Christian religion.

1:3–4 As a medical doctor, Luke knew the importance of being thorough. He used his skills in observation and analysis to thoroughly investigate the stories about Jesus. His diagnosis? The gospel of Jesus Christ is true! You can read Luke's account of Jesus' life with confidence that it was written by a clear thinker and a thoughtful researcher. Because the gospel is founded on historical truth, our spiritual growth must involve careful, disciplined, and thorough investigation of God's Word so that we can understand how God has acted in history. If this kind of study is not part of your life, find a pastor, teacher, or even a book to help you get started and to guide you in this important part of Christian growth.

1:5 This was Herod the Great, confirmed by the Roman Senate as king of the Jews. Only half Jewish himself and eager to please his Roman superiors, Herod expanded and beautified the Jerusalem temple—but he placed a Roman eagle over the entrance. When he helped the Jews, it was for political purposes and not because he cared about their God. Herod the Great later ordered a massacre of infants in a futile attempt to kill the infant Jesus, whom some were calling the new "king of the Jews" (Matthew 2:16–18).

1:5 A Jewish priest was a minister of God who worked at the temple managing its upkeep, teaching the people the Scriptures, and directing the worship services. At this time there were about 20,000 priests throughout the country—far too many to minister in the temple at one time. Therefore the priests were divided into 24 separate groups of about 1,000 each, according to David's directions (1 Chronicles 24:3–19).

Zacharias was a member of the Abijah division, on duty this particular week. Each morning a priest was to enter the holy place in the temple and burn incense. Lots were cast to decide who would enter the sacred room, and one day the lot fell to Zacharias. But it was not by chance that Zacharias was on duty and that he was chosen that day to enter the holy place—perhaps a once-in-a-lifetime opportunity. God was guiding the events of history to prepare the way for Jesus to come to earth.

1:6 Zacharias and Elizabeth didn't merely go through the motions in following God's laws; they backed up their outward compliance with inward obedience. Unlike the religious leaders whom Jesus called hypocrites, Zacharias and Elizabeth did not stop with the letter of the law. Their obedience was from the heart, and that is why they are called "righteous in the sight of God."

1:9 Incense was burned in the temple twice daily. When the people saw the smoke from the burning incense, they prayed. The smoke drifting heavenward symbolized their prayers ascending to God's throne.

10 And the whole multitude of the people were in prayer outside at the hour of the
incense offering.
11 And an angel of the Lord appeared to him, standing to the right of the altar of incense.
12 Zacharias was troubled when he saw *the angel,* and fear gripped him.
13 But the angel said to him, "Do not be afraid, Zacharias, for your petition has been
heard, and your wife Elizabeth will bear you a son, and you will give him the name John.
14 "You will have joy and gladness, and many will rejoice at his birth.
15 "For he will be great in the sight of the Lord; and he will drink no wine or liquor, and
he will be filled with the Holy Spirit while yet in his mother's womb.
16 "And he will turn many of the sons of Israel back to the Lord their God.
17 "It is he who will go *as a forerunner* before Him in the spirit and power of Elijah, TO
TURN THE HEARTS OF THE FATHERS BACK TO THE CHILDREN, and the disobedient to
the attitude of the righteous, so as to make ready a people prepared for the Lord."
18 Zacharias said to the angel, "How will I know this *for certain?* For I am an old man
and my wife is advanced in years."
19 The angel answered and said to him, "I am Gabriel, who stands in the presence of
God, and I have been sent to speak to you and to bring you this good news.
20 "And behold, you shall be silent and unable to speak until the day when these things
take place, because you did not believe my words, which will be fulfilled in their proper
time."
21 The people were waiting for Zacharias, and were wondering at his delay in the
temple.
22 But when he came out, he was unable to speak to them; and they realized that he
had seen a vision in the temple; and he kept making signs to them, and remained mute.
23 When the days of his priestly service were ended, he went back home.
24 After these days Elizabeth his wife became pregnant, and she kept herself in seclu-
sion for five months, saying,

1:10 Lev 16:17
1:11 Luke 2:9; Acts 5:19
1:12 Luke 2:9
1:13 Matt 14:27; Luke 1:30; Luke 1:60, 63
1:15 Num 6:3; Judg 13:4; Matt 11:18; Luke 7:33
1:16 Matt 3:2, 6; Luke 3:3
1:17 Luke 1:76; Matt 11:14; Mal 4:6
1:18 Gen 17:17
1:19 Dan 8:16; 9:21; Luke 1:26; Matt 18:10
1:22 Luke 1:62

1:11–12 Angels are spirit beings who live in God's presence and do his will. Only two angels are mentioned by name in Scripture—Michael and Gabriel—but there are many who act as God's messengers. Here, Gabriel (1:19) delivered a special message to Zacharias. This was not a dream or a vision. The angel appeared in visible form and spoke audible words to the priest.

1:13 Zacharias, while burning incense on the altar, was also praying, perhaps for a son or for the coming of the Messiah. In either case, his prayer was answered. He would soon have a son, who would prepare the way for the Messiah. God answers prayer in his own way and in his own time. He worked in an "impossible" situation—Zacharias's wife was barren—to bring about the fulfillment of all the prophecies concerning the Messiah. If we want to have our prayers answered, we must be open to what God can do in impossible situations. And we must wait for God to work in his way, in his time.

1:13 *John* means "the LORD is gracious," and *Jesus* means "the LORD saves." Both names were prescribed by God, not chosen by human parents. Throughout the Gospels, God acts graciously and saves his people. He will not withhold salvation from anyone who sincerely comes to him.

1:15 John was set apart for special service to God. He may have been forbidden to drink wine as part of the Nazirite vow, an ancient vow of consecration to God (see Numbers 6:1–8). Samson (Judges 13) was under the Nazirite vow, and Samuel may have been also (1 Samuel 1:11).

1:15 This is Luke's first mention of the Holy Spirit, the third person of the Trinity; Luke refers to the Holy Spirit more than any other Gospel writer. Because Luke also wrote the book of Acts, we know he was thoroughly informed about the work of the Holy Spirit. Luke recognized and emphasized the Holy Spirit's work in directing the founding of Christianity and in guiding the early church. The presence of the Spirit is God's gift given to the entire church at Pentecost. Prior to that, God's Spirit was given to the faithful for special tasks. We need the Holy Spirit's help to do God's work effectively.

1:17 John's role was to be almost identical to that of an Old Testament prophet—to encourage people to turn away from sin and back to God. John is often compared to the great prophet Elijah, who was known for standing up to evil rulers (Malachi 4:5; Matthew 11:14; 17:10–13). See Elijah's Profile in 1 Kings 18.

1:17 In preparing people for the Messiah's arrival, John would do "heart transplants." He would take stony hearts and exchange them for hearts that were soft, pliable, trusting, and open to change. (See Ezekiel 11:19–20 and 36:25–29 for more on "heart transplants.") Are you as open to God as you should be? Or do you need a change of heart?

1:18 When told he would have a son, Zacharias doubted the angel's word. From Zacharias's human perspective, his doubts were understandable—but with God, anything is possible. Although Zacharias and Elizabeth were past the age of childbearing, God gave them a child. It is easy to doubt or misunderstand what God wants to do in our lives. Even God's people sometimes make the mistake of trusting their intellect or experience rather than God. When tempted to think that one of God's promises is impossible, remember his work throughout history. God's power is not confined by narrow perspective or bound by human limitations. Trust him completely.

1:20 Zacharias thought it incredible that he and his wife, at their old age, could conceive a child. But what God promises, he delivers. And God delivers *on time!* You can have complete confidence that God will keep his promises. Their fulfillments may not be the next day, but they will be "in their proper time." If you are waiting for God to answer some request or to fill some need, remain patient. No matter how impossible God's promises may seem, what he has said in his Word will come true at the right time.

1:21 The people were waiting outside for Zacharias to come out and pronounce the customary blessing upon them as found in Numbers 6:24–26.

1:25 Gen 30:23; Is 4:1; 25:8

25 "This is the way the Lord has dealt with me in the days when He looked *with favor*
upon *me,* to take away my disgrace among men."

An Angel Promises the Birth of Jesus to Mary
(5)

1:26 Luke 1:19; Matt 2:23

1:27 Matt 1:18; Matt 1:16, 20; Luke 2:4

26 Now in the sixth month the angel Gabriel was sent from God to a city in Galilee
called Nazareth,
27 to a virgin engaged to a man whose name was Joseph, of the descendants of David;
and the virgin's name was Mary.
28 And coming in, he said to her, "Greetings, favored one!
The Lord *is* with you."

ZACHARIAS

Zacharias was told before anyone else that God was setting in motion his own visit to earth. Zacharias and his wife, Elizabeth, were known for their personal holiness. They were well suited to doing a special work for God. But they shared the pain of not having children, and in Jewish culture this was considered not having God's blessing. Zacharias and Elizabeth were old, and they had stopped even asking for children.

This trip to the temple in Jerusalem for Zacharias's turn at duty had included an unexpected blessing. Zacharias was chosen to be the priest who would enter the holy place to offer incense to God for the people. Suddenly, much to his surprise and terror, he found himself face to face with an angel. The angel's message was too good to be true! But Zacharias did not respond to the news of the coming Savior as much as he expressed doubts about his own ability to father the child the angel promised him. His age spoke more loudly than God's promise. As a result, God prevented Zacharias from speaking until the promise became reality.

The record of the prayer in Luke 1 is our last glimpse of Zacharias. Like so many of God's most faithful servants, he passed quietly from the scene once his part was done. He becomes our hero for those times when we doubt God and yet are willing to obey. We gain hope from Zacharias's story that God can do great things through anyone who is available to him.

Strengths and accomplishments:
- Known as a righteous man
- Was a priest before God
- One of the few people to be directly addressed by an angel
- Fathered John the Baptist

Weakness and mistake:
- Momentarily doubted the angel's promise of a son because of his own old age

Lessons from his life:
- Physical limitations do not limit God
- God accomplishes his will, sometimes in unexpected ways

Vital statistics:
- Occupation: Priest
- Relatives: Wife: Elizabeth. Son: John the Baptist

Key verses:
"They were both righteous in the sight of God, walking blamelessly in all the commandments and requirements of the Lord. But they had no child, because Elizabeth was barren, and they were both advanced in years" (Luke 1:6–7).

Zacharias's story is told in Luke 1.

1:25 Zacharias and Elizabeth were both faithful people, and yet they were suffering. Some Jews at that time did not believe in a bodily resurrection, so their hope of immortality was in their children. In addition, children cared for their parents in their old age and added to the family's financial security and social status. Children were considered a blessing, and childlessness was seen as a curse. Zacharias and Elizabeth had been childless for many years, and at this time they were too old to expect any change in their situation. They felt humiliated and hopeless. But God was waiting for the right time to encourage them and take away their disgrace.

1:26 Gabriel appeared not only to Zacharias and to Mary but also to the prophet Daniel more than 500 years earlier (Daniel 8:15–17; 9:21). Each time Gabriel appeared, he brought important messages from God.

1:26 Nazareth, Joseph's and Mary's hometown, was a long way from Jerusalem, the center of Jewish life and worship. Located on a major trade route, Nazareth was frequently visited by Gentile merchants and Roman soldiers. It was known for its independent and aloof attitude. Jesus was born in Bethlehem but grew up in Nazareth. Nevertheless, the people of Nazareth would reject him as the Messiah (4:22–30).

1:27–28 Mary was young, poor, female—all characteristics that, to the people of her day, would make her seem unusable by God for any major task. But God chose Mary for one of the most important acts of obedience he has ever demanded of anyone. You may feel that your ability, experience, or education makes you an unlikely candidate for God's service. Don't limit God's choices. He can use you if you trust him.

29 But she was very perplexed at *this* statement, and kept pondering what kind of salutation this was.
30 The angel said to her, "Do not be afraid, Mary; for you have found favor with God.
31 "And behold, you will conceive in your womb and bear a son, and you shall name
Him Jesus.
32 "He will be great and will be called the Son of the Most High; and the Lord God will
give Him the throne of His father David;
33 and He will reign over the house of Jacob forever, and His kingdom will have
no end."
34 Mary said to the angel, "How can this be, since I am a virgin?"
35 The angel answered and said to her, "The Holy Spirit will come upon you, and the
power of the Most High will overshadow you; and for that reason the holy Child shall be
called the Son of God.
36 "And behold, even your relative Elizabeth has also conceived a son in her old age;
and she who was called barren is now in her sixth month.
37 "For nothing will be impossible with God."
38 And Mary said, "Behold, the [4]bondslave of the Lord; may it be done to me according to your word." And the angel departed from her.

1:29 Luke 1:12
1:30 Matt 14:27; Luke 1:13
1:31 Is 7:14; Matt 1:21, 25; Luke 2:21
1:32 Mark 5:7; Luke 1:35, 76; 6:35; Acts 7:48; 2 Sam 7:12, 13, 16; Is 9:7
1:33 Matt 1:1; 2 Sam 7:13, 16; Ps 89:36, 37; Dan 2:44; 7:14, 18, 27; Matt 28:18
1:35 Matt 1:18; Luke 1:32; Mark 1:24; Matt 4:3; John 1:34, 49; 20:31
1:37 Gen 18:14; Jer 32:17; Matt 19:26

Mary Visits Elizabeth
(6)

39 Now at this time Mary arose and went in a hurry to the hill country, to a city of
Judah,
40 and entered the house of Zacharias and greeted Elizabeth.
41 When Elizabeth heard Mary's greeting, the baby leaped in her womb; and Elizabeth was filled with the Holy Spirit.
42 And she cried out with a loud voice and said, "Blessed *are* you among women, and
blessed *is* the fruit of your womb!

1:39 Josh 20:7; 21:11; Luke 1:65
1:41 Luke 1:67; Acts 2:4; 4:8; 9:17

4 I.e. female slave

1:30–31 God's favor does not automatically bring instant success or fame. His blessing on Mary, the honor of being the mother of the Messiah, would lead to much pain: Her peers would ridicule her; her fiancé would come close to leaving her; her son would be rejected and murdered. But through her son would come the world's only hope, and this is why Mary has been praised by countless generations as the young girl who "found favor with God." Her submission was part of God's plan to bring about our salvation. If sorrow weighs you down and dims your hope, think of Mary and wait patiently for God to finish working out his plan.

1:31–33 *Jesus*, a Greek form of the Hebrew name *Joshua*, was a common name meaning "the LORD saves." Just as Joshua had led Israel into the promised land (see Joshua 1:1–2), so Jesus would lead his people into eternal life. The symbolism of his name was not lost on the people of his day, who took names seriously and saw them as a source of power. In Jesus' name people were healed, demons were banished, and sins were forgiven.

1:32–33 Centuries earlier, God had promised David that David's kingdom would last forever (2 Samuel 7:16). This promise was fulfilled in the coming of Jesus, a direct descendant of David, whose reign will continue throughout eternity.

1:34 The birth of Jesus to a virgin is a miracle that many people find hard to believe. These three facts can aid our faith: (1) Luke was a medical doctor, and he knew perfectly well how babies are made. It would have been just as hard for him to believe in a virgin birth as it is for us, and yet he reports it as fact. (2) Luke was a painstaking researcher who based his Gospel on eyewitness accounts. Tradition holds that he talked with Mary about the events he recorded in the first two chapters. This is Mary's story, not a fictional invention. (3) Christians and Jews, who worship God as the Creator of the universe, should believe that God has the power to create a child in a virgin's womb.

1:35 Jesus was born without the sin that entered the world through Adam. He was born holy, just as Adam was created sinless. In contrast to Adam, who disobeyed God, Jesus obeyed God and was thus able to face sin's consequences in our place and make us acceptable to God (Romans 5:14–19).

1:38 A young unmarried girl who became pregnant risked disaster. Unless the father of the child agreed to marry her, she would probably remain unmarried for life. If her own father rejected her, she could be forced into begging or prostitution in order to earn her living. And Mary, with her story about being made pregnant by the Holy Spirit, risked being considered crazy as well. Still Mary said, despite the possible risks, "May it be done to me according to your word." When Mary said that, she didn't know about the tremendous opportunity she would have. She only knew that God was asking her to serve him, and she willingly obeyed. Don't wait to see the bottom line before offering your life to God. Offer yourself willingly, even when the outcome seems disastrous.

1:38 God's announcement of a child to be born was met with various responses throughout Scripture. Sarah, Abraham's wife, laughed (Genesis 18:9–15). Zacharias doubted (Luke 1:18). By contrast, Mary submitted. She believed the angel's words and agreed to bear the child, even under humanly impossible circumstances. God is able to do the impossible. Our response to his demands should not be laughter, or doubt, but willing acceptance.

1:41–43 Apparently the Holy Spirit told Elizabeth that Mary's child was the Messiah because Elizabeth called her young relative "the mother of my Lord" as she greeted her. As Mary rushed off to visit her relative, she must have been wondering if the events of the last few days were real. Elizabeth's greeting must have strengthened her faith. Mary's pregnancy may have seemed impossible, but her wise relative believed in the Lord's faithfulness and rejoiced in Mary's blessed condition.

1:42–43 Even though she herself was pregnant with a long-awaited son, Elizabeth could have envied Mary, whose son would be even greater than her own. Instead she was filled with joy that the mother of her Lord would visit her. Have you ever envied people

1:43 Luke 2:11
1:45 Luke 1:20, 48
1:46 1 Sam 2:1-10; Ps 34:2f
1:47 Ps 35:9; Hab 3:18; 1 Tim 1:1; 2:3; Titus 1:3; 2:10; 3:4; Jude 25
1:48 Ps 138:6; Luke 1:45
1:50 Ps 103:17
1:51 Ps 98:1; 118:15
1:52 Job 5:11
1:53 Ps 107:9
1:55 Gen 17:19; Ps 132:11; Gal 3:16; Gen 17:7

43 "And how has it *happened* to me, that the mother of my Lord would come to me?
44 "For behold, when the sound of your greeting reached my ears, the baby leaped in
my womb for joy.
45 "And blessed *is* she who believed that there would be a fulfillment of what had been
spoken to her by the Lord."
46 And Mary said:
"My soul exalts the Lord,
47 And my spirit has rejoiced in God my Savior.
48 "For He has had regard for the humble state of His bondslave;
For behold, from this time on all generations will count me blessed.
49 "For the Mighty One has done great things for me;
And holy is His name.
50 "AND HIS MERCY IS UPON GENERATION AFTER GENERATION
TOWARD THOSE WHO FEAR HIM.
51 "He has done mighty deeds with His arm;
He has scattered *those who were* proud in the thoughts of their heart.
52 "He has brought down rulers from *their* thrones,
And has exalted those who were humble.
53 "HE HAS FILLED THE HUNGRY WITH GOOD THINGS;
And sent away the rich empty-handed.
54 "He has given help to Israel His servant,
In remembrance of His mercy,
55 As He spoke to our fathers,
To Abraham and his descendants forever."
56 And Mary stayed with her about three months, and *then* returned to her home.

GOD'S UNUSUAL METHODS
One of the best ways to understand God's willingness to communicate to people is to note the various methods, some of them quite unexpected, that he has used to give his message. Following is a sample of his methods and the people he contacted.

Person/Group	*Method*	*Reference*
Jacob, Zacharias, Mary, shepherds	Angels	Genesis 32:22–32 Luke 1:13, 30; 2:10
Jacob, Joseph, a baker, a cupbearer, Pharaoh, Isaiah, Joseph, the magi	Dreams	Genesis 28:10–22; 37:5–10; 40:5; 41:7–8 Isaiah 1:1 Matthew 1:20; 2:12–13
Belshazzar	Writing on the wall	Daniel 5:5–9
Balaam	Talking donkey	Numbers 22:21–35
People of Israel	Pillar of cloud and fire	Exodus 13:21–22
Jonah	Being swallowed by a fish	Jonah 2
Abraham, Moses, Jesus at his baptism, Paul	Verbally	Genesis 12:1–4 Exodus 7:8 Matthew 3:13–17 Acts 18:9
Moses	Fire	Exodus 3:2
Us	God's Son	Hebrews 1:1–2

whom God has apparently singled out for special blessing? A cure for jealousy is to rejoice with those people, realizing that God uses his people in ways best suited to his purpose.

1:46–55 This song is often called the *Magnificat*, the first word in the Latin translation of this passage. Mary's song has often been used as the basis for choral music and hymns. Like Hannah, the mother of Samuel (1 Samuel 2:1–10), Mary glorified God in song for what he was going to do for the world through her. Notice that in both songs, God is pictured as a champion of the poor, the oppressed, and the despised.

1:48 When Mary said, "From this time on all generations will count me blessed," was she being proud? No, she was recognizing and accepting the gift God had given her. If Mary had denied her incredible position, she would have been throwing God's blessing back at him. Pride is refusing to accept God's gifts or taking credit for what God has done; humility is accepting the gifts and using them to praise and serve God. Don't deny, belittle, or ignore your gifts. Thank God for them and use them to his glory.

1:54–55 God kept his promise to Abraham to be merciful to God's people forever (Genesis 22:16–18). Christ's birth fulfilled the promise, and Mary understood this. She was not surprised when her special son eventually announced that he was the Messiah. She had known Jesus' mission from before his birth. Some of God's promises to Israel are found in 2 Samuel 22:50–51; Psalms 89:2–4; 103:17–18; Micah 7:18–20.

1:56 Because travel was not easy, long visits were customary. Mary must have been a great help to Elizabeth, who was experiencing the discomforts of a first pregnancy in old age.

John the Baptist Is Born
(7)

57 Now the time had come for Elizabeth to give birth, and she gave birth to a son.
58 Her neighbors and her relatives heard that the Lord had displayed His great mercy
toward her; and they were rejoicing with her.
59 And it happened that on the eighth day they came to circumcise the child, and they
were going to call him Zacharias, after his father.
60 But his mother answered and said, "No indeed; but he shall be called John."
61 And they said to her, "There is no one among your relatives who is called by that
name."
62 And they made signs to his father, as to what he wanted him called.
63 And he asked for a tablet and wrote as follows, "His name is John." And they were
all astonished.
64 And at once his mouth was opened and his tongue *loosed,* and he *began* to speak in
praise of God.
65 Fear came on all those living around them; and all these matters were being talked
about in all the hill country of Judea.
66 All who heard them kept them in mind, saying, "What then will this child *turn out to*
be?" For the hand of the Lord was certainly with him.
67 And his father Zacharias was filled with the Holy Spirit, and prophesied, saying:
68 "Blessed *be* the Lord God of Israel,
For He has visited us and accomplished redemption for His people,
69 And has raised up a horn of salvation for us
In the house of David His servant—
70 As He spoke by the mouth of His holy prophets from of old—
71 Salvation FROM OUR ENEMIES,
And FROM THE HAND OF ALL WHO HATE US;
72 To show mercy toward our fathers,
And to remember His holy covenant,
73 The oath which He swore to Abraham our father,
74 To grant us that we, being rescued from the hand of our enemies,
Might serve Him without fear,
75 In holiness and righteousness before Him all our days.
76 "And you, child, will be called the prophet of the Most High;
For you will go on BEFORE THE LORD TO PREPARE HIS WAYS;
77 To give to His people *the* knowledge of salvation
By the forgiveness of their sins,
78 Because of the tender mercy of our God,
With which the Sunrise from on high will visit us,
79 TO SHINE UPON THOSE WHO SIT IN DARKNESS AND THE SHADOW OF DEATH,
To guide our feet into the way of peace."

1:58 Gen 19:19

1:59 Gen 17:12; Lev 12:3; Luke 2:21; Phil 3:5

1:62 Luke 1:22

1:63 Luke 1:13, 60

1:66 Acts 11:21

1:67 Luke 1:41; Acts 2:4, 8; 9:17; Joel 2:28

1:68 1 Kin 1:48; Ps 41:13; 72:18; 106:48; Luke 1:71; 2:38; Heb 9:12

1:69 1 Sam 2:1, 10; Ps 18:2; 89:17; 132:17; Ezek 29:21; Matt 1:1

1:70 Rom 1:2; Acts 3:21

1:71 Ps 106:10

1:72 Mic 7:20; Ps 105:8f, 42; 106:45

1:73 Gen 22:16ff; Heb 6:13

1:75 Eph 4:24

1:76 Luke 1:32; Mal 3:1; Matt 11:10; Mark 1:2; Luke 7:27

1:77 Jer 31:34; Mark 1:4

1:78 Mal 4:2; Eph 5:14; 2 Pet 1:19

1:79 Is 9:2; Is 59:8; Matt 4:16

1:59 The circumcision ceremony was an important event to the family of a Jewish baby boy. God commanded circumcision when he was beginning to form his holy nation (Genesis 17:4–14), and he reaffirmed it through Moses (Leviticus 12:1–3). This ceremony was a time of joy when friends and family members celebrated the baby's becoming part of God's covenant nation.

1:59 Family lines and family names were important to the Jews. The people naturally assumed the child would receive Zacharias's name or at least a family name. Thus they were surprised that both Elizabeth and Zacharias wanted to name the boy John, as the angel had told them to do (see 1:13).

1:62 Zacharias's relatives talked to him by signs, because he was apparently deaf as well as speechless and had not heard what his wife had said.

1:67–79 Zacharias praised God with his first words after months of silence. In a song that is often called the *Benedictus* after the first words in the Latin translation of this passage, Zacharias prophesied the coming of a Savior who would redeem his people, and he predicted that his son John would prepare the Messiah's way. All the Old Testament prophecies were coming true—no wonder Zacharias praised God! The Messiah would come in Zacharias's lifetime, and his son had been chosen to pave the way.

1:71 The Jews were eagerly awaiting the Messiah, but they thought he would come to save them from the powerful Roman empire. They were ready for a military Savior, but not for a peaceful Messiah who would conquer sin.

1:72–73 This was God's promise to Abraham to bless all peoples through him (see Genesis 12:3). It would be fulfilled through the Messiah, Abraham's descendant.

1:76 Zacharias had just recalled hundreds of years of God's sovereign work in history, beginning with Abraham and going on into eternity. Then, in tender contrast, he personalized the story. His son had been chosen for a key role in the drama of the ages. Although God has unlimited power, he chooses to work through frail humans who begin as helpless babies. Don't minimize what God can do through those who are faithful to him.

1:80 Luke 2:40

80 And the child continued to grow and to become strong in spirit, and he lived in the deserts until the day of his public appearance to Israel.

Jesus Is Born in Bethlehem
(9)

2:1 Matt 22:17; Luke 3:1; Matt 24:14
2:2 Matt 4:24
2:4 Luke 1:27
2:7 Matt 1:25

2 Now in those days a decree went out from Caesar Augustus, that a census be taken
of all [5]the inhabited earth.
2 This was the first census taken while [6]Quirinius was governor of Syria.
3 And everyone was on his way to register for the census, each to his own city.
4 Joseph also went up from Galilee, from the city of Nazareth, to Judea, to the city of
David which is called Bethlehem, because he was of the house and family of David,
5 in order to register along with Mary, who was engaged to him, and was with child.
6 While they were there, the days were completed for her to give birth.
7 And she gave birth to her firstborn son; and she wrapped Him in cloths, and laid
Him in a manger, because there was no room for them in the inn.

5 I.e. the Roman empire **6** Gr *Kyrenios*

DOUBTERS IN THE BIBLE

Doubter	*Doubtful Moment*	*Reference*
Abraham	When God told him he would be a father in old age	Genesis 17:17
Sarah	When she heard she would be a mother in old age	Genesis 18:12
Moses	When God told him to return to Egypt to lead the people	Exodus 3:10–15
Israelites	Whenever they faced difficulties in the wilderness	Exodus 16:1–3
Gideon	When told he would be a judge and leader	Judges 6:14–23
Zacharias	When told he would be a father in old age	Luke 1:18
Thomas	When told Jesus had risen from the dead	John 20:24–25

Many of the people God used to accomplish great things started out as real doubters. With all of them, God showed great patience. Honest doubt was not a bad starting point as long as they didn't stay there. How great a part does doubt have in your willingness to trust God?

1:80 Why did John live out in the desert? Prophets used the isolation of the uninhabited desert to enhance their spiritual growth and to focus their message on God. By being in the desert, John remained separate from the economic and political powers so that he could aim his message against them. He also remained separate from the hypocritical religious leaders of his day. His message was different from theirs, and his life proved it.

2:1 Luke is the only Gospel writer who related the events he recorded to world history. His account was addressed to a predominantly Greek audience that would have been interested in and familiar with the political situation. Palestine was under the rule of the Roman empire; Emperor Caesar Augustus, the first Roman emperor, was in charge. The Roman rulers, considered to be like gods, stood in contrast to the tiny baby in a manger who was truly God in the flesh.

2:1 A Roman census was taken to aid military conscription or tax collection. The Jews didn't have to serve in the Roman army, but they could not avoid paying taxes. Augustus's decree went out in God's perfect timing and according to God's perfect plan to bring his Son into the world.

2:3–6 The government forced Joseph to make a long trip just to pay his taxes. His fiancée, who had to go with him, was going to have a baby any moment. But when they arrived in Bethlehem, they couldn't even find a place to stay. When we do God's will, we are not guaranteed a comfortable life. But we are promised that everything, even our discomfort, has meaning in God's plan.

2:4 God controls all history. By the decree of Emperor Augustus, Jesus was born in the very town prophesied for his birth (Micah 5:2), even though his parents did not live there.

2:4 Joseph and Mary were both descendants of David. The Old Testament is filled with prophecies that the Messiah would be born in David's royal line (see, for example, Isaiah 11:1; Jeremiah 33:15; Ezekiel 37:24; Hosea 3:5).

2:7 Bands of cloth were used to keep a baby warm and give it a sense of security. These cloths were believed to protect its internal organs. The custom of wrapping infants this way is still practiced in many Mideastern countries.

2:7 This mention of the manger is the basis for the traditional belief that Jesus was born in a stable. Stables were often caves with feeding troughs (mangers) carved into the rock walls. Despite popular Christmas card pictures, the surroundings were dark and dirty. This was not the atmosphere the Jews expected as the birthplace of the Messiah King. They thought their promised Messiah would be born in royal surroundings. We should not limit God by our expectations. He is at work wherever he is needed in our sin-darkened and dirty world.

2:7 Although our first picture of Jesus is as a baby in a manger, it must not be our last. The Christ-child in the manger has been made into a beautiful Christmas scene, but we cannot leave him there. This tiny, helpless baby lived an amazing life, died for us, ascended to heaven, and will come back to this earth as King of kings. Christ will rule the world and judge all people according to their decisions about him. Do you still picture Jesus as a baby in a manger—or is he your Lord? Make sure you don't underestimate Jesus. Let him grow up in your life.

Shepherds Visit Jesus
(10)
8 In the same region there were *some* shepherds staying out in the fields and keeping
watch over their flock by night.
9 And an angel of the Lord suddenly stood before them, and the glory of the Lord
shone around them; and they were terribly frightened.
10 But the angel said to them, "Do not be afraid; for behold, I bring you good news of
great joy which will be for all the people;
11 for today in the city of David there has been born for you a Savior, who is [7]Christ
the Lord.
12 "This *will be* a sign for you: you will find a baby wrapped in cloths and lying in a
manger."
13 And suddenly there appeared with the angel a multitude of the heavenly host praising God and saying,
14 "Glory to God in the highest,
And on earth peace among men [8]with whom He is pleased."
15 When the angels had gone away from them into heaven, the shepherds *began* saying to one another, "Let us go straight to Bethlehem then, and see this thing that has
happened which the Lord has made known to us."
16 So they came in a hurry and found their way to Mary and Joseph, and the baby as
He lay in the manger.
17 When they had seen this, they made known the statement which had been told them
about this Child.
18 And all who heard it wondered at the things which were told them by the shepherds.
19 But Mary treasured all these things, pondering them in her heart.
20 The shepherds went back, glorifying and praising God for all that they had heard
and seen, just as had been told them.

2:9 Luke 1:11; Acts 5:19; Luke 24:4; Acts 12:7
2:10 Matt 14:27
2:11 Matt 1:21; John 4:42; Acts 5:31; Matt 1:16; 16:16, 20; John 11:27; Luke 1:43; Acts 2:36; 10:36
2:12 1 Sam 2:34; 2 Kin 19:29; 20:8f; Is 7:11, 14
2:14 Matt 21:9; Luke 19:38; Luke 3:22; Eph 1:9; Phil 2:13
2:19 Luke 2:51
2:20 Matt 9:8

Mary And Joseph Bring Jesus to the Temple
(11)
21 And when eight days had passed, before His circumcision, His name was *then* called
Jesus, the name given by the angel before He was conceived in the womb.

2:21 Gen 17:12; Lev 12:3; Luke 1:59; Matt 1:21, 25; Luke 1:31

7 I.e. Messiah 8 Lit *of good pleasure;* or *of good will*

2:8 God continued to reveal his Son, but not to those we might expect. Luke records that Jesus' birth was announced to shepherds in the fields. These may have been the shepherds who supplied the lambs for the temple sacrifices that were performed for the forgiveness of sin. Here the angels invited these shepherds to greet the Lamb of God (John 1:36), who would take away the sins of the whole world forever.

2:8–15 What a birth announcement! The shepherds were terrified, but their fear turned to joy as the angels announced the Messiah's birth. First the shepherds ran to see the baby; then they spread the word. Jesus is *your* Messiah, *your* Savior. Do you look forward to meeting him in prayer and in his Word each day? Have you discovered a Lord so wonderful that you can't help sharing your joy with your friends?

2:9–10 The greatest event in history had just happened! The Messiah had been born! For ages the Jews had waited for this, and when it finally occurred, the announcement came to humble shepherds. The Good News about Jesus is that he comes to all, including the plain and the ordinary. He comes to anyone with a heart humble enough to accept him. Whoever you are, whatever you do, you can have Jesus in your life. Don't think you need extraordinary qualifications—he accepts you as you are.

2:11–14 Some of the Jews were waiting for a savior to deliver them from Roman rule; others hoped the Christ (Messiah) would deliver them from physical ailments. But Jesus, while healing their illnesses and establishing a spiritual kingdom, delivered them from sin. His work is more far-reaching than anyone could imagine. Christ paid the price for sin and opened the way to peace with God. He offers us more than temporary political or physical changes—he offers us new hearts that will last for eternity.

THE JOURNEY TO BETHLEHEM
Caesar's decree for a census of the entire Roman empire made it necessary for Joseph and Mary to leave their hometown, Nazareth, and journey the 70 miles to the Judean village of Bethlehem.

2:14 The story of Jesus' birth resounds with music that has inspired composers for 2,000 years. The angels' song is an all-time favorite. Often called the *Gloria* after its first word in the Latin translation, it is the basis of modern choral works, traditional Christmas carols, and ancient liturgical chants.

2:21–24 Jewish families went through several ceremonies soon after a baby's birth: (1) *Circumcision.* Every boy was circumcised

2:22 Lev 12:6-8
2:23 Ex 13:2, 12; Num 3:13; 8:17
2:24 Lev 5:11; 12:8
2:25 Luke 1:6; Mark 15:43; Luke 2:38; 23:51
2:26 Matt 2:12; Ps 89:48; John 8:51; Heb 11:5
2:29 Luke 2:26
2:30 Ps 119:166, 174; Is 52:10; Luke 3:6
2:32 Is 9:2; 42:6; 49:6, 9; 51:4; 60:1-3; Matt 4:16; Acts 13:47; 26:23
2:33 Matt 12:46

22 And when the days for their purification according to the law of Moses were completed, they brought Him up to Jerusalem to present Him to the Lord
23 (as it is written in the Law of the Lord, "EVERY *firstborn* MALE THAT OPENS THE
WOMB SHALL BE CALLED HOLY TO THE LORD"),
24 and to offer a sacrifice according to what was said in the Law of the Lord, "A PAIR
OF TURTLEDOVES OR TWO YOUNG PIGEONS."
25 And there was a man in Jerusalem whose name was Simeon; and this man was
righteous and devout, looking for the consolation of Israel; and the Holy Spirit was upon
him.
26 And it had been revealed to him by the Holy Spirit that he would not see death before
he had seen the Lord's Christ.
27 And he came in the Spirit into the temple; and when the parents brought in the child
Jesus, to carry out for Him the custom of the Law,
28 then he took Him into his arms, and blessed God, and said,
29 "Now Lord, You are releasing Your bond-servant to depart in peace,
According to Your word;
30 For my eyes have seen Your salvation,
31 Which You have prepared in the presence of all peoples,
32 A LIGHT OF REVELATION TO THE GENTILES,
And the glory of Your people Israel."
33 And His father and mother were amazed at the things which were being said
about Him.

TO FEAR OR NOT TO FEAR

Person	*Reference*
Abraham	Genesis 15:1
Moses	Numbers 21:34; Deuteronomy 3:2
Joshua	Joshua 8:1
Jeremiah	Lamentations 3:57
Daniel	Daniel 10:12, 19
Zacharias	Luke 1:13
Mary	Luke 1:30
Shepherds	Luke 2:10
Peter	Luke 5:10
Paul	Acts 27:23–24
John	Revelation 1:17–18

People in the Bible who were confronted by God or his angels all had one consistent response—fear. To each of them, God's response was always the same—don't be afraid. As soon as they sensed that God accepted them and wanted to communicate with them, their fear subsided. He had given them freedom to be his friends. Has he given you the same freedom?

and named on the eighth day after birth (Leviticus 12:3; Luke 1:59–60). Circumcision symbolized the Jews' separation from Gentiles and their unique relationship with God (see the second note on 1:59). (2) *Redemption of the firstborn.* A firstborn son was presented to God one month after birth (Exodus 13:2, 11–16; Numbers 18:15–16). The ceremony included buying back—"redeeming"—the child from God through an offering. Thus the parents acknowledged that the child belonged to God, who alone has the power to give life. (3) *Purfication of the mother.* For 40 days after the birth of a son and 80 days after the birth of a daughter, the mother was ceremonially unclean and could not enter the temple. At the end of her time of separation, the parents were to bring a lamb for a burnt offering and a dove or pigeon for a sin offering. The priest would sacrifice these animals and declare her to be clean. If a lamb was too expensive, the parents could bring a second dove or pigeon instead. This is what Mary and Joseph did.

Jesus was God's Son, but his family carried out these ceremonies according to God's law. Jesus was not born above the law; instead, he fulfilled it perfectly.

2:28–32 When Mary and Joseph brought Jesus to the temple to be consecrated to God, they met an old man who told them what their child would become. Simeon's song is often called the *Nunc Dimittis*, because these are the first words of its Latin translation. Simeon could die in peace because he had seen the Messiah.

2:32 The Jews were well acquainted with the Old Testament prophecies that spoke of the Messiah's blessings to their nation. They did not always give equal attention to the prophecies saying that he would bring salvation to the entire world, not just the Jews (see, for example, Isaiah 49:6). Many thought that Christ had come to save only his own people. Luke made sure his Greek audience understood that Christ had come to save *all* who believe, Gentiles as well as Jews.

2:33 Joseph and Mary were amazed for three reasons: Simeon said that Jesus was a gift from God, Simeon recognized Jesus as the Messiah, and Simeon said Jesus would be a light to the entire world. This was at least the second time that Mary had been greeted with a prophecy about her son; the first time was when Elizabeth welcomed her as the mother of her Lord (1:42–45).

34 And Simeon blessed them and said to Mary His mother, "Behold, this *Child* is appointed for the fall and rise of many in Israel, and for a sign to be opposed—
35 and a sword will pierce even your own soul—to the end that thoughts from many
hearts may be revealed."
36 And there was a prophetess, Anna the daughter of Phanuel, of the tribe of Asher.
She was advanced in years and had lived with *her* husband seven years after her marriage,
37 and then as a widow to the age of eighty-four. She never left the temple, serving
night and day with fastings and prayers.
38 At that very moment she came up and *began* giving thanks to God, and continued
to speak of Him to all those who were looking for the redemption of Jerusalem.
39 When they had performed everything according to the Law of the Lord, they returned to Galilee, to their own city of Nazareth.
40 The Child continued to grow and become strong, increasing in wisdom; and the grace
of God was upon Him.

2:34 Matt 12:46; Matt 21:44; 1 Cor 1:23; 2 Cor 2:16; 1 Pet 2:8

2:36 Luke 2:38; Acts 21:9; Josh 19:24; 1 Tim 5:9

2:37 Luke 5:33; Acts 13:3; 14:23; 1 Tim 5:5

2:38 Luke 1:68; 2:25

2:39 Matt 2:23; Luke 1:26; 2:51; 4:16

2:40 Luke 1:80; 2:52

Jesus Speaks with the Religious Teachers
(15)

41 Now His parents went to Jerusalem every year at the Feast of the Passover.
42 And when He became twelve, they went up *there* according to the custom of the
Feast;
43 and as they were returning, after spending the full number of days, the boy Jesus
stayed behind in Jerusalem. But His parents were unaware of it,
44 but supposed Him to be in the caravan, and went a day's journey; and they *began*
looking for Him among their relatives and acquaintances.
45 When they did not find Him, they returned to Jerusalem looking for Him.
46 Then, after three days they found Him in the temple, sitting in the midst of the teachers, both listening to them and asking them questions.
47 And all who heard Him were amazed at His understanding and His answers.

2:41 Ex 12:11; 23:15; Deut 16:1-6

2:43 Ex 12:15

2:47 Matt 7:28; 13:54; 22:33; Mark 1:22; 6:2; 11:18; Luke 4:32; John 7:15

2:34–35 Simeon prophesied that Jesus would have a paradoxical effect on Israel. Some would fall because of him (see Isaiah 8:14–15), while others would rise (see Malachi 4:2). With Jesus, there would be no neutral ground: People would either joyfully accept him or totally reject him. As Jesus' mother, Mary would be grieved by the widespread rejection he would face. This is the first note of sorrow in Luke's Gospel.

2:36 Although Simeon and Anna were very old, they had never lost their hope that they would see the Messiah. Led by the Holy Spirit, they were among the first to bear witness to Jesus. In the Jewish culture, elders were respected, so because of Simeon's and Anna's age, their prophecies carried extra weight. Our society, however, values youthfulness over wisdom, and potential contributions by the elderly are often ignored. As Christians, we should reverse those values wherever we can. Encourage older people to share their wisdom and experience. Listen carefully when they speak. Offer them your friendship and help them find ways to continue to serve God.

2:36–37 Anna was called a prophetess, indicating that she was unusually close to God. Prophets did not necessarily predict the future. Their main role was to speak for God, proclaiming his truth.

2:39 Did Mary and Joseph return immediately to Nazareth, or did they remain in Bethlehem for a time (as implied in Matthew 2)? Apparently there is a gap of several years between verses 38 and 39—ample time for them to find a place to live in Bethlehem, flee to Egypt to escape Herod's wrath, and return to Nazareth when it was safe to do so.

2:40 Jesus was filled with wisdom, which is not surprising since he stayed in close contact with his heavenly Father. James 1:5 says God gives wisdom generously to all who ask. Like Jesus, we can grow in wisdom by walking with God.

2:41–42 According to God's law, every male was required to go to Jerusalem three times a year for the great festivals (Deuteronomy 16:16). In the spring, the Passover was celebrated, followed immediately by the week-long Feast of Unleavened Bread. Passover commemorated the night of the Jews' escape from Egypt when God had killed the Egyptian firstborn but had passed over Israelite homes (see Exodus 12:21–36). Passover was the most important of the three annual festivals.

2:43–45 At age 12, Jesus was considered almost an adult, and so he didn't spend a lot of time with his parents during the feast. Those who attended these feasts often traveled in caravans for protection from robbers along the Palestine roads. It was customary for the women and children to travel at the front of the caravan, with the men bringing up the rear. A 12-year-old boy conceivably could have been in either group, and both Mary and Joseph assumed Jesus was with the other one. But when the caravan left Jerusalem, Jesus stayed behind, absorbed in his discussion with the religious leaders.

2:46–47 The temple courts were famous throughout Judea as a place of learning. The apostle Paul studied in Jerusalem, perhaps in the temple courts, under Gamaliel, one of its foremost teachers (Acts 22:3). At the time of the Passover, the greatest rabbis of the land would assemble to teach and to discuss great truths among themselves. The coming Messiah would no doubt have been a popular discussion topic, for everyone was expecting him soon. Jesus would have been eager to listen and to ask probing questions. It was not his youth, but the depth of his wisdom, that astounded these teachers.

2:48 Matt 12:46; Luke 2:49; 3:23; 4:22

2:49 John 4:34; 5:36

2:50 Mark 9:32; Luke 9:45; 18:34

48 When they saw Him, they were astonished; and His mother said to Him, "Son, why
have You treated us this way? Behold, Your father and I have been anxiously looking
for You."
49 And He said to them, "Why is it that you were looking for Me? Did you not know
that I had to be in My Father's *house?*"
50 But they did not understand the statement which He had made to them.

ELIZABETH

In societies like Israel, in which a woman's value was largely measured by her ability to bear children, to be aging and without children often led to personal hardship and public shame. For Elizabeth, a childless old age was a painful and lonely time during which she remained faithful to God.

Both Elizabeth and Zacharias came from priestly families. For two weeks each year, Zacharias had to go to the temple in Jerusalem to attend to his priestly duties. After one of those trips, Zacharias returned home excited, but speechless. He had to write down his good news, because he couldn't give it any other way. And what a wonderful surprise he had for his wife—their faded dream would become an exciting reality! Soon Elizabeth became pregnant, and she knew her child was a long-hoped-for gift from God.

News traveled fast among the family. Seventy miles to the north, in Nazareth, Elizabeth's relative, Mary, also unexpectedly became pregnant. Within days after the angel's message that she would bear the Messiah, Mary went to visit Elizabeth. They were instantly bound together by the unique gifts God had given them. Elizabeth knew that Mary's son would be even greater than her own, for John would be the messenger for Mary's son.

When the baby was born, Elizabeth insisted on his God-given name: John. Zacharias's written agreement freed his tongue, and everyone in town wondered what would become of this obviously special child.

Elizabeth whispered her praise as she cared for God's gift. Knowing about Mary must have made her marvel at God's timing. Things had worked out even better than she could have planned. We too need to remember that God is in control of every situation. When did you last pause to recognize God's timing in the events of your life?

Strengths and accomplishments:
- Known as a deeply spiritual woman
- Showed no doubts about God's ability to fulfill his promise
- Mother of John the Baptist
- The first woman besides Mary to hear of the coming Savior

Lessons from her life:
- God does not forget those who have been faithful to him
- God's timetable and methods do not have to conform to what we expect

Vital statistics:
- Occupation: Homemaker
- Relatives: Husband: Zacharias. Son: John the Baptist. Relative: Mary
- Contemporaries: Joseph, Herod the Great

Key verses:
"How has it happened to me, that the mother of my Lord would come to me? For behold, when the sound of your greeting reached my ears, the baby leaped in my womb for joy. And blessed is she who believed that there would be a fulfillment of what had been spoken to her by the Lord" (Luke 1:43–45).

Elizabeth's story is told in Luke 1:5–80.

2:48 Mary had to let go of her child and let him become a man, God's Son, the Messiah. Fearful that she hadn't been careful enough with this God-given child, she searched frantically for him. But she was looking for a boy, not the young man who was in the temple astounding the religious leaders with his questions. It is hard to let go of people or projects we have nurtured. It is both sweet and painful to see our children as adults, our students as teachers, our subordinates as managers, our inspirations as institutions. But when the time comes to step back and let go, we must do so in spite of the hurt. Then our protegés can exercise their wings, take flight, and soar to the heights God intended for them.

2:49–50 This is the first mention of Jesus' awareness that he was God's Son. But even though he knew his real Father, he did not reject his earthly parents. He went back to Nazareth with them and lived under their authority for another 18 years. God's people do not despise human relationships or family responsibilities. If the Son of God obeyed his human parents, how much more should we honor our family members! Don't use commitment to God's work to justify neglecting your family.

2:50 Jesus' parents didn't understand what he meant about his Father's house. They didn't realize he was making a distinction between his earthly father and his heavenly Father. Jesus knew that he had a unique relationship with God. Although Mary and Joseph knew he was God's Son, they didn't understand what his mission would involve. Besides, they had to raise him, along with his brothers and sisters (Matthew 13:55–56), as a normal child. They knew he was unique, but they did not know what was going on in his mind.

51 And He went down with them and came to Nazareth, and He continued in subjection to them; and His mother treasured all *these* things in her heart.
52 And Jesus kept increasing in wisdom and stature, and in favor with God and men.

2:51 Luke 2:39; Matt 12:46; Luke 2:19

2:52 Luke 2:40

John the Baptist Prepares the Way for Jesus
(16/Matthew 3:1-12; Mark 1:1-8)

3 Now in the fifteenth year of the reign of Tiberius Caesar, when Pontius Pilate was
governor of Judea, and Herod was tetrarch of Galilee, and his brother Philip was
tetrarch of the region of Ituraea and Trachonitis, and Lysanias was tetrarch of Abilene,
2 in the high priesthood of Annas and Caiaphas, the word of God came to John, the
son of Zacharias, in the wilderness.
3 And he came into all the district around the Jordan, preaching a baptism of repentance for the forgiveness of sins;
4 as it is written in the book of the words of Isaiah the prophet,
"THE VOICE OF ONE CRYING IN THE WILDERNESS,
'MAKE READY THE WAY OF THE LORD,
MAKE HIS PATHS STRAIGHT.
5 'EVERY RAVINE WILL BE FILLED,
AND EVERY MOUNTAIN AND HILL WILL BE BROUGHT LOW;
THE CROOKED WILL BECOME STRAIGHT,
AND THE ROUGH ROADS SMOOTH;
6 AND ALL FLESH WILL SEE THE SALVATION OF GOD.' "
7 So he *began* saying to the crowds who were going out to be baptized by him, "You
brood of vipers, who warned you to flee from the wrath to come?
8 "Therefore bear fruits in keeping with repentance, and do not begin to say to your-

3:1 Matt 27:2; Matt 14:1

3:2 John 18:13, 24; Acts 4:6; Matt 26:3

3:3 Matt 3:5

3:4 Is 40:3

3:5 Is 40:4

3:6 Is 40:5; Luke 2:30

3:7 Matt 12:34; 23:33

3:8 Luke 5:21; 13:25, 26; 14:9; John 8:33

2:52 The Bible does not record any events of the next 18 years of Jesus' life, but Jesus undoubtedly was learning and maturing. As the oldest in a large family, he assisted Joseph in his carpentry work. Joseph may have died during this time, leaving Jesus to provide for the family. The normal routines of daily life gave Jesus a solid understanding of the Judean people.

2:52 The second chapter of Luke shows us that although Jesus was unique, he had a normal childhood and adolescence. In terms of development, he went through the same progression we do. He grew physically and mentally, he related to other people, and he was loved by God. A full human life is not unbalanced. It was important to Jesus—and it should be important to all believers—to develop fully and harmoniously in each of these key areas: physical, mental, social, and spiritual.

3:1 Tiberius, the Roman emperor, ruled from A.D. 14 to 37. Pilate was the Roman governor responsible for the province of Judea; Herod (Antipas) and Philip were half brothers and sons of the cruel Herod the Great, who had been dead more than 20 years. Antipas, Philip, Pilate, and Lysanias apparently had equal powers in governing their separate territories. All were subject to Rome and responsible for keeping peace in their respective lands.

3:2 Under Jewish law there was only one high priest. He was appointed from Aaron's line, and he held his position for life. By this time, however, the religious system had been corrupted, and the Roman government was appointing its own religious leaders to maintain greater control over the Jews. Apparently the Roman authorities had deposed the Jewish-appointed Annas and had replaced him with Annas's son-in-law, Caiaphas. Nevertheless, Annas retained his title (see Acts 4:6) and probably also much of the power it carried. Because the Jews believed the high priest's position to be for life, they would have continued to call Annas their high priest.

3:2 This is John the Baptist, whose birth story is told in chapter 1. See his Profile in John 1.

3:2 Pilate, Herod, and Caiaphas were the most powerful leaders in Palestine, but they were upstaged by a wilderness prophet from rural Judea. God chose to speak through the loner John the Baptist, who has gone down in history as greater than any of the rulers of his day. How often we judge people by our culture's standards—power, wealth, beauty—and miss the truly great people through whom God works! Greatness is not measured by what you have, but by your faith in God. Like John, give yourself entirely to God so God's power can work through you.

3:3 Repentance has two sides—turning away from sins and turning toward God. To be truly repentant, we must do both. We can't just say we believe and then live any way we choose (see 3:7–8), and neither can we simply live a morally correct life without a personal relationship with God, because that cannot bring forgiveness from sin. Determine to rid your life of any sins God points out, and put your trust in him alone to guide you.

3:4–5 In John's day, before a king took a trip, messengers would tell those he was planning to visit to prepare the roads for him. Similarly John told his listeners to make their lives ready so the Lord could come to them. To prepare for Jesus' coming to us, we must focus on him, listen to his words, and respond obediently to his directions.

3:6 This book was written to a non-Jewish audience. Luke quoted from Isaiah to show that salvation is for all people, not just the Jews (Isaiah 40:3–5; 52:10). John the Baptist called all mankind to prepare to meet Jesus. That includes you, no matter what your standing is with religious organizations and authorities. Don't let feelings of being an outsider cause you to hold back. No one who wants to follow Jesus is an outsider in God's kingdom.

3:7 What motivates your faith—fear of the future, or a desire to be a better person in a better world? Some people wanted to be baptized by John so they could escape eternal punishment, but they didn't turn to God for salvation. John had harsh words for such people. He knew that God values reformation above ritual. Is your faith motivated by a desire for a new, changed life, or is it only like a vaccination or insurance policy against possible disaster?

3:8 Many of John's hearers were shocked when he said that being Abraham's descendants was not enough for God. The religious leaders relied more on their family lines than on their faith for their standing with God. For them, religion was inherited. But a personal relationship with God is not handed down from parents to children. Everyone has to commit to it on his or her own. Don't rely on

3:9 Matt 7:19; Luke 13:6-9
3:10 Luke 3:12, 14; Acts 2:37, 38
3:11 Is 58:7; 1 Tim 6:17, 18; James 2:14-20

selves, 'We have Abraham for our father,' for I say to you that from these stones God is
able to raise up children to Abraham.
9 "Indeed the axe is already laid at the root of the trees; so every tree that does not
bear good fruit is cut down and thrown into the fire."
10 And the crowds were questioning him, saying, "Then what shall we do?"
11 And he would answer and say to them, "The man who has two tunics is to share
with him who has none; and he who has food is to do likewise."

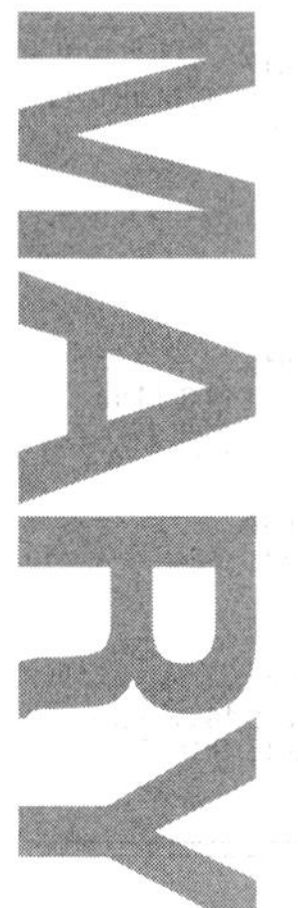

Motherhood is a painful privilege. Young Mary of Nazareth had the unique privilege of being mother to the very Son of God. Yet the pains and pleasures of her motherhood can be understood by mothers everywhere. Mary was the only human present at Jesus' birth who also witnessed his death. She saw him arrive as her baby son, and she watched him die as her Savior.

Until Gabriel's unexpected visit, Mary's life was quite satisfactory. She had recently become engaged to a carpenter, Joseph, and was anticipating married life. But her life was about to change forever.

Angels don't usually make appointments before visiting. As if she were being congratulated for winning the grand prize in a contest she had never entered, Mary found the angel's greeting puzzling and his presence frightening. What she heard next was the news almost every woman in Israel hoped to hear—that her child would be the Messiah, God's promised Savior. Mary did not doubt the message, but rather asked how pregnancy would be possible. Gabriel told her the baby would be God's Son. Her answer was the one God waits in vain to hear from so many other people: "Behold, the bondslave of the Lord; may it be done to me according to your word" (Luke 1:38). Later, her song of joy shows us how well she knew God, for her thoughts were filled with his words from the Old Testament.

Within a few weeks of his birth, Jesus was taken to the temple to be dedicated to God. There Joseph and Mary were met by two devout people, Simeon and Anna, who recognized the child as the Messiah and praised God. Simeon directed some words to Mary that must have come to her mind many times in the years that followed: "A sword will pierce even your own soul" (Luke 2:35). A big part of her painful privilege of motherhood would be to see her son rejected and crucified by the people he came to save.

We can imagine that even if she had known all she would suffer as Jesus' mother, Mary would still have given the same response. Are you, like Mary, available to be used by God?

Strengths and accomplishments:
- The mother of Jesus, the Messiah
- The one human who was with Jesus from birth to death
- Willing to be available to God
- Knew and applied Old Testament Scriptures

Lessons from her life:
- God's best servants are often ordinary people available to him
- God's plans involve extraordinary events in ordinary people's lives
- A person's character is revealed by his or her response to the unexpected

Vital statistics:
- Where: Nazareth, Bethlehem
- Occupation: Homemaker
- Relatives: Husband: Joseph. Relatives: Zacharias and Elizabeth. Children: Jesus, James, Joseph, Judas, Simon, and daughters

Key verse:
" 'Behold, the bondslave of the Lord; may it be done to me according to your word.' And the angel departed from her" (Luke 1:38).

Mary's story is told throughout the Gospels. She is also mentioned in Acts 1:14.

someone else's faith for your salvation. Put your own faith in Jesus, and then exercise it every day.

3:8–9 Confession of sins and a changed life are inseparable. Faith without deeds is dead (James 2:14–26). Jesus' harshest words were to the respectable religious leaders who lacked the desire for real change. They wanted to be known as religious authorities, but they didn't want to change their hearts and minds. Thus their lives were unproductive. Repentance must be tied to action, or it isn't real. Following Jesus means more than saying the right words; it means acting on what he says.

3:11–14 John's message demanded at least three specific responses: (1) share what you have with those who need it, (2) whatever your job is, do it well and with fairness, and (3) be content with what you're earning. John had no time to address comforting messages to those who lived careless or selfish lives—he was calling the people to right living. What changes can you make in sharing what you have, doing your work honestly and well, and being content?

12 And *some* tax collectors also came to be baptized, and they said to him, "Teacher,
what shall we do?"
13 And he said to them, "Collect no more than what you have been ordered to."
14 *Some* soldiers were questioning him, saying, "And *what about* us, what shall we do?"
And he said to them, "Do not take money from anyone by force, or accuse *anyone* falsely, and be content with your wages."
15 Now while the people were in a state of expectation and all were wondering in their
hearts about John, as to whether he was the Christ,
16 John answered and said to them all, "As for me, I baptize you with water; but One
is coming who is mightier than I, and I am not fit to untie the thong of His sandals; He
will baptize you with the Holy Spirit and fire.
17 "His winnowing fork is in His hand to thoroughly clear His threshing floor, and to
gather the wheat into His barn; but He will burn up the chaff with unquenchable fire."
18 So with many other exhortations he preached the gospel to the people.

3:12 Luke 7:29
3:14 Ex 20:16; 23:1; Phil 4:11
3:15 John 1:19f
3:16 Matt 3:11, 12; Mark 1:7, 8
3:17 Is 30:24; Mark 9:43, 48

Herod Puts John in Prison
(26)

19 But when Herod the tetrarch was reprimanded by him because of Herodias, his
brother's wife, and because of all the wicked things which Herod had done,
20 Herod also added this to them all: he locked John up in prison.

3:19 Matt 14:3; Mark 6:17; Matt 14:1; Luke 3:1
3:20 John 3:24

John Baptizes Jesus
(17/Matthew 3:13-17; Mark 1:9-11)

21 Now when all the people were baptized, Jesus was also baptized, and while He was
praying, heaven was opened,

3:21 Matt 14:23; Luke 5:16; 9:18, 28f

3:12 Tax collectors were notorious for their dishonesty. Romans gathered funds for their government by farming out the collection privilege. Tax collectors earned their own living by adding a sizable sum—whatever they could get away with—to the total and keeping this money for themselves. Unless the people revolted and risked Roman retaliation, they had to pay whatever was demanded. Obviously they hated the tax collectors, who were generally dishonest, greedy, and ready to betray their own countrymen for cold cash. Yet, said John, God would accept even these men; God desires to pour out mercy on those who confess, and then to give strength to live changed lives.

3:12–14 John's message took root in unexpected places—among the poor, the dishonest, and even the hated occupation army. These people were painfully aware of their needs. Too often we confuse respectability with right living. They are not the same. Respectability can even hinder right living if it keeps us from seeing our need for God. If you had to choose, would you protect your character or your reputation?

3:14 These soldiers were the Roman troops sent to keep peace in this distant province. Many of them oppressed the poor and used their power to take advantage of all the people. John called them to repent and change their ways.

3:15 There had not been a prophet in Israel for more than 400 years. It was widely believed that when the Messiah came, prophecy would reappear (Joel 2:28–29; Malachi 3:1; 4:5). When John burst onto the scene, the people were excited. He was obviously a great prophet, and they were sure that the eagerly awaited age of the Messiah had come. Some, in fact, thought John himself was the Messiah. John spoke like the prophets of old, saying that the people must turn from their sin to avoid punishment and turn to God to experience his mercy and approval. This is a message for all times and places, but John spoke it with particular urgency—he was preparing the people for the coming Messiah.

3:16 John's baptism with water symbolized the washing away of sins. His baptism coordinated with his message of repentance and reformation. Jesus' baptism with fire includes the power needed to do God's will. The baptism with the Holy Spirit was fulfilled at Pentecost (Acts 2) when the Holy Spirit came upon believers in the form of tongues of fire, empowering them to proclaim Jesus' resurrection in many languages. The baptism with fire also symbolizes the work of the Holy Spirit in bringing God's judgment on those who refuse to repent.

3:17 John warned of impending judgment by comparing those who refuse to live for God to chaff, the useless outer husk of the grain. By contrast, he compared those who repent and reform their lives to the nourishing wheat itself. The winnowing fork was a pitchfork used to toss wheat so that the kernels would separate from the blades. Those who refuse to be used by God will be discarded because they have no value in furthering God's work. Those who repent and believe, however, hold great value in God's eyes because they are beginning a new life of productive service for him.

3:19–20 In these two verses Luke flashes forward to continue his explanation about John the Baptist. See the Harmony of the Gospels for the chronological order of events.

3:19–20 This is Herod Antipas (see Mark 6 for his Profile). Herodias was Herod's niece and also his brother's wife. She treacherously plotted John the Baptist's death (Matthew 14:1–12). The Herods were a murderous and deceitful family. Rebuking a tyrannical Roman official who could imprison and execute him was extremely dangerous, yet that is what John did. Herod seemingly had the last word, but the story is not finished. At the last judgment, Herod, not John, will be the one in danger.

3:21 Luke emphasizes Jesus' human nature. Jesus was born to humble parents, a birth unannounced except to shepherds and foreigners. This baptism recorded here was the first public declaration of Jesus' ministry. Instead of going to Jerusalem and identifying with the established religious leaders, Jesus went to a river and identified himself with those who were repenting of sin. When Jesus, at age 12, visited the temple, he understood his mission (2:49). Eighteen years later, at his baptism, he began carrying it out. And as Jesus prayed, God spoke and confirmed his decision to act. God was breaking into human history through Jesus the Christ.

3:21–22 If baptism was a sign of repentance from sin, why did Jesus ask to be baptized? Several explanations are often given:

3:22 Ps 2:7; Is 42:1; Matt 3:17; 17:5; Mark 1:11; Luke 9:35; 2 Pet 1:17

22 and the Holy Spirit descended upon Him in bodily form like a dove, and a voice
came out of heaven, "You are My beloved Son, in You I am well-pleased."

The Ancestors of Jesus
(3/Matthew 1:1-17)

3:23 Matt 4:17; Acts 1:1; Matt 1:16

23 When He began His ministry, Jesus Himself was about thirty years of age, being, as
was supposed, the son of Joseph, the son of Eli,
24 the son of Matthat, the son of Levi, the son of Melchi, the son of Jannai, the son of
Joseph,
25 the son of Mattathias, the son of Amos, the son of Nahum, the son of Hesli, the son
of Naggai,
26 the son of Maath, the son of Mattathias, the son of Semein, the son of Josech, the
son of Joda,

3:27 Matt 1:12

27 the son of Joanan, the son of Rhesa, the son of Zerubbabel, the son of Shealtiel, the
son of Neri,
28 the son of Melchi, the son of Addi, the son of Cosam, the son of Elmadam, the son
of Er,
29 the son of Joshua, the son of Eliezer, the son of Jorim, the son of Matthat, the son
of Levi,
30 the son of Simeon, the son of Judah, the son of Joseph, the son of Jonam, the son of
Eliakim,
31 the son of Melea, the son of Menna, the son of Mattatha, the son of Nathan, the
son of David,

3:32 Matt 1:1-6

32 the son of Jesse, the son of Obed, the son of Boaz, the son of Salmon, the son of
Nahshon,
33 the son of Amminadab, the son of Admin, the son of Ram, the son of Hezron, the
son of Perez, the son of Judah,

3:34 Gen 11:26-30; 1 Chr 1:24-27

34 the son of Jacob, the son of Isaac, the son of Abraham, the son of Terah, the son of
Nahor,
35 the son of Serug, the son of Reu, the son of Peleg, the son of Heber, the son of Shelah,

3:36 Gen 5:3-32; 1 Chr 1:1-4

36 the son of Cainan, the son of Arphaxad, the son of Shem, the son of Noah, the son
of Lamech,
37 the son of Methuselah, the son of Enoch, the son of Jared, the son of Mahalaleel,
the son of Cainan,
38 the son of Enosh, the son of Seth, the son of Adam, the son of God.

---

(1) Jesus' baptism was one step in fulfilling his earthly mission of identifying with our humanity and sin; (2) by endorsing the rite of baptism, Jesus was giving us an example to follow; (3) Jesus was announcing the beginning of his public ministry; (4) Jesus was being baptized for the sins of the nation. The Holy Spirit's appearance in the form of a dove showed that God's plan for salvation was centered in Jesus. Jesus was the perfect human who didn't need baptism for repentance, but he was baptized anyway on our behalf.

3:21–22 This is one of several places in Scripture where all the members of the Trinity are mentioned—Father, Son, and Holy Spirit. In the traditional words of the church, the one God exists in three persons but one substance, coeternal and coequal. No amount of explanation can adequately portray the power and intricacy of this unique relationship. There are no perfect analogies in nature because there is no other relationship like the Trinity.

3:23 Imagine the Savior of the world working in a small-town carpenter's shop until he was 30 years old! It seems incredible that Jesus would have been content to remain in Nazareth all that time, but he patiently trusted the Father's timing for his life and ministry. Thirty was the prescribed age for priests to begin their ministry (Numbers 4:3). Joseph was 30 years old when he began serving the king of Egypt (Genesis 41:46), and David was 30 years old when he began to reign over Judah (2 Samuel 5:4). Age 30, then, was a good time to begin an important task in the Jewish culture. Like Jesus, we need to resist the temptation to jump ahead before receiving the Spirit's direction. Are you waiting and wondering what your next step should be? Don't jump ahead—trust God's timing.

3:23 Eli may have been Joseph's father-in-law. If that were the case, this would be Mary's genealogy that Luke may have received personally from her. It is fitting that Luke would show Mary's genealogy because of the prominence he gives women in his Gospel.

3:23–38 Matthew's genealogy goes back to Abraham and shows that Jesus was related to all Jews (Matthew 1). Luke's genealogy goes back to Adam, showing that Jesus is related to all human beings. This is consistent with Luke's picture of Jesus as the Savior of the whole world.

Satan Tempts Jesus in the Wilderness
(18/Matthew 4:1-11; Mark 1:12-13)

4 Jesus, full of the Holy Spirit, returned from the Jordan and was led around by the 4:1
Spirit in the wilderness Luke 3:3
2 for forty days, being tempted by the devil. And He ate nothing during those days, 4:2
and when they had ended, He became hungry. Ex 34:28; 1 Kin 19:8
3 And the devil said to Him, "If You are the Son of God, tell this stone to become 4:4
bread." Deut 8:3
4 And Jesus answered him, "It is written, 'MAN SHALL NOT LIVE ON BREAD ALONE.' "
5 And he led Him up and showed Him all the kingdoms of the world in a moment of 4:5
time. Matt 4:8-10; Matt 24:14
6 And the devil said to Him, "I will give You all this domain and its glory; for it has 4:6
been handed over to me, and I give it to whomever I wish. 1 John 5:19
7 "Therefore if You worship before me, it shall all be Yours."
8 Jesus answered him, "It is written, 'YOU SHALL WORSHIP THE LORD YOUR GOD 4:8
AND SERVE HIM ONLY.' " Deut 6:13; 10:20; Matt 4:10
9 And he led Him to Jerusalem and had Him stand on the pinnacle of the temple,
and said to Him, "If You are the Son of God, throw Yourself down from here; 4:9 Matt 4:5-7
10 for it is written,
'HE WILL COMMAND HIS ANGELS CONCERNING YOU TO GUARD YOU,' 4:10 Ps 91:11
11 and,
'ON *their* HANDS THEY WILL BEAR YOU UP,
SO THAT YOU WILL NOT STRIKE YOUR FOOT AGAINST A STONE.' " 4:11 Ps 91:12

4:1 Sometimes we feel that if the Holy Spirit leads us, it will always be "beside quiet waters" (Psalm 23:2). But that is not necessarily true. He led Jesus into the wilderness for a long and difficult time of testing, and he may also lead us into difficult situations. When facing trials, first make sure you haven't brought them on yourself through sin or unwise choices. If you find no sin to confess or unwise behavior to change, then ask God to strengthen you for your test. Finally, be careful to follow faithfully wherever the Holy Spirit leads.

4:1 Temptation will often come after a high point in our spiritual lives or ministries (see 1 Kings 18; 19 for Elijah's story of great victory followed by despair). Remember that Satan chooses the times for his attacks. We need to be on our guard in times of victory just as much as in times of discouragement. See the third note on Matthew 4:1ff for a comment on how Satan tempts us when we're vulnerable.

4:1–2 The devil, who tempted Adam and Eve in the garden, also tempted Jesus in the wilderness. Satan is a real being, a created but rebellious fallen angel, and not a symbol or an idea. He constantly fights against God and those who follow and obey God. Jesus was a prime target for the devil's temptations. Satan succeeded with Adam and Eve, and he hoped to succeed with Jesus too.

4:1–13 Knowing and obeying God's Word is an effective weapon against temptation, the only *offensive* weapon provided in the Christian's "armor" (Ephesians 6:17). Jesus used Scripture to counter Satan's attacks, and you can too. But to use it effectively you must have faith in God's promises, because Satan also knows Scripture and is adept at twisting it to suit his purpose. Obeying the Scriptures is more important than simply having a verse to quote, so read them daily and apply them to your life. Then your "sword" will always be sharp.

4:2 Why was it necessary for Jesus to be tempted? First, temptation is part of the human experience. For Jesus to be fully human, for him to understand us completely, he had to face temptation (see Hebrews 4:15). Second, Jesus had to undo Adam's work. Adam, though created perfect, gave in to temptation and passed sin on to the whole human race. Jesus, by contrast, resisted Satan. His victory offers salvation to all of Adam's descendants (see Romans 5:12–19).

4:3 Satan may tempt us to doubt Christ's true identity. He knows that once we begin to question whether or not Jesus is God, it's far easier to get us to do what he wants. Times of questioning can help us sort out our beliefs and strengthen our faith, but those times can also be dangerous. If you are dealing with doubt, realize that you are especially vulnerable to temptation. Even as you search for answers, protect yourself by meditating on the unshakable truths of God's Word.

4:3 Sometimes what we are tempted to do isn't wrong in itself. Turning stones into bread wasn't necessarily bad. The sin was not in the act but in the reason behind it. The devil was trying to get Jesus to take a shortcut, to solve Jesus' immediate problem at the expense of his long-range goals, to seek comfort at the sacrifice of his discipline. Satan often works that way—persuading us to take action, even right action, for the wrong reason or at the wrong time. The fact that something is not wrong in itself does not mean that it is good for you at a given time. Many people sin by attempting to fulfill legitimate desires outside of God's will or ahead of his timetable. First ask, "Is the Holy Spirit leading me to do this? Or is Satan trying to get me off the track?"

4:3ff Often we are tempted not through our weaknesses, but through our strengths. The devil tempted Jesus where he was strong. Jesus had power over stones, the kingdoms of the world, and even angels, and Satan wanted him to use that power without regard to his mission. When we give in to the devil and wrongly use our strengths, we become proud and self-reliant. Trusting in our own powers, we feel little need of God. To avoid this trap, we must realize that all our strengths are God's gifts to us, and we must dedicate those strengths to his service.

4:6–7 The devil arrogantly hoped to succeed in his rebellion against God by diverting Jesus from his mission and winning his worship. "This world is mine, not God's," he was saying, "and if you hope to do anything worthwhile here, you'd better recognize that fact." Jesus didn't argue with Satan about who owns the world, but Jesus refused to validate Satan's claim by worshiping him. Jesus knew that he would redeem the world through giving up his life on the cross, not through making an alliance with a corrupt angel.

4:9–11 Here the devil misinterpreted Scripture. The intention of Psalm 91 is to show God's protection of his people, not to incite them to use God's power for sensational or foolish displays.

4:12 Deut 6:16

12 And Jesus answered and said to him, "It is said,
'YOU SHALL NOT PUT THE LORD YOUR GOD TO THE TEST.' "
13 When the devil had finished every temptation, he left Him until an opportune time.

B. MESSAGE AND MINISTRY OF JESUS, THE SAVIOR (4:14—21:38)

Luke accurately records the actions and teachings of Christ, helping us understand the way of salvation. There is much unique material in Luke, especially the parables of Jesus. Jesus came to teach us how to live and how to find salvation. How carefully, then, we should study the words and life of our Savior.

1. Jesus' ministry in Galilee

Jesus Preaches in Galilee
(30/Matthew 4:12-17; Mark 1:14-15; John 4:43-45)

4:14 Matt 4:12; Matt 9:26; Luke 4:37

4:15 Matt 4:23

14 And Jesus returned to Galilee in the power of the Spirit, and news about Him spread
through all the surrounding district.
15 And He *began* teaching in their synagogues and was praised by all.

Jesus Is Rejected at Nazareth
(32)

4:16 Luke 2:39, 51; Matt 13:54; Mark 6:1f; Acts 13:14-16

16 And He came to Nazareth, where He had been brought up; and as was His custom,
He entered the synagogue on the Sabbath, and stood up to read.
17 And the book of the prophet Isaiah was handed to Him. And He opened the book
and found the place where it was written,

4:18 Is 61:1; Matt 11:5; 12:18; John 3:34

18 "THE SPIRIT OF THE LORD IS UPON ME,
BECAUSE HE ANOINTED ME TO PREACH THE GOSPEL TO THE POOR.
HE HAS SENT ME TO PROCLAIM RELEASE TO THE CAPTIVES,
AND RECOVERY OF SIGHT TO THE BLIND,
TO SET FREE THOSE WHO ARE OPPRESSED,

4:19 Is 61:2; Lev 25:10

4:20 Luke 4:17; Matt 26:55

19 TO PROCLAIM THE FAVORABLE YEAR OF THE LORD."
20 And He closed the book, gave it back to the attendant and sat down; and the eyes of
all in the synagogue were fixed on Him.
21 And He began to say to them, "Today this Scripture has been fulfilled in your
hearing."

4:22 Matt 13:55; Mark 6:3; John 6:42

22 And all were speaking well of Him, and wondering at the gracious words which were
falling from His lips; and they were saying, "Is this not Joseph's son?"

4:13 Christ's defeat of the devil in the wilderness was decisive but not final. Throughout his ministry, Jesus would confront Satan in many forms. Too often we see temptation as once and for all. In reality, we need to be constantly on guard against the devil's ongoing attacks. Where are you most susceptible to temptation right now? How are you preparing to withstand it?

4:16 Synagogues were very important in Jewish religious life. During the exile when the Jews no longer had their temple, synagogues were established as places of worship on the Sabbath and as schools for young boys during the week. Synagogues continued to exist even after the temple was rebuilt. A synagogue could be set up in any town where there were at least ten Jewish families. It was administered by one leader and an assistant. At the synagogue, the leader often would invite a visiting rabbi to read from the Scriptures and to teach.

4:16 Jesus went to the synagogue "as was His custom." Even though he was the perfect Son of God, and his local synagogue undoubtedly left much to be desired, Jesus attended services every week. His example makes our excuses for not attending church sound weak and self-serving. Make regular worship a part of your life.

4:17–21 Jesus was quoting from Isaiah 61:1–2. Isaiah pictures the deliverance of Israel from exile in Babylon as a Year of Jubilee when all debts are canceled, all slaves are freed, and all property is returned to original owners (Leviticus 25). But the release from Babylonian exile had not brought the fulfillment the people had expected; they were still a conquered and oppressed people. So Isaiah must have been referring to a future Messianic age. Jesus boldly announced, "Today this Scripture has been fulfilled in your hearing." Jesus was proclaiming himself as the One who would bring this Good News to pass, but in a way that the people would not yet be able to grasp.

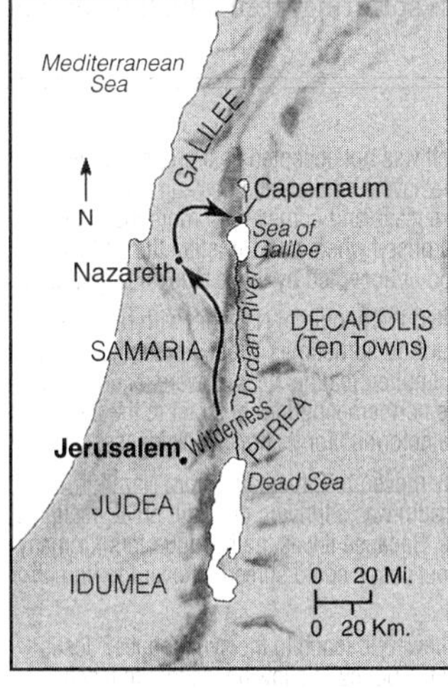

JESUS' TEMPTATION AND RETURN TO GALILEE
Jesus was tempted by Satan in the rough Judean wilderness before returning to his boyhood home, Nazareth. John's Gospel tells of Jesus' journeys in Galilee, Samaria, and Judea (see John 1—4) before he moved to Capernaum to set up his base of operations (see Matthew 4:12–13).

23 And He said to them, "No doubt you will quote this proverb to Me, 'Physician, heal
yourself! Whatever we heard was done at Capernaum, do here in your hometown as
well.' "
24 And He said, "Truly I say to you, no prophet is welcome in his hometown.
25 "But I say to you in truth, there were many widows in Israel in the days of Elijah,
when the sky was shut up for three years and six months, when a great famine came over
all the land;
26 and yet Elijah was sent to none of them, but only to Zarephath, *in the land* of Sidon,
to a woman who was a widow.
27 "And there were many lepers in Israel in the time of Elisha the prophet; and none of
them was cleansed, but only Naaman the Syrian."
28 And all *the people* in the synagogue were filled with rage as they heard these things;
29 and they got up and drove Him out of the city, and led Him to the brow of the hill
on which their city had been built, in order to throw Him down the cliff.
30 But passing through their midst, He went His way.

4:23 Matt 4:13; Mark 1:21ff; 2:1ff; Luke 4:35ff; John 4:46ff; Mark 6:1; Luke 2:39, 51; 4:16
4:24 Matt 13:57; Mark 6:4; John 4:44
4:25 1 Kin 17:1; 18:1; James 5:17
4:26 1 Kin 17:9; Matt 11:21
4:27 2 Kin 5:1-14
4:29 Num 15:35; Acts 7:58; Heb 13:12
4:30 John 10:39

Jesus Teaches with Great Authority
(34/Mark 1:21-28)

31 And He came down to Capernaum, a city of Galilee, and He was teaching them on
the Sabbath;
32 and they were amazed at His teaching, for His message was with authority.
33 In the synagogue there was a man possessed by the spirit of an unclean demon, and
he cried out with a loud voice,
34 "Let us alone! What business do we have with each other, Jesus of Nazareth? Have
You come to destroy us? I know who You are—the Holy One of God!"
35 But Jesus rebuked him, saying, "Be quiet and come out of him!" And when the
demon had thrown him down in the midst *of the people*, he came out of him without doing
him any harm.
36 And amazement came upon them all, and they *began* talking with one another saying, "What is this message? For with authority and power He commands the unclean
spirits and they come out."
37 And the report about Him was spreading into every locality in the surrounding
district.

4:31 Matt 4:13; Luke 4:23
4:32 Matt 7:28; Luke 4:36; John 7:46
4:34 Matt 8:29; Mark 1:24
4:35 Matt 8:26; Mark 4:39; Luke 4:39, 41; 8:24
4:36 Luke 4:32
4:37 Luke 4:14

Jesus Heals Peter's Mother-in-law and Many Others
(35/Matthew 8:14-17; Mark 1:29-34)

38 Then He got up and *left* the synagogue, and entered Simon's home. Now Simon's
mother-in-law was suffering from a high fever, and they asked Him to help her.

4:38 Matt 4:24

4:24 Even Jesus himself was not accepted as a prophet in his hometown. Many people have a similar attitude—an expert is anyone who carries a briefcase and comes from more than 200 miles away. Don't be surprised when your Christian life and faith are not easily understood or accepted by those who know you well.

4:28 Jesus' remarks filled the people of Nazareth with rage because he was saying that God sometimes chose to reach Gentiles rather than Jews. Jesus implied that his hearers were as unbelieving as the citizens of the northern kingdom of Israel in the days of Elijah and Elisha, a time notorious for its great wickedness.

4:31 Jesus had recently moved to Capernaum from Nazareth (Matthew 4:13). Capernaum was a thriving city with great wealth as well as great decadence. Because it was the headquarters for many Roman troops, word about Jesus could spread all over the Roman empire.

4:31 Why was Jesus allowed to teach in the synagogues? Jesus was taking advantage of the policy of allowing visitors to teach. Itinerant rabbis were always welcome to speak to those gathered each Sabbath in the synagogues. The apostle Paul also profited from this practice (see Acts 13:5; 14:1).

4:33 A man possessed by a demon was in the synagogue where Jesus was teaching. This man made his way into the place of worship and verbally abused Jesus. It is naive to think that we will be sheltered from evil in the church. Satan is happy to invade our presence wherever and whenever he can. But Jesus' authority is much greater than Satan's; and where Jesus is present, demons cannot stay for long.

4:34–36 The people were amazed at Jesus' authority to drive out demons—evil spirits ruled by Satan and sent to harass people and tempt them to sin. Demons are fallen angels who have joined Satan in rebellion against God. Demons can cause a person to become mute, deaf, blind, or insane. Jesus faced many demons during his time on earth, and he always exerted authority over them. Not only did the unclean spirit leave this man; Luke records that the man was not even injured.

4:36 Evil permeates our world, and it is no wonder that people are often fearful. But Jesus' power is far greater than Satan's. The first step toward conquering fear of evil is to recognize Jesus' authority and power. He has overcome all evil, including Satan himself.

4:39 Luke 4:35, 41

39 And standing over her, He rebuked the fever, and it left her; and she immediately
got up and waited on them.

4:40 Mark 5:23; Matt 4:23

40 While the sun was setting, all those who had any *who were* sick with various diseases
brought them to Him; and laying His hands on each one of them, He was healing them.

4:41 Matt 4:3; Luke 4:35; Matt 8:16; Mark 1:34

41 Demons also were coming out of many, shouting, "You are the Son of God!" But
rebuking them, He would not allow them to speak, because they knew Him to be the
Christ.

Jesus Preaches throughout Galilee
(36/Matthew 4:23-25; Mark 1:35-39)

42 When day came, Jesus left and went to a secluded place; and the crowds were searching for Him, and came to Him and tried to keep Him from going away from them.

4:43 Mark 1:38

43 But He said to them, "I must preach the kingdom of God to the other cities also, for
I was sent for this purpose."

4:44 Matt 4:23

44 So He kept on preaching in the synagogues of [9]Judea.

Jesus Provides Miraculous Catch of Fish
(37)

5:1 Matt 4:18-22; Mark 1:16-20; John 1:40-42; Num 34:11; Deut 3:17; Josh 12:3; 13:27; Matt 4:18

5 Now it happened that while the crowd was pressing around Him and listening to the
word of God, He was standing by the lake of Gennesaret;
2 and He saw two boats lying at the edge of the lake; but the fishermen had gotten
out of them and were washing their nets.

5:3 Matt 13:2; Mark 3:9, 10; 4:1

3 And He got into one of the boats, which was Simon's, and asked him to put out a
little way from the land. And He sat down and *began* teaching the people from the boat.

5:4 John 21:6

4 When He had finished speaking, He said to Simon, "Put out into the deep water
and let down your nets for a catch."

5:5 Luke 8:24; 9:33, 49; 17:13; John 21:3

5 Simon answered and said, "Master, we worked hard all night and caught nothing,
but I will do as You say *and* let down the nets."

5:6 John 21:6

6 When they had done this, they enclosed a great quantity of fish, and their nets *began* to break;
7 so they signaled to their partners in the other boat for them to come and help them.
And they came and filled both of the boats, so that they began to sink.
8 But when Simon Peter saw *that,* he fell down at Jesus' feet, saying, "Go away from
me Lord, for I am a sinful man, O Lord!"

9 I.e. the country of the Jews (including Galilee)

4:39 Jesus healed Simon's (Peter's) mother-in-law so completely that not only did the fever leave, but her strength was restored, and immediately she got up and took care of others' needs. What a beautiful attitude of service she showed! God gives us health so that we may serve others.

4:40 The people came to Jesus when the sun was setting because this was the Sabbath (4:31), their day of rest. Sabbath lasted from sunset on Friday to sunset on Saturday. The people didn't want to break the law that prohibited travel on the Sabbath, so they waited until the Sabbath hours were over before coming to Jesus. Then, as Luke the physician notes, they came with all kinds of diseases, and Jesus healed each one.

4:41 Why didn't Jesus want the demons to reveal who he was? (1) Jesus commanded them to remain silent to show his authority over them. (2) Jesus wanted his listeners to believe he was the Messiah because of his words, not because of the demons' words. (3) Jesus was going to reveal his identity according to God's timetable, and he would not be pushed by Satan's evil plans. The demons called Jesus "Son of God" or "the Holy One of God" (4:35) because they knew he was the Christ. But Jesus was going to show himself to be the suffering servant before he became the great King. To reveal his identity as King too soon would stir up the crowds with the wrong expectations of what he had come to do.

4:42 Jesus had to get up very early just to get some time alone. If Jesus needed solitude for prayer and refreshment, how much more is this true for us? Don't become so busy that life turns into a flurry of activity leaving no room for quiet fellowship alone with God. No matter how much you have to do, you should always have time for prayer.

4:43 The kingdom of God was good news! It was Good News to the Jews because they had been awaiting the coming of the promised Messiah ever since the Babylonian captivity. It is Good News for us also because it means freedom from slavery to sin and selfishness. The kingdom of God is here and now because the Holy Spirit lives in the hearts of believers. Yet it is also in the future because Jesus will return to reign over a perfect kingdom where sin and evil no longer exist.

5:1 The lake of Gennesaret was also known as the Sea of Galilee or the Sea of Tiberias.

5:2 Fishermen on the Sea of Galilee used nets, often bell-shaped nets with lead weights around the edges. A net would be thrown flat onto the water, and the lead weights would cause it to sink around the fish. Then the fishermen would pull on a cord, drawing the net around the fish. Nets had to be kept in good condition, so they were washed to remove weeds and then mended.

5:8 Simon Peter was awestruck at this miracle, and his first response was to feel his own insignificance in comparison to this man's greatness. Peter knew that Jesus had healed the sick and driven out demons, but he was amazed that Jesus cared about his day-to-day routine and understood his needs. God is interested not only in saving us, but also in helping us in our daily activities.

9 For amazement had seized him and all his companions because of the catch of fish
which they had taken;
10 and so also *were* James and John, sons of Zebedee, who were partners with Simon.
And Jesus said to Simon, "Do not fear, from now on you will be catching men."
11 When they had brought their boats to land, they left everything and followed Him.

5:10 Matt 14:27; 2 Tim 2:26

5:11 Matt 4:20, 22; 19:29; Mark 1:18, 20; Luke 5:28

Jesus Heals a Man with Leprosy
(38/Matthew 8:1-4; Mark 1:40-45)

12 While He was in one of the cities, behold, *there was* a man covered with leprosy;
and when he saw Jesus, he fell on his face and implored Him, saying, "Lord, if You are
willing, You can make me clean."
13 And He stretched out His hand and touched him, saying, "I am willing; be cleansed."
And immediately the leprosy left him.
14 And He ordered him to tell no one, "But go and show yourself to the priest and
make an offering for your cleansing, just as Moses commanded, as a testimony to them."
15 But the news about Him was spreading even farther, and large crowds were gathering to hear *Him* and to be healed of their sicknesses.
16 But Jesus Himself would *often* slip away to the wilderness and pray.

5:14 Lev 13:49; 14:2ff

5:15 Matt 9:26

5:16 Matt 14:23; Mark 1:35; Luke 6:12

Jesus Heals a Paralytic
(39/Matthew 9:1-8; Mark 2:1-12)

17 One day He was teaching; and there were *some* Pharisees and teachers of the law
sitting *there,* who had come from every village of Galilee and Judea and *from* Jerusalem;
and the power of the Lord was *present* for Him to perform healing.
18 And *some* men *were* carrying on a bed a man who was paralyzed; and they were trying to bring him in and to set him down in front of Him.
19 But not finding any *way* to bring him in because of the crowd, they went up on the
roof and let him down through the tiles with his stretcher, into the middle *of the crowd,*
in front of Jesus.
20 Seeing their faith, He said, "Friend, your sins are forgiven you."

5:17 Matt 15:1; Luke 2:46; Mark 1:45; Mark 5:30; Luke 6:19; 8:46

5:19 Matt 24:17; Mark 2:4

5:20 Matt 9:2

5:11 There are two requirements for coming to God. Like Peter, we must recognize our own sinfulness. Then, like these fishermen, we must realize that we can't save ourselves. If we know that we need help, and if we know that Jesus is the only One who can help us, we will be ready to leave everything and follow him.

5:11 This was the disciples' second call. After the first call (Matthew 4:18–22; Mark 1:16–20), Peter, Andrew, James, and John had gone back to fishing. They continued to watch Jesus, however, as he established his authority in the synagogue, healed the sick, and drove out demons. Here he also established his authority in their lives—he met them on their level and helped them in their work. From this point on, they left their nets and remained with Jesus. For us, following Jesus means more than just acknowledging him as Savior. We must leave our past behind and commit our future to him.

5:12 Leprosy was a feared disease because there was no known cure for it, and some forms of it were highly contagious. Leprosy had a similar emotional impact and terror associated with it as AIDS does today. (Sometimes called Hansen's disease, leprosy still exists today in a less contagious form that can be treated.) The priests monitored the disease, banishing lepers who were in a contagious stage to prevent the spread of infection and readmitting lepers whose disease was in remission. Because leprosy destroys the nerve endings, lepers often would unknowingly damage their fingers, toes, and noses. This man with leprosy had an advanced case, so he undoubtedly had lost much bodily tissue. Still, he believed that Jesus could heal every trace of the disease.

5:13 Lepers were considered untouchable because people feared contracting their disease. Yet Jesus reached out and touched the leper to heal him. We may consider certain people who are diseased or disabled to be untouchable or repulsive. We must not be afraid to reach out and touch them with God's love. Whom do you know that needs God's touch of love?

5:16 People were flocking to hear Jesus preach and to have their diseases healed, but Jesus made sure he often withdrew to quiet, solitary places to pray. Many things clamor for our attention, and we often run ourselves ragged attending to them. Like Jesus, however, we should take time to withdraw to a quiet and deserted place to pray. Strength comes from God, and we can only be strengthened by spending time with him.

5:17 The religious leaders spent much time defining and discussing the huge body of religious tradition that had been accumulating for more than 400 years since the Jews' return from exile. They were so concerned with these man-made traditions, in fact, that they often lost sight of Scripture. Here these leaders felt threatened because Jesus challenged their sincerity and because the people were flocking to him.

5:18–19 In Bible times, houses were built of stone and had flat roofs made of mud mixed with straw. Outside stairways led to the roof. These men carried their friend up the stairs to the roof where they took apart as much of the mud and straw mixture as was necessary to lower him in front of Jesus.

5:18–20 It wasn't the paralytic's faith that impressed Jesus, but the faith of his friends. Jesus responded to their faith and healed the man. For better or worse, our faith affects others. We cannot make another person a Christian, but we can do much through our words, actions, and love to give him or her a chance to respond. Look for opportunities to bring your friends to the living Christ.

5:21 Luke 3:8; Luke 7:49; Is 43:25

21 The scribes and the Pharisees began to reason, saying, "Who is this *man* who speaks
blasphemies? Who can forgive sins, but God alone?"
22 But Jesus, aware of their reasonings, answered and said to them, "Why are you reasoning in your hearts?
23 "Which is easier, to say, 'Your sins have been forgiven you,' or to say, 'Get up and
walk'?

5:24 Matt 4:24

24 "But, so that you may know that the Son of Man has authority on earth to forgive
sins,"—He said to the paralytic—"I say to you, get up, and pick up your stretcher and go
home."

5:25 Matt 9:8

25 Immediately he got up before them, and picked up what he had been lying on, and
went home glorifying God.

5:26 Matt 9:8; Luke 1:65; 7:16

26 They were all struck with astonishment and *began* glorifying God; and they were
filled with fear, saying, "We have seen remarkable things today."

Jesus Eats with Sinners at Matthew's House
(40/Matthew 9:9-13; Mark 2:13-17)

5:27 Matt 9:9

27 After that He went out and noticed a tax collector named Levi sitting in the tax booth,
and He said to him, "Follow Me."

5:28 Luke 5:11

28 And he left everything behind, and got up and *began* to follow Him.

5:29 Matt 9:9; Luke 15:1

29 And Levi gave a big reception for Him in his house; and there was a great crowd of
tax collectors and other *people* who were reclining *at the table* with them.

5:30 Mark 2:16; Luke 15:2; Acts 23:9

30 The Pharisees and their scribes *began* grumbling at His disciples, saying, "Why do
you eat and drink with the tax collectors and sinners?"

5:31 Matt 9:12, 13; Mark 2:17

31 And Jesus answered and said to them, "*It is* not those who are well who need a
physician, but those who are sick.
32 "I have not come to call the righteous but sinners to repentance."

Religious Leaders Ask Jesus about Fasting
(41/Matthew 9:14-17; Mark 2:18-22)

5:33 Matt 9:14; Mark 2:18

33 And they said to Him, "The disciples of John often fast and offer prayers, the *disciples* of the Pharisees also do the same, but Yours eat and drink."
34 And Jesus said to them, "You cannot make the attendants of the bridegroom fast
while the bridegroom is with them, can you?

5:35 Matt 9:15; Mark 2:20; Luke 17:22

35 "But *the* days will come; and when the bridegroom is taken away from them, then
they will fast in those days."
36 And He was also telling them a parable: "No one tears a piece of cloth from a new
garment and puts it on an old garment; otherwise he will both tear the new, and the piece
from the new will not match the old.

5:21 When Jesus told the paralytic his sins were forgiven, the Jewish leaders accused Jesus of blasphemy—claiming to be God or to do what only God can do. In Jewish law, blasphemy was punishable by death (Leviticus 24:16). In labeling Jesus' claim to forgive sins blasphemous, the religious leaders showed they did not understand that Jesus *is* God, and he has God's power to heal both the body and the soul. Forgiveness of sins was a sign that the Messianic age had come (Isaiah 40:2; Joel 2:32; Micah 7:18–19; Zechariah 13:1).

5:27 For more about Levi (who was also named Matthew), the disciple and author of the Gospel of Matthew, see his Profile in Matthew 9.

5:28–29 Levi responded as Jesus would want all his followers to do—he followed his Lord immediately, and he called his friends together to meet him too. Levi left a lucrative, though probably dishonest, tax-collecting business to follow Jesus. Then he held a reception for his fellow tax collectors and other notorious "sinners" so they could meet Jesus too. Levi, who left behind a material fortune in order to gain a spiritual fortune, was proud to be associated with Jesus.

5:30–32 The Pharisees wrapped their sin in respectability. They made themselves appear good by publicly doing good deeds and pointing at the sins of others. Jesus chose to spend time not with these proud, self-righteous religious leaders, but with people who sensed their own sin and knew that they were not good enough for God. In order to come to God, we must repent; and in order to renounce our sin, we must recognize it for what it is.

5:35 Jesus knew his death was coming. After that time, fasting would be in order. Although he was fully human, Jesus knew he was God and knew why he had come—to die for the sins of the world.

5:36–39 "Wineskins" were goatskins sewed together at the edges to form watertight bags. Because new wine expands as it ages, it had to be put in new, pliable wineskins. A used skin, having become more rigid, would burst and spill the wine. Like old wineskins, the Pharisees were too rigid to accept Jesus, who could not be contained in their traditions or rules. Christianity required new approaches, new traditions, new structures. Our church programs and ministries should not be so structured that they have no room for a fresh touch of the Spirit, a new method, or a new idea. We, too, must be careful that our hearts do not become so rigid that they prevent us from accepting the new way of thinking that Christ brings. We need to keep our hearts pliable so we can accept Jesus' life-changing message.

37 "And no one puts new wine into old wineskins; otherwise the new wine will burst the
skins and it will be spilled out, and the skins will be ruined.
38 "But new wine must be put into fresh wineskins.
39 "And no one, after drinking old *wine* wishes for new; for he says, 'The old is good
enough.' "

The Disciples Pick Grain on the Sabbath
(45/Matthew 12:1-8; Mark 2:23-28)

6 Now it happened that He was passing through *some* grainfields on a Sabbath; and **6:1**
His disciples were picking the heads of grain, rubbing them in their hands, and eat- Deut 23:25
ing *the grain.* **6:2**
2 But some of the Pharisees said, "Why do you do what is not lawful on the Sabbath?" Matt 12:2
3 And Jesus answering them said, "Have you not even read what David did when he **6:3**
was hungry, he and those who were with him, 1 Sam 21:6
4 how he entered the house of God, and took and ate the [10]consecrated bread which **6:4**
is not lawful for any to eat except the priests alone, and gave it to his companions?" Lev 24:9
5 And He was saying to them, "The Son of Man is Lord of the Sabbath."

Jesus Heals a Man's Hand on the Sabbath
(46/Matthew 12:9-14; Mark 3:1-6)

6 On another Sabbath He entered the synagogue and was teaching; and there was a **6:6**
man there whose right hand was withered. Luke 6:1; Matt 4:23
7 The scribes and the Pharisees were watching Him closely *to see* if He healed on the **6:7**
Sabbath, so that they might find *reason* to accuse Him. Mark 3:2
8 But He knew what they were thinking, and He said to the man with the withered **6:8**
hand, "Get up and come forward!" And he got up and came forward. Matt 9:4
9 And Jesus said to them, "I ask you, is it lawful to do good or to do harm on the
Sabbath, to save a life or to destroy it?"
10 After looking around at them all, He said to him, "Stretch out your hand!" And he **6:10**
did *so;* and his hand was restored. Mark 3:5
11 But they themselves were filled with rage, and discussed together what they might
do to Jesus.

10 Or *showbread;* lit *loaves of presentation*

6:1–2 In Jewish legal tradition, there were 39 categories of activities forbidden on the Sabbath—and harvesting was one of them. The Pharisees even went so far as to describe different methods of harvesting. One method was to rub the heads of grain between the hands, as the disciples were doing here. God's law said farmers were to leave the edges of their fields unplowed so travelers and the poor could eat from this bounty (Deuteronomy 23:25), so the disciples were not guilty of stealing grain. Neither were they breaking the Sabbath by doing their daily work on it. In fact, though they may have been violating the Pharisees' rules, they were not breaking any divine law.

6:2 The Pharisees thought their religious system had all the answers. They could not accept Jesus because he did not fit into their system. We could miss Christ for the same reason. Beware of thinking that you or your church has all the answers. No religious system is big enough to contain Christ completely or to fulfill perfectly all his desires for the world.

6:3–5 Each week 12 consecrated loaves of bread, representing the 12 tribes of Israel, were placed on a table in the temple. This bread was called the bread of the Presence. After its use in the temple, it was to be eaten only by priests. Jesus, accused of Sabbath-breaking, referred to a well-known story about David (1 Samuel 21:1–6). On one occasion, when fleeing from Saul, David and his men ate this consecrated bread. Their need was more important than ceremonial regulations. Jesus was appealing to the same principle: Human need is more important than human regulations and rules. By comparing himself and his disciples with David and his men, Jesus was saying, "If you condemn me, you must also condemn David."

6:5 When Jesus said he was "Lord of the Sabbath," he meant that he had the authority to overrule the Pharisees' traditions and regulations because he had created the Sabbath. The Creator is always greater than the creation.

6:6–7 According to the tradition of the religious leaders, no healing could be done on the Sabbath. Healing, they argued, was practicing medicine, and a person could not practice his or her profession on the Sabbath. It was more important for the religious leaders to protect their laws than to free a person from painful suffering.

6:11 Jesus' enemies were furious. Not only had he read their minds; he also flouted their laws and exposed the hatred in their hearts. It is ironic that it was their hatred, combined with their zeal for the law, that drove them to plot murder—an act that was clearly against the law.

Jesus Selects the Twelve Disciples
(48/Mark 3:13-19)

6:12 Matt 5:1; Matt 14:23; Luke 5:16; 9:18, 28

6:13 Matt 10:2-4; Acts 1:13; Mark 6:30

6:15 Matt 9:9

12 It was at this time that He went off to the mountain to pray, and He spent the whole
night in prayer to God.
13 And when day came, He called His disciples to Him and chose twelve of them, whom
He also named as apostles:
14 Simon, whom He also named Peter, and Andrew his brother; and James and John;
and Philip and Bartholomew;
15 and Matthew and Thomas; James *the son* of Alphaeus, and Simon who was called
the Zealot;
16 Judas *the son* of James, and Judas Iscariot, who became a traitor.

Jesus Gives the Beatitudes
(49/Matthew 5:1-12)

6:17 Luke 6:12; Matt 4:25; Mark 3:7, 8; Matt 11:21

6:19 Matt 9:21; 14:36; Mark 3:10; Luke 5:17

6:20 Matt 5:3

6:22 1 Pet 4:14; John 9:22; 16:2

6:23 Mal 4; 2 Chr 36:16; Acts 7:52

6:24 Luke 16:25; James 5:1; Matt 6:2

17 Jesus came down with them and stood on a level place; and *there was* a large crowd
of His disciples, and a great throng of people from all Judea and Jerusalem and the coastal
region of Tyre and Sidon,
18 who had come to hear Him and to be healed of their diseases; and those who were
troubled with unclean spirits were being cured.
19 And all the people were trying to touch Him, for power was coming from Him and
healing *them* all.
20 And turning His gaze toward His disciples, He *began* to say, "Blessed *are* you *who*
are poor, for yours is the kingdom of God.
21 "Blessed *are* you who hunger now, for you shall be satisfied. Blessed *are* you who weep
now, for you shall laugh.
22 "Blessed are you when men hate you, and ostracize you, and insult you, and scorn
your name as evil, for the sake of the Son of Man.
23 "Be glad in that day and leap *for joy,* for behold, your reward is great in heaven. For
in the same way their fathers used to treat the prophets.
24 "But woe to you who are rich, for you are receiving your comfort in full.
25 "Woe to you who are well-fed now, for you shall be hungry. Woe *to you* who laugh
now, for you shall mourn and weep.

6:12 The Gospel writers note that before every important event in Jesus' life, he took time to go off by himself and pray. This time Jesus was preparing to choose his inner circle, the 12 disciples. Make sure that all your important decisions are grounded in prayer.

6:13 Jesus had many *disciples* (learners), but he chose only 12 *apostles* (messengers). The apostles were his inner circle, to whom he gave special training and whom he sent out with his own authority. These were the men who started the Christian church. In the Gospels these 12 men are usually called the disciples, but in the book of Acts they are called apostles.

6:13–16 Jesus selected "ordinary" men with a mixture of backgrounds and personalities to be his disciples. Today, God calls "ordinary" people together to build his church, teach salvation's message, and serve others out of love. Alone we may feel unqualified to serve Christ effectively, but together we make up a group strong enough to serve God in any way. Ask for patience to accept the diversity of people in your church, and build on the variety of strengths represented in your group.

6:14–16 The disciples are not always listed by the same names. For example, Peter is sometimes called Simon or Cephas. Matthew is also known as Levi. Bartholomew is thought to be the same person as Nathanael (John 1:45). Judas the son of James is also called Thaddaeus.

6:19 Once word of Jesus' healing power spread, crowds gathered just to touch him. For many, he had become a symbol of good fortune, a lucky charm, or a magician. Instead of desiring God's pardon and love, they only wanted physical healing or a chance to see spectacular events. Some people still see God as a cosmic magician and consider prayer as a way to get God to do his tricks. But God is not a magician—he is the Master. Prayer is not a way for us to control God; it is a way for us to put ourselves under his control.

6:20ff This may be Luke's account of the sermon that Matthew records in Matthew 5—7, or it may be that Jesus gave similar sermons on several different occasions. Some believe that this was not one sermon, but a composite based on Jesus' customary teachings.

6:20–23 These verses are called the *Beatitudes,* from the Latin word meaning "blessing." They describe what it means to be Christ's follower; they are standards of conduct; they contrast kingdom values with worldly values, showing what Christ's followers can expect from the world and what God will give them; they contrast fake piety with true humility; and finally, they show how Old Testament expectations are fulfilled in God's kingdom.

6:21 Some believe that the hunger about which Jesus spoke is a hunger for righteousness (Matthew 5:6). Others say this is physical hunger. In any case, in a nation where riches were seen as a sign of God's favor, Jesus startled his hearers by pronouncing blessings on the hungry. In doing so, however, he was in line with an ancient tradition. The Old Testament is filled with texts proclaiming God's concern for the poor and needy. See, for example, 1 Samuel 2:5; Psalm 146:7; Isaiah 58:6–7; and Jesus' own mother's prayer in Luke 1:53.

6:24 If you are trying to find fulfillment only through riches, wealth may be the only reward you will ever get—and it does not last. We should not seek comfort now at the expense of eternal life.

26"Woe *to you* when all men speak well of you, for their fathers used to treat the false
prophets in the same way.

6:26 Matt 7:15

Jesus Teaches about Loving Enemies
(57/Matthew 5:43-48)

27"But I say to you who hear, love your enemies, do good to those who hate you,
28 bless those who curse you, pray for those who mistreat you.
29"Whoever hits you on the cheek, offer him the other also; and whoever takes away
your coat, do not withhold your shirt from him either.
30"Give to everyone who asks of you, and whoever takes away what is yours, do not
demand it back.
31"Treat others the same way you want them to treat you.
32"If you love those who love you, what credit is *that* to you? For even sinners love those
who love them.
33"If you do good to those who do good to you, what credit is *that* to you? For even
sinners do the same.
34"If you lend to those from whom you expect to receive, what credit is *that* to you?
Even sinners lend to sinners in order to receive back the same *amount.*
35"But love your enemies, and do good, and lend, expecting nothing in return; and your
reward will be great, and you will be sons of the Most High; for He Himself is kind to
ungrateful and evil *men.*
36"Be merciful, just as your Father is merciful.

6:27 Matt 5:44; Luke 6:35
6:28 Matt 5:44; Luke 6:35
6:29 Matt 5:39-42
6:31 Matt 7:12
6:32 Matt 5:46
6:34 Matt 5:42
6:35 Luke 6:27; Matt 5:9; Luke 1:32

Jesus Teaches about Criticizing Others
(63/Matthew 7:1-6)

37"Do not judge, and you will not be judged; and do not condemn, and you will not be
condemned; pardon, and you will be pardoned.
38"Give, and it will be given to you. They will pour into your lap a good measure—
pressed down, shaken together, *and* running over. For by your standard of measure it
will be measured to you in return."
39 And He also spoke a parable to them: "A blind man cannot guide a blind man, can
he? Will they not both fall into a pit?
40"A pupil is not above his teacher; but everyone, after he has been fully trained, will
be like his teacher.
41"Why do you look at the speck that is in your brother's eye, but do not notice the log
that is in your own eye?
42"Or how can you say to your brother, 'Brother, let me take out the speck that is in
your eye,' when you yourself do not see the log that is in your own eye? You hypocrite,

6:37 Matt 6:14; Luke 23:16; Acts 3:13
6:38 Mark 4:24; Ps 79:12; Is 65:6, 7; Jer 32:18
6:39 Matt 15:14
6:40 Matt 10:24; John 13:16; 15:20

6:26 There were many false prophets in Old Testament times. They were praised by kings and crowds because their predictions—prosperity and victory in war—were exactly what the people wanted to hear. But popularity is no guarantee of truth, and human flattery does not bring God's approval. Sadness lies ahead for those who chase after the crowd's praise rather than God's truth.

6:27 The Jews despised the Romans because they oppressed God's people, but Jesus told the people to love these enemies. Such words turned many away from Christ. But Jesus wasn't talking about having affection for enemies; he was talking about an act of the will. You can't "fall into" this kind of love—it takes conscious effort. Loving our enemies means acting in their best interests. We can pray for them, and we can think of ways to help them. Jesus loved the whole world, even though the world was in rebellion against God. Jesus asks us to follow his example by loving our enemies. Grant your enemies the same respect and rights as you desire for yourself.

6:35 Love means action. One way to put love to work is to take the initiative in meeting specific needs. This is easy to do with people who love us, people whom we trust; but love means doing this even to those who dislike us or plan to hurt us. The money we give others should be considered a gift, not a high-interest loan that will help us more than them. Give as though you are giving to God.

6:37–38 A forgiving spirit demonstrates that a person has received God's forgiveness. Jesus uses the picture of measuring grain in a basket to ensure the full amount. If we are critical rather than compassionate, we will also receive criticism. If we treat others generously, graciously, and compassionately, however, these qualities will come back to us in full measure. We are to love others, not judge them.

6:39–40 Make sure you're following the right teachers and leaders, because you will go no farther than they do. Look for leaders who will show you more about faith and whose guidance you can trust.

6:41 Jesus doesn't mean we should ignore wrongdoing, but we should not be so worried about others' sins that we overlook our own. We often rationalize our sins by pointing out the same mistakes in others. What kinds of specks in others' eyes are the easiest for you to criticize? Remember your own "logs" when you feel like criticizing, and you may find that you have less to say.

6:42 We should not be so afraid of the label *hypocrite* that we stand still in our Christian life, hiding our faith and making no attempts to grow. A person who tries to do right but often fails is not a hypocrite. Neither are those who fulfill their duty even when they don't feel like doing it—it is often necessary and good to set aside our desires in order to do what needs doing. It is not hypocri-

first take the log out of your own eye, and then you will see clearly to take out the speck that is in your brother's eye.

Jesus Teaches about Fruit in People's Lives
(66/Matthew 7:15-20)

43 "For there is no good tree which produces bad fruit, nor, on the other hand, a bad tree which produces good fruit.

6:44 Matt 7:16; 12:33

44 "For each tree is known by its own fruit. For men do not gather figs from thorns, nor do they pick grapes from a briar bush.

6:45 Matt 12:35; Matt 12:34

45 "The good man out of the good treasure of his heart brings forth what is good; and the evil *man* out of the evil *treasure* brings forth what is evil; for his mouth speaks from that which fills his heart.

Jesus Teaches about Those Who Build Houses on Rock and Sand
(67/Matthew 7:21-29)

6:46 Mal 1:6; Matt 7:21

6:47 James 1:22ff

46 "Why do you call Me, 'Lord, Lord,' and do not do what I say?
47 "Everyone who comes to Me and hears My words and acts on them, I will show you whom he is like:
48 he is like a man building a house, who dug deep and laid a foundation on the rock; and when a flood occurred, the torrent burst against that house and could not shake it, because it had been well built.
49 "But the one who has heard and has not acted *accordingly,* is like a man who built a house on the ground without any foundation; and the torrent burst against it and immediately it collapsed, and the ruin of that house was great."

A Roman Centurion Demonstrates Faith
(68/Matthew 8:5-13)

7:1 Matt 7:28

7:3 Matt 8:5

7 When He had completed all His discourse in the hearing of the people, He went to Capernaum.
2 And a centurion's slave, who was highly regarded by him, was sick and about to die.
3 When he heard about Jesus, he sent some Jewish elders asking Him to come and save the life of his slave.
4 When they came to Jesus, they earnestly implored Him, saying, "He is worthy for You to grant this to him;
5 for he loves our nation and it was he who built us our synagogue."
6 Now Jesus *started* on His way with them; and when He was not far from the house, the centurion sent friends, saying to Him, "Lord, do not trouble Yourself further, for I am not worthy for You to come under my roof;
7 for this reason I did not even consider myself worthy to come to You, but *just* say the word, and my servant will be healed.

---

sy to be weak in faith. A hypocrite is a person who puts on religious behavior in order to gain attention, approval, acceptance, or admiration from others.

6:45 Jesus reminds us that our speech and actions reveal our true underlying beliefs, attitudes, and motivations. The good impressions we try to make cannot last if our hearts are deceptive. What is in your heart will come out in your speech and behavior.

6:46–49 Obeying God is like building a house on a strong, solid foundation that stands firm when storms come. When life is calm, our foundations don't seem to matter. But when crises come, our foundations are tested. Be sure your life is built on the solid foundation of knowing and trusting Jesus Christ.

6:49 Why would people build a house without a foundation? Perhaps to save time and avoid the hard work of preparing a stone foundation. Possibly because the waterfront scenery is more attractive or because beach houses have higher social status than cliff houses. Perhaps because they want to join their friends who have already settled in sandy areas. Maybe because they haven't heard about the violent storms coming, or because they have discounted the reports, or for some reason they think disaster can't happen to them. Whatever their reason, those with no foundation are shortsighted, and they will be sorry. When you find yourself listening but not obeying, what are your reasons?

7:2 A *centurion* was a Roman army officer in charge of 100 men. This man came to Jesus not as a last resort or magic charm, but because he believed Jesus was sent from God. Apparently the centurion recognized that the Jews possessed God's message for mankind—it is recorded that he loved the nation and built the synagogue. Thus, in his time of need, it was natural for him to turn to Jesus.

7:3 Why did the centurion send Jewish elders to Jesus instead of going himself? Since he was well aware of the Jewish hatred for Roman soldiers, he may not have wanted to interrupt a Jewish gathering. As an army captain, he daily delegated work and sent groups on missions, so this was how he chose to get his message to Jesus.

7:3 Matthew 8:5 says the Roman centurion visited Jesus himself, while Luke 7:3 says he sent Jewish elders to present his request to Jesus. In dealing with the messengers, Jesus was dealing with the centurion. For his Jewish audience, Matthew emphasized the man's faith. For his Gentile audience, Luke highlighted the good relationship between the Jewish elders and the Roman centurion.

8 "For I also am a man placed under authority, with soldiers under me; and I say to
this one, 'Go!' and he goes, and to another, 'Come!' and he comes, and to my slave, 'Do
this!' and he does it."
9 Now when Jesus heard this, He marveled at him, and turned and said to the crowd
that was following Him, "I say to you, not even in Israel have I found such great faith."
10 When those who had been sent returned to the house, they found the slave in good
health.

7:9 Matt 8:10; Luke 7:50

Jesus Raises a Widow's Son from the Dead
(69)

11 Soon afterwards He went to a city called Nain; and His disciples were going along
with Him, accompanied by a large crowd.
12 Now as He approached the gate of the city, a dead man was being carried out, the
only son of his mother, and she was a widow; and a sizeable crowd from the city was with
her.
13 When the Lord saw her, He felt compassion for her, and said to her, "Do not weep."
14 And He came up and touched the coffin; and the bearers came to a halt. And He
said, "Young man, I say to you, arise!"
15 The dead man sat up and began to speak. And *Jesus* gave him back to his mother.
16 Fear gripped them all, and they *began* glorifying God, saying, "A great prophet has
arisen among us!" and, "God has visited His people!"
17 This report concerning Him went out all over Judea and in all the surrounding
district.

7:13 Luke 7:19; 10:1; 11:1, 39; 12:42; 13:15; 17:5, 6; 18:6; 19:8; 22:61; 24:34; John 4:1; 6:23; 11:2

7:16 Luke 5:26; Matt 9:8; Matt 21:11; Luke 7:39

7:17 Matt 9:26

Jesus Eases John's Doubt
(70/Matthew 11:1-19)

18 The disciples of John reported to him about all these things.
19 Summoning two of his disciples, John sent them to the Lord, saying, "Are You the
Expected One, or do we look for someone else?"

7:19 Luke 7:13; 10:1; 11:1, 39; 12:42; 13:15; 17:5, 6; 18:6; 19:8; 22:61; 24:34; John 4:1; 6:23; 11:2

7:9 The Roman centurion didn't come to Jesus, and he didn't expect Jesus to come to him. Just as this officer did not need to be present to have his orders carried out, so Jesus didn't need to be present to heal. The centurion's faith was especially amazing because he was a Gentile who had not been brought up to know a loving God.

7:11–15 The widow's situation was serious. She had lost her husband, and here her only son was dead—her last means of support. The crowd of mourners would go home, and she would be left penniless and alone. The widow was probably past the age of childbearing and would not marry again. Unless a relative came to her aid, her future was bleak. She would be an easy prey for swindlers, and she would likely be reduced to begging for food. In fact, as Luke repeatedly emphasizes, this woman was just the kind of person Jesus had come to help—and help her he did. Jesus has the power to bring hope out of any tragedy.

JESUS RAISES A WIDOW'S SON
Jesus traveled to Nain and met a funeral procession leaving the village. A widow's only son had died, leaving her virtually helpless, but Jesus brought the young man back to life. This miracle, recorded only in Luke, reveals Jesus' compassion for people's needs.

7:11–17 This story illustrates salvation. The whole world was dead in sin (Ephesians 2:1), just as the widow's son was dead. Being dead, we could do nothing to help ourselves—we couldn't even ask for help. But God had compassion on us, and he sent Jesus to raise us to life with him (Ephesians 2:4–7). The dead man did not earn his second chance at life, and we cannot earn our new life in Christ. But we can accept God's gift of life, praise God for it, and use our lives to do his will.

7:12 Honoring the dead was important in Jewish tradition. A funeral procession—the relatives of the dead person following the body that was wrapped and carried on a kind of stretcher—would make its way through town, and bystanders would be expected to join the procession. In addition, hired mourners would cry aloud and draw attention to the procession. The family's mourning would continue for 30 days.

7:16 The people thought of Jesus as a prophet because, like the Old Testament prophets, he boldly proclaimed God's message and sometimes raised the dead. Both Elijah and Elisha raised children from the dead (1 Kings 17:17–24; 2 Kings 4:18–37). The people were correct in thinking that Jesus was a prophet, but he was much more—he is God himself.

7:18–23 John was confused because the reports he received about Jesus were unexpected and incomplete. John's doubts were natural, and Jesus didn't rebuke him for them. Instead, Jesus responded in a way that John would understand: Jesus explained that he had accomplished what the Messiah was supposed to accomplish. God can handle our doubts, and he welcomes our questions. Do you have questions about Jesus—about who he is or what he expects of you? Admit them to yourself and to God, and begin

20 When the men came to Him, they said, "John the Baptist has sent us to You, to ask,
'Are You the Expected One, or do we look for someone else?' "

7:21 Matt 4:23; Mark 3:10

21 At that very time He cured many *people* of diseases and afflictions and evil spirits;
and He gave sight to many *who were* blind.

7:22 Is 35:5; Is 61:1

22 And He answered and said to them, "Go and report to John what you have seen
and heard: *the* BLIND RECEIVE SIGHT, *the* lame walk, *the* lepers are cleansed, and *the*
deaf hear, *the* dead are raised up, *the* POOR HAVE THE GOSPEL PREACHED TO THEM.
23 "Blessed is he who does not take offense at Me."
24 When the messengers of John had left, He began to speak to the crowds about John,
"What did you go out into the wilderness to see? A reed shaken by the wind?
25 "But what did you go out to see? A man dressed in soft clothing? Those who are
splendidly clothed and live in luxury are *found* in royal palaces!
26 "But what did you go out to see? A prophet? Yes, I say to you, and one who is more
than a prophet.

7:27 Mal 3:1; Matt 11:10; Mark 1:2

27 "This is the one about whom it is written,
'BEHOLD, I SEND MY MESSENGER AHEAD OF YOU,
WHO WILL PREPARE YOUR WAY BEFORE YOU.'
28 "I say to you, among those born of women there is no one greater than John; yet he
who is least in the kingdom of God is greater than he."

7:29 Luke 7:35; Matt 21:32; Luke 3:12; Acts 18:25; 19:3

7:30 Matt 22:35

29 When all the people and the tax collectors heard *this,* they acknowledged God's
justice, having been baptized with the baptism of John.
30 But the Pharisees and the [11]lawyers rejected God's purpose for themselves, not having been baptized by John.
31 "To what then shall I compare the men of this generation, and what are they like?
32 "They are like children who sit in the market place and call to one another, and they
say, 'We played the flute for you, and you did not dance; we sang a dirge, and you did
not weep.'

7:33 Luke 1:15

33 "For John the Baptist has come eating no bread and drinking no wine, and you say,
'He has a demon!'
34 "The Son of Man has come eating and drinking, and you say, 'Behold, a gluttonous
man and a drunkard, a friend of tax collectors and sinners!'

7:35 Luke 7:29

35 "Yet wisdom is vindicated by all her children."

A Sinful Woman Anoints Jesus' Feet
(72)

7:37 Matt 26:6-13; Mark 14:3-9; John 12:1-8

36 Now one of the Pharisees was requesting Him to dine with him, and He entered the
Pharisee's house and reclined *at the table.*
37 And there was a woman in the city who was a sinner; and when she learned that He

11 I.e. experts in the Mosaic Law

---

looking for answers. Only as you face your doubts honestly can you begin to resolve them.

7:20–22 The proofs listed here for Jesus' being the Messiah are significant. They consist of observable deeds, not theories—actions that Jesus' contemporaries saw and reported for us to read today. The prophets had said that the Messiah would do these very acts (see Isaiah 35:5–6; 61:1). These physical proofs helped John—and will help all of us—to recognize who Jesus is.

7:28 Of all people, no one fulfilled his God-given purpose better than John. Yet in God's kingdom, all who come after John have a greater spiritual heritage because they have clearer knowledge of the purpose of Jesus' death and resurrection. John was the last to function like the Old Testament prophets, the last to prepare the people for the coming Messianic age. Jesus was not contrasting the man John with individual Christians; he was contrasting life before Christ with life in the fullness of Christ's kingdom.

7:29–30 The tax collectors (who embodied evil in most people's minds) and common people heard John's message and repented. In contrast, the Pharisees and scribes—religious leaders—rejected his words. Wanting to live their own way, they justified their own point of view and refused to listen to other ideas. Rather than trying to force your plans on God, try to discover his plan for you.

7:31–35 The religious leaders hated anyone who spoke the truth and exposed their own hypocrisy, and they did not bother to be consistent in their faultfinding. They criticized John the Baptist because he fasted and drank no wine; they criticized Jesus because he ate heartily and drank wine with tax collectors and "sinners." Their real objection to both men, of course, had nothing to do with dietary habits. What the Pharisees and lawyers couldn't stand was being exposed for their hypocrisy.

7:33–34 The Pharisees weren't troubled by their inconsistency toward John the Baptist and Jesus. They were good at justifying their "wisdom." Most of us can find compelling reasons to do or believe whatever suits our purposes. If we do not examine our ideas in the light of God's truth, however, we may be just as obviously self-serving as the Pharisees.

7:35 Wisdom's children were the followers of Jesus and John. These followers lived changed lives. Their righteous living demonstrated the wisdom that Jesus and John taught.

7:36 A similar incident occurred later in Jesus' ministry (see Matthew 26:6–13; Mark 14:3–9; John 12:1–11).

7:37 Alabaster vials were carved, expensive, and beautiful.

was reclining *at the table* in the Pharisee's house, she brought an alabaster vial of perfume,
38 and standing behind *Him* at His feet, weeping, she began to wet His feet with her
tears, and kept wiping them with the hair of her head, and kissing His feet and anointing
them with the perfume.
39 Now when the Pharisee who had invited Him saw this, he said to himself, "If this
man were a prophet He would know who and what sort of person this woman is who is
touching Him, that she is a sinner."
40 And Jesus answered him, "Simon, I have something to say to you." And he replied,
"Say it, Teacher."
41 "A moneylender had two debtors: one owed five hundred [12]denarii, and the other
fifty.
42 "When they were unable to repay, he graciously forgave them both. So which of them
will love him more?"
43 Simon answered and said, "I suppose the one whom he forgave more." And He said
to him, "You have judged correctly."
44 Turning toward the woman, He said to Simon, "Do you see this woman? I entered
your house; you gave Me no water for My feet, but she has wet My feet with her tears
and wiped them with her hair.
45 "You gave Me no kiss; but she, since the time I came in, has not ceased to kiss My
feet.
46 "You did not anoint My head with oil, but she anointed My feet with perfume.
47 "For this reason I say to you, her sins, which are many, have been forgiven, for she
loved much; but he who is forgiven little, loves little."
48 Then He said to her, "Your sins have been forgiven."
49 Those who were reclining *at the table* with Him began to say to themselves, "Who is
this *man* who even forgives sins?"
50 And He said to the woman, "Your faith has saved you; go in peace."

Women Accompany Jesus and the Disciples

(73)

8 Soon afterwards, He *began* going around from one city and village to another, proclaiming and preaching the kingdom of God. The twelve were with Him,
2 and *also* some women who had been healed of evil spirits and sicknesses: Mary who
was called Magdalene, from whom seven demons had gone out,
3 and Joanna the wife of Chuza, Herod's steward, and Susanna, and many others who
were contributing to their support out of their private means.

7:39 Luke 7:16; John 4:19
7:41 Matt 18:28; Mark 6:37
7:42 Matt 18:25
7:44 Gen 18:4; 19:2; 43:24; Judg 19:21; 1 Tim 5:10
7:45 2 Sam 15:5
7:46 2 Sam 12:20; Ps 23:5; Eccl 9:8; Dan 10:3
7:48 Matt 9:2; Mark 2:5, 9; Luke 5:20, 23
7:49 Luke 5:21
7:50 Matt 9:22; Luke 17:19; 18:42; Mark 5:34; Luke 8:48
8:1 Matt 4:23
8:2 Matt 27:55; Mark 15:40, 41; Luke 23:49, 55; Matt 27:56; Mark 16:9
8:3 Matt 14:1; Matt 20:8

12 The denarius was equivalent to a day's wages

7:38 Although the woman was not an invited guest, she entered the house anyway and knelt behind Jesus at his feet. In Jesus' day, it was customary to recline while eating. Dinner guests would lie on couches with their heads near the table, propping themselves up on one elbow and stretching their feet out behind them. The woman could easily anoint Jesus' feet without approaching the table.

7:44ff Again Luke contrasts the Pharisees with sinners—and again the sinners come out ahead. Simon had committed several social errors in neglecting to wash Jesus' feet (a courtesy extended to guests because sandaled feet got very dirty), anoint his head with oil, and offer him the kiss of greeting. Did Simon perhaps feel that he was too good to treat Jesus as an equal? The sinful woman, by contrast, lavished tears, expensive perfume, and kisses on her Savior. In this story it is the grateful prostitute, and not the stingy religious leader, whose sins were forgiven. Although it is God's grace through faith that saves us, and not acts of love or generosity, this woman's act demonstrated her true faith, and Jesus honored her faith.

7:47 Overflowing love is the natural response to forgiveness and the appropriate consequence of faith. But only those who realize the depth of their sin can appreciate the complete forgiveness God offers them. Jesus has rescued all of his followers, whether they were once extremely wicked or conventionally good, from eternal death. Do you appreciate the wideness of God's mercy? Are you grateful for his forgiveness?

7:49–50 The Pharisees believed that only God could forgive sins, so they wondered why this man Jesus was saying that the woman's sins were forgiven. They did not grasp the fact that Jesus was indeed God.

8:2–3 Jesus lifted women up from the agony of degradation and servitude to the joy of fellowship and service. In Jewish culture, women were not supposed to learn from rabbis. By allowing these women to travel with him, Jesus was showing that all people are equal under God. These women supported Jesus' ministry with their own money. They owed a great debt to him because he had driven demons out of some and had healed others.

8:2–3 Here we catch a glimpse of a few of the people behind the scenes in Jesus' ministry. The ministry of those in the foreground is often supported by those whose work is less visible but just as essential. Offer your resources to God, whether or not you will be on center stage.

Jesus Tells the Parable of the Four Soils
(77/Matthew 13:1-9; Mark 4:1-9)

4 When a large crowd was coming together, and those from the various cities were
journeying to Him, He spoke by way of a parable:
5 "The sower went out to sow his seed; and as he sowed, some fell beside the road, and
it was trampled under foot and the birds of the air ate it up.
6 "Other *seed* fell on rocky *soil,* and as soon as it grew up, it withered away, because it
had no moisture.
7 "Other *seed* fell among the thorns; and the thorns grew up with it and choked it out.
8 "Other *seed* fell into the good soil, and grew up, and produced a crop a hundred times
as great." As He said these things, He would call out, "He who has ears to hear, let him
hear."

8:8 Matt 11:15; Mark 7:16; Luke 14:35; Rev 2:7, 11, 17, 29; 3:6, 13, 22; 13:9

Jesus Explains the Parable of the Four Soils
(78/Matthew 13:10-23; Mark 4:10-25)

9 His disciples *began* questioning Him as to what this parable meant.
10 And He said, "To you it has been granted to know the mysteries of the kingdom of
God, but to the rest *it is* in parables, so that SEEING THEY MAY NOT SEE, AND HEARING
THEY MAY NOT UNDERSTAND.
11 "Now the parable is this: the seed is the word of God.

8:10 Matt 13:11; Is 6:9; Matt 13:14; Acts 28:26

8:11 1 Pet 1:23

JESUS AND WOMEN

Jesus talks to a Samaritan woman at the well	John 4:1–26
Jesus raises a widow's son from the dead	Luke 7:11–17
A sinful woman anoints Jesus' feet	Luke 7:36–50
The adulterous woman	John 8:1–11
The group of women travels with Jesus	Luke 8:1–3
Jesus visits Mary and Martha	Luke 10:38–42
Jesus heals a crippled woman	Luke 13:10–17
Jesus heals the daughter of a Gentile woman	Mark 7:24–30
Weeping women follow Jesus on his way to the cross	Luke 23:27–31
Jesus' mother and other women gather at the cross	John 19:25–27
Jesus appears to Mary Magdalene	Mark 16:9–11
Jesus appears to other women after his resurrection	Matthew 18:8–10

As a non-Jew recording the words and works of Jesus' life, Luke demonstrates a special sensitivity to other "outsiders" with whom Jesus came into contact. For instance, Luke records five events involving women that are not mentioned in the other Gospels. In first-century Jewish culture, women were usually treated as second-class citizens with few of the rights men had. But Jesus crossed those barriers, and Luke showed the special care Jesus had for women. Jesus treated all people with equal respect. The above passages tell of his encounters with women.

8:4 Jesus often communicated spiritual truth through *parables*—short stories or descriptions that take a familiar object or situation and give it a startling new twist. By linking the known with the hidden and forcing listeners to think, parables can point to spiritual truths. A parable compels listeners to discover the truth for themselves, and it conceals the truth from those too lazy or dull to understand it. In reading Jesus' parables, we must be careful not to read too much into them. Most have only one point and one meaning.

8:5 Why would a farmer allow precious seed to land on the road, on rocks, or among thorns? This is not an irresponsible farmer scattering seeds at random. He is using the acceptable method of hand-seeding a large field—tossing it by handfuls as he walks through the field. His goal is to get as much seed as possible to take root in good soil, but there is inevitable waste as some falls or is blown into less productive areas. That some of the seed produced no crop was not the fault of the faithful farmer or of the seed. The yield depended on the condition of the soil where the seed fell. It is our responsibility to spread the seed (God's message), but we should not give up when some of our efforts fail. Remember, not every seed falls on good soil.

8:10 Why didn't the crowds understand Jesus' words? Perhaps they were looking for a military leader or a political Messiah and could not fit his gentle teaching style into their preconceived idea. Perhaps they were afraid of pressure from religious leaders and did not want to look too deeply into Jesus' words. God told Isaiah that people would hear without understanding and see without perceiving (Isaiah 6:9), and that kind of reaction confronted Jesus. The parable of the sower was an accurate picture of the people's reaction to the rest of his parables.

8:11–15 "Road" people, like many of the religious leaders, refused to believe God's message. "Rocky soil" people, like many in the crowds who followed Jesus, believed his message but never got around to doing anything about it. "Thorn" people, overcome by worries and the lure of materialism, left no room in their lives for God. "Good soil" people, in contrast to all the other groups, followed Jesus no matter what the cost. Which type of soil are you?

12 "Those beside the road are those who have heard; then the devil comes and takes
away the word from their heart, so that they will not believe and be saved.
13 "Those on the rocky *soil are* those who, when they hear, receive the word with joy;
and these have no *firm* root; they believe for a while, and in time of temptation fall away.
14 "The *seed* which fell among the thorns, these are the ones who have heard, and as
they go on their way they are choked with worries and riches and pleasures of *this* life,
and bring no fruit to maturity.
15 "But the *seed* in the good soil, these are the ones who have heard the word in an honest
and good heart, and hold it fast, and bear fruit with perseverance.
16 "Now no one after lighting a lamp covers it over with a container, or puts it under a **8:16** Matt 5:15; Mark 4:21; Luke 11:33
bed; but he puts it on a lampstand, so that those who come in may see the light.
17 "For nothing is hidden that will not become evident, nor *anything* secret that will not
be known and come to light. **8:17** Matt 10:26; Mark 4:22; Luke 12:2
18 "So take care how you listen; for whoever has, to him *more* shall be given; and who-
ever does not have, even what he thinks he has shall be taken away from him." **8:18** Matt 13:12; 25:29; Luke 19:26

Jesus Describes His True Family
(76/Matthew 12:46-50; Mark 3:31-35)

19 And His mother and brothers came to Him, and they were unable to get to Him
because of the crowd.
20 And it was reported to Him, "Your mother and Your brothers are standing outside,
wishing to see You."
21 But He answered and said to them, "My mother and My brothers are these who **8:21** Luke 11:28
hear the word of God and do it."

Jesus Calms the Storm
(87/Matthew 8:23-27; Mark 4:35-41)

22 Now on one of *those* days Jesus and His disciples got into a boat, and He said to **8:22** Luke 5:1f; 8:23
them, "Let us go over to the other side of the lake." So they launched out.
23 But as they were sailing along He fell asleep; and a fierce gale of wind descended **8:23** Luke 5:1f; 8:22
on the lake, and they *began* to be swamped and to be in danger.
24 They came to Jesus and woke Him up, saying, "Master, Master, we are perishing!" **8:24** Luke 5:5; Luke 4:39
And He got up and rebuked the wind and the surging waves, and they stopped, and it
became calm.
25 And He said to them, "Where is your faith?" They were fearful and amazed, saying

HEALING A DEMON-POSSESSED MAN
As he traveled through Galilee, Jesus told many parables and met many people, as recorded in Matthew and Mark. Later, from Capernaum, Jesus and the disciples set out in a boat, only to encounter a fierce storm. Jesus calmed the storm and, when they landed, exorcised a "legion" of demons.

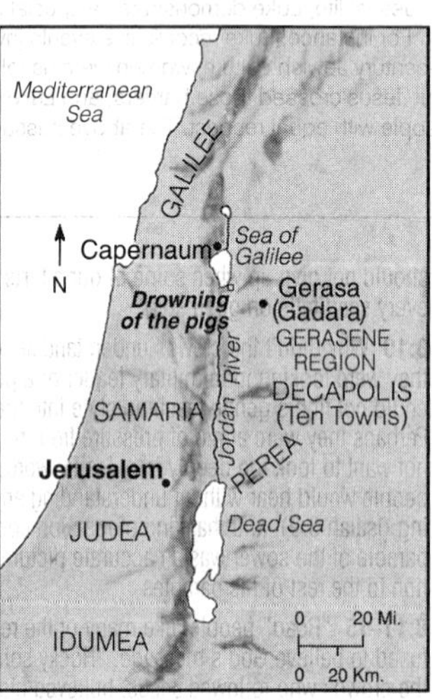

8:16–17 When the light of the truth about Jesus illuminates us, it is our duty to shine that light to help others. Our witness for Christ should be public, not hidden. We should not keep the benefits for ourselves alone but pass them on to others. In order to be helpful, we need to be well placed. Seek opportunities to be there when unbelievers need help.

8:18 Applying God's Word helps us grow. This is a principle of growth in physical, mental, and spiritual life. For example, a muscle, when exercised, will grow stronger, but an unused muscle will grow weak and flabby. If you are not growing stronger, you are growing weaker; it is impossible for you to stand still. How are you using what God has taught you?

8:21 Jesus' true family are those who hear *and* obey his words. Hearing without obeying is not enough. As Jesus loved his mother (see John 19:25–27), so he loves us. Christ offers us an intimate family relationship with him.

8:23 The Sea of Galilee (actually a large lake) is even today the scene of fierce storms, sometimes with waves as high as 20 feet. Jesus' disciples were not frightened without cause. Even though several of them were expert fishermen and knew how to handle a boat, their peril was real.

8:25 When caught in the storms of life, it is easy to think that God has lost control and that we're at the mercy of the winds of fate. In reality, God is sovereign. He controls the history of the world as well as our personal destinies. Just as Jesus calmed the waves, he can calm whatever storms you may face.

to one another, "Who then is this, that He commands even the winds and the water, and
they obey Him?"

Jesus Sends the Demons into a Herd of Swine
(88/Matthew 8:28-34; Mark 5:1-20)

26 Then they sailed to the country of the Gerasenes, which is opposite Galilee.
27 And when He came out onto the land, He was met by a man from the city who was
possessed with demons; and who had not put on any clothing for a long time, and was
not living in a house, but in the tombs.
8:28 Matt 8:29; Mark 5:7
28 Seeing Jesus, he cried out and fell before Him, and said in a loud voice, "What business do we have with each other, Jesus, Son of the Most High God? I beg You, do not
torment me."
29 For He had commanded the unclean spirit to come out of the man. For it had seized
him many times; and he was bound with chains and shackles and kept under guard, and
yet he would break his bonds and be driven by the demon into the desert.
8:30 Matt 26:53
30 And Jesus asked him, "What is your name?" And he said, "Legion"; for many demons had entered him.
8:31 Rom 10:7; Rev 9:1f, 11; 11:7; 17:8; 20:1, 3
31 They were imploring Him not to command them to go away into the abyss.
32 Now there was a herd of many swine feeding there on the mountain; and *the demons* implored Him to permit them to enter the swine. And He gave them permission.
8:33 Luke 5:1f; 8:22
33 And the demons came out of the man and entered the swine; and the herd rushed
down the steep bank into the lake and was drowned.
34 When the herdsmen saw what had happened, they ran away and reported it in the
city and *out* in the country.
8:35 Luke 10:39
35 *The people* went out to see what had happened; and they came to Jesus, and found
the man from whom the demons had gone out, sitting down at the feet of Jesus, clothed
and in his right mind; and they became frightened.
8:36 Matt 4:24
36 Those who had seen it reported to them how the man who was demon-possessed
had been made well.
37 And all the people of the country of the Gerasenes and the surrounding district asked
Him to leave them, for they were gripped with great fear; and He got into a boat and
returned.
38 But the man from whom the demons had gone out was begging Him that he might
accompany Him; but He sent him away, saying,

8:26 The country of the Gerasenes was a Gentile region southeast of the Sea of Galilee, home of the Decapolis, or the Ten Cities. These were Greek cities that belonged to no country and were self-governing. Although Jews would not have raised pigs because the Jewish religion labeled them unclean, the Gentiles had no such aversion.

8:27–28 These demons recognized Jesus and his authority immediately. They knew who Jesus was and what his great power could do to them. Demons, Satan's messengers, are powerful and destructive. Still active today, they attempt to distort and destroy people's relationship with God. Demons and demon-possession are real. It is vital that believers recognize the power of Satan and his demons, but we shouldn't let curiosity lead us to get involved with demonic forces (Deuteronomy 18:10–12). Demons are powerless against those who trust in Jesus. If we resist the devil, he will leave us alone (James 4:7).

8:29–31 The demons begged Jesus to spare them from the abyss, which is also mentioned in Revelation 9:1 and 20:1–3 as the place of confinement for Satan and his messengers. The demons, of course, knew all about this place of confinement, and they didn't want to go there.

8:30 The demons' name was Legion. A legion was the largest unit in the Roman army, having between 3,000 and 6,000 soldiers. The man was possessed by not one, but many demons.

8:33 Why didn't Jesus just destroy these demons—or send them to the abyss? Because the time for such work had not yet come. He healed many people of the destructive effects of demon-possession, but he did not yet destroy demons. The same question could be asked today—why doesn't Jesus stop all the evil in the world? His time for that has not yet come. But it will come. The book of Revelation portrays the future victory of Jesus over Satan, his demons, and all evil.

8:33–37 The demons destroyed the pigs, which hurt the finances of those tending the pigs, but can swine and money compare with a human life? A man had been freed from the devil's power, but the people thought only about their livestock. People have always tended to value financial gain above needy people. Throughout history, most wars have been fought to protect economic interests. Much injustice and oppression, both at home and abroad, is the direct result of some individual's or company's urge to get rich. People are continually being sacrificed to the god of money. Don't think more highly of "pigs" than of people. Think carefully about how your decisions will affect other human beings, and be willing to choose a simpler life-style if it will keep other people from being harmed.

8:38–39 Often Jesus asked those he healed to be quiet about the healing, but he urged this man to return to his family and tell them what God had done for him. Why? (1) Jesus knew the man would be an effective witness to those who knew his previous condition and could attest to the miraculous healing. (2) Jesus wanted to expand his ministry by introducing his message into this Gentile area. (3) Jesus knew that the Gentiles, since they were not expecting a Messiah, would not divert his ministry by trying to crown him king. When God touches your life, don't be afraid to share the wonderful events with your family and friends.

39 “Return to your house and describe what great things God has done for you.” So he
went away, proclaiming throughout the whole city what great things Jesus had done
for him.

Jesus Heals a Bleeding Woman and Restores a Girl to Life
(89/Matthew 9:18-26; Mark 5:21-43)

40 And as Jesus returned, the people welcomed Him, for they had all been waiting **8:40**
for Him. Matt 9:1; Mark 5:21
41 And there came a man named Jairus, and he was an official of the synagogue; and **8:41**
he fell at Jesus' feet, and *began* to implore Him to come to his house; Mark 5:22; Luke 8:49
42 for he had an only daughter, about twelve years old, and she was dying. But as He
went, the crowds were pressing against Him.
43 And a woman who had a hemorrhage for twelve years, and could not be healed by
anyone,
44 came up behind Him and touched the fringe of His cloak, and immediately her
hemorrhage stopped.
45 And Jesus said, “Who is the one who touched Me?” And while they were all deny- **8:45**
ing it, Peter said, “Master, the people are crowding and pressing in on You.” Luke 5:5
46 But Jesus said, “Someone did touch Me, for I was aware that power had gone out **8:46**
of Me.” Luke 5:17
47 When the woman saw that she had not escaped notice, she came trembling and fell
down before Him, and declared in the presence of all the people the reason why she had
touched Him, and how she had been immediately healed.
48 And He said to her, “Daughter, your faith has made you well; go in peace.” **8:48**
49 While He was still speaking, someone ☆came from *the house of* the synagogue offi- Matt 9:22; Mark 5:34; Luke 7:50
cial, saying, “Your daughter has died; do not trouble the Teacher anymore.”
50 But when Jesus heard *this,* He answered him, “Do not be afraid *any longer;* only **8:49** Luke 8:41
believe, and she will be made well.”
51 When He came to the house, He did not allow anyone to enter with Him, except **8:50** Mark 5:36
Peter and John and James, and the girl's father and mother.
52 Now they were all weeping and lamenting for her; but He said, “Stop weeping, for **8:52**
she has not died, but is asleep.” Matt 11:17; Luke 23:27; John 11:13
53 And they *began* laughing at Him, knowing that she had died.
54 He, however, took her by the hand and called, saying, “Child, arise!”
55 And her spirit returned, and she got up immediately; and He gave orders for *something* to be given her to eat.
56 Her parents were amazed; but He instructed them to tell no one what had happened. **8:56** Matt 8:4

Jesus Sends out the Twelve Disciples
(93/Matthew 10:1-16; Mark 6:7-13)

9 And He called the twelve together, and gave them power and authority over all the **9:1**
demons and to heal diseases. Matt 10:5; Mark 6:7

8:41 The synagogue was the local center of worship. The synagogue official was responsible for administration, building maintenance, and worship supervision. It would have been quite unusual for a respected synagogue official to fall at the feet of an itinerant preacher and beg him to heal his daughter. Jesus honored this man's humble faith (8:50, 54–56).

8:43–48 Many people surrounded Jesus as he made his way toward Jairus's house. It was virtually impossible to get through the multitude, but one woman fought her way desperately through the crowd in order to touch Jesus. As soon as she did so, she was healed. What a difference there is between the crowds that are curious about Jesus and the few who reach out and touch him! Today, many people are vaguely familiar with Jesus, but nothing in their lives is changed or bettered by this passing acquaintance. It is only faith that releases God's healing power. Are you just curious about God, or do you reach out to him in faith, knowing that his mercy will bring healing to your body, soul, and spirit?

8:45 It isn't that Jesus didn't know who had touched him; it's that he wanted the woman to step forward and identify herself. Jesus wanted to teach her that his cloak did not contain magical properties, but that her faith in him had healed her. He may also have wanted to teach the crowds a lesson. According to Jewish law, a man who touched a menstruating woman became ceremonially unclean (Leviticus 15:19–28). This was true whether her bleeding was normal or, as in this woman's case, the result of illness. To protect themselves from such defilement, Jewish men carefully avoided touching, speaking to, or even looking at women. By contrast, Jesus proclaimed to hundreds of people that this "unclean" woman had touched him—and then he healed her. In Jesus' mind, this suffering woman was not to be overlooked. As God's creation, she deserved attention and respect.

8:56 Jesus told the parents not to talk about their daughter's healing because he knew the facts would speak for themselves. Besides, Jesus was concerned for his ministry. He did not want to be known as just a miracle-worker; he wanted people to listen to his words that would heal their broken spiritual lives.

9:1–10 Note Jesus' methods of leadership. He empowered his disciples (9:1), gave them specific instructions so they knew what

9:2 Matt 10:7
9:3 Luke 10:4-12; 22:35; Matt 10:10; Mark 6:8; Luke 22:35f
9:5 Luke 10:11; Acts 13:51
9:6 Mark 6:12; Luke 8:1

2 And He sent them out to proclaim the kingdom of God and to perform healing.
3 And He said to them, "Take nothing for *your* journey, neither a staff, nor a bag, nor
bread, nor money; and do not *even* have two tunics apiece.
4 "Whatever house you enter, stay there until you leave that city.
5 "And as for those who do not receive you, as you go out from that city, shake the
dust off your feet as a testimony against them."
6 Departing, they *began* going throughout the villages, preaching the gospel and healing everywhere.

Herod Kills John the Baptist
(95/Matthew 14:1-12; Mark 6:14-29)

9:7 Matt 14:1; Luke 3:1; 13:31; 23:7; Matt 14:2
9:8 Matt 16:14
9:9 Luke 23:8

7 Now Herod the tetrarch heard of all that was happening; and he was greatly perplexed, because it was said by some that John had risen from the dead,
8 and by some that Elijah had appeared, and by others that one of the prophets of old
had risen again.
9 Herod said, "I myself had John beheaded; but who is this man about whom I hear
such things?" And he kept trying to see Him.

Jesus Feeds Five Thousand
(96/Matthew 14:13-21; Mark 6:30-44; John 6:1-15)

9:10 Matt 11:21

10 When the apostles returned, they gave an account to Him of all that they had done.
Taking them with Him, He withdrew by Himself to a city called Bethsaida.
11 But the crowds were aware of this and followed Him; and welcoming them, He
began speaking to them about the kingdom of God and curing those who had need of
healing.
12 Now the day was ending, and the twelve came and said to Him, "Send the crowd

---

to do (9:3–4), told them how to deal with tough times (9:5), and held them accountable (9:10). As you lead others, study the Master Leader's pattern. Which of these elements do you need to incorporate into your leadership?

9:2 Jesus announced his kingdom by both preaching and healing. If he had limited himself to preaching, people might have seen his kingdom as spiritual only. On the other hand, if he had healed without preaching, people might not have realized the spiritual importance of his mission. Most of his listeners expected a Messiah who would bring wealth and power to their nation; they preferred material benefits to spiritual discernment. The truth about Jesus is that he is both God and man, both spiritual and physical; and the salvation that he offers is both for the soul and the body. Any group or teaching that emphasizes soul at the expense of body, or body at the expense of soul, is in danger of distorting Jesus' Good News.

9:3–4 Why were the disciples instructed to depend on others while they went from town to town preaching the gospel? Their purpose was to blanket Judea with Jesus' message, and by traveling light they could move quickly. Their dependence on others had other good effects as well: (1) It clearly showed that the Messiah had not come to offer wealth to his followers; (2) it forced the disciples to rely on God's power and not on their own provision; (3) it involved the villagers and made them more eager to hear the message. This was an excellent approach for the disciples' short-term mission; it was not intended, however, to be a permanent way of life for them.

9:4 The disciples were told to stay in only one home in each town because they were not to offend their hosts by moving to a home that was more comfortable or socially prominent. To remain in one home was not a burden for the homeowner, because the disciples' stay in each community was short.

9:5 Shaking the dust of unaccepting towns from their feet had deep cultural implications. Pious Jews would do this after passing through Gentile cities to show their separation from Gentile practices. If the disciples shook the dust of a *Jewish* town from their feet, it would show their separation from Jews who rejected their Messiah. This action also showed that the disciples were not responsible for how the people responded to their message. Neither are we responsible if we have carefully and truthfully presented Christ, but our message is rejected. Like the disciples, we must move on to others whom God desires to reach.

9:7 For more information on Herod, also known as Herod Antipas, see his Profile in Mark 6.

9:7–8 It was so difficult for the people to accept Jesus as the Son of God that they tried to come up with other solutions—most of which sound quite unbelievable to us. Many thought that he must be someone who had come back to life, perhaps John the Baptist or another prophet. Some suggested that he was Elijah, the great prophet who did not die but was taken to heaven in a chariot of fire (2 Kings 2:1–11). Very few found the correct answer, as Peter did (9:20). For many people today, it is still not easy to accept Jesus as the fully human yet fully divine Son of God. People are still trying to find alternate explanations—a great prophet, a radical political leader, a self-deceived rabble-rouser. None of these explanations can account for Jesus' miracles or, especially, his glorious resurrection—so these realities too have to be explained away. In the end, the attempts to explain away Jesus are far more difficult to believe than the truth.

9:9 For the story of how Herod had John beheaded, see Mark 6:14–29.

9:10–11 Jesus had tried to slip quietly away from the crowds, but they found out where he was going and followed him. Instead of showing impatience at this interruption, Jesus welcomed the people and ministered to their needs. How do you see people who interrupt your schedule—as nuisances, or as the reason for your life and ministry?

9:11 The kingdom of God was a focal point of Jesus' teaching. He explained that it was not just a future kingdom; it was among them, embodied in him, the Messiah. Even though the kingdom will not be complete until Jesus comes again in glory, we do not have to wait to taste it. The kingdom of God begins in the hearts of those who believe in Jesus (17:21). It is as present with us today as it was with the Judeans almost 2,000 years ago.

away, that they may go into the surrounding villages and countryside and find lodging
and get something to eat; for here we are in a desolate place."
13 But He said to them, "You give them *something* to eat!" And they said, "We have
no more than five loaves and two fish, unless perhaps we go and buy food for all these
people."
14 (For there were about five thousand men.) And He said to His disciples, "Have them
sit down *to eat* in groups of about fifty each."
15 They did so, and had them all sit down.
16 Then He took the five loaves and the two fish, and looking up to heaven, He blessed
them, and broke *them,* and kept giving *them* to the disciples to set before the people.
17 And they all ate and were satisfied; and the broken pieces which they had left over
were picked up, twelve baskets *full.*

Peter Says Jesus Is the Messiah
(109/Matthew 16:13-20; Mark 8:27-30)

18 And it happened that while He was praying alone, the disciples were with Him, and
He questioned them, saying, "Who do the people say that I am?"
19 They answered and said, "John the Baptist, and others *say* Elijah; but others, that
one of the prophets of old has risen again."
20 And He said to them, "But who do you say that I am?" And Peter answered and
said, "The Christ of God."

Jesus Predicts His Death the First Time
(110/Matthew 16:21-28; Mark 8:31—9:1)

21 But He warned them and instructed *them* not to tell this to anyone,
22 saying, "The Son of Man must suffer many things and be rejected by the elders and
chief priests and scribes, and be killed and be raised up on the third day."
23 And He was saying to *them* all, "If anyone wishes to come after Me, he must deny
himself, and take up his cross daily and follow Me.
24 "For whoever wishes to save his life will lose it, but whoever loses his life for My sake,
he is the one who will save it.
25 "For what is a man profited if he gains the whole world, and loses or forfeits himself?

9:14 Mark 6:39
9:17 Matt 14:20
9:18 Matt 14:23; Luke 6:12; 9:28
9:20 John 6:68f
9:21 Matt 8:4; 16:20; Mark 8:30
9:22 Matt 16:21; Luke 9:44
9:23 Matt 10:38; Luke 14:27
9:24 Matt 10:39; Luke 17:33; John 12:25
9:25 Heb 10:34

9:13–14 When the disciples expressed concern about where the crowd of thousands would eat, Jesus offered a surprising solution—"You give them something to eat!" The disciples protested, focusing their attention on what they didn't have (food and money). Do you think God would ask you to do something that you and he together couldn't handle? Don't let your lack of resources blind you to seeing God's power.

9:16–17 Why did Jesus bother to feed these people? He could just as easily have sent them on their way. But Jesus does not ignore needs. He is concerned with every aspect of our lives—the physical as well as the spiritual. As we work to bring wholeness to people's lives, we must never ignore the fact that all of us have both physical and spiritual needs. It is impossible to minister effectively to one type of need without considering the other.

9:18–20 The Christian faith goes beyond knowing what others believe. It requires us to hold beliefs for ourselves. When Jesus asks, "Who do you say that I am?" he wants us to take a stand. Who do *you* say Jesus is?

9:21 Jesus told his disciples not to tell anyone that he was the Christ because at this point they didn't fully understand the significance of that confession—nor would anyone else. Everyone still expected the Messiah to come as a conquering king. But even though Jesus was the Messiah, he still had to suffer, be rejected by the leaders, be killed, and rise from the dead. When the disciples saw all this happen to Jesus, they would understand what the Messiah had come to do. Only then would they be equipped to share the gospel around the world.

9:22 This was the turning point in Jesus' instruction to his disciples. From then on he began teaching clearly and specifically what they could expect, so that they would not be surprised when it happened. He explained that he would not *now* be the conquering Messiah because he first had to suffer, die, and rise again. But one day he would return in great glory to set up his eternal kingdom.

9:23 Christians follow their Lord by imitating his life and obeying his commands. To take up the cross meant to carry your own cross to the place where you would be killed. Many Galileans had been killed that way by the Romans. Applied to the disciples, it meant to identify completely with Christ's message, even if it meant death. We must deny our selfish desires to use our time and money our own way and to choose our own direction in life without regard to Christ. Following Christ is costly now, but in the long run it is well worth the pain and effort.

9:23–26 People are willing to pay a high price for something they value. Is it any surprise that Jesus would demand this much commitment from his followers? There are at least three conditions that must be met by people who want to follow Jesus. We must be willing to deny self, to take up our crosses, and to follow him. Anything less is superficial lip service.

9:24–25 If this present life is most important to you, you will do everything you can to protect it. You will not want to do anything that might endanger your safety, health, or comfort. By contrast, if following Jesus is most important, you may find yourself in unsafe, unhealthy, and uncomfortable places. You will risk death, but you will not fear it because you know that Jesus will raise you to eternal life. Nothing material can compensate for the loss of eternal life. Jesus' disciples are not to use their lives on earth for their own pleasure—they should spend their lives serving God and people.

26 "For whoever is ashamed of Me and My words, the Son of Man will be ashamed of
him when He comes in His glory, and *the glory* of the Father and of the holy angels.
27 "But I say to you truthfully, there are some of those standing here who will not taste
death until they see the kingdom of God."

Jesus Is Transfigured on the Mountain
(111/Matthew 17:1-13; Mark 9:2-13)

28 Some eight days after these sayings, He took along Peter and John and James, and
went up on the mountain to pray.
29 And while He was praying, the appearance of His face became different, and His
clothing *became* white *and* gleaming.
30 And behold, two men were talking with Him; and they were Moses and Elijah,
31 who, appearing in glory, were speaking of His departure which He was about to
accomplish at Jerusalem.
32 Now Peter and his companions had been overcome with sleep; but when they were
fully awake, they saw His glory and the two men standing with Him.
33 And as these were leaving Him, Peter said to Jesus, "Master, it is good for us to be
here; let us make three tabernacles: one for You, and one for Moses, and one for Elijah"—not realizing what he was saying.
34 While he was saying this, a cloud formed and *began* to overshadow them; and they
were afraid as they entered the cloud.
35 Then a voice came out of the cloud, saying, "This is My Son, *My* Chosen One; listen
to Him!"
36 And when the voice had spoken, Jesus was found alone. And they kept silent, and
reported to no one in those days any of the things which they had seen.

Jesus Heals a Demon-Possessed Boy
(112/Matthew 17:14-21; Mark 9:14-29)

37 On the next day, when they came down from the mountain, a large crowd met Him.
38 And a man from the crowd shouted, saying, "Teacher, I beg You to look at my son,
for he is my only *boy,*

9:26 Matt 10:33; Luke 12:9
9:27 Matt 16:28
9:28 Matt 17:1; Matt 5:1; Luke 3:21; 5:16; 6:12; 9:18
9:29 Luke 3:21; 5:16; 6:12; 9:18; Mark 16:12
9:31 2 Pet 1:15
9:32 Matt 26:43; Mark 14:40
9:33 Luke 5:5; 9:49; Matt 17:4; Mark 9:5; Mark 9:6
9:35 2 Pet 1:17f; Is 42:1; Matt 3:17; 12:18; Mark 1:11; Luke 3:22
9:36 Matt 17:9; Mark 9:9f

9:26 Luke's Greek audience would have found it difficult to understand a God who could die, just as Jesus' Jewish audience would have been perplexed by a Messiah who would let himself be captured. Both would be ashamed of Jesus if they did not look past his death to his glorious resurrection and second coming. Then they would see Jesus not as a loser but as the Lord of the universe, who through his death brought salvation to all people.

9:27 When Jesus said some would not die without seeing the kingdom, he was referring (1) to Peter, James, and John, who would witness the transfiguration eight days later, or in a broader sense (2) to all who would witness the resurrection and ascension, or (3) to all who would take part in the spread of the church after Pentecost. Jesus' listeners were not going to have to wait for another, future Messiah—the kingdom was among them, and it would soon come in power.

9:29–30 Jesus took Peter, James, and John to the top of a mountain to show them who he really was—not just a great prophet, but God's own Son. Moses, representing the law, and Elijah, representing the prophets, appeared with Jesus. Then God's voice singled out Jesus as the long-awaited Messiah who possessed divine authority. Jesus would fulfill both the law and the Prophets (Matthew 5:17).

9:33 When Peter suggested making three tabernacles (shelters), he may have been thinking of the Feast of Booths, where shelters were set up to commemorate the exodus, God's deliverance from slavery in Egypt. Peter wanted to keep Moses and Elijah with them. But this was not what God wanted. Peter's desire to build tabernacles for Jesus, Moses, and Elijah may also show his understanding that real faith is built on three cornerstones: the law, the prophets, and Jesus. But Peter grew in his understanding, and eventually he would write of Jesus as the "choice stone, a precious corner stone" of the church (1 Peter 2:6).

9:33 Peter, James, and John experienced a wonderful moment on the mountain, and they didn't want to leave. Sometimes we too have such an inspiring experience that we want to stay where we are—away from the reality and problems of our daily lives. Knowing that struggles await us in the valley encourages us to linger on the mountaintop. Yet staying on top of a mountain prohibits our ministering to others. Instead of becoming spiritual giants, we would soon become dwarfed by our self-centeredness. We need times of retreat and renewal, but only so we can return to minister to the world. Our faith must make sense off the mountain as well as on it.

9:35 As God's Son, Jesus has God's power and authority; thus his words should be our final authority. If a person's teaching is true, it will agree with Jesus' teachings. Test everything you hear against Jesus' words, and you will not be led astray. Don't be hasty to seek advice and guidance from merely human sources and thereby neglect Christ's message.

9:35 God clearly identified Jesus as his Son before saying that Peter and the others were to listen to Jesus and not to their own ideas and desires. The ability to follow Jesus comes from confidence about who he is. If we believe he is God's Son, then we surely will want to do what he says.

9:37–39 As the disciples came down from the mountain with Jesus, they passed from a reassuring experience of God's presence to a frightening experience of evil. The beauty they had just seen must have made the ugliness seem even uglier. As our spiritual vision improves and allows us to see and understand God better, we will also be able to see and understand evil better. We would be overcome by its horror if we did not have Jesus with us to take us through it safely.

39 and a spirit seizes him, and he suddenly screams, and it throws him into a convulsion with foaming *at the mouth;* and only with difficulty does it leave him, mauling him
as it leaves.
40 "I begged Your disciples to cast it out, and they could not."
41 And Jesus answered and said, "You unbelieving and perverted generation, how long
shall I be with you and put up with you? Bring your son here."
42 While he was still approaching, the demon slammed him *to the ground* and threw
him into a convulsion. But Jesus rebuked the unclean spirit, and healed the boy and gave
him back to his father.
43 And they were all amazed at the greatness of God.

9:43 2 Pet 1:16

Jesus Predicts his Death the Second Time
(113/Matthew 17:22-23; Mark 9:30-32)

But while everyone was marveling at all that He was doing, He said to His disciples,
44 "Let these words sink into your ears; for the Son of Man is going to be delivered into
the hands of men."
45 But they did not understand this statement, and it was concealed from them so that
they would not perceive it; and they were afraid to ask Him about this statement.

9:44 Luke 9:22
9:45 Mark 9:32

The Disciples Argue about Who Would Be the Greatest
(115/Matthew 18:1-6; Mark 9:33-37)

46 An argument started among them as to which of them might be the greatest.
47 But Jesus, knowing what they were thinking in their heart, took a child and stood
him by His side,
48 and said to them, "Whoever receives this child in My name receives Me, and whoever receives Me receives Him who sent Me; for the one who is least among all of you,
this is the one who is great."

9:46 Luke 22:24
9:47 Matt 9:4
9:48 Matt 10:40; Luke 10:16; John 13:20; Luke 22:26

The Disciples Forbid Another to Use Jesus' Name
(116/Mark 9:38-41)

49 John answered and said, "Master, we saw someone casting out demons in Your name;
and we tried to prevent him because he does not follow along with us."
50 But Jesus said to him, "Do not hinder *him;* for he who is not against you is for you."

9:49 Luke 5:5; 9:33
9:50 Matt 12:30; Luke 11:23

2. Jesus' ministry on the way to Jerusalem

Jesus Teaches about the Cost of Following Him
(122/Matthw 8:18-22)

51 When the days were approaching for His ascension, He was determined to go to
Jerusalem;
52 and He sent messengers on ahead of Him, and they went and entered a village of
the Samaritans to make arrangements for Him.

9:51 Mark 16:19; Luke 13:22; 17:11; 18:31; 19:11, 28
9:52 Matt 10:5; Luke 10:33; 17:16; John 4:4

9:40 Why couldn't the disciples drive out the evil spirit? For a possible answer, see the note on Mark 9:18.

9:45–46 The disciples didn't understand Jesus' words about his death. They still thought of Jesus as only an earthly king, and they were concerned about their places in the kingdom he would set up. So they ignored Jesus' words about his death and began arguing about who would be the greatest.

9:48 Our care for others is a measure of our greatness. How much concern do you show to others? This is a vital question that can accurately measure your greatness in God's eyes. How have you expressed your care for others lately, especially the helpless, the needy, the poor—those who can't return your love and concern? Your honest answer to that question will give you a good idea of your real greatness.

9:49–50 The disciples were jealous. Nine of them together were unable to drive out a single evil spirit (9:40), but when they saw a man who was not one of their group driving out demons, they told him to stop. Our pride is hurt when someone else succeeds where we have failed, but Jesus says there is no room for such jealousy in the spiritual warfare of his kingdom. Share Jesus' open-arms attitude to Christian workers outside your group.

9:51 Although Jesus knew he would face persecution and death in Jerusalem, he was determined to go there. That kind of resolve should characterize our lives too. When God gives us a course of action, we must move steadily toward our destination, no matter what potential hazards await us there.

9:53 John 4:9
9:54 Mark 3:17; 2 Kin 1:9-16

53 But they did not receive Him, because He was traveling toward Jerusalem.
54 When His disciples James and John saw *this,* they said, "Lord, do You want us to
command fire to come down from heaven and consume them?"
55 But He turned and rebuked them, [and said, "You do not know what kind of spirit
you are of;
56 for the Son of Man did not come to destroy men's lives, but to save them."] And
they went on to another village.
57 As they were going along the road, someone said to Him, "I will follow You wherever You go."
58 And Jesus said to him, "The foxes have holes and the birds of the air *have* nests, but
the Son of Man has nowhere to lay His head."
59 And He said to another, "Follow Me." But he said, "Lord, permit me first to go and
bury my father."
60 But He said to him, "Allow the dead to bury their own dead; but as for you, go and
proclaim everywhere the kingdom of God."
61 Another also said, "I will follow You, Lord; but first permit me to say good-bye to
those at home."
62 But Jesus said to him, "No one, after putting his hand to the plow and looking back,
is fit for the kingdom of God."

9:57 Luke 9:51; Matt 8:19-22
9:58 Matt 8:20
9:59 Matt 8:22
9:60 Matt 4:23
9:61 1 Kin 19:20
9:62 Phil 3:13

Jesus Sends Out Seventy-two Messengers
(130)

10 Now after this the Lord appointed seventy others, and sent them in pairs ahead of
Him to every city and place where He Himself was going to come.
2 And He was saying to them, "The harvest is plentiful, but the laborers are few; therefore beseech the Lord of the harvest to send out laborers into His harvest.
3 "Go; behold, I send you out as lambs in the midst of wolves.
4 "Carry no money belt, no bag, no shoes; and greet no one on the way.
5 "Whatever house you enter, first say, 'Peace *be* to this house.'
6 "If a man of peace is there, your peace will rest on him; but if not, it will return
to you.

10:1 Luke 7:13; Luke 9:1f, 52; Mark 6:7
10:2 Matt 9:37, 38; John 4:35
10:3 Matt 10:16
10:4 Matt 10:9-14; Mark 6:8-11; Luke 9:3-5

9:53 After Assyria invaded Israel, the northern kingdom, and resettled it with its own people (2 Kings 17:24–41), the mixed race that developed became known as the Samaritans. "Purebred" Jews hated these "half-breeds," and the Samaritans in turn hated the Jews. So many tensions arose between the two peoples that Jewish travelers between Galilee and southern Judea often walked around rather than through Samaritan territory, even though this lengthened their trip considerably. Jesus held no such prejudices, and he sent messengers ahead to get things ready in a Samaritan village. But the village refused to welcome these Jewish travelers.

9:54 When James and John were rejected by the Samaritan village, they didn't want to stop at shaking the dust from their feet (9:5). They wanted to retaliate by calling down fire from heaven on the people, as Elijah did on the servants of a wicked king of Israel (2 Kings 1). When others reject or scorn us, we too may feel like retaliating. We must remember that judgment belongs to God, and we must not expect him to use his power to carry out our personal vendettas.

9:59 Luke does not tell us whether the father is already dead or whether he's terminally ill. It seems likely that if the father were dead, the son would have been fulfilling the burial duties. Jesus was proclaiming that true discipleship requires instant action. Jesus did not teach people to forsake responsibilities to family, but he often gave commands to people in light of their real motives. Perhaps this man wanted to delay following Christ and used his father as an excuse. There is a cost to following Jesus, and each of us must be ready to serve, even when it requires sacrifice.

9:62 What does Jesus want from us? Total dedication, not half-hearted commitment. We can't pick and choose among Jesus' ideas and follow him selectively; we have to accept the cross along with the crown, judgment as well as mercy. We must count the cost and be willing to abandon everything else that has given us security. With our focus on Jesus, we should allow nothing to distract us from the manner of living that he calls good and true.

10:1–2 Far more than 12 people had been following Jesus. Here Jesus designated a group of 70 to prepare a number of towns for Jesus' later visit. These disciples were not unique in their qualifications. They were not better educated, more capable, or of higher status than other followers of Jesus. What equipped them for this mission was their awareness of Jesus' power and their vision to reach all the people. It is important to dedicate our skills to God's kingdom, but we must also be equipped with his power and have a clear vision of what he wants us to do.

10:2 Jesus was sending 35 teams of two to reach the multitudes. These teams were not to try to do the job without help; rather, they were to ask God for more workers. Some people, as soon as they understand the gospel, want to go to work immediately contacting unsaved people. This story suggests a different approach: Begin by mobilizing people to pray. And before praying for unsaved people, pray that other concerned disciples will join you in reaching out to them.

10:2 In Christian service, there is no unemployment. God has work enough for everyone. Don't just sit back and watch others work—look for ways to help with the harvest.

10:3 Jesus said he was sending his disciples out "as lambs in the midst of wolves." They would have to be careful because they would surely meet with opposition. We too are sent into the world like lambs among wolves. Be alert, and remember to face your enemies not with aggression but with love and gentleness. A dangerous mission requires sincere commitment.

7 "Stay in that house, eating and drinking what they give you; for the laborer is worthy
of his wages. Do not keep moving from house to house.
8 "Whatever city you enter and they receive you, eat what is set before you;
9 and heal those in it who are sick, and say to them, 'The kingdom of God has come
near to you.'
10 "But whatever city you enter and they do not receive you, go out into its streets
and say,
11 'Even the dust of your city which clings to our feet we wipe off *in protest* against you;
yet be sure of this, that the kingdom of God has come near.'
12 "I say to you, it will be more tolerable in that day for Sodom than for that city.
13 "Woe to you, Chorazin! Woe to you, Bethsaida! For if the miracles had been performed in Tyre and Sidon which occurred in you, they would have repented long ago,
sitting in sackcloth and ashes.
14 "But it will be more tolerable for Tyre and Sidon in the judgment than for you.
15 "And you, Capernaum, will not be exalted to heaven, will you? You will be brought
down to Hades!
16 "The one who listens to you listens to Me, and the one who rejects you rejects Me;
and he who rejects Me rejects the One who sent Me."

The Seventy-two Messengers Return
(131)

17 The seventy returned with joy, saying, "Lord, even the demons are subject to us in
Your name."
18 And He said to them, "I was watching Satan fall from heaven like lightning.
19 "Behold, I have given you authority to tread on serpents and scorpions, and over all
the power of the enemy, and nothing will injure you.
20 "Nevertheless do not rejoice in this, that the spirits are subject to you, but rejoice
that your names are recorded in heaven."
21 At that very time He rejoiced greatly in the Holy Spirit, and said, "I praise You,
O Father, Lord of heaven and earth, that You have hidden these things from *the* wise

10:7 Matt 10:10; 1 Cor 9:14; 1 Tim 5:18
10:9 Matt 3:2; 10:7
10:11 Matt 10:14; Mark 6:11; Luke 9:5; Acts 13:51; Matt 3:2
10:12 Gen 19:24-28; Matt 10:15; 11:24
10:13 Ezek 26:1-28:26; Joel 3:4-8; Matt 11:21; Rev 11:3
10:14 Matt 11:21
10:15 Is 14:13-15; Matt 4:13; 11:23
10:16 Matt 10:40; Mark 9:37; Luke 9:48; John 13:20
10:17 Mark 16:17
10:18 Matt 4:10
10:19 Ps 91:13; Mark 16:18
10:21 Matt 11:25-27

10:7 Jesus' direction to stay in one house avoided certain problems. Shifting from house to house could offend the families who first took them in. Some families might begin to compete for the disciples' presence, and some might think they weren't good enough to hear their message. If the disciples appeared not to appreciate the hospitality offered them, the town might not accept Jesus when he followed them there. In addition, by staying in one place, the disciples did not have to worry continually about getting good accommodations. They could settle down and do their appointed task.

10:7 Jesus told his disciples to accept hospitality graciously because their work entitled them to it. Ministers of the gospel deserve to be supported, and it is our responsibility to make sure they have what they need. There are several ways to encourage those who serve God in his church. First, see that they have an adequate salary. Second, see that they are supported emotionally; plan a time to express appreciation for something they have done. Third, lift their spirits with special surprises from time to time. Our ministers deserve to know we are giving to them cheerfully and generously.

10:8–9 Jesus gave two rules for the disciples to follow as they traveled. They were to eat what was set before them—that is, they were to accept hospitality without being picky—and they were to heal the sick. Because of the healings, people would be willing to listen to the gospel.

10:12 Sodom was an evil city that God destroyed because of its great sinfulness (Genesis 19). The city's name is often used to symbolize wickedness and immorality. Sodom will suffer at judgment day, but cities who saw the Messiah and rejected him will suffer even more.

10:13 Chorazin was a city near the Sea of Galilee, probably about two miles north of Capernaum. Tyre and Sidon were cities destroyed by God as punishment for their wickedness (see Ezekiel 26—28).

10:15 Capernaum was Jesus' base for his Galilean ministry. The city was located at an important crossroads used by traders and the Roman army, so a message proclaimed in Capernaum was likely to go far. But many people of Capernaum did not understand Jesus' miracles or believe his teaching, and the city was included among those who would be judged for rejecting him.

10:17–20 The disciples had seen tremendous results as they ministered in Jesus' name and with his authority. They were elated by the victories they had witnessed, and Jesus shared their enthusiasm. He helped them get their priorities right, however, by reminding them of their most important victory—that their names were written in heaven. This honor was more important than any of their accomplishments. As we see God's wonders at work in and through us, we should not lose sight of the greatest wonder of all—our heavenly citizenship.

10:18–19 Jesus may have been looking ahead to his victory over Satan at the cross. John 12:31–32 indicates that Satan would be judged and driven out at the time of Jesus' death. On the other hand, Jesus may have been warning his disciples against pride. Perhaps he was referring to Isaiah 14:12–17, which begins, "How you have fallen from heaven, O star of the morning, son of the dawn!" Some interpreters identify this verse with Satan and explain that Satan's pride led to all the evil we see on earth today. To Jesus' disciples, who were thrilled with their power over evil spirits ("serpents and scorpions"), he may have been giving this stern warning: "Yours is the kind of pride that led to Satan's downfall. Be careful!"

10:21 Jesus thanked God that spiritual truth was for everyone, and not just for the elite. Many of life's rewards seem to go to the intelligent, the rich, the good-looking, or the powerful, but the kingdom of God is equally available to all, regardless of position or abilities.

and intelligent and have revealed them to infants. Yes, Father, for this way was well-pleasing in Your sight.
22 "All things have been handed over to Me by My Father, and no one knows who the
Son is except the Father, and who the Father is except the Son, and anyone to whom the
Son wills to reveal *Him.*"
23 Turning to the disciples, He said privately, "Blessed *are* the eyes which see the things
you see,

10:22 John 3:35; John 10:15
10:23 Matt 13:16, 17

JAMES

Jesus singled out three of his 12 disciples for special training. James, his brother John, and Peter made up this inner circle. Each eventually played a key role in the early church. Peter became a great speaker, John became a major writer, and James was the first of the 12 disciples to die for the faith.

The fact that his name is always mentioned before John's indicates that James was the older brother. Zebedee, their father, owned a fishing business where they worked along with Peter and Andrew. When Peter, Andrew, and John left Galilee to see John the Baptist, James stayed back with the boats and fishing nets. Later, when Jesus called them, James was as eager as his partners to follow.

James enjoyed being in the inner circle of Jesus' disciples, but he misunderstood Jesus' purpose. He and his brother even tried to secure their role in Jesus' kingdom by asking Jesus to promise them each a special position. Like the other disciples, James had a limited view of what Jesus was doing on earth, picturing only an earthly kingdom that would overthrow Rome and restore Israel's former glory. But above all, James wanted to be with Jesus. He had found the right leader, even though he was still on the wrong timetable. It took Jesus' death and resurrection to correct his view.

James was the first of the 12 disciples to die for the gospel. He was willing to die because he knew Jesus had conquered death, the doorway to eternal life. Our expectations about life will be limited if this life is all we can see. Jesus promised eternal life to those willing to trust him. If we believe this promise, he will give us the courage to stand for him even during dangerous times.

Strengths and accomplishments:
- One of the 12 disciples
- One of a special inner circle of three with Peter and John
- First of the 12 disciples to be killed for his faith

Weaknesses and mistakes:
- Two outbursts from James indicate struggles with temper (Luke 9:54) and selfishness (Mark 10:37). Both times, he and his brother, John, spoke as one

Lesson from his life:
- Loss of life is not too heavy a price to pay for following Jesus

Vital statistics:
- Where: Galilee
- Occupations: Fisherman, disciple
- Relatives: Father: Zebedee. Mother: Salome. Brother: John
- Contemporaries: Jesus, Pilate, Herod Agrippa

Key verses:
"James and John, the two sons of Zebedee, came up to Jesus, saying, 'Teacher, we want You to do for us whatever we ask of You.' And He said to them, 'What do you want Me to do for you?' They said to Him, 'Grant that we may sit, one on Your right and one on Your left, in Your glory' " (Mark 10:35–37).

James's story is told in the Gospels. He is also mentioned in Acts 1:13 and 12:2.

We come to Jesus not through strength or brains, but through childlike trust. Jesus is not opposed to engaging in scholarly pursuits; he is opposed to spiritual pride (being wise in one's own eyes). Join Jesus in thanking God that we all have equal access to him. Trust in God's grace, not in your personal qualifications, for your citizenship in the kingdom.

10:22 Christ's mission was to reveal God the Father to people. His words brought difficult ideas down to earth. He explained God's love through parables, teachings, and, most of all, his life. By examining Jesus' actions, principles, and attitudes, we can understand God more clearly.

10:23–24 The disciples had a fantastic opportunity—they were eyewitnesses of Christ, the Son of God. But for many months they took Jesus for granted, not really listening to him or obeying him. We also have a privileged position, with knowledge of 2,000 years of church history, availability of the Bible in hundreds of languages and translations, and access to many excellent pastors and speakers. Yet often we take these for granted. Remember, with privilege comes responsibility. Because we are privileged to know so much about Christ, we must be careful to follow him.

24 for I say to you, that many prophets and kings wished to see the things which you
see, and did not see *them,* and to hear the things which you hear, and did not hear *them.*"

Jesus Tells the Parable of the Good Samaritan
(132)

25 And a lawyer stood up and put Him to the test, saying, "Teacher, what shall I do to
inherit eternal life?"
26 And He said to him, "What is written in the Law? How does it read to you?"
27 And he answered, "YOU SHALL LOVE THE LORD YOUR GOD WITH ALL YOUR
HEART, AND WITH ALL YOUR SOUL, AND WITH ALL YOUR STRENGTH, AND WITH ALL
YOUR MIND; AND YOUR NEIGHBOR AS YOURSELF."
28 And He said to him, "You have answered correctly; DO THIS AND YOU WILL LIVE."
29 But wishing to justify himself, he said to Jesus, "And who is my neighbor?"
30 Jesus replied and said, "A man was going down from Jerusalem to Jericho, and fell
among robbers, and they stripped him and beat him, and went away leaving him half dead.
31 "And by chance a priest was going down on that road, and when he saw him, he passed
by on the other side.
32 "Likewise a Levite also, when he came to the place and saw him, passed by on the
other side.
33 "But a Samaritan, who was on a journey, came upon him; and when he saw him, he
felt compassion,
34 and came to him and bandaged up his wounds, pouring oil and wine on *them;* and
he put him on his own beast, and brought him to an inn and took care of him.
35 "On the next day he took out two [13]denarii and gave them to the innkeeper and said,
'Take care of him; and whatever more you spend, when I return I will repay you.'
36 "Which of these three do you think proved to be a neighbor to the man who fell into
the robbers' *hands?*"
37 And he said, "The one who showed mercy toward him." Then Jesus said to him,
"Go and do the same."

Jesus Visits Mary and Martha
(133)

38 Now as they were traveling along, He entered a village; and a woman named Martha welcomed Him into her home.

10:25 Mark 12:28-31; Matt 19:16-19; Matt 22:35
10:27 Deut 6:5; Lev 19:18
10:28 Lev 18:5; Ezek 20:11; Matt 19:17
10:29 Luke 16:15
10:30 Luke 18:31; 19:28
10:33 Matt 10:5; Luke 9:52
10:38 Luke 10:40f; John 11:1, 5, 19ff, 30, 39; 12:2

13 The denarius was equivalent to a day's wages

10:24 Old Testament men of God such as David and the prophet Isaiah made many God-inspired predictions that Jesus fulfilled. As Peter later wrote, these prophets wondered what their words meant and when they would be fulfilled (1 Peter 1:10–13). In Jesus' words, they "wished to see the things which you see"—the coming of God's kingdom.

10:27 This lawyer was quoting Deuteronomy 6:5 and Leviticus 19:18. He correctly understood that the law demanded total devotion to God and love for one's neighbor. Jesus talked more about these laws elsewhere (see Matthew 19:16–22 and Mark 10:17–22).

10:27–37 The lawyer treated the wounded man as a topic for discussion; the robbers, as an object to exploit; the priest, as a problem to avoid; and the Levite, as an object of curiosity. Only the Samaritan treated him as a person to love.

10:27–37 From the parable we learn three principles about loving our neighbor: (1) Lack of love is often easy to justify, even though it is never right; (2) our neighbor is anyone of any race, creed, or social background who is in need; and (3) love means acting to meet the person's need. Wherever you live, there are needy people close by. There is no good reason for refusing to help.

10:33 There was deep hatred between Jews and Samaritans. The Jews saw themselves as pure descendants of Abraham, while the Samaritans were a mixed race produced when Jews from the northern kingdom intermarried with other peoples after Israel's exile. To this lawyer, the person least likely to act correctly would be the Samaritan. In fact, he could not bear to say "Samaritan" in answer to Jesus' question. This lawyer's attitude betrayed his lack of the very thing that he had earlier said the law commanded—love.

10:38–42 Mary and Martha both loved Jesus. On this occasion

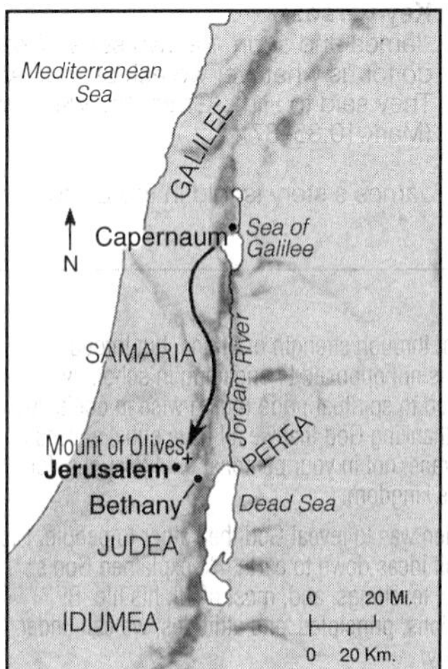

JESUS VISITS MARY AND MARTHA
After teaching throughout Galilee, Jesus returned to Jerusalem for the Feast of Booths (John 7:2ff). He spoke in Jerusalem and then visited his friends Mary and Martha in Bethany, a tiny village on the eastern slope of the Mount of Olives.

10:39 Luke 10:42; John 11:1f, 19f, 28, 31f, 45; 12:3; Luke 8:35; Acts 22:3

10:40 Luke 10:38, 41; John 11:1, 5, 19ff, 30, 39; 12:2

10:41 Luke 10:38, 40; John 11:1, 5, 19ff, 30, 39; 12:2; Matt 6:25

10:42 Ps 27:4; John 6:27; Luke 10:39; John 11:1f, 19f, 28, 31f, 45; 12:3

11:2 Matt 6:9-13

11:3 Acts 17:11

11:4 Luke 13:4

11:8 Luke 18:1-5

11:9 Matt 7:7-11

39 She had a sister called Mary, who was seated at the Lord's feet, listening to His word.
40 But Martha was distracted with all her preparations; and she came up *to Him* and
said, "Lord, do You not care that my sister has left me to do all the serving alone? Then
tell her to help me."
41 But the Lord answered and said to her, "Martha, Martha, you are worried and bothered about so many things;
42 but *only* one thing is necessary, for Mary has chosen the good part, which shall not
be taken away from her."

Jesus Teaches His Disciples about Prayer
(134)

11 It happened that while Jesus was praying in a certain place, after He had finished,
one of His disciples said to Him, "Lord, teach us to pray just as John also taught
his disciples."
2 And He said to them, "When you pray, say:
'[14]Father, hallowed be Your name.
Your kingdom come.
3 'Give us each day our daily bread.
4 'And forgive us our sins,
For we ourselves also forgive everyone who is indebted to us.
And lead us not into temptation.' "
5 Then He said to them, "Suppose one of you has a friend, and goes to him at midnight and says to him, 'Friend, lend me three loaves;
6 for a friend of mine has come to me from a journey, and I have nothing to set before him';
7 and from inside he answers and says, 'Do not bother me; the door has already been
shut and my children and I are in bed; I cannot get up and give you *anything.*'
8 "I tell you, even though he will not get up and give him *anything* because he is his
friend, yet because of his persistence he will get up and give him as much as he needs.
9 "So I say to you, ask, and it will be given to you; seek, and you will find; knock, and it
will be opened to you.

14 Later mss add phrases from Matt 6:9-13 to make the two passages closely similar

---

A COLLECTION OF ATTITUDES

To the lawyer, the wounded man was a subject to discuss.

To the robbers, the wounded man was someone to use and exploit.

To the religious men, the wounded man was a problem to be avoided.

To the innkeeper, the wounded man was a customer to serve for a fee.

To the Samaritan, the wounded man was a human being worth being cared for and loved.

To Jesus, all of them and all of us were worth dying for.

Confronting the needs of others brings out various attitudes in us. Jesus used the story of the good but despised Samaritan to make clear what attitude was acceptable to him. If we are honest, we often will find ourselves in the place of the lawyer, needing to learn again who our neighbor is. Note these different attitudes toward the wounded man.

---

they were both serving him. But Martha thought Mary's style of serving was inferior to hers. She didn't realize that in her desire to serve, she was actually neglecting her guest. Are you so busy doing things *for* Jesus that you're not spending any time *with* him? Don't let your service become self-serving.

10:41–42 Jesus did not blame Martha for being concerned about household chores. He was only asking her to set priorities. It is possible for service to Christ to degenerate into mere busywork that is no longer full of devotion to God.

11:1–4 Notice the order in this prayer. First Jesus praised God; then he made his requests. Praising God first puts us in the right frame of mind to tell him about our needs. Too often our prayers are more like shopping lists than conversations.

11:2–13 These verses focus on three aspects of prayer: its content (11:2–4), our persistence (11:5–10), and God's faithfulness (11:11–13).

11:3 God's provision is daily, not all at once. We cannot store it up and then cut off communication with God. And we dare not be self-satisfied. If you are running low on strength, ask yourself—how long have I been away from the Source?

11:4 When Jesus taught his disciples to pray, he made forgiveness the cornerstone of their relationship with God. God has forgiven our sins; we must now forgive those who have wronged us. To remain unforgiving shows we have not understood that we ourselves deeply need to be forgiven. Think of some people who have wronged you. Have you forgiven them? How will God deal with you if he treats you as you treat others?

11:8 Persistence, or boldness, in prayer overcomes our insensitivity, not God's. To practice persistence does more to change our hearts and minds than his, and it helps us understand and express the intensity of our need. Persistence in prayer helps us recognize God's work.

10 "For everyone who asks, receives; and he who seeks, finds; and to him who knocks,
it will be opened.
11 "Now suppose one of you fathers is asked by his son for a fish; he will not give him a
snake instead of a fish, will he?
12 "Or *if* he is asked for an egg, he will not give him a scorpion, will he?
13 "If you then, being evil, know how to give good gifts to your children, how much more
will *your* heavenly Father give the Holy Spirit to those who ask Him?"

11:13 Matt 7:11; Luke 18:7f

Jesus Answers Hostile Accusations
(135)

14 And He was casting out a demon, and it was mute; when the demon had gone out,
the mute man spoke; and the crowds were amazed.
15 But some of them said, "He casts out demons by Beelzebul, the ruler of the demons."
16 Others, to test *Him,* were demanding of Him a sign from heaven.
17 But He knew their thoughts and said to them, "Any kingdom divided against itself
is laid waste; and a house *divided* against itself falls.
18 "If Satan also is divided against himself, how will his kingdom stand? For you say
that I cast out demons by Beelzebul.
19 "And if I by Beelzebul cast out demons, by whom do your sons cast them out? So
they will be your judges.
20 "But if I cast out demons by the finger of God, then the kingdom of God has come
upon you.
21 "When a strong *man,* fully armed, guards his own house, his possessions are undisturbed.
22 "But when someone stronger than he attacks him and overpowers him, he takes away
from him all his armor on which he had relied and distributes his plunder.
23 "He who is not with Me is against Me; and he who does not gather with Me, scatters.
24 "When the unclean spirit goes out of a man, it passes through waterless places seeking rest, and not finding any, it says, 'I will return to my house from which I came.'
25 "And when it comes, it finds it swept and put in order.
26 "Then it goes and takes *along* seven other spirits more evil than itself, and they go in
and live there; and the last state of that man becomes worse than the first."

11:14 Matt 12:22, 24; Matt 9:32-34

11:15 Matt 9:34; Matt 10:25

11:16 Matt 12:38; 16:1; Mark 8:11

11:17 Matt 12:25-29; Mark 3:23-27

11:18 Matt 4:10; Matt 10:25

11:19 Matt 10:25

11:20 Ex 8:19; Matt 3:2

11:23 Matt 12:30; Mark 9:40

11:24 Matt 12:43-45

11:13 Even though good fathers make mistakes, they treat their children well. How much better our perfect heavenly Father treats his children! The most important gift he could ever give us is the Holy Spirit (Acts 2:1–4), whom he promised to give all believers after his death, resurrection, and return to heaven (John 15:26).

11:14–23 A similar and possibly separate event is reported in Matthew 12:22–45 and Mark 3:20–30. The event described by Luke happened in Judea while the other took place in Galilee. According to Luke, Jesus spoke to the crowds; in Matthew and Mark, he accused the Pharisees.

11:15–20 There are two common interpretations of these verses. (1) Some of the Pharisees' followers drove out demons. If this was so, the Pharisees' accusations were becoming more desperate. To accuse Jesus of being empowered by Beelzebul, the prince of demons (or Satan himself), because Jesus was driving out demons was also to say that the Pharisees' own followers were doing Satan's work. Jesus turned the religious leaders' accusation against them. (2) Another possibility is that the Pharisees' followers were *not* driving out demons; and even if they tried, they did not succeed. Jesus first dismissed their claim as absurd (Why would the devil drive out his own demons?). Then he engaged in a little irony ("By whom do your sons cast them out?"). Finally he concluded that his work of driving out demons proves that the kingdom of God has arrived.

Satan, who had controlled the kingdom of this world for thousands of years, was now being controlled and overpowered by Jesus and the kingdom of heaven. Jesus' kingdom began to come into power at Jesus' birth, grew as he resisted the wilderness temptations, established itself through his teachings and healings, blossomed in victory at his resurrection and at Pentecost, and will become permanent and universal at his second coming. Though these two interpretations may differ, they arrive at the same conclusion—the kingdom of God has arrived with the coming of Jesus Christ.

11:21–22 Jesus may have been referring to Isaiah 49:24–26. Regardless of how great Satan's power is, Jesus is stronger still. He will bind Satan and dispose of him for eternity (see Revelation 20:2, 10).

11:23 How does this verse relate to 9:50: "He who is not against you is for you"? In the earlier passage, Jesus was talking about a person who was driving out demons in Jesus' name. Those who fight evil, he was saying, are on the same side as one driving out demons in Jesus' name. Here, by contrast, he was talking about the conflict between God and the devil. In this battle, if a person is not on God's side, he or she is on Satan's. There is no neutral ground. Because God has already won the battle, why be on the losing side? If you aren't actively for Christ, you are against him.

11:24–26 Jesus was illustrating an unfortunate human tendency—our desire to reform often does not last long. In Israel's history, almost as soon as a good king would pull down idols, a bad king would set them up again. It is not enough to be emptied of evil; we must then be filled with the power of the Holy Spirit to accomplish God's new purpose in our lives (see also Matthew 12:43–45; Galatians 5:22).

11:27 Luke 23:29
27 While Jesus was saying these things, one of the women in the crowd raised her voice
and said to Him, "Blessed is the womb that bore You and the breasts at which You
nursed."

11:28 Luke 8:21
28 But He said, "On the contrary, blessed are those who hear the word of God and
observe it."

MARTHA

Many older brothers and sisters have an irritating tendency to take charge, a habit developed while growing up. We can easily see this pattern in Martha, the older sister of Mary and Lazarus. She was used to being in control.

The fact that Martha, Mary, and Lazarus are remembered for their hospitality takes on added significance when we note that hospitality was a social requirement in their culture. It was considered shameful to turn anyone away from your door. Apparently Martha's family met this requirement very well.

Martha worried about details. She wished to please, to serve, to do the right thing—but she often succeeded in making everyone around her uncomfortable. Perhaps as the oldest she feared shame if her home did not measure up to expectations. She tried to do everything she could to make sure that wouldn't happen. As a result, she found it hard to relax and enjoy her guests, and even harder to accept Mary's lack of cooperation in all the preparations. Martha's frustration was so intense that she finally asked Jesus to settle the matter. He gently corrected her attitude and showed her that her priorities, though good, were not the best. The personal attention she gave her guests should be more important than the comforts she tried to provide for them.

Later, following her brother Lazarus's death, Martha could hardly help being herself. When she heard Jesus was finally coming, she rushed out to meet him and expressed her inner conflict of disappointment and hope. Jesus pointed out that her hope was too limited. He was not only Lord beyond death, he was Lord over death—the resurrection and the life! Moments later, Martha again spoke without thinking, pointing out that four-day-old corpses are well on their way to decomposition. Her awareness of details sometimes kept her from seeing the whole picture, but Jesus was consistently patient with her.

In our last picture of Martha, she is once again serving a meal to Jesus and his disciples. She has not stopped serving. But the Bible records her silence this time. She has begun to learn what her younger sister already knew—that worship begins with silence and listening.

Strengths and accomplishments:
- Known as a hospitable homemaker
- Believed in Jesus with growing faith
- Had a strong desire to do everything exactly right

Weaknesses and mistakes:
- Expected others to agree with her priorities
- Was overly concerned with details
- Tended to feel sorry for herself when her efforts were not recognized
- Limited Jesus' power to this life

Lessons from her life:
- Getting caught up in details can make us forget the main reasons for our actions
- There is a proper time to listen to Jesus and a proper time to work for him

Vital statistics:
- Where: Bethany
- Relatives: Sister: Mary. Brother: Lazarus

Key verse:
"But Martha was distracted with all her preparations; and she came up to Him and said, 'Lord, do You not care that my sister has left me to do all the serving alone? Then tell her to help me' " (Luke 10:40).

Martha's story is told in Luke 10:38–42 and John 11:17–45.

11:27–28 Jesus was speaking to people who put extremely high value on family ties. Their genealogies were important guarantees that they were part of God's chosen people. A man's value came from his ancestors, and a woman's value came from the sons she bore. Jesus' response to the woman meant that a person's obedience to God is more important than his or her place on the family tree. The patient work of consistent obedience is even more important than the honor of bearing a respected son.

Jesus Warns against Unbelief
(136)

29 As the crowds were increasing, He began to say, "This generation is a wicked generation; it seeks for a sign, and *yet* no sign will be given to it but the sign of Jonah.
30 "For just as Jonah became a sign to the Ninevites, so will the Son of Man be to this
generation.
31 "The Queen of the South will rise up with the men of this generation at the judgment and condemn them, because she came from the ends of the earth to hear the
wisdom of Solomon; and behold, something greater than Solomon is here.
32 "The men of Nineveh will stand up with this generation at the judgment and condemn it, because they repented at the preaching of Jonah; and behold, something greater than Jonah is here.

11:29 Matt 12:39-42; Matt 16:4; Mark 8:12; Matt 12:38; Luke 11:16
11:30 Jon 3:4
11:31 1 Kin 10:1-10; 2 Chr 9:1-12
11:32 Jon 3:5

Jesus Teaches about the Light Within
(137)

33 "No one, after lighting a lamp, puts it away in a cellar nor under a basket, but on the
lampstand, so that those who enter may see the light.
34 "The eye is the lamp of your body; when your eye is clear, your whole body also is full
of light; but when it is bad, your body also is full of darkness.
35 "Then watch out that the light in you is not darkness.
36 "If therefore your whole body is full of light, with no dark part in it, it will be wholly
illumined, as when the lamp illumines you with its rays."

11:33 Matt 5:15; Mark 4:21; Luke 8:16
11:34 Matt 6:22, 23

Jesus Criticizes the Religious Leaders
(138)

37 Now when He had spoken, a Pharisee ☆asked Him to have lunch with him; and He
went in, and reclined *at the table.*
38 When the Pharisee saw it, he was surprised that He had not first ceremonially washed
before the meal.
39 But the Lord said to him, "Now you Pharisees clean the outside of the cup and of
the platter; but inside of you, you are full of robbery and wickedness.
40 "You foolish ones, did not He who made the outside make the inside also?
41 "But give that which is within as charity, and then all things are clean for you.
42 "But woe to you Pharisees! For you pay tithe of mint and rue and every *kind of* garden herb, and *yet* disregard justice and the love of God; but these are the things you should
have done without neglecting the others.

11:38 Matt 15:2; Mark 7:3f
11:39 Luke 7:13; Matt 23:25f
11:40 Luke 12:20; 1 Cor 15:36
11:41 Luke 12:33; 16:9; Mark 7:19; Titus 1:15
11:42 Matt 23:23; Lev 27:30; Luke 18:12

11:29–30 What was the sign of Jonah? God had asked Jonah to preach repentance to the Gentiles (non-Jews). Jesus was affirming Jonah's message. Salvation is not only for Jews, but for all people. Matthew 12:40 adds another explanation: Jesus would die and rise after three days, just as the prophet Jonah was rescued after three days in the belly of the great fish.

11:29–32 The cruel, warlike men of Nineveh, capital of Assyria, repented when Jonah preached to them—and Jonah did not even care about them. The pagan Queen of the South (Sheba) praised the God of Israel when she heard Solomon's wisdom, and Solomon was full of faults. By contrast, Jesus, the perfect Son of God, had come to people that he loved dearly—but they rejected him. Thus God's chosen people made themselves more liable to judgment than either a notoriously wicked nation or a powerful pagan queen. Compare 10:12–15 where Jesus says the evil cities of Sodom, Tyre, and Sidon will be judged less harshly than the cities in Judea and Galilee that rejected Jesus' message.

11:31–32 The Ninevites and the Queen of the South had turned to God with far less evidence than Jesus was giving his listeners—and far less than we have today. We have eyewitness reports of the risen Jesus, the continuing power of the Holy Spirit unleashed at Pentecost, easy access to the Bible, and knowledge of 2,000 years of Christ's acts through his church. With the knowledge and insight available to us, our response to Christ ought to be even more complete and wholehearted.

11:33–36 The lamp is Christ; the eye represents spiritual understanding and insight. Evil desires make the eye less sensitive and blot out the light of Christ's presence. If you have a hard time seeing God at work in the world and in your life, check your vision. Are any sinful desires blinding you to Christ?

11:37–39 This washing was done not for health reasons, but as a symbol of washing away any contamination from touching anything unclean. Not only did the Pharisees make a public show of their washing, but they also commanded everyone else to follow a practice originally intended only for the priests.

11:41 The Pharisees loved to think of themselves as "clean," but their stinginess toward God and the poor proved that they were not as clean as they thought. How do you use the resources God has entrusted to you? Are you generous in meeting the needs around you? Your generosity reveals much about the purity of your heart.

11:42 It is easy to rationalize not helping others because we have already given to the church, but a person who follows Jesus should share with needy neighbors. While tithing is important to the life of the church, our compassion must not stop there. Where we can help, we should help.

11:42–52 Jesus criticized the Pharisees and the scribes harshly because they (1) washed their outsides but not their insides, (2) remembered to give a tenth of even their garden herbs, but neglected justice, (3) loved praise and attention, (4) loaded people down with burdensome religious demands, (5) would not accept

43 "Woe to you Pharisees! For you love the chief seats in the synagogues and the respectful greetings in the market places.
44 "Woe to you! For you are like concealed tombs, and the people who walk over *them*
are unaware *of it*."
45 One of the [15]lawyers ☆said to Him in reply, "Teacher, when You say this, You insult
us too."
46 But He said, "Woe to you lawyers as well! For you weigh men down with burdens
hard to bear, while you yourselves will not even touch the burdens with one of your fingers.
47 "Woe to you! For you build the tombs of the prophets, and *it was* your fathers *who*
killed them.
48 "So you are witnesses and approve the deeds of your fathers; because it was they who
killed them, and you build *their tombs*.
49 "For this reason also the wisdom of God said, 'I will send to them prophets and apostles, and *some* of them they will kill and *some* they will persecute,
50 so that the blood of all the prophets, shed since the foundation of the world, may be
charged against this generation,
51 from the blood of Abel to the blood of Zechariah, who was killed between the altar
and the house *of God;* yes, I tell you, it shall be charged against this generation.'
52 "Woe to you lawyers! For you have taken away the key of knowledge; you yourselves
did not enter, and you hindered those who were entering."
53 When He left there, the scribes and the Pharisees began to be very hostile and to
question Him closely on many subjects,
54 plotting against Him to catch *Him* in something He might say.

Jesus Speaks against Hypocrisy
(139)

12 Under these circumstances, after so many thousands of people had gathered together that they were stepping on one another, He began saying to His disciples
first *of all,* "Beware of the leaven of the Pharisees, which is hypocrisy.
2 "But there is nothing covered up that will not be revealed, and hidden that will not
be known.
3 "Accordingly, whatever you have said in the dark will be heard in the light, and what
you have whispered in the inner rooms will be proclaimed upon the housetops.

11:43 Matt 23:6f; Mark 12:38f; Luke 14:7; 20:46
11:44 Matt 23:27
11:45 Matt 22:35; Luke 11:46, 52
11:46 Matt 22:35; Luke 11:45, 52; Matt 23:4
11:47 Matt 23:29ff
11:49 1 Cor 1:24, 30; Col 2:3; Matt 23:34-36
11:50 Matt 25:34
11:51 Gen 4:8; 2 Chr 24:20, 21
11:52 Matt 22:35; Luke 11:45, 46; Matt 23:13
11:54 Mark 3:2; Luke 20:20; Acts 23:21; Mark 12:13
12:1 Matt 16:6, 11f; Mark 8:15
12:2 Matt 10:26; Mark 4:22; Luke 8:17
12:3 Matt 10:27; 24:17

15 I.e. experts in the Mosaic Law

the truth about Jesus, and (6) prevented others from believing the truth as well. They went wrong by focusing on outward appearances and ignoring the inner condition of their hearts. We do the same when our service comes from a desire to be seen rather than from a pure heart and out of a love for others. People may sometimes be fooled, but God isn't. Don't be a Christian on the outside only. Bring your inner life under God's control, and your outer life will naturally reflect him.

11:44 The Old Testament laws said a person who touched a grave was unclean (Numbers 19:16). Jesus accused the Pharisees of making others unclean by their spiritual rottenness. Like concealed tombs hidden in a field, the Pharisees corrupted everyone who came in contact with them.

11:46 These "burdens" were the details the Pharisees had added to God's law. To the commandment, "Remember the sabbath day, to keep it holy" (Exodus 20:8), for example, they had added instructions regarding how far a person could walk on the Sabbath, which kinds of knots could be tied, and how much weight could be carried. Healing a person was considered unlawful work on the Sabbath, although rescuing a trapped animal was permitted (14:5). No wonder Jesus condemned their additions to the law.

11:49 God's prophets have been persecuted and murdered throughout history. But this generation was rejecting more than a human prophet—they were rejecting God himself. This quotation is not from the Old Testament. Jesus, the greatest Prophet of all, was directly giving them God's message.

11:51 Abel's death is recorded in Genesis 4:8. For more about him, see his Profile in Genesis 6. Zechariah's death is recorded in 2 Chronicles 24:20–22 (the last book in the Hebrew canon). Why would all these sins come upon this particular generation? Because they were rejecting the Messiah himself, the One to whom all their history and prophecy were pointing.

11:52 How did the lawyers take away the "key of knowledge"? Through their erroneous interpretations of Scripture and their added man-made rules, they made God's truth hard to understand and practice. On top of that, these men were bad examples, arguing their way out of the demanding rules they placed on others. Caught up in a religion of their own making, they could no longer lead the people to God. They had closed the door of God's love to the people and had thrown away the key.

11:53–54 The scribes and the Pharisees hoped to arrest Jesus for blasphemy, heresy, and lawbreaking. They were enraged by Jesus' words about them, but they couldn't arrest him for merely speaking words. They had to find a legal way to get rid of Jesus.

12:1–2 As Jesus watched the huge crowds waiting to hear him, he warned his disciples against hypocrisy—trying to appear good when one's heart is far from God. The Pharisees could not keep their attitudes hidden forever. Their selfishness would act like leaven, and soon they would expose themselves for what they really were—power-hungry impostors, not devoted religious leaders. It is easy to be angry at the blatant hypocrisy of the Pharisees, but each of us must resist the temptation to settle for the appearance of respectability when our hearts are far from God.

4 "I say to you, My friends, do not be afraid of those who kill the body and after that
have no more that they can do.
5 "But I will warn you whom to fear: fear the One who, after He has killed, has authority to cast into hell; yes, I tell you, fear Him!
6 "Are not five sparrows sold for two cents? *Yet* not one of them is forgotten before God.
7 "Indeed, the very hairs of your head are all numbered. Do not fear; you are more
valuable than many sparrows.
8 "And I say to you, everyone who confesses Me before men, the Son of Man will confess him also before the angels of God;
9 but he who denies Me before men will be denied before the angels of God.
10 "And everyone who speaks a word against the Son of Man, it will be forgiven him;
but he who blasphemes against the Holy Spirit, it will not be forgiven him.
11 "When they bring you before the synagogues and the rulers and the authorities, do
not worry about how or what you are to speak in your defense, or what you are to say;
12 for the Holy Spirit will teach you in that very hour what you ought to say."

Jesus Tells the Parable of the Rich Fool
(140)

13 Someone in the crowd said to Him, "Teacher, tell my brother to divide the *family*
inheritance with me."
14 But He said to him, "Man, who appointed Me a judge or arbitrator over you?"
15 Then He said to them, "Beware, and be on your guard against every form of greed;
for not *even* when one has an abundance does his life consist of his possessions."
16 And He told them a parable, saying, "The land of a rich man was very productive.
17 "And he began reasoning to himself, saying, 'What shall I do, since I have no place
to store my crops?'

12:4 John 15:13-15
12:5 Heb 10:31; Matt 5:22
12:6 Matt 10:29
12:7 Matt 10:30
12:8 Matt 10:32; Luke 15:10; Rom 10:9
12:9 Matt 10:33; Luke 9:26; Luke 15:10
12:10 Matt 12:31, 32; Mark 3:28-30
12:11 Matt 10:17; Matt 6:25; 10:19; Mark 13:11; Luke 12:22; 21:14
12:12 Matt 10:20; Luke 21:15
12:14 Mic 6:8; Rom 2:1, 3; 9:20
12:15 1 Tim 6:6-10

12:4–5 Fear of opposition or ridicule can weaken our witness for Christ. Often we cling to peace and comfort, even at the cost of our walk with God. Jesus reminds us here that we should fear God, who controls eternal, not merely temporal, consequences. Don't allow fear of a person or group to keep you from standing up for Christ.

12:7 Our true value is God's estimate of our worth, not our peers'. Other people evaluate and categorize us according to how we perform, what we achieve, and how we look. But God cares for us, as he does for all of his creatures, because we belong to him. So we can face life without fear.

12:8–9 We deny Jesus when we (1) hope no one will think we are Christians; (2) decide *not* to speak up for what is right; (3) are silent about our relationship with God; (4) blend into society; (5) accept our culture's non-Christian values. By contrast, we confess him when we (1) live moral, upright, Christ-honoring lives; (2) look for opportunities to share our faith with others; (3) help others in need; (4) take a stand for justice; (5) love others; (6) acknowledge our loyalty to Christ; (7) use our lives and resources to carry out his desires rather than our own.

12:10 Jesus said that blasphemy against the Holy Spirit is unforgivable. This has worried many sincere Christians, but it does not need to. The unforgivable sin means attributing to Satan the work that the Holy Spirit accomplishes (see the notes on Matthew 12:31–32; Mark 3:28–29). Thus it is deliberate and ongoing rejection of the Holy Spirit's work and even of God himself. A person who has committed this sin has shut himself or herself off from God so thoroughly that he or she is unaware of any sin at all. A person who fears having committed it shows, by his or her very concern, that he or she has not sinned in this way.

12:11–12 The disciples knew they could never dominate a religious dispute with the well-educated Jewish leaders. Nevertheless, they would not be left unprepared. Jesus promised that the Holy Spirit would supply the needed words. The disciples' testimony might not make them look impressive, but it would still point out God's work in the world through Jesus' life. We need to pray for opportunities to speak for God, and then trust him to help us with our words. This promise of the Spirit's help, however, does not compensate for lack of preparation. Remember that these disciples had three years of teaching and practical application. We too must study God's Word. Then God will bring his truths to mind when we most need them, helping us present them in the most effective way.

12:13ff Problems like this were often brought to rabbis for them to settle. Jesus' response, though not directly to the topic, is not a change of subject. Rather, Jesus is pointing to a higher issue—a correct attitude toward the accumulation of wealth. Life is more than material goods; far more important is our relationship with God. Jesus put his finger on this questioner's heart. When we bring problems to God in prayer, he often does the same—showing us how we need to change and grow in our attitude toward the problem. This answer is often not the one we were looking for, but it is more effective in helping us trace God's hand in our lives.

12:15 Jesus says that the good life has nothing to do with being wealthy, so be on guard against greed (desire for what we don't have). This is the exact opposite of what society usually says. Advertisers spend millions of dollars to entice us to think that if we buy more and more of their products, we will be happier, more fulfilled, more comfortable. How do you respond to the constant pressure to buy? Learn to tune out expensive enticements and concentrate instead on the truly good life—living in a relationship with God and doing his work.

12:16–21 The rich man in Jesus' story died before he could begin to use what was stored in his big barns. Planning for retirement—preparing for life *before* death—is wise, but neglecting life *after* death is disastrous. If you accumulate wealth only to enrich yourself, with no concern for helping others, you will enter eternity empty-handed.

12:19 Eccl 11:9

12:20 Jer 17:11; Luke 11:40; Job 27:8; Ps 39:6

12:21 Luke 12:33

12:22 Matt 6:25-33

12:24 Job 38:41; Luke 12:18

12:25 Ps 39:5

12:27 1 Kin 10:4-7; 2 Chr 9:3-6

12:28 Matt 6:30

12:29 Matt 6:31

12:31 Matt 6:33

12:32 Matt 14:27; John 21:15-17; Eph 1:5, 9

12:33 Matt 19:21; Luke 11:41; 18:22; Matt 6:20; Luke 12:21

12:34 Matt 6:21

12:35 Matt 25:1ff

Eph 6:14; 1 Pet 1:13

12:37 Matt 24:42; Luke 17:8; John 13:4

18 "Then he said, 'This is what I will do: I will tear down my barns and build larger ones,
and there I will store all my grain and my goods.
19 'And I will say to my soul, "Soul, you have many goods laid up for many years *to
come;* take your ease, eat, drink *and* be merry." '
20 "But God said to him, 'You fool! This *very* night your soul is required of you; and
now who will own what you have prepared?'
21 "So is the man who stores up treasure for himself, and is not rich toward God."

Jesus Warns about Worry
(141)

22 And He said to His disciples, "For this reason I say to you, do not worry about *your*
life, *as to* what you will eat; nor for your body, *as to* what you will put on.
23 "For life is more than food, and the body more than clothing.
24 "Consider the ravens, for they neither sow nor reap; they have no storeroom nor barn,
and *yet* God feeds them; how much more valuable you are than the birds!
25 "And which of you by worrying can add a *single* [16]hour to his [17]life's span?
26 "If then you cannot do even a very little thing, why do you worry about other matters?
27 "Consider the lilies, how they grow: they neither toil nor spin; but I tell you, not even
Solomon in all his glory clothed himself like one of these.
28 "But if God so clothes the grass in the field, which is *alive* today and tomorrow is
thrown into the furnace, how much more *will He clothe* you? You men of little faith!
29 "And do not seek what you will eat and what you will drink, and do not keep
worrying.
30 "For all these things the nations of the world eagerly seek; but your Father knows
that you need these things.
31 "But seek His kingdom, and these things will be added to you.
32 "Do not be afraid, little flock, for your Father has chosen gladly to give you the
kingdom.
33 "Sell your possessions and give to charity; make yourselves money belts which do not
wear out, an unfailing treasure in heaven, where no thief comes near nor moth destroys.
34 "For where your treasure is, there your heart will be also.

Jesus Warns about Preparing for His Coming
(142)

35 "Be dressed in readiness, and *keep* your lamps lit.
36 "Be like men who are waiting for their master when he returns from the wedding
feast, so that they may immediately open *the door* to him when he comes and knocks.
37 "Blessed are those slaves whom the master will find on the alert when he comes; truly

16 Lit *cubit* (approx 18 in.) **17** Or *height*

12:18–20 Why do you save money? To retire? To buy more expensive cars or toys? To be secure? Jesus challenges us to think beyond earthbound goals and to use what we have been given for God's kingdom. Faith, service, and obedience are the way to become rich toward God.

12:22–34 Jesus commands us not to worry. But how can we avoid it? Only faith can free us from the anxiety caused by greed and covetousness. It is good to work and plan responsibly; it is bad to dwell on all the ways our planning could go wrong. Worry is pointless because it can't fill any of our needs; worry is foolish because the Creator of the universe loves us and knows what we need. He promises to meet all our real needs, but not necessarily all our desires.

12:31 Seeking the kingdom of God means making Jesus the Lord and King of your life. He must control every area—your work, play, plans, relationships. Is the kingdom only one of your many concerns, or is it central to all you do? Are you holding back any areas of your life from God's control? As Lord and Creator, he wants to help provide what you need as well as guide how you use what he provides.

12:33 Money seen as an end in itself quickly traps us and cuts us off from both God and the needy. The key to using money wisely is to see how much we can use for God's purposes, not how much we can accumulate for ourselves. Does God's love touch your wallet? Does your money free you to help others? If so, you are storing up lasting treasures in heaven. If your financial goals and possessions hinder you from giving generously, loving others, or serving God, sell what you must to bring your life into perspective.

12:34 If you concentrate your money in your business, your thoughts will center on making the business profitable. If you direct it toward other people, you will become concerned with their welfare. Where do you put your time, money, and energy? What do you think about most? How should you change the way you use your resources in order to reflect kingdom values more accurately?

12:35–40 Jesus repeatedly said that he would leave this world but would return at some future time (see Matthew 24; 25; John 14:1–3). He also said that a kingdom is being prepared for his followers. Many Greeks envisioned this as a heavenly, idealized, spiritual kingdom. Jews—like Isaiah and John, the writer of Revelation—saw it as a restored earthly kingdom.

I say to you, that he will gird himself *to serve,* and have them recline *at the table,* and will come up and wait on them.
38 "Whether he comes in the [18]second watch, or even in the [19]third, and finds *them* so, blessed are those *slaves.*
39 "But be sure of this, that if the head of the house had known at what hour the thief was coming, he would not have allowed his house to be broken into.
40 "You too, be ready; for the Son of Man is coming at an hour that you do not expect."
41 Peter said, "Lord, are You addressing this parable to us, or to everyone *else* as well?"
42 And the Lord said, "Who then is the faithful and sensible steward, whom his master will put in charge of his servants, to give them their rations at the proper time?
43 "Blessed is that slave whom his master finds so doing when he comes.
44 "Truly I say to you that he will put him in charge of all his possessions.
45 "But if that slave says in his heart, 'My master will be a long time in coming,' and begins to beat the slaves, *both* men and women, and to eat and drink and get drunk;
46 the master of that slave will come on a day when he does not expect *him* and at an hour he does not know, and will cut him in pieces, and assign him a place with the unbelievers.
47 "And that slave who knew his master's will and did not get ready or act in accord with his will, will receive many lashes,
48 but the one who did not know *it,* and committed deeds worthy of a flogging, will receive but few. From everyone who has been given much, much will be required; and to whom they entrusted much, of him they will ask all the more.

12:38 Matt 24:43
12:39 Matt 24:43, 44; Matt 6:19
12:40 Mark 13:33; Luke 21:36
12:41 Luke 12:47, 48
12:42 Luke 7:13; Matt 24:45; Luke 16:1ff
12:43 Luke 12:42
12:47 Deut 25:2; James 4:17
12:48 Lev 5:17; Num 15:29f; Matt 13:12

Jesus Warns about Coming Division
(143)

49 "I have come to cast fire upon the earth; and how I wish it were already kindled!
50 "But I have a baptism to undergo, and how distressed I am until it is accomplished!
51 "Do you suppose that I came to grant peace on earth? I tell you, no, but rather division;
52 for from now on five *members* in one household will be divided, three against two and two against three.
53 "They will be divided, father against son and son against father, mother against daughter and daughter against mother, mother-in-law against daughter-in-law and daughter-in-law against mother-in-law."

12:50 Mark 10:38
12:51 Matt 10:34-36
12:53 Mic 7:6; Matt 10:21

Jesus Warns about the Future Crisis
(144)

54 And He was also saying to the crowds, "When you see a cloud rising in the west, immediately you say, 'A shower is coming,' and so it turns out.

12:54 Matt 16:2f

18 I.e. 9 p.m. to midnight **19** I.e. midnight to 3 a.m.

12:40 Christ's return at an unexpected time is not a trap, a trick by which God hopes to catch us off guard. In fact, God is delaying his return so more people will have the opportunity to follow him (see 2 Peter 3:9). Before Christ's return, we have time to live out our beliefs and to reflect Jesus' love as we relate to others.

People who are ready for their Lord's return are (1) not hypocritical, but sincere (12:1); (2) not fearful, but ready to witness (12:4–9); (3) not worried, but trusting (12:25–26); (4) not greedy, but generous (12:34); (5) not lazy, but diligent (12:37). May your life be more like Christ's so that when he comes, you will be ready to greet him joyfully.

12:42–44 Jesus promises a reward for those who have been faithful to the Master. While we sometimes experience immediate and material rewards for our obedience to God, this is not always the case. If so, we would be tempted to boast about our achievements and do good only for what we get. Jesus said that if we look for rewards now, we will lose them later (see Mark 8:36). Our heavenly rewards will be the most accurate reflection of what we have done on earth, and they will be far greater than we can imagine.

12:48 Jesus has told us how to live until he comes: We must watch for him, work diligently, and obey his commands. Such attitudes are especially necessary for leaders. Watchful and faithful leaders will be given increased opportunities and responsibilities. The more resources, talents, and understanding we have, the more we are responsible to use them effectively. God will not hold us responsible for gifts he has not given us, but all of us have enough gifts and duties to keep us busy until Jesus comes.

12:50 The "baptism" to which Jesus referred was his coming crucifixion. Jesus was dreading the physical pain, of course, but even worse would be the spiritual pain of complete separation from God that would accompany his death for the sins of the world.

12:51–53 In these strange and unsettling words, Jesus revealed that his coming often results in conflict. He demands a response, so intimate groups may be torn apart when some choose to follow him and others refuse to do so. There is no middle ground with Jesus. Loyalties must be declared and commitments made, sometimes to the point of severing other relationships. Are you willing to risk your family's approval in order to gain eternal life?

12:54–57 For most of recorded history, the world's principal

12:55 Matt 20:12
55 "And when *you see* a south wind blowing, you say, 'It will be a hot day,' and it turns out *that way.*

12:56 Matt 16:3
56 "You hypocrites! You know how to analyze the appearance of the earth and the sky, but why do you not analyze this present time?

12:57 Luke 21:30
57 "And why do you not even on your own initiative judge what is right?

12:58 Matt 5:25, 26
58 "For while you are going with your opponent to appear before the magistrate, on *your* way *there* make an effort to settle with him, so that he may not drag you before the judge, and the judge turn you over to the officer, and the officer throw you into prison.

12:59 Mark 12:42
59 "I say to you, you will not get out of there until you have paid the very last cent."

Jesus Calls the People to Repent
(145)

13:1 Matt 27
13 Now on the same occasion there were some present who reported to Him about
the Galileans whose blood Pilate had mixed with their sacrifices.

13:2 John 9:2f
2 And Jesus said to them, "Do you suppose that these Galileans were *greater* sinners
than all *other* Galileans because they suffered this *fate?*
3 "I tell you, no, but unless you repent, you will all likewise perish.

13:4 Neh 3:15; Is 8:6; John 9:7, 11; Matt 6:12; Luke 11:4
4 "Or do you suppose that those eighteen on whom the tower in Siloam fell and killed
them were *worse* culprits than all the men who live in Jerusalem?
5 "I tell you, no, but unless you repent, you will all likewise perish."

13:6 Matt 21:19
6 And He *began* telling this parable: "A man had a fig tree which had been planted in
his vineyard; and he came looking for fruit on it and did not find any.

13:7 Matt 3:10; 7:19; Luke 3:9
7 "And he said to the vineyard-keeper, 'Behold, for three years I have come looking
for fruit on this fig tree without finding any. Cut it down! Why does it even use up the
ground?'

SEVEN SABBATH MIRACLES

Jesus sends a demon out of a man	Mark 1:21–28
Jesus heals Peter's mother-in-law	Mark 1:29–31
Jesus heals a lame man by Bethesda Pool	John 5:1–18
Jesus heals a man with a withered hand	Mark 3:1–6
Jesus restores a crippled woman	Luke 13:10–17
Jesus heals a man with dropsy	Luke 14:1–6
Jesus heals a man born blind	John 9:1–16

Over the centuries, the Jewish religious leaders had added rule after rule to God's law. For example, God's law said the Sabbath is a day of rest (Exodus 20:10–11). But the religious leaders added to that law, creating one that said, "you cannot heal on the Sabbath" because that is "work." Seven times Jesus healed people on the Sabbath. In doing this, he was challenging these religious leaders to look beneath their rules to their true purpose—to honor God by helping those in need. Would God have been pleased if Jesus had ignored these people?

occupation was farming. The farmer depended directly on the weather for his livelihood. He needed just the right amounts of sun and rain—not too much, not too little—to make his living, and he grew skilled at interpreting natural signs. Jesus was announcing an earthshaking event that would be much more important than the year's crops—the coming of God's kingdom. Like a rainstorm or a sunny day, there were signs that the kingdom would soon arrive. But Jesus' hearers, though skilled at interpreting weather signs, were intentionally ignoring the signs of the times.

13:1–5 Pilate may have killed the Galileans because he thought they were rebelling against Rome; those killed by the tower in Siloam may have been working for the Romans on an aqueduct there. The Pharisees, who were opposed to using force to deal with Rome, would have said that the Galileans deserved to die for rebelling. The Zealots, a group of anti-Roman terrorists, would have said the aqueduct workers deserved to die for cooperating. Jesus said that neither the Galileans nor the workers should be blamed for their calamity. And instead of blaming others, everyone should look to his or her own day of judgment.

13:5 Whether a person is killed in a tragic accident or miraculously survives is not a measure of righteousness. Everyone has to die; that's part of being human. But not everyone needs to stay dead. Jesus promises that those who believe in him will not perish but have eternal life (John 3:16).

13:6–9 In the Old Testament, a fruitful tree was often used as a symbol of godly living (see, for example, Psalm 1:3 and Jeremiah 17:7–8). Jesus pointed out what would happen to the other kind of tree—the kind that took valuable time and space and still produced nothing for the patient gardener. This was one way Jesus warned his listeners that God would not tolerate forever their lack of productivity. (Luke 3:9 records John the Baptist's version of the same message.) Have you been enjoying God's special treatment without giving anything in return? If so, respond to the Gardener's patient care, and begin to bear the fruit God has created you to produce.

8 "And he answered and said to him, 'Let it alone, sir, for this year too, until I dig around
it and put in fertilizer;
9 and if it bears fruit next year, *fine;* but if not, cut it down.' "

Jesus Heals the Crippled Woman
(146)

10 And He was teaching in one of the synagogues on the Sabbath.
11 And there was a woman who for eighteen years had had a sickness caused by a spirit; and she was bent double, and could not straighten up at all.
12 When Jesus saw her, He called her over and said to her, "Woman, you are freed
from your sickness."
13 And He laid His hands on her; and immediately she was made erect again and *began* glorifying God.
14 But the synagogue official, indignant because Jesus had healed on the Sabbath, *began*
saying to the crowd in response, "There are six days in which work should be done; so
come during them and get healed, and not on the Sabbath day."
15 But the Lord answered him and said, "You hypocrites, does not each of you on the
Sabbath untie his ox or his donkey from the stall and lead him away to water *him?*
16 "And this woman, a daughter of Abraham as she is, whom Satan has bound for eighteen long years, should she not have been released from this bond on the Sabbath day?"
17 As He said this, all His opponents were being humiliated; and the entire crowd was
rejoicing over all the glorious things being done by Him.

13:10 Matt 4:23
13:11 Luke 13:16
13:13 Mark 5:23; Matt 9:8
13:14 Mark 5:22; Matt 12:2; Luke 14:3; Ex 20:9; Deut 5:13
13:15 Luke 7:13; Luke 14:5
13:16 Luke 19:9; Matt 4:10; Luke 13:11
13:17 Luke 18:43

Jesus Teaches about the Kingdom of God
(147)

18 So He was saying, "What is the kingdom of God like, and to what shall I compare it?
19 "It is like a mustard seed, which a man took and threw into his own garden; and it
grew and became a tree, and THE BIRDS OF THE AIR NESTED IN ITS BRANCHES."
20 And again He said, "To what shall I compare the kingdom of God?
21 "It is like leaven, which a woman took and hid in three pecks of flour until it was all
leavened."

13:18 Matt 13:31, 32; Mark 4:30-32; Matt 13:24; Luke 13:20
13:19 Ezek 17:23
13:20 Matt 13:24; Luke 13:18
13:21 Matt 13:33

Jesus Teaches about Entering the Kingdom
(153)

22 And He was passing through from one city and village to another, teaching, and
proceeding on His way to Jerusalem.
23 And someone said to Him, "Lord, are there *just* a few who are being saved?" And
He said to them,
24 "Strive to enter through the narrow door; for many, I tell you, will seek to enter and
will not be able.

13:22 Luke 9:51
13:24 Matt 7:13

13:10–17 Why was healing considered work? The religious leaders saw healing as part of a doctor's profession, and practicing one's profession on the Sabbath was prohibited. The synagogue official could not see beyond the law to Jesus' compassion in healing this crippled woman. Jesus shamed him and the other leaders by pointing out their hypocrisy. They would untie their animals and care for them, but they refused to rejoice when a human being was freed from Satan's bondage.

13:15–16 The Pharisees hid behind their own set of laws to avoid love's obligations. We too can use the letter of the law to rationalize away our obligation to care for others (for example, by tithing regularly and then refusing to help a needy neighbor). But people's needs are more important than rules and regulations. Take time to help others, even if doing so might compromise your public image.

13:16 In our fallen world, disease and disability are common. Their causes are many and often multiple—inadequate nutrition, contact with a source of infection, lowered defenses, and even direct attack by Satan. Whatever the immediate cause of our illness, we can trace its original source to Satan, the author of all the evil in our world. The good news is that Jesus is more powerful than any devil or any disease. He often brings physical healing in this life; and when he returns, he will put an end to all disease and disability.

13:18–21 The general expectation among Jesus' hearers was that the Messiah would come as a great king and leader, freeing the nation from Rome and restoring Israel's former glory. But Jesus said his kingdom was beginning quietly. Like the tiny mustard seed that grows into an enormous tree, or the spoonful of leaven that makes the bread dough double in size, the kingdom of God would eventually push outward until the whole world was changed.

13:22 This is the second time Luke reminds us that Jesus was intentionally going to Jerusalem (the other time is in 9:51). Jesus knew he was on his way to die, but he continued preaching to large crowds. The prospect of death did not deter Jesus from his mission.

13:24–25 Finding salvation requires more concentrated effort than most people are willing to put forth. Obviously we cannot save ourselves—there is no way we can work ourselves into God's favor.

13:25 Matt 25:10; Matt 7:22; 25:11; Matt 7:23; 25:12; Luke 13:27
13:26 Luke 3:8
13:27 Luke 13:25; Ps 6:8; Matt 25:41
13:28 Matt 8:12; 22:13; 25:30
13:29 Matt 8:11
13:30 Matt 19:30; 20:16; Mark 10:31

25 "Once the head of the house gets up and shuts the door, and you begin to stand
outside and knock on the door, saying, 'Lord, open up to us!' then He will answer and
say to you, 'I do not know where you are from.'
26 "Then you will begin to say, 'We ate and drank in Your presence, and You taught in
our streets';
27 and He will say, 'I tell you, I do not know where you are from; DEPART FROM ME,
ALL YOU EVILDOERS.'
28 "In that place there will be weeping and gnashing of teeth when you see Abraham
and Isaac and Jacob and all the prophets in the kingdom of God, but yourselves being
thrown out.
29 "And they will come from east and west and from north and south, and will recline *at
the table* in the kingdom of God.
30 "And behold, *some* are last who will be first and *some* are first who will be last."

Jesus Grieves over Jerusalem
(154)

13:31 Matt 14:1; Luke 3:1; 9:7; 23:7
13:32 Heb 2:10; 5:9; 7:28
13:33 John 11:9; Matt 21:11
13:34 Matt 23:37-39; Luke 19:41; Matt 23:37
13:35 Ps 118:26; Matt 21:9; Luke 19:38

31 Just at that time some Pharisees approached, saying to Him, "Go away, leave here,
for Herod wants to kill You."
32 And He said to them, "Go and tell that fox, 'Behold, I cast out demons and perform
cures today and tomorrow, and the third *day* I reach My goal.'
33 "Nevertheless I must journey on today and tomorrow and the next *day;* for it cannot
be that a prophet would perish outside of Jerusalem.
34 "O Jerusalem, Jerusalem, *the city* that kills the prophets and stones those sent to her!
How often I wanted to gather your children together, just as a hen *gathers* her brood
under her wings, and you would not *have it!*
35 "Behold, your house is left to you *desolate;* and I say to you, you will not see Me until
the time comes when you say, 'BLESSED IS HE WHO COMES IN THE NAME OF THE LORD!' "

Jesus Heals a Man with Dropsy
(155)

14:1 Mark 3:2

14 It happened that when He went into the house of one of the leaders of the Pharisees on *the* Sabbath to eat bread, they were watching Him closely.
2 And there in front of Him was a man suffering from dropsy.

The effort we must put out "to enter through the narrow door" is earnestly desiring to know Jesus and diligently striving to follow him whatever the cost. We dare not put off making this decision because the door will not stay open forever.

13:26–27 The kingdom of God will not necessarily be populated with the people we expect to find there. Some perfectly respectable religious leaders claiming allegiance to Jesus will not be there because secretly they were morally corrupt.

13:27 The people were eager to know who would be in God's kingdom. Jesus explained that although many people know something about God, only a few have acknowledged their sins and accepted his forgiveness. Just listening to Jesus' words or admiring his miracles is not enough—we must turn from sin and trust in God to save us.

13:29 God's kingdom will include people from every part of the world. Israel's rejection of Jesus as Messiah would not stop God's plan. True Israel includes all people who believe in God. This was an important fact for Luke to stress as he was directing his Gospel to a Gentile audience (see also Romans 4:16–25; Galatians 3:6–9).

13:30 There will be many surprises in God's kingdom. Some who are despised now will be greatly honored then; some influential people here will be left outside the gates. Many "great" people on this earth (in God's eyes) are virtually ignored by the rest of the world. What matters to God is not a person's earthly popularity, status, wealth, heritage, or power, but his or her commitment to Christ. How do your values match what the Bible tells you to value? Put God in first place, and you will join people from all over the world who will take their places at the feast in the kingdom of heaven.

13:31–33 The Pharisees weren't interested in protecting Jesus from danger. They were trying to trap him themselves. The Pharisees urged Jesus to leave because they wanted to stop him from going to Jerusalem, not because they feared Herod. But Jesus' life, work, and death were not to be determined by Herod or the Pharisees. His life was planned and directed by God himself, and his mission would unfold in God's time and according to God's plan.

13:33–34 Why was Jesus focusing on Jerusalem? Jerusalem, the city of God, symbolized the entire nation. It was Israel's largest city and the nation's spiritual and political capital, and Jews from around the world visited it frequently. But Jerusalem had a history of rejecting God's prophets (1 Kings 19:10; 2 Chronicles 24:19; Jeremiah 2:30; 26:20–23), and it would reject the Messiah just as it had rejected his forerunners.

14:1–6 Earlier Jesus had been invited to a Pharisee's home for discussion (7:36). This time a prominent Pharisee invited Jesus to his home specifically to trap him into saying or doing something for which he could be arrested. It may be surprising to see Jesus on the Pharisees' turf after he had denounced them so many times. But he was not afraid to face them, even though he knew that their purpose was to trick him into breaking their laws.

14:2 Luke, the physician, identifies this man's disease—he was suffering from *dropsy*, an abnormal accumulation of fluid in bodily tissues and cavities.

3 And Jesus answered and spoke to the lawyers and Pharisees, saying, "Is it lawful to
heal on the Sabbath, or not?"
4 But they kept silent. And He took hold of him and healed him, and sent him away.
5 And He said to them, "Which one of you will have a son or an ox fall into a well, and
will not immediately pull him out on a Sabbath day?"
6 And they could make no reply to this.

14:3 Matt 22:35; Matt 12:2; Luke 13:14
14:5 Matt 12:11; Luke 13:15
14:6 Matt 22:46; Luke 20:40

Jesus Teaches about Seeking Honor (156)

7 And He *began* speaking a parable to the invited guests when He noticed how they
had been picking out the places of honor *at the table,* saying to them,
8 "When you are invited by someone to a wedding feast, do not take the place of hon-
or, for someone more distinguished than you may have been invited by him,
9 and he who invited you both will come and say to you, 'Give *your* place to this man,'
and then in disgrace you proceed to occupy the last place.
10 "But when you are invited, go and recline at the last place, so that when the one who
has invited you comes, he may say to you, 'Friend, move up higher'; then you will have
honor in the sight of all who are at the table with you.
11 "For everyone who exalts himself will be humbled, and he who humbles himself will
be exalted."
12 And He also went on to say to the one who had invited Him, "When you give a luncheon or a dinner, do not invite your friends or your brothers or your relatives or rich
neighbors, otherwise they may also invite you in return and *that* will be your repayment.
13 "But when you give a reception, invite *the* poor, *the* crippled, *the* lame, *the* blind,
14 and you will be blessed, since they do not have *the means* to repay you; for you will
be repaid at the resurrection of the righteous."

14:7 Matt 23:6
14:8 Prov 25:6, 7
14:9 Luke 3:8
14:10 Prov 25:6, 7
14:11 2 Sam 22:28; Prov 29:23; Matt 23:12; Luke 1:52; 18:14; James 4:10
14:14 John 5:29; Acts 24:15; Rev 20:4, 5

Jesus Tells the Parable of the Great Feast (157)

15 When one of those who were reclining *at the table* with Him heard this, he said to
Him, "Blessed is everyone who will eat bread in the kingdom of God!"
16 But He said to him, "A man was giving a big dinner, and he invited many;
17 and at the dinner hour he sent his slave to say to those who had been invited, 'Come;
for everything is ready now.'

14:15 Rev 19:9
14:16 Matt 22:2-14

14:7–11 Jesus advised people not to rush for the best places at a feast. People today are just as eager to raise their social status, whether by being with the right people, dressing for success, or driving the right car. Whom do you try to impress? Rather than aiming for prestige, look for a place where you can serve. If God wants you to serve on a wider scale, he will invite you to take a higher place.

14:7–14 Jesus taught two lessons here. First, he spoke to the guests, telling them not to seek places of honor. Service is more important in God's kingdom than status. Second, he told the host not to be exclusive about whom he invites. God opens his kingdom to everyone.

14:11 How can we humble ourselves? Some people try to give the appearance of humility in order to manipulate others. Others think that humility means putting themselves down. Truly humble people compare themselves only with Christ, realize their sinfulness, and understand their limitations. On the other hand, they also recognize their gifts and strengths and are willing to use them as Christ directs. Humility is not self-degradation; it is realistic assessment and commitment to serve.

14:15–24 The man sitting at the table with Jesus saw the glory of God's kingdom, but he did not yet understand how to get in. In Jesus' story, many people turned down the invitation to the banquet because the timing was inconvenient. We too can resist or delay responding to God's invitation, and our excuses may sound reasonable—work duties, family responsibilities, financial needs, or whatever they may be. Nevertheless, God's invitation is the most important event in our lives, no matter how inconveniently it may be timed. Are you making excuses to avoid responding to God's call? Jesus reminds us that the time will come when God will pull his invitation and offer it to others—then it will be too late to get into the banquet.

14:16ff It was customary to send two invitations to a party—the first to announce the event, the second to tell the guests that everything was ready. The guests in Jesus' story insulted the host by making excuses when he issued the second invitation. In Israel's history, God's first invitation came from Moses and the prophets; the second came from his Son. The religious leaders accepted the first invitation. They believed that God had called them to be his people, but they insulted God by refusing to accept his Son. Thus, as the master in the story sent his servant into the streets to invite the needy to his banquet, so God sent his Son to the whole world of needy people to tell them that God's kingdom had arrived and was ready for them.

14:16ff In this chapter we read Jesus' words against seeking status, and in favor of hard work and even suffering. Let us not lose sight of the end result of all our humility and self-sacrifice—a joyous banquet with our Lord! God never asks us to suffer for the sake of suffering. He never asks us to give up something good unless he plans to replace it with something even better. Jesus is not calling us to join him in a labor camp but in a feast—the marriage supper of the Lamb (Revelation 19:6–9), when God and his beloved church will be joined forever.

18 "But they all alike began to make excuses. The first one said to him, 'I have bought
a piece of land and I need to go out and look at it; please consider me excused.'
19 "Another one said, 'I have bought five yoke of oxen, and I am going to try them out;
please consider me excused.'
14:20 Deut 24:5; 1 Cor 7:33
20 "Another one said, 'I have married a wife, and for that reason I cannot come.'
21 "And the slave came *back* and reported this to his master. Then the head of the household became angry and said to his slave, 'Go out at once into the streets and lanes of the
city and bring in here the poor and crippled and blind and lame.'
22 "And the slave said, 'Master, what you commanded has been done, and still there is
room.'
23 "And the master said to the slave, 'Go out into the highways and along the hedges,
and compel *them* to come in, so that my house may be filled.
24 'For I tell you, none of those men who were invited shall taste of my dinner.' "

Jesus Teaches about the Cost of Being a Disciple
(158)

25 Now large crowds were going along with Him; and He turned and said to them,
14:26 Matt 10:37
26 "If anyone comes to Me, and does not [20]hate his own father and mother and wife
and children and brothers and sisters, yes, and even his own life, he cannot be My
disciple.
14:27 Matt 10:38; 16:24; Mark 8:34; Luke 9:23
27 "Whoever does not carry his own cross and come after Me cannot be My disciple.
28 "For which one of you, when he wants to build a tower, does not first sit down and
calculate the cost to see if he has enough to complete it?
29 "Otherwise, when he has laid a foundation and is not able to finish, all who observe
it begin to ridicule him,
30 saying, 'This man began to build and was not able to finish.'
14:31 Prov 20:18
31 "Or what king, when he sets out to meet another king in battle, will not first sit down
and consider whether he is strong enough with ten thousand *men* to encounter the one
coming against him with twenty thousand?
32 "Or else, while the other is still far away, he sends a delegation and asks for terms of
peace.
14:33 Phil 3:7; Heb 11:26
33 "So then, none of you can be My disciple who does not give up all his own possessions.
14:34 Matt 5:13; Mark 9:50
34 "Therefore, salt is good; but if even salt has become tasteless, with what will it be
seasoned?
14:35 Matt 11:15
35 "It is useless either for the soil or for the manure pile; it is thrown out. He who has
ears to hear, let him hear."

20 I.e. by comparison of his love for Me

14:27 Jesus' audience was well aware of what it meant to carry one's own cross. When the Romans led a criminal to his execution site, he was forced to carry the cross on which he would die. This showed his submission to Rome and warned observers that they had better submit too. Jesus spoke this teaching to get the crowds to think through their enthusiasm for him. He encouraged those who were superficial either to go deeper or to turn back. Following Christ means total submission to him—perhaps even to the point of death.

14:28–30 When a builder doesn't count the cost or estimates it inaccurately, his building may be left half completed. Will your Christian life be only half built and then abandoned because you did not count the cost of commitment to Jesus? What are those costs? Christians may face loss of social status or wealth. They may have to give up control over their money, their time, or their career. They may be hated, separated from their family, and even put to death. Following Christ does not mean a trouble-free life. We must carefully count the cost of becoming Christ's disciples so that we will know what we are getting into and won't be tempted later to turn back.

14:34 Salt can lose its flavor. When it gets wet and then dries, nothing is left but a tasteless residue. Many Christians blend into the world and avoid the cost of standing up for Christ. But Jesus says if Christians lose their distinctive saltiness, they become worthless. Just as salt flavors and preserves food, so we are to preserve the good in the world, help keep it from spoiling, and bring new flavor to life. This requires careful planning, willing sacrifice, and unswerving commitment to Christ's kingdom. Being "salty" is not easy, but if a Christian fails in this function, he or she fails to represent Christ in the world. How salty are you?

Jesus Tells the Parable of the Lost Sheep
(159)

15 Now all the tax collectors and the sinners were coming near Him to listen to Him. **15:1** Luke 5:29
2 Both the Pharisees and the scribes *began* to grumble, saying, "This man receives
sinners and eats with them." **15:2** Matt 9:11
3 So He told them this parable, saying,
4 "What man among you, if he has a hundred sheep and has lost one of them, does not **15:4** Matt 18:12-14; Luke 15:4-7
leave the ninety-nine in the open pasture and go after the one which is lost until he
finds it?
5 "When he has found it, he lays it on his shoulders, rejoicing.
6 "And when he comes home, he calls together his friends and his neighbors, saying to
them, 'Rejoice with me, for I have found my sheep which was lost!'
7 "I tell you that in the same way, there will be *more* joy in heaven over one sinner who
repents than over ninety-nine righteous persons who need no repentance.

Jesus Tells the Parable of the Lost Coin
(160)

8 "Or what woman, if she has ten silver coins and loses one coin, does not light a lamp
and sweep the house and search carefully until she finds it?
9 "When she has found it, she calls together her friends and neighbors, saying, 'Rejoice with me, for I have found the coin which I had lost!'
10 "In the same way, I tell you, there is joy in the presence of the angels of God over **15:10** Matt 10:32; Luke 15:7
one sinner who repents."

Jesus Tells the Parable of the Lost Son
(161)

11 And He said, "A man had two sons.
12 "The younger of them said to his father, 'Father, give me the share of the estate that **15:12** Deut 21:17; Mark 12:44; Luke 15:30
falls to me.' So he divided his wealth between them.
13 "And not many days later, the younger son gathered everything together and went
on a journey into a distant country, and there he squandered his estate with loose living.
14 "Now when he had spent everything, a severe famine occurred in that country, and
he began to be impoverished.
15 "So he went and hired himself out to one of the citizens of that country, and he sent
him into his fields to feed swine.

15:2 Why were the Pharisees and scribes bothered that Jesus associated with these people? The religious leaders were always careful to stay "clean" according to Old Testament law. In fact, they went well beyond the law in their avoidance of certain people and situations and in their ritual washings. By contrast, Jesus took their concept of "cleanness" lightly. He risked defilement by touching those who had leprosy and by neglecting to wash in the Pharisees' prescribed manner, and he showed complete disregard for their sanctions against associating with certain classes of people. He came to offer salvation to sinners, to show that God loves them. Jesus didn't worry about the accusations. Instead he continued going to those who needed him, regardless of the effect these rejected people might have on his reputation. What keeps you away from people who need Christ?

15:3–6 It may seem foolish for the shepherd to leave 99 sheep to go search for just one. But the shepherd knew that the 99 would be safe in the sheepfold, whereas the lost sheep was in danger. Because each sheep was of high value, the shepherd knew that it was worthwhile to search diligently for the lost one. God's love for each individual is so great that he seeks each one out and rejoices when he or she is "found." Jesus associated with sinners because he wanted to bring the lost sheep—people considered beyond hope—the gospel of God's kingdom. Before you were a believer, God sought you; and his love is still seeking those who are yet lost.

15:4, 5 We may be able to understand a God who would forgive sinners who come to him for mercy. But a God who tenderly searches for sinners and then joyfully forgives them must possess an extraordinary love! This is the kind of love that prompted Jesus to come to earth to search for lost people and save them. This is the kind of extraordinary love that God has for you. If you feel far from God, don't despair. He is seaching for you.

15:8–10 Palestinian women received ten silver coins as a wedding gift. Besides their monetary value, these coins held sentimental value like that of a wedding ring, and to lose one would be extremely distressing. Just as a woman would rejoice at finding her lost coin or ring, so the angels would rejoice over a repentant sinner. Each individual is precious to God. He grieves over every loss and rejoices whenever one of his children is found and brought into the kingdom. Perhaps we would have more joy in our churches if we shared Jesus' love and concern for the lost.

15:12 The younger son's share of the estate would have been one-third, with the older son receiving two-thirds (Deuteronomy 21:17). In most cases he would have received this at his father's death, although fathers sometimes chose to divide up their inheritance early and retire from managing their estates. What is unusual here is that the younger one initiated the division of the estate. This showed arrogant disregard for his father's authority as head of the family.

15:15–16 According to Moses' law, pigs were unclean animals (Leviticus 11:2–8; Deuteronomy 14:8). This meant that pigs could not be eaten or used for sacrifices. To protect themselves from defilement, Jews would not even touch pigs. For a Jew to stoop to

16 "And he would have gladly filled his stomach with the pods that the swine were eating, and no one was giving *anything* to him.
17 "But when he came to his senses, he said, 'How many of my father's hired men have
more than enough bread, but I am dying here with hunger!
18 'I will get up and go to my father, and will say to him, "Father, I have sinned against
heaven, and in your sight;
19 I am no longer worthy to be called your son; make me as one of your hired men." '

15:20 Gen 45:14; 46:29; Acts 20:37

20 "So he got up and came to his father. But while he was still a long way off, his father
saw him and felt compassion *for him,* and ran and embraced him and kissed him.
21 "And the son said to him, 'Father, I have sinned against heaven and in your sight; I
am no longer worthy to be called your son.'

15:22 Zech 3:4; Rev 6:11; Gen 41:42

22 "But the father said to his slaves, 'Quickly bring out the best robe and put it on him,
and put a ring on his hand and sandals on his feet;
23 and bring the fattened calf, kill it, and let us eat and celebrate;

15:24 Matt 8:22; Luke 9:60; 15:32; Rom 11:15; Eph 2:1, 5; 5:14; Col 2:13; 1 Tim 5:6

24 for this son of mine was dead and has come to life again; he was lost and has been
found.' And they began to celebrate.
25 "Now his older son was in the field, and when he came and approached the house,
he heard music and dancing.
26 "And he summoned one of the servants and *began* inquiring what these things
could be.
27 "And he said to him, 'Your brother has come, and your father has killed the fattened
calf because he has received him back safe and sound.'
28 "But he became angry and was not willing to go in; and his father came out and *began* pleading with him.
29 "But he answered and said to his father, 'Look! For so many years I have been serving you and I have never neglected a command of yours; and *yet* you have never given
me a young goat, so that I might celebrate with my friends;

15:30 Prov 29:3; Luke 15:12

30 but when this son of yours came, who has devoured your wealth with prostitutes,
you killed the fattened calf for him.'
31 "And he said to him, 'Son, you have always been with me, and all that is mine is yours.

15:32 Luke 15:24

32 'But we had to celebrate and rejoice, for this brother of yours was dead and *has begun* to live, and *was* lost and has been found.' "

---

feeding swine was a great humiliation, and for this young man to eat food that the swine had touched was to be degraded beyond belief. The younger son had truly sunk to the depths.

15:17 The younger son, like many who are rebellious and immature, wanted to be free to live as he pleased, and he had to hit bottom before he came to his senses. It often takes great sorrow and tragedy to cause people to look to the only One who can help them. Are you trying to live life your own way, selfishly pushing aside any responsibility or commitment that gets in your way? Stop and look before you hit bottom. You will save yourself and your family much grief.

15:20 In the two preceding stories, the seeker actively looked for the coin and the sheep, which could not return by themselves. In this story, the father watched and waited. He was dealing with a human being with a will of his own, but he was ready to greet his son if he returned. In the same way, God's love is constant and patient and welcoming. He will search for us and give us opportunities to respond, but he will not force us to come to him. Like the father in this story, God waits patiently for us to come to our senses.

15:24 The sheep was lost because it may have foolishly wandered away (15:4); the coin was lost through no fault of its own (15:8); and the son left out of selfishness (15:12). God's great love reaches out and finds sinners no matter why or how they got lost.

15:25–31 It was hard for the older brother to accept his younger brother when he returned, and it is just as difficult to accept "younger brothers" today. People who repent after leading notoriously sinful lives are often held in suspicion; churches are sometimes unwilling to admit them to membership. Instead, we should rejoice like the angels in heaven when an unbeliever repents and turns to God. Like the father, accept repentant sinners wholeheartedly and give them the support and encouragement that they need to grow in Christ.

15:30 In the story of the lost son, the father's response is contrasted with the older brother's. The father forgave because he was filled with love. The son refused to forgive because he was bitter about the injustice of it all. His resentment rendered him just as lost to the father's love as his younger brother had been. Don't let anything keep you from forgiving others. If you are refusing to forgive people, you are missing a wonderful opportunity to experience joy and share it with others. Make your joy grow: Forgive somebody who has hurt you.

15:32 In Jesus' story, the older brother represented the Pharisees, who were angry and resentful that sinners were being welcomed into God's kingdom. After all, the Pharisees must have thought, we have sacrificed and done *so much* for God. How easy it is to resent God's gracious forgiveness of others whom we consider to be far worse sinners than ourselves. But when our self-righteousness gets in the way of rejoicing when others come to Jesus, we are no better than the Pharisees.

Jesus Tells the Parable of the Shrewd Manager
(162)

16 Now He was also saying to the disciples, "There was a rich man who had a manager, and this *manager* was reported to him as squandering his possessions.
2 "And he called him and said to him, 'What is this I hear about you? Give an accounting of your management, for you can no longer be manager.'
3 "The manager said to himself, 'What shall I do, since my master is taking the management away from me? I am not strong enough to dig; I am ashamed to beg.
4 'I know what I shall do, so that when I am removed from the management people
will welcome me into their homes.'
5 "And he summoned each one of his master's debtors, and he *began* saying to the first,
'How much do you owe my master?'
6 "And he said, 'A hundred measures of oil.' And he said to him, 'Take your bill, and
sit down quickly and write fifty.'
7 "Then he said to another, 'And how much do you owe?' And he *said, 'A hundred
measures of wheat.' He said to him, 'Take your bill, and write eighty.'
8 "And his master praised the unrighteous manager because he had acted shrewdly;
for the sons of this age are more shrewd in relation to their own kind than the sons of
light.
9 "And I say to you, make friends for yourselves by means of the [21]wealth of unrighteousness, so that when it fails, they will receive you into the eternal dwellings.
10 "He who is faithful in a very little thing is faithful also in much; and he who is unrighteous in a very little thing is unrighteous also in much.
11 "Therefore if you have not been faithful in the *use of* unrighteous wealth, who will
entrust the true *riches* to you?
12 "And if you have not been faithful in *the use of* that which is another's, who will give
you that which is your own?
13 "No servant can serve two masters; for either he will hate the one and love the other,
or else he will be devoted to one and despise the other. You cannot serve God and wealth."
14 Now the Pharisees, who were lovers of money, were listening to all these things and
were scoffing at Him.
15 And He said to them, "You are those who justify yourselves in the sight of men, but
God knows your hearts; for that which is highly esteemed among men is detestable in
the sight of God.
16 "The Law and the Prophets *were proclaimed* until John; since that time the gospel of
the kingdom of God has been preached, and everyone is forcing his way into it.

16:1 Luke 15:13
16:8 Matt 12:32; Luke 20:34; John 12:36; Eph 5:8; 1 Thess 5:5
16:9 Matt 19:21; Luke 11:41; 12:33; Matt 6:24; Luke 16:11, 13; Luke 16:4
16:10 Matt 25:21, 23
16:11 Luke 16:9
16:13 Matt 6:24; Luke 16:9
16:14 2 Tim 3:2; Luke 23:35
16:15 Luke 10:29; 18:9, 14; 1 Sam 16:7; Prov 21:2; Acts 1:24; Rom 8:27
16:16 Matt 11:12f; Matt 4:23

21 Gr *mammon* , fr Aram *mamona* , signifying riches, wealth, etc, personified as an object of worship

---

16:1–8 Our use of money is a good test of the lordship of Christ. (1) Let us use our resources wisely because they belong to God, and not to us. (2) Money can be used for good or evil; let us use ours for good. (3) Money has a lot of power, so we must use it carefully and thoughtfully. (4) We must use our material goods in a way that will foster faith and obedience (see 12:33–34).

16:9 We are to make wise use of the financial opportunities we have, not to earn heaven, but so that heaven ("eternal dwellings") will be a welcome experience for those we help. If we use our money to help those in need or to help others find Christ, our earthly investment will bring eternal benefit. When we obey God's will, the unselfish use of possessions will follow.

16:10–11 Our integrity often meets its match in money matters. God calls us to be honest even in small details we could easily rationalize away. Heaven's riches are far more valuable than earthly wealth. But if we are not trustworthy with our money here (no matter how much or little we have), we will be unfit to handle the vast riches of God's kingdom. Don't let your integrity slip in small matters, and it will not fail you in crucial decisions either.

16:13 Money has the power to take God's place in your life. It can become your master. How can you tell if you are a slave to money? (1) Do you think and worry about it frequently? (2) Do you give up doing what you should do or would like to do in order to make more money? (3) Do you spend a great deal of your time caring for your possessions? (4) Is it hard for you to give money away? (5) Are you in debt?

Money is a hard master and a deceptive one. Wealth promises power and control, but often it cannot deliver. Great fortunes can be made—and lost—overnight, and no amount of money can provide health, happiness, or eternal life. How much better it is to let God be your Master. His servants have peace of mind and security, both now and forever.

16:14 Because the Pharisees loved money, they took exception to Jesus' teaching. We live in an age that measures people's worth by how much money they make. Do we laugh at Jesus' warnings against serving money? Do we try to explain them away? Do we apply them to someone else—the Pharisees, for example? Unless we take Jesus' statements seriously, we may be acting like Pharisees ourselves.

16:15 The Pharisees acted piously to get praise from others, but God knew what was in their hearts. They considered their wealth to be a sign of God's approval. God detested their wealth because it caused them to abandon true spirituality. Though prosperity may earn people's praise, it must never substitute for devotion and service to God.

16:16–17 John the Baptist's ministry was the dividing line between the Old and New Testaments (John 1:15–18). With the arrival of Jesus came the realization of all the prophets' hopes. Jesus

16:17 Matt 5:18

17 "But it is easier for heaven and earth to pass away than for one stroke of a letter of
the Law to fail.

16:18 Matt 5:32; 1 Cor 7:10, 11

18 "Everyone who divorces his wife and marries another commits adultery, and he who
marries one who is divorced from a husband commits adultery.

Jesus Tells about the Rich Man and the Beggar
(163)

19 "Now there was a rich man, and he habitually dressed in purple and fine linen, joyously living in splendor every day.

16:20 Acts 3:2

20 "And a poor man named Lazarus was laid at his gate, covered with sores,
21 and longing to be fed with the *crumbs* which were falling from the rich man's table;
besides, even the dogs were coming and licking his sores.

16:22 John 1:18; 13:23

22 "Now the poor man died and was carried away by the angels to Abraham's bosom;
and the rich man also died and was buried.

16:23 Matt 11:23

23 "In Hades he lifted up his eyes, being in torment, and ☆saw Abraham far away and
Lazarus in his bosom.

16:24 Luke 3:8; 16:30; 19:9; Matt 25:41

24 "And he cried out and said, 'Father Abraham, have mercy on me, and send Lazarus
so that he may dip the tip of his finger in water and cool off my tongue, for I am in agony
in this flame.'

16:25 Luke 6:24

25 "But Abraham said, 'Child, remember that during your life you received your good
things, and likewise Lazarus bad things; but now he is being comforted here, and you
are in agony.
26 'And besides all this, between us and you there is a great chasm fixed, so that those
who wish to come over from here to you will not be able, and *that* none may cross over
from there to us.'
27 "And he said, 'Then I beg you, father, that you send him to my father's house—

16:28 Acts 2:40; 8:25; 10:42; 18:5; 20:21ff; 23:11; 28:23; Gal 5:3; Eph 4:17; 1 Thess 2:11; 4:6

28 for I have five brothers—in order that he may warn them, so that they will not also
come to this place of torment.'

16:29 Luke 4:17; John 5:45-47; Acts 15:21

29 "But Abraham ☆said, 'They have Moses and the Prophets; let them hear them.'

16:30 Luke 3:8; 16:24; 19:9

30 "But he said, 'No, father Abraham, but if someone goes to them from the dead, they
will repent!'
31 "But he said to him, 'If they do not listen to Moses and the Prophets, they will not be
persuaded even if someone rises from the dead.' "

Jesus Tells about Forgiveness and Faith
(164)

17:1 Matt 18:7; 1 Cor 11:19; 1 Tim 4:1

17 He said to His disciples, "It is inevitable that stumbling blocks come, but woe to
him through whom they come!

17:2 Matt 18:6; Mark 9:42; 1 Cor 8:12

2 "It would be better for him if a millstone were hung around his neck and he were
thrown into the sea, than that he would cause one of these little ones to stumble.

---

emphasized that his kingdom fulfilled the law (the Old Testament); it did not cancel it (Matthew 5:17). His was not a new system but the culmination of the old. The same God who worked through Moses was working through Jesus.

16:18 Most religious leaders of Jesus' day permitted a man to divorce his wife for nearly any reason. Jesus' teaching about divorce went beyond Moses' (Deuteronomy 24:1–4). Stricter than any of the then-current schools of thought, Jesus' teachings shocked his hearers (see Matthew 19:10) just as they shake today's readers. Jesus says in no uncertain terms that marriage is a lifetime commitment. To leave your spouse for another person may be legal, but it is adultery in God's eyes. As you think about marriage, remember that God intends it to be a permanent commitment.

16:19–31 The Pharisees considered wealth to be a proof of a person's righteousness. Jesus startled them with this story where a diseased beggar is rewarded and a rich man is punished. The rich man did not go to hell because of his wealth but because he was selfish, refusing to feed Lazarus, take him in, or care for him. The rich man was hardhearted in spite of his great blessings. The amount of money we have is not as important as the way we use it. What is your attitude toward your money and possessions? Do you hoard them selfishly, or do you use them to help others?

16:20 This Lazarus should not be confused with the Lazarus whom Jesus raised from the dead in John 11.

16:29–31 The rich man thought that his five brothers would surely believe a messenger who had been raised from the dead. But Jesus said that if they did not believe Moses and the prophets, who spoke constantly of the duty to care for the poor, not even a resurrection would convince them. Notice the irony in Jesus' statement; on his way to Jerusalem to die, he was fully aware that even when he had risen from the dead, most of the religious leaders would not accept him. They were set in their ways, and neither Scripture nor God's Son himself would shake them loose.

17:1–3 Jesus may have been directing this warning at the religious leaders who taught their converts their own hypocritical ways (see Matthew 23:15). They were perpetuating an evil system. A person who teaches others has a solemn responsibility (James 3:1). Like physicians, a teacher should keep this ancient oath in mind: "First, do no harm."

3 "Be on your guard! If your brother sins, rebuke him; and if he repents, forgive him.
4 "And if he sins against you seven times a day, and returns to you seven times, saying,
'I repent,' forgive him."
5 The apostles said to the Lord, "Increase our faith!"
6 And the Lord said, "If you had faith like a mustard seed, you would say to this
mulberry tree, 'Be uprooted and be planted in the sea'; and it would obey you.
7 "Which of you, having a slave plowing or tending sheep, will say to him when he has
come in from the field, 'Come immediately and sit down to eat'?
8 "But will he not say to him, 'Prepare something for me to eat, and *properly* clothe
yourself and serve me while I eat and drink; and afterward you may eat and drink'?
9 "He does not thank the slave because he did the things which were commanded,
does he?
10 "So you too, when you do all the things which are commanded you, say, 'We are
unworthy slaves; we have done *only* that which we ought to have done.' "

Jesus Heals Ten Men with Leprosy
(169)

11 While He was on the way to Jerusalem, He was passing between Samaria and
Galilee.
12 As He entered a village, ten leprous men who stood at a distance met Him;
13 and they raised their voices, saying, "Jesus, Master, have mercy on us!"
14 When He saw them, He said to them, "Go and show yourselves to the priests." And
as they were going, they were cleansed.
15 Now one of them, when he saw that he had been healed, turned back, glorifying
God with a loud voice,
16 and he fell on his face at His feet, giving thanks to Him. And he was a Samaritan.

17:3 Matt 18:15
17:4 Matt 18:21f
17:5 Mark 6:30; Luke 7:13
17:6 Luke 7:13; Matt 13:31; 17:20; Mark 4:31; Luke 13:19; Luke 19:4
17:8 Luke 12:37
17:11 Luke 9:51; Luke 9:52ff; John 4:3f
17:12 Lev 13:45f
17:13 Luke 5:5
17:14 Lev 14:1-32; Matt 8:4; Luke 5:14
17:15 Matt 9:8
17:16 Matt 10:5

17:3–4 To rebuke does not mean to point out every sin we see; it means to bring sin to a person's attention with the purpose of restoring him or her to God and to fellow humans. When you feel you must rebuke another Christian for a sin, check your attitudes before you speak. Do you love the person? Are you willing to forgive? Unless rebuke is tied to forgiveness, it will not help the sinning person.

17:5–6 The disciples' request was genuine; they wanted the faith necessary for such radical forgiveness. But Jesus didn't directly answer their question because the amount of faith is not as important as its genuineness. What is faith? It is total dependence on God and a willingness to do his will. Faith is not something we use to put on a show for others. It is complete and humble obedience to God's will, readiness to do whatever he calls us to do. The amount of faith isn't as important as the right kind of faith—faith in our all-powerful God.

17:6 A mustard seed is small, but it is alive and growing. Like a tiny seed, a small amount of genuine faith in God will take root and grow. Almost invisible at first, it will begin to spread, first under the ground and then visibly. Although each change will be gradual and imperceptible, soon this faith will have produced major results that will uproot and destroy competing loyalties. We don't need more faith; a tiny seed of faith is enough, if it is alive and growing.

17:7–10 If we have obeyed God, we have only done our duty and should regard it as a privilege. Do you sometimes feel that you deserve extra credit for serving God? Remember, obedience is not something extra we do; it is our duty. Jesus is not rendering our service as meaningless or useless, nor is he doing away with rewards. He is attacking unwarranted self-esteem and spiritual pride.

17:11–14 People who had leprosy were required to try to stay away from other people and to announce their presence if they had to come near. Sometimes leprosy went into remission. If a leper thought his leprosy had gone away, he was supposed to present himself to a priest who could declare him clean (Leviticus 14). Jesus sent the ten leprous men to the priest *before* they were healed—and they went! They responded in faith, and Jesus healed them on the way. Is your trust in God so strong that you act on what he says even before you see evidence that it will work?

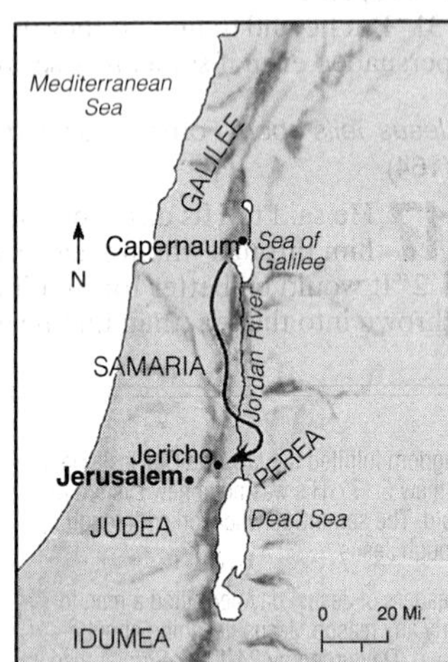

LAST TRIP FROM GALILEE
Jesus left Galilee for the last time—he would not return before his death. He passed through Samaria, met and healed 10 men who had leprosy, and continued to Jerusalem. He spent some time east of the Jordan (Mark 10:1) before going to Jericho (Luke 19:1).

17:16 Jesus healed all ten leprous men, but only one returned to thank him. It is possible to receive God's great gifts with an ungrateful spirit—nine of the ten men did so. Only the thankful man, however, learned that his faith had played a role in his healing; and only grateful Christians grow in understanding God's grace. God does not demand that we thank him, but he is pleased when we do so. And he uses our responsiveness to teach us more about himself.

17:16 Not only was this man a leper; he was also a Samaritan—a race despised by the Jews as idolatrous half-breeds (see the note on 10:33). Once again Luke is pointing out that God's grace is for everybody.

17:18 Matt 9:8
17:19 Matt 9:22; Luke 18:42
17:20 Luke 19:11; Acts 1:6; Luke 14:1
17:21 Luke 17:23
17:22 Matt 9:15; Mark 2:20; Luke 5:35
17:23 Matt 24:23; Mark 13:21; Luke 21:8
17:24 Matt 24:27
17:25 Matt 16:21; Luke 9:22
17:26 Matt 24:37-39; Gen 6:5-8; 7
17:28 Gen 19
17:30 Matt 16:27; 1 Cor 1:7; Col 3:4; 2 Thess 1:7; 1 Pet 1:7; 4:13; 1 John 2:28
17:31 Matt 24:17, 18; Mark 13:15f; Luke 21:21
17:32 Gen 19:26
17:33 Matt 10:39
17:35 Matt 24:41
17:36 Matt 24:40
17:37 Matt 24:28

17 Then Jesus answered and said, "Were there not ten cleansed? But the nine—where
are they?
18 "Was no one found who returned to give glory to God, except this foreigner?"
19 And He said to him, "Stand up and go; your faith [22]has made you well."

Jesus Teaches about the Coming of the Kingdom of God (170)

20 Now having been questioned by the Pharisees as to when the kingdom of God was
coming, He answered them and said, "The kingdom of God is not coming with signs to
be observed;
21 nor will they say, 'Look, here *it is!*' or, 'There *it is!*' For behold, the kingdom of God
is in your midst."
22 And He said to the disciples, "The days will come when you will long to see one of
the days of the Son of Man, and you will not see it.
23 "They will say to you, 'Look there! Look here!' Do not go away, and do not run after
them.
24 "For just like the lightning, when it flashes out of one part of the sky, shines to the
other part of the sky, so will the Son of Man be in His day.
25 "But first He must suffer many things and be rejected by this generation.
26 "And just as it happened in the days of Noah, so it will be also in the days of the Son
of Man:
27 they were eating, they were drinking, they were marrying, they were being given in
marriage, until the day that Noah entered the ark, and the flood came and destroyed
them all.
28 "It was the same as happened in the days of Lot: they were eating, they were drinking, they were buying, they were selling, they were planting, they were building;
29 but on the day that Lot went out from Sodom it rained fire and brimstone from
heaven and destroyed them all.
30 "It will be just the same on the day that the Son of Man is revealed.
31 "On that day, the one who is on the housetop and whose goods are in the house must
not go down to take them out; and likewise the one who is in the field must not turn
back.
32 "Remember Lot's wife.
33 "Whoever seeks to keep his life will lose it, and whoever loses *his life* will preserve it.
34 "I tell you, on that night there will be two in one bed; one will be taken and the other
will be left.
35 "There will be two women grinding at the same place; one will be taken and the other will be left.
36 ["[23]Two men will be in the field; one will be taken and the other will be left."]
37 And answering they ☆said to Him, "Where, Lord?" And He said to them, "Where
the body *is,* there also the vultures will be gathered."

22 Lit *has saved you* **23** Early mss do not contain this v

---

17:20–21 The Pharisees asked when God's kingdom would come, not knowing that it had already arrived. The kingdom of God is not like an earthly kingdom with geographical boundaries. Instead, it begins with the work of God's Spirit in people's lives and in relationships. Still today we must resist looking to institutions or programs for evidence of the progress of God's kingdom. Instead, we should look for what God is doing in people's hearts.

17:23–24 Many will claim to be the Messiah and many will claim that Jesus has returned—and people will believe them. Jesus warns us never to take such reports seriously, no matter how convincing they may sound. When Jesus returns, his power and presence will be evident to everyone. No one will need to spread the message because all will see for themselves.

17:23–36 Life will be going on as usual on the day Christ returns. There will be no warning. Most people will be going about their everyday tasks, indifferent to the demands of God. They will be as surprised by Christ's return as the people in Noah's day were by the flood (Genesis 6—8) or the people in Lot's day by the destruction of Sodom (Genesis 19). We don't know the time of Christ's return, but we do know that he is coming. He may come today, tomorrow, or centuries in the future. Whenever he comes, we must be morally and spiritually ready. Live as if Jesus were returning today.

17:26–35 Jesus warned against false security. We are to abandon the values and attachments of this world in order to be ready for Christ's return. His return will happen suddenly, and when he comes, there will be no second chances. Some will be taken to be with him; the rest will be left behind.

17:37 To answer the disciples' question, Jesus quoted a familiar proverb. One vulture circling overhead does not mean much, but a gathering of vultures means that a dead body is nearby. Likewise, one sign of the end may not be significant, but when many signs occur, the second coming is near.

Jesus Tells the Parable of the Persistent Widow
(171)

18 Now He was telling them a parable to show that at all times they ought to pray and
not to lose heart,
2 saying, "In a certain city there was a judge who did not fear God and did not respect man.
3 "There was a widow in that city, and she kept coming to him, saying, 'Give me legal
protection from my opponent.'
4 "For a while he was unwilling; but afterward he said to himself, 'Even though I do
not fear God nor respect man,
5 yet because this widow bothers me, I will give her legal protection, otherwise by
continually coming she will wear me out.' "
6 And the Lord said, "Hear what the unrighteous judge ☆said;
7 now, will not God bring about justice for His elect who cry to Him day and night,
and will He delay long over them?
8 "I tell you that He will bring about justice for them quickly. However, when the Son
of Man comes, will He find faith on the earth?"

Jesus Tells the Parable of Two Men Who Prayed
(172)

9 And He also told this parable to some people who trusted in themselves that they
were righteous, and viewed others with contempt:
10 "Two men went up into the temple to pray, one a Pharisee and the other a tax collector.
11 "The Pharisee stood and was praying this to himself: 'God, I thank You that I am not
like other people: swindlers, unjust, adulterers, or even like this tax collector.
12 'I fast twice a week; I pay tithes of all that I get.'
13 "But the tax collector, standing some distance away, was even unwilling to lift up his
eyes to heaven, but was beating his breast, saying, 'God, be merciful to me, the sinner!'
14 "I tell you, this man went to his house justified rather than the other; for everyone
who exalts himself will be humbled, but he who humbles himself will be exalted."

Jesus Blesses Little Children
(174/Matthew 19:13-15; Mark 10:13-16)

15 And they were bringing even their babies to Him so that He would touch them, but
when the disciples saw it, they *began* rebuking them.
16 But Jesus called for them, saying, "Permit the children to come to Me, and do not
hinder them, for the kingdom of God belongs to such as these.
17 "Truly I say to you, whoever does not receive the kingdom of God like a child will not
enter it *at all.*"

18:1 Luke 11:5-10; 2 Cor 4:1
18:2 Luke 18:4; 20:13; Heb 12:9
18:4 Luke 18:2; 20:13; Heb 12:9
18:5 Luke 11:8; 1 Cor 9:27
18:6 Luke 7:13
18:7 Rev 6:10; Matt 24:22; Rom 8:33; Col 3:12; 2 Tim 2:10; Titus 1:1; 2 Pet 3:9
18:8 Luke 17:26ff
18:9 Luke 16:15; Rom 14:3, 10
18:10 1 Kin 10:5; 2 Kin 20:5, 8; Acts 3:1
18:11 Matt 6:5; Mark 11:25; Luke 22:41
18:12 Matt 9:14; Luke 11:42
18:13 Matt 6:5; Mark 11:25; Luke 22:41; Ezra 9:6; Luke 23:48
18:14 Matt 23:12; Luke 14:11
18:17 Matt 18:3; 19:14; Mark 10:15; 1 Cor 14:20; 1 Pet 2:2

18:1 To persist in prayer and not give up does not mean endless repetition or painfully long prayer sessions. Always praying means keeping our requests constantly before God as we live for him day by day, believing he will answer. When we live by faith, we are not to give up. God may delay answering, but his delays always have good reasons. As we persist in prayer we grow in character, faith, and hope.

18:3 Widows and orphans were among the most vulnerable of all God's people, and both Old Testament prophets and New Testament apostles insisted that these needy people be properly cared for. See, for example, Exodus 22:22–24; Isaiah 1:17; 1 Timothy 5:3; James 1:27.

18:6–7 If unrighteous judges respond to constant pressure, how much more will a great and loving God respond to us. If we know he loves us, we can believe he will hear our cries for help.

18:10 The people who lived near Jerusalem often went to the temple to pray. The temple was the center of their worship.

18:11–14 The Pharisee did not go to the temple to pray to God but to announce to all within earshot how good he was. The tax collector went recognizing his sin and begging for mercy. Self-righteousness is dangerous. It leads to pride, causes a person to despise others, and prevents him or her from learning anything from God. The tax collector's prayer should be our prayer because we all need God's mercy every day. Don't let pride in your achievements cut you off from God.

18:15–17 It was customary for a mother to bring her children to a rabbi for a blessing, and that is why these mothers gathered around Jesus. The disciples, however, thought the children were unworthy of the Master's time—less important than whatever else he was doing. But Jesus welcomed them, because little children have the kind of faith and trust needed to enter God's kingdom. It is important that we introduce our children to Jesus and that we ourselves approach him with childlike attitudes of acceptance, faith, and trust.

Jesus Speaks to the Rich Young Man
(175/Matthew 19:16-30; Mark 10:17-31)

18:18 Luke 10:25-28

18 A ruler questioned Him, saying, "Good Teacher, what shall I do to inherit eternal
life?"

18:20 Ex 20:12-16; Deut 5:16-20

19 And Jesus said to him, "Why do you call Me good? No one is good except God alone.
20 "You know the commandments, 'DO NOT COMMIT ADULTERY, DO NOT MURDER,
DO NOT STEAL, DO NOT BEAR FALSE WITNESS, HONOR YOUR FATHER AND MOTHER.' "
21 And he said, "All these things I have kept from *my* youth."

18:22 Matt 19:21; Luke 12:33; Matt 6:20

22 When Jesus heard *this,* He said to him, "One thing you still lack; sell all that you
possess and distribute it to the poor, and you shall have treasure in heaven; and come,
follow Me."
23 But when he had heard these things, he became very sad, for he was extremely rich.

18:24 Matt 19:23; Mark 10:23f

18:25 Matt 19:24; Mark 10:25

24 And Jesus looked at him and said, "How hard it is for those who are wealthy to enter
the kingdom of God!
25 "For it is easier for a camel to go through the eye of a needle than for a rich man to
enter the kingdom of God."
26 They who heard it said, "Then who can be saved?"

18:27 Matt 19:26

27 But He said, "The things that are impossible with people are possible with God."

18:28 Luke 5:11

28 Peter said, "Behold, we have left our own *homes* and followed You."

18:29 Matt 6:33; 19:29; Mark 10:29f

29 And He said to them, "Truly I say to you, there is no one who has left house or wife
or brothers or parents or children, for the sake of the kingdom of God,

18:30 Matt 12:32

30 who will not receive many times as much at this time and in the age to come, eternal
life."

Jesus Predicts His Death the Third Time
(177/Matthew 20:17-19; Mark 10:32-34)

18:31 Luke 9:51; Ps 22; Is 53

31 Then He took the twelve aside and said to them, "Behold, we are going up to Jerusalem, and all things which are written through the prophets about the Son of Man will
be accomplished.

18:32 Matt 16:21

32 "For He will be handed over to the Gentiles, and will be mocked and mistreated and
spit upon,
33 and after they have scourged Him, they will kill Him; and the third day He will rise
again."

18:34 Mark 9:32; Luke 9:45

34 But the disciples understood none of these things, and *the meaning of* this statement
was hidden from them, and they did not comprehend the things that were said.

18:18ff This ruler sought reassurance, some way of knowing for sure that he had eternal life. He wanted Jesus to measure and grade his qualifications, or to give him some task he could do to assure his own immortality. So Jesus gave him a task—the one thing the rich ruler knew he could not do. "Then who can be saved?" the bystanders asked. "No one can, by his or her own achievements," Jesus' answer implied. "The things that are impossible with people are possible with God." Salvation cannot be earned—it is God's gift (see Ephesians 2:8–10).

18:18–19 Jesus' question to the ruler who came and called him "Good Teacher" was, in essence, "Do you know who I am?" Undoubtedly the man did not catch the implications of Jesus' reply—that the man was right in calling him good because Jesus truly is God.

18:22–23 This man's wealth made his life comfortable and gave him power and prestige. When Jesus told him to sell everything he owned, Jesus was touching the very basis of his security and identity. The man did not understand that he would be even more secure if he followed Jesus than he was with all his wealth. Jesus does not ask all believers to sell everything they have, although this may be his will for some. He does ask us all, however, to get rid of anything that has become more important than God. If your basis for security has shifted from God to what you own, it would be better for you to get rid of those possessions.

18:24–27 Because money represents power, authority, and success, often it is difficult for wealthy people to realize their need and their powerlessness to save themselves. The rich in talent or intelligence suffer the same difficulty. Unless God reaches down into their lives, they will not come to him. Jesus surprised some of his hearers by offering salvation to the poor; he may surprise some people today by offering it to the rich. It is difficult for a self-sufficient person to realize his or her need and come to Jesus, but "The things that are impossible with people are possible with God."

18:26–30 Peter and the other disciples had paid a high price—leaving their homes and jobs—to follow Jesus. But Jesus reminded Peter that following him has its benefits as well as its sacrifices. Any believer who has had to give up something to follow Christ will be paid back in this life as well as in the next. For example, if you must give up a secure job, you will find that God offers a secure relationship with himself now and forever. If you must give up your family's approval, you will gain the love of the family of God. The disciples had begun to pay the price of following Jesus, and Jesus said they would be rewarded. Don't dwell on what you have given up; think about what you have gained and give thanks for it. You can never outgive God.

18:31–34 Some predictions about what would happen to Jesus are found in Psalm 41:9 (betrayal); Psalm 22:16–18 and Isaiah 53:4–7 (crucifixion); Psalm 16:10 (resurrection). The disciples didn't understand Jesus, apparently because they focused on what he said about his death and ignored what he said about his resurrection. Even though Jesus spoke plainly, they would not grasp the significance of his words until they saw the risen Christ face-to-face.

Jesus Heals a Blind Beggar
(179/Matthew 20:29-34; Mark 10:46-52)

35 As Jesus was approaching Jericho, a blind man was sitting by the road begging.
36 Now hearing a crowd going by, he *began* to inquire what this was.
37 They told him that Jesus of Nazareth was passing by.
38 And he called out, saying, "Jesus, Son of David, have mercy on me!"
39 Those who led the way were sternly telling him to be quiet; but he kept crying out
all the more, "Son of David, have mercy on me!"
40 And Jesus stopped and commanded that he be brought to Him; and when he came
near, He questioned him,
41 "What do you want Me to do for you?" And he said, "Lord, *I want* to regain my sight!"
42 And Jesus said to him, "Receive your sight; your faith has made you well."
43 Immediately he regained his sight and *began* following Him, glorifying God; and
when all the people saw it, they gave praise to God.

18:35 Matt 20:29; Mark 10:46; Luke 19:1
18:38 Matt 9:27; Luke 18:39
18:39 Luke 18:38
18:42 Matt 9:22
18:43 Matt 9:8; Luke 9:43; 13:17; 19:37

Jesus Brings Salvation to Zaccheus's Home
(180)

19 He entered Jericho and was passing through.
2 And there was a man called by the name of Zaccheus; he was a chief tax collector and he was rich.
3 Zaccheus was trying to see who Jesus was, and was unable because of the crowd, for
he was small in stature.
4 So he ran on ahead and climbed up into a sycamore tree in order to see Him, for He
was about to pass through that way.
5 When Jesus came to the place, He looked up and said to him, "Zaccheus, hurry and
come down, for today I must stay at your house."
6 And he hurried and came down and received Him gladly.
7 When they saw it, they all *began* to grumble, saying, "He has gone to be the guest of
a man who is a sinner."
8 Zaccheus stopped and said to the Lord, "Behold, Lord, half of my possessions I will
give to the poor, and if I have defrauded anyone of anything, I will give back four times
as much."
9 And Jesus said to him, "Today salvation has come to this house, because he, too, is
a son of Abraham.
10 "For the Son of Man has come to seek and to save that which was lost."

19:1 Luke 18:35
19:4 1 Kin 10:27; 1 Chr 27:28; 2 Chr 1:15; 9:27; Ps 78:47; Is 9:10; Luke 17:6
19:8 Luke 7:13; Luke 3:14; Ex 22:1; Lev 6:5; Num 5:7; 2 Sam 12:6
19:9 Luke 3:8; 13:16; Rom 4:16; Gal 3:7
19:10 Matt 18:11

18:35 Beggars often waited along the roads near cities, because that was where they were able to contact the most people. Usually disabled in some way, beggars were unable to earn a living. Medical help was not available for their problems, and people tended to ignore their obligation to care for the needy (Leviticus 25:35–38). Thus beggars had little hope of escaping their degrading way of life. But this blind beggar took hope in the Messiah. He shamelessly cried out for Jesus' attention, and Jesus said that his faith allowed him to see. No matter how desperate your situation may seem, if you call out to Jesus in faith, he will help you.

18:38 The blind man called Jesus "Son of David," a title for the Messiah (Isaiah 11:1–3). This means that he understood Jesus to be the long-awaited Messiah. A poor and blind beggar could *see* that Jesus was the Messiah, while the religious leaders who saw his miracles were blinded to his identity and refused to recognize him as the Messiah.

19:1–10 To finance their great world empire, the Romans levied heavy taxes on all nations under their control. The Jews opposed these taxes because they supported a secular government and its pagan gods, but they were still forced to pay. Tax collectors were among the most unpopular people in Israel. Jews by birth, they chose to work for Rome and were considered traitors. Besides, it was common knowledge that tax collectors were making themselves rich by gouging their fellow Jews. No wonder the people muttered when Jesus went home with the tax collector Zaccheus. But despite the fact that Zaccheus was both a cheater and a turncoat, Jesus loved him; and in response, the little tax collector was converted. In every society, certain groups of people are considered "untouchable" because of their political views, their immoral behavior, or their life-style. We should not give in to social pressure to avoid these people. Jesus loves them, and they need to hear his Good News.

19:8 Judging from the crowd's reaction to him, Zaccheus must have been a very crooked tax collector. But after he met Jesus, he realized that his life needed straightening out. By giving to the poor and making restitution—with generous interest—to those he had cheated, Zaccheus demonstrated inward change by outward action. It is not enough to follow Jesus in your head or heart alone. You must show your faith by changed behavior. Has your faith resulted in action? What changes do you need to make?

19:9–10 When Jesus said Zaccheus was a son of Abraham and yet was lost, he must have shocked his hearers in at least two ways. They would not have liked to acknowledge that this unpopular tax collector was a fellow son of Abraham, and they would not have wished to admit that sons of Abraham could be lost. But a person is not saved by a good heritage or condemned by a bad one; faith is more important than genealogy. Jesus still loves to bring the lost into his kingdom, no matter what their background or previous way of life. Through faith, the lost can be forgiven and made new.

Jesus Tells the Parable of the King's Ten Servants (181)

19:11 Luke 9:51; Luke 17:20

19:12 Matt 25:14-30

19:17 Luke 16:10

11 While they were listening to these things, Jesus went on to tell a parable, because
He was near Jerusalem, and they supposed that the kingdom of God was going to appear immediately.
12 So He said, "A nobleman went to a distant country to receive a kingdom for himself, and *then* return.
13 "And he called ten of his slaves, and gave them ten [24]minas and said to them, 'Do
business *with this* until I come *back.*'
14 "But his citizens hated him and sent a delegation after him, saying, 'We do not want
this man to reign over us.'
15 "When he returned, after receiving the kingdom, he ordered that these slaves, to
whom he had given the money, be called to him so that he might know what business
they had done.
16 "The first appeared, saying, 'Master, your mina has made ten minas more.'
17 "And he said to him, 'Well done, good slave, because you have been faithful in a very
little thing, you are to be in authority over ten cities.'
18 "The second came, saying, 'Your mina, master, has made five minas.'
19 "And he said to him also, 'And you are to be over five cities.'
20 "Another came, saying, 'Master, here is your mina, which I kept put away in a hand-
kerchief;
21 for I was afraid of you, because you are an exacting man; you take up what you did
not lay down and reap what you did not sow.'
22 "He ☆said to him, 'By your own words I will judge you, you worthless slave. Did you
know that I am an exacting man, taking up what I did not lay down and reaping what I
did not sow?
23 'Then why did you not put my money in the bank, and having come, I would have
collected it with interest?'
24 "Then he said to the bystanders, 'Take the mina away from him and give it to the one
who has the ten minas.'

24 A mina is equal to about 100 days' wages

GOSPEL ACCOUNTS FOUND ONLY IN LUKE

Luke 1:5–80	Special events leading up to birth of John the Baptist and Jesus
Luke 2:1–52	Events from Jesus' childhood
Luke 3:19–20	Herod puts John in prison
Luke 4:16–30	Jesus is rejected at Nazareth
Luke 5:1–11	Jesus provides a miraculous catch of fish
Luke 7:11–17	Jesus raises a widow's son from the dead
Luke 7:36–50	A sinful woman anoints Jesus' feet
Luke 8:1–3	Women travel with Jesus
Luke 10:1—18:14	Events, miracles, and teachings during the months prior to Christ's death
Luke 19:1–27	Jesus meets Zaccheus and later tells the parable of the king's ten slaves
Luke 23:6–12	Jesus' trial before Herod
Luke 24:44–49	Some of Jesus' last words before his ascension

19:11ff The people still hoped for a political leader who would set up an earthly kingdom and get rid of Roman domination. Jesus' parable showed that his kingdom would not take this form right away. First he would go away for a while, and his followers would need to be faithful and productive during his absence. Upon his return, Jesus would inaugurate a kingdom more powerful and just than anything they could expect.

19:11ff This story showed Jesus' followers what they were to do during the time between Jesus' departure and his second coming. Because we live in that time period, it applies directly to us. We have been given excellent resources to build and expand God's kingdom. Jesus expects us to use these talents so that they multiply and the kingdom grows. He asks each of us to account for what we do with his gifts. While awaiting the coming of the kingdom of God in glory, we must do Christ's work.

19:20–27 Why was the king so hard on this man who had not increased the money? He punished the man because (1) he didn't share his master's interest in the kingdom; (2) he didn't trust his master's intentions; (3) his only concern was for himself, and (4) he did nothing to use the money. Like the king in this story, God has given you gifts to use for the benefit of his kingdom. Do you want the kingdom to grow? Do you trust God to govern it fairly? Are you as concerned for others' welfare as you are for your own? Are you willing to use faithfully what he has entrusted to you?

25 "And they said to him, 'Master, he has ten minas *already.*'
26 "I tell you that to everyone who has, more shall be given, but from the one who does
not have, even what he does have shall be taken away.
27 "But these enemies of mine, who did not want me to reign over them, bring them
here and slay them in my presence."

19:26 Matt 13:12; Mark 4:25; Luke 8:18
19:27 Luke 19:14; Matt 22:7; Luke 20:16

3. Jesus' ministry in Jerusalem

Jesus Rides into Jerusalem on a Donkey
(183/Matthew 21:1-11; Mark 11:1-11; John 12:12-19)

28 After He had said these things, He was going on ahead, going up to Jerusalem.
29 When He approached Bethphage and Bethany, near the mount that is called Olivet,
He sent two of the disciples,
30 saying, "Go into the village ahead of *you;* there, as you enter, you will find a colt
tied on which no one yet has ever sat; untie it and bring it *here.*
31 "If anyone asks you, 'Why are you untying it?' you shall say, 'The Lord has need
of it.' "
32 So those who were sent went away and found it just as He had told them.
33 As they were untying the colt, its owners said to them, "Why are you untying the
colt?"
34 They said, "The Lord has need of it."
35 They brought it to Jesus, and they threw their coats on the colt and put Jesus *on it.*
36 As He was going, they were spreading their coats on the road.
37 As soon as He was approaching, near the descent of the Mount of Olives, the whole
crowd of the disciples began to praise God joyfully with a loud voice for all the miracles
which they had seen,
38 shouting:
"BLESSED IS THE KING WHO COMES IN THE NAME OF THE LORD;
Peace in heaven and glory in the highest!"
39 Some of the Pharisees in the crowd said to Him, "Teacher, rebuke Your disciples."
40 But Jesus answered, "I tell you, if these become silent, the stones will cry out!"
41 When He approached *Jerusalem,* He saw the city and wept over it,
42 saying, "If you had known in this day, even you, the things which make for peace!
But now they have been hidden from your eyes.

19:28 Mark 10:32; Luke 9:51
19:29 Matt 21:17; Luke 21:37; Acts 1:12
19:35 Matt 21:4-9; Mark 11:7-10; John 12:12-15
19:37 Matt 21:1; Luke 19:29; Luke 18:43
19:38 Ps 118:26; Matt 2:2; 25:34; Matt 21:9; Luke 2:14
19:39 Matt 21:15f
19:40 Hab 2:11
19:41 Luke 13:34, 35

19:30–35 By this time Jesus was extremely well known. Everyone coming to Jerusalem for the Passover feast had heard of him, and, for a time, the popular mood was favorable toward him. "The Lord has need of it" was all the disciples had to say, and the colt's owners gladly turned their animal over to them.

19:35–38 Christians celebrate this event on Palm Sunday. The people lined the road, praising God, waving palm branches, and spreading their coats in front of the colt as it passed before them. "Long live the King" was the meaning behind their joyful shouts, because they knew that Jesus was intentionally fulfilling the prophecy in Zechariah 9:9: "Behold, your king is coming to you; He is just and endowed with salvation, humble, and mounted on a donkey, even on a colt, the foal of a donkey." To announce that he was indeed the Messiah, Jesus chose a *time* when all Israel would be gathered at Jerusalem, a *place* where huge crowds could see him, and a *way* of proclaiming his mission that was unmistakable. The people went wild. They were sure their liberation was at hand.

19:38 The people who were praising God for giving them a king had the wrong idea about Jesus. They expected him to be a national leader who would restore their nation to its former glory, and thus they were deaf to the words of their prophets and blind to Jesus' real mission. When it became apparent that Jesus was not going to fulfill their hopes, many people would turn against him.

19:39–40 The Pharisees thought the crowd's words were sacrilegious and blasphemous. They didn't want someone challenging their power and authority, and they didn't want a revolt that would bring the Roman army down on them. So they asked Jesus to keep his people quiet. But Jesus said that if the people were quiet, the stones would immediately cry out. Why? Not because Jesus was setting up a powerful political kingdom, but because he was establishing God's eternal kingdom, a reason for the greatest celebration of all.

19:41–44 The Jewish leaders had rejected their King (19:47). They had gone too far. They had refused God's offer of salvation in

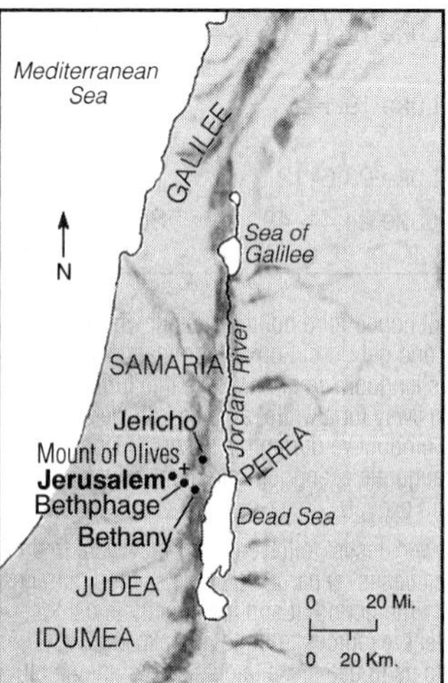

LAST WEEK IN JERUSALEM
As they approached Jerusalem from Jericho (19:1), Jesus and the disciples came to the villages of Bethany and Bethphage, nestled on the eastern slope of the Mount of Olives, only a few miles outside Jerusalem. Jesus stayed in Bethany during the nights of that last week, entering Jerusalem during the day.

19:43 Eccl 9:14; Is 29:3; 37:33; Jer 6:6; Ezek 4:2; 26:8; Luke 21:20

19:44 Matt 24:2; Mark 13:2; Luke 21:6; 1 Pet 2:12

43 "For the days will come upon you when your enemies will throw up a barricade against
you, and surround you and hem you in on every side,
44 and they will level you to the ground and your children within you, and they will not
leave in you one stone upon another, because you did not recognize the time of your
visitation."

Jesus Clears the Temple Again
(184/Matthew 21:12-17; Mark 11:12-19)

19:45 John 2:13-16

19:46 Is 56:7; Jer 7:11; Matt 21:13; Mark 11:17; Jer 7:11

19:47 Matt 26:55; Luke 21:37; Luke 20:19

45 Jesus entered the temple and began to drive out those who were selling,
46 saying to them, "It is written, 'AND MY HOUSE SHALL BE A HOUSE OF PRAYER,' but
you have made it a ROBBERS' DEN."
47 And He was teaching daily in the temple; but the chief priests and the scribes and
the leading men among the people were trying to destroy Him,
48 and they could not find anything that they might do, for all the people were hanging
on to every word He said.

Religious Leaders Challenge Jesus' Authority
(189/Matthew 21:23-27; Mark 11:27-33)

20:1 Matt 26:55; Luke 8:1; Acts 4:1; 6:12

20:6 Matt 11:9; Luke 7:29, 30

20 On one of the days while He was teaching the people in the temple and preaching
the gospel, the chief priests and the scribes with the elders confronted *Him,*
2 and they spoke, saying to Him, "Tell us by what authority You are doing these things,
or who is the one who gave You this authority?"
3 Jesus answered and said to them, "I will also ask you a question, and you tell Me:
4 "Was the baptism of John from heaven or from men?"
5 They reasoned among themselves, saying, "If we say, 'From heaven,' He will say,
'Why did you not believe him?'
6 "But if we say, 'From men,' all the people will stone us to death, for they are convinced that John was a prophet."
7 So they answered that they did not know where *it came* from.
8 And Jesus said to them, "Nor will I tell you by what authority I do these things."

Jesus Tells the Parable of the Wicked Vine-growers
(191/Matthew 21:33-46; Mark 12:1-12)

9 And He began to tell the people this parable: "A man planted a vineyard and rented
it out to vine-growers, and went on a journey for a long time.
10 "At the *harvest* time he sent a slave to the vine-growers, so that they would give him
some of the produce of the vineyard; but the vine-growers beat him and sent him away
empty-handed.
11 "And he proceeded to send another slave; and they beat him also and treated him
shamefully and sent him away empty-handed.
12 "And he proceeded to send a third; and this one also they wounded and cast out.

Jesus Christ when they were visited by God himself ("the time of your visitation"), and soon their nation would suffer. God did not turn away from the Jewish people who obeyed him, however. He continues to offer salvation to the people he loves, both Jews and Gentiles. Eternal life is within your reach—accept it while the opportunity is still offered.

19:43–44 About 40 years after Jesus said these words, they came true. In A.D. 66, the Jews revolted against Roman control. Three years later Titus, son of the Emperor Vespasian, was sent to crush the rebellion. Roman soldiers attacked Jerusalem and broke through the northern wall but still couldn't take the city. Finally they laid siege to it, and in A.D. 70 they were able to enter the severely weakened city and burn it. Six hundred thousand Jews were killed during Titus's onslaught.

19:47 Who were the "leading men among the people"? This group probably included wealthy leaders in politics, commerce, and law. They had several reasons for wanting to get rid of Jesus. He had damaged business in the temple by driving the merchants out. In addition, he was preaching against injustice, and his teachings often favored the poor over the rich. Further, his great popularity was in danger of attracting Rome's attention, and the leaders of Israel wanted as little as possible to do with Rome.

20:1–8 This group of leaders wanted to get rid of Jesus, so they tried to trap him with their question. If Jesus would answer that his authority came from God—if he stated openly that he was the Messiah and the Son of God—they would accuse him of blasphemy and bring him to trial. Jesus did not let himself be caught. Instead, he turned the question on them. Thus he exposed their motives and avoided their trap.

20:9–16 The characters in this story are easily identified. Even the religious leaders understood it. The owner of the vineyard is God; the vineyard is Israel; the vine-growers are the religious leaders; the slaves are the prophets and priests God sent to Israel; the son is the Messiah, Jesus; and the others are the Gentiles. Jesus' parable indirectly answered the religious leaders' question about his authority; it also showed them that he knew about their plan to kill him.

13 "The owner of the vineyard said, 'What shall I do? I will send my beloved son; perhaps they will respect him.'
14 "But when the vine-growers saw him, they reasoned with one another, saying, 'This is the heir; let us kill him so that the inheritance will be ours.'
15 "So they threw him out of the vineyard and killed him. What, then, will the owner of the vineyard do to them?
16 "He will come and destroy these vine-growers and will give the vineyard to others." When they heard it, they said, "May it never be!"
17 But Jesus looked at them and said, "What then is this that is written:
'THE STONE WHICH THE BUILDERS REJECTED,
THIS BECAME THE CHIEF CORNER *stone*'?
18 "Everyone who falls on that stone will be broken to pieces; but on whomever it falls, it will scatter him like dust."
19 The scribes and the chief priests tried to lay hands on Him that very hour, and they feared the people; for they understood that He spoke this parable against them.

20:13 Luke 18:2

20:16 Matt 21:41; Mark 12:9; Luke 19:27; Rom 3:4, 6, 31; 6:2, 15; 7:7, 13; 9:14; 11:1, 11; 1 Cor 6:15; Gal 2:17; 3:21; 6:14

20:17 Ps 118:22; Eph 2:20; 1 Pet 2:6

20:18 Matt 21:44

20:19 Luke 19:47

Religious Leaders Question Jesus about Paying Taxes
(193/Matthew 22:15-22; Mark 12:13-17)

20 So they watched Him, and sent spies who pretended to be righteous, in order that they might catch Him in some statement, so that they *could* deliver Him to the rule and the authority of the governor.
21 They questioned Him, saying, "Teacher, we know that You speak and teach correctly, and You are not partial to any, but teach the way of God in truth.
22 "Is it lawful for us to pay taxes to Caesar, or not?"
23 But He detected their trickery and said to them,
24 "Show Me a [25]denarius. Whose likeness and inscription does it have?" They said, "Caesar's."
25 And He said to them, "Then render to Caesar the things that are Caesar's, and to God the things that are God's."
26 And they were unable to catch Him in a saying in the presence of the people; and being amazed at His answer, they became silent.

20:20 Mark 3:2; Luke 11:54; 20:26; Matt 27:2

20:22 Matt 17:25; Luke 23:2

20:25 Matt 22:21; Mark 12:17

20:26 Luke 11:54

Religious Leaders Question Jesus about the Resurrection
(194/Matthew 22:23-33; Mark 12:18-27)

27 Now there came to Him some of the Sadducees (who say that there is no resurrection),
28 and they questioned Him, saying, "Teacher, Moses wrote for us that IF A MAN'S BROTHER DIES, having a wife, AND HE IS CHILDLESS, HIS BROTHER SHOULD MARRY THE WIFE AND RAISE UP CHILDREN TO HIS BROTHER.
29 "Now there were seven brothers; and the first took a wife and died childless;
30 and the second

20:27 Acts 23:8

20:28 Deut 25:5

25 The denarius was a day's wages

20:17–19 Quoting Psalm 118:22, Jesus showed the unbelieving leaders that even their rejection of the Messiah had been prophesied in Scripture. Ignoring the corner stone was dangerous. A person could be tripped or crushed (judged and punished). Jesus' comments were veiled, but the religious leaders had no trouble interpreting them. They immediately wanted to arrest him.

20:20–26 Jesus turned his enemies' attempt to trap him into a powerful lesson: As God's followers, we have legitimate obligations to both God and the government. But it is important to keep our priorities straight. When the two authorities conflict, our duty to God always must come before our duty to the government.

20:21 These spies, pretending to be honest men, flattered Jesus before asking him their trick question, hoping to catch him off guard. But Jesus knew what they were trying to do and stayed out of their trap. Beware of flattery. With God's help, you can detect it and avoid the trap that often follows.

20:22 This was a loaded question. The Jews were enraged at having to pay taxes to Rome, thus supporting the pagan government and its gods. They hated the system that allowed tax collectors to charge exorbitant rates and keep the extra for themselves. If Jesus said they should pay taxes, they would call him a traitor to their nation and their religion. But if he said they should not, they could report him to Rome as a rebel. Jesus' questioners thought they had him this time, but he outwitted them again.

20:24 The denarius was the usual pay for one day's work.

20:27–38 The Sadducees, a group of conservative religious leaders, honored only the Pentateuch—Genesis through Deuteronomy—as Scripture. They also did not believe in a resurrection of the dead because they could find no mention of it in those books. The Sadducees decided to try their hand at tricking Jesus, so they brought him a question that had always stumped the Pharisees. After addressing their question about marriage, Jesus answered their *real* question about resurrection. Basing his answer on the writings of Moses—an authority they respected—he upheld belief in resurrection.

31 and the third married her; and in the same way all seven died, leaving no children.
32 "Finally the woman died also.
33 "In the resurrection therefore, which one's wife will she be? For all seven had married her."
34 **34** Jesus said to them, "The sons of this age marry and are given in marriage,
35 but those who are considered worthy to attain to that age and the resurrection from the dead, neither marry nor are given in marriage;
36 for they cannot even die anymore, because they are like angels, and are sons of God, being sons of the resurrection.
37 "But that the dead are raised, even Moses showed, in the *passage about the burning* bush, where he calls the Lord THE GOD OF ABRAHAM, AND THE GOD OF ISAAC, AND THE GOD OF JACOB.
38 "Now He is not the God of the dead but of the living; for all live to Him."
39 Some of the scribes answered and said, "Teacher, You have spoken well."
40 For they did not have courage to question Him any longer about anything.

20:34 Matt 12:32; Luke 16:8
20:35 Matt 12:32; Luke 16:8
20:36 Rom 8:16f; 1 John 3:1, 2
20:37 Mark 12:26; Ex 3:6
20:38 Matt 22:32; Mark 12:27; Rom 14:8
20:40 Matt 22:46; Luke 14:6

Religious Leaders Cannot Answer Jesus' Question
(196/Matthew 22:41-46; Mark 12:35-37)

41 Then He said to them, "How *is it that* they say [26]the Christ is David's son?
42 "For David himself says in the book of Psalms,
'THE LORD SAID TO MY LORD,
"SIT AT MY RIGHT HAND,
43 UNTIL I MAKE YOUR ENEMIES A FOOTSTOOL FOR YOUR FEET." '
44 "Therefore David calls Him 'Lord,' and how is He his son?"

20:41 Matt 22:41-46; Mark 12:35-37; Matt 9:27
20:42 Ps 110:1
20:43 Ps 110:1

Jesus Warns against the Religious Leaders
(197/Matthew 23:1-12; Mark 12:38-40)

45 And while all the people were listening, He said to the disciples,
46 "Beware of the scribes, who like to walk around in long robes, and love respectful greetings in the market places, and chief seats in the synagogues and places of honor at banquets,
47 who devour widows' houses, and for appearance's sake offer long prayers. These will receive greater condemnation."

20:46 Luke 11:43; 14:7

26 I.e. the Messiah

20:34–35 Jesus' statement does not mean that people will not recognize their partners in heaven. It simply means that we must not think of heaven as an extension of life as we now know it. Our relationships in this life are limited by time, death, and sin. We don't know everything about our resurrection life, but Jesus affirms that relationships will be different from what we are used to here and now.

20:37–38 The Sadducees came to Jesus with a trick question. Not believing in the resurrection, they wanted Jesus to say something they could refute. Even so, Jesus did not ignore or belittle their question. He answered it, and then he went beyond it to the real issue. When people ask you tough religious questions—"How can a loving God allow people to starve?" "If God knows what I'm going to do, do I have any free choice?"—follow Jesus' example. First answer the question to the best of your ability; then look for the real issue—hurt over a personal tragedy, for example, or difficulty in making a decision. Often the spoken question is only a test, not of your ability to answer hard questions, but of your willingness to listen and care.

20:41–44 The Pharisees and Sadducees had asked their questions. Then Jesus turned the tables and asked them a question that went right to the heart of the matter—what they thought about the Messiah's identity. The Pharisees knew that the Messiah would be a descendant of David, but they did not understand that he would be more than a human descendant—he was God in the flesh. Jesus quoted from Psalm 110:1 to show that David knew that the Messiah would be both human and divine. The Pharisees expected only a human ruler to restore Israel's greatness as in the days of David and Solomon.

The central issue of life is what we believe about Jesus. Other spiritual questions are irrelevant unless we first decide to believe that Jesus is who he said he is. The Pharisees and Sadducees could not do this. They remained confused over Jesus' identity.

20:45–47 The scribes loved the benefits associated with their position, and they sometimes cheated the poor in order to get even more benefits. Every job has its rewards, but gaining rewards should never become more important than doing the job faithfully. God will punish people who use their position of responsibility to cheat others. Whatever resources you have been given, use them to help others and not just yourself.

20:47 How strange to think that the scribes would receive the worst punishment. But behind their appearance of holiness and respectability, they were arrogant, crafty, selfish, and uncaring. Jesus exposed their evil hearts. He showed that despite their pious words, they were neglecting God's laws and doing as they pleased. Religious deeds do not cancel sin. Jesus said that God's most severe judgment awaited these scribes because they should have been living examples of mercy and justice.

A Poor Widow Gives All She Has
(200/Mark 12:41-44)

21 And He looked up and saw the rich putting their gifts into the treasury.
2 And He saw a poor widow putting in two small copper coins. **21:2**
3 And He said, "Truly I say to you, this poor widow put in more than all *of them;* Mark 12:42
4 for they all out of their surplus put into the offering; but she out of her poverty put **21:4**
in all that she had to live on." Mark 12:44

Jesus Tells about the Future
(201/Matthew 24:1-25; Mark 13:1-23)

5 And while some were talking about the temple, that it was adorned with beautiful
stones and votive gifts, He said,
6 "*As for* these things which you are looking at, the days will come in which there will **21:6**
not be left one stone upon another which will not be torn down." Luke 19:44
7 They questioned Him, saying, "Teacher, when therefore will these things happen? **21:8**
And what *will be* the sign when these things are about to take place?" John 8:24; Luke 17:23
8 And He said, "See to it that you are not misled; for many will come in My name,
saying, 'I am *He,*' and, 'The time is near.' Do not go after them.
9 "When you hear of wars and disturbances, do not be terrified; for these things must
take place first, but the end *does* not *follow* immediately."
10 Then He continued by saying to them, "Nation will rise against nation and kingdom
against kingdom,
11 and there will be great earthquakes, and in various places plagues and famines; and
there will be terrors and great signs from heaven.
12 "But before all these things, they will lay their hands on you and will persecute you, **21:12**
delivering you to the synagogues and prisons, bringing you before kings and governors Matt 10:19-22; Mark 13:11-13
for My name's sake.
13 "It will lead to an opportunity for your testimony. **21:13**
14 "So make up your minds not to prepare beforehand to defend yourselves; Phil 1:12
15 for I will give you utterance and wisdom which none of your opponents will be able **21:14**
to resist or refute. Luke 12:11
16 "But you will be betrayed even by parents and brothers and relatives and friends, and **21:15**
they will put *some* of you to death, Luke 12:12
17 and you will be hated by all because of My name. **21:18**
18 "Yet not a hair of your head will perish. Matt 10:30; Luke 12:7

21:1–2 Jesus was in the area of the temple called the court of women. The treasury was located there or in an adjoining walkway. In this area were seven boxes in which worshipers could deposit their temple tax and six boxes for freewill offerings like the one this woman gave. Not only was she poor; as a widow she had few resources for making money. Her small gift was a sacrifice, but she gave it willingly.

21:1–4 This widow gave all she had to live on, in contrast to the way most of us handle our money. When we consider giving a certain percentage of our income a great accomplishment, we resemble those who gave "out of their surplus." Here, Jesus was admiring generous and sacrificial giving. As believers, we should consider increasing our giving—whether of money, time, or talents—to a point beyond convenience or safety.

21:5–6 The temple the disciples were admiring was not Solomon's temple—that had been destroyed by the Babylonians in the seventh century B.C. This temple had been built by Ezra after the return from exile in the sixth century B.C., desecrated by the Seleucids in the second century B.C., reconsecrated by the Maccabees soon afterward, and enormously expanded by Herod the Great over a 46-year period. It was a beautiful, imposing structure with a significant history, but Jesus said that it would be completely destroyed. This happened in A.D. 70 when the Roman army burned Jerusalem.

21:7ff Jesus did not leave his disciples unprepared for the difficult years ahead. He warned them about false messiahs, natural disasters, and persecutions; but he assured them that he would be with them to protect them and make his kingdom known through them. In the end, Jesus promised that he would return in power and glory to save them. Jesus' warnings and promises to his disciples also apply to us as we look forward to his return.

21:12–13 These persecutions soon began. Luke recorded many of them in the book of Acts. Paul wrote from prison that he suffered gladly because it helped him know Christ better and do Christ's work for the church (Philippians 3:10; Colossians 1:24). The early church thrived despite intense persecution. In fact, late in the second century the church father Tertullian wrote, "The blood of Christians is seed," because opposition helped spread Christianity.

21:14–19 Jesus warned that in the coming persecutions his followers would be betrayed by their family members and friends. Christians of every age have had to face this possibility. It is reassuring to know that even when we feel completely abandoned, the Holy Spirit will stay with us. He will comfort us, protect us, and give us the words we need. This assurance can give us the courage and hope to stand firm for Christ no matter how difficult the situation.

21:18 Jesus was *not* saying that believers would be exempt from physical harm or death during the persecutions. Remember that most of the disciples were martyred. Rather he was saying that none of his followers would suffer spiritual or eternal loss. On earth, everyone will die, but believers in Jesus will be saved for eternal life.

21:19 Matt 10:22; 24:13; Rom 2:7; 5:3f; Heb 10:36; James 1:3; 2 Pet 1:6
21:20 Luke 19:43
21:21 Luke 17:31
21:22 Is 63:4; Dan 9:24-27; Hos 9:7
21:23 Dan 8:19; 1 Cor 7:26
21:24 Gen 34:26; Ex 17:13; Heb 11:34; Is 63:18; Dan 8:13; Rev 11:2; Rom 11:25

19 "By your endurance you will gain your lives.
20 "But when you see Jerusalem surrounded by armies, then recognize that her desolation is near.
21 "Then those who are in Judea must flee to the mountains, and those who are in the
midst of the city must leave, and those who are in the country must not enter the city;
22 because these are days of vengeance, so that all things which are written will be fulfilled.
23 "Woe to those who are pregnant and to those who are nursing babies in those days;
for there will be great distress upon the land and wrath to this people;
24 and they will fall by the edge of the sword, and will be led captive into all the nations; and Jerusalem will be trampled under foot by the Gentiles until the times of the
Gentiles are fulfilled.

Jesus Tells about His Return
(202/Matthew 24:26-35; Mark 13:24-31)

21:27 Matt 16:27; 24:30; 26:64; Mark 13:26; Dan 7:13; Rev 1:7
21:28 Luke 18:7
21:30 Luke 12:57
21:31 Matt 3:2

25 "There will be signs in sun and moon and stars, and on the earth dismay among nations, in perplexity at the roaring of the sea and the waves,
26 men fainting from fear and the expectation of the things which are coming upon
the world; for the powers of the heavens will be shaken.
27 "Then they will see THE SON OF MAN COMING IN A CLOUD with power and great
glory.
28 "But when these things begin to take place, straighten up and lift up your heads,
because your redemption is drawing near."
29 Then He told them a parable: "Behold the fig tree and all the trees;
30 as soon as they put forth *leaves*, you see it and know for yourselves that summer is
now near.
31 "So you also, when you see these things happening, recognize that the kingdom of
God is near.

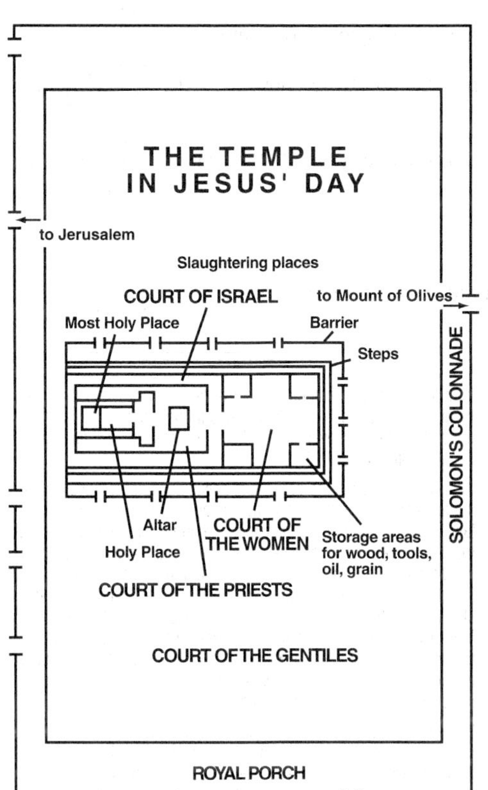

21:24 The "times of the Gentiles" began with Babylon's destruction of Jerusalem in 586 B.C. and the exile of the Jewish people. Israel was no longer an independent nation but was under the control of Gentile rulers. In Jesus' day, Israel was governed by the Roman empire, and a Roman general would destroy the city in A.D. 70. Jesus was saying that the domination of God's people by his enemies would continue until God decided to end it. The "times of the Gentiles" refers not just to the repeated destructions of Jerusalem, but also to the continuing and mounting persecution of God's people until the end.

21:28 The picture of the coming persecutions and natural disasters is gloomy, but ultimately it is a cause not for worry but for great joy. When believers see these events happening, they will know that the return of their Messiah is near, and they can look forward to his reign of justice and peace. Rather than being terrified by what is happening in our world, we should confidently await Christ's return to bring justice and restoration to his people.

32 "Truly I say to you, this generation will not pass away until all things take place.
33 "Heaven and earth will pass away, but My words will not pass away.

Jesus Tells about Remaining Watchful
(203/Matthew 24:36-51; Mark 13:32-37)

34 "Be on guard, so that your hearts will not be weighted down with dissipation and
drunkenness and the worries of life, and that day will not come on you suddenly like a
trap;
35 for it will come upon all those who dwell on the face of all the earth.
36 "But keep on the alert at all times, praying that you may have strength to escape all
these things that are about to take place, and to stand before the Son of Man."
37 Now during the day He was teaching in the temple, but at evening He would go out
and spend the night on the mount that is called Olivet.
38 And all the people would get up early in the morning *to come* to Him in the temple
to listen to Him.

21:33 Matt 5:18; Luke 16:17
21:34 Matt 24:42-44; Mark 4:19; Luke 12:40, 45; 1 Thess 5:2ff
21:36 Mark 13:33; Luke 12:40; Luke 1:19; Rev 7:9; 8:2; 11:4
21:37 Matt 26:55; Luke 19:47; Mark 11:19; Matt 21:1
21:38 John 8:2

C. DEATH AND RESURRECTION OF JESUS, THE SAVIOR (22:1—24:35)

The perfect man was a high ideal in Greek culture. Written with Greeks in mind, Luke's Gospel shows how Jesus was the perfect man given as the perfect sacrifice for the sin of all mankind. Christ is the ideal human—the perfect model for us to follow. We must stand in awe of his character, which met humanity's highest ideals as well as God's demand for an atonement for sin. He is, at one and the same time, our model and our Savior.

Religious Leaders Plot to Kill Jesus
(207/Matthew 26:1-5; Mark 14:1-2)

Judas Agrees to Betray Jesus
(208/Matthew 26:14-16; Mark 14:10-11)

22 Now the Feast of Unleavened Bread, which is called the Passover, was approaching.
2 The chief priests and the scribes were seeking how they might put Him to death; for
they were afraid of the people.
3 And Satan entered into Judas who was called Iscariot, belonging to the number of
the twelve.
4 And he went away and discussed with the chief priests and officers how he might
betray Him to them.
5 They were glad and agreed to give him money.
6 So he consented, and *began* seeking a good opportunity to betray Him to them apart
from the crowd.

Disciples Prepare for the Passover
(209/Matthew 26:17-19; Mark 14:12-16)

7 Then came the *first* day of Unleavened Bread on which the Passover *lamb* had to be
sacrificed.

22:1 Matt 26:2-5; Mark 14:1, 2; Ex 12:1-27; John 11:55; 13:1
22:2 Matt 12:14
22:3 Matt 26:14-16; Mark 14:10, 11; Matt 4:10; John 13:2, 27
22:4 1 Chr 9:11; Neh 11:11; Luke 22:52; Acts 4:1; 5:24, 26
22:7 Mark 14:12

21:34–36 Jesus told the disciples to keep a constant watch for his return. Although nearly 2,000 years have passed since he spoke these words, their truth remains: Christ is coming again, and we need to watch and be spiritually fit. This means working faithfully at the tasks God has given us. Don't let your mind and spirit be dulled by careless living, drinking, or the foolish pursuit of pleasure. Don't let life's anxieties overburden you, so that you will be ready to move at God's command.

21:36 Only days after telling the disciples to pray that they might escape persecution, Jesus himself asked God to spare him the agonies of the cross, if that was God's will (22:41–42). It is abnormal to *want* to suffer, but as Jesus' followers we are willing to suffer if by doing so we can help build God's kingdom. We have two wonderful promises to help us as we suffer: God will always be with us (Matthew 28:20), and he will one day rescue us and give us eternal life (Revelation 21:1–4).

22:1 All Jewish males over the age of 12 were required to go to Jerusalem for the Passover festival, followed by a seven-day festival called the Feast of Unleavened Bread. For these feasts, Jews from all over the Roman empire converged on Jerusalem to celebrate one of the most important events in their history. To learn more about the Passover and the Feast of Unleavened Bread, see the first note on Mark 14:1.

22:3 Satan's part in the betrayal of Jesus does not remove any of the responsibility from Judas. Disillusioned because Jesus was talking about dying rather than about setting up his kingdom, Judas may have been trying to force Jesus' hand and make him use his power to prove he was the Messiah. Or perhaps Judas, not understanding Jesus' mission, no longer believed that Jesus was God's chosen one. (For more information on Judas, see his Profile in Mark 14.) Whatever Judas thought, Satan assumed that Jesus' death would end Jesus' mission and thwart God's plan. Like Judas, he did not know that Jesus' death and resurrection were the most important parts of God's plan all along.

22:7–8 The Passover meal included the sacrifice of a lamb because of the association with the Jews' exodus from Egypt. When the Jews were getting ready to leave, God told them to kill a lamb and paint its blood on the doorposts of their houses. They then

8 And Jesus sent Peter and John, saying, "Go and prepare the Passover for us, so that
we may eat it."
9 They said to Him, "Where do You want us to prepare it?"
10 And He said to them, "When you have entered the city, a man will meet you carrying a pitcher of water; follow him into the house that he enters.
11 "And you shall say to the owner of the house, 'The Teacher says to you, "Where is
the guest room in which I may eat the Passover with My disciples?" '
12 "And he will show you a large, furnished upper room; prepare it there."
13 And they left and found *everything* just as He had told them; and they prepared the
Passover.

Jesus and the Disciples Have the Last Supper
(211/Matthew 26:20-30; Mark 14:17-26; John 13:21-30)

14 When the hour had come, He reclined *at the table,* and the apostles with Him.
15 And He said to them, "I have earnestly desired to eat this Passover with you before
I suffer;
16 for I say to you, I shall never again eat it until it is fulfilled in the kingdom of God."
17 And when He had taken a cup *and* given thanks, He said, "Take this and share it
among yourselves;
18 for I say to you, I will not drink of the fruit of the vine from now on until the kingdom of God comes."
19 And when He had taken *some* bread *and* given thanks, He broke it and gave it to
them, saying, "This is My body which is given for you; do this in remembrance of Me."
20 And in the same way *He took* the cup after they had eaten, saying, "This cup which
is poured out for you is the new covenant in My blood.
21 "But behold, the hand of the one betraying Me is with Mine on the table.
22 "For indeed, the Son of Man is going as it has been determined; but woe to that man
by whom He is betrayed!"
23 And they began to discuss among themselves which one of them it might be who
was going to do this thing.

22:8 Acts 3:1, 11; 4:13, 19; 8:14; Gal 2:9

22:14 Matt 26:20; Mark 14:17; Mark 6:30

22:16 Luke 14:15; 22:18, 30; Rev 19:9

22:17 1 Cor 11:23-25; 1 Cor 10:16; Matt 14:19

22:18 Matt 26:29; Mark 14:25

22:19 Matt 14:19

22:20 Matt 26:28; Mark 14:24; Ex 24:8; Jer 31:31; 1 Cor 11:25; 2 Cor 3:6; Heb 8:8, 13; 9:15

22:21 Matt 26:21-24; Mark 14:18-21; Ps 41:9; John 13:18, 21, 22, 26

22:22 Acts 2:23; 4:28; 10:42; 17:31

---

were to prepare the meat for food. Peter and John had to buy and prepare the lamb as well as the unleavened bread, herbs, wine, and other ceremonial food.

22:10 Ordinarily women, not men, went to the well and brought home the water. So this man would have stood out in the crowd.

22:14–18 The Passover commemorated Israel's escape from Egypt when the blood of a lamb painted on their doorposts saved their firstborn sons from death. This event foreshadowed Jesus' work on the cross. As the spotless Lamb of God, his blood would be spilled in order to save his people from the penalty of death brought by sin.

22:17, 20 Luke mentions two cups of wine, while Matthew and Mark mention only one. In the traditional Passover meal, the wine is served four times. Christ spoke the words about his body and his blood when he offered the fourth and last cup.

22:17–20 Christians differ in their interpretation of the meaning of the commemoration of the Lord's Supper. There are three main views: (1) The bread and wine actually become Christ's body and blood; (2) the bread and wine remain unchanged, yet Christ is spiritually present by faith in and through them; (3) the bread and wine, which remain unchanged, are lasting memorials of Christ's sacrifice. No matter which view they favor, all Christians agree that the Lord's Supper commemorates Christ's death on the cross for our sins and points to the coming of his kingdom in glory. When we partake of it, we show our deep gratitude for Christ's work on our behalf, and our faith is strengthened.

22:19 Jesus asked the disciples to eat the broken bread "in remembrance of Me." He wanted them to remember his sacrifice, the basis for forgiveness of sins, and also his friendship that they could continue to enjoy through the work of the Holy Spirit. Although the exact meaning of Communion has been strongly debated throughout church history, Christians still take bread and wine in remembrance of their Lord and Savior, Jesus Christ. Do not neglect participating in the Lord's Supper. Let it remind you of what Christ did for you.

22:20 In Old Testament times, God agreed to forgive people's sins if they brought animals for the priests to sacrifice. When this sacrificial system was inaugurated, the agreement between God and man was sealed with the blood of animals (Exodus 24:8). But animal blood did not in itself remove sin (only God can forgive sin), and animal sacrifices had to be repeated day by day and year after year. Jesus instituted a "new covenant" or agreement between humans and God. Under this new covenant, Jesus would die in the place of sinners. Unlike the blood of animals, his blood (because he is God) would truly remove the sins of all who put their faith in him. And Jesus' sacrifice would never have to be repeated; it would be good for all eternity (Hebrews 9:23–28). The prophets looked forward to this new covenant that would fulfill the old sacrificial agreement (Jeremiah 31:31–34), and John the Baptist called Jesus "the Lamb of God who takes away the sin of the world" (John 1:29).

22:21 From the accounts of Mark and John we know that the betrayer was Judas Iscariot. Although the other disciples were confused by Jesus' words, Judas knew what he meant.

24 And there arose also a dispute among them *as to* which one of them was regarded
to be greatest.
25 And He said to them, "The kings of the Gentiles lord it over them; and those who
have authority over them are called 'Benefactors.'
26 "But *it is* not this way with you, but the one who is the greatest among you must become like the youngest, and the leader like the servant.
27 "For who is greater, the one who reclines *at the table* or the one who serves? Is it not
the one who reclines *at the table?* But I am among you as the one who serves.
28 "You are those who have stood by Me in My trials;
29 and just as My Father has granted Me a kingdom, I grant you
30 that you may eat and drink at My table in My kingdom, and you will sit on thrones
judging the twelve tribes of Israel.

Jesus Predicts Peter's Denial
(212/John 13:31-38)

31 "Simon, Simon, behold, Satan has demanded *permission* to sift you like wheat;
32 but I have prayed for you, that your faith may not fail; and you, when once you have
turned again, strengthen your brothers."
33 But he said to Him, "Lord, with You I am ready to go both to prison and to death!"
34 And He said, "I say to you, Peter, the rooster will not crow today until you have
denied three times that you know Me."
35 And He said to them, "When I sent you out without money belt and bag and sandals, you did not lack anything, did you?" They said, "*No,* nothing."
36 And He said to them, "But now, whoever has a money belt is to take it along, likewise also a bag, and whoever has no sword is to sell his coat and buy one.
37 "For I tell you that this which is written must be fulfilled in Me, 'AND HE WAS NUM-
BERED WITH TRANSGRESSORS'; for that which refers to Me has *its* fulfillment."
38 They said, "Lord, look, here are two swords." And He said to them, "It is enough."

Jesus Agonizes in the Garden
(223/Matthew 26:36-46; Mark 14:32-42)

39 And He came out and proceeded as was His custom to the Mount of Olives; and
the disciples also followed Him.
40 When He arrived at the place, He said to them, "Pray that you may not enter into
temptation."
41 And He withdrew from them about a stone's throw, and He knelt down and *began*
to pray,

22:24 Mark 9:34; Luke 9:46
22:25 Matt 20:25-28; Mark 10:42-45
22:26 Matt 23:11; Mark 9:35; Luke 9:48; 1 Pet 5:5
22:27 Luke 12:37; Matt 20:28; John 13:12-15
22:28 Heb 2:18; 4:15
22:29 Matt 5:3; 2 Tim 2:12
22:30 Luke 22:16; Matt 5:3; 2 Tim 2:12; Matt 19:28
22:31 Job 1:6-12; 2:1-6; Matt 4:10; Amos 9:9
22:32 John 17:9, 15; John 21:15-17
22:33 Matt 26:33-35; Mark 14:29-31
22:35 Matt 10:9f; Mark 6:8; Luke 9:3ff; 10:4
22:37 Is 53:12; John 17:4; 19:30
22:39 John 18:1; Luke 21:37; Matt 21:1
22:40 Matt 6:13; Luke 22:46
22:41 Luke 18:11

22:24 The most important event in human history was about to take place, and the disciples were still arguing about their prestige in the kingdom! Looking back, we say, "This was no time to worry about status." But the disciples, wrapped up in their own concerns, did not perceive what Jesus had been trying to tell them about his approaching death and resurrection. What are your major concerns today? Twenty years from now, as you look back, will these worries look petty and inappropriate? Get your eyes off yourself and get ready for Christ's coming into human history for the second time.

22:24–27 The world's system of leadership is very different from leadership in God's kingdom. Worldly leaders are often selfish and arrogant as they claw their way to the top. (Some kings in the ancient world gave themselves the title "Benefactor.") But among Christians, the leader is to be the one who *serves* best. There are different styles of leadership—some lead through public speaking, some through administering, some through relationships—but every Christian leader needs a servant's heart. Ask the people you lead how you can serve them better.

22:31–32 Satan wanted to crush Simon Peter and the other disciples like grains of wheat. He hoped to find only chaff and blow it away. But Jesus assured Peter that his faith, although it would falter, would not be destroyed. It would be renewed, and Peter would become a powerful leader.

22:33–34 Jesus predicted that Judas would betray him, and he said that calamity awaited the traitor (22:22). Jesus then predicted that Peter would deny that he knew Jesus, but later Peter would repent and receive a commission to feed Jesus' lambs (John 21:15). Betraying and denying—one is just about as bad as the other. But the two men had entirely different fates because one repented.

22:35–38 Here Jesus reversed his earlier advice regarding how to travel (9:3). The disciples were to bring bags, money, and swords. They would be facing hatred and persecution and would need to be prepared. When Jesus said "It is enough," he may have meant it was not time to think of using swords. In either case, mention of a sword vividly communicated the trials they were soon to face.

22:39 The Mount of Olives was located just to the east of Jerusalem. Jesus went up the southwestern slope to an olive grove called Gethsemane, which means "oil press."

22:40 Jesus asked the disciples to pray that they would not fall into temptation because he knew that he would soon be leaving them. Jesus also knew that they would need extra strength to face the temptations ahead—temptations to run away or to deny their relationship with him. They were about to see Jesus die. Would they still think he was the Messiah? The disciples' strongest temptation would undoubtedly be to think they had been deceived.

22:41–42 Was Jesus trying to get out of his mission? It is never wrong to express our true feelings to God. Jesus exposed his dread

22:42 Matt 20:22; Matt 26:39
22:43 Matt 4:11
22:44 Heb 5:7
22:46 Luke 22:40

42 saying, "Father, if You are willing, remove this cup from Me; yet not My will, but
Yours be done."
43 Now an angel from heaven appeared to Him, strengthening Him.
44 And being in agony He was praying very fervently; and His sweat became like drops
of blood, falling down upon the ground.
45 When He rose from prayer, He came to the disciples and found them sleeping from
sorrow,
46 and said to them, "Why are you sleeping? Get up and pray that you may not enter
into temptation."

Jesus Is Betrayed and Arrested
(224/Matthew 26:47-56; Mark 14:43-52; John 18:1-11)

22:49 Luke 22:38
22:52 Luke 22:4; Luke 22:37

47 While He was still speaking, behold, a crowd *came,* and the one called Judas, one of
the twelve, was preceding them; and he approached Jesus to kiss Him.
48 But Jesus said to him, "Judas, are you betraying the Son of Man with a kiss?"
49 When those who were around Him saw what was going to happen, they said, "Lord,
shall we strike with the sword?"
50 And one of them struck the slave of the high priest and cut off his right ear.
51 But Jesus answered and said, "Stop! No more of this." And He touched his ear and
healed him.
52 Then Jesus said to the chief priests and officers of the temple and elders who had
come against Him, "Have you come out with swords and clubs as you would against a
robber?

JESUS' TRIAL
Jesus' trial was actually a series of hearings, carefully controlled to accomplish the death of Jesus. The verdict was predecided, but certain "legal" procedures were necessary. A lot of effort went into condemning and crucifying an innocent man. Jesus went through an unfair trial in our place so that we would not have to face a fair trial and receive the well-deserved punishment for our sins.

Event	*Probable reasons*	*References*
Trial before Annas (powerful ex-high priest)	Although no longer the high priest, he may have still wielded much power	John 18:13–23
Trial before Caiaphas (the ruling high priest)	To gather evidence for the full Council hearing to follow	Matthew 26:57–68 Mark 14:53–65 Luke 22:54, 63–65 John 18:24
Trial before the Council (Sanhedrin)	Formal religious trial and condemnation to death	Matthew 27:1 Mark 15:1 Luke 22:66–71
Trial before Pilate (highest Roman authority)	All death sentences needed Roman approval	Matthew 27:2, 11–14 Mark 15:1–5 Luke 23:1–6 John 18:28–38
Trial before Herod (ruler of Galilee)	A courteous and guilt-sharing act by Pilate because Jesus was from Galilee, Herod's district	Luke 23:7–12
Trial before Pilate	Pilate's last effort to avoid condemning an obviously innocent man	Matthew 27:15–26 Mark 15:6–15 Luke 23:13–25 John 18:39—19:16

of the coming trials, but he also reaffirmed his commitment to do what God wanted. The cup he spoke of meant the terrible agony he knew he would endure—not only the horror of the crucifixion but, even worse, the total separation from God that he would have to experience in order to die for the world's sins.

22:44 Only Luke tells us that Jesus' sweat resembled drops of blood. Jesus was in extreme agony, but he did not give up or give in. He went ahead with the mission for which he had come.

22:46 These disciples were asleep. How tragic it is that many Christians act as if they are sound asleep when it comes to devotion to Christ and service for him. Don't be found insensitive to or unprepared for Christ's work.

22:47 A kiss was and still is the traditional greeting among men in certain parts of the world. In this case, it was also the agreed-upon signal to point out Jesus (Matthew 26:48). It is ironic that a gesture of greeting would be the means of betrayal. It was a hollow gesture because of Judas's treachery. Have any of your religious practices become empty gestures? We still betray Christ when our acts of service or giving are insincere or carried out merely for show.

22:50 We learn from the Gospel of John that the man who cut off the slave's ear was Peter (John 18:10).

53 "While I was with you daily in the temple, you did not lay hands on Me; but this hour
and the power of darkness are yours."

Peter Denies Knowing Jesus
(227/Matthew 26:69-75; Mark 14:66-72; John 18:25-27)

54 Having arrested Him, they led Him *away* and brought Him to the house of the high
priest; but Peter was following at a distance.
55 After they had kindled a fire in the middle of the courtyard and had sat down together, Peter was sitting among them.
56 And a servant-girl, seeing him as he sat in the firelight and looking intently at him,
said, "This man was with Him too."
57 But he denied *it,* saying, "Woman, I do not know Him."
58 A little later, another saw him and said, "You are *one* of them too!" But Peter said,
"Man, I am not!"
59 After about an hour had passed, another man *began* to insist, saying, "Certainly this
man also was with Him, for he is a Galilean too."
60 But Peter said, "Man, I do not know what you are talking about." Immediately, while
he was still speaking, a rooster crowed.
61 The Lord turned and looked at Peter. And Peter remembered the word of the
Lord, how He had told him, "Before a rooster crows today, you will deny Me three
times."
62 And he went out and wept bitterly.
63 Now the men who were holding Jesus in custody were mocking Him and beating Him,
64 and they blindfolded Him and were asking Him, saying, "Prophesy, who is the one
who hit You?"
65 And they were saying many other things against Him, blaspheming.

22:54 Matt 26:57; Mark 14:53; Matt 26:58; Mark 14:54; John 18:15

22:55 Matt 26:3

22:58 John 18:26

22:59 Matt 26:73; Mark 14:70

22:61 Luke 7:13; Luke 22:34

22:63 Matt 26:67f; Mark 14:65; John 18:22f

22:64 Matt 26:68; Mark 14:65

22:65 Matt 27:39

22:53 The religious leaders had not arrested Jesus in the temple for fear of a riot. Instead, they came secretly at night, under the influence of the prince of darkness, Satan himself. Although it looked as if Satan was getting the upper hand, everything was proceeding according to God's plan. It was time for Jesus to die.

22:54 Jesus was immediately taken to the high priest's house, even though this was the middle of the night. The Jewish leaders were in a hurry—they wanted to complete the execution before the Sabbath and get on with the Passover celebration. This residence was a palace with outer walls enclosing a courtyard where servants and soldiers warmed themselves around a fire.

22:55 Peter's experiences in the next few hours would change his life. He would change from a halfhearted follower to a repentant disciple, and finally to the kind of person Christ could use to build his church. For more information on Peter, see his Profile in Matthew 26.

22:62 Peter wept bitterly, not only because he realized that he had denied his Lord, the Messiah, but also because he had turned away from a very dear friend, a person who had loved and taught him for three years. Peter had said that he would *never* deny Christ, despite Jesus' prediction (Mark 14:29–31; Luke 22:33–34). But when frightened, he went against all he had boldly promised. Unable to stand up for his Lord for even 12 hours, he had failed as a disciple and as a friend. We need to be aware of our own breaking points and not become overconfident or self-sufficient. If we fail him, we must remember that Christ can use those who recognize their failure. From this humiliating experience Peter learned much that would help him later when he assumed leadership of the young church.

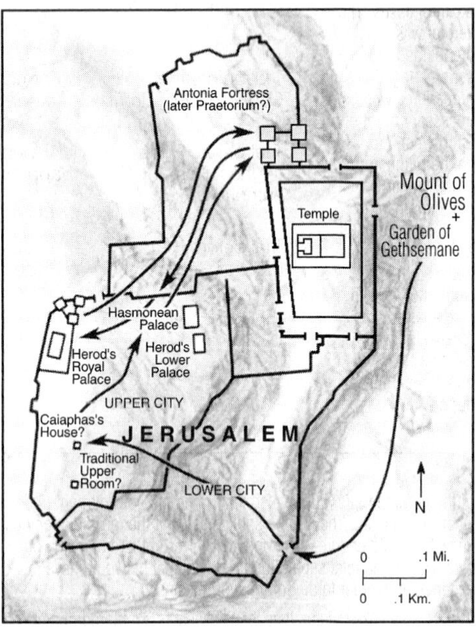

JESUS' TRIAL Taken from Gethsemane, Jesus first appeared before the Jewish Council, which had convened at daybreak at Caiaphas's house. From there he went to Pilate, the Roman governor; then to Herod, tetrarch of Galilee, who was visiting in Jerusalem; and back to Pilate, who, in desperation, sentenced Jesus to die.

The Council of Religious Leaders Condemns Jesus
(228/Matthew 27:1-2; Mark 15:1)

66 When it was day, the [27]Council of elders of the people assembled, both chief priests
and scribes, and they led Him away to their council *chamber*, saying,
67 "If You are the Christ, tell us." But He said to them, "If I tell you, you will not believe;
68 and if I ask a question, you will not answer.
69 "But from now on THE SON OF MAN WILL BE SEATED AT THE RIGHT HAND of the power OF GOD."
70 And they all said, "Are You the Son of God, then?" And He said to them, "Yes, I am."
71 Then they said, "What further need do we have of testimony? For we have heard it
ourselves from His own mouth."

Jesus Stands Trial before Pilate
(230/Matthew 27:11-14; Mark 15:2-5; John 18:28-37)

23 Then the whole body of them got up and brought Him before Pilate.
2 And they began to accuse Him, saying, "We found this man misleading our
nation and forbidding to pay taxes to Caesar, and saying that He Himself is Christ, a King."
3 So Pilate asked Him, saying, "Are You the King of the Jews?" And He answered
him and said, "*It is as* you say."
4 Then Pilate said to the chief priests and the crowds, "I find no guilt in this man."
5 But they kept on insisting, saying, "He stirs up the people, teaching all over Judea,
starting from Galilee even as far as this place."

Jesus Stands Trial before Herod
(231)

6 When Pilate heard it, he asked whether the man was a Galilean.
7 And when he learned that He belonged to Herod's jurisdiction, he sent Him to
Herod, who himself also was in Jerusalem at that time.
8 Now Herod was very glad when he saw Jesus; for he had wanted to see Him for a
long time, because he had been hearing about Him and was hoping to see some sign
performed by Him.
9 And he questioned Him at some length; but He answered him nothing.
10 And the chief priests and the scribes were standing there, accusing Him vehemently.
11 And Herod with his soldiers, after treating Him with contempt and mocking Him,
dressed Him in a gorgeous robe and sent Him back to Pilate.

27 Or *Sanhedrin*

22:66 Matt 27:1f; Mark 15:1; John 18:28; Acts 22:5; Matt 5:22

22:67 Matt 26:63-66; Mark 14:61-63; John 18:19-21

22:69 Matt 26:64; Mark 14:62; 16:19; Ps 110:1

22:70 Matt 4:3; Matt 26:64; 27:11; Luke 23:3

23:1 Matt 27:2; Mark 15:1; John 18:28

23:2 Luke 23:14; Luke 20:22; John 18:33ff; 19:12; Acts 17:7

23:3 Luke 22:70

23:4 Matt 27:23; Mark 15:14; Luke 23:14, 22; John 18:38; 19:4, 6

23:5 Matt 4:12

23:7 Matt 14:1; Mark 6:14; Luke 3:1; 9:7; 13:31

23:8 Luke 9:9

23:9 Matt 27:12, 14; Mark 15:5; John 19:9

23:11 Matt 27:28

22:70 Jesus in effect agreed that he was the Son of God when he simply turned the high priest's question around by saying, "Yes, I am." And Jesus identified himself with God by using a familiar title for God found in the Old Testament: "I am" (Exodus 3:14). The high priest recognized Jesus' claim and accused him of blasphemy. For any other human this claim would have been blasphemy, but in this case it was true. Blasphemy, the sin of claiming to be God or of attacking God's authority and majesty in any way, was punishable by death. The Jewish leaders had the evidence they wanted.

23:1 Pilate was the Roman governor of Judea, where Jerusalem was located. He seemed to take special pleasure in harassing the Jews. For example, Pilate had taken money from the temple treasury and had used it to build an aqueduct. And he had insulted the Jewish religion by bringing imperial images into the city. As Pilate well knew, such acts could backfire. If the people were to lodge a formal complaint against his administration, Rome might remove him from his post. Pilate was already beginning to feel insecure in his position when the Jewish leaders brought Jesus to trial. Would he continue to badger the Jews and risk his political future, or would he give in to their demands and condemn a man who, he was quite sure, was innocent? That was the question facing Pilate that springtime Friday morning nearly 2,000 years ago. For more about Pilate, see his Profile in Mark 15.

23:7 Herod, also called Herod Antipas, was in Jerusalem that weekend for the Passover celebration. (This was the Herod who killed John the Baptist.) Pilate hoped to pass Jesus off on Herod because he knew that Jesus had lived and worked in Galilee. But Herod was not much help. He was curious about Jesus and enjoyed making fun of him. But when Herod sent Jesus back to Pilate, it was with the verdict of "not guilty." For more about Herod Antipas, see his Profile in Mark 6.

12 Now Herod and Pilate became friends with one another that very day; for before
they had been enemies with each other.

23:12
Acts 4:27

Pilate Hands Jesus Over to Be Crucified
(232/Matthew 27:15-26; Mark 15:6-15; John 18:38—19:16)

13 Pilate summoned the chief priests and the rulers and the people,
14 and said to them, "You brought this man to me as one who incites the people to
rebellion, and behold, having examined Him before you, I have found no guilt in this
man regarding the charges which you make against Him.
15 "No, nor has Herod, for he sent Him back to us; and behold, nothing deserving death
has been done by Him.
16 "Therefore I will punish Him and release Him."
17 [[28]Now he was obliged to release to them at the feast one prisoner.]
18 But they cried out all together, saying, "Away with this man, and release for us Barabbas!"
19 (He was one who had been thrown into prison for an insurrection made in the city,
and for murder.)
20 Pilate, wanting to release Jesus, addressed them again,
21 but they kept on calling out, saying, "Crucify, crucify Him!"
22 And he said to them the third time, "Why, what evil has this man done? I have found
in Him no guilt *demanding* death; therefore I will punish Him and release Him."
23 But they were insistent, with loud voices asking that He be crucified. And their voices
began to prevail.

23:13
Luke 23:35; John 7:26, 48; 12:42; Acts 3:17; 4:5, 8; 13:27

23:14
Luke 23:2; Luke 23:4

23:15
Luke 9:9

23:16
Matt 27:26; Mark 15:15; Luke 23:22; John 19:1; Acts 16:37

23:22
Luke 23:16

28 Early mss do not contain this v

23:12 Herod was the part-Jewish ruler of Galilee and Perea. Pilate was the Roman governor of Judea and Samaria. Those four provinces, together with several others, had been united under Herod the Great. But when Herod died in 4 B.C., the kingdom was divided among his sons, each of whom was called "tetrarch" (meaning "ruler of a fourth part of a region"). Archelaus, the son who had received Judea and Samaria, was removed from office within ten years, and his provinces were then ruled by a succession of Roman governors, of whom Pilate was the fifth.

Herod Antipas had two advantages over Pilate: He came from a hereditary, part-Jewish monarchy, and he had held his position much longer. But Pilate had two advantages over Herod: He was a Roman citizen and an envoy of the emperor, and his position was created to replace that of Herod's ineffective half brother. It is not surprising that the two men were uneasy around each other. Jesus' trial, however, brought them together. Because Pilate had recognized Herod's authority over Galilee, Herod stopped feeling threatened by the Roman politician. And because neither man knew what to do in this predicament, their common problem united them.

23:13–25 Pilate wanted to release Jesus, but the crowd loudly demanded his death; so Pilate sentenced Jesus to die. No doubt Pilate did not want to risk losing his position, which may already have been shaky, by allowing a riot to occur in his province. As a career politician, he knew the importance of compromise, and he saw Jesus more as a political threat than as a human being with rights and dignity.

When the stakes are high, it is difficult to stand up for what is right, and it is easy to see our opponents as problems to be solved rather than as people to be respected. Had Pilate been a man of real courage, he would have released Jesus no matter what the consequences. But the crowd roared, and Pilate buckled. We are like Pilate when we know what is right but decide not to do it. When you have a difficult decision to make, don't discount the effects of peer pressure. Realize beforehand that the right decision could have unpleasant consequences: social rejection, career derailment, public ridicule. Then think of Pilate and resolve to stand up for what is right no matter what other people pressure you to do.

23:15 Jesus was tried six times, by both Jewish and Roman authorities, but he was never convicted of a crime deserving death. Even when condemned to execution, he had been convicted of no felony. Today, no one can find fault in Jesus. But just like Pilate, Herod, and the religious leaders, many still refuse to acknowledge him as Lord.

23:18–19 Barabbas had been part of a rebellion against the Roman government (Mark 15:7). As a political insurgent, he was no doubt a hero among some of the Jews. How ironic it is that Barabbas, who was released, was guilty of the very crime Jesus was accused of (23:14).

23:18–19 Who was Barabbas? Jewish men had names that identified them with their fathers. Simon Peter, for example, is called Simon Barjona (Matthew 16:17), meaning son of Jonah. Barabbas is never identified by his given name, and this name is not much help either—*bar-abbas* means "son of *Abba*" (or "son of daddy"). He could have been anybody's son—and that's just the point. Barabbas, son of an unnamed father, committed a crime. Because Jesus died in his place, this man was set free. We too are sinners and criminals who have broken God's holy law. Like Barabbas, we deserve to die. But Jesus has died in our place, for our sins, and we have been set free. We don't have to be "very important people" to accept our freedom in Christ. In fact, thanks to Jesus, God adopts us all as his own sons and daughters and gives us the right to call him *Abba*—"daddy" (see Galatians 4:4–6).

23:22 When Pilate said he would have Jesus punished, he was referring to a punishment that could have killed Jesus. The usual procedure was to bare the upper half of the victim's body and tie his hands to a pillar before whipping him with a three-pronged whip. The number of lashes was determined by the severity of the crime; up to 40 were permitted under Jewish law. After being flogged, Jesus also endured other agonies as recorded in Matthew and Mark. He was slapped, struck with fists, and mocked. A crown of thorns was placed on his head, and he was beaten with a stick and stripped before being hung on the cross.

23:23–24 Pilate did not want to give Jesus the death sentence. He thought the Jewish leaders were simply jealous men who wanted to get rid of a rival. When they threatened to report Pilate to Caesar (John 19:12), however, Pilate became frightened. Historical records indicate that Pilate had already been warned by Roman authorities about tensions in this region. The last thing he needed was a riot in

24 And Pilate pronounced sentence that their demand be granted.
25 And he released the man they were asking for who had been thrown into prison for
insurrection and murder, but he delivered Jesus to their will.

Jesus Is Led away to Be Crucified
(234/Matthew 27:32-34; Mark 15:21-24; John 19:17)

23:26 Matt 27:32
26 When they led Him away, they seized a man, Simon of Cyrene, coming in from the
country, and placed on him the cross to carry behind Jesus.

23:27 Luke 8:52
27 And following Him was a large crowd of the people, and of women who were mourning and lamenting Him.
28 But Jesus turning to them said, "Daughters of Jerusalem, stop weeping for Me, but
weep for yourselves and for your children.

23:29 Matt 24:19; Luke 11:27; 21:23
29 "For behold, the days are coming when they will say, 'Blessed are the barren, and the
wombs that never bore, and the breasts that never nursed.'

23:30 Hos 10:8; Is 2:19, 20; Rev 6:16
30 "Then they will begin TO SAY TO THE MOUNTAINS, 'FALL ON US,' AND TO THE HILLS,
'COVER US.'
31 "For if they do these things when the tree is green, what will happen when it is dry?"

Jesus Is Placed on the Cross
(235/Matthew 27:35-44; Mark 15:25-32; John 19:18-27)

23:32 Matt 27:38; Mark 15:27; John 19:18
32 Two others also, who were criminals, were being led away to be put to death
with Him.
33 When they came to the place called The Skull, there they crucified Him and the
criminals, one on the right and the other on the left.

23:34 Matt 11:25; Luke 22:42; Ps 22:18; John 19:24
34 But Jesus was saying, "Father, forgive them; for they do not know what they are
doing." And they cast lots, dividing up His garments among themselves.

Jerusalem at Passover time, when the city was crowded with Jews from all over the empire. So Pilate turned Jesus over to the mob to do with as they pleased.

23:27–29 Luke alone mentions the tears of the Jewish women while Jesus was being led through the streets to his execution. Jesus told them not to weep for him but for themselves. He knew that in only about 40 years, Jerusalem and the temple would be destroyed by the Romans.

23:31 This proverb is difficult to interpret. Some feel it means: If the innocent Jesus (green tree) suffered at the hands of the Romans, what would happen to the guilty Jews (dry tree)?

23:32–33 The place called The Skull, or Golgotha, was probably a hill outside Jerusalem along a main road. The Romans executed people publicly as examples to the people.

23:32–33 When James and John asked Jesus for the places of honor next to him in his kingdom, he told them they didn't know what they were asking (Mark 10:35–39). Here, as Jesus was preparing to inaugurate his kingdom through his death, the places on his right and on his left were taken by dying men—criminals. As Jesus explained to his two position-conscious disciples, a person who wants to be close to Jesus must be prepared to suffer and die. The way to the kingdom is the way of the cross.

23:34 Jesus asked God to forgive the people who were putting him to death—Jewish leaders, Roman politicians and soldiers, bystanders—and God answered that prayer by opening up the way of salvation even to Jesus' murderers. The Roman centurion and soldiers who witnessed the crucifixion said, "Truly this was the Son of God" (Matthew 27:54). Soon many priests were converted to the Christian faith (Acts 6:7). Because we are all sinners, we all played a part in putting Jesus to death. The gospel—the Good News—is that God is gracious. He will forgive us and give us new life through his Son.

23:34 Roman soldiers customarily divided up the clothing of executed criminals among themselves. When they cast lots for Jesus' clothes, they fulfilled the prophecy in Psalm 22:18.

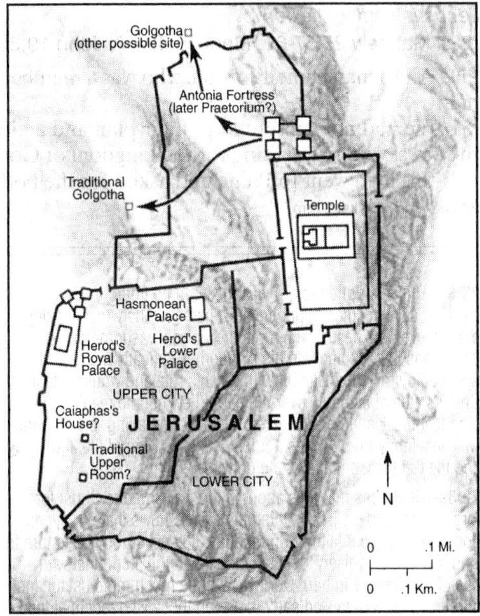

JESUS LED AWAY TO DIE As Jesus was led away through the streets of Jerusalem, he could no longer carry his cross, and Simon of Cyrene was given the burden. Jesus was crucified, along with common criminals, on a hill outside Jerusalem.

35 And the people stood by, looking on. And even the rulers were sneering at Him,
saying, "He saved others; let Him save Himself if this is the Christ of God, His Chosen
One."
36 The soldiers also mocked Him, coming up to Him, offering Him sour wine,
37 and saying, "If You are the King of the Jews, save Yourself!"
38 Now there was also an inscription above Him, "THIS IS THE KING OF THE
JEWS."
39 One of the criminals who were hanged *there* was hurling abuse at Him, saying, "Are
You not the Christ? Save Yourself and us!"
40 But the other answered, and rebuking him said, "Do you not even fear God, since
you are under the same sentence of condemnation?
41 "And we indeed *are suffering* justly, for we are receiving what we deserve for our deeds;
but this man has done nothing wrong."
42 And he was saying, "Jesus, remember me when You come in Your kingdom!"
43 And He said to him, "Truly I say to you, today you shall be with Me in Paradise."

Jesus Dies on the Cross

(236/Matthew 27:45-56; Mark 15:33-41; John 19:28-37)

44 It was now about [29]the sixth hour, and darkness fell over the whole land until [30]the
ninth hour,
45 because the sun was obscured; and the veil of the temple was torn in two.
46 And Jesus, crying out with a loud voice, said, "Father, INTO YOUR HANDS I COM-
MIT My SPIRIT." Having said this, He breathed His last.
47 Now when the centurion saw what had happened, he *began* praising God, saying,
"Certainly this man was innocent."
48 And all the crowds who came together for this spectacle, when they observed what
had happened, *began* to return, beating their breasts.
49 And all His acquaintances and the women who accompanied Him from Galilee were
standing at a distance, seeing these things.

Jesus Is Laid in the Tomb

(237/Matthew 27:57-61; Mark 15:42-47; John 19:38-42)

50 And a man named Joseph, who was a member of the Council, a good and righteous
man
51 (he had not consented to their plan and action), *a man* from Arimathea, a city of
the Jews, who was waiting for the kingdom of God;
52 this man went to Pilate and asked for the body of Jesus.

23:35 Luke 23:13; Matt 27:43
23:36 Matt 27:48
23:37 Matt 27:43
23:38 Matt 27:37; Mark 15:26; John 19:19
23:39 Matt 27:44; Mark 15:32; Luke 23:35, 37
23:43 2 Cor 12:4; Rev 2:7
23:45 Ex 26:31-33; Matt 27:51
23:46 Matt 27:50; Mark 15:37; John 19:30; Ps 31:5
23:47 Matt 27:54; Mark 15:39; Matt 9:8
23:48 Luke 8:52; 18:13
23:49 Matt 27:55f; Mark 15:40f; Luke 8:2; John 19:25
23:50 Mark 15:43
23:51 Mark 15:43; Luke 2:25

29 I.e. noon **30** I.e. 3 p.m.

23:38 This inscription (sign) was meant to be ironic. A king, stripped and executed in public view, had obviously lost his kingdom forever. But Jesus, who turns the world's wisdom upside down, was just coming into his kingdom. His death and resurrection would strike the deathblow to Satan's rule and would establish Christ's eternal authority over the earth. Few people reading the sign that bleak afternoon understood its real meaning, but the sign was absolutely true. All was not lost. Jesus is King of the Jews—and the Gentiles, and the whole universe.

23:39–43 As this man was about to die, he turned to Christ for forgiveness, and Christ accepted him. This shows that our deeds don't save us—our faith in Christ does. It is never too late to turn to God. Even in his misery, Jesus had mercy on this criminal who decided to believe in him. Our lives will be much more useful and fulfilling if we turn to God early, but even those who repent at the very last moment will be with God in paradise.

23:42–43 The dying criminal had more faith than the rest of Jesus' followers put together. Although the disciples continued to love Jesus, their hopes for the kingdom were shattered. Most of them had gone into hiding. As one of his followers sadly said two days later, "We were hoping that it was He who was going to redeem Israel" (24:21). By contrast, the criminal looked at the man who was dying next to him and said, "Jesus, remember me when You come in Your kingdom!" By all appearances, the kingdom was finished. How awe-inspiring is the faith of this man who alone saw beyond the present shame to the coming glory!

23:44 Darkness covered the entire land for about three hours in the middle of the day. All nature seemed to mourn over the stark tragedy of the death of God's Son.

23:45 This significant event symbolized Christ's work on the cross. The temple had three parts: the courts for all the people; the holy place, where only priests could enter; and the holy of holies, where the high priest alone could enter once a year to atone for the sins of the people. It was in the holy of holies that the ark of the covenant, and God's presence with it, rested. The veil that was torn was the one that closed off the holy of holies from view. At Christ's death, the barrier between God and man was split in two. Now all people can approach God directly through Christ (Hebrews 9:1–14; 10:19–22).

23:50–52 Joseph of Arimathea was a wealthy and honored member of the Jewish Council. He was also a secret disciple of Jesus (John 19:38). The disciples who had publicly followed Jesus fled, but Joseph boldly took a stand that could cost him dearly. He cared enough about Jesus to ask for his body so he could give it a proper burial.

53 And he took it down and wrapped it in a linen cloth, and laid Him in a tomb cut into
the rock, where no one had ever lain.

23:54 Matt 27:62; Mark 15:42

54 It was the preparation day, and the Sabbath was about to begin.
55 Now the women who had come with Him out of Galilee followed, and saw the tomb
and how His body was laid.

23:55 Luke 23:49

56 Then they returned and prepared spices and perfumes.
And on the Sabbath they rested according to the commandment.

23:56 Mark 16:1; Luke 24:1; Ex 20:10f; Deut 5:14

Jesus Rises from the Dead
(239/Matthew 28:1-7; Mark 16:1-8; John 20:1-9)

24 But on the first day of the week, at early dawn, they came to the tomb bringing
the spices which they had prepared.
2 And they found the stone rolled away from the tomb,

24:3 Luke 7:13; Acts 1:21

3 but when they entered, they did not find the body of the Lord Jesus.

24:4 John 20:12; Luke 2:9; Acts 12:7

4 While they were perplexed about this, behold, two men suddenly stood near them
in dazzling clothing;
5 and as *the women* were terrified and bowed their faces to the ground, *the men* said
to them, "Why do you seek the living One among the dead?

24:6 Mark 16:6; Matt 17:22f; Mark 9:30f; Luke 9:44; 24:44

6 "He is not here, but He has risen. Remember how He spoke to you while He was still
in Galilee,

24:7 Matt 16:21; Luke 24:46

7 saying that the Son of Man must be delivered into the hands of sinful men, and be
crucified, and the third day rise again."

24:8 John 2:22

8 And they remembered His words,
9 and returned from the tomb and reported all these things to the eleven and to all
the rest.

24:10 Matt 27:56; Mark 6:30

10 Now they were Mary Magdalene and Joanna and Mary the *mother* of James; also
the other women with them were telling these things to the apostles.

23:53 The tomb was likely a man-made cave cut out of one of the many limestone hills in the area around Jerusalem. Such a tomb was large enough to walk into. After burial, a large stone would have been rolled across the entrance (John 20:1).

23:55 The Galilean women followed Joseph to the tomb, so they knew exactly where to find Jesus' body when they returned after the Sabbath with their spices and perfumes. These women could not do "great" things for Jesus—they were not permitted to stand up before the Jewish council or the Roman governor and testify on his behalf—but they did what they could. They stayed at the cross when most of the disciples had fled, and they got ready to anoint their Lord's body. Because of their devotion, they were the first to know about the resurrection. As believers, we may feel we can't do much for Jesus. But we are called to take advantage of the opportunities given us, doing what we *can* do and not worrying about what we cannot do.

24:1 The women brought spices to the tomb as we would bring flowers—as a sign of love and respect. The women went home and kept Sabbath as the law required, from sundown Friday to sundown Saturday, before gathering up their spices and perfumes and returning to the tomb.

24:1–9 The two angels (appearing as men "in dazzling clothing") asked the women why they were looking in a tomb for someone who was alive. Often we run into people who are looking for God among the dead. They study the Bible as a mere historical document and go to church as if going to a memorial service. But Jesus is not among the dead—he lives! He reigns in the hearts of Christians, and he is the head of his church. Do you look for Jesus among the living? Do you expect him to be active in the world and in the church? Look for signs of his power—they are all around you.

24:4 We learn from Matthew and John that these two men in dazzling clothes were angels. When angels appeared to people, they looked like humans.

24:6–7 The angels reminded the women that Jesus had accurately predicted all that had happened to him (9:22, 44; 18:31–33).

24:6–7 The resurrection of Jesus from the dead is the central fact of Christian history. On it, the church is built; without it, there would be no Christian church today. Jesus' resurrection is unique. Other religions have strong ethical systems, concepts about paradise and afterlife, and various holy Scriptures. Only Christianity has a God who became human, literally died for his people, and was raised again in power and glory to rule his church forever.

Why is the resurrection so important? (1) Because Christ was raised from the dead, we know that the kingdom of heaven has broken into earth's history. Our world is now headed for redemption, not disaster. God's mighty power is at work destroying sin, creating new lives, and preparing us for Jesus' second coming. (2) Because of the resurrection, we know that death has been conquered, and we too will be raised from the dead to live forever with Christ. (3) The resurrection gives authority to the church's witness in the world. Look at the early evangelistic sermons in the book of Acts: The apostles' most important message was the proclamation that Jesus Christ had been raised from the dead! (4) The resurrection gives meaning to the church's regular feast, the Lord's Supper. Like the disciples on the Emmaus Road, we break bread with our risen Lord, who comes in power to save us. (5) The resurrection helps us find meaning even in great tragedy. No matter what happens to us as we walk with the Lord, the resurrection gives us hope for the future. (6) The resurrection assures us that Christ is alive and ruling his kingdom. He is not legend; he is alive and real. (7) God's power that brought Jesus back from the dead is available to us so that we can live for him in an evil world.

Christians can look very different from one another, and they can hold widely varying beliefs about politics, life-style, and even theology. But one central belief unites and inspires all true Christians—Jesus Christ rose from the dead! (For more on the importance of the resurrection, see 1 Corinthians 15:12–58.)

11 But these words appeared to them as nonsense, and they would not believe them. **24:11** Mark 16:11
12 But Peter got up and ran to the tomb; stooping and looking in, he ☆saw the linen
wrappings only; and he went away to his home, marveling at what had happened. **24:12** John 20:3-6; John 20:10

Jesus Appears to Two Believers Traveling on the Road
(243/Mark 16:12-13)

13 And behold, two of them were going that very day to a village named Emmaus, which **24:13** Mark 16:12
was [31]about seven miles from Jerusalem.
14 And they were talking with each other about all these things which had taken place.
15 While they were talking and discussing, Jesus Himself approached and *began* traveling with them.
16 But their eyes were prevented from recognizing Him.
17 And He said to them, "What are these words that you are exchanging with one **24:16** Luke 24:31; John 20:14; 21:4
another as you are walking?" And they stood still, looking sad.
18 One *of them*, named Cleopas, answered and said to Him, "Are You the only one
visiting Jerusalem and unaware of the things which have happened here in these days?"
19 And He said to them, "What things?" And they said to Him, "The things about Jesus **24:19** Mark 1:24; Matt 21:11
the Nazarene, who was a prophet mighty in deed and word in the sight of God and all
the people,
20 and how the chief priests and our rulers delivered Him to the sentence of death, **24:20** Luke 23:13
and crucified Him.
21 "But we were hoping that it was He who was going to redeem Israel. Indeed, besides **24:21** Luke 1:68
all this, it is the third day since these things happened.
22 "But also some women among us amazed us. When they were at the tomb early in **24:22** Luke 24:1ff
the morning,
23 and did not find His body, they came, saying that they had also seen a vision of angels who said that He was alive.
24 "Some of those who were with us went to the tomb and found it just exactly as the
women also had said; but Him they did not see."

31 Lit *60 stadia;* one stadion was about 600 ft

24:11–12 People who hear about the resurrection for the first time may need time before they can comprehend this amazing story. Like the disciples, they may pass through four stages of belief. (1) At first, they may think it is a fairy tale, impossible to believe. (2) Like Peter, they may check out the facts but still be puzzled about what happened. (3) Only when they encounter Jesus personally will they be able to accept the fact of the resurrection. (4) Then, as they commit themselves to Jesus and devote their lives to serving him, they will begin fully to understand the reality of his presence with them.

24:12 From John 20:3–4, we learn that another disciple ran to the tomb with Peter. That other disciple was almost certainly John, the author of the fourth Gospel.

24:13ff The two disciples returning to Emmaus at first missed the significance of history's greatest event because they were too focused on their disappointments and problems. In fact, they didn't recognize Jesus when he was walking beside them. To compound the problem, they were walking in the wrong direction—away from the fellowship of believers in Jerusalem. We are likely to miss Jesus and withdraw from the strength found in other believers when we become preoccupied with our dashed hopes and frustrated plans. Only when we are looking for Jesus in our midst will we experience the power and help he can bring.

24:18 The news about Jesus' crucifixion had spread throughout Jerusalem. Because this was Passover week, Jewish pilgrims visiting the city from all over the Roman empire now knew about his death. This was not a small, insignificant event, affecting only the disciples—the whole nation was interested.

24:21 The disciples from Emmaus were counting on Jesus to redeem Israel—that is, to rescue the nation from its enemies. Most Jews believed that the Old Testament prophecies pointed to a military and political Messiah; they didn't realize that the Messiah had come to redeem people from slavery to sin. When Jesus died, therefore, they lost all hope. They didn't understand that Jesus' death offered the greatest hope possible.

24:24 These disciples knew that the tomb was empty but didn't understand that Jesus had risen, and they were filled with sadness. Despite the women's witness, which was verified by other disciples, and despite the Biblical prophecies of this very event, they still didn't believe. Today the resurrection still catches people by surprise. In spite of 2,000 years of evidence and witness, many people refuse to believe. What more will it take? For these disciples it took the living, breathing Jesus in their midst. For many people today, it takes the presence of living, breathing Christians.

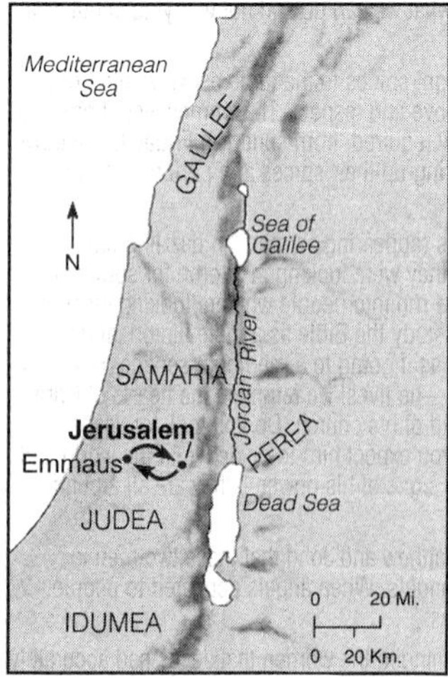

ON THE ROAD TO EMMAUS
After Jesus' death, two of his followers were walking from Jerusalem back toward Emmaus when a stranger joined them. During dinner in Emmaus, Jesus revealed himself to them and then disappeared. They immediately returned to Jerusalem to tell the disciples the good news that Jesus was alive!

24:25 Matt 26:24
24:26 Luke 24:7, 44ff; Heb 2:10; 1 Pet 1:11
24:27 Acts 13:27
24:28 Mark 6:48
24:30 Matt 14:19
24:31 Luke 24:16
24:32 Luke 24:45
24:33 Mark 16:13; Acts 1:14
24:34 Luke 24:6; 1 Cor 15:5

25 And He said to them, "O foolish men and slow of heart to believe in all that the
prophets have spoken!
26 "Was it not necessary for the Christ to suffer these things and to enter into His
glory?"
27 Then beginning with Moses and with all the prophets, He explained to them the
things concerning Himself in all the Scriptures.
28 And they approached the village where they were going, and He acted as though
He were going farther.
29 But they urged Him, saying, "Stay with us, for it is *getting* toward evening, and the
day is now nearly over." So He went in to stay with them.
30 When He had reclined *at the table* with them, He took the bread and blessed *it,* and
breaking *it,* He *began* giving *it* to them.
31 Then their eyes were opened and they recognized Him; and He vanished from their
sight.
32 They said to one another, "Were not our hearts burning within us while He was
speaking to us on the road, while He was explaining the Scriptures to us?"
33 And they got up that very hour and returned to Jerusalem, and found gathered together the eleven and those who were with them,
34 saying, "The Lord has really risen and has appeared to Simon."
35 They *began* to relate their experiences on the road and how He was recognized by
them in the breaking of the bread.

Jesus Appears to the Disciples Behind Locked Doors
(244/John 20:19-23)

24:36 Mark 16:14
24:37 Matt 14:26; Mark 6:49
24:39 1 John 1:1
24:41 Luke 24:11; John 21:5
24:43 Acts 10:41

36 While they were telling these things, He Himself stood in their midst and ☆said to
them, "Peace be to you."
37 But they were startled and frightened and thought that they were seeing a spirit.
38 And He said to them, "Why are you troubled, and why do doubts arise in your hearts?
39 "See My hands and My feet, that it is I Myself; touch Me and see, for a spirit does
not have flesh and bones as you see that I have."
40 And when He had said this, He showed them His hands and His feet.
41 While they still could not believe *it* because of their joy and amazement, He said to
them, "Have you anything here to eat?"
42 They gave Him a piece of a broiled fish;
43 and He took it and ate *it* before them.

24:25 Why did Jesus call these disciples foolish? Even though they well knew the Biblical prophecies, they failed to understand that Christ's suffering was his path to glory. They could not understand why God did not intervene to save Jesus from the cross. They were so caught up in the world's admiration of political power and military might that they were unprepared for the reversal of values in God's kingdom—that the last will be first, and that life grows out of death. The world has not changed its values: A suffering servant is no more popular today than 2,000 years ago. But we have not only the witness of the Old Testament prophets; we have also the witness of the New Testament apostles and the history of the Christian church all pointing to Jesus' victory over death. Will we step outside the values of our culture and put our faith in Jesus? Or will we foolishly continue to be baffled by his Good News?

24:25–27 After the two disciples had explained their sadness and confusion, Jesus responded by going to Scripture and applying it to his ministry. When we are puzzled by questions or problems, we too can go to Scripture and find authoritative help. If we, like these two disciples, do not understand what the Bible means, we can turn to other believers who know the Bible and have the wisdom to apply it to our situation.

24:27 Beginning with the promised offspring in Genesis (Genesis 3:15) and going through the suffering servant in Isaiah (Isaiah 53), the pierced one in Zechariah (Zechariah 12:10), and the messenger of the covenant in Malachi (Malachi 3:1), Jesus reintroduced these disciples to the Old Testament. Christ is the thread woven through all the Scriptures, the central theme that binds them together. Following are several key passages Jesus may have mentioned on this walk to Emmaus: Genesis 3; 12; Psalms 22; 69; 110; Isaiah 53; Jeremiah 31; Zechariah 9; 13; Malachi 3.

24:33–34 Paul also mentions that Jesus appeared to Peter alone (1 Corinthians 15:5). This appearance is not further described in the Gospels. Jesus showed individual concern for Peter because Peter felt completely unworthy after disowning his Lord. But Peter repented, and Jesus approached him and forgave him. Soon God would use Peter in building Christ's church (see the first half of the book of Acts).

24:36–43 Jesus' body wasn't just a figment of the imagination or the appearance of a ghost—the disciples touched him, and he ate food. On the other hand, his body wasn't merely a restored human body like Lazarus's (John 11)—he was able to appear and disappear. Jesus' resurrected body was immortal. This is the kind of body we will be given at the resurrection of the dead (see 1 Corinthians 15:42–50).

Jesus Appears to the Disciples in Jerusalem
(249)

44 Now He said to them, "These are My words which I spoke to you while I was still
with you, that all things which are written about Me in the Law of Moses and the Prophets and the Psalms must be fulfilled."
45 Then He opened their minds to understand the Scriptures,
46 and He said to them, "Thus it is written, that the Christ would suffer and rise again
from the dead the third day,
47 and that repentance for forgiveness of sins would be proclaimed in His name to all
the nations, beginning from Jerusalem.
48 "You are witnesses of these things.
49 "And behold, I am sending forth the promise of My Father upon you; but you are to
stay in the city until you are clothed with power from on high."

Jesus Ascends into Heaven
(250/Mark 16:19-20)

50 And He led them out as far as Bethany, and He lifted up His hands and blessed
them.
51 While He was blessing them, He parted from them and was carried up into heaven.
52 And they, after worshiping Him, returned to Jerusalem with great joy,
53 and were continually in the temple praising God.

24:44 Luke 9:22, 44f; 18:31-34; 22:37; Luke 24:27; Ps 2:7ff; Ps 16:10 [Acts 2:27]; Ps 22:1-18; Ps 69:1-21; Ps 72; 110:1 Ps 118:22f

24:45 Luke 24:32; Acts 16:14; 1 John 5:20

24:46 Luke 24:26, 44; Luke 24:7

24:47 Acts 5:31; 10:43; 13:38; 26:18; Matt 28:19

24:48 Acts 1:8, 22; 2:32; 3:15; 4:33; 5:32; 10:39, 41; 13:31; 1 Pet 5:1

24:49 John 14:26; Acts 1:4

24:50

24:44 Many days may have elapsed between verses 43 and 44 because Jesus and his followers traveled to Galilee and back before he returned to heaven (Matthew 28:16; John 21). In his second book, Acts, Luke makes it clear that Jesus spent 40 days with his disciples between his resurrection and ascension.

24:44–46 The law of Moses, the prophets, and the Psalms is a way to describe the entire Old Testament. In other words, the entire Old Testament points to the Messiah. For example, his role as prophet was foretold in Deuteronomy 18:15–20; his sufferings were prophesied in Psalm 22 and Isaiah 53; his resurrection was predicted in Psalm 16:9–11 and Isaiah 53:10–11.

24:45 Jesus opened these people's minds to understand the Scriptures. The Holy Spirit does this in our lives today when we study the Bible. Have you ever wondered how to understand a difficult Bible passage? Besides reading surrounding passages, asking other people, and consulting reference works, pray that the Holy Spirit will open your mind to understand, giving you the needed insight to put God's Word into action in your life.

24:47 Luke wrote to the Greek-speaking world. He wanted them to know that Christ's message of God's love and forgiveness should go to all the world. We must never ignore the worldwide scope of Christ's gospel. God wants all the world to hear the Good News of salvation.

24:50–53 As the disciples stood and watched, Jesus began rising into the air, and soon he disappeared into heaven. Seeing Jesus leave must have been frightening, but the disciples knew that Jesus would keep his promise to be with them through the Holy Spirit. This same Jesus, who lived with the disciples, who died and was buried, and who rose from the dead, loves us and promises to be with us always. We can get to know him better through studying the Scriptures, praying, and allowing the Holy Spirit to make us more like Jesus.

24:51 Jesus' physical presence left the disciples when he returned to heaven (Acts 1:9), but the Holy Spirit soon came to comfort them and empower them to spread the gospel of salvation (Acts 2:1–4). Today Jesus' work of salvation is completed, and he is sitting at God's right hand, where he has authority over heaven and earth.

24:53 Luke's Gospel portrays Jesus as the perfect example of a life lived according to God's plan—as a child living in obedience to his parents and yet amazing the religious leaders in the temple, as an adult serving God and others through preaching and healing, and finally as a condemned man suffering without complaint. This emphasis was well suited to Luke's Greek audience, who placed high value on being an example and improving oneself, and who often discussed the meaning of perfection. The Greeks, however, had a difficult time understanding the spiritual importance of the physical world. To them, the spiritual was always more important than the physical. To help them understand the God-man who united the spiritual and the physical, Luke emphasized that Jesus was not a phantom human but a real human being who healed people and fed them because he was concerned with their physical health as well as the state of their souls.

As believers living according to God's plan, we too should obey our Lord in every detail as we seek to restore people's bodies and souls to the health and salvation God has in store for them. If we want to know how to live a perfect life, we can look to Jesus as our example.

KEY PLACES IN JOHN

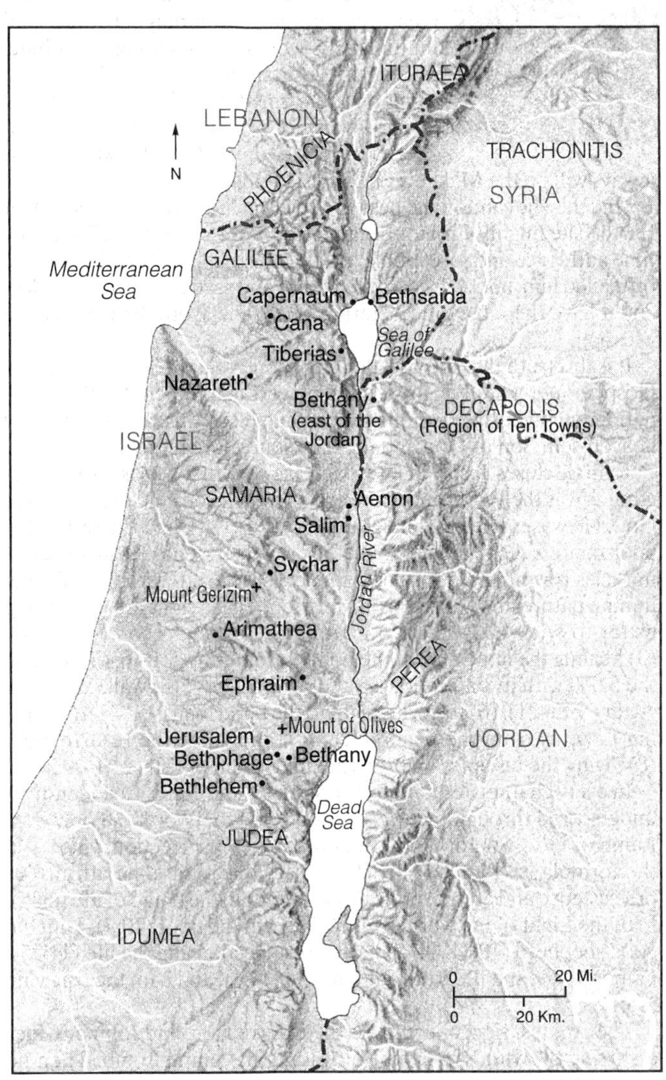

The broken lines (—·—·) indicate modern boundaries.

John's story begins as John the Baptist ministers near Bethany east of the Jordan (1:28ff). Jesus also begins his ministry, talking to some of the men who would later become his 12 disciples. Jesus' ministry in Galilee began with a visit to a wedding in Cana (2:1ff). Then he went to Capernaum, which became his new home (2:12). He journeyed to Jerusalem for the special festivals (2:13) and there met with Nicodemus, a religious leader (3:1ff). When Jesus left Judea, he traveled through Samaria and ministered to the Samaritans (4:1ff). Jesus did miracles in Galilee (4:46ff) and in Judea and Jerusalem (5:1ff). We follow him as he fed 5,000 near Bethsaida beside the Sea of Galilee (6:1ff), walked on the water to his frightened disciples (6:16ff), preached through Galilee (7:1), returned to Jerusalem (7:2ff), preached beyond the Jordan in Perea (10:40), raised Lazarus from the dead in Bethany (11:1ff), and finally entered Jerusalem for the last time to celebrate the Passover with his disciples and give them key teachings about what was to come and how they should act. His last hours before his crucifixion were spent in the city (13:1ff), in a grove of olive trees (the Garden of Gethsemane) (18:1ff), and finally in various buildings in Jerusalem during his trial (18:12ff). He would be crucified, but he would rise again as he had promised.

JOHN

Herod the Great begins to rule 37 B.C.	Jesus is born 6/5 B.C.	Escape to Egypt 5/4 B.C.	Herod the Great dies 4 B.C.	Return to Nazareth 4/3 B.C.	Judea becomes a Roman province A.D. 6

VITAL STATISTICS

PURPOSE:
To prove conclusively that Jesus is the Son of God and that all who believe in him will have eternal life

AUTHOR:
John the apostle, son of Zebedee, brother of James, called a "Son of Thunder"

TO WHOM WRITTEN:
New Christians and searching non-Christians

DATE WRITTEN:
Probably A.D. 85–90

SETTING:
Written after the destruction of Jerusalem in A.D. 70 and before John's exile to the island of Patmos

KEY VERSES:
"Therefore many other signs Jesus also performed in the presence of the disciples, which are not written in this book; but these have been written so that you may believe that Jesus is the Christ, the Son of God; and that believing you may have life in His name" (20:30–31).

KEY PEOPLE:
Jesus, John the Baptist, the disciples, Mary, Martha, Lazarus, Jesus' mother, Pilate, Mary Magdalene

KEY PLACES:
Judean countryside, Samaria, Galilee, Bethany, Jerusalem

SPECIAL FEATURES:
Of the eight miracles recorded, six are unique (among the Gospels) to John, as is the "Upper Room Discourse" (chapters 14—17). Over 90 percent of John is unique to his Gospel— John does not contain a genealogy or any record of Jesus' birth, childhood, temptation, transfiguration, appointment of the disciples, nor any account of Jesus' parables, ascension, or great commission.

HE SPOKE, and galaxies whirled into place, stars burned the heavens, and planets began orbiting their suns—words of awesome, unlimited, unleashed power. He spoke again, and the waters and lands were filled with plants and creatures, running, swimming, growing, and multiplying—words of animating, breathing, pulsing life. Again he spoke, and man and woman were formed, thinking, speaking, and loving—words of personal and creative glory. Eternal, infinite, unlimited—he was, is, and always will be the Maker and Lord of all that exists.

And then he came in the flesh to a speck in the universe called planet Earth. The mighty Creator became a part of the creation, limited by time and space and susceptible to aging, sickness, and death. But love propelled him, and so he came to rescue and save those who were lost and to give them the gift of eternity. He is the Word; he is Jesus, the Messiah.

It is this truth that the apostle John brings to us in this book. John's Gospel is not a life of Christ; it is a powerful argument for the incarnation, a conclusive demonstration that Jesus was, and is, the very heaven-sent Son of God and the only source of eternal life.

John discloses Jesus' identity with his very first words, "In the beginning was the Word, and the Word was with God, and the Word was God. He was in the beginning with God" (1:1–2); and the rest of the book continues the theme. John, the eyewitness, chose eight of Jesus' miracles (or miraculous signs, as he calls them) to reveal his divine/human nature and his life-giving mission. These signs are (1) turning water to wine (2:1–11), (2) healing the official's son (4:46–54), (3) healing the lame man at the pool of Bethesda (5:1–9), (4) feeding the 5,000 with just a few loaves and fish (6:1–14), (5) walking on the water (6:15–21), (6) restoring sight to the blind man (9:1–41), (7) raising Lazarus from the dead (11:1–44), and, after the resurrection, (8) giving the disciples an overwhelming catch of fish (21:1–14).

In every chapter Jesus' deity is revealed. And Jesus' true identity is underscored through the titles he is given—the Word, the only Son, Lamb of God, Son of God, true bread, life, resurrection, vine. And the formula is "I am." When Jesus uses this phrase, he affirms his preexistence and eternal deity. Jesus says, I am the bread of life (6:35); I am the Light of the world (8:12; 9:5); I am the door (10:7); I am the good shepherd (10:11, 14); *I am* the resurrection and the life (11:25); I am the way, and the truth, and the life (14:6); and I am the true vine (15:1).

The greatest sign, of course, is the resurrection, and John provides a stirring eyewitness account of finding the empty tomb. Then he records various post-resurrection appearances by Jesus.

John, the devoted follower of Christ, has given us a personal and powerful look at Jesus Christ, the eternal Son of God. As you read his story, commit yourself to believe in and follow him.

Tiberius Caesar becomes emperor 14	Pontius Pilate appointed governor 26	Jesus begins his ministry 26/27	Jesus and Nicodemus 27	Jesus chooses twelve disciples 28	Jesus feeds 5,000 29	Jesus is crucified, rises again, and ascends 30

THE BLUEPRINT

A. BIRTH AND PREPARATION OF JESUS, THE SON OF GOD (1:1—2:12)

John makes it clear that Jesus is not just a man; he is the eternal Son of God. He is the Light of the world because he offers this gift of eternal life to all people. How blind and foolish to call Jesus nothing more than an unusually good man or moral teacher. Yet we sometimes act as if this were true when we casually toss around his words and go about living our own way. If Jesus is the eternal Son of God, we should pay attention to his divine identity and life-giving message.

B. MESSAGE AND MINISTRY OF JESUS, THE SON OF GOD (2:13—12:50)
1. Jesus encounters belief and unbelief from the people
2. Jesus encounters conflict with the religious leaders
3. Jesus encounters crucial events in Jerusalem

Jesus meets with individuals, preaches to great crowds, trains his disciples, and debates with the religious leaders. The message that he is the Son of God receives a mixed reaction. Some worship him, some are puzzled, some shrink back, and some move to silence him. We see the same varied reactions today. Times have changed, but people's hearts remain hard. May we see ourselves in these encounters Jesus had with people, and may our response be to worship and follow him.

C. DEATH AND RESURRECTION OF JESUS, THE SON OF GOD (13:1—21:25)
1. Jesus teaches his disciples
2. Jesus completes his mission

Jesus carefully instructed the disciples how to continue to believe even after his death, yet they could not take it in. After he died and the first reports came back that Jesus was alive, the disciples could not believe it. Thomas is especially remembered as one who refused to believe even when he heard the eyewitness accounts from other disciples. May we not be like Thomas, demanding a physical face-to-face encounter, but may we accept the eyewitness testimony of the disciples that John has recorded in this Gospel.

MEGATHEMES

THEME	EXPLANATION	IMPORTANCE
Jesus Christ, Son of God	John shows us that Jesus is unique as God's special Son, yet he is fully God. Because he is fully God, Jesus is able to reveal God to us clearly and accurately.	Because Jesus is God's Son, we can perfectly trust what he says. By trusting him, we can gain an open mind to understand God's message and fulfill his purpose in our lives.
Eternal Life	Because Jesus is God, he lives forever. Before the world began, he lived with God, and he will reign forever with him. In John we see Jesus revealed in power and magnificence even before his resurrection.	Jesus offers eternal life to us. We are invited to begin living in a personal, eternal relationship with him now. Although we must grow old and die, by trusting him we can have a new life that lasts forever.
Belief	John records eight specific signs, or miracles, that show the nature of Jesus' power and love. We see his power over everything created, and we see his love of all people. These signs encourage us to believe in him.	Believing is active, living, and continuous trust in Jesus as God. When we believe in his life, his words, his death, and his resurrection, we are cleansed from sin and receive power to follow him. But we must respond to him by believing.
Holy Spirit	Jesus taught his disciples that the Holy Spirit would come after he ascended from earth. The Holy Spirit would then indwell, guide, counsel, and comfort those who follow Jesus. Through the Holy Spirit, Christ's presence and power are multiplied in all who believe.	Through God's Holy Spirit, we are drawn to him in faith. We must know the Holy Spirit to understand all Jesus taught. We can experience Jesus' love and guidance as we allow the Holy Spirit to do his work in us.

Resurrection	On the third day after he died, Jesus rose from the dead. This was verified by his disciples and many eyewitnesses. This reality changed the disciples from frightened deserters to dynamic leaders in the new church. This fact is the foundation of the Christian faith.	We can be changed as the disciples were and have confidence that our bodies will one day be raised to live with Christ forever. The same power that raised Christ to life can give us the ability to follow Christ each day.

A. BIRTH AND PREPARATION OF JESUS, THE SON OF GOD (1:1—2:11)

In this Gospel, John provides clear evidence that Jesus is the Son of God and that by believing in him we may have eternal life. John also provides unique material about Jesus' birth. He did not come into being when he was born, because he is eternal.

God Became a Human Being

(2)

1 In the beginning was the Word, and the Word was with God, and the Word was God.
2 He was in the beginning with God.
3 All things came into being through Him, and apart from Him nothing came into
being that has come into being.
4 In Him was life, and the life was the Light of men.
5 The Light shines in the darkness, and the darkness did not [1]comprehend it.
6 There [2]came a man sent from God, whose name was John.
7 He came as a witness, to testify about the Light, so that all might believe through
him.
8 He was not the Light, but *he came* to testify about the Light.
9 There was the true Light [3]which, coming into the world, enlightens every man.

1 Or *overpower* 2 Or *came into being* 3 Or *which enlightens every person coming into the world*

1:1 Gen 1:1; Col 1:17; 1 John 1:1; John 1:14; Rev 19:13; John 17:5; 1 John 1:2; Phil 2:6

1:3 John 1:10; 1 Cor 8:6; Col 1:16; Heb 1:2

1:4 John 5:26; 11:25; 14:6; John 8:12; 9:5; 12:46

1:5 John 3:19

1:6 Matt 3:1

1:7 John 1:15, 19, 32; 3:26; 5:33; John 1:12; Acts 19:4; Gal 3:26

1:9 1 John 2:8

1:1 What Jesus taught and what he did are tied inseparably to who he is. John shows Jesus as fully human and fully God. Although Jesus took upon himself full humanity and lived as a man, he never ceased to be the eternal God who has always existed, the Creator and Sustainer of all things, and the source of eternal life. This is the truth about Jesus, and the foundation of all truth. If we cannot or do not believe this basic truth, we will not have enough faith to trust our eternal destiny to him. That is why John wrote this Gospel—to build faith and confidence in Jesus Christ so that we may believe that he truly was and is the Son of God (20:30–31).

1:1 John wrote to believers everywhere, both Jews and non-Jews (Gentiles). As one of Jesus' 12 disciples, John was an eyewitness, so his story is accurate. His book is not a biography (like the book of Luke); it is a thematic presentation of Jesus' life. Many in John's original audience had a Greek background. Greek culture encouraged worship of many mythological gods, whose supernatural characteristics were as important to Greeks as genealogies were to Jews. John shows that Jesus is not only different from but superior to these gods of mythology.

1:1ff What does John mean by *the Word? The Word* was a term used by theologians and philosophers, both Jews and Greeks, in many different ways. In Hebrew Scripture, *the Word* was an agent of creation (Psalm 33:6), the source of God's message to his people through the prophets (Hosea 1:2), and God's law, his standard of holiness (Psalm 119:11). In Greek philosophy, *the Word* was the principle of reason that governed the world, or the thought still in the mind, while in Hebrew thought, *the Word* was another expression for God. John's description shows clearly that he is speaking of Jesus (see especially 1:14)—a human being he knew and loved, but at the same time the Creator of the universe, the ultimate revelation of God, the living picture of God's holiness, the One in whom "all things hold together" (Colossians 1:17). To Jewish readers, "the Word was God" was blasphemous. To Greek readers, "the Word became flesh" (1:14) was unthinkable. To John, this new understanding of the Word was gospel, the Good News of Jesus Christ.

1:3 When God created, he made something from nothing. Because we are created beings, we have no basis for pride. Remember that you exist only because God made you, and you have special gifts only because God gave them to you. With God you are something valuable and unique; apart from God you are nothing, and if you try to live without him, you will be abandoning the purpose for which you were made.

1:3–5 Do you ever feel that your life is too complex for God to understand? Remember, God created the entire universe, and nothing is too difficult for him. God created you; he is alive today, and his love is bigger than any problem you may face.

1:4–5 "The darkness did not comprehend it" means the darkness of evil never has and never will overcome or extinguish God's light. Jesus Christ is the Creator of life, and his life brings light to mankind. In his light, we see ourselves as we really are (sinners in need of a Savior). When we follow Jesus, the true Light, we can avoid walking blindly and falling into sin. He lights the path ahead of us so we can see how to live. He removes the darkness of sin from our lives. Have you allowed the light of Christ to shine into your life? Let Christ guide your life, and you'll never need to stumble in darkness.

1:6–8 In this book, the name *John* refers to John the Baptist. For more information on John the Baptist, see his Profile in this chapter.

1:8 We, like John the Baptist, are not the source of God's light; we merely reflect that light. Jesus Christ is the true Light; he helps us see our way to God and shows us how to walk along that way. But Christ has chosen to reflect his light through his followers to an unbelieving world, perhaps because unbelievers are not able to bear the full blazing glory of his light firsthand. The word *witness* indicates our role as reflectors of Christ's light. We are never to present ourselves as the light to others, but are always to point them to Christ, the Light.

1:10 1 Cor 8:6; Col 1:16; Heb 1:2

1:12 John 11:52; Gal 3:26; John 1:7; 3:18; 1 John 3:23; 5:13

1:13 John 3:5f; James 1:18; 1 Pet 1:23; 1 John 2:29; 3:9

10 He was in the world, and the world was made through Him, and the world did not
know Him.
11 He came to His [4]own, and those who were His own did not receive Him.
12 But as many as received Him, to them He gave the right to become children of God,
even to those who believe in His name,
13 who were born, not of blood nor of the will of the flesh nor of the will of man, but
of God.

4 Or *own things, possessions, domain*

JOHN THE BAPTIST

There's no getting around it—John the Baptist was unique. He wore odd clothes and ate strange food and preached an unusual message to the Judeans who went out to the wastelands to see him.

But John did not aim at uniqueness for its own sake. Instead, he aimed at obedience. He knew he had a specific role to play in the world—announcing the coming of the Savior—and he put all his energies into this task. Luke tells us that John was in the desert when God's word of direction came to him. John was ready and waiting. The angel who had announced John's birth to Zacharias had made it clear this child was to be a Nazirite—one set apart for God's service. John remained faithful to that calling.

This wild-looking man had no power or position in the Jewish political system, but he spoke with almost irresistible authority. People were moved by his words because he spoke the truth, challenging them to turn from their sins and baptizing them as a symbol of their repentance. They responded by the hundreds. But even as people crowded to him, he pointed beyond himself, never forgetting that his main role was to announce the coming of the Savior.

The words of truth that moved many to repentance goaded others to resistance and resentment. John even challenged Herod to admit his sin. Herodias, the woman Herod had married illegally, decided to get rid of this desert preacher. Although she was able to have him killed, she was not able to stop his message. The One John had announced was already on the move. John had accomplished his mission.

God has given each of us a purpose for living, and we can trust him to guide us. John did not have the complete Bible as we know it today, but he focused his life on the truth he knew from the available Old Testament Scriptures. Likewise we can discover in God's Word the truths he wants us to know. And as these truths work in us, others will be drawn to him. God can use you in a way he can use no one else. Let him know your willingness to follow him today.

Strengths and accomplishments:
- The God-appointed messenger to announce the arrival of Jesus
- A preacher whose theme was repentance
- A fearless confronter
- Known for his remarkable life-style
- Uncompromising

Lessons from his life:
- God does not guarantee an easy or safe life to those who serve him
- Doing what God desires is the greatest possible life investment
- Standing for the truth is more important than life itself

Vital statistics:
- Where: Judea
- Occupation: Prophet
- Relatives: Father: Zacharias. Mother: Elizabeth. Distant relative: Jesus
- Contemporaries: Herod, Herodias

Key verse:
"Truly I say to you, among those born of women there has not arisen anyone greater than John the Baptist! Yet the one who is least in the kingdom of heaven is greater than he" (Matthew 11:11).

John's story is told in all four Gospels. His coming was predicted in Isaiah 40:3 and Malachi 4:5; and he is mentioned in Acts 1:5, 22; 10:37; 11:16; 13:24–25; 18:25; 19:3–4.

1:10–11 Although Christ created the world, the people he created didn't recognize him (1:10). Even the people chosen by God to prepare the rest of the world for the Messiah rejected him (1:11), although the entire Old Testament pointed to his coming.

1:12–13 All who welcome Jesus Christ as Lord of their lives are reborn spiritually, receiving new life from God. Through faith in Christ, this new birth changes us from the inside out—rearranging our attitudes, desires, and motives. Being born makes you physically alive and places you in your parents' family (1:13). Being born of God makes you spiritually alive and puts you in God's family (1:12). Have you asked Christ to make you a new person? This fresh start in life is available to all who believe in Christ.

14 And the Word became flesh, and dwelt among us, and we saw His glory, glory as of
the only begotten from the Father, full of grace and truth.
15 John ☆testified about Him and cried out, saying, "This was He of whom I said, 'He
who comes after me has a higher rank than I, for He existed before me.' "
16 For of His fullness we have all received, and grace upon grace.
17 For the Law was given through Moses; grace and truth were realized through Jesus
Christ.
18 No one has seen God at any time; the only begotten God who is in the bosom of the
Father, He has explained *Him.*

John the Baptist Declares His Mission
(19)

19 This is the testimony of John, when the Jews sent to him priests and Levites from
Jerusalem to ask him, "Who are you?"
20 And he confessed and did not deny, but confessed, "I am not the Christ."
21 They asked him, "What then? Are you Elijah?" And he ☆said, "I am not." "Are you
the Prophet?" And he answered, "No."
22 Then they said to him, "Who are you, so that we may give an answer to those who
sent us? What do you say about yourself?"
23 He said, "I am A VOICE OF ONE CRYING IN THE WILDERNESS, 'MAKE STRAIGHT
THE WAY OF THE LORD,' as Isaiah the prophet said."
24 Now they had been sent from the Pharisees.
25 They asked him, and said to him, "Why then are you baptizing, if you are not the
Christ, nor Elijah, nor the Prophet?"
26 John answered them saying, "I baptize [5]in water, *but* among you stands One whom
you do not know.

5 The Gr here can be translated *in, with* or *by*

1:14
1 Tim 3:16; Heb 2:14; 1 John 1:1f; 4:2; 2 John 7; Rev 21:3; Luke 9:32; John 2:11; 17:22

1:15
John 1:7; Matt 3:11

1:16
Eph 1:23; 3:19; 4:13; Col 1:19; 2:9

1:17
Rom 5:21; 6:14; John 8:32; 14:6; 18:37

1:18
Col 1:15; 1 Tim 6:16; 1 John 4:12; John 3:16, 18; 1 John 4:9; Luke 16:22; John 13:23; John 3:11

1:20
Luke 3:15f

1:21
Matt 11:14; 16:14; 21:11; John 1:25

1:23
Is 40:3; Matt 3:3; Mark 1:3; Luke 3:4

1:25
Matt 21:11; John 1:21

1:26
Matt 3:11; Mark 1:8; Luke 3:16; Acts 1:5

1:14 "The Word became flesh" means becoming human. By doing so, Christ became (1) *the perfect teacher*—in Jesus' life we see how God thinks and therefore how we should think (Philippians 2:5–11); (2) *the perfect example*—as a model of what we are to become, he shows us how to live and gives us the power to live that way (1 Peter 2:21); (3) *the perfect sacrifice*—Jesus came as a sacrifice for all sins, and his death satisfied God's requirements for the removal of sin (Colossians 1:15–23).

1:14 "The only begotten from the Father" means Jesus is God's only and unique Son. The emphasis is on unique. Jesus is one of a kind and enjoys a relationship with God unlike all believers who are called "children" and said to be "born of God."

1:14 When Christ was born, God became a man. He was not part man and part God; he was completely human and completely divine (Colossians 2:9). Before Christ came, people could know God partially. After Christ came, people could know God fully because he became visible and tangible in Christ. Christ is the perfect expression of God in human form. The two most common errors people make about Jesus are to minimize his humanity or to minimize his divinity. Jesus is both God and man.

1:17 Law and grace are both aspects of God's nature that he uses in dealing with us. Moses emphasized God's law and justice, while Jesus Christ came to highlight God's mercy, love, and forgiveness. Moses could only be the giver of the law, while Christ came to fulfill the law (Matthew 5:17). The nature and will of God were revealed in the law; now the nature and will of God are revealed in Jesus Christ. Rather than coming through cold stone tablets, God's revelation ("truth") now comes through a person's life. As we get to know Christ better, our understanding of God will increase.

1:18 God communicated through various people in the Old Testament, usually prophets who were told to give specific messages. But no one ever *saw* God. "The only begotten God" is a title showing that Jesus is both God and the Father's unique Son. In Christ, God revealed his nature and essence in a way that could be seen and touched. In Christ, God became a man who lived on earth.

1:19 The priests and Levites were respected religious leaders in Jerusalem. Priests served in the temple, and Levites assisted them. The leaders that came to see John were Pharisees (1:24), a group that both John the Baptist and Jesus often denounced. Many of them outwardly obeyed God's laws to look pious, while inwardly their hearts were filled with pride and greed. The Pharisees believed that their own oral traditions were just as important as God's inspired Word. For more information on the Pharisees, see the charts in Matthew 3 and Mark 2.

These leaders came to see John the Baptist for several reasons: (1) Their duty as guardians of the faith caused them to want to investigate any new preaching (Deuteronomy 13:1–5; 18:20–22). (2) They wanted to find out if John had the credentials of a prophet. (3) John had quite a following, and it was growing. They were probably jealous and wanted to see why this man was so popular.

1:21–23 In the Pharisees' minds, there were four options regarding John the Baptist's identity: He was (1) the prophet foretold by Moses (Deuteronomy 18:15), (2) Elijah (Malachi 4:5), (3) the Messiah, or (4) a false prophet. John denied being the first three personages. Instead he called himself, in the words of the Old Testament prophet Isaiah, "a voice of one crying in the wilderness, 'Make straight the way of the LORD' " (see Isaiah 40:3). The leaders kept pressing John to say who he was because people were expecting the Messiah to come (Luke 3:15). But John emphasized only *why* he had come—to prepare the way for the Messiah. The Pharisees missed the point. They wanted to know who John was, but John wanted them to know who Jesus was.

1:25–26 John was baptizing Jews. The Essenes (a strict, monastic sect of Judaism) practiced baptism for purification, but normally only non-Jews (Gentiles) were baptized when they converted to Judaism. When the Pharisees questioned John's authority to baptize, they were asking who gave John the right to treat God's chosen people like Gentiles. John said, "I baptize in water"—he was merely helping the people perform a symbolic act of repentance. But soon One would come who would truly *forgive* sins, something only the Son of God—the Messiah—could do.

1:27 Matt 3:11; John 1:30; Mark 1:7; Luke 3:16
1:28 John 3:26; 10:40
1:29 Is 53:7; John 1:36; Acts 8:32; 1 Pet 1:19; Rev 5:6, 8, 12f; 6:1; Matt 1:21; 1 John 3:5
1:30 Matt 3:11; John 1:27; John 1:15
1:32 John 1:7; Matt 3:16; Mark 1:10; Luke 3:22
1:33 Matt 3:11; Mark 1:8; Luke 3:16; Acts 1:5
1:34 Matt 4:3; John 1:49
1:35 John 1:29
1:36 John 1:29
1:38 Matt 23:7f; John 1:49

27 "*It is* He who comes after me, the thong of whose sandal I am not worthy to untie."
28 These things took place in Bethany beyond the Jordan, where John was baptizing.

John the Baptist Proclaims Jesus as the Messiah
(20)

29 The next day he ☆saw Jesus coming to him and ☆said, "Behold, the Lamb of God
who takes away the sin of the world!
30 "This is He on behalf of whom I said, 'After me comes a Man who has a higher rank
than I, for He existed before me.'
31 "I did not recognize Him, but so that He might be manifested to Israel, I came baptizing [6]in water."
32 John testified saying, "I have seen the Spirit descending as a dove out of heaven,
and He remained upon Him.
33 "I did not recognize Him, but He who sent me to baptize [6]in water said to me, 'He
upon whom you see the Spirit descending and remaining upon Him, this is the One who
baptizes in the Holy Spirit.'
34 "I myself have seen, and have testified that this is the Son of God."

The First Disciples Follow Jesus
(21)

35 Again the next day John was standing with two of his disciples,
36 and he looked at Jesus as He walked, and ☆said, "Behold, the Lamb of God!"
37 The two disciples heard him speak, and they followed Jesus.
38 And Jesus turned and saw them following, and ☆said to them, "What do you seek?"
They said to Him, "Rabbi (which translated means Teacher), where are You staying?"
39 He ☆said to them, "Come, and you will see." So they came and saw where He was
staying; and they stayed with Him that day, for it was about the [7]tenth hour.

6 The Gr here can be translated *in, with* or *by* **7** Perhaps 10 a.m. (Roman time)

1:27 John the Baptist said he was not even worthy to be Christ's slave, to perform the humble task of untying his shoes. But according to Luke 7:28, Jesus said that John was the greatest of all prophets. If such a great person felt inadequate even to be Christ's slave, how much more should we lay aside our pride to serve Christ! When we truly understand who Christ is, our pride and self-importance melt away.

1:29 Every morning and evening, a lamb was sacrificed in the temple for the sins of the people (Exodus 29:38–42). Isaiah 53:7 prophesied that the Messiah, God's servant, would be led to the slaughter like a lamb. To pay the penalty for sin, a life had to be given—and God chose to provide the sacrifice himself. The sins of the world were removed when Jesus died as the perfect sacrifice. This is the way our sins are forgiven (1 Corinthians 5:7). The "sin of the world" means everyone's sin, the sin of each individual. Jesus paid the price of *your* sin by his death. You can receive forgiveness by confessing your sin to him and asking for his forgiveness.

1:30 Although John the Baptist was a well-known preacher who attracted large crowds, he was content for Jesus to take the higher place. This is true humility, the basis for greatness in preaching, teaching, or any other work we do for Christ. When you are content to do what God wants you to do and let Jesus Christ be honored for it, God will do great things through you.

1:31–34 At Jesus' baptism, John the Baptist had declared Jesus to be the Messiah. At that time God had given John a sign to show him that Jesus truly had been sent from God (1:33). John and Jesus were related (see Luke 1:36), so John probably knew who he was. But it wasn't until Jesus' baptism that John understood that Jesus was the Messiah. Jesus' baptism is described in Matthew 3:13–17; Mark 1:9–11; and Luke 3:21–22.

1:33 John the Baptist's baptism in water was preparatory, because it was for repentance and symbolized the washing away of sins. Jesus, by contrast, would baptize with the Holy Spirit. He would send the Holy Spirit upon all believers, empowering them to live and to teach the message of salvation. This outpouring of the Spirit came after Jesus had risen from the dead and ascended into heaven (see 20:22; Acts 2).

1:34 John the Baptist's job was to point people to Jesus, their long-awaited Messiah. Today people are looking for someone to give them security in an insecure world. Our job is to point them to Christ and to show that he is the one whom they seek.

1:35ff These new disciples used several names for Jesus: Lamb of God (1:36), Rabbi (1:38), Messiah (1:41), Son of God (1:49), and King of Israel (1:49). As they got to know Jesus, their appreciation for him grew. The more time we spend getting to know Christ, the more we will understand and appreciate who he is. We may be drawn to him for his teaching, but we will come to know him as the Son of God. Although these disciples made this verbal shift in a few days, they would not fully understand Jesus until three years later (Acts 2). What they so easily professed had to be worked out in experience. We may find that words of faith come easily, but deep appreciation for Christ comes with living by faith.

1:37 One of the two disciples was Andrew (1:40). The other was probably John, the writer of this book. Why did these disciples leave John the Baptist? Because that's what John wanted them to do—he was pointing the way to Jesus, the one John had prepared them to follow. These were Jesus' first disciples, along with Simon Peter (1:42) and Nathanael (1:45).

1:38 When the two disciples began to follow Jesus, he asked them, "What do you seek?" Following Christ is not enough; we must follow him for the right reasons. To follow Christ for our own purposes would be asking Christ to follow us—to align with us to support and advance our cause, not his. We must examine our motives for following him. Are we seeking his glory or ours?

40 One of the two who heard John *speak* and followed Him, was Andrew, Simon Peter's
brother.
41 He ☆found first his own brother Simon and ☆said to him, "We have found the Messiah" (which translated means Christ).
42 He brought him to Jesus. Jesus looked at him and said, "You are Simon the son of
John; you shall be called Cephas" (which is translated Peter).
43 The next day He purposed to go into Galilee, and He ☆found Philip. And Jesus ☆said
to him, "Follow Me."
44 Now Philip was from Bethsaida, of the city of Andrew and Peter.
45 Philip ☆found Nathanael and ☆said to him, "We have found Him of whom Moses in
the Law and *also* the Prophets wrote—Jesus of Nazareth, the son of Joseph."
46 Nathanael said to him, "Can any good thing come out of Nazareth?" Philip ☆said to
him, "Come and see."
47 Jesus saw Nathanael coming to Him, and ☆said of him, "Behold, an Israelite indeed,
in whom there is no deceit!"
48 Nathanael ☆said to Him, "How do You know me?" Jesus answered and said to him,
"Before Philip called you, when you were under the fig tree, I saw you."
49 Nathanael answered Him, "Rabbi, You are the Son of God; You are the King of
Israel."
50 Jesus answered and said to him, "Because I said to you that I saw you under the fig
tree, do you believe? You will see greater things than these."
51 And He ☆said to him, "Truly, truly, I say to you, you will see the heavens opened
and the angels of God ascending and descending on the Son of Man."

1:40 Matt 4:18-22; Mark 1:16-20; Luke 5:2-11

1:41 Dan 9:25; John 4:25

1:42 Matt 16:17; John 21:15-17; 1 Cor 1:12; 3:22; 9:5; 15:5; Gal 1:18; 2:9, 11

1:43 Matt 4:12; 8:22

1:44 Matt 10:3; John 6:5, 7; 12:21f; 14:8f; Matt 11:21

1:45 Luke 24:27; Matt 2:23; Luke 2:48; 3:23; 4:22; John 6:42

1:46 John 7:41, 52

1:47 Rom 9:4

1:49 Matt 2:2; 27:42; Mark 15:32; John 12:13

1:51 Matt 3:16; Luke 3:21; Acts 7:56; 10:11; Rev 19:11; Matt 8:20

Jesus Turns Water into Wine
(22)

2 On the third day there was a wedding in Cana of Galilee, and the mother of Jesus
was there;
2 and both Jesus and His disciples were invited to the wedding.
3 When the wine ran out, the mother of Jesus ☆said to Him, "They have no wine."

2:1 John 2:11; 4:46; 21:2; Matt 12:46

1:40–42 Andrew accepted John the Baptist's testimony about Jesus and immediately went to tell his brother, Simon, about him. There was no question in Andrew's mind that Jesus was the Messiah. Not only did he tell his brother, but he was also eager to introduce others to Jesus (see 6:8–9; 12:22).

1:42 Jesus saw not only who Simon was, but who he would become. That is why he gave him a new name—Cephas in Aramaic, Peter in Greek (the name means "a rock"). Peter is not presented as rock-solid throughout the Gospels, but he became a solid rock in the days of the early church, as we learn in the book of Acts. By giving Simon a new name, Jesus introduced a change in character. For more on Simon Peter, see his Profile in Matthew 26.

1:46 Nazareth was despised by the Jews because a Roman army garrison was located there. Some have speculated that an aloof attitude or a poor reputation in morals and religion on the part of the people of Nazareth led to Nathanael's harsh comment. Nathanael's hometown was Cana, about four miles from Nazareth.

1:46 When Nathanael heard that the Messiah was from Nazareth, he was surprised. Philip responded, "Come and see." Fortunately for Nathanael, he went to meet Jesus and became a disciple. If he had stuck to his prejudice without investigating further, he would have missed the Messiah! Don't let people's stereotypes about Christ cause them to miss his power and love. Invite them to come and see who Jesus really is.

1:47–49 Jesus knew about Nathanael before the two ever met. Jesus also knows what we are really like. An honest person will feel comfortable with the thought that Jesus knows him or her through and through. A dishonest person will feel uncomfortable. You can't pretend to be something you're not. God knows the real you and wants *you* to follow him.

1:51 This is a reference to Jacob's dream recorded in Genesis 28:12. As the unique God-man, Jesus would be the ladder between heaven and earth. Jesus is not saying that this would be a physical experience (that they would see the ladder with their eyes) like the transfiguration, but that they would have spiritual insight into Jesus' true nature and purpose for coming.

2:1–2 Jesus was on a mission to save the world, the greatest mission in the history of mankind. Yet he took time to attend a wedding and take part in its festivities. We may be tempted to think we should not take time out from our "important" work for social occasions. But maybe these social occasions are part of our mission. Jesus valued these wedding festivities because they involved people, and Jesus came to be with people. Our mission can often be accomplished in joyous times of celebration with others. Bring balance to your life by bringing Jesus into times of pleasure as well as times of work.

2:1–3 Weddings in Jesus' day were week-long festivals. Banquets would be prepared for many guests, and the week would be spent celebrating the new life of the married couple. Often the whole town was invited, and everybody would come—it was considered an insult to refuse an invitation to a wedding. To accommodate many people, careful planning was needed. To run out of wine was more than embarrassing; it broke the strong unwritten laws of hospitality. Jesus was about to respond to a heartfelt need.

2:4 John 19:26; Matt 8:29; John 7:6, 8, 30; 8:20

2:5 Matt 12:46

2:6 Mark 7:3f; John 3:25

2:9 John 4:46

2:10 Matt 24:49; Luke 12:45; Acts 2:15; 1 Cor 11:21; Eph 5:18; 1 Thess 5:7; Rev 17:2, 6

2:11 John 2:23; 3:2; 4:54; 6:2, 14, 26, 30; 7:31; 9:16; 10:41; 11:47; 12:18, 37; 20:30; John 1:43; John 1:14

2:12 Matt 4:13; Matt 12:46; John 2:2

4 And Jesus ☆said to her, "Woman, what does that have to do with us? My hour has
not yet come."
5 His mother ☆said to the servants, "Whatever He says to you, do it."
6 Now there were six stone waterpots set there for the Jewish custom of purification,
containing twenty or thirty gallons each.
7 Jesus ☆said to them, "Fill the waterpots with water." So they filled them up to the
brim.
8 And He ☆said to them, "Draw *some* out now and take it to the [8]headwaiter." So
they took it *to him.*
9 When the headwaiter tasted the water which had become wine, and did not know
where it came from (but the servants who had drawn the water knew), the headwaiter
☆called the bridegroom,
10 and ☆said to him, "Every man serves the good wine first, and when *the people* have
drunk freely, *then he serves* the poorer *wine; but* you have kept the good wine until now."
11 This beginning of *His* signs Jesus did in Cana of Galilee, and manifested His glory,
and His disciples believed in Him.
12 After this He went down to Capernaum, He and His mother and *His* brothers and
His disciples; and they stayed there a few days.

8 Or *steward*

JESUS' FIRST TRAVELS
After his baptism by John in the Jordan River and the temptation by Satan in the wilderness (see the map in Mark 1), Jesus returned to Galilee. He visited Nazareth, Cana, and Capernaum, and then returned to Jerusalem for the Passover.

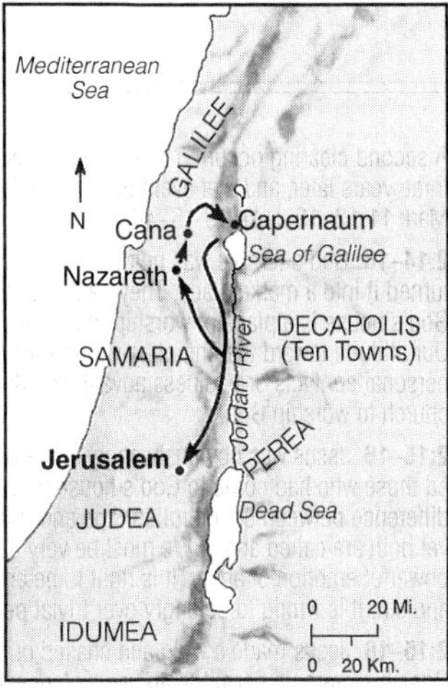

2:4 Mary was probably not asking Jesus to do a miracle; she was simply hoping that her son would help solve this major problem and find some wine. Tradition says that Joseph, Mary's husband, was dead, so she probably was used to asking for her son's help in certain situations. Jesus' answer to Mary is difficult to understand, but maybe that is the point. Although Mary did not understand what Jesus was going to do, she trusted him to do what was right. Those who believe in Jesus but run into situations they cannot understand must continue to trust that he will work in the best way.

2:5 Mary submitted to Jesus' way of doing things. She recognized that Jesus was more than her human son—he was the Son of God. When we bring our problems to Christ, we may think we know how he should take care of them. But he may have a completely different plan. Like Mary, we should submit and allow him to deal with the problem as he sees best.

2:6 The six stone waterpots were normally used for ceremonial washing. When full, the pots would hold 20 to 30 gallons. According to the Jews' ceremonial law, people became symbolically unclean by touching objects of everyday life. Before eating, the Jews would pour water over their hands to cleanse themselves of any bad influences associated with what they had touched.

2:10 People look everywhere but to God for excitement and meaning. For some reason, they expect God to be dull and lifeless. Just as the wine Jesus made was the best, so life in him is better than life on our own. Why wait until everything else runs out before trying God? Why save the best until last?

2:11 When the disciples saw Jesus' miracle, they believed. The miracle showed his power over nature and revealed the way he would go about his ministry—helping others, speaking with authority, and being in personal touch with people.

2:11 Miracles are not merely superhuman events, but events that demonstrate God's power. Almost every miracle Jesus did was a renewal of fallen creation—restoring sight, making the lame walk, even restoring life to the dead. Believe in Christ not because he is a superman but because he is the God who continues his creation, even in those of us who are poor, weak, crippled, orphaned, blind, deaf, or with some other desperate need for re-creation.

2:12 Capernaum became Jesus' home base during his ministry in Galilee. Located on a major trade route, it was an important city in the region, with a Roman garrison and a customs station. At Capernaum, Matthew was called to be a disciple (Matthew 9:9). The city was also the home of several other disciples (Matthew 4:13–19) and a royal official (4:46). It had at least one major synagogue. Although Jesus made this city his base of operations in Galilee, he condemned it for the people's unbelief (Matthew 11:23; Luke 10:15).

B. MESSAGE AND MINISTRY OF JESUS, THE SON OF GOD (2:12—12:50)

John stresses the deity of Christ. He gives us seven miracles that serve as signs that Jesus is the Messiah. In this section he records Jesus describing himself as the bread of life, the water of life, the light of the world, the door, and the good shepherd. John provides teachings of Jesus found nowhere else. This is the most theological of the four Gospels.

1. Jesus encounters belief and unbelief from the people

Jesus Clears the Temple

(23)

13 The Passover of the Jews was near, and Jesus went up to Jerusalem.
14 And He found in the temple those who were selling oxen and sheep and doves, and
the money changers seated *at their tables*.
15 And He made a scourge of cords, and drove *them* all out of the temple, with the
sheep and the oxen; and He poured out the coins of the money changers and overturned
their tables;
16 and to those who were selling the doves He said, "Take these things away; stop
making My Father's house a place of business."
17 His disciples remembered that it was written, "ZEAL FOR YOUR HOUSE WILL CON-
SUME ME."
18 The Jews then said to Him, "What sign do You show us as your authority for doing
these things?"
19 Jesus answered them, "Destroy this temple, and in three days I will raise it up."
20 The Jews then said, "It took forty-six years to build this temple, and will You raise
it up in three days?"
21 But He was speaking of the temple of His body.

2:13 Deut 16:1-6; John 5:1; 6:4; 11:55; Luke 2:41; John 2:23

2:14 John 2:14-16; Matt 21:12ff; Mark 11:15, 17; Luke 19:45f; Mal 3:1ff

2:16 Matt 21:12; Luke 2:49

2:17 John 2:2; Ps 69:9

2:18 John 1:19; Matt 12:38

2:19 Matt 26:61; 27:40; Mark 14:58; 15:29; Acts 6:14

2:20 John 1:19; Ezra 5:16

2:21 1 Cor 6:19

2:13 The Passover celebration took place yearly at the temple in Jerusalem. Every Jewish male was expected to make a pilgrimage to Jerusalem during this time (Deuteronomy 16:16). This was a week-long festival—the Passover was one day, and the Feast of Unleavened Bread lasted the rest of the week. The entire week commemorated the freeing of the Jews from slavery in Egypt (Exodus 12:1–13).

2:13 Jerusalem was both the religious and the political seat of Palestine, and the place where the Messiah was expected to arrive. The temple was located there, and many Jewish families from all over the world would travel to Jerusalem during the key feasts. The temple was on an imposing site, a hill overlooking the city. Solomon had built the first temple on this same site almost 1,000 years earlier (949 B.C.), but his temple had been destroyed by the Babylonians (2 Kings 25). The temple was rebuilt in 515 B.C., and Herod the Great had enlarged and remodeled it.

2:14 The temple area was always crowded during Passover with thousands of out-of-town visitors. The religious leaders crowded it even further by allowing money changers and merchants to set up booths in the court of the Gentiles. They rationalized this practice as a convenience for the worshipers and as a way to make money for temple upkeep. But the religious leaders did not seem to care that the court of the Gentiles was so full of merchants that foreigners found it difficult to worship. And worship was the main purpose for visiting the temple. No wonder Jesus was angry!

2:14 The temple tax had to be paid in local currency, so foreigners had to have their money changed. But the money changers often would charge exorbitant exchange rates. The people also were required to make sacrifices for sins. Because of the long journey, many could not bring their own animals. Some who brought animals would have them rejected for imperfections. So animal merchants would do a flourishing business in the temple courtyard. The price of sacrificial animals was much higher in the temple area than elsewhere. Jesus was angry at the dishonest, greedy practices of the money changers and merchants, and he particularly disliked their presence on the temple grounds. They were making a mockery of God's house of worship.

2:14ff John records this first clearing, or cleansing, of the temple. A second clearing occurred at the end of Jesus' ministry, about three years later, and that event is recorded in Matthew 21:12–17; Mark 11:12–19; Luke 19:45–48.

2:14–16 God's temple was being misused by people who had turned it into a marketplace. They had forgotten, or didn't care, that God's house is a place of worship, not a place for making a profit. Our attitude toward the church is wrong if we see it as a place for personal contacts or business advantage. Make sure you attend church to worship God.

2:15–16 Jesus was obviously angry at the merchants who exploited those who had come to God's house to worship. There is a difference between uncontrolled rage and righteous indignation—yet both are called anger. We must be very careful how we use the powerful emotion of anger. It is right to be angry about injustice and sin; it is wrong to be angry over trivial personal offenses.

2:15–16 Jesus made a whip and chased out the money changers. Does his example permit us to use violence against wrongdoers? Certain authority is granted to some, but not to all. For example, the authority to use weapons and restrain people is granted to police officers, but not to the general public. The authority to imprison people is granted to judges, but not to individual citizens. Jesus had God's authority, something we cannot have. While we want to live like Christ, we should never try to claim his authority where it has not been given to us.

2:17 Jesus took the evil acts in the temple as an insult against God, and thus he did not deal with them halfheartedly. He was consumed with righteous anger against such flagrant disrespect for God.

2:19–20 The Jews understood Jesus to mean the temple out of which he had just driven the merchants and money changers. This was the temple Zerubbabel had built over 500 years earlier, but Herod the Great had begun remodeling it, making it much larger and far more beautiful. It had been 46 years since this remodeling had started (20 B.C.), and it still wasn't completely finished. They understood Jesus' words to mean that this imposing building could be torn down and rebuilt in three days, and they were startled.

2:21–22 Jesus was not talking about the temple made of stones, but about his body. His listeners didn't realize it, but Jesus was

2:22 Ps 16:10; Luke 24:26f; John 20:9; Acts 13:33
2:24 Acts 1:24; 15:8
2:25 Matt 9:4; John 1:42, 47; 6:61, 64; 13:11
3:1 John 7:50; 19:39; Luke 23:13
3:2 Matt 23:7; John 3:26; John 2:11; John 9:33; 10:38; 14:10f; Acts 2:22; 10:38
3:3 2 Cor 5:17; 1 Pet 1:23; Matt 19:24; 21:31; Mark 9:47; 10:14f; John 3:5
3:5 Matt 19:24; 21:31; Mark 9:47; 10:14f; John 3:3

22 So when He was raised from the dead, His disciples remembered that He said this;
and they believed the Scripture and the word which Jesus had spoken.
23 Now when He was in Jerusalem at the Passover, during the feast, many believed in
His name, observing His signs which He was doing.
24 But Jesus, on His part, was not entrusting Himself to them, for He knew all men,
25 and because He did not need anyone to testify concerning man, for He Himself knew
what was in man.

Nicodemus Visits Jesus at Night
(24)

3 Now there was a man of the Pharisees, named Nicodemus, a ruler of the Jews;
2 this man came to Jesus by night and said to Him, "Rabbi, we know that You have
come from God *as* a teacher; for no one can do these signs that You do unless God is
with him."
3 Jesus answered and said to him, "Truly, truly, I say to you, unless one is born again
he cannot see the kingdom of God."
4 Nicodemus ☆said to Him, "How can a man be born when he is old? He cannot enter
a second time into his mother's womb and be born, can he?"
5 Jesus answered, "Truly, truly, I say to you, unless one is born of water and the Spirit
he cannot enter into the kingdom of God.

---

greater than the temple (Matthew 12:6). His words would take on meaning for his disciples after his resurrection. That Christ so perfectly fulfilled this prediction became the strongest proof for his claims to be God.

2:23–25 The Son of God knows all about human nature. Jesus was well aware of the truth of Jeremiah 17:9, which states, "The heart is more deceitful than all else and is desperately sick; who can understand it?" Jesus was discerning, and he knew that the faith of some followers was superficial. Some of the same people claiming to believe in Jesus at this time would later yell "Crucify him!" It's easy to believe when it is exciting and everyone else believes the same way. But keep your faith firm even when it isn't popular to follow Christ.

3:1 Nicodemus was a Pharisee and a member of the ruling Council (called the Sanhedrin). The Pharisees were a group of religious leaders whom Jesus and John the Baptist often criticized for being hypocrites (see the note on Matthew 3:7 for more on the Pharisees). Most Pharisees were intensely jealous of Jesus because he undermined their authority and challenged their views. But Nicodemus was searching, and he believed that Jesus had some answers. A learned teacher himself, he came to Jesus to be taught. No matter how intelligent and well educated you are, you must come to Jesus with an open mind and heart so he can teach you the truth about God.

3:1ff Nicodemus came to Jesus personally, although he could have sent one of his assistants. He wanted to examine Jesus for himself to separate fact from rumor. Perhaps Nicodemus was afraid of what his peers, the Pharisees, would say about his visit, so he came after dark. Later, when he understood that Jesus was truly the Messiah, he spoke up boldly in his defense (7:50–51). Like Nicodemus, we must examine Jesus for ourselves—others cannot do it for us. Then, if we believe he is who he says, we will want to speak up for him.

3:3 What did Nicodemus know about the kingdom? From the Bible he knew it would be ruled by God, it would be restored on earth, and it would incorporate God's people. Jesus revealed to this devout Pharisee that the kingdom would come to the whole world (3:16), not just the Jews, and that Nicodemus wouldn't be a part of it unless he was personally born again (3:5). This was a revolutionary concept: The kingdom is personal, not national or ethnic, and its entrance requirements are repentance and spiritual rebirth. Jesus later taught that God's kingdom has *already begun* in the hearts of believers (Luke 17:21). It will be fully realized when Jesus

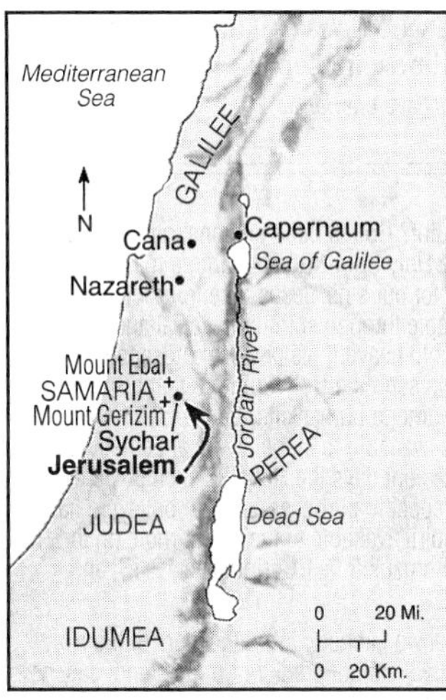

THE VISIT IN SAMARIA
Jesus went to Jerusalem for the Passover, cleared the temple, and talked with Nicodemus, a religious leader, about eternal life. He then left Jerusalem and traveled in Judea. On his way to Galilee, he visited Sychar and other villages in Samaria. Unlike most Jews of the day, he did not try to avoid the region of Samaria.

returns again to judge the world and abolish evil forever (Revelation 21; 22).

3:5–6 "Of water and the Spirit" could refer to (1) the contrast between physical birth (water) and spiritual birth (Spirit), or (2) being regenerated by the Spirit and signifying that rebirth by Christian baptism. The water may also represent the cleansing action of God's Holy Spirit (Titus 3:5). Nicodemus undoubtedly would have been familiar with God's promise in Ezekiel 36:25–26. Jesus was explaining the importance of a spiritual rebirth, saying that people don't enter the kingdom by living a better life, but by being spiritually reborn.

6 "That which is born of the flesh is flesh, and that which is born of the Spirit is spirit.
7 "Do not be amazed that I said to you, 'You must be born again.'
8 "The wind blows where it wishes and you hear the sound of it, but do not know where
it comes from and where it is going; so is everyone who is born of the Spirit."
9 Nicodemus said to Him, "How can these things be?"
10 Jesus answered and said to him, "Are you the teacher of Israel and do not understand these things?
11 "Truly, truly, I say to you, we speak of what we know and testify of what we have seen,
and you do not accept our testimony.
12 "If I told you earthly things and you do not believe, how will you believe if I tell you
heavenly things?
13 "No one has ascended into heaven, but He who descended from heaven: the Son
of Man.
14 "As Moses lifted up the serpent in the wilderness, even so must the Son of Man be
lifted up;
15 so that whoever [9]believes will in Him have eternal life.
16 "For God so loved the world, that He gave His only begotten Son, that whoever believes in Him shall not perish, but have eternal life.
17 "For God did not send the Son into the world to judge the world, but that the world
might be saved through Him.
18 "He who believes in Him is not judged; he who does not believe has been judged
already, because he has not believed in the name of the only begotten Son of God.
19 "This is the judgment, that the Light has come into the world, and men loved the
darkness rather than the Light, for their deeds were evil.
20 "For everyone who does evil hates the Light, and does not come to the Light for fear
that his deeds will be exposed.

9 Or *believes in Him will have eternal life*

3:10 Luke 2:46; 5:17

3:11 John 1:18; 7:16f; 8:26, 28; 12:49

3:13 Acts 2:34; Rom 10:6; Eph 4:9; John 6:38, 42; Matt 8:20

3:14 Num 21:9; Matt 8:20; John 8:28

3:15 John 20:31; 1 John 5:11-13

3:16 Rom 5:8; Eph 2:4; 2 Thess 2:16; Rom 8:32; 1 John 4:9

3:17 Luke 19:10; John 8:15; 12:47; 1 John 4:14

3:18 Mark 16:16; John 5:24; John 1:18; 1 John 4:9

3:19 John 1:4; 8:12; 9:5; 12:46; John 7:7

3:20 John 3:20, 21; Eph 5:11, 13

3:6 Who is the Holy Spirit? God is three persons in one—the Father, the Son, and the Holy Spirit. God became a man in Jesus so that Jesus could die for our sins. Jesus rose from the dead to offer salvation to all people through spiritual renewal and rebirth. When Jesus ascended into heaven, his physical presence left the earth, but he promised to send the Holy Spirit so that his spiritual presence would still be among humankind (see Luke 24:49). The Holy Spirit first became available to all believers at Pentecost (Acts 2). Whereas in Old Testament days the Holy Spirit empowered specific individuals for specific purposes, now all believers have the power of the Holy Spirit available to them. For more on the Holy Spirit, read 14:16–28; Romans 8:9; 1 Corinthians 12:13; and 2 Corinthians 1:22.

3:8 Jesus explained that we cannot control the work of the Holy Spirit. He works in ways we cannot predict or understand. Just as you did not control your physical birth, so you cannot control your spiritual birth. It is a gift from God through the Holy Spirit (Romans 8:16; 1 Corinthians 2:10–12; 1 Thessalonians 1:5–6).

3:10–11 This Jewish teacher of the Bible knew the Old Testament thoroughly, but he didn't understand what it said about the Messiah. Knowledge is not salvation. You should know the Bible, but even more important, you should understand the God whom the Bible reveals and the salvation that God offers.

3:14–15 When the Israelites were wandering in the wilderness, God sent a plague of serpents to punish the people for their rebellious attitudes. Those doomed to die from snakebite could be healed by obeying God's command to look up at the elevated bronze serpent and by believing that God would heal them if they did (see Numbers 21:8–9). Similarly, our salvation happens when we look up to Jesus, believing he will save us. God has provided this way for us to be healed of sin's deadly bite.

3:16 The entire gospel comes to a focus in this verse. God's love is not static or self-centered; it reaches out and draws others in. Here God sets the pattern of true love, the basis for all love relationships—when you love someone dearly, you are willing to give freely to the point of self-sacrifice. God paid dearly with the life of his Son, the highest price he could pay. Jesus accepted our punishment, paid the price for our sins, and then offered us the new life that he had bought for us. When we share the gospel with others, our love must be like Jesus'—willingly giving up our own comfort and security so that others might join us in receiving God's love.

3:16 Some people are repulsed by the idea of eternal life because their lives are miserable. But eternal life is not an extension of a person's miserable, mortal life; eternal life is God's life embodied in Christ given to all believers now as a guarantee that they will live forever. In eternal life there is no death, sickness, enemy, evil, or sin. When we don't know Christ, we make choices as though this life is all we have. In reality, this life is just the introduction to eternity. Receive this new life by faith and begin to evaluate all that happens from an eternal perspective.

3:16 To "believe" is more than intellectual agreement that Jesus is God. It means to put our trust and confidence in him that he alone can save us. It is to put Christ in charge of our present plans and eternal destiny. Believing is both trusting his words as reliable, and relying on him for the power to change. If you have never trusted Christ, let this promise of everlasting life be yours—and believe.

3:18 People often try to protect themselves from their fears by putting their faith in something they do or have: good deeds, skill or intelligence, money or possessions. But only God can save us from the one thing that we really need to fear—eternal condemnation. We believe in God by recognizing the insufficiency of our own efforts to find salvation and by asking him to do his work in us. When Jesus talks about unbelievers, he means those who reject or ignore him completely, not those who have momentary doubts.

3:19–21 Many people don't want their lives exposed to God's light because they are afraid of what will be revealed. They don't want to be changed. Don't be surprised when these same people are threatened by your desire to obey God and do what is right, because they are afraid that the light in you may expose some of the darkness in their lives. Rather than giving in to discouragement, keep praying that they will come to see how much better it is to live in light than in darkness.

3:21 1 John 1:6

21 "But he who practices the truth comes to the Light, so that his deeds may be manifested as having been wrought in God."

John the Baptist Tells More about Jesus
(25)

3:22 John 2:2; John 4:1, 2

3:24 Matt 4:12; 14:3; Mark 6:17; Luke 3:20

3:25 John 2:6

3:26 Matt 23:7; John 3:2; John 1:28; John 1:7

22 After these things Jesus and His disciples came into the land of Judea, and there
He was spending time with them and baptizing.
23 John also was baptizing in Aenon near Salim, because there was much water there;
and *people* were coming and were being baptized—
24 for John had not yet been thrown into prison.
25 Therefore there arose a discussion on the part of John's disciples with a Jew about
purification.
26 And they came to John and said to him, "Rabbi, He who was with you beyond the
Jordan, to whom you have testified, behold, He is baptizing and all are coming to Him."

NICODEMUS

God specializes in finding and changing people we consider out of reach. It took awhile for Nicodemus to come out of the dark, but God was patient with this "undercover" believer.

Afraid of being discovered, Nicodemus made an appointment to see Jesus at night. Daylight conversations between Pharisees and Jesus tended to be antagonistic, but Nicodemus really wanted to learn. He probably got a lot more than he expected—a challenge to a new life! We know very little about Nicodemus, but we know that he left that evening's encounter a changed man. He came away with a whole new understanding of both God and himself.

Nicodemus next appears as part of the Jewish Council. As the group discussed ways to eliminate Jesus, Nicodemus raised the question of justice. Although his objection was overruled, he had spoken up. He had begun to change.

Our last picture of Nicodemus shows him joining Joseph of Arimathea in asking for Jesus' body in order to provide for its burial. Realizing what he was risking, Nicodemus was making a bold move. He was continuing to grow.

God looks for steady growth, not instant perfection. How well does your present level of spiritual growth match up with how long you have known Jesus?

Strengths and accomplishments:
- One of the few religious leaders who believed in Jesus
- A member of the powerful Jewish Council
- A Pharisee who was attracted by Jesus' character and miracles
- Joined with Joseph of Arimathea in burying Jesus

Weakness and mistake:
- Limited by his fear of being publicly exposed as Jesus' follower

Lessons from his life:
- Unless we are born again, we can never be part of the kingdom of God
- God is able to change those we might consider unreachable
- God is patient, but persistent
- If we are available, God can use us

Vital statistics:
- Where: Jerusalem
- Occupation: Religious leader
- Contemporaries: Jesus, Annas, Caiaphas, Pilate, Joseph of Arimathea

Key verse:
"Nicodemus said to Him, 'How can a man be born when he is old? He cannot enter a second time into his mother's womb and be born, can he?' " (John 3:4).

Nicodemus's story is told in John 3:1–21; 7:50–52; and 19:39–40.

3:25ff Some people look for points of disagreement so they can sow seeds of discord, discontent, and doubt. John the Baptist ended this theological argument by focusing on his devotion to Christ. It is divisive to try to force others to believe our way. Instead, let's witness about what Christ has done for us. How can anyone argue with us about that?

3:26 John the Baptist's disciples were disturbed because people were following Jesus instead of John. It is easy to grow jealous of the popularity of another person's ministry. But we must remember that our true mission is to influence people to follow Christ, not us.

27 John answered and said, "A man can receive nothing unless it has been given him
from heaven.
28 "You yourselves are my witnesses that I said, 'I am not the Christ,' but, 'I have been
sent ahead of Him.'
29 "He who has the bride is the bridegroom; but the friend of the bridegroom, who stands
and hears him, rejoices greatly because of the bridegroom's voice. So this joy of mine
has been made full.
30 "He must increase, but I must decrease.
31 "He who comes from above is above all, he who is of the earth is from the earth and
speaks of the earth. He who comes from heaven is above all.
32 "What He has seen and heard, of that He testifies; and no one receives His testimony.
33 "He who has received His testimony has set his seal to *this,* that God is true.
34 "For He whom God has sent speaks the words of God; for He gives the Spirit without measure.
35 "The Father loves the Son and has given all things into His hand.
36 "He who believes in the Son has eternal life; but he who does not obey the Son will
not see life, but the wrath of God abides on him."

Jesus Talks to a Woman at the Well
(27)

4 Therefore when the Lord knew that the Pharisees had heard that Jesus was making
and baptizing more disciples than John
2 (although Jesus Himself was not baptizing, but His disciples were),
3 He left Judea and went away again into Galilee.
4 And He had to pass through Samaria.
5 So He ☆came to a city of Samaria called Sychar, near the parcel of ground that Jacob gave to his son Joseph;
6 and Jacob's well was there. So Jesus, being wearied from His journey, was sitting
thus by the well. It was about [10]the sixth hour.

10 Perhaps 6 p.m. Roman time or noon Jewish time

3:27 1 Cor 4:7; Heb 5:4; James 1:17

3:28 John 1:20, 23

3:29 Matt 9:15; 25:1; John 15:11; 16:24; 17:13; Phil 2:2; 1 John 1:4; 2 John 12

3:31 Matt 28:18; John 3:13; 8:23; 1 Cor 15:47; 1 John 4:5

3:33 John 6:27; Rom 4:11; 15:28; 1 Cor 9:2; 2 Cor 1:22; Eph 1:13; 4:30; 2 Tim 2:19; Rev 7:3-8

3:34 Matt 12:18; Luke 4:18; Acts 1:2; 10:38

3:35 Matt 28:18; John 5:20; 17:2; Matt 11:27; Luke 10:22

3:36 Acts 14:2; Heb 3:18

4:1 Luke 7:13; 1 Cor 1:17

4:5 Luke 9:52; Gen 33:19; Josh 24:32; Gen 48:22; John 4:12

3:27 Why did John the Baptist continue to baptize after Jesus came onto the scene? Why didn't he become a disciple too? John explained that because God had given him his work, he had to continue it until God called him to do something else. John's main purpose was to point people to Christ. Even with Jesus beginning his own ministry, John could still turn people to Jesus.

3:30 John's willingness to decrease in importance shows unusual humility. Pastors and other Christian leaders can be tempted to focus more on the success of their ministries than on Christ. Beware of those who put more emphasis on their own achievements than on God's kingdom.

3:31–35 Jesus' testimony was trustworthy because he had come from heaven and was speaking of what he had seen there. His words were the very words of God. Your whole spiritual life depends on your answer to one question, "Who is Jesus Christ?" If you accept Jesus as only a prophet or teacher, you have to reject his teaching, for he claimed to be God's Son, even God himself. The heartbeat of John's Gospel is the dynamic truth that Jesus Christ is God's Son, the Messiah, the Savior, who was from the beginning and will continue to live forever. This same Jesus has invited us to accept him and live with him eternally. When we understand who Jesus is, we are compelled to believe what he said.

3:34 God's Spirit was upon Jesus without limit or measure. Thus Jesus was the highest revelation of God to humanity (Hebrews 1:2).

3:36 Jesus says that whoever believes in him *has* (not *will have*) eternal life. To receive eternal life is to join in God's life, which by nature is eternal. Thus, eternal life begins at the moment of spiritual rebirth.

3:36 John, the author of this Gospel, has been demonstrating that Jesus is the true Son of God. Jesus sets before us the greatest choice in life. We are responsible to decide today whom we will obey (Joshua 24:15), and God wants us to choose him and life (Deuteronomy 30:15–20). The wrath of God is God's final judgment and rejection of the sinner. To put off the choice is to choose not to follow Christ. Indecision is a fatal decision.

4:1–3 Already opposition was rising against Jesus, especially from the Pharisees. They resented Jesus' popularity as well as his message, which challenged much of their teachings. Because Jesus was just beginning his ministry, it wasn't yet time to confront these leaders openly; so he left Jerusalem and traveled north toward Galilee.

4:4 After the northern kingdom, with its capital at Samaria, fell to the Assyrians, many Jews were deported to Assyria, and foreigners were brought in to settle the land and help keep the peace (2 Kings 17:24). The intermarriage between those foreigners and the remaining Jews resulted in a mixed race, impure in the opinion of Jews who lived in the southern kingdom. Thus the pure Jews hated this mixed race called Samaritans because they felt that their fellow Jews who had intermarried had betrayed their people and nation. The Samaritans had set up an alternate center for worship on Mount Gerizim (4:20) to parallel the temple at Jerusalem, but it had been destroyed 150 years earlier. The Jews did everything they could to avoid traveling through Samaria. But Jesus had no reason to live by such cultural restrictions. The route through Samaria was shorter, and that was the route he took.

4:5–7 Jacob's well was on the property originally owned by Jacob (Genesis 33:18–19). It was not a spring-fed well, but a well into which water seeped from rain and dew, collecting at the bottom. Wells were almost always located outside the city along the main road. Twice each day, morning and evening, women came to draw water. This woman came at about the sixth hour (meaning at noon), however, probably to avoid meeting people who knew her reputation. Jesus gave this woman an extraordinary message about fresh and pure water that would quench her spiritual thirst forever.

7 There ☆came a woman of Samaria to draw water. Jesus ☆said to her, "Give Me a
drink."
8 For His disciples had gone away into the city to buy food.
9 Therefore the Samaritan woman ☆said to Him, "How is it that You, being a Jew,
ask me for a drink since I am a Samaritan woman?" (For Jews have no dealings with
Samaritans.)
10 Jesus answered and said to her, "If you knew the gift of God, and who it is who says
to you, 'Give Me a drink,' you would have asked Him, and He would have given you
living water."
11 She ☆said to Him, "Sir, You have nothing to draw with and the well is deep; where
then do You get that living water?
12 "You are not greater than our father Jacob, are You, who gave us the well, and drank
of it himself and his sons and his cattle?"
13 Jesus answered and said to her, "Everyone who drinks of this water will thirst again;
14 but whoever drinks of the water that I will give him shall never thirst; but the water
that I will give him will become in him a well of water springing up to eternal life."
15 The woman ☆said to Him, "Sir, give me this water, so I will not be thirsty nor come
all the way here to draw."
16 He ☆said to her, "Go, call your husband and come here."
17 The woman answered and said, "I have no husband." Jesus ☆said to her, "You have
correctly said, 'I have no husband';
18 for you have had five husbands, and the one whom you now have is not your husband; this you have said truly."
19 The woman ☆said to Him, "Sir, I perceive that You are a prophet.
20 "Our fathers worshiped in this mountain, and you *people* say that in Jerusalem is the
place where men ought to worship."
21 Jesus ☆said to her, "Woman, believe Me, an hour is coming when neither in this
mountain nor in Jerusalem will you worship the Father.
22 "You worship what you do not know; we worship what we know, for salvation is from
the Jews.

4:9 Luke 9:52; Ezra 4:3-6, 11ff; Matt 10:5; John 8:48; Acts 10:28

4:10 Jer 2:13; John 4:14; 7:37f; Rev 7:17; 21:6; 22:1, 17

4:11 Jer 2:13; John 4:14; 7:37f; Rev 7:17; 21:6; 22:1, 17

4:12 John 4:6

4:14 John 6:35; 7:38; Matt 25:46; John 6:27

4:15 John 6:35

4:19 Matt 21:11; Luke 7:16, 39; 24:19; John 6:14; 7:40; 9:17

4:20 Gen 33:20; John 4:12; Deut 11:29; Josh 8:33; Luke 9:53

4:21 John 4:23; 5:25, 28; 16:2, 32; Mal 1:11; 1 Tim 2:8

4:22 2 Kin 17:28-41; Is 2:3; Rom 3:1f; 9:4f

4:7–9 This woman (1) was a Samaritan, a member of the hated mixed race, (2) was known to be living in sin, and (3) was in a public place. No respectable Jewish man would talk to a woman under such circumstances. But Jesus did. The gospel is for every person, no matter what his or her race, social position, or past sins. We must be prepared to share this gospel at any time and in any place. Jesus crossed all barriers to share the gospel, and we who follow him must do no less.

4:10 What did Jesus mean by "living water?" In the Old Testament, many verses speak of thirsting after God as one thirsts for water (Psalm 42:1; Isaiah 55:1; Jeremiah 2:13; Zechariah 13:1). God is called the fountain of life (Psalm 36:9) and the fountain of living water (Jeremiah 17:13). In saying he would bring living water that could forever quench a person's thirst for God, Jesus was claiming to be the Messiah. Only the Messiah could give this gift that satisfies the soul's desire.

4:13–15 Many spiritual functions parallel physical functions. As our bodies hunger and thirst, so do our souls. But our souls need *spiritual* food and water. The woman confused the two kinds of water, perhaps because no one had ever talked with her about her spiritual hunger and thirst before. We would not think of depriving our bodies of food and water when they hunger or thirst. Why then should we deprive our souls? The living Word, Jesus Christ, and the written Word, the Bible, can satisfy our hungry and thirsty souls.

4:15 The woman mistakenly believed that if she received the water Jesus offered, she would not have to return to the well each day. She was interested in Jesus' message because she thought it could make her life easier. But if that were always the case, people would accept Christ's message for the wrong reasons. Christ did not come to take away challenges, but to change us on the inside and to empower us to deal with problems from God's perspective.

4:15 The woman did not immediately understand what Jesus was talking about. It takes time to accept something that changes the very foundations of your life. Jesus allowed the woman time to ask questions and put pieces together for herself. Sharing the gospel will not always have immediate results. When you ask people to let Jesus change their lives, give them time to weigh the matter.

4:16–20 When this woman discovered that Jesus knew all about her private life, she quickly changed the subject. Often people become uncomfortable when the conversation is too close to home, and they try to talk about something else. As we witness, we should gently guide the conversation back to Christ. His presence exposes sin and makes people squirm, but only Christ can forgive sins and give new life.

4:20–24 The woman brought up a popular theological issue—the correct place to worship. But her question was a smoke screen to keep Jesus away from her deepest need. Jesus directed the conversation to a much more important point: The *location* of worship is not nearly as important as the *attitude* of the worshipers.

4:21–24 "God is spirit" means he is not a physical being limited to one place. He is present everywhere and can be worshiped anywhere, at any time. It is not where we worship that counts, but how we worship. Is your worship genuine and true? Do you have the Holy Spirit's help? How does the Holy Spirit help us worship? The Holy Spirit prays for us (Romans 8:26), teaches us the words of Christ (14:26), and tells us we are loved (Romans 5:5).

4:22 When Jesus said, "salvation is from the Jews," he meant that only through the Jewish Messiah would the whole world find salvation. God had promised that through the Jewish race the whole earth would be blessed (Genesis 12:3). The Old Testament prophets had called the Jews to be a light to the other nations of the world, bringing them to a knowledge of God; and they had predicted the Messiah's coming. The woman at the well may have known of these passages and was expecting the Messiah, but she didn't realize that she was talking to him!

23 "But an hour is coming, and now is, when the true worshipers will worship the Father
in spirit and truth; for such people the Father seeks to be His worshipers.
24 "God is spirit, and those who worship Him must worship in spirit and truth."
25 The woman ☆said to Him, "I know that Messiah is coming (He who is called Christ);
when that One comes, He will declare all things to us."
26 Jesus ☆said to her, "I who speak to you am *He.*"

Jesus Tells about the Spiritual Harvest
(28)

27 At this point His disciples came, and they were amazed that He had been speaking
with a woman, yet no one said, "What do You seek?" or, "Why do You speak with her?"
28 So the woman left her waterpot, and went into the city and ☆said to the men,
29 "Come, see a man who told me all the things that I *have* done; this is not the Christ,
is it?"
30 They went out of the city, and were coming to Him.
31 Meanwhile the disciples were urging Him, saying, "Rabbi, eat."
32 But He said to them, "I have food to eat that you do not know about."
33 So the disciples were saying to one another, "No one brought Him *anything* to eat,
did he?"
34 Jesus ☆said to them, "My food is to do the will of Him who sent Me and to accomplish His work.
35 "Do you not say, 'There are yet four months, and *then* comes the harvest'? Behold, I
say to you, lift up your eyes and look on the fields, that they are white for harvest.
36 "Already he who reaps is receiving wages and is gathering fruit for life eternal; so
that he who sows and he who reaps may rejoice together.
37 "For in this *case* the saying is true, 'One sows and another reaps.'
38 "I sent you to reap that for which you have not labored; others have labored and you
have entered into their labor."

Many Samaritans Believe in Jesus
(29)

39 From that city many of the Samaritans believed in Him because of the word of the
woman who testified, "He told me all the things that I *have* done."
40 So when the Samaritans came to Jesus, they were asking Him to stay with them;
and He stayed there two days.
41 Many more believed because of His word;
42 and they were saying to the woman, "It is no longer because of what you said that
we believe, for we have heard for ourselves and know that this One is indeed the Savior
of the world."

Jesus Preaches in Galilee
(30/Matthew 4:12-17; Mark 1:14-15; Luke 4:14-15)

43 After the two days He went forth from there into Galilee.
44 For Jesus Himself testified that a prophet has no honor in his own country.
45 So when He came to Galilee, the Galileans received Him, having seen all the things
that He did in Jerusalem at the feast; for they themselves also went to the feast.

4:23 John 4:21; 5:25, 28; 16:2, 32; Phil 3:3
4:24 Phil 3:3
4:25 Dan 9:25; John 1:41; Matt 1:16; 27:17, 22; Luke 2:11
4:26 John 8:24, 28, 58; 9:37; 13:19
4:27 John 4:8
4:29 John 4:17f; Matt 12:23; John 7:26, 31
4:31 Matt 23:7; 26:25, 49; Mark 9:5; 11:21; 14:45; John 1:38, 49; 3:2, 26; 6:25; 9:2; 11:8
4:33 Luke 6:13-16; John 1:40-49; 2:2
4:34 John 5:30; 6:38; John 5:36; 17:4; 19:28, 30
4:35 Matt 9:37, 38; Luke 10:2
4:36 Prov 11:18; 1 Cor 9:17f; Rom 1:13; Matt 19:29; John 3:36; 4:14; 5:24; Rom 2:7; 6:23
4:37 Job 31:8; Mic 6:15
4:39 John 4:5, 30; John 4:29
4:42 Matt 1:21; Luke 2:11; John 1:29; Acts 5:31; 13:23; 1 Tim 4:10; 1 John 4:14
4:43 John 4:40
4:44 Matt 13:57; Mark 6:4; Luke 4:24
4:45 John 2:23

4:34 The "food" about which Jesus was speaking was his spiritual nourishment. It includes more than Bible study, prayer, and attending church. Spiritual nourishment also comes from doing God's will and helping to bring his work of salvation to completion. We are nourished not only by what we take in, but also by what we give out for God. In 17:4, Jesus refers to completing God's work on earth.

4:35 Sometimes Christians excuse themselves from witnessing by saying that their family or friends aren't ready to believe. Jesus, however, makes it clear that around us a continual harvest waits to be reaped. Don't let Jesus find you making excuses. Look around. You will find people ready to hear God's Word.

4:36–38 The wages Jesus offers are the joy of working for him and seeing the harvest of believers. These wages come to sower and reaper alike because both find joy in seeing new believers come into Christ's kingdom. The phrase "others have labored" (4:38) may refer to the Old Testament prophets and to John the Baptist, who paved the way for the gospel.

4:39 The Samaritan woman immediately shared her experience with others. Despite her reputation, many took her invitation and came out to meet Jesus. Perhaps there are sins in our past of which we're ashamed. But Christ changes us. As people see these changes, they become curious. Use these opportunities to introduce them to Christ.

Jesus Heals a Government Official's Son
(31)

4:46 John 2:1; John 2:9; Luke 4:23; John 2:12

4:47 John 4:3, 54

4:48 Dan 4:2f; 6:27; Matt 24:24; Mark 13:22; Acts 2:19, 22, 43; 4:30; 5:12; 6:8; 7:36; 14:3; 15:12; Rom 15:19; 1 Cor 1:22; 2 Cor 12:12; 2 Thess 2:9; Heb 2:4

4:50 Matt 8:13

4:53 Acts 11:14

4:54 John 2:11; John 4:45f

46 Therefore He came again to Cana of Galilee where He had made the water wine.
And there was a royal official whose son was sick at Capernaum.
47 When he heard that Jesus had come out of Judea into Galilee, he went to Him and
was imploring *Him* to come down and heal his son; for he was at the point of death.
48 So Jesus said to him, "Unless you *people* see signs and wonders, you *simply* will not
believe."
49 The royal official ☆said to Him, "Sir, come down before my child dies."
50 Jesus ☆said to him, "Go; your son lives." The man believed the word that Jesus spoke
to him and started off.
51 As he was now going down, *his* slaves met him, saying that his son was living.
52 So he inquired of them the hour when he began to get better. Then they said to
him, "Yesterday at the [11]seventh hour the fever left him."
53 So the father knew that *it was* at that hour in which Jesus said to him, "Your son
lives"; and he himself believed and his whole household.
54 This is again a second sign that Jesus performed when He had come out of Judea
into Galilee.

Jesus Heals a Lame Man by the Pool
(42)

5:1 Deut 16:1; John 2:13

5:2 Neh 3:1, 32; 12:39; John 19:13, 17, 20; 20:16; Acts 21:40; Rev 9:11; 16:16

5 After these things there was a feast of the Jews, and Jesus went up to Jerusalem.
2 Now there is in Jerusalem by the sheep *gate* a pool, which is called in Hebrew Bethesda, having five porticoes.
3 In these lay a multitude of those who were sick, blind, lame, and withered, [[12]wait-
ing for the moving of the waters;
4 for an angel of the Lord went down at certain seasons into the pool and stirred up
the water; whoever then first, after the stirring up of the water, stepped in was made
well from whatever disease with which he was afflicted.]
5 A man was there who had been ill for thirty-eight years.
6 When Jesus saw him lying *there*, and knew that he had already been a long time *in
that condition,* He ☆said to him, "Do you wish to get well?"

11 Perhaps 7 p.m. Roman time or 1 p.m. Jewish time **12** Early mss do not contain the remainder of v 3, nor v 4

4:46–49 This royal official was probably an officer in Herod's service. He had walked 20 miles to see Jesus and addressed him as "Sir," putting himself under Jesus even though he had legal authority over Jesus.

4:48 This miracle was more than a favor to one official; it was a sign to all the people. John's Gospel was written to all humankind to urge faith in Christ. Here a government official had faith that Jesus could do what he claimed. The official believed; *then* he saw a miraculous sign.

4:50 This royal official not only believed Jesus could heal; he also obeyed Jesus by returning home, thus demonstrating his faith. It isn't enough for us to say we believe that Jesus can take care of our problems. We need to act as if he can. When you pray about a need or problem, live as though you believe Jesus can do what he says.

4:51 Jesus' miracles were not mere illusions, the product of wishful thinking. Although the official's son was 20 miles away, he was healed when Jesus spoke the word. Distance was no problem because Christ has mastery over space. We can never put so much space between ourselves and Christ that he can no longer help us.

4:53 Notice how the official's faith grew. First, he believed enough to ask Jesus to help his son. Second, he believed Jesus' assurance that his son would live, and he acted on it. Third, he and his whole house believed in Jesus. Faith is a gift that grows as we use it.

5:1 Three feasts required all Jewish males to come to Jerusalem: (1) the Feast of Passover and Unleavened Bread, (2) the Feast of Weeks (also called Pentecost), and (3) the Feast of Booths.

5:6 After 38 years, this man's problem had become a way of life. No one had ever helped him. He had no hope of ever being healed and no desire to help himself. The man's situation looked hopeless. But no matter how trapped you feel in your infirmities, God can minister to your deepest needs. Don't let a problem or hardship cause you to lose hope. God may have special work for you to do in spite of your condition, or even because of it. Many have ministered effectively to hurting people because they have triumphed over their own hurts.

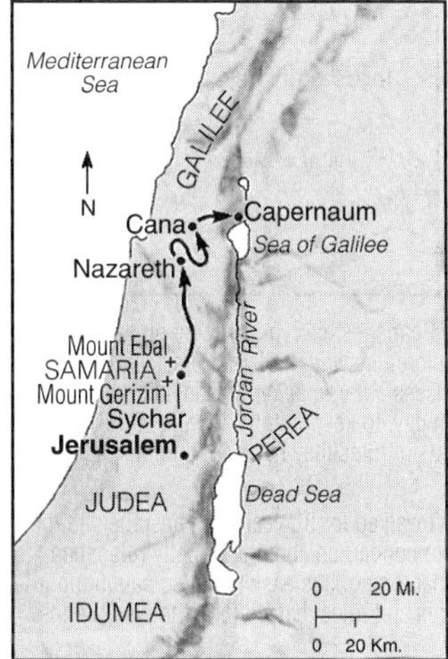

JESUS RETURNS TO GALILEE
Jesus stayed in Sychar for two days, then went on to Galilee. He visited Nazareth and various towns in Galilee before arriving in Cana. From there he spoke the word of healing, and a royal official's son in Capernaum was healed. The Gospel of Matthew tells us Jesus then settled in Capernaum (Matthew 4:12–13).

7 The sick man answered Him, "Sir, I have no man to put me into the pool when the
water is stirred up, but while I am coming, another steps down before me."
8 Jesus ☆said to him, "Get up, pick up your pallet and walk."
9 Immediately the man became well, and picked up his pallet and *began* to walk.
Now it was the Sabbath on that day.
10 So the Jews were saying to the man who was cured, "It is the Sabbath, and it is not
permissible for you to carry your pallet."
11 But he answered them, "He who made me well was the one who said to me, 'Pick
up your pallet and walk.' "
12 They asked him, "Who is the man who said to you, 'Pick up *your pallet* and walk'?"
13 But the man who was healed did not know who it was, for Jesus had slipped away
while there was a crowd in *that* place.
14 Afterward Jesus ☆found him in the temple and said to him, "Behold, you have become well; do not sin anymore, so that nothing worse happens to you."
15 The man went away, and told the Jews that it was Jesus who had made him well.
16 For this reason the Jews were persecuting Jesus, because He was doing these things
on the Sabbath.
17 But He answered them, "My Father is working until now, and I Myself am working."
18 For this reason therefore the Jews were seeking all the more to kill Him, because
He not only was breaking the Sabbath, but also was calling God His own Father, making
Himself equal with God.

5:7 John 5:4
5:8 Matt 9:6; Mark 2:11; Luke 5:24
5:9 John 9:14
5:10 John 1:19; 5:15, 16, 18; Neh 13:19; Jer 17:21f; Matt 12:2; Luke 6:2; John 7:23; 9:16
5:14 Mark 2:5; John 8:11; Ezra 9:14
5:15 John 1:19; 5:16, 18
5:16 John 1:19; 5:10, 15, 18
5:18 John 1:19; 5:15, 16; John 5:16; 7:1; John 10:33; 19:7

Jesus Claims to be God's Son
(43)

19 Therefore Jesus answered and was saying to them, "Truly, truly, I say to you, the
Son can do nothing of Himself, unless *it is* something He sees the Father doing; for whatever the Father does, these things the Son also does in like manner.

5:19 Matt 26:39; John 5:30; 6:38; 8:28; 12:49; 14:10

JESUS TEACHES IN JERUSALEM
Between chapters 4 and 5 of John, Jesus ministered throughout Galilee, especially in Capernaum. He had been calling certain men to follow him, but it wasn't until after this trip to Jerusalem (5:1) that he chose his 12 disciples from among them.

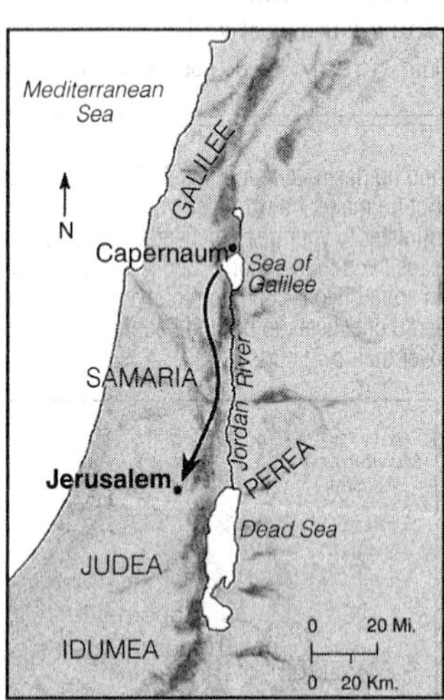

5:10 According to the Pharisees, carrying a pallet on the Sabbath was work and was therefore unlawful. It did not break an Old Testament law, but the Pharisees' *interpretation* of God's command to "remember the sabbath day, to keep it holy" (Exodus 20:8). This was just one of hundreds of rules they had added to the Old Testament law.

5:10 A man who hadn't walked for 38 years had been healed, but the Pharisees were more concerned about their petty rules than the life and health of a human being. It is easy to get so caught up in our man-made structures and rules that we forget the people involved. Are your guidelines for living God-made or man-made? Are they helping people, or have they become needless stumbling blocks?

5:14 This man had been lame, or paralyzed, and suddenly he could walk. This was a great miracle. But he needed an even greater miracle—to have his sins forgiven. The man was delighted to be physically healed, but he had to turn from his sins and seek God's forgiveness to be spiritually healed. God's forgiveness is the greatest gift you will ever receive. Don't neglect his gracious offer.

5:16 The Jewish leaders saw both a mighty miracle of healing and a broken rule. They threw the miracle aside as they focused their attention on the broken rule, because the rule was more important to them than the miracle. God is prepared to work in our lives, but we can shut out his miracles by limiting our views about how he works.

5:17 If God stopped every kind of work on the Sabbath, nature would fall into chaos, and sin would overrun the world. Genesis 2:2 says that God rested on the seventh day, but this can't mean that he stopped doing good. Jesus wanted to teach that when the opportunity to do good presents itself, it should not be ignored, even on the Sabbath.

5:17ff Jesus was identifying himself with God, his Father. There could be no doubt as to his claim to be God. Jesus does not leave us the option to believe in God while ignoring God's Son (5:23). The Pharisees also called God their Father, but they realized Jesus was claiming a unique relationship with him. In response to Jesus' claim, the Pharisees had two choices: to believe him, or to accuse him of blasphemy. They chose the second.

5:19–23 Because of his unity with God, Jesus lived as God wanted him to live. Because of our identification with Jesus, we must honor him and live as he wants us to live. The questions "What would Jesus do?" and "What would Jesus have me do?" may help us make the right choices.

20 "For the Father loves the Son, and shows Him all things that He Himself is doing;
and *the Father* will show Him greater works than these, so that you will marvel.
21 "For just as the Father raises the dead and gives them life, even so the Son also gives
life to whom He wishes.
22 "For not even the Father judges anyone, but He has given all judgment to the Son,
23 so that all will honor the Son even as they honor the Father. He who does not honor
the Son does not honor the Father who sent Him.
24 "Truly, truly, I say to you, he who hears My word, and believes Him who sent Me, has
eternal life, and does not come into judgment, but has passed out of death into life.
25 "Truly, truly, I say to you, an hour is coming and now is, when the dead will hear the
voice of the Son of God, and those who hear will live.
26 "For just as the Father has life in Himself, even so He gave to the Son also to have
life in Himself;
27 and He gave Him authority to execute judgment, because He is *the* Son of Man.
28 "Do not marvel at this; for an hour is coming, in which all who are in the tombs will
hear His voice,
29 and will come forth; those who did the good *deeds* to a resurrection of life, those
who committed the evil *deeds* to a resurrection of judgment.
30 "I can do nothing on My own initiative. As I hear, I judge; and My judgment is just,
because I do not seek My own will, but the will of Him who sent Me.

Jesus Supports His Claim
(44)

31 "If I *alone* testify about Myself, My testimony is not true.
32 "There is another who testifies of Me, and I know that the testimony which He gives
about Me is true.
33 "You have sent to John, and he has testified to the truth.
34 "But the testimony which I receive is not from man, but I say these things so that you
may be saved.
35 "He was the lamp that was burning and was shining and you were willing to rejoice
for a while in his light.
36 "But the testimony which I have is greater than *the testimony of* John; for the works
which the Father has given Me to accomplish—the very works that I do—testify about
Me, that the Father has sent Me.
37 "And the Father who sent Me, He has testified of Me. You have neither heard His
voice at any time nor seen His form.
38 "You do not have His word abiding in you, for you do not believe Him whom He
sent.

5:20 Matt 3:17; John 3:35; 2 Pet 1:17
5:21 Rom 4:17; 8:11; John 11:25
5:22 Acts 10:42; 17:31
5:23 Luke 10:16; 1 John 2:23
5:24 John 3:18; 12:44; 20:31; 1 John 5:13
5:25 Luke 15:24; John 6:60; 8:43, 47; 9:27
5:26 John 1:4; 6:57
5:27 John 9:39; Acts 10:42; 17:31
5:28 John 4:21; John 11:24; 1 Cor 15:52
5:29 Dan 12:2; Matt 25:46; Acts 24:15
5:30 John 5:19; 8:16; John 4:34; 6:38
5:31 John 8:14
5:34 1 John 5:9
5:35 2 Pet 1:19; Mark 1:5
5:36 Matt 11:4
5:37 Matt 3:17; Mark 1:11; Luke 3:22; 24:27; John 8:18
5:38 John 3:17

5:24 "Eternal life"—living forever with God—begins when you accept Jesus Christ as Savior. At that moment, new life begins in you (2 Corinthians 5:17). It is a completed transaction. You still will face physical death, but when Christ returns again, your body will be resurrected to live forever (1 Corinthians 15).

5:25 In saying that the dead will hear his voice, Jesus was talking about the spiritually dead who hear, understand, and accept him. Those who accept Jesus, the Word, will have eternal life. Jesus was also talking about the physically dead. He raised several dead people while he was on earth, and at his second coming all the "dead in Christ" will rise to meet him (1 Thessalonians 4:16).

5:26 God is the source and Creator of life, for there is no life apart from God, here or hereafter. The life in us is a gift from him (see Deuteronomy 30:20; Psalm 36:9). Because Jesus is eternally existent with God, the Creator, he too is "the life" (14:6) through whom we may live eternally (see 1 John 5:11).

5:27 The Old Testament mentioned three signs of the coming Messiah. In this chapter, John shows that Jesus has fulfilled all three signs. All power and authority are given to him as the Son of Man (cf. 5:27 with Daniel 7:13–14). The lame and sick are healed (cf. 5:20, 26 with Isaiah 35:6; Jeremiah 31:8–9). The dead are raised to life (cf. 5:21, 28 with Deuteronomy 32:39; 1 Samuel 2:6; 2 Kings 5:7).

5:29 Those who have rebelled against Christ will be resurrected too, but to hear God's judgment against them and to be sentenced to eternity apart from him. There are those who wish to live well on earth, ignore God, and then see death as final rest. Jesus does not allow unbelieving people to see death as the end of it all. There is a judgment to face.

5:31ff Jesus claimed to be equal with God (5:18), to give eternal life (5:24), to be the source of life (5:26), and to judge sin (5:27). These statements make it clear that Jesus was claiming to be divine—an almost unbelievable claim, but one that was supported by another witness, John the Baptist.

39 "[13]You search the Scriptures because you think that in them you have eternal life; it
is these that testify about Me;
40 and you are unwilling to come to Me so that you may have life.
41 "I do not receive glory from men;
42 but I know you, that you do not have the love of God in yourselves.
43 "I have come in My Father's name, and you do not receive Me; if another comes in
his own name, you will receive him.
44 "How can you believe, when you receive glory from one another and you do not seek
the glory that is from the *one and* only God?
45 "Do not think that I will accuse you before the Father; the one who accuses you is
Moses, in whom you have set your hope.
46 "For if you believed Moses, you would believe Me, for he wrote about Me.
47 "But if you do not believe his writings, how will you believe My words?"

Jesus Feeds Five Thousand

(96/Matthew 14:13-21; Mark 6:30-44; Luke 9:10-17)

6 After these things Jesus went away to the other side of the Sea of Galilee (or Tiberias).
2 A large crowd followed Him, because they saw the signs which He was performing
on those who were sick.
3 Then Jesus went up on the mountain, and there He sat down with His disciples.
4 Now the Passover, the feast of the Jews, was near.
5 Therefore Jesus, lifting up His eyes and seeing that a large crowd was coming to
Him, ☆said to Philip, "Where are we to buy bread, so that these may eat?"
6 This He was saying to test him, for He Himself knew what He was intending to do.
7 Philip answered Him, "Two hundred [14]denarii worth of bread is not sufficient for
them, for everyone to receive a little."
8 One of His disciples, Andrew, Simon Peter's brother, ☆said to Him,
9 "There is a lad here who has five barley loaves and two fish, but what are these for so
many people?"
10 Jesus said, "Have the people sit down." Now there was much grass in the place. So
the men sat down, in number about five thousand.
11 Jesus then took the loaves, and having given thanks, He distributed to those who
were seated; likewise also of the fish as much as they wanted.
12 When they were filled, He ☆said to His disciples, "Gather up the leftover fragments
so that nothing will be lost."

13 Or (a command) *Search the Scriptures!* **14** The denarius was equivalent to a day's wages

5:39 John 7:52; Rom 2:17ff; Luke 24:25, 27; Acts 13:27
5:41 1 Thess 2:6
5:43 Matt 24:5
5:44 Rom 2:29; John 17:3; 1 Tim 1:17
5:45 John 9:28; Rom 2:17ff
5:46 Luke 24:27
5:47 Luke 16:29, 31
6:1 Matt 4:18; Luke 5:1
6:3 Matt 5:1; Mark 3:13; Luke 6:12; 9:28
6:4 Deut 16:1; John 2:13
6:5 John 1:43
6:6 2 Cor 13:5; Rev 2:2
6:7 John 1:43
6:9 John 6:11; 21:9, 10, 13
6:10 Matt 14:21
6:11 Matt 15:36; John 6:9; 21:9, 10, 13
6:12 John 2:2

5:39–40 The religious leaders knew what the Bible said but failed to apply its words to their lives. They knew the teachings of the Scriptures but failed to see the Messiah to whom the Scriptures pointed. They knew the rules but missed the Savior. Entrenched in their own religious system, they refused to let the Son of God change their lives. Don't become so involved in "religion" that you miss Christ.

5:41 Whose praise do you seek? The religious leaders enjoyed great prestige in Israel, but their stamp of approval meant nothing to Jesus. He was concerned about God's approval. This is a good principle for us. If even the highest officials in the world approve of our actions and God does not, we should be concerned. But if God approves, even though others don't, we should be content.

5:45 The Pharisees prided themselves on being the true followers of their ancestor Moses. They were trying to follow every one of his laws to the letter, and they even added some of their own. Jesus' warning that Moses would accuse them stung them to fury. Moses wrote about Jesus (Genesis 3:15; Numbers 21:9; 24:17; Deuteronomy 18:15), yet the religious leaders refused to believe Jesus when he came.

6:5 If anyone knew where to get food, it would have been Philip because he was from Bethsaida, a town about nine miles away (1:44). Jesus was testing Philip to strengthen his faith. By asking for a human solution (knowing that there was none), Jesus highlighted the powerful and miraculous act that he was about to perform.

6:5–7 When Jesus asked Philip where they could buy a great amount of bread, Philip started assessing the probable cost. Jesus wanted to teach him that financial resources are not the most important ones. We can limit what God does in us by assuming what is and is not possible. Is there some impossible task that you believe God wants you to do? Don't let your estimate of what can't be done keep you from taking on the task. God can do the miraculous; trust him to provide the resources.

6:8–9 The disciples are contrasted with the youngster who brought what he had. They certainly had more resources than the boy, but they knew they didn't have enough, so they didn't give anything at all. The boy gave what little he had, and it made all the difference. If we offer nothing to God, he will have nothing to use. But he can take what little we have and turn it into something great.

6:8–9 In performing his miracles, Jesus usually preferred to work through people. Here he took what a young child offered and used it to accomplish one of the most spectacular miracles recorded in the Gospels. Age is no barrier to Christ. Never think you are too young or old to be of service to him.

6:13 Matt 14:20
6:14 Matt 11:3; 21:11; John 1:21
6:15 John 18:36f

13 So they gathered them up, and filled twelve baskets with fragments from the five
barley loaves which were left over by those who had eaten.
14 Therefore when the people saw the sign which He had performed, they said, "This
is truly the Prophet who is to come into the world."
15 So Jesus, perceiving that they were intending to come and take Him by force to make
Him king, withdrew again to the mountain by Himself alone.

Jesus Walks on Water
(97/Matthew 14:22-33; Mark 6:45-52)

6:16 John 2:2
6:17 Mark 6:45; John 6:24, 59

16 Now when evening came, His disciples went down to the sea,
17 and after getting into a boat, they *started to* cross the sea to Capernaum. It had already become dark, and Jesus had not yet come to them.

THE CLAIMS OF CHRIST
Those who read the life of Christ are faced with one unavoidable question—was Jesus God? Part of any reasonable conclusion has to include the fact that he did claim to be God. We have no other choice but to agree or disagree with his claim. Eternal life is at stake in the choice.

Jesus claimed to be:	*Matthew*	*Mark*	*Luke*	*John*
the fulfillment of Old Testament prophecies	5:17; 14:33; 16:16–17; 26:31, 53–56; 27:43	14:21, 61–62	4:16–21; 7:18–23; 18:31; 22:37; 24:44	2:22; 5:45–47; 6:45; 7:40; 10:34–36; 13:18; 15:25; 20:9
the Son of Man	8:20; 12:8; 16:27; 19:28; 20:18–19; 24:27, 44; 25:31; 26:2, 45, 64	8:31, 38; 9:9; 10:45; 14:41	6:22; 7:33–34; 12:8; 17:22; 18:8, 31; 19:10; 21:36	1:51; 3:13–14; 6:27, 53; 12:23, 34
the Son of God	11:27; 14:33; 16:16–17; 27:43	3:11–12; 14:61–62	8:28; 10:22	1:18; 3:35–36; 5:18–26; 6:40; 10:36; 11:4; 17:1; 19:7
the Messiah/ the Christ	23:9–10; 26:63–64	8:29–30	4:41; 23:1–2; 24:25–27	4:25–26; 10:24–25; 11:27
Teacher/Master	26:18			13:13–14
One with authority to forgive		2:1–12	7:48–49	
Lord		5:19		13:13–14; 20:28
Savior			19:10	3:17; 10:9

JESUS WALKS ON THE WATER
Jesus fed the 5,000 on a hill near the Sea of Galilee at Bethsaida. The disciples set out across the sea toward Capernaum. But they encountered a storm—and Jesus came walking to them on the water! The boat landed at Gennesaret (Mark 6:53); from there they went back to Capernaum.

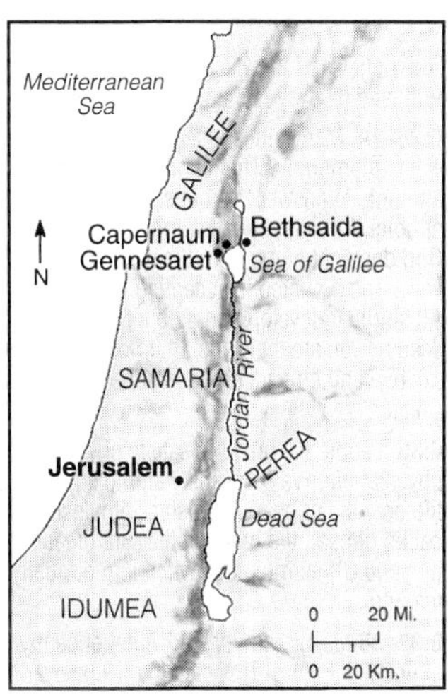

6:13 There is a lesson in the leftovers. God gives in abundance. He takes whatever we can offer him in time, ability, or resources and multiplies its effectiveness beyond our wildest expectations. If you take the first step in making yourself available to God, he will show you how greatly you can be used to advance the work of his kingdom.

6:14 "The Prophet" is the one prophesied by Moses (Deuteronomy 18:15).

18 The sea *began* to be stirred up because a strong wind was blowing.
19 Then, when they had rowed about three or four miles, they ☆saw Jesus walking on
the sea and drawing near to the boat; and they were frightened.
20 But He ☆said to them, "It is I; do not be afraid."
21 So they were willing to receive Him into the boat, and immediately the boat was at
the land to which they were going.

Jesus Is the True Bread from Heaven
(99)

22 The next day the crowd that stood on the other side of the sea saw that there was no
other small boat there, except one, and that Jesus had not entered with His disciples
into the boat, but *that* His disciples had gone away alone.
23 There came other small boats from Tiberias near to the place where they ate the
bread after the Lord had given thanks.
24 So when the crowd saw that Jesus was not there, nor His disciples, they themselves
got into the small boats, and came to Capernaum seeking Jesus.
25 When they found Him on the other side of the sea, they said to Him, "Rabbi, when
did You get here?"
26 Jesus answered them and said, "Truly, truly, I say to you, you seek Me, not because
you saw signs, but because you ate of the loaves and were filled.
27 "Do not work for the food which perishes, but for the food which endures to eternal
life, which the Son of Man will give to you, for on Him the Father, God, has set His seal."
28 Therefore they said to Him, "What shall we do, so that we may work the works
of God?"
29 Jesus answered and said to them, "This is the work of God, that you believe in Him
whom He has sent."
30 So they said to Him, "What then do You do for a sign, so that we may see, and believe You? What work do You perform?
31 "Our fathers ate the manna in the wilderness; as it is written, 'HE GAVE THEM BREAD
OUT OF HEAVEN TO EAT.' "
32 Jesus then said to them, "Truly, truly, I say to you, it is not Moses who has given you
the bread out of heaven, but it is My Father who gives you the true bread out of heaven.
33 "For the bread of God is [15]that which comes down out of heaven, and gives life to the
world."
34 Then they said to Him, "Lord, always give us this bread."
35 Jesus said to them, "I am the bread of life; he who comes to Me will not hunger, and
he who believes in Me will never thirst.
36 "But I said to you that you have seen Me, and yet do not believe.
37 "All that the Father gives Me will come to Me, and the one who comes to Me I will
certainly not cast out.

6:20 Matt 14:27
6:22 John 6:2; John 6:15ff
6:23 John 6:1; Luke 7:13; John 6:11
6:24 Matt 14:34; Mark 6:53; John 6:17, 59
6:25 Matt 23:7
6:26 John 6:24; John 6:2, 14, 30
6:27 Is 55:2; John 3:15f; 4:14; 6:40, 47, 54; 10:28; 17:2f; Matt 8:20; John 6:53, 62; John 3:33
6:29 1 Thess 1:3; James 2:22; 1 John 3:23; Rev 2:26; John 3:17
6:30 Matt 12:38; John 6:2, 14, 26
6:31 Ex 16:4, 15, 21; Num 11:8; John 6:49, 58; Ps 78:24; Ex 16:4, 15; Neh 9:15; Ps 105:40
6:33 John 6:41, 50
6:34 John 4:15
6:35 John 6:48, 51; John 4:14
6:36 John 6:26
6:37 John 6:39; 17:2, 24

15 Or *He who comes*

6:18 The Sea of Galilee is 650 feet below sea level, 150 feet deep, and surrounded by hills. These physical features make it subject to sudden windstorms that would cause extremely high waves. Such storms were expected on this lake, but they were nevertheless frightening. When Jesus came to the disciples during a storm, walking on the water (three and a half miles from shore), he told them not to be afraid. We often face spiritual and emotional storms and feel tossed about like a small boat on a big lake. In spite of terrifying circumstances, if we trust our lives to Christ for his safekeeping, he will give us peace in any storm.

6:18–19 The disciples, terrified, probably thought they were seeing a ghost (Mark 6:49). But if they had thought about all they had already seen Jesus do, they could have accepted this miracle. They were frightened—they didn't expect Jesus to come, and they weren't prepared for his help. Faith is a mind-set that *expects* God to act. When we act on this expectation, we can overcome our fears.

6:26 Jesus criticized the people who followed him only for the physical and temporal benefits and not for the satisfying of their spiritual hunger. Many people use religion to gain prestige, comfort, or even political votes. But those are self-centered motives. True believers follow Jesus simply because they know he has the truth and his way is the way to live.

6:28–29 Many sincere seekers for God are puzzled about what he wants them to do. The religions of the world are humankind's attempts to answer this question. But Jesus' reply is brief and simple: We must believe on him whom God has sent. Satisfying God does not come from the work we *do,* but from whom we *believe.* The first step is accepting that Jesus is who he claims to be. All spiritual development is built on this affirmation. Declare to Jesus, "You are the Christ, the Son of the living God" (Matthew 16:16), and embark on a life of belief that is satisfying to your Creator.

6:35 People eat bread to satisfy physical hunger and to sustain physical life. We can satisfy spiritual hunger and sustain spiritual life only by a right relationship with Jesus Christ. No wonder he called himself the bread of life. But bread must be eaten to sustain life, and Christ must be invited into our daily walk to sustain spiritual life.

6:37–38 Jesus did not work independently of God the Father, but in union with him. This should give us even more assurance of

38 "For I have come down from heaven, not to do My own will, but the will of Him who
sent Me.
39 "This is the will of Him who sent Me, that of all that He has given Me I lose nothing,
but raise it up on the last day.
40 "For this is the will of My Father, that everyone who beholds the Son and believes in
Him will have eternal life, and I Myself will raise him up on the last day."

The Jews Disagree That Jesus Is from Heaven
(100)

41 Therefore the Jews were grumbling about Him, because He said, "I am the bread
that came down out of heaven."
42 They were saying, "Is not this Jesus, the son of Joseph, whose father and mother we
know? How does He now say, 'I have come down out of heaven'?"
43 Jesus answered and said to them, "Do not grumble among yourselves.
44 "No one can come to Me unless the Father who sent Me draws him; and I will raise
him up on the last day.
45 "It is written in the prophets, 'AND THEY SHALL ALL BE TAUGHT OF GOD.' Everyone
who has heard and learned from the Father, comes to Me.
46 "Not that anyone has seen the Father, except the One who is from God; He has seen
the Father.
47 "Truly, truly, I say to you, he who believes has eternal life.
48 "I am the bread of life.
49 "Your fathers ate the manna in the wilderness, and they died.
50 "This is the bread which comes down out of heaven, so that one may eat of it and
not die.
51 "I am the living bread that came down out of heaven; if anyone eats of this bread, he
will live forever; and the bread also which I will give for the life of the world is My flesh."
52 Then the Jews *began* to argue with one another, saying, "How can this man give us
His flesh to eat?"
53 So Jesus said to them, "Truly, truly, I say to you, unless you eat the flesh of the Son
of Man and drink His blood, you have no life in yourselves.
54 "He who eats My flesh and drinks My blood has eternal life, and I will raise him up
on the last day.
55 "For My flesh is true food, and My blood is true drink.

6:38 John 3:13; Matt 26:39; John 4:34

6:39 John 17:12; 10:9; Matt 10:15; John 6:40, 44, 54; 11:24

6:40 John 12:45; 14:17, 19; John 3:16; Matt 10:15; John 6:39, 44, 54; 11:24

6:41 John 1:19; 6:52

6:42 Luke 4:22; John 7:27f

6:44 Jer 31:3; Hos 11:4; John 6:65; 12:32

6:45 Acts 7:42; 13:40; Heb 8:11; Is 54:13; Jer 31:34; Phil 3:15; 1 Thess 4:9; 1 John 2:27

6:46 John 1:18

6:47 John 3:36; 5:24; 6:51, 58; 11:26

6:50 John 3:36; 5:24; 6:47, 51, 58; 11:26

6:51 John 3:36; 5:24; 6:47, 58; 11:26; John 1:29; 3:14f; Heb 10:10; 1 John 4:10; John 6:53-56

6:52 John 9:16; 10:19

---

being welcomed into God's presence and being protected by him. Jesus' purpose was to do the will of God, not to satisfy Jesus' human desires. When we follow Jesus, we should have the same purpose.

6:39 Jesus said he would not lose even one person whom the Father had given him. Thus anyone who makes a sincere commitment to believe in Jesus Christ as Savior is secure in God's promise of eternal life. Christ will not let his people be overcome by Satan and lose their salvation (see also 17:12; Philippians 1:6).

6:40 Those who put their faith in Christ will be resurrected from physical death to eternal life with God when Christ comes again (see 1 Corinthians 15:52; 1 Thessalonians 4:16).

6:41 When John says *Jews,* he is referring to the Jewish leaders who were hostile to Jesus, not to Jews in general. John himself was a Jew, and so was Jesus.

6:41 The religious leaders grumbled because they could not accept Jesus' claim of divinity. They saw him only as a carpenter from Nazareth. They refused to believe that Jesus was God's divine Son, and they could not tolerate his message. Many people reject Christ because they say they cannot believe he is the Son of God. In reality, the demands that Christ makes for their loyalty and obedience are what they can't accept. So to protect themselves from the message, they reject the messenger.

6:44 God, not man, plays the most active role in salvation. When someone chooses to believe in Jesus Christ as Savior, he or she does so only in response to the urging of God's Holy Spirit. God does the urging; then we decide whether or not to believe. Thus no one can believe in Jesus without God's help.

6:45 Jesus was alluding to an Old Testament view of the Messianic kingdom in which all people are taught directly by God (Isaiah 54:13; Jeremiah 31:31–34). He was stressing the importance of not merely hearing, but learning. We are taught by God through the Bible, our experiences, the thoughts the Holy Spirit brings, and relationships with other Christians. Are you open to God's teaching?

6:47 *Believes* as used here means "continues to believe." We do not believe merely once; we keep on believing in and trusting Jesus.

6:47ff The religious leaders frequently asked Jesus to prove to them why he was better than the prophets they already had. Jesus here referred to the manna that Moses had given their ancestors in the wilderness (see Exodus 16). This bread was physical and temporal. The people ate it, and it sustained them for a day. But they had to get more bread every day, and this bread could not keep them from dying. Jesus, who is much greater than Moses, offers himself as the spiritual bread from heaven that satisfies completely and leads to eternal life.

6:51 How can Jesus give us his flesh as bread to eat? To eat living bread means to accept Christ into our lives and become united with him. We are united with Christ in two ways: (1) by believing in his death (the sacrifice of his flesh) and resurrection and (2) by devoting ourselves to living as he requires, depending on his teaching for guidance and trusting in the Holy Spirit for power.

56 "He who eats My flesh and drinks My blood abides in Me, and I in him.
57 "As the living Father sent Me, and I live because of the Father, so he who eats Me, he
also will live because of Me.
58 "This is the bread which came down out of heaven; not as the fathers ate and died;
he who eats this bread will live forever."
59 These things He said in the synagogue as He taught in Capernaum.

Many Disciples Desert Jesus
(101)

60 Therefore many of His disciples, when they heard *this* said, "This is a difficult statement; who can listen to it?"
61 But Jesus, conscious that His disciples grumbled at this, said to them, "Does this
cause you to stumble?
62 "*What* then if you see the Son of Man ascending to where He was before?
63 "It is the Spirit who gives life; the flesh profits nothing; the words that I have spoken
to you are spirit and are life.
64 "But there are some of you who do not believe." For Jesus knew from the beginning
who they were who did not believe, and who it was that would betray Him.
65 And He was saying, "For this reason I have said to you, that no one can come to Me
unless it has been granted him from the Father."
66 As a result of this many of His disciples withdrew and were not walking with Him
anymore.
67 So Jesus said to the twelve, "You do not want to go away also, do you?"
68 Simon Peter answered Him, "Lord, to whom shall we go? You have words of eternal life.
69 "We have believed and have come to know that You are the Holy One of God."
70 Jesus answered them, "Did I Myself not choose you, the twelve, and *yet* one of you
is a devil?"
71 Now He meant Judas *the son* of Simon Iscariot, for he, one of the twelve, was going
to betray Him.

2. Jesus encounters conflict with the religious leaders

Jesus' Brothers Ridicule Him
(121)

7 After these things Jesus was walking in Galilee, for He was unwilling to walk in Judea because the Jews were seeking to kill Him.
2 Now the feast of the Jews, the Feast of Booths, was near.

6:56 John 15:4f; 17:23
6:57 Matt 16:16; John 5:26; John 3:17
6:58 John 3:36; 5:24; 6:47, 51; 11:26
6:60 John 2:2; 6:66; 7:3
6:61 John 6:64; Matt 11:6
6:62 Matt 8:20; Mark 16:19; John 3:13
6:63 2 Cor 3:6; John 6:68
6:64 John 2:25; Matt 10:4; John 13:11
6:65 Matt 13:11; John 3:27
6:66 John 2:2; 7:3
6:67 Matt 10:2; John 2:2
6:68 Matt 16:16; John 6:63; 12:49f; 17:8
6:69 Mark 1:24; 8:29; Luke 9:20
6:70 Matt 10:2; John 2:2; 6:71; 20:24
6:71 John 12:4; 13:2, 26; Mark 14:10; Matt 10:2; John 2:2; 20:24
7:1 John 4:3; 6:1; 11:54; John 5:18; 7:19; 8:37, 40; 11:53

6:56 This was a shocking message—to eat flesh and drink blood sounded cannibalistic. The idea of drinking any blood, let alone human blood, was repugnant to the religious leaders because the law forbade it (Leviticus 17:10–11). Jesus was not talking about literal blood, of course. He was saying that his life had to become their own, but they could not accept this concept. The apostle Paul later used the body and blood imagery in talking about communion (see 1 Corinthians 11:23–26).

6:63, 65 The Holy Spirit gives spiritual life; without the work of the Holy Spirit we cannot even see our need for new life (14:17). All spiritual renewal begins and ends with God. He reveals truth to us, lives within us, and then enables us to respond to that truth.

6:66 Why did Jesus' words cause many of his followers to desert him? (1) They may have realized that he wasn't going to be the conquering Messiah-King they expected. (2) He refused to give in to their self-centered requests. (3) He emphasized faith, not deeds. (4) His teachings were difficult to understand, and some of his words were offensive. As we grow in our faith, we may be tempted to turn away because Jesus' lessons are difficult. Will your response be to give up, ignore certain teachings, or reject Christ? Instead, ask God to show you what the teachings mean and how they apply to your life. Then have the courage to act on God's truth.

6:67 There is no middle ground with Jesus. When he asked the disciples if they would also leave, he was showing that they could either accept or reject him. Jesus was not trying to repel people with his teachings. He was simply telling the truth. The more the people heard Jesus' real message, the more they divided into two camps—the honest seekers who wanted to understand more, and those who rejected Jesus because they didn't like what they had heard.

6:67–68 After many of Jesus' followers had deserted him, he asked the 12 disciples if they were also going to leave. Peter replied, "To whom shall we go?" In his straightforward way, Peter answered for all of us—there is no other way. Though there are many philosophies and self-styled authorities, Jesus alone has the words of eternal life. People look everywhere for eternal life and miss Christ, the only source. Stay with him, especially when you are confused or feel alone.

6:70 In response to Jesus' message, some people left; others stayed and truly believed; and some, like Judas, stayed but tried to use Jesus for personal gain. Many people today turn away from Christ. Others pretend to follow, going to church for status, approval of family and friends, or business contacts. But there are only two real responses to Jesus—you either accept him or reject him. How have you responded to Christ?

6:71 For more information on Judas, see his Profile in Mark 14.

7:2 The Feast of Booths is described in Leviticus 23:33ff. This event occurred in October, about six months after the Passover

7:3 Matt 12:46; Mark 3:21; John 6:60
7:5 Matt 12:46; Mark 3:21; John 7:3, 10
7:6 Matt 26:18
7:7 John 15:18f; John 3:19f
7:10 Matt 12:46; Mark 3:21; John 7:3, 5
7:11 John 11:56
7:13 John 9:22; 12:42; 19:38; 20:19
7:14 Matt 26:55; John 7:28
7:15 John 1:19; 7:11, 13, 35; Acts 26:24
7:16 John 3:11
7:17 John 3:21; 8:43f
7:18 John 5:41; 8:50, 54; 12:43
7:19 John 1:17; Mark 11:18; John 7:1
7:20 Matt 11:18; John 8:48f, 52; 10:20

3 Therefore His brothers said to Him, "Leave here and go into Judea, so that Your
disciples also may see Your works which You are doing.
4 "For no one does anything in secret when he himself seeks to be *known* publicly. If
You do these things, show Yourself to the world."
5 For not even His brothers were believing in Him.
6 So Jesus ☆said to them, "My time is not yet here, but your time is always opportune.
7 "The world cannot hate you, but it hates Me because I testify of it, that its deeds are
evil.
8 "Go up to the feast yourselves; I do not go up to this feast because My time has not
yet fully come."
9 Having said these things to them, He stayed in Galilee.

Jesus Teaches Openly at the Temple
(123)

10 But when His brothers had gone up to the feast, then He Himself also went up, not
publicly, but as if, in secret.
11 So the Jews were seeking Him at the feast and were saying, "Where is He?"
12 There was much grumbling among the crowds concerning Him; some were saying,
"He is a good man"; others were saying, "No, on the contrary, He leads the people astray."
13 Yet no one was speaking openly of Him for fear of the Jews.
14 But when it was now the midst of the feast Jesus went up into the temple, and *began*
to teach.
15 The Jews then were astonished, saying, "How has this man become learned, having
never been educated?"
16 So Jesus answered them and said, "My teaching is not Mine, but His who sent Me.
17 "If anyone is willing to do His will, he will know of the teaching, whether it is of God
or *whether* I speak from Myself.
18 "He who speaks from himself seeks his own glory; but He who is seeking the glory of
the One who sent Him, He is true, and there is no unrighteousness in Him.
19 "Did not Moses give you the Law, and *yet* none of you carries out the Law? Why do
you seek to kill Me?"
20 The crowd answered, "You have a demon! Who seeks to kill You?"

---

celebration mentioned in John 6:2–5. The feast commemorated the days when the Israelites wandered in the wilderness and lived in booths (Leviticus 23:43).

7:3–5 Jesus' brothers had a difficult time believing in him. Some of these brothers would eventually become leaders in the church (James, for example), but for several years they were embarrassed by Jesus. After Jesus died and rose again, they finally believed. We today have every reason to believe because we have the full record of Jesus' miracles, death, and resurrection. We also have the evidence of what the gospel has done in people's lives through the centuries. Don't miss this opportunity to believe in God's Son.

7:7 Because the world hated Jesus, we who follow him can expect that many people will hate us as well. If circumstances are going too well, ask if you are following Christ as you should. We can be grateful when life goes well, but we must make sure it is not at the cost of following Jesus halfheartedly or not at all.

7:10 Jesus came with the greatest gift ever offered, so why did he often act secretly? The religious leaders hated him, and many would refuse his gift of salvation, no matter what he said or did. The more Jesus taught and worked publicly, the more these leaders would cause trouble for him and his followers. So it was necessary for Jesus to teach and work as quietly as possible. Many people today have the privilege of teaching, preaching, and worshiping publicly with little persecution. These believers should be grateful and make the most of their opportunities to proclaim the gospel.

7:13 The religious leaders had a great deal of power over the common people. Apparently these leaders couldn't do much to Jesus at this time, but they threatened anyone who might publicly support him. Excommunication from the synagogue was one of the reprisals for believing in Jesus (9:22). To a Jew, this was a severe punishment.

7:13 Everyone was talking about Jesus! But when it came time to speak up for him in public, no one said a word. All were afraid. Fear can stifle our witness. Although many people talk about Christ in church, when it comes to making a public statement about their faith, they are often embarrassed. Jesus says that he will acknowledge us before God if we acknowledge him before others (Matthew 10:32). Be courageous! Speak up for Christ!

7:16–18 Those who attempt to know God's will and do it will know intuitively that Jesus was telling the truth about himself. Have you ever listened to religious speakers and wondered if they were telling the truth? Test them: (1) Their words should agree with, not contradict, the Bible; (2) their words should point to God and his will, not to themselves.

7:19 The Pharisees spent their days trying to achieve holiness by keeping the meticulous rules that they had added to God's laws. Jesus' accusation that they didn't keep Moses' law stung them deeply. In spite of their pompous pride in themselves and their rules, they did not even fulfill a legalistic religion, for they were living far below what the law of Moses required. Murder was certainly against the law. Jesus' followers should do *more* than the moral law requires, not by adding to its requirements, but by going beyond and beneath the mere do's and don't's of the law to the spirit of the law.

7:20 Most of the people were probably not aware of the plot to kill Jesus (5:18). There was a small group looking for the right opportunity to kill him, but most were still trying to decide what they believed about him.

21 Jesus answered them, "I did one deed, and you all marvel.
22"For this reason Moses has given you circumcision (not because it is from Moses,
but from the fathers), and on *the* Sabbath you circumcise a man.
23"If a man receives circumcision on *the* Sabbath so that the Law of Moses will not be
broken, are you angry with Me because I made an entire man well on *the* Sabbath?
24"Do not judge according to appearance, but judge with righteous judgment."
25 So some of the people of Jerusalem were saying, "Is this not the man whom they
are seeking to kill?
26"Look, He is speaking publicly, and they are saying nothing to Him. The rulers do
not really know that this is the Christ, do they?
27"However, we know where this man is from; but whenever the Christ may come, no
one knows where He is from."
28 Then Jesus cried out in the temple, teaching and saying, "You both know Me and
know where I am from; and I have not come of Myself, but He who sent Me is true,
whom you do not know.
29"I know Him, because I am from Him, and He sent Me."
30 So they were seeking to seize Him; and no man laid his hand on Him, because His
hour had not yet come.
31 But many of the crowd believed in Him; and they were saying, "When the Christ
comes, He will not perform more signs than those which this man has, will He?"

Religious Leaders Attempt to Arrest Jesus
(124)

32 The Pharisees heard the crowd muttering these things about Him, and the chief
priests and the Pharisees sent officers to seize Him.
33 Therefore Jesus said, "For a little while longer I am with you, then I go to Him who
sent Me.
34"You will seek Me, and will not find Me; and where I am, you cannot come."
35 The Jews then said to one another, "Where does this man intend to go that we will
not find Him? He is not intending to go to the Dispersion among the Greeks, and teach
the Greeks, is He?
36"What is this statement that He said, 'You will seek Me, and will not find Me; and
where I am, you cannot come'?"
37 Now on the last day, the great *day* of the feast, Jesus stood and cried out, saying, "If
anyone is thirsty, let him come to Me and drink.
38"He who believes in Me, as the Scripture said, 'From his innermost being will flow
rivers of living water.' "
39 But this He spoke of the Spirit, whom those who believed in Him were to receive;
for the Spirit was not yet *given,* because Jesus was not yet glorified.
40 *Some* of the people therefore, when they heard these words, were saying, "This
certainly is the Prophet."

7:21 John 5:2-9, 16; 7:23
7:22 Lev 12:3; Gen 17:10ff; 21:4; Acts 7:8
7:23 Matt 12:2; John 5:9
7:26 Luke 23:13; John 3:1
7:27 John 6:42; 7:41f
7:28 John 8:42
7:29 Matt 11:27; John 8:55; 17:25; John 6:46; John 3:17
7:31 John 2:23; 8:30; 10:42; 11:45; 12:11, 42; John 7:26; John 2:11
7:32 Matt 26:58; John 7:45f; Matt 12:14
7:33 John 12:35; 13:33; 14:19; 16:16-19; John 14:12, 28
7:35 Acts 14:1; 17:4; 18:4; Rom 1:16
7:36 John 8:21; 13:33
7:37 John 4:10, 14; 6:35
7:38 Is 44:3; 55:1; 58:11; John 4:10
7:39 Joel 2:28; John 1:33; John 20:22; Acts 1:4f; 2:4, 33; 19:2; John 12:16, 23; 13:31f; 16:14; 17:1
7:40 Matt 21:11; John 1:21

7:21–23 According to Moses' law, circumcision was to be performed eight days after a baby's birth (Genesis 17:9–14; Leviticus 12:3). This rite was carried out on all Jewish males to demonstrate their identity as part of God's covenant people. If the eighth day after birth was a Sabbath, the circumcision would still be performed (even though it was considered work). While the religious leaders allowed certain exceptions to Sabbath laws, they allowed none to Jesus, who was simply showing mercy to those who needed healing.

7:26 This chapter shows the many reactions people had toward Jesus. They called him a good man (7:12), a deceiver (7:12), a demon (7:20), the Christ (7:26), and the Prophet (7:40). We must make up our own minds about who Jesus is, knowing that whatever we decide will have eternal consequences.

7:27 There was a popular tradition that the Messiah would simply appear. But those who believed this tradition were ignoring the Scriptures that clearly predicted the Messiah's birthplace (Micah 5:2).

7:37 Jesus' words, "come to Me and drink," alluded to the theme of many Bible passages that talk about the Messiah's life-giving blessings (Isaiah 12:2–3; 44:3–4; 58:11). In promising to give the Holy Spirit to all who believed, Jesus was claiming to be the Messiah, for that was something only the Messiah could do.

7:38 Jesus used the term *living water* in 4:10 to indicate eternal life. Here he uses the term to refer to the Holy Spirit. The two go together: Wherever the Holy Spirit is accepted, he brings eternal life. Jesus teaches more about the Holy Spirit in chapters 14—16. The Holy Spirit empowered Jesus' followers at Pentecost (Acts 2) and has since been available to all who believe in Jesus as Savior.

7:40–44 The crowd was asking questions about Jesus. Some believed, others were hostile, and others disqualified Jesus as the Messiah because he was from Nazareth, not Bethlehem (Micah 5:2). But he *was* born in Bethlehem (Luke 2:1–7), although he grew up in Nazareth. If they had looked more carefully, they would not have jumped to the wrong conclusions. When you search for God's truth, make sure you look carefully and thoughtfully at the Bible with an open heart and mind. Don't jump to conclusions before knowing more of what the Bible says.

41 Others were saying, "This is the Christ." Still others were saying, "Surely the Christ
is not going to come from Galilee, is He?
42 "Has not the Scripture said that the Christ comes from the descendants of David,
and from Bethlehem, the village where David was?"
43 So a division occurred in the crowd because of Him.
44 Some of them wanted to seize Him, but no one laid hands on Him.
45 The officers then came to the chief priests and Pharisees, and they said to them,
"Why did you not bring Him?"
46 The officers answered, "Never has a man spoken the way this man speaks."
47 The Pharisees then answered them, "You have not also been led astray, have you?
48 "No one of the rulers or Pharisees has believed in Him, has he?
49 "But this crowd which does not know the Law is accursed."
50 Nicodemus (he who came to Him before, being one of them) ☆said to them,
51 "Our Law does not judge a man unless it first hears from him and knows what he is
doing, does it?"
52 They answered him, "You are not also from Galilee, are you? Search, and see that
no prophet arises out of Galilee."

Jesus Forgives an Adulterous Woman
(125)

53 [[16]Everyone went to his home.
8 But Jesus went to the Mount of Olives.
2 Early in the morning He came again into the temple, and all the people were coming to Him; and He sat down and *began* to teach them.
3 The scribes and the Pharisees ☆brought a woman caught in adultery, and having set
her in the center *of the court*,
4 they ☆said to Him, "Teacher, this woman has been caught in adultery, in the very
act.
5 "Now in the Law Moses commanded us to stone such women; what then do You say?"
6 They were saying this, testing Him, so that they might have grounds for accusing
Him. But Jesus stooped down and with His finger wrote on the ground.
7 But when they persisted in asking Him, He straightened up, and said to them, "He
who is without sin among you, let him *be the* first to throw a stone at her."
8 Again He stooped down and wrote on the ground.

16 Later mss add the story of the adulterous woman, numbering it as John 7:53-8:11

7:41 John 1:46; 7:52
7:42 Ps 89:4; Mic 5:2; Matt 1:1; 2:5f; Luke 2:4ff
7:43 John 9:16; 10:19
7:46 John 7:32; Matt 7:28
7:47 John 7:12
7:48 John 12:42; Luke 23:13; John 7:26
7:50 John 3:1; 19:39
7:51 Ex 23:1; Deut 17:6; 19:15; Prov 18:13; Acts 23:3
7:52 John 1:46; 7:41
8:1 Matt 21:1
8:2 Matt 26:55; John 8:20
8:5 Lev 20:10; Deut 22:22f
8:6 Matt 16:1; 19:3; 22:18, 35; Mark 8:11; 10:2; 12:15; Luke 10:25; 11:16; Mark 3:2
8:7 John 8:10; Matt 7:1; Rom 2:1; Deut 17:7

7:44–46 Although the Romans ruled Palestine, they gave the Jewish religious leaders authority over minor civil and religious affairs. The religious leaders supervised their own temple guards and gave the officers power to arrest anyone causing a disturbance or breaking any of their ceremonial laws. Because these leaders had developed hundreds of trivial laws, it was almost impossible for anyone, even the leaders themselves, not to break, neglect, or ignore at least a few of them some of the time. But these temple guards couldn't find one reason to arrest Jesus. And as they listened to Jesus to try to find evidence, they couldn't help hearing the wonderful words he said.

7:46–49 The Jewish leaders saw themselves as an elite group that alone had the truth, and they resisted the truth about Christ because it wasn't *theirs* to begin with. It is easy to think that we have the truth and that those who disagree with us do not have any truth at all. But God's truth is available to everyone. Don't copy the Pharisees' self-centered and narrow attitude.

7:50–52 This passage offers additional insight into Nicodemus, the Pharisee who visited Jesus at night (chapter 3). Apparently Nicodemus had become a secret believer. Since most of the Pharisees hated Jesus and wanted to kill him, Nicodemus risked his reputation and high position when he spoke up for Jesus. His statement was bold, and the Pharisees immediately became suspicious. After Jesus' death, Nicodemus brought spices for his body (19:39). That is the last time he is mentioned in Scripture.

7:51 Nicodemus confronted the Pharisees with their failure to keep their own laws. The Pharisees were losing ground—the temple guards came back impressed by Jesus (7:46), and one of the Pharisees' own, Nicodemus, was defending him. With their hypocritical motives being exposed and their prestige slowly eroding, they began to move to protect themselves. Pride would interfere with their ability to reason, and soon they would become obsessed with getting rid of Jesus just to save face. What was good and right no longer mattered.

8:3–6 The Jewish leaders had already disregarded the law by arresting the woman without the man. The law required that both parties to adultery be stoned (Leviticus 20:10; Deuteronomy 22:22). The leaders were using the woman as a trap so they could trick Jesus. If Jesus said the woman should not be stoned, they would accuse him of violating Moses' law. If he urged them to execute her, they would report him to the Romans, who did not permit the Jews to carry out their own executions (18:31).

8:7 This is a significant statement about judging others. Because Jesus upheld the legal penalty for adultery, stoning, he could not be accused of being against the law. But by saying that only a sinless person could throw the first stone, he highlighted the importance of compassion and forgiveness. When others are caught in sin, are you quick to pass judgment? To do so is to act as though you have never sinned. It is God's role to judge, not ours. Our role is to show forgiveness and compassion.

8:8 It is uncertain whether Jesus was merely ignoring the accusers by writing on the ground, listing their sins, or writing out the Ten Commandments.

9 When they heard it, they *began* to go out one by one, beginning with the older ones,
and He was left alone, and the woman, where she was, in the center *of the court*.
10 Straightening up, Jesus said to her, "Woman, where are they? Did no one condemn
you?"
11 She said, "No one, Lord." And Jesus said, "I do not condemn you, either. Go. From
now on sin no more."]

Jesus Is the Light of the World
(126)

12 Then Jesus again spoke to them, saying, "I am the Light of the world; he who follows Me will not walk in the darkness, but will have the Light of life."
13 So the Pharisees said to Him, "You are testifying about Yourself; Your testimony is
not true."
14 Jesus answered and said to them, "Even if I testify about Myself, My testimony is
true, for I know where I came from and where I am going; but you do not know where I
come from or where I am going.
15 "You judge according to the flesh; I am not judging anyone.
16 "But even if I do judge, My judgment is true; for I am not alone *in it*, but I and the
Father who sent Me.
17 "Even in your law it has been written that the testimony of two men is true.
18 "I am He who testifies about Myself, and the Father who sent Me testifies about Me."
19 So they were saying to Him, "Where is Your Father?" Jesus answered, "You know
neither Me nor My Father; if you knew Me, you would know My Father also."
20 These words He spoke in the treasury, as He taught in the temple; and no one seized
Him, because His hour had not yet come.

Jesus Warns of Coming Judgment
(127)

21 Then He said again to them, "I go away, and you will seek Me, and will die in your
sin; where I am going, you cannot come."
22 So the Jews were saying, "Surely He will not kill Himself, will He, since He says,
'Where I am going, you cannot come'?"
23 And He was saying to them, "You are from below, I am from above; you are of this
world, I am not of this world.
24 "Therefore I said to you that you will die in your sins; for unless you believe that I am
He, you will die in your sins."

8:11 John 3:17; John 5:14

8:12 John 1:4; 9:5; 12:35; Matt 5:14

8:13 John 5:31

8:14 John 18:37; Rev 1:5; 3:14; John 8:42; 13:3; 16:28

8:15 1 Sam 16:7; John 7:24; John 3:17

8:16 John 5:30

8:17 Deut 17:6; 19:15; Matt 18:16

8:18 John 5:37; 1 John 5:9

8:19 John 7:28; 8:55; 14:7, 9; 16:3

8:20 Mark 12:41, 43; Luke 21:1; John 7:14; 8:2; John 7:30

8:21 John 7:34

8:22 John 1:19; 8:48, 52, 57; John 7:35

8:23 John 3:31; 1 John 4:5; John 17:14, 16

8:24 John 8:21; Matt 24:5; Mark 13:6; Luke 21:8; John 4:26; 8:28, 58; 13:19

8:9 When Jesus said that only someone who had not sinned should throw the first stone, the leaders slipped quietly away, from oldest to youngest. Evidently the older men were more aware of their sins than the younger. Age and experience often temper youthful self-righteousness. But whatever your age, take an honest look at your life. Recognize your sinful nature, and look for ways to help others rather than hurt them.

8:11 Jesus didn't condemn the woman accused of adultery, but neither did he ignore or condone her sin. He told her to leave her life of sin. Jesus stands ready to forgive any sin in your life, but confession and repentance mean a change of heart. With God's help we can accept Christ's forgiveness and stop our wrongdoing.

8:12 To understand what Jesus meant by *the Light of the world*, see the notes on 1:4–5.

8:12 Jesus was speaking in the part of the temple where the offerings were put (8:20), where candles burned to symbolize the pillar of fire that led the people of Israel through the wilderness (Exodus 13:21–22). In this context, Jesus called himself the Light of the world. The pillar of fire represented God's presence, protection, and guidance. Jesus brings God's presence, protection, and guidance. Is he the Light of *your* world?

8:12 What does it mean to follow Christ? As a soldier follows his captain, so we should follow Christ, our commander. As a slave follows his master, so we should follow Christ, our Lord. As we follow the advice of a trusted counselor, so we should follow Jesus' commands to us in Scripture. As we follow the laws of our nation, so we should follow the laws of the kingdom of heaven.

8:13–14 The Pharisees thought Jesus was either a lunatic or a liar. Jesus provided them with a third alternative: He was telling the truth. Because most of the Pharisees refused to consider the third alternative, they never recognized him as Messiah and Lord. If you are seeking to know who Jesus is, do not close any door before looking through it honestly. Only with an open mind will you know the truth that he is Messiah and Lord.

8:13–18 The Pharisees argued that Jesus' claim was legally invalid because he had no other witnesses. Jesus responded that his confirming witness was God himself. Jesus and the Father made two witnesses, the number required by the law (Deuteronomy 19:15).

8:20 The temple treasury was located in the court of women. In this area, 13 collection boxes were set up to receive money offerings. Seven of the boxes were for the temple tax; the other six were for freewill offerings. On another occasion, a widow placed her money in one of these boxes, and Jesus taught a profound lesson from her action (Luke 21:1–4).

8:24 People will die in their sins if they reject Christ, because they are rejecting the only way to be rescued from sin. Sadly, many are so taken up with the values of this world that they are blind to the priceless gift Christ offers. Where are you looking? Don't focus on this world's values and miss what is most valuable—eternal life with God.

25 So they were saying to Him, "Who are You?" Jesus said to them, "What have I been
saying to you *from* the beginning?
26 "I have many things to speak and to judge concerning you, but He who sent Me is
true; and the things which I heard from Him, these I speak to the world."
27 They did not realize that He had been speaking to them about the Father.
28 So Jesus said, "When you lift up the Son of Man, then you will know that I am *He,*
and I do nothing on My own initiative, but I speak these things as the Father taught Me.
29 "And He who sent Me is with Me; He has not left Me alone, for I always do the things
that are pleasing to Him."
30 As He spoke these things, many came to believe in Him.

Jesus Speaks about God's True Children
(128)

31 So Jesus was saying to those Jews who had believed Him, "If you continue in My
word, *then* you are truly disciples of Mine;
32 and you will know the truth, and the truth will make you free."
33 They answered Him, "We are Abraham's descendants and have never yet been
enslaved to anyone; how is it that You say, 'You will become free'?"
34 Jesus answered them, "Truly, truly, I say to you, everyone who commits sin is the
slave of sin.
35 "The slave does not remain in the house forever; the son does remain forever.
36 "So if the Son makes you free, you will be free indeed.
37 "I know that you are Abraham's descendants; yet you seek to kill Me, because My
word has no place in you.
38 "I speak the things which I have seen with *My* Father; therefore you also do the things
which you heard from *your* father."
39 They answered and said to Him, "Abraham is our father." Jesus ☆said to them, "If
you are Abraham's children, do the deeds of Abraham.
40 "But as it is, you are seeking to kill Me, a man who has told you the truth, which I
heard from God; this Abraham did not do.
41 "You are doing the deeds of your father." They said to Him, "We were not born of
fornication; we have one Father: God."
42 Jesus said to them, "If God were your Father, you would love Me, for I proceeded
forth and have come from God, for I have not even come on My own initiative, but He
sent Me.
43 "Why do you not understand what I am saying? *It is* because you cannot hear My
word.
44 "You are of *your* father the devil, and you want to do the desires of your father. He
was a murderer from the beginning, and does not stand in the truth because there is no
truth in him. Whenever he speaks a lie, he speaks from his own *nature,* for he is a liar
and the father of lies.
45 "But because I speak the truth, you do not believe Me.

8:26 John 3:33; 7:28; 12:49; 15:15
8:28 John 3:14; 12:32; Matt 24:5; Mark 13:6; Luke 21:8; John 4:26; 13:19; John 3:11; 5:19
8:29 John 4:34
8:30 John 7:31
8:31 John 15:7; 2 John 9; John 2:2
8:32 John 1:14, 17; John 8:36; Rom 8:2; 2 Cor 3:17; Gal 5:1, 13; James 2:12; 1 Pet 2:16
8:33 Matt 3:9; Luke 3:8
8:34 Rom 6:16; 2 Pet 2:19
8:35 Gen 21:10; Gal 4:30; Luke 15:31
8:37 Matt 3:9; John 7:1
8:39 Matt 3:9; John 8:37; Rom 9:7; Gal 3:7
8:40 John 7:1; 8:37
8:41 Is 63:16; 64:8
8:42 1 John 5:1; John 13:3; 16:28, 30; 17:8; John 7:28
8:43 John 5:25
8:44 1 John 3:8; John 7:17; Gen 3:4; 1 John 3:8, 15; 1 John 2:4
8:45 John 18:37

8:32 Jesus himself is the truth that sets us free (8:36). He is the source of truth, the perfect standard of what is right. He frees us from the consequences of sin, from self-deception, and from deception by Satan. He shows us clearly the way to eternal life with God. Thus Jesus does not give us freedom to do what we want, but freedom to follow God. As we seek to serve God, Jesus' perfect truth frees us to be all that God meant us to be.

8:34–35 Sin has a way of enslaving us, controlling us, dominating us, and dictating our actions. Jesus can free you from this slavery that keeps you from becoming the person God created you to be. If sin is restraining, mastering, or enslaving you, Jesus can break its power over your life.

8:41 Jesus made a distinction between hereditary children and *true* children. The religious leaders were hereditary children of Abraham (founder of the Jewish nation) and therefore claimed to be children of God. But their actions showed them to be true children of the devil, for they lived under the devil's guidance. True children of Abraham (faithful followers of God) would not act as they did. Your church membership and family connections will not make you a true child of God. Your true father is the one you imitate and obey.

8:43 The religious leaders were unable to understand because they refused to listen. Satan used their stubbornness, pride, and prejudices to keep them from believing in Jesus.

8:44–45 The attitudes and actions of these leaders clearly identified them as followers of the devil. They may not have been conscious of this, but their hatred of truth, their lies, and their murderous intentions indicated how much control the devil had over them. They were his tools in carrying out his plans; they spoke the very same language of lies. Satan still uses people to obstruct God's work (Genesis 4:8; Romans 5:12; 1 John 3:12).

46 "Which one of you convicts Me of sin? If I speak truth, why do you not believe Me?
47 "He who is of God hears the words of God; for this reason you do not hear *them,*
because you are not of God."

Jesus States He Is Eternal
(129)

48 The Jews answered and said to Him, "Do we not say rightly that You are a Samaritan and have a demon?"
49 Jesus answered, "I do not have a demon; but I honor My Father, and you dishonor Me.
50 "But I do not seek My glory; there is One who seeks and judges.
51 "Truly, truly, I say to you, if anyone keeps My word he will never see death."
52 The Jews said to Him, "Now we know that You have a demon. Abraham died, and
the prophets *also;* and You say, 'If anyone keeps My word, he will never taste of death.'
53 "Surely You are not greater than our father Abraham, who died? The prophets died
too; whom do You make Yourself out *to be?*"
54 Jesus answered, "If I glorify Myself, My glory is nothing; it is My Father who glorifies Me, of whom you say, 'He is our God';
55 and you have not come to know Him, but I know Him; and if I say that I do not
know Him, I will be a liar like you, but I do know Him and keep His word.
56 "Your father Abraham rejoiced to see My day, and he saw *it* and was glad."
57 So the Jews said to Him, "You are not yet fifty years old, and have You seen
Abraham?"
58 Jesus said to them, "Truly, truly, I say to you, before Abraham was born, I am."
59 Therefore they picked up stones to throw at Him, but Jesus hid Himself and went
out of the temple.

Jesus Heals the Man Who Was Born Blind
(148)

9 As He passed by, He saw a man blind from birth.
2 And His disciples asked Him, "Rabbi, who sinned, this man or his parents, that
he would be born blind?"
3 Jesus answered, "*It was* neither *that* this man sinned, nor his parents; but *it was* so
that the works of God might be displayed in him.

8:46 John 18:37
8:47 1 John 4:6
8:48 John 1:19; Matt 10:5; John 4:9
8:49 John 7:20
8:50 John 5:41; 8:54
8:51 Matt 16:28; Luke 2:26; Heb 2:9; 11:5
8:52 John 1:19; 7:20; 14:23; 15:20; 17:6
8:53 John 4:12
8:54 John 7:39
8:55 John 7:29
8:56 Matt 13:17; Heb 11:13
8:57 John 1:19
8:58 Ex 3:14; John 1:1; 17:5, 24
8:59 Matt 12:14; John 10:31; 11:8
9:2 Matt 23:7; Luke 13:2; John 9:34; Acts 28:4; Ex 20:5
9:3 John 11:4

8:46 No one could accuse Jesus of a single sin. People who hated him and wanted him dead scrutinized his behavior but could find nothing wrong. Jesus proved he was God in the flesh by his sinless life. He is the only perfect example for us to follow.

8:46–47 In a number of places Jesus intentionally challenged his listeners to test him. He welcomed those who wanted to question his claims and character as long as they were willing to follow through on what they discovered. Jesus' challenge clarifies the two most frequent reasons that people miss when encountering him: (1) They never accept his challenge to test him, or (2) they test him but are not willing to believe what they discover. Have you made either of those mistakes?

8:51 To keep Jesus' word means to hear his words and obey them. When Jesus says those who obey won't die, he is talking about spiritual death, not physical death. Even physical death, however, will eventually be overcome. Those who follow Christ will be raised to live eternally with him.

8:56 God told Abraham, the father of the Jewish nation, that through him all nations would be blessed (Genesis 12:1–7; 15:1–21). Abraham had been able to see this through the eyes of faith. Jesus, a descendant of Abraham, blessed all people through his death, resurrection, and offer of salvation.

8:58 This is one of the most powerful statements uttered by Jesus. When he said that he existed before Abraham was born, he undeniably proclaimed his divinity. Not only did Jesus say that he existed before Abraham; he also applied God's holy name (*I Am*—Exodus 3:14) to himself. This claim demands a response. It cannot be ignored. The Jewish leaders tried to stone Jesus for blasphemy because he claimed equality with God. But Jesus *is* God. How have you responded to Jesus, the Son of God?

8:59 In accordance with the law in Leviticus 24:16, the religious leaders were ready to stone Jesus for claiming to be God. They well understood what Jesus was claiming, and because they didn't believe him, they charged him with blasphemy. It is ironic that *they* were really the blasphemers, cursing and attacking the very God they claimed to serve!

9:1ff In chapter 9, we see four different reactions to Jesus. The neighbors revealed surprise and skepticism; the Pharisees showed disbelief and prejudice; the parents believed but kept quiet for fear of excommunication; and the healed man showed consistent, growing faith.

9:2–3 A common belief in Jewish culture was that calamity or suffering was the result of some great sin. But Christ used this man's suffering to teach about faith and to glorify God. We live in a fallen world where good behavior is not always rewarded and bad behavior not always punished. Therefore, innocent people sometimes suffer. If God took suffering away whenever we asked, we would follow him for comfort and convenience, not out of love and devotion. Regardless of the reasons for our suffering, Jesus has the power to help us deal with it. When you suffer from a disease, tragedy, or disability, try not to ask, "Why did this happen to me?" or "What did I do wrong?" Instead, ask God to give you strength for the trial and a clearer perspective on what is happening.

4 "We must work the works of Him who sent Me as long as it is day; night is coming
when no one can work.
5 "While I am in the world, I am the Light of the world."
6 When He had said this, He spat on the ground, and made clay of the spittle, and
applied the clay to his eyes,
7 and said to him, "Go, wash in the pool of Siloam" (which is translated, Sent). So he
went away and washed, and came *back* seeing.
8 Therefore the neighbors, and those who previously saw him as a beggar, were saying, "Is not this the one who used to sit and beg?"
9 Others were saying, "This is he," *still* others were saying, "No, but he is like him."
He kept saying, "I am the one."
10 So they were saying to him, "How then were your eyes opened?"
11 He answered, "The man who is called Jesus made clay, and anointed my eyes, and
said to me, 'Go to Siloam and wash'; so I went away and washed, and I received sight."
12 They said to him, "Where is He?" He ☆said, "I do not know."

Religious Leaders Question the Blind Man
(149)

13 They ☆brought to the Pharisees the man who was formerly blind.
14 Now it was a Sabbath on the day when Jesus made the clay and opened his eyes.
15 Then the Pharisees also were asking him again how he received his sight. And he
said to them, "He applied clay to my eyes, and I washed, and I see."
16 Therefore some of the Pharisees were saying, "This man is not from God, because
He does not keep the Sabbath." But others were saying, "How can a man who is a sinner
perform such signs?" And there was a division among them.
17 So they ☆said to the blind man again, "What do you say about Him, since He opened
your eyes?" And he said, "He is a prophet."
18 The Jews then did not believe *it* of him, that he had been blind and had received
sight, until they called the parents of the very one who had received his sight,
19 and questioned them, saying, "Is this your son, who you say was born blind? Then
how does he now see?"
20 His parents answered them and said, "We know that this is our son, and that he was
born blind;
21 but how he now sees, we do not know; or who opened his eyes, we do not know. Ask
him; he is of age, he will speak for himself."
22 His parents said this because they were afraid of the Jews; for the Jews had already
agreed that if anyone confessed Him to be Christ, he was to be put out of the synagogue.
23 For this reason his parents said, "He is of age; ask him."
24 So a second time they called the man who had been blind, and said to him, "Give
glory to God; we know that this man is a sinner."
25 He then answered, "Whether He is a sinner, I do not know; one thing I do know,
that though I was blind, now I see."
26 So they said to him, "What did He do to you? How did He open your eyes?"
27 He answered them, "I told you already and you did not listen; why do you want to
hear *it* again? You do not want to become His disciples too, do you?"

9:4 John 7:33; 11:9; 12:35; Gal 6:10
9:5 Matt 5:14; John 1:4; 8:12; 12:46
9:6 Mark 7:33; 8:23
9:7 Neh 3:15; Is 8:6; Luke 13:4; John 9:11; 2 Kin 5:13f; Is 29:18; 35:5; 42:7; Matt 11:5; John 11:37
9:8 Acts 3:2, 10
9:11 John 9:7
9:14 John 5:9
9:15 John 9:10
9:16 Matt 12:2; Luke 13:14; John 5:10; 7:23; John 2:11; John 6:52; 7:12, 43; 10:19
9:17 John 9:15; Deut 18:15; Matt 21:11
9:18 John 1:19; 9:22
9:22 John 7:13; John 7:45-52; Luke 6:22; John 12:42; 16:2
9:23 John 9:21
9:24 Josh 7:19; Ezra 10:11; Rev 11:13; John 9:16
9:27 John 9:15; John 5:25

9:7 The pool of Siloam was built by Hezekiah. His workers constructed an underground tunnel from a spring outside the city walls to carry water into the city. Thus the people could always get water without fear of being attacked. This was especially important during times of siege (see 2 Kings 20:20; 2 Chronicles 32:30).

9:13–17 While the Pharisees conducted investigations and debated about Jesus, people were being healed and lives were being changed. The Pharisees' skepticism was based not on insufficient evidence, but on jealousy of Jesus' popularity and his influence on the people.

9:14–16 The Jewish Sabbath, Saturday, was the weekly holy day of rest. The Pharisees had made a long list of specific do's and don't's regarding the Sabbath. Kneading the clay and healing the man were considered work and therefore were forbidden. Jesus may have purposely made the clay in order to emphasize his teaching about the Sabbath—that it is right to care for others' needs even if it involves working on a day of rest.

9:25 By now the man who had been blind had heard the same questions over and over. He did not know how or why he was healed, but he knew that his life had been miraculously changed, and he was not afraid to tell the truth. You don't need to know all the answers in order to share Christ with others. It is important to tell them how he has changed your life. Then trust that God will use your words to help others believe in him too.

28 They reviled him and said, "You are His disciple, but we are disciples of Moses.
29 "We know that God has spoken to Moses, but as for this man, we do not know where
He is from."
30 The man answered and said to them, "Well, here is an amazing thing, that you do
not know where He is from, and *yet* He opened my eyes.
31 "We know that God does not hear sinners; but if anyone is God-fearing and does
His will, He hears him.
32 "Since the beginning of time it has never been heard that anyone opened the eyes of
a person born blind.
33 "If this man were not from God, He could do nothing."
34 They answered him, "You were born entirely in sins, and are you teaching us?" So
they put him out.

Jesus Teaches about Spiritual Blindness
(150)

35 Jesus heard that they had put him out, and finding him, He said, "Do you believe in
the Son of Man?"
36 He answered, "Who is He, Lord, that I may believe in Him?"
37 Jesus said to him, "You have both seen Him, and He is the one who is talking
with you."
38 And he said, "Lord, I believe." And he worshiped Him.
39 And Jesus said, "For judgment I came into this world, so that those who do not see
may see, and that those who see may become blind."
40 Those of the Pharisees who were with Him heard these things and said to Him, "We
are not blind too, are we?"
41 Jesus said to them, "If you were blind, you would have no sin; but since you say, 'We
see,' your sin remains.

Jesus Is the Good Shepherd
(151)

10 "Truly, truly, I say to you, he who does not enter by the door into the fold of the
sheep, but climbs up some other way, he is a thief and a robber.
2 "But he who enters by the door is a shepherd of the sheep.
3 "To him the doorkeeper opens, and the sheep hear his voice, and he calls his own
sheep by name and leads them out.
4 "When he puts forth all his own, he goes ahead of them, and the sheep follow him
because they know his voice.
5 "A stranger they simply will not follow, but will flee from him, because they do not
know the voice of strangers."
6 This figure of speech Jesus spoke to them, but they did not understand what those
things were which He had been saying to them.
7 So Jesus said to them again, "Truly, truly, I say to you, I am the door of the sheep.

9:28 John 5:45; Rom 2:17
9:29 John 8:14
9:31 Job 27:8f; 35:13; Ps 34:15f; 66:18; 145:19; Prov 15:29; 28:9; Is 1:15; James 5:16ff
9:33 John 3:2; 9:16
9:34 John 9:2; John 9:22, 35; 3 John 10
9:35 John 9:22, 34; 3 John 10; Matt 4:3
9:36 Rom 10:14
9:37 John 4:26
9:38 Matt 8:2
9:39 John 3:19; 5:22, 27; Luke 4:18; Matt 13:13; 15:14
9:40 Rom 2:19
9:41 John 15:22, 24; Prov 26:12
10:1 John 10:8
10:2 John 10:11f
10:3 John 10:4f, 16, 27; John 10:9
10:4 John 10:5, 16, 27
10:5 John 10:4, 16, 27
10:6 John 16:25, 29; 2 Pet 2:22
10:7 John 10:1f, 9

9:28, 34 The man's new faith was severely tested by some of the authorities. He was reviled and evicted from the synagogue. Persecution may come when you follow Jesus. You may lose friends; you may even lose your life. But no one can ever take away the eternal life that Jesus gives you.

9:38 The longer this man experienced his new life through Christ, the more confident he became in the One who had healed him. He gained not only physical sight but also spiritual sight as he recognized Jesus first as a prophet (9:17), then as his Lord. When you turn to Christ, you begin to see him differently. The longer you walk with him, the better you will understand who he is. Peter tells us to "grow in the grace and knowledge of our Lord and Savior Jesus Christ" (2 Peter 3:18). If you want to know more about Jesus, keep walking with him.

9:40–41 The Pharisees were shocked that Jesus thought they were spiritually blind. Jesus countered by saying that it was only blindness (stubbornness and stupidity) that could excuse their behavior. To those who remained open and recognized how sin had truly blinded them from knowing the truth, he gave spiritual understanding and insight. But he rejected those who had become complacent, self-satisfied, and blind.

10:1 At night, sheep were often gathered into a sheep fold to protect them from thieves, weather, or wild animals. The sheep folds were caves, sheds, or open areas surrounded by walls made of stones or branches. The shepherd often slept in the fold to protect the sheep. Just as a shepherd cares for his sheep, so Jesus, the good shepherd, cares for his flock (those who follow him). The prophet Ezekiel, in predicting the coming of the Messiah, called him a shepherd (Ezekiel 34:23).

10:7 In the sheep fold, the shepherd functioned as a door, letting the sheep in and protecting them. Jesus is the door to God's salvation for us. He offers access to safety and security. Christ is our protector. Some people resent that Jesus is the door, the only way of access to God. But Jesus is God's Son—why should we seek any other way or want to customize a different approach to God? (See also the note on 14:6.)

8 "All who came before Me are thieves and robbers, but the sheep did not hear them.
9 "I am the door; if anyone enters through Me, he will be saved, and will go in and out
and find pasture.
10 "The thief comes only to steal and kill and destroy; I came that they may have life,
and have *it* abundantly.
11 "I am the good shepherd; the good shepherd lays down His life for the sheep.
12 "He who is a hired hand, and not a shepherd, who is not the owner of the sheep, sees
the wolf coming, and leaves the sheep and flees, and the wolf snatches them and scatters
them.
13 "*He flees* because he is a hired hand and is not concerned about the sheep.
14 "I am the good shepherd, and I know My own and My own know Me,
15 even as the Father knows Me and I know the Father; and I lay down My life for the
sheep.
16 "I have other sheep, which are not of this fold; I must bring them also, and they will
hear My voice; and they will become one flock *with* one shepherd.
17 "For this reason the Father loves Me, because I lay down My life so that I may take
it again.
18 "No one has taken it away from Me, but I lay it down on My own initiative. I have
authority to lay it down, and I have authority to take it up again. This commandment I
received from My Father."
19 A division occurred again among the Jews because of these words.
20 Many of them were saying, "He has a demon and is insane. Why do you listen
to Him?"
21 Others were saying, "These are not the sayings of one demon-possessed. A demon
cannot open the eyes of the blind, can he?"

Religious Leaders Surround Jesus at the Temple
(152)

22 At that time the Feast of the Dedication took place at Jerusalem;
23 it was winter, and Jesus was walking in the temple in the portico of Solomon.

10:8 Jer 23:1f; Ezek 34:2ff; John 10:1
10:10 John 5:40
10:11 Is 40:11; Ezek 34:11-16, 23; Heb 13:20; 1 Pet 5:4; Rev 7:17; 15:13; 1 John 3:16
10:15 Matt 11:27; Luke 10:22; John 10:11
10:16 Is 56:8; John 11:52; 17:20f; Eph 2:13-18; 1 Pet 2:25; Ezek 34:23; 37:24
10:17 John 10:11, 15, 18
10:18 Matt 26:53; John 2:19; 5:26; John 10:11, 15, 17; John 14:31; 15:10; Phil 2:8; Heb 5:8
10:19 John 7:43; 9:16
10:20 John 7:20; Mark 3:21
10:21 Matt 4:24; Ex 4:11; John 9:32f
10:23 Acts 3:11; 5:12

10:10 In contrast to the thief who takes life, Jesus gives life. The life he gives right now is abundantly richer and fuller. It is eternal, yet it begins immediately. Life in Christ is lived on a higher plane because of his overflowing forgiveness, love, and guidance. Have you taken Christ's offer of life?

10:11–12 A hired hand tends the sheep for money, while the shepherd does it for love. The shepherd owns the sheep and is committed to them. Jesus is not merely doing a job; he is committed to love us and even lay down his life for us. False teachers and false prophets do not have this commitment.

10:16 The "other sheep" were non-Jews. Jesus came to save Gentiles as well as Jews. This is an insight into his worldwide mission—to die for the sins of the world. People tend to want to restrict God's blessings to their own group, but Jesus refuses to be limited by the fences we build.

10:17–18 Jesus' death and resurrection, as part of God's plan for the salvation of the world, were under God's full control. No one could kill Jesus without his consent.

10:19–20 If Jesus had been merely a man, his claims to be God would have proven him insane. But his miracles proved his words true—he really was God. The Jewish leaders could not see beyond their own prejudices, and they looked at Jesus only from a human perspective—Jesus confined in a human box. But Jesus was not limited by their restricted vision.

10:22–23 The Feast of the Dedication commemorated the cleansing of the temple under Judas Maccabeus in 165 B.C. after Antiochus Epiphanes had defiled it by sacrificing a pig on the altar of burnt offering. The feast was celebrated toward the end of December. This is also the present-day Feast of Lights called Hanukkah.

10:23 The portico of Solomon was a roofed walkway supported by large stone columns, just inside the walls of the temple courtyard.

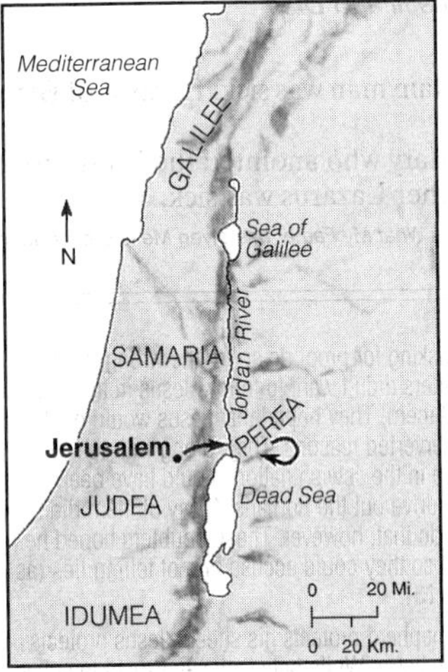

MINISTRY EAST OF THE JORDAN
Jesus had been in Jerusalem for the Feast of Booths (7:2); then he preached in various towns, probably in Judea, before returning to Jerusalem for Hanukkah. He again angered the religious leaders, who tried to arrest him, but he left the city and went to the region east of the Jordan to preach.

24 The Jews then gathered around Him, and were saying to Him, "How long will You
keep us in suspense? If You are the Christ, tell us plainly."
25 Jesus answered them, "I told you, and you do not believe; the works that I do in My
Father's name, these testify of Me.
26 "But you do not believe because you are not of My sheep.
27 "My sheep hear My voice, and I know them, and they follow Me;
28 and I give eternal life to them, and they will never perish; and no one will snatch
them out of My hand.
29 "[17]My Father, who has given *them* to Me, is greater than all; and no one is able to
snatch *them* out of the Father's hand.
30 "I and the Father are one."
31 The Jews picked up stones again to stone Him.
32 Jesus answered them, "I showed you many good works from the Father; for which
of them are you stoning Me?"
33 The Jews answered Him, "For a good work we do not stone You, but for blasphemy; and because You, being a man, make Yourself out *to be* God."
34 Jesus answered them, "Has it not been written in your Law, 'I SAID, YOU ARE GODS'?
35 "If he called them gods, to whom the word of God came (and the Scripture cannot
be broken),
36 do you say of Him, whom the Father sanctified and sent into the world, 'You are
blaspheming,' because I said, 'I am the Son of God'?
37 "If I do not do the works of My Father, do not believe Me;
38 but if I do them, though you do not believe Me, believe the works, so that you may
know and understand that the Father is in Me, and I in the Father."
39 Therefore they were seeking again to seize Him, and He eluded their grasp.
40 And He went away again beyond the Jordan to the place where John was first baptizing, and He was staying there.
41 Many came to Him and were saying, "While John performed no sign, yet everything
John said about this man was true."
42 Many believed in Him there.

3. Jesus encounters crucial events in Jerusalem

Lazarus Becomes Ill and Dies
(165)

11 Now a certain man was sick, Lazarus of Bethany, the village of Mary and her sister
Martha.
2 It was the Mary who anointed the Lord with ointment, and wiped His feet with her
hair, whose brother Lazarus was sick.

17 One early ms reads *What My Father has given Me is greater than all*

10:24 John 1:19; 10:31, 33; Luke 22:67; John 16:25
10:25 John 8:56, 58; John 5:36; 10:38
10:26 John 8:47
10:28 John 17:2f; 1 John 2:25; 5:11; John 6:37, 39
10:31 John 8:59
10:33 John 5:18
10:34 John 8:17; John 12:34; 15:25; Rom 3:19; 1 Cor 14:21
10:36 Jer 1:5; John 6:69; John 3:17; 5:17f; 10:30
10:37 John 10:25; 15:24
10:38 John 14:10f, 20; 17:21, 23
10:39 John 7:30; Luke 4:30; John 8:59
10:40 John 1:28
10:41 John 2:11; John 1:27, 30, 34; 3:27-30
10:42 John 7:31
11:1 Matt 21:17; John 11:18; Luke 10:38; John 11:5, 19ff
11:2 Luke 7:38; John 12:3; Luke 7:13; John 11:3, 21, 32; 13:13f

10:24 Many people asking for proof do so for the wrong reasons. Most of these questioners didn't want to follow Jesus in the way that he wanted to lead them. They hoped that Jesus would declare himself Messiah for perverted reasons. They, along with the disciples and everyone else in the Jewish nation, would have been delighted to have him drive out the Romans. Many of them didn't think he was going to do that, however. These doubters hoped he would identify himself so they could accuse him of telling lies (as the Pharisees did in 8:13).

10:28–29 Just as a shepherd protects his sheep, Jesus protects his people from eternal harm. While believers can expect to suffer on earth, Satan cannot harm their souls or take away their eternal life with God. There are many reasons to be afraid here on earth because this is the devil's domain (1 Peter 5:8). But if you choose to follow Jesus, he will give you everlasting safety.

10:30 This is the clearest statement of Jesus' divinity he ever made. Jesus and his Father are not the same person, but they are one in essence and nature. Thus Jesus is not merely a good teacher—he is God. His claim to be God was unmistakable. The religious leaders wanted to kill him because their laws said that anyone claiming to be God should die. Nothing could persuade them that Jesus' claim was true.

10:31 The Jewish leaders attempted to carry out the directive found in Leviticus 24:16 regarding those who blaspheme (claim to be God). They intended to stone Jesus.

10:34–36 Jesus referred to Psalm 82:6, where the Israelite rulers and judges are called "gods" (see also Exodus 4:16; 7:1). If God called the Israelite leaders gods because they were agents of God's revelation and will, how could it be blasphemy for Jesus to call himself the Son of God? Jesus was rebuking the religious leaders, because he is the Son of God in a unique, unparalleled relationship of oneness with the Father.

10:35 "The Scripture cannot be broken" is a clear statement of the truth of the Bible. If we accept Christ as Lord, we also must accept his testimony to the Bible as God's Word.

11:1 The village of Bethany was located about two miles east of Jerusalem on the road to Jericho. It was near enough to Jerusalem for Jesus and the disciples to be in danger, but far enough away so as not to attract attention prematurely.

11:3 Luke 7:13; John 11:2, 21, 32; 13:13
11:4 John 9:3; 10:38; 11:40
11:7 John 10:40
11:8 Matt 23:7; John 8:59; 10:31
11:9 Luke 13:33; John 9:4; 12:35
11:11 John 11:3; Matt 27:52; Mark 5:39; John 11:13; Acts 7:60

3 So the sisters sent *word* to Him, saying, "Lord, behold, he whom You love is sick."
4 But when Jesus heard *this*, He said, "This sickness is not to end in death, but for the
glory of God, so that the Son of God may be glorified by it."
5 Now Jesus loved Martha and her sister and Lazarus.
6 So when He heard that he was sick, He then stayed two days *longer* in the place where
He was.
7 Then after this He ☆said to the disciples, "Let us go to Judea again."
8 The disciples ☆said to Him, "Rabbi, the Jews were just now seeking to stone You,
and are You going there again?"
9 Jesus answered, "Are there not twelve hours in the day? If anyone walks in the day,
he does not stumble, because he sees the light of this world.
10 "But if anyone walks in the night, he stumbles, because the light is not in him."
11 This He said, and after that He ☆said to them, "Our friend Lazarus has fallen asleep;
but I go, so that I may awaken him out of sleep."

THE NAMES OF JESUS IN THE BOOK OF JOHN
In different settings, Jesus gave himself names that pointed to special roles he was ready to fulfill for people. Some of these refer back to the Old Testament promises of the Messiah. Others were ways to help people understand him.

Reference	Name	Significance
6:27	Son of Man	Jesus' favorite reference to himself. It emphasized his humanity—but the way he used it, it was a claim to divinity.
6:35	Bread of life	Refers to his life-giving role—that he is the only source of eternal life.
8:12	Light of the world	Light is a symbol of spiritual truth. Jesus is the universal answer for man's need of spiritual truth.
10:7	Door for the sheep	Jesus is the only way into God's kingdom.
10:11	Good shepherd	Jesus appropriated the prophetic images of the Messiah pictured in the Old Testament. This is a claim to divinity, focusing on Jesus' love and guidance.
11:25	The resurrection and the life	Not only is Jesus the source of life, he is the power over death.
14:6	The way and the truth and the life	Jesus is the method, the message, and the meaning for all people. With this title he summarized his purpose in coming to earth.
15:1	The true vine	This title has an important second part, "you are the branches." As in so many of his other names, Jesus reminds us that just as branches gain life from the vine and cannot live apart from it, so we are completely dependent on Christ for spiritual life.

JESUS RAISES LAZARUS
Jesus had been preaching in the villages beyond the Jordan, probably in Perea, when he received the news of Lazarus's sickness. Jesus did not leave immediately, but waited two days before returning to Judea. He knew Lazarus would be dead when he arrived in Bethany, but he was going to do a great miracle.

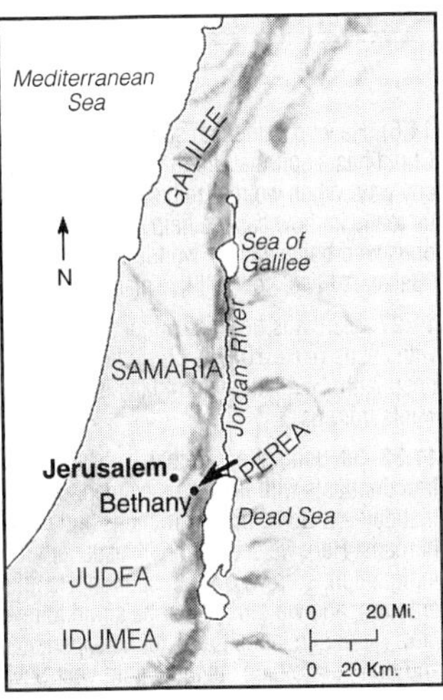

11:3 As their brother grew very sick, Mary and Martha turned to Jesus for help. They believed in his ability to help because they had seen his miracles. We too know of Jesus' miracles, both from Scripture and through changed lives we have seen. When we need extraordinary help, Jesus offers extraordinary resources. We should not hesitate to ask him for assistance.

11:4 Any trial a believer faces can ultimately bring glory to God because God can bring good out of any bad situation (Genesis 50:20; Romans 8:28). When trouble comes, do you grumble, complain, and blame God, or do you see your problems as opportunities to honor him?

11:5–7 Jesus loved this family and often stayed with them. He knew their pain but did not respond immediately. His delay had a specific purpose. God's timing, especially his delays, may make us think he is not answering or is not answering the way we want. But he will meet all our needs according to his perfect schedule and purpose (Philippians 4:19). Patiently await his timing.

11:9–10 *Day* pictures the knowledge of God's will and *night* the absence of this knowledge. When we move ahead in darkness, we will be likely to stumble.

12 The disciples then said to Him, "Lord, if he has fallen asleep, he will recover."
13 Now Jesus had spoken of his death, but they thought that He was speaking of literal
sleep.
14 So Jesus then said to them plainly, "Lazarus is dead,
15 and I am glad for your sakes that I was not there, so that you may believe; but let us
go to him."
16 Therefore Thomas, who is called Didymus, said to *his* fellow disciples, "Let us also
go, so that we may die with Him."

Jesus Comforts Mary and Martha
(166)

17 So when Jesus came, He found that he had already been in the tomb four days.
18 Now Bethany was near Jerusalem, about two miles off;
19 and many of the Jews had come to Martha and Mary, to console them concerning
their brother.
20 Martha therefore, when she heard that Jesus was coming, went to meet Him, but
Mary stayed at the house.
21 Martha then said to Jesus, "Lord, if You had been here, my brother would not have
died.
22 "Even now I know that whatever You ask of God, God will give You."
23 Jesus ☆said to her, "Your brother will rise again."
24 Martha ☆said to Him, "I know that he will rise again in the resurrection on the last
day."
25 Jesus said to her, "I am the resurrection and the life; he who believes in Me will live
even if he dies,
26 and everyone who lives and believes in Me will never die. Do you believe this?"
27 She ☆said to Him, "Yes, Lord; I have believed that You are the Christ, the Son of
God, *even* He who comes into the world."
28 When she had said this, she went away and called Mary her sister, saying secretly,
"The Teacher is here and is calling for you."
29 And when she heard it, she ☆got up quickly and was coming to Him.
30 Now Jesus had not yet come into the village, but was still in the place where Martha
met Him.
31 Then the Jews who were with her in the house, and consoling her, when they saw
that Mary got up quickly and went out, they followed her, supposing that she was going
to the tomb to weep there.
32 Therefore, when Mary came where Jesus was, she saw Him, and fell at His feet, saying
to Him, "Lord, if You had been here, my brother would not have died."
33 When Jesus therefore saw her weeping, and the Jews who came with her *also* weeping, He was deeply moved in spirit and was troubled,
34 and said, "Where have you laid him?" They ☆said to Him, "Lord, come and see."

11:13 Matt 9:24; Luke 8:52
11:16 Matt 10:3; Mark 3:18; Luke 6:15; John 14:5; 20:26-28; Acts 1:13; John 20:24; 21:2
11:17 John 11:39
11:18 John 11:1
11:19 John 1:19; 11:8; John 11:1; 1 Sam 31:13; 1 Chr 10:12; Job 2:11; John 11:31
11:20 Luke 10:38-42
11:21 John 11:2; John 11:32, 37
11:22 John 9:31; 11:41f
11:24 Dan 12:2; John 5:28f; Acts 24:15
11:25 John 1:4; 5:26; 6:39f; Rev 1:18
11:26 John 6:47, 50, 51; 8:51
11:27 Matt 16:16; Luke 2:11; John 6:14
11:28 John 11:30; Matt 26:18; Mark 14:14; Luke 22:11; John 13:13
11:30 John 11:20
11:31 John 11:19, 33; John 11:19
11:33 John 11:19; John 11:38; John 12:27; 13:21

11:14–15 If Jesus had been with Lazarus during the final moments of Lazarus's sickness, he might have healed him rather than let him die. But Lazarus died so that Jesus' power over death could be shown to his disciples and others. The raising of Lazarus was an essential display of his power, and the resurrection from the dead is a crucial belief of Christian faith. Jesus not only raised himself from the dead (10:18), but he has the power to raise others.

11:16 We often remember Thomas as "the doubter," because he doubted Jesus' resurrection. But here he demonstrated love and courage. The disciples knew the dangers of going with Jesus to Jerusalem, and they tried to talk him out of it. Thomas merely expressed what all of them felt. When their objections failed, they were willing to go and even die with Jesus. They may not have understood why Jesus would be killed, but they were loyal. There are unknown dangers in doing God's work. It is wise to consider the high cost of being Jesus' disciple.

11:25–26 Jesus has power over life and death as well as power to forgive sins. This is because he is the Creator of life (see John 14:6). He who *is* life can surely restore life. Whoever believes in Christ has a spiritual life that death cannot conquer or diminish in any way. When we realize his power and how wonderful his offer to us really is, how can we help but commit our lives to him! To those of us who believe, what wonderful assurance and certainty we have: "Because I live, you will live also" (14:19).

11:27 Martha is best known for being too busy to sit down and talk with Jesus (Luke 10:38–42). But here we see her as a woman of deep faith. Her statement of faith is exactly the response that Jesus wants from us.

11:33–38 John stresses that we have a God who cares. This portrait contrasts with the Greek concept of God that was popular in that day—a God with no emotions and no messy involvement with humans. Here we see many of Jesus' emotions—compassion, indignation, sorrow, even frustration. He often expressed deep emotion, and we must never be afraid to reveal our true feelings to him. He understands them, for he experienced them. Be honest, and don't try to hide anything from your Savior. He cares.

35 Jesus wept.
36 So the Jews were saying, "See how He loved him!"
37 But some of them said, "Could not this man, who opened the eyes of the blind man,
have kept this man also from dying?"

Jesus Raises Lazarus from the Dead
(167)

38 So Jesus, again being deeply moved within, ☆came to the tomb. Now it was a cave,
and a stone was lying against it.
39 Jesus ☆said, "Remove the stone." Martha, the sister of the deceased, ☆said to Him,
"Lord, by this time there will be a stench, for he has been *dead* four days."
40 Jesus ☆said to her, "Did I not say to you that if you believe, you will see the glory
of God?"
41 So they removed the stone. Then Jesus raised His eyes, and said, "Father, I thank
You that You have heard Me.
42 "I knew that You always hear Me; but because of the people standing around I said
it, so that they may believe that You sent Me."
43 When He had said these things, He cried out with a loud voice, "Lazarus, come
forth."
44 The man who had died came forth, bound hand and foot with wrappings, and his
face was wrapped around with a cloth. Jesus ☆said to them, "Unbind him, and let
him go."

Religious Leaders Plot to Kill Jesus
(168)

45 Therefore many of the Jews who came to Mary, and saw what He had done, believed in Him.
46 But some of them went to the Pharisees and told them the things which Jesus had
done.
47 Therefore the chief priests and the Pharisees convened a council, and were saying,
"What are we doing? For this man is performing many signs.
48 "If we let Him *go on* like this, all men will believe in Him, and the Romans will come
and take away both our place and our nation."
49 But one of them, Caiaphas, who was high priest that year, said to them, "You know
nothing at all,
50 nor do you take into account that it is expedient for you that one man die for the
people, and that the whole nation not perish."
51 Now he did not say this on his own initiative, but being high priest that year, he
prophesied that Jesus was going to die for the nation,
52 and not for the nation only, but in order that He might also gather together into
one the children of God who are scattered abroad.
53 So from that day on they planned together to kill Him.
54 Therefore Jesus no longer continued to walk publicly among the Jews, but went away
from there to the country near the wilderness, into a city called Ephraim; and there He
stayed with the disciples.

11:35 Luke 19:41; John 11:33
11:36 John 11:19; John 11:3
11:37 John 9:7
11:38 Matt 27:60; Mark 15:46; Luke 24:2; John 20:1
11:39 John 11:17
11:40 John 11:4, 23ff
11:41 Matt 27:60; Mark 15:46; Luke 24:2; John 20:1; John 17:1; Acts 7:55; Matt 11:25
11:42 John 12:30; 17:21; John 3:17
11:44 John 19:40; John 20:7
11:45 John 7:31; John 11:19; 12:17f
John 2:23
11:46 John 7:32, 45; 11:57
11:47 John 7:32, 45; 11:57; Matt 26:3; Matt 5:22; John 2:11
11:48 Matt 24:15
11:49 Matt 26:3; John 11:51; 18:13
11:50 John 18:14
11:51 John 18:13
11:52 John 10:16
11:53 Matt 26:4
11:54 John 7:1; 2 Chr 13:19

11:35 When Jesus saw the weeping and wailing, he too wept openly. Perhaps he empathized with their grief, or perhaps he was troubled at their unbelief. In either case, Jesus showed that he cares enough for us to weep with us in our sorrow.

11:38 Tombs at this time were usually caves carved in the limestone rock of a hillside. A tomb was often large enough for people to walk inside. Several bodies would be placed in one tomb. After burial, a large stone was rolled across the entrance to the tomb.

11:44 Jesus raised others from the dead, including Jairus's daughter (Matthew 9:18–26; Mark 5:41–42; Luke 8:40–56) and a widow's son (Luke 7:11–15).

11:45–53 Even when confronted point-blank with the power of Jesus' deity, some refused to believe. These eyewitnesses not only rejected Jesus; they plotted his murder. They were so hardened that they preferred to reject God's Son rather than admit that they were wrong. Beware of pride. If we allow it to grow, it can lead us into enormous sin.

11:48 The Jewish leaders knew that if they didn't stop Jesus, the Romans would discipline them. Rome gave partial freedom to the Jews as long as they were quiet and obedient. Jesus' miracles often caused a disturbance. The leaders feared that Rome's displeasure would bring additional hardship to their nation.

11:51 John regarded Caiaphas's statement as a prophecy. As high priest, Caiaphas was used by God to explain Jesus' death even though Caiaphas didn't realize what he was doing.

55 Now the Passover of the Jews was near, and many went up to Jerusalem out of the
country before the Passover to purify themselves.
56 So they were seeking for Jesus, and were saying to one another as they stood in the
temple, "What do you think; that He will not come to the feast at all?"
57 Now the chief priests and the Pharisees had given orders that if anyone knew where
He was, he was to report it, so that they might seize Him.

11:55 Matt 26:1f; Mark 14:1; Luke 22:1; John 2:13; 12:1; 13:1; Num 9:10; 2 Chr 30:17f; John 18:28

11:56 John 7:11

11:57 John 11:47

A Woman Anoints Jesus with Perfume
(182/Matthew 26:6-13; Mark 14:3-9)

12 Jesus, therefore, six days before the Passover, came to Bethany where Lazarus was,
whom Jesus had raised from the dead.
2 So they made Him a supper there, and Martha was serving; but Lazarus was one of
those reclining *at the table* with Him.
3 Mary then took a pound of very costly perfume of pure nard, and anointed the feet
of Jesus and wiped His feet with her hair; and the house was filled with the fragrance of
the perfume.
4 But Judas Iscariot, one of His disciples, who was intending to betray Him, ☆said,
5 "Why was this perfume not sold for [18]three hundred denarii and given to poor
people?"
6 Now he said this, not because he was concerned about the poor, but because he was
a thief, and as he had the money box, he used to pilfer what was put into it.
7 Therefore Jesus said, "Let her alone, so that she may keep [19]it for the day of My
burial.
8 "For you always have the poor with you, but you do not always have Me."
9 The large crowd of the Jews then learned that He was there; and they came, not for
Jesus' sake only, but that they might also see Lazarus, whom He raised from the dead.
10 But the chief priests planned to put Lazarus to death also;
11 because on account of him many of the Jews were going away and were believing in
Jesus.

12:1 John 11:55; 12:20; Matt 21:17; John 11:43f

12:2 Luke 10:38

12:3 Luke 7:37f; John 11:2; Mark 14:3

12:4 John 6:71

12:6 John 13:29; Luke 8:3

12:7 John 19:40

12:8 Deut 15:11; Matt 26:11; Mark 14:7

12:9 Mark 12:37

12:11 John 11:45f; 12:18; John 7:31; 11:42

18 Equivalent to 11 months' wages **19** I.e. the custom of preparing the body for burial

---

TIME WITH THE DISCIPLES
Lazarus's return to life became the last straw for the religious leaders, who were bent on killing Jesus. So Jesus stopped his public ministry and took his disciples away from Jerusalem to Ephraim. From there they returned to Galilee for a while (see the map in Luke 17).

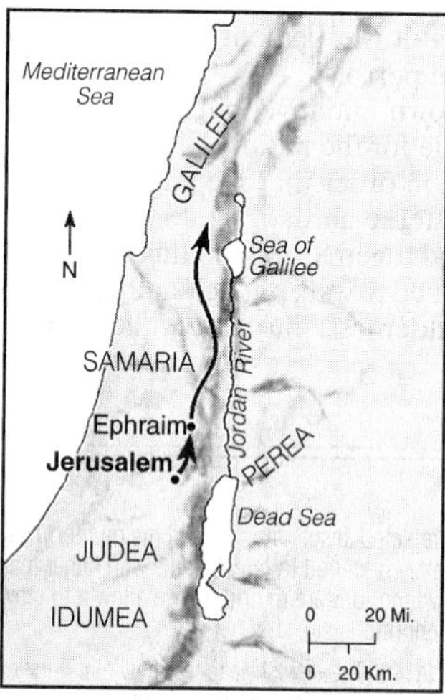

12:3 Pure nard was a fragrant ointment imported from the mountains of India. Thus it was very expensive. The amount Mary used was worth a year's wages.

12:4–6 Judas often dipped into the disciples' money bag for his own use. Quite likely, Jesus knew what Judas was doing (2:24–25; 6:64) but never did or said anything about it. Similarly, when we choose the way of sin, God may not immediately do anything to stop us, but this does not mean he approves of our actions. What we deserve will come.

12:5–6 Judas used a pious phrase to hide his true motives. But Jesus knew what was in his heart. Judas's life had become a lie, and the devil was entering him (13:27). Satan is the father of lies, and a lying character opens the door to his influence. Jesus' knowledge of us should make us want to keep our actions consistent with our words. Because we have nothing to fear with him, we should have nothing to hide.

12:7–8 This act and Jesus' response to it do not teach us to ignore the poor so we can spend money extravagantly for Christ. This was a unique act for a specific occasion—an anointing that anticipated Jesus' burial and a public declaration of faith in him as Messiah. Jesus' words should have taught Judas a valuable lesson about the worth of money. Unfortunately, Judas did not take heed; soon he would sell his Master's life for 30 pieces of silver.

12:10–11 The chief priests' blindness and hardness of heart caused them to sink ever deeper into sin. They rejected the Messiah and planned to kill him, and then plotted to murder Lazarus as well. One sin leads to another. From the Jewish leaders' point of view, they could accuse Jesus of blasphemy because he claimed equality with God. But Lazarus had done nothing of the kind. They wanted Lazarus dead simply because he was a living witness to Jesus' power. This is a warning to us to avoid sin. Sin leads to more sin, a downward spiral that can be stopped only by repentance and the power of the Holy Spirit to change our behavior.

Jesus Rides into Jerusalem on a Donkey
(183/Matthew 21:1-11; Mark 11:1-11; Luke 19:28-44)

12:12 John 12:1
12:13 Ps 118:26; John 1:49
12:15 Zech 9:9

12 On the next day the large crowd who had come to the feast, when they heard that
Jesus was coming to Jerusalem,
13 took the branches of the palm trees and went out to meet Him, and *began* to shout,
"Hosanna! BLESSED IS HE WHO COMES IN THE NAME OF THE LORD, even the King of
Israel."
14 Jesus, finding a young donkey, sat on it; as it is written,
15 "FEAR NOT, DAUGHTER OF ZION; BEHOLD, YOUR KING IS COMING, SEATED ON A
DONKEY'S COLT."

CAIAPHAS

Caiaphas was the leader of the religious group called the Sadducees. Educated and wealthy, they were politically influential in the nation. As the elite group, they were on fairly good terms with Rome. They hated Jesus because he endangered their secure life-styles and taught a message they could not accept. A kingdom in which leaders *served* had no appeal to them.

Caiaphas's usual policy was to remove any threats to his power by whatever means necessary. For Caiaphas, whether Jesus should die was not in question; the only point to be settled was *when* his death should take place. Not only did Jesus have to be captured and tried; the Jewish Council also needed Roman approval before they could carry out the death sentence. Caiaphas's plans were unexpectedly helped by Judas's offer to betray Christ.

Caiaphas did not realize that his schemes were actually part of a wonderful plan God was carrying out. Caiaphas's willingness to sacrifice another man to preserve his own security was clearly selfish. By contrast, Jesus' willingness to die for us was a clear example of loving self-sacrifice. Caiaphas thought he had won the battle as Jesus hung on the cross, but he did not count on the resurrection!

Caiaphas's mind was closed. He couldn't accept the resurrection even when the evidence was overwhelming, and he attempted to silence those whose lives had been forever changed by the risen Christ (Matthew 28:12–13). Caiaphas represents those people who will not believe because they think it will cost them too much to accept Jesus as Lord. They choose the fleeting power, prestige, and pleasures of this life instead of the eternal life God offers those who receive his Son. What is your choice?

Strength and accomplishment:
- High priest for 18 years

Weaknesses and mistakes:
- One of those most directly responsible for Jesus' death
- Used his office as a means to power and personal security
- Planned Jesus' capture, carried out his illegal trial, pressured Pilate to approve the crucifixion, attempted to prevent the resurrection, and later tried to cover up the fact of the resurrection
- Kept up religious appearances while compromising with Rome
- Involved in the later persecution of Christians

Lessons from his life:
- God uses even the twisted motives and actions of his enemies to bring about his will
- When we cover selfish motives with spiritual objectives and words, God still sees our intentions

Vital statistics:
- Where: Jerusalem
- Occupation: High priest
- Relative: Father-in-law: Annas
- Contemporaries: Jesus, Pilate, Herod Antipas

Key verses:
"But one of them, Caiaphas, who was high priest that year, said to them, 'You know nothing at all, nor do you take into account that it is expedient for you that one man die for the people, and that the whole nation not perish' " (John 11:49–50).

12:13 Jesus began his last week on earth by riding into Jerusalem on a donkey under a canopy of palm branches, with crowds hailing him as their king. To announce that he was indeed the Messiah, Jesus chose a *time* when all Israel would be gathered at Jerusalem, a *place* where huge crowds could see him, and a *way* of proclaiming his mission that was unmistakable. On Palm Sunday we celebrate Jesus' Triumphal Entry into Jerusalem.

12:13 The people who were praising God for giving them a king had the wrong idea about Jesus. They were sure he would be a national leader who would restore their nation to its former glory, and thus they were deaf to the words of their prophets and blind to Jesus' real mission. When it became apparent that Jesus was not going to fulfill their hopes, many people turned against him.

16 These things His disciples did not understand at the first; but when Jesus was glorified, then they remembered that these things were written of Him, and that they had
done these things to Him.
17 So the people, who were with Him when He called Lazarus out of the tomb and
raised him from the dead, continued to testify *about Him*.
18 For this reason also the people went and met Him, because they heard that He had
performed this sign.
19 So the Pharisees said to one another, "You see that you are not doing any good;
look, the world has gone after Him."

Jesus Explains Why He Must Die
(185)

20 Now there were some Greeks among those who were going up to worship at the
feast;
21 these then came to Philip, who was from Bethsaida of Galilee, and *began to* ask him,
saying, "Sir, we wish to see Jesus."
22 Philip ☆came and ☆told Andrew; Andrew and Philip ☆came and ☆told Jesus.
23 And Jesus ☆answered them, saying, "The hour has come for the Son of Man to be
glorified.
24 "Truly, truly, I say to you, unless a grain of wheat falls into the earth and dies, it remains alone; but if it dies, it bears much fruit.
25 "He who loves his life loses it, and he who hates his life in this world will keep it to
life eternal.
26 "If anyone serves Me, he must follow Me; and where I am, there My servant will be
also; if anyone serves Me, the Father will honor him.
27 "Now My soul has become troubled; and what shall I say, 'Father, save Me from this
hour'? But for this purpose I came to this hour.
28 "Father, glorify Your name." Then a voice came out of heaven: "I have both glorified it, and will glorify it again."
29 So the crowd *of people* who stood by and heard it were saying that it had thundered;
others were saying, "An angel has spoken to Him."
30 Jesus answered and said, "This voice has not come for My sake, but for your sakes.
31 "Now judgment is upon this world; now the ruler of this world will be cast out.

12:16 Mark 9:32; John 2:22; 14:26
12:17 John 11:42
12:18 Luke 19:37
12:22 John 1:44
12:23 Matt 26:45; Mark 14:35, 41; John 13:1; 17:1; John 7:39; 12:16; 13:32
12:24 Rom 14:9; 1 Cor 15:36
12:25 Matt 10:39; 16:25; Mark 8:35; Luke 9:24; 17:33
12:26 John 14:3; 17:24; 2 Cor 5:8; Phil 1:23; 1 Thess 4:17; Ps 91:15; Luke 12:37
12:27 Matt 26:38; Mark 14:34; John 11:33
12:28 Matt 11:25; Matt 3:17; 17:5; Mark 1:11; 9:7; Luke 3:22
12:29 Acts 23:9
12:30 John 11:42
12:31 John 3:19; 9:39; 14:30; 16:11; 2 Cor 4:4; Eph 2:2; 6:12

12:16 After Jesus' resurrection, the disciples understood for the first time many of the prophecies that they had missed along the way. Jesus' words and actions took on new meaning and made more sense. In retrospect, the disciples saw how Jesus had led them into a deeper and better understanding of his truth. Stop now and think about the events in your life leading up to where you are now. How has God led you to this point? As you grow older, you will look back and see God's involvement more clearly than you do now.

12:18 The people flocked to Jesus because they had heard about his great miracle in raising Lazarus from the dead. Their adoration was short-lived and their commitment shallow, for in a few days they would do nothing to stop his crucifixion. Devotion based only on curiosity or popularity fades quickly.

12:20–21 These Greeks probably were converts to the Jewish faith. They may have gone to Philip because, though he was a Jew, he had a Greek name.

12:23–25 This is a beautiful picture of the necessary sacrifice of Jesus. Unless a grain of wheat is buried in the ground, it will not become a blade of wheat producing many more seeds. Jesus had to die to pay the penalty for our sin, but also to show his power over death. His resurrection proves he has eternal life. Because Jesus is God, Jesus can give this same eternal life to all who believe in him.

12:25 We must be so committed to living for Christ that we "hate" our lives by comparison. This does not mean that we long to die or that we are careless or destructive with the life God has given, but that we are willing to die if doing so will glorify Christ. We must deny the tyrannical rule of our own self-centeredness. By laying aside our striving for advantage, security, and pleasure, we can serve God lovingly and freely. Releasing control of our lives and transferring control to Christ bring eternal life and genuine joy.

12:26 Many believed that Jesus came for the Jews only. But when Jesus said, "If anyone serves Me," he was talking to these Greeks as well. No matter who the sincere seekers are, Jesus welcomes them. His message is for everyone. Don't allow social or racial differences to become barriers to the gospel. Take the Good News to all people.

12:27 Jesus knew his crucifixion lay ahead, and because he was human he dreaded it. He knew he would have to take the sins of the world on himself, and he knew this would separate him from his Father. He wanted to be delivered from this horrible death, but he knew that God sent him into the world to die for our sins, in our place. Jesus said no to his human desires in order to obey his Father and glorify him. Although we will never have to face such a difficult and awesome task, we are still called to obedience. Whatever the Father asks, we should do his will and bring glory to his name.

12:31 The ruler of this world is Satan, an angel who rebelled against God. Satan is real, not symbolic, and is constantly working against God and those who obey him. Satan tempted Eve in the garden and persuaded her to sin; he tempted Jesus in the wilderness and did not persuade him to fall (Matthew 4:1–11). Satan has great power, but people can be delivered from his reign of spiritual darkness because of Christ's victory on the cross. Satan is powerful, but Jesus is much more powerful. Jesus' resurrection shattered Satan's deathly power (Colossians 1:13–14). To overcome Satan we need faithful allegiance to God's Word, determination to stay away from sin, and the support of other believers.

32 "And I, if I am lifted up from the earth, will draw all men to Myself."
33 But He was saying this to indicate the kind of death by which He was to die.
34 The crowd then answered Him, "We have heard out of the Law that the Christ is to
remain forever; and how can You say, 'The Son of Man must be lifted up'? Who is this
Son of Man?"
35 So Jesus said to them, "For a little while longer the Light is among you. Walk while
you have the Light, so that darkness will not overtake you; he who walks in the darkness
does not know where he goes.
36 "While you have the Light, believe in the Light, so that you may become sons of Light."
These things Jesus spoke, and He went away and hid Himself from them.

Most of the People Do Not Believe in Jesus
(186)

37 But though He had performed so many signs before them, *yet* they were not believing in Him.
38 *This was* to fulfill the word of Isaiah the prophet which he spoke: "LORD, WHO HAS
BELIEVED OUR REPORT? AND TO WHOM HAS THE ARM OF THE LORD BEEN REVEALED?"
39 For this reason they could not believe, for Isaiah said again,
40 "HE HAS BLINDED THEIR EYES AND HE HARDENED THEIR HEART, SO THAT THEY

12:32 John 3:14; 8:28; 12:34; John 6:44
12:33 John 18:32; 21:19
12:34 John 10:34; Ps 110:4; Is 9:7; Ezek 37:25; Dan 7:14; Matt 8:20; John 3:14; 8:28; 12:32
12:35 John 7:33; 9:4; John 12:46; 1 John 2:10; Gal 6:10; Eph 5:8; 1 John 1:6; 2:11
12:36 John 12:46; Luke 16:8; John 8:12; John 8:59
12:38 Is 53:1; Rom 10:16
12:40 Is 6:10; Matt 13:14f; Mark 6:52

GREAT EXPECTATIONS
Wherever he went, Jesus exceeded people's expectations.

What was expected	*What Jesus did*	*Reference*
A man looked for healing	Jesus also forgave his sins	Mark 2:1–12
The disciples were expecting an ordinary day of fishing	They found the Savior	Luke 5:1–11
A widow was resigned to bury her dead son	Jesus restored her son to life	Luke 7:11–17
The religious leaders wanted a miracle	Jesus offered them the Creator of miracles	Matthew 12:38–45
A woman who wanted to be healed touched Jesus	Jesus helped her see it was her faith that had healed her	Mark 5:25–34
The disciples thought the crowd should be sent home because there was no food	Jesus used a small meal to feed thousands, and there were leftovers!	John 6:1–15
The crowds looked for a political leader to set up a new kingdom to overthrow Rome's control	Jesus offered them an eternal, spiritual kingdom to overthrow sin's control	A theme throughout the Gospels
The disciples wanted to eat the Passover meal with Jesus, their Master	Jesus washed their feet, showing that he was also their servant	John 13:1–20
The religious leaders wanted Jesus killed and got their wish	But Jesus rose from the dead!	John 11:53; 19:30; 20:1–29

12:32–34 The crowd could not believe what Jesus was saying about the Messiah. They were waving palm branches for a victorious Messiah who would set up a political, earthly kingdom that would never end. From their reading of certain Scriptures, they thought the Messiah would never die (Psalms 89:35–36; 110:4; Isaiah 9:7). Other passages, however, showed that he would (Isaiah 53:5–9). Jesus' words did not mesh with their concept of the Messiah. First he had to suffer and die—then he would one day set up his eternal kingdom. What kind of Messiah, or Savior, are you seeking? Beware of trying to force Jesus into your own mold—he won't fit.

12:35–36 Jesus said he would be with them in person for only a short time, and they should take advantage of his presence while they had it. Like a light shining in a dark place, he would point out the way they should walk. If they walked in his light, they would become "sons of Light," revealing the truth and pointing people to God. As Christians, we are to be Christ's light bearers, letting his light shine through us. How brightly is your light shining? Can others see Christ in your actions?

12:37–38 Jesus had performed many miracles, but most people still didn't believe in him. Likewise, many today won't believe despite all God does. Don't be discouraged if your witness for Christ doesn't turn as many to him as you'd like. Your job is to continue as a faithful witness. You are responsible to reach out to others, but they are responsible for their own decisions.

12:39–41 People in Jesus' time, like those in the time of Isaiah, would not believe despite the evidence (12:37). As a result, God hardened their hearts. Does that mean God intentionally prevented these people from believing in him? No, he simply confirmed their own choices. After a lifetime of resisting God, they had become so set in their ways that they wouldn't even try to understand Jesus' message. For such people, it is virtually impossible to come to God—their hearts have been permanently hardened. Other instances of hardened hearts because of constant stubbornness are recorded in Exodus 9:12, Romans 1:24–28, and 2 Thessalonians 2:8–12.

WOULD NOT SEE WITH THEIR EYES AND PERCEIVE WITH THEIR HEART, AND BE CON-
VERTED AND I HEAL THEM."
41 These things Isaiah said because he saw His glory, and he spoke of Him.
42 Nevertheless many even of the rulers believed in Him, but because of the Pharisees
they were not confessing *Him,* for fear that they would be put out of the synagogue;
43 for they loved the approval of men rather than the approval of God.

Jesus Summarizes His Message
(187)

44 And Jesus cried out and said, "He who believes in Me, does not believe in Me but
in Him who sent Me.
45 "He who sees Me sees the One who sent Me.
46 "I have come *as* Light into the world, so that everyone who believes in Me will not
remain in darkness.
47 "If anyone hears My sayings and does not keep them, I do not judge him; for I did
not come to judge the world, but to save the world.
48 "He who rejects Me and does not receive My sayings, has one who judges him; the
word I spoke is what will judge him at the last day.
49 "For I did not speak on My own initiative, but the Father Himself who sent Me has
given Me a commandment *as to* what to say and what to speak.
50 "I know that His commandment is eternal life; therefore the things I speak, I speak
just as the Father has told Me."

12:41 Is 6:1ff; Luke 24:27
12:42 John 7:48; 12:11; Luke 23:13; John 7:13; John 9:22
12:43 John 5:41, 44
12:44 Matt 10:40; John 5:24
12:45 John 14:9
12:46 John 1:4; 3:19; 8:12; 9:5; 12:35f
12:47 John 3:17; 8:15f
12:48 Luke 10:16; Deut 18:18f; John 5:45ff; 8:47; Matt 10:15; John 6:39; Acts 17:31; 1 Pet 1:5; 2 Pet 3:3, 7; Heb 10:25
12:49 John 3:11; 7:16; 8:26, 28, 38; 14:10, 24; John 14:31; 17:8
12:50 John 6:68; John 5:19; 8:28

C. DEATH AND RESURRECTION OF JESUS, THE SON OF GOD (13:1—21:25)

John begins his Gospel with eternity and ends with Jesus coming to earth again. He features Jesus teaching his disciples privately just before his arrest and death. We see, clearly, the deep love Jesus has for the believer, and the peace that comes from faith. Knowing the love Jesus has for believers, we too should believe and allow Jesus to forgive our sins. Only then will we experience peace in a world filled with turmoil.

1. Jesus teaches his disciples

Jesus Washes the Disciples' Feet
(210)

13 Now before the Feast of the Passover, Jesus knowing that His hour had come that
He would depart out of this world to the Father, having loved His own who were
in the world, He loved them to the end.
2 During supper, the devil having already put into the heart of Judas Iscariot, *the son*
of Simon, to betray Him,

13:1 John 2:13; 11:55; John 12:23; John 13:3; 16:28
13:2 John 6:70; 13:27; John 6:71

12:42–43 Along with those who refused to believe, many believed but refused to admit it. This is just as bad, and Jesus had strong words for such people (see Matthew 10:32–33). People who will not take a stand for Jesus are afraid of rejection or ridicule. Many Jewish leaders wouldn't admit to faith in Jesus because they feared excommunication from the synagogue (which was their livelihood) and loss of their prestigious place in the community. But the praise of others is fickle and short-lived. We should be much more concerned about God's eternal acceptance than about the temporary approval of other people.

12:45 We often wonder what God is like. How can we know the Creator when he doesn't make himself visible? Jesus said plainly that those who see him see God, because he *is* God. If you want to know what God is like, study the person and words of Jesus Christ.

12:48 The purpose of Jesus' first mission on earth was not to judge people, but to show them the way to find salvation and eternal life. When he comes again, one of his main purposes will be to judge people for how they lived on earth. Christ's words that we would *not* accept and obey will condemn us. On the day of judgment, those who accepted Jesus and lived his way will be raised to eternal life (1 Corinthians 15:51–57; 1 Thessalonians 4:15–18; Revelation 21:1–8), and those who rejected Jesus and lived any way they pleased will face eternal punishment (Revelation 20:11–15). Decide now which side you'll be on, for the consequences of your decision last forever.

13:1 Jesus knew he would be betrayed by one of his disciples, denied by another, and deserted by all of them for a time. Still "He loved them to the end." God knows us completely, as Jesus knew his disciples (2:24–25; 6:64). He knows the sins we have committed and the ones we will yet commit. Still, he loves us. How do you respond to that kind of love?

13:1ff Chapters 13—17 tell us what Jesus said to his disciples on the night before his death. These words were all spoken in one evening when, with only the disciples as his audience, he gave final instructions to prepare them for his death and resurrection, events that would change their lives forever.

13:1–3 For more information on Judas Iscariot, see his Profile in Mark 14.

13:1–17 Jesus was the model servant, and he showed his servant attitude to his disciples. Washing guests' feet was a job for a household servant to carry out when guests arrived. But Jesus wrapped a towel around his waist, as the lowliest slave would do, and washed and dried his disciples' feet. If even he, God in the flesh, is willing to serve, we his followers must also be servants, willing to serve in any way that glorifies God. Are you willing to follow Christ's example of serving? Whom can you serve today? There is a special blessing for those who not only agree that humble service is Christ's way, but who also follow through and do it (13:17).

13:3 John 3:35; John 8:42

13:4 Luke 12:37; 17:8

13:5 Gen 18:4; 19:2; 43:24; Judg 19:21; Luke 7:44; 1 Tim 5:10

13:8 Ps 51:2, 7; Ezek 36:25; Acts 22:16; 1 Cor 6:11; Heb 10:22; Deut 12:12; 2 Sam 20:1; 1 Kin 12:16

13:10 John 15:3; Eph 5:26

3 *Jesus,* knowing that the Father had given all things into His hands, and that He had
come forth from God and was going back to God,
4 ☆got up from supper, and ☆laid aside His garments; and taking a towel, He girded
Himself.
5 Then He ☆poured water into the basin, and began to wash the disciples' feet and to
wipe them with the towel with which He was girded.
6 So He ☆came to Simon Peter. He ☆said to Him, "Lord, do You wash my feet?"
7 Jesus answered and said to him, "What I do you do not realize now, but you will
understand hereafter."
8 Peter ☆said to Him, "Never shall You wash my feet!" Jesus answered him, "If I do
not wash you, you have no part with Me."
9 Simon Peter ☆said to Him, "Lord, *then wash* not only my feet, but also my hands
and my head."
10 Jesus ☆said to him, "He who has bathed needs only to wash his feet, but is completely clean; and you are clean, but not all *of you.*"

JOHN

Being loved is the most powerful motivation in the world! Our ability to love is often shaped by our experience of love. We usually love others as we have been loved.

Some of the greatest statements about God's loving nature were written by a man who experienced God's love in a unique way. John, Jesus' disciple, expressed his relationship to the Son of God by calling himself "the disciple whom Jesus loved" (John 21:20). Although Jesus' love is clearly communicated in all the Gospels, in John's Gospel it is a central theme. Because his own experience of Jesus' love was so strong and personal, John was sensitive to those words and actions of Jesus that illustrated how the One who *is* love loved others.

Jesus knew John fully and loved him fully. He gave John and his brother James the nickname "Sons of Thunder," perhaps from an occasion when the brothers asked Jesus for permission to "command fire to come down from heaven" (Luke 9:54) on a village that had refused to welcome Jesus and the disciples. In John's Gospel and letters, we see the great God of love, while the thunder of God's justice bursts from the pages of Revelation.

Jesus confronts each of us as he confronted John. We cannot know the depth of Jesus' love unless we are willing to face the fact that he knows us completely. Otherwise we are fooled into believing he must love the people we pretend to be, not the sinners we actually are. John and all the disciples convince us that God is able and willing to accept us as we are. Being aware of God's love is a great motivator for change. His love is not given in exchange for our efforts; his love frees us to really live. Have you accepted that love?

Strengths and accomplishments:
- Before following Jesus, one of John the Baptist's disciples
- One of the 12 disciples and, with Peter and James, one of the inner three, closest to Jesus
- Wrote five New Testament books: the Gospel of John; 1, 2, and 3 John; and Revelation

Weaknesses and mistakes:
- Along with James, shared a tendency to outbursts of selfishness and anger
- Asked for a special position in Jesus' kingdom

Lessons from his life:
- Those who realize how much they are loved are able to love much
- When God changes a life, he does not take away personality characteristics, but puts them to effective use in his service

Vital statistics:
- Occupations: Fisherman, disciple
- Relatives: Father: Zebedee. Mother: Salome. Brother: James
- Contemporaries: Jesus, Pilate, Herod

Key verses:
"Beloved, I am not writing a new commandment to you, but an old commandment which you have had from the beginning; the old commandment is the word which you have heard. On the other hand, I am writing a new commandment to you, which is true in Him and in you, because the darkness is passing away and the true Light is already shining" (1 John 2:7–8).

John's story is told throughout the Gospels, Acts, and Revelation.

13:6–7 Imagine being Peter and watching Jesus wash the others' feet, all the while moving closer to you. Seeing his Master behave like a slave must have confused Peter. He still did not understand Jesus' teaching that to be a leader, a person must be a servant. This is not a comfortable passage for leaders who find it hard to serve those beneath them. How do you treat those who work under you (whether children, employees, or volunteers)?

11 For He knew the one who was betraying Him; for this reason He said, "Not all of
you are clean."
12 So when He had washed their feet, and taken His garments and reclined *at the table*
again, He said to them, "Do you know what I have done to you?
13 "You call Me Teacher and Lord; and you are right, for *so* I am.
14 "If I then, the Lord and the Teacher, washed your feet, you also ought to wash one
another's feet.
15 "For I gave you an example that you also should do as I did to you.
16 "Truly, truly, I say to you, a slave is not greater than his master, nor *is* one who is sent
greater than the one who sent him.
17 "If you know these things, you are blessed if you do them.
18 "I do not speak of all of you. I know the ones I have chosen; but *it is* that the Scripture may be fulfilled, 'HE WHO EATS MY BREAD HAS LIFTED UP HIS HEEL AGAINST ME.'
19 "From now on I am telling you before *it* comes to pass, so that when it does occur,
you may believe that I am *He*.
20 "Truly, truly, I say to you, he who receives whomever I send receives Me; and he who
receives Me receives Him who sent Me."

Jesus and the Disciples Have the Last Supper
(211/Matthew 26:20-30; Mark 14:17-26; Luke 22:14-30)

21 When Jesus had said this, He became troubled in spirit, and testified and said, "Truly,
truly, I say to you, that one of you will betray Me."
22 The disciples *began* looking at one another, at a loss *to know* of which one He was
speaking.
23 There was reclining on Jesus' bosom one of His disciples, whom Jesus loved.
24 So Simon Peter ☆gestured to him, and ☆said to him, "Tell *us* who it is of whom He is
speaking."
25 He, leaning back thus on Jesus' bosom, ☆said to Him, "Lord, who is it?"
26 Jesus then ☆answered, "That is the one for whom I shall dip the morsel and give it
to him." So when He had dipped the morsel, He ☆took and ☆gave it to Judas, *the son* of
Simon Iscariot.
27 After the morsel, Satan then entered into him. Therefore Jesus ☆said to him, "What
you do, do quickly."
28 Now no one of those reclining *at the table* knew for what purpose He had said this
to him.
29 For some were supposing, because Judas had the money box, that Jesus was saying
to him, "Buy the things we have need of for the feast"; or else, that he should give something to the poor.
30 So after receiving the morsel he went out immediately; and it was night.

Jesus Predicts Peter's Denial
(212/Luke 22:31-38)

31 Therefore when he had gone out, Jesus ☆said, "Now is the Son of Man glorified,
and God is glorified in Him;
32 if God is glorified in Him, God will also glorify Him in Himself, and will glorify Him
immediately.

13:11 John 6:64; 13:2
13:12 John 13:4
13:13 John 11:28; John 11:2; 1 Cor 12:3; Phil 2:11
13:14 John 11:2; 1 Cor 12:3; Phil 2:11
13:15 1 Pet 5:3
13:16 Matt 10:24; Luke 6:40; John 15:20; 2 Cor 8:23; Phil 2:25
13:17 Matt 7:24ff; Luke 11:28; James 1:25
13:18 John 13:10f; John 6:70; 15:16, 19; John 15:25; 17:12; 18:32; 19:24, 36; Ps 41:9; Matt 26:21ff; Mark 14:18f; Luke 22:21ff; John 13:21, 22, 26
13:19 John 14:29; 16:4; John 8:24
13:20 Matt 10:40; Mark 9:37; Luke 9:48; 10:16; Gal 4:14
13:21 John 11:33
13:23 John 1:18; John 19:26; 20:2; 21:7, 20
13:25 John 21:20
13:26 John 6:71
13:27 Matt 4:10; Luke 22:3; John 13:2
13:29 John 12:6
13:31 Matt 8:20; John 7:39; John 14:13; 17:4; 1 Pet 4:11
13:32 John 17:1

13:12ff Jesus did not wash his disciples' feet just to get them to be nice to each other. His far greater goal was to extend his mission on earth after he was gone. These men were to move into the world serving God, serving each other, and serving all people to whom they took the message of salvation.

13:22 Judas was not the obvious betrayer. After all, he was the one the disciples trusted to keep the money (12:6; 13:29).

13:26 The honored guest at a meal was often singled out in this way.

13:27 Satan's part in the betrayal of Jesus does not remove any of the responsibility from Judas. Disillusioned because Jesus was talking about dying rather than setting up his kingdom, Judas may have been trying to force Jesus' hand and make him use his power to prove he was the Messiah. Or perhaps Judas, not understanding Jesus' mission, no longer believed Jesus was God's chosen one. Whatever Judas thought, Satan assumed that Jesus' death would end his mission and thwart God's plan. Like Judas, Satan did not know that Jesus' death was the most important part of God's plan all along.

13:27–38 John describes these few moments in clear detail. We can see that Jesus knew exactly what was going to happen. He knew about Judas and about Peter, but he did not change the situation, nor did he stop loving them. In the same way, Jesus knows exactly what you will do to hurt him. Yet he still loves you unconditionally and will forgive you whenever you ask for it. Judas couldn't understand this, and his life ended tragically. Peter understood, and despite his shortcomings, his life ended triumphantly because he never let go of his faith in the One who loved him.

33 "Little children, I am with you a little while longer. You will seek Me; and as I said to
the Jews, now I also say to you, 'Where I am going, you cannot come.'
34 "A new commandment I give to you, that you love one another, even as I have loved
you, that you also love one another.
35 "By this all men will know that you are My disciples, if you have love for one
another."
36 Simon Peter ☆said to Him, "Lord, where are You going?" Jesus answered, "Where
I go, you cannot follow Me now; but you will follow later."
37 Peter ☆said to Him, "Lord, why can I not follow You right now? I will lay down my
life for You."
38 Jesus ☆answered, "Will you lay down your life for Me? Truly, truly, I say to you, a
rooster will not crow until you deny Me three times.

Jesus Is the Way to the Father
(213)

14 "Do not let your heart be troubled; [20]believe in God, believe also in Me.
2 "In My Father's house are many dwelling places; if it were not so, I would have
told you; for I go to prepare a place for you.
3 "If I go and prepare a place for you, I will come again and receive you to Myself, that
where I am, *there* you may be also.
4 "And you know the way where I am going."
5 Thomas ☆said to Him, "Lord, we do not know where You are going, how do we know
the way?"
6 Jesus ☆said to him, "I am the way, and the truth, and the life; no one comes to the
Father but through Me.
7 "If you had known Me, you would have known My Father also; from now on you
know Him, and have seen Him."
8 Philip ☆said to Him, "Lord, show us the Father, and it is enough for us."
9 Jesus ☆said to him, "Have I been so long with you, and *yet* you have not come to
know Me, Philip? He who has seen Me has seen the Father; how *can* you say, 'Show us
the Father'?
10 "Do you not believe that I am in the Father, and the Father is in Me? The words that

13:33 1 John 2:1; John 7:33; John 7:34
13:34 John 15:12, 17; 1 John 2:7f; 3:11, 23; Matt 5:44; Gal 5:14; 1 Thess 4:9; Heb 13:1
13:35 1 John 3:14; 4:20
13:36 John 21:18
13:37 Matt 26:33-35; Mark 14:29-31; Luke 22:33-34
13:38 Mark 14:30; John 18:27
14:1 John 14:27; 16:22
14:2 John 13:33, 36
14:3 John 12:26
14:5 John 11:16
14:6 John 10:9; Rom 5:2; Eph 2:18; Heb 10:20; John 1:14; John 1:4; 11:25; 1 John 5:20
14:9 John 1:14; 12:45; Col 1:15; Heb 1:3
14:10 John 10:38; 14:11, 20; John 5:19; 14:24

20 Or *you believe in God*

13:34 To love others was not a new commandment (see Leviticus 19:18), but to love others as much as Christ loved others was revolutionary. Now we are to love others based on Jesus' sacrificial love for us. Such love will not only bring unbelievers to Christ; it will also keep believers strong and united in a world hostile to God. Jesus was a living example of God's love, as we are to be living examples of Jesus' love.

13:34–35 Jesus says that our Christlike love will show we are his disciples. Do people see petty bickering, jealousy, and division in your church? Or do they know you are Jesus' followers by your love for one another?

13:35 Love is more than simply warm feelings; it is an attitude that reveals itself in action. How can we love others as Jesus loves us? By helping when it's not convenient, by giving when it hurts, by devoting energy to others' welfare rather than our own, by absorbing hurts from others without complaining or fighting back. This kind of loving is hard to do. That is why people notice when you do it and know you are empowered by a supernatural source. The Bible has another beautiful description of love in 1 Corinthians 13.

13:37–38 Peter proudly told Jesus that he was ready to die for him. But Jesus corrected him. He knew Peter would deny that he knew Jesus that very night to protect himself (18:25–27). In our enthusiasm, it is easy to make promises, but God knows the extent of our commitment. Paul tells us not to think of ourselves more highly than we ought (Romans 12:3). Instead of bragging, demonstrate your commitment step by step as you grow in your knowledge of God's Word and in your faith.

14:1–3 Jesus' words show that the way to eternal life, though unseen, is secure—as secure as your trust in Jesus. He has already prepared the way to eternal life. The only issue that may still be unsettled is your willingness to believe.

14:2–3 There are few verses in Scripture that describe eternal life, but these few verses are rich with promises. Here Jesus says, "I go to prepare a place for you," and "I will come again." We can look forward to eternal life because Jesus has promised it to all who believe in him. Although the details of eternity are unknown, we need not fear because Jesus is preparing for us and will spend eternity with us.

14:5–6 This is one of the most basic and important passages in Scripture. How can we know the way to God? Only through Jesus. Jesus is the way because he is both God and man. By uniting our lives with his, we are united with God. Trust Jesus to take you to the Father, and all the benefits of being God's child will be yours.

14:6 Jesus says he is the *only* way to God the Father. Some people may argue that this way is too narrow. In reality, it is wide enough for the whole world, if the world chooses to accept it. Instead of worrying about how limited it sounds to have only one way, we should be saying, "Thank you, God, for providing a sure way to get to you!"

14:6 As the *way,* Jesus is our path to the Father. As the *truth,* he is the reality of all God's promises. As the *life,* he joins his divine life to ours, both now and eternally.

14:9 Jesus is the visible, tangible image of the invisible God. He is the complete revelation of what God is like. Jesus explained to Philip, who wanted to see the Father, that to know Jesus is to know God. The search for God, for truth and reality, ends in Christ. (See also Colossians 1:15; Hebrews 1:1–4.)

I say to you I do not speak on My own initiative, but the Father abiding in Me does His
works.
11 "Believe Me that I am in the Father and the Father is in Me; otherwise believe because of the works themselves.
12 "Truly, truly, I say to you, he who believes in Me, the works that I do, he will do also;
and greater *works* than these he will do; because I go to the Father.
13 "Whatever you ask in My name, that will I do, so that the Father may be glorified in
the Son.
14 "If you ask Me anything in My name, I will do *it.*
15 "If you love Me, you will keep My commandments.

Jesus Promises the Holy Spirit
(214)

16 "I will ask the Father, and He will give you another Helper, that He may be with you
forever;
17 *that is* the Spirit of truth, whom the world cannot receive, because it does not see
Him or know Him, *but* you know Him because He abides with you and will be in you.
18 "I will not leave you as orphans; I will come to you.
19 "After a little while the world will no longer see Me, but you *will* see Me; because I
live, you will live also.
20 "In that day you will know that I am in My Father, and you in Me, and I in you.
21 "He who has My commandments and keeps them is the one who loves Me; and he
who loves Me will be loved by My Father, and I will love him and will disclose Myself
to him."
22 Judas (not Iscariot) ☆said to Him, "Lord, what then has happened that You are going to disclose Yourself to us and not to the world?"
23 Jesus answered and said to him, "If anyone loves Me, he will keep My word; and
My Father will love him, and We will come to him and make Our abode with him.
24 "He who does not love Me does not keep My words; and the word which you hear is
not Mine, but the Father's who sent Me.
25 "These things I have spoken to you while abiding with you.

14:11 John 10:38; 14:10, 20; John 5:36

14:12 John 4:37f; 5:20; John 7:33; 14:28

14:13 Matt 7:7; John 13:31

14:14 John 15:16; 16:23f

14:16 John 7:39; 14:26; 15:26; 16:7; Rom 8:26; 1 John 2:1

14:17 John 15:26; 16:13; 1 John 4:6; 5:7; 1 Cor 2:14

14:19 John 7:33; John 16:16, 22; John 6:57

14:20 John 16:23, 26

14:21 1 John 5:3; 2 John 6; John 14:23; 16:27

14:22 Luke 6:16; Acts 1:13; Acts 10:40, 41

14:23 John 15:10; 1 John 5:3; 2 John 6; John 8:51; 1 John 2:5; Eph 3:17; 1 John 2:24; Rev 3:20; 21:3

14:24 John 7:16; 14:10

14:12–13 Jesus is not saying that his disciples would do more amazing miracles—after all, raising the dead is about as amazing as you can get. Rather, the disciples, working in the power of the Holy Spirit, would carry the gospel of God's kingdom out of Palestine and into the whole world.

14:14 When Jesus says we can ask for anything, we must remember that our asking must be in his name—that is, according to God's character and will. God will not grant requests contrary to his nature or his will, and we cannot use his name as a magic formula to fulfill our selfish desires. If we are sincerely following God and seeking to do his will, then our requests will be in line with what he wants, and he will grant them. (See also 15:16; 16:23.)

14:15–16 Jesus was soon going to leave the disciples, but he would remain with them. How could this be? The Helper—the Spirit of God himself—would come after Jesus was gone to care for and guide the disciples. The regenerating power of the Spirit came on the disciples just before Jesus' ascension (20:22), and the Spirit was poured out on all the believers at Pentecost (Acts 2), shortly after Jesus ascended to heaven. The Holy Spirit is the very presence of God within us and all believers, helping us live as God wants and building Christ's church on earth. By faith we can appropriate the Spirit's power each day.

14:16 The word translated "Helper" combines the ideas of comfort and counsel. The Holy Spirit is a powerful person on our side, working for and with us.

14:17ff The following chapters teach these truths about the Holy Spirit: He will be with us forever (14:16); the world at large cannot accept him (14:17); he lives with us and in us (14:17); he teaches us (14:26); he reminds us of Jesus' words (14:26; 15:26); he convicts us of sin, shows us God's righteousness, and announces God's judgment on evil (16:8); he guides into truth and gives insight into future events (16:13); he brings glory to Christ (16:14). The Holy Spirit has been active among people from the beginning of time, but after Pentecost (Acts 2) he came to live in all believers. Many people are unaware of the Holy Spirit's activities, but to those who hear Christ's words and understand the Spirit's power, the Spirit gives a whole new way to look at life.

14:18 When Jesus said, "I will come to you," he meant it. Although Jesus ascended to heaven, he sent the Holy Spirit to live in believers, and to have the Holy Spirit is to have Jesus himself.

14:19–21 Sometimes people wish they knew the future so they could prepare for it. God has chosen not to give us this knowledge. He alone knows what will happen, but he tells us all we need to know to [prepare for the future. When we live by his standards, he will not leave us; he will come to us, he will be in us, and he will show himself to us. God knows what will happen and, because he will be with us through it all, we need not fear. We don't have to know the future to have faith in God; we have to have faith in God to be secure about the future.

14:21 Jesus said that his followers show their love for him by obeying him. Love is more than lovely words; it is commitment and conduct. If you love Christ, then prove it by obeying what he says in his Word.

14:22–23 Because the disciples were still expecting Jesus to establish an earthly kingdom and overthrow Rome, they found it hard to understand why he did not tell the world at large that he was the Messiah. Not everyone, however, could understand Jesus' message. Ever since Pentecost, the gospel of the kingdom has been proclaimed in the whole world, and yet not everyone is receptive to it. Jesus saves the deepest revelations of himself for those who love and obey him.

14:26
Luke 24:49; John 1:33; 15:26; 16:7; Acts 2:33; John 16:13f; 1 John 2:20, 27; John 2:22

14:27
John 16:33; 20:19; Phil 4:7; Col 3:15

14:28
John 10:29; Phil 2:6

14:29
John 13:19

14:30
John 12:31

14:31
John 10:18; 12:49; John 13:1; 18:1

15:1
Ps 80:8ff; Is 5:1ff; Ezek 19:10ff; Matt 21:33ff; Matt 15:13; Rom 11:17; 1 Cor 3:9

15:3
John 13:10; 17:17; Eph 5:26

15:4
John 6:56; 15:4-7; 1 John 2:6

26"But the Helper, the Holy Spirit, whom the Father will send in My name, He will
teach you all things, and bring to your remembrance all that I said to you.
27"Peace I leave with you; My peace I give to you; not as the world gives do I give to
you. Do not let your heart be troubled, nor let it be fearful.
28"You heard that I said to you, 'I go away, and I will come to you.' If you loved Me,
you would have rejoiced because I go to the Father, for the Father is greater than I.
29"Now I have told you before it happens, so that when it happens, you may believe.
30"I will not speak much more with you, for the ruler of the world is coming, and he
has nothing in Me;
31 but so that the world may know that I love the Father, I do exactly as the Father
commanded Me. Get up, let us go from here.

Jesus Teaches about the Vine and the Branches
(215)

15 "I am the true vine, and My Father is the vinedresser.
2 "Every branch in Me that does not bear fruit, He takes away; and every *branch*
that bears fruit, He [21]prunes it so that it may bear more fruit.
3"You are already clean because of the word which I have spoken to you.
4"Abide in Me, and I in you. As the branch cannot bear fruit of itself unless it abides
in the vine, so neither *can* you unless you abide in Me.
5"I am the vine, you are the branches; he who abides in Me and I in him, he bears
much fruit, for apart from Me you can do nothing.
6"If anyone does not abide in Me, he is thrown away as a branch and dries up; and
they gather them, and cast them into the fire and they are burned.

21 Lit *cleans;* used to describe pruning

14:26 Jesus promised the disciples that the Holy Spirit would help them remember what he had been teaching them. This promise ensures the validity of the New Testament. The disciples were eyewitnesses of Jesus' life and teachings, and the Holy Spirit helped them remember without taking away their individual perspectives. We can be confident that the Gospels are accurate records of what Jesus taught and did (see 1 Corinthians 2:10–14). The Holy Spirit can help us in the same way. As we study the Bible, we can trust him to plant truth in our mind, convince us of God's will, and remind us when we stray from it.

14:27 The end result of the Holy Spirit's work in our lives is deep and lasting peace. Unlike worldly peace, which is usually defined as the absence of conflict, this peace is confident assurance in any circumstance; with Christ's peace, we have no need to fear the present or the future. If your life is full of stress, allow the Holy Spirit to fill you with Christ's peace (see Philippians 4:6–7 for more on experiencing God's peace).

14:27–29 Sin, fear, uncertainty, doubt, and numerous other forces are at war within us. The peace of God moves into our hearts and lives to restrain these hostile forces and offer comfort in place of conflict. Jesus says he will give us that peace if we are willing to accept it from him.

14:28 As God the Son, Jesus willingly submits to God the Father. On earth, Jesus also submitted to many of the physical limitations of his humanity (Philippians 2:6).

14:30–31 Although Satan, the ruler of this world, was unable to overpower Jesus (Matthew 4), he still had the arrogance to try. Satan's power exists only because God allows him to act. But because Jesus is sinless, Satan has no power over him. If we obey Jesus and align ourselves closely with God's purposes, Satan can have no power over us.

14:31 "Let us go from here" suggests that chapters 15—17 may have been spoken en route to the Garden of Gethsemane. Another view is that Jesus was asking the disciples to get ready to leave the upper room, but they did not actually do so until 18:1.

15:1 The grapevine is a prolific plant; a single vine bears many grapes. In the Old Testament, grapes symbolized Israel's fruitfulness in doing God's work on the earth (Psalm 80:8; Isaiah 5:1–7; Ezekiel 19:10–14). In the Passover meal, the fruit of the vine symbolized God's goodness to his people.

15:1ff Christ is the vine, and God is the vinedresser who cares for the branches to make them fruitful. The branches are all those who claim to be followers of Christ. The fruitful branches are true believers who by their living union with Christ produce much fruit. But those who become unproductive—those who turn back from following Christ after making a superficial commitment—will be separated from the vine. Unproductive followers are as good as dead and will be cut off and tossed aside.

15:2–3 Jesus makes a distinction between two kinds of pruning: (1) separating and (2) cutting back branches. Fruitful branches are cut back to promote growth. In other words, God must sometimes discipline us to strengthen our character and faith. But branches that don't bear fruit are cut off at the trunk because not only are they worthless, but they often infect the rest of the tree. People who won't bear fruit for God or who try to block the efforts of God's followers will be cut off from his life-giving power.

15:5 Fruit is not limited to soulwinning. In this chapter, answered prayer, joy, and love are mentioned as fruit (15:7, 11–12). Galatians 5:22–24 and 2 Peter 1:5–8 describe additional fruit: qualities of Christian character.

15:5–6 Abiding in Christ means (1) believing that he is God's Son (1 John 4:15), (2) receiving him as Savior and Lord (John 1:12), (3) doing what God says (1 John 3:24), (4) continuing to believe the gospel (1 John 2:24), and (5) relating in love to the community of believers, Christ's body (John 15:12).

15:5–8 Many people try to be good, honest people who do what is right. But Jesus says that the only way to live a truly good life is to stay close to him, like a branch attached to the vine. Apart from Christ our efforts are unfruitful. Are you receiving the nourishment and life offered by Christ, the vine? If not, you are missing a special gift he has for you.

7 "If you abide in Me, and My words abide in you, ask whatever you wish, and it will be
done for you.
8 "My Father is glorified by this, that you bear much fruit, and *so* prove to be My disciples.
9 "Just as the Father has loved Me, I have also loved you; abide in My love.
10 "If you keep My commandments, you will abide in My love; just as I have kept My
Father's commandments and abide in His love.
11 "These things I have spoken to you so that My joy may be in you, and *that* your joy
may be made full.
12 "This is My commandment, that you love one another, just as I have loved you.
13 "Greater love has no one than this, that one lay down his life for his friends.
14 "You are My friends if you do what I command you.
15 "No longer do I call you slaves, for the slave does not know what his master is doing;
but I have called you friends, for all things that I have heard from My Father I have made
known to you.
16 "You did not choose Me but I chose you, and appointed you that you would go and
bear fruit, and *that* your fruit would remain, so that whatever you ask of the Father in
My name He may give to you.
17 "This I command you, that you love one another.

Jesus Warns about the World's Hatred
(216)

18 "If the world hates you, you know that it has hated Me before *it hated* you.
19 "If you were of the world, the world would love its own; but because you are not of
the world, but I chose you out of the world, because of this the world hates you.
20 "Remember the word that I said to you, 'A slave is not greater than his master.' If
they persecuted Me, they will also persecute you; if they kept My word, they will keep
yours also.
21 "But all these things they will do to you for My name's sake, because they do not
know the One who sent Me.
22 "If I had not come and spoken to them, they would not have sin, but now they have
no excuse for their sin.
23 "He who hates Me hates My Father also.
24 "If I had not done among them the works which no one else did, they would not have
sin; but now they have both seen and hated Me and My Father as well.
25 "But *they have done this* to fulfill the word that is written in their Law, 'THEY HATED
ME WITHOUT A CAUSE.'
26 "When the Helper comes, whom I will send to you from the Father, *that is* the Spirit
of truth who proceeds from the Father, He will testify about Me,
27 and you *will* testify also, because you have been with Me from the beginning.

15:7 Matt 7:7; John 15:16
15:8 Matt 5:16; John 8:31
15:9 John 3:35; 17:23
15:10 John 14:15; John 8:29
15:11 John 17:13; John 3:29
15:12 John 13:34; 1 John 3:23; 2 John 5
15:13 Rom 5:7f; John 10:11
15:14 Luke 12:4; Matt 12:50
15:16 John 6:70; 13:18; 15:19; John 15:5; John 14:13; 15:7; 16:23
15:18 1 John 3:13
15:19 Matt 10:22; 24:9
15:20 John 13:16; 1 Cor 4:12; 2 Cor 4:9; 2 Tim 3:12; John 8:51
15:21 Matt 10:22; 24:9; Mark 13:13; Luke 21:12, 17; Acts 4:17; 5:41; 9:14; 26:9; 1 Pet 4:14; Rev 2:3
15:24 John 5:36; 10:37
15:25 Ps 35:19; 69:4
15:27 Luke 24:48; John 19:35; 21:24

15:8 When a vine bears "much fruit," God is glorified, for daily he sent the sunshine and rain to make the crops grow, and constantly he nurtured each tiny plant and prepared it to blossom. What a moment of glory for the Lord of the harvest when the harvest is brought into the barns, mature and ready for use! He made it all happen! This farming analogy shows how God is glorified when people come into a right relationship with him and begin to "bear much fruit" in their lives.

15:11 When things are going well, we feel elated. When hardships come, we sink into depression. But true joy transcends the rolling waves of circumstance. Joy comes from a consistent relationship with Jesus Christ. When our lives are intertwined with his, he will help us walk through adversity without sinking into debilitating lows and manage prosperity without moving into deceptive highs. The joy of living with Jesus Christ daily will keep us level-headed, no matter how high or low our circumstances.

15:12–13 We are to love each other as Jesus loved us, and he loved us enough to give his life for us. We may not have to die for someone, but there are other ways to practice sacrificial love: listening, helping, encouraging, giving. Think of someone in particular who needs this kind of love today. Give all the love you can, and then try to give a little more.

15:15 Because Jesus Christ is Lord and Master, he should call us slaves; instead he calls us friends. How comforting and reassuring to be chosen as Christ's friends. Because he is Lord and Master, we owe him our unqualified obedience, but most of all, Jesus asks us to obey him because we love him.

15:16 Jesus made the first choice—to love and to die for us, to invite us to live with him forever. We make the next choice—to accept or reject his offer. Without *his* choice, we would have no choice to make.

15:17 Christians will get plenty of hatred from the world; from each other we need love and support. Do you allow small problems to get in the way of loving other believers? Jesus commands that you love them, and he will give you the strength to do it.

15:26 Once again Jesus offers hope. The Holy Spirit gives strength to endure the unreasonable hatred and evil in our world and the hostility many have toward Christ. This is especially comforting for those facing persecution.

15:26 Jesus uses two names for the Holy Spirit—*Helper* and *Spirit of truth.* The word *Helper* conveys the helping, encouraging,

16 "These things I have spoken to you so that you may be kept from stumbling.
2 "They will make you outcasts from the synagogue, but an hour is coming for
everyone who kills you to think that he is offering service to God.
3 "These things they will do because they have not known the Father or Me.
4 "But these things I have spoken to you, so that when their hour comes, you may remember that I told you of them. These things I did not say to you at the beginning, because I was with you.

Jesus Teaches about the Holy Spirit
(217)

5 "But now I am going to Him who sent Me; and none of you asks Me, 'Where are You
going?'
6 "But because I have said these things to you, sorrow has filled your heart.
7 "But I tell you the truth, it is to your advantage that I go away; for if I do not go away,
the Helper will not come to you; but if I go, I will send Him to you.
8 "And He, when He comes, will convict the world concerning sin and righteousness
and judgment;
9 concerning sin, because they do not believe in Me;
10 and concerning righteousness, because I go to the Father and you no longer see Me;
11 and concerning judgment, because the ruler of this world has been judged.
12 "I have many more things to say to you, but you cannot bear *them* now.
13 "But when He, the Spirit of truth, comes, He will guide you into all the truth; for He
will not speak on His own initiative, but whatever He hears, He will speak; and He will
disclose to you what is to come.
14 "He will glorify Me, for He will take of Mine and will disclose *it* to you.
15 "All things that the Father has are Mine; therefore I said that He takes of Mine and
will disclose *it* to you.

Jesus Teaches about Using His Name in Prayer
(218)

16 "A little while, and you will no longer see Me; and again a little while, and you will
see Me."
17 *Some* of His disciples then said to one another, "What is this thing He is telling us,
'A little while, and you will not see Me; and again a little while, and you will see Me';
and, 'because I go to the Father'?"
18 So they were saying, "What is this that He says, 'A little while'? We do not know
what He is talking about."

16:1 John 15:18-27; Matt 11:6
16:2 John 9:22; John 4:21; 16:25; Is 66:5; Acts 26:9-11; Rev 6:9
16:3 John 8:19, 55; 15:21; 17:25; Acts 3:17; 1 John 3:1
16:4 John 13:19; Luke 1:2
16:5 John 7:33; 16:10, 17, 28; John 13:36; 14:5
16:6 John 14:1; 16:22
16:7 John 14:16; John 14:26
16:9 John 15:22, 24
16:10 Acts 3:14; 7:52; 17:31; 1 Pet 3:18; John 16:5
16:11 John 12:31
16:13 John 14:17; John 14:26
16:14 John 7:39
16:15 John 17:10
16:16 John 7:33; John 14:18-24; 16:16-24; John 16:22
16:17 John 16:16; John 16:5

and strengthening work of the Spirit. *Spirit of truth* points to the teaching, illuminating, and reminding work of the Spirit. The Holy Spirit ministers to both the head and the heart, and both dimensions are important.

16:1–16 In his last moments with his disciples, Jesus (1) warned them about further persecution, (2) told them where, when, and why he was going, and (3) assured them that they would not be left alone, but that the Spirit would come. Jesus knew what lay ahead, and he did not want the disciples' faith shaken or destroyed. God wants you to know you are not alone. You have the Holy Spirit to comfort you, teach you truth, and help you.

16:2 Saul (who later became Paul), under the authority of the high priest, went through the land hunting down and persecuting Christians, convinced that he was doing the right thing (Acts 9:1–2; 26:9–11).

16:5 Although the disciples had asked Jesus about his death (13:36; 14:5), they had never wondered about its meaning. They were mostly concerned about themselves. If Jesus went away, what would become of them?

16:7 Unless Jesus did what he came to do, there would be no gospel. If he did not die, he could not remove our sins; he could not rise again and defeat death. If he did not go back to the Father, the Holy Spirit would not come. Christ's presence on earth was limited to one place at a time. His leaving meant he could be present to the whole world through the Holy Spirit.

16:8–11 Three important tasks of the Holy Spirit are (1) convicting the world of its sin and calling it to repentance, (2) revealing the standard of God's righteousness to anyone who believes, because Christ would no longer be physically present on earth, and (3) demonstrating Christ's judgment over Satan.

16:9 According to Jesus, not believing in him is *sin.*

16:10–11 Christ's death on the cross made a personal relationship with God available to us. When we confess our sin, God declares us righteous and delivers us from judgment for our sins.

16:13 The truth into which the Holy Spirit guides us is the truth about Christ. The Spirit also helps us through patient practice to discern right from wrong.

16:13 Jesus said the Holy Spirit would tell them "what is to come"—the nature of their mission, the opposition they would face, and the final outcome of their efforts. They didn't fully understand these promises until the Holy Spirit came after Jesus' death and resurrection. Then the Holy Spirit revealed truths to the disciples that they wrote down in the books that now form the New Testament.

16:16 Jesus was referring to his death, now only a few hours away, and his resurrection three days later.

19 Jesus knew that they wished to question Him, and He said to them, "Are you delib-
erating together about this, that I said, 'A little while, and you will not see Me, and again
a little while, and you will see Me'?
20 "Truly, truly, I say to you, that you will weep and lament, but the world will rejoice;
you will grieve, but your grief will be turned into joy.
21 "Whenever a woman is in labor she has pain, because her hour has come; but when
she gives birth to the child, she no longer remembers the anguish because of the joy that
a child has been born into the world.
22 "Therefore you too have grief now; but I will see you again, and your heart will rejoice, and no one *will* take your joy away from you.
23 "In that day you will not question Me about anything. Truly, truly, I say to you, if you
ask the Father for anything in My name, He will give it to you.
24 "Until now you have asked for nothing in My name; ask and you will receive, so that
your joy may be made full.
25 "These things I have spoken to you in figurative language; an hour is coming when I
will no longer speak to you in figurative language, but will tell you plainly of the Father.
26 "In that day you will ask in My name, and I do not say to you that I will request of the
Father on your behalf;
27 for the Father Himself loves you, because you have loved Me and have believed that
I came forth from the Father.
28 "I came forth from the Father and have come into the world; I am leaving the world
again and going to the Father."
29 His disciples ☆said, "Lo, now You are speaking plainly and are not using a figure of
speech.
30 "Now we know that You know all things, and have no need for anyone to question
You; by this we believe that You came from God."
31 Jesus answered them, "Do you now believe?
32 "Behold, an hour is coming, and has *already* come, for you to be scattered, each to
his own *home,* and to leave Me alone; and *yet* I am not alone, because the Father is
with Me.
33 "These things I have spoken to you, so that in Me you may have peace. In the world
you have tribulation, but take courage; I have overcome the world."

Jesus Prays for Himself
(219)

17 Jesus spoke these things; and lifting up His eyes to heaven, He said, "Father, the
hour has come; glorify Your Son, that the Son may glorify You,
2 even as You gave Him authority over all flesh, that to all whom You have given Him,
He may give eternal life.

16:19 Mark 9:32; John 6:61
16:20 Mark 16:10; Luke 23:27; John 20:20
16:23 John 14:20; 15:16
16:24 John 14:14; John 3:29; 15:11
16:25 Matt 13:34; John 10:6
16:26 John 14:20; 16:23
16:27 John 14:21, 23; John 2:11
16:28 John 8:42; John 13:1, 3
16:29 Matt 13:34; John 10:6; 16:25
16:30 John 2:11; 8:42
16:32 John 4:23; Zech 13:7; Matt 26:31; John 19:27; John 8:29
16:33 John 14:27; John 15:18ff; Matt 9:2; Rom 8:37; 2 Cor 2:14; 4:7ff; 6:4ff; Rev 3:21; 12:11
17:1 John 11:41; John 7:39; 13:31f
17:2 John 3:35; John 10:28; John 6:37, 39; 17:6, 9, 24

16:20 What a contrast between the disciples and the world! The world rejoiced as the disciples wept, but the disciples would see him again (in three days) and rejoice. The world's values are often the opposite of God's values. This can cause Christians to feel like misfits. But even if life is difficult now, one day we will rejoice. Keep your eye on the future and on God's promises!

16:23–27 Jesus is talking about a new relationship between the believer and God. Previously, people approached God through priests. After Jesus' resurrection, any believer could approach God directly. A new day has dawned and now all believers are priests, talking with God personally and directly (see Hebrews 10:19–23). We approach God, not because of our own merit, but because Jesus, our great high priest, has made us acceptable to God.

16:30 The disciples believed Jesus' words because they were convinced that he knew everything. But their belief was only a first step toward the great faith they would receive when the Holy Spirit came to live in them.

16:31–33 As Christians, we should expect continuing tension with an unbelieving world that is "out of sync" with Christ, his gospel, and his people. At the same time, we can expect our relationship with Christ to produce peace and comfort because we are "in sync" with him.

16:32 The disciples scattered after Jesus was arrested (see Mark 14:50).

16:33 Jesus summed up all he had told them this night, tying together themes from 14:27–29; 16:1–4; and 16:9–11. With these words he told his disciples to take courage. In spite of the inevitable struggles they would face, they would not be alone. Jesus does not abandon us to our struggles either. If we remember that the ultimate victory has already been won, we can claim the peace of Christ in the most troublesome times.

17:1ff This entire chapter is Jesus' prayer. From it, we learn that the world is a tremendous battleground where the forces under Satan's power and those under God's authority are at war. Satan and his forces are motivated by bitter hatred for Christ and his forces. Jesus prayed for his disciples, including those of us who follow him today. He prayed that God would keep his chosen believers safe from Satan's power, setting them apart and making them pure and holy, uniting them through his truth.

3 "This is eternal life, that they may know You, the only true God, and Jesus Christ
whom You have sent.
4 "I glorified You on the earth, having accomplished the work which You have given
Me to do.
5 "Now, Father, glorify Me together with Yourself, with the glory which I had with You
before the world was.

Jesus Prays for His Disciples
(220)

6 "I have manifested Your name to the men whom You gave Me out of the world; they
were Yours and You gave them to Me, and they have kept Your word.
7 "Now they have come to know that everything You have given Me is from You;
8 for the words which You gave Me I have given to them; and they received *them* and
truly understood that I came forth from You, and they believed that You sent Me.
9 "I ask on their behalf; I do not ask on behalf of the world, but of those whom You
have given Me; for they are Yours;
10 and all things that are Mine are Yours, and Yours are Mine; and I have been glorified in them.
11 "I am no longer in the world; and *yet* they themselves are in the world, and I come to
You. Holy Father, keep them in Your name, *the name* which You have given Me, that
they may be one even as We *are*.
12 "While I was with them, I was keeping them in Your name which You have given
Me; and I guarded them and not one of them perished but the son of perdition, so that
the Scripture would be fulfilled.
13 "But now I come to You; and these things I speak in the world so that they may have
My joy made full in themselves.
14 "I have given them Your word; and the world has hated them, because they are not
of the world, even as I am not of the world.
15 "I do not ask You to take them out of the world, but to keep them from the evil *one*.
16 "They are not of the world, even as I am not of the world.
17 "Sanctify them in the truth; Your word is truth.
18 "As You sent Me into the world, I also have sent them into the world.
19 "For their sakes I sanctify Myself, that they themselves also may be sanctified in truth.

17:3 John 5:44
17:4 John 10:01; Luke 22:37; John 4:34
17:5 John 1:1; 8:58; Phil 2:6
17:6 John 6:37, 39; John 8:51
17:8 John 8:42; 16:27, 30
17:9 Luke 22:32; John 14:16; John 6:37, 39
17:11 John 13:1; John 7:33; Phil 2:9; Rev 19:12; Rom 12:5; Gal 3:28
17:12 John 6:39; 18:9; Ps 41:9; John 13:18
17:13 John 7:33; John 15:11; John 3:29
17:14 John 15:19
17:15 Matt 5:37
17:17 John 15:3
17:18 John 3:17; Matt 10:5; John 4:38; 20:21
17:19 John 15:3; 2 Cor 7:14; Col 1:6; 1 John 3:18

17:3 How do we get eternal life? Jesus tells us clearly here—by knowing God the Father himself through his Son, Jesus Christ. Eternal life requires entering into a personal relationship with God in Jesus Christ. When we admit our sin and turn away from it, Christ's love lives in us by the Holy Spirit.

17:5 Before Jesus came to earth, he was one with God. At this point, when his mission on earth was almost finished, Jesus was asking his Father to restore him to his original place of honor and authority. Jesus' resurrection and ascension—and Stephen's dying exclamation (Acts 7:56)—attest that Jesus did return to his exalted position at the right hand of God.

17:10 What did Jesus mean when he said, "I have been glorified in them"? God's glory is the revelation of his character and presence. The lives of Jesus' disciples reveal his character, and he is present to the world through them. Does your life reveal Jesus' character and presence?

17:11 Jesus was asking that the disciples be united in harmony and love as the Father, Son, and Holy Spirit are united—the strongest of all unions. (See the note on 17:21–23.)

17:12 Judas was "the son of perdition," who was lost because he betrayed Jesus (see Psalm 41:9).

17:13 Joy is a common theme in Christ's teachings—he wants us to be joyful (see 15:11; 16:24, 33). The key to immeasurable joy is living in intimate contact with Christ, the source of all joy. When we do, we will experience God's special care and protection and see the victory God brings even when defeat seems certain.

17:14 The world hates Christians because Christians' values differ from the world's. Because Christ's followers don't cooperate with the world by joining in their sin, they are living accusations against the world's immorality. The world follows Satan's agenda, and Satan is the avowed enemy of Jesus and his people.

17:17 A follower of Christ becomes sanctified (set apart for sacred use, cleansed and made holy) through believing and obeying the Word of God (Hebrews 4:12). He or she has already accepted forgiveness through Christ's sacrificial death (Hebrews 7:26–27). But daily application of God's Word has a purifying effect on our minds and hearts. Scripture points out sin, motivates us to confess, renews our relationship with Christ, and guides us back to the right path.

17:18 Jesus didn't ask God to take believers *out* of the world but instead to use them *in* the world. Because Jesus sends us into the world, we should not try to escape from the world, nor should we avoid all relationships with non-Christians. We are called to be salt and light (Matthew 5:13–16), and we are to do the work that God sent us to do.

Jesus Prays for Future Believers
(221)

20 "I do not ask on behalf of these alone, but for those also who believe in Me through
their word;
21 that they may all be one; even as You, Father, *are* in Me and I in You, that they also
may be in Us, so that the world may believe that You sent Me.
22 "The glory which You have given Me I have given to them, that they may be one, just
as We are one;
23 I in them and You in Me, that they may be perfected in unity, so that the world may
know that You sent Me, and loved them, even as You have loved Me.
24 "Father, I desire that they also, whom You have given Me, be with Me where I am, so
that they may see My glory which You have given Me, for You loved Me before the foundation of the world.
25 "O righteous Father, although the world has not known You, yet I have known You;
and these have known that You sent Me;
26 and I have made Your name known to them, and will make it known, so that the
love with which You loved Me may be in them, and I in them."

17:21 John 10:38; 17:11, 23; John 17:8; John 3:17; 17:3, 8, 18, 23, 25

17:22 John 1:14; 17:24

17:23 John 10:38; 17:11, 21; John 3:17; 17:3, 8, 18, 21, 25; John 16:27

17:24 John 17:2; John 12:26; John 1:14; 17:22; Matt 25:34; John 17:5

17:25 John 17:11; 1 John 1:9; John 7:29; 15:21; John 3:17; 17:3, 8, 18, 21, 23

17:26 John 17:6; John 15:9

2. Jesus completes his mission

Jesus Is Betrayed and Arrested
(224/Matthew 26:47-56; Mark 14:43-52; Luke 22:47-53)

18 When Jesus had spoken these words, He went forth with His disciples over the
ravine of the Kidron, where there was a garden, in which He entered with His disciples.
2 Now Judas also, who was betraying Him, knew the place, for Jesus had often met
there with His disciples.
3 Judas then, having received the *Roman* cohort and officers from the chief priests
and the Pharisees, ☆came there with lanterns and torches and weapons.
4 So Jesus, knowing all the things that were coming upon Him, went forth and ☆said
to them, "Whom do you seek?"

18:1 Matt 26:30, 36; Mark 14:26, 32; Luke 22:39; John 18:26

18:2 Luke 21:37; 22:39

18:3 Acts 10:1; John 7:32; 18:12, 18; Matt 25:1

18:4 John 6:64; 13:1, 11; John 18:7

17:20 Jesus prayed for all who would follow him, including you and others you know. He prayed for unity (17:11), protection from the evil one (17:15), and sanctity (holiness) (17:17). Knowing that Jesus prayed for us should give us confidence as we work for his kingdom.

17:21–23 Jesus' great desire for his disciples was that they would become one. He wanted them unified as a powerful witness to the reality of God's love. Are you helping to unify the body of Christ, the church? You can pray for other Christians, avoid gossip, build others up, work together in humility, give your time and money, exalt Christ, and refuse to get sidetracked arguing over divisive matters.

17:21–23 Jesus prayed for unity among the believers based on the believers' unity with him and the Father. Christians can know unity among themselves if they are living in union with God. For example, each branch living in union with the vine is united with all other branches doing the same.

18:3 The officers from the chief priests and Pharisees were probably members of the temple guard; they were Jews given authority by the religious leaders to make arrests for minor infractions. The soldiers in the cohort may have been a small contingent of Roman soldiers who did not participate in the arrest but accompanied the temple guard to make sure matters didn't get out of control.

18:4–5 John does not record Judas's kiss of greeting (Matthew 26:49; Mark 14:45; Luke 22:47–48), but Judas's kiss marked a turning point for the disciples. With Jesus' arrest, each one's life would be radically different. For the first time, Judas openly betrayed Jesus before the other disciples. For the first time, Jesus' loyal disciples ran away from him (Matthew 26:56). The band of disciples would undergo severe testing before they were transformed from hesitant followers to dynamic leaders.

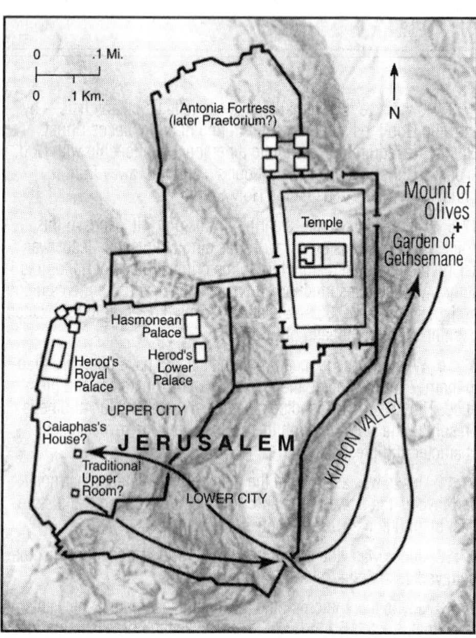

BETRAYAL IN THE GARDEN After eating the Passover meal in the upper room, Jesus and his disciples went to Gethsemane, where Judas led the temple guard to arrest Jesus. Jesus was then taken to Caiaphas's house for his first of many trials.

5 They answered Him, "Jesus the Nazarene." He ☆said to them, "I am *He.*" And Judas also, who was betraying Him, was standing with them.
6 So when He said to them, "I am *He,*" they drew back and fell to the ground.
7 Therefore He again asked them, "Whom do you seek?" And they said, "Jesus the
Nazarene."
8 Jesus answered, "I told you that I am *He;* so if you seek Me, let these go their way,"
9 to fulfill the word which He spoke, "Of those whom You have given Me I lost not
one."
10 Simon Peter then, having a sword, drew it and struck the high priest's slave, and cut
off his right ear; and the slave's name was Malchus.
11 So Jesus said to Peter, "Put the sword into the sheath; the cup which the Father has
given Me, shall I not drink it?"

18:7 John 18:4

18:9 John 17:12

18:10 Matt 26:51; Mark 14:47

18:11 Matt 20:22; 26:39; Mark 14:36; Luke 22:42

THE SIX STAGES OF JESUS' TRIAL

Although Jesus' trial lasted less than 18 hours, he was taken to six different hearings.

BEFORE JEWISH AUTHORITIES	Preliminary Hearing before Annas (John 18:12–24)	Because the office of high priest was for life, Annas was still the "official" high priest in the eyes of the Jews, even though the Romans had appointed another. Thus Annas still carried much weight among the Council.
	Hearing before Caiaphas (Matthew 26:57–68)	Like the hearing before Annas, this hearing was conducted at night in secrecy. It was full of illegalities that made a mockery of justice (see the chart in Matthew 27—28).
	Trial before the Council (Matthew 27:1–2)	Just after daybreak, 70 members of the Jewish Council met to rubber-stamp their approval of the previous hearings to make them appear legal. The purpose of this trial was not to determine justice, but to justify their own preconceptions of Jesus' guilt.
BEFORE ROMAN AUTHORITIES	First Hearing before Pilate (Luke 23:1–5)	The religious leaders had condemned Jesus to death on religious grounds, but only the Roman government could grant the death penalty. Thus, they took Jesus to Pilate, the Roman governor, and accused him of treason and rebellion, crimes for which the Roman government gave the death penalty. Pilate saw at once that Jesus was innocent, but he was afraid about the uproar being caused by the religious leaders.
	Hearing before Herod (Luke 23:6–12)	Because Jesus' home was in the region of Galilee, Pilate sent Jesus to Herod Agrippa, the ruler of Galilee, who was in Jerusalem for the Passover celebration. Herod was eager to see Jesus do a miracle, but when Jesus remained silent, Herod wanted nothing to do with him and sent him back to Pilate.
	Last Hearing before Pilate (Luke 23:13–25)	Pilate didn't like the religious leaders. He wasn't interested in condemning Jesus because he knew Jesus was innocent. However, he knew that another uprising in his district might cost him his job. First he tried to compromise with the religious leaders by having Jesus beaten, an illegal action in itself. But finally he gave in and handed Jesus over to be executed. Pilate's self-interest was stronger than his sense of justice.

18:6 The men may have been startled by the boldness of Jesus' question, or by the words "I am He," a declaration of his divinity (Exodus 3:14). Or perhaps they were overcome by his obvious power and authority.

18:10–11 Trying to protect Jesus, Peter pulled a sword and wounded the high priest's slave. But Jesus told Peter to put away his sword and allow God's plan to unfold. At times it is tempting to take matters into our own hands, to force the issue. Most often such moves lead to sin. Instead we must trust God to work out his plan. Think of it—if Peter had had his way, Jesus would not have gone to the cross, and God's plan of redemption would have been thwarted.

18:11 The cup means the suffering, isolation, and death that Jesus would have to endure in order to atone for the sins of the world.

Annas Questions Jesus
(225)

12 So the *Roman* cohort and the commander and the officers of the Jews, arrested Jesus
and bound Him,
13 and led Him to Annas first; for he was father-in-law of Caiaphas, who was high priest
that year.
14 Now Caiaphas was the one who had advised the Jews that it was expedient for one
man to die on behalf of the people.
15 Simon Peter was following Jesus, and *so was* another disciple. Now that disciple was
known to the high priest, and entered with Jesus into the court of the high priest,
16 but Peter was standing at the door outside. So the other disciple, who was known to
the high priest, went out and spoke to the doorkeeper, and brought Peter in.
17 Then the slave-girl who kept the door ☆said to Peter, "You are not also *one* of this
man's disciples, are you?" He ☆said, "I am not."
18 Now the slaves and the officers were standing *there,* having made a charcoal fire,
for it was cold and they were warming themselves; and Peter was also with them, standing and warming himself.
19 The high priest then questioned Jesus about His disciples, and about His teaching.
20 Jesus answered him, "I have spoken openly to the world; I always taught in synagogues and in the temple, where all the Jews come together; and I spoke nothing in
secret.
21 "Why do you question Me? Question those who have heard what I spoke to them;
they know what I said."
22 When He had said this, one of the officers standing nearby struck Jesus, saying, "Is
that the way You answer the high priest?"
23 Jesus answered him, "If I have spoken wrongly, testify of the wrong; but if rightly,
why do you strike Me?"
24 So Annas sent Him bound to Caiaphas the high priest.

Peter Denies Knowing Jesus
(227/Matthew 6:69-75; Mark 14:66-72; Luke 22:54-65)

25 Now Simon Peter was standing and warming himself. So they said to him, "You are
not also *one* of His disciples, are you?" He denied *it,* and said, "I am not."

18:12 John 18:12f; Matt 26:57ff; John 18:3

18:13 Luke 3:2; John 18:24; Matt 26:3; John 11:49, 51

18:14 John 11:50

18:15 Matt 26:58; Mark 14:54; Luke 22:54; Matt 26:3; John 18:24, 28

18:16 Matt 26:69f; Mark 14:66-68; Luke 22:55-57

18:17 Acts 12:13; John 18:25

18:18 John 18:3; John 21:9; Mark 14:54, 67

18:19 Matt 26:59-68; Mark 14:55-65; Luke 22:63-71

18:20 John 7:26; 8:26; Matt 4:23; John 6:59; Matt 26:55

18:22 John 18:3; John 19:3

18:23 Matt 5:39; Acts 23:2-5

18:24 John 18:13

18:12–13 Jesus was immediately taken to the high priest's residence, even though this was the middle of the night. The religious leaders were in a hurry—they wanted to complete the execution before the Sabbath and get on with the Passover celebration. This residence was a palace whose outer walls enclosed a courtyard where servants and soldiers would warm themselves around a fire.

18:13 Both Annas and Caiaphas had been high priests. Annas was Israel's high priest from A.D. 6 to 15, when he was deposed by Roman rulers. Caiaphas, Annas's son-in-law, was appointed high priest from A.D. 18 to 36/37. According to Jewish law, the office of high priest was held for life. Many Jews therefore still considered Annas the high priest and still called him by that title. But although Annas retained much authority among the Jews, Caiaphas made the final decisions.

Both Caiaphas and Annas cared more about their political ambitions than about their responsibility to lead the people to God. Though religious leaders, they had become evil. As the nation's spiritual leaders, they should have been sensitive to God's revelation. They should have known that Jesus was the Messiah about whom the Scriptures spoke, and they should have pointed the people to him. But when deceitful men and women pursue evil, they want to eliminate all opposition. Instead of honestly evaluating Jesus' claims based on their knowledge of Scripture, these religious leaders sought to further their own selfish ambitions and were even willing to kill God's Son, if that's what it took, to do it.

18:15–16 The other disciple is probably John, the author of this Gospel. He knew the high priest and identified himself to the girl at the door. Because of his connections, John got himself and Peter into the courtyard. But Peter refused to identify himself as Jesus' follower. Peter's experiences in the next few hours would change his life. For more information about Peter, see his Profile in Matthew 26.

18:19ff During the night, Jesus had a pre-trial hearing before Annas before he was taken to Caiaphas and the entire Council (Mark 14:53–65). The religious leaders knew they had no grounds for charging Jesus, so they tried to build evidence against him by using false witnesses (Mark 14:55–59).

18:22–27 We can easily get angry at the Council for their injustice in condemning Jesus, but we must remember that Peter and the rest of the disciples also contributed to Jesus' pain by deserting and denying him (Matthew 26:56, 75). While most of us are not like the religious leaders, we are all like the disciples, for all of us have been guilty of denying that Christ is Lord in vital areas of our lives or of keeping secret our identity as believers in times of pressure. Don't excuse yourself by pointing at others whose sins seem worse than yours. Instead, come to Jesus for forgiveness and healing.

18:25 The other three Gospels say that Peter's three denials happened near a fire in the courtyard outside Caiaphas's palace. John places the first denial outside Annas's home and the other two denials outside Caiaphas's home. This was very likely the same courtyard. The high priest's residence was large, and Annas and Caiaphas undoubtedly lived near each other.

18:25–27 Imagine standing outside while Jesus, your Lord and Master, is questioned. Imagine watching this man, whom you have come to believe is the long-awaited Messiah, being abused and

18:26 John 18:10; John 18:1

26 One of the slaves of the high priest, being a relative of the one whose ear Peter cut
off, ☆said, "Did I not see you in the garden with Him?"
27 Peter then denied *it* again, and immediately a rooster crowed.

18:27 John 13:38

Jesus Stands Trial before Pilate
(230/Matthew 27:11-14; Mark 15:2-5; Luke 23:1-5)

18:28 Matt 27:2; Mark 15:1; Luke 23:1; John 18:13; Matt 27:27; John 18:33; 19:9; John 11:55; Acts 11:3

28 Then they ☆led Jesus from Caiaphas into the [22]Praetorium, and it was early; and
they themselves did not enter into the Praetorium so that they would not be defiled, but
might eat the Passover.
29 Therefore Pilate went out to them and ☆said, "What accusation do you bring against
this Man?"
30 They answered and said to him, "If this Man were not an evildoer, we would not
have delivered Him to you."
31 So Pilate said to them, "Take Him yourselves, and judge Him according to your law."
The Jews said to him, "We are not permitted to put anyone to death,"

18:32 Matt 20:19; 26:2; Mark 10:33f; Luke 18:32f; John 3:14; 8:28; 12:32f

32 to fulfill the word of Jesus which He spoke, signifying by what kind of death He was
about to die.
33 Therefore Pilate entered again into the Praetorium, and summoned Jesus and said
to Him, "Are You the King of the Jews?"

18:33 John 18:28, 29; 19:9; Luke 23:3; John 19:12

34 Jesus answered, "Are you saying this on your own initiative, or did others tell you
about Me?"
35 Pilate answered, "I am not a Jew, am I? Your own nation and the chief priests delivered You to me; what have You done?"

22 I.e. governor's official residence

---

beaten. Naturally Peter was confused and afraid. It is a serious sin to deny Christ, but Jesus forgave Peter (21:15–17). No sin is too great for Jesus to forgive if you are truly repentant. He will forgive even your worst sin if you turn from it and ask his pardon.

18:27 This fulfilled Jesus' words to Peter after he promised he would never deny him (Mark 14:31; John 13:38).

18:28 By Jewish law, entering the house of a Gentile would cause a Jewish person to be ceremonially defiled. As a result, he could not take part in worship at the temple or celebrate the feasts until he was restored to a state of "cleanness." Afraid of being defiled, these men stayed outside the house where they had taken Jesus for trial. They kept the ceremonial requirements of their religion while harboring murder and treachery in their hearts.

18:29 This Roman governor, Pilate, was in charge of Judea (the region where Jerusalem was located) from A.D. 26 to 36. Pilate was unpopular with the Jews because he had raided the temple treasuries for money to build an aqueduct. He did not like the Jews, but when Jesus, the King of the Jews, stood before him, Pilate found him innocent.

18:30 Pilate knew what was going on; he knew that the religious leaders hated Jesus, and he did not want to act as their executioner. They could not sentence him to death themselves—permission had to come from a Roman leader. But Pilate initially refused to sentence Jesus without sufficient evidence. Jesus' life became a pawn in a political power struggle.

18:31ff Pilate made four attempts to deal with Jesus: (1) He tried to put the responsibility on someone else (18:31); (2) he tried to find a way of escape so he could release Jesus (18:39); (3) he tried to compromise by having Jesus scourged (flogged) rather than handing him over to die (19:1–3); and (4) he tried a direct appeal to the sympathy of the accusers (19:15). Everyone has to decide what to do with Jesus. Pilate tried to let everyone else decide for him—and in the end, he lost.

18:32 This prediction is recorded in Matthew 20:19. Crucifixion was a common method of execution for criminals who were not Roman citizens.

18:34 If Pilate was asking this question in his role as the Roman governor, he would have been inquiring whether Jesus was setting up a rebel government. But the Jews were using the word *king* to mean their religious ruler, the Messiah. Israel was a captive nation, under the authority of the Roman empire. A rival king might have threatened Rome; a Messiah could have been a purely religious leader.

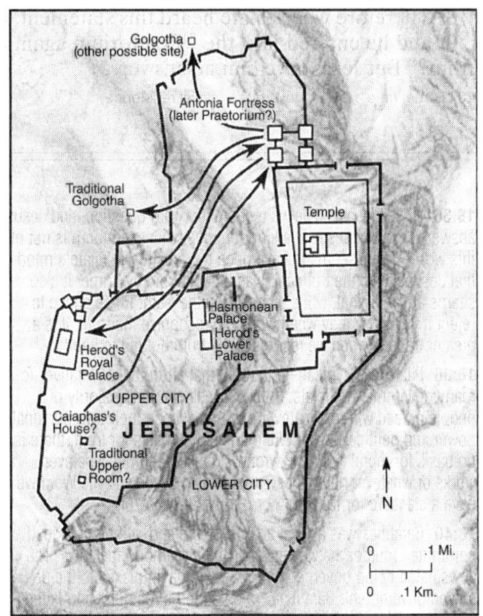

JESUS' TRIAL AND CRUCIFIXION Jesus was taken from trial before the Jewish Council to trial before the Roman governor, Pilate, in Pilate's palace. Pilate sent him to Herod (Luke 23:5–12), but Herod just returned Jesus to Pilate. Responding to threats from the mob, Pilate finally turned Jesus over to be crucified.

36 Jesus answered, "My kingdom is not of this world. If My kingdom were of this world,
then My servants would be fighting so that I would not be handed over to the Jews; but
as it is, My kingdom is not [23]of this realm."
37 Therefore Pilate said to Him, "So You are a king?" Jesus answered, "You say *cor-*
rectly that I am a king. For this I have been born, and for this I have come into the world,
to testify to the truth. Everyone who is of the truth hears My voice."

Pilate Hands Jesus Over to Be Crucified

(232/Matthew 27:15-26; Mark 15:6-15; Luke 23:13-25)

38 Pilate ☆said to Him, "What is truth?"
And when he had said this, he went out again to the Jews and ☆said to them, "I find no
guilt in Him.
39 "But you have a custom that I release someone for you at the Passover; do you wish
then that I release for you the King of the Jews?"
40 So they cried out again, saying, "Not this Man, but Barabbas." Now Barabbas was a
robber.
19 Pilate then took Jesus and scourged Him.
2 And the soldiers twisted together a crown of thorns and put it on His head, and
put a purple robe on Him;
3 and they *began* to come up to Him and say, "Hail, King of the Jews!" and to give
Him slaps *in the face.*
4 Pilate came out again and ☆said to them, "Behold, I am bringing Him out to you so
that you may know that I find no guilt in Him."
5 Jesus then came out, wearing the crown of thorns and the purple robe. *Pilate* ☆said
to them, "Behold, the Man!"
6 So when the chief priests and the officers saw Him, they cried out saying, "Crucify,
crucify!" Pilate ☆said to them, "Take Him yourselves and crucify Him, for I find no guilt
in Him."
7 The Jews answered him, "We have a law, and by that law He ought to die because
He made Himself out *to be* the Son of God."
8 Therefore when Pilate heard this statement, he was *even* more afraid;
9 and he entered into the [24]Praetorium again and ☆said to Jesus, "Where are You
from?" But Jesus gave him no answer.

18:36 Matt 26:53; Luke 17:21; John 6:15

18:37 Matt 27:11; Mark 15:2; Luke 22:70; 23:3; John 1:14; 3:32; 8:14; John 8:47; 1 John 4:6

18:38 John 18:33; 19:4; Luke 23:4; John 19:4, 6

18:40 Acts 3:14

19:1 Matt 27:26

19:2 Matt 27:27-30; Mark 15:16-19

19:3 Matt 27:29; Mark 15:18; John 18:22

19:4 John 18:33, 38; Luke 23:4; John 18:38; 19:6

19:5 John 19:2

19:6 Matt 26:58; John 18:3; Luke 23:4; John 18:38; 19:4

19:7 Lev 24:16; Matt 26:63-66; John 5:18; 10:33

19:9 John 18:33; Matt 26:63; 27:12, 14; John 18:34-37

23 Lit *from here* **24** I.e. governor's official residence

18:36–37 Pilate asked Jesus a straightforward question, and Jesus answered clearly. Jesus is a king, but one whose kingdom is not of this world. There seems to have been no question in Pilate's mind that Jesus spoke the truth and was innocent of any crime. It also seems apparent that, while recognizing the truth, Pilate chose to reject it. It is a tragedy when we fail to recognize the truth. It is a greater tragedy when we recognize the truth but fail to heed it.

18:38 Pilate was cynical; he thought that all truth was relative. To many government officials, truth was whatever the majority of people agreed with or whatever helped advance their own personal power and political goals. When there is no basis for truth, there is no basis for moral right and wrong. Justice becomes whatever works or whatever helps those in power. In Jesus and his Word we have a standard for truth and for our moral behavior.

18:40 Barabbas was a rebel against Rome and, although he had committed murder, he was probably a hero among the Jews. The Jews hated being governed by Rome and paying taxes to the despised government. Barabbas, who had led a rebellion and failed, was released instead of Jesus, the only One who could truly help Israel. For more on Barabbas, see the note on Luke 23:17–19.

19:1ff To grasp the full picture of Jesus' crucifixion, read John's perspective along with the other three accounts in Matthew 27, Mark 15, and Luke 23. Each writer adds meaningful details, but each has the same message—Jesus died on the cross, in fulfillment of Old Testament prophecy, so that we could be saved from our sins and given eternal life.

19:1–3 Scourging could have killed Jesus. The usual procedure was to bare the upper half of the victim's body and tie his hands to a pillar before whipping him with a three-pronged whip. The number of lashes was determined by the severity of the crime; up to 40 were permitted under Jewish law (Deuteronomy 25:3). After being scourged, Jesus also endured other agonies recorded here and in the other Gospels.

19:2–5 The soldiers went beyond their orders to whip Jesus—they also mocked his claim to royalty by placing a crown on his head and a royal robe on his shoulders.

19:7 The truth finally came out—the religious leaders had not brought Jesus to Pilate because he was causing rebellion against Rome, but because they thought he had broken their religious laws. Blasphemy, one of the most serious crimes in Jewish law, deserved the death penalty. Accusing Jesus of blasphemy would give credibility to their case in the eyes of Jews; accusing Jesus of treason would give credibility to their case in the eyes of the Romans. They didn't care which accusation Pilate listened to, as long as he would cooperate with them in killing Jesus.

19:11 Rom 13:1; John 18:13f, 28ff; Acts 3:13

19:12 Luke 23:2; John 18:33ff

19:13 Matt 27:19; John 5:2; 19:17, 20

10 So Pilate ☆said to Him, "You do not speak to me? Do You not know that I have
authority to release You, and I have authority to crucify You?"
11 Jesus answered, "You would have no authority over Me, unless it had been given
you from above; for this reason he who delivered Me to you has *the* greater sin."
12 As a result of this Pilate made efforts to release Him, but the Jews cried out saying,
"If you release this Man, you are no friend of Caesar; everyone who makes himself out
to be a king opposes Caesar."
13 Therefore when Pilate heard these words, he brought Jesus out, and sat down on
the judgment seat at a place called The Pavement, but in Hebrew, Gabbatha.

MARY MAGDALENE

The absence of women among the 12 disciples has bothered a few people. But it is clear that there were many women among Jesus' followers. It is also clear that Jesus did not treat women as others in his culture did; he treated them with dignity, as people with worth.

Mary of Magdala was an early follower of Jesus who certainly deserves to be called a disciple. An energetic, impulsive, caring woman, she not only traveled with Jesus, but also contributed to the needs of the group. She was present at the crucifixion and was on her way to anoint Jesus' body on Sunday morning when she discovered the empty tomb. Mary was the first to see Jesus after his resurrection.

Mary Magdalene is a heartwarming example of thankful living. Her life was miraculously freed by Jesus when he drove seven demons out of her. In every glimpse we have of her, she was acting out her appreciation for the freedom Christ had given her. That freedom allowed her to stand under Christ's cross when all the disciples except John were hiding in fear. After Jesus' death, she intended to give his body every respect. Like the rest of Jesus' followers, she never expected his bodily resurrection—but she was overjoyed to discover it.

Mary's faith was not complicated, but it was direct and genuine. She was more eager to believe and obey than to understand everything. Jesus honored her childlike faith by appearing to her first and by entrusting her with the first message of his resurrection.

Strengths and accomplishments:
- Contributed to the needs of Jesus and his disciples
- One of the few faithful followers present at Jesus' death on the cross
- First to see the risen Christ

Weakness and mistake:
- Jesus had to drive seven demons out of her

Lessons from her life:
- Those who are obedient grow in understanding
- Women are vital to Jesus' ministry
- Jesus relates to women as he created them—as equal reflectors of God's image

Vital statistics:
- Where: Magdala
- Occupation: We are not told, but she seems to have been wealthy
- Contemporaries: Jesus, the 12 disciples, Mary, Martha, Lazarus, Jesus' mother Mary

Key verse:
"Now after He had risen early on the first day of the week, He first appeared to Mary Magdalene, from whom He had cast out seven demons" (Mark 16:9).

Mary Magdalene's story is told in Matthew 27—28; Mark 15—16; Luke 23—24; and John 19—20. She is also mentioned in Luke 8:2.

19:10 Throughout the trial we see that Jesus was in control, not Pilate or the religious leaders. Pilate vacillated, the Jewish leaders reacted out of hatred and anger, but Jesus remained composed. He knew the truth, he knew God's plan, and he knew the reason for his trial. Despite the pressure and persecution, Jesus remained unmoved. It was really Pilate and the religious leaders who were on trial, not Jesus. When you are questioned or ridiculed because of your faith, remember that, while you may be on trial before your accusers, they are on trial before God.

19:11 When Jesus said the man who delivered him to Pilate was guiltier than Pilate, he was not excusing Pilate for reacting to the political pressure placed on him. Pilate was responsible for his decision about Jesus. Caiaphas and the other religious leaders were guilty of a greater sin because they premeditated Jesus' murder.

19:12–13 These words pressured Pilate into allowing Jesus to be crucified. As Roman governor of the area, Pilate was expected to keep the peace. Because Rome could not afford to keep large numbers of troops in the outlying regions, they maintained control by crushing rebellions immediately with brute force. Pilate was afraid that reports to Caesar of insurrection in his region would cost Pilate his job and perhaps even his life. When we face a tough decision, we can take the easy way out, or we can stand for what is right regardless of the cost. If we know the good we ought to do and don't do it, we sin (James 4:17).

19:13 The Pavement was part of the Tower of Antonia bordering the northwest corner of the temple complex.

14 Now it was the day of preparation for the Passover; it was about the [25]sixth hour.
And he ☆said to the Jews, "Behold, your King!"
15 So they cried out, "Away with *Him,* away with *Him,* crucify Him!" Pilate ☆said to
them, "Shall I crucify your King?" The chief priests answered, "We have no king but
Caesar."
16 So he then handed Him over to them to be crucified.

Jesus Is Led Away to Be Crucified
(234/Matthew 27:32-34; Mark 15:21-24; Luke 23:26-31)

Jesus Is Placed on the Cross
(235/Matthew 27:35-44; Mark 15:25-32; Luke 23:32-43)

17 They took Jesus, therefore, and He went out, bearing His own cross, to the place
called the Place of a Skull, which is called in Hebrew, Golgotha.
18 There they crucified Him, and with Him two other men, one on either side, and
Jesus in between.
19 Pilate also wrote an inscription and put it on the cross. It was written, "JESUS THE
NAZARENE, THE KING OF THE JEWS."
20 Therefore many of the Jews read this inscription, for the place where Jesus was crucified was near the city; and it was written in Hebrew, Latin *and* in Greek.
21 So the chief priests of the Jews were saying to Pilate, "Do not write, 'The King of
the Jews'; but that He said, 'I am King of the Jews.' "
22 Pilate answered, "What I have written I have written."
23 Then the soldiers, when they had crucified Jesus, took His outer garments and made
four parts, a part to every soldier and *also* the [26]tunic; now the tunic was seamless, woven in one piece.
24 So they said to one another, "Let us not tear it, but cast lots for it, *to decide* whose
it shall be"; *this was* to fulfill the Scripture: "THEY DIVIDED MY OUTER GARMENTS
AMONG THEM, AND FOR MY CLOTHING THEY CAST LOTS."
25 Therefore the soldiers did these things.
But standing by the cross of Jesus were His mother, and His mother's sister, Mary the
wife of Clopas, and Mary Magdalene.
26 When Jesus then saw His mother, and the disciple whom He loved standing nearby,
He ☆said to His mother, "Woman, behold, your son!"
27 Then He ☆said to the disciple, "Behold, your mother!" From that hour the disciple
took her into his own *household.*

25 Perhaps 6 a.m. **26** Gr *khiton,* the garment worn next to the skin

19:14 Matt 27:62; John 19:31, 42; Matt 27:45; Mark 15:25
19:15 Luke 23:18
19:16 Matt 27:26; Mark 15:15; Luke 23:25
19:18 Luke 23:32
19:19 Matt 27:37; Mark 15:26; Luke 23:38
19:20 John 19:13
19:21 John 19:14, 19
19:22 Gen 43:14; Esth 4:16
19:23 Matt 27:35; Mark 15:24; Luke 23:34; Acts 12:4
19:24 Ex 28:32; Matt 27:35; Mark 15:24; Luke 23:34; John 19:28, 36f; Ps 22:18
19:25 Matt 27:55f; Mark 15:40f; Luke 23:49; Matt 12:46; Luke 8:2; John 20:1, 18
19:26 John 13:23; John 2:4
19:27 Luke 18:28; John 1:11; 16:32; Acts 21:6

19:15 The Jewish leaders were so desperate to get rid of Jesus that, despite their intense hatred for Rome, they shouted, "We have no king but Caesar." How ironic that they feigned allegiance to Rome while rejecting their own Messiah! Their own words condemned them, for God was to be their only true King, and they had abandoned every trace of loyalty to him. The priests had truly lost their reasons for existence—instead of turning people to God, they claimed allegiance to Rome in order to kill their Messiah.

19:17 This place called *Golgotha,* "the Place of a Skull," was probably a hill outside Jerusalem along a main road. Many executions took place here so the Romans could use them as an example to the people.

19:18 Crucifixion was a Roman form of execution. The condemned man was forced to carry his cross along a main road to the execution site, as a warning to the people. Types of crosses and methods of crucifixion varied. Jesus was nailed to his cross; some people were tied with ropes. Death came by suffocation because the weight of the body made breathing difficult as the victim lost strength. Crucifixion was a hideously slow and painful death.

19:19 This inscription was meant to be ironic. A king, stripped nearly naked and executed in public view, had obviously lost his kingdom forever. But Jesus, who turns the world's wisdom upside down, was just coming into his kingdom. His death and resurrection would strike the deathblow to Satan's rule and would establish Jesus' eternal authority over the earth. Few people reading the sign that bleak afternoon understood its real meaning, but the sign was absolutely true. All was not lost. Jesus was King of the Jews—and the Gentiles, and the whole universe.

19:20 The inscription was written in three languages: Hebrew for the native Jews, Latin for the Roman occupation forces, and Greek for foreigners and Jews visiting from other lands.

19:23–24 Roman soldiers in charge of crucifixions customarily took for themselves the clothes of the condemned men. They divided Jesus' clothing, casting lots to determine who would get his seamless tunic, the most valuable piece of clothing. This fulfilled the prophecy in Psalm 22:18.

19:25–27 Even while dying on the cross, Jesus was concerned about his family. He instructed John to care for Mary, Jesus' mother. Our families are precious gifts from God, and we should value and care for them under all circumstances. Neither Christian work nor key responsibilities in any job or position excuse us from caring for our families. What can you do today to show your love to your family?

19:27 Jesus asked his close friend John, the writer of this Gospel, to care for Jesus' mother, Mary, whose husband, Joseph, must have been dead by this time. Why didn't Jesus assign this task to his brothers? As the oldest son, Jesus entrusted his mother to a person who stayed with him at the cross—and that was John.

Jesus Dies on the Cross
(236/Matthew 27:45-56; Mark 15:33-41; Luke 23:44-49)

19:28 John 13:1; 17:4; John 19:24, 36f; Ps 69:21

28 After this, Jesus, knowing that all things had already been accomplished, to fulfill
the Scripture, ☆said, "I am thirsty."
29 A jar full of sour wine was standing there; so they put a sponge full of the sour wine
upon *a branch of* hyssop and brought it up to His mouth.

19:30 John 17:4; Matt 27:50; Mark 15:37; Luke 23:46

30 Therefore when Jesus had received the sour wine, He said, "It is finished!" And He
bowed His head and gave up His spirit.

19:31 John 19:14, 42; Deut 21:23; Josh 8:29; 10:26f; Ex 12:16

31 Then the Jews, because it was the day of preparation, so that the bodies would not
remain on the cross on the Sabbath (for that Sabbath was a high day), asked Pilate that
their legs might be broken, and *that* they might be taken away.

19:32 John 19:18

32 So the soldiers came, and broke the legs of the first man and of the other who was
crucified with Him;
33 but coming to Jesus, when they saw that He was already dead, they did not break
His legs.

19:34 1 John 5:6, 8

34 But one of the soldiers pierced His side with a spear, and immediately blood and
water came out.

19:35 John 15:27; 21:24

35 And he who has seen has testified, and his testimony is true; and he knows that he
is telling the truth, so that you also may believe.

19:36 John 19:24, 28; Ex 12:46; Num 9:12; Ps 34:20

36 For these things came to pass to fulfill the Scripture, "NOT A BONE OF HIM SHALL
BE BROKEN."
37 And again another Scripture says, "THEY SHALL LOOK ON HIM WHOM THEY
PIERCED."

19:37 Zech 12:10; Rev 1:7

Jesus Is Laid in the Tomb
(237/Matthew 27:57-61; Mark 15:42-47; Luke 23:50-56)

19:38 John 7:13

19:39 John 3:1; Mark 16:1; Ps 45:8; Prov 7:17; Song 4:14; Matt 2:11; John 12:3

38 After these things Joseph of Arimathea, being a disciple of Jesus, but a secret *one*
for fear of the Jews, asked Pilate that he might take away the body of Jesus; and Pilate
granted permission. So he came and took away His body.
39 Nicodemus, who had first come to Him by night, also came, bringing a mixture of
myrrh and aloes, about a hundred pounds *weight*.

19:29 This sour wine was a cheap wine that the Roman soldiers drank while waiting for those crucified to die.

19:30 Until this time, a complicated system of sacrifices had atoned for sins. Sin separates people from God, and only through the sacrifice of an animal, a substitute, could people be forgiven and become clean before God. But people sin continually, so frequent sacrifices were required. Jesus, however, became the final and ultimate sacrifice for sin. The word *finished* is the same as "paid in full." Jesus came to *finish* God's work of salvation (4:34; 17:4), to pay the full penalty for our sins. With his death, the complex sacrificial system ended because Jesus took all sin upon himself. Now we can freely approach God because of what Jesus did for us. Those who believe in Jesus' death and resurrection can live eternally with God and escape the penalty that comes from sin.

19:31 It was against God's law to leave the body of a dead person exposed overnight (Deuteronomy 21:23), and it was also against the law to work after sundown on Friday, when the Sabbath began. This is why the religious leaders urgently wanted to get Jesus' body off the cross and buried by sundown.

19:31–35 These Romans were experienced soldiers. They knew from many previous crucifixions whether a man was dead or alive. There was no question that Jesus was dead when they checked him, so they decided not to break his legs as they had done to the other victims. Piercing his side and seeing the sudden flow of blood and water (indicating that the sac surrounding the heart and the heart itself had been pierced) was further proof of his death. Some people say Jesus didn't really die, that he only passed out—and that's how he came back to life. But we have the witness of an impartial party, the Roman soldiers, that Jesus died on the cross (see Mark 15:44–45).

19:32 The Roman soldiers would break victims' legs to hasten the death process. When a person hung on a cross, death came by suffocation, but the victim could push against the cross with his legs to hold up his body and keep breathing. With broken legs, he would suffocate almost immediately.

19:34–35 The graphic details of Jesus' death are especially important in John's record because he was an eyewitness.

19:36–37 Jesus died as the lambs for the Passover meal were being slain. Not a bone was to be broken in these sacrificial lambs (Exodus 12:46; Numbers 9:12). Jesus, the Lamb of God, was the perfect sacrifice for the sins of the world (1 Corinthians 5:7).

19:38–39 Four people were changed in the process of Jesus' death. The criminal, dying on the cross beside Jesus, asked Jesus to include him in his kingdom (Luke 23:39–43). The Roman centurion proclaimed that surely Jesus was the Son of God (Mark 15:39). Joseph and Nicodemus, members of the Jewish Council and secret followers of Jesus (7:50–52), came out of hiding. These men were changed more by Jesus' death than by his life. They realized who Jesus was, and that realization brought out their belief, proclamation, and action. When confronted with Jesus and his death, we should be changed—to believe, proclaim, and act.

19:38–42 Joseph of Arimathea and Nicodemus were secret followers of Jesus. They were afraid to make this allegiance known because of their positions in the Jewish community. Joseph was a leader and honored member of the Jewish Council. Nicodemus, also a member of the Council, had come to Jesus by night (3:1) and later tried to defend him before the other religious leaders (7:50–52). Yet they risked their reputations to provide for Jesus' burial. Are you a secret believer? Do you hide your faith from your friends and fellow workers? This is an appropriate time to step out of hiding and let others know whom you follow.

40 So they took the body of Jesus and bound it in linen wrappings with the spices, as is
the burial custom of the Jews.
41 Now in the place where He was crucified there was a garden, and in the garden a
new tomb in which no one had yet been laid.
42 Therefore because of the Jewish day of preparation, since the tomb was nearby, they
laid Jesus there.

19:40 Matt 26:12; Mark 14:8; John 11:44; Luke 24:12; John 20:5, 7

19:41 Matt 27:60; Luke 23:53

19:42 John 19:14, 31; John 19:20, 41

Jesus Rises from the Dead
(239/Matthew 28:1-7; Mark 16:1-8; Luke 24:1-12)

20 Now on the first *day* of the week Mary Magdalene ☆came early to the tomb, while
it ☆was still dark, and ☆saw the stone *already* taken away from the tomb.
2 So she ☆ran and ☆came to Simon Peter and to the other disciple whom Jesus loved,
and ☆said to them, "They have taken away the Lord out of the tomb, and we do not know
where they have laid Him."
3 So Peter and the other disciple went forth, and they were going to the tomb.
4 The two were running together; and the other disciple ran ahead faster than Peter
and came to the tomb first;
5 and stooping and looking in, he ☆saw the linen wrappings lying *there;* but he did not
go in.
6 And so Simon Peter also ☆came, following him, and entered the tomb; and he ☆saw
the linen wrappings lying *there,*
7 and the face-cloth which had been on His head, not lying with the linen wrappings,
but rolled up in a place by itself.
8 So the other disciple who had first come to the tomb then also entered, and he saw
and believed.
9 For as yet they did not understand the Scripture, that He must rise again from the
dead.

20:1 John 19:25; 20:18; Matt 27:60, 66; 28:2; Mark 15:46; 16:3f; Luke 24:2; John 11:38

20:2 John 13:23; John 20:13

20:3 Luke 24:12; John 20:3-10

20:5 John 20:11; John 19:40

20:7 John 11:44; John 19:40

20:8 John 20:4

20:9 Matt 22:29; John 2:22; Luke 24:26ff, 46

Jesus Appears to Mary Magdalene
(240/Mark 16:9-11)

10 So the disciples went away again to their own homes.
11 But Mary was standing outside the tomb weeping; and so, as she wept, she stooped
and looked into the tomb;
12 and she ☆saw two angels in white sitting, one at the head and one at the feet, where
the body of Jesus had been lying.
13 And they ☆said to her, "Woman, why are you weeping?" She ☆said to them, "Because they have taken away my Lord, and I do not know where they have laid Him."

20:10 Luke 24:12

20:11 Mark 16:5; John 20:5

20:12 Matt 28:2f; Mark 16:5; Luke 24:4

19:42 This tomb was probably a cave carved out of the stone hillside. It was large enough for a person to walk into, so Joseph and Nicodemus carried Jesus' body into it. A large stone was rolled in front of the entrance.

19:42 As they buried Jesus, Nicodemus and Joseph had to hurry to avoid working on the Sabbath, which began Friday evening at sundown.

20:1 Other women came to the tomb along with Mary Magdalene. The other Gospel accounts give their names. For more information on Mary Magdalene, see her Profile in chapter 19.

20:1 The stone was not rolled away from the entrance to the tomb so Jesus could get out. He could have left easily without moving the stone. It was rolled away so others could get *in* and see that Jesus was gone.

20:1ff People who hear about the resurrection for the first time may need time before they can comprehend this amazing story. Like Mary and the disciples, they may pass through four stages of belief. (1) At first, they may think the story is a fabrication, impossible to believe (20:2). (2) Like Peter, they may check out the facts and still be puzzled about what happened (20:6). (3) Only when they encounter Jesus personally are they able to accept the fact of the resurrection (20:16). (4) Then, as they commit themselves to the risen Lord and devote their lives to serving him, they begin to understand fully the reality of his presence with them (20:28).

20:7 The graveclothes (linen wrappings) were left as if Jesus had passed right through them. The face-cloth was still rolled up in the shape of a head, and it was at about the right distance from the wrappings that had enveloped Jesus' body. A grave robber couldn't possibly have made off with Jesus' body and left the linens as if they were still shaped around it.

20:9 As further proof that the disciples did not fabricate this story, we find that Peter and John were surprised that Jesus was not in the tomb. When John saw the linen wrappings looking like an empty cocoon from which Jesus had emerged, he believed that Jesus had risen. It wasn't until after they had seen the empty tomb that they remembered what the Scriptures and Jesus had said—he would die, but he would also rise again!

20:9 Jesus' resurrection is the key to the Christian faith. Why? (1) Just as he said, Jesus rose from the dead. We can be confident, therefore, that he will accomplish all he has promised. (2) Jesus' bodily resurrection shows us that the living Christ, not a false prophet or imposter, is ruler of God's eternal kingdom. (3) We can be certain of our own resurrection because Jesus was resurrected. Death is not the end—there is future life. (4) The divine power that brought Jesus back to life is now available to us to bring our spiritually dead selves back to life. (5) The resurrection is the basis for the church's witness to the world.

20:14 Matt 28:9; Mark 16:9; John 21:4

20:15 John 20:13

20:16 John 5:2; Matt 23:7; Mark 10:51

20:17 Matt 28:10; Mark 12:26; 16:19; John 7:33

14 When she had said this, she turned around and ☆saw Jesus standing *there,* and did not know that it was Jesus.
15 Jesus ☆said to her, "Woman, why are you weeping? Whom are you seeking?" Supposing Him to be the gardener, she ☆said to Him, "Sir, if you have carried Him away, tell me where you have laid Him, and I will take Him away."
16 Jesus ☆said to her, "Mary!" She turned and ☆said to Him in Hebrew, "Rabboni!" (which means, Teacher).
17 Jesus ☆said to her, "Stop clinging to Me, for I have not yet ascended to the Father; but go to My brethren and say to them, 'I ascend to My Father and your Father, and My God and your God.' "

THOMAS

Thomas, so often remembered as "Doubting Thomas," deserves to be respected for his faith. He was a doubter, but his doubts had a purpose—he wanted to know the truth. Thomas did not idolize his doubts; he gladly believed when given reasons to do so. He expressed his doubts fully and had them answered completely. Doubting was only his way of responding, not his way of life.

Although our glimpses of Thomas are brief, his character comes through with consistency. He struggled to be faithful to what he knew, despite what he felt. At one point, when it was plain to everyone that Jesus' life was in danger, only Thomas put into words what most were feeling, "Let us also go, so that we may die with Him" (John 11:16). He didn't hesitate to follow Jesus.

We don't know why Thomas was absent the first time Jesus appeared to the disciples after the resurrection, but he was reluctant to believe their witness to Christ's resurrection. Not even ten friends could change his mind!

We can doubt without having to live a doubting way of life. Doubt encourages rethinking. Its purpose is more to sharpen the mind than to change it. Doubt can be used to pose the question, get an answer, and push for a decision. But doubt was never meant to be a permanent condition. Doubt is one foot lifted, poised to step forward or backward. There is no motion until the foot comes down.

When you experience doubt, take encouragement from Thomas. He didn't stay in his doubt, but allowed Jesus to bring him to belief. Take encouragement also from the fact that countless other followers of Christ have struggled with doubts. The answers God gave them may help you too. Don't settle into doubts, but move on from them to decision and belief. Find another believer with whom you can share your doubts. Silent doubts rarely find answers.

Strengths and accomplishments:
- One of Jesus' 12 disciples
- Intense both in doubt and belief
- Was a loyal and honest man

Weaknesses and mistakes:
- Along with the others, abandoned Jesus at his arrest
- Refused to believe the others' claims to have seen Christ and demanded proof
- Struggled with a pessimistic outlook

Lessons from his life:
- Jesus does not reject doubts that are honest and directed toward belief
- Better to doubt out loud than to disbelieve in silence

Vital statistics:
- Where: Galilee, Judea, Samaria
- Occupation: Disciple of Jesus
- Contemporaries: Jesus, other disciples, Herod, Pilate

Key verses:
"Then He said to Thomas, 'Reach here with your finger, and see My hands; and reach here your hand and put it into My side; and do not be unbelieving, but believing.' Thomas answered and said to Him, 'My Lord and my God!' " (John 20:27–28).

Thomas's story is told in the Gospels. He is also mentioned in Acts 1:13.

20:17 Mary did not want to lose Jesus again. She had not yet understood the resurrection. Perhaps she thought this was his promised second coming (14:3). But Jesus did not want to be detained at the tomb. If he did not ascend to heaven, the Holy Spirit could not come. Both he and Mary had important work to do.

18 Mary Magdalene ☆came, announcing to the disciples, "I have seen the Lord," and
that He had said these things to her.

Jesus Appears to the Disciples behind Locked Doors
(244/Luke 24:36-43)

19 So when it was evening on that day, the first *day* of the week, and when the doors
were shut where the disciples were, for fear of the Jews, Jesus came and stood in their
midst and ☆said to them, "Peace *be* with you."
20 And when He had said this, He showed them both His hands and His side. The disciples then rejoiced when they saw the Lord.
21 So Jesus said to them again, "Peace *be* with you; as the Father has sent Me, I also
send you."
22 And when He had said this, He breathed on them and ☆said to them, "Receive the
Holy Spirit.
23 "If you forgive the sins of any, *their sins* have been forgiven them; if you retain the
sins of any, they have been retained."

Jesus Appears to the Disciples Including Thomas
(245/Mark 16:14)

24 But Thomas, one of the twelve, called Didymus, was not with them when Jesus came.
25 So the other disciples were saying to him, "We have seen the Lord!" But he said to
them, "Unless I see in His hands the imprint of the nails, and put my finger into the place
of the nails, and put my hand into His side, I will not believe."
26 After eight days His disciples were again inside, and Thomas with them. Jesus ☆came,
the doors having been shut, and stood in their midst and said, "Peace *be* with you."
27 Then He ☆said to Thomas, "Reach here with your finger, and see My hands; and
reach here your hand and put it into My side; and do not be unbelieving, but believing."
28 Thomas answered and said to Him, "My Lord and my God!"

20:18 John 20:1; Mark 16:10; Luke 24:10, 23

20:19 John 7:13; Luke 24:36; John 14:27; 20:21, 26

20:20 Luke 24:39, 40; John 19:34; John 16:20, 22

20:21 Luke 24:36; John 14:27; 20:19, 26; John 17:18

20:23 Matt 16:19; 18:18

20:24 John 11:16; John 6:67

20:25 John 20:20; Mark 16:11

20:26 Luke 24:36; John 14:27; 20:19, 21

20:27 Luke 24:40; John 20:25

20:18 Mary didn't recognize Jesus at first. Her grief had blinded her; she couldn't see him because she didn't expect to see him. Then he spoke her name, and immediately she recognized him. Imagine the love that flooded her heart when she heard her Savior saying her name. Jesus is near you, and he is calling your name. Can you, like Mary, regard him as your Lord?

20:18 Mary did not meet the risen Christ until she had discovered the empty tomb. She responded with joy and obedience by going to tell the disciples. We cannot meet Christ until we discover that he is indeed alive, that his tomb is empty. Are you filled with joy by this good news, and do you share it with others?

20:21 Jesus again identified himself with his Father. He told the disciples by whose authority he did his work. Then he passed the job to his disciples of spreading the gospel of salvation around the world. Whatever God has asked you to do, remember: (1) Your authority comes from God, and (2) Jesus has demonstrated by words and actions how to accomplish the job he has given you. As the Father sent Jesus, Jesus sends his followers . . . and you.

20:22 This may have been a special filling of the Holy Spirit for the disciples, a foretaste of what all believers would experience from the time of Pentecost (Acts 2) and forever after. To do God's work, we need the guidance and power of the Holy Spirit. We must avoid trying to do his work in our own strength.

20:22 There is life in the breath of God. Man was created but did not come alive until God breathed into him the breath of life (Genesis 2:7). God's first breath made man different from all other forms of creation. Now, through the breath of Jesus, God imparted eternal, spiritual life. With this inbreathing came the power to do God's will on earth.

20:23 Jesus was giving the disciples their Spirit-powered and Spirit-guided mission—to preach the Good News about Jesus so people's sins might be forgiven. The disciples did not have the power to forgive sins (only God can forgive sins), but Jesus gave them the privilege of telling new believers that their sins *have been* forgiven because they have accepted Jesus' message (see the notes on Matthew 16:19 and 18:18). All believers have this same privilege. We can announce the forgiveness of sin with certainty when we ourselves find repentance and faith.

20:24–29 Have you ever wished you could actually see Jesus, touch him, and hear his words? Are there times you want to sit down with him and get his advice? Thomas wanted Jesus' physical presence. But God's plan is wiser. He has not limited himself to one physical body; he wants to be present with you at all times. Even now he is with you in the form of the Holy Spirit. You can talk to him, and you can find his words to you in the pages of the Bible. He can be as real to you as he was to Thomas.

20:25–28 Jesus wasn't hard on Thomas for his doubts. Despite his skepticism, Thomas was still loyal to the believers and to Jesus himself. Some people need to doubt before they believe. If doubt leads to questions, questions lead to answers, and the answers are accepted, then doubt has done good work. It is when doubt becomes stubbornness and stubbornness becomes a life-style that doubt harms faith. When you doubt, don't stop there. Let your doubt deepen your faith as you continue to search for the answer.

20:27 Jesus' resurrected body was unique. It was not the same kind of flesh and blood Lazarus had when he came back to life. Jesus' body was no longer subject to the same laws of nature as before his death. He could appear in a locked room; yet he was not a ghost or apparition because he could be touched and could eat. Jesus' resurrection was *literal* and *physical*—he was not a disembodied spirit.

29 Jesus ☆said to him, "Because you have seen Me, have you believed? Blessed *are* they
who did not see, and *yet* believed."
30 Therefore many other signs Jesus also performed in the presence of the disciples,
which are not written in this book;
31 but these have been written so that you may believe that Jesus is the Christ, the Son
of God; and that believing you may have life in His name.

Jesus Appears to the Disciples While Fishing
(246)

21 After these things Jesus manifested Himself again to the disciples at the Sea of
Tiberias, and He manifested *Himself* in this way.
2 Simon Peter, and Thomas called Didymus, and Nathanael of Cana in Galilee, and
the *sons* of Zebedee, and two others of His disciples were together.
3 Simon Peter ☆said to them, "I am going fishing." They ☆said to him, "We will also
come with you." They went out and got into the boat; and that night they caught nothing.
4 But when the day was now breaking, Jesus stood on the beach; yet the disciples did
not know that it was Jesus.
5 So Jesus ☆said to them, "Children, you do not have any fish, do you?" They answered
Him, "No."
6 And He said to them, "Cast the net on the right-hand side of the boat and you will
find *a catch*." So they cast, and then they were not able to haul it in because of the great
number of fish.
7 Therefore that disciple whom Jesus loved ☆said to Peter, "It is the Lord." So when
Simon Peter heard that it was the Lord, he put his outer garment on (for he was stripped
for work), and threw himself into the sea.
8 But the other disciples came in the little boat, for they were not far from the land,
but about one hundred yards away, dragging the net *full* of fish.
9 So when they got out on the land, they ☆saw a charcoal fire *already* laid and fish
placed on it, and bread.

20:29 1 Pet 1:8
20:30 John 21:25; John 2:11
20:31 John 19:35; Matt 4:3; John 3:15
21:1 Mark 16:12; John 21:14; John 20:19, 26; John 6:1
21:2 John 11:16; John 1:45ff; John 2:1; Matt 4:21; Mark 1:19; Luke 5:10
21:3 Luke 5:5
21:4 Luke 24:16; John 20:14
21:5 Luke 24:41
21:6 Luke 5:4ff
21:7 John 13:23; 21:20
21:9 John 18:18; John 6:9, 11; 21:10, 13

JESUS' APPEARANCES AFTER HIS RESURRECTION

Mary Magdalene	Mark 16:9–11; John 20:10–18
The other women at the tomb	Matthew 28:8–10
Peter in Jerusalem	Luke 24:34; 1 Corinthians 15:5
The two travelers on the road	Mark 16:12–13
Ten disciples behind closed doors	Mark 16:14; Luke 24:36–43; John 20:19–25
All the disciples, with Thomas (excluding Judas Iscariot)	John 10:26–31; 1 Corinthians 15:5
Seven disciples while fishing	John 21:1–14
Eleven disciples on the mountain	Matthew 28:16–20
A crowd of 500	1 Corinthians 15:6
Jesus' brother James	1 Corinthians 15:7
Those who watched Jesus ascend into heaven	Luke 24:44–49; Acts 1:3–8

The truth of Christianity rests heavily on the resurrection. If Jesus rose from the grave, who saw him? How trustworthy were the witnesses? Those who claimed to have seen the risen Jesus went on to turn the world upside down. Most of them also died for being followers of Christ. People rarely die for halfhearted belief. These are the people who saw Jesus risen from the grave.

20:29 Some people think they would believe in Jesus if they could see a definite sign or miracle. But Jesus says we are blessed if we can believe without seeing. We have all the proof we need in the words of the Bible and the testimony of believers. A physical appearance would not make Jesus any more real to us than he is now.

20:30–31 To understand the life and mission of Jesus more fully, all we need to do is study the Gospels. John tells us that his Gospel records only a few of the many events in Jesus' life on earth. But the gospel includes everything we need to know to believe that Jesus is the Christ, the Son of God, through whom we receive eternal life.

21:1ff This chapter tells how Jesus commissioned Peter. Perhaps Peter needed special encouragement after his denial—he may have felt completely worthless. Verses 1–14 set the scene for Jesus' conversation with Peter.

21:7 Only John ("that disciple whom Jesus loved") recognized Jesus in the dim morning light, undoubtedly because Jesus had performed a similar miracle earlier (Luke 5:1–11).

10 Jesus ☆said to them, "Bring some of the fish which you have now caught."
11 Simon Peter went up and drew the net to land, full of large fish, a hundred and fifty-
three; and although there were so many, the net was not torn.
12 Jesus ☆said to them, "Come *and* have breakfast." None of the disciples ventured to
question Him, "Who are You?" knowing that it was the Lord.
13 Jesus ☆came and ☆took the bread and ☆gave *it* to them, and the fish likewise.
14 This is now the third time that Jesus was manifested to the disciples, after He was
raised from the dead.

Jesus Talks with Peter
(247)

15 So when they had finished breakfast, Jesus ☆said to Simon Peter, "Simon, *son* of
John, do you love Me more than these?" He ☆said to Him, "Yes, Lord; You know that I
love You." He ☆said to him, "Tend My lambs."
16 He ☆said to him again a second time, "Simon, *son* of John, do you love Me?" He
☆said to Him, "Yes, Lord; You know that I love You." He ☆said to him, "Shepherd My
sheep."
17 He ☆said to him the third time, "Simon, *son* of John, do you love Me?" Peter was
grieved because He said to him the third time, "Do you love Me?" And he said to Him,
"Lord, You know all things; You know that I love You." Jesus ☆said to him, "Tend My
sheep.
18 "Truly, truly, I say to you, when you were younger, you used to gird yourself and walk
wherever you wished; but when you grow old, you will stretch out your hands and someone else will gird you, and bring you where you do not wish to *go.*"
19 Now this He said, signifying by what kind of death he would glorify God. And when
He had spoken this, He ☆said to him, "Follow Me!"
20 Peter, turning around, ☆saw the disciple whom Jesus loved following *them;* the one
who also had leaned back on His bosom at the supper and said, "Lord, who is the one
who betrays You?"
21 So Peter seeing him ☆said to Jesus, "Lord, and what about this man?"
22 Jesus ☆said to him, "If I want him to remain until I come, what *is that* to you? You
follow Me!"
23 Therefore this saying went out among the brethren that that disciple would not die;
yet Jesus did not say to him that he would not die, but *only,* "If I want him to remain until
I come, what *is that* to you?"

21:10 John 6:9, 11; 21:9, 13

21:12 John 21:15

21:13 John 21:9; John 6:9, 11; 21:9, 10

21:14 John 20:19, 26

21:15 John 21:12; Matt 26:33; Mark 14:29; John 13:37; Luke 12:32

21:16 Matt 2:6; Acts 20:28; 1 Pet 5:2; Rev 7:17

21:17 John 13:38; John 16:30; John 21:15, 16

21:19 John 12:33; 18:32; 2 Pet 1:14; Matt 8:22; 16:24; John 21:22

21:20 John 21:7; John 13:25

21:22 Matt 16:27f; 1 Cor 4:5; 11:26; James 5:7; Rev 2:25; Matt 8:22; 16:24; John 21:19

21:23 Acts 1:15; Matt 16:27f; 1 Cor 4:5; 11:26; James 5:7; Rev 2:25

21:15–17 In this beach scene, Jesus led Peter through an experience that would remove the cloud of his denial. Peter had denied Jesus three times. Three times Jesus asked Peter if he loved him. When Peter answered yes, Jesus told him to feed his sheep. It is one thing to say you love Jesus, but the real test is willingness to serve him. Peter had repented, and here Jesus was asking him to commit his life. Peter's life changed when he finally realized who Jesus was. His occupation changed from fisherman to evangelist; his identity changed from impetuous to "rock;" and his relationship to Jesus changed—he was forgiven, and he finally understood the significance of Jesus' words about his death and resurrection.

21:15–17 Jesus asked Peter three times if he loved him. The first time Jesus asked, "Do you love (Greek *agape:* volitional, self-sacrificial love) Me more than these?" The second time, Jesus focused on Peter alone and still used the word translated into Greek, *agape.* The third time, Jesus used the word translated into Greek, *phileo* (signifying affection, affinity, or brotherly love) and asked, in effect, "Are you even my friend?" Each time Peter responded with the word translated into Greek as *phileo.* Jesus doesn't settle for quick, superficial answers. He has a way of getting to the heart of the matter. Peter had to face his true feelings and motives when Jesus confronted him. How would you respond if Jesus asked you, "Do you love me?" Do you really love Jesus? Are you even his friend?

21:18–19 This was a prediction of Peter's death by crucifixion. Tradition indicates that Peter was crucified for his faith—upside down because he did not feel worthy of dying as his Lord did. Despite what Peter's future held, Jesus told him to follow him. We may be uncertain and fearful about our future. But if we know God is in control, we can confidently follow Christ.

21:21–22 Peter asked Jesus how John would die. Jesus replied that Peter should not concern himself with that. We tend to compare our lives to others, whether to rationalize our own level of devotion to Christ or to question God's justice. Jesus responds to us as he did to Peter: "What is that to you? You follow Me!"

21:23 Early church history reports that after John spent several years as an exile on the island of Patmos, he returned to Ephesus where he died as an old man, near the end of the first century.

21:24 John 15:27

24 This is the disciple who is testifying to these things and wrote these things, and we
know that his testimony is true.

21:25 John 20:30

25 And there are also many other things which Jesus did, which if they ☆were written
in detail, I suppose that even the world itself ☆would not contain the books that ☆would
be written.

21:25 John's stated purpose for writing his Gospel was to show that Jesus was the Son of God. He clearly and systematically presented the evidence for Jesus' claims. When evidence is presented in the courtroom, those who hear it must make a choice. Those who read the Gospel of John must also make a choice—is Jesus the Son of God, or isn't he? You are the jury. The evidence has been clearly presented. You must decide. Read John's Gospel and believe!

250 EVENTS IN THE LIFE OF CHRIST A HARMONY OF THE GOSPELS

Each of the four books in the Bible that tells the story of Jesus Christ—Matthew, Mark, Luke, and John—stands alone, emphasizing a unique aspect of Jesus' life. But when these are blended into one complete account, or harmonized, we gain new insights about the life of Christ.

This harmony combines the four Gospels into a single chronological account of Christ's life on earth. It includes every chapter and verse of each Gospel, leaving nothing out.

The harmony is divided into 250 events. The title of each event is identical to the title found in the corresponding Gospel. Parallel passages found in more than one Gospel have identical titles, helping you to identify them quickly.

Each of the 250 events in the harmony is numbered. The number of the event corresponds to the number next to the title in the Bible text. When reading one of the Gospel accounts, you will notice, at times, that some numbers are missing or out of sequence. The easiest way to locate these events is to refer to the harmony.

In addition, if you are looking for a particular event in the life of Christ, the harmony can help you locate it more rapidly than paging through all four Gospels. Each of the 250 events has a distinctive title keyed to the main emphasis of the passage to help you locate and remember the events.

This harmony will help you to better visualize the travels of Jesus, study the four Gospels comparatively, and appreciate the unity of their message.

I. BIRTH AND PREPARATION OF JESUS CHRIST

		Matthew	*Mark*	*Luke*	*John*
1	Luke's purpose in writing			1:1-4	
2	God became a human being				1:1-18
3	The ancestors of Jesus	1:1-17		3:23-38	
4	An angel promises the birth of John to Zacharias			1:5-25	
5	An angel promises the birth of Jesus to Mary			1:26-38	
6	Mary visits Elizabeth			1:39-56	
7	John the Baptist is born			1:57-80	
8	An angel appears to Joseph	1:18-25			
9	Jesus is born in Bethlehem			2:1-7	
10	Shepherds visit Jesus			2:8-20	
11	Mary and Joseph bring Jesus to the temple			2:21-40	
12	Visitors arrive from eastern lands	2:1-12			
13	The escape to Egypt	2:13-18			
14	The return to Nazareth	2:19-23			
15	Jesus speaks with the religious teachers			2:41-52	
16	John the Baptist prepares the way for Jesus	3:1-12	1:1-8	3:1-18	
17	John baptizes Jesus	3:13-17	1:9-11	3:21-22	
18	Satan tempts Jesus in the wilderness	4:1-11	1:12-13	4:1-13	
19	John the Baptist declares his mission				1:19-28
20	John the Baptist proclaims Jesus as the Messiah				1:29-34
21	The first disciples follow Jesus				1:35-51
22	Jesus turns water into wine				2:1-12

II. MESSAGE AND MINISTRY OF JESUS CHRIST

		Matthew	Mark	Luke	John
23	Jesus clears the temple				2:12-25
24	Nicodemus visits Jesus at night				3:1-21
25	John the Baptist tells more about Jesus				3:22-36
26	Herod puts John in prison			3:19-20	
27	Jesus talks to a woman at the well				4:1-26
28	Jesus tells about the spiritual harvest				4:27-38
29	Many Samaritans believe in Jesus				4:39-42
30	Jesus preaches in Galilee	4:12-17	1:14-15	4:14-15	4:43-45
31	Jesus heals a government official's son				4:46-54
32	Jesus is rejected at Nazareth			4:16-30	
33	Four fishermen follow Jesus	4:18-22	1:16-20		
34	Jesus teaches with great authority		1:21-28	4:31-37	
35	Jesus heals Peter's mother-in-law and many others	8:14-17	1:29-34	4:38-41	
36	Jesus preaches throughout Galilee	4:23-25	1:35-39	4:42-44	
37	Jesus provides miraculous catch of fish			5:1-11	
38	Jesus heals a man with leprosy	8:1-4	1:40-45	5:12-16	
39	Jesus heals a paralytic	9:1-8	2:1-12	5:17-26	
40	Jesus eats with sinners at Matthew's house	9:9-13	2:13-17	5:27-32	
41	Religious leaders ask Jesus about fasting	9:14-17	2:18-22	5:33-39	
42	Jesus heals a lame man by the pool				5:1-18
43	Jesus claims to be God's Son				5:19-30
44	Jesus supports his claim				5:31-47
45	The disciples pick grain on the Sabbath	12:1-8	2:23-28	6:1-5	
46	Jesus heals a man's hand on the Sabbath	12:9-14	3:1-6	6:6-11	
47	Large crowds follow Jesus	12:15-21	3:7-12		
48	Jesus selects the twelve disciples		3:13-19	6:12-16	
49	Jesus gives the Beatitudes	5:1-12		6:17-26	
50	Jesus teaches about salt and light	5:13-16			
51	Jesus teaches about the law	5:17-20			
52	Jesus teaches about anger	5:21-26			
53	Jesus teaches about lust	5:27-30			
54	Jesus teaches about divorce	5:31-32			
55	Jesus teaches about vows	5:33-37			
56	Jesus teaches about retaliation	5:38-42			
57	Jesus teaches about loving enemies	5:43-48		6:27-36	
58	Jesus teaches about giving to the needy	6:1-4			
59	Jesus teaches about prayer	6:5-15			
60	Jesus teaches about fasting	6:16-18			
61	Jesus teaches about money	6:19-24			
62	Jesus teaches about worry	6:25-34			
63	Jesus teaches about criticizing others	7:1-6		6:37-42	
64	Jesus teaches about asking, seeking, knocking	7:7-12			
65	Jesus teaches about the way to heaven	7:13-14			
66	Jesus teaches about fruit in people's lives	7:15-20		6:43-45	
67	Jesus teaches about those who build houses on rock and sand	7:21-29		6:46-49	
68	A Roman centurion demonstrates faith	8:5-13		7:1-10	
69	Jesus raises a widow's son from the dead			7:11-17	
70	Jesus eases John's doubt	11:1-19		7:18-35	
71	Jesus promises rest for the soul	11:20-30			
72	A sinful woman anoints Jesus' feet			7:36-50	
73	Women accompany Jesus and the disciples			8:1-3	
74	Religious leaders accuse Jesus of being under Satan's power	12:22-37	3:20-30		
75	Religious leaders ask Jesus for a miracle	12:38-45			
76	Jesus describes his true family	12:46-50	3:31-35	8:19-21	
77	Jesus tells the parable of the four soils	13:1-9	4:1-9	8:4-8	
78	Jesus explains the parable of the four soils	13:10-23	4:10-25	8:9-18	
79	Jesus tells the parable of the growing seed		4:26-29		
80	Jesus tells the parable of the weeds	13:24-30			
81	Jesus tells the parable of the mustard seed	13:31-32	4:30-34		
82	Jesus tells the parable of the yeast	13:33-35			
83	Jesus explains the parable of the weeds	13:36-43			
84	Jesus tells the parable of hidden treasure	13:44			
85	Jesus tells the parable of the pearl merchant	13:45-46			
86	Jesus tells the parable of the fishing net	13:47-52			
87	Jesus calms the storm	8:23-27	4:35-41	8:22-25	
88	Jesus sends the demons into a herd of swine	8:28-34	5:1-20	8:26-39	

		Matthew	Mark	Luke	John
89	Jesus heals a bleeding woman and restores a girl to life	9:18-26	5:21-43	8:40-56	
90	Jesus heals the blind and mute	9:27-34			
91	The people of Nazareth refuse to believe	13:53-58	6:1-6		
92	Jesus urges the disciples to pray for workers	9:35-38			
93	Jesus sends out the twelve disciples	10:1-16	6:7-13	9:1-6	
94	Jesus prepares the disciples for persecution	10:17-42			
95	Herod kills John the Baptist	14:1-12	6:14-29	9:7-9	
96	Jesus feeds five thousand	14:13-21	6:30-44	9:10-17	6:1-15
97	Jesus walks on water	14:22-33	6:45-52		6:16-21
98	Jesus heals all who touch him	14:34-36	6:53-56		
99	Jesus is the true bread from heaven				6:22-40
100	The Jews disagree that Jesus is from heaven				6:41-59
101	Many disciples desert Jesus				6:60-71
102	Jesus teaches about inner purity	15:1-20	7:1-23		
103	Jesus sends a demon out of a girl	15:21-28	7:24-30		
104	The crowd marvels at Jesus' healings	15:29-31	7:31-37		
105	Jesus feeds four thousand	15:32-39	8:1-10		
106	Religious leaders ask for a sign in the sky	16:1-4	8:11-13		
107	Jesus warns against wrong teaching	16:5-12	8:14-21		
108	Jesus restores sight to a blind man		8:22-26		
109	Peter says Jesus is the Messiah	16:13-20	8:14-21		
110	Jesus predicts his death the first time	16:21-28	8:31—9:1	9:21-27	
111	Jesus is transfigured on the mountain	17:1-13	9:2-13	9:28-36	
112	Jesus heals a demon-possessed boy	17:14-21	9:14-29	9:37-43	
113	Jesus predicts his death the second time	17:22-23	9:30-32	9:44-45	
114	Peter finds the coin in the fish's mouth	17:24-27			
115	The disciples argue about who would be the greatest	18:1-6	9:33-37	9:46-48	
116	The disciples forbid another to use Jesus' name		9:38-41	9:49-50	
117	Jesus warns against temptation	18:7-9	9:42-50		
118	Jesus warns against looking down on others	18:10-14			
119	Jesus teaches how to treat a believer who sins	18:15-20			
120	Jesus tells the parable of the unforgiving debtor	18:21-35			
121	Jesus' brothers ridicule him				7:1-9
122	Jesus teaches about the cost of following him	8:18-22		9:51-62	
123	Jesus teaches openly at the temple				7:10-31
124	Religious leaders attempt to arrest Jesus				7:32-52
125	Jesus forgives an adulterous woman				7:53-8:11
126	Jesus is the light of the world				8:12-20
127	Jesus warns of coming judgment				8:21-30
128	Jesus speaks about God's true children				8:31-47
129	Jesus states he is eternal				8:48-59
130	Jesus sends out seventy-two messengers			10:1-16	
131	The seventy-two messengers return			10:17-24	
132	Jesus tells the parable of the Good Samaritan			10:25-37	
133	Jesus visits Mary and Martha			10:38-42	
134	Jesus teaches his disciples about prayer			11:1-13	
135	Jesus answers hostile accusations			11:14-28	
136	Jesus warns against unbelief			11:29-32	
137	Jesus teaches about the light within			11:33-36	
138	Jesus criticizes the religious leaders			11:37-54	
139	Jesus speaks against hypocrisy			12:1-12	
140	Jesus tells the parable of the rich fool			12:13-21	
141	Jesus warns about worry			12:22-34	
142	Jesus warns about preparing for his coming			12:35-48	
143	Jesus warns about coming division			12:49-53	
144	Jesus warns about the future crisis			12:54-59	
145	Jesus calls the people to repent			13:1-9	
146	Jesus heals the crippled woman			13:10-17	
147	Jesus teaches about the kingdom of God			13:18-21	
148	Jesus heals the man who was born blind				9:1-12
149	Religious leaders question the blind man				9:13-34
150	Jesus teaches about spiritual blindness				9:35-41
151	Jesus is the good shepherd				10:1-21
152	Religious leaders surround Jesus at the temple				10:22-42
153	Jesus teaches about entering the kingdom			13:22-30	
154	Jesus grieves over Jerusalem			13:31-35	
155	Jesus heals a man with dropsy			14:1-6	
156	Jesus teaches about seeking honor			14:7-14	
157	Jesus tells the parable of the great feast			14:15-24	

		Matthew	Mark	Luke	John
158	Jesus teaches about the cost of being a disciple			14:25-35	
159	Jesus tells the parable of the lost sheep			15:1-7	
160	Jesus tells the parable of the lost coin			15:8-10	
161	Jesus tells the parable of the lost son			15:11-32	
162	Jesus tells the parable of the shrewd manager			16:1-18	
163	Jesus tells about the rich man and the beggar			16:19-31	
164	Jesus tells about forgiveness and faith			17:1-10	
165	Lazarus becomes ill and dies				11:1-16
166	Jesus comforts Mary and Martha				11:17-37
167	Jesus raises Lazarus from the dead				11:38-44
168	Religious leaders plot to kill Jesus				11:45-57
169	Jesus heals ten men with leprosy			17:11-19	
170	Jesus teaches about the coming of the kingdom of God			17:20-37	
171	Jesus tells the parable of the persistent widow			18:1-8	
172	Jesus tells the parable of two men who prayed			18:9-14	
173	Jesus teaches about marriage and divorce	19:1-12	10:1-12		
174	Jesus blesses little children	19:13-15	10:13-16	18:15-17	
175	Jesus speaks to the rich young man	19:16-30	10:17-31	18:18-30	
176	Jesus tells the parable of the workers paid equally	20:1-16			
177	Jesus predicts his death the third time	20:17-19	10:32-34	18:31-34	
178	Jesus teaches about serving others	20:20-28	10:35-45		
179	Jesus heals a blind beggar	20:29-34	10:46-52	18:35-43	
180	Jesus brings salvation to Zaccheus's home			19:1-10	
181	Jesus tells the parable of the king's ten servants			19:11-27	
182	A woman anoints Jesus with perfume	26:6-13	14:3-9		12:1-11
183	Jesus rides into Jerusalem on a donkey	21:1-11	11:1-11	19:28-44	12:12-19
184	Jesus clears the temple again	21:12-17	11:12-19	19:45-48	
185	Jesus explains why he must die				12:20-36
186	Most of the people do not believe in Jesus				12:37-43
187	Jesus summarizes his message				12:44-50
188	Jesus says the disciples can pray for anything	21:18-22	11:20-26		
189	Religious leaders challenge Jesus' authority	21:23-27	11:27-33	20:1-8	
190	Jesus tells the parable of the two sons	21:28-32			
191	Jesus tells the parable of the wicked vine-growers	21:33-46	12:1-12	20:9-19	
192	Jesus tells the parable of the wedding feast	22:1-14			
193	Religious leaders question Jesus about paying taxes	22:15-22	12:13-17	20:20-26	
194	Religious leaders question Jesus about the resurrection	22:23-33	12:18-27	20:27-40	
195	Religious leaders question Jesus about the greatest commandment	22:34-40	12:28-34		
196	Religious leaders cannot answer Jesus' question	22:41-46	12:35-37	20:41-44	
197	Jesus warns against the religious leaders	23:1-12	12:38-40	20:45-47	
198	Jesus condemns the religious leaders	23:13-36			
199	Jesus grieves over Jerusalem again	23:37-39			
200	A poor widow gives all she has		12:41-44	21:1-4	
201	Jesus tells about the future	24:1-25	13:1-23	21:5-24	
202	Jesus tells about his return	24:26-35	13:24-31	21:25-33	
203	Jesus tells about remaining watchful	24:36-51	13:32-37	21:34-38	
204	Jesus tells the parable of the ten virgins	25:1-13			
205	Jesus tells the parable of the loaned money	25:14-30			
206	Jesus tells about the final judgment	25:31-46			

III. DEATH AND RESURRECTION OF JESUS CHRIST

		Matthew	Mark	Luke	John
207	Religious leaders plot to kill Jesus	26:1-5	14:1-2	22:1-2	
208	Judas agrees to betray Jesus	26:14-16	14:10-11	22:3-6	
209	Disciples prepare for the Passover	26:17-19	14:12-16	22:7-13	
210	Jesus washes the disciples' feet				13:1-20
211	Jesus and the disciples have the Last Supper	26:20-30	14:17-26	22:14-30	13:21-30
212	Jesus predicts Peter's denial			22:31-38	13:31-38
213	Jesus is the way to the Father				14:1-14
214	Jesus promises the Holy Spirit				14:15-31
215	Jesus teaches about the vine and the branches				15:1-17
216	Jesus warns about the world's hatred				15:18- 16:4
217	Jesus teaches about the Holy Spirit				16:5-15
218	Jesus teaches about using his name in prayer				16:16-33
219	Jesus prays for himself				17:1-5

		Matthew	Mark	Luke	John
220	Jesus prays for his disciples				17:6-19
221	Jesus prays for future believers				17:20-26
222	Jesus again predicts Peter's denial	26:31-35	14:27-31		
223	Jesus agonizes in the garden	26:36-46	14:32-42	22:39-46	
224	Jesus is betrayed and arrested	26:47-56	14:43-52	22:47-53	18:1-11
225	Annas questions Jesus				18:12-24
226	Caiaphas questions Jesus	26:57-68	14:53-65		
227	Peter denies knowing Jesus	26:69-75	14:66-72	22:54-65	18:25-27
228	The council of religious leaders condemns Jesus	27:1-2	15:1	22:66-71	
229	Judas kills himself	27:3-10			
230	Jesus stands trial before Pilate	27:11-14	15:2-5	23:1-5	18:28-37
231	Jesus stands trial before Herod			23:6-12	
232	Pilate hands Jesus over to be crucified	27:15-26	15:6-15	23:13-25	18:38- 19:16
233	Roman soldiers mock Jesus	27:27-31	15:16-20		
234	Jesus is led away to be crucified	27:32-34	15:21-24	23:26-31	19:17
235	Jesus is placed on the cross	27:35-44	15:25-32	23:32-43	19:18-27
236	Jesus dies on the cross	27:45-56	15:33-41	23:44-49	19:28-37
237	Jesus is laid in the tomb	27:57-61	15:42-47	23:50-56	19:38-42
238	Guards are posted at the tomb	27:62-66			
239	Jesus rises from the dead	28:1-7	16:1-8	24:1-12	20:1-9
240	Jesus appears to Mary Magdalene		16:9-11		20:10-18
241	Jesus appears to the women	28:8-10			
242	Religious leaders bribe the guards	28:11-15			
243	Jesus appears to two believers traveling on the road		16:12-13	24:13-35	
244	Jesus appears to the disciples behind locked doors			24:36-43	20:19-23
245	Jesus appears to the disciples including Thomas		16:14		20:24-31
246	Jesus appears to the disciples while fishing				21:1-14
247	Jesus talks with Peter				21:15-25
248	Jesus gives the Great Commission	28:16-20	16:15-18		
249	Jesus appears to the disciples in Jerusalem			24:44-49	
250	Jesus ascends into heaven		16:19-20	24:50-53	

THE PARABLES OF JESUS

I. Teaching Parables

A. About the Kingdom of God
1. The Soils (Matthew 13:3-8; Mark 4:4-8; Luke 8:5-8)
2. The Weeds (Matthew 13:24-30)
3. The Mustard Seed (Matthew 13:31-32; Mark 4:30-32; Luke 13:18-19)
4. The Yeast (Matthew 13:33; Luke 13:20-21)
5. The Treasure (Matthew 13:44)
6. The Pearl (Matthew 13:45-46)
7. The Fishing Net (Matthew 13:47-50)
8. The Growing Wheat (Mark 4:26-29)

B. About Service and Obedience
1. The Workers in the Harvest (Matthew 20:1-16)
2. The Loaned Money (Matthew 25:14-30)
3. The Nobleman's Servants (Luke 19:11-27)
4. The Servant's Role (Luke 17:7-10)

C. About Prayer
1. The Friend at Midnight (Luke 11:5-8)
2. The Unjust Judge (Luke 18:1-8)

D. About Neighbors
1. The Good Samaritan (Luke 10:30-37)

E. About Humility
1. The Wedding Feast (Luke 14:7-11)
2. The Proud Pharisee and the Corrupt Tax Collector (Luke 18:9-14)

F. About Wealth
1. The Rich Fool (Luke 12:16-21)
2. The Great Feast (Luke 14:16-24)
3. The Shrewd Manager (Luke 16:1-9)

II. Gospel Parables
   A. About God's Love
      1. The Lost Sheep (Matthew 18:12-14; Luke 15:3-7)
      2. The Lost Coin (Luke 15:8-10)
      3. The Lost Son (Luke 15:11-32)
   B. About Thankfulness
      1. The Forgiven Debts (Luke 7:41-43)

III. Parables of Judgment and the Future
   A. About Christ's Return
      1. The Ten Virgins (Matthew 25:1-13)
      2. The Wise and Faithful Servants (Matthew 24:45-51; Luke 12:42-48)
      3. The Traveling Owner of the House (Mark 13:34-37)
   B. About God's Values
      1. The Two Sons (Mat 21:28-32)
      2. The Wicked Vine-growers (Mat 21:33-34; Mark 12:1-9; Luke 20:9-16)
      3. The Unproductive Fig Tree (Luke 13:6-9)
      4. The Marriage Feast (Matthew 22:1-14)
      5. The Unforgiving Servant (Matthew 18:23-35)

THE MIRACLES OF JESUS

John and the other Gospel writers were able to record only a fraction of the people who were touched and healed by Jesus. But enough of Jesus' words and works have been saved so that we also might be able to know him and be his disciples in this day. There follows a listing of the miracles that are included in the Gospels. They were supernatural events that pointed people to God, and they were acts of love by One who is love.

	Matthew	*Mark*	*Luke*	*John*
Five thousand people are fed	14:15-21	6:35-44	9:12-17	6:5-14
Calming the storm	8:23-27	4:35-41	8:22-25	
Demons sent into the swine	8:28-34	5:1-20	8:26-39	
Jairus's daughter raised	9:18-26	5:22-24, 35-43	8:41-42, 49-56	
A sick woman is healed	9:20-22	5:25-34	8:43-48	
Jesus heals a paralytic	9:1-8	2:1-12	5:17-26	
A leper is healed at Gennesaret	8:1-4	1:40-45	5:12-15	
Peter's mother-in-law healed	8:14-17	1:29-31	4:38-39	
A shriveled hand is restored	12:9-13	3:1-5	6:6-11	
A boy with an evil spirit is healed	17:14-21	9:14-29	9:37-42	
Jesus walks on the water	14:22-33	6:45-52		6:17-21
Blind Bartimaeus receives sight	20:29-34	10:46-52	18:35-43	
A girl is freed from a demon	15:21-28	7:24-30		
Four thousand are fed	15:32-38	8:1-9		
Cursing the fig tree	21:18-22	11:12-14, 20-24		
A centurion's servant is healed	8:5-13		7:1-10	
An evil spirit is sent out of a man		1:23-27	4:33-36	
A mute demoniac is healed	12:22	11:14		
Two blind men find sight	9:27-31			
Jesus heals the mute man	9:32-33			
A coin in a fish's mouth	17:24-27			
A deaf and mute man is healed		7:31-37		
A blind man sees at Bethsaida		8:22-26		
The first miraculous catch of fish			5:1-11	
A widow's son is raised			7:11-16	
A crippled woman is healed			13:10-17	
Jesus heals a sick man			14:1-6	
Ten lepers are healed			17:11-19	
Jesus restores a man's ear			22:49-51	
Jesus turns water into wine				2:1-11
An official's son is healed at Cana				4:46-54
A lame man is healed				5:1-16
Jesus heals a man born blind				9:1-7
Lazarus is raised from the dead				11:1-45
The second miraculous catch of fish				21:1-14

MESSIANIC PROPHECIES AND FULFILLMENTS

For the Gospel writers, one of the main reasons for believing in Jesus was the way his life fulfilled the Old Testament prophecies about the Messiah. Following is a list of some of the main prophecies.

	Old Testament Prophecies	*New Testament Fulfillment*
1. Messiah was to be born in Bethlehem	Micah 5:2	Matthew 2:1-6; Luke 2:1-20
2. Messiah was to be born of a virgin	Isaiah 7:14	Matthew 1:18-25; Luke 1:26-38
3. Messiah was to be a prophet like Moses	Deuteronomy 18:15, 18-19	John 7:40
4. Messiah was to enter Jerusalem in triumph	Zechariah 9:9	Matthew 21:1-9; John 12:12-16
5. Messiah was to be rejected by his own people	Isaiah 53:1, 3; Psalm 118:22	Matthew 26:3-4; John 12:37-43; Acts 4:1-12
6. Messiah was to be betrayed by one of his followers	Psalm 41:9	Matthew 26:14-16, 47-50; Luke 22:19-23
7. Messiah was to be tried and condemned	Isaiah 53:8	Luke 23:1-25; Matthew 27:1-2
8. Messiah was to be silent before his accusers	Isaiah 53:7	Matthew 27:12-14; Mark 15:3-4; Luke 23:8-10
9. Messiah was to be struck and spat on by his enemies	Isaiah 50:6	Matthew 26:67; 27:30; Mark 14:65
10. Messiah was to be mocked and insulted	Psalm 22:7-8	Matthew 27:39-44; Luke 23:11, 35
11. Messiah was to die by crucifixion	Psalm 22:14, 16-17	Matthew 27:31; Mark 15:20, 25
12. Messiah was to suffer with criminals and pray for his enemies	Isaiah 53:12	Matthew 27:38; Mark 15:27-28; Luke 23:32-34
13. Messiah was to be given vinegar and gall	Psalm 69:21	Matthew 27:34; John 19:28-30
14. Others were to cast lots for Messiah's garments	Psalm 22:18	Matthew 27:35; John 19:23-24
15. Messiah's bones were not to be broken	Exodus 12:46	John 19:31-36
16. Messiah was to die as a sacrifice for sin	Isaiah 53:5-6, 8, 10-12	John 1:29; John 11:49-52; Acts 10:43; Acts 13:38-39
17. Messiah was to be raised from the dead	Psalm 16:10	Acts 2:22-32; Matthew 28:1-10
18. Messiah is now at God's right hand	Psalm 110:1	Mark 16:19; Luke 24:50-51

COMPARISON OF THE FOUR GOSPELS

All four Gospels present the life and teachings of Jesus. Each book, however, focuses on a unique facet of Jesus and his character. To understand more about the specific characteristics of Jesus, read any one of the four Gospels.

	Matthew	*Mark*	*Luke*	*John*
Jesus is . . .	The promised King	The Servant of God	The Son of Man	The Son of God
The original readers were . . .	Jews	Gentiles, Romans	Greeks	Christians throughout the world
Significant themes . . .	Jesus is the Messiah because he fulfilled Old Testament prophecy	Jesus backed up his words with action	Jesus was God but also fully human	Belief in Jesus is required for salvation
Character of the writer . . .	Teacher	Storyteller	Historian	Theologian
Greatest emphasis is on . . .	Jesus' sermons and words	Jesus' miracles and actions	Jesus' humanity	The principles of Jesus' teaching

ACTS

Jesus crucified; Pentecost; church begun A.D. 30	Stephen martyred; Paul's conversion 35	Paul returns to Tarsus 38	Barnabas goes to find Paul 43	James martyred; Peter in prison 44	Paul's first missionary journey 46–48	Jerusalem council 50	Paul's second missionary journey 50–52

VITAL STATISTICS

PURPOSE:
To give an accurate account of the birth and growth of the Christian church

AUTHOR:
Luke (a Gentile physician)

TO WHOM WRITTEN:
Theophilus and all lovers of God

DATE WRITTEN:
Between A.D. 63 and 70

SETTING:
Acts is the connecting link between Christ's life and the life of the church, between the Gospels and the Letters

KEY VERSE:
"But you will receive power when the Holy Spirit has come upon you; and you shall be My witnesses both in Jerusalem, and in all Judea and Samaria, and even to the remotest part of the earth" (1:8).

KEY PEOPLE:
Peter, John, James, Stephen, Philip, Paul, Barnabas, Cornelius, James (Jesus' brother), Timothy, Lydia, Silas, Titus, Apollos, Agabus, Ananias, Felix, Festus, Agrippa, Luke

KEY PLACES:
Jerusalem, Samaria, Lydda, Joppa, Antioch, Cyprus, Pisidian Antioch, Iconium, Lystra, Derbe, Philippi, Thessalonica, Berea, Athens, Corinth, Ephesus, Caesarea, Malta, Rome

SPECIAL FEATURES:
Acts is a sequel to the Gospel of Luke. Because Acts ends so abruptly, Luke may have planned to write a third book, continuing the story.

WITH a flick of a match, friction occurs and a spark leaps from match to tinder. A small flame burns the edges and grows, fueled by wood and air. Heat builds, and soon the kindling is licked by reddish orange tongues. Higher and wider it spreads, consuming the wood. The flame has become a fire.

Nearly 2,000 years ago, a match was struck in Palestine. At first, just a few in that corner of the world were touched and warmed; but the fire spread beyond Jerusalem and Judea out to the world and to all people. Acts provides an eyewitness account of the flame and fire—the birth and spread of the church. Beginning in Jerusalem with a small group of disciples, the message traveled across the Roman empire. Empowered by the Holy Spirit, this courageous band preached, taught, healed, and demonstrated love in synagogues, schools, homes, marketplaces, and courtrooms, and on streets, hills, ships, and desert roads—wherever God sent them, lives and history were changed.

Written by Luke as a sequel to his Gospel, Acts is an accurate historical record of the early church. But Acts is also a theological book, with lessons and living examples of the work of the Holy Spirit, church relationships and organization, the implications of grace, and the law of love. And Acts is an apologetic work, building a strong case for the validity of Christ's claims and promises.

The book of Acts begins with the outpouring of the promised Holy Spirit and the commencement of the proclamation of the gospel of Jesus Christ. This Spirit-inspired evangelism began in Jerusalem and eventually spread to Rome, covering most of the Roman empire. The gospel first went to the Jews, but they, as a nation, rejected it. A remnant of Jews, of course, gladly received the Good News. But the continual rejection of the gospel by the vast majority of the Jews led to the ever-increasing proclamation of the gospel to the Gentiles. This was according to Jesus' plan: The gospel was to go from Jerusalem, to Judea, to Samaria, and to the remotest part of the earth (1:8). This, in fact, is the pattern that the Acts narrative follows. The glorious proclamation began in Jerusalem (chapters 1—7), went to Judea and Samaria (chapters 8 and following), and to the countries beyond Judea (11:19; 13:4 and on to the end of Acts). The second half of Acts is focused primarily on Paul's missionary journeys to many countries north of the Mediterranean Sea. He, with his companions, took the gospel first to the Jews and then to the Gentiles. Some of the Jews believed, and many of the Gentiles received the Good News with joy. New churches were started, and new believers began to grow in the Christian life.

As you read Acts, put yourself in the place of the disciples: Identify with them as they are filled with the Holy Spirit, and experience the thrill of seeing thousands respond to the gospel message. Sense their commitment as they give every ounce of talent and treasure to Christ. And as you read, watch the Spirit-led boldness of these first-century believers, who through suffering and in the face of death take every opportunity to tell of their crucified and risen Lord. Then decide to be a twentieth-century version of those men and women of God.

Paul's third missionary journey 53–57	Nero becomes emperor 54	Paul imprisoned in Caesarea 57–59	Paul's journey to Rome 59	Paul released from prison 62	Paul martyred 67?	Rome destroys Jerusalem 70

THE BLUEPRINT

A. PETER'S MINISTRY (1:1—12:25)
1. Establishment of the church
2. Expansion of the church

After the resurrection of Jesus Christ, Peter preached boldly and performed many miracles. Peter's actions demonstrate vividly the source and effects of Christian power. Because of the Holy Spirit, God's people were empowered so they could accomplish their tasks. The Holy Spirit is still available to empower believers today. We should turn to the Holy Spirit to give us the strength, courage, and insight to accomplish our work for God.

B. PAUL'S MINISTRY (13:1—28:31)
1. First missionary journey
2. The council at Jerusalem
3. Second missionary journey
4. Third missionary journey
5. Paul on trial

Paul's missionary adventures show us the progress of Christianity. The gospel could not be confined to one corner of the world. This was a faith that offered hope to all humanity. We, too, should venture forth and share in this heroic task to witness for Christ in all the world.

MEGATHEMES

THEME	EXPLANATION	IMPORTANCE
Church Beginnings	Acts is the history of how Christianity was founded and organized and solved its problems. The community of believers began by faith in the risen Christ and in the power of the Holy Spirit, who enabled them to witness, to love, and to serve.	New churches are continually being founded. By faith in Jesus Christ and through the power of the Holy Spirit, the church can be a vibrant agent for change. As we face new problems, Acts gives important remedies for solving them.
Holy Spirit	The church did not start or grow by its own power or enthusiasm. The disciples were empowered by God's Holy Spirit. He was the promised Counselor and Guide sent when Jesus went to heaven.	The Holy Spirit's work demonstrated that Christianity was supernatural. Thus, the church became more Holy Spirit conscious than problem conscious. By faith, any believer can claim the Holy Spirit's power to do Christ's work.
Church Growth	Acts presents the history of a dynamic, growing community of believers from Jerusalem to Syria, Africa, Asia, and Europe. In the first century, Christianity spread from believing Jews to non-Jews in 39 cities and 30 countries, islands, or provinces.	When the Holy Spirit works, there is movement, excitement, and growth. He gives us the motivation, energy, and ability to get the gospel to the whole world. How are you fitting into God's plan for spreading Christianity? What is your place in this movement?
Witnessing	Peter, John, Philip, Paul, Barnabas, and thousands more witnessed to their new faith in Christ. By personal testimony, preaching, or defense before authorities, they told the story with boldness and courage to groups of all sizes.	We are God's people, chosen to be part of his plan to reach the world. In love and by faith, we can have the Holy Spirit's help as we witness or preach. Witnessing is also beneficial to us because it strengthens our faith as we confront those who challenge it.
Opposition	Through imprisonment, beatings, plots, and riots, Christians were persecuted by both Jews and Gentiles. But the opposition became a catalyst for the spread of Christianity. Growth during times of oppression showed that Christianity was not the work of humans, but of God.	God can work through any opposition. When persecution from hostile unbelievers comes, realize that it has come because you have been a faithful witness and you have looked for the opportunity to present the Good News about Christ. Seize the opportunities that opposition brings.

KEY PLACES IN ACTS

Modern names and boundaries are shown in gray.

The apostle Paul, whose missionary journeys fill much of this book, traveled tremendous distances as he tirelessly spread the gospel across much of the Roman empire. His combined trips, by land and sea, equal more than 13,000 air miles.

1 Judea Jesus ascended to heaven from the Mount of Olives, outside Jerusalem, and his followers returned to the city to await the infilling of the Holy Spirit, which occurred at Pentecost. Peter gave a powerful sermon that was heard by Jews from across the empire. The Jerusalem church grew, but Stephen was martyred for his faith by Jewish leaders who did not believe in Jesus (1:1—7:60).

2 Samaria After Stephen's death, persecution of Christians intensified, but it caused the believers to leave Jerusalem and spread the gospel to other cities in the empire. Philip took the gospel into Samaria, and even to a man from Ethiopia (8:1–40).

3 Syria Paul (Saul) began his story as a persecutor of Christians, only to be met by Jesus himself on the road to Damascus. He became a believer, but his new faith caused opposition, so he returned to Tarsus, his home, for safety. Barnabas sought out Paul in Tarsus and brought him to the church in Antioch of Syria, where they worked together. Meanwhile, Peter had received a vision that led him to Caesarea, where he presented the gospel to a Gentile family, who became believers (9:1—12:25).

4 Cyprus and Galatia Paul and Barnabas were dedicated by the church in Antioch of Syria for God's work of spreading the gospel to other cities. They set off on their first missionary journey through Cyprus and Galatia (13:1—14:28).

5 Jerusalem Controversy between Jewish Christians and Gentile Christians over the matter of keeping the law led to a special council, with delegates from the churches in Antioch and Jerusalem meeting in Jerusalem. Together, they resolved the conflict and the news was taken back to Antioch (15:1–35).

6 Macedonia Barnabas traveled to Cyprus while Paul took a second missionary journey. He revisited the churches in Galatia and headed toward Ephesus, but the Holy Spirit said no. So he turned north toward Bithynia and Pontus but again was told not to go. He then received the "Macedonian call," and followed the Spirit's direction into the cities of Macedonia (15:36—17:14).

7 Achaia Paul traveled from Macedonia to Athens and Corinth in Achaia, then traveled by ship to Ephesus before returning to Caesarea, Jerusalem, and finally back to Antioch (17:15—18:22).

8 Ephesus Paul's third missionary journey took him back through Cilicia and Galatia, this time straight to Ephesus in Asia. He visited other cities in Asia before going back to Macedonia and Achaia. He returned to Jerusalem by ship, despite his knowledge that arrest awaited him there (18:23—23:30).

9 Caesarea Paul was arrested in Jerusalem and taken to Antipatris, then on to Caesarea under Roman guard. Paul always took advantage of any opportunity to share the gospel, and he did so before many Gentile leaders. Because Paul appealed to Caesar, he began the long journey to Rome (23:31—26:32).

10 Rome After storms, layovers in Crete, and shipwreck on the island of Malta, Paul arrived in Sicily and finally in Italy, where he traveled by land, under guard, to his long-awaited destination: Rome, the capital of the empire (27:1—28:31).

1:1
Luke 1:3; Luke 3:23

1:2
Mark 16:19; Acts 1:9, 11, 22; Matt 28:19f; Mark 16:15; John 20:21f; Mark 6:30; John 13:18; Acts 10:41

1:3
Matt 28:17; Mark 16:12, 14; Luke 24:34, 36; John 20:19, 26; 21:1, 14; 1 Cor 15:5-7; Acts 8:12; 19:8; 28:23, 31

1:4
Luke 24:49; John 14:16, 26; 15:26

1:5
Matt 3:11; Mark 1:8; Luke 3:16; John 1:33; Acts 2:1-4

1:6
Matt 17:11; Mark 9:12; Luke 17:20; 19:11

A. PETER'S MINISTRY (1:1—12:25)

The book of Acts begins where the Gospels leave off, reporting on the actions of the apostles and the work of the Holy Spirit. Beginning in Jerusalem, the church is established and grows rapidly, then faces intense persecution, which drives the believers out into the surrounding areas. Through this dispersion, Samaritans and Gentiles hear the Good News and believe.

1. Establishment of the church

Introduction

1 The first account I composed, Theophilus, about all that Jesus began to do and teach,
2 until the day when He was taken up *to heaven*, after He had by the Holy Spirit
given orders to the apostles whom He had chosen.
3 To these He also presented Himself alive after His suffering, by many convincing
proofs, appearing to them over *a period of* forty days and speaking of the things concerning the kingdom of God.
4 Gathering them together, He commanded them not to leave Jerusalem, but to wait
for what the Father had promised, "Which," *He said,* "you heard of from Me;
5 for John baptized with water, but you will be baptized with the Holy Spirit not many
days from now."
6 So when they had come together, they were asking Him, saying, "Lord, is it at this
time You are restoring the kingdom to Israel?"

1:1 The book of Acts continues the story Luke began in his Gospel, covering the 30 years after Jesus was taken up into heaven. During that short time the church was established, and the gospel of salvation was taken throughout the world, even to the capital of the Roman empire. Those preaching the gospel, though ordinary people with human frailties and limitations, were empowered by the Holy Spirit to take the Good News all over the world (17:6). Throughout the book of Acts we learn about the nature of the church and how we today are also to go about turning our world upside down.

1:1 Luke's first account was the Gospel of Luke; that book was also addressed to Theophilus, whose name means "one who loves God." (See note on Luke 1:3.)

1:1ff Verses 1–11 are the bridge between the events recorded in the Gospels and the events marking the beginning of the church. Jesus spent 40 days teaching his disciples, and they were changed drastically. Before, they had argued with each other, deserted their Lord, and one (Peter) even lied about knowing Jesus. Here, in a series of meetings with the living, resurrected Christ, the disciples had many questions answered. They became convinced about the resurrection, learned about the kingdom of God, and learned about their power source—the Holy Spirit. By reading the Bible, we can sit with the resurrected Christ in his school of discipleship. By believing in him, we can receive his power through the Holy Spirit to be new people. By joining with other Christians in Christ's church, we can take part in doing his work on earth.

1:1–3 Luke says that the disciples were eyewitnesses to all that had happened to Jesus Christ—his life before his crucifixion ("suffering"), and the 40 days after his resurrection as he taught them more about the kingdom of God. Today there are still people who doubt Jesus' resurrection. But Jesus appeared to the disciples on many occasions after his resurrection, proving that he was alive. Look at the change the resurrection made in the disciples' lives. At Jesus' death, they scattered—they were disillusioned, and they feared for their lives. After seeing the resurrected Christ, they were fearless and risked everything to spread the Good News about him around the world. They faced imprisonment, beatings, rejection, and martyrdom, yet they never compromised their mission. These men would not have risked their lives for something they knew was a fraud. They knew Jesus was raised from the dead, and the early church was fired with their enthusiasm to tell others. It is important to know this so we can have confidence in their testimony. Twenty centuries later we can still be confident that our faith is based on fact.

1:3 Jesus explained that with his coming, the kingdom of God was inaugurated. When he returned to heaven, God's kingdom would remain in the hearts of all believers through the presence of the Holy Spirit. But the kingdom of God will not be fully realized until Jesus Christ comes again to judge all people and remove all evil from the world. Before that time, believers are to work to spread God's kingdom across the world. The book of Acts records how this work was begun. What the early church started, we must continue.

1:4–5 The *Trinity* is a description of the unique relationship of God the Father, the Son, and the Holy Spirit. If Jesus had stayed on earth, his physical presence would have limited the spread of the gospel, because physically he could be in only one place at a time. After Christ was taken up into heaven, he would be spiritually present everywhere through the Holy Spirit. The Holy Spirit was sent so that God would be with and within his followers after Christ returned to heaven. The Spirit would comfort them, guide them to know his truth, remind them of Jesus' words, give them the right words to say, and fill them with power (see John 14—16).

1:5 At Pentecost (2:1–4) the Holy Spirit was made available to all who believed in Jesus. We receive the Holy Spirit (are baptized with him) when we receive Jesus Christ. The baptism of the Holy Spirit must be understood in the light of his total work in Christians.

(1) The Spirit marks the beginning of the Christian experience. We cannot belong to Christ without his Spirit (Romans 8:9); we cannot be united to Christ without his Spirit (1 Corinthians 6:17); we cannot be adopted as his children without his Spirit (Romans 8:14–17; Galatians 4:6–7); we cannot be in the body of Christ except by baptism in the Spirit (1 Corinthians 12:13).

(2) The Spirit is the power of our new lives. He begins a lifelong process of change as we become more like Christ (Galatians 3:3; Philippians 1:6). When we receive Christ by faith, we begin an immediate personal relationship with God. The Holy Spirit works in us to help us become like Christ.

(3) The Spirit unites the Christian community in Christ (Ephesians 2:19–22). The Holy Spirit can be experienced by all, and he works through all (1 Corinthians 12:11; Ephesians 4:4).

1:6 During the years of Jesus' ministry on earth, the disciples continually wondered about his kingdom. When would it come? What would their role be? In the traditional view, the Messiah would be an earthly conqueror who would free Israel from Rome. But the kingdom Jesus spoke about was first of all a *spiritual* kingdom established in the hearts and lives of believers (Luke 17:21). God's presence and power dwell in believers in the person of the Holy Spirit.

7 He said to them, "It is not for you to know times or epochs which the Father has
fixed by His own authority;
8 but you will receive power when the Holy Spirit has come upon you; and you shall
be My witnesses both in Jerusalem, and in all Judea and Samaria, and even to the remotest part of the earth."

The Ascension

9 And after He had said these things, He was lifted up while they were looking on,
and a cloud received Him out of their sight.
10 And as they were gazing intently into the sky while He was going, behold, two men
in white clothing stood beside them.
11 They also said, "Men of Galilee, why do you stand looking into the sky? This Jesus,
who has been taken up from you into heaven, will come in just the same way as you have
watched Him go into heaven."

The Upper Room

12 Then they returned to Jerusalem from the mount called Olivet, which is near Jerusalem, a Sabbath day's journey away.
13 When they had entered *the city*, they went up to the upper room where they were
staying; that is, Peter and John and James and Andrew, Philip and Thomas, Bartholomew and Matthew, James *the son* of Alphaeus, and Simon the Zealot, and Judas *the son*
of James.
14 These all with one mind were continually devoting themselves to prayer, along with
the women, and Mary the mother of Jesus, and with His brothers.
15 At this time Peter stood up in the midst of the brethren (a gathering of about one
hundred and twenty persons was there together), and said,

1:7 Matt 24:36; Mark 13:32

1:8 Acts 2:1-4; Luke 24:48; John 15:27; Acts 8:1, 5, 14; Matt 28:19; Mark 16:15; Rom 10:18; Col 1:23

1:9 Luke 24:50, 51

1:10 Luke 24:4; John 20:12

1:11 Acts 2:7; 13:31; Matt 16:27f; Acts 3:21

1:12 Luke 24:52; Matt 21:1

1:13 Mark 14:15; Luke 22:12; Acts 9:37, 39; 20:8; Matt 10:2-4; Mark 3:16-19; Luke 6:14-16; John 14:22

1:14 Acts 2:42; 6:4; Rom 12:12; Eph 6:18; Col 4:2; Luke 8:2f; Matt 12:46

1:6–7 Like other Jews, the disciples chafed under their Roman rulers. They wanted Jesus to free Israel from Roman power and then become their king. Jesus replied that God the Father sets the timetable for all events—worldwide, national, and personal. If you want changes that God isn't making immediately, don't become impatient. Instead, trust God's timetable.

1:8 Power from the Holy Spirit is not limited to strength beyond the ordinary—that power also involves courage, boldness, confidence, insight, ability, and authority. The disciples would need all these gifts to fulfill their mission. If you believe in Jesus Christ, you can experience the power of the Holy Spirit in your life.

1:8 Jesus promised the disciples that they would receive power to witness after they received the Holy Spirit. Notice the progression: (1) They would receive the Holy Spirit, (2) he would give them power, and (3) they would witness with extraordinary results. Often we try to reverse the order and witness by our own power and authority. Witnessing is not showing what we can do for God. It is showing and telling what God has done for us.

1:8 Jesus had instructed his disciples to witness to people of all nations about him (Matthew 28:19, 20). But they were told to wait first for the Holy Spirit (Luke 24:49). God has important work for you to do for him, but you must do it by the power of the Holy Spirit. We often like to get on with the job, even if it means running ahead of God. But waiting is sometimes part of God's plan. Are you waiting and listening for God's complete instructions, or are you running ahead of his plans? We need God's timing and power to be truly effective.

1:8 This verse describes a series of ever-widening circles. The gospel was to spread, geographically, from Jerusalem, into Judea and Samaria, and finally to the whole world. It would begin with the devout Jews in Jerusalem and Samaria, spread to the mixed race in Samaria, and finally be offered to the Gentiles in the uttermost parts of the earth. God's gospel has not reached its final destination if someone in your family, your workplace, your school, or your community hasn't heard about Jesus Christ. Make sure that you are contributing in some way to the ever-widening circle of God's loving message.

1:9 It was important for the disciples to see Jesus taken up into heaven. Then they knew without a doubt that he was God and that his home was in heaven.

1:9–11 After 40 days with his disciples (1:3), Jesus returned to heaven. The two men dressed in white were angels who proclaimed to the disciples that one day Jesus would return in the same way he went—bodily and visibly. History is not haphazard or cyclical; it is moving toward a specific point—the return of Jesus to judge and rule over the earth. We should be ready for his sudden return (1 Thessalonians 5:2), not by standing around "looking into the sky," but by working hard to share the gospel so that others will be able to share in God's great blessings.

1:12–13 After Christ was taken up into heaven, the disciples immediately returned to Jerusalem and had a prayer meeting. Jesus had said they would be baptized with the Holy Spirit in a few days, so they waited and prayed. When you face a difficult task, an important decision, or a baffling dilemma, don't rush into the work and just hope it comes out the way it should. Instead, your first step should be to pray for the Holy Spirit's power and guidance.

1:13 A "Zealot" could mean anyone zealous for the Jewish law. The Zealots may have been a radical political party working for the violent overthrow of Roman rule in Israel.

1:14 At this time, Jesus' brothers were with the disciples. During Jesus' lifetime, they did not believe he was the Messiah (John 7:5), but his resurrection must have convinced them. Jesus' special appearance to James, one of his brothers, may have been an especially significant event in their conversion (see 1 Corinthians 15:7).

1:15–26 This was the first church business meeting. The small group of 11 had already grown to more than 120. The main order of business was to appoint a new disciple, or apostle, as the 12 were now called. While the apostles waited, they were doing what they could—praying, seeking God's guidance, and getting organized. Waiting for God to work does not mean sitting around doing nothing. We must do what we can, while we can, as long as we don't run ahead of God.

A JOURNEY THROUGH THE BOOK OF ACTS

Beginning with a brief summary of Jesus' last days on earth with his disciples, his ascension, and the selection of a replacement for Judas Iscariot, Luke moves quickly to his subject—the spread of the gospel and the growth of the church. Pentecost, highlighted by the filling of the Holy Spirit (2:1–13) and Peter's powerful sermon (2:14–42), was the beginning. Then the **Jerusalem** church grew daily through the bold witness of Peter and John and the love of the believers (2:43—4:37). The infant church was not without problems, however, with external opposition (resulting in imprisonment, beatings, and death) and internal deceit and complaining. Greek-speaking Jewish believers were appointed to help with the administration of the church to free the apostles to preach. Stephen and Philip were among the first deacons, and Stephen became the church's first martyr (5:1–8:3).

Instead of stopping Christianity, opposition and persecution served as catalysts for its spread because the believers took the message with them wherever they fled (8:4). Soon there were converts throughout **Samaria** and even in **Ethiopia** (8:5—40).

At this point, Luke introduces us to a bright young Jew, zealous for the Law and intent on ridding Judaism of the Jesus heresy. But on the way to **Damascus** to capture believers, Saul was converted when he was confronted in person by the risen Christ (9:1–9). Through the ministry of Ananias and the sponsorship of Barnabas, Saul (Paul) was welcomed into the fellowship and then sent to **Tarsus** for safety (9:10–30).

Meanwhile, the church continued to thrive throughout **Judea**, **Galilee**, and **Samaria**. Luke recounts Peter's preaching and how Peter healed Aeneas in Lydda and Dorcas in **Joppa** (9:31–43). While in Joppa, Peter learned through a vision that he could take the gospel to the "unclean" Gentiles. Peter understood, and he faithfully shared the truth with Cornelius, whose entire household became believers (chapter 10). This was startling news to the Jerusalem church; but when Peter told his story, they praised God for his plan for all people to hear the Good News (11:1–18). This pushed the church into even wider circles as the message was preached to Greeks in **Antioch**, where Barnabas went to encourage the believers. Then he went on to **Tarsus** to find Saul (11:20–26).

To please the Jewish leaders, Herod joined in the persecution of the Jerusalem church, killing James (John's brother) and imprisoning Peter. But God freed Peter, and Peter walked from prison to a prayer meeting on his behalf at John Mark's house (chapter 12).

Here Luke shifts the focus to Paul's ministry. Commissioned by the Antioch church for a missionary tour (13:1–3), Paul and Barnabas took the gospel to **Cyprus** and south **Galatia** with great success (13:4—14:28). But the Jewish-Gentile controversy still smoldered, and with so many Gentiles responding to Christ, the controversy threatened to divide the church. So a council met in Jerusalem to rule on the relationship of Gentile Christians to the Old Testament laws. After hearing both sides, James (Jesus' brother and the leader of the Jerusalem church) resolved the issue and sent messengers to the churches with the decision (15:1–31).

After the council, Paul and Silas preached in **Antioch**. Then they left for **Syria** and **Cilicia** as Barnabas and Mark sailed for **Cyprus** (15:36–41). On this second missionary journey, Paul and Silas traveled throughout **Macedonia** and **Achaia**, establishing churches in **Philippi**, **Thessalonica**, **Berea**, **Corinth**, and **Ephesus** before returning to **Antioch** (16:1—18:21). Luke also tells of the ministry of Apollos (18:24–28).

On Paul's third missionary trip he traveled through **Galatia**, **Phrygia**, **Macedonia**, and **Achaia**, encouraging and teaching the believers (19:1—21:9). During this time, he felt compelled to go to **Jerusalem**; and although he was warned by Agabus and others of impending imprisonment (21:10–12), he continued his journey in that direction.

While in Jerusalem, Paul was accosted in the temple by an angry mob and taken into protective custody by the Roman commander (21:17—22:29). Now we see Paul as a prisoner and on trial before the Jewish Council (23:1–9), Governor Felix (23:23—24:27), and Festus and Agrippa (25:1—26:32). In each case, Paul gave a strong and clear witness for his Lord.

Because Paul appealed to Caesar, however, he was sent to **Rome** for the final hearing of his case. But on the way the ship was destroyed in a storm, and the sailors and prisoners had to swim ashore. Even in this circumstance Paul shared his faith (27:1—28:10). Eventually the journey continued and Paul arrived in Rome, where he was held under house arrest while awaiting trial (28:11–31).

Luke ends Acts abruptly with the encouraging word that Paul had freedom in his captivity to talk to visitors and guards: "preaching the kingdom of God and teaching concerning the Lord Jesus Christ with all openness, unhindered" (28:31).

16 "Brethren, the Scripture had to be fulfilled, which the Holy Spirit foretold by the
mouth of David concerning Judas, who became a guide to those who arrested Jesus.
17 "For he was counted among us and received his share in this ministry."
18 (Now this man acquired a field with the price of his wickedness, and falling headlong, he burst open in the middle and all his intestines gushed out.
19 And it became known to all who were living in Jerusalem; so that in their own language that field was called Hakeldama, that is, Field of Blood.)
20 "For it is written in the book of Psalms,

'LET HIS HOMESTEAD BE MADE DESOLATE,
AND LET NO ONE DWELL IN IT';

and,

'LET ANOTHER MAN TAKE HIS OFFICE.'

21 "Therefore it is necessary that of the men who have accompanied us all the time that
the Lord Jesus went in and out among us—
22 beginning with the baptism of John until the day that He was taken up from us—
one of these *must* become a witness with us of His resurrection."
23 So they put forward two men, Joseph called Barsabbas (who was also called Justus), and Matthias.
24 And they prayed and said, "You, Lord, who know the hearts of all men, show which
one of these two You have chosen
25 to occupy this ministry and apostleship from which Judas turned aside to go to his
own place."
26 And they drew lots for them, and the lot fell to Matthias; and he was added to the
eleven apostles.

1:16 John 13:18; 17:12; Mark 14:43; Luke 22:47; John 18:3
1:17 John 6:70f
1:18 Matt 27:3-10; Matt 26:14f
1:19 Acts 21:40
1:20 Ps 69:25; Ps 109:8
1:21 Luke 24:3
1:22 Matt 3:16; Mark 1:1-4, 9; Luke 3:21; Mark 16:19
1:24 Acts 6:6; 13:3; 14:23; 1 Sam 16:7; Jer 17:10; Acts 15:8; Rom 8:27
1:25 Acts 1:17; Rom 1:5; 1 Cor 9:2; Gal 2:8

The Day of Pentecost

2 When the day of Pentecost had come, they were all together in one place.
2 And suddenly there came from heaven a noise like a violent rushing wind, and it
filled the whole house where they were sitting.
3 And there appeared to them tongues as of fire distributing themselves, and they
rested on each one of them.
4 And they were all filled with the Holy Spirit and began to speak with other tongues,
as the Spirit was giving them utterance.

2:1 Lev 23:15f; Acts 20:16; 1 Cor 16:8
2:2 Acts 4:31
2:4 Matt 10:20; Acts 1:5, 8; 4:8, 31; 6:3, 5; 7:55; 8:17; 9:17; 11:15; 13:9, 52; Mark 16:17; 1 Cor 12:10f; 14:21

1:16–17 How could someone who had been with Jesus daily betray him? Judas received the same calling and teaching as everyone else. But he chose to reject Christ's warning as well as his offers of mercy. Judas hardened his heart and joined in the plot with Jesus' enemies to put him to death. Judas remained unrepentant to the end, and he finally committed suicide. Although Jesus predicted this would happen, it was Judas's choice. Those privileged to be *close* to the truth are not necessarily *committed* to the truth. See Judas's Profile in Mark 14 for more information on his life.

1:18 Matthew says that Judas hanged himself (Matthew 27:5); Acts says that he fell. The traditional explanation is that when Judas hanged himself, the rope or branch broke, Judas fell, and his body burst open.

1:21–22 There were many who consistently followed Jesus throughout his ministry on earth. The 12 disciples were his inner circle, but others shared the disciples' deep love for and commitment to Jesus.

1:21–25 The apostles had to choose a replacement for Judas Iscariot. They outlined specific criteria for making the choice. When the "finalists" had been chosen, the apostles prayed, asking God to guide the selection process. This gives us a good example of how to proceed when we are making important decisions. Set up criteria consistent with the Bible, examine the alternatives, and pray for wisdom and guidance to reach a wise decision.

1:26 The disciples became *apostles. Disciple* means follower or learner, and *apostle* means messenger or missionary. These men now had the special assignment of spreading the Good News of Jesus' death and resurrection.

2:1 Held 50 days after Passover, Pentecost was also called the Feast of Weeks. It was one of three major annual feasts (Deuteronomy 16:16), a festival of thanksgiving for the harvested crops. Jesus was crucified at Passover time, and he ascended 40 days after his resurrection. The Holy Spirit came 50 days after the resurrection, ten days after the ascension. Jews of many nations gathered in Jerusalem for this festival. Thus Peter's speech (2:14ff) was given to an international audience, and it resulted in a worldwide harvest of new believers—the first converts to Christianity.

2:3–4 This was a fulfillment of John the Baptist's words about the Holy Spirit's baptizing with fire (Luke 3:16), and of the prophet Joel's words about the outpouring of the Holy Spirit (Joel 2:28–29).

Why tongues of fire? Tongues symbolize speech and the communication of the gospel. Fire symbolizes God's purifying presence, which burns away the undesirable elements of our lives and sets our hearts aflame to ignite the lives of others. On Mount Sinai, God confirmed the validity of the Old Testament law with fire from heaven (Exodus 19:16–18). At Pentecost, God confirmed the validity of the Holy Spirit's ministry by sending fire. At Mount Sinai, fire had come down on one place; at Pentecost, fire came down on many believers, symbolizing that God's presence is now available to all who believe in him.

2:3–4 God made his presence known to this group of believers in a spectacular way—violent wind, fire, and his Holy Spirit. Would you like God to reveal himself to you in such recognizable ways? He may do so, but be wary of forcing your expectations on God. In 1 Kings 19:10–13, Elijah also needed a message from God. There was a great wind, then an earthquake, and finally a fire. But God's message came in a "gentle blowing." God may use dramatic methods to work in your life—or he may speak in gentle whispers. Wait patiently and always listen.

2:5 Luke 2:25; Acts 8:2
2:6 Acts 2:2
2:7 Acts 2:12; Matt 26:73; Acts 1:11
2:9 1 Pet 1:1; Acts 18:2; Acts 6:9; 16:6; 19:10; 20:4; 21:27; 24:18; 27:2; Rom 16:5; 1 Cor 16:19; 2 Cor 1:8; 2 Tim 1:15; Rev 1:4
2:10 Acts 16:6; 18:23; Acts 13:13; 14:24; 15:38; 27:5; Matt 27:32; Acts 17:21; Matt 23:15
2:12 Acts 2:7
2:13 1 Cor 14:23
2:14 Acts 1:26
2:15 1 Thess 5:7
2:17 Joel 2:28-32

5 Now there were Jews living in Jerusalem, devout men from every nation under heaven.
6 And when this sound occurred, the crowd came together, and were bewildered because each one of them was hearing them speak in his own language.
7 They were amazed and astonished, saying, "Why, are not all these who are speaking Galileans?
8 "And how is it that we each hear *them* in our own language to which we were born?
9 "Parthians and Medes and Elamites, and residents of Mesopotamia, Judea and Cappadocia, Pontus and Asia,
10 Phrygia and Pamphylia, Egypt and the districts of Libya around Cyrene, and visitors from Rome, both Jews and [1]proselytes,
11 Cretans and Arabs—we hear them in our *own* tongues speaking of the mighty deeds of God."
12 And they all continued in amazement and great perplexity, saying to one another, "What does this mean?"
13 But others were mocking and saying, "They are full of sweet wine."

Peter's Sermon

14 But Peter, taking his stand with the eleven, raised his voice and declared to them: "Men of Judea and all you who live in Jerusalem, let this be known to you and give heed to my words.
15 "For these men are not drunk, as you suppose, for it is *only* the [2]third hour of the day;
16 but this is what was spoken of through the prophet Joel:
17 'AND IT SHALL BE IN THE LAST DAYS,' God says,
'THAT I WILL POUR FORTH OF MY SPIRIT ON ALL MANKIND;
AND YOUR SONS AND YOUR DAUGHTERS SHALL PROPHESY,
AND YOUR YOUNG MEN SHALL SEE VISIONS,
AND YOUR OLD MEN SHALL DREAM DREAMS;
18 EVEN ON MY BONDSLAVES, BOTH MEN AND WOMEN,
I WILL IN THOSE DAYS POUR FORTH OF MY SPIRIT
And they shall prophesy.
19 'AND I WILL GRANT WONDERS IN THE SKY ABOVE
AND SIGNS ON THE EARTH BELOW,

1 I.e. Gentile converts to Judaism **2** I.e. 9 a.m.

2:4–11 These people literally spoke in other languages—a miraculous attention-getter for the international crowd gathered in town for the feast. All the nationalities represented recognized their own languages being spoken. But more than miraculous speaking drew people's attention; they saw the presence and power of the Holy Spirit. The apostles continued to minister in the power of the Holy Spirit wherever they went.

2:7–8 Christianity is not limited to any race or group of people. Christ offers salvation to all people without regard to nationality. Visitors in Jerusalem were surprised to hear the apostles and other believers speaking in languages other than their own, the languages of other nationalities, but they need not have been. God works all kinds of miracles to spread the gospel, using many languages as he calls all kinds of people to become his followers. No matter what your race, color, nationality, or language, God speaks to you. Are you listening?

2:9–11 Why are all these places mentioned? This is a list of many lands from which Jews came to the festivals in Jerusalem. These Jews were not living in Palestine because they had been dispersed throughout the world through captivities and persecutions. Very likely, some of the Jews who responded to Peter's message returned to their homelands with God's Good News of salvation. Thus God prepared the way for the spread of the gospel. As you read Acts, you will see how the way was often prepared for Paul and other messengers by people who became believers at Pentecost. The church at Rome, for example, was probably begun by such Jewish believers.

2:14 Peter had been an unstable leader during Jesus' ministry, letting his bravado be his downfall, even denying that he knew Jesus (John 18:15–18, 25–27). But Christ had forgiven and restored him (John 21). This was a new Peter, humble but bold. His confidence came from the Holy Spirit, who made him a powerful and dynamic speaker. Have you ever felt as if you've made such bad mistakes that God could never forgive and use you? No matter what sins you have committed, God promises to forgive you and make you useful for his kingdom. Allow him to forgive you and use you effectively to serve him.

2:14ff Peter tells the people why they should listen to the testimony of the believers: because the Old Testament prophecies had been entirely fulfilled in Jesus (2:14–21), because Jesus is the Messiah (2:25–36), and because the risen Christ could change their lives (2:37–40).

2:15 Peter answered accusations that they were all drunk (2:13) by saying it was much too early in the day for that.

2:16–21 Not everything mentioned in Joel 2:28–29 was happening that particular morning. The "last days" include all the days between Christ's first and second comings and is another way of saying "from now on." "The great and glorious day of the Lord" (2:20) denotes the whole Christian age. Even Moses yearned for the Lord to put his Spirit on everyone (Numbers 11:29). At Pentecost the Holy Spirit was released throughout the entire world—to men, women, slaves, Jews, Gentiles. Now *everyone* can receive the Spirit. This was a revolutionary thought for first-century Jews.

BLOOD, AND FIRE, AND VAPOR OF SMOKE.
20 'THE SUN WILL BE TURNED INTO DARKNESS
AND THE MOON INTO BLOOD,
BEFORE THE GREAT AND GLORIOUS DAY OF THE LORD SHALL COME.
21 'AND IT SHALL BE THAT EVERYONE WHO CALLS ON THE NAME OF THE LORD
WILL BE SAVED.'
22 "Men of Israel, listen to these words: Jesus the Nazarene, a man attested to you by
God with miracles and wonders and signs which God performed through Him in your
midst, just as you yourselves know—
23 this *Man*, delivered over by the predetermined plan and foreknowledge of God, you
nailed to a cross by the hands of godless men and put *Him* to death.
24 "But God raised Him up again, putting an end to the agony of death, since it was
impossible for Him to be held in its power.
25 "For David says of Him,
'I SAW THE LORD ALWAYS IN MY PRESENCE;
FOR HE IS AT MY RIGHT HAND, SO THAT I WILL NOT BE SHAKEN.
26 'THEREFORE MY HEART WAS GLAD AND MY TONGUE EXULTED;
MOREOVER MY FLESH ALSO WILL LIVE IN HOPE;
27 BECAUSE YOU WILL NOT ABANDON MY SOUL TO HADES,
NOR ALLOW YOUR HOLY ONE TO UNDERGO DECAY.
28 'YOU HAVE MADE KNOWN TO ME THE WAYS OF LIFE;
YOU WILL MAKE ME FULL OF GLADNESS WITH YOUR PRESENCE.'
29 "Brethren, I may confidently say to you regarding the patriarch David that he both
died and was buried, and his tomb is with us to this day.
30 "And so, because he was a prophet and knew that GOD HAD SWORN TO HIM WITH
AN OATH TO SEAT *one* OF HIS DESCENDANTS ON HIS THRONE,
31 he looked ahead and spoke of the resurrection of [3]the Christ, that HE WAS NEITHER
ABANDONED TO HADES, NOR DID His flesh SUFFER DECAY.
32 "This Jesus God raised up again, to which we are all witnesses.
33 "Therefore having been exalted to the right hand of God, and having received from
the Father the promise of the Holy Spirit, He has poured forth this which you both see
and hear.
34 "For it was not David who ascended into heaven, but he himself says:
'THE LORD SAID TO MY LORD,
"SIT AT MY RIGHT HAND,
35 UNTIL I MAKE YOUR ENEMIES A FOOTSTOOL FOR YOUR FEET." '
36 "Therefore let all the house of Israel know for certain that God has made Him both
Lord and Christ—this Jesus whom you crucified."

The Ingathering

37 Now when they heard *this*, they were pierced to the heart, and said to Peter and the
rest of the apostles, "Brethren, what shall we do?"
38 Peter *said* to them, "Repent, and each of you be baptized in the name of Jesus Christ
for the forgiveness of your sins; and you will receive the gift of the Holy Spirit.

3 I.e. the Messiah

2:21 Rom 10:13
2:22 Acts 3:6; 4:10; 10:38; John 3:2
2:23 Luke 22:22; Acts 3:18; 4:28; 1 Pet 1:20; Matt 27:35; Mark 15:24; Luke 23:33; 24:20; John 19:18; Acts 3:13
2:24 Matt 28:5, 6; Mark 16:6; Luke 24:5, 6
2:25 Ps 16:8-11
2:27 Matt 11:23; Acts 2:31; Acts 13:35
2:30 Matt 22:43; Ps 132:11; 2 Sam 7:12f; Ps 89:3f
2:31 Matt 11:23
2:32 Acts 2:24; 3:15, 26; 4:10; 5:30; 10:40; 13:30, 33, 34, 37; 17:31; Rom 4:24; 6:4; 8:11; 10:9; 1 Cor 6:14; 15:15; 2 Cor 4:14; Gal 1:1; Eph 1:20; Col 2:12; 1 Thess 1:10; Heb 13:20; 1 Pet 1:21
2:33 Mark 16:19; John 7:39; Gal 3:14
2:34 Ps 110:1; Matt 22:44f
2:36 Ezek 36:22, 32, 37; 45:6; Luke 2:11
2:37 Luke 3:10, 12, 14
2:38 Mark 1:15; Luke 24:47; Acts 3:19; 5:31; 20:21; Mark 16:16

2:23 Everything that happened to Jesus was under God's control. His plans were never disrupted by the Roman government or the Jewish officials. This was especially comforting to those facing oppression during the time of the early Christian church.

2:24 Peter began with a public proclamation of the resurrection at a time when it could be verified by many witnesses. This was a powerful statement, because many of the people listening to Peter's words had been in Jerusalem 50 days earlier at Passover and may have seen or heard about the crucifixion and resurrection of this "great teacher." Jesus' resurrection was the ultimate sign that what he said about himself was true. Without the resurrection, we would have no reason to believe in Jesus (1 Corinthians 15:14).

2:25–32 Peter quoted from Psalm 16:8–11—a psalm written by David. He explained that David was not writing about himself, because David died and was buried (2:29). Instead, he wrote as a prophet (2:30) who spoke of the Messiah who would be resurrected. The audience understood "decay" (2:27) to mean the grave. The emphasis here is that Jesus' body was *not* left to decay but was in fact resurrected and glorified.

2:33 He "has poured forth this which you both see and hear" could be paraphrased, "gave Jesus the authority to send the Holy Spirit, with the results you are seeing and hearing today."

2:37 After Peter's powerful, Spirit-filled message, the people were deeply moved and asked, "What shall we do?" This is the basic question we must ask. It is not enough to be sorry for our sins—we must let God forgive them, and then we must live like forgiven people. Has God spoken to you through his Word or through the words of another believer? Like Peter's audience, ask God what you should do, and then obey.

2:38–39 If you want to follow Christ, you must repent and be

2:39 Is 44:3; 54:13; 57:19; Joel 2:32; Rom 9:4; Eph 2:12
2:40 Luke 16:28; Deut 32:5; Matt 17:17
2:41 Acts 3:23; 7:14; 27:37; Rom 13:1
2:42 Acts 1:14; Luke 24:30; Acts 2:46; 20:7; 1 Cor 10:16
2:44 Acts 4:32, 37; 5:2
2:45 Matt 19:21
2:46 Acts 5:42; Luke 24:30; 1 Cor 10:16
2:47 Acts 5:13
3:1 Luke 22:8; Acts 3:3, 4, 11; Ps 55:17; Matt 27:45; Acts 10:30
3:2 Acts 14:8; Luke 16:20; John 9:8; Acts 3:10
3:3 Luke 22:8; Acts 3:1

39 "For the promise is for you and your children and for all who are far off, as many as
the Lord our God will call to Himself."
40 And with many other words he solemnly testified and kept on exhorting them, saying, "Be saved from this perverse generation!"
41 So then, those who had received his word were baptized; and that day there were
added about three thousand [4]souls.
42 They were continually devoting themselves to the apostles' teaching and to fellowship, to the breaking of bread and to prayer.
43 Everyone kept feeling a sense of awe; and many wonders and signs were taking place
through the apostles.
44 And all those who had believed [5]were together and had all things in common;
45 and they *began* selling their property and possessions and were sharing them with
all, as anyone might have need.
46 Day by day continuing with one mind in the temple, and breaking bread from house
to house, they were taking their meals together with gladness and sincerity of heart,
47 praising God and having favor with all the people. And the Lord was adding to their
number day by day those who were being saved.

Healing the Lame Beggar

3 Now Peter and John were going up to the temple at the [6]ninth *hour,* the hour of prayer.
2 And a man who had been lame from his mother's womb was being carried along,
whom they used to set down every day at the gate of the temple which is called Beautiful, in order to beg [7]alms of those who were entering the temple.
3 When he saw Peter and John about to go into the temple, he *began* asking to receive alms.
4 But Peter, along with John, fixed his gaze on him and said, "Look at us!"
5 And he *began* to give them his attention, expecting to receive something from them.

4 I.e. persons **5** One early ms does not contain *were* and *and* **6** I.e. 3 p.m. **7** Or *a gift of charity*

---

baptized. To repent means to *turn from* sin, changing the direction of your life from selfishness and rebellion against God's laws. At the same time, you must *turn to* Christ, depending on him for forgiveness, mercy, guidance, and purpose. We cannot save ourselves—only God can save us. Baptism identifies us with Christ and with the community of believers. It is a condition of discipleship and a sign of faith.

2:40–43 About 3,000 people became new believers when Peter preached the Good News about Christ. These new Christians were united with the other believers, taught by the apostles, and included in the prayer meetings and fellowship. New believers in Christ need to be in groups where they can learn God's Word, pray, and mature in the faith. If you have just begun a relationship with Christ, seek out other believers for fellowship, prayer, and teaching. This is the way to grow.

2:42 "Breaking of bread" refers to communion services that were celebrated in remembrance of Jesus and were patterned after the Last Supper that Jesus had with his disciples before his death (Matthew 26:26–29).

2:44 Recognizing the other believers as brothers and sisters in the family of God, the Christians in Jerusalem shared all they had so that all could benefit from God's gifts. It is tempting—especially if we have material wealth—to cut ourselves off from one another, each taking care of his or her own interests, each providing for and enjoying his or her own little piece of the world. But as part of God's spiritual family, it is our responsibility to help one another in every way possible. God's family works best when its members work together.

2:46 A common misconception about the first Christians (who were Jews) was that they rejected the Jewish religion. But these believers saw Jesus' message and resurrection as the fulfillment of everything they knew and believed from the Old Testament. The Jewish believers at first did not separate from the rest of the Jewish community. They still went to the temple and synagogues for worship and instruction in the Scriptures. But their belief in Jesus created great friction with Jews who didn't believe that Jesus was the Messiah. Thus, believing Jews were forced to meet in private homes for communion, prayer, and teaching about Christ. By the end of the first century, many of these Jewish believers were excommunicated from their synagogues.

2:47 A healthy Christian community attracts people to Christ. The Jerusalem church's zeal for worship and brotherly love was contagious. A healthy, loving church will grow in numbers. What are you doing to make your church the kind of place that will attract others to Christ?

3:1 The Jews observed three times of prayer—morning (9:00 a.m.), afternoon (3:00 p.m.), and evening (sunset). At these times devout Jews and Gentiles who believed in God often went to the temple to pray. Peter and John were going to the temple at 3:00 p.m.

3:2 The gate called Beautiful was an entrance to the temple, not to the city. It was one of the favored entrances, and many people passed through it on their way to worship. The lame man was begging where he would be seen by the most people.

3:2 Giving money to beggars was considered praiseworthy in the Jewish religion. So the beggar wisely placed himself where pious people might see him on their way to worship at the temple.

3:5–6 The lame man asked for money, but Peter gave him something much better—the use of his legs. We often ask God to solve a small problem, but he wants to give us a whole new life and help for *all* our problems. When we ask God for help, he may say, "I've got something even better for you." Ask God for what you want, but don't be surprised when he gives you what you really *need.*

6 But Peter said, "I do not possess silver and gold, but what I do have I give to you: In
the name of Jesus Christ the Nazarene—walk!"
7 And seizing him by the right hand, he raised him up; and immediately his feet and
his ankles were strengthened.
8 With a leap he stood upright and *began* to walk; and he entered the temple with
them, walking and leaping and praising God.
9 And all the people saw him walking and praising God;
10 and they were taking note of him as being the one who used to sit at the Beautiful
Gate of the temple to *beg* alms, and they were filled with wonder and amazement at what
had happened to him.

Peter's Second Sermon

11 While he was clinging to Peter and John, all the people ran together to them at the
so-called portico of Solomon, full of amazement.
12 But when Peter saw *this*, he replied to the people, "Men of Israel, why are you amazed
at this, or why do you gaze at us, as if by our own power or piety we had made him walk?
13 "The God of Abraham, Isaac and Jacob, the God of our fathers, has glorified His
servant Jesus, *the one* whom you delivered and disowned in the presence of Pilate, when
he had decided to release Him.
14 "But you disowned the Holy and Righteous One and asked for a murderer to be
granted to you,
15 but put to death the Prince of life, *the one* whom God raised from the dead, *a fact* to
which we are witnesses.
16 "And on the basis of faith in His name, *it is* the name of Jesus which has strengthened this man whom you see and know; and the faith which *comes* through Him has giv-
en him this perfect health in the presence of you all.
17 "And now, brethren, I know that you acted in ignorance, just as your rulers did also.
18 "But the things which God announced beforehand by the mouth of all the prophets,
that His Christ would suffer, He has thus fulfilled.
19 "Therefore repent and return, so that your sins may be wiped away, in order that
times of refreshing may come from the presence of the Lord;

3:6 Acts 2:22; 3:16; 4:10

3:8 Acts 14:10

3:9 Acts 4:16, 21

3:10 John 9:8; Acts 3:2

3:11 Luke 22:8; John 10:23; Acts 5:12

3:13 Matt 20:19; John 19:11; Acts 2:23; Matt 27:2; Luke 23:4

3:14 Mark 1:24; Acts 4:27; 7:52; 2 Cor 5:21; Matt 27:20; Mark 15:11; Luke 23:18, 25

3:15 Acts 5:31; Heb 2:10; 12:2; Acts 2:24; Luke 24:48

3:17 Luke 23:34; John 15:21; Acts 13:27; 26:9; Eph 4:18; Luke 23:13

3:18 Acts 2:23; Luke 24:27; Acts 17:3; 26:23

3:19 Acts 2:38; 26:20; 2 Thess 1:7; Heb 4:1ff

3:6 "In the name of Jesus Christ" means "by the authority of Jesus Christ." The apostles were doing this healing through the Holy Spirit's power, not their own.

3:7–10 In his excitement, the formerly lame man began to jump and walk around. He also praised God! And then others were also awed by God's power. Don't forget to thank people who help you, but also remember to praise God for his care and protection.

3:11 The portico of Solomon was a covered porch or entrance with columns.

3:11ff Peter had an audience, and he capitalized on the opportunity to share Jesus Christ. He clearly presented his message by telling (1) who Jesus is, (2) how the Jews had rejected him, (3) why their rejection was fatal, and (4) what they needed to do to change the situation. Peter told the crowd that they still had a choice; God still offered them the opportunity to believe and receive Jesus as their Messiah and as their Lord. Displays of God's mercy and grace, such as the healing of this crippled man, often create teachable moments. Pray to have courage like Peter to see these opportunities and to use them to speak up for Christ.

3:13–14 Pilate had decided to release Jesus, but the people had clamored to have Barabbas, a murderer, released instead (see John 19:1–16). When Peter said "You delivered and disowned" him, he meant it literally. Jesus' trial and death had occurred right there in Jerusalem only weeks earlier. It wasn't an event of the distant past—most of these people had heard about it, and some may very well have taken part in condemning Jesus.

3:15 The religious leaders thought they had put an end to Jesus when they crucified him. But their confidence was shaken when Peter told them that Jesus was alive again and that this time they could not harm him. Peter's message emphasized that (1) the people and their religious leaders killed Jesus (3:17), (2) God brought him back to life, and (3) the apostles were witnesses to this fact. After pointing out the sin and injustice of these leaders, Peter showed the significance of the resurrection, God's triumph and power over death.

3:16 Jesus, not the apostles, received the glory for the healing of the crippled man. In those days a man's name represented his character; it stood for his authority and power. By using Jesus' name, Peter showed who gave him the authority and power to heal. The apostles did not emphasize what *they* could do, but what God could do through them. Jesus' name is not to be used as magic—it must be used in faith. When we pray in Jesus' name, we must remember that it is Christ himself, not merely the sound of his name, who gives our prayers their power.

3:18 These prophecies are found in Psalm 22 and Isaiah 50:6 and Isaiah 53. Peter was explaining the kind of Messiah God had sent to earth. The Jews expected a great ruler, not a suffering servant.

3:19 John the Baptist prepared the way for Jesus by preaching repentance. The apostles' message of salvation also included the call to repentance—acknowledging personal sin and turning away from it. Many people want the benefits of being identified with Christ without admitting their own disobedience and turning from sin. The key to forgiveness is confessing your sin and turning from it (see 2:38).

3:19–20 When we repent, God promises not only to wipe out our sins, but to bring spiritual refreshment. Repentance may at first seem painful because it is hard to give up certain sins. But God will give you a better way. As Hosea promised, "So let us know, let us press on to know the LORD. His going forth is as certain as the dawn; and He will come to us like the rain, like the spring rain watering the earth" (Hosea 6:3). Do you feel a need to be refreshed?

20 and that He may send Jesus, the Christ appointed for you,
21 whom heaven must receive until *the* period of restoration of all things about which
God spoke by the mouth of His holy prophets from ancient time.
22 "Moses said, 'THE LORD GOD WILL RAISE UP FOR YOU A PROPHET LIKE ME FROM
YOUR BRETHREN; TO HIM YOU SHALL GIVE HEED to everything He says to you.
23 'And it will be that every soul that does not heed that prophet shall be utterly destroyed from among the people.'
24 "And likewise, all the prophets who have spoken, from Samuel and *his* successors
onward, also announced these days.
25 "It is you who are the sons of the prophets and of the covenant which God made with
your fathers, saying to Abraham, 'AND IN YOUR SEED ALL THE FAMILIES OF THE EARTH
SHALL BE BLESSED.'
26 "For you first, God raised up His Servant and sent Him to bless you by turning every
one *of you* from your wicked ways."

Peter and John Arrested

4 As they were speaking to the people, the priests and the captain of the temple *guard*
and the Sadducees came up to them,
2 being greatly disturbed because they were teaching the people and proclaiming in
Jesus the resurrection from the dead.
3 And they laid hands on them and put them in jail until the next day, for it was already evening.
4 But many of those who had heard the message believed; and the number of the men
came to be about five thousand.
5 On the next day, their rulers and elders and scribes were gathered together in Jerusalem;
6 and Annas the high priest *was there,* and Caiaphas and John and Alexander, and all
who were of high-priestly descent.

3:21 Acts 1:11; Matt 17:11; Rom 8:21; Luke 1:70

3:22 Deut 18:15, 18; Acts 7:37

3:23 Deut 18:19; Acts 2:41; Lev 23:29

3:24 Luke 24:27; Acts 17:3; 26:23

3:25 Acts 2:39; Rom 9:4f; Gen 22:18

3:26 Matt 15:24; John 4:22; Acts 13:46; Rom 1:16; 2:9f; Acts 2:24

4:1 Luke 22:4; Matt 3:7; Luke 20:1; Acts 6:12

4:2 Acts 3:15; 17:18

4:3 Acts 5:18

4:4 Acts 2:41

4:5 Luke 23:13; Acts 4:8

4:6 Luke 3:2; Matt 26:3

3:21 The time when God will restore everything refers to the second coming, the Last Judgment, and the removal of sin from the world.

3:21–22 Most Jews thought that Joshua was this prophet predicted by Moses (Deuteronomy 18:15). Peter was saying that the prophet was Jesus Christ. Peter wanted to show them that their long-awaited Messiah had come! He and all the apostles were calling the Jewish nation to realize what they had done to their Messiah, to repent, and to believe. From this point on in Acts, we see many Jews rejecting the gospel. So the message went also to the Gentiles, many of whom were open to receive Jesus.

3:24 The prophet Samuel lived during the transition between the judges and the kings of Israel, and he was seen as the first in a succession of prophets. He anointed David king, founding David's royal line, from which the Messiah eventually came. All the prophets pointed to a future Messiah. For more on Samuel, see his Profile in 1 Samuel 8.

3:25 God promised Abraham that he would bless the world through Abraham's descendants, the Jewish race (Genesis 12:3), from which the Messiah would come. God intended the Jewish nation to be a separate and holy nation that would teach the world about God, introduce the Messiah, and then carry on his work in the world. After the days of Solomon, the nation gave up its mission to tell the world about God. Here too, in apostolic times as well as in the time Jesus spent on earth, Israel rejected its Messiah.

4:1 These priests may have been chief priests, who had special influence and were often close relatives of the high priests. The captain of the temple guard was the leader of the guards who were set around the temple to ensure order. The Sadducees were members of a small but powerful Jewish religious sect that did not believe in the resurrection of the dead. They were the religious leaders who stood to gain financially by cooperating with the Romans. Most of those who engineered and carried out Jesus' arrest and crucifixion were from these three groups.

4:2–3 Peter and John spoke to the people during the afternoon prayer time. The Sadducees moved in quickly to investigate. Because they did not believe in the resurrection, they were understandably disturbed with what the apostles were saying. Peter and John were refuting one of their fundamental beliefs and thus threatening their authority as religious teachers. Even though the nation was under Roman rule, the Sadducees had almost unlimited power over the temple grounds. Thus they were able to arrest Peter and John for no other reason than teaching something that contradicted their beliefs.

4:3 Not often will sharing the gospel send us to jail as it did Peter and John. Still, we run risks in trying to win others to Christ. We might be willing to face a night in jail if it would bring 5,000 people to Christ, but shouldn't we also be willing to suffer for the sake of even one? What do you risk in witnessing—rejection, persecution? Whatever the risks, realize that nothing done for God is ever wasted.

4:5–6 The rulers, elders, and scribes made up the Jewish Council—the same Council that had condemned Jesus to death (Luke 22:66). It had 70 members plus the current high priest, who presided over the group. The Sadducees held a majority in this ruling group. These were the wealthy, intellectual, and powerful men of Jerusalem. Jesus' followers stood before this Council just as he had.

4:6 Annas had been deposed as high priest by the Romans, who then appointed Caiaphas, Annas's son-in-law, in his place. But because the Jews considered the office of high priest a lifetime position, they still called Annas by that title and gave him respect and authority within the Council. Annas and Caiaphas had played significant roles in Jesus' trial (John 18:24, 28). It did not please them that the man they thought they had sacrificed for the good of the nation (John 11:49–51) had followers who were just as persistent and who promised to be just as troublesome as he had been.

7 When they had placed them in the center, they *began to* inquire, "By what power,
or in what name, have you done this?"
8 Then Peter, filled with the Holy Spirit, said to them, "Rulers and elders of the **4:8** Acts 2:4; 13:9; Luke
people, 23:13; Acts 4:5
9 if we are on trial today for a benefit done to a sick man, as to how this man has been
made well, **4:9** Acts 3:7f
10 let it be known to all of you and to all the people of Israel, that by the name of Jesus
Christ the Nazarene, whom you crucified, whom God raised from the dead—by this *name* **4:10** Acts 2:22; 3:6; Acts
this man stands here before you in good health. 2:24
11 "He is the STONE WHICH WAS REJECTED by you, THE BUILDERS, *but* WHICH BECAME **4:11** Matt 21:42; Ps
THE CHIEF CORNER *stone.* 118:22; Mark 9:12
12 "And there is salvation in no one else; for there is no other name under heaven that
has been given among men by which we must be saved." **4:12** Matt 1:21; Acts 10:43; 1 Tim 2:5

Threat and Release

13 Now as they observed the confidence of Peter and John and understood that they **4:13** Acts 4:31; Luke
were uneducated and untrained men, they were amazed, and *began* to recognize them 22:8; Acts 4:19;
as having been with Jesus. John 7:15
14 And seeing the man who had been healed standing with them, they had nothing to
say in reply.
15 But when they had ordered them to leave the Council, they *began* to confer with **4:15** Matt 5:22
one another,
16 saying, "What shall we do with these men? For the fact that a noteworthy miracle **4:16** John 11:47; Acts
has taken place through them is apparent to all who live in Jerusalem, and we cannot 3:7-10
deny it.
17 "But so that it will not spread any further among the people, let us warn them to speak **4:17** John 15:21
no longer to any man in this name."
18 And when they had summoned them, they commanded them not to speak or teach **4:18** Acts 5:28f
at all in the name of Jesus.
19 But Peter and John answered and said to them, "Whether it is right in the sight of **4:19** Acts 4:13; Acts 5:28f
God to give heed to you rather than to God, you be the judge;
20 for we cannot stop speaking about what we have seen and heard." **4:20** 1 Cor 9:16
21 When they had threatened them further, they let them go (finding no basis on which
to punish them) on account of the people, because they were all glorifying God for what **4:21** Acts 5:26; Matt 9:8
had happened;
22 for the man was more than forty years old on whom this miracle of healing had been
performed.

4:7 The Council asked Peter and John by what power they had healed the man (3:6–7) and by what authority they preached (3:12–26). The actions and words of Peter and John threatened these religious leaders who, for the most part, were more interested in their reputations and positions than in God. Through the help of the Holy Spirit (Mark 13:11), Peter spoke boldly before the Council, actually putting the Council on trial by showing them that the One they had crucified had risen again. Instead of being defensive, the apostles went on the offensive, boldly speaking out for God and presenting the gospel to these leaders.

4:11 The corner stone unites two walls at the corner of a building and holds the building together. Peter said that the Jews rejected Jesus, but now Christ has become the corner stone of the church (Psalm 118:22; Mark 12:10; 1 Peter 2:7). Without him there would be no church, because it wouldn't be able to stand.

4:12 Many people react negatively to the fact that there is no other name than that of Jesus to call on for salvation. Yet this is not something the church decided; it is the specific teaching of Jesus himself (John 14:6). If God designated Jesus to be the Savior of the world, no one else can be his equal. Christians are to be open-minded on many issues, but not on how we are saved from sin. No other religious teacher could die for our sins; no other religious teacher came to earth as God's only Son; no other religious teacher rose from the dead. Our focus should be on Jesus, whom God offered as the way to have an eternal relationship with himself. There is no other name or way!

4:13 Knowing that Peter and John were unschooled, the Council was amazed at what being with Jesus had done for them. A changed life convinces people of Christ's power. One of your greatest testimonies is the difference others see in your life and attitudes since you have believed in Christ.

4:13–18 Although the evidence was overwhelming and irrefutable (changed lives and a healed man), the religious leaders refused to believe in Christ and continued to try to suppress the truth. Don't be surprised if some people reject you and your positive witness for Christ. When minds are closed, even the clearest presentation of the facts can't open them. But don't give up either. Pray for those people and continue to spread the gospel.

4:20 We sometimes may be afraid to share our faith in Christ because people might feel uncomfortable and might reject us. But Peter and John's zeal for the Lord was so strong that they could not keep quiet, even when threatened. If your courage to witness for God has weakened, pray that your boldness may increase. Remember Jesus' promise, "Everyone who confesses Me before men, I will also confess him before My Father who is in heaven" (Matthew 10:32).

23 When they had been released, they went to their own *companions* and reported all
that the chief priests and the elders had said to them.
24 And when they heard *this*, they lifted their voices to God with one accord and said,
"O Lord, it is You who MADE THE HEAVEN AND THE EARTH AND THE SEA, AND ALL
THAT IS IN THEM,
25 who by the Holy Spirit, *through* the mouth of our father David Your servant, said,
'WHY DID THE [8]GENTILES RAGE,
AND THE PEOPLES DEVISE FUTILE THINGS?
26 'THE KINGS OF THE EARTH TOOK THEIR STAND,
AND THE RULERS WERE GATHERED TOGETHER
AGAINST THE LORD AND AGAINST HIS CHRIST.'
27 "For truly in this city there were gathered together against Your holy servant Jesus,
whom You anointed, both Herod and Pontius Pilate, along with the Gentiles and the
peoples of Israel,
28 to do whatever Your hand and Your purpose predestined to occur.
29 "And now, Lord, take note of their threats, and grant that Your bond-servants may
speak Your word with all confidence,
30 while You extend Your hand to heal, and signs and wonders take place through the
name of Your holy servant Jesus."
31 And when they had prayed, the place where they had gathered together was shak-
en, and they were all filled with the Holy Spirit and *began* to speak the word of God with
boldness.

Sharing among Believers

32 And the congregation of those who believed were of one heart and soul; and not
one *of them* claimed that anything belonging to him was his own, but all things were
common property to them.
33 And with great power the apostles were giving testimony to the resurrection of the
Lord Jesus, and abundant grace was upon them all.
34 For there was not a needy person among them, for all who were owners of land or
houses would sell them and bring the proceeds of the sales
35 and lay them at the apostles' feet, and they would be distributed to each as any had
need.
36 Now Joseph, a Levite of Cyprian birth, who was also called Barnabas by the apostles (which translated means Son of Encouragement),

8 Or *nations*

4:24 Ex 20:11; Neh 9:6; Ps 146:6
4:25 Acts 1:16; Ps 2:1
4:26 Ps 2:2; Dan 9:24f; Luke 4:18; Acts 10:38; Heb 1:9
4:27 Acts 3:13; 4:30; Matt 14:1; Luke 23:7-11; Matt 27:2; Mark 15:1; Luke 23:1, 12; John 18:28, 29; Matt 20:19
4:28 Acts 2:23
4:29 Phil 1:14; Acts 4:13, 31; 14:3
4:30 John 4:48; Acts 3:13; 4:27
4:31 Acts 2:1; Acts 2:4; Phil 1:14; Acts 4:13; 14:3
4:32 Acts 2:44
4:33 Acts 1:8; Luke 24:48
4:34 Matt 19:21; Acts 2:45
4:35 Acts 4:37; 5:2; Acts 2:45; 6:1
4:36 1 Cor 9:6; Gal 2:1, 9, 13; Col 4:10; Acts 2:40; 11:23; 13:15; 1 Cor 14:3; 1 Thess 2:3

4:24–30 Notice how the believers prayed. First they praised God; then they told God their specific problem and asked for his help. They did not ask God to remove the problem, but to help them deal with it. This is a model for us to follow when we pray. We may ask God to remove our problems, and he may choose to do so. But we must recognize that often he will leave the problem in place and give us the strength and courage to deal with it.

4:27 This Herod was Herod Antipas, appointed by the Romans to rule over the territory of Galilee. For more information on Herod, see his Profile in Mark 6. Pontius Pilate was the Roman governor over Judea. He bowed to pressure from the crowd and sentenced Jesus to death. For more information on Pilate, see his Profile in Mark 15.

4:28 God is the sovereign Lord of all events who rules history to fulfill his purpose. What his will determines, his power carries out. No army, government, or council can stand in God's way.

4:29–31 Boldness is not reckless impulsiveness. Boldness requires courage to press on through our fears and do what we know is right. How can we be more bold? Like the disciples, we need to pray with others for that courage. To gain boldness, you can (1) pray for the power of the Holy Spirit to give you courage, (2) look for opportunities in your family and neighborhood to talk about Christ, (3) realize that rejection, social discomfort, and embarrassment are not necessarily persecution, and (4) start where you are by being bolder in small ways.

4:32 Differences of opinion are inevitable among human personalities and can actually be helpful, if handled well. But spiritual unity is essential—loyalty, commitment, and love for God and his Word. Without spiritual unity, the church could not survive. Paul wrote the letter of 1 Corinthians to urge the church in Corinth toward greater unity.

4:32 None of these Christians felt that what they had was their own, and so they were able to give and share, eliminating poverty among them. They would not let a brother or sister suffer when others had plenty. How do you feel about your possessions? We should adopt the attitude that everything we have comes from God, and we are only sharing what is already his.

4:32–35 The early church was able to share possessions and property as a result of the unity brought by the Holy Spirit working in and through the believers' lives. This way of living is different from communism because (1) the sharing was voluntary; (2) it didn't involve *all* private property, but only as much as was needed; (3) it was not a membership requirement in order to be a part of the church. The spiritual unity and generosity of these early believers attracted others to them. This organizational structure is not a Biblical command, but it offers vital principles for us to follow.

4:36 Barnabas (Joseph) was a respected leader of the church. He was a Levite by birth, a member of the Jewish tribe that carried out temple duties. But his family had moved to Cyprus, so Barnabas didn't serve in the temple. He traveled with Paul on Paul's first missionary journey (13:1ff). For more information on Barnabas, see his Profile in chapter 13.

37 and who owned a tract of land, sold it and brought the money and laid it at the apostles' feet.

4:37 Acts 4:35; 5:2

Fate of Ananias and Sapphira

5 But a man named Ananias, with his wife Sapphira, sold a piece of property,
2 and kept back *some* of the price for himself, with his wife's full knowledge, and
bringing a portion of it, he laid it at the apostles' feet.
3 But Peter said, "Ananias, why has Satan filled your heart to lie to the Holy Spirit
and to keep back *some* of the price of the land?
4 "While it remained *unsold,* did it not remain your own? And after it was sold, was it
not under your control? Why is it that you have conceived this deed in your heart? You
have not lied to men but to God."
5 And as he heard these words, Ananias fell down and breathed his last; and great
fear came over all who heard of it.
6 The young men got up and covered him up, and after carrying him out, they
buried him.
7 Now there elapsed an interval of about three hours, and his wife came in, not knowing what had happened.
8 And Peter responded to her, "Tell me whether you sold the land for such and such
a price?" And she said, "Yes, that was the price."
9 Then Peter *said* to her, "Why is it that you have agreed together to put the Spirit of
the Lord to the test? Behold, the feet of those who have buried your husband are at the
door, and they will carry you out *as well.*"
10 And immediately she fell at his feet and breathed her last, and the young men came
in and found her dead, and they carried her out and buried her beside her husband.
11 And great fear came over the whole church, and over all who heard of these things.
12 At the hands of the apostles many signs and wonders were taking place among the
people; and they were all with one accord in Solomon's portico.
13 But none of the rest dared to associate with them; however, the people held them
in high esteem.
14 And all the more believers in the Lord, multitudes of men and women, were constantly added to *their number,*
15 to such an extent that they even carried the sick out into the streets and laid them
on cots and pallets, so that when Peter came by at least his shadow might fall on any one
of them.

5:2 Acts 5:3; Acts 4:35, 37

5:3 Matt 4:10; Luke 22:3; John 13:2, 27; Acts 5:4, 9; Acts 5:2

5:4 Acts 5:3, 9

5:5 Ezek 11:13; Acts 5:10; Acts 2:43; 5:11

5:6 John 19:40

5:8 Acts 5:2

5:9 Acts 15:10; Acts 5:3, 4

5:10 Ezek 11:13; Acts 5:5

5:11 Acts 2:43; 5:5

5:12 John 4:48; John 10:23; Acts 3:11

5:13 Acts 2:47; 4:21

5:14 2 Cor 6:15; Acts 2:47; 11:24

5:15 Acts 19:12

5:1ff In Acts 5:1—8:3 we see both internal and external problems facing the early church. Inside, there were dishonesty (5:1–11) and adminstrative headaches (6:1–7). Outside, the church was being pressured by persecution. While church leaders were careful and sensitive in dealing with the internal problems, there was not much they could do to prevent the external pressures. Through it all, the leaders kept their focus on what was most important—spreading the gospel of Jesus Christ.

5:3 Even after the Holy Spirit had come, the believers were not immune to Satan's temptations. Although Satan had been defeated by Christ at the cross, he was still actively trying to make the believers stumble—as he does today (Ephesians 6:12; 1 Peter 5:8). Satan's overthrow is inevitable, but it will not occur until the last days, when Christ returns to judge the world (Revelation 20:10).

5:3ff The sin Ananias and Sapphira committed was not stinginess or holding back part of the money—it was their choice whether or not to sell the land and how much to give. Their sin was lying to God and God's people—saying they gave the whole amount but holding back some for themselves and trying to make themselves appear more generous than they really were. This act was judged harshly because dishonesty, greed, and covetousness are destructive in a church, preventing the Holy Spirit from working effectively. All lying is bad, but when we lie to try to deceive God and his people about our relationship with him, we destroy our testimony about Christ.

5:11 God's judgment on Ananias and Sapphira produced shock and fear among the believers, making them realize how seriously God regards sin in the church.

5:12 Solomon's portico was part of the temple complex built by King Herod the Great in an attempt to strengthen his relationship with the Jews. A portico is an entrance or porch supported by columns. Jesus taught and performed miracles in the temple many times. When the apostles went to the temple, they were undoubtedly in close proximity to the same religious leaders who had conspired to put Jesus to death.

5:13 Although many people greatly respected the apostles, they did not dare join them in the temple or work beside them. Some may have been afraid to face the same kind of persecution the apostles had just faced (4:17), while others may have feared a similar fate as the one that fell on Ananias and Sapphira.

5:14 What makes Christianity attractive? It is easy to be drawn to churches because of programs, good speakers, size, beautiful facilities, or fellowship. People were attracted to the early church by expressions of God's power at work; the generosity, sincerity, honesty, and unity of the members; and the character of the leaders. Have our standards slipped? God wants to add believers to his church, not just newer and better programs or larger and fancier facilities.

5:15 People who passed within Peter's shadow were healed, not by Peter's shadow, but by God's power working through Peter.

5:17 Acts 15:5; Matt 3:7; Acts 4:1

5:18 Acts 4:3

5:19 Matt 1:20, 24; 2:13, 19; 28:2; Luke 1:11; 2:9; Acts 8:26; 10:3; 12:7, 23; 27:23

5:20 John 6:63, 68

5:21 John 8:2; Acts 4:6; Matt 5:22; Acts 5:27, 34, 41

5:22 Matt 26:58; Acts 5:26

5:24 Acts 4:1; 5:26

5:26 Acts 5:24; Acts 5:22; Acts 4:21; 5:13

5:27 Matt 5:22; Acts 5:21, 34, 41

5:28 Acts 4:18; Matt 23:35; 27:25; Acts 2:23, 36; 3:14f; 7:52

5:29 Acts 4:19

5:30 Acts 3:13; Acts 2:24; Acts 10:39; 13:29; Gal 3:13; 1 Pet 2:24

5:31 Acts 2:33; Acts 3:15; Luke 2:11; Luke 24:47; Acts 2:38

16 Also the people from the cities in the vicinity of Jerusalem were coming together,
bringing people who were sick [9]or afflicted with unclean spirits, and they were all being
healed.

Imprisonment and Release

17 But the high priest rose up, along with all his associates (that is the sect of the Sadducees), and they were filled with jealousy.
18 They laid hands on the apostles and put them in a public jail.
19 But during the night an angel of the Lord opened the gates of the prison, and taking them out he said,
20 "Go, stand and speak to the people in the temple the whole message of this Life."
21 Upon hearing *this,* they entered into the temple about daybreak and *began* to teach.
Now when the high priest and his associates came, they called the Council together,
even all the Senate of the sons of Israel, and sent *orders* to the prison house for them to
be brought.
22 But the officers who came did not find them in the prison; and they returned and
reported back,
23 saying, "We found the prison house locked quite securely and the guards standing
at the doors; but when we had opened up, we found no one inside."
24 Now when the captain of the temple *guard* and the chief priests heard these words,
they were greatly perplexed about them as to what would come of this.
25 But someone came and reported to them, "The men whom you put in prison are
standing in the temple and teaching the people!"
26 Then the captain went along with the officers and *proceeded* to bring them *back*
without violence (for they were afraid of the people, that they might be stoned).
27 When they had brought them, they stood them before the Council. The high priest
questioned them,
28 saying, "We gave you strict orders not to continue teaching in this name, and yet,
you have filled Jerusalem with your teaching and intend to bring this man's blood upon
us."
29 But Peter and the apostles answered, "We must obey God rather than men.
30 "The God of our fathers raised up Jesus, whom you had put to death by hanging Him
on a cross.
31 "He is the one whom God exalted to His right hand as a Prince and a Savior, to grant
repentance to Israel, and forgiveness of sins.

9 Lit *and*

5:16 What did these miraculous healings do for the early church? (1) They attracted new believers. (2) They confirmed the truth of the apostles' teaching. (3) They demonstrated that the power of the Messiah who had been crucified and risen was now with his followers.

5:17 The religious leaders were jealous—Peter and the apostles were already commanding more respect than they had ever received. The difference, however, was that the religious leaders demanded respect and reverence for themselves; the apostles' goal was to bring respect and reverence to God. The apostles were respected not because they demanded it, but because they deserved it.

5:17–18 The apostles experienced power to do miracles, great boldness in preaching, and God's presence in their lives, yet they were not free from hatred and persecution. They were arrested, put in jail, beaten, and slandered by community leaders. Faith in God does not make troubles disappear; it makes troubles appear less frightening because it puts them in the right perspective. Don't expect everyone to react favorably when you share something as dynamic as your faith in Christ. Some will be jealous, afraid, or threatened. Expect some negative reactions, and remember that you must be more concerned about serving God than about the reactions of people (see 5:29).

5:21 "All the Senate of the sons of Israel" refers to the entire group, the 70 men of the Council (also called the Sanhedrin). This was going to be no small trial. The religious leaders would do anything to stop these apostles from challenging their authority, threatening their secure position, and exposing their hypocritical motives to the people.

5:21 The temple at daybreak was a busy place. Many people stopped at the temple to pray and worship at sunrise. The apostles were already there, ready to tell them the good news of new life in Jesus Christ.

5:21 Suppose someone threatened to kill you if you didn't stop talking about God. You might be tempted to keep quiet. But after being threatened by powerful leaders, arrested, jailed, and miraculously released, the apostles went back to preaching. This was nothing less than God's power working through them (4:13)! When we are convinced of the truth of Christ's resurrection and have experienced the presence and power of his Holy Spirit, we can have the confidence to speak out for Christ.

5:29 The apostles knew their priorities. While we should try to live at peace with everyone (Romans 12:18), conflict with the world and its authorities is sometimes inevitable for a Christian (John 15:18). There will be situations where you cannot obey both God and man. Then you must obey God and trust his Word. Let Jesus' words in Luke 6:22 encourage you: "Blessed are you when men hate you, and ostracize you, and insult you, and scorn your name as evil, for the sake of the Son of Man."

32 "And we are witnesses [10]of these things; and *so is* the Holy Spirit, whom God has
given to those who obey Him."

Gamaliel's Counsel

33 But when they heard this, they were cut to the quick and intended to kill them.
34 But a Pharisee named Gamaliel, a teacher of the Law, respected by all the people,
stood up in the Council and gave orders to put the men outside for a short time.
35 And he said to them, "Men of Israel, take care what you propose to do with these
men.
36 "For some time ago Theudas rose up, claiming to be somebody, and a group of about
four hundred men joined up with him. But he was killed, and all who followed him were
dispersed and came to nothing.
37 "After this man, Judas of Galilee rose up in the days of the census and drew away
some people after him; he too perished, and all those who followed him were scattered.
38 "So in the present case, I say to you, stay away from these men and let them alone,
for if this plan or action is of men, it will be overthrown;
39 but if it is of God, you will not be able to overthrow them; or else you may even be
found fighting against God."
40 They took his advice; and after calling the apostles in, they flogged them and ordered them not to speak in the name of Jesus, and *then* released them.
41 So they went on their way from the presence of the Council, rejoicing that they had
been considered worthy to suffer shame for *His* name.
42 And every day, in the temple and from house to house, they kept right on teaching
and preaching Jesus *as* the Christ.

Choosing of the Seven

6 Now at this time while the disciples were increasing *in number,* a complaint arose on
the part of the [11]Hellenistic *Jews* against the *native* Hebrews, because their widows
were being overlooked in the daily serving *of food.*

5:32 Luke 24:48; John 15:26; Acts 15:28; Rom 8:16; Heb 2:4
5:33 Acts 2:37; 7:54
5:34 Acts 22:3; Luke 2:46; 5:17; Acts 5:21
5:36 Acts 8:9; Gal 2:6; 6:3
5:37 Luke 2:2
5:38 Mark 11:30
5:39 Prov 21:30; Acts 11:17
5:40 Matt 10:17
5:41 Acts 5:21; 1 Pet 4:14, 16; John 15:21
5:42 Acts 2:46; Acts 8:35; 11:20; 17:18; Gal 1:16
6:1 Acts 11:26; Acts 2:47; 6:7; Acts 9:29; 11:20; 2 Cor 11:22; Phil 3:5; Acts 9:39, 41; 1 Tim 5:3; Acts 4:35; 11:29

10 One early ms adds *in Him* **11** Jews who adopted the Gr language and much of Gr culture through acculturation

---

5:34 The Pharisees were the other major party in the Jewish Council with the Sadducees (5:17). The Pharisees were the strict keepers of the law—not only God's law, but hundreds of other rules they had added to God's law. They were careful about outward purity, but many had hearts full of impure motives. Jesus confronted the Pharisees often during his ministry on earth.

5:34 Gamaliel was an unexpected ally for the apostles, although he probably did not support their teachings. He was a distinguished member of the Council and a teacher. While Gamaliel may have saved the apostles' lives, his real intentions probably were to prevent a division in the Council and to avoid arousing the Romans. The apostles were popular among the people, and killing them might start a riot. Gamaliel's advice to the Council gave the apostles some breathing room to continue their work. The Council decided to wait, hoping that this would all fade away harmlessly. They couldn't have been more wrong. Ironically, Paul, later one of the greatest apostles, was one of Gamaliel's students (22:3).

5:39 Gamaliel presented some sound advice about reacting to religious movements. Unless disciples in these groups endorse obviously dangerous doctrines or practices, it is often wiser to be tolerant rather than repressive. Sometimes only time will tell if they are merely the work of humans or if God is trying to say something through them. The next time a group promotes differing religious ideas, consider Gamaliel's advice, just in case you "be found fighting against God."

5:40–42 Peter and John were warned repeatedly not to preach, but they continued in spite of the threats. We, too, should live as Christ has asked us to, sharing our faith no matter what the cost. We may not be beaten or thrown in jail, but we may be ridiculed, ostracized, or slandered. To what extent are you willing to suffer for the sake of sharing the gospel with others?

5:41 Have you ever thought of persecution as a blessing, as something worth rejoicing about? This beating suffered by Peter and John was the first time any of the apostles had been physically abused for their faith. These men knew how Jesus had suffered, and they praised God that he had allowed them to be persecuted like their Lord. If you are mocked or persecuted for your faith, it isn't because you're doing something wrong, but because God has counted you "worthy to suffer shame for His name."

5:42 Home Bible studies are not new. As the believers needed to grow in their new faith, home Bible studies met their needs, as well as serving as a means to introduce new people to the Christian faith. During later times of persecution, meeting in homes became the primary method of passing on Bible knowledge. Christians throughout the world still use this approach when under persecution and as a way to build up believers.

6:1 When we read the descriptions of the early church—the miracles, the sharing and generosity, the fellowship—we may wish we could have been a part of this "perfect" church. In reality, the early church had problems just as we do today. No church has ever been or will ever be perfect until Christ and his followers are united at his second coming. All churches have problems. If your church's shortcomings distress you, ask yourself: "Would a perfect church allow me to be a member?" Then do what you can to make your church better. A church does not have to be perfect to be faithful.

6:1ff Another internal problem developed in the early church. The Hebraic Jews, native Jewish Christians, spoke Aramaic, a Semitic language. The Hellenistic Jews, Greek-speaking Christians, were probably Jews from other lands who were converted at Pentecost. The Greek-speaking Christians complained that their widows were being unfairly treated. This favoritism was probably not intentional, but was more likely caused by the language barrier. To correct the situation, the apostles put seven respected Greek-speaking men in charge of the food distribution program. This solved the problem and allowed the apostles to keep their focus on teaching and preaching the Good News about Jesus.

6:3 John 21:23; Acts 1:15; Acts 2:4
6:4 Acts 1:14
6:5 Acts 6:3; 11:24; Acts 8:5ff; 21:8; Matt 23:15; Acts 11:19
6:6 Acts 1:24; Num 8:10; 27:18; Deut 34:9; Mark 5:23; Acts 8:17ff; 9:17; 13:3; 19:6; 1 Tim 4:14; 2 Tim 1:6; Heb 6:2
6:7 Acts 12:24; 19:20; Acts 13:8; 14:22; Gal 1:23; 6:10; Jude 3, 20
6:9 Matt 27:32; Gal 1:21; Acts 16:6; 19:10; 21:27; 24:18
6:12 Luke 20:1; Acts 4:1; Matt 5:22
6:13 Matt 26:59-61; Acts 7:58; Matt 24:15; Acts 21:28; 25:8
6:14 Matt 26:61; Acts 15:1; 21:21; 26:3; 28:17
6:15 Matt 5:22

2 So the twelve summoned the congregation of the disciples and said, "It is not desirable for us to neglect the word of God in order to serve tables.

3 "Therefore, brethren, select from among you seven men of good reputation, full of the Spirit and of wisdom, whom we may put in charge of this task.

4 "But we will devote ourselves to prayer and to the ministry of the word."

5 The statement found approval with the whole congregation; and they chose Stephen, a man full of faith and of the Holy Spirit, and Philip, Prochorus, Nicanor, Timon, Parmenas and Nicolas, a [12]proselyte from Antioch.

6 And these they brought before the apostles; and after praying, they laid their hands on them.

7 The word of God kept on spreading; and the number of the disciples continued to increase greatly in Jerusalem, and a great many of the priests were becoming obedient to the faith.

8 And Stephen, full of grace and power, was performing great wonders and signs among the people.

9 But some men from what was called the Synagogue of the Freedmen, *including* both Cyrenians and Alexandrians, and some from Cilicia and Asia, rose up and argued with Stephen.

10 But they were unable to cope with the wisdom and the Spirit with which he was speaking.

11 Then they secretly induced men to say, "We have heard him speak blasphemous words against Moses and *against* God."

12 And they stirred up the people, the elders and the scribes, and they came up to him and dragged him away and brought him before the Council.

13 They put forward false witnesses who said, "This man incessantly speaks against this holy place and the Law;

14 for we have heard him say that this Nazarene, Jesus, will destroy this place and alter the customs which Moses handed down to us."

15 And fixing their gaze on him, all who were sitting in the Council saw his face like the face of an angel.

12 I.e. a Gentile convert to Judaism

6:2 "The twelve" are the 11 original disciples and Matthias, who was chosen to replace Judas Iscariot (1:26).

6:2–4 As the early church increased in size, so did its needs. One great need was to organize the distribution of food to the poor. The apostles needed to focus on preaching, so they chose others to administer the food program. Each person has a vital part to play in the life of the church (see 1 Corinthians 12). If you are in a position of leadership and find yourself overwhelmed by responsibilities, determine *your* God-given abilities and priorities and then find others to help. If you are not in leadership, you have gifts that can be used by God in various areas of the church's ministry. Offer these gifts in service to him.

6:3 This administrative task was not taken lightly. Notice the requirements for the men who were to handle the food program: full of the Holy Spirit and wisdom. People who carry heavy responsibilities and work closely with others should have these qualities. We must look for spiritually mature and wise men and women to lead our churches.

6:4 The apostles' priorities were correct. The ministry of the Word should never be neglected because of administrative burdens. Pastors should not try, or be expected to try, to do everything. Instead, the work of the church should be spread out among its members.

6:6 Spiritual leadership is serious business and must not be taken lightly by the church or its leaders. In the early church, the chosen men were ordained or commissioned (set apart by prayer and laying on of hands) by the apostles. Laying hands on someone, an ancient Jewish practice, was a way to set a person apart for special service (see Numbers 27:23; Deuteronomy 34:9).

6:7 Jesus had told the apostles that they were to witness first in Jerusalem (1:8). In a short time, their message had infiltrated the entire city and all levels of society. Even some priests were being converted, an obvious violation of the wishes of the Council that would endanger their position.

6:7 The word of God spread like ripples on a pond where, from a single center, each wave touches the next, spreading wider and farther. The gospel still spreads this way today. You don't have to change the world single-handedly—it is enough just to be part of the wave, touching those around you, who in turn will touch others until all have felt the movement. Don't ever feel that your part is insignificant or unimportant.

6:8–10 The most important prerequisite for any kind of Christian service is to be filled with faith and the power of the Holy Spirit. By the Spirit's power, Stephen was a wise servant (6:3), miracle worker (6:8), and evangelist (6:10). By the Spirit's power, you can exercise the gifts God has given you.

6:9 The Freedmen was a group of Jewish slaves who had been freed by Rome and had formed their own synagogue in Jerusalem.

6:11 These men lied about Stephen, causing him to be arrested and brought before the Jewish Council. The Sadducees, the dominant party in the Council, accepted and studied only the writings of Moses (Genesis through Deuteronomy). In their view, to speak blasphemy against Moses was a crime. But from Stephen's speech (chapter 7), we learn that this accusation was false. Stephen based his review of Israel's history on Moses' writings.

6:14 When Stephen was brought before the Council of religious leaders, the accusation against him was the same that the religious leaders had used against Jesus (Matthew 26:59–61). The group falsely accused Stephen of wanting to change Moses' customs, because they knew that the Sadducees, who controlled the Council, believed *only* in Moses' laws.

Stephen's Defense

7 The high priest said, "Are these things so?"
2 And he said, "Hear me, brethren and fathers! The God of glory appeared to our
father Abraham when he was in Mesopotamia, before he lived in Haran,
3 and said to him, 'LEAVE YOUR COUNTRY AND YOUR RELATIVES, AND COME INTO
THE LAND THAT I WILL SHOW YOU.'
4 "Then he left the land of the Chaldeans and settled in Haran. From there, after his
father died, *God* had him move to this country in which you are now living.
5 "But He gave him no inheritance in it, not even a foot of ground, and *yet,* even when
he had no child, He promised that HE WOULD GIVE IT TO HIM AS A POSSESSION, AND TO
HIS DESCENDANTS AFTER HIM.
6 "But God spoke to this effect, that his DESCENDANTS WOULD BE ALIENS IN A FOR-
EIGN LAND, AND THAT THEY WOULD BE ENSLAVED AND MISTREATED FOR FOUR HUN-
DRED YEARS.
7 " 'AND WHATEVER NATION TO WHICH THEY WILL BE IN BONDAGE I MYSELF WILL
JUDGE,' said God, 'AND AFTER THAT THEY WILL COME OUT AND [13]SERVE ME IN THIS
PLACE.'
8 "And He gave him the covenant of circumcision; and so *Abraham* became the father
of Isaac, and circumcised him on the eighth day; and Isaac *became the father of* Jacob,
and Jacob *of* the twelve patriarchs.
9 "The patriarchs became jealous of Joseph and sold him into Egypt. *Yet* God was with
him,
10 and rescued him from all his afflictions, and granted him favor and wisdom in the
sight of Pharaoh, king of Egypt, and he made him governor over Egypt and all his household.
11 "Now a famine came over all Egypt and Canaan, and great affliction *with it,* and our
fathers could find no food.
12 "But when Jacob heard that there was grain in Egypt, he sent our fathers *there* the
first time.
13 "On the second *visit* Joseph made himself known to his brothers, and Joseph's family
was disclosed to Pharaoh.
14 "Then Joseph sent *word* and invited Jacob his father and all his relatives to come to
him, seventy-five persons *in all.*
15 "And Jacob went down to Egypt and *there* he and our fathers died.
16 "*From there* they were removed to Shechem and laid in the tomb which Abraham
had purchased for a sum of money from the sons of Hamor in Shechem.
17 "But as the time of the promise was approaching which God had assured to Abraham, the people increased and multiplied in Egypt,
18 until THERE AROSE ANOTHER KING OVER EGYPT WHO KNEW NOTHING ABOUT
JOSEPH.

13 Or *worship*

7:2 Acts 22:1; Ps 29:3; 1 Cor 2:8; Gen 11:31; 15:7
7:3 Gen 12:1
7:4 Gen 11:31; 15:7; Gen 12:4, 5
7:5 Gen 12:7; 13:15; 15:18; 17:8
7:6 Gen 15:13f
7:7 Ex 3:12
7:8 Gen 17:10ff Gen 21:2-4; Gen 25:26; Gen 29:31ff; 30:5ff; 35:23ff; Acts 2:29
7:9 Gen 37:11, 28; 39:2, 21f; 45:4
7:10 Gen 39:21; 41:40-46; Ps 105:21
7:11 Gen 41:54f; 42:5
7:12 Gen 42:2
7:13 Gen 45:1-4; Gen 45:16
7:14 Gen 45:9, 10, 17, 18; Gen 46:26f; Ex 1:5; Deut 10:22; Acts 2:41
7:15 Gen 46:1-7; 49:33; Ex 1:6
7:16 Gen 23:16; 33:19; 50:13; Josh 24:32
7:17 Gen 15:13; Ex 1:7f

7:1 This high priest was probably Caiaphas, the same man who had earlier questioned and condemned Jesus (John 18:24).

7:2ff Stephen launched into a long speech about Israel's relationship with God. From Old Testament history he showed that the Jews had constantly rejected God's message and his prophets, and that this Council had rejected the Messiah, God's Son. He made three main points: (1) Israel's history is the history of God's acts in the world; (2) people worshiped God long before there was a temple, because God does not live in a temple; (3) Jesus' death was just one more example of Israel's rebellion against and rejection of God.

7:2ff Stephen didn't really defend himself. Instead, he took the offensive, seizing the opportunity to summarize his teaching about Jesus. Stephen was accusing these religious leaders of failing to obey God's laws—the laws they prided themselves in following so meticulously. This was the same accusation that Jesus had leveled against them. When we witness for Christ, we don't need to be on the defensive. Instead we can simply share our faith.

7:8 Circumcision was a sign of the promise or covenant made between God, Abraham, and the entire nation of Israel (Genesis 17:9–13). Because Stephen's speech summarized Israel's history, he summarized how this covenant fared during that time. Stephen pointed out that God always had kept his side of the promise, but Israel had failed again and again to uphold its end. Although the Jews in Stephen's day still circumcised their baby boys, they failed to obey God. The people's hearts were far from God. Their lack of faith and lack of obedience meant that they had failed to keep their part of the covenant.

7:17 Stephen's review of Jewish history gives a clear testimony of God's faithfulness and sovereignty. Despite the continued failures of his chosen people and the swirling world events, God was working out his plan. When faced by a confusing array of circumstances, remember that: (1) God is in control—nothing surprises him; (2) this world is not all there is—it will pass away, but God is eternal; (3) God is just, and he will make things right—punishing the wicked and rewarding the faithful; (4) God wants to use you (like Joseph, Moses, and Stephen) to make a difference in the world.

7:19 Ex 1:10f, 16ff; Ex 1:22
19 "It was he who took shrewd advantage of our race and mistreated our fathers so that
they would expose their infants and they would not survive.
7:20 Ex 2:2; Heb 11:23
20 "It was at this time that Moses was born; and he was lovely in the sight of God, and
he was nurtured three months in his father's home.
7:21 Ex 2:5f, 10
21 "And after he had been set outside, Pharaoh's daughter took him away and nurtured
him as her own son.
7:22 1 Kin 4:30; Is 19:11
22 "Moses was educated in all the learning of the Egyptians, and he was a man of power
in words and deeds.
7:23 Ex 2:11f; Heb 11:24-26
23 "But when he was approaching the age of forty, it entered his mind to visit his brethren, the sons of Israel.
24 "And when he saw one *of them* being treated unjustly, he defended him and took
vengeance for the oppressed by striking down the Egyptian.
25 "And he supposed that his brethren understood that God was granting them deliverance through him, but they did not understand.
7:26 Ex 2:13f
26 "On the following day he appeared to them as they were fighting together, and he
tried to reconcile them in peace, saying, 'Men, you are brethren, why do you injure one
another?'

STEPHEN

Around the world, the gospel has most often taken root in places prepared by the blood of martyrs. Before people can *give* their lives for the gospel, however, they must first *live* their lives for the gospel. One way God trains his servants is to place them in insignificant positions. Their desire to serve Christ is translated into the reality of serving others. Stephen was an effective administrator and messenger before becoming a martyr.

Stephen was named among the managers of food distribution in the early church. Long before violent persecution broke out against Christians, there was already social ostracism. Jews who accepted Jesus as Messiah were usually cut off from their families. As a result, the believers depended on each other for support. The sharing of homes, food, and resources was both a practical and necessary mark of the early church. Eventually, the number of believers made it necessary to organize the sharing. People were being overlooked. There were complaints. Those chosen to help manage were chosen for their integrity, wisdom, and sensitivity to God.

Stephen, besides being a good administrator, was also a powerful speaker. When confronted in the temple by various antagonistic groups, Stephen's logic in responding was convincing. This is clear from the defense he made before the Council. He presented a summary of the Jews' own history and made powerful applications that stung his listeners. During his defense Stephen must have known he was speaking his own death sentence. Members of the Council could not stand to have their evil motives exposed. They stoned him to death while he prayed for their forgiveness. His final words show how much like Jesus he had become in a short time. His death had a lasting impact on young Saul (Paul) of Tarsus, who would move from being a violent persecutor of Christians to being one of the greatest champions of the gospel the church has known.

Stephen's life is a continual challenge to all Christians. Because he was the first to die for the faith, his sacrifice raises questions: How many risks do we take in being Jesus' followers? Would we be willing to die for him? Are we really willing to live for him?

Strengths and accomplishments:
- One of seven leaders chosen to supervise food distribution to the needy in the early church
- Known for his spiritual qualities of faith, wisdom, grace, and power, and for the Spirit's presence in his life
- Outstanding leader, teacher, and debater
- First to give his life for the gospel

Lessons from his life:
- Striving for excellence in small assignments prepares one for greater responsibilities
- Real understanding of God always leads to practical and compassionate actions toward people

Vital statistics:
- Church responsibilities: Deacon—distributing food to the needy
- Contemporaries: Paul, Caiaphas, Gamaliel, the apostles

Key verses:
"They went on stoning Stephen as he called on the Lord and said, 'Lord Jesus, receive my spirit!' Then falling on his knees, he cried out with a loud voice, 'Lord, do not hold this sin against them!' Having said this, he fell asleep" (Acts 7:59–60).

Stephen's story is told in Acts 6:3—8:2. He is also mentioned in Acts 11:19; 22:20.

27 "But the one who was injuring his neighbor pushed him away, saying, 'WHO MADE YOU A RULER AND JUDGE OVER US?
28 'YOU DO NOT MEAN TO KILL ME AS YOU KILLED THE EGYPTIAN YESTERDAY, DO YOU?'
29 "At this remark, MOSES FLED AND BECAME AN ALIEN IN THE LAND OF MIDIAN, where he became the father of two sons.
30 "After forty years had passed, AN ANGEL APPEARED TO HIM IN THE WILDERNESS OF MOUNT Sinai, IN THE FLAME OF A BURNING THORN BUSH.
31 "When Moses saw it, he marveled at the sight; and as he approached to look *more* closely, there came the voice of the Lord:
32 'I AM THE GOD OF YOUR FATHERS, THE GOD OF ABRAHAM AND ISAAC AND JACOB.' Moses shook with fear and would not venture to look.
33 "BUT THE LORD SAID TO HIM, 'TAKE OFF THE SANDALS FROM YOUR FEET, FOR THE PLACE ON WHICH YOU ARE STANDING IS HOLY GROUND.
34 'I HAVE CERTAINLY SEEN THE OPPRESSION OF MY PEOPLE IN EGYPT AND HAVE HEARD THEIR GROANS, AND I HAVE COME DOWN TO RESCUE THEM; COME NOW, AND I WILL SEND YOU TO EGYPT.'
35 "This Moses whom they disowned, saying, 'WHO MADE YOU A RULER AND A JUDGE?' is the one whom God sent *to be* both a ruler and a deliverer with the help of the angel who appeared to him in the thorn bush.
36 "This man led them out, performing wonders and signs in the land of Egypt and in the Red Sea and in the wilderness for forty years.
37 "This is the Moses who said to the sons of Israel, 'GOD WILL RAISE UP FOR YOU A PROPHET LIKE ME FROM YOUR BRETHREN.'
38 "This is the one who was in the congregation in the wilderness together with the angel who was speaking to him on Mount Sinai, and *who was* with our fathers; and he received living oracles to pass on to you.
39 "Our fathers were unwilling to be obedient to him, but repudiated him and in their hearts turned back to Egypt,
40 SAYING TO AARON, 'MAKE FOR US GODS WHO WILL GO BEFORE US; FOR THIS MOSES WHO LED US OUT OF THE LAND OF EGYPT—WE DO NOT KNOW WHAT HAPPENED TO HIM.'
41 "At that time they made a calf and brought a sacrifice to the idol, and were rejoicing in the works of their hands.
42 "But God turned away and delivered them up to serve the host of heaven; as it is written in the book of the prophets, 'IT WAS NOT TO ME THAT YOU OFFERED VICTIMS AND SACRIFICES FORTY YEARS IN THE WILDERNESS, WAS IT, O HOUSE OF ISRAEL?
43 'YOU ALSO TOOK ALONG THE TABERNACLE OF MOLOCH AND THE STAR OF THE GOD ROMPHA, THE IMAGES WHICH YOU MADE TO WORSHIP. I ALSO WILL REMOVE YOU BEYOND BABYLON.'
44 "Our fathers had the tabernacle of testimony in the wilderness, just as He who spoke to Moses directed *him* to make it according to the pattern which he had seen.
45 "And having received it in their turn, our fathers brought it in with Joshua upon dispossessing the nations whom God drove out before our fathers, until the time of David.

7:27 Ex 2:14; Acts 7:35
7:28 Ex 2:14
7:29 Ex 2:15, 22; Ex 18:3, 4
7:30 Ex 3:1f; Is 63:9
7:32 Ex 3:6; Matt 22:32
7:33 Ex 3:5; Josh 5:15
7:34 Ex 3:7f; Ex 3:10
7:35 Ex 2:14; Acts 7:27
7:36 Ex 12:41; 33:1; Heb 8:9; Ex 7:3; 14:21; John 4:48; Ex 16:35; Num 14:33; Ps 95:8-10; Acts 7:42; 13:18; Heb 3:8f
7:37 Deut 18:15, 18; Acts 3:22
7:38 Ex 19:17; Acts 7:53; Deut 32:47; Heb 4:12; Rom 3:2; Heb 5:12; 1 Pet 4:11
7:39 Num 14:3f
7:40 Ex 32:1, 23
7:41 Ex 32:4, 6; Rev 9:20
7:42 Josh 24:20; Is 63:10; Jer 19:13; Ezek 20:39; Amos 5:25; Acts 7:36
7:43 Amos 5:26, 27
7:44 Ex 25:8, 9; 38:21; Ex 25:40
7:45 Deut 32:49; Josh 3:14ff; 18:1; 23:9; 24:18; Ps 44:2f

7:37 The Jews originally thought this "prophet" was Joshua. But Moses was prophesying about the coming Messiah (Deuteronomy 18:15). Peter also quoted this verse in referring to the Messiah (3:22).

7:38 Stephen used the word *ekklesia* (translated "congregation") to describe the people of God in the wilderness. This word means "called out ones" and was used by the first-century Christians to describe their own community. Stephen's point was that the giving of the law through Moses to the Jews was the sign of the covenant. By *obedience,* then, would they continue to be God's covenant people. But because they disobeyed (7:39), they broke the covenant and forfeited their right to be the chosen people.

7:38 From Galatians 3:19 and Hebrews 2:2, it appears that God had given the Law to Moses through angels. Exodus 31:18 says God wrote the Ten Commandments himself ("written by the finger of God"). Apparently God used angelic messengers as mediators to deliver his Law to Moses.

7:42 The *host of heaven* refers to their practice of worshiping deities associated with stars and planets.

7:43 Here Stephen gave more details of the idolatry referred to in 7:40. These were idols worshiped by Israel during their wilderness wanderings (Exodus 32:4). Moloch was the god associated with child sacrifice, and Rompha was an Egyptian god. Amos also names Assyrian deities worshiped by Israel (Amos 5:25–27).

7:44–50 Stephen had been accused of speaking against the temple (6:13). Although he recognized the importance of the temple, he knew that it was not more important than God. God is not limited; he doesn't live only in a house of worship, but wherever hearts of faith are open to receive him (Isaiah 66:1–2). Solomon knew this when he prayed at the dedication of the temple (2 Chronicles 6:18). God wants to live in us. Is he living in you?

7:46 2 Sam 7:8ff; Ps 132:1-5; Acts 13:22; 2 Sam 7:1-16; 1 Chr 17:1-14
7:47 1 Kin 6:1-38; 8:20; 2 Chr 3:1-17
7:49 Is 66:1; Matt 5:34f
7:50 Is 66:2
7:51 Ex 32:9; 33:3, 5; Lev 26:41; Num 27:14; Is 63:10
7:52 2 Chr 36:15f; Matt 5:12; 23:31, 37; Acts 3:14; 22:14; 1 John 2:1; Acts 3:14; 5:28
7:53 Deut 33:2; Gal 3:19; Heb 2:2
7:54 Acts 5:33
7:55 Acts 2:4; John 11:41; Mark 16:19
7:56 John 1:51; Matt 8:20
7:58 Acts 6:13; Acts 22:20; Acts 8:1; 26:10
7:59 Acts 9:14, 21; 22:16; Rom 10:12-14; 1 Cor 1:2; 2 Tim 2:22

46 "*David* found favor in God's sight, and asked that he might find a dwelling place for
the [14]God of Jacob.
47 "But it was Solomon who built a house for Him.
48 "However, the Most High does not dwell in *houses* made by *human* hands; as the
prophet says:
49 'HEAVEN IS MY THRONE,
AND EARTH IS THE FOOTSTOOL OF MY FEET;
WHAT KIND OF HOUSE WILL YOU BUILD FOR ME?' says the Lord,
'OR WHAT PLACE IS THERE FOR MY REPOSE?
50 'WAS IT NOT MY HAND WHICH MADE ALL THESE THINGS?'
51 "You men who are stiff-necked and uncircumcised in heart and ears are always resisting the Holy Spirit; you are doing just as your fathers did.
52 "Which one of the prophets did your fathers not persecute? They killed those who
had previously announced the coming of the Righteous One, whose betrayers and murderers you have now become;
53 you who received the law as ordained by angels, and *yet* did not keep it."

Stephen Put to Death

54 Now when they heard this, they were cut to the quick, and they *began* gnashing their
teeth at him.
55 But being full of the Holy Spirit, he gazed intently into heaven and saw the glory of
God, and Jesus standing at the right hand of God;
56 and he said, "Behold, I see the heavens opened up and the Son of Man standing at
the right hand of God."
57 But they cried out with a loud voice, and covered their ears and rushed at him with
one impulse.
58 When they had driven him out of the city, they *began* stoning *him;* and the witnesses
laid aside their robes at the feet of a young man named Saul.
59 They went on stoning Stephen as he called on *the Lord* and said, "Lord Jesus, receive my spirit!"

14 The earliest mss read *house* instead of *God;* the Septuagint reads *God*

THE EFFECTS OF STEPHEN'S DEATH

Stephen's death was not in vain. Below are some of the events that were by-products (either directly or indirectly) of the persecution that began with Stephen's martyrdom.

1. Philip's evangelistic tour (Acts 8:4–40)
2. Paul's (Saul's) conversion (Acts 9:1–30)
3. Peter's missionary tour (Acts 9:32—11:18)
4. The church in Antioch in Syria founded (Acts 11:19–26)

7:52 Indeed many prophets were persecuted and killed: Uriah (Jeremiah 26:20–23); Jeremiah (Jeremiah 38:1–6); Isaiah (tradition says he was killed by King Manasseh; see 2 Kings 21:16); Amos (Amos 7:10–13); Zechariah (not the author of the Bible book, but the son of Jehoiada the priest, 2 Chronicles 24:20–22); Elijah (1 Kings 19:1–2). Jesus also told a parable about how the Jews had constantly rejected God's messages and persecuted his messengers (Luke 20:9–19). The Righteous One refers to the Messiah.

7:55–58 Stephen saw the glory of God, and Jesus the Messiah standing at God's right hand. Stephen's words are similar to Jesus' words spoken before the Council (Matthew 26:64; Mark 14:62; Luke 22:69). Stephen's vision supported Jesus' claim and angered the Jewish leaders who had condemned Jesus to death for blasphemy. They would not tolerate Stephen's words, so they dragged him out and killed him. People may not kill us for witnessing about Christ, but they will let us know they don't want to hear the truth and will often try to silence us. Keep honoring God in your conduct and words; though many may turn against you and your message, some will follow Christ. Remember, Stephen's death made a profound impact on Paul, who later became the world's greatest missionary. Even those who oppose you now may later turn to Christ.

7:58 Saul is also called Paul (see 13:9), the great missionary who wrote many of the letters in the New Testament. Saul was his Hebrew name; Paul, his Greek name, was used as he began his ministry to the Gentiles. When Luke introduces him, Paul was hating and persecuting Jesus' followers. This is a great contrast to the Paul about whom Luke will write for most of the rest of the book of Acts—a devoted follower of Christ and a gifted gospel preacher. Paul was uniquely qualified to talk to the Jews about Jesus because he had once persecuted those who believed in Jesus, and he understood how the opposition felt. Paul is a powerful example of how no one is impossible for God to reach and change.

7:59 The penalty for blasphemy, speaking irreverently about God, was death by stoning (Leviticus 24:14). The religious leaders, who were furious, had Stephen stoned without a trial. They did not understand that Stephen's words were true, because they were not seeking the truth. They only wanted support for their own views.

60 Then falling on his knees, he cried out with a loud voice, "Lord, do not hold this sin
against them!" Having said this, he fell asleep.

7:60 Luke 22:41; Matt 5:44; Luke 23:34; Dan 12:2; Matt 27:52; John 11:11f; Acts 13:36; 1 Cor 15:6, 18, 20; 1 Thess 4:13ff; 2 Pet 3:4

Saul Persecutes the Church

8 Saul was in hearty agreement with putting him to death.

2. Expansion of the church

And on that day a great persecution began against the church in Jerusalem, and they
were all scattered throughout the regions of Judea and Samaria, except the apostles.
2 *Some* devout men buried Stephen, and made loud lamentation over him.
3 But Saul *began* ravaging the church, entering house after house, and dragging off
men and women, he would put them in prison.

8:1 Acts 7:58; 22:20; 26:10; Acts 9:31; Acts 8:4; 11:19; Acts 1:8; 8:5, 14; 9:31

8:3 Acts 9:1, 13, 21; 22:4, 19; 26:10f; 1 Cor 15:9; Gal 1:13; Phil 3:6; 1 Tim 1:13; James 2:6

Philip in Samaria

4 Therefore, those who had been scattered went about preaching the word.
5 Philip went down to the city of Samaria and *began* proclaiming Christ to them.
6 The crowds with one accord were giving attention to what was said by Philip, as they
heard and saw the signs which he was performing.
7 For *in the case of* many who had unclean spirits, they were coming out *of them* shouting with a loud voice; and many who had been paralyzed and lame were healed.
8 So there was much rejoicing in that city.
9 Now there was a man named Simon, who formerly was practicing magic in the city
and astonishing the people of Samaria, claiming to be someone great;

8:5 Acts 6:5; 8:26, 30

8:7 Mark 16:17; Matt 4:24

8:8 John 4:40-42; Acts 8:39

8:9 Acts 8:11; 13:6; Acts 5:36

PHILIP'S MINISTRY
To escape persecution in Jerusalem, Philip fled to Samaria, where he continued preaching the gospel. While he was there, an angel commanded him to meet an Ethiopian official on the road between Jerusalem and Gaza. The man became a believer before continuing on to Ethiopia. Philip then went from Azotus to Caesarea.

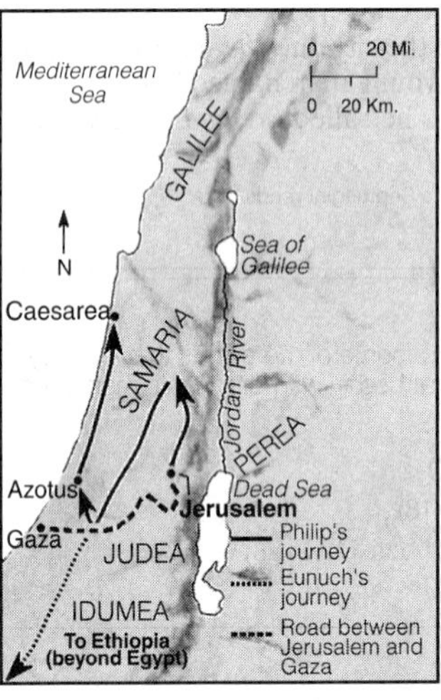

7:60 As Stephen died, he spoke words very similar to Jesus' words on the cross (Luke 23:34). The early believers were glad to suffer as Jesus had suffered because that meant they were counted worthy (5:41). Stephen was ready to suffer like Jesus, even to the point of asking forgiveness for his murderers. Such a forgiving response comes only from the Holy Spirit. The Spirit can also help us respond as Stephen did with love for our enemies (Luke 6:27). How would you react if someone hurt you because of what you believed?

8:1–4 Persecution forced the Christians out of Jerusalem and into Judea and Samaria—thus fulfilling the second part of Jesus' command (see 1:8). The persecution helped spread the gospel. God would bring great results from the believers' suffering.

8:4 Persecution forced the believers out of their homes in Jerusalem, and along with them went the gospel. Sometimes we have to become uncomfortable before we'll move. We may not want to experience it, but discomfort may be the best thing for us because God may be working through our hurts. When you are tempted to complain about uncomfortable or painful circumstances, stop and ask if God might be preparing you for a special task.

8:5 This is not the apostle Philip (see John 1:43–44), but a Greek-speaking Jew, "full of the Spirit and of wisdom" (6:3), who was one of the seven deacons chosen to help with the food distribution program in the church (6:5).

8:5 Israel had been divided into three main regions—Galilee in the north, Samaria in the middle, and Judea in the south. The city of Samaria (in the region of Samaria) had been the capital of the northern kingdom of Israel in the days of the divided kingdom, before it was conquered by Assyria in 722 B.C. During that war, the Assyrian king took many captives, leaving only the poorest people in the land and resettling it with foreigners. These foreigners intermarried with the Jews who were left, and the mixed race became known as Samaritans. The Samaritans were considered half-breeds by the "pure" Jews in the southern kingdom of Judah, and there was intense hatred between the two groups. But Jesus himself went into Samaria (John 4), and he commanded his followers to spread the gospel there (1:8).

8:7 Jesus encountered and drove out many unclean spirits (demons) during his ministry on earth. Demons, or unclean spirits, are ruled by Satan. Most scholars believe that they are fallen angels who joined Satan in his rebellion against God, and who can cause a person to be mute, deaf, blind, or insane. Demons also tempt people to sin. Although they can be powerful, they are not able to read our minds and cannot be everywhere at once. Demons are real and active, but Jesus has authority over them; and he gave this authority to his followers. Although Satan is allowed to work in our world, God is in complete control. He can drive out demons and end their destructive work in people's lives. Eventually Satan and his demons will be thrown into the lake of fire, forever ending their evil work in the world (Revelation 20:10).

8:9–11 In the days of the early church, sorcerers and magicians were numerous and influential. They worked wonders, performed healings and exorcisms, and practiced astrology. Their wonders may simply have been magic tricks, or the sorcerers may have been empowered by Satan (Matthew 24:24; 2 Thessalonians 2:9). Simon had done so many wonders that some even thought that he was the Messiah; but his powers did not come from God (see 8:18–24).

8:10 Acts 14:11; 28:6
8:11 Acts 8:9; 13:6
8:12 Acts 1:3; 8:4; Acts 2:38
8:13 Acts 8:6; Acts 19:11
8:14 Acts 8:1; Luke 22:8
8:15 Acts 2:38; 19:2
8:16 Matt 28:19; Acts 19:2; Acts 2:38; 10:48
8:17 Mark 5:23; Acts 6:6; Acts 2:4

10 and they all, from smallest to greatest, were giving attention to him, saying, "This
man is what is called the Great Power of God."
11 And they were giving him attention because he had for a long time astonished them
with his magic arts.
12 But when they believed Philip preaching the good news about the kingdom of God
and the name of Jesus Christ, they were being baptized, men and women alike.
13 Even Simon himself believed; and after being baptized, he continued on with Philip, and as he observed signs and great miracles taking place, he was constantly amazed.
14 Now when the apostles in Jerusalem heard that Samaria had received the word of
God, they sent them Peter and John,
15 who came down and prayed for them that they might receive the Holy Spirit.
16 For He had not yet fallen upon any of them; they had simply been baptized in the
name of the Lord Jesus.
17 Then they *began* laying their hands on them, and they were receiving the Holy
Spirit.
18 Now when Simon saw that the Spirit was bestowed through the laying on of the
apostles' hands, he offered them money,

MISSIONARIES OF THE NEW TESTAMENT AND THEIR JOURNEYS

Name	*Journey's Purpose*	*Scripture Reference in Acts*
Philip	One of the first to preach the gospel outside Jerusalem	8:4–40
Peter and John	Visited new Samaritan believers to encourage them	8:14–25
Paul (journey to Damascus)	Set out to capture Christians but was captured by Christ	9:1–25
Peter	Led by God to one of the first Gentile families to become Christians—Cornelius's family	9:32—10:48
Barnabas	Went to Antioch as an encourager; traveled on to Troas to bring Paul back to Jerusalem from Antioch	11:25-30
Barnabas, Paul, John Mark	Left Antioch for Cyprus, Pamphylia, and Galatia on the first missionary journey	13:1—14:28
Barnabas and John Mark	After a break with Paul, they left Antioch for Cyprus	15:36–41
Paul, Silas, Timothy, Luke	Left Antioch to revisit churches in Galatia, then traveled on to Asia, Macedonia, and Achaia on a second missionary journey	15:36—18:22
Apollos	Left Alexandria for Ephesus; learned the complete gospel story from Priscilla and Aquila; preached in Athens and Corinth	18:24–28
Paul, Timothy, Erastus	Third major missionary journey revisiting churches in Galatia, Asia, Macedonia, and Achaia	18:23; 19:1—21:14

8:14 Peter and John were sent to Samaria to find out whether or not the Samaritans were truly becoming believers. The Jewish Christians, even the apostles, were still unsure whether Gentiles (non-Jews) and half-Jews could receive the Holy Spirit. It wasn't until Peter's experience with Cornelius (chapter 10) that the apostles became fully convinced that the Holy Spirit was for all people. It was John who had asked Jesus if they should call down fire from heaven to burn up a Samaritan village that refused to welcome them (Luke 9:51–55). Here he and Peter went to the Samaritans to pray with them.

8:15–17 This was a crucial moment for the spread of the gospel and for the growth of the church. Peter and John had to go to Samaria to help keep this new group of believers from becoming separated from other believers. When Peter and John saw the Lord working in these people, they were assured that the Holy Spirit worked through *all* believers—Gentiles and mixed races as well as "pure" Jews.

8:15–17 Many scholars believe that God chose to have a dramatic filling of his Spirit as a sign at this special moment in history—the spread of the gospel into Samaria through the powerful, effective preaching of believers. Normally, the Holy Spirit enters a person's life at conversion. This was a special event. The pouring out of the Spirit would happen again with Cornelius and his family (10:44–47), a sign that the uncircumcised Gentiles could receive the gospel.

8:18–23 "Everything has a price" seems to be true in our world of bribes, wealth, and materialism. Simon thought he could buy the Holy Spirit's power, but Peter harshly rebuked him. The only way to receive God's power is to do what Peter told Simon to do—turn from sin, ask God for forgiveness, and be filled with his Spirit. No amount of money can buy salvation, forgiveness of sin, or God's power. These are only gained by repentance and belief in Christ as Savior.

19 saying, "Give this authority to me as well, so that everyone on whom I lay my hands
may receive the Holy Spirit."
20 But Peter said to him, "May your silver perish with you, because you thought you
could obtain the gift of God with money!
21 "You have no part or portion in this matter, for your heart is not right before God.
22 "Therefore repent of this wickedness of yours, and pray the Lord that, if possible,
the intention of your heart may be forgiven you.
23 "For I see that you are in the gall of bitterness and in the bondage of iniquity."
24 But Simon answered and said, "Pray to the Lord for me yourselves, so that nothing
of what you have said may come upon me."

An Ethiopian Receives Christ

25 So, when they had solemnly testified and spoken the word of the Lord, they started
back to Jerusalem, and were preaching the gospel to many villages of the Samaritans.
26 But an angel of the Lord spoke to Philip saying, "Get up and go south to the road
that descends from Jerusalem to Gaza." (This is a desert *road.*)
27 So he got up and went; and there was an Ethiopian eunuch, a court official of
Candace, queen of the Ethiopians, who was in charge of all her treasure; and he had
come to Jerusalem to worship,
28 and he was returning and sitting in his chariot, and was reading the prophet Isaiah.
29 Then the Spirit said to Philip, "Go up and join this chariot."
30 Philip ran up and heard him reading Isaiah the prophet, and said, "Do you understand what you are reading?"
31 And he said, "Well, how could I, unless someone guides me?" And he invited Philip to come up and sit with him.
32 Now the passage of Scripture which he was reading was this:
"HE WAS LED AS A SHEEP TO SLAUGHTER;
AND AS A LAMB BEFORE ITS SHEARER IS SILENT,
SO HE DOES NOT OPEN HIS MOUTH.
33 "IN HUMILIATION HIS JUDGMENT WAS TAKEN AWAY;
WHO WILL RELATE HIS GENERATION?
FOR HIS LIFE IS REMOVED FROM THE EARTH."
34 The eunuch answered Philip and said, "Please *tell me,* of whom does the prophet
say this? Of himself or of someone else?"
35 Then Philip opened his mouth, and beginning from this Scripture he preached Jesus
to him.
36 As they went along the road they came to some water; and the eunuch ☆said, "Look!
Water! What prevents me from being baptized?"
37 [[15]And Philip said, "If you believe with all your heart, you may." And he answered
and said, "I believe that Jesus Christ is the Son of God."]

15 Early mss do not contain this v

8:20 2 Kin 5:16; Is 55:1; Dan 5:17; Matt 10:8; Acts 2:38

8:21 Deut 10:9; 12:12; Eph 5:5; Ps 78:37

8:22 Is 55:7

8:23 Is 58:6

8:24 Gen 20:7; Ex 8:8; Num 21:7; James 5:16

8:25 Luke 16:28; Acts 13:12; Acts 8:40; Matt 10:5

8:26 Acts 5:19; 8:29; Acts 8:5; Gen 10:19

8:27 Ps 68:31; 87:4; Is 56:3ff; 1 Kin 8:41f; John 12:20

8:29 Acts 8:39; 10:19; 11:12; 13:2; 16:6, 7; 20:23; 21:11; 28:25; Heb 3:7

8:32 Is 53:7

8:33 Is 53:8

8:35 Matt 5:2; Luke 24:27; Acts 17:2; 18:28; 28:23; Acts 5:42

8:36 Acts 10:47

8:24 The last time a parent or friend rebuked you, were you hurt, angry, or defensive? Learn a lesson from Simon and his reaction to what Peter told him. He exclaimed, "Pray to the Lord for me." If you are rebuked for a serious mistake, it is for your good. Admit your error, repent quickly, and ask for prayer.

8:26 Philip was having a successful preaching ministry to great crowds in Samaria (8:5–8), but he obediently left that ministry to travel on a desert road. Because Philip went where God sent him, Ethiopia was opened up to the gospel. Follow God's leading, even if it seems like a demotion. At first you may not understand his plans, but the results will prove that God's way is right.

8:27 Ethiopia was located in Africa south of Egypt. The eunuch was obviously very dedicated to God because he had traveled such a long distance to worship in Jerusalem. The Jews had contact with Ethiopia (known as Cush) in ancient days (Psalm 68:31; Jeremiah 38:7), so this man may have been a Gentile convert to Judaism. Because he was in charge of the treasury of Ethiopia, this man's conversion brought Christianity into the power structures of another government. This is the beginning of the witness "to the remotest part of the earth" (1:8). See the prophecy in Isaiah 56:3–5 for words about foreigners and eunuchs.

8:29–35 Philip found the Ethiopian man reading Scripture. Taking advantage of this opportunity to explain the gospel, Philip asked the man if he understood what he was reading. Philip (1) followed the Spirit's leading, (2) began the discussion from where the man was (immersed in the prophecies of Isaiah), and (3) explained how Jesus Christ fulfilled Isaiah's prophecies. When we share the gospel, we should start where the other person's concerns are focused. Then we can bring the gospel to bear on those concerns.

8:30–31 The eunuch asked Philip to explain a passage of Scripture that he did not understand. When we have trouble understanding the Bible, we should ask others to help us. We must never let our insecurity or pride get in the way of understanding God's Word.

8:35 Some think that the Old Testament is not relevant today, but Philip led this man to faith in Jesus Christ by using the Old Testament. Jesus Christ is found in the pages of both the Old and New Testaments. God's entire Word is applicable to all people in all ages. Don't avoid or neglect to use the Old Testament. It too is God's Word.

8:39 2 Cor 12:2
8:40 Acts 9:30; 10:1, 24; 11:11; 12:19; 18:22; 21:8, 16; 23:23, 33; 25:1, 4, 6, 13
9:1 Acts 9:1-22; 22:3-16; 26:9-18
9:2 Matt 10:17; Gen 14:15; 2 Cor 11:32; Gal 1:17; John 14:6; Acts 18:25f; 19:9, 23; 22:4; 24:14, 22
9:3 1 Cor 15:8
9:4 Acts 22:7; 26:14
9:7 Acts 26:14; John 12:29f; Acts 22:9
9:8 Acts 9:18; 22:11; Gen 14:15; 2 Cor 11:32; Gal 1:17
9:10 Gen 14:15; 2 Cor 11:32; Gal 1:17; Acts 22:12; Acts 10:3, 17, 19; 11:5; 12:9; 16:9f; 18:9
9:11 Acts 9:30; 11:25; 21:39; 22:3

38 And he ordered the chariot to stop; and they both went down into the water, Philip
as well as the eunuch, and he baptized him.
39 When they came up out of the water, the Spirit of the Lord snatched Philip away;
and the eunuch no longer saw him, but went on his way rejoicing.
40 But Philip found himself at Azotus, and as he passed through he kept preaching the
gospel to all the cities until he came to Caesarea.

The Conversion of Saul

9 Now Saul, still breathing threats and murder against the disciples of the Lord, went
to the high priest,
2 and asked for letters from him to the synagogues at Damascus, so that if he found
any belonging to the Way, both men and women, he might bring them bound to Jerusalem.
3 As he was traveling, it happened that he was approaching Damascus, and suddenly
a light from heaven flashed around him;
4 and he fell to the ground and heard a voice saying to him, "Saul, Saul, why are you
persecuting Me?"
5 And he said, "Who are You, Lord?" And He *said,* "I am Jesus whom you are persecuting,
6 but get up and enter the city, and it will be told you what you must do."
7 The men who traveled with him stood speechless, hearing the voice but seeing
no one.
8 Saul got up from the ground, and though his eyes were open, he could see nothing;
and leading him by the hand, they brought him into Damascus.
9 And he was three days without sight, and neither ate nor drank.
10 Now there was a disciple at Damascus named Ananias; and the Lord said to him in
a vision, "Ananias." And he said, "Here I am, Lord."
11 And the Lord *said* to him, "Get up and go to the street called Straight, and inquire
at the house of Judas for a man from Tarsus named Saul, for he is praying,

---

8:38 Baptism was a sign of identification with Christ and with the Christian community. Although there were no witnesses besides Philip, it was still important for the eunuch to take this step.

8:39–40 Why was Philip suddenly transported to a different city? This miraculous sign showed the urgency of bringing the Gentiles to belief in Christ. Azotus is Ashdod, one of the ancient Philistine capitals. Philip probably lived in Caesarea for the next 20 years (21:8).

9:2 Saul (later called Paul) was so zealous for his Jewish beliefs that he began a persecution campaign against anyone who believed in Christ ("any belonging to the Way"). Why would the Jews in Jerusalem want to persecute Christians as far away as Damascus? There are several possibilities: (1) to seize the Christians who had fled, (2) to prevent the spread of Christianity to other major cities, (3) to keep the Christians from causing any trouble with Rome, (4) to advance Saul's career and build his reputation as a true Pharisee, zealous for the law, (5) to unify the factions of Judaism by giving them a common enemy.

9:2–5 As Saul traveled to Damascus, pursuing Christians, he was confronted by the risen Christ and brought face-to-face with the truth of the gospel. Sometimes God breaks into a life in a spectacular manner, and sometimes conversion is a quiet experience. Beware of people who insist that you must have a particular type of conversion experience. The right way to come to faith in Jesus is whatever way God brings *you.*

9:3 Damascus, a key commercial city, was located about 175 miles northeast of Jerusalem in the Roman province of Syria. Several trade routes linked Damascus to other cities throughout the Roman world. Saul may have thought that by stamping out Christianity in Damascus, he could prevent its spread to other areas.

9:3–5 Paul refers to this experience as the start of his new life in Christ (1 Corinthians 9:1; 15:8; Galatians 1:15–16). At the center of this wonderful experience was Jesus Christ. Paul did not see a vision; he saw the risen Christ himself (9:17). Paul acknowledged

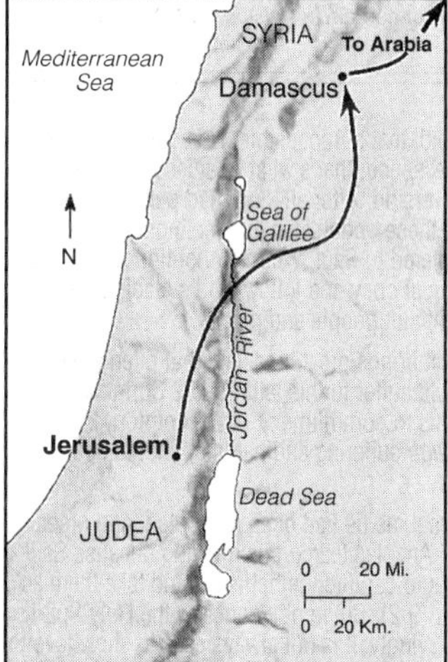

SAUL TRAVELS TO DAMASCUS
Many Christians fled Jerusalem when persecution began after Stephen's death, seeking refuge in other cities and countries. Saul tracked them down, even traveling 150 miles to Damascus in Syria to bring Christians back in chains to Jerusalem. But as he neared the ancient city, he discovered that God had other plans for him (9:15).

Jesus as Lord, confessed his own sin, surrendered his life to Christ, and resolved to obey him. True conversion comes from a personal encounter with Jesus Christ and leads to a new life in relationship with him.

9:5 Saul thought he was pursuing heretics, but he was persecuting Jesus himself. Anyone who persecutes believers today is also guilty of persecuting Jesus (see Matthew 25:40, 45), because believers are the body of Christ on earth.

12 and he has seen [16]in a vision a man named Ananias come in and lay his hands on
him, so that he might regain his sight."
13 But Ananias answered, "Lord, I have heard from many about this man, how much
harm he did to Your saints at Jerusalem;
14 and here he has authority from the chief priests to bind all who call on Your name."
15 But the Lord said to him, "Go, for he is a chosen [17]instrument of Mine, to bear My
name before the Gentiles and kings and the sons of Israel;
16 for I will show him how much he must suffer for My name's sake."
17 So Ananias departed and entered the house, and after laying his hands on him said,
"Brother Saul, the Lord Jesus, who appeared to you on the road by which you were coming, has sent me so that you may regain your sight and be filled with the Holy Spirit."
18 And immediately there fell from his eyes something like scales, and he regained his
sight, and he got up and was baptized;
19 and he took food and was strengthened.

Saul Begins to Preach Christ

Now for several days he was with the disciples who were at Damascus,
20 and immediately he *began* to proclaim Jesus in the synagogues, saying, "He is the
Son of God."
21 All those hearing him continued to be amazed, and were saying, "Is this not he who
in Jerusalem destroyed those who called on this name, and *who* had come here for the
purpose of bringing them bound before the chief priests?"
22 But Saul kept increasing in strength and confounding the Jews who lived at Damascus by proving that this *Jesus* is the Christ.
23 When many days had elapsed, the Jews plotted together to do away with him,
24 but their plot became known to Saul. They were also watching the gates day and
night so that they might put him to death;
25 but his disciples took him by night and let him down through *an opening in* the wall,
lowering him in a large basket.
26 When he came to Jerusalem, he was trying to associate with the disciples; but they
were all afraid of him, not believing that he was a disciple.

16 A few early mss do not contain *in a vision* **17** Or *vessel*

9:12 Mark 5:23; Acts 6:6
9:14 Acts 7:59
9:15 Eph 3:7; Acts 22:21; 26:17; Rom 1:5; 11:13; 15:16; Gal 1:16; 2:7ff; Eph 3:1, 8; 1 Tim 2:7; 2 Tim 4:17; Acts 25:22f; 26:1, 32; 2 Tim 4:17
9:16 Acts 20:23; 21:4, 11, 13; 2 Cor 6:4f; 11:23-27; 1 Thess 3:3
9:17 Mark 5:23; Acts 6:6; 9:12; Acts 22:13; Acts 2:4
9:19 Acts 26:20; Acts 9:26, 38; 11:26
9:20 Acts 13:5, 14; 14:1; 16:13; 17:2, 10; 18:4, 19; 19:8; Matt 4:3; Acts 9:22; 13:33
9:21 Acts 8:3; 9:13; Gal 1:13, 23; Acts 9:14
9:23 Gal 1:17, 18; 1 Thess 2:16
9:24 Acts 20:3, 19; 23:12, 30; 25:3; 2 Cor 11:32f
9:26 Acts 22:17-20; 26:20

9:13–14 "Not him, Lord; that's impossible. He could never become a Christian!" In essence, that's what Ananias said when God told him of Saul's conversion. After all, Saul had pursued believers to their death. Despite these understandable feelings, Ananias obeyed God and ministered to Saul. We must not limit God—he can do anything. We must obey and follow God's leading, even when he leads us to difficult people and places.

9:15–16 Faith in Christ brings great blessings but often great suffering too. Paul would suffer for his faith (see 2 Corinthians 11:23–27). God calls us to commitment, not to comfort. He promises to be with us *through* suffering and hardship, not to spare us from them.

9:17 Ananias found Saul, as he had been instructed, and greeted him as "Brother Saul." Ananias feared this meeting because Saul had come to Damascus to capture the believers and take them as prisoners to Jerusalem (9:2). But in obedience to the Holy Spirit, Ananias greeted Saul lovingly. It is not always easy to show love to others, especially when we are afraid of them or doubt their motives. Nevertheless, we must follow Jesus' command (John 13:34) and Ananias's example, showing loving acceptance to other believers.

9:17–18 Although there is no mention of a special filling of the Holy Spirit for Saul, his changed life and subsequent accomplishments bear strong witness to the Holy Spirit's presence and power in his life. Evidently, the Holy Spirit filled Saul when he received his sight and was baptized. See the second note on 8:15–17 for more on the filling of the Holy Spirit.

9:20 Immediately after receiving his sight and spending some time with the believers in Damascus, Saul went to the synagogue to tell the Jews about Jesus Christ. Some Christians counsel new believers to wait until they are thoroughly grounded in their faith before attempting to share the gospel. Saul took time alone to learn about Jesus before beginning his worldwide ministry, but he did not wait to witness. Although we should not rush into a ministry unprepared, we do not need to wait before telling others what has happened to us.

9:21–22 Saul's arguments were powerful because he was a brilliant scholar. But what was more convincing was his changed life. People knew that what he taught was real because they could see the evidence in the way he lived. It is important to know what the Bible teaches and how to defend the faith, but your words should be backed up with a changed life.

9:23 According to Galatians 1:17–18, Paul left Damascus and traveled to Arabia, the desert region just southeast of Damascus, where he lived for three years. It is unclear whether his three-year stay occurred between verses 22 and 23 or between verses 25 and 26. Some commentators say that "many days" could mean a long period of time. They suggest that when Paul returned to Damascus, the governor under Aretas ordered his arrest (2 Corinthians 11:32) in an effort to keep peace with influential Jews.

The other possibility is that Paul's night escape occurred during his first stay in Damascus, just after his conversion, when the Pharisees were especially upset over his defection from their ranks. He would have fled to Arabia to spend time alone with God and to let the Jewish religious leaders cool down. Regardless of which theory is correct, there was a period of at least three years between Paul's conversion (9:3–6) and his trip to Jerusalem (9:26).

9:26–27 It is difficult to change your reputation, and Saul had a terrible reputation with the Christians. But Barnabas, a Jewish

9:27 Acts 4:36; Acts 9:3-6; Acts 9:20, 22; Acts 4:13, 29; 9:29

9:28 Acts 4:13, 29; 9:29

9:29 Acts 6:1

9:30 Acts 1:15; Acts 8:40; Gal 1:21; Acts 9:11

9:31 Acts 5:11; 8:1; 16:5

27 But Barnabas took hold of him and brought him to the apostles and described to
them how he had seen the Lord on the road, and that He had talked to him, and how at
Damascus he had spoken out boldly in the name of Jesus.
28 And he was with them, moving about freely in Jerusalem, speaking out boldly in the
name of the Lord.
29 And he was talking and arguing with the Hellenistic *Jews;* but they were attempting
to put him to death.
30 But when the brethren learned *of it,* they brought him down to Caesarea and sent
him away to Tarsus.
31 So the church throughout all Judea and Galilee and Samaria enjoyed peace, being
built up; and going on in the fear of the Lord and in the comfort of the Holy Spirit, it
continued to increase.

PHILIP

Jesus' last words to his followers were a command to take the gospel everywhere, but they seemed reluctant to leave Jerusalem. It took intense persecution to scatter the believers from Jerusalem and into Judea and Samaria, where Jesus had instructed them to go. Philip, one of the deacons in charge of food distribution, left Jerusalem and, like most Jewish Christians, spread the gospel wherever he went; but unlike most of them, he did not limit his audience to other Jews. He went directly to Samaria, the last place many Jews would go, due to age-old prejudice.

The Samaritans responded in large numbers. When word got back to Jerusalem, Peter and John were sent to evaluate Philip's ministry. They quickly became involved themselves, seeing firsthand God's acceptance of those who previously were considered unacceptable.

In the middle of all this success and excitement, God directed Philip out to the desert for an appointment with an Ethiopian eunuch, another foreigner, who had been in Jerusalem. Philip went immediately. His effectiveness in sharing the gospel with this man placed a Christian in a significant position in a distant country, and may well have had an effect on an entire nation.

Philip ended up in Caesarea, where events allowed him to be Paul's host many years later. Paul, who as the leading persecutor of the Christians had been instrumental in pushing Philip and others out of Jerusalem, had himself become an effective believer. The conversion of the Gentiles begun by Philip was continued across the entire Roman empire by Paul.

Whether or not you are a follower of Christ, Philip's life presents a challenge. To those still outside the gospel, he is a reminder that the gospel is for you also. To those who have accepted Christ, he is a reminder that we are not free to disqualify anyone from hearing about Jesus. How much like Philip would your neighbors say you are?

Strengths and accomplishments:
- One of the seven organizers of food distribution in the early church
- Became an evangelist, one of the first traveling missionaries
- One of the first to obey Jesus' command to take the gospel to all people
- A careful student of the Bible who could explain its meaning clearly

Lessons from his life:
- God finds great and various uses for those willing to obey wholeheartedly
- The gospel is universal Good News
- The whole Bible, not just the New Testament, helps us understand more about Jesus
- Both mass response (the Samaritans) and individual response (the man from Ethiopia) to the gospel are valuable

Vital statistics:
- Occupations: Deacon, evangelist
- Relatives: Four daughters
- Contemporaries: Paul, Stephen, the apostles

Key verse:
"Then Philip opened his mouth, and beginning from this Scripture he preached Jesus to him" (Acts 8:35).

Philip's story is told in Acts 6:1–7; 8:5–40; 21:8–10.

convert (mentioned in 4:36), became the bridge between Saul and the apostles. New Christians (especially those with tarnished reputations) need sponsors, people who will come alongside, encourage, teach, and introduce them to other believers. Find ways that you can become a Barnabas to new believers.

9:27 Galatians 1:18–19 explains that Paul was in Jerusalem only 15 days and that he met only with Peter and James.

9:29–30 In these short sentences we can see two characteristics of Paul, even as a new believer in Christ: He was bold, and he stirred up controversy. These would characterize Paul's ministry the rest of his life. The Hellenistic Jews were Greek-speaking Jews.

9:30 Saul's visit to Tarsus helped quiet conflicts with the Jews and allowed him time to prove his commitment. After Saul, the most zealous persecutor, was converted, the church enjoyed a brief time of peace. "Brethren" refers to fellow Christians, members of God's family.

Peter's Ministry

32 Now as Peter was traveling through all *those regions,* he came down also to the saints
who lived at Lydda.
33 There he found a man named Aeneas, who had been bedridden eight years, for he
was paralyzed.
34 Peter said to him, "Aeneas, Jesus Christ heals you; get up and make your bed."
Immediately he got up.
35 And all who lived at Lydda and Sharon saw him, and they turned to the Lord.
36 Now in Joppa there was a disciple named Tabitha (which translated *in Greek* is called

9:32 Acts 9:13

9:35 Acts 2:47; 9:42; 11:21

9:36 Josh 19:46; 2 Chr 2:16; Ezra 3:7; Jon 1:3; Acts 9:38, 42f; 10:5, 8, 23, 32; 11:5, 13

GREAT ESCAPES IN THE BIBLE

Who escaped	*Reference*	*What happened*	*What the escape accomplished*	*Application*
Jacob	Genesis 31:1–55	Fled from his father-in-law, Laban, after almost 20 years of service	Allowed Jacob to return home for Isaac's death and for reconciliation with Esau, his brother	A time away from home often puts the really important things into perspective
Moses	Exodus 2:11–15	Fled Egypt after killing an Egyptian in defense of a fellow Israelite	Saved his own life and began another part of God's training	God fits even our mistakes into his plan
Israelites	Exodus 12:28–42	Escaped Egypt after 430 years, most of that time in slavery	God confirmed his choice of Abraham's descendants	God will not forget his promises
Spies	Joshua 2:1–24	Escaped searchers in Jericho by hiding in Rahab's house	Prepared the destruction of Jericho and preserved Rahab, who would become one of David's ancestors—as well as an ancestor of Jesus	God's plan weaves lives together in a pattern beyond our understanding
Ehud	Judges 3:15–30	Assassinated the Moabite King Eglon, but escaped undetected	Broke the control of Moab over Israel and began 80 years of peace	Punishments by God are often swift and deadly
Samson	Judges 16:1–3	Escaped a locked city by ripping the gates from their hinges	Merely postponed Samson's self-destruction because of his lack of self-control	Without dependence on God and his guidance, even great ability is wasted
Elijah	1 Kings 19:1–18	Fled into the wilderness out of fear of Queen Jezebel	Preserved Elijah's life, but also displayed his human weakness	Even at moments of real success, our personal weaknesses are our greatest challenges
Saul (Paul)	Acts 9:23–25	Lowered over the wall in a basket to get out of Damascus	Saved this new Christian for great service to God	God has a purpose for every life, which leads to a real adventure for those willing to cooperate
Peter	Acts 12:1–11	Freed from prison by an angel	Saved Peter for God's further plans for his life	God can use extraordinary means to carry out his plan—often when we least expect it
Paul and Silas	Acts 16:22–40	Chains loosened and doors opened by an earthquake, but they chose not to leave the prison	Pointed out the powerlessness of humans before God	When our dependence and attention are focused on God rather than our problems, he is able to offer help in unexpected ways

9:36 The important harbor city of Joppa sits 125 feet above sea level overlooking the Mediterranean Sea. Joppa was the town into which the cedars of Lebanon had been floated to be shipped to Jerusalem and used in the temple construction (2 Chronicles 2:16; Ezra 3:7). The prophet Jonah left the port of Joppa on his ill-fated trip (Jonah 1:3).

9:36–42 Dorcas made an enormous impact on her community by "abounding with deeds of kindness and charity," by making tunics

Dorcas); this woman was abounding with deeds of kindness and charity which she continually did.

9:37 Acts 1:13; 9:39

37 And it happened at that time that she fell sick and died; and when they had washed her body, they laid it in an upper room.

PAUL

No person, apart from Jesus himself, shaped the history of Christianity like the apostle Paul. Even before he was a believer, his actions were significant. His frenzied persecution of Christians following Stephen's death got the church started in obeying Christ's final command to take the gospel worldwide. Paul's personal encounter with Jesus changed his life. He never lost his fierce intensity, but from then on it was channeled for the gospel.

Paul was very religious. His training under Gamaliel was the finest available. His intentions and efforts were sincere. He was a good Pharisee, who knew the Bible and sincerely believed that this Christian movement was dangerous to Judaism. Thus Paul hated the Christian faith and persecuted Christians without mercy.

Paul got permission to travel to Damascus to capture Christians and bring them back to Jerusalem. But God stopped him in his hurried tracks on the Damascus road. Paul personally met Jesus Christ, and his life was never again the same.

Until Paul's conversion, little had been done about carrying the gospel to non-Jews. Philip had preached in Samaria and to an Ethiopian man; Cornelius, a Gentile, was converted under Peter; and in Antioch in Syria, some Greeks had joined the believers. When Barnabas was sent from Jerusalem to check on this situation, he went to Tarsus to find Paul and bring him to Antioch, and together they worked among the believers there. They were then sent on a missionary journey, the first of three Paul would take, that would carry the gospel across the Roman empire.

The thorny issue of whether Gentile believers had to obey Jewish laws before they could become Christians caused many problems in the early church. Paul worked hard to convince the Jews that Gentiles were acceptable to God, but he spent even more time convincing the Gentiles that they were acceptable to God. The lives Paul touched were changed and challenged by meeting Christ through him.

God did not waste any part of Paul—his background, his training, his citizenship, his mind, or even his weaknesses. Are you willing to let God do the same for you? You will never know all he can do with you until you allow him to have all that you are!

Strengths and accomplishments:
- Transformed by God from a persecutor of Christians to a preacher for Christ
- Preached for Christ throughout the Roman empire on three missionary journeys
- Wrote letters to various churches, which became part of the New Testament
- Was never afraid to face an issue head-on and deal with it
- Was sensitive to God's leading and, despite his strong personality, always did as God directed
- Is often called the apostle to the Gentiles

Weaknesses and mistakes:
- Witnessed and approved of Stephen's stoning
- Set out to destroy Christianity by persecuting Christians

Lessons from his life:
- The Good News is that forgiveness and eternal life are a gift of God's grace received through faith in Christ and available to all people
- Obedience results from a relationship with God, but obedience will never create or earn that relationship
- Real freedom doesn't come until we no longer have to prove our freedom
- God does not waste our time—he will use our past and present so we may serve him with our future

Vital statistics:
- Where: Born in Tarsus, but became a world traveler for Christ
- Occupations: Trained as a Pharisee, learned the tent-making trade, served as a missionary
- Contemporaries: Gamaliel, Stephen, the apostles, Luke, Barnabas, Timothy

Key verses:
"For to me, to live is Christ and to die is gain. But if I am to live on in the flesh, this will mean fruitful labor for me; and I do not know which to choose. But I am hard-pressed from both directions, having the desire to depart and be with Christ, for that is very much better; yet to remain on in the flesh is more necessary for your sake" (Philippians 1:21–24).

Paul's story is told in Acts 7:58—28:31 and throughout his New Testament letters.

and other clothing (9:39). When she died, the room was filled with mourners, very likely many of the people she had helped. And when she was brought back to life, the news raced through the town. God uses great preachers like Peter and Paul, but he also uses those who have gifts of kindness like Dorcas. Rather than wishing you had other gifts, make good use of the gifts God has given you.

38 Since Lydda was near Joppa, the disciples, having heard that Peter was there, sent
two men to him, imploring him, "Do not delay in coming to us."
39 So Peter arose and went with them. When he arrived, they brought him into the
upper room; and all the widows stood beside him, weeping and showing all the [18]tunics
and garments that Dorcas used to make while she was with them.
40 But Peter sent them all out and knelt down and prayed, and turning to the body, he
said, "Tabitha, arise." And she opened her eyes, and when she saw Peter, she sat up.
41 And he gave her his hand and raised her up; and calling the saints and widows, he
presented her alive.
42 It became known all over Joppa, and many believed in the Lord.
43 And Peter stayed many days in Joppa with a tanner *named* Simon.

Cornelius's Vision

10 Now *there was* a man at Caesarea named Cornelius, a centurion of what was called
the Italian [19]cohort,
2 a devout man and one who feared God with all his household, and gave many [20]alms
to the *Jewish* people and prayed to God continually.
3 About the [21]ninth hour of the day he clearly saw in a vision an angel of God who
had *just* come in and said to him, "Cornelius!"
4 And fixing his gaze on him and being much alarmed, he said, "What is it, Lord?"
And he said to him, "Your prayers and [22]alms have ascended as a memorial before God.
5 "Now dispatch *some* men to Joppa and send for a man *named* Simon, who is also
called Peter;
6 he is staying with a tanner *named* Simon, whose house is by the sea."
7 When the angel who was speaking to him had left, he summoned two of his servants
and a devout soldier of those who were his personal attendants,
8 and after he had explained everything to them, he sent them to Joppa.
9 On the next day, as they were on their way and approaching the city, Peter went up
on the housetop about the [23]sixth hour to pray.
10 But he became hungry and was desiring to eat; but while they were making preparations, he fell into a trance;

18 Or *inner garments* **19** Or *battalion* **20** Or *gifts of charity* **21** I.e. 3 p.m. **22** Or *deeds of charity* **23** I.e. noon

9:38 Acts 11:26
9:39 Acts 1:13
9:40 Matt 9:25; Luke 22:41; Acts 7:60; Mark 5:41
9:41 Acts 6:1
9:42 Jon 1:3; Acts 9:38, 42f; 10:5, 8, 23, 32; 11:5, 13; Acts 9:35
9:43 Acts 9:38, 42f; 10:5, 8, 23, 32
10:1 Acts 8:40; 10:24; Matt 27:27; Mark 15:16; John 18:3, 12; Acts 21:31; 27:1
10:2 Acts 10:22, 35; 13:16, 26; Luke 7:4f
10:3 Acts 3:1; Acts 9:10; 10:17, 19; Acts 5:19
10:4 Acts 3:4; Rev 8:4; Matt 26:13; Phil 4:18; Heb 6:10
10:5 Acts 9:36
10:9 Acts 10:9-32; 11:5-14; Matt 24:17; Ps 55:17; Acts 10:3
10:10 Acts 11:5; 22:17

SAUL'S RETURN TO TARSUS
At least three years elapsed between Acts 9:22 and 9:26. After time alone in Arabia (see Galatians 1:16–18), Saul (Paul) returned to Damascus and then to Jerusalem. The apostles were reluctant to believe that this former persecutor could have become one of them. He escaped to Caesarea, where he caught a ship and returned to Tarsus.

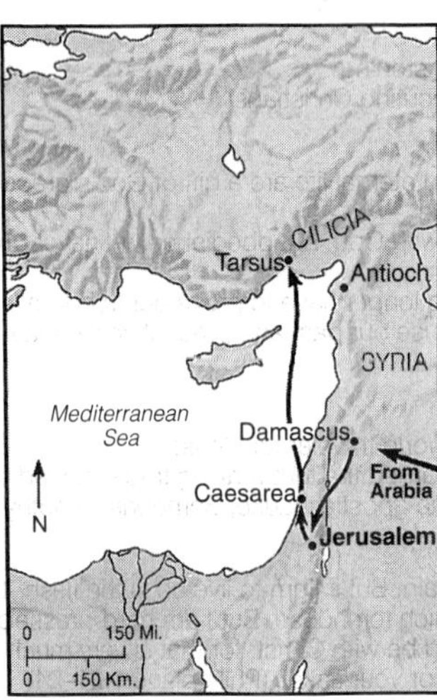

9:43 In Joppa, Peter stayed at the home of Simon, a tanner. Tanners made animal hides into leather. It is significant that Peter was at Simon's house, because tanning involved contact with dead animals, and Jewish law considered it an "unclean" job. Peter was already beginning to break down his prejudice against people who were not of his kind and customs that did not adhere to Jewish religious traditions.

10:1 This Caesarea, sometimes called Palestinian Caesarea, was located on the coast of the Mediterranean Sea, 32 miles north of Joppa. The largest and most important port city on the Mediterranean in Palestine, it served as the capital of the Roman province of Judea. This was the first city to have Gentile Christians and a non-Jewish church.

10:1 This Roman officer was a *centurion,* a commander of 100 soldiers. Although stationed in Caesarea, Cornelius would probably return soon to Rome. Thus his conversion was a major stepping-stone for spreading the gospel to the empire's capital city.

10:2 "What will happen to the heathen who have never heard about Christ?" This question is often asked about God's justice. Cornelius wasn't a believer in Christ, but he was seeking God, and he was reverent and generous. Therefore God sent Peter to tell Cornelius about Christ. Cornelius is an example that God "is a rewarder of those who seek Him" (Hebrews 11:6). Those who sincerely seek God will find him! God made Cornelius's knowledge complete.

10:4 God saw Cornelius's sincere faith. His prayers and generous giving were a "memorial before God," a sacrificial offering to the Lord. God answers the sincere prayers of those who seek him by sending the right person or the right information at the right time.

11 and he ☆saw the sky opened up, and an [24]object like a great sheet coming down,
lowered by four corners to the ground,
12 and there were in it all *kinds of* four-footed animals and [25]crawling creatures of the
earth and birds of the air.
13 A voice came to him, "Get up, Peter, kill and eat!"
14 But Peter said, "By no means, Lord, for I have never eaten anything unholy and
unclean."
15 Again a voice *came* to him a second time, "What God has cleansed, no *longer* consider unholy."
16 This happened three times, and immediately the object was taken up into the sky.
17 Now while Peter was greatly perplexed in mind as to what the vision which he had
seen might be, behold, the men who had been sent by Cornelius, having asked directions for Simon's house, appeared at the gate;
18 and calling out, they were asking whether Simon, who was also called Peter, was
staying there.
19 While Peter was reflecting on the vision, the Spirit said to him, "Behold, three men
are looking for you.
20 "But get up, go downstairs and accompany them without misgivings, for I have sent
them Myself."
21 Peter went down to the men and said, "Behold, I am the one you are looking for;
what is the reason for which you have come?"
22 They said, "Cornelius, a centurion, a righteous and God-fearing man well spoken
of by the entire nation of the Jews, was *divinely* directed by a holy angel to send for you
to come to his house and hear a message from you."
23 So he invited them in and gave them lodging.

Peter at Caesarea

And on the next day he got up and went away with them, and some of the brethren
from Joppa accompanied him.
24 On the following day he entered Caesarea. Now Cornelius was waiting for them and
had called together his relatives and close friends.
25 When Peter entered, Cornelius met him, and fell at his feet and worshiped *him.*
26 But Peter raised him up, saying, "Stand up; I too am *just* a man."
27 As he talked with him, he entered and ☆found many people assembled.
28 And he said to them, "You yourselves know how unlawful it is for a man who is a
Jew to associate with a foreigner or to visit him; and *yet* God has shown me that I should
not call any man unholy or unclean.
29 "That is why I came without even raising any objection when I was sent for. So I ask
for what reason you have sent for me."

24 Or *vessel* **25** Or *reptiles*

10:11 John 1:51

10:14 Matt 8:2ff; John 4:11ff; Acts 9:5; 22:8; Lev 11:20-25; Deut 14:4-20; Ezek 4:14; Dan 1:8; Acts 10:28

10:15 Matt 15:11; Mark 7:19; Rom 14:14; 1 Cor 10:25ff; 1 Tim 4:4f; Titus 1:15

10:17 Acts 10:3; Acts 10:8

10:19 Acts 10:3; Acts 8:29

10:20 Acts 15:7-9

10:22 Acts 10:2; Matt 2:12; Mark 8:38; Luke 9:26; Rev 14:10; Acts 11:14

10:23 Acts 10:45; 11:12; Acts 1:15; Acts 9:36

10:24 Acts 8:40; 10:1

10:25 Matt 8:2

10:26 Acts 14:15; Rev 19:10; 22:8f

10:27 Acts 10:24

10:28 John 4:9; 18:28; Acts 11:3; Acts 10:14f, 35; 15:9

PETER'S MINISTRY
Peter traveled to the ancient crossroads town of Lydda, where he healed crippled Aeneas. The believers in Joppa, an old port city, sent for him after a wonderful woman died. Peter went and brought her back to life. While in Joppa, Peter had a vision that led him to take the gospel to Cornelius, a Gentile, in Caesarea.

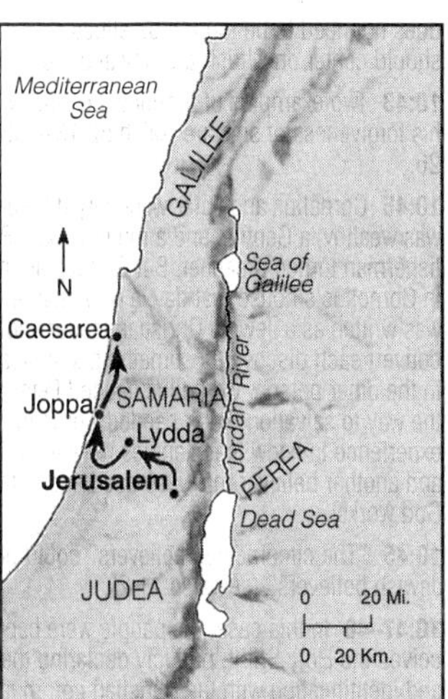

10:12 According to Jewish law, certain foods were forbidden to be eaten (see Leviticus 11). The food laws made it difficult for Jews to eat with Gentiles without risking defilement. In fact, the Gentiles themselves were often seen as "unclean." Peter's vision meant that he should not look upon the Gentiles as inferior people whom God would not redeem. Before having the vision, Peter would have thought that a Gentile Roman officer could not accept Christ. Afterward, he understood that it was his responsibility to go with the messengers into a Gentile home and tell Cornelius the Good News of salvation in Jesus Christ.

10:26 This act of worship could have caused Peter to become arrogant. After all, a Roman centurion was bowing before him. Instead, Peter pointed Cornelius to Christ. We too should remember our mortality whenever we are flattered or honored, and use the opportunity to give glory to God.

30 Cornelius said, "Four days ago to this hour, I was praying in my house during the
[26]ninth hour; and behold, a man stood before me in shining garments,
31 and he ☆said, 'Cornelius, your prayer has been heard and your alms have been remembered before God.
32 'Therefore send to Joppa and invite Simon, who is also called Peter, to come to you;
he is staying at the house of Simon *the* tanner by the sea.'
33 "So I sent for you immediately, and you have been kind enough to come. Now then,
we are all here present before God to hear all that you have been commanded by the
Lord."

Gentiles Hear Good News

34 Opening his mouth, Peter said:
"**I** most certainly understand *now* that God is not one to show partiality,
35 but in every nation the man who fears Him and does what is right is welcome
to Him.
36 "The word which He sent to the sons of Israel, preaching peace through Jesus Christ
(He is Lord of all)—
37 you yourselves know the thing which took place throughout all Judea, starting from
Galilee, after the baptism which John proclaimed.
38 "*You know of* Jesus of Nazareth, how God anointed Him with the Holy Spirit and
with power, and *how* He went about doing good and healing all who were oppressed by
the devil, for God was with Him.
39 "We are witnesses of all the things He did both in the land of the Jews and in Jerusalem. They also put Him to death by hanging Him on a cross.
40 "God raised Him up on the third day and granted that He become visible,
41 not to all the people, but to witnesses who were chosen beforehand by God, *that is,*
to us who ate and drank with Him after He arose from the dead.
42 "And He ordered us to preach to the people, and solemnly to testify that this is the
One who has been appointed by God as Judge of the living and the dead.
43 "Of Him all the prophets bear witness that through His name everyone who believes
in Him receives forgiveness of sins."
44 While Peter was still speaking these words, the Holy Spirit fell upon all those who
were listening to the message.
45 All the circumcised believers who came with Peter were amazed, because the gift of
the Holy Spirit had been poured out on the Gentiles also.
46 For they were hearing them speaking with tongues and exalting God. Then Peter
answered,
47 "Surely no one can refuse the water for these to be baptized who have received the
Holy Spirit just as we *did,* can he?"

26 I.e. 3 to 4 p.m.

10:30 Acts 10:9, 22f; Acts 3:1; 10:3; Acts 10:3-6, 30-32

10:32 John 4:9; 18:28; Acts 11:3

10:34 Matt 5:2; Deut 10:17; 2 Chr 19:7; Rom 2:11; Gal 2:6; Eph 6:9; Col 3:25; 1 Pet 1:17

10:36 Acts 13:32; Luke 1:79; 2:14; Rom 5:1; Eph 2:17; Matt 28:18; Acts 2:36; Rom 10:12

10:38 Acts 2:22; Acts 4:26; Matt 4:23; John 3:2

10:39 Luke 24:48; Acts 10:41; Acts 5:30

10:40 Acts 2:24

10:41 John 14:19, 22; 15:27; Luke 24:48

10:42 Acts 1:2; Luke 16:28; Luke 22:22; John 5:22, 27; Acts 17:31; 2 Tim 4:1; 1 Pet 4:5

10:43 Acts 3:18; Luke 24:47; Acts 2:38; 4:12

10:44 Acts 11:15; 15:8

10:45 Acts 10:23; Acts 2:33, 38

10:46 Mark 16:17; Acts 2:4; 19:6

10:47 Acts 8:36; Acts 2:4; 10:44f; 11:17; 15:8

10:34–35 Perhaps the greatest barrier to the spread of the gospel in the first century was the Jewish-Gentile conflict. Most of the early believers were Jewish, and to them it was scandalous even to think of associating with Gentiles. But God told Peter to take the gospel to a Roman, and Peter obeyed despite his background and personal feelings. (Later Peter struggled with this again—see Galatians 2:11–14.) God was making it clear that the Good News of Christ is for everyone! We should not allow any barrier—language, culture, prejudice, geography, economic level, or educational level—to keep us from telling others about Christ.

10:35 In every nation there are hearts restless for God, ready to receive the gospel—but someone must take it to them. Seeking God is not enough—people must find him. How then shall seekers find God without someone to point the way? Is God asking you to show someone the way to him? (See Romans 10:14–15.)

10:37–43 Peter's brief and powerful sermon contains a concise statement of the gospel: Jesus' perfect life of servanthood; his death on the cross; his resurrection, personally witnessed and experienced by Peter; Jesus' fulfillment of the Scriptures; and the necessity of personal faith in him. A sermon or witness for Christ does not need to be long to be effective. It should be Spirit-led and should center on Christ, the way and the truth and the life.

10:43 Two examples of prophets bearing witness about Jesus and his forgiveness of sins are Isaiah 52:13—53:12 and Ezekiel 36:25–26.

10:45 Cornelius and Peter were very different people. Cornelius was wealthy, a Gentile, and a military man. Peter was a Jewish fisherman turned preacher. But God's plan included both of them. In Cornelius's house that day, a new chapter in Christian history was written as a Jewish Christian leader and a Gentile Christian convert each discovered something significant about God at work in the other person. Cornelius needed Peter and his gospel to know the way to salvation. Peter needed Cornelius and his salvation experience to know that Gentiles were included in God's plan. You and another believer may also need each other to understand how God works!

10:45 "The circumcised believers" could be translated, "the Jewish believers" (see also 11:2).

10:47–48 In this case, the people were baptized *after* they received the Holy Spirit, publicly declaring their allegiance to Christ and identification with the Christian community.

11:28 Acts 21:10; Matt 24:14; Acts 18:2

11:29 John 2:2; Acts 1:15; 6:1f; 9:19, 25, 26, 38; 11:26; 13:52; 14:20, 22, 28; Acts 11:1

28 One of them named Agabus stood up and *began* to indicate by the Spirit that there
would certainly be a great famine all over the world. And this took place in the *reign* of
Claudius.
29 And in the proportion that any of the disciples had means, each of them determined
to send *a contribution* for the relief of the brethren living in Judea.
30 And this they did, sending it in charge of Barnabas and Saul to the elders.

CORNELIUS

The early days of Christianity were exciting as God's Spirit moved and people's lives were changed. Converts were pouring in from surprising backgrounds. Even the dreaded Saul (Paul) became a Christian, and non-Jews were responding to the Good News about Jesus. Among the first of these was the Roman centurion, Cornelius.

Because of frequent outbreaks of violence, Roman soldiers had to be stationed to keep peace throughout Israel. But most Romans, hated as conquerors, did not get along well in the nation. As an army officer, Cornelius was in a difficult position. He represented Rome, but his home was in Caesarea. During his years in Israel, he had himself been conquered by the God of Israel. He had a reputation as a godly man who put his faith into action, and he was respected by the Jews.

Four significant aspects of Cornelius's character are noted in Acts. He actively sought God, he revered God, he was generous in meeting other people's needs, and he prayed. God told him to send for Peter, because Peter would give him more knowledge about the God he was already seeking to please.

When Peter entered Cornelius's home, Peter broke a whole list of Jewish rules. Peter confessed he wasn't comfortable, but here was an eager audience and he couldn't hold back his message. He had no sooner started sharing the gospel when God gave overwhelming approval by filling that Roman family with his Holy Spirit. Peter saw he had no choice but to baptize them and welcome them as equals in the growing Christian church. Another step had been taken in carrying the gospel to the whole world.

Cornelius is a welcome example of God's willingness to use extraordinary means to reach those who desire to know him. He does not play favorites, and he does not hide from those who want to find him. God sent his Son because he loves the whole world—and that includes Peter, Cornelius, and you.

Strengths and accomplishments:
- A godly and generous Roman
- Although an officer in the occupying army, he seems to have been well-respected by the Jews
- He responded to God and encouraged his family to do the same
- His conversion helped the young church realize that the Good News was for all people, both Jews and Gentiles

Lessons from his life:
- God reaches those who want to know him
- The gospel is open to all people
- There are people everywhere to believe
- When we are willing to seek the truth and be obedient to the light God gives us, God will reward us richly

Vital statistics:
- Where: Caesarea
- Occupation: Roman centurion
- Contemporaries: Peter, Philip, the apostles

Key verse:
"A devout man and one who feared God with all his household, and gave many alms to the Jewish people and prayed to God continually" (Acts 10:2).

Cornelius's story is told in Acts 10:1—11:18.

11:28–29 There were serious food shortages during the reign of the Roman emperor Claudius (A.D. 41–54) because of a drought that had extended across much of the Roman empire for many years. It is significant that the church in Antioch assisted the church in Jerusalem. The daughter church had grown enough to be able to help the established church.

11:29 The people of Antioch were motivated to give generously because they cared about the needs of others. This is the "cheerful" giving that the Bible commends (2 Corinthians 9:7). Reluctant giving reflects a lack of concern for people. Focus your concern on the needy, and you will be motivated to give.

11:30 Elders were appointed to manage the affairs of the congregation. At this point, not much is known about their responsibilities, but it appears that their main role was to respond to the believers' needs.

Peter's Arrest and Deliverance

12 Now about that time Herod the king laid hands on some who belonged to the church
in order to mistreat them.
2 And he had James the brother of John put to death with a sword.
3 When he saw that it pleased the Jews, he proceeded to arrest Peter also. Now it was
during the days of Unleavened Bread.
4 When he had seized him, he put him in prison, delivering him to four squads of
soldiers to guard him, intending after the Passover to bring him out before the people.
5 So Peter was kept in the prison, but prayer for him was being made fervently by the
church to God.
6 On the very night when Herod was about to bring him forward, Peter was sleeping
between two soldiers, bound with two chains, and guards in front of the door were watching over the prison.
7 And behold, an angel of the Lord suddenly appeared and a light shone in the cell;
and he struck Peter's side and woke him up, saying, "Get up quickly." And his chains fell
off his hands.
8 And the angel said to him, "Gird yourself and put on your sandals." And he did so.
And he ☆said to him, "Wrap your cloak around you and follow me."
9 And he went out and continued to follow, and he did not know that what was being
done by the angel was real, but thought he was seeing a vision.
10 When they had passed the first and second guard, they came to the iron gate that
leads into the city, which opened for them by itself; and they went out and went along
one street, and immediately the angel departed from him.
11 When Peter came to himself, he said, "Now I know for sure that the Lord has sent
forth His angel and rescued me from the hand of Herod and from all that the Jewish
people were expecting."
12 And when he realized *this,* he went to the house of Mary, the mother of John who
was also called Mark, where many were gathered together and were praying.
13 When he knocked at the door of the gate, a servant-girl named Rhoda came to
answer.
14 When she recognized Peter's voice, because of her joy she did not open the gate,
but ran in and announced that Peter was standing in front of the gate.
15 They said to her, "You are out of your mind!" But she kept insisting that it was so.
They kept saying, "It is his angel."
16 But Peter continued knocking; and when they had opened *the door,* they saw him
and were amazed.

12:2 Matt 4:21; 20:23; Mark 10:39

12:3 Acts 24:27; 25:9; Ex 12:15; 23:15; Acts 20:6

12:4 John 19:23; Ex 12:1-27; Mark 14:1; Acts 12:3

12:6 Acts 21:33

12:7 Acts 5:19; Luke 2:9; 24:4; Acts 16:26

12:9 Acts 9:10

12:10 Acts 5:19; 16:26

12:11 Luke 15:17; Dan 3:28; 6:22

12:12 Acts 12:25; 13:5, 13; 15:37, 39; Col 4:10; 2 Tim 4:11; Philem 24; 1 Pet 5:13; Acts 12:5

12:13 John 18:16f

12:14 Luke 24:41

12:15 Matt 18:10

12:1 This King Herod was Herod Agrippa I, the son of Aristobulus and grandson of Herod the Great. His sister was Herodias, who was responsible for the death of John the Baptist (see Mark 6:17–28). Herod Agrippa I was partly Jewish. The Romans had appointed him to rule over most of Palestine, including the territories of Galilee, Perea, Judea, and Samaria. He persecuted the Christians in order to please the Jewish leaders who opposed them, hoping that would solidify his position. Agrippa I died suddenly in A.D. 44 (see 12:20–23). His death was also recorded by the historian Josephus.

12:2 James and John were two of the original 12 disciples who followed Jesus. They had asked Jesus for special recognition in his kingdom (Mark 10:35–40). Jesus said that to be a part of his kingdom would mean suffering with Jesus (drink from the same cup—Mark 10:38–39). James and John did indeed suffer—Herod executed James, and later John was exiled (see Revelation 1:9).

12:2–11 Why did God allow James to die and yet miraculously save Peter? Life is full of difficult questions like this. Why is one child physically disabled and another child athletically gifted? Why do people die seemingly before realizing their potential? These are questions we cannot possibly answer in this life because we do not see all that God sees. He has chosen to allow evil in this world for a time. But we can trust God's leading because he has promised to destroy all evil eventually. In the meantime, we know that God will help us use our suffering to strengthen us and glorify him. For more on this question, see the notes on Job 1:1ff; 2:10; 3:23–26.

12:3 Peter was arrested during the Feast of Unleavened Bread, the week-long festival directly following Passover. This was a strategic move, since more Jews were in the city than usual, and Herod could impress the most people.

12:5 Herod's plan undoubtedly was to execute Peter, but the believers were praying for Peter's safety. The earnest prayer of the church significantly affected the outcome of these events. Prayer changes things, so pray often and with confidence.

12:7 God sent an angel to rescue Peter. Angels are God's messengers. They are divinely created beings with supernatural powers, and they sometimes take on human appearance in order to talk to people. Angels should not be worshiped, because they are not divine. They are God's servants, just as we are.

12:12 John Mark wrote the Gospel of Mark. His mother's house was large enough to accommodate a meeting of many believers. An upstairs room in this house may have been the location of Jesus' last supper with his disciples (Luke 22:8ff).

12:13–15 The prayers of the group of believers were answered, even as they prayed. But when the answer arrived at the door, they didn't believe it. We should be people of faith who believe that God answers the prayers of those who seek his will. When you pray, believe you'll get an answer. And when the answer comes, don't be surprised; be thankful!

12:17
Acts 13:16; 19:33; 21:40; Mark 6:3; Acts 15:13; 21:18; 1 Cor 15:7; Gal 1:19; 2:9, 12; Acts 1:15

12:19
Acts 16:27; 27:42; Acts 8:40

17 But motioning to them with his hand to be silent, he described to them how the Lord
had led him out of the prison. And he said, "Report these things to James and the brethren." Then he left and went to another place.
18 Now when day came, there was no small disturbance among the soldiers *as to* what
could have become of Peter.
19 When Herod had searched for him and had not found him, he examined the guards
and ordered that they be led away *to execution.* Then he went down from Judea to Caesarea and was spending time there.

HEROD AGRIPPA I

For good or evil, families have lasting and powerful influence on their children. Traits and qualities are passed on to the next generation, and often the mistakes and sins of the parents are repeated by the children. Four generations of the Herod family are mentioned in the Bible. Each leader left his evil mark: Herod the Great murdered Bethlehem's children; Herod Antipas was involved in Jesus' trial and John the Baptist's execution; Herod Agrippa I murdered the apostle James; and Herod Agrippa II was one of Paul's judges.

Herod Agrippa I related fairly well to his Jewish subjects. Because he had a Jewish grandmother of royal blood (Mariamne), he was grudgingly accepted by the people. Although as a youth he had been temporarily imprisoned by the emperor Tiberias, he was now trusted by Rome and got along well with the emperors Caligula and Claudius.

An unexpected opportunity for Herod to gain new favor with the Jews was created by the Christian movement. Gentiles began to be accepted into the church in large numbers. Many Jews had been tolerating this new movement as a sect within Judaism, but its rapid growth alarmed them. Persecution of Christians was revived, and even the apostles were not spared. James was killed, and Peter was thrown into prison.

But soon, Herod made a fatal error. During a visit to Caesarea, the people called him a god, and he accepted their praise. Herod was immediately struck with a painful disease, and he died within a week.

Like his grandfather, uncle, and son after him, Herod Agrippa I came close to the truth but missed it. Because religion was important only as an aspect of politics, he had no reverence and no qualms about taking praise that only God should receive. His mistake is a common one. Whenever we are proud of our own abilities and accomplishments, not recognizing them as gifts from God, we repeat Herod's sin.

Strengths and accomplishments:
- Capable administrator and negotiator
- Managed to maintain good relations with the Jews in his region and with Rome

Weaknesses and mistakes:
- Arranged the murder of the apostle James
- Imprisoned Peter with plans to execute him
- Allowed the people to praise him as a god

Lessons from his life:
- Those who set themselves against God are doomed to ultimate failure
- There is great danger in accepting praise that only God deserves
- Family traits can influence children toward great good or great evil

Vital statistics:
- Where: Jerusalem
- Occupation: Roman-appointed king of the Jews
- Relatives: Grandfather: Herod the Great. Father: Aristobulus. Uncle: Herod Antipas. Sister: Herodias. Wife: Cypros. Son: Herod Agrippa II. Daughters: Bernice, Mariamne, Drusilla
- Contemporaries: Emperors Tiberias, Caligula, and Claudius. James, Peter, the apostles.

Key verse:
"Immediately an angel of the Lord struck him because he did not give God the glory, and he was eaten by worms and died" (Acts 12:23).

Herod Agrippa I's story is told in Acts 12:1–23.

12:17 This James was Jesus' brother, who became a leader in the Jerusalem church (15:13; Galatians 1:19). The James who was killed (12:2) was John's brother and one of the original 12 disciples.

12:19 Under Roman law, guards who allowed a prisoner to escape were subject to the same punishment the prisoner was to receive. Thus these 16 guards were sentenced to death.

12:19 The Jews considered Jerusalem their capital, but the Romans made Caesarea their headquarters in Palestine. That is where Herod Agrippa I lived.

Death of Herod

20 Now he was very angry with the people of Tyre and Sidon; and with one accord they
came to him, and having won over Blastus the king's chamberlain, they were asking for
peace, because their country was fed by the king's country.
21 On an appointed day Herod, having put on his royal apparel, took his seat on the
rostrum and *began* delivering an address to them.
22 The people kept crying out, "The voice of a god and not of a man!"
23 And immediately an angel of the Lord struck him because he did not give God the
glory, and he was eaten by worms and died.
24 But the word of the Lord continued to grow and to be multiplied.
25 And Barnabas and Saul returned from Jerusalem when they had fulfilled their mission, taking along with *them* John, who was also called Mark.

12:20 Matt 11:21; 1 Kin 5:11; Ezra 3:7; Ezek 27:17

12:23 2 Sam 24:16; 2 Kin 19:35; Acts 5:19

12:24 Acts 6:7; 19:20

12:25 Acts 4:36; 13:1ff; Acts 11:30; Acts 12:12

B. PAUL'S MINISTRY (13:1—28:31)

The book focuses now on the ministry to the Gentiles and the spread of the church around the world, and Paul replaces Peter as the central figure in the book. Paul completes three missionary journeys and ends up being imprisoned in Jerusalem and transported to Rome. The book of Acts ends abruptly, showing that the history of the church is not yet complete. We are to be a part of the sequel.

1. First missionary journey

13 Now there were at Antioch, in the church that was *there*, prophets and teachers:
Barnabas, and Simeon who was called Niger, and Lucius of Cyrene, and Manaen
who had been brought up with Herod the tetrarch, and Saul.
2 While they were ministering to the Lord and fasting, the Holy Spirit said, "Set apart
for Me Barnabas and Saul for the work to which I have called them."
3 Then, when they had fasted and prayed and laid their hands on them, they sent them
away.
4 So, being sent out by the Holy Spirit, they went down to Seleucia and from there
they sailed to Cyprus.

13:1 Acts 11:19; Acts 11:26; Acts 11:27; 15:32; 19:6; 21:9; 1 Cor 11:4f; 13:2, 8f; 14:29, 32, 37; Rom 12:6f; 1 Cor 12:28f; Eph 4:11; James 3:1; Acts 4:36; Matt 27:32; Acts 11:20; Matt 14:1

13:2 Acts 8:29; 13:4; Acts 4:36; Acts 9:15

13:3 Acts 1:24; Acts 6:6; Acts 13:4; 14:26

13:4 Acts 13:2f; Acts 4:36

MINISTRY IN CYPRUS
The leaders of the church in Antioch chose Paul and Barnabas to take the gospel westward. Along with John Mark, they boarded ship at Seleucia and set out across the Mediterranean for Cyprus. They preached in Salamis, the largest city, and went across the island to Paphos.

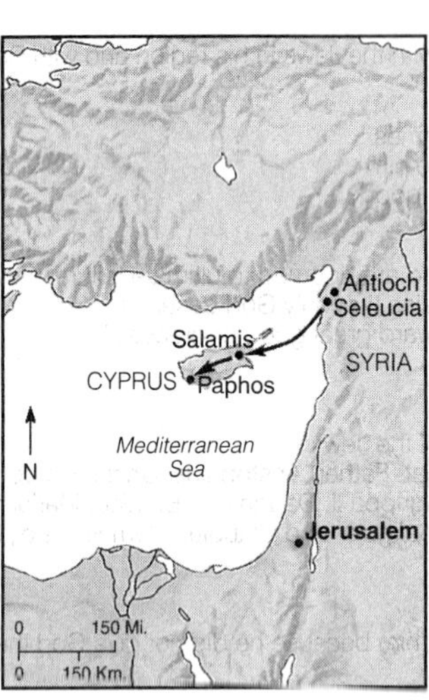

12:20 These coastal cities, Tyre and Sidon, were free and self-governing but economically dependent on Judea (see the map in the introduction to Acts for their location). We don't know why Herod had quarreled with them, but now representatives from those cities were trying to appease him through his personal servant.

12:23 Herod died a horrible death accompanied by intense pain; he was literally eaten alive, from the inside out, by worms. To be eaten by worms was considered to be one of the most disgraceful ways to die. Pride is a serious sin, and in this case, God chose to punish it immediately. God does not immediately punish all sin, but he *will* bring all to judgment (Hebrews 9:27). Accept Christ's offer of forgiveness today. No one can afford to wait.

12:25 John Mark was Barnabas's cousin (Colossians 4:10). His mother, Mary, often opened her home to the apostles (12:12), so John Mark would have been exposed to most of the great men and teachings of the early church. Later, John Mark joined Paul and Barnabas on their first missionary journey, but for unknown reasons, he left them in the middle of the trip. John Mark was criticized by Paul for abandoning the mission (15:37–39), but he wrote the Gospel of Mark and was later acclaimed by Paul as a vital help in the growth of the early church (2 Timothy 4:11).

13:1 What variety there is in the church! The common thread among these five men was their deep faith in Christ. We must never exclude anyone whom Christ has called to follow him.

13:2–3 The church set apart Barnabas and Saul to the work God had for them. To *set apart* means to dedicate for a special purpose. We too should dedicate our pastors, missionaries, and Christian workers for their tasks. We can also dedicate ourselves to use our time, money, and talents for God's work. Ask God what he wants you to set apart for him.

13:2–3 This was the beginning of Paul's first missionary journey. The church was involved in sending Paul and Barnabas, but it was God's plan. Why did Paul and Barnabas go where they did? (1) The Holy Spirit led them. (2) They followed the communication routes of the Roman empire—this made travel easier. (3) They visited key population and cultural centers to reach as many people as possible. (4) They went to cities with synagogues, speaking first to the Jews in hopes that they would see Jesus as the Messiah and help spread the Good News to everyone.

13:4 Located in the Mediterranean Sea, the island of Cyprus, with a large Jewish population, was Barnabas's home. Their first stop was in familiar territory.

13:5 Acts 9:20; 12:12
13:6 Acts 8:9; Matt 7:15
13:7 Acts 18:12; 19:38
13:8 Acts 8:9; Acts 13:7, 12; 18:12; 19:38; Acts 6:7
13:9 Acts 2:4; 4:8

5 When they reached Salamis, they *began* to proclaim the word of God in the synagogues of the Jews; and they also had John as their helper.
6 When they had gone through the whole island as far as Paphos, they found a magician, a Jewish false prophet whose name was Bar-Jesus,
7 who was with the proconsul, Sergius Paulus, a man of intelligence. This man summoned Barnabas and Saul and sought to hear the word of God.
8 But Elymas the magician (for so his name is translated) was opposing them, seeking to turn the proconsul away from the faith.
9 But Saul, who was also *known as* Paul, filled with the Holy Spirit, fixed his gaze
on him,

JOHN MARK

Mistakes are effective teachers. Their consequences have a way of making lessons painfully clear. But those who learn from their mistakes are likely to develop wisdom. John Mark was a good learner who just needed some time and encouragement.

Mark was eager to do the right thing, but he had trouble staying with a task. In his Gospel, Mark mentions a young man (probably referring to himself) who fled in such fear during Jesus' arrest that he left his clothes behind. This tendency to run was to reappear later when Paul and Barnabas took him as their assistant on their first missionary journey. At their second stop, Mark left them and returned to Jerusalem. It was a decision Paul did not easily accept. In preparing for their second journey two years later, Barnabas again suggested Mark as a traveling companion, but Paul flatly refused. As a result, the team was divided. Barnabas took Mark with him, and Paul chose Silas. Barnabas was patient with Mark, and the young man repaid his investment. Paul and Mark were later reunited, and the older apostle became a close friend of the young disciple.

Mark was a valuable companion to three early Christian leaders—Barnabas, Paul, and Peter. The material in Mark's Gospel seems to have come mostly from Peter. Mark's role as a serving assistant allowed him to be an observer. He heard Peter's accounts of the years with Jesus over and over, and he was one of the first to put Jesus' life in writing.

Barnabas played a key role in Mark's life. He stood beside the young man despite his failure, giving him patient encouragement. Mark challenges us to learn from our mistakes and appreciate the patience of others. Is there a Barnabas in your life you need to thank for his or her encouragement to you?

Strengths and accomplishments:
- Wrote the Gospel of Mark
- He and his mother provided their home as one of the main meeting places for the Christians in Jerusalem
- Persisted beyond his youthful mistakes
- Was an assistant and traveling companion to three of the greatest early missionaries

Weaknesses and mistakes:
- Probably the nameless young man described in the Gospel of Mark who fled in panic when Jesus was arrested
- Left Paul and Barnabas for unknown reasons during the first missionary journey

Lessons from his life:
- Personal maturity usually comes from a combination of time and mistakes
- Mistakes are not usually as important as what can be learned from them
- Effective living is not measured as much by what we accomplish as by what we overcome in order to accomplish it
- Encouragement can change a person's life

Vital statistics:
- Where: Jerusalem
- Occupations: Missionary-in-training, Gospel writer, traveling companion
- Relatives: Mother: Mary. Cousin: Barnabas
- Contemporaries: Paul, Peter, Timothy, Luke, Silas

Key verse:
"Only Luke is with me. Pick up Mark and bring him with you, for he is useful to me for service" (Paul writing in 2 Timothy 4:11).

John Mark's story is told in Acts 12:23—13:13 and 15:36–39. He is also mentioned in Colossians 4:10; 2 Timothy 4:11; Philemon 24; 1 Peter 5:13.

13:6–7 A proconsul was a high Roman official. Here he functioned as the governor of the island. Such leaders often kept private sorcerers. Bar-Jesus realized that if Sergius Paulus believed in Jesus, he would soon be out of a job.

13:9–10 Here is where Saul is first called Paul.

10 and said, "You who are full of all deceit and fraud, you son of the devil, you enemy
of all righteousness, will you not cease to make crooked the straight ways of the Lord?
11 "Now, behold, the hand of the Lord is upon you, and you will be blind and not see
the sun for a time." And immediately a mist and a darkness fell upon him, and he went
about seeking those who would lead him by the hand.
12 Then the proconsul believed when he saw what had happened, being amazed at the
teaching of the Lord.
13 Now Paul and his companions put out to sea from Paphos and came to Perga in
Pamphylia; but John left them and returned to Jerusalem.
14 But going on from Perga, they arrived at Pisidian Antioch, and on the Sabbath day
they went into the synagogue and sat down.
15 After the reading of the Law and the Prophets the synagogue officials sent to them,
saying, "Brethren, if you have any word of exhortation for the people, say it."
16 Paul stood up, and motioning with his hand said,
"Men of Israel, and you who fear God, listen:
17 "The God of this people Israel chose our fathers and made the people great during
their stay in the land of Egypt, and with an uplifted arm He led them out from it.
18 "For a period of about forty years He put up with them in the wilderness.
19 "When He had destroyed seven nations in the land of Canaan, He distributed their
land as an inheritance—*all of which took* about four hundred and fifty years.
20 "After these things He gave *them* judges until Samuel the prophet.
21 "Then they asked for a king, and God gave them Saul the son of Kish, a man of the
tribe of Benjamin, for forty years.
22 "After He had removed him, He raised up David to be their king, concerning whom
He also testified and said, 'I HAVE FOUND DAVID the son of Jesse, A MAN AFTER MY
HEART, who will do all My will.'

13:10 Matt 13:38; John 8:44; Hos 14:9; 2 Pet 2:15

13:13 Acts 2:10; 14:24; 15:38; 27:5

13:15 Acts 15:21; 2 Cor 3:14f; Mark 5:22

13:17 Ex 6:1, 6; 13:14, 16; Deut 7:6-8; Acts 7:17ff; Ex 1:7; Ex 12:51

13:18 Num 14:34; Acts 7:36; Deut 1:31

13:19 Acts 7:45; Deut 7:1; Josh 14:1; 19:51; Ps 78:55; Judg 11:26; 1 Kin 6:1

13:20 Judg 2:16; 1 Sam 3:20; Acts 3:24

13:21 1 Sam 8:5; 1 Sam 9:1f; 10:1, 21

13:22 1 Sam 15:23, 26, 28; 16:1, 13; 1 Sam 13:14; Ps 89:20; Acts 7:46

13:10 The Holy Spirit led Paul to confront Bar-Jesus with his sin. There is a time to be nice and a time to confront. Ask God to show you the difference and to give you the courage to do what is right.

13:13 No reason is given why John Mark left Paul and Barnabas. Some suggestions are: (1) He was homesick; (2) he resented the change in leadership from Barnabas (his cousin) to Paul; (3) he became ill (an illness that may have affected all of them—see Galatians 4:13); (4) he was unable to withstand the rigors and dangers of the missionary journey; (5) he may have planned to go only that far but had not communicated this to Paul and Barnabas. Paul implicitly accused John Mark of lacking courage and commitment, refusing to take him along on another journey (see 15:37–38). It is clear from Paul's later letters, however, that he grew to respect Mark (Colossians 4:10), and that he needed Mark in his work (2 Timothy 4:11).

13:14 This is Pisidian Antioch, not the Antioch of Syria where there was already a flourishing church (11:26). This Antioch, in the region of Pisidia, was a hub of good roads and trade, with a large Jewish population.

13:14 When they went to a new city to witness for Christ, Paul and Barnabas went first to the synagogue. The Jews who were there believed in God and diligently studied the Scriptures. Tragically, however, many could not accept Jesus as the promised Messiah because they had the wrong idea of what kind of Messiah he would be. He was not, as they desired, a military king who would overthrow Rome's control, but a servant king who would defeat sin in people's hearts. (Only later, when Christ returns, will he judge the nations of the world.) Paul and Barnabas did not separate themselves from the synagogues but tried to show clearly that the very Scriptures the Jews studied pointed to Jesus.

13:14–15 What happened in a synagogue service? First the *Shema* was recited (this is Deuteronomy 6:4, which Jews repeated several times daily). Certain prayers were spoken; then there was a reading from the law (the books of Genesis through Deuteronomy), a reading from the prophets intending to illustrate the law, and a sermon. A synagogue official decided who was to lead the service and give the sermon. A different person was chosen to lead each week. Since it was customary for the synagogue leader to invite visiting rabbis to speak, Paul and Barnabas usually had an open door when they first went to a synagogue. But as soon as they spoke about Jesus as Messiah, the door would slam shut. They were usually not invited back by the religious leaders, and sometimes they were thrown out of town!

13:16ff Paul's message to the Jews in the synagogue in Antioch began with an emphasis on God's covenant with Israel. This was a point of agreement, because all Jews were proud to be God's chosen people. Then Paul went on to explain how the gospel fulfilled the covenant. Some Jews found this message hard to swallow.

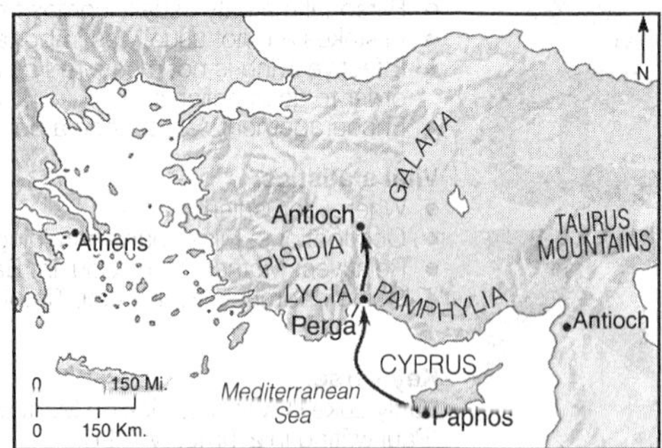

MINISTRY IN PAMPHYLIA AND GALATIA Paul, Barnabas, and John Mark left Paphos and landed at Perga in the humid region of Pamphylia, a narrow strip of land between the sea and the Taurus Mountains. John Mark left them in Perga, but Paul and Barnabas traveled up the steep road into the higher elevation of Pisidia in Galatia. When the Jews rejected his message, Paul preached to Gentiles, and the Jews drove Paul and Barnabas out of the Pisidian city of Antioch.

13:23 Luke 2:11

13:24 Mark 1:1-4; Luke 3:3

13:25 Matt 3:11; Luke 3:16; John 1:20, 27

23 "From the descendants of this man, according to promise, God has brought to Israel
a Savior, Jesus,
24 after John had proclaimed before His coming a baptism of repentance to all the
people of Israel.
25 "And while John was completing his course, he kept saying, 'What do you suppose

BARNABAS

Every group needs an "encourager," because everyone needs encouragement at one time or another. However, the value of encouragement is often missed because it tends to be private rather than public. In fact, people most need encouragement when they feel most alone. A man named Joseph was such an encourager that he earned the nickname "Son of Encouragement," or Barnabas, from the Jerusalem Christians.

Barnabas was drawn to people he could encourage, and he was a great help to those around him. It is delightful that wherever Barnabas encouraged Christians, non-Christians flocked to become believers!

Barnabas's actions were crucial to the early church. In a way, we can thank him for most of the New Testament. God used his relationship with Paul at one point and with Mark at another to keep these two men going when either might have failed. Barnabas did wonders with encouragement!

When Paul arrived in Jerusalem for the first time following his conversion, the local Christians were understandably reluctant to welcome him. They thought his story was a trick to capture more Christians. Only Barnabas proved willing to risk his life to meet with Paul and then convince the others that their former enemy was now a vibrant believer in Jesus. We can only wonder what might have happened to Paul without Barnabas.

It was Barnabas who encouraged Mark to go with him and Paul to Antioch. Mark joined them on their first missionary journey, but decided during the trip to return home. Later, Barnabas wanted to invite Mark to join them for another journey, but Paul would not agree. As a result, the partners went separate ways, Barnabas with Mark and Paul with Silas. This actually doubled the missionary effort. Barnabas's patient encouragement was confirmed by Mark's eventual effective ministry. Paul and Mark were later reunited in missionary efforts.

As Barnabas's life shows, we are rarely in a situation where there isn't someone we can encourage. Our tendency, however, is to criticize instead. It may be important at times to point out someone's shortcomings, but before we have the right to do this, we must build that person's trust through encouragement. Are you prepared to encourage those with whom you come in contact today?

Strengths and accomplishments:
- One of the first to sell possessions to help the Christians in Jerusalem
- First to travel with Paul as a missionary team
- Was an encourager, as his nickname shows, and thus one of the most quietly influential people in the early days of Christianity
- Called an apostle, although not one of the original 12

Weakness and mistake:
- With Peter, temporarily stayed aloof from Gentile believers until Paul corrected him

Lessons from his life:
- Encouragement is one of the most effective ways to help
- Sooner or later, true obedience to God will involve risk
- There is always someone who needs encouragement

Vital statistics:
- Where: Cyprus, Jerusalem, Antioch
- Occupations: Missionary, teacher
- Relatives: Aunt: Mary. Cousin: John Mark
- Contemporaries: Peter, Silas, Paul, Herod Agrippa I

Key verses:
"When he arrived and witnessed the grace of God, he rejoiced and began to encourage them all with resolute heart to remain true to the Lord; for he was a good man, and full of the Holy Spirit and of faith. And considerable numbers were brought to the Lord" (Acts 11:23–24).

Barnabas's story is told in Acts 4:36–37; 9:27—15:39. He is also mentioned in 1 Corinthians 9:6; Galatians 2:1, 9, 13; Colossians 4:10.

13:23–31 Paul began where his listeners were and then introduced them to Christ. Because Paul was speaking to devout Jews, he began with the covenant, Abraham, David, and other familiar themes. Later, when speaking to the Greek philosophers in Athens (17:22–32), he would begin by talking about what he had observed in their city. In both cases, however, he centered the sermon around Christ and emphasized the resurrection. When you share the Good News, begin where your audience is—then tell them about Christ.

that I am? I am not *He.* But behold, one is coming after me the sandals of whose feet I
am not worthy to untie.'
26 "Brethren, sons of Abraham's family, and those among you who fear God, to us the
message of this salvation has been sent.
27 "For those who live in Jerusalem, and their rulers, recognizing neither Him nor
the utterances of the prophets which are read every Sabbath, fulfilled *these* by condemning *Him.*
28 "And though they found no ground for *putting Him to* death, they asked Pilate that
He be executed.
29 "When they had carried out all that was written concerning Him, they took Him down
from the cross and laid Him in a tomb.
30 "But God raised Him from the dead;
31 and for many days He appeared to those who came up with Him from Galilee to
Jerusalem, the very ones who are now His witnesses to the people.
32 "And we preach to you the good news of the promise made to the fathers,
33 that God has fulfilled this *promise* to our children in that He raised up Jesus, as it is
also written in the second Psalm, 'YOU ARE MY SON; TODAY I HAVE BEGOTTEN YOU.'
34 "*As for the fact* that He raised Him up from the dead, no longer to return to decay,
He has spoken in this way: 'I WILL GIVE YOU THE HOLY *and* SURE *blessings* OF DAVID.'
35 "Therefore He also says in another *Psalm,* 'YOU WILL NOT ALLOW YOUR HOLY ONE
TO UNDERGO DECAY.'
36 "For David, after he had served the purpose of God in his own generation, fell asleep,
and was laid among his fathers and underwent decay;
37 but He whom God raised did not undergo decay.
38 "Therefore let it be known to you, brethren, that through Him forgiveness of sins is
proclaimed to you,
39 and through Him everyone who believes is freed from all things, from which you
could not be freed through the Law of Moses.
40 "Therefore take heed, so that the thing spoken of in the Prophets may not come
upon *you:*
41 'BEHOLD, YOU SCOFFERS, AND MARVEL, AND PERISH;
FOR I AM ACCOMPLISHING A WORK IN YOUR DAYS,
A WORK WHICH YOU WILL NEVER BELIEVE, THOUGH SOMEONE SHOULD
DESCRIBE IT TO YOU.' "
42 As Paul and Barnabas were going out, the people kept begging that these things
might be spoken to them the next Sabbath.
43 Now when *the meeting of* the synagogue had broken up, many of the Jews and of the
God-fearing proselytes followed Paul and Barnabas, who, speaking to them, were urging
them to continue in the grace of God.

13:26 John 6:68

13:27 Luke 23:13; Acts 3:17; Luke 24:27

13:28 Matt 27:22, 23; Mark 15:13, 14; Luke 23:21-23; John 19:15; Acts 3:14

13:29 Acts 26:22; Acts 5:30; Matt 27:57-61; Mark 15:42-47; Luke 23:50-56; John 19:38-42

13:30 Acts 2:24; 13:33, 34

13:31 Acts 1:3; Luke 24:48

13:32 Acts 5:42; 14:15; Rom 1:2; 4:13; 9:4

13:33 Acts 2:24; Ps 2:7

13:34 Acts 2:24; Is 55:3

13:35 Ps 16:10; Acts 2:27

13:36 Acts 2:29; 20:27; 1 Kin 2:10; Acts 8:1

13:38 Luke 24:47; Acts 2:38

13:39 Acts 10:43; Rom 3:28; 10:4

13:40 Luke 24:44; John 6:45; Acts 7:42

13:41 Hab 1:5

13:43 Acts 13:50; 16:14; 17:4, 17; 18:7; Matt 23:15; Acts 11:23

13:38–39 This is the Good News of the gospel: that forgiveness of sins and freedom from guilt are available through faith in Christ to all people—including *you.* Have you received this forgiveness? Are you refreshed by it each day?

13:42–45 The Jewish leaders undoubtedly brought theological arguments against Paul and Barnabas, but Luke tells us that the real reason for their hostility was that "they were filled with jealousy." When we see others succeeding where we haven't, or receiving the affirmation we crave, it is hard to rejoice with them. Jealousy is our natural reaction. But how tragic it is when our own jealous feelings make us try to stop God's work. If a work is God's work, rejoice in it—no matter who is doing it.

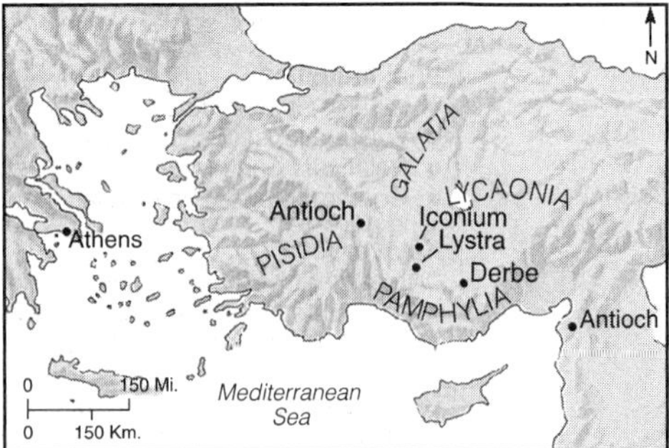

CONTINUED MINISTRY IN GALATIA Paul and Barnabas, thrown out of Antioch in Pisidia, descended the mountains, going east into Lycaonia. They went first to Iconium, a commercial center on the road between Asia and Syria. After preaching there, they had to flee to Lystra, 25 miles south. Paul was stoned in Lystra, but he and Barnabas traveled the 50 miles to Derbe, a border town. The pair then boldly retraced their steps.

13:45
Acts 13:50; 14:2, 4, 5, 19; 1 Thess 2:16

13:46
Acts 18:6; 19:9; 22:21; 26:20; 28:28

13:47
Is 42:6; 49:6; Luke 2:32

13:48
Acts 13:12; Rom 8:28ff; Eph 1:4f, 11

13:50
Acts 13:45; 14:2, 4, 5, 19; 1 Thess 2:14ff; Acts 17:4, 17; 18:7; Mark 15:43

13:51
Matt 10:14; Mark 6:11; Luke 9:5; 10:11

13:52
Acts 2:4

14:1
Acts 13:51; 14:19, 21; 16:2; 2 Tim 3:11; John 7:35; Acts 18:4

14:2
1 Thess 2:14ff; John 3:36; Acts 1:15

14:3
Acts 4:29f; 20:32; Heb 2:4; John 4:48

14:5
Acts 13:45, 50; 1 Thess 2:14ff

14:6
2 Tim 3:11; Acts 14:20; 16:1; 20:4

14:7
Acts 16:10

14:8
Acts 14:6, 21; 16:1f; 2 Tim 3:11; Acts 3:2

Paul Turns to the Gentiles

44 The next Sabbath nearly the whole city assembled to hear the word of the Lord.
45 But when the Jews saw the crowds, they were filled with jealousy and *began* contradicting the things spoken by Paul, and were blaspheming.
46 Paul and Barnabas spoke out boldly and said, "It was necessary that the word of
God be spoken to you first; since you repudiate it and judge yourselves unworthy of eternal
life, behold, we are turning to the Gentiles.
47 "For so the Lord has commanded us,
'I HAVE PLACED YOU AS A LIGHT FOR THE GENTILES,
THAT YOU MAY BRING SALVATION TO THE END OF THE EARTH.' "
48 When the Gentiles heard this, they *began* rejoicing and glorifying the word of the
Lord; and as many as had been appointed to eternal life believed.
49 And the word of the Lord was being spread through the whole region.
50 But the Jews incited the devout women of prominence and the leading men of the
city, and instigated a persecution against Paul and Barnabas, and drove them out of their
district.
51 But they shook off the dust of their feet *in protest* against them and went to
Iconium.
52 And the disciples were continually filled with joy and with the Holy Spirit.

Acceptance and Opposition

14 In Iconium they entered the synagogue of the Jews together, and spoke in such a
manner that a large number of people believed, both of Jews and of Greeks.
2 But the Jews who disbelieved stirred up the minds of the Gentiles and embittered
them against the brethren.
3 Therefore they spent a long time *there* speaking boldly *with reliance* upon the Lord,
who was testifying to the word of His grace, granting that signs and wonders be done by
their hands.
4 But the people of the city were divided; and some sided with the Jews, and some
with the apostles.
5 And when an attempt was made by both the Gentiles and the Jews with their rulers,
to mistreat and to stone them,
6 they became aware of it and fled to the cities of Lycaonia, Lystra and Derbe, and
the surrounding region;
7 and there they continued to preach the gospel.
8 At Lystra a man was sitting who had no strength in his feet, lame from his mother's
womb, who had never walked.

13:46 Why was it necessary for the gospel to go first to the Jews? God planned that through the Jewish nation *all* the world would come to know God (Genesis 12:3). Paul, a Jew himself, loved his people (Romans 9:1–5) and wanted to give them every opportunity to join him in proclaiming God's salvation. Unfortunately, many Jews did not recognize Jesus as Messiah, and they did not understand that God was offering salvation to anyone, Jew or Gentile, who comes to him through faith in Christ.

13:47 God had planned for Israel to be this light (Isaiah 49:6). Through Israel came Jesus, the light of the nations (Luke 2:32). This light would spread out and enlighten the Gentiles.

13:50 Instead of accepting the truth, the Jewish leaders stirred up opposition and ran Paul and Barnabas out of town. When confronted by a disturbing truth, people often turn away and refuse to listen. When God's Spirit points out needed changes in our lives, we must listen to him. Otherwise we may be pushing the truth so far away that it no longer affects us.

13:51 Often Jews would shake the dust off their feet when leaving a Gentile town, on the way back to their own land. This symbolized cleansing themselves from the contamination of those who did not worship God. For Paul and Barnabas to do this to Jews demonstrated that Jews who reject the gospel are not truly part of Israel and are no better than pagans.

13:51 Jesus had told his disciples to shake from their feet the dust of any town that would not accept or listen to them (Mark 6:11). The disciples were not to blame if the message was rejected, as long as they had faithfully presented it. When we share Christ carefully and sensitively, God does not hold us responsible for the other person's decision.

14:3–4 We may wish we could perform a miraculous act that would convince everyone once and for all that Jesus is the Lord. But we see here that even if we could perform a miracle, it wouldn't convince everyone. God gave these men power to do great wonders as confirmation of the message of grace, but people were still divided. Don't spend your time and energy wishing for miracles. Sow your seeds of Good News on the best ground you can find in the best way you can, and leave the convincing to the Holy Spirit.

14:6 Iconium (14:1), Lystra, and Derbe were three cities Paul visited in the southern part of the region of Galatia. Paul probably wrote a letter to these churches—the letter to the Galatians—because many Jewish Christians were claiming that non-Jewish Christians couldn't be saved unless they followed Jewish laws and customs. Paul's letter refuted this and brought the believers back to a right understanding of faith in Jesus (see Galatians 3:3, 5). Paul may have written his letter soon after leaving the region (see the note on 14:28).

9 This man was listening to Paul as he spoke, who, when he had fixed his gaze on him
and had seen that he had faith to be made well,
10 said with a loud voice, "Stand upright on your feet." And he leaped up and *began* to
walk.
11 When the crowds saw what Paul had done, they raised their voice, saying in the
Lycaonian language, "The gods have become like men and have come down to us."
12 And they *began* calling Barnabas, Zeus, and Paul, Hermes, because he was the chief
speaker.
13 The priest of Zeus, whose *temple* was just outside the city, brought oxen and gar-
lands to the gates, and wanted to offer sacrifice with the crowds.
14 But when the apostles Barnabas and Paul heard of it, they tore their robes and rushed
out into the crowd, crying out
15 and saying, "Men, why are you doing these things? We are also men of the same
nature as you, and preach the gospel to you that you should turn from these [29]vain things
to a living God, WHO MADE THE HEAVEN AND THE EARTH AND THE SEA AND ALL THAT
IS IN THEM.
16 "In the generations gone by He permitted all the nations to go their own ways;
17 and yet He did not leave Himself without witness, in that He did good and gave you
rains from heaven and fruitful seasons, satisfying your hearts with food and gladness."
18 *Even* saying these things, with difficulty they restrained the crowds from offering
sacrifice to them.
19 But Jews came from Antioch and Iconium, and having won over the crowds, they
stoned Paul and dragged him out of the city, supposing him to be dead.
20 But while the disciples stood around him, he got up and entered the city. The next
day he went away with Barnabas to Derbe.
21 After they had preached the gospel to that city and had made many disciples, they
returned to Lystra and to Iconium and to Antioch,

29 I.e. idols

14:9 Acts 3:4; 10:4; Matt 9:28
14:10 Acts 3:8
14:11 Acts 8:10; 28:6
14:13 Dan 2:46
14:14 Num 14:6; Matt 26:65; Mark 14:63
14:15 Acts 10:26; James 5:17; Acts 13:32; 1 Cor 8:4; Matt 16:16; Ex 20:11; Ps 146:6; Acts 4:24; 17:24; Rev 14:7
14:16 Acts 17:30; Ps 81:12; Mic 4:5
14:17 Acts 17:26f; Rom 1:19f; Deut 11:14; Job 5:10; Ps 65:10f
14:19 Acts 13:45, 50; 1 Thess 2:14ff; 2 Cor 11:25; 2 Tim 3:11
14:20 Acts 11:26; 14:22
14:21 Acts 2:47; 13:51; 14:1, 19; Acts 13:14; 14:26

14:11 "The Lycaonian language" refers to their local dialect.

14:11–12 Zeus and Hermes (also known as Jupiter and Mercury) were two popular gods in the Roman world. People from Lystra claimed that these gods had once visited their city. According to legend, no one offered them hospitality except an old couple, so Zeus and Hermes killed the rest of the people and rewarded the old couple. When the citizens of Lystra saw the miracles of Paul and Barnabas, they assumed that the gods were revisiting them. Remembering the story of what had happened to the previous citizens, they immediately honored Paul and Barnabas and showered them with gifts.

14:15–18 Responding to the people of Lystra, Paul and Barnabas reminded them that God never leaves himself "without witness." Rain and crops, for example, are evidence of his goodness. Later Paul wrote that this evidence in nature leaves people without an excuse for unbelief (Romans 1:20). When in doubt about God, look around and you will see abundant evidence that he is at work in our world.

14:18–19 Only days after the people in Lystra had thought that Paul and Barnabas were gods and wanted to offer sacrifices to them, they stoned Paul and left him for dead. That's human nature. Jesus understood how fickle crowds can be (John 2:24–25). When many people approve of us, we feel good, but that should never cloud our thinking or affect our decisions. We should not live to please the crowd—especially in our spiritual lives. Be like Jesus. Know the nature of the crowd and don't put your trust in it. Put your trust in God alone.

14:18–20 Paul and Barnabas were persistent in their preaching of the Good News, considering the cost to themselves to be nothing in comparison with obedience to Christ. They had just narrowly escaped being stoned in Iconium (14:1–7), but Jews from Antioch and Iconium tracked Paul down, stoned him, and left him for dead. But Paul got up and went back into the city to preach the Good News. That's true commitment! Being a disciple of Christ calls for total commitment. As Christians, we no longer belong to ourselves but to our Lord, for whom we are called to suffer.

14:21–22 Paul and Barnabas returned to visit the believers in all the cities where they had recently been threatened and physically attacked. These men knew the dangers they faced, yet they believed that they had a responsibility to encourage the new believers. No matter how inconvenient or uncomfortable the task may seem, we must always support new believers who need our help and encouragement. It was not convenient or comfortable for Jesus to go to the cross for us!

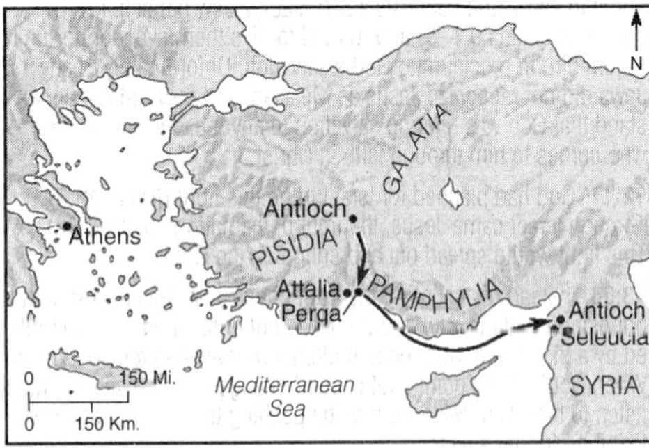

THE END OF THE FIRST JOURNEY From Antioch in Pisidia, Paul and Barnabas went down the mountains back to Pamphylia on the coast. Stopping first in Perga, where they had landed, they went west to Attalia, the main port that sent goods from Asia to Syria and Egypt. There they found a ship bound for Seleucia, the port of Antioch in Syria. This ended their first missionary journey.

14:22 Mark 10:30; John 15:18, 20; 16:33; Acts 9:16; 1 Thess 3:3; 2 Tim 3:12; 1 Pet 2:21; Rev 1:9

14:23 Titus 1:5; Acts 11:30; Acts 1:24; 13:3; Acts 20:32

14:24 Acts 13:13

14:27 Acts 15:3, 4, 12; 21:19; 1 Cor 16:9; 2 Cor 2:12; Col 4:3; Rev 3:8

15:1 Acts 1:15; 15:3, 22, 32; Lev 12:3; 1 Cor 7:18; Gal 2:11, 14; 5:2f; Acts 6:14

15:2 Gal 2:2; Acts 11:30; 15:4, 6, 22, 23; 16:4

15:3 Rom 15:24; 1 Cor 16:6, 11; 2 Cor 1:16; Titus 3:13; 3 John 6

15:5 1 Cor 7:18; Gal 2:11, 14; 5:2f

15:6 Acts 11:30; 16:4

15:7 Acts 10:19f; 20:24

22 strengthening the souls of the disciples, encouraging them to continue in the faith,
and *saying,* "Through many tribulations we must enter the kingdom of God."
23 When they had appointed elders for them in every church, having prayed with fasting, they commended them to the Lord in whom they had believed.
24 They passed through Pisidia and came into Pamphylia.
25 When they had spoken the word in Perga, they went down to Attalia.
26 From there they sailed to Antioch, from which they had been commended to the grace of God for the work that they had accomplished.
27 When they had arrived and gathered the church together, they *began* to report all things that God had done with them and how He had opened a door of faith to the Gentiles.
28 And they spent a long time with the disciples.

2. The council at Jerusalem

15 Some men came down from Judea and *began* teaching the brethren, "Unless you are circumcised according to the custom of Moses, you cannot be saved."
2 And when Paul and Barnabas had great dissension and debate with them, *the brethren* determined that Paul and Barnabas and some others of them should go up to Jerusalem to the apostles and elders concerning this issue.
3 Therefore, being sent on their way by the church, they were passing through both Phoenicia and Samaria, describing in detail the conversion of the Gentiles, and were bringing great joy to all the brethren.
4 When they arrived at Jerusalem, they were received by the church and the apostles and the elders, and they reported all that God had done with them.
5 But some of the sect of the Pharisees who had believed stood up, saying, "It is necessary to circumcise them and to direct them to observe the Law of Moses."
6 The apostles and the elders came together to look into this matter.
7 After there had been much debate, Peter stood up and said to them, "Brethren, you

---

14:23 Part of the reason that Paul and Barnabas risked their lives to return to these cities was to organize the churches' leadership. They were not just following up on a loosely knit group; they were helping the believers get organized with spiritual leaders who could help them grow. Churches grow under Spirit-led leaders, both laypersons and pastors. Pray for your church leaders and support them; and if God puts his finger on you, humbly accept the responsibility of a leadership role in your church.

14:28 Paul probably wrote his letter to the Galatians while he was staying in Antioch (A.D. 48 or 49) after completing his first missionary journey. There are several theories as to what part of Galatia Paul was addressing, but most agree that Iconium, Lystra, and Derbe were part of that region for whom the letter is intended. Galatians was probably written before the Jerusalem council (Acts 15), because in the letter the question of whether Gentile believers should be required to follow Jewish law was not yet resolved. The council met to solve that problem.

15:1 The real problem for the Jewish Christians was not whether Gentiles could be saved, but whether Gentiles had to adhere to the laws of Moses. The test of following these laws was circumcision. The Jewish Christians were worried because soon there would be more Gentile than Jewish Christians. And they were afraid of weakening moral standards among believers if they did not follow Jewish laws. Paul, Barnabas, and the other church leaders believed that the Old Testament law was very important, but it was not a prerequisite to salvation. The law cannot save; only by grace through faith in Jesus Christ can a person be saved.

15:1ff The delegates to the council at Jerusalem came from the churches in Jerusalem and Antioch. The conversion of Gentiles was raising an urgent question for the early church—do the Gentiles have to adhere to the laws of Moses and other Jewish traditions to be saved? One group of Jewish Christians insisted that following the law, including submitting to the rite of circumcision, was necessary for salvation. The Gentiles, however, did not think they needed to become Jewish first in order to become Christians. So Paul and Barnabas discussed this problem with the leaders of the church. The council upheld the convictions expressed by Paul and Barnabas that following the Jewish laws, including being circumcised, was not essential for salvation.

15:2 The question of whether the Gentile believers should obey the law of Moses to be saved was an important one. The controversy intensified largely due to the success of the new Gentile churches. The conservatives in the Jerusalem church were led by converted Pharisees (15:5) who preferred a legalistic religion to one based on faith alone. If the conservatives had won, the Gentiles would have been required to be circumcised and converted to Judaism. This would have seriously confined Christianity to simply being another sect within Judaism. There is something of a "Pharisee" in each one of us. We may unwittingly mistake upholding tradition, structure, and legal requirements for obeying God. Make sure the gospel brings freedom and life to those you are trying to reach.

15:2ff It is helpful to see how the churches in Antioch and Jerusalem resolved their conflict: (1) The church in Antioch sent a delegation to help seek a solution; (2) the delegates met with the church leaders to give their reports and set another date to continue the discussion; (3) Paul and Barnabas gave their report; (4) James summarized the reports and drew up the decision; (5) everyone agreed to abide by the decision; (6) the council sent a letter with delegates back to Antioch to report the decision.

This is a wise way to handle conflicts within the church. Problems must be confronted, and all sides of the argument must be given a fair hearing. The discussion should be held in the presence of leaders who are spiritually mature and trustworthy to make wise decisions. Everyone should then abide by the decisions.

know that in the early days God made a choice among you, that by my mouth the Gentiles would hear the word of the gospel and believe.
8 "And God, who knows the heart, testified to them giving them the Holy Spirit, just
as He also did to us;
9 and He made no distinction between us and them, cleansing their hearts by faith.
10 "Now therefore why do you put God to the test by placing upon the neck of the disciples a yoke which neither our fathers nor we have been able to bear?
11 "But we believe that we are saved through the grace of the Lord Jesus, in the same
way as they also are."
12 All the people kept silent, and they were listening to Barnabas and Paul as they were
relating what signs and wonders God had done through them among the Gentiles.

James's Judgment

13 After they had stopped speaking, James answered, saying, "Brethren, listen to me.
14 "Simeon has related how God first concerned Himself about taking from among the
Gentiles a people for His name.
15 "With this the words of the Prophets agree, just as it is written,
16 'AFTER THESE THINGS I will return,
AND I WILL REBUILD THE TABERNACLE OF DAVID WHICH HAS FALLEN,
AND I WILL REBUILD ITS RUINS,
AND I WILL RESTORE IT,
17 SO THAT THE REST OF MANKIND MAY SEEK THE LORD,
AND ALL THE GENTILES WHO ARE CALLED BY MY NAME,'
18 SAYS THE LORD, WHO MAKES THESE THINGS KNOWN FROM LONG AGO.
19 "Therefore it is my judgment that we do not trouble those who are turning to God
from among the Gentiles,
20 but that we write to them that they abstain from things contaminated by idols and
from fornication and from what is strangled and from blood.
21 "For Moses from ancient generations has in every city those who preach him, since
he is read in the synagogues every Sabbath."
22 Then it seemed good to the apostles and the elders, with the whole church, to choose
men from among them to send to Antioch with Paul and Barnabas—Judas called Barsabbas, and Silas, leading men among the brethren,

15:8 Acts 1:24; 10:44, 47
15:9 Acts 10:28, 34; 11:12; Acts 10:43
15:10 Acts 5:9; Matt 23:4; Gal 5:1
15:11 Rom 3:24; 5:15; 2 Cor 13:14; Eph 2:5-8
15:12 Acts 14:27; 15:3, 4; John 4:48
15:14 Acts 15:7; 2 Pet 1:1
15:16 Amos 9:11; Jer 12:15
15:17 Amos 9:12; Deut 28:10; Is 63:19; Jer 14:9; Dan 9:19; James 2:7
15:18 Amos 9:12; Is 45:21
15:20 Ex 34:15-17; 1 Cor 8:7, 13; 10:7f, Deut 12:16, 23; 15:23; 1 Sam 14:33
15:21 2 Cor 3:14f
15:22 Acts 11:20; 16:19, 25, 29; 17:4, 10, 14f; 18:5; 2 Cor 1:19; 1 Thess 1:1; 2 Thess 1:1; 1 Pet 5:12; Acts 15:1

THE JERUSALEM COUNCIL
A dispute arose when some Judeans taught that Gentile believers had to be circumcised to be saved. Paul and Barnabas went to Jerusalem to discuss this situation with the leaders there. After the Jerusalem council made its decision, Paul and Barnabas returned to Antioch with the news.

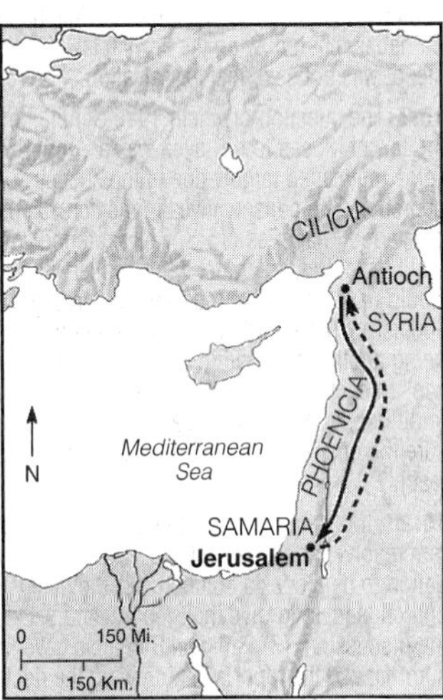

15:10 If the law was a yoke that the Jews could not bear, how did having the law help them throughout their history? Paul wrote that the law was a guide that pointed out their sins so they could repent and return to God and right living (see Galatians 3:24, 25). It was, and still is, impossible to obey the law completely.

15:13 This James is Jesus' brother. He became the leader of the church in Jerusalem and wrote the book of James.

15:14 Simeon is another name for Peter.

15:20–21 James' judgment was that Gentile believers did not have to be circumcised, but they should stay away from things (mainly referring to food) polluted by idols, from fornication (sexual immorality—a common part of idol worship), and from eating meat of strangled animals and from consuming blood (reflecting the Biblical teaching that the life is in the blood—Leviticus 17:14). If Gentile Christians would abstain from these practices, they would please God and get along better with their Jewish brothers and sisters in Christ. Of course, there were other actions inappropriate for believers, but the Jews were especially concerned about these four. This compromise helped the church grow unhindered by the cultural differences of Jews and Gentiles. When we share our message across cultural and economic boundaries, we must be sure that the requirements for faith we set up are God's, not people's.

15:22 Apostleship was not a church office but a position and function based on specific gifts. Elders were appointed to lead and manage the church. In this meeting, apostles submitted to the judgment of an elder—James, Jesus' brother.

15:22 Later Silas accompanied Paul on Paul's second missionary journey in place of Barnabas, who visited different cities with John Mark.

15:23 Acts 11:20; Matt 4:24; Acts 15:41; Gal 1:21; Acts 6:9; Acts 23:26; James 1:1; 2 John 10f

15:24 Gal 1:7; 5:10

15:26 Acts 9:23ff; 14:19

15:27 Acts 15:22, 32; Acts 15:22

15:28 Acts 15:25; Acts 5:32; 15:8; Acts 15:19

15:29 Acts 15:20

23 and they sent this letter by them,
"The apostles and the brethren who are elders, to the brethren in Antioch and Syria
and Cilicia who are from the Gentiles, greetings.
24 "Since we have heard that some of our number to whom we gave no instruction have
disturbed you with *their* words, unsettling your souls,
25 it seemed good to us, having become of one mind, to select men to send to you with
our beloved Barnabas and Paul,
26 men who have risked their lives for the name of our Lord Jesus Christ.
27 "Therefore we have sent Judas and Silas, who themselves will also report the same
things by word *of mouth*.
28 "For it seemed good to the Holy Spirit and to us to lay upon you no greater burden
than these essentials:
29 that you abstain from things sacrificed to idols and from blood and from things strangled and from fornication; if you keep yourselves free from such things, you will do
well. Farewell."

THE FIRST CHURCH CONFERENCE

Group	Position	Reasons
Judaizers (some Jewish Christians)	Gentiles must become Jewish first to be eligible for salvation	1. They were devout, practicing Jews who found it difficult to set aside a tradition of gaining merit with God by keeping the Law. 2. They thought grace was too easy for the Gentiles. 3. They were afraid of seeming too non-Jewish in the practice of their new faith—which could lead to death. 4. The demands on the Gentiles were a way of maintaining control and authority in the movement.
Gentile Christians	Faith in Christ as Savior is the only requirement for salvation	1. To submit to Jewish demands would be to doubt what God had already done for them by grace alone. 2. They resisted exchanging a system of Jewish rituals for their pagan rituals—neither of which had power to save. 3. They sought to obey Christ by baptism (rather than by circumcision) as a sign of their new faith.
Peter and James	Faith is the only requirement, but there must be evidence of change by rejecting the old life-style	1. They tried to distinguish between what was true from God's Word and what was just human tradition. 2. They had Christ's command to preach to all the world. 3. They wanted to preserve unity. 4. They saw that Christianity could never survive as just a sect within Judaism.

As long as most of the first Christians were Jewish, there was little difficulty in welcoming new believers; however, Gentiles (non-Jews) began to accept Jesus' offer of salvation. The evidence in their lives and the presence of God's Spirit in them showed that God was accepting them. Some of the early Christians believed that non-Jewish Christians needed to meet certain conditions before they could be worthy to accept Christ. The issue could have destroyed the church, so a conference was called in Jerusalem and the issue was formally settled there, although it continued to be a problem for many years following. Above is an outline of the three points of view at the conference.

15:23–29 This letter answered their questions and brought great joy to the Gentile Christians in Antioch (15:31). Beautifully written, it appeals to the Holy Spirit's guidance and explains what is to be done as though the readers already knew it. It is helpful when believers learn to be careful not only in what they say, but also in how they say it. We may be correct in our content, but we can lose our audience by our tone of voice or by our attitude.

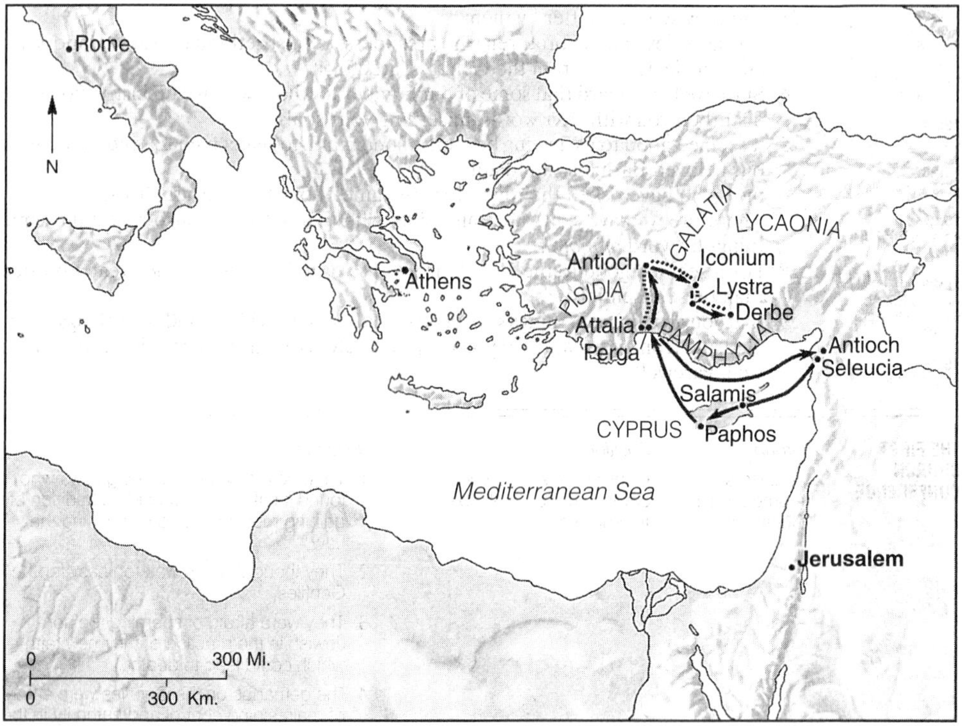

PAUL'S FIRST MISSIONARY JOURNEY (ACTS 13:1—14:28)

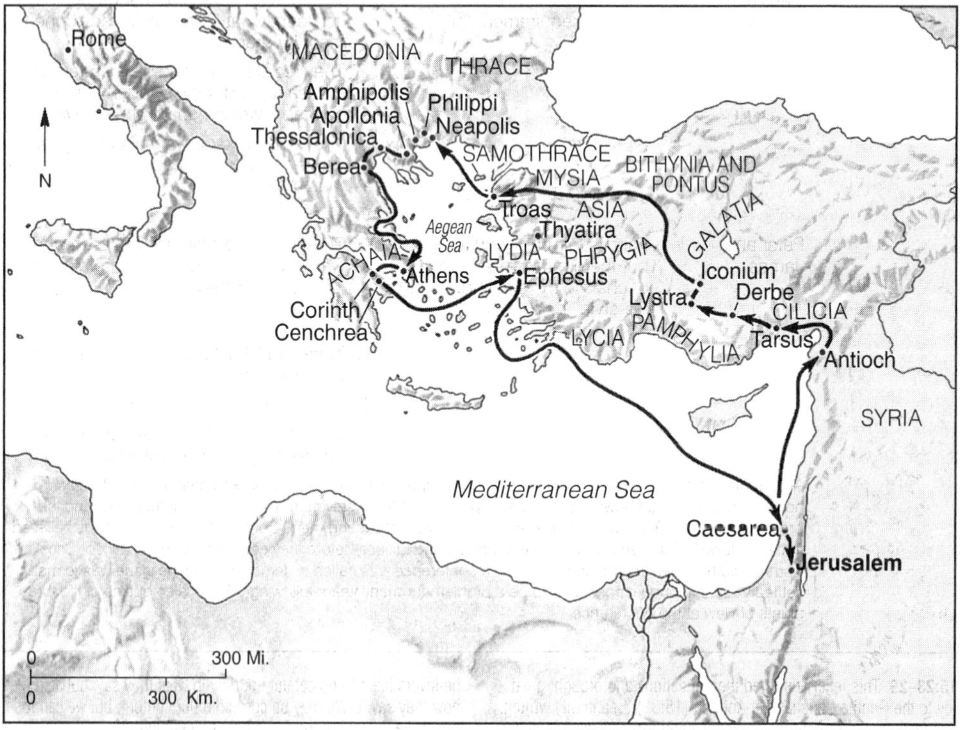

PAUL'S SECOND MISSIONARY JOURNEY (ACTS 15:36—18:22)

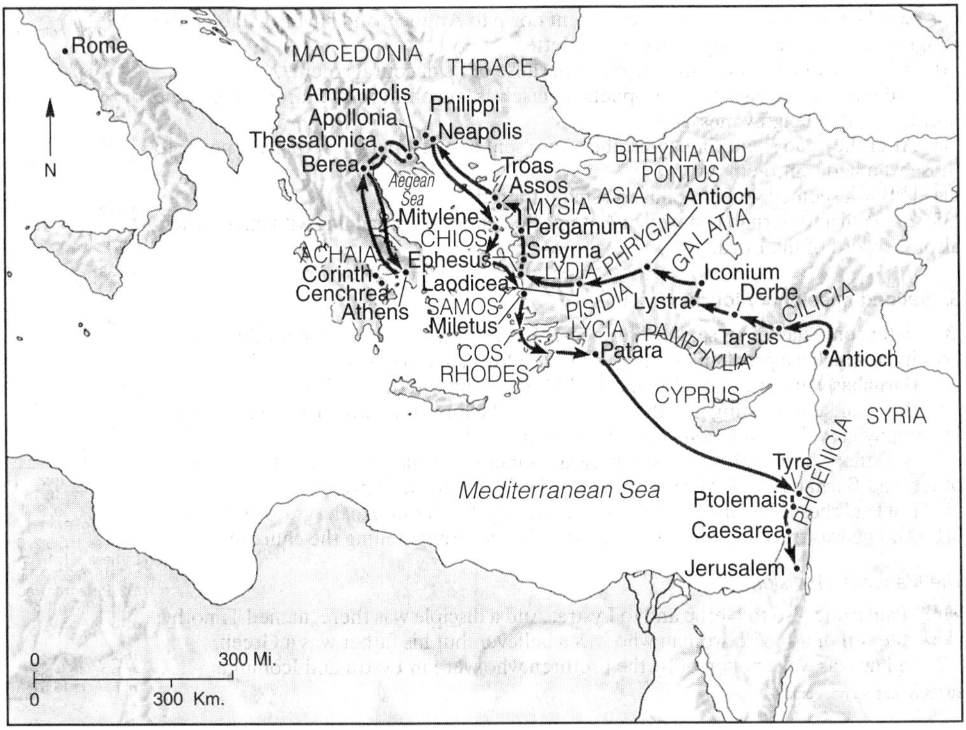

PAUL'S THIRD MISSIONARY JOURNEY (ACTS 18:23—21:16)

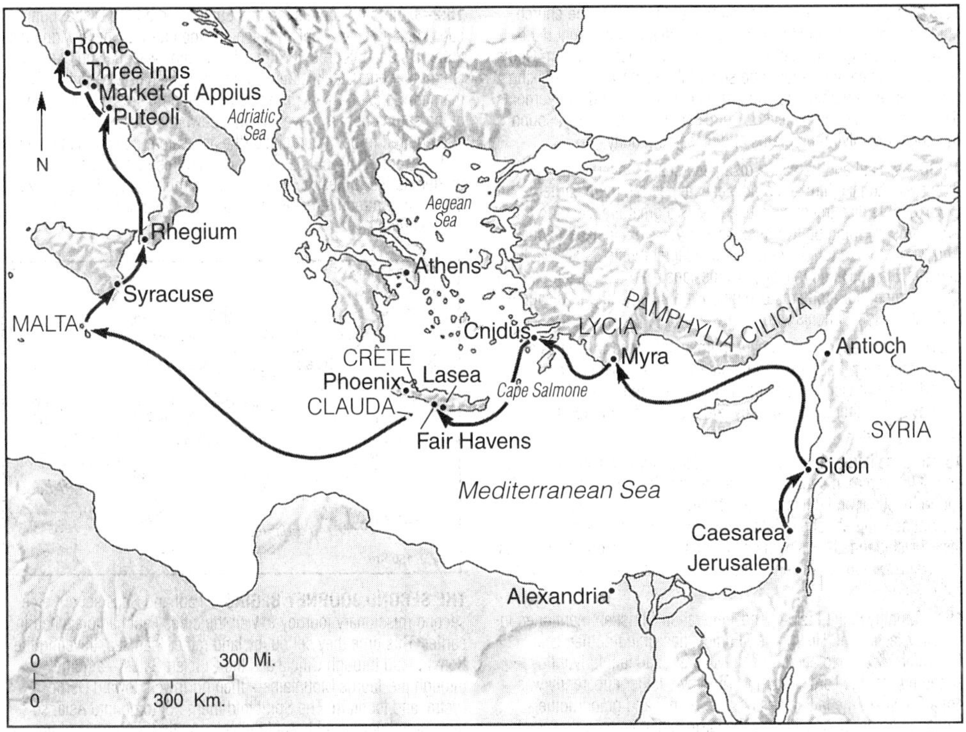

PAUL'S JOURNEY TO ROME (ACTS 21:17—28:31)

30 So when they were sent away, they went down to Antioch; and having gathered the
congregation together, they delivered the letter.
31 When they had read it, they rejoiced because of its encouragement.
32 Judas and Silas, also being prophets themselves, encouraged and strengthened the
brethren with a lengthy message.
33 After they had spent time *there*, they were sent away from the brethren in peace to
those who had sent them out.
34 [30But it seemed good to Silas to remain there.]
35 But Paul and Barnabas stayed in Antioch, teaching and preaching with many others
also, the word of the Lord.

3. Second missionary journey

36 After some days Paul said to Barnabas, "Let us return and visit the brethren in every city in which we proclaimed the word of the Lord, *and see* how they are."
37 Barnabas wanted to take John, called Mark, along with them also.
38 But Paul kept insisting that they should not take him along who had deserted them
in Pamphylia and had not gone with them to the work.
39 And there occurred such a sharp disagreement that they separated from one another, and Barnabas took Mark with him and sailed away to Cyprus.
40 But Paul chose Silas and left, being committed by the brethren to the grace of the Lord.
41 And he was traveling through Syria and Cilicia, strengthening the churches.

The Macedonian Vision

16 Paul came also to Derbe and to Lystra. And a disciple was there, named Timothy,
the son of a Jewish woman who was a believer, but his father was a Greek,
2 and he was well spoken of by the brethren who were in Lystra and Iconium.

30 Early mss do not contain this v

15:32 Acts 13:1; Acts 15:1

15:33 Mark 5:34; Acts 16:36; 1 Cor 16:11; Heb 11:31

15:35 Acts 12:25; Acts 8:4; Acts 13:12

15:36 Acts 13:4, 13, 14, 51; 14:6, 24f

15:38 Acts 13:13

15:39 Acts 12:12; 15:37; Col 4:10; Acts 4:36

15:40 Acts 11:23; 14:26

16:1 Acts 14:6; Acts 17:14f; 18:5; 19:22; 20:4; Rom 16:21; 1 Cor 4:17; 16:10; 2 Cor 1:1, 19; Phil 1:1; 2:19; Col 1:1; 1 Thess 1:1; 3:2, 6; 2 Thess 1:1; 1 Tim 1:2, 18; 6:20; 2 Tim 1:2; Philem 1; Heb 13:23; 2 Tim 1:5; 3:15

16:2 Acts 16:40; Acts 14:6; Acts 13:51

15:31 The debate over circumcision could have split the church, but Paul, Barnabas, and the Jews in Antioch made the right decision—they sought counsel from the church leaders and from God's Word. Our differences should be settled the same way, by seeking wise counsel and abiding by the decisions. Don't let disagreements divide you from other believers. Third-party assistance is a sound method for resolving problems and preserving unity.

15:36–39 Paul and Barnabas disagreed sharply over Mark. Paul didn't want to take him along because he had left them earlier (13:13). This disagreement caused the two great preachers to form two teams, opening up two missionary endeavors instead of one. God works even through conflict and disagreements. Later, Mark became vital to Paul's ministry (Colossians 4:10). Christians do not always agree, but problems can be solved by agreeing to disagree and letting God work his will.

15:40 Paul's second missionary journey, this time with Silas as his partner, began approximately three years after his first one ended. The two visited many of the cities covered on Paul's first journey, plus others. This journey laid the groundwork for the church in Greece.

15:40 Silas had been involved in the Jerusalem council and was one of the two men chosen to represent the Jerusalem church by taking the letter and decision back to Antioch (15:22). Paul, from the Antioch church, chose Silas, from the Jerusalem church, and they traveled together to many cities to spread the Good News. This teamwork demonstrated the church's unity after the decision at the Jerusalem council.

16:1 Timothy is the first second-generation Christian mentioned in the New Testament. His mother, Eunice, and grandmother, Lois (2 Timothy 1:5), had become believers and had faithfully influenced him for the Lord. Although Timothy's father apparently was not a Christian, the faithfulness of his mother and grandmother prevailed. Never underestimate the far-reaching consequences of raising one small child to love the Lord.

16:2–3 Timothy and his mother, Eunice, were from Lystra. Eunice had probably heard Paul's preaching when he was there during his first missionary journey (14:6–18). Timothy was the son of a Jewish mother and Greek father—to the Jews, a half-breed like a Samaritan. So Paul asked Timothy to be circumcised to remove some of the stigma he may have had with Jewish believers. Timothy was not required to be circumcised (the Jerusalem council had decided that—chapter 15), but he voluntarily did this to overcome any barriers to his witness for Christ. Sometimes we need to go beyond the minimum requirements in order to help our audience receive our testimony.

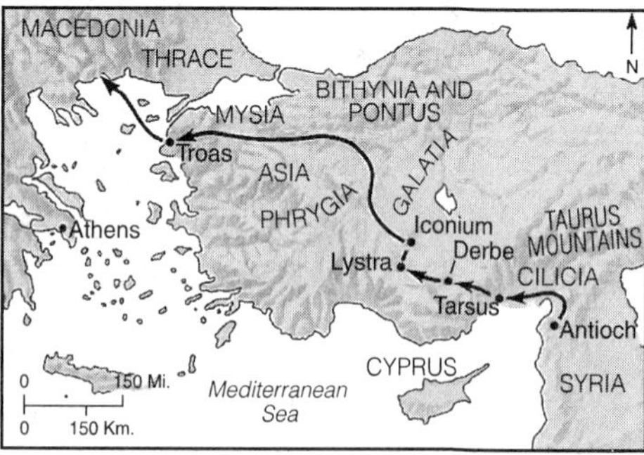

THE SECOND JOURNEY BEGINS Paul and Silas set out on a second missionary journey to visit the cities Paul had preached in earlier. This time they set out by land rather than sea, traveling the Roman road through Cilicia and the Cilician Gates—a gorge through the Taurus Mountains—then northwest toward Derbe, Lystra, and Iconium. The Spirit told them not to go into Asia, so they turned northward toward Bithynia. Again the Spirit said no, so they turned west through Mysia to the harbor city of Troas.

16:3 Gal 2:3
16:4 Acts 15:28f
Acts 15:2; Acts 11:30
16:5 Acts 9:31; Acts 2:47

3 Paul wanted this man to go with him; and he took him and circumcised him because
of the Jews who were in those parts, for they all knew that his father was a Greek.
4 Now while they were passing through the cities, they were delivering the decrees
which had been decided upon by the apostles and elders who were in Jerusalem, for them
to observe.
5 So the churches were being strengthened in the faith, and were increasing in number daily.

SILAS

The lives of the first Christian missionaries can be described with many words, but "boring" is not one of them. There were days of great excitement as men and women who had never heard of Jesus responded to the gospel. There were dangerous journeys over land and sea. Health risks and hunger were part of the daily routine. And there was open and hostile resistance to Christianity in many cities. Silas was one of the first missionaries, and he found out that serving Jesus Christ was certainly not boring!

Silas's name appears in Acts at the end of the first church council on the Jewish/Gentile problem. The majority of early Christians were Jews who realized that Jesus was the fulfillment of God's Old Testament promises to his people; however, the universal application of those promises had been overlooked. Thus, many felt that becoming Jewish was a prerequisite to becoming a Christian. The idea that God could accept a Gentile pagan was too incredible. But Gentiles began to accept Christ as Savior, and the transformation of their lives and the presence of God's Spirit confirmed their conversions. Some Jews were still reluctant, though, and insisted these new Christians take on various Jewish customs. The issue came to a boiling point at the Jerusalem meeting, but was peacefully resolved. Silas was one of the representatives from Jerusalem sent with Paul and Barnabas back to Antioch with an official letter of welcome and acceptance to the Gentile Christians. Having fulfilled this mission, Silas returned to Jerusalem. Within a short time, however, he was back in Antioch at Paul's request to join him on his second missionary journey.

Paul, Silas, and Timothy began a far-ranging ministry that included some exciting adventures. Paul and Silas spent a night singing in a Philippian jail after being severely beaten. An earthquake, the loosing of their chains, and the resulting panic led to the conversion of their jailer. Later, they narrowly missed another beating in Thessalonica, prevented by an evening escape. In Berea there was more trouble, but Silas and Timothy stayed to teach the young believers while Paul traveled on to Athens. The team was finally reunited in Corinth. In each place they visited, they left behind a small group of Christians.

Silas leaves the story as suddenly as he entered it. Peter mentions him as the co-author of 1 Peter, but we do not know when he joined Peter. He was an effective believer before leaving Jerusalem, and he doubtless continued to minister after his work with Paul was completed. He took advantage of opportunities to serve God and was not discouraged by the setbacks and opposition he met along the way. Silas, though not the most famous of the early missionaries, was certainly a hero worth imitating.

Strengths and accomplishments:
- A leader in the Jerusalem church
- Represented the church in carrying the "acceptance letter" prepared by the Jerusalem council to the Gentile believers in Antioch
- Was closely associated with Paul from the second missionary journey on
- When in jail with Paul in Philippi, sang songs of praise to God
- Worked as a writing secretary for both Paul and Peter

Lessons from his life:
- Partnership is a significant part of effective ministry
- God never guarantees that his servants will not suffer
- Obedience to God will often mean giving up what makes us feel secure

Vital statistics:
- Where: Roman citizen living in Jerusalem
- Occupation: One of the first career missionaries
- Contemporaries: Paul, Timothy, Peter, Mark, Barnabas

Key verses:
"It seemed good to us, having become of one mind, to select men to send to you with our beloved Barnabas and Paul, men who have risked their lives for the name of our Lord Jesus Christ. Therefore we have sent Judas and Silas, who themselves will also report the same things by word of mouth" (Acts 15:25–27).

Silas's story is told in Acts 15:22—19:10. He is also mentioned in 2 Corinthians 1:19; 1 Thessalonians 1:1; 2 Thessalonians 1:1; 1 Peter 5:12.

6 They passed through the Phrygian and Galatian region, having been forbidden by
the Holy Spirit to speak the word in Asia;
7 and after they came to Mysia, they were trying to go into Bithynia, and the Spirit of
Jesus did not permit them;
8 and passing by Mysia, they came down to Troas.
9 A vision appeared to Paul in the night: a man of Macedonia was standing and appealing to him, and saying, "Come over to Macedonia and help us."
10 When he had seen the vision, immediately we sought to go into Macedonia, concluding that God had called us to preach the gospel to them.
11 So putting out to sea from Troas, we ran a straight course to Samothrace, and on
the day following to Neapolis;
12 and from there to Philippi, which is a leading city of the district of Macedonia, a
Roman colony; and we were staying in this city for some days.
13 And on the Sabbath day we went outside the gate to a riverside, where we were
supposing that there would be a place of prayer; and we sat down and began speaking to
the women who had assembled.

First Convert in Europe

14 A woman named Lydia, from the city of Thyatira, a seller of purple fabrics, a worshiper of God, was listening; and the Lord opened her heart to respond to the things
spoken by Paul.
15 And when she and her household had been baptized, she urged us, saying, "If you
have judged me to be faithful to the Lord, come into my house and stay." And she prevailed upon us.

16:6 Acts 18:23; 1 Cor 16:1; Gal 1:2; 3:1; 2 Tim 4:10; 1 Pet 1:1; Acts 2:9

16:7 1 Pet 1:1; Luke 24:49; Acts 8:29; Rom 8:9; Gal 4:6; Phil 1:19; 1 Pet 1:11

16:9 Acts 9:10; 18:5; 19:21f, 29; 20:1, 3; 27:2; Rom 15:26

16:10 Acts 9:10; 20:5-15; 21:1-18; 27:1-28:16; Acts 14:7

16:12 Acts 20:6; Phil 1:1; 1 Thess 2:2

16:13 Acts 13:14

16:14 Rev 1:11; 2:18, 24; Acts 13:43; 18:7; Luke 24:45

16:15 Acts 11:14

16:6 We don't know how the Holy Spirit told Paul that he and his companions should not go into Asia. It may have been through a prophet, a vision, an inner conviction, or some other circumstance. To know God's will does not mean we must hear his voice. He leads in different ways. When seeking God's will, (1) make sure your plan is in harmony with God's Word; (2) ask mature Christians for their advice; (3) check your own motives (are you seeking to do what you want or what you think God wants?); and (4) pray for God to open and close the doors as he desires.

16:7–9 The "Spirit of Jesus" is another name for the Holy Spirit. The Holy Spirit had closed the door twice for Paul, so Paul must have wondered which geographical direction to take in spreading the gospel. Then, in a vision (16:9), Paul was given definite direction, and he and his companions obediently traveled into Macedonia. The Holy Spirit guides us to the right places, but he also guides us away from the wrong places. As we seek God's will, it is important to know what God wants us to do and where he wants us to go, but it is equally important to know what God does not want us to do and where he does not want us to go.

16:10 The use of the pronoun *we* indicates that Luke, the author of the Gospel of Luke and of this book, joined Paul, Silas, and Timothy on their journey. He was an eyewitness to most of the remaining incidents in this book.

16:12 Philippi was the key city in the region of Macedonia (northern Greece today). Paul founded a church during this visit (A.D. 50–51). Later Paul wrote a letter to the church, the book of Philippians, probably from a prison in Rome (A.D. 61). The letter was personal and tender, showing Paul's deep love for and friendship with the believers there. In it he thanked them for a gift they had sent, alerted them to a coming visit by Timothy and Epaphroditus, urged the church to clear up any disunity, and encouraged the believers not to give in to persecution.

16:13 Inscribed on the arches outside the city of Philippi was a prohibition against bringing an unrecognized religion into the city; therefore, this prayer meeting was held outside the city, beside the river.

16:13–14 After following the Holy Spirit's leading into Macedonia, Paul made his first evangelistic contact with a small group of women. Paul never allowed gender or cultural boundaries to keep him from preaching the gospel. He preached to these women, and Lydia, an influential merchant, believed. This opened the way for ministry in that region. God often worked in and through women in the early church.

16:14 Lydia was a seller of purple fabrics, so she was probably wealthy. Purple cloth was valuable and expensive. It was often worn as a sign of nobility or royalty.

16:14ff Luke highlights the stories of three individuals who became believers through Paul's ministry in Philippi: Lydia, the influential businesswoman (16:14), the demon-possessed slave girl (16:16–18), and the jailer (16:27–30). The gospel was affecting all strata of society, just as it does today.

16:15 Why was Lydia's household baptized after Lydia responded in faith to the gospel? Baptism was a public sign of identification with Christ and the Christian community. Although all members of her household may not have chosen to follow Christ (we don't know), it was now a Christian home.

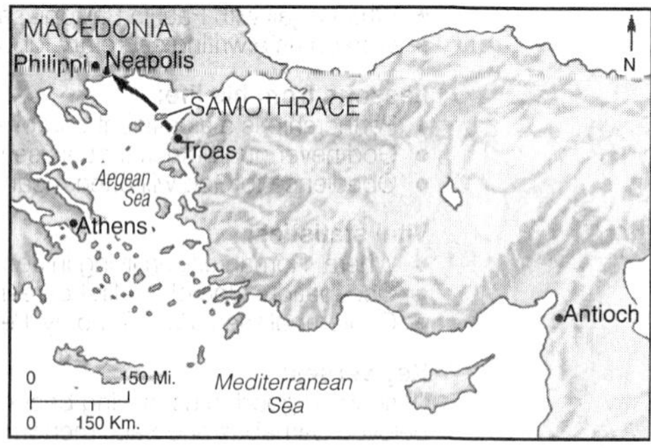

PAUL TRAVELS TO MACEDONIA At Troas, Paul received the Macedonian call (16:9), and he, Silas, Timothy, and Luke boarded a ship. They sailed to the island of Samothrace, then on to Neapolis, the port for the city of Philippi. Philippi sat on the Egnatian Way, a main transportation artery connecting the eastern provinces with Italy.

16 It happened that as we were going to the place of prayer, a slave-girl having a spirit
of divination met us, who was bringing her masters much profit by fortune-telling.
17 Following after Paul and us, she kept crying out, saying, "These men are bond-
servants of the Most High God, who are proclaiming to you the way of salvation."
18 She continued doing this for many days. But Paul was greatly annoyed, and turned
and said to the spirit, "I command you in the name of Jesus Christ to come out of her!"
And it came out at that very moment.
19 But when her masters saw that their hope of profit was gone, they seized Paul and
Silas and dragged them into the market place before the authorities,
20 and when they had brought them to the chief magistrates, they said, "These men
are throwing our city into confusion, being Jews,
21 and are proclaiming customs which it is not lawful for us to accept or to observe,
being Romans."

Paul and Silas Imprisoned

22 The crowd rose up together against them, and the chief magistrates tore their robes
off them and proceeded to order *them* to be beaten with rods.
23 When they had struck them with many blows, they threw them into prison, commanding the jailer to guard them securely;
24 and he, having received such a command, threw them into the inner prison and fastened their feet in the stocks.
25 But about midnight Paul and Silas were praying and singing hymns of praise to God,
and the prisoners were listening to them;
26 and suddenly there came a great earthquake, so that the foundations of the prison
house were shaken; and immediately all the doors were opened and everyone's chains
were unfastened.
27 When the jailer awoke and saw the prison doors opened, he drew his sword and was
about to kill himself, supposing that the prisoners had escaped.
28 But Paul cried out with a loud voice, saying, "Do not harm yourself, for we are all
here!"

16:16 Acts 16:13; Lev 19:31; 20:6, 27; Deut 18:11; 1 Sam 28:3, 7; 2 Kin 21:6; 1 Chr 10:13; Is 8:19

16:17 Mark 5:7

16:18 Mark 16:17

16:19 Acts 16:16; 19:25f; Acts 15:22, 40; 16:25, 29; Acts 8:3; 17:6f; 21:30; James 2:6

16:21 Esth 3:8; Acts 16:12

16:22 2 Cor 11:25; 1 Thess 2:2

16:23 Acts 16:27, 36

16:24 Job 13:27; 33:11; Jer 20:2f; 29:26

16:25 Acts 16:19; Eph 5:19

16:26 Acts 4:31; Acts 12:10; Acts 12:7

16:27 Acts 16:23, 36; Acts 12:19

THE BOOKS OF THE NEW TESTAMENT: WHEN WERE THEY WRITTEN?

Book	Approximate Date	Book	Approximate Date
Galatians	49	1 Timothy	64
James	49	Titus	64
1, 2 Thessalonians	51/52	1 Peter	64/65
1, 2 Corinthians	55	Jude	65
Romans	57	2 Timothy	66/67
Mark	58/60	Acts	66/68
Ephesians	60	2 Peter	66/68
Colossians	60	Hebrews	68/70
Philemon	60	John	85
Philippians	61	1, 2, 3 John	85/90
Matthew	61/64	Revelation	95
Luke	61/64		

16:16 This girl's fortune-telling ability came from evil spirits. Fortune-telling was a common practice in Greek and Roman culture. There were many superstitious methods by which people thought they could foretell future events, from interpreting omens in nature to communicating with the spirits of the dead. This young slave girl had an evil spirit, and she made her master rich by interpreting signs and telling people their fortunes. The master was exploiting her unfortunate condition for personal gain.

16:17–18 What the slave girl said was true, although the source of her knowledge was a demon. Why did a demon announce the truth about Paul, and why did this annoy Paul? If Paul accepted the demon's words, he would appear to be linking the gospel with demon-related activities. This would damage his message about Christ. Truth and evil do not mix.

16:22–25 Paul and Silas were stripped, beaten, and placed in stocks in the inner cell. Despite this dismal situation, they praised God, praying and singing as the other prisoners listened. No matter what our circumstances, we should praise God. Others may come to Christ because of our example.

16:24 Stocks were made of two boards joined with iron clamps, leaving holes just big enough for the ankles. The prisoner's legs were placed across the lower board, and then the upper board was closed over them. Sometimes both wrists and ankles were placed in stocks. Paul and Silas, who had committed no crime and were peaceful men, were put in stocks designed for holding the most dangerous prisoners in absolute security.

16:27 The jailer drew his sword to kill himself because jailers were responsible for their prisoners and would be held accountable for their escape.

29 And he called for lights and rushed in, and trembling with fear he fell down before
Paul and Silas,
30 and after he brought them out, he said, "Sirs, what must I do to be saved?"

16:29 Acts 16:19
16:30 Acts 2:37; 22:10

The Jailer Converted

31 They said, "Believe in the Lord Jesus, and you will be saved, you and your household."
32 And they spoke the word of the Lord to him together with all who were in his house.
33 And he took them that *very* hour of the night and washed their wounds, and immediately he was baptized, he and all his *household.*
34 And he brought them into his house and set food before them, and rejoiced greatly,
having believed in God with his whole household.
35 Now when day came, the chief magistrates sent their policemen, saying, "Release
those men."
36 And the jailer reported these words to Paul, *saying,* "The chief magistrates have sent
to release you. Therefore come out now and go in peace."
37 But Paul said to them, "They have beaten us in public without trial, men who are
Romans, and have thrown us into prison; and now are they sending us away secretly? No
indeed! But let them come themselves and bring us out."
38 The policemen reported these words to the chief magistrates. They were afraid when
they heard that they were Romans,
39 and they came and appealed to them, and when they had brought them out, they
kept begging them to leave the city.
40 They went out of the prison and entered *the house of* Lydia, and when they saw the
brethren, they encouraged them and departed.

16:31 Mark 16:16; Acts 11:14; 16:15
16:33 Acts 16:25
16:34 Acts 11:14; 16:15
16:36 Acts 16:27; Acts 15:33
16:37 Acts 22:25-29
16:38 Acts 22:29
16:39 Matt 8:34
16:40 Acts 16:14; Acts 1:15; 16:2

Paul at Thessalonica

17 Now when they had traveled through Amphipolis and Apollonia, they came to
Thessalonica, where there was a synagogue of the Jews.
2 And according to Paul's custom, he went to them, and for three Sabbaths reasoned
with them from the Scriptures,

17:1 Acts 17:11, 13; 20:4; 27:2; Phil 4:16; 1 Thess 1:1; 2 Thess 1:1; 2 Tim 4:10
17:2 Acts 9:20; 17:10, 17; Acts 13:14; Acts 8:35

16:30–31 Paul and Silas's reputation in Philippi was well known. When the jailer realized his own true condition and need, he risked everything to find the answer. The Christian Good News of salvation is simply expressed: Believe in the Lord Jesus, and you will be saved (see Romans 10:9; 1 Corinthians 12:3; Ephesians 2:8–9; Philippians 2:11). When we recognize Jesus as Lord and trust in him with our entire life, salvation is assured to us. If you have never trusted in Jesus to save you, do so quickly. Your life can be filled with joy, just as the jailer's was (16:34).

16:31–34 Paul and Silas took the family unit seriously. So the offer of salvation was made to the jailer's entire household—family and servants. Yet it was not the jailer's faith that saved them; they all needed to come to Jesus in faith and believe in him in the same way the jailer had. Yet his entire family did believe and all were saved. Pray that God will use you to introduce Jesus to your family and that they will come to believe in him.

16:37 Paul refused to take his freedom and run. He wanted to teach the rulers in Philippi a lesson and to protect the other believers from the treatment he and Silas had received. The word would spread that Paul and Silas had been found innocent and freed by the leaders, expressing the truth that believers should not be persecuted especially if they were Roman citizens.

16:38 Roman citizenship carried with it certain privileges. These Philippian authorities were alarmed because it was illegal to whip a Roman citizen. In addition, every citizen had the right to a fair trial—which Paul and Silas had not been given.

17:1 Thessalonica was one of the wealthiest and most influential cities in Macedonia. This is the first city Paul visited where his teachings attracted a large group of socially prominent citizens. The church he planted grew quickly, but in A.D. 50–51 Paul was forced out of the city by a mob (17:5–6, 10). Paul later sent Timothy back to Thessalonica to see how the Christians were doing. Soon afterward, Paul wrote two letters to the Thessalonian believers (1 and 2 Thessalonians), encouraging them to remain faithful and to refuse to listen to false teachers who tried to refute their beliefs.

MINISTRY IN MACEDONIA
Luke stayed in Philippi while Paul, Silas, and Timothy continued on the Egnatian Way to Amphipolis, Apollonia, and Thessalonica. But trouble arose in Thessalonica, and they fled to Berea. When their enemies from Thessalonica pursued them, Paul set out by sea to Athens, leaving Silas and Timothy to encourage the believers.

17:1–2 A synagogue, a group of Jews who gathered for teaching and prayer, could be established wherever there were ten Jewish males. Paul's regular practice was to preach in synagogues as long as the Jews allowed it. Often those who weren't Jews would come to these services and hear Paul's preaching. For a description of a synagogue service, see the note on 13:14–15.

17:3 Acts 3:18; John 20:9; Acts 9:22; 18:5, 28

17:4 Acts 14:4; 15:22, 40; Acts 13:43; John 7:35; Acts 13:50

17:5 1 Thess 2:14ff; Rom 16:21

3 explaining and giving evidence that the Christ had to suffer and rise again from the
dead, and *saying,* "This Jesus whom I am proclaiming to you is the Christ."
4 And some of them were persuaded and joined Paul and Silas, along with a large
number of the God-fearing Greeks and a number of the leading women.
5 But the Jews, becoming jealous and taking along some wicked men from the market place, formed a mob and set the city in an uproar; and attacking the house of Jason,
they were seeking to bring them out to the people.

One of the essential qualities of a good doctor is compassion. People need to know that their doctor cares. Even if he or she doesn't know what is wrong or isn't sure what to do, real concern is always a doctor's good medicine. Doctor Luke was a person of compassion.

Although we know few facts of his life, Luke has left us a strong impression of himself by what he wrote. In his Gospel, he emphasizes Jesus Christ's compassion. He vividly recorded both the power demonstrated by Christ's life and the care with which Christ treated people. Luke highlighted the relationships Jesus had with women. His writing in Acts is full of sharp verbal pictures of real people caught up in the greatest events of history.

Luke was also a doctor. He had a traveling medical practice as Paul's companion. Since the gospel was often welcomed with whips and stones, the doctor was undoubtedly seldom without patients. It is even possible that Paul's "thorn in the flesh" was some kind of physical ailment that needed Luke's regular attention. Paul deeply appreciated Luke's skills and faithfulness.

God also made special use of Luke as the historian of the early church. Repeatedly, the details of Luke's descriptions have been proven accurate. The first words in his Gospel indicate his interest in the truth.

Luke's compassion reflected his Lord's. Luke's skill as a doctor helped Paul. His passion for the facts as he recorded the life of Christ, the spread of the early church, and the lives of Christianity's missionaries gives us dependable sources for the basis of our faith. He accomplished all this while staying out of the spotlight. Perhaps his greatest example is the challenge to greatness even when we are not the center of attention.

Strengths and accomplishments:
- A humble, faithful, and useful companion of Paul
- A well-educated and trained physician
- A careful and exact historian
- Writer of both the Gospel of Luke and the book of Acts

Lessons from his life:
- The words we leave behind will be a lasting picture of who we are
- Even the most successful person needs the personal care of others
- Excellence is shown by how we work when no one is noticing

Vital statistics:
- Where: Probably met Paul in Troas
- Occupations: Doctor, historian, traveling companion
- Contemporaries: Paul, Timothy, Silas, Peter

Key verses:
"Many have undertaken to compile an account of the things accomplished among us, just as they were handed down to us by those who from the beginning were eyewitnesses and servants of the word. It seemed fitting for me as well, having investigated everything carefully from the beginning, to write it out for you in consecutive order, most excellent Theophilus; so that you may know the exact truth about the things you have been taught" (Luke 1:1–4).

Luke includes himself in the *we* sections of Acts 16—28. He is also mentioned in Luke 1:3; Acts 1:1; Colossians 4:14; 2 Timothy 4:11; Philemon 24.

17:2–3 When Paul spoke in the synagogues, he wisely began by talking about Old Testament writings and explaining how the Messiah fulfilled them, moving from the known to the unknown. This is a good strategy for us. When we witness for Christ, we should begin where people are, affirming the truth they do know, and then we can present Christ, the One who is truth.

17:5 The Jewish leaders didn't refute the theology of Paul and Silas, but they were jealous of the popularity of these itinerant preachers. Their motives for causing the riot were rooted in personal jealousy, not doctrinal purity.

6 When they did not find them, they *began* dragging Jason and some brethren before
the city authorities, shouting, "These men who have upset [31]the world have come here
also;
7 and Jason has welcomed them, and they all act contrary to the decrees of Caesar,
saying that there is another king, Jesus."
8 They stirred up the crowd and the city authorities who heard these things.
9 And when they had received a pledge from Jason and the others, they released them.

Paul at Berea

10 The brethren immediately sent Paul and Silas away by night to Berea, and when
they arrived, they went into the synagogue of the Jews.
11 Now these were more noble-minded than those in Thessalonica, for they received
the word with great eagerness, examining the Scriptures daily *to see* whether these things
were so.
12 Therefore many of them believed, along with a number of prominent Greek wom-
en and men.
13 But when the Jews of Thessalonica found out that the word of God had been proclaimed by Paul in Berea also, they came there as well, agitating and stirring up the crowds.
14 Then immediately the brethren sent Paul out to go as far as the sea; and Silas and
Timothy remained there.
15 Now those who escorted Paul brought him as far as Athens; and receiving a command for Silas and Timothy to come to him as soon as possible, they left.

Paul at Athens

16 Now while Paul was waiting for them at Athens, his spirit was being provoked within him as he was observing the city full of idols.
17 So he was reasoning in the synagogue with the Jews and the God-fearing *Gentiles,*
and in the market place every day with those who happened to be present.
18 And also some of the Epicurean and Stoic philosophers were conversing with him.
Some were saying, "What would this idle babbler wish to say?" Others, "He seems to be
a proclaimer of strange deities,"—because he was preaching Jesus and the resurrection.
19 And they took him and brought him to the Areopagus, saying, "May we know what
this new teaching is which you are proclaiming?
20 "For you are bringing some strange things to our ears; so we want to know what these
things mean."

31 Lit *the inhabited earth*

17:6 Acts 16:19f; Matt 24:14; Acts 17:31

17:7 Luke 10:38; James 2:25; Luke 23:2

17:9 Acts 17:5

17:10 Acts 1:15; 17:6, 14f; Acts 17:4; Acts 17:13; 20:4; Acts 17:1f

17:11 Acts 17:1

17:12 Acts 2:47; Mark 15:43; Acts 13:50

17:13 Acts 17:1; Acts 17:10; 20:4

17:14 Acts 1:15; 17:6, 10; Acts 15:22; 17:4, 10; Acts 16:1

17:15 Acts 15:3; Acts 17:16, 21f; 18:1; 1 Thess 3:1; Acts 17:14; Acts 18:5

17:16 Acts 17:15, 21f; 18:1; 1 Thess 3:1

17:17 Acts 9:20; 17:2; Acts 17:4

17:18 1 Cor 1:20; 4:10; Acts 4:2; 17:31f

17:19 Acts 23:19; Acts 17:22; Mark 1:27

17:6 We don't know much about Jason except that he evidently was the local host and sponsor of Paul and Silas; thus he took the heat for all the problems. Jason is just one of many "unsung heroes" who faithfully played their part to help spread the gospel. Because of Jason's courage, Paul and Silas were able to minister more effectively. You may not receive much attention (in fact you may receive only grief) for your service for Christ. But God wants to use you. Lives will be changed because of your courage and faithfulness.

17:6 What a reputation these early Christians had! The power of the gospel revolutionized lives, broke down all social barriers, threw open prison doors, caused people to care deeply for one another, and stirred them to worship God. Our world needs to be turned upside down, to be transformed. The gospel is not in the business of merely improving programs and encouraging good conduct, but of dynamically transforming lives. Take courage and ask God how you can help spread his Good News all over *your* world.

17:7 The Jewish leaders had difficulty manufacturing an accusation that would be heard by the city government. The Romans did not care about theological disagreements between the Jews and these preachers. Treason, however, was a serious offense in the Roman empire. Although Paul and Silas were not advocating rebellion against Roman law, their loyalty to another king sounded suspicious.

17:8–9 Jason posted a pledge—putting up cash for freedom. By doing so, he promised that the trouble would cease or his own property and possibly his own life would be taken.

17:11 How do you evaluate sermons and teachings? The people in Berea opened the Scriptures for themselves and searched for truths to verify or disprove the message they heard. Always compare what you hear with what the Bible says. A preacher or teacher who gives God's true message will never contradict or explain away anything that is found in God's Word.

17:15 Athens, with its magnificent buildings and many gods, was a center for Greek culture, philosophy, and education. Philosophers and educated men were always ready to hear something new, so they invited Paul to speak to them at the meeting of the Areopagus (17:18–19).

17:18 The Epicureans and Stoics were the dominant philosophers in Greek culture. The Epicureans believed that seeking happiness or pleasure was the primary goal of life. By contrast, the Stoics placed thinking above feeling and tried to live in harmony with nature and reason, suppressing their desire for pleasure. Thus they were very disciplined.

17:19 For a time the Council or Court (here called the Areopagus) met on a low hill in Athens near the Acropolis. As Paul stood there and spoke about the one true God, his audience could look down on the city and see the many idols representing gods that Paul knew were worthless.

17:21 Acts 2:10
17:22 Acts 17:15; Acts 25:19
17:23 2 Thess 2:4; John 4:22
17:24 Is 42:5; Acts 14:15; Deut 10:14; Ps 115:16; Matt 11:25; 1 Kin 8:27; Acts 7:48
17:25 Job 22:2; Ps 50:10-12
17:26 Mal 2:10; Deut 32:8; Job 12:23
17:27 Deut 4:7; Jer 23:23f; Acts 14:17
17:28 Job 12:10; Dan 5:23
17:29 Is 40:18ff; Rom 1:23
17:30 Acts 14:16; Rom 3:25; Acts 17:23; Luke 24:47; Acts 26:20; Titus 2:11f
17:31 Matt 10:15; Ps 9:8; 96:13; 98:9; John 5:22, 27; Acts 10:42; Matt 24:14; Acts 17:6; Luke 22:22; Acts 2:24

21 (Now all the Athenians and the strangers visiting there used to spend their time in
nothing other than telling or hearing something new.)

Sermon on Mars Hill

22 So Paul stood in the midst of the Areopagus and said, "Men of Athens, I observe
that you are very religious in all respects.
23 "For while I was passing through and examining the objects of your worship, I also
found an altar with this inscription, 'TO AN UNKNOWN GOD.' Therefore what you
worship in ignorance, this I proclaim to you.
24 "The God who made the world and all things in it, since He is Lord of heaven and
earth, does not dwell in temples made with hands;
25 nor is He served by human hands, as though He needed anything, since He Himself
gives to all *people* life and breath and all things;
26 and He made from one *man* every nation of mankind to live on all the face of the
earth, having determined *their* appointed times and the boundaries of their habitation,
27 that they would seek God, if perhaps they might grope for Him and find Him, though
He is not far from each one of us;
28 for in Him we live and move and exist, as even some of your own poets have said,
'For we also are His children.'
29 "Being then the children of God, we ought not to think that the Divine Nature is like
gold or silver or stone, an image formed by the art and thought of man.
30 "Therefore having overlooked the times of ignorance, God is now declaring to men
that all *people* everywhere should repent,
31 because He has fixed a day in which He will judge the world in righteousness through
a Man whom He has appointed, having furnished proof to all men by raising Him from
the dead."
32 Now when they heard of the resurrection of the dead, some *began* to sneer, but others said, "We shall hear you again concerning this."
33 So Paul went out of their midst.
34 But some men joined him and believed, among whom also were Dionysius the
Areopagite and a woman named Damaris and others with them.

17:22 Paul was well prepared to speak to this group. He came from Tarsus, an educational center, and had the training and knowledge to present his beliefs clearly and persuasively. Paul was a rabbi, taught by the finest scholar of his day, Gamaliel, and he had spent much of his life thinking and reasoning through the Scriptures.

It is not enough to teach or preach with conviction. Like Paul, we must be prepared. The more we know about the Bible, what it means, and how to apply it to our lives, the more convincing our words will be. This does not mean that we should avoid presenting the gospel until we feel adequately prepared. We should work with what we know, but always want to know more in order to reach more people and answer their questions and arguments more effectively.

17:22ff Paul's address is a good example of how to communicate the gospel. Paul did not begin by reciting Jewish history, as he usually did, for this would have been meaningless to his Greek audience. He began by building a case for the One true God, using examples they understood (17:22–23). Then he established common ground by emphasizing what they agreed on about God (17:24–29). Finally he moved his message to the person of Christ, centering on the resurrection (17:30–31). When you witness to others, you can use Paul's approach: Use examples, establish common ground, and then move people toward a decision about Jesus Christ.

17:23 The Athenians had built an idol to the unknown god for fear of missing blessings or receiving punishment. Paul's opening statement to the men of Athens was about their unknown god. Paul was not endorsing this god, but using the inscription as a point of entry for his witness to the One true God.

17:23 Paul explained the One true God to these educated men of Athens; although these men were, in general, very religious, they did not know God. Today we have a "Christian" society, but to most people, God is still unknown. We need to proclaim who he is and make clear what he did for all mankind through his Son Jesus Christ. We cannot assume that even religious people around us truly know Jesus or understand the importance of faith in him.

17:27–28 God is known in his creation, and he is close to every one of us. But he is not trapped in his creation—he is transcendent. God is the Creator, not the creation. This means that God is sovereign and in control, while at the same time he is close and personal. Let the Creator of the universe rule your life.

17:30–31 Paul did not leave his message unfinished. He confronted his listeners with Jesus' resurrection and its meaning to all people—either blessing or punishment. The Greeks had no concept of judgment. Most of them preferred worshiping many gods instead of just one, and the concept of resurrection was unbelievable and offensive to them. Paul did not hold back the truth, however, no matter what they might think of it. Paul often changed his approach to fit his audience, but he never changed his basic message.

17:32–34 Paul's speech received a mixed reaction: Some sneered, some kept searching for more information, and a few believed. Don't hesitate to tell others about Christ because you fear that some will not believe you. Don't expect a unanimously positive response to your witnessing. Even if only a few believe, it's worth the effort.

Paul at Corinth

18 After these things he left Athens and went to Corinth.
2 And he found a Jew named Aquila, a native of Pontus, having recently come
from Italy with his wife Priscilla, because Claudius had commanded all the Jews to leave
Rome. He came to them,
3 and because he was of the same trade, he stayed with them and they were working,
for by trade they were tent-makers.
4 And he was reasoning in the synagogue every Sabbath and trying to persuade Jews
and Greeks.
5 But when Silas and Timothy came down from Macedonia, Paul *began* devoting himself completely to the word, solemnly testifying to the Jews that Jesus was the Christ.
6 But when they resisted and blasphemed, he shook out his garments and said to them,
"Your blood *be* on your own heads! I am clean. From now on I will go to the Gentiles."
7 Then he left there and went to the house of a man named Titius Justus, a worshiper
of God, whose house was next to the synagogue.
8 Crispus, the leader of the synagogue, believed in the Lord with all his household,
and many of the Corinthians when they heard were believing and being baptized.
9 And the Lord said to Paul in the night by a vision, "Do not be afraid *any longer*, but
go on speaking and do not be silent;
10 for I am with you, and no man will attack you in order to harm you, for I have many
people in this city."

18:2 Rom 16:3; 1 Cor 16:19; 2 Tim 4:19; Acts 2:9; Acts 27:1, 6; Heb 13:24; Acts 11:28

18:3 1 Cor 4:12; 9:14f; 2 Cor 11:7; 12:13; 1 Thess 2:9; 4:11; 2 Thess 3:8

18:5 Acts 15:22; 16:1; Acts 16:9; Luke 16:28; Acts 20:21

18:6 Matt 27:25; Acts 20:26; Acts 13:46

18:7 Acts 13:43; 16:14

18:8 1 Cor 1:14; Mark 5:22; Acts 11:14; Acts 18:1; 19:1; 1 Cor 1:2; 2 Cor 1:1, 23; 6:11; 2 Tim 4:20

18:9 Acts 9:10

MINISTRY IN CORINTH AND EPHESUS
Paul left Athens and traveled on to Corinth, one of the greatest commercial centers of the empire, located on a narrow neck of land offering direct passage between the Aegean and Adriatic seas. When Paul left from the port of Corinth at Cenchrea, he visited Ephesus. He then traveled to Caesarea, from where he went on to Jerusalem to report on his trip before returning to Antioch.

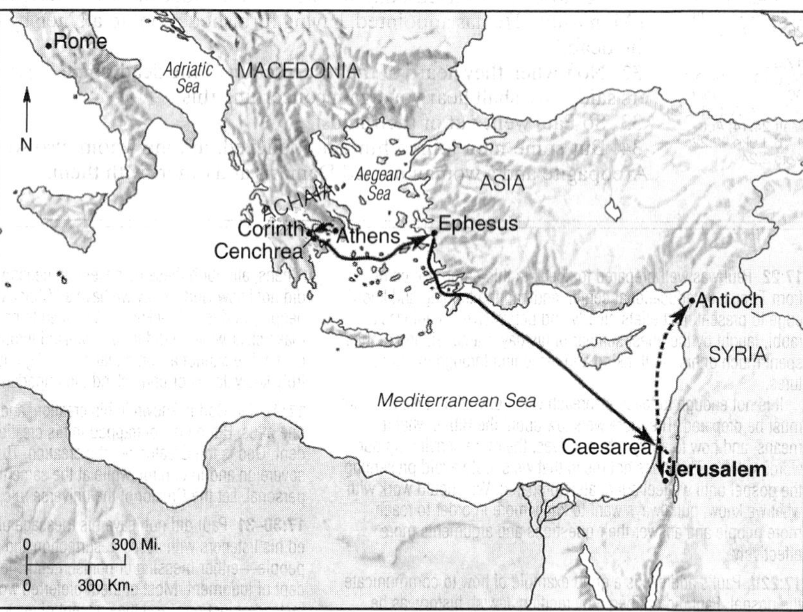

18:1 Corinth was the political and commercial center of Greece, surpassing Athens in importance. It had a reputation for great wickedness and immorality. A temple to Aphrodite—goddess of love and war—had been built on the large hill behind the city. In this popular religion, people worshiped the goddess by giving money to the temple and taking part in sexual acts with male and female temple prostitutes. Paul found Corinth a challenge and a great ministry opportunity. Later, he would write a series of letters to the Corinthians dealing in part with the problems of immorality. First and Second Corinthians are two of those letters.

18:2–3 Each Jewish boy learned a trade and tried to earn his living with it. Paul and Aquila had been trained in tent-making, cutting and sewing the woven cloth of goats' hair into tents. Tents were used to house soldiers, and so these tents may have been sold to the Roman army. As a tent-maker, Paul was able to go wherever God led him, carrying his livelihood with him. The word "tent-maker" in Greek was also used to describe a leather worker.

18:6 Paul told the Jews he had done all he could for them. Because they rejected Jesus as their Messiah, he would go to the Gentiles, who would be more receptive.

18:10 In a vision, Christ told Paul that he had many people in Corinth. Sometimes we can feel alone or isolated, especially when we see wickedness all around us and when we are persecuted for our faith. Usually, however, there are others in the neighborhood or community who also follow Christ. Ask God to lead you to them.

18:10–11 Others who became Christians in Corinth were Phoebe (Romans 16:1—Cenchrea was the port city of Corinth), Tertius (Romans 16:22), Erastus (Romans 16:23), Quartus (Romans

18:12 Rom 15:26; 1 Cor 16:15; 2 Cor 1:1; 9:2; 11:10; 1 Thess 1:7f; 1 Thess 2:14ff; Matt 27:19

18:13 John 19:7

18:14 Matt 5:2

11 And he settled *there* a year and six months, teaching the word of God among them.
12 But while Gallio was proconsul of Achaia, the Jews with one accord rose up against
Paul and brought him before the judgment seat,
13 saying, "This man persuades men to worship God contrary to the law."
14 But when Paul was about to open his mouth, Gallio said to the Jews, "If it were a
matter of wrong or of vicious crime, O Jews, it would be reasonable for me to put up
with you;

AQUILA, PRISCILLA

Some couples know how to make the most of life. They complement each other, capitalize on each other's strengths, and form an effective team. Their united efforts affect those around them. Aquila and Priscilla, also called Prisca, were such a couple. They are never mentioned separately in the Bible. In marriage and ministry, they were together.

Prisca and Aquila met Paul in Corinth during his second missionary journey. They had just been expelled from Rome by Emperor Claudius's decree against Jews. Their home was as movable as the tents they made to support themselves. They opened their home to Paul, and he joined them in tent-making. He shared with them his wealth of spiritual wisdom.

Prisca and Aquila made the most of their spiritual education. They listened carefully to sermons and evaluated what they heard. When they heard Apollos speak, they were impressed by his ability, but realized that his information was not complete. Instead of open confrontation, the couple quietly took Apollos home and shared with him what he needed to know. Until then, Apollos had only John the Baptist's message about Christ. Prisca and Aquila told him about Jesus' life, death, and resurrection, and the reality of God's indwelling Spirit. He continued to preach powerfully—but now with the full story.

As for Prisca and Aquila, they went on using their home as a warm place for training and worship. Back in Rome years later, they hosted one of the house churches that developed.

In an age when the focus is mostly on what happens *between* husband and wife, Aquila and Prisca are an example of what can happen *through* husband and wife. Their effectiveness together speaks about their relationship with each other. Their hospitality opened the doorway of salvation to many. The Christian home is still one of the best tools for spreading the gospel. Do guests find Christ in your home?

Strengths and accomplishments:
- Outstanding husband/wife team who ministered in the early church
- Supported themselves by tent-making while serving Christ
- Close friends of Paul
- Explained to Apollos the full message of Christ

Lessons from their lives:
- Couples can have an effective ministry together
- The home is a valuable tool for evangelism
- Every believer needs to be well educated in the faith, whatever his or her role in the church

Vital statistics:
- Where: Originally from Rome, moved to Corinth, then Ephesus
- Occupation: Tent-makers
- Contemporaries: Emperor Claudius, Paul, Timothy, Apollos

Key verses:
"Greet Prisca and Aquila, my fellow workers in Christ Jesus, who for my life risked their own necks, to whom not only do I give thanks, but also all the churches of the Gentiles" (Romans 16:3–4).

Their story is told in Acts 18. They are also mentioned in Romans 16:3–5; 1 Corinthians 16:19; 2 Timothy 4:19.

16:23), Chloe (1 Corinthians 1:11), Gaius (1 Corinthians 1:14), Stephanas and his household (1 Corinthians 16:15), Fortunatus (1 Corinthians 16:17), and Achaicus (1 Corinthians 16:17).

18:11 During the year and a half that Paul stayed in wicked Corinth, he established a church and wrote two letters to the believers in Thessalonica (the books of 1 and 2 Thessalonians). Although Paul had been in Thessalonica for only a short time (17:1–15), he commended the believers there for their loving deeds, strong faith, and endurance inspired by hope. While encouraging them to stay away from immorality, he dealt with the themes of salvation, suffering, and the second coming of Jesus Christ. Paul told them to continue to work hard while they awaited Christ's return.

18:12 Gallio was proconsul of Achaia (modern Greece) and the brother of Seneca the philosopher. He came to power in A.D. 51–52.

18:13 Paul was charged with promoting a religion not approved by Roman law. This charge amounted to treason. Paul was not encouraging obedience to a human king other than Caesar (see 17:7), nor was he speaking against the Roman empire. Instead he was speaking about Christ's eternal kingdom.

18:14–16 This was an important judicial decision for the spread of the gospel in the Roman empire. Judaism was a recognized religion under Roman law. As long as Christians were seen as part of Judaism, the court refused to hear cases brought against them. If they had claimed to be a new religion, they could easily have been outlawed by the government. In effect Gallio was saying, "I don't understand all your terminology and finer points of theology. Handle the matter yourself and don't bother me."

15 but if there are questions about words and names and your own law, look after it
yourselves; I am unwilling to be a judge of these matters."
16 And he drove them away from the judgment seat.
17 And they all took hold of Sosthenes, the leader of the synagogue, and *began* beating
him in front of the judgment seat. But Gallio was not concerned about any of these things.
18 Paul, having remained many days longer, took leave of the brethren and put out to
sea for Syria, and with him were Priscilla and Aquila. In Cenchrea he had his hair cut,
for he was keeping a vow.
19 They came to Ephesus, and he left them there. Now he himself entered the synagogue and reasoned with the Jews.
20 When they asked him to stay for a longer time, he did not consent,
21 but taking leave of them and saying, "I will return to you again if God wills," he set
sail from Ephesus.
22 When he had landed at Caesarea, he went up and greeted the church, and went down
to Antioch.

4. Third missionary journey

23 And having spent some time *there,* he left and passed successively through the Galatian region and Phrygia, strengthening all the disciples.
24 Now a Jew named Apollos, an Alexandrian by birth, an eloquent man, came to
Ephesus; and he was mighty in the Scriptures.
25 This man had been instructed in the way of the Lord; and being fervent in spirit, he
was speaking and teaching accurately the things concerning Jesus, being acquainted only
with the baptism of John;
26 and he began to speak out boldly in the synagogue. But when Priscilla and Aquila
heard him, they took him aside and explained to him the way of God more accurately.
27 And when he wanted to go across to Achaia, the brethren encouraged him and wrote
to the disciples to welcome him; and when he had arrived, he greatly helped those who
had believed through grace,
28 for he powerfully refuted the Jews in public, demonstrating by the Scriptures that
Jesus was the Christ.

Paul at Ephesus

19 It happened that while Apollos was at Corinth, Paul passed through the upper country and came to Ephesus, and found some disciples.
2 He said to them, "Did you receive the Holy Spirit when you believed?" And they
said to him, "No, we have not even heard whether there is a Holy Spirit."

18:15 Acts 23:29; 25:19
18:16 Matt 27:19
18:17 1 Cor 1:1; Matt 27:19
18:18 Mark 6:46; Acts 1:15; 18:27; Matt 4:24; Rom 16:1; Num 6:2, 5, 9, 18; Acts 21:24
18:21 Mark 6:46; Rom 1:10; 15:32; 1 Cor 4:19; 16:7; Heb 6:3; James 4:15; 1 Pet 3:17; 1 Cor 15:32; 16:8
18:22 Acts 8:40; Acts 11:19
18:23 Acts 16:6
18:24 Acts 19:1; 1 Cor 1:12; 3:5, 6, 22; 4:6; 16:12; Titus 3:13
18:25 Acts 9:2; 18:26; Luke 7:29; Acts 19:3
18:27 Acts 11:26
18:28 Acts 8:35; Acts 18:5
19:1 1 Cor 1:12; 3:5, 6, 22; 4:6; 16:12; Titus 3:13; Acts 18:21, 24; 19:17, 26, 28, 34f; 20:16f; 21:29; 1 Cor 15:32; 16:8; Eph 1:1; 1 Tim 1:3; 2 Tim 1:18; 4:12; Rev 1:11; 2:1
19:2 Acts 8:15f; 11:16f; John 7:39

18:17 Crispus had been the leader of the synagogue, but he and his family were converted and joined the Christians (18:8). Sosthenes was chosen to take his place. The mob could have been Greeks venting their feelings against the Jews for causing turmoil, or the crowd may have included some Jews. In any case, they beat Sosthenes for losing the case and leaving the synagogue worse off than before. A person named Sosthenes is mentioned in 1 Corinthians 1:1, and many believe this was the same man who, in time, became a convert and a companion of Paul.

18:18 This vow Paul took was probably a temporary Nazirite vow that ended with shaving of the head and offering the hair as a sacrifice (Numbers 6:18).

18:22 This verse marks the end of Paul's second missionary journey and the beginning of the third, which lasted from A.D. 53–57. Leaving the church at Antioch (his home base), Paul headed toward Ephesus, but along the way he revisited the churches in Galatia and Phrygia (18:23). The heart of this trip was a lengthy stay (two to three years) in Ephesus. Before returning to Jerusalem, he also visited believers in Macedonia and Greece.

18:24–26 Apollos had heard only what John the Baptist had said about Jesus (see Luke 3:1–18), so his message was not the complete story. John focused on repentance from sin, the first step. But the whole message is to repent from sin and then believe in Christ. Apollos did not know about Jesus' life, crucifixion, and resurrection. Nor did he know about the coming of the Holy Spirit. Priscilla and Aquila explained the way of salvation to him.

18:27–28 Apollos was from Alexandria in Egypt, the second most important city in the Roman empire, and the home of a great university. There was a thriving Jewish population in Alexandria. Apollos was a scholar, orator, and debater; and after his knowledge about Christ was made more complete, God greatly used these gifts to strengthen and encourage the church. Reason is a powerful tool in the right hands and in the right situation. Apollos used the gift of reason to convince many in Greece of the truth of the gospel. You don't have to turn off your mind when you turn to Christ. If you have an ability in logic or debate, use it to bring others to God.

18:27–28 Not all the work of a minister or missionary is drudgery, setback, or suffering. Chapter 18 is triumphant, showing victories in key cities and the addition of exciting new leaders such as Priscilla, Aquila, and Apollos to the church. Rejoice in the victories Christ brings, and don't let the hazards create a negative mind-set.

19:1 Ephesus was the capital and leading business center of the Roman province of Asia (part of present-day Turkey). A hub of sea and land transportation, it ranked with Antioch in Syria and Alexandria in Egypt as one of the great cities on the Mediterranean Sea. Paul stayed in Ephesus for a little over two years. There he wrote his

19:3 Luke 7:29; Acts 18:25
19:4 Matt 3:11; Mark 1:4, 7, 8; Luke 3:16; John 1:26, 27; Acts 13:24; John 1:7
19:5 Acts 8:12, 16; 10:48
19:6 Acts 6:6; 8:17; Mark 16:17; Acts 2:4; 10:46; Acts 13:1
19:8 Acts 9:20; 18:26; Acts 1:3
19:9 Acts 14:4; Acts 9:2; 19:23; Acts 11:26
19:10 Acts 16:6; Acts 13:12
19:11 Acts 8:13
19:12 Mark 16:17
19:13 Matt 12:27; Luke 11:19

3 And he said, "Into what then were you baptized?" And they said, "Into John's baptism."
4 Paul said, "John baptized with the baptism of repentance, telling the people to believe in Him who was coming after him, that is, in Jesus."
5 When they heard this, they were baptized in the name of the Lord Jesus.
6 And when Paul had laid his hands upon them, the Holy Spirit came on them, and
they *began* speaking with tongues and prophesying.
7 There were in all about twelve men.
8 And he entered the synagogue and continued speaking out boldly for three months,
reasoning and persuading *them* about the kingdom of God.
9 But when some were becoming hardened and disobedient, speaking evil of the Way
before the people, he withdrew from them and took away the disciples, reasoning daily
in the school of Tyrannus.
10 This took place for two years, so that all who lived in Asia heard the word of the
Lord, both Jews and Greeks.

Miracles at Ephesus

11 God was performing extraordinary miracles by the hands of Paul,
12 so that handkerchiefs or aprons were even carried from his body to the sick, and the
diseases left them and the evil spirits went out.
13 But also some of the Jewish exorcists, who went from place to place, attempted to
name over those who had the evil spirits the name of the Lord Jesus, saying, "I adjure
you by Jesus whom Paul preaches."
14 Seven sons of one Sceva, a Jewish chief priest, were doing this.
15 And the evil spirit answered and said to them, "I recognize Jesus, and I know about
Paul, but who are you?"

---

first letter to the Corinthians to counter several problems the church in Corinth was facing. Later, while imprisoned in Rome, Paul wrote a letter to the Ephesian church (the book of Ephesians).

19:2–4 John's baptism was a sign of repentance from sin only, not a sign of new life in Christ. Like Apollos (18:24–26), these Ephesian believers needed further instruction on the message and ministry of Jesus Christ. They believed in Jesus as the Messiah, but they did not understand the significance of his death and resurrection or the work of the Holy Spirit. Becoming a Christian involves turning from sin (repentance) and turning to Christ (faith). These "believers" were incomplete.

In the book of Acts, believers received the Holy Spirit in a variety of ways. Usually the Holy Spirit would fill a person as soon as he or she professed faith in Christ. Here that filling happened later because these disciples' knowledge was incomplete. God was confirming to these believers, who did not initially know about the Holy Spirit, that they were a part of the church. The Holy Spirit's filling endorsed them as believers.

Pentecost was the formal outpouring of the Holy Spirit on the church. The other outpourings in the book of Acts were God's way of uniting new believers to the church. The mark of the true church is not merely right doctrine, but right actions, the true evidence of the Holy Spirit's work.

PAUL TAKES A THIRD JOURNEY What prompted Paul's third journey may have been the need to correct any misunderstandings in the churches Paul had planted. So he hurried north, then west, returning to many of the cities he had previously visited. This time, however, he stayed on a more direct westward route toward Ephesus.

19:6 When Paul laid his hands on these disciples, they received the Holy Spirit, just as the disciples did at Pentecost, and there were outward, visible signs of the Holy Spirit's presence. This also happened when the Holy Spirit came on Gentiles (non-Jews, see 10:45–47).

19:9 Paul spoke in a lecture hall at this school. Such halls were used in the morning for teaching philosophy, but they were empty during the hot part of the day (about 11 a.m. to 4 p.m.). Because many people did not work during those hours, they would come to hear Paul's preaching.

19:10 "Asia" refers to Asia Minor or modern-day Turkey. During this time, Paul and his coworkers spread the gospel throughout the land.

19:13 These Jews traveled from town to town making a living by claiming to heal and drive out demons. Often they would recite a whole list of names in their incantation to be sure of including the right deity. Here they were trying to use Jesus' name in an effort to match Paul's power.

19:13–16 Many Ephesians engaged in exorcism and occult practices for profit (see 19:18–19). The sons of Sceva were impressed by Paul's work, whose power to drive out demons came from God's Holy Spirit, not from witchcraft, and was obviously more powerful than theirs. They discovered, however, that no one can control or duplicate God's power. These men were calling on the name of Jesus without knowing the person. The power to change people comes from Christ. It cannot be tapped by reciting his name like a magic charm. God works his power only through those he chooses.

16 And the man, in whom was the evil spirit, leaped on them and subdued all of them
and overpowered them, so that they fled out of that house naked and wounded.
17 This became known to all, both Jews and Greeks, who lived in Ephesus; and fear
fell upon them all and the name of the Lord Jesus was being magnified.
18 Many also of those who had believed kept coming, confessing and disclosing their
practices.
19 And many of those who practiced magic brought their books together and *began*
burning them in the sight of everyone; and they counted up the price of them and found
it fifty thousand pieces of silver.
20 So the word of the Lord was growing mightily and prevailing.
21 Now after these things were finished, Paul purposed in the spirit to go to Jerusalem
after he had passed through Macedonia and Achaia, saying, "After I have been there, I
must also see Rome."
22 And having sent into Macedonia two of those who ministered to him, Timothy and
Erastus, he himself stayed in Asia for a while.
23 About that time there occurred no small disturbance concerning the Way.
24 For a man named Demetrius, a silversmith, who made silver shrines of Artemis, was
bringing no little business to the craftsmen;
25 these he gathered together with the workmen of similar *trades,* and said, "Men, you
know that our prosperity depends upon this business.
26 "You see and hear that not only in Ephesus, but in almost all of Asia, this Paul has
persuaded and turned away a considerable number of people, saying that gods made with
hands are no gods *at all.*
27 "Not only is there danger that this trade of ours fall into disrepute, but also that the
temple of the great goddess Artemis be regarded as worthless and that she whom all of
Asia and the world worship will even be dethroned from her magnificence."
28 When they heard *this* and were filled with rage, they *began* crying out, saying, "Great
is Artemis of the Ephesians!"
29 The city was filled with the confusion, and they rushed with one accord into the
theater, dragging along Gaius and Aristarchus, Paul's traveling companions from Macedonia.
30 And when Paul wanted to go into the assembly, the disciples would not let him.
31 Also some of the [32]Asiarchs who were friends of his sent to him and repeatedly urged
him not to venture into the theater.

32 I.e. political or religious officials of the province of Asia

19:17 Acts 18:19
19:19 Luke 15:8
19:20 Acts 6:7; 12:24
19:21 Acts 20:16, 22; 21:15; Rom 15:25; 2 Cor 1:16; Acts 20:1; 1 Cor 16:5; Acts 16:9; 19:22, 29; Rom 15:26; 1 Thess 1:7f; Acts 18:12; Acts 23:11; Rom 15:24, 28
19:22 Acts 16:9; 19:21, 29; Acts 13:5; 19:29; 20:34; 2 Cor 8:19; Acts 16:1; Rom 16:23; 2 Tim 4:20
19:24 Acts 16:16, 19f
19:26 Acts 18:19; Acts 19:10; Deut 4:28; Ps 115:4; Is 44:10-20; Jer 10:3ff; Acts 17:29; 1 Cor 8:4; 10:19; Rev 9:20
19:27 Matt 24:14
19:28 Acts 18:19
19:29 Acts 20:4; Acts 20:4; 27:2; Col 4:10; Philem 24; Acts 13:5; 19:22; 20:34; 2 Cor 8:19; Acts 16:9; 19:22
19:30 Acts 19:9

19:18–19 Ephesus was a center for black magic and other occult practices. The people cooked up magical formulas to give them wealth, happiness, and success in marriage. Superstition and sorcery were commonplace. God clearly forbids such practices (Deuteronomy 18:9–13). You cannot be a believer and hold on to the occult, black magic, or sorcery. Once you begin to dabble in these areas, it is extremely easy to become obsessed by them because Satan is very powerful. But God's power is even greater (1 John 4:4; Revelation 20:10). If you are mixed up in the occult, learn a lesson from the Ephesians and get rid of anything that could keep you trapped in such practices.

19:21 Why did Paul say he had to go to Rome? Wherever he went, he could see Rome's influence. Paul wanted to take the message of Christ to the world's center of influence and power.

19:22 Paul mentions Timothy in more detail in the books of 1 and 2 Timothy. Erastus was a committed follower of Christ who was not only Paul's helpful assistant, but also Corinth's city treasurer (see Romans 16:23).

19:23 "The Way" refers to those who followed the way of Christ—the Christians.

19:24 Artemis was a goddess of fertility. She was represented by a carved female figure with many breasts. A large statue of her (which was said to have come from heaven, 19:35) was in the great temple at Ephesus. That temple was one of the wonders of the ancient world. The festival of Artemis involved wild orgies and carousing. Obviously the religious and commercial life of Ephesus reflected the city's worship of this pagan deity.

19:25–27 When Paul preached in Ephesus, Demetrius and his fellow craftsmen did not quarrel with his doctrine. Their anger boiled because his preaching threatened their profits. They made silver statues of the Ephesian goddess Artemis. The craftsmen knew that if people started believing in God and discarding the idols, their livelihood would suffer.

19:27 Demetrius's strategy for stirring up a riot was to appeal to his fellow workmen's love of money and then to encourage them to hide their greed behind the mask of patriotism and religious loyalty. The rioters couldn't see the selfish motives for their rioting—instead they saw themselves as heroes for the sake of their land and beliefs.

19:29 Paul often sought others to help him in his work. On this occasion, his traveling companions were Aristarchus (who would accompany him on other journeys; see 20:3–4 and 27:1–2), and Gaius (probably not the same Gaius mentioned in Romans 16:23 or 1 Corinthians 1:14).

19:30 Paul wanted to go to the theater to speak up and defend his companions, but the other believers wouldn't let him go, fearing for his safety.

19:31 These Asiarchs were government officials, responsible for the religious and political order of the region. Paul's message had reached all levels of society, crossing all social barriers and giving Paul friends in high places.

19:32 Acts 21:34 32 So then, some were shouting one thing and some another, for the assembly was in
confusion and the majority did not know for what reason they had come together.
19:33 Acts 12:17 33 Some of the crowd concluded *it was* Alexander, since the Jews had put him forward;
and having motioned with his hand, Alexander was intending to make a defense to the
assembly.
34 But when they recognized that he was a Jew, a *single* outcry arose from them all as
they shouted for about two hours, "Great is Artemis of the Ephesians!"
19:35 Acts 18:19 35 After quieting the crowd, the town clerk ☆said, "Men of Ephesus, what man is there
after all who does not know that the city of the Ephesians is guardian of the temple of
the great Artemis and of the *image* which fell down from heaven?
36 "So, since these are undeniable facts, you ought to keep calm and to do nothing rash.

APOLLOS

Some people have an amazing natural talent for public speaking. Some even have a great message to go along with it. When Apollos arrived in Ephesus shortly after Paul's departure, he made an immediate impact. He spoke boldly in public, interpreting and applying the Old Testament Scriptures effectively. He debated opponents of Christianity forcefully and effectively. It didn't take long for him to be noticed by Priscilla (also called Prisca; see Romans 16:3) and Aquila.

The couple quickly realized that Apollos did not have the whole story. His preaching was based on the Old Testament and John the Baptist's message. He was probably urging people to repent and prepare for the coming Messiah. Priscilla and Aquila took him home with them and brought him up to date on all that had happened. As they told him of the life of Jesus, his death and resurrection, and the coming of the Holy Spirit, Apollos must have seen Scripture after Scripture become clear. He was filled with new energy and boldness now that he had the complete gospel.

Apollos next decided to travel to Achaia. His friends in Ephesus were able to send along a glowing letter of introduction. He quickly became the verbal champion of the Christians in Corinth, debating the opponents of the gospel in public. As often happens, Apollos's abilities eventually created a problem. Some of the Corinthians began to follow Apollos rather than his message. Paul had to confront the Corinthians about their divisiveness. They had been forming little groups named after their favorite preacher. Apollos left Corinth and hesitated to return. Paul wrote warmly of Apollos as a fellow minister who had "watered" the seeds of the gospel that Paul had planted in Corinth. Paul last mentions Apollos briefly to Titus. Apollos was still a traveling representative of the gospel who deserved Titus's help.

Although his natural abilities could have made him proud, Apollos proved himself willing to learn. God used Priscilla and Aquila, fresh from months of learning from Paul, to give Apollos the complete gospel. Because Apollos did not hesitate to be a student, he became an even better teacher. How much does your willingness to learn affect God's efforts to help you become all he wants you to be?

Strengths and accomplishments:
- A gifted and persuasive preacher and apologist in the early church
- Willing to be taught
- One of the possible candidates for the unknown author of Hebrews

Lessons from his life:
- Effective communication of the gospel includes an accurate message delivered with God's power
- A clear verbal defense of the gospel can be a real encouragement to believers, while convincing non-believers of its truth

Vital statistics:
- Where: From Alexandria in Egypt
- Occupations: Traveling preacher, apologist
- Contemporaries: Priscilla, Aquila, Paul

Key verses:
"This man had been instructed in the way of the Lord; and being fervent in spirit, he was speaking and teaching accurately the things concerning Jesus, being acquainted only with the baptism of John; and he began to speak out boldly in the synagogue. But when Priscilla and Aquila heard him, they took him aside and explained to him the way of God more accurately" (Acts 18:25–26).

Apollos's story is told in Acts 18:24–28; 19:1. He is also mentioned in 1 Corinthians 1:12; 3:4–6, 22; 4:1, 6; 16:12; Titus 3:13.

19:33–34 The mob had become anti-Jewish as well as anti-Christian. This Alexander may have been pushed forward by the Jews as a spokesman to explain that the Jews had no part in the Christian community, and thus were not involved in the economic problem of the silversmiths.

37 "For you have brought these men *here* who are neither robbers of temples nor blasphemers of our goddess.
38 "So then, if Demetrius and the craftsmen who are with him have a complaint against
any man, the courts are in session and proconsuls are *available;* let them bring charges
against one another.
39 "But if you want anything beyond this, it shall be settled in the lawful assembly.
40 "For indeed we are in danger of being accused of a riot in connection with today's
events, since there is no *real* cause *for it*, and in this connection we will be unable to account for this disorderly gathering."
41 After saying this he dismissed the assembly.

Paul in Macedonia and Greece

20 After the uproar had ceased, Paul sent for the disciples, and when he had exhorted them and taken his leave of them, he left to go to Macedonia.
2 When he had gone through those districts and had given them much exhortation,
he came to Greece.
3 And *there* he spent three months, and when a plot was formed against him by the
Jews as he was about to set sail for Syria, he decided to return through Macedonia.
4 And he was accompanied by Sopater of Berea, *the son* of Pyrrhus, and by Aristarchus and Secundus of the Thessalonians, and Gaius of Derbe, and Timothy, and Tychicus and Trophimus of Asia.
5 But these had gone on ahead and were waiting for us at Troas.
6 We sailed from Philippi after the days of Unleavened Bread, and came to them at
Troas within five days; and there we stayed seven days.
7 On the first day of the week, when we were gathered together to break bread, Paul
began talking to them, intending to leave the next day, and he prolonged his message
until midnight.
8 There were many lamps in the upper room where we were gathered together.
9 And there was a young man named Eutychus sitting on the window sill, sinking into

19:37 Rom 2:22

19:38 Acts 13:7

20:1 Acts 11:26; Acts 19:21; Acts 16:9; 20:3

20:3 Acts 9:23f; 20:19; Matt 4:24; Acts 16:9; 20:1

20:4 Acts 17:10; Acts 19:29; Acts 17:1; Acts 14:6; Acts 16:1; Eph 6:21; Col 4:7; 2 Tim 4:12; Titus 3:12; Acts 21:29; 2 Tim 4:20; Acts 16:6; 20:16, 18

20:5 Acts 16:10; 20:5-15; Acts 16:8

20:6 Acts 16:10; 20:5-15; Acts 16:12; Acts 12:3; Acts 16:8

20:7 1 Cor 16:2; Rev 1:10; Acts 16:10; 20:5-15; Acts 2:42; 20:11

20:8 Matt 25:1; Acts 1:13

19:38 A proconsul served as a civil magistrate or governor of a Roman province.

19:40 The city of Ephesus was under the domination of the Roman empire. The main responsibility of the local city leaders was simply to maintain peace and order. If they failed to control the people, Rome would remove the appointed officials from office. The entire town could also be put under martial law, taking away many civic freedoms.

19:41 The riot in Ephesus convinced Paul that it was time to move on. But it also showed that the law still provided some protection for Christians as they challenged the worship of the goddess Artemis and the most idolatrous religion in Asia.

20:1–3 While in Greece, Paul spent much of his time in Corinth. From there he wrote the letter to the Romans. Although Paul had not yet been to Rome, believers had already started a church there (2:10; 18:2). Paul wrote to tell the church that he planned to visit the Roman believers. The letter to the Romans is a theological essay on the meaning of faith and salvation, an explanation of the relation between Jews and Gentiles in Christ, and a list of practical guidelines for the church.

20:4 These men who were traveling with Paul represented churches that Paul had started in Asia. Each man was carrying an offering from his home church to be given to the believers in Jerusalem. By having each man deliver the gift, the gifts had a personal touch, and the unity of the believers was strengthened. This was also an effective way to teach the church about giving, because the men were able to report back to their churches the way God was working through their giving. Paul discussed this gift in one of his letters to the Corinthian church (see 2 Corinthians 8:1–21).

20:5–6 The use of *us* and *we* shows that this is where Luke again joins the group. The last *we* was in chapter 16.

THROUGH MACEDONIA AND ACHAIA
A riot in Ephesus sent Paul to Troas, then through Macedonia to the region of Achaia. In Achaia he went to Corinth to deal with problems there. Paul had planned to sail from Corinth straight to Antioch in Syria, but a plot against his life was discovered. So he retraced his steps through Macedonia.

20:6 Jewish believers celebrated the Passover (which was immediately followed by the Feast of Unleavened Bread) according to Moses' instructions (see Exodus 12:43–51) even if they couldn't be at Jerusalem for the occasion.

20:8–9 The many lamps were candles in lanterns. The combination of the heat from the candles and the gathered number of people in an upstairs room probably made the room very warm. This no doubt helped Eutychus fall asleep, as well as the fact that Paul spoke for a long time. Eutychus was probably somewhere in the range of 8–14 years old (the age of a "young man").

20:10 1 Kin 17:21; 2 Kin 4:34; Matt 9:23f; Mark 5:39
20:11 Acts 2:42; 20:7
20:13 Acts 16:10; 20:5-15
20:15 Acts 20:17; 2 Tim 4:20
20:16 Acts 18:19; Acts 16:6; 20:4, 18; Acts 19:21; 20:6, 22; 1 Cor 16:8; Acts 2:1
20:17 Acts 18:19; Acts 11:30
20:18 Acts 18:19; 19:1, 10; 20:4, 16
20:19 Acts 20:3
20:20 Acts 20:27
20:21 Luke 16:28; Acts 18:5; 20:23, 24; Acts 2:38; 11:18; 26:20; Acts 24:24; 26:18; Eph 1:15; Col 2:5; Philem 5
20:22 Acts 17:16; 20:16
20:23 Acts 8:29; Luke 16:28; Acts 18:5; 20:21, 24; Acts 9:16; 21:33

a deep sleep; and as Paul kept on talking, he was overcome by sleep and fell down from
the third floor and was picked up dead.
10 But Paul went down and fell upon him, and after embracing him, he said, "Do not
be troubled, for his life is in him."
11 When he had gone *back* up and had broken the bread and eaten, he talked with
them a long while until daybreak, and then left.
12 They took away the boy alive, and were greatly comforted.

Troas to Miletus

13 But we, going ahead to the ship, set sail for Assos, intending from there to take Paul
on board; for so he had arranged it, intending himself to go by land.
14 And when he met us at Assos, we took him on board and came to Mitylene.
15 Sailing from there, we arrived the following day opposite Chios; and the next day
we crossed over to Samos; and the day following we came to Miletus.
16 For Paul had decided to sail past Ephesus so that he would not have to spend time
in Asia; for he was hurrying to be in Jerusalem, if possible, on the day of Pentecost.

Farewell to Ephesus

17 From Miletus he sent to Ephesus and called to him the elders of the church.
18 And when they had come to him, he said to them,
"You yourselves know, from the first day that I set foot in Asia, how I was with you the
whole time,
19 serving the Lord with all humility and with tears and with trials which came upon
me through the plots of the Jews;
20 how I did not shrink from declaring to you anything that was profitable, and teaching you publicly and from house to house,
21 solemnly testifying to both Jews and Greeks of repentance toward God and faith in
our Lord Jesus Christ.
22 "And now, behold, bound in spirit, I am on my way to Jerusalem, not knowing what
will happen to me there,
23 except that the Holy Spirit solemnly testifies to me in every city, saying that bonds
and afflictions await me.

PAUL TRAVELS FROM TROAS TO MILETUS From Troas, Paul traveled overland to Assos, then boarded a ship to Mitylene and Samos on its way to Miletus. He summoned the elders of the Ephesian church to say farewell to them, because he knew he would probably not see them again.

20:16 Paul had missed attending the Passover in Jerusalem, so he was especially interested in arriving on time for Pentecost, which was 50 days after Passover. He was carrying with him gifts for the Jerusalem believers from churches in Asia and Greece (see Romans 15:25–26; 1 Corinthians 16:1ff; 2 Corinthians 8–9). The Jerusalem church was experiencing difficult times. Paul may have been anxious to deliver this gift to the believers at Pentecost because it was a day of celebration and thanksgiving to God for his provision.

20:18–21 The way of the believer is not an easy road; being a Christian does not solve or remove all problems. Paul served humbly and "with tears," but he never quit, never gave up. The message of salvation was so important that he never missed an opportunity to share it. And although he preached his message in different ways to fit different audiences, the message remained the same—turning away from sin and turning to Christ by faith. The Christian life will have its rough times, its tears, and its sorrows, as well as its joys, but we should always be ready to tell others what good things God has done for us. His blessings far outweigh life's difficulties.

20:22 "Bound in spirit" could be paraphrased, "drawn irresistably by the Holy Spirit."

20:23 The Holy Spirit showed Paul that he would be imprisoned and experience suffering. Even knowing this, Paul did not shrink from fulfilling his mission. His strong character was a good example to the Ephesian elders, some of whom would also suffer for Christ.

24 "But I do not consider my life of any account as dear to myself, so that I may finish
my course and the ministry which I received from the Lord Jesus, to testify solemnly of
the gospel of the grace of God.
25 "And now, behold, I know that all of you, among whom I went about preaching the
kingdom, will no longer see my face.
26 "Therefore, I testify to you this day that I am innocent of the blood of all men.
27 "For I did not shrink from declaring to you the whole purpose of God.
28 "Be on guard for yourselves and for all the flock, among which the Holy Spirit has
made you overseers, to shepherd the church of God which He purchased with His own
blood.
29 "I know that after my departure savage wolves will come in among you, not sparing
the flock;
30 and from among your own selves men will arise, speaking perverse things, to draw
away the disciples after them.
31 "Therefore be on the alert, remembering that night and day for a period of three
years I did not cease to admonish each one with tears.
32 "And now I commend you to God and to the word of His grace, which is able to build
you up and to give *you* the inheritance among all those who are sanctified.
33 "I have coveted no one's silver or gold or clothes.
34 "You yourselves know that these hands ministered to my *own* needs and to the men
who were with me.
35 "In everything I showed you that by working hard in this manner you must help the
weak and remember the words of the Lord Jesus, that He Himself said, 'It is more blessed
to give than to receive.' "
36 When he had said these things, he knelt down and prayed with them all.
37 And they *began* to weep aloud and embraced Paul, and repeatedly kissed him,
38 grieving especially over the word which he had spoken, that they would not see his
face again. And they were accompanying him to the ship.

20:24 2 Tim 4:7; Acts 1:17; Luke 16:28
20:25 Matt 4:23; Acts 28:31
20:27 Acts 13:36
20:28 Luke 12:32; John 21:15-17; Acts 20:29; 1 Pet 5:2f; Matt 16:18; Rom 16:16; 1 Cor 10:32; Eph 1:7, 14; Titus 2:14; 1 Pet 1:19; 2:9; Rev 5:9
20:29 Matt 7:15; Luke 12:32; John 21:15-17; 1 Pet 5:2f
20:30 Acts 11:26
20:31 Acts 19:8, 10; 24:17
20:32 Eph 1:14; 5:5; Col 1:12; 3:24; Heb 9:15; 1 Pet 1:4
20:33 1 Cor 9:4-18; 2 Cor 11:7-12; 12:14-18; 1 Thess 2:5f
20:34 Acts 18:3; Acts 19:22
20:36 Luke 22:41
20:37 Luke 15:20

Paul Sails from Miletus

21 When we had parted from them and had set sail, we ran a straight course to Cos
and the next day to Rhodes and from there to Patara;
2 and having found a ship crossing over to Phoenicia, we went aboard and set sail.
3 When we came in sight of Cyprus, leaving it on the left, we kept sailing to Syria and
landed at Tyre; for there the ship was to unload its cargo.
4 After looking up the disciples, we stayed there seven days; and they kept telling Paul
through the Spirit not to set foot in Jerusalem.
5 When our days there were ended, we left and started on our journey, while they all,
with wives and children, escorted us until *we were* out of the city. After kneeling down on
the beach and praying, we said farewell to one another.
6 Then we went on board the ship, and they returned home again.

21:1 Acts 16:11
21:2 Acts 11:19; 21:3
21:4 Acts 11:26; 20:23
21:5 Acts 15:3; Luke 22:41; Acts 9:40

20:24 We often feel that life is a failure unless we're getting a lot out of it: recognition, fun, money, success. But Paul considered life worth *nothing* unless he used it for God's work. What he put *into* life was far more important than what he got out. Which is more important to you—what you get out of life, or what you put into it?

20:24 Single-mindedness is a quality needed by anyone who wishes to do God's work. Paul was a single-minded person, and the most important goal of his life was to tell others about Christ (Philippians 3:7–13). It is no wonder that Paul was the greatest missionary who ever lived. God is looking for more men and women who focus on that one great task God has given them to do.

20:31, 36–38 Paul's relationship with these believers is a beautiful example of Christian fellowship. He had cared for them and loved them, even cried over their needs. They responded with love and care for him and sorrow over his leaving. They had prayed together and comforted one another. Like Paul, you can build strong relationships with other Christians by sharing, caring, sorrowing, rejoicing, and praying with them. You will gather others around you only by giving yourself away to them.

20:33 Paul was satisfied with whatever he had, wherever he was, as long as he could do God's work. Examine your attitudes toward wealth and comfort. If you focus more on what you don't have than on what you do have, it's time to reexamine your priorities and put God's work back in first place.

20:34 Paul was a tent-maker, and he supported himself with this trade. Paul worked not in order to become rich, but to be free from being dependent on anyone. He supported himself and others who traveled with him (he also mentions this in some of his letters; see Philippians 4:11–13; 1 Thessalonians 2:9).

20:35 These words of Jesus are not recorded in the Gospels. Obviously, not all of Jesus' words were written down (John 21:25); this saying may have been passed on orally through the apostles.

21:4 Did Paul disobey the Holy Spirit by going to Jerusalem? No. More likely, the Holy Spirit warned these believers about the suffering that Paul would face in Jerusalem. They drew the conclusion that he should not go there because of that danger. This is supported by 21:10–12 where the local believers, after hearing that Paul would be turned over to the Romans, begged him to turn back.

21:7 Acts 12:20; 21:3; Acts 1:15; 21:17
21:8 Acts 8:40; 21:16; Acts 6:5; 8:5; Eph 4:11; 2 Tim 4:5
21:9 Luke 2:36; Acts 13:1; 1 Cor 11:5
21:10 Acts 11:28
21:11 1 Kin 22:11; Is 20:2; Jer 13:1-11; 19:1, 11; John 18; Acts 8:29; Acts 9:16; 21:33; Matt 20:19
21:13 Acts 20:24; Acts 5:41; 9:16
21:14 Luke 22:42
21:16 Acts 21:4; Acts 8:40; Acts 4:36; 21:3; Acts 15:7
21:17 Acts 1:15; 21:7
21:18 Acts 12:17; Acts 11:30

7 When we had finished the voyage from Tyre, we arrived at Ptolemais, and after greeting the brethren, we stayed with them for a day.
8 On the next day we left and came to Caesarea, and entering the house of Philip the evangelist, who was one of the seven, we stayed with him.
9 Now this man had four virgin daughters who were prophetesses.
10 As we were staying there for some days, a prophet named Agabus came down from Judea.
11 And coming to us, he took Paul's belt and bound his own feet and hands, and said, "This is what the Holy Spirit says: 'In this way the Jews at Jerusalem will bind the man who owns this belt and deliver him into the hands of the Gentiles.' "
12 When we had heard this, we as well as the local residents *began* begging him not to go up to Jerusalem.
13 Then Paul answered, "What are you doing, weeping and breaking my heart? For I am ready not only to be bound, but even to die at Jerusalem for the name of the Lord Jesus."
14 And since he would not be persuaded, we fell silent, remarking, "The will of the Lord be done!"

5. Paul on trial

Paul at Jerusalem

15 After these days we got ready and started on our way up to Jerusalem.
16 *Some* of the disciples from Caesarea also came with us, taking us to Mnason of Cyprus, a disciple of long standing with whom we were to lodge.
17 After we arrived in Jerusalem, the brethren received us gladly.
18 And the following day Paul went in with us to James, and all the elders were present.

PAUL RETURNS TO JERUSALEM The ship sailed from Miletus to Cos, Rhodes, and Patara. Paul and his companions then boarded a cargo ship bound for Phoenicia. They passed Cyprus and landed at Tyre, then Ptolemais, and finally Caesarea, where Paul disembarked and returned by land to Jerusalem.

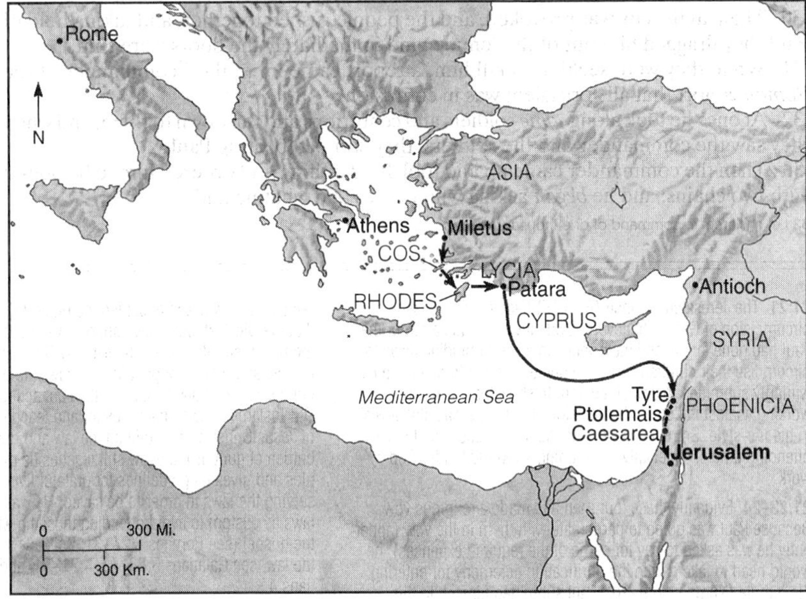

21:8 This is the Philip mentioned in 6:5 and 8:26–40.

21:9 Obviously the gift of prophecy was given to both men and women. Women actively participated in God's work (2:17; Philippians 4:3). Other women who prophesied include Miriam (Exodus 15:20), Deborah (Judges 4:4), Huldah (2 Kings 22:14), Noadiah (Nehemiah 6:14), Isaiah's wife (Isaiah 8:3), and Anna (Luke 2:36–38).

21:10 Fifteen years earlier, Agabus had predicted the famine in Jerusalem (11:27–29).

21:13–14 Paul knew he would be imprisoned in Jerusalem. Although his friends pleaded with him to not go there, he knew that he had to because God wanted him to. No one enjoys pain, but a faithful disciple wants above all else to please God. Our desire to please God should overshadow our desire to avoid hardship and suffering. When we really want to do God's will, we must accept all that comes with it—even the pain. Then we can say with Paul, "The will of the Lord be done!"

21:18 James, Jesus' brother, was the leader of the Jerusalem church (15:13–21; Galatians 1:19; 2:9). He was called an apostle even though he wasn't one of the original 12 who followed Jesus.

19 After he had greeted them, he *began* to relate one by one the things which God had
done among the Gentiles through his ministry.
20 And when they heard it they *began* glorifying God; and they said to him, "You see,
brother, how many thousands there are among the Jews of those who have believed, and
they are all zealous for the Law;
21 and they have been told about you, that you are teaching all the Jews who are among
the Gentiles to forsake Moses, telling them not to circumcise their children nor to walk
according to the customs.
22 "What, then, is *to be done?* They will certainly hear that you have come.
23 "Therefore do this that we tell you. We have four men who are under a vow;
24 take them and purify yourself along with them, and pay their expenses so that they
may shave their heads; and all will know that there is nothing to the things which they
have been told about you, but that you yourself also walk orderly, keeping the Law.
25 "But concerning the Gentiles who have believed, we wrote, having decided that they
should abstain from meat sacrificed to idols and from blood and from what is strangled
and from fornication."
26 Then Paul took the men, and the next day, purifying himself along with them, went
into the temple giving notice of the completion of the days of purification, until the sacrifice was offered for each one of them.

Paul Seized in the Temple

27 When the seven days were almost over, the Jews from Asia, upon seeing him in the
temple, *began* to stir up all the crowd and laid hands on him,
28 crying out, "Men of Israel, come to our aid! This is the man who preaches to all
men everywhere against our people and the Law and this place; and besides he has even
brought Greeks into the temple and has defiled this holy place."
29 For they had previously seen Trophimus the Ephesian in the city with him, and they
supposed that Paul had brought him into the temple.
30 Then all the city was provoked, and the people rushed together, and taking hold of
Paul they dragged him out of the temple, and immediately the doors were shut.
31 While they were seeking to kill him, a report came up to the [33]commander of the
Roman cohort that all Jerusalem was in confusion.
32 At once he took along *some* soldiers and centurions and ran down to them; and when
they saw the commander and the soldiers, they stopped beating Paul.
33 Then the commander came up and took hold of him, and ordered him to be bound
with two chains; and he *began* asking who he was and what he had done.

33 I.e. chiliarch, in command of one thousand troops

21:19 Acts 14:27; Acts 1:17

21:20 Matt 9:8; Acts 15:1; 22:3; Rom 10:2; Gal 1:14

21:21 Acts 21:28; Acts 15:19ff; 1 Cor 7:18f; Acts 6:14

21:23 Num 6:13-21; Acts 18:18

21:24 John 11:55; Acts 21:26; 24:18; Acts 18:18

21:25 Acts 15:19f, 29

21:26 John 11:55; Acts 21:24; 24:18; Num 6:13; Acts 24:18

21:27 Num 6:9, 13-20; Acts 20:19; 24:18; Acts 16:6

21:28 Acts 6:13; Matt 24:15; Acts 6:13f; 24:6

21:29 Acts 20:4; Acts 18:19

21:30 2 Kin 11:15; Acts 16:19; 26:21

21:32 Acts 23:27

21:33 Acts 20:23; 21:11; 22:29; 26:29; 28:20; Eph 6:20; 2 Tim 1:16; 2:9; Acts 12:6

21:21 The Jerusalem council (Acts 15) had settled the issue of circumcision of Gentile believers. Evidently there was a rumor that Paul had gone far beyond their decision, even forbidding Jews to circumcise their children. This, of course, was not true, and so Paul willingly submitted to Jewish custom to show that he was not working against the council's decision and that he was still Jewish in his life-style. Sometimes we must go the second mile to avoid offending others, especially when doing so would hinder God's work.

21:23–24 Evidently these four men had made a religious vow. Because Paul was going to participate with them in the vow (apparently he was asked to pay for some of the required expenses), he would need to take part in the purification ceremony for entering the temple (Numbers 6:9–20). Paul submitted himself to this Jewish custom to keep peace in the Jerusalem church. Although Paul was a man of strong convictions, he was willing to compromise on non-essential points, becoming all things to all people so that he might save some (1 Corinthians 9:19–23). Often a church is split over disagreements about minor issues or traditions. Like Paul, we should remain firm on Christian essentials but flexible on non-essentials. Of course, no one should violate his or her true convictions, but sometimes we need to exercise the gift of mutual submission for the sake of the gospel.

21:23–24 There are two ways to think of the Jewish laws. Paul rejected one way and accepted the other. (1) Paul rejected the idea that the Old Testament laws bring salvation to those who keep them. Our salvation is freely given by God's gracious act. We receive salvation through faith. The laws are of no value for salvation except to show us our sin. (2) Paul accepted the view that the Old Testament laws prepare us for and teach us about the coming of Jesus Christ. Christ fulfilled the law and released us from its burden of guilt. But the law still teaches us many valuable principles and gives us guidelines for grateful living. Paul was not observing the laws in order to be saved. He was simply keeping the laws as custom to avoid offending those he wished to reach with the gospel (see Romans 3:21–31; 7:4–6; 13:9–10). For more on the law, see Galatians 3:23–29; 4:21–31, and the chart in Galatians 4.

21:28–29 These Jews knew how effective Paul's work had been in Asia. Their strategy was to discredit Paul so that his work would be weakened. Be alert when you hear accusations against God's workers. Someone may be trying to discredit them or to hinder their work. Keep an open mind and pray for the workers. They will be strengthened by your support.

21:31 Because Jerusalem was under Roman control, an uproar in the city would be investigated by Roman authorities. The commander of the troops at this time was Claudius Lysias (23:26). This commander was head of a cohort (a special group, part of a legion) of Roman soldiers. He was the senior Roman official in Jerusalem.

34 But among the crowd some were shouting one thing *and* some another, and when
he could not find out the facts because of the uproar, he ordered him to be brought into
the barracks.
35 When he got to the stairs, he was carried by the soldiers because of the violence of
the mob;
36 for the multitude of the people kept following them, shouting, "Away with him!"
37 As Paul was about to be brought into the barracks, he said to the commander, "May
I say something to you?" And he ☆said, "Do you know Greek?
38 "Then you are not the Egyptian who some time ago stirred up a revolt and led the
four thousand men of the Assassins out into the wilderness?"
39 But Paul said, "I am a Jew of Tarsus in Cilicia, a citizen of no insignificant city; and
I beg you, allow me to speak to the people."
40 When he had given him permission, Paul, standing on the stairs, motioned to the
people with his hand; and when there was a great hush, he spoke to them in the Hebrew
dialect, saying,

Paul's Defense before the Jews

22 "Brethren and fathers, hear my defense which I now *offer* to you."
2 And when they heard that he was addressing them in the Hebrew dialect, they
became even more quiet; and he ☆said,
3 "I am a Jew, born in Tarsus of Cilicia, but brought up in this city, educated under
Gamaliel, strictly according to the law of our fathers, being zealous for God just as you
all are today.
4 "I persecuted this Way to the death, binding and putting both men and women into
prisons,
5 as also the high priest and all the Council of the elders can testify. From them I also
received letters to the brethren, and started off for Damascus in order to bring even those
who were there to Jerusalem as prisoners to be punished.
6 "But it happened that as I was on my way, approaching Damascus about noontime,
a very bright light suddenly flashed from heaven all around me,
7 and I fell to the ground and heard a voice saying to me, 'Saul, Saul, why are you
persecuting Me?'
8 "And I answered, 'Who are You, Lord?' And He said to me, 'I am Jesus the Nazarene, whom you are persecuting.'
9 "And those who were with me saw the light, to be sure, but did not understand the
voice of the One who was speaking to me.
10 "And I said, 'What shall I do, Lord?' And the Lord said to me, 'Get up and go on
into Damascus, and there you will be told of all that has been appointed for you to do.'
11 "But since I could not see because of the brightness of that light, I was led by the
hand by those who were with me and came into Damascus.
12 "A certain Ananias, a man who was devout by the standard of the Law, *and* well spoken of by all the Jews who lived there,

21:34 Acts 19:32; Acts 21:37; 22:24; 23:10, 16, 32

21:36 Luke 23:18; John 19:15; Acts 22:22

21:37 Acts 21:34; 22:24; 23:10, 16, 32

21:38 Acts 5:36; Matt 24:26

21:39 Acts 9:11; 22:3; Acts 6:9

21:40 Acts 21:35; Acts 12:17; John 5:2; Acts 1:19; 22:2; 26:14

22:1 Acts 7:2

22:3 Acts 9:1-22; 22:3-16; 26:9-18; Acts 6:9; Acts 5:34; Acts 23:6; 26:5; Phil 3:6; Acts 21:20

22:4 Acts 8:3; 22:19f; 26:9-11; Acts 9:2

22:5 Acts 9:1; Luke 22:66; Acts 5:21; 1 Tim 4:14; Acts 9:2; Acts 2:29; 3:17; 13:26; 23:1; 28:17, 21; Rom 9:3

22:6 Acts 9:3-8; 26:12-18

22:8 Acts 26:9

22:9 Acts 26:13; Acts 9:7

22:10 Acts 16:30

22:11 Acts 9:8

22:12 Acts 9:10; Acts 6:3; 10:22

21:37–38 By speaking in Greek, Paul showed that he was a cultured, educated man and not just a common rebel starting riots in the streets. The language grabbed the commander's attention and gave Paul protection and the opportunity to give his defense.

21:37–38 The historian Josephus wrote of an Egyptian who led a revolt of 4,000 people in Jerusalem in A.D. 54 and then disappeared. The commander assumed that Paul was this rebel.

21:40—22:2 Paul was probably speaking in Aramaic, the common language among Palestinian Jews. He used Aramaic not only to communicate in the language of his listeners, but also to show that he was a devout Jew and had respect for the Jewish laws and customs. Paul spoke Greek to the Roman officials and Aramaic to the Jews. To minister to people most effectively, use their language.

22:3 Gamaliel was the most honored rabbi of the first century. He was well known and respected as an expert on religious law and as a voice for moderation (5:34). Paul was showing his credentials as a well-educated man trained under the most respected Jewish rabbi.

22:3 By saying that at one time he was as zealous for God as any of his listeners, Paul was acknowledging their sincere motives behind their desire to kill him and recognizing that he would have done the same to Christian leaders a few years earlier. Paul always tried to establish a common point of contact with his audience before launching into a full-scale defense of Christianity. When you witness for Christ, first identify yourself with your audience. They are much more likely to listen if they feel a common bond with you.

22:6ff After gaining a hearing and establishing common ground with his audience, Paul gave his testimony. He shared how he had come to faith in Christ. Sound reasoning is good, but it is also important to simply share what Christ has done in our lives. But no matter how we present the message, not everyone will accept it, as Paul knew. We must faithfully and responsibly present the gospel, and leave the results to God.

13 came to me, and standing near said to me, 'Brother Saul, receive your sight!' And at
that very time I looked up at him.
14 "And he said, 'The God of our fathers has appointed you to know His will and to see
the Righteous One and to hear an utterance from His mouth.
15 'For you will be a witness for Him to all men of what you have seen and heard.
16 'Now why do you delay? Get up and be baptized, and wash away your sins, calling on
His name.'
17 "It happened when I returned to Jerusalem and was praying in the temple, that I fell
into a trance,
18 and I saw Him saying to me, 'Make haste, and get out of Jerusalem quickly, because
they will not accept your testimony about Me.'
19 "And I said, 'Lord, they themselves understand that in one synagogue after another
I used to imprison and beat those who believed in You.
20 'And when the blood of Your witness Stephen was being shed, I also was standing by
approving, and watching out for the coats of those who were slaying him.'
21 "And He said to me, 'Go! For I will send you far away to the Gentiles.' "
22 They listened to him up to this statement, and *then* they raised their voices and said,
"Away with such a fellow from the earth, for he should not be allowed to live!"
23 And as they were crying out and throwing off their cloaks and tossing dust into
the air,
24 the [34]commander ordered him to be brought into the barracks, stating that he should
be examined by scourging so that he might find out the reason why they were shouting
against him that way.
25 But when they stretched him out with thongs, Paul said to the centurion who was
standing by, "Is it lawful for you to scourge a man who is a Roman and uncondemned?"
26 When the centurion heard *this,* he went to the commander and told him, saying,
"What are you about to do? For this man is a Roman."
27 The commander came and said to him, "Tell me, are you a Roman?" And he said,
"Yes."
28 The commander answered, "I acquired this citizenship with a large sum of money."
And Paul said, "But I was actually born *a citizen.*"
29 Therefore those who were about to examine him immediately let go of him; and the
commander also was afraid when he found out that he was a Roman, and because he
had put him in chains.
30 But on the next day, wishing to know for certain why he had been accused by the
Jews, he released him and ordered the chief priests and all the Council to assemble, and
brought Paul down and set him before them.

Paul before the Council

23 Paul, looking intently at the Council, said, "Brethren, I have lived my life with a
perfectly good conscience before God up to this day."
2 The high priest Ananias commanded those standing beside him to strike him on
the mouth.

34 I.e. chiliarch, in command of one thousand troops

22:13 Acts 9:17; Acts 9:18
22:14 Acts 3:13; Acts 9:15; 26:16; Acts 9:17; 26:16; 1 Cor 9:1; 15:8; Acts 7:52
22:15 Acts 23:11; 26:16; Acts 22:14
22:16 Acts 9:18; Acts 2:38; 1 Cor 6:11; Eph 5:26; Heb 10:22; Acts 7:59
22:17 Acts 9:26; 26:20; Acts 10:10
22:18 Acts 9:29
22:19 Acts 8:3; 22:4; Matt 10:17; Acts 26:11
22:20 Acts 7:58f; 8:1; 26:10
22:21 Acts 9:15
22:22 Acts 21:36; 1 Thess 2:16; Acts 25:24
22:23 Acts 7:58; 2 Sam 16:13
22:24 Acts 21:34; Acts 22:29
22:25 Acts 16:37
22:29 Acts 22:24; Acts 16:38; Acts 21:33
22:30 Acts 23:28; Acts 21:33; Matt 5:22
23:1 Acts 22:30; 23:6, 15, 20, 28; Acts 22:5; Acts 24:16; 2 Cor 1:12; 2 Tim 1:3
23:2 Acts 24:1; John 18:22

22:21–22 These people listened intently to Paul, but the word *Gentiles* brought out all their anger and exposed their pride. They were supposed to be a light to the Gentiles, telling them about the one true God. But they had renounced that mission by becoming separatist and exclusive. God's plan, however, would not be thwarted; the Gentiles were hearing the Good News through Jewish Christians such as Paul and Peter.

22:25–28 Paul's question stopped the centurion because, by law, a Roman citizen could not be punished until he had been proven guilty of a crime. Paul was born a Roman citizen, whereas the commander had purchased his citizenship. Buying citizenship was a common practice and a good source of income for the Roman government. Bought citizenship was considered inferior to citizenship by birth.

22:30 Paul used his times of persecution as an opportunity for him to witness. Even his enemies were creating a platform for him to address the entire Jewish Council. If we are sensitive to the Holy Spirit's leading, we will see increased opportunities to share our faith, even in the face of opposition.

23:2–5 Josephus, a respected first-century historian, described Ananias as profane, greedy, and hot-tempered. Paul's outburst came as a result of the illegal command that Ananias had given. Ananias had violated Jewish law by assuming that Paul was guilty without a trial and ordering his punishment (see Deuteronomy 19:15). Paul didn't recognize Ananias as the high priest, probably because Ananias's command broke the law he was pledged to represent. As Christians, we are to represent Christ. When those around us say, "I didn't know you were a Christian," we have failed to represent him as we should. We are not merely Christ's followers; we are his representatives to others.

3 Then Paul said to him, "God is going to strike you, you whitewashed wall! Do you
sit to try me according to the Law, and in violation of the Law order me to be struck?"
4 But the bystanders said, "Do you revile God's high priest?"
5 And Paul said, "I was not aware, brethren, that he was high priest; for it is written,
'YOU SHALL NOT SPEAK EVIL OF A RULER OF YOUR PEOPLE.' "
6 But perceiving that one group were Sadducees and the other Pharisees, Paul *began*
crying out in the Council, "Brethren, I am a Pharisee, a son of Pharisees; I am on trial
for the hope and resurrection of the dead!"
7 As he said this, there occurred a dissension between the Pharisees and Sadducees,
and the assembly was divided.
8 For the Sadducees say that there is no resurrection, nor an angel, nor a spirit, but
the Pharisees acknowledge them all.
9 And there occurred a great uproar; and some of the scribes of the Pharisaic party
stood up and *began* to argue heatedly, saying, "We find nothing wrong with this man;
suppose a spirit or an angel has spoken to him?"
10 And as a great dissension was developing, the [35]commander was afraid Paul would
be torn to pieces by them and ordered the troops to go down and take him away from
them by force, and bring him into the barracks.
11 But on the night *immediately* following, the Lord stood at his side and said, "Take
courage; for as you have solemnly witnessed to My cause at Jerusalem, so you must witness at Rome also."

A Conspiracy to Kill Paul

12 When it was day, the Jews formed a conspiracy and bound themselves under an oath,
saying that they would neither eat nor drink until they had killed Paul.
13 There were more than forty who formed this plot.
14 They came to the chief priests and the elders and said, "We have bound ourselves
under a solemn oath to taste nothing until we have killed Paul.
15 "Now therefore, you and the Council notify the commander to bring him down to
you, as though you were going to determine his case by a more thorough investigation;
and we for our part are ready to slay him before he comes near *the place.*"
16 But the son of Paul's sister heard of their ambush, and he came and entered the
barracks and told Paul.
17 Paul called one of the centurions to him and said, "Lead this young man to the commander, for he has something to report to him."
18 So he took him and led him to the commander and ☆said, "Paul the prisoner
called me to him and asked me to lead this young man to you since he has something to
tell you."
19 The commander took him by the hand and stepping aside, *began* to inquire of him
privately, "What is it that you have to report to me?"
20 And he said, "The Jews have agreed to ask you to bring Paul down tomorrow to the
Council, as though they were going to inquire somewhat more thoroughly about him.
21 "So do not listen to them, for more than forty of them are lying in wait for him who

23:3 Matt 23:27; Lev 19:15; Deut 25:2; John 7:51
23:5 Ex 22:28
23:6 Matt 3:7; 22:23; Acts 22:30; 23:1, 15, 20, 28; Acts 22:5; Acts 26:5; Phil 3:5; Acts 24:15, 21; 26:8
23:8 Matt 22:23; Mark 12:18; Luke 20:27
23:9 Mark 2:16; Luke 5:30; Acts 23:29; John 12:29; Acts 22:6ff
23:10 Acts 21:34; 23:16, 32
23:11 Acts 18:9; Matt 9:2; Acts 19:21; Luke 16:28; Acts 28:23
23:12 Acts 9:23; 23:30; 1 Thess 2:16; Acts 23:14, 21
23:14 Acts 23:12, 21
23:15 Acts 22:30; 23:1, 6, 20, 28
23:16 Acts 21:34; 23:10, 32
23:18 Eph 3:1
23:20 Acts 23:14f; Acts 22:30; 23:1, 6, 15, 28
23:21 Acts 23:12, 14; Luke 11:54

35 I.e. chiliarch, in command of one thousand troops

23:6–8 The Sadducees and Pharisees were two groups of religious leaders, but with strikingly different beliefs. The Pharisees believed in a bodily resurrection, but the Sadducees did not. The Sadducees adhered only to Genesis through Deuteronomy, which contain no explicit teaching on resurrection. Paul's words moved the debate away from himself and toward their festering controversy about the resurrection. The Jewish Council was split.

23:6–8 Paul's sudden insight that the Council was a mixture of Sadducees and Pharisees is an example of the power that Jesus promised to believers (Mark 13:9–11). God will help us when we are under fire for our faith. Like Paul, we should always be ready to present our testimony. The Holy Spirit will give us power to speak boldly.

23:14–15 When the Pharisee/Sadducee controversy died down, the religious leaders refocused their attention on Paul. To these leaders, politics and position had become more important than God. They were ready to plan another murder, just as they had done with Jesus. But as always, God was in control.

23:16 This is the only Biblical reference to Paul's family. Some scholars believe that Paul's family had disowned Paul when he became a Christian. Paul wrote of having suffered the loss of everything for Christ (Philippians 3:8). Paul's nephew was able to see Paul, even though Paul was in protective custody, because Roman prisoners were accessible to their relatives and friends who could bring them food and other amenities.

23:16–22 It is easy to overlook children, assuming that they aren't old enough to do much for the Lord. But a young boy played an important part in protecting Paul's life. God can use anyone, of any age, who is willing to yield to him. Jesus made it clear that children are important (Matthew 18:2–6). Give children the importance God gives them.

have bound themselves under a curse not to eat or drink until they slay him; and now
they are ready and waiting for the promise from you."
22 So the commander let the young man go, instructing him, "Tell no one that you have
notified me of these things."

Paul Moved to Caesarea

23 And he called to him two of the centurions and said, "Get two hundred soldiers
ready by [36]the third hour of the night to proceed to Caesarea, with seventy horsemen
and two hundred spearmen."
24 *They were* also to provide mounts to put Paul on and bring him safely to Felix the
governor.
25 And he wrote a letter having this form:
26 "Claudius Lysias, to the most excellent governor Felix, greetings.
27 "When this man was arrested by the Jews and was about to be slain by them, I came
up to them with the troops and rescued him, having learned that he was a Roman.
28 "And wanting to ascertain the charge for which they were accusing him, I brought
him down to their Council;
29 and I found him to be accused over questions about their Law, but under no accusation deserving death or imprisonment.
30 "When I was informed that there would be a plot against the man, I sent him to you
at once, also instructing his accusers to bring charges against him before you."
31 So the soldiers, in accordance with their orders, took Paul and brought him by night
to Antipatris.
32 But the next day, leaving the horsemen to go on with him, they returned to the barracks.
33 When these had come to Caesarea and delivered the letter to the governor, they
also presented Paul to him.
34 When he had read it, he asked from what province he was, and when he learned
that he was from Cilicia,
35 he said, "I will give you a hearing after your accusers arrive also," giving orders for
him to be kept in Herod's [37]Praetorium.

Paul before Felix

24 After five days the high priest Ananias came down with some elders, with an attorney *named* Tertullus, and they brought charges to the governor against Paul.
2 After *Paul* had been summoned, Tertullus began to accuse him, saying *to the governor,*

23:23 Acts 8:40; 23:33
23:24 Acts 23:26, 33; 24:1, 3, 10; 25:14
23:26 Luke 1:3; Acts 24:3; 26:25; Acts 15:23
23:27 Acts 21:32f
Acts 22:25-29
23:28 Acts 22:30; Acts 23:10; Acts 23:1
23:29 Acts 18:15; 25:19; Acts 23:9; 25:25; 26:31; 28:18
23:30 Acts 23:20f; Acts 9:24; 23:12; Acts 23:35; 24:19; 25:16
23:32 Acts 23:23; Acts 23:10
23:33 Acts 8:40; 23:23; Acts 23:24, 26; 24:1, 3, 10; 25:14
23:34 Acts 25:1; Acts 6:9; 21:39
23:35 Acts 23:30; 24:19; 25:16; Acts 24:27
24:1 Acts 24:11; Acts 23:2; Acts 23:24

36 I.e. 9 p.m. **37** I.e. governor's official residence

IMPRISONMENT IN CAESAREA
Paul brought news of his third journey to the elders of the Jerusalem church, who rejoiced at his ministry. But Paul's presence soon stirred up the Jews, who persuaded the Romans to arrest him. A plot to kill Paul was uncovered, so Paul was taken by night to Antipatris and then transferred to the provincial prison in Caesarea.

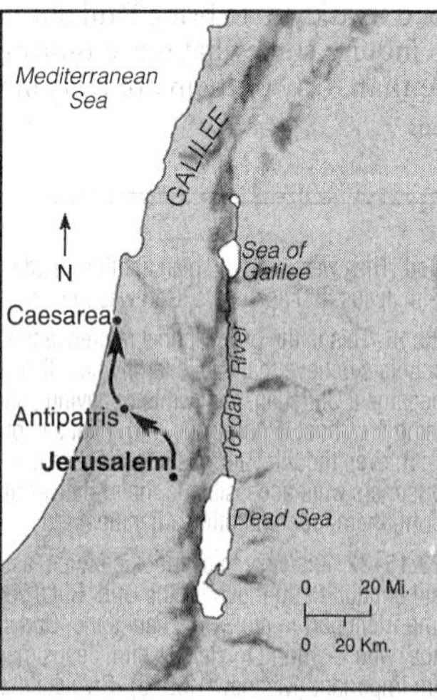

23:23–24 The Roman commander ordered Paul sent to Caesarea. Jerusalem was the seat of Jewish government, but Caesarea was the Roman headquarters for the area. God works in amazing and amusing ways. There were infinite possibilities of ways God could use to get Paul to Caesarea, but he chose to use the Roman army to deliver Paul from his enemies. God's ways are not our ways. Ours are limited; his are not. Don't limit God by asking him to respond your way. When God intervenes, anything can happen, so much more and so much better than you could ever anticipate.

23:26 Felix was the Roman governor or procurator of Judea from A.D. 52 to 59. This was the same position Pontius Pilate had held. While the Jews were given much freedom to govern themselves, the governor ran the army, kept the peace, and gathered the taxes.

23:26 How did Luke know what was written in the letter from Claudius Lysias? In his concern for historical accuracy, Luke used many sources to make sure that his writings were correct (see Luke 1:1 4). This letter was probably read aloud in court when Paul came before Felix to answer the Jews' accusations. Also, because Paul was a Roman citizen, a copy may have been given to him as a courtesy.

24:1 The accusers arrived—Ananias, the high priest; Tertullus, the lawyer; and several Jewish leaders. They traveled 60 miles to Caesarea, the Roman center of government, to bring their false accusations against Paul. Their murder plot had failed (23:12–15), but they persisted in trying to kill him. This attempt at murder was both premeditated and persistent.

"Since we have through you attained much peace, and since by your providence reforms are being carried out for this nation,
24:3 Acts 23:26; 26:25 3 we acknowledge *this* in every way and everywhere, most excellent Felix, with all thankfulness.
4 "But, that I may not weary you any further, I beg you to grant us, by your kindness, a
brief hearing.
24:5 Acts 15:5; 24:14 5 "For we have found this man a real pest and a fellow who stirs up dissension among
all the Jews throughout [38]the world, and a ringleader of the sect of the Nazarenes.
24:6 Acts 21:28 6 "And he even tried to desecrate the temple; and then we arrested him. [[39]We wanted
to judge him according to our own Law.
7 "But Lysias the commander came along, and with much violence took him out of our
hands,
8 ordering his accusers to come before you.] By examining him yourself concerning
all these matters you will be able to ascertain the things of which we accuse him."
24:9 1 Thess 2:16 9 The Jews also joined in the attack, asserting that these things were so.
24:10 Acts 23:24 **10** When the governor had nodded for him to speak, Paul responded:
"Knowing that for many years you have been a judge to this nation, I cheerfully make
my defense,
24:11 Acts 21:18, 27; 24:1 11 since you can take note of the fact that no more than twelve days ago I went up to
Jerusalem to worship.

38 Lit *the inhabited earth* **39** The early mss do not contain the remainder of v 6, v 7, nor the first part of v 8

UNSUNG HEROES IN ACTS

When we think of the success of the early church, we often think of the work of the apostles. But the church could have died if it hadn't been for the unsung heroes, the men and women who through some small but committed act moved the church forward.

Hero	*Reference*	*Heroic action*
Lame man	3:9–12	After his healing, he praised God. With the crowds gathering to see what happened, Peter used the opportunity to tell many about Jesus.
Five deacons	6:2–5	Everyone has heard of Stephen and many know of Philip, but there were five other men chosen to be deacons. They not only laid the foundation for service in the church, but their hard work also gave the apostles the time they needed to preach the gospel.
Ananias	9:10–19	He had the responsibility of being the first to demonstrate Christ's love to Saul (Paul) after his conversion.
Cornelius	10:30–35	His example showed Peter that the gospel was for all people, Jews and Gentiles.
Rhoda	12:13–15	Her persistence brought Peter inside Mary's home where he would be safe.
James	15:13–21	He took command of the Jerusalem council and had the courage and discernment to help form a decision that would affect literally millions of Christians over many generations.
Lydia	16:13–15	She opened her home to Paul, from which he led many to Christ and founded a church in Philippi.
Jason	17:5–9	He risked his life for the gospel by allowing Paul to stay in his home. He stood up for what was true and right, even though he faced persecution for it.
Paul's nephew	23:16–24	He saved Paul's life by telling officials of a murder plot.
Julius	27:1, 43	He spared Paul when the other soldiers wanted to kill him.

24:2ff Tertullus was a special orator called to present the religious leaders' case before the Roman governor. He made three accusations against Paul: (1) He was a pest, stirring up riots among the Jews around the world; (2) he was the ringleader of an unrecognized religious sect, which was against Roman law; and (3) he had tried to desecrate the temple. The religious leaders hoped that these accusations would persuade Felix to execute Paul in order to keep the peace in Palestine.

24:5 While the charge that Paul was a pest was insulting to Paul, it was too vague to be a substantial legal charge. The Nazarene sect referred to the Christians—named here after Jesus' hometown of Nazareth.

24:10ff Tertullus and the religious leaders seemed to have a strong argument against Paul, but Paul refuted their accusations point by point. Paul was also able to present the gospel message through his defense. Paul's accusers were unable to present specific evidence to support their general accusations. For example, Paul was accused of starting trouble among the Jews in the province of Asia (24:18–19), but the Jews in the province of Asia (western Turkey) were not present to confirm this. This is another example of Paul using every opportunity to witness for Christ (see 24:14, 24).

12 "Neither in the temple, nor in the synagogues, nor in the city *itself* did they find me
carrying on a discussion with anyone or causing a riot.
13 "Nor can they prove to you *the charges* of which they now accuse me.
14 "But this I admit to you, that according to the Way which they call a sect I do serve
the God of our fathers, believing everything that is in accordance with the Law and that
is written in the Prophets;
15 having a hope in God, which these men cherish themselves, that there shall certainly be a resurrection of both the righteous and the wicked.
16 "In view of this, I also do my best to maintain always a blameless conscience *both*
before God and before men.
17 "Now after several years I came to bring [40]alms to my nation and to present offerings;
18 in which they found me *occupied* in the temple, having been purified, without *any*
crowd or uproar. But *there were* some Jews from Asia—
19 who ought to have been present before you and to make accusation, if they should
have anything against me.
20 "Or else let these men themselves tell what misdeed they found when I stood before
the Council,
21 other than for this one statement which I shouted out while standing among them,
'For the resurrection of the dead I am on trial before you today.' "
22 But Felix, having a more exact knowledge about the Way, put them off, saying, "When
Lysias the [41]commander comes down, I will decide your case."
23 Then he gave orders to the centurion for him to be kept in custody and *yet* have
some freedom, and not to prevent any of his friends from ministering to him.
24 But some days later Felix arrived with Drusilla, his wife who was a Jewess, and sent
for Paul and heard him *speak* about faith in Christ Jesus.
25 But as he was discussing righteousness, self-control and the judgment to come, Felix became frightened and said, "Go away for the present, and when I find time I will
summon you."
26 At the same time too, he was hoping that money would be given him by Paul; therefore he also used to send for him quite often and converse with him.
27 But after two years had passed, Felix was succeeded by Porcius Festus, and wishing
to do the Jews a favor, Felix left Paul imprisoned.

Paul before Festus

25 Festus then, having arrived in the province, three days later went up to Jerusalem
from Caesarea.
2 And the chief priests and the leading men of the Jews brought charges against Paul,
and they were urging him,
3 requesting a concession against Paul, that he might have him brought to Jerusalem
(*at the same time,* setting an ambush to kill him on the way).
4 Festus then answered that Paul was being kept in custody at Caesarea and that he
himself was about to leave shortly.

24:12 Acts 25:8; Acts 24:18
24:14 Acts 9:2; 24:22; Acts 15:5; 24:5; Acts 3:13; Acts 25:8; 26:4ff, 22f; 28:23
24:15 Dan 12:2; John 5:28f; 11:24
24:17 Acts 20:31; Acts 11:29f; Rom 15:25-28; 1 Cor 16:1-4; 2 Cor 8:1-4; 9:1, 2, 12; Gal 2:10
24:18 Acts 21:26; Acts 24:12; Acts 21:27
24:19 Acts 23:30
24:20 Matt 5:22
24:21 Acts 23:6; 24:15
24:22 Acts 24:14
24:23 Acts 23:35; Acts 28:16; Acts 23:16
24:24 Acts 20:21
24:25 Titus 2:12; Gal 5:23; Titus 1:8; 2 Pet 1:6; Acts 10:42
24:26 Acts 24:17
24:27 Acts 25:1, 4, 9, 12; 26:24f, 32; Acts 12:3; 25:9; Acts 23:35; 25:14
25:1 Acts 23:34; Acts 8:40; 25:4, 6, 13
25:2 Acts 24:1; 25:15
25:4 Acts 25:16; Acts 24:23; Acts 8:40; 25:1, 6, 13

40 Or *gifts to charity* **41** I.e. chiliarch, in command of one thousand troops

---

24:22 Felix had been governor for six years and would have known about the Christians ("the Way"), a topic of conversation among the Romans leaders. The Christians' peaceful life-styles had already proven to the Romans that Christians didn't go around starting riots.

24:25 Paul's talk with Felix became so personal that Felix grew fearful. Felix, like Herod Antipas (Mark 6:17–18), had taken another man's wife. Paul's words were interesting until they focused on "righteousness, self-control, and the judgment to come." Many people will be glad to discuss the gospel with you as long as it doesn't touch their lives too personally. When it does, some will resist or run. But this is what the gospel is all about—God's power to change lives. The gospel is not effective until it moves from principles and doctrine into a life-changing dynamic. When someone resists or runs from your witness, you have undoubtedly succeeded in making the gospel personal.

24:27 Felix lost his job as governor and was called back to Rome. Porcius Festus took over as governor in late 59 or early 60. He was more just than Felix, who had kept Paul in prison for two years, in hopes that perhaps Paul would bribe him, and that by detaining Paul, the Jews would be kept happy. When Festus came into office, he immediately ordered Paul's trial to resume.

24:27 The Jews were in the majority, and the Roman political leaders wanted to defer to them to help keep the peace. Paul seemed to incite problems among the Jews everywhere he went. By keeping him in prison, Felix left office on good terms with the Jews.

25:1–9 Although two years had passed, the Jewish leaders still were looking for a way to kill Paul. They told Festus about Paul and tried to convince him to hold the trial in Jerusalem (so they could prepare an ambush). But God and Paul thwarted their schemes again.

5 "Therefore," he ☆said, "let the influential men among you go there with me, and if
there is anything wrong about the man, let them prosecute him."
6 After he had spent not more than eight or ten days among them, he went down to
Caesarea, and on the next day he took his seat on the tribunal and ordered Paul to be
brought.
7 After Paul arrived, the Jews who had come down from Jerusalem stood around him,
bringing many and serious charges against him which they could not prove,
8 while Paul said in his own defense, "I have committed no offense either against the
Law of the Jews or against the temple or against Caesar."
9 But Festus, wishing to do the Jews a favor, answered Paul and said, "Are you willing
to go up to Jerusalem and stand trial before me on these *charges?*"
10 But Paul said, "I am standing before Caesar's tribunal, where I ought to be tried. I
have done no wrong to *the* Jews, as you also very well know.
11 "If, then, I am a wrongdoer and have committed anything worthy of death, I do not
refuse to die; but if none of those things is *true* of which these men accuse me, no one
can hand me over to them. I appeal to Caesar."
12 Then when Festus had conferred with his council, he answered, "You have appealed
to Caesar, to Caesar you shall go."
13 Now when several days had elapsed, King Agrippa and Bernice arrived at Caesarea
and paid their respects to Festus.
14 While they were spending many days there, Festus laid Paul's case before the king,
saying, "There is a man who was left as a prisoner by Felix;
15 and when I was at Jerusalem, the chief priests and the elders of the Jews brought
charges against him, asking for a sentence of condemnation against him.
16 "I answered them that it is not the custom of the Romans to hand over any man before the accused meets his accusers face to face and has an opportunity to make his
defense against the charges.
17 "So after they had assembled here, I did not delay, but on the next day took my seat
on the tribunal and ordered the man to be brought before me.
18 "When the accusers stood up, they *began* bringing charges against him not of such
crimes as I was expecting,
19 but they *simply* had some points of disagreement with him about their own religion
and about a dead man, Jesus, whom Paul asserted to be alive.
20 "Being at a loss how to investigate such matters, I asked whether he was willing to go
to Jerusalem and there stand trial on these matters.
21 "But when Paul appealed to be held in custody for [42]the Emperor's decision, I ordered him to be kept in custody until I send him to Caesar."
22 Then Agrippa *said* to Festus, "I also would like to hear the man myself." "Tomorrow," he ☆said, "you shall hear him."

25:6 Acts 8:40; 25:1, 4, 13; Matt 27:19; Acts 25:10, 17
25:7 Acts 24:5f; Acts 24:13
25:8 Acts 6:13; 24:12; 28:17
25:9 Acts 12:3; 24:27; Acts 25:20
25:10 Matt 27:19; Acts 25:6, 17
25:11 Acts 25:21, 25; 26:32; 28:19
25:13 Acts 8:40; 25:1, 4, 6
25:14 Acts 24:27
25:15 Acts 24:1; 25:2
25:16 Acts 25:4f; Acts 23:30
25:17 Matt 27:19; Acts 25:6, 10
25:19 Acts 18:15; 23:29; Acts 17:22
25:20 Acts 25:9
25:21 Acts 25:11f
25:22 Acts 9:15

42 Lit *the Augustus's* (in this case Nero)

25:10–11 Every Roman citizen had the right to appeal to Caesar. This didn't mean that Caesar himself would hear the case, but that the citizen's case would be tried by the highest courts in the empire. Festus saw Paul's appeal as a way to send him out of the country and thus pacify the Jews. Paul wanted to go to Rome to preach the gospel (Romans 1:10), and he knew that his appeal would give him the opportunity. To go to Rome as a prisoner was better than not to go there at all.

25:11 Paul knew that he was innocent of the charges against him and could appeal to Caesar's judgment. He knew his rights as a Roman citizen and as an innocent person. Paul had met his responsibilities as a Roman, and so he had the opportunity to claim Rome's protection. The good reputation and clear conscience that result from our walk with God can help us remain guiltless before God and blameless before the world.

25:13 This was Herod Agrippa II, son of Herod Agrippa I, and a descendant of Herod the Great. He had power over the temple, controlled the temple treasury, and could appoint and remove the high priest. Bernice was the sister of Herod Agrippa II. She married her uncle, Herod Chalcis, became a mistress to her brother Agrippa II, and then became mistress to the emperor Vespasian's son, Titus. Here Agrippa and Bernice were making an official visit to Festus. Agrippa, of Jewish descent, could help clarify Paul's case for Roman governor. Agrippa and Festus were anxious to cooperate in governing their neighboring territories.

25:19 Even though Festus knew little about Christianity, he somehow sensed that the resurrection was central to Christian belief.

Paul before Agrippa

23 So, on the next day when Agrippa came together with Bernice amid great pomp,
and entered the auditorium [43]accompanied by the commanders and the prominent men
of the city, at the command of Festus, Paul was brought in.
24 Festus ☆said, "King Agrippa, and all you gentlemen here present with us, you see
this man about whom all the people of the Jews appealed to me, both at Jerusalem and
here, loudly declaring that he ought not to live any longer.
25 "But I found that he had committed nothing worthy of death; and since he himself
appealed to the Emperor, I decided to send him.
26 "Yet I have nothing definite about him to write to my lord. Therefore I have brought
him before you *all* and especially before you, King Agrippa, so that after the investigation has taken place, I may have something to write.
27 "For it seems absurd to me in sending a prisoner, not to indicate also the charges
against him."

Paul's Defense before Agrippa

26 Agrippa said to Paul, "You are permitted to speak for yourself." Then Paul
stretched out his hand and *proceeded* to make his defense:
2 "In regard to all the things of which I am accused by the Jews, I consider myself fortunate, King Agrippa, that I am about to make my defense before you today;
3 especially because you are an expert in all customs and questions among *the* Jews;
therefore I beg you to listen to me patiently.
4 "So then, all Jews know my manner of life from my youth up, which from the beginning was spent among my *own* nation and at Jerusalem;
5 since they have known about me for a long time, if they are willing to testify, that I
lived *as* a Pharisee according to the strictest sect of our religion.
6 "And now I am standing trial for the hope of the promise made by God to our fathers;
7 *the promise* to which our twelve tribes hope to attain, as they earnestly serve *God*
night and day. And for this hope, O King, I am being accused by Jews.
8 "Why is it considered incredible among you *people* if God does raise the dead?
9 "So then, I thought to myself that I had to do many things hostile to the name of
Jesus of Nazareth.
10 "And this is just what I did in Jerusalem; not only did I lock up many of the saints in
prisons, having received authority from the chief priests, but also when they were being
put to death I cast my vote against them.
11 "And as I punished them often in all the synagogues, I tried to force them to blaspheme; and being furiously enraged at them, I kept pursuing them even to foreign
cities.
12 "While so engaged as I was journeying to Damascus with the authority and commission of the chief priests,
13 at midday, O King, I saw on the way a light from heaven, brighter than the sun, shining
all around me and those who were journeying with me.
14 "And when we had all fallen to the ground, I heard a voice saying to me in the Hebrew dialect, 'Saul, Saul, why are you persecuting Me? It is hard for you to kick against
the goads.'
15 "And I said, 'Who are You, Lord?' And the Lord said, 'I am Jesus whom you are
persecuting.
16 'But get up and stand on your feet; for this purpose I have appeared to you, to appoint you a minister and a witness not only to the things which you have seen, but also to
the things in which I will appear to you;

25:23 Acts 25:13; 26:30
25:24 Acts 25:2, 7; Acts 22:22
25:25 Luke 23:4; Acts 23:29; Acts 25:11f
26:1 Acts 9:15
26:3 Acts 6:14; 25:19; 26:7
26:4 Gal 1:13f; Phil 3:5
26:5 Acts 23:6; Phil 3:5; Acts 22:3; Acts 15:5
26:6 Acts 24:15; 28:20; Acts 13:32
26:7 James 1:1; Acts 24:15; 28:20; Acts 26:2
26:8 Acts 23:6
26:9 John 16:2; 1 Tim 1:13; John 15:21
26:10 Acts 8:3; 9:13; Acts 9:1f; Acts 22:20
26:11 Matt 10:17; Acts 22:19; Acts 9:1; Acts 22:5
26:12 Acts 26:12-18; 9:3-8; 22:6-11
26:14 Acts 9:7; Acts 21:40
26:16 Ezek 2:1; Dan 10:11; Acts 22:14; Luke 1:2; Acts 22:15

43 Lit *and with*

25:23ff Paul was in prison, but that didn't stop him from making the most of his situation. Military officers and prominent city leaders met in the palace room with Agrippa to hear this case. Paul saw this new audience as yet another opportunity to present the gospel. Rather than complain about your present situation, look for ways to use every opportunity to serve God and share him with others. Your problems may be opportunities in disguise.

26:3ff This speech is a good example of Paul's powerful oratory. Beginning with a compliment to Agrippa, he told his story, including the resurrection of Christ, and the royal audience was spellbound.

26:14 An oxgoad was a sharp stick used to prod cattle. "It is hard for you to kick against the goads" (oxgoads) means, "You are only hurting yourself."

26:17 Jer 1:8, 19; 1 Chr 16:35; Acts 9:15

26:18 Is 35:5; 42:7, 16; Eph 5:8; Col 1:13; 1 Pet 2:9; John 1:5; Eph 5:8; Col 1:12f; 1 Thess 5:5; 1 Pet 2:9; Matt 4:10; Luke 24:47; Acts 2:38; Acts 20:32; Acts 20:21

26:20 Acts 9:19ff; 22:17-20; Acts 9:15; 13:46; Acts 3:19; Matt 3:8; Luke 3:8

26:21 Acts 21:27, 30

26:22 Luke 16:28; Acts 10:43; 24:14

26:23 Matt 26:24; Acts 3:18; 1 Cor 15:20, 23; Col 1:18; Rev 1:5; Is 42:6; 49:6; Luke 2:32; 2 Cor 4:4

26:24 John 7:15; 2 Tim 3:15

26:25 Acts 23:26; 24:3

26:28 Acts 11:26

26:29 Acts 21:33

26:30 Acts 25:23

26:31 Acts 23:29

26:32 Acts 28:18; Acts 25:11

27:1 [we] Acts 16:10; 27:1-28; Acts 25:12, 25; Acts 18:2; 27:6; Acts 10:1

17 rescuing you from the *Jewish* people and from the Gentiles, to whom I am sending you,

18 to open their eyes so that they may turn from darkness to light and from the dominion of Satan to God, that they may receive forgiveness of sins and an inheritance among those who have been sanctified by faith in Me.'

19 "So, King Agrippa, I did not prove disobedient to the heavenly vision,

20 but *kept* declaring both to those of Damascus first, and *also* at Jerusalem and *then* throughout all the region of Judea, and *even* to the Gentiles, that they should repent and turn to God, performing deeds appropriate to repentance.

21 "For this reason *some* Jews seized me in the temple and tried to put me to death.

22 "So, having obtained help from God, I stand to this day testifying both to small and great, stating nothing but what the Prophets and Moses said was going to take place;

23 that the Christ was to suffer, *and* that by reason of *His* resurrection from the dead He would be the first to proclaim light both to the *Jewish* people and to the Gentiles."

24 While *Paul* was saying this in his defense, Festus ☆said in a loud voice, "Paul, you are out of your mind! *Your* great learning is driving you mad."

25 But Paul ☆said, "I am not out of my mind, most excellent Festus, but I utter words of sober truth.

26 "For the king knows about these matters, and I speak to him also with confidence, since I am persuaded that none of these things escape his notice; for this has not been done in a corner.

27 "King Agrippa, do you believe the Prophets? I know that you do."

28 Agrippa *replied* to Paul, "In a short time you will persuade me to become a Christian."

29 And Paul *said*, "I would wish to God, that whether in a short or long time, not only you, but also all who hear me this day, might become such as I am, except for these chains."

30 The king stood up and the governor and Bernice, and those who were sitting with them,

31 and when they had gone aside, they *began* talking to one another, saying, "This man is not doing anything worthy of death or imprisonment."

32 And Agrippa said to Festus, "This man might have been set free if he had not appealed to Caesar."

Paul Is Sent to Rome

27 When it was decided that we would sail for Italy, they proceeded to deliver Paul and some other prisoners to a centurion of the Augustan [44]cohort named Julius.

2 And embarking in an Adramyttian ship, which was about to sail to the regions along the coast of Asia, we put out to sea accompanied by Aristarchus, a Macedonian of Thessalonica.

44 Or *battalion*

26:17–18 Paul took every opportunity to remind his audience that the Gentiles have an equal share in God's inheritance. This inheritance is the promise and blessing of the covenant that God made with Abraham (see Ephesians 2:19; 1 Peter 1:3–4). Paul's mission was to preach the Good News to the Gentiles.

26:24 Paul was risking his life for a message that was offensive to the Jews and unbelievable to the Gentiles. Jesus received the same response to his message (Mark 3:21; John 10:20). To a worldly, materialistic mind, it seems insane to risk so much to gain what seems to be so little. But as you follow Christ, you soon discover that temporary possessions look so small next to even the smallest eternal reward.

26:26 Paul was appealing to the *facts*—people were still alive who had heard Jesus and seen his miracles, the empty tomb could still be seen, and the Christian message was turning the world upside down (17:6). The history of Jesus' life and the early church are facts that are still open for us to examine. We still have eyewitness accounts of Jesus' life recorded in the Bible as well as historical and archaeological records of the early church to study. Examine the events and facts as verified by many witnesses. Strengthen your faith with the truth of these accounts.

26:28–29 Agrippa responded to Paul's presentation with a sarcastic remark. Paul didn't react to the brush-off, but made a personal appeal to which he hoped all his listeners would respond. Paul's response is a good example for us as we tell others about God's plan of salvation. A sincere personal appeal or personal testimony can show the depth of our concern and break through hardened hearts.

26:28–29 Paul's heart is revealed here in his words: He was more concerned for the salvation of these strangers than for the removal of his own chains. Ask God to give you a burning desire to see others come to Christ—a desire so strong that it overshadows your problems.

27:1–2 Use of the pronoun *we* indicates that Luke accompanied Paul on this journey. Aristarchus is the man who was dragged into the theater at the beginning of the riot in Ephesus (19:29; 20:4; Philemon 24).

27:1–3 Julius, a hardened Roman centurion, was assigned to guard Paul. Obviously he had to remain close to Paul at all times. Through this contact, Julius developed a respect for Paul. He gave Paul a certain amount of freedom (27:3) and later spared his life (27:43). How would your character look, up close and personal?

3 The next day we put in at Sidon; and Julius treated Paul with consideration and allowed him to go to his friends and receive care.
4 From there we put out to sea and sailed under the shelter of Cyprus because the
winds were contrary.
5 When we had sailed through the sea along the coast of Cilicia and Pamphylia, we
landed at Myra in Lycia.
6 There the centurion found an Alexandrian ship sailing for Italy, and he put us
aboard it.
7 When we had sailed slowly for a good many days, and with difficulty had arrived off
Cnidus, since the wind did not permit us *to go* farther, we sailed under the shelter of
Crete, off Salmone;
8 and with difficulty sailing past it we came to a place called Fair Havens, near which
was the city of Lasea.
9 When considerable time had passed and the voyage was now dangerous, since even
the [45]fast was already over, Paul *began* to admonish them,
10 and said to them, "Men, I perceive that the voyage will certainly be with damage
and great loss, not only of the cargo and the ship, but also of our lives."
11 But the centurion was more persuaded by the pilot and the captain of the ship than
by what was being said by Paul.
12 Because the harbor was not suitable for wintering, the majority reached a decision
to put out to sea from there, if somehow they could reach Phoenix, a harbor of Crete,
facing southwest and northwest, and spend the winter *there.*
13 When a moderate south wind came up, supposing that they had attained their purpose, they weighed anchor and *began* sailing along Crete, close *inshore.*

Shipwreck

14 But before very long there rushed down from the land a violent wind, called [46]Eura-
quilo;
15 and when the ship was caught *in it* and could not face the wind, we gave way *to it* and
let ourselves be driven along.
16 Running under the shelter of a small island called Clauda, we were scarcely able to
get the *ship's* boat under control.
17 After they had hoisted it up, they used supporting cables in undergirding the ship;
and fearing that they might run aground on *the shallows* of Syrtis, they let down the sea
anchor and in this way let themselves be driven along.
18 The next day as we were being violently storm-tossed, they began to jettison the cargo;
19 and on the third day they threw the ship's tackle overboard with their own hands.
20 Since neither sun nor stars appeared for many days, and no small storm was assail-
ing *us,* from then on all hope of our being saved was gradually abandoned.
21 When they had gone a long time without food, then Paul stood up in their midst
and said, "Men, you ought to have followed my advice and not to have set sail from Crete
and incurred this damage and loss.
22 "*Yet* now I urge you to keep up your courage, for there will be no loss of life among
you, but *only* of the ship.
23 "For this very night an angel of the God to whom I belong and whom I serve stood
before me,
24 saying, 'Do not be afraid, Paul; you must stand before Caesar; and behold, God has
granted you all those who are sailing with you.'

27:3 Matt 11:21; Acts 27:43; Acts 24:23
27:4 Acts 4:36; Acts 27:7
27:5 Acts 6:9; Acts 13:13
27:6 Acts 28:11; Acts 18:2; 27:1
27:7 Acts 27:4; Acts 2:11; 27:12f, 21; Titus 1:5, 12
27:8 Acts 27:13
27:9 Lev 16:29-31; 23:27-29; Num 29:7
27:10 Acts 27:21
27:11 Rev 18:17
27:12 Acts 2:11; 27:13, 21; Titus 1:5, 12
27:13 Acts 27:8; Acts 2:11; 27:12f, 21; Titus 1:5, 12
27:14 Mark 4:37
27:17 Acts 27:26, 29
27:18 Jon 1:5; Acts 27:38
27:21 Acts 27:10; Acts 27:7
27:22 Acts 27:25, 36
27:23 Acts 5:19; Rom 1:9; Acts 18:9; 23:11; 2 Tim 4:17
27:24 Acts 23:11; Acts 27:31, 42, 44

45 I.e. Day of Atonement in September or October, which was a dangerous time of year for navigation **46** I.e. a northeaster

---

27:9 The "fast" was the day of atonement. Ships in ancient times had no compasses and navigated by the stars. Overcast weather made sailing almost impossible and very dangerous. Sailing was doubtful in September and impossible by November. This event occurred in October (A.D. 59).

27:12 Although this was not the best time to sail, the pilot and the captain of the ship didn't want to spend the winter in Lasea, and so the pilot took a chance. At first the winds and weather were favorable, but then the deadly storm arose.

27:17 The measures they took to survive included passing cables under the ship to hold it together. Syrtis was on the northern coast of Africa.

27:21 Why would Paul talk to the crew this way? Paul was not taunting them with an "I told you so," but was reminding them that, with God's guidance, he had predicted this very problem (27:10). In the future, they listened to him (27:30–32) and their lives were spared because of it.

27:25 Acts 27:22, 36
27:26 Acts 27:17, 29; Acts 28:1
27:29 Acts 27:17, 26
27:30 Acts 27:16
27:32 John 2:15

25 "Therefore, keep up your courage, men, for I believe God that it will turn out exactly
as I have been told.
26 "But we must run aground on a certain island."
27 But when the fourteenth night came, as we were being driven about in the Adriatic
Sea, about midnight the sailors *began* to surmise that they were approaching some land.
28 They took soundings and found *it to be* twenty fathoms; and a little farther on they
took another sounding and found *it to be* fifteen fathoms.
29 Fearing that we might run aground somewhere on the rocks, they cast four anchors
from the stern and wished for daybreak.
30 But as the sailors were trying to escape from the ship and had let down the *ship's*
boat into the sea, on the pretense of intending to lay out anchors from the bow,
31 Paul said to the centurion and to the soldiers, "Unless these men remain in the ship,
you yourselves cannot be saved."
32 Then the soldiers cut away the ropes of the *ship's* boat and let it fall away.
33 Until the day was about to dawn, Paul was encouraging them all to take some food,
saying, "Today is the fourteenth day that you have been constantly watching and going
without eating, having taken nothing.

HEROD AGRIPPA II

Like great-grandfather, like grandfather, like father, like son—this tells the story of Herod Agrippa II. He inherited the effects of generations of powerful men with flawed personalities. Each son followed his father in weaknesses, mistakes, and missed opportunities. Each generation had a confrontation with God, but each failed to realize the importance of the decision. Herod Agrippa's great-uncle, Herod Antipas, actually met Jesus during his trial, but failed to see Jesus for who he was. Agrippa II heard the gospel from Paul, but considered the message mild entertainment. He found it humorous that Paul actually tried to convince him to become a Christian.

Like so many before and after, Agrippa II stopped within hearing distance of the kingdom of God. He left himself without excuse. He heard the gospel but decided it wasn't worth responding to personally. Unfortunately, his mistake isn't uncommon. Many who read his story also will not believe. Their problem, like his, is not really that the gospel isn't convincing or that they don't need to know God personally; it is that they choose not to respond.

What has been your response to the gospel? Has it turned your life around and given you the hope of eternal life, or has it been a message to resist or reject? Perhaps it has just been entertainment. It may seem like too great a price to give God control of your life, but it is an even greater price by far to live eternally apart from him because you have chosen not to be his child.

Strengths and accomplishments:
- Last of the Herod dynasty that ruled parts of Palestine from 40 B.C. to A.D. 100
- Continued his father's success in mediating between Rome and Palestine
- Continued the family tradition of building and improving cities

Weaknesses and mistakes:
- Was not convinced by the gospel and consciously rejected it
- Carried on an incestuous relationship with his sister Bernice

Lessons from his life:
- Families pass on both positive and negative influences to children
- There are no guarantees of multiple opportunities to respond to God

Vital statistics:
- Occupation: Ruler of northern and eastern Palestine
- Relatives: Great-grandfather: Herod the Great. Father: Herod Agrippa I. Great-uncle: Herod Antipas. Sisters: Bernice, Drusilla
- Contemporaries: Paul, Felix, Festus, Peter, Luke

Key verse:
"Agrippa replied to Paul, 'In a short time you will persuade me to become a Christian' " (Acts 26:28).

Herod Agrippa II's story is told in Acts 25:13—26:32.

27:27 The Adriatic Sea referred to the central part of the Mediterranean Sea between Italy, Crete, and the northern coast of Africa.

27:28 Soundings were made by throwing a weighted, marked line into the water. When the lead hit the bottom, sailors could tell the depth of the water from the marks on the rope.

34 "Therefore I encourage you to take some food, for this is for your preservation, for
not a hair from the head of any of you will perish."
35 Having said this, he took bread and gave thanks to God in the presence of all, and
he broke it and began to eat.
36 All of them were encouraged and they themselves also took food.
37 All of us in the ship were two hundred and seventy-six persons.
38 When they had eaten enough, they *began* to lighten the ship by throwing out the
wheat into the sea.
39 When day came, they could not recognize the land; but they did observe a bay with
a beach, and they resolved to drive the ship onto it if they could.
40 And casting off the anchors, they left them in the sea while at the same time they
were loosening the ropes of the rudders; and hoisting the foresail to the wind, they were
heading for the beach.
41 But striking a reef where two seas met, they ran the vessel aground; and the prow
stuck fast and remained immovable, but the stern *began* to be broken up by the force *of*
the waves.
42 The soldiers' plan was to kill the prisoners, so that none *of them* would swim away
and escape;
43 but the centurion, wanting to bring Paul safely through, kept them from their intention, and commanded that those who could swim should jump overboard first and get to
land,
44 and the rest *should follow*, some on planks, and others on various things from the
ship. And so it happened that they all were brought safely to land.

Safe at Malta

28 When they had been brought safely through, then we found out that the island
was called Malta.
2 The natives showed us extraordinary kindness; for because of the rain that had set
in and because of the cold, they kindled a fire and received us all.
3 But when Paul had gathered a bundle of sticks and laid them on the fire, a viper
came out because of the heat and fastened itself on his hand.
4 When the natives saw the creature hanging from his hand, they *began* saying to one
another, "Undoubtedly this man is a murderer, and though he has been saved from the
sea, justice has not allowed him to live."
5 However he shook the creature off into the fire and suffered no harm.
6 But they were expecting that he was about to swell up or suddenly fall down dead.
But after they had waited a long time and had seen nothing unusual happen to him, they
changed their minds and *began* to say that he was a god.
7 Now in the neighborhood of that place were lands belonging to the leading man of
the island, named Publius, who welcomed us and entertained us courteously three days.
8 And it happened that the father of Publius was lying *in bed* afflicted with *recurrent*
fever and dysentery; and Paul went in *to see* him and after he had prayed, he laid his
hands on him and healed him.
9 After this had happened, the rest of the people on the island who had diseases were
coming to him and getting cured.
10 They also honored us with many marks of respect; and when we were setting sail,
they supplied *us* with all we needed.

27:34 Matt 10:30
27:35 Matt 14:19
27:36 Acts 27:22, 25
27:37 Acts 2:41
27:38 Jon 1:5; Acts 27:18
27:39 Acts 28:1
27:40 Acts 27:29
27:42 Acts 12:19
27:43 Acts 27:3
27:44 Acts 27:22, 31
28:1 [they] Acts 16:10; 27:1; Acts 27:39; Acts 27:26
28:2 Acts 28:4; Rom 1:14; 1 Cor 14:11; Col 3:11; Rom 14:1
28:4 Acts 28:2; Luke 13:2, 4
28:5 Mark 16:18
28:6 Acts 14:11
28:8 Acts 9:40; James 5:14f; Matt 9:18; Mark 5:23; 6:5

27:42–43 The soldiers would pay with their own lives if any of their prisoners escaped. Their instinctive reaction was to kill the prisoners so they wouldn't get away. Julius, the centurion, was impressed with Paul and wanted to save his life. Julius was the highest ranking official and therefore he could make this decision. This act preserved Paul for his later ministry in Rome and fulfilled Paul's prediction that all the people on the ship would be saved (27:22).

28:1 The island of Malta is 60 miles south of Sicily. It had excellent harbors and was ideally located for trade.

28:2 The natives on Malta were of Phoenician ancestry.

28:3 God had promised safe passage to Paul (27:23–25), and he would let nothing stop his servant. The poisonous viper that bit Paul was unable to harm him. Our lives are in God's hands, to continue on or to come to an end in his good timing. God still had work for Paul to do.

28:6 These people were very superstitious and believed in many gods. When they saw that Paul was unhurt by the poisonous viper, they thought he was a god. A similar assessment is reported in 14:11–18.

28:7–8 Paul continued to minister to others, even as a shipwrecked prisoner. On this trip alone, his centurion, the leading man of Malta, and many others were affected. It is no wonder that the gospel spread like wildfire.

Paul Arrives at Rome

11 At the end of three months we set sail on an Alexandrian ship which had wintered
at the island, and which had the Twin Brothers for its figurehead.
12 After we put in at Syracuse, we stayed there for three days.
13 From there we sailed around and arrived at Rhegium, and a day later a south wind
sprang up, and on the second day we came to Puteoli.
14 There we found *some* brethren, and were invited to stay with them for seven days;
and thus we came to Rome.
15 And the brethren, when they heard about us, came from there as far as the Market
of Appius and Three Inns to meet us; and when Paul saw them, he thanked God and
took courage.
16 When we entered Rome, Paul was allowed to stay by himself, with the soldier who
was guarding him.
17 After three days Paul called together those who were the leading men of the Jews,
and when they came together, he *began* saying to them, "Brethren, though I had done
nothing against our people or the customs of our fathers, yet I was delivered as a prisoner from Jerusalem into the hands of the Romans.
18 "And when they had examined me, they were willing to release me because there
was no ground for putting me to death.
19 "But when the Jews objected, I was forced to appeal to Caesar, not that I had any
accusation against my nation.

28:11 Acts 27:6
28:14 John 21:23; Acts 1:15; 6:3; 9:30; 28:15; Rom 1:13
28:15 Acts 1:15; 10:23; 11:1, 12, 29; 12:17
28:16 Acts 24:23
28:17 Acts 13:50; 25:2; Acts 22:5; Acts 25:8; Acts 6:14
28:18 Acts 22:24; Acts 26:32; Acts 23:29; 25:25; 26:31
28:19 Acts 25:11, 21, 25; 26:32

PAUL'S JOURNEY TO ROME

One of Paul's most important journeys was to Rome, but he didn't get there the way he expected. It turned out to be more of a legal journey than a missionary journey because, through a series of legal trials and transactions, Paul was delivered to Rome where his presentation of the gospel would penetrate even into the walls of the emperor's palace. Sometimes when our plans don't work out as we want them to, they work out even better than we expected.

Reference	*What happened*
21:30–34	When Paul arrived in Jerusalem, a riot broke out. Seeing the riot, Roman soldiers put Paul into protective custody. Paul asked for a chance to defend himself to the people. His speech was interrupted by the crowd when he told about what God was doing in the lives of Gentiles.
22:24–25	A Roman commander ordered a beating to get a confession from Paul. Paul claimed Roman citizenship and escaped the whip.
22:30	Paul was brought before the Jewish Council. Because of his Roman citizenship, he was rescued from the religious leaders who wanted to kill him.
23:10	The Roman commander put Paul back under protective custody.
23:21–24	Due to a plot to kill Paul, the commander transferred him to Caesarea, which was under Governor Felix's control.
23:35	Paul was in prison until the Jews arrived to accuse him. Paul defended himself before Felix.
24:25–26	Paul was in prison for two years, speaking occasionally to Felix and Drusilla.
24:27	Felix was replaced by Festus.
25:1, 10	New accusations were brought against Paul—Jews wanted him back in Jerusalem for a trial. Paul claimed his right to a hearing before Caesar.
25:12	Festus promised to send him to Rome.
25:13–14	Festus discussed Paul's case with Herod Agrippa II.
26:1	Agrippa and Festus heard Paul speak. Paul again told his story.
26:24–28	Agrippa interrupted with a sarcastic rejection of the gospel.
26:30–32	Group consensus was that Paul was guilty of nothing and could have been released if he had not appealed to Rome.
27:1–2	Paul left for Rome, courtesy of the Roman empire.

28:15 Where did the Roman believers (brethren) come from? The gospel message had spread to Rome by various methods. Many Jews who lived in Rome visited Jerusalem for religious festivals. Some were present at Pentecost (2:10), believed in Jesus, and brought the message back to Rome. Also, Paul had written his letter to the Romans before he visited there.

28:15 The Market of Appius was a town about 43 miles south of Rome; Three Inns was located about 35 miles south of Rome. An inn was a shop, or a place that provided food and lodging for travelers. The Christians openly went to meet Paul and encourage him.

28:17 The decree of Claudius expelling Jews from Rome (18:2) must have been temporary, because Jewish leaders were back in Rome.

28:17–20 Paul wanted to preach the gospel in Rome, and he eventually got there—in chains, through shipwreck, and after many trials. Although he may have wished for an easier passage, he knew that God had blessed him greatly in allowing him to meet the believers in Rome and preach the message to both Jews and Gentiles in that great city. In all things, God worked for Paul's good (Romans 8:28). You can trust him to do the same for you. God may not make you comfortable or secure, but he will provide the opportunity to do his work.

20 "For this reason, therefore, I requested to see you and to speak with you, for I am
wearing this chain for the sake of the hope of Israel."
21 They said to him, "We have neither received letters from Judea concerning you,
nor have any of the brethren come here and reported or spoken anything bad about you.
22 "But we desire to hear from you what your views are; for concerning this sect, it is
known to us that it is spoken against everywhere."
23 When they had set a day for Paul, they came to him at his lodging in large numbers;
and he was explaining to them by solemnly testifying about the kingdom of God and trying
to persuade them concerning Jesus, from both the Law of Moses and from the Prophets, from morning until evening.
24 Some were being persuaded by the things spoken, but others would not believe.
25 And when they did not agree with one another, they *began* leaving after Paul had
spoken one *parting* word, "The Holy Spirit rightly spoke through Isaiah the prophet to
your fathers,
26 saying,

'GO TO THIS PEOPLE AND SAY,
"YOU WILL KEEP ON HEARING, BUT WILL NOT UNDERSTAND;
AND YOU WILL KEEP ON SEEING, BUT WILL NOT PERCEIVE;
27 FOR THE HEART OF THIS PEOPLE HAS BECOME DULL,
AND WITH THEIR EARS THEY SCARCELY HEAR,
AND THEY HAVE CLOSED THEIR EYES;
OTHERWISE THEY MIGHT SEE WITH THEIR EYES,
AND HEAR WITH THEIR EARS,
AND UNDERSTAND WITH THEIR HEART AND RETURN,
AND I WOULD HEAL THEM." '

28 "Therefore let it be known to you that this salvation of God has been sent to the
Gentiles; they will also listen."

28:20 Acts 21:33; Acts 26:6f
28:21 Acts 3:17; 22:5; 28:14; Rom 9:3
28:22 Acts 24:14; 1 Pet 2:12; 3:16; 4:14, 16
28:23 Philem 22; Luke 16:28; Acts 1:3; 23:11; Acts 8:35
28:24 Acts 14:4
28:26 Is 6:9; Matt 13:14f
28:27 Is 6:10
28:28 Ps 98:3; Luke 2:30; Acts 13:26; Acts 9:15; 13:46

47 Early mss do not contain this v

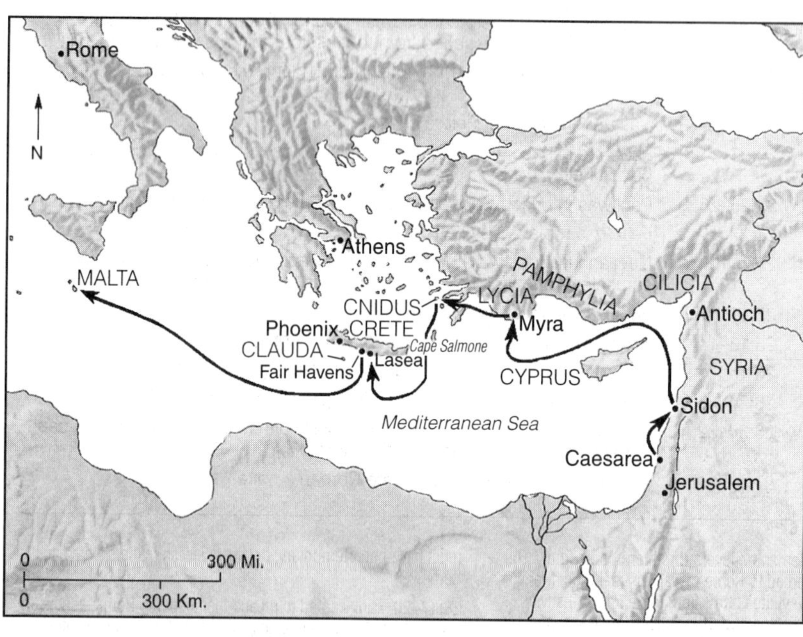

THE TRIP TOWARD ROME
Paul began his 2,000-mile trip to Rome at Caesarea. To avoid the open seas, the ship followed the coastline. At Myra, Paul was put on a vessel bound for Italy. It arrived with difficulty at Cnidus, then went to Crete, landing at the port of Fair Havens. The next stop was Phoenix, but the ship was blown south around the island of Clauda, then drifted for two weeks until it was shipwrecked on the island of Malta.

28:22 Christians were denounced everywhere by the Romans because they were seen as a threat to the Roman establishment. They believed in one God, whereas the Romans had many gods, including Caesar. The Christians were committed to an authority higher than Caesar.

28:23 Paul used the Old Testament to teach the Jews that Jesus was the Messiah, the fulfillment of God's promises. The book of Romans, written ten years earlier, reveals the ongoing dialogue that Paul had with the Jews in Rome.

29 [47When he had spoken these words, the Jews departed, having a great dispute among
themselves.]
30 And he stayed two full years in his own rented quarters and was welcoming all who
came to him,
31 preaching the kingdom of God and teaching concerning the Lord Jesus Christ with
all openness, unhindered.

28:31 Matt 4:23; Acts 20:25; 28:23; 2 Tim 2:9

PAUL ARRIVES IN ROME
The shipwreck occurred on Malta, where the ship's company spent three months. Finally, another ship gave them passage for the 100 miles to Syracuse, capital of Sicily, then sailed on to Rhegium, finally dropping anchor at Puteoli. Paul was taken to the Market of Appius and to Three Inns before arriving in Rome.

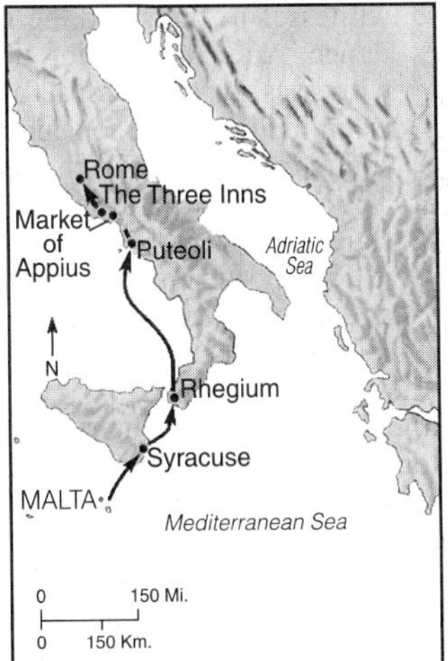

28:30 While Paul was under house arrest, he did more than speak to the Jews. He wrote letters, commonly called his Prison Letters, to the Ephesians, Colossians, and Philippians. He also wrote personal letters, such as the one to Philemon. Luke was with Paul in Rome (2 Timothy 4:11). Timothy often visited him (Philippians 1:1; Colossians 1:1; Philemon 1), as did Tychicus (Ephesians 6:21), Epaphroditus (Philippians 4:18), and Mark (Colossians 4:10). Paul witnessed to the whole Roman guard (Philippians 1:13) and was involved with the Roman believers.

28:30 Tradition says that Paul was released after two years of house arrest in Rome and then set off on a fourth missionary journey. Some reasons for this tradition are as follows: (1) Luke does not give us an account of his trial before Caesar, and Luke was a detailed chronicler; (2) the prosecution had two years to bring the case to trial, and time may have run out; (3) in his letter to the Philippians, written during his imprisonment in Rome, Paul implied that he would soon be released and would do further traveling; (4) Paul mentions several places where he intended to take the gospel, but he never visited those places in his first three journeys; and (5) early Christian literature talks plainly about other travels by Paul.

It may be that during Paul's time of freedom, he continued to travel extensively, even going to Spain (see Romans 15:24, 28) and back to the churches in Greece. The books of 1 Timothy and Titus were written during this time. Later, Paul was imprisoned again, probably in Rome, where he wrote his last letter (2 Timothy).

28:31 Why does the book of Acts end here and so abruptly? The book is not about the life of Paul, but about the spread of the gospel, and that has been clearly presented. God apparently thought it was not necessary for someone to write an additional book describing the continuing history of the early church. Now that the gospel had been preached and established at the center of trade and government, it would spread across the world.

28:31 The book of Acts deals with the history of the Christian church and its expansion in ever-widening circles touching Jerusalem, Antioch, Ephesus, and Rome—the most influential cities in the western world. Acts also shows the mighty miracles and testimonies of the heroes and martyrs of the early church—Peter, Stephen, James, Paul. All the ministry was prompted and held together by the Holy Spirit working in the lives of ordinary people—merchants, travelers, slaves, jailers, church leaders, males, females, Gentiles, Jews, rich, poor. Many unsung heroes of the faith continued the work, through the Holy Spirit, in succeeding generations, changing the world with a changeless message—that Jesus Christ is Savior and Lord for all who call on him. Today we can be the unsung heroes in the continuing story of the spread of the gospel. It is that same message that we Christians are to take to our world so that many more may hear and believe.

ROMANS

VITAL STATISTICS

PURPOSE:
To introduce Paul to the Romans and to give a sample of his message before he arrives in Rome

AUTHOR:
Paul

TO WHOM WRITTEN:
The Christians in Rome and believers everywhere

DATE WRITTEN:
About A.D. 57, from Corinth, as Paul was preparing for his visit to Jerusalem

SETTING:
Apparently Paul had finished his work in the east, and he planned to visit Rome on his way to Spain after first bringing a collection to Jerusalem for the poor Christians there (15:23–28). The Roman church was mostly Jewish but also contained a great number of Gentiles.

KEY VERSE:
"Therefore, having been justified by faith, we have peace with God through our Lord Jesus Christ" (5:1).

KEY PEOPLE:
Paul, Phoebe

KEY PLACE:
Rome

SPECIAL FEATURES:
Paul wrote Romans as an organized and carefully presented statement of his faith—it does not have the form of a typical letter. He does, however, spend considerable time greeting people in Rome at the end of the letter.

KNOWLEDGEABLE and experienced, the district attorney makes his case. Calling key witnesses to the stand, he presents the evidence. After discrediting the testimonies of witnesses for the defense by skillfully cross-examining them, he concludes with an airtight summary and stirring challenge for the jury. The announced verdict is no surprise. "Guilty" states the foreman, and justice is served.

The apostle Paul was intelligent, articulate, and committed to his calling. Like a skilled lawyer, he presented the case for the gospel clearly and forthrightly in his letter to the believers in Rome.

Paul had heard of the church at Rome, but he had never been there, nor had any of the other apostles. Evidently the church had been started by Jews who had come to faith during Pentecost (Acts 2). They spread the gospel on their return to Rome, and the church grew.

Although many barriers separated them, Paul felt a bond with these believers in Rome. They were his brothers and sisters in Christ, and he longed to see them face to face. He had never met most of the believers there, yet he loved them. He sent this letter to introduce himself and to make a clear declaration of the faith.

After a brief introduction, Paul presents the facts of the gospel (1:3) and declares his allegiance to it (1:16–17). He continues by building an airtight case for the lostness of humanity and the necessity for God's intervention (1:18—3:20).

Then Paul presents the Good News: Salvation is available to all, regardless of a person's identity, sin, or heritage. We are saved by *grace* (unearned, undeserved favor from God) through *faith* (complete trust) in Christ and his finished work. Through him we can stand before God justified, "not guilty" (3:21—5:21). With this foundation Paul moves directly into a discussion of the freedom that comes from being saved—freedom from the power of sin (6:1–23), freedom from the domination of the Law (7:1–25), freedom to become like Christ and discover God's limitless love (8:1–39).

Speaking directly to his Jewish brothers and sisters, Paul shares his concern for them and explains how they fit into God's plan (9:1—11:12). God has made the way for Jews and Gentiles to be united in the body of Christ; both groups can praise God for his wisdom and love (11:13–36).

Paul explains what it means to live in complete submission to Christ: Use spiritual gifts to serve others (12:3–8), genuinely love others (12:9–21), and be good citizens (13:1–14). Freedom must be guided by love as we build each other up in the faith, being sensitive and helpful to those who are weak (14:1—15:4). Paul stresses unity, especially between Gentiles and Jews (15:5–13). He concludes by reviewing his reasons for writing, outlining his personal plans (15:22–33), greeting his friends, and giving a few final thoughts and greetings from his traveling companions (16:1–27).

As you read Romans, reexamine your commitment to Christ, and reconfirm your relationships with other believers in Christ's body.

THE BLUEPRINT

A. WHAT TO BELIEVE (1:1—11:36)
1. Sinfulness of humankind
2. Forgiveness of sin through Christ
3. Freedom from sin's grasp
4. Israel's past, present, and future

Paul clearly sets forth the foundations of the Christian faith. All people are sinful; Christ died to forgive sin; we are made right with God through faith; this begins a new life with a new relationship with God. Like a sports team that constantly reviews the basics, we will be greatly helped in our faith by keeping close to these foundations. If we study Romans carefully, we will never be at a loss to know what to believe.

B. HOW TO BEHAVE (12:1—16:27)
1. Personal responsibility
2. Personal notes

Paul gives clear, practical guidelines for the believers in Rome. The Christian life is not abstract theology unconnected with life, but it has practical implications that will affect how we choose to behave each day. It is not enough merely to know the gospel; we must let it transform our life and let God impact every aspect of our lives.

MEGATHEMES

THEME	EXPLANATION	IMPORTANCE
Sin	Sin means refusing to do God's will and failing to do all that God wants. Since Adam's rebellion against God, our nature is to disobey him. Our sin cuts us off from God. Sin causes us to want to live our own way rather than God's way. Because God is morally perfect, just, and fair, he is right to condemn sin.	Each person has sinned, either by rebelling against God or by ignoring his will. No matter what our background or how hard we try to live good and moral lives, we cannot earn salvation or remove our sin. Only Christ can save us.
Salvation	Our sin points out our need to be forgiven and cleansed. Although we don't deserve it, God, in his kindness, reached out to love and forgive us. He provides the way for us to be saved. Christ's death paid the penalty for our sin.	It is good news that God saves us from our sin. But in order to enter into a wonderful new relationship with God, we must believe that Jesus died for us and that he forgives all our sin.
Growth	By God's power, believers are sanctified—made holy. This means we are set apart from sin, enabled to obey and to become more like Christ. When we are growing in our relationship with Christ, the Holy Spirit frees us from the demands of the Law and from fear of judgment.	Because we are free from sin's control, the Law's demands, and fear of God's punishment, we can grow in our relationship with Christ. By trusting in the Holy Spirit and allowing him to help us, we can overcome sin and temptation.
Sovereignty	God oversees and cares about his people—past, present, and future. God's ways of dealing with people are always fair. Because God is in charge of all creation, he can save whomever he wills.	Because of God's mercy, both Jews and Gentiles can be saved. We all must respond to his mercy and accept his gracious offer of forgiveness. Because he is sovereign, let him reign in your heart.
Service	When our purpose is to give credit to God for his love, power, and perfection in all we do, we can serve him properly. Serving him unifies all believers and enables them to show love and sensitivity to others.	None of us can be fully Christlike by ourselves—it takes the entire body of Christ to fully express Christ. By actively and vigorously building up other believers, Christians can be a symphony of service to God.

A. WHAT TO BELIEVE (1:1—11:36)

Paul begins his message to the Romans by vividly portraying the sinfulness of all humankind, explaining how forgiveness is available through faith in Christ, and showing what believers experience in life through their new faith. In this section, we learn of the centrality of faith to becoming a Christian and to living the Christian life. Apart from faith, we have no hope in life.

1. Sinfulness of humankind

The Gospel Exalted

1 Paul, a bond-servant of Christ Jesus, called *as* an apostle, set apart for the gospel
of God,
2 which He promised beforehand through His prophets in the holy Scriptures,
3 concerning His Son, who was born of a descendant of David according to the flesh,
4 who was declared the Son of God with power [1]by the resurrection from the dead,
according to the Spirit of holiness, Jesus Christ our Lord,

1:1 1 Cor 1:1; 9:1; 2 Cor 1:1; Acts 9:15; 13:2; Gal 1:15; Mark 1:14; Rom 15:16

1:2 Titus 1:2; Luke 1:70; Rom 3:21; 16:26

1:3 Matt 1:1; John 1:14; Rom 4:1; 9:3, 5; 1 Cor 10:18

1:4 Matt 4:3

1 Or *as a result of*

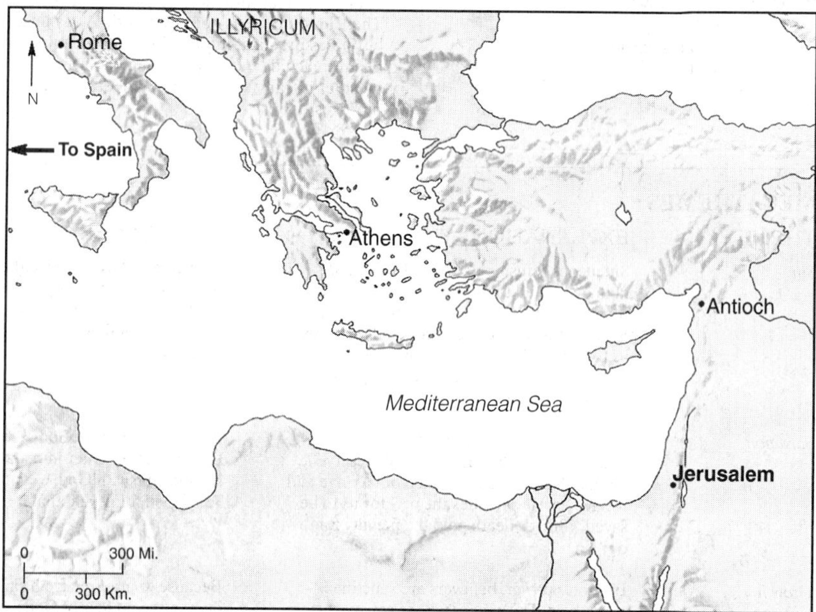

THE GOSPEL GOES TO ROME
When Paul wrote his letter to the church in Rome, he had not yet been there, but he had taken the gospel "from Jerusalem and round about as far as Illyricum" (15:19). He planned to visit and preach in Rome one day and hoped to continue to take the gospel farther west—even to Spain.

1:1 Paul wrote this letter to the church in Rome. Neither he nor the other church leaders, James and Peter, had yet been to Rome. Most likely, the Roman church had been established by believers who had been at Jerusalem for Pentecost (Acts 2:10) and travelers who had heard the Good News in other places and had brought it back to Rome (for example, Priscilla and Aquila, Acts 18:2; Romans 16:3–5). Paul wrote the letter to the Romans during his ministry in Corinth (at the end of his third missionary journey just before returning to Jerusalem; Acts 20:3; Romans 15:25) to encourage the believers and to express his desire to visit them someday (within three years he would). The Roman church had no New Testament because the Gospels were not yet being circulated in their final written form. Thus, this letter may well have been the first piece of Christian literature the Roman believers had seen. Written to both Jewish and Gentile Christians, the letter to the Romans is a systematic presentation of the Christian faith.

1:1 When Paul, a devout Jew who had at first persecuted the Christians, became a believer, God used him to spread the gospel throughout the world. Although it was as a prisoner, Paul did eventually preach in Rome (Acts 28), perhaps even to Caesar himself. Paul's Profile is found in Acts 9.

1:1 Paul humbly calls himself a bond-servant of Jesus Christ and an apostle ("one who is sent"). For a Roman citizen—which Paul was—to choose to be a servant was unthinkable. But Paul chose to be completely dependent on and obedient to his beloved Master. What is your attitude toward Christ, your Master? Our willingness to serve and obey Jesus Christ enables us to be useful and usable servants to do work for him—work that really matters.

1:2 Some of the prophecies predicting the Good News regarding Jesus Christ are Genesis 12:3; Psalms 16:10; 40:6–10; 118:22; Isaiah 11:1ff; Zechariah 9:9–11; 12:10; Malachi 4:1–6.

1:3–4 Paul states that Jesus is the Son of God, the promised Messiah, and the resurrected Lord. Paul calls Jesus a descendant of King David to emphasize that Jesus truly had fulfilled the Old Testament Scriptures predicting that the Messiah would come from David's line. With this statement of faith, Paul declares his agreement with the teaching of all Scripture and of the apostles.

1:3–5 Here Paul summarizes the Good News about Jesus Christ, who (1) came as a human by natural descent, (2) was part of the Jewish royal line through David, (3) died and was raised from the dead, and (4) opened the door for God's grace and kindness to be

1:6 Jude 1; Rev 17:14

1:8 1 Cor 1:4; Eph 1:15f; Phil 1:3f; Col 1:3f; 1 Thess 1:2; 2:13

1:9 Rom 9:1; Acts 24:14; 2 Tim 1:3; Eph 1:16; Phil 1:3f

1:10 Acts 18:21; Rom 15:32

1:11 Acts 19:21; Rom 15:23

1:13 Rom 11:25; 1 Cor 10:1; 12:1; 2 Cor 1:8; 1 Thess 4:13; Acts 1:15; Rom 7:1; 1 Cor 1:10; 14:20, 26; Gal 3:15; Acts 19:21; Rom 15:22f; John 4:36; 15:16; Phil 1:22; Col 1:6

1:14 1 Cor 9:16

5 through whom we have received grace and apostleship to bring about *the* obedience
of faith among all the Gentiles for His name's sake,
6 among whom you also are the called of Jesus Christ;
7 to all who are beloved of God in Rome, called *as* saints: Grace to you and peace
from God our Father and the Lord Jesus Christ.
8 First, I thank my God through Jesus Christ for you all, because your faith is being
proclaimed throughout the whole world.
9 For God, whom I serve in my spirit in the *preaching of the* gospel of His Son, is my
witness *as to* how unceasingly I make mention of you,
10 always in my prayers making request, if perhaps now at last by the will of God I may
succeed in coming to you.
11 For I long to see you so that I may impart some spiritual gift to you, that you may be
established;
12 that is, that I may be encouraged together with you *while* among you, each of us by
the other's faith, both yours and mine.
13 I do not want you to be unaware, brethren, that often I have planned to come to
you (and have been prevented so far) so that I may obtain some fruit among you also,
even as among the rest of the Gentiles.
14 I am [2]under obligation both to Greeks and to barbarians, both to the wise and to
the foolish.

2 Lit *debtor*

poured out on us. The book of Romans is an expansion of these themes.

1:5–6 Christians have both a privilege and a great responsibility. Paul and the apostles received forgiveness ("grace") as an undeserved privilege. But they also received the responsibility to share the message of God's forgiveness with others. God also graciously forgives our sins when we believe in him as Lord. In doing this, we are committing ourselves to begin a new life. Paul's new life also involved a God-given responsibility—to witness about God's Good News to the world as a missionary. God may or may not call you to be an overseas missionary, but he does call you (and all believers) to witness to and be an example of the changed life that Jesus Christ has begun in you.

1:6–7 Paul says that those who become Christians are invited by Jesus Christ to (1) become part of God's family and (2) be holy people ("saints," set apart, dedicated for his service). What a wonderful expression of what it means to be a Christian! In being reborn into God's family we have the greatest experience of love and the greatest inheritance. Because of all that God has done for us, we strive to be his holy people.

1:6–12 Paul showed his love for the Roman Christians by expressing God's love for them and his own gratitude and prayers for them. To have an effect on people's lives, you first need to love them and believe in them. Paul's passion to teach these people began with his love for them. Thank God for your Christian brothers and sisters, and let them know how deeply you care for them.

1:7 Rome was the capital of the Roman empire that had spread over most of Europe, North Africa, and the Near East. In New Testament times, Rome was experiencing a golden age. The city was wealthy, literary, and artistic. It was a cultural center, but it was also morally decadent. The Romans worshiped many pagan gods, and even some of the emperors were worshiped. In stark contrast to the Romans, the followers of Christ believed in only one God and lived by his high moral standards.

1:7 Christianity was at odds with the Romans' dependence on military strength. Many Romans were naively pragmatic, believing that any means to accomplish the intended task was good. And for them, nothing worked better than physical might. The Romans trusted in their strong military power to protect them against all enemies. Christians in every age need to be reminded that God is the only permanent source of our security and salvation, and at the same time he is "our Father"!

1:8 Paul uses the phrase "I thank my God through Jesus Christ" to emphasize the point that Christ is the one and only mediator between God and humans. Through Christ, God sends his love and forgiveness to us; through Christ, we send our thanks to God (see 1 Timothy 2:5).

1:8 The Roman Christians, at the Western world's political power center, were highly visible. Fortunately, their reputation was excellent; their strong faith was making itself known around the world. When people talk about your congregation or your denomination, what do they say? Are their comments accurate? Would you rather they noticed other features? What is the best way to get the public to recognize your faith?

1:9–10 When you pray continually about a concern, don't be surprised at how God answers. Paul prayed to visit Rome so he could teach the Christians there. When he finally arrived in Rome, it was as a prisoner (see Acts 28:16). Paul prayed for a safe trip, and he did arrive safely—after getting arrested, slapped in the face, shipwrecked, and bitten by a poisonous snake. God's ways of answering our prayers are often far from what we expect. When you sincerely pray, God will answer—although sometimes with timing and in ways you do not expect.

1:11–12 Paul prayed for the chance to visit these Christians so that he could encourage them with his gift of faith and be encouraged by theirs. As God's missionary, he could help them understand the meaning of the Good News about Jesus. As God's devoted people, they could offer him fellowship and comfort. When Christians gather, everyone should give *and* receive. Our mutual faith gives us a common language and a common purpose for encouraging one another.

1:13 By the end of his third missionary journey, Paul had traveled through Syria, Galatia, Asia, Macedonia, and Achaia. The churches in these areas were made up mostly of Gentile believers.

1:14 The terms *Greeks* and *barbarians* refer to those of the Greek culture and those not of the Greek culture. *Wise* and *foolish* refer to educated and uneducated people. What was Paul's obligation? After his experience with Christ on the road to Damascus (Acts 9), his whole life was consumed with spreading the Good News of salvation. His obligation was to Christ for being his Savior, and he was obligated to the entire world. He met his obligation by proclaiming Christ's salvation to *all* people—both Jews and Gentiles, across all cultural, social, racial, and economic lines. We also are obligated to Christ because he took on the punishment we deserve for our sin. Although we cannot repay Christ for all he has done, we can demonstrate our gratitude by showing his love to others.

15 So, for my part, I am eager to preach the gospel to you also who are in Rome.
16 For I am not ashamed of the gospel, for it is the power of God for salvation to everyone who believes, to the Jew first and also to the Greek.
17 For in it *the* righteousness of God is revealed from faith to faith; as it is written, "BUT THE RIGHTEOUS *man* SHALL LIVE BY FAITH."

Unbelief and Its Consequences

18 For the wrath of God is revealed from heaven against all ungodliness and unrighteousness of men who suppress the truth in unrighteousness,
19 because that which is known about God is evident within them; for God made it evident to them.
20 For since the creation of the world His invisible attributes, His eternal power and divine nature, have been clearly seen, being understood through what has been made, so that they are without excuse.

1:15 Rom 15:20

1:16 Mark 8:38; 2 Tim 1:8, 12, 16; 1 Cor 1:18, 24; Acts 3:26; Rom 2:9; John 7:35

1:17 Rom 3:21; 9:30; Phil 3:9; Hab 2:4; Gal 3:11; Heb 10:38

1:18 Rom 5:9; Eph 5:6; Col 3:6; 2 Thess 2:6f

1:19 Acts 14:17; 17:24ff

1:20 Mark 10:6

1:16 Paul was not ashamed because his message was the gospel of Christ, the Good News. It was a message of salvation, it had life-changing power, and it was for everyone. When you are tempted to be ashamed, remember what the Good News is all about. If you focus on God and on what God is doing in the world rather than on your own inadequacy, you won't be ashamed or embarrassed.

1:16 Why did the message go to the Jews first? They had been God's special people for more than 2,000 years, ever since God chose Abraham and promised great blessings to his descendants (Genesis 12:1–3). God did not choose the Jews because they deserved to be chosen (Deuteronomy 7:7–8; 9:4–6), but because he wanted to show his love and mercy to them, teach them, and prepare them to welcome his Messiah into the world. God chose them, not to play favorites, but so that they would tell the world about his plan of salvation.

For centuries the Jews had been learning about God by obeying his laws, keeping his feasts, and living according to his moral principles. Often they would forget God's promises and requirements; often they would have to be disciplined; but still they had a precious heritage of belief in the One true God. Of all the people on earth, the Jews should have been the most ready to welcome the Messiah and to understand his mission and message—and some of them were (see Luke 2:25, 36–38). Of course, the disciples and the great apostle Paul were faithful Jews who recognized in Jesus God's most precious gift to the human race.

1:16 Jews and Christians alike stood against the idolatrous Roman religions, and Roman officials often confused the two groups. This was especially easy to do since the Christian church in Rome could have been originally composed of Jewish converts who had attended the Feast of Pentecost (see Acts 2:1ff). By the time Paul wrote this letter to the Romans, however, many Gentiles had joined the church. The Jews and the Gentiles needed to know the relationship between Judaism and Christianity.

1:17 The gospel shows us both how righteous God is in his plan for us to be saved, and also how we may be made fit for eternal life. By trusting Christ, our relationship with God is made right. "From faith to faith" God declares us to be righteous because of faith and faith alone.

1:17 Paul is quoting Habakkuk 2:4. Habakkuk may have understood "shall live" to mean this present life only. But Paul extends this statement to include eternal life. As we trust God, we are saved; we find life both now and forever.

1:18 Why is God angry at sinful people? Because they have substituted the truth about him with a fantasy of their own imagination (1:25). They have stifled the truth God naturally reveals to all people in order to believe anything that supports their own self-centered life-styles. God cannot tolerate sin because his nature is morally perfect. He cannot ignore or condone such willful rebellion. God wants to remove the sin and restore the sinner—and he is able to, as long as the sinner does not stubbornly distort or reject the truth. But his anger erupts against those who persist in sinning. Make sure you are not pursuing a fantasy rather than the true God. Don't suppress the truth about him merely to protect your own life-style.

1:18ff Romans 1:18—3:20 develops Paul's argument that no one can claim by their own efforts or merit to be good in God's sight—not the masses, not the Romans, not even the Jews. All people everywhere deserve God's condemnation for their sin.

1:18–20 Does anyone have an excuse for not believing in God? The Bible answers an emphatic *no.* God has revealed what he is like in and through his creation. Every person, therefore, either accepts or rejects God. Don't be fooled. When the day comes for God to judge your response to him, no excuses will be accepted. Begin today to give your devotion and worship to him.

1:18–20 In these verses, Paul answers a common objection: How could a loving God send anyone to hell, especially someone who has never heard about Christ? In fact, says Paul, God has revealed himself plainly in the creation to *all* people. And yet people reject even this basic knowledge of God. Also, everyone has an inner sense of what God requires, but they choose not to live up to it. Put another way, people's moral standards are always better than their behavior. If people suppress God's truth in order to live their own way, they have no excuse. They know the truth, and they will have to endure the consequences of ignoring it.

1:18–20 Some people wonder why we need missionaries if people can know about God through nature (the creation). The answer: (1) Although people know that God exists, they suppress that truth by their wickedness and thus refuse a relationship with him. Missionaries sensitively expose their error and point them to a new beginning. (2) Although people may believe there is a God, they refuse to commit themselves to him. Missionaries help persuade them, both through loving words and caring actions. (3) Missionaries convince people who reject God of the dangerous consequences of their actions. (4) Missionaries help the church obey the Great Commission of our Lord (Matthew 28:19–20). (5) Most important, though nature reveals God, people need to be told about Jesus and how, through him, they can have a personal relationship with God.

Knowing that God exists is not enough. People must learn that God is loving. They must understand what he did to demonstrate his love for us (5:8). They must be shown how to accept God's forgiveness of their sins. (See also 10:14–15.)

1:20 What kind of God does nature reveal? Nature shows us a God of might, intelligence, and intricate detail; a God of order and beauty; a God who controls powerful forces. That is *general* revelation. Through *special* revelation (the Bible and the coming of Jesus), we learn about God's love and forgiveness, and the promise of eternal life. God has graciously given us both sources that we might fully believe in him.

1:20 God reveals his divine nature and personal qualities through creation, even though creation's testimony has been distorted by the fall. Adam's sin resulted in a divine curse upon the whole

1:21 Eph 4:17f

1:22 Jer 10:14; 1 Cor 1:20

1:23 Ps 106:20; Jer 2:11; Acts 17:29

1:24 Rom 1:26, 28; Eph 4:19; Eph 2:3

1:25 2 Cor 11:31

21 For even though they knew God, they did not [3]honor Him as God or give thanks,
but they became futile in their speculations, and their foolish heart was darkened.
22 Professing to be wise, they became fools,
23 and exchanged the glory of the incorruptible God for an image in the form of corruptible man and of birds and four-footed animals and [4]crawling creatures.
24 Therefore God gave them over in the lusts of their hearts to impurity, so that their bodies would be dishonored among them.
25 For they exchanged the truth of God for a lie, and worshiped and served the creature rather than the Creator, who is blessed forever. Amen.

3 Lit *glorify* **4** Or *reptiles*

FAITH

Faith is a word with many meanings. It can mean faithfulness (Matthew 24:45). It can mean absolute trust, as shown by some of the people who came to Jesus for healing (Luke 7:2–10). It can mean confident hope (Hebrews 11:1). Or, as James points out, it can even mean a barren belief that does not result in good deeds (James 2:14–26). What does Paul mean when, in Romans, he speaks of saving faith?

We must be very careful to understand faith as Paul uses the word, because he ties faith so closely to salvation. It is not something we must do in order to earn salvation—if that were true, then faith would be just one more deed, and Paul clearly states that human deeds can never save us (Galatians 2:16). Instead, faith is a gift God gives us because he is saving us (Ephesians 2:8). It is God's grace, not our faith, that saves us. In his mercy, however, when he saves us he gives us faith—a relationship with his Son that helps us become like him. Through the faith he gives us, he carries us from death into life (John 5:24).

Even in Old Testament times, grace, not deeds, was the basis of salvation. As Hebrews points out. "It is impossible for the blood of bulls and goats to take away sins" (Hebrews 10:4). God intended for his people to look beyond the animal sacrifices to him, but all too often they, instead, put their confidence in fulfilling the requirements of the Law—that is, performing the required sacrifices. When Jesus triumphed over death, he canceled the charges against us and opened the way to the Father (Colossians 2:12–15). Because he is merciful, he offers us faith. How tragic if we turn faith into a deed and try to develop it on our own! We can never come to God through our own faith, any more than his Old Testament people could come through their own sacrifices. Instead, we must accept his gracious offer with thanksgiving and allow him to plant the seed of faith within us.

natural order (Genesis 3:17–19); thorns and thistles were an immediate result, and natural disasters have been common from Adam's day to ours. In Romans 8:19–21, Paul says that nature itself is eagerly awaiting its own redemption from the effects of sin (see Revelation 22:3).

1:21–23 How could intelligent people turn to idolatry? Idolatry begins when people reject what they know about God. Instead of looking to him as the Creator and sustainer of life, they see themselves as the center of the universe. They soon invent "gods" that are convenient projections of their own selfish plans and decrees. These gods may be wooden figures, but they may also be goals or things we pursue such as money, power, or comfort. They may even be misrepresentations of God himself—making God in our image, instead of the reverse. The common denominator is this—idolaters worship the things God made rather than God himself. Is there anything you feel you can't live without? Is there any priority greater than God? Do you have a dream you would sacrifice everything to realize? Does God take first place? Do you worship God or idols of your own making?

1:21–32 Paul clearly portrays the inevitable downward spiral into sin. First, people reject God; next, they make up their own ideas of what a god should be and do; then they fall into sin—sexual sin, greed, hatred, envy, murder, strife, deceit, malice, gossip. Finally, they grow to hate God and encourage others to do so. God does not cause this steady progression toward evil. Rather, when people reject him, he allows them to live as they choose. God gives them over or permits them to experience the natural consequences of their sin. Once caught in the downward spiral, no one can pull himself or herself out. Sinners must trust Christ alone to put them on the path of escape.

1:23 When Paul says that men exchanged the glory of God for images of birds, animals, and reptiles, he seems to deliberately state man's wickedness in the terms used in the Genesis narrative of Adam's fall (see Genesis 1:20–26). When we worship the creature instead of the Creator, we lose sight of our own identity as those who are higher than the animals—made in the image of God.

1:24–32 These people chose to reject God, and God allowed them to do it. God does not usually stop us from making choices that are against his will. He lets us declare our supposed independence from him, even though he knows that in time we will become slaves to our own rebellious choices—we will lose our freedom not to sin. Does life without God look like freedom to you? Look more closely. There is no worse slavery than slavery to sin.

1:25 People tend to believe lies that reinforce their own selfish, personal beliefs. Today, more than ever, we need to be careful about the input we allow to form our beliefs. With TV, music, movies, and the rest of the media often presenting sinful life-styles and unwholesome values, we find ourselves constantly bombarded by attitudes and beliefs that are totally opposed to the Bible. Be careful about what you allow to form your opinions. The Bible is the only standard of truth. Evaluate all other opinions in light of its teachings.

26 For this reason God gave them over to degrading passions; for their women exchanged the natural function for that which is unnatural,
27 and in the same way also the men abandoned the natural function of the woman
and burned in their desire toward one another, men with men committing indecent acts
and receiving in their own persons the due penalty of their error.
28 And just as they did not see fit to acknowledge God any longer, God gave them over
to a depraved mind, to do those things which are not proper,
29 being filled with all unrighteousness, wickedness, greed, evil; full of envy, murder,
strife, deceit, malice; *they are* gossips,
30 slanderers, haters of God, insolent, arrogant, boastful, inventors of evil, disobedient to parents,
31 without understanding, untrustworthy, unloving, unmerciful;
32 and although they know the ordinance of God, that those who practice such things
are worthy of death, they not only do the same, but also give hearty approval to those
who practice them.

The Impartiality of God

2 Therefore you have no excuse, everyone of you who passes judgment, for in that which
you judge another, you condemn yourself; for you who judge practice the same things.
2 And we know that the judgment of God rightly falls upon those who practice such
things.
3 But do you suppose this, O man, when you pass judgment on those who practice
such things and do the same *yourself,* that you will escape the judgment of God?
4 Or do you think lightly of the riches of His kindness and tolerance and patience,
not knowing that the kindness of God leads you to repentance?

1:29 2 Cor 12:20

1:30 Ps 5:5; 2 Tim 3:2

1:31 2 Tim 3:3

1:32 Rom 6:21; Luke 11:48; Acts 8:1; 22:20

2:1 Rom 1:20; Luke 12:14; Rom 2:3; 9:20; 2 Sam 12:5-7; Matt 7:1; Luke 6:37; Rom 14:22

2:3 Luke 12:14; Rom 2:1; 9:20

2:4 Rom 9:23; 11:33; 2 Cor 8:2; Eph 1:7, 18; 2:7; Phil 4:19; Col 1:27; 2:2; Titus 3:6; Rom 11:22; Rom 3:25; Ex 34:6; Rom 9:22; 1 Tim 1:16; 1 Pet 3:20; 2 Pet 3:9, 15

1:26–27 God's plan for natural sexual relationships is his ideal for his creation. Unfortunately, sin distorts the natural use of God's gifts. Sin often means not only denying God, but also denying the way we are made. When people say that any sex act is acceptable as long as nobody gets hurt, they are fooling themselves. In the long run (and often in the short run), sin hurts people—individuals, families, whole societies. How sad it is that people who worship the things God made instead of the Creator so often distort and destroy the very things they claim to value!

1:26, 27 Homosexuality (to exchange or abandon natural relations of sex) was as widespread in Paul's day as it is in ours. Many pagan practices encouraged it. God is willing to receive anyone who comes to him in faith, and Christians should love and accept others no matter what their background. Yet, homosexuality is strictly forbidden in Scripture (Leviticus 18:22). Homosexuality is considered an acceptable practice by many in our world today—even by some churches. But society does not set the standard for God's law. Many homosexuals believe that their desires are normal and that they have a right to express them. But God does not obligate nor encourage us to fulfill all our desires (even normal ones). Those desires that violate his laws must be controlled.

If you have these desires, you can and must resist acting upon them. Consciously avoid places or activities you know will kindle temptations of this kind. Don't underestimate the power of Satan to tempt you, nor the potential for serious harm if you yield to these temptations. Remember, God can and will forgive sexual sins just as he forgives other sins. Surrender yourself to the grace and mercy of God, asking him to show you the way out of sin and into the light of his freedom and his love. Prayer, Bible study, and strong support in a Christian church can help you to gain strength to resist these powerful temptations. If you are already deeply involved in homosexual behavior, seek help from a trustworthy, professional, pastoral counselor.

1:32 How were these people aware of God's death penalty? Human beings, created in God's image, have a basic moral nature and a conscience. This truth is understood beyond religious circles. Psychologists, for example, say that the rare person who has no conscience has a serious personality disorder that is extremely difficult to treat. Most people instinctively know when they do wrong—but they may not care. Some people will even risk an early death for the freedom to indulge their desires now. "I know it's wrong, but I really want it," they say; or, "I know it's dangerous, but it's worth the risk." For such people, part of the "fun" is going against God's law, the community's moral standards, common sense, or their own sense of right and wrong. But deep down inside they know that sin deserves the punishment of death (6:23).

2:1 Whenever we find ourselves feeling justifiably angry about someone's sin, we should be careful. We need to speak out against sin, but we must do so in a spirit of humility. Often the sins we notice most clearly in others are the ones that have taken root in us. If we look closely at ourselves, we may find that we are committing the same sins in more socially acceptable forms. For example, a person who gossips may be very critical of others who gossip about him or her.

2:1ff When Paul's letter was read in the Roman church, no doubt many heads nodded as he condemned idol worshipers, homosexual practices, and violent people. But what surprise his listeners must have felt when he turned on them and said in effect, "You have no excuse. You are just as bad!" Paul was emphatically stressing that *nobody* is good enough to save himself or herself. If we want to avoid punishment and live eternally with Christ, all of us, whether we have been murderers and molesters or whether we have been honest, hardworking, solid citizens, must depend totally on God's grace. Paul is not discussing whether some sins are worse than others. Any sin is enough to lead us to depend on Jesus Christ for salvation and eternal life. We have all sinned repeatedly, and there is no way apart from Christ to be saved from sin's consequences.

2:4 In his kindness, God holds back his judgment, giving people time to repent. It is easy to mistake God's patience for approval of the wrong way we are living. Self-evaluation is difficult, and it is even more difficult to expose our conduct to God and let him tell us where we need to change. But as Christians we must pray constantly that God will point out our sins, so that he can heal them. Unfortunately, we are more likely to be amazed at God's patience with others than humbled at his patience with us.

5 But because of your stubbornness and unrepentant heart you are storing up wrath
for yourself in the day of wrath and revelation of the righteous judgment of God,
6 who WILL RENDER TO EACH PERSON ACCORDING TO HIS DEEDS:
7 to those who by perseverance in doing good seek for glory and honor and immortality, eternal life;
8 but to those who are selfishly ambitious and do not obey the truth, but obey unrighteousness, wrath and indignation.
9 *There will be* tribulation and distress for every soul of man who does evil, of the Jew
first and also of the Greek,
10 but glory and honor and peace to everyone who does good, to the Jew first and also
to the Greek.
11 For there is no partiality with God.
12 For all who have sinned without the Law will also perish without the Law, and all
who have sinned under the Law will be judged by the Law;
13 for *it is* not the hearers of the Law *who* are just before God, but the doers of the
Law will be justified.
14 For when Gentiles who do not have the Law do instinctively the things of the Law,
these, not having the Law, are a law to themselves,
15 in that they show the work of the Law written in their hearts, their conscience bearing witness and their thoughts alternately accusing or else defending them,
16 on the day when, according to my gospel, God will judge the secrets of men through
Christ Jesus.

The Jew Is Condemned by the Law

17 But if you bear the name "Jew" and rely upon the Law and boast in God,
18 and know *His* will and approve the things that are essential, being instructed out of
the Law,
19 and are confident that you yourself are a guide to the blind, a light to those who are
in darkness,
20 a corrector of the foolish, a teacher of the immature, having in the Law the embodi-
ment of knowledge and of the truth,
21 you, therefore, who teach another, do you not teach yourself? You who preach that
one shall not steal, do you steal?
22 You who say that one should not commit adultery, do you commit adultery? You
who abhor idols, do you rob temples?

2:5 2 Cor 5:10; 2 Thess 1:5; Jude 6

2:6 Ps 62:12; Prov 24:12; Matt 16:27

2:7 Luke 8:15; Heb 10:36; Rom 2:10; Heb 2:7; 1 Pet 1:7; 1 Cor 15:42, 50, 53f; Eph 6:24; 2 Tim 1:10; Matt 25:46

2:8 2 Cor 12:20; Gal 5:20; Phil 1:17; 2:3; James 3:14, 16; 2 Thess 2:12

2:9 1 Pet 4:17

2:10 Heb 2:7; 1 Pet 1:7

2:11 Acts 10:34

2:12 1 Cor 9:21

2:13 Matt 7:21, 24ff; John 13:17; James 1:22

2:14 Acts 10:35

2:16 Rom 16:25; 1 Cor 15:1; Gal 1:11; 1 Tim 1:11; 2 Tim 2:8; Acts 10:42

2:20 Rom 3:31; 2 Tim 1:13

2:21 Matt 23:3ff

2:5–11 Although God does not usually punish us immediately for sin, his eventual judgment is certain. We don't know exactly when it will happen, but we know that no one will escape that final encounter with the Creator. For more on judgment, see John 12:48 and Revelation 20:11–15.

2:7 Paul says that those who patiently and persistently *do* God's will find eternal life. He is not contradicting his previous statement that salvation comes by faith alone (1:16–17). We are not saved by good deeds, but when we commit our lives fully to God, we want to please him and do his will. As such, our good deeds are a grateful *response* to what God has done, not a prerequisite to earning his grace.

2:12–15 People are condemned not for what they don't know, but for what they do with what they know. Those who know God's written Word and his law will be judged by them. Those who have never seen a Bible still know right from wrong, and they will be judged because they did not keep even those standards that their own consciences dictated. Our modern-day sense of fair play and the rights of the individual often balks at God's judgment. But keep in mind that people violate the very standards they create for themselves.

2:12–15 If you traveled around the world, you would find evidence in every society and culture of God's moral law. For example, all cultures prohibit murder, and yet in all societies that law has been broken. We belong to a stubborn race. We know what's right, but we insist on doing what's wrong. It is not enough to know what's right; we must also do it. Admit to yourself and to God that you fit the human pattern and frequently fail to live up to your own standards (much more to God's standards). That's the first step to forgiveness and healing.

2:17ff Paul continues to argue that all stand guilty before God. After describing the fate of the unbelieving, pagan Gentiles, he moves to that of the religiously privileged. Despite their knowledge of God's will, they are guilty because they too have refused to live by their beliefs. Those of us who have grown up in Christian families are the religiously privileged of today. Paul's condemnation applies to us if we do not live up to what we know.

2:21–22 Paul explained to the Jews that they needed to teach *themselves,* not others, by their law. They knew the law so well that they had learned how to excuse their own actions while criticizing others. But the law is more than legalistic minimum requirements—it is a guideline for living according to God's will. It is also a reminder that we cannot please God without a proper relationship to him. As Jesus pointed out, even withholding what rightfully belongs to someone else is stealing (Mark 7:9–13), and looking on another person with lustful, adulterous intent is adultery (Matthew 5:27–28). Before we accuse others, we must look at ourselves and see if that sin, in any form, exists within us.

2:21–27 These verses are a scathing criticism of hypocrisy. It is much easier to tell others how to behave than to behave properly ourselves. It is easier to say the right words than to allow them to take root in our lives. Do you ever advise others to do something you are unwilling to do yourself? Make sure that your actions match your words.

23 You who boast in the Law, through your breaking the Law, do you dishonor God?
24 For "THE NAME OF GOD IS BLASPHEMED AMONG THE GENTILES BECAUSE OF
YOU," just as it is written.
25 For indeed circumcision is of value if you practice the Law; but if you are a transgressor of the Law, your circumcision has become uncircumcision.
26 So if the uncircumcised man keeps the requirements of the Law, will not his uncircumcision be regarded as circumcision?
27 And he who is physically uncircumcised, if he keeps the Law, will he not judge you
who though having the letter *of the Law* and circumcision are a transgressor of the Law?
28 For he is not a Jew who is one outwardly, nor is circumcision that which is outward
in the flesh.
29 But he is a Jew who is one inwardly; and circumcision is that which is of the heart,
by the Spirit, not by the letter; and his praise is not from men, but from God.

All the World Guilty

3 Then what advantage has the Jew? Or what is the benefit of circumcision?
2 Great in every respect. First of all, that they were entrusted with the oracles of
God.
3 What then? If some did not believe, their unbelief will not nullify the faithfulness of
God, will it?
4 May it never be! Rather, let God be found true, though every man *be found* a liar, as
it is written,

"THAT YOU MAY BE JUSTIFIED IN YOUR WORDS,
AND PREVAIL WHEN YOU ARE JUDGED."

5 But if our unrighteousness demonstrates the righteousness of God, what shall we
say? The God who inflicts wrath is not unrighteous, is He? (I am speaking in human
terms.)
6 May it never be! For otherwise, how will God judge the world?
7 But if through my lie the truth of God abounded to His glory, why am I also still
being judged as a sinner?
8 And why not *say* (as we are slanderously reported and as some claim that we say),
"Let us do evil that good may come"? Their condemnation is just.

2:23 Mic 3:11; John 5:45; Rom 2:17; 9:4
2:24 Is 52:5; Ezek 36:20ff 2 Pet 2:2
2:26 1 Cor 7:19; Rom 3:30; Eph 2:11; Rom 2:25, 27; 8:4
2:27 Rom 3:30; Eph 2:11; Matt 12:41
2:28 John 8:39; Rom 2:17; 9:6; Gal 6:15
2:29 Phil 3:3; Col 2:11; Deut 30:6; Rom 2:27; 7:6; 2 Cor 3:6; John 5:44; 12:43; 1 Cor 4:5; 2 Cor 10:18
3:2 Rom 9:4; Acts 7:38
3:3 Rom 10:16; Heb 4:2
3:4 Luke 20:16; Rom 3:6, 31; Ps 116:11; Rom 3:7; Ps 51:4
3:5 Rom 5:8; 2 Cor 6:4; 7:11; Rom 4:1; 7:7; 8:31; 9:14, 30; Rom 6:19; 1 Cor 9:8; 15:32; Gal 3:15
3:6 Luke 20:16
3:8 Rom 6:1

2:24 If you claim to be one of God's people, your life should reflect what God is like. When you disobey God, you dishonor his name. People may even blaspheme or profane God's name because of you. What do people think about God from watching your life?

2:25–29 *Circumcision* refers to the sign of God's special covenant with his people. Submitting to this rite was required for all Jewish males (Genesis 17:9–14). According to Paul, being a Jew (being circumcised) meant nothing if the person didn't obey God's laws. On the other hand, the Gentiles (the uncircumcised) would receive God's love and approval if they kept the law's requirements. Paul goes on to explain that a real Jew (one who pleases God) is not someone who has been circumcised (a Jew "outwardly") but someone whose heart is right with God and obeys him (a Jew "inwardly").

2:28–29 To be a Jew meant you were in God's family, an heir to all his promises. Yet Paul made it clear that membership in God's family is based on internal, not external, qualities. All whose hearts are right with God are real Jews—that is, part of God's family (see also Galatians 3:7). Attending church or being baptized, confirmed, or accepted for membership is not enough, just as submitting to circumcision was not enough for the Jews. God desires our heartfelt devotion and obedience. (See also Deuteronomy 10:16; Jeremiah 4:4 for more on "circumcision of the heart.")

3:1ff In this chapter Paul contends that everyone stands guilty before God. Paul has dismantled the common excuses of people who refuse to admit they are sinners: (1) "There is no God" or "I follow my conscience"—1:18–32; (2) "I'm not as bad as other people"—2:1–16; (3) "I'm a church member" or "I'm a religious person"—2:17–29. No one will be exempt from God's judgment on sin. Every person must accept that he or she is sinful and condemned before God. Only then can we understand and receive God's wonderful gift of salvation.

3:1ff What a depressing picture Paul is painting! All of us—pagan Gentiles, humanitarians, and religious people—are condemned by our own actions. The law, which God gave to show the way to live, holds up our evil deeds to public view. Is there any hope for us? Yes, says Paul. The law condemns us, it is true, but the law is not the basis of our hope. God himself is. He, in his righteousness and wonderful love, offers us eternal life. We receive our salvation not through law but through faith in Jesus Christ. We do not—cannot—earn it; we accept it as a gift from our loving heavenly Father.

3:2 The Jewish nation had many advantages. (1) They were entrusted with God's laws ("the oracles of God," Exodus 19; 20; Deuteronomy 4:8). (2) They were the race through whom the Messiah came to earth (Isaiah 11:1–10; Matthew 1:1–17). (3) They were the beneficiaries of covenants with God himself (Genesis 17:1–16; Exodus 19:3–6). But these privileges did not make them better than anyone else (see 3:9). In fact, because of them the Jews were even more responsible to live up to God's requirements.

3:5–8 Some may think they don't have to worry about sin because (1) it's God's job to forgive; (2) God is so loving that he won't judge us; (3) sin isn't so bad—it teaches us valuable lessons, or (4) we need to stay in touch with the culture around us. It is far too easy to take God's grace for granted. But God cannot overlook sin. Sinners, no matter how many excuses they make, will have to answer to God for their sin.

9 What then? Are we better than they? Not at all; for we have already charged that
both Jews and Greeks are all under sin;
10 as it is written,
"THERE IS NONE RIGHTEOUS, NOT EVEN ONE;
11 THERE IS NONE WHO UNDERSTANDS,
THERE IS NONE WHO SEEKS FOR GOD;
12 ALL HAVE TURNED ASIDE, TOGETHER THEY HAVE BECOME USELESS;
THERE IS NONE WHO DOES GOOD,
THERE IS NOT EVEN ONE."
13 "THEIR THROAT IS AN OPEN GRAVE,
WITH THEIR TONGUES THEY KEEP DECEIVING,"
"THE POISON OF ASPS IS UNDER THEIR LIPS";
14 "WHOSE MOUTH IS FULL OF CURSING AND BITTERNESS";
15 "THEIR FEET ARE SWIFT TO SHED BLOOD,
16 DESTRUCTION AND MISERY ARE IN THEIR PATHS,
17 AND THE PATH OF PEACE THEY HAVE NOT KNOWN."
18 "THERE IS NO FEAR OF GOD BEFORE THEIR EYES."
19 Now we know that whatever the Law says, it speaks to those who are under the Law,
so that every mouth may be closed and all the world may become accountable to God;
20 because by the works of the Law no flesh will be justified in His sight; for through
the Law *comes* the knowledge of sin.

3:9 Rom 3:1; Rom 2:1-29; Rom 1:18-32; Rom 3:19, 23; 11:32; Gal 3:22

3:10 Ps 14:1-3; 53:1-3

3:13 Ps 5:9; Ps 140:3

3:14 Ps 10:7

3:15 Is 59:7f

3:18 Ps 36:1

3:19 John 10:34; Rom 2:12; Rom 3:9

3:20 Ps 143:2; Acts 13:39; Gal 2:16; Rom 4:15; 5:13, 20; 7:7

3:21 Rom 1:17; 9:30; Acts 10:43; Rom 1:2

3:22 Rom 1:17; 9:30; Rom 4:5; Acts 3:16; Gal 2:16, 20; 3:22; Eph 3:12; Rom 4:11, 16; 10:4; Rom 10:12; Gal 3:28; Col 3:11

3:23 Rom 3:9

2. Forgiveness of sin through Christ

Justification by Faith

21 But now apart from the Law *the* righteousness of God has been manifested, being
witnessed by the Law and the Prophets,
22 even *the* righteousness of God through faith in Jesus Christ for all those who believe; for there is no distinction;
23 for all have sinned and fall short of the glory of God,

SALVATION'S FREEWAY		
	Romans 3:23	Everyone has sinned.
	Romans 6:23	The penalty for our sin is death.
	Romans 5:8	Jesus Christ died for sin.
	Romans 10:8–10	To be forgiven for our sin, we must believe and confess that Jesus is Lord. Salvation comes through Jesus Christ.

3:10–12 Paul is referring to Psalm 14:1–3. "There is none righteous" means "no one is innocent." Every person is valuable in God's eyes because God created us in his image and he loves us. But no one is righteous (that is, no one can earn right standing with God). Though valuable, we have fallen into sin. But God, through Jesus his Son, has redeemed us and offers to forgive us if we return to him in faith.

3:10–18 Paul uses these Old Testament references to show that humanity in general, in its present sinful condition, is unacceptable before God. Have you ever thought to yourself, "Well, I'm not too bad. I'm a pretty good person"? Look at these verses and see if any of them apply to you. Have you ever lied? Have you ever hurt someone's feelings by your words or tone of voice? Are you bitter toward anyone? Do you become angry with those who strongly disagree with you? In thought, word, and deed you, like everyone else in the world, stand guilty before God. We must remember who we are in his sight—alienated sinners. Don't deny that you are a sinner. Instead, allow your desperate need to point you toward Christ.

3:19 The last time someone accused you of wrongdoing, what was your reaction? Denial, argument, and defensiveness? The Bible tells us the world stands silent and accountable before Almighty God. No excuses or arguments are left. Have you reached the point with God where you are ready to hang up your defenses and await his decision? If you haven't, stop now and admit your sin to him. If you have, the following verses are truly good news for you!

3:20, 31 In these verses we see two functions of God's law. First, it shows us where we go wrong. Because of the law, we know that we are helpless sinners and that we must come to Jesus Christ for mercy. Second, the moral code revealed in the law can serve to guide our actions by holding up God's moral standards. We do not earn salvation by keeping the law (no one except Christ ever kept or could keep God's law perfectly), but we do please God when our lives conform to his revealed will for us.

3:21–29 After all this bad news about our sinfulness and God's condemnation, Paul gives the wonderful news. There is a way to be declared not guilty—by trusting Jesus Christ to take away our sins. Trusting means putting our confidence in Christ to forgive our sins, to make us right with God, and to empower us to live the way he taught us. God's solution is available to all of us regardless of our background or past behavior.

3:23 Some sins seem bigger than others because their obvious consequences are much more serious. Murder, for example, seems to us to be worse than hatred, and adultery seems worse than lust. But this does not mean that because we do lesser sins we deserve eternal life. All sin makes us sinners, and all sin cuts us off from our holy God. All sin, therefore, leads to death (because it disqualifies us from living with God), regardless of how great or small it seems. Don't minimize "little" sins or overrate "big" sins. They all separate us from God, but they all can be forgiven.

24 being justified as a gift by His grace through the redemption which is in Christ Jesus;
25 whom God displayed publicly as a propitiation in His blood through faith. *This was*
to demonstrate His righteousness, because in the forbearance of God He passed over
the sins previously committed;
26 for the demonstration, *I say,* of His righteousness at the present time, so that He
would be just and the justifier of the one who has faith in Jesus.
27 Where then is boasting? It is excluded. By what kind of law? Of works? No, but by
a law of faith.
28 For we maintain that a man is justified by faith apart from works of the Law.
29 Or is God *the God* of Jews only? Is He not *the God* of Gentiles also? Yes, of Gentiles also,
30 since indeed God who will justify the circumcised by faith and the uncircumcised
through faith is one.
31 Do we then nullify the Law through faith? May it never be! On the contrary, we
establish the Law.

Justification by Faith Evidenced in Old Testament

4 What then shall we say that Abraham, our forefather according to the flesh, has
found?
2 For if Abraham was justified by works, he has something to boast about, but not
before God.
3 For what does the Scripture say? "ABRAHAM BELIEVED GOD, AND IT WAS CREDIT-
ED TO HIM AS RIGHTEOUSNESS."
4 Now to the one who works, his wage is not credited as a favor, but as what is due.
5 But to the one who does not work, but believes in Him who justifies the ungodly, his
faith is credited as righteousness,

3:24 Rom 4:4f; Eph 1:7; Col 1:14; Heb 9:15

3:25 1 John 2:2; 4:10; 1 Cor 5:7; Heb 9:14, 28; 1 Pet 1:19

3:27 Rom 2:17, 23; 4:2; 1 Cor 1:29ff; Rom 9:31

3:28 Acts 13:39; Rom 3:20, 21; Eph 2:9; James 2:20, 24, 26

3:29 Acts 10:34f; Rom 9:24; 10:12; 15:9; Gal 3:28

3:30 Rom 10:12; Gal 3:20; Rom 3:22; 4:11f, 16; Gal 3:8

3:31 Luke 20:16; Rom 3:4; Matt 5:17; Rom 3:4, 6; 8:4

4:3 Gen 15:6; Rom 4:9, 22; Gal 3:6

4:4 Rom 11:6

4:5 John 6:29

3:24 *Justified* means to be declared not guilty. When a judge in a court of law declares the defendant not guilty, all the charges are removed from his record. Legally, it is as if the person had never been accused. When God forgives our sins, our record is wiped clean. From his perspective, it is as though we had never sinned.

3:24 Redemption refers to Christ setting sinners free from slavery to sin. In Old Testament times, a person's debts could result in his being sold as a slave. The next of kin could redeem him—buy his freedom. Christ purchased our freedom, and the price was his life.

3:25 Christ is our propitiation. In other words, he died in our place, for our sins. God is justifiably angry at sinners. They have rebelled against him and cut themselves off from his life-giving power. But God declares Christ's death to be the appropriate, designated sacrifice for our sin. Christ then stands in our place, having paid the penalty of death for our sin, and he completely satisfies God's demands. His sacrifice brings pardon, deliverance, and freedom.

3:25 What happened to people who lived before Christ came and died for sin? If God condemned them, was he being unfair? If he saved them, was Christ's sacrifice unnecessary? Paul shows that God forgave all human sin at the cross of Jesus. Old Testament believers looked forward in faith to Christ's coming and were saved, even though they did not know Jesus' name or the details of his earthly life. Unlike the Old Testament believers, you know about the God who loved the world so much that he gave his own Son (John 3:16). Have you put your trust in him?

3:27–28 Most religions prescribe specific duties that must be performed to make a person acceptable to a god. Christianity is unique in teaching that the good deeds we do will not make us right with God. No amount of human achievement or progress in personal development will close the gap between God's moral perfection and our imperfect daily performance. Good deeds are important, but they will not earn us eternal life. We are saved only by trusting in what God has done for us (see Ephesians 2:8–10).

3:28 Why does God save us by faith alone? (1) Faith eliminates the pride of human effort, because faith is not a deed that we do. (2) Faith exalts what God has done, not what people do. (3) Faith admits that we can't keep the law or measure up to God's standards—we need help. (4) Faith is based on our relationship with God, not our performance for God.

3:31 There were some misunderstandings between the Jewish and Gentile Christians in Rome. Worried Jewish Christians were asking Paul, "Does faith wipe out everything Judaism stands for? Does it cancel our Scriptures, put an end to our customs, declare that God is no longer working through us?" (This is essentially the question used to open chapter 3.) "Absolutely not!" says Paul. When we understand the way of salvation through faith, we understand the Jewish religion better. We know why Abraham was chosen, why the law was given, why God worked patiently with Israel for centuries. Faith does not wipe out the Old Testament. Rather, it makes God's dealings with the Jewish people understandable. In chapter 4, Paul will expand on this theme (see also 5:20–21; 8:3–4; 13:9–10; Galatians 3:24–29; and 1 Timothy 1:8 for more on this concept).

4:1–3 The Jews were proud to be called children of Abraham. Paul uses Abraham as a good example of someone who was saved by faith. By emphasizing faith, Paul is not saying that God's laws are unimportant (4:13) but that it is impossible to be saved simply by obeying them. For more about Abraham, see his Profile in Genesis 18.

4:4 This verse means that if a person could earn right standing with God by being good, the granting of that gift wouldn't be a free act; it would be an obligation. Our self reliance is futile; all we can do is cast ourselves on God's mercy and grace.

4:5 When some people learn that they are saved by God through faith, they start to worry. "Do I have enough faith?" they wonder, "Is my faith strong enough to save me?" These people miss the point. It is Jesus Christ who saves us, not *our* feelings or actions, and he is strong enough to save us no matter how weak our faith is. Jesus offers us salvation as a gift because he loves us, not because we have earned it through our powerful faith. What, then, is the role of faith? Faith is believing and trusting in Jesus Christ, and reaching out to accept his wonderful gift of salvation.

6 just as David also speaks of the blessing on the man to whom God credits righteousness apart from works:
7 "BLESSED ARE THOSE WHOSE LAWLESS DEEDS HAVE BEEN FORGIVEN,
AND WHOSE SINS HAVE BEEN COVERED.
8 "BLESSED IS THE MAN WHOSE SIN THE LORD WILL NOT TAKE INTO ACCOUNT."
9 Is this blessing then on the circumcised, or on the uncircumcised also? For we say,
"FAITH WAS CREDITED TO ABRAHAM AS RIGHTEOUSNESS."
10 How then was it credited? While he was circumcised, or uncircumcised? Not while
circumcised, but while uncircumcised;
11 and he received the sign of circumcision, a seal of the righteousness of the faith which
he had while uncircumcised, so that he might be the father of all who believe without
being circumcised, that righteousness might be credited to them,
12 and the father of circumcision to those who not only are of the circumcision, but
who also follow in the steps of the faith of our father Abraham which he had while uncircumcised.
13 For the promise to Abraham or to his descendants that he would be heir of the world
was not through the Law, but through the righteousness of faith.
14 For if those who are of the Law are heirs, faith is made void and the promise is
nullified;
15 for the Law brings about wrath, but where there is no law, there also is no violation.
16 For this reason *it is* by faith, in order that *it may be* in accordance with grace, so that
the promise will be guaranteed to all the descendants, not only to those who are of the
Law, but also to those who are of the faith of Abraham, who is the father of us all,
17 (as it is written, "A FATHER OF MANY NATIONS HAVE I MADE YOU") in the presence
of Him whom he believed, *even* God, who gives life to the dead and calls into being that
which does not exist.

4:7 Ps 32:1
4:8 Ps 32:2; 2 Cor 5:19
4:9 Rom 3:30; Rom 4:3; Gen 15:6
4:11 Gen 17:10f; John 3:33; Luke 19:9; Rom 4:16f; Rom 3:22; 4:16
4:13 Rom 9:8; Gal 3:16, 29; Gen 17:4-6; 22:17f
4:14 Gal 3:18
4:15 Rom 7:7, 10-25; 1 Cor 15:56; Gal 3:10; Rom 3:20
4:16 Rom 3:24; Rom 4:11; 9:8; 15:8; Gal 3:7; Luke 19:9; Rom 4:11
4:17 Gen 17:5; John 5:21; Is 48:13; 51:2; 1 Cor 1:28

CRUCIAL CONCEPTS IN ROMANS

ELECTION Romans 9:10–13	God's choice of an individual or group for a specific purpose or destiny.
JUSTIFICATION Romans 4:25; 5:18	God's act of declaring us "not guilty" for our sins.
PROPITIATION Romans 3:25	The removal of God's punishment for sin through the perfect sacrifice of Jesus Christ.
REDEMPTION Romans 3:24; 8:23	Jesus Christ has paid the price so we can go free. The price of sin is death; Jesus paid he price.
SANCTIFICATION Romans 5:2; 15:16	Becoming more and more like Jesus Christ through the work of the Holy Spirit.
GLORIFICATION Romans 8:18–19, 30	The ultimate state of the believer after death when he or she becomes like Christ (1 John 3:2).

4:6–8 What can we do to get rid of guilt? King David was guilty of terrible sins—adultery, murder, lying—and yet he experienced the joy of forgiveness. We too can have this joy when we (1) quit denying our guilt and recognize that we have sinned, (2) admit our guilt to God and ask for his forgiveness, and (3) let go of our guilt and believe that God has forgiven us. This can be difficult when a sin has taken root and grown over many years, when it is very serious, or when it involves others. We must remember that Jesus is willing and able to forgive every sin. In view of the tremendous price he paid on the cross, it is arrogant to think that any of our sins are too great for him to cover. Even though our faith is weak, our conscience is sensitive, and our memory haunts us, God's Word declares that sins confessed are sins forgiven (1 John 1:9).

4:10 Circumcision was a sign to others and a personal seal or certification for the Jews that they were God's special people. Circumcision of all Jewish boys set the Jewish people apart from the nations who worshiped other gods; thus it was a very important ceremony. God gave the blessing and the command for this ceremony to Abraham (Genesis 17:9–14).

4:10–12 Rituals did not earn any reward for Abraham; he had been blessed long before the circumcision ceremony was introduced. Abraham found favor with God by faith alone, before he was circumcised. Genesis 12:1–4 tells of God's call to Abraham when he was 75 years old; the circumcision ceremony was introduced when he was 99 (Genesis 17:1–14). Ceremonies and rituals serve as reminders of our faith, and they instruct new and younger believers. But we should not think that they give us any special merit before God. They are outward signs and seals that demonstrate inward belief and trust. The focus of our faith should be on Christ and his saving actions, not on our own actions.

4:16 Paul explains that Abraham had pleased God through Abraham's faith alone, before he had ever heard about the rituals that would become so important to the Jewish people. We too are saved by faith plus nothing. It is not by loving God and doing good that we are saved; neither is it by faith plus love or by faith plus good deeds. We are saved only through faith in Christ, trusting him to forgive all our sins. For more on Abraham, see his Profile in Genesis 18.

4:17 The promise (or covenant) God gave Abraham stated that Abraham would be the father of many nations (Genesis 17:2–4) and that the entire world would be blessed through him (Genesis 12:3). This promise was fulfilled in Jesus Christ. Jesus was from Abraham's line, and truly the whole world was blessed through him.

18 In hope against hope he believed, so that he might become a father of many nations
according to that which had been spoken, "SO SHALL YOUR DESCENDANTS BE."
19 Without becoming weak in faith he contemplated his own body, now as good as dead
since he was about a hundred years old, and the deadness of Sarah's womb;
20 yet, with respect to the promise of God, he did not waver in unbelief but grew strong
in faith, giving glory to God,
21 and being fully assured that what God had promised, He was able also to perform.
22 Therefore IT WAS ALSO CREDITED TO HIM AS RIGHTEOUSNESS.
23 Now not for his sake only was it written that it was credited to him,
24 but for our sake also, to whom it will be credited, as those who believe in Him who
raised Jesus our Lord from the dead,
25 *He* who was delivered over because of our transgressions, and was raised because
of our justification.

Results of Justification

5 Therefore, having been justified by faith, we have peace with God through our Lord
Jesus Christ,
2 through whom also we have obtained our introduction by faith into this grace in
which we stand; and we exult in hope of the glory of God.
3 And not only this, but we also exult in our tribulations, knowing that tribulation brings
about perseverance;
4 and perseverance, proven character; and proven character, hope;
5 and hope does not disappoint, because the love of God has been poured out within
our hearts through the Holy Spirit who was given to us.
6 For while we were still helpless, at the right time Christ died for the ungodly.
7 For one will hardly die for a righteous man; though perhaps for the good man someone would dare even to die.

4:18 Rom 4:17; Gen 15:5
4:19 Heb 11:12
4:22 Gen 15:6; Rom 4:3
4:23 Rom 15:4
4:24 Rom 10:9; 1 Pet 1:21; Acts 2:24
4:25 Is 53:4, 5; Rom 5:6, 8; 8:32; Gal 2:20; Eph 5:2
5:2 Eph 2:18; 3:12; Heb 10:19f; 1 Pet 3:18; 1 Cor 15:1
5:3 Matt 5:12; James 1:2f; Luke 21:19
5:4 Luke 21:19; Phil 2:22; James 1:12
5:5 Ps 119:116; Rom 9:33; Heb 6:18f; Gal 4:6; Titus 3:6
5:6 Rom 5:8, 10; Gal 4:4; Rom 4:25; 5:8; 8:32; Gal 2:20; Eph 5:2

4:21 Abraham never doubted that God would fulfill his promise. Abraham's life was marked by mistakes, sins, and failures as well as by wisdom and goodness, but he consistently trusted God. His faith was strengthened by the obstacles he faced, and his life was an example of faith in action. If he had looked only at his own resources for subduing Canaan and founding a nation, he would have given up in despair. But Abraham looked to God, obeyed him, and waited for God to fulfill his word.

4:25 When we believe, an exchange takes place. We give Christ our sins, and he gives us his righteousness and forgiveness (see 2 Corinthians 5:21). There is nothing we can do to earn this. Only through Christ can we receive God's righteousness. What an incredible bargain this is for us! But sadly, many still choose to pass up this gift to continue "enjoying" their sin.

5:1 We now have peace *with God,* which may differ from peaceful feelings such as calmness and tranquility. Peace with God means that we have been reconciled with him. There is no more hostility between us, no sin blocking our relationship with him. Peace with God is possible only because Jesus paid the price for our sins through his death on the cross.

5:1–5 These verses introduce a section that contains some difficult concepts. To understand the next four chapters, it helps to keep in mind the two-sided reality of the Christian life. On the one hand, we are complete in Christ (our acceptance with him is secure). On the other hand, we are growing in Christ (we are becoming more and more like him). At one and the same time we have the status of kings and the duties of slaves. We feel both the presence of Christ and the pressure of sin. We enjoy the peace that comes from being made right with God, but we still face daily problems that often help us grow. If we remember these two sides of the Christian life, we will not grow discouraged as we face temptations and problems. Instead, we will learn to depend on the power available to us from Christ, who lives in us by the Holy Spirit.

5:2 Paul states that, as believers, we now stand in a place of highest privilege ("this grace in which we stand"). Not only has God declared us not guilty; he has drawn us close to himself. Instead of being enemies, we have become his friends—in fact, his own children (John 15:15; Galatians 4:5).

5:2–5 As Paul states clearly in 1 Corinthians 13:13, faith, hope, and love are at the heart of the Christian life. Our relationship with God begins with *faith,* which helps us realize that we are delivered from our past by Christ's death. *Hope* grows as we learn all that God has in mind for us; it gives us the promise of the future. And God's *love* fills our lives and gives us the ability to reach out to others.

5:3–4 For first-century Christians, suffering was the rule rather than the exception. Paul tells us that in the future we will *become,* but until then we must *overcome.* This means we will experience difficulties that help us grow. We rejoice in suffering not because we like pain or deny its tragedy, but because we know God is using life's difficulties and Satan's attacks to build our character. The problems that we run into will develop our perseverance—which in turn will strengthen our character, deepen our trust in God, and give us greater confidence about the future. You probably find your patience tested in some way every day. Thank God for those opportunities to grow, and deal with them in his strength (see also James 1:2–4; 1 Peter 1:6–7).

5:5–6 All three members of the Trinity are involved in salvation. The Father loved us so much that he sent his Son to bridge the gap between us (John 3:16). The Father and the Son send the Holy Spirit to fill our lives with love and to enable us to live by his power (Acts 1:8). With all this loving care, how can we do less than serve him completely!

5:6 We were weak and helpless because we could do nothing on our own to save ourselves. Someone had to come and rescue us. Not only did Christ come at a good time in history; he came at exactly the right time—according to God's own schedule. God controls all history, and he controlled the timing, methods, and results of Jesus' death.

5:8 Rom 3:5; John 3:16; 15:13; Rom 8:39; Gal 2:20; Eph 5:2

5:9 Rom 3:25; Rom 1:18; 1 Thess 1:10

5:10 Rom 8:34; Heb 7:25; 1 John 2:1

5:11 2 Cor 5:18f

5:12 1 Cor 15:56; James 1:15; 1 Cor 15:22

5:14 Hos 6:7; 1 Cor 15:45

5:15 Acts 15:11

5:16 1 Cor 11:32

5:17 Gen 2:17; 3:6, 19; Rom 5:12, 15, 16; 1 Cor 15:21f; 2 Tim 2:12; Rev 22:5

8 But God demonstrates His own love toward us, in that while we were yet sinners,
Christ died for us.
9 Much more then, having now been justified by His blood, we shall be saved from
the wrath *of God* through Him.
10 For if while we were enemies we were reconciled to God through the death of His
Son, much more, having been reconciled, we shall be saved by His life.
11 And not only this, but we also exult in God through our Lord Jesus Christ, through
whom we have now received the reconciliation.
12 Therefore, just as through one man sin entered into the world, and death through
sin, and so death spread to all men, because all sinned—
13 for until the Law sin was in the world, but sin is not imputed when there is no law.
14 Nevertheless death reigned from Adam until Moses, even over those who had not
sinned in the likeness of the offense of Adam, who is a [5]type of Him who was to come.
15 But the free gift is not like the transgression. For if by the transgression of the one
the many died, much more did the grace of God and the gift by the grace of the one
Man, Jesus Christ, abound to the many.
16 The gift is not like *that which came* through the one who sinned; for on the one hand
the judgment *arose* from one *transgression* resulting in condemnation, but on the other
hand the free gift *arose* from many transgressions resulting in justification.
17 For if by the transgression of the one, death reigned through the one, much more

5 Or *foreshadowing*

WHAT WE HAVE AS CHILDREN

What we have as Adam's children	*What we have as God's children*
Ruin 5:9	Rescue 5:8
Sin 5:12, 15, 21	Righteousness 5:18
Death 5:12, 16, 21	Eternal life 5:17, 21
Separation from God 5:18	Relationship with God 5:11, 19
Disobedience 5:12, 19	Obedience 5:19
Judgment 5:18	Deliverance 5:10–11
Law 5:20	Grace 5:20

5:8 *While we were yet sinners*—these are amazing words. God sent Jesus Christ to die for us, not because we were good enough, but because he loved us. Whenever you feel uncertain about God's love for you, remember that he loved you even before you turned to him. If God loved you when you were a rebel, he can surely strengthen you, now that you love him in return.

5:9–10 The love that caused Christ to die is the same love that sends the Holy Spirit to live in us and guide us every day. The power that raised Christ from the dead is the same power that saved you and is available to you in your daily life. Be assured that, having begun a life with Christ, you have a reserve of power and love to call on each day, for help to meet every challenge or trial. You can pray for God's power and love as you need it.

5:11 God is holy, and he will not be associated with sin. All people are sinful and so they are separated from God. In addition, all sin deserves punishment. Instead of punishing us with the death we deserve, however, Christ took our sins upon himself and took our punishment by dying on the cross. Now we can "exult in God." Through faith in *Christ's* work, we become close to God (reconciled) rather than being enemies and outcasts.

5:12 How can we be declared guilty for something Adam did thousands of years ago? Many feel it isn't right for God to judge us because of Adam's sin. Yet each of us confirms our solidarity with Adam by our own sins each day. We are made of the same stuff and are prone to rebel, and we are judged for the sins *we* commit. Because we are sinners, it isn't fairness we need—it's mercy.

5:13–14 Paul has shown that keeping the law does not bring salvation. Here he adds that breaking the law is not what brings death. Death is the result of Adam's sin and of the sins we all commit, even if they don't resemble Adam's. Paul reminds his readers that for thousands of years the law had not yet been explicitly given, and yet people died. The law was added, he explains in 5:20, to help people see their sinfulness, to show them the seriousness of their offenses, and to drive them to God for mercy and pardon. This was true in Moses' day, and it is still true today. Sin is a deep discrepancy between who we are and who we were created to be. The law points out our sin and places the responsibility for it squarely on our shoulders. But the Law offers no remedy. When we are convicted of sin, we must turn to Jesus Christ for healing.

5:14 Adam is a type; he is the counterpart of Christ. Just as Adam was a representative of created humanity, so Christ is the representative of a new spiritual humanity.

5:15–19 We were all born into Adam's physical family—the family line that leads to certain death. All of us have reaped the results of Adam's sin. We have inherited his guilt, a sinful nature (the tendency to sin), and God's punishment. Because of Jesus, however, we can trade judgment for forgiveness. We can trade our sin for Jesus' righteousness. Christ offers us the opportunity to be born into his spiritual family—the family line that begins with forgiveness and leads to eternal life. If we do nothing, we have death through Adam; but if we come to God by faith, we have life through Christ. Which family line do you now belong to?

5:17 What a promise this is to those who love Christ! We can reign over sin's power, over death's threats, and over Satan's attacks. Eternal life is ours now and forever. In the power and protection of Jesus Christ, we can overcome temptation. See 8:17 for more on our privileged position in Christ.

those who receive the abundance of grace and of the gift of righteousness will reign in
life through the One, Jesus Christ.
18 So then as through one transgression there resulted condemnation to all men, even
so through one act of righteousness there resulted justification of life to all men.
19 For as through the one man's disobedience the many were made sinners, even so
through the obedience of the One the many will be made righteous.
20 The Law came in so that the transgression would increase; but where sin increased,
grace abounded all the more,
21 so that, as sin reigned in death, even so grace would reign through righteousness to
eternal life through Jesus Christ our Lord.

3. Freedom from sin's grasp

Believers Are Dead to Sin, Alive to God

6 What shall we say then? Are we to continue in sin so that grace may increase?
2 May it never be! How shall we who died to sin still live in it?
3 Or do you not know that all of us who have been baptized into Christ Jesus have
been baptized into His death?
4 Therefore we have been buried with Him through baptism into death, so that as
Christ was raised from the dead through the glory of the Father, so we too might walk in
newness of life.
5 For if we have become united with *Him* in the likeness of His death, certainly we
shall also be *in the likeness* of His resurrection,
6 knowing this, that our old self was crucified with *Him,* in order that our body of sin
might be done away with, so that we would no longer be slaves to sin;
7 for he who has died is freed from sin.
8 Now if we have died with Christ, we believe that we shall also live with Him,
9 knowing that Christ, having been raised from the dead, is never to die again; death
no longer is master over Him.
10 For the death that He died, He died to sin once for all; but the life that He lives, He
lives to God.

5:18 Rom 3:25; Rom 4:25
5:19 Rom 11:32; Phil 2:8
5:20 Rom 3:20; 7:7f; Gal 3:19; Rom 6:1
5:21 Rom 5:12, 14; John 1:17; Rom 6:23
6:2 Luke 20:16; Rom 7:4, 6; Gal 2:19; Col 2:20; 3:3; 1 Pet 2:24
6:3 Matt 28:19; Acts 2:38; 8:16; 19:5; Gal 3:27
6:4 Col 2:12; Acts 2:24; Rom 7:6; 2 Cor 5:17; Gal 6:15; Eph 4:23f; Col 3:10
6:5 2 Cor 4:10; Phil 3:10f; Col 2:12; 3:1
6:6 Eph 4:22; Col 3:9; Gal 2:20; 5:24; 6:14
6:7 1 Pet 4:1
6:8 Rom 6:4; 2 Cor 4:10; 2 Tim 2:11
6:9 Acts 2:24; Rev 1:18

5:20 As a sinner, separated from God, you see his law from below, as a ladder to be climbed to get to God. Perhaps you have repeatedly tried to climb it, only to fall to the ground every time you have advanced one or two rungs. Or perhaps the sheer height of the ladder seems so overwhelming that you have never even started up. In either case, what relief you should feel to see Jesus offering with open arms to lift you above the ladder of the law, to take you directly to God! Once Jesus lifts you into God's presence, you are free to obey—out of love, not necessity, and through God's power, not your own. You know that if you stumble, you will not fall back to the ground. Instead, you will be caught and held in Christ's loving arms.

6:1—8:39 This section deals with *sanctification*—the change God makes in our lives as we grow in the faith. Chapter 6 explains that believers are free from sin's control. Chapter 7 discusses the continuing struggle believers have with sin. Chapter 8 describes how we can have victory over sin.

6:1–2 If God loves to forgive, why not give him more to forgive? If forgiveness is guaranteed, do we have the freedom to sin as much as we want? Paul's forceful answer is *May it never be!* Such an attitude—deciding ahead of time to take advantage of God—shows that a person does not understand the seriousness of sin. God's forgiveness does not make sin less serious; his Son's death for sin shows us the dreadful seriousness of sin. Jesus paid with his life so we could be forgiven. The availability of God's mercy must not become an excuse for careless living and moral laxness.

6:1–4 In the church of Paul's day, immersion was the usual form of baptism—that is, new Christians were completely "buried" in water. They understood this form of baptism to symbolize the death and burial of the old way of life. Coming up out of the water symbolized resurrection to new life with Christ. If we think of our old, sinful life as dead and buried, we have a powerful motive to resist sin. We can consciously choose to treat the desires and temptations of the old nature as if they were dead. Then we can continue to enjoy our wonderful new life with Jesus (see Galatians 3:27 and Colossians 2:12 and 3:1–4 for more on this concept).

6:5ff We can enjoy our new life in Christ because we are united with him in his death and resurrection. Our evil desires, our bondage to sin, and our love of sin died with him. Now, united by faith with him in his resurrection life, we have unbroken fellowship with God and freedom from sin's hold on us. For more on the difference between our new life in Christ and our old sinful nature, read Ephesians 4:21–24 and Colossians 3:3–15.

6:6 The power and penalty of sin died with Christ on the cross. Our "old self," our sinful nature, died once and for all, so we are freed from its power. The "body of sin" is not the human body, but our rebellious sin-loving nature inherited from Adam. Though our body willingly cooperates with our sinful nature, we must not regard the body as evil. It is the sin in us that is evil. And it is this power of sin at work in our body that is defeated. Paul has already stated that through faith in Christ we stand acquitted, "not guilty" before God. Here Paul emphasizes that we need no longer live under sin's power. God does not take us out of the world or make us robots—we will still feel like sinning, and sometimes we will sin. The difference is that before we were saved we were slaves to our sinful nature, but now we can choose to live for Christ (see Galatians 2:20).

6:8 Because of Christ's death and resurrection, his followers need never fear death. That assurance frees us to enjoy fellowship with him and to do his will. This will affect all our activities—work and worship, play, Bible study, quiet times, and times of caring for others. When you know that you don't have to fear death, you will experience a new vigor in life.

6:11 Rom 6:2; 7:4, 6; Gal 2:19; Col 2:20; 3:3
6:13 Rom 12:1; 2 Cor 5:14f; 1 Pet 2:24
6:14 Rom 8:2, 12; Rom 6:12; Rom 5:18; 7:4
6:15 Rom 6:1; Luke 20:16; Rom 6:2
6:16 John 8:34; 2 Pet 2:19
6:17 Rom 1:8; 2 Cor 2:14; 2 Tim 1:13
6:18 John 8:32
6:19 Rom 3:5; Rom 6:13
6:21 Jer 12:13; Ezek 16:63; Rom 7:5
6:22 John 8:32; Rom 6:18; 8:2; 1 Cor 7:22; 1 Pet 2:16

11 Even so consider yourselves to be dead to sin, but alive to God in Christ Jesus.
12 Therefore do not let sin reign in your mortal body so that you obey its lusts,
13 and do not go on presenting the members of your body to sin *as* instruments of
unrighteousness; but present yourselves to God as those alive from the dead, and your
members *as* instruments of righteousness to God.
14 For sin shall not be master over you, for you are not under law but under grace.
15 What then? Shall we sin because we are not under law but under grace? May it
never be!
16 Do you not know that when you present yourselves to someone *as* slaves for obedience, you are slaves of the one whom you obey, either of sin resulting in death, or of
obedience resulting in righteousness?
17 But thanks be to God that though you were slaves of sin, you became obedient from
the heart to that form of teaching to which you were committed,
18 and having been freed from sin, you became slaves of righteousness.
19 I am speaking in human terms because of the weakness of your flesh. For just as
you presented your members as slaves to impurity and to lawlessness, resulting in *further*
lawlessness, so now present your members as slaves to righteousness, resulting in sanctification.
20 For when you were slaves of sin, you were free in regard to righteousness.
21 Therefore what benefit were you then deriving from the things of which you are
now ashamed? For the outcome of those things is death.
22 But now having been freed from sin and enslaved to God, you derive your benefit,
resulting in sanctification, and the outcome, eternal life.

WHAT HAS GOD DONE ABOUT SIN?

He has given us . . .		*Principle*	*Importance*
New life	6:2–3	Sin's power is broken.	We can be certain that sin's power is broken.
	6:4	Sin-loving nature is buried.	
	6:6	You are no longer under sin's control.	
New nature	6:5	Now you share his new life.	We can see ourselves as unresponsive to the old power and alive to the new.
	6:11	Look upon your old self as dead; instead be alive to God.	
New freedom	6:12	Do not let sin control you.	We can commit ourselves to obey Christ in perfect freedom.
	6:13	Give yourselves completely to God.	
	6:14	You are free.	
	6:16	You can choose your own master.	

6:11 "Consider yourselves to be dead to sin" means that we should regard our old sinful nature as dead and unresponsive to sin. Because of our union and identification with Christ, we are no longer obligated to carry out those old motives, desires, and goals. So let us consider ourselves to be what God has in fact made us. We have a new start, and the Holy Spirit will help us become in our daily experience what Christ has declared us to be.

6:14–15 If we're no longer under the law but under grace, are we now free to sin and disregard the Ten Commandments? Paul says, "May it never be!" When we were under the law, sin was our master—the law does not justify us or help us overcome sin. But now that we are bound to Christ, he is our Master, and he gives us power to do good rather than evil.

6:16–18 In certain skilled crafts, an apprentice works under a master, who trains, shapes, and molds his apprentice in the finer points of his craft. All people choose a master and pattern themselves after him. Without Jesus, we would have no choice—we would have to apprentice ourselves to sin, and the results would be guilt, suffering, and separation from God. Thanks to Jesus, however, we can now choose God as our Master. Following him, we can enjoy new life and learn how to work for him. Are you still serving your first master, sin? Or have you apprenticed yourself to God?

6:17 To be obedient from the heart means to give yourself fully to God, to love him "with all your heart, and with all your soul, and with all your mind" (Matthew 22:37). And yet so often our efforts to know and obey God's commands can best be described as "half-hearted." How do you rate your heart's obedience? God wants to give you the power to obey him with all your heart.

6:17 The "form of teaching" delivered to them is the Good News that Jesus died for their sins and was raised to give them new life. Many believe that this refers to the early church's statement of faith found in 1 Corinthians 15:1–11.

6:19–22 It is impossible to be neutral. Every person has a master—either God or sin. A Christian is not someone who cannot sin, but someone who is no longer a slave to sin. He or she belongs to God.

23 For the wages of sin is death, but the free gift of God is eternal life in Christ Jesus
our Lord.

Believers United to Christ

7 Or do you not know, brethren (for I am speaking to those who know the law), that
the law has jurisdiction over a person as long as he lives?
2 For the married woman is bound by law to her husband while he is living; but if her
husband dies, she is released from the law concerning the husband.
3 So then, if while her husband is living she is joined to another man, she shall be called
an adulteress; but if her husband dies, she is free from the law, so that she is not an adulteress though she is joined to another man.
4 Therefore, my brethren, you also were made to die to the Law through the body of
Christ, so that you might be joined to another, to Him who was raised from the dead, in
order that we might bear fruit for God.
5 For while we were in the flesh, the sinful passions, which were *aroused* by the Law,
were at work in the members of our body to bear fruit for death.
6 But now we have been released from the Law, having died to that by which we were
bound, so that we serve in newness of the [6]Spirit and not in oldness of the letter.
7 What shall we say then? Is the Law sin? May it never be! On the contrary, I would
not have come to know sin except through the Law; for I would not have known about
coveting if the Law had not said, "YOU SHALL NOT COVET."
8 But sin, taking opportunity through the commandment, produced in me coveting
of every kind; for apart from the Law sin *is* dead.
9 I was once alive apart from the Law; but when the commandment came, sin became
alive and I died;
10 and this commandment, which was to result in life, proved to result in death for me;
11 for sin, taking an opportunity through the commandment, deceived me and through
it killed me.

6 Or *spirit*

6:23 Rom 1:32; 5:12; 6:16, 21; 8:6, 13; Gal 6:8; Matt 25:46; Rom 5:21; 8:38, 39
7:1 Rom 1:13
7:2 1 Cor 7:39
7:4 Rom 6:2; 7:6; Rom 8:2; Gal 2:19; 5:18; Col 1:22
7:5 Rom 8:8f; 2 Cor 10:3; Rom 7:7f
Rom 6:13, 21, 23
7:6 Rom 7:2; Rom 6:2; Rom 6:4; Rom 2:29
7:7 Rom 3:5; Luke 20:16; Rom 3:20; 4:15; 5:20; Ex 20:17; Deut 5:21
7:8 Rom 7:11; Rom 3:20; 7:11; 1 Cor 15:56
7:10 Lev 18:5; Luke 10:28; Rom 10:5; Gal 3:12
7:11 Rom 7:8; Rom 3:20; 7:8; Gen 3:13

6:23 You are free to choose between two masters, but you are not free to manipulate the consequences of your choice. Each of the two masters pays with his own kind of currency. The currency of sin is death. That is all you can expect or hope for in life without God. Christ's currency is eternal life—new life with God that begins on earth and continues forever with God. What choice have you made?

6:23 Eternal life is a free gift from God. If it is a gift, then it is not something that we earn, nor something that must be paid back. Consider the foolishness of someone who receives a gift given out of love and then offers to pay for it. A gift cannot be purchased by the recipient. A more appropriate response to a loved one who offers a gift is graceful acceptance with gratitude. Our salvation is a gift of God, not something of our own doing (Ephesians 2:8–9). He saved us because of his mercy, not because of any righteous things that we have done (Titus 3:5). How much more we should accept with thanksgiving the gift that God has freely given to us.

7:1ff Paul shows that the law is powerless to save the sinner (7:7–14), the lawkeeper (7:15–22), and even the person with a new nature (7:23–25). The sinner is condemned by the law; the lawkeeper can't live up to it; and the person with the new nature finds his or her obedience to the law sabotaged by the effects of the old nature. Once again, Paul declares that salvation cannot be found by obeying the law. No matter who we are, only Jesus Christ can set us free.

7:2–6 Paul uses marriage to illustrate our relationship to the law. When a spouse dies, the law of marriage no longer applies. Because we have died with Christ, the law can no longer condemn us. We rose again when Christ was resurrected and, as new people, we "belong" to Christ. His Spirit enables us to produce good fruit for God. We now serve not by obeying a set of rules, but out of renewed hearts and minds that overflow with love for God.

7:4 When a person dies to the old life and belongs to Christ, a new life begins. An unbeliever's mind-set is centered on his or her own personal gratification. Those who don't follow Christ have only their own self-determination as their source of power. By contrast, God is at the center of a Christian's life. God supplies the power for the Christian's daily living. Believers find that their whole way of looking at the world changes when they come to Christ.

7:6 Some people try to earn their way to God by keeping a set of rules (obeying the Ten Commandments, attending church faithfully, or doing good deeds), but all they earn for their efforts is frustration and discouragement. However, because of Christ's sacrifice, the way to God is already open, and we can become his children simply by putting our faith in him. No longer trying to reach God by keeping rules, we can become more and more like Jesus as we live with him day by day. Let the Holy Spirit turn your eyes away from your own performance and toward Jesus. He will free you to serve him out of love and gratitude. This is living "in newness of the Spirit."

7:6 Keeping the rules, laws, and customs of Christianity doesn't save us. Even if we could keep our actions pure, we would still be doomed because our hearts and minds are perverse and rebellious. Like Paul, we can find no relief in the synagogue or church until we look to Jesus Christ himself for our salvation—which he gives us freely. When we do come to Jesus, we are flooded with relief and gratitude. Will we keep the rules any better? Most likely, but we will be motivated by love and gratitude, not by the desire to get God's approval. We will not be merely submitting to an external code, but willingly and lovingly seeking to do God's will.

7:9–11 Where there is no law, there is no sin, because people cannot know that their actions are sinful unless a law forbids those actions. God's law makes people realize that they are sinners doomed to die, yet it offers no help. Sin is real, and it is dangerous. Imagine a sunny day at the beach. You plunge into the surf; then you notice a sign on the pier: "No swimming. Sharks in water." Your day is ruined. Is it the sign's fault? Are you angry with the people who put it up? The law is like the sign. It is essential, and

7:12 Rom 7:16; 1 Tim 1:8
7:13 Luke 20:16
7:14 1 Cor 3:1; 1 Kin 21:20, 25; 2 Kin 17:17; Rom 6:6; Gal 4:3; Rom 3:9
7:15 John 15:15; Rom 7:19; Gal 5:17
7:16 Rom 7:12; 1 Tim 1:8
7:18 John 3:6
7:21 Rom 7:23, 25; 8:2
7:22 2 Cor 4:16; Eph 3:16; 1 Pet 3:4
7:23 Rom 6:19; Gal 5:17; James 4:1; 1 Pet 2:11; Rom 7:25
7:24 Rom 6:6; Col 2:11
7:25 1 Cor 15:57

12 So then, the Law is holy, and the commandment is holy and righteous and good.
13 Therefore did that which is good become *a cause of* death for me? May it never be!
Rather it was sin, in order that it might be shown to be sin by effecting my death through
that which is good, so that through the commandment sin would become utterly sinful.

The Conflict of Two Natures

14 For we know that the Law is spiritual, but I am of flesh, sold into bondage to sin.
15 For what I am doing, I do not understand; for I am not practicing what I *would* like
to *do,* but I am doing the very thing I hate.
16 But if I do the very thing I do not want *to do,* I agree with the Law, *confessing* that
the Law is good.
17 So now, no longer am I the one doing it, but sin which dwells in me.
18 For I know that nothing good dwells in me, that is, in my flesh; for the willing is
present in me, but the doing of the good *is* not.
19 For the good that I want, I do not do, but I practice the very evil that I do not want.
20 But if I am doing the very thing I do not want, I am no longer the one doing it, but
sin which dwells in me.
21 I find then the principle that evil is present in me, the one who wants to do good.
22 For I joyfully concur with the law of God in the inner man,
23 but I see a different law in the members of my body, waging war against the law of
my mind and making me a prisoner of the law of sin which is in my members.
24 Wretched man that I am! Who will set me free from the body of this death?
25 Thanks be to God through Jesus Christ our Lord! So then, on the one hand I myself
with my mind am serving the law of God, but on the other, with my flesh the law of sin.

---

we are grateful for it—but it doesn't get rid of the sharks.

7:11–12 Sin deceives people by misusing the Law. The Law was holy, expressing God's nature and will for people. In the Garden of Eden (Genesis 3), the serpent deceived Eve by taking her focus off the freedom she had and putting it on the one restriction God had made. Ever since then, we have all been rebels. Sin looks good to us precisely because God has said it is wrong. Instead of paying attention to his warnings, we use them as a "to do" list. When we are tempted to rebel, we need to look at the law from a wider perspective—in the light of God's grace and mercy. If we focus on his great love for us, we will understand that he only restricts us from actions and attitudes that ultimately will harm us.

7:14 "I am of flesh, sold into bondage to sin" may be a reference to the old nature that seeks to rebel and be independent of God. If I, being a Christian, try to struggle with sin in my own strength, I am slipping into the grasp of sin's power.

7:15 Paul shares three lessons that he learned in trying to deal with his old sinful desires. (1) Knowledge is not the answer (7:9). Paul felt fine as long as he did not understand what the Law demanded. When he learned the truth, he knew he was doomed. (2) Self-determination (struggling in one's own strength) doesn't succeed (7:15). Paul found himself sinning in ways that weren't even attractive to him. (3) Becoming a Christian does not stamp out all sin and temptation from a person's life (7:22–25).

Being born again takes a moment of faith, but becoming like Christ is a lifelong process. Paul compares Christian growth to a strenuous race or fight (1 Corinthians 9:24–27; 2 Timothy 4:7). Thus, as Paul has been emphasizing since the beginning of this letter, *no one* in the world is innocent; no one deserves to be saved—not the pagan who doesn't know God's laws, not the Christian or Jew who knows them and tries to keep them. All of us must depend totally on the work of Christ for our salvation. We cannot earn it by our good behavior.

7:15 This is more than the cry of one desperate man—it describes the experience of any Christian struggling against sin or trying to please God by keeping rules and laws without the Spirit's help. We must never underestimate the power of sin. We must never attempt to fight it in our own strength. Satan is a crafty tempter, and we have an amazing ability to make excuses. Instead of trying to overcome sin with human willpower, we must take hold of the tremendous power of Christ that is available to us. This is God's provision for victory over sin—he sends the Holy Spirit to live in us and give us power. And when we fall, he lovingly reaches out to help us up.

7:17–20 "The devil made me do it." This sounds like a good excuse, but we are responsible for our actions. We must never use the power of sin or Satan as an excuse, because they are defeated enemies. Without Christ's help, sin is stronger than we are, and sometimes we are unable to defend ourselves against its attacks. That is why we should never stand up to sin all alone. Jesus Christ, who has conquered sin once and for all, promises to fight by our side. If we look to him for help, we will not have to give in to sin.

7:23–25 The "law in the members of my body" is the sin deep within us. This is our vulnerability to sin; it refers to everything within us that is more loyal to our old way of selfish living than to God.

7:23–25 This inward struggle with sin was as real for Paul as it is for us. From Paul we learn what to do about it. Whenever Paul felt lost, he would return to the beginning of his spiritual life, remembering that he had already been freed by Jesus Christ. When you feel confused and overwhelmed by sin's appeal, follow Paul's example: Thank God that he has given you freedom through Jesus Christ. Let the reality of Christ's power lift you up to real victory over sin.

Deliverance from Bondage

8 Therefore there is now no condemnation for those who are in Christ Jesus.
2 For the law of the Spirit of life in Christ Jesus has set you free from the law of sin
and of death.
3 For what the Law could not do, weak as it was through the flesh, God *did:* sending
His own Son in the likeness of sinful flesh and *as an offering* for sin, He condemned sin
in the flesh,
4 so that the requirement of the Law might be fulfilled in us, who do not walk according to the flesh but according to the Spirit.
5 For those who are according to the flesh set their minds on the things of the flesh,
but those who are according to the Spirit, the things of the Spirit.
6 For the mind set on the flesh is death, but the mind set on the Spirit is life and peace,
7 because the mind set on the flesh is hostile toward God; for it does not subject itself
to the law of God, for it is not even able *to do so,*
8 and those who are in the flesh cannot please God.
9 However, you are not in the flesh but in the Spirit, if indeed the Spirit of God dwells
in you. But if anyone does not have the Spirit of Christ, he does not belong to Him.
10 If Christ is in you, though the body is dead because of sin, yet the spirit is alive because of righteousness.
11 But if the Spirit of Him who raised Jesus from the dead dwells in you, He who raised
Christ Jesus from the dead will also give life to your mortal bodies [7]through His Spirit
who dwells in you.
12 So then, brethren, we are under obligation, not to the flesh, to live according to the
flesh—
13 for if you are living according to the flesh, you must die; but if by the Spirit you are
putting to death the deeds of the body, you will live.
14 For all who are being led by the Spirit of God, these are sons of God.

7 One early ms reads *because of*

8:1 Rom 5:16
8:2 1 Cor 15:45; John 8:32, 36; Rom 6:14, 18; 7:4
8:3 Acts 13:39; Heb 10:1ff; Rom 7:18f; Heb 7:18; Phil 2:7
8:4 Luke 1:6; Rom 2:26
8:5 Gal 5:19-21
8:6 Gal 6:8; Rom 6:21
8:7 James 4:4
8:9 1 Cor 3:16; 6:19; 2 Cor 6:16; Gal 4:6; Phil 1:19; 2 Tim 1:14; 1 John 4:13
8:10 Gal 2:20; Eph 3:17; Col 1:27
8:11 Acts 2:24; Rom 6:4; John 5:21
8:13 Rom 8:6; Col 3:5
8:14 Matt 5:9; John 1:12; 2 Cor 6:18; Gal 3:26; 1 John 3:1

8:1 "Not guilty; let him go free"—what would those words mean to you if you were on death row? The fact is that the whole human race *is* on death row, justly condemned for repeatedly breaking God's holy law. Without Jesus we would have no hope at all. But thank God! He has declared us not guilty and has offered us freedom from sin and power to do his will.

8:2 This Spirit of life is the Holy Spirit. He was present at the creation of the world (Genesis 1:2), and he is the power behind the rebirth of every Christian. He gives us the power we need to live the Christian life. For more about the Holy Spirit, read the notes on John 3:6; Acts 1:3; 1:4, 5; 1:5.

8:3 Jesus gave himself as a *sacrifice* ("an offering") for our sins. In Old Testament times, animal sacrifices were continually offered at the temple. The sacrifices showed the Israelites the seriousness of sin: Blood had to be shed before sins could be pardoned (see Leviticus 17:11). But animal blood could not really remove sins (Hebrews 10:4). The sacrifices could only point to Jesus' sacrifice, which paid the penalty for all sins.

8:5–6 Paul divides people into two categories—those who let themselves be controlled by their sinful natures, and those who follow after the Holy Spirit. All of us would be in the first category if Jesus hadn't offered us a way out. Once we have said yes to Jesus, we will want to continue following him, because his way brings life and peace. Daily we must consciously choose to center our lives on God. Use the Bible to discover God's guidelines, and then follow them. In every perplexing situation ask yourself, "What would Jesus want me to do?" When the Holy Spirit points out what is right, do it eagerly. For more on our sinful natures versus our new life in Christ, see 6:6–8, Ephesians 4:22–24; Colossians 3:3–15.

8:9 Have you ever worried about whether or not you really are a Christian? A Christian is anyone who has the Spirit of God living in him or her. If you have sincerely trusted Christ for your salvation and acknowledged him as Lord, then the Holy Spirit has come into your life, and you are a Christian. You won't know that the Holy Spirit has come if you are waiting for a certain feeling; you will know he has come because Jesus promised he would. When the Holy Spirit is working within you, you will believe that Jesus Christ is God's Son and that eternal life comes through him (1 John 5:5); you will begin to act as Christ directs (Romans 8:5; Galatians 5:22–23); you will find help in your daily problems and in your praying (Romans 8:26–27); you will be empowered to serve God and do his will (Acts 1:8; Romans 12:6ff); and you will become part of God's plan to build up his church (Ephesians 4:12–13).

8:11 The Holy Spirit is God's promise or guarantee of eternal life for those who believe in him. The Spirit is in us now by faith, and by faith we are certain to live with Christ forever. See Romans 8:23; 1 Corinthians 6:14; 2 Corinthians 4:14; 1 Thessalonians 4:14.

8:13 "Putting to death the deeds of the body" means regarding as dead the power of sin in your body (see 6:11; Galatians 5:24). When we regard sin's appeal as dead and lifeless, we can ignore temptation when it comes.

8:14–17 Paul uses adoption or "sonship" to illustrate the believer's new relationship with God. In Roman culture, the adopted person lost all rights in his old family and gained all the rights of a legitimate child in his new family. He became a full heir to his new father's estate. Likewise, when a person becomes a Christian, he or she gains all the privileges and responsibilities of a child in God's family. One of these outstanding privileges is being led by the Spirit (see Galatians 4:5–6). We may not always feel as though we belong to God, but the Holy Spirit is our witness. His inward presence reminds us of who we are and encourages us with God's love (5:5).

8:14–17 We are no longer cringing and fearful slaves; instead, we are the Master's children. What a privilege! Because we are God's children, we share in great treasures as fellow heirs. God has already given us his best gifts: his Son, forgiveness, and eternal life; and he encourages us to ask him for whatever we need.

8:15 Gal 4:5f; Mark 14:36
8:16 Matt 5:9; John 1:12; 1 John 3:1; Rev 21:7
8:17 Titus 3:7; Heb 1:14; Rev 21:7; 2 Cor 1:5
8:18 Col 3:4; Titus 2:13; 1 Pet 1:5; 5:1
8:19 Phil 1:20; 1 Cor 1:7f; Col 3:4; 1 Pet 1:7, 13; 1 John 3:1; Rev 21:7
8:20 Gen 3:17-19; Ps 39:5f; Eccl 1:2
8:21 2 Pet 3:13; Rev 21:1
8:23 Gal 5:5; Rom 7:24
8:24 Titus 3:7; Rom 4:18; 2 Cor 5:7; Heb 11:1
8:25 1 Thess 1:3
8:26 Matt 20:22; 2 Cor 12:8; John 14:16
8:27 Ps 139:1f; Luke 16:15; Acts 1:24

15 For you have not received a spirit of slavery leading to fear again, but you have received a spirit of adoption as sons by which we cry out, "Abba! Father!"
16 The Spirit Himself testifies with our spirit that we are children of God,
17 and if children, heirs also, heirs of God and fellow heirs with Christ, if indeed we
suffer with *Him* so that we may also be glorified with *Him.*
18 For I consider that the sufferings of this present time are not worthy to be compared
with the glory that is to be revealed to us.
19 For the anxious longing of the creation waits eagerly for the revealing of the sons
of God.
20 For the creation was subjected to futility, not willingly, but because of Him who
subjected it, [8]in hope
21 that the creation itself also will be set free from its slavery to corruption into the
freedom of the glory of the children of God.
22 For we know that the whole creation groans and suffers the pains of childbirth together until now.
23 And not only this, but also we ourselves, having the first fruits of the Spirit, even we
ourselves groan within ourselves, waiting eagerly for *our* adoption as sons, the redemption of our body.
24 For in hope we have been saved, but hope that is seen is not hope; for who hopes
for what he *already* sees?
25 But if we hope for what we do not see, with perseverance we wait eagerly for it.

Our Victory in Christ

26 In the same way the Spirit also helps our weakness; for we do not know how to pray
as we should, but the Spirit Himself intercedes for *us* with groanings too deep for words;
27 and He who searches the hearts knows what the mind of the Spirit is, because He
intercedes for the saints according to *the will of* God.

8 Or *in hope; because the creation*

8:17 There is a price for being identified with Jesus. Along with the great treasures, Paul mentions the suffering that Christians must face. What kinds of suffering are we to endure? For first-century believers, there was economic and social persecution, and some even faced death. We too must pay a price for following Jesus. In many parts of today's world, Christians face pressures just as severe as those faced by Christ's first followers. Even in countries where Christianity is tolerated or encouraged, Christians must not become complacent. To live as Jesus did—serving others, giving up one's own rights, resisting pressures to conform to the world—always exacts a price. Nothing we suffer, however, can compare to the great price that Jesus paid to save us.

8:19–22 Sin has caused all creation to fall from the perfect state in which God created it. So the world is subject to frustration and bondage to decay so that it cannot fulfill its intended purpose. One day all creation will be liberated and transformed. Until that time it waits in eager expectation for the resurrection of God's children.

8:19–22 Christians see the world as it is—physically decaying and spiritually infected with sin. But Christians do not need to be pessimistic, because they have hope for future glory. They look forward to the new heaven and new earth that God has promised, and they wait for God's new order that will free the world of sin, sickness, and evil. In the meantime, Christians go with Christ into the world where they heal people's bodies and souls and fight the evil effects of sin in the world.

8:23 We will be resurrected with bodies, glorified bodies like the body Christ now has in heaven (see 1 Corinthians 15:25–58). We have the "first fruits," the first installment or down payment of the Holy Spirit as a guarantee of our resurrection life (see 2 Corinthians 1:22; 5:5; Ephesians 1:14).

8:24–25 It is natural for children to trust their parents, even though parents sometimes fail to keep their promises. Our heavenly Father, however, never makes promises he won't keep. Nevertheless, his plan may take more time than we expect. Rather than acting like impatient children as we wait for God's will to unfold, we should place our confidence in God's goodness and wisdom.

8:24–25 In Romans, Paul presents the idea that salvation is past, present, and future. It is past because we *were* saved the moment we believed in Jesus Christ as Savior (3:21–26; 5:1–11; 6:1–11, 22–23); our new life (eternal life) begins at that moment. And it is present because we *are being* saved; this is the process of sanctification (see the note on 6:1—8:39). But at the same time, we have not fully received all the benefits and blessings of salvation that will be ours when Christ's new kingdom is completely established. That's our future salvation. While we can be confident of our salvation, we still look ahead with hope and trust toward that complete change of body and personality that lies beyond this life, when we will be like Christ (1 John 3:2).

8:26–27 As a believer, you are not left to your own resources to cope with problems. Even when you don't know the right words to pray, the Holy Spirit prays with and for you, and God answers. With God helping you pray, you don't need to be afraid to come before him. Ask the Holy Spirit to intercede for you "according to the will of God." Then, when you bring your requests to God, trust that he will always do what is best.

28 And we know that [9]God causes all things to work together for good to those who
love God, to those who are called according to *His* purpose.
29 For those whom He foreknew, He also predestined *to become* conformed to the
image of His Son, so that He would be the firstborn among many brethren;
30 and these whom He predestined, He also called; and these whom He called, He
also justified; and these whom He justified, He also glorified.
31 What then shall we say to these things? If God *is* for us, who *is* against us?
32 He who did not spare His own Son, but delivered Him over for us all, how will He
not also with Him freely give us all things?
33 Who will bring a charge against God's elect? God is the one who justifies;
34 who is the one who condemns? Christ Jesus is He who died, yes, rather who was
[10]raised, who is at the right hand of God, who also intercedes for us.
35 Who will separate us from the love of [11]Christ? Will tribulation, or distress, or persecution, or famine, or nakedness, or peril, or sword?
36 Just as it is written,

"FOR YOUR SAKE WE ARE BEING PUT TO DEATH ALL DAY LONG;
WE WERE CONSIDERED AS SHEEP TO BE SLAUGHTERED."

37 But in all these things we overwhelmingly conquer through Him who loved us.
38 For I am convinced that neither death, nor life, nor angels, nor principalities, nor
things present, nor things to come, nor powers,
39 nor height, nor depth, nor any other created thing, will be able to separate us from
the love of God, which is in Christ Jesus our Lord.

8:28 1 Cor 1:9; Gal 1:6, 15; 5:8; Eph 1:11
8:29 1 Cor 8:3; 2 Tim 1:9; 1 Pet 1:2, 20
8:30 1 Cor 1:9; Gal 1:6, 15; 5:8; Eph 1:11; 3:11; 2 Thess 2:14; Heb 9:15; 1 Pet 2:9
8:31 Rom 3:5; 4:1; Ps 118:6; Matt 1:23
8:32 John 3:16; Rom 5:8
8:33 Luke 18:7; Is 50:8f
8:34 Rom 5:6f; Acts 2:24
8:35 2 Cor 4:8; 1 Cor 4:11; 2 Cor 11:26f
8:36 Ps 44:22; Acts 20:24; 1 Cor 4:9
8:37 John 16:33; Eph 5:2; Rev 1:5
8:38 1 Cor 15:24; Eph 1:21; 1 Pet 3:22
9:1 2 Cor 11:10; Gal 1:20; 1 Tim 2:7

4. Israel's past, present, and future

Solicitude for Israel

9 I am telling the truth in Christ, I am not lying, my conscience testifies with me in the
Holy Spirit,

9 One early ms reads *all things work together for good* 10 One early ms reads *raised from the dead* 11 Two early mss read *God*

8:28 God works in "all things"—not just isolated incidents—for our good. This does not mean that all that happens to us is good. Evil is prevalent in our fallen world, but God is able to turn every circumstance around for our long-range good. Note that God is not working to make us happy, but to fulfill his purpose. Note also that this promise is not for everybody. It can be claimed only by those who love God and are called according to his purpose. Those who are "called" are those the Holy Spirit convinces and enables to receive Christ. Such people have a new perspective, a new mind-set on life. They trust in God, not life's treasures; they look for their security in heaven, not on earth; they learn to accept, not resent, pain and persecution because God is with them.

8:29 God's ultimate goal for us is to make us like Christ (1 John 3:2). As we become more and more like him, we discover our true selves, the persons we were created to be. How can we be conformed to Christ's likeness? By reading and heeding the Word, by studying his life on earth through the Gospels, by being filled with his Spirit, and by doing his work in the world.

8:29–30 Some believe these verses mean that before the beginning of the world, God chose certain people to receive his gift of salvation. They point to verses like Ephesians 1:11 that says we are "predestined according to His purpose who works all things after the counsel of his will." Others believe that God *foreknew* those who would respond to him and upon those he set his mark (predestined). What is clear is that God's *purpose* for people was not an afterthought; it was settled before the foundation of the world. People are to serve and honor God. If you have believed in Christ, you can rejoice in the fact that God has always known you. God's love is eternal. His wisdom and power are supreme. He will guide and protect you until you one day stand in his presence.

8:30 *Called* means summoned or invited. For more on justification and glorification, see the chart in chapter 3.

8:31–34 Do you ever think that because you aren't good enough for God, he will not save you? Do you ever feel as if salvation is for everyone else but you? Then these verses are especially for you. If God gave his Son for you, he isn't going to hold back the gift of salvation! If Christ gave his life for you, he isn't going to turn around and condemn you! He will not withhold anything you need to live for him. The book of Romans is more than a theological explanation of God's redeeming grace—it is a letter of comfort and confidence addressed to you.

8:34 Paul says that Jesus is interceding for us in heaven. God has acquitted us and has removed our sin and guilt, so it is Satan, not God, who accuses us. When he does, Jesus, the advocate for our defense, stands at God's right hand to present our case. For more on the concept of Christ as our advocate, see the notes on Hebrews 4:14; 15.

8:35–36 These words were written to a church that would soon undergo terrible persecution. In just a few years, Paul's hypothetical situations would turn into painful realities. This passage reaffirms God's profound love for his people. No matter what happens to us, no matter where we are, we can never be lost to his love. Suffering should not drive us away from God, but help us to identify with him further and allow his love to reach us and heal us.

8:35–39 These verses contain one of the most comforting promises in all Scripture. Believers have always had to face hardships in many forms: persecution, illness, imprisonment, even death. These could cause them to fear that they have been abandoned by Christ. But Paul exclaims that it is *impossible* to be separated from Christ. His death for us is proof of his unconquerable love. Nothing can stop Christ's constant presence with us. God tells us how great his love is so that we will feel totally secure in him. If we believe these overwhelming assurances, we will not be afraid.

8:38 *Powers* are unseen forces of evil in the universe, forces like Satan and his fallen angels (see Ephesians 6:12). In Christ we are super-conquerors, and his love will protect us from any such forces.

9:1–3 Paul expressed concern for his Jewish "brethren" by saying that he would willingly take their punishment if that could save

9:3 Gal 1:8f; Rom 1:3; 11:14; Eph 6:5
9:4 Heb 9:1, 6; Acts 2:39; 13:32; Eph 2:12
9:5 Rom 1:3; Col 1:16-19; John 1:1
9:6 John 1:47; Rom 2:28f; Gal 6:16
9:7 John 8:33, 39; Gal 4:23; Gen 21:12
9:8 Gal 3:29
9:9 Gen 18:10
9:10 Rom 5:3; Gen 25:21
9:12 Gen 25:23
9:13 Mal 1:2f
9:14 Luke 20:16
9:15 Ex 33:19
9:16 Gal 2:2; Eph 2:8
9:17 Ex 9:16
9:18 Ex 4:21; 7:3; 9:12; Josh 11:20; John 12:40; Rom 11:7, 25
9:19 Rom 11:19; 1 Cor 15:35; James 2:18
9:20 Rom 2:1; 2 Tim 2:20

2 that I have great sorrow and unceasing grief in my heart.
3 For I could wish that I myself were accursed, *separated* from Christ for the sake of
my brethren, my kinsmen according to the flesh,
4 who are Israelites, to whom belongs the adoption as sons, and the glory and the
covenants and the giving of the Law and the *temple* service and the promises,
5 whose are the fathers, and from whom is the Christ according to the flesh, who is
over all, God blessed forever. Amen.
6 But *it is* not as though the word of God has failed. For they are not all Israel who are
descended from Israel;
7 nor are they all children because they are Abraham's descendants, but: "THROUGH
ISAAC YOUR DESCENDANTS WILL BE NAMED."
8 That is, it is not the children of the flesh who are children of God, but the children
of the promise are regarded as descendants.
9 For this is the word of promise: "AT THIS TIME I WILL COME, AND SARAH SHALL
HAVE A SON."
10 And not only this, but there was Rebekah also, when she had conceived *twins* by
one man, our father Isaac;
11 for though *the twins* were not yet born and had not done anything good or bad, so
that God's purpose according to *His* choice would stand, not because of works but because of Him who calls,
12 it was said to her, "THE OLDER WILL SERVE THE YOUNGER."
13 Just as it is written, "JACOB I LOVED, BUT ESAU I HATED."
14 What shall we say then? There is no injustice with God, is there? May it never be!
15 For He says to Moses, "I WILL HAVE MERCY ON WHOM I HAVE MERCY, AND I WILL
HAVE COMPASSION ON WHOM I HAVE COMPASSION."
16 So then it *does* not *depend* on the man who wills or the man who runs, but on God
who has mercy.
17 For the Scripture says to Pharaoh, "FOR THIS VERY PURPOSE I RAISED YOU UP, TO
DEMONSTRATE MY POWER IN YOU, AND THAT MY NAME MIGHT BE PROCLAIMED
THROUGHOUT THE WHOLE EARTH."
18 So then He has mercy on whom He desires, and He hardens whom He desires.
19 You will say to me then, "Why does He still find fault? For who resists His will?"
20 On the contrary, who are you, O man, who answers back to God? The thing molded
will not say to the molder, "Why did you make me like this," will it?
21 Or does not the potter have a right over the clay, to make from the same lump one
vessel for honorable use and another for common use?
22 What if God, although willing to demonstrate His wrath and to make His power
known, endured with much patience vessels of wrath prepared for destruction?

---

them. While the only one who can save us is Christ, Paul showed a rare depth of love. Like Jesus, he was willing to sacrifice for others. How concerned are you for those who don't know Christ? Are you willing to sacrifice your time, money, energy, comfort, and safety to see them come to faith in Jesus?

9:4 The Jews viewed God's choosing of Israel in the Old Testament as being like adoption. They were undeserving and without rights as natural children. Yet God adopted them and granted them the status of his sons and daughters.

9:6 God's word in the form of beautiful covenant promises came to Abraham. Covenant people, the true children of Abraham, are not just his biological descendants. They are all those who trust in God and in what Jesus Christ has done for them. (See also 2:29; Galatians 3:7.)

9:11 The Jews were proud of the fact that their lineage came from Isaac, whose mother was Sarah (Abraham's legitimate wife), rather than Ishmael, whose mother was Hagar (Sarah's maid). Paul asserts that no one can claim to be chosen by God because of his or her heritage or good deeds. God freely chooses to save whomever he wills. The doctrine of election teaches that it is God's sovereign choice to save us by his goodness and mercy, and not by our own merit.

9:12–14 Was it right for God to choose Jacob, the younger, to be over Esau? In Malachi 1:2–3, the statement "Jacob I loved, but Esau I hated" refers to the nations of Israel and Edom rather than to the individual brothers. God chose Jacob to continue the family line of the faithful because he knew his heart was for God. But he did not exclude Esau from knowing and loving him. Keep in mind the kind of God we worship: He is sovereign; he is not arbitrary; in all things he works for our good; he is trustworthy; he will save all who believe in him. When we understand these qualities of God, we know that his choices are good even if we don't understand all his reasons.

9:17–18 Paul quotes from Exodus 9:16, where God foretold how Pharaoh would be used to declare God's power. Paul uses this argument to show that salvation was God's proper work, not man's. God's judgment on Pharaoh's sin was to harden his heart, to confirm his disobedience, so that the consequences of his rebellion would be his own punishment.

9:21 With this illustration, Paul is not saying that some of us are worth more than others, but simply that the Creator has control over the created object. The created object, therefore, has no right to demand anything from its Creator—its very existence depends on him. Keeping this perspective removes any temptation to have pride in personal achievement.

23 And *He did so* to make known the riches of His glory upon vessels of mercy, which
He prepared beforehand for glory,
24 *even* us, whom He also called, not from among Jews only, but also from among
Gentiles.
25 As He says also in Hosea,
"I WILL CALL THOSE WHO WERE NOT MY PEOPLE, 'MY PEOPLE,'
AND HER WHO WAS NOT BELOVED, 'BELOVED.' "
26 "AND IT SHALL BE THAT IN THE PLACE WHERE IT WAS SAID TO THEM, 'YOU ARE
NOT MY PEOPLE,'
THERE THEY SHALL BE CALLED SONS OF THE LIVING GOD."
27 Isaiah cries out concerning Israel, "THOUGH THE NUMBER OF THE SONS OF ISRAEL
BE LIKE THE SAND OF THE SEA, IT IS THE REMNANT THAT WILL BE SAVED;
28 FOR THE LORD WILL EXECUTE HIS WORD ON THE EARTH, THOROUGHLY AND
QUICKLY."
29 And just as Isaiah foretold,
"UNLESS THE LORD OF SABAOTH HAD LEFT TO US A POSTERITY,
WE WOULD HAVE BECOME LIKE SODOM, AND WOULD HAVE RESEMBLED
GOMORRAH."
30 What shall we say then? That Gentiles, who did not pursue righteousness, attained
righteousness, even the righteousness which is by faith;
31 but Israel, pursuing a law of righteousness, did not arrive at *that* law.
32 Why? Because *they did* not *pursue it* by faith, but as though *it were* by works. They
stumbled over the stumbling stone,
33 just as it is written,
"BEHOLD, I LAY IN ZION A STONE OF STUMBLING AND A ROCK OF OFFENSE,
AND HE WHO BELIEVES IN HIM WILL NOT BE DISAPPOINTED."

The Word of Faith Brings Salvation

10 Brethren, my heart's desire and my prayer to God for them is for *their* salvation.
2 For I testify about them that they have a zeal for God, but not in accordance
with knowledge.
3 For not knowing about God's righteousness and seeking to establish their own, they
did not subject themselves to the righteousness of God.

9:23 Rom 2:4; Eph 3:16; Acts 9:15; Rom 8:29f

9:24 Rom 8:28; Rom 3:29

9:25 Hos 2:23; 1 Pet 2:10

9:26 Hos 1:10; Matt 16:16

9:27 Is 10:22; Gen 22:17; Hos 1:10; Rom 11:5

9:28 Is 10:23

9:29 Is 1:9; James 5:4; Deut 29:23; Is 13:19; Jer 49:18; 50:40; Amos 4:11

9:30 Rom 9:14; Rom 1:17; 3:21f; 10:6; Gal 2:16; 3:24; Phil 3:9; Heb 11:7

9:31 Is 51:1; Rom 9:30; 10:2f, 20; 11:7; Gal 5:4

9:32 Is 8:14; 1 Pet 2:6, 8

9:33 Is 28:16; Is 8:14; Rom 10:11; Rom 5:5

10:2 Acts 21:20

10:3 Rom 1:17; Is 51:1; Rom 10:2f, 20; 11:7

9:25–26 About seven hundred years before Jesus' birth, Hosea told of God's intention to restore his people. Paul applies Hosea's message to God's intention to bring Gentiles into his family after the Jews rejected his plan. Verse 25 is a quotation from Hosea 2:23 and verse 26 is from Hosea 1:10.

9:27–29 Isaiah prophesied that only a small number—a remnant—of God's original people, the Jews, would be saved. Paul saw this happening in every city where he preached. Even though he went to the Jews first, relatively few ever accepted the message. Verses 27 and 28 are based on Isaiah 10:22–23; and 9:29 is from Isaiah 1:9.

9:31–33 Sometimes we are like these people, trying to get right with God by keeping his laws. We may think that attending church, doing church work, giving offerings, and being nice will be enough. After all, we've played by the rules, haven't we? But Paul's words sting—this approach never succeeds. Paul explains that God's plan is not for those who try to earn his favor by being good; it is for those who realize that they can never be good enough and so must depend on Christ. We can be saved only by putting our faith in what Jesus Christ has done. If we do that, we will never "be disappointed."

9:32 The Jews had a worthy goal—to honor God. But they tried to achieve it the wrong way—by rigid and painstaking obedience to the law. Thus some of them became more dedicated to the law than to God. They thought that if they kept the law, God would have to accept them as his people. But God cannot be controlled. The Jews did not see that their Scriptures, the Old Testament, taught salvation by faith, and not by human effort (see Genesis 15:6).

9:32 The "stumbling stone" was Jesus. The Jews did not believe in him, because he didn't meet their expectations for the Messiah. Some people still stumble over Christ because salvation by faith doesn't make sense to them. They would rather try to earn their way to God, or else they expect God simply to overlook their sins. Others stumble over Christ because his values are the opposite of the world's. He asks for humility, and many are unwilling to humble themselves before him. He requires obedience, and many refuse to put their wills at his disposal.

10:1 What will happen to the Jewish people who believe in God but not in Christ? Since they believe in the same God, won't they be saved? If that were true, Paul would not have worked so hard and sacrificed so much to teach them about Christ. Because Jesus is the most complete revelation of God, we cannot fully know God apart from Christ; and because God appointed Jesus to bring God and man together, we cannot come to God by another path. The Jews, like everyone else, can find salvation only through Jesus Christ (John 14:6; Acts 4:12). Like Paul, we should wish that all Jews might be saved. We should pray for them and lovingly share the Good News with them.

10:3–5 Rather than living by faith in God, the Jews established customs and traditions (in addition to God's law) to try to make themselves acceptable in God's sight. But human effort, no matter how sincere, can never substitute for the righteousness God offers us by faith. The only way to *earn* salvation is to be perfect—and that is impossible. We can only hold out our empty hands and receive salvation as a gift.

4 For Christ is the end of the law for righteousness to everyone who believes.
5 For Moses writes that the man who practices the righteousness which is based on
law shall live by that righteousness.
6 But the righteousness based on faith speaks as follows: "DO NOT SAY IN YOUR HEART,
'WHO WILL ASCEND INTO HEAVEN?' (that is, to bring Christ down),
7 or 'WHO WILL DESCEND INTO THE ABYSS?' (that is, to bring Christ up from the
dead)."
8 But what does it say? "THE WORD IS NEAR YOU, in your mouth and in your heart"—
that is, the word of faith which we are preaching,
9 that if you confess with your mouth Jesus *as* Lord, and believe in your heart that
God raised Him from the dead, you will be saved;
10 for with the heart a person believes, resulting in righteousness, and with the mouth
he confesses, resulting in salvation.
11 For the Scripture says, "WHOEVER BELIEVES IN HIM WILL NOT BE DISAPPOINTED."
12 For there is no distinction between Jew and Greek; for the same *Lord* is Lord of all,
abounding in riches for all who call on Him;
13 for "WHOEVER WILL CALL ON THE NAME OF THE LORD WILL BE SAVED."
14 How then will they call on Him in whom they have not believed? How will they
believe in Him whom they have not heard? And how will they hear without a preacher?
15 How will they preach unless they are sent? Just as it is written, "HOW BEAUTIFUL
ARE THE FEET OF THOSE WHO BRING GOOD NEWS OF GOOD THINGS!"
16 However, they did not all heed the good news; for Isaiah says, "LORD, WHO HAS
BELIEVED OUR REPORT?"
17 So faith *comes* from hearing, and hearing by the word of Christ.
18 But I say, surely they have never heard, have they? Indeed they have;
"THEIR VOICE HAS GONE OUT INTO ALL THE EARTH,
AND THEIR WORDS TO THE ENDS OF THE WORLD."
19 But I say, surely Israel did not know, did they? First Moses says,
"I WILL MAKE YOU JEALOUS BY THAT WHICH IS NOT A NATION,
BY A NATION WITHOUT UNDERSTANDING WILL I ANGER YOU."
20 And Isaiah is very bold and says,
"I WAS FOUND BY THOSE WHO DID NOT SEEK ME,
I BECAME MANIFEST TO THOSE WHO DID NOT ASK FOR ME."
21 But as for Israel He says, "ALL THE DAY LONG I HAVE STRETCHED OUT MY HANDS
TO A DISOBEDIENT AND OBSTINATE PEOPLE."

10:4 Rom 7:1-4; Gal 3:24; 4:5; Rom 3:22
10:5 Lev 18:5; Neh 9:29; Ezek 20:11, 13, 21
10:6 Deut 30:12
10:7 Luke 8:31; Heb 13:20
10:9 Matt 10:32; Luke 12:8; 1 Cor 12:3; Phil 2:11
10:11 Is 28:16; Rom 9:33
10:12 Acts 10:36
10:13 Joel 2:32; Acts 2:21
10:14 Eph 2:17; 4:21; Acts 8:31; Titus 1:3
10:15 Is 52:7; Rom 1:15; 15:20
10:16 Rom 3:3; Is 53:1; John 12:38
10:17 Gal 3:2, 5; Col 3:16
10:18 Ps 19:4; Col 1:6, 23; 1 Thess 1:8
10:19 Deut 32:21
10:20 Is 65:1; Rom 9:30
10:21 Is 65:2

10:4 Christ is the "end of the law" in two ways. He fulfills the purpose and goal of the law (Matthew 5:17) in that he perfectly exemplified God's desires on earth. But he is also the termination of the law because in comparison to Christ, the law is powerless to save.

10:5 In order to be saved by the law, a person would have to live a perfect life, not sinning once. Why did God give the law when he knew people couldn't keep it? According to Paul, one reason the law was given was to show people how guilty they are (Galatians 3:19). The law was a shadow of Christ—that is, the sacrificial system educated the people so that when the true sacrifice came, they would be able to understand his work (Hebrews 10:1–4). The system of ceremonial laws was to last until the coming of Christ. The law points to Christ, the reason for all those animal sacrifices.

10:6–8 Paul adapts Moses' farewell challenge from Deuteronomy 30:11–14 to apply to Christ. Christ has provided our salvation through his incarnation (coming to earth) and resurrection (coming back from the dead). God's salvation is right in front of us. He will come to us wherever we are. All we need to do is to respond and accept his gift of salvation. The *abyss* as used here refers to the grave or Hades, the place of the dead.

10:8–12 Have you ever been asked, "How do I become a Christian?" These verses give you the beautiful answer—salvation is as close as your own mouth and heart. People think it must be a complicated process, but it is not. If we believe in our hearts and say with our mouths that Christ is the risen Lord, we will be saved.

10:11 This verse must be read in context. Paul is not saying Christians will never be put to shame or be disappointed. There will be times when people will let us down and when circumstances will take a turn for the worse. Paul is saying that God will keep his side of the bargain—those who call on him will be saved. God will never fail to provide righteousness to those who believe.

10:14–15 We must take God's great message of salvation to others so that they can respond to the Good News. How will your loved ones and neighbors hear it unless someone tells them? Is God calling you to take a part in making his message known in your community? Think of one person who needs to hear the Good News, and think of something you can do to help him or her hear it. Then take that step as soon as possible.

10:18–20 Many Jews who looked for the Messiah refused to believe in him when he came. God offered his salvation to the Gentiles ("that which is not a nation" and "a nation without understanding"); thus many Gentiles who didn't even know about a Messiah found and believed in him. Some religious people are spiritually blind, while those who have never been in a church are sometimes the most responsive to God's message. Because appearances are deceiving, and we can't see into people's hearts, beware of judging beforehand who will respond to the gospel and who will not.

Israel Is Not Cast Away

11 I say then, God has not rejected His people, has He? May it never be! For I too am
an Israelite, a descendant of Abraham, of the tribe of Benjamin.
2 God has not rejected His people whom He foreknew. Or do you not know what the
Scripture says in *the passage about* Elijah, how he pleads with God against Israel?
3 "Lord, THEY HAVE KILLED YOUR PROPHETS, THEY HAVE TORN DOWN YOUR AL-
TARS, AND I ALONE AM LEFT, AND THEY ARE SEEKING MY LIFE."
4 But what is the divine response to him? "I HAVE KEPT for Myself SEVEN THOUSAND
MEN WHO HAVE NOT BOWED THE KNEE TO BAAL."
5 In the same way then, there has also come to be at the present time a remnant according to *God's* gracious choice.
6 But if it is by grace, it is no longer on the basis of works, otherwise grace is no longer
grace.
7 What then? What Israel is seeking, it has not obtained, but those who were chosen
obtained it, and the rest were hardened;
8 just as it is written,
"GOD GAVE THEM A SPIRIT OF STUPOR,
EYES TO SEE NOT AND EARS TO HEAR NOT,
DOWN TO THIS VERY DAY."
9 And David says,
"LET THEIR TABLE BECOME A SNARE AND A TRAP,
AND A STUMBLING BLOCK AND A RETRIBUTION TO THEM.
10 "LET THEIR EYES BE DARKENED TO SEE NOT,
AND BEND THEIR BACKS FOREVER."
11 I say then, they did not stumble so as to fall, did they? May it never be! But by their
transgression salvation *has come* to the Gentiles, to make them jealous.
12 Now if their transgression is riches for the world and their failure is riches for the
Gentiles, how much more will their fulfillment be!
13 But I am speaking to you who are Gentiles. Inasmuch then as I am an apostle of
Gentiles, I magnify my ministry,
14 if somehow I might move to jealousy my fellow countrymen and save some of them.
15 For if their rejection is the reconciliation of the world, what will *their* acceptance be
but life from the dead?

11:1 1 Sam 12:22; Jer 31:37; 33:24-26; Luke 20:16; 2 Cor 11:22; Phil 3:5
11:2 Ps 94:14; Rom 8:29
11:3 1 Kin 19:10, 14
11:4 1 Kin 19:18
11:5 2 Kin 19:4; Rom 9:27
11:7 Rom 9:31; Mark 6:52; Rom 9:18; 11:25; 2 Cor 3:14
11:8 Deut 29:4; Is 29:10; Matt 13:13f
11:9 Ps 69:22
11:10 Ps 69:23
11:11 Rom 11:1; Luke 20:16; Acts 28:28
11:12 Rom 11:25
11:13 Acts 9:15
11:14 Gen 29:14; 2 Sam 19:12f; 1 Cor 1:21; 7:16; 9:22; 1 Tim 1:15; 2:4; 2 Tim 1:9
11:15 Rom 5:11; Luke 15:24, 32

11:1ff In this chapter Paul points out that not *all* Jews have rejected God's message of salvation. There is still a faithful remnant (11:5). Paul himself, after all, was a Jew, and so were Jesus' disciples and nearly all of the early Christian missionaries.

11:2 Elijah was a great reforming prophet who challenged the northern kingdom of Israel to repent. See his Profile in 1 Kings 18 for more information.

11:2 God chose the Jews ("His people whom He foreknew") to be the people through whom the rest of the world could find salvation. But this did not mean the entire Jewish nation would be saved; only those who were faithful to God (the remnant) were considered true Jews (11:5). We are saved through faith in Christ, not because we are part of a nation, religion, or family. On whom or on what are you depending for salvation?

11:6 Do you think it's easier for God to love you when you're good? Do you secretly suspect that God chose you because you deserved it? Do you think some people's behavior is so bad that God couldn't possibly save them? If you ever think this way, you don't entirely understand that salvation is by grace, a free gift. It cannot be earned, in whole or in part; it can only be accepted with thankfulness and praise.

11:7 "The rest were hardened" was God's punishment for their sin. It was a confirmation of their own stubbornness. In judging them, God removed their ability to see and hear, and to repent; thus they would experience the consequences of their rebellion.

11:8–10 These verses describe the punishment for hardened hearts predicted by the prophet Isaiah (Isaiah 6:9–13). If people refuse to hear God's Good News, they eventually will be unable to understand it. Paul saw this happening in the Jewish congregations he visited on his missionary journeys. (Verse 8 is based on Deuteronomy 29:4 and Isaiah 29:10. Verses 9 and 10 are from Psalm 69:22–23.)

11:11ff Paul had a vision of a church where all Jews and Gentiles would be united in their love of God and in obedience to Christ. While respecting God's law, this ideal church would look to Christ alone for salvation. A person's ethnic background and social status would be irrelevant (see Galatians 3:28)—what mattered would be his or her faith in Christ.

But Paul's vision has not yet been realized. Many Jewish people rejected the gospel. They depended on their heritage for salvation, and they did not have the heart of obedience that was so important to the Old Testament prophets and to Paul. Once Gentiles became dominant in many of the Christian churches, they began rejecting Jews and even persecuting them. Unfortunately, this practice has recurred through the centuries.

True Christians should not persecute others. Both Gentiles and Jews have done so much to damage the cause of the God they claim to serve that Paul's vision often seems impossible to fulfill. Yet God chose the Jews, just as he chose the Gentiles, and he is still working to unite Jew and Gentile in a new Israel, a new Jerusalem, ruled by his Son (see Ephesians 2:11–22).

11:13–15 Paul was appointed as a missionary to the Gentiles. He reminded his Jewish brothers of this fact, hoping that they too would want to be saved. The Jews had been rejected, and thus Gentiles were being offered salvation. But when a Jew comes to Christ, there is great rejoicing, as if a dead person had come back to life.

11:16 Num 15:18f
11:17 Jer 11:16; John 15:2; Eph 2:11ff
11:18 John 4:22
11:20 Rom 5:2; 1 Cor 10:12; 2 Cor 1:24; Rom 12:16; 1 Tim 6:17; 1 Pet 1:17
11:22 Rom 2:4; 1 Cor 15:2; Heb 3:6, 14; John 15:2
11:23 2 Cor 3:16
11:25 Rom 1:13; Matt 13:11; Rom 16:25; 1 Cor 2:7-10; Eph 3:3-5, 9; Luke 21:24; John 10:16
11:26 Is 59:20
11:27 Is 59:21; Jer 31:33, 34; Heb 8:10
11:28 Rom 5:10; Rom 9:5
11:29 Rom 8:28; 1 Cor 1:26; Eph 1:18; 4:1, 4; Phil 3:14; 2 Thess 1:11; 2 Tim 1:9; Heb 3:1; 2 Pet 1:10
11:32 Rom 3:9; Gal 3:22f
11:33 Rom 2:4; Eph 3:8; Job 5:9; 11:7; 15:8

16 If the first piece *of dough* is holy, the lump is also; and if the root is holy, the branches
are too.
17 But if some of the branches were broken off, and you, being a wild olive, were grafted in among them and became partaker with them of the rich root of the olive tree,
18 do not be arrogant toward the branches; but if you are arrogant, *remember that* it is
not you who supports the root, but the root *supports* you.
19 You will say then, "Branches were broken off so that I might be grafted in."
20 Quite right, they were broken off for their unbelief, but you stand by your faith. Do
not be conceited, but fear;
21 for if God did not spare the natural branches, He will not spare you, either.
22 Behold then the kindness and severity of God; to those who fell, severity, but to
you, God's kindness, if you continue in His kindness; otherwise you also will be cut off.
23 And they also, if they do not continue in their unbelief, will be grafted in, for God is
able to graft them in again.
24 For if you were cut off from what is by nature a wild olive tree, and were grafted
contrary to nature into a cultivated olive tree, how much more will these who are the
natural *branches* be grafted into their own olive tree?
25 For I do not want you, brethren, to be uninformed of this mystery—so that you will
not be wise in your own estimation—that a partial hardening has happened to Israel until
the fullness of the Gentiles has come in;
26 and so all Israel will be saved; just as it is written,
"THE DELIVERER WILL COME FROM ZION,
HE WILL REMOVE UNGODLINESS FROM JACOB."
27 "THIS IS MY COVENANT WITH THEM,
WHEN I TAKE AWAY THEIR SINS."
28 From the standpoint of the gospel they are enemies for your sake, but from the standpoint of *God's* choice they are beloved for the sake of the fathers;
29 for the gifts and the calling of God are irrevocable.
30 For just as you once were disobedient to God, but now have been shown mercy
because of their disobedience,
31 so these also now have been disobedient, that because of the mercy shown to you
they also may now be shown mercy.
32 For God has shut up all in disobedience so that He may show mercy to all.
33 Oh, the depth of the riches both of the wisdom and knowledge of God! How unsearchable are His judgments and unfathomable His ways!

11:17–24 Speaking to Gentile Christians, Paul warns them not to feel superior because God rejected some Jews. Abraham's faith is like the root of a productive tree, and the Jewish people are the tree's natural branches. Because of faithlessness, the Jews were the broken branches. Gentile believers have been grafted into the tree like a wild olive shoot. Both Jews and Gentiles share the tree's nourishment based on faith in God; neither can rest on heritage or culture for salvation.

11:22 "Continue in His kindness" refers to steadfast perseverance in faith. Steadfastness is a proof of the reality of faith and a by-product of salvation, not a means to it.

11:26 Some say the phrase "And so all Israel will be saved" means that the majority of Jews in the final generation before Christ's return will turn to Christ for salvation. Others say that Paul is using the term *Israel* for the "spiritual" nation of Israel made up of everyone—Jew and Gentile—who has received salvation through faith in Christ. Thus *all Israel* (or all believers) will receive God's promised gift of salvation. Still others say that *all Israel* means Israel as a whole will have a role in Christ's kingdom. Their identity as a people won't be discarded. God chose the nation of Israel, and he has never rejected it. He also chose the church, through Jesus Christ, and he will never reject it either. This does not mean, of course, that all Jews or all church members will be saved. It is possible to belong to a nation or to an organization without ever responding in faith. But just because some people have rejected Christ does not mean that God stops working with either Israel or the church. He continues to offer salvation freely to all. Still others say that the phrase "and so" means "in this way" or "this is how," referring to the necessity of faith in Christ.

11:28–32 In this passage Paul shows how the Jews and the Gentiles benefit each other. Whenever God shows mercy to one group, the other shares the blessing. In God's original plan, the Jews would be the source of God's blessing to the Gentiles (see Genesis 12:3). When the Jews neglected this mission, God blessed the Gentiles anyway through the Jewish Messiah. He still maintained his love for the Jews because of his promises to Abraham, Isaac, and Jacob ("for the sake of the fathers"). But someday the faithful Jews will share in God's mercy. God's plans will not be thwarted: He will "show mercy to all." For a beautiful picture of Jews and Gentiles experiencing rich blessings, see Isaiah 60.

11:29 The privileges and invitation of God given to Israel can never be withdrawn.

11:33 This doxology is a prayer of praise to God for the wisdom of his plan. Although God's method and means are beyond our comprehension, God himself is not arbitrary. He governs the universe and our lives in perfect wisdom, justice, and love.

34 For WHO HAS KNOWN THE MIND OF THE LORD, OR WHO BECAME HIS COUN-
SELOR?
35 Or WHO HAS FIRST GIVEN TO HIM THAT IT MIGHT BE PAID BACK TO HIM AGAIN?
36 For from Him and through Him and to Him are all things. To Him *be* the glory forever. Amen.

B. HOW TO BEHAVE (12:1—16:27)

Moving from the theological to the practical, Paul gives guidelines for living as a redeemed people in a fallen world. We are to give ourselves to Christ as living sacrifices, obey the government, love our neighbors, and take special care of those who are weak in the faith. He closes with personal remarks. Throughout this section, we learn how to live our faith each day.

1. Personal responsibility

Dedicated Service

12 Therefore I urge you, brethren, by the mercies of God, to present your bodies a
living and holy sacrifice, acceptable to God, *which is* your spiritual service of worship.
2 And do not be conformed to this world, but be transformed by the renewing of your
mind, so that you may prove what the will of God is, that which is good and acceptable
and perfect.
3 For through the grace given to me I say to everyone among you not to think more
highly of himself than he ought to think; but to think so as to have sound judgment, as
God has allotted to each a measure of faith.
4 For just as we have many members in one body and all the members do not have
the same function,
5 so we, who are many, are one body in Christ, and individually members one of another.

11:34 Is 40:13f; 1 Cor 2:16

11:35 Job 35:7; 41:11

11:36 1 Cor 8:6; 11:12; Col 1:16; Heb 2:10; Rom 16:27; Eph 3:21; Phil 4:20; 1 Tim 1:17; 2 Tim 4:18; 1 Pet 4:11; 5:11; 2 Pet 3:18

12:1 1 Cor 1:10; 2 Cor 10:1-4; Eph 4:1; 1 Pet 2:11; Rom 6:13, 16, 19; 1 Cor 6:20; Heb 13:15

12:2 1 Pet 1:14; Matt 13:22; Gal 1:4; 1 John 2:15; Eph 4:23; Titus 3:5; Eph 5:10, 17; Col 1:9

12:3 1 Cor 3:10; 15:10; Gal 2:9; Eph 3:7f; 1 Cor 7:17; 2 Cor 10:13; Eph 4:7; 1 Pet 4:11

12:4 1 Cor 12:12-14; Eph 4:4, 16

12:5 1 Cor 10:17, 33; 1 Cor 12:20, 27; Eph 4:12, 25

11:34–35 The implication of these questions is that no one has fully understood the mind of the Lord. No one has been his counselor. And God owes nothing to any one of us. Isaiah and Jeremiah asked similar questions to show that we are unable to give advice to God or criticize his ways (Isaiah 40:13; Jeremiah 23:18). God alone is the possessor of absolute power and absolute wisdom.

11:36 In the final analysis, all of us are absolutely dependent on God. He is the source of all things, including ourselves. He is the power that sustains and rules the world that we live in. And God works out all things to bring glory to himself. The all-powerful God deserves our praise.

12:1 When sacrificing an animal according to God's law, a priest would kill the animal, cut it in pieces, and place it on the altar. Sacrifice was important, but even in the Old Testament God made it clear that obedience from the heart was much more important (see 1 Samuel 15:22; Psalm 40:6; Amos 5:21–24). God wants us to offer ourselves, not animals, as *living* sacrifices—daily laying aside our own desires to follow him, putting all our energy and resources at his disposal and trusting him to guide us. We do this out of gratitude that our sins have been forgiven.

12:1–2 God has good, acceptable, and perfect plans for his children. He wants us to be transformed people with renewed minds, living to honor and obey him. Because he wants only what is best for us, and because he gave his Son to make our new lives possible, we should joyfully give ourselves as living sacrifices for his service.

12:2 Christians are called to "not be conformed to this world," with its behavior and customs that are usually selfish and often corrupting. Many Christians wisely decide that much worldly behavior is off limits for them. Our refusal to conform to this world's values, however, must go even deeper than the level of behavior and customs—it must be firmly planted in our minds—"be transformed by the renewing of your mind." It is possible to avoid most worldly customs and still be proud, covetous, selfish, stubborn, and arrogant. Only when the Holy Spirit renews, reeducates, and redirects our minds are we truly transformed (see 8:5).

12:3 Healthy self-esteem is important because some of us think too little of ourselves; on the other hand, some of us overestimate ourselves. The key to an honest and accurate evaluation is knowing the basis of our self-worth—our identity in Christ. Apart from him, we aren't capable of very much by eternal standards; in him, we are valuable and capable of worthy service. Evaluating yourself by the worldly standards of success and achievement can cause you to think too much about your worth in the eyes of others and thus miss your true value in God's eyes.

12:4–5 Paul uses the concept of the human body to teach how Christians should live and work together. Just as the parts of the body function under the direction of the brain, so Christians are to work together under the command and authority of Jesus Christ (see 1 Corinthians 12:12–31; Ephesians 4:1–16).

12:4–8 God gives us gifts so we can build up his church. To use them effectively, we must (1) realize that all gifts and abilities come from God; (2) understand that not everyone has the same gifts; (3) know who we are and what we do best; (4) dedicate our gifts to God's service and not to our personal success; (5) be willing to utilize our gifts wholeheartedly, not holding back anything from God's service.

12:6 1 Cor 7:7; 12:4; 1 Pet 4:10; Acts 13:1

12:7 Acts 6:1; 13:1; 1 Cor 12:28; 14:26

12:9 2 Cor 6:6; 1 Tim 1:5

12:10 John 13:34; Phil 2:3

12:12 Rom 5:2; Heb 10:32

12:13 Rom 15:25; 1 Cor 16:15; 2 Cor 9:1

12:14 Matt 5:44

12:16 1 Pet 3:8; Prov 3:7

12:17 Prov 20:22; 24:29

12:19 Deut 32:35

6 Since we have gifts that differ according to the grace given to us, *each of us is to*
exercise them accordingly: if prophecy, according to the proportion of his faith;
7 if service, in his serving; or he who teaches, in his teaching;
8 or he who exhorts, in his exhortation; he who gives, with [12]liberality; he who leads,
with diligence; he who shows mercy, with cheerfulness.
9 *Let* love *be* without hypocrisy. Abhor what is evil; cling to what is good.
10 *Be* devoted to one another in brotherly love; give preference to one another in
honor;
11 not lagging behind in diligence, fervent in spirit, serving the Lord;
12 rejoicing in hope, persevering in tribulation, devoted to prayer,
13 contributing to the needs of the saints, practicing hospitality.
14 Bless those who persecute [13]you; bless and do not curse.
15 Rejoice with those who rejoice, and weep with those who weep.
16 Be of the same mind toward one another; do not be haughty in mind, but associate
with the lowly. Do not be wise in your own estimation.
17 Never pay back evil for evil to anyone. Respect what is right in the sight of all men.
18 If possible, so far as it depends on you, be at peace with all men.
19 Never take your own revenge, beloved, but leave room for the wrath *of God,* for it
is written, "VENGEANCE IS MINE, I WILL REPAY," says the Lord.

12 Or *simplicity* **13** Two early mss do not contain *you*

12:6 God's gifts differ in nature, power, and effectiveness according to his wisdom and graciousness, not according to our faith. The "measure of faith" (12:3) or the "proportion to his faith" means that God will give spiritual power necessary and appropriate to carry out each responsibility. We cannot, by our own effort or willpower, drum up more faith and thus be more effective teachers or servants. These are God's gifts to his church, and he gives faith and power as he wills. Our role is to be faithful and to seek ways to serve others with what Christ has given us.

12:6 *Prophecy* in Scripture is not always predicting the future. Often it means preaching God's messages (1 Corinthians 14:1–3).

12:6–8 Look at this list of gifts and imagine the kinds of people who would have each gift. Prophets are often bold and articulate. Servers (those in ministry) are faithful and loyal. Teachers are clear thinkers. Encouragers (those who exhort) know how to motivate others. Givers are generous and trusting. Leaders are good organizers and managers. Those who show mercy are caring people who are happy to give their time to others. It would be difficult for one person to embody all these gifts. An assertive prophet would not usually make a good counselor, and a generous giver might fail as a leader. When you identify your own gifts (and this list is far from complete), ask how you can use them to build up God's family. At the same time, realize that your gifts can't do the work of the church all alone. Be thankful for people whose gifts are completely different from yours. Let your strengths balance their weaknesses, and be grateful that their abilities make up for your deficiencies. Together you can build Christ's church.

12:9 Most of us have learned how to pretend to love others—how to speak kindly, avoid hurting their feelings, and appear to take an interest in them. We may even be skilled in pretending to feel moved with compassion when we hear of others' needs, or to become indignant when we learn of injustice. But God calls us to real and sincere love that goes far beyond pretense and politeness. Sincere love requires concentration and effort. It means helping others become better people. It demands our time, money, and personal involvement. No individual has the capacity to express love to a whole community, but the body of Christ in your town does. Look for people who need your love, and look for ways you and your fellow believers can love your community for Christ.

12:10 We can honor others in one of two ways. One involves ulterior motives. We honor our bosses so they will reward us, our employees so they will work harder, the wealthy so they will contribute to our cause, the powerful so they will use their power for us and not against us. God's other way involves love. As Christians, we honor people because they have been created in God's image, because they are our brothers and sisters in Christ, and because they have a unique contribution to make to Christ's church. Does God's way of honoring others sound too difficult for your competitive nature? Why not try to outdo one another in showing honor? Put others first!

12:13 Christian hospitality differs from social entertaining. Entertaining focuses on the host—the home must be spotless; the food must be well prepared and abundant; the host must appear relaxed and good-natured. Hospitality, by contrast, focuses on the guests. Their needs—whether for a place to stay, nourishing food, a listening ear, or acceptance—are the primary concern. Hospitality can happen in a messy home. It can happen around a dinner table where the main dish is canned soup. It can even happen while the host and the guest are doing chores together. Don't hesitate to offer hospitality just because you are too tired, too busy, or not wealthy enough to entertain.

12:17–21 These verses summarize the core of Christian living. If we love someone the way Christ loves us, we will be willing to forgive. If we have experienced God's grace, we will want to pass it on to others. And remember, grace is *undeserved* favor. By giving an enemy a drink, we're not excusing his misdeeds. We're recognizing him, forgiving him, and loving him in spite of his sins—just as Christ did for us.

12:19–21 In this day of constant lawsuits and incessant demands for legal rights, Paul's command sounds almost impossible. When someone hurts you deeply, instead of giving him what he deserves, Paul says to befriend him. Why does Paul tell us to forgive our enemies? (1) Forgiveness may break a cycle of retaliation and lead to mutual reconciliation. (2) It may make the enemy feel ashamed and change his or her ways. (3) By contrast, repaying evil for evil hurts you just as much as it hurts your enemy. Even if your enemy never repents, forgiving him or her will free you of a heavy load of bitterness.

12:19–21 Forgiveness involves both attitudes and actions. If you find it difficult to *feel* forgiving toward someone who has hurt you, try responding with kind actions. If appropriate, tell this person that you would like to heal your relationship. Lend a helping hand. Send him or her a gift. Smile at him or her. Many times you will discover that right actions lead to right feelings.

20"BUT IF YOUR ENEMY IS HUNGRY, FEED HIM, AND IF HE IS THIRSTY, GIVE HIM A
DRINK; FOR IN SO DOING YOU WILL HEAP BURNING COALS ON HIS HEAD."
21 Do not be overcome by evil, but overcome evil with good.

Be Subject to Government

13 Every person is to be in subjection to the governing authorities. For there is no
authority except from God, and those which exist are established by God.
2 Therefore whoever resists authority has opposed the ordinance of God; and they
who have opposed will receive condemnation upon themselves.
3 For rulers are not a cause of fear for good behavior, but for evil. Do you want to
have no fear of authority? Do what is good and you will have praise from the same;
4 for it is a minister of God to you for good. But if you do what is evil, be afraid; for it
does not bear the sword for nothing; for it is a minister of God, an avenger who brings
wrath on the one who practices evil.
5 Therefore it is necessary to be in subjection, not only because of wrath, but also for
conscience' sake.
6 For because of this you also pay taxes, for *rulers* are servants of God, devoting themselves to this very thing.
7 Render to all what is due them: tax to whom tax *is due;* custom to whom custom;
fear to whom fear; honor to whom honor.
8 Owe nothing to anyone except to love one another; for he who loves his neighbor
has fulfilled *the* law.
9 For this, "YOU SHALL NOT COMMIT ADULTERY, YOU SHALL NOT MURDER, YOU
SHALL NOT STEAL, YOU SHALL NOT COVET," and if there is any other commandment, it
is summed up in this saying, "YOU SHALL LOVE YOUR NEIGHBOR AS YOURSELF."
10 Love does no wrong to a neighbor; therefore love is the fulfillment of *the* law.

12:20 2 Kin 6:22; Prov 25:21f; Matt 5:44; Luke 6:27

13:1 Acts 2:41; Titus 3:1; 1 Pet 2:13f; Dan 2:21; 4:17; John 19:11

13:3 1 Pet 2:14

13:4 1 Thess 4:6

13:5 Eccl 8; 1 Pet 2:13, 19

13:7 Matt 22:21; Mark 12:17; Luke 20:25; Luke 20:22; 23:2; Matt 17:25

13:8 Matt 7:12; 22:39f; John 13:34; Rom 13:10; Gal 5:14; James 2:8

13:9 Ex 20:13ff; Deut 5:17ff; Lev 19:18; Matt 19:19

13:10 Matt 7:12; 22:39f; John 13:34; Rom 13:8; Gal 5:14; James 2:8

12:20 What does it mean to "heap burning coals" on someone's head? This may refer to an Egyptian tradition of carrying a pan of burning charcoal on one's head as a public act of repentance. By referring to this proverb, Paul was saying that we should treat our enemies with kindness so that they will become ashamed and turn from their sins. The best way to get rid of enemies is to turn them into friends.

13:1 Are there times when we should not submit to the government? We should never allow government to force us to disobey God. Jesus and his apostles never disobeyed the government for personal reasons; when they disobeyed, it was in order to follow their higher loyalty to God. Their disobedience was not cheap: They were threatened, beaten, thrown into jail, tortured, and executed for their convictions. Like them, if we are compelled to disobey, we must be ready to accept the consequences.

13:1ff Christians understand Romans 13 in different ways. All Christians agree that we are to live at peace with the state as long as the state allows us to live by our religious convictions. For hundreds of years, however, there have been at least three interpretations of how we are to do this.

(1) Some Christians believe that the state is so corrupt that Christians should have as little to do with it as possible. Although they should be good citizens as long as they can do so without compromising their beliefs, they should not work for the government, vote in elections, or serve in the military.

(2) Others believe that God has given the state authority in certain areas and the church authority in others. Christians can be loyal to both and can work for either. They should not, however, confuse the two. In this view, church and state are concerned with two totally different spheres—the spiritual and the physical—and thus complement each other but do not work together.

(3) Still others believe that Christians have a responsibility to make the state better. They can do this politically, by electing Christian or other high-principled leaders. They can also do this morally, by serving as an influence for good in society. In this view, church and state ideally work together for the good of all.

None of these views advocate rebelling against or refusing to obey the government's laws or regulations unless those laws clearly require you to violate the moral standards revealed by God. Wherever we find ourselves, we must be responsible citizens, as well as responsible Christians.

13:3–4 When civil rulers are unjust, upright people are afraid. In these verses, Paul is talking about officials who are doing their duty. When these officials are just, people who are doing right have nothing to fear.

13:8 Why is love for others considered something that is owed? We are permanently in debt to Christ for the lavish love he has poured out on us. The only way we can even begin to repay this debt is by loving others in turn. Because Christ's love will always be infinitely greater than ours, we will always have the obligation to love our neighbors.

13:9 Somehow many of us have gotten the idea that self-love is wrong. But if this were the case, it would be pointless to love our neighbors as ourselves. But Paul explains what he means by self-love. Even if you have low self-esteem, you probably don't willingly let yourself go hungry. You clothe yourself reasonably well. You make sure there's a roof over your head if you can. You try not to let yourself be cheated or injured. And you get angry if someone tries to ruin your marriage. This is the kind of love we need to have for our neighbors. Do we see that others are fed, clothed, and housed as well as they can be? Are we concerned about issues of social justice? Loving others as ourselves means to be actively working to see that their needs are met. Interestingly, people who focus on others rather than on themselves rarely suffer from low self-esteem.

13:10 Christians must obey the law of love, which supersedes both religious and civil laws. How easy it is to excuse our indifference to others merely because we have no legal obligation to help them, and even to justify harming them if our actions are technically legal! But Jesus does not leave loopholes in the law of love. Whenever love demands it, we are to go beyond human legal requirements and imitate the God of love. See James 2:8–9; 4:11 and 1 Peter 2:16–17 for more about this law of love.

13:11 James 5:8; 1 Pet 4:7; 2 Pet 3:9, 11; 1 John 2:18; Rev 1:3; 22:10; Mark 13:37; 1 Cor 15:34

13:12 Heb 10:25; 1 John 2:8; Eph 6:11, 13; 1 Thess 5:8

13:13 1 Thess 4:12; Luke 21:34; Gal 5:21; Eph 5:18; 1 Pet 4:3

13:14 Col 3:10, 12; Gal 5:16; 1 Pet 2:11

14:1 Acts 28:2; 1 Cor 8:9ff; 9:22

14:2 1 Cor 8:9ff; 9:22

14:3 Col 2:16; Acts 28:2

14:4 James 4:12

14:5 Gal 4:10; Luke 1:1

14:6 1 Cor 10:30; 1 Tim 4:3f

11 *Do* this, knowing the time, that it is already the hour for you to awaken from sleep; for now [14]salvation is nearer to us than when we believed.
12 The night is almost gone, and the day is near. Therefore let us lay aside the deeds of darkness and put on the armor of light.
13 Let us behave properly as in the day, not in carousing and drunkenness, not in sexual promiscuity and sensuality, not in strife and jealousy.
14 But put on the Lord Jesus Christ, and make no provision for the flesh in regard to *its* lusts.

Principles of Conscience

14 Now accept the one who is weak in faith, *but* not for *the purpose of* passing judgment on his opinions.
2 One person has faith that he may eat all things, but he who is weak eats vegetables *only.*
3 The one who eats is not to regard with contempt the one who does not eat, and the one who does not eat is not to judge the one who eats, for God has accepted him.
4 Who are you to judge the servant of another? To his own master he stands or falls; and he will stand, for the Lord is able to make him stand.
5 One person regards one day above another, another regards every day *alike.* Each person must be fully convinced in his own mind.
6 He who observes the day, observes it for the Lord, and he who eats, does so for the Lord, for he gives thanks to God; and he who eats not, for the Lord he does not eat, and gives thanks to God.
7 For not one of us lives for himself, and not one dies for himself;

14 Or *our salvation is nearer than when*

13:12–14 The *night* refers to the present evil time. The *day* refers to the time of Christ's return. Some people are surprised that Paul lists strife and jealousy with the gross and obvious sins of carousing, drunkenness, and sexual promiscuity. Like Jesus in his Sermon on the Mount (Matthew 5—7), Paul considers attitudes as important as actions. Just as hatred leads to murder, so jealousy leads to strife and lust to adultery. When Christ returns, he wants to find his people clean on the inside as well as on the outside.

13:14 How do we put on the Lord Jesus Christ? First we identify with Christ by being baptized (Galatians 3:27). This shows our solidarity with other Christians and with the death, burial, and resurrection of Jesus Christ. Second, we exemplify the qualities Jesus showed while he was here on earth (love, humility, truth, service). In a sense, we role-play what Jesus would do in our situation (see Ephesians 4:24–32; Colossians 3:10–17). We also must not give our desires any opportunity to lead us into sin. Avoid those situations that open the door to gratifying sinful desires.

14:1 Who is weak in faith and who is strong? We are all weak in some areas and strong in others. Our faith is strong in an area if we can survive contact with sinners without falling into their patterns. It is weak in an area if we must avoid certain activities, people, or places in order to protect our spiritual life. It is important to take a self-inventory in order to find out our strengths and weaknesses. Whenever in doubt, we should ask, "Can I do that without sinning? Can I influence others for good, rather than being influenced by them?"

In areas of strength, we should not fear being defiled by the world; rather we should go and serve God. In areas of weakness, we need to be cautious. If we have a strong faith but shelter it, we are not doing Christ's work in the world. If we have a weak faith but expose it, we are being extremely foolish.

14:1 This verse assumes there will be differences of opinion in the church (disputable matters). Paul says we are not to quarrel about issues that are matters of opinion. Differences should not be feared or avoided, but accepted and handled with love. Don't expect everyone, even in the best possible church, to agree on every subject. Through sharing ideas we can come to a fuller understanding of what the Bible teaches. Accept, listen to, and respect others. Differences of opinion need not cause division. They can be a source of learning and richness in our relationships.

14:1ff What is weak faith? Paul is speaking about immature faith that has not yet developed the muscle it needs to stand against external pressures. For example, if a person who once worshiped idols were to become a Christian, he might understand perfectly well that Christ saved him through faith and that idols have no real power. Still, because of his past associations, he might be badly shaken if he knowingly ate meat that had been used in idol worship as part of a pagan ritual. If a person who once worshiped God on the required Jewish holy days were to become a Christian, he might well know that Christ saved him through faith, not through his keeping of the law. Still, when the feast days came, he might feel empty and unfaithful if he didn't dedicate those days to God.

Paul responds to both weak brothers in love. Both are acting according to their consciences, but their honest scruples do not need to be made into rules for the church. Certainly some issues are central to the faith and worth fighting for—but many are based on individual differences and should not be legislated. Our principle should be: in essentials, unity; in nonessentials, liberty; in everything, love.

14:2 Eating "all things" may refer to freedom from dietary restrictions, or it may refer to eating meat offered to idols, while the person weaker in the faith eats only vegetables and refuses to eat meat that has been offered to idols. But how would Christians end up eating meat that had been offered to idols? The ancient system of sacrifice was at the center of the religious, social, and domestic life of the Roman world. After a sacrifice was presented to a god in a pagan temple, only part of it was burned. The remainder was often sent to the market to be sold. Thus a Christian might easily—even unknowingly—buy such meat in the marketplace or eat it at the home of a friend. Should a Christian question the source of his meat? Some thought there was nothing wrong with eating meat that had been offered to idols because idols were worthless and phony. Others carefully checked the source of their meat or gave up meat altogether, in order to avoid a guilty conscience. The problem was especially acute for Christians who had once been idol worshipers. For them, such a strong reminder of their pagan days might weaken their newfound faith. Paul also deals with this problem in 1 Corinthians 8.

8 for if we live, we live for the Lord, or if we die, we die for the Lord; therefore whether
we live or die, we are the Lord's.
9 For to this end Christ died and lived again, that He might be Lord both of the dead
and of the living.
10 But you, why do you judge your brother? Or you again, why do you regard your
brother with contempt? For we will all stand before the judgment seat of God.
11 For it is written,

"AS I LIVE, SAYS THE LORD, EVERY KNEE SHALL BOW TO ME,
AND EVERY TONGUE SHALL GIVE PRAISE TO GOD."

12 So then each one of us will give an account of himself to God.
13 Therefore let us not judge one another anymore, but rather determine this—not to
put an obstacle or a stumbling block in a brother's way.
14 I know and am convinced in the Lord Jesus that nothing is unclean in itself; but to
him who thinks anything to be unclean, to him it is unclean.
15 For if because of food your brother is hurt, you are no longer walking according to
love. Do not destroy with your food him for whom Christ died.
16 Therefore do not let what is for you a good thing be spoken of as evil;
17 for the kingdom of God is not eating and drinking, but righteousness and peace and
joy in the Holy Spirit.
18 For he who in this *way* serves Christ is acceptable to God and approved by men.
19 So then [15]we pursue the things which make for peace and the building up of one
another.
20 Do not tear down the work of God for the sake of food. All things indeed are clean,
but they are evil for the man who eats and gives offense.
21 It is good not to eat meat or to drink wine, or *to do anything* by which your brother
stumbles.
22 The faith which you have, have as your own conviction before God. Happy is he
who does not condemn himself in what he approves.
23 But he who doubts is condemned if he eats, because *his eating is* not from faith; and
whatever is not from faith is sin.

Self-denial on Behalf of Others

15 Now we who are strong ought to bear the weaknesses of those without strength
and not *just* please ourselves.
2 Each of us is to please his neighbor for his good, to his edification.

15 Later mss read *let us pursue*

14:8 Luke 20:38; Phil 1:20; 1 Thess 5:10
14:9 Rev 1:18; 2:8; Matt 28:18; 1 Thess 5:10
14:10 Luke 18:9
14:11 Is 45:23; Phil 2:10f
14:12 Matt 12:36; 16:27
14:13 Matt 7:1; 1 Cor 8:13
14:14 Acts 10:15
14:15 Eph 5:2; 1 Cor 8:11
14:16 1 Cor 10:30
14:17 Gal 5:22
14:18 Rom 16:18; 2 Cor 8:21; Phil 4:8; 1 Pet 2:12
14:19 Ps 34:14; Rom 12:18; 1 Cor 7:15; 2 Tim 2:22; Heb 12:14; Rom 15:2
14:20 Acts 10:15; 1 Cor 8:9-12
14:21 1 Cor 8:13
15:1 1 Thess 5:14
15:2 1 Cor 9:22; 10:23; 14:3f, 26; 2 Cor 12:19; Eph 4:12, 29

14:10–12 Each person is accountable to Christ, not to others. While the church must be uncompromising in its stand against activities that are expressly forbidden by Scripture (adultery, homosexuality, murder, theft), it should not create additional rules and regulations and give them equal standing with God's law. Many times Christians base their moral judgments on opinion, personal dislikes, or cultural bias rather than on the Word of God. When they do this, they show that their own faith is weak—they do not think that God is powerful enough to guide his children. When we stand before God's court of justice ("judgment seat"), we won't be worried about what our Christian neighbor has done (see 2 Corinthians 5:10).

14:13 Both strong and weak Christians can cause their brothers and sisters to stumble. The strong but insensitive Christian may flaunt his or her freedom and intentionally offend others' consciences. The scrupulous but weak Christian may try to fence others in with petty rules and regulations, thus causing dissension. Paul wants his readers to be both strong in the faith and sensitive to others' needs. Because we are all strong in some areas and weak in others, we need constantly to monitor the effects of our behavior on others.

14:13ff Some Christians use an invisible weaker brother to support their own opinions, prejudices, or standards. "You must live by these standards," they say, "or you will be offending the weaker brother." In truth, the person would often be offending no one but the speaker. While Paul urges us to be sensitive to those whose faith may be harmed by our actions, we should not sacrifice our liberty in Christ just to satisfy the selfish motives of those who are trying to force their opinions on us. Neither fear them nor criticize them, but follow Christ as closely as you can.

14:14 At the Jerusalem council (Acts 15), the Jewish church in Jerusalem asked the Gentile church in Antioch not to eat meat that had been sacrificed to idols. Paul was at the Jerusalem council, and he accepted this request not because he felt that eating such meat was wrong in itself, but because this practice would deeply offend many Jewish believers. Paul did not think the issue was worth dividing the church over; his desire was to promote unity.

14:20–21 Sin is not just a private matter. Everything we do affects others, and we have to think of them constantly. God created us to be interdependent, not independent. We who are strong in our faith must, without pride or condescension, treat others with love, patience, and self-restraint.

14:23 We try to steer clear of actions forbidden by Scripture, of course, but sometimes Scripture is silent. Then we should follow our consciences. "Whatever is not from faith is sin" means that to go against a conviction will leave a person with a guilty or uneasy conscience. When God shows us that something is wrong for us, we should avoid it. But we should not look down on other Christians who exercise their freedom in those areas.

15:2 If we merely set out to please our neighbors, we will be people-pleasers. Paul was opposed to that (see Galatians 1:10). But we are to set aside willfulness and self-pleasing actions for the

3 For even Christ did not please Himself; but as it is written, "THE REPROACHES OF
THOSE WHO REPROACHED YOU FELL ON ME."
4 For whatever was written in earlier times was written for our instruction, so that
through perseverance and the encouragement of the Scriptures we might have hope.
5 Now may the God who gives perseverance and encouragement grant you to be of
the same mind with one another according to Christ Jesus,
6 so that with one accord you may with one voice glorify the God and Father of our
Lord Jesus Christ.
7 Therefore, accept one another, just as Christ also accepted us to the glory of God.
8 For I say that Christ has become a servant to the circumcision on behalf of the truth
of God to confirm the promises *given* to the fathers,
9 and for the Gentiles to glorify God for His mercy; as it is written,
"THEREFORE I WILL GIVE PRAISE TO YOU AMONG THE GENTILES,
AND I WILL SING TO YOUR NAME."
10 Again he says,
"REJOICE, O GENTILES, WITH HIS PEOPLE."
11 And again,
"PRAISE THE LORD ALL YOU GENTILES,
AND LET ALL THE PEOPLES PRAISE HIM."
12 Again Isaiah says,
"THERE SHALL COME THE ROOT OF JESSE,
AND HE WHO ARISES TO RULE OVER THE GENTILES,
IN HIM SHALL THE GENTILES HOPE."
13 Now may the God of hope fill you with all joy and peace in believing, so that you
will abound in hope by the power of the Holy Spirit.

2. Personal notes

14 And concerning you, my brethren, I myself also am convinced that you yourselves
are full of goodness, filled with all knowledge and able also to admonish one another.
15 But I have written very boldly to you on some points so as to remind you again,
because of the grace that was given me from God,
16 to be a minister of Christ Jesus to the Gentiles, ministering as a priest the gospel of
God, so that *my* offering of the Gentiles may become acceptable, sanctified by the Holy
Spirit.
17 Therefore in Christ Jesus I have found reason for boasting in things pertaining to
God.
18 For I will not presume to speak of anything except what Christ has accomplished
through me, resulting in the obedience of the Gentiles by word and deed,
19 in the power of signs and wonders, in the power of the Spirit; so that from Jerusalem and round about as far as Illyricum I have fully preached the gospel of Christ.
20 And thus I aspired to preach the gospel, not where Christ was *already* named, so
that I would not build on another man's foundation;
21 but as it is written,

15:3 2 Cor 8:9; Ps 69:9
15:4 Rom 4:23f; 2 Tim 3:16
15:5 2 Cor 1:3; Rom 12:16
15:6 Rev 1:6
15:8 Matt 15:24; Acts 3:26; Rom 4:16; 2 Cor 1:20
15:9 Rom 3:29; 11:30f; Matt 9:8; 2 Sam 22:50; Ps 18:49
15:10 Deut 32:43
15:11 Ps 117:1
15:12 Is 11:10; Rev 5:5
15:13 1 Thess 1:5
15:14 Eph 5:9; 2 Thess 1:11; 1 Cor 1:5; 8:1
15:15 Rom 12:3
15:16 Acts 9:15; Rom 11:13; 12:1; Eph 5:2; Phil 2:17
15:17 Phil 3:3; Heb 2:17; 5:1
15:18 Acts 15:12; 21:19; Rom 1:5; 2 Cor 3:5
15:19 John 4:48; Rom 15:13; 1 Cor 2:4; 1 Thess 1:5; Acts 22:17-21; Acts 20:1f
15:20 Rom 1:15; 10:15; 15:16; 1 Cor 3:10; 2 Cor 10:15f
15:21 Is 52:15

---

sake of building others up for good. Our Christian convictions must not be a disguise for coldhearted treatment of our brothers and sisters.

15:4 The knowledge of the Scriptures affects our attitude toward the present and the future. The more we know about what God has done in years past, the greater the confidence we have about what he will do in the days ahead. We should read our Bibles diligently to increase our trust that God's will is best for us.

15:5–7 To accept Jesus' lordship in all areas of life means to share his values and his perspective. Just as we take Jesus' view on the authority of Scripture, the nature of heaven, and the resurrection, we are to have his attitude of love toward other Christians as well (have "the same mind"). As we grow in faith and come to know Jesus better, we will become more capable of maintaining this attitude of loving unity throughout each day. Christ's attitude is explained in more detail in Philippians 2.

15:8 This verse means that Jesus came to bring the truth to the Jews and to show that God is true to his promises.

15:12 The *Root of Jesse* refers to Christ as the heir from the family line of Jesse, David's father (1 Samuel 16:1).

15:17 Paul did not glory in what he had done, but in what God had done through him. Being proud of God's work is not a sin—it is worship. If you are not sure whether your pride is selfish or holy, ask yourself this question: Are you just as proud of what God is doing through other people as of what he is doing through you?

15:19 Illyricum was a Roman territory on the Adriatic Sea between present-day Italy and Greece. See the map in chapter 1.

15:20–22 Paul wanted to visit the church at Rome, but he had delayed his visit because he had heard many good reports about the believers there and he knew they were doing well on their own. It was more important for him to preach in areas that had not yet heard the Good News.

“THEY WHO HAD NO NEWS OF HIM SHALL SEE,
AND THEY WHO HAVE NOT HEARD SHALL UNDERSTAND.”
22 For this reason I have often been prevented from coming to you;
23 but now, with no further place for me in these regions, and since I have had for many
years a longing to come to you
24 whenever I go to Spain—for I hope to see you in passing, and to be helped on my
way there by you, when I have first enjoyed your company for a while—
25 but now, I am going to Jerusalem serving the saints.
26 For Macedonia and Achaia have been pleased to make a contribution for the poor
among the saints in Jerusalem.
27 Yes, they were pleased *to do so,* and they are indebted to them. For if the Gentiles
have shared in their spiritual things, they are indebted to minister to them also in material things.
28 Therefore, when I have finished this, and have put my seal on this fruit of theirs, I
will go on by way of you to Spain.
29 I know that when I come to you, I will come in the fullness of the blessing of Christ.
30 Now I urge you, brethren, by our Lord Jesus Christ and by the love of the Spirit, to
strive together with me in your prayers to God for me,
31 that I may be rescued from those who are disobedient in Judea, and *that* my service
for Jerusalem may prove acceptable to the saints;
32 so that I may come to you in joy by the will of God and find *refreshing* rest in your
company.
33 Now the God of peace be with you all. Amen.

Greetings and Love Expressed

16 I commend to you our sister Phoebe, who is a servant of the church which is at
Cenchrea;
2 that you receive her in the Lord in a manner worthy of the saints, and that you help
her in whatever matter she may have need of you; for she herself has also been a helper
of many, and of myself as well.
3 Greet Prisca and Aquila, my fellow workers in Christ Jesus,
4 who for my life risked their own necks, to whom not only do I give thanks, but also
all the churches of the Gentiles;
5 also *greet* the church that is in their house. Greet Epaenetus, my beloved, who is the
first convert to Christ from Asia.

15:22 Rom 1:13; 1 Thess 2:18
15:24 Rom 15:28; Acts 15:3; Rom 1:12
15:25 Acts 19:21
15:26 Acts 16:9; 1 Cor 16:5; 2 Cor 1:16; 2:13; 7:5; 8:1; 9:2, 4; 11:9; Phil 4:15; 1 Thess 1:7f; 4:10; 1 Tim 1:3; Acts 18:12; 19:21
15:27 1 Cor 9:11
15:28 John 3:33
15:30 Gal 5:22; Col 1:8; 2 Cor 1:11; Col 4:12
15:31 2 Cor 1:10; 2 Thess 3:2; 2 Tim 3:11; 4:17; 2 Cor 8:4; 9:1; Acts 9:13, 15
15:32 Rom 15:23; Acts 18:21; Rom 1:10
16:1 2 Cor 3:1; Acts 18:18
16:2 Phil 2:29; Acts 9:13
16:3 Acts 18:2; Rom 8:1ff; 16:7, 9, 10; 2 Cor 5:17; 12:2
16:5 1 Cor 16:19; Col 4:15; Philem 2; 1 Cor 16:15; Acts 16:6

15:23–24 Paul was referring to the completion of his work in Corinth, the city from which he most likely wrote this letter. Most of Paul's three-month stay in Achaia (see Acts 20:3) was probably spent in Corinth. He believed that he had accomplished what God wanted him to do there, and he was looking forward to taking the gospel to new lands west of Rome. When Paul eventually went to Rome, however, it was as a prisoner (see Acts 28). Tradition says that Paul was released for a time, and that he used this opportunity to go to Spain to preach the Good News. This journey is not mentioned in the book of Acts.

15:27 If the Gentiles had received the gospel ("spiritual things") originally from Jerusalem, surely they would want to offer financial help ("material things").

15:28 Paul's future plan was to go to Spain because Spain was at the very western end of the civilized world. He wanted to extend Christianity there. Also, Spain had many great minds and influential leaders in the Roman world (Lucan, Martial, Hadrian), and perhaps Paul thought Christianity would advance greatly in such an atmosphere.

15:30 Too often we view prayer as a time for comfort, reflection, or making our requests known to God. But here Paul urges believers to join in his struggle by means of prayer. Prayer is also a weapon in all believers' armor as we intercede for others who join in the fight against Satan. Do your prayers reflect that urgency?

15:33 This phrase sounds like it should signal the end of the book, and it does pronounce the end of Paul's teaching. He concludes his letter, then, with personal greetings and remarks.

16:1–2 Phoebe was known as a servant (the Greek word used here is often translated "deaconess") and a helper. Apparently she was a wealthy person who helped support Paul's ministry. Phoebe was highly regarded in the church, and she may have delivered this letter from Corinth to Rome. This provides evidence that women had important roles in the early church. Cenchrea, the town where Phoebe lived, was the eastern port of Corinth, six miles from the city center.

16:3 Prisca (Priscilla) and Aquila were a married couple who had become Paul's close friends. They, along with all other Jews, had been expelled from Rome by the emperor (Acts 18:2–3) and had moved to Corinth. There they met Paul and invited him to live with them. They were Christians before they met Paul, and probably told him much about the Roman church. Like Paul, Priscilla and Aquila were missionaries. They helped believers in Ephesus (Acts 18:18–28), in Rome when they were allowed to return, and again at Ephesus (2 Timothy 4:19).

16:5ff Paul's personal greetings went to Romans and Greeks, Jews and Gentiles, men and women, prisoners and prominent citizens. The church's base was broad: It crossed cultural, social, and economic lines. From this list we learn that the Christian community was mobile. Though Paul had not yet been to Rome, he had met these people in other places on his journeys.

16:7
Rom 9:3; 16:11, 21; Col 4:10; Philem 23

16:9
Rom 8:1ff; 16:3, 7, 10; 2 Cor 5:17; 12:2; Gal 1:22

16:13
Mark 15:21

16:16
1 Cor 16:20; 2 Cor 13:12; 1 Thess 5:26; 1 Pet 5:14

16:17
1 Tim 1:3; 6:3; Matt 7:15; Gal 1:8f; 2 Thess 3:6, 14; Titus 3:10; 2 John 10

16:18
Rom 14:18; Phil 3:19; Col 2:4; 2 Pet 2:3

16:20
Rom 15:33; Matt 4:10; 1 Cor 16:23; 2 Cor 13:14; Gal 6:18; Phil 4:23; 1 Thess 5:28; 2 Thess 3:18; Rev 22:21

16:21
Acts 16:1; [Acts 13:1]; [Acts 17:5]; [Acts 20:4]; Rom 9:3; 16:7, 11

16:22
1 Cor 16:21; Gal 6:11; Col 4:18; 2 Thess 3:17

16:23
[Acts 19:29; 20:4]; 1 Cor 1:14; Acts 19:22; 2 Tim 4:20

16:25
Eph 3:20; Jude 24; Col 1:26f; 2:2; 4:3; 1 Tim 3:16; 2 Tim 1:9; Titus 1:2

16:26
Rom 1:2; Rom 1:5

6 Greet Mary, who has worked hard for you.
7 Greet Andronicus and Junias, my kinsmen and my fellow prisoners, who are outstanding among the apostles, who also were in Christ before me.
8 Greet Ampliatus, my beloved in the Lord.
9 Greet Urbanus, our fellow worker in Christ, and Stachys my beloved.
10 Greet Apelles, the approved in Christ. Greet those who are of the *household* of
Aristobulus.
11 Greet Herodion, my kinsman. Greet those of the *household* of Narcissus, who are
in the Lord.
12 Greet Tryphaena and Tryphosa, workers in the Lord. Greet Persis the beloved, who
has worked hard in the Lord.
13 Greet Rufus, a choice man in the Lord, also his mother and mine.
14 Greet Asyncritus, Phlegon, Hermes, Patrobas, Hermas and the brethren with them.
15 Greet Philologus and Julia, Nereus and his sister, and Olympas, and all the saints
who are with them.
16 Greet one another with a holy kiss. All the churches of Christ greet you.
17 Now I urge you, brethren, keep your eye on those who cause dissensions and hindrances contrary to the teaching which you learned, and turn away from them.
18 For such men are slaves, not of our Lord Christ but of their own appetites; and by
their smooth and flattering speech they deceive the hearts of the unsuspecting.
19 For the report of your obedience has reached to all; therefore I am rejoicing over
you, but I want you to be wise in what is good and innocent in what is evil.
20 The God of peace will soon crush Satan under your feet.
The grace of our Lord Jesus be with you.
21 Timothy my fellow worker greets you, and *so do* Lucius and Jason and Sosipater,
my kinsmen.
22 I, Tertius, who write this letter, greet you in the Lord.
23 Gaius, host to me and to the whole church, greets you. Erastus, the city treasurer
greets you, and Quartus, the brother.
24 [[16]The grace of our Lord Jesus Christ be with you all. Amen.]
25 Now to Him who is able to establish you according to my gospel and the preaching
of Jesus Christ, according to the revelation of the mystery which has been kept secret for
long ages past,
26 but now is manifested, and by the Scriptures of the prophets, according to the commandment of the eternal God, has been made known to all the nations, *leading* to obedience of faith;
27 to the only wise God, through Jesus Christ, be the glory forever. Amen.

16 Early mss do not contain this v

16:7 The fact that Andronicus and Junias were "outstanding among the apostles" could mean they had distinguished themselves as apostles. They may have been a husband and wife team. Paul's references to them as relatives (see also 16:21) could mean that they were from the same tribe as Paul.

16:17–20 When we read books or listen to sermons, we should check the content of what is written or said and not be fooled by smooth style. Christians who study God's Word will not be fooled, even though superficial listeners may easily be taken in. For an example of believers who carefully checked God's Word, see Acts 17:10–12.

16:21 Timothy was a key person in the growth of the early church, traveling with Paul on his second missionary journey (Acts 16:1–3). Later Paul wrote two letters to him as he worked to strengthen the churches in Ephesus—1 and 2 Timothy. See his Profile in the book of 1 Timothy.

16:25–27 Paul exclaims that it is wonderful to be alive when the mystery, God's secret—his way of saving the Gentiles—is becoming known throughout the world! All the Old Testament prophecies were coming true, and God was using Paul as his instrument to tell this Good News.

16:25–27 As Jerusalem was the center of Jewish life, Rome was the world's political, religious, social, and economic center. There the major governmental decisions were made, and from there the gospel spread to the ends of the earth. The church in Rome was a cosmopolitan mixture of Jews, Gentiles, slaves, free people, men, women, Roman citizens, and world travelers; therefore, it had potential for both great influence and great conflict.

Paul had not yet been to Rome to meet all the Christians there, and, of course, he has not yet met us. We too live in a cosmopolitan setting with the entire world open to us. We also have the potential for both widespread influence and wrenching conflict. We should listen carefully to and apply Paul's teaching about unity, service, and love.

1 CORINTHIANS

VITAL STATISTICS

PURPOSE:
To identify problems in the Corinthian church, to offer solutions, and to teach the believers how to live for Christ in a corrupt society

AUTHOR:
Paul

TO WHOM WRITTEN:
The church in Corinth and Christians everywhere

DATE WRITTEN:
Approximately A.D. 55, near the end of Paul's three-year ministry in Ephesus, during his third missionary journey

SETTING:
Corinth was a major cosmopolitan city, a seaport and major trade center—the most important city in Achaia. It was also filled with idolatry and immorality. The church was largely made up of Gentiles. Paul had established this church on his second missionary journey.

KEY VERSE:
"Now I exhort you, brethren, by the name of our Lord Jesus Christ, that you all agree and that there be no divisions among you, but that you be made complete in the same mind and in the same judgment" (1:10).

KEY PEOPLE:
Paul, Timothy, members of Chloe's household

KEY PLACES:
Worship meetings in Corinth

SPECIAL FEATURES:
This is a strong, straightforward letter.

ON A bed of grass, a chameleon's skin turns green. On the earth, it becomes brown. The animal changes to match the environment. Many creatures blend into nature with God-given camouflage suits to aid their survival. It's natural to fit in and adapt to the environment. But followers of Christ are *new creations,* born from above and changed from within, with values and life-styles that confront the world and clash with accepted morals. True believers don't blend in very well.

The Christians in Corinth were struggling with their environment. Surrounded by corruption and every conceivable sin, they felt the pressure to adapt. They knew they were free in Christ, but what did this freedom mean? How should they view idols or sexuality? What should they do about marriage, women in the church, and the gifts of the Spirit? These were more than theoretical questions—the church was being undermined by immorality and spiritual immaturity. The believers' faith was being tried in the crucible of immoral Corinth, and some of them were failing the test.

Paul heard of their struggles and wrote this letter to address their problems, heal their divisions, and answer their questions. Paul confronted them with their sin and their need for corrective action and clear commitment to Christ.

After a brief introduction (1:1–9), Paul immediately turns to the question of unity (1:10—4:21). He emphasizes the clear and simple gospel message around which all believers should rally; he explains the role of church leaders; and he urges them to grow up in their faith.

Paul then deals with the immorality of certain church members and the issue of lawsuits among Christians (5:1—6:8). He tells them to exercise church discipline and to settle their internal matters themselves. Because so many of the problems in the Corinthian church involved sex, Paul denounces sexual sin in the strongest possible terms (6:9–20).

Next, Paul answers some questions that the Corinthians had. Because prostitution and immorality were pervasive, marriages in Corinth were in shambles, and Christians weren't sure how to react. Paul gives pointed and practical answers (7:1–40). Concerning the question of meat sacrificed to idols, Paul suggests that they show complete commitment to Christ and sensitivity to other believers, especially weaker brothers and sisters (8:1—11:2).

Paul goes on to talk about worship, and he carefully explains the role of women, the Lord's Supper, and spiritual gifts (11:3—14:40). Sandwiched in the middle of this section is his magnificent description of the greatest gift—love (chapter 13). Then Paul concludes with a discussion of the resurrection (15:1–58), some final thoughts, greetings, and a benediction (16:1–24).

In this letter Paul confronted the Corinthians about their sins and shortcomings. And 1 Corinthians calls all Christians to be careful not to blend in with the world and accept its values and life-styles. We must live Christ-centered, blameless, loving lives that make a difference for God. As you read 1 Corinthians, examine your values in light of complete commitment to Christ.

THE BLUEPRINT

A. PAUL ADDRESSES CHURCH PROBLEMS (1:1—6:20) 1. Divisions in the church 2. Disorder in the church	Without Paul's presence, the Corinthian church had fallen into divisiveness and disorder. This resulted in many problems, which Paul addressed squarely. We must be concerned for unity and order in our local churches, but we should not mistake inactivity for order and cordiality for unity. We, too, must squarely address problems in our churches.
B. PAUL ANSWERS CHURCH QUESTIONS (7:1—16:24) 1. Instruction on Christian marriage 2. Instruction on Christian freedom 3. Instruction on public worship 4. Instruction on the resurrection	The Corinthians had sent Paul a list of questions, and he answered them in a way meant to correct abuses in the church and to show how important it is that they live what they believe. Paul gives us a Christian approach to problem solving. He analyzed the problem thoroughly to uncover the underlying issue and then highlighted the Biblical values that should guide our actions.

MEGATHEMES

THEME	EXPLANATION	IMPORTANCE
Loyalties	The Corinthians were rallying around various church leaders and teachers—Peter, Paul, and Apollos. These loyalties led to intellectual pride and created a spirit of division in the church.	Our loyalty to human leaders or human wisdom must never divide Christians into camps. We must care for our fellow believers, not fight with them. Your allegiance must be to Christ. Let him lead you.
Immorality	Paul received a report of uncorrected sexual sin in the church at Corinth. The people had grown indifferent to immorality. Others had misconceptions about marriage. We are to live morally, keeping our bodies for God's service at all times.	Christians must never compromise with sinful ideas and practices. We should not blend in with people around us. You must live up to God's standard of morality and not condone immoral behavior, even if society accepts it.
Freedom	Paul taught freedom of choice on practices not expressly forbidden in Scripture. Some believers felt certain actions—like eating the meat of animals used in pagan rituals—were corrupt by association. Others felt free to participate in such actions without feeling that they had sinned.	We are free in Christ, yet we must not abuse our Christian freedom by being inconsiderate and insensitive to others. We must never encourage others to do something they feel is wrong just because we have done it. Let love guide your behavior.
Worship	Paul addressed disorder in worship. People were taking the Lord's Supper without first confessing sin. There was misuse of spiritual gifts and confusion over women's roles in the church.	Worship must be carried out properly and in an orderly manner. Everything we do to worship God should be done in a manner worthy of his high honor. Make sure that worship is harmonious, useful, and edifying to all believers.
Resurrection	Some people denied that Christ rose from the dead. Others felt that people would not physically be resurrected. Christ's resurrection assures us that we will have new, living bodies after we die. The hope of the resurrection forms the secret of Christian confidence.	Since we will be raised again to life after we die, our life is not in vain. We must stay faithful to God in our morality and our service. We are to live today knowing we will spend eternity with Christ.

A. PAUL ADDRESSES CHURCH PROBLEMS (1:1—6:20)

Through various sources, Paul had received reports of problems in the Corinthian church, including jealousy, divisiveness, sexual immorality, and failure to discipline members. Churches today must also address the problems they face. We can learn a great deal by observing how Paul handled these delicate situations.

Appeal to Unity

1 Paul, called *as* an apostle of Jesus Christ by the will of God, and Sosthenes our brother,
2 To the church of God which is at Corinth, to those who have been sanctified in
Christ Jesus, saints by calling, with all who in every place call on the name of our Lord
Jesus Christ, their *Lord* and ours:

1:1 Rom 1:1; Rom 1:10; 2 Tim 1:1; Acts 18:17; Acts 1:15

1:2 1 Cor 10:32; Acts 18:1; Rom 1:7; 8:28; Acts 7:59

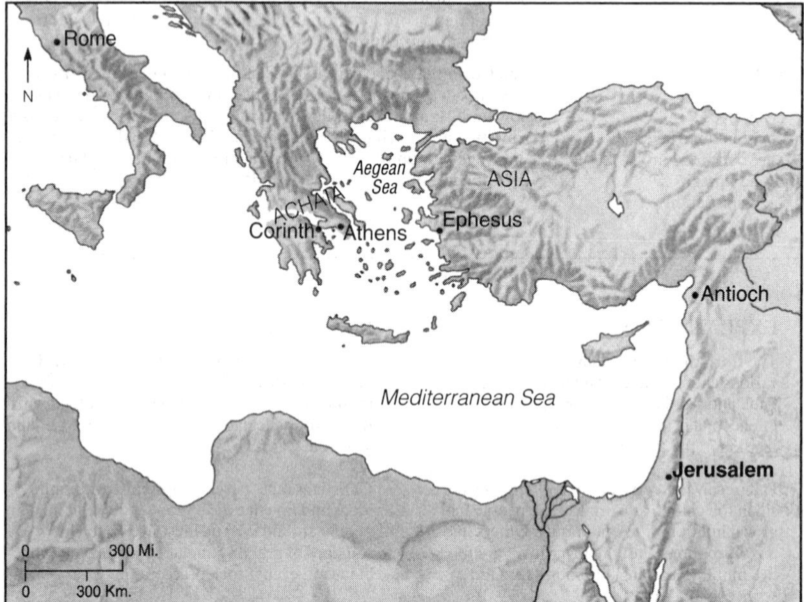

CORINTH AND EPHESUS
Paul wrote this letter to Corinth during his three-year visit in Ephesus on his third missionary journey. The two cities sat across from each other on the Aegean Sea—both were busy and important ports. Titus may have carried this letter from Ephesus to Corinth (2 Corinthians 12:18).

1:1 Paul wrote this letter to the church in Corinth while he was visiting Ephesus during his third missionary journey (Acts 19:1—20:1). Corinth and Ephesus faced each other across the Aegean Sea. Paul knew the Corinthian church well because he had spent 18 months in Corinth during his second missionary journey (Acts 18:1–18). While in Ephesus, he had heard about problems in Corinth (1:11). About the same time, a delegation from the Corinthian church had visited Paul to ask his advice about their conflicts (16:17). Paul's purpose for writing was to correct those problems and to answer questions church members had asked in a previous letter (7:1).

1:1 Paul was given a special calling from God to preach about Jesus Christ. Each Christian has a job to do, a role to take, or a contribution to make. One assignment may seem more spectacular than another, but all are necessary to carry out God's greater plans for his church and for his world (12:12–27). Be available to God by placing your gifts at his service. Then as you discover what he calls you to do, be ready to do it.

1:1 Sosthenes may have been Paul's secretary who wrote down this letter as Paul dictated it. He was probably the Jewish synagogue leader in Corinth (Acts 18:17) who had been beaten during an attack on Paul, and then later became a believer. Sosthenes was well known to the members of the Corinthian church, and so Paul included his familiar name in the opening of the letter.

1:2 Corinth, a giant cultural melting pot with a great diversity of wealth, religions, and moral standards, had a reputation for being fiercely independent and as decadent as any city in the world. The Romans had destroyed Corinth in 146 B.C. after a rebellion. But in 46 B.C., the Roman Emperor Julius Caesar rebuilt it because of its strategic seaport. By Paul's day (A.D. 50), the Romans had made Corinth the capital of Achaia (present-day Greece). It was a large city, offering Rome great profits through trade as well as the military protection of its ports. But the city's prosperity made it ripe for all sorts of corruption. Idolatry flourished, and there were more than a dozen pagan temples employing at least a thousand prostitutes. Corinth's reputation was such that prostitutes in other cities began to be called "Corinthian girls."

1:2 A personal invitation makes a person feel wanted and welcome. We are "saints by calling." God personally invites us to be citizens of his eternal kingdom. But Jesus Christ, God's Son, is the only one who can bring us into this glorious kingdom because he is the only one who removes our sins. *Sanctified* means that we are chosen or set apart by Christ for his service. We accept God's invitation by accepting his Son, Jesus Christ, and by trusting in the work he did on the cross to forgive our sins.

1:2 By including a salutation to "all who in every place call on the name of our Lord Jesus Christ," Paul is making it clear that this is not a private letter. Although it deals with specific issues facing the church at Corinth, all believers can learn from it. The Corinthian church included a great cross section of believers—wealthy mer-

1:5
2 Cor 9:11; Rom 15:14; 2 Cor 8:7

1:6
2 Thess 1:10; 1 Tim 2:6; 2 Tim 1:8; Rev 1:2

1:7
Luke 17:30; Rom 8:19, 23; Phil 3:20; 2 Pet 3:12

1:8
Rom 8:19; Phil 1:6; 2 Cor 1:14; 2:16; 1 Thess 5:2; 2 Thess 2:2

1:9
1 Cor 10:13; 2 Cor 1:18; 1 Thess 5:24; 2 Thess 3:3; Rom 8:28; 1 John 1:3

1:10
Rom 12:1; Rom 1:13; 1 Cor 11:18

3 Grace to you and peace from God our Father and the Lord Jesus Christ.
4 I thank [1]my God always concerning you for the grace of God which was given you in
Christ Jesus,
5 that in everything you were enriched in Him, in all speech and all knowledge,
6 even as the testimony concerning Christ was confirmed in you,
7 so that you are not lacking in any gift, awaiting eagerly the revelation of our Lord
Jesus Christ,
8 who will also confirm you to the end, blameless in the day of our Lord Jesus Christ.
9 God is faithful, through whom you were called into fellowship with His Son, Jesus
Christ our Lord.

1. Divisions in the church

10 Now I exhort you, brethren, by the name of our Lord Jesus Christ, that you all agree
and that there be no divisions among you, but that you be made complete in the same
mind and in the same judgment.
11 For I have been informed concerning you, my brethren, by Chloe's *people,* that there
are quarrels among you.

1 Two early mss do not contain *my*

HIGHLIGHTS OF 1 CORINTHIANS

The Meaning of the Cross 1:18—2:16	Be considerate of one another because of what Christ has done for us. There is no place for pride or a know-it-all attitude. We are to have the mind of Christ.
The Story of the Last Supper 11:23–29	The Last Supper is a time of reflection on Christ's final words to his disciples before he died on the cross; we must celebrate this in an orderly and correct manner.
The Poem of Love 13:1–13	Love is to guide all we do. We have different gifts, abilities, likes, dislikes—but we are called, without exception, to love.
The Christian's Destiny 15:42–58	We are promised by Christ, who died for us, that, as he came back to life after death, so our perishable bodies will be exchanged for heavenly bodies. Then we will live and reign with Christ.

---

chants, common laborers, former temple prostitutes, and middle-class families. Because of the wide diversity of people and backgrounds, Paul takes great pains to stress the need for both spiritual unity and Christlike character.

1:3 Grace is God's free gift of salvation given to us in Christ. Receiving it brings us peace (see Romans 5:1). In a world of noise, confusion, and relentless pressures, people long for peace. Many give up the search, thinking it impossible to find, but true peace of heart and mind is available to us through faith in Jesus Christ.

1:4–6 In this letter, Paul wrote some strong words to the Corinthians, but he began on a positive note of thanksgiving. He affirmed their privilege of belonging to the Lord and receiving his grace, the power God gave them to speak out for him and understand his truth, and the reality of their spiritual gifts. When we must correct others, it helps to begin by affirming what God has already accomplished in them.

1:7 The Corinthian church members had all the spiritual gifts they needed to live the Christian life, to witness for Christ, and to stand against the paganism and immorality of Corinth. But instead of using what God had given them, they were arguing over which gifts were more important. Paul addresses this issue in depth in chapters 12—14.

1:7–9 Paul guaranteed the Corinthian believers that God would consider them "blameless" when Christ returns (see Ephesians 1:7–10). This guarantee was not because of their great gifts or their shining performance, but because of what Jesus Christ accomplished for them through his death and resurrection. *All* who believe in the Lord Jesus will be considered blameless when Jesus Christ returns (see also 1 Thessalonians 3:13; Hebrews 9:28). If you have faith in Christ, even if it is weak, you *are* and *will be* saved.

1:10 Paul founded the church in Corinth on his second missionary journey. Eighteen months after he left, arguments and divisions arose, and some church members slipped back into an immoral life-style. Paul wrote this letter to address the problems, to clear up confusion about right and wrong, and to remove the immorality among them. The Corinthian people had a reputation for jumping from fad to fad; Paul wanted to keep Christianity from degenerating into just another fad.

1:10 By saying "brethren," Paul is emphasizing that all Christians are part of God's family. Believers share a unity that runs even deeper than that of blood brothers and sisters.

1:10–11 To "agree," allow for "no divisions," and "be made complete in the same mind and in the same judgment" do not require everyone to believe in exactly the same way. There is a difference between having opposing viewpoints and being divisive. A group of people will not completely agree on every issue, but they can work together harmoniously if they agree on what truly matters—Jesus Christ is Lord of all. In your church, speak and behave in a way that will reduce arguments and increase harmony. Petty differences should never divide Christians.

12 Now I mean this, that each one of you is saying, "I am of Paul," and "I of Apollos,"
and "I of Cephas," and "I of Christ."
13 Has Christ been divided? Paul was not crucified for you, was he? Or were you baptized in the name of Paul?
14 [2]I thank God that I baptized none of you except Crispus and Gaius,
15 so that no one would say you were baptized in my name.
16 Now I did baptize also the household of Stephanas; beyond that, I do not know
whether I baptized any other.
17 For Christ did not send me to baptize, but to preach the gospel, not in cleverness of
speech, so that the cross of Christ would not be made void.

The Wisdom of God

18 For the word of the cross is foolishness to those who are perishing, but to us who
are being saved it is the power of God.
19 For it is written,
"I WILL DESTROY THE WISDOM OF THE WISE,
AND THE CLEVERNESS OF THE CLEVER I WILL SET ASIDE."
20 Where is the wise man? Where is the scribe? Where is the debater of this age? Has
not God made foolish the wisdom of the world?
21 For since in the wisdom of God the world through its wisdom did not *come to* know
God, God was well-pleased through the foolishness of the message preached to save those
who believe.
22 For indeed Jews ask for signs and Greeks search for wisdom;
23 but we preach [3]Christ crucified, to Jews a stumbling block and to Gentiles foolishness,
24 but to those who are the called, both Jews and Greeks, Christ the power of God and
the wisdom of God.

2 Two early mss read *I give thanks that* 3 I.e. Messiah

1:12 John 1:42; 1 Cor 3:22; 9:5; 15:5
1:13 Matt 28:19; Acts 2:38
1:14 Acts 18:8; Rom 16:23
1:17 2 Cor 10:10; 11:6
1:18 Acts 2:47; 2 Cor 2:15; 4:3; 2 Thess 2:10; Rom 1:16
1:19 Is 29:14
1:20 1 Cor 2:6, 8; 3:18, 19; Rom 1:20ff
1:21 John 12:31; 1 Cor 1:27f; 6:2; 11:32; Luke 12:32; Gal 1:15
1:22 Matt 12:38
1:23 1 Cor 2:2; Gal 3:1; 5:11; Luke 2:34; 1 Pet 2:8
1:24 Rom 8:28; Rom 1:16; 1 Cor 1:18; Luke 11:49; 1 Cor 1:30

1:12ff In this large and diverse Corinthian church, the believers favored different preachers. Because there was as yet no written New Testament, the believers depended heavily on preaching and teaching for spiritual insight into the meaning of the Old Testament. Some followed Paul, who had founded their church; some who had heard Peter (Cephas) in Jerusalem followed him; while others listened only to Apollos, an eloquent and popular preacher who had had a dynamic ministry in Corinth (Acts 18:24; 19:1). Although these three preachers were united in their message, their personalities attracted different people. At this time the church was in danger of dividing. By mentioning Jesus Christ ten times in the first ten verses, Paul makes it clear who it is all preachers and teachers should emphasize. God's message is much more important than any human messenger.

1:12–13 Paul wondered whether the Corinthians' quarrels had "divided" Christ. This is a graphic picture of what happens when the church (the body of Christ) is divided. With the many churches and styles of worship available today, we could get caught up in the same game of "my preacher is better than yours!" To do so would divide Christ again. But Christ is not divided, and his true followers should not allow anything to divide them. Don't let your appreciation for any teacher, preacher, or author lead you into intellectual pride. Our allegiance must be to Christ and to the unity that he desires.

1:17 When Paul said that Christ didn't send him to baptize, he wasn't minimizing the importance of baptism. Baptism was commanded by Jesus himself (Matthew 28:19) and practiced by the early church (Acts 2:41). Paul was emphasizing that no one person should do everything. Paul's gift was preaching, and that's what he did. Christian ministry should be a team effort; no preacher or teacher is a complete link between God and people, and no individual can do all that the apostles did. We must be content with the contribution God has given us to make, and carry it out wholeheartedly. (For more on different gifts, see chapters 12 and 13.)

1:17 Some speakers use impressive words, but they are weak on content. Paul stressed solid content and practical help for his listeners. He wanted them to be impressed with his *message,* not just his style (see 2:1–5). You don't need to be a great speaker with a large vocabulary to share the gospel effectively. The persuasive power is in the story, not the storyteller. Paul was not against those who carefully prepare what they say (see 2:6), but against those who try to impress others only with their own knowledge or speaking ability.

1:19 Paul summarizes Isaiah 29:14 to emphasize a point Jesus often made: God's way of thinking is not like the world's way (normal human wisdom). And God offers eternal life, which the world can never give. We can spend a lifetime accumulating human wisdom and yet never learn how to have a personal relationship with God. We must come to the crucified and risen Christ to receive eternal life and the joy of a personal relationship with our Savior.

1:22–24 Many Jews considered the Good News of Jesus Christ to be foolish, because they thought the Messiah would be a conquering king accompanied by signs and miracles. Jesus had not restored David's throne as they expected. Besides, he was executed as a criminal, and how could a criminal be a savior? Greeks, too, considered the gospel foolish: They did not believe in a bodily resurrection, they did not see in Jesus the powerful characteristics of their mythological gods, and they thought no reputable person would be crucified. To them, death was defeat, not victory.

The Good News of Jesus Christ still sounds foolish to many. Our society worships power, influence, and wealth. Jesus came as a humble, poor servant, and he offers his kingdom to those who have faith, not to those who do all kinds of good deeds to try to earn his gifts. This looks foolish to the world, but Christ is our power, the only way we can be saved. Knowing Christ personally is the greatest wisdom anyone could have.

25 Because the foolishness of God is wiser than men, and the weakness of God is stronger than men.
26 For consider your calling, brethren, that there were not many wise according to the
flesh, not many mighty, not many noble;
27 but God has chosen the foolish things of the world to shame the wise, and God has
chosen the weak things of the world to shame the things which are strong,
28 and the base things of the world and the despised God has chosen, the things that
are not, so that He may nullify the things that are,
29 so that no man may boast before God.
30 But by His doing you are in Christ Jesus, who became to us wisdom from God, and
righteousness and sanctification, and redemption,
31 so that, just as it is written, "LET HIM WHO BOASTS, BOAST IN THE LORD."

Paul's Reliance upon the Spirit

2 And when I came to you, brethren, I did not come with superiority of speech or of
wisdom, proclaiming to you the [4]testimony of God.
2 For I determined to know nothing among you except Jesus Christ, and Him crucified.
3 I was with you in weakness and in fear and in much trembling,
4 and my message and my preaching were not in persuasive words of wisdom, but in
demonstration of the Spirit and of power,
5 so that your faith would not rest on the wisdom of men, but on the power of God.
6 Yet we do speak wisdom among those who are mature; a wisdom, however, not of
this age nor of the rulers of this age, who are passing away;
7 but we speak God's wisdom in a mystery, the hidden *wisdom* which God predestined before the ages to our glory;
8 *the wisdom* which none of the rulers of this age has understood; for if they had understood it they would not have crucified the Lord of glory;

4 One early ms reads *mystery*

1:25 2 Cor 13:4
1:26 Rom 11:29; Matt 11:25; 1 Cor 1:20
1:27 James 2:5
1:28 1 Cor 2:6; 2 Thess 2:8; Heb 2:14
1:30 2 Cor 5:21; Phil 3:9; 1 Thess 5:23; Rom 3:24
1:31 Jer 9:23
2:2 1 Cor 1:23; Gal 6:14
2:3 1 Cor 4:10; 2 Cor 11:30; 12:5, 9f; 13:9
2:4 Rom 15:19; 1 Cor 4:20
2:5 2 Cor 4:7; 6:7; 12:9
2:6 Eph 4:13; Phil 3:15
2:7 Rom 11:25; 16:25f; Heb 1:2; 11:3
2:8 1 Cor 1:26; 2:6; Matt 13:22; 1 Cor 1:20; Acts 7:2; James 2:1

1:25 The message of Christ's death for sins sounds foolish to those who don't believe. Death seems to be the end of the road, the ultimate weakness. But Jesus did not stay dead. His resurrection demonstrated his power even over death. And he will save us from eternal death and give us everlasting life if we trust him as Savior and Lord. This sounds so simple that many people won't accept it. They try other ways to obtain eternal life (being good, being wise, etc.). But all their attempts will not work. The "foolish" people who simply accept Christ's offer are actually the wisest of all, because they alone will live eternally with God.

1:27 Is Christianity against rational thinking? Christians clearly do believe in using their minds to weigh the evidence and make wise choices. Paul is declaring that no amount of human knowledge can replace or bypass Christ's work on the cross. If it could, Christ would be accessible only to the intellectually gifted and well educated, and not to ordinary people or to children.

1:28–31 Paul continues to emphasize that the way to receive salvation is so simple that *any* person who wants to can understand it. Skill and wisdom do not get a person into God's kingdom—simple faith does—so no one can boast that his or her achievements helped him or her secure eternal life. Salvation is totally from God through Jesus' death. There is *nothing* we can do to earn our salvation; we need only accept what Jesus has already done for us.

1:30 God is the source of and the reason for our personal and living relationship with Christ. Our union and identification with Christ results in our having God's wisdom and knowledge (Colossians 2:3), possessing right standing with God (*righteousness,* 2 Corinthians 5:21), being holy (*sanctification,* 1 Thessalonians 4:3–7), and having the penalty for our sins paid by Jesus (*redemption,* Mark 10:45).

2:1 Paul is referring to his first visit to Corinth during his second missionary journey (A.D. 51), when he founded the church (Acts 18:1ff).

2:1–5 A brilliant scholar, Paul could have overwhelmed his listeners with intellectual arguments. Instead he shared the simple message of Jesus Christ by allowing the Holy Spirit to guide his words. In sharing the gospel with others, we should follow Paul's example and keep our message simple and basic. The Holy Spirit will give power to our words and use them to bring glory to Jesus.

2:4 Paul's confidence was not in his keen intellect or speaking ability but in his knowledge that the Holy Spirit was helping and guiding him. Paul is not denying the importance of study and preparation for preaching—he had a thorough education in the Scriptures. Effective preaching must combine studious preparation with reliance on the work of the Holy Spirit. Don't use Paul's statement as an excuse for not studying or preparing.

2:7 God's "mystery, the hidden wisdom" was his offer of salvation to all people. Originally unknown to humanity, this plan became crystal clear when Jesus rose from the dead. His resurrection proved that he had power over sin and death and could offer us this power as well (see also 1 Peter 1:10–12 and the first note on Romans 16:25–27). God's plan, however, is still hidden to unbelievers because they either refuse to accept it, choose to ignore it, or simply haven't heard about it.

2:8 Jesus was misunderstood and rejected by those whom the world considered wise and great. He was put to death by the rulers in Palestine—the high priest, King Herod, Pilate, and the Pharisees and Sadducees. Jesus' rejection by these rulers had been predicted in Isaiah 53:3 and Zechariah 12:10–11.

9 but just as it is written,
"THINGS WHICH EYE HAS NOT SEEN AND EAR HAS NOT HEARD,
AND *which* HAVE NOT ENTERED THE HEART OF MAN,
ALL THAT GOD HAS PREPARED FOR THOSE WHO LOVE HIM."
10 [5]For to us God revealed *them* through the Spirit; for the Spirit searches all things,
even the depths of God.
11 For who among men knows the *thoughts* of a man except the spirit of the man which
is in him? Even so the *thoughts* of God no one knows except the Spirit of God.
12 Now we have received, not the spirit of the world, but the Spirit who is from God,
so that we may know the things freely given to us by God,
13 which things we also speak, not in words taught by human wisdom, but in those taught
by the Spirit, combining spiritual *thoughts* with spiritual *words.*
14 But a natural man does not accept the things of the Spirit of God, for they are foolishness to him; and he cannot understand them, because they are spiritually appraised.
15 But he who is spiritual appraises all things, yet he himself is appraised by no one.
16 FOR WHO HAS KNOWN THE MIND OF THE LORD, THAT HE WILL INSTRUCT HIM?
But we have the mind of Christ.

Foundations for Living

3 And I, brethren, could not speak to you as to spiritual men, but as to men of flesh, as
to infants in Christ.
2 I gave you milk to drink, not solid food; for you were not yet able *to receive it.* Indeed, even now you are not yet able,
3 for you are still fleshly. For since there is jealousy and strife among you, are you not
fleshly, and are you not walking like mere men?
4 For when one says, "I am of Paul," and another, "I am of Apollos," are you not
mere men?
5 What then is Apollos? And what is Paul? Servants through whom you believed, even
as the Lord gave *opportunity* to each one.
6 I planted, Apollos watered, but God was causing the growth.
7 So then neither the one who plants nor the one who waters is anything, but God
who causes the growth.

5 One early ms reads *But*

2:9 Is 64:4; 65:17
2:10 Matt 11:25; 13:11; 16:17; Gal 1:12; Eph 3:3, 5; John 14:26; Rom 11:33ff
2:11 Prov 20:27
2:12 Rom 8:15; 1 Cor 1:27
2:13 1 Cor 1:17; 2:1, 4
2:14 1 Cor 15:44, 46
2:15 Gal 6:1
2:16 Is 40:13; Rom 11:34; John 15:15
3:1 Gal 6:1; Rom 7:14
3:2 Heb 5:12f; 1 Pet 2:2; John 16:12
3:3 Rom 13:13; 1 Cor 1:10f; 11:18
3:5 Rom 15:16; 2 Cor 3:3, 6; 4:1; 5:18; 6:4; Eph 3:7; Col 1:25; 1 Tim 1:12; Rom 12:6; 1 Cor 3:10
3:6 1 Cor 4:15; 9:1; 15:1; 2 Cor 10:14f; Acts 18:24-27; 1 Cor 1:12; 1 Cor 15:10

2:9 We cannot imagine all that God has in store for us, both in this life and for eternity. He will create a new heaven and a new earth (Isaiah 65:17; Revelation 21:1), and we will live with him forever. Until then, his Holy Spirit comforts and guides us. Knowing the wonderful and eternal future that awaits us gives us hope and courage to press on in this life, to endure hardship, and to avoid giving in to temptation. This world is not all there is. The best is yet to come.

2:10 The "depths of God" refers to God's unfathomable nature and his wonderful plan—Jesus' death and resurrection—and to the promise of salvation, revealed only to those who believe that what God says is true. Those who believe in Christ's death and resurrection and put their faith in him will know all they need to know to be saved. This knowledge, however, can't be grasped by even the wisest people unless they accept God's message. All who reject God's message are foolish, no matter how wise the world thinks they are.

2:13 Paul's words are authoritative because their source was the Holy Spirit. Paul was not merely giving his own personal views or his personal impression of what God had said. Under the inspiration of the Holy Spirit, he wrote the very thoughts and words of God.

2:14–15 Non-Christians cannot understand God, and they cannot grasp the concept that God's Spirit lives in believers. Don't expect most people to approve of or understand your decision to follow Christ. It all seems so silly to them. Just as a tone-deaf person cannot appreciate fine music, the person who rejects God cannot understand God's beautiful message. With the lines of communication broken, he or she won't be able to hear what God is saying to him or her.

2:15–16 No one can comprehend God (Romans 11:34), but through the guidance of the Holy Spirit, believers have insight into some of God's plans, thoughts, and actions—they, in fact, have the "mind of Christ." Through the Holy Spirit we can begin to know God's thoughts, talk with him, and expect his answers to our prayers. Are you spending enough time with Christ to have his very mind in you? An intimate relationship with Christ comes only from spending time consistently in his presence and in his Word. Read Philippians 2:5ff for more on the mind of Christ.

3:1–3 Paul called the Corinthians infants in the Christian life because they were not yet spiritually healthy and mature. The proof was that they quarreled like children, allowing divisions to distract them. Immature Christians are "worldly," controlled by their own desires; mature believers are in tune with God's desires. How much influence do your desires have on your life? Your goal should be to let God's desires be yours. Being controlled by your own desires will stunt your growth.

3:6 Paul planted the seed of the gospel message in people's hearts. He was a missionary pioneer; he brought the message of salvation. Apollos's role was to water—to help the believers grow stronger in the faith. Paul founded the church in Corinth, and Apollos built on that foundation. Tragically, the believers in Corinth had split into factions, pledging loyalty to different teachers (see 1:11–13). After the preachers' work is completed, God keeps on making Christians grow. Our leaders should certainly be respected, but we should never place them on pedestals that create barriers between people or set them up as a substitute for Christ.

3:7–9 God's work involves many different individuals with a variety

3:8 Gal 6:4
3:9 Matt 15:13; 1 Cor 3:16; Eph 2:20-22; Col 2:7; 1 Pet 2:5
3:10 Rom 12:3; 1 Cor 15:10; Rom 15:20; 1 Cor 3:11f
3:11 Is 28:16; Eph 2:20; 1 Pet 2:4ff
3:13 2 Thess 1:7-10; 2 Tim 1:12, 18; 4:8
3:15 Job 23:10; Ps 66:10, 12; Jude 23
3:16 Rom 6:16; Rom 8:9
3:18 Is 5:21; 1 Cor 8:2; Gal 6:3; 1 Cor 1:20
3:19 1 Cor 1:20; Job 5:13
3:20 Ps 94:11
3:21 1 Cor 4:6; Rom 8:32
3:22 Rom 8:38
3:23 1 Cor 15:23; 2 Cor 10:7; Gal 3:29

8 Now he who plants and he who waters are one; but each will receive his own reward
according to his own labor.
9 For we are God's fellow workers; you are God's field, God's building.
10 According to the grace of God which was given to me, like a wise master builder I
laid a foundation, and another is building on it. But each man must be careful how he
builds on it.
11 For no man can lay a foundation other than the one which is laid, which is Jesus
Christ.
12 Now if any man builds on the foundation with gold, silver, precious stones, wood,
hay, straw,
13 each man's work will become evident; for the day will show it because it is *to be* revealed with fire, and the fire itself will test the quality of each man's work.
14 If any man's work which he has built on it remains, he will receive a reward.
15 If any man's work is burned up, he will suffer loss; but he himself will be saved, yet
so as through fire.
16 Do you not know that you are a temple of God and *that* the Spirit of God dwells
in you?
17 If any man destroys the temple of God, God will destroy him, for the temple of God
is holy, and that is what you are.
18 Let no man deceive himself. If any man among you thinks that he is wise in this age,
he must become foolish, so that he may become wise.
19 For the wisdom of this world is foolishness before God. For it is written, "*He is* THE
ONE WHO CATCHES THE WISE IN THEIR CRAFTINESS";
20 and again, "THE LORD KNOWS THE REASONINGS of the wise, THAT THEY ARE
USELESS."
21 So then let no one boast in men. For all things belong to you,
22 whether Paul or Apollos or Cephas or the world or life or death or things present or
things to come; all things belong to you,
23 and you belong to Christ; and Christ belongs to God.

---

of gifts and abilities. There are no superstars in this task, only team members performing their own special roles. We can become useful members of God's team by setting aside our desires to receive glory for what we do. Don't seek the praise that comes from people—it is comparatively worthless. Instead, seek approval from God.

3:10–11 The foundation of the church—of all believers—is Jesus Christ. Paul laid this foundation (by preaching Christ) when he began the church at Corinth. Whoever builds the church—officers, teachers, preachers, parents, and others—must build with high-quality materials (right doctrine and right living, 3:12ff) that meet God's standards. Paul is not criticizing Apollos, but challenging future church leaders to have sound preaching and teaching.

3:10–17 In the church built on Jesus Christ, each church member would be mature, spiritually sensitive, and doctrinally sound. However, the Corinthian church was filled with those whose work was "wood, hay, straw," members who were immature, insensitive to one another, and vulnerable to wrong doctrine (3:1–4). No wonder they had so many problems. Local church members should be deeply committed to Christ. Can your Christian character stand the test?

3:11 A building is only as solid as its foundation. The foundation of our lives is Jesus Christ; he is our base, our reason for being. Everything we are and do must fit into the pattern provided by him. Are you building your life on the only real and lasting foundation, or are you building on a faulty foundation such as wealth, security, success, or fame?

3:13–15 Two sure ways to destroy a building are to tamper with the foundation and to build with inferior materials. The church must be built on Christ, not on any other person or principle. Christ will evaluate each minister's contribution to the life of the church, and the day of judgment ("the day") will reveal the sincerity of each person's work. God will determine whether or not they have been faithful to Jesus' instructions. Good work will be rewarded; unfaithful or inferior work will be discounted. The idea that the builder "will be saved, yet so as through fire" means that unfaithful workers will be saved, but like people escaping from a burning building. All their possessions (accomplishments) will be lost.

3:16–17 Just as our bodies are a "temple of the Holy Spirit" (6:19), the local church or Christian community is God's temple. Just as the Jews' temple in Jerusalem was not to be destroyed, the church is not to be spoiled and ruined by divisions, controversy, or other sins as members come together to worship God.

3:18–21 Paul was not telling the Corinthian believers to neglect the pursuit of knowledge. He was warning them that if worldly wisdom holds them back from God, it is not wisdom at all. God's way of thinking is far more valuable, even though it may seem foolish to the world (1:27). The Corinthians were using so-called worldly wisdom to evaluate their leaders and teachers. Their pride made them value the presentation of the message more than its content.

3:22 Paul says that both life and death are ours. While nonbelievers are victims of life, swept along by its current and wondering if there is meaning to it, believers can use life well because they understand its true purpose. Nonbelievers can only fear death. For believers, however, death holds no terrors because Christ has conquered all fears (see 1 John 4:18). Death is only the beginning of eternal life with God.

Servants of Christ

4 Let a man regard us in this manner, as servants of Christ and stewards of the mysteries of God.
2 In this case, moreover, it is required of stewards that one be found trustworthy.
3 But to me it is a very small thing that I may be examined by you, or by *any* human
court; in fact, I do not even examine myself.
4 For I am conscious of nothing against myself, yet I am not by this acquitted; but the
one who examines me is the Lord.
5 Therefore do not go on passing judgment before [6]the time, *but wait* until the Lord
comes who will both bring to light the things hidden in the darkness and disclose the
motives of *men's* hearts; and then each man's praise will come to him from God.
6 Now these things, brethren, I have figuratively applied to myself and Apollos for
your sakes, so that in us you may learn not to exceed what is written, so that no one of
you will become arrogant in behalf of one against the other.
7 For who regards you as superior? What do you have that you did not receive? And
if you did receive it, why do you boast as if you had not received it?
8 You are already filled, you have already become rich, you have become kings
without us; and indeed, *I* wish that you had become kings so that we also might reign
with you.
9 For, I think, God has exhibited us apostles last of all, as men condemned to death;
because we have become a spectacle to the world, both to angels and to men.
10 We are fools for Christ's sake, but you are prudent in Christ; we are weak, but you
are strong; you are distinguished, but we are without honor.
11 To this present hour we are both hungry and thirsty, and are poorly clothed, and
are roughly treated, and are homeless;
12 and we toil, working with our own hands; when we are reviled, we bless; when we
are persecuted, we endure;
13 when we are slandered, we try to conciliate; we have become as the scum of the world,
the dregs of all things, *even* until now.
14 I do not write these things to shame you, but to admonish you as my beloved children.
15 For if you were to have countless tutors in Christ, yet *you would* not *have* many fathers, for in Christ Jesus I became your father through the gospel.
16 Therefore I exhort you, be imitators of me.

6 I.e. the appointed time of judgment

4:1 Luke 1:2; 1 Cor 9:17; Titus 1:7; 1 Pet 4:10; Rom 11:25

4:4 Acts 23:1; 2 Cor 1:12; Ps 143:2; Rom 2:13

4:5 John 21:22; Rom 2:16; 1 Cor 3:13; Rom 2:29

4:6 1 Cor 1:19, 31; 3:19f; 8:1; 13:4

4:7 John 3:27; Rom 12:3, 6; 1 Pet 4:10

4:9 Rom 8:36; 1 Cor 15:31; 2 Cor 11:23; Heb 10:33

4:10 Acts 17:18; 26:24; 1 Cor 1:18; 1 Cor 1:19f; 3:18; 2 Cor 11:19; 1 Cor 2:3; 2 Cor 13:9

4:11 Rom 8:35; 2 Cor 11:23-27

4:12 Acts 18:3; 1 Pet 3:9; John 15:20; Rom 8:35

4:15 Gal 3:24f; 1 Cor 1:30; Num 11:12; 1 Cor 3:8; Gal 4:19; Philem 10; 1 Cor 9:12, 14, 18, 23; 15:1

4:16 1 Cor 11:1; Phil 3:17; 4:9; 1 Thess 1:6; 2 Thess 3:9

4:1–2 Paul urged the Corinthians to think of him, Peter (Cephas), and Apollos not as leaders of factions, but as servants of Christ entrusted with the secret things of God (see the note on 2:7). A servant does what his master tells him to do. We must do what God tells us to do in the Bible and through his Holy Spirit. Each day God presents us with needs and opportunities that challenge us to do what we know is right.

4:5 It is tempting to judge fellow Christians, evaluating whether or not they are good followers of Christ. But only God knows a person's heart, and he is the only One with the right to judge. Paul's warning to the Corinthians should also warn us. We are to confront those who are sinning (see 5:12–13), but we must not judge who is a better servant for Christ. When you judge someone, you invariably consider yourself better—and that is arrogant.

4:6–7 How easy it is for us to become attached to a spiritual leader. When someone has helped us, it's natural to feel loyalty. But Paul warns against having such pride in our favorite leaders that we cause divisions in the church. Any true spiritual leader is a representative of Christ and has nothing to offer that God hasn't given him or her. Don't let your loyalty cause strife, slander, or broken relationships. Make sure that your deepest loyalties are to Christ and not to his human agents. Those who spend more time debating church leadership than declaring Christ's message don't have Christ as their top priority.

4:6–13 The Corinthians had split into various cliques, each following its favorite preacher (Paul, Apollos, Peter, etc.). Each clique really believed it was the only one to have the whole truth, and thus felt spiritually proud. But Paul told the groups not to boast about being tied to a particular preacher because each preacher was simply a humble servant who had suffered for the same message of salvation in Jesus Christ. No preacher of God has more status than another.

4:15 In Paul's day, a tutor was a slave who was assigned as a special caretaker of a child. Paul was portraying his special affection for the Corinthians (greater than a slave) and his special role (more than a tutor). In an attempt to unify the church, Paul appealed to his relationship with them. By *father,* he meant he was the church's founder. Because he started the church, he could be trusted to have its best interests at heart. Paul's tough words were motivated by love—like the love a good father has for his children (see also 1 Thessalonians 2:11).

4:16 Paul told the Corinthians to imitate him. He was able to make this statement because he walked close to God, spent time in God's Word and in prayer, and was aware of God's presence in his life at all times. God was Paul's example; therefore, Paul's life could be an example to other Christians. Paul wasn't expecting others to imitate everything he did, but they should imitate those aspects of his beliefs and conduct that were modeling Christ's way of living.

17 For this reason I have sent to you Timothy, who is my beloved and faithful child in
the Lord, and he will remind you of my ways which are in Christ, just as I teach everywhere in every church.
18 Now some have become arrogant, as though I were not coming to you.
19 But I will come to you soon, if the Lord wills, and I shall find out, not the words of
those who are arrogant but their power.
20 For the kingdom of God does not consist in words but in power.
21 What do you desire? Shall I come to you with a rod, or with love and a spirit of
gentleness?

2. Disorder in the church

Immorality Rebuked

5 It is actually reported that there is immorality among you, and immorality of such a
kind as does not exist even among the Gentiles, that someone has his father's wife.
2 You have become arrogant and have not mourned instead, so that the one who had
done this deed would be removed from your midst.
3 For I, on my part, though absent in body but present in spirit, have already judged
him who has so committed this, as though I were present.
4 In the name of our Lord Jesus, when you are assembled, and I with you in spirit,
with the power of our Lord Jesus,
5 *I have decided* to deliver such a one to Satan for the destruction of his flesh, so that
his spirit may be saved in the day of the Lord [7]Jesus.
6 Your boasting is not good. Do you not know that a little leaven leavens the whole
lump *of dough?*
7 Clean out the old leaven so that you may be a new lump, just as you are *in fact* unleavened. For Christ our Passover also has been sacrificed.
8 Therefore let us celebrate the feast, not with old leaven, nor with the leaven of malice
and wickedness, but with the unleavened bread of sincerity and truth.

7 Two early mss do not contain *Jesus*

4:17 1 Cor 16:10; Acts 16:1; 1 Cor 4:14; 1 Tim 1:2, 18; 2 Tim 1:2; 1 Cor 7:17; 14:33; 16:1; Titus 1:5

4:19 Acts 19:21; 20:2; 1 Cor 11:34; 16:5f; 16:7-9; 2 Cor 1:15f

4:21 2 Cor 1:23; 2:1, 3; 12:20; 13:2, 10

5:2 1 Cor 4:6; 2 Cor 7:7-10; 1 Cor 5:13

5:3 Col 2:5; 1 Thess 2:17

5:4 2 Thess 3:6; John 20:23; 2 Cor 2:10; 13:3, 10

5:5 Prov 23:14; Luke 22:31; 1 Tim 1:20; Matt 4:10; 1 Cor 1:8

5:6 1 Cor 5:2; James 4:16; Rom 6:16; Hos 7:4; Matt 16:6, 12; Gal 5:9

5:7 Mark 14:12; 1 Pet 1:19

5:8 Ex 12:19; 13:7; Deut 16:3

4:17 Timothy had traveled with Paul on Paul's second missionary journey (see Acts 16:1–3) and was a key person in the growth of the early church. Timothy may have delivered this letter to Corinth, but more likely he arrived there shortly after the letter came (see 16:10). Timothy's role was to see that Paul's advice was received, read, and implemented. Then he was to return to Paul and report on the church's progress.

4:18–20 Some people talk a lot about faith, but that's all it is—talk. They may know all the right words to say, but their lives don't reflect God's power. Paul says that the kingdom of God is to be *lived,* not just discussed. There is a big difference between knowing the right words and living them out. Don't be content to have the right answers about Christ. Let your life show that God's power is really working in you.

4:19 It is not known whether Paul ever returned to Corinth, but it is likely. In 2 Corinthians 2:1, he writes that he decided not to come "in sorrow again," implying that he had had a previous painful confrontation with the Corinthian believers (see 2 Corinthians 12:14; 13:1; and the note on 2 Corinthians 2:1).

5:1ff The church must discipline flagrant sin among its members—such sins, left unchecked, can polarize and paralyze a church. The correction, however, should never be vengeful. Instead, it should be given to help bring about a cure. There was a specific sin in the church, but the Corinthian believers had refused to deal with it. In this case, a man was having an affair with his mother (or stepmother), and the church members were trying to ignore the situation. Paul was telling the church that it had a responsibility to maintain the standards of morality found in God's commandments. God tells us not to judge others. But he also tells us not to tolerate flagrant sin because leaving that sin undisciplined will have a dangerous influence on other believers (5:6).

5:5 To "deliver such a one to Satan" means to exclude him from the fellowship of believers. Without the spiritual support of Christians, this man would be left alone with his sin and Satan, and perhaps this emptiness would drive him to repentance. "For the destruction of his flesh" states the hope that the experience would bring him to God to destroy his sinful nature through repentance. Putting someone out of the church should be a last resort in disciplinary action. It should not be done out of vengeance, but out of love, just as parents punish children to correct and restore them. The church's role should be to help, not hurt, offenders, motivating them to repent of their sins and to return to the fellowship of the church.

5:6 Paul was writing to those who wanted to ignore this church problem. They didn't realize that allowing public sin to exist in the church affects all its members. Paul does not expect anyone to be sinless—all believers struggle with sin daily. Instead, he is speaking against those who deliberately sin, feel no guilt, and refuse to repent. This kind of sin cannot be tolerated in the church because it affects others. We have a responsibility to other believers. Leaven (yeast) makes bread dough rise. A little bit affects the whole batch. Blatant sins, left uncorrected, confuse and divide the congregation. While believers should encourage, pray for, and build up one another, they must also be intolerant of sin that jeopardizes the spiritual health of the church.

5:7–8 As the Hebrews prepared for their exodus from slavery in Egypt, they were commanded to prepare bread without leaven (yeast) because they didn't have time to wait for it to rise. And because leaven also was a symbol of sin, they were commanded to sweep all of it out of the house (Exodus 12:15; 13:7). Christ is our Passover lamb, the perfect sacrifice for our sin. Because he has delivered us from the slavery of sin, we should have nothing to do with the sins of the past ("old leaven").

9 I wrote you in my letter not to associate with immoral people;
10 I *did* not at all *mean* with the immoral people of this world, or with the covetous and
swindlers, or with idolaters, for then you would have to go out of the world.
11 But actually, I wrote to you not to associate with any so-called brother if he is an
immoral person, or covetous, or an idolater, or a reviler, or a drunkard, or a swindler—
not even to eat with such a one.
12 For what have I to do with judging outsiders? Do you not judge those who are within *the church?*
13 But those who are outside, God judges. REMOVE THE WICKED MAN FROM AMONG
YOURSELVES.

5:9 2 Cor 6:14; Eph 5:11; 2 Thess 3:6
5:11 Acts 1:15; 2 Thess 3:6; 1 Cor 10:7, 14, 20f
5:12 Mark 4:11
5:13 Deut 13:5; 17:7, 12; 21:21; 22:21; 1 Cor 5:2

Lawsuits Discouraged

6 Does any one of you, when he has a case against his neighbor, dare to go to law before the unrighteous and not before the saints?
2 Or do you not know that the saints will judge the world? If the world is judged by
you, are you not competent *to constitute* the smallest law courts?
3 Do you not know that we will judge angels? How much more matters of this life?
4 So if you have law courts dealing with matters of this life, do you appoint them as
judges who are of no account in the church?
5 I say *this* to your shame. *Is it* so, *that* there is not among you one wise man who will
be able to decide between his brethren,
6 but brother goes to law with brother, and that before unbelievers?
7 Actually, then, it is already a defeat for you, that you have lawsuits with one another. Why not rather be wronged? Why not rather be defrauded?
8 On the contrary, you yourselves wrong and defraud. *You do* this even to *your*
brethren.
9 Or do you not know that the unrighteous will not inherit the kingdom of God? Do
not be deceived; neither fornicators, nor idolaters, nor adulterers, nor [8]effeminate, nor
homosexuals,

8 I.e. effeminate by perversion

6:1 Matt 18:17
6:2 Rom 6:16; Dan 7:18, 22, 27; Matt 19:28; 1 Cor 1:20
6:5 1 Cor 4:14; 15:34; Acts 1:15; 9:13; 1 Cor 6:1
6:6 2 Cor 6:14f; 1 Tim 5:8
6:7 Matt 5:39f
6:8 1 Thess 4:6
6:9 Rom 6:16; Acts 20:32; Luke 21:8; 1 Cor 15:33; Gal 6:7; James 1:16; 1 John 3:7; Rom 13:13; 1 Cor 5:11; Gal 5:19-21; Eph 5:5; 1 Tim 1:10

5:9 Paul is referring to an earlier letter to the Corinthian church, often called the lost letter because it has not been preserved.

5:10–11 Paul makes it clear that we should not disassociate ourselves from unbelievers—otherwise, we could not carry out Christ's command to tell them about salvation (Matthew 28:18–20). But we are to distance ourselves from the person who claims to be a Christian, yet indulges in sins explicitly forbidden in Scripture and then rationalizes his or her actions. By rationalizing sin, a person harms others for whom Christ died and dims the image of God in himself or herself. A church that includes such people is hardly fit to be the light of the world. To do so would distort the picture of Christ it presents to the world. Church leaders must be ready to correct, in love, for the sake of spiritual unity.

5:12 The Bible consistently tells us not to criticize people by gossiping or making rash judgments. At the same time, however, we are to judge and deal with sin that can hurt others. Paul's instructions should not be used to handle trivial matters or to take revenge; nor should they be applied to individual problems between believers. These verses are instructions for dealing with open sin in the church, with a person who claims to be a Christian and yet who sins without remorse. The church is to confront and discipline such a person in love. Also see the notes on 4:5 and 5:1ff.

6:1–6 In chapter 5, Paul explained what to do with open immorality in the congregation. In chapter 6, he teaches how the congregation should handle smaller problems between believers. Society has set up a legal system where disagreements can be resolved in courts. But Paul declares that disagreeing Christians should not have to go to a secular court to resolve their differences. As Christians, we have the Holy Spirit and the mind of Christ, so why should we turn to those who lack God's wisdom? Because of all that we have been given as believers, and because of the authority that we will have in the future to judge the world and the angels, we should be able to deal with disputes among ourselves. The *saints* are believers. See John 5:22 and Revelation 3:21 for more on judging the world. Judging angels is mentioned in 2 Peter 2:4 and Jude 6.

6:6–8 Why did Paul say that Christians should not take their disagreements to unbelivers in secular courts? (1) If the judge and jury are not Christians, they are not likely to be sensitive to Christian values. (2) The basis for going to court is often revenge; this should never be a Christian's motive. (3) Lawsuits make the church look bad, causing unbelievers to focus on its problems rather than on its purpose.

6:9–11 Paul is describing characteristics of unbelievers. He doesn't mean that fornicators, idolaters, adulterers, male prostitutes (effeminate), homosexuals, thieves, greedy people (covetous), drunkards, revilers, or swindlers are automatically and irrevocably excluded from heaven. Christians come out of all kinds of different backgrounds, including these. They may still struggle with evil desires, but they should not continue in these practices. In 6:11, Paul clearly states that even those who sin in these ways can have their lives changed by Christ. However, those who say that they are Christians but persist in those practices with no sign of remorse will not inherit the kingdom of God. Such people need to reevaluate their lives to see if they truly believe in Christ.

6:9–11 In a permissive society it is easy for Christians to overlook or tolerate some immoral behaviors (greed, drunkenness, etc.) while remaining outraged at others (homosexuality, thievery). We must not participate in sin or condone it in any way, nor may we be selective about what we condemn or excuse. Staying away from more "acceptable" forms of sin is difficult, but it is no harder for us than it was for the Corinthians. God expects his followers in any age to have high standards.

6:10 Acts 20:32; 1 Cor 15:50; Gal 5:21; Eph 5:5

6:11 1 Cor 12:2; Eph 2:2f; Col 3:5-7; Titus 3:3-7; Rom 8:30

6:12 1 Cor 10:23

6:13 Matt 15:17; Gal 5:24; Eph 5:23

6:14 Acts 2:24; John 6:39f; 1 Cor 15:23

6:15 Eph 5:30; Luke 20:16

10 nor thieves, nor *the* covetous, nor drunkards, nor revilers, nor swindlers, will inherit
the kingdom of God.
11 Such were some of you; but you were washed, but you were sanctified, but you were
justified in the name of the Lord Jesus Christ and in the Spirit of our God.

The Body Is the Lord's

12 All things are lawful for me, but not all things are profitable. All things are lawful
for me, but I will not be mastered by anything.
13 Food is for the stomach and the stomach is for food, but God will do away with both
of them. Yet the body is not for immorality, but for the Lord, and the Lord is for the
body.
14 Now God has not only raised the Lord, but will also raise us up through His power.
15 Do you not know that your bodies are members of Christ? Shall I then take away
the members of Christ and make them members of a prostitute? May it never be!

CHURCH DISCIPLINE The church, at times, must exercise discipline toward members who have sinned. But church discipline must be handled carefully, straightforwardly, and lovingly.

Situations	*Steps* (Matthew 18:15–17)
Unintentional error and/or private sin	1. Go to the brother or sister; show the fault to him or her in private.
Public sins and/or those done flagrantly and arrogantly	2. If he/she does not listen, go with one or two witnesses.
	3. If he/she refuses to listen, take the matter before the church.

After these steps have been carried out, the next steps are:

1. Remove the one in error from the fellowship (1 Corinthians 5:2–13).
2. The church gives united disapproval, but forgiveness and comfort are in order if he/she chooses to repent (2 Corinthians 2:5–8).
3. Do not associate with the disobedient person; and if you must, speak to him/her as one who needs a warning (2 Thessalonians 3:14–15).
4. After two warnings, reject the person from the fellowship (Titus 3:10).

6:11 Paul emphasizes God's action in making believers new people. The three aspects of God's work are all part of our salvation: Our sins were washed away, we were set apart for special use ("sanctified"), and we were pronounced not guilty ("justified") for our sins.

6:12 Apparently the church had been quoting and misapplying the words "all things are lawful for me." Some Christians in Corinth were excusing their sins by saying that (1) Christ had taken away all sin, and so they had complete freedom to live as they pleased, or (2) what they were doing was not strictly forbidden by Scripture. Paul answered both these excuses. (1) While Christ has taken away our sin, this does not give us freedom to go on doing what we know is wrong. The New Testament specifically forbids many sins (see 6:9–10) that were originally prohibited in the Old Testament (see Romans 12:9–21; 13:8–10). (2) Some actions are not sinful in themselves, but they are not appropriate because they can control our lives and lead us away from God. (3) Some actions may hurt others. Anything we do that hurts rather than helps others is not right.

6:12–13 Many of the world's religions teach that the soul or spirit is important but the body is not; and Christianity has sometimes been influenced by these ideas. In truth, however, Christianity takes very seriously the realm of the physical. We worship a God who created a physical world and pronounced it good. He promises us a new earth where real people have transformed physical lives—not a pink cloud where disembodied souls listen to harp music. At the heart of Christianity is the story of God himself taking on flesh and blood and coming to live with us, offering both physical healing and spiritual restoration.

We humans, like Adam, are a combination of dust and spirit. Just as our spirits affect our bodies, so our physical bodies affect our spirits. We cannot commit sin with our bodies without damaging our souls because our bodies and souls are inseparably joined. In the new earth we will have resurrection bodies that are not corrupted by sin. Then we will enjoy the fullness of our salvation.

6:12–13 Freedom is a mark of the Christian faith—freedom from sin and guilt, and freedom to use and enjoy anything that comes from God. But Christians should not abuse this freedom and hurt themselves or others. Drinking too much leads to alcoholism, and gluttony leads to obesity. Be careful that what God has allowed you to enjoy doesn't grow into a bad habit that controls you. For more about Christian freedom and everyday behavior, read chapter 8.

6:13 Sexual immorality is a temptation that is always before us. In movies and on television, sex outside marriage is treated as a normal, even desirable, part of life, while marriage is often shown as confining and joyless. We can even be looked down on by others if we are suspected of being pure. But God does not forbid sexual sin just to be difficult. He knows its power to destroy us physically and spiritually. No one should underestimate the power of sexual immorality. It has devastated countless lives and destroyed families, churches, communities, and even nations. God wants to protect us from damaging ourselves and others, and so he offers to fill us—our loneliness, our desires—with himself.

6:15–17 This teaching about sexual immorality and prostitutes was especially important for the Corinthian church because the temple of the love goddess Aphrodite was in Corinth. This temple employed more than a thousand prostitutes as priestesses, and sex was part of the worship ritual. Paul clearly stated that Christians are to have no part in sexual immorality, even if it is acceptable and popular in our culture.

16 Or do you not know that the one who joins himself to a prostitute is one body *with*
her? For He says, "THE TWO SHALL BECOME ONE FLESH."
17 But the one who joins himself to the Lord is one spirit *with Him.*
18 Flee immorality. Every *other* sin that a man commits is outside the body, but the
immoral man sins against his own body.
19 Or do you not know that your body is a temple of the Holy Spirit who is in you,
whom you have from God, and that you are not your own?
20 For you have been bought with a price: therefore glorify God in your body.

6:16 1 Cor 6:3; Gen 2:24; Matt 19:5; Mark 10:8; Eph 5:31

6:17 John 17:21-23; Rom 8:9-11; 1 Cor 6:15; Gal 2:20

6:18 1 Cor 6:9; 2 Cor 12:21; Eph 5:3; Col 3:5; Heb 13:4

6:19 1 Cor 6:3; John 2:21; 1 Cor 3:16; 2 Cor 6:16; Rom 14:7f

6:20 Acts 20:28; 1 Cor 7:23; 1 Pet 1:18f; 2 Pet 2:1; Rev 5:9; Rom 12:1; Phil 1:20

B. PAUL ANSWERS CHURCH QUESTIONS (7:1—16:24)

After discussing disorder in the church, Paul moves to the list of questions that the Corinthians had sent him, including subjects of marriage, singleness, eating meat offered to idols, propriety in worship, orderliness in the Lord's Supper, spiritual gifts, and the resurrection. Questions that plague churches today are remarkably similar to these, so we can receive specific guidance in these areas from the letter.

1. Instruction on Christian marriage

Teaching on Marriage

7 Now concerning the things about which you wrote, it is good for a man not to touch
a woman.
2 But because of immoralities, each man is to have his own wife, and each woman is
to have her own husband.
3 The husband must fulfill his duty to his wife, and likewise also the wife to her husband.
4 The wife does not have authority over her own body, but the husband *does;* and likewise also the husband does not have authority over his own body, but the wife *does.*
5 Stop depriving one another, except by agreement for a time, so that you may devote yourselves to prayer, and come together again so that Satan will not tempt you
because of your lack of self-control.
6 But this I say by way of concession, not of command.
7 [9]Yet I wish that all men were even as I myself am. However, each man has his own
gift from God, one in this manner, and another in that.

7:1 1 Cor 7:8, 26

7:5 Ex 19:15; 1 Sam 21:5; Matt 4:10

7:6 2 Cor 8:8

7:7 1 Cor 7:8; 9:5; Matt 19:11f; Rom 12:6; 1 Cor 12:4, 11

9 One early ms reads *For*

6:18 Christians are free to be all they can be for God, but they are not free *from* God. God created sex to be a beautiful and essential ingredient of marriage, but sexual sin—sex outside the marriage relationship—*always* hurts someone. It hurts God because it shows that we prefer following our own desires instead of the leading of the Holy Spirit. It hurts others because it violates the commitment so necessary to a relationship. It often brings disease to our bodies. And it deeply affects our personalities, which respond in anguish when we harm ourselves physically and spiritually.

6:19–20 What did Paul mean when he said that our bodies belong to God? Many people say they have the right to do whatever they want with their own bodies. Although they think that this is freedom, they are really enslaved to their own desires. When we become Christians, the Holy Spirit fills and lives in us. Therefore, we no longer own our bodies. "Bought with a price" refers to slaves purchased at auction. Christ's death freed us from sin, but also obligates us to his service. If you live in a building owned by someone else, you try not to violate the building's rules. Because your body belongs to God, you must not violate his standards for living.

7:1 The Corinthians had written to Paul, asking him several questions relating to the Christian life and problems in the church. The first question was whether it was good to be married. Paul answers this and other questions in the remainder of this letter.

7:1ff Christians in Corinth were surrounded by sexual temptation. The city had a reputation even among pagans for sexual immorality and religious prostitution. It was to this kind of society that Paul delivered these instructions on sex and marriage. The Corinthians needed special, specific instructions because of their culture's immoral standards. For more on Paul's teaching about marriage, see Ephesians 5.

7:3–5 Sexual temptations are difficult to withstand because they appeal to the normal and natural desires that God has given us. Marriage provides God's way to satisfy these natural sexual desires and to strengthen the partners against temptation. Married couples have the responsibility to care for each other; therefore, husbands and wives should not withhold themselves sexually from one another but should fulfill each other's needs and desires. (See also the note on 10:13.)

7:3–11 The Corinthian church was in turmoil because of the immorality of the culture around them. Some Greeks, in rejecting immorality, rejected sex and marriage altogether. The Corinthian Christians wondered if this was what they should do also, so they asked Paul several questions: "Because sex is perverted, shouldn't we also abstain in marriage?" "If my spouse is unsaved, should I seek a divorce?" "Should unmarried people and widows remain unmarried?" Paul answered many of these questions by saying, "For now, stay put. Be content in the situation where God has placed you. If you're married, don't seek to be single. If you're single, don't seek to be married. Live God's way, one day at a time, and he will show you what to do."

7:4 Spiritually, our bodies belong to God when we become Christians because Jesus Christ bought us by paying the price to release us from sin (see 6:19–20). Physically, our bodies belong to our spouses because God designed marriage so that, through the union of husband and wife, the two become one (Genesis 2:24). Paul stressed complete equality in sexual relationships. Neither male nor female should seek dominance or autonomy.

7:7 Both marriage and singleness are gifts from God. One is not morally better than the other, and both are valuable to accomplishing God's purposes. It is important for us, therefore, to accept our present situation. When Paul said he wished that all people were

7:8
1 Cor 7:1, 26; 1 Cor 7:7; 9:5

7:9
1 Tim 5:14

7:10
Mal 2:16; Matt 5:32; 19:3-9; Mark 10:2-12; Luke 16:18; 1 Cor 7:6

7:12
1 Cor 7:6; 2 Cor 11:17

7:14
Ezra 9:2; Mal 2:15

7:15
Rom 14:19

7:16
Rom 11:14; 1 Pet 3:1

7:17
Rom 12:3; 1 Cor 4:17; 1 Cor 11:16; 14:33; 2 Cor 8:18; 11:28; Gal 1:22; 1 Thess 2:14; 2 Thess 1:4

7:18
Acts 15:1ff

7:19
Rom 2:27, 29; Gal 3:28; 5:6; 6:15; Col 3:11; Rom 2:25

8 But I say to the unmarried and to widows that it is good for them if they remain
even as I.
9 But if they do not have self-control, let them marry; for it is better to marry than to
burn *with passion*.
10 But to the married I give instructions, not I, but the Lord, that the wife should not
leave her husband
11 (but if she does leave, she must remain unmarried, or else be reconciled to her husband), and that the husband should not divorce his wife.
12 But to the rest I say, not the Lord, that if any brother has a wife who is an unbeliever, and she consents to live with him, he must not divorce her.
13 And a woman who has an unbelieving husband, and he consents to live with her,
she must not send her husband away.
14 For the unbelieving husband is sanctified through his wife, and the unbelieving wife
is sanctified through her believing husband; for otherwise your children are unclean, but
now they are holy.
15 Yet if the unbelieving one leaves, let him leave; the brother or the sister is not under
bondage in such *cases,* but God has called [10]us to peace.
16 For how do you know, O wife, whether you will save your husband? Or how do you
know, O husband, whether you will save your wife?
17 Only, as the Lord has assigned to each one, as God has called each, in this manner
let him walk. And so I direct in all the churches.
18 Was any man called *when he was already* circumcised? He is not to become uncircumcised. Has anyone been called in uncircumcision? He is not to be circumcised.
19 Circumcision is nothing, and uncircumcision is nothing, but *what matters is* the keeping of the commandments of God.

10 One early ms reads *you*

---

like him (i.e., unmarried), he was expressing his desire that more people would devote themselves *completely* to the ministry without the added concerns of spouse and family, as he had done. He was not criticizing marriage—after all, it is God's created way of providing companionship and populating the earth.

7:9 Sexual pressure is not the best motive for getting married, but it is better to marry the right person than to "burn with passion." Many new believers in Corinth thought that all sex was wrong, and so engaged couples were deciding not to get married. In this passage, Paul was telling couples who wanted to marry that they should not frustrate their normal sexual drives by avoiding marriage. This does not mean, however, that people who have trouble controlling themselves should marry the first person who comes along. It is better to deal with the pressure of desire than to deal with an unhappy marriage.

7:12 Paul's instructions about the permanence of marriage (7:10) comes from the Old Testament (Genesis 2:24) and from Jesus (Mark 10:2–12). His suggestion in this verse is based on God's command, and Paul applies it to the situation the Corinthians were facing. Paul ranked the instructions above the suggestion because one is an eternal principle while the other is a specific application. Nevertheless, for people in similar situations, Paul's suggestion is the best advice they will get. Paul was a man of God, an apostle, and he had the mind of Christ.

7:12–14 Because of their desire to serve Christ, some people in the Corinthian church thought they ought to divorce their pagan spouses and marry Christians. But Paul affirmed the marriage commitment. God's ideal is for marriages to stay together—even when one spouse is not a believer. The Christian spouse should try to win the other to Christ. It would be easy to rationalize leaving; however, Paul makes a strong case for staying with the unbelieving spouse and being a positive influence on the marriage. Paul, like Jesus, believed that marriage is permanent (see Mark 10:1–9).

7:14 The blessings that flow to believers don't stop there, but extend to others. God regards the marriage as "sanctified" (set apart for his use) by the presence of one Christian spouse. The other does not receive salvation automatically, but is helped by this relationship. The children of such a marriage are to be regarded as "holy" (because of God's blessing on the family unit) until they are old enough to decide for themselves.

7:15–16 This verse is misused by some as a loophole to get out of marriage. But Paul's statements were given to encourage the Christian spouse to try to get along with the unbeliever and make the marriage work. If, however, the unbelieving spouse insisted on leaving, Paul said to let him or her go. The only alternative would be for the Christian to deny his or her faith to preserve the marriage, and that would be worse than dissolving the marriage. Paul's chief purpose in writing this was to urge the married couples to seek unity, not separation (see 7:17; 1 Peter 3:1–2).

7:17 Apparently the Corinthians were ready to make wholesale changes without thinking through the ramifications. Paul was writing to say that people should be Christians where they are. You can do God's work and demonstrate your faith *anywhere.* If you became a Christian after marriage, and your spouse is not a believer, remember that you don't have to be married to a Christian to live for Christ. Don't assume that you are in the wrong place, or stuck with the wrong person. You may be just where God wants you (see 7:20).

7:18–19 The ceremony of circumcision was an important part of the Jews' relationship with God. In fact, before Christ came, circumcision was commanded by God for those who claimed to follow him (Genesis 17:9–14). But after Christ's death, circumcision was no longer necessary (Acts 15; Romans 4:9–11; Galatians 5:2–4; Colossians 2:11). Pleasing God and obeying him is more important than observing traditional ceremonies.

20 Each man must remain in that condition in which he was called.
21 Were you called while a slave? Do not worry about it; but if you are able also to
become free, rather do that.
22 For he who was called in the Lord while a slave, is the Lord's freedman; likewise he
who was called while free, is Christ's slave.
23 You were bought with a price; do not become slaves of men.
24 Brethren, each one is to remain with God in that *condition* in which he was called.
25 Now concerning virgins I have no command of the Lord, but I give an opinion as
one who by the mercy of the Lord is trustworthy.
26 I think then that this is good in view of the present distress, that it is good for a man
to remain as he is.
27 Are you bound to a wife? Do not seek to be released. Are you released from a wife?
Do not seek a wife.
28 But if you marry, you have not sinned; and if a virgin marries, she has not sinned.
Yet such will have trouble in this life, and I am trying to spare you.
29 But this I say, brethren, the time has been shortened, so that from now on those
who have wives should be as though they had none;
30 and those who weep, as though they did not weep; and those who rejoice, as though
they did not rejoice; and those who buy, as though they did not possess;
31 and those who use the world, as though they did not make full use of it; for the form
of this world is passing away.
32 But I want you to be free from concern. One who is unmarried is concerned about
the things of the Lord, how he may please the Lord;
33 but one who is married is concerned about the things of the world, how he may please
his wife,
34 and *his interests* are divided. The woman who is unmarried, and the virgin, is concerned about the things of the Lord, that she may be holy both in body and spirit; but
one who is married is concerned about the things of the world, how she may please her
husband.
35 This I say for your own benefit; not to put a restraint upon you, but to promote what
is appropriate and *to secure* undistracted devotion to the Lord.
36 But if any man thinks that he is acting unbecomingly toward his virgin *daughter,* if
she is past her youth, and if it must be so, let him do what he wishes, he does not sin; let
her marry.
37 But he who stands firm in his heart, being under no constraint, but has authority

7:20
1 Cor 7:24

7:22
John 8:32, 36; Philem 16; Eph 6:6; Col 3:24; 1 Pet 2:16

7:23
1 Cor 6:20

7:24
1 Cor 7:20

7:25
1 Cor 7:6; 2 Cor 4:1; 1 Tim 1:13, 16

7:26
Luke 21:23; 2 Thess 2:2; 1 Cor 7:1, 8

7:29
Rom 13:11f; 1 Cor 7:31

7:31
1 Cor 9:18; 1 Cor 7:29; 1 John 2:17

7:32
1 Tim 5:5

7:20 Often we are so concerned about what we *could* be doing for God somewhere else that we miss great opportunities right where we are. Paul says that when someone becomes a Christian, he or she should usually continue with the work he or she has previously been doing—provided it isn't immoral or unethical. Every job can become Christian work when you realize that the purpose of your life is to honor, serve, and speak out for Christ. Because God has placed you where you are, look carefully for opportunities to serve him there.

7:23 Slavery was common throughout the Roman empire. Some Christians in the Corinthian church were undoubtedly slaves. Paul said that although the Christian slaves were slaves to other human beings, they were free from the power of sin in their lives. People today are slaves to sin until they commit their lives to Christ, who alone can conquer sin's power. Sin, pride, and fear no longer have any claim over us, just as a slave owner no longer has power over the slaves he has sold. The Bible says we become Christ's slaves when we become Christians (Romans 6:18), but this actually means we gain our freedom, because sin no longer controls us.

7:26 Paul probably foresaw the impending persecution that the Roman government would soon bring upon Christians. He gave this practical advice because being unmarried would mean less suffering and more freedom to throw one's life into the cause of Christ (7:29), even to the point of fearlessly dying for him. Paul's advice reveals his single-minded devotion to spreading the Good News.

7:28 Many people naively think that marriage will solve all their problems. Here are some problems marriage won't solve: (1) loneliness, (2) sexual temptation, (3) satisfaction of one's deepest emotional needs, (4) elimination of life's difficulties. Marriage alone does not hold two people together, but commitment does—commitment to Christ and to each other despite conflicts and problems. As wonderful as it is, marriage does not automatically solve every problem. Whether married or single, we must be content with our situation and focus on Christ, not on loved ones, to help address our problems.

7:29 Paul urges all believers to make the most of their time before Christ's return. Every person in every generation should have this sense of urgency about telling the Good News to others. Life is short—there's not much time!

7:29–31 Paul urges believers not to regard marriage, home, or financial security as the ultimate goals of life. As much as possible, we should live unhindered by the cares of this world, not getting involved with burdensome mortgages, budgets, investments, or debts that might keep us from doing God's work. A married man or woman, as Paul points out (7:33–34), must take care of earthly responsibilities—but they should make every effort to keep them modest and manageable.

7:32–34 Some single people feel tremendous pressure to be married. They think their lives can be complete only with a spouse. But Paul underlines one advantage of being single—the potential of a greater focus on Christ and his work. If you are unmarried, use your special opportunity to serve Christ wholeheartedly.

7:39 Rom 7:2; 2 Cor 6:14
8:1 Acts 15:20; Rom 14:19
8:2 1 Cor 3:18; 1 Cor 13:8-12; 1 Tim 6:4
8:3 Ps 1:6; Jer 1:5; Amos 3:2; Rom 8:29; 11:2; Gal 4:9
8:4 Acts 15:20; 1 Cor 8:1, 7, 10; Acts 14:15; 1 Cor 10:19; Gal 4:8; Deut 4:35, 39; 6:4; 1 Cor 8:6
8:5 2 Thess 2:4
8:6 Deut 4:35, 39; 6:4; Is 46:9; Jer 10:6, 7; 1 Cor 8:4; Mal 2:10; Eph 4:6; Rom 11:36; John 13:13; 1 Cor 1:2; Eph 4:5; 1 Tim 2:5; John 1:3; Col 1:16
8:8 Rom 14:17
8:9 1 Cor 10:28; Gal 5:13; Rom 14:1; 1 Cor 8:10f
8:10 1 Cor 8:4ff; Acts 15:20
8:11 1 Cor 8:4ff; Rom 14:15, 20
8:12 Matt 18:6; Rom 14:20; Matt 25:45
8:13 Rom 14:21; 1 Cor 10:32; 2 Cor 6:3; 11:29

over his own will, and has decided this in his own heart, to keep his own virgin *daughter,*
he will do well.
38 So then both he who gives his own virgin *daughter* in marriage does well, and he
who does not give her in marriage will do better.
39 A wife is bound as long as her husband lives; but if her husband is dead, she is free
to be married to whom she wishes, only in the Lord.
40 But in my opinion she is happier if she remains as she is; and I think that I also have
the Spirit of God.

2. Instruction on Christian freedom

Take Care with Your Liberty

8 Now concerning things sacrificed to idols, we know that we all have knowledge.
Knowledge makes arrogant, but love edifies.
2 If anyone supposes that he knows anything, he has not yet known as he ought to
know;
3 but if anyone loves God, he is known by Him.
4 Therefore concerning the eating of things sacrificed to idols, we know that [11]there
is no such thing as an idol in the world, and that there is no God but one.
5 For even if there are so-called gods whether in heaven or on earth, as indeed there
are many gods and many lords,
6 yet for us there is *but* one God, the Father, from whom are all things and we *exist* for
Him; and one Lord, Jesus Christ, by whom are all things, and we *exist* through Him.
7 However not all men have this knowledge; but some, being accustomed to the idol
until now, eat *food* as if it were sacrificed to an idol; and their conscience being weak is
defiled.
8 But food will not commend us to God; we are neither the worse if we do not eat,
nor the better if we do eat.
9 But take care that this liberty of yours does not somehow become a stumbling block
to the weak.
10 For if someone sees you, who have knowledge, dining in an idol's temple, will not
his conscience, if he is weak, be strengthened to eat things sacrificed to idols?
11 For through your knowledge he who is weak is ruined, the brother for whose sake
Christ died.
12 And so, by sinning against the brethren and wounding their conscience when it is
weak, you sin against Christ.
13 Therefore, if food causes my brother to stumble, I will never eat meat again, so that
I will not cause my brother to stumble.

11 Lit *nothing is an idol in the world;* i.e. an idol has no real existence

---

7:38 When Paul says the unmarried person does even better, he is talking about the potential time available for service to God. The single person does not have the responsibility of caring for a spouse and raising a family. Singleness, however, does not ensure service to God—involvement in service depends on the commitment of the individual.

7:40 Paul's advice comes from the Holy Spirit, who guides and equips both single and married people to fulfill their roles.

8:1 Meat bought in the marketplace was likely to have been symbolically offered to an idol in one of the many pagan temples. Animals were brought to a temple, killed before an idol as part of a pagan religious ceremony, and eaten at a feast in the idol's temple or taken to butchers who sold the meat in the marketplace. The believers wondered if, by eating such meat, they were somehow participating in the worship of pagan idols.

8:1–3 Love is more important than knowledge. Knowledge can make us look good and feel important, but we can all too easily develop an arrogant, know-it-all attitude. Many people with strong opinions are unwilling to listen to and learn from God and others. We can obtain God's knowledge only by loving him (see James 3:17–18). And we can know and be known by God only when we model him by showing love (1 John 4:7–8).

8:4–9 Paul addressed these words to believers who weren't bothered by eating meat that had been sacrificed to idols. Although idols were phony, and the pagan ritual of sacrificing to them was meaningless, eating such meat offended Christians with more sensitive consciences. Paul said, therefore, that if a weaker or less mature believer misunderstood their actions, they should, out of consideration, avoid eating meat offered to idols.

8:10–13 Christian freedom does not mean that anything goes. It means that our salvation is not determined by good deeds or legalistic rules, but by the free gift of God (Ephesians 2:8–9). Christian freedom, then, is inseparably tied to Christian responsibility. New believers are often very sensitive to what is right or wrong, what they should or shouldn't do. Some actions may be perfectly all right for us to do, but may harm a Christian brother or sister who is still young in the faith and learning what the Christian life is all about. We must be careful not to offend a sensitive or younger Christian or, by our example, to cause him or her to sin. When we love others, our freedom should be less important to us than strengthening the faith of a brother or sister in Christ.

Paul's Use of Liberty

9 Am I not free? Am I not an apostle? Have I not seen Jesus our Lord? Are you not
my work in the Lord?
2 If to others I am not an apostle, at least I am to you; for you are the seal of my apostleship in the Lord.
3 My defense to those who examine me is this:
4 Do we not have a right to eat and drink?
5 Do we not have a right to take along a believing wife, even as the rest of the apostles and the brothers of the Lord and Cephas?
6 Or do only Barnabas and I not have a right to refrain from working?
7 Who at any time serves as a soldier at his own expense? Who plants a vineyard and
does not eat the fruit of it? Or who tends a flock and does not use the milk of the flock?
8 I am not speaking these things according to human judgment, am I? Or does not
the Law also say these things?
9 For it is written in the Law of Moses, "YOU SHALL NOT MUZZLE THE OX WHILE HE
IS THRESHING." God is not concerned about oxen, is He?
10 Or is He speaking altogether for our sake? Yes, for our sake it was written, because
the plowman ought to plow in hope, and the thresher *to thresh* in hope of sharing *the*
crops.
11 If we sowed spiritual things in you, is it too much if we reap material things
from you?
12 If others share the right over you, do we not more? Nevertheless, we did not use
this right, but we endure all things so that we will cause no hindrance to the gospel of
Christ.
13 Do you not know that those who perform sacred services eat the *food* of the temple,
and those who attend regularly to the altar have their share from the altar?
14 So also the Lord directed those who proclaim the gospel to get their living from the
gospel.
15 But I have used none of these things. And I am not writing these things so that it
will be done so in my case; for it would be better for me to die than have any man make
my boast an empty one.
16 For if I preach the gospel, I have nothing to boast of, for I am under compulsion;
for woe is me if I do not preach the gospel.
17 For if I do this voluntarily, I have a reward; but if against my will, I have a stewardship entrusted to me.
18 What then is my reward? That, when I preach the gospel, I may offer the gospel
without charge, so as not to make full use of my right in the gospel.
19 For though I am free from all *men,* I have made myself a slave to all, so that I may
win more.
20 To the Jews I became as a Jew, so that I might win Jews; to those who are under the

9:2 John 3:33; 2 Cor 3:2f; Acts 1:25

9:4 1 Cor 9:14; 1 Thess 2:6, 9; 2 Thess 3:8f

9:5 1 Cor 7:7f; Matt 12:46; Matt 8:14; John 1:42

9:7 2 Cor 10:4; 1 Tim 1:18; 2 Tim 2:3f

9:9 Deut 25:4; 1 Tim 5:18; Deut 22:1-4; Prov 12:10

9:10 Rom 4:23f; 2 Tim 2:6

9:11 Rom 15:27; 1 Cor 9:14

9:12 Acts 18:3; 20:33; 1 Cor 4:15; 9:14, 16, 18, 23; 2 Cor 2:12

9:14 Matt 10:10; Luke 10:7; 1 Tim 5:18

9:15 Acts 18:3; 20:33; 2 Cor 11:10

9:16 Acts 9:15; Rom 1:14; 1 Cor 4:15; 2 Cor 2:12

9:17 John 4:36; 1 Cor 3:8; 9:18

9:18 John 4:36; 1 Cor 3:8; 9:17; Acts 18:3; 2 Cor 11:7; 12:13; 1 Cor 7:31; 9:12

9:19 1 Cor 9:1; 2 Cor 4:5; Gal 5:13; Matt 18:15; 1 Pet 3:1

9:20 Acts 16:3; 21:23-26; Rom 11:14; Gal 2:19

9:1 Some Corinthians were questioning Paul's authority and rights as an apostle, so Paul gave his credentials—he actually saw and talked with the resurrected Christ, who called him to be an apostle (see Acts 9:3–18). Such credentials make the advice he gives in this letter more persuasive. In 2 Corinthians 10—13, Paul defends his apostleship in greater detail.

9:1 Changed lives were the evidence that God was using Paul. Does your faith have an impact on others? You can be a life-changer, helping others grow spiritually, if you dedicate yourself to being used by God and letting him make you effective.

9:4ff Paul uses himself as an illustration of giving up personal rights. Paul had the right to hospitality, to be married, and to be paid for his work. But he willingly gave up these rights to win people to Christ. When your focus is on living for Christ, your rights become comparatively unimportant.

9:4–10 Jesus said that workers deserve their wages (Luke 10:7). Paul echoes this thought and urges the church to be sure to pay their Christian workers. We have the responsibility to care for our pastors, teachers, and other spiritual leaders. It is our duty to see that those who serve us in the ministry are fairly and adequately compensated.

9:5 The brothers of Jesus attained leadership status in the church at Jerusalem. James (one of the "brothers of the Lord"), for example, led the way to an agreement at the Jerusalem council in Acts 15 and wrote the book of James.

9:13 As part of their pay, priests in the temple would receive a portion of the offerings as their food (see Numbers 18:8–24).

9:16 Preaching the gospel was Paul's gift and calling, and he said he couldn't stop preaching even if he wanted to. Paul was driven by the desire to do what God wanted, using his gifts for God's glory. What special gifts has God given you? Are you motivated, like Paul, to honor God with your gifts?

9:19–27 In 9:19–22 Paul asserts that he has freedom to do anything; in 9:24–27 he emphasizes a life of strict discipline. The Christian life involves both freedom and discipline. The goals of Paul's life were to glorify God and bring people to Christ. Thus he stayed free of any philosophical position or material entanglement that might sidetrack him, while he strictly disciplined himself to carry out his goal. For Paul, both freedom and discipline were important tools to be used in God's service.

9:21
Rom 2:12, 14; Gal 2:3; 3:2; 1 Cor 7:22

9:22
2 Cor 11:29; 1 Cor 10:33; Rom 11:14

9:24
Col 2:18; Gal 2:2; 2 Tim 4:7; Heb 12:1

9:25
Eph 6:12; 1 Tim 6:12; 2 Tim 2:5; 4:7; James 1:12; 1 Pet 5:4; Rev 2:10; 3:11

9:26
Gal 2:2; 2 Tim 4:7; Heb 12:1; 1 Cor 14:9

9:27
Rom 8:13

10:1
Rom 1:13; Ex 13:21; Ps 105:39; Ex 14:22

10:2
Rom 6:3; 1 Cor 1:13; Gal 3:27

10:3
Ex 16:4, 35; Deut 8:3

Law, as under the Law though not being myself under the Law, so that I might win those
who are under the Law;
21 to those who are without law, as without law, though not being without the law of
God but under the law of Christ, so that I might win those who are without law.
22 To the weak I became weak, that I might win the weak; I have become all things to
all men, so that I may by all means save some.
23 I do all things for the sake of the gospel, so that I may become a fellow partaker
of it.
24 Do you not know that those who run in a race all run, but *only* one receives the prize?
Run in such a way that you may win.
25 Everyone who competes in the games exercises self-control in all things. They then
do it to receive a perishable wreath, but we an imperishable.
26 Therefore I run in such a way, as not without aim; I box in such a way, as not beating
the air;
27 but I discipline my body and make it my slave, so that, after I have preached to others, I myself will not be disqualified.

Avoid Israel's Mistakes

10 For I do not want you to be unaware, brethren, that our fathers were all under the
cloud and all passed through the sea;
2 and all were baptized into Moses in the cloud and in the sea;
3 and all ate the same spiritual food;
4 and all drank the same spiritual drink, for they were drinking from a spiritual rock
which followed them; and the rock was Christ.

STRONGER, WEAKER BELIEVERS

Advice to:	
Stronger believer	Don't be proud of your maturity; don't flaunt your freedom. Act in love so you do not cause a weaker believer to stumble.
Weaker believer	Although you may not feel the same freedom in some areas as in others, take your time, pray to God, but do not force others to adhere to your stipulations. You would hinder other believers by making up rules and standards for how everyone ought to behave. Make sure your convictions are based on God's Word, and are not simply an expression of your opinions.
Pastors and leaders	Teach correctly from God's Word, helping Christians understand what is right and wrong in God's eyes, and helping them see that they can have varied opinions on other issues and still be unified. Don't allow potential problems to get out of hand, causing splits and divisions.

Paul advises those who are more mature in the faith about how they must care about their brothers and sisters in Christ who have more tender consciences; those "weaker" brothers and sisters are advised concerning their growth; and pastors and leaders are instructed on how to deal with the conflicts that easily could arise between these groups.

9:22–23 Paul gives several important principles for ministry: (1) Find common ground with those you contact, (2) avoid a know-it-all attitude, (3) make others feel accepted, (4) be sensitive to their needs and concerns, and (5) look for opportunities to tell them about Christ. These principles are just as valid for us as they were for Paul.

9:24–27 Winning a race requires purpose and discipline. Paul uses this illustration to explain that the Christian life takes hard work, self-denial, and grueling preparation. As Christians, we are running toward our heavenly reward. The essential disciplines of prayer, Bible study, and worship equip us to run with vigor and stamina. Don't merely observe from the grandstand; don't just turn out to jog a couple of laps each morning. Train diligently—your spiritual progress depends upon it.

9:25 At times we must even give up something good in order to do what God wants. Each person's special duties determine the discipline and denial that he or she must accept. Without a goal, discipline is nothing but self-punishment. With the goal of pleasing God, our denial seems like nothing compared to the eternal, imperishable reward that will be ours.

9:27 When Paul says he might be disqualified, he does not mean that he could lose his salvation, but rather that he could lose his privilege of telling others about Christ. It is easy to tell others how to live and then not to take our own advice. We must be careful to practice what we preach.

10:1ff In chapter 9 Paul used himself as an example of a mature Christian who disciplines himself to better serve God. In chapter 10, he uses Israel as an example of spiritual immaturity, shown in their overconfidence and lack of self-discipline.

10:1–5 The cloud and the sea mentioned here refer to Israel's escape from slavery in Egypt when God led them by a cloud and brought them safely through the Red Sea (Exodus 14). The spiritual food and drink are the miraculous provisions God gave as they traveled through the wilderness (Exodus 15; 16).

10:2 "Baptized into Moses" means that just as we are united in Christ by baptism, so the Israelites were united under Moses' leadership in the events of the exodus.

5 Nevertheless, with most of them God was not well-pleased; for they were laid low
in the wilderness.
6 Now these things happened as examples for us, so that we would not crave evil things
as they also craved.
7 Do not be idolaters, as some of them were; as it is written, "THE PEOPLE SAT DOWN
TO EAT AND DRINK, AND STOOD UP TO PLAY."
8 Nor let us act immorally, as some of them did, and twenty-three thousand fell in
one day.
9 Nor let us try the Lord, as some of them did, and were destroyed by the serpents.
10 Nor grumble, as some of them did, and were destroyed by the destroyer.
11 Now these things happened to them as an example, and they were written for our
instruction, upon whom the ends of the ages have come.
12 Therefore let him who thinks he stands take heed that he does not fall.
13 No temptation has overtaken you but such as is common to man; and God is faithful, who will not allow you to be tempted beyond what you are able, but with the temptation will provide the way of escape also, so that you will be able to endure it.
14 Therefore, my beloved, flee from idolatry.
15 I speak as to wise men; you judge what I say.
16 Is not the cup of blessing which we bless a sharing in the blood of Christ? Is not the
bread which we break a sharing in the body of Christ?
17 Since there is one bread, we who are many are one body; for we all partake of the
one bread.
18 Look at the nation Israel; are not those who eat the sacrifices sharers in the altar?
19 What do I mean then? That a thing sacrificed to idols is anything, or that an idol is
anything?
20 *No,* but *I say* that the things which the Gentiles sacrifice, they sacrifice to demons
and not to God; and I do not want you to become sharers in demons.
21 You cannot drink the cup of the Lord and the cup of demons; you cannot partake
of the table of the Lord and the table of demons.
22 Or do we provoke the Lord to jealousy? We are not stronger than He, are we?
23 All things are lawful, but not all things are profitable. All things are lawful, but not
all things edify.

10:6 Num 11:4, 34
10:7 Ex 32:4; 1 Cor 5:11; 10:14
10:8 Num 25:1ff
10:9 Num 21:5f
10:11 Rom 4:23; 13:11
10:12 Rom 11:20; 2 Pet 3:17
10:13 1 Cor 1:9; 2 Pet 2:9
10:14 Heb 6:9; 1 John 5:21
10:16 Matt 26:27f; Mark 14:23f; Luke 22:20; Acts 2:42; 1 Cor 11:23f
10:17 Rom 12:5; 1 Cor 12:12f, 27; Eph 4:4
10:19 1 Cor 8:4
10:20 Gal 4:8; Rev 9:20
10:21 2 Cor 6:16; Is 65:11
10:23 1 Cor 6:12; Rom 14:19

10:7–10 The incident referred to in 10:7 is when the Israelites made a golden calf and worshiped it in the wilderness (Exodus 32). The incident in 10:8 is recorded in Numbers 25:1–9 when the Israelites worshiped Baal of Peor and engaged in sexual immorality with Moabite women. The reference in 10:9 is to the Israelites' complaint about their food (Numbers 21:5–6). They put the Lord to the test by seeing how far they could go. In 10:10, Paul refers to the incident when the people complained against Moses and Aaron, and the plague that resulted (Numbers 14:2, 36; 16:41–50). The destroyer is referred to in Exodus 12:23.

10:11 Today's pressures make it easy to ignore or forget the lessons of the past. But Paul cautions us to remember the lessons the Israelites learned about God so we can avoid repeating their errors. The key to remembering is to study the Bible regularly so that these lessons remind us of how God wants us to live. We need not repeat their mistakes!

10:13 In a culture filled with moral depravity and sin-inducing pressures, Paul gave strong encouragement to the Corinthians about temptation. He said: (1) Wrong desires and temptations happen to everyone, so don't feel you've been singled out; (2) others have resisted temptation, and so can you; (3) any temptation can be resisted because God will help you resist it. God helps you resist temptation by helping you (1) recognize those people and situations that give you trouble, (2) run from anything you know is wrong, (3) choose to do only what is right, (4) pray for God's help, and (5) seek friends who love God and can offer help when you are tempted. Running from a tempting situation is your first step on the way to victory (see 2 Timothy 2:22).

10:14 Idol worship was the major expression of religion in Corinth. There were several pagan temples in the city, and they were very popular. The statues of wood or stone were not evil in themselves, but people gave them credit for what only God could do, such as providing good weather, crops, and children. Idolatry is still a serious problem today, but it takes a different form. We don't put our trust in statues of wood and stone, but in paper money and plastic cards. Trusting anything for what God alone provides is idolatry. Our modern idols are those symbols of power, pleasure, or prestige that we so highly regard. When we understand contemporary parallels to idolatry, Paul's words to "flee from idolatry" become much more meaningful.

10:16–21 The idea of unity and fellowship with God through eating a sacrifice was strong in Judaism and Christianity as well as in paganism. In Old Testament days, when a Jew offered a sacrifice, he ate a part of that sacrifice as a way of restoring his unity with God, against whom he had sinned (Deuteronomy 12:17–18). Similarly, Christians participate in Christ's once-for-all sacrifice when they eat the bread and drink the wine symbolizing his body and blood. Recent converts from paganism could not help being affected if they knowingly ate with pagans in their feasts the meat offered to idols.

10:21 As followers of Christ we must give him our total allegiance. We cannot, as Paul explains, have a part in "the table of the Lord and the table of demons." Eating at the Lord's table means communing with Christ and identifying with his death. Eating at the demons' table means identifying with Satan by worshiping or promoting pagan (or evil) activities. Are you trying to lead two lives, following the desires of both Christ and the crowd? The Bible says that you can't do both at the same time.

10:23–24 Sometimes it's hard to know when to defer to the weaker believer. Paul gives a simple rule of thumb to help in making the decision—we should be sensitive and gracious. While some

10:24 Rom 15:2; Phil 2:21
10:25 Acts 10:15; 1 Cor 8:7
10:26 Ps 24:1; 50:12
10:27 Luke 10:8
10:29 Rom 14:16
10:31 Col 3:17; 1 Pet 4:11
10:32 Gal 1:13; Phil 3:6; 1 Tim 3:5, 15
10:33 Rom 15:2; 1 Cor 9:22; Gal 1:10

24 Let no one seek his own *good,* but that of his neighbor.
25 Eat anything that is sold in the meat market without asking questions for conscience' sake;
26 FOR THE EARTH IS THE LORD'S, AND ALL IT CONTAINS.
27 If one of the unbelievers invites you and you want to go, eat anything that is set before you without asking questions for conscience' sake.
28 But if anyone says to you, "This is meat sacrificed to idols," do not eat *it,* for the sake of the one who informed *you,* and for conscience' sake;
29 I mean not your own conscience, but the other *man's;* for why is my freedom judged by another's conscience?
30 If I partake with thankfulness, why am I slandered concerning that for which I give thanks?
31 Whether, then, you eat or drink or whatever you do, do all to the glory of God.
32 Give no offense either to Jews or to Greeks or to the church of God;
33 just as I also please all men in all things, not seeking my own profit but the *profit* of the many, so that they may be saved.

WHY WE DON'T GIVE UP
Perseverance, persistence, the prize! The Christian life was never promised as an easy way to live; instead, Paul constantly reminds us that we must have a purpose and a plan because times will be difficult and Satan will attack. But we never persevere without the promise of a prize—a promise God will keep.

Reference	*The Purpose*	*The Plan*	*The Prize*
1 Corinthians 9:24–27	• Run to get the prize • Run straight to the goal	• Deny yourself whatever is potentially harmful • Discipline your body, training it	• A crown (wreath) that will last forever
Galatians 6:7–10	• Don't lose heart in doing good • Don't get discouraged and give up • Do good to everyone	• Sow to please the Spirit	• Reap eternal life
Ephesians 6:10–20	• Put on the full armor of God • Pray at all times	• Use all the pieces of God's armor provided for you	• Standing firm against the schemes of the devil
Philippians 3:12–14	• Press on toward the day when you will be all God wants you to be	• Forget the past; strain toward what is ahead	• The prize for which God calls us heavenward
2 Timothy 2:1–13	• Entrust these great truths to faithful people who will teach them to others • Be strong in Christ's grace, even when your faith is faltering	• Suffer hardship like a soldier, and don't get involved in worldly affairs • Follow the Lord's rules, as an athlete must do in order to win • Work hard, like a farmer who tends his crops for the harvest	• We will live with Christ; we will reign with him • He always remains faithful to us and always carries out his promises

actions may not be wrong, they may not be in the best interest of others. While we have freedom in Christ, we shouldn't exercise our freedom at the cost of hurting a Christian brother or sister. We are not to consider only ourselves, but we must be sensitive to others. For more on the proper attitude toward a weaker believer, see the notes on 8:10–13 and Romans 14.

10:25–27 Paul gave one answer to the dilemma—to buy whatever meat is sold at the market without asking whether it was offered to idols. It doesn't matter anyway, and no one's conscience would be troubled. When we become too worried about our every action, we become legalistic and cannot enjoy life. Everything belongs to God, and he has given us all things to enjoy. If we know something is a problem, then we can deal with it, but we don't need to go looking for problems.

10:28–33 Why should we be limited by another person's conscience? Simply because we are to do all things for God's glory, even our eating and drinking. Nothing we do should cause another believer to stumble. We do what is best for others, so that they might be saved. On the other hand, Christians should not make a career out of being the weaker person with oversensitive consciences. Christian leaders and teachers should carefully teach about the freedom we have in matters not expressly forbidden by Scripture.

10:31 God's love must so permeate our motives that all we do will be for his glory. Keep this as a guiding principle by asking, "Is this action glorifying God?" or "How can I honor God through this action?"

10:33 Paul's criterion for all his actions was not what he liked best, but what was best for those around him. The opposite attitude would be: (1) being insensitive and doing what we want, no matter who is hurt by it; (2) being oversensitive and doing nothing, for fear that someone may be displeased; (3) being a "yes person" by going along with everything, trying to gain approval from people rather than from God. In this age of "me first" and "looking out for number one," Paul's startling statement is a good standard. If we make the good of others one of our primary goals, we will develop a serving attitude that pleases God.

3. Instruction on public worship

Christian Order

11 Be imitators of me, just as I also am of Christ.
2 Now I praise you because you remember me in everything and hold firmly to
the traditions, just as I delivered them to you.
3 But I want you to understand that Christ is the head of every man, and the man is
the head of a woman, and God is the head of Christ.
4 Every man who has *something* on his head while praying or prophesying disgraces
his head.
5 But every woman who has her head uncovered while praying or prophesying disgraces her head, for she is one and the same as the woman whose head is shaved.
6 For if a woman does not cover her head, let her also have her hair cut off; but if it is
disgraceful for a woman to have her hair cut off or her head shaved, let her cover her
head.
7 For a man ought not to have his head covered, since he is the image and glory of
God; but the woman is the glory of man.
8 For man does not originate from woman, but woman from man;
9 for indeed man was not created for the woman's sake, but woman for the man's sake.
10 Therefore the woman ought to have *a symbol of* authority on her head, because of
the angels.
11 However, in the Lord, neither is woman independent of man, nor is man independent of woman.
12 For as the woman originates from the man, so also the man *has his birth* through the
woman; and all things originate from God.
13 Judge for yourselves: is it proper for a woman to pray to God *with her head* uncovered?

11:1
1 Cor 4:16; Phil 3:17

11:2
1 Cor 11:17, 22; 1 Cor 4:17; 15:2; 1 Thess 1:6; 3:6; 2 Thess 2:15; 3:6

11:3
Eph 1:22; 4:15; 5:23; Col 1:18; 2:19; Gen 3:16; Eph 5:23; 1 Cor 3:23

11:4
Acts 13:1; 1 Thess 5:20

11:5
Luke 2:36; Acts 21:9; 1 Cor 14:34; Deut 21:12

11:7
Gen 1:26; 5:1; 9:6; James 3:9

11:8
Gen 2:21-23; 1 Tim 2:13

11:9
Gen 2:18

11:12
2 Cor 5:18; Rom 11:36

11:13
Luke 12:57

11:1 Why did Paul say, "Be imitators of me"? Paul wasn't being arrogant—he did not think of himself as sinless. At this time, however, the Corinthian believers did not know much about the life and ministry of Christ. Paul could not tell them to imitate Jesus, because the Gospels had not yet been written, so they did not know what Jesus was like. The best way to point these new Christians to Christ was to point them to a Christian whom they trusted (see also Galatians 4:12; Philippians 3:17; 1 Thessalonians 1:6; 2:14; 2 Thessalonians 3:7, 9). Paul had been in Corinth almost two years and had built a relationship of trust with many of these new believers.

11:2ff In this section Paul's main concern is irreverence in worship. We need to read it in the context of the situation in Corinth. The matter of wearing hats or head coverings, although seemingly insignificant, had become a big problem because two cultural backgrounds were colliding. Jewish women always covered their heads in worship. For a woman to uncover her head in public was a sign of loose morals. On the other hand, Greek women may have been used to worshiping without head coverings.

In this letter Paul had already spoken about divisions and disorder in the church. Both are involved in this issue. Paul's solution comes from his desire for unity among church members and for appropriateness in the worship service. He accepted God's sovereignty in creating the rules for relationships.

11:2–16 This section focuses primarily on proper attitudes and conduct in worship, not on the marriage relationship or on the role of women in the church. While Paul's specific instructions may be cultural (women covering their heads in worship), the principles behind his specific instructions are timeless, principles like respect for spouse, reverence and appropriateness in worship, and focus of all of life on God. If anything you do can easily offend members and divide the church, then change your ways to promote church unity. Thus Paul told the women who were not wearing head coverings to wear them, not because it was a Scriptural command, but because it kept the congregation from dividing over a petty issue that served only to take people's minds off Christ.

11:3 In the phrase, "the man is the head of a woman," *head* is not used to indicate control or supremacy, but rather, "the source of." Because man was created first, the woman derives her existence from man, as man does from Christ and Christ from God. Evidently Paul was correcting some excesses in worship that the emancipated Corinthian women were engaging in.

11:3 Submission is a key element in the smooth functioning of any business, government, or family. God ordained submission in certain relationships to prevent chaos. It is essential to understand that submission is not surrender, withdrawal, or apathy. It does not mean inferiority, because God created all people in his image and because all have equal value. Submission is mutual commitment and cooperation.

Thus God calls for submission among *equals.* He did not make the man superior; he made a way for the man and woman to work together. Jesus Christ, although equal with God the Father, submitted to him to carry out the plan for salvation. Likewise, although equal to man under God, the wife should submit to her husband for the sake of their marriage and family. Submission between equals is submission by choice, not by force. We serve God in these relationships by willingly submitting to others in our church, to our spouses, and to our government leaders.

11:9–11 God created lines of authority in order for his created world to function smoothly. Although there must be lines of authority, even in marriage, there should *not* be lines of superiority. God created men and women with unique and complementary characteristics. One sex is not better than the other. We must not let the issue of authority and submission become a wedge to destroy oneness in marriage. Instead, we should use our unique gifts to strengthen our marriages and to glorify God.

11:10 "The woman ought to have a symbol of authority on her head, because of the angels" may mean that the woman should wear a covering on her head as a sign that she is under the man's authority. This is a fact even the angels understand as they observe Christians in worship. See the note on 11:2ff for an explanation of head coverings.

14 Does not even nature itself teach you that if a man has long hair, it is a dishonor
to him,
15 but if a woman has long hair, it is a glory to her? For her hair is given to her for a
covering.
16 But if one is inclined to be contentious, we have no other practice, nor have the
churches of God.
17 But in giving this instruction, I do not praise you, because you come together not
for the better but for the worse.
18 For, in the first place, when you come together as a church, I hear that divisions
exist among you; and in part I believe it.
19 For there must also be factions among you, so that those who are approved may
become evident among you.
20 Therefore when you meet together, it is not to eat the Lord's Supper,
21 for in your eating each one takes his own supper first; and one is hungry and another is drunk.
22 What! Do you not have houses in which to eat and drink? Or do you despise the
church of God and shame those who have nothing? What shall I say to you? Shall I praise
you? In this I will not praise you.

The Lord's Supper

23 For I received from the Lord that which I also delivered to you, that the Lord Jesus
in the night in which He was betrayed took bread;

11:16 1 Cor 4:5; 9:1-3, 6; 1 Cor 7:17

11:17 1 Cor 11:2, 22

11:18 1 Cor 1:10; 3:3

11:19 Matt 18:7; Luke 17:1; 1 Tim 4:1; 2 Pet 2:1; Deut 13:3; 1 John 2:19

11:21 Jude 12

11:22 1 Cor 10:32; James 2:6; 1 Cor 11:2, 17

11:23 1 Cor 15:3; Gal 1:12; Col 3:24; Matt 26:26-28; Mark 14:22-24; Luke 22:17-20; 1 Cor 10:16

MAKING CHOICES IN SENSITIVE ISSUES

If I choose one course of action:

. . . does it help my witness for Christ? (9:19–22)

. . . am I motivated by a desire to help others to know Christ? (9:23; 10:33)

. . . does it help me do my best? (9:25)

. . . is it against a specific command in Scripture and would thus cause me to sin? (10:12)

. . . is it the best and most beneficial course of action? (10:23, 33)

. . . am I thinking only of myself, or do I truly care about the other person? (10:24)

. . . am I acting lovingly or selfishly? (10:28–31)

. . . does it glorify God? (10:31)

. . . will it cause someone else to sin? (10:32)

All of us make hundreds of choices every day. Most choices have no right or wrong attached to them—like what you wear or what you eat. But we always face decisions that carry a little more weight. We don't want to do wrong, and we don't want to cause others to do wrong, so how can we make such decisions?

11:14–15 In talking about head coverings and length of hair, Paul is saying that believers should look and behave in ways that are honorable within their own culture. In many cultures long hair on men is considered appropriate and masculine. In Corinth, it was thought to be a sign of male prostitution in the pagan temples. And women with short hair were labeled prostitutes. Paul was saying that in the Corinthian culture, Christian women should keep their hair long. If short hair on women was a sign of prostitution, then a Christian woman with short hair would find it even more difficult to be a believable witness for Jesus Christ. Paul wasn't saying we should adopt all the practices of our culture, but that we should avoid appearances and behavior that detract from our ultimate goal of being believable witnesses for Jesus Christ while demonstrating our Christian faith.

11:17–34 The Lord's Supper (11:20) is a visible representation of the Good News of the death of Christ for our sins. It reminds us of Christ's death and the glorious hope of his return. Our participation in it strengthens our faith through fellowship with Christ and with other believers.

11:19 Paul allows that there might be differences among church members. When they develop into self willed divisions, they are destructive to the congregation. Those who cause division only serve to highlight those who are genuine believers.

11:21–22 When the Lord's Supper was celebrated in the early church, it included a feast or fellowship meal followed by the celebration of Communion. In the church in Corinth, the fellowship meal had become a time when some ate and drank excessively while others went hungry. There was little sharing and caring. This certainly did not demonstrate the unity and love that should characterize the church, nor was it a preparation for Communion. Paul condemned these actions and reminded the church of the real purpose of the Lord's Supper.

24 and when He had given thanks, He broke it and said, "This is My body, which is for
you; do this in remembrance of Me."
25 In the same way *He took* the cup also after supper, saying, "This cup is the new covenant in My blood; do this, as often as you drink *it,* in remembrance of Me."
26 For as often as you eat this bread and drink the cup, you proclaim the Lord's death
until He comes.
27 Therefore whoever eats the bread or drinks the cup of the Lord in an unworthy
manner, shall be guilty of the body and the blood of the Lord.
28 But a man must examine himself, and in so doing he is to eat of the bread and drink
of the cup.
29 For he who eats and drinks, eats and drinks judgment to himself if he does not judge
the body rightly.
30 For this reason many among you are weak and sick, and a number sleep.
31 But if we judged ourselves rightly, we would not be judged.
32 But when we are judged, we are disciplined by the Lord so that we will not be condemned along with the world.
33 So then, my brethren, when you come together to eat, wait for one another.
34 If anyone is hungry, let him eat at home, so that you will not come together for judgment. The remaining matters I will arrange when I come.

The Use of Spiritual Gifts

12 Now concerning spiritual *gifts,* brethren, I do not want you to be unaware.
2 You know that when you were pagans, *you were* led astray to the mute idols,
however you were led.

11:25 1 Cor 10:16; Ex 24:6-8; Luke 22:20; 2 Cor 3:6
11:26 John 21:22; 1 Cor 4:5
11:27 Heb 10:29
11:28 Matt 26:22; 2 Cor 13:5; Gal 6:4
11:30 Acts 7:60
11:32 Rev 3:19; 1 Cor 1:20
11:34 1 Cor 4:17; 7:17; 16:1; 1 Cor 4:19
12:1 Rom 1:13
12:2 1 Cor 6:11; Eph 2:11f; 1 Pet 4:3; 1 Thess 1:9; Ps 115:5; Is 46:7; Jer 10:5; Hab 2:18f

---

11:24–25 What does the Lord's Supper mean? The early church remembered that Jesus instituted the Lord's Supper on the night of the Passover meal (Luke 22:13–20). Just as Passover celebrated deliverance from slavery in Egypt, so the Lord's Supper celebrates deliverance from sin by Christ's death.

Christians pose several different possibilities for what Christ meant when he said, "This is My body." (1) Some believe that the wine and bread actually become Christ's physical blood and body. (2) Others believe that the bread and wine remain unchanged, but Christ is spiritually present with the bread and wine. (3) Still others believe that the bread and wine symbolize Christ's body and blood. Christians generally agree, however, that participating in the Lord's Supper is an important element in the Christian faith and that Christ's presence, however we understand it, strengthens us spiritually.

11:25 What is this new covenant? In the old covenant, people could approach God only through the priests and the sacrificial system. Jesus' death on the cross ushered in the new covenant or agreement between God and us. Now all people can personally approach God and communicate with him. The people of Israel first entered into this agreement after their exodus from Egypt (Exodus 24), and it was designed to point to the day when Jesus Christ would come. The new covenant completes, rather than replaces, the old covenant, fulfilling everything the old covenant looked forward to (see Jeremiah 31:31–34). Eating the bread and drinking the cup show that we are remembering Christ's death for us and renewing our commitment to serve him.

11:25 Jesus said, "Do this, as often as you drink it, in remembrance of Me." How do we remember Christ in the Lord's Supper? By thinking about what he did and why he did it. If the Lord's Supper becomes just a ritual or a pious habit, it no longer remembers Christ, and it loses its significance.

11:27ff Paul gives specific instructions on how the Lord's Supper should be observed. (1) We should take the Lord's Supper thoughtfully because we are proclaiming that Christ died for our sins (11:26). (2) We should take it worthily, with due reverence and respect (11:27). (3) We should examine ourselves for any unconfessed sin or resentful attitude (11:28). We are to be properly prepared, based on our belief in and love for Christ. (4) We should be considerate of others (11:33), waiting until everyone is there and then eating in an orderly and unified manner.

11:27–34 When Paul said that no one should take the Lord's Supper in an unworthy manner, he was speaking to the church members who were rushing into it without thinking of its meaning. Those who did so were "guilty of the body and the blood of the Lord." Instead of honoring his sacrifice, they were sharing in the guilt of those who crucified Christ. In reality, *no one* is worthy to take the Lord's Supper. We are all sinners saved by grace. This is why we should prepare ourselves for Communion through healthy introspection, confession of sin, and resolution of differences with others. These actions remove the barriers that affect our relationship with Christ and with other believers. Awareness of your sin should not keep you away from Communion but should drive you to participate in it.

11:29 "If he does not judge the body rightly" means not understanding what the Lord's Supper means and not distinguishing it from a normal meal. Those who do so condemn themselves (see 11:27).

11:30 "Sleep" is another way of describing death. That some of the people had died may have been a special supernatural judgment on the Corinthian church. This type of disciplinary judgment highlights the seriousness of the Communion service. The Lord's Supper is not to be taken lightly; this new covenant cost Jesus his life. It is not a meaningless ritual, but a sacrament given by Christ to help strengthen our faith.

11:34 People should come to this meal desiring to fellowship with other believers and prepare for the Lord's Supper to follow, not to fill up on a big dinner. "If anyone is hungry, let him eat at home" means that they should eat dinner beforehand, so as to come to the fellowship meal in the right frame of mind.

12:1ff The spiritual gifts given to each person by the Holy Spirit are special abilities that are to be used to minister to the needs of the body of believers. This chapter is not an exhaustive list of spiritual gifts (see Romans 12; Ephesians 4; 1 Peter 4:10–11 for more examples). There are many gifts, people have different gifts, some people have more than one gift, and one gift is not superior to another. All spiritual gifts come from the Holy Spirit, and their purpose is to build up Christ's body, the church.

12:1ff Instead of building up and unifying the Corinthian church,

12:3 Matt 22:43; 1 John 4:2f; Rev 1:10; Rom 9:3; John 13:13; Rom 10:9
12:4 Rom 12:6f; 1 Cor 12:11; Eph 4:4ff, 11; Heb 2:4
12:6 1 Cor 15:28; Eph 1:23; 4:6
12:7 Eph 4:12
12:8 1 Cor 2:6; 2 Cor 1:12; Rom 15:14; 1 Cor 2:11, 16; 2 Cor 2:14; 4:6; 8:7; 11:6
12:9 1 Cor 13:2; 2 Cor 4:13
12:10 1 Cor 12:28f; Gal 3:5; 1 Cor 11:4; 13:2, 8; 1 Cor 14:29; 1 John 4:1; Mark 16:17; 1 Cor 12:28, 30; 13:1; 14:2ff; 1 Cor 12:30; 14:26
12:11 1 Cor 12:4
12:12 Rom 12:4f; 1 Cor 10:17; 1 Cor 12:27
12:13 Eph 2:18; Rom 3:22; Gal 3:28; Eph 2:13-18; Col 3:11; John 7:37-39
12:18 Rom 12:6

3 Therefore I make known to you that no one speaking by the Spirit of God says, "Jesus
is accursed"; and no one can say, "Jesus is Lord," except by the Holy Spirit.
4 Now there are varieties of gifts, but the same Spirit.
5 And there are varieties of ministries, and the same Lord.
6 There are varieties of effects, but the same God who works all things in all *persons.*
7 But to each one is given the manifestation of the Spirit for the common good.
8 For to one is given the word of wisdom through the Spirit, and to another the word
of knowledge according to the same Spirit;
9 to another faith by the same Spirit, and to another gifts of healing by the one Spirit,
10 and to another the effecting of miracles, and to another prophecy, and to another
the distinguishing of spirits, to another *various* kinds of tongues, and to another the interpretation of tongues.
11 But one and the same Spirit works all these things, distributing to each one individually just as He wills.
12 For even as the body is one and *yet* has many members, and all the members of the
body, though they are many, are one body, so also is Christ.
13 For by one Spirit we were all baptized into one body, whether Jews or Greeks, whether slaves or free, and we were all made to drink of one Spirit.
14 For the body is not one member, but many.
15 If the foot says, "Because I am not a hand, I am not *a part* of the body," it is not for
this reason any the less *a part* of the body.
16 And if the ear says, "Because I am not an eye, I am not *a part* of the body," it is not
for this reason any the less *a part* of the body.
17 If the whole body were an eye, where would the hearing be? If the whole were hearing, where would the sense of smell be?
18 But now God has placed the members, each one of them, in the body, just as He
desired.
19 If they were all one member, where would the body be?
20 But now there are many members, but one body.
21 And the eye cannot say to the hand, "I have no need of you"; or again the head to
the feet, "I have no need of you."
22 On the contrary, it is much truer that the members of the body which seem to be
weaker are necessary;

---

the issue of spiritual gifts was splitting it. Spiritual gifts had become symbols of spiritual power, causing rivalries because some people thought they were more "spiritual" than others because of their gifts. This was a terrible misuse of spiritual gifts because their purpose is always to help the church function more effectively, not to divide it. We can be divisive if we insist on using our gift our own way without being sensitive to others. We must never use gifts as a means of manipulating others or serving our own self-interest.

12:3 Anyone can claim to speak for God, and the world is full of false teachers. Paul gives us a test to help us discern whether or not a messenger is really from God: Does he or she confess Christ as Lord? Don't naively accept the words of all who claim to speak for God; test their credentials by finding out what they teach about Christ.

12:9 All Christians have faith. Some, however, have the spiritual gift of faith, which is an unusual measure of trust in the Holy Spirit's power.

12:10–11 "Prophecy" is not just a prediction about the future; it can also mean preaching God's Word with power. "Distinguishing of spirits" means the ability to discern whether a person who claims to speak for God is actually doing so, or is speaking by an evil spirit. (Paul discusses tongues and their interpretation in more detail in chapter 14.) No matter what gift(s) a person has, each gift is given by the Holy Spirit. The Holy Spirit decides which gifts each one of us should have. We are responsible to use and sharpen our gifts, but we can take no credit for what God has freely given us.

12:12 Paul compares the body of Christ to a human body. Each part has a specific function that is necessary to the body as a whole. The parts are different for a purpose, and in their differences they must work together. Christians must avoid two common errors: (1) being too proud of their abilities, or (2) thinking they have nothing to give to the body of believers. Instead of comparing ourselves to one another, we should use our different gifts, together, to spread the Good News of salvation.

12:13 The church is composed of many types of people from a variety of backgrounds with a multitude of gifts and abilities. It is easy for these differences to divide people, as was the case in Corinth. But despite the differences, all believers have one thing in common—faith in Christ. On this essential truth the church finds unity. All believers are baptized by one Holy Spirit into one body of believers, the church. We don't lose our individual identities, but we have an overriding oneness in Christ. When a person becomes a Christian, the Holy Spirit takes up residence, and he or she is born into God's family. "We were all made to drink of one Spirit" means that the same Holy Spirit completely fills our innermost beings. As members of God's family, we may have different interests and gifts, but we have a common goal.

12:14–24 Using the analogy of the body, Paul emphasizes the importance of each church member (see the note on 12:12). If a seemingly insignificant part is taken away, the whole body becomes less effective. Thinking that your gift is more important than someone else's is an expression of spiritual pride. We should not look down on those who seem unimportant, and we should not be jealous of others who have impressive gifts. Instead, we should use the gifts we have been given and encourage others to use theirs. If we don't, the body of believers will be less effective.

23 and those *members* of the body which we deem less honorable, on these we bestow
more abundant honor, and our less presentable members become much more presentable,
24 whereas our more presentable members have no need *of it.* But God has *so* composed the body, giving more abundant honor to that *member* which lacked,
25 so that there may be no division in the body, but *that* the members may have the
same care for one another.
26 And if one member suffers, all the members suffer with it; if *one* member is honored, all the members rejoice with it.
27 Now you are Christ's body, and individually members of it.
28 And God has appointed in the church, first apostles, second prophets, third teachers, then miracles, then gifts of healings, helps, administrations, *various* kinds of tongues.
29 All are not apostles, are they? All are not prophets, are they? All are not teachers,
are they? All are not *workers of* miracles, are they?
30 All do not have gifts of healings, do they? All do not speak with tongues, do they?
All do not interpret, do they?
31 But earnestly desire the greater gifts.
And I show you a still more excellent way.

The Excellence of Love

13 If I speak with the tongues of men and of angels, but do not have love, I have become a noisy gong or a clanging cymbal.
2 If I have *the gift of* prophecy, and know all mysteries and all knowledge; and if I have
all faith, so as to remove mountains, but do not have love, I am nothing.
3 And if I give all my possessions to feed *the poor,* and if I surrender my body [12]to be
burned, but do not have love, it profits me nothing.
4 Love is patient, love is kind *and* is not jealous; love does not brag *and* is not arrogant,
5 does not act unbecomingly; it does not seek its own, is not provoked, does not take
into account a wrong *suffered,*
6 does not rejoice in unrighteousness, but rejoices with the truth;
7 bears all things, believes all things, hopes all things, endures all things.
8 Love never fails; but if *there are gifts of* prophecy, they will be done away; if *there are*
tongues, they will cease; if *there is* knowledge, it will be done away.
9 For we know in part and we prophesy in part;
10 but when the perfect comes, the partial will be done away.
11 When I was a child, I used to speak like a child, think like a child, reason like a child;
when I became a man, I did away with childish things.

12 Early mss read *that I may boast*

12:27
1 Cor 1:2; 12:12; Eph 1:23; 4:12; Col 1:18, 24; 2:19; Rom 12:5; Eph 5:30

12:28
1 Cor 12:18; 1 Cor 10:32; Eph 4:11; Acts 13:1; Eph 2:20; 3:5; Acts 13:1; 1 Cor 12:10, 29; 1 Cor 12:9, 30; Rom 12:8; 1 Cor 12:10

12:30
1 Cor 12:10

12:31
1 Cor 14:1, 39

13:1
1 Cor 12:10; 2 Cor 12:4; Rev 14:2; Ps 150:5

13:2
Matt 7:22; Acts 13:1; 1 Cor 11:4; 13:8; 14:1, 39; 1 Cor 14:2; 15:51; Rom 15:14; 1 Cor 12:9; Matt 17:20; 21:21; Mark 11:23

13:3
Matt 6:2; Dan 3:28

13:4
Prov 10:12; 17:9; 1 Thess 5:14; 1 Pet 4:8; Acts 7:9; 1 Cor 4:6

13:5
1 Cor 10:24; Phil 2:21; 2 Cor 5:19

13:6
2 Thess 2:12; 2 John 4; 3 John 3f

13:7
1 Cor 9:12

13:8
1 Cor 13:2; 1 Cor 13:1

13:9
1 Cor 8:2; 13:12

12:25–26 What is your response when a fellow Christian is honored? How do you respond when someone is suffering? We are called to rejoice with those who rejoice and weep with those who weep (Romans 12:15). Too often, unfortunately, we are jealous of those who rejoice and apathetic toward those who weep. Believers are in the world together—there is no such thing as private or individualistic Christianity. We shouldn't stop with enjoying only our own relationship with God; we need to get involved in the lives of others.

12:30 Paul discusses the subject of speaking in and interpreting tongues in more detail in chapter 14.

12:31 The greater gifts are those that are more beneficial to the body of Christ. Paul has already made it clear that one gift is not superior to another, but he urges the believers to discover how they can serve Christ's body with the gifts God has given them. Your spiritual gifts are not for your own self-advancement. They were given to you for serving God and enhancing the spiritual growth of the body of believers.

13:1ff In chapter 12 Paul gave evidence of the Corinthians' lack of love in the utilization of spiritual gifts, chapter 13 defines real love, and chapter 14 shows how love works. Love is more important than all the spiritual gifts exercised in the church body. Great faith, acts of dedication or sacrifice, and miracle-working power produce very little without love. Love makes our actions and gifts useful. Although people have different gifts, love is available to everyone.

13:4–7 Our society confuses love and lust. Unlike lust, God's kind of love is directed outward toward others, not inward toward ourselves. It is utterly unselfish. This kind of love goes against our natural inclinations. It is possible to practice this love only if God helps us set aside our own desires and instincts, so that we can give love while expecting nothing in return. Thus the more we become like Christ, the more love we will show to others.

13:10 God gives us spiritual gifts for our lives on earth in order to build up, serve, and strengthen fellow Christians. The spiritual gifts are for the church. In eternity, we will be made perfect and complete and will be in the very presence of God. We will no longer need the spiritual gifts, so they will come to an end.

12 For now we see in a mirror dimly, but then face to face; now I know in part, but then
I will know fully just as I also have been fully known.
13 But now faith, hope, love, abide these three; but the greatest of these is love.

Prophecy a Superior Gift

14 Pursue love, yet desire earnestly spiritual *gifts,* but especially that you may prophesy.
2 For one who speaks in a tongue does not speak to men but to God; for no one understands, but in *his* spirit he speaks mysteries.
3 But one who prophesies speaks to men for edification and exhortation and consolation.
4 One who speaks in a tongue edifies himself; but one who prophesies edifies the
church.
5 Now I wish that you all spoke in tongues, but *even* more that you would prophesy;
and greater is one who prophesies than one who speaks in tongues, unless he interprets,
so that the church may receive edifying.
6 But now, brethren, if I come to you speaking in tongues, what will I profit you
unless I speak to you either by way of revelation or of knowledge or of prophecy or of
teaching?
7 Yet *even* lifeless things, either flute or harp, in producing a sound, if they do not
produce a distinction in the tones, how will it be known what is played on the flute or on
the harp?
8 For if the bugle produces an indistinct sound, who will prepare himself for battle?
9 So also you, unless you utter by the tongue speech that is clear, how will it be known
what is spoken? For you will be speaking into the air.
10 There are, perhaps, a great many kinds of languages in the world, and no *kind* is
without meaning.
11 If then I do not know the meaning of the language, I will be to the one who speaks
a barbarian, and the one who speaks will be a barbarian to me.
12 So also you, since you are zealous of spiritual *gifts,* seek to abound for the edification of the church.
13 Therefore let one who speaks in a tongue pray that he may interpret.
14 For if I pray in a tongue, my spirit prays, but my mind is unfruitful.
15 What is *the outcome* then? I will pray with the spirit and I will pray with the mind
also; I will sing with the spirit and I will sing with the mind also.

13:12 2 Cor 5:7; Phil 3:12; James 1:23; 1 John 3:2; 1 Cor 8:3
13:13 Gal 5:6
14:2 Mark 16:17; 1 Cor 12:10, 28, 30; 13:1; 14:18ff; 1 Cor 13:2
14:3 Rom 14:19; Acts 4:36
14:4 Mark 16:17; 1 Cor 12:10, 28, 30; 13:1; 14:18ff, 26f; Rom 14:19; 1 Cor 14:5, 12, 17, 26; 1 Cor 13:2
14:5 Mark 16:17; 1 Cor 12:10, 28, 30; 13:1; 14:18ff, 26f; Num 11:29; Rom 14:19
14:6 1 Cor 14:26; Eph 1:17; 1 Cor 12:8; 1 Cor 13:2; Acts 2:42; Rom 6:17
14:8 Num 10:9; Jer 4:19; Ezek 33:3-6; Joel 2:1
14:9 1 Cor 9:26
14:11 Acts 28:2
14:12 Rom 14:19
14:15 Acts 21:22; 1 Cor 14:26; Eph 5:19; Col 3:16

13:12 Paul offers a glimpse into the future to give us hope that one day we will be complete when we see God face to face. This truth should strengthen our faith—we don't have all the answers now, but one day we will. Someday we will see Christ in person and be able to see with God's perspective.

13:13 In morally corrupt Corinth, love had become a mixed-up term with little meaning. Today people are still confused about love. Love is the greatest of all human qualities, and it is an attribute of God himself (1 John 4:8). Love involves unselfish service to others; to show it gives evidence that you care. *Faith* is the foundation and content of God's message; *hope* is the attitude and focus; *love* is the action. When faith and hope are in line, you are free to love completely because you understand how God loves.

14:1 Prophesying may involve predicting future events, but its main purpose is to communicate God's message to people, providing insight, warning, correction, and encouragement.

14:2 The gift of speaking in a tongue was a concern of the Corinthian church because the use of the gift had caused disorder in worship. Speaking in tongues is a legitimate gift of the Holy Spirit, but the Corinthian believers were using it as a sign of spiritual superiority rather than as a means to spiritual unity. Spiritual gifts are beneficial only when they are properly used to help everyone in the church. We should not exercise them only to make *ourselves* feel good.

14:2ff Paul makes several points about speaking in tongues: (1) It is a spiritual gift from God (14:2); (2) it is a desirable gift even though it isn't a requirement of faith (12:28–31); (3) it is less important than prophecy and teaching (14:4). Although Paul himself spoke in tongues, he stresses prophecy (preaching) because it benefits the whole church, while speaking in tongues primarily benefits the speaker. Public worship must be understandable and edifying to the whole church.

14:5–12 As musical instruments must play each note in order for the music to be clear, so Paul says words preached in the hearers' language are clearer and more helpful. There are many languages in the world (14:10), and people who speak different languages can rarely understand each other. It is the same with speaking in tongues. Although this gift is helpful to many people in private worship, and helpful in public worship with interpretation, Paul says he would rather speak five words that his hearers can understand than 10,000 that they cannot (14:19).

14:13–20 If a person has the gift of speaking in tongues, he should also pray for the gift of knowing what he has said (interpretation) so he can tell people afterwards. This way, the entire church will be edified by this gift.

14:15 There is a proper place for the intellect in Christianity. In praying and singing, both the mind and the spirit are to be fully engaged. When we sing, we should also think about the meaning of the words. When we pour out our feelings to God in prayer, we should not turn off our capacity to think. True Christianity is neither barren intellectualism nor thoughtless emotionalism. See also Ephesians 1:17–18; Philippians 1:9–11; Colossians 1:9.

16 Otherwise if you bless in the spirit *only,* how will the one who fills the place of the
ungifted say the "Amen" at your giving of thanks, since he does not know what you are
saying?
17 For you are giving thanks well enough, but the other person is not edified.
18 I thank God, I speak in tongues more than you all;
19 however, in the church I desire to speak five words with my mind so that I may instruct others also, rather than ten thousand words in a tongue.

Instruction for the Church

20 Brethren, do not be children in your thinking; yet in evil be infants, but in your thinking be mature.
21 In the Law it is written, "BY MEN OF STRANGE TONGUES AND BY THE LIPS OF
STRANGERS I WILL SPEAK TO THIS PEOPLE, AND EVEN SO THEY WILL NOT LISTEN TO
ME," says the Lord.
22 So then tongues are for a sign, not to those who believe but to unbelievers; but prophecy *is for a sign*, not to unbelievers but to those who believe.
23 Therefore if the whole church assembles together and all speak in tongues, and
ungifted men or unbelievers enter, will they not say that you are mad?
24 But if all prophesy, and an unbeliever or an ungifted man enters, he is convicted by
all, he is called to account by all;
25 the secrets of his heart are disclosed; and so he will fall on his face and worship God,
declaring that God is certainly among you.
26 What is *the outcome* then, brethren? When you assemble, each one has a psalm, has
a teaching, has a revelation, has a tongue, has an interpretation. Let all things be done
for edification.
27 If anyone speaks in a tongue, *it should be* by two or at the most three, and *each* in
turn, and one must interpret;
28 but if there is no interpreter, he must keep silent in the church; and let him speak to
himself and to God.
29 Let two or three prophets speak, and let the others pass judgment.
30 But if a revelation is made to another who is seated, the first one must keep silent.
31 For you can all prophesy one by one, so that all may learn and all may be exhorted;
32 and the spirits of prophets are subject to prophets;
33 for God is not *a God* of confusion but of peace, as in all the churches of the saints.
34 The women are to keep silent in the churches; for they are not permitted to speak,
but are to subject themselves, just as the Law also says.
35 If they desire to learn anything, let them ask their own husbands at home; for it is
improper for a woman to speak in church.
36 Was it from you that the word of God *first* went forth? Or has it come to you only?
37 If anyone thinks he is a prophet or spiritual, let him recognize that the things which
I write to you are the Lord's commandment.

14:16 Deut 27:15-26; 1 Chr 16:36; Neh 5:13; 8:6; Ps 106:48; Jer 11:5; 28:6; Rev 5:14; 7:12; Matt 15:36

14:17 Rom 14:19; 1 Cor 14:4, 5, 12, 26

14:20 Rom 1:13; Eph 4:14; Heb 5:12f; Ps 131:2; Matt 18:3; Rom 16:19; 1 Pet 2:2

14:21 John 10:34; 1 Cor 14:34; Is 28:11f

14:22 1 Cor 14:1

14:23 Acts 2:13

14:24 1 Cor 14:1; John 16:8

14:25 John 4:19; Luke 17:16; Is 45:14; Dan 2:47; Zech 8:23; Acts 4:13

14:26 1 Cor 14:15; Rom 1:13; 1 Cor 12:8-10; Eph 5:19; 1 Cor 14:6; 1 Cor 14:2; 1 Cor 12:10; 14:5, 13, 27f; Rom 14:19

14:27 1 Cor 14:2; 1 Cor 12:10; 14:5, 13, 26ff

14:29 1 Cor 13:2; 14:32, 37; 1 Cor 12:10

14:33 1 Cor 14:40; 1 Cor 4:17; 7:17; Acts 9:13

14:34 1 Cor 11:5, 13; 1 Tim 2:11f; 1 Pet 3:1; 1 Cor 14:21

14:37 2 Cor 10:7; 1 Cor 2:15; 1 John 4:6

14:22–25 The way the Corinthians were speaking in tongues was helping no one because believers did not understand what was being said, and unbelievers thought that the people speaking in tongues were crazy. Speaking in tongues was supposed to be a *sign* to unbelievers (as it was in Acts 2). After speaking in tongues, believers were supposed to explain what was said and give the credit to God. The unsaved people would then be convinced of a spiritual reality and motivated to look further into the Christian faith. While this is one way to reach unbelievers, Paul says that clear preaching is usually better (14:5)

14:26ff Everything done in worship services must be beneficial to the worshipers. This principle touches every aspect—singing, preaching, and the exercise of spiritual gifts. Those contributing to the service (singers, speakers, readers) must have love as their chief motivation, speaking useful words or participating in a way that will strengthen the faith of other believers.

14:33 In worship, everything must be done properly and in an orderly manner. Even when the gifts of the Holy Spirit are being exercised, there is no excuse for disorder. When there is chaos, the church is not allowing God to work among believers as he would like.

14:34–35 Does this mean that women should not speak in church services today? It is clear from 11:5 that women prayed and prophesied in public worship. It is also clear in chapters 12—14 that women are given spiritual gifts and are encouraged to exercise them in the body of Christ. Women have much to contribute and can participate in worship services.

In the Corinthian culture, women were not allowed to confront men in public. Apparently some of the women who had become Christians thought that their Christian freedom gave them the right to question the men in public worship. This was causing division in the church. In addition, women of that day did not receive formal religious education as did the men. Women may have been raising questions in the worship services that could have been answered at home without disrupting the services. Paul was asking the women not to flaunt their Christian freedom during worship. The purpose of Paul's words was to promote unity, not to teach about women's role in the church.

14:39
1 Cor 12:31
15:1
Rom 2:16; 1 Cor 3:6; 4:15; Rom 5:2; 11:20; 2 Cor 1:24
15:2
Rom 11:22; Gal 3:4
15:3
1 Cor 11:23; John 1:29; Gal 1:4; Heb 5:1, 3; 1 Pet 2:24
15:4
Matt 16:21; John 2:20ff; Acts 2:24
15:5
Luke 24:34; 1 Cor 1:12; Mark 16:14; John 20:19
15:6
Acts 7:60
15:7
Luke 24:33, 36
15:8
Acts 9:3-8; 22:6-11
15:9
2 Cor 12:11; Eph 3:8; 1 Tim 1:15; Acts 8:3
15:10
Rom 12:3; 2 Cor 11:23; Col 1:29
15:12
Acts 17:32; 23:8; 2 Tim 2:18
15:14
1 Thess 4:14

38 But if anyone does not recognize *this*, he [13]is not recognized.
39 Therefore, my brethren, desire earnestly to prophesy, and do not forbid to speak in
tongues.
40 But all things must be done properly and in an orderly manner.

4. Instruction on the resurrection

The Fact of Christ's Resurrection

15 Now I make known to you, brethren, the gospel which I preached to you, which
also you received, in which also you stand,
2 by which also you are saved, if you hold fast the word which I preached to you, unless you believed in vain.
3 For I delivered to you as of first importance what I also received, that Christ died
for our sins according to the Scriptures,
4 and that He was buried, and that He was raised on the third day according to the
Scriptures,
5 and that He appeared to Cephas, then to the twelve.
6 After that He appeared to more than five hundred brethren at one time, most of
whom remain until now, but some have fallen asleep;
7 then He appeared to James, then to all the apostles;
8 and last of all, as to one untimely born, He appeared to me also.
9 For I am the least of the apostles, and not fit to be called an apostle, because I persecuted the church of God.
10 But by the grace of God I am what I am, and His grace toward me did not prove
vain; but I labored even more than all of them, yet not I, but the grace of God with me.
11 Whether then *it was* I or they, so we preach and so you believed.
12 Now if Christ is preached, that He has been raised from the dead, how do some
among you say that there is no resurrection of the dead?
13 But if there is no resurrection of the dead, not even Christ has been raised;
14 and if Christ has not been raised, then our preaching is vain, your faith also is vain.

13 Two early mss read *is not to be recognized*

14:40 Worship is vital to the life of an individual and to the whole church. Our church services should be conducted in an orderly way so that we can worship, be taught, and be prepared to serve God. Those who are responsible for planning worship should make sure it has order and direction rather than chaos and confusion.

15:2 Most churches contain people who do not yet believe. Some are moving in the direction of belief, and others are simply pretending. Imposters, however, are not to be removed (see Matthew 13:28–29), for that is the Lord's work alone. The Good News about Jesus Christ will save us *if* we firmly believe it and faithfully follow it.

15:5–8 There will always be people who say that Jesus didn't rise from the dead. Paul assures us that many people saw Jesus after his resurrection: Peter; the disciples (the Twelve); more than 500 Christian believers (most of whom were still alive when Paul wrote this, although some had died); James (Jesus' brother); all the apostles; and finally Paul himself. The resurrection is an historical fact. Don't be discouraged by doubters who deny the resurrection. Be filled with hope because of the knowledge that one day you, and they, will see the living proof when Christ returns. (For more evidence on the resurrection, see the chart in Mark 16.)

15:7 This James is Jesus' brother, who at first did not believe that Jesus was the Messiah (John 7:5). After seeing the resurrected Christ, he became a believer and ultimately a leader of the church in Jerusalem (Acts 15:13). James wrote the New Testament book of James.

15:8–9 Paul's most important credential to be an apostle was that he was an eyewitness of the risen Christ (see Acts 9:3–6). "Untimely born" means that his was a special case. The other apostles saw Christ in the flesh. Paul was in the next generation of believers—yet Christ appeared to him.

15:9–10 As a zealous Pharisee, Paul had been an enemy of the Christian church—even to the point of capturing and persecuting believers (see Acts 9:1–3). Thus he felt unworthy to be called an apostle of Christ. Though undoubtedly the most influential of the apostles, Paul was deeply humble. He knew that he had worked hard and accomplished much, but only because God had poured kindness and grace upon him. True humility is not convincing yourself that you are worthless, but recognizing God's work in you. It is having God's perspective on who you are and acknowledging his grace in developing your abilities.

15:10 Paul wrote of working harder than the other apostles. This was not an arrogant boast because he knew that his power came from God and that it really didn't matter who worked hardest. Because of his prominent position as a Pharisee, Paul's conversion made him the object of even greater persecution than the other apostles; thus he had to work harder to preach the same message.

15:12ff Most Greeks did not believe that people's bodies would be resurrected after death. They saw the afterlife as something that happened only to the soul. According to Greek philosophers, the soul was the real person, imprisoned in a physical body, and at death the soul was released. There was no immortality for the body, but the soul entered an eternal state. Christianity, by contrast, affirms that the body and soul will be united after resurrection. The church at Corinth was in the heart of Greek culture. Thus many believers had a difficult time believing in a bodily resurrection. Paul wrote this part of his letter to clear up this confusion about the resurrection.

15:13–18 The resurrection of Christ is the center of the Christian faith. Because Christ rose from the dead as he promised, we know that what he said is true—he is God. Because he rose, we have certainty that our sins are forgiven. Because he rose, he lives and represents us to God. Because he rose and defeated death, we know we will also be raised.

15 Moreover we are even found *to be* false witnesses of God, because we testified against
God that He raised [14]Christ, whom He did not raise, if in fact the dead are not raised.
16 For if the dead are not raised, not even Christ has been raised;
17 and if Christ has not been raised, your faith is worthless; you are still in your sins.
18 Then those also who have fallen asleep in Christ have perished.
19 If we have hoped in Christ in this life only, we are of all men most to be pitied.

The Order of Resurrection

20 But now Christ has been raised from the dead, the first fruits of those who are asleep.
21 For since by a man *came* death, by a man also *came* the resurrection of the dead.
22 For as in Adam all die, so also in Christ all will be made alive.
23 But each in his own order: Christ the first fruits, after that those who are Christ's at
His coming,
24 then *comes* the end, when He hands over the kingdom to the God and Father, when
He has abolished all rule and all authority and power.
25 For He must reign until He has put all His enemies under His feet.
26 The last enemy that will be abolished is death.
27 For HE HAS PUT ALL THINGS IN SUBJECTION UNDER HIS FEET. But when He says,
"All things are put in subjection," it is evident that He is excepted who put all things in
subjection to Him.
28 When all things are subjected to Him, then the Son Himself also will be subjected
to the One who subjected all things to Him, so that God may be all in all.
29 Otherwise, what will those do who are baptized for the dead? If the dead are not
raised at all, why then are they baptized for them?
30 Why are we also in danger every hour?
31 I affirm, brethren, by the boasting in you which I have in Christ Jesus our Lord, I
die daily.
32 If from human motives I fought with wild beasts at Ephesus, what does it profit me?
If the dead are not raised, LET US EAT AND DRINK, FOR TOMORROW WE DIE.
33 Do not be deceived: "Bad company corrupts good morals."
34 Become sober-minded as you ought, and stop sinning; for some have no knowledge
of God. I speak *this* to your shame.
35 But someone will say, "How are the dead raised? And with what kind of body do
they come?"

14 I.e. the Messiah

15:17 Rom 4:25
15:18 1 Cor 15:6; 1 Thess 4:16; Rev 14:13
15:19 1 Cor 4:9; 2 Tim 3:12
15:20 Acts 2:24; 1 Pet 1:3; 1 Thess 4:16; Rev 14:13
15:21 Rom 5:12
15:23 Acts 26:23; 1 Thess 2:19
15:24 2 Pet 1:11; Eph 5:20; Rom 8:38
15:26 2 Tim 1:10; Rev 20:14; 21:4
15:27 Ps 8:6; Matt 11:27; 28:18; Eph 1:22
15:28 Phil 3:21; 1 Cor 3:23; 12:6
15:30 2 Cor 11:26
15:31 Rom 8:36
15:32 2 Cor 1:8; Acts 18:19; 1 Cor 16:8
15:33 1 Cor 6:9
15:34 Rom 13:11; Matt 22:29; Acts 26:8

15:19 Why does Paul say believers should be pitied if there were only earthly value to Christianity? In Paul's day, Christianity often brought a person persecution, ostracism from family, and, in many cases, poverty. There were few tangible benefits from being a Christian in that society. It was certainly not a step up the social or career ladder. Even more important, however, is the fact that if Christ had not been resurrected from death, Christians could not be forgiven for their sins and would have no hope of eternal life.

15:20 First fruits were the first part of the harvest that faithful Jews brought to the temple as an offering (Leviticus 23:10ff). Although Christ was not the first to rise from the dead (he raised Lazarus and others), he was the first to never die again. He is the forerunner for us, the proof of our eventual resurrection to eternal life.

15:21 Death came into the world as a result of Adam and Eve's sin. In Romans 5:12–21, Paul explained why Adam's sin brought sin to all people, how death and sin spread to all humans because of this first sin, and the parallel between Adam's death and Christ's death.

15:24–28 This is not a chronological sequence of events, and no specific time for these events is given. Paul's point is that the resurrected Christ will conquer all evil, including death. See Revelation 20:14 for words about the final destruction of death.

15:25–28 Although God the Father and God the Son are equal, each has a special work to do and an area of sovereign control (15:28). Christ is not inferior to the Father, but his work is to defeat all evil on earth. First he defeated sin and death on the cross, and in the final days he will defeat Satan and all evil. World events may seem out of control and justice may seem scarce. But God is in control, allowing evil to remain for a time until he sends Jesus to earth again. Then Christ will present to God a perfect new world.

15:29 Some believers were baptized on behalf of others who had died unbaptized. Nothing more is known about this practice, but it obviously affirms a belief in resurrection. Paul is not promoting baptism for the dead; he is illustrating his argument that the resurrection is a reality.

15:30–34 If death ended it all, enjoying the moment would be all that matters. But Christians know that there is life beyond the grave and that our life on earth is only a preparation for our life that will never end. What you do today matters for eternity. In light of eternity, sin is a foolish gamble.

15:31–32 "I die daily" refers to Paul's daily exposure to danger. There is no evidence that Paul actually "fought with wild beasts at Ephesus," but rather he was referring to the savage opposition he had faced.

15:33 Keeping company with those who deny the resurrection could corrupt good Christian character. Don't let your relationships with unbelievers lead you away from Christ or cause your faith to waver.

15:35ff Paul launches into a discussion about what our resurrected bodies will be like. If you could select your own body, what kind would you choose—strong, athletic, beautiful? Paul explains that we will be recognized in our resurrected bodies, yet they will be

15:36 Luke 11:40; John 12:24
15:38 Gen 1:11
15:42 Dan 12:3; Matt 13:43; Rom 8:21; 1 Cor 15:50; Gal 6:8; Rom 2:7
15:43 Phil 3:21; Col 3:4
15:44 1 Cor 2:14; 1 Cor 15:50
15:45 Gen 2:7; Rom 5:14; John 5:21; 6:57f; Rom 8:2
15:47 John 3:31; Gen 2:7; 3:19
15:48 Phil 3:20f
15:49 Gen 5:3; Rom 8:29
15:50 Matt 16:17; John 3:5f; 1 Cor 6:9; Rom 2:7
15:51 1 Cor 13:2; 2 Cor 5:2, 4
15:52 Matt 24:31; John 5:28; 1 Thess 4:15, 17
15:53 Rom 2:7; 2 Cor 5:4
15:54 Is 25:8

36 You fool! That which you sow does not come to life unless it dies;
37 and that which you sow, you do not sow the body which is to be, but a bare grain,
perhaps of wheat or of something else.
38 But God gives it a body just as He wished, and to each of the seeds a body of
its own.
39 All flesh is not the same flesh, but there is one *flesh* of men, and another flesh of
beasts, and another flesh of birds, and another of fish.
40 There are also heavenly bodies and earthly bodies, but the glory of the heavenly is
one, and the *glory* of the earthly is another.
41 There is one glory of the sun, and another glory of the moon, and another glory of
the stars; for star differs from star in glory.
42 So also is the resurrection of the dead. It is sown a perishable *body*, it is raised an
imperishable *body;*
43 it is sown in dishonor, it is raised in glory; it is sown in weakness, it is raised in
power;
44 it is sown a natural body, it is raised a spiritual body. If there is a natural body, there
is also a spiritual *body.*
45 So also it is written, "The first MAN, Adam, BECAME A LIVING SOUL." The last Adam
became a life-giving spirit.
46 However, the spiritual is not first, but the natural; then the spiritual.
47 The first man is from the earth, earthy; the second man is from heaven.
48 As is the earthy, so also are those who are earthy; and as is the heavenly, so also are
those who are heavenly.
49 Just as we have borne the image of the earthy, [15]we will also bear the image of the
heavenly.

The Mystery of Resurrection

50 Now I say this, brethren, that flesh and blood cannot inherit the kingdom of God;
nor does the perishable inherit the imperishable.
51 Behold, I tell you a mystery; we will not all sleep, but we will all be changed,
52 in a moment, in the twinkling of an eye, at the last trumpet; for the trumpet will
sound, and the dead will be raised imperishable, and we will be changed.
53 For this perishable must put on the imperishable, and this mortal must put on immortality.
54 But when this perishable will have put on the imperishable, and this mortal will have

15 Two early mss read *let us also*

---

better than we can imagine, for they will be made to live forever. We will still have our own personalities and individualities, but these will be perfected through Christ's work. The Bible does not reveal everything that our resurrected bodies will be able to do, but we know they will be perfect, without sickness or disease (see Philippians 3:21).

15:35ff Paul compares the resurrection of our bodies with the growth in a garden. Seeds placed in the ground don't grow unless they "die" first. The plant that grows looks very different from the seed because God gives it a new "body." There are different kinds of bodies—people, animals, fish, birds. Even the angels in heaven have bodies that are different in beauty and glory. Our resurrected bodies will be very different in some ways, but not all, from our earthly bodies.

15:42–44 Our present bodies are perishable and prone to decay. Our resurrection bodies will be transformed. These spiritual bodies will not be limited by the laws of nature. This does not necessarily mean we'll be superpeople, but our bodies will be different from and more capable than our present earthly bodies. Our spiritual bodies will not be weak, will never get sick, and will never die.

15:45 The "last Adam" refers to Christ. Because Christ rose from the dead, he is a life-giving spirit. This means that he entered into a new form of existence (see the note on 2 Corinthians 3:17). He is the source of the spiritual life that will result in our resurrection. Christ's new glorified human body now suits his new glorified life—just as Adam's human body was suitable to his natural life. When we are resurrected, God will give us a transformed, eternal body suited to our new eternal life.

15:50–53 We all face limitations. Those who have physical, mental, or emotional disabilities are especially aware of this. Some may be blind, but they can see a new way to live. Some may be deaf, but they can hear God's Good News. Some may be lame, but they can walk in God's love. In addition, they have the encouragement that those disabilities are only temporary. Paul tells us that we all will be given new bodies when Christ returns and that these bodies will be without disabilities, never to die or become sick. This can give us hope in our suffering.

15:51–52 "We will not all sleep" means that Christians alive at that day will not have to die but will be transformed immediately. A trumpet blast will usher in the new heaven and earth. The Jews would understand the significance of this because trumpets were always blown to signal the start of great festivals and other extraordinary events (Numbers 10:10).

15:54–56 Satan seemed to be victorious in the Garden of Eden (Genesis 3) and at the cross of Jesus. But God turned Satan's apparent victory into defeat when Jesus Christ rose from the dead (Colossians 2:15; Hebrews 2:14–15). Thus death is no longer a source of dread or fear. Christ overcame it, and one day we will also. The law will no longer make sinners out of us who cannot keep it. Death has been defeated, and we have hope beyond the grave.

put on immortality, then will come about the saying that is written, "DEATH IS SWAL-
LOWED UP in victory.
55 "O DEATH, WHERE IS YOUR VICTORY? O DEATH, WHERE IS YOUR STING?"
56 The sting of death is sin, and the power of sin is the law;
57 but thanks be to God, who gives us the victory through our Lord Jesus Christ.
58 Therefore, my beloved brethren, be steadfast, immovable, always abounding in the
work of the Lord, knowing that your toil is not *in* vain in the Lord.

Instructions and Greetings

16 Now concerning the collection for the saints, as I directed the churches of Galatia,
so do you also.
2 On the first day of every week each one of you is to put aside and save, as he may
prosper, so that no collections be made when I come.
3 When I arrive, whomever you may approve, I will send them with letters to carry
your gift to Jerusalem;
4 and if it is fitting for me to go also, they will go with me.
5 But I will come to you after I go through Macedonia, for I am going through Macedonia;
6 and perhaps I will stay with you, or even spend the winter, so that you may send me
on my way wherever I may go.
7 For I do not wish to see you now *just* in passing; for I hope to remain with you for
some time, if the Lord permits.
8 But I will remain in Ephesus until Pentecost;
9 for a wide door for effective *service* has opened to me, and there are many adversaries.
10 Now if Timothy comes, see that he is with you without cause to be afraid, for he is
doing the Lord's work, as I also am.
11 So let no one despise him. But send him on his way in peace, so that he may come
to me; for I expect him with the brethren.
12 But concerning Apollos our brother, I encouraged him greatly to come to you with
the brethren; and it was not at all *his* desire to come now, but he will come when he has
opportunity.
13 Be on the alert, stand firm in the faith, act like men, be strong.
14 Let all that you do be done in love.
15 Now I urge you, brethren (you know the household of Stephanas, that they were
the first fruits of Achaia, and that they have devoted themselves for ministry to the saints),
16 that you also be in subjection to such men and to everyone who helps in the work
and labors.
17 I rejoice over the coming of Stephanas and Fortunatus and Achaicus, because they
have supplied what was lacking on your part.
18 For they have refreshed my spirit and yours. Therefore acknowledge such men.

15:55 Hos 13:14
15:56 Rom 5:12; Rom 3:20; 4:15; 7:8
15:57 Rom 7:25; 8:37; Heb 2:14f; 1 John 5:4; Rev 21:4
15:58 2 Pet 3:14
16:2 Acts 20:7; 2 Cor 9:4f
16:3 2 Cor 3:1; 8:18f
16:5 1 Cor 4:19; Rom 15:26; Acts 19:21
16:9 Acts 14:27; 19:9
16:10 Acts 16:1; 1 Cor 4:17; 2 Cor 1:1; 1 Cor 15:58
16:11 1 Tim 4:12; Titus 2:15; Acts 15:3
16:12 Acts 18:24; 1 Cor 1:12; 3:5f
16:13 Matt 24:42; 1 Cor 15:1; Gal 5:1; Phil 1:27; 4:1; 1 Thess 3:8; 2 Thess 2:15; 1 Sam 4:9; 2 Sam 10:12; Ps 31:24; Eph 3:16; 6:10; Col 1:11
16:14 1 Cor 14:1
16:16 1 Thess 5:12; Heb 13:17
16:17 2 Cor 7:6f; 2 Cor 11:9; Phil 2:30
16:18 2 Cor 7:13; Philem 7, 20; Phil 2:29; 1 Thess 5:12

15:58 Paul says that because of the resurrection, nothing we do is in vain. Sometimes we hesitate to do good because we don't see any results. But if we can maintain a heavenly perspective, we will understand that we often will not see the good that results from our efforts. If we truly believe that Christ has won the ultimate victory, that fact must affect the way we live right now. Don't let discouragement over an apparent lack of results keep you from working. Do the good that you have opportunity to do, knowing that your work will have eternal results.

16:1ff Paul had just said that no good work is ever in vain (15:58). In this chapter he mentions some practical deeds that have value for all Christians.

16:1–4 The Christians in Jerusalem were suffering from poverty and famine, so Paul was collecting money for them (Romans 15:25–31; 2 Corinthians 8:4; 9:1ff). He suggested that believers set aside a certain amount each week and give it to the church until he arrived to take it on to Jerusalem. Paul had planned to go straight to Corinth from Ephesus, but he changed his mind (2 Corinthians 1; 2). When he finally arrived, he took the gift and delivered it to the Jerusalem church (Acts 21:18; 24:17).

16:10–11 Paul was sending Timothy ahead to Corinth. Paul respected Timothy and had worked closely with him (Philippians 2:22; 1 Timothy 1:2). Although Timothy was young, Paul encouraged the Corinthian church to welcome him because he was doing the Lord's work. God's work is not limited by age. Paul wrote two personal letters to Timothy that have been preserved in the Bible (1 and 2 Timothy).

16:12 Apollos, who had preached in Corinth, was doing evangelistic work in Greece (see Acts 18:24–28; 1 Corinthians 3:3ff). Apollos didn't go to Corinth right away, partly because he knew of the factions there and didn't want to cause any more divisions.

16:13–14 As the Corinthians awaited Paul's next visit, they were directed to (1) be on the alert against spiritual dangers, (2) stand firm in the faith, (3) behave courageously, (4) be strong, and (5) do everything with love. Today, as we wait for the return of Christ, we should follow the same instructions.

16:19 Acts 16:6; Acts 18:2; Rom 16:5

16:21 Gal 6:11; Col 4:18; 2 Thess 3:17; Philem 19

16:22 Rom 9:3; Phil 4:5; Rev 22:20

19 The churches of Asia greet you. Aquila and Prisca greet you heartily in the Lord,
with the church that is in their house.
20 All the brethren greet you. Greet one another with a holy kiss.
21 The greeting is in my own hand—Paul.
22 If anyone does not love the Lord, he is to be accursed. Maranatha.
23 The grace of the Lord Jesus be with you.
24 My love be with you all in Christ Jesus. Amen.

PHYSICAL AND RESURRECTION BODIES

Physical Bodies	*Resurrection Bodies*
Perishable	Imperishable
Sown in dishonor	Raised in glory
Sown in weakness	Raised in power
Natural	Spiritual
From the dust	From heaven

We all have bodies—each looks different, each has different strengths and weaknesses. But as physical, earthly bodies, they are all alike. All believers are promised life after death and bodies like Christ's (15:49)—resurrection bodies.

16:19 Aquila and Prisca (Priscilla) were tentmakers (or leather workers) whom Paul had met in Corinth (Acts 18:1–3). They followed Paul to Ephesus and lived there with him, helping to teach others about Jesus (Romans 16:3–5). Many in the Corinthian church would have known this Christian couple. They are also mentioned in Acts 18:18, 26; Romans 16:3; 2 Timothy 4:19.

16:20 Kissing was a normal way of greeting each other in Paul's day. Paul encouraged the "holy kiss" as a way to greet Christians, and a way to help break down the divisions in this church.

16:21 Paul had a helper, or secretary, who wrote down this letter while he dictated. Paul wrote the final words, however, in his own handwriting. This is similar to adding a handwritten postscript (P.S.) to a typewritten letter. It also served to verify that this was a genuine letter from the apostle, and not a forgery.

16:22 The Lord Jesus Christ is coming back to earth again. To Paul, this was a glad hope, the very best he could look forward to. He was not afraid of seeing Christ—he could hardly wait! Do you share Paul's eager anticipation? Those who love Christ are looking forward to that wonderful time of his return (Titus 2:13). To those who did not love the Lord, however, Paul says, let them be cursed.

16:24 The church at Corinth was a church in trouble. Paul lovingly and forcefully confronted their problems and pointed them back to Christ. He dealt with divisions and conflicts, selfishness, inconsiderate use of freedom, disorder in worship, misuse of spiritual gifts, and wrong attitudes about the resurrection.

In every church, there are enough problems to create tensions and divisions. We should not ignore or gloss over problems in our churches or in our lives. Instead, like Paul, we should deal with problems head on as they arise. The lesson for us in 1 Corinthians is that unity and love in a church are far more important than leaders and labels.

2 CORINTHIANS

VITAL STATISTICS

PURPOSE:
To affirm Paul's ministry, defend his authority as an apostle, and refute the false teachers in Corinth

AUTHOR:
Paul

TO WHOM WRITTEN:
The church in Corinth and Christians everywhere

DATE WRITTEN:
Approximately A.D. 55–57, from Macedonia

SETTING:
Paul had already written three letters to the Corinthians (two are now lost). In 1 Corinthians (the second of these letters), he used strong words to correct and teach. Most of the church had responded in the right spirit; there were, however, those who were denying Paul's authority and questioning his motives.

KEY VERSE:
"We are ambassadors for Christ, as though God were making an appeal through us; we beg you on behalf of Christ, be reconciled to God" (5:20).

KEY PEOPLE:
Paul, Timothy, Titus, false teachers

KEY PLACES:
Corinth, Jerusalem

SPECIAL FEATURES:
This is an intensely personal and autobiographical letter.

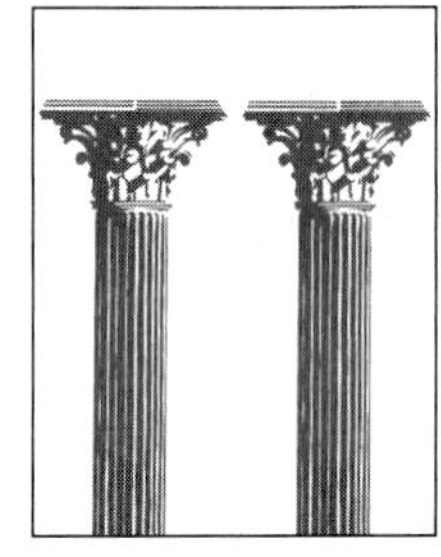

SLITHERING through the centuries, the serpent whispers his smooth-tongued promises, beguiling, deceiving, and tempting—urging men and women to reject God and to follow Satan. Satan's emissaries have been many—false prophets contradicting God's ancient spokesmen, "pious" leaders hurling blasphemous accusations, and heretical teachers infiltrating churches. And the deception continues. Our world is filled with cults, "isms," and ideologies, all claiming to provide the way to God.

Paul constantly struggled with those who would mislead God's people, and he poured his life into spreading the Good News to the uttermost parts of the world. During three missionary trips and other travels, he proclaimed Christ, made converts, and established churches. But often young believers were easy prey for false teachers. False teachers were a constant threat to the gospel and the early church. So Paul had to spend much time warning and correcting these new Christians.

The church at Corinth was weak. Surrounded by idolatry and immorality, they struggled with their Christian faith and life-style. Through personal visits and letters, Paul tried to instruct them in the faith, resolve their conflicts, and solve some of their problems. First Corinthians was sent to deal with specific moral issues in the church and to answer questions about sex, marriage, and tender consciences. That letter confronted the issues directly and was well received by most. But there were false teachers who denied Paul's authority and slandered him. Paul then wrote 2 Corinthians to defend his position and to denounce those who were twisting the truth.

Second Corinthians must have been a difficult letter for Paul to write because he had to list his credentials as an apostle. Paul was reluctant to do so as a humble servant of Christ, but he knew it was necessary. Paul also knew that most of the believers in Corinth had taken his previous words to heart and were beginning to mature in their faith. He affirmed their commitment to Christ.

Second Corinthians begins with Paul reminding his readers of (1) his relationship to them—Paul had always been honest and straightforward with them (1:12–14), (2) his itinerary—he was planning to visit them again (1:15—2:3), and (3) his previous letter (2:4–11). Paul then moves directly to the subject of false teachers (2:17), and he reviews his ministry among the Corinthians to demonstrate the validity of his message and to urge them not to turn away from the truth (3:1—7:16).

Paul next turns to the issue of collecting money for the poor Christians in Jerusalem. He tells them how others have given, and he urges them to show their love in a tangible way as well (8:1—9:15). Paul then gives a strong defense of his authority as a genuine apostle while pointing out the deceptive influence of the false apostles (10:1—13:10).

As you read this intensely personal letter, listen to Paul's words of love and exhortation, and be committed to the truth of God's Word and prepared to reject all false teaching.

THE BLUEPRINT

1. Paul explains his actions (1:1—2:11)
2. Paul defends his ministry (2:12—7:16)
3. Paul defends the collection (8:1—9:15)
4. Paul defends his authority (10:1—13:14)

In responding to the attacks on his character and authority, Paul explains the nature of Christian ministry and, as an example, openly shares about his ministry. This is an important letter for all who wish to be involved in any kind of Christian ministry, because it has much to teach us about how we should handle our ministries today. Like Paul, those involved in ministry should be blameless, sincere, confident, caring, open, and willing to suffer for the sake of Christ.

MEGATHEMES

THEME	EXPLANATION	IMPORTANCE
Trials	Paul experienced great suffering, persecution, and opposition in his ministry. He even struggled with a personal weakness—a "thorn" in the flesh. Through it all, Paul affirmed God's faithfulness.	God is faithful. His strength is sufficient for any trial. When trials come, they keep us from pride and teach us dependence on God. He comforts us so we can comfort others.
Church Discipline	Paul defends his role in church discipline. Neither immorality nor false teaching could be ignored. The church was to be neither too lax nor too severe in administering discipline. The church was to restore the corrected person when he or she repented.	The goal of all discipline in the church should be correction, not vengeance. For churches to be effective, they must confront and solve problems, not ignore them. In everything, we must act in love.
Hope	To encourage the Corinthians as they faced trials, Paul reminded them that they would receive new bodies in heaven. This would be a great victory in contrast to their present suffering.	To know we will receive new bodies offers us hope. No matter what adversity we face, we can keep going. Our faithful service will result in triumph.
Giving	Paul organized a collection of funds for the poor in the Jerusalem church. Many of the Asian churches gave money. Paul explains and defends his beliefs about giving, and he urges the Corinthians to follow through on their previous commitment.	Like the Corinthians, we should follow through on our financial commitments. Our giving must be generous, sacrificial, well planned, and based on need. Our generosity not only helps those in need but enables them to thank God.
Sound Doctrine	False teachers were challenging Paul's ministry and authority as an apostle. Paul asserts his authority in order to preserve correct Christian doctrine. His sincerity, his love for Christ, and his concern for the people were his defense.	We should share Paul's concern for correct teaching in our churches. But in so doing, we must share his motivation—love for Christ and people—and his sincerity.

1. Paul explains his actions

Introduction

1 Paul, an apostle of Christ Jesus by the will of God, and Timothy *our* brother,
To the church of God which is at Corinth with all the saints who are throughout
Achaia:
2 Grace to you and peace from God our Father and the Lord Jesus Christ.
3 Blessed *be* the God and Father of our Lord Jesus Christ, the Father of mercies and
God of all comfort,
4 who comforts us in all our affliction so that we will be able to comfort those who are
in any affliction with the comfort with which we ourselves are comforted by God.
5 For just as the sufferings of Christ are ours in abundance, so also our comfort is
abundant through Christ.
6 But if we are afflicted, it is for your comfort and salvation; or if we are comforted, it
is for your comfort, which is effective in the patient enduring of the same sufferings which
we also suffer;
7 and our hope for you is firmly grounded, knowing that as you are sharers of our
sufferings, so also you are *sharers* of our comfort.
8 For we do not want you to be unaware, brethren, of our affliction which came *to us*
in Asia, that we were burdened excessively, beyond our strength, so that we despaired
even of life;
9 indeed, we had the sentence of death within ourselves so that we would not trust in
ourselves, but in God who raises the dead;
10 who delivered us from so great a *peril of* death, and will deliver *us,* He on whom we
have set our hope. And He will yet deliver us,
11 you also joining in helping us through your prayers, so that thanks may be given by
many persons on our behalf for the favor bestowed on us through *the prayers of* many.

1:1 Acts 16:1; 1 Cor 16:10; 2 Cor 1:19; 1 Cor 10:32; Acts 18:1; Acts 18:12
1:2 Rom 1:7
1:3 Eph 1:3; 1 Pet 1:3; Rom 15:5
1:4 Is 51:12; 66:13; 2 Cor 7:6, 7, 13
1:5 2 Cor 4:10; Phil 3:10; Col 1:24
1:6 2 Cor 4:15; 12:15; Eph 3:1, 13; 2 Tim 2:10
1:7 Rom 8:17
1:8 Rom 1:13; Acts 19:23; 1 Cor 15:32; Acts 16:6
1:10 Rom 15:31; 1 Tim 4:10
1:11 Rom 15:30; Phil 1:19; Philem 22; 2 Cor 4:15; 9:11f

1:1 Paul visited Corinth on his second missionary journey and founded a church there (Acts 18:1ff). He later wrote several letters to the believers in Corinth, two of which are included in the Bible. Paul's first letter to the Corinthians is lost (1 Corinthians 5:9–11), his second letter to them is our book of 1 Corinthians, his third letter is lost (2:6–9; 7:12), and his fourth letter is our book of 2 Corinthians. Second Corinthians was written less than a year after 1 Corinthians.

Paul wrote 1 Corinthians to deal with divisions in the church. When his advice was not taken and their problems weren't solved, Paul visited Corinth a second time. That visit was painful both for Paul and for the church (2:1). He then planned a third visit, but delayed it and wrote 2 Corinthians instead. After writing 2 Corinthians, Paul visited Corinth once more (Acts 20:2–3).

1:1 Paul had great respect for Timothy (see also Philippians 2:19–20; 1 Timothy 1:2), one of his traveling companions (Acts 16:1–3). Timothy had accompanied Paul to Corinth on his second missionary journey, and Paul had recently sent him there to minister (1 Corinthians 4:17; 16:10). Timothy's report to Paul about the crisis in the Corinthian church prompted Paul to make an unplanned visit to the church to deal with the problem in person (see 2:1). For more information on Timothy, see his Profile in 1 Timothy.

1:1 The Romans had made Corinth the capital of Achaia (the southern half of present-day Greece). The city was a flourishing trade center because of its seaport. With the thousands of merchants and sailors who disembarked there each year, it had developed a reputation as one of the most immoral cities in the ancient world; its many pagan temples encouraged the practice of sexual immorality along with idol worship. In fact, the Greek word "to Corinthianize" came to mean "to practice sexual immorality." A Christian church in the city would face many pressures and conflicts. For more information on Corinth, see the first note on 1 Corinthians 1:2.

1:3–5 Many think that when God comforts us, our troubles should go away. But if that were always so, people would turn to God only out of a desire to be relieved of pain and not out of love for him. We must understand that being *comforted* can also mean receiving strength, encouragement, and hope to deal with our troubles. The more we suffer, the more comfort God gives us. If you are feeling overwhelmed, allow God to comfort you. Remember that every trial you endure will help you comfort other people who are suffering similar troubles.

1:5 The "sufferings of Christ" are those afflictions we experience as we do Christ's ministry. At the same time, Christ suffers with his people, since they are united with him. In Acts 9:4–5 Christ asked Paul why he was persecuting him. This implies that Christ suffered with the early Christians when they were persecuted.

1:6–7 Paul explains that he and his companions suffered greatly for bringing "comfort and salvation" to the Corinthians. But just as God comforted Paul, God would also comfort the Corinthian believers when they suffered for their faith. He would give them the strength to endure.

1:8–10 Paul does not give details about their afflictions in Asia, although his accounts of all three missionary journeys record many difficult trials he faced (Acts 13:2—14:28; 15:40—21:17). He does write that they felt that they were going to die, and realized that they could do nothing to help themselves—they simply had to rely on God.

1:8–10 We often depend on our own skills and abilities when life seems easy, but we turn to God when we feel unable to help ourselves. Depending on God is a realization of our own powerlessness without him and our need for his constant touch in our lives. God is our source of power, and we receive his help by keeping in touch with him. With this attitude of dependence, problems will drive us to God rather than away from him. Learn how to rely on God daily.

1:11 Paul requested prayer for himself and his companions as they traveled to spread God's message. Pray for pastors, teachers, missionaries, and others who are spreading the gospel. Satan will challenge anyone making a real difference for God.

1:12 Acts 23:1; 1 Thess 2:10; Heb 13:18; 2 Cor 2:17; 1 Cor 1:17; James 3:15
1:15 1 Cor 4:19; Rom 1:11; 15:29
1:16 Acts 19:21; 1 Cor 16:5-7; Acts 19:21; Rom 15:26
1:17 2 Cor 10:2f; 11:18
1:19 Matt 4:3; 16:16; 26:63; Acts 15:22
1:20 Rom 15:8; Heb 13:8; 1 Cor 14:16; Rev 3:14
1:21 1 Cor 1:8; 1 John 2:20, 27
1:22 John 3:33; Rom 8:16; 2 Cor 5:5; Eph 1:14

Paul's Integrity

12 For our proud confidence is this: the testimony of our conscience, that in holiness
and godly sincerity, not in fleshly wisdom but in the grace of God, we have conducted
ourselves in the world, and especially toward you.
13 For we write nothing else to you than what you read and understand, and I hope
you will understand until the end;
14 just as you also partially did understand us, that we are your reason to be proud as
you also are ours, in the day of our Lord Jesus.
15 In this confidence I intended at first to come to you, so that you might twice receive
a blessing;
16 that is, to pass your way into Macedonia, and again from Macedonia to come to
you, and by you to be helped on my journey to Judea.
17 Therefore, I was not vacillating when I intended to do this, was I? Or what I purpose, do I purpose according to the flesh, so that with me there will be yes, yes and no,
no *at the same time?*
18 But as God is faithful, our word to you is not yes and no.
19 For the Son of God, Christ Jesus, who was preached among you by us—by me and
Silvanus and Timothy—was not yes and no, but is yes in Him.
20 For as many as are the promises of God, in Him they are yes; therefore also through
Him is our Amen to the glory of God through us.
21 Now He who establishes us with you in Christ and anointed us is God,
22 who also sealed us and gave *us* the Spirit in our hearts as a pledge.

DIFFERENCES BETWEEN 1 AND 2 CORINTHIANS

The two letters to the Corinthian church that are found in the Bible are very different, with different tones and focuses.

1 Corinthians	*2 Corinthians*
Practical	Personal
Focuses on the character of the Corinthian church	Focuses on Paul as he bares his soul and tells of his love for the Corinthian church
Deals with questions on marriage, freedom, spiritual gifts, and order in the church	Deals with the problem of false teachers, whereby Paul defends his authority and the truth of his message
Paul instructs in matters concerning the church's well-being	Paul gives his testimony because he knows that acceptance of his advice is vital to the church's well-being
Contains advice to help the church combat the pagan influences in the wicked city of Corinth	Contains testimony to help the church combat the havoc caused by false teachers

1:12–14 Paul knew the importance of holiness and sincerity in word and action, especially in a situation as in Corinth, where constructive criticism was necessary. So Paul did not come with impressive human knowledge (fleshly wisdom). God wants us to be real and transparent in all our relationships. If we aren't, we may end up lowering ourselves to spreading rumors, gossiping, and second-guessing.

1:15–17 Paul had recently made a brief, unscheduled visit to Corinth that was very painful for him and the church (see 2:1). After that visit, he told the church when he would return. But Paul changed his original travel plans. Instead of sailing from Ephesus to Corinth before going to Macedonia, he traveled from Ephesus directly to Macedonia, where he wrote a letter to the Corinthians that caused him much anguish and them much sorrow (7:8–9). He had made his original plans thinking that the church would have solved its problems. When the time came for Paul's scheduled trip to Corinth, however, the crisis had not been fully resolved (although progress was being made in some areas; 7:11–16). So he wrote a letter instead (2:3–4; 7:8) because another visit may have only made matters worse. Thus Paul stayed away from Corinth because he was concerned over the church's unity, not because he was fickle.

1:17–20 Paul's change of plans caused some of his accusers to say that he couldn't be trusted, hoping to undermine his authority. Paul said that he was not the type of person to say yes when he means no. Paul explained that it was not indecision but concern for their feelings that forced him to change his plans. The reason for his trip—to bring joy (1:24)—could not be accomplished with the present crisis. Paul didn't want to visit them only to rebuke them severely (1:23). Just as the Corinthians could trust God to keep his promises, they could trust Paul as God's representative to keep his. He would still visit them, but at a better time.

1:19–20 All of God's promises of what the Messiah would be like are fulfilled in Christ ("in Him they are yes"). Jesus was completely faithful in his ministry; he never sinned (1 Peter 3:18); he faithfully died for us (Hebrews 2:9); and now he faithfully intercedes for us (Romans 8:34; Hebrews 4:14–15). Because Jesus Christ is faithful, Paul wanted to be faithful in his ministry.

1:21–22 Paul mentions two gifts God gives when we become believers: (1) a *seal of ownership* to show who our Master is, and (2) the Holy Spirit, who guarantees that we belong to him and will receive all his benefits (Ephesians 1:13–14). The Holy Spirit guarantees that salvation is ours now, and that we will receive so much more when Christ returns. The great comfort and power the Holy Spirit gives in this life are a foretaste or down payment ("pledge") of the benefits of our eternal life in God's presence. With the privilege of belonging to God comes the responsibility of identifying ourselves as his faithful servants. Don't be ashamed to let others know that you are his.

23 But I call God as witness to my soul, that to spare you I did not come again to Corinth.
24 Not that we lord it over your faith, but are workers with you for your joy; for in your faith you are standing firm.

1:23 Rom 1:9; Gal 1:20; 1 Cor 4:21
1:24 2 Cor 4:5; 11:20; 1 Pet 5:3; Rom 11:20; 1 Cor 15:1

Reaffirm Your Love

2 But I determined this for my own sake, that I would not come to you in sorrow again.
2 For if I cause you sorrow, who then makes me glad but the one whom I made sorrowful?
3 This is the very thing I wrote you, so that when I came, I would not have sorrow from those who ought to make me rejoice; having confidence in you all that my joy would be *the joy* of you all.
4 For out of much affliction and anguish of heart I wrote to you with many tears; not so that you would be made sorrowful, but that you might know the love which I have especially for you.
5 But if any has caused sorrow, he has caused sorrow not to me, but in some degree—in order not to say too much—to all of you.
6 Sufficient for such a one is this punishment which *was inflicted* by the majority,
7 so that on the contrary you should rather forgive and comfort *him*, otherwise such a one might be overwhelmed by excessive sorrow.
8 Wherefore I urge you to reaffirm *your* love for him.
9 For to this end also I wrote, so that I might put you to the test, whether you are obedient in all things.
10 But one whom you forgive anything, I *forgive* also; for indeed what I have forgiven, if I have forgiven anything, *I did it* for your sakes in the presence of Christ,
11 so that no advantage would be taken of us by Satan, for we are not ignorant of his schemes.

2:1 1 Cor 4:21
2:2 2 Cor 7:8
2:3 2 Cor 2:9; 7:8, 12; 1 Cor 4:21; 2 Cor 12:21; Gal 5:10; 2 Thess 3:4; Philem 21
2:4 2 Cor 2:9; 7:8, 12
2:5 1 Cor 5:1f
2:6 1 Cor 5:4f; 2 Cor 7:11
2:7 Gal 6:1; Eph 4:32
2:9 2 Cor 8:2; Phil 2:22; 2 Cor 7:15; 10:6
2:10 1 Cor 5:4; 2 Cor 4:6
2:11 Matt 4:10; Luke 22:31; 2 Cor 4:4; 1 Pet 5:8

2. Paul defends his ministry

12 Now when I came to Troas for the gospel of Christ and when a door was opened for me in the Lord,
13 I had no rest for my spirit, not finding Titus my brother; but taking my leave of them, I went on to Macedonia.

2:13 2 Cor 7:5; 2 Cor 7:6, 13f; 8:6, 16, 23; 12:18; Gal 2:1, 3; 2 Tim 4:10; Titus 1:4; Mark 6:46; Rom 15:26

1:23 The Corinthian church had written to Paul with questions about their faith (see 1 Corinthians 7:1). In response, Paul had written 1 Corinthians. But the church did not follow his instructions.

Paul had planned to visit them again, but instead he wrote a letter that caused sorrow (7:8–9) to give them another chance to change their ways. He didn't want to visit and repeat the same advice for the same problems. He wrote the emotional letter to encourage them to follow the advice that he had already given in previous letters and visits.

2:1 Paul's words, "I would not come to you in sorrow again," indicate that he had already made one difficult trip to Corinth (see the notes on 1:1; 1:15–17) since founding the church. Paul had gone there to deal with those in the church who had been attacking and undermining his authority as an apostle of Jesus Christ, thus confusing other believers.

2:3 Paul's last letter, referred to here, was not the book of 1 Corinthians, but a letter written between 1 and 2 Corinthians, just after his unplanned, painful visit (2:1). Paul refers to this letter again in 7:8.

2:4 Paul did not enjoy reprimanding his friends and fellow believers, but he cared enough about the Corinthians to confront them with their wrongdoing. Proverbs 27:6 says: "Faithful are the wounds of a friend, but deceitful are the kisses of an enemy." Sometimes our friends make choices that we know are wrong. If we ignore their behavior and let them continue in it, we won't be showing love to them. We show love by honestly sharing our concerns in order to help these friends do and be their very best for God. When we don't make any move to help, we show that we are more concerned about being well liked than about what will happen to them.

2:5–11 Paul explained that it was time to forgive the man who had been punished by the church and had subsequently repented. He needed forgiveness, acceptance, and comfort. Satan would gain an advantage if they permanently separated this man from the congregation rather than forgiving and restoring him. This may have been the man who had required the disciplinary action described in 1 Corinthians 5, or he may have been the chief opponent of Paul who had caused Paul the anguish described in 2:1–11. The sorrowful letter had finally brought about the repentance of the Corinthians (7:8–14), and their discipline of the man had led to his repentance. Church discipline should seek restoration. Two mistakes in church discipline should be avoided—being too lenient and not correcting mistakes, or being too harsh and not forgiving the sinner. There is a time to confront and a time to comfort.

2:11 We use church discipline to help keep the church pure and to help wayward people repent. But Satan tries to harm the church by tempting it to use discipline in an unforgiving way. This causes those exercising discipline to become proud of their purity, and it causes the person who is being disciplined to become bitter and perhaps leave the church entirely. We must remember that our purpose in discipline is to *restore* a person to the fellowship, not to destroy him or her. We must be cautious that personal anger is not vented under the guise of church discipline.

2:13 Titus was a Greek convert whom Paul greatly loved and trusted (the book of Titus is a letter that Paul wrote to him). Titus was

2:14 Rom 1:8; 6:17; 1 Cor 15:57; 2 Cor 8:16; 9:15; Col 2:15
2:15 Eph 5:2; Phil 4:18; 1 Cor 1:18
2:16 1 Pet 2:7f; 2 Cor 3:5f
2:17 2 Cor 4:2; Gal 1:6-9; 1 Cor 5:8; 1 Thess 2:4; 1 Pet 4:11

14 But thanks be to God, who always leads us in triumph in Christ, and manifests
through us the sweet aroma of the knowledge of Him in every place.
15 For we are a fragrance of Christ to God among those who are being saved and among
those who are perishing;
16 to the one an aroma from death to death, to the other an aroma from life to life.
And who is adequate for these things?
17 For we are not like many, [1]peddling the word of God, but as from sincerity, but as
from God, we speak in Christ in the sight of God.

1 Or *corrupting*

PAUL SEARCHES FOR TITUS
Paul had searched for Titus, hoping to meet him in Troas and receive news about the Corinthian church. When he did not find Titus in Troas, he went on to Macedonia (2:13), most likely to Philippi, where he found Titus.

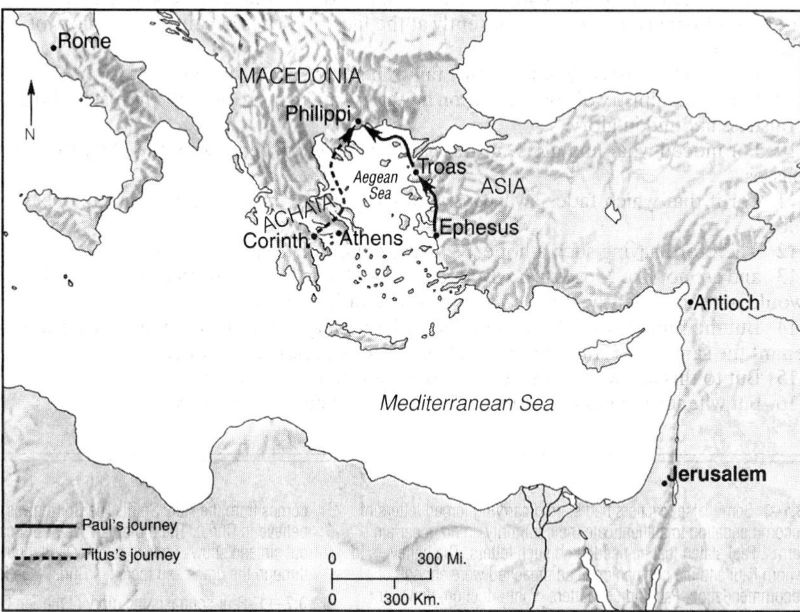

one of the men responsible for collecting the money for the poverty-stricken Jerusalem church (8:6). Paul may also have sent Titus with the sorrowful letter. On his way to Macedonia, Paul was supposed to meet Titus in Troas. When Paul didn't find him there, he was worried for Titus's safety and left Troas to search for him in Macedonia. There Paul found him (7:6), and the good news that Paul received (7:8–16) led to this letter. Paul would send Titus back to Corinth with this letter (8:16–17).

2:14ff In the middle of discussing his unscheduled trip to Macedonia, Paul thanked God for his ministry, his relationship with the Corinthian believers, and the way God had used him to help others wherever he went, despite difficulties (2:14—7:4). In 7:5, Paul resumed his story of his trip to Macedonia.

2:14–16 In a Roman triumphal procession, the Roman general would display his treasures and captives amidst a cloud of incense burned for the gods. To the victors, the aroma was sweet; to the captives in the parade, it was the smell of slavery and death. When Christians preach the gospel, it is Good News to some and repulsive news to others. Believers recognize the life-giving fragrance of the message. To nonbelievers, however, it smells foul, like death—their own.

2:16–17 Paul asks "who is adequate" for the task of representing Christ. Our adequacy is always from God (1 Corinthians 15:10; 2 Corinthians 3:5). He has already commissioned and sent us (see Matthew 28:18–20). He has given us the Holy Spirit to enable us to speak with Christ's power. He keeps his eye on us, protecting us as we work for him. So, if we realize that God makes us competent and useful, we can overcome our feelings of inadequacy. Serving Christ, therefore, requires that we focus on what he can do through us, not on what we can't do by ourselves.

2:17 Some preachers in Paul's day were "peddlers" of God's Word, preaching without understanding God's message or caring about what happened to their listeners. They weren't concerned about furthering God's kingdom—they just wanted money. Today there are still religious teachers who care only about money, and not about truth. Those who truly speak for God should have sincerity and integrity and should never preach for selfish reasons (1 Timothy 6:5–10).

Ministers of a New Covenant

3 Are we beginning to commend ourselves again? Or do we need, as some, letters of
commendation to you or from you?
2 You are our letter, written in our hearts, known and read by all men;
3 being manifested that you are a letter of Christ, cared for by us, written not with ink
but with the Spirit of the living God, not on tablets of stone but on tablets of human
hearts.
4 Such confidence we have through Christ toward God.
5 Not that we are adequate in ourselves to consider anything as *coming* from ourselves,
but our adequacy is from God,
6 who also made us adequate *as* servants of a new covenant, not of the letter but of
the Spirit; for the letter kills, but the Spirit gives life.
7 But if the ministry of death, in letters engraved on stones, came with glory, so that
the sons of Israel could not look intently at the face of Moses because of the glory of his
face, fading *as* it was,
8 how will the ministry of the Spirit fail to be even more with glory?
9 For if the ministry of condemnation has glory, much more does the ministry of righteousness abound in glory.
10 For indeed what had glory, in this case has no glory because of the glory that surpasses *it.*
11 For if that which fades away *was* with glory, much more that which remains *is* in
glory.
12 Therefore having such a hope, we use great boldness in *our* speech,
13 and *are* not like Moses, *who* used to put a veil over his face so that the sons of Israel
would not look intently at the end of what was fading away.
14 But their minds were hardened; for until this very day at the reading of the old covenant the same veil remains unlifted, because it is removed in Christ.
15 But to this day whenever Moses is read, a veil lies over their heart;
16 but whenever a person turns to the Lord, the veil is taken away.

3:1 2 Cor 5:12; 10:12, 18; 12:11; Acts 18:27; 1 Cor 16:3

3:2 1 Cor 9:2

3:3 2 Cor 3:6; Matt 16:16; Ex 24:12; 31:18; 32:15f; 2 Cor 3:7; Prov 3:3; 7:3; Jer 17:1; Jer 31:33; Ezek 11:19; 36:26

3:4 Eph 3:12

3:5 1 Cor 15:10

3:6 1 Cor 3:5; Jer 31:31; Luke 22:20; Rom 2:29; John 6:63; Rom 7:6

3:7 Rom 4:15; 5:20; 7:5f; Gal 3:10, 21f; Ex 24:12; 31:18; 32:15

3:9 Heb 12:18-21; Rom 1:17; 3:21f

3:12 2 Cor 7:4; Acts 4:13, 29; 2 Cor 7:4; Eph 6:19; 1 Thess 2:2

3:14 Rom 11:7; 2 Cor 4:4; Acts 13:15; 2 Cor 3:6

3:1–3 Some false teachers had started carrying forged letters of recommendation to authenticate their authority. In no uncertain terms, Paul stated that he needed no such letters. The believers to whom Paul and his companions had preached were enough of a recommendation. Paul did use letters of introduction, however, many times. He wrote them on behalf of Phoebe (Romans 16:1–2) and Timothy (1 Corinthians 16:10–11). These letters helped Paul's trusted companions and friends find a welcome in various churches.

3:3 Paul uses powerful imagery from famous Old Testament passages predicting the promised day of new hearts and new beginnings for God's people (see Jeremiah 31:33; Ezekiel 11:19; 36:26). No human minister can take credit for this process of conversion. It is the work of God's Spirit. We do not become believers by following some manual or using some technique. Our conversion is a result of God's implanting his Spirit in our hearts, giving us new power to live for him.

3:4–5 Paul was not boasting; he gave God the credit for all his accomplishments. While the false teachers boasted of their own power and prestige, Paul expressed his humility before God. No one can claim to be adequate without God's help. No one is competent to carry out the responsibilities of God's calling in his or her own strength. Without the Holy Spirit's enabling, our natural talent can carry us only so far. As Christ's witnesses, we need the character and special strength that only God gives.

3:6 "The letter kills, but the Spirit gives life" means that trying to be saved by keeping the Old Testament laws will end in death. Only by believing in the Lord Jesus Christ can a person receive eternal life through the Holy Spirit. No one but Jesus has ever fulfilled the law perfectly, and thus the whole world is condemned to death. The law makes people realize their sin, but it cannot give life. Under the new covenant, which means promise or agreement, eternal life comes from the Holy Spirit. The Spirit gives new life to all who believe in Christ. The moral law (Ten Commandments) still points out sin and shows us how to obey God, but forgiveness comes only through the grace and mercy of Christ (see Romans 7:10—8:2).

3:7–11 Paul contrasts the glory of the Ten Commandments with the glory of the life-giving Spirit. If the law that leads to death was glorious, how much more glorious is God's plan to give us life through his Spirit! The sacrifice of Jesus Christ is far superior to the Old Testament system of sacrifice (see Hebrews 8; 10 for a more complete discussion). If Christianity is superior to the Judaism of the Old Testament, which was the highest form of religion on earth, it will surely be superior to any other religion we may come across. Because God's plan is wonderful by comparison to any other, we dare not reject it or treat it casually.

3:9 Paul is saying that if the old covenant (the ministry of condemnation) had its glory (and certainly it did), just imagine the glory of the new covenant (the ministry of righteousness). The law was wonderful because, although it condemned us, it pointed us to Christ. But in the new covenant, the law and the promise are fulfilled. Christ has come—by faith we can be justified (made right with God)!

3:13–18 When Moses came down Mount Sinai with the Ten Commandments, his face glowed from being in God's presence (Exodus 34:29–35). Moses had to put on a veil to keep the people from being terrified by the brightness of his face. Paul adds that this veil kept them from seeing the radiance fade away. Moses and his veil illustrate the fading of the old system and the veiling of the people's minds and understanding by their pride, hardness of heart, and refusal to repent. The veil kept them from understanding the references to Christ in the Scriptures. When anyone becomes a Christian, Christ removes the veil (3:16), giving eternal life and freedom from trying to be saved by keeping laws. And without the veil, we can be like mirrors reflecting God's glory.

17 Now the Lord is the Spirit, and where the Spirit of the Lord is, *there* is liberty.
18 But we all, with unveiled face, beholding as in a mirror the glory of the Lord, are
being transformed into the same image from glory to glory, just as from the Lord, the
Spirit.

Paul's Apostolic Ministry

4 Therefore, since we have this ministry, as we received mercy, we do not lose heart,
2 but we have renounced the things hidden because of shame, not walking in craftiness or adulterating the word of God, but by the manifestation of truth commending
ourselves to every man's conscience in the sight of God.
3 And even if our gospel is veiled, it is veiled to those who are perishing,
4 in whose case the god of this world has blinded the minds of the unbelieving so that
they might not see the light of the gospel of the glory of Christ, who is the image of God.
5 For we do not preach ourselves but Christ Jesus as Lord, and ourselves as your bond-
servants for Jesus' sake.
6 For God, who said, "Light shall shine out of darkness," is the One who has shone in
our hearts to give the Light of the knowledge of the glory of God in the face of Christ.
7 But we have this treasure in earthen vessels, so that the surpassing greatness of the
power will be of God and not from ourselves;
8 *we are* afflicted in every way, but not crushed; perplexed, but not despairing;
9 persecuted, but not forsaken; struck down, but not destroyed;
10 always carrying about in the body the dying of Jesus, so that the life of Jesus also
may be manifested in our body.
11 For we who live are constantly being delivered over to death for Jesus' sake, so that
the life of Jesus also may be manifested in our mortal flesh.
12 So death works in us, but life in you.
13 But having the same spirit of faith, according to what is written, "I BELIEVED, THERE-
FORE I SPOKE," we also believe, therefore we also speak,
14 knowing that He who raised the Lord Jesus will raise us also with Jesus and will
present us with you.

3:17 John 8:32; Gal 5:1
3:18 1 Cor 13:12; John 17:22, 24
4:1 1 Cor 3:5; 1 Cor 7:25; Luke 18:1; Eph 3:13; 2 Thess 3:13
4:2 Rom 6:21; 1 Cor 4:5; 2 Cor 2:17
4:3 2 Cor 2:12; 1 Cor 2:6ff; 2 Cor 3:14
4:4 John 12:31; Matt 13:22; 2 Cor 3:14; John 1:18; Phil 2:6; Col 1:15; Heb 1:3
4:6 Gen 1:3; 2 Pet 1:19
4:7 2 Tim 2:20; Judg 7:2; 1 Cor 2:5
4:8 2 Cor 1:8; 7:5; 2 Cor 6:12; Gal 4:20
4:9 John 15:20
4:10 Gal 6:17; Rom 6:8
4:13 Ps 116:10
4:14 Acts 2:24; 1 Thess 4:14; Luke 21:36

3:17 Those who were trying to be saved by keeping the Old Testament law were soon tied up in rules and ceremonies. But now, through the Holy Spirit, God provides freedom from sin and condemnation (Romans 8:1). When we trust Christ to save us, he removes our heavy burden of trying to please him and our guilt for failing to do so. By trusting Christ we are loved, accepted, forgiven, and freed to live for him. "Where the Spirit of the Lord is, there is liberty."

3:18 The glory that the Spirit imparts to the believer is more excellent and lasts longer than the glory that Moses experienced. By gazing at the nature of God with unveiled minds, we can be more like him. In the gospel, we see the truth about Christ, and it transforms us morally as we understand and apply it. Through learning about Christ's life, we can understand how wonderful God is and what he is really like. As our knowledge deepens, the Holy Spirit helps us to change. Becoming Christlike is a progressive experience (see Romans 8:29; Galatians 4:19; Philippians 3:21; 1 John 3:2). The more closely we follow Christ, the more we will be like him.

4:2 Preachers, teachers, and anyone else who talks about Jesus Christ must remember that they stand in God's presence—he hears every word. When you tell people about Christ, be careful not to distort the message to please your audience. Proclaim the truth of God's Word.

4:3–4 The gospel is open and revealed to everyone, except to those who refuse to believe. Satan is "the god of this world." His work is to deceive, and he has blinded those who don't believe in Christ (see 11:14–15). The allure of money, power, and pleasure blinds people to the light of Christ's gospel. Those who reject Christ and prefer their own pursuits have unknowingly made Satan their god.

4:5 The focus of Paul's preaching was Christ and not himself. When you witness, tell people about what Christ has done, and not about your abilities and accomplishments. People must be introduced to Christ, not to you. And if you hear someone preaching himself or his own ideas rather than Christ, beware—he is a false teacher.

4:5 Paul willingly served the Corinthian church even though the people must have deeply disappointed him. Serving people requires a sacrifice of time and personal desires. Being Christ's follower means serving others, even when they do not measure up to our expectations.

4:7 The supremely valuable message of salvation in Jesus Christ has been entrusted by God to frail and fallible human beings ("earthen vessels"). Paul's focus, however, was not on the perishable container but on its priceless contents—God's power dwelling in us. Though we are weak, God uses us to spread his Good News, and he gives us power to do his work. Knowing that the power is his, not ours, should keep us from pride and motivate us to keep daily contact with God, our power source. Our responsibility is to let people see God through us.

4:8–12 Paul reminds us that though we may think we are at the end of the rope, we are never at the end of hope. Our perishable bodies are subject to sin and suffering, but God never abandons us. Because Christ has won the victory over death, we have eternal life. All our risks, humiliations, and trials are opportunities for Christ to demonstrate his power and presence in and through us.

15 For all things *are* for your sakes, so that the grace which is spreading to more and
more people may cause the giving of thanks to abound to the glory of God.
16 Therefore we do not lose heart, but though our outer man is decaying, yet our inner
man is being renewed day by day.
17 For momentary, light affliction is producing for us an eternal weight of glory far
beyond all comparison,
18 while we look not at the things which are seen, but at the things which are not seen;
for the things which are seen are temporal, but the things which are not seen are eternal.

The Temporal and Eternal

5 For we know that if the earthly tent which is our house is torn down, we have a building from God, a house not made with hands, eternal in the heavens.
2 For indeed in this *house* we groan, longing to be clothed with our dwelling from
heaven,
3 inasmuch as we, having put it on, will not be found naked.
4 For indeed while we are in this tent, we groan, being burdened, because we do not
want to be unclothed but to be clothed, so that what is mortal will be swallowed up by
life.
5 Now He who prepared us for this very purpose is God, who gave to us the Spirit as
a pledge.
6 Therefore, being always of good courage, and knowing that while we are at home in
the body we are absent from the Lord—
7 for we walk by faith, not by sight—
8 we are of good courage, I say, and prefer rather to be absent from the body and to
be at home with the Lord.
9 Therefore we also have as our ambition, whether at home or absent, to be pleasing
to Him.
10 For we must all appear before the judgment seat of Christ, so that each one may be

4:15 Rom 8:28; 2 Cor 1:6; 1 Cor 9:19
4:16 Rom 7:22; Is 40:29, 31; Col 3:10
4:17 Rom 8:18
4:18 Rom 8:24; 2 Cor 5:7; Heb 11:1, 13
5:1 2 Cor 4:7; 2 Pet 1:13f Mark 14:58; Acts 7:48
5:2 Rom 8:23; 2 Cor 5:4; 1 Cor 15:53f
5:4 2 Cor 5:2; 1 Cor 15:53f
5:6 Heb 11:13f
5:7 1 Cor 13:12
5:8 Phil 1:23; John 12:26
5:9 Rom 14:18; Col 1:10; 1 Thess 4:1
5:10 Matt 16:27; Acts 10:42; Rom 2:16

4:15–18 Paul had faced sufferings, trials, and distress as he preached the Good News. But he knew that they would one day be over, and he would obtain God's rest and rewards. As we face great troubles, it's easy to focus on the pain rather than on our ultimate goal. Just as athletes concentrate on the finish line and ignore their discomfort, we too must focus on the reward for our faith and the joy that lasts forever. No matter what happens to us in this life, we have the assurance of eternal life, when all suffering will end and all sorrow will flee away (Isaiah 35:10).

4:16 It is easy to lose heart and quit. We all have faced problems in our relationships or in our work that have caused us to want to think about laying down the tools and walking away. Rather than giving up when persecution wore him down, Paul concentrated on experiencing the inner strength from the Holy Spirit (Ephesians 3:16). Don't let fatigue, pain, or criticism force you off the job. Renew your commitment to serving Christ. Don't forsake your eternal reward because of the intensity of today's pain. Your very weakness allows the resurrection power of Christ to strengthen you moment by moment.

4:17 Our troubles should not diminish our faith or disillusion us. We should realize that there is a purpose in our suffering. Problems and human limitations have several benefits: (1) They remind us of Christ's suffering for us, (2) they keep us from pride, (3) they cause us to look beyond this brief life, (4) they prove our faith to others, and (5) they give God the opportunity to demonstrate his power. See your troubles as opportunities!

4:18 Our ultimate hope when we are experiencing terrible illness, persecution, or pain is the realization that this life is not all there is—there is life after death! Knowing that we will live forever with God in a place without sin and suffering can help us live above the pain that we face in this life.

5:1–10 Paul contrasts our earthly bodies ("earthly tent") and our future resurrection bodies ("a building from God, a house not made with hands, eternal in the heavens"). Paul clearly states that our present bodies make us groan, but when we die we will not be spirits without bodies ("be found naked"). We will have new bodies that will be perfect for our everlasting life.

Paul wrote as he did because the church at Corinth was in the heart of Greek culture, and many believers had difficulty with the concept of bodily resurrection. Greeks did not believe in a bodily resurrection. Most saw the afterlife as something that happened only to the soul, with the real person imprisoned in a physical body. They believed that at death the soul is released—there is no immortality for the body, and the soul enters an eternal state. But the Bible teaches that the body and soul are not permanently separated.

Paul describes our resurrected bodies in more detail in 1 Corinthians 15:46–58. We will still have personalities and recognizable characteristics in our resurrected bodies, but through Christ's work, our bodies will be better than we can imagine. The Bible does not tell us everything about our resurrected bodies, but we know they will be perfect, without sickness, disease, or pain (see Philippians 3:21; Revelation 21:4).

5:5 The Holy Spirit within us is our pledge, our guarantee, that God will give us everlasting bodies at the resurrection (1:22). We have eternity in us now! This truth should give us great courage and patience to endure anything we might experience.

5:6–8 Paul was not afraid to die, because he was confident of spending eternity with Christ. Of course, facing the unknown may cause us anxiety, and leaving loved ones hurts deeply, but if we believe in Jesus Christ, we can share Paul's hope and confidence of eternal life with Christ.

5:8 For those who believe in Christ, death is only a prelude to eternal life with God. We will continue to live. Let this hope give you confidence and inspire you to faithful service.

5:9–10 While eternal life is a free gift given on the basis of God's grace (Ephesians 2:8–9), each of us will still be judged by Christ. This judgment will reward us for how we have lived. God's gracious gift of salvation does not free us from the requirement for faithful obedience. All Christians must give account for how they

recompensed for his deeds in the body, according to what he has done, whether good
or bad.
11 Therefore, knowing the fear of the Lord, we persuade men, but we are made manifest to God; and I hope that we are made manifest also in your consciences.
12 We are not again commending ourselves to you but *are* giving you an occasion to be
proud of us, so that you will have *an answer* for those who take pride in appearance and
not in heart.
13 For if we are beside ourselves, it is for God; if we are of sound mind, it is for you.
14 For the love of Christ controls us, having concluded this, that one died for all, therefore all died;
15 and He died for all, so that they who live might no longer live for themselves, but
for Him who died and rose again on their behalf.
16 Therefore from now on we recognize no one according to the flesh; even though we
have known Christ according to the flesh, yet now we know *Him in this way* no longer.
17 Therefore if anyone is in Christ, *he is* a new creature; the old things passed away;
behold, new things have come.
18 Now all *these* things are from God, who reconciled us to Himself through Christ
and gave us the ministry of reconciliation,
19 namely, that God was in Christ reconciling the world to Himself, not counting their
trespasses against them, and He has committed to us the word of reconciliation.
20 Therefore, we are ambassadors for Christ, as though God were making an appeal
through us; we beg you on behalf of Christ, be reconciled to God.
21 He made Him who knew no sin *to be* sin on our behalf, so that we might become the
righteousness of God in Him.

Their Ministry Commended

6 And working together *with Him,* we also urge you not to receive the grace of God in
vain—
2 for He says,
"AT THE ACCEPTABLE TIME I LISTENED TO YOU,
AND ON THE DAY OF SALVATION I HELPED YOU."
Behold, now is "THE ACCEPTABLE TIME," behold, now is "THE DAY OF SALVATION"—
3 giving no cause for offense in anything, so that the ministry will not be discredited,

5:11 Heb 10:31; 12:29; Jude 23; 2 Cor 4:2
5:12 2 Cor 3:1; 2 Cor 1:14; Phil 1:26
5:13 Mark 3:21; 2 Cor 11:1, 16ff; 12:11
5:14 Acts 18:5; Rom 5:15; 6:6f; Gal 2:20; Col 3:3
5:15 Rom 14:7-9
5:16 John 8:15; 2 Cor 11:18; Phil 3:4
5:17 Rom 6:4; Gal 6:15; Is 43:18f; 65:17; Eph 4:24; Rev 21:4f
5:18 1 Cor 11:12; Rom 5:10; Col 1:20; 1 Cor 3:5
5:19 Col 2:9; Rom 4:8; 1 Cor 13:5
5:20 Mal 2:7; Eph 6:20; 2 Cor 6:1; Rom 5:10; Col 1:20
5:21 Acts 3:14; Heb 4:15; 7:26; 1 Pet 2:22
6:1 1 Cor 3:9; 2 Cor 5:20; Acts 11:23
6:2 Is 49:8

---

have lived (see Matthew 16:27; Romans 14:10–12; 1 Corinthians 3:10–15).

5:12 Those who "take pride in appearance and not in heart" are the false preachers (see 2:17) who were concerned only about getting ahead in this world. They were preaching the gospel for money and popularity, while Paul and his companions were preaching out of concern for eternity. You can identify false preachers by finding out what really motivates them. If they are more concerned about themselves than about Christ, avoid them and their message.

5:13–15 Everything that Paul and his companions did was to honor God. Christ's love controlled their lives. Because Christ died for us, we also are dead to our old lives. Like Paul, we should no longer live to please ourselves; we should spend our lives pleasing Christ, who died for us and rose from the grave.

5:17 Christians are brand-new people on the *inside.* The Holy Spirit gives them new life, and they are not the same anymore. We are not reformed, rehabilitated, or reeducated—we are re-created (new creatures), living in vital union with Christ (Colossians 2:6–7). At conversion we are not merely turning over a new leaf; we are beginning a new life under a new Master.

5:18–19 God brings us back to himself (reconciles us) by blotting out our sins (see also Ephesians 2:13–18) and making us righteous. We are no longer God's enemies, or strangers or foreigners to him, when we trust in Christ. Because we have been reconciled to God, we have the privilege of encouraging others to do the same, and thus we are those who have the "word of reconciliation."

5:20 An ambassador is an official representative on behalf of one country to another. As believers, we are Christ's ambassadors, sent with his message of reconciliation to the world. An ambassador of reconciliation has an important responsibility. We dare not take this responsibility lightly. How well are you fulfilling your commission as Christ's ambassador?

5:21 When we trust in Christ, we make an exchange—our sin for his righteousness. Our sin was poured into Christ at his crucifixion. His righteousness is poured into us at our conversion. This is what Christians mean by Christ's atonement for sin. In the world, bartering works only when two people exchange goods of relatively equal value. But God offers to trade his righteousness for our sin—something of immeasurable worth for something completely worthless. How grateful we should be for his kindness to us.

6:1 How could the Corinthian believers toss aside God's message ("receive the grace of God in vain")? Perhaps they were doubting Paul and his words, confused by the false teachers who taught a different message. The people heard God's message but did not let it affect what they said and did. How often does God's message reach you in vain?

6:2 God offers salvation to all people. Many people put off a decision for Christ, thinking that there will be a better time—but they could easily miss their opportunity altogether. There is no time like the present to receive God's forgiveness. Don't let anything hold you back from coming to Christ.

6:3 In everything he did, Paul always considered what his actions communicated about Jesus Christ. If you are a believer, you are a minister for God. In the course of each day, non-Christians observe you. Don't let your careless or undisciplined actions be another person's excuse for rejecting Christ.

4 but in everything commending ourselves as servants of God, in much endurance, in
afflictions, in hardships, in distresses,
5 in beatings, in imprisonments, in tumults, in labors, in sleeplessness, in hunger,
6 in purity, in knowledge, in patience, in kindness, in the Holy Spirit, in genuine love,
7 in the word of truth, in the power of God; by the weapons of righteousness for the
right hand and the left,
8 by glory and dishonor, by evil report and good report; *regarded* as deceivers and yet
true;
9 as unknown yet well-known, as dying yet behold, we live; as punished yet not put to
death,
10 as sorrowful yet always rejoicing, as poor yet making many rich, as having nothing
yet possessing all things.
11 Our mouth has spoken freely to you, O Corinthians, our heart is opened wide.
12 You are not restrained by us, but you are restrained in your own affections.
13 Now in a like exchange—I speak as to children—open wide *to us* also.
14 Do not be bound together with unbelievers; for what partnership have righteousness and lawlessness, or what fellowship has light with darkness?
15 Or what harmony has Christ with Belial, or what has a believer in common with an
unbeliever?
16 Or what agreement has the temple of God with idols? For we are the temple of the
living God; just as God said,
"I WILL DWELL IN THEM AND WALK AMONG THEM;
AND I WILL BE THEIR GOD, AND THEY SHALL BE MY PEOPLE.
17 "Therefore, COME OUT FROM THEIR MIDST AND BE SEPARATE," says the Lord.
"AND DO NOT TOUCH WHAT IS UNCLEAN;
And I will welcome you.
18 "And I will be a father to you,
And you shall be sons and daughters to Me,"
Says the Lord Almighty.

Paul Reveals His Heart

7 Therefore, having these promises, beloved, let us cleanse ourselves from all defilement of flesh and spirit, perfecting holiness in the fear of God.
2 Make room for us *in your hearts;* we wronged no one, we corrupted no one, we took
advantage of no one.
3 I do not speak to condemn you, for I have said before that you are in our hearts to
die together and to live together.
4 Great is my confidence in you; great is my boasting on your behalf. I am filled with
comfort; I am overflowing with joy in all our affliction.

6:4 Rom 3:5; 1 Cor 3:5; 2 Tim 2:24f; Acts 9:16; 2 Cor 4:8-11
6:5 Acts 16:23; Acts 19:23ff; 1 Cor 4:11
6:6 Rom 12:9
6:7 2 Cor 2:17; 4:2; 1 Cor 2:5; Rom 13:12; 2 Cor 10:4; Eph 6:11ff
6:8 2 Cor 12:16; Matt 27:63; 2 Cor 1:18; 4:2; 1 Thess 2:3f
6:9 Rom 8:36; 2 Cor 1:8, 10; 4:11
6:10 John 16:22; 2 Cor 7:4; Phil 2:17; 4:4
6:13 Gal 4:12; 1 Cor 4:14
6:14 1 Cor 5:9f; 6:6; Eph 5:7, 11; 1 John 1:6
6:15 1 Cor 10:21; Acts 5:14; 1 Pet 1:21
6:16 Matt 16:16; Ex 29:45
6:17 Is 52:11; Rev 18:4
6:18 Rom 8:14
7:1 Heb 6:9; 1 Pet 1:15f
7:3 2 Cor 6:11f; Phil 1:7
7:4 Phil 1:26; 2 Thess 1:4; 2 Cor 1:4; 2 Cor 6:10

6:7 See Romans 13:2; 2 Corinthians 10:3–5; and Ephesians 6:10–18 for more about the weapons of righteousness. Weapons for the right hand are offensive weapons; those for the left hand are defensive. No soldier is fully prepared for battle without both.

6:8–10 What a difference it makes to know Jesus! He cares for us in spite of what the world thinks. Christians don't have to give in to public opinion and pressure. Paul stood faithful to God whether people praised him or condemned him. He remained active, joyous, and content in the most difficult hardships. Don't let circumstances or people's expectations control you. Be firm as you stand true to God, and refuse to compromise his standards for living.

6:11–13 "Our heart is opened wide" and "you are not restrained by us" mean that Paul had told the Corinthian believers his true feelings for them, clearly revealing how much he loved them. The Corinthians were reacting coldly to Paul's words, but Paul explained that his harsh words came from his love for them. It is easy to react against those whom God has placed over us in leadership, rather than to accept their exhortations as a sign of their love for us. We need an open rather than a closed heart toward God's messengers.

6:14–18 Paul urges believers not to form binding relationships with nonbelievers, because this might weaken their Christian commitment, integrity, or standards. It would be a mismatch. Earlier, Paul had explained that this did not mean isolating oneself from nonbelievers (see 1 Corinthians 5:9–10). Paul even tells Christians to stay with their nonbelieving spouses (1 Corinthians 7:12–13). Paul wants believers to be active in their witness for Christ to nonbelievers, but they should not lock themselves into personal or business relationships that could cause them to compromise the faith. Believers should do everything in their power to avoid situations that could force them to divide their loyalties.

6:15 Belial is a name that Paul uses for Satan. For those who have discovered God's light, there can be no fellowship or compromise with the darkness (1 Corinthians 10:20–21).

6:17 Separation from the world involves more than keeping our distance from sinners; it means staying close to God (see 7:1–2). It involves more than avoiding entertainment that leads to sin; it extends into how we spend our time and money. There is no way to separate ourselves totally from all sinful influences. Nevertheless, we are to resist the sin around us, without either giving up or giving in.

7:1 Purifying ourselves is a twofold action: turning *away* from sin and turning *toward* God. "Perfecting holiness" means that the Corinthians were to have nothing to do with paganism. They were to make a clean break with their past and give themselves to God alone.

7:5 Rom 15:26; 2 Cor 2:13; 2 Cor 4:8; Deut 32:25

7:6 2 Cor 1:3f; 2 Cor 7:13; 2 Cor 2:13; 7:13f

7:8 2 Cor 2:2

7:10 Acts 11:18

7:11 2 Cor 7:7; 2 Cor 2:6; Rom 3:5

7:12 2 Cor 2:3, 9; 7:8; 1 Cor 5:1f

7:13 2 Cor 7:6; 2 Cor 2:13; 7:6, 14; 1 Cor 16:18

7:14 2 Cor 7:4; 8:24; 9:2f; 10:8; Phil 1:26; 2 Thess 1:4; 2 Cor 2:13; 7:6, 13

7:15 2 Cor 2:9; 1 Cor 2:3; Phil 2:12

7:16 2 Cor 2:3

8:1 2 Cor 8:5; Acts 16:9

8:2 Rom 2:4

8:3 1 Cor 16:2; 2 Cor 8:11

8:4 Acts 24:17; Rom 15:25f; Rom 15:31; 2 Cor 8:19f; 9:1, 12f

5 For even when we came into Macedonia our flesh had no rest, but we were afflicted
on every side: conflicts without, fears within.
6 But God, who comforts the depressed, comforted us by the coming of Titus;
7 and not only by his coming, but also by the comfort with which he was comforted in
you, as he reported to us your longing, your mourning, your zeal for me; so that I rejoiced even more.
8 For though I caused you sorrow by my letter, I do not regret it; though I did regret
it—*for* I see that that letter caused you sorrow, though only for a while—
9 I now rejoice, not that you were made sorrowful, but that you were made sorrowful
to *the point of* repentance; for you were made sorrowful according to *the will of* God, so
that you might not suffer loss in anything through us.
10 For the sorrow that is according to *the will of* God produces a repentance without
regret, *leading* to salvation, but the sorrow of the world produces death.
11 For behold what earnestness this very thing, this godly sorrow, has produced in you:
what vindication of yourselves, what indignation, what fear, what longing, what zeal, what
avenging of wrong! In everything you demonstrated yourselves to be innocent in the
matter.
12 So although I wrote to you, *it was* not for the sake of the offender nor for the sake
of the one offended, but that your earnestness on our behalf might be made known to
you in the sight of God.
13 For this reason we have been comforted.
And besides our comfort, we rejoiced even much more for the joy of Titus, because his
spirit has been refreshed by you all.
14 For if in anything I have boasted to him about you, I was not put to shame; but as
we spoke all things to you in truth, so also our boasting before Titus proved to be *the*
truth.
15 His affection abounds all the more toward you, as he remembers the obedience of
you all, how you received him with fear and trembling.
16 I rejoice that in everything I have confidence in you.

3. Paul defends the collection

Great Generosity

8 Now, brethren, we *wish to* make known to you the grace of God which has been giv-
en in the churches of Macedonia,
2 that in a great ordeal of affliction their abundance of joy and their deep poverty
overflowed in the wealth of their liberality.
3 For I testify that according to their ability, and beyond their ability, *they gave* of their
own accord,
4 begging us with much urging for the favor of participation in the support of the saints,

---

7:5 Here Paul resumed the story that he left in 2:13, where he said he went to Macedonia to look for Titus. Though Paul still had many problems and hardships to face, he found comfort and joy in the progress of the ministry.

7:8ff "My letter" refers to the third letter (now lost) that Paul had written to the Corinthians. Apparently it had caused the people to begin to change. For an explanation of the chronology of Paul's letters to Corinth, see the first note on 1:1.

7:10 "Sorrow that is according to the will of God produces a repentance without regret, leading to salvation" refers to the sorrow for our sins that results in changed behavior. Many people are sorry only for the effects of their sins or for being caught ("sorrow of the world"). Compare Peter's remorse and repentance with Judas's bitterness and act of suicide. Both denied Christ. One repented and was restored to faith and service; the other took his own life.

7:11 It is difficult to be confronted with our sin, and even more difficult to get rid of sin. Paul praised the Corinthians for clearing up an especially troublesome situation (see the note on 2:5–11). Do you tend to be defensive when confronted? Don't let pride keep you from admitting your sins. Accept correction as a tool for your growth, and do all you can to correct problems that are pointed out to you.

8:1ff Paul, writing from Macedonia, hoped that news of the generosity of these churches would encourage the Corinthian believers and motivate them to solve their problems and unite in fellowship.

8:2–5 During his third missionary journey, Paul had collected money for the impoverished believers in Jerusalem. The churches in Macedonia—Philippi, Thessalonica, and Berea—had given money even though they were poor, and they had given more than Paul expected. This was sacrificial giving—they were poor themselves, but they wanted to help. The point of giving is not so much the amount we give, but why and how we give. God does not want gifts given grudgingly. Instead, he wants us to give as these churches did—out of dedication to Christ, love for fellow believers, the joy of helping those in need, as well as the fact that it was simply the good and right thing to do. How well does your giving measure up to the standards set by the Macedonian churches?

8:3–6 The kingdom of God spreads through believers' concern and eagerness to help others. Here we see several churches joining to help others beyond their own circle of friends and their own city. Explore ways that you might link up with a ministry outside your city, either through your church or through a Christian organization. By joining with other believers to do God's work, you increase Christian unity and help the kingdom grow.

5 and *this,* not as we had expected, but they first gave themselves to the Lord and to us by the will of God.

6 So we urged Titus that as he had previously made a beginning, so he would also complete in you this gracious work as well.

7 But just as you abound in everything, in faith and utterance and knowledge and in all earnestness and in the [2]love we inspired in you, *see* that you abound in this gracious work also.

8 I am not speaking *this* as a command, but as proving through the earnestness of others the sincerity of your love also.

9 For you know the grace of our Lord Jesus Christ, that though He was rich, yet for your sake He became poor, so that you through His poverty might become rich.

10 I give *my* opinion in this matter, for this is to your advantage, who were the first to begin a year ago not only to do *this,* but also to desire *to do it.*

11 But now finish doing it also, so that just as *there was* the readiness to desire it, so *there may be* also the completion of it by your ability.

12 For if the readiness is present, it is acceptable according to what *a person* has, not according to what he does not have.

13 For *this* is not for the ease of others *and* for your affliction, but by way of equality—

14 at this present time your abundance *being a supply* for their need, so that their abundance also may become *a supply* for your need, that there may be equality;

15 as it is written, "HE WHO *gathered* MUCH DID NOT HAVE TOO MUCH, AND HE WHO *gathered* LITTLE HAD NO LACK."

16 But thanks be to God who puts the same earnestness on your behalf in the heart of Titus.

17 For he not only accepted our appeal, but being himself very earnest, he has gone to you of his own accord.

18 We have sent along with him the brother whose fame in *the things of* the gospel *has spread* through all the churches;

19 and not only *this,* but he has also been appointed by the churches to travel with us in this gracious work, which is being administered by us for the glory of the Lord Himself, and *to show* our readiness,

20 taking precaution so that no one will discredit us in our administration of this generous gift;

2 Lit *love from us in you;* one early ms reads *your love for us*

8:6 Acts 24:17; Rom 15:25f

8:7 2 Cor 9:8; Rom 15:14; 1 Cor 1:5; 12:8

8:8 1 Cor 7:6

8:9 2 Cor 13:14; Matt 20:28; 2 Cor 6:10; Phil 2:6f

8:10 1 Cor 7:25, 40; 1 Cor 16:2f; 2 Cor 9:2

8:11 2 Cor 8:12, 19; 9:2

8:12 Mark 12:43f; Luke 21:3, 4; 2 Cor 9:7

8:14 Acts 4:34; 2 Cor 9:12

8:15 Ex 16:18

8:16 2 Cor 2:14; Rev 17:17; 2 Cor 2:13; 8:6, 23

8:17 2 Cor 8:6; 12:18

8:18 1 Cor 16:3; 2 Cor 12:18; 2 Cor 2:12; 1 Cor 4:17; 7:17

8:19 Rom 5:3; Acts 14:23; 1 Cor 16:3f; 2 Cor 8:4, 6

8:7–8 The Corinthian believers excelled in everything—they had faith, good preaching (utterance), much knowledge, much earnestness, much love. Paul wanted them to also be leaders in giving. Giving is a natural response of love. Paul did not order the Corinthians to give, but he encouraged them to prove that their love was sincere. When you love someone, you want to give him or her your time and attention and to provide for his or her needs. If you refuse to help, your love is not as genuine as you say.

8:9 There is no evidence that Jesus was any poorer than most first-century Palestinians; rather, Jesus became poor by giving up his rights as God and becoming human. In his incarnation God voluntarily became man—the wholly human person, Jesus of Nazareth. As a man, Jesus was subject to place, time, and other human limitations. He did not give up his eternal power when he became human, but he did set aside his glory and his rights (see the note on Philippians 2:5–7). In response to the Father's will, he limited his power and knowledge. Christ became "poor" when he became human, because he set aside so much. Yet by doing so, he made us "rich" because we received salvation and eternal life.

What made Jesus' humanity unique was his freedom from sin. In his full humanity, we can see everything about God's character that can be conveyed in human terms. The incarnation is explained further in these Bible passages: John 1:1–14; Romans 1:2–5; Philippians 2:6–11; 1 Timothy 3:16; Hebrews 2:14; 1 John 1:1–3.

8:10–15 The Corinthian church had money, and apparently they had planned to collect money for the Jerusalem churches a year previously (see also 9:2). Paul challenges them to act on their plans. Four principles of giving emerge here: (1) Your willingness to give cheerfully is more important than the amount you give; (2) you should strive to fulfill your financial commitments; (3) if you give to others in need, they will, in turn, help you when you are in need; (4) you should give as a response to Christ, not for anything you can get out of it. How you give reflects your devotion to Christ.

8:12 How do you decide how much to give? What about differences in the financial resources Christians have? Paul gives the Corinthian church several principles to follow: (1) Each person should follow through on previous promises (8:10–11; 9:3); (2) each person should give as much as he or she is able (8:12; 9:6); (3) each person must make up his or her own mind how much to give (9:7); and (4) each person should give in proportion to what God has given him or her (9:10). God gives to us so that we can give to others.

8:12 Paul says that we should give of what we have, not what we don't have. Sacrificial giving must be responsible. Paul wants believers to give generously, but not to the extent that those who depend on the givers (their families, for example) must go without having their basic needs met. Give until it hurts, but don't give so that it hurts your family and/or relatives who need your financial support.

8:18–21 Another "brother" was traveling with Paul and Titus, a man who was elected by the churches to also take the large financial gift to Jerusalem. Paul explained that by traveling together there could be no suspicion and people would know that the gift was being handled honestly. The church did not need to worry that the bearers of the collection would misuse the money.

8:21 Rom 12:17; Prov 3:4; Rom 14:18
8:23 2 Cor 8:6; Philem 17; 2 Cor 8:18, 22; John 13:16; Phil 2:25; 1 Cor 11:7
8:24 2 Cor 7:4
9:1 1 Thess 4:9; 2 Cor 8:4
9:2 2 Cor 7:4; Rom 15:26; Acts 18:12; 2 Cor 8:10
9:3 2 Cor 7:4; 1 Cor 16:2
9:4 Rom 15:26
9:5 2 Cor 9:3; Gen 33:11; Judg 1:15; 2 Cor 9:6; Phil 4:17; 2 Cor 12:17f
9:6 Prov 11:24f; 22:9; Gal 6:7, 9
9:7 Deut 15:10; 1 Chr 29:17; Rom 12:8; 2 Cor 8:12; Ex 25:2
9:8 Eph 3:20
9:9 Ps 112:9
9:10 Is 55:10; Hos 10:12

21 for we have regard for what is honorable, not only in the sight of the Lord, but also
in the sight of men.
22 We have sent with them our brother, whom we have often tested and found diligent
in many things, but now even more diligent because of *his* great confidence in you.
23 As for Titus, *he is* my partner and fellow worker among you; as for our brethren,
they are messengers of the churches, a glory to Christ.
24 Therefore openly before the churches, show them the proof of your love and of our
reason for boasting about you.

God Gives Most

9 For it is superfluous for me to write to you about this ministry to the saints;
2 for I know your readiness, of which I boast about you to the Macedonians, *namely,* that Achaia has been prepared since last year, and your zeal has stirred up most of
them.
3 But I have sent the brethren, in order that our boasting about you may not be made
empty in this case, so that, as I was saying, you may be prepared;
4 otherwise if any Macedonians come with me and find you unprepared, we—not to
speak of you—will be put to shame by this confidence.
5 So I thought it necessary to urge the brethren that they would go on ahead to you
and arrange beforehand your previously promised bountiful gift, so that the same would
be ready as a bountiful gift and not affected by covetousness.
6 Now this *I say,* he who sows sparingly will also reap sparingly, and he who sows bountifully will also reap bountifully.
7 Each one *must do* just as he has purposed in his heart, not grudgingly or under compulsion, for God loves a cheerful giver.
8 And God is able to make all grace abound to you, so that always having all sufficiency in everything, you may have an abundance for every good deed;
9 as it is written,

"HE SCATTERED ABROAD, HE GAVE TO THE POOR,
HIS RIGHTEOUSNESS ENDURES FOREVER."

10 Now He who supplies seed to the sower and bread for food will supply and multiply
your seed for sowing and increase the harvest of your righteousness;

PRINCIPLES OF CONFRONTATION IN 2 CORINTHIANS

Method	*Reference*
Be firm and bold	7:9; 10:2
Affirm all you see that is good	7:4
Be accurate and honest	7:14; 8:21
Know the facts	11:22–27
Follow up after the confrontation	7:13; 12:14
Be gentle after being firm	7:15; 13:11–13
Speak words that reflect Christ's message, not your own ideas	10:3; 10:12–13; 12:19
Use discipline only when all else fails	13:2

Sometimes rebuke is necessary, but it must be used with caution. The purpose of any rebuke, confrontation, or discipline is to help people, not hurt them.

9:3–5 Paul reminded the Corinthians to fulfill the commitment that they had already made (see also 8:10–12). They had said that they would collect a financial gift to send to the church in Jerusalem. Paul was sending a few men ahead of him to make sure their gift was ready, so it would be a real gift and not look like people had to give under pressure at the last minute ("ready as a bountiful gift and not affected by covetousness"). He was holding them accountable to keep their promise, so that neither Paul nor the Corinthians would be embarrassed.

9:6–8 People may hesitate to give generously to God if they worry about having enough money left over to meet their own needs. Paul assured the Corinthians that God was able to meet their needs. The person who gives only a little will receive only a little in return. Don't let a lack of faith keep you from giving freely and generously.

9:7 Our attitude when we give is more important than the amount we give. We don't have to be embarrassed if we can give only a small gift. God is concerned about *how* we give from the resources we have (see Mark 12:41–44). According to that standard, the giving of the Macedonian churches would be difficult to match (8:3).

9:10 God gives us resources to use and invest for him. Paul uses the illustration of seed to explain that the resources God gives us are not to be hidden, foolishly devoured, or thrown away. Instead, they should be cultivated in order to produce more crops. When we invest what God has given us in his work, he will provide us with even more to give in his service.

11 you will be enriched in everything for all liberality, which through us is producing
thanksgiving to God.
12 For the ministry of this service is not only fully supplying the needs of the saints, but
is also overflowing through many thanksgivings to God.
13 Because of the proof given by this ministry, they will glorify God for *your* obedience
to your confession of the gospel of Christ and for the liberality of your contribution to
them and to all,
14 while they also, by prayer on your behalf, yearn for you because of the surpassing
grace of God in you.
15 Thanks be to God for His indescribable gift!

4. Paul defends his authority

Paul Describes Himself

10 Now I, Paul, myself urge you by the meekness and gentleness of Christ—I who am
meek when face to face with you, but bold toward you when absent!
2 I ask that when I am present I *need* not be bold with the confidence with which I
propose to be courageous against some, who regard us as if we walked according to the
flesh.
3 For though we walk in the flesh, we do not war according to the flesh,
4 for the weapons of our warfare are not of the flesh, but divinely powerful for the
destruction of fortresses.
5 *We are* destroying speculations and every lofty thing raised up against the knowledge of God, and *we are* taking every thought captive to the obedience of Christ,
6 and we are ready to punish all disobedience, whenever your obedience is complete.
7 You are looking at things as they are outwardly. If anyone is confident in himself
that he is Christ's, let him consider this again within himself, that just as he is Christ's, so
also are we.
8 For even if I boast somewhat further about our authority, which the Lord gave for
building you up and not for destroying you, I will not be put to shame,
9 for I do not wish to seem as if I would terrify you by my letters.
10 For they say, "His letters are weighty and strong, but his personal presence is unim-
pressive and his speech contemptible."
11 Let such a person consider this, that what we are in word by letters when absent,
such persons *we are* also in deed when present.
12 For we are not bold to class or compare ourselves with some of those who commend

9:11 1 Cor 1:5; 2 Cor 1:11
9:12 2 Cor 8:14
9:13 Rom 15:31; 2 Cor 8:4; Matt 9:8; 1 Tim 6:12f; Heb 3:1; 4:14
9:15 2 Cor 2:14; Rom 5:15f
10:1 Gal 5:2; Eph 3:1; Col 1:23; Rom 12:1; Matt 11:29; 1 Cor 4:21; Phil 4:5; 1 Cor 2:3f; 2 Cor 10:10
10:2 1 Cor 4:21; 2 Cor 13:2, 10; 1 Cor 4:18f; Rom 8:4; 2 Cor 1:17
10:3 Rom 8:4; 2 Cor 1:17
10:4 1 Cor 9:7; 2 Cor 6:7; 1 Tim 1:18; Jer 1:10; 2 Cor 10:8; 13:10
10:5 Is 2:11f; 2 Cor 9:13
10:7 John 7:24; 2 Cor 5:12; 1 Cor 1:12; 14:37; 1 Cor 9:1; 2 Cor 11:23; Gal 1:12
10:8 2 Cor 7:4; 2 Cor 13:10
10:10 1 Cor 2:3; 2 Cor 12:7; Gal 4:13f
10:12 2 Cor 3:1; 10:18

9:12–15 Paul emphasizes the spiritual rewards for those who give generously to God's work. We should not expect to become wealthy through giving. Those who receive your gifts will be helped, will praise God, and will pray for you. As you bless others, you will be blessed.

10:1–2 Paul's opponents questioned his authority. From 7:8–16 we know that the majority of Corinthian believers sided with Paul. However, a minority continued to slander him, saying that he was bold in his letters but had no authority in person. Chapters 10—13 are Paul's response to this charge.

10:3–6 We, like Paul, are merely weak humans, but we don't need to use human plans and methods to win our battles. God's mighty weapons are available to us as we fight against Satan's "fortresses." The Christian must choose whose methods to use, God's or the world's. Paul assures us that God's mighty weapons—prayer, faith, hope, love, God's Word, the Holy Spirit—are powerful and effective (see Ephesians 6:13–18)! These weapons can break down the proud human arguments against God and the walls that Satan builds to keep people from finding God. When dealing with the pride that keeps people from a relationship with Christ, we may be tempted to use our own methods. But nothing can break down these barriers like God's weapons.

10:5 Paul uses military terminology to describe this warfare against sin and Satan. God must be the commander in chief—even our thoughts must be submitted to his control as we live for him.

10:7–9 Those who opposed Paul portrayed him as weak and powerless, but Paul reminded the Corinthians that he claimed the power and authority of Christ. False teachers were encouraging the believers to ignore Paul, but Paul explained that the words in his letters were to be taken seriously. Paul had authority because he and his companions were the first to bring the Good News to Corinth (10:14). On the basis of this authority over them, Paul wrote to them to help them grow.

10:10 Some said that Paul's speaking amounted to nothing. Greece was known for its eloquent and persuasive orators. Evidently, some were judging Paul by comparing him to other speakers they had heard, and Paul was perhaps not the most powerful preacher (although he was an excellent debater). But Paul responded obediently to God's call and thus introduced Christianity to the Roman empire. Moses and Jeremiah also had problems with speaking (see Exodus 4:10–12; Jeremiah 1:6). Preaching ability is not the first prerequisite of a great leader!

10:12–13 Paul criticized the false teachers who were trying to prove their goodness by comparing themselves with others rather than with God's standards. When we compare ourselves with others, we may feel pride because we think we're better. But when we measure ourselves against God's standards, it becomes obvious that we have no basis for pride. Don't worry about other people's accomplishments. Instead, continually ask: How does my life measure up to what God wants? How does my life compare to Jesus Christ?

10:13 Rom 12:3
10:14 1 Cor 3:6; 2 Cor 2:12
10:15 Rom 15:20; 2 Thess 1:3; Acts 5:13
10:16 2 Cor 11:7; Acts 19:21; Rom 15:20
10:17 Jer 9:24; 1 Cor 1:31
10:18 Rom 2:29; 1 Cor 4:5
11:1 Matt 17:17; 2 Cor 11:4, 16, 19f
11:2 Hos 2:19f; Eph 5:26f; 2 Cor 4:14
11:3 Gen 3:4, 13; John 8:44; 1 Thess 3:5; 1 Tim 2:14; Rev 12:9, 15
11:4 1 Cor 3:11; Rom 8:15; Gal 1:6
11:5 2 Cor 12:11; Gal 2:6

themselves; but when they measure themselves by themselves and compare themselves
with themselves, they are without understanding.
13 But we will not boast beyond *our* measure, but within the measure of the sphere
which God apportioned to us as a measure, to reach even as far as you.
14 For we are not overextending ourselves, as if we did not reach to you, for we were
the first to come even as far as you in the gospel of Christ;
15 not boasting beyond *our* measure, *that is,* in other men's labors, but with the hope
that as your faith grows, we will be, within our sphere, enlarged even more by you,
16 so as to preach the gospel even to the regions beyond you, *and* not to boast in what
has been accomplished in the sphere of another.
17 But HE WHO BOASTS IS TO BOAST IN THE LORD.
18 For it is not he who commends himself that is approved, but he whom the Lord
commends.

Paul Defends His Apostleship

11 I wish that you would bear with me in a little foolishness; but indeed you are bearing with me.
2 For I am jealous for you with a godly jealousy; for I betrothed you to one husband,
so that to Christ I might present you *as* a pure virgin.
3 But I am afraid that, as the serpent deceived Eve by his craftiness, your minds will
be led astray from the simplicity and purity *of devotion* to Christ.
4 For if one comes and preaches another Jesus whom we have not preached, or you
receive a different spirit which you have not received, or a different gospel which you
have not accepted, you bear *this* beautifully.
5 For I consider myself not in the least inferior to the most eminent apostles.

NEEDS FOR A FUND-RAISING PROJECT

Information	8:4
Definite purpose	8:4
Readiness and willingness	9:7
Dedication	8:5
Leadership	8:7
Enthusiasm	8:7–8, 11
Persistence	8:2–12
Honesty and integrity	8:21
Accountability	9:3
Someone to keep it moving	8:18–22

The topic of fund-raising is not one to be avoided or one that should embarrass us, but all fund-raising efforts should be planned and conducted responsibly.

10:17–18 When we do something well, we want to tell others and be recognized. But recognition is dangerous—it can lead to inflated pride. How much better it is to seek the praise of God rather than the praise of people. Then, when we receive praise, we will be free to give God the credit. What should you change about the way you live in order to receive God's commendation?

11:1 Paul asked the Corinthian believers to bear with him as he talked a little "foolishness." In other words, Paul felt foolish rehearsing his credentials as a preacher of the gospel (11:16–21). But he thought that he had to do this in order to silence the false teachers (11:13).

11:2 Paul was anxious that the church's love should be for Christ alone, just as a pure virgin saves her love for one man only. By "virgin" he meant one who was unaffected by false doctrine.

11:3 The Corinthians' simple and pure devotion to Christ was being threatened by false teaching. Paul did not want the believers to lose their single-minded love for Christ. Keeping Christ first in our lives can be very difficult when we have so many distractions threatening to sidetrack our faith. Just as Eve lost her focus by listening to the serpent, we too can lose our focus by letting our lives become overcrowded and confused. Is there anything that weakens your commitment to keep Christ first in your life? How can you minimize the distractions that threaten your devotion to him?

11:3–4 The Corinthian believers fell for smooth talk and messages that sounded good and seemed to make sense. Today there are many false teachings that seem to make sense. Don't believe someone simply because he or she sounds like an authority or says words you like to hear. Search the Bible and check his or her teachings against God's Word. The Bible should be your authoritative guide. Don't listen to any "authoritative preacher" who contradicts God's Word.

11:4 The false teachers distorted the truth about Jesus and ended up preaching a different Jesus, a different spirit than the Holy Spirit, and a different gospel than God's way of salvation. Because the Bible is God's infallible Word, those who teach anything different from what it says are both mistaken and misleading.

11:5 Paul was saying that these marvelous teachers ("the most eminent apostles") were no better than he was. They may have been more eloquent speakers, but they spoke lies and were servants of Satan.

6 But even if I am unskilled in speech, yet I am not *so* in knowledge; in fact, in every
way we have made *this* evident to you in all things.
7 Or did I commit a sin in humbling myself so that you might be exalted, because I
preached the gospel of God to you without charge?
8 I robbed other churches by taking wages *from them* to serve you;
9 and when I was present with you and was in need, I was not a burden to anyone; for
when the brethren came from Macedonia they fully supplied my need, and in everything
I kept myself from being a burden to you, and will continue to do so.
10 As the truth of Christ is in me, this boasting of mine will not be stopped in the regions of Achaia.
11 Why? Because I do not love you? God knows *I do!*
12 But what I am doing I will continue to do, so that I may cut off opportunity from
those who desire an opportunity to be regarded just as we are in the matter about which
they are boasting.
13 For such men are false apostles, deceitful workers, disguising themselves as apostles of Christ.
14 No wonder, for even Satan disguises himself as an angel of light.
15 Therefore it is not surprising if his servants also disguise themselves as servants of
righteousness, whose end will be according to their deeds.
16 Again I say, let no one think me foolish; but if *you do,* receive me even as foolish, so
that I also may boast a little.
17 What I am saying, I am not saying as the Lord would, but as in foolishness, in this
confidence of boasting.
18 Since many boast according to the flesh, I will boast also.
19 For you, being *so* wise, tolerate the foolish gladly.
20 For you tolerate it if anyone enslaves you, anyone devours you, anyone takes advantage of you, anyone exalts himself, anyone hits you in the face.
21 To *my* shame I *must* say that we have been weak *by comparison.*
But in whatever respect anyone *else* is bold—I speak in foolishness—I am just as bold
myself.
22 Are they Hebrews? So am I. Are they Israelites? So am I. Are they descendants of
Abraham? So am I.
23 Are they servants of Christ?—I speak as if insane—I more so; in far more labors, in
far more imprisonments, beaten times without number, often in danger of death.

11:6 1 Cor 1:17; 12:8; Eph 3:4; 2 Cor 4:2
11:7 2 Cor 12:13; Rom 1:1; 2 Cor 2:12; Acts 18:3; 1 Cor 9:18
11:8 1 Cor 4:12; 9:6; Phil 4:15, 18
11:9 Acts 18:5; Rom 15:26; Phil 4:15-18
11:10 Rom 1:9; 9:1; 2 Cor 1:23; Gal 2:20
11:11 2 Cor 12:15; Rom 1:9; 2 Cor 2:17
11:13 Acts 20:30; Gal 1:7; 2:4; Phil 1:15
11:14 Matt 4:10; Eph 6:12
11:15 Rom 2:6; 3:8
11:17 1 Cor 7:12, 25
11:18 Phil 3:3f; 2 Cor 5:16
11:20 Gal 2:4; 4:3, 9; 5:1; Mark 12:40
11:22 Acts 6:1; Phil 3:5; Rom 9:4; Gal 3:16
11:23 Acts 16:23; 2 Cor 6:5; Rom 8:36

11:6 Paul, a brilliant thinker, was not a trained, spellbinding speaker. Although his ministry was effective (see Acts 17), he had not been trained in the Greek schools of oratory and speechmaking, as many of the false teachers probably had been. Paul believed in a simple presentation of the gospel (see 1 Corinthians 1:17), and some people thought this showed simple-mindedness. Thus Paul's speaking performance was often used against him by false teachers. In all our teaching and preaching, content is far more important than the presentation. A simple, clear presentation that helps listeners understand will be of great value.

11:7 The Corinthians may have thought that preachers could be judged by how much money they demanded. A good speaker would charge a large sum, a fair speaker would be a little cheaper, and a poor speaker would speak for free. The false teachers may have argued that because Paul asked no fee for his preaching, he must have been an amateur, with little authority or competence. Believers today must be careful not to assume that every speaker who is well known and demands a large honorarium is superior at explaining and applying God's Word.

11:7–12 Paul could have asked the Corinthian church for financial support. Jesus himself taught that those who minister for God should be supported by the people to whom they minister (Matthew 10:10). But Paul thought that asking for support in Corinth might be misunderstood. There were many false teachers who hoped to make a good profit from preaching (2:17), and Paul might look like one of them. Paul separated himself completely from those false teachers in order to silence those who only claimed to do God's work.

11:14–15 One Jewish writing (the Apocalypse of Moses) says that the story of Eve's temptation includes Satan masquerading as an angel. Paul may have been thinking of this story, or he could have been referring to Satan's typical devices. In either case, nothing could be more deceitful than Satan, the prince of darkness (Ephesians 6:12; Colossians 1:13) disguising himself as an angel of light. In the same way, when the false teachers were claiming to represent Christ as servants of righteousness, they were lying shamelessly.

11:14–15 Satan and his servants can deceive us by appearing to be attractive, good, and moral. Many unsuspecting people follow smooth-talking, Bible-quoting leaders into cults that alienate them from their families and lead them into the practice of immorality and deceit. Don't be fooled by external appearances. Our impressions alone are not an accurate indicator of who is or isn't a true follower of Christ; so it helps to ask these questions: (1) Do the teachings confirm Scripture (Acts 17:11)? (2) Does the teacher affirm and proclaim that Jesus Christ is God who came into the world as a man to save people from their sins (1 John 4:1–3)? (3) Is the teacher's life-style consistent with Biblical morality (Matthew 12:33–37)?

11:22–23 Paul presented his credentials to counteract the charges that the false teachers were making against him. He felt foolish boasting like this, but his list of credentials would silence any doubts about his authority. Paul wanted to keep the Corinthians from slipping under the spell of the false teachers and turning away from the gospel. Paul also gave a list of his credentials in his letter to the Philippians (see Philippians 3:4–8).

11:25
Acts 16:22; 14:19

11:26
Acts 9:23; 13:45, 50; 14:5; 17:5, 13; 18:12; 20:3, 19; 21:27; 23:10, 12; 25:3; 1 Thess 2:15

11:27
1 Thess 2:9; 2 Thess 3:8; 1 Cor 4:11; Phil 4:12; 2 Cor 6:5

24 Five times I received from the Jews thirty-nine *lashes.*
25 Three times I was beaten with rods, once I was stoned, three times I was shipwrecked,
a night and a day I have spent in the deep.
26 *I have been* on frequent journeys, in dangers from rivers, dangers from robbers,
dangers from *my* countrymen, dangers from the Gentiles, dangers in the city, dangers in
the wilderness, dangers on the sea, dangers among false brethren;
27 *I have been* in labor and hardship, through many sleepless nights, in hunger and thirst,
often without food, in cold and exposure.

PAUL'S CREDENTIALS
One of Paul's biggest problems with the church in Corinth was his concern that they viewed him as no more than a blustering preacher; thus, they were not taking seriously his advice in his letters and on his visits. Paul addressed this attitude in the letter of 2 Corinthians, pointing out his credentials as an apostle of Christ and why the Corinthians should take his advice.

1:1, 21; 4:1	Commissioned by God
1:18; 4:2	Spoke truthfully
1:12	Acted in holiness, sincerity, and dependence on God alone in his dealings with them
1:13–14	Was straightforward and sincere in his letters
1:22	Had God's Holy Spirit
2:4; 6:11; 11:11	Loved the Corinthian believers
2:17	Spoke with sincerity and Christ's power
3:2–3	Worked among them and changed their lives
3:4; 12:6	Lived as an example to the believers
4:1, 16	Did not lose heart
4:2	Taught the Bible with integrity
4:5	Had Christ as the center of his message
4:8–12; 6:4–5, 9–10	Endured persecution as he taught the Good News
5:18–20	Was Christ's ambassador, called to tell the Good News
6:3–4	Tried to live an exemplary life so others would not be kept from God
6:6	Led a pure life, understood the gospel, and displayed patience with the Corinthians
6:7	Was truthful and filled with God's power
6:8	Stood true to God first and always
7:2; 11:7–9	Never corrupted or exploited anyone
8:20–21	Handled their offering for the Jerusalem believers in a responsible, blameless manner
10:1–6	Used God's weapons, not his own, for God's work
10:7–8	Was confident that he belonged to Christ
10:12–13	Would boast not in himself but in the Lord
10:14–15	Had authority because he taught them the Good News
11:23–33	Endured pain and danger as he fulfilled his calling
12:2–4	Was blessed with an astounding vision
12:7–10	Was constantly humbled by a "thorn" in the flesh that God refused to take away
12:12	Did miracles among them
12:19	Was always motivated to strengthen others spiritually
13:4	Was filled with God's power
13:5–6	Passed the test
13:9	Was always concerned that his spiritual children become mature believers

11:23–29 Paul was angry that the false teachers had impressed and deceived the Corinthians (11:13–15). Therefore, he had to reestablish his credibility and authority by listing the trials he had endured in his service for Christ. Some of these trials are recorded in the book of Acts (Acts 14:19; 16:22–24). Because Paul wrote this letter during his third missionary journey (Acts 18:23—21:17), his trials weren't over. He would experience yet further difficulties and humiliations for the cause of Christ (see Acts 21:30–33; 22:24 30). Paul was sacrificing his life for the gospel, something the false teachers would never do. The trials and hurts we experience for Christ's sake build our character, demonstrate our faith, and prepare us for further service to the Lord.

11:25 Sea travel was not as safe as it is today. Paul had been shipwrecked three times, and he would face another accident on his voyage to Rome (see Acts 27). By this time, Paul had probably made at least eight or nine voyages.

28 Apart from *such* external things, there is the daily pressure on me *of* concern for all
the churches.
29 Who is weak without my being weak? Who is led into sin without my intense concern?
30 If I have to boast, I will boast of what pertains to my weakness.
31 The God and Father of the Lord Jesus, He who is blessed forever, knows that I am
not lying.
32 In Damascus the ethnarch under Aretas the king was guarding the city of the Dam-
ascenes in order to seize me,
33 and I was let down in a basket through a window in the wall, and *so* escaped his
hands.

Paul's Vision

12 Boasting is necessary, though it is not profitable; but I will go on to visions and
revelations of the Lord.
2 I know a man in Christ who fourteen years ago—whether in the body I do not know,
or out of the body I do not know, God knows—such a man was caught up to the third
heaven.
3 And I know how such a man—whether in the body or apart from the body I do not
know, God knows—
4 was caught up into Paradise and heard inexpressible words, which a man is not permitted to speak.
5 On behalf of such a man I will boast; but on my own behalf I will not boast, except
in regard to *my* weaknesses.
6 For if I do wish to boast I will not be foolish, for I will be speaking the truth; but I
refrain *from this,* so that no one will credit me with more than he sees *in* me or hears
from me.

A Thorn in the Flesh

7 Because of the surpassing greatness of the revelations, for this reason, to keep me
from exalting myself, there was given me a thorn in the flesh, a messenger of Satan to
torment me—to keep me from exalting myself!
8 Concerning this I implored the Lord three times that it might leave me.
9 And He has said to me, "My grace is sufficient for you, for power is perfected in
weakness." Most gladly, therefore, I will rather boast about my weaknesses, so that the
power of Christ may dwell in me.
10 Therefore I am well content with weaknesses, with insults, with distresses, with
persecutions, with difficulties, for Christ's sake; for when I am weak, then I am strong.

11:28 1 Cor 7:17
11:29 1 Cor 8:9, 13; 9:22
11:30 1 Cor 2:3
11:31 Rom 1:25; 2 Cor 11:11
11:32 Acts 9:2; Acts 9:24
11:33 Acts 9:25
12:1 2 Cor 11:16, 18, 30; 12:5, 9; 1 Cor 14:6; 2 Cor 12:7; Gal 1:12; 2:2; Eph 3:3
12:2 Rom 16:7; Acts 8:39; 1 Thess 4:17; Rev 12:5; Eph 4:10; Heb 4:14
12:3 2 Cor 11:11
12:4 Acts 8:39; 2 Cor 12:2; 1 Thess 4:17; Rev 12:5; Luke 23:43
12:5 1 Cor 2:3
12:6 2 Cor 5:13; 11:16f
12:7 Matt 4:10; 1 Cor 5:5
12:8 Matt 26:44
12:9 1 Cor 2:5; Eph 3:16; Phil 4:13; 1 Cor 2:3
12:10 Rom 5:3; 8:35; 2 Cor 6:4; 2 Thess 1:4; 2 Tim 3:11; 2 Cor 5:15, 20

11:28–29 Not only did Paul face beatings and dangers, he also carried the daily concern for the young churches, worrying that they were staying true to the gospel and free from false teachings and inner strife. Paul was concerned for individuals in the churches he served. If God has placed you in a position of leadership and authority, treat people with Paul's kind of empathy and concern.

11:32 King Aretas, king of the Nabateans (Edomites) from 9 B.C. to A.D. 40, had appointed a governor to oversee the Nabatean segment of the population in Damascus. Somehow the Jews in Damascus had been able to enlist this governor to help them try to capture Paul (see Acts 9:22–25). Paul gave a "for instance" here, describing his escape from Damascus in a basket lowered from a window in the city wall. Paul recounted this incident to show what he had endured for Christ. The false teachers couldn't make such claims.

12:2–3 Paul continued his "boasting" by telling about visions and revelations he had received from the Lord. "I know a man in Christ" means that he was speaking about himself. He explained that he didn't know if he was taken up in his body or in his spirit, but he was in paradise ("the third heaven"). This incident cannot be positively identified with a recorded event in Paul's career, although some think this may have been when he was stoned and left for dead (Acts 14:19, 20). Paul told about this incident to show that he had been uniquely touched by God.

12:7–8 We don't know what Paul's thorn in the flesh was, because he doesn't tell us. Some have suggested that it was malaria, epilepsy, or a disease of the eyes (see Galatians 4:13–15). Whatever the case, it was a chronic and debilitating problem, which at times kept him from working. This thorn was a hindrance to his ministry, and he prayed for its removal; but God refused. Paul was a very self-sufficient person, so this thorn must have been difficult for him. It kept Paul humble, reminded him of his need for constant contact with God, and benefited those around him as they saw God at work in his life.

12:9 Although God did not remove Paul's physical affliction, he promised to demonstrate his power in Paul. The fact that God's power is displayed in weak people should give us courage. Though we recognize our limitations, we will not congratulate ourselves and rest at that. Instead, we will turn to God to seek pathways for effectiveness. We must rely on God for our effectiveness rather than simply on our own energy, effort, or talent. Our weakness not only helps develop Christian character; it also deepens our worship, because in admitting our weakness, we affirm God's strength.

12:10 When we are strong in abilities or resources, we are tempted to do God's work on our own, and that can lead to pride. When we are weak, allowing God to fill us with *his* power, then we are stronger than we could ever be on our own. God does not intend for us to seek to be weak, passive, or ineffective—life provides enough

12:11 2 Cor 5:13; 11:16f; 12:6; 1 Cor 15:10; 2 Cor 11:5; 1 Cor 3:7; 13:2; 15:9

12:12 John 4:48; Rom 15:19; 1 Cor 9:1

12:13 1 Cor 9:12, 18; 2 Cor 11:9; 12:14

12:14 2 Cor 1:15; 13:1, 2; 1 Cor 9:12, 18; 10:24, 33; 1 Cor 4:14f; Gal 4:19

12:15 Rom 9:3; 2 Cor 1:6; Phil 2:17; Col 1:24; 1 Thess 2:8; 2 Tim 2:10; 2 Cor 11:11

12:16 2 Cor 11:9; 11:20

12:19 Rom 9:1; 2 Cor 2:17; Rom 14:19; 2 Cor 10:8; 1 Thess 5:11; Heb 6:9

12:20 Gal 5:20; Rom 2:8; James 4:11; 1 Pet 2:1; Rom 1:29;

12:21 1 Cor 6:9, 18; Gal 5:19; Col 3:5

13:1 2 Cor 12:14; Deut 17:6; 19:15; Matt 18:16

13:2 2 Cor 12:21; 1 Cor 4:21; 2 Cor 1:23

13:3 2 Cor 10:1, 10; Matt 10:20; 1 Cor 5:4

13:4 Phil 2:7f; 1 Pet 3:18; Rom 1:4; 6:4; 1 Cor 6:14; 1 Cor 2:3

11 I have become foolish; you yourselves compelled me. Actually I should have been
commended by you, for in no respect was I inferior to the most eminent apostles, even
though I am a nobody.
12 The signs of a true apostle were performed among you with all perseverance, by
signs and wonders and miracles.
13 For in what respect were you treated as inferior to the rest of the churches, except
that I myself did not become a burden to you? Forgive me this wrong!
14 Here for this third time I am ready to come to you, and I will not be a burden to
you; for I do not seek what is yours, but you; for children are not responsible to save up
for *their* parents, but parents for *their* children.
15 I will most gladly spend and be expended for your souls. If I love you more, am I to
be loved less?
16 But be that as it may, I did not burden you myself; nevertheless, crafty fellow that I
am, I took you in by deceit.
17 *Certainly* I have not taken advantage of you through any of those whom I have sent
to you, have I?
18 I urged Titus *to go,* and I sent the brother with him. Titus did not take any advantage of you, did he? Did we not conduct ourselves in the same spirit *and walk* in the same
steps?
19 All this time you have been thinking that we are defending ourselves to you. *Actually,* it is in the sight of God that we have been speaking in Christ; and all for your
upbuilding, beloved.
20 For I am afraid that perhaps when I come I may find you to be not what I wish and
may be found by you to be not what you wish; that perhaps *there will be* strife, jealousy,
angry tempers, disputes, slanders, gossip, arrogance, disturbances;
21 I am afraid that when I come again my God may humiliate me before you, and I
may mourn over many of those who have sinned in the past and not repented of the
impurity, immorality and sensuality which they have practiced.

Examine Yourselves

13 This is the third time I am coming to you. EVERY FACT IS TO BE CONFIRMED BY
THE TESTIMONY OF TWO OR THREE WITNESSES.
2 I have previously said when present the second time, and though now absent I say
in advance to those who have sinned in the past and to all the rest *as well,* that if I come
again I will not spare *anyone,*
3 since you are seeking for proof of the Christ who speaks in me, and who is not weak
toward you, but mighty in you.
4 For indeed He was crucified because of weakness, yet He lives because of the

---

hindrances and setbacks without us creating them. When those obstacles come, we must depend on God. Only his power will make us effective for him and will help us do work that has lasting value.

12:11–15 Paul was not merely revealing his feelings; he was defending his authority as an apostle of Jesus Christ. Paul was hurt that the church in Corinth doubted and questioned him, so he defended himself for the cause of the gospel, not to satisfy his ego. When you are "put on trial," do you think only about saving your reputation or are you more concerned about what people will think about Christ?

12:13 Paul explained that the only thing he did for the other churches that he didn't do in Corinth was to become a burden—to ask the believers to feed and house him. When he said, "Forgive me this wrong," he was clearly being sarcastic. He actually did more for the Corinthians than for any other church, but still they misunderstood him.

12:14 Paul had founded the church in Corinth on his first visit there (Acts 18:1). He subsequently made a second visit (2:1). He was planning what would be his third visit (see also 13:1). Paul explained that, as before, he didn't want to be paid, fed, or housed; he only wanted the believers to be nourished with the spiritual food he would feed them.

12:16–19 Although Paul asked nothing of the Corinthian believers, some doubters were still saying that Paul must have been crafty and made money from them somehow. But Paul again explained that everything he did for the believers was for their edification, not to enrich himself.

12:20–21 After reading this catalog of sins, it is hard to believe that these are the people that Paul said possessed great gifts and excelled as leaders (8:7). Paul feared that the practices of wicked Corinth had invaded the congregation. He wrote sternly, hoping that they would straighten out their lives before he arrived. We must live differently from unbelievers, not letting secular society dictate how we are to treat others. Don't let culture invade your practices at church.

13:2 When Paul arrived the third time in Corinth, he would not be lenient toward unrepentant sinners. His actions could include (1) confronting and publicly denouncing their behavior; (2) exercising church discipline by calling them before the church leaders; or (3) excommunicating them from the church.

power of God. For we also are weak [3]in Him, yet we will live with Him because of the
power of God *directed* toward you.
5 Test yourselves *to see* if you are in the faith; examine yourselves! Or do you not recognize this about yourselves, that Jesus Christ is in you—unless indeed you fail the test?
6 But I trust that you will realize that we ourselves do not fail the test.
7 Now we pray to God that you do no wrong; not that we ourselves may appear approved, but that you may do what is right, even though we may appear unapproved.
8 For we can do nothing against the truth, but *only* for the truth.
9 For we rejoice when we ourselves are weak but you are strong; this we also pray for,
that you be made complete.
10 For this reason I am writing these things while absent, so that when present I *need*
not use severity, in accordance with the authority which the Lord gave me for building
up and not for tearing down.
11 Finally, brethren, rejoice, be made complete, be comforted, be like-minded, live in
peace; and the God of love and peace will be with you.
12 Greet one another with a holy kiss.
13 All the saints greet you.
14 The grace of the Lord Jesus Christ, and the love of God, and the fellowship of the
Holy Spirit, be with you all.

3 One early ms reads *with Him*

13:5 John 6:6; 1 Cor 11:28; 1 Cor 9:27

13:9 2 Cor 12:10; 13:4; 1 Cor 1:10; 2 Cor 13:11; Eph 4:12; 1 Thess 3:10

13:10 2 Cor 2:3; Titus 1:13; 1 Cor 5:4; 2 Cor 10:8

13:11 1 Thess 4:1; 2 Thess 3:1; 1 Cor 1:10; 2 Cor 13:9; Eph 4:12; 1 Thess 3:10; Rom 12:16; Mark 9:50; Rom 15:33; Eph 6:23

13:12 Rom 16:16

13:13 Phil 4:22

13:14 Rom 16:20; 2 Cor 8:9; Rom 5:5; Jude 21; Phil 2:1

13:5 The Corinthians were called to examine and test themselves to see if they really were Christians. Just as we get physical checkups, Paul urges us to give ourselves spiritual checkups. We should look for a growing awareness of Christ's presence and power in our lives. Only then will we know if we are true Christians or merely imposters. If we're not taking active steps to grow closer to God, we are drawing further away from him.

13:8–9 Just as parents want their children to grow into mature adults, so Paul wanted the Corinthians to grow into mature believers. As we share the gospel, our goal should be not merely to see others profess faith or begin attending church, but to see them become mature in their faith. Don't set your sights too low.

13:11 Paul's closing words—what he wanted the Corinthians to remember about the needs facing their church—are still fitting for the church today. When these qualities are not present, there are problems that must be dealt with. These traits do not come to a church by glossing over problems, conflicts, and difficulties. They are not produced by neglect, denial, withdrawal, or bitterness. They are the by-products of the extremely hard work of solving problems. Just as Paul and the Corinthians had to hammer out difficulties to bring peace, so we must *apply* the principles of God's Word and not just hear them.

13:14 Paul's farewell blessing invokes all three members of the Trinity—Father (God), Son (Lord Jesus Christ), and Holy Spirit. Although the term *Trinity* is not explicitly used in Scripture, verses such as this one show that it was believed and experienced through knowing God's grace, love, and fellowship. See Luke 1:35—the angel Gabriel's announcement of Jesus' birth to Mary; Matthew 3:17—the Father's voice was heard at the baptism of Jesus; and Matthew 28:19—Jesus' commission to the disciples.

13:14 Paul was dealing with an ongoing problem in the Corinthian church. He could have refused to communicate until they cleared up their situation, but he loved them and reached out to them again with the love of Christ. Love, however, means that sometimes we must confront those we care about. Both authority and personal concern are needed in dealing with people who are ruining their lives with sin. But there are several wrong approaches in confronting others, and these can further break relationships rather than heal them. We can be legalistic and blast people away with the laws they should be obeying. We can turn away from them because we don't want to face the situation. We can isolate them by gossiping about their problem and turning others against them as well. Or, like Paul, we can seek to build relationships by taking a better approach—sharing, communicating, and caring. This is a difficult approach that can drain us emotionally, but it is the best way for the other person, and it is the only Christlike way to deal with others' sin.

GALATIANS

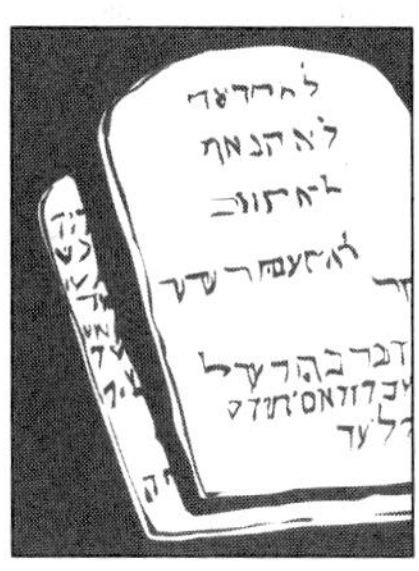

A FAMILY, executing their carefully planned escape at midnight, dashing for the border . . . a man standing outside prison walls, gulping fresh air, awash in the new sun . . . a young woman with every trace of the ravaging drug gone from her system . . . they are FREE! With fresh anticipation, they can begin life anew.

Whether fleeing oppression, stepping out of prison, or breaking a strangling habit, freedom means life. There is nothing so exhilarating as knowing that the past is forgotten and that new options await. People yearn to be free.

The book of Galatians is the charter of Christian freedom. In this profound letter, Paul proclaims the reality of our liberty in Christ—freedom from the Law and the power of sin, and freedom to serve our living Lord.

Most of the first converts and early leaders in the church were Jewish Christians who proclaimed Jesus as their Messiah. As Jewish Christians, they struggled with a dual identity: Their Jewishness constrained them to be strict followers of the Law; their newfound faith in Christ invited them to celebrate a holy liberty. They wondered how Gentiles (non-Jews) could be part of the kingdom of heaven.

This controversy tore the early church. Judaizers—an extremist Jewish faction within the church—taught that Gentile Christians had to submit to Jewish laws and traditions *in addition to* believing in Christ. As a missionary to the Gentiles, Paul had to confront this issue many times.

Galatians was written, therefore, to refute the Judaizers and to call believers back to the pure gospel. The Good News is for all people—Jews and Gentiles alike. Salvation is by God's grace through faith in Christ Jesus *and nothing else.* Faith in Christ means true freedom.

After a brief introduction (1:1–5), Paul addresses those who were accepting the Judaizers' perverted gospel (1:6–9). He summarizes the controversy, including his personal confrontation with Peter and other church leaders (1:10—2:16). He then demonstrates that salvation is by faith alone by alluding to his conversion (2:17–21), appealing to his readers' own experience of the gospel (3:1–5), and showing how the Old Testament teaches about grace (3:6–20). Next, he explains the purpose of God's laws and the relationship between Law, God's promises, and Christ (3:21—4:31).

Having laid the foundation, Paul builds his case for Christian liberty. We are saved by faith, not by keeping the Law (5:1–12); our freedom means that we are free to love and serve one another, not to do wrong (5:13–26); and Christians should carry each other's burdens and be kind to each other (6:1–10). In 6:11–18, Paul takes the pen into his own hand and shares his final thoughts.

As you read Galatians, try to understand this first-century conflict between grace and Law, or faith and deeds, but also be aware of modern parallels. Like Paul, defend the truth of the gospel and reject all those who would add to or twist this truth. You are *free* in Christ—step into the light and celebrate!

VITAL STATISTICS

PURPOSE:
To refute the Judaizers (who taught that Gentile believers must obey the Jewish Law in order to be saved), and to call Christians to faith and freedom in Christ

AUTHOR:
Paul

TO WHOM WRITTEN:
The churches in southern Galatia, founded on Paul's first missionary journey (including Iconium, Lystra, Derbe), and Christians everywhere

DATE WRITTEN:
Approximately A.D. 49, from Antioch, prior to the Jerusalem council (A.D. 50)

SETTING:
The most pressing controversy in the early church was the relationship of new believers, particularly Gentiles, to the Jewish laws. This was especially a problem for the converts and for the young churches that Paul had founded on his first missionary journey. Paul wrote to correct this problem. Later, at the council in Jerusalem, the conflict was officially resolved by the church leaders.

KEY VERSE:
"It was for freedom that Christ set us free; therefore keep standing firm and do not be subject again to a yoke of slavery" (5:1).

KEY PEOPLE:
Paul, Peter, Barnabas, Titus, Abraham, false teachers

KEY PLACES:
Galatia, Jerusalem

SPECIAL FEATURES:
This letter is not addressed to any specific body of believers and was probably circulated to several churches in Galatia.

THE BLUEPRINT

1. Authenticity of the gospel (1:1—2:21)
2. Superiority of the gospel (3:1—4:31)
3. Freedom of the gospel (5:1—6:18)

In response to attacks from false teachers, Paul wrote to defend his apostleship and the authority of the gospel. The Galatians were beginning to turn from faith to legalism. The struggle between the gospel and legalism is still a relevant issue. Many today would have us return to trying to earn God's favor through following rituals or obeying a set of rules. As Christians, we are not boxed in but set free. To preserve our freedom, we must stay close to Christ and resist any who promote subtle ways for us to earn our salvation.

MEGATHEMES

THEME	EXPLANATION	IMPORTANCE
Law	A group of Jewish teachers insisted that non-Jewish believers must obey Jewish law and traditional rules. They believed a person was saved by following the law of Moses (with emphasis on circumcision, the sign of the covenant), in addition to faith in Christ. Paul opposed them by showing that the law can't save anyone.	We can't be saved by keeping the Old Testament law, even the Ten Commandments. The law served as a guide to point out our need to be forgiven. Christ fulfilled the obligations of the law for us. We must turn to him to be saved. He alone can make us right with God.
Faith	We are saved from God's judgment and penalty for sin by God's gracious gift to us. We receive salvation by faith—trusting in him—not in anything else. Becoming a Christian is in no way based on our initiative, wise choice, or good character. We can be right with God only by believing in him.	Your acceptance with God comes by believing in Christ alone. You must never add to or twist this truth. We are saved by faith, not by the good that we do. Have you placed your whole trust and confidence in Christ? He alone can forgive you and bring you into a relationship with God.
Freedom	Galatians is our charter of Christian freedom. We are not under the jurisdiction of Jewish laws and traditions nor under the authority of Jerusalem. Faith in Christ brings true freedom from sin and from the futile attempt to be right with God by keeping the Law.	We are free in Christ, and yet freedom is a privilege. We are not free to disobey Christ or practice immorality, but we are free to serve the risen Christ. Let us use our freedom to love and to serve, not to do wrong.
Holy Spirit	We become Christians through the work of the Holy Spirit. He brings new life; even our faith to believe is a gift from him. The Holy Spirit instructs, guides, leads, and gives us power. He ends our bondage to evil desires, and he creates in us love, joy, peace, and many other wonderful changes.	When the Holy Spirit leads us, he produces his fruit in us. Just as we are saved by faith, not deeds, we also grow by faith. By believing, we can have the Holy Spirit within us, helping us live for Christ. Obey Christ by following the Holy Spirit's leading.

1. Authenticity of the gospel

Introduction

1 Paul, an apostle (not *sent* from men nor through the agency of man, but through Jesus
Christ and God the Father, who raised Him from the dead),
2 and all the brethren who are with me,

1:1 2 Cor 1:1; Gal 1:11f; Acts 9:15; Gal 1:15f; Acts 2:24

1:2 Phil 4:21; Acts 16:6; 1 Cor 16:1

1:1 Paul and Barnabas had just completed their first missionary journey (Acts 13:2—14:28). They had visited Iconium, Lystra, and Derbe, cities in the Roman province of Galatia (present-day Turkey). Upon returning to Antioch, Paul was accused by some Jewish Christians of diluting Christianity to make it more appealing to Gentiles. These Jewish Christians disagreed with Paul's statements that Gentiles did not have to follow many of the religious laws that the Jews had obeyed for centuries. Some of Paul's accusers had even followed him to those Galatian cities and had told the Gentile converts they had to be circumcised and follow all the Jewish laws and customs in order to be saved. According to those men, Gentiles had to first become Jews in order to become Christians.

In response to this threat, Paul wrote this letter to the Galatian churches. In it, he explains that following the Old Testament laws or the Jewish laws will not bring salvation. A person is saved by grace through faith. Paul wrote this letter about A.D. 49, shortly before the meeting of the Jerusalem council, which settled the law versus grace controversy (Acts 15).

1:1 Paul was called to be an apostle by Jesus Christ and God the Father. He presented his credentials at the very outset of this letter because some people in Galatia were questioning his authority.

1:4
Gal 2:20; Matt 13:22; Rom 12:2; 2 Cor 4:4; Phil 4:20

1:5
Rom 11:36

1:6
Gal 5:8; 2 Cor 11:4; Gal 1:7, 11; 2:2, 7; 5:14; 1 Tim 1:3

1:7
Acts 15:24; Gal 5:10

1:8
2 Cor 11:14; Rom 9:3

1:9
Acts 18:23; Rom 16:17; Rom 9:3

1:10
1 Cor 10:33; 1 Thess 2:4; Rom 1:1; Phil 1:1

To the churches of Galatia:
3 Grace to you and peace from God our Father and the Lord Jesus Christ,
4 who gave Himself for our sins so that He might rescue us from this present evil age,
according to the will of our God and Father,
5 to whom *be* the glory forevermore. Amen.

Perversion of the Gospel

6 I am amazed that you are so quickly deserting Him who called you by the grace of
Christ, for a different gospel;
7 which is *really* not another; only there are some who are disturbing you and want to
distort the gospel of Christ.
8 But even if we, or an angel from heaven, should preach to you a gospel contrary to
what we have preached to you, he is to be accursed!
9 As we have said before, so I say again now, if any man is preaching to you a gospel
contrary to what you received, he is to be accursed!
10 For am I now seeking the favor of men, or of God? Or am I striving to please men?
If I were still trying to please men, I would not be a bond-servant of Christ.

1:1 For more information about Paul's life, see his Profile in Acts 9. Paul had been a Christian for about 15 years at this time.

1:2 In Paul's time, *Galatia* was the Roman province located in the center section of present-day Turkey. Much of the region rests on a large and fertile plateau, and large numbers of people had moved to the region because of its favorable agriculture. One of Paul's goals during his missionary journeys was to visit regions with large population centers in order to reach as many people as possible.

1:3–5 God's plan all along was to save us by Jesus' death. We have been rescued from the power of this present evil age—a world ruled by Satan and full of cruelty, tragedy, temptation, and deception. Being rescued from this evil age doesn't mean that we are taken out of it, but that we are no longer enslaved to it. You were saved to live for God. Does your life reflect your gratitude for being rescued? Have you transferred your loyalty from this world to Christ?

1:6 Some people were preaching "a different gospel." They were teaching that to be saved, Gentile believers had to follow Jewish laws and customs, especially the rite of circumcision. Faith in Christ was not enough. This message undermined the truth of the Good News that salvation is a gift, not a reward for certain deeds. Jesus Christ has made this gift available to all people, not just to Jews. Beware of people who say that we need more than simple faith in Christ to be saved. When people set up additional requirements for salvation, they deny the power of Christ's death on the cross (see 3:1–5).

1:7 There is only one way given to us by God to be forgiven of sin—through believing in Jesus Christ as Savior and Lord. No other person, method, or ritual can give eternal life. Attempting to be open-minded and tolerant, some people assert that all religions are equally valid paths to God. In a free society, people have the right to their religious opinions, but this doesn't guarantee that their ideas are right. God does not accept man-made religion as a substitute for faith in Jesus Christ. He has provided just one way—Jesus Christ (John 14:6).

1:7 Those who had disturbed the Galatian believers and distorted the gospel were zealous Jewish Christians who believed that the Old Testament practices such as circumcision and dietary restrictions were required of all believers. Because these teachers wanted to turn the Gentile Christians into Jews, they were called *Judaizers.* Some time after the letter to the Galatians was sent, Paul met with the apostles in Jerusalem to discuss this matter further (see Acts 15).

1:7 Most of the Galatian Christians were Greeks who were unfamiliar with Jewish laws and customs. The Judaizers were an extreme faction of Jewish Christians. Both groups believed in Christ, but their life-styles differed considerably. We do not know why the Judaizers may have traveled no small distance to teach their mistaken notions to the new Gentile converts. They may have been motivated by (1) a sincere wish to integrate Judaism with the new Christian faith, (2) a sincere love for their Jewish heritage, or (3) a jealous desire to destroy Paul's authority. Whether or not these Judaizers were sincere, their teaching threatened these new churches and had to be countered. When Paul called their teaching a distortion of the gospel, he was not rejecting everything Jewish. He himself was a Jew who worshiped in the temple and attended the religious festivals. But he was concerned that *nothing* get in the way of the simple truth of his message—that salvation, for Jews and Gentiles alike, is through faith in Jesus Christ alone.

1:7 A twisting of the truth is more difficult to spot than an outright lie. The Judaizers were twisting the truth about Christ. They claimed to follow him, but they denied that Jesus' work on the cross was sufficient for salvation. There will always be people who distort the Good News. Either they do not understand what the Bible teaches, or they are uncomfortable with the truth as it stands. How can we tell when people are twisting the truth? Before accepting the teachings of any group, find out what the group teaches about Jesus Christ. If their teaching does not match the truth in God's Word, then it is distorted.

1:8–9 Paul strongly denounced the Judaizers' distortion of the gospel of Christ. He said that even if an angel from heaven comes preaching another message, that angel should be "accursed." If an angel came preaching another message, he would not be from heaven, no matter how he looked. In 2 Corinthians 11:14–15, Paul warned that Satan masquerades as an angel of light. Here he invoked a curse on any angel who spreads a false gospel—a fitting response to an emissary of hell. Paul extended that curse to include himself if he should distort the gospel. His message must never change, for the truth of the gospel never changes. Paul used strong language because he was dealing with a life-and-death issue.

1:10 Do you spend your life trying to please everybody? Paul had to speak harshly to the Christians in Galatia because they were in serious danger. He did not apologize for his straightforward words, knowing that he could not serve Christ faithfully if he allowed the Galatian Christians to remain on the wrong track. Whose approval are you seeking—others' or God's? Pray for the courage to seek God's approval above anyone else's.

Paul Defends His Ministry

11 For I would have you know, brethren, that the gospel which was preached by me is
not according to man.
12 For I neither received it from man, nor was I taught it, but *I received it* through a
revelation of Jesus Christ.
13 For you have heard of my former manner of life in Judaism, how I used to persecute the church of God beyond measure and tried to destroy it;
14 and I was advancing in Judaism beyond many of my contemporaries among my
countrymen, being more extremely zealous for my ancestral traditions.
15 But when God, who had set me apart *even* from my mother's womb and called me
through His grace, was pleased

1:11
Rom 2:16; 1 Cor 15:1; 1 Cor 3:4; 9:8

1:12
1 Cor 2:10; 2 Cor 12:1; Gal 1:16; 2:2

1:13
Acts 26:4f; Acts 8:3; 22:4, 5; 1 Cor 10:32

1:14
Acts 22:3; Jer 9:14; Matt 15:2; Mark 7:3

1:15
Acts 9:15; Rom 1:1; Gal 1:6

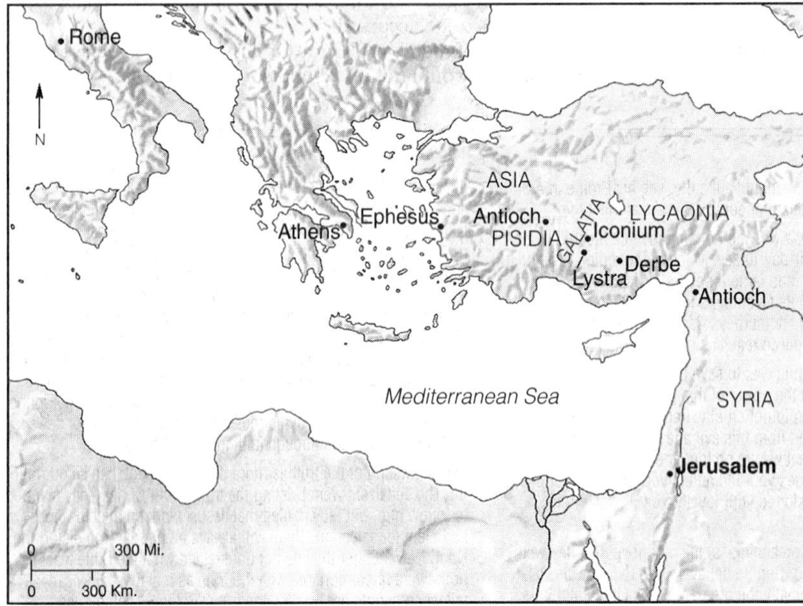

CITIES IN GALATIA
Paul visited several cities in Galatia on each of his three missionary journeys. On his first journey he went through Antioch in Pisidia, Iconium, Lystra, and Derbe, and then retraced his steps; on his second journey he went by land from Antioch of Syria through the four cities in Galatia; on his third journey he also went through those cities on the main route to Ephesus.

1:11ff Why should the Galatians have listened to Paul instead of the Judaizers? Paul answered this implicit question by furnishing his credentials: His message was received directly from Christ (1:12); he had been an exemplary Jew (1:13–14); he had had a special conversion experience (1:15–16; see also Acts 9:1–9); he had been confirmed and accepted in his ministry by the other apostles (1:18–19; 2:1–9). Paul also presented his credentials to the Corinthian and Philippian churches (2 Corinthians 11; 12; Philippians 3:4–9).

1:12 We do not know the details of this revelation. Paul is referring to something other than his experience on the road to Damascus. His point is that his words are more than his own speculations or ideas.

1:13–14 Paul had been one of the most religious Jews of his day, scrupulously keeping the law and relentlessly persecuting Christians (see Acts 9:1–2). Before his conversion Paul had been even more zealous for the law than the Judaizers. He had surpassed his contemporaries in religious knowledge and practice. Paul had been sincere in his zeal—but wrong. When he met Jesus Christ, his life changed. He then directed all his energies toward building up the Christian church.

1:14 The word *Judaism* refers not only to nationality but also to religion. To be fully Jewish, a person must have descended from Abraham. In addition, a faithful Jew adhered to the Jewish laws. *Gentiles* (1:16) are non-Jews, whether in nationality or religion. In Paul's day, Jews thought of all Gentiles as pagans. Jews avoided Gentiles, believing that contact with Gentiles brought spiritual corruption. Although Gentiles could become Jews in religion by undergoing circumcision and by following Jewish laws and customs, they were never fully accepted.

Many Jews had difficulty understanding that God's message is for Jews and Gentiles alike. Some Jews thought that Gentiles had to become Jews before they could become Christians. But God planned to save both Jews and Gentiles. He had revealed this plan through Old Testament prophets (see, for example, Genesis 12:3; Isaiah 42:6; 66:19), and he had fulfilled it through Jesus Christ; he was proclaiming it to the Gentiles through Paul.

1:15–16 Because God was guiding his ministry, Paul wasn't doing anything that God hadn't already planned and given him power to do. Similarly, God told Jeremiah that God had called him, even before he was born, to do special work for God (Jeremiah 1:5). God knows you intimately as well, and he chose you to be his even before you were born (see Psalm 139). He wants you to draw close to him and to fulfill the purpose he has for your life.

1:15–24 Paul tells of his conversion to show that his message came directly from God. God commissioned him to preach the Good News to the Gentiles. After his call, Paul did not consult with anyone; instead he spent three years in Arabia. Then he spoke with

1:16 Acts 9:15; Gal 2:9; Acts 9:20; Matt 16:17

1:17 Acts 9:19-22

1:19 Matt 12:46; Acts 12:17

1:20 Rom 9:1; 2 Cor 1:23; 11:31

1:21 Acts 9:30; 15:23, 41

1:22 1 Cor 7:17; 1 Thess 2:14; Rom 16:7

1:23 Acts 6:7; Gal 6:10; Acts 9:21

2:1 Acts 15:2; Acts 4:36

2:2 Acts 15:2; Rom 9:16; 1 Cor 9:24ff; Gal 5:7; Phil 2:16

2:4 Gal 1:7; 2 Pet 2:1; Jude 4; Gal 5:1, 13; James 1:25

16 to reveal His Son in me so that I might preach Him among the Gentiles, I did not
immediately consult with flesh and blood,
17 nor did I go up to Jerusalem to those who were apostles before me; but I went away
to Arabia, and returned once more to Damascus.
18 Then three years later I went up to Jerusalem to become acquainted with Cephas,
and stayed with him fifteen days.
19 But I did not see any other of the apostles except James, the Lord's brother.
20 (Now in what I am writing to you, I assure you before God that I am not lying.)
21 Then I went into the regions of Syria and Cilicia.
22 I was *still* unknown by sight to the churches of Judea which were in Christ;
23 but only, they kept hearing, "He who once persecuted us is now preaching the faith
which he once tried to destroy."
24 And they were glorifying God because of me.

The Council at Jerusalem

2 Then after an interval of fourteen years I went up again to Jerusalem with Barnabas,
taking Titus along also.
2 It was because of a revelation that I went up; and I submitted to them the gospel
which I preach among the Gentiles, but *I did so* in private to those who were of reputation, for fear that I might be running, or had run, in vain.
3 But not even Titus, who was with me, though he was a Greek, was compelled to be
circumcised.
4 But *it was* because of the false brethren secretly brought in, who had sneaked in to
spy out our liberty which we have in Christ Jesus, in order to bring us into bondage.

Peter and James, but he had no other contact with Jewish Christians for several more years. During those years, Paul preached to the Gentiles the message God had given him. His Good News did not come from human insight; it came from God.

1:18 This was Paul's first visit to Jerusalem as a Christian, as recorded in Acts 9:26–30.

1:21 Because of opposition in Jerusalem (see Acts 9:29–30), Paul had gone to Syria and Cilicia. In those remote areas, he had no opportunity to receive instruction from the apostles.

1:24 Paul's changed life had brought praise from those who saw him or heard about him. His new life had astonished them. They had praised God because only God could have turned this zealous persecutor of Christians into a Christian himself. We may not have had as dramatic a change as Paul, but still our new lives should honor God in every way. When people look at you, do they recognize that God has made changes in you? If not, perhaps you are not living as you should.

2:1 Paul was converted around A.D. 35. The 14 years he mentions are probably calculated from the time of his conversion. Therefore, this trip to Jerusalem was not his first. Most likely, he made his first trip to Jerusalem around A.D. 38 (see Acts 9:26–30), and other trips to Jerusalem in approximately A.D. 44 (Acts 11:29–30; Galatians 2:1–10), A.D. 49/50 (Acts 15), A.D. 52 (Acts 18:22, where *the church* refers to the church in Jerusalem), and A.D. 57 (Acts 21:15ff). Paul probably visited Jerusalem on several other occasions as well.

2:1 Barnabas and Titus were two of Paul's close friends. Barnabas and Paul visited Galatia together on their first missionary journey. Paul wrote a personal letter to Titus, a faithful believer and church leader serving on the island of Crete (see the book of Titus). For more information on Barnabas, see his Profile in Acts 13. For more information on Titus, see the letter Paul wrote to him in the New Testament.

2:1 After his conversion, Paul spent many years preparing for the ministry to which God had called him. This preparation period included time alone with God (1:16–17), as well as time conferring with other Christians. Often new Christians, in their zeal, want to begin a full-time ministry without investing the necessary time studying the Bible and learning from qualified teachers. We need not wait to share Christ with our friends, but we may need more preparation before embarking on a special ministry, whether volunteer or paid. While we wait for God's timing, we should continue to study, learn, and grow.

2:2 God told Paul, through a revelation, to confer with the church leaders in Jerusalem about the message he was preaching to the Gentiles, so they would understand and approve of what he was doing. The essence of Paul's message to both Jews and Gentiles was that God's salvation is offered to all people regardless of race, sex, nationality, wealth, social standing, educational level, or anything else. Anyone can be forgiven by trusting in Christ (see Romans 10:8–13).

2:2–3 Even though God had specifically sent him to the Gentiles (Acts 9:15–16), Paul needed to discuss his gospel message with the leaders of the Jerusalem church (Acts 15). This meeting prevented a major split in the church, and it formally acknowledged the apostles' approval of Paul's preaching. Sometimes we avoid conferring with others because we fear that problems or arguments may develop. Instead, we should openly discuss our plans and actions with friends, counselors, and advisers. Good communication helps everyone understand the situation better, it reduces gossip, and it builds unity in the church.

2:3–5 When Paul took Titus, a Greek Christian, to Jerusalem, the Judaizers (false brethren) said that Titus should be circumcised. Paul adamantly refused to give in to their demands. The apostles agreed that circumcision was an unnecessary rite for Gentile converts. Several years later, Paul circumcised Timothy, another Greek Christian (Acts 16:3). Unlike Titus, however, Timothy was half Jewish. Paul did not deny Jews the right to be circumcised; he was simply saying that Gentiles should not be asked to become Jews before becoming Christians.

2:4 These false brothers were most likely from the party of the Pharisees (Acts 15:5). These were the strictest religious leaders of Judaism, some of whom had been converted. We don't know if these were representatives of well-meaning converts or of those trying to distort Christianity. Most commentators agree that neither Peter nor James had any part in this conspiracy.

5 But we did not yield in subjection to them for even an hour, so that the truth of the
gospel would remain with you.
6 But from those who were of high reputation (what they were makes no difference
to me; God shows no partiality)—well, those who were of reputation contributed nothing to me.
7 But on the contrary, seeing that I had been entrusted with the gospel to the uncircumcised, just as Peter *had been* to the circumcised
8 (for He who effectually worked for Peter in *his* apostleship to the circumcised effectually worked for me also to the Gentiles),
9 and recognizing the grace that had been given to me, James and Cephas and John,
who were reputed to be pillars, gave to me and Barnabas the right hand of fellowship, so
that we *might go* to the Gentiles and they to the circumcised.
10 *They* only *asked* us to remember the poor—the very thing I also was eager to do.

2:5 Gal 1:6; Col 1:5
2:6 2 Cor 11:5; 12:11; Acts 10:34
2:7 1 Cor 9:17; 1 Thess 2:4; 1 Tim 1:11; Acts 9:15; Gal 1:16
2:8 Acts 1:25
2:9 2 Cor 11:5; 12:11; Gal 6:3; 1 Tim 3:15; Rev 3:12; Acts 4:36
2:10 Acts 24:17

Peter (Cephas) Opposed by Paul

11 But when Cephas came to Antioch, I opposed him to his face, because he stood
condemned.
12 For prior to the coming of certain men from James, he used to eat with the Gentiles; but when they came, he *began* to withdraw and hold himself aloof, fearing the party of the circumcision.
13 The rest of the Jews joined him in hypocrisy, with the result that even Barnabas was
carried away by their hypocrisy.
14 But when I saw that they were not straightforward about the truth of the gospel, I
said to Cephas in the presence of all, "If you, being a Jew, live like the Gentiles and not
like the Jews, how *is it that* you compel the Gentiles to live like Jews?
15 "We *are* Jews by nature and not sinners from among the Gentiles;

2:11 Acts 11:19; 15:1
2:12 Acts 12:17; Acts 11:2
2:13 Acts 4:36; Gal 2:1, 9
2:14 Heb 12:13; Gal 1:6; 2:5; Col 1:5
2:15 Phil 3:4f; 1 Sam 15:18; Luke 24:7

2:5 We normally think of taking a stand against those who might lead us into immoral behavior, but Paul had to take a hard line against the most "moral" of people. We must not give in to those who make the keeping of man-made standards a condition for salvation, even when such people are morally upright or in respected positions.

2:6 It's easy to rate people on the basis of their official status and to be intimidated by powerful people. But Paul was not intimidated by "those who were of reputation" because all believers are equal in Christ. We should show respect for our spiritual leaders, but our ultimate allegiance must be to Christ. We are to serve him with our whole being. God doesn't rate us according to our status; he looks at the attitude of our hearts (1 Samuel 16:7).

2:7–9 The church leaders ("pillars")—James, Peter, and John—realized that God was using Paul to reach the Gentiles, just as Peter was being used so greatly to reach the Jews. After hearing Paul's message, they gave Paul and Barnabas their approval ("the right hand of fellowship") to continue working among the Gentiles.

2:10 The apostles were referring to the poor of Jerusalem. While many Gentile converts were financially comfortable, the Jerusalem church had suffered from the effects of a severe famine in Palestine (see Acts 11:28–30) and was struggling. So on his journeys, Paul had gathered funds for the Jewish Christians (Acts 24:17; Romans 15:25–29; 1 Corinthians 16:1–4; 2 Corinthians 8). The need for believers to care for the poor is a constant theme in Scripture. But often we do nothing, caught up in meeting our own needs and desires. Perhaps we don't see enough poverty to remember the needs of the poor. The world is filled with poor people, here and in other countries. What can you do to help?

2:11 This was Antioch in Syria (distinguished from Antioch in Pisidia), a major trade center in the ancient world. Heavily populated by Greeks, it eventually became a strong Christian center. In Antioch the believers were first called Christians (Acts 11:26). Antioch in Syria became the headquarters for the Gentile church and was Paul's base of operations.

2:11ff The Judaizers accused Paul of watering down the gospel to make it easier for Gentiles to accept, while Paul accused the Judaizers of nullifying the truth of the gospel by adding conditions to it. The basis of salvation was the issue—is salvation through Christ alone, or does it come through Christ *and* adherence to the law? The argument came to a climax when Peter, Paul, the Judaizers, and some Gentile Christians all gathered together in Antioch to share a meal. Peter probably thought that by staying away from the Gentiles, he was promoting harmony—he did not want to offend James and the Jewish Christians. James had a very prominent position and presided over the Jerusalem council (Acts 15). But Paul charged that Peter's action violated the gospel. By joining the Judaizers, Peter implicitly was supporting their claim that Christ was not sufficient for salvation. Compromise is an important element in getting along with others, but we should never compromise the truth of God's Word. If we feel we have to change our Christian beliefs to match those of our companions, we are on dangerous ground.

2:11–12 Although Peter was a leader of the church, he was acting like a hypocrite. He knew better, yet he was driven by fear of what James and the others would think. Proverbs 29:25 says, "The fear of man brings a snare." Paul knew that he had to confront Peter before his actions damaged the church. So Paul publicly opposed Peter. Note, however, that Paul did not go to the other leaders, nor did he write letters to the churches telling them not to follow Peter's example. Instead, he opposed Peter face-to-face. Sometimes sincere Christians, even Christian leaders, make mistakes. And it may take other sincere Christians to get them back on track. If you are convinced that someone is doing harm to himself/herself or the church, try the direct approach. There is no place for backstabbing in the body of Christ.

2:15–16 If observing the Jewish laws cannot justify us, why should we still obey the Ten Commandments and other Old Testament laws? We know that Paul was not saying the law is bad, because in another letter he wrote, "the Law is holy" (Romans 7:12). Instead, he is saying that the law can never make us acceptable to God. The law still has an important role to play in the life of a Christian. The law: (1) guards us from sin by giving us standards for behavior; (2) convicts us of sin, leaving us the opportunity to

2:16 Acts 13:39; Gal 3:11; Rom 3:22; 9:30; Ps 143:2; Rom 3:20

2:17 Gal 2:15; Luke 20:16; Gal 3:21

2:18 Rom 3:5

2:19 Rom 6:2; 7:4; 1 Cor 9:20

2:20 Rom 6:6; Gal 5:24; 6:14; Rom 8:10; Matt 4:3; Rom 8:37; Gal 1:4

2:21 Gal 3:21

3:1 Gal 1:2; 1 Cor 1:23; Gal 5:11

16 nevertheless knowing that a man is not justified by the works of the Law but through
faith in Christ Jesus, even we have believed in Christ Jesus, so that we may be justified
by faith in Christ and not by the works of the Law; since by the works of the Law no flesh
will be justified.
17 "But if, while seeking to be justified in Christ, we ourselves have also been found
sinners, is Christ then a minister of sin? May it never be!
18 "For if I rebuild what I have *once* destroyed, I prove myself to be a transgressor.
19 "For through the Law I died to the Law, so that I might live to God.
20 "I have been crucified with Christ; and it is no longer I who live, but Christ lives in
me; and the *life* which I now live in the flesh I live by faith in the Son of God, who loved
me and gave Himself up for me.
21 "I do not nullify the grace of God, for if righteousness *comes* through the Law, then
Christ died needlessly."

2. Superiority of the gospel

Faith Brings Righteousness

3 You foolish Galatians, who has bewitched you, before whose eyes Jesus Christ was
publicly portrayed *as* crucified?

THE MARKS OF THE TRUE GOSPEL AND OF FALSE GOSPELS

Marks of a false gospel		*Marks of the true gospel*	
2:21	Treats Christ's death as meaningless	1:11–12	Teaches that the source of the gospel is God
3:12	Says people must obey the Law in order to be saved	2:20	Knows that life is obtained through death; we trust in the God who loved us and died for us so that we might die to sin and live for him
4:10	Tries to find favor with God by observing certain rituals	3:14	Explains that all believers have the Holy Spirit through faith
5:4	Counts on keeping laws to erase sin	3:21–22	Declares that we cannot be saved by keeping laws; the only way of salvation is through faith in Christ, which is available to all
		3:26–28	Says that all believers are one in Christ, so there is no basis for discrimination of any kind
		5:24–25	Proclaims that we are free from the grip of sin and that the Holy Spirit's power fills and guides us

ask for God's forgiveness; (3) drives us to trust in the sufficiency of Christ, because we can never keep the Ten Commandments perfectly. The law cannot possibly save us. But after we have become Christians, it can guide us to live as God requires.

2:17–19 Through studying the Old Testament Scriptures, Paul realized that he could not be saved by obeying God's laws. The prophets knew that God's plan of salvation did not rest on keeping the Law (see the chart in chapter 4 for references). Because we have all been infected by sin, we cannot keep God's laws perfectly. Fortunately, God has provided a way of salvation that depends on Jesus Christ, not on our own efforts. Even though we know this truth, we must guard against the temptation of using service, good deeds, charitable giving, or any other effort as a substitute for faith.

2:20 How have we been crucified with Christ? *Legally,* God looks at us as if we had died with Christ. Because our sins died with him, we are no longer condemned (Colossians 2:13–15). *Relationally,* we have become one with Christ, and his experiences are ours. Our Christian life began when, in unity with him, we died to our old life (see Romans 6:5–11). *In our daily life,* we must regularly crucify sinful desires that keep us from following Christ. This too is a kind of dying with him (Luke 9:23–25).

And yet the focus of Christianity is not dying, but living. Because we have been crucified with Christ, we have also been raised with him (Romans 6:5). *Legally,* we have been reconciled with God (2 Corinthians 5:19) and are free to grow into Christ's likeness (Romans 8:29). And *in our daily life,* we have Christ's resurrection power as we continue to fight sin (Ephesians 1:19–20). We are no longer alone, for Christ lives in us—he is our power for living and our hope for the future (Colossians 1:27).

2:21 Believers today may still be in danger of acting as if Christ died needlessly. How? By replacing Jewish legalism with their own brand of Christian legalism, they are giving people extra laws to obey. By believing they can earn God's favor by what they do, they are not trusting completely in Christ's work on the cross. By struggling to appropriate God's power to change them (sanctification), they are not resting in God's power to save them (justification). If we could be saved by being good, then Christ did not have to die. But the cross is the only way to salvation.

3:1 The Galatian believers had become fascinated by the false teachers' arguments, almost as though they had been bewitched. Magic was common in Paul's day (Acts 8:9–11; 13:6–7). Magicians used both optical illusions and Satan's power to perform miracles, and people were drawn into the magicians' mysterious rites without recognizing their dangerous source.

2 This is the only thing I want to find out from you: did you receive the Spirit by the
works of the Law, or by hearing with faith?
3 Are you so foolish? Having begun by the Spirit, are you now being perfected by the
flesh?
4 Did you suffer so many things in vain—if indeed it was in vain?
5 So then, does He who provides you with the Spirit and works miracles among you,
do it by the works of the Law, or by hearing with faith?
6 Even so Abraham BELIEVED GOD, AND IT WAS RECKONED TO HIM AS RIGHT-
EOUSNESS.
7 Therefore, be sure that it is those who are of faith who are sons of Abraham.
8 The Scripture, foreseeing that God would justify the Gentiles by faith, preached the
gospel beforehand to Abraham, *saying*, "ALL THE NATIONS WILL BE BLESSED IN YOU."
9 So then those who are of faith are blessed with Abraham, the believer.
10 For as many as are of the works of the Law are under a curse; for it is written,
"CURSED IS EVERYONE WHO DOES NOT ABIDE BY ALL THINGS WRITTEN IN THE BOOK
OF THE LAW, TO PERFORM THEM."
11 Now that no one is justified by the Law before God is evident; for, "THE RIGHTEOUS
MAN SHALL LIVE BY FAITH."
12 However, the Law is not of faith; on the contrary, "HE WHO PRACTICES THEM SHALL
LIVE BY THEM."
13 Christ redeemed us from the curse of the Law, having become a curse for us—for it
is written, "CURSED IS EVERYONE WHO HANGS ON A TREE"—
14 in order that in Christ Jesus the blessing of Abraham might come to the Gentiles,
so that we would receive the promise of the Spirit through faith.

Intent of the Law

15 Brethren, I speak in terms of human relations: even though it is *only* a man's covenant, yet when it has been ratified, no one sets it aside or adds conditions to it.
16 Now the promises were spoken to Abraham and to his seed. He does not say, "And
to seeds," as *referring* to many, but *rather* to one, "And to your seed," that is, Christ.
17 What I am saying is this: the Law, which came four hundred and thirty years later,
does not invalidate a covenant previously ratified by God, so as to nullify the promise.

3:2 Rom 10:17
3:4 1 Cor 15:2
3:5 2 Cor 9:10; Phil 1:19; 1 Cor 12:10; Rom 10:17
3:6 Rom 4:3; Gen 15:6
3:7 Luke 19:9; Gal 6:16
3:8 Gen 12:3
3:10 Deut 27:26
3:11 Gal 2:16; Hab 2:4; Rom 1:17; Heb 10:38
3:12 Lev 18:5; Rom 10:5
3:13 Gal 4:5; Deut 21:23; Acts 5:30
3:14 Rom 4:9, 16; Gal 3:28; Gal 3:2; Acts 2:33; Eph 1:13
3:15 Acts 1:15; Rom 1:13; Gal 6:18; Rom 3:5; Heb 6:16
3:16 Luke 1:55; Rom 4:13, 16; 9:4
3:17 Gen 15:13f; Ex 12:40; Acts 7:6

3:2–3 The believers in Galatia, some of whom may have been in Jerusalem at Pentecost and received the Holy Spirit there, knew that they hadn't received God's Spirit by obeying the Jewish laws. Paul stressed that just as they began their Christian lives in the power of the Spirit, so they should grow by the Spirit's power. The Galatians had taken a step backward when they had decided to insist on keeping the Jewish laws. We must realize that we grow spiritually because of God's work in us by his Spirit, not by following special rules.

3:5 The Galatians knew that they had received the Holy Spirit when they believed, not when they obeyed the law. People still feel insecure in their faith, because faith alone seems too easy. People still try to get closer to God by following rules. While certain disciplines (Bible study, prayer) and service may help us grow, they must not take the place of the Holy Spirit in us or become ends in themselves. By asking these questions, Paul hoped to get the Galatians to focus again on Christ as the foundation of their faith.

3:5 The Holy Spirit gives Christians great power to live for God. Some Christians want more than this. They want to live in a state of perpetual excitement. The tedium of everyday living leads them to conclude that something is wrong spiritually. Often the Holy Spirit's greatest work is teaching us to persist, to keep on doing what is right even when it no longer seems interesting or exciting. The Galatians quickly turned from Paul's Good News to the teachings of the newest teachers in town; what they needed was the Holy Spirit's gift of persistence. If the Christian life seems ordinary, you may need the Spirit to stir you up. Every day offers a challenge to live for Christ.

3:6–9 The main argument of the Judaizers was that Gentiles had to become Jews in order to become Christians. Paul exposed the flaw in this argument by showing that real children of Abraham are those who have faith, not those who keep the law. Abraham himself was saved by his faith (Genesis 15:6). All believers in every age and from every nation share Abraham's blessing. This is a comforting promise to us, a great heritage for us, and a solid foundation for living.

3:10 Paul quoted Deuteronomy 27:26 to prove that, contrary to what the Judaizers claimed, the law cannot justify and save—it can only condemn. Breaking even one commandment brings a person under condemnation. And because everyone has broken the commandments, everyone stands condemned. The law can do nothing to reverse the condemnation (Romans 3:20–24). But Christ took the curse of the law upon himself when he hung on the cross. He did this so we wouldn't have to bear our own punishment. The only condition is that we accept Christ's death on our behalf as the means to be saved (Colossians 1:20–23).

3:11 Trying to be right with God ("justified") by our own effort doesn't work. Good intentions such as "I'll do better next time" or "I'll never do that again" usually end in failure. Paul points to Habakkuk's declaration (Habakkuk 2:4) that by trusting God—believing in his provision for our sins and living each day in his power—we can break this cycle of failure.

3:17 God kept his promise to Abraham (Genesis 17:7, 8)—he has not revoked it, though thousands of years have passed. He saved Abraham through his faith, and he blessed the world through Abraham by sending the Messiah as one of Abraham's descendants. Circumstances may change, but God remains constant and does not break his promises. He has promised to forgive our sins through Jesus Christ, and we can be sure that he will do so.

3:18 Rom 4:14; Heb 6:14
3:19 Rom 5:20; Acts 7:53; Ex 20:19
3:20 1 Tim 2:5; Heb 8:6; 9:15; 12:24
3:21 Luke 20:16
3:22 Rom 11:32
3:24 1 Cor 4:15; Gal 2:16
3:26 Rom 8:14; Gal 4:5
3:27 Matt 28:19; Rom 6:3; 1 Cor 10:2; Rom 13:14

18 For if the inheritance is based on law, it is no longer based on a promise; but God
has granted it to Abraham by means of a promise.
19 Why the Law then? It was added because of transgressions, having been ordained
through angels by the agency of a mediator, until the seed would come to whom the
promise had been made.
20 Now a mediator is not for one *party only;* whereas God is *only* one.
21 Is the Law then contrary to the promises of God? May it never be! For if a law had
been given which was able to impart life, then righteousness would indeed have been
based on law.
22 But the Scripture has shut up everyone under sin, so that the promise by faith in
Jesus Christ might be given to those who believe.
23 But before faith came, we were kept in custody under the law, being shut up to the
faith which was later to be revealed.
24 Therefore the Law has become our tutor *to lead us* to Christ, so that we may be
justified by faith.
25 But now that faith has come, we are no longer under a tutor.
26 For you are all sons of God through faith in Christ Jesus.
27 For all of you who were baptized into Christ have clothed yourselves with Christ.

JUDAIZERS VERSUS PAUL

What the Judaizers said about Paul	*Paul's defense*
They said he was distorting the truth.	He received his message from Christ himself (1:11–12).
They said he was a traitor to the Jewish faith.	Paul was one of the most dedicated Jews of his time. Yet, in the midst of one of his most zealous acts, God transformed him through a revelation of the Good News about Jesus (1:13–16; Acts 9:1–30).
They said he compromised and watered down his message for the Gentiles.	The other apostles declared that the message Paul preached was the true gospel (2:1–10).
They said he was disregarding the Law of Moses.	Far from degrading the Law, Paul puts the Law in its proper place. He says it shows people where they have sinned, and it points them to Christ (3:19–29).

As the debate raged between the Gentile Christians and the Judaizers, Paul found it necessary to write to the churches in Galatia. The Judaizers were trying to undermine Paul's authority, and they taught a false gospel. In reply, Paul defended his authority as an apostle and the truth of his message. The debate over Jewish laws and Gentile Christians was officially resolved at the Jerusalem council (Acts 15), yet it continued to be a point of contention after that time.

3:18–19 The law has two functions. On the positive side, it reveals the nature and will of God and shows people how to live. On the negative side, it points out people's sins and shows them that it is impossible to please God by trying to obey all his laws completely. God's promise to Abraham dealt with Abraham's faith; the law focuses on actions. The covenant with Abraham shows that faith is the only way to be saved; the law shows how to obey God in grateful response. Faith does not annul the law; but the more we know God, the more we see how sinful we are. Then we are driven to depend on our faith in Christ alone for our salvation.

3:19–20 When God gave his promise to Abraham, he did it by himself alone, without angels or Moses as mediators. Although it is not mentioned in Exodus, Jews believed that the Ten Commandments had been given to Moses by angels (Stephen referred to this in his speech, see Acts 7:38, 53). Paul was showing the superiority of salvation and growth by faith over trying to be saved by keeping the Jewish laws. Christ is the best and only way given by God for us to come to him (1 Timothy 2:5).

3:21–22 Before faith in Christ delivered us, we were imprisoned by sin, beaten down by past mistakes, and choked by desires that we knew were wrong. God knew we were sin's prisoners, but he provided a way of escape—faith in Jesus Christ. Without Christ, everyone is held in sin's grasp, and only those who place their faith in Christ ever get out of it. Look to Christ—he is reaching out to set you free.

3:24–25 "The Law has become our tutor" is like the supervision given by a tutor to a young child. We no longer need that kind of supervision. The law teaches us the *need* for salvation; God's grace *gives* us that salvation. The Old Testament still applies today. In it, God reveals his nature, his will for humanity, his moral laws, and his guidelines for living. But we cannot be saved by keeping that law; we must trust in Christ.

3:26–27 In Roman society, a youth coming of age laid aside the robe of childhood and put on a new toga. This represented his move into adult citizenship with full rights and responsibilities. Paul combined this cultural understanding with the concept of baptism. By becoming Christians and being baptized, the Galatian believers were becoming spiritually grown up and ready to take on the privileges and responsibilities of the more mature. Paul was saying that they had laid aside the old clothes of the law, and were putting on Christ's new robe of righteousness (see 2 Corinthians 5:21; Ephesians 4:23–24).

28 There is neither Jew nor Greek, there is neither slave nor free man, there is neither
male nor female; for you are all one in Christ Jesus.
29 And if you belong to Christ, then you are Abraham's descendants, heirs according
to promise.

Sonship in Christ

4 Now I say, as long as the heir is a child, he does not differ at all from a slave although
he is owner of everything,
2 but he is under guardians and managers until the date set by the father.
3 So also we, while we were children, were held in bondage under the elemental things
of the world.
4 But when the fullness of the time came, God sent forth His Son, born of a woman,
born under the Law,
5 so that He might redeem those who were under the Law, that we might receive the
adoption as sons.
6 Because you are sons, God has sent forth the Spirit of His Son into our hearts, crying, "Abba! Father!"
7 Therefore you are no longer a slave, but a son; and if a son, then an heir through
God.
8 However at that time, when you did not know God, you were slaves to those which
by nature are no gods.
9 But now that you have come to know God, or rather to be known by God, how is it
that you turn back again to the weak and worthless elemental things, to which you desire
to be enslaved all over again?
10 You observe days and months and seasons and years.
11 I fear for you, that perhaps I have labored over you in vain.
12 I beg of you, brethren, become as I *am*, for I also *have become* as you *are*. You have
done me no wrong;
13 but you know that it was because of a bodily illness that I preached the gospel to
you the first time;
14 and that which was a trial to you in my bodily condition you did not despise or loathe,
but you received me as an angel of God, as Christ Jesus *Himself*.

3:28 Rom 3:22; 1 Cor 12:13; Col 3:11; John 17:11; Eph 2:15; Rom 8:1; Gal 3:26; 4:14; 5:6, 24

3:29 Rom 4:13; 1 Cor 3:23; Rom 9:8; Gal 3:18; 4:28

4:3 Gal 2:4; 4:8f, 24f; Heb 5:12

4:4 Mark 1:15; John 1:14; Rom 1:3; 8:3; Phil 2:7; Luke 2:21f

4:5 Rom 8:14; Gal 3:26

4:6 Acts 16:7; Rom 5:5; 8:9, 16; 2 Cor 3:17; Mark 14:36; Rom 8:15

4:7 Rom 8:17

4:8 1 Cor 1:21; Eph 2:12; 1 Thess 4:5; 2 Thess 1:8; 1 Cor 8:4f; 10:20

4:9 1 Cor 8:3; Col 2:20; Gal 4:3

4:10 Rom 14:5; Col 2:16

4:12 Gal 6:18; 2 Cor 6:11

4:14 Matt 10:40; 1 Thess 2:13; Gal 3:26

3:28 Some Jewish males greeted each new day by praying, "Lord, I thank you that I am not a Gentile, a slave, or a woman." The role of women was enhanced by Christianity. Faith in Christ transcends these differences and makes all believers one in Christ. Make sure you do not impose distinctions that Christ has removed. Because all believers are his heirs, no one is more privileged than or superior to anyone else.

3:28 It's our natural inclination to feel uncomfortable around people who are different from us and to gravitate toward those who are similar to us. But when we allow our differences to separate us from our fellow believers, we are disregarding clear Biblical teaching. Make a point to seek out and appreciate people who are not just like you and your friends. You may find that you have a lot in common with them.

3:29 The original promise to Abraham was intended for the whole world, not just for Abraham's descendants (see Genesis 12:3). All believers participate in this promise and are blessed as children of Abraham.

4:3 7 The "elemental things of the world" are the elementary stages of religious practice, whether in the Jewish or pagan religion. Paul uses the illustration of slavery to show that before Christ came and died for sins, people were in bondage to the law. Thinking they could be saved by it, they became enslaved to trying—and failing—to keep it. But we who were once slaves are now God's very own children who have an intimate relationship with him. Because of Christ, there is no reason to be afraid of God. We can come boldly into his presence, knowing that he will welcome us as his family members.

4:4 "When the fullness of the time came," God sent Jesus to earth to die for our sins. For centuries the Jews had been wondering when their Messiah would come—but God's timing was perfect. We may sometimes wonder if God will ever respond to our prayers. But we must never doubt him or give up hope. At the right time he will respond. Are you waiting for God's timing? Trust his judgment and trust that he has your best interests in mind.

4:4–5 Jesus was born of a woman—he was human. He was born as a Jew—he was subject to God's law and fulfilled it perfectly. Thus Jesus was the perfect sacrifice because, although he was fully human, he never sinned. His death bought freedom for us who were enslaved to sin so that we could be adopted into God's family.

4:5–7 Under Roman law, an adopted child was guaranteed all legal rights to his father's property, even if he was formerly a slave. He was not a second-class son; he was equal to all other sons, biological or adopted, in his father's family. *Abba* is an Aramaic word for father. It was used by Christ in his prayer in Mark 14:36. As adopted children of God, we share with Jesus all rights to God's resources. As God's heirs, we can claim what he has provided for us our full identity as his children (see Romans 8:15–17).

4:13–14 Paul's illness was a sickness that he was enduring while he visited the Galatian churches. The world is often callous to people's pain and misery. Paul commended the Galatians for not scorning him, even though his condition was a trial to them (he didn't explain what was wrong with him). Such caring was what Jesus meant when he called us to serve the homeless, hungry, sick, and imprisoned as if they were Jesus himself (Matthew 25:34–40). Do you avoid those in pain or those facing difficulty—or are you willing to care for them as if they were Jesus Christ himself?

4:16 Amos 5:10	15 Where then is that sense of blessing you had? For I bear you witness that, if possi- ble, you would have plucked out your eyes and given them to me.
4:18 Gal 4:13f	16 So have I become your enemy by telling you the truth? 17 They eagerly seek you, not commendably, but they wish to shut you out so that you will seek them.
4:19 1 John 2:1; 1 Cor 4:15; Eph 4:13	18 But it is good always to be eagerly sought in a commendable manner, and not only when I am present with you.
4:20 2 Cor 4:8	19 My children, with whom I am again in labor until Christ is formed in you— 20 but I could wish to be present with you now and to change my tone, for I am per- plexed about you.
4:21 Luke 16:29	

Bond and Free

4:22 Gen 16:15; Gen 21:2	21 Tell me, you who want to be under law, do you not listen to the law?
4:23 Rom 9:7; Gal 4:29; Gen 17:16ff; 18:10ff; 21:1; Gal 4:28; Heb 11:11	22 For it is written that Abraham had two sons, one by the bondwoman and one by the free woman. 23 But the son by the bondwoman was born according to the flesh, and the son by the free woman through the promise.
4:24 1 Cor 10:11; Deut 33:2; Gal 4:3	24 This is allegorically speaking, for these *women* are two covenants: one *proceeding* from Mount Sinai bearing children who are to be slaves; she is Hagar.

WHAT IS THE LAW?
Part of the Jewish law included those laws found in the Old Testament. When Paul says that non–Jews (Gentiles) are no longer bound by these laws, he is not saying that the Old Testament laws do not apply to us today. He is saying certain types of laws may not apply to us. In the Old Testament there were three categories of laws:

Ceremonial law	This kind of law relates specifically to Israel's worship (see, for example, Leviticus 1:1–13). Its primary purpose was to point forward to Jesus Christ. Therefore, these laws were no longer necessary after Jesus' death and resurrection. While we are no longer bound by ceremonial laws, the principles behind them—to worship and love a holy God—still apply. The Jewish Christians often accused the Gentile Christians of violating the ceremonial law.
Civil law	This type of law dictated Israel's daily living (see Deuteronomy 24:10–11, for example). Because modern society and culture are so radically different, some of these guidelines cannot be followed specifically. But the principles behind the commands should guide our conduct. At times, Paul asked Gentile Christians to follow some of these laws, not because they had to, but in order to promote unity.
Moral law	This sort of law is the direct command of God—for example, the Ten Commandments (Exodus 20:1–17). It requires strict obedience. It reveals the nature and will of God, and it still applies to us today. We are to obey this moral law not to obtain salvation, but to live in ways pleasing to God.

4:15 Have you lost your joy? Paul sensed that the Galatians had lost the joy of their salvation because of legalism. Legalism can take away joy because (1) it makes people feel guilty rather than loved; (2) it produces self-hatred rather than humility; (3) it stresses performance over relationship; (4) it points out how far short we fall rather than how far we've come because of what Christ did for us. If you feel guilty and inadequate, check your focus. Are you living by faith in Christ or by trying to live up to the demands and expectations of others?

4:16 Paul did not gain great popularity when he rebuked the Galatians for turning away from their first faith in Christ. Human nature hasn't changed much—we still get angry when we're scolded. But don't write off someone who challenges you. There may be truth in what he or she says. Receive his or her words with humility; carefully think them over. If you discover that you need to change an attitude or action, take steps to do it.

4:17 "They wish to shut you out" refers to false teachers who claimed to be religious authorities and experts in Judaism and Christianity. Appealing to the believers' desire to do what was right, they drew quite a following. Paul said, however, that they were wrong and that their motives were selfish. False teachers are often respectable and persuasive. That is why all teachings should be checked against the Bible.

4:19 Paul led many people to Christ and helped them mature spiritually. Perhaps one reason for his success as a spiritual father was the deep concern he felt for his spiritual children; he compared his pain over their faithlessness to the pain of childbirth. We should have the same intense care for those to whom we are spiritual parents. When you lead people to Christ, remember to stand by them to help them grow.

4:21ff People are saved because of their faith in Christ, not because of what they do. Paul contrasted those who are enslaved to the law (represented by Hagar, the bondwoman) with those who are free from the law (represented by Sarah, the free woman). Hagar's abuse of Sarah (Genesis 16:4) was like the persecution that the Gentile Christians were getting from the Judaizers who insisted on keeping the law in order to be saved. Eventually Sarah triumphed because God kept his promise to give her a son, just as those who worship Christ in faith will also triumph.

4:24 Paul explained that what happened to Sarah and Hagar is an allegory or picture of the relationship between God and mankind. Paul was using a type of argument that was common in his day and that was probably being used against him by his opponents.

25 Now this Hagar is Mount Sinai in Arabia and corresponds to the present Jerusalem, for she is in slavery with her children.
26 But the Jerusalem above is free; she is our mother.
27 For it is written,

"REJOICE, BARREN WOMAN WHO DOES NOT BEAR;
BREAK FORTH AND SHOUT, YOU WHO ARE NOT IN LABOR;
FOR MORE NUMEROUS ARE THE CHILDREN OF THE DESOLATE
THAN OF THE ONE WHO HAS A HUSBAND."

28 And you brethren, like Isaac, are children of promise.
29 But as at that time he who was born according to the flesh persecuted him *who was*
born according to the Spirit, so it is now also.
30 But what does the Scripture say?

"CAST OUT THE BONDWOMAN AND HER SON,
FOR THE SON OF THE BONDWOMAN SHALL NOT BE AN HEIR WITH THE SON OF
THE FREE WOMAN."

31 So then, brethren, we are not children of a bondwoman, but of the free woman.

3. Freedom of the gospel

Walk by the Spirit

5 It was for freedom that Christ set us free; therefore keep standing firm and do not
be subject again to a yoke of slavery.
2 Behold I, Paul, say to you that if you receive circumcision, Christ will be of no benefit to you.
3 And I testify again to every man who receives circumcision, that he is under obligation to keep the whole Law.
4 You have been severed from Christ, you who are seeking to be justified by law; you
have fallen from grace.
5 For we through the Spirit, by faith, are waiting for the hope of righteousness.
6 For in Christ Jesus neither circumcision nor uncircumcision means anything, but
faith working through love.
7 You were running well; who hindered you from obeying the truth?
8 This persuasion *did* not *come* from Him who calls you.
9 A little leaven leavens the whole lump *of dough.*
10 I have confidence in you in the Lord that you will adopt no other view; but the one
who is disturbing you will bear his judgment, whoever he is.
11 But I, brethren, if I still preach circumcision, why am I still persecuted? Then the
stumbling block of the cross has been abolished.
12 I wish that those who are troubling you would even mutilate themselves.

4:26 Heb 12:22; Rev 3:12; 21:2, 10

4:27 Is 54:1

4:28 Rom 9:7ff; Gal 3:29

4:30 Gen 21:10, 12; John 8:35

5:1 John 8:32, 36; Rom 8:15; 2 Cor 3:17; Gal 2:4; 5:13; 1 Cor 16:13; Acts 15:10; Gal 2:4

5:2 2 Cor 10:1; Acts 15:1; Gal 5:3, 6, 11

5:3 Luke 16:28; Acts 15:1; Rom 2:25

5:4 Heb 12:15; 2 Pet 3:17

5:5 Rom 8:23; 1 Cor 1:7

5:6 Gal 3:26; 1 Cor 7:19; Gal 6:15; Col 1:4f; 1 Thess 1:3; James 2:18, 20, 22

5:7 Gal 2:2

5:8 Rom 8:28; Gal 1:6

5:9 1 Cor 5:6

5:10 2 Cor 2:3; Gal 5:7; Phil 3:15; Gal 1:7; 5:12

5:11 Gal 4:29; 6:12; Rom 9:33; 1 Cor 1:23

5:12 Gal 2:4; 5:10; Deut 23:1

5:1 Christ died to set us free from sin and from a long list of laws and regulations. Christ came to set us free—not free to do whatever we want because that would lead us back into slavery to our selfish desires. Rather, thanks to Christ, we are now free and able to do what was impossible before—to live unselfishly. Those who appeal to their freedom so that they can have their own way or indulge their own desires are falling back into sin. But it is also wrong to put a burden of lawkeeping on Christians. We must stand against those who would enslave us with rules, methods, or special conditions for being saved or growing in Christ.

5:2–4 Trying to be saved by keeping the law and being saved by grace are two entirely different approaches. "Christ will be of no benefit to you" means that Christ's provision for our salvation will not help us if we are trying to save ourselves. Obeying the law does not make it any easier for God to save us. All we can do is accept his gracious gift through faith. Our deeds of service must never be used to try to earn God's love or favor.

5:3–4 Circumcision was a symbol of having the right background and doing everything required by religion. No amount of work, discipline, or moral behavior can save us. If a person were counting on finding favor with God by being circumcised, he would also have to obey the rest of God's law completely. Trying to save ourselves by keeping all God's laws only separates us from God.

5:6 We are saved by faith, not by deeds. But love for others and for God is the response of those whom God has forgiven. God's forgiveness is complete, and Jesus said that those who are forgiven much love much (Luke 7:47). Because faith expresses itself through love, you can check your love for others as a way to monitor your faith.

5:9 A little leaven (yeast) causes a whole lump of dough to rise. It only takes one wrong person to infect all the others.

5:11 Persecution proved that Paul was preaching the true gospel. If he had taught what the false teachers were teaching, no one would be offended. But because he was teaching the truth, he was persecuted by both Jews and Judaizers. Have friends or loved ones rejected you because you have taken a stand for Christ? Jesus said not to be surprised if the world hates you, because it hated him (John 15:18–19). Just as Paul continued to faithfully proclaim the message about Christ, you should continue doing the ministry God has given you—in spite of the obstacles others may put in your way.

5:13 1 Pet 2:16; 1 Cor 9:19; Eph 5:21

5:14 Matt 7:12; 22:40; John 13:34

5:15 Gal 5:20; Phil 3:2

5:16 Rom 8:4; 13:14

13 For you were called to freedom, brethren; only *do* not *turn* your freedom into an
opportunity for the flesh, but through love serve one another.
14 For the whole Law is fulfilled in one word, in the *statement*, "YOU SHALL LOVE YOUR
NEIGHBOR AS YOURSELF."
15 But if you bite and devour one another, take care that you are not consumed by one
another.
16 But I say, walk by the Spirit, and you will not carry out the desire of the flesh.

THREE DISTORTIONS OF CHRISTIANITY

Almost from the beginning there were forces at work within Christianity that could have destroyed or sidetracked the movement. Of these, three created many problems then and have continued to reappear in other forms even today. The three aberrations are contrasted to true Christianity.

Group	*Their definition of a Christian*	*Their genuine concern*	*The danger*	*Application question*
Judaized Christianity	Christians are Jews who have recognized Jesus as the promised Savior. Therefore any Gentile desiring to become a Christian must first become a Jew.	Having a high regard for the Scriptures and God's choice of Jews as his people, they did not want to see God's commands overlooked or broken.	Tends to add human traditions and standards to God's Law. Also subtracts from the Scriptures God's clear concern for all nations.	Do you appreciate God's choice of a unique people through whom he offered forgiveness and eternal life to all peoples?
Legalized Christianity	Christians are those who live by a long list of "don'ts." God's favor is earned by good behavior.	Recognized that real change brought about by God should lead to changes in behavior.	Tends to make God's love something to earn rather than to accept freely. Would reduce Christianity to a set of impossible rules and transform the Good News into bad news.	As important as change in action is, can you see that God may be desiring different changes in you than in others?
Lawless Christianity	Christians live above the Law. They need no guidelines. God's Word is not as important as our personal sense of God's guidance.	Recognized that forgiveness from God cannot be based on our ability to live up to his perfect standards. It must be received by faith as a gift made possible by Christ's death on the cross.	Forgets that Christians are still human and fail consistently when trying to live only by what they "feel" God wants.	Do you recognize the ongoing need for God's expressed commands as you live out your gratitude for his great salvation?
True Christianity	Christians are those who believe inwardly and outwardly that Jesus' death has allowed God to offer them forgiveness and eternal life as a gift. They have accepted that gift through faith and are seeking to live a life of obedient gratitude for what God has done for them.	Christianity is both private and public, with heart-belief and mouth-confession. Our relationship to God and the power he provides result in obedience. Having received the gift of forgiveness and eternal life, we are now daily challenged to live that life with his help.	Avoids the above dangers.	How would those closest to you describe your Christianity? Do they think you live so that God will accept you or do they know that you live *because* God has accepted you in Christ?

5:13 Paul distinguishes between freedom to sin and freedom to serve. Freedom or license to sin is no freedom at all, because it enslaves you to Satan, others, or your own sinful nature. Christians, by contrast, should not be slaves to sin, because they are free to do right and to glorify God through loving service to others.

5:14–15 When we are not motivated by love, we become critical of others. We stop looking for good in them and see only their faults. Soon the unity of believers is broken. Have you talked behind someone's back? Have you focused on others' shortcomings instead of their strengths? Remind yourself of Jesus' command to love others as you love yourself (Matthew 22:39). When you begin to feel critical of someone, make a list of that person's positive qualities. If there are problems that need to be addressed, it is better to confront in love than to gossip.

5:16–18 If your desire is to have the qualities listed in 5:22–23, then you know that the Holy Spirit is leading you. At the same time, be careful not to confuse your subjective feelings with the Spirit's leading. Being led by the Holy Spirit involves the desire to hear, the readiness to obey God's Word, and the sensitivity to discern between your feelings and his promptings. Live each day controlled and guided by the Holy Spirit. Then the words of Christ will be in your mind, the love of Christ will be behind your actions, and the power of Christ will help you control your selfish desires.

17 For the flesh sets its desire against the Spirit, and the Spirit against the flesh; for
these are in opposition to one another, so that you may not do the things that you please.
18 But if you are led by the Spirit, you are not under the Law.
19 Now the deeds of the flesh are evident, which are: immorality, impurity, sensuality,
20 idolatry, sorcery, enmities, strife, jealousy, outbursts of anger, disputes, dissensions,
factions,
21 envying, drunkenness, carousing, and things like these, of which I forewarn you, just
as I have forewarned you, that those who practice such things will not inherit the kingdom of God.
22 But the fruit of the Spirit is love, joy, peace, patience, kindness, goodness, faithfulness,
23 gentleness, self-control; against such things there is no law.
24 Now those who belong to Christ Jesus have crucified the flesh with its passions and
desires.

5:17 Rom 7:15ff
5:18 Rom 6:14; 7:4
5:19 1 Cor 6:9, 18; 2 Cor 12:21
5:20 Rom 2:8; James 3:14ff; 1 Cor 11:19
5:21 Rom 13:13
5:22 Matt 7:16ff; Eph 5:9; Rom 5:1-5; 1 Cor 13:4; Col 3:12-15
5:24 Gal 3:26; Rom 6:6

VICES AND VIRTUES
The Bible mentions many specific actions and attitudes that are either right or wrong. Look at the list included here. Are there a number of characteristics from the wrong column that are influencing you?

VICES (Neglecting God and others)	*VIRTUES* (The by-products of living for God)
Sexual immorality *(5:19)*	Love *(5:22)*
Impurity *(5:19)*	Joy *(5:22)*
Passion *(Colossians 3:5)*	Peace *(5:22)*
Enmities *(5:20)*	Patience *(5:22)*
Strife *(5:20)*	Kindness *(5:22)*
Jealousy *(5:20)*	Goodness *(5:22)*
Anger *(5:20)*	Faithfulness *(5:22)*
Disputes *(5:20)*	Gentleness *(5:23)*
Dissensions *(5:20)*	Self-control *(5:23)*
Arrogance *(2 Corinthians 12:20)*	
Envy *(5:21)*	
Murder *(Revelation 22:12–16)*	
Idolatry *(5:20; Ephesians 5:5)*	
Sorcery *(5:20)*	
Drunkenness *(5:21)*	
Carousing *(Luke 15:13; Galatians 5:21)*	
Fraud *(1 Corinthians 6:8)*	
Adultery *(1 Corinthians 6:9–10)*	
Homosexuality *(1 Corinthians 6:9–10)*	
Coveting *(1 Corinthians 6:9–10; Ephesians 5:5)*	
Stealing *(1 Corinthians 6:9–10)*	
Lying *(Revelation 22:12–16)*	

5:17 Paul describes the two forces conflicting within us—the Spirit and the flesh (our evil desires or inclinations that stem from our bodies; see also 5:16, 19, 24). Paul is not saying that these forces are equal—the Holy Spirit is infinitely stronger. But if we rely on our own wisdom, we will make wrong choices. If we try to follow the Spirit by our own human effort, we will fail. Our only way to freedom from our evil desires is through the empowering of the Holy Spirit (see Romans 8:9; Ephesians 4:23–24; Colossians 3:3–8).

5:19–21 We all have evil desires, and we can't ignore them. In order for us to follow the Holy Spirit's guidance, we must deal with them decisively (crucify them—5:24). These desires include obvious sins such as sexual immorality and sorcery. They also include less obvious sins such as strife, jealousy, and anger. Those who ignore such sins or refuse to deal with them reveal that they have not received the gift of the Spirit that leads to a transformed life.

5:22–23 The fruit of the Spirit is the spontaneous work of the Holy Spirit in us. The Spirit produces these character traits that are found in the nature of Christ. They are the by-products of Christ's control—we can't obtain them by *trying* to get them without his help. If we want the fruit of the Spirit to grow in us, we must join our lives to his (see John 15:4–5). We must know him, love him, remember him, and imitate him. As a result, we will fulfill the intended purpose of the law—to love God and our neighbors. Which of these qualities do you want the Spirit to produce in you?

5:23 Because the God who sent the law also sent the Spirit, the by-products of the Spirit-filled life are in perfect harmony with the intent of God's law. A person who exhibits the fruit of the Spirit fulfills the law far better than a person who observes the rituals but has little love in his or her heart.

5:24 In order to accept Christ as Savior, we need to turn from our sins and willingly nail our sinful nature to the cross. This doesn't mean, however, that we will never see traces of its evil desires again. As Christians we still have the capacity to sin, but we have been set free from sin's power over us and no longer have to give in to it. We must daily commit our sinful tendencies to God's control, daily crucify them, and moment by moment draw on the Spirit's power to overcome them (see 2:20; 6:14).

6:1 1 Thess 4:1; 1 Cor 2:15; 2 Cor 2:7; 2 Thess 3:15; Heb 12:13; James 5:19f
6:2 1 Cor 9:21; James 1:25; 2:12; 2 Pet 3:2
6:3 Acts 5:36; 1 Cor 3:18; 2 Cor 12:11
6:5 Prov 9:12; Rom 14:12; 1 Cor 3:8
6:6 1 Cor 9:11, 14; 2 Tim 4:2
6:8 Rom 6:21; 8:11; James 3:18
6:9 Matt 10:22; Heb 12:3, 5; James 5:7f
6:10 Prov 3:27; John 12:35; Eph 2:19; Heb 3:6; 1 Pet 2:5

25 If we live by the Spirit, let us also walk by the Spirit.
26 Let us not become boastful, challenging one another, envying one another.

Bear One Another's Burdens

6 Brethren, even if anyone is caught in any trespass, you who are spiritual, restore such
a one in a spirit of gentleness; *each one* looking to yourself, so that you too will not
be tempted.
2 Bear one another's burdens, and thereby fulfill the law of Christ.
3 For if anyone thinks he is something when he is nothing, he deceives himself.
4 But each one must examine his own work, and then he will have *reason for* boasting
in regard to himself alone, and not in regard to another.
5 For each one will bear his own load.
6 The one who is taught the word is to share all good things with the one who
teaches *him*.
7 Do not be deceived, God is not mocked; for whatever a man sows, this he will
also reap.
8 For the one who sows to his own flesh will from the flesh reap corruption, but the
one who sows to the Spirit will from the Spirit reap eternal life.
9 Let us not lose heart in doing good, for in due time we will reap if we do not grow
weary.
10 So then, while we have opportunity, let us do good to all people, and especially to
those who are of the household of the faith.

OUR WRONG DESIRES VERSUS THE FRUIT OF THE SPIRIT

The will of the Holy Spirit is in constant opposition to our sinful desires. The two are on opposite sides of the spiritual battle.

Our wrong desires are:	*The fruits of the spirit are:*
Evil	Good
Destructive	Productive
Easy to ignite	Difficult to ignite
Difficult to stifle	Easy to stifle
Self-centered	Self-giving
Oppressive and possessive	Liberating and nurturing
Decadent	Uplifting
Sinful	Holy
Deadly	Abundant life

5:25 God is interested in every part of our lives, not just the spiritual part. As we live by the Holy Spirit's power, we need to submit every aspect of our lives to God—emotional, physical, social, intellectual, vocational. Paul says that because we're saved, we should live like it! The Holy Spirit is the source of your new life, so keep in step with his leading. Don't let anything or anyone else determine your values and standards in any area of your life.

5:26 Everyone needs a certain amount of approval from others. But those who go out of their way to secure honors or to win popularity with a lot of people become conceited and show they are not following the Holy Spirit's leading. Those who look to God for approval won't need to envy others. Because we are God's sons and daughters, we have his Holy Spirit as the loving guarantee of his approval.

6:1–3 No Christian should ever think that he or she is totally independent and doesn't need help from others, and no one should feel excused from the task of helping others. The body of Christ—the church—functions only when the members work together for the common good. Do you know someone who needs help? Is there a Christian brother or sister who needs correction or encouragement? Humbly and gently reach out to that person (John 13:34–35).

6:4 When you do your very best, you feel good about the results. There is no need to compare yourself with others. People make comparisons for many reasons. Some point out others' flaws in order to feel better about themselves. Others simply want reassurance that they are doing well. When you are tempted to compare, look at Jesus Christ. His example will inspire you to do your very best, and his loving acceptance will comfort you when you fall short of your expectations.

6:6 Paul says that students should take care of the material needs of their teachers (1 Corinthians 9:7–12). It is easy to receive the benefit of good Bible teaching and then to take our spiritual leaders for granted, ignoring their financial and physical needs. We should care for our teachers, not grudgingly or reluctantly, but with a generous spirit, showing honor and appreciation for all they have done (1 Timothy 5:17–18).

6:7–8 It would certainly be a surprise if you planted corn and pumpkins came up. It's a natural law to reap what we sow. It's true in other areas too. If you gossip about your friends, you will lose their friendship. Every action has results. If you plant to please your own desires, you'll reap a crop of sorrow and evil. If you plant to please God, you'll reap joy and everlasting life. What kind of seeds are you sowing?

6:9–10 It is discouraging to continue to do right and receive no word of thanks or see no tangible results. But Paul challenged the Galatians and he challenges us to keep on doing good and to trust God for the results. In due time, we will reap a harvest of blessing.

11 See with what large letters I am writing to you with my own hand.
12 Those who desire to make a good showing in the flesh try to compel you to be circumcised, simply so that they will not be persecuted for the cross of Christ.
13 For those who [1]are circumcised do not even keep the Law themselves, but they desire to have you circumcised so that they may boast in your flesh.
14 But may it never be that I would boast, except in the cross of our Lord Jesus Christ,
through which the world has been crucified to me, and I to the world.
15 For neither is circumcision anything, nor uncircumcision, but a new creation.
16 And those who will walk by this rule, peace and mercy *be* upon them, and upon the
Israel of God.
17 From now on let no one cause trouble for me, for I bear on my body the brand-
marks of Jesus.
18 The grace of our Lord Jesus Christ be with your spirit, brethren. Amen.

1 Two early mss read *have been*

6:12 Acts 15:1; Gal 5:11

6:13 Rom 2:25; Phil 3:3

6:14 Gal 2:20; Col 2:20; Rom 6:2, 6

6:15 Rom 2:26, 28; 1 Cor 7:19; 2 Cor 5:17

6:16 Rom 9:6; Gal 3:7

6:17 2 Cor 4:10; 11:23; Rev 13:16

6:18 Rom 16:20

6:11 Up to this point, Paul had probably dictated the letter to a scribe. Here he takes the pen into his own hand to write his final, personal greetings. Paul did this in other letters as well, to add emphasis to his words and to validate that the letter was genuine.

6:13 Some of the Judaizers were emphasizing circumcision as proof of holiness—but ignoring the other Jewish laws. People often choose a certain principle or prohibition and make it the measure of faith. Some may abhor drunkenness but ignore gluttony. Others may despise promiscuity but tolerate prejudice. The Bible in its entirety is our rule of faith and practice. We cannot pick and choose the mandates we will follow.

6:14 The world is full of enticements. Daily we are confronted with subtle cultural pressures and overt propaganda. The only way to escape these destructive influences is to ask God to help crucify our interest in them, just as Paul did. How much do the interests of this world matter to you? (See 2:20 and 5:24 for more on this concept.)

6:15 It is easy to get caught up with the externals. Beware of those who emphasize actions that we should or shouldn't do, with no concern for the inward condition of the heart. Living a good life without an inward change leads to a shallow or empty spiritual walk. What matters to God is that we be completely changed from the inside out (2 Corinthians 5:17).

6:18 Paul's letter to the Galatians boldly declares the freedom of the Christian. Doubtless these early Christians in Galatia wanted to grow in the Christian life, but they were being misled by those who said this could be done only by keeping certain Jewish laws.

How strange it would be for a prisoner who had been set free to walk back into his or her cell and refuse to leave! How strange for an animal, released from a trap, to go back inside it! How sad for a believer to be freed from the bondage of sin, only to return to rigid conformity to a set of rules and regulations!

If you believe in Jesus Christ, you have been set free. Instead of going back into some form of slavery, whether to legalism or to sin, use your freedom to live for Christ and serve him as he desires.

EPHESIANS

OUR churches come in all styles and shapes—secret meetings in homes; wide-open gatherings in amphitheaters; worship services packing thousands into a sanctuary while an overflow crowd watches on closed-circuit television; handfuls who kneel in urban storefronts. Buildings will vary, but the church is not confined to four walls. The church of Jesus Christ is *people,* his people, of every race and nation, who love Christ and are committed to serving him.

The "church age" began at Pentecost (Acts 2). Born in Jerusalem, the church spread rapidly through the ministry of the apostles and the early believers. Fanned by persecution, the gospel flame then spread to other cities and nations. On three courageous journeys, Paul and his associates established local assemblies in scores of Gentile cities.

One of the most prominent of those churches was at Ephesus. It was established in A.D. 53 on Paul's homeward journey to Jerusalem. But Paul returned a year later, on his third missionary trip, and stayed there for three years, preaching and teaching with great effectiveness (Acts 19:1–20). At another time, Paul met with the Ephesian elders, and he sent Timothy to serve as their leader (1 Timothy 1:3). Just a few years later, Paul was sent as a prisoner to Rome. In Rome, he was visited by messengers from various churches, including Tychicus of Ephesus. Paul wrote this letter to the church and sent it with Tychicus. Not written to counteract heresy or to confront any specific problem, Ephesians is a letter of encouragement. In it Paul describes the nature and appearance of the church, and he challenges believers to function as the living body of Christ on earth.

After a warm greeting (1:1–2), Paul affirms the nature of the church—the glorious fact that believers in Christ have been showered with God's kindness (1:3–8), chosen for greatness (1:9–12), marked with the Holy Spirit (1:13–14), filled with the Spirit's power (1:15–23), freed from sin's curse and bondage (2:1–10), and brought near to God (2:11–18). As part of God's "household," we stand with the prophets, apostles, Jews, Gentiles, and Christ himself (2:19—3:13). Then, as though overcome with emotion by remembering all that God has done, Paul challenges the Ephesians to live close to Christ, and he breaks into spontaneous praise (3:14–21).

Paul then turns his attention to the implications of being in the body of Christ, the church. Believers should have unity in their commitment to Christ and their use of spiritual gifts (4:1–16). They should have the highest moral standards (4:17—6:9). For the individual, this means rejecting pagan practices (4:17—5:20), and for the family, this means mutual submission and love (5:21—6:9).

Paul then reminds them that the church is in a constant battle with the forces of darkness and that they should use every spiritual weapon at their disposal (6:10–17). He concludes by asking for their prayers, commissioning Tychicus, and giving a benediction (6:18–24).

As you read this masterful description of the church, thank God for the diversity and unity in his family, pray for your brothers and sisters across the world, and draw close to those in your local church.

VITAL STATISTICS

PURPOSE:
To strengthen the believers in Ephesus in their Christian faith by explaining the nature and purpose of the church, the body of Christ

AUTHOR:
Paul

TO WHOM WRITTEN:
The church at Ephesus, and all believers everywhere

DATE WRITTEN:
Approximately A.D. 60, from Rome, during Paul's imprisonment there

SETTING:
The letter was not written to confront any heresy or problem in the churches. It was sent with Tychicus to strengthen and encourage the churches in the area. Paul had spent over three years with the Ephesian church. As a result, he was very close to them. Paul met with the elders of the Ephesian church at Miletus (Acts 20:17–38)—a meeting that was filled with great sadness because he was leaving them for what he thought would be the last time. Because there are no specific references to people or problems in the Ephesian church and because the words "in Ephesus" (1:1) are not present in some early manuscripts, Paul may have intended this to be a circular letter to be read to all the churches in the area.

KEY VERSES:
"There is one body and one Spirit, just as also you were called in one hope of your calling; one Lord, one faith, one baptism, one God and Father of all who is over all and through all and in all" (4:4–6).

KEY PEOPLE:
Paul, Tychicus

SPECIAL FEATURES:
Several pictures of the church are presented: body, temple, mystery, new man, bride, and soldier. This letter was probably distributed to many of the early churches.

THE BLUEPRINT

1. Unity in Christ (1:1—3:21)
2. Unity in the body of Christ (4:1—6:24)

In this letter, Paul explains the wonderful things that we have received through Christ and refers to the church as a body, a temple, a bride, and a soldier. These all illustrate unity of purpose and show how each individual member is a part that must work together with all the other parts. In our own life, we should work to eradicate all backbiting, gossip, criticism, jealousy, anger, and bitterness, because these are barriers to unity in the church.

MEGATHEMES

THEME	EXPLANATION	IMPORTANCE
God's Purpose	According to God's eternal, loving plan, he directs, carries out, and sustains our salvation.	When we respond to Christ's love by trusting in him, his purpose becomes our mission. Have you committed yourself to fulfilling God's purpose?
Christ the Center	Christ is exalted as the center of the universe and the focus of history. He is the head of the body, the church. He is the Creator and sustainer of all creation.	Because Christ is central to everything, his power must be central in us. Begin by placing all your priorities under his control.
Living Church	Paul describes the nature of the church. The church, under Christ's control, is a living body, a family, a dwelling. God gives believers special abilities by his Holy Spirit to build the church.	We are part of Christ's body, and we must live in vital union with him. Our conduct must be consistent with this living relationship. Use your God-given abilities to equip believers for service. Fulfill your role in the living church.
New Family	Because God through Christ paid our penalty for sin and forgave us, we have been reconciled—brought near to him. We are a new society, a new family. Being united with Christ means we are to treat one another as family members.	We are one family in Christ, so there should be no barriers, no divisions, no basis for discrimination. We all belong to him, so we should live in harmony with one another.
Christian Conduct	Paul encourages all Christians to wise, dynamic Christian living, for with privileges goes family responsibility. As a new community, we are to live by Christ's new standards.	God provides his Holy Spirit to enable us to live his way. To utilize the Spirit's power, we must lay aside our evil desires and draw on the power of his new life. Submit your will to Christ, and seek to love others.

1. Unity in Christ

The Blessings of Redemption

1 Paul, an apostle of Christ Jesus by the will of God,
To the saints who are [1]at Ephesus and *who are* faithful in Christ Jesus:
2 Grace to you and peace from God our Father and the Lord Jesus Christ.

1:1 2 Cor 1:1; Rom 8:1; 1 Cor 1:1; Acts 9:13; Acts 18:19; Col 1:2

1:2 Rom 1:7

1 Three early mss do not contain *at Ephesus*

1:1 Paul wrote this letter to the Ephesian believers and all other believers to give them in-depth teaching about how to nurture and maintain the unity of the church. He wanted to put this important information in written form because he was in prison for preaching the gospel and could not visit the churches himself. The words "at Ephesus" are not present in some early manuscripts; therefore, this was very likely a circular letter—it was first sent to Ephesus and then circulated to neighboring local churches. Paul mentions no particular problems or local situations, and he offers no personal greetings.

1:1 Paul had been a Christian for nearly 30 years. He had taken three missionary trips and established churches all around the Mediterranean Sea. When he wrote Ephesians, Paul was under house arrest in Rome (see Acts 28:16ff). Though a prisoner, he was free to have visitors and write letters. For more information on Paul, see his Profile in Acts 9.

1:1 Ephesus was one of the five major cities in the Roman empire, along with Rome, Corinth, Antioch, and Alexandria. Paul first visited Ephesus on his second missionary journey (Acts 18:19–21). During his third missionary journey, he stayed there for almost three years (Acts 19). Paul later met again with the elders of the Ephesian church at Miletus (Acts 20:16–38). Ephesus was a commercial, political, and religious center for all of Asia Minor. The temple to the Greek goddess Artemis (Diana is her Roman equivalent) was located there.

1:1 "Faithful in Christ Jesus"—what an excellent reputation! Such a label would be an honor for any believer. What would it take for others to characterize you as faithful to Christ Jesus? Hold fast to your faith, one day at a time; faithfully obey God, even in the details of life. Then, like the Ephesians, you will be known as a person who is faithful to the Lord.

1:3
2 Cor 1:3

1:4
Eph 2:10; 2 Thess 2:13f; Matt 25:34; Eph 5:27; Col 1:22; Eph 4:2, 15, 16; 5:2

1:5
Rom 8:14ff; Phil 2:13; Col 1:19

1:6
Eph 1:12, 14; Matt 3:17

3 Blessed *be* the God and Father of our Lord Jesus Christ, who has blessed us with
every spiritual blessing in the heavenly *places* in Christ,
4 just as He chose us in Him before the foundation of the world, that we would be
holy and blameless before [2]Him. In love
5 He predestined us to adoption as sons through Jesus Christ to Himself, according
to the kind intention of His will,
6 to the praise of the glory of His grace, which He freely bestowed on us in the Beloved.

2 Or *Him, in love*

LOCATION OF EPHESUS
Ephesus was a strategic city, ranking in importance with Alexandria in Egypt and Antioch of Syria as a port. It lay on the most western edge of Asia Minor (modern-day Turkey), the most important port on the Aegean Sea on the main route from Rome to the east.

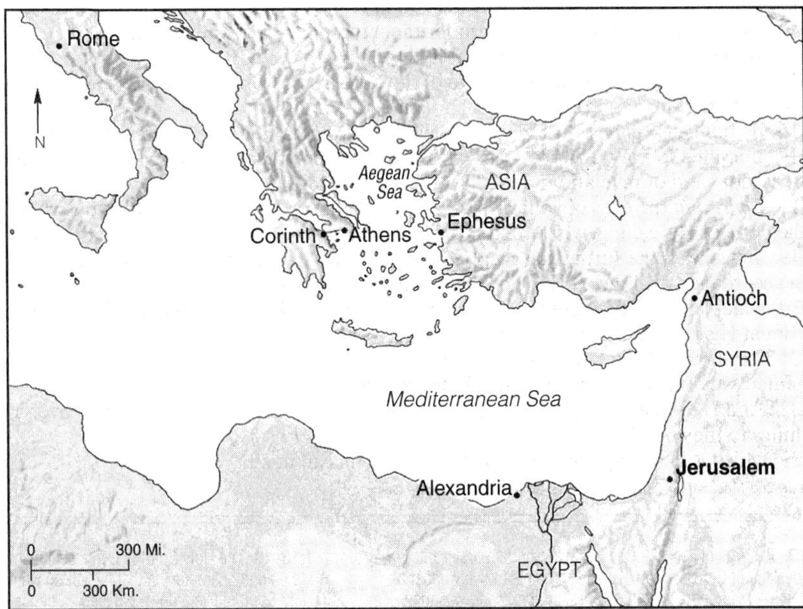

1:3 "Who has blessed us with every spiritual blessing in the heavenly places" means that in Christ we have all the benefits of knowing God—being chosen for salvation, being adopted as his children, forgiveness, insight, the gifts of the Spirit, power to do God's will, the hope of living forever with Christ. Because we have an intimate relationship with Christ, we can enjoy these blessings now. The *heavenly places* means that these blessings are eternal, not temporal. The blessings come from Christ's spiritual realm, not the earthly realm of the goddess Artemis. Other references to the heavenly places in this letter include 1:20; 2:6; 3:10. Such passages reveal Christ in his victorious, exalted role as ruler of all.

1:4 Paul says that God "chose us in Him" to emphasize that salvation depends totally on God. We are not saved because we deserve it, but because God is gracious and freely gives salvation. We did not influence God's decision to save us; he saved us according to his plan. Thus there is no way to take credit for our salvation or to allow room for pride. The mystery of salvation originated in the timeless mind of God long before we existed. It is hard to understand how God could accept us. But because of Christ, we are holy and blameless in his sight. God chose us, and when we belong to him through Jesus Christ, God looks at us as if we had never sinned. All we can do is express our thanks for his wonderful love.

1:5 "Predestined" means marked out beforehand. This is another way of saying that salvation is God's work and not our own doing. In his infinite love, God has adopted us as his own children. Through Jesus' sacrifice, he has brought us into his family and made us heirs along with Jesus (Romans 8:17). In Roman law, adopted children had the same rights and privileges as biological children, even if they had been slaves. Paul uses this term to show how strong our relationship to God is. Have you entered into this loving relationship with God? For more on the meaning of adoption, see Galatians 4:5–7.

1:6 "Freely bestowed on us in the Beloved" means that God graciously accepts us (though we don't deserve it) now that we belong to his dearly loved Son.

7 In Him we have redemption through His blood, the forgiveness of our trespasses,
according to the riches of His grace
8 which He lavished on us. In all wisdom and insight
9 He made known to us the mystery of His will, according to His kind intention which
He purposed in Him
10 with a view to an administration suitable to the fullness of the times, *that is*, the
summing up of all things in Christ, things in the heavens and things on the earth. In Him
11 also we have obtained an inheritance, having been predestined according to His
purpose who works all things after the counsel of His will,
12 to the end that we who were the first to hope in [3]Christ would be to the praise of His
glory.
13 In Him, you also, after listening to the message of truth, the gospel of your salvation—having also believed, you were sealed in Him with the Holy Spirit of promise,
14 who is given as a pledge of our inheritance, with a view to the redemption of *God's*
own possession, to the praise of His glory.
15 For this reason I too, having heard of the faith in the Lord Jesus which *exists* among
you and [4]your love for all the saints,
16 do not cease giving thanks for you, while making mention *of you* in my prayers;
17 that the God of our Lord Jesus Christ, the Father of glory, may give to you a spirit
of wisdom and of revelation in the knowledge of Him.
18 *I pray that* the eyes of your heart may be enlightened, so that you will know what is
the hope of His calling, what are the riches of the glory of His inheritance in the saints,
19 and what is the surpassing greatness of His power toward us who believe. *These are*
in accordance with the working of the strength of His might
20 which He brought about in Christ, when He raised Him from the dead and seated
Him at His right hand in the heavenly *places*,
21 far above all rule and authority and power and dominion, and every name that is
named, not only in this age but also in the one to come.
22 And He put all things in subjection under His feet, and gave Him as head over all
things to the church,
23 which is His body, the fullness of Him who fills all in all.

1:7 Col 1:14; Rom 3:24; 1 Cor 1:30; Eph 1:14; Acts 20:28
1:9 Rom 11:25; Eph 3:3; 1 Cor 1:21; Gal 1:15; Rom 8:28
1:10 Mark 1:15; Phil 2:9f; Col 1:16, 20
1:11 Rom 8:28f; Eph 3:11; Rom 9:11
1:14 2 Cor 1:22
1:15 Col 1:4; Eph 3:18
1:16 Rom 1:8f; Col 1:9
1:17 John 20:17; Rom 15:6; Acts 7:2
1:18 Eph 4:4; Rom 11:29; Eph 1:7; Col 1:12
1:19 Eph 3:7; Col 1:29
1:20 Acts 2:24
1:21 Matt 28:18; Col 1:16; Phil 2:9
1:22 Ps 8:6; Col 1:18
1:23 1 Cor 12:27

3 I.e. the Messiah **4** Three early mss do not contain *your love*

1:7 To speak of Jesus' blood was an important first-century way of speaking of Christ's death. His death points to two wonderful truths—redemption and forgiveness. *Redemption* was the price paid to gain freedom for a slave (Leviticus 25:47–54). Through his death, Jesus paid the price to release us from slavery to sin. *Forgiveness* was granted in Old Testament times on the basis of the shedding of animals' blood (Leviticus 17:11). Now we are forgiven on the basis of the shedding of Jesus' blood—he died as the perfect and final sacrifice. (See also Romans 5:9; Ephesians 2:13; Colossians 1:20; Hebrews 9:22; 1 Peter 1:19.)

1:7–8 Grace is God's voluntary and loving favor given to those he saves. We can't earn salvation, nor do we deserve it. No religious, intellectual, or moral effort can gain it, because it comes only from God's mercy and love. Without God's grace, no person can be saved. To receive it, we must acknowledge that we cannot save ourselves, that only God can save us, and that our only way to receive this loving favor is through faith in Christ.

1:9–10 God was not intentionally keeping his plan ("the mystery of His will") a secret, but his plan for the world could not be fully understood until Christ rose from the dead. His purpose for sending Christ was to unite Jews and Gentiles in one body with Christ as the head. Many people still do not understand God's plan; but when the time is right ("the fullness of the times"), he will bring us together to be with him forever. Then everyone will understand. On that day, all people will bow to Jesus as Lord, either because they love him or because they fear his power (see Philippians 2:10–11).

1:11 God's purpose is to offer salvation to the world, just as he planned to do long ago. God is sovereign; he is in charge. When your life seems chaotic, rest in this truth: Jesus is Lord, and God is in control. God's purpose to save you cannot be thwarted, no matter what evil Satan may bring.

1:13–14 The Holy Spirit is God's seal that we belong to him and his pledge guaranteeing that he will do what he has promised. The Holy Spirit is like a down payment, a deposit, a validating signature on the contract. The presence of the Holy Spirit in us demonstrates the genuineness of our faith, proves that we are God's children, and secures eternal life for us. His power works in us to transform us now, and what we experience now is a taste of the total change we will experience in eternity.

1:16–17 Paul prayed that the Ephesians would know Christ better. Christ is our model, and the more we know of him, the more we will be like him. Study Jesus' life in the Gospels to see what he was like on earth nearly 2,000 years ago, and get to know him in prayer now. Personal knowledge of Christ will change your life.

1:18 The hope we have is not a vague feeling that the future will be positive, but it is complete assurance of certain victory through God. This complete certainty comes to us through the Holy Spirit who is working in us. For more on hope, see Romans 8:23–24; Ephesians 4:4; Colossians 1:5; 1 Thessalonians 1:3; 1 Peter 3:15.

1:19–20 The world fears the power of the atom, yet we belong to the God of the universe who not only created that atomic power but also raised Jesus Christ from the dead. God's incomparably great power is available to help you. There is nothing too difficult for him.

1:20–22 Having been raised from the dead, Christ is now the head of the church, the ultimate authority over the world. Jesus is the Messiah, God's Anointed One, the One Israel longed for, the One who would set their broken world right. As Christians we can be confident that God has won the final victory and is in control of everything. We need not fear any dictator or nation, or even death or Satan himself. The contract has been signed and sealed; we are waiting just a short while for delivery. Paul says, in Romans 8:37–39, that nothing can separate us from God and his love.

2:1 Eph 2:5; Col 2:13
2:2 Eph 1:21; John 12:31; Eph 6:12
2:3 Gal 5:16f; Rom 2:14; Gal 2:15; Rom 5:9; Col 1:21; 2 Pet 2:14; Rom 5:12
2:4 Eph 1:7; John 3:16
2:5 Eph 2:1; Acts 15:11

Made Alive in Christ

2 And you were dead in your trespasses and sins,
2 in which you formerly walked according to the course of this world, according to
the prince of the power of the air, of the spirit that is now working in the sons of disobedience.
3 Among them we too all formerly lived in the lusts of our flesh, indulging the desires
of the flesh and of the mind, and were by nature children of wrath, even as the rest.
4 But God, being rich in mercy, because of His great love with which He loved us,
5 even when we were dead in our transgressions, made us alive together [5]with Christ
(by grace you have been saved),

5 Two early mss read *in Christ*

OUR TRUE IDENTITY IN CHRIST

Romans 3:24	We are justified (declared "not guilty" of sin).
Romans 8:1	No condemnation awaits us.
Romans 8:2	We are set free from the law of sin and death.
1 Corinthians 1:2	We are sanctified and made acceptable in Jesus Christ.
1 Corinthians 1:30	We are righteous and holy in Christ.
1 Corinthians 15:22	We will be made alive at the resurrection.
2 Corinthians 5:17	We are new creatures.
2 Corinthians 5:21	We receive God's righteousness.
Galatians 3:28	We are one in Christ with all other believers.
Ephesians 1:3	We are blessed with every spiritual blessing in Christ.
Ephesians 1:4	We are holy, blameless, and covered with God's love.
Ephesians 1:5–6	We are adopted as God's children.
Ephesians 1:7	Our sins are taken away, and we are forgiven.
Ephesians 1:10–11	We will be brought under Christ's headship.
Ephesians 1:13	We are marked as belonging to God by the Holy Spirit.
Ephesians 2:6	We have been raised up to sit with Christ in glory.
Ephesians 2:10	We are God's work of art.
Ephesians 2:13	We have been brought near to God.
Ephesians 3:6	We share in the promise in Christ.
Ephesians 3:12	We can come with freedom and confidence into God's presence.
Ephesians 5:29–30	We are members of Christ's body, the church.
Colossians 2:10	We have been given fullness in Christ.
Colossians 2:11	We are set free from our sinful nature.
2 Timothy 2:10	We will have eternal glory.

1:22–23 *Fullness* refers to Christ filling the church with gifts and blessings. The church should be the full expression of Christ, who himself fills everything (see 3:19). When reading Ephesians, it is important to remember that it was written primarily to the entire church, not merely to an individual. Christ is the head and we are the body of his church (Paul uses this metaphor in Romans 12:4–5; 1 Corinthians 12:12–27; and Colossians 3:15 as well as throughout the book of Ephesians). The image of the body shows the church's unity. Each member is involved with all the others as they go about doing Christ's work on earth. We should not attempt to work, serve, or worship merely on our own. We need the entire body.

2:2 "The prince of the power of the air" was understood by Paul's readers to mean Satan. They believed that Satan and the evil spiritual forces inhabited the region between earth and sky. Satan is thus pictured as ruling an evil spiritual kingdom—the demons and those who are against Christ. *Satan* means "the accuser." He is also called the devil (4:27). In the resurrection, Christ was victorious over Satan and his power. Therefore, Jesus Christ is the permanent ruler of the whole world; Satan is only the temporary ruler of the part of the world that chooses to follow him.

2:3 The fact that all people, without exception, commit sin proves that without Christ we have a sinful nature. We are lost in sin and cannot save ourselves. Does this mean only Christians do good? Of course not—many people do good to others. On a relative scale, many are moral, kind, and law-abiding. Comparing these people to criminals, we would say that they are very good indeed. But on God's absolute scale, *no one* is good enough to earn salvation ("you were dead in your trespasses and sins," 2:1). Only through being united with Christ's perfect life can we become good in God's sight. "Children of wrath" refers to those who are to receive God's wrath because of their rejection of Christ.

2:4–5 In the previous verses Paul wrote about our old sinful nature (2:1–3). Here Paul emphasizes that we do not need to live any longer under sin's power. The penalty of sin and its power over us were miraculously destroyed by Christ on the cross. Through faith in Christ we stand acquitted, or not guilty, before God (Romans 3:21–22). God does not take us out of the world or make us robots—we will still feel like sinning, and sometimes we will sin. The difference is that before we became Christians, we were dead in sin and were slaves to our sinful nature. But now we are alive with Christ (see also Galatians 2:20).

6 and raised us up with Him, and seated us with Him in the heavenly *places* in Christ
Jesus,
7 so that in the ages to come He might show the surpassing riches of His grace in kindness toward us in Christ Jesus.
8 For by grace you have been saved through faith; and that not of yourselves, *it is* the
gift of God;
9 not as a result of works, so that no one may boast.
10 For we are His workmanship, created in Christ Jesus for good works, which God
prepared beforehand so that we would walk in them.
11 Therefore remember that formerly you, the Gentiles in the flesh, who are called
"Uncircumcision" by the so-called "Circumcision," *which is* performed in the flesh by
human hands—
12 *remember* that you were at that time separate from Christ, excluded from the commonwealth of Israel, and strangers to the covenants of promise, having no hope and
without God in the world.
13 But now in Christ Jesus you who formerly were far off have been brought near by
the blood of Christ.
14 For He Himself is our peace, who made both *groups into* one and broke down the
barrier of the dividing wall,
15 by abolishing in His flesh the enmity, *which is* the Law of commandments *contained*
in ordinances, so that in Himself He might make the two into one new man, *thus* establishing peace,
16 and might reconcile them both in one body to God through the cross, by it having
put to death the enmity.
17 AND HE CAME AND PREACHED PEACE TO YOU WHO WERE FAR AWAY, AND PEACE
TO THOSE WHO WERE NEAR;

2:6 Col 2:12; Eph 1:20
2:7 Rom 2:4; Eph 1:7
2:8 1 Pet 1:5; John 4:10
2:9 1 Cor 1:29
2:10 Col 3:10; Titus 2:14
2:11 Eph 5:8; Rom 2:28f; Col 2:11
2:12 Rom 9:4; Col 1:21; Gal 4:8; 1 Thess 4:5
2:13 Rom 3:25; Col 1:20
2:14 Eph 2:15; Col 3:15
2:15 Eph 2:16; Col 1:21f; 2:14, 20; Gal 3:28; Col 3:10; Is 9:6; Eph 2:14; Col 3:15
2:16 2 Cor 5:18; Col 1:20, 22; 1 Cor 10:17
2:17 Is 57:19; Rom 10:14; Acts 10:36

2:6 Because of Christ's resurrection, we know that our bodies will also be raised from the dead (1 Corinthians 15:2–23) and that we have been given the power to live as Christians now (1:19). These ideas are combined in Paul's image of sitting with Christ in "the heavenly places" (see the note on 1:3). Our eternal life with Christ is certain because we are united in his powerful victory.

2:8–9 When someone gives you a gift, do you say, "That's very nice—now how much do I owe you?" No, the appropriate response to a gift is "Thank you." Yet how often Christians, even after they have been given the gift of salvation, feel obligated to try to work their way to God. Because our salvation and even our faith are gifts, we should respond with gratitude, praise, and joy.

2:8–10 We become Christians through God's unmerited grace, not as the result of any effort, ability, intelligent choice, or act of service on our part. However, out of gratitude for this free gift, we will seek to help and serve others with kindness, love, and gentleness, and not merely to please ourselves. While no action or work we do can help us obtain salvation, God's intention is that our salvation will result in acts of service. We are not saved merely for our own benefit but to serve Christ and build up the church (4:12).

2:10 We are God's workmanship (work of art, masterpiece). Our salvation is something only God can do. It is his powerful, creative work in us. If God considers us his works of art, we dare not treat ourselves or others with disrespect or as inferior work.

2:11–13 Pious Jews ("the Circumcision") considered all non-Jews (the "Uncircumcision") ceremonially unclean. They thought of themselves as pure and clean because of their national heritage and religious ceremonies. Paul pointed out that Jews and Gentiles alike were unclean before God and needed to be cleansed by Christ. In order to realize how great a gift salvation is, we need to remember our former natural, unclean condition. Have you ever felt separate, excluded, hopeless? These verses are for you. No one is alienated from Christ's love or from the body of believers.

2:11–13 Jews and Gentiles alike could be guilty of spiritual pride—Jews for thinking their faith and traditions elevated them above everyone else, Gentiles for trusting in their achievements, power, or position. Spiritual pride blinds us to our own faults and magnifies the faults of others. Be careful not to become proud of your salvation. Instead, humbly thank God for what he has done, and encourage others who might be struggling in their faith.

2:11–16 Before Christ's coming, Gentiles and Jews kept apart from one another. Jews considered Gentiles beyond God's saving power and therefore without hope. Gentiles resented Jewish claims. Christ revealed the total sinfulness of both Jews and Gentiles, and then he offered his salvation to both. Only Christ breaks down the walls of prejudice, reconciles all believers to God, and unifies us in one body.

2:14ff Christ has destroyed the barriers people build between themselves. Because these walls have been removed, we can have real unity with people who are not like us. This is true reconciliation. Because of Christ's death, we are all one (2:14); our hostility against each other has been put to death (2:16); we can all have access to the Father by the Holy Spirit (2:18); we are no longer strangers or aliens to God (2:19); and we are all being built into a holy temple with Christ as our corner stone (2:20–21).

2:14–22 There are many barriers that can divide us from other Christians: age, appearance, intelligence, political persuasion, economic status, race, theological perspective. One of the best ways to stifle Christ's love is to be friendly with only those people that we like. Fortunately, Christ has knocked down the barriers and has unified all believers in one family. His cross should be the focus of our unity. The Holy Spirit helps us look beyond the barriers to the unity we are called to enjoy.

2:15 By his death, Christ ended the angry resentment between Jews and Gentiles, caused by the Jewish laws that favored the Jews and excluded the Gentiles. Christ died to abolish that whole system of Jewish laws. Then he took the two groups that had been opposed to each other and made them parts of himself. "One new man" means that Christ made a single entity or person out of the two. Thus he fused all believers together to become one in himself.

2:17–18 The Jews were near to God because they already knew of him through the Scriptures and worshiped him in their religious ceremonies. The Gentiles were far away because they knew little or

18 for through Him we both have our access in one Spirit to the Father.
19 So then you are no longer strangers and aliens, but you are fellow citizens with the
saints, and are of God's household,
20 having been built on the foundation of the apostles and prophets, Christ Jesus Himself being the corner *stone*,
21 in whom the whole building, being fitted together, is growing into a holy temple in
the Lord,
22 in whom you also are being built together into a dwelling of God in the Spirit.

Paul's Stewardship

3 For this reason I, Paul, the prisoner of Christ Jesus for the sake of you Gentiles—
2 if indeed you have heard of the stewardship of God's grace which was given to
me for you;
3 that by revelation there was made known to me the mystery, as I wrote before in
brief.
4 By referring to this, when you read you can understand my insight into the mystery
of Christ,
5 which in other generations was not made known to the sons of men, as it has now
been revealed to His holy apostles and prophets in the Spirit;
6 *to be specific*, that the Gentiles are fellow heirs and fellow members of the body,
and fellow partakers of the promise in Christ Jesus through the gospel,
7 of which I was made a minister, according to the gift of God's grace which was given
to me according to the working of His power.

2:18 Eph 4:4; Col 1:12

2:19 Phil 3:20; Heb 12:22f; Gal 6:10

2:20 1 Cor 3:10; Rev 21:14; 1 Cor 12:28; Eph 3:5; Luke 20:17

2:22 1 Cor 3:9, 16; 2 Cor 6:16; Eph 3:17

3:1 Acts 23:18

3:3 Rom 11:25; 16:25; Heb 13:22; 1 Pet 5:12

3:4 2 Cor 11:6; Rom 11:25; 16:25

3:5 1 Cor 12:28

3:6 Gal 3:29; Eph 2:16

3:7 Col 1:23, 25; 1 Cor 3:5; Acts 9:15

OUR LIVES BEFORE AND AFTER CHRIST

Before	*After*
Dead in transgressions	Made alive with Christ
Children of wrath	Shown God's mercy and given salvation
Followed the ways of the world	Stand for Christ and truth
God's enemies	God's children
Enslaved to Satan	Free in Christ to love, serve, and sit with him
Followed our evil thoughts and desires	Raised up with Christ to glory

nothing about God. Because neither group could be saved by good deeds, knowledge, or sincerity, both needed to hear about the salvation available through Jesus Christ. Both Jews and Gentiles are now free to come to God through Christ. You have been brought near to him (2:13).

2:19–22 A church building is sometimes called God's house. In reality, God's household is not a building, but a group of people. He lives in us and shows himself to a watching world through us. People can see that God is love and that Christ is Lord as we live in harmony with each other and in accordance with what God says in his Word. We are citizens of God's kingdom and members of his household.

2:20 What does it mean to be built on the foundation of the apostles and prophets? It means that the church is not built on modern ideas, but rather on the spiritual heritage given to us by the early apostles and prophets of the Christian church.

3:1 Paul was under house arrest in Rome for preaching about Christ. The religious leaders in Jerusalem, who felt threatened by Christ's teachings and didn't believe he was the Messiah, pressured the Romans to arrest Paul and bring him to trial for treason and for causing rebellion among the Jews. Paul had appealed for his case to be heard by the emperor, and he was awaiting trial (see Acts 28:16–31). Even though he was under arrest, Paul maintained his firm belief that God was in control of all that happened to him. Do circumstances make you wonder if God has lost control of this world? Like Paul, remember that no matter what happens, God directs the world's affairs.

3:2–3 "The stewardship of God's grace" means the special trust or commitment that Paul had been given. He had been assigned the special work of preaching the Good News to the Gentiles, God's great plan shown to Paul in a revelation. "As I wrote before in brief" may refer to a previous letter that was not preserved by the church, or it may refer to an earlier part of this letter (especially 1:9ff; 2:11ff).

3:5–6 God's plan was hidden from previous generations, not because God wanted to keep something from his people, but because he would reveal it to everyone in his perfect timing. God planned to have Jews and Gentiles comprise one body, the church. It was known in the Old Testament that the Gentiles would receive salvation (Isaiah 49:6); but it was never revealed in the Old Testament that all Gentile and Jewish believers would become equal in the body of Christ. Yet this equality was accomplished when Jesus destroyed the "dividing wall" and created the "one new man" (2:14–15).

3:7 When Paul became a servant of the gospel, God gave him the ability to share effectively the gospel of Christ. You may not be an apostle or even an evangelist, but God will give you opportunities to tell others about Christ. And with the opportunities he will provide the ability, courage, and power. Whenever an opportunity presents itself, make yourself available to God as his servant. As you focus on the other person and his or her needs, God will communicate your caring attitude. Your words will be natural, loving, and compelling.

8 To me, the very least of all saints, this grace was given, to preach to the Gentiles the
unfathomable riches of Christ,
9 and to bring to light what is the administration of the mystery which for ages has
been hidden in God who created all things;
10 so that the manifold wisdom of God might now be made known through the church
to the rulers and the authorities in the heavenly *places.*
11 *This was* in accordance with the eternal purpose which He carried out in Christ Jesus
our Lord,
12 in whom we have boldness and confident access through faith in Him.
13 Therefore I ask you not to lose heart at my tribulations on your behalf, for they are
your glory.
14 For this reason I bow my knees before the Father,
15 from whom every family in heaven and on earth derives its name,
16 that He would grant you, according to the riches of His glory, to be strengthened
with power through His Spirit in the inner man,
17 so that Christ may dwell in your hearts through faith; *and* that you, being rooted
and grounded in love,
18 may be able to comprehend with all the saints what is the breadth and length and
height and depth,
19 and to know the love of Christ which surpasses knowledge, that you may be filled
up to all the fullness of God.
20 Now to Him who is able to do far more abundantly beyond all that we ask or think,
according to the power that works within us,
21 to Him *be* the glory in the church and in Christ Jesus to all generations forever and
ever. Amen.

2. Unity in the body of Christ

Unity of the Spirit

4 Therefore I, the prisoner of the Lord, implore you to walk in a manner worthy of the
calling with which you have been called,

3:8 1 Cor 15:9; Acts 9:15; Rom 2:4
3:9 Col 1:26f; 4:3; Col 3:3; Rev 4:11
3:10 Rom 11:33; 1 Pet 1:12; Eph 1:21; 6:12; Col 2:10, 15
3:11 Eph 1:11; Gal 5:24
3:12 2 Cor 3:4; Heb 4:16; 10:19, 35; 1 John 2:28; 3:21; Eph 2:18
3:13 2 Cor 4:1; Eph 3:1
3:16 1 Cor 16:13; Phil 4:13; Col 1:11; Rom 7:22
3:17 John 14:23; Rom 8:9f; 1 Cor 3:6; Col 2:7; Col 1:23
3:19 Rom 8:35, 39; Phil 4:7; Col 2:10; Eph 1:23
3:20 Rom 16:25; 2 Cor 9:8; Eph 3:7
3:21 Rom 11:36
4:1 Eph 2:10; Col 1:10; 2:6; 1 Thess 2:12

3:8 When Paul describes himself as "the very least of all saints," he means that without God's help, he would never be able to do God's work. Yet God chose him to share the gospel with the Gentiles and gave him the power to do it. If we feel that our role is minor, we may be right—except that we have forgotten what a difference God makes. How does God want to use you? Draw on his power, do your part, and faithfully perform the special role God has called you to play in his plan.

3:9 "The administration of the mystery" refers to the way God's great plan is carried out through the church and to Paul's work to demonstrate and teach God's great purpose in Christ (see 3:2).

3:10 The "rulers and the authorities in the heavenly places" are either angels who are witnesses to these events (see 1 Peter 1:12), or hostile spiritual forces opposed to God (2:2; 6:12).

3:12 It is an awesome privilege to be able to approach God with freedom and confidence. Most of us would be apprehensive in the presence of a powerful ruler. But thanks to Christ, by faith we can enter directly into God's presence through prayer. We know we'll be welcomed with open arms because we are God's children through our union with Christ. Don't be afraid of God. Talk with him about everything. He is waiting to hear from you.

3:13 Why should Paul's suffering make the Ephesians feel honored ("they are your glory")? If Paul had not preached the gospel, he would not be in jail—but then the Ephesians would not have heard the Good News and been converted either. Just as a mother endures the pain of childbirth in order to bring new life into the world, Paul endured the pain of persecution in order to bring new believers to Christ. Obeying Christ is never easy. He calls you to take up your cross and follow him (Matthew 16:24)—that is, to be willing to endure pain so that God's message of salvation can reach the entire world. We should feel honored that others have suffered and sacrificed for us so that we might reap the benefit.

3:14–15 The family of God includes all who have believed in him in the past, all who believe in the present, and all who will believe in the future. We are all a family because we have the same Father. He is the source of all creation, the rightful owner of everything. God promises his love and power to his family, the church (3:16–21). If we want to receive God's blessings, it is important that we stay in contact with other believers in the body of Christ. Those who isolate themselves from God's family and try to go it alone cut themselves off from God's power.

3:17–19 God's love is total, says Paul. It reaches every corner of our experience. It is *wide*—it covers the breadth of our own experience, and it reaches out to the whole world. God's love is *long*—it continues the length of our lives. It is *high*—it rises to the heights of our celebration and elation. His love is *deep*—it reaches to the depths of discouragement, despair, and even death. When you feel shut out or isolated, remember that you can never be lost to God's love. For another prayer about God's immeasurable and inexhaustible love, see Paul's words in Romans 8:38–39.

3:19 "The fullness of God" is fully expressed only in Christ (Colossians 2:9–10). In union with Christ and through his empowering Spirit, we are complete. We have all the fullness of God available to us. But we must appropriate that fullness through faith and through prayer as we daily live for him. Paul's prayer for the Ephesians is also for you. You can ask the Holy Spirit to fill every aspect of your life to the fullest.

3:20–21 This *doxology*—prayer of praise to God—ends Part One of Ephesians. In the first section, Paul described the timeless role of the church. In Part Two (chapters 4—6), he will explain how church members should live in order to bring about the unity God wants. As in most of his books, Paul first lays a doctrinal foundation and then makes practical applications of the truths he has presented.

4:1–2 God has chosen us to be Christ's representatives on earth.

4:2 Col 3:12f; Eph 1:4
4:4 1 Cor 12:4ff; Eph 2:16, 18; Eph 1:18
4:5 1 Cor 8:6
4:6 Rom 11:36
4:7 1 Cor 12:7, 11; Eph 3:2; Rom 12:3
4:8 Ps 68:18; Col 2:15
4:9 John 3:13; Is 44:23
4:10 Eph 1:20f; Heb 4:14
4:11 1 Cor 12:28; Acts 21:8; Acts 13:1

2 with all humility and gentleness, with patience, showing tolerance for one another
in love,
3 being diligent to preserve the unity of the Spirit in the bond of peace.
4 *There is* one body and one Spirit, just as also you were called in one hope of your
calling;
5 one Lord, one faith, one baptism,
6 one God and Father of all who is over all and through all and in all.
7 But to each one of us grace was given according to the measure of Christ's gift.
8 Therefore it says,
"WHEN HE ASCENDED ON HIGH,
HE LED CAPTIVE A HOST OF CAPTIVES,
AND HE GAVE GIFTS TO MEN."
9 (Now this *expression,* "He ascended," what does it mean except that He also had
descended into the lower parts of the earth?
10 He who descended is Himself also He who ascended far above all the heavens, so
that He might fill all things.)
11 And He gave some *as* apostles, and some *as* prophets, and some *as* evangelists, and
some *as* pastors and teachers,

THE ONENESS OF ALL BELIEVERS

Believers are one in:	*Our unity is experienced in:*
Body	The fellowship of believers—the church
Spirit	The Holy Spirit, who activates the fellowship
Hope	That glorious future to which we are all called
Lord	Christ, to whom we all belong
Faith	Our singular commitment to Christ
Baptism	Baptism—the sign of entry into the church
God	God, who is our Father who keeps us for eternity

Too often believers are separated because of minor differences in doctrine. But Paul here shows those areas where Christians must agree to attain true unity. When believers have this unity of spirit, petty differences should never be allowed to dissolve that unity.

In light of this truth, Paul challenges us to live lives worthy of the calling we have received—the awesome privilege of being called Christ's very own. This includes being humble, gentle, patient, understanding, and peaceful. People are watching your life. Can they see Christ in you? How well are you doing as his representative?

4:1–6 "There is one body," says Paul. Unity does not just happen; we have to work at it. Often differences among people can lead to division, but this should not be true in the church. Instead of concentrating on what divides us, we should remember what unites us: *one* body, *one* Spirit, *one* hope, *one* Lord, *one* faith, *one* baptism, *one* God! Have you learned to appreciate people who are different from you? Can you see how their differing gifts and viewpoints can help the church as it does God's work? Learn to enjoy the way we members of Christ's body complement one another. (See 1 Corinthians 12:12–13 for more on this thought.)

4:2 No one is ever going to be perfect here on earth, so we must accept and love other Christians in spite of their faults. When we see faults in fellow believers, we should be patient and gentle. Is there someone whose actions or personality really annoys you? Rather than dwelling on that person's weaknesses or looking for faults, pray for him or her. Then do even more—spend time together and see if you can learn to like him or her.

4:3 To build unity is one of the Holy Spirit's important roles. He leads, but we have to be willing to be led and to do our part to keep the peace. We do that by focusing on God, not on ourselves. For more about who the Holy Spirit is and what he does, see the notes on John 3:6; Acts 1:5; and Ephesians 1:13–14.

4:4–7 All believers in Christ belong to one body; all are united under one head, Christ himself (see 1 Corinthians 12:12–26). Each believer has God-given abilities that can strengthen the whole body. Your special ability may seem small or large, but it is yours to use in God's service. Ask God to use your unique gifts to contribute to the strength and health of the body of believers.

4:6 God is *over all*—this shows his overruling care (transcendence). He is *through all and in all*—this shows his active presence in the world and in the lives of believers (immanence). Any view of God that violates either his transcendence or his immanence does not paint a true picture of God.

4:8 In Psalm 68:18, God is pictured as a conqueror marching to the gates and taking tribute from the fallen city. Paul uses that picture to teach that Christ, in his crucifixion and resurrection, was victorious over Satan. When Christ ascended to heaven, he gave gifts to the church, some of which Paul discusses in 4:11–13.

4:9 The "lower parts of the earth" may be (1) the earth itself (lowly by comparison to heaven), (2) the grave, or (3) Hades (many believe Hades is the resting place of souls between death and resurrection). However we understand it, Christ is Lord of the whole universe, past, present, and future. Nothing or no one is hidden from him. The Lord of all came to earth and faced death to rescue all people. No one is beyond his reach.

4:11–12 Our oneness in Christ does not destroy our individuality. The Holy Spirit has given each Christian special gifts for building up the church. Now that we have these gifts, it is crucial to use them. Are you spiritually mature, exercising the gifts God has given you? If you know what your gifts are, look for opportunities to serve. If you don't know, ask God to show you, perhaps with the help of your minister or Christian friends. Then, as you begin to recognize your special area of service, use your gifts to strengthen and encourage the church.

12 for the equipping of the saints for the work of service, to the building up of the body
of Christ;
13 until we all attain to the unity of the faith, and of the knowledge of the Son of God,
to a mature man, to the measure of the stature which belongs to the fullness of Christ.
14 As a result, we are no longer to be children, tossed here and there by waves and
carried about by every wind of doctrine, by the trickery of men, by craftiness in deceitful
scheming;
15 but speaking the truth in love, we are to grow up in all *aspects* into Him who is the
head, *even* Christ,
16 from whom the whole body, being fitted and held together by what every joint supplies, according to the proper working of each individual part, causes the growth of the
body for the building up of itself in love.

The Christian's Walk

17 So this I say, and affirm together with the Lord, that you walk no longer just as the
Gentiles also walk, in the futility of their mind,
18 being darkened in their understanding, excluded from the life of God because of
the ignorance that is in them, because of the hardness of their heart;
19 and they, having become callous, have given themselves over to sensuality for the
practice of every kind of impurity with greediness.
20 But you did not learn Christ in this way,
21 if indeed you have heard Him and have been taught in Him, just as truth is in Jesus,
22 that, in reference to your former manner of life, you lay aside the old self, which is
being corrupted in accordance with the lusts of deceit,
23 and that you be renewed in the spirit of your mind,
24 and put on the new self, which in *the likeness of* God has been created in righteousness and holiness of the truth.
25 Therefore, laying aside falsehood, SPEAK TRUTH EACH ONE *of you* WITH HIS NEIGH-
BOR, for we are members of one another.
26 BE ANGRY, AND *yet* DO NOT SIN; do not let the sun go down on your anger,

4:12 1 Cor 12:27
4:13 Eph 1:17; Phil 3:10; 1 Cor 14:20; Col 1:28; Heb 5:14
4:14 Jude 12; 1 Cor 3:19; 2 Cor 4:2
4:16 Rom 12:4f; Col 2:19
4:17 Col 2:4; Rom 1:21; 2 Pet 2:18
4:18 Rom 1:21; 1 Cor 2:8; Heb 5:2; 9:7; 1 Pet 1:14
4:19 Rom 1:24; Col 3:5
4:22 Col 3:8; Heb 12:1; James 1:21; 1 Pet 2:1; Rom 6:6
4:23 Rom 12:2
4:24 Rom 13:14; Rom 6:4; 7:6; 12:2; 2 Cor 5:17; Col 3:10
4:25 Col 3:8; Heb 12:1; James 1:21; 1 Pet 2:1; Zech 8:16; Col 3:9; Rom 12:5
4:26 Ps 4:4

4:12–13 God has given his church an enormous responsibility—to make disciples in every nation (Matthew 28:18–20). This involves preaching, teaching, healing, nurturing, giving, administering, building, and many other tasks. If we had to fulfill this command as individuals, we might as well give up without trying—it would be impossible. But God calls us as members of his body. Some of us can do one task; some can do another. Together we can obey God more fully than any of us could alone. It is a human tendency to overestimate what we can do by ourselves and to underestimate what we can do as a group. But as the body of Christ, we can accomplish more together than we would dream possible working by ourselves. Working together, the church can express the fullness of Christ (see the note on 3:19).

4:14–16 Christ is the truth (John 14:6), and the Holy Spirit who guides the church is the Spirit of truth (John 16:13). Satan, by contrast, is the father of lies (John 8:44). As followers of Christ, we must be committed to the truth. This means both that our words should be honest and that our actions should reflect Christ's integrity. Speaking the truth in love is not always easy, convenient, or pleasant, but it is necessary if the church is going to do Christ's work in the world.

4:15–16 Some Christians fear that any mistake will destroy their witness for the Lord. They see their own weaknesses, and they know that many non-Christians seem to have stronger character than they do. How can we grow up into Christ? The answer is that Christ forms us into a body—into a group of individuals who are united in their purpose and in their love for one another and for the Lord. If an individual stumbles, the rest of the group is there to pick him or her up and help him or her walk with God again. If an individual sins, he or she can find restoration through the church (Galatians 6:1) even as the rest of the body continues to witness to God's truth. As part of Christ's body, do you reflect part of Christ's character and carry out your special role in his work?

4:17 Living "in the futility of their mind" refers to the natural tendency of human beings to think their way away from God. Intellectual pride, rationalizations, and excuses all keep people from God. Don't be surprised if people can't grasp the gospel. The gospel will seem foolish to those who forsake faith and rely on their own understanding.

4:17–24 People should be able to see a difference between Christians and non-Christians because of the way Christians live. We are to live as children of Light (5:8). Paul told the Ephesians to leave behind the old life of sin, since they were followers of Christ. Living the Christian life is a process. Although we have a new nature, we don't automatically think all good thoughts and express all right attitudes when we become new people in Christ. But if we keep listening to God, we will be changing all the time. As you look back over last year, do you see a process of change for the better in your thoughts, attitudes, and actions? Although change may be slow, it comes as you trust God to change you. For more about our new nature as believers, see Romans 6:6; 8:9; Galatians 5:16–26; Colossians 3:3–8.

4:22–24 Our old way of life before we believed in Christ is completely in the past. We should put it behind us like old clothes to be thrown away. This is both a once-for-all decision when we decide to accept Christ's gift of salvation (2:8–10) and also a daily conscious commitment. We are not to be driven by desire and impulse. We must put on the new role, head in the new direction, and have the new way of thinking that the Holy Spirit gives.

4:25 Lying to each other disrupts unity by creating conflicts and destroying trust. It tears down relationships and leads to open warfare in a church.

4:26–27 The Bible doesn't tell us that we shouldn't feel angry, but it points out that it is important to handle our anger properly. If vented thoughtlessly, anger can hurt others and destroy relationships. If bottled up inside, it can cause us to become bitter and

4:27 Rom 12:19

4:28 Acts 20:35; 1 Cor 4:12; Gal 6:10; Titus 3:8, 14; Luke 3:11; 1 Thess 4:12

4:29 Matt 12:34; Eph 5:4; Col 3:8

4:30 1 Thess 5:19

4:31 Rom 3:14; Col 3:8, 19; 1 Pet 2:1

4:32 1 Cor 13:4; Col 3:12f; 1 Pet 3:8

5:1 Matt 5:48; Luke 6:36; Eph 4:32

5:2 Rom 14:15; Col 3:14; John 13:34

5:4 Col 3:8; Rom 1:28

5:5 1 Cor 6:9; Col 3:5

5:6 Col 2:8; Rom 1:18

5:8 Eph 2:2; Acts 26:18; Col 1:12f; John 12:36; Rom 13:12

5:9 Gal 5:22; Rom 15:14

5:11 1 Cor 5:9; 2 Cor 6:14; Rom 13:12

27 and do not give the devil an opportunity.
28 He who steals must steal no longer; but rather he must labor, performing with his
own hands what is good, so that he will have *something* to share with one who has need.
29 Let no unwholesome word proceed from your mouth, but only such *a word* as is
good for edification according to the need *of the moment,* so that it will give grace to
those who hear.
30 Do not grieve the Holy Spirit of God, by whom you were sealed for the day of redemption.
31 Let all bitterness and wrath and anger and clamor and slander be put away from
you, along with all malice.
32 Be kind to one another, tender-hearted, forgiving each other, just as God in Christ
also has forgiven [6]you.

Be Imitators of God

5 Therefore be imitators of God, as beloved children;
2 and walk in love, just as Christ also loved [7]you and gave Himself up for us, an
offering and a sacrifice to God as a fragrant aroma.
3 But immorality or any impurity or greed must not even be named among you, as is
proper among saints;
4 and *there must be no* filthiness and silly talk, or coarse jesting, which are not fitting,
but rather giving of thanks.
5 For this you know with certainty, that no immoral or impure person or covetous
man, who is an idolater, has an inheritance in the kingdom of Christ and God.
6 Let no one deceive you with empty words, for because of these things the wrath of
God comes upon the sons of disobedience.
7 Therefore do not be partakers with them;
8 for you were formerly darkness, but now you are Light in the Lord; walk as children
of Light
9 (for the fruit of the Light *consists* in all goodness and righteousness and truth),
10 trying to learn what is pleasing to the Lord.
11 Do not participate in the unfruitful deeds of darkness, but instead even expose them;
12 for it is disgraceful even to speak of the things which are done by them in secret.

6 Two early mss read *us* **7** One early ms reads *us*

---

destroy us from within. Paul tells us to deal with our anger immediately in a way that builds relationships rather than destroys them. If we nurse our anger, we will give Satan an opportunity to divide us. Are you angry with someone right now? What can you do to resolve your differences? Don't let the day end before you begin to work on mending your relationship.

4:28–32 We can grieve the Holy Spirit by the way we live. Paul warns us against unwholesome language, bitterness, improper use of anger, clamor, slander, and bad attitudes toward others. Instead of acting that way, we should be forgiving, just as God has forgiven us. Are you grieving or pleasing God with your attitudes and actions? Act in love toward your brothers and sisters in Christ, just as God acted in love by sending his Son to die for your sins.

4:30 The Holy Spirit within us is a seal or guarantee that we belong to God. For more on this thought, see the note on 1:13–14.

4:32 This is Christ's law of forgiveness as taught in the Gospels (Matthew 6:14–15; 18:35; Mark 11:25). We also see it in the Lord's Prayer—"Forgive us our debts, as we also have forgiven our debtors." God does not forgive us *because* we forgive others, but solely because of his great mercy. As we come to understand his mercy, however, we will want to be like him. Having received forgiveness, we will pass it on to others. Those who are unwilling to forgive have not become one with Christ, who was willing to forgive even those who crucified him (Luke 23:34).

5:1–2 Just as children imitate their parents, so we should imitate Christ. His great love for us led him to sacrifice himself so that we might live. Our love for others should be of the same kind—a love that goes beyond affection to self-sacrificing service.

5:4 Obscenity and coarse joking are so common that we begin to take them for granted. Paul cautions, however, that improper language should have no place in the Christian's conversation because it does not reflect God's gracious presence in us. How can we praise God and remind others of his goodness when we are speaking coarsely?

5:5–7 Paul is not forbidding all contact with unbelievers. Jesus taught his followers to befriend sinners and lead them to him (Luke 5:30–32). Instead, Paul is speaking against condoning the lifestyle of people who make excuses for bad behavior and recommend its practice to others—whether they are in the church or outside of it. Such people can quickly pollute the church and endanger its unity and purpose. We must befriend unbelievers if we are to lead them to Christ, but we must be wary of those who are viciously evil, immoral, or opposed to all that Christianity stands for. Such people are more likely to influence us for evil than we are likely to influence them for good.

5:8 As children of Light, your actions should reflect your faith. You should live above reproach morally so that you will reflect God's goodness to others. Jesus stressed this truth in the Sermon on the Mount (Matthew 5:15–16).

5:10–14 It is important to avoid the "unfruitful deeds of darkness" (any pleasure or activity that results in sin), but we must go even further. Paul instructs us to expose these deeds, because our silence may be interpreted as approval. God needs people who will take a stand for what is right. Christians must lovingly speak out for what is true and right.

13 But all things become visible when they are exposed by the light, for everything that
becomes visible is light.
14 For this reason it says,
"Awake, sleeper,
And arise from the dead,
And Christ will shine on you."
15 Therefore be careful how you walk, not as unwise men but as wise,
16 making the most of your time, because the days are evil.
17 So then do not be foolish, but understand what the will of the Lord is.
18 And do not get drunk with wine, for that is dissipation, but be filled with the Spirit,
19 speaking to one another in psalms and hymns and spiritual songs, singing and making melody with your heart to the Lord;
20 always giving thanks for all things in the name of our Lord Jesus Christ to God, even
the Father;
21 and be subject to one another in the fear of Christ.

Marriage Like Christ and the Church

22 Wives, *be subject* to your own husbands, as to the Lord.
23 For the husband is the head of the wife, as Christ also is the head of the church, He
Himself *being* the Savior of the body.
24 But as the church is subject to Christ, so also the wives *ought to be* to their husbands
in everything.
25 Husbands, love your wives, just as Christ also loved the church and gave Himself up
for her,

5:14 Is 26:19; 51:17; 52:1; 60:1
5:15 Eph 5:2; Col 4:5
5:16 Col 4:5; Gal 1:4
5:17 Rom 12:2; Col 1:9; 1 Thess 4:3
5:18 Rom 13:13; 1 Cor 5:11; 1 Thess 5:7
5:19 Col 3:16; 1 Cor 14:26; Acts 16:25
5:20 Rom 1:8; Col 3:17
5:21 Gal 5:13; Phil 2:3; 1 Pet 5:5; 2 Cor 5:11
5:22 Col 3:18-4:1; 1 Cor 14:34f; Titus 2:5
5:23 1 Cor 11:3; Eph 1:22; 1 Cor 6:13
5:25 Col 3:19; 1 Pet 3:7

5:14 This is not a direct quote from Scripture but was probably taken from a hymn well known to the Ephesians. The hymn seems to have been based on Isaiah 26:19; 51:17; 52:1; 60:1; and Malachi 4:2. Paul was appealing to the Ephesians to wake up and realize the dangerous condition into which some of them had been slipping.

5:15–16 By saying, "the days are evil," Paul was communicating his sense of urgency because of evil's pervasiveness. We need the same sense of urgency because our days are also difficult. We must keep our standards high, act wisely, and do good whenever we can.

5:18 Paul contrasts getting drunk with wine, which produces a temporary "high," to being filled with the Spirit, which produces lasting joy. Getting drunk with wine is associated with the old way of life and its selfish desires. In Christ, we have a better joy, higher and longer lasting, to cure our depression, monotony, or tension. We should not be concerned with how much of the Holy Spirit we have, but how much of us the Holy Spirit has. Submit yourself daily to his leading and draw constantly on his power.

5:20 When you feel down, you may find it difficult to give thanks. Take heart— in all things God works for our good if we love him and are called according to his purpose (Romans 8:28). Thank God, not for your problems, but for the strength he is building in you through the difficult experiences of your life. You can be sure that God's perfect love will see you through.

5:21–22 Being subject (submitting) to another person is an often misunderstood concept. It does not mean becoming a doormat. Christ—at whose name "every knee will bow, of those who are in heaven and on earth and under the earth" (Philippians 2:10)—subjected his will to the Father, and we honor Christ by following his example. When we subject ourselves to God, we become more willing to obey his command to submit to others, that is, to subordinate our rights to theirs. In a marriage relationship, both husband and wife are called to be subject to one another. For the wife, this means willingly following her husband's leadership in Christ. For the husband, it means putting aside his own interests in order to care for his wife. Submission is rarely a problem in homes where both partners have a strong relationship with Christ and where each is concerned for the happiness of the other.

5:22–24 In Paul's day, women, children, and slaves were to submit (be subject) to the head of the family—slaves would submit until they were freed, male children until they grew up, and women and girls their whole lives. Paul emphasized the equality of all believers in Christ (Galatians 3:28), but he did not suggest overthrowing Roman society to achieve it. Instead, he counseled all believers to submit to one another by choice—wives to husbands and also husbands to wives; slaves to masters and also masters to slaves; children to parents and also parents to children. This kind of mutual submission preserves order and harmony in the family while it increases love and respect among family members.

5:22–24 Although some people have distorted Paul's teaching on submission by giving unlimited authority to husbands, we cannot get around it—Paul told wives to submit to their husbands. The fact that a teaching is not popular is no reason to discard it. According to the Bible, the man is the spiritual head of the family, and his wife should acknowledge his leadership. But real spiritual leadership involves service. Just as Christ served the disciples, even to the point of washing their feet, so the husband is to serve his wife. A wise and Christ-honoring husband will not take advantage of his leadership role, and a wise and Christ-honoring wife will not try to undermine her husband's leadership. Either approach causes disunity and friction in marriage.

5:22–28 Why did Paul tell wives to be subject and husbands to love? Perhaps Christian women, newly freed in Christ, found submission difficult; perhaps Christian men, used to the Roman custom of giving unlimited power to the head of the family, were not used to treating their wives with respect and love. Of course both husbands and wives should submit to each other (5:21), just as both should love each other.

5:25ff Some Christians have thought that Paul was negative about marriage because of the counsel he gave in 1 Corinthians 7:32–38. These verses in Ephesians, however, show a high view of marriage. Here marriage is not a practical necessity or a cure for lust, but a picture of the relationship between Christ and his church! Why the apparent difference? Paul's counsel in 1 Corinthians was designed for a state of emergency during a time of persecution and crisis. Paul's counsel to the Ephesians is more the Biblical ideal for marriage. Marriage, for Paul, is a holy union, a living symbol, a precious relationship that needs tender, self-sacrificing care.

26 so that He might sanctify her, having cleansed her by the washing of water with the
word,
27 that He might present to Himself the church in all her glory, having no spot or wrinkle or any such thing; but that she would be holy and blameless.
28 So husbands ought also to love their own wives as their own bodies. He who loves
his own wife loves himself;
29 for no one ever hated his own flesh, but nourishes and cherishes it, just as Christ
also *does* the church,
30 because we are members of His body.
31 FOR THIS REASON A MAN SHALL LEAVE HIS FATHER AND MOTHER AND SHALL BE
JOINED TO HIS WIFE, AND THE TWO SHALL BECOME ONE FLESH.
32 This mystery is great; but I am speaking with reference to Christ and the church.
33 Nevertheless, each individual among you also is to love his own wife even as himself, and the wife must *see to it* that she respects her husband.

Family Relationships

6 Children, obey your parents in the Lord, for this is right.
2 HONOR YOUR FATHER AND MOTHER (which is the first commandment with a
promise),
3 SO THAT IT MAY BE WELL WITH YOU, AND THAT YOU MAY LIVE LONG ON THE
EARTH.
4 Fathers, do not provoke your children to anger, but bring them up in the discipline
and instruction of the Lord.
5 Slaves, be obedient to those who are your masters according to the flesh, with fear
and trembling, in the sincerity of your heart, as to Christ;
6 not by way of eyeservice, as men-pleasers, but as slaves of Christ, doing the will of
God from the heart.
7 With good will render service, as to the Lord, and not to men,

5:26 Titus 2:14; Heb 10:10, 14, 29; 13:12; Titus 3:5; John 15:3; 17:17; Rom 10:8f; Eph 6:17

5:27 2 Cor 4:14; 11:2; Col 1:22; Eph 1:4

5:28 1 Pet 3:7

5:30 1 Cor 6:15; 12:27

5:31 Gen 2:24; Matt 19:5

5:33 1 Pet 3:2, 5f

6:1 Col 3:20

6:2 Ex 20:12; Deut 5:16

6:4 Col 3:21; Deut 6:7

6:5 Col 3:22; 1 Tim 6:1; Titus 2:9; 1 Cor 2:3; Eph 5:22

6:6 Col 3:22; Gal 1:10; 1 Cor 7:22; Mark 3:35

6:7 Col 3:23

5:25–30 Paul devotes twice as many words to telling husbands to love their wives as to telling wives to be subject to their husbands. How should a man love his wife? (1) He should be willing to sacrifice everything for her. (2) He should make her well-being of primary importance. (3) He should care for her as he cares for his own body. No wife needs to fear submitting to a man who treats her in this way.

5:26–27 Christ's death sanctifies and cleanses the church. He cleanses us from the old ways of sin and sets us apart for his special sacred service (Hebrews 10:29; 13:12). Christ cleansed the church by the "washing" of baptism. Through baptism we are prepared for entrance into the church just as ancient Near Eastern brides were prepared for marriage by a ceremonial bath. It is God's Word that cleanses us (John 17:17; Titus 3:5).

5:31–33 The union of husband and wife merges two persons in such a way that little can affect one without also affecting the other. Oneness in marriage does not mean losing your personality in the personality of the other. Instead, it means caring for your spouse as you care for yourself, learning to anticipate his or her needs, helping the other person become all he or she can be. The creation story tells of God's plan that husband and wife should be one (Genesis 2:24), and Jesus also referred to this plan (Matthew 19:4–6).

6:1–2 There is a difference between obeying and honoring. To obey means to do as one is told; to honor means to respect and love. Children are not commanded to disobey God in obeying their parents. Adult children are not asked to be subservient to domineering parents. Children are to obey while under their parents' care, but the responsibility to honor parents is for life.

6:1–4 If our faith in Christ is real, it will usually prove itself at home, in our relationships with those who know us best. Children and parents have a responsibility to each other. Children should honor their parents even if the parents are demanding and unfair. Parents should care gently for their children, even if the children are disobedient and unpleasant. Ideally, of course, Christian parents and Christian children will relate to each other with thoughtfulness and love. This will happen if both parents and children put the others' interests above their own—that is, if they submit to one another.

6:3 Some societies honor their elders. They respect their wisdom, defer to their authority, and pay attention to their comfort and happiness. This is how Christians should act. Where elders are respected, long life is a blessing, not a burden to them.

6:4 The purpose of parental discipline is to help children grow, not to provoke them to anger or discouragement (see also Colossians 3:21). Parenting is not easy—it takes lots of patience to raise children in a loving, Christ-honoring manner. But frustration and anger should not be causes for discipline. Instead, parents should act in love, treating their children as Jesus treats the people he loves. This is vital to children's development and to their understanding of what Christ is like.

6:5 Slaves played a significant part in this society. There were several million of them in the Roman empire at this time. Because many slaves and owners had become Christians, the early church had to deal straightforwardly with the question of master/slave relations. Paul's statement neither condemns nor condones slavery. Instead, it tells masters and slaves how to live together in Christian households. In Paul's day, women, children, and slaves had few rights. In the church, however, they had freedoms that society denied them. Paul tells husbands, parents, and masters to be caring.

6:6–8 Paul's instructions encourage responsibility and integrity on the job. Christian employees should do their jobs as if Jesus Christ were their supervisor. And Christian employers should treat their employees fairly and with respect. Can you be trusted to do your best, even when the boss is not around? Do you work hard and with enthusiasm? Do you treat your employees as people, not machines? Remember that no matter whom you work for, and no matter who works for you, the One you ultimately should want to please is your Father in heaven.

8 knowing that whatever good thing each one does, this he will receive back from the
Lord, whether slave or free.
9 And masters, do the same things to them, and give up threatening, knowing that
both their Master and yours is in heaven, and there is no partiality with Him.

6:8 Col 3:24f; 1 Cor 12:13; Col 3:11
6:9 John 13:13; Col 4:1

The Armor of God

10 Finally, be strong in the Lord and in the strength of His might.
11 Put on the full armor of God, so that you will be able to stand firm against the schemes
of the devil.
12 For our struggle is not against flesh and blood, but against the rulers, against the
powers, against the world forces of this darkness, against the spiritual *forces* of wickedness in the heavenly *places.*
13 Therefore, take up the full armor of God, so that you will be able to resist in the evil
day, and having done everything, to stand firm.
14 Stand firm therefore, HAVING GIRDED YOUR LOINS WITH TRUTH, and HAVING PUT
ON THE BREASTPLATE OF RIGHTEOUSNESS,
15 and having shod YOUR FEET WITH THE PREPARATION OF THE GOSPEL OF PEACE;

6:10 1 Cor 16:13; 2 Tim 2:1; Eph 1:19
6:11 Rom 13:12
6:12 Eph 1:21; 2:2; 3:10; Acts 26:18
6:13 Eph 6:11; James 4:7; Eph 5:16
6:14 Is 11:5; 59:17; Rom 13:12; 1 Thess 5:8
6:15 Is 52:7; Rom 10:15

Piece of Armor	*Use*	*Application*
Belt	Truth	Satan fights with lies, and sometimes his lies *sound* like truth; but only believers have God's truth, which can defeat Satan's lies.
Breastplate	Righteousness	Satan often attacks our hearts—the seat of our emotions, self-worth, and trust. God's righteousness is the breastplate that protects our hearts and ensures his approval. He approves of us because he loves us and sent his Son to die for us.
Footgear	Readiness to spread the Good News	Satan wants us to think that telling the Good News others the Good News is a worthless and hopeless task—the size of the task is too big and the negative responses are too much to handle. But the footgear God gives us is the motivation to continue to proclaim the true peace that is available in God—news everyone needs to hear.
Shield	Faith	What *we* see are Satan's attacks in the form of insults, setbacks, and temptations. But the shield of faith protects us from Satan's flaming arrows. With God's perspective, we can see beyond our circumstances and know that ultimate victory is ours.
Helmet	Salvation	Satan wants to make us doubt God, Jesus, and our salvation. The helmet protects our minds from doubting God's saving work for us.
Sword	The Spirit, the Word of God	The sword is the only weapon of *offense* in this list of armor. There are times when we need to take the offensive against Satan. When we are tempted, we need to trust in the truth of God's Word.

GOD'S ARMOR FOR US
We are engaged in a spiritual battle—all believers find themselves subject to Satan's attacks because they are no longer on Satan's side. Thus, Paul tells us to use every piece of God's armor to resist Satan's attacks and to stand true to God in the midst of those attacks.

6:9 Although Christians may be at different levels in earthly society, we are all equal before God. He does not play favorites; no one is more important than anyone else. Paul's letter to Philemon stresses the same point: Philemon, the master, and Onesimus, his slave, were brothers in Christ.

6:10–17 In the Christian life we battle against rulers and spiritual forces (the powerful evil forces of fallen angels headed by Satan, who is a vicious fighter; see 1 Peter 5:8). To withstand their attacks, we must depend on God's strength and use every piece of his armor. Paul is not only giving this counsel to the church, the body of Christ, but to all individuals within the church. The whole body needs to be armed. As you do battle against "the world forces of this darkness," fight in the strength of the church, whose power comes from the Holy Spirit.

6:12 These who are not "flesh and blood" are demons over whom Satan has control. They are not mere fantasies—they are very real. We face a powerful army whose goal is to defeat Christ's church. When we believe in Christ, these beings become our enemies, and they try every device to turn us away from him and back to sin. Although we are assured of victory, we must engage in the struggle until Christ returns, because Satan is constantly battling against all who are on the Lord's side. We need supernatural power to defeat Satan, and God has provided this by giving us his Holy Spirit within us and his armor surrounding us. If you feel discouraged, remember Jesus' words to Peter: "Upon this rock I will build My church; and the gates of Hades will not overpower it" (Matthew 16:18).

6:16
1 Thess 5:8; Ps 7:13; 120:4; Matt 5:37

6:17
Is 59:17; Is 49:2; Hos 6:5; Heb 4:12

6:18
Phil 4:6; Luke 18:1; Col 1:3; 4:2; 1 Thess 5:17; Rom 8:26f

6:19
Col 4:3; 1 Thess 5:25; 2 Cor 6:11

6:22
Col 4:8; Col 2:2

6:23
Rom 15:33; Gal 6:16; 2 Thess 3:16; 1 Pet 5:14; Gal 5:6; 1 Thess 5:8

16 in addition to all, taking up the shield of faith with which you will be able to extinguish all the flaming arrows of the evil *one.*
17 And take THE HELMET OF SALVATION, and the sword of the Spirit, which is the word
of God.
18 With all prayer and petition pray at all times in the Spirit, and with this in view, be
on the alert with all perseverance and petition for all the saints,
19 and *pray* on my behalf, that utterance may be given to me in the opening of my mouth,
to make known with boldness the mystery of the gospel,
20 for which I am an ambassador in chains; that [8]in *proclaiming* it I may speak boldly,
as I ought to speak.
21 But that you also may know about my circumstances, how I am doing, Tychicus, the
beloved brother and faithful minister in the Lord, will make everything known to you.
22 I have sent him to you for this very purpose, so that you may know about us, and
that he may comfort your hearts.
23 Peace be to the brethren, and love with faith, from God the Father and the Lord
Jesus Christ.
24 Grace be with all those who love our Lord Jesus Christ with incorruptible *love.*

8 Two early mss read *I may speak it boldly*

6:18 How can anyone pray at all times? One way is to make quick, brief prayers your habitual response to every situation you meet throughout the day. Another way is to order your life around God's desires and teachings so that your very life becomes a prayer. You don't have to isolate yourself from other people and from daily work in order to pray constantly. You can make prayer your life and your life a prayer while living in a world that needs God's powerful influence. Praying "for all the saints" means praying for all believers in Christ; so pray for the Christians you know and for the church around the world.

6:19–20 Undiscouraged and undefeated, Paul wrote powerful letters of encouragement from prison. Paul did not ask the Ephesians to pray that his chains would be removed, but that he would continue to speak fearlessly for Christ in spite of them. God can use us in any circumstance to do his will. Even as we pray for a change in our circumstances, we should also pray that God will accomplish his plan through us right where we are. Knowing God's eternal purpose for us will help us through the difficult times.

6:21 Tychicus is also mentioned in Acts 20:4, Colossians 4:7, 2 Timothy 4:12, and Titus 3:12.

6:24 This letter was written to the church at Ephesus, but it was also meant for circulation among other churches. In this letter Paul highlights the supremacy of Christ, gives information on both the nature of the church and on how church members should live, and stresses the unity of all believers—male, female, parent, child, master, slave—regardless of sex, nationality, or social rank. The home and the church are difficult places to live the Christian life, because our real self comes through to those who know us well. Close relationships between imperfect people can lead to trouble—or to increased faith and deepened dependence on God. We can build unity in our churches through willing submission to Christ's leadership and humble service to one another.

PHILIPPIANS

VITAL STATISTICS

PURPOSE:
To thank the Philippians for the gift they had sent Paul and to strengthen these believers by showing them that true joy comes from Jesus Christ alone

AUTHOR:
Paul

TO WHOM WRITTEN:
All the Christians at Philippi, and all believers everywhere

DATE WRITTEN:
Approximately A.D. 61, from Rome during Paul's imprisonment there

SETTING:
Paul and his companions began the church at Philippi on his second missionary journey (Acts 16:11–40). This was the first church established on the European continent. The Philippian church had sent a gift with Epaphroditus (one of their members) to be delivered to Paul (4:18). Paul was in a Roman prison at the time. He wrote this letter to thank them for their gift and to encourage them in their faith.

KEY VERSE:
"Rejoice in the Lord always; again I will say, rejoice!" (4:4).

KEY PEOPLE:
Paul, Timothy, Epaphroditus, Euodia, and Syntyche

KEY PLACE:
Philippi

THE WORD *happiness* evokes visions of unwrapping gifts on Christmas morning, strolling hand in hand with the one you love, being surprised on your birthday, responding with unbridled laughter to a comedian, or vacationing in an exotic locale. Everyone wants to be happy; we make chasing this elusive ideal a lifelong pursuit: spending money, collecting things, and searching for new experiences. But if happiness depends on our circumstances, what happens when the toys rust, loved ones die, health deteriorates, money is stolen, and the party's over? Often happiness flees and despair sets in.

In contrast to *happiness* stands *joy.* Running deeper and stronger, joy is the quiet, confident assurance of God's love and work in our life—that he will be there no matter what! Happiness depends on happenings, but joy depends on Christ.

Philippians is Paul's joy letter. The church in that Macedonian city had been a great encouragement to Paul. The Philippian believers had enjoyed a very special relationship with Paul, so he wrote them a personal expression of his love and affection. They had brought him great joy (4:1). Philippians is also a joyful book because it emphasizes the real joy of the Christian life. The concept of *rejoicing* or *joy* appears sixteen times in four chapters, and the pages radiate this positive message, culminating in the exhortation to "Rejoice in the Lord always; again I will say, rejoice!" (4:4).

In a life dedicated to serving Christ, Paul had faced excruciating poverty, abundant wealth, and everything in between. He even wrote this joyful letter from prison. Whatever the circumstances, Paul had learned to be content (4:11–12), finding real joy as he focused all of his attention and energy on knowing Christ (3:8) and obeying him (3:12–13).

Paul's desire to know Christ above all else is wonderfully expressed in the following words: "I count all things to be loss in view of the surpassing value of knowing Christ Jesus my Lord, for whom I have suffered the loss of all things, and count them but rubbish so that I may gain Christ, and may be found in Him . . . that I may know Him and the power of His resurrection and the fellowship of His sufferings, being conformed to His death" (3:8–10). May we share Paul's aspiration and seek to know Jesus Christ more and more. Rejoice with Paul in Philippians, and rededicate yourself to finding joy in Christ.

THE BLUEPRINT

1. Joy in suffering (1:1–30)
2. Joy in serving (2:1–30)
3. Joy in believing (3:1—4:1)
4. Joy in giving (4:2–23)

Although Paul was writing from prison, joy is a dominant theme in this letter. The secret of his joy is grounded in his relationship with Christ. People today desperately want to be happy but are tossed and turned by daily successes, failures, and inconveniences. Christians are to be joyful in every circumstance, even when things are going badly, even when we feel like complaining, even when no one else is joyful. Christ still reigns, and we still know him, so we can rejoice at all times.

MEGATHEMES

THEME	EXPLANATION	IMPORTANCE
Humility	Christ showed true humility when he laid aside his rights and privileges as God to become human. He poured out his life to pay the penalty we deserve. Laying aside self-interest is essential to all our relationships.	We are to take Christ's attitude in serving others. We must renounce personal recognition and merit. When we give up our self-interest, we can serve with joy, love, and kindness.
Self-sacrifice	Christ suffered and died so we might have eternal life. With courage and faithfulness, Paul sacrificed himself for the ministry. He preached the gospel even while he was in prison.	Christ gives us power to lay aside our personal needs and concerns. To utilize his power, we must imitate those leaders who show self-denying concern for others. We dare not be self-centered.
Unity	In every church, in every generation, there are divisive influences (issues, loyalties, and conflicts). In the midst of hardships, it is easy to turn on one another. Paul encouraged the Philippians to agree with one another, stop complaining, and work together.	As believers, we should not contend with one another but unite against a mutual enemy. When we are unified in love, Christ's strength is most abundant. Keep before you the ideals of teamwork, consideration of others, and unselfishness.
Christian Living	Paul shows us how to live successful Christian lives. We can become mature by being so identified with Christ that his attitude of humility and self-sacrifice becomes ours. Christ is both our source of power and our guide.	Developing our character begins with God's work in us. But growth also requires self-discipline, obedience to God's Word, and concentration on our part.
Joy	Believers can have profound contentment, serenity, and peace no matter what happens. This joy comes from knowing Christ personally and from depending on his strength rather than our own.	We can have joy, even in hardship. Joy does not come from outward circumstances but from inward strength. As Christians, we must not rely on what we have or what we experience to give us joy but on Christ within us.

1. Joy in suffering

Thanksgiving

1 Paul and Timothy, bond-servants of Christ Jesus,
To all the saints in Christ Jesus who are in Philippi, including the overseers and
deacons:
2 Grace to you and peace from God our Father and the Lord Jesus Christ.
3 I thank my God in all my remembrance of you,
4 always offering prayer with joy in my every prayer for you all,
5 in view of your participation in the gospel from the first day until now.
6 *For I am* confident of this very thing, that He who began a good work in you will
perfect it until the day of Christ Jesus.
7 For it is only right for me to feel this way about you all, because I have you in my
heart, since both in my imprisonment and in the defense and confirmation of the gospel,
you all are partakers of grace with me.
8 For God is my witness, how I long for you all with the affection of Christ Jesus.
9 And this I pray, that your love may abound still more and more in real knowledge
and all discernment,

1:3
Rom 1:8

1:5
Acts 2:42; Phil 4:15; Phil 1:7; 2:22; 4:3, 15; Acts 16:12-40; Phil 2:12; 4:15

1:6
1 Cor 1:8; Phil 1:10; 2:16

1:7
2 Pet 1:13; 2 Cor 7:3; Acts 21:33; Eph 6:20; Phil 1:13f, 17; Phil 1:16; Phil 1:5, 12, 16, 27; 2:22; 4:3, 15

1:8
Rom 1:9; Gal 3:26

1:9
1 Thess 3:12; Col 1:9

1:1 This is a personal letter to the Philippians, not intended for general circulation to all the churches as was the letter to the Ephesians. Paul wanted to thank the believers for helping him when he had a need. He also wanted to tell them why he could be full of joy despite his imprisonment and upcoming trial. In this uplifting letter, Paul counseled the Philippians about humility and unity and warned them about potential problems.

1:1 On Paul's first missionary journey, he visited towns close to his headquarters in Antioch of Syria. On his second and third journeys, he traveled even farther. Because of the great distance between the congregations that Paul had founded, he could no longer personally oversee them all. Thus he was compelled to write letters to teach and encourage the believers. Fortunately, Paul had a staff of volunteers (including Timothy, Mark, and Epaphras) who personally delivered these letters and often remained with the congregations for a while to teach and encourage them.

1:1 For more information on Paul, see his Profile in Acts 9. Timothy's Profile is found in 1 Timothy 6.

1:1 The Roman colony of Philippi was located in northern Greece (called Macedonia in Paul's day). Philip II of Macedon (the father of Alexander the Great) took the town from ancient Thrace in about 357 B.C., enlarged and strengthened it, and gave it his name. This thriving commercial center sat at the crossroads between Europe and Asia. In about A.D. 50, Paul, Silas, Timothy, and Luke crossed the Aegean Sea from Asia Minor and landed at Philippi (Acts 16:11–40). The church in Philippi consisted mostly of Gentile (non-Jewish) believers. Because they were not familiar with the Old Testament, Paul did not specifically quote any Old Testament passages in this letter.

1:1 Overseers (bishops or pastors) and deacons led the early Christian churches. The qualifications and duties of the overseers are explained in detail in 1 Timothy 3:1–7 and Titus 1:5–9. The qualifications and duties of deacons are spelled out in 1 Timothy 3:8–13. The saints are all those who believe in Christ.

1:4 This is the first of many times Paul used the word *joy* in his letter. The Philippians were remembered with joy and thanksgiving whenever Paul prayed. By helping Paul, they were helping Christ's cause. The Philippians were willing to be used by God for whatever he wanted them to do. When others think about you, what comes to their minds? Are you remembered with joy by them? Do your acts of kindness lift up others?

1:4–5 The Philippians first heard the gospel about ten years earlier when Paul and his companions visited Philippi (during Paul's second missionary journey) and founded the church there.

1:5 When Paul said that the Philippians had been participating in the gospel, he was pointing out their valuable contribution in spreading God's message. They contributed through their practical help when Paul was in Philippi, and through their financial support when he was in prison. As we help our ministers, missionaries, and evangelists through prayer, hospitality, and financial donations, we become partners with them.

1:6 The God who began a good work in us continues it throughout our lifetime and will finish it when we meet him face-to-face. God's work *for* us began when Christ died on the cross in our place. His work *in* us began when we first believed. Now the Holy Spirit lives in us, enabling us to be more like Christ every day. Paul is describing the process of Christian growth and maturity that began when we accepted Jesus and continues until Christ returns.

1:6 Do you sometimes feel as though you aren't making progress in your spiritual life? When God starts a project, he completes it! As with the Philippians, God will help you grow in grace until he has completed his work in your life. When you are discouraged, remember that God won't give up on you. He promises to finish the work he has begun. When you feel incomplete, unfinished, or distressed by your shortcomings, remember God's promise and provision. Don't let your present condition rob you of the joy of knowing Christ or keep you from growing closer to him.

1:7 When he said "imprisonment," Paul was probably referring to his imprisonment in Philippi, recorded in Acts 16:22–36. In verses 13 and 14, Paul speaks of his Roman imprisonment. Wherever Paul was, even in prison, he faithfully preached the Good News. Remember Paul's inspiring example when hindrances, small or large, slow down your work for God.

1:7–8 Have you ever longed to see a friend with whom you share fond memories? Paul had such a longing to see the Christians at Philippi. His love and affection for them was based not merely on past experiences, but also on the unity that comes when believers draw upon Christ's love. All Christians are part of God's family and thus share equally in the transforming power of his love. Do you feel a deep love for fellow Christians, friends and strangers alike? Let Christ's love motivate you to love other Christians and to express that love in your actions toward them.

1:9 Often the best way to influence someone is to pray for him or her. Paul's prayer for the Philippians was that they would be unified in love. Their love was to result in greater knowledge of Christ and deeper insight (moral discernment). Their love was not based on feelings but on what Christ had done for them. As you grow in Christ's love, your heart and mind must grow together. Is your love and insight growing?

1:10
Rom 2:18; 1 Cor 1:8; Phil 1:6; 2:16

1:11
James 3:18

1:12
Luke 21:13; Phil 1:5, 7, 16, 27; 2:22; 4:3, 15

1:13
Phil 1:7; 2 Tim 2:9; Acts 28:30

1:14
Phil 1:7; 2 Tim 2:9; Acts 4:31; 2 Cor 3:12; 7:4; Phil 1:20

10 so that you may approve the things that are excellent, in order to be sincere and
blameless until the day of Christ;
11 having been filled with the fruit of righteousness which *comes* through Jesus Christ,
to the glory and praise of God.

The Gospel Is Preached

12 Now I want you to know, brethren, that my circumstances have turned out for the
greater progress of the gospel,
13 so that my imprisonment in *the cause of* Christ has become well known throughout
the whole [1]praetorian guard and to everyone else,
14 and that most of the brethren, trusting in the Lord because of my imprisonment,
have far more courage to speak the word of God without fear.

1 Or *governor's palace*

LOCATION OF PHILIPPI
Philippi sat on the Egnatian Way, the main transportation route in Macedonia, an extension of the Appian Way, which joined the eastern empire with Italy.

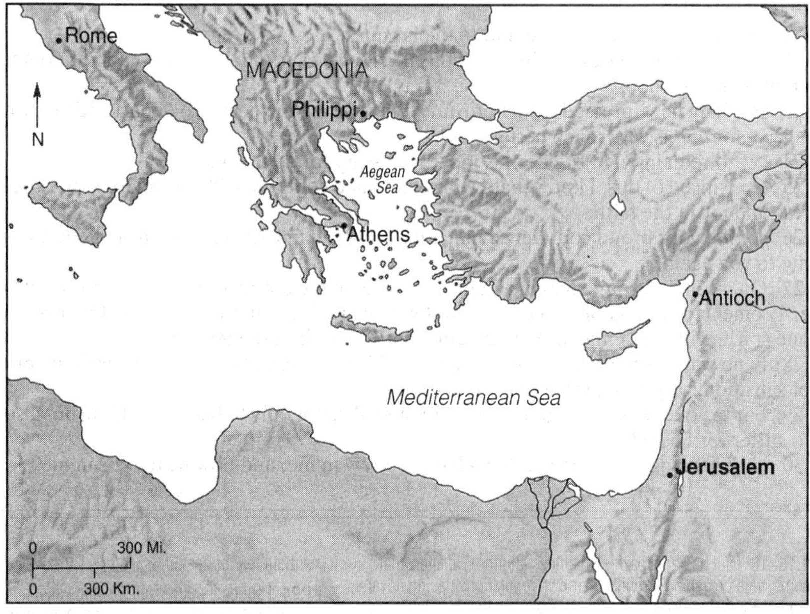

1:10 Paul prayed that the Philippian believers would "approve the things that are excellent"—in other words, that they would have the ability to differentiate between right and wrong, good and bad, vital and trivial. We ought to pray for moral discernment so we can maintain our Christian morals and values. Hebrews 5:14 emphasizes the need for discernment.

1:10 The "day of Christ" refers to the time when God will judge the world through Jesus Christ. We should live each day as though he could return at any moment.

1:11 The "fruit of righteousness" includes all of the character traits flowing from a right relationship with God. There is no other way for us to gain this fruit of righteousness than through Christ. See Galatians 5:22–23 for the "fruit of the Spirit."

1:12–14 Being imprisoned would cause many people to become bitter or to give up, but Paul saw it as one more opportunity to spread the Good News of Christ. Paul realized that his current circumstances weren't as important as what he did with them. Turning a bad situation into a good one, he reached out to the Roman soldiers who made up the palace guard and encouraged those Christians who were afraid of persecution. We may not be in prison, but we still have plenty of opportunities to be discouraged—times of indecision, financial burdens, family conflict, church conflict, or the loss of our jobs. How we act in such situations will reflect what we believe. Like Paul, look for ways to demonstrate your faith even in bad situations. Whether or not the situation improves, your faith will grow stronger.

1:13 How did Paul end up in a Roman prison? While he was visiting Jerusalem, some Jews had him arrested for preaching the gospel, but he appealed to Caesar to hear his case (Acts 21:15—25:12). He was then escorted by soldiers to Rome, where he was placed under house arrest while awaiting trial—not a trial for breaking civil law, but for proclaiming the Good News of Christ. At that time, the Roman authorities did not consider this to be a serious charge. A few years later, however, Rome would take a different view of Christianity and make every effort to stamp it out of existence. Paul's house arrest allowed him some degree of freedom. He could have visitors, continue to preach, and write letters such as this one. A brief record of Paul's time in Rome is found in Acts 28:11–31. The "whole praetorian guard" refers to the elite troops housed in the emperor's palace.

1:14 When we speak the word of God without fear, or live faithfully for him during difficult situations, we encourage others to do the same. Be an encouragement by the way that you live.

15 Some, to be sure, are preaching Christ even from envy and strife, but some also from
good will;
16 the latter *do it* out of love, knowing that I am appointed for the defense of the
gospel;
17 the former proclaim Christ out of selfish ambition rather than from pure motives,
thinking to cause me distress in my imprisonment.
18 What then? Only that in every way, whether in pretense or in truth, Christ is proclaimed; and in this I rejoice.
Yes, and I will rejoice,
19 for I know that this will turn out for my deliverance through your prayers and the
provision of the Spirit of Jesus Christ,
20 according to my earnest expectation and hope, that I will not be put to shame in
anything, but *that* with all boldness, Christ will even now, as always, be exalted in my body, whether by life or by death.

1:15 2 Cor 11:13
1:16 Phil 2:22; 4:3, 15
1:17 Rom 2:8; 2 Tim 2:9
1:19 2 Cor 1:11; Acts 16:7
1:20 Rom 8:19; Rom 5:5; 1 Pet 4:16; Acts 4:31; 2 Cor 3:12; 7:4; Phil 1:14; 1 Cor 6:20; Rom 14:8
1:21 Gal 2:20
1:22 Rom 1:13
1:23 2 Cor 5:8; 2 Tim 4:6; John 12:26
1:25 Phil 2:24
1:26 2 Cor 5:12; 7:4; Phil 2:16
1:27 Eph 4:1; Phil 1:5; 1 Cor 16:13; Phil 4:1; Acts 4:32; Jude 3
1:28 2 Thess 1:5
1:29 Matt 5:11, 12; Acts 14:22
1:30 Col 1:29; 2:1; 1 Thess 2:2; 1 Tim 6:12; 2 Tim 4:7

To Live Is Christ

21 For to me, to live is Christ and to die is gain.
22 But if *I am* to live *on* in the flesh, this *will mean* fruitful labor for me; and I do not
know which to choose.
23 But I am hard-pressed from both *directions,* having the desire to depart and be with
Christ, for *that* is very much better;
24 yet to remain on in the flesh is more necessary for your sake.
25 Convinced of this, I know that I will remain and continue with you all for your progress and joy in the faith,
26 so that your proud confidence in me may abound in Christ Jesus through my coming to you again.
27 Only conduct yourselves in a manner worthy of the gospel of Christ, so that whether I come and see you or remain absent, I will hear of you that you are standing firm in one spirit, with one mind striving together for the faith of the gospel;
28 in no way alarmed by *your* opponents—which is a sign of destruction for them, but
of salvation for you, and that *too,* from God.
29 For to you it has been granted for Christ's sake, not only to believe in Him, but also
to suffer for His sake,
30 experiencing the same conflict which you saw in me, and now hear *to be* in me.

1:15–18 Paul had an amazingly selfless attitude. He knew that some were preaching to build their own reputations, taking advantage of Paul's imprisonment to try to make a name for themselves. Regardless of the motives of these preachers, Paul rejoiced that the gospel was being preached. Some Christians serve for the wrong reasons. Paul wouldn't condone, nor does God excuse, their motives, but we should be glad if God uses their message, regardless of their motives.

1:19–21 This was not Paul's final imprisonment in Rome. But he didn't know that. Awaiting trial, he knew he could either be released or executed. However, he trusted Christ to work it out for his deliverance. Paul's prayer was that when he stood trial, he would speak courageously for Christ and not be timid or ashamed. Whether he lived or died, he wanted to exalt Christ. As it turned out, he was released from this imprisonment but arrested again two or three years later. Only faith in Christ could sustain Paul in such adversity.

1:20–21 To those who don't believe in God, life on earth is all there is, and so it is natural for them to strive for this world's values—money, popularity, power, pleasure, and prestige. For Paul, however, to live meant to develop eternal values and to tell others about Christ, who alone could help them see life from an eternal perspective. Paul's whole purpose in life was to speak out boldly for Christ and to become more like him. Thus Paul could confidently say that dying would be even better than living, because in death he would be removed from worldly troubles, and he would see Christ face-to-face (1 John 3:2–3). If you're not ready to die, then you're not ready to live. Make certain of your eternal destiny; then you will be free to serve—devoting your life to what really counts, without fear of death.

1:24 Paul had a purpose for living when he served the Philippians and others. We also need a purpose for living that goes beyond providing for our own physical needs. Whom can you serve or help? What is your purpose for living?

1:27 Paul encourages the believers to be unified, as they are "standing firm in one spirit, with one mind striving together for the faith of the gospel." How sad that much time and effort is lost in some churches by fighting against one another instead of uniting against the real opposition! It takes a courageous church to resist in-fighting and to maintain the common purpose of serving Christ.

1:29 Paul considered it a privilege to suffer for Christ. We do not by nature consider suffering a privilege. Yet when we suffer, if we faithfully represent Christ, our message and example affect us and others for good (see Acts 5:41). Suffering has these additional benefits: (1) It takes our eyes off of earthly comforts; (2) it weeds out superficial believers; (3) it strengthens the faith of those who endure; (4) it serves as an example to others who may follow us. When we suffer for our faith, it doesn't mean that we have done something wrong. In fact, the opposite is often true—it verifies that we have been faithful. Use suffering to build your character. Don't resent it or let it tear you down.

1:30 Throughout his life Paul suffered for spreading the gospel. Like the Philippians, we are in conflict with anyone who would discredit the saving message of Christ. All true believers are in this fight together, uniting against the same enemy for a common cause.

2:1 2 Cor 13:14; Col 3:12

2:2 Rom 12:16; Phil 4:2

2:3 Gal 5:26; Rom 12:10; Eph 5:21

2:4 Rom 15:1f

2:5 Matt 11:29

2:6 John 1:1; John 5:18; 10:33; 14:28

2:7 2 Cor 8:9; Matt 20:28; John 1:14; Rom 8:3; Gal 4:4; Heb 2:17

2:8 2 Cor 8:9; Matt 26:39; John 10:18; Rom 5:19; Heb 5:8

2. Joy in serving

Be Like Christ

2 Therefore if there is any encouragement in Christ, if there is any consolation of love,
if there is any fellowship of the Spirit, if any affection and compassion,
2 make my joy complete by being of the same mind, maintaining the same love, united in spirit, intent on one purpose.
3 Do nothing from selfishness or empty conceit, but with humility of mind regard one
another as more important than yourselves;
4 do not *merely* look out for your own personal interests, but also for the interests of
others.
5 Have this attitude in yourselves which was also in Christ Jesus,
6 who, although He existed in the form of God, did not regard equality with God a
thing to be grasped,
7 but [2]emptied Himself, taking the form of a bond-servant, *and* being made in the
likeness of men.
8 Being found in appearance as a man, He humbled Himself by becoming obedient
to the point of death, even death on a cross.

2 I.e. laid aside His privileges

2:1–5 Many people—even Christians—live only to make a good impression on others or to please themselves. But "selfishness or empty conceit" brings discord. Paul therefore stressed spiritual unity, asking the Philippians to love one another and to be one in spirit and purpose. When we work together, caring for the problems of others as if they were our problems, we demonstrate Christ's example of putting others first, and we experience unity. Don't be so concerned about making a good impression or meeting your own needs that you strain relationships in God's family.

2:3 Selfishness can ruin a church, but genuine humility can build it. Being humble involves having a true perspective about ourselves (see Romans 12:3). It does not mean that we should put ourselves down. Before God, we are sinners, saved only by God's grace, but we *are* saved and therefore have great worth in God's kingdom. We are to lay aside selfishness and treat others with respect and common courtesy. Considering others' interests as more important than our own links us with Christ, who was a true example of humility.

2:4 Philippi was a cosmopolitan city. The composition of the church reflected great diversity, with people from a variety of backgrounds and walks of life. Acts 16 gives us some indication of the diverse makeup of this church. The church included Lydia, a Jewish convert from Asia and a wealthy businesswoman (Acts 16:14); the slave girl (Acts 16:16–17), probably a native Greek; and the jailer serving this colony of the empire, probably a Roman (Acts 16:25–36). With so many different backgrounds among the members, unity must have been difficult to maintain. Although there is no evidence of division in the church, its unity had to be safeguarded (3:2; 4:2). Paul encourages us to guard against any selfishness, prejudice, or jealousy that might lead to dissension. Showing genuine interest in others is a positive step forward in maintaining unity among believers.

2:5 Jesus Christ was humble, willing to give up his rights in order to obey God and serve people. Like Christ, we should have a servant's attitude, serving out of love for God and for others, not out of guilt or fear. Remember, you can choose your attitude. You can approach life expecting to be served, or you can look for opportunities to serve others. See Mark 10:45 for more on Christ's attitude of servanthood.

2:5–7 The *incarnation* was the act of the preexistent Son of God voluntarily assuming a human body and human nature. Without ceasing to be God, he became a human being, the man called Jesus. He did not give up his deity to become human, but he set aside the right to his glory and power. In submission to the Father's will, Christ limited his power and knowledge. Jesus of Nazareth was subject to place, time, and many other human limitations. What made his humanity unique was his freedom from sin. In his full humanity, Jesus showed us everything about God's character that can be conveyed in human terms. The incarnation is explained further in these passages: John 1:1–14; Romans 1:2–5; 2 Corinthians 8:9; 1 Timothy 3:16; Hebrews 2:14; and 1 John 1:1–3.

2:5–11 These verses are probably from a hymn sung by the early Christian church. The passage holds many parallels to the prophecy of the suffering servant in Isaiah 53. As a hymn, it was not meant to be a complete statement about the nature and work of Christ. Several key characteristics of Jesus Christ, however, are praised in this passage: (1) Christ has always existed with God; (2) Christ is equal to God because he *is* God (John 1:1ff; Colossians 1:15–19); (3) though Christ is God, he became a man in order to fulfill God's plan of salvation for all people; (4) Christ did not just have the appearance of being a man—he actually became human to identify with our sins; (5) Christ voluntarily laid aside his divine rights and privileges out of love for his Father; (6) Christ died on the cross for our sins so we wouldn't have to face eternal death; (7) God glorified Christ because of his obedience; (8) God raised Christ to his original position at the Father's right hand, where he will reign forever as our Lord and Judge. How can we do anything less than praise Christ as our Lord and dedicate ourselves to his service!

2:5–11 Often people excuse selfishness, pride, or evil by claiming their rights. They think, "I can cheat on this test; after all, I deserve to pass this class," or "I can spend all this money on myself—I worked hard for it," or "I can get an abortion; I have a right to control my own body." But as believers, we should have a different attitude, one that enables us to lay aside our rights in order to serve others. If we say we follow Christ, we must also say we want to live as he lived. We should develop his attitude of humility as we serve, even when we are not likely to get recognition for our efforts. Are you selfishly clinging to your rights, or are you willing to serve?

2:8 Death on a cross (crucifixion) was the form of capital punishment that Romans used for notorious criminals. It was excruciatingly painful and humiliating. Prisoners were nailed or tied to a cross and left to die. Death might not come for several days, and it usually came by suffocation when the weight of the weakened body made breathing more and more difficult. Jesus died as One who was cursed (Galatians 3:13). How amazing that the perfect man should die this most shameful death so that we would not have to face eternal punishment!

9 For this reason also, God highly exalted Him, and bestowed on Him the name which
is above every name,
10 so that at the name of Jesus EVERY KNEE WILL BOW, of those who are in heaven and
on earth and under the earth,
11 and that every tongue will confess that Jesus Christ is Lord, to the glory of God the
Father.
12 So then, my beloved, just as you have always obeyed, not as in my presence only,
but now much more in my absence, work out your salvation with fear and trembling;
13 for it is God who is at work in you, both to will and to work for *His* good pleasure.
14 Do all things without grumbling or disputing;
15 so that you will prove yourselves to be blameless and innocent, children of God above
reproach in the midst of a crooked and perverse generation, among whom you appear
as lights in the world,
16 holding fast the word of life, so that in the day of Christ I will have reason to glory
because I did not run in vain nor toil in vain.
17 But even if I am being poured out as a drink offering upon the sacrifice and service
of your faith, I rejoice and share my joy with you all.
18 You too, *I urge you,* rejoice in the same way and share your joy with me.

Timothy and Epaphroditus

19 But I hope in the Lord Jesus to send Timothy to you shortly, so that I also may be
encouraged when I learn of your condition.
20 For I have no one *else* of kindred spirit who will genuinely be concerned for your
welfare.
21 For they all seek after their own interests, not those of Christ Jesus.
22 But you know of his proven worth, that he served with me in the furtherance of the
gospel like a child *serving* his father.
23 Therefore I hope to send him immediately, as soon as I see how things *go* with me;

2:9 Heb 1:9; Matt 28:18; Acts 2:33; Heb 2:9; Eph 1:21

2:10 Is 45:23; Rom 14:11; Eph 1:10

2:11 John 13:13; Rom 10:9; 14:9

2:12 Phil 1:5, 6; 4:15; Heb 5:9; 2 Cor 7:15

2:13 Rom 12:3; 1 Cor 12:6; 15:10; Heb 13:21; Eph 1:5

2:14 1 Cor 10:10; 1 Pet 4:9

2:15 Matt 5:45; Eph 5:1; Matt 5:14-16

2:16 Phil 1:6; Gal 2:2; Is 49:4; Gal 4:11; 1 Thess 3:5

2:17 2 Cor 12:15; 2 Tim 4:6; Num 28:6, 7; Rom 15:16

2:20 1 Cor 16:10; 2 Tim 3:10

2:21 1 Cor 10:24

2:9–11 At the last judgment even those who are condemned will recognize Jesus' authority and right to rule. People can choose to regard Jesus as Lord now as a step of willing and loving commitment, or be forced to acknowledge him as Lord when he returns. Christ may return at any moment. Are you prepared to meet him?

2:12 The words *so then* tie this verse to the previous section. "Work out your salvation," in light of the preceding exhortation to unity, may mean that the entire church was to work together to rid themselves of divisions and discord. The Philippian Christians needed to be especially careful to obey Christ, now that Paul wasn't there to continually remind them about what was right. We too must be careful about what we believe and how we live, especially when we are on our own. In the absence of cherished Christian leaders, we must focus our attention and devotion even more on Christ so that we won't be sidetracked.

2:13 What do we do when we don't feel like obeying? God has not left us alone in our struggles to do his will. He wants to come alongside us and be within us to help. God helps us *want* to obey him and then gives us the *power* to do what he wants. The secret to a changed life is to submit to God's control and let him work. Next time, ask God to help you *want* to do his will.

2:13 To be like Christ, we must train ourselves to think like Christ. To change our desires to be more like Christ's, we need the power of the indwelling Spirit (1:19), the influence of faithful Christians, obedience to God's Word (not just exposure to it), and sacrificial service. Often it is in *doing* God's will that we gain the *desire* to do it (see 4:8–9). Do what he wants and trust him to change your desires.

2:14–16 Why are complaining and arguing so harmful? If all that people know about a church is that its members constantly argue, complain, and gossip, they get a false impression of Christ and the gospel. Belief in Christ should unite those who trust him. If your church is always complaining and arguing, it lacks the unifying power of Jesus Christ. Stop arguing with other Christians or complaining about people and conditions within the church and let the world see Christ.

2:14–16 Our lives should be characterized by moral purity, patience, and peacefulness, so that we will be "lights" in a dark and depraved world. A transformed life is an effective witness to the power of God's Word. Are you shining brightly, or are you clouded by complaining and arguing? Shine out for God.

2:17 The drink offering was an important part of the sacrificial system of the Jews (for an explanation, see Numbers 28:7). Because this church had little Jewish background, the drink offering may refer to the wine poured out to pagan deities prior to important public events. Paul regarded his life as a sacrifice.

2:17 Even if he had to die, Paul was content, knowing that he had helped the Philippians live for Christ. When you're totally committed to serving Christ, sacrificing to build the faith of others brings a joyous reward.

2:19 Timothy was with Paul in Rome when Paul wrote this letter. He traveled with Paul on his second missionary journey when the church at Philippi was begun. For more information on Timothy, see his Profile in 1 Timothy .

2:21 Paul observed that most believers are too preoccupied with their own needs to spend time working for Christ. Don't let your schedule and concerns crowd out your Christian service to and love for others.

2:22 Just as a skilled workman trains an apprentice, Paul was preparing Timothy to carry on the ministry in his absence. Who are you apprenticing for God's work? For more information, see Timothy's Profile in 1 Timothy .

2:23 Paul was in prison (either awaiting his trial or its verdict) for preaching about Christ. He was telling the Philippians that when he learned of the court's decision, he would send Timothy to them with the news and that he was ready to accept whatever came (1:21–26).

2:24 Phil 1:25

2:25 Phil 4:18; Rom 16:3, 9, 21; Phil 4:3; Philem 1, 24; 2; John 13:16; 2 Cor 8:23

2:29 Rom 16:2; 1 Cor 16:18

2:30 Acts 20:24; 1 Cor 16:17; Phil 4:10

3:1 Phil 2:18; 4:4

3:2 Ps 22:16, 20; Gal 5:15; Rev 22:15; 2 Cor 11:13

3:3 Rom 2:29; 9:6; Gal 6:15; Gal 5:25; Rom 15:17; Gal 6:14; Rom 8:39; Phil 1:1; 3:12

24 and I trust in the Lord that I myself also will be coming shortly.
25 But I thought it necessary to send to you Epaphroditus, my brother and fellow worker
and fellow soldier, who is also your messenger and minister to my need;
26 because he was longing [3]for you all and was distressed because you had heard that
he was sick.
27 For indeed he was sick to the point of death, but God had mercy on him, and not on
him only but also on me, so that I would not have sorrow upon sorrow.
28 Therefore I have sent him all the more eagerly so that when you see him again you
may rejoice and I may be less concerned *about you.*
29 Receive him then in the Lord with all joy, and hold men like him in high regard;
30 because he came close to death for the work of Christ, risking his life to complete
what was deficient in your service to me.

3. Joy in believing

The Goal of Life

3 Finally, my brethren, rejoice in the Lord. To write the same things *again* is no trouble to me, and it is a safeguard for you.
2 Beware of the dogs, beware of the evil workers, beware of the false circumcision;
3 for we are the *true* circumcision, who worship in the Spirit of God and glory in Christ
Jesus and put no confidence in the flesh,

3 One early ms reads *to see you all*

THREE STAGES OF PERFECTION

1. Perfect Relationship	We are perfect because of our eternal union with the infinitely perfect Christ. When we become his children, we are declared "not guilty," and thus righteous, because of what Christ, God's beloved Son, has done for us. This perfection is absolute and unchangeable, and it is this perfect relationship that guarantees that we will one day be "completely perfect" (below). See Colossians 2:8–10; Hebrews 10:8–14.
2. Perfect Progress	We can grow and mature spiritually as we continue to trust Christ, learn more about him, draw closer to him, and obey him. Our progress is changeable (in contrast to our relation ship, above) because it depends on our daily walk—at times in life we mature more than at other times. But we are growing toward perfection if we "press on" (Philippians 3:12). These good deeds do not perfect us; rather, as God perfects us, we do good deeds for him. See Philippians 3:1–15.
3. Completely Perfect	When Christ returns to take us into his eternal kingdom, we will be glorified and made completely perfect. See Philippians 3:20–21.

All phases of perfection are grounded in faith in Christ and what he has done, not what we can do for him. We cannot perfect ourselves; only God can work in and through us to "perfect it until the day of Christ Jesus" (1:6).

2:25 Epaphroditus delivered money from the Philippians to Paul; then he returned with this thank-you letter to Philippi. Epaphroditus may have been an elder in Philippi (2:25–30; 4:18) who, while staying with Paul, became ill (2:27, 30). After Epaphroditus recovered, he returned home. He is mentioned only in Philippians.

2:29–30 The world honors those who are intelligent, beautiful, rich, and powerful. What kind of people should the church honor? Paul indicates that we should honor those who give their lives for the sake of Christ, going where we cannot go ourselves. Our missionaries do that for us today by providing ministry where we are not able to go.

3:1 As a safeguard, Paul reviewed the basics with these believers. The Bible is our safeguard both morally and theologically. When we read it individually and publicly in church, it alerts us to corrections we need to make in our thoughts, attitudes, and actions.

3:2–3 These "dogs" and "evil workers" were very likely *Judaizers*—Jewish Christians who wrongly believed that it was essential for Gentiles to follow all the Old Testament Jewish laws, especially submission to the rite of circumcision, in order to receive salvation. Many Judaizers were motivated by spiritual pride. Because they had invested so much time and effort in keeping their laws, they couldn't accept the fact that all their efforts couldn't bring them a step closer to salvation.

Paul criticized the Judaizers because they looked at Christianity backwards—thinking that what they *did* (*circumcision*—cutting or mutilating the flesh) made them believers rather than the free gift of grace given by Christ. What believers do is a *result* of faith, not a *prerequisite* to faith. This had been confirmed by the early church leaders at the Jerusalem council 11 years earlier (Acts 15). Who are the Judaizers of our day? They are those who say that people must add something else to simple faith. No person should add anything to Christ's offer of salvation by grace through faith.

3:2–3 It is easy to place more emphasis on religious effort ("confidence in the flesh") than on internal faith, but God values the attitude of our hearts above all else. Don't judge people's spirituality by their fulfillment of duties or by their level of human activity. And don't think that you will satisfy God by feverishly doing his work. God notices all you do for him and will reward you for it, but only if it comes as a loving response to his free gift of salvation.

4 although I myself might have confidence even in the flesh. If anyone else has a mind
to put confidence in the flesh, I far more:
5 circumcised the eighth day, of the nation of Israel, of the tribe of Benjamin, a Hebrew of Hebrews; as to the Law, a Pharisee;
6 as to zeal, a persecutor of the church; as to the righteousness which is in the Law,
found blameless.
7 But whatever things were gain to me, those things I have counted as loss for the
sake of Christ.
8 More than that, I count all things to be loss in view of the surpassing value of knowing Christ Jesus my Lord, for whom I have suffered the loss of all things, and count them
but rubbish so that I may gain Christ,

3:4 2 Cor 5:16; 11:18

3:5 Luke 1:59; Rom 11:1; 2 Cor 11:22; Rom 11:1; Acts 22:3; 23:6; 26:5

3:6 Acts 8:3; 22:4, 5; 26:9-11; Phil 2:15

3:7 Luke 14:33

3:8 2 Pet 1:3; Rom 8:39; Phil 1:1; 3:12

TRAINING FOR THE CHRISTIAN LIFE

As a great amount of training is needed for athletic activities, so we must train diligently for the Christian life. Such training takes time, dedication, energy, continued practice, and vision. We must all commit ourselves to the Christian life, but we must first know the rules as prescribed in God's Word (2 Timothy 2:5).

Reference	*Metaphors*	*Training*	*Our Goal as Believers*
1 Corinthians 9:24–27	Race	Go into strict training in order to get the prize.	We train ourselves to run the race of life. So we keep our eyes on Christ—the goal—and don't get sidetracked or slowed down. When we do this, we will win a reward in Christ's kingdom.
Philippians 3:13–14	Race	Focus all your energies toward winning the race.	Living the Christian life demands all of our energy. We can forget the past and strain for the goal because we know Christ promises eternity with him at the race's end.
1 Timothy 4:7–10	Exercise	Spiritual exercise will help you grow in faith and character.	As we must repeat exercises to tone our bodies, so we must steadily repeat spiritual exercises to be spiritually fit. When we do this, we will be better Christians, living in accordance with God's will. Such a life will attract others to Christ and pay dividends in this present life and the next.
2 Timothy 4:7–8	Fight, Race (Course)	Fighting the good fight and persevering to the end.	The Christian life is a fight against evil forces from without and temptation from within. If we stay true to God through it all, he promises an end, a rest, and a crown.

3:4–6 At first glance, it looks like Paul is boasting about his achievements. But he is actually doing the opposite, showing that human achievements, no matter how impressive, cannot earn a person salvation and eternal life with God. Paul had impressive credentials: upbringing, nationality, family background, inheritance, orthodoxy, activity, and morality (see 2 Corinthians 11; Galatians 1:13–24, for more of his credentials). However, his conversion to faith in Christ (Acts 9) wasn't based on what he had done, but on God's grace. Paul did not depend on his deeds to please God because even the most impressive credentials fall short of God's holy standards. Are you depending on Christian parents, church affiliation, or just being good to make you right with God? Credentials, accomplishments, or reputation cannot earn salvation. Salvation comes only through faith in Christ.

3:5 Paul belonged to the tribe of Benjamin, a heritage greatly esteemed among the Jews. From this tribe had come Israel's first king, Saul (1 Samuel 10:20–24). The tribes of Benjamin and Judah were the only two tribes to return to Israel after the exile (Ezra 4:1). Paul was also a Pharisee, a member of a very devout Jewish sect that scrupulously kept its own numerous rules in addition to the laws of Moses. Jewish listeners would have been impressed by both of these credentials.

3:6 Why did Paul, a devout Jewish leader, persecute the church? Agreeing with the leaders of the religious establishment, Paul thought that Christianity was heretical and blasphemous. Because Jesus did not meet his expectations of what the Messiah would be like, Paul assumed that Jesus' claims were false—and therefore wicked. In addition, he saw Christianity as a political menace because it threatened to disrupt the fragile harmony between the Jews and the Roman government.

3:7 When Paul spoke of his "gain," he was referring to his credentials, credits, and successes. After showing that he could beat the Judaizers at their own game (being proud of who they were and what they had done), Paul showed that it was the wrong game. Be careful of considering past achievements so important that they get in the way of your relationship with Christ.

3:8 After Paul considered everything he had accomplished in his life, he said that it was all "rubbish" when compared with the greatness of knowing Christ. This is a profound statement about values: A person's relationship with Christ is more important than anything else. To know Christ should be our ultimate goal. Consider your values. Do you place anything above your relationship with Christ? If your priorities are wrong, how will you reorder them?

3:9 Rom 10:5; Rom 9:30; 1 Cor 1:30

3:10 John 17:3; Eph 4:13; Rom 8:17; Rom 6:5; 8:36; Gal 6:17

3:12 1 Cor 9:24f; 1 Tim 6:12, 19; Acts 9:5f

3:14 1 Cor 9:24; Heb 6:1

3:15 Matt 5:48; 1 Cor 2:6; Gal 5:10; John 6:45; 1 Thess 4:9

3:17 1 Cor 4:16; 11:1; Phil 4:9; 1 Pet 5:3

3:18 2 Cor 11:13; Acts 20:31; Gal 6:14

3:19 Titus 1:12; Rom 8:5f; Col 3:2

9 and may be found in Him, not having a righteousness of my own derived from *the*
Law, but that which is through faith in Christ, the righteousness which *comes* from God
on the basis of faith,
10 that I may know Him and the power of His resurrection and the fellowship of His
sufferings, being conformed to His death;
11 in order that I may attain to the resurrection from the dead.
12 Not that I have already obtained *it* or have already become perfect, but I press on
so that I may lay hold of that for which also I was laid hold of by Christ Jesus.
13 Brethren, I do not regard myself as having laid hold of *it* yet; but one thing *I do:*
forgetting what *lies* behind and reaching forward to what *lies* ahead,
14 I press on toward the goal for the prize of the upward call of God in Christ Jesus.
15 Let us therefore, as many as are perfect, have this attitude; and if in anything you
have a different attitude, God will reveal that also to you;
16 however, let us keep living by that same *standard* to which we have attained.
17 Brethren, join in following my example, and observe those who walk according to
the pattern you have in us.
18 For many walk, of whom I often told you, and now tell you even weeping, *that they*
are enemies of the cross of Christ,
19 whose end is destruction, whose god is *their* appetite, and *whose* glory is in their
shame, who set their minds on earthly things.

3:9 No amount of lawkeeping, self-improvement, discipline, or religious effort can make us right with God. Righteousness comes only from God. We are made righteous (receive right standing with him) by trusting in Christ. He exchanges our sin and shortcomings for his complete righteousness. See 2 Corinthians 5:21 for more on Christ's gift of righteousness.

3:9–10 Paul gave up everything—family, friendship, and freedom—in order to know Christ and his resurrection power. We too have access to this knowledge and this power, but we may have to make sacrifices to enjoy it fully. What are you willing to give up in order to know Christ? A crowded schedule in order to set aside a few minutes each day for prayer and Bible study? Your friend's approval? Some of your plans or pleasures? Whatever it is, knowing Christ is more than worth the sacrifice.

3:10 When we are united with Christ by trusting in him, we experience the power that raised him from the dead. That same mighty power will help us live morally renewed and regenerated lives. But before we can walk in newness of life, we must also die to sin. Just as the resurrection gives us Christ's power to live for him, so his crucifixion marks the death of our old sinful nature. We can't know the victory of the resurrection without personally applying the crucifixion.

3:11 When Paul wrote, "in order that I may attain to the resurrection from the dead" he was not implying uncertainty or doubt. He was unsure of the way that he would meet God, whether by execution or by natural death. He did not doubt that he would be raised, but attainment of it was within God's power and not his own.

3:11 Just as Christ was exalted after his resurrection, so we will one day share Christ's glory (Revelation 22:1–7). Paul knew that he might die soon, but he had faith that he would be raised to life again.

3:12–14 Paul says that his goal is to know Christ, to be like Christ, and to be all Christ has in mind for him. This goal absorbs all Paul's energy. This is a helpful example for us. We should not let anything take our eyes off our goal—knowing Christ. With the single-mindedness of an athlete in training, we must lay aside everything harmful and forsake anything that may distract us from being effective Christians. What is holding you back?

3:13–14 Paul had reason to forget what was behind—he had held the coats of those who stoned Stephen, the first Christian martyr (Acts 7:57, 58, Paul is called Saul here). We have all done things for which we are ashamed, and we live in the tension of what we have been and what we want to be. Because our hope is in Christ, however, we can let go of past guilt and look forward to what God will help us become. Don't dwell on your past. Instead, grow in the knowledge of God by concentrating on your relationship with him *now.* Realize that you are forgiven, and then move on to a life of faith and obedience. Look forward to a fuller and more meaningful life because of your hope in Christ.

3:15–16 Sometimes trying to live a perfect Christian life can be so difficult that it leaves us drained and discouraged. We may feel so far from perfect that we can never please God with our lives. Paul used *perfect* (3:12) to mean mature or complete, not flawless in every detail. Those who are mature should press on in the Holy Spirit's power, knowing that Christ will reveal and fill in any discrepancy between what we are and what we should be. Christ's provision is no excuse for lagging devotion, but it provides relief and assurance for those who feel driven.

3:16 Christian maturity involves acting on the guidance that you have already received. We can always make excuses that we still have so much to learn. The instruction for us is to live up to what we already know and live out what we have already learned. We do not have to be sidetracked by an unending search for truth.

3:17 Paul challenged the Philippians to pursue Christlikeness by following Paul's example. This did not mean, of course, that they should copy everything he did; he had just stated that he was not perfect (3:12). But as he focused his life on being like Christ, so should they. The Gospels may not yet have been in circulation, so Paul could not tell them to read the Bible to see what Christ was like. Therefore he urged them to imitate him. That Paul could tell people to follow his example is a testimony to his character. Can you do the same? What kind of follower would a new Christian become if he or she imitated you?

3:17–21 Paul criticized not only the Judaizers (see the first note on 3:2–3), but also the self-indulgent Christians, people who claim to be Christians but don't live up to Christ's model of servanthood and self-sacrifice. These people satisfy their own desires before even thinking about the needs of others. Freedom in Christ does not mean freedom to be selfish. It means taking every opportunity to serve and to become the best person you can be.

20 For our citizenship is in heaven, from which also we eagerly wait for a Savior, the
Lord Jesus Christ;
21 who will transform the body of our humble state into conformity with the body of
His glory, by the exertion of the power that He has even to subject all things to Himself.

Think of Excellence

4 Therefore, my beloved brethren whom I long *to see,* my joy and crown, in this way
stand firm in the Lord, my beloved.

4. Joy in giving

2 I urge Euodia and I urge Syntyche to live in harmony in the Lord.
3 Indeed, true companion, I ask you also to help these women who have shared my
struggle in *the cause of* the gospel, together with Clement also and the rest of my fellow
workers, whose names are in the book of life.
4 Rejoice in the Lord always; again I will say, rejoice!
5 Let your gentle *spirit* be known to all men. The Lord is near.
6 Be anxious for nothing, but in everything by prayer and supplication with thanksgiving let your requests be made known to God.
7 And the peace of God, which surpasses all comprehension, will guard your hearts
and your minds in Christ Jesus.
8 Finally, brethren, whatever is true, whatever is honorable, whatever is right, whatever is pure, whatever is lovely, whatever is of good repute, if there is any excellence and
if anything worthy of praise, dwell on these things.
9 The things you have learned and received and heard and seen in me, practice these
things, and the God of peace will be with you.

3:20 Eph 2:19; Phil 1:27; Col 3:1; Heb 12:22; 1 Cor 1:7
3:21 1 Cor 15:43-53; Rom 8:29; Col 3:4; 1 Cor 15:43, 49; Eph 1:19; 1 Cor 15:28
4:2 Phil 2:2
4:3 Luke 10:20
4:5 Heb 10:37; James 5:8f
4:6 Matt 6:25; Eph 6:18; 1 Tim 2:1; 5:5
4:7 Is 26:3; John 14:27; Phil 4:9; Col 3:15; 1 Pet 1:5; 2 Cor 10:5; Phil 1:1; 4:19, 21
4:8 Rom 14:18; 1 Pet 2:12
4:9 Phil 3:17; Rom 15:33

3:20 Citizens of Philippi had the same rights and privileges as the citizens of Rome, because Philippi was a Roman colony. Likewise, we Christians will one day experience all the special privileges of our heavenly citizenship, because we belong to Christ. Let us not be so tied to this life that we would be sorry to see Christ return.

3:21 The phrase "the body of our humble state" does not imply any negative attitude toward the human body. However, the bodies we will receive when we are raised from the dead will be glorious, like Christ's resurrected body. Those who struggle with pain, physical limitations, or disabilities can have wonderful hope in the resurrection. For a more detailed discussion of our new bodies, see 1 Corinthians 15:35ff and 2 Corinthians 5:1–10.

4:1 How do we "stand firm in the Lord"? This refers to what Paul has just taught in 3:20–21. The way to stand firm is to keep our eyes on Christ, to remember that this world is not our home, and to focus on the fact that Christ will bring everything under his control.

4:2–3 Paul did not warn the Philippian church of doctrinal errors, but he did address some relational problems. These two women had been workers for Christ in the church. Their broken relationship was no small matter, because many had become believers through their efforts. It is possible to believe in Christ, work hard for his kingdom, and yet have broken relationships with others who are committed to the same cause. But there is no excuse for remaining unreconciled. Do you need to be reconciled to someone today?

4:3 The identity of this "true companion" remains a mystery. It could be Epaphroditus, the bearer of this letter, or a comrade of Paul in prison. It could also be someone named Syzygus, another way to understand the word for "companion."

4:3 Those "whose names are in the book of life" are all who are marked for salvation through their faith in Christ (see also Luke 10:17–20; Revelation 20:11–15).

4:4 It seems strange that a man in prison would be telling a church to rejoice. But Paul's attitude teaches us an important lesson: Our inner attitudes do not have to reflect our outward circumstances. Paul was full of joy because he knew that no matter what happened to him, Jesus Christ was with him. Several times in this letter, Paul urged the Philippians to be joyful, probably because they needed to hear this. It's easy to get discouraged about unpleasant circumstances or to take unimportant events too seriously. If you haven't been joyful lately, you may not be looking at life from the right perspective.

4:4–5 Ultimate joy comes from Christ dwelling within us. Christ is near, and at his second coming we will fully realize this ultimate joy. He who lives within us will fulfill his final purposes for us.

4:5 We are to be gentle (reasonable, fair minded, and charitable) to those outside the church, and not just to fellow believers. This means we are not to seek revenge against those who treat us unfairly, nor are we to be overly vocal about our personal rights.

4:6–7 Imagine being "anxious for nothing"! It seems like an impossibility—we all have worries on the job, in our homes, at school. But Paul's advice is to turn our worries into prayers. Do you want to worry less? Then pray more! Whenever you start to worry, stop and pray.

4:7 God's peace is different from the world's peace (see John 14:27). True peace is not found in positive thinking, in absence of conflict, or in good feelings. It comes from knowing that God is in control. Our citizenship in Christ's kingdom is sure, our destiny is set, and we can have victory over sin. Let God's peace guard your heart against anxiety.

4:8 What we put into our minds determines what comes out in our words and actions. Paul tells us to program our minds with thoughts that are true, honorable, right, pure, lovely, of good repute, excellent, and praiseworthy. Do you have problems with impure thoughts and daydreams? Examine what you are putting into your mind through television, books, conversations, movies, and magazines. Replace harmful input with wholesome material. Above all, read God's Word and pray. Ask God to help you focus your mind on what is good and pure. It takes practice, but it can be done.

4:9 It's not enough to hear or read the Word of God, or even to know it well. We must also put it into practice. How easy it is to listen to a sermon and forget what the preacher said. How easy it is to read the Bible and not think about how to live differently. How easy it is to debate what a passage means and not live out that meaning. Exposure to God's Word is not enough. It must lead to obedience.

4:10 2 Cor 11:9; Phil 2:30
4:11 2 Cor 9:8; 1 Tim 6:6, 8; Heb 13:5
4:12 1 Cor 4:11; 2 Cor 11:9
4:13 2 Cor 12:9; Eph 3:16; Col 1:11
4:14 Heb 10:33; Rev 1:9
4:15 Phil 1:5; Rom 15:26
4:16 Acts 17:1; 1 Thess 2:9
4:17 1 Cor 9:11f; 2 Cor 9:5
4:18 2 Cor 2:14; Eph 5:2
4:19 2 Cor 9:8; Rom 2:4
4:20 Gal 1:4; Rom 11:36
4:23 Rom 16:20; 2 Tim 4:22

God's Provisions

10 But I rejoiced in the Lord greatly, that now at last you have revived your concern
for me; indeed, you were concerned *before,* but you lacked opportunity.
11 Not that I speak from want, for I have learned to be content in whatever circumstances I am.
12 I know how to get along with humble means, and I also know how to live in prosperity; in any and every circumstance I have learned the secret of being filled and going
hungry, both of having abundance and suffering need.
13 I can do all things through Him who strengthens me.
14 Nevertheless, you have done well to share *with me* in my affliction.
15 You yourselves also know, Philippians, that at the first preaching of the gospel, after I left Macedonia, no church shared with me in the matter of giving and receiving but
you alone;
16 for even in Thessalonica you sent *a gift* more than once for my needs.
17 Not that I seek the gift itself, but I seek for the profit which increases to your account.
18 But I have received everything in full and have an abundance; I am amply supplied,
having received from Epaphroditus what you have sent, a fragrant aroma, an acceptable
sacrifice, well-pleasing to God.
19 And my God will supply all your needs according to His riches in glory in Christ
Jesus.
20 Now to our God and Father *be* the glory forever and ever. Amen.
21 Greet every saint in Christ Jesus. The brethren who are with me greet you.
22 All the saints greet you, especially those of Caesar's household.
23 The grace of the Lord Jesus Christ be with your spirit.

4:10 In 1 Corinthians 9:11–18, Paul wrote that he didn't accept gifts from the Corinthian church because he didn't want to be accused of preaching only to get money. But Paul maintained that it was a church's responsibility to support God's ministers (1 Corinthians 9:14). He accepted the Philippians' gift because they gave it willingly and because he was in need.

4:10–14 Are you content in any circumstances you face? Paul knew how to be content whether he had plenty or whether he was in need. The secret was drawing on Christ's power for strength. Do you have great needs, or are you discontented because you don't have what you want? Learn to rely on God's promises and Christ's power to help you be content. If you always want more, ask God to remove that desire and teach you contentment in every circumstance. He will supply all your needs, but in a way that he knows is best for you (see the note on 4:19 for more on God supplying our needs).

4:12–13 Paul was content because he could see life from God's point of view. He focused on what he was supposed to *do,* not what he felt he should *have.* Paul had his priorities straight, and he was grateful for everything God had given him. Paul had detached himself from the nonessentials so that he could concentrate on the eternal. Often the desire for more or better possessions is really a longing to fill an empty place in a person's life. To what are you drawn when you feel empty inside? How can you find true contentment? The answer lies in your perspective, your priorities, and your source of power.

4:13 Can we really do everything? The power we receive in union with Christ is sufficient to do his will and to face the challenges that arise from our commitment to doing it. He does not grant us superhuman ability to accomplish anything we can imagine without regard to his interests. As we contend for the faith we will face troubles, pressures, and trials. As they come, ask Christ to strengthen you.

4:14 The Philippians shared in Paul's financial support while he was in prison.

4:17 When we give to those in need, there is not only benefit to the receiver, but we are benefited as well. It was not the Philippians' gift, but their spirit of love and devotion that Paul appreciated most.

4:18 Paul was not referring to a sin offering but to a thanksgiving offering, "a fragrant aroma, an acceptable sacrifice, well-pleasing to God" (Leviticus 7:12–15 contains the instructions for thank offerings). Although the Greek and Roman Christians were not Jews, and they had not offered sacrifices according to the Old Testament laws, they were well acquainted with the pagan rituals of offering sacrifices.

4:19 We can trust that God will always meet our needs. Whatever we need on earth he will always supply, even if it is the courage to face death as Paul did. Whatever we need in heaven he will supply. We must remember, however, the difference between our wants and our needs. Most people want to feel good and avoid discomfort or pain. We may not get all that we want. By trusting in Christ, our attitudes and appetites can change from wanting everything to accepting his provision and power to live for him.

4:22 There were many Christians in Rome; some were even in Caesar's household. Perhaps Paul, while awaiting trial, was making converts of the Roman civil service! Paul sent greetings from these Roman Christians to the believers at Philippi. The gospel had spread to all strata of society, linking people who had no other bond but Christ. The Roman Christians and the Philippian Christians were brothers and sisters because of their unity in Christ. Believers today are also linked to others across cultural, economic, and social barriers. Because all believers are brothers and sisters in Christ, let us live like God's true family.

4:23 In many ways the Philippian church was a model congregation. It was made up of many different kinds of people who were learning to work together. But Paul recognized that problems could arise, so in his thank-you letter he prepared the Philippians for difficulties that could crop up within a body of believers. Though a prisoner in Rome, Paul had learned the true secret of joy and peace—imitating Christ and serving others. By focusing our minds on Christ we will learn unity, humility, joy, and peace. We will also be motivated to live for him. We can live confidently for him because we have "the grace of the Lord Jesus Christ" with us.

COLOSSIANS

VITAL STATISTICS

PURPOSE:
To combat errors in the church and to show that believers have everything they need in Christ

AUTHOR:
Paul

TO WHOM WRITTEN:
The church at Colosse, a city in Asia Minor, and all believers everywhere

DATE WRITTEN:
Approximately A.D. 60, during Paul's imprisonment in Rome

SETTING:
Paul had never visited Colosse. Evidently the church had been founded by Epaphras and other converts from Paul's missionary travels. The church, however, had been infiltrated by religious relativism, with some believers attempting to combine elements of paganism and secular philosophy with Christian doctrine. Paul confronts these false teachings and affirms the sufficiency of Christ.

KEY VERSES:
"For in Him all the fullness of Deity dwells in bodily form, and in Him you have been made complete, and He is the head over all rule and authority" (2:9–10).

KEY PEOPLE:
Paul, Timothy, Tychicus, Onesimus, Aristarchus, Mark, Epaphras

KEY PLACES:
Colosse, Laodicea (4:15–16)

SPECIAL FEATURES:
Christ is presented as having absolute supremacy and sole sufficiency. Colossians has similarities to Ephesians, probably because it was written at about the same time, but it has a different emphasis.

REMOVE the head coach, and the team flounders; break the fuel line, and the car won't run; unplug the electrical appliance, and it has no power. Whether for leadership, power, or life, connections are vital!

Colossians is a book of connections. Writing from prison in Rome, Paul combatted false teachings, which had infiltrated the Colossian church. The problem was "syncretism," combining ideas from other philosophies and religions (such as paganism, strains of Judaism, and Greek thought) with Christian truth. The resulting heresy later became known as "Gnosticism," emphasizing special knowledge (*gnosis* in Greek) and denying Christ as God and Savior. To combat this devious error, Paul stressed Christ's deity—his connection with the Father—and his sacrificial death on the cross for sin. Only by being connected with Christ through faith can anyone have eternal life, and only through a continuing connection with him can anyone have power for living. Christ is God incarnate and the *only* way to forgiveness and peace with God the Father. Paul also emphasized believers' connections with each other as Christ's body on earth.

Paul's introduction to the Colossians includes a greeting, a note of thanksgiving, and a prayer for spiritual wisdom and strength for these brothers and sisters in Christ (1:1–12). He then moves into a doctrinal discussion of the person and work of Christ (1:13–23), stating that Christ is "the image of the invisible God" (1:15), the Creator (1:16), "head of the body, the church" (1:18), and "the firstborn from the dead" (1:18). His death on the cross makes it possible for us to stand in the presence of God (1:22).

Paul then explains how the world's teachings are totally empty when compared with God's plan, and he challenges the Colossians to reject shallow answers and to live in union with Christ (1:24—2:23).

Against this theological backdrop, Paul turns to practical considerations—what the divinity, death, and resurrection of Jesus should mean to all believers (3:1—4:6). Because our eternal destiny is sure, heaven should fill our thoughts (3:1–4), sexual impurity and other worldly lusts should not be named among us (3:5–8), and truth, love, and peace should mark our life (3:9–15). Our love for Christ should also translate into love for others—friends, fellow believers, spouses, children, parents, slaves, and masters (3:16—4:1). We should constantly communicate with God through prayer (4:2–4), and we should take every opportunity to tell others the Good News (4:5–6). In Christ we have everything we need for salvation and for living the Christian life.

Paul had probably never visited Colosse, so he concludes this letter with personal comments about their common Christian associations, providing a living lesson of the connectedness of the body of Christ.

Read Colossians as a book for an embattled church in the first century, but read it also for its timeless truths. Gain a fresh appreciation for Christ as the *fullness* of God and the *only* source for living the Christian life. Know that he is your leader, head, and power source, and make sure of your connection to him.

THE BLUEPRINT

1. What Christ has done (1:1—2:23)
2. What Christians should do (3:1—4:18)

In this letter Paul clearly teaches that Christ has paid for sin, that Christ has reconciled us to God, and that Christ gives us the pattern and the power to grow spiritually. Because Christ is the exact likeness of God, when we learn what he is like, we see what we need to become. Since Christ is Lord over all creation, we should crown him Lord over our life. Since Christ is the head of the body, his church, we should nurture our vital connection to him.

MEGATHEMES

THEME	EXPLANATION	IMPORTANCE
Christ Is God	Jesus Christ is God in the flesh, Lord of all creation, and Lord of the new creation. He is the expressed reflection of the invisible God. He is eternal, preexistent, omnipotent, equal with the Father. He is supreme and complete.	Because Christ is supreme, our life must be Christ-centered. To recognize him as God means to regard our relationship with him as most vital and to make his interests our top priority.
Christ Is Head of the Church	Because Christ is God, he is the head of the church, his true believers. Christ is the founder, the leader, and the highest authority on earth. He requires first place in all our thoughts and activities.	To acknowledge Christ as our head, we must welcome his leadership in all we do or think. No person, group, or church can regard any loyalty as more critical than that of loyalty to Christ.
Union with Christ	Because our sin has been forgiven and we have been reconciled to God, we have a union with Christ that can never be broken. In our faith connection with him, we identify with his death, burial, and resurrection.	We should live in constant contact and communication with God. When we do, we all will be unified with Christ and with one another.
Man-Made Religion	False teachers were promoting a heresy that stressed self-made rules (legalism). They also sought spiritual growth by discipline of the body (asceticism) and visions (mysticism). This search created pride in their self-centered efforts.	We must not cling to our own ideas and try to blend them into Christianity. Nor should we let our hunger for a more fulfilling Christian experience cause us to trust in a teacher, a group, or a system of thought more than in Christ himself. Christ is our hope and our true source of wisdom.

1. What Christ has done

Thankfulness for Spiritual Attainments

1 Paul, an apostle of Jesus Christ by the will of God, and Timothy our brother,
2 To the saints and faithful brethren in Christ *who are* at Colossae: Grace to you
and peace from God our Father.
3 We give thanks to God, the Father of our Lord Jesus Christ, praying always for you,
4 since we heard of your faith in Christ Jesus and the love which you have for all the
saints;
5 because of the hope laid up for you in heaven, of which you previously heard in the
word of truth, the gospel
6 which has come to you, just as in all the world also it is constantly bearing fruit and
increasing, even as *it has been doing* in you also since the day you heard *of it* and understood the grace of God in truth;
7 just as you learned *it* from Epaphras, our beloved fellow bond-servant, who is a faithful servant of Christ on our behalf,
8 and he also informed us of your love in the Spirit.
9 For this reason also, since the day we heard *of it*, we have not ceased to pray for you
and to ask that you may be filled with the knowledge of His will in all spiritual wisdom
and understanding,

1:2 Acts 9:13; Rom 1:7
1:3 Rom 1:8; Rom 15:6; 2 Cor 1:3
1:4 Eph 1:15; Gal 5:6; Eph 6:18
1:5 Acts 23:6; 2 Tim 4:8; Eph 1:13
1:6 Rom 10:18; Rom 1:13; Eph 4:21
1:7 Col 4:12; Col 4:7
1:8 Rom 15:30
1:9 Col 1:4; Eph 1:16; Phil 1:9; Eph 1:17

1:1 Colossians, along with Philippians, Ephesians, and Philemon, is called a *Prison Letter* because Paul wrote it from prison in Rome. This prison was actually a house where Paul was kept under close guard at all times (probably chained to a soldier) but given certain freedoms not offered to most prisoners. He was allowed to write letters and to see any visitors he wanted to see.

1:1 Paul was an apostle "by the will of God." Paul often would establish his credentials as chosen and sent by God because he had not been one of the original 12 disciples. *Apostle* means chosen and sent by God as a missionary or ambassador. *By the will of God* means that he was appointed; this was not just a matter of his own personal aspirations.

1:1 Paul mentions Timothy in other New Testament letters as well: 2 Corinthians, Philippians, 1 and 2 Thessalonians, and Philemon. Paul also wrote two letters to Timothy (1 and 2 Timothy). For more information on these men, two of the greatest missionaries of the early church, see Paul's Profile in Acts 9 and Timothy's Profile in 1 Timothy.

1:2 The city of Colossae was 100 miles east of Ephesus on the Lycus River. It was not as influential as the nearby city of Laodicea, but as a trading center it was a crossroads for ideas and religions. Colossae had a large Jewish population—many Jews had fled there when they were forced out of Jerusalem under the persecutions of Antiochus III and IV, almost 200 years before Christ. The church in Colossae had been founded by Epaphras (1:7), one of Paul's converts. Paul had not yet visited this church. His purpose in writing was to refute heretical teachings about Christ that had been causing confusion among the Christians there.

1:2–3 Letters in Paul's day frequently would begin with identifying the writer and the readers, followed by a greeting of peace. Paul usually would add Christian elements to his greetings, reminding his readers of his call by God to spread the gospel, emphasizing that the authority for his words came from God, and giving thanks for God's blessings.

1:4–5 Throughout this letter Paul combats a heresy similar to *Gnosticism* (see the notes on 1:9–14; 1:15–23; 2:4ff). Gnostics believed that it took special knowledge to be accepted by God; for them, even for those who claimed to be Christians, Christ alone was not the way of salvation (1:20). In his introductory comments, therefore, Paul commended the Colossians for their faith, love, and hope—three main emphases of Christianity (1 Corinthians 13:13). He deliberately omitted the word *knowledge* because of the "special knowledge" aspect of the heresy. It is not *what* we know that brings salvation, but *whom* we know. Knowing Christ is knowing God.

1:5 When Paul says that our hope is laid up in heaven, he is emphasizing the security of the believer. Because we know that our future destination and salvation are sure, we are free to live for Christ and love others (1 Peter 1:3–4). When you find yourself doubting or wavering in your faith or love, remember your destination—heaven.

1:6 Wherever Paul went, he preached the gospel—to Gentile audiences, to hostile Jewish leaders, and even to his Roman guards. Whenever people believed in the message that Paul spoke, they were changed. God's Word is not just for our information, it is for our transformation! Becoming a Christian means beginning a whole new relationship with God, not just turning over a new leaf or determining to do right. New believers have a changed purpose, direction, attitude, and behavior. They are no longer seeking to serve themselves, but they are bearing fruit for God. How is the gospel reaching others through your life?

1:7 Epaphras had founded the church at Colossae while Paul was living in Ephesus (Acts 19:10). Epaphras may have been converted in Ephesus, and then he returned to Colossae, his hometown. For some reason, he visited Rome and, while there, told Paul about the problem with the Colossian heresy. This prompted Paul to write this letter. Epaphras is also mentioned in Philemon 23 (the Colossian church met in Philemon's house).

1:8 Because of their love for one another, Christians can have an impact that goes far beyond their neighborhoods and communities. Christian love comes from the Holy Spirit (see Galatians 5:22). The Bible speaks of it as an action and attitude, not just an emotion. Love is a by-product of our new life in Christ (see Romans 5:5; 1 Corinthians 13). Christians have no excuse for not loving, because Christian love is a decision to *act* in the best interests of others.

1:9–14 Paul was exposing a heresy in the Colossian church that was similar to *Gnosticism* (see the note on 2:4ff for more information). Gnostics valued the accumulation of knowledge, but Paul pointed out that knowledge in itself is empty. To be worth anything, it must lead to a changed life and right living. His prayer for the Colossians has two dimensions: (1) that they might be filled with the knowledge of God's will through all spiritual wisdom and understanding, and (2) that they would bear fruit in every good work, growing in the knowledge of God. Knowledge is not merely to be accumulated; it should give us direction for living. Paul wanted the Colossians to be wise, but he also wanted them to *use* their knowledge. Knowledge of God is not a secret that only a few can discover; it is open to everyone. God wants us to learn more about him, and also to put belief into practice by helping others.

1:10 Eph 4:1; Eph 5:10; Rom 1:13
1:11 1 Cor 16:13; Eph 4:2
1:12 Eph 2:18; Acts 20:32; Acts 26:18

10 so that you will walk in a manner worthy of the Lord, to please *Him* in all respects,
bearing fruit in every good work and increasing in the knowledge of God;
11 strengthened with all power, according to His glorious might, for the attaining of
all steadfastness and patience; joyously
12 giving thanks to the Father, who has qualified us to share in the inheritance of the
saints in Light.

The Incomparable Christ

1:13 Eph 6:12; Eph 1:6
1:14 Rom 3:24

13 For He rescued us from the domain of darkness, and transferred us to the kingdom
of His beloved Son,
14 in whom we have redemption, the forgiveness of sins.

THE COLOSSIAN HERESY
Paul answered the various tenets of the Colossian heresy that threatened the church. This heresy was a "mixed bag," containing elements from several different heresies, some of which contradicted each other (as the chart shows).

The Heresy	*Reference*	*Paul's Answer*
Spirit is good; matter is evil.	1:15–20	God created heaven and earth for his glory.
One must follow ceremonies, rituals, and restrictions in order to be saved or perfected.	2:11, 16–23; 3:11	These were only shadows that ended when Christ came. He is all you need to be saved.
One must deny the body and live in strict asceticism.	2:20–23	Asceticism is no help in conquering evil thoughts and desires; instead, it leads to pride.
Angels must be worshiped.	2:18	Angels are not to be worshiped; Christ alone is worthy of worship.
Christ could not be both human and divine.	1:15–20; 2:2–3	Christ is God in the flesh; he is the eternal One, head of the body, first in everything, supreme.
One must obtain "secret knowledge" in order to be saved or perfected—and this was not available to everyone.	2:2–18	God's secret is Christ, and he has been revealed to all.
One must adhere to human wisdom, tradition, and philosophies.	2:4, 8–10; 3:15–17	By themselves, these can be misleading and shallow because they have human origin; instead, we should remember what Christ taught and follow his words as our ultimate authority.
It is even better to combine aspects of several religions.	2:10	You have everything when you have Christ; he is all-sufficient.
There is nothing wrong with immorality.	3:1–11	Get rid of sin and evil because you have been chosen by God to live a new life as a representative of the Lord Jesus.

1:9–14 Sometimes we wonder how to pray for missionaries and other leaders we have never met. Paul had never met the Colossians, but he faithfully prayed for them. His prayers teach us how to pray for others, whether we know them or not. We can request that they (1) understand God's will, (2) gain spiritual wisdom, (3) please and honor God, (4) bear good fruit, (5) grow in the knowledge of God, (6) be filled with God's strength, (7) have great endurance and patience, (8) stay full of Christ's joy, and (9) give thanks always. All believers have these same basic needs. When you don't know how to pray for someone, use Paul's prayer pattern for the Colossians.

1:12–14 Paul lists five benefits God gives all believers through Christ: (1) He made us qualified to share his inheritance (see also 2 Corinthians 5:21); (2) he rescued us from Satan's dominion of darkness and made us his children (see also 2:15); (3) he brought us into his eternal kingdom (see also Ephesians 1:5–6); (4) he redeemed us—bought our freedom from sin and judgment (see also Hebrews 9:12); and (5) he forgave all our sins (see also Ephesians 1:7). Thank God for what you have received in Christ.

1:13 The Colossians feared the unseen forces of darkness, but Paul says that true believers have been transferred from darkness to light, from slavery to freedom, from guilt to forgiveness, and from the power of Satan to the power of God. We have been rescued from a rebel kingdom to serve the rightful King. Our conduct should reflect our new allegiance.

15 He is the image of the invisible God, the firstborn of all creation.
16 For by Him all things were created, *both* in the heavens and on earth, visible and
invisible, whether thrones or dominions or rulers or authorities—all things have been
created through Him and for Him.
17 He is before all things, and in Him all things hold together.
18 He is also head of the body, the church; and He is the beginning, the firstborn from
the dead, so that He Himself will come to have first place in everything.

1:15 2 Cor 4:4; John 1:1; Rom 8:29

1:16 Eph 1:10; Eph 1:20f

1:17 John 1:1; 8:58

1:18 Eph 1:22; Rev 3:14

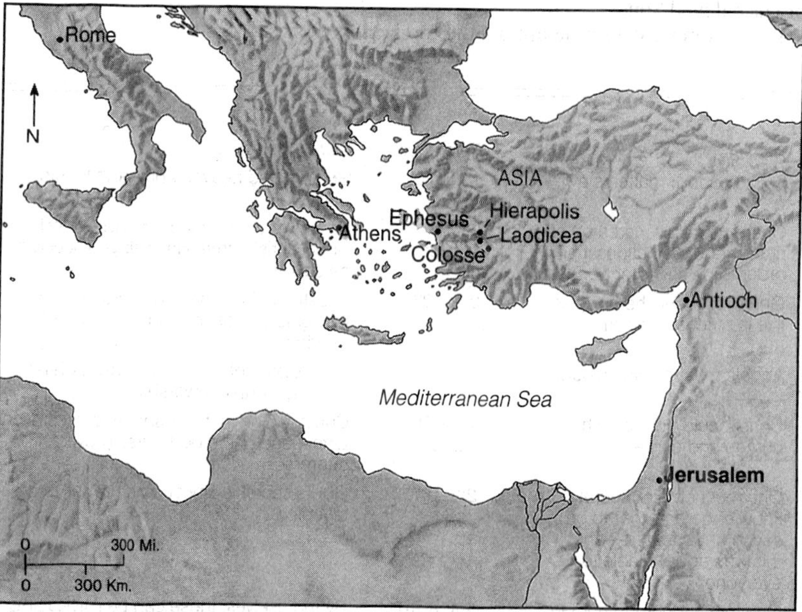

LOCATION OF COLOSSAE
Paul had no doubt been through Laodicea on his third missionary journey, as it lay on the main route to Ephesus, but he had never been to Colossae (Colosse). Though a large city with a significant population, Colosse was smaller and less important than the nearby cities of Laodicea and Hierapolis.

1:15–16 This is one of the strongest statements about the divine nature of Christ found anywhere in the Bible. Jesus is not only equal to God (Philippians 2:6); he *is* God (John 10:30, 38; 12:45; 14:1–11). As the image of the invisible God, he is the exact representation of God. He not only reflects God, but he reveals God to us (John 1:18; 14:9); as the firstborn over all creation, he has all the priority and authority of the firstborn prince in a king's household. He came from heaven, not from the dust of the earth (1 Corinthians 15:47), and he is Lord of all (Romans 9:5; 10:11–13; Revelation 1:5; 17:14). He is completely holy (Hebrews 7:26–28; 1 Peter 1:19; 2:22; 1 John 3:5), and he has authority to judge the world (Romans 2:16; 2 Corinthians 5:10; 2 Timothy 4:1). Therefore, Christ is supreme over all creation, including the spirit world. We, like the Colossian believers, must believe in the deity of Jesus Christ (that Jesus is God) or our Christian faith is hollow, misdirected, and meaningless. This is a central truth of Christianity. We must oppose those who say that Jesus was merely a prophet or a good teacher.

1:15–23 In the Colossian church there were several misconceptions about Christ that Paul directly refuted:

(1) Believing that matter is evil, false teachers argued that God would not have come to earth as a true human being in bodily form. Paul stated that Christ is the image—the exact likeness—of God, and is himself God, and yet he died on the cross as a human being. (2) They believed that God did not create the world, because he would not have created evil. Paul proclaimed that Jesus Christ, who was also God in the flesh, is the Creator of both heaven and earth. (3) They said that Christ was not the unique Son of God, but rather one of many intermediaries between God and people. Paul explained that Christ existed before anything else and is the firstborn of those resurrected. (4) They refused to see Christ as the source of salvation, insisting that people could find God only through special and secret knowledge. In contrast Paul openly proclaimed the way of salvation to be through Christ alone. Paul continued to bring the argument back to Christ. When we share the gospel, we too must keep the focus on Christ.

1:16 Because the false teachers believed that the physical world was evil, they thought that God himself could not have created it. If Christ were God, they reasoned, he would be in charge only of the spiritual world. But Paul explained that all the rulers, powers, thrones, and authorities of both the spiritual and physical worlds were created by and are under the authority of Christ himself. This includes not only the government but also the spiritual world that the heretics were so concerned about. Christ has no equal and no rival. He is the Lord of all.

1:17 God is not only the Creator of the world, but he is also its Sustainer. In him, everything is held together, protected, and prevented from disintegrating into chaos. Because Christ is the Sustainer of all life, none of us is independent from him. We are all his servants who must daily trust him for protecting us, caring for us, and sustaining us.

1:18 Christ is the "firstborn from the dead." Jesus was raised from death, and his resurrection proves his lordship over the material world. All who trust in Christ will also defeat death and rise again to live eternally with him (1 Corinthians 15:20; 1 Thessalonians 4:14). Because of Christ's death on the cross, he has been exalted and elevated to the status that was rightfully his (see Philippians 2:5–11). Because Christ is spiritually supreme in the universe, surely

1:19 Eph 1:5; John 1:16
1:20 Eph 2:16; Rom 5:1
1:21 Rom 5:10; Eph 2:3
1:22 2 Cor 5:18; Eph 2:16; Rom 7:4
1:23 Eph 3:17; Col 2:7; Mark 16:15; Eph 3:7
1:24 Rom 8:17; 2 Cor 1:5; 12:15; Phil 2:17
1:25 Col 1:23; Eph 3:2
1:26 Rom 16:25f

19 For it was the *Father's* good pleasure for all the fullness to dwell in Him,
20 and through Him to reconcile all things to Himself, having made peace through the
blood of His cross; through Him, *I say*, whether things on earth or things in heaven.
21 And although you were formerly alienated and hostile in mind, *engaged* in evil deeds,
22 yet He has now reconciled you in His fleshly body through death, in order to present you before Him holy and blameless and beyond reproach—
23 if indeed you continue in the faith firmly established and steadfast, and not moved
away from the hope of the gospel that you have heard, which was proclaimed in all creation under heaven, and of which I, Paul, was made a minister.
24 Now I rejoice in my sufferings for your sake, and in my flesh I do my share on behalf
of His body, which is the church, in filling up what is lacking in Christ's afflictions.
25 Of *this church* I was made a minister according to the stewardship from God bestowed on me for your benefit, so that I might fully carry out the *preaching of* the word
of God,
26 *that is,* the mystery which has been hidden from the *past* ages and generations, but
has now been manifested to His saints,

HOW TO PRAY FOR OTHER CHRISTIANS
How many people in your life could be touched if you prayed in this way?

1. Be thankful for their faith and changed lives (1:3).
2. Ask God to help them know what he wants them to do (1:9).
3. Ask God to give them deep spiritual understanding (1:9).
4. Ask God to help them live for him (1:10).
5. Ask God to give them more knowledge of himself (1:10).
6. Ask God to give them strength for endurance (1:11).
7. Ask God to fill them with joy, strength, and thankfulness (1:11).

---

we should give him first place in all our thoughts and activities. See the second note on Luke 24:6–7 for more about the significance of Christ's resurrection.

1:19 By this statement, Paul was refuting the Greek idea that Jesus could not be human and divine at the same time. Christ is fully human; he is also fully divine. Christ has always been God and always will be God. When we have Christ we have all of God in human form. Don't diminish any aspect of Christ—either his humanity or his divinity.

1:20 Christ's death provided a way for all people to come to God. It cleared away the sin that keeps us from having a right relationship with our Creator. This does not mean that everyone has been saved, but that the way has been cleared for anyone who will trust Christ to be saved. We can have peace with God and be reconciled to him by accepting Christ, who died in our place. Is there a distance between you and the Creator? Be reconciled to God. Come to him through Christ.

1:21 Because we were alienated from God, we were strangers to his way of thinking and were "hostile in mind." Sin corrupted our way of thinking about God. Wrong thinking leads to sin, which further perverts and destroys our thoughts about him. When we were out of harmony with God, our natural condition was to be totally hostile to his standards. See Romans 1:21–32 for more on the perverted thinking of unbelievers.

1:21–22 *No one* is good enough to save himself or herself. If we want to live eternally with Christ, we must depend totally on God's grace. This is true whether we have been murderers or honest, hardworking citizens. We have all sinned repeatedly, and *any* sin is enough to cause us to come to Jesus Christ for salvation and eternal life. Apart from Christ, there is no way for our sin to be forgiven and removed.

1:22 In order to answer the accusation that Jesus was only a spirit and not a true human being, Paul explained that Jesus' physical body actually died. Jesus suffered death fully as a human so that we could be assured that he died in our place. Jesus faced death as God so we can be assured that his sacrifice was complete and that he truly removed our sin.

1:22–23 The way to be free from sin is to trust Jesus Christ to take it away. We must remain "established and steadfast" in the truth of the gospel, putting our confidence in Jesus alone to forgive our sins, to make us right with God, and to empower us to live the way he desires. When a judge in a court of law declares the defendant not guilty, the person has been acquitted of all the accusations or charges. Legally, it is as if he or she had never been accused. When God forgives our sins, our record is wiped clean. From his perspective, it is as though we had never sinned. God's solution is available to you. No matter what you have done or what you have been like, God's forgiveness is for you.

1:24 When Paul says, "filling up what is lacking in Christ's afflictions," he does not mean that Christ's suffering was inadequate to save him, nor does he mean that there is a predetermined amount of suffering that must be paid by all believers. Paul could be saying that suffering is unavoidable in bringing the Good News of Christ to the world. It is called Christ's suffering, because all Christians are related to Christ. When we suffer, Christ feels it with us. But this suffering can be endured joyfully because it changes lives and brings people into God's kingdom (see 1 Peter 4:1–2, 12–19). For more about how Paul could rejoice despite his suffering, see the note on Philippians 1:29.

1:26–27 The false teachers in the Colossian church believed that spiritual perfection was a secret and hidden plan that only a few privileged people could discover. Their secret plan was meant to be exclusive. Paul said that he was proclaiming the word of God in its fullness, not just a part of the plan. He also called God's plan a "mystery which has been hidden from the past ages and generations," not in the sense that only a few would understand, but because it was hidden until Christ came. Through Christ it was made open to all. God's secret plan is "Christ in you, the hope of glory"—God planned to have his Son, Jesus Christ, live in the hearts of all who believe in him—even Gentiles like the Colossians. Do you know Christ? He is not hidden if you will come to him.

27 to whom God willed to make known what is the riches of the glory of this mystery
among the Gentiles, which is Christ in you, the hope of glory.
28 We proclaim Him, admonishing every man and teaching every man with all wisdom,
so that we may present every man complete in Christ.
29 For this purpose also I labor, striving according to His power, which mightily works
within me.

You Are Built Up in Christ

2 For I want you to know how great a struggle I have on your behalf and for those who
are at Laodicea, and for all those who have not personally seen my face,
2 that their hearts may be encouraged, having been knit together in love, and *attain-*
ing to all the wealth that comes from the full assurance of understanding, *resulting* in a
true knowledge of God's mystery, *that is,* Christ *Himself,*
3 in whom are hidden all the treasures of wisdom and knowledge.
4 I say this so that no one will delude you with persuasive argument.
5 For even though I am absent in body, nevertheless I am with you in spirit, rejoicing
to see your good discipline and the stability of your faith in Christ.
6 Therefore as you have received Christ Jesus the Lord, *so* walk in Him,
7 having been firmly rooted *and now* being built up in Him and established [1]in your
faith, just as you were instructed, *and* overflowing with gratitude.
8 See to it that no one takes you captive through philosophy and empty deception,
according to the tradition of men, according to the elementary principles of the world,
rather than according to Christ.
9 For in Him all the fullness of Deity dwells in bodily form,

1 Or *by*

1:27 Matt 13:11; Eph 1:7, 18; 3:16; Rom 8:10
1:28 Acts 20:31; Matt 5:48; Eph 4:13
1:29 1 Cor 15:10; Eph 1:19; Col 2:12
2:2 1 Cor 14:31; Eph 6:22; 3:16; Matt 13:11; Rom 16:25f
2:3 Is 11:2; Rom 11:33
2:4 Eph 4:17
2:5 1 Cor 5:3; 1 Cor 14:40; 1 Pet 5:9
2:6 Gal 3:26; Col 1:10
2:7 Eph 3:17; 1 Cor 3:9; Eph 2:20; 1 Cor 1:8
2:8 1 Cor 8:9; 10:12; Gal 5:15; Heb 3:12
2:9 2 Cor 5:19; Col 1:19

1:28–29 The word *complete* means mature, not flawless. Paul wanted to see each believer mature spiritually. Like Paul, we must work wholeheartedly like an athlete, but we should not strive in our own strength alone. We have the power of God's Spirit working in us. We can learn and grow daily, motivated by love, and not by fear or pride, knowing that God gives the energy to become mature.

1:28–29 Christ's message is for everyone; so everywhere Paul and Timothy went they brought the Good News to all who would listen. An effective presentation of the gospel includes *admonishing* (warning) and teaching. The warning is that, without Christ, people are doomed to eternal separation from God. The teaching is that salvation is available through faith in Christ. As Christ works in you, tell others about him, warning and teaching them in love. Who do you know that needs to hear this message?

2:1 Laodicea was located a few miles northwest of Colossae. Like the church at Colossae, the Laodicean church was probably founded by one of Paul's converts while Paul was staying in Ephesus (Acts 19:10). The city was a wealthy center of trade and commerce, but later Christ would criticize the believers at Laodicea for their lukewarm commitment (Revelation 3:14–22). The fact that Paul wanted this letter to be passed on to the Laodicean church (4:16) indicates that false teaching may have spread there as well. Paul was counting on ties of love to bring the churches together to stand against this heresy and to encourage each other to remain true to God's plan of salvation in Christ. Our churches should be encouraging, unified communities committed to carrying out Christ's work.

2:4ff The problem that Paul was combating in the Colossian church was similar to *Gnosticism* (from the Greek word for *knowledge*). This *heresy* (a teaching contrary to Biblical doctrine) undermined Christianity in several basic ways: (1) It insisted that important secret knowledge was hidden from most believers; Paul, however, said that Christ provides all the knowledge we need. (2) It taught that the body was evil; Paul countered that God himself lived in a body—that is, he was embodied in Jesus Christ. (3) It contended that Christ only seemed to be human, but was not; Paul insisted that Jesus is fully human and fully God.

Gnosticism became fashionable in the second century. Even in Paul's day, these ideas sounded attractive to many, and exposure to such teachings could easily seduce a church that didn't know Christian doctrine well. Similar teachings still pose significant problems for many in the church today. We combat heresy by becoming thoroughly acquainted with God's Word through personal study and sound Bible teaching.

2:6–7 Receiving Christ as Lord of your life is the beginning of life with Christ. But you must continue to follow his leadership by being rooted, built up, and established in the faith. Christ wants to guide you and help you with your daily problems. You can live for Christ by (1) committing your life and submitting your will to him (Romans 12:1–2); (2) seeking to learn from him, his life, and his teachings (3:16); and (3) recognizing the Holy Spirit's power in you (Acts 1:8; Galatians 5:22).

2:7 Paul uses the illustration of our being rooted in Christ. Just as plants draw nourishment from the soil through their roots, so we draw our life-giving strength from Christ. The more we draw our strength from him, the less we will be fooled by those who falsely claim to have life's answers. If Christ is our strength, we will be free from human regulations.

2:8 Paul writes against any philosophy of life based only on human ideas and experiences. Paul himself was a gifted philosopher, so he is not condemning philosophy. He is condemning teaching that credits humanity, not Christ, with being the answer to life's problems. That approach becomes a false religion. There are many man-made approaches to life's problems that totally disregard God. To resist heresy you must use your mind, keep your eyes on Christ, and study God's Word.

2:9 Again Paul asserts Christ's deity. "In Him all the fullness of Deity dwells in bodily form" means that all of God was in Christ's human body. When we have Christ we have everything we need for salvation and right living. See the note on 1:15–16 for more on the divine nature of Christ.

2:10 Eph 3:19; Eph 1:21f; 1 Cor 15:24

2:11 Rom 2:29; 6:6; 7:24; Gal 5:24; Col 3:5

2:12 Rom 6:4f; Eph 2:6

2:13 Eph 2:1; Eph 2:5

2:14 Eph 2:15; Col 2:20; 1 Pet 2:24

2:15 Eph 4:8; John 12:31; 1 Cor 15:24

10 and in Him you have been made complete, and He is the head over all rule and
authority;
11 and in Him you were also circumcised with a circumcision made without hands, in
the removal of the body of the flesh by the circumcision of Christ;
12 having been buried with Him in baptism, in which you were also raised up with Him
through faith in the working of God, who raised Him from the dead.
13 When you were dead in your transgressions and the uncircumcision of your flesh,
He made you alive together with Him, having forgiven us all our transgressions,
14 having canceled out the certificate of debt consisting of decrees against us, which
was hostile to us; and He has taken it out of the way, having nailed it to the cross.
15 When He had disarmed the rulers and authorities, He made a public display of them,
having triumphed over them through Him.

SALVATION THROUGH FAITH

	Religion by Self-effort	*Salvation by Faith*
Goal	Please God by our own good deeds	Trust in Christ and then live to please God
Means	Practice, diligent service, discipline, and obedience, in hope of reward	Confess, submit, and commit yourself to Christ's control
Power	Good, honest effort through self-determination	The Holy Spirit helps us do good work for Christ's kingdom
Control	Self-motivation; self-control	Christ is in us; we are in Christ
Results	Chronic guilt, apathy, depression, failure, constant desire for approval	Joy, thankfulness, love, guidance, service, forgiveness

Salvation by faith in Christ sounds too easy for many people. They would rather think that they have done something to save themselves. Their religion becomes one of self-effort that leads either to disappointment or pride, but finally to eternal death. Christ's simple way is the only way, and it alone leads to eternal life.

2:10 When we know Jesus Christ, we don't need to seek God by means of other religions, cults, or unbiblical philosophies as the Colossians were doing. Christ alone holds the answers to the true meaning of life, because he *is* life. Christ is the unique source of knowledge and power for the Christian life. No Christian needs anything in addition to what Christ has provided to be saved. We are complete in him.

2:11 Jewish males were circumcised as a sign of the Jews' covenant with God (Genesis 17:9–14). With the death of Christ, circumcision was no longer necessary. So now our commitment to God is written on our hearts, not our bodies. Christ sets us free from our evil desires by a spiritual operation, not a bodily one. God removes the old nature and gives us a new self.

2:11–12 In this passage, circumcision is related to baptism; therefore, some see baptism as the New Testament sign of the covenant, identifying the person with the covenant community. Baptism parallels the death, burial, and resurrection of Christ, and it also portrays the death and burial of our sinful old way of life followed by resurrection to new life in Christ. Remembering that our old sinful life is dead and buried with Christ gives us a powerful motive to resist sin. Not wanting the desires of our past to come back to power again, we can consciously choose to treat our desires as if they were dead. Then we can continue to enjoy our wonderful new life with Christ (see Galatians 3:27 and Colossians 3:1–4).

2:13–15 Before we believed in Christ, our nature was evil. We disobeyed, rebelled, and ignored God (even at our best, we did not love him with all our heart, soul, and mind). The Christian, however, has a new self. God has crucified the old rebellious nature (Romans 6:6) and replaced it with a new loving nature (3:9–10). The penalty of sin died with Christ on the cross. God has declared us not guilty, and we need no longer live under sin's power. God does not take us out of the world or make us robots—we will still feel like sinning, and sometimes we will sin. The difference is that before we were saved, we were slaves to our sinful nature, but now we are free to live for Christ (see Galatians 2:20).

2:14 The certificate of debt that was canceled was the legal demands of the Old Testament law. The law opposed us by its demands for payment for our sin. Though no one can be saved by merely keeping that code, the moral truths and principles in the Old Testament still teach and guide today.

2:14 We can enjoy our new life in Christ because we have joined him in his death and resurrection. Our evil desires, our bondage to sin, and our love of sin died with him. Now, joining him in his resurrection life, we may have unbroken fellowship with God and freedom from sin. Our debt for sin has been paid in full; our sins are swept away and forgotten by God; and we can be clean and new. For more on the difference between our new life in Christ and our old sinful nature, read Ephesians 4:23–24 and Colossians 3:3–15.

2:15 Who are these rulers and authorities? Several suggestions have been made, including (1) demonic powers, (2) the gods of the powerful nations, (3) angels (highly regarded by the heretical teachers), or (4) the government of Rome. These powers and authorities were probably not the demonic forces in 2:10. More likely they are the angels who were mediators of the law (Galatians 3:19). The Colossian false teachers were encouraging worship of angels. But at his death, Christ surpassed the position and authority of any angel. So rather than fear angels or worship them, we are to view them as deposed rulers. Paul meant no disrespect toward angels, but he showed that they are not to be compared with Jesus Christ. Some scholars believe these powers are the powers of Rome. By his resurrection, Christ stripped the power away from a world empire that seemed to temporarily defeat him.

16 Therefore no one is to act as your judge in regard to food or drink or in respect to
a festival or a new moon or a Sabbath day—
17 things which are a *mere* shadow of what is to come; but the substance belongs to
Christ.
18 Let no one keep defrauding you of your prize by delighting in self-abasement and
the worship of the angels, taking his stand on *visions* he has seen, inflated without cause
by his fleshly mind,
19 and not holding fast to the head, from whom the entire body, being supplied and
held together by the joints and ligaments, grows with a growth which is from God.
20 If you have died with Christ to the elementary principles of the world, why, as if you
were living in the world, do you submit yourself to decrees, such as,
21 "Do not handle, do not taste, do not touch!"
22 (which all *refer to* things destined to perish with use)—in accordance with the commandments and teachings of men?
23 These are matters which have, to be sure, the appearance of wisdom in self-made
religion and self-abasement and severe treatment of the body, *but are* of no value against
fleshly indulgence.

2:16 Rom 14:3; Mark 7:19; Heb 9:10; Mark 2:27f; Gal 4:10

2:17 Heb 8:5; 10:1

2:18 1 Cor 9:24; Phil 3:14; Col 2:23; 1 Cor 4:6; Rom 8:7

2:19 Eph 1:22; Eph 1:23; 4:16

2:20 Rom 6:2; Col 2:8; Gal 4:9; Col 2:14, 16

2:23 Col 2:18; 1 Tim 4:3; Rom 13:14; 1 Tim 4:8

2:16 "Food or drink" probably refers to the Jewish dietary laws. The festivals mentioned are Jewish holy days celebrated annually, monthly (new moon), and weekly (the Sabbath). These rituals distinguished the Jews from their pagan neighbors. Failure to observe them could be easily noticed by those who were keeping track of what others did. But we should not let ourselves be judged by the opinions of others, because Christ has set us free.

2:16–17 Paul told the Colossian Christians not to let others criticize their diet or their religious ceremonies. Instead of outward observance, believers should focus on faith in Christ alone. Our worship, traditions and ceremonies can help bring us close to God, but we should never criticize fellow Christians whose traditions and ceremonies differ from ours. More important than how we worship is that we worship Christ. Don't let anyone judge you. You are responsible to Christ.

2:17 Old Testament laws, holidays, and festivals pointed toward Christ. Paul calls them a "shadow" of the reality that was to come—Christ himself. When Christ came, he dispelled the shadow. If we have Christ, we have what we need to know and please God.

2:18 The false teachers were proud of their humility! This false humility (self-abasement) brought attention and praise to themselves rather than to God. True humility means seeing ourselves as we really are from God's perspective, and acting accordingly. People today practice false humility when they talk negatively about themselves so that others will think they are spiritual. False humility is self-centered; true humility is God-centered.

2:18 The false teachers were claiming that God was far away and could be approached only through various levels of angels. They taught that people had to worship angels in order, eventually, to reach God. This is unscriptural; the Bible teaches that angels are God's servants, and it forbids worshiping them (Exodus 20:3–4; Revelation 22:8–9). As you grow in your Christian faith, let God's Word be your guide, not the opinions of other people.

2:18 The expression "fleshly mind" means that these people had a self-made religion. The false teachers were trying to deny the significance of the body by saying that it was evil, but their desire for attention from others showed that, in reality, they were obsessed with the physical realm.

2:19 The fundamental problem with the false teachers was that they were not connected to Christ, the head of the body of believers. If they had been joined to him, they could not have taught false doctrine or lived immorally. Anyone who teaches about God without being connected to him by faith should not be trusted.

2:20 The "elementary principles" are the beliefs of pagans. See 2:8 for more on Paul's view of non-Christian philosophy.

2:20; 3:1 How do we die with Christ, and how are we raised with him? When a person becomes a Christian, he or she is given new life through the power of the Holy Spirit. See the notes on 2:11–12 and 2:13–15 for further information.

2:20–23 People should be able to see a difference between the way Christians and non-Christians live. Still, we should not expect instant maturity in new Christians. Christian growth is a lifelong process. Although we have a new self, we don't automatically think all good thoughts and have all pure attitudes when we become new people in Christ. But if we keep listening to God, we will be changing all the time. As you look over the last year, what changes for the better have you seen in your thoughts and attitudes? Change may be slow, but your life will change significantly if you trust God to change you.

2:20–23 We cannot reach up to God by following rules of self-denial, by observing rituals, or by practicing religion. Paul isn't saying all rules are bad (see the note on Galatians 2:15–16). But no keeping of laws or rules will earn salvation. The Good News is that God reaches down to human beings, and he asks for our response. Self-made religions focus on human effort; Christianity focuses on Christ's work. Believers must put aside sinful desires, but doing so is the by-product of our new life in Christ, not the reason for our new life. Our salvation does not depend on our own discipline and rule-keeping, but on the power of Christ's death and resurrection.

2:22–23 We can guard against self-made religions by asking these questions about any religious group: (1) Does it stress man-made rules and taboos rather than God's grace? (2) Does it foster a critical spirit toward others, or does it exercise discipline discreetly and lovingly? (3) Does it stress formulas, secret knowledge, or special visions more than the Word of God? (4) Does it elevate self-righteousness, honoring those who keep the rules, rather than elevating Christ? (5) Does it neglect Christ's universal church, claiming to be an elite group? (6) Does it teach humiliation of the body as a means to spiritual growth rather than focusing on the growth of the whole person? (7) Does it disregard the family rather than holding it in high regard as the Bible does?

2:23 To the Colossians, the discipline demanded by the false teachers seemed good, and legalism still attracts many people today. Following a long list of religious rules requires strong self-discipline and can make a person appear moral, but religious rules cannot change a person's heart. Only the Holy Spirit can do that.

3:1
Col 2:12; Ps 110:1

3:2
Matt 16:23; Phil 3:19, 20

3:3
Rom 6:2; 2 Cor 5:14; Col 2:20

3:4
1 Cor 1:7; Phil 3:21; 1 Pet 1:13; 1 John 2:28; 3:2

3:5
Mark 7:21f; 1 Cor 6:9f, 18; 2 Cor 12:21; Gal 5:19f; Eph 4:19; 5:3, 5

3:6
Rom 1:18; Eph 5:6

3:8
Eph 4:22; Eph 4:31

2. What Christians should do

Put On the New Self

3 Therefore if you have been raised up with Christ, keep seeking the things above, where
Christ is, seated at the right hand of God.
2 Set your mind on the things above, not on the things that are on earth.
3 For you have died and your life is hidden with Christ in God.
4 When Christ, who is our life, is revealed, then you also will be revealed with Him in
glory.
5 Therefore consider the members of your earthly body as dead to immorality, impurity, passion, evil desire, and greed, which amounts to idolatry.
6 For it is because of these things that the wrath of God will come [2]upon the sons of
disobedience,
7 and in them you also once walked, when you were living in them.
8 But now you also, put them all aside: anger, wrath, malice, slander, *and* abusive
speech from your mouth.
9 Do not lie to one another, since you laid aside the old self with its *evil* practices,

2 Two early mss do not contain *upon the sons of disobedience*

FROM DEATH TO LIFE

The Bible uses many illustrations to teach what happens when we choose to let Jesus be Lord of our lives. Following are some of the most vivid pictures:

1. Because Christ died for us, we have been crucified with him.	Romans 6:2–13; 7:4–6 2 Corinthians 5:14 Galatians 2:20; 5:24; 6:14 Colossians 2:20; 3:3–5 1 Peter 2:24
2. Our old, rebellious nature died with Christ.	Romans 6:6; 7:4–6 Colossians 3:9–10
3. Christ's resurrection guarantees our new life now and eternal life with him later.	Romans 6:4, 11 Colossians 2:12, 13; 3:1, 3

This process is acted out in baptism (Colossians 2:12), based on our faith in Christ: (1) The old sinful nature dies (crucified); (2) We are ready to receive a new life (buried); (3) Christ gives us new life (resurrected).

3:1ff In chapter 2, Paul exposed the wrong reasons for self-denial. In chapter 3, he explains true Christian behavior—putting on the new self by accepting Christ and regarding the earthly nature as dead. We change our moral and ethical behavior by letting Christ live within us, so that he can shape us into what we *should* be.

3:1–2 Setting our minds on things above means striving to put heaven's priorities into daily practice. Setting our minds on things above means concentrating on the eternal rather than the temporal. See Philippians 4:9 and Colossians 3:15 for more on Christ's rule in our hearts and minds.

3:2–3 "For you have died" means that we should have as little desire for this world as a dead person would have. The Christian's real home is where Christ lives (John 14:2–3). This truth gives us a different perspective on our lives here on earth. To "set your mind on the things above" means to look at life from God's perspective and to seek what he desires. This is the antidote to materialism; we gain the proper perspective on material goods when we take God's view of them. The more we regard the world around us as God does, the more we will live in harmony with him. We must not become too attached to what is only temporary.

3:3 What does it mean that a believer's life is "hidden with Christ"? *Hidden* means concealed and safe. This is not only a future hope, but an accomplished fact right now. Our service and conduct do not earn our salvation, but they are results of our salvation. Take heart that your salvation is sure, and live each day for Christ.

3:4 Christ gives us power to live for him now, and he gives us hope for the future—he will return. In the rest of this chapter Paul explains how Christians should act *now* in order to be prepared for Christ's return.

3:5 We should consider ourselves dead and unresponsive to sexual immorality, impurity, passion, evil desires, and greed. Just like diseased limbs of a tree, these practices must be cut off before they destroy us. We must make a conscious, daily decision to remove anything that supports or feeds these desires and to rely on the Holy Spirit's power.

3:6 The "wrath of God" refers to God's judgment on these kinds of behavior, culminating with future and final punishment of evil. When tempted to sin, remember that you must one day stand before God.

3:8–10 We must rid ourselves of all evil practices and immorality. Then we can commit ourselves to what Christ teaches. Paul was appealing to the commitment the believers had made and urging them to remain true to their confession of faith. They were to rid themselves of the old life and "put on" the new way of living given by Christ and guided by the Holy Spirit. If you have made such a commitment to Christ, are you remaining true to it?

3:9 Lying to one another disrupts unity by destroying trust. It tears down relationships and may lead to serious conflict in a church. So don't exaggerate statistics, pass on rumors or gossip, or say things to build up your own image. Be committed to telling the truth.

10 and have put on the new self who is being renewed to a true knowledge according
to the image of the One who created him—
11 *a renewal* in which there is no *distinction between* Greek and Jew, circumcised and
uncircumcised, [3]barbarian, Scythian, slave and freeman, but Christ is all, and in all.
12 So, as those who have been chosen of God, holy and beloved, put on a heart of compassion, kindness, humility, gentleness and patience;
13 bearing with one another, and forgiving each other, whoever has a complaint against
anyone; just as the Lord forgave you, so also should you.
14 Beyond all these things *put on* love, which is the perfect bond of unity.
15 Let the peace of Christ rule in your hearts, to which indeed you were called in one
body; and be thankful.
16 Let the word of [4]Christ richly dwell within you, with all wisdom teaching and admonishing one another with psalms *and* hymns *and* spiritual songs, singing with thankfulness in your hearts to God.
17 Whatever you do in word or deed, *do* all in the name of the Lord Jesus, giving thanks
through Him to God the Father.

Family Relations

18 Wives, be subject to your husbands, as is fitting in the Lord.
19 Husbands, love your wives and do not be embittered against them.
20 Children, be obedient to your parents in all things, for this is well-pleasing to the
Lord.

3 I.e. those who were not Greeks, either by birth or by culture 4 One early ms reads *the Lord*

3:10 Eph 4:24; Rom 12:2; Rom 8:29; Eph 2:10
3:11 1 Cor 7:19; Gal 5:6; Acts 28:2
3:12 Eph 4:24; Gal 5:22f; Phil 2:1; Eph 4:2
3:13 Eph 4:2; Rom 15:7
3:14 Eph 4:3; John 17:23; Heb 6:1
3:15 Eph 2:16
3:16 Rom 10:17; Eph 5:26; 1 Thess 1:8; Col 1:28
3:17 1 Cor 10:31
3:18 Eph 5:22-6:9
3:19 Eph 5:25; 1 Pet 3:7
3:20 Eph 6:1

3:10 What does it mean to "put on the new self"? It means that your conduct should match your faith. If you are a Christian, you should act like it. To be a Christian means more than just making good resolutions and having good intentions; it means taking the right actions. This is a straightforward step that is as simple as putting on your clothes.

3:10 Every Christian is in a continuing education program. The more we know of Christ and his work, the more we are being changed to be like him. Because this process is lifelong, we must never stop learning and obeying. There is no justification for drifting along, but there is an incentive to find the rich treasures of growing in him. It takes practice, ongoing review, patience, and concentration to keep in line with his will.

3:11 The Christian church should have no barriers of nationality, race, education level, social standing, wealth, gender, religion, or power. Christ breaks down all barriers and accepts all people who come to him. Nothing should keep us from telling others about Christ or accepting into our fellowship any and all believers (Ephesians 2:14–15). Christians should be building bridges, not walls.

3:12–17 Paul offers a strategy to help us live for God day by day: (1) imitate Christ's compassionate, forgiving attitude (3:12–13); (2) let love guide your life (3:14); (3) let the peace of Christ rule in your heart (3:15); (4) always be thankful (3:15); (5) keep God's word in you at all times (3:16); (6) live as Jesus Christ's representative (3:17).

3:13 The key to forgiving others is remembering how much God has forgiven you. Is it difficult for you to forgive someone who has wronged you a little when God has forgiven you so much? Realizing God's infinite love and forgiveness can help you love and forgive others.

3:14 All the virtues that Paul encourages us to develop are perfectly bound together by love. As we clothe ourselves with these virtues, the last garment we are to put on is love, which holds all of the others in place. To practice any list of virtues without practicing love will lead to distortion, fragmentation, and stagnation (1 Corinthians 13:3).

3:14–15 Christians should live in peace. To live in peace does not mean that suddenly all differences in opinion are eliminated, but it does require that loving Christians work together despite their differences. Such love is not a feeling, but a decision to meet others' needs (see 1 Corinthians 13). To live in love leads to peace between individuals and among the members of the body of believers. Do problems in your relationships with other Christians cause open conflicts or mutual silence? Consider what you can do to heal those relationships with love.

3:15 The word *rule* comes from the language of athletics: Paul tells us to let Christ's peace be umpire or referee in our hearts. Our hearts are the center of conflict because there our feelings and desires clash—our fears and hopes, distrust and trust, jealousy and love. How can we deal with these constant conflicts and live as God wants? Paul explains that we must decide between conflicting elements by using the rule of peace—which choice will promote peace in our souls and in our churches? For more on the peace of Christ, see Philippians 4:9.

3:16 Although the early Christians had access to the Old Testament and freely used it, they did not yet have the New Testament or any other Christian books to study. Their stories and teachings about Christ were memorized and passed on from person to person. Sometimes the teachings were set to music, and so music became an important part of Christian worship and education.

3:17 Doing "all in the name of the Lord Jesus" means bringing honor to Christ in every aspect and activity of daily living. As a Christian, you represent Christ at all times—wherever you go and whatever you say. What impression do people have of Christ when they see or talk with you? What changes would you make in your life in order to honor Christ?

3:18—4:1 Paul gives rules for three sets of household relationships: (1) husbands and wives, (2) parents and children, and (3) masters and slaves. In each case there is mutual responsibility to submit and love, to obey and encourage, to work hard and be fair. Examine your family and work relationships. Do you relate to others as God intended? See Ephesians 5:21—6:9 for similar instructions.

3:19 Christian marriage involves mutual submission, subordinating our personal desires for the good of the loved one, and submitting ourselves to Christ as Lord. For more on submission, see the notes on Ephesians 5:21–33.

3:20–21 Children must be handled with care. They need firm discipline administered in love. Don't alienate them by nagging, deriding, or destroying their self-respect so that they lose heart.

21 Fathers, do not exasperate your children, so that they will not lose heart.
22 Slaves, in all things obey those who are your masters on earth, not with external
service, as those who *merely* please men, but with sincerity of heart, fearing the Lord.
23 Whatever you do, do your work heartily, as for the Lord rather than for men,
24 knowing that from the Lord you will receive the reward of the inheritance. It is the
Lord Christ whom you serve.
25 For he who does wrong will receive the consequences of the wrong which he has
done, and that without partiality.

Fellow Workers

4 Masters, grant to your slaves justice and fairness, knowing that you too have a Master in heaven.
2 Devote yourselves to prayer, keeping alert in it with *an attitude of* thanksgiving;
3 praying at the same time for us as well, that God will open up to us a door for the
word, so that we may speak forth the mystery of Christ, for which I have also been imprisoned;
4 that I may make it clear in the way I ought to speak.
5 Conduct yourselves with wisdom toward outsiders, making the most of the opportunity.
6 Let your speech always be with grace, *as though* seasoned with salt, so that you will
know how you should respond to each person.
7 As to all my affairs, Tychicus, *our* beloved brother and faithful servant and fellow
bond-servant in the Lord, will bring you information.

3:21 Eph 6:4
3:22 Eph 6:5; Eph 6:6
3:23 Eph 6:7
3:24 Eph 6:8; Acts 20:32
3:25 Eph 6:8; Acts 10:34
4:1 Eph 6:9
4:2 Acts 1:14; Eph 6:18
4:3 Eph 6:19; Acts 14:27; 2 Tim 4:2
4:4 Eph 6:20
4:5 Eph 5:15
4:6 Eph 4:29; Mark 9:50; 1 Pet 3:15
4:7 Acts 20:4; 2 Tim 4:12; Eph 6:21

SINS VERSUS SIGNS OF LOVE

Sins of Sexual Attitude and Behavior	*Sins of Speech*	*Signs of Love*
Evil desires	Anger expressed	Compassion
Sexual immorality	Wrath	Kindness
Impurity	Malice	Humility
Passion	Slander	Gentleness
Greed	Abusive speech	Patience
	Lying	Forgiveness

In Colossians 3:5 Paul tells us to put to death the things found in list 1. In 3:8 he tells us to rid ourselves of the things found in list 2. In 3:12 we're told to practice the things found in list 3. List 1 deals with sins of sexual attitudes and behavior—they are particularly destructive because of what they do to destroy any group or church. List 2 deals with sins of speech—these are the relationship-breakers. List 3 contains the relationship-builders, which we are to express as members of Christ's body.

3:22—4:1 Paul does not condemn or condone slavery, but explains that Christ transcends all divisions between people. Slaves are told to work hard as though their master were Christ himself (3:22–25); but masters should be just and fair (4:1). Perhaps Paul was thinking specifically of Onesimus and Philemon—the slave and master whose conflict lay behind the letter to Philemon (see the book of Philemon). Philemon was a slave owner in the Colossian church, and Onesimus had been his slave (4:9).

3:23 Since the creation, God has given us work to do. If we could regard our work as an act of worship or service to God, such an attitude would take some of the drudgery and boredom out of it. We could work without complaining or resentment if we would treat our job problems as the cost of discipleship.

4:1 Masters were to provide what was just and fair. Similarly today, employers should pay fair wages and treat their employees justly. And leaders should take care of their volunteers and not abuse them. If you have responsibility over others, make sure you do what is just and fair—you are accountable to your Master in heaven.

4:2 Have you ever grown tired of praying for something or someone? Paul says we should "devote" ourselves to prayer and be "alert" in prayer. Our persistence is an expression of our faith that God answers our prayers. Faith shouldn't die if the answers come slowly, for the delay may be God's way of working his will in our lives. When you feel tired of praying, know that God is present, always listening, always answering—maybe not in ways you had hoped, but in ways that he knows are best.

4:3 The "mystery of Christ" is Christ's Good News of salvation, the gospel. The whole focus of Paul's life was to tell others about Christ, explaining and preaching this wonderful mystery.

4:4 Paul asked for prayer that he could proclaim the Good News about Christ clearly, and we can request prayer to do the same. No matter what approach to evangelism we use, whether emphasizing life-style and example or whether building relationships, we should never obscure the message of the gospel.

4:5 We should be wise in our contacts with non-Christians ("outsiders"), making the most of our opportunities to tell them the Good News of salvation. What opportunities do you have?

4:6 When we tell others about Christ, it is important always to be gracious in what we say. No matter how much sense the message makes, we lose our effectiveness if we are not courteous. Just as we like to be respected, we must respect others if we want them to listen to what we have to say. "Seasoned with salt" means that what we say should be "tasty" and should encourage further dialogue.

4:7 Tychicus was one of Paul's personal representatives and probably the bearer of the letters to the Colossians and Ephesians (see also Ephesians 6:21–22). He accompanied Paul to Jerusalem with the collection for the church (Acts 20:4).

8 *For* I have sent him to you for this very purpose, that you may know about our circumstances and that he may encourage your hearts;
9 and with him Onesimus, *our* faithful and beloved brother, who is one of your *num-*
ber. They will inform you about the whole situation here.
10 Aristarchus, my fellow prisoner, sends you his greetings; and *also* Barnabas's cousin Mark (about whom you received instructions; if he comes to you, welcome him);
11 and *also* Jesus who is called Justus; these are the only fellow workers for the kingdom of God who are from the circumcision, and they have proved to be an encouragement to me.
12 Epaphras, who is one of your number, a bondslave of Jesus Christ, sends you his
greetings, always laboring earnestly for you in his prayers, that you may stand perfect
and fully assured in all the will of God.
13 For I testify for him that he has a deep concern for you and for those who are in
Laodicea and Hierapolis.
14 Luke, the beloved physician, sends you his greetings, and *also* Demas.
15 Greet the brethren who are in Laodicea and also [5]Nympha and the church that is in
her house.
16 When this letter is read among you, have it also read in the church of the Laodiceans; and you, for your part read my letter *that is coming* from Laodicea.

5 Or *Nymphas* (masc)

4:8 Eph 6:22; Col 2:2
4:9 Philem 10; Col 1:7
4:10 Acts 19:29; 27:2; Philem 24; Rom 16:7; Acts 4:36; 12:12, 25; 15:37, 39; 2 Tim 4:11
4:11 Rom 16:3; Acts 11:2
4:12 Col 1:7; Philem 23; Col 4:9; Rom 15:30; Col 1:28
4:14 2 Tim 4:11; Philem 24; 2 Tim 4:10
4:15 Col 2:1; 4:13, 16; Rom 16:5
4:16 1 Thess 5:27; 2 Thess 3:14; Col 2:1; 4:13, 15

RULES OF SUBMISSION

Wives, be subject to your husbands (3:18).	*Husbands*, love your wives and don't be embittered against them (3:19).
Children, be obedient to your parents (3:20).	*Parents*, don't exasperate your children so that they lose heart (3:21).
Slaves, obey your masters (3:22).	*Masters*, grant your slaves justice and fairness (4:1).
(*Employees*, work hard for your employers.)	(*Employers*, be just and fair with your employees.)

The New Testament includes many instructions concerning relationships. Most people read these instructions for the other person and ignore the ones that apply to themselves. But you can't control another person's behavior, only your own. Start by following your own instructions and not insisting on the obedience of others first.

4:10 Aristarchus was a Thessalonian who accompanied Paul on his third missionary journey. He was with Paul in the riot at Ephesus (Acts 19:29). He and Tychicus were with Paul in Greece (Acts 20:4). Aristarchus went to Rome with Paul (Acts 27:2). Mark started out with Paul and Barnabas on their first missionary journey (Acts 12:25), but he left in the middle of the trip for unknown reasons (Acts 13:13). Barnabas and Mark were relatives, and when Paul refused to take Mark on another journey, Barnabas and Mark journeyed together to preach the Good News (Acts 15:37–41). Mark also worked with Peter (Acts 12:12–13; 1 Peter 5:13). Later, Mark and Paul were reconciled (Philemon 24). Mark wrote the Gospel of Mark. His Profile is in Acts 13.

4:12 Epaphras founded the Colossian church (see the note on 1:7), and his report to Paul in Rome caused Paul to write this letter. Epaphras was a hero of the Colossian church, one of the believers who helped keep the church together despite growing troubles. His earnest prayers for the believers show his deep love and concern for them.

4:13 Laodicea was located a few miles northwest of Colossae; Hierapolis was about five miles north of Laodicea. See the note on 2:1 for more about Laodicea.

4:14 Luke spent much time with Paul, not only accompanying him on most of his third missionary journey, but sitting with him in the prison at Rome. Luke wrote the Gospel of Luke and the book of Acts. His Profile is in Acts 17. Demas was faithful for a while, but then he deserted Paul, having "loved this present world" (2 Timothy 4:10).

4:15 The early Christians often met in homes. Church buildings were not common until the third century.

4:16 Some suggest that the letter from Laodicea may be the book of Ephesians, because the letter to the Ephesians was circulated to all the churches in Asia Minor. It is also possible that there was a special letter to the Laodiceans, of which we have no record today. Paul wrote several letters that have been lost (see, for example, 2 Corinthians 2:3 and note).

4:17
Philem 2; 2 Tim 4:5

4:18
1 Cor 16:21; Heb 13:3; 1 Tim 6:21; 2 Tim 4:22; Titus 3:15; Heb 13:25

17 Say to Archippus, "Take heed to the ministry which you have received in the Lord,
that you may fulfill it."
18 I, Paul, write this greeting with my own hand. Remember my imprisonment. Grace
be with you.

4:17 Paul's letter to Philemon is also addressed to Archippus (Philemon 2). Paul called him a "fellow soldier." He may have been a Roman soldier who had become a member of the Colossian church, or he may have been Philemon's son.

4:17 Paul encouraged Archippus to make sure that he completed the work he had received in the Lord. There are many ways for us to leave our work unfinished. We can easily get sidetracked morally, we can become exhausted and stop, we can get mad and quit, or we can let it slide and leave it up to others. We should see to it that we finish God's assignments, completing the work we have received.

4:18 Paul usually dictated his letters to a scribe, and then often ended with a short note in his own handwriting (see also 1 Corinthians 16:21; Galatians 6:11). This assured the recipients that false teachers were not writing letters in Paul's name. It also gave the letters a personal touch.

4:18 To understand the letter to the Colossians, we need to know that the church was facing pressure from a heresy that promised deeper spiritual life through secret knowledge (an early form of Gnosticism). The false teachers were destroying faith in Christ by undermining Christ's humanity and divinity.

Paul makes it clear in Colossians that Christ alone is the source of our spiritual life, the Head of the body of believers. Christ is Lord of both the physical and spiritual worlds. The path to deeper spiritual life is not through religious duties, special knowledge, or secrets; it is only through a clear connection with the Lord Jesus Christ. We must never let anything come between us and our Savior.

1 THESSALONIANS

VITAL STATISTICS

PURPOSE:
To strengthen the Thessalonian Christians in their faith and give them the assurance of Christ's return

AUTHOR:
Paul

TO WHOM WRITTEN:
The church at Thessalonica, and all believers everywhere

DATE WRITTEN:
Approximately A.D. 51 from Corinth; one of Paul's earliest letters

SETTING:
The church at Thessalonica was very young, having been established only two or three years before this letter was written. The Thessalonian Christians needed to mature in their faith. In addition, there was a misunderstanding concerning Christ's second coming—some thought Christ would return immediately, and thus they were confused when their loved ones died because they expected Christ to return beforehand. Also, believers were being persecuted.

KEY VERSE:
"For if we believe that Jesus died and rose again, even so God will bring with Him those who have fallen asleep in Jesus" (4:14).

KEY PEOPLE:
Paul, Timothy, Silas

KEY PLACE:
Thessalonica

SPECIAL FEATURES:
Paul received from Timothy a favorable report about the Thessalonians. However, Paul wrote this letter to correct their misconceptions about the resurrection and the second coming of Christ.

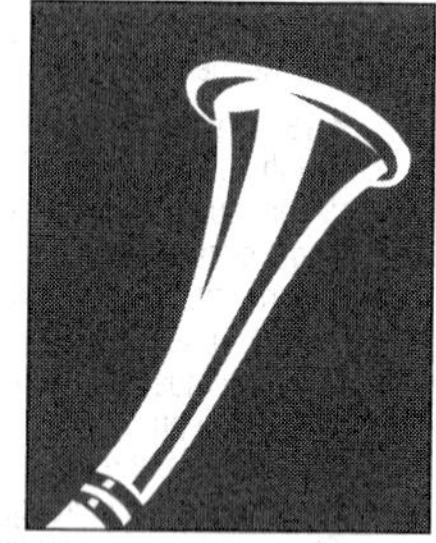

SLOWLY they walk, one by one, scattering the leaves and trampling the grass under measured and heavy steps. The minister's words still echoing in their minds, they hear workmen moving toward the terrible place, preparing to cover the casket of their loved one. Death, the enemy, has torn the bonded relationships of family and friends, leaving only memories . . . and tears . . . and loneliness.

But like a golden shaft of sun piercing the winter sky, a singular truth shatters the oppressive gloom: Death is not the end! Christ is the victor over death, and there is hope of the resurrection through him.

As with every member of the human family, first-century Christians came face to face with their mortality. Many of them met early deaths at the hands of those who hated Christ and all allied with him. Whether at the hands of zealous Jews (like Paul before his conversion), angry Greeks, or ruthless Roman authorities, persecution included stonings, beatings, crucifixions, torture, and death. To be a follower of Christ meant to give up everything.

Paul established the church in Thessalonica during his second missionary journey (in about A.D. 51). He wrote this letter a short time later to encourage the young believers there. He wanted to assure them of his love, to praise them for their faithfulness during persecution, and to remind them of their hope—the sure return of their Lord and Savior.

Paul begins this letter with a note of affirmation, thanking God for the strong faith and good reputation of the Thessalonians (1:1–10). Then Paul reviews their relationship—how he and his companions brought the gospel to them (2:1–12), how they accepted the message (2:13–16), and how he longed to be with them again (2:17–20). Because of his concern, Paul sent Timothy to encourage them in their faith (3:1–13).

Paul then presents the core of his message—exhortation and comfort. He challenges them to please God in their daily living by avoiding sexual immorality (4:1–8), loving each other (4:9–10), and living as good citizens in a sinful world (4:11–12).

Paul comforts the Thessalonians by reminding them of the hope of the resurrection (4:13–18). Then he warns them to be prepared at all times, for Jesus Christ could return at any moment. When Christ returns, those Christians who are alive and those who have died will be raised to new life (5:1–11).

Paul then gives the Thessalonians a handful of reminders on how to prepare themselves for the second coming: Admonish the unruly (5:14), encourage the fainthearted (5:14), help the weak (5:14), be patient with everyone (5:14), be kind to everyone (5:15), rejoice always (5:16), pray without ceasing (5:17), give thanks (5:18), examine everything that is taught (5:20–21), and abstain from evil (5:22). Paul concludes his letter with two benedictions and a request for prayer.

As you read this letter, listen carefully to Paul's practical advice for Christian living. And when burdened by grief and overwhelmed by sorrow, take hope in the reality of Christ's return, the resurrection, and eternal life!

THE BLUEPRINT

1. Faithfulness to the Lord (1:1—3:13)
2. Watchfulness for the Lord (4:1—5:28)

Paul and his companions were faithful to bring the gospel to the Thessalonians in the midst of persecution. The Thessalonians had only recently become Christians, and yet they had remained faithful to the Lord, despite the fact that the apostles were not with them. Others have been faithful in bringing God's Word to us. We must remain faithful and live in the expectation that Christ will return at any time.

MEGATHEMES

THEME	EXPLANATION	IMPORTANCE
Persecution	Paul and the new Christians at Thessalonica experienced persecution because of their faith in Christ. We can expect trials and troubles as well. We need to stand firm in our faith in the midst of trials, being strengthened by the Holy Spirit.	The Holy Spirit helps us to remain strong in faith, able to show genuine love to others and maintain our moral character even when we are being persecuted, slandered, or oppressed.
Paul's Ministry	Paul expressed his concern for this church even while he was being slandered. Paul's commitment to share the gospel in spite of difficult circumstances is a model we should follow.	Paul not only delivered his message, but gave of himself. In our ministries, we must become like Paul—faithful and bold, yet sensitive and self-sacrificing.
Hope	One day all believers, both those who are alive and those who have died, will be united with Christ. To those Christians who die before Christ's return, there is hope—the hope of the resurrection of the body.	If we believe in Christ, we will live with him forever. All those who belong to Jesus Christ—from throughout history—will be present with him at his second coming. We can be confident that we will be with loved ones who have trusted in Christ.
Being Prepared	No one knows the time of Christ's return. We are to live moral and holy lives, ever watchful for his coming. Believers must not neglect daily responsibilities, but always work and live to please the Lord.	The gospel is not only what we believe but also what we must live. The Holy Spirit leads us in faithfulness, so we can avoid lust and fraud. Live as though you expect Christ's return at any time. Don't be caught unprepared.

1. Faithfulness to the Lord

Thanksgiving for These Believers

1 Paul and Silvanus and Timothy,
To the church of the Thessalonians in God the Father and the Lord Jesus Christ:
Grace to you and peace.
2 We give thanks to God always for all of you, making mention *of you* in our prayers;
3 constantly bearing in mind your work of faith and labor of love and steadfastness of
hope in our Lord Jesus Christ in the presence of our God and Father,
4 knowing, brethren beloved by God, *His* choice of you;
5 for our gospel did not come to you in word only, but also in power and in the Holy
Spirit and with full conviction; just as you know what kind of men we proved to be among
you for your sake.
6 You also became imitators of us and of the Lord, having received the word in much
tribulation with the joy of the Holy Spirit,
7 so that you became an example to all the believers in Macedonia and in Achaia.
8 For the word of the Lord has sounded forth from you, not only in Macedonia and
Achaia, but also in every place your faith toward God has gone forth, so that we have no
need to say anything.
9 For they themselves report about us what kind of a reception we had with you, and
how you turned to God from idols to serve a living and true God,
10 and to wait for His Son from heaven, whom He raised from the dead, *that is* Jesus,
who rescues us from the wrath to come.

1:1 Acts 16:1
1:2 Rom 1:8
1:3 John 6:29; 1 Cor 13:13; Rom 8:25
1:4 Rom 1:7; 2 Thess 2:13; 2 Pet 1:10
1:5 1 Cor 9:14; Rom 15:19; Luke 1:1
1:6 Acts 17:5-10; 2 Tim 4:2; Acts 13:52; 2 Cor 6:10; Gal 5:22
1:8 Col 3:16; 2 Thess 3:1; Rom 10:18
1:9 1 Thess 2:1; Acts 14:15; 1 Cor 12:2; Matt 16:16
1:10 Matt 16:27f; 1 Cor 1:7; Acts 2:24; Rom 5:9; Matt 3:7; 1 Thess 2:16; 5:9

1:1 Paul and his companions probably arrived in Thessalonica in the early summer of A.D. 50. They planted the first Christian church in that city, but had to leave in a hurry because their lives were threatened (Acts 17:1–10). At the first opportunity, probably when he stopped at Corinth, Paul sent Timothy back to Thessalonica to see how the new believers were doing. Timothy returned to Paul with good news: the Christians in Thessalonica were remaining firm in the faith and were unified. But the Thessalonians did have some questions about their new faith. Paul had not had time to answer all their questions during his brief visit, and in the meantime, other questions had arisen. So Paul wrote this letter to answer their questions and to commend them on their faithfulness to Christ.

1:1 For more information on Paul, see his Profile in Acts 9. Timothy's Profile is in 1 Timothy. Silas accompanied Paul on his second missionary journey (Acts 15:36—17:15). He helped Paul establish the church in Thessalonica (Acts 17:1–9). He is also mentioned in 2 Corinthians 1:19, 2 Thessalonians 1:1, and in 1 Peter 5:12. Silas's Profile is found in Acts 16.

1:1 Thessalonica was the capital and largest city (about 200,000 population) of the Roman province of Macedonia. The most important Roman highway (the Egnatian Way)—extending from Rome all the way to the Orient—went through Thessalonica. This highway, along with the city's thriving seaport, made Thessalonica one of the wealthiest and most flourishing trade centers in the Roman empire. Recognized as a free city, Thessalonica was allowed self-rule and was exempted from most of the restrictions placed by Rome on other cities in the empire. However, with its international flavor came many pagan religions and cultural influences that challenged the faith of the young Christians there.

1:3 The Thessalonians had stood firm when they were persecuted (1:6; 3:1–4, 7–8). Paul commended these young Christians for their work of faith, labor of love, and steadfastness of hope. These characteristics are the marks of effective Christians in any age.

1:5 The gospel came "in power;" it had a powerful effect on the Thessalonians. Whenever the Bible is heard and obeyed, lives are changed! Christianity is more than a collection of interesting facts; it is the power of God to every one who believes. What has God's power done in your life since you first believed?

1:5 The Holy Spirit changes people when they believe the gospel. When we tell others about Christ, we must depend on the Holy Spirit to open their eyes and convince them that they need salvation. God's power changes people—not our cleverness or persuasion. Without the work of the Holy Spirit, our words are meaningless. The Holy Spirit not only convicts people of sin but also assures them of the truth of the gospel. (For more information on the Holy Spirit, see John 14:23–26; 15:26–27; and the notes on John 3:6 and Acts 1:5.)

1:5 Paul wrote, "You know what kind of men we proved to be among you for your sake." The Thessalonians could see that what Paul, Silas, and Timothy were preaching was true because these men lived it. Does your life confirm or contradict what you say you believe?

1:6 The word, the message of salvation, had been welcomed with joy, but had brought the Thessalonians much tribulation because it led to persecution from both Jews and Gentiles (3:2–4; Acts 17:5). Having believed the gospel message and accepted new life in Christ, apparently many Thessalonians believed that they would be protected from death until Christ returned. Then, when believers began to die under persecution, some Thessalonian Christians started to question their faith. Many of Paul's comments throughout this letter were addressed to these people, as he explained what happens when believers die (see 4:13ff).

1:9–10 All of us should respond to the Good News as the Thessalonians did: *turn* to God, *serve* God, and *wait* for his Son, Christ, to return from heaven. We should turn from sin to God because Christ is coming to judge the earth. We should be fervent in our service because we have little time before Christ returns. We should be prepared for Christ to return because we don't know when he will come.

1:10 Paul emphasized Christ's second coming throughout this book. Because the Thessalonian church was being persecuted, Paul encouraged them to look forward to the deliverance that Christ would bring. A believer's hope is in the return of Jesus, our great God and Savior (Titus 2:13). Our perspective on life remains incomplete without this hope. Just as surely as Christ was raised from the dead and ascended into heaven, he will return (Acts 1:11).

2:2
Acts 14:5; 16:19-24; Phil 1:30; Acts 16:22-24

2:3
Acts 13:15; 2 Thess 2:11; 1 Thess 4:7

2:4
2 Cor 2:17; Gal 2:7; Gal 1:10; Rom 8:27

2:5
Acts 20:33; 2 Pet 2:3; Rom 1:9

2:6
John 5:41, 44; 2 Cor 4:5; 1 Cor 9:1f

Paul's Ministry

2 For you yourselves know, brethren, that our coming to you was not in vain,
2 but after we had already suffered and been mistreated in Philippi, as you know,
we had the boldness in our God to speak to you the gospel of God amid much opposition.
3 For our exhortation does not *come* from error or impurity or by way of deceit;
4 but just as we have been approved by God to be entrusted with the gospel, so we
speak, not as pleasing men, but God who examines our hearts.
5 For we never came with flattering speech, as you know, nor with a pretext for greed—
God is witness—
6 nor did we seek glory from men, either from you or from others, even though as
apostles of Christ we might have asserted our authority.

LOCATION OF THESSALONICA
After Paul visited Thessalonica on his second missionary journey, he went on to Berea, Athens, and Corinth (Acts 17—18). From Corinth, Paul wrote his two letters to the Thessalonian church.

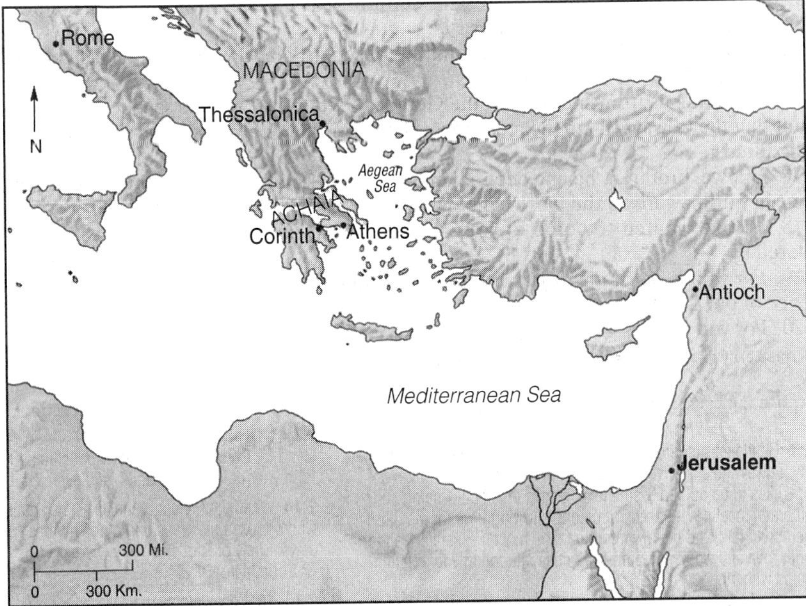

2:1 "Our coming to you" refers to Paul's first visit to Thessalonica (see Acts 17:1–9).

2:2 The Thessalonians knew that Paul had been imprisoned in Philippi just prior to coming to Thessalonica (see Acts 16:11—17:1). Fear of imprisonment did not keep Paul from preaching the gospel. If God wants us to do something, he will give us the strength and courage to do it despite any obstacles that may come our way.

2:3 This pointed statement may be a response to accusations from the Jewish leaders who had stirred up the crowds (Acts 17:5). Paul did not seek money, fame, or popularity by sharing the gospel. He demonstrated the sincerity of his motives by showing that he and Silas had suffered for sharing the gospel in Philippi. People become involved in ministry for a variety of reasons, not all of them good or pure. When their bad motives are exposed, all of Christ's work suffers. When you get involved in ministry, do so out of love for Christ and others.

2:4–8 In trying to persuade people, we may be tempted to alter our position just enough to make our message more palatable or to use flattery or praise. Paul never changed his *message* to make it more acceptable, but he did tailor his *methods* to each audience. Although our presentation must be altered to be appropriate to the situation, the truth of the gospel must never be compromised.

2:5 It's disgusting to hear a person "butter up" someone. Flattery is phony, and it is a false cover-up for a person's real intentions. Christians should not be flatterers. Those who proclaim God's truth have a special responsibility to be honest. Are you honest and straightforward in your words and actions? Or do you tell people what they want to hear in order to get what you want or to get ahead?

2:6–8 When Paul was with the Thessalonians, he didn't flatter them, didn't seek their praise, and didn't become a burden to them. He and Silas completely focused their efforts on presenting God's message of salvation to the Thessalonians. This was important! The Thessalonian believers had their lives changed by God, not Paul; it was Christ's message they believed, not Paul's. When we witness for Christ, our focus should not be on the impressions we make. As true ministers of Christ, we should point to him, not to ourselves.

7 But we proved to be [1]gentle among you, as a nursing *mother* tenderly cares for her
own children.
8 Having so fond an affection for you, we were well-pleased to impart to you not only
the gospel of God but also our own lives, because you had become very dear to us.
9 For you recall, brethren, our labor and hardship, *how* working night and day so as
not to be a burden to any of you, we proclaimed to you the gospel of God.
10 You are witnesses, and *so is* God, how devoutly and uprightly and blamelessly we
behaved toward you believers;
11 just as you know how we *were* exhorting and encouraging and imploring each one of
you as a father *would* his own children,
12 so that you would walk in a manner worthy of the God who calls you into His own
kingdom and glory.
13 For this reason we also constantly thank God that when you received the word of
God which you heard from us, you accepted *it* not *as* the word of men, but *for* what it
really is, the word of God, which also performs its work in you who believe.
14 For you, brethren, became imitators of the churches of God in Christ Jesus that are
in Judea, for you also endured the same sufferings at the hands of your own countrymen, even as they *did* from the Jews,
15 who both killed the Lord Jesus and the prophets, and drove us out. They are not
pleasing to God, but hostile to all men,
16 hindering us from speaking to the Gentiles so that they may be saved; with the result that they always fill up the measure of their sins. But wrath has come upon them [2]to
the utmost.
17 But we, brethren, having been taken away from you for a short while—in person,
not in spirit—were all the more eager with great desire to see your face.
18 For we wanted to come to you—I, Paul, more than once—and *yet* Satan hindered us.
19 For who is our hope or joy or crown of exultation? Is it not even you, in the presence of our Lord Jesus at His coming?
20 For you are our glory and joy.

1 Three early mss read *babes* 2 Or *forever* or *altogether;* lit *to the end*

2:7 2 Tim 2:24; Gal 4:19; 1 Thess 2:11
2:8 2 Cor 12:15; 1 John 3:16; Rom 1:1
2:9 Phil 4:16; 2 Thess 3:8; Acts 18:3
2:11 Luke 16:28; 1 Cor 4:14
2:12 Eph 4:1; Rom 8:28; 2 Cor 4:6; 1 Pet 5:10
2:13 Rom 10:17; Heb 4:2; Matt 10:20; Gal 4:14
2:14 1 Cor 7:17; 10:32; Gal 1:22; Acts 17:5
2:15 Luke 24:20; Acts 2:23; Matt 5:12
2:16 Acts 9:23; 13:45, 50; 18:12; 21:21f, 27; 25:2, 7; 1 Cor 10:33; Gen 15:16; Dan 8:23; Matt 23:32
2:17 1 Cor 5:3
2:18 Rom 15:22; Phil 4:16; Matt 4:10
2:19 Phil 4:1; Matt 16:27
2:20 2 Cor 1:14

2:7 Gentleness is often overlooked as a personal trait in our society. Power and assertiveness gain more respect, even though no one likes to be bullied. Gentleness is love in action—being considerate, meeting the needs of others, allowing time for the other person to talk, and being willing to learn. It is an essential trait for both men and women. Maintain a gentle attitude in your relationships with others.

2:9 Although Paul had the right to receive financial support from the people he taught, he supported himself as a tent-maker (Acts 18:3) so that he wouldn't be a burden to the new Thessalonian believers.

2:11 No loving father would neglect the safety of his children, allowing them to walk into circumstances that might be harmful or fatal. In the same way, we must take new believers under our wing until they are mature enough to stand firm in their faith. We must help new Christians become strong enough to influence others for the sake of the gospel.

2:11–12 By his words and example, Paul encouraged the Thessalonians to live in such a way that would be worthy of God. Is there anything about your daily life that would embarrass God? What do people think of God from watching you?

2:13 In the New Testament, *the word of God* usually refers to the preaching of the gospel, the Old Testament, or Jesus Christ himself. Today we often apply it only to the Bible. Remember that Jesus Christ himself is the Word (John 1:1).

2:14 Just as the Jewish Christians in Jerusalem were persecuted by other Jews, so the Gentile Christians in Thessalonica were persecuted by their fellow Gentiles. Persecution is discouraging, especially when it comes from your own people. When you take a stand for Christ, you may face opposition, disapproval, and ridicule from your neighbors, friends, and even family members.

2:14 When Paul refers to the Jews, he is talking about certain Jews who opposed his preaching of the gospel. He does not mean all Jews. Many of Paul's converts were Jewish. Paul himself was a Jew (2 Corinthians 11:22).

2:15–16 Why were so many Jews opposed to Christianity? (1) Although the Jewish religion had been declared legal by the Roman government, it still had a tenuous relationship with the government. At this time, Christianity was viewed as a sect of Judaism. The Jews were afraid that reprisals leveled against the Christians might be expanded to include them. (2) The Jewish leaders thought Jesus was a false prophet, and they didn't want his teachings to spread. (3) They feared that if many Jews were drawn away, their own political position might be weakened. (4) They were proud of their special status as God's chosen people, and they resented the fact that Gentiles could be full members within the Christian church.

2:18 Satan is real. He is called "the god of this world" (2 Corinthians 4:4) and "the prince of the power of the air" (Ephesians 2:2). We don't know exactly what hindered Paul from returning to Thessalonica—opposition, illness, travel complications, or a direct attack by Satan—but Satan worked in some way to keep him away. Many of the difficulties that prevent us from accomplishing God's work can be attributed to Satan (see Ephesians 6:12).

2:20 The ultimate reward for Paul's ministry was not money, prestige, or fame, but new believers whose lives had been changed by God through the preaching of the gospel. This was why he longed to see them. No matter what ministry God has given to you, your highest reward and greatest joy should be those who come to believe in Christ and are growing in him.

Encouragement of Timothy's Visit

3 Therefore when we could endure *it* no longer, we thought it best to be left behind at
Athens alone,
2 and we sent Timothy, our brother and God's fellow worker in the gospel of Christ,
to strengthen and encourage you as to your faith,
3 so that no one would be disturbed by these afflictions; for you yourselves know that
we have been destined for this.
4 For indeed when we were with you, we *kept* telling you in advance that we were going
to suffer affliction; and so it came to pass, as you know.
5 For this reason, when I could endure *it* no longer, I also sent to find out about your
faith, for fear that the tempter might have tempted you, and our labor would be in vain.
6 But now that Timothy has come to us from you, and has brought us good news of
your faith and love, and that you always think kindly of us, longing to see us just as we
also long to see you,
7 for this reason, brethren, in all our distress and affliction we were comforted about
you through your faith;
8 for now we *really* live, if you stand firm in the Lord.
9 For what thanks can we render to God for you in return for all the joy with which we
rejoice before our God on your account,
10 as we night and day keep praying most earnestly that we may see your face, and may
complete what is lacking in your faith?
11 Now may our God and Father Himself and Jesus our Lord direct our way to you;
12 and may the Lord cause you to increase and abound in love for one another, and
for all people, just as we also *do* for you;
13 so that He may establish your hearts without blame in holiness before our God and
Father at the coming of our Lord Jesus with all His saints.

3:1 1 Thess 3:5; Acts 17:15f

3:2 2 Cor 1:1; Col 1:1

3:3 Acts 9:16; 14:22

3:5 Phil 2:19; 1 Thess 3:1; 1 Thess 3:2; Matt 4:3; 2 Cor 6:1; Phil 2:16

3:6 Acts 18:5; 1 Thess 1:3; 1 Cor 11:2

3:8 1 Cor 16:13

3:10 2 Tim 1:3; 1 Thess 2:17; 2 Cor 13:9

3:11 2 Thess 2:16; Gal 1:4; 1 Thess 3:13; 1 Thess 4:16; 5:23; 2 Thess 2:16; 3:16; Rev 21:3

3:12 Phil 1:9; 1 Thess 4:1, 10; 2 Thess 1:3

3:13 1 Cor 1:8; 1 Thess 3:2; Luke 1:6; Gal 1:4; 1 Thess 2:19; Matt 25:31; Mark 8:38; 2 Thess 1:7

3:1–3 Some think that troubles are always caused by sin or a lack of faith. Trials may be a part of God's plan for believers. Experiencing problems and persecutions can build character (James 1:2–4), perseverance (Romans 5:3–5), and sensitivity toward others who also face trouble (2 Corinthians 1:3–7). Problems are unavoidable for God's people. Your troubles may be a sign of effective Christian living.

3:1–4 Because Paul could not return to Thessalonica (2:18), he sent Timothy as his representative. According to Acts 17:10, Paul left Thessalonica and went to Berea. When trouble broke out in Berea, some Christians took Paul to Athens, while Silas and Timothy stayed behind (Acts 17:13–15). Then Paul directed Silas and Timothy to join him in Athens. Later Paul sent Timothy to encourage the Thessalonian Christians to be strong in their faith in the face of persecution and other troubles.

3:4 Some people turn to God with the hope of escaping suffering on earth. But God doesn't promise that. Instead he gives us power to grow through our sufferings. The Christian life involves obedience to Christ despite temptations and hardships.

3:5 Satan ("the tempter") is the most powerful of the evil spirits. His power can affect both the spiritual world (Ephesians 2:1–3; 6:10–12) and the physical world (2 Corinthians 12:7–10). Satan even tempted Jesus (Matthew 4:1–11). But Jesus defeated Satan when he died on the cross for our sins and rose again to bring us new life. At the proper time God will overthrow Satan forever (Revelation 20:7–10).

3:7–8 During persecution or pressure, believers should encourage one another. Christians who stand firm in the Lord encourage both ministers and teachers (who can see the benefit of their work in those who remain faithful), and also those who are new in their faith (who can learn from the steadfastness of the mature).

3:9–10 It brings great joy to a Christian to see another person come to faith in Christ and mature in that faith. Paul experienced this joy countless times. He thanked God for those who had come to know Christ and for their strong faith. He also prayed for their continued growth. If there are new Christians who have brought you joy, thank God for them and support them as they continue to grow in the faith.

3:11 Paul wanted to return to Thessalonica. We have no record that he was able to do so; but when he was traveling through Asia on his third journey, he was joined by Aristarchus and Secundus, who were from Thessalonica (Acts 20:4–5).

3:11–13 "The coming of our Lord Jesus with all His saints" refers to the second coming of Christ when he will establish his eternal kingdom. At that time, Christ will gather all believers, those who have died and those who are alive, into one united family under his rule. All believers from all times, including these Thessalonians, will be with Christ in his kingdom.

3:12 If we are full of God's love, it will overflow to others. It's not enough merely to be courteous to others; we must actively and persistently show love to them. Our love should be growing continually. If your capacity to love has remained unchanged for some time, ask God to fill you again with his never-ending supply. Then look for opportunities to express his love.

2. Watchfulness for the Lord

Sanctification and Love

4 Finally then, brethren, we request and exhort you in the Lord Jesus, that as you received from us *instruction* as to how you ought to walk and please God (just as you
actually do [3]walk), that you excel still more.
2 For you know what commandments we gave you [4]by *the authority of* the Lord Jesus.
3 For this is the will of God, your sanctification; *that is,* that you abstain from sexual
immorality;
4 that each of you know how to possess his own [5]vessel in sanctification and honor,
5 not in lustful passion, like the Gentiles who do not know God;
6 *and* that no man transgress and defraud his brother in the matter because the
Lord is *the* avenger in all these things, just as we also told you before and solemnly
warned *you.*
7 For God has not called us for the purpose of impurity, but in sanctification.
8 So, he who rejects *this* is not rejecting man but the God who gives His Holy Spirit
to you.
9 Now as to the love of the brethren, you have no need for *anyone* to write to you, for
you yourselves are taught by God to love one another;
10 for indeed you do practice it toward all the brethren who are in all Macedonia. But
we urge you, brethren, to excel still more,
11 and to make it your ambition to lead a quiet life and attend to your own business
and work with your hands, just as we commanded you,
12 so that you will behave properly toward outsiders and not be in any need.

Those Who Died in Christ

13 But we do not want you to be uninformed, brethren, about those who are asleep, so
that you will not grieve as do the rest who have no hope.
14 For if we believe that Jesus died and rose again, even so God will bring with Him
those who have fallen asleep in Jesus.
15 For this we say to you by the word of the Lord, that we who are alive and remain
until the coming of the Lord, will not precede those who have fallen asleep.
16 For the Lord Himself will descend from heaven with a shout, with the voice of *the*
archangel and with the trumpet of God, and the dead in Christ will rise first.

3 Or *conduct yourselves* **4** Lit *through the Lord* **5** I.e. body; or wife

4:1 2 Cor 13:11; 2 Thess 3:1; Gal 6:1; Eph 4:1; 2 Cor 5:9; Phil 1:9
4:4 1 Cor 7:2, 9; 2 Cor 4:7; 1 Pet 3:7
4:5 Rom 1:26; Gal 4:8
4:6 1 Cor 6:8; 2 Cor 7:11; Rom 12:19; 13:4; Heb 2:6
4:7 1 Pet 1:15
4:8 Rom 5:5; 2 Cor 1:22; Gal 4:6; 1 John 3:24
4:9 John 13:34; Rom 12:10; 2 Cor 9:1
4:11 2 Thess 3:12; 1 Pet 4:15; Acts 18:3; Eph 4:28
4:12 Rom 13:13; Col 4:5; Mark 4:11; Eph 4:28
4:13 Rom 1:13; Acts 7:60; Eph 2:3
4:14 Rom 14:9; 2 Cor 4:14; 1 Cor 15:18
4:15 2 Cor 12:1; Gal 1:12; 1 Cor 15:52
4:16 2 Thess 1:7; Matt 24:31; 1 Cor 15:23; 2 Thess 2:1; Rev 14:13

4:1–8 Sexual standards were very low in the Roman empire, and in many societies today they are not any higher. The temptation to engage in sexual intercourse outside the marriage relationship has always been powerful. Giving in to that temptation can have disastrous results. Sexual sins always hurt someone: individuals, families, businesses, churches. Besides the physical consequences, there are also spiritual consequences. For more on why sexual sin is so harmful, see the note on 1 Corinthians 6:18.

4:1–8 Sexual desires and activities must be placed under Christ's control. God created sex for procreation and pleasure, and as an expression of love between a husband and wife. Sexual experience must be limited to the marriage relationship to avoid hurting ourselves, our relationship to God, and our relationships with others.

4:3 *Sanctification,* being made holy, is the process of living the Christian life. The Holy Spirit works in us, conforming us into the image of Christ (Romans 8:29).

4:11–12 There is more to Christian living than simply loving other Christians. We must be responsible in all areas of life. Some of the Thessalonian Christians had adopted a life of idleness, depending on others for handouts. Some Greeks looked down on manual labor. So Paul told the Thessalonians to work hard and live a quiet life. You can't be effective in sharing your faith with others if they don't respect you. Whatever you do, do it faithfully and be a positive force in society.

4:13ff The Thessalonians were wondering why many of their fellow believers had fallen asleep (died) and what would happen to them when Christ returned. Paul wanted the Thessalonians to understand that death is not the end of the story. When Christ returns, all believers—dead and alive—will be reunited, never to suffer or die again.

4:15 What does Paul mean when he says, "by the word of the Lord"? Either this was something that the Lord had revealed directly to Paul, or it was a teaching of Jesus that had been passed along orally by the apostles and other Christians.

4:15–18 Knowing exactly *when* the dead will be raised, in relation to the other events at the second coming, is not as important as knowing why Paul wrote these words—to challenge believers to comfort and encourage one another when loved ones die. This passage can be a great comfort when any believer dies. The same love that should unite believers in this life (4:9) will unite believers when Christ returns and reigns for eternity.

4:15–18 Because Jesus Christ came back to life, so will all believers. All Christians, including those living when Christ returns, will live with Christ forever. Therefore, we need not despair when loved ones die or world events take a tragic turn. God will turn our tragedies to triumphs, our poverty to riches, our pain to glory, and our defeat to victory. All believers throughout history will stand reunited in God's very presence, safe and secure. As Paul comforted the Thessalonians with the promise of the resurrection, so we should comfort and reassure each other with this great hope.

4:16 An *archangel* is a high or holy angel appointed to a special task. Michael is the only archangel mentioned in the New Testament (see Jude 9).

17 Then we who are alive and remain will be caught up together with them in the clouds
to meet the Lord in the air, and so we shall always be with the Lord.
18 Therefore comfort one another with these words.

The Day of the Lord

5 Now as to the times and the epochs, brethren, you have no need of anything to be
written to you.
2 For you yourselves know full well that the day of the Lord will come just like a thief
in the night.
3 While they are saying, "Peace and safety!" then destruction will come upon them
suddenly like labor pains upon a woman with child, and they will not escape.
4 But you, brethren, are not in darkness, that the day would overtake you like a thief;
5 for you are all sons of light and sons of day. We are not of night nor of darkness;
6 so then let us not sleep as others do, but let us be alert and [6]sober.
7 For those who sleep do their sleeping at night, and those who get drunk get drunk
at night.
8 But since we are of *the* day, let us be [6]sober, having put on the breastplate of faith
and love, and as a helmet, the hope of salvation.
9 For God has not destined us for wrath, but for obtaining salvation through our Lord
Jesus Christ,
10 who died for us, so that whether we are awake or asleep, we will live together
with Him.
11 Therefore encourage one another and build up one another, just as you also are
doing.

Christian Conduct

12 But we request of you, brethren, that you appreciate those who diligently labor among
you, and have charge over you in the Lord and give you instruction,
13 and that you esteem them very highly in love because of their work. Live in peace
with one another.

6 Or *self-controlled*

4:17 1 Cor 15:52; 2 Cor 12:2; Rev 11:12; John 12:26

5:1 Acts 1:7

5:2 1 Cor 1:8; Luke 21:34; 2 Pet 3:10; Rev 3:3; 16:15

5:3 John 16:21

5:4 Acts 26:18; 1 John 2:8; Luke 21:34; 1 Thess 5:2; 2 Pet 3:10; Rev 3:3; 16:15

5:5 Luke 16:8; Acts 26:18; 1 John 2:8

5:6 Rom 13:11; Eph 2:3; 1 Pet 1:13

5:7 Acts 2:15; 2 Pet 2:13

5:8 Rom 8:24

5:9 2 Thess 2:13f

5:10 Rom 14:9

5:11 Eph 4:29

5:12 1 Cor 16:18; 1 Tim 5:17; Rom 16:6, 12; Heb 13:17

THE EVENTS OF CHRIST'S RETURN

1. Christ will return visibly, with a loud command.
2. There will be an unmistakable cry from an angel.
3. There will be a trumpet fanfare such as has never been heard.
4. Believers in Christ who are dead will rise from their graves.
5. Believers who are alive will be caught up in the clouds to meet Christ.

While Christians have often disagreed about what events will lead up to the return of Christ, there has been less disagreement about what will happen once Christ does return.

5:1 "The times and the epochs" refers to the knowledge of what will happen in the future, specifically to the return of Christ.

5:1–3 Efforts to determine the date of Christ's return are foolish. Don't be misled by anyone who claims to know. We are told here that no one knows and that even believers will be surprised. The Lord will return suddenly and unexpectedly, warns Paul, so be ready! Because no one knows when Jesus will come back to earth, we should be ready at all times. Suppose he were to return today. How would he find you living? Are you ready to meet him? Live each day prepared to welcome Christ.

5:2 The "day of the Lord" is a future time when God will intervene directly and dramatically in world affairs. Predicted and discussed often in the Old Testament (Isaiah 13:6–12; Joel 2:28–32; Zephaniah 1:14–18), the day of the Lord will include both punishment and blessing. Christ will judge sin and set up his eternal kingdom.

5:8 For more about the Christian's armor, see Ephesians 6:13–17.

5:9–11 As you near the end of a long race, your legs ache, your throat burns, and your whole body cries out for you to stop. This is when friends and fans are most valuable. Their encouragement helps you push through the pain to the finish line. In the same way, Christians are to encourage one another. A word of encouragement offered at the right moment can be the difference between finishing well and collapsing along the way. Look around you. Be sensitive to others' need for encouragement, and offer supportive words or actions.

5:12 "Those who diligently labor among you, and have charge over you in the Lord" probably refers to elders and deacons in the church.

5:12–13 How can you show respect to and "esteem very highly" your pastor and other church leaders? Express your appreciation, tell them how you have been helped by their leadership and teaching, and thank them for their ministry in your life. If you say nothing, how will they know where you stand? Remember, they need and deserve your support and love.

14 We urge you, brethren, admonish the unruly, encourage the fainthearted, help the
weak, be patient with everyone.
15 See that no one repays another with evil for evil, but always seek after that which is
good for one another and for all people.
16 Rejoice always;
17 pray without ceasing;
18 in everything give thanks; for this is God's will for you in Christ Jesus.
19 Do not quench the Spirit;

5:14 Rom 15:1; 1 Cor 13:4

5:15 Matt 5:44; Rom 12:17; 1 Pet 3:9

5:16 Phil 4:4

5:18 Eph 5:20

CHECKLIST FOR ENCOURAGERS

The command to "encourage" others is found throughout the Bible. In 1 Thessalonians 5:11–23, Paul gives many specific examples of how we can encourage others.

Reference	*Example*	*Suggested Application*
5:11	Build up one another.	Point out to someone a quality you appreciate in him or her.
5:12	Respect leaders.	Look for ways to cooperate.
5:13	Highly esteem leaders.	Hold back your next critical comment about those in positions of responsibility. Say "thank you" to your leaders for their efforts.
5:13	Live in peace.	Search for ways to get along with others.
5:14	Admonish the unruly.	Challenge someone to join you in a project.
5:14	Encourage the fainthearted.	Encourage those who are timid by reminding them of God's promises.
5:14	Help the weak.	Support those who are weak by loving them and praying for them.
5:14	Be patient.	Think of a situation that tries your patience and plan ahead of time how you can stay calm.
5:15	Resist revenge.	Instead of planning to get even with those who mistreat you, do good to them.
5:16	Rejoice always.	Remember that even in the midst of turmoil, God is in control.
5:17	Pray without ceasing.	God is always with you—talk to him.
5:18	Give thanks.	Make a list of all the gifts God has given you, giving thanks to God for each one.
5:19	Do not quench the Spirit.	Cooperate with the Spirit the next time he prompts you to participate in a Christian meeting.
5:20	Do not despise prophecy.	Receive God's word from those who speak for him.
5:22	Avoid every kind of evil.	Avoid situations where you will be drawn into temptation.
5:23	Count on God's constant help.	Realize that the Christian life is to be lived not in our own strength but through God's power.

5:14 Don't loaf around with the unruly; admonish them. Don't yell at the fainthearted and weak; encourage and help them. At times it's difficult to distinguish between faintheartedness and weakness. Two people may be doing nothing—one out of shyness and the other out of fear of doing something wrong. The key to ministry is sensitivity: sensing the condition of each person and offering the appropriate remedy for each situation. You can't effectively help until you know the problem. You can't apply the medicine until you know where the wound is.

5:16–18 Our joy, prayers, and thankfulness should not fluctuate with our circumstances or feelings. Obeying these three commands—rejoice, pray without ceasing, and give thanks—often goes against our natural inclinations. When we make a conscious decision to do what God says, however, we will begin to see people in a new perspective. When we do God's will, we will find it easier to be joyful and thankful.

5:17 We cannot spend all our time on our knees, but it is possible to have a prayerful attitude at all times. This attitude is built upon acknowledging our dependence on God, realizing his presence within us, and determining to obey him fully. Then we will find it natural to pray frequent, spontaneous, short prayers. A prayerful attitude is not a substitute for regular times of prayer but should be an outgrowth of those times.

5:18 Paul was not teaching that we should thank God *for* everything that happens to us, but *in* everything. Evil does not come from God, so we should not thank him for it. But when evil strikes, we can still be thankful for God's presence and for the good that he will accomplish through the distress.

5:19 By warning us not to "quench the Spirit," Paul means that we should not ignore or toss aside the gifts the Holy Spirit gives. Here, he mentions prophecy (5:20); in 1 Corinthians 14:39, he mentions tongues. Sometimes spiritual gifts are controversial, and they may cause division in a church. Rather than trying to solve the problems, some Christians prefer to smother the gifts. This impoverishes the church. We should not stifle the Holy Spirit's work in anyone's life but encourage the full expression of these gifts to benefit the whole body of Christ.

5:20 1 Cor 14:31
5:21 1 Cor 14:29; 1 John 4:1; Rom 12:9
5:23 Rom 15:33; James 1:4; 2 Pet 3:14
5:24 1 Cor 1:9; 2 Thess 3:3; 1 Thess 2:12
5:25 Eph 6:19; 2 Thess 3:1; Heb 13:18
5:26 Rom 16:16

20 do not despise prophetic [7]utterances.
21 But examine everything *carefully;* hold fast to that which is good;
22 abstain from every [8]form of evil.
23 Now may the God of peace Himself sanctify you entirely; and may your spirit and
soul and body be preserved complete, without blame at the coming of our Lord Jesus
Christ.
24 Faithful is He who calls you, and He also will bring it to pass.
25 Brethren, pray for us[9].
26 Greet all the brethren with a holy kiss.
27 I adjure you by the Lord to have this letter read to all the brethren.
28 The grace of our Lord Jesus Christ be with you.

7 Or *gifts* **8** Or *appearance* **9** Two early mss add *also*

5:20–21 We shouldn't make fun of those who don't agree with what we believe ("despise prophetic utterances"), but we should always "examine everything," checking their words against the Bible. We are on dangerous ground if we scoff at a person who speaks the truth. Instead we should carefully check out what people say, accepting what is true and rejecting what is false.

5:22–24 As Christians, we cannot avoid every kind of evil because we live in a sinful world. We can, however, make sure that we don't give evil a foothold by avoiding tempting situations and concentrating on obeying God.

5:23 The spirit, soul, and body refer not so much to the distinct parts of a person as to the entire being of a person. This expression is Paul's way of saying that God must be involved in *every* aspect of our lives. It is wrong to think that we can separate our spiritual lives from everything else, obeying God only in some ethereal sense or living for him only one day each week. Christ must control *all* of us, not just a "religious" part.

5:27 For every Christian to hear this letter, it had to be read in a public meeting—there were not enough copies to circulate. Paul wanted to make sure that everyone had the opportunity to hear his message because he was answering important questions and offering needed encouragement.

5:28 The Thessalonian church was young, and they needed help and encouragement. Both the persecution they faced and the temptations of their pagan culture were potential problems for these new Christians. Paul wrote, therefore, to strengthen their faith and bolster their resistance to persecution and temptation. We too have a responsibility to help new believers, and to make sure that they continue in their faith and don't become sidetracked by wrong beliefs or practices. First Thessalonians can better equip us to help our brothers and sisters in Christ.

2 THESSALONIANS

VITAL STATISTICS

PURPOSE:
To clear up the confusion about the second coming of Christ

AUTHOR:
Paul

TO WHOM WRITTEN:
The church at Thessalonica, and all believers everywhere

DATE WRITTEN:
Approximately A.D. 51 or 52, a few months after 1 Thessalonians, from Corinth

SETTING:
Many in the church were confused about the timing of Christ's return. Because of mounting persecution, they thought the day of the Lord must be imminent, and they interpreted Paul's first letter to say that the second coming would be at any moment. In light of this misunderstanding, many persisted in being idle and disorderly, with the excuse of waiting for Christ's return.

KEY VERSE:
"May the Lord direct your hearts into the love of God and into the steadfastness of Christ" (3:5).

KEY PEOPLE:
Paul, Silas, Timothy

KEY PLACE:
Thessalonica

SPECIAL FEATURES:
This is a follow-up letter to 1 Thessalonians. In this letter, Paul indicates various events that must precede the second coming of Christ.

"BUT I thought he said . . . ," "I'm sure he meant . . . ," "It is clear to me that we should . . . ," "I disagree. I think we must . . ."

Effective communication is difficult; often the message sent is *not* the message received in the home, marketplace, neighborhood, or church. Even when clearly stated or written, words can be misinterpreted and misunderstood, especially when filtered through the sieve of prejudices and preconceptions.

Paul faced this problem with the Thessalonians. He had written them earlier to help them grow in the faith, comforting and encouraging them by affirming the reality of Christ's return. Just a few months later, however, word came from Thessalonica that some had misunderstood Paul's teaching about the second coming. His announcement that Christ could come at any moment had caused some to stop working and just wait, rationalizing their idleness by pointing to Paul's teaching. Adding fuel to this fire was the continued persecution of the church. Many felt that indeed this must be the "day of the Lord."

Responding quickly, Paul sent a second letter to this young church. In it he gave further instruction concerning the second coming and the day of the Lord (2:1–2). Second Thessalonians, therefore, continues the subject of 1 Thessalonians and is a call to continued courage and consistent conduct.

The letter begins with Paul's trademark—a personal greeting and a statement of thanksgiving for their faith (1:1–3). He mentions their perseverance in spite of their persecution and trials (1:4) and uses this situation to broach the subject of Christ's return. At that time, Christ will vindicate the righteous who endure and will punish the wicked (1:5–12).

Paul then directly answers the misunderstanding concerning the timing of the events of the end times. He tells them not to listen to rumors and reports that the day of the Lord has already begun (2:1–2), because a number of events must occur before Christ returns (2:3–12). Meanwhile, they should stand firm for Christ's truth (2:13–15), receive God's encouragement and hope (2:16–17), pray for strength and for the spread of the Lord's message (3:1–5), and warn those who are unruly, meaning idle (3:6–15). Paul ends with personal greetings and a benediction (3:16–18).

Almost 2,000 years later, we stand much closer to the time of Christ's return; but we also would be wrong to see his imminent appearance as an excuse for idle waiting and heavenward gazing. Being prepared for his coming means spreading the gospel, reaching out to those in need, and building the church, his body. As you read 2 Thessalonians, then, see clearly the reality of his return and your responsibility to live for him until that day.

THE BLUEPRINT

1. The bright hope of Christ's return (1:1—2:17)
2. Living in the light of Christ's return (3:1–18)

Paul wrote to encourage those who were facing persecution and to correct a misunderstanding about the timing of Christ's return. The teaching about the Lord's return promoted unruliness (idleness) in this young church. The imminent coming of Christ should never make us idle; we should be even more busy—living purely, using our time well, and working for his kingdom. We must work not only during easy times when it is convenient but also during difficult times. Christians must patiently watch for Christ's return and work for him while they wait.

MEGATHEMES

THEME	EXPLANATION	IMPORTANCE
Persecution	Paul encouraged the church to persevere in spite of troubles and trials. God will bring victory to his faithful followers and judge those who persecute them.	God promises to reward our faith by giving us his power and helping us bear persecution. Suffering for our faith will strengthen us to serve Christ. We must be faithful to him.
Christ's Return	Since Paul had said that the Lord could come at any moment, some of the Thessalonian believers had stopped working in order to wait for Christ.	Christ will return and bring total victory to all who trust in him. If we are ready, we need not be concerned about *when* he will return. We should stand firm, keep working, and wait for Christ.
Great Rebellion	Before Christ's return, there will be a great rebellion against God led by the man of lawlessness (the antichrist). God will remove all the restraints on evil before he brings judgment on the rebels. The antichrist will attempt to deceive many.	We should not be afraid when we see evil increase. God is in control, no matter how evil the world becomes. God guards us during Satan's attacks. We can have victory over evil by remaining faithful to God.
Persistence	Because church members had quit working and become unruly and disobedient, Paul chastised them for their idleness. He called on them to show courage and true Christian conduct.	We must never get so tired of doing right that we quit. We can be persistent by making the most of our time and talents. Our endurance will be rewarded.

1. The bright hope of Christ's return

Thanksgiving for Faith and Perseverance

1 Paul and Silvanus and Timothy,
To the church of the Thessalonians in God our Father and the Lord Jesus Christ:
2 Grace to you and peace from God the Father and the Lord Jesus Christ.
3 We ought always to give thanks to God for you, brethren, as is *only* fitting, because
your faith is greatly enlarged, and the love of each one of you toward one another grows
ever greater;
4 therefore, we ourselves speak proudly of you among the churches of God for your
perseverance and faith in the midst of all your persecutions and afflictions which you
endure.
5 *This is* a plain indication of God's righteous judgment so that you will be considered
worthy of the kingdom of God, for which indeed you are suffering.
6 For after all it is *only* just for God to repay with affliction those who afflict you,
7 and *to give* relief to you who are afflicted and to us as well when the Lord Jesus will
be revealed from heaven with His mighty angels in flaming fire,
8 dealing out retribution to those who do not know God and to those who do not obey
the gospel of our Lord Jesus.
9 These will pay the penalty of eternal destruction, away from the presence of the Lord
and from the glory of His power,
10 when He comes to be glorified in His saints on that day, and to be marveled at among
all who have believed—for our testimony to you was believed.
11 To this end also we pray for you always, that our God will count you worthy of your
calling, and fulfill every desire for goodness and the work of faith with power,
12 so that the name of our Lord Jesus will be glorified in you, and you in Him, according
to the grace of our God and *the* Lord Jesus Christ.

1:3 Rom 1:8; Eph 5:20; 1 Thess 1:2;
1:4 2 Cor 7:4; 1 Thess 2:19; 1 Cor 7:17
1:5 Phil 1:28; Luke 20:35; 2 Thess 1:11
1:6 Ex 23:22; Col 3:25; Heb 6:10
1:7 Luke 17:30; 1 Thess 4:16; Matt 25:41; 1 Cor 3:13; Heb 10:27; 12:29
1:8 Gal 4:8; Rom 2:8
1:9 Phil 3:19; 1 Thess 5:3; Is 2:10, 19, 21
1:10 1 Thess 2:12; 1 Cor 1:6; 1 Thess 2:1
1:11 Col 1:9; Rom 15:14; 1 Thess 1:3
1:12 Is 24:15; 66:5; Mal 1:11; Phil 2:9ff

1:1 Paul wrote this letter from Corinth less than a year after he wrote 1 Thessalonians. He and his companions, Timothy and Silas, had visited Thessalonica on Paul's second missionary journey (Acts 17:1–10). They established the church there, but Paul had to leave suddenly because of persecution. This prompted him to write his first letter (1 Thessalonians), which contains words of comfort and encouragement. Paul then heard how the Thessalonians had responded to this letter. The good news was that they were continuing to grow in their faith. But the bad news was that false teachings about Christ's return were spreading, leading many to quit their jobs and wait for the end of the world. So Paul wrote to them again. While the purpose of Paul's first letter was to comfort the Thessalonians with the assurance of Christ's second coming, the purpose of his second letter is to correct false teaching about the second coming.

1:1 Paul, Silvanus (Silas), and Timothy were together in Corinth (Acts 18:5). Paul wrote this letter on behalf of all three of them. Paul often included Timothy as a co-sender of his letters (see Philippians 1:1; Colossians 1:1; 1 Thessalonians 1:1). For more information about Paul, see his Profile in Acts 9. Timothy's Profile is found in 1 Timothy, and Silas's Profile is in Acts 16.

1:1 Thessalonica was the capital and largest city of the Roman province of Macedonia. The most important Roman highway—extending from Rome to the Orient—went through Thessalonica. This highway, along with the city's thriving seaport, made Thessalonica one of the wealthiest and most flourishing trade centers in the Roman empire. Recognized as a free city, Thessalonica was allowed self-rule and was exempted from most of the restrictions placed by Rome on other cities. Because of this open climate, however, the city had many pagan religions and cultural influences that challenged the Christians' faith.

1:3 Regardless of the contents of Paul's letters, his style was affirming. Paul began most of his letters by stating what he most appreciated about his readers and the joy he felt because of their faith in God. We also should look for ways to encourage and build up other believers.

1:4 The keys to surviving persecution and trials are perseverance and faith. When we are faced with crushing troubles, we can have faith that God is using our trials for our good and for his glory. Knowing that God is fair and just will give us patience in our suffering because we know that he has not forgotten us. In God's perfect timing, he will relieve our suffering and punish those who persecute us. Can you trust God's timing?

1:4–6 Paul had been persecuted during his first visit to Thessalonica (Acts 17:5–9). No doubt those who had responded to his message and had become Christians were continuing to be persecuted by both Jews and Gentiles. In Paul's first letter to the Thessalonians, he said that Christ's return would bring deliverance from persecution and judgment on the persecutors. But this caused the people to expect Christ's return right away to rescue and vindicate them. So Paul had to point out that while waiting for God's kingdom, believers could and should learn perseverance and faith from their suffering.

1:5 As we live for Christ, we will experience troubles because we are trying to be God's people in a perverse world. Some people say that troubles are the result of sin or lack of faith, but Paul teaches that they may be a part of God's plan for believers. Our problems can help us look upward and forward, instead of inward (Mark 13:35–36; Philippians 3:13–14); they can build strong character (Romans 5:3–4); and they can provide us with opportunities to comfort others who also are struggling (2 Corinthians 1:3–5). Your troubles may be an indication that you are taking a stand for Christ.

1:5–7 There are two dimensions of the relief mentioned by Paul. We can gain relief in knowing that our sufferings are strengthening us, making us ready for Christ's kingdom. We can also gain relief in the fact that one day everyone will stand before God; at that time, wrongs will be righted, judgment will be pronounced, and evil will be terminated.

1:7–9 The "eternal destruction" that Paul describes is the lake of fire (see Revelation 20:14)—the place of eternal separation from God. Those people who are separated from God in eternity no longer have any hope for salvation.

1:11–12 Our "calling" from God, as Christians, is to become like Christ (Romans 8:29). This is a gradual, lifelong process that will

2:1
1 Thess 2:19; Mark 13:27; 1 Thess 4:15-17

2:2
1 Cor 14:32; 1 John 4:1; 1 Thess 5:2; 2 Thess 3:17; 1 Cor 1:8; 1 Cor 7:26

2:3
Eph 5:6; 1 Tim 4:1; Dan 7:25; 8:25; 11:36; Rev 13:5ff; John 17:12

2:4
1 Cor 8:5; Is 14:14

Man of Lawlessness

2 Now we request you, brethren, with regard to the coming of our Lord Jesus Christ and our gathering together to Him,
2 that you not be quickly shaken from your composure or be disturbed either by a spirit or a message or a letter as if from us, to the effect that the day of the Lord has come.
3 Let no one in any way deceive you, for *it will not come* unless the [1]apostasy comes first, and the man of lawlessness is revealed, the son of destruction,
4 who opposes and exalts himself above every so-called god or object of worship, so that he takes his seat in the temple of God, displaying himself as being God.

1 Or *falling away* from the faith

LOCATION OF THESSALONICA
After Paul visited Thessalonica on his second missionary journey, he went on to Berea, Athens, and Corinth (Acts 17—18). From Corinth, Paul wrote his two letters to the Thessalonian church.

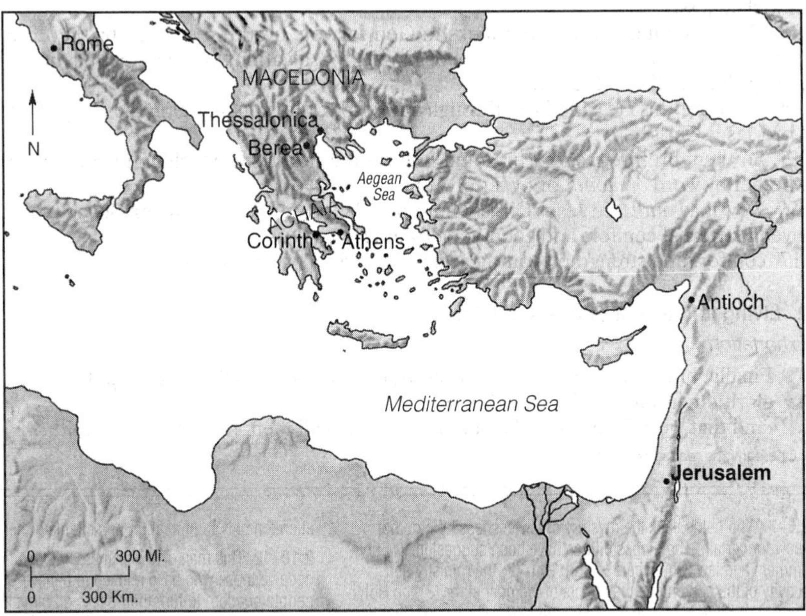

be completed when we see Christ face to face (1 John 3:2). To be "worthy" of this calling means to *want* to do what is right and good (as Christ would). We aren't perfect yet, but we're moving in that direction as God works in us.

2:1ff Paul describes the end of the world and Christ's second coming. He says that great suffering and trouble lie ahead, but evil will not prevail, because Christ will return to judge all people. Although Paul presents a few signs of the end times, his emphasis, like Jesus' (Mark 13), is the need for each person to prepare for Christ's return by living rightly day by day. If we are ready, we won't have to be concerned about the preceding events or the timing of Christ's return. God controls all events. (See 1 Thessalonians 4 and 5 for Paul's earlier teaching on this subject.)

2:1–2 In the Bible, the *day of the Lord* is used in two ways: It can mean the end times (beginning with Christ's birth and continuing until today), and it can mean the final judgment day (in the future). Because some false teachers were saying that judgment day had come, many believers were waiting expectantly for their vindication and for relief from suffering. But judgment day had not yet come; other events would have to happen first.

2:2 "A spirit or a message or a letter" could refer to the fact that false teaching had come from: (1) someone claiming to have had a divine revelation, (2) someone passing on a teaching as though it were from Paul, or (3) someone distributing a letter supposedly written by Paul.

2:3 Throughout history there have been individuals who epitomized evil and who were hostile to everything Christ stands for (see 1 John 2:18; 4:3; 2 John 7). These antichrists have lived in every generation and will continue to work their evil. Then just before Christ's second coming, "the man of lawlessness . . . the son of destruction," a completely evil man, will arise. He will be Satan's tool, equipped with Satan's power (2:9). This lawless man will be *the* antichrist.

It is dangerous, however, to label any person as the antichrist and to try to predict Christ's coming based on that assumption. Paul mentions the antichrist, not so we might identify him specifically, but so we might be ready for anything that threatens our faith. If our faith is strong, we don't need to be afraid of what lies ahead, because we know that this lawless man has already been defeated by God, no matter how powerful he becomes or how terrible our situation seems. God is in control, and he will be victorious over the antichrist. Our task is to be prepared for Christ's return and to spread the gospel so that even more people will also be prepared.

2:3ff When Paul first wrote to the Thessalonians, they were in danger of losing hope in the second coming. Then they shifted to the opposite extreme—some of them thought that Jesus would be coming at any minute. Paul tried to restore the balance by describing certain events that would happen before Christ's return.

5 Do you not remember that while I was still with you, I was telling you these things?
6 And you know what restrains him now, so that in his time he will be revealed.
7 For the mystery of lawlessness is already at work; only he who now restrains *will do*
so until he is taken out of the way.
8 Then that lawless one will be revealed whom the Lord will slay with the breath of
His mouth and bring to an end by the appearance of His coming;
9 *that is,* the one whose coming is in accord with the activity of Satan, with all power
and signs and false wonders,
10 and with all the deception of wickedness for those who perish, because they did not
receive the love of the truth so as to be saved.
11 For this reason God will send upon them a deluding influence so that they will believe what is false,
12 in order that they all may be judged who did not believe the truth, but took pleasure
in wickedness.
13 But we should always give thanks to God for you, brethren beloved by the Lord,
because God has chosen you [2]from the beginning for salvation through sanctification by
the Spirit and faith in the truth.
14 It was for this He called you through our gospel, that you may gain the glory of our
Lord Jesus Christ.
15 So then, brethren, stand firm and hold to the traditions which you were taught,
whether by word *of mouth* or by letter from us.
16 Now may our Lord Jesus Christ Himself and God our Father, who has loved us and
given us eternal comfort and good hope by grace,
17 comfort and strengthen your hearts in every good work and word.

2. Living in the light of Christ's return

Exhortation

3 Finally, brethren, pray for us that the word of the Lord will spread rapidly and be
glorified, just as *it did* also with you;
2 and that we will be rescued from perverse and evil men; for not all have faith.

2 One early ms reads *first fruits*

2:5 1 Thess 3:4

2:7 Rev 17:5, 7

2:8 Dan 7:25; 8:25; 11:36; Rev 13:5ff; Is 11:4; Rev 2:16; 19:15; 1 Tim 6:14; 2 Tim 1:10; 4:1, 8; Titus 2:13

2:9 Matt 4:10; Matt 24:24; John 4:48

2:10 1 Cor 1:18

2:11 Rom 1:28; 1 Thess 2:3; 2 Tim 4:4

2:12 Rom 2:8; Rom 1:32

2:13 1 Thess 1:4; Eph 1:4ff; 1 Cor 1:21; 1 Thess 2:12; 5:9; 1 Pet 1:5

2:14 1 Thess 1:5

2:15 1 Cor 16:13; 1 Cor 11:2; 2 Thess 3:6

2:16 John 3:16; Titus 3:7; 1 Pet 1:3

2:17 1 Thess 3:2, 13

3:1 1 Thess 4:1; 5:25

2:6–7 Who holds back the mystery of lawlessness? We do not know for certain. Three possibilities have been suggested: (1) government and law, which help to curb evil; (2) the ministry and activity of the church and the effects of the gospel; or (3) the Holy Spirit. The Bible is not clear on who this restrainer is, only that he will not restrain forever. But we should not fear this time when the restraint is removed—God is far stronger than the man of lawlessness, and God will save his people.

2:7 "The mystery of lawlessness is already at work" means that the work that this antichrist will do is already going on. *Mystery* means something no one can discover, but something God will reveal. *Lawlessness* is the hidden, subtle, underlying force from which all sin springs. Civilization still has a veneer of decency through law enforcement, education, science, and reason. Although we are horrified by criminal acts, we have yet to see the real horror of complete lawlessness. This will happen when "he who now restrains [possibly the Holy Spirit]. . . is taken out of the way." Why will God allow this to happen? To show people and nations their own sinfulness, and to show them by bitter experience the true alternative to the lordship of Christ. People totally without God can act no better than vicious animals. Lawlessness, to a certain extent, is already going on, but the man of lawlessness has not yet been revealed.

2:9 This man of lawlessness will use "power and signs and false wonders" to deceive and draw a following. Miracles from God can help strengthen our faith and lead people to Christ, but all miracles are not necessarily from God. Christ's miracles were significant, not just because of their power, but because of their purpose—to help, to heal, and to point us to God. The man of lawlessness will have power to do amazing things, but his power will be from Satan. He will use this power to destroy and to lead people away from God and toward himself. If any so-called religious personality draws attention only to himself or herself, his or her work is not from God.

2:10–12 This man of lawlessness with his power and wonders will deceive those who have refused to believe God's truth. God gives people freedom to turn their backs on him and believe Satan's lies. If they say no to the truth, they will experience the consequences of their sin.

2:13 Paul consistently taught that salvation begins and ends with God. We can do nothing to be saved on our own merit—we must accept God's gift of salvation (see the note on Ephesians 1:4). There is no other way to receive forgiveness from sin. Paul is encouraging the Thessalonian believers by reminding them that they were chosen by God from the beginning. *Sanctification* is the process of Christian growth through which the Holy Spirit makes us like Christ (Romans 8:29). See the note on 1:11–12.

2:14 God worked through Paul and his companions to tell the Good News so that people could share in Christ's glory. It may seem strange that God works through us—fallible, unfaithful, untrustworthy human creatures. But he has given us the fantastic privilege of accomplishing his great mission—telling the world how to find salvation.

2:15 Paul knew that the Thessalonians would face pressure from persecutions, false teachers, worldliness, and apathy to waver from the truth and to leave the faith. So he urged them to "stand firm" and hold on to the truth they had been taught both through his letters and in person. We also may face persecution, false teachings, worldliness, and apathy. We should hold on to the truth of Christ's teachings because our lives depend on it. Never forget the reality of Christ's life and love!

3:1–3 Beneath the surface of the routine of daily life, a fierce struggle among invisible spiritual powers is being waged. Our main defense is prayer that God will protect us from the evil one and that

3:2 Rom 15:31
3:3 1 Cor 1:9; 1 Thess 5:24; Matt 5.37
3:4 2 Cor 2:3
3:6 1 Cor 5:4; Rom 16:17; 1 Cor 5:11; 1 Cor 11:2
3:7 1 Thess 1:6
3:8 1 Cor 9:4; 1 Thess 2:9; Acts 18:3
3:9 1 Cor 9:4f
3:10 1 Thess 4:11
3:11 1 Tim 5:13
3:12 1 Thess 4:1
3:13 2 Cor 4:1; Gal 6:9
3:14 Col 4:16
3:15 Gal 6:1
3:17 1 Cor 16:21
3:18 Rom 16:20

3 But the Lord is faithful, and He will strengthen and protect you from the evil *one.*
4 We have confidence in the Lord concerning you, that you are doing and will *contin-*
ue to do what we command.
5 May the Lord direct your hearts into the love of God and into the steadfastness of
Christ.
6 Now we command you, brethren, in the name of our Lord Jesus Christ, that you
keep away from every brother who leads an unruly life and not according to the tradition which you received from us.
7 For you yourselves know how you ought to follow our example, because we did not
act in an undisciplined manner among you,
8 nor did we eat anyone's bread without paying for it, but with labor and hardship we
kept working night and day so that we would not be a burden to any of you;
9 not because we do not have the right *to this,* but in order to offer ourselves as a model
for you, so that you would follow our example.
10 For even when we were with you, we used to give you this order: if anyone is not
willing to work, then he is not to eat, either.
11 For we hear that some among you are leading an undisciplined life, doing no work
at all, but acting like busybodies.
12 Now such persons we command and exhort in the Lord Jesus Christ to work in quiet
fashion and eat their own bread.
13 But as for you, brethren, do not grow weary of doing good.
14 If anyone does not obey our instruction in this letter, take special note of that person and do not associate with him, so that he will be put to shame.
15 *Yet* do not regard him as an enemy, but admonish him as a brother.
16 Now may the Lord of peace Himself continually grant you peace in every circumstance. The Lord be with you all!
17 I, Paul, write this greeting with my own hand, and this is a distinguishing mark in
every letter; this is the way I write.
18 The grace of our Lord Jesus Christ be with you all.

---

he will strengthen us. (See also comments on Ephesians 6:10–19 concerning our armor for spiritual warfare.) The following guidelines can help you prepare for and survive satanic attacks: (1) Take the threat of spiritual attack seriously; (2) pray for strength and help from God; (3) study the Bible to recognize Satan's style and tactics; (4) memorize Scripture so it will be a source of help no matter where you are; (5) associate with those who speak the truth; and (6) practice what you are taught by spiritual leaders.

3:6–10 Paul was writing here about the person who is lazy and unruly. Paul explained that when he and his companions were in Thessalonica, they worked hard, buying what they needed rather than becoming a burden to any of the believers. The rule they followed was, "If anyone is not willing to work, then he is not to eat, either." There's a difference between leisure and laziness. Relaxation and recreation provide a necessary and much needed balance to our lives; but when it is time to work, Christians should jump right in. We should make the most of our talent and time, doing all we can to provide for ourselves and our dependents. Rest when you should be resting, and work when you should be working.

3:6–15 Some people in the Thessalonian church were falsely teaching that because Christ would return any day, people should set aside their responsibilities, quit work, do no future planning, and just wait for the Lord. But their lack of activity only led them into sin. They became a burden to the church, which was supporting them; they wasted time that could have been used for helping others; and they became "busybodies" (3:11). These church members may have thought that they were being more spiritual by not working, but Paul tells them to be responsible and get back to work. Being ready for Christ means obeying him in every area of life. Because we know that Christ is coming, we must live in such a way that our faith and our daily practice will please him when he arrives.

3:11–12 A "busybody" is a gossip. An idle person who doesn't work ends up filling his or her time with less than helpful activities, like gossip. Rumors and hearsay are tantalizing, exciting to hear, and make us feel like insiders. But they tear people down. If you often find your nose in other people's business, you may be underemployed. Look for a task to do for Christ or for your family, and get to work.

3:14–15 Paul counseled the church to stop supporting financially and associating with those who persisted in their idleness. Hunger and loneliness can be very effective ways to make the idle person become productive. Paul was not advising coldness or cruelty, but the kind of tough love that a person would show a brother or sister.

3:18 The book of 2 Thessalonians is especially meaningful for those who are being persecuted or are under pressure because of their faith. In chapter 1 we are told what suffering can do for us. In chapter 2 we are assured of final victory. In chapter 3 we are encouraged to continue living responsibly in spite of difficult circumstances. Christ's return is more than a doctrine; it is a promise. It is not just for the future; it has a vital impact on how we live now.

1 TIMOTHY

VITAL STATISTICS

PURPOSE:
To give encouragement and instruction to Timothy, a young leader

AUTHOR:
Paul

TO WHOM WRITTEN:
Timothy, young church leaders, and all believers everywhere

DATE WRITTEN:
Approximately A.D. 64, from Rome or Macedonia (possibly Philippi), probably just prior to Paul's final imprisonment in Rome

SETTING:
Timothy was one of Paul's closest companions. Paul had sent Timothy to the church at Ephesus to counter the false teaching that had arisen there (1:3–4). Timothy probably served for a time as a leader in the church at Ephesus. Paul hoped to visit Timothy (3:14–15; 4:13), but in the meantime, he wrote this letter to give Timothy practical advice about the ministry.

KEY VERSE:
"Let no one look down on your youthfulness, but rather in speech, conduct, love, faith and purity, show yourself an example of those who believe" (4:12).

KEY PEOPLE:
Paul, Timothy

KEY PLACE:
Ephesus

SPECIAL FEATURES:
First Timothy is a personal letter and a handbook of church administration and discipline.

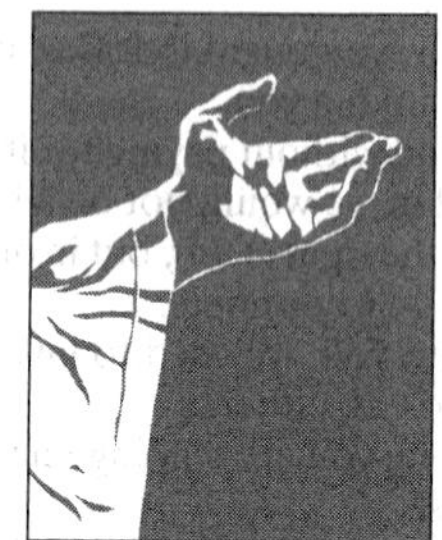

WITHOUT trying, we model our values. Parents in particular demonstrate to their children what they consider important and valuable. "Like father, like son" is not just a well-worn cliché; it is a truth repeated in our homes. And experience proves that children often follow the life-styles of their parents, repeating their successes and mistakes.

Timothy is a prime example of one who was influenced by godly relatives. His mother, Eunice, and grandmother Lois were Jewish believers who helped shape his life and promote his spiritual growth (2 Timothy 1:5; 3:15). The first "second generation" Christian mentioned in the New Testament, Timothy became Paul's protegé and pastor of the church at Ephesus. As a young minister, Timothy faced all sorts of pressures, conflicts, and challenges from the church and his surrounding culture. To counsel and encourage Timothy, Paul sent this very personal letter.

Paul wrote 1 Timothy in about A.D. 64, probably just prior to his final Roman imprisonment. Because he had appealed to Caesar, Paul was sent as a prisoner to Rome (see Acts 25—28). Most scholars believe that Paul was released in about A.D. 62 (possibly because the "statute of limitations" had expired), and that during the next few years he was able to travel. During this time, he wrote 1 Timothy and Titus. Soon, however, Emperor Nero began his campaign to eliminate Christianity. It is believed that during this time Paul was imprisoned again and eventually executed. During this second Roman imprisonment, Paul wrote 2 Timothy. Titus and the two letters to Timothy comprise what are called the "Pastoral Letters."

Paul's first letter to Timothy affirms their relationship (1:2). Paul begins his fatherly advice, warning Timothy about false teachers (1:3–11) and urging him to hold on to his faith in Christ (1:12–20). Next, Paul considers public worship, emphasizing the importance of prayer (2:1–7) and order in church meetings (2:8–15). This leads to a discussion of the qualifications of church leaders—elders and deacons. Here Paul lists specific criteria for each office (3:1–16).

Paul speaks again about false teachers, telling Timothy how to recognize them and respond to them (4:1–16). Next, he gives practical advice on pastoral care to the young and old (5:1–2), widows (5:3–16), elders (5:17–25), and slaves (6:1–2). Paul concludes by exhorting Timothy to guard his motives (6:3–10), to stand firm in his faith (6:11–12), to live above reproach (6:13–16), and to minister faithfully (6:17–21).

First Timothy holds many lessons. If you are a church leader, take note of Paul's relationship with this young disciple—his careful counsel and guidance. Measure yourself against the qualifications that Paul gives for overseers and deacons. If you are young in the faith, follow the example of godly Christian leaders like Timothy, who imitated Paul's life. If you are a parent, remind yourself of the profound effect a Christian home can have on family members. A faithful mother and grandmother led Timothy to Christ, and Timothy's ministry helped change the world.

THE BLUEPRINT

1. Instructions on right belief (1:1–20)
2. Instructions for the church (2:1—3:16)
3. Instructions for elders (4:1—6:21)

Paul advised Timothy on such practical topics as qualifications for church leaders, public worship, confronting false teaching, and how to treat various groups of people within the church. Right belief and right behavior are critical for anyone who desires to lead or serve effectively in the church. We should all believe rightly, participate in church actively, and minister to one another lovingly.

MEGATHEMES

THEME	EXPLANATION	IMPORTANCE
Sound Doctrine	Paul instructed Timothy to preserve the Christian faith by teaching sound doctrine and modeling right living. Timothy had to oppose false teachers, who were leading church members away from belief in salvation by faith in Jesus Christ alone.	We must know the truth in order to defend it. We must cling to the belief that Christ came to save us. We should stay away from those who twist the words of the Bible for their own purposes.
Public Worship	Prayer in public worship must be done with a proper attitude toward God and fellow believers.	Christian character must be evident in every aspect of worship. We must rid ourselves of any anger, resentment, or offensive behavior that might disrupt worship or damage church unity.
Church Leadership	Paul gives specific instructions concerning the qualifications for church leaders so that the church might honor God and operate smoothly.	Church leaders must be wholly committed to Christ. If you are a new or young Christian, don't be anxious to become a leader in the church. Seek to develop your Christian character first. Be sure to seek God, not your own ambition.
Personal Discipline	It takes discipline to be a leader in the church. Timothy, like all pastors, had to guard his motives, minister faithfully, and live above reproach. Any pastor must keep morally and spiritually fit.	To stay in good spiritual shape, you must discipline yourself to study God's Word and to obey it. Put your spiritual abilities to work!
Caring Church	The church has a responsibility to care for the needs of all its members, especially the sick, the poor, and the widowed. Caring must go beyond good intentions.	Caring for the family of believers demonstrates our Christlike attitude and exhibits genuine love to nonbelievers.

1. Instructions on right belief

Misleadings in Doctrine and Living

1 Paul, an apostle of Christ Jesus according to the commandment of God our Savior,
and of Christ Jesus, *who is* our hope,
2 To Timothy, *my* true child in *the* faith: Grace, mercy *and* peace from God the Father and Christ Jesus our Lord.
3 As I urged you upon my departure for Macedonia, remain on at Ephesus so that
you may instruct certain men not to teach strange doctrines,
4 nor to pay attention to myths and endless genealogies, which give rise to mere speculation rather than *furthering* the administration of God which is by faith.
5 But the goal of our instruction is love from a pure heart and a good conscience and
a sincere faith.
6 For some men, straying from these things, have turned aside to fruitless discussion,
7 wanting to be teachers of the Law, even though they do not understand either what
they are saying or the matters about which they make confident assertions.
8 But we know that the Law is good, if one uses it lawfully,
9 realizing the fact that law is not made for a righteous person, but for those who are
lawless and rebellious, for the ungodly and sinners, for the unholy and profane, for those
who kill their fathers or mothers, for murderers
10 and immoral men and homosexuals and kidnappers and liars and perjurers, and
whatever else is contrary to sound teaching,

1:1 Col 1:27

1:4 1 Tim 4:7; 2 Tim 4:4; Titus 1:14; 2 Pet 1:16; Eph 3:2

1:5 2 Tim 2:22; 2 Tim 1:3; 1 Pet 3:16, 21

1:6 Titus 1:10

1:7 James 3:1; Luke 2:46

1:8 Rom 7:12, 16

1:9 Gal 5:23; Titus 1:6, 10; 1 Pet 4:18; Jude 15; 1 Tim 4:7; 6:20; Heb 12:16

1:10 1 Cor 6:9; Rev 18:13; 21:8, 27; 22:15; Matt 5:33; 1 Tim 4:6; 6:3; 2 Tim 4:3; Titus 1:9, 13; 2:1, 2

1:1 This letter was written to Timothy in A.D. 64 or 65, after Paul's first imprisonment in Rome (Acts 28:16–31). Apparently Paul had been out of prison for several years, and during that time he had revisited many churches in Asia and Macedonia. When he and Timothy returned to Ephesus, they found widespread false teaching in the church. Paul had warned the Ephesian elders to be on guard against the false teachers who inevitably would come after he had left (Acts 20:17–31). Paul sent Timothy to lead the Ephesian church while he moved on to Macedonia. From there Paul wrote this letter of encouragement and instruction to help Timothy deal with the difficult situation in the Ephesian church. Later, Paul was arrested again and brought back to a Roman prison.

1:1 Paul calls himself an *apostle,* meaning "one who is sent." Paul was sent by Jesus Christ to bring the message of salvation to the Gentiles (Acts 9:1–20). For more information on Paul, see his Profile in Acts 9.

1:1 How was Paul an apostle "according to the commandment of God"? In Acts 13:2, the Holy Spirit, through the prophets, said, "Set apart for Me Barnabas and Saul [Paul] for the work to which I have called them." From Romans 16:25–26 and Titus 1:3 it is obvious that Paul regarded his commission as directly from God.

1:3–4 Paul first visited Ephesus on his second missionary journey (Acts 18:19–21). Later, on his third missionary journey, he stayed there for almost three years (Acts 19; 20). Ephesus, along with Rome, Corinth, Antioch, and Alexandria, was one of the major cities in the Roman empire. It was a center for the commerce, politics, and religions of Asia Minor, and the location of the temple dedicated to the goddess Artemis (Diana).

1:3–4 The church at Ephesus may have been plagued by the same heresy that was threatening the church at Colosse—the teaching that to be acceptable to God, a person had to discover certain hidden knowledge and had to worship angels (Colossians 2:8, 18). Thinking that it would aid in their salvation, some Ephesians constructed mythical stories based on Old Testament history or genealogies. The false teachers were motivated by their own interests rather than Christ's. They embroiled the church in endless and irrelevant questions and controversies, taking precious time away from the study of the truth. Today we could also enter into worthless and irrelevant discussions, but such disputes quickly crowd out the life-changing message of Christ. Stay away from religious speculation and pointless theological arguments. Such exercises may seem harmless at first, but they have a way of sidetracking us from the central message of the gospel—the person and work of Jesus Christ. And they expend time we should use to share the gospel with others. You should avoid anything that keeps you from doing God's work.

1:3–11 There are many leaders and authorities today who demand allegiance, some of whom would even have us turn from Christ to follow them. When they seem to know the Bible, their influence can be dangerously subtle. How can you recognize false teaching? (1) It promotes controversies instead of helping people come to Jesus (1:4). (2) It is often initiated by those whose motivation is to make a name for themselves (1:7). (3) It will be contrary to the true teaching of the Scriptures (1:6–7; 4:1–3). To protect yourself from the deception of false teachers, you should learn what the Bible teaches and remain steadfast in your faith in Christ alone.

1:5 The false teachers were motivated by a spirit of curiosity and a desire to gain power and prestige. By contrast, genuine Christian teachers are motivated by sincere faith and a desire to do what is right. It may be exciting to impress people with our great knowledge, but high status based on falsehood is ultimately empty.

1:6 Arguing about details of the Bible can send us off on interesting but irrelevant tangents and cause us to miss the intent of God's message. The false teachers at Ephesus constructed vast speculative systems and then argued about the minor details of their wholly imaginary ideas. We should allow nothing to distract us from the Good News of salvation in Jesus Christ, the main point of Scripture. We should know what the Bible says, apply it to our lives daily, and teach it to others. When we do this, we will be able to evaluate all teachings in light of the central truth about Jesus. Don't focus on the minute details of the Bible to the exclusion of the main point God is teaching you.

1:7 Paul was writing against those who were engaging in philosophical speculation based on the Pentateuch (the first five books of the Old Testament, written by Moses).

1:7–11 The false teachers wanted to become famous as teachers of God's law, but they didn't even understand the law's purpose. The law was not meant to give believers a list of commands for every occasion, but to show unbelievers their sin and bring them to God. For more of what Paul taught about our relationship to law, see Romans 5:20–21; 13:9–10; Galatians 3:24–29.

1:10 There are those who attempt to legitimize homosexuality as

1:12 Gal 3:26; Acts 9:22
1:13 Acts 8:3
1:14 Rom 5:20; 1 Cor 3:10; 2 Cor 4:15; Titus 2:2
1:15 Luke 15:2ff; 19:10; Rom 11:14
1:16 1 Cor 7:25; Eph 2:7
1:17 Rev 15:3; 1 Tim 6:16; Col 1:15; John 5:44; 1 Tim 6:15
1:18 1 Tim 4:14; 2 Cor 10:4
1:19 2 Tim 2:18
1:20 2 Tim 2:17; 4:14; Heb 12:5ff

11 according to the glorious gospel of the blessed God, with which I have been entrusted.
12 I thank Christ Jesus our Lord, who has strengthened me, because He considered
me faithful, putting me into service,
13 even though I was formerly a blasphemer and a persecutor and a violent aggressor.
Yet I was shown mercy because I acted ignorantly in unbelief;
14 and the grace of our Lord was more than abundant, with the faith and love which
are *found* in Christ Jesus.
15 It is a trustworthy statement, deserving full acceptance, that Christ Jesus came into
the world to save sinners, among whom I am foremost *of all.*
16 Yet for this reason I found mercy, so that in me as the foremost, Jesus Christ might
demonstrate His perfect patience as an example for those who would believe in Him for
eternal life.
17 Now to the King eternal, immortal, invisible, the only God, *be* honor and glory forever and ever. Amen.
18 This command I entrust to you, Timothy, *my* son, in accordance with the prophecies previously made concerning you, that by them you fight the good fight,
19 keeping faith and a good conscience, which some have rejected and suffered shipwreck in regard to their faith.
20 Among these are Hymenaeus and Alexander, whom I have handed over to Satan,
so that they will be taught not to blaspheme.

---

an acceptable alternative life-style. Even some Christians say people have a right to choose their sexual preference. But the Bible specifically calls homosexual behavior sin (see Leviticus 18:22; Romans 1:18–32; 1 Corinthians 6:9–11). We must be careful, however, to condemn only the practice, and not the people. Those who commit homosexual acts are not to be feared, ridiculed, or hated. They can be forgiven and their lives can be transformed. The church should be a haven of forgiveness and healing for repentant homosexuals without compromising its stance against homosexual behavior. For more on this subject see the notes on Romans 1:26–27.

1:12–17 People can feel so guilt-ridden by their past that they think God could never forgive and accept them. But consider Paul's past. He had scoffed at the teachings of Jesus ("a blasphemer") and hunted down and murdered God's people ("a persecutor and a violent aggressor") before coming to faith in Christ (Acts 9:1–9). God forgave Paul and used Paul mightily for his kingdom. No matter how shameful your past, God also can forgive and use you.

1:14 We may feel that our faith in God and our love for Christ and for others is inadequate. But we can be confident that Christ will help our faith and love grow as our relationship with him deepens.

1:15 Here Paul summarizes the Good News: Jesus came into the world to save sinners, and no sinner is beyond his saving power. (See Luke 5:32 for Jesus' purpose for being on earth.) Jesus didn't come merely to show us how to live a better life or to challenge us to be better people. He came to offer us salvation that leads to eternal life. Have you accepted his offer?

1:15 Paul calls himself "the foremost" of sinners. We think of Paul as a great hero of the faith, but Paul never saw himself that way, because he remembered his life before he met Christ. The more Paul understood God's grace, the more he was aware of his own sinfulness. Humility and gratitude should mark the life of every Christian. Never forget that you too are a sinner saved by grace.

1:17 This verse is a typical doxology given by Paul as a natural, emotional response to these reflections about the mercy of God. Paul was so moved by God's love that he was able to praise God spontaneously.

1:18 Paul highly valued the gift of prophecy (1 Corinthians 14:1). Through prophecy important messages of warning and encouragement came to the church. Just as pastors are ordained and set apart for ministry in church today, Timothy had been set apart for ministry when elders laid their hands on him (see 4:14). Apparently at this ceremony, several believers had prophesied about Timothy's gifts and strengths. These words from the Lord must have encouraged Timothy throughout his ministry.

1:19 How can you keep a good conscience? Treasure your faith in Christ more than anything else and do what you know is right. Each time you deliberately ignore your conscience, you are hardening your heart. Over a period of time your capacity to tell right from wrong will diminish. As you walk with God, he will speak to you through your conscience, letting you know the difference between right and wrong. Be sure to act on those inner tugs so that you do what is right—then your conscience will remain clear.

1:20 We don't know who Alexander was—he may have been an associate of Hymenaeus. Hymenaeus's error is explained in 2 Timothy 2:17–18. He weakened people's faith by teaching that the resurrection had already occurred. Paul says that he handed Hymenaeus over to Satan, meaning that Paul had removed him from the fellowship of the church. Paul did this so that Hymenaeus would see his error and repent. The ultimate purpose of this punishment was correction. The church today is too often lax in disciplining Christians who deliberately sin. Deliberate disobedience should be responded to quickly and sternly to prevent the entire congregation from being affected. But discipline must be done in a way that tries to bring the offender back to Christ and into the loving embrace of the church. The definition of discipline includes these words: strengthening, purifying, training, correcting, perfecting. Condemnation, suspicion, withholding of forgiveness, or permanent exile should not be a part of church discipline.

2. Instructions for the church

A Call to Prayer

2 First of all, then, I urge that entreaties *and* prayers, petitions *and* thanksgivings, be
made on behalf of all men,
2 for kings and all who are in authority, so that we may lead a tranquil and quiet life
in all godliness and dignity.
3 This is good and acceptable in the sight of God our Savior,
4 who desires all men to be saved and to come to the knowledge of the truth.
5 For there is one God, *and* one mediator also between God and men, *the* man Christ
Jesus,
6 who gave Himself as a ransom for all, the testimony *given* at the proper time.
7 For this I was appointed a preacher and an apostle (I am telling the truth, I am not
lying) as a teacher of the Gentiles in faith and truth.
8 Therefore I want the men in every place to pray, lifting up holy hands, without wrath
and dissension.

Women Instructed

9 Likewise, *I want* women to adorn themselves with proper clothing, modestly and
discreetly, not with braided hair and gold or pearls or costly garments,
10 but rather by means of good works, as is proper for women making a claim to godliness.
11 A woman must quietly receive instruction with entire submissiveness.

2:1 Eph 6:18
2:2 Ezra 6:10; Rom 13:1
2:3 Luke 1:47
2:4 John 3:17; 1 Tim 4:10; Titus 2:11; 2 Pet 3:9; Rom 11:14; 2 Tim 2:25
2:5 Rom 3:30; 10:12; 1 Cor 8:4; Gal 3:20; Matt 1:1; Rom 1:3
2:6 Matt 20:28; Gal 1:4; 1 Cor 1:6
2:7 Acts 9:15
2:8 Titus 3:8; John 4:21; 1 Cor 1:2; 2 Cor 2:14; 1 Thess 1:8; James 4:8
2:9 1 Pet 3:3
2:11 1 Cor 14:34; Titus 2:5

2:1–4 Although God is all-powerful and all-knowing, he has chosen to let us help him change the world through our prayers. How this works is a mystery to us because of our limited understanding, but it is a reality. Paul urges us to pray for each other and for our leaders in government. Our earnest prayers will have powerful results (James 5:16).

2:2 Paul's command to pray for kings was remarkable considering that Nero, a notoriously cruel ruler, was emperor at this time (A.D. 54–68). When Paul wrote this letter, persecution was a growing threat to believers. Later, when Nero needed a scapegoat for the great fire that destroyed much of Rome in A.D. 64, he blamed the Roman Christians so as to take the focus off himself. Then persecution erupted throughout the Roman empire. Not only were Christians denied certain privileges in society, but some were even publicly butchered, burned, or fed to animals.

2:2 When our lives are going along peacefully and quietly, it is difficult to remember to pray for those in authority, because we often take good government for granted. It's easier to remember to pray when we experience problems. But we should pray for those in authority around the world so that their societies will be conducive to the spread of the gospel.

2:4 Both Peter and Paul said that God wants all to be saved (see 2 Peter 3:9). This does not mean that all *will* be saved, because the Bible makes it clear that many reject Christ (Matthew 25:31–46; John 12:44–50; Hebrews 10:26–29). The gospel message has a universal scope; it is not directed only to people of one race, one sex, or one national background. God loves the whole world and sent his Son to save sinners. Never assume that anyone is outside God's mercy or beyond the reach of his offer of salvation.

2:5–6 We human beings are separated from God by sin, and only one person in the universe is our mediator and can stand between us and God and bring us together again—Jesus, who is both God and man. Jesus' sacrifice brought new life to all people. Have you let him bring you to the Father?

2:6 Jesus gave his life as a ransom for our sin (Mark 10:45). A ransom was the price paid to release a slave from captivity. Jesus, our mediator, gave his life in exchange for ours. By his death, he paid our penalty for sin.

2:7 Paul describes himself as a preacher. He was given the special privilege of announcing the gospel to the Gentiles. He gives his credentials as an apostle in 1 Corinthians 15:7–11.

2:8 Besides displeasing God, wrath and dissension make prayer difficult. That is why Jesus said that we should interrupt our prayers, if necessary, to make peace with others (Matthew 5:23, 24). God wants us to obey him immediately and thoroughly. Our goal should be to have a right relationship with God and also with others.

2:9–10 Apparently some Christian women were trying to gain respect by looking beautiful rather than by becoming Christlike in character. Some may have thought that they could win unbelieving husbands to Christ through their appearance (see Peter's counsel to such women in 1 Peter 3:1–6). It is not unscriptural for a woman to want to be attractive. Beauty, however, begins inside a person. A gentle, modest, loving character gives a light to the face that cannot be duplicated by the best cosmetics and jewelry in the world. A carefully groomed and well-decorated exterior is artificial and cold unless inner beauty is present.

2:9–15 To understand these verses, we must understand the situation in which Paul and Timothy worked. In first-century Jewish culture, women were not allowed to study. When Paul said that women should *learn* in quietness and full submission, he was offering them an amazing new opportunity. Paul did not want the Ephesian women to teach because they didn't yet have enough knowledge or experience. The Ephesian church had a particular problem with false teachers. Evidently the women were especially susceptible to the false teachings (2 Timothy 3:1–9), because they did not yet have enough Biblical knowledge to discern the truth. In addition, some of the women were apparently flaunting their newfound Christian freedom by wearing inappropriate clothing (2:9). Paul was telling Timothy not to put anyone (in this case, women) into a position of leadership who was not yet mature in the faith (see 5:22). The same principle applies to churches today (see the note on 3:6).

TIMOTHY

Painful lessons are usually doorways to new opportunities. Even the apostle Paul had much to learn. Shortly after his disappointing experience with John Mark, Paul recruited another eager young man, Timothy, to be his assistant. Paul's intense personality may have been too much for John Mark to handle. It could easily have created the same problem for Timothy. But Paul seems to have learned a lesson in patience from his old friend Barnabas. As a result, Timothy became a "son" to Paul.

Timothy probably became a Christian after Paul's first missionary visit to Lystra (Acts 16:1–5). Timothy already had solid Jewish training in the Scriptures from his mother and grandmother. By Paul's second visit, Timothy had grown into a respected disciple of Jesus. He did not hesitate to join Paul and Silas on their journey. His willingness to be circumcised as an adult is clearly a mark of his commitment. (Timothy's mixed Greek/Jewish background could have created problems on their missionary journeys, because many of their audiences would be made up of Jews who were concerned about the strict keeping of this tradition. Timothy's submission to the rite of circumcision helped to avoid that potential problem.)

Beyond the tensions created by his mixed racial background, Timothy seemed to struggle with a naturally timid character and a sensitivity to his youthfulness. Unfortunately, many who share Timothy's character traits are quickly written off as too great a risk to deserve much responsibility. By God's grace, Paul saw great potential in Timothy. Paul demonstrated his confidence in Timothy by entrusting him with important responsibilities. Paul sent Timothy as his personal representative to Corinth during a particularly tense time (1 Corinthians 4:14–17). Although Timothy was apparently ineffective in that difficult mission, Paul did not give up on him. Timothy continued to travel with Paul.

Our last pictures of Timothy come from the most personal letters in the New Testament: 1 and 2 Timothy. The aging apostle Paul was near the end of his life, but his burning desire to continue his mission had not dimmed. Paul was writing to one of his closest friends—they had traveled, suffered, cried, and laughed together. They shared the intense joy of seeing people respond to the Good News and the agonies of seeing the gospel rejected and distorted. Paul left Timothy in Ephesus to oversee the young church there (1 Timothy 1:3–4). He wrote to encourage Timothy and give him needed direction. These letters have provided comfort and help to countless other "Timothys" through the years. When you face a challenge that seems beyond your abilities, read 1 and 2 Timothy, and remember that others have shared your experience.

Strengths and accomplishments:
- Became a believer after Paul's first missionary journey and joined him for his other two journeys
- Was a respected Christian in his hometown
- Was Paul's special representative on several occasions
- Received two personal letters from Paul
- Probably knew Paul better than any other person, becoming like a son to Paul

Weaknesses and mistakes:
- Struggled with a timid and reserved nature
- Allowed others to look down on his youthfulness
- Was apparently unable to correct some of the problems in the church at Corinth when Paul sent him there

Lessons from his life:
- Youthfulness should not be an excuse for ineffectiveness
- Our inadequacies and inabilities should not keep us from being available to God

Vital statistics:
- Where: Lystra
- Occupations: Missionary, pastor
- Relatives: Mother: Eunice. Grandmother: Lois. Greek father
- Contemporaries: Paul, Silas, Luke, Mark, Peter, Barnabas

Key verses:
"For I have no one else of kindred spirit who will genuinely be concerned for your welfare. For they all seek after their own interests, not those of Christ Jesus. But you know of his [Timothy's] proven worth, that he served with me in the furtherance of the gospel like a child serving his father" (Philippians 2:20–22).

Timothy's story is told in Acts, starting in chapter 16. He is also mentioned in Romans 16:21; 1 Corinthians 4:17; 16:10–11; 2 Corinthians 1:1, 19; Philippians 1:1; 2:19–23; Colossians 1:1; 1 Thessalonians 1:1–10; 2:3–4; 3:2–6; 1 and 2 Timothy; Philemon 1; Hebrews 13:23.

12 But I do not allow a woman to teach or exercise authority over a man, but to remain
quiet.
13 For it was Adam who was first created, *and* then Eve.
14 And *it was* not Adam *who* was deceived, but the woman being deceived, fell into
transgression.
15 But *women* will be preserved through the bearing of children if they continue in faith
and love and sanctity with self-restraint.

Overseers and Deacons

3 It is a trustworthy statement: if any man aspires to the office of overseer, it is a fine
work he desires *to do.*
2 An overseer, then, must be above reproach, the husband of one wife, temperate,
prudent, respectable, hospitable, able to teach,
3 not addicted to wine or pugnacious, but gentle, peaceable, free from the love of
money.
4 *He must be* one who manages his own household well, keeping his children under
control with all dignity
5 (but if a man does not know how to manage his own household, how will he take
care of the church of God?),
6 *and* not a new convert, so that he will not become conceited and fall into the condemnation incurred by the devil.

2:12 1 Cor 14:34; Titus 2:5
2:13 Gen 2:7, 22; 3:16; 1 Cor 11:8ff
2:14 2 Cor 11:3
2:15 1 Tim 1:14
3:1 Acts 20:28
3:2 1 Tim 3:2-4; Titus 1:6-8; 1 Tim 5:9; 1 Tim 3:8, 11; Titus 2:2; Rom 12:13; Heb 13:2; 1 Pet 4:9; 2 Tim 2:24
3:3 Titus 1:7; Heb 13:5
3:5 1 Cor 10:32
3:6 1 Tim 6:4; 2 Tim 3:4

2:12 Some interpret this passage to mean that women should never teach in the assembled church; however, commentators point out that Paul did not forbid women from ever teaching. Paul's commended co-worker, Priscilla, taught Apollos, the great preacher (Acts 18:24–26). In addition, Paul frequently mentioned other women who held positions of responsibility in the church. Phoebe worked in the church (Romans 16:1). Mary, Tryphena, and Tryphosa were the Lord's workers (Romans 16:6, 12), as were Euodia and Syntyche (Philippians 4:2). Paul was very likely prohibiting the Ephesian women, not all women, from teaching (see the note on 2:9–15).

2:12 In Paul's reference to women remaining quiet, the word *quiet* expresses an attitude of serenity and composure. (A different Greek word is usually used to convey "complete silence.") In addition, Paul himself acknowledges that women publicly prayed and prophesied (1 Corinthians 11:5). Apparently, however, the women in the Ephesian church were abusing their newly acquired Christian freedom. Because these women were new converts, they did not yet have the necessary experience, knowledge, or Christian maturity to teach those who already had extensive Scriptural education.

2:13–14 In previous letters Paul had discussed male/female roles in marriage (Ephesians 5:21–33; Colossians 3:18–19). Here he talks about male/female roles within the church. Some scholars see these verses about Adam and Eve as an illustration of what was happening in the Ephesian church. Just as Eve had been deceived in the Garden of Eden, so the women in the church were being deceived by false teachers. And just as Adam was the first human created by God, so the men in the church in Ephesus should be the first to speak and teach, because they had more training. This view, then, stresses that Paul's teaching here is not universal, but applies to churches with similar problems. Other scholars, however, contend that the roles Paul points out are God's design for his created order—God established these roles to maintain harmony in both the family and the church.

2:14 Paul is not excusing Adam for his part in the fall (Genesis 3:6–7, 17–19). On the contrary, in his letter to the Romans Paul places the primary blame for humanity's sinful nature on Adam (Romans 5:12–21).

2:15 There are several ways to understand the phrase, being "preserved through the bearing of children": (1) Man sinned and so men were condemned to painful labor. Woman sinned and so women were condemned to pain in childbearing. Both men and women, however, can be saved through trusting Christ and obeying him. (2) Women who fulfill their God-given roles are demonstrating true commitment and obedience to Christ. One of the most important roles for a wife and mother is to care for her family. (3) The childbearing mentioned here refers to the birth of Jesus Christ. Women (and men) are saved spiritually because of the most important birth, that of Christ himself. (4) From the lessons learned through the trials of childbearing, women can develop qualities that teach them about love, trust, submission, and service.

3:1 To be a church leader ("overseer") is a heavy responsibility because the church belongs to the living God. Church leaders should not be elected because they are popular, nor should they be allowed to push their way to the top. Instead they should be chosen by the church because of their respect for the truth, both in what they believe and in how they live.

3:1–13 The word *overseer* can refer to a pastor, church leader, or presiding elder. It is good to want to be a spiritual leader, but the standards are high. Paul enumerates some of the qualifications here. Do you hold a position of spiritual leadership, or would you like to be a leader some day? Check yourself against Paul's standard of excellence. Those with great responsibility must meet high expectations.

3:1–13 The lists of qualifications for church office show that living a blameless and pure life requires effort and self-discipline. All believers, even if they never plan to be church leaders, should strive to follow these guidelines because they are consistent with what God says is true and right. The strength to live according to God's will comes from Christ.

3:2 When Paul says that each overseer should have only one wife, he is prohibiting both polygamy and promiscuity. This does not prohibit an unmarried person from becoming an elder or a widowed elder from remarrying.

3:4–5 Christian workers and volunteers sometimes make the mistake of thinking their work is so important that they are justified in ignoring their families. Spiritual leadership, however, must begin at home. If a man is not willing to care for, discipline, and teach his children, he is not qualified to lead the church. Don't allow your volunteer activities to detract from your family responsibilities.

3:6 New believers should become secure and strong in the faith before taking leadership roles in the church. Too often, when the church is desperate for workers, new believers are placed in positions of responsibility prematurely. New faith needs time to mature. New believers should have a place of service, but they should not be put into leadership positions until they are firmly grounded in

3:7 2 Cor 8:21; Mark 4:11; 1 Tim 6:9; 2 Tim 2:26

3:8 Phil 1:1; 1 Tim 5:23; Titus 2:3; Titus 1:7; 1 Pet 5:2

3:9 1 Tim 1:5, 19

3:10 1 Tim 5:22

3:11 2 Tim 3:3; Titus 2:3

3:12 Phil 1:1; 1 Tim 3:2; 1 Tim 3:4

3:13 Matt 25:21

3:15 1 Cor 3:16; 2 Cor 6:16; Eph 2:21f; 1 Pet 2:5; 4:17; Gal 2:9; 2 Tim 2:19

3:16 Rom 16:25; John 1:14; Rom 3:4; Luke 2:13; 24:4; 1 Pet 1:12; Rom 16:26; 2 Cor 1:19; Col 1:23; 2 Thess 1:10; Mark 16:19

4:1 1 Cor 2:10f; 2 Thess 2:3ff; 2 Tim 3:1; 2 Pet 3:3; Jude 18; 1 John 4:6; James 3:15

4:2 Eph 4:19

7 And he must have a good reputation with those outside *the church,* so that he will
not fall into reproach and the snare of the devil.
8 Deacons likewise *must be* men of dignity, not double-tongued, or addicted to much
wine or fond of sordid gain,
9 *but* holding to the mystery of the faith with a clear conscience.
10 These men must also first be tested; then let them serve as deacons if they are beyond reproach.
11 Women *must* likewise *be* dignified, not malicious gossips, but temperate, faithful in
all things.
12 Deacons must be husbands of *only* one wife, *and* good managers of *their* children
and their own households.
13 For those who have served well as deacons obtain for themselves a high standing
and great confidence in the faith that is in Christ Jesus.
14 I am writing these things to you, hoping to come to you before long;
15 but in case I am delayed, *I write* so that you will know how one ought to conduct
himself in the household of God, which is the church of the living God, the pillar and
support of the truth.
16 By common confession, great is the mystery of godliness:

He who was revealed in the flesh,
Was vindicated in the Spirit,
Seen by angels,
Proclaimed among the nations,
Believed on in the world,
Taken up in glory.

3. Instructions for leaders

Apostasy

4 But the Spirit explicitly says that in later times some will fall away from the faith,
paying attention to deceitful spirits and doctrines of demons,
2 by means of the hypocrisy of liars seared in their own conscience as with a branding
iron,

---

their faith, with a solid Christian life-style and a knowledge of the Word of God.

3:6–7 Younger believers who are selected for office need to beware of the damaging effects of pride. Pride can seduce our emotions and cloud our reason. It can make those who are immature susceptible to the influence of unscrupulous people. Pride and conceit were the devil's downfall, and he uses pride to trap others.

3:8–13 *Deacon* means "one who serves." This position was possibly begun by the apostles in the Jerusalem church (Acts 6:1–6) to care for the physical needs of the congregation, especially the needs of the Greek-speaking widows. Deacons were leaders in the church, and their qualifications resemble those of the overseers. In some churches today, the office of deacon has lost its importance. New Christians are often asked to serve in this position, but that is not the New Testament pattern. Paul says that potential deacons should first be tested before they are asked to serve.

3:11 *Women* can refer to women helpers or deaconesses. It could also mean wives of deacons, or female leaders of the church (such as Phoebe, the deaconess mentioned in Romans 16:1). In either case, Paul expected the behavior of prominent women in the church to be just as responsible and blameless as that of prominent men.

3:16 In this short hymn, Paul affirms the humanity and divinity of Christ. By so doing he reveals the heart of the gospel, "the mystery of godliness" (the secret of how we become godly). "Revealed in the flesh"—Jesus was a man; Jesus' incarnation is the basis of our being right with God. "Was vindicated in the Spirit"—Jesus' resurrection showed that the Holy Spirit's power was in him (Romans 8:11). "Seen by angels" and "taken up in glory"—Jesus is divine. We can't please God on our own; we must depend on Christ. As a man, Jesus lived a perfect life, and so he is a perfect example of how to live. As God, Jesus gives us the power to do what is right. It is possible to live a godly life—through following Christ.

4:1 The "later times" began with Christ's resurrection and will continue until his return when he will set up his kingdom and judge all humanity.

4:1–2 False teachers were and still are a threat to the church. Jesus and the apostles repeatedly warned against them (see, for example, Mark 13:21–23; Acts 20:28–31; 2 Thessalonians 2:1–12; 2 Peter 3:3–7). The danger that Timothy faced in Ephesus seems to have come from certain people in the church who were following some Greek philosophers who taught that the body was evil and that only the soul mattered. The false teachers refused to believe that the God of creation was good, because his very contact with the physical world would have soiled him. Though these Greek-influenced church members honored Jesus, they could not believe he was truly human. Paul knew that their teachings, if left unchecked, would greatly distort Christian truth.

It is not enough that a teacher appears to know what he is talking about, is disciplined and moral, or says that he is speaking for God. If his words contradict the Bible, his teaching is false. Like Timothy, we must guard against any teaching that causes believers to dilute or reject any aspect of their faith. Such false teaching can be very direct or extremely subtle.

4:1–5 Paul said the false teachers were hypocritical liars who encouraged people to follow "deceitful spirits and doctrines of demons." Satan deceives people by offering a clever imitation of the real thing. The false teachers gave stringent rules (such as forbidding people to marry or to eat certain foods). This made them appear self-disciplined and righteous. Their strict disciplines for the body, however, could not remove sin (see Colossians 2:20–23). We must not be unduly impressed by a teacher's style or credentials; we must look to his teaching about Jesus Christ. His conclusions about Christ show the source of his message.

3 *men* who forbid marriage *and advocate* abstaining from foods which God has created to be gratefully shared in by those who believe and know the truth.
4 For everything created by God is good, and nothing is to be rejected if it is received
with gratitude;
5 for it is sanctified by means of the word of God and prayer.

A Good Minister's Discipline

6 In pointing out these things to the brethren, you will be a good servant of Christ
Jesus, *constantly* nourished on the words of the faith and of the sound doctrine which
you have been following.
7 But have nothing to do with worldly fables fit only for old women. On the other
hand, discipline yourself for the purpose of godliness;
8 for bodily discipline is only of little profit, but godliness is profitable for all things,
since it holds promise for the present life and *also* for the *life* to come.
9 It is a trustworthy statement deserving full acceptance.
10 For it is for this we labor and strive, because we have fixed our hope on the living
God, who is the Savior of all men, especially of believers.
11 Prescribe and teach these things.
12 Let no one look down on your youthfulness, but *rather* in speech, conduct, love, faith
and purity, show yourself an example of those who believe.
13 Until I come, give attention to the *public* reading *of Scripture,* to exhortation and
teaching.
14 Do not neglect the spiritual gift within you, which was bestowed on you through
prophetic utterance with the laying on of hands by the presbytery.
15 Take pains with these things; be *absorbed* in them, so that your progress will be evident to all.
16 Pay close attention to yourself and to your teaching; persevere in these things, for
as you do this you will ensure salvation both for yourself and for those who hear you.

Honor Widows

5 Do not sharply rebuke an older man, but *rather* appeal to *him* as a father, *to* the younger men as brothers,
2 the older women as mothers, *and* the younger women as sisters, in all purity.

4:3 Heb 13:4; Col 2:16, 23; Gen 1:29; 9:3; Rom 14:6; 1 Cor 10:30f; 1 Tim 4:4
4:4 1 Cor 10:26; Rom 14:6
4:5 Gen 1:25, 31; Heb 11:3
4:6 Acts 1:15; 2 Cor 11:23; 1 Tim 1:10; Luke 1:3; Phil 2:20, 22; 2 Tim 3:10
4:7 1 Tim 1:4; 2 Tim 3:5
4:8 Col 2:23; 1 Tim 4:7; 6:3, 5f; 2 Tim 3:5; Matt 6:33; 12:32; Mark 10:30
4:10 2 Cor 1:10; 1 Tim 6:17; 1 Tim 3:15; John 4:42; 1 Tim 2:4
4:12 1 Cor 16:11; Titus 2:15; Titus 2:7; 1 Pet 5:3; 1 Tim 1:14
4:13 1 Tim 3:14; 2 Tim 3:15ff
4:14 1 Tim 1:18; Acts 6:6; 1 Tim 5:22; 2 Tim 1:6; Acts 11:30
4:16 Acts 20:28
5:1 Lev 19:32; Titus 2:2

4:4–5 In opposition to the false teachers, Paul affirmed that everything God created is good (see Genesis 1). We should ask for God's blessing on his created gifts that give us pleasure and thank him for them. This doesn't mean that we should abuse what God has made (for example, gluttony abuses God's gift of good food, lust abuses God's gift of love, and murder abuses God's gift of life). Instead of abusing, we should enjoy these gifts by using them to serve and honor God. Have you thanked God for the good gifts he has given? Are you using the gifts in ways pleasing to you *and* to God?

4:7–10 Are you in shape both physically and spiritually? In our society, much emphasis is placed on physical fitness, but spiritual health (godliness) is even more important. Our physical health is susceptible to disease and injury, but faith can sustain us through these tragedies. To train ourselves to be godly, we must develop our faith by using our God-given abilities in the service of the church (see 4:14–16). Are you developing your spiritual muscles?

4:10 Christ is the Savior for all, but his salvation becomes effective only for those who trust him.

4:12 Timothy was a young pastor. It would have been easy for older Christians to look down on him because of his youth. He had to earn the respect of his elders by setting an example in his speech, life, love, faith, and purity. Regardless of your age, God can use you. Whether you are young or old, don't think of your age as a handicap. Live so others can see Christ in you.

4:13 The Scripture that Paul mentions is in fact the Old Testament. We must make sure to emphasize the entire Bible, both the Old and the New Testaments. There are rich rewards in studying the people, events, prophecies, and principles of the Old Testament.

4:14 Timothy's commission as a church leader was confirmed by prophecy (see also 1:18) and by the laying on of hands by the presbytery (elders) of the church. He was not a self-appointed leader. If you aspire to church leadership, seek the counsel of mature Christians who know you well and who will hold you accountable.

4:14–15 As a young leader in a church that had a lot of problems, Timothy may have felt intimidated. But the elders and prophets encouraged him and charged him to use his spiritual gift responsibly. Highly skilled and talented athletes lose their abilities if their muscles aren't toned by constant use, and we will lose our spiritual gifts if we don't put them to work. Our talents are improved by exercise, but failing to use them causes them to waste away from lack of practice and nourishment. What gifts and abilities has God given you? Use them regularly in serving God and others. (See Romans 12:1–8; 2 Timothy 1:6–8 for more on using well the abilities God has given us.)

4:16 We know the importance of watching our lives closely. We must be on constant guard against falling into sin that can so easily destroy us. Yet we must watch what we believe ("teaching") just as closely. Wrong beliefs can quickly lead us into sin and heresy. We should be on guard against those who would persuade us that how we live is more important than what we believe. We should persevere in both.

5:2 Men in the ministry can avoid improper attitudes toward women by treating them as family members. If men see women as fellow members in God's family, they will protect them and help them grow spiritually.

5:3 Acts 6:1; 9:39, 41

5:4 Eph 6:2; 1 Tim 2:3

5:5 Acts 6:1; 9:39, 41; 1 Tim 5:3, 16; 1 Cor 7:34; 1 Pet 3:5; Luke 2:37; 1 Tim 2:1; 2 Tim 1:3

5:6 James 5:5; Luke 15:24; 2 Tim 3:6; Rev 3:1

5:8 2 Tim 2:12; Titus 1:16; 2 Pet 2:1; Jude 4

5:10 Acts 9:36; 1 Tim 6:18; Titus 2:7; 3:8; 1 Pet 2:12; 1 Tim 3:2; Luke 7:44

5:11 Rev 18:7

5:13 3 John 10; 2 Thess 3:11; Titus 1:11

5:14 1 Cor 7:9; 1 Tim 4:3; Titus 2:5; 1 Tim 6:1

5:15 1 Tim 1:20; Matt 4:10

3 Honor widows who are widows indeed;
4 but if any widow has children or grandchildren, they must first learn to practice piety in regard to their own family and to make some return to their parents; for this is acceptable in the sight of God.
5 Now she who is a widow indeed and who has been left alone, has fixed her hope on God and continues in entreaties and prayers night and day.
6 But she who gives herself to wanton pleasure is dead even while she lives.
7 Prescribe these things as well, so that they may be above reproach.
8 But if anyone does not provide for his own, and especially for those of his household, he has denied the faith and is worse than an unbeliever.
9 A widow is to be put on the list only if she is not less than sixty years old, *having been* the wife of one man,
10 having a reputation for good works; *and* if she has brought up children, if she has shown hospitality to strangers, if she has washed the saints' feet, if she has assisted those in distress, *and* if she has devoted herself to every good work.
11 But refuse *to put* younger widows *on the list*, for when they feel sensual desires in disregard of Christ, they want to get married,
12 *thus* incurring condemnation, because they have set aside their previous pledge.
13 At the same time they also learn *to be* idle, as they go around from house to house; and not merely idle, but also gossips and busybodies, talking about things not proper *to mention.*
14 Therefore, I want younger *widows* to get married, bear children, keep house, *and* give the enemy no occasion for reproach;
15 for some have already turned aside to follow Satan.
16 If any woman who is a believer has *dependent* widows, she must assist them and the church must not be burdened, so that it may assist those who are widows indeed.

5:3ff Paul wanted Christian families to be as self-supporting as possible. He insisted that children and grandchildren take care of the widows in their families (5:4); he suggested that younger widows remarry and start new families (5:14); and he ordered the church not to support lazy members who refused to work (2 Thessalonians 3:10). Nevertheless, when necessary, the believers pooled their resources (Acts 2:44–47); they gave generously to help disaster-ridden churches (1 Corinthians 16:1–4), and they took care of a large number of widows (Acts 6:1–6). The church has always had limited resources, and it has always had to balance financial responsibility with generosity. It only makes sense for members to work as hard as they can and to be as independent as possible, so they can adequately care for themselves and for less fortunate members. When church members are both responsible and generous, everyone's needs will be met.

5:3–5 Because there were no pensions, no social security, no life insurance, and few honorable jobs for women, widows were usually unable to support themselves. The responsibility for caring for the helpless naturally falls first on their families, the people whose lives are most closely linked with theirs. Paul stresses the importance of families caring for the needs of widows and not leaving this responsibility for the church—so the church can care for those widows who have no families. A widow who had no children or other family members to support her was doomed to poverty. From the beginning, the church took care of its widows, who in turn gave valuable service to the church.

The church should support those who have no families and should also help the elderly, young, disabled, ill, or poverty-stricken with their emotional and spiritual needs. Often families who are caring for their own helpless members have heavy burdens. They may need extra money, a listening ear, a helping hand, or a word of encouragement. Interestingly, those who are helped often turn around and help others, turning the church into more of a caring community. Don't wait for people to ask. Take the initiative and look for ways to serve them.

5:8 Almost everyone has relatives, family of some kind. Family relationships are so important in God's eyes, Paul says, that a person who neglects his or her family responsibilities has denied the faith. Are you doing your part to meet the needs of those included in your family circle?

5:9–16 Apparently some older widows had been "put on the list" of widows, meaning that they had taken a vow committing themselves to work for the church in exchange for financial support. Paul lists a few qualifications for these church workers—these widows should be at least 60 years old, should have been faithful to their husbands, and should be well known for their kind deeds. Younger widows should not be included in this group because they might desire to marry again and thus have to break their pledge (5:11–12).

Three out of four wives today eventually are widowed, and many of the older women in our churches have lost their husbands. Does your church provide an avenue of service for these women? Could you help match their gifts and abilities with your church's needs? Often their maturity and wisdom can be of great service in the church.

5:10 "Wash[ing] the saints' feet" means helping and serving other believers with humility, following the example of Jesus, who washed the feet of his disciples at the Last Supper (John 13:1–17).

5:15 "Turned aside to follow Satan" refers to the immoral conduct that identified these women with their pagan neighbors.

Concerning Elders

17 The elders who rule well are to be considered worthy of double honor, especially
those who work hard at preaching and teaching.
18 For the Scripture says, "YOU SHALL NOT MUZZLE THE OX WHILE HE IS THRESH-
ING," and "The laborer is worthy of his wages."
19 Do not receive an accusation against an elder except on the basis of two or three
witnesses.
20 Those who continue in sin, rebuke in the presence of all, so that the rest also will be
fearful *of sinning.*
21 I solemnly charge you in the presence of God and of Christ Jesus and of *His* chosen
angels, to maintain these *principles* without bias, doing nothing in a *spirit of* partiality.
22 Do not lay hands upon anyone *too* hastily and thereby share *responsibility for* the
sins of others; keep yourself free from sin.
23 No longer drink water *exclusively,* but use a little wine for the sake of your stomach
and your frequent ailments.
24 The sins of some men are quite evident, going before them to judgment; for others,
their *sins* follow after.
25 Likewise also, deeds that are good are quite evident, and those which are otherwise
cannot be concealed.

Instructions to Those Who Minister

6 All who are under the yoke as slaves are to regard their own masters as worthy of all
honor so that the name of God and *our* doctrine will not be spoken against.
2 Those who have believers as their masters must not be disrespectful to them because they are brethren, but must serve them all the more, because those who partake of
the benefit are believers and beloved. Teach and preach these *principles.*
3 If anyone advocates a different doctrine and does not agree with sound words, those
of our Lord Jesus Christ, and with the doctrine conforming to godliness,

5:17 Acts 11:30; 1 Tim 4:14; 5:19; Rom 12:8; 1 Thess 5:12
5:18 Deut 25:4; 1 Cor 9:9; Lev 19:13; Deut 24:15; Matt 10:10; Luke 10:7; 1 Cor 9:14
5:19 Acts 11:30; 1 Tim 4:14; 5:17; Deut 17:6; 19:15; Matt 18:16
5:20 Gal 2:14; Eph 5:11; 2 Tim 4:2; 2 Cor 7:11
5:21 Luke 9:26; 1 Tim 6:13; 2 Tim 2:14; 4:1
5:22 1 Tim 3:10; 4:14; Eph 5:11; 1 Tim 3:2-7
5:24 Rev 14:13
5:25 Prov 10:9
6:1 Eph 6:5; Titus 2:9; 1 Pet 2:18; Titus 2:5
6:2 Acts 1:15; Gal 3:28; Philem 16

5:17–18 Faithful church leaders should be supported and appreciated. Too often they are targets for criticism because the congregation has unrealistic expectations. How do you treat your church leaders? Do you enjoy finding fault, or do you show your appreciation? Do they receive enough financial support to allow them to live without worry and to provide for the needs of their families? Jesus and Paul emphasized the importance of supporting those who lead and teach us (see Galatians 6:6 and the notes on Luke 10:7 and 1 Corinthians 9:4–10).

5:17–18 Preaching and teaching are closely related. Preaching is proclaiming the Word of God and confronting listeners with the truth of Scripture. Teaching is explaining the truth in Scripture, helping learners understand difficult passages, and helping them apply God's Word to daily life. Paul says that these elders are worthy of double honor. Unfortunately, however, we often take them for granted by not providing adequately for their needs or by subjecting them to heavy criticism. Think of how you can honor your preachers and teachers.

5:19–21 Church leaders are not exempt from sin, faults, and mistakes. But they are often criticized for the wrong reasons—minor imperfections, failure to meet someone's expectations, personality clashes. Thus Paul said that accusations should not even be heard unless two or three witnesses confirm them. Sometimes church leaders should be confronted about their behavior, and sometimes they should be rebuked. But all rebuking must be done fairly and lovingly, and for the purpose of restoration.

5:21 "Chosen angels" are all those angels who did not rebel against God like Satan did.

5:21 We must be constantly on guard against favoritism, against giving preferential treatment to some and ignoring others. We live in a society that plays favorites. It's easy to give special treatment to those who are gifted, intelligent, rich, or beautiful without realizing what we are doing. Make sure you honor people for who they are in Christ, not for who they are in the world.

5:22 Paul says that a church should never be hasty about choosing its leaders, especially the pastor, because we may overlook major problems or sins. It is a serious responsibility to choose church leaders. They must have strong faith and be morally upright, having the qualities described in 3:1–13 and Titus 1:5–9. Not everyone who wants to be a church leader is eligible. Be certain of an applicant's qualifications before asking him or her to take a leadership position.

5:23 It is unclear why Paul gave this advice to Timothy. Perhaps contaminated water had led to Timothy's indigestion and so he should stop drinking only water. Whatever the reason, this statement is not an invitation to overindulgence or alcoholism.

5:24–25 Paul instructs Timothy to choose church leaders carefully because sometimes their sins are not obvious and it takes time for them to be revealed. Church leaders should live lives that are above reproach.

6:1–2 In Paul's culture there was a great social and legal gulf separating masters and slaves. But as Christians, masters and slaves became spiritual equals, brothers and sisters in Christ Jesus (Galatians 3:28). Paul did not speak against the institution of slavery, but he gave guidelines for Christian slaves and Christian masters. His counsel for the master/slave relationship can be applied to the employer/employee relationship today. Employees should work hard, showing respect for their employers. In turn, employers should be fair (Ephesians 6:5–9; Colossians 3:22–25). Our work should reflect our faithfulness to and love for Christ.

6:3–5 Paul told Timothy to stay away from those who just wanted to make money from preaching, and from those who strayed from the sound teachings of the gospel into quarrels that caused strife in the church. A person's understanding of the finer points of theology should not become the basis for lording it over others or for making money. Stay away from people who just want to argue.

6:4 Acts 18:15

6:5 2 Pet 2:3

6:6 Luke 12:15-21; Phil 4:11; Heb 13:5

6:7 Job 1:21; Eccl 5:15

6:8 Prov 30:8

6:9 Prov 15:27; 23:4; 28:20; Luke 12:21

6:10 Col 3:5; 1 Tim 3:3; 6:9; James 5:19

6:11 2 Tim 2:22

6:12 1 Cor 9:25f; Phil 1:30; Col 3:15; 2 Cor 9:13

6:13 Matt 27:2; John 18:37

6:14 2 Thess 2:8

6:15 Deut 10:17; Rev 17:14; 19:16

6:16 Ps 104:2; James 1:17

6:17 Matt 12:32Ps 62:10; Luke 12:20

6:18 1 Tim 5:10; Rom 12:8; Eph 4:28

4 he is conceited *and* understands nothing; but he has a morbid interest in controversial questions and disputes about words, out of which arise envy, strife, abusive language,
evil suspicions,
5 and constant friction between men of depraved mind and deprived of the truth, who
suppose that godliness is a means of gain.
6 But godliness *actually* is a means of great gain when accompanied by contentment.
7 For we have brought nothing into the world, so we cannot take anything out of it
either.
8 If we have food and covering, with these we shall be content.
9 But those who want to get rich fall into temptation and a snare and many foolish
and harmful desires which plunge men into ruin and destruction.
10 For the love of money is a root of all sorts of evil, and some by longing for it have
wandered away from the faith and pierced themselves with many griefs.
11 But flee from these things, you man of God, and pursue righteousness, godliness,
faith, love, perseverance *and* gentleness.
12 Fight the good fight of faith; take hold of the eternal life to which you were called,
and you made the good confession in the presence of many witnesses.
13 I charge you in the presence of God, who gives life to all things, and of Christ Jesus,
who testified the good confession before Pontius Pilate,
14 that you keep the commandment without stain or reproach until the appearing of
our Lord Jesus Christ,
15 which He will bring about at the proper time—He who is the blessed and only Sovereign, the King of kings and Lord of lords,
16 who alone possesses immortality and dwells in unapproachable light, whom no man
has seen or can see. To Him *be* honor and eternal dominion! Amen.
17 Instruct those who are rich in this present world not to be conceited or to fix their
hope on the uncertainty of riches, but on God, who richly supplies us with all things to
enjoy.
18 *Instruct them* to do good, to be rich in good works, to be generous and ready to share,
19 storing up for themselves the treasure of a good foundation for the future, so that
they may take hold of that which is life indeed.
20 O Timothy, guard what has been entrusted to you, avoiding worldly *and* empty chatter *and* the opposing arguments of what is falsely called "knowledge"—
21 which some have professed and thus gone astray from the faith.
Grace be with you.

6:6 This statement is the key to spiritual growth and personal fulfillment. We should honor God and center our desires on him ("godliness," see Matthew 6:33), and we should be content with what God is doing in our lives (see Philippians 4:11–13).

6:6–10 Despite overwhelming evidence to the contrary, most people still believe that money brings happiness. Rich people craving greater riches can be caught in an endless cycle that only ends in ruin and destruction. How can you keep away from the love of money? Paul gives us some guidelines: (1) Realize that one day riches will all be gone (6:7, 17); (2) be content with what you have (6:8); (3) monitor what you are willing to do to get more money (6:9–10); (4) love people more than money (6:11); (5) love God's work more than money (6:11); (6) freely share what you have with others (6:18). (See Proverbs 30:7–9 for more on avoiding the love of money.)

6:8 It is often helpful to distinguish between *needs* and *wants.* We may have all we need to live but let ourselves become anxious and discontented over what we merely want. Like Paul, we can choose to be content without having all that we want. The only alternative is to be a slave to our desires.

6:10 Greed leads to all kinds of evil: marriage problems, robbery, blowups in partnerships. To master greed, you must control it at its root. Get rid of the desire to be rich.

6:11–12 Paul uses active and forceful verbs to describe the Christian life: *flee, pursue, fight, take hold.* Some think Christianity is a passive religion that advocates waiting for God to act. But we must have an *active* faith, obeying God with courage and doing what we know is right. Is it time for action on your part? Don't wait—get going!

6:13 Jesus' trial before Pilate is recorded in the Gospels: Matthew 27:11–26; Mark 15:1–15; Luke 23:1–25; John 18:28—19:16.

6:13–16 Paul concludes with a charge to Timothy to keep "the commandment," referring to the commands Christ has given to his church, or perhaps to Timothy's promise to serve Christ. Timothy's own confession of faith is compared with Christ's before Pilate.

6:17–19 Ephesus was a wealthy city, and the Ephesian church probably had many wealthy members. Paul advised Timothy to deal with any potential problems by teaching that having riches carries great responsibility. Those who have money must be generous, but they may not be arrogant just because they have a lot to give. They must be careful not to put their hope in money instead of in the living God for their security. Even if we don't have material wealth, we can be rich in good deeds. No matter how poor we are, we have something to share with someone.

6:21 The book of 1 Timothy provides guiding principles for local churches, including rules for public worship and qualifications for overseers (elders, pastors), deacons, and special church workers (widows). Paul tells the church leaders to correct incorrect doctrine and to deal lovingly and fairly with all people in the church. The church is not organized simply for the sake of organization, but so that Christ can be honored and glorified. While studying these guidelines, don't lose sight of what is most important in the life of the church—knowing God, working together in loving harmony, and taking God's Good News to the world.

2 TIMOTHY

VITAL STATISTICS

PURPOSE:
To give final instructions and encouragement to Timothy, pastor of the church at Ephesus

AUTHOR:
Paul

TO WHOM WRITTEN:
Timothy and all Christians everywhere

DATE WRITTEN:
Approximately A.D. 66 or 67, from prison in Rome. After a year or two of freedom, Paul was arrested again and executed under Emperor Nero.

SETTING:
Paul was virtually alone in prison; only Luke was with him. Paul wrote this letter to pass the torch to the new generation of church leaders. He also asked for visits from his friends and for his scrolls, especially the parchments—possibly parts of the Old Testament, the Gospels, and other Biblical manuscripts.

KEY VERSE:
"Be diligent to present yourself approved to God as a workman who does not need to be ashamed, accurately handling the word of truth" (2:15).

KEY PEOPLE:
Paul, Timothy, Luke, Mark, and others

KEY PLACES:
Rome, Ephesus

SPECIAL FEATURES:
Because this is Paul's last letter, it reveals his heart and his priorities—sound doctrine, steadfast faith, confident endurance, and lasting love.

"FAMOUS last words" is more than a cliché. When notable men and women of influence are about to die, the world waits to hear their final words of insight and wisdom. Then those quotes are repeated worldwide. This is also true with a dying loved one. Gathered at his or her side, the family strains to hear every whispered syllable of blessing, encouragement, and advice, knowing that this will be the final message.

One of the most knowledgeable, influential, and beloved men of history is the apostle Paul. And we have his famous last words.

Paul was facing death. He was not dying of a disease in a sterile hospital with loved ones gathered nearby. He was very much alive, but his condition was terminal. Convicted as a follower of Jesus of Nazareth, Paul sat in a cold Roman prison, cut off from the world, with just a visitor or two and his writing materials. Paul knew that soon he would be executed (4:6), and so he wrote his final thoughts to his "son" Timothy, passing to him the torch of leadership, reminding him of what was truly important, and encouraging him in the faith. Imagine how Timothy must have read and reread every word; this was the last message from his beloved mentor, Paul. Because of the situation and the recipient, this is the most intimate and moving of all Paul's letters and his last.

Paul's introduction is tender, and every phrase exudes the love he has for Timothy (1:1–5). He then reminds Timothy of the qualities necessary for a faithful minister of Jesus Christ (1:6—2:13). Timothy should remember his call and use his gifts with boldness (1:6–12), keep to the truth (1:13–18), prepare others to follow him in the ministry (2:1–2), be disciplined and ready to endure suffering (2:3–7), and keep his eyes and mind focused on Christ (2:8–13). Paul challenges Timothy to hold to sound doctrine, reject error and avoid godless chatter, correctly handle the word of truth (2:14–19), and keep his life pure (2:20–26).

Next, Paul warns Timothy of the opposition that he and other believers would face in the last days from self-centered people who use the church for their own gain and teach false doctrines (3:1–9). Paul tells Timothy to be prepared for these unfaithful people by remembering his example (3:10–11), understanding the real source of the opposition (3:12–13), and finding strength and power in the Word of God (3:14–17). Then Paul gives Timothy a stirring charge: to preach the Word (4:1–4) and to fulfill his ministry until the end (4:5–8).

Paul concludes with personal requests and items of information. In these final words, he reveals his loneliness and his strong love for his brothers and sisters in Christ (4:9–22).

There has never been another person like Paul, the missionary apostle. He was a man of deep faith, undying love, constant hope, tenacious conviction, and profound insight. And he was inspired by the Holy Spirit to give us God's message. As you read 2 Timothy, know that you are reading the last words of this great man of God—his last words to Timothy and to all who would claim to follow Christ. Recommit yourself to stand courageously for the truth, knowing the Word and being empowered by the Holy Spirit.

THE BLUEPRINT

1. Foundations of Christian service (1:1—2:26)
2. Difficult times for Christian service (3:1—4:22)

Paul gives helpful advice to Timothy to remain solidly grounded in Christian service and to endure suffering during the difficult days to come. It is easy for us to serve Christ for the wrong reasons: because it is exciting, rewarding, or personally enriching. Without a proper foundation, however, we will find it easy to quit during difficult times. All believers need a strong foundation for their service, because Christian service does not get easier as we grow older, and it will become no easier as the time of Christ's return grows closer.

MEGATHEMES

THEME	EXPLANATION	IMPORTANCE
Boldness	In the face of opposition and persecution, Timothy was to carry out his ministry without fear or shame. Paul urged him to utilize boldly the gifts of preaching and teaching that the Holy Spirit had given him.	The Holy Spirit helps us to be wise and strong. God honors our confident testimony even when we suffer. To get over our fear of what people might say or do, we must take our eyes off of people and look only to God.
Faithfulness	Christ was faithful to all of us in dying for our sin. Paul was a faithful minister even when he was in prison. Paul urged Timothy to maintain not only sound doctrine but also loyalty, diligence, and endurance.	We can count on opposition, suffering, and hardship as we serve Christ. But this shows that our faithfulness is having an effect on others. As we trust Christ, he counts us worthy to suffer, and he will give us the strength we need to be steadfast.
Preaching and Teaching	Paul and Timothy were active in preaching and teaching the Good News about Jesus Christ. Paul encouraged Timothy not only to carry the torch of truth but also to train others, passing on to them sound doctrine and enthusiasm for Christ's mission.	We must prepare people to transmit God's Word to others so that they in turn might pass it on. Does your church carefully train others to teach?
Error	In the final days before Christ returns, there will be false teachers, spiritual dropouts, and heretics. The remedy for error is to have a solid program for teaching Christians.	Because of deception and false teaching, we must be disciplined and ready to reject error. Know the Word of God as your sure defense against error and confusion.

1. Foundations of Christian service

Timothy Charged to Guard His Trust

1:1 2 Cor 1:1; Gal 3:26; 1 Cor 1:1; 1 Tim 6:19

1:2 Acts 16:1; 1 Tim 1:2; 1 Tim 1:2; 2 Tim 2:1; Titus 1:4; Rom 1:7

1 Paul, an apostle of Christ Jesus by the will of God, according to the promise of life in Christ Jesus,
2 To Timothy, my beloved son: Grace, mercy *and* peace from God the Father and
Christ Jesus our Lord.

1:1 This letter has a somber tone. Paul was imprisoned for the last time, and he knew he would soon die. Unlike Paul's first imprisonment in Rome, when he was in a house (Acts 28:16, 23, 30) where he continued to teach, this time he was probably confined to a cold dungeon, awaiting his death (4:6–8). Emperor Nero had begun a major persecution in A.D. 64 as part of his plan to pass the blame for the great fire of Rome from himself to the Christians. This persecution spread across the empire and included social ostracism, public torture, and murder. As Paul was waiting to die, he wrote a letter to his dear friend Timothy, a younger man who was like a son to him (1:2). Written in approximately A.D. 66/67, these are the last words we have from Paul.

1:2 Paul's second letter to Timothy was written about two to four years after his first letter. Timothy had been Paul's traveling companion on the second and third missionary journeys, and Paul had left him in Ephesus to help the church there (1 Timothy 1:3, 4). For more information on Timothy, see his Profile in 1 Timothy. For more information on the great missionary, Paul, see his Profile in Acts 9.

3 I thank God, whom I serve with a clear conscience the way my forefathers did, as I
constantly remember you in my prayers night and day,
4 longing to see you, even as I recall your tears, so that I may be filled with joy.
5 For I am mindful of the sincere faith within you, which first dwelt in your grandmother Lois and your mother Eunice, and I am sure that *it is* in you as well.
6 For this reason I remind you to kindle afresh the gift of God which is in you through
the laying on of my hands.
7 For God has not given us a spirit of timidity, but of power and love and discipline.
8 Therefore do not be ashamed of the testimony of our Lord or of me His prisoner,
but join with *me* in suffering for the gospel according to the power of God,
9 who has saved us and called us with a holy calling, not according to our works, but
according to His own purpose and grace which was granted us in Christ Jesus from all
eternity,
10 but now has been revealed by the appearing of our Savior Christ Jesus, who abolished death and brought life and immortality to light through the gospel,
11 for which I was appointed a preacher and an apostle and a teacher.
12 For this reason I also suffer these things, but I am not ashamed; for I know whom I
have believed and I am convinced that He is able to guard what I have entrusted to Him
until that day.
13 Retain the standard of sound words which you have heard from me, in the faith and
love which are in Christ Jesus.

1:3 Rom 1:8; Acts 23:1; 24:16; 1 Tim 1:5
1:6 1 Tim 4:14
1:7 John 14:27; Rom 8:15
1:8 Mark 8:38; Rom 1:16; 2 Tim 1:16; 2:3, 9; 4:5
1:9 Rom 8:28ff; 11:29; Rom 16:25; Eph 1:4
1:10 Rom 16:26; 2 Thess 2:8; 2 Tim 4:1, 8
1:11 1 Tim 2:7
1:12 Titus 3:8; 1 Tim 6:20
1:13 Titus 1:9; Rom 2:20; 6:17; 1 Tim 1:10; 2 Tim 2:2

1:3 Paul constantly prayed for Timothy, his friend, his fellow traveler, his son in the faith, and a strong leader in the Christian church. Although the two men were separated from each other, their prayers provided a source of mutual encouragement. We too should pray consistently for others, especially for those who do God's work.

1:4 We don't know when Paul and Timothy last parted, but it was probably when Paul was arrested and taken to Rome for his second imprisonment. The tears they shed at parting revealed the depth of their relationship.

1:5 Timothy's mother and grandmother, Eunice and Lois, were early Christian converts, possibly through Paul's ministry in their home city, Lystra (Acts 16:1). They had communicated their strong Christian faith to Timothy, even though his father was probably not a believer. Don't hide your light at home: Our families are fertile fields for planting gospel seeds. Let your parents, children, spouse, brothers, and sisters know of your faith in Jesus, and be sure they see Christ's love, helpfulness, and joy in you.

1:6 At the time of his ordination, Timothy had received special gifts of the Spirit to enable him to serve the church (see 1 Timothy 4:14). In telling Timothy to "kindle afresh the gift of God," Paul was encouraging him to persevere. Timothy did not need new revelations or new gifts; he needed the courage and self-discipline to hang on to the truth and to use the gifts he had already received (see 1:13–14). If Timothy would step out boldly in faith and proclaim the gospel once again, the Holy Spirit would go with him and give him power. When you use the gifts God has given you, you will find that God will give you the power you need.

1:6 Clearly Timothy's spiritual gift had been given to him when Paul and the elders had laid their hands on him and set him apart for ministry (see 1 Timothy 4:14). God gives all Christians gifts to use to build up the body of Christ (see 1 Corinthians 12:4–31), and he gives special gifts to some through church leaders, who serve as God's instruments.

1:6–7 Timothy was experiencing great opposition to his message and to himself as a leader. His youth, his association with Paul, and his leadership had come under fire from believers and nonbelievers alike. Paul urged him to be bold. When we allow people to intimidate us, we neutralize our effectiveness for God. The power of the Holy Spirit can help us overcome our fear of what some might say or do to us, so that we can continue to do God's work.

1:7 Paul mentions three characteristics of the effective Christian leader: power, love, and discipline. These are available to us because the Holy Spirit lives in us. Follow his leading each day so that your life will more fully exhibit these characteristics. See Galatians 5:22–23 for a list of the by-products of the Holy Spirit living in us.

1:8 In this time of mounting persecution, Timothy may have been afraid to continue preaching the gospel. His fears were based on fact, because believers were being arrested and executed. Paul told Timothy to expect suffering—Timothy, like Paul, would be jailed for preaching the gospel (Hebrews 13:23). But Paul promised Timothy that God would give him strength and that he would be ready when it was his turn to suffer. Even when there is no persecution, it can be difficult to share our faith in Christ. Fortunately we, like Paul and Timothy, can call on the Holy Spirit to give us courage. Don't be ashamed to testify.

1:9–10 In these verses Paul gives a brief summary of the gospel. God loves us, called us, and sent Christ to die for us. We can have eternal life through faith in him, because he broke the power of death with his resurrection. We do not deserve to be saved, but God offers us salvation anyway. What we must do is believe in him and accept his offer.

1:12 Paul was in prison, but that did not stop his ministry. He carried it on through others like Timothy. Paul had lost all his material possessions, but he would never lose his faith. He trusted God to use him regardless of his circumstances. If your situation looks bleak, give your concerns to Christ. He will guard your faith and safely guard all you have entrusted to him until the day of his return. For more on our security in Christ, see Romans 8:38–39.

1:12 The phrase "guard what I have entrusted to Him" could mean: (1) Paul knew that God would guard the souls of those converted through his preaching; (2) Paul trusted God to guard his own soul until Christ's second coming; or (3) Paul was confident that, though he was in prison and facing death, God would carry out the gospel ministry through others such as Timothy. Paul may have expressed his confidence to encourage Timothy, who was undoubtedly discouraged by the problems in Ephesus and fearful of persecution. Even in prison, Paul knew that God was still in control. No matter what setbacks or problems we face, we can trust fully in God.

1:13–14 Timothy was in a time of transition. He had been Paul's bright young helper; soon he would be on his own as leader of a church in a difficult environment. Although his responsibilities were changing, Timothy was not without help. He had everything he

1:14 Rom 8:9; 1 Tim 6:20; 2 Tim 1:12
1:15 Acts 2:9; 2 Tim 4:10
1:16 Eph 6:20
1:18 1 Cor 1:8; 3:13; Acts 18:19; 1 Tim 1:3
2:1 2 Tim 1:2; Eph 6:10
2:2 1 Tim 1:12; 2 Cor 2:14ff; 3:5
2:3 2 Tim 1:8; 1 Cor 9:7; 1 Tim 1:18
2:4 2 Pet 2:20
2:5 1 Cor 9:25
2:8 Acts 2:24; Matt 1:1
2:9 Phil 1:7; Luke 23:32; 1 Thess 1:8; Acts 28:31
2:10 Col 1:24; Luke 18:7; Titus 1:1; 2 Cor 1:6; 1 Thess 5:9; 2 Cor 4:17; 1 Pet 5:10

14 Guard, through the Holy Spirit who dwells in us, the treasure which has been entrusted to *you.*
15 You are aware of the fact that all who are in Asia turned away from me, among
whom are Phygelus and Hermogenes.
16 The Lord grant mercy to the house of Onesiphorus, for he often refreshed me and
was not ashamed of my chains;
17 but when he was in Rome, he eagerly searched for me and found me—
18 the Lord grant to him to find mercy from the Lord on that day—and you know very
well what services he rendered at Ephesus.

Be Strong

2 You therefore, my son, be strong in the grace that is in Christ Jesus.
2 The things which you have heard from me in the presence of many witnesses, entrust these to faithful men who will be able to teach others also.
3 Suffer hardship with *me,* as a good soldier of Christ Jesus.
4 No soldier in active service entangles himself in the affairs of everyday life, so that
he may please the one who enlisted him as a soldier.
5 Also if anyone competes as an athlete, he does not win the prize unless he competes according to the rules.
6 The hard-working farmer ought to be the first to receive his share of the crops.
7 Consider what I say, for the Lord will give you understanding in everything.
8 Remember Jesus Christ, risen from the dead, descendant of David, according to
my gospel,
9 for which I suffer hardship even to imprisonment as a criminal; but the word of God
is not imprisoned.
10 For this reason I endure all things for the sake of those who are chosen, so that they
also may obtain the salvation which is in Christ Jesus *and* with *it* eternal glory.

---

needed to face the future, if he would hold on tightly to the Lord's resources. When you are facing difficult transitions, it is good to follow Paul's advice to Timothy and look back at your experience. Who is the foundation of your faith? How can you build on that foundation? What gifts has the Holy Spirit given you? Use the gifts you have already been given.

1:15, 16 Nothing more is known about Phygelus and Hermogenes, who evidently opposed Paul's ministry. These men serve as a warning that even leaders can fall. Onesiphorus was mentioned as a positive example in contrast to these men.

2:1 How can someone be strong in grace? Grace means undeserved favor. Just as we are saved by grace (Ephesians 2:8–9), we should live by grace (Colossians 2:6). This means trusting completely in Christ and *his* power, and not trying to live for Christ in our strength alone. Receive and utilize Christ's power. He will give you the strength to do his work.

2:2 If the church were to consistently follow this advice, it would expand exponentially as well-taught believers would teach others and commission them, in turn, to teach still others. Disciples need to be equipped to pass on their faith; our work is not done until new believers are able to make disciples of others (see Ephesians 4:12–13).

2:3–7 As Timothy preached and taught, he would face suffering, but he should be able to endure. Paul used comparisons with soldiers, athletes, and farmers who must discipline themselves and be willing to sacrifice to achieve the results they want. Like soldiers, we have to give up worldly security and endure rigorous discipline. Like athletes, we must train hard and follow the rules. Like farmers, we must work extremely hard and be patient. But we keep going despite suffering because of the thought of victory, the vision of winning, and the hope of harvest. We will see that our suffering is worthwhile when we achieve our goal of glorifying God, winning people to Christ, and one day living eternally with him.

2:7 Paul told Timothy to consider his words, and God would give him understanding. God speaks through the Bible, his Word, but we need to be open and receptive to him. As you read the Bible, ask God to show you his timeless truths and the application to your life. Then consider what you have read by thinking it through and meditating on it. God will give you understanding.

2:8 False teachers were a problem in Ephesus (see Acts 20:29–30; 1 Timothy 1:3–11). At the heart of false teaching is an incorrect view of Christ. In Timothy's day many asserted that Christ was divine but not human—God but not man. These days we often hear that Jesus was human but not divine—man but not God. Either view destroys the Good News that Jesus Christ has taken our sins on himself and has reconciled us to God. In this verse, Paul firmly states that Jesus is fully man ("descendant of David") and fully God ("risen from the dead"). This is an important doctrine for all Christians. For more on this key concept see the note on Philippians 2:5–7.

2:9 Paul was in chains in prison because of the gospel he preached. The truth about Jesus is no more popular in our day than in Paul's, but it still reaches receptive hearts. When Paul said that Jesus was God, he angered the Jews who had condemned Jesus for blasphemy, but many Jews became followers of Christ (1 Corinthians 1:24). He angered the Romans who worshiped the emperor as god, but even some in Caesar's household turned to Jesus (Philippians 4:22). When Paul said Jesus was human, he angered the Greeks who thought divinity was soiled if it had any contact with humanity; still many Greeks accepted the faith (Acts 11:20–21). The truth that Jesus is one person with two united natures has never been easy to understand, but it is being believed by people every day. Despite the opposition, continue to proclaim Christ. Some will listen and believe.

2:10 When Paul says "obtain the salvation," is he contradicting grace? As Paul taught in Ephesians 2:8–9, salvation is not something that can be earned. Paul is referring to being faithful to the end, not to a way to earn salvation.

12 Indeed, all who desire to live godly in Christ Jesus will be persecuted.
13 But evil men and impostors will proceed *from bad* to worse, deceiving and being
deceived.
14 You, however, continue in the things you have learned and become convinced of,
knowing from whom you have learned *them*,
15 and that from childhood you have known the sacred writings which are able to give
you the wisdom that leads to salvation through faith which is in Christ Jesus.
16 All Scripture is inspired by God and profitable for teaching, for reproof, for correction,
tion, for training in righteousness;
17 so that the man of God may be adequate, equipped for every good work.

3:12 John 15:20; Acts 14:22; 2 Cor 4:9f
3:13 2 Tim 2:16; Titus 3:3
3:15 Rom 2:27; Ps 119:98f; 1 Cor 1:21
3:16 2 Pet 1:20f
3:17 1 Tim 6:11; 2 Tim 2:21; Heb 13:21

"Preach the Word"

4 I solemnly charge *you* in the presence of God and of Christ Jesus, who is to judge the
living and the dead, and by His appearing and His kingdom:
2 preach the word; be ready in season *and* out of season; reprove, rebuke, exhort, with
great patience and instruction.
3 For the time will come when they will not endure sound doctrine; but *wanting* to
have their ears tickled, they will accumulate for themselves teachers in accordance to
their own desires,
4 and will turn away their ears from the truth and will turn aside to myths.
5 But you, be sober in all things, endure hardship, do the work of an evangelist, fulfill
your ministry.

4:1 Acts 10:42; 2 Thess 2:8
4:2 Gal 6:6; Col 4:3; 1 Thess 1:6; 1 Tim 5:20; Titus 1:13
4:4 2 Thess 2:11; Titus 1:14; 1 Tim 1:4
4:5 1 Pet 1:13; Eph 4:12; Col 4:17

3:12 In this charge, Paul told Timothy that people who obey God and live for Christ will be persecuted. Don't be surprised when people misunderstand, criticize, and even try to hurt you because of what you believe and how you live. Don't give up. Continue to live as you know you should. God is the only one you need to please.

3:13 Don't expect false teachers and evil people to reform and change on their own. Left alone, they will go from bad to worse. If you have the opportunity, correct them so as to bring them back to faith in Christ. Fight for the truth, especially to protect younger Christians.

3:14 Besieged by false teachers and the inevitable pressures of a growing ministry, Timothy could easily have abandoned his faith or modified his doctrine. Once again Paul counseled Timothy to look to his past and to hold to the basic teachings about Jesus that are eternally true. Like Timothy, we are surrounded by false teachings. But we must not allow our society to distort or crowd out God's eternal truth. Spend time every day reflecting on the foundation of your Christian faith found in God's Word, the great truths that build up your life.

3:15 Timothy was one of the first second-generation Christians: He became a Christian not because an evangelist preached a powerful sermon but because his mother and grandmother taught him the holy Scriptures when he was a small child (1:5). A parent's work is vitally important. At home and in church, we should realize that teaching small children is both an opportunity and a responsibility. Jesus wanted little children to come to him (Matthew 19:13–15). Like Timothy's mother and grandmother, Eunice and Lois, do your part in leading children to Christ.

3:15 For Timothy, the "sacred writings" meant the Old Testament—Genesis to Malachi. The Old Testament is important because it points to Jesus Christ. At the same time, faith in Christ makes the whole Bible intelligible.

3:16 The Bible is not a collection of stories, fables, myths, or merely human ideas about God. It is not a human book. Through the Holy Spirit, God revealed his person and plan to certain believers, who wrote down his message for his people (2 Peter 1:20–21). This process is known as *inspiration.* The writers wrote from their own personal, historical, and cultural contexts. Although they used their own minds, talents, languages, and styles, they wrote what God wanted them to write. Scripture is completely trustworthy because God was in control of its writing. Its words are entirely authoritative for our faith and lives. The Bible is "God-breathed." Read it, and use its teachings to guide your conduct.

3:16–17 The whole Bible is God's inspired Word. Because it is inspired and trustworthy, we should *read* it and *apply* it to our lives. The Bible is our standard for testing everything else that claims to be true. It is our safeguard against false teaching and our source of guidance for how we should live. It is our only source of knowledge about how we can be saved. God wants to show you what is true and equip you to live for him. How much time do you spend in God's Word? Read it regularly to discover God's truth and to become confident in your life and faith. Develop a plan for reading the whole Bible, not just the familiar passages.

3:17 In our zeal for the *truth* of Scripture, we must never forget its *purpose*—to equip us to do good. We should not study God's Word simply to increase our knowledge or to prepare us to win arguments. We should study the Bible so that we will know how to do Christ's work in the world. Our knowledge of God's Word is not useful unless it strengthens our faith and leads us to do good.

4:1–2 It was important for Timothy to preach the gospel so that the Christian faith could spread throughout the world. We believe in Christ today because people like Timothy were faithful to their mission. It is still vitally important for believers to spread the gospel. Half the people who have ever lived are alive today, and most of them do not know Christ. He is coming soon, and he wants to find his faithful believers ready for him. It may be inconvenient to take a stand for Christ or to tell others about his love, but preaching the Word of God is the most important responsibility the church and its members have been given. Be prepared for, courageous in, and sensitive to God-given opportunities to tell the Good News.

4:2 "Be ready in season and out of season" means to always be ready to serve God in any situation, whether or not it is convenient. Be sensitive to the opportunities God gives you.

4:2 Paul told Timothy to "reprove, rebuke and exhort." It is difficult to accept correction, to be told we have to change. But no matter how much the truth hurts, we must be willing to listen to it so we can more fully obey God.

4:5 To keep cool when you are jarred and jolted by people or circumstances, don't react quickly. In any work of ministry that you undertake, keeping your head makes you morally alert to temptation, resistant to pressure, and vigilant when facing heavy responsibility.

6 For I am already being poured out as a drink offering, and the time of my departure
has come.
7 I have fought the good fight, I have finished the course, I have kept the faith;
8 in the future there is laid up for me the crown of righteousness, which the Lord, the
righteous Judge, will award to me on that day; and not only to me, but also to all who
have loved His appearing.

Personal Concerns

9 Make every effort to come to me soon;
10 for Demas, having loved this present world, has deserted me and gone to Thessalonica; Crescens *has gone* to Galatia, Titus to Dalmatia.
11 Only Luke is with me. Pick up Mark and bring him with you, for he is useful to me
for service.
12 But Tychicus I have sent to Ephesus.
13 When you come bring the cloak which I left at Troas with Carpus, and the books,
especially the parchments.
14 Alexander the coppersmith did me much harm; the Lord will repay him according
to his deeds.
15 Be on guard against him yourself, for he vigorously opposed our teaching.
16 At my first defense no one supported me, but all deserted me; may it not be counted against them.
17 But the Lord stood with me and strengthened me, so that through me the proclamation might be fully accomplished, and that all the Gentiles might hear; and I was rescued out of the lion's mouth.

4:6
Phil 2:17; Phil 1:23; 2 Pet 1:14

4:7
1 Cor 9:25f; Phil 1:30; 1 Tim 1:18; 6:12; Acts 20:24; 1 Cor 9:24

4:8
Col 1:5; 1 Pet 1:4; 1 Cor 9:25; James 1:12; Phil 3:11

4:10
Col 4:14; 1 Tim 6:17; 2 Cor 2:13; 8:23; Gal 2:3; Titus 1:4

4:12
Acts 20:4; Eph 6:21

4:13
Acts 16:8

4:14
Rom 2:6; 12:19

4:16
Acts 7:60; 1 Cor 13:5

4:17
1 Tim 1:12; 2 Tim 2:1; Titus 1:3; Acts 9:15; Phil 1:12ff; Rom 15:31;

4:5–8 As he neared the end of his life, Paul could confidently say he had been faithful to his call. Thus he faced death calmly, knowing that he would be rewarded by Christ. Is your life preparing you for death? Do you share Paul's confident expectation of meeting Christ? The good news is that the heavenly reward is not just for giants of the faith, like Paul, but for all who are eagerly looking forward to Jesus' second coming. Paul gave these words to encourage Timothy, and us, that no matter how difficult the fight seems—keep fighting. When we are with Jesus Christ, we will discover that it was all worth it.

4:6 A drink offering consisted of wine poured out on an altar as a sacrifice to God (see Genesis 35:14; Exodus 29:41). Its fragrance was considered pleasing to God. Paul viewed his life as an offering to God.

4:8 In Roman athletic games, a laurel wreath was given to the winners. A symbol of triumph and honor, it was the most coveted prize in ancient Rome. This is probably what Paul was referring to when he spoke of a "crown." But his would be a crown of righteousness. See 2 Corinthians 5:10 and the note on Matthew 19:27 for more on the rewards awaiting us for our faith and deeds. Although Paul would not receive an earthly reward, he would be rewarded in heaven. Whatever we may face—discouragement, persecution, or death—we know our reward is with Christ in heaven.

4:9–10 Paul was virtually alone and probably lonely. No one had been there at his trial to speak in his defense (4:16), and Demas had left the faith (4:10). Only Luke had returned (4:11).

4:10 Demas had been one of Paul's co-workers (Colossians 4:14; Philemon 24), but he had deserted Paul because he "loved this present world." In other words, Demas loved worldly values and worldly pleasures. There are two ways to love the world. God loves the world as he created it and as it could be if it were rescued from evil. Others, like Demas, love the world as it is, sin and all. Do you love the world as it could be if justice were done, the hungry were fed, and people loved one another? Or do you love what the world has to offer—wealth, power, pleasure—even if gaining it means hurting people and neglecting the work God has given you to do?

4:11 Crescens and Titus had left, but not for the same reasons as Demas. Paul did not criticize or condemn them.

4:11–12 Mentioning Demas reminded Paul of more faithful co-workers. Only Luke was with Paul, and Paul was feeling lonely. Tychicus, one of his most trusted companions (Acts 20:4; Ephesians 6:21; Colossians 4:7; Titus 3:12), had already left for Ephesus. Paul missed his young helpers Timothy and Mark. Mark had left Paul and Barnabas on the first missionary journey, and this had greatly upset Paul (Acts 13:13; 15:36–41). But later Mark proved to be a worthy helper, and Paul recognized him as a good friend and trusted Christian leader (Colossians 4:10; Philemon 24). Mark wrote the Gospel of Mark.

4:13 Paul's arrest probably occurred so suddenly that he was not allowed to return home to gather his personal belongings. Because he was a prisoner in a damp and chilly dungeon, Paul asked Timothy to bring him his cloak. Even more than the cloak, Paul wanted his parchments. These may have included parts of the Old Testament, the Gospels, copies of his own letters, or other important documents.

4:14–15 Alexander may have been a witness against Paul at his trial. He may have been the Alexander mentioned in 1 Timothy 1:20.

4:17 With his mentor in prison and his church in turmoil, Timothy was probably not feeling very brave. Paul may have been subtly telling Timothy that the Lord had called Timothy to preach and would give him the courage to continue to do so. God always gives us the strength to do what he has commanded. This strength may not be evident, however, until we step out in faith and actually begin doing the task.

4:17 Some have seen this as a reference to Nero throwing Christians to the lions in the Coliseum. More likely, it is Paul's way of describing his deliverance at his first defense (see, for example, Psalm 22:21; Daniel 6:22).

18 The Lord will rescue me from every evil deed, and will bring me safely to His heavenly kingdom; to Him *be* the glory forever and ever. Amen.
19 Greet Prisca and Aquila, and the household of Onesiphorus.
20 Erastus remained at Corinth, but Trophimus I left sick at Miletus.
21 Make every effort to come before winter. Eubulus greets you, also Pudens and Linus
and Claudia and all the brethren.
22 The Lord be with your spirit. Grace be with you.

4:18 Rom 11:36; 2 Pet 3:18

4:20 Acts 19:22; Rom 16:23; Acts 18:1

4:22 Gal 6:18; Phil 4:23; Philem 25; Col 4:18

4:18 Here Paul was affirming his belief in eternal life after death. Paul knew the end was near, and he was ready for it. Paul was confident in God's power even as he faced death. Anyone facing a life and death struggle can be comforted knowing that God will bring each believer safely through death to his heavenly kingdom.

4:19–20 Prisca (Priscilla) and Aquila were fellow Christian leaders with whom Paul had lived and worked (Acts 18:2–3). Onesiphorus visited and encouraged Paul in jail. Erastus was one of Paul's trusted companions (Acts 19:22), as was Trophimus (Acts 20:4; 21:29).

4:19–22 Paul ended the final chapter in his book and in his life by greeting those who were closest to him. Although Paul had spent most of his life traveling, he had developed close and lasting friendships. Too often we rush through our days, barely touching anyone's life. Like Paul, take time to weave your life into others through deep relationships.

4:22 As Paul reached the end of his life, he could look back and know he had been faithful to God's call. Now it was time to pass the torch to the next generation, preparing leaders to take his place so that the world would continue to hear the life-changing message of Jesus Christ. Timothy was Paul's living legacy, a product of Paul's faithful teaching, discipleship, and example. Because of Paul's work with many believers, including Timothy, the world is full of believers today who are also carrying on the work. What legacy will you leave behind? Whom are you training to carry on your work? It is our responsibility to do all we can do to keep the gospel message alive for the next generation.

TITUS

THE VACUUM produced when a strong leader departs can devastate a movement, organization, or institution. Having been dependent on his or her skill, style, and personality, associates and subordinates flounder or vie for control. Soon efficiency and vitality are lost, and decline and demise follow. Often this pattern is repeated in churches. Great speakers and teachers gather a following, and soon a church is flourishing. It is alive, vital, and effective. Lives are being changed and people led into the kingdom. But when this person leaves or dies, with him or her goes the drive and the heart of the organization.

People flocked to hear Paul's teaching. Educated, articulate, motivated, and filled with the Holy Spirit, this man of God faithfully proclaimed the Good News throughout the Roman empire; lives were changed and churches begun. But Paul knew that the church must be built on Christ, not on a person. And he knew that eventually he would not be there to build, encourage, discipline, and teach. So he trained young pastors to assume leadership in the churches after he was gone. Paul urged them to center their lives and preaching on the Word of God (2 Timothy 3:16–17) and to train others to carry on the ministry (2 Timothy 2:2).

Titus was a Greek believer. Taught and nurtured by Paul, he stood before the leaders of the church in Jerusalem as a living example of what Christ was doing among the Gentiles (Galatians 2:1–3). Like Timothy, he was one of Paul's trusted traveling companions and closest friends. Later he became Paul's special ambassador (2 Corinthians 7:5–16) and eventually the overseer of the churches on Crete (Titus 1:5). Slowly and carefully, Paul developed Titus into a mature Christian and a responsible leader. The letter to Titus was a step in this discipleship process. As with Timothy, Paul told Titus how to organize and lead the churches.

Paul begins with a longer than usual greeting and introduction, outlining the leadership progression: Paul's ministry (1:1–3), Titus's responsibilities (1:4–5), and those leaders whom Titus would appoint and train (1:5). Paul then lists pastoral qualifications (1:6–9) and contrasts faithful elders with the false leaders and teachers (1:10–16).

Next, Paul emphasizes the importance of good deeds in the life of the Christian, telling Titus how to relate to the various age groups in the church (2:2–6). He urges Titus to be a good example of a mature believer (2:7–8) and to teach with courage and conviction (2:9–15). He then discusses the general responsibilities of Christians in society: Titus should remind the people of these (3:1–8), and he should avoid divisive arguments (3:9–11). Paul concludes with a few matters of itinerary and personal greetings (3:12–15).

Paul's letter to Titus is brief, but it is an important link in the discipleship process, helping a young man grow into leadership in the church. As you read this pastoral letter, you will gain insight into the organization and life of the early church, and you will find principles for structuring contemporary churches. But you should also see how to be a responsible Christian leader. Read the letter to Titus and determine, like Paul, to train men and women to lead and teach others.

VITAL STATISTICS

PURPOSE:
To advise Titus in his responsibility of supervising the churches on the island of Crete

AUTHOR:
Paul

TO WHOM WRITTEN:
Titus, a Greek, probably converted to Christ through Paul's ministry (he had become Paul's special representative to the island of Crete), and all believers everywhere

DATE WRITTEN:
Approximately A.D. 64, around the same time 1 Timothy was written; probably from Macedonia when Paul traveled between his Roman imprisonments

SETTING:
Paul sent Titus to organize and oversee the churches on Crete. This letter tells Titus how to do this job.

KEY VERSE:
"For this reason I left you in Crete, that you would set in order what remains and appoint elders in every city as I directed you" (1:5).

KEY PEOPLE:
Paul, Titus

KEY PLACES:
Crete, Nicopolis

SPECIAL FEATURES:
Titus is very similar to 1 Timothy with its instructions to church leaders.

THE BLUEPRINT

1. Leadership in the church (1:1–16)
2. Right living in the church (2:1–15)
3. Right living in society (3:1–15)

Paul calls for church order and right living on an island known for laziness, gluttony, lying, and evil. The Christians are to be self-disciplined as individuals, and they must be orderly as people who form one body, the church. We need to obey this message in our day when discipline is not respected or rewarded by our society. Although others may not appreciate our efforts, we must live upright lives, obey the government, and control our speech. We should live together peacefully in the church and be living examples of our faith to contemporary society.

MEGATHEMES

THEME	EXPLANATION	IMPORTANCE
A Good Life	The Good News of salvation is that we can't be saved by living a good life; we are saved only by faith in Jesus Christ. But the gospel transforms people's lives, so that they eventually perform good deeds. Our service won't save us, but we are saved to serve.	A good life is a witness to the gospel's power. As Christians, we must have commitment and discipline to serve. Are you putting your faith into action by serving others?
Character	Titus's responsibility in Crete was to appoint elders to maintain proper organization and discipline, so Paul listed the qualities needed for the eldership. Their conduct in their homes revealed their fitness for service in the church.	It's not enough to be educated or to have a loyal following to be Christ's kind of leader. You must have self-control, spiritual and moral fitness, and Christian character. Who you are is just as important as what you can do.
Church Relationships	Church teaching must relate to various groups. Older Christians were to teach and to be examples to younger men and women. People of every age and group have a lesson to learn and a role to play.	Right living and right relationships go along with right doctrine. Treat relationships with other believers as an outgrowth of your faith.
Citizenship	Christians must be good citizens in society, not just in church. Believers must obey the government and work honestly.	How you fulfill your civic duties is a witness to the watching world. Your community life should reflect Christ's love as much as your church life does.

1. Leadership in the church

Salutation

1 Paul, a bond-servant of God and an apostle of Jesus Christ, for the faith of those
chosen of God and the knowledge of the truth which is according to godliness,
2 in the hope of eternal life, which God, who cannot lie, promised long ages ago,
3 but at the proper time manifested, *even* His word, in the proclamation with which I
was entrusted according to the commandment of God our Savior,

1:1 Rom 1:1; 1 Tim 6:3
1:2 2 Tim 1:1; Titus 3:7; 2 Tim 2:13; Heb 6:18; Rom 1:2
1:3 1 Tim 2:6; Rom 16:25; 2 Tim 4:17; 1 Tim 1:11; 1 Tim 1:1; Luke 1:47

1:1 Paul wrote this letter between his first and second imprisonments in Rome (before he wrote 2 Timothy) to guide Titus in working with the churches on the island of Crete. Paul had visited Crete with Titus and had left him there to minister (1:5). There was a strong pagan influence on this small island because Crete may have been a training center for Roman soldiers. Therefore, the church in Crete needed strong Christian leadership.

1:1 In one short phrase, Paul gives us insight into his reason for living. He calls himself a bond-servant of God—that is, one who was committed to obeying God. This obedience led him to spend his life telling others about Christ. How would you describe your purpose in life? To what are you devoted? For more information on Paul, see his Profile in Acts 9.

1:1 Paul called himself "an apostle." Even though Paul was not one of the original 12, he was specially called by God to bring the Good News to the Gentiles (see Acts 9:1–16 for an account of his call). The word *apostle* means messenger or missionary. "Those chosen of God" refers to God's choice of his people, the church.

1:2 Apparently lying was commonplace in Crete (1:12). Paul made it clear at the start that God does not lie. The foundation of our faith is trust in God's character. Because God *is* truth, he is the *source* of all truth, and he cannot lie. Believing in him leads to *godliness,* living a God-honoring life-style (1:1). The eternal life that God has promised will be ours, because he keeps his promises. Build your faith on the foundation of a trustworthy God who never lies.

1:3 God is called "our Savior," as is Jesus Christ (1:4). "God" here refers to the Father. Jesus did the work of salvation by dying for our sins and, therefore, he is our Savior. God planned the work of salvation, and he forgives our sins. Both the Father and the Son acted to save us from our sins.

1:4
2 Cor 2:13; 8:23; Gal 2:3; 2 Tim 4:10

1:5
Acts 27:7; Titus 1:12; Acts 14:23; Acts 11:30

1:6
1 Tim 3:2-4; Eph 5:18; Titus 1:10

1:7
1 Tim 3:2; 1 Cor 4:1; 2 Pet 2:10

1:8
1 Tim 3:2; 2 Tim 3:3

1:9
2 Thess 2:15; 1 Tim 1:19; 2 Tim 1:13

4 To Titus, my true child in a common faith: Grace and peace from God the Father
and Christ Jesus our Savior.

Qualifications of Elders

5 For this reason I left you in Crete, that you would set in order what remains and
appoint elders in every city as I directed you,
6 *namely,* if any man is above reproach, the husband of one wife, having children who
believe, not accused of dissipation or rebellion.
7 For the overseer must be above reproach as God's steward, not self-willed, not quick-
tempered, not addicted to wine, not pugnacious, not fond of sordid gain,
8 but hospitable, loving what is good, sensible, just, devout, self-controlled,
9 holding fast the faithful word which is in accordance with the teaching, so that he
will be able both to exhort in sound doctrine and to refute those who contradict.

TITUS GOES TO CRETE
Tradition says that after Paul was released from prison in Rome (before his second and final Roman imprisonment), he and Titus traveled together for a while. They stopped in Crete and when it was time for Paul to go, he left Titus behind to help the churches there.

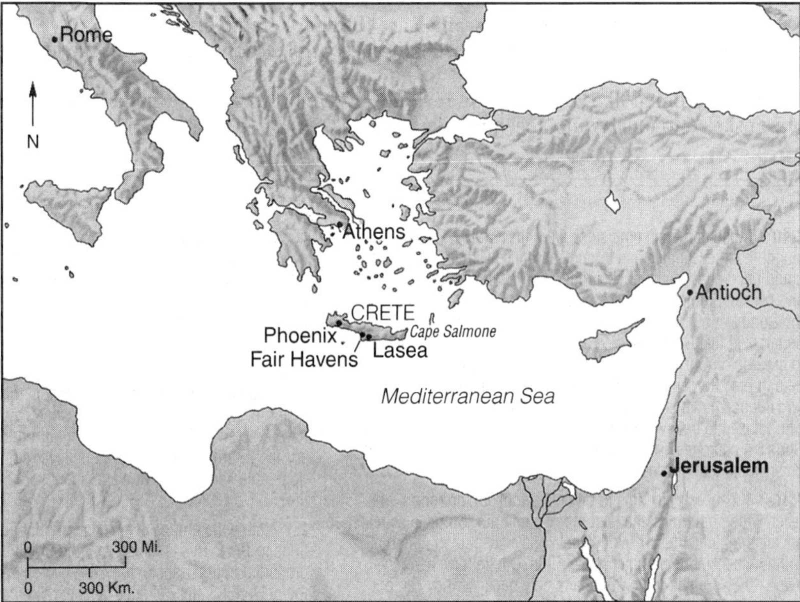

1:4 Titus, a Greek, was one of Paul's most trusted and dependable co-workers. Paul sent Titus to Corinth on several special missions to help the church in its troubles (2 Corinthians 7; 8). Paul and Titus also traveled together to Jerusalem (Galatians 2:3) and Crete (1:5). Paul left Titus in Crete to lead the new churches springing up on the island. Titus is last mentioned by Paul in 2 Timothy 4:10, in Paul's last recorded letter. Titus had leadership ability, so Paul gave him leadership responsibility, urging him to use his abilities well.

1:5 Crete, a small island in the Mediterranean Sea, had a large population of Jews. The churches there were probably founded by Cretan Jews who had been in Jerusalem at Pentecost (Acts 2:11) more than 30 years before Paul wrote this letter.

1:5 What remained to be finished refers to establishing correct teaching and appointing elders in every town.

1:5 Paul had appointed elders in various churches during his journeys (Acts 14:23). He could not stay in each church, but he knew that these new churches needed strong spiritual leadership. The men chosen were to lead the churches by teaching sound doctrine, helping believers mature spiritually, and equipping them to live for Jesus Christ despite opposition.

1:5–9 Paul briefly described some qualifications that the elders or overseers should have. Paul had given Timothy a similar set of instructions for the church in Ephesus (see 1 Timothy 3:1–7; 5:22). Notice that most of the qualifications involve character, not knowledge or skill. A person's life-style and relationships provide a window into his or her character. Consider these qualifications as you evaluate a person for a position of leadership in your church. It is important to have leaders who can effectively preach God's Word, but it is even more important to have those who can live out God's Word and be examples for others to follow.

10 For there are many rebellious men, empty talkers and deceivers, especially those of the circumcision,
11 who must be silenced because they are upsetting whole families, teaching things they should not *teach* for the sake of sordid gain.
12 One of themselves, a prophet of their own, said, "Cretans are always liars, evil beasts, lazy gluttons."
13 This testimony is true. For this reason reprove them severely so that they may be sound in the faith,
14 not paying attention to Jewish myths and commandments of men who turn away from the truth.
15 To the pure, all things are pure; but to those who are defiled and unbelieving, nothing is pure, but both their mind and their conscience are defiled.
16 They profess to know God, but by *their* deeds they deny *Him*, being detestable and disobedient and worthless for any good deed.

1:10 2 Cor 11:13; Titus 1:6; 1 Tim 1:6; Acts 11:2

1:11 1 Tim 5:4; 2 Tim 3:6; 1 Tim 5:13; 1 Tim 6:5

1:12 Acts 2:11; 27:7

1:13 1 Tim 5:20; 2 Tim 4:2; 2 Cor 13:10

1:14 1 Tim 1:4; Col 2:22; 2 Tim 4:4

1:15 Luke 11:41; Rom 14:20; Rom 14:14, 23; 1 Tim 6:5

1:16 1 John 2:4; 1 Tim 5:8; Rev 21:8; 2 Tim 3:8; 2 Tim 3:17

2. Right living in the church

Duties of the Older and Younger

2 But as for you, speak the things which are fitting for sound doctrine.
2 Older men are to be temperate, dignified, sensible, sound in faith, in love, in perseverance.
3 Older women likewise are to be reverent in their behavior, not malicious gossips nor enslaved to much wine, teaching what is good,

2:2 Philem 9; 1 Tim 3:2; 1 Tim 1:2, 14

2:3 1 Tim 3:11; 1 Tim 3:8

1:10 "Those of the circumcision" were the *Judaizers,* Jews who taught that the Gentiles had to obey all the Jewish laws before they could become Christians. This regulation confused new Christians and caused problems in many churches where Paul had preached the Good News. Paul wrote letters to several churches to help them understand that Gentile believers did not have to become Jews first in order to be Christians—God accepts anyone who comes to him in faith (see Romans 1:17; Galatians 3:2–7). Although the Jerusalem council had dealt with this issue (see Acts 15), devout Jews who refused to believe in Jesus still tried to cause problems in the Christian churches. Church leaders must be alert and take action on anything that divides Christians.

1:10–14 Paul warned Titus to be on the lookout for people who teach wrong doctrines and lead others into error. Some false teachers are simply confused—they speak their misguided opinions without checking them against the Bible. Others have evil motives—they pretend to be Christians only because they can get more money ("sordid gain"), additional business, or a feeling of power from being a leader in the church. Jesus and the apostles repeatedly warned against false teachers (see Mark 13:22; Acts 20:29; 2 Thessalonians 2:3–12; 2 Peter 3:3–7) because their teachings attack the foundations of truth and integrity upon which the Christian faith is built. You can recognize false teachers because they will (1) focus more attention on themselves than on Christ; (2) ask you to do something that will compromise or dilute your faith; (3) de-emphasize the divine nature of Christ or the inspiration of the Bible; or (4) urge believers to make decisions based more on human judgment than on prayer and Biblical guidelines.

1:12 Paul was quoting a line from a poem by Epimenides, a poet and philosopher who had lived in Crete 600 years earlier. Some Cretans had a bad reputation and were known for lying. Paul used this familiar phrase to make the point that Titus's ministry and leadership were very much needed.

1:15 Some people see good all around them, while others see nothing but evil. What is the difference? Our souls become filters through which we perceive goodness or evil. The pure (those who have Christ in control of their lives) learn to see goodness and purity even in this evil world. But defiled and unbelieving people find evil in everything because their evil minds and hearts color even the good they see and hear. Whatever you choose to fill your mind with will affect the way you think and act. Turn your thoughts to God and his Word, and you will discover more and more goodness, even in this evil world. A mind filled with good has little room for what is evil (see Philippians 4:8).

1:16 Many people claim to know God. How can we know if they really do? We will not know for certain in this life, but a glance at their life-styles will quickly tell us what they value and whether they have ordered their lives around kingdom priorities. Our conduct speaks volumes about what we believe (see 1 John 2:4–6). What do people know about God and about your faith by watching your life?

2:1 Notice the emphasis on "sound doctrine" in Paul's instructions to Titus. This is the *content* of our faith. Believers must be grounded in the truths of the Bible—then they won't be swayed by the powerful oratory of false teachers, the possible devastation of tragic circumstances, or the pull of emotions. Learn the Bible, study theology, apply Biblical principles, and *do* what you learn.

2:1–8 Having people of all ages in the church makes it strong, but it also brings potential for problems. Paul gave Titus counsel on how to help various groups of people. The older people should teach the younger by words *and* by example. This is how values are passed on from generation to generation. Does your church carry out this basic function?

2:2, 5 Self-control (being sensible) was an important aspect in early Christianity. The Christian community was made up of people from differing backgrounds and viewpoints, making conflict inevitable. Christians existed in a pagan and often hostile world. To stay above reproach, men and women needed wisdom and discernment to be discreet, and to master their wills, tongues, and passions so that Christ would not be dishonored. How's your self-control?

2:3–5 Women who were new Christians were to learn how to have harmony in the home by watching older women who had been Christians for some time. We have the same need today. Younger wives and mothers should learn to live in a Christian manner—loving their husbands and caring for their children—through observing exemplary women of God. If you are of an age or position where people look up to you, make sure that your example is motivating younger believers to live in a way that honors God.

2:5 1 Tim 5:14; Eph 5:22; 1 Tim 6:1
2:6 1 Tim 5:1
2:7 1 Tim 4:12
2:8 2 Thess 3:14; 1 Pet 2:12
2:9 Eph 6:5; 1 Tim 6:1
2:11 2 Tim 1:10; Titus 3:4; 1 Tim 2:4
2:12 1 Tim 6:9; Titus 3:3
2:13 2 Thess 2:8; 1 Tim 1:1; 2 Tim 1:2; Titus 1:4; 2 Pet 1:1
2:14 1 Pet 1:18f; 1 John 1:7; Eph 1:11; 1 Pet 2:9
2:15 1 Tim 4:13; 5:20; 2 Tim 4:2
3:1 2 Tim 2:14; Rom 13:1; 2 Tim 2:21
3:2 1 Tim 3:3; 1 Pet 2:18; 2 Tim 2:25

4 so that they may encourage the young women to love their husbands, to love their
children,
5 *to be* sensible, pure, workers at home, kind, being subject to their own husbands, so
that the word of God will not be dishonored.
6 Likewise urge the young men to be sensible;
7 in all things show yourself to be an example of good deeds, *with* purity in doctrine,
dignified,
8 sound *in* speech which is beyond reproach, so that the opponent will be put to shame,
having nothing bad to say about us.
9 *Urge* bondslaves to be subject to their own masters in everything, to be well-pleasing, not argumentative,
10 not pilfering, but showing all good faith so that they will adorn the doctrine of God
our Savior in every respect.
11 For the grace of God has appeared, bringing salvation to all men,
12 instructing us to deny ungodliness and worldly desires and to live sensibly, righteously
and godly in the present age,
13 looking for the blessed hope and the appearing of the glory of our great God and
Savior, Christ Jesus,
14 who gave Himself for us to redeem us from every lawless deed, and to purify for
Himself a people for His own possession, zealous for good deeds.
15 These things speak and exhort and reprove with all authority. Let no one disregard you.

3. Right living in society

Godly Living

3 Remind them to be subject to rulers, to authorities, to be obedient, to be ready for
every good deed,
2 to malign no one, to be peaceable, gentle, showing every consideration for all men.

2:6 This advice given to young men was very important. In ancient Greek society, the role of the husband/father was not viewed as a nurturing role, but merely as a functional one. Many young men today have been raised in families where fathers have neglected their responsibilities to their wives and children. Husbands and fathers who are good examples of Christian living are important role models for young men who need to *see* how it is done.

2:7 When Paul encouraged Titus, and through Titus other young men, to be serious, he wanted them to be reverent and purposeful. Christianity should never be intentionally boring or gloomy. Don't let the seriousness of the gospel cause you to repel others by your grim disposition.

2:7–8 Paul urged Titus to be a good example to those around him so that others might see Titus's good deeds and imitate him. Paul's life would give his words greater impact. If you want someone to act a certain way, be sure that you live that way yourself. Then you will earn the right to be heard, and your life will reinforce what you teach.

2:8 Paul counseled Titus to be above criticism in how he taught. This quality of integrity comes from careful Bible study and listening before speaking. This is especially important when teaching or confronting others about spiritual or moral issues. If we are impulsive, unreasonable, and confusing, we are likely to start arguments rather than to convince people of the truth.

2:9–10 Slavery was common in Paul's day. Paul did not condemn slavery in any of his letters, but he advised slaves and masters to be loving and responsible in their conduct (see also Ephesians 6:5–9). The standards set by Paul can help any employee/employer relationship. Employees should always do their best work and be trustworthy, not just when the employer is watching. Businesses lose millions of dollars a year to employee theft and timewasting. If all Christian employees would follow Paul's advice at work, what a transformation it would make!

2:11–14 The power to live as a Christian comes from the Holy Spirit. Because Christ died and rescued us from sin, we are free from sin's control. God gives us the power and understanding to live according to his will and to do good. Then we will look forward to Christ's wonderful return with eager expectation and hope.

2:12 It is not enough to renounce sin and evil desires; we must also live actively for God. To fight against ungodliness and worldly desires we must say no to temptation, but we must also say yes to active service for Christ.

2:14 Christ's redeeming us opens the way for him to purify us. *Redeem* means to purchase our release from the captivity of sin with a ransom (see Mark 10:45 for more on Christ as our ransom). We are not only free from the sentence of death for our sin, but we are also purified from sin's influence as we grow in Christ.

2:15 Paul told Titus to teach the Scriptures as well as to live them. We must also teach, encourage, and correct others when necessary. It is easy to feel afraid when others are older, more influential in the community, or wealthier. Like Titus, we should not let ourselves be threatened when we are trying to minister to others or provide leadership in the church.

3:1–2 As Christians, our first allegiance is to Jesus as Lord, but we must obey our government and its leaders as well. Christians are not above the law. Obeying the civil law is only the beginning of our Christian responsibility; we must do what we can to be good citizens. In a democracy, this means participation and willingness to serve. (See Acts 5:29 and Romans 13:1ff for more on the Christian's attitude toward government.)

3 For we also once were foolish ourselves, disobedient, deceived, enslaved to various
lusts and pleasures, spending our life in malice and envy, hateful, hating one another.
4 But when the kindness of God our Savior and *His* love for mankind appeared,
5 He saved us, not on the basis of deeds which we have done in righteousness, but
according to His mercy, by the washing of regeneration and renewing by the Holy Spirit,
6 whom He poured out upon us richly through Jesus Christ our Savior,
7 so that being justified by His grace we would be made heirs according to *the* hope of
eternal life.
8 This is a trustworthy statement; and concerning these things I want you to speak
confidently, so that those who have believed God will be careful to engage in good deeds.
These things are good and profitable for men.
9 But avoid foolish controversies and genealogies and strife and disputes about the
Law, for they are unprofitable and worthless.
10 Reject a factious man after a first and second warning,
11 knowing that such a man is perverted and is sinning, being self-condemned.

Personal Concerns

12 When I send Artemas or Tychicus to you, make every effort to come to me at Nicopolis, for I have decided to spend the winter there.
13 Diligently help Zenas the lawyer and Apollos on their way so that nothing is lacking
for them.
14 Our people must also learn to engage in good deeds to meet pressing needs, so that
they will not be unfruitful.
15 All who are with me greet you. Greet those who love us in *the* faith.
Grace be with you all.

3:3 Rom 11:30; Col 3:7; Rom 1:29

3:4 Rom 2:4; Eph 2:7

3:5 Rom 11:14; Eph 2:4; 1 Pet 1:3; John 3:5; Eph 5:26; 1 Pet 3:21; Rom 12:2

3:6 Rom 5:5; Rom 2:4

3:7 Matt 25:34; Mark 10:17; Rom 8:17

3:10 2 John 10; Rom 16:17; Matt 18:15f

3:12 Acts 20:4; Eph 6:21f; Col 4:7f; 2 Tim 4:12; 2 Tim 4:9

3:13 Matt 22:35; Acts 18:24; 1 Cor 16:12

3:14 Rom 12:13; Phil 4:16; Matt 7:19; Phil 1:11; Col 1:10

3:15 Acts 20:34; 1 Tim 1:2; Col 4:18

3:3 Following a life of pleasure and giving in to every sensual desire leads to slavery. Many think freedom consists in doing anything they want. But this path leads to a slavish addiction to sensual gratification. A person is no longer free, but is a slave to what his or her body dictates (2 Peter 2:19). Christ frees us from the desires and control of sin. Have you been released?

3:3–8 Paul summarized what Christ does for us when he saves us. We move from a life full of sin to one where we are led by God's Holy Spirit. *All* our sins, not merely some, are washed away. Washing refers to the water of baptism, which is a sign of salvation. In becoming a Christian, the believer acknowledges Christ as Lord and recognizes Christ's saving work. We gain eternal life with *all* its treasures. We have *renewal* by the Holy Spirit, and he continually renews our hearts. None of this occurs because we earned or deserved it; it is all God's gift.

3:4–6 All three persons of the Trinity are mentioned in these verses because all three participate in the work of salvation. Based upon the redemptive work of his Son, the Father forgives and sends the Holy Spirit to wash away our sins and continually renew us.

3:9 Paul warned Titus, as he warned Timothy, not to get involved in foolish and unprofitable arguments (2 Timothy 2:14). This does not mean we should refuse to study, discuss, and examine different interpretations of difficult Bible passages. Paul is warning against petty quarrels, not honest discussion that leads to wisdom. As foolish arguments develop, it is best to turn the discussion back to a helpful direction or politely excuse yourself.

3:9 The false teachers were basing their heresies on genealogies and speculations about the law (see 1 Timothy 1:3–4). Similar to the methods used by false teachers in Ephesus and Colossae, they were building their case on genealogies of angels. We should avoid false teachers, not even bothering to react to their pretentious positions. Our overreaction can sometimes give more attention to their points of view.

3:9–11 A person must be warned when he or she is causing division that threatens the unity of the church. This warning should not be a heavy-handed action, but it is intended to correct the individual's divisive nature and restore him or her to fellowship. A person who refuses to be corrected should be put outside the fellowship. As Paul said, that person is "self-condemned"—he or she is sinning and knows it. (See also Matthew 18:15–18 and 2 Thessalonians 3:14–15 for help in handling such problems in the church.)

3:12 The city of Nicopolis was on the western coast of Greece. Artemas or Tychicus would take over Titus's work on the island of Crete so Titus could meet Paul in Nicopolis. Tychicus was one of Paul's trusted companions (Acts 20:4; Ephesians 6:21; Colossians 4:7). Titus would have to leave soon because sea travel was dangerous in the winter months.

3:13 Apollos was a famous Christian preacher. A native of Alexandria in North Africa, he became a Christian in Ephesus and was trained by Aquila and Priscilla (Acts 18:24–28; 1 Corinthians 1:12).

3:15 The letters of Paul to Titus and Timothy are his last writings and mark the end of his life and ministry. These letters are rich treasures for us today because they give vital information for church leadership. They provide a strong model for elders, pastors, and other Christian leaders as they develop younger leaders to carry on the work, following Paul's example of preparing Timothy and Titus to carry on his ministry. For practical guidelines on church leadership and problem solving, carefully study the principles found in these letters.

PHILEMON

AT THE foreman's signal, the giant ball is released, and with dynamite force and a reverberating crash, it meets the wall, snapping bricks like twigs and scattering pieces of mortar. Repeatedly, the powerful pendulum works, and soon the barrier has been reduced to rubble. Then it is carted away so that construction can begin.

Life has many walls and fences that divide, separate, and compartmentalize. Not made of wood or stone, they are personal obstructions, blocking people from each other and from God. But Christ came as the great wall remover, tearing down the sin partition that separates us from God and blasting the barriers that keep us from each other. His death and resurrection opened the way to eternal life to bring all who believe into the family of God (see Ephesians 2:14–18).

Roman, Greek, and Jewish cultures were littered with barriers, as society assigned people to classes and expected them to stay in their place—men and women, slave and free, rich and poor, Jews and Gentiles, Greeks and barbarians, pious and pagan. But with the message of Christ, the walls came down, and Paul could declare, "There is no distinction between Greek and Jew, circumcised and uncircumcised, barbarian, Scythian, slave and freeman, but Christ is all, and in all" (Colossians 3:11).

This life-changing truth forms the backdrop for the letter to Philemon. One of three personal letters in the Bible, the letter to Philemon is Paul's personal plea for a slave. Onesimus "belonged" to Philemon, a member of the Colossian church and Paul's friend. But Onesimus, the slave, had stolen from his master and run away. He ran to Rome, where he met Paul, and there he responded to the Good News and came to faith in Christ (10). So Paul writes to Philemon and reintroduces Onesimus to him, explaining that he is sending him back, not just as a slave but as a brother (11–12, 16). Tactfully he asks Philemon to accept and forgive his brother (10, 14–15, 20). The barriers of the past and the new ones erected by Onesimus's desertion and theft should divide them no longer—they are one in Christ.

This small book is a masterpiece of grace and tact and a profound demonstration of the power of Christ and of true Christian fellowship in action. What barriers are in your home, neighborhood, and church? What separates you from fellow believers? Is it race? status? wealth? education? personality? As with Philemon, God calls you to seek unity, breaking down those walls and embracing your brothers and sisters in Christ.

VITAL STATISTICS

PURPOSE:
To convince Philemon to forgive his runaway slave, Onesimus, and to accept him as a brother in the faith

AUTHOR:
Paul

TO WHOM WRITTEN:
Philemon, who was probably a wealthy member of the Colossian church, and all believers

DATE WRITTEN:
Approximately A.D. 60, during Paul's first imprisonment in Rome, at about the same time Ephesians and Colossians were written

SETTING:
Slavery was very common in the Roman empire, and evidently some Christians had slaves. Paul does not condemn the institution of slavery in his writings, but he makes a radical statement by calling this slave Philemon's brother in Christ.

KEY VERSES:
"For perhaps he was for this reason separated from you for a while, that you would have him back forever, no longer as a slave, but more than a slave, a beloved brother, especially to me, but how much more to you, both in the flesh and in the Lord" (15–16).

KEY PEOPLE:
Paul, Philemon, Onesimus

KEY PLACES:
Colossae, Rome

SPECIAL FEATURES:
This is a private, personal letter to a friend.

THE BLUEPRINT

1. Paul's appreciation of Philemon (1–7)
2. Paul's appeal for Onesimus (8–25)

Paul pleads on behalf of Onesimus, a runaway slave. Paul's intercession for him illustrates what Christ has done for us. As Paul interceded for a slave, so Christ intercedes for us, slaves to sin. As Onesimus was reconciled to Philemon, so we are reconciled to God through Christ. As Paul offered to pay the debts of a slave, so Christ paid our debt of sin. Like Onesimus, we must return to God our Master and serve him.

MEGATHEMES

THEME	EXPLANATION	IMPORTANCE
Forgiveness	Philemon was Paul's friend and the legal owner of the slave Onesimus. Paul asked him not to punish Onesimus but to forgive and restore him as a new Christian brother.	Christian relationships must be full of forgiveness and acceptance. Can you forgive those who have wronged you?
Barriers	Slavery was widespread in the Roman empire, but no one is lost to God or beyond his love. Slavery was a barrier between people, but Christian love and fellowship are to overcome such barriers.	In Christ we are one family. No walls of racial, economic or political differences should separate us. Let Christ work through you to remove barriers between Christian brothers and sisters.
Respect	Paul was a friend of both Philemon and Onesimus. He had the authority as an apostle to tell Philemon what to do. Yet Paul chose to appeal to his friend in Christian love rather than to order him what to do.	Tactful persuasion accomplishes a great deal more than commands when dealing with people. Remember to exhibit courtesy and respect in your relationships.

1. Paul's appreciation of Philemon

Salutation

1 Paul, a prisoner of Christ Jesus, and Timothy our brother,
To Philemon our beloved *brother* and fellow worker,
2 and to Apphia our sister, and to Archippus our fellow soldier, and to the church in
your house:
3 Grace to you and peace from God our Father and the Lord Jesus Christ.

Philemon's Love and Faith

4 I thank my God always, making mention of you in my prayers,
5 because I hear of your love and of the faith which you have toward the Lord Jesus
and toward all the saints;

1:1 Phil 1:1; Eph 3:1; Gal 3:26; 2 Cor 1:1; Col 1:1; Phil 2:25; Philem 24

1:2 Rom 16:1; Col 4:17; Phil 2:25; 2 Tim 2:3; Rom 16:5

1:3 Rom 1:7

1:4 Rom 1:8f

1:5 Eph 1:15; Col 1:4; 1 Thess 3:6

---

1 Paul wrote this letter from Rome in about A.D. 60, when he was under house arrest (see Acts 28:30–31). Onesimus was a domestic slave who belonged to Philemon, a wealthy man and a member of the church in Colossae. Onesimus had run away from Philemon and had made his way to Rome where he met Paul, who apparently led him to Christ (verse 10). Paul convinced Onesimus that running from his problems wouldn't solve them, and he persuaded Onesimus to return to his master. Paul wrote this letter to Philemon to ask him to be reconciled to his runaway slave.

1 For more information on Paul's life, see his Profile in Acts 9. Timothy's name is included with Paul's in 2 Corinthians, 1 Thessalonians, 2 Thessalonians, Philippians, Colossians, and Philemon—the last three of these letters are from a group known as the "Prison Letters." Timothy was one of Paul's trusted companions; Paul wrote two letters to him—1 and 2 Timothy.

1 Philemon was a Greek landowner living in Colossae. He had been converted under Paul's ministry, and the Colossian church met in his home. Onesimus was one of Philemon's slaves.

2 Apphia may have been Philemon's wife. Archippus may have been Philemon's son, or perhaps an elder in the Colossian church. In either case, Paul included him as a recipient of the letter, possibly so Archippus could read the letter with Philemon and encourage him to take Paul's advice.

2 The early churches often would meet in people's homes. Because of sporadic persecutions and the great expense involved, church buildings were typically not constructed at this time.

4–7 Paul reflected on Philemon's faith and love. Philemon had opened his heart and his home to the church. We should do likewise, opening ourselves and our homes to others, offering Christian fellowship to refresh people's hearts.

1:6 Phil 1:9; Col 1:9; 3:10
1:7 2 Cor 7:4, 13; 1 Cor 16:18; Philem 20
1:8 2 Cor 3:12; 1 Thess 2:6; Eph 5:4
1:9 Rom 12:1; Titus 2:2; Philem 1; Gal 3:26; 1 Tim 1:12; Philem 23
1:10 Rom 12:1; 1 Cor 4:14f; Col 4:9
1:13 Phil 1:7; Philem 10
1:14 2 Cor 9:7; 1 Pet 5:2
1:15 Gen 45:5, 8
1:16 1 Cor 7:22; Matt 23:8; 1 Tim 6:2; Eph 6:5; Col 3:22
1:17 2 Cor 8:23
1:19 1 Cor 16:21; 2 Cor 10:1; Gal 5:2; 2 Cor 9:4
1:20 Philem 7
1:21 2 Cor 2:3

6 *and I pray* that the fellowship of your faith may become effective [1]through the knowledge of every good thing which is in you for Christ's sake.
7 For I have come to have much joy and comfort in your love, because the hearts of
the saints have been refreshed through you, brother.

2. Paul's appeal for Onesimus

8 Therefore, though I have enough confidence in Christ to order you *to do* what is
proper,
9 yet for love's sake I rather appeal *to you*—since I am such a person as Paul, the aged,
and now also a prisoner of Christ Jesus—

Plea for Onesimus, a Free Man

10 I appeal to you for my child [2]Onesimus, whom I have begotten in my imprisonment,
11 who formerly was useless to you, but now is useful both to you and to me.
12 I have sent him back to you in person, that is, *sending* my very heart,
13 whom I wished to keep with me, so that on your behalf he might minister to me in
my imprisonment for the gospel;
14 but without your consent I did not want to do anything, so that your goodness would
not be, in effect, by compulsion but of your own free will.
15 For perhaps he was for this reason separated *from you* for a while, that you would
have him back forever,
16 no longer as a slave, but more than a slave, a beloved brother, especially to me, but
how much more to you, both in the flesh and in the Lord.
17 If then you regard me a partner, accept him as *you would* me.
18 But if he has wronged you in any way or owes you anything, charge that to my account;
19 I, Paul, am writing this with my own hand, I will repay it (not to mention to you that
you owe to me even your own self as well).
20 Yes, brother, let me benefit from you in the Lord; refresh my heart in Christ.
21 Having confidence in your obedience, I write to you, since I know that you will do
even more than what I say.

1 Or *in* **2** I.e. useful

8–9 Because Paul was an elder and an apostle, he could have used his authority with Philemon, commanding him to deal kindly with his runaway slave. But Paul based his request not on his own authority, but on Philemon's Christian commitment. Paul wanted Philemon's heartfelt, not grudging, obedience. When you know something is right and you have the power to demand it, do you appeal to your authority or to the other person's commitment? Here Paul provides a good example of how to deal with a possible conflict between Christian friends.

10 A master had the legal right to kill a runaway slave, so Onesimus feared for his life. Paul wrote this letter to Philemon to help him understand his new relationship with Onesimus. Onesimus was now a Christian brother, not a mere possession. "My child . . . whom I have begotten" means that Onesimus had become a Christian.

10ff From his prison cell, Paul had led Onesimus to the Lord. Paul asked Philemon to forgive his runaway slave who had become a Christian, and even going beyond forgiveness, to accept Onesimus as a brother. As Christians, we should forgive as we have been forgiven (Matthew 6:12; Ephesians 4:31–32). True forgiveness means that we treat the one we've forgiven as we would want to be treated. Is there someone you say you have forgiven, but who still needs your kindness?

11–15 *Onesimus* means "useful." Paul used a play on words, saying that Onesimus had not been much use to Philemon in the past, but had become very useful to both Philemon and Paul. Although Paul wanted to keep Onesimus with him, he was sending Onesimus back, requesting that Philemon accept him not only as a forgiven runaway servant, but also as a brother in Christ.

15–16 Slavery was widespread throughout the Roman empire. In these early days, Christians did not have the political power to change the slavery system. Paul didn't condemn or condone slavery, but he worked to transform relationships. The gospel begins to change social structures by changing the *people* within those structures. (See also 1 Corinthians 7:20–24; Ephesians 6:5–9; Colossians 3:22—4:1 for more on master/slave relationships.)

16 What a difference Onesimus's status as a Christian made in his relationship to Philemon. He was no longer merely a slave, but he was also a brother. That meant that both Onesimus and Philemon were members of God's family—equals in Christ. A Christian's status as a member of God's family transcends all other distinctions among believers. Do you look down on any fellow Christians? Remember, they are your equals before Christ (Galatians 3:28). How you treat your brothers and sisters in Christ's family reflects your true Christian commitment.

17–19 Paul genuinely loved Onesimus. Paul showed his love by personally guaranteeing payment for any stolen goods or wrongs for which Onesimus might be responsible. Paul's investment in the life of this new believer certainly encouraged and strengthened Onesimus's faith. Are there young believers who need you to demonstrate such self-sacrifice toward them? Be grateful when you can invest in the lives of others, helping them with Bible study, prayer, encouragement, support, and friendship.

19 Philemon owed himself to Paul, meaning that Paul had led Philemon to Christ. Because Paul was Philemon's spiritual father, he was hoping that Philemon would feel a debt of gratitude that he would repay by accepting Onesimus with a spirit of forgiveness.

22 At the same time also prepare me a lodging, for I hope that through your prayers I
will be given to you.
23 Epaphras, my fellow prisoner in Christ Jesus, greets you,
24 *as do* Mark, Aristarchus, Demas, Luke, my fellow workers.
25 The grace of the Lord Jesus Christ be with your spirit.[3]

3 One early ms adds *Amen*

1:22
Acts 28:23; Heb 13:19

1:23
Col 1:7; 4:12

1:24
Acts 12:12, 25

1:25
Gal 6:18; 2 Tim 4:22

22 Paul was released from prison soon after writing this letter, but the Bible doesn't say whether or not he returned to Colossae.

23 Epaphras was well known to the Colossians because he had founded the church there (Colossians 1:7). He was a hero to this church, helping to hold it together in spite of growing persecution and struggles with false doctrine. His report to Paul about the problems in Colossae had prompted Paul to write his letter to the Colossians. Epaphras's greetings to and prayers for the Colossian Christians reveal his deep love for them (Colossians 4:12–13). He may have been in prison with Paul for preaching the gospel.

24 Mark, Aristarchus, Demas, and Luke are also mentioned in Colossians 4:10, 14. Mark had accompanied Paul and Barnabas on their first missionary journey (Acts 12:25ff). Mark also wrote the Gospel of Mark. Luke had accompanied Paul on his third missionary journey and was the writer of the Gospel of Luke and the book of Acts. Demas had been faithful to Paul for a while but then deserted him (see 2 Timothy 4:10).

25 Paul urged Philemon to be reconciled to his slave, receiving him as a brother and fellow member of God's family. *Reconciliation* means reestablishing relationship. Christ has reconciled us to God and to others. Many barriers come between people—race, social status, sex, personality differences—but Christ can break down these barriers. Jesus Christ changed Onesimus's relationship to Philemon from slave to brother. Christ can transform our most hopeless relationships into deep and loving friendships.

HEBREWS

CONSCIENTIOUS consumers shop for value, the best products for the money. Wise parents desire only the best for their children, nourishing their growing bodies, minds, and spirits. Individuals with integrity seek the best investment of time, talents, and treasures. In every area, to settle for less would be wasteful, foolish, and irresponsible. Yet it is a natural pull to move toward what is convenient and comfortable.

Judaism was not second-rate or easy. Divinely designed, it was the best religion, expressing true worship and devotion to God. The commandments, the rituals, and the prophets described God's promises and revealed the way to forgiveness and salvation. But Christ came, fulfilling the Law and the Prophets, conquering sin, shattering all barriers to God, freely providing eternal life.

This message was difficult for Jews to accept. Although they had sought the Messiah for centuries, they were entrenched in thinking and worshiping in traditional forms. Following Jesus seemed to repudiate their marvelous heritage and Scriptures. With caution and questions they listened to the gospel, but many rejected it and sought to eliminate this "heresy." Those who did accept Jesus as the Messiah often found themselves slipping back into familiar routines, trying to live a hybrid faith.

Hebrews is a masterful document written to Jews who were evaluating Jesus or struggling with this new faith. The message of Hebrews is that Jesus is better, Christianity is superior, Christ is supreme and completely sufficient for salvation.

Hebrews begins by emphasizing that the old (Judaism) and the new (Christianity) are both religions revealed by God (1:1–3). In the doctrinal section that follows (1:4—10:18), the writer shows how Jesus is superior to angels (1:4—2:18), superior to their leaders (3:1—4:13), and superior to their priests (4:14—7:28). Christianity surpasses Judaism because it has a better covenant (8:1–13), a better sanctuary (9:1–10), and a more sufficient sacrifice for sins (9:11—10:18).

Having established the superiority of Christianity, the writer moves on to the practical implications of following Christ. The readers are exhorted to hold on to their new faith, encourage each other, and look forward to Christ's return (10:19–25). They are warned about the consequences of rejecting Christ's sacrifice (10:26–31) and reminded of the rewards for faithfulness (10:32–39). Then the author explains how to live by faith, giving illustrations of the faithful men and women in Israel's history (11:1–40) and giving encouragement and exhortation for daily living (12:1–17). This section ends by comparing the old covenant with the new (12:18–29). The writer concludes with moral exhortations (13:1–17), a request for prayer (13:18–19), and a benediction and greetings (13:20–25).

Whatever you are considering as the focus of life, Christ is better. He is the perfect revelation of God, the final and complete sacrifice for sin, the compassionate and understanding mediator, and the *only* way to eternal life. Read Hebrews and begin to see history and life from God's perspective. Then give yourself unreservedly and completely to Christ.

VITAL STATISTICS

PURPOSE:
To present the sufficiency and superiority of Christ

AUTHOR:
Paul, Luke, Barnabas, Apollos, Silas, Philip, Priscilla, and others have been suggested because the name of the author is not given in the Biblical text itself. Whoever it was speaks of Timothy as "brother" (13:23).

TO WHOM WRITTEN:
Hebrew Christians (perhaps second-generation Christians, see 2:3) who may have been considering a return to Judaism, perhaps because of immaturity, stemming from a lack of understanding of Biblical truths; and all believers in Christ.

DATE WRITTEN:
Probably before the destruction of the temple in Jerusalem in A.D. 70, because the religious sacrifices and ceremonies are referred to in the book, but no mention is made of the temple's destruction

SETTING:
These Jewish Christians were probably undergoing fierce persecution, socially and physically, both from Jews and from Romans. Christ had not returned to establish his kingdom, and the people needed to be reassured that Christianity was true and that Jesus was indeed the Messiah.

KEY VERSE:
"And He is the radiance of His glory and the exact representation of His nature, and upholds all things by the word of His power. When He had made purification of sins, He sat down at the right hand of the Majesty on high" (1:3).

KEY PEOPLE:
Old Testament men and women of faith (chapter 11)

SPECIAL FEATURES:
Although Hebrews is called a "letter" (13:22), it has the form and the content of a sermon.

THE BLUEPRINT

A. THE SUPERIORITY OF CHRIST (1:1—10:18) 1. Christ is greater than the angels 2. Christ is greater than Moses 3. Christ is greater than the Old Testament priesthood 4. The new covenant is greater than the old	The superiority of Christ over everyone and everything is clearly demonstrated by the author. Christianity supersedes all other religions and can never be surpassed. Where can one find anything better than Christ? Living in Christ is having the best there is in life. All competing religions are deceptions or cheap imitations.
B. THE SUPERIORITY OF FAITH (10:19—13:25)	Jews who had become Christians in the first century were tempted to fall back into Judaism because of uncertainty, the security of custom, and persecution. Today believers are also tempted to fall back into legalism, fulfilling minimum religious requirements rather than pressing on in genuine faith. We must strive to live by faith each day.

MEGATHEMES

THEME	EXPLANATION	IMPORTANCE
Christ Is Superior	Hebrews reveals Jesus' true identity as God. Jesus is the ultimate authority. He is greater than any religion or any angel. He is superior to any Jewish leader (such as Abraham, Moses, or Joshua) and superior to any priest. He is the complete revelation of God.	Jesus alone can forgive our sin. He has secured our forgiveness and salvation by his death on the cross. We can find peace with God and real meaning for life by believing in Christ. We should not accept any alternative to or substitute for him.
High Priest	In the Old Testament, the high priest represented the Jews before God. Jesus Christ links us with God. There is no other way to reach God. Because Jesus Christ lived a sinless life, he is the perfect substitute to die for our sin. He is our perfect representative with God.	Jesus guarantees our access to God the Father. He intercedes for us so we can boldly come to the Father with our needs. When we are weak, we can come confidently to God for forgiveness and ask for his help.
Sacrifice	Christ's sacrifice was the ultimate fulfillment of all that the Old Testament sacrifices represented—God's forgiveness for sin. Because Christ is the perfect sacrifice for our sin, our sins are completely forgiven—past, present, and future.	Christ removed sin, which barred us from God's presence and fellowship. But we must accept his sacrifice for us. By believing in him, we are no longer guilty but cleansed and made whole. His sacrifice clears the way for us to have eternal life.
Maturity	Though we are saved from sin when we believe in Christ, we are given the task of going on and growing in our faith. Through our relationship with Christ, we can live blameless lives, be set aside for his special use, and develop maturity.	The process of maturing in our faith takes time. Daily commitment and service produce maturity. When we are mature in our faith, we are not easily swayed or shaken by temptations or worldly concerns.
Faith	Faith is confident trust in God's promises. God's greatest promise is that we can be saved through Jesus.	If we trust in Jesus Christ for our complete salvation, he will transform us completely. A life of obedience and complete trust is pleasing to God.
Endurance	Faith enables Christians to face trials. Genuine faith includes the commitment to stay true to God when we are under fire. Endurance builds character and leads to victory.	We can have victory in our trials if we don't give up or turn our back on Christ. Stay true to Christ and pray for endurance.

1:1 John 9:29; 16:13; Acts 2:30; 3:21; Num 12:6, 8; Joel 2:28

1:2 Matt 13:39; 1 Pet 1:20; John 9:29; John 5:26, 27; Heb 3:6; 5:8; 7:28; Ps 2:8; Matt 28:18; Mark 12:7; Rom 8:17; John 1:3; 1 Cor 8:6; Col 1:16; 1 Cor 2:7; Heb 11:3

1:3 2 Cor 4:4; Col 1:17; Titus 2:14; Heb 9:14; Mark 16:19

1:4 Eph 1:21

1:5 Ps 2:7; Acts 13:33; Heb 5:5; 2 Sam 7:14

A. THE SUPERIORITY OF CHRIST (1:1—10:18)

The relationship of Christianity to Judaism was a critical issue in the early church. The author clears up confusion by carefully explaining how Christ is superior to angels, Moses, and high priests. The new covenant is shown to be far superior to the old. This can be of great encouragement to us and help us avoid drifting away from our faith in Christ.

1. Christ is greater than the angels

God's Final Word in His Son

1 God, after He spoke long ago to the fathers in the prophets in many portions and in
many ways,
2 in these last days has spoken to us in His Son, whom He appointed heir of all things,
through whom also He made the world.
3 And He is the radiance of His glory and the exact representation of His nature, and
upholds all things by the word of His power. When He had made purification of sins, He
sat down at the right hand of the Majesty on high,
4 having become as much better than the angels, as He has inherited a more excellent name than they.
5 For to which of the angels did He ever say,
"YOU ARE MY SON,
TODAY I HAVE BEGOTTEN YOU"?

CHRIST AND THE ANGELS

Hebrews passage	Old Testament passage	How Christ is superior to angels
1:5–6	Psalm 2:7	Christ is called "Son" of God, a title never given to an angel.
1:7, 14	Psalm 104:4	Angels are important, but are still only servants under God.
1:8–9	Psalm 45:6	Christ's kingdom is forever.
1:10	Psalm 102:25	Christ is the Creator of the world.
1:13	Psalm 110:1	Christ is given unique honor by God.

The writer of Hebrews quotes from the Old Testament repeatedly in demonstrating Christ's greatness in comparison to the angels. This audience of first-century Jewish Christians had developed an imbalanced belief in angels and their role. Christ's lordship is affirmed without disrespect to God's valued angelic messengers.

1:1 The book of Hebrews describes in detail how Jesus Christ not only fulfills the promises and prophecies of the Old Testament, but how Jesus Christ is better than everything in the Jewish system of thought. The Jews accepted the Old Testament, but most of them rejected Jesus as the long-awaited Messiah. The recipients of this letter seem to have been Jewish Christians. They were well-versed in Scripture, and they had professed faith in Christ. Whether through doubt, persecution, or false teaching, however, they may have been in danger of giving up their Christian faith and returning to Judaism.

The authorship of this book is uncertain. Several names have been suggested, including Luke, Barnabas, Apollos, Priscilla, and Paul. Most scholars do not believe that Paul was the author, because the writing style of Hebrews is quite different from that of his letters. In addition, Paul identified himself in his other letters and appealed to his authority as an apostle, whereas this writer of Hebrews, who never gives his or her name, appeals to eyewitnesses of Jesus' ministry for authority. Nevertheless, the author of Hebrews evidently knew Paul well. Hebrews was probably written by one of Paul's close associates who often heard him preach.

1:1–2 God used many approaches to send his messages to people in Old Testament times. He spoke to Isaiah in visions (Isaiah 6), to Jacob in a dream (Genesis 28:10–22), and to Abraham and Moses personally (Genesis 18; Exodus 31:18). Jewish people familiar with these stories would not have found it hard to believe that God was still revealing his will, but it was astonishing for them to think that God had revealed *himself* by speaking through his Son, Jesus Christ. Jesus is the fulfillment and culmination of God's revelation through the centuries. When we know him, we have all we need to be saved from our sin and to have a perfect relationship with God.

1:2–3 Not only is Jesus the exact representation of God, but he is God himself—the very God who spoke in Old Testament times. He is eternal; he worked with the Father in creating the world (John 1:3; Colossians 1:16). He is the full revelation of God. You can have no clearer view of God than by looking at Christ. Jesus Christ is the complete expression of God in a human body.

1:3 The book of Hebrews links God's saving power with his creative power. In other words, the power that brought the universe into being and that keeps it operating is the very power that removes (makes purification for) our sins. How mistaken we would be to ever think that God couldn't forgive us. No sin is too big for the Ruler of the universe to handle. He can and will forgive us when we come to him through his Son. That Jesus *sat down* means that the work was complete. Christ's sacrifice was final.

1:4 The name Jesus inherited that is more excellent is "Son of God." This name given to him by his Father is greater than the names and titles of the angels.

1:4ff False teachers in many of the early churches taught that God could be approached only through angels. Instead of worshiping God directly, followers of these heretics revered angels. Hebrews clearly denounces such teaching as false. Some thought of Jesus as the highest angel of God. But Jesus is not a superior angel; and, in any case, angels are not to be worshiped (see Colossians 2:18; Revelation 19:1–10). We should not regard any intermediaries or authorities as greater than Christ. Jesus is God. He alone deserves our worship.

1:5–6 Jesus is God's firstborn Son. In Jewish families the firstborn son held the place of highest privilege and responsibility. The Jewish Christians reading this message would understand that as God's firstborn, Jesus was superior to any created being.

And again,
"I WILL BE A FATHER TO HIM
AND HE SHALL BE A SON TO ME"?
6 And when He again brings the firstborn into the world, He says,
"AND LET ALL THE ANGELS OF GOD WORSHIP HIM."
7 And of the angels He says,
"WHO MAKES HIS ANGELS WINDS,
AND HIS MINISTERS A FLAME OF FIRE."
8 But of the Son *He says,*
"YOUR THRONE, O GOD, IS FOREVER AND EVER,
AND THE RIGHTEOUS SCEPTER IS THE SCEPTER OF [1]HIS KINGDOM.
9 "YOU HAVE LOVED RIGHTEOUSNESS AND HATED LAWLESSNESS;
THEREFORE GOD, YOUR GOD, HAS ANOINTED YOU
WITH THE OIL OF GLADNESS ABOVE YOUR COMPANIONS."
10 And,
"YOU, LORD, IN THE BEGINNING LAID THE FOUNDATION OF THE EARTH,
AND THE HEAVENS ARE THE WORKS OF YOUR HANDS;
11 THEY WILL PERISH, BUT YOU REMAIN;
AND THEY ALL WILL BECOME OLD LIKE A GARMENT,
12 AND LIKE A MANTLE YOU WILL ROLL THEM UP;
LIKE A GARMENT THEY WILL ALSO BE CHANGED.
BUT YOU ARE THE SAME,
AND YOUR YEARS WILL NOT COME TO AN END."
13 But to which of the angels has He ever said,
"SIT AT MY RIGHT HAND,
UNTIL I MAKE YOUR ENEMIES
A FOOTSTOOL FOR YOUR FEET"?
14 Are they not all ministering spirits, sent out to render service for the sake of those
who will inherit salvation?

1:6 Heb 10:5; Matt 24:14; Ps 97:7
1:7 Ps 104:4
1:8 Ps 45:6
1:9 Ps 45:7; John 10:17; Phil 2:9; Heb 2:9; Is 61:1, 3
1:10 Ps 102:25
1:11 Ps 102:26; Is 51:6; Heb 8:13
1:12 Ps 102:26, 27; Heb 13:8
1:13 Ps 110:1; Matt 22:44; Heb 1:3; Josh 10:24; Heb 10:13
1:14 Ps 103:20f; Dan 7:10; Matt 25:34; Mark 10:17; Titus 3:7; Heb 6:12; Rom 11:14; 1 Cor 1:21; Heb 2:3; 5:9; 9:28
2:1 Prov 3:21
2:2 Heb 1:1; Acts 7:53; Heb 10:28; Heb 10:35; 11:26
2:3 Heb 10:29; 12:25; Rom 11:14; 1 Cor 1:21; Heb 1:14; 5:9; 9:28; Heb 1:1; Mark 16:20; Luke 1:2; 1 John 1:1

Give Heed

2 For this reason we must pay much closer attention to what we have heard, so that we
do not drift away *from it.*
2 For if the word spoken through angels proved unalterable, and every transgression
and disobedience received a just penalty,
3 how will we escape if we neglect so great a salvation? After it was at the first spoken
through the Lord, it was confirmed to us by those who heard,

1 Late mss read *Your*

1:10–12 The author of Hebrews quotes Psalm 102:25–27. In the quotation, he regards God as the speaker and applies the words to the Son Jesus. The earth and the heavens rolled up reveals that the earth is not permanent or indestructible (a position held by many Greek and Roman philosophies). Jesus' authority is established over all of creation, so we dare not treat any created object or earthly resource as more important than he is.

1:11–12 Because the readers of Hebrews had experienced the rejection of their fellow Jews, they often felt isolated. Many were tempted to exchange the changeless Christ for their familiar old faith. The writer of Hebrews warned them not to do this: Christ is our *only* security in a changing world. Whatever may happen in this world, Christ remains forever changeless. If we trust him, we are absolutely secure, because we stand on the firmest foundation in the universe—Jesus Christ. A famous hymn captures this truth: "On Christ the solid rock I stand, all other ground is sinking sand."

1:12 What does it mean that Christ is changeless ("you are the same")? It means that Christ's character will never change. He persistently shows his love to us. He is always fair, just, and merciful to us who are so undeserving. Be thankful that Christ is changeless—he will always help you when you need it and offer forgiveness when you fall.

1:14 Angels are God's messengers, spiritual beings created by God and under his authority (Colossians 1:16). They have several functions: serving believers (1:14), protecting the helpless (Matthew 18:10), proclaiming God's messages (Revelation 14:6–12), and executing God's judgment (Acts 12:1–23; Revelation 20:1–3).

2:1–3 The author called his readers to pay close attention to the truth they had heard so that they wouldn't drift away into false teachings. Paying careful attention is hard work. It involves focusing our minds, bodies, and senses. Listening to Christ means not merely hearing, but also obeying (see James 1:22–25). We must listen carefully and be ready to carry out his instructions.

2:2–3 "The word spoken through angels" refers to the teaching that angels, as messengers for God, had brought the law to Moses (see Galatians 3:19). A central theme of Hebrews is that Christ is infinitely greater than all other proposed ways to God. The author was saying that the faith of his Jewish readers was good, but faith must point to Christ. Just as Christ is greater than angels, so Christ's message is more important than theirs. No one will escape God's punishment if he or she is indifferent to the salvation offered by Christ.

2:3 Eyewitnesses to Jesus' ministry had handed down his teachings to the readers of this book. These readers were second-generation believers who had not seen Christ in the flesh. They are like us; we have not seen Jesus personally. We base our belief in Jesus

4 God also testifying with them, both by signs and wonders and by various miracles
and by gifts of the Holy Spirit according to His own will.

Earth Subject to Man

5 For He did not subject to angels the world to come, concerning which we are
speaking.
6 But one has testified somewhere, saying,
"WHAT IS MAN, THAT YOU REMEMBER HIM?
OR THE SON OF MAN, THAT YOU ARE CONCERNED ABOUT HIM?
7 "YOU HAVE MADE HIM FOR A LITTLE WHILE LOWER THAN THE ANGELS;
YOU HAVE CROWNED HIM WITH GLORY AND HONOR,
[2]AND HAVE APPOINTED HIM OVER THE WORKS OF YOUR HANDS;
8 YOU HAVE PUT ALL THINGS IN SUBJECTION UNDER HIS FEET."
For in subjecting all things to him, He left nothing that is not subject to him. But now we
do not yet see all things subjected to him.

Jesus Briefly Humbled

9 But we do see Him who was made for a little while lower than the angels, *namely,*
Jesus, because of the suffering of death crowned with glory and honor, so that by the
grace of God He might taste death for everyone.
10 For it was fitting for Him, for whom are all things, and through whom are all things,
in bringing many sons to glory, to perfect the author of their salvation through sufferings.
11 For both He who sanctifies and those who are sanctified are all from one *Father;* for
which reason He is not ashamed to call them brethren,

2 Two early mss do not contain *And...hands*

2:4 John 4:48; Mark 6:14; 1 Cor 12:4, 11; Eph 4:7; Eph 1:5

2:5 Matt 24:14; Heb 6:5

2:6 Heb 4:4; Ps 8:4

2:7 Ps 8:5, 6

2:8 Ps 8:6; 1 Cor 15:27; 1 Cor 15:25

2:9 Heb 2:7; Acts 2:33; 3:13; 1 Pet 1:21; Phil 2:9; Heb 1:9; John 3:16; Matt 16:28; John 8:52; Heb 7:25

2:10 Luke 24:26; Rom 11:36; Heb 5:9; 7:28; Acts 3:15; 5:31

2:11 Heb 13:12; Heb 10:10; Acts 17:28; Matt 25:40; Mark 3:34f; John 20:17

LESSONS FROM CHRIST'S HUMANITY

Christ is the perfect human		
	leader	and he wants to lead you
	model	and he is worth imitating
	sacrifice	and he died for you
	conqueror	and he conquered death to give you eternal life
	high priest	and he is merciful, loving, and understanding

God, in Christ, became a living, breathing human being. Hebrews points out many reasons why this is so important.

on the eyewitness accounts recorded in the Bible. See John 20:29 for Jesus' encouragement to those who believe without ever having seen him.

2:4 "God also testifying with them" continues the thought from 2:3. Those who had heard Jesus speak and then had passed on his words also had the truth of their words confirmed by "signs and wonders and by various miracles and by gifts of the Holy Spirit." In the book of Acts, miracles and gifts of the Spirit authenticated the gospel wherever it was preached (see Acts 9:31–42; 14:1–20). Paul, who discussed spiritual gifts in Romans 12, 1 Corinthians 12—14, and Ephesians 4, taught that their purpose is to build up the church, making it strong and mature. When we see the gifts of the Spirit in an individual or congregation, we know that God is truly present. As we receive God's gifts, we should thank him for them and put them to use in the church.

2:8–9 God put Jesus in charge of everything, and Jesus revealed himself to us. We do not yet see Jesus reigning on earth, but we can picture him in his heavenly glory. When you are confused by present events and anxious about the future, remember Jesus' true position and authority. He is Lord of all, and one day he will rule on earth as he does now in heaven. This truth can give stability to your decisions day by day.

2:9–10 God's grace to us led Christ to his death. Jesus did not come into the world to gain status or political power, but to suffer and die so that we could have eternal life ("bringing many sons to glory"). If it is difficult for us to identify with Christ's servant attitude, perhaps we need to evaluate our own motives. Are we more interested in power or participation, domination or service, getting or giving?

2:10 How was Jesus made perfect through suffering? Jesus' suffering made him a perfect leader, or pioneer, of our salvation (see the notes on 5:8 and 5:9). Jesus did not need to suffer for his own salvation, because he was God in human form. His perfect obedience (which led him down the road of suffering) demonstrates that he was the complete sacrifice for us. Through suffering, Jesus completed the work necessary for our own salvation. Our suffering can make us more sensitive servants of God. People who have known pain are able to reach out with compassion to others who hurt. If you have suffered, ask God how your experience can be used to help others.

2:11–13 We who have been set apart for God's service, cleansed, and made holy (sanctified) by Jesus now have the same Father he has, so he has made us his brothers and sisters. Various psalms look forward to Christ and his work in the world. Here the writer quotes a portion of Psalm 22, a Messianic psalm. Because God has adopted all believers as his children, Jesus calls them his brothers and sisters.

12 saying,
"I WILL PROCLAIM YOUR NAME TO MY BRETHREN,
IN THE MIDST OF THE CONGREGATION I WILL SING YOUR PRAISE."
13 And again,
"I WILL PUT MY TRUST IN HIM."
And again,
"BEHOLD, I AND THE CHILDREN WHOM GOD HAS GIVEN ME."
14 Therefore, since the children share in flesh and blood, He Himself likewise also
partook of the same, that through death He might render powerless him who had the
power of death, that is, the devil,
15 and might free those who through fear of death were subject to slavery all their lives.
16 For assuredly He does not give help to angels, but He gives help to the descendant
of Abraham.
17 Therefore, He had to be made like His brethren in all things, so that He might become a merciful and faithful high priest in things pertaining to God, to make propitiation for the sins of the people.
18 For since He Himself was tempted in that which He has suffered, He is able to come to the aid of those who are tempted.

2:12 Ps 22:22

2:13 Is 8:17; Is 8:18

2:14 Matt 16:17; John 1:14; 1 Cor 15:54-57; 2 Tim 1:10; John 12:31; 1 John 3:8

2:15 Rom 8:15

2:17 Phil 2:7; Heb 2:14; Heb 4:15f; 5:2; Heb 3:1; 4:14f; 5:5, 10; 6:20; 7:26, 28; 8:1, 3; 9:11; 10:21; Rom 15:17; Heb 5:1; Dan 9:24; 1 John 2:2; 4:10

2:18 Heb 4:15

2. Christ is greater than Moses

Jesus Our High Priest

3 Therefore, holy brethren, partakers of a heavenly calling, consider Jesus, the Apostle and High Priest of our confession;
2 He was faithful to Him who appointed Him, as Moses also was in all His house.
3 For He has been counted worthy of more glory than Moses, by just so much as the
builder of the house has more honor than the house.
4 For every house is built by someone, but the builder of all things is God.

3:1 Acts 1:15; Heb 2:11; 3:12; 10:19; 13:22; Phil 3:14; John 17:3; Heb 2:17; 4:14f; 5:5, 10; 6:20; 7:26, 28; 8:1, 3; 9:11; 10:21; 2 Cor 9:13; Heb 4:14; 10:23

3:2 Ex 40:16; Num 12:7; Heb 3:5

3:3 2 Cor 3:7-11

2:14–15 Jesus had to become human ("flesh and blood") so that he could die and rise again, in order to destroy the devil's power over death (Romans 6:5–11). Only then could Christ deliver those who had lived in constant fear of death, and free them to live for him. When we belong to God, we need not fear death, because we know that death is only the doorway into eternal life (1 Corinthians 15).

2:14–15 Christ's death and resurrection set us free from the fear of death because death has been defeated. Every person must die, but death is not the end; instead, it is the doorway to a new life. All who dread death should have the opportunity to know the hope that Christ's victory brings. How can you share this truth with those close to you?

2:16–17 In the Old Testament, the high priest was the mediator between God and his people. His job was to regularly offer animal sacrifices according to the law and to intercede with God for forgiveness for the people's sins. Jesus Christ is now our high priest. He came to earth as a human being; therefore, he understands our weaknesses and shows mercy to us. He has *once and for all* paid the penalty for our sins by his own sacrificial death (propitiation), and he can be depended on to restore our broken relationship with God. We are released from sin's domination over us when we commit ourselves fully to Christ, trusting completely in what he has done for us (see the note on 4:14 for more about Jesus as the great high priest).

2:18 Knowing that Christ suffered pain and faced temptation helps us face our trials. Jesus understands our struggles because he faced them as a human being. We can trust Christ to help us survive suffering and overcome temptation. When you face trials, go to Jesus for strength and patience. He understands your needs and is able to help (see 4:14–16).

3:1 This verse would have been especially meaningful to Jewish Christians. For Jews, the highest human authority was the high priest. For Christians, the highest human authorities were God's apostles. Jesus, God's Apostle (meaning "one who is sent") and High Priest, is the ultimate authority in the church.

3:1–6 The author uses different pictures to explain Jesus' relationship to believers: he is (1) the Apostle ("one who is sent") of God, to whom we should listen; (2) our High Priest, through whom we come to God the Father; and (3) the ruler of God's house ("faithful to Him . . . in all His house"), whom we should obey. The Bible is filled with different names for and pictures of Jesus Christ, and each one reveals something more about his nature and ministry. What do these images teach you about your relationship with Christ?

3:2–3 To the Jewish people, Moses was a great hero; he had led their ancestors, the Israelites, from Egyptian bondage to the border of the promised land. He also had written the first five books of the Old Testament, and he was the prophet through whom God had given the Law; therefore, Moses was the greatest prophet in the Scriptures. But Jesus is worthy of greater honor as the central figure of faith than Moses, who was merely a human servant. Jesus is more than human; he is God himself (1:3). As Moses led the people of Israel out of Egyptian bondage, so Christ leads us out of sin's slavery. Why settle for Moses, the author of Hebrews asks, when you can have Jesus Christ, who appointed Moses?

5 Now Moses was faithful in all His house as a servant, for a testimony of those things
which were to be spoken later;
6 but Christ *was faithful* as a Son over His house—whose house we are, if we hold fast
our confidence and the boast of our hope firm until the end.
7 Therefore, just as the Holy Spirit says,
"TODAY IF YOU HEAR HIS VOICE,
8 DO NOT HARDEN YOUR HEARTS AS WHEN THEY PROVOKED ME,
AS IN THE DAY OF TRIAL IN THE WILDERNESS,
9 WHERE YOUR FATHERS TRIED *ME* BY TESTING *ME*,
AND SAW MY WORKS FOR FORTY YEARS.
10 "THEREFORE I WAS ANGRY WITH THIS GENERATION,
AND SAID, 'THEY ALWAYS GO ASTRAY IN THEIR HEART,
AND THEY DID NOT KNOW MY WAYS';
11 AS I SWORE IN MY WRATH,
'THEY SHALL NOT ENTER MY REST.' "

The Peril of Unbelief

12 Take care, brethren, that there not be in any one of you an evil, unbelieving heart
that falls away from the living God.
13 But encourage one another day after day, as long as it is *still* called "Today," so that
none of you will be hardened by the deceitfulness of sin.
14 For we have become partakers of Christ, if we hold fast the beginning of our assurance firm until the end,
15 while it is said,
"TODAY IF YOU HEAR HIS VOICE,
DO NOT HARDEN YOUR HEARTS, AS WHEN THEY PROVOKED ME."
16 For who provoked *Him* when they had heard? Indeed, did not all those who came
out of Egypt *led* by Moses?
17 And with whom was He angry for forty years? Was it not with those who sinned,
whose bodies fell in the wilderness?
18 And to whom did He swear that they would not enter His rest, but to those who
were disobedient?
19 *So* we see that they were not able to enter because of unbelief.

3:5 Heb 3:2; Ex 14:31; Num 12:7; Deut 18:18f; Heb 1:1

3:6 Heb 1:2; 1 Cor 3:16; 1 Tim 3:15; Rom 11:22; Heb 3:14; 4:14; Eph 3:12; Heb 4:16; 10:19, 35; Heb 6:11; 7:19; 10:23

3:7 Acts 28:25; Heb 9:8; 10:15; Ps 95:7; Heb 3:15; 4:7

3:8 Ps 95:8

3:9 Ps 95:9-11; Acts 7:36

3:11 Ps 95:11; Heb 4:3, 5

3:12 Matt 16:16; Heb 9:14; 10:31; 12:22

3:13 Heb 10:24f; Eph 4:22

3:15 Ps 95:7f; Heb 3:7

3:16 Jer 32:29; 44:3, 8; Num 14:2, 11, 30; Deut 1:35, 36, 38

3:17 Num 14:29; 1 Cor 10:5

3:18 Num 14:23; Deut 1:34f; Heb 4:2

3:19 John 3:18, 36; Rom 11:23; Heb 3:12

3:5 Moses was faithful to God's calling not only to deliver Israel but also to prepare the way for the Messiah ("a testimony of those things which were to be spoken later"). All the Old Testament believers also served to prepare the way. Thus, knowing the Old Testament is the best foundation for understanding the New Testament. In reading the Old Testament, we see (1) how God used people to accomplish his purposes, (2) how God used events and personalities to illustrate important truths, (3) how, through prophets, God announced the Messiah, and (4) how, through the system of sacrifices, God prepared people to understand the Messiah's work. If you include the Old Testament in your regular Bible reading, the New Testament will grow clearer and more meaningful to you.

3:6 Because Christ lives in us as believers, we can remain confident and hopeful to the end. We are not saved by being steadfast and firm in our faith, but our courage and hope do reveal that our faith is real. Without this enduring faithfulness, we could easily be blown away by the winds of temptation, false teaching, or persecution. (See also 3:14.)

3:7–15 In many places, the Bible warns us not to "harden" our hearts. This means stubbornly setting ourselves against God so that we are no longer able to turn to him for forgiveness. The Israelites became hardhearted when they disobeyed God's command to conquer the promised land (here called "when they provoked Me," see Numbers 13; 14; 20; and Psalm 95). Be careful to obey God's Word, and do not allow your heart to become hardened.

3:11 God's *rest* has several meanings in Scripture: (1) the seventh day of creation and the weekly Sabbath commemorating it (Genesis 2:2; Hebrews 4:4–9); (2) the promised land of Canaan (Deuteronomy 12:8–12; Psalm 95); (3) peace with God now because of our relationship with Christ through faith (Matthew 12:28; Hebrews 4:1, 3, 8–11); and (4) our future eternal life with Christ (Hebrews 4:8–11). All of these meanings were probably familiar to the Jewish Christian readers of Hebrews.

3:12–14 Our hearts turn away from the living God when we stubbornly refuse to believe him. If we persist in our unbelief, God will eventually leave us alone in our sin. But God can give us new hearts, new desires, and new spirits (Ezekiel 36:22–27). To prevent having an unbelieving heart, stay in fellowship with other believers, talk daily about your mutual faith, be aware of the deceitfulness of sin (it attracts but also destroys), and encourage each other with love and concern.

3:15–19 The Israelites failed to enter the promised land because they did not believe in God's protection, and they did not believe that God would help them conquer the giants in the land (see Numbers 14; 15). So God sent them into the wilderness to wander for 40 years. This was an unhappy alternative to the wonderful gift he had planned for them. Lack of trust in God always prevents us from receiving his best.

The Believer's Rest

4 Therefore, let us fear if, while a promise remains of entering His rest, any one of you
may seem to have come short of it.
2 For indeed we have had good news preached to us, just as they also; but the word
they heard did not profit them, because it was not united by faith in those who heard.
3 For we who have believed enter that rest, just as He has said,
"AS I SWORE IN MY WRATH,
THEY SHALL NOT ENTER MY REST,"
although His works were finished from the foundation of the world.
4 For He has said somewhere concerning the seventh *day:* "AND GOD RESTED ON THE
SEVENTH DAY FROM ALL HIS WORKS";
5 and again in this *passage*, "THEY SHALL NOT ENTER MY REST."
6 Therefore, since it remains for some to enter it, and those who formerly had good
news preached to them failed to enter because of disobedience,
7 He again fixes a certain day, "Today," saying through David after so long a time just
as has been said before,
"TODAY IF YOU HEAR HIS VOICE,
DO NOT HARDEN YOUR HEARTS."
8 For if Joshua had given them rest, He would not have spoken of another day after
that.
9 So there remains a Sabbath rest for the people of God.
10 For the one who has entered His rest has himself also rested from his works, as God
did from His.
11 Therefore let us be diligent to enter that rest, so that no one will fall, through *following* the same example of disobedience.
12 For the word of God is living and active and sharper than any two-edged sword, and
piercing as far as the division of soul and spirit, of both joints and marrow, and able to
judge the thoughts and intentions of the heart.
13 And there is no creature hidden from His sight, but all things are open and laid bare
to the eyes of Him with whom we have to do.

4:1 2 Cor 6:1; Gal 5:4; Heb 12:15
4:2 Rom 10:17; Gal 3:2; 1 Thess 2:13
4:3 Ps 95:11; Heb 3:11; Matt 25:34
4:4 Heb 2:6; Gen 2:2; Ex 20:11; 31:17
4:5 Ps 95:11; Heb 3:11
4:6 Heb 3:18; 4:11
4:7 Heb 3:7f; Ps 95:7f
4:8 Josh 22:4
4:10 Rev 14:13; Gen 2:2; Heb 4:4
4:11 2 Pet 2:6; Heb 3:18; 4:6
4:12 Jer 23:29; Eph 5:26; Heb 6:5; 1 Pet 1:23; Acts 7:38; 1 Thess 2:13; Eph 6:17; 1 Thess 5:23; John 12:48; 1 Cor 14:24f
4:13 2 Chr 16:9; Ps 33:13-15; Job 26:6

4:1–3 Some of the Jewish Christians who received this letter may have been on the verge of turning back from their promised rest in Christ, just as the people in Moses' day had turned back from the promised land. In both cases, the difficulties of the present moment overshadowed the reality of God's promise, and the people doubted that God would fulfill his promises. When we trust our own efforts instead of Christ's power, we too are in danger of turning back. Our own efforts are never adequate; only Christ can see us through.

4:2 The Israelites of Moses' day illustrate a problem facing many who fill our churches today. They know a great deal about Christ, but they do not know him personally—they don't combine their knowledge with faith. Let the Good News about Christ benefit your life. Believe in him and then act on what you know. Trust in Christ and do what he says.

4:4 God rested on the seventh day, not because he was tired, but to indicate the completion of creation. The world was perfect, and God was well satisfied with it. This rest is a foretaste of our eternal joy when creation will be renewed and restored, every mark of sin will be removed, and the world will be made perfect again. Our Sabbath-rest in Christ begins when we trust him to complete his good and perfect work in us (see the note on 3:11).

4:6–7 God had given the Israelites the opportunity to enter Canaan, but they disobeyed and failed to enter (Numbers 13; 14). Now God offers us the opportunity to enter his ultimate place of rest—he invites us to come to Christ. To enter his rest, you must believe that God has this relationship in mind for you; you must stop trying to create it; you must trust in Christ for it; and you must determine to obey him. *Today* is the best time to find peace with God. Tomorrow may be too late.

4:8–11 God wants us to enter his rest. For the Israelites of Moses' time, this rest was the earthly rest to be found in the promised land. For Christians, it is peace with God now and eternal life on a new earth later. We do not need to wait for the next life to enjoy God's rest and peace; we may have it daily now! Our daily rest in the Lord will not end with death, but will become an eternal rest in the place that Christ is preparing for us (John 14:1–4).

4:11 If Jesus has provided for our rest through faith, why must we "be diligent to enter that rest"? This is not the struggle of doing good in order to appreciate and benefit from salvation, nor is it a mystical struggle to overcome selfishness. It refers to making every effort to obtain what God has already provided. Salvation is not to be taken for granted; to appropriate the gift God offers requires decision and commitment.

4:12 The Word of God is not simply a collection of words from God, a vehicle for communicating ideas; it is living, life-changing, and dynamic as it works in us. With the incisiveness of a surgeon's knife, God's Word reveals who we are and what we are not. It penetrates the core of our moral and spiritual life. It discerns what is within us, both good and evil. The demands of God's Word require decisions. We must not only listen to the Word; we must also let it shape our lives.

4:13 Nothing can be hidden from God. He knows about everyone everywhere, and everything about us is wide open to his all-seeing eyes. God sees all we do and knows all we think. Even when we are unaware of his presence, he is there. When we try to hide from him, he sees us. We can have no secrets from God. It is comforting to realize that although God knows us intimately, he still loves us.

4:14 Heb 2:17; Eph 4:10; Heb 6:20; 8:1; 9:24; Matt 4:3; Heb 1:2; 6:6; 7:3; 10:29
4:15 Heb 2:17; 2 Cor 5:21; Heb 7:26
4:16 Heb 7:19; Heb 3:6
5:1 Ex 28:1; Heb 2:17; Heb 7:27; 8:3f; 9:9; 10:11; 1 Cor 15:3
5:2 Heb 2:18; 4:15; Eph 4:18; Heb 9:7; James 5:19; 1 Pet 2:25; Heb 7:28
5:3 1 Cor 15:3; Heb 7:27; 10:12; Lev 9:7
5:4 Num 16:40; 18:7; 2 Chr 26:18; Ex 28:1; 1 Chr 23:13
5:5 John 8:54; Heb 2:17; 5:10; Heb 1:1, 5; Ps 2:7
5:6 Ps 110:4; Heb 7:17

3. Christ is greater than the Old Testament priesthood

14 Therefore, since we have a great high priest who has passed through the heavens,
Jesus the Son of God, let us hold fast our confession.
15 For we do not have a high priest who cannot sympathize with our weaknesses, but
One who has been tempted in all things as *we are, yet* without sin.
16 Therefore let us draw near with confidence to the throne of grace, so that we may
receive mercy and find grace to help in time of need.

The Perfect High Priest

5 For every high priest taken from among men is appointed on behalf of men in things
pertaining to God, in order to offer both gifts and sacrifices for sins;
2 he can deal gently with the ignorant and misguided, since he himself also is beset
with weakness;
3 and because of it he is obligated to offer *sacrifices* for sins, as for the people, so also
for himself.
4 And no one takes the honor to himself, but *receives it* when he is called by God, even
as Aaron was.
5 So also Christ did not glorify Himself so as to become a high priest, but He who said
to Him,
"YOU ARE MY SON,
TODAY I HAVE BEGOTTEN YOU";
6 just as He says also in another *passage,*
"YOU ARE A PRIEST FOREVER
ACCORDING TO THE ORDER OF MELCHIZEDEK."

THE CHOICES OF MATURITY
One way to evaluate spiritual maturity is by looking at the choices we make. The writer of Hebrews notes many of the ways those choices change with personal growth.

Mature choices	*Versus*	*Immature choices*
Teaching others	rather than . . .	just being taught.
Developing depth of understanding	rather than . . .	struggling with the basics.
Self-evaluation	rather than . . .	self-criticism.
Seeking unity	rather than . . .	promoting disunity.
Desiring spiritual challenges	rather than . . .	desiring entertainment.
Careful study and observation	rather than . . .	opinions and half-hearted efforts.
Active faith	rather than . . .	cautious apathy and doubt.
Confidence	rather than . . .	fear.
Feelings and experiences evaluated in the light of God's Word	rather than . . .	experiences evaluated according to feelings.

4:14 Christ is superior to the priests, and his priesthood is superior to their priesthood. To the Jews, the high priest was the highest religious authority in the land. He alone entered the holy of holies in the temple once a year to make atonement for the sins of the whole nation (Leviticus 16). Like the high priest, Jesus mediates between God and us. As humanity's representative, he intercedes for us before God. As God's representative, he assures us of God's forgiveness. Jesus has more authority than the Jewish high priests because he is truly God and truly man. Unlike the high priest who could go before God only once a year, Christ is always at God's right hand, interceding for us. He is always available to hear us when we pray.

4:15 Jesus is like us because he experienced a full range of temptations throughout his life as a human being. We can be comforted knowing that Jesus faced temptation—he can sympathize with us. We can be encouraged knowing that Jesus faced temptation without giving in to sin. He shows us that we do not have to sin when facing the seductive lure of temptation. Jesus is the only perfect human being who has ever lived.

4:16 Prayer is our approach to God, and we are to come "with confidence." Some Christians approach God meekly with heads hung low, afraid to ask him to meet their needs. Others pray flippantly, giving little thought to what they say. Come with reverence because he is your King. But also come with bold assurance because he is your Friend and Counselor.

5:4–6 This chapter stresses both Christ's divine appointment and his humanity. The writer uses two Old Testament verses to show Christ's divine appointment—Psalms 2:7 and 110:4. At the time this book was written, the Romans selected the high priest in Jerusalem. In the Old Testament, however, God chose Aaron, and only Aaron's descendants could be high priests. Christ, like Aaron, was chosen and called by God.

5:6 Melchizedek was a priest of Salem (now called Jerusalem). His Profile is found in Genesis 16. Melchizedek's position is explained in Hebrews 7.

7 In the days of His flesh, He offered up both prayers and supplications with loud
crying and tears to the One able to save Him from death, and He was heard because of
His piety.
8 Although He was a Son, He learned obedience from the things which He suffered.
9 And having been made perfect, He became to all those who obey Him the source of
eternal salvation,
10 being designated by God as a high priest according to the order of Melchizedek.
11 Concerning [3]him we have much to say, and *it is* hard to explain, since you have become dull of hearing.
12 For though by this time you ought to be teachers, you have need again for someone
to teach you the elementary principles of the oracles of God, and you have come to need
milk and not solid food.
13 For everyone who partakes *only* of milk is not accustomed to the word of righteousness, for he is an infant.
14 But solid food is for the mature, who because of practice have their senses trained
to discern good and evil.

5:7 Matt 26:39, 42, 44; Mark 14:36, 39; Luke 22:41, 44; Matt 27:46, 50; Mark 15:34, 37
5:8 Heb 1:2; Phil 2:8
5:9 Heb 2:10
5:10 Heb 2:17; 5:5
5:12 Gal 4:3; Heb 6:1; Acts 7:38; 1 Cor 3:2; 1 Pet 2:2
5:13 1 Cor 3:1; 14:20; 1 Pet 2:2
5:14 1 Cor 2:6; 1 Tim 4:7; Rom 14:1ff

The Peril of Falling Away

6 Therefore leaving the elementary teaching about the Christ, let us press on to maturity, not laying again a foundation of repentance from dead works and of faith toward God,
2 of instruction about washings and laying on of hands, and the resurrection of the
dead and eternal judgment.
3 And this we will do, if God permits.
4 For in the case of those who have once been enlightened and have tasted of the
heavenly gift and have been made partakers of the Holy Spirit,
5 and have tasted the good word of God and the powers of the age to come,

3 Lit *whom* or *which*

6:1 Phil 3:13f; Heb 9:14
6:2 John 3:25; Acts 19:3f; Acts 6:6
6:3 Acts 18:21
6:4 2 Cor 4:4, 6; Heb 10:32; John 4:10; Eph 2:8; Gal 3:2
6:5 1 Pet 2:3; Eph 6:17

5:7 Jesus was in great agony as he prepared to face death (Luke 22:41–44). Although Jesus cried out to God, asking to be delivered, he was prepared to suffer humiliation, separation from his Father, and death in order to do God's will. At times we will undergo trials, not because we want to suffer, but because we want to obey God. Let Jesus' obedience sustain and encourage you in times of trial. You will be able to face anything if you know that Jesus Christ is with you.

5:7 Have you ever felt that God didn't hear your prayers? Be sure you are praying with reverent submission (piety), willing to do what God wants. God responds to his obedient children.

5:8 Jesus' human life was not a script that he passively followed. It was a life that he chose freely (John 10:17–18). It was a continuous process of making the will of God the Father his own. Jesus chose to obey, even though obedience led to suffering and death. Because Jesus obeyed perfectly, even under great trial, he can help us obey, no matter how difficult obedience seems to be.

5:9 Christ was always morally perfect. By obeying, he demonstrated his perfection to us, not to God or to himself. In the Bible, *perfection* usually means completeness or maturity. By sharing our experience of suffering, Christ shared our human experience completely. He is now able to offer eternal salvation to those who obey him. See Philippians 2:5–11 for Christ's attitude as he took on human form.

5:12–13 These Jewish Christians were immature. Some of them should have been teaching others, but they had not even applied the basics to their own lives. They were reluctant to move beyond age-old traditions, established doctrines, and discussion of the basics. They wouldn't be able to understand the high-priestly role of Christ unless they moved out of their comfortable position, cut some of their Jewish ties, and stopped trying to blend in with their culture. Commitment to Christ moves people out of their comfort zones.

5:12–14 In order to grow from infant Christians to mature Christians, we must learn discernment. We must train our consciences, our senses, our minds, and our bodies to distinguish good from evil. Can you recognize temptation before it traps you? Can you tell the difference between a correct use of Scripture and a mistaken one?

5:14 Our capacity to feast on deeper knowledge of God ("solid food") is determined by our spiritual growth. Too often we want God's banquet before we are spiritually capable of digesting it. As you grow in the Lord and put into practice what you have learned, your capacity to understand will also grow.

6:1–2 Certain elementary teachings are essential for all believers to understand. Those basics include the importance of faith, the foolishness of trying to be saved by good deeds, the meaning of baptism and spiritual gifts, and the facts of resurrection and eternal life. To go on to maturity in our understanding, we need to move beyond (but not away from) the elementary teachings to a more complete understanding of the faith. And this is what the author intends for them to do (6:3). Mature Christians should be teaching new Christians the basics. Then, acting on what they know, the mature will learn even more from God's Word.

6:3 These Christians needed to move beyond the basics of their faith to an understanding of Christ as the perfect high priest and the fulfillment of all the Old Testament prophecies. Rather than arguing about the respective merits of Judaism and Christianity, they needed to depend on Christ and live effectively for him.

6:4–6 In the first century, a pagan who investigated Christianity and then went back to paganism made a clean break with the church. But for Jewish Christians who decided to return to Judaism, the break was less obvious. Their life-style remained relatively unchanged. But by deliberately turning away from Christ, they were cutting themselves off from God's forgiveness. Those who persevere in believing are true saints; those who continue to reject Christ are unbelievers, no matter how well they behave.

6:6 Matt 19:26; Heb 10:26f; 2 Pet 2:21; 1 John 5:16; Heb 10:29

6:7 2 Tim 2:6

6 and *then* have fallen away, it is impossible to renew them again to repentance, since
they again crucify to themselves the Son of God and put Him to open shame.
7 For ground that drinks the rain which often falls on it and brings forth vegetation
useful to those for whose sake it is also tilled, receives a blessing from God;

ABRAHAM IN THE NEW TESTAMENT

Abraham was an ancestor of Jesus Christ	Matthew 1:1–2, 17 Luke 3:23–24	Jesus Christ was human; he was born into the line of Abraham, whom God had chosen to be the father of a great nation through which the whole world would be blessed. We are blessed because of what Jesus Christ, Abraham's descendant, did for us.
Abraham was the father of the Jewish nation	Matthew 3:9 Luke 3:8 Acts 13:26 Romans 4:1; 11:1 2 Corinthians 11:22 Hebrews 6:13–14	God wanted to set apart a nation for himself, a nation that would tell the world about him. He began with a man of faith who, though old and childless, believed God's promise of innumerable descendants. We can trust God to do the impossible when we have faith.
Abraham, because of his faith, now sits in the kingdom with Christ.	Matthew 8:11 Luke 13:28 Luke 16:23–31	Abraham followed God, and now he is enjoying his reward—eternity with God. We will one day meet Abraham, because we have been promised eternity as well.
God *is* Abraham's God; thus Abraham is alive with God	Matthew 22:32 Mark 12:26 Luke 20:37 Acts 7:32	As Abraham lives forever, we will live forever, because we, like Abraham, have chosen the life of faith.
Abraham received great promises from God	Luke 1:55, 72–73 Acts 3:25; 7:17–18; Galatians 3:6, 14–16 Hebrews 6:13–15	Many of the promises God made to Abraham seemed impossible to be realized, but Abraham trusted God. The promises to believers in God's Word also seem too incredible to believe, but we can trust God to keep all his promises.
Abraham followed God	Acts 7:2–8 Hebrews 11:8, 17–19	Abraham followed God's leading from his homeland to an unknown territory, which became the Jews' promised land. When we follow God, even before he makes all his plans clear to us, we will never be disappointed.
God blessed Abraham because of his faith	Romans 4 Galatians 3:6–9, 14–29; Hebrews 11:8, 17–19 James 2:21–24	Abraham showed faith in times of disappointment, trial, and testing. Because of Abraham's faith, God counted him righteous and called him his "friend." God accepts us because of our faith.
Abraham is the father of all those who come to God by faith	Romans 9:6–8 Galatians 3:6–9, 14–29	The Jews are Abraham's children, and Christ was his descendant. We are Christ's brothers and sisters; thus all believers are Abraham's children and God's children. Abraham was righteous because of his faith; we are made righteous through faith in Christ. The promises made to Abraham apply to us because of Christ.

6:6 This verse points to the danger of the Hebrew Christians returning to Judaism and thus committing apostasy. Some apply this verse today to superficial believers who renounce their Christianity, or to unbelievers who come close to salvation and then turn away. Either way, those who reject Christ will not be saved. Christ died once for all. He will not be crucified again. Apart from his cross, there is no other possible way of salvation. However, the author does not indicate that his readers were in danger of renouncing Christ (see 6:9). He is warning against hardness of heart that would make repentance inconceivable for the sinner.

6:7–8 Land that produces a good crop receives loving care, but land that produces thorns and thistles has to be burned so the farmer can start over. An unproductive Christian life falls under God's condemnation. We are not saved by deeds or conduct, but what we do is the *evidence* of our faith.

8 but if it yields thorns and thistles, it is worthless and close to being cursed, and it
ends up being burned.

Better Things for You

9 But, beloved, we are convinced of better things concerning you, and things that
accompany salvation, though we are speaking in this way.
10 For God is not unjust so as to forget your work and the love which you have shown
toward His name, in having ministered and in still ministering to the saints.
11 And we desire that each one of you show the same diligence so as to realize the full
assurance of hope until the end,
12 so that you will not be sluggish, but imitators of those who through faith and patience inherit the promises.
13 For when God made the promise to Abraham, since He could swear by no one greater, He swore by Himself,
14 saying, "I WILL SURELY BLESS YOU AND I WILL SURELY MULTIPLY YOU."
15 And so, having patiently waited, he obtained the promise.
16 For men swear by one greater *than themselves*, and with them an oath *given* as confirmation is an end of every dispute.
17 In the same way God, desiring even more to show to the heirs of the promise the
unchangeableness of His purpose, interposed with an oath,
18 so that by two unchangeable things in which it is impossible for God to lie, we
who have taken refuge would have strong encouragement to take hold of the hope set
before us.
19 This hope we have as an anchor of the soul, a *hope* both sure and steadfast and one
which enters within the veil,
20 where Jesus has entered as a forerunner for us, having become a high priest forever
according to the order of Melchizedek.

Melchizedek's Priesthood Like Christ's

7 For this Melchizedek, king of Salem, priest of the Most High God, who met Abraham as he was returning from the slaughter of the kings and blessed him,
2 to whom also Abraham apportioned a tenth part of all *the spoils*, was first of all, by
the translation *of his name*, king of righteousness, and then also king of Salem, which is
king of peace.
3 Without father, without mother, without genealogy, having neither beginning of days
nor end of life, but made like the Son of God, he remains a priest perpetually.

6:8 Gen 3:17f

6:9 1 Cor 10:14; 2 Cor 7:1; 12:19; 1 Pet 2:11; 2 Pet 3:1; 1 John 2:7; Jude 3

6:10 Acts 10:4; 1 Thess 1:3; Rom 15:25; Heb 10:32-34

6:11 Heb 10:22; Heb 3:6

6:12 Heb 13:7; 2 Thess 1:4; James 1:3; Rev 13:10; Heb 1:14

6:13 Gal 3:15, 18; Gen 22:16; Luke 1:73

6:14 Gen 22:17

6:15 Gen 12:4; 21:5

6:16 Gal 3:15; Ex 22:11

6:17 Prov 19:21; Heb 6:18

6:18 Num 23:19; Titus 1:2; Heb 3:6; 7:19

6:19 Ps 39:7; 62:5; Acts 23:6; Rom 4:18; 5:4, 5; 1 Cor 13:13; Col 1:27; 1 Pet 1:3; Lev 16:2, 15; Heb 9:3, 7

6:20 John 14:2; Heb 4:14; Ps 110:4; Heb 2:17; 5:6

7:1 Gen 14:18-20; Heb 7:6; Mark 5:7

6:10 It's easy to get discouraged, thinking that God has forgotten us. But God is never unjust. He never forgets or overlooks our hard work for him. Presently you may not be receiving rewards and acclaim, but God knows your efforts of love and ministry. Let God's love for you and his intimate knowledge of your service for him bolster you as you face disappointment and rejection here on earth.

6:11–12 Hope keeps the Christian from becoming lazy or feeling bored. Like an athlete, train hard and run well, remembering the reward that lies ahead (Philippians 3:14).

6:15 Abraham waited patiently—it was 25 years from the time God had promised him a son (Genesis 17:16) to Isaac's birth (Genesis 21:1–3). Because our trials and temptations are often so intense, they seem to last for an eternity. Both the Bible and the testimony of mature Christians encourage us to wait for God to act in his timing, even when our needs seem too great to wait any longer.

6:17 God's promises are unchanging and trustworthy because God is unchanging and trustworthy. When promising Abraham a son, God took an oath in his own name. The oath was as good as God's name, and God's name was as good as his divine nature.

6:18–19 These two unchangeable things are God's nature and his promise. God embodies all truth; therefore, he cannot lie. Because God is truth, you can be secure in his promises; you don't need to wonder if he will change his plans. Our hope is secure and immovable, anchored in God, just as a ship anchor holds firmly to the seabed. To the true seeker who comes to God in belief, God gives an unconditional promise of acceptance. When you ask God with openness, honesty, and sincerity to save you from your sins, *he will do it.* This truth should give you encouragement, assurance, and confidence.

6:19–20 This veil hung across the entrance from the holy place to the holy of holies, the two innermost rooms of the temple. This veil prevented anyone from entering, gazing into, or even getting a fleeting glimpse of the interior of the holy of holies (see also 9:1–8). The high priest could enter there only once a year to stand before God's presence and atone for the sins of the entire nation. But Christ is in God's presence at all times, not just once a year, as the high priest who can continually intercede for us.

7:2ff The writer of Hebrews uses this story from Genesis 14:18–20 to show that Christ is even greater than Abraham, father of the Jewish nation, and Levi (Abraham's descendant). Therefore, the Jewish priesthood (made up of Levi's descendants) was inferior to Melchizedek's priesthood (a type of Christ's priesthood).

7:3–10 Melchizedek was a priest of the Most High God (see the note on Genesis 14:18 and his Profile in Genesis 16). He is said to remain a priest forever (see also Psalm 110:4), because his priesthood has no record of beginning or ending—he was a priest of God in Salem (Jerusalem) long before the nation of Israel and the regular priesthood began.

4 Now observe how great this man was to whom Abraham, the patriarch, gave a tenth
of the choicest spoils.
5 And those indeed of the sons of Levi who receive the priest's office have commandment in the Law to collect a tenth from the people, that is, from their brethren, although
these are descended from Abraham.
6 But the one whose genealogy is not traced from them collected a tenth from Abraham and blessed the one who had the promises.
7 But without any dispute the lesser is blessed by the greater.
8 In this case mortal men receive tithes, but in that case one *receives them*, of whom it
is witnessed that he lives on.
9 And, so to speak, through Abraham even Levi, who received tithes, paid tithes,
10 for he was still in the loins of his father when Melchizedek met him.
11 Now if perfection was through the Levitical priesthood (for on the basis of it the
people received the Law), what further need *was there* for another priest to arise according to the order of Melchizedek, and not be designated according to the order of
Aaron?
12 For when the priesthood is changed, of necessity there takes place a change of law
also.
13 For the one concerning whom these things are spoken belongs to another tribe, from
which no one has officiated at the altar.
14 For it is evident that our Lord was descended from Judah, a tribe with reference to
which Moses spoke nothing concerning priests.
15 And this is clearer still, if another priest arises according to the likeness of Melchizedek,
16 who has become *such* not on the basis of a law of physical requirement, but according to the power of an indestructible life.
17 For it is attested *of Him*,
"YOU ARE A PRIEST FOREVER
ACCORDING TO THE ORDER OF MELCHIZEDEK."
18 For, on the one hand, there is a setting aside of a former commandment because of
its weakness and uselessness
19 (for the Law made nothing perfect), and on the other hand there is a bringing in of
a better hope, through which we draw near to God.
20 And inasmuch as *it was* not without an oath
21 (for they indeed became priests without an oath, but He with an oath through the
One who said to Him,
"THE LORD HAS SWORN
AND WILL NOT CHANGE HIS MIND,
'YOU ARE A PRIEST FOREVER' ");
22 so much the more also Jesus has become the guarantee of a better covenant.
23 The *former* priests, on the one hand, existed in greater numbers because they were
prevented by death from continuing,
24 but Jesus, on the other hand, because He continues forever, holds His priesthood
permanently.

7:4 Acts 2:29; 7:8f; Gen 14:20
7:5 Num 18:21, 26; 2 Chr 31:4f
7:6 Heb 7:3; Heb 7:1f; Rom 4:13
7:8 Heb 5:6; 6:20
7:11 Heb 7:18f; 8:7; Heb 9:6; 10:1; Heb 5:6; 7:17
7:13 Heb 7:14; Heb 7:11
7:14 Num 24:17; Is 11:1; Mic 5:2; Matt 2:6; Rev 5:5
7:16 Heb 9:10; Heb 9:14
7:17 Ps 110:4; Heb 5:6; 6:20; 7:21
7:18 Rom 8:3; Gal 3:21; Heb 7:11
7:19 Acts 13:39; Rom 3:20; 7:7f; Gal 2:16; 3:21; Heb 9:9; 10:1; Heb 3:6; Lam 3:57; Heb 4:16; 7:25; 10:1, 22; James 4:8
7:21 Ps 110:4; Heb 5:6; 7:17; Num 23:19; 1 Sam 15:29; Rom 11:29; Heb 7:23f, 28
7:22 Ps 119:122; Is 38:14; Heb 8:6
7:24 Is 9:7; John 12:34; Rom 9:5; Heb 7:23f, 28

7:7 "The lesser is blessed by the greater" means a person who has the power to bless is always greater than the person that he or she blesses.

7:11–17 Jesus' high-priestly role was superior to that of any priest of Levi, because the Messiah was a priest of a higher order (Psalm 110:4). If the Jewish priests and their laws had been able to save people, why would God need to send Christ as a priest, who came not from the tribe of Levi (the priestly tribe), but from the tribe of Judah? The animal sacrifices had to be repeated, and they offered only temporary forgiveness; but Christ's sacrifice was offered once, and it offers total and permanent forgiveness. Under the new covenant, the Levitical priesthood was canceled in favor of Christ's role as high priest. Because Christ is our high priest, we need to pay attention to him. No minister, leader, or Christian friend can substitute for Christ's work and for his role in our salvation.

7:18–19 The law was not intended to save people, but to point out sin (see Romans 3:20; 5:20) and to point toward Christ (see Galatians 3:24–25). Salvation comes through Christ, whose sacrifice brings forgiveness for our sins. Being ethical, working diligently to help others, and giving to charitable causes are all commendable, but all of our good deeds cannot save us or make us right with God. There is a "better hope."

7:22–24 This "better covenant" is also called the new covenant or testament. It is new and better because it allows us to go directly to God through Christ. We no longer need to rely on sacrificed animals and mediating priests to obtain God's forgiveness. This new covenant is better because, while all human priests die, Christ lives forever. Priests and sacrifices could not save people, but Christ truly saves. You have access to Christ. He is available to you, but do you go to him with your needs?

25 Therefore He is able also to save forever those who draw near to God through Him,
since He always lives to make intercession for them.
26 For it was fitting for us to have such a high priest, holy, innocent, undefiled, separated from sinners and exalted above the heavens;
27 who does not need daily, like those high priests, to offer up sacrifices, first for His
own sins and then for the *sins* of the people, because this He did once for all when He
offered up Himself.
28 For the Law appoints men as high priests who are weak, but the word of the oath,
which came after the Law, *appoints* a Son, made perfect forever.

4. The new covenant is greater than the old

A Better Ministry

8 Now the main point in what has been said *is this:* we have such a high priest, who has
taken His seat at the right hand of the throne of the Majesty in the heavens,
2 a minister in the sanctuary and in the true tabernacle, which the Lord pitched, not
man.
3 For every high priest is appointed to offer both gifts and sacrifices; so it is necessary
that this *high priest* also have something to offer.
4 Now if He were on earth, He would not be a priest at all, since there are those who
offer the gifts according to the Law;
5 who serve a copy and shadow of the heavenly things, just as Moses was warned *by
God* when he was about to erect the tabernacle; for, "SEE," He says, "THAT YOU MAKE
all things ACCORDING TO THE PATTERN WHICH WAS SHOWN YOU ON THE MOUNTAIN."
6 But now He has obtained a more excellent ministry, by as much as He is also the
mediator of a better covenant, which has been enacted on better promises.

A New Covenant

7 For if that first *covenant* had been faultless, there would have been no occasion sought
for a second.
8 For finding fault with them, He says,
"BEHOLD, DAYS ARE COMING, SAYS THE LORD,

7:25 1 Cor 1:21; Heb 7:19; Rom 8:34; Heb 9:24

7:26 Heb 2:17; 1 Pet 2:22; Heb 4:14

7:27 Lev 9:7; Heb 5:3; Eph 5:2; Heb 9:14, 28; 10:10, 12

7:28 Heb 5:2; Heb 1:2

8:1 Col 3:1; Heb 2:17; 3:1; Ps 110:1; Heb 1:3

8:2 Heb 10:11; Heb 9:11, 24; Ex 33:7

8:3 Heb 2:17; Rom 4:25; 5:6, 8; Gal 2:20; Eph 5:2; Heb 5:1; 8:4

8:4 Heb 5:1; 7:27; 8:3; 9:9; 10:11

8:5 Heb 9:23; Col 2:17; Heb 10:1; Matt 2:12; Heb 11:7; 12:25; Ex 25:40

8:6 1 Tim 2:5; Luke 22:20; Heb 7:22; 8:8; 9:15; 12:24

8:8 Jer 31:31; Luke 22:20; 2 Cor 3:6

7:25 No one can add to what Jesus did to save us; our past, present, and future sins are all forgiven, and Jesus is with the Father as a sign that our sins are forgiven. If you are a Christian, remember that Christ has paid the price for your sins once and for all. (See also 9:24–28.)

7:25 As our high priest, Christ is our advocate, the mediator between us and God. He looks after our interests and intercedes for us with God. The Old Testament high priest went before God once a year to plead for the forgiveness of the nation's sins; Christ makes perpetual intercession before God for us. Christ's continuous presence in heaven with the Father assures us that our sins have been paid for and forgiven (see Romans 8:33–34; Hebrews 2:17–18; 4:15–16; 9:24). This wonderful assurance frees us from guilt and from fear of failure.

7:27 In Old Testament times when animals were sacrificed, they were cut into pieces, the parts were washed, the fat was burned, the blood was sprinkled, and the meat was boiled. Blood was demanded as atonement for sins, and God accepted animal blood to cover the people's sins (Leviticus 17:11). Because of the sacrificial system, the Israelites were generally aware that sin costs someone something and that they themselves were sinful. Many people take Christ's work on the cross for granted. They don't realize how costly it was for Jesus to secure our forgiveness—it cost him his life and painful, temporary separation from his Father (Matthew 27:46; 1 Peter 1:18–19).

7:27 Because Jesus died *once for all,* he brought the sacrificial system to an end. He forgave sins—past, present, and future. The Jews did not need to go back to the old system because Christ, the perfect sacrifice, completed the work of redemption. You don't have to look for another way to have your sins forgiven—Christ was the final sacrifice for you.

7:28 As we better understand the Jewish sacrificial system, we see that Jesus' death served as the perfect atonement for our sins. His death brings us eternal life. How callous, how cold, how stubborn it would be to refuse God's greatest gift.

8:4 Under the old Jewish system, priests were chosen only from the tribe of Levi, and sacrifices were offered daily on the altar for forgiveness of sins (see 7:12–14). This system would not have allowed Jesus to be a priest, because he was from the tribe of Judah. But his perfect sacrifice ended all need for further priests and sacrifices.

The use of the present tense, "there are those who offer the gifts" indicates that this book was written before A.D. 70 when the temple in Jerusalem was destroyed, ending the sacrifices.

8:5 The pattern for the tabernacle built by Moses was given by God. It was a pattern of the spiritual reality of Christ's sacrifice, and thus it looked forward to the future reality. There is no tabernacle in heaven of which the earthly one is a copy, but rather the earthly tabernacle was an expression of eternal, theological principles. Because the temple at Jerusalem had not yet been destroyed, using the worship system there as an example would have had a great impact on this original audience.

8:8–12 This passage is a quotation of Jeremiah 31:31–34, which compares the new covenant with the old. The old covenant was the covenant of law between God and Israel. The new and better way is the covenant of grace—Christ's offer to forgive our sins and bring us to God through his sacrificial death. This covenant is new in extent—it goes beyond Israel and Judah to include all the Gentile nations. It is new in application because it is written on our hearts and in our minds. It offers a new way to forgiveness, not through animal sacrifice but through faith. Have you entered into this new covenant and begun walking in the better way?

WHEN I WILL EFFECT A NEW COVENANT
WITH THE HOUSE OF ISRAEL AND WITH THE HOUSE OF JUDAH;
9 NOT LIKE THE COVENANT WHICH I MADE WITH THEIR FATHERS
ON THE DAY WHEN I TOOK THEM BY THE HAND
TO LEAD THEM OUT OF THE LAND OF EGYPT;
FOR THEY DID NOT CONTINUE IN MY COVENANT,
AND I DID NOT CARE FOR THEM, SAYS THE LORD.
10 "FOR THIS IS THE COVENANT THAT I WILL MAKE WITH THE HOUSE OF ISRAEL
AFTER THOSE DAYS, SAYS THE LORD:
I WILL PUT MY LAWS INTO THEIR MINDS,
AND I WILL WRITE THEM ON THEIR HEARTS.
AND I WILL BE THEIR GOD,
AND THEY SHALL BE MY PEOPLE.
11 "AND THEY SHALL NOT TEACH EVERYONE HIS FELLOW CITIZEN,
AND EVERYONE HIS BROTHER, SAYING, 'KNOW THE LORD,'
FOR ALL WILL KNOW ME,
FROM THE LEAST TO THE GREATEST OF THEM.
12 "FOR I WILL BE MERCIFUL TO THEIR INIQUITIES,
AND I WILL REMEMBER THEIR SINS NO MORE."
13 When He said, "A new *covenant*," He has made the first obsolete. But whatever is
becoming obsolete and growing old is ready to disappear.

8:9 Ex 19:5; 24:6-8; Deut 5:2, 3; Jer 31:32

8:10 Jer 31:33; Rom 11:27; Heb 10:16; 2 Cor 3:3

8:11 Jer 31:34; Is 54:13; John 6:45; 1 John 2:27

8:12 Is 43:25; Jer 31:34; 50:20; Mic 7:18, 19; Heb 10:17

8:13 Luke 22:20; 2 Cor 3:6; Heb 7:22; 8:6, 8; 9:15; 12:24; 2 Cor 5:17; Heb 1:11

The Old and New Covenants

Like pointing out the similarities and differences between the photograph of a person and the actual person, the writer of Hebrews shows the connection between the old Mosaic covenant and the new Messianic covenant. He proves that the old covenant was a shadow of the real Christ.

Reference	*The Old Covenant under Moses*	*The New Covenant in Christ*	*Application*
8:3-4	Gifts and sacrifices by those guilty of sin	Self-sacrifice by the guiltless Christ	Christ died for you
8:5-6; 10-12	Focused on a physical building where one goes to worship	Focuses on the reign of Christ in believers' hearts	God is directly involved in your life
8:5-6; 10-12	A shadow	A reality	Not temporal, but eternal
8:6	Limited promises	Limitless promises	We can trust God's promises to us
8:8-9	Failed agreement by people	Faithful agreement by Christ	Christ has kept the agreement where people couldn't
9:1	External standards and rules	Internal standards—a new heart	God sees both actions and motives—we are accountable to God, not rules
9:7	Limited access to God	Unlimited access to God	God is personally available
9:9-10	Legal cleansing	Personal cleansing	God's cleansing is complete
9:11-14; 24-28	Continual sacrifice	Conclusive sacrifice	Christ's sacrifice was perfect and final
9:22	Forgiveness earned	Forgiveness freely given	We have true and complete forgiveness
9:24-28	Repeated yearly	Completed by Christ's death	Christ's death can be applied to your sin
9:26	Available to some	Available to all	Available to you

8:10 If our hearts are not changed, following God's rules will be unpleasant and difficult. We will rebel against being told how to live. The Holy Spirit, however, gives us new desires, helping us *want* to obey God (see Philippians 2:12–13). With new hearts, we find that serving God is our greatest joy.

8:10–11 Under God's new covenant, God's Law is inside us. It is no longer an external set of rules and principles. The Holy Spirit reminds us of Christ's words, activates our consciences, influences our motives and desires, and makes us want to obey. Now doing God's will is something we desire with all our heart and mind.

The Old and the New

9 Now even the first *covenant* had regulations of divine worship and the earthly sanctuary.

2 For there was a tabernacle prepared, the outer one, in which *were* the lampstand and the table and the sacred bread; this is called the holy place.

3 Behind the second veil there was a tabernacle which is called the Holy of Holies,

4 having a golden altar of incense and the ark of the covenant covered on all sides with gold, in which was a golden jar holding the manna, and Aaron's rod which budded, and the tables of the covenant;

5 and above it *were* the cherubim of glory overshadowing the mercy seat; but of these things we cannot now speak in detail.

6 Now when these things have been so prepared, the priests are continually entering the outer tabernacle performing the divine worship,

7 but into the second, only the high priest *enters* once a year, not without *taking* blood, which he offers for himself and for the sins of the people committed in ignorance.

8 The Holy Spirit *is* signifying this, that the way into the holy place has not yet been disclosed while the outer tabernacle is still standing,

9 which *is* a symbol for the present time. Accordingly both gifts and sacrifices are offered which cannot make the worshiper perfect in conscience,

10 since they *relate* only to food and drink and various washings, regulations for the body imposed until a time of reformation.

11 But when Christ appeared *as* a high priest of the good things [4]to come, *He entered* through the greater and more perfect tabernacle, not made with hands, that is to say, not of this creation;

12 and not through the blood of goats and calves, but through His own blood, He entered the holy place once for all, having obtained eternal redemption.

13 For if the blood of goats and bulls and the ashes of a heifer sprinkling those who have been defiled sanctify for the cleansing of the flesh,

14 how much more will the blood of Christ, who through the eternal Spirit offered Himself without blemish to God, cleanse your conscience from dead works to serve the living God?

15 For this reason He is the mediator of a new covenant, so that, since a death has taken place for the redemption of the transgressions that were *committed* under the first covenant, those who have been called may receive the promise of the eternal inheritance.

16 For where a covenant is, there must of necessity be the death of the one who made it.

17 For a covenant is valid *only* when men are dead, [5]for it is never in force while the one who made it lives.

18 Therefore even the first *covenant* was not inaugurated without blood.

4 Two early mss read *that have come* 5 Two early mss read *for is it then...lives?*

9:1 Heb 9:10; Ex 25:8

9:2 Ex 25:8, 9; 26:1-30; Ex 25:23-29; Lev 24:5ff; Matt 12:4

9:3 Ex 26:31-33; 40:3

9:4 Ex 30:1-5; Ex 25:10ff; 37:1ff; Ex 16:32f; Num 17:10; Ex 31:18; 32:15; Deut 9:9, 11, 15; 10:3-5

9:5 Ex 25:18ff

9:7 Heb 9:3; Lev 16:12ff; Ex 30:10; Lev 16:34; Heb 10:3; Heb 5:3; Num 15:25; Heb 5:2

9:8 Heb 3:7; John 14:6

9:10 Lev 11:2ff; Col 2:16; Num 6:3; Lev 11:25; Num 19:13; Mark 7:4; Heb 7:16

9:11 Heb 2:17; Heb 10:1; 2 Cor 4:18; Heb 12:27; 13:14

9:12 Lev 4:3; 16:6, 15; Heb 9:14; 13:12; Heb 7:27; Heb 5:9

9:13 Lev 16:15; Num 19:9, 17f

9:14 1 Cor 15:45; 1 Pet 3:18; Eph 5:2; Heb 7:27; 10:10, 12; Acts 15:9; Titus 2:14; Heb 1:3; 10:2, 22; Heb 6:1; Matt 16:16; Heb 3:12

9:15 Heb 8:8; Matt 22:3ff; Rom 8:28f; Heb 3:1

9:5 *Cherubim* are mighty angels.

9:6–8 The high priest could enter the holy of holies (9:3; or the "the second," 9:7), the innermost room of the tabernacle, one day each year to atone for the nation's sins. The holy of holies was a small room that contained the ark of the covenant (a gold-covered chest containing the original stone tablets on which the Ten Commandments were written, a jar of manna, and Aaron's staff). The top of the chest served as the "atonement cover" (the altar) on which the blood would be sprinkled by the high priest on the day of atonement. The holy of holies was the most sacred spot on earth for the Jews. Only the high priest could enter—the other priests and the common people were forbidden to come into the room. Their only access to God was through the high priest, who would offer a sacrifice and use the animal's blood to atone first for his own sins and then for the people's sins (see also 10:19).

9:10 The people had to keep the Old Testament dietary laws and ceremonial cleansing laws until Christ came with God's new and better way.

9:12 This imagery comes from the day of atonement rituals described in Leviticus 16. *Redemption* refers to the process of paying the price (ransom) to free a slave. Through his own death, Christ freed us from the slavery of sin forever.

9:12–14 Though you know Christ, you may believe that you have to work hard to make yourself good enough for God. But rules and rituals have never cleansed people's hearts. By Jesus' blood alone (1) we have our consciences cleansed, (2) we are freed from death's sting and can live to serve God, and (3) we are freed from sin's power. If you are carrying a load of guilt because you are finding that you can't be good enough for God, take another look at Jesus' death and what it means for you. Christ can heal your conscience and deliver you from the frustration of trying to earn God's favor.

9:13–14 When the people sacrificed animals, God considered the people's faith and obedience, cleansed them from sin, and made them *ceremonially* acceptable according to Old Testament law. But Christ's sacrifice transforms our lives and hearts and makes us clean on the inside. His sacrifice is infinitely more effective than animal sacrifices. No barrier of sin or weakness on our part can stifle his forgiveness.

9:15 People in Old Testament times were saved through Christ's sacrifice, although that sacrifice had not yet happened. In offering unblemished animal sacrifices, they were anticipating Christ's coming and his death for sin. There was no point in returning to the sacrificial system now that Christ had come and had become the final, perfect sacrifice.

19 For when every commandment had been spoken by Moses to all the people according to the Law, he took the blood of the calves and the goats, with water and scarlet wool
and hyssop, and sprinkled both the book itself and all the people,
20 saying, "THIS IS THE BLOOD OF THE COVENANT WHICH GOD COMMANDED YOU."
21 And in the same way he sprinkled both the tabernacle and all the vessels of the
ministry with the blood.
22 And according to the Law, *one may* almost *say*, all things are cleansed with blood,
and without shedding of blood there is no forgiveness.
23 Therefore it was necessary for the copies of the things in the heavens to be cleansed
with these, but the heavenly things themselves with better sacrifices than these.
24 For Christ did not enter a holy place made with hands, a *mere* copy of the true one,
but into heaven itself, now to appear in the presence of God for us;
25 nor was it that He would offer Himself often, as the high priest enters the holy place
year by year with blood that is not his own.
26 Otherwise, He would have needed to suffer often since the foundation of the world;
but now once at the consummation of the ages He has been manifested to put away sin
by the sacrifice of Himself.
27 And inasmuch as it is appointed for men to die once and after this *comes* judgment,
28 so Christ also, having been offered once to bear the sins of many, will appear a second time for salvation without *reference to* sin, to those who eagerly await Him.

One Sacrifice of Christ Is Sufficient

10 For the Law, since it has *only* a shadow of the good things to come *and* not the
very form of things, [6]can never, by the same sacrifices which they offer continually
year by year, make perfect those who draw near.
2 Otherwise, would they not have ceased to be offered, because the worshipers, having once been cleansed, would no longer have had consciousness of sins?
3 But in those *sacrifices* there is a reminder of sins year by year.
4 For it is impossible for the blood of bulls and goats to take away sins.

6 Two early mss read *they can*

9:19 Heb 1:1 Lev 14:4, 7; Num 19:6, 18; Ex 24:7
9:20 Ex 24:8; Matt 26:28
9:21 Ex 24:6; 40:9; Lev 8:15, 19; 16:14-16
9:22 Lev 5:11f; Lev 17:11
9:23 Heb 8:5
9:24 Heb 4:14; 8:2; Matt 18:10; Heb 7:25
9:26 Matt 25:34; Heb 4:3; Heb 7:27; 9:12; Matt 13:39; Heb 1:2
9:27 Gen 3:19; 2 Cor 5:10; 1 John 4:17
9:28 1 Pet 2:24; Acts 1:11; Heb 5:9; Heb 4:15; 1 Cor 1:7; Titus 2:13
10:1 Heb 8:5; Heb 9:11; Rom 8:3; Heb 7:19
10:2 1 Pet 2:19
10:3 Heb 9:7
10:4 Heb 9:12f

9:22 Why does forgiveness require the shedding of blood? This is no arbitrary decree on the part of a bloodthirsty God, as some have suggested. There is no greater symbol of life than blood; blood keeps us alive. Jesus shed his blood—gave his life—for our sins so that we wouldn't have to experience spiritual death, eternal separation from God. Jesus is the source of life, not death. He gave his own life to pay our penalty for us so that we might live. After shedding his blood for us, Christ rose from the grave and proclaimed victory over sin and death.

9:23 In a way that we don't fully understand, the earthly tabernacle was a copy and symbol of heavenly realities. This cleansing of the heavenly things can best be understood as referring to Christ's spiritual work for us in heaven (see the note on 8:5).

9:24 Among references to priests, tabernacles, sacrifices, and other ideas unfamiliar to us, we come to this description of Christ as our mediator, appearing in God's presence on our behalf. We can relate to this role and be encouraged by it. Christ is on our side at God's side. He is our Lord and Savior. He is not there to convince or remind God that our sins are forgiven, but to present both our needs and our service for him as an offering (see 7:25).

9:24–28 All people die physically, but Christ died so that we would not have to die spiritually. We can have wonderful confidence in his saving work for us, doing away with sin—past, present, and future. He has forgiven our past sin—when he died on the cross, he sacrificed himself once for all (9:26); he has given us the Holy Spirit to help us deal with present sin; he appears for us now in heaven as our high priest (9:24); and he promises to return (9:28) and raise us to eternal life in a world where sin will be banished.

9:26 The "consummation of the ages" refers to the time of Christ's coming to earth in fulfillment of the Old Testament prophecies. Christ ushered in the new era of grace and forgiveness. We are still living in the "consummation of the ages." The day of the Lord has begun and will be completed at Christ's return.

10:3 When people gathered for the offering of sacrifices on the day of atonement, they were reminded of their sins, and they undoubtedly felt guilty all over again. What they needed most was forgiveness—the permanent, powerful, sin-destroying forgiveness we have from Christ. When we confess a sin to him, we need never think of it again. Christ has forgiven us, and the sin no longer exists. See 1 John 1:9.

10:4 Animal sacrifices could not take away sins; they provided only a temporary way to deal with sin until Jesus came to deal with sin permanently. How, then, were people forgiven in Old Testament times? Because Old Testament believers were following God's command to offer sacrifices, he graciously forgave them when, by faith, they made their sacrifices. But that practice looked forward to Christ's perfect sacrifice. Christ's way was superior to the Old Testament way because the old way only pointed to what Christ would do to take away sins.

5 Therefore, when He comes into the world, He says,
"SACRIFICE AND OFFERING YOU HAVE NOT DESIRED,
BUT A BODY YOU HAVE PREPARED FOR ME;
6 IN WHOLE BURNT OFFERINGS AND *sacrifices* FOR SIN YOU HAVE TAKEN NO
PLEASURE.
7 "THEN I SAID, 'BEHOLD, I HAVE COME
(IN THE SCROLL OF THE BOOK IT IS WRITTEN OF ME)
TO DO YOUR WILL, O GOD.' "
8 After saying above, "SACRIFICES AND OFFERINGS AND WHOLE BURNT OFFERINGS
AND *sacrifices* FOR SIN YOU HAVE NOT DESIRED, NOR HAVE YOU TAKEN PLEASURE *in*
them" (which are offered according to the Law),
9 then He said, "BEHOLD, I HAVE COME TO DO YOUR WILL." He takes away the first
in order to establish the second.
10 By this will we have been sanctified through the offering of the body of Jesus Christ
once for all.
11 Every priest stands daily ministering and offering time after time the same sacrifices, which can never take away sins;
12 but He, having offered one sacrifice for sins for all time, SAT DOWN AT THE RIGHT
HAND OF GOD,
13 waiting from that time onward UNTIL HIS ENEMIES BE MADE A FOOTSTOOL FOR
HIS FEET.
14 For by one offering He has perfected for all time those who are sanctified.
15 And the Holy Spirit also testifies to us; for after saying,
16 "THIS IS THE COVENANT THAT I WILL MAKE WITH THEM
AFTER THOSE DAYS, SAYS THE LORD:
I WILL PUT MY LAWS UPON THEIR HEART,
AND ON THEIR MIND I WILL WRITE THEM,"
He then says,
17 "AND THEIR SINS AND THEIR LAWLESS DEEDS
I WILL REMEMBER NO MORE."
18 Now where there is forgiveness of these things, there is no longer *any* offering
for sin.

10:5 Heb 1:6; Ps 40:6; Heb 2:14; 5:7; 1 Pet 2:24

10:6 Ps 40:6

10:7 Ps 40:7, 8; Ezra 6:2; Jer 36:2; Ezek 2:9; 3:1f

10:8 Ps 40:6; Heb 10:5f; Mark 12:33; Rom 8:3

10:9 Ps 40:7, 8; Heb 10:7

10:10 John 17:19; Eph 5:26; Heb 2:11; 10:14, 29; 13:12; John 6:51; Eph 5:2; Heb 7:27; 9:14, 28; 10:12; 1 Pet 2:24; Heb 7:27

10:11 Heb 5:1; Mic 6:6-8

10:12 Ps 110:1; Heb 1:3

10:13 Ps 110:1; Heb 1:13

10:14 Heb 10:1; Heb 10:12

10:15 Heb 3:7

10:16 Jer 31:33; Heb 8:10

10:17 Jer 31:34; Heb 8:12

10:5–10 This quotation is not cited in any other New Testament book. However, it is a central teaching of the Old Testament that God desires obedience and a right heart, not empty compliance to the sacrifice system (see the chart in Hosea 7). The writer of Hebrews applies to Christ the words of the psalmist in Psalm 40:6–8. Christ came to offer his body on the cross for us as a sacrifice that is completely acceptable to God. God's new and living way for us to please him is not by keeping laws or even by abstaining from sin. It is by coming to him in faith to be forgiven, and then following him in loving obedience.

10:5–10 The costly sacrifice of an animal's life impressed upon the sinner the seriousness of his or her own sin before God. Because Jesus shed his own blood for us, his sacrifice is infinitely greater than any Old Testament offering. Considering the immeasurable gift he gave us, we should respond by giving him our devotion and service.

10:9 Setting aside the first system in order to establish a far better one meant doing away with the system of sacrifices contained in the ceremonial law. It didn't mean eliminating God's *moral* law (the Ten Commandments). The ceremonial law prepared people for Christ's coming. With Christ's death and resurrection, that system was no longer needed. And through Christ we can fulfill the moral law as we let him live in us.

10:11–12 Christ's work is contrasted with the work of the Jewish priests. The priests' work was never finished, so they always had to stand and offer sacrifices; Christ's sacrifice (dying in our place) is finished, so he is seated. The priests repeated the sacrifices often; Christ sacrificed once for all. The sacrifice system couldn't completely remove sin; Christ's sacrifice effectively cleansed us.

10:12 If the Jewish readers of this book were to return to the old Jewish system, they would be implying that Christ's sacrifice wasn't enough to forgive their sins. Adding anything to his sacrifice or taking anything from it denies its validity. Any system to gain salvation through good deeds is essentially rejecting the significance of Christ's death and spurning the Holy Spirit's work. Beware of anyone who tells you that Christ's sacrifice still leaves you incomplete or that something else is needed to make you acceptable to God. When we believe in Christ, he makes us completely right with God. Our loving relationship leads us to follow him in willing obedience and service. He is pleased with our service, but we cannot be saved by our good deeds.

10:14 We have been made perfect, yet we are being made holy (sanctified). Through his death and resurrection, Christ, once for all, made his believers perfect in God's sight. At the same time, he is making them holy (progressively cleansed and set apart for his special use) in their daily pilgrimage here. We should not be surprised, ashamed, or shocked that we still need to grow. God is not finished with us. We can encourage this growth process by deliberately applying Scripture to all areas of our lives, by accepting the discipline and guidance Christ provides, and by giving him control of our desires and goals.

10:17 The writer concludes his argument with this powerful statement that God will remember our sins no more. Christ forgives completely, so there is no need to confess our past sins repeatedly. As believers, we can be confident that the sins we confess and renounce are forgiven and forgotten.

10:19 Heb 3:6; 9:25
10:20 Heb 9:8; Heb 6:19
10:21 Heb 2:17; 1 Tim 3:15; Heb 3:6
10:22 Heb 7:19; 10:1; 1 Pet 1:2; Acts 22:16; 1 Cor 6:11; Eph 5:26; Titus 3:5; 1 Pet 3:21
10:23 Heb 3:1; 1 Cor 1:9; 10:13; Heb 11:11
10:24 Heb 13:1; Titus 3:8
10:25 Acts 2:42; 1 Cor 3:13
10:26 Num 15:30; Heb 6:4-8; 2 Pet 2:20f; 1 Tim 2:4
10:27 John 5:29; Heb 9:27; Is 26:11
10:28 Deut 17:2-6; 19:15; Matt 18:16; Heb 2:2
10:29 Ex 24:8; Matt 26:28; Heb 13:20; Eph 5:26; Heb 9:13f; Rev 1:5; 1 Cor 6:11
10:30 Deut 32:35
10:31 2 Cor 5:11; Matt 16:16; Heb 3:12
10:33 Phil 4:14; 1 Thess 2:14
10:34 Heb 9:15; 11:16; 13:14; 1 Pet 1:4f

B. THE SUPERIORITY OF FAITH (10:19—13:25)

Moving from argument to instruction, the author cites many examples of those who have demonstrated faith throughout history. Living by faith is far better than merely fulfilling rituals and rules. This can challenge us to grow in faith and to live in obedience to God each day.

A New and Living Way

19 Therefore, brethren, since we have confidence to enter the holy place by the blood
of Jesus,
20 by a new and living way which He inaugurated for us through the veil, that is, His
flesh,
21 and since *we have* a great priest over the house of God,
22 let us draw near with a sincere heart in full assurance of faith, having our hearts
sprinkled *clean* from an evil conscience and our bodies washed with pure water.
23 Let us hold fast the confession of our hope without wavering, for He who promised
is faithful;
24 and let us consider how to stimulate one another to love and good deeds,
25 not forsaking our own assembling together, as is the habit of some, but encouraging
one another; and all the more as you see the day drawing near.

Christ or Judgment

26 For if we go on sinning willfully after receiving the knowledge of the truth, there no
longer remains a sacrifice for sins,
27 but a terrifying expectation of judgment and THE FURY OF A FIRE WHICH WILL
CONSUME THE ADVERSARIES.
28 Anyone who has set aside the Law of Moses dies without mercy on *the testimony of*
two or three witnesses.
29 How much severer punishment do you think he will deserve who has trampled under foot the Son of God, and has regarded as unclean the blood of the covenant by which
he was sanctified, and has insulted the Spirit of grace?
30 For we know Him who said, "VENGEANCE IS MINE, I WILL REPAY." And again, "THE
LORD WILL JUDGE HIS PEOPLE."
31 It is a terrifying thing to fall into the hands of the living God.
32 But remember the former days, when, after being enlightened, you endured a great
conflict of sufferings,
33 partly by being made a public spectacle through reproaches and tribulations, and
partly by becoming sharers with those who were so treated.
34 For you showed sympathy to the prisoners and accepted joyfully the seizure of your
property, knowing that you have for yourselves a better possession and a lasting one.

10:19 The holy of holies in the temple was sealed from view by a veil (10:20). Only the high priest could enter this holy room, and he did so only once a year on the day of atonement when he offered the sacrifice for the nation's sins. But Jesus' death removed the veil, and all believers may walk into God's presence at any time (see also 6:19–20).

10:22–25 We have significant privileges associated with our new life in Christ: (1) We have personal access to God through Christ and can draw near to him without an elaborate system (10:22); (2) we may grow in faith, overcome doubts and questions, and deepen our relationship with God (10:23); (3) we may enjoy encouragement from one another (10:24); (4) we may worship together (10:25).

10:25 To neglect Christian meetings is to give up the encouragement and help of other Christians. We gather together to share our faith and to strengthen one another in the Lord. As we get closer to the "day" when Christ will return, we will face many spiritual struggles, and even times of persecution. Anti-Christian forces will grow in strength. Difficulties should never be excuses for missing church services. Rather, as difficulties arise, we should make an even greater effort to be faithful in attendance.

10:26 When people deliberately reject Christ's offer of salvation, they reject God's most precious gift. They ignore the leading of the Holy Spirit, the one who communicates to us God's saving love. This warning was given to Jewish Christians who were tempted to reject Christ for Judaism, but it applies to anyone who rejects Christ for another religion or, having understood Christ's atoning work, deliberately turns away from it (see also Numbers 15:30–31 and Mark 3:28–30). The point is that there is no other acceptable sacrifice for sin than the death of Christ on the cross. If someone deliberately rejects the sacrifice of Christ after clearly understanding the gospel teaching about it, then there is no way for that person to be saved, because God has not provided any other name under heaven by which we can be saved (see Acts 4:12).

10:31 This judgment is for those who have rejected God's mercy. For those who accept Christ's love and accept his salvation, the coming judgment is no cause for worry. Being saved through his grace, they have nothing to fear (see 1 John 4:18).

10:32–36 Hebrews encourages believers to persevere in their Christian faith and conduct when facing persecution and pressure. We don't usually think of suffering as good for us, but it can build our character and our patience. During times of great stress, we may feel God's presence more clearly and find help from Christians we never thought would care. Knowing that Jesus is with us in our suffering and that he will return one day to put an end to all pain helps us grow in our faith and our relationship with him (see Romans 5:3–5).

35 Therefore, do not throw away your confidence, which has a great reward.
36 For you have need of endurance, so that when you have done the will of God, you
may receive what was promised.
37 FOR YET IN A VERY LITTLE WHILE,
HE WHO IS COMING WILL COME, AND WILL NOT DELAY.
38 BUT MY RIGHTEOUS ONE SHALL LIVE BY FAITH;
AND IF HE SHRINKS BACK, MY SOUL HAS NO PLEASURE IN HIM.
39 But we are not of those who shrink back to destruction, but of those who have faith
to the preserving of the soul.

The Triumphs of Faith

11 Now faith is the assurance of *things* hoped for, the conviction of things not seen.
2 For by it the men of old gained approval.
3 By faith we understand that the worlds were prepared by the word of God, so that
what is seen was not made out of things which are visible.
4 By faith Abel offered to God a better sacrifice than Cain, through which he obtained
the testimony that he was righteous, God testifying about his gifts, and through faith,
though he is dead, he still speaks.
5 By faith Enoch was taken up so that he would not see death; AND HE WAS NOT FOUND
BECAUSE GOD TOOK HIM UP; for he obtained the witness that before his being taken up
he was pleasing to God.
6 And without faith it is impossible to please *Him*, for he who comes to God must
believe that He is and *that* He is a rewarder of those who seek Him.
7 By faith Noah, being warned *by God* about things not yet seen, in reverence prepared an ark for the salvation of his household, by which he condemned the world, and
became an heir of the righteousness which is according to faith.
8 By faith Abraham, when he was called, obeyed by going out to a place which he was
to receive for an inheritance; and he went out, not knowing where he was going.
9 By faith he lived as an alien in the land of promise, as in a foreign *land*, dwelling in
tents with Isaac and Jacob, fellow heirs of the same promise;

10:36 Luke 21:19; Heb 12:1; Mark 3:35; Heb 9:15

10:37 Hab 2:3; Heb 10:25; Rev 22:20; Matt 11:3

10:38 Hab 2:4; Rom 1:17; Gal 3:11

11:1 Heb 3:14; Heb 3:6; Rom 8:24; 2 Cor 4:18; 5:7

11:3 John 1:3; Heb 1:2; Gen ch 1; Ps 33:6, 9; Heb 6:5; 2 Pet 3:5; Rom 4:17

11:4 Gen 4:4; Gen 4:8-10; Heb 12:24

11:5 Gen 5:21-24; Luke 2:26; John 8:51; Heb 2:9

11:7 Gen 6:13-22; Heb 8:5; Heb 11:1; Heb 5:7; 1 Pet 3:20; Gen 6:9; Ezek 14:14, 20; Rom 4:13; 9:30

11:8 Gen 12:1-4; Acts 7:2-4; Gen 12:7

11:9 Acts 7:5; Gen 12:8; 13:3, 18; 18:1, 9; Heb 6:17

10:35–38 The writer encourages his readers not to abandon their faith in times of persecution, but to show by their endurance that their faith is real. Faith means resting in what Christ has done for us in the past, but it also means trusting him for what he will do for us in the present and in the future (see Romans 8:12–25; Galatians 3:10–13).

11:1 Do you remember how you felt when you were very young and your birthday approached? You were excited and anxious. You knew you would certainly receive gifts and other special treats. But some things would be a surprise. Birthdays combine assurance and anticipation, and so does faith! Faith is the conviction based on past experience that God's new and fresh surprises will surely be ours.

11:1 Two words describe faith: *assurance* and *conviction.* These two qualities need a secure beginning and ending point. The beginning point of faith is believing in God's character—he *is* who he says. The end point is believing in God's promises—he will *do* what he says. When we believe that God will fulfill his promises even though we don't see those promises materializing yet, we demonstrate true faith (see John 20:24–31).

11:3 God called the universe into existence out of nothing; he declared that it was to be, and it was. Our faith is in the God who created the entire universe by his Word. God's Word has awesome power. When he speaks, do you listen and respond? How can you better prepare yourself to respond to God's Word?

11:4 Cain and Abel were Adam and Eve's first two sons. Abel offered a sacrifice that pleased God, while Cain's sacrifice was unacceptable. Abel's Profile is found in Genesis 6. Cain's Profile is in Genesis 7. Abel's sacrifice (an animal substitute) was more acceptable to God, both because it was a blood sacrifice and, most important, because of Abel's attitude when he offered it.

11:6 Believing that God exists is only the beginning; even the demons believe that much (James 2:19–20). God will not settle for mere acknowledgment of his existence. He wants a personal, dynamic relationship with you that will transform your life. Those who seek God will find that they are rewarded with his intimate presence.

11:6 Sometimes we wonder about the fate of those who haven't heard of Christ and have not even had a Bible to read. God assures us that all who honestly seek him—who act in faith on the knowledge of God that they possess—will be rewarded. When you tell others the gospel, encourage them to be honest and diligent in their search for truth. Those who hear the gospel are responsible for what they have heard (see 2 Corinthians 6:1–2).

11:7 Noah experienced rejection because he was different from his neighbors. God commanded him to build a huge boat in the middle of dry land, and although God's command seemed foolish, Noah obeyed. Noah's obedience made him appear strange to his neighbors, just as the new beliefs of Jewish Christians undoubtedly made them stand out. As you obey God, don't be surprised if others regard you as "different." Your obedience makes their disobedience stand out. Remember, if God asks you to do something, he will give you the necessary strength to carry out that task. For more information on Noah, see his Profile in Genesis 8.

11:8–10 Abraham's life was filled with faith. At God's command, he left home and went to another land—obeying without question (Genesis 12:1ff). He believed the covenant that God made with him (Genesis 12:2–3; 13:14–16; 15:1–6). In obedience to God, Abraham was even willing to sacrifice his son Isaac (Genesis 22:1–19). Do not be surprised if God asks you to give up secure, familiar surroundings in order to carry out his will. For further information on Abraham, see his Profile in Genesis 18.

11:10 Rev 21:14ff
11:11 Gen 17:19; 18:11-14; 21:2; Heb 10:23
11:12 Rom 4:19; Gen 15:5; 22:17; 32:12
11:13 Gen 23:4; 47:9; 1 Chr 29:15; Ps 39:12; Eph 2:19; 1 Pet 1:1; 2:11
11:15 Gen 24:6-8
11:16 2 Tim 4:18; Mark 8:38; Heb 2:11; Gen 26:24; 28:13; Ex 3:6; Rev 21:2
11:17 Gen 22:1-10
11:18 Gen 21:12; Rom 9:7
11:19 Rom 4:21; Heb 9:9
11:21 Gen 48:1, 5, 16, 20; Gen 47:31; 1 Kin 1:47
11:22 Gen 50:24f; Ex 13:19
11:23 Ex 2:2; Ex 1:16, 22

10 for he was looking for the city which has foundations, whose architect and builder
is God.
11 By faith even Sarah herself received ability to conceive, even beyond the proper time
of life, since she considered Him faithful who had promised.
12 Therefore there was born even of one man, and him as good as dead at that, *as many*
descendants AS THE STARS OF HEAVEN IN NUMBER, AND INNUMERABLE AS THE SAND
WHICH IS BY THE SEASHORE.
13 All these died in faith, without receiving the promises, but having seen them and
having welcomed them from a distance, and having confessed that they were strangers
and exiles on the earth.
14 For those who say such things make it clear that they are seeking a country of
their own.
15 And indeed if they had been thinking of that *country* from which they went out, they
would have had opportunity to return.
16 But as it is, they desire a better *country*, that is, a heavenly one. Therefore God is
not ashamed to be called their God; for He has prepared a city for them.
17 By faith Abraham, when he was tested, offered up Isaac, and he who had received
the promises was offering up his only begotten *son;*
18 *it was he* to whom it was said, "IN ISAAC YOUR DESCENDANTS SHALL BE CALLED."
19 He considered that God is able to raise *people* even from the dead, from which he
also received him back as a type.
20 By faith Isaac blessed Jacob and Esau, even regarding things to come.
21 By faith Jacob, as he was dying, blessed each of the sons of Joseph, and worshiped,
leaning on the top of his staff.
22 By faith Joseph, when he was dying, made mention of the exodus of the sons of Israel, and gave orders concerning his bones.
23 By faith Moses, when he was born, was hidden for three months by his parents,
because they saw he was a beautiful child; and they were not afraid of the king's edict.

11:11–12 Sarah was Abraham's wife. They were unable to have children through many years of their marriage. God promised Abraham a son, but Sarah doubted that she could become pregnant in her old age. At first she laughed, but afterward she believed (Genesis 18). For more information on Sarah, see her Profile in Genesis 19.

11:13 That we are "strangers and exiles" may be an awareness forced on us by circumstances. It may come late in life or as the result of difficult times. But this world is not our home. We cannot live here forever (see also 1 Peter 1:1). It is best for us not to be so attached to this world's desires and possessions that we can't move out at God's command.

11:13–16 These people of faith died without receiving all that God had promised, but they never lost their vision of heaven ("a better country . . . a heavenly one"). Many Christians become frustrated and defeated because their needs, wants, expectations, and demands are not immediately met when they believe in Christ. They become impatient and want to quit. Are you discouraged because the achievement of your goal seems far away? Take courage from these heroes of faith who lived and died without seeing the fruit of their faith on earth and yet continued to believe (see 11:36–39).

11:17–19 Abraham was willing to give up his son when God commanded him to do so (Genesis 22:1–19). God did not let Abraham take Isaac's life, because God had given the command in order to test Abraham's faith. Instead of taking Abraham's son, God gave Abraham a whole nation of descendants through Isaac. If you are afraid to trust God with your most prized possession, dream, or person, pay attention to Abraham's example. Because Abraham was willing to give up everything for God, he received back more than he could have imagined. What we receive, however, is not always immediate, or in the form of material possessions. Material things should be among the least satisfying of rewards. Our best and greatest rewards await us in eternity.

11:20 Isaac was the son who had been promised to Abraham and Sarah in their old age. It was through Isaac that God fulfilled his promise to eventually give Abraham countless descendants. Isaac had twin sons, Jacob and Esau. God chose the younger son, Jacob, to continue the fulfillment of his promise to Abraham. For more information on Isaac, see his Profile in Genesis 22.

11:21 Jacob was Isaac's son and Abraham's grandson. Jacob's sons became the fathers of Israel's 12 tribes. Even when Jacob (also called "Israel") was dying in a strange land, he believed the promise that Abraham's descendants would be like the sand on the seashore and that Israel would become a great nation (Genesis 48:1–22). True faith helps us see beyond the grave. For more information on Jacob and Esau, see their Profiles in Genesis 25 and 27.

11:22 Joseph, one of Jacob's sons, was sold into slavery by his jealous brothers (Genesis 37). Eventually, Joseph was sold again, this time to an official of the Pharaoh of Egypt. Because of Joseph's faithfulness to God, however, he was given a top-ranking position in Egypt. Although Joseph could have used that position to build a personal empire, he remembered God's promise to Abraham. After he had been reconciled to his brothers, Joseph brought his family to be near him and requested that his bones be taken to the promised land when the Jews eventually left Egypt (Genesis 50:24–25). Faith means trusting in God and doing what he wants, regardless of the circumstances or consequences. For more information on Joseph, see his Profile in Genesis 37.

11:23 Moses' parents trusted God to protect their son's life. They were not merely proud parents; they were believers who had faith that God would care for him. As a parent, have you trusted God enough to take care of your children? God has a plan for every person, and your important task is to pray for your children and prepare them to do the work God has planned for them to do. Faith allows us to entrust even our children to God.

24 By faith Moses, when he had grown up, refused to be called the son of Pharaoh's
daughter,
25 choosing rather to endure ill-treatment with the people of God than to enjoy the
passing pleasures of sin,
26 considering the reproach of Christ greater riches than the treasures of Egypt; for
he was looking to the reward.
27 By faith he left Egypt, not fearing the wrath of the king; for he endured, as seeing
Him who is unseen.
28 By faith he kept the Passover and the sprinkling of the blood, so that he who destroyed the firstborn would not touch them.
29 By faith they passed through the Red Sea as though *they were passing* through dry
land; and the Egyptians, when they attempted it, were drowned.
30 By faith the walls of Jericho fell down after they had been encircled for seven days.
31 By faith Rahab the harlot did not perish along with those who were disobedient,
after she had welcomed the spies in peace.
32 And what more shall I say? For time will fail me if I tell of Gideon, Barak, Samson,
Jephthah, of David and Samuel and the prophets,
33 who by faith conquered kingdoms, performed *acts of* righteousness, obtained promises, shut the mouths of lions,
34 quenched the power of fire, escaped the edge of the sword, from weakness were
made strong, became mighty in war, put foreign armies to flight.
35 Women received *back* their dead by resurrection; and others were tortured, not
accepting their release, so that they might obtain a better resurrection;
36 and others experienced mockings and scourgings, yes, also chains and imprisonment.
37 They were stoned, they were sawn in two, [7]they were tempted, they were put to death
with the sword; they went about in sheepskins, in goatskins, being destitute, afflicted, ill-
treated
38 (*men* of whom the world was not worthy), wandering in deserts and mountains and
caves and holes in the ground.

7 One early ms does not contain *they were tempted*

11:24 Ex 2:10, 11ff
11:27 Ex 2:15; 12:50f
11:28 Ex 12:21ff; 1 Cor 10:10
11:29 Ex 14:22-29
11:30 Josh 6:15f
11:31 Josh 2:9ff; 6:23; James 2:25
11:33 Judg ch 4, 7, 11, 14; 2 Sam 5:17-20; 8:1f; 10:12; 1 Sam 12:4; 2 Sam 8:15; 2 Sam 7:11f; 1 Sam 17:34ff; Dan 6:22
11:34 Dan 3:23ff; Ex 18:4
11:35 1 Kin 17:23; 2 Kin 4:36f
11:36 Gen 39:20; 1 Kin 22:27; 2 Chr 18:26; Jer 20:2; 37:15
11:37 1 Kin 21:13; 2 Chr 24:21; 2 Sam 12:31; 1 Chr 20:3; 2 Kin 2:8, 13f; Zech 13:4; Heb 11:25; 13:3
11:38 1 Kin 18:4, 13; 19:9

11:24–28 Moses became one of Israel's greatest leaders, a prophet and a lawgiver. But when he was born, his people were slaves in Egypt, and the Egyptian officials had ordered that all Hebrew baby boys were to be killed. Moses was spared, however, and Pharaoh's daughter raised Moses in Pharaoh's own household (Exodus 1; 2)! It took faith for Moses to give up his place in the palace, but he could do it because he saw the fleeting nature of great wealth and prestige. It is easy to be deceived by the temporary benefits of wealth, popularity, status, and achievement, and to be blind to the long-range benefits of God's kingdom. Faith helps us look beyond the world's value system to see the eternal values of God's kingdom. For more information on Moses, see his Profile in Exodus 14.

11:31 When Joshua planned the conquest of Jericho, he sent spies to investigate the fortifications of the city. The spies met Rahab, who had two strikes against her—she was a Gentile and a prostitute (harlot). But she showed that she had faith in God by welcoming the spies and by trusting God to spare her and her family when the city was destroyed. Faith helps us turn around and do what is right regardless of our past or the disapproval of others. For more information on Rahab, see her Profile in Joshua 3.

11:32–35 The Old Testament records the lives of the various people who experienced these great victories. Joshua and Deborah conquered kingdoms (the book of Joshua; Judges 4; 5). Nehemiah performed an act of righteousness (the book of Nehemiah). Daniel was saved from the mouths of lions (Daniel 6). Shadrach, Meshach, and Abednego were kept from harm in the furious flames of a fiery furnace (Daniel 3). Elijah escaped the edge of the swords of evil Queen Jezebel's henchmen (1 Kings 19:2ff). Hezekiah regained strength after sickness (2 Kings 20). Gideon was mighty in war (Judges 7). A widow's son was brought back to life by the prophet Elisha (2 Kings 4:8–37).

We, too, can experience victory through faith in Christ. Our victories over oppressors may be like those of the Old Testament saints, but more likely our victories will be directly related to the role God wants us to play. Even though our bodies deteriorate and die, we will live forever because of Christ. In the promised resurrection, even death will be defeated and Christ's victory will be made complete.

11:32–40 These verses summarize the lives of other great men and women of faith. Some experienced outstanding victories, even over the threat of death. But others were severely mistreated, tortured, and even killed. Having a steadfast faith in God does not guarantee a happy, carefree life. On the contrary, our faith almost guarantees us some form of abuse from the world. While we are on earth, we may never see the purpose of our suffering. But we know that God will keep his promises to us. Do you believe that God will keep his promises to you?

11:35–39 Many think that pain is the exception in the Christian life. When suffering occurs, they say, "Why me?" They feel as though God deserted them, or perhaps they accuse him of not being as dependable as they thought. In reality, however, we live in an evil world filled with suffering, even for believers. But God is still in control. He allows some Christians to become martyrs for the faith, and he allows others to survive persecution. Rather than asking, "Why me?" it is much more helpful to ask, "Why not me?" Our faith and the values of this world are on a collision course. If we expect pain and suffering to come, we will not be shocked when it hits. But we can also take comfort in knowing that Jesus also suffered. He understands our fears, our weaknesses, and our disappointments (see 2:16–18; 4:14–16). He promised never to leave us (Matthew 28:18–20), and he intercedes on our behalf (7:24–25). In times of pain, persecution, or suffering we should trust confidently in Christ.

11:40 Heb 11:16; Rev 6:11
12:1 Rom 13:12; Eph 4:22; 1 Cor 9:24; Gal 2:2; Heb 10:36
12:2 Heb 2:10; Phil 2:8f; Heb 2:9; 1 Cor 1:18, 23; Heb 13:13; Heb 1:3
12:3 Rev 2:3; Gal 6:9; Heb 12:5
12:4 Heb 10:32ff; 13:13; Phil 2:8
12:5 Job 5:17; Prov 3:11; Heb 12:3
12:6 Prov 3:12; Ps 119:75; Rev 3:19
12:7 Deut 8:5; 2 Sam 7:14; Prov 13:24; 19:18; 23:13f
12:8 1 Pet 5:9
12:9 Luke 18:2; Num 16:22; 27:16; Rev 22:6; Is 38:16
12:10 2 Pet 1:4
12:11 1 Pet 1:6; Is 32:17; 2 Tim 4:8; James 3:17f
12:12 Is 35:3

39 And all these, having gained approval through their faith, did not receive what was
promised,
40 because God had provided something better for us, so that apart from us they would
not be made perfect.

Jesus, the Example

12 Therefore, since we have so great a cloud of witnesses surrounding us, let us also
lay aside every encumbrance and the sin which so easily entangles us, and let us
run with endurance the race that is set before us,
2 fixing our eyes on Jesus, the author and perfecter of faith, who for the joy set before
Him endured the cross, despising the shame, and has sat down at the right hand of the
throne of God.
3 For consider Him who has endured such hostility by sinners against Himself, so that
you will not grow weary and lose heart.

A Father's Discipline

4 You have not yet resisted to the point of shedding blood in your striving against sin;
5 and you have forgotten the exhortation which is addressed to you as sons,
"MY SON, DO NOT REGARD LIGHTLY THE DISCIPLINE OF THE LORD,
NOR FAINT WHEN YOU ARE REPROVED BY HIM;
6 FOR THOSE WHOM THE LORD LOVES HE DISCIPLINES,
AND HE SCOURGES EVERY SON WHOM HE RECEIVES."
7 It is for discipline that you endure; God deals with you as with sons; for what son is
there whom *his* father does not discipline?
8 But if you are without discipline, of which all have become partakers, then you are
illegitimate children and not sons.
9 Furthermore, we had earthly fathers to discipline us, and we respected them; shall
we not much rather be subject to the Father of spirits, and live?
10 For they disciplined us for a short time as seemed best to them, but He *disciplines*
us for *our* good, so that we may share His holiness.
11 All discipline for the moment seems not to be joyful, but sorrowful; yet to those who
have been trained by it, afterwards it yields the peaceful fruit of righteousness.
12 Therefore, strengthen the hands that are weak and the knees that are feeble,

---

11:39–40 Hebrews 11 has been called faith's hall of fame. No doubt the author surprised his readers by this conclusion: These mighty Jewish heroes did not receive God's total reward, because they died before Christ came. In God's plan, they and the Christian believers (who were also enduring much testing) would be rewarded together. Once again Hebrews shows that Christianity offers a better way than Judaism.

11:40 There is a solidarity among believers (see 12:23). Old and New Testament believers will be glorified together. Not only are we one in the body of Christ with all those alive, but we are also one with all those who ever lived. It takes all of us to be perfect in him.

12:1 This "cloud of witnesses" is composed of the people described in chapter 11. Their faithfulness is a constant encouragement to us. We do not struggle alone, and we are not the first to struggle with the problems we face. Others have run the race and won, and their witness stirs us to run and win also. What an inspiring heritage we have!

12:1–4 The Christian life involves hard work. It requires us to give up whatever endangers our relationship with God, to run patiently, and to struggle against sin with the power of the Holy Spirit. To live effectively, we must keep our eyes on Jesus. We will stumble if we look away from him to stare at ourselves or at the circumstances surrounding us. We should be running for Christ, not ourselves, and we must always keep him in sight.

12:3 When we face hardship and discouragement, it is easy to lose sight of the big picture. But we're not alone; there is help. Many have already made it through life, enduring far more difficult circumstances than we have experienced. Suffering is the training ground for Christian maturity. It develops our patience and makes our final victory sweet.

12:4 These readers were facing difficult times of persecution, but none of them had yet died for their faith. Because they were still alive, the writer urged them to continue to run their race. Just as Christ did not give up, neither should they.

12:5–11 Who loves his child more—the father who allows the child to do what will harm him, or the one who corrects, trains, and even punishes the child to help him learn what is right? It's never pleasant to be corrected and disciplined by God, but his discipline is a sign of his deep love for us. When God corrects you, see it as proof of his love and ask him what he is trying to teach you.

12:11 We may respond to discipline in several ways: (1) We can accept it with resignation; (2) we can accept it with self-pity, thinking we really don't deserve it; (3) we can be angry and resentful toward God; or (4) we can accept it gratefully, as the appropriate response we owe a loving Father.

12:12–13 God is not only a disciplining parent but also a demanding coach who pushes us to our limits and requires our lives to be disciplined. Although we may not feel strong enough to push on to victory, we will be able to accomplish it as we follow Christ and draw on his strength. Then we can use our growing strength to help those around us who are weak and struggling.

12:12–13 The word *therefore* is a clue that what follows is important! We must not live with only our own survival in mind. Others will follow our example, and we have a responsibility to them if we are living for Christ, as we claim to be. Does your example make it easier for others to believe in and follow Christ, and to mature in him? Or would those who follow you end up confused and misled?

13 and make straight paths for your feet, so that *the limb* which is lame may not be put
out of joint, but rather be healed.
14 Pursue peace with all men, and the sanctification without which no one will see the
Lord.
15 See to it that no one comes short of the grace of God; that no root of bitterness
springing up causes trouble, and by it many be defiled;
16 that *there be* no immoral or godless person like Esau, who sold his own birthright
for a *single* meal.
17 For you know that even afterwards, when he desired to inherit the blessing, he was
rejected, for he found no place for repentance, though he sought for it with tears.

Contrast of Sinai and Zion

18 For you have not come to *a mountain* that can be touched and to a blazing fire, and
to darkness and gloom and whirlwind,
19 and to the blast of a trumpet and the sound of words which *sound was such that* those
who heard begged that no further word be spoken to them.
20 For they could not bear the command, "IF EVEN A BEAST TOUCHES THE MOUNTAIN,
IT WILL BE STONED."
21 And so terrible was the sight, *that* Moses said, "I AM FULL OF FEAR and trembling."
22 But you have come to Mount Zion and to the city of the living God, the heavenly
Jerusalem, and to myriads of angels,
23 to the general assembly and church of the firstborn who are enrolled in heaven, and
to God, the Judge of all, and to the spirits of *the* righteous made perfect,
24 and to Jesus, the mediator of a new covenant, and to the sprinkled blood, which
speaks better than *the blood* of Abel.

The Unshaken Kingdom

25 See to it that you do not refuse Him who is speaking. For if those did not escape
when they refused him who warned *them* on earth, much less *will* we *escape* who turn
away from Him who *warns* from heaven.
26 And His voice shook the earth then, but now He has promised, saying, "YET ONCE
MORE I WILL SHAKE NOT ONLY THE EARTH, BUT ALSO THE HEAVEN."
27 This *expression*, "Yet once more," denotes the removing of those things which can
be shaken, as of created things, so that those things which cannot be shaken may remain.
28 Therefore, since we receive a kingdom which cannot be shaken, let us show gratitude, by which we may offer to God an acceptable service with reverence and awe;
29 for our God is a consuming fire.

12:14 Matt 5:8; Heb 9:28
12:15 2 Cor 6:1; Gal 5:4; Heb 4:1; Deut 29:18; Titus 1:15
12:16 Heb 13:4; 1 Tim 1:9; Gen 25:33f
12:17 Gen 27:30-40
12:18 2 Cor 3:7-13; Ex 19:12, 16ff; 20:18; Deut 4:11; 5:22
12:19 Ex 19:16, 19; 20:18; Matt 24:31
12:20 Ex 19:12f
12:21 Deut 9:19
12:22 Rev 14:1; Eph 2:19; Heb 3:12; Gal 4:26; Heb 11:16; Rev 5:11
12:23 Ex 4:22; Heb 2:12; Luke 10:20; Gen 18:25; Ps 50:6; 94:2
12:24 1 Tim 2:5; Heb 8:6; Gen 4:10; Heb 11:4
12:25 Ex 20:22
12:26 Ex 19:18; Judg 5:4f; Hag 2:6
12:27 Is 34:4; 54:10; 65:17; Rom 8:19, 21; 1 Cor 7:31
12:28 Dan 2:44; Heb 13:15, 21

12:14 The readers were familiar with the ceremonial cleansing ritual that prepared them for worship, and they knew that they had to be holy or clean in order to enter the temple. Sin always blocks our vision of God; so if we want to see God, we must renounce sin and obey him (see Psalm 24:3–4). Holiness (sanctification) is coupled with living in peace. A right relationship with God leads to right relationships with fellow believers. Although we will not always feel loving toward all other believers, we must pursue peace as we become more Christlike.

12:15 Like a small root that grows into a great tree, bitterness springs up in our hearts and overshadows even our deepest Christian relationships. A "root of bitterness" comes when we allow disappointment to grow into resentment, or when we nurse grudges over past hurts. Bitterness brings with it jealousy, dissension, and immorality. When the Holy Spirit fills us, however, he can heal the hurt that causes bitterness.

12:16–17 Esau's story shows us that mistakes and sins sometimes have lasting consequences (Genesis 25:29–34; 27:36). Even repentance and forgiveness do not always eliminate sin's consequences. How often do you make decisions based on what you want now, rather than on what you need in the long run? Evaluate the long-range effects of your decisions and actions.

12:18–24 What a contrast between the people's terrified approach to God at Mount Sinai and their joyful approach at Mount Zion! What a difference Jesus has made! Before Jesus came, God seemed distant and threatening. After Jesus came, God welcomes us through Christ into his presence. Accept God's invitation!

12:22 As Christians, we are citizens of the heavenly Jerusalem right now, because Christ rules our lives, the Holy Spirit is always with us, and we experience close fellowship with other believers. The full and ultimate rewards and reality of the heavenly Jerusalem are depicted in Revelation 21.

12:27–29 Eventually the world will crumble, and only God's kingdom will last. Those who follow Christ are part of this unshakable kingdom, and they will withstand the shaking, sifting, and burning. When we feel unsure about the future, we can take confidence from these verses. No matter what happens here, our future is built on a solid foundation that cannot be destroyed. Don't put your confidence in what will be destroyed; instead, build your life on Christ and his unshakable kingdom. (See Matthew 7:24–29 for the importance of building on a solid foundation.)

12:29 There is a big difference between the flame of a candle and the roaring blast of a forest fire. We cannot even stand near a raging fire. Even with sophisticated fire-fighting equipment, a consuming fire is often beyond human control. God is not within our control either. We cannot force him to do anything for us through our prayers. He cannot be contained. Yet, he is a God of compassion.

13:1 Rom 12:10; 1 Thess 4:9; 1 Pet 1:22
13:2 Matt 25:35; Rom 12:13; 1 Pet 4:9; Gen 18:1ff; 19:1f
13:3 Matt 25:36
13:4 1 Cor 7:38; 1 Tim 4:3; 1 Cor 6:9
13:5 Deut 31:6, 8; Josh 1:5
13:6 Ps 118:6
13:7 Luke 5:1; Heb 6:12
13:8 2 Cor 1:19
13:9 Eph 4:14; 5:6; Jude 12; 2 Cor 1:21
13:10 1 Cor 10:18
13:11 Ex 29:14; Lev 4:12, 21; 9:11; 16:27; Num 19:3, 7

The Changeless Christ

13 Let love of the brethren continue.
2 Do not neglect to show hospitality to strangers, for by this some have entertained angels without knowing it.
3 Remember the prisoners, as though in prison with them, *and* those who are ill-treated, since you yourselves also are in the body.
4 Marriage *is to be held* in honor among all, and the *marriage* bed *is to be* undefiled;
for fornicators and adulterers God will judge.
5 *Make sure that* your character is free from the love of money, being content with
what you have; for He Himself has said, "I WILL NEVER DESERT YOU, NOR WILL I EVER
FORSAKE YOU,"
6 so that we confidently say,
"THE LORD IS MY HELPER, I WILL NOT BE AFRAID.
WHAT WILL MAN DO TO ME?"
7 Remember those who led you, who spoke the word of God to you; and considering
the result of their conduct, imitate their faith.
8 Jesus Christ *is* the same yesterday and today and forever.
9 Do not be carried away by varied and strange teachings; for it is good for the heart
to be strengthened by grace, not by foods, through which those who were so occupied
were not benefited.
10 We have an altar from which those who serve the tabernacle have no right to eat.
11 For the bodies of those animals whose blood is brought into the holy place by the
high priest *as an offering* for sin, are burned outside the camp.
12 Therefore Jesus also, that He might sanctify the people through His own blood,
suffered outside the gate.
13 So, let us go out to Him outside the camp, bearing His reproach.
14 For here we do not have a lasting city, but we are seeking *the city* which is to come.

He has saved us from sin, and he will save us from death. But everything that is worthless and sinful will be consumed by the fire of his wrath. Only what is good, dedicated to God, and righteous will remain.

13:1–5 Real love for others produces tangible actions: (1) hospitality to strangers (13:2); (2) empathy for those who are in prison and those who have been mistreated (13:3); (3) respect for your marriage vows (13:4); and (4) contentment with what you have (13:5). Make sure that your love runs deep enough to affect your hospitality, empathy, fidelity, and contentment.

13:2 Three Old Testament people "entertained angels without knowing it": (1) Abraham (Genesis 18:1ff), (2) Gideon (Judges 6:11ff), and (3) Manoah (Judges 13:2ff). Some people say they cannot be hospitable because their homes are not large enough or nice enough. But even if you have no more than a table and two chairs in a rented room, there are people who would be grateful to spend time in your home. Are there visitors to your church with whom you could share a meal? Do you know single people who would enjoy an evening of conversation? Is there any way your home could meet the needs of traveling missionaries? Hospitality simply means making other people feel comfortable and at home.

13:3 We are to have empathy for those in prison, especially for (but not limited to) Christians imprisoned for their faith. Jesus said that his true followers would represent him as they visit those in prison (Matthew 25:36).

13:5 How can we learn to be content? Strive to live with less rather than desiring more; give away out of your abundance rather than accumulating more; relish what you have rather than resent what you're missing. See God's love expressed in what he has provided, and remember that money and possessions will all pass away. (See Philippians 4:11 for more on contentment, and 1 John 2:17 for the futility of earthly desires.)

13:5–6 We become content when we realize God's sufficiency for our needs. Christians who become materialistic are saying by their actions that God can't take care of them—or at least that he won't take care of them the way they want. Insecurity can lead to the love of money, whether we are rich or poor. The only antidote is to trust God to meet all our needs.

13:7 If you are a Christian, you owe much to others who have taught you and modeled for you what you needed to know about the gospel and Christian living. Continue following the good examples of those who have invested themselves in you by investing your life through evangelism, service, and Christian education.

13:8 Though human leaders have much to offer, we must keep our eyes on Christ, our ultimate leader. Unlike any human leaders, he will never change. Christ has been and will be the same forever. In a changing world we can trust our unchanging Lord.

13:9 Apparently some were teaching that keeping the Old Testament ceremonial laws and rituals (such as not eating certain foods) was important to salvation. But these laws were useless for conquering a person's evil thoughts and desires (Colossians 2:23). The laws could influence conduct, but they could not change the heart. Lasting changes in conduct begin when the Holy Spirit lives in each person.

13:13 The Jewish Christians were being ridiculed and persecuted by Jews who didn't believe in Jesus the Messiah. Most of the book of Hebrews tells them how Christ is greater than the sacrificial system. Here the writer drives home the point of his lengthy argument: It may be necessary to leave the "camp" and suffer with Christ. To be outside the camp meant to be unclean—in the days of the exodus, those who were ceremonially unclean had to stay outside the camp. But Jesus suffered humiliation and uncleanness outside the Jerusalem gates on their behalf. The time had come for Jewish Christians to declare their loyalty to Christ above any other loyalty, to choose to follow the Messiah whatever suffering that might entail. They needed to move outside the safe confinement of their past, their traditions, and their ceremonies to live for Christ. What holds you back from complete loyalty to Jesus Christ?

13:14 We should not be attached to this world, because all that we are and have here is temporary. Only our relationship with God and our service to him will last. Don't store up your treasures here; store them in heaven (Matthew 6:19–21)

God-pleasing Sacrifices

15 Through Him then, let us continually offer up a sacrifice of praise to God, that is,
the fruit of lips that give thanks to His name.
16 And do not neglect doing good and sharing, for with such sacrifices God is pleased.
17 Obey your leaders and submit *to them*, for they keep watch over your souls as those
who will give an account. Let them do this with joy and not with grief, for this would be
unprofitable for you.
18 Pray for us, for we are sure that we have a good conscience, desiring to conduct
ourselves honorably in all things.
19 And I urge *you* all the more to do this, so that I may be restored to you the sooner.

Benediction

20 Now the God of peace, who brought up from the dead the great Shepherd of the
sheep through the blood of the eternal covenant, *even* Jesus our Lord,
21 equip you in every good thing to do His will, working in us that which is pleasing in
His sight, through Jesus Christ, to whom *be* the glory forever and ever. Amen.
22 But I urge you, brethren, bear with this word of exhortation, for I have written to
you briefly.
23 Take notice that our brother Timothy has been released, with whom, if he comes
soon, I will see you.
24 Greet all of your leaders and all the saints. Those from Italy greet you.
25 Grace be with you all.

13:15 1 Pet 2:5; Lev 7:12; Is 57:19; Hos 14:2

13:16 Rom 12:13; Phil 4:18

13:17 1 Cor 16:16; Is 62:6; Ezek 3:17; Acts 20:28

13:18 1 Thess 5:25; Acts 24:16; 1 Tim 1:5

13:19 Philem 22

13:20 Rom 15:33; Acts 2:24; Rom 10:7; Is 63:11; John 10:11; Is 55:3; Jer 32:40; Ezek 37:26

13:21 1 Pet 5:10; Phil 2:13; Heb 12:28; 1 John 3:22; Rom 11:36

13:22 Acts 13:15

13:24 Acts 9:13; Acts 18:2

13:15–16 Since these Jewish Christians, because of their witness to the Messiah, no longer worshiped with other Jews, they should consider praise and acts of service their sacrifices—ones they could offer anywhere, anytime. This must have reminded them of the prophet Hosea's words, "Take away all iniquity and receive us graciously, that we may present the fruit of our lips" (Hosea 14:2). A "sacrifice of praise" today would include thanking Christ for his sacrifice on the cross and telling others about it. Acts of kindness and sharing are particularly pleasing to God, even when they go unnoticed by others.

13:17 The task of church leaders is to help people mature in Christ. Cooperative followers greatly ease the burden of leadership. Does your conduct give your leaders reason to report joyfully about you?

13:18–19 The writer recognizes the need for prayer. Christian leaders are especially vulnerable to criticism from others, pride (if they succeed), depression (if they fail), and Satan's constant efforts to destroy their work for God. They desperately need our prayers! For whom should you regularly pray?

13:21 This verse includes two significant results of Christ's death and resurrection. God works in us to make us the kind of people that would please him, and he equips us to do the kind of *work* that would please him. Let God change you from within and then use you to help others.

13:23 We have no record of Timothy's imprisonment, but we know that he had been in prison because it states here that he had been released. For more about Timothy, see his Profile in 1 Timothy 2.

13:24–25 Hebrews is a call to Christian maturity. It was addressed to first-century Jewish Christians, but it applies to Christians of any age or background. Christian maturity means making Christ the beginning and end of our faith. To grow in maturity, we must center our lives on him, not depending on religious ritual, not falling back into sin, not trusting in ourselves, and not letting anything come between us and Christ. Christ is sufficient and superior.

THE INHERITANCE Our promised inheritance comes from our loving Father. We cannot earn an inheritance; it is a gift. The word *inheritance* is described in various ways in Scripture.		
	The promised land	Numbers 32:19; Deuteronomy 12:9; 15:4; 19:10; Joshua 11:23; Psalm 105:11
	God himself	Psalm 16:5
	Eternal life	Daniel 12:13; Matthew 19:29; Mark 10:17; Titus 3:7
	The earth	Matthew 5:5
	The kingdom of God	Matthew 25:34; 1 Corinthians 15:50; Ephesians 5:5
	Glory with Christ	Romans 8:17
	Sealed by the Holy Spirit	Ephesians 1:13–14
	A reward	Colossians 3:24
	Salvation	Hebrews 1:14
	Eternal inheritance	Hebrews 9:15
	A blessing	1 Peter 3:9
	Holy city, new Jerusalem	Revelation 21:2–7

JAMES

VITAL STATISTICS

PURPOSE:
To expose hypocritical practices and to teach right Christian behavior

AUTHOR:
James, Jesus' brother, a leader in the Jerusalem church

TO WHOM WRITTEN:
First-century Jewish Christians residing in Gentile communities outside Palestine, and all Christians everywhere

DATE WRITTEN:
Probably A.D. 49, prior to the Jerusalem council held in A.D. 50

SETTING:
This letter expresses James's concern for persecuted Christians who were once part of the Jerusalem church

KEY VERSE:
"But someone may well say, 'You have faith and I have works; show me your faith without the works, and I will show you my faith by my works' " (2:18).

"MIRACULOUS!" . . . "Revolutionary!" . . . "Greatest ever!" We are inundated by a flood of extravagant claims as we channel surf the television or flip magazine pages. The messages leap out at us. The products assure that they are new, improved, fantastic, and capable of changing our life. For only a few dollars, we can have "cleaner clothes," "whiter teeth," "glamorous hair," and "tastier food." Automobiles, perfume, diet drinks, and mouthwash are guaranteed to bring happiness, friends, and the good life. And just before an election, no one can match the politicians' promises. But talk is cheap, and too often we soon realize that the boasts were hollow, quite far from the truth.

"Jesus is the answer!" . . . "Believe in God!" . . . "Follow me to church!" Christians also make great claims but are often guilty of belying them with their actions. Professing to trust God and to be his people, they cling tightly to the world and its values. Possessing all the right answers, they contradict the gospel with their lives.

With energetic style and crisp, well-chosen words, James confronts this conflict head-on. It is not enough to talk the Christian faith, he says; we must live it. "What use is it, my brethren, if someone says he has faith but he has no works? Can that faith save him?" (2:14). The proof of the reality of our faith is a changed life.

Genuine faith will inevitably produce good works. This is the central theme of James's letter, around which he supplies practical advice on living the Christian life.

James begins his letter by outlining some general characteristics of the Christian life (1:1–27). Next, he exhorts Christians to act justly in society (2:1–13). He follows this practical advice with a theological discourse on the relationship between faith and action (2:14–26). Then James shows the importance of controlling one's speech (3:1–12). In 3:13–18, James distinguishes two kinds of wisdom—earthly and heavenly. Then he encourages his readers to turn from evil desires and obey God (4:1–12). James reproves those who trust in their own plans and possessions (4:13—5:6). Finally, he exhorts his readers to be patient with each other (5:7–11), to be straightforward in their promises (5:12), to pray for each other (5:13–18), and to help each other remain faithful to God (5:19–20).

This letter could be considered a how-to book on Christian living. Confrontation, challenges, and a call to commitment await you in its pages. Read James and become a *doer* of the Word (1:22–25).

THE BLUEPRINT

1. Genuine religion (1:1–27)
2. Genuine faith (2:1—3:12)
3. Genuine wisdom (3:13—5:20)

James wrote to Jewish Christians who had been scattered throughout the Mediterranean world because of persecution. In their hostile surroundings they were tempted to let intellectual agreement pass for true faith. This letter can have rich meaning for us as we are reminded that genuine faith transforms lives. We are encouraged to put our faith into action. It is easy to say we have faith, but true faith will produce loving actions toward others.

MEGATHEMES

THEME	EXPLANATION	IMPORTANCE
Living Faith	James wants believers not only to hear the truth but also to put it into action. He contrasts empty faith (claims without conduct) with faith that works. Commitment to love and to serve others is evidence of true faith.	Living faith makes a difference. Make sure your faith is more than just a statement; it should also result in action. Seek ways of putting your faith to work.
Trials	In the Christian life there are trials and temptations. Successfully overcoming these adversities produces maturity and strong character.	Don't resent troubles when they come. Pray for wisdom; God will supply all you need to face persecution or adversity. He will give you patience and keep you strong in times of trial.
Law of Love	We are saved by God's gracious mercy, not by keeping the law. But Christ gave us a special command: "You shall love your neighbor as yourself" (Matthew 19:19). We are to love and serve those around us.	Keeping the law of love shows that our faith is vital and real. When we show love to others, we are overcoming our own selfishness.
Wise Speech	Wisdom shows itself in wise speech. God holds us responsible for the results of our destructive words. The wisdom of God that helps control the tongue can help control all our actions.	Accepting God's wisdom will affect your speech. Your words will convey true humility and lead to peace. Think before you speak and allow God to give you self-control.
Wealth	James taught Christians not to compromise with worldly attitudes about wealth. Because the glory of wealth fades, Christians should store up God's treasures through sincere service. Christians must not show partiality to the wealthy or be prejudiced against the poor.	All of us are accountable for how we use what we have. We should not hoard wealth but be generous toward others. In addition, we should not be impressed by the wealthy nor look down on those who are poor.

1. Genuine religion

Testing Your Faith

1 James, a bond-servant of God and of the Lord Jesus Christ,
To the twelve tribes who are dispersed abroad: Greetings.
2 Consider it all joy, my brethren, when you encounter various trials,
3 knowing that the testing of your faith produces endurance.
4 And let endurance have *its* perfect result, so that you may be perfect and complete,
lacking in nothing.
5 But if any of you lacks wisdom, let him ask of God, who gives to all generously and
without reproach, and it will be given to him.
6 But he must ask in faith without any doubting, for the one who doubts is like the
surf of the sea, driven and tossed by the wind.
7 For that man ought not to expect that he will receive anything from the Lord,
8 *being* a double-minded man, unstable in all his ways.
9 But the brother of humble circumstances is to glory in his high position;
10 and the rich man *is to glory* in his humiliation, because like flowering grass he will
pass away.
11 For the sun rises with a scorching wind and withers the grass; and its flower falls off
and the beauty of its appearance is destroyed; so too the rich man in the midst of his
pursuits will fade away.

1:2 Matt 5:12; 1 Pet 1:6
1:3 1 Pet 1:7; Heb 6:12
1:4 Luke 21:19; Matt 5:48; Col 4:12
1:5 1 Kin 3:9ff; James 3:17; Matt 7:7
1:6 Matt 21:21; Mark 11:23; Acts 10:20; Matt 14:28-31; Eph 4:14
1:8 James 4:8; 2 Pet 2:14
1:9 Luke 14:11
1:10 1 Cor 7:31; 1 Pet 1:24
1:11 Matt 20:12

1:1 The writer of this letter, a leader of the church in Jerusalem (see Acts 12:17; 15:13), was James, Jesus' brother, not James the apostle. The book of James was one of the earliest letters, probably written before A.D. 50. After Stephen was martyred (Acts 7:55—8:3), persecution increased, and Christians in Jerusalem were scattered throughout the Roman world. There were thriving Jewish-Christian communities in Rome, Alexandria, Cyprus, and cities in Greece and Asia Minor. Because these early believers did not have the support of established Christian churches, James wrote to them as a concerned leader, to encourage them in their faith during those difficult times.

1:2–3 James doesn't say *if* you face trials, but *when* you face them. He assumes that we will have trials and that it is possible to profit from them. The point is not to pretend to be happy when we face pain, but to have a positive outlook ("consider it all joy") because of what trials can produce in our lives. James tells us to turn our hardships into times of learning. Tough times can teach us perseverance. For other passages dealing with perseverance (also called patience and steadfastness), see Romans 2:7; 5:3–5; 8:24, 25; 2 Corinthians 6:3–7; 2 Peter 1:2–9.

1:2–4 We can't really know the depth of our character until we see how we react under pressure. It is easy to be kind to others when everything is going well, but can we still be kind when others are treating us unfairly? God wants to make us mature and complete, not to keep us from all pain. Instead of complaining about our struggles, we should see them as opportunities for growth. Thank God for promising to be with you in rough times. Ask him to help you solve your problems or to give you the strength to endure them. Then be patient. God will not leave you alone with your problems; he will stay close and help you grow.

1:5 By *wisdom,* James is talking not only about knowledge, but about the ability to make wise decisions in difficult circumstances. Whenever we need wisdom, we can pray to God, and he will generously supply what we need. Christians don't have to grope around in the dark, hoping to stumble upon answers. We can ask for God's wisdom to guide our choices.

1:5 *Wisdom* means practical discernment. It begins with respect for God, leads to right living, and results in increased ability to tell right from wrong. God is willing to give us this wisdom, but we will be unable to receive it if our goals are self-centered instead of God-centered. To learn God's will, we need to read his Word and ask him to show us how to obey it. Then we must do what he tells us.

1:6 To "ask in faith without any doubting" means not only believing in the existence of God, but also believing in his loving care. It includes relying on God and expecting that he will hear and answer when we pray. We must put away our critical attitude when we come to him. God does not grant every thoughtless or selfish request. We must have confidence that God will align our desires with his purposes. For more on this concept, read the note on Matthew 21:22.

1:6 A mind that wavers is not completely convinced that God's way is best. It treats God's Word like any human advice, and it retains the option to disobey. It vacillates between allegiance to subjective feelings, the world's ideas, and God's commands. If your faith is new, weak, or struggling, remember that you can trust God. Then be loyal to him. To stabilize your wavering or doubtful mind, commit yourself wholeheartedly to God.

1:6–8 If you have ever seen the constant rolling of huge waves at sea, you know how restless they are—subject to the forces of wind, gravity, and tide. Doubt leaves a person as unsettled as the restless waves. If you want to stop being tossed about, rely on God to show you what is best for you. Ask him for wisdom, and trust that he will give it to you. Then your decisions will be sure and solid.

1:9 Christians who aren't in high positions in this world should be glad, because they are great in the Lord's eyes. This "brother of humble circumstances" is a person without status or wealth. Such people are often overlooked, even in our churches today, but they are not overlooked by God.

1:9–11 The poor should be glad that riches mean nothing to God; otherwise these people would be considered unworthy. The rich should be glad that money means nothing to God, because money is easily lost. We find true wealth by developing our spiritual life, not by developing our financial assets. God is interested in what is lasting (our souls), not in what is temporary (our money and possessions). See Mark 4:18–19 for Jesus' words on this subject. Strive to treat each person as Christ would treat him or her.

1:10–11 If wealth, power, and status mean nothing to God, why do we attribute so much importance to them and so much honor to those who possess them? Do your material possessions give you goals and your only reason for living? If they were gone, what would be left? What you have in your heart, not your bank account, matters to God and endures for eternity.

12 Blessed is a man who perseveres under trial; for once he has been approved, he will
receive the crown of life which *the Lord* has promised to those who love Him.
13 Let no one say when he is tempted, "I am being tempted by God"; for God cannot
be tempted by evil, and He Himself does not tempt anyone.
14 But each one is tempted when he is carried away and enticed by his own lust.
15 Then when lust has conceived, it gives birth to sin; and when sin is accomplished, it
brings forth death.
16 Do not be deceived, my beloved brethren.
17 Every good thing given and every perfect gift is from above, coming down from the
Father of lights, with whom there is no variation or shifting shadow.
18 In the exercise of His will He brought us forth by the word of truth, so that we would
be a kind of first fruits among His creatures.
19 [1]*This* you know, my beloved brethren. But everyone must be quick to hear, slow to
speak *and* slow to anger;
20 for the anger of man does not achieve the righteousness of God.
21 Therefore, putting aside all filthiness and *all* that remains of wickedness, in humility receive the word implanted, which is able to save your souls.
22 But prove yourselves doers of the word, and not merely hearers who delude themselves.
23 For if anyone is a hearer of the word and not a doer, he is like a man who looks at
his natural face in a mirror;
24 for *once* he has looked at himself and gone away, he has immediately forgotten what
kind of person he was.

1 Or *Know* this

1:12 Luke 6:22; James 5:11; 1 Pet 3:14; 1 Cor 2:9; 8:3
1:13 Gen 22:1
1:15 Rom 5:12; 6:23
1:17 John 3:3; James 3:15, 17
1:18 John 1:13; James 1:15; 1 Pet 1:3, 23; 2 Cor 6:7; Eph 1:13
1:19 1 John 2:21; Acts 1:15; Prov 10:19; 17:27
1:20 Matt 5:22; Eph 4:26
1:21 Eph 4:22; 1 Pet 2:1; Eph 1:13
1:22 Matt 7:24-27; Luke 6:46-49; Rom 2:13
1:23 1 Cor 13:12

CHAPTER SUMMARY OF THE BOOK OF JAMES

Chapter 1	Confident Stand	What a Christian has
Chapter 2	Compassionate Service	What a Christian does
Chapter 3	Careful Speech	What a Christian says
Chapter 4	Contrite Submission	What a Christian feels
Chapter 5	Concerned Sharing	What a Christian gives

1:12 The crown of life is like the victory wreath given to winning athletes (see 1 Corinthians 9:25). God's crown of life is not glory and honor here on earth, but the reward of eternal life—living with God forever. The way to be in God's winners' circle is by loving him and staying faithful even under pressure.

1:12–15 Temptation comes from evil desires inside us, not from God. It begins with an evil thought and becomes sin when we dwell on the thought and allow it to become an action. Like a snowball rolling downhill, sin grows more destructive the more we let it have its way. The best time to stop a temptation is before it is too strong or moving too fast to control. See Matthew 4:1–11; 1 Corinthians 10:13; and 2 Timothy 2:22 for more about escaping temptation.

1:13–14 People who live for God often wonder why they still have temptations. Does God tempt them? God *tests* people, but he does not *tempt* them by trying to seduce them into sin. God allows Satan to tempt people, however, in order to refine their faith and to help them grow in their dependence on Christ. We can resist the temptation to sin by turning to God for strength and choosing to obey his Word.

1:13–15 It is easy to blame others and make excuses for evil thoughts and wrong actions. Excuses include: (1) It's the other person's fault; (2) I couldn't help it; (3) everybody's doing it; (4) it was just a mistake; (5) nobody's perfect; (6) the devil made me do it; (7) I was pressured into it; (8) I didn't know it was wrong; (9) God is tempting me. A person who makes excuses is trying to shift the blame from himself or herself to something or someone else. A Christian, on the other hand, accepts responsibility for his or her wrongs, confesses them, and asks God for forgiveness.

1:17 The Bible often compares goodness with light and evil with darkness. For other passages where God is pictured as light, see Psalm 27:1, Isaiah 60:19–22, John 1:1–14.

1:18 First-century Christians were the first generation to believe in Jesus Christ as Messiah. James called them "a kind of first fruits among His creatures." The Jewish leaders would be well aware of the practice of offering the first crops to ripen just prior to harvest as an act of worship, and also as a blessing on the rest of the harvest (see Deuteronomy 26:9–11). In 1 Corinthians 15:20, Paul refers to Christ as the first fruits of those who have died.

1:19 When we talk too much and listen too little, we communicate to others that we think our ideas are much more important than theirs. James wisely advises us to reverse this process. Put a mental stopwatch on your conversations and keep track of how much you talk and how much you listen. When people talk with you, do they feel that their viewpoints and ideas have value?

1:19–20 These verses speak of anger that erupts when our egos are bruised—*"I* am hurt;" *"My* opinions are not being heard." When injustice and sin occur, we *should* become angry because others are being hurt. But we should not become angry when we fail to win an argument or when we feel offended or neglected. Selfish anger never helps anybody.

1:21 James advises us to get rid of all that is wrong in our lives and "in humility receive" the salvation message we have received ("the word implanted"), because it alone can save us.

1:22–25 It is important to listen to what God's Word says, but it is much more important to obey it, to *do* what it says. We can measure the effectiveness of our Bible study time by the effect it has on our behavior and attitudes. Do you put into action what you have studied?

25 But one who looks intently at the perfect law, the *law* of liberty, and abides by it, not
having become a forgetful hearer but an effectual doer, this man will be blessed in what
he does.
26 If anyone thinks himself to be religious, and yet does not bridle his tongue but deceives his *own* heart, this man's religion is worthless.
27 Pure and undefiled religion in the sight of *our* God and Father is this: to visit orphans and widows in their distress, *and* to keep oneself unstained by the world.

1:25 John 8:32; Rom 8:2; Gal 2:4; 6:2; James 2:12; 1 Pet 2:16; John 13:17

1:26 Ps 39:1; 141:3

1:27 Rom 2:13; Gal 3:11; Matt 25:36; Eph 2:2; Titus 2:12; James 4:4; 2 Pet 1:4; 2:20; 1 John 2:15-17

2. Genuine faith

The Sin of Partiality

2 My brethren, do not hold your faith in our glorious Lord Jesus Christ with *an attitude of* personal favoritism.
2 For if a man comes into your assembly with a gold ring and dressed in fine clothes,
and there also comes in a poor man in dirty clothes,
3 and you pay special attention to the one who is wearing the fine clothes, and say,
"You sit here in a good place," and you say to the poor man, "You stand over there, or
sit down by my footstool,"
4 have you not made distinctions among yourselves, and become judges with evil
motives?
5 Listen, my beloved brethren: did not God choose the poor of this world *to be* rich in
faith and heirs of the kingdom which He promised to those who love Him?
6 But you have dishonored the poor man. Is it not the rich who oppress you and personally drag you into court?

2:1 James 1:16; Heb 12:2; Acts 7:2; 1 Cor 2:8; Acts 10:34; James 2:9

2:2 Luke 23:11; James 2:3; Zech 3:3f

2:4 Luke 18:6; John 7:24

2:5 James 1:16; Job 34:19; 1 Cor 1:27f; Luke 12:21; Rev 2:9; Matt 5:3; 25:34

2:6 Acts 8:3; 16:19

1:25 It seems paradoxical that a law could give us freedom, but God's law points out sin in us and gives us the opportunity to ask for God's forgiveness (see Romans 7:7–8). As Christians, we are saved by God's grace, and salvation frees us from sin's control. As believers, we are free to live as God created us to live. Of course, this does not mean that we are free to do as we please (see 1 Peter 2:16). We are now free to obey God.

1:26 See the notes in chapter 3 for more on bridling the tongue. No matter how spiritual we may think we are, we all could control our speech more effectively.

1:27 In the first century, orphans and widows had very little means of economic support. Unless a family member was willing to care for them, they were reduced to begging, selling themselves as slaves, or starving. By caring for these powerless people, the church put God's Word into practice. When we give with no hope of receiving in return, we show what it means to serve others.

1:27 To keep ourselves unstained by the world, we need to commit ourselves to Christ's ethical and moral system, not the world's. We are not to adapt to the world's value system, which is based on money, power, and pleasure. True faith means nothing if we are contaminated with such values.

2:1ff In this chapter James argues against favoritism and for the necessity of good works. He presents three principles of faith: (1) Commitment is an essential part of faith. You cannot be a Christian simply by affirming the right doctrines or agreeing with Biblical facts (2:19). You must commit your mind and heart to Christ. (2) Right actions are the natural by-products of true faith. A genuine Christian will have a changed life (2:18). (3) Faith without good works doesn't do anybody any good—it is useless (2:14–17). James's teachings are consistent with Paul's teaching that we receive salvation by faith alone. Paul emphasizes the purpose of faith—to bring salvation. James emphasizes the results of faith—a changed life.

2:1–7 James condemns acts of favoritism. Often we treat a well-dressed, impressive-looking person better than someone who looks shabby. We do this because we would rather identify with successful people than with apparent failures. The irony, as James reminds us, is that the supposed winners may have gained their impressive life-style at our expense. In addition, the rich find it difficult to identify with the Lord Jesus, who came as a humble servant. Are you easily impressed by status, wealth, or fame? Are you partial to the "haves" while ignoring the "have nots"? This attitude is sinful. God views all people as equals, and if he favors anyone, it is the poor and the powerless. We should follow his example.

2:2–4 Why is it wrong to judge a person by his or her economic status? Wealth may indicate intelligence, wise decisions, and hard work. On the other hand, it may mean only that a person had the good fortune of being born into a wealthy family. Or it can even be the sign of greed, dishonesty, and selfishness. By honoring someone just because he or she dresses well, we are making appearance more important than character. Sometimes we do this because: (1) Poverty makes us uncomfortable; we don't want to face our responsibilities to those who have less than we do; (2) we want to be wealthy too, and we hope to use the rich person as a means to that end; (3) we want the rich person to join our church and help support it financially. All these motives are selfish; they view neither the rich nor the poor person as a human being in need of fellowship. If we say that Christ is our Lord, then we must live as he requires, showing no favoritism and loving all people regardless of whether they are rich or poor.

2:2–4 We are often partial to the rich because we mistakenly assume that riches are a sign of God's blessing and approval. But God does not promise us earthly rewards or riches; in fact, Christ calls us to be ready to suffer for him and give up everything in order to hold on to eternal life (Matthew 6:19–21; 19:28–30; Luke 12:14–34; Romans 8:15–21; 1 Timothy 6:17–19). We will have untold riches in eternity if we are faithful in our present life (Luke 6:35; John 12:23–25; Galatians 6:7–10; Titus 3:4–8).

2:5 When James speaks about the poor, he is talking about those who have no money and also about those whose simple values are despised by much of our affluent society. Perhaps the "poor" people prefer serving to managing, human relationships to financial security, peace to power. This does not mean that the poor will automatically go to heaven and the rich to hell. Poor people, however, are usually more aware of their powerlessness. Thus it is often easier for them to acknowledge their need for salvation. One of the greatest barriers to salvation for the rich is pride. For the poor, bitterness can often bar the way to acceptance of salvation.

2:8 Matt 7:12; Lev 19:18
2:9 Acts 10:34
2:10 James 3:2; 2 Pet 1:10; Jude 24; Matt 5:19; Gal 5:3
2:11 Ex 20:14; Deut 5:18
2:12 James 1:25
2:13 Prov 21:13; Matt 5:7; 18:32-35; Luke 6:37f
2:15 Matt 25:35f; Luke 3:11
2:16 1 John 3:17f
2:17 Gal 5:6; James 2:20
2:18 Rom 9:19; Rom 3:28; 4:6; Heb 11:33; James 3:13
2:19 Matt 8:29; Mark 1:24; 5:7; Luke 4:34

7 Do they not blaspheme the fair name by which you have been called?
8 If, however, you are fulfilling the royal law according to the Scripture, "YOU SHALL
LOVE YOUR NEIGHBOR AS YOURSELF," you are doing well.
9 But if you show partiality, you are committing sin *and* are convicted by the law as
transgressors.
10 For whoever keeps the whole law and yet stumbles in one *point,* he has become guilty
of all.
11 For He who said, "DO NOT COMMIT ADULTERY," also said, "DO NOT COMMIT MUR-
DER." Now if you do not commit adultery, but do commit murder, you have become a
transgressor of the law.
12 So speak and so act as those who are to be judged by *the* law of liberty.
13 For judgment *will be* merciless to one who has shown no mercy; mercy triumphs over
judgment.

Faith and Works

14 What use is it, my brethren, if someone says he has faith but he has no works? Can
that faith save him?
15 If a brother or sister is without clothing and in need of daily food,
16 and one of you says to them, "Go in peace, be warmed and be filled," and yet you
do not give them what is necessary for *their* body, what use is that?
17 Even so faith, if it has no works, is dead, *being* by itself.
18 But someone may *well* say, "You have faith and I have works; show me your faith
without the works, and I will show you my faith by my works."
19 You believe that [2]God is one. You do well; the demons also believe, and shudder.

2 One early ms reads *there is one God*

SHOWING FAVORITISM
Why it is wrong to show favoritism to the wealthy:

1. It is inconsistent with Christ's teachings.
2. It results from evil thoughts.
3. It insults people made in God's image.
4. It is a by-product of selfish motives.
5. It goes against the Biblical definition of love.
6. It shows a lack of mercy to those less fortunate.
7. It is hypocritical.
8. It is sin.

2:8 The *royal law* is the law of our great King Jesus Christ, who said, "Love one another, just as I have loved you" (John 15:12). This law, originally summarized in Leviticus 19:18, is the basis for all the laws of how people should relate to one another. Christ reinforced this truth in Matthew 22:37–40, and Paul taught it in Romans 13:8 and Galatians 5:14.

2:8–9 We must treat all people as we would want to be treated. We should not ignore the rich, because then we would be withholding our love. But we must not favor them for what they can do for us, while ignoring the poor who can offer us seemingly so little in return.

2:10 Christians must not use this verse to justify sinning. We dare not say: "Because I can't keep every demand of God, why even try?" James reminds us that if we've broken just one law, we are sinners. We can't decide to keep part of God's law and ignore the rest. You can't break the law a little bit; if you have broken it at all, you need Christ to pay for your sin. Measure yourself, not someone else, against God's standards. Ask for forgiveness where you need it, and then renew your effort to put your faith into practice.

2:12 As Christians we are saved by God's free gift (grace) through faith, not by keeping the law. But as Christians, we are also required to obey Christ. The apostle Paul taught that "we must all appear before the judgment seat of Christ" (2 Corinthians 5:10) to be judged for our conduct. God's grace does not cancel our duty to obey him; it gives our obedience a new basis. The law is no longer an external set of rules, but it is "the law of liberty"—one we joyfully and willingly carry out, because we love God and because we have the power of his Holy Spirit to carry it out (see 1:25).

2:13 Only God in his mercy can forgive our sins. We can't earn forgiveness by forgiving others. But when we withhold forgiveness from others after having received it ourselves, we show that we don't understand or appreciate God's mercy toward us (see Matthew 6:14–15; 18:21ff; Ephesians 4:31–32).

2:14 When someone claims to have faith, what he or she may have is intellectual assent—agreement with a set of Christian teachings—and as such it would be incomplete faith. True faith transforms our conduct as well as our thoughts. If our lives remain unchanged, we don't truly believe the truths we claim to believe.

2:17 We cannot earn our salvation by serving and obeying God. But such actions show that our commitment to God is real. Works of loving service are not a substitute for, but rather a verification of, our faith in Christ.

2:18 At first glance, this verse seems to contradict Romans 3:28: "Man is justified by faith apart from works of the Law." Deeper investigation, however, shows that the teachings of James and Paul are not at odds. While it is true that our good works can never earn salvation, true faith always results in a changed life and good works. Paul speaks against those who try to be saved by works instead of true faith; James speaks against those who confuse mere intellectual assent with true faith. After all, even demons know who Jesus is, but they don't obey him (2:19). True faith involves a commitment of your whole self to God.

20 But are you willing to recognize, you foolish fellow, that faith without works is useless?
21 Was not Abraham our father justified by works when he offered up Isaac his son on
the altar?
22 You see that faith was working with his works, and as a result of the works, faith was
perfected;
23 and the Scripture was fulfilled which says, "AND ABRAHAM BELIEVED GOD, AND IT
WAS RECKONED TO HIM AS RIGHTEOUSNESS," and he was called the friend of God.
24 You see that a man is justified by works and not by faith alone.
25 In the same way, was not Rahab the harlot also justified by works when she received
the messengers and sent them out by another way?
26 For just as the body without *the* spirit is dead, so also faith without works is dead.

The Tongue Is a Fire

3 Let not many *of you* become teachers, my brethren, knowing that as such we will
incur a stricter judgment.
2 For we all stumble in many *ways.* If anyone does not stumble in what he says, he is
a perfect man, able to bridle the whole body as well.
3 Now if we put the bits into the horses' mouths so that they will obey us, we direct
their entire body as well.
4 Look at the ships also, though they are so great and are driven by strong winds, are
still directed by a very small rudder wherever the inclination of the pilot desires.
5 So also the tongue is a small part of the body, and *yet* it boasts of great things.
See how great a forest is set aflame by such a small fire!
6 And the tongue is a fire, the *very* world of iniquity; the tongue is set among our
members as that which defiles the entire body, and sets on fire the course of *our* life, and
is set on fire by hell.
7 For every species of beasts and birds, of reptiles and creatures of the sea, is tamed
and has been tamed by the human race.
8 But no one can tame the tongue; *it is* a restless evil *and* full of deadly poison.
9 With it we bless *our* Lord and Father, and with it we curse men, who have been made
in the likeness of God;
10 from the same mouth come *both* blessing and cursing. My brethren, these things
ought not to be this way.

2:20 Rom 9:20; 1 Cor 15:36; Gal 5:6; James 2:17, 26
2:21 Gen 22:9, 10, 12, 16-18
2:22 John 6:29; Heb 11:17; 1 Thess 1:3
2:23 Gen 15:6; Rom 4:3; 2 Chr 20:7; Is 41:8
2:25 Heb 11:31; Josh 2:4, 6, 15
2:26 Gal 5:6; James 2:17, 20
3:1 Matt 23:8; Rom 2:20f; 1 Tim 1:7; James 1:16; 3:10
3:2 James 2:10; Matt 12:34-37; James 3:2-12; James 1:4; James 1:26
3:3 Ps 32:9
3:5 Ps 12:3f; 73:8f; Prov 26:20f
3:6 Ps 120:2, 3; Prov 16:27; Matt 12:36f; 15:11, 18f; Matt 5:22
3:8 Ps 140:3; Eccl 10:11; Rom 3:13
3:9 James 1:27; Gen 1:26; 1 Cor 11:7

2:21–24 James says that Abraham was considered "righteous" for what he *did.* Paul says he was justified because he *believed* God (Romans 4:1–5). James and Paul are not contradicting but complementing each other. Let's not conclude that the truth is a blending of these two statements. We are not justified by what we do in any way. True faith always results in works, but the works do not justify us. Faith brings us salvation; active obedience demonstrates that our faith is genuine.

2:25 Rahab lived in Jericho, a city the Israelites conquered as they entered the promised land (Joshua 2). When Israel's spies came to the city, she hid them and helped them escape. In this way she demonstrated faith in God's purpose for Israel. As a result, she and her family were saved when the city was destroyed. Hebrews 11:31 lists Rahab among the heroes of faith.

3:1 Teaching was a highly valued and respected profession in Jewish culture, and many Jews who embraced Christianity wanted to become teachers. James warned that although it is good to aspire to teach, the teachers' responsibility is great because their words and example affect others' spiritual lives. If you are in a teaching or leadership role, how are you affecting those you lead?

3:2–3 What you say and what you *don't* say are both important. Proper speech is not only saying the right words at the right time, but it is also controlling your desire to say what you shouldn't. Examples of an unbridled tongue include gossiping, putting others down, bragging, manipulating, false teaching, exaggerating, complaining, flattering, and lying. Before you speak, ask, "Is what I want to say true? Is it necessary? Is it kind?"

3:6 James compares the damage the tongue can do to a raging fire—the tongue's wickedness has its source in hell itself. The uncontrolled tongue can do terrible damage. Satan uses the tongue to divide people and pit them against one another. Idle and hateful words are damaging because they spread destruction quickly, and no one can stop the results once they are spoken. We dare not be careless with what we say, thinking we can apologize later, because even if we do, the scars remain. A few words spoken in anger can destroy a relationship that took years to build. Before you speak, remember that words are like fire—you can neither control nor reverse the damage they can do.

3:8 If no human being can tame the tongue, why bother trying? Even if we may not achieve perfect control of our tongues, we can still learn enough control to reduce the damage our words can do. It is better to fight a fire than to go around setting new ones! Remember that we are not fighting the tongue's fire in our own strength. The Holy Spirit will give us increasing power to monitor and control what we say, so that when we are offended, the Spirit will remind us of God's love, and we won't react in a hateful manner. When we are criticized, the Spirit will heal the hurt, and we won't lash out.

3:9–12 Our contradictory speech often puzzles us. At times our words are right and pleasing to God, but at other times they are violent and destructive. Which of these speech patterns reflects our true identity? The tongue gives us a picture of our basic human nature. We were made in God's image, but we have also fallen into sin. God works to change us from the inside out. When the Holy Spirit purifies a heart, he gives self-control so that the person will speak words that please God.

3:12 Matt 7:16
3:13 1 Pet 2:12
3:14 1 Tim 2:4; James 1:18; 5:19
3:15 James 1:17; 1 Cor 2:6; 3:19; 2 Thess 2:9f; 1 Tim 4:1; Rev 2:24
3:16 Rom 2:8; 2 Cor 12:20; James 3:14
3:17 James 1:17; 2 Cor 7:11; James 4:8; Matt 5:9; Heb 12:11; Titus 3:2; Luke 6:36
3:18 Gal 6:8; Phil 1:11
4:1 Titus 3:9; Rom 7:23
4:2 James 5:6; 1 John 3:15
4:3 1 John 3:22; 5:14
4:4 James 1:27; Rom 8:7; 1 John 2:15; Matt 6:24; John 15:19
4:5 Num 23:19; 1 Cor 6:19; 2 Cor 6:16
4:6 Is 54:7f; Matt 13:12; Ps 138:6; Prov 3:34

11 Does a fountain send out from the same opening *both* fresh and bitter *water?*
12 Can a fig tree, my brethren, produce olives, or a vine produce figs? Nor *can* salt
water produce fresh.

3. Genuine wisdom

Wisdom from Above

13 Who among you is wise and understanding? Let him show by his good behavior his
deeds in the gentleness of wisdom.
14 But if you have bitter jealousy and selfish ambition in your heart, do not be arrogant and *so* lie against the truth.
15 This wisdom is not that which comes down from above, but is earthly, natural, demonic.
16 For where jealousy and selfish ambition exist, there is disorder and every evil thing.
17 But the wisdom from above is first pure, then peaceable, gentle, reasonable, full of
mercy and good fruits, unwavering, without hypocrisy.
18 And the seed whose fruit is righteousness is sown in peace by those who make peace.

Things to Avoid

4 What is the source of quarrels and conflicts among you? Is not the source your pleasures that wage war in your members?
2 You lust and do not have; *so* you commit murder. You are envious and cannot obtain; *so* you fight and quarrel. You do not have because you do not ask.
3 You ask and do not receive, because you ask with wrong motives, so that you may
spend *it* on your pleasures.
4 You adulteresses, do you not know that friendship with the world is hostility toward
God? Therefore whoever wishes to be a friend of the world makes himself an enemy
of God.
5 Or do you think that the Scripture speaks to no purpose: "[3]He jealously desires the
Spirit which He has made to dwell in us"?
6 But He gives a greater grace. Therefore *it* says, "GOD IS OPPOSED TO THE PROUD,
BUT GIVES GRACE TO THE HUMBLE."

3 Or *The spirit which He has made to dwell in us lusts with envy*

3:13–18 Have you ever known anyone who claimed to be wise but who acted foolishly? True wisdom can be measured by the depth of a person's character. Just as you can identify a tree by the type of fruit it produces, you can evaluate your wisdom by the way you act. Foolishness leads to disorder, but wisdom leads to peace and goodness. Are you tempted to escalate the conflict, pass on the gossip, or fan the fire of discord? Careful, winsome speech and wise, loving words are the seeds of peace. God loves peacemakers (Matthew 5:9).

3:14–15 "Bitter jealousy and selfish ambition" are inspired by the devil. It is easy for us to be drawn into wrong desires by the pressures of society and sometimes even by well-meaning Christians. By listening to advice like, "Assert yourself," "Go for it," "Set high goals," we can be drawn into greed and destructive competitiveness. Seeking God's wisdom delivers us from the need to compare ourselves to others and to want what they have.

4:1–3 Quarrels and conflicts among believers are always harmful. James explains that these quarrels result from evil desires battling within us—we want more possessions, more money, higher status, more recognition. When we want badly enough to fulfill these desires, we fight in order to do so. Instead of aggressively grabbing what we want, we should submit ourselves to God, ask God to help us get rid of our selfish desires, and trust him to give us what we really need.

4:2–3 James mentions the most common problems in prayer: not asking, asking for the wrong things, asking for the wrong reasons. Do you talk to God at all? When you do, what do you talk about? Do you ask only to satisfy your desires? Do you seek God's approval for what you already plan to do? Your prayers will become powerful when you allow God to change your desires so that they perfectly correspond to his will for you (1 John 3:21–22).

4:3–4 There is nothing wrong with wanting a pleasurable life. God gives us good gifts that he wants us to enjoy (1:17; Ephesians 4:7; 1 Timothy 4:4–5). But having friendship with the world involves seeking pleasure at others' expense or at the expense of obeying God. Pleasure that keeps us from pleasing God is sinful; pleasure from God's rich bounty is good.

4:4–6 The cure for evil desires is humility (see Proverbs 16:18–19; 1 Peter 5:5–6). Pride makes us self-centered and leads us to conclude that we deserve all we can see, touch, or imagine. It creates greedy appetites for far more than we need. We can be released from our self-centered desires by humbling ourselves before God, realizing that all we really need is his approval. When the Holy Spirit fills us, we see that this world's seductive attractions are only cheap substitutes for what God has to offer.

4:5 This verse may mean that because of our fallen nature, we have a tendency toward jealousy. James is not quoting a specific verse or passage—he is summing up a teaching of Scripture. See Romans 6:6–8 and Galatians 5:17–21 for more on the human tendency toward jealousy and discontent.

7 Submit therefore to God. Resist the devil and he will flee from you.
8 Draw near to God and He will draw near to you. Cleanse your hands, you sinners;
and purify your hearts, you double-minded.
9 Be miserable and mourn and weep; let your laughter be turned into mourning and
your joy to gloom.
10 Humble yourselves in the presence of the Lord, and He will exalt you.
11 Do not speak against one another, brethren. He who speaks against a brother or
judges his brother, speaks against the law and judges the law; but if you judge the law,
you are not a doer of the law but a judge *of it.*
12 There is *only* one Lawgiver and Judge, the One who is able to save and to destroy;
but who are you who judge your neighbor?
13 Come now, you who say, "Today or tomorrow we will go to such and such a city,
and spend a year there and engage in business and make a profit."
14 Yet you do not know what your life will be like tomorrow. You are *just* a vapor that
appears for a little while and then vanishes away.
15 Instead, *you ought* to say, "If the Lord wills, we will live and also do this or that."
16 But as it is, you boast in your arrogance; all such boasting is evil.
17 Therefore, to one who knows *the* right thing to do and does not do it, to him it is sin.

4:7 1 Pet 5:6; Eph 4:27
4:8 1 Tim 2:8; 1 Pet 1:22; 1 John 3:3; James 1:8
4:9 Luke 6:25
4:10 Luke 1:52
4:11 2 Cor 12:20; Matt 7:1; Rom 14:4; James 2:8
4:12 Matt 10:28; Rom 14:4
4:13 James 5:1; Prov 27:1; Luke 12:18-20
4:15 Acts 18:21
4:17 Luke 12:47; John 9:41; 2 Pet 2:21

Misuse of Riches

5 Come now, you rich, weep and howl for your miseries which are coming upon you.
2 Your riches have rotted and your garments have become moth-eaten.
3 Your gold and your silver have rusted; and their rust will be a witness against you
and will consume your flesh like fire. It is in the last days that you have stored up your
treasure!
4 Behold, the pay of the laborers who mowed your fields, *and* which has been withheld by you, cries out *against you;* and the outcry of those who did the harvesting has
reached the ears of the Lord of Sabaoth.

5:1 James 4:13; Luke 6:24; 1 Tim 6:9
5:2 Matt 6:19f
5:4 Mal 3:5; Ex 2:23; Deut 24:15; Job 31:38f; Rom 9:29

4:7 Although God and the devil are at war, we don't have to wait until the end to see who will win. God has *already* defeated Satan (Revelation 12:10–12), and when Christ returns, the devil and all he stands for will be eliminated forever (Revelation 20:10–15). Satan is here now, however, and he is trying to win us over to his evil cause. With the Holy Spirit's power, we can resist the devil, and he will flee from us.

4:7–10 How can you draw near to God? James gives five ways: (1) *Submit to God* (4:7). Yield to his authority and will, commit your life to him and his control, and be willing to follow him. (2) *Resist the devil* (4:7). Don't allow Satan to entice and tempt you. (3) *Cleanse your hands . . . and purify your hearts* (that is, lead a pure life) (4:8). Be cleansed from sin, replacing your desire to sin with your desire to experience God's purity. (4) *Be miserable and mourn and weep* in sincere sorrow for your sins (4:9). Don't be afraid to express deep heartfelt sorrow for what you have done. (5) *Humble yourself in the presence of the Lord,* and he will lift you up (4:10; 1 Peter 5:6).

4:10 Humbling ourselves means recognizing that our worth comes from God alone. To be humble involves working with his power according to his guidance, not with our own independent effort. Although we do not deserve God's favor, he reaches out to us in love and gives us worth and dignity, despite our human shortcomings.

4:11–12 Jesus summarized the law as love for God and neighbor (Matthew 22:37–40), and Paul said that love demonstrated toward a neighbor would fully satisfy the law (Romans 13:6–10). When we fail to love, we are actually breaking God's law. Examine your attitude and actions toward others. Do you build people up or tear them down? When you're ready to criticize someone, remember God's law of love and say something good instead. Saying something beneficial to others will cure you of finding fault and increase your ability to obey God's law of love.

4:13–16 It is good to have goals, but goals will disappoint us if we leave God out of them. There is no point in making plans as though God does not exist, because the future is in his hands. What would you like to be doing ten years from now? One year from now? Tomorrow? How will you react if God steps in and rearranges your plans? Plan ahead, but hold your plans loosely. Put God's desires at the center of your planning; he will never disappoint you.

4:14 Life is short no matter how many years we live. Don't be deceived into thinking that you have lots of remaining time to live for Christ, to enjoy your loved ones, or to do what you know you should. Live for God today! Then, no matter when your life ends, you will have fulfilled God's plan for you.

4:17 We tend to think that *doing* wrong is sin. But James tells us that sin is also *not* doing right. (These two kinds of sin are sometimes called sins of commission and sins of omission.) It is a sin to lie; it can also be a sin to know the truth and not tell it. It is a sin to speak evil of someone; it is also a sin to avoid him or her when you know he or she needs your friendship. We should be willing to help as the Holy Spirit guides us. If God has directed you to do a kind act, to render a service, or to restore a relationship, do it. You will experience a renewed and refreshed vitality to your Christian faith.

5:1–6 James proclaims the worthlessness of riches, not the worthlessness of the rich. Today's money will be worthless when Christ returns, so we should spend our time accumulating the kind of treasures that will be worthwhile in God's eternal kingdom. Money is not the problem; Christian leaders need money to live and to support their families; missionaries need money to help them spread the gospel; churches need money to do their work effectively. It is the *love* of money that leads to evil (1 Timothy 6:10) and causes some people to oppress others in order to get more. This is a warning to all Christians who are tempted to adopt worldly standards rather than God's standards (Romans 12:1–2) as well as an encouragement to all those who are oppressed by the rich. Also read Matthew 6:19–21 to see what Jesus says about riches.

5 You have lived luxuriously on the earth and led a life of wanton pleasure; you have
fattened your hearts in a day of slaughter.
6 You have condemned and put to death the righteous *man;* he does not resist you.

Exhortation

7 Therefore be patient, brethren, until the coming of the Lord. The farmer waits for
the precious produce of the soil, being patient about it, until it gets the early and late
rains.
8 You too be patient; strengthen your hearts, for the coming of the Lord is near.
9 Do not complain, brethren, against one another, so that you yourselves may not be
judged; behold, the Judge is standing right at the door.
10 As an example, brethren, of suffering and patience, take the prophets who spoke in
the name of the Lord.
11 We count those blessed who endured. You have heard of the endurance of Job and
have seen the outcome of the Lord's dealings, that the Lord is full of compassion and *is*
merciful.
12 But above all, my brethren, do not swear, either by heaven or by earth or with any
other oath; but your yes is to be yes, and your no, no, so that you may not fall under
judgment.
13 Is anyone among you suffering? *Then* he must pray. Is anyone cheerful? He is to
sing praises.

5:5 1 Tim 5:6; 2 Pet 2:13; Jer 12:3; 25:34

5:6 James 4:2; Heb 10:38; 1 Pet 4:18

5:7 John 21:22; 1 Thess 2:19; Gal 6:9

5:8 1 Thess 2:19; Rom 13:11, 12; 1 Pet 4:7

5:9 James 4:11; James 5:7, 10; 1 Cor 4:5

5:10 Matt 5:12

5:11 Matt 5:10; 1 Pet 3:14; Job 1:21f; 2:10; Job 42:10, 12

5:12 James 1:16; Matt 5:34-37

5:13 Ps 50:15; 1 Cor 14:15; Col 3:16

SPEECH	*When our speech is motivated by:*	*It is full of:*
	Satan	Bitter jealousy Selfish ambition Earthly concerns and desires Unspiritual thoughts and ideas Disorder Evil
	God and his wisdom	Mercy Love for others Peace Consideration for others Submission Sincerity, impartiality Righteousness

5:6 *The righteous man* is a defenseless person, probably a poor laborer. Poor people who could not pay their debts were thrown in prison or forced to sell all their possessions. At times, they were even forced to sell their family members into slavery. With no opportunity to work off their debts, poor people often died of starvation. God called this murder. Hoarding money, exploiting employees, and living self-indulgently will not escape God's notice.

5:7–8 The farmer must wait patiently for his crops to grow; he cannot hurry the process. But he does not take the summer off and hope that all goes well in the fields. There is much work to do to ensure a good harvest. In the same way, we must wait patiently for Christ's return. We cannot make him come back any sooner. But while we wait, there is much work that we can do to advance God's kingdom. Both the farmer and the Christian must live by faith, looking toward the future reward for their labors. Don't live as if Christ will never come. Work faithfully to build his kingdom—the King *will* come when the time is right.

5:9 When things go wrong, we tend to complain against and blame others for our miseries (see the second note on Genesis 3:11–13). Blaming others is easier than owning our share of the responsibility, but it can be both destructive and sinful. Before you judge others for their shortcomings, remember that Christ the Judge will come to evaluate each of us (Matthew 7:1–5; 25:31–46). He will not let us get away with shifting the blame to others.

5:10–11 Many prophets suffered and were persecuted, such as Moses, Elijah, and Jeremiah. For a complete list of those persecuted, see the chart in 2 Chronicles 19. For more on the topic of suffering, see the notes on Job 1:1ff; 2:10; 3:23–26; 4:7–8; 42:17; and Job's Profile in Job 2.

5:12 A person with a reputation for exaggeration or lying often can't get anyone to believe him on his word alone. Christians should never become like that. Always be honest so that others will believe your simple yes or no. By avoiding lies, half-truths, and omissions of the truth, you will become known as a trustworthy person.

14 Is anyone among you sick? *Then* he must call for the elders of the church and they
are to pray over him, anointing him with oil in the name of the Lord;
15 and the prayer offered in faith will [4]restore the one who is sick, and the Lord will
raise him up, and if he has committed sins, they will be forgiven him.
16 Therefore, confess your sins to one another, and pray for one another so that you
may be healed. The effective prayer of a righteous man can accomplish much.
17 Elijah was a man with a nature like ours, and he prayed earnestly that it would not
rain, and it did not rain on the earth for three years and six months.

4 Or *save*

5:14 Acts 11:30; Mark 6:13; 16:18

5:15 James 1:6; 1 Cor 1:21; James 5:20; John 6:39; 2 Cor 4:14

5:16 Matt 3:6; Mark 1:5; Acts 19:18; Heb 12:13; 1 Pet 2:24; Gen 18:23-32; John 9:31

FAITH THAT WORKS

James offers a larger number of similarities to the Sermon on the Mount than any other book in the New Testament. James relied heavily on Jesus' teachings.

Lesson	*Reference*
When your life is full of various trials, be glad. A reward awaits you.	James 1:2 Matthew 5:10–12
You are to be perfect, complete, and lacking in nothing.	James 1:4 Matthew 5:48
Ask God, and he will answer.	James 1:5; 5:15 Matthew 7:7–12
Those who are humble (who don't amount to much by the world's standards) should rejoice in their position as those whom God loves.	James 1:9 Matthew 5:3
Watch out for your anger . . . it can be dangerous.	James 1:20 Matthew 5:22
Be merciful to others, as God is merciful to you. Matthew 5:7; 6:14	James 2:13
Your faith must express itself in helping others. Matthew 7:21–23	James 2:14–16
Blessed are the peacemakers; they sow in peace and reap a harvest of righteousness.	James 3:17–18 Matthew 5:9
You cannot serve God and money, pleasures, or evil. Friendship with the world is hostility toward God.	James 4:4 Matthew 6:24
When we humble ourselves and realize our need for God, he will come to us and lift us up.	James 4:10 Matthew 5:3–4
Don't slander or speak against others; it speaks against God's command to love one another.	James 4:11 Matthew 7:1–2
Treasures on earth will only rot and fade away—we must store up eternal treasures in heaven.	James 5:2–3 Matthew 6:19
Be patient in suffering, as God's prophets were patient. Matthew 5:12	James 5:10
Be honest in your speech so you can say a simple "yes" or "no" and always be trusted.	James 5:12 Matthew 5:33–37

5:14–15 James is referring to someone who is incapacitated physically. In Scripture, oil was both a medicine (see the parable of the Good Samaritan in Luke 10:30–37) and a symbol of the Spirit of God (as used in anointing kings, see 1 Samuel 16:1–13). Thus oil can represent both the medical and the spiritual spheres of life. Christians should not separate the physical and the spiritual—Jesus Christ is Lord over both the body and the spirit.

5:14–15 People in the church are not alone. Members of Christ's body should be able to count on others for support and prayer, especially when they are sick or suffering. The elders should be on call to respond to the illness of any member, and the church should stay alert to pray for the needs of all its members.

5:15 "The prayer offered in faith" does not refer to the faith of the sick person, but to the faith of the people praying. God heals, faith doesn't, and all prayers are subject to God's will. But our prayers are part of God's healing process. That is why God often waits for our prayers of faith before intervening to heal a person.

5:16 Christ has made it possible for us to go directly to God for forgiveness. But confessing our sins to each other still has an important place in the life of the church. (1) If we have sinned against an individual, we must ask him or her to forgive us. (2) If our sin has affected the church, we must confess it publicly. (3) If we need loving support as we struggle with a sin, we should confess that sin to those who are able to provide that support. (4) If, after confessing a private sin to God, we still don't feel his forgiveness, we may wish to confess that sin to a fellow believer and hear him or her assure us of God's pardon. In Christ's kingdom, every believer is a priest to other believers (1 Peter 2:9).

5:16–18 The Christian's most powerful resource is communion with God through prayer. The results are often greater than we thought were possible. Some people see prayer as a last resort to be tried when all else fails. This approach is backward. Prayer should come first. Because God's power is infinitely greater than ours, it only makes sense to rely on it—especially because God encourages us to do so.

5:17 For more about the great prophet Elijah, read his Profile in 1 Kings 18.

5:18
1 Kin 18:42

5:19
Matt 18:15; Gal 6.1

5:20
Rom 11:14

18 Then he prayed again, and the sky poured rain and the earth produced its fruit.
19 My brethren, if any among you strays from the truth and one turns him back,
20 let him know that he who turns a sinner from the error of his way will save his soul
from death and will cover a multitude of sins.

5:19–20 Clearly this person who has strayed from the truth is a believer who has fallen into sin—one who is no longer living a life consistent with his or her beliefs. Christians disagree over whether or not it is possible for people to lose their salvation, but all agree that those who move away from their faith are in serious trouble and need to repent. James urges Christians to help backsliders return to God. By taking the initiative, praying for the person, and acting in love, we can meet the person where he or she is and bring him or her back to God and his forgiveness.

5:20 The book of James emphasizes faith in action. Right living is the evidence and result of faith. The church must serve with compassion, speak lovingly and truthfully, live in obedience to God's commands, and love one another. The body of believers ought to be an example of heaven on earth, drawing people to Christ through love for God and each other. If we truly believe God's Word, we will *live* it day by day. God's Word is not merely something we read or think about, but something we do. Belief, faith, and trust must have hands and feet—ours!

1 PETER

VITAL STATISTICS

PURPOSE:
To offer encouragement to suffering Christians

AUTHOR:
Peter

TO WHOM WRITTEN:
Jewish Christians driven out of Jerusalem and scattered throughout Asia Minor, and all believers everywhere

DATE WRITTEN:
Approximately A.D. 62–64, possibly from Rome

SETTING:
Peter was probably in Rome when the great persecution under Emperor Nero began. (Eventually Peter was executed during this persecution.) Throughout the Roman Empire, Christians were being tortured and killed for their faith, and the church in Jerusalem was being scattered.

KEY VERSE:
"So that the proof of your faith, being more precious than gold which is perishable, even though tested by fire, may be found to result in praise and glory and honor at the revelation of Jesus Christ" (1:7).

KEY PEOPLE:
Peter, Silas, Mark

KEY PLACES:
Jerusalem, Rome, and the regions of Pontus, Galatia, Cappadocia, Asia Minor, and Bithynia

SPECIAL FEATURES:
Peter used several images that were very special to him because Jesus had used them when he revealed certain truths to Peter. Peter's name (which means "rock") had been given to him by Jesus. Peter's conception of the church—a spiritual house composed of living stones built upon Christ as the foundation— came from Christ. Jesus encouraged Peter to care for the church as a shepherd tending the flock. Thus, it is not surprising to see Peter using living stones (2:5–9) and shepherds and sheep (2:25; 5:2, 4) to describe the church.

CRUSHED, overwhelmed, devastated, torn—these waves of feelings wash over those who suffer, obliterating hope and threatening to destroy them. Suffering has many forms—physical abuse, debilitating disease, social ostracism, persecution. The pain and anguish tempt a person to turn back, to surrender, to give in.

Many first-century followers of Christ were suffering and being abused and persecuted for believing in and obeying Jesus. Beginning in Jerusalem at the hands of their Jewish brothers, the persecution spread to the rest of the world—wherever Christians gathered. It climaxed when Rome determined to rid the empire of the "Christ-ones"—those who would not bow to Caesar.

Peter knew persecution firsthand. Beaten and jailed, Peter had been threatened often. He had seen fellow Christians die and the church scattered. But he knew Christ, and nothing could shake his confidence in his risen Lord. So Peter wrote to the church scattered and suffering for the faith, giving comfort and hope, and urging continued loyalty to Christ.

Peter begins by thanking God for salvation (1:2–6). He explains to his readers that trials will refine their faith (1:7–9). They should believe in spite of their circumstances; for many in past ages believed in God's plan of salvation, even the prophets of old who wrote about it but didn't understand it. But now salvation has been revealed in Christ (1:10–13).

In response to such a great salvation, Peter commands them to live holy lives (1:14–16), to reverently fear and trust God (1:17–21), to be honest and loving (2:1–3), and to become like Christ (2:1–3).

Jesus Christ, as "the living cornerstone" upon whom the church is to be built (2:4, 6), is also the stone that was rejected, causing those who are disobedient to stumble and fall (2:7–8). But the church, built upon this stone, is to be God's holy priesthood (2:9–10).

Next, Peter explains how believers should live during difficult times (2:11—4:11). Christians should be above reproach (2:12–17), imitating Christ in all their social roles—masters and servants, husbands and wives, church members and neighbors (2:18—3:17). Christ should be our model for obedience to God in the midst of great suffering (3:18—4:11).

Peter then outlines the right attitude to have about persecution: Expect it (4:12), be thankful for the privilege of suffering for Christ (4:13–18), and trust God for deliverance (4:19).

Next, Peter gives some special instructions: Elders should care for God's flock (5:1–4), younger men should be submissive to those who are older (5:5–6), and everyone should trust God and resist Satan (5:7–11).

Peter concludes by introducing Silas and by sending personal greetings, possibly from the church in Rome, and from Mark (5:12–14).

When you suffer for doing what is right, remember that following Christ is a costly commitment. When persecuted for your faith, rejoice that you have been counted worthy to suffer for Christ. He suffered for us; as his followers, we should expect nothing less. As you read 1 Peter, remember that trials will come to refine your faith. When they come, remain faithful to God.

THE BLUEPRINT

1. God's great blessings to his people (1:1—2:10)
2. The conduct of God's people in the midst of suffering (2:11—4:19)
3. The shepherding of God's people in the midst of suffering (5:1–14)

Peter wrote to Jewish Christians who were experiencing persecution for their faith. He wrote to comfort them with the hope of eternal life and to challenge them to continue living holy lives. Those who suffer for being Christians become partners with Christ in his suffering. As we suffer, we must remember that Christ is both our hope in the midst of suffering and our example of how to endure suffering faithfully.

MEGATHEMES

THEME	EXPLANATION	IMPORTANCE
Salvation	Our salvation is a gracious gift from God. God chose us out of his love for us, Jesus died to pay the penalty for our sin, and the Holy Spirit cleansed us from sin when we believed. Eternal life is a wonderful gift for those who trust in Christ.	Our safety and security are in God. If we experience joy in relationship with Christ now, how much greater will our joy be when he returns and we see him face to face. Such a hope should motivate us to serve Christ with greater commitment.
Persecution	Peter offers faithful believers comfort and hope. We should expect ridicule, rejection, and suffering because we are Christians. Persecution makes us stronger because it refines our faith. We can face persecution victoriously, as Christ did, if we rely on him.	Christians still suffer for what they believe. We should expect persecution, but we don't have to be terrified by it. The fact that we will live eternally with Christ should give us the confidence, patience, and hope to stand firm even when we are persecuted.
God's Family	We are privileged to belong to God's family, a community with Christ as the founder and foundation. Everyone in this community is related—we are all brothers and sisters, loved equally by God.	Because Christ is the foundation of our family, we must be devoted, loyal, and faithful to him. By obeying him, we show that we are his children. We must accept the challenge to live differently from the society around us.
Family Life	Peter encouraged the wives of unbelievers to submit to their husbands' authority as a means of winning them to Christ. He urged all family members to treat others with sympathy, love, compassion, and humility.	We must treat our families lovingly. Though it's never easy, willing service is the best way to influence loved ones. To gain the strength we need for self-discipline and submission, we need to pray for God's help.
Judgment	God will judge everyone with perfect justice. We all will face God. He will punish evildoers and those who persecute God's people. Those who love him will be rewarded with life forever in his presence.	Because all are accountable to God, we can leave judgment of others to him. We must not hate or resent those who persecute us. We should realize that we will be held responsible for how we live each day.

1. God's great blessings to his people

A Living Hope, and a Sure Salvation

1 Peter, an apostle of Jesus Christ,
To those who reside as aliens, scattered throughout Pontus, Galatia, Cappadocia,
Asia, and Bithynia, who are chosen
2 according to the foreknowledge of God the Father, by the sanctifying work of the
Spirit, to obey Jesus Christ and be sprinkled with His blood: May grace and peace be
yours in the fullest measure.
3 Blessed be the God and Father of our Lord Jesus Christ, who according to His great
mercy has caused us to be born again to a living hope through the resurrection of Jesus
Christ from the dead,
4 to *obtain* an inheritance *which is* imperishable and undefiled and will not fade away,
reserved in heaven for you,
5 who are protected by the power of God through faith for a salvation ready to be
revealed in the last time.

1:2 Rom 8:29; 1 Pet 1:20; 2 Thess 2:13; Heb 10:22; 12:24; 2 Pet 1:2

1:3 2 Cor 1:3; Gal 6:16; Titus 3:5; James 1:18

1:4 Acts 20:32; Rom 8:17; Col 3:24; 1 Pet 5:4; 2 Tim 4:8

1:5 John 10:28; Phil 4:7; Eph 2:8; 1 Cor 1:21; 2 Thess 2:13; 1 Pet 4:13; 5:1

1:1 The apostle Peter wrote this letter to encourage believers who would likely face trials and persecution under Emperor Nero. During most of the first century, Christians were not hunted down and killed throughout the Roman empire. They could, however, expect social and economic persecution from three main sources: the Romans, the Jews, and their own families. All would very likely be misunderstood; some would be harassed; a few would be tortured and even put to death.

The legal status of Christians in the Roman empire was unclear. Many Romans still thought of Christians as members of a Jewish sect, and because the Jewish religion was legal, they considered Christianity legal also—as long as Christians complied with the empire's laws. However, if Christians refused to worship the emperor or join the army, or if they were involved in civil disturbances (such as the one in Ephesus recorded in Acts 19:23ff), they might be punished by the civil authorities.

Many Jews did not appreciate being legally associated with Christians. As the book of Acts frequently records, Jews occasionally harmed Christians physically, drove them out of town, or attempted to turn Roman officials against them. Saul, later the great apostle Paul, was an early Jewish persecutor of Christians.

Another source of persecution was the Christian's own family. Under Roman law, the head of the household had absolute authority over all its members. Unless the ruling male became a Christian, the wife, children and servants who were believers might well face extreme hardship. If they were sent away, they would have no place to turn but the church; if they were beaten, no court of law would uphold their interests.

Peter may have been writing especially for new Christians and those planning to be baptized. Peter wanted to warn them about what lay ahead, and they needed his encouraging words to help them face opposition. This letter is still helpful for any Christians facing trials. Many Christians around the world are living under governments more repressive than the Roman empire of the first century. Christians everywhere are subject to misunderstanding, ridicule, and even harassment by unbelieving friends, employers, and family members. None of us is exempt from catastrophe, pain, illness, and death—trials that, like persecution, make us lean heavily on God's grace. For today's readers, as well as for Peter's original audience, the theme of this letter is *hope.*

1:1 Peter (also called Simon and Cephas) was one of the 12 disciples chosen by Jesus (Mark 1:16–18; John 1:42) and, with James and John, was part of the inner group that Jesus singled out for special training and fellowship. Peter was one of the first to recognize Jesus as the Messiah, God's Son, and Jesus gave him a special leadership role in the church (Matthew 16:16–19; Luke 22:31–32; John 21:15–19). Although during Jesus' trial Peter denied knowing Jesus, Peter repented and became a great apostle. For more information on Peter, see his Profile in Matthew 27.

1:1 This letter is addressed to "aliens," or to the Jewish Christians scattered throughout the world as a result of persecution against believers in and around Jerusalem. The first believers and leaders of the early church were Jews. When they became Christians, they didn't give up their Jewish heritage, just as you didn't give up your nationality when you became a follower of Christ. Because of persecution, these believers had been scattered throughout the Roman world (this scattering is described in Acts 8:1–4). Persecution didn't stop the spread of the gospel; instead, persecution served as a way to introduce the Good News to the whole empire. Thus the churches to whom Peter wrote also included Gentile Christians.

1:2 Peter encouraged his readers by this strong declaration that they were *chosen* by God the Father. At one time, only the nation of Israel could claim to be God's chosen people; but through Christ, all believers—Jews and Gentiles—belong to God. Our salvation and security rest in the free and merciful choice of almighty God; no trials or persecutions can take away the eternal life he gives to those who believe in him.

1:2 This verse mentions all three members of the Trinity—God the Father, God the Son (Jesus Christ), and God the Holy Spirit. All members of the Trinity work to bring about our salvation. The Father chose us before we chose him (Ephesians 1:4). Jesus Christ the Son died for us while we were still sinners (Romans 5:6–10). The Holy Spirit brings us the benefits of salvation and sets us apart (sanctifies us) for God's service (2 Thessalonians 2:13).

1:3 The term *born again* refers to spiritual birth (regeneration)—the Holy Spirit's act of bringing believers into God's family. Jesus used this concept of new birth when he explained salvation to Nicodemus (see John 3).

1:3–6 Do you need encouragement? Peter's words offer joy and hope in times of trouble, and he bases his confidence on what God has done for us in Christ Jesus. We're called into a *living* hope of eternal life (1:3). Our hope is not only for the future; eternal life begins when we trust Christ and join God's family. No matter what pain or trial we face in this life, we know that it is not our final experience. Eventually we will live with Christ forever.

1:4 The Jews had looked forward to an inheritance in the promised land of Canaan (Numbers 32:19; Deuteronomy 2:12; 19:9). Christians now look forward to a family inheritance in the eternal city of God. God has reserved the inheritance; it will never fade or decay; it will be unstained by sin. The best part is that *you* have an inheritance if you have trusted Christ as your Savior.

1:5 God will help us remain true to our faith through whatever difficult times we must face. The "last time" is the judgment day of Christ described in Romans 14:10 and Revelation 20:11–15. We may have to endure trials, persecution, or violent death, but our souls cannot be harmed if we have accepted Christ's gift of salvation. We know we will receive the promised rewards.

1:6 Rom 5:2; 1 Pet 5:10; 1 Pet 3:17; James 1:2; 1 Pet 4:12

1:7 James 1:3; 1 Cor 3:13; Rom 2:7; Luke 17:30; 1 Pet 1:13

1:9 Rom 6:22

1:10 Matt 13:17; Luke 10:24; Matt 26:24; 1 Pet 1:13

1:11 2 Pet 1:21; Matt 26:24

1:12 1 Tim 3:16

6 In this you greatly rejoice, even though now for a little while, if necessary, you have
been distressed by various trials,
7 so that the proof of your faith, *being* more precious than gold which is perishable,
even though tested by fire, may be found to result in praise and glory and honor at the
revelation of Jesus Christ;
8 and though you have not seen Him, you love Him, and though you do not see Him
now, but believe in Him, you greatly rejoice with joy inexpressible and full of glory,
9 obtaining as the outcome of your faith the salvation of [1]your souls.
10 As to this salvation, the prophets who prophesied of the grace that *would come* to
you made careful searches and inquiries,
11 seeking to know what person or time the Spirit of Christ within them was indicating
as He predicted the sufferings of Christ and the glories to follow.
12 It was revealed to them that they were not serving themselves, but you, in these things

1 One early ms does not contain *your*

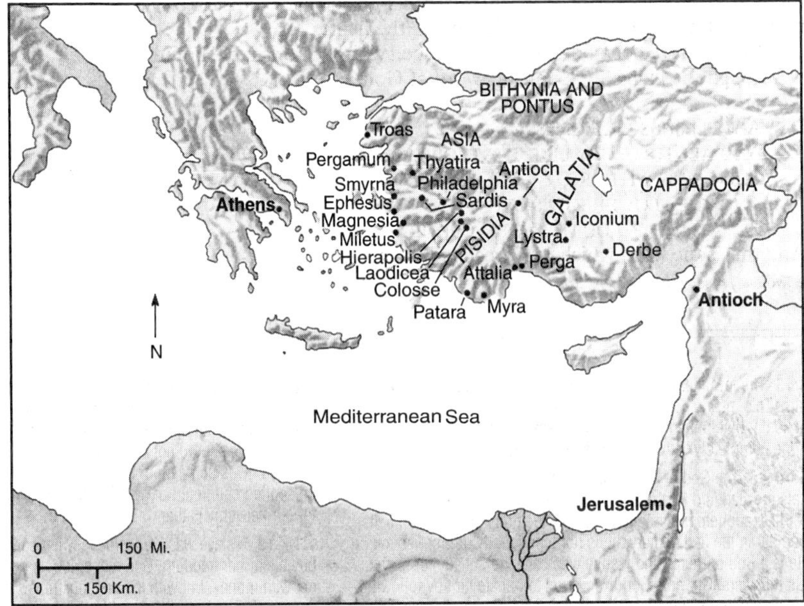

THE CHURCHES OF PETER'S LETTER
Peter addressed his letter to the churches located throughout Pontus, Galatia, Cappadocia, Asia, and Bithynia. Paul had evangelized many of these areas; other areas had churches that were begun by the Jews who were in Jerusalem on the day of Pentecost and heard Peter's powerful sermon (see Acts 2:9–11).

1:6 Why were Christians the target of persecution? (1) They refused to worship the emperor as a god and thus were viewed as atheists and traitors. (2) They refused to worship at pagan temples, so business for these moneymaking enterprises dropped wherever Christianity took hold. (3) They didn't support the Roman ideals of self, power, and conquest, and the Romans scorned the Christian ideal of self-sacrificing service. (4) They exposed and rejected the horrible immorality of pagan culture.

1:6–7 Peter mentions suffering several times in this letter: 1:6–7; 3:13–17; 4:12–19; 5:9. When he speaks of trials, he is not talking about natural disasters or the experience of God's punishments, but the response of an unbelieving world to people of faith. All believers face such trials when they let their light shine into the darkness. We must accept trials as part of the refining process that burns away impurities and prepares us to meet Christ. Trials teach us patience (Romans 5:3–4; James 1:2–3) and help us grow to be the kind of people God wants.

1:7 As gold is heated, impurities float to the top and can be skimmed off. Steel is tempered or strengthened by heating it in fire. Likewise, our trials, struggles, and persecutions refine and strengthen our faith, making us useful to God.

1:10–12 Although the plan of salvation was a mystery to the Old Testament prophets, they still suffered persecution, and some even died for God. In contrast, some Jewish Christians who read Peter's letter had seen Jesus for themselves and knew why he came. They based their assurance on Jesus' death and resurrection. With their firsthand knowledge and personal experience of Jesus, their faith could be even stronger than that of the Old Testament prophets.

1:11 The Spirit of Christ is another name for the Holy Spirit. Before Jesus left his ministry on earth to return to heaven, he promised to send the Holy Spirit, the Helper, to teach, help, and guide his followers (John 14:15–17, 26; 16:7). The Holy Spirit would tell them all about Jesus and would reveal his glory (John 15:26; 16:14). The Old Testament prophets, writing under the Holy Spirit's inspiration (2 Peter 1:20–21), described the coming of the Messiah. The New Testament apostles, through the inspiration of the same Spirit, preached the crucified and risen Lord.

which now have been announced to you through those who preached the gospel to you
by the Holy Spirit sent from heaven—things into which angels long to look.
13 Therefore, prepare your minds for action, keep sober *in spirit,* fix your hope completely on the grace to be brought to you at the revelation of Jesus Christ.
14 As obedient children, do not be conformed to the former lusts *which were yours* in
your ignorance,
15 but like the Holy One who called you, be holy yourselves also in all *your* behavior;
16 because it is written, "YOU SHALL BE HOLY, FOR I AM HOLY."
17 If you address as Father the One who impartially judges according to each one's
work, conduct yourselves in fear during the time of your stay *on earth;*
18 knowing that you were not redeemed with perishable things like silver or gold from
your futile way of life inherited from your forefathers,
19 but with precious blood, as of a lamb unblemished and spotless, *the blood* of Christ.
20 For He was foreknown before the foundation of the world, but has appeared in these
last times for the sake of you
21 who through Him are believers in God, who raised Him from the dead and gave
Him glory, so that your faith and hope are in God.
22 Since you have in obedience to the truth purified your souls for a sincere love of the
brethren, fervently love one another from [2]the heart,
23 for you have been born again not of seed which is perishable but imperishable, *that
is,* through the living and enduring word of God.
24 For,
"ALL FLESH IS LIKE GRASS,
AND ALL ITS GLORY LIKE THE FLOWER OF GRASS.
THE GRASS WITHERS,
AND THE FLOWER FALLS OFF,
25 BUT THE WORD OF THE LORD ENDURES FOREVER."
And this is the word which was preached to you.

2 Two early mss read *a clean heart*

1:13 Eph 6:14; 1 Thess 5:6, 8; 2 Tim 4:5

1:14 Rom 12:2; Eph 4:18

1:15 1 Thess 4:7; 1 John 3:3; 2 Cor 7:1; James 3:13

1:16 Lev 11:44f; 19:2

1:17 Matt 16:27; 2 Cor 7:1; Heb 12:28

1:18 Titus 2:14; Heb 9:12

1:19 Acts 20:28; 1 Pet 1:2; John 1:29

1:20 1 Pet 1:2; Rev 13:8

1:21 Rom 4:24; 10:9; John 17:5, 24; 1 Tim 3:16; Heb 2:9

1:22 James 4:8; John 13:34; Rom 12:10; Heb 13:1

1:23 John 3:3; 1 Pet 1:3

1:24 Is 40:6ff; James 1:10f

1:25 Is 40:8; Heb 6:5

1:13 The imminent return of Christ should motivate us to live for him. This means being mentally alert ("prepare your minds for action"), disciplined ("keep sober in spirit"), and focused ("fix your hope completely"). Are you ready to meet Christ?

1:14–16 The God of Israel and of the Christian church is holy—he sets the standard for morality. Unlike the Roman gods, he is not warlike, adulterous, or spiteful. Unlike the gods of the pagan cults popular in the first century, he is not bloodthirsty or promiscuous. He is a God of mercy and justice who cares personally for each of his followers. Our holy God expects us to imitate him by following his high moral standards. Like him, we should be both merciful and just; like him, we should sacrifice ourselves for others.

1:15–16 After people commit their lives to Christ, they usually still feel a pull back to their old ways. Peter tells us to be like our heavenly Father—holy in all our behavior. Holiness means being totally devoted or dedicated to God, set aside for his special use and set apart from sin and its influence. We're to be set apart and different, not blending in with the crowd, yet not being different just for the sake of being different. What makes us different are God's qualities in our lives. Our focus and priorities must be his. All this is in direct contrast to our old ways (1:14). We cannot become holy on our own, but God gives us his Holy Spirit to help us obey and to give us power to overcome sin. Don't use the excuse that you can't help slipping into sin. Call on God's power to free you from sin's grip.

1:17 "Fear" is not the fear of a slave for a ruthless master, but the healthy respect of a believer for the all-powerful God. Because God is the Judge of all the earth, we dare not ignore him or treat him casually. We should not assume that our privileged status as God's children gives us freedom to do whatever we want. We should not be spoiled children, but grateful children who love to show respect for our heavenly Father.

1:18–19 A slave was "redeemed" when someone paid money to buy his or her freedom. God redeemed us from the tyranny of sin, not with money, but with the precious blood of his own Son (Romans 6:6–7; 1 Corinthians 6:20; Colossians 2:13–14; Hebrews 9:12). We cannot escape from sin on our own; only the life of God's Son can free us.

1:20 Christ's sacrifice for our sins was not an afterthought, not something God decided to do when the world spun out of control. This plan was set in motion by the all-knowing, eternal God long before the world was created. What a comfort it must have been to Jewish believers to know that Christ's coming and his work of salvation were planned by God long before the world began. This assured them that the law was not being scrapped because it didn't work, but that both the law *and* the coming of Christ were part of God's eternal plan.

1:22 "Sincere love" involves selfless giving; a self-centered person can't truly love. God's love and forgiveness free you to take your eyes off yourselves and to meet others' needs. By sacrificing his life, Christ showed that he truly loves you. Now you can love others by following his example and giving of yourself sacrificially.

1:24–25 Quoting Isaiah 40:6–8, Peter reminds believers that everything in this life—possessions, accomplishments, people—will eventually fade away and disappear. Only God's will, Word, and work are permanent. We must stop grasping the temporary and begin focusing our time, money, and energy on the permanent—the Word of God and our eternal life in Christ.

2:1 Eph 4:22, 25, 31; James 1:21
2:2 1 Cor 3:2; Eph 4:15f
2:3 Heb 6:5; Ps 34:8; Titus 3:4
2:4 1 Pet 2:7
2:5 1 Cor 3:9; Gal 6:10; 1 Pet 2:9; Rev 1:6; Rom 15:16; Heb 13:15
2:6 Is 28:16; Rom 9:32; Eph 2:20
2:7 2 Cor 2:16; 1 Pet 2:7, 8; Ps 118:22
2:8 Is 8:14; 1 Cor 1:23; Gal 5:11; Rom 9:22
2:9 Is 43:20f; Deut 10:15; Is 61:6; 66:21; Titus 2:14; Is 9:2; 42:16; Acts 26:18; 2 Cor 4:6
2:10 Hos 1:10; 2:23; Rom 9:25; 10:19

As Newborn Babes

2 Therefore, putting aside all malice and all deceit and hypocrisy and envy and all slander,
2 like newborn babies, long for the pure milk of the word, so that by it you may grow
in respect to salvation,
3 if you have tasted the kindness of the Lord.

As Living Stones

4 And coming to Him as to a living stone which has been rejected by men, but is choice
and precious in the sight of God,
5 you also, as living stones, are being built up as a spiritual house for a holy priesthood, to offer up spiritual sacrifices acceptable to God through Jesus Christ.
6 For *this* is contained in Scripture:
"BEHOLD, I LAY IN ZION A CHOICE STONE, A PRECIOUS CORNER *stone*,
AND HE WHO BELIEVES IN HIM WILL NOT BE DISAPPOINTED."
7 This precious value, then, is for you who believe; but for those who disbelieve,
"THE STONE WHICH THE BUILDERS REJECTED,
THIS BECAME THE VERY CORNER *stone*,"
8 and,
"A STONE OF STUMBLING AND A ROCK OF OFFENSE";
for they stumble because they are disobedient to the word, and to this *doom* they were
also appointed.
9 But you are A CHOSEN RACE, A royal PRIESTHOOD, A HOLY NATION, A PEOPLE FOR
God's OWN POSSESSION, so that you may proclaim the excellencies of Him who has called
you out of darkness into His marvelous light;
10 for you once were NOT A PEOPLE, but now you are THE PEOPLE OF GOD; you had
NOT RECEIVED MERCY, but now you have RECEIVED MERCY.

2:2–3 One characteristic all children share is that they want to grow up—to be like big brother or sister or like their parents. When we are born again, we become spiritual newborn babies. If we are healthy, we will yearn to grow. How sad it is that some people never grow up. The need for milk is a natural instinct for a baby, and it signals the desire for nourishment that will lead to growth. Once we see our need for God's Word and begin to find nourishment in Christ, our spiritual appetite will increase, and we will start to mature. How strong is your desire for God's Word?

2:4–8 In describing the church as God's spiritual house, Peter drew on several Old Testament texts familiar to his Jewish Christian readers: Psalm 118:22; Isaiah 8:14; 28:16. Peter's readers would have understood the living stones to be Israel; then Peter applied the image of "stone" to Christ. Once again Peter showed that the church does not cancel the Jewish heritage, but fulfills it.

2:4–8 Peter portrays the church as a living, spiritual house, with Christ as the foundation and cornerstone and each believer as a stone. Paul portrays the church as a body, with Christ as the head and each believer as a member (see, for example, Ephesians 4:15–16). Both pictures emphasize *community.* One stone is not a temple or even a wall; one body part is useless without the others. In our individualistic society, it is easy to forget our interdependence with other Christians. When God calls you to a task, remember that he is also calling others to work with you. Together your individual efforts will be multiplied. Look for those people and join with them to build a beautiful house for God.

2:6 Christians will sometimes be put to shame or face disappointment in this life, but their trust in God is never misplaced. God will not let them down. We can safely put our confidence in him because the eternal life he promises is certain.

2:6–8 No doubt Peter often thought of Jesus' words to him right after he confessed that Jesus was "the Christ, the Son of the living God": "You are Peter, and upon this rock I will build My church; and the gates of Hades will not overpower it" (Matthew 16:16–18). What is the stone that really counts in the building of the church? Peter answers: Christ himself. What are the characteristics of Christ, the corner stone? (1) He is completely trustworthy; (2) he is precious to believers; (3) and, though rejected by some, he is the most important part of the church.

2:8 Jesus Christ is called "a stone of stumbling and a rock of offense." Some will stumble over Christ because they reject him or refuse to believe that he is who he says he is. But Psalm 118:22 says that "the stone which the builders rejected has become the chief corner stone," the most important part of God's building, the church. In the same way today, people who refuse to believe in Christ have made the greatest mistake of their lives. They have stumbled over the one person who could save them and give meaning to their lives, and they have fallen into God's hands for judgment.

2:9 Christians sometimes speak of "the priesthood of all believers." In Old Testament times, people did not approach God directly. A priest acted as intermediary between God and sinful human beings. With Christ's victory on the cross, that pattern changed. Now we can come directly into God's presence without fear (Hebrews 4:16), and we are given the responsibility of bringing others to him also (2 Corinthians 5:18–21). When we are united with Christ as members of his body, we join in his priestly work of reconciling God and man.

2:9–10 People often base their self-concept on their accomplishments. But our relationship with Christ is far more important than our jobs, successes, wealth, or knowledge. We have been chosen by God as his very own, and we have been called to represent him to others. Remember that your value comes from being one of God's children, not from what you can achieve. You have worth because of what *God does,* not because of what you do.

2. The conduct of God's people in the midst of suffering

11 Beloved, I urge you as aliens and strangers to abstain from fleshly lusts which wage
war against the soul.
12 Keep your behavior excellent among the Gentiles, so that in the thing in which they
slander you as evildoers, they may because of your good deeds, as they observe *them,*
glorify God in the day of [3]visitation.

Honor Authority

13 Submit yourselves for the Lord's sake to every human institution, whether to a king
as the one in authority,
14 or to governors as sent by him for the punishment of evildoers and the praise of
those who do right.
15 For such is the will of God that by doing right you may silence the ignorance of foolish men.
16 *Act* as free men, and do not use your freedom as a covering for evil, but *use it* as
bondslaves of God.
17 Honor all people, love the brotherhood, fear God, honor the king.
18 Servants, be submissive to your masters with all respect, not only to those who are
good and gentle, but also to those who are unreasonable.
19 For this *finds* favor, if for the sake of conscience toward God a person bears up under
sorrows when suffering unjustly.
20 For what credit is there if, when you sin and are harshly treated, you endure it with
patience? But if when you do what is right and suffer *for it* you patiently endure it, this
finds favor with God.

Christ Is Our Example

21 For you have been called for this purpose, since Christ also suffered for you, leaving you an example for you to follow in His steps,

3 I.e. Christ's coming again in judgment

2:11 Heb 6:9; 1 Pet 4:12; Rom 12:1; Lev 25:23; Ps 39:12; Eph 2:19; Heb 11:13; 1 Pet 1:17; Rom 13:14; Gal 5:16, 24; James 4:1

2:12 2 Cor 8:21; Phil 2:15; Titus 2:8; 1 Pet 2:15; 3:16; Acts 28:22; Matt 5:16; 9:8; John 13:31; 1 Pet 4:11, 16; Is 10:3; Luke 19:44

2:13 Rom 13:1

2:14 Rom 13:4; Rom 13:3

2:16 John 8:32; James 1:25; Rom 6:22; 1 Cor 7:22

2:17 Rom 12:10; 13:7; 1 Pet 1:22; Prov 24:21; Matt 22:21; 1 Pet 2:13

2:18 Eph 6:5; James 3:17

2:19 Rom 13:5

2:21 Acts 14:22; 1 Pet 3:9; 1 Pet 3:18; 4:1, 13; Matt 11:29; 16:24

2:11 As believers, we are "aliens and strangers" in this world, because our real home is with God. Heaven is not the pink-cloud-and-harp existence popular in cartoons. Heaven is where God lives. Life in heaven operates according to God's principles and values, and it is eternal and unshakable. Heaven came to earth in the symbolism of the Jewish sanctuary (the tabernacle and temple) where God's presence dwelt. It came in a fuller way in the person of Jesus Christ, "God with us." It permeated the entire world as the Holy Spirit came to live in every believer.

Someday, after God judges and destroys all sin, the kingdom of heaven will rule every corner of this earth. John saw this day in a vision, and he cried out, "Behold, the tabernacle of God is among men, and He will dwell among them, and they shall be His people, and God Himself will be among them" (Revelation 21:3). Our true loyalty should be to our citizenship in heaven, not to our citizenship here, because the earth will be destroyed. Our loyalty should be to God's truth, his way of life, and his dedicated people. Because we are loyal to God, we often will feel like strangers in a world that would prefer to ignore God.

2:12 Peter's advice sounds like Jesus' in Matthew 5:16: If your actions are above reproach, even hostile people will end up praising God. Peter's readers were scattered among unbelieving Gentiles who were inclined to believe and spread vicious lies about Christians. Attractive, gracious, and upright behavior on the part of Christians could show these rumors to be false and could even win some of the unsaved critics to the Lord's side. Don't write off people because they misunderstand Christianity; instead, show them Christ by your life. The day may come when those who criticize you will praise God with you.

2:13–17 When Peter told his readers to submit to the civil authorities, he was speaking of the Roman empire under Nero, a notoriously cruel tyrant. Obviously he was not telling believers to compromise their consciences; as Peter had told the high priest years before, "We must obey God rather than men" (Acts 5:29). But in most aspects of daily life, it was possible and desirable for Christians to live according to the law of their land. Today, some Christians live in freedom while others live under repressive governments. All are commanded to cooperate with the rulers as far as conscience will allow. We are to do this "for the Lord's sake"—so that his Good News and his people will be respected. If we are to be persecuted, it should be for obeying God, and not for breaking moral or civil laws. For more about the Christian's relationship to government, see the note on Romans 13:1ff.

2:16 We are free from keeping the law as a way to earn salvation. However we are still to obey, out of gratitude for our free salvation, the teachings of the Ten Commandments, for they are an expression of God's will for us.

2:18–21 Many Christians were household servants. It would be easy for them to submit to masters who were gentle and kind. But Peter encouraged loyalty and perseverance even in the face of unjust treatment. In the same way, we should submit to our employers, whether they are considerate or harsh. By so doing, we may win them to Christ by our good example. Paul gave similar advice in his letters (see Ephesians 6:5–9; Colossians 3:22–25), as did Jesus (Matthew 5:46; Luke 6:32–36).

2:21–22 We may suffer for many reasons. Some suffering is the direct result of our own sin; some happens because of our foolishness; and some is the result of living in a fallen world. Peter is writing about suffering that comes as a result of doing good. Christ never sinned, and yet he suffered so that we could be set free. When we follow Christ's example and live for others, we too may suffer. Our goal should be to face suffering as he did—with patience, calmness, and confidence that God is in control of the future.

2:21–25 Peter had learned about suffering from Jesus. He knew that Jesus' suffering was part of God's plan (Matthew 16:21–23;

2:22 Is 53:9; 2 Cor 5:21
2:23 Is 53:7; Heb 12:3; 1 Pet 3:9
2:24 Is 53:4, 11; 1 Cor 15:3; Heb 9:28; Acts 5:30; Rom 6:2, 13; Is 53:5; Heb 12:13; James 5:16
2:25 Is 53:6; John 10:11; 1 Pet 5:4
3:1 1 Pet 3:7; Eph 5:22; Col 3:18; 1 Cor 9:19
3:3 Is 3:18ff; 1 Tim 2:9
3:4 Rom 7:22
3:5 1 Tim 5:5; 1 Pet 1:3
3:6 Gen 18:12; 1 Pet 3:14

22 WHO COMMITTED NO SIN, NOR WAS ANY DECEIT FOUND IN HIS MOUTH;
23 and while being reviled, He did not revile in return; while suffering, He uttered no
threats, but kept entrusting *Himself* to Him who judges righteously;
24 and He Himself bore our sins in His body on the cross, so that we might die to sin
and live to righteousness; for by His wounds you were healed.
25 For you were continually straying like sheep, but now you have returned to the Shepherd and Guardian of your souls.

Godly Living

3 In the same way, you wives, be submissive to your own husbands so that even if any
of them are disobedient to the word, they may be won without a word by the behavior of their wives,
2 as they observe your chaste and respectful behavior.
3 Your adornment must not be *merely* external—braiding the hair, and wearing gold
jewelry, or putting on dresses;
4 but *let it be* the hidden person of the heart, with the imperishable quality of a gentle
and quiet spirit, which is precious in the sight of God.
5 For in this way in former times the holy women also, who hoped in God, used to
adorn themselves, being submissive to their own husbands;
6 just as Sarah obeyed Abraham, calling him lord, and you have become her children
if you do what is right without being frightened by any fear.

SUBMISSION
Submission is:

Functional	a distinguishing of our roles and the work we are called to do
Relational	a loving acknowledgment of another's value as a person
Reciprocal	a mutual, humble cooperation with one another
Universal	an acknowledgement by the church of the all-encompassing lordship of Jesus Christ

Submission is voluntarily cooperating with anyone out of love and respect for God first, and then secondly, out of love and respect for that person. Submitting to nonbelievers is difficult, but it is a vital part of leading them to Jesus Christ. We are not called to submit to nonbelievers to the point that we compromise our relationship with God, but we must look for every opportunity to humbly serve in the power of God's Spirit.

Luke 24:25–27, 44–47) and was intended to save us (Matthew 20:28; 26:28). He also knew that all who follow Jesus must be prepared to suffer (Mark 8:34–35). Peter learned these truths from Jesus and passed them on to us.

2:24 Christ died for *our* sins, in *our* place, so we would not have to suffer the punishment we deserve. This is called *substitutionary atonement.*

3:1ff When a man became a Christian, he usually would bring his whole family into the church with him (see, for example, the story of the conversion of the Philippian jailer in Acts 16:29–33). By contrast, a woman who became a Christian usually came into the church alone. Under Roman law, the husband and father had absolute authority over all members of his household, including his wife. Demanding her rights as a free woman in Christ could endanger her marriage if her husband disapproved. Peter reassured Christian women who were married to unbelievers that they did not need to preach to their husbands. Under the circumstances, their best approach would be one of loving service: They should show their husbands the kind of self-giving love that Christ showed the church. By being exemplary wives, they would please their husbands. At the very least, the men would then allow them to continue practicing their "strange" religion. At best, their husbands would join them and become Christians too.

3:1–7 A changed life speaks loudly and clearly, and it is often the most effective way to influence a family member. Peter instructs Christian wives to develop inner beauty rather than being overly concerned about their outward appearance. Their husbands will be won over by their love rather than by their looks. Live your Christian faith quietly and consistently in your home, and your family will see Christ in you.

3:3 We should not be obsessed by fashion, but neither should we be so unconcerned that we do not bother to care for ourselves. Hygiene, neatness, and grooming are important, but even more important are a person's attitude and inner spirit. True beauty begins inside.

3:5 To be *submissive* means to cooperate voluntarily with someone else out of love and respect for God and for that person. Ideally, submission is mutual ("Be subject to one another in the fear of Christ"—Ephesians 5:21). Even when it is one-sided, however, the expression of submission can be an effective Christian strategy. Jesus Christ submitted to death so that we could be saved; we may sometimes have to submit to unpleasant circumstances so that others will see Christ in us. (Christian submission never requires us to disobey God or to participate in what our conscience forbids.) One-sided submission requires tremendous strength. We could not do it without the power of the Holy Spirit working in us.

7 You husbands in the same way, live with *your wives* in an understanding way, as with
someone weaker, since she is a woman; and show her honor as a fellow heir of the grace
of life, so that your prayers will not be hindered.
8 To sum up, all of you be harmonious, sympathetic, brotherly, kindhearted, and humble in spirit;
9 not returning evil for evil or insult for insult, but giving a blessing instead; for you
were called for the very purpose that you might inherit a blessing.
10 For,
"THE ONE WHO DESIRES LIFE, TO LOVE AND SEE GOOD DAYS,
MUST KEEP HIS TONGUE FROM EVIL AND HIS LIPS FROM SPEAKING DECEIT.
11 "HE MUST TURN AWAY FROM EVIL AND DO GOOD;
HE MUST SEEK PEACE AND PURSUE IT.
12 "FOR THE EYES OF THE LORD ARE TOWARD THE RIGHTEOUS,
AND HIS EARS ATTEND TO THEIR PRAYER,
BUT THE FACE OF THE LORD IS AGAINST THOSE WHO DO EVIL."
13 Who is there to harm you if you prove zealous for what is good?
14 But even if you should suffer for the sake of righteousness, you are blessed. AND
DO NOT FEAR THEIR INTIMIDATION, AND DO NOT BE TROUBLED,
15 but [4]sanctify Christ as Lord in your hearts, always *being* ready to make a defense to
everyone who asks you to give an account for the hope that is in you, yet with gentleness
and reverence;
16 and keep a good conscience so that in the thing in which you are slandered, those
who revile your good behavior in Christ will be put to shame.
17 For it is better, if God should will it so, that you suffer for doing what is right rather
than for doing what is wrong.

4 I.e. set apart

3:7 Eph 5:25; Col 3:19; 1 Thess 4:4

3:8 Rom 12:16; 1 Pet 1:22; Eph 4:32; Eph 4:2; Phil 2:3; 1 Pet 5:5

3:9 Rom 12:17; 1 Thess 5:15; 1 Cor 4:12; 1 Pet 2:23; Luke 6:28; Rom 12:14; 1 Cor 4:12; 1 Pet 2:21; Gal 3:14; Heb 6:14; 12:17

3:10 Ps 34:12, 13

3:13 Prov 16:7

3:14 Matt 5:10; 1 Pet 2:19ff; 4:15f; James 5:11; Is 8:12f

3:15 1 Pet 1:3; Col 4:6; 2 Tim 2:25; 1 Pet 1:17

3:16 1 Tim 1:5; Heb 13:18; 1 Pet 3:21; 1 Pet 2:12, 15

3:17 1 Pet 2:20; 4:15f; Acts 18:21; 1 Pet 1:6; 2:15; 4:19

3:7 When Peter calls women the "weaker" partners, he does not imply moral or intellectual inferiority, but he is recognizing women's physical limitations. Women in his day, if unprotected by men, were vulnerable to attack, abuse, and financial disaster. Women's lives may be easier today, but women are still vulnerable to criminal attack and family abuse. And in spite of increased opportunities in the workplace, most women still earn considerably less than most men, and the vast majority of the nations' poor are single mothers and their children. A man who honors his wife as a member of the weaker sex will protect, respect, help, and stay with her. He will not expect her to work full-time outside the home and full-time at home; he will lighten her load wherever he can. He will be sensitive to her needs, and he will relate to her with courtesy, consideration, insight, and tact.

3:7 If a man is not considerate and respectful of his wife, his prayers will be hindered, because a living relationship with God depends on right relationships with others. Jesus said that if you have a problem with a fellow believer, you must make it right with that person before coming to worship (Matthew 5:23–24). This principle carries over into family relationships. If men use their position to mistreat their wives, their relationship with God will suffer.

3:8 Peter lists five key elements that should characterize any group of believers: (1) harmony—pursuing the same goals; (2) sympathy—being responsive to others' needs; (3) brotherly love—seeing and treating each other as brothers and sisters; (4) kindhearted—being affectionately sensitive and caring; and (5) humble in spirit—being willing to encourage one another and rejoice in each other's successes. These five qualities go a long way toward helping believers serve God effectively.

3:8–9 Peter developed the qualities of kindheartedness and humility the hard way. In his early days with Christ, these attitudes did not come naturally to his impulsive, strong-willed personality (see Mark 8:31–33; John 13:6–9 for examples of Peter's blustering). But the Holy Spirit changed Peter, molding his strong personality to God's use, and teaching him tenderness and humility.

3:9 In our fallen world, it is often deemed acceptable by some to tear people down verbally or to get back at them if we feel hurt. Peter, remembering Jesus' teaching to turn the other cheek (Matthew 5:39), encourages his readers to pay back wrongs by praying for the offenders. In God's kingdom, revenge is unacceptable behavior, as is insulting a person, no matter how indirectly it is done. Rise above getting back at those who hurt you. Instead of reacting angrily to these people, pray for them.

3:10 For more about controlling your tongue, see the notes in James 3:2–18.

3:11 Too often we see peace as merely the absence of conflict, and we think of peacemaking as a passive role. But an effective peacemaker actively pursues peace. He or she builds good relationships, knowing that peace is a by-product of commitment. The peacemaker anticipates problems and deals with them before they occur. When conflicts arise, he or she brings them into the open and deals with them before they grow unmanageable. Making peace can be harder work than waging war, but it results not in death but in life and happiness.

3:14–15 Rather than fear our enemies, we are to quietly trust in God as the Lord of all. We must believe that Christ is truly in control of all events. When he rules our thoughts and emotions, we cannot be shaken by anything our enemies may do.

3:15 Some Christians believe that faith is a personal matter that should be kept to oneself. It is true that we shouldn't be boisterous or obnoxious in sharing our faith, but we should always be ready to give an answer, gently and respectfully, when asked about our faith, our life-style, or our Christian perspective. Can others see your hope in Christ? Are you prepared to tell them what Christ has done in your life?

3:16 You may not be able to keep people from slandering you, but you can at least stop supplying them with ammunition. As long as you do what is right, their accusations will be empty and will only embarrass them. Keep your conduct above criticism!

3:18 1 Pet 2:21; Heb 9:26, 28; 10:10; Rom 5:2; Eph 3:12

3:20 Rom 2:4; Gen 6:3, 5, 13f; Heb 11:7; Gen 8:18; 2 Pet 2:5; Acts 2:41; 1 Pet 1:9, 22; 2:25; 4:19

3:21 Acts 16:33; Titus 3:5; Heb 9:14; 10:22; 1 Tim 1:5; Heb 13:18; 1 Pet 3:16; 1 Pet 1:3

3:22 Mark 16:19; Heb 4:14; 6:20; Rom 8:38f; Heb 1:6

4:1 1 Pet 2:21; Eph 6:13; Rom 6:7

4:2 1 Pet 1:14; Mark 3:35

4:3 1 Cor 12:2; Rom 13:13; Eph 2:2; 4:17ff

4:4 Eph 5:18; 1 Pet 3:16

4:5 Acts 10:42; Rom 14:9; 2 Tim 4:1

18 For Christ also died for sins once for all, *the* just for *the* unjust, so that He might
bring us to God, having been put to death in the flesh, but made alive in the spirit;
19 in which also He went and made proclamation to the spirits *now* in prison,
20 who once were disobedient, when the patience of God kept waiting in the days of
Noah, during the construction of the ark, in which a few, that is, eight persons, were
brought safely through *the* water.
21 Corresponding to that, baptism now saves you—not the removal of dirt from the
flesh, but an appeal to God for a good conscience—through the resurrection of Jesus
Christ,
22 who is at the right hand of God, having gone into heaven, after angels and authorities and powers had been subjected to Him.

Keep Fervent in Your Love

4 Therefore, since Christ has [5]suffered in the flesh, arm yourselves also with the same
purpose, because he who has suffered in the flesh has ceased from sin,
2 so as to live the rest of the time in the flesh no longer for the lusts of men, but for
the will of God.
3 For the time already past is sufficient *for you* to have carried out the desire of the
Gentiles, having pursued a course of sensuality, lusts, drunkenness, carousing, drinking
parties and abominable idolatries.
4 In *all* this, they are surprised that you do not run with *them* into the same excesses
of dissipation, and they malign *you;*
5 but they will give account to Him who is ready to judge the living and the dead.
6 For the gospel has for this purpose been preached even to those who are dead, that
though they are judged in the flesh as men, they may live in the spirit according to *the
will of* God.

5 I.e. suffered death

3:18–20 The meaning of preaching "to the spirits now in prison" is not completely clear, and commentators have explained it in different ways. The traditional interpretation is that Christ, between his death and resurrection, announced salvation to God's faithful followers who had been waiting for their salvation during the whole Old Testament era. Matthew records that when Jesus died, "many bodies of the saints who had fallen asleep were raised; and coming out of the tombs after His resurrection they entered the holy city and appeared to many" (Matthew 27:52–53). A few commentators think that this passage says that Christ's Spirit was in Noah as Noah preached to those imprisoned by sin (but now in hell). Still others hold that Christ went to Hades to proclaim his victory and final condemnation to the fallen angels imprisoned there since Noah's day (see 2 Peter 2:4).

In any case, the passage shows that Christ's Good News of salvation and victory is not limited. It has been preached in the past as well as in the present; it has gone to the dead as well as to the living. God has given everyone the opportunity to come to him, but this does not imply a second chance for those who reject Christ in this life.

3:21 Peter says that Noah's salvation *through the water* symbolized baptism, a ceremony involving water. In baptism we identify with Jesus Christ, who separates us from the lost and gives us new life. It is not the ceremony that saves us, but faith in Christ's death and resurrection. Baptism is the symbol of the transformation that happens in the hearts of those who believe (Romans 6:3–5; Galatians 3:27; Colossians 2:12). By identifying themselves with Christ through baptism, Peter's readers could resist turning back, even under the pressure of persecution. Public baptism would keep them from the temptation to renounce their faith.

4:1–2 Some people will do anything to avoid pain. As followers of Christ, however, we should be willing and prepared to do God's will and to suffer for it if necessary. Sin loses its power to defeat us in our suffering if we focus on Christ and what he wants us to do. When our bodies are in pain or our lives are in jeopardy, our real values show up clearly, and sinful pleasures seem less important. If anyone suffers for doing good and still faithfully obeys in spite of suffering, that person has made a clean break with sin.

4:3–4 A person whose life changes radically at conversion may experience contempt from his or her old friends. He may be scorned not only because he refuses to participate in certain activities, but also because his priorities have changed and he is now heading in the opposite direction. His very life incriminates their sinful activities. Mature Christians should help new believers resist such pressures of opposition by encouraging them to be faithful to Christ. *Dissipation* refers to wasteful expenditure and intemperate pursuit of pleasure, especially drinking to excess.

4:5 The basis of salvation is our belief in Jesus (Acts 16:31), but the basis for judgment is how we have lived. Those who inflict persecution are marked for punishment when they stand before God. Believers have nothing to fear, however, because Jesus will be the final Judge over all (John 5:22; 2 Timothy 4:1).

4:5–6 Many people in the early church had concerns about life after death. In Thessalonica, Christians worried that loved ones who died before Christ's return might never see Christ (1 Thessalonians 4:13–18). Peter's readers needed to be reminded that the dead (both the faithful and their oppressors) would be judged. The judgment will be perfectly fair, he pointed out, because even the dead have heard the gospel (see also 3:18–19). The Good News was first announced when Jesus Christ preached on the earth, but it has been operating since before the creation of the world (Ephesians 1:4), and it affects all people, the dead as well as the living.

7 The end of all things is near; therefore, be of sound judgment and sober *spirit* for
the purpose of prayer.
8 Above all, keep fervent in your love for one another, because love covers a multitude of sins.
9 Be hospitable to one another without complaint.
10 As each one has received a *special* gift, employ it in serving one another as good
stewards of the manifold grace of God.
11 Whoever speaks, *is to do so* as one who is speaking the utterances of God; whoever
serves *is to do so* as one who is serving by the strength which God supplies; so that in all
things God may be glorified through Jesus Christ, to whom belongs the glory and dominion forever and ever. Amen.

Share the Sufferings of Christ

12 Beloved, do not be surprised at the fiery ordeal among you, which comes upon you
for your testing, as though some strange thing were happening to you;
13 but to the degree that you share the sufferings of Christ, keep on rejoicing, so that
also at the revelation of His glory you may rejoice with exultation.
14 If you are reviled for the name of Christ, you are blessed, because the Spirit of glory
and of God rests on you.
15 Make sure that none of you suffers as a murderer, or thief, or evildoer, or a troublesome meddler;
16 but if *anyone suffers* as a Christian, he is not to be ashamed, but is to glorify God in
this name.
17 For *it is* time for judgment to begin with the household of God; and if *it begins* with
us first, what *will be* the outcome for those who do not obey the gospel of God?
18 AND IF IT IS WITH DIFFICULTY THAT THE RIGHTEOUS IS SAVED, WHAT WILL
BECOME OF THE GODLESS MAN AND THE SINNER?
19 Therefore, those also who suffer according to the will of God shall entrust their souls
to a faithful Creator in doing what is right.

4:7 Rom 13:11; Heb 9:26; James 5:8; 1 John 2:18; 1 Pet 1:13

4:8 James 5:20

4:9 1 Tim 3:2; Heb 13:2; Phil 2:14

4:11 1 Thess 2:4; Titus 2:1, 15; Heb 13:7; Acts 7:38; Eph 1:19; Rev 1:6; 5:13

4:13 Rom 8:17; 2 Cor 1:5; 4:10; Phil 3:10

4:14 John 15:21; Heb 11:26; 1 Pet 4:16

4:15 1 Pet 2:19f; 3:17; 1 Thess 4:11; 2 Thess 3:11; 1 Tim 5:13

4:16 Acts 5:41; 28:22; James 2:7

4:17 1 Tim 3:15; Heb 3:6; 1 Pet 2:5; Rom 2:9; 2 Thess 1:8; Rom 1:1

4:18 Prov 11:31; Luke 23:31; 1 Tim 1:9

4:7–9 We should live expectantly because Christ is coming. Getting ready to meet Christ involves continually growing in love for God and for others (see Jesus' summary of the Law in Matthew 22:37–40). It is important to pray regularly, and it is also important to reach out to needy people. Your possessions, status, and power will mean nothing in God's kingdom, but you will spend eternity with other people. Invest your time and talents where they will make an eternal difference.

4:9 For more about hospitality, see the note on Romans 12:13.

4:10–11 Some people, well aware of their abilities (gifts), believe that they have the right to use their abilities as they please. Others feel that they have no special talents at all. Peter addresses both groups in these verses. Everyone has some gifts; find yours and use them. All our abilities should be used in serving others; none are for our own exclusive enjoyment. Peter mentions speaking and serving. Paul lists these and other abilities in Romans 12:6–8; 1 Corinthians 12:8–11; Ephesians 4:11.

4:11 How is God glorified when we use our gifts? When we use them as he directs, to help others, they will see Jesus in us and praise him for the help they have received. Peter may have been thinking of Jesus' words: "Let your light shine before men in such a way that they may see your good works, and glorify your Father who is in heaven" (Matthew 5:16).

4:14–16 Again Peter brings to mind Jesus' words: "Blessed are you when people insult you and persecute you, and falsely say all kinds of evil against you because of Me" (Matthew 5:11). Christ will send his Spirit to strengthen those who are persecuted for their faith. This does not mean that all suffering is the result of good Christian conduct. Sometimes a person will grumble, "He's just picking on me because I'm a Christian," when it's obvious to everyone else that the person's own unpleasant behavior is the cause of his or her problems. It may take careful thought or wise counsel to determine the real cause of our suffering. We can be assured, however, that whenever we suffer because of our loyalty to Christ, he will be with us all the way.

4:16 It is not shameful to suffer for being a Christian. When Peter and John were persecuted for preaching the Good News, they rejoiced because such persecution was a mark of God's approval of their work (Acts 5:41). Don't seek out suffering, and don't try to avoid it. Instead, keep on doing what is right regardless of the suffering it might bring.

4:17–18 This refers not to final judgment but to God's refining discipline (Hebrews 12:7). God often allows believers to sin and then experience the consequences. He does this for several reasons: (1) to show us our potential for sinning, (2) to encourage us to turn from sin and more constantly depend on him, (3) to prepare us to face other, even stronger temptations in the future, and (4) to help us stay faithful and keep on trusting him. If believers need earthly discipline (judgment) from God, how much more will unbelievers receive it? If it is hard for the righteous to be saved (only because of God's mercy), what chance do those have who reject Christ?

4:19 God created the world, and he has faithfully ordered it and kept it since the creation. Because we know that God is faithful, we can count on him to fulfill his promises to us. If God can oversee the forces of nature, surely he can see us through the trials we face.

3. The shepherding of God's people in the midst of suffering

Serve God Willingly

5 Therefore, I exhort the elders among you, as *your* fellow elder and witness of the
sufferings of Christ, and a partaker also of the glory that is to be revealed,
2 shepherd the flock of God among you, exercising oversight not under compulsion,
but voluntarily, according to *the will of* God; and not for sordid gain, but with eagerness;
3 nor yet as lording it over those allotted to your charge, but proving to be examples
to the flock.
4 And when the Chief Shepherd appears, you will receive the unfading crown of
glory.
5 You younger men, likewise, be subject to *your* elders; and all of you, clothe yourselves with humility toward one another, for GOD IS OPPOSED TO THE PROUD, BUT GIVES
GRACE TO THE HUMBLE.
6 Therefore humble yourselves under the mighty hand of God, that He may exalt you
at the proper time,
7 casting all your anxiety on Him, because He cares for you.
8 Be of sober *spirit,* be on the alert. Your adversary, the devil, prowls around like a
roaring lion, seeking someone to devour.
9 But resist him, firm in *your* faith, knowing that the same experiences of suffering
are being accomplished by your brethren who are in the world.
10 After you have suffered for a little while, the God of all grace, who called you to His
eternal glory in Christ, will Himself perfect, confirm, strengthen *and* establish you.
11 To Him *be* dominion forever and ever. Amen.

5:2 John 21:16; Acts 20:28; Philem 14

5:3 Phil 3:17; 1 Thess 1:7; 2 Thess 3:9; 1 Tim 4:12; Titus 2:7

5:4 1 Pet 2:25; 1 Pet 1:4; 1 Cor 9:25

5:5 Luke 22:26; 1 Tim 5:1; Eph 5:21; 1 Pet 3:8; Prov 3:34

5:6 Matt 23:12; Luke 14:11; 18:14; James 4:10

5:7 Ps 55:22; Matt 6:25

5:8 1 Pet 1:13; Matt 24:42; James 4:7; 2 Tim 4:17

5:10 2 Cor 4:17; 2 Tim 2:10; 1 Cor 1:10; Heb 13:21

5:11 Rom 11:36; 1 Pet 4:11

5:1 Elders were church officers providing supervision, protection, discipline, instruction, and direction for the other believers. *Elder* simply means "older." Both Greeks and Jews gave positions of great honor to wise older men, and the Christian church continued this pattern of leadership. Elders carried great responsibility, and they were expected to be good examples.

5:1–2 Peter, one of Jesus' 12 disciples, was one of the three who saw Christ's glory at the transfiguration (Mark 9:1–13; 2 Peter 1:16–18). Often the spokesman for the apostles, Peter witnessed Jesus' death and resurrection, preached at Pentecost, and became a pillar of the Jerusalem church. But writing to the elders, he identified himself as a fellow elder, not a superior. He asked them to "shepherd the flock of God," exactly what Jesus had told him to do (John 21:15–17). Peter was taking his own advice as he worked along with the other elders in caring for God's faithful people. His identification with the elders is a powerful example of Christian leadership, where authority is based on service, not power (Mark 10:42–45).

5:2–5 Peter describes several characteristics of good leaders in the church: (1) they realize they are caring for God's flock, not their own; (2) They lead out of eagerness to serve, not out of obligation; (3) they are concerned for what they can give, not for what they can get; (4) they lead by example, not force. All of us lead others in some way. Whatever our role, our leadership should be in line with these characteristics.

5:4 The Chief Shepherd is Jesus Christ. This refers to his second coming, when he will judge all people.

5:5 Both young and old can benefit from Peter's instructions. Pride often keeps older people from trying to understand young people and keeps young people from listening to those who are older. Peter told both young and old to be humble and to serve each other. Young men should follow the leadership of older men, who should lead by example. Respect those who are older than you, listen to those younger than you, and be humble enough to admit that you can learn from each other.

5:6 We often worry about our position and status, hoping to get proper recognition for what we do. But Peter advises us to remember that God's recognition counts more than human praise. God is able and willing to bless us according to his timing. Humbly obey God regardless of present circumstances, and in his good time—either in this life or in the next—he will exalt you.

5:7 Carrying your worries, stresses, and daily struggles by yourself shows that you have not trusted God fully with your life. It takes humility, however, to recognize that God cares, to admit your need, and to let others in God's family help you. Sometimes we think that struggles caused by our own sin and foolishness are not God's concern. But when we turn to God in repentance, he will bear the weight even of those struggles. Letting God have your anxieties calls for action, not passivity. Don't submit to circumstances, but to the Lord who controls circumstances.

5:8–9 Lions attack sick, young, or straggling animals; they choose victims who are alone or not alert. Peter warns us to watch out for Satan when we are suffering or being persecuted. Feeling alone, weak, helpless, and cut off from other believers, so focused on our troubles that we forget to watch for danger, we are especially vulnerable to Satan's attacks. During times of suffering, seek other Christians for support. Keep your eyes on Christ, and resist the devil. Then, says James, "he will flee from you" (James 4:7).

5:10 When we are suffering, we often feel as though our pain will never end. Peter gave these faithful Christians the wider perspective. In comparison with eternity, their suffering would last only "a little while." Some of Peter's readers would be strengthened and delivered in their own lifetimes. Others would be released from their suffering through death. All of God's faithful followers are assured of an eternal life with Christ where there will be no suffering (Revelation 21:4).

12 Through Silvanus, our faithful brother (for so I regard *him),* I have written to you
briefly, exhorting and testifying that this is the true grace of God. Stand firm in it!
13 She who is in Babylon, chosen together with you, sends you greetings, and *so does*
my son, Mark.
14 Greet one another with a kiss of love.
Peace be to you all who are in Christ.

5:12
2 Cor 1:19; Heb 13:22; Acts 11:23; 1 Pet 1:13; 4:10; 1 Cor 15:1

5:13
Acts 12:12, 25; 15:37, 39; Col 4:10; Philem 24

5:12 Silvanus (Silas) was one of the men chosen to deliver the letter from the Jerusalem council to the church in Antioch (Acts 15:22). He accompanied Paul on his second missionary journey (Acts 15:40—18:11), is mentioned by Paul in the salutation of Paul's letters to the Thessalonians (1 Thessalonians 1:1; 2 Thessalonians 1:1), and ministered with Timothy in Corinth (2 Corinthians 1:19).

5:13 *Babylon* has been broadly understood by believers to be a reference to Rome. Just as the nation of Israel had been under captivity to Babylon, so the Christians as the new Israel were exiles in a foreign land.

5:13 Mark, also called John Mark, was known to many of this letter's readers because he had traveled widely (Acts 12:25—13:13; 15:36–41) and was recognized as a leader in the church (Colossians 4:10; Philemon 24). Mark was probably with the disciples at the time of Jesus' arrest (Mark 14:51–52). Tradition holds that Peter was Mark's main source of information when Mark wrote his Gospel.

5:14 Peter wrote this letter just before the cruel Emperor Nero began persecuting Christians in Rome and throughout the empire. Afraid for his life, Peter had three times denied even knowing Jesus (John 18:15–27). But here, having learned how to stand firm in an evil world, he encouraged other Christians who were facing persecution for their faith. Peter himself lived by the words he wrote because he was martyred for his faith. Those who stand for Christ will be persecuted because the world is ruled by Christ's greatest enemy. But just as the small group of early believers stood against persecution, so we must be willing to stand for our faith with the patience, endurance, and courage that Peter exhibited.

2 PETER

WARNINGS have many forms: lights, signs, sights, sounds, smells, feelings, and written words. With varied focus, their purpose is the same—to advise alertness and give notice of imminent danger. Responses to these warnings will also vary—from disregard and neglect to evasive or corrective action. How a person reacts to a warning is usually determined by the situation and the source. One reacts differently to an impending storm than to an onrushing automobile, and the counsel of a trusted friend is heeded more than advice from a stranger or the fearful imaginings of a child.

Second Peter is a letter of warning—from an authority none other than the courageous, experienced, and faithful apostle. And it is the last communication from this great warrior of Christ. Soon thereafter he would die, martyred for his faith.

Previously Peter had written to comfort and encourage believers in the midst of suffering and persecution—an external onslaught. But three years later, in this letter containing his last words, he wrote to warn them of an internal attack—complacency and heresy. He spoke of holding fast to the nonnegotiable facts of the faith, of growing and maturing in the faith, and of rejecting all who would distort the truth. To follow this advice would ensure Christ-honoring individuals and Christ-centered churches.

After a brief greeting (1:1), Peter gives the antidote for stagnancy and shortsightedness in the Christian life (1:2–11). Then he explains that his days are numbered (1:12–15) and that the believers should listen to his messages and the words of Scripture (1:16–21).

Next, Peter gives a blunt warning about false teachers (2:1–22). They will become prevalent in the last days (2:1–2), they will do or say anything for money (2:3), they will spurn the things of God (2:2, 10–11), they will do whatever they feel like doing (2:12–17), they will be proud and boastful (2:18–19), and they will be judged and punished by God (2:3–10, 20–22).

Peter concludes his brief letter by explaining why he has written it (3:1–18): to remind them of the words of the prophets and apostles that predicted the coming of false teachers, to give the reasons for the delay in Christ's return (3:1–13), and to encourage them to beware of heresies and to grow in their faith (3:14–18).

Addressed to those who have received "a faith of the same kind as ours," 2 Peter could have been written to us. Our world is filled with false prophets and teachers, who claim to have the truth and who clamor for attention and allegiance. Listen carefully to Peter's message and heed his warning. Determine to grow in your knowledge of Christ and to reject all those who preach anything inconsistent with God's Word.

VITAL STATISTICS

PURPOSE:
To warn Christians about false teachers and to exhort them to grow in their faith in and knowledge of Christ

AUTHOR:
Peter

TO WHOM WRITTEN:
The church at large and all believers everywhere

DATE WRITTEN:
Approximately A.D. 67, three years after 1 Peter was written, possibly from Rome

SETTING:
Peter knew that his time on earth was limited (1:13–14), so he wrote about what was on his heart, warning believers of what would happen when he was gone—especially about the presence of false teachers. He reminded his readers of the unchanging truth of the gospel.

KEY VERSE:
"His divine power has granted to us everything pertaining to life and godliness, through the true knowledge of Him who called us by His own glory and excellence." (1:3).

KEY PEOPLE:
Peter, Paul

SPECIAL FEATURES:
The date and destination are uncertain, and the authorship has been disputed. Because of this, 2 Peter was the last book admitted to the canon of the New Testament Scripture. Also, there are similarities between 2 Peter and Jude.

THE BLUEPRINT

1. Guidance for growing Christians (1:1–21)
2. Danger to growing Christians (2:1–22)
3. Hope for growing Christians (3:1–18)

While Peter wrote his first letter to teach about handling persecution (trials from without), he wrote this letter to teach about handling heresy (trials from within). False teachers are often subtly deceitful. Believers today must still be vigilant against falling into false doctrine, heresy, and cult activity. This letter gives us clues to help detect false teaching.

MEGATHEMES

THEME	EXPLANATION	IMPORTANCE
Diligence	If our faith is real, it will be evident in our godly behavior. If people are diligent in Christian growth, they won't backslide or be deceived by false teachers.	Growth is essential. It begins with faith and culminates in love for others. To keep growing we need to know God, keep on following him, and remember what he taught us. We must remain diligent in faithful obedience and Christian growth.
False Teachers	Peter warns the church to beware of false teachers. These teachers were proud of their position, promoted sexual sin, and advised against keeping the Ten Commandments. Peter countered them by pointing to the Spirit-inspired Scriptures as our authority.	Christians need discernment to be able to resist false teachers. God can rescue us from their lies if we stay true to his Word, the Bible, and reject those who distort the truth.
Christ's Return	One day Christ will create a new heaven and earth, where we will live forever. As Christians, our hope is in this promise. But with Christ's return comes his judgment on all who refuse to believe.	The cure for complacency, lawlessness, and heresy is found in the confident assurance that Christ will return. God is still giving unbelievers time to repent. To be ready, Christians must keep on trusting and resist the pressure to give up waiting for Christ's return.

1. Guidance for growing Christians

Growth in Christian Virtue

1 Simon Peter, a bond-servant and apostle of Jesus Christ,
To those who have received a faith of the same kind as ours, by the righteousness of
our God and Savior, Jesus Christ:
2 Grace and peace be multiplied to you in the knowledge of God and of Jesus our
Lord;
3 seeing that His divine power has granted to us everything pertaining to life and
godliness, through the true knowledge of Him who called us by His own glory and excellence.
4 For by these He has granted to us His precious and magnificent promises, so that
by them you may become partakers of *the* divine nature, having escaped the corruption
that is in the world by lust.

1:1 Rom 1:1; Phil 1:1; James 1:1; Jude 1; 1 Pet 1:1; Rom 1:12; 2 Cor 4:13; Titus 1:4; Rom 3:21-26; Titus 2:13

1:2 Rom 1:7; 1 Pet 1:2; John 17:3; Phil 3:8; 2 Pet 1:3, 8; 2:20; 3:18

1:3 1 Pet 1:5; John 17:3; Phil 3:8; 2 Pet 1:2, 8; 2:20; 3:18; 1 Thess 2:12; 2 Thess 2:14; 1 Pet 5:10

1:4 2 Pet 3:9, 13; Eph 4:13, 24; Heb 12:10; 1 John 3:2; 2 Pet 2:18, 20; 2 Pet 2:19; James 1:27

1:1 First Peter was written just before the time that the Roman Emperor Nero began his persecution of Christians. Second Peter was written two or three years later (between A.D. 66–68), after persecution had intensified. First Peter was a letter of encouragement to the Christians who suffered, but 2 Peter focuses on the church's internal problems, especially on the false teachers who were causing people to doubt their faith and turn away from Christianity. Second Peter combats their heresies by denouncing the evil motives of the false teachers and reaffirming Christianity's truths—the authority of Scripture, the primacy of faith, and the certainty of Christ's return.

1:2 Many believers want an abundance of God's grace and peace, but they are unwilling to put forth the effort to get to know him better through Bible study and prayer. To enjoy the privileges God offers us freely, we have "the knowledge of God and of Jesus our Lord."

1:3–4 The power to grow doesn't come from within us, but from God. Because we don't have the resources to be truly godly, God allows us to "become partakers of the divine nature" in order to keep us from sin and help us live for him. When we are born again, God by his Spirit empowers us with his own moral goodness. See John 3:6; 14:17–23; 2 Corinthians 5:21; and 1 Peter 1:22–23.

1:5 Col 2:3; 2 Pet 1:2
1:6 Acts 24:25; Luke 21:19; 2 Pet 1:3
1:7 Rom 12:10; 1 Pet 1:22
1:8 Col 1:10; John 17:3; Phil 3:8; 2 Pet 1:2, 3
1:9 1 John 2:11; Eph 5:26; Titus 2:14
1:10 Matt 22:14; Rom 11:29; 1 Thess 1:4; James 2:10
1:11 2 Tim 4:18; 2 Pet 2:20; 3:18; Rom 2:4
1:12 Col 1:5f; 2 John 2
1:13 Phil 1:7; 2 Cor 5:1
1:14 2 Cor 5:1; 2 Tim 4:6; John 13:36; 21:19
1:16 1 Thess 2:19; Matt 17:1ff; Mark 9:2ff; Luke 9:28ff
1:17 Matt 17:5; Mark 9:7; Luke 9:35; Heb 1:3

5 Now for this very reason also, applying all diligence, in your faith supply moral excellence, and in *your* moral excellence, knowledge,
6 and in *your* knowledge, self-control, and in *your* self-control, perseverance, and in *your* perseverance, godliness,
7 and in *your* godliness, brotherly kindness, and in *your* brotherly kindness, love.
8 For if these *qualities* are yours and are increasing, they render you neither useless nor unfruitful in the true knowledge of our Lord Jesus Christ.
9 For he who lacks these *qualities* is blind *or* short-sighted, having forgotten *his* purification from his former sins.
10 Therefore, brethren, be all the more diligent to make certain about His calling and choosing you; for as long as you practice these things, you will never stumble;
11 for in this way the entrance into the eternal kingdom of our Lord and Savior Jesus Christ will be abundantly supplied to you.
12 Therefore, I will always be ready to remind you of these things, even though you *already* know *them*, and have been established in the truth which is present with *you.*
13 I consider it right, as long as I am in this *earthly* dwelling, to stir you up by way of reminder,
14 knowing that the laying aside of my *earthly* dwelling is imminent, as also our Lord Jesus Christ has made clear to me.
15 And I will also be diligent that at any time after my departure you will be able to call these things to mind.

Eyewitnesses

16 For we did not follow cleverly devised tales when we made known to you the power and coming of our Lord Jesus Christ, but we were eyewitnesses of His majesty.
17 For when He received honor and glory from God the Father, such an utterance as this was made to Him by the Majestic Glory, "This is My beloved Son with whom I am well-pleased"—

1:5–9 Faith must be more than belief in certain facts; it must result in action, growth in Christian character, and the practice of moral discipline, or it will die away (James 2:14–17). Peter lists several of faith's actions: learning to know God better, developing perseverance, doing God's will, loving others. These actions do not come automatically; they require hard work. They are not optional; all of them must be a continual part of the Christian life. We don't finish one and start on the next, but we work on them all together. God empowers and enables us, but he also gives us the responsibility to learn and to grow. We should not be surprised at or resentful of the process.

1:6 False teachers were saying that self-control was not needed because works do not help the believer anyway (2:19). It is true that works cannot save us, but it is absolutely false to think they are unimportant. We are saved so that we can grow to resemble Christ and so that we can serve others. God wants to produce his character in us. But to do this, he demands our discipline and effort. As we obey Christ who guides us by his Spirit, we will develop self-control, not only with respect to food and drink, but also with respect to our emotions.

1:9 Our faith must go beyond what we believe; it must become a dynamic part of all we do, resulting in good fruit and spiritual maturity. Salvation does not depend on good works, but it results in good works. A person who claims to be saved while remaining unchanged does not understand faith or what God has done for him or her.

1:10 Peter wanted to rouse the complacent believers who had listened to the false teachers and believed that because salvation is not based on good works they could live any way they wanted. If you truly belong to the Lord, Peter wrote, your hard work will prove it. If you're not working to develop the qualities listed in 1:5–7, maybe you don't belong to him. If you are the Lord's—and your hard work backs up your claim to be chosen by God ("His calling and choosing you")—you will never be led astray by the lure of false teaching or glamorous sin.

1:12–15 Outstanding coaches constantly review the basics of the sport with their teams, and good athletes can execute the fundamentals consistently well. We must not neglect the basics of our faith when we go on to study deeper truths. Just as an athlete needs constant practice, we need constant reminders of the fundamentals of our faith and of how we came to believe in the first place. Don't allow yourself to be bored or impatient with messages on the basics of the Christian life. Instead, take the attitude of an athlete who continues to practice and refine the basics even as he or she learns more advanced skills.

1:13–14 Peter knew that he would die soon. Many years before, Christ had prepared Peter for the kind of death Peter would face (see John 21:18–19). At this time, Peter knew that his death was at hand. Peter was martyred for the faith in about A.D. 68. According to one tradition, he was crucified upside down, at his own request, because he did not feel worthy to die in the same manner as his Master.

1:16–18 Peter is referring to the transfiguration where Jesus' divine identity was revealed to him and two other disciples, James and John (see Matthew 17:1–8; Mark 9:2–8; Luke 9:28–36).

1:16–21 This section is a strong statement on the inspiration of Scripture. Peter affirms that the Old Testament prophets wrote God's messages. He puts himself and the other apostles in the same category, because they also proclaim God's truth. The Bible is not a collection of fables or human ideas about God. It is God's very words given *through* people *to* people. Peter emphasized his authority as an eyewitness as well as the God-inspired authority of Scripture to prepare the way for his harsh words against the false teachers. If these wicked men were contradicting the apostles and the Bible, their message could not be from God.

18 and we ourselves heard this utterance made from heaven when we were with Him
on the holy mountain.
19 *So* we have the prophetic word *made* more sure, to which you do well to pay attention as to a lamp shining in a dark place, until the day dawns and the morning star arises
in your hearts.
20 But know this first of all, that no prophecy of Scripture is *a matter* of one's own interpretation,
21 for no prophecy was ever made by an act of human will, but men moved by the Holy
Spirit spoke from God.

2. Danger to growing Christians

The Rise of False Prophets

2 But false prophets also arose among the people, just as there will also be false teachers among you, who will secretly introduce destructive heresies, even denying the
Master who bought them, bringing swift destruction upon themselves.
2 Many will follow their sensuality, and because of them the way of the truth will be
maligned;
3 and in *their* greed they will exploit you with false words; their judgment from long
ago is not idle, and their destruction is not asleep.
4 For if God did not spare angels when they sinned, but cast them into hell and committed them to pits of darkness, reserved for judgment;
5 and did not spare the ancient world, but preserved Noah, a preacher of righteousness, with seven others, when He brought a flood upon the world of the ungodly;
6 and *if* He condemned the cities of Sodom and Gomorrah to destruction by reducing *them* to ashes, having made them an example to those who would live ungodly *lives*
thereafter;
7 and *if* He rescued righteous Lot, oppressed by the sensual conduct of unprincipled men
8 (for by what he saw and heard *that* righteous man, while living among them, felt *his*
righteous soul tormented day after day by *their* lawless deeds),
9 *then* the Lord knows how to rescue the godly from temptation, and to keep the
unrighteous under punishment for the day of judgment,
10 and especially those who indulge the flesh in *its* corrupt desires and despise authority.

1:18 Ex 3:5; Josh 5:15
1:19 Heb 2:2; Ps 119:105; Luke 1:78; Rev 22:16; 2 Cor 4:6
1:20 2 Pet 3:3; Rom 12:6
1:21 Luke 1:70; Acts 1:16; 3:18
2:1 Matt 7:15; 1 Tim 4:1; Gal 2:4; Jude 4; 1 Cor 11:19
2:2 2 Pet 2:7, 18; Jude 4; Acts 16:17; 22:4; 24:14; Rom 2:24
2:3 1 Tim 6:5; Jude 16; 2 Cor 2:17; 1 Thess 2:5; Rom 16:18
2:4 Jude 6; Rev 20:1f
2:5 Gen 6:8, 9; 1 Pet 3:20; 2 Pet 3:6
2:6 Gen 19:24; Jude 7; Is 1:9; Matt 10:15; 11:23; Rom 9:29
2:7 Gen 19:5ff; Jude 4
2:8 Heb 11:4
2:9 1 Cor 10:13; Rev 3:10; Matt 10:15; Jude 6
2:10 2 Pet 3:3; Jude 16

1:19 Christ is the "morning star," and when he returns, he will shine in his full glory. Until that day we have Scripture as a light and the Holy Spirit to illuminate Scripture for us and guide us as we seek the truth. For more on Christ as the morning star, see Luke 1:78; Ephesians 5:14; Revelation 2:28; 22:16.

1:20–21 "Men moved by the Holy Spirit spoke from God" means that Scripture did not come from the creative work of the prophets' own invention or interpretation. God inspired the writers, so their message is authentic and reliable. God used the talents, education, and cultural background of each writer (they were not mindless robots); and God cooperated with the writers in such a way as to ensure that the message he intended was faithfully communicated in the very words they wrote.

2:1 Jesus had told the disciples that false teachers would come (Matthew 24:11; Mark 13:22–23). Peter had heard these words, and at this time he was seeing them come true. Just as false prophets had contradicted the true prophets in Old Testament times (see, for example, Jeremiah 23:16–40; 28:1–17), telling people only what they wanted to hear, so false teachers were twisting Christ's teachings and the words of his apostles. These teachers were belittling the significance of Jesus' life, death, and resurrection. Some claimed that Jesus couldn't be God; others claimed that he couldn't have been a real man. These teachers allowed and even encouraged all kinds of wrong and immoral acts, especially sexual sin. We must be careful to avoid false teachers today. Any book, tape series, or TV message must be evaluated according to God's Word. Beware of special meanings or interpretations that belittle Christ or his work.

2:3 Teachers should be paid by the people they teach, but these false teachers were attempting to make more money by distorting the truth and saying what people wanted to hear. They were more interested in making money than in teaching truth. Peter and Paul both condemned greedy, lying teachers (see 1 Timothy 6:5). Before you send money to any cause, evaluate it carefully. Is the teacher or preacher clearly serving God or promoting his/her own interests? Will the money be used to promote valid ministry, or will it merely finance further promotions?

2:4–6 If God did not spare angels, or people who lived before the flood, or the citizens of Sodom and Gomorrah, he would not spare these false teachers. Some people would have us believe that God will save all people because he is so loving. But it is foolish to think that he will cancel the last judgment. These three examples should warn us clearly that God judges sin and that unrepentant sinners cannot escape.

2:7–9 Just as God rescued Lot from Sodom, so he is able to rescue us from the temptations and trials we face in a wicked world. Lot was not sinless, but he put his trust in God and was spared when Sodom was destroyed. For more information on Lot, see his Profile in Genesis 14. God also will judge those who cause the temptations and trials, so we need never worry about justice being done.

2:10–12 The *angelic majesties* may be angels, all the glories of the unseen world, or, more probably, fallen angels. A similar passage is found in Jude 8–10. Whoever they are, the false teachers slandered the spiritual realities they did not understand, taking Satan's power lightly and claiming to have the ability to judge evil.

2:11 Jude 9

2:12 Jude 10; Jer 12:3; Col 2:22

2:13 Rom 13:13; 1 Thess 5:7; 1 Cor 11:21; Jude 12

2:14 James 1:8; 2 Pet 3:16; Eph 2:3

2:15 Acts 13:10; Num 22:5, 7; Deut 23:4; Neh 13:2; Jude 11

2:16 Num 22:21, 23, 28, 30ff

2:17 Jude 12; Jude 13

2:18 Jude 16; Eph 4:17; 2 Pet 1:4; 2:20

2:19 John 8:34; Rom 6:16

2:20 2 Pet 1:11; 3:18; 2 Tim 2:4; Matt 12:45; Luke 11:26

2:21 Ezek 18:24; Heb 6:4ff; 10:26f; James 4:17; Gal 6:2; 1 Tim 6:14; 2 Pet 3:2; Jude 3

2:22 Prov 26:11

3:1 1 Pet 2:11; 2 Pet 3:8, 14, 17; 2 Pet 1:13

3:2 Jude 17; Luke 1:70; Acts 3:21; Eph 3:5; Gal 6:2; 1 Tim 6:14

Daring, self-willed, they do not tremble when they revile angelic majesties,
11 whereas angels who are greater in might and power do not bring a reviling judgment against them before the Lord.
12 But these, like unreasoning animals, born as creatures of instinct to be captured and
killed, reviling where they have no knowledge, will in the destruction of those creatures
also be destroyed,
13 suffering wrong as the wages of doing wrong. They count it a pleasure to revel in
the daytime. They are stains and blemishes, reveling in their [1]deceptions, as they carouse
with you,
14 having eyes full of adultery that never cease from sin, enticing unstable souls, having a heart trained in greed, accursed children;
15 forsaking the right way, they have gone astray, having followed the way of Balaam,
the *son* of Beor, who loved the wages of unrighteousness;
16 but he received a rebuke for his own transgression, *for* a mute donkey, speaking with
a voice of a man, restrained the madness of the prophet.
17 These are springs without water and mists driven by a storm, for whom the black
darkness has been reserved.
18 For speaking out arrogant *words* of vanity they entice by fleshly desires, by sensuality, those who barely escape from the ones who live in error,
19 promising them freedom while they themselves are slaves of corruption; for by what
a man is overcome, by this he is enslaved.
20 For if, after they have escaped the defilements of the world by the knowledge of the
Lord and Savior Jesus Christ, they are again entangled in them and are overcome, the
last state has become worse for them than the first.
21 For it would be better for them not to have known the way of righteousness, than
having known it, to turn away from the holy commandment handed on to them.
22 It has happened to them according to the true proverb, "A DOG RETURNS TO ITS
OWN VOMIT," and, "A sow, after washing, *returns* to wallowing in the mire."

3. Hope for growing Christians

Purpose of This Letter

3 This is now, beloved, the second letter I am writing to you in which I am stirring up
your sincere mind by way of reminder,
2 that you should remember the words spoken beforehand by the holy prophets and
the commandment of the Lord and Savior *spoken* by your apostles.

1 One early ms reads *love feasts*

Many in our world today mock the supernatural. They deny the reality of the spiritual world and claim that only what can be seen and felt is real. Like the false teachers of Peter's day, they are fools who will be proven wrong in the end. Don't take Satan and his supernatural powers of evil lightly, and don't become arrogant about how defeated he will be. Although Satan will be destroyed completely, he is at work now trying to render Christians complacent and ineffective.

2:13–14 This carousing may have been taking place during the feast that preceded the celebration of the Lord's Supper. The false teachers, although they were sinning openly, took part in these meals with everyone else in the church. In one of the greatest of hypocritical acts, they attended a sacred feast designed to promote love and unity among believers, while at the same time they gossiped and slandered those who disagreed with their opinions. As Paul told the Corinthians, "Therefore whoever eats the bread or drinks the cup of the Lord in an unworthy manner, shall be guilty of the body and the blood of the Lord" (1 Corinthians 11:27). These men were guilty of more than false teaching and promoting evil pleasures; they were guilty of leading others away from God's Son, Jesus.

2:15 Balaam was hired by a pagan king to curse Israel. He did what God told him to do for a time (Numbers 22—24), but eventually his evil motives and desire for money won out (Numbers 25:1–3; 31:16). Like the false teachers of Peter's day, Balaam used religion for personal advancement, a sin that God does not take lightly.

2:19 A person is a slave to whatever controls him or her. Many believe that freedom means doing anything we want. But no one is ever completely free in that sense. If we refuse to follow God, we will follow our own sinful desires and become enslaved to what our bodies want. If we submit our lives to Christ, he will free us from slavery to sin. Christ frees us to serve him, a freedom that results in our ultimate good.

2:20–22 Peter is speaking of a person who has learned about Christ and how to be saved, and has even been positively influenced by Christians, but then rejects the truth and returns to his or her sin. This person is worse off than before, because he or she has rejected the only way out of sin, the only way of salvation. Like a person sinking in quicksand who refuses to grab the rope thrown to him or her, the one who turns away from Christ casts aside his or her only means of escape (see the note on Luke 11:24–26).

The Coming Day of the Lord

3 Know this first of all, that in the last days mockers will come with *their* mocking,
following after their own lusts,
4 and saying, "Where is the promise of His coming? For *ever* since the fathers fell
asleep, all continues just as it was from the beginning of creation."
5 For when they maintain this, it escapes their notice that by the word of God *the*
heavens existed long ago and *the* earth was formed out of water and by water,
6 through which the world at that time was destroyed, being flooded with water.
7 But by His word the present heavens and earth are being reserved for fire, kept for
the day of judgment and destruction of ungodly men.
8 But do not let this one *fact* escape your notice, beloved, that with the Lord one day
is like a thousand years, and a thousand years like one day.
9 The Lord is not slow about His promise, as some count slowness, but is patient toward you, not wishing for any to perish but for all to come to repentance.

A New Heaven and Earth

10 But the day of the Lord will come like a thief, in which the heavens will pass away
with a roar and the elements will be destroyed with intense heat, and the earth and its
works will be [2]burned up.
11 Since all these things are to be destroyed in this way, what sort of people ought you
to be in holy conduct and godliness,
12 looking for and hastening the coming of the day of God, because of which the heavens will be destroyed by burning, and the elements will melt with intense heat!
13 But according to His promise we are looking for new heavens and a new earth, in
which righteousness dwells.
14 Therefore, beloved, since you look for these things, be diligent to be found by Him
in peace, spotless and blameless,
15 and regard the patience of our Lord *as* salvation; just as also our beloved brother
Paul, according to the wisdom given him, wrote to you,

3:3 2 Pet 1:20; 1 Tim 4:1; Heb 1:2; Jude 18; 2 Pet 2:10
3:4 2 Pet 3:12; Acts 7:60; Mark 10:6
3:6 2 Pet 2:5; Gen 7:11, 12, 21f
3:7 2 Thess 1:7; Heb 12:29; Matt 10:15; 1 Cor 3:13; Jude 7
3:8 2 Pet 3:1; Ps 90:4
3:9 Hab 2:3; Rom 13:11; Heb 10:37; Rom 2:4; Rev 2:21
3:10 1 Cor 1:8; Matt 24:43; Luke 12:39; 1 Thess 5:2; Rev 3:3; 16:15; Matt 24:35; Rev 21:1
3:12 1 Cor 1:7; Mic 1:4
3:13 Rom 8:21; Rev 21:27
3:14 1 Cor 15:58; 2 Pet 1:10; Phil 2:15; 1 Thess 5:23; 1 Tim 6:14; James 1:27
3:15 Acts 9:17; 15:25; 1 Cor 3:10; Eph 3:3

2 Two early mss read *discovered*

3:3–4 "In the last days" mockers will say that Jesus is never coming back, but Peter refutes their argument by explaining God's mastery over time. The "last days" is the time between Christ's first and second comings; thus we, like Peter, live in the last days. We must do the work to which God has called us and believe that he will return as he promised.

3:7 In Noah's day the earth was judged by water; at the second coming it will be judged by fire. This fire is described in Revelation 19:20; 20:10–15.

3:8–9 God may have seemed slow to these believers as they faced persecution every day and longed to be delivered. But God is not slow; he just is not on *our* timetable (Psalm 90:4). Jesus is waiting so that more sinners will repent and turn to him. We must not sit and wait for Christ to return, but we should live with the realization that time is short and that we have important work to do. Be ready to meet Christ any time, even today; yet plan your course of service as though he may not return for many years.

3:10–11 The day of the Lord is the day of God's judgment on the earth. Here it is used in reference to Christ's return. Christ's second coming will be sudden and terrible for those who do not believe in him. But if we are morally clean and spiritually alert, it won't come as a surprise. For other prophetic pictures of the day of the Lord, see Isaiah 34:4; Joel 3:15–16; Matthew 24; Mark 13; Luke 21; Revelation 6:12–17. Realizing that the earth is going to be burned up, we should put our confidence in what is lasting and eternal and not be bound to earth and its treasures or pursuits. Do you spend more of your time piling up possessions, or striving to develop Christlike character?

3:13 God's purpose for people is not destruction but re-creation (see Isaiah 66:22; Revelation 21; 22). God will purify the heavens and earth with fire; then he will create them anew. We can joyously look forward to the restoration of God's good world.

3:14 We should not become lazy and complacent because Christ has not yet returned. Instead, we should live in eager expectation of his coming. What would you like to be doing when Christ returns? That is how you should be living each day.

3:15–16 By the time of Peter's writing, Paul's letters already had a widespread reputation. Notice that Peter spoke of Paul's letters as if they were on a level with "the rest of the Scriptures." Already the early church was thinking of Paul's letters as inspired by God.

3:15–18 Peter and Paul had very different backgrounds and personalities, and they preached from different viewpoints. Paul emphasized salvation by grace, not law, while Peter preferred to talk about Christian life and service. The two men did not contradict each other, however, and they always held each other in high esteem. The false teachers intentionally misused Paul's writings by distorting them to condone lawlessness. No doubt this made the teachers popular, because people always like to have their favorite sins justified, but the net effect was to totally destroy Paul's message. Paul may have been thinking of teachers like these when he wrote in Romans 6:15: "What then? Shall we sin because we are not under law but under grace? May it never be!" Peter warned his readers to avoid the mistakes of those wicked teachers by growing in the grace and knowledge of Jesus. The better we know Jesus, the less attractive false teaching will be.

3:16
Heb 5:11; 2 Pet 2:14; 2 Pet 3:2

3:17
2 Pet 2:18; 2 Pet 2:7; Rev 2:5

3:18
2 Pet 1:2; 2:20; Rom 11:36; 2 Tim 4:18; Rev 1:6

16 as also in all *his* letters, speaking in them of these things, in which are some things
hard to understand, which the untaught and unstable distort, as *they do* also the rest of
the Scriptures, to their own destruction.
17 You therefore, beloved, knowing this beforehand, be on your guard so that you are
not carried away by the error of unprincipled men and fall from your own steadfastness,
18 but grow in the grace and knowledge of our Lord and Savior Jesus Christ. To Him
be the glory, both now and to the day of eternity. Amen.

3:18 Peter concludes this brief letter as he began, by urging his readers to grow in the grace and knowledge of the Lord and Savior Jesus Christ—to get to know him better and better. This is the most important step in refuting false teachers. No matter where we are in our spiritual journey, no matter how mature we are in our faith, the sinful world always will challenge our faith. We still have much room for growth. If every day we find some way to draw closer to Christ, we will be prepared to stand for truth in any and all circumstances.

1 JOHN

VITAL STATISTICS

PURPOSE:
To reassure Christians in their faith and to counter false teachings

AUTHOR:
The apostle John

TO WHOM WRITTEN:
The letter is untitled and was written to no particular church. It was sent as a pastoral letter to several Gentile congregations. It was also written to all believers everywhere.

DATE WRITTEN:
Probably between A.D. 85 and 90 from Ephesus

SETTING:
John was an older man and perhaps the only surviving apostle at this time. He had not yet been banished to the island of Patmos, where he would live in exile. As an eyewitness of Christ, he wrote authoritatively to give this new generation of believers assurance and confidence in God and in their faith.

KEY VERSE:
"These things I have written to you who believe in the name of the Son of God, so that you may know that you have eternal life" (5:13).

KEY PEOPLE:
John, Jesus

SPECIAL FEATURES:
John is the apostle of love, and love is mentioned throughout this letter. There are a number of similarities between this letter and John's Gospel—in vocabulary, style, and main ideas. John uses brief statements and simple words, and he features sharp contrasts—light and darkness, truth and error, God and Satan, life and death, love and hate.

"A GOOD man . . . yes . . . perhaps one of the best who ever lived . . . but just a man," say many. Others disagree, claiming that he suffered from delusions of grandeur—a "messiah complex." And the argument rages over the true identity of this man called Jesus. Suggestions have ranged from "simple teacher" to "egomaniac" and "misguided fool." Whoever he was, all would agree that Jesus left his mark on history.

Hearing these discussions, even Christians can begin to wonder and doubt. Is Jesus really God? Did he come to save sinners like us? Does God care about me?

First John was written to dispel doubts and to build assurance by presenting a clear picture of Christ. Entering history, Jesus was and is God in the flesh and God in focus—seen, heard, and touched by the author of this letter, John the apostle. John walked and talked with Jesus, saw him heal, heard him teach, watched him die, met him arisen, and saw him ascend. John knew God—he had lived with him and had seen him work. And John enjoyed fellowship with the Father and the Son all the days of his life.

The elder statesman in the church, John wrote this letter to his "dear children." In it he presented God as light, as love, and as life. He explained in simple and practical terms what it means to have fellowship with God.

At the same time, false teachers had entered the church, denying the incarnation of Christ. John wrote to correct their serious errors. So John's letter is a model for us to follow as we combat modern heresies.

John opens this letter by giving his credentials as an eyewitness of the Incarnation and by stating his reason for writing (1:1–4). He then presents God as "light," symbolizing absolute purity and holiness (1:5–7), and he explains how believers can walk in the light and have fellowship with God (1:8–10). If they do sin, Christ is their defender (2:1–2). John urges them to obey Christ fully and to love all the members of God's family (2:3–17). He warns his readers of "antichrists" and the antichrist who will try to lead them away from the truth (2:18–29).

In the next section, John presents God as "love"—giving, dying, forgiving, and blessing (3:1—4:21). God *is* love, and because God loves us, he calls us his children and makes us like Christ (3:1–2). This truth should motivate us to live close to him (3:3–6). We can be sure of our family relationship with God when our life is filled with good works and love for others (3:7–24). Again, John warns of false teachers who twist the truth. We should reject these false teachers (4:1–6) as we continue to live in God's love (4:7–21).

In the last section, John presents God as "life" (5:1–21). God's life is in his Son. To have his Son is to have eternal life.

Do you know God? Do you know Christ? Do you know that you have eternal life? First John was written to help you know the reality of God in your life through faith in Christ, to assure you that you have eternal life, and to encourage you to remain in fellowship with the God who is light and love. Read this letter written by one overwhelmed by God's love, and with renewed confidence, pass on his love to others.

THE BLUEPRINT

1. God is light (1:1—2:29)
2. God is love (3:1—4:21)
3. God is life (5:1–21)

John wrote about the most vital aspects of faith so that his readers would know Christian truth from error. He emphasizes the basics of faith so that we can be confident in our faith. In our dark world, God is light. In our cold world, God brings the warmth of love. In our dying world, God brings life. When we lack confidence, these truths bring us certainty.

MEGATHEMES

THEME	EXPLANATION	IMPORTANCE
Sin	Even Christians sin. Sin requires God's forgiveness, and Christ's death provides it for us. Determining to live according to God's standards in the Bible shows that our life is being transformed.	We cannot deny our sin nature, maintain that we are "above" sinning, or minimize the consequences of sin in our relationship with God. We must resist the attraction of sin, yet we must confess when we do sin.
Love	Christ commands us to love others as he loved us. This love is evidence that we are truly saved. God is the Creator of love; he cares that his children love each other.	Love means putting others first and being unselfish. Love is action—showing others we care—not just saying it. To show love we must give sacrificially of our time and money to meet the needs of others.
Family of God	We become God's children by believing in Christ. God's life in us enables us to love our fellow family members.	How we treat others shows who our Father is. Live as a faithful, loving family member.
Truth and Error	Teaching that the physical body does not matter, false teachers encouraged believers to throw off moral restraints. They also taught that Christ wasn't really a man and that we must be saved by having some special mystical knowledge. The result was that people became indifferent to sin.	God is truth and light, so the more we get to know him, the better we can keep focused on the truth. Don't be led astray by any teaching that denies Christ's deity or humanity. Check the message; test the claims.
Assurance	God is in control of heaven and earth. Because his word is true, we can have assurance of eternal life and victory over sin. By faith we can be certain of our eternal destiny with him.	Assurance of our relationship with God is a promise, but it is also a way of life. We build our confidence by trusting in God's Word and in Christ's provision for our sin.

1. God is light

Introduction, The Incarnate Word

1 What was from the beginning, what we have heard, what we have seen with our eyes,
what we have looked at and touched with our hands, concerning the Word of Life—
2 and the life was manifested, and we have seen and testify and proclaim to you the
eternal life, which was with the Father and was manifested to us—
3 what we have seen and heard we proclaim to you also, so that you too may have
fellowship with us; and indeed our fellowship is with the Father, and with His Son Jesus
Christ.
4 These things we write, so that our joy may be made complete.

God Is Light

5 This is the message we have heard from Him and announce to you, that God is Light,
and in Him there is no darkness at all.
6 If we say that we have fellowship with Him and *yet* walk in the darkness, we lie and
do not practice the truth;
7 but if we walk in the Light as He Himself is in the Light, we have fellowship with
one another, and the blood of Jesus His Son cleanses us from all sin.
8 If we say that we have no sin, we are deceiving ourselves and the truth is not in us.

1:1 John 19:35; 2 Pet 1:16; John 1:14; 1 John 4:14; Luke 24:39; John 20:27

1:2 1 John 3:5, 8; 5:20; John 19:35; John 15:27; 1 John 4:14; John 10:28; 17:3; John 1:1

1:3 John 19:35; 2 Pet 1:16; 1 John 1:1; John 17:3, 21

1:5 John 1:19; 1 John 3:11; 1 Tim 6:16

1:6 John 8:55; John 3:21

1:7 Titus 2:14

1:8 James 3:2; John 8:44; 1 John 2:4

1:1 First John was written by John, one of Jesus' original 12 disciples. He was probably "the disciple whom Jesus loved" (John 21:20) and, along with Peter and James, he had a special relationship with Jesus. This letter was written between A.D. 85–90 from Ephesus, before John's exile to the island of Patmos (see Revelation 1:9). Jerusalem had been destroyed in A.D. 70, and Christians were scattered throughout the empire. By the time John wrote this letter, Christianity had been around for more than a generation. It had faced and survived severe persecution. The main problem confronting the church at this time was declining commitment: Many believers were conforming to the world's standards, failing to stand up for Christ, and compromising their faith. False teachers were plentiful, and they were accelerating the church's downward slide away from the Christian faith.

John wrote this letter to put believers back on track, to show the difference between light and darkness (truth and error), and to encourage the church to grow in genuine love for God and for one another. He also wrote to assure true believers that they possessed eternal life and to help them know that their faith was genuine—so they could enjoy all the benefits of being God's children. For more about John, see his Profile in John 13.

1:1–5 John opens his first letter to the churches similar to the way he began his Gospel, emphasizing that Christ ("the Word of Life") is eternal, that God came into the world as a human, that he, John, was an eyewitness to Jesus' life, and that Jesus brings light and life.

1:3 As an eyewitness to Jesus' ministry, John was qualified to teach the truth about him. The readers of this letter had not seen and heard Jesus themselves, but they could trust that what John wrote was accurate. We are like those second- and third-generation Christians. Though we have not personally seen, heard, or touched Jesus, we have the New Testament record of his eyewitnesses, and we can trust that they spoke the truth about him. See John 20:29.

1:3–4 John writes about having fellowship with other believers. There are three principles behind true Christian fellowship. First, our fellowship is grounded in the testimony of God's Word. Without this underlying strength, togetherness is impossible. Second, it is mutual, depending on the unity of believers. Third, it is renewed daily through the Holy Spirit. True fellowship combines social and spiritual interaction, and it is made possible only through a living relationship with Christ.

1:5–6 Light represents what is good, pure, true, holy, and reliable. Darkness represents what is sinful and evil. The statement "God is Light" means that God is perfectly holy and true and that he alone can guide us out of the darkness of sin. Light is also related to truth in that light exposes whatever exists, whether it is good or bad. In the dark, good and evil look alike; in the light, they can be clearly distinguished. Just as darkness cannot exist in the presence of light, sin cannot exist in the presence of a holy God. If we want to have a relationship with God, we must put aside our sinful ways of living. To claim that we belong to him but then to go out and live for ourselves is hypocrisy. Christ will expose and judge such deceit.

1:6 Here John was confronting the first of three claims of the false teachers: that we can have fellowship with God and still walk in darkness. False teachers who thought that the physical body was evil or worthless taught one of two approaches to behavior: Either they insisted on denying bodily desires through rigid discipline, or they approved of gratifying every physical lust because the body was going to be destroyed anyway. Obviously the second approach was more popular! Here John is saying that no one can claim to be a Christian and still live in evil and immorality. We can't love God and court sin at the same time.

1:7 How does Jesus' blood cleanse us from every sin? In Old Testament times, believers symbolically transferred their sins to an animal, which they then sacrificed (see a description of this ceremony in Leviticus 4). The animal died in their place to pay for their sin and to allow them to continue living in God's favor. God graciously forgave them because of their faith in him, and because they obeyed his commandments concerning the sacrifice. Those sacrifices anticipated the day when Christ would completely remove sin. Real cleansing from sin came with Jesus, the "Lamb of God who takes away the sin of the world" (John 1:29). Sin, by its very nature, brings death—that is a fact as certain as the law of gravity. Jesus did not die for his own sins; he had none. Instead, by a transaction that we may never fully understand, he died for the sins of the world. When we commit our lives to Christ and thus identify ourselves with him, his death becomes ours. He has paid the penalty for our sins, and his blood has cleansed us. Just as Christ rose from the grave, so we rise to a new life of fellowship with him (Romans 6:4).

1:8 Here John was attacking the second claim of the false teachers: that people have no natural tendency toward sin, that they "have no sin," and that they were then incapable of sinning. This idea is at best self-deception and at worst a bald-faced lie. The false teachers refused to take sin seriously. They wanted to be considered Christians, but they saw no need to confess and repent. The death of Christ did not mean much to them because they didn't think they needed it. Instead of repenting and being purified by Christ's blood, they were encouraging sin among believers. In this

1:10 John 3:33

2:1 John 13:33; 1 John 2:12, 28; 3:7, 18; 4:4; 5:21; John 14:16

2:2 1 John 4:10; John 4:42; 11:51f

2:3 1 John 2:5; 3:24; 4:13; 5:2; 1 John 2:4; 3:6; 4:7f; John 14:15; 15:10

2:4 1 John 3:6; 4:7

2:5 John 14:23; 1 John 2:3; 3:24; 4:13; 5:2

9 If we confess our sins, He is faithful and righteous to forgive us our sins and to cleanse
us from all unrighteousness.
10 If we say that we have not sinned, we make Him a liar and His word is not in us.

Christ Is Our Advocate

2 My little children, I am writing these things to you so that you may not sin. And if
anyone sins, we have an [1]Advocate with the Father, Jesus Christ the righteous;
2 and He Himself is the propitiation for our sins; and not for ours only, but also for
those of the whole world.
3 By this we know that we have come to know Him, if we keep His commandments.
4 The one who says, "I have come to know Him," and does not keep His commandments, is a liar, and the truth is not in him;
5 but whoever keeps His word, in him the love of God has truly been perfected. By
this we know that we are in Him:

1 Gr *Paracletos,* one called alongside to help; or *Intercessor*

JOHN COUNTERS FALSE TEACHINGS

John counters two major threads in the false teachings of the heretics in this letter:

1:6, 8, 10	They denied the reality of sin. John says that if we continue in sin, we can't claim to belong to God. If we say we have no sin, we are only fooling ourselves and refusing to accept the truth.
2:22; 4:1–3	They denied that Jesus was the Messiah—God in the flesh. John said that if we believe that Jesus was God incarnate and trust him for our salvation, we are children of God.

life we are always capable of sinning, so we should never let down our guard.

1:8–10 The false teachers not only denied that sin breaks our fellowship with God (1:6) and that they had a sinful nature (1:8), but they also denied that their conduct involved any sin at all (1:10). That was a lie that ignored one basic truth: All people are sinners by nature and by practice. At conversion all our sins are forgiven—past, present, and future. Yet even after we become Christians, we still sin and still need to confess. This kind of confession is not offered to gain God's acceptance, but to remove the barrier to fellowship that our sin has put between us and him. It is difficult, however, for many people to admit their faults and shortcomings, even to God. It takes humility and honesty to recognize our weaknesses, and most of us would rather pretend that we are strong. But we need not fear revealing our sins to God—he knows them already. He will not push us away, no matter what we've done. Instead he will draw us to himself.

1:9 Confession is supposed to free us to enjoy fellowship with Christ. It should ease our consciences and lighten our cares. But some Christians do not understand how it works. They feel so guilty that they confess the same sins over and over; then they wonder if they might have forgotten something. Other Christians believe that God forgives them when they confess, but if they died with unconfessed sins, they would be forever lost. These Christians do not understand that God *wants* to forgive us. He allowed his beloved Son to die just so he could offer us pardon. When we come to Christ, he forgives all the sins we have committed or will ever commit. We don't need to confess the sins of the past all over again, and we don't need to fear that God will reject us if we don't keep our slate perfectly clean. Of course we should continue to confess our sins, but not because failure to do so will make us lose our salvation. Our relationship with Christ is secure. Instead, we should confess so that we can enjoy maximum fellowship and joy with him.

True confession also involves a commitment not to continue in sin. We wouldn't be genuinely confessing our sins to God if we planned to commit them again and just wanted temporary forgiveness. We should also pray for strength to defeat temptation the next time we face it.

1:9 If God has forgiven us for our sins because of Christ's death, why must we confess our sins? In admitting our sins and receiving Christ's cleansing, we are: (1) agreeing with God that our sin truly is sin and that we are willing to turn from it, (2) ensuring that we don't conceal our sins from him and consequently from ourselves, and (3) recognizing our tendency to sin and relying on his power to overcome it.

2:1 John uses the address "little children" in a warm, fatherly way. He is not talking down to his readers but is showing affection for them. At this writing, John was a very old man. He had spent almost all his life in ministry, and many of his readers were indeed his spiritual children.

2:1–2 To people who are feeling guilty and condemned, John offers reassurance. They know they have sinned, and Satan (called "the accuser" in Revelation 12:10) is demanding the death penalty. When you feel this way, don't give up hope—the best defense attorney in the universe is pleading your case. Jesus Christ, your Advocate, your defender, is the Judge's Son. He has already suffered your penalty in your place. You can't be tried for a case that is no longer on the docket. United with Christ, you are as safe as he is. Don't be afraid to ask Christ to plead your case—he has already won it (see Romans 8:33–34; Hebrews 7:24–25).

2:2 Jesus Christ is the propitiation for our sins (see also 4:10). He can stand before God as our mediator because his death satisfied the wrath of God against sin and paid the death penalty for our sin. Thus Christ both satisfies God's requirement and removes our sin. In him we are forgiven and purified.

2:2 Sometimes it is difficult to forgive those who wrong us. Imagine how hard it would be to forgive everyone, no matter what they had done! This is what God has done in Jesus. No one, no matter what he or she has done, is beyond forgiveness. All a person has to do is turn from his or her sin, receive Christ's forgiveness, and commit his or her life to him.

2:3–6 How can you be sure that you belong to Christ? This passage gives two ways to know: If you do what Christ says and live as Christ wants. What does Christ tell us to do? John answers in 3:23: "Believe in the name of His Son Jesus Christ, and love one another." True Christian faith results in loving behavior; that is why John says that the way we act can give us assurance that we belong to Christ.

6 the one who says he abides in Him ought himself to walk in the same manner as He
walked.
7 Beloved, I am not writing a new commandment to you, but an old commandment
which you have had from the beginning; the old commandment is the word which you
have heard.
8 On the other hand, I am writing a new commandment to you, which is true in Him
and in you, because the darkness is passing away and the true Light is already shining.
9 The one who says he is in the Light and *yet* hates his brother is in the darkness
until now.
10 The one who loves his brother abides in the Light and there is no cause for stumbling in him.
11 But the one who hates his brother is in the darkness and walks in the darkness, and
does not know where he is going because the darkness has blinded his eyes.
12 I am writing to you, little children, because your sins have been forgiven you for His
name's sake.
13 I am writing to you, fathers, because you know Him who has been from the beginning. I am writing to you, young men, because you have overcome the evil one. I have
written to you, children, because you know the Father.
14 I have written to you, fathers, because you know Him who has been from the beginning. I have written to you, young men, because you are strong, and the word of God
abides in you, and you have overcome the evil one.

Do Not Love the World

15 Do not love the world nor the things in the world. If anyone loves the world, the
love of the Father is not in him.
16 For all that is in the world, the lust of the flesh and the lust of the eyes and the boastful
pride of life, is not from the Father, but is from the world.
17 The world is passing away, and *also* its lusts; but the one who does the will of God
lives forever.

2:6 John 13:15; 15:10

2:7 Heb 6:9; 1 John 3:2, 21; 4:1, 7, 11; John 13:34; 1 John 3:11, 23; 4:21; 2 John 5

2:8 John 13:34; Rom 13:12; Eph 5:8; 1 Thess 5:4f; John 1:9

2:9 1 John 2:11; 3:15; 4:20; Acts 1:15

2:10 John 11:9; 1 John 2:10, 11

2:11 1 John 2:9; 3:15; 4:20; John 12:35; 1 John 1:6; 2 Cor 4:4; 2 Pet 1:9

2:13 1 John 1:1; John 16:33; 1 John 2:14

2:14 1 John 1:10; 2:13

2:15 Rom 12:2; James 1:27; James 4:4

2:16 Rom 13:14; Eph 2:3; 1 Pet 2:11; Prov 27:20; James 4:16

2:6 To "walk . . . as He walked" or to live as Christ did doesn't mean choosing 12 disciples, performing great miracles, and being crucified. We cannot merely copy Christ's life—much of what Jesus did had to do with his identity as God's Son, the fulfillment of his special role in dying for sin, and the cultural context of the first-century Roman world. To walk today as Christ did we must obey his teachings and follow his example of complete obedience to God and loving service to people.

2:7–8 The commandment to love others is both old and new. It is old because it comes from the Old Testament (Leviticus 19:18). It is new because Jesus interpreted it in a radically new way (John 13:34–35). In the Christian church, love is not only expressed by showing respect; it is also expressed through self-sacrifice and servanthood (John 15:13). In fact, it can be defined as "selfless giving," reaching beyond friends to enemies and persecutors (Matthew 5:43–48). Love should be the unifying force and the identifying mark of the Christian community. Love is the key to walking in the light, because we cannot grow spiritually while we hate others. Our growing relationship with God will result in growing relationships with others.

2:9–11 Does this mean that if you dislike someone you aren't a Christian? These verses are not talking about disliking a disagreeable Christian brother or sister. There will always be people we will not like as well as others. John's words focus on the attitude that causes us to ignore or despise others, to treat them as irritants, competitors, or enemies. Christian love is not a feeling but a choice. We can choose to be concerned with people's well-being and treat them with respect, whether or not we feel affection toward them. If we choose to love others, God will help us express our love.

2:12–14 John was writing to believers of all ages, his "little children" who had experienced forgiveness through Jesus. The older men ("fathers") were mature in the faith and had a long-standing relationship with Christ. The young men had struggled with Satan's temptations and had won. The boys and girls had learned about Christ and were just beginning their spiritual journey. Each stage of life in the Christian pilgrimage builds upon the other. As children learn about Christ, they grow in their ability to win battles with temptation. As young adults move from victory to victory, they grow in their relationship with Christ. Older adults, having known Christ for years, have developed the wisdom needed to teach young people and start the cycle all over again. Has your Christian growth reached the maturity level appropriate for your stage in life?

2:15–16 Some people think that worldliness is limited to external behavior—the people we associate with, the places we go, the activities we enjoy. Worldliness is also internal because it begins in the heart and is characterized by three attitudes: (1) *the lust of the flesh*—preoccupation with gratifying physical desires; (2) *the lust of the eyes*—craving and accumulating things, bowing to the god of materialism; and (3) *the boastful pride of life*—obsession with one's status or importance. When the serpent tempted Eve (Genesis 3:6), he tempted her in these areas. Also, when the devil tempted Jesus in the wilderness, these were his three areas of attack (see Matthew 4:1–11).

By contrast, God values self-control, a spirit of generosity, and a commitment to humble service. It is possible to give the impression of avoiding worldly pleasures while still harboring worldly attitudes in one's heart. It is also possible, like Jesus, to love sinners and spend time with them while maintaining a commitment to the values of God's kingdom. What values are most important to you? Do your actions reflect the world's values or God's values?

2:17 When our attachment to possessions is strong, it's hard to believe that what we want will one day pass away. It may be even harder to believe that the person who does the will of God will live forever. But this was John's conviction based on the facts of Jesus' life, death, resurrection, and promises. Knowing that this evil world and our desires for its pleasures will end can give us courage to control our greedy, self-indulgent behavior and to continue doing God's will.

2:18 Matt 24:5, 24; 2 John 7
2:19 Acts 20:30
2:20 Acts 10:38; Prov 28:5; Matt 13:11
2:21 James 1:19
2:22 1 John 4:3; 2 John 7; Matt 24:5, 24
2:23 John 8:19; 16:3; 17:3; 1 John 4:15
2:24 2 John 9

18 Children, it is the last hour; and just as you heard that antichrist is coming, even
now many antichrists have appeared; from this we know that it is the last hour.
19 They went out from us, but they were not *really* of us; for if they had been of us, they
would have remained with us; but *they went out,* so that it would be shown that they all
are not of us.
20 But you have an anointing from the Holy One, and you all know.
21 I have not written to you because you do not know the truth, but because you do
know it, and because no lie is of the truth.
22 Who is the liar but the one who denies that Jesus is the Christ? This is the antichrist, the one who denies the Father and the Son.
23 Whoever denies the Son does not have the Father; the one who confesses the Son
has the Father also.
24 As for you, let that abide in you which you heard from the beginning. If what you
heard from the beginning abides in you, you also will abide in the Son and in the Father.

A BOOK OF CONTRASTS
One of the distinct features of John's writing style was his habit of noting both sides of a conflict. He wrote to show the difference between real Christianity and anything else. Here are some of his favorite contrasts.

Contrast between:	*Passage*
Light and darkness	1:5
The new command and the old command	2:7–8
Loving the Father and loving the world	2:15–16
Christ and antichrist	2:18
Truth and lies	2:20–21
Children of God and children of the devil	3:1–10
Eternal life and eternal death	3:14
Love and hatred	3:15–16
True teaching and false teaching	4:1–3
Love and fear	4:18–19
Having life and not having life	5:11–12

2:18–23 John is talking about the last days, the time between Christ's first and second comings. The first-century readers of 1 John lived in the last days, and so do we. During this time, antichrists (false teachers who pretend to be Christians and who lure weak members away from Christ) will appear. Finally, just before the world ends, one great antichrist will arise (Revelation 13; 19:20; 20:10). We do not need to fear these evil people, however. The Holy Spirit shows us their errors, so we will not be deceived. However, we must teach God's Word clearly and carefully to the peripheral, weak members among us so that they won't fall prey to these teachers who "come to you in sheep's clothing, but inwardly are ravenous wolves" (Matthew 7:15).

2:19 The antichrists were not total strangers to the church; they once had been in the church, but they did not really belong to it. John does not say why they left; it is clear that their reasons for joining in the first place were wrong. Some people may call themselves Christians for less than the best reasons. Perhaps going to church is a family tradition. Maybe they like the social and business contacts they make there. Or possibly going to church is a long-standing habit, and they have never stopped to ask themselves why they do it. What is your main reason for being a Christian? Unless it is a Christ-centered reason, you may not really belong. You don't have to settle for less than the best. You can become personally acquainted with Jesus Christ and become a loyal, trustworthy follower.

2:20 *Anointing* usually refers to the pouring out of special olive oil. Oil was used to consecrate kings and special servants for service (1 Samuel 16:1, 13), and also was used by the church when someone was sick (James 5:14). "You have an anointing from the Holy One" could read, "The Holy Spirit has been given to you by the Father and the Son." When a person becomes a Christian, he or she receives the Holy Spirit. One way the Holy Spirit helps the believer and the church is by communicating truth. Jesus is the truth (John 14:6), and the Holy Spirit guides believers to him (John 16:13). People who are opposed to Christ are also opposed to his truth, and the Holy Spirit is not working in their lives. When we are led by the Spirit, we can stand against false teachers and the antichrist. Ask the Spirit to guide you each day (see 2:27).

2:22–23 Apparently the antichrists in John's day were claiming faith in God while denying and opposing Christ. To do so, John firmly states, is impossible. Because Jesus is God's Son and the Messiah, to deny Christ is to reject God's way of revealing himself to the world. A person who accepts Christ as God's Son, however, accepts God the Father at the same time. The two are one and cannot be separated. Many cultists today call themselves Christians, but they deny that Jesus is divine. We must expose these heresies and oppose such teachings so that the weak believers among us do not succumb to their teachings.

2:24 These Christians had heard the gospel, very likely from John himself. They knew that Christ was God's Son, that he died for their sins and was raised to give them new life, and that he would return and establish his kingdom in its fullness. But their fellowship was being infiltrated by teachers who denied these basic doctrines of the Christian faith, and some of the believers were in danger of succumbing to false arguments. John encouraged them to hold on to the Christian truth they heard at the beginning of their walk with Christ. It is important to grow in our knowledge of the Lord, to deepen our understanding through careful study, and to teach these truths to others. But no matter how much we learn, we must never abandon the basic truths about Christ. Jesus will always be God's Son, and his sacrifice for our sins is permanent. No truth will ever contradict these teachings in the Bible.

The Promise Is Eternal Life

25 This is the promise which He Himself made to us: eternal life.
26 These things I have written to you concerning those who are trying to deceive you.
27 As for you, the anointing which you received from Him abides in you, and you have
no need for anyone to teach you; but as His anointing teaches you about all things, and
is true and is not a lie, and just as it has taught you, you abide in Him.
28 Now, little children, abide in Him, so that when He appears, we may have confidence and not shrink away from Him in shame at His coming.
29 If you know that He is righteous, you know that everyone also who practices righteousness is born of Him.

2. God is love

Children of God Love One Another

3 See how great a love the Father has bestowed on us, that we would be called children of God; and *such* we are. For this reason the world does not know us, because
it did not know Him.
2 Beloved, now we are children of God, and it has not appeared as yet what we will
be. We know that when He appears, we will be like Him, because we will see Him just as
He is.
3 And everyone who has this hope *fixed* on Him purifies himself, just as He is pure.
4 Everyone who practices sin also practices lawlessness; and sin is lawlessness.
5 You know that He appeared in order to take away sins; and in Him there is no sin.
6 No one who abides in Him sins; no one who sins has seen Him or knows Him.
7 Little children, make sure no one deceives you; the one who practices righteousness is righteous, just as He is righteous;
8 the one who practices sin is of the devil; for the devil has sinned from the beginning.
The Son of God appeared for this purpose, to destroy the works of the devil.

2:25 John 3:15; 6:40
2:27 John 14:16; 1 John 2:20; 1 Cor 2:12
2:28 1 John 2:1; Luke 17:30; Col 3:4; 1 John 3:2; Eph 3:12; 1 John 3:21; 4:17; 5:14; Mark 8:38; 1 Thess 2:19
2:29 John 7:18; John 1:13; 3:3
3:1 John 3:16; 1 John 4:10; John 1:12; 1 John 3:2, 10; John 15:18, 21; 16:3
3:2 1 John 2:28; Rom 8:29; 2 Pet 1:4; John 17:24; 2 Cor 3:18
3:3 Rom 15:12; 1 Pet 1:3; John 17:19
3:5 1 John 1:2; 3:8; John 1:29; 1 Pet 1:18-20; 1 John 2:2
3:6 1 John 3:9; 1 John 2:3; 3 John 11
3:8 Matt 4:3; 1 John 3:5; John 12:31; 16:11

2:26–27 Christ had promised to send the Holy Spirit to teach his followers and to remind them of all that Christ had taught (John 14:26). As a result, Christians have the Holy Spirit within them ("the anointing") to keep them from going astray. In addition, they have the God-inspired Scriptures, against which they can test questionable teachings. To stay true to Christ, we must follow his Word and his Spirit. Let the Holy Spirit help you discern truth from error. For more about who the Holy Spirit is and what he does, see the notes on John 3:6; Acts 1:5; and Ephesians 1:13–14.

2:27 Christ lives (abides) in us through the Holy Spirit, and we also live in Christ. This means that we place our total trust in him, rely on him for guidance and strength, and live as he wants us to live. It implies a personal, life-giving relationship. John uses the same idea in John 15:5, where he speaks of Christ as the vine and his followers as the branches (see also 3:24; 4:15).

2:28–29 The visible proof of being a Christian is right behavior. Many people do good deeds but don't have faith in Jesus Christ. Others claim to have faith but rarely produce good deeds. A deficit in either faith or right behavior will be a cause for shame when Christ returns. Because true faith always results in good deeds, those who claim to have faith *and* who consistently do what is right are true believers. Good deeds cannot produce salvation (see Ephesians 2:8–9), but they are necessary proof that true faith is actually present (James 2:14–17).

3:1 As believers, our self-worth is based on the fact that God loves us and calls us his children. We are his children *now,* not just sometime in the distant future. Knowing that we are his children should encourage us to live as Jesus did. For other references about being part of God's family, see Romans 8:14–17; Galatians 3:26–27; 4:6–7.

3:1ff Verse 1 tells us who we are—members of God's family ("children of God"). Verse 2 tells us who we are becoming—reflections of God. The rest of the chapter tells us what we have as we grow to resemble God: (1) victory over sin (3:4–9); (2) love for others (3:10–18); and (3) confidence before God (3:19–24).

3:2–3 The Christian life is a process of becoming more and more like Christ (see Romans 8:29). This process will not be complete until we see Christ face-to-face (1 Corinthians 13:12; Philippians 3:21), but knowing that it is our ultimate destiny should motivate us to purify ourselves. To purify means to keep morally straight, free from the corruption of sin. God also purifies us, but there is action we must take to remain morally fit (see 1 Timothy 5:22; James 4:8; 1 Peter 1:22).

3:4ff There is a difference between committing a sin and continuing to sin. Even the most faithful believers sometimes commit sins, but they do not cherish a particular sin and choose to commit it. A believer who commits a sin repents, confesses, and finds forgiveness. A person who practices sin, by contrast, is not sorry for what he or she is doing. Thus this person never confesses and never receives forgiveness. Such a person is in opposition to God, no matter what religious claims he or she makes.

3:5 Under the Old Testament sacrifice system, a lamb without blemish was offered as a sacrifice for sin. Jesus is "the Lamb of God who takes away the sin of the world" (John 1:29). Because Jesus lived a perfect life and sacrificed himself for our sins, we can be completely forgiven (2:2). We can look back to his death for us and know that we need never suffer eternal death (1 Peter 1:18–20).

3:8–9 We all have areas where temptation is strong and habits are hard to conquer. These weaknesses give the devil a foothold, so we must deal with our areas of vulnerability. If we are struggling with a particular sin, however, these verses are not directed at us, even if for the time we seem to keep on sinning. John is not talking about people whose victories are still incomplete; he is talking about people who make a practice of sinning and look for ways to justify it.

Three steps are necessary to find victory over prevailing sin: (1) seek the power of the Holy Spirit and God's Word; (2) stay away

3:9 1 John 2:29; 4:7; 5:1, 4, 18; 3 John 11; 1 Pet 1:23
3:10 John 8:44; 1 John 3:8; Rom 13:8ff; Col 3:14; 1 Tim 1:5
3:11 1 John 1:5; 1 John 2:7; John 13:4f
3:12 Gen 4:8; Matt 5:37; John 8:40, 41
3:13 John 15:18; 17:14
3:14 John 5:24; 13:35
3:15 Matt 5:21f
3:16 John 10:11; 15:13
3:18 1 John 2:1; 3:7; 2 John 1; 3 John 1
3:21 1 John 2:28; 5:14
3:22 1 John 2:3; John 8:29; Heb 13:21
3:23 John 1:12; 2:23; 3:18; 13:34; 15:12

9 No one who is born of God practices sin, because His seed abides in him; and he
cannot sin, because he is born of God.
10 By this the children of God and the children of the devil are obvious: anyone
who does not practice righteousness is not of God, nor the one who does not love his
brother.
11 For this is the message which you have heard from the beginning, that we should
love one another;
12 not as Cain, *who* was of the evil one and slew his brother. And for what reason did
he slay him? Because his deeds were evil, and his brother's were righteous.
13 Do not be surprised, brethren, if the world hates you.
14 We know that we have passed out of death into life, because we love the brethren.
He who does not love abides in death.
15 Everyone who hates his brother is a murderer; and you know that no murderer has
eternal life abiding in him.
16 We know love by this, that He laid down His life for us; and we ought to lay down
our lives for the brethren.
17 But whoever has the world's goods, and sees his brother in need and closes his heart
against him, how does the love of God abide in him?
18 Little children, let us not love with word or with tongue, but in deed and truth.
19 We will know by this that we are of the truth, and will assure our heart before Him
20 in whatever our heart condemns us; for God is greater than our heart and knows all
things.
21 Beloved, if our heart does not condemn us, we have confidence before God;
22 and whatever we ask we receive from Him, because we keep His commandments
and do the things that are pleasing in His sight.
23 This is His commandment, that we believe in the name of His Son Jesus Christ, and
love one another, just as He commanded us.

---

from tempting situations; and (3) seek the help of the body of Christ—be open to their willingness to hold you accountable and to pray for you.

3:9 "No one who is born of God practices sin" means that true believers do not make a practice of sinning, nor do they become indifferent to God's moral law. All believers still sin, but they are working to gain victory over sin. "His seed abides in him" means that true believers do not make a practice of sinning because God's new life has been born into them.

3:9 We are "born of God" when the Holy Spirit lives in us and gives us Jesus' new life. Being born again is more than a fresh start; it is a rebirth, receiving a new family name based on Christ's death for us. When this happens, God forgives us and totally accepts us; the Holy Spirit gives us new minds and hearts, lives in us, and begins helping us to become like Christ. Our perspective changes too because we have a mind that is renewed day by day by the Holy Spirit (see Romans 12:2; Ephesians 4:22–24). So we must begin to think and act differently. See John 3:1–21 for more on being born again.

3:12–13 Cain killed his brother, Abel, when God accepted Abel's offering and not his (Genesis 4:1–16). Abel's offering showed that Cain was not giving his best to God, and Cain's jealous anger drove him to murder. People who are morally upright expose and shame those who aren't. If we live for God, the world will often hate us, because we make them painfully aware of their immoral way of living.

3:15 John echoes Jesus' teaching that whoever hates another person is a murderer at heart (Matthew 5:21–22). Christianity is a religion of the heart; outward compliance alone is not enough. Bitterness against someone who has wronged you is an evil cancer within you and will eventually destroy you. Don't let a "root of bitterness" (Hebrews 12:15) grow in you or your church.

3:16 Real love is an action, not a feeling. It produces selfless, sacrificial giving. The greatest act of love is giving oneself for others. How can we lay down our lives? By serving others with no thought of receiving anything in return. Sometimes it is easier to say we'll die for others than to truly live for them—this involves putting others' desires first. Jesus taught this same principle of love in John 15:13.

3:17–18 These verses give an example of how to lay down our lives for others—to help those in need. This is strikingly similar to James's teaching (James 2:14–17). How clearly do your actions say you really love others? Are you as generous as you should be with your money, possessions, and time?

3:19–20 Many are afraid that they don't love others as they should. They feel guilty because they think they are not doing enough to show proper love to Christ. Their consciences bother them. John has these people in mind in this letter. How do we escape the gnawing accusations of our consciences? Not by ignoring them or rationalizing our behavior, but by setting our hearts on God's love. When we feel guilty, we should remind ourselves that God knows our motives as well as our actions. His voice of assurance is stronger than the accusing voice of our conscience. If we are in Christ, he will not condemn us (Romans 8:1; Hebrews 9:14–15). So if you are living for the Lord but feeling that you are not good enough, remind yourself that God is greater than your conscience.

3:21–22 If your conscience is clear, you can come to God without fear, confident that your requests will be heard. John reaffirms Jesus' promise that whatever we ask for will be given to us (Matthew 7:7; see also Matthew 21:22; John 9:31; 15:7). You will receive if you obey and do what pleases him because you will then be asking in line with God's will. Of course this does not mean that you can have anything you want, like instant riches. If you are truly seeking God's will, there are some requests you will not make.

3:23 In the Bible, a person's name stands for his or her character. It represents who he or she really is. We are to believe not only in Jesus' words, but also in his very person as the Son of God. Moreover, to believe "in the name" means to pattern your life after Christ's, to become more like him by uniting yourself with him. And if we are living like Christ, we will "love one another."

24 The one who keeps His commandments abides in Him, and He in him. We know by this that He abides in us, by the Spirit whom He has given us.

Testing the Spirits

4 Beloved, do not believe every spirit, but test the spirits to see whether they are from
God, because many false prophets have gone out into the world.
2 By this you know the Spirit of God: every spirit that confesses that Jesus Christ has
come in the flesh is from God;
3 and every spirit that does not confess Jesus is not from God; this is the *spirit* of the
antichrist, of which you have heard that it is coming, and now it is already in the world.
4 You are from God, little children, and have overcome them; because greater is He
who is in you than he who is in the world.
5 They are from the world; therefore they speak *as* from the world, and the world listens to them.
6 We are from God; he who knows God listens to us; he who is not from God does
not listen to us. By this we know the spirit of truth and the spirit of error.

God Is Love

7 Beloved, let us love one another, for love is from God; and everyone who loves is
born of God and knows God.
8 The one who does not love does not know God, for God is love.
9 By this the love of God was manifested in us, that God has sent His only begotten
Son into the world so that we might live through Him.
10 In this is love, not that we loved God, but that He loved us and sent His Son *to be*
the propitiation for our sins.

3:24 John 6:56; 10:38; 1 John 2:6, 24; 4:15; John 14:17

4:1 1 Cor 12:10; 1 Thess 5:20f; 2 Thess 2:2

4:2 1 John 1:2

4:3 2 John 7; 2 Thess 2:3-7; 1 John 2:18

4:4 1 John 2:1; 3:20; John 12:31

4:5 John 15:19; 17:14

4:6 John 8:47; 10:3ff; 18:37; 1 Cor 14:37; John 14:17

4:7 1 John 2:7; 1 John 3:11; 1 John 5:1; 1 John 2:29

4:9 John 9:3; 1 John 4:16; John 3:16

4:10 Rom 5:8, 10; 1 John 4:19; John 3:16f

3:24 The mutual relationship, abiding in Christ as he abides in us, shows itself in Christians who keep these three essential commands: (1) Believe in Christ, (2) love the brothers and sisters, and (3) live morally upright lives. The Spirit's presence is not only spiritual and mystical, but it is also practical. Our conduct verifies his presence.

4:1–2 "Do not believe every spirit, but test the spirits" means that we shouldn't believe everything we hear just because someone says it is a message inspired by God. There are many ways to test teachers to see if their message is truly from the Lord. One is to check to see if their words match what God says in the Bible. Other tests include their commitment to the body of believers (2:19), their life-style (3:23–24), and the fruit of their ministry (4:6). But the most important test of all, says John, is what they believe about Christ. Do they teach that Jesus is fully God and fully man? Our world is filled with voices claiming to speak for God. Give them these tests to see if they are indeed speaking God's truth.

4:1–3 Some people believe everything they read or hear. Unfortunately, many ideas printed and taught are not true. Christians should have faith, but they should not be gullible. Verify every message you hear, even if the person who brings it says it's from God. If the message is truly from God, it will be consistent with Christ's teachings.

4:3 The antichrist will be a person who epitomizes all that is evil, and he will be readily received by an evil world. He is more fully described in 2 Thessalonians 2:3–12 and Revelation 13. The "spirit of the antichrist" is already here (see the note on 2:18–23).

4:4 It is easy to be frightened by the wickedness we see all around us and overwhelmed by the problems we face. Evil is obviously much stronger than we are. John assures us, however, that God is even stronger. He will conquer all evil—and his Spirit and his Word live in our hearts!

4:6 False teachers are popular with the world because, like the false prophets of the Old Testament, they tell people what they want to hear. John warns that Christians who faithfully teach God's Word will not win any popularity contests in the world. People don't want to hear their sins denounced; they don't want to listen to demands that they change their behavior. A false teacher will be well received by non-Christians.

4:7ff Everyone believes that love is important, but love is usually thought of as a feeling. In reality, love is a choice and an action, as 1 Corinthians 13:4–7 shows. God is the source of our love: He loved us enough to sacrifice his Son for us. Jesus is our example of what it means to love; everything he did in life and death was supremely loving. The Holy Spirit gives us the power to love; he lives in our hearts and makes us more and more like Christ. God's love always involves a choice and an action, and our love should be like his. How well do you display your love for God in the choices you make and the actions you take?

4:8 John says, "God is love," not "Love is God." Our world, with its shallow and selfish view of love, has turned these words around and contaminated our understanding of love. The world thinks that love is what makes a person feel good and that it is all right to sacrifice moral principles and others' rights in order to obtain such "love." But that isn't real love; it is the exact opposite—selfishness. And God is not that kind of "love." Real love is like God, who is holy, just, and perfect. If we truly know God, we will love as he does.

4:9 Jesus is God's *only* Son. While all believers are sons and daughters of God, only Jesus lives in this special unique relationship (see John 1:18; 3:16).

4:9–10 Love explains (1) why God creates—because he loves, he creates people to love; (2) why God cares—because he loves them, he cares for sinful people; (3) why we are free to choose—God wants a loving response from us; (4) why Christ died—his love for us caused him to seek a solution to the problem of sin; and (5) why we receive eternal life—God's love expresses itself to us forever.

4:10 Nothing sinful or evil can exist in God's presence. He is absolute goodness. He cannot overlook, condone, or excuse sin as though it never happened. He loves us, but his love does not make him morally lax. If we trust in Christ, however, we will not have to bear the penalty for our sins (1 Peter 2:24). We will be acquitted (Romans 5:18) by his atoning sacrifice.

4:11 1 John 2:7
4:12 John 1:18; 1 Tim 6:16; 1 John 2:5
4:13 Rom 8:9; 1 John 3:24
4:14 John 15:27; 1 John 1:2; John 3:17; 4:42; 1 John 2:2
4:15 1 John 3:23; 1 John 2:24; 3:24
4:16 John 6:69; John 9:3
4:17 1 John 2:5
4:20 1 John 1:6; 3:17; 1 Pet 1:8

11 Beloved, if God so loved us, we also ought to love one another.
12 No one has seen God at any time; if we love one another, God abides in us, and His
love is perfected in us.
13 By this we know that we abide in Him and He in us, because He has given us of His
Spirit.
14 We have seen and testify that the Father has sent the Son *to be* the Savior of the
world.
15 Whoever confesses that Jesus is the Son of God, God abides in him, and he in God.
16 We have come to know and have believed the love which God has for us. God is
love, and the one who abides in love abides in God, and God abides in him.
17 By this, love is perfected with us, so that we may have confidence in the day of judgment; because as He is, so also are we in this world.
18 There is no fear in love; but perfect love casts out fear, because fear involves punishment, and the one who fears is not perfected in love.
19 We love, because He first loved us.
20 If someone says, "I love God," and hates his brother, he is a liar; for the one who
does not love his brother whom he has seen, cannot love God whom he has not seen.

HEREISIES

Most of the eyewitnesses to Jesus' ministry had died by the time John composed this letter. Some of the second or third-generation Christians began to have doubts about what they had been taught about Jesus. Some Christians with a Greek background had a hard time believing that Jesus was human as well as divine, because in Platonic thought the spirit was all-important. The body was only a prison from which one desired to escape. Heresies developed from a uniting of this kind of Platonic thought and Christianity.

A particularly widespread false teaching, later called Docetism (from a Greek word meaning "to seem"), held that Jesus was actually a spirit who only appeared to have a body. In reality he cast no shadow and left no footprints; he was God, but not man. Another heretical teaching, related to Gnosticism (from a Greek word meaning "knowledge"), held that all physical matter was evil, the spirit was good, and only the intellectually enlightened could enjoy the benefits of religion. Both groups found it hard to believe in a Savior who was fully human.

John answers these false teachers as an eyewitness to Jesus' life on earth. He saw Jesus, talked with him, touched him—he knew that Jesus was more than a mere spirit. In the very first sentence of his letter, John establishes that Jesus had been alive before the world began and also that he lived as a man among men and women. In other words, he was both divine and human.

Through the centuries, many heretics have denied that Jesus was both God and man. In John's day people had trouble believing he was human; today more people have problems seeing him as God. But Jesus' divine-human nature is the pivotal issue of Christianity. Before you accept what religious teachers say about any topic, listen carefully to what they believe about Jesus. To deny either his divinity or his humanity is to consider him less than Christ, the Savior.

4:12 If no one has ever seen God, how can we ever know him? John in his Gospel said, "The only begotten God who is in the bosom of the Father, He has explained Him" (John 1:18). Jesus is the complete expression of God in human form, and he has revealed God to us. When we love one another, the invisible God reveals himself to others through us, and his love is made complete.

4:12 Some people enjoy being with others. They make friends with strangers easily and always are surrounded by many friends. Other people are shy or reserved. They have a few friends, but they are uncomfortable talking with people they don't know or mingling in crowds. Shy people don't need to become extroverts in order to love others. John isn't telling us *how many* people to love, but *how much* to love the people we already know. Our job is to love faithfully the people God has given us to love, whether there are two or two hundred of them. If God sees that we are ready to love others, he will bring them to us. No matter how shy we are, we don't need to be afraid of the love commandment. God provides us the strength to do what he asks.

4:13 When we become Christians, we receive the Holy Spirit. God's presence in our lives is proof that we really belong to him. He also gives us the power to love (Romans 5:5; 8:9; 2 Corinthians 1:22). Rely on that power as you reach out to others. As you do so, you will gain confidence. See also Romans 8:16.

4:17 The day of judgment is that time when all people will appear before Christ and be held accountable for their actions. With God living in us through Christ, we have no reason to fear this day, because we have been saved from punishment. Instead, we can look forward to the day of judgment, because it will mean the end of sin and the beginning of a face-to-face relationship with Jesus Christ.

4:18 If we ever are afraid of the future, eternity, or God's judgment, we can remind ourselves of God's love. We know that he loves us perfectly (Romans 8:38–39). We can resolve our fears first by focusing on his immeasurable love for us, and then by allowing him to love others through us. His love will quiet your fears and give you confidence.

4:19 God's love is the source of all human love, and it spreads like fire. In loving his children, God kindles a flame in their hearts. In turn, they love others, who are warmed by God's love through them.

4:20–21 It is easy to say we love God when that love doesn't cost us anything more than weekly attendance at religious services. But the real test of our love for God is how we treat the people right in front of us—our family members and fellow believers. We cannot truly love God while neglecting to love those who are created in his image.

21 And this commandment we have from Him, that the one who loves God should love
his brother also.

3. God is life

Overcoming the World

5 Whoever believes that Jesus is the [2]Christ is born of God, and whoever loves the
Father loves the *child* born of Him.
2 By this we know that we love the children of God, when we love God and observe
His commandments.
3 For this is the love of God, that we keep His commandments; and His commandments are not burdensome.
4 For whatever is born of God overcomes the world; and this is the victory that has
overcome the world—our faith.
5 Who is the one who overcomes the world, but he who believes that Jesus is the Son
of God?
6 This is the One who came by water and blood, Jesus Christ; not with the water only,
but with the water and with the blood. It is the Spirit who testifies, because the Spirit is
the truth.
7 For there are three that testify:
8 [3]the Spirit and the water and the blood; and the three are in agreement.
9 If we receive the testimony of men, the testimony of God is greater; for the testimony of God is this, that He has testified concerning His Son.
10 The one who believes in the Son of God has the testimony in himself; the one who
does not believe God has made Him a liar, because he has not believed in the testimony
that God has given concerning His Son.
11 And the testimony is this, that God has given us eternal life, and this life is in
His Son.
12 He who has the Son has the life; he who does not have the Son of God does not
have the life.

This Is Written That You May Know

13 These things I have written to you who believe in the name of the Son of God, so
that you may know that you have eternal life.
14 This is the confidence which we have before Him, that, if we ask anything according
to His will, He hears us.
15 And if we know that He hears us *in* whatever we ask, we know that we have the
requests which we have asked from Him.

4:21 Lev 19:18; Matt 5:43f; 22:37ff; John 13:34; 1 John 3:11

5:1 1 John 2:22f; 4:2, 15; John 1:3; 3:3

5:2 1 John 2:5; 3:14

5:3 John 14:15; 2 John 6; 1 John 2:3; Matt 11:30; 23:4

5:4 John 1:13; 3:3; 1 John 2:29; 5:1, 18; 1 John 2:13; 4:4

5:6 John 19:34; Matt 3:16f; John 15:26; 16:13-15

5:7 Matt 18:16

5:9 John 5:34, 37; 8:18; Matt 3:17; John 5:32, 37

5:10 Rom 8:16; Gal 4-6; Rev 12:17; John 3:18, 33; 1 John 1:10

5:11 John 3:36; 1 John 1:2; 2:25; 4:9; 5:13, 20; John 1:4

5:12 John 3:15f, 36

5:13 John 20:31; 1 John 3:23; 1 John 1:2; 2:25; 4:9; 5:11, 20

5:14 1 John 2:28; 3:21f; Matt 7:7; John 14:13; 1 John 3:22

5:15 1 John 5:18-20

2 I.e. Messiah 3 A few late mss add ...*in heaven, the Father, the Word, and the Holy Spirit, and these three are one. And there are three that testify on earth, the Spirit*

5:1–2 When we become Christians, we become part of God's family, with fellow believers as our brothers and sisters. It is God who determines who the other family members are, not us. We are simply called to accept and love them. How well do you treat your fellow family members?

5:3–4 Jesus never promised that obeying him would be easy. But the hard work and self-discipline of serving Christ are no burden to those who love him. And if our load starts to feel heavy, we can always trust Christ to help us bear it (see Matthew 11:28–30).

5:6–8 The phrase "came by water and blood" may refer to Jesus' baptism and his crucifixion. At this time, there was a false teaching in circulation that said Jesus was "the Christ" only between his baptism and his death—that is, he was merely human until he was baptized, at which time "the Christ" then descended upon him but then later left him before his death on the cross. But if Jesus died only as a man, he could not have taken upon himself the sins of the world, and Christianity would be an empty religion. Only an act of God could take away the punishment that we deserve for our sin.

5:7–9 The Gospels twice record God's clear declaration that Jesus was his Son—at Jesus' baptism (Matthew 3:16–17), and at his transfiguration (Matthew 17:5).

5:12 Whoever believes in God's Son has eternal life. He is all you need. You don't need to *wait* for eternal life, because it begins the moment you believe. You don't need to *work* for it, because it is already yours. You don't need to *worry* about it, because you have been given eternal life by God himself—and it is guaranteed.

5:13 Some people *hope* that they will receive eternal life. John says we can *know* we have it. Our certainty is based on God's promise that he has given us eternal life through his Son. This is true whether you feel close to God or far away from him. Eternal life is not based on feelings, but on facts. You can know that you have eternal life if you believe God's truth. If you aren't sure that you are a Christian, ask yourself: "Have I honestly committed my life to him as my Savior and Lord?" If so, you know by faith that you are indeed a child of God.

5:14–15 The emphasis here is on God's will, not our will. When we communicate with God, we don't demand what we want; rather we discuss with him what *he* wants for us. If we align our prayers to his will, he will listen; and we can be certain that if he listens, he will give us a definite answer. Start praying with confidence!

5:16 James 5:15
5:18 James 1:27; Jude 21; John 14:30
5:19 1 John 4:6; John 12:31; 17:15
5:20 John 8:42; Luke 24:45; John 17:3; Rev 3:7; John 1:18; 14:9; 1 John 2:23
5:21 1 John 2:1

16 If anyone sees his brother committing a sin not *leading* to death, he shall ask and
God will for him give life to those who commit sin not *leading* to death. There is a sin
leading to death; I do not say that he should make request for this.
17 All unrighteousness is sin, and there is a sin not *leading* to death.
18 We know that no one who is born of God sins; but He who was born of God keeps
him, and the evil one does not touch him.
19 We know that we are of God, and that the whole world lies in *the power of* the evil
one.
20 And we know that the Son of God has come, and has given us understanding so that
we may know Him who is true; and we are in Him who is true, in His Son Jesus Christ.
This is the true God and eternal life.
21 Little children, guard yourselves from idols.

5:16–17 Commentators differ widely in their thoughts about what this sin that leads to death is, and whether the death it causes is physical or spiritual. Paul wrote that some Christians had died because they took Communion "in an unworthy manner" (1 Corinthians 11:27–30), and Ananias and Sapphira were struck dead when they lied to God (Acts 5:1–11). Blasphemy against the Holy Spirit results in spiritual death (Mark 3:29), and the book of Hebrews describes the spiritual death of the person who turns against Christ (Hebrews 6:4–6). John was probably referring to the people who had left the Christian fellowship and joined the antichrists. By rejecting the only way of salvation, these people were putting themselves out of reach of prayer. In most cases, however, even if we knew what the terrible sin is, we would have no sure way of knowing whether a certain person had committed it. Therefore we should continue praying for our loved ones and for our Christian brothers and sisters, leaving the judgment up to God. Note that John says, "I do not say that he should make request for this," rather than "You cannot pray about that." He recognized the lack of certainty.

5:18–19 Christians commit sins, of course, but they ask God to forgive them, and then they continue serving him. God has freed believers from their slavery to Satan, and he keeps them safe from Satan's continued attacks. The rest of the world does not have the Christian's freedom to obey God. Unless they come to Christ in faith, they have no choice but to obey Satan. There is no middle ground; people either belong to God and obey him, or they live under Satan's control.

5:21 An idol is anything that substitutes for the true faith, anything that robs Christ of his full deity and humanity, any human idea that claims to be more authoritative than the Bible, any loyalty that replaces God at the center of our lives.

5:21 John presents a clear picture of Christ. What we think about Jesus Christ is central to our teaching, preaching, and living. Jesus is the God-man, fully God and fully human at the same time. He came to earth to die in our place for our sins. Through faith in him, we are given eternal life and the power to do his will. What is your answer to the most important question you could ever ask—who is Jesus Christ?

2 JOHN

VITAL STATISTICS

PURPOSE:
To emphasize the basics of following Christ—truth and love—and to warn against false teachers

AUTHOR:
The apostle John

TO WHOM WRITTEN:
To "the chosen lady and her children"—or possibly to a local church and all believers everywhere

DATE WRITTEN:
About the same time as 1 John, approximately A.D. 90 from Ephesus

SETTING:
Evidently this woman and her family were involved in one of the churches that John was overseeing—they had developed a strong friendship with John. John was warning her of the false teachers who were becoming prevalent in some of the churches.

KEY VERSE:
"And this is love, that we walk according to His commandments. This is the commandment, just as you have heard from the beginning, that you should walk in it" (6).

KEY PEOPLE:
John, the chosen lady, and her children

TRUTH and love are frequently discussed in our world but seldom practiced.

From politicians to salesmen, people conveniently ignore or conceal facts and use words to enhance positions or sell products. Perjury is common, and integrity and credibility are endangered species. Words, twisted in meaning and torn from context, have become mere tools for ego building. It is not surprising that we have to "swear" to tell the truth.

And what about love? Our world is filled with its words: Popular songs, greeting cards, media counselors, and romantic novels shower us with notions and dreams of ethereal, idyllic relationships and feelings. Real love, however, is scarce—selfless giving, caring, sharing, and even dying. We yearn to love and be loved but see few living examples of real love. Plentiful are those who grasp, hoard, and watch out for "number one."

Christ is the antithesis of society's prevailing values, that is, falsehood and self-centeredness—for *he is truth and love* in person. Therefore, all who claim loyalty to him must be committed to these ideals—following the truth and living the truth, reflecting love and acting with love toward one another.

The apostle John had seen Truth and Love firsthand—he had been with Jesus. So affected was this disciple that all of his writings, from the Gospel to the book of Revelation, are filled with this theme: Truth and love are vital to the Christian and are inseparable in the Christian life. Second John, his brief letter to a dear friend, is no different. John says to live in the truth and obey God (4), watch out for deceivers (7), and love God and each other (6).

Second John will take just a few minutes to read, but its message should last a lifetime. As you reflect on these few paragraphs penned by the wise and aged follower of Christ, recommit yourself to being a person of truth, of love, and of obedience.

THE BLUEPRINT

1. Watch out for false teachers (1–11)
2. John's final words (12–13)

False teachers were a dangerous problem for the church to which John was writing. His warning against showing hospitality to false teachers may sound harsh and unloving to many today. Yet these men were teaching heresy that could seriously harm many believers—for eternity.

MEGATHEMES

THEME	EXPLANATION	IMPORTANCE
Truth	Following God's Word, the Bible, is essential to Christian living because God is truth. Christ's true followers consistently obey his truth.	To be loyal to Christ's teaching, we must seek to know the Bible, but we may never twist its message to our own needs or purposes or encourage others who misuse it.
Love	Christ's command is for Christians to love one another. This is the basic ingredient of true Christianity.	To obey Christ fully, we must believe his command to love others. Helping, giving, and meeting needs put love into practice.
False Leaders	We must be wary of religious leaders who are not true to Christ's teaching. We should not give them a platform to spread false teaching.	Don't encourage those who are opposed to Christ. Politely remove yourself from association with false leaders. Be aware of what is being taught in your church.

1:1
1 John 3:18; 2 John 3; 3 John 1; John 8:32; 1 Tim 2:4

1:2
2 Pet 1:12; 1 John 1:8; John 14:16

1:3
Rom 1:7; 1 Tim 1:2

1:4
3 John 3f

1:5
1 John 2:7; John 13:34, 35; 15:12, 17; 1 John 3:11; 4:7, 11

1:6
1 John 2:5; 5:3; 1 John 2:24; 1 John 2:7

1:7
1 John 2:19; 4:1; 1 John 4:2f

1:8
Mark 13:9; 1 Cor 3:8; Heb 10:35

1. Watch out for false teachers

Walk According to His Commandments

1 The elder to the chosen lady and her children, whom I love in truth; and not only I,
but also all who know the truth,
2 for the sake of the truth which abides in us and will be with us forever:
3 Grace, mercy *and* peace will be with us, from God the Father and from Jesus Christ,
the Son of the Father, in truth and love.
4 I was very glad to find *some* of your children walking in truth, just as we have received commandment *to do* from the Father.
5 Now I ask you, lady, not as though *I were* writing to you a new commandment, but
the one which we have had from the beginning, that we love one another.
6 And this is love, that we walk according to His commandments. This is the commandment, just as you have heard from the beginning, that you should walk in it.
7 For many deceivers have gone out into the world, those who do not acknowledge
Jesus Christ *as* coming in the flesh. This is the deceiver and the antichrist.
8 Watch yourselves, that you do not lose what we have accomplished, but that you
may receive a full reward.

---

1 The "elder" is John, one of Jesus' 12 disciples and the writer of the Gospel of John, three letters, and the book of Revelation. For more information about John, see his Profile in John 13. This letter was written shortly after 1 John to warn about false teachers. The salutation, "to the chosen lady and her children," could refer to a specific woman, or to a church whose identity is no longer known. John may have written this from Ephesus.

1–4 The "truth" is the truth about Jesus Christ, as opposed to the lies of the false teachers (see 1 John 2:21–23).

5–6 The statement that Christians should love one another is a recurrent New Testament theme. Yet love for one's neighbor is an old command, first appearing in the third book of Moses (Leviticus 19:18). We can show love in many ways: by avoiding prejudice and discrimination, by accepting people, by listening, helping, giving, serving, and refusing to judge. Knowing God's command is not enough. We must put it into practice, walking "according to His commandments." (See also Matthew 22:37–39 and 1 John 2:7–8.)

7 In John's day, many false teachers taught that spirit was good and matter was evil; therefore, they reasoned that Jesus could not have been both God and man. In strong terms, John warns against this kind of teaching. There are still many false teachers who promote an understanding of Jesus that is not Biblical. These teachers are dangerous because they distort the truth and undermine the foundations of Christian faith. They may use the right words but change the meanings. The way your teachers live shows a lot about what they believe about Christ. For more on testing teachers, see 1 John 4:1.

8 To "receive a full reward" refers not to salvation but to the rewards of loyal service. All who value the truth and persistently hold to it will win their full reward. Those who live for themselves and justify their self-centeredness by teaching false doctrines will lose that reward (see Matthew 7:21–23).

9 Anyone who goes too far and does not abide in the teaching of Christ, does not have
God; the one who abides in the teaching, he has both the Father and the Son.
10 If anyone comes to you and does not bring this teaching, do not receive him into
your house, and do not give him a greeting;
11 for the one who gives him a greeting participates in his evil deeds.

1:9 John 7:16; 8:31; 1 John 2:23

1:10 1 Kin 13:16f; Rom 16:17; 2 Thess 3:6, 14; Titus 3:10

1:11 Eph 5:11; 1 Tim 5:22; Jude 23

2. John's final words

12 Though I have many things to write to you, I do not want to *do so* with paper and
ink; but I hope to come to you and speak face to face, so that your joy may be made full.
13 The children of your chosen sister greet you.

1:12 3 John 13, 14; John 3:29; 1 John 1:4

1:13 2 John 1

10 John instructed the believers not to show hospitality to false teachers. They were to do nothing that would encourage the heretics in their propagation of falsehoods. In addition, if believers were to invite them in, such action would show that they were approving of what the false teachers said and did. It may seem rude to turn people away, even if they are teaching heresy, but how much better it is to be faithful to God than merely courteous to people! John is condemning the support of those who are dedicated to opposing the true teachings of God, not condemning hospitality to unbelievers. John adds that a person who supports a false teacher in any way shares in the teacher's evil deeds.

13 False teaching is serious business, and we dare not overlook it. It is so serious that John wrote this letter to warn against it. There are so many false teachings in our world that we might be tempted to take many of them lightly. Instead, we should realize the dangers they pose and actively refuse to give heresies any foothold.

3 JOHN

BY special invitation or with a surprise knock, company arrives and with them comes the promise of soiled floors, extra laundry, dirty dishes, altered schedules, personal expense, and inconvenience. From sharing a meal to providing a bed, hospitality costs . . . in time, energy, and money. But how we treat others reflects our true values—what is really important to us. Do we see people as objects or inconveniences, or as unique creations of a loving God? And which is more important to God, a person or a carpet? Perhaps the most effective way to demonstrate God's values and Christ's love to others is to invite and welcome guests into our home.

For Gaius, hospitality was a habit, and his reputation for friendship and generosity, especially to traveling teachers and missionaries (5), had spread. To affirm and thank Gaius for his Christian life-style, and to encourage him in his faith, John wrote this personal note.

John's format for this letter centers around three men: Gaius, the example of one who follows Christ and loves others (1–8); Diotrephes, the self-proclaimed church leader who does not reflect God's values (9–11); and Demetrius, who also follows the truth (12). John encourages Gaius to practice hospitality, continue to walk in the truth, and do what is right.

Although this is a personal letter, we can "look over the shoulder" of Gaius and apply its lessons to our life. As you read 3 John, with which man do you identify? Are you a Gaius, generously giving to others? a Demetrius, loving the truth? or a Diotrephes, looking out for yourself and your "things"? Determine to reflect Christ's values in your relationships, opening your home and touching others with his love.

VITAL STATISTICS

PURPOSE:
To commend Gaius for his hospitality and to encourage him in his Christian life

AUTHOR:
The apostle John

TO WHOM WRITTEN:
Gaius, a prominent Christian in one of the churches known to John, and to all Christians

DATE WRITTEN:
Approximately A.D. 90 from Ephesus

SETTING:
Church leaders traveled from town to town helping to establish new congregations. They depended on the hospitality of fellow believers. Gaius was one who welcomed these leaders into his home.

KEY VERSE:
"Beloved, you are acting faithfully in whatever you accomplish for the brethren, and especially when they are strangers" (5).

KEY PEOPLE:
John, Gaius, Diotrephes, Demetrius

THE BLUEPRINT

1. God's children live by the standards of the gospel
   (1–12)
2. John's final words
   (13–15)

John wrote to commend Gaius, who was taking care of traveling teachers and missionaries, and to warn against people like Diotrephes, who was proud and refused to listen to spiritual leaders in authority. If we are to live in the truth of the gospel, we must look for ways to support pastors, Christian workers, and missionaries today. All Christians should work together to support God's work both at home and around the world.

MEGATHEMES

THEME	EXPLANATION	IMPORTANCE
Hospitality	John wrote to encourage those who were kind to others. Genuine hospitality for traveling Christian workers was needed then and is still important today.	Faithful Christian teachers and missionaries need our support. Whenever you can extend hospitality to others, it will make you a partner in their ministry.
Pride	Diotrephes not only refused to offer hospitality but also set himself up as a church boss. Pride disqualified him from being a real leader.	Christian leaders must shun pride and its effects on them. Be careful not to misuse your position of leadership.
Faithfulness	Gaius and Demetrius were commended for their faithful work in the church. They were held up as examples of faithful, selfless servants.	Don't take for granted Christian workers who serve faithfully. Be sure to encourage them so they won't grow weary of serving.

---

1. God's children live by the standards of the gospel

You Walk in the Truth

1 The elder to the beloved Gaius, whom I love in truth.
2 Beloved, I pray that in all respects you may prosper and be in good health, just as
your soul prospers.
3 For I was very glad when brethren came and testified to your truth, *that is,* how you
are walking in truth.
4 I have no greater joy than this, to hear of my children walking in the truth.
5 Beloved, you are acting faithfully in whatever you accomplish for the brethren, and
especially *when they are* strangers;
6 and they have testified to your love before the church. You will do well to send them
on their way in a manner worthy of God.
7 For they went out for the sake of the Name, accepting nothing from the Gentiles.
8 Therefore we ought to support such men, so that we may be fellow workers with the
truth.
9 I wrote something to the church; but Diotrephes, who loves to be first among them,
does not accept what we say.

1:1 1 John 3:18; 2 John 1

1:3 2 John 4; Acts 1:15; Gal 6:10; 3 John 5, 10

1:4 1 Cor 4:14f; 2 Cor 6:13; Gal 4:19; 1 Thess 2:11; 1 Tim 1:2; 2 Tim 1:2

1:5 Acts 1:15; Gal 6:10

1:6 Acts 15:3; Titus 3:13; Col 1:10; 1 Thess 2:12

1:7 John 15:21; Acts 5:41; Phil 2:9; Acts 20:33, 35

---

1 This letter gives us an important glimpse into the life of the early church. Third John, addressed to Gaius, is about the need for showing hospitality to traveling preachers and other believers. It also warns against a would-be church dictator.

1 The "elder," John, was one of Jesus' 12 disciples and the writer of the Gospel of John, three letters, and the book of Revelation. For more information about John, see his Profile in John 13. We have no further information about Gaius, but he is someone whom John loved dearly. Perhaps Gaius had shared his home and hospitality with John at some time during John's travels. If so, John would have appreciated his actions, because traveling preachers depended on expressions of hospitality to survive (see Matthew 10:11–16).

2 John was concerned for Gaius's physical *and* spiritual well-being. This was the opposite of the popular heresy that taught the separation of spirit and matter and despised the physical side of life. Today, many people still fall into this way of thinking. This non-Christian attitude logically leads to one of two responses: neglect of the body and physical health, or indulgence of the body's sinful desires. God is concerned for both your body and your soul. As a responsible Christian, you should neither neglect nor indulge yourself, but care for your physical needs and discipline your body so that you are at your best for God's service.

4 John wrote about "my children" because, as a result of his preaching, he was the spiritual father of many, including Gaius.

5 In the church's early days, traveling prophets, evangelists, and teachers ("the brethren") were helped on their way by people like Gaius who housed and fed them. Hospitality is a lost art in many churches today. We would do well to invite more people for meals—fellow church members, young people, traveling missionaries, those in need, visitors. This is an active and much-appreciated way to show your love. In fact it is probably more important today. Because of our individualistic, self-centered society, there are many lonely people who wonder if anyone cares whether they live or die. If you find such a lonely person, show him or her that *you* care!

7 The traveling missionaries neither asked for nor accepted anything from nonbelievers because they didn't want anyone questioning their motives for preaching. God's true preachers do not preach to make money but to express their love for God. It is the church's responsibility to care for Christian workers; this should never be left to nonbelievers.

7–8 When you help someone who is spreading the gospel, you are in a very real way a partner in the ministry. This is the other side of the principle in 2 John 10 (see the note there). Not everyone should go to the mission field; those who work for Christ at home are vital to the ministry of those who go and who need support. We can support missionaries by praying for them and by giving them our money, hospitality, and time.

9 This letter to which John refers was neither 1 nor 2 John, but another letter that no longer exists.

9–10 All we know about Diotrephes is that he wanted to control the church. John denounced (1) his refusal to have anything to do with other spiritual leaders, (2) his slander of the leaders, (3) his bad

1:10
2 John 12; 2 John 10; 3 John 5; Acts 1:15; Gal 6:10; 3 John 3, 5; John 9:34

1:11
Ps 34:14; 37:27; 1 John 2:29; 3:10; 1 John 3:6

1:12
Acts 6:3; 1 Tim 3:7; John 19:35; 21:24

1:13
2 John 12

1:14
John 20:19, 21, 26; Eph 6:23; 1 Pet 5:14; John 10:3

10 For this reason, if I come, I will call attention to his deeds which he does, unjustly
accusing us with wicked words; and not satisfied with this, he himself does not receive
the brethren, either, and he forbids those who desire *to do so* and puts *them* out of the
church.
11 Beloved, do not imitate what is evil, but what is good. The one who does good is of
God; the one who does evil has not seen God.
12 Demetrius has received a *good* testimony from everyone, and from the truth itself;
and we add our testimony, and you know that our testimony is true.

2. John's final words

13 I had many things to write to you, but I am not willing to write *them* to you with pen
and ink;
14 but I hope to see you shortly, and we will speak face to face.
15 Peace *be* to you. The friends greet you. Greet the friends by name.

---

example in refusing to welcome any gospel teachers, and (4) his attempt to excommunicate those who opposed his leadership. Sins such as pride, jealousy, and slander are still present in the church, and when a leader makes a habit of encouraging sin and discouraging right actions, he must be stopped. If no one speaks up, great harm can come to the church. We must confront sin in the church; if we try to avoid it, it will continue to grow. A true Christian leader is a servant, not an autocrat!

12 We know nothing about Demetrius except that he may have carried this letter from John to Gaius. The book of Acts mentions an Ephesian silversmith named Demetrius who opposed Paul (Acts 19:24ff), but this is probably another man. In contrast to the corrupt Diotrephes, Demetrius had a high regard for truth. John personified truth as a witness to Demetrius's character and teaching. In other words, if truth could speak, it would speak on Demetrius's behalf. When Demetrius arrived, Gaius certainly opened his home to him.

14 Whereas 2 John emphasizes the need to refuse hospitality to false teachers, 3 John urges continued hospitality to those who teach the truth. Hospitality is a strong sign of support for people and their work. It means giving them of your resources so their stay will be comfortable and their work and travel easier. Actively look for creative ways to show hospitality to God's workers. It may be in the form of a letter of encouragement, a gift, financial support, an open home, or prayer.

JUDE

VITAL STATISTICS

PURPOSE:
To remind the church of the need for constant vigilance—to keep strong in the faith and to oppose heresy

AUTHOR:
Jude, brother of Jesus and James

TO WHOM WRITTEN:
Jewish Christians and all believers everywhere

DATE WRITTEN:
Approximately A.D. 65

SETTING:
From the first century on, the church has been threatened by heresy and false teaching; we must always be on our guard.

KEY VERSE:
"Beloved, while I was making every effort to write you about our common salvation, I felt the necessity to write to you appealing that you contend earnestly for the faith which was once for all handed down to the saints" (3).

KEY PEOPLE:
Jude, James, Jesus

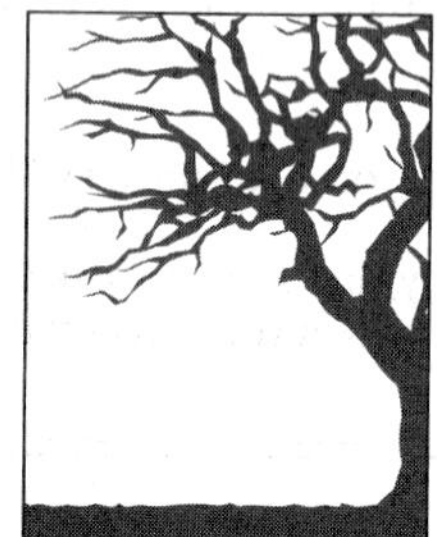

TO PROTECT from harm, to guard from attack, to repulse enemies—for centuries rugged defenders have built walls, launched missiles, and waged wars, expending material and human resources in the battle to save nations and cities. And with total commitment and courageous abandon, individuals have fought for their families. It is a rule of life that we fight for survival, defending with all our strength what is most precious to us, from every real or imagined attack.

God's Word and the gift of eternal life have infinite value and have been entrusted to Christ's faithful followers. There are many people who live in opposition to God and his followers. They twist God's truth, seeking to deceive and destroy the unwary. But God's truth must go forth, carried and defended by those who have committed their lives to God's Son. It is an important task, an awesome responsibility, and a profound privilege to have this commission.

This was Jude's message to Christians everywhere. Opposition would come and godless teachers would arise, but Christians should "contend earnestly for the faith" (3) by rejecting all falsehood and immorality (4–19), remembering God's mighty acts of rescue and punishment (5–11, 14–16) and the warnings of the apostles (17–19). His readers are to build up their own faith through prayer (20), keeping close to Christ (21), helping others (22–23), and hating sin (23). Then Jude concludes with a glorious benediction of praise to God (24–25).

How much do you value God's Word, the fellowship of the church, and obedience to Jesus Christ? There are many false teachers waiting to destroy your Christ-centered life, the credibility of God's Word, and the unity of the body of Christ. Read Jude and determine to stand firm in your faith and defend God's truth at all costs. *Nothing* is more valuable.

THE BLUEPRINT

1. The danger of false teachers (1–16)
2. The duty to fight for God's truth (17–25)

Jude wrote to motivate Christians everywhere to action. He wanted them to recognize the dangers of false teaching, to protect themselves and other believers, and to win back those who had already been deceived. Jude was writing against godless teachers who were saying that Christians could do as they pleased without fear of God's punishment. While few teach this heresy openly in the church today, many in the church act as though this were true. This letter contains a warning against living a nominal Christian life.

MEGATHEMES

THEME	EXPLANATION	IMPORTANCE
False Teachers	Jude warns against false teachers and leaders who reject the lordship of Christ, undermine the faith of others, and lead them astray. These leaders and any who follow them will be punished.	We must staunchly defend Christian truth. Make sure that you avoid leaders and teachers who distort the Bible to suit their own purposes. Genuine servants of God will faithfully portray Christ in their words and conduct.
Apostasy	Jude also warns against apostasy—turning away from Christ. We are to remember that God punishes rebellion against him. We must be careful not to drift away from a faithful commitment to Christ.	Those who do not seek to know the truth in God's Word are susceptible to apostasy. Christians must guard against any false teachings that would distract them from the truth preached by the apostles and written in God's Word.

1:1
Matt 13:55; Mark 6:3; Rom 1:1; Rom 1:6f; John 17:11f; 1 Pet 1:5; Jude 21

1:3
Heb 6:9; Jude 1, 17, 20; Titus 1:4; 1 Tim 6:12; Acts 6:7; 2 Pet 2:21; Acts 9:13

1:4
Gal 2:4; 2 Tim 3:6; 1 Pet 2:8; Acts 11:23; 2 Pet 2:7; 2 Tim 2:12; Titus 1:16; 2 Pet 2:1; 1 John 2:22

1. The danger of false teachers

The Warnings of History to the Ungodly

1 Jude, a bond-servant of Jesus Christ, and brother of James,
To those who are the called, beloved in God the Father, and kept for Jesus Christ:
2 May mercy and peace and love be multiplied to you.
3 Beloved, while I was making every effort to write you about our common salvation,
I felt the necessity to write to you appealing that you contend earnestly for the faith which
was once for all handed down to the saints.
4 For certain persons have crept in unnoticed, those who were long beforehand marked
out for this condemnation, ungodly persons who turn the grace of our God into licen-
tiousness and deny our only Master and Lord, Jesus Christ.

1 Jude's letter focuses on *apostasy*—when people turn away from God's truth and embrace false teachings. Jude reminded his readers of God's judgment on those who had left the faith in the past. This letter is a warning against false teachers—in this case, probably Gnostic teachers (see the note on Colossians 2:4ff for a description of the Gnostic heresy). Gnostics opposed two of the basic tenets of Christianity—the incarnation of Christ and the call to Christian ethics. Jude wrote to combat these false teachings and to encourage true doctrine and right conduct.

1 Jude was a brother of James, who was one of the leaders in the early church. Both of these men were Jesus' half brothers. Mary was their mother, and Joseph was their father. Although Mary was Jesus' true mother, God was Jesus' true Father.

3 Jude emphasizes the important relationship between correct doctrine and true faith. The truth of the Bible must not be compromised, because it gives us the real facts about Jesus and salvation. The Bible is inspired by God and should never be twisted or manipulated; when it is, we can become confused over right and wrong and lose sight of the only path that leads to eternal life. Before writing about salvation, then, Jude felt he had to set his readers back on the right track, calling them back to the basics of their faith. Then the way to salvation would be clearer. *Saints* refers to all believers.

4 Even some of our churches today have false ("ungodly") teachers who "crept in unnoticed" and are twisting the Bible's teachings to justify their own opinions, life-style, or wrong behavior. In doing this, they may gain temporary freedom to do as they wish, but they will discover that in distorting Scripture they are playing with fire. God will judge them for excusing, tolerating, and promoting sin.

4 Some people avoid studying the Bible because they think theology is dry and boring. Those who refuse to learn correct doctrine, however, are susceptible to false teaching because they are not fully grounded in God's truth. We must understand the basic doctrines of our faith so that we can recognize false doctrines and prevent wrong teaching from undermining our faith and hurting others.

4 Many first-century false teachers were teaching that Christians could do whatever they liked without fear of God's punishment. They had a light view of God's holiness and his justice. Paul refuted this same kind of false teaching in Romans 6:1–23. Even today, some Christians minimize the sinfulness of sin, believing that how they live has little to do with their faith. But what a person truly believes will show up in how he or she acts. Those who truly have faith will show it by their deep respect for God and their sincere desire to live according to the principles in his Word.

5 Now I desire to remind you, though you know all things once for all, that [1]the Lord,
after saving a people out of the land of Egypt, subsequently destroyed those who did not
believe.
6 And angels who did not keep their own domain, but abandoned their proper abode,
He has kept in eternal bonds under darkness for the judgment of the great day,
7 just as Sodom and Gomorrah and the cities around them, since they in the same
way as these indulged in gross immorality and went after strange flesh, are exhibited as
an example in undergoing the punishment of eternal fire.
8 Yet in the same way these men, also by dreaming, defile the flesh, and reject authority, and revile angelic majesties.
9 But Michael the archangel, when he disputed with the devil and argued about the
body of Moses, did not dare pronounce against him a railing judgment, but said, "The
Lord rebuke you!"
10 But these men revile the things which they do not understand; and the things which
they know by instinct, like unreasoning animals, by these things they are destroyed.
11 Woe to them! For they have gone the way of Cain, and for pay they have rushed
headlong into the error of Balaam, and perished in the rebellion of Korah.
12 These are the men who are hidden reefs in your love feasts when they feast with
you without fear, caring for themselves; clouds without water, carried along by winds;
autumn trees without fruit, doubly dead, uprooted;
13 wild waves of the sea, casting up their own shame like foam; wandering stars, for
whom the black darkness has been reserved forever.
14 *It was* also about these men *that* Enoch, *in* the seventh *generation* from Adam, prophesied, saying, "Behold, the Lord came with many thousands of His holy ones,
15 to execute judgment upon all, and to convict all the ungodly of all their ungodly deeds
which they have done in an ungodly way, and of all the harsh things which ungodly sinners have spoken against Him."
16 These are grumblers, finding fault, following after their *own* lusts; they speak arrogantly, flattering people for the sake of *gaining an* advantage.

1 Two early mss read *Jesus*

1:5 2 Pet 1:12f; 3:1f; 1 John 2:20; Ex 12:51; 1 Cor 10:5-10; Heb 3:16f

1:6 2 Pet 2:4; 2 Pet 2:9

1:7 Gen 19:24f; 2 Pet 2:6; Deut 29:23; Hos 11:8; 2 Pet 2:2; 2 Pet 2:6; Matt 25:41; 2 Thess 1:8f; 2 Pet 3:7

1:8 2 Pet 2:10

1:9 Dan 10:13, 21; 12:1; Rev 12:7; 1 Thess 4:16; 2 Pet 2:11; Deut 34:6; Zech 3:2

1:10 2 Pet 2:12; Phil 3:19

1:11 Gen 4:3-8; 2 Pet 2:15; Rev 2:14; Num 16:1-3, 31-35

1:12 1 Cor 11:20ff; Eph 4:14; Matt 15:13

1:14 Gen 5:18, 21ff; Deut 33:2; Dan 7:10; Matt 16:27; Heb 12:22

1:15 2 Pet 2:6ff; 1 Tim 1:9

1:16 2 Pet 2:18; 2 Pet 2:3

5–7 Jude gave three examples of rebellion: (1) the children of Israel—who, although they were delivered from Egypt, refused to trust God and enter the promised land (Numbers 14:26–39); (2) the angels—although they were once pure, holy, and living in God's presence, some gave in to pride and joined Satan to rebel against God (2 Peter 2:4); and (3) the cities of Sodom and Gomorrah—the inhabitants were so full of sin that God wiped them off the face of the earth (Genesis 19:1–29). If the chosen people, angels, and sinful cities were punished, how much more would these false teachers be severely judged?

7 Many people don't want to believe that God sentences people to "eternal fire" for rejecting him. But this is clearly taught in Scripture. Sinners who don't seek forgiveness from God will face eternal separation from him. Jude gives this warning to all who rebel against, ignore, or reject God.

8 The "angelic majesties" here are probably angels. Just as the men of Sodom insulted angels (Genesis 19), these false teachers scoffed at any authority. For information on the danger of insulting even the fallen angels, see the note on 2 Peter 2:10–12.

9 This incident is not recorded in any other place in Scripture. Moses' death is recorded in Deuteronomy 34. Here Jude may have been making use of an ancient book called *The Assumption of Moses*.

10 False teachers claimed that they possessed secret knowledge that gave them authority. Their "knowledge" of God was esoteric—mystical and beyond human understanding. The nature of God *is* beyond our understanding, but God, in his grace, has chosen to reveal himself to us—in his Word, and supremely in Jesus Christ. Therefore, we must seek to know all we can about what he has revealed, even though we cannot fully comprehend God with our finite human minds. Beware of those who claim to have all the answers and who belittle what they do not understand.

11 Jude gives three examples of men who did whatever they wanted (verse 10)—Cain, who murdered his brother out of vengeful jealousy (Genesis 4:1–16); Balaam, who prophesied out of greed, not out of obedience to God's command (Numbers 22—24); and Korah, who rebelled against God's divinely appointed leaders, wanting the power for himself (Numbers 16:1–35). These stories illustrate attitudes that are typical of false teachers—pride, selfishness, jealousy, greed, lust for power, and disregard of God's will.

12 When the Lord's Supper was celebrated in the early church, believers ate a full meal before taking part in Communion with the sharing of the bread and wine. The meal was called a "love feast," and it was designed to be a sacred time of fellowship to prepare one's heart for Communion. However, the false teachers were joining these love feasts, becoming "hidden reefs" in what should have been a time of rejoicing in the Lord. In several of the churches, however, this meal had turned into a time of gluttony and drunken revelry. In Corinth, for example, some people hastily gobbled food while others went hungry (1 Corinthians 11:20–22). No church function should be an occasion for selfishness, gluttony, greed, disorder, or other sins that destroy unity or take one's mind away from the real purpose for gathering together.

12 The false teachers were "doubly dead." They were useless "trees" because they weren't producing fruit; because they weren't even believers, they would be rooted up and burned.

14 Enoch is mentioned briefly in Genesis 5:21–24. This quotation is from an apocryphal book called the book of Enoch.

14 Other places where Jesus is mentioned as coming with angels ("holy ones") are Matthew 16:27 and 24:31. Daniel 7:10 speaks of God judging humanity in the presence of ten thousand times ten thousand angels.

1:17 Jude 3; 2 Pet 3:2; Heb 2:3

1:18 Acts 20:29; 1 Tim 4:1; 2 Tim 3:1f; 4:3

1:19 1 Cor 2:14f; James 3:15

1:20 1 Thess 5:11; Eph 6:18

1:21 Titus 2:13; Heb 9:28; 2 Pet 3:12

1:24 Rom 16:25; 2 Cor 4:14; 1 Pet 4:13

1:25 John 5:44; 1 Tim 1:17; Luke 1:47; Rom 11:36; Heb 13:8

2. The duty to fight for God's truth

Keep Yourselves in the Love of God

17 But you, beloved, ought to remember the words that were spoken beforehand by
the apostles of our Lord Jesus Christ,
18 that they were saying to you, "In the last time there will be mockers, following after
their own ungodly lusts."
19 These are the ones who cause divisions, worldly-minded, devoid of the Spirit.
20 But you, beloved, building yourselves up on your most holy faith, praying in the Holy
Spirit,
21 keep yourselves in the love of God, waiting anxiously for the mercy of our Lord Jesus
Christ to eternal life.
22 And have mercy on some, who are doubting;
23 save others, snatching them out of the fire; and on some have mercy with fear, hating even the garment polluted by the flesh.
24 Now to Him who is able to keep you from stumbling, and to make you stand in the
presence of His glory blameless with great joy,
25 to the only God our Savior, through Jesus Christ our Lord, *be* glory, majesty, dominion and authority, before all time and now and forever. Amen.

---

17 Other apostles also warned about false teachers—see Acts 20:29; 1 Timothy 4:1; 2 Timothy 3:1–5; 2 Peter 2:1–3; 2 John 7.

18 The *last time* is a common phrase referring to the time between Jesus' first and second comings. We live in the last times.

20 "Praying in the Holy Spirit" means to pray in the power and strength of the Holy Spirit. He prays for us (Romans 8:26–27), opens our minds to Jesus (John 14:26), and teaches us about him (John 15:26).

21 To "keep yourselves in the love of God" means to live close to God and his people, not listening to false teachers who would try to pull you away from him (John 15:9–10).

22–23 Effective witnessing saves people from God's judgment. We witness to some through our compassion and kindness; to others we witness as if we were snatching them from the eternal fire. To hate "even the garment polluted by the flesh" means that we are to hate the sin, but we must witness to and love the sinner. Unbelievers, no matter how successful they seem by worldly standards, are lost and in need of salvation. We should not take witnessing lightly—it is a matter of life and death.

23 In trying to find common ground with those to whom we witness, we must be careful not to fall into the quicksand of compromise. When reaching out to others, we must be sure that our own footing is safe and secure. Be careful not to become so much like non-Christians that no one can tell who you are or what you believe. Influence them for Christ—don't allow them to influence you to sin!

24–25 As the letter begins, so it ends—with assurance. God keeps believers from falling prey to false teachers. Although false teachers are widespread and dangerous, we don't have to be afraid if we trust God and are rooted and grounded in him.

24–25 To be sinless and perfect ("blameless") will be the ultimate condition of the believer when he or she finally sees Christ face to face. When Christ appears, and we are given our new bodies, we will be like Christ (1 John 3:2). Coming into Christ's presence will be more wonderful than we could ever imagine!

24–25 The audience to whom Jude wrote was vulnerable to heresies and to temptations toward immoral living. Jude encouraged the believers to remain firm in their faith and trust in God's promises for their future. This was all the more important because they were living in a time of increased apostasy. We too are living in the last days, much closer to the end than were the original readers of this letter. We too are vulnerable to doctrinal error. We too are tempted to give in to sin. Although there is much false teaching around us, we need not be afraid or give up in despair—God can keep us from falling, and he guarantees that if we remain faithful, he will bring us into his presence and give us everlasting joy.

REVELATION

VITAL STATISTICS

PURPOSE:
To reveal the full identity of Christ and to give warning and hope to believers

AUTHOR:
The apostle John

TO WHOM WRITTEN:
The seven churches in Asia and all believers everywhere

DATE WRITTEN:
Approximately A.D. 95 from Patmos

SETTING:
Most scholars believe that the seven churches of Asia to whom John writes were experiencing the persecution that took place under Emperor Domitian (A.D. 90–95). It seems that the Roman authorities had exiled John to the island of Patmos (off the coast of Asia). John, who had been an eyewitness of the incarnate Christ, had a vision of the glorified Christ. God also revealed to him what would take place in the future—judgment and the ultimate triumph of God over evil.

KEY VERSE:
"Blessed is he who reads and those who hear the words of the prophecy, and heed the things which are written in it; for the time is near" (1:3).

KEY PEOPLE:
John, Jesus

KEY PLACES:
Patmos, the seven churches, the new Jerusalem

SPECIAL FEATURES:
Revelation is written in "apocalyptic" form—a type of Jewish literature that uses symbolic imagery to communicate hope (in the ultimate triumph of God) to those in the midst of persecution. The events are ordered according to literary, rather than strictly chronological, patterns.

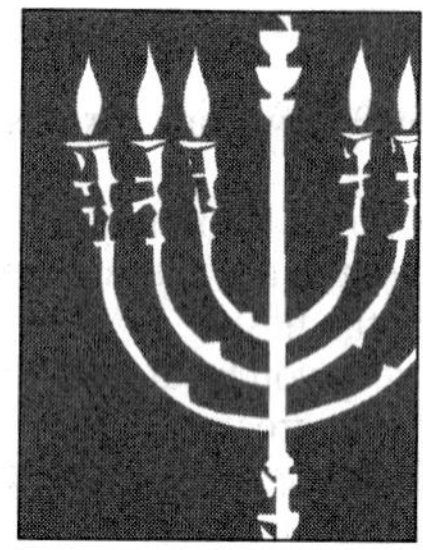

WITH tiny wrinkles and cries, he entered the world and, wrapped in strips of cloth, took his first nap on a bed of straw. Subject to time and to parents, he grew to manhood in Roman-occupied Palestine, his gentle hands becoming strong and calloused in Joseph's woodworking shop. As a man, he walked through the countryside and city, touching individuals, preaching to crowds, and training 12 men to carry on his work. At every step he was hounded by those seeking to rid the world of his influence. Finally, falsely accused and tried, he was condemned to a disgraceful execution by foreign hands. And he died—spat upon, cursed, pierced by nails, and hung heavenward for all to deride. Jesus, the God-man, gave his life completely so that all might live.

At God's appointed time, the risen and ascended Lord Jesus will burst onto the world scene. Then everyone will know that Jesus is Lord of the universe! Those who love him will rejoice, greeting their Savior with hearts overflowing into songs of praise. But his enemies will be filled with fear. Allied with Satan, the enemies of Christ will marshal their legions against Christ and his armies. But who can withstand God's wrath? Christ will win the battle and reign victorious forever! Jesus, the humble suffering servant, is also the powerful, conquering King and Judge.

Revelation is a book of hope. John, the beloved apostle and eyewitness of Jesus, proclaimed that the victorious Lord would surely return to vindicate the righteous and judge the wicked. But Revelation is also a book of warning. Things were not as they should have been in the churches, so Christ called the members to commit themselves to live in righteousness.

Although Jesus gave this revelation of himself to John nearly 2,000 years ago, it still stands as a comfort and challenge to God's people today. We can take heart as we understand John's vision of hope: Christ will return to rescue his people and settle accounts with all who defy him.

John begins this book by explaining how he received this revelation from God (1:1–20). He then records specific messages from Jesus to the seven churches in Asia (2:1—3:22). Suddenly, the scene shifts as a mosaic of dramatic and majestic images bursts into view before John's eyes. This series of visions portrays the future rise of evil, culminating in the antichrist (4:1—18:24). Then follows John's recounting of the triumph of the King of kings, the wedding of the Lamb, the final judgment, and the coming of the new Jerusalem (19:1—22:5). Revelation concludes with the promise of Christ's soon return (22:6–21), and John breathes a prayer that has been echoed by Christians through the centuries: "Amen. Come, Lord Jesus" (22:20).

As you read the book of Revelation, marvel with John at the wondrous panorama of God's revealed plan. Listen as Christ warns the churches, and root out any sin that blocks your relationship with him. Be full of hope, knowing that God is in control, Christ's victory is assured, and all who trust him will be saved.

THE BLUEPRINT

A. LETTERS TO THE CHURCHES (1:1—3:22)	The vision John received opens with instructions for him to write to seven churches. He both commends them for their strengths and warns them about their flaws. Each letter was directed to a church then in existence but also speaks to conditions in the church throughout history. Both in the church and in our individual lives, we must constantly fight against the temptation to become loveless, immoral, lenient, compromising, lifeless, or casual about our faith. The letters make it clear how our Lord feels about these qualities.
B. MESSAGE FOR THE CHURCH (4:1—22:21) 1. Worshiping God in heaven 2. Opening the seven seals 3. Sounding the seven trumpets 4. Observing the great conflict 5. Pouring out the seven plagues 6. Seizing the final victory 7. Making all things new	This revelation is both a warning to Christians who have grown apathetic and an encouragement to those who are faithfully enduring the struggles in this world. It reassures us that good will triumph over evil, gives us hope as we face difficult times, and gives guidance when we are wavering in our faith. Christ's message to the church is a message of hope for all believers in every generation.

MEGATHEMES

THEME	EXPLANATION	IMPORTANCE
God's Sovereignty	God is sovereign. He is greater than any power in the universe. God is not to be compared with any leader, government, or religion. He controls history for the purpose of uniting true believers in loving fellowship with him.	Though Satan's power may temporarily increase, we are not to be led astray. God is all-powerful. He is in control. He will bring his true family safely into eternal life. Because he cares for us, we can trust him with our very life.
Christ's Return	Christ came to earth as a "Lamb," the symbol of his perfect sacrifice for our sin. He will return as the triumphant "Lion," the rightful ruler and conqueror. He will defeat Satan, settle accounts with all those who reject him, and bring his faithful people into eternity.	Assurance of Christ's return gives suffering Christians the strength to endure. We can look forward to his return as king and judge. Since no one knows the time when he will appear, we must be ready at all times by keeping our faith strong.
God's Faithful People	John wrote to encourage the church to resist the demands to worship the Roman emperor. He warns all God's faithful people to be devoted only to Christ. Revelation identifies who the faithful people are and what they should be doing until Christ returns.	You can take your place in the ranks of God's faithful people by believing in Christ. Victory is sure for those who resist temptation and make loyalty to Christ their top priority.
Judgment	One day God's anger toward sin will be fully and completely unleashed. Satan will be defeated with all of his agents. False religion will be destroyed. God will reward the faithful with eternal life, but all who refuse to believe in him will face eternal punishment.	Evil and injustice will not prevail forever. God's final judgment will put an end to these. We need to be certain of our commitment to Jesus if we want to escape this great final judgment. No one who rejects Christ will escape God's punishment.
Hope	One day God will create a new heaven and a new earth. All believers will live with him forever in perfect peace and security. Those who have already died will be raised to life. These promises for the future bring us hope.	Our great hope is that what Christ promises will come true. When we have confidence in our final destination, we can follow Christ with unwavering dedication no matter what we must face. We can be encouraged by hoping in Christ's return.

A. LETTERS TO THE CHURCHES (1:1—3:22)

Near the end of his life, John received a vision from Christ, which he recorded for the benefit of the seven churches in Asia and for Christians throughout history. This book contains a beautiful promise of blessing for those who listen to its words and do what it says.

The Revelation of Jesus Christ

1 The Revelation of Jesus Christ, which God gave Him to show to His bond-servants,
the things which must soon take place; and He sent and communicated *it* by His angel
to His bond-servant John,
2 who testified to the word of God and to the testimony of Jesus Christ, *even* to all
that he saw.
3 Blessed is he who reads and those who hear the words of the prophecy, and heed
the things which are written in it; for the time is near.

Message to the Seven Churches

4 John to the seven churches that are in Asia: Grace to you and peace, from Him who
is and who was and who is to come, and from the seven Spirits who are before His throne,
5 and from Jesus Christ, the faithful witness, the firstborn of the dead, and the ruler
of the kings of the earth. To Him who loves us and released us from our sins by His
blood—

1:1 John 17:8; Rev 5:7; Rev 22:6; Dan 2:28f; Rev 1:19; Rev 17:1; 19:9f; 21:9; 22:16; Rev 1:4, 9; 22:8

1:2 Rev 1:9; 6:9; 12:17; 20:4; 1 Cor 1:6

1:3 Luke 11:28; Rom 13:11; Rev 3:11; 22:7, 10, 12

1:4 Rev 1:1, 9; 22:8; Rev 1:11, 20; Acts 2:9; Rom 1:7; Rev 1:8, 17; 4:8; 16:5; Is 11:2; Rev 3:1; 4:5; 5:6; 8:2

1:5 Rev 3:14; 19:11; 1 Cor 15:20; Col 1:18; Rev 17:14; 19:16; Rom 8:37

1:1 Revelation is a book about the future *and* about the present. It offers future hope to all believers, especially those who have suffered for their faith, by proclaiming Christ's final victory over evil and the reality of eternal life with him. It also gives present guidance as it teaches us about Jesus Christ and how we should live for him now. Through graphic pictures we learn that (1) Jesus Christ is coming again, (2) evil will be judged, and (3) the dead will be raised to judgment, resulting in eternal life or eternal destruction.

1:1 According to tradition, John, the author, was the only one of Jesus' original twelve disciples who was not killed for the faith. He also wrote the Gospel of John and the letters of 1, 2, and 3 John. When he wrote Revelation, John was in exile on the island of Patmos in the Aegean Sea, sent there by the Romans for his witness about Jesus Christ. For more information on John, see his Profile in John 13.

1:1 This book is the revelation *of, concerning,* and *from* Jesus Christ. God gave the revelation of his plan to Jesus Christ, who, in turn, revealed it to John. The book of Revelation unveils Christ's full identity and God's plan for the end of the world, and it focuses on Jesus Christ, his second coming, his victory over evil, and the establishment of his kingdom. As you read and study Revelation, don't focus so much on the timetable of the events or the details of John's imagery that you miss the main message—the infinite love, power, and justice of the Lord Jesus Christ.

1:1 The book of Revelation is *apocalyptic* (meaning uncovered, unveiled, or revealed) in style. This style of ancient literature usually featured spectacular and mysterious imagery, and such literature was written under the name of an ancient hero. John was acquainted with Jewish apocalyptic works, but his book is different in several ways: (1) He uses his own name rather than the name of an ancient hero; (2) he denounces evil and exhorts people to high Christian standards; (3) he offers hope rather than gloom. John was not a psychic attempting to predict the future; he was a prophet of God describing what God had shown him.

1:1 For more about angels, see the note on 5:11.

1:1 Jesus gave his message to John in a vision, allowing John to see and record certain future events so they could be an encouragement to all believers. The vision includes many signs and symbols that convey the essence of what is to happen. What John saw, in most cases, was indescribable, so he used illustrations to show what it was *like.* When reading this symbolic language, we don't have to understand every detail—John himself didn't. Instead, realize that John's imagery shows us that Christ is indeed the glorious and victorious Lord of all.

1:1–3 The book of Revelation reveals future events, but there is not the gloomy pessimism we might expect. The drama of these unfolding events is spectacular, but there is nothing to fear if you are on the winning side. When you think about the future, walk with confidence because Christ, the victor, walks with you.

1:3 Revelation is a book of prophecy that is both *prediction* (foretelling future events) and *proclamation* (preaching about who God is and what he will do). Prophecy is more than telling the future. Behind the predictions are important principles about God's character and promises. As we read, we will get to know God better so that we can trust him completely.

1:3 The typical news reports—filled with violence, scandal, and political haggling—are depressing, and we may wonder where the world is heading. God's plan for the future, however, provides inspiration and encouragement because we know he will intervene in history to conquer evil. John encourages churches to read this book aloud so everyone can hear it, apply it ("heed the things which are written in it"), and be assured of the fact that God will triumph.

1:3 When John says, "the time is near," he is urging his readers to be ready at all times for the Last Judgment and the establishment of God's kingdom. We do not know when these events will occur, but we must always be prepared. They will happen quickly, and there will be no second chance to change sides.

1:4 Jesus told John to write to seven churches that knew and trusted him and had read his earlier letters (see 1:11). The letters were addressed so that they could be read and passed on in a systematic fashion, following the main Roman road clockwise around the province of Asia (now called Turkey).

1:4 The "seven Spirits" is another name for the Holy Spirit. The number seven is used throughout Revelation to symbolize completeness and perfection. For more about the Holy Spirit, see the notes on John 3:6 and Acts 1:5.

1:4–6 The Trinity—the Father ("Him who is and who was and who is to come"), the Holy Spirit ("the seven Spirits"), and the Son (Jesus Christ)—is the source of all truth (John 14:6, 17; 1 John 2:27; Revelation 19:11). Thus we can be assured that John's message is reliable and is God's Word to us.

1:5 Others had risen from the dead—people whom the prophets, Jesus, and the apostles had brought back to life during their ministries—but later those people died again. Jesus was the first who rose from the dead in an imperishable body (1 Corinthians 15:20), never to die again. He is the firstborn from the dead.

1:5–6 Many hesitate to witness about their faith in Christ because

1:6 Rev 5:10; 20:6

1:7 Dan 7.13, 1 Thess 4:17; Zech 12:10-14; John 19:37; Luke 23:28

6 and He has made us *to be* a kingdom, priests to His God and Father—to Him *be* the glory and the dominion forever and ever. Amen.
7 BEHOLD, HE IS COMING WITH THE CLOUDS, and every eye will see Him, even those who pierced Him; and all the tribes of the earth will mourn over Him. So it is to be. Amen.

A JOURNEY THROUGH THE BOOK OF REVELATION

Revelation is a complex book, and it has baffled interpreters for centuries. We can avoid a great deal of confusion by understanding the literary structure of this book. This approach will allow us to understand the individual scenes within the overall structure of Revelation and keep us from getting unnecessarily bogged down in the details of each vision. John gives hints throughout the book to indicate a change of scene, a change of subject, or a flashback to an earlier scene.

In chapter 1, John relates the circumstances that led to the writing of this book (1:1–20). In chapters 2 and 3 Jesus gives special messages to the seven churches of Asia Minor (2:1—3:22).

Suddenly John is caught up into heaven, where he sees a vision of God Almighty on his throne. All of Christ's followers and the heavenly angels are worshiping God (4:1–11). John watches as God gives a book with seven seals to the worthy Lamb, Jesus Christ (5:1–14). The Lamb begins to open the seals one by one. As each seal is opened, a new vision appears.

As the first four seals are opened, riders appear on horses of different colors—war, famine, disease, and death are in their path (6:1–8). As the fifth seal is opened, John sees those in heaven who have been martyred for their faith in Christ (6:9–11).

A set of contrasting images appears at the opening of the sixth seal. On one side, there is a huge earthquake, stars falling from the sky, and the sky rolling up like a scroll (6:12–17). On the other side, multitudes are before the great throne, worshiping and praising God and the Lamb (7:1–17).

Finally, the seventh seal is opened (8:1–5), unveiling a series of God's judgments announced by seven angels with seven trumpets. The first four angels bring hail, fire, a burning mountain, and a falling star—the sun and the moon are darkened (8:6–13). The fifth trumpet announces the coming of locusts with the power to sting (9:1–12). The sixth trumpet heralds the coming of an army of warriors on horses (9:13–21). In 10:1–11, John is given a little book to eat. Following this, John is commanded to measure the temple of God (11:1–2). He sees two witnesses who proclaim God's judgment on the earth for three and a half years (11:3–14).

Finally, the seventh trumpet sounds, calling the rival forces of good and evil to the final battle. On one side is Satan and his forces; on the other side stands Jesus Christ with his forces (11:15—13:18). In the midst of this call to battle, John sees three angels announcing the final judgment (14:6–13). Two angels begin to reap this harvest of judgment on the earth (14:14–20). Following on the heels of these two angels are seven more angels who pour out God's judgment on the earth from seven bowls (15:1—16:21). One of these angels from the group of seven reveals to John a vision of a "great harlot" called Babylon (symbolizing the Roman empire) riding a scarlet beast (17:1–18). After the defeat of Babylon (18:1–24), a great multitude in heaven shouts praise to God for his mighty victory (19:1–10).

The final three chapters of the book of Revelation catalogue the events that finalize Christ's victory over the enemy: Satan's 1,000-year imprisonment (20:1–10), the final judgment (20:11–15), and the creation of a new earth and a new Jerusalem (21:1—22:6). An angel then gives John final instructions concerning the visions John has seen and what to do once he has written them all down (22:7–11).

Revelation concludes with the promise of Christ's soon return, an offer to drink of the water of life that flows through the great street of the new Jerusalem, and a warning to those who read the book (22:12–21). May we pray with John, "Amen. Come, Lord Jesus" (22:20).

The Bible ends with a message of warning and hope for men and women of every generation. Christ is victorious, and all evil has been done away with. As you read the book of Revelation, marvel at God's grace in the salvation of the saints and his power over the evil forces of Satan, and remember the hope of this victory to come.

they don't feel the change in their lives has been spectacular enough. But you qualify as a witness for Jesus because of what he has done for you, not because of what you have done for him. Christ demonstrated his great love by setting us free from our sins through his death on the cross ("released us from our sins by His blood"), guaranteeing us a place in his kingdom, and making us priests to administer God's love to others. The fact that the all-powerful God has offered eternal life to you is nothing short of spectacular.

1:5–7 Jesus is portrayed as an all-powerful King, victorious in battle, glorious in peace. He is not just a humble earthly teacher, he is the glorious God. When you read John's description of the vision, keep in mind that his words are not just good advice; they are truth from the King of kings. Don't just read his words for their interesting and amazing portrayal of the future. Let the truth about Christ penetrate your life, deepen your faith in him, and strengthen your commitment to follow him no matter what the cost.

1:7 John is announcing the return of Jesus to earth (see also Matthew 24; Mark 13; 1 Thessalonians 4:15–18). Jesus' second coming will be *visible* and *victorious.* All people will see him arrive (Mark 13:26), and they will *know* it is Jesus. When he comes, he will conquer evil and judge all people according to their deeds (20:11–15).

1:7 "Those who pierced Him" could refer to the Roman soldiers who pierced Jesus' side as he hung on the cross or to the Jews who were responsible for his death. John saw Jesus' death with his own eyes, and he never forgot the horror of it (see John 19:34–35; see also Zechariah 12:10).

8 "I am the Alpha and the Omega," says the Lord God, "who is and who was and who
is to come, the Almighty."

The Patmos Vision

9 I, John, your brother and fellow partaker in the tribulation and kingdom and perseverance *which are* in Jesus, was on the island called Patmos because of the word of God
and the testimony of Jesus.
10 I was [1]in the Spirit on the Lord's day, and I heard behind me a loud voice like *the*
sound of a trumpet,
11 saying, "Write in a book what you see, and send *it* to the seven churches: to Ephesus
and to Smyrna and to Pergamum and to Thyatira and to Sardis and to Philadelphia and
to Laodicea."
12 Then I turned to see the voice that was speaking with me. And having turned I saw
seven golden lampstands;
13 and in the middle of the lampstands *I saw* one like [2]a son of man, clothed in a robe
reaching to the feet, and girded across His chest with a golden sash.
14 His head and His hair were white like white wool, like snow; and His eyes were like
a flame of fire.
15 His feet *were* like burnished bronze, when it has been made to glow in a furnace,
and His voice *was* like the sound of many waters.
16 In His right hand He held seven stars, and out of His mouth came a sharp two-edged
sword; and His face was like the sun shining in its strength.
17 When I saw Him, I fell at His feet like a dead man. And He placed His right hand
on me, saying, "Do not be afraid; I am the first and the last,
18 and the living One; and I was dead, and behold, I am alive forevermore, and I have
the keys of death and of Hades.
19 "Therefore write the things which you have seen, and the things which are, and the
things which will take place after these things.
20 "As for the mystery of the seven stars which you saw in My right hand, and the seven

1 Or *in spirit* 2 Or *the Son of Man*

1:8 Is 41:4; Rev 21:6
1:9 2 Thess 3:5; Rev 3:10; Rev 1:2
1:10 Matt 22:43; Rev 4:2; 17:3; 21:10
1:12 Ex 25:37; 37:23; Zech 4:2; Rev 1:20; 2:1
1:13 Rev 2:1; Ezek 1:26; Dan 7:13; 10:16; Rev 14:14; Dan 10:5; Rev 15:6
1:14 Dan 7:9; 10:6; Rev 2:18; 19:12
1:15 Ezek 1:7; Dan 10:6; Rev 2:18; Ezek 1:24; 43:2; Rev 14:2; 19:6
1:16 Rev 1:20; 2:1; 3:1; Is 49:2; Heb 4:12; Rev 2:12, 16; 19:15; Matt 17:2; Rev 10:1
1:17 Dan 8:17; 10:9, 10; Is 41:4; 44:6; 48:12; Rev 2:8; 22:13
1:18 Luke 24:5; Rev 4:9f; Rom 6:9; Rev 2:8; 10:6; 15:7; Job 38:17; Matt 11:23; 16:19; Rev 9:1; 20:1

1:8 Alpha and Omega are the first and last letters of the Greek alphabet. The Lord God is the beginning and the end. God the Father is the eternal Lord and Ruler of the past, present, and future (see also 4:8; Isaiah 44:6; 48:12–15). Without him you have nothing that is eternal, nothing that can change your life, nothing that can save you from sin. Is the Lord your reason for living, "the Alpha and the Omega" of your life? Honor the One who is the beginning and the end of all existence, wisdom, and power.

1:9 Patmos was a small rocky island in the Aegean Sea, about 50 miles offshore from the city of Ephesus on the Asia Minor seacoast (see map).

1:9 The Christian church was facing severe persecution. Almost all believers were socially, politically, or economically suffering because of this empire-wide persecution, and some were even being killed for their faith. John was exiled to Patmos because he refused to stop preaching the gospel. We may not face persecution for our faith as the early Christians did, but even with our freedom few of us have the courage to share God's Word with others. If we hesitate to share our faith during easy times, how will we do during times of persecution?

1:12–13 The seven golden lampstands are the seven churches in Asia (1:11, 20), and Jesus stands among them. No matter what the churches face, Jesus protects them with his all-encompassing love and reassuring power. Through his Spirit, Jesus Christ is still among the churches today. When a church faces persecution, it should remember Christ's deep love and compassion. When a church is wracked by internal strife and conflict, it should remember Christ's concern for purity and his intolerance of sin.

1:13–14 This man "like a son of man" is Jesus himself. The title *Son of Man* occurs many times in the New Testament in reference to Jesus as the Messiah. John recognized Jesus because he lived with him for three years and had seen him both as the Galilean preacher and as the glorified Son of God at the transfiguration (Matthew 17:1–8). Here Jesus appears as the mighty Son of Man. His white hair indicates his wisdom and divine nature (see also Daniel 7:9); his blazing eyes symbolize judgment of all evil; the golden sash around his chest reveals him as the high priest who goes into God's presence to obtain forgiveness of sin for those who have believed in him.

1:16 The sword in Jesus' mouth symbolizes the power and force of his message. His words of judgment are as sharp as swords (Isaiah 49:2; Hebrews 4:12).

1:17–18 As the Roman government stepped up its persecution of Christians, John must have wondered if the church could survive and stand against the opposition. But Jesus appeared in glory and splendor, reassuring John that he and his fellow believers had access to God's strength to face these trials. If you are facing difficult problems, remember that the power available to John and the early church is also available to you (see 1 John 4:4).

1:17–18 Our sins have convicted and sentenced us, but Jesus holds the keys of death and Hades. He alone can free us from eternal bondage to Satan. He alone has the power and authority to set us free from sin's control. Believers don't have to fear Hades or death, because Christ holds the keys to both. All we must do is turn from sin and turn to him in faith. When we attempt to control our lives and disregard God, we set a course that leads directly to hell. But when we place our lives in Christ's hands, he restores us now and resurrects us later to an eternal, peaceful relationship with him.

1:20 Who are the "angels of the seven churches"? Some say that they are angels designated to guard the churches; others say that they are elders or pastors of the local churches. Because the seven letters in chapters 2 and 3 contain reprimands, it is doubtful that these angels are heavenly messengers. If these are earthly leaders or messengers, they are accountable to God for the churches they represent.

golden lampstands: the seven stars are the angels of the seven churches, and the seven lampstands are the seven churches.

Message to Ephesus

2:1 Rev 1:11; Rev 1:16; Rev 1:12f

2:2 Rev 2:19; 3:1, 8, 15; John 6:6; 1 John 4:1; 2 Cor 11:13

2 "To the angel of the church in Ephesus write:
The One who holds the seven stars in His right hand, the One who walks among the
seven golden lampstands, says this:
2 'I know your deeds and your toil and perseverance, and that you cannot tolerate evil
men, and you put to the test those who call themselves apostles, and they are not, and
you found them *to be* false;

INTERPRETING THE BOOK OF REVELATION
Over the centuries, four main approaches to interpreting the book of Revelation have developed. Each approach has had capable supporters, but none has proved itself the only way to read this book. However, the most basic application question for each approach can be summarized by asking yourself, "Will this help me become a better follower of Jesus Christ today?"

Approach	*Description*	*Challenge*	*Caution*
PRETERIST VIEW	John is writing to encourage Christians in his own day who are experiencing persecution from the Roman empire.	To gain the same kind of encouragement John's first readers gained from the vivid images of God's sovereignty.	Do not forget that most Biblical prophecy has both an immediate and a future application.
FUTURIST VIEW	Except for the first three chapters, John is describing events that will occur at the end of history.	To see in contemporary events many of the characteristics John describes and realize that the end could come at any time.	Do not assume that we have "figured out" the future, since Jesus said that no one will know the day of his return before it happens.
HISTORICIST VIEW	The book of Revelation is a presentation of history from John's day until the second coming of Christ and beyond.	To note the consistency of human evil throughout history and recognize that names may change but the rebellion against God has not.	Be careful before identifying current events or leaders as fulfilling aspects of the book of Revelation.
IDEALIST VIEW	The book of Revelation is a symbolic representation of the continual struggle of good and evil. It does not refer to any particular historical events. It is applicable at any point in history.	Read the book to gain insight into the past, to prepare for the future, and to live obediently and confidently in the present.	Do not avoid the book because it is difficult. Try to understand Revelation within its broader literary context.

2:1 Ephesus was the capital of Asia Minor, a center of land and sea trade, and, along with Alexandria and Antioch in Syria, one of the three most influential cities in the eastern part of the Roman empire. The temple to Artemis, one of the ancient wonders of the world, was located in this city, and a major industry was the manufacture of images of this goddess (see Acts 19:21–41). Paul ministered in Ephesus for three years and warned the Ephesians that false teachers would come and try to draw people away from the faith (see Acts 20:29–31). False teachers did indeed cause problems in the Ephesian church, but the church resisted them, as we can see from Paul's letter to them (see the book of Ephesians). John spent much of his ministry in this city and knew that they had resisted false teaching (2:2).

2:1 The one who "walks among the seven golden lampstands" (the seven churches) is Jesus (1:11–13). He holds the "seven stars in His right hand" (messengers of the churches), indicating his power and authority over the churches and their leaders. Ephesus had become a large, proud church, and Jesus' message would remind them that he alone is the head of the body of believers.

2:1ff Does God care about your church? If you are tempted to doubt it, look more closely at these seven letters. The Lord of the universe knew each of these churches and its precise situation. In each letter, Jesus told John to write about specific people, places, and events. He praised believers for their successes and told them how to correct their failures. Just as Jesus cared for each of these churches, he cares for yours. He wants it to reach its greatest potential. The group of believers with whom you worship and serve is God's vehicle for changing the world. Take it seriously—God does.

2:2 Over a long period of time, the church in Ephesus had steadfastly refused to tolerate sin among its members. This was not easy in a city noted for immoral sexual practices associated with the worship of the goddess Artemis. We also are living in times of widespread sin and sexual immorality. It is popular to be open-minded toward many types of sin, calling them personal choices or alternative life-styles. But when the body of believers begins to tolerate sin in the church, it is lowering the standards and compromising the church's witness. Remember that God's approval is infinitely more important than the world's.

2:2–3 Christ commended the church at Ephesus for (1) working hard, (2) persevering, (3) resisting sin, (4) critically examining the claims of false apostles, and (5) enduring hardships without becoming weary. Every church should have these characteristics. But these good efforts should spring from our love for Jesus Christ. Both Jesus and John stressed love for one another as an authentic proof of the gospel (John 13:34; 1 John 3:18–19). In the battle to maintain sound teaching and moral and doctrinal purity, it is possible to lose a charitable spirit. Prolonged conflict can weaken or destroy our patience and affection. In defending the faith, guard against any structure or rigidity that weakens love.

3 and you have perseverance and have endured for My name's sake, and have not grown weary.
4 'But I have *this* against you, that you have left your first love.
5 'Therefore remember from where you have fallen, and repent and do the deeds you
did at first; or else I am coming to you and will remove your lampstand out of its place—
unless you repent.
6 'Yet this you do have, that you hate the deeds of the Nicolaitans, which I also hate.
7 'He who has an ear, let him hear what the Spirit says to the churches. To him who
overcomes, I will grant to eat of the tree of life which is in the Paradise of God.'

2:3 John 15:21
2:4 Jer 2:2; Matt 24:12
2:5 Rev 2:16, 22; 3:3, 19; Heb 10:32
2:7 Matt 11:15; Gen 2:9; 3:22; Prov 3:18; 11:30; 13:12; 15:4; Rev 22:2, 14; Ezek 28:13; 31:8f

Message to Smyrna

8 "And to the angel of the church in Smyrna write:
The first and the last, who was dead, and has come to life, says this:
9 'I know your tribulation and your poverty (but you are rich), and the blasphemy by
those who say they are Jews and are not, but are a synagogue of Satan.
10 'Do not fear what you are about to suffer. Behold, the devil is about to cast some of
you into prison, so that you will be tested, and you will have tribulation for ten days. Be
faithful until death, and I will give you the crown of life.

2:8 Rev 1:11; Is 44:6
2:9 Rev 1:9; 2 Cor 6:10
2:10 Rev 3:10; 13:14ff; Dan 1:12, 14

2:4 Paul had once commended the church at Ephesus for its love for God and others (Ephesians 1:15), but many of the church founders had died, and many of the second-generation believers had lost their zeal for God. They were a busy church—the members did much to benefit themselves and the community—but they were acting out of the wrong motives. Work for God must be motivated by love for God or it will not last.

2:4–5 Just as when a man and woman fall in love, so also new believers rejoice at their newfound forgiveness. But when we lose sight of the seriousness of sin, we begin to lose the thrill of our forgiveness (see 2 Peter 1:9). In the first steps of your Christian life, you may have had enthusiasm without knowledge. Do you now have knowledge without enthusiasm? Both are necessary if we are to keep love for God intense and untarnished (see Hebrews 10:32, 35). Do you love God with the same fervor as when you were a new Christian?

2:5 For Jesus to "remove your lampstand out of its place" would mean your church would cease to be an effective church. Just as the seven-branched candlestick in the temple gave light for the priests to see, the churches were to give light to their surrounding communities. But Jesus warned them that their lights could go out. In fact, Jesus himself would extinguish any light that did not fulfill its purpose. The church had to repent of its sins.

2:6 The Nicolaitans were believers who compromised their faith in order to enjoy some of the sinful practices of Ephesian society. The name *Nicolaitans* is held by some to be roughly the Greek equivalent of the Hebrew word for "Balaamites." Balaam was a prophet who induced the Israelites to carry out their lustful desires (see 2:14 and Numbers 31:16). When we want to take part in an activity that we know is wrong, we may make excuses to justify our behavior, saying that it isn't as bad as it seems or that it won't hurt our faith. Christ has strong words for those who look for excuses to sin.

2:6 Through John, Jesus commended the church at Ephesus for hating the wicked deeds of the Nicolaitans. Note that they didn't hate the people, just their sinful actions. We should accept and love all people and refuse to tolerate all evil. God cannot tolerate sin, and he expects us to stand against it. The world needs Christians who will stand for God's truth and point people toward right living.

2:7 To overcome is to be victorious by believing in Christ, persevering, remaining faithful, and living as one who follows Christ. Such a life brings great rewards (21:7).

2:7 Two trees were in the Paradise of God (the Garden of Eden)—the tree of life and the tree of the knowledge of good and evil (see Genesis 2:9). Eating from the tree of life brought eternal life with God; eating from the tree of knowledge brought realization of good and evil. When Adam and Eve ate from the tree of knowledge, they disobeyed God's command. So they were excluded from Eden and barred from eating from the tree of life. Eventually, evil will be destroyed and believers will be brought into a restored Paradise. In the new earth, everyone will eat from the tree of life and will live forever.

2:8 The city of Smyrna was about 25 miles north of Ephesus. It was nicknamed "Port of Asia" because it had an excellent harbor on the Aegean Sea. The church in this city struggled against two hostile forces: a Jewish population strongly opposed to Christianity, and a non-Jewish population that was loyal to Rome and supported emperor worship. Persecution and suffering were inevitable in an environment like this.

2:9–10 Persecution comes from Satan, not from God. Satan, the devil, will cause believers to be thrown into prison and even killed. But believers need not fear death, because it will only result in their receiving the crown of life. Satan may harm their earthly bodies, but he can do them no spiritual harm. The "synagogue of Satan" means that these Jews were serving Satan's purposes, not God's, when they gathered to worship. "Ten days" means that although persecution would be intense, it would be relatively short. It would have a definite beginning and end, and God would remain in complete control.

2:9–11 Pain is part of life, but it is never easy to suffer, no matter what the cause. Jesus commended the church at Smyrna for its faith in suffering. He then encouraged the believers that they need not fear the future if they remained faithful. If you are experiencing difficult times, don't let them turn you away from God. Instead let them draw you toward greater faithfulness. Trust God and remember your heavenly reward (see also 22:12–14).

2:10 Smyrna was famous for its athletic games. A crown was the victory wreath, the trophy for the champion at the games. If we have been faithful, we will receive the prize of victory—eternal life (James 1:12). The message to the Smyrna church was to remain faithful during their suffering because God is in control and his promises are reliable. Jesus never says that by being faithful to him we will avoid troubles, suffering, and persecution. Rather, we must be faithful to him *in* our sufferings. Only then will our faith prove to be genuine. We remain faithful by keeping our eyes on Christ and on what he promises us now and in the future (see Philippians 3:13–14; 2 Timothy 4:8).

2:11 Matt 11:15; Rev 2:7, 17, 29; 3:6, 13, 22; 13:9; 21:7; Rev 20:6, 14; 21:8

2:13 Matt 4:10; Rev 2:24; 1 Tim 5:8; Rev 14:12; Acts 22:20; Rev 1:5; 11:3; 17:6

2:14 Num 31:16; 2 Pet 2:15; Num 25:1f; Acts 15:29; 1 Cor 10:20

11 'He who has an ear, let him hear what the Spirit says to the churches. He who overcomes will not be hurt by the second death.'

Message to Pergamum

12 "And to the angel of the church in Pergamum write:
The One who has the sharp two-edged sword says this:
13 'I know where you dwell, where Satan's throne is; and you hold fast My name, and
did not deny My faith even in the days of Antipas, My witness, My faithful one, who was
killed among you, where Satan dwells.
14 'But I have a few things against you, because you have there some who hold the teaching of Balaam, who kept teaching Balak to put a stumbling block before the sons of Israel, to eat things sacrificed to idols and to commit *acts of* immorality.

THE SEVEN CHURCHES

The seven churches were located on a major Roman road. A letter carrier would leave the island of Patmos (where John was exiled), arriving first at Ephesus. He would travel north to Smyrna and Pergamum, turn southeast to Thyatira, and continue on to Sardis, Philadelphia, and Laodicea—in the exact order in which the letters were dictated.

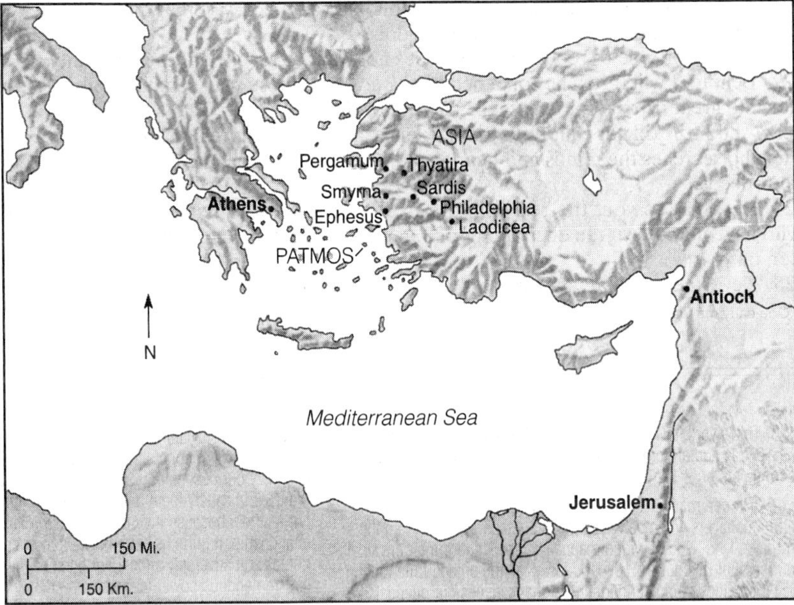

2:11 Believers and unbelievers alike experience physical death. All people will be resurrected, but believers will be resurrected to eternal life with God while unbelievers will be resurrected to be punished with a second death, eternal separation from God (see also 20:14; 21:8, 27; 22:15).

2:12 The city of Pergamum was built on a hill 1,000 feet above the surrounding countryside, creating a natural fortress. It was a sophisticated city, a center of Greek culture and education, with a 200,000-volume library. But it was also the center of four cults, and it rivaled Ephesus in its worship of idols. The city's chief god was Asclepius, whose symbol was a serpent, and who was considered the god of healing. People came to Pergamum from all over the world to seek healing from this god.

2:12 Just as the Romans used their swords for authority and judgment, Jesus' sharp, two-edged sword represents God's ultimate authority and judgment. It may also represent God's future separation of believers from unbelievers. Unbelievers cannot experience the eternal rewards of living in God's kingdom.

2:13 As the center for four idolatrous cults (Zeus, Dionysius, Asclepius, and Athene), Pergamum was called the city "where Satan's throne is." Surrounded by worship of Satan and the Roman emperor as god, the church at Pergamum refused to renounce their faith, even when Satan's worshipers martyred one of their members. Standing firm against the strong pressures and temptations of society is never easy, but the alternative is deadly (2:11).

2:13–15 It was not easy to be a Christian in Pergamum. Believers experienced great pressure to compromise or leave the faith. (For information on the Nicolaitans, see the first note on 2:6.) Nothing is known about Antipas except that he did *not* compromise. He was faithful, and he died for his faith. Apparently, however, some in the church were tolerating those who taught or practiced what Christ opposed. Compromise can be defined as a blending of the qualities of two different things or a concession of principles. Cooperate with people as much as you can, but avoid any alliance, partnership, or participation that could lead to immoral practices.

2:14 There is room for differences of opinion among Christians in some areas, but there is no room for heresy and moral impurity. Your town might not participate in idol feasts, but it probably has pornography, sexual sin, cheating, gossiping, and lying. Don't tolerate sin by bowing to the pressure to be open-minded.

2:14–16 Balak was a king who feared the large number of Israelites traveling through his country, so he hired Balaam to pronounce a curse on them. Balaam refused at first, but an offer of money changed his mind (Numbers 22—24). Later Balaam influenced the Israelites to turn to idol worship (Numbers 31:16; also see 2 Peter 2:15; Jude 11). Here Christ rebuked the church for tolerating those who, like Balaam, lead people away from God

15 'So you also have some who in the same way hold the teaching of the Nicolaitans.
16 'Therefore repent; or else I am coming to you quickly, and I will make war against
them with the sword of My mouth.
17 'He who has an ear, let him hear what the Spirit says to the churches. To him who
overcomes, to him I will give *some* of the hidden manna, and I will give him a white stone,
and a new name written on the stone which no one knows but he who receives it.'

Message to Thyatira

18 "And to the angel of the church in Thyatira write:
The Son of God, who has eyes like a flame of fire, and His feet are like burnished bronze,
says this:
19 'I know your deeds, and your love and faith and service and perseverance, and that
your deeds of late are greater than at first.
20 'But I have *this* against you, that you tolerate the woman Jezebel, who calls herself a
prophetess, and she teaches and leads My bond-servants astray so that they commit *acts
of* immorality and eat things sacrificed to idols.
21 'I gave her time to repent, and she does not want to repent of her immorality.
22 'Behold, I will throw her on a bed *of sickness*, and those who commit adultery with
her into great tribulation, unless they repent of [3]her deeds.
23 'And I will kill her children with pestilence, and all the churches will know that I am
He who searches the minds and hearts; and I will give to each one of you according to
your deeds.
24 'But I say to you, the rest who are in Thyatira, who do not hold this teaching,
who have not known the deep things of Satan, as they call them—I place no other burden on you.
25 'Nevertheless what you have, hold fast until I come.

3 One early ms reads *their*

2:16 Rev 22:7, 20; 2 Thess 2:8; Rev 1:16

2:17 Rev 2:7; Ex 16:33; John 6:49f; Is 56:5; 62:2; 65:15; Rev 14:3; 19:12

2:18 Rev 1:11; 2:24; Matt 4:3; Rev 1:14f

2:19 Rev 2:2

2:20 Rev 2:14; 1 Kin 16:31; 21:25; 2 Kin 9:7, 22, 30; Acts 15:29; 1 Cor 10:20

2:21 Rom 2:4; 2 Pet 3:9; Rom 2:5; Rev 9:20f; 16:9, 11

2:22 Rev 17:2; 18:9

2:23 Ps 7:9; 26:2; 139:1; Jer 11:20; 17:10; Matt 16:27; Luke 16:15; Acts 1:24; Rom 8:27; Ps 62:12

2:24 Rev 2:18; 1 Cor 2:10; Acts 15:28

2:16 This sword is God's judgment against rebellious nations (19:15, 21) and all forms of sin. See also the note on 1:16 and the second note on 2:12.

2:17 "Hidden manna" suggests the spiritual nourishment that the faithful believers will receive. As the Israelites traveled toward the promised land, God provided manna from heaven for their physical nourishment (Exodus 16:13–18). Jesus, as the bread of life (John 6:51), provides spiritual nourishment that satisfies our deepest hunger.

2:17 It is unclear what the white stones are or exactly what the names on each will be. Because they relate to the hidden manna, they may be symbols of the believer's eternal nourishment, or eternal life. The stones are significant because each will bear the new name of every person who truly believes in Christ. They are the evidence that a person has been accepted by God and declared worthy to receive eternal life. A person's name represented his or her character. God will give us new names and new hearts.

2:18 Thyatira was a working man's town, with many trade guilds for cloth making, dyeing, and pottery. Lydia, Paul's first convert in Philippi was a merchant from Thyatira (Acts 16:14). The city was basically secular, with no focus on any particular religion.

2:19 The believers in Thyatira were commended for growing in good deeds. We should not feel satisfied when our church only rejoices in the salvation of its members or in the comfort of gathering for worship. We should grow in love, faith, and acts of service. Because the times are critical, we must spend our days wisely and faithfully.

2:20 A woman in the church in Thyatira was teaching that immorality was not a serious matter for believers. Her name may have been Jezebel, or John may have used the name Jezebel to symbolize the kind of evil she was promoting. Jezebel, a pagan queen of Israel, was considered the most evil woman who ever lived (see 1 Kings 19:1–2; 21:1–15; 2 Kings 9:7–10, 30–37; and her Profile in 1 Kings 21).

2:20 Why is sexual immorality serious? Sex outside marriage always hurts someone. It hurts God because it shows that we prefer to satisfy our desires our own way instead of according to God's Word, or to satisfy them now instead of waiting for his timing. It hurts others because it violates the commitment so necessary to a relationship. It hurts us because it often brings disease to our bodies and adversely affects our personalities. Sexual immorality has tremendous power to destroy families, churches, and communities because it destroys the integrity on which these relationships are built. God wants to protect us from hurting ourselves and others; thus we are to have no part in sexual immorality, even if our culture accepts it.

2:20 In pagan temples, meat was often offered to idols. Then the meat that wasn't burned was sold to shoppers in the temple marketplace. Eating meat offered to idols wasn't wrong in itself, but it could violate the principle of sensitivity toward weaker Christian brothers and sisters who would be bothered by it (see 1 Corinthians 8 and the note on Romans 14:2). Jezebel was obviously more concerned about her own selfish pleasure and freedom than about the needs and concerns of fellow believers.

2:21 Jezebel was unwilling to repent. "Repent" means to change our mind and direction from following our way to following God's way, from sin and its disastrous consequences to God and eternal life. In his mercy, God has given us time in his mercy to decide to follow him. Only our stubborn willfulness stands in the way.

2:23 We cannot hide from Christ; he knows what is in our hearts and minds, and still he loves us. The sins we try to hide from God need to be confessed to him.

2:24–25 The "deep things of Satan" were either false teaching advocated by heretics, or secret insights by so-called believers "guaranteed" to promote deeper spiritual life. We should hold tightly to the basics of our Christian faith and view with caution and counsel any new teaching that turns us away from the Bible, the fellowship of our church, or our basic confession of faith.

26 'He who overcomes, and he who keeps My deeds until the end, TO HIM I WILL GIVE
AUTHORITY OVER THE NATIONS;
27 AND HE SHALL RULE THEM WITH A ROD OF IRON, AS THE VESSELS OF THE POTTER
ARE BROKEN TO PIECES, as I also have received *authority* from My Father;
28 and I will give him the morning star.
29 'He who has an ear, let him hear what the Spirit says to the churches.'

Message to Sardis

3 "To the angel of the church in Sardis write:
He who has the seven Spirits of God and the seven stars, says this: 'I know your deeds,
that you have a name that you are alive, but you are dead.
2 'Wake up, and strengthen the things that remain, which were about to die; for I have
not found your deeds completed in the sight of My God.
3 'So remember what you have received and heard; and keep *it,* and repent. Therefore if you do not wake up, I will come like a thief, and you will not know at what hour I
will come to you.
4 'But you have a few people in Sardis who have not soiled their garments; and they
will walk with Me in white, for they are worthy.
5 'He who overcomes will thus be clothed in white garments; and I will not erase his
name from the book of life, and I will confess his name before My Father and before His
angels.
6 'He who has an ear, let him hear what the Spirit says to the churches.'

2:26 Rev 2:7; Matt 10:22; Heb 3:6; Ps 2:8; Rev 3:21; 20:4

2:27 Ps 2:9; Rev 12:5; 19:15; Is 30:14; Jer 19:11

2:28 1 John 3:2; Rev 22:16

3:3 Rev 2:5; 1 Thess 5:2; 2 Pet 3:10; Rev 16:15; Matt 24:43; Luke 12:39f

3:4 Rev 11:13; Rev 1:11; Jude 23; Eccl 9:8

3:5 Rev 2:7; Rev 3:4; Ex 32:32f; Ps 69:28; Luke 10:20; Rev 13:8; 17:8; 20:12, 15; 21:27; Matt 10:32; Luke 12:8

3:6 Rev 2:7

THE NAMES OF JESUS IN THE BOOK OF REVELATION

Reference	*Jesus' Name*	*Reference*	*Jesus' Name*
1:8	The Alpha and the Omega	5:5	Root of David
1:8	Lord God	5:6	Lamb
1:8	The Almighty	7:17	Shepherd
1:13	Son of man	12:10	Christ
1:17	The First and the Last	19:11	Faithful and True
1:18	The Living One	19:13	The Word of God
2:18	Son of God	19:16	King of kings
3:14	The faithful and true Witness	19:16	Lord of lords
4:11	Creator	22:16	Bright Morning Star
5:5	Lion from the tribe of Judah		

Scattered among the vivid images of the book of Revelation is a large collection of names for Jesus. Each one tells something of his character and highlights a particular aspect of his role within God's plan of redemption.

2:26–27 Christ says that those who overcome (those who remain faithful until the end and continue to please God) will rule over Christ's enemies and reign with him as he judges evil (see also Psalm 2:8–9; Isaiah 30:14; Jeremiah 19:11; 1 Corinthians 6:2–3; Revelation 12:5; 19:15; 20:3–4 for more about God's judgment).

2:28 Christ is called the morning star in 2:28; 22:16; and 2 Peter 1:19. A morning star appears just before dawn, when the night is coldest and darkest. When the world is at its bleakest point, Christ will burst onto the scene, exposing evil with his light of truth and bringing his promised reward.

3:1 The wealthy city of Sardis was actually in two locations. The older section of the city was on a mountain, and, when its population outgrew the spot, a newer section was built in the valley below.

3:1 The "seven Spirits of God" is another name for the Holy Spirit. The seven stars are the messengers, or leaders, of the churches (see 2:1).

3:1 The problem in the Sardis church was not heresy, but spiritual death. In spite of its reputation for being active, Sardis was infested with sin. Its deeds were evil and its clothes soiled. The Spirit has no words of commendation for this church that looked so good on the outside but was so corrupt on the inside.

3:3 The church at Sardis was urged to obey the Christian truth they had heard when they first believed in Christ, to get back to the basics of the faith. It is important to grow in our knowledge of the Lord, to deepen our understanding through careful study. But no matter how much we learn, we must never abandon the basic truths about Jesus. Jesus will always be God's Son, and his sacrifice for our sins is permanent. No new truth from God will ever contradict these Biblical teachings.

3:5 To be "clothed in white garments" means to be set apart for God and made pure. Christ promises future honor and eternal life to those who stand firm in their faith. The names of all believers are registered in the book of life. This book symbolizes God's knowledge of who belongs to him. All such people are guaranteed a listing in the book of life and are introduced to the hosts of heaven as belonging to Christ (see Luke 12:8–9).

Message to Philadelphia

7 "And to the angel of the church in Philadelphia write:
He who is holy, who is true, who has the key of David, who opens and no one will shut,
and who shuts and no one opens, says this:
8 'I know your [4]deeds. Behold, I have put before you an open door which no one can
shut, because you have a little power, and have kept My word, and have not denied My
name.
9 'Behold, I will cause *those* of the synagogue of Satan, who say that they are Jews and
are not, but lie—I will make them come and bow down at your feet, and *make them* know
that I have loved you.
10 'Because you have kept the word of My perseverance, I also will keep you from the
hour of testing, that *hour* which is about to come upon the whole world, to test those
who dwell on the earth.
11 'I am coming quickly; hold fast what you have, so that no one will take your crown.
12 'He who overcomes, I will make him a pillar in the temple of My God, and he will
not go out from it anymore; and I will write on him the name of My God, and the name
of the city of My God, the new Jerusalem, which comes down out of heaven from My
God, and My new name.
13 'He who has an ear, let him hear what the Spirit says to the churches.'

Message to Laodicea

14 "To the angel of the church in Laodicea write:
The Amen, the faithful and true Witness, the [5]Beginning of the creation of God, says
this:
15 'I know your deeds, that you are neither cold nor hot; I wish that you were cold or hot.
16 'So because you are lukewarm, and neither hot nor cold, I will spit you out of My
mouth.
17 'Because you say, "I am rich, and have become wealthy, and have need of nothing,"
and you do not know that you are wretched and miserable and poor and blind and
naked,
18 I advise you to buy from Me gold refined by fire so that you may become rich, and

3:8 Rev 3:1; Acts 14:27; Rev 2:13

3:10 John 17:6; Rev 3:8; Rev 1:9; 2 Tim 2:12; 2 Pet 2:9; Rev 2:10; Matt 24:14; Rev 16:14; Rev 6:10; 8:13; 11:10; 13:8, 14; 17:8

3:11 Rev 1:3; 22:7, 12, 20; Rev 2:25; Rev 2:10

3:12 Rev 3:5; 1 Kin 7:21; Jer 1:18; Gal 2:9; Rev 14:1; 22:4; Ezek 48:35; Gal 4:26; Heb 13:14; Rev 21:2, 10; Is 62:2; Rev 2:17

3:13 Rev 3:6

3:14 Rev 1:11; 2 Cor 1:20; Rev 1:5; 3:7; Gen 49:3; Deut 21:17; Prov 8:22; John 1:3; Col 1:18; Rev 21:6; 22:13

3:15 Rev 3:1; Rom 12:11

3:17 Hos 12:8; Zech 11:5; Matt 5:3; 1 Cor 4:8

3:18 Is 55:1; Matt 13:44

4 Or *deeds (behold...shut), that you have* **5** I.e. Origin or Source

3:7 Philadelphia was founded by the citizens of Pergamum. The community was built in a frontier area as a gateway to the central plateau of Asia Minor. Philadelphia's residents kept barbarians out of the region and brought in Greek culture and language. The city was destroyed by an earthquake in A.D. 17, and aftershocks kept the people so worried that most of them lived outside the city limits.

3:7 The key of David represents Christ's authority to open the door of invitation into his future kingdom. After the door is opened, no one can close it—salvation is assured. Once it is closed, no one can open it—judgment is certain.

3:10 Some believe that "I also will keep you from the hour of testing" means there will be a future time of great tribulation from which true believers will be spared. Others interpret this to mean that the church will go through the time of tribulation and that God will keep them strong in the midst of it. Still others believe this refers to times of great distress in general, the church's suffering through the ages. Whatever the case, our emphasis should be on patiently obeying God no matter what we may face.

3:11 Christians have differing gifts, abilities, experience, and maturity. God doesn't expect us all to be and act the same, but he does expect us to "hold fast" to what we have, to persevere in using our resources for him. The Philadelphians are commended for their effort to obey (3:8) and encouraged to hold tightly to whatever strength they have. You may be a new believer and feel that your faith and spiritual strength are little. Use what you have to live for Christ, and God will commend you.

3:12 The new Jerusalem is the future dwelling of the people of God (21:2). We will have a new citizenship in God's future kingdom. Everything will be new, pure, and secure.

3:14 Laodicea was the wealthiest of the seven cities, known for its banking industry, manufacture of wool, and a medical school that produced eye salve. But the city had always had a problem with its water supply. At one time an aqueduct was built to bring water to the city from hot springs. But by the time the water reached the city, it was neither hot nor refreshingly cool—only lukewarm. The church had become as bland as the tepid water that came into the city.

3:15 Lukewarm water makes a disgusting drink. The church in Laodicea had become lukewarm and thus distasteful and repugnant. The believers didn't take a stand for anything; indifference had led to idleness. By neglecting to do anything for Christ, the church had become hardened and self-satisfied, and it was destroying itself. There is nothing more disgusting than a halfhearted, in-name-only Christian who is self-sufficient. Don't settle for following God halfway. Let Christ fire up your faith and get you into the action.

3:17 Some believers falsely assume that numerous material possessions are a sign of God's spiritual blessing. Laodicea was a wealthy city, and the church was also wealthy. But what the Laodiceans could see and buy had become more valuable to them than what is unseen and eternal. Wealth, luxury, and ease can make people feel confident, satisfied, and complacent. But no matter how much you possess or how much money you make, you have nothing if you don't have a vital relationship with Christ. How does your current level of wealth affect your spiritual desire? Instead of centering your life primarily on comfort and luxury, find your true riches in Christ.

3:18 Laodicea was known for its great wealth—but Christ told the Laodiceans to buy their gold from him (real spiritual treasures). The city was proud of its cloth and dyeing industries—but Christ told

white garments so that you may clothe yourself, and *that* the shame of your nakedness
will not be revealed; and eye salve to anoint your eyes so that you may see.
19 'Those whom I love, I reprove and discipline; therefore be zealous and repent.
20 'Behold, I stand at the door and knock; if anyone hears My voice and opens the door,
I will come in to him and will dine with him, and he with Me.
21 'He who overcomes, I will grant to him to sit down with Me on My throne, as I also
overcame and sat down with My Father on His throne.
22 'He who has an ear, let him hear what the Spirit says to the churches.' "

3:19 Prov 3:12; 1 Cor 11:32; Heb 12:6; Rev 2:5
3:20 Matt 24:33; James 5:9; Luke 12:36; John 10:3; John 14:23
3:21 Rev 2:7; Matt 19:28; 2 Tim 2:12; Rev 2:26; 20:4; John 16:33; Rev 5:5; 6:2; 17:14
3:22 Rev 2:7

B. MESSAGE FOR THE CHURCH (4:1—22:21)

Moving from the conditions within the churches in Asia to the future of the universal church, John sees the course of coming events in a way similar to Daniel and Ezekiel. Many of these passages contain clear spiritual teachings, but others seem beyond our ability to understand. The clear teaching of this book is that God will defeat all evil in the end. We must live in obedience to Jesus Christ, the coming Conqueror and Judge.

1. Worshiping God in heaven

Scene in Heaven

4 After these things I looked, and behold, a door *standing* open in heaven, and the
first voice which I had heard, like *the sound* of a trumpet speaking with me, said,
"Come up here, and I will show you what must take place after these things."

4:1 Rev 1:12ff, 19; Ezek 1:1; Rev 19:11; Rev 1:10; Rev 11:12

THE LETTERS TO THE SEVEN CHURCHES

Church	*Reference*	*Commendation*	*Rebuke*	*Action*
Ephesus	2:1–7	Hard work, perseverance	Forsaken first love	Remember and repent
Smyrna	2:8–11	Suffered persecution, poverty	None	Don't fear, be faithful
Pergamum	2:12–17	True to faith	Compromise	Repent
Thyatira	2:18–29	Love, faith, service	Immorality	Repent
Sardis	3:1–6	Effective	Superficial	Wake up, repent
Philadelphia	3:7–13	Faithful	None	Hold on
Laodicea	3:14–22	None	Lukewarm	Be earnest and repent

This summary of the letters to the seven churches shows us the qualities our churches should seek and those we should avoid.

them to purchase white garments from him (his righteousness). Laodicea prided itself on its precious eye salve that healed many eye problems—but Christ told them to get medicine from him to heal their eyes so they could see the truth (John 9:39). Christ was showing the Laodiceans that true value was not in material possessions, but in a right relationship with God. Their possessions and achievements were valueless compared with the everlasting future of Christ's kingdom.

3:19 God would discipline this lukewarm church unless it turned from its indifference toward him. God's purpose in discipline is not to punish, but to bring people back to him. Are you lukewarm in your devotion to God? God may discipline you to help you out of your uncaring attitude, but he uses only loving discipline. You can avoid God's discipline by drawing near to him again through confession, service, worship, and studying his Word. Just as the spark of love can be rekindled in marriage, so the Holy Spirit can reignite our zeal for God when we allow him to work in our hearts.

3:20 The Laodicean church was complacent and rich. They felt self-satisfied, but they didn't have Christ's presence among them. Christ knocked at the door of their hearts, but they were so busy enjoying worldly pleasures that they didn't notice that he was trying to enter. The pleasures of this world—money, security, material possessions—can be dangerous, because their temporary satisfaction makes us indifferent to God's offer of lasting satisfaction. If you find yourself feeling indifferent to church, to God, or to the Bible, you have begun to shut God out of your life. Leave the door of your heart constantly open to God, and you won't need to worry about hearing his knock. Letting him in is your only hope for lasting fulfillment.

3:20 Jesus is knocking on the door of our hearts every time we sense we should turn to him. Jesus wants to have fellowship with us, and he wants us to open up to him. He is patient and persistent in trying to get through to us—not breaking and entering, but knocking. He allows us to decide whether or not to open our lives to him. Do you intentionally keep his life-changing presence and power on the other side of the door?

3:22 At the end of each letter to these churches, the believers were urged to listen and take to heart what was written to them. Although a different message was addressed to each church, all the messages contain warnings and principles for everyone. Which letter speaks most directly to your church? Which has the greatest bearing on your own spiritual condition at this time? How will you respond?

4:1 Chapters 4 and 5 record glimpses into Christ's glory. Here we see into the throne room of heaven. God is on the throne and orchestrating all the events that John will record. The world is not spinning out of control; the God of creation will carry out his plans as Christ initiates the final battle with the forces of evil. John shows us heaven before showing us earth so that we will not be frightened by future events.

4:1 The voice John had first heard that sounded like a trumpet blast was the voice of Christ (see 1:10–11).

2 Immediately I was [6]in the Spirit; and behold, a throne was standing in heaven, and
One sitting on the throne.
3 And He who was sitting *was* like a jasper stone and a sardius in appearance; and
there was a rainbow around the throne, like an emerald in appearance.
4 Around the throne *were* twenty-four thrones; and upon the thrones *I saw* twenty-
four elders sitting, clothed in white garments, and golden crowns on their heads.

The Throne and Worship of the Creator

5 Out from the throne come flashes of lightning and sounds and peals of thunder.
And *there were* seven lamps of fire burning before the throne, which are the seven Spirits
of God;
6 and before the throne *there was something* like a sea of glass, like crystal; and in the
center and around the throne, four living creatures full of eyes in front and behind.
7 The first creature *was* like a lion, and the second creature like a calf, and the third
creature had a face like that of a man, and the fourth creature *was* like a flying eagle.
8 And the four living creatures, each one of them having six wings, are full of eyes
around and within; and day and night they do not cease to say,
"HOLY, HOLY, HOLY *is* THE LORD GOD, THE ALMIGHTY, WHO WAS AND WHO IS AND
WHO IS TO COME."
9 And when the living creatures give glory and honor and thanks to Him who sits on
the throne, to Him who lives forever and ever,
10 the twenty-four elders will fall down before Him who sits on the throne, and will
worship Him who lives forever and ever, and will cast their crowns before the throne,
saying,
11 "Worthy are You, our Lord and our God, to receive glory and honor and power; for
You created all things, and because of Your will they existed, and were created."

The Book with Seven Seals

5 I saw in the right hand of Him who sat on the throne a book written inside and on
the back, sealed up with seven seals.
2 And I saw a strong angel proclaiming with a loud voice, "Who is worthy to open the
book and to break its seals?"
3 And no one in heaven or on the earth or under the earth was able to open the book
or to look into it.
4 Then I *began* to weep greatly because no one was found worthy to open the book or
to look into it;

6 Or *in spirit*

4:2 Rev 1:10; 1 Kin 22:19; Is 6:1; Ezek 1:26; Dan 7:9

4:3 Rev 21:11; Rev 21:20; Ezek 1:28

4:4 Rev 11:16; Rev 4:10; 5:6, 8, 14; 19:4; Matt 19:28; Rev 20:4

4:5 Rev 8:5; 11:19; 16:18

4:6 Ezek 1:22; Rev 15:2; 21:18, 21; Rev 4:4; Ezek 1:5; Rev 4:8f; 5:6; 6:1, 6; 7:11; 14:3; 15:7; 19:4; Ezek 1:18; 10:12

4:7 Ezek 1:10; 10:14

4:8 Ezek 1:5; Rev 5:6; 6:1, 6; 7:11; 14:3; 15:7; 19:4; Is 6:2; Ezek 1:18; 10:12; Rev 14:11; Is 6:3

4:10 Dan 4:34; 12:7; Rev 4:4; 10:6; 15:7

4:11 Rev 1:6; 5:12; Acts 14:15; Rev 10:6; 14:7

5:1 Rev 4:9; 5:7, 13; Ezek 2:9, 10; Is 29:11; Dan 12:4

5:2 Rev 10:1; 18:21

5:3 Phil 2:10; Rev 5:13

4:2 Four times in the book of Revelation John says he was "in the Spirit" (1:10; 4:2; 17:3; 21:10). This expression means that the Holy Spirit was giving him a vision—showing him situations and events he could not have seen with mere human eyesight. All true prophecy comes from God through the Holy Spirit (2 Peter 1:20–21).

4:4 Who are these 24 elders? Because there were 12 tribes of Israel in the Old Testament and 12 apostles in the New Testament, the 24 elders in this vision probably represent all the redeemed of God for all time (both before and after Christ's death and resurrection). They symbolize all those—both Jews and Gentiles—who are now part of God's family. The 24 elders show us that *all* the redeemed of the Lord are worshiping him.

4:5 In Revelation, lightning and thunder are connected with significant events in heaven. They remind us of the lightning and thunder at Mount Sinai when God gave the people his laws (Exodus 19:16). The Old Testament often uses such imagery to reflect God's power and majesty (Psalm 77:18).

4:5 The "seven Spirits of God" is another name for the Holy Spirit. See also Zechariah 4:2–6, where the seven lamps are equated with the one Spirit.

4:6 Glass was very rare in New Testament times, and crystal-clear glass was virtually impossible to find (see 1 Corinthians 13:12). The "sea of glass" highlights both the magnificence and holiness of God.

4:6–7 Just as the Holy Spirit is seen symbolically in the seven lighted lamps, so the "four living creatures" represent the attributes (the qualities and character) of God. These creatures were not real animals. Like the cherubim (the highest order of the angels), they guard God's throne, lead others in worship, and proclaim God's holiness. God's attributes symbolized in the animal-like appearance of these four creatures are majesty and power (the lion), faithfulness (the calf), intelligence (the man), and sovereignty (the eagle). The Old Testament prophet Ezekiel saw four similar creatures in one of his visions (Ezekiel 1:5–10).

4:11 The point of this chapter is summed up in this verse: All creatures in heaven and earth will praise and honor God because he is the Creator and Sustainer of everything.

5:1 In John's day, books were written on scrolls—pieces of papyrus or vellum up to 30 feet long, rolled up and sealed with clay or wax. The book that John sees contains the full account of what God has in store for the world. The seven seals indicate the importance of its contents. The seals are located throughout the scroll so that as each one is broken, more of the scroll can be read to reveal another phase of God's plan for the end of the world. Only Christ is worthy to break the seals and open the book (5:3–5).

5:1ff Chapter 5 continues the glimpse into heaven begun in chapter 4.

5:5
Gen 49:9; Heb 7:14; Is 11:1, 10; Rom 15:12; Rev 22:16

5:6
Rev 4:4; 5:8, 14; John 1:29; Rev 5:8, 12f; 13:8; Rev 5:9, 12; 13:8; Dan 8:3f; Zech 3:9; 4:10; Rev 1:4

5 and one of the elders *said to me, "Stop weeping; behold, the Lion that is from the
tribe of Judah, the Root of David, has overcome so as to open the book and its seven
seals."
6 And I saw [7]between the throne (with the four living creatures) and the elders a Lamb
standing, as if slain, having seven horns and seven eyes, which are the seven Spirits of
God, sent out into all the earth.
7 And He came and took the book out of the right hand of Him who sat on the throne.

7 Lit *in the middle of the throne and of the four living creatures, and in the middle of the elders*

EVENTS IN REVELATION DESCRIBED ELSEWHERE IN THE BIBLE

Other Reference	*Revelation Reference*	*Event*
Ezekiel 1:22–28	4:2–3; 10:1–3	Glowing rainbow around God's throne
Isaiah 53:7	5:6–8	Christ is pictured as a lamb
Psalm 96	5:9–14	New song
Zechariah 1:7–11; 6:1–8	6:1–8	Horses and riders
Isaiah 2:19–22	6:12; 8:5; 11:13	Earthquake
Joel 2:28–32; Acts 2:14–21	6:12	Moon turns blood red
Mark 13:21–25	6:13	Stars falling from the sky
Isaiah 34:1–4	6:14	Sky rolled up like a scroll
Zephaniah 1:14–18; 1 Thessalonians 5:1–3	6:15–17	God's inescapable wrath
Jeremiah 49:35–39	7:1	Four winds of judgment
Luke 8:26–34	9:1–2; 17:3–8	Abyss (bottomless pit)
Joel 1:2—2:11	9:3–11	Plague of locusts
Luke 21:20–24	11:1–2	Trampling of the holy city of Jerusalem
Zechariah 4	11:3–6	Two olive trees as witnesses
Daniel 7	13:1–10	A beast coming out of the sea
2 Thessalonians 2:7–14	13:11–15	Wondrous signs and miracles done by the evil beast
Jeremiah 25:15–29	14:9–12	Drinking the cup of God's wrath
Isaiah 21:1–10	18:2–3	"Babylon" falls
Matthew 22:1–14	19:5–8	Marriage supper of the Lamb
Ezekiel 38; 39	20:7–10	Conflict with Gog and Magog
John 5:19–30	20:11–15	Judging of all people
Ezekiel 37:21–28	21:3	God lives among mankind
Isaiah 25:1–8	21:4	Our tears will be wiped away forever
Genesis 2:8–14	22:1–2	Tree of life
1 Corinthians 13:11–12	22:3–5	We will see God face to face
Daniel 7:18–28	22:5	Believers will reign with God forever

5:5 The Lion, Jesus, proved himself worthy to break the seals and open the book by living a perfect life of obedience to God, dying on the cross for the sins of the world, and rising from the dead to show his power and authority over evil and death. Only Christ conquered sin, death, hell, and Satan himself; so only he can be trusted with the world's future. The Root of David refers to Jesus being from David's family line, thus fulfilling the promise of the Messiah in the Old Testament.

5:5–6 Jesus Christ is pictured as both a lion (symbolizing his authority and power) and a lamb (symbolizing his submission to God's will). One of the elders calls John to look at the lion, but when John looks he sees a lamb. Christ the Lamb was the perfect sacrifice for the sins of all mankind; therefore, only he can save us from the terrible events revealed by the book. Christ the Lamb won the greatest battle of all. He defeated all the forces of evil by dying on the cross. The role of Christ the Lion will be to lead the battle where Satan is finally defeated (19:19–21). Christ the Lion is victorious because of what Christ the Lamb has already done. We will participate in his victory not because of our effort or goodness, but because he has promised eternal life to all who believe in him.

5:6 John sees the lamb "as if slain;" the wounds inflicted on Jesus' body during his trial and crucifixion could still be seen (see John 20:24–31). Jesus was called the Lamb of God by John the Baptist (John 1:29). In the Old Testament, lambs were sacrificed to atone for sins: the Lamb of God died as the final sacrifice for all sins (see Isaiah 53:7; Hebrews 10:1–12, 18).

5:6 The horns symbolize strength and power (see 1 Kings 22:11; Zechariah 1:18). Although Christ is a sacrificial lamb, he is in no way weak. He was killed, but now he lives in God's strength and power. In Zechariah 4:2–10, the eyes are equated with the seven lamps and the one Spirit.

8 When He had taken the book, the four living creatures and the twenty-four elders
fell down before the Lamb, each one holding a harp and golden bowls full of incense,
which are the prayers of the saints.
9 And they ☆sang a new song, saying,
"Worthy are You to take the book and to break its seals; for You were slain, and purchased for God with Your blood *men* from every tribe and tongue and people and
nation.
10 "You have made them *to be* a kingdom and priests to our God; and they will reign
upon the earth."

Angels Exalt the Lamb

11 Then I looked, and I heard the voice of many angels around the throne and the living creatures and the elders; and the number of them was myriads of myriads, and thousands of thousands,
12 saying with a loud voice,
"Worthy is the Lamb that was slain to receive power and riches and wisdom and might
and honor and glory and blessing."
13 And every created thing which is in heaven and on the earth and under the earth
and on the sea, and all things in them, I heard saying,
"To Him who sits on the throne, and to the Lamb, *be* blessing and honor and glory
and dominion forever and ever."
14 And the four living creatures kept saying, "Amen." And the elders fell down and
worshiped.

2. Opening the seven seals

The Book Opened; The First Seal—The False Christ

6 Then I saw when the Lamb broke one of the seven seals, and I heard one of the four
living creatures saying as with a voice of thunder, "Come."
2 I looked, and behold, a white horse, and he who sat on it had a bow; and a crown
was given to him, and he went out conquering and to conquer.

The Second Seal—War

3 When He broke the second seal, I heard the second living creature saying, "Come."
4 And another, a red horse, went out; and to him who sat on it, it was granted to take
peace from the earth, and that *men* would slay one another; and a great sword was given
to him.

5:8 Rev 4:6; 5:6, 11, 14; John 1:29; Rev 5:6, 12f; 13:8; Rev 14:2; 15:2; Rev 15:7; Ps 141:2; Rev 8:3f

5:9 Ps 33:3; 40:3; 98:1; 149:1; Is 42:10; Rev 14:3; 15:3; Rev 4:11; Rev 5:6, 12; 13:8; 1 Cor 6:20; Rev 14:3f; Dan 3:4; 5:19

5:10 Rev 1:6; Rev 3:21; 20:4

5:11 Dan 7:10; Heb 12:22; Jude 14; Rev 9:16

5:12 Rev 1:6; 4:11; 5:9; John 1:29; Rev 5:6, 13; 13:8

5:13 Phil 2:10; John 1:29; Rom 11:36; Rev 1:6

5:14 Rev 4:6; 5:6, 8, 11; 1 Cor 14:16; Rev 7:12; 19:4; Rev 4:4; 5:6, 8; Rev 4:10

6:1 John 1:29; Rev 5:6, 12f; 13:8; Rev 5:1; Rev 4:6; Rev 14:2; 19:6

6:2 Zech 1:8; 6:3f; Rev 19:11; Zech 6:11; Rev 9:7; 14:14; 19:12; Rev 3:21

6:3 Rev 4:7

6:4 Zech 1:8; 6:2; Matt 10:34

5:9–10 People from every nation are praising God before his throne. God's message of salvation and eternal life is not limited to a specific culture, race, or country. Anyone who comes to God in repentance and faith is accepted by him and will be part of his kingdom. Don't allow prejudice or bias to keep you from sharing Christ with others. Christ welcomes all people into his kingdom.

5:9–10 The song of God's people praises Christ's work. He (1) was slain, (2) purchased them with his blood, (3) gathered them into a kingdom, (4) made them priests, and (5) appointed them to reign on the earth. Jesus has already died and paid the penalty for sin. He is now gathering us into his kingdom and making us priests. In the future we will reign with him. Worship God and praise him for what he has done, what he is doing, and what he will do for all who trust in him. When we realize the glorious future that awaits us, we will find the strength to face our present difficulties.

5:10 The believers' song praises Christ for bringing them into the kingdom and making them kings and priests. While now we are sometimes despised and mocked for our faith (John 15:17–27), in the future we will reign over all the earth (Luke 22:29–30). Christ's death made all believers priests of God—the channels of blessing between God and mankind (1 Peter 2:5–9).

5:11 Angels are spiritual beings created by God who help carry out his work on earth. They bring messages (Luke 1:26–28), protect God's people (Daniel 6:22), offer encouragement (Genesis 16:7ff), give guidance (Exodus 14:19), bring punishment (2 Samuel 24:16), patrol the earth (Ezekiel 1:9–14), and fight the forces of evil (2 Kings 6:16–18; Revelation 20:1). There are both good and evil angels (12:7), but because evil angels are allied with Satan, they have considerably less power and authority than good angels. Eventually, the main role of the good angels will be to offer continuous praise to God (see also 19:1–3).

5:14 The scene in chapter 5 shows us that only the Lamb, Jesus Christ, is worthy to open the book (the events of history). Jesus, not Satan, holds the future. Jesus Christ is in control, and he alone is worthy to set into motion the events of the last days of history.

6:1ff This is the first of three seven-part judgments. The trumpets (chapters 8; 9) and the bowls (chapter 16) are the other two. As each seal is opened, Christ the Lamb sets in motion events that will bring about the end of human history. This book is not completely opened until the seventh seal is broken (8:1). The contents of the book reveal mankind's depravity and portray God's authority over the events of human history.

6:2ff Four horses appear as the first four seals are opened. The horses represent God's judgment of people's sin and rebellion. God is directing human history—even using his enemies to accomplish his purposes. The four horses are a foretaste of the final judgments yet to come. Some view this chapter as a parallel to the Olivet Discourse (see Matthew 24). The imagery of four horses is also found in Zechariah 6:1–8.

6:2–8 Each of the four horses is a different color. Some assume

6:5
Rev 4:7; Zech 6:2, 6; Ezek 4:16

6:8
Zech 6:3; Prov 5:5; Hos 13:14; Matt 11:23; Rev 1:18; 20:13f; Jer 14:12; 15:2f; 24:10; 29:17f; Ezek 5:12, 17; 14:21; 29:5

6:9
Ex 29:12; Lev 4:7; John 16:2; Rev 14:18; 16:7; Rev 20:4; Rev 1:2, 9; Rev 12:17

6:10
Zech 1:12; Luke 2:29; 2 Pet 2:1; Rev 3:7; Deut 32:43; Ps 79:10; Luke 18:7; Rev 19:2; Rev 3:10

6:11
Rev 3:4, 5; 7:9; 2 Thess 1:7; Heb 4:10; Rev 14:13; Heb 11:40; Acts 20:24; 2 Tim 4:7

6:12
Matt 24:7; Rev 8:5; 11:13; 16:18; Is 13:10; Joel 2:10, 31; 3:15; Matt 24:29; Mark 13:24; Is 50:3; Matt 11:21

6:13
Matt 24:29; Mark 13:25; Rev 8:10; 9:1; Is 34:4

6:14
Is 34:4; 2 Pet 3:10; Rev 20:11; 21:1; Is 54:10; Jer 4:24; Ezek 38:20; Nah 1:5; Rev 16:20

The Third Seal—Famine

5 When He broke the third seal, I heard the third living creature saying, "Come." I
looked, and behold, a black horse; and he who sat on it had a pair of scales in his hand.
6 And I heard *something* like a voice in the center of the four living creatures saying,
"A [8]quart of wheat for a [9]denarius, and three quarts of barley for a denarius; and do not
damage the oil and the wine."

The Fourth Seal—Death

7 When the Lamb broke the fourth seal, I heard the voice of the fourth living creature saying, "Come."
8 I looked, and behold, an ashen horse; and he who sat on it had the name Death;
and Hades was following with him. Authority was given to them over a fourth of the earth,
to kill with sword and with famine and with pestilence and by the wild beasts of the earth.

The Fifth Seal—Martyrs

9 When the Lamb broke the fifth seal, I saw underneath the altar the souls of those
who had been slain because of the word of God, and because of the testimony which
they had maintained;
10 and they cried out with a loud voice, saying, "How long, O Lord, holy and true, will
You refrain from judging and avenging our blood on those who dwell on the earth?"
11 And there was given to each of them a white robe; and they were told that they should
rest for a little while longer, until *the number of* their fellow servants and their brethren
who were to be killed even as they had been, would be completed also.

The Sixth Seal—Terror

12 I looked when He broke the sixth seal, and there was a great earthquake; and the
sun became black as sackcloth *made* of hair, and the whole moon became like blood;
13 and the stars of the sky fell to the earth, as a fig tree casts its unripe figs when shak-
en by a great wind.
14 The sky was split apart like a scroll when it is rolled up, and every mountain and
island were moved out of their places.
15 Then the kings of the earth and the great men and the [10]commanders and the rich
and the strong and every slave and free man hid themselves in the caves and among the
rocks of the mountains;

8 Gr *choenix;* i.e. a dry measure almost equal to a qt **9** The denarius was equivalent to a day's wages
10 I.e. chiliarchs, in command of one thousand troops

---

that the white horse represents victory and that its rider must be Christ (because Christ later rides to victory on a white horse—19:11). But because the other three horses relate to judgment and destruction, this rider on a white horse would most likely not be Christ. The four are part of the unfolding judgment of God, and it would be premature for Christ to ride forth as conqueror. The other horses represent different kinds of judgment: red for warfare and bloodshed; black for famine; ashen for death. The high prices of wheat and barley illustrate famine conditions. But the worst is yet to come.

6:8 It is not clear whether Hades was on a separate horse than Death or merely rode along with Death, but the riders described in verses 2–8 are commonly referred to as the four horsemen of the Apocalypse.

6:8 The four riders are given power over one-fourth of the earth, indicating that God is still limiting his judgment—it is not yet complete. With these judgments there is still time for unbelievers to turn to Christ and away from their sin. In this case, the limited punishment not only demonstrates God's wrath on sin, but also his merciful love in giving people yet another opportunity to turn to him before he brings final judgment.

6:9 The altar represents the altar of sacrifice in the temple, where animals were sacrificed to atone for sins. Instead of the animals' blood at the base of the altar, John saw the souls of martyrs who had died for preaching the gospel. These martyrs were told that still more would lose their lives for their belief in Christ (6:11). In the face of warfare, famine, persecution, and death, Christians will be called on to stand firmly for what they believe. Only those who endure to the end will be rewarded by God (Mark 13:13).

6:9–11 The martyrs are eager for God to bring justice to the earth, but they are told to wait. God is not waiting until a certain number is reached, but he is promising that those who suffer and die for their faith will not be forgotten. Rather, they will be singled out by God for special honor. We may wish for justice immediately, as these martyrs did, but we must be patient. God works according to his own timetable, and he promises justice. No suffering for the sake of God's kingdom, however, is wasted.

6:12 The sixth seal changes the scene back to the physical world. The first five judgments were directed toward specific areas, but this judgment is universal. Everyone will be afraid when the earth itself trembles.

6:15–17 At the sight of God sitting on the throne, all human beings, great and small, will be terrified, calling for the mountains to fall on them so that they will not have to face the judgment of the Lamb. This vivid picture was not intended to frighten believers. For them, the Lamb is a gentle Savior. But those kings, great men, and commanders who previously showed no fear of God and arrogantly flaunted their unbelief will find that they were wrong, and in that day they will have to face God's wrath. No one who has rejected God can survive the day of his wrath, but those who belong to Christ will receive a reward rather than punishment. Do you belong to Christ? If so, you need not fear these final days.

16 and they ☆said to the mountains and to the rocks, "Fall on us and hide us from the
presence of Him who sits on the throne, and from the wrath of the Lamb;
17 for the great day of their wrath has come, and who is able to stand?"

6:16 Hos 10:8; Luke 23:30; Rev 9:6; Rev 4:9; 5:1; Mark 3:5

6:17 Is 63:4; Jer 30:7; Joel 1:15; 2:1f, 11, 31; Zeph 1:14f; Rev 16:14; Ps 76:7; Nah 1:6; Mal 3:2; Luke 21:36

An Interlude

7 After this I saw four angels standing at the four corners of the earth, holding back
the four winds of the earth, so that no wind would blow on the earth or on the sea or
on any tree.
2 And I saw another angel ascending from the rising of the sun, having the seal of the
living God; and he cried out with a loud voice to the four angels to whom it was granted
to harm the earth and the sea,
3 saying, "Do not harm the earth or the sea or the trees until we have sealed the bond-
servants of our God on their foreheads."

7:1 Rev 9:14; Is 11:12; Ezek 7:2; Rev 20:8; Jer 49:36; Dan 7:2; Zech 6:5; Matt 24:31; Rev 7:3; 8:7; 9:4

7:2 Is 41:2; Rev 7:3; 9:4; Matt 16:16; Rev 9:14

A Remnant of Israel—144,000

4 And I heard the number of those who were sealed, one hundred and forty-four thousand sealed from every tribe of the sons of Israel:
5 from the tribe of Judah, twelve thousand *were* sealed, from the tribe of Reuben twelve
thousand, from the tribe of Gad twelve thousand,
6 from the tribe of Asher twelve thousand, from the tribe of Naphtali twelve thousand, from the tribe of Manasseh twelve thousand,
7 from the tribe of Simeon twelve thousand, from the tribe of Levi twelve thousand,
from the tribe of Issachar twelve thousand,
8 from the tribe of Zebulun twelve thousand, from the tribe of Joseph twelve thousand, from the tribe of Benjamin, twelve thousand *were* sealed.

7:3 Rev 6:6; John 3:33; Rev 7:3-8; Ezek 9:4, 6; Rev 13:16; 14:1, 9; 20:4; 22:4

7:4 Rev 9:16; Rev 14:1, 3

A Multitude from the Tribulation

9 After these things I looked, and behold, a great multitude which no one could count,
from every nation and *all* tribes and peoples and tongues, standing before the throne
and before the Lamb, clothed in white robes, and palm branches *were* in their hands;
10 and they cry out with a loud voice, saying,

7:9 Rev 5:9; Rev 7:15; Rev 22:3; Rev 6:11; 7:14; Lev 23:40

7:10 Ps 3:8; Rev 12:10; 19:1; Rev 22:3

7:1ff The sixth seal has been opened, and the people of the earth have tried to hide from God, saying, "Who is able to stand?" (6:12–17). Just when all hope seems lost, four angels hold back the four winds of judgment until God's people are sealed as his own. Only then will God open the seventh seal (8:1).

7:2 A seal on a scroll or document identified and protected its contents. God places his own seal on his followers, identifying them as his own and guaranteeing his protection over their souls. This shows how valuable we are to him. Our physical bodies may be beaten, maimed, or even destroyed, but *nothing* can harm our souls when we have been sealed by God. See Ephesians 1:13 for the seal of the Holy Spirit.

7:3 God's seal is placed on the foreheads of his servants. This seal is the exact opposite of the mark of the beast explained in 13:16. These two marks place the people in two distinct categories—those owned by God and those owned by Satan.

7:4–8 The number 144,000 is 12 x 12 x 1,000, symbolizing completeness—*all* God's followers will be brought safely to him; not one will be overlooked or forgotten. God seals these believers either by withdrawing them from the earth (this is called the Rapture) or by giving them special strength and courage to make it through this time of great persecution. Even though many believers have to undergo persecution, the seal does not necessarily guarantee protection from physical harm—many will die (see 6:11)—but God will protect them from spiritual harm. No matter what happens, they will be brought to their reward of eternal life. Their destiny is secure. These believers will not fall away from God even though they may undergo intense persecution.

This is not saying that 144,000 individuals must be sealed before the persecution comes, but that when persecution begins, the faithful will have already been sealed (marked by God), and they will remain true to him until the end.

7:4–8 This is a different list from the usual listing of the 12 tribes in the Old Testament, because it is a symbolic list of God's true followers. (1) Judah is mentioned first because Judah is both the tribe of David and of Jesus the Messiah (Genesis 49:8–12; Matthew 1:1). (2) Levi had no tribal allotment because of the Levites' work for God in the temple (Deuteronomy 18:1), but here the tribe is given a place as a reward for faithfulness. (3) Dan is not mentioned because it was known for rebellion and idolatry, traits unacceptable for God's followers (Genesis 49:17). (4) The two tribes representing Joseph (usually called Ephraim and Manasseh, after Joseph's sons) are here called Joseph and Manasseh because of Ephraim's rebellion. See Genesis 49 for the story of the beginning of these 12 tribes.

7:9 Who is this great multitude? While some interpreters identify it as the martyrs described in 6:9, it may also be the same group as the 144,000 just mentioned (7:4–8). The 144,000 were sealed by God before the great time of persecution; the great multitude was brought to eternal life, as God had promised. Before, they were being prepared; now, they are victorious. This multitude in heaven is composed of all those who remained faithful to God throughout the generations. No true believer ever need worry about which group he or she will be in. God includes and protects each of us, and we are guaranteed a place in his presence.

7:10 People try many methods to remove the guilt of sin—good works, intellectual pursuits, and even casting blame on others. The multitude in heaven however, praises God, saying that salvation comes from him and from the Lamb. Salvation from sin's penalty can come only through Jesus Christ. Have you had the guilt of sin removed in the only way possible?

"Salvation to our God who sits on the throne, and to the Lamb."
11 And all the angels were standing around the throne and *around* the elders and the
four living creatures; and they fell on their faces before the throne and worshiped God,
12 saying,
"Amen, blessing and glory and wisdom and thanksgiving and honor and power and
might, *be* to our God forever and ever. Amen."
13 Then one of the elders answered, saying to me, "These who are clothed in the white
robes, who are they, and where have they come from?"
14 I said to him, "My lord, you know." And he said to me, "These are the ones who
come out of the great tribulation, and they have washed their robes and made them white
in the blood of the Lamb.
15 "For this reason, they are before the throne of God; and they serve Him day and night
in His temple; and He who sits on the throne will spread His tabernacle over them.
16 "They will hunger no longer, nor thirst anymore; nor will the sun beat down on them,
nor any heat;
17 for the Lamb in the center of the throne will be their shepherd, and will guide them
to springs of the water of life; and God will wipe every tear from their eyes."

The Seventh Seal—the Trumpets

8 When the Lamb broke the seventh seal, there was silence in heaven for about half
an hour.
2 And I saw the seven angels who stand before God, and seven trumpets were given
to them.
3 Another angel came and stood at the altar, holding a golden censer; and much incense was given to him, so that he might add it to the prayers of all the saints on the
golden altar which was before the throne.
4 And the smoke of the incense, with the prayers of the saints, went up before God
out of the angel's hand.
5 Then the angel took the censer and filled it with the fire of the altar, and threw it to
the earth; and there followed peals of thunder and sounds and flashes of lightning and
an earthquake.

3. Sounding the seven trumpets

6 And the seven angels who had the seven trumpets prepared themselves to sound
them.
7 The first sounded, and there came hail and fire, mixed with blood, and they were
thrown to the earth; and a third of the earth was burned up, and a third of the trees were
burned up, and all the green grass was burned up.

7:12 Rev 5:14; Rev 5:12
7:13 Acts 3:12; Rev 7:9
7:14 Dan 12:1; Matt 24:21; Mark 13:19; Zech 3:3-5; Rev 22:14; Rev 6:11; 7:9; Heb 9:14; 1 John 1:7
7:15 Rev 7:9; Rev 4:8f; 22:3; Rev 11:19; 21:22; Rev 4:9; Lev 26:11; Ezek 37:27; John 1:14; Rev 21:3
7:17 Ps 23:1f; Matt 2:6; John 10:11; John 4:14; Rev 21:6; 22:1; Is 25:8; Matt 5:4; Rev 21:4
8:1 Rev 5:1; 6:1, 3, 5, 7, 9, 12
8:2 Rev 1:4; 8:6-13; 9:1, 13; 11:15; 1 Cor 15:52; 1 Thess 4:16
8:3 Rev 7:2; Amos 9:1; Rev 6:9; Heb 9:4; Ex 30:1; Rev 5:8; Ex 30:3; Num 4:11; Rev 8:5; 9:13
8:5 Lev 16:12; Ezek 10:2; Ex 19:16; Rev 4:5; 11:19; 16:18; Rev 6:12
8:6 Rev 8:2
8:7 Ex 9:23ff; Is 28:2; Ezek 38:22; Joel 2:30; Zech 13:8, 9; Rev 8:7-12; 9:15, 18; 12:4; Rev 9:4

7:11 More information about the elders is found in the note on 4:4. The four living creatures are explained further in the note on 4:6–7.

7:14 "The great tribulation" has been explained in several ways. Some believe it refers to the suffering of believers through the ages; others believe that there is a specific time of intense tribulation yet to come. In either case, these believers come through their times of suffering by remaining loyal to God. Because they remain faithful, God will give them eternal life with him (7:17).

7:14 It is difficult to imagine how blood could make any cloth white, but the blood of Jesus Christ is the world's greatest purifier because it removes the stain of sin. White symbolizes sinless perfection or holiness, which can be given to people only by the death of the sinless Lamb of God on our behalf. This is a picture of how we are saved through faith (see Isaiah 1:18; Romans 3:21–26).

7:16–17 God will provide for his children's needs in their eternal home where there will be no hunger, thirst, or pain, and he will wipe away all tears. When you are suffering or torn apart by sorrow, take comfort in this promise of complete protection and relief.

7:17 In verses 1–8 we see the believers receiving a seal to protect them through a time of great tribulation and suffering; in verses 9–17 we see the believers finally with God in heaven. All who have been faithful through the ages are singing before God's throne. Their tribulations and sorrows are over: no more tears for sin, for all sins are forgiven; no more tears for suffering, for all suffering is over; no more tears for death, for all believers have been resurrected to die no more.

8:1–2 When the seventh seal is opened, the seven trumpet judgments are revealed. In the same way, the seventh trumpet will announce the seven bowl judgments in 11:15 and 16:1–21. The trumpet judgments, like the seal judgments, are only partial. God's final and complete judgment has not yet come.

8:3 A censer filled with live coals was used in temple worship. Incense was poured on the coals, and the sweet-smelling smoke drifted upwards, symbolizing believers' prayers ascending to God (see Exodus 30:7–9).

8:6 The trumpet blasts have three purposes: (1) to warn that judgment is certain, (2) to call the forces of good and evil to battle, and (3) to announce the return of the King, the Messiah. These warnings urge us to make sure our faith is firmly fixed on Christ.

8:7–12 Since only one-third of the earth is destroyed by these trumpet judgments, this is only a partial judgment from God. His full wrath is yet to be unleashed.

8 The second angel sounded, and *something* like a great mountain burning with fire
was thrown into the sea; and a third of the sea became blood,
9 and a third of the creatures which were in the sea and had life, died; and a third of
the ships were destroyed.
10 The third angel sounded, and a great star fell from heaven, burning like a torch,
and it fell on a third of the rivers and on the springs of waters.
11 The name of the star is called Wormwood; and a third of the waters became wormwood, and many men died from the waters, because they were made bitter.
12 The fourth angel sounded, and a third of the sun and a third of the moon and a
third of the stars were struck, so that a third of them would be darkened and the day
would not shine for a third of it, and the night in the same way.
13 Then I looked, and I heard an eagle flying in midheaven, saying with a loud voice,
"Woe, woe, woe to those who dwell on the earth, because of the remaining blasts of the
trumpet of the three angels who are about to sound!"

The Fifth Trumpet—the Bottomless Pit

9 Then the fifth angel sounded, and I saw a star from heaven which had fallen to the
earth; and the key of the bottomless pit was given to him.
2 He opened the bottomless pit, and smoke went up out of the pit, like the smoke of
a great furnace; and the sun and the air were darkened by the smoke of the pit.
3 Then out of the smoke came locusts upon the earth, and power was given them, as
the scorpions of the earth have power.
4 They were told not to hurt the grass of the earth, nor any green thing, nor any tree,
but only the men who do not have the seal of God on their foreheads.
5 And they were not permitted to kill anyone, but to torment for five months; and
their torment was like the torment of a scorpion when it stings a man.
6 And in those days men will seek death and will not find it; they will long to die, and
death flees from them.
7 The appearance of the locusts was like horses prepared for battle; and on their heads
appeared to be crowns like gold, and their faces were like the faces of men.
8 They had hair like the hair of women, and their teeth were like *the teeth* of lions.
9 They had breastplates like breastplates of iron; and the sound of their wings was
like the sound of chariots, of many horses rushing to battle.
10 They have tails like scorpions, and stings; and in their tails is their power to hurt
men for five months.

8:8 Rev 8:7-12; 9:15, 18
8:9 Rev 8:7-12; 9:15, 18; 12:4; Is 2:16
8:10 Rev 8:7-12; 9:15, 18; 12:4; Rev 14:7; 16:4
8:11 Zech 13:8, 9; Rev 8:7-12; 9:15, 18; 12:4; Jer 9:15; 23:15
8:12 Ex 10:21ff; Is 13:10; Ezek 32:7; Joel 2:10, 31; 3:15
8:13 Rev 14:6; 19:17; Rev 9:12; 11:14; 12:12; Rev 3:10; Rev 8:2
9:1 Rev 8:2; Rev 8:10; Rev 1:18; Luke 8:31; Rev 9:2, 11
9:3 Ex 10:12-15; Rev 9:7; 2 Chr 10:11, 14; Ezek 2:6; Rev 9:5
9:4 Rev 6:6; Rev 8:7; Ezek 9:4; Rev 7:2, 3
9:5 Rev 9:10; 2 Chr 10:11, 14; Ezek 2:6
9:6 Job 3:21; 7:15; Jer 8:3; Rev 6:16
9:8 Joel 1:6
9:9 Jer 47:3; Joel 2:5
9:10 2 Chr 10:11, 14; Ezek 2:6; Rev 9:3, 5

8:11 Wormwood is a plant with a very bitter taste, and it stands for the bitterness of God's judgment.

8:13 Habakkuk used the image of an eagle to symbolize swiftness and destruction (see Habakkuk 1:8). The picture here is of a strong, powerful bird flying over all the earth, warning of the terrors yet to come. While both believers and unbelievers experience the terrors described in verses 7–12, "those who dwell on the earth" are the unbelievers who will meet spiritual harm through the next three trumpet judgments. God has guaranteed believers protection from spiritual harm (7:2–3).

8:13 In 6:10, the martyrs call out to God, "How long . . . will You refrain from judging and avenging our blood?" As we see the world's wickedness, we too may cry out to God, "How long?" In the following chapters, the judgment comes at last. We may be distressed and impatient, but God has his plan and his timing, and we must learn to trust him to know what is best. Judgment is coming—be sure of that. Thank God for the time he has given you to turn from sin. Use the available time to work to help others turn to him.

9:1 It is not known whether this "star" that fell from heaven is Satan, a fallen angel, Christ, or a good angel. Most likely it is a good angel, because the key to the bottomless pit is normally held by Christ (1:17–18), and it was temporarily given to this other being from heaven (see also 20:1). This being, whoever he may be, is still under God's control and authority. The bottomless pit represents the place of the demons and of Satan, the king of demons (9:11). See also Luke 8:31 for another reference to the bottomless pit (also called the abyss).

9:3 The prophet Joel described a locust plague as a foreshadowing of the "day of the LORD," meaning God's coming judgment (Joel 2:1–10). In the Old Testament, locusts were symbols of destruction because they destroyed vegetation. Here, however, they symbolize an invasion of demons called to torture people who do not believe in God. The limitations placed on the demons (they could only torment people for five months) show that they are under God's authority.

9:3ff Most likely these locusts are demons—evil spirits ruled by Satan who tempt people to sin. They were not created by Satan, because God is the Creator of all; rather, they are fallen angels who joined Satan in his rebellion. God limits what they can do; they can do nothing without his permission. Their main purpose on earth is to prevent, distort, or destroy people's relationship with God. Because they are corrupt and degenerate, their appearance reflects the distortion of their spirits. While it is important to recognize their evil activity so we can stay away from them, we must avoid any curiosity about or involvement with demonic forces or with the occult.

9:11 Luke 8:31; Rev 9:1, 2; John 5:2; Rev 16:16; Job 26:6; 28:22; 31:12; Ps 88:11; Prov 15:11

9:12 Rev 8:13; 11:14

9:13 Ex 30:2f, 10; Rev 8:3

9:14 Rev 7:1; Gen 15:18; Deut 1:7; Josh 1:4; Rev 16:12

9:15 Rev 20:7; Rev 8:7; 9:18

9:16 Rev 5:11; Rev 7:4

9:17 Dan 8:2; 9:21; Rev 9:18; 14:10; 19:20; 20:10; 21:8; Rev 11:5

9:18 Rev 8:7; 9:15; Rev 9:17

9:20 Rev 2:21; Deut 4:28; Jer 1:16; Mic 5:13; Acts 7:41; 1 Cor 10:20; Ps 115:4-7; 135:15-17; Dan 5:23

9:21 Rev 9:20; Is 47:9, 12; Rev 18:23; Rev 17:2, 4, 5

10:1 Rev 5:2; Rev 18:1; 20:1; Rev 4:3; Matt 17:2; Rev 1:16; Rev 1:15

10:2 Rev 5:1; 10:8-10

11 They have as king over them, the angel of the abyss; his name in Hebrew is [11]Abad-
don, and in the Greek he has the name Apollyon.
12 The first woe is past; behold, two woes are still coming after these things.

The Sixth Trumpet—Army from the East

13 Then the sixth angel sounded, and I heard a voice from the [12]four horns of the gold-
en altar which is before God,
14 one saying to the sixth angel who had the trumpet, "Release the four angels who
are bound at the great river Euphrates."
15 And the four angels, who had been prepared for the hour and day and month and
year, were released, so that they would kill a third of mankind.
16 The number of the armies of the horsemen was two hundred million; I heard the
number of them.
17 And this is how I saw in the vision the horses and those who sat on them: *the riders*
had breastplates *the color* of fire and of hyacinth and of brimstone; and the heads of the
horses are like the heads of lions; and out of their mouths proceed fire and smoke and
brimstone.
18 A third of mankind was killed by these three plagues, by the fire and the smoke and
the brimstone which proceeded out of their mouths.
19 For the power of the horses is in their mouths and in their tails; for their tails are
like serpents and have heads, and with them they do harm.
20 The rest of mankind, who were not killed by these plagues, did not repent of the
works of their hands, so as not to worship demons, and the idols of gold and of silver and
of brass and of stone and of wood, which can neither see nor hear nor walk;
21 and they did not repent of their murders nor of their sorceries nor of their immorality nor of their thefts.

The Angel and the Little Book

10 I saw another strong angel coming down out of heaven, clothed with a cloud; and
the rainbow was upon his head, and his face was like the sun, and his feet like pillars of fire;
2 and he had in his hand a little book which was open. He placed his right foot on the
sea and his left on the land;
3 and he cried out with a loud voice, as when a lion roars; and when he had cried out,
the seven peals of thunder uttered their voices.

11 I.e. destruction **12** Two early mss do not contain *four*

9:11 The locust-demons have a leader whose name in Hebrew and in Greek means *destroyer.* It may be a play on words by John to show that those who worshiped the great god Apollo worshiped only a demon.

9:13 The altar in the temple had four projections, one at each corner, and these were called the horns of the altar (see Exodus 27:2).

9:14 The word *angels* here means fallen angels or demons. These four unidentified demons will be exceedingly evil and destructive. But note that they do not have the power to release themselves and do their evil work on earth. Instead, they are held back by God and will be released at a specific time, doing only what he allows them to do.

9:15 Here one-third of all people are killed. In 6:7–8, one-fourth of mankind was killed. Thus, over one-half of the people in the world will have been killed by God's great judgments. Even more would have been killed if God had not set limits on the destruction.

9:16 In John's day, this number of mounted troops in an army was inconceivable, but today there are countries and alliances that could easily amass this many soldiers. This huge army, led by the four demons, will be sent out to destroy one-third of the earth's population. But the judgment is still not complete.

9:20–21 These people were so hardhearted that even plagues did not drive them to God. People don't usually fall into immorality and evil suddenly—they slip into it a little bit at a time until, hardly realizing what has happened, they are irrevocably mired in their wicked ways. Any person who allows sin to take root in his or her life can find himself or herself in this predicament. Temptation entertained today becomes sin tomorrow, then a habit the next day, then death and separation from God forever (see James 1:15). To think you could never become this evil is the first step toward a hard heart. Acknowledge your need to confess your sin before God.

10:1–6 The purpose of this strong angel is clear—to announce the final judgments on the earth. His right foot on the sea and left foot on the land (10:2) indicate that his words deal with all creation, not just a limited part as did the seal and trumpet judgments. The seventh trumpet (11:15) will usher in the seven bowl judgments, which will bring an end to the present world. When this universal judgment comes, God's truth will prevail.

10:2 We see two books in Revelation. The first contains a revelation of judgments against evil (5:1ff). The contents of the second little book are not indicated, but it also may contain a revelation of judgment.

4 When the seven peals of thunder had spoken, I was about to write; and I heard a
voice from heaven saying, "Seal up the things which the seven peals of thunder have
spoken and do not write them."
5 Then the angel whom I saw standing on the sea and on the land lifted up his right
hand to heaven,
6 and swore by Him who lives forever and ever, WHO CREATED HEAVEN AND THE
THINGS IN IT, AND THE EARTH AND THE THINGS IN IT, AND THE SEA AND THE THINGS IN
IT, that there will be delay no longer,
7 but in the days of the voice of the seventh angel, when he is about to sound, then the
mystery of God is finished, as He preached to His servants the prophets.
8 Then the voice which I heard from heaven, *I heard* again speaking with me, and
saying, "Go, take the book which is open in the hand of the angel who stands on the sea
and on the land."
9 So I went to the angel, telling him to give me the little book. And he ☆said to me,
"Take it and eat it; it will make your stomach bitter, but in your mouth it will be sweet as
honey."
10 I took the little book out of the angel's hand and ate it, and in my mouth it was sweet
as honey; and when I had eaten it, my stomach was made bitter.
11 And they ☆said to me, "You must prophesy again concerning many peoples and
nations and tongues and kings."

The Two Witnesses

11 Then there was given me a measuring rod like a staff; and someone said, "Get up
and measure the temple of God and the altar, and those who worship in it.
2 "Leave out the court which is outside the temple and do not measure it, for it has
been given to the nations; and they will tread under foot the holy city for forty-two months.
3 "And I will grant *authority* to my two witnesses, and they will prophesy for twelve
hundred and sixty days, clothed in sackcloth."
4 These are the two olive trees and the two lampstands that stand before the Lord of
the earth.
5 And if anyone wants to harm them, fire flows out of their mouth and devours their
enemies; so if anyone wants to harm them, he must be killed in this way.
6 These have the power to shut up the sky, so that rain will not fall during the days of
their prophesying; and they have power over the waters to turn them into blood, and to
strike the earth with every plague, as often as they desire.

10:4 Rev 1:11, 19; Rev 10:8; Dan 8:26; 12:4, 9; Rev 22:10

10:6 Gen 14:22; Ex 6:8; Num 14:30; Ezek 20:5; Rev 4:9; Ex 20:11; Rev 4:11; Rev 6:11; 12:12; 16:17; 21:6

10:7 Rev 11:15; Amos 3:7; Rom 16:25

10:9 Jer 15:16; Ezek 2:8; 3:1-3

10:11 Rev 11:1; Ezek 37:4, 9; Rev 5:9; Rev 17:10, 12

11:1 Ezek 40:3-42:20; Zech 2:1; Rev 21:15f

11:2 Ezek 40:17, 20; Luke 21:24; Is 52:1; Matt 4:5; 27:53; Rev 21:2, 10; 22:19; Dan 7:25; 12:7; Rev 12:6; 13:5

11:3 Rev 1:5; 2:13; Dan 7:25; 12:7; Rev 12:6; 13:5; Gen 37:34; 2 Sam 3:31; 1 Kin 21:27; 2 Kin 19:1f; Neh 9:1; Esth 4:1; Ps 69:11; Joel 1:13; Jon 3:5f, 8

11:5 2 Kin 1:10-12; Jer 5:14; Rev 9:17f; Num 16:29, 35

11:6 1 Kin 17:1; Luke 4:25; Rev 11:3; Ex 7:17ff; Rev 8:8

10:4 Throughout history people have wanted to know what would happen in the future, and God reveals some of it in this book. But John was stopped from revealing certain parts of his vision. An angel also told the prophet Daniel that some visions he saw were not to be revealed yet to everyone (Daniel 12:9), and Jesus told his disciples that the time of the end is known by no one but God (Mark 13:32–33). God has revealed all we need to know to live for him now. In our desire to be ready for the end, we must not place more emphasis on speculation about the last days than on living for God while we wait.

10:7 When God's plan for human history is completely revealed, all prophecy will be fulfilled. The end of the age will have arrived (see 11:15 and Ephesians 1:9–10).

10:9–10 The prophet Ezekiel had a vision in which he was told to eat a scroll filled with judgments against the nation of Israel (Ezekiel 3:1ff). The taste was sweet in his mouth, but the scroll's contents brought destruction—just like the book John was told to eat. God's Word is sweet to us as believers because it brings encouragement, but it sours our stomach because of the coming judgment we must pronounce on unbelievers.

11:1ff This temple is most likely a symbol of the church (all true believers), because there will be no temple in the new Jerusalem (21:22). John measured the temple to show that God is building walls of protection around his people to spare them from spiritual harm, and that there is a place reserved for all believers who remain faithful to God.

11:2 Those worshiping inside the temple will be protected spiritually, but those outside will face great suffering. This is a way of saying that true believers will be protected through persecution, but those who refuse to believe will be destroyed.

11:3 These two witnesses bear strong resemblance to Moses and Elijah, two of God's mighty prophets. With God's power, Moses called plagues down upon the nation of Egypt (see Exodus 8—11). Elijah defeated the prophets of Baal (1 Kings 18). Both of these men appeared with Christ at his transfiguration (see Matthew 17:1–7).

11:3 In the book of Revelation, numbers are likely to have symbolic rather than literal meanings. The 42 months or 1,260 days equal 3 1/2 years. As half of the perfect number 7, 3 1/2 can indicate incompletion, imperfection, or even evil. Notice the events predicted for this time period: There is trouble (Daniel 12:7), the holy city is trampled (11:2), the woman takes refuge in the wilderness (12:6), and the devil-inspired beast exercises his authority (13:5). Some commentators link the 3 1/2 years with the period of famine in the days of Elijah (Luke 4:25; James 5:17). Since Malachi predicted the return of Elijah before the Last Judgment (Malachi 4:5), and since the events in Daniel and Revelation pave the way for the second coming, perhaps John was making this connection. It is possible, of course, that the 3 1/2 years are literal. If so, we will clearly recognize when the 3 1/2 years are over! Whether symbolic or literal, however, they indicate that evil's reign will have a definite end.

11:7 Rev 13:1ff; 17:8; Rev 9:1; Dan 7:21; Rev 13:7

11:8 Rev 14:8; 16:19; 17:18; 18:2, 10, 16, 18, 19, 21; Is 1:9, 10; 3:9; Jer 23:14; Ezek 16:46, 49; Ezek 23:3, 8, 19, 27

11:9 Rev 5:9; 10:11; 1 Kin 13:22; Ps 79:2f

11:10 Rev 3:10; Neh 8:10, 12; Esth 9:19, 22

11:11 Ezek 37:5, 9, 10, 14

11:12 Rev 4:1; 2 Kin 2:11; Acts 1:9

11:13 Rev 6:12; 8:5; 11:19; 16:18; John 9:24; Rev 14:7; 16:9; 19:7; Rev 16:11

11:15 Rev 8:2; 10:7; Rev 16:17; 19:1; Rev 12:10; Ps 2:2; Acts 4:26; Ex 15:18; Dan 2:44; 7:14, 27; Luke 1:33

11:17 Rev 1:8; Rev 19:6

11:18 Ps 2:1; Ps 2:5; 110:5; Dan 7:10; Rev 20:12; Rev 10:7; 16:6; Ps 115:13; Rev 13:16; 19:5

11:19 Rev 4:1; 15:5; Heb 9:4; Rev 4:5; 8:5; 16:18; Rev 16:21

7 When they have finished their testimony, the beast that comes up out of the abyss
will make war with them, and overcome them and kill them.
8 And their dead bodies *will lie* in the street of the great city which [13]mystically is called
Sodom and Egypt, where also their Lord was crucified.
9 Those from the peoples and tribes and tongues and nations *will* look at their dead
[14]bodies for three and a half days, and will not permit their dead bodies to be laid in a
tomb.
10 And those who dwell on the earth *will* rejoice over them and celebrate; and they
will send gifts to one another, because these two prophets tormented those who dwell
on the earth.
11 But after the three and a half days, the breath of life from God came into them, and
they stood on their feet; and great fear fell upon those who were watching them.
12 And they heard a loud voice from heaven saying to them, "Come up here." Then
they went up into heaven in the cloud, and their enemies watched them.
13 And in that hour there was a great earthquake, and a tenth of the city fell; seven
thousand people were killed in the earthquake, and the rest were terrified and gave glory
to the God of heaven.
14 The second woe is past; behold, the third woe is coming quickly.

The Seventh Trumpet—Christ's Reign Foreseen

15 Then the seventh angel sounded; and there were loud voices in heaven, saying,
"The kingdom of the world has become *the kingdom* of our Lord and of His [15]Christ;
and He will reign forever and ever."
16 And the twenty-four elders, who sit on their thrones before God, fell on their faces
and worshiped God,
17 saying,
"We give You thanks, O Lord God, the Almighty, who are and who were, because You
have taken Your great power and have begun to reign.
18 "And the nations were enraged, and Your wrath came, and the time *came* for the
dead to be judged, and *the time* to reward Your bond-servants the prophets and the saints
and those who fear Your name, the small and the great, and to destroy those who destroy the earth."
19 And the temple of God which is in heaven was opened; and the ark of His covenant
appeared in His temple, and there were flashes of lightning and sounds and peals of
thunder and an earthquake and a great hailstorm.

13 Lit *spiritually* **14** Lit *body* **15** I.e. Messiah

11:7 This beast could be Satan or an agent of Satan.

11:8–9 Jerusalem, once the great city and the capital of Israel, is now enemy territory. It is compared with Sodom and with Egypt, both well known for their evil. At the time of John's writing, Jerusalem had been destroyed by the Romans in 70 A.D., nearly a million Jews had been slaughtered, and the temple treasures had been carried off to Rome.

11:10 The whole world rejoices at the deaths of these two witnesses who have caused trouble by saying what the people didn't want to hear—words about their sin, their need for repentance, and the coming punishment. Sinful people hate those who call attention to their sin and who urge them to repent. They hated Christ, and they hate his followers (1 John 3:13). When you obey Christ and take a stand against sin, be prepared to experience the world's hatred. But remember that the great reward awaiting you in heaven far outweighs any suffering that you face now.

11:15 The seventh trumpet is sounded, announcing the arrival of the King. There is now no turning back. The coming judgments are no longer partial, but complete in their destruction. God is in control, and he unleashes his full wrath on the evil world that refuses to turn to him (9:20–21). When his wrath begins, there will be no escape.

11:16 For more on the 24 elders, see the note on 4:4.

11:18 In the Bible, God gives rewards to his people according to what they deserve. Throughout the Old Testament, obedience often brought reward in this life (Deuteronomy 28), but obedience and immediate reward are not always linked. If they were, good people would always be rich, and suffering would always be a sign of sin. If we were quickly rewarded for every faithful deed, we would soon think we were pretty good. Before long, we would be doing many good deeds for purely selfish reasons. While it is true that God will reward us for our earthly deeds (see 20:12), our greatest reward will be eternal life in his presence.

11:19 In Old Testament days, the ark of the covenant was the most sacred treasure of the Israelite nation. For more information about the ark, see the note on Exodus 37:1.

4. Observing the great conflict

The Woman, Israel

12 A great sign appeared in heaven: a woman clothed with the sun, and the moon
under her feet, and on her head a crown of twelve stars;
2 and she was with child; and she ☆cried out, being in labor and in pain to give birth.

The Red Dragon, Satan

3 Then another sign appeared in heaven: and behold, a great red dragon having sev-
en heads and ten horns, and on his heads *were* seven diadems.
4 And his tail ☆swept away a third of the stars of heaven and threw them to the earth.
And the dragon stood before the woman who was about to give birth, so that when she
gave birth he might devour her child.

The Male Child, Christ

5 And she gave birth to a son, a male *child*, who is to rule all the nations with a rod of
iron; and her child was caught up to God and to His throne.
6 Then the woman fled into the wilderness where she ☆had a place prepared by God,
so that there she would be nourished for one thousand two hundred and sixty days.

The Angel, Michael

7 And there was war in heaven, Michael and his angels waging war with the dragon.
The dragon and his angels waged war,
8 and they were not strong enough, and there was no longer a place found for them in
heaven.
9 And the great dragon was thrown down, the serpent of old who is called the devil
and Satan, who deceives the whole world; he was thrown down to the earth, and his angels
were thrown down with him.

12:1 Matt 24:30; Rev 12:3; Rev 11:19; Gal 4:26; Ps 104:2; Song 6:10

12:2 Is 26:17; 66:6-9; Mic 4:9f

12:3 Rev 12:1; 15:1; Is 27:1; Rev 12:4, 7, 9, 13, 16f; 13:2, 4, 11; 16:13; 20:2; Dan 7:7, 20, 24; Rev 13:1; 17:12, 16; Rev 19:12

12:4 Rev 8:7, 12; Dan 8:10; Is 27:1; Rev 12:3, 7, 9, 13, 16f; 13:2, 4, 11; 16:13; 20:2; Matt 2:16

12:5 Is 66:7; Ps 2:9; Rev 2:27; 2 Cor 12:2ff

12:7 Dan 10:13, 21; 12:1; Jude 9; Rev 12:3; Matt 25:41

12:9 Rev 12:3; Gen 3:1; 2 Cor 11:3; Rev 12:15; 20:2; Matt 4:10; 25:41; Rev 13:14; 20:3, 8, 10; Luke 10:18; John 12:31

12:1—14:20 The seventh trumpet (11:15) ushers in the bowl judgments (15:1—16:21), but in the intervening chapters (12—14), John sees the conflict between God and Satan. He sees the source of all sin, evil, persecution, and suffering on the earth, and he understands why the great battle between the forces of God and Satan must soon take place. In these chapters the nature of evil is exposed, and Satan is seen in all his wickedness.

12:1–6 The woman represents God's faithful people who have been waiting for the Messiah; the crown of 12 stars represents the 12 tribes of Israel. God set apart the Jews for himself (Romans 9:4–5), and that nation gave birth to the Messiah. The male child (12:5) is Jesus, born to a devout Jew named Mary (Luke 1:26–33). Evil King Herod immediately tried to destroy the infant Jesus (Matthew 2:13–20). Herod's desire to kill this newborn king, whom he saw as a threat to his throne, was motivated by Satan (the red dragon), who wanted to kill the world's Savior. The heavenly pageant of Revelation 12 shows that Christ's quiet birth in the town of Bethlehem had cosmic significance.

12:3–4 The enormous red dragon, Satan, has seven heads, ten horns, and seven diadems (crowns), representing his power and the kingdoms of the world over which he rules. The stars that plunged to earth with him are usually considered to be the angels who fell with Satan and became his demons. According to Hebrew tradition, one-third of all the angels in heaven fell with Satan. For more on demons, see the notes on 9:3ff and Mark 5:1–20.

12:6 The wilderness represents a place of spiritual refuge and protection from Satan. Because God aided the woman's escape into the wilderness, we can be sure that he offers security to all true believers. Satan always attacks God's people, but God keeps them spiritually secure. Some will experience physical harm, but all will be protected from spiritual harm. God will not let Satan take the souls of God's true followers.

12:6 The 1,260 days (3 1/2 years) is the same length of time that the dragon is allowed to exercise his authority (13:5) and that the holy city is trampled (see the second note on 11:3).

12:7 This event fulfills Daniel 12:1ff. Michael is a high-ranking angel. One of his responsibilities is to guard God's community of believers.

12:7ff Much more happened at Christ's birth, death, and resurrection than most people realize. A war between the forces of good and evil was under way. With Christ's resurrection, Satan's ultimate defeat was assured. Some believe that Satan's fall to earth took place at Jesus' resurrection or ascension and that the 1,260 days (3 1/2 years) is a symbolic way of referring to the time between Christ's first and second comings. Others say that Satan's defeat will occur in the middle of a literal seven-year tribulation period, following the rapture of the church and preceding the second coming of Christ and the beginning of Christ's 1,000-year reign. Whatever the case, we must remember that Christ is victorious—Satan has already been defeated because of Christ's death on the cross (12:10–12).

12:9 The devil is not a symbol or legend; he is very real. Originally Satan was an angel of God, but through his own pride he became corrupt. The devil is God's enemy, and he constantly tries to hinder God's work, but he is limited by God's power and can do only what he is permitted to do (Job 1:6—2:8). The name *Satan* means "accuser" (12:10). He actively looks for people to attack (1 Peter 5:8–9). Satan likes to pursue believers who are vulnerable in their faith, who are spiritually weak, or who are isolated from other believers.

Even though God permits the devil to do his work in this world, God is still in control. And Jesus has complete power over Satan—he defeated Satan when he died and rose again for the sins of mankind. One day Satan will be bound forever, never again to do his evil work (see 20:10).

12:10 Rev 11:15; Rev 7:10; Job 1:11; 2:5; Zech 3:1; Luke 22:31; 1 Pet 5:8

12:11 John 16:33; 1 John 2:13; Rev 15:2; Rev 7:14; Rev 6:9; Luke 14:26; Rev 2:10

12:12 Ps 96:11; Is 44:23; Rev 18:20; Rev 13:6; Rev 8:13; Rev 12:9

12:13 Rev 12:3; Rev 12:5

12:14 Ex 19:4; Deut 32:11; Is 40:31; Rev 12:6; Dan 7:25; 12:7

12:15 Gen 3:1; 2 Cor 11:3; Rev 12:9; 20:2

12:17 Rev 11:7; 13:7; Gen 3:15; 1 John 2:3; Rev 1:2; 6:9; 14:12; 19:10

10 Then I heard a loud voice in heaven, saying,
"Now the salvation, and the power, and the kingdom of our God and the authority of
His Christ have come, for the accuser of our brethren has been thrown down, he who
accuses them before our God day and night.
11 "And they overcame him because of the blood of the Lamb and because of the word
of their testimony, and they did not love their life even when faced with death.
12 "For this reason, rejoice, O heavens and you who dwell in them. Woe to the earth
and the sea, because the devil has come down to you, having great wrath, knowing that
he has *only* a short time."
13 And when the dragon saw that he was thrown down to the earth, he persecuted the
woman who gave birth to the male *child*.
14 But the two wings of the great eagle were given to the woman, so that she could fly
into the wilderness to her place, where she ☆was nourished for a time and times and half
a time, from the presence of the serpent.
15 And the serpent poured water like a river out of his mouth after the woman, so that
he might cause her to be swept away with the flood.
16 But the earth helped the woman, and the earth opened its mouth and drank up the
river which the dragon poured out of his mouth.
17 So the dragon was enraged with the woman, and went off to make war with the rest
of her children, who keep the commandments of God and hold to the testimony of Jesus.

SATAN'S WORK IN THE WORLD		
	His hatred for Christ	12:13
	His hatred for God's people	12:17
	His power and authority	13:2
	His popularity among unbelievers	13:4
	His blasphemy against God	13:6
	His war against believers	13:7
	His ability to deceive	13:14

12:10 Many believe that until this time Satan still had access to God (see the note on Job 1:7ff). But here his access is forever barred (see also 9:1). He can no longer accuse people before God (see how Satan made accusations about Job before God in Job 1:6ff).

12:11 The critical blow to Satan came when the Lamb, Jesus Christ, shed his blood for our sins. The victory is won by sacrifice—Christ's death in our place to pay the penalty for our sin, and the sacrifices we make because of our faith in him. As we face the battle with Satan, we should not fear it or try to escape from it, but we should loyally serve Christ, who alone brings victory (see Romans 8:34–39).

12:12 The devil begins to step up his persecution because he knows that "he has only a short time." We are living in the last days, and Satan's work has become more intense. Even though the devil is very powerful, as we can see by the condition of our world, he is always under God's control. One of the reasons God allows Satan to work evil and bring temptation is so that those who pretend to be Christ's followers will be weeded out from Christ's true believers. Knowing that the last great confrontation with Jesus is near, Satan is desperately trying to recruit as great an enemy force as possible for this final battle.

12:17 While the woman (12:1) represents faithful Jews and the child (12:5) represents Christ, the rest of her offspring could be either Jewish believers or, most likely, all believers.

12:17 The apostle Paul tells us that we are in a spiritual battle (Ephesians 6:10–12). John says that the war is still being waged, but the outcome has already been determined. Satan and his followers have been defeated and will be destroyed. Nevertheless, Satan is battling daily to bring more into his ranks and to keep his own from defecting to God's side. Those who belong to Christ have gone into battle on God's side, and he has guaranteed them victory. God will not lose the war, but we must make certain not to lose the battle for our own souls. Don't waver in your commitment to Christ. A great spiritual battle is being fought, and there is no time for indecision.

The Beast from the Sea

13 And the dragon stood on the sand of the seashore.
Then I saw a beast coming up out of the sea, having ten horns and seven heads,
and on his horns *were* ten diadems, and on his heads *were* blasphemous names.
2 And the beast which I saw was like a leopard, and his feet were like *those* of a bear,
and his mouth like the mouth of a lion. And the dragon gave him his power and his throne
and great authority.
3 *I saw* one of his heads as if it had been slain, and his fatal wound was healed. And
the whole earth was amazed *and followed* after the beast;
4 they worshiped the dragon because he gave his authority to the beast; and
they worshiped the beast, saying, "Who is like the beast, and who is able to wage war
with him?"
5 There was given to him a mouth speaking arrogant words and blasphemies, and
authority to act for forty-two months was given to him.
6 And he opened his mouth in blasphemies against God, to blaspheme His name and
His tabernacle, *that is*, those who dwell in heaven.
7 It was also given to him to make war with the saints and to overcome them, and
authority over every tribe and people and tongue and nation was given to him.
8 All who dwell on the earth will worship him, *everyone* whose name has not been [16]writ-
ten from the foundation of the world in the book of life of the Lamb who has been slain.
9 If anyone has an ear, let him hear.
10 If anyone [17]*is destined* for captivity, to captivity he goes; if anyone kills with the sword,
with the sword he must be killed. Here is the perseverance and the faith of the saints.

16 Or *written in the book...slain from the foundation of the world* **17** Or leads *into captivity*

13:1 Dan 7:3; Rev 11:7; 13:14, 15; 15:2; 16:13; 17:8; Rev 12:3; Rev 12:3; 17:12; Dan 7:8; 11:36; Rev 17:3

13:2 Dan 7:5; Dan 7:4; Rev 12:3; 13:4, 12; Rev 2:13; 16:10

13:4 Rev 12:3; 13:2, 12; Rev 18:18

13:5 Dan 7:8, 11, 20, 25; 11:36; 2 Thess 2:3f; Rev 11:2

13:6 Rev 7:15; 12:12

13:7 Dan 7:21; Rev 11:7; Rev 5:9

13:8 Rev 3:10; 13:12, 14; Rev 3:5; Matt 25:34; Rev 17:8; Ps 69:28; Rev 5:6

13:10 Is 33:1; Jer 15:2; 43:11; Gen 9:6; Matt 26:52; Rev 11:18; Heb 6:12; Rev 14:12

13:1 This beast was initially identified with Rome, because the Roman empire, in its early days, encouraged an evil life-style, persecuted believers, and opposed God and his followers. But the beast also symbolizes the antichrist—not Satan, but someone under Satan's power and control. This antichrist looks like a combination of the four beasts that Daniel saw centuries earlier in a vision (Daniel 7). As the dragon (12:17) is in opposition to God, so the beast from the sea is against Christ and may be seen as Satan's false messiah. The early Roman empire was strong and also anti-Christ (or against Christ's standards); many other individual powers throughout history have been anti-Christ. Many Christians believe that Satan's evil will culminate in a final antichrist, one who will focus all the powers of evil against Jesus Christ and his followers.

13:1ff Chapter 13 introduces Satan's (the dragon's) two evil accomplices: (1) the beast out of the sea (13:1ff) and (2) the beast out of the earth (13:11ff). Together, the three evil beings form an unholy trinity in direct opposition to the holy Trinity of God the Father, God the Son, and God the Holy Spirit.

When Satan tempted Jesus in the wilderness, he wanted Jesus to show his power by turning stones into bread, to do miracles by jumping from a high place, and to gain political power by worshiping him (see Matthew 4:1–11). Satan's plan was to rule the world through Jesus, but Jesus refused to do Satan's bidding. Thus Satan turns to the fearsome beasts described in Revelation. To the beast out of the sea he gives political power. To the beast out of the earth he gives power to do miracles. Both beasts work together to capture the control of the whole world. This unholy trinity—the dragon, the beast out of the sea, and the false prophet (see 16:13)—unite in a desperate attempt to overthrow God, but their efforts are doomed to failure. See what becomes of them in 19:19–21 and 20:10.

13:3ff Because the beast, the antichrist, is a false messiah, he will be a counterfeit of Christ and will even stage a false resurrection (13:14). People will follow and worship him because they will be awed by his power and miracles (13:3–4). He will unite the world under his leadership (13:7–8), and he will control the world economy (13:16–17). People are impressed by power and will follow those who display it forcefully or offer it to their followers. But those who follow the beast will only be fooling themselves: he will use his power to manipulate others, to point to himself, and to promote evil plans. God, by contrast, uses his infinitely greater power to love and to build up. Don't be misled by claims of great miracles or reports about a resurrection or reincarnation of someone claiming to be Christ. When Jesus returns, he will reveal himself to everyone (Matthew 24:23–28).

13:5 The power given to the beast will be limited by God. He will allow the beast to exercise authority only for a short time. Even while the beast is in power, God will still be in control (11:15; 12:10–12).

13:7 The beast will conquer God's people and rule over them, but he will not be able to harm them spiritually. He will establish worldwide dominance and demand that everyone worship him. And many *will* worship him—everyone except true believers. Refusal to worship the beast will result in temporary suffering for God's people, but they will be rewarded with eternal life in the end.

13:8 See the note on 3:5 for more information on the book of life.

13:10 In this time of persecution, being faithful to Christ could bring imprisonment and even execution. Some believers will be hurt or killed. But all that the beast and his followers will be able to do to believers is harm them physically; no spiritual harm will come to those whose faith in God is sincere. All believers will enter God's presence perfected and purified by the blood of the Lamb (7:9–17).

13:10 The times of great persecution that John saw will provide an opportunity for believers to exercise patient endurance and faithfulness. The tough times we face right now are also opportunities for spiritual growth. Don't fall into Satan's trap and turn away from God when hard times come. Instead, use those tough times as opportunities for growth.

13:11 Dan 8:3; Rev 13:4
13:12 Rev 13:4; Rev 13:14; 19:20; Rev 13:8; Rev 13:15; 14:9, 11; 16:2; 19:20; 20:4; Rev 13:3
13:13 Luke 9:54; Rev 11:5; 20:9
13:14 Rev 12:9; Rev 13:8; 2 Thess 2:9f; Rev 13:12; 19:20; Rev 13:3
13:15 Dan 3:3ff; Rev 13:12; 14:9, 11; 16:2; 19:20; 20:4
13:16 Rev 11:18; 19:5, 18; Gal 6:17; Rev 7:3; 14:9; 20:4
13:17 Gal 6:17; Rev 7:3; 14:9; 20:4; Rev 14:11; Rev 15:2
13:18 Rev 17:9; Rev 21:17
14:1 Rev 5:6; Ps 2:6; Heb 12:22; Rev 7:4; 14:3; Rev 3:12; Ezek 9:4; Rev 7:3
14:2 Rev 1:15; Rev 6:1; Rev 5:8
14:3 Rev 5:9; Rev 4:6; Rev 4:4; Rev 2:17

The Beast from the Earth

11 Then I saw another beast coming up out of the earth; and he had two horns like a
lamb and he spoke as a dragon.
12 He exercises all the authority of the first beast in his presence. And he makes the
earth and those who dwell in it to worship the first beast, whose fatal wound was healed.
13 He performs great signs, so that he even makes fire come down out of heaven to the
earth in the presence of men.
14 And he deceives those who dwell on the earth because of the signs which it was giv-
en him to perform in the presence of the beast, telling those who dwell on the earth to
make an image to the beast who ☆had the wound of the sword and has come to life.
15 And it was given to him to give breath to the image of the beast, so that the image
of the beast would even [18]speak and cause as many as do not worship the image of the
beast to be killed.
16 And he causes all, the small and the great, and the rich and the poor, and the free
men and the slaves, to be given a mark on their right hand or on their forehead,
17 and *he provides* that no one will be able to buy or to sell, except the one who has the
mark, *either* the name of the beast or the number of his name.
18 Here is wisdom. Let him who has understanding calculate the number of the beast,
for the number is that of a man; and his number is [19]six hundred and sixty-six.

The Lamb and the 144,000 on Mount Zion

14 Then I looked, and behold, the Lamb *was* standing on Mount Zion, and with Him
one hundred and forty-four thousand, having His name and the name of His Father written on their foreheads.
2 And I heard a voice from heaven, like the sound of many waters and like the sound
of loud thunder, and the voice which I heard *was* like *the sound* of harpists playing on
their harps.
3 And they ☆sang a new song before the throne and before the four living creatures
and the elders; and no one could learn the song except the one hundred and forty-four
thousand who had been purchased from the earth.

18 One early ms reads *speak, and he will cause* **19** One early ms reads 616

13:11ff The first beast came out of the sea (13:1), but this second beast comes out of the earth. Later identified as the false prophet (16:13; 19:20), he is a counterfeit of the Holy Spirit. He seems to do good, but the purpose of his miracles is to deceive.

13:14 Throughout the Bible we see miracles performed as proofs of God's power, love, and authority. But here we see counterfeit miracles performed to deceive. This is a reminder of Pharaoh's magicians, who duplicated Moses' signs in Egypt. True signs and miracles point us to Jesus Christ, but miracles alone can be deceptive. That is why we must ask with respect to each miracle we see: Is this consistent with what God says in the Bible? The second beast here gains influence through the signs and wonders that he can perform on behalf of the first beast. The second beast orders the people to worship an image in honor of the first beast—a direct flouting of the second commandment (Exodus 20:4–6). Allowing the Bible to guide our faith and practice will keep us from being deceived by false signs, however convincing they appear to be. Any teaching that contradicts God's Word is false.

13:16–18 This mark of the beast is designed to mock the seal that God places on his followers (7:2–3). Just as God marks his people to save them, so Satan's beast marks his people to save them from the persecution that Satan will inflict upon God's followers. Identifying this particular mark is not as important as identifying the purpose of the mark. Those who accept it show their allegiance to Satan, their willingness to operate within the economic system he promotes, and their rebellion against God. To refuse the mark means to commit oneself entirely to God, preferring death to compromising one's faith in Christ.

13:16–17 In every generation, Christians need to maintain a healthy skepticism about society's pleasures and rewards. In our educational, economic, and civic structures, there are incentives and rewards. Cooperating Christians must always support what is good and healthy about our society, but we must stand against sin. In some cases, such as Satan's system described here, the system or structure becomes so evil that there is no way to cooperate with it.

13:18 The meaning of this number has been discussed more than that of any other part of the book of Revelation. The three sixes have been said to represent many things, including the number of man or the unholy trinity of Satan, the first beast, and the false prophet (16:13). If the number seven is considered to be the perfect number in the Bible, and if three sevens represent complete perfection, then the number 666 falls completely short of perfection. The first readers of this book probably applied the number to the Emperor Nero, who symbolized all the evils of the Roman empire. (The Greek letters of Nero's name represent numbers that total 666.) Whatever specific application the number is given, the number symbolizes the worldwide dominion and complete evil of this unholy trinity designed to undo Christ's work and overthrow him.

14:1ff Chapter 13 described the onslaught of evil that will occur when Satan and his helpers control the world. Chapter 14 gives a glimpse into eternity to show believers what awaits them if they endure. The Lamb is the Messiah. Mount Zion, often another name for Jerusalem, the capital of Israel, is contrasted with the worldly empire. The 144,000 represent believers who have endured persecutions on earth and now are ready to enjoy the eternal benefits and blessings of life with God forever. The three angels contrast the destiny of believers with that of unbelievers.

4 These are the ones who have not been defiled with women, for they [20]have kept
themselves chaste. These *are* the ones who follow the Lamb wherever He goes. These
have been purchased from among men as first fruits to God and to the Lamb.
5 And no lie was found in their mouth; they are blameless.

Vision of the Angel with the Gospel

6 And I saw another angel flying in midheaven, having an eternal gospel to preach to
those who live on the earth, and to every nation and tribe and tongue and people;
7 and he said with a loud voice, "Fear God, and give Him glory, because the hour of
His judgment has come; worship Him who made the heaven and the earth and sea and
springs of waters."
8 And another angel, a second one, followed, saying, "Fallen, fallen is Babylon the
great, she who has made all the nations drink of the wine of the passion of her immorality."

Doom for Worshipers of the Beast

9 Then another angel, a third one, followed them, saying with a loud voice, "If anyone worships the beast and his image, and receives a mark on his forehead or on his
hand,
10 he also will drink of the wine of the wrath of God, which is mixed in full strength in
the cup of His anger; and he will be tormented with fire and brimstone in the presence
of the holy angels and in the presence of the Lamb.
11 "And the smoke of their torment goes up forever and ever; they have no rest day and
night, those who worship the beast and his image, and whoever receives the mark of his
name."
12 Here is the perseverance of the saints who keep the commandments of God and
their faith in Jesus.
13 And I heard a voice from heaven, saying, "Write, 'Blessed are the dead who die in
the Lord from now on!' " "Yes," says the Spirit, "so that they may rest from their labors,
for their deeds follow with them."

20 Lit *are chaste men*

14:4 Matt 19:12; 2 Cor 11:2; Eph 5:27; Rev 3:4; Rev 3:4; 7:17; 17:14; Rev 5:9; Heb 12:23; James 1:18

14:5 Ps 32:2; Zeph 3:13; Mal 2:6; John 1:47; 1 Pet 2:22; Heb 9:14; 1 Pet 1:19; Jude 24

14:6 Rev 8:13; 1 Pet 1:25; Rev 10:7; Rev 3:10; Rev 5:9

14:7 Rev 15:4; Rev 11:13; Rev 4:11; Rev 8:10

14:8 Is 21:9; Jer 51:8; Rev 18:2; Dan 4:30; Rev 16:19; 17:5; 18:10; Jer 51:7; Rev 17:2, 4; 18:3

14:9 Rev 13:12; 14:11; Rev 13:14f

14:11 Is 34:8-10; Rev 18:9, 18; 19:3; Rev 4:8; Rev 13:12; 14:9; Rev 13:17

14:12 Rev 13:10; Rev 12:17; Rev 2:13

14:13 Rev 20:6; 1 Cor 15:18; 1 Thess 4:16; Rev 2:7; 22:17; Heb 4:9ff; Rev 6:11; 1 Tim 5:25

14:4 These people are true believers whose robes have been washed and made white in Christ's blood (7:14) through his death ("purchased from among men"). In the Old Testament, idolatry was often portrayed as spiritual adultery (see the book of Hosea). Their purity is best understood symbolically, meaning that they are free from involvement with the pagan world system. These believers are spiritually pure; they have remained faithful to Christ, they have followed him exclusively, and they have received God's reward for staying committed to him. "First fruits" refers to the act of dedicating the first part of the harvest as holy to God (Exodus 23:19; see also James 1:18).

14:6–7 Some believe that this is a final, worldwide appeal to all people to recognize the One true God. No one will have the excuse of never hearing God's truth. Others, however, see this as an announcement of judgment rather than as an appeal. The people of the world have had their chance to proclaim their allegiance to God, and now God's great judgment is about to begin. If you are reading this, you have already heard God's truth. You know that God's final judgment will not be put off forever. Have you joyfully received the everlasting Good News? Have you confessed your sins and trusted in Christ to save you? If so, you have nothing to fear from God's judgment. The Judge of all the earth is your Savior!

14:8 Babylon was the name of both an evil city and an immoral empire, a world center for idol worship. Babylon ransacked Jerusalem and carried the people of Judah into captivity (see 2 Kings 24 and 2 Chronicles 36). Just as Babylon was the Jews' worst enemy, the Roman empire was the worst enemy of the early Christians. John, who probably did not dare speak against Rome openly, applied the name *Babylon* to this enemy of God's people (Rome)—and, by extension, to all God's enemies of all times.

14:9–11 Those who worship the beast, accept his mark on their foreheads, and operate according to his world economic system will ultimately face God's judgment. Our world values money, power, and pleasure over God's leadership. To get what the world values, many people deny God and violate Christian principles. Thus they must drink of the wine of God's wrath (see Psalm 75; Isaiah 51:17).

14:11 The ultimate result of sin is unending separation from God. Because human beings are created in God's image with an inborn thirst for fellowship with him, separation from God will be the ultimate torment and misery. Sin always brings misery, but in this life we can choose to repent and restore our relationship with God. In eternity there will no longer be opportunity for repentance. If in this life we choose to be independent of God, in the next life we will be separated from him forever. Nobody is forced to choose eternal separation from God, and nobody suffers this fate by accident. Jesus invites all of us to open the door of our hearts to him (3:20). If we do this, we will enjoy everlasting fellowship with him.

14:12 This news about God's ultimate triumph should encourage God's people to remain faithful through every trial and persecution. They can do this, God promises, by trusting in Jesus and obeying the commands found in his Word. The secret to enduring, therefore, is trust and obedience. Trust God to give you patience to endure even the small trials you face daily; obey him even when obedience is unattractive or dangerous.

14:13 While it is true that money, fame, and belongings can't be taken with us from this life, God's people *can* produce fruit that survives even death. God will remember our love, kindness, and faithfulness, and those who accept Christ through our witness will join us in the new earth. Be sure that your values are in line with God's values, and decide today to produce fruit that lasts forever.

The Reapers

14 Then I looked, and behold, a white cloud, and sitting on the cloud *was* one like [21]a
son of man, having a golden crown on His head and a sharp sickle in His hand.
15 And another angel came out of the temple, crying out with a loud voice to Him who
sat on the cloud, "Put in your sickle and reap, for the hour to reap has come, because the
harvest of the earth is ripe."
16 Then He who sat on the cloud swung His sickle over the earth, and the earth was
reaped.
17 And another angel came out of the temple which is in heaven, and he also had a
sharp sickle.
18 Then another angel, the one who has power over fire, came out from the altar; and
he called with a loud voice to him who had the sharp sickle, saying, "Put in your sharp
sickle and gather the clusters from the vine of the earth, because her grapes are ripe."
19 So the angel swung his sickle to the earth and gathered *the clusters from* the vine of
the earth, and threw them into the great wine press of the wrath of God.
20 And the wine press was trodden outside the city, and blood came out from the wine
press, up to the horses' bridles, for a distance of [22]two hundred miles.

5. Pouring out the seven plagues

A Scene of Heaven

15 Then I saw another sign in heaven, great and marvelous, seven angels who had
seven plagues, *which are* the last, because in them the wrath of God is finished.
2 And I saw something like a sea of glass mixed with fire, and those who had been
victorious over the beast and his image and the number of his name, standing on the sea
of glass, holding harps of God.
3 And they ☆sang the song of Moses, the bond-servant of God, and the song of the
Lamb, saying,
"Great and marvelous are Your works,
O Lord God, the Almighty;
Righteous and true are Your ways,
King of the [23]nations!
4 "Who will not fear, O Lord, and glorify Your name?
For You alone are holy;
For ALL THE NATIONS WILL COME AND WORSHIP BEFORE YOU,
FOR YOUR RIGHTEOUS ACTS HAVE BEEN REVEALED."
5 After these things I looked, and the temple of the tabernacle of testimony in heav-
en was opened,
6 and the seven angels who had the seven plagues came out of the temple, clothed in
[24]linen, clean *and* bright, and girded around their chests with golden sashes.

21 Or *the Son of Man* **22** Lit *sixteen hundred stadia;* a stadion was approx 600 ft **23** Two early mss read *ages*
24 One early ms reads *stone*

14:14 Matt 17:5; Dan 7:13; Rev 1:13; Ps 21:3; Rev 6:2

14:15 Rev 11:19; 14:17; 15:6; 16:17; Joel 3:13; Mark 4:29; Rev 14:18; Jer 51:33; Matt 13:39-41

14:17 Rev 11:19; 14:15; 15:6; 16:17

14:18 Rev 16:8; Rev 6:9; 8:3; Joel 3:13; Mark 4:29; Rev 14:15; Joel 3:13

14:19 Is 63:2f; Rev 19:15

14:20 Is 63:3; Lam 1:15; Rev 19:15; Heb 13:12; Rev 11:8; Gen 49:11; Deut 32:14

15:1 Rev 12:1, 3; Rev 15:6-8; 16:1; 17:1; 21:9; Lev 26:21; Rev 9:20

15:2 Rev 4:6; Rev 12:11; Rev 13:1; Rev 13:14f; Rev 13:17; Rev 5:8

15:3 Ex 15:1ff; Josh 22:5; Heb 3:5; Rev 5:9f, 12f; Deut 32:3f; Ps 111:2; 139:14; Hos 14:9; Rev 1:8; 1 Tim 1:17

15:4 Jer 10:7; Rev 14:7; Ps 86:9; Is 66:23; Rev 19:8

15:5 Rev 11:19; Ex 38:21; Num 1:50; Heb 8:5; Rev 13:6

15:6 Rev 15:1; Rev 14:15; Rev 1:13

14:14–16 This is an image of judgment: Christ is separating the faithful from the unfaithful like a farmer harvesting his crops. This is a time of joy for the Christians who have been persecuted and martyred—they will receive their long-awaited reward. Christians should not fear the Last Judgment. Jesus said, "Truly, truly, I say to you, an hour is coming and now is, when the dead will hear the voice of the Son of God, and those who hear will live" (John 5:24).

14:19 A wine press was a large vat or trough where grapes were collected and then smashed. The juice flowed out of a duct that led into a large holding vat. The wine press is often used in the Bible as a symbol of God's wrath and judgment against sin (Isaiah 63:3–6; Lamentations 1:15; Joel 3:12–13).

14:20 The distance of 200 miles is approximately the north-south length of Palestine.

15:1 The seven last plagues are also called the seven bowl judgments. They actually begin in chapter 16. Unlike the previous plagues, these are universal, and they will culminate in the abolition of all evil ("in them the wrath of God is finished") and the end of the world.

15:2 This is similar to the "sea of glass" described in 4:6, located before the throne of God. Here it is mixed with fire to represent wrath and judgment. Those who stand beside it are victorious over Satan and his evil beast.

15:3–4 The song of Moses celebrated Israel's deliverance from Egypt (Exodus 15). The song of the Lamb celebrates the ultimate deliverance of God's people from the power of Satan.

15:5–8 The *tabernacle of testimony* is a Greek translation for the Hebrew "tent of meeting" (see Exodus 40:34–35). The imagery brings us back to the time of the exodus in the wilderness when the ark of the covenant (the symbol of God's presence among his people) resided in the tabernacle. The angels coming out of the temple are clothed in clean, shining linen with golden sashes around their chests. Their garments, reminiscent of the high priest's clothing, show that they are free from corruption, immorality, and injustice. The smoke that fills the temple is the manifestation of God's glory and power. There is no escape from this judgment.

7 Then one of the four living creatures gave to the seven angels seven golden bowls full of the wrath of God, who lives forever and ever.
8 And the temple was filled with smoke from the glory of God and from His power; and no one was able to enter the temple until the seven plagues of the seven angels were finished.

Six Bowls of Wrath

16 Then I heard a loud voice from the temple, saying to the seven angels, "Go and pour out on the earth the seven bowls of the wrath of God."
2 So the first *angel* went and poured out his bowl on the earth; and it became a loath-
some and malignant sore on the people who had the mark of the beast and who worshiped his image.
3 The second *angel* poured out his bowl into the sea, and it became blood like *that* of
a dead man; and every living [25]thing in the sea died.
4 Then the third *angel* poured out his bowl into the rivers and the springs of waters;
and they became blood.
5 And I heard the angel of the waters saying, "Righteous are You, who are and who
were, O Holy One, because You judged these things;
6 for they poured out the blood of saints and prophets, and You have given them blood
to drink. They deserve it."
7 And I heard the altar saying, "Yes, O Lord God, the Almighty, true and righteous
are Your judgments."
8 The fourth *angel* poured out his bowl upon the sun, and it was given to it to scorch
men with fire.
9 Men were scorched with fierce heat; and they blasphemed the name of God who
has the power over these plagues, and they did not repent so as to give Him glory.
10 Then the fifth *angel* poured out his bowl on the throne of the beast, and his kingdom became darkened; and they gnawed their tongues because of pain,
11 and they blasphemed the God of heaven because of their pains and their sores; and
they did not repent of their deeds.
12 The sixth *angel* poured out his bowl on the great river, the Euphrates; and its water
was dried up, so that the way would be prepared for the kings from the east.

Armageddon

13 And I saw *coming* out of the mouth of the dragon and out of the mouth of the beast
and out of the mouth of the false prophet, three unclean spirits like frogs;
14 for they are spirits of demons, performing signs, which go out to the kings of the
whole world, to gather them together for the war of the great day of God, the Almighty.
15 ("Behold, I am coming like a thief. Blessed is the one who stays awake and keeps
his clothes, so that he will not walk about naked and men will not see his shame.")

25 Lit *soul*

16:1 Rev 11:19; Rev 15:1; Ps 79:6; Jer 10:25; Ezek 22:31; Zeph 3:8; Rev 16:2ff

16:2 Rev 8:7; Ex 9:9-11; Deut 28:35; Rev 16:11; Rev 13:15-17; 14:9

16:3 Ex 7:17-21; Rev 8:8f; 11:6

16:4 Rev 8:10; Ex 7:17-20; Ps 78:44; Rev 11:6

16:6 Rev 17:6; 18:24; Is 49:26; Luke 11:49-51

16:8 Rev 6:12; Rev 14:18

16:10 Rev 13:2; Ex 10:21f; Is 8:22; Rev 8:12; 9:2

16:12 Rev 9:14; Is 11:15f; 44:27; Jer 51:36; Is 41:2, 25; 46:11; Rev 7:2

16:13 Rev 12:3; Rev 13:1; Rev 13:11, 14; 19:20; 20:10; Rev 18:2; Ex 8:6

16:14 1 Tim 4:1; Rev 13:13; Rev 3:10; 1 Kin 22:21-23; Rev 17:14; 19:19; 20:8; Rev 6:17

16:15 Matt 24:43f; Luke 12:39f; Rev 3:3, 11; Luke 12:37; Rev 3:18

15:8 Our eternal reign with Christ won't begin until all evil is destroyed by his judgment. The faithful must wait for his timetable to be revealed.

16:1ff The bowl judgments are God's final and complete judgments on the earth. The end has come. There are many similarities between the bowl judgments and the trumpet judgments (8:6—11:19), but there are three main differences: (1) These judgments are complete, whereas the trumpet judgments are partial; (2) the trumpet judgments still give unbelievers the opportunity to repent, but the bowl judgments do not; and (3) mankind is indirectly affected by several of the trumpet judgments but directly attacked by all the bowl judgments.

16:7 The significance of the altar itself responding is that *everyone and everything* will be praising God, acknowledging his righteousness and perfect justice.

16:9–21 We know that the people realize that these judgments come from God because they curse him for sending them. But they still refuse to recognize God's authority and repent of their sins. Christians should not be surprised at the hostility and hardness of heart of unbelievers. Even when the power of God is fully and completely revealed, many will still refuse to repent. If you find yourself ignoring God more and more, turn back to him now before your heart becomes too hard to repent (see the note on 9:20–21 for more on hard hearts).

16:12 The Euphrates River was a natural protective boundary against the empires to the east (Babylon, Assyria, Persia). If it dried up, nothing could hold back invading armies. The armies from the east symbolize unhindered judgment.

16:13–14 These spirits of demons performing miraculous signs who come out of the mouths of the unholy trinity unite the rulers of the world for battle against God. The imagery of the demons coming out of the mouths of the three evil rulers signifies the verbal enticements and propaganda that will draw many people to their evil cause. For more about demons, see the note on 9:3ff.

16:15 Christ will return unexpectedly (1 Thessalonians 5:1–6), so we must be ready when he returns. We can prepare ourselves by standing firm in temptation and by being committed to God's moral standards. In what ways does your life show either your readiness or your lack of preparation for Christ's return?

16:16
Rev 19:19; Rev 9:11; Judg 5:19; 2 Kin 23:29f; 2 Chr 35:22; Zech 12:11

16:17
Eph 2:2; Rev 11:15; Rev 14:15; Rev 10:6; 21:6

16:18
Rev 4:5; Rev 6:12; Dan 12:1; Matt 24:21

16:21
Rev 8:7; 11:19; Rev 16:9, 11; Ex 9:18-25

17:1
Rev 1:1; 21:9; Rev 15:1; Rev 15:7; Rev 16:19; Is 1:21; Jer 2:20; Nah 3:4; Rev 17:5, 15f; 19:2; Jer 51:13; Rev 17:15

17:2
Rev 2:22; 18:3, 9; Rev 3:10; 17:8; Rev 14:8

17:3
Rev 21:10; Rev 1:10; Rev 12:6, 14; Matt 27:28; Rev 18:12, 16; Rev 13:1; Rev 12:3; 17:7, 9, 12, 16

17:4
Ezek 28:13; Rev 18:12, 16; Jer 51:7; Rev 18:6

17:5
2 Thess 2:7; Rev 1:20; 17:7; Rev 14:8; 16:19; Rev 17:2

17:6
Rev 16:6

17:7
2 Thess 2:7; Rev 1:20; 17:5; Rev 17:3

16 And they gathered them together to the place which in Hebrew is called [26]Har-
Magedon.

Seventh Bowl of Wrath

17 Then the seventh *angel* poured out his bowl upon the air, and a loud voice came out
of the temple from the throne, saying, "It is done."
18 And there were flashes of lightning and sounds and peals of thunder; and there was
a great earthquake, such as there had not been since man came to be upon the earth, so
great an earthquake *was it, and* so mighty.
19 The great city was split into three parts, and the cities of the nations fell. Babylon
the great was remembered before God, to give her the cup of the wine of His fierce wrath.
20 And every island fled away, and the mountains were not found.
21 And huge hailstones, about [27]one hundred pounds each, ☆came down from heaven
upon men; and men blasphemed God because of the plague of the hail, because its plague
☆was extremely severe.

6. Seizing the final victory

The Doom of Babylon

17 Then one of the seven angels who had the seven bowls came and spoke with me,
saying, "Come here, I will show you the judgment of the great harlot who sits on
many waters,
2 with whom the kings of the earth committed *acts of* immorality, and those who dwell
on the earth were made drunk with the wine of her immorality."
3 And he carried me away [28]in the Spirit into a wilderness; and I saw a woman sitting
on a scarlet beast, full of blasphemous names, having seven heads and ten horns.
4 The woman was clothed in purple and scarlet, and adorned with gold and precious
stones and pearls, having in her hand a gold cup full of abominations and of the unclean
things of her immorality,
5 and on her forehead a name *was* written, a mystery, "BABYLON THE GREAT,
THE MOTHER OF HARLOTS AND OF THE ABOMINATIONS OF THE EARTH."
6 And I saw the woman drunk with the blood of the saints, and with the blood of the
witnesses of Jesus. When I saw her, I wondered greatly.
7 And the angel said to me, "Why do you wonder? I will tell you the mystery of the
woman and of the beast that carries her, which has the seven heads and the ten horns.
8 "The beast that you saw was, and is not, and is about to come up out of the abyss and

26 Two early mss read *Armageddon* **27** Lit *the weight of a talent* **28** Or *in spirit*

16:16 This battlefield called Har-Magedon (also called Armageddon) is near the city of Megiddo (southeast of the modern port of Haifa), which guarded a large plain in northern Israel. It is a strategic location near a prominent international highway leading north from Egypt through Israel, along the coast, and on to Babylon. Megiddo overlooked the entire plain southward toward Galilee and westward toward the mountains of Gilboa.

16:16 Sinful people will unite to fight against God in a final display of rebellion. Many are already united against Christ and his people—those who stand for truth, peace, justice, and morality. Your personal battle with evil foreshadows the great battle pictured here, where God will meet evil and destroy it once and for all. Be strong and courageous as you battle against sin and evil: You are fighting on the winning side.

16:17–21 For more information on Babylon and what it represents in Revelation, see the note on 14:8. The city's division into three sections is a symbol of its complete destruction.

17:1ff The destruction of Babylon mentioned in 16:17–21 is now described in greater detail. The "great harlot," called Babylon, represents the early Roman empire with its many gods and the blood of Christian martyrs on its hands. The water stands for either sea commerce or a well-watered (well-provisioned) city. The great harlot represents the seductiveness of the governmental system that uses immoral means to gain its own pleasure, prosperity, and advantage. In contrast to the harlot, Christ's bride, the church, is pure and obedient (19:6–9). The wicked city of Babylon contrasts with the heavenly city of Jerusalem (21:10—22:5). The original readers probably rather quickly identified Babylon with Rome, but Babylon also symbolizes any system that is hostile to God (see 17:5).

17:3 The scarlet beast is either the dragon of 12:3 or the beast from the sea described in 13:1.

17:6 Throughout history, people have been killed for their faith. Over the last century, millions have been killed by oppressive governments, and many of those victims were believers. The woman's drunkenness shows her pleasure in her evil accomplishments and her false feeling of triumph over the church. But every martyr who has fallen before her sword has only served to strengthen the faith of the church.

17:8 In chapter 12 we met the dragon (Satan). In chapter 13 we saw the beast from the sea and the power he received from Satan. In chapters 14—16 we see God's great judgments. In this chapter, a scarlet beast similar to the beast and the dragon appears as an ally of the great prostitute. The phrase, "was and is not and will come" means that the beast was alive, died, and then came back to life. The beast's resurrection symbolizes the persistence of evil. This resurgence of evil power will convince many to join forces with the beast, but those who choose the side of evil condemn themselves to the devil's fate—eternal torment.

17:8 For more information on the book of life, see the note on 3:5.

[29]go to destruction. And those who dwell on the earth, whose name has not been written
in the book of life from the foundation of the world, will wonder when they see the beast,
that he was and is not and will come.
9 "Here is the mind which has wisdom. The seven heads are seven mountains on which
the woman sits,
10 and they are seven kings; five have fallen, one is, the other has not yet come; and
when he comes, he must remain a little while.
11 "The beast which was and is not, is himself also an eighth and is *one* of the seven, and
he goes to destruction.
12 "The ten horns which you saw are ten kings who have not yet received a kingdom,
but they receive authority as kings with the beast for one hour.
13 "These have one purpose, and they give their power and authority to the beast.

Victory for the Lamb

14 "These will wage war against the Lamb, and the Lamb will overcome them, because
He is Lord of lords and King of kings, and those who are with Him *are the* called and
chosen and faithful."
15 And he ☆said to me, "The waters which you saw where the harlot sits, are peoples
and multitudes and nations and tongues.
16 "And the ten horns which you saw, and the beast, these will hate the harlot and will
make her desolate and naked, and will eat her flesh and will burn her up with fire.
17 "For God has put it in their hearts to execute His purpose by having a common purpose, and by giving their kingdom to the beast, until the words of God will be fulfilled.
18 "The woman whom you saw is the great city, which reigns over the kings of the earth."

Babylon Is Fallen

18 After these things I saw another angel coming down from heaven, having great
authority, and the earth was illumined with his glory.
2 And he cried out with a mighty voice, saying, "Fallen, fallen is Babylon the great!
She has become a dwelling place of demons and a prison of every unclean spirit, and a
prison of every unclean and hateful bird.
3 "For all the nations [30]have drunk of the wine of the passion of her immorality, and
the kings of the earth have committed *acts of* immorality with her, and the merchants of
the earth have become rich by the wealth of her sensuality."
4 I heard another voice from heaven, saying, "Come out of her, my people, so that
you will not participate in her sins and receive of her plagues;

17:9 Rev 13:18; Rev 17:3
17:10 Rev 10:11
17:11 Rev 13:3, 12, 14; 17:8; Rev 13:10; 17:8
17:12 Dan 7:24; Rev 12:3; 13:1; 17:16; Rev 18:10, 17, 19
17:13 Rev 17:17
17:14 Rev 16:14; Rev 3:21; 1 Tim 6:15; Rev 19:16; Rev 2:10f; Matt 22:14
17:15 Is 8:7; Jer 47:2; Rev 17:1; Rev 5:9
17:16 Rev 17:12; Rev 18:17, 19; Ezek 16:37, 39; Rev 19:18; Rev 18:8
17:17 2 Cor 8:16; Rev 17:13; Rev 10:7
17:18 Rev 11:8; 16:19
18:1 Rev 17:1, 7; Rev 10:1; Ezek 43:2
18:2 Is 21:9; Jer 51:8; Rev 14:8; Is 13:21f; 34:11, 13-15; Jer 50:39; 51:37; Zeph 2:14f; Rev 16:13
18:4 Is 52:11; Jer 50:8; 51:6, 9, 45; 2 Cor 6:17

29 One early ms reads *is going* **30** Two early ancient mss read *have fallen by*

17:9–11 Here John is referring to Rome, the city famous for its seven mountains. Many say that this city also symbolized all evil in the world—any person, religion, group, government, or structure that opposed Christ. Whatever view is taken of the seven mountains and seven kings, this section indicates the climax of Satan's struggle against God. Evil's power is limited, and its destruction is on the horizon.

17:12 The ten horns represent kings of nations yet to arise. Rome will be followed by other powers. Rome is a good example of how the antichrist's system will work, demanding complete allegiance and ruling by raw power, oppression, and slavery. Whoever the ten kings are, they will give their power to the antichrist and will make war against the Lamb.

17:16 In a dramatic turn of events, the harlot's allies turn on her and destroy her. This is how evil operates. Destructive by its very nature, it discards its own adherents when they cease to serve its purposes. An unholy alliance is an uneasy alliance because each partner puts its own interests first.

17:17 No matter what happens, we must trust that God is still in charge, that God overrules all the plans and intrigues of the evil one, and that God's plans will happen just as he says. God even uses people opposed to him as tools to execute his will. Although he allows evil to permeate this present world, the new earth will never know sin.

18:1ff This chapter shows the complete destruction of Babylon, John's metaphorical name for the evil world power and all it represents. Everything that tries to block God's purposes will come to a violent end. For more information on how the book of Revelation uses the name *Babylon,* see the note on 14:8.

18:2–3 Merchants in the Roman empire grew rich by exploiting the sinful pleasures of their society. Many business people today do the same thing. Businesses and governments are often based on greed, money, and power. Many bright individuals are tempted to take advantage of an evil system to enrich themselves. Christians are warned to stay free from the lure of money, status, and the good life. We are to live according to the values Christ exemplified: service, giving, self-sacrifice, obedience, and truth.

18:4–8 The people of Babylon had lived in luxury and pleasure. The city boasted, "I sit as a queen . . . and never see mourning." The powerful, wealthy people of this world are susceptible to this same attitude. A person who is financially comfortable often feels invulnerable, secure, and in control, feeling no need for God or anyone else. This kind of attitude defies God, and his judgment against it is harsh. We are told to avoid Babylon's sins. If you are financially secure, don't become complacent and deluded by the myth of self-sufficiency. Use your resources to help others and advance God's kingdom.

18:5 Jer 51:9; Rev 16:19
18:6 Ps 137:8; Jer 50:15, 29; Rev 17:4
18:7 Ezek 28:2-8; 1 Tim 5:11; Rev 18:3, 9; Is 47:7f; Zeph 2:15
18:9 Rev 17:2; 18:3; 1 Tim 5:11; Rev 18:3, 7; Ezek 26:16f; 27:35; Rev 14:11; 18:18; 19:3
18:10 Rev 18:15, 17; Rev 18:16, 19; Rev 11:8; 16:19; Rev 17:12; 18:8, 17, 19
18:11 Ezek 27:9-25; Rev 18:3, 15, 19, 23; Ezek 27:27-34
18:12 Ezek 27:12-22; Rev 17:4
18:13 1 Chr 5:21; Ezek 27:13; 1 Tim 1:10
18:15 Rev 18:3; Rev 18:12, 13; Rev 18:10
18:17 Rev 18:10; Rev 17:16; 18:19; Ezek 27:28f
18:18 Ezek 27:30; Rev 18:9; Ezek 27:32; Rev 13:4; Rev 18:10
18:19 Josh 7:6; Job 2:12; Lam 2:10; Rev 18:10; Rev 18:3, 15; Rev 17:16; 18:17

5 for her sins have piled up as high as heaven, and God has remembered her iniquities.
6 "Pay her back even as she has paid, and give back *to her* double according to her deeds;
in the cup which she has mixed, mix twice as much for her.
7 "To the degree that she glorified herself and lived sensuously, to the same degree
give her torment and mourning; for she says in her heart, 'I SIT *as* A QUEEN AND I AM
NOT A WIDOW, and will never see mourning.'
8 "For this reason in one day her plagues will come, pestilence and mourning and famine, and she will be burned up with fire; for the Lord God who judges her is strong.

Lament for Babylon

9 "And the kings of the earth, who committed *acts of* immorality and lived sensuously
with her, will weep and lament over her when they see the smoke of her burning,
10 standing at a distance because of the fear of her torment, saying, 'Woe, woe, the
great city, Babylon, the strong city! For in one hour your judgment has come.'
11 "And the merchants of the earth weep and mourn over her, because no one buys
their cargoes any more—
12 cargoes of gold and silver and precious stones and pearls and fine linen and purple
and silk and scarlet, and every *kind of* citron wood and every article of ivory and every
article *made* from very costly wood and bronze and iron and marble,
13 and cinnamon and spice and incense and perfume and frankincense and wine and
olive oil and fine flour and wheat and cattle and sheep, and *cargoes* of horses and chariots and slaves and human lives.
14 "The fruit you long for has gone from you, and all things that were luxurious and
splendid have passed away from you and *men* will no longer find them.
15 "The merchants of these things, who became rich from her, will stand at a distance
because of the fear of her torment, weeping and mourning,
16 saying, 'Woe, woe, the great city, she who was clothed in fine linen and purple and
scarlet, and adorned with gold and precious stones and pearls;
17 for in one hour such great wealth has been laid waste!' And every shipmaster and
every passenger and sailor, and as many as make their living by the sea, stood at a distance,
18 and were crying out as they saw the smoke of her burning, saying, 'What *city* is like
the great city?'
19 "And they threw dust on their heads and were crying out, weeping and mourning,
saying, 'Woe, woe, the great city, in which all who had ships at sea became rich by her
wealth, for in one hour she has been laid waste!'

HOW CAN A PERSON KEEP AWAY FROM THE EVIL SYSTEM?
Here are some suggestions:

1. People must always be more important than products.
2. Keep away from pride in your own programs, plans, and successes.
3. Remember that God's will and Word must never be compromised.
4. People must always be considered above the making of money.
5. Do what is right, no matter what the cost.
6. Be involved in businesses that provide worthwhile products or services—not just things that feed the world's desires.

18:9–10 Those who are tied to the world's system will lose everything when it collapses. What they have worked for a lifetime to build up will be destroyed in one hour. Those who work only for material rewards will have nothing when they die or when their possessions are destroyed. What can we take with us to the new earth? Our faith, our Christian character, and our relationships with other believers. These are more important than any amount of money, power, or pleasure.

18:9–19 Those who are in control of various parts of the economic system will mourn at Babylon's fall. The political leaders will mourn because they were the overseers of Babylon's wealth and were in a position to enrich themselves greatly. The merchants will mourn because Babylon, the greatest customer for their goods, will be gone. The sea captains will no longer have anywhere to bring their goods because the merchants will have nowhere to sell them. The fall of the evil world system affects all who enjoyed and depended on it. No one will remain unaffected by Babylon's fall.

18:11–13 This list of various merchandise illustrates the extreme materialism of this society. Few of these goods are necessities—most are luxuries. The society had become so self-indulgent that people were willing to use evil means to gratify their desires. Even people had become commodities.

18:11–19 God's people should not live for money, because money will be worthless in eternity. And they should keep on guard constantly against greed, a sin that is always ready to take over their lives.

20 "Rejoice over her, O heaven, and you saints and apostles and prophets, because God
has pronounced judgment for you against her."
21 Then a strong angel took up a stone like a great millstone and threw it into the sea,
saying, " So will Babylon, the great city, be thrown down with violence, and will not be
found any longer.
22 "And the sound of harpists and musicians and flute-players and trumpeters will not
be heard in you any longer; and no craftsman of any craft will be found in you any longer; and the sound of a mill will not be heard in you any longer;
23 and the light of a lamp will not shine in you any longer; and the voice of the bridegroom and bride will not be heard in you any longer; for your merchants were the great
men of the earth, because all the nations were deceived by your sorcery.
24 "And in her was found the blood of prophets and of saints and of all who have been
slain on the earth."

The Fourfold Hallelujah

19 After these things I heard something like a loud voice of a great multitude in heaven,
saying,
"**H**allelujah! Salvation and glory and power belong to our God;
2 BECAUSE HIS JUDGMENTS ARE TRUE AND RIGHTEOUS; for He has judged the great
harlot who was corrupting the earth with her immorality, and HE HAS AVENGED THE
BLOOD OF HIS BOND-SERVANTS ON HER."
3 And a second time they said, "Hallelujah! HER SMOKE RISES UP FOREVER AND
EVER."
4 And the twenty-four elders and the four living creatures fell down and worshiped
God who sits on the throne saying, "Amen. Hallelujah!"
5 And a voice came from the throne, saying,
"**G**ive praise to our God, all you His bond-servants, you who fear Him, the small and
the great."
6 Then I heard *something* like the voice of a great multitude and like the sound of
many waters and like the sound of mighty peals of thunder, saying,
"**H**allelujah! For the Lord our God, the Almighty, reigns.

Marriage of the Lamb

7 "Let us rejoice and be glad and give the glory to Him, for the marriage of the Lamb
has come and His bride has made herself ready."
8 It was given to her to clothe herself in fine linen, bright *and* clean; for the fine linen
is the righteous acts of the saints.
9 Then he ☆said to me, "Write, 'Blessed are those who are invited to the marriage
supper of the Lamb.' " And he ☆said to me, "These are true words of God."
10 Then I fell at his feet to worship him. But he ☆said to me, "Do not do that; I am a
fellow servant of yours and your brethren who hold the testimony of Jesus; worship God.
For the testimony of Jesus is the spirit of prophecy."

18:20 Jer 51:48; Rev 12:12; Luke 11:49f; Rev 6:10; 18:6ff; 19:2

18:21 Rev 5:2; 10:1; Jer 51:63f; Rev 18:10; Ezek 26:21

18:22 Is 24:8; Ezek 26:13; Matt 9:23; Eccl 12:4; Jer 25:10

18:23 Jer 7:34; 16:9; Is 23:8; Rev 6:15; 18:3; Nah 3:4; Rev 9:21

18:24 Rev 16:6; 17:6; Matt 23:35

19:1 Jer 51:48; Rev 11:15; 19:6; Ps 104:35; Rev 19:3, 4, 6; Rev 7:10; Rev 4:11

19:2 Ps 19:9; Rev 6:10; Rev 16:7; Rev 17:1; Deut 32:43; 2 Kin 9:7; Rev 16:6; 18:20

19:3 Ps 104:35; Rev 19:1, 4, 6; Is 34:10; Rev 14:11

19:5 Ps 22:23; 115:13; 134:1; 135:1; Rev 11:18

19:6 Jer 51:48; Rev 11:15; 19:1; Ezek 1:24; Rev 1:15; Rev 6:1; Ps 93:1; 97:1; 99:1; Rev 1:8

19:7 Rev 11:13; Matt 22:2; 25:10; Luke 12:36; John 3:29; Eph 5:23, 32; Rev 19:9; Matt 1:20; Rev 21:2, 9

19:10 Rev 22:8; Acts 10:26; Rev 22:9; Rev 1:1f; Rev 12:17

19:1ff Praise is the heartfelt response to God by those who love him. The more you get to know God and realize what he has done, the more you will respond with praise. Praise is at the heart of true worship. Let your praise of God flow out of your realization of who he is and how much he loves you.

19:1–2 The identity of this great harlot is explained in the note on 17:1ff.

19:1–8 A great multitude in heaven initiates the chorus of praise to God for his victory (19:1–3). Then the 24 elders (identified in the note on 4:4) join the chorus (19:4). Finally, the great choir of heaven once again praises God—the wedding of the Lamb has come (19:6–8). See Matthew 25:1–13 where Christ compares the coming of his kingdom to a wedding for which we must be prepared.

19:7–8 This is the culmination of human history—the judgment of the wicked and the wedding of the Lamb and his bride, the church. The church consists of all faithful believers from all time. The bride's clothing stands in sharp contrast to the gaudy clothing of the great prostitute of 17:4 and 18:16. The bride's clothing is the righteous acts of the saints. These righteous acts are not religious deeds done by believers to their merit, but they reflect the work of Christ to save us (7:9, 14).

19:10 The angel did not accept John's homage and worship because only God is worthy of worship. Like John, it would be easy for us to become overwhelmed by this prophetic pageant. But Jesus is the central focus of God's revelation and his redemptive plan (as announced by the prophets). As you read the book of Revelation, don't get bogged down in all the details of the awesome visions; remember that the overarching theme in all the visions is the ultimate victory of Jesus Christ over evil.

19:11 Ezek 1:1; John 1:51; Rev 4:1; Rev 6:2; 19:19, 21; Rev 3:14; Ps 96:13; Is 11:4

19:12 Dan 10:6; Rev 1:14; Rev 6:2; 12:3; Rev 2:17; 19:16

19:13 Is 63:3; John 1:1

19:14 Rev 19:8; Rev 3:4; 19:8

19:16 Rev 2:17; 19:12; Rev 17:14

19:17 Rev 19:21; Rev 8:13; 1 Sam 17:44; Jer 12:9; Ezek 39:17

19:19 Rev 11:7; 13:1; Rev 16:14, 16; Rev 19:11, 21

The Coming of Christ

11 And I saw heaven opened, and behold, a white horse, and He who sat on it *is* called
Faithful and True, and in righteousness He judges and wages war.
12 His eyes *are* a flame of fire, and on His head *are* many diadems; and He has a name
written *on Him* which no one knows except Himself.
13 *He is* clothed with a robe dipped in blood, and His name is called The Word of God.
14 And the armies which are in heaven, clothed in fine linen, white *and* clean, were
following Him on white horses.
15 From His mouth comes a sharp sword, so that with it He may strike down the nations, and He will rule them with a rod of iron; and He treads the wine press of the fierce
wrath of God, the Almighty.
16 And on His robe and on His thigh He has a name written, "KING OF KINGS, AND
LORD OF LORDS."
17 Then I saw an angel standing in the sun, and he cried out with a loud voice, saying
to all the birds which fly in midheaven, "Come, assemble for the great supper of God,
18 so that you may eat the flesh of kings and the flesh of [31]commanders and the flesh
of mighty men and the flesh of horses and of those who sit on them and the flesh of all
men, both free men and slaves, and small and great."
19 And I saw the beast and the kings of the earth and their armies assembled to make
war against Him who sat on the horse and against His army.

31 I.e. chiliarchs, in command of one thousand troops

THE BEGINNING AND THE END
The Bible records for us the beginning of the world and the end of the world. The story of mankind, from beginning to end—from the fall into sin to redemption and God's ultimate victory over evil—is found in the pages of the Bible.

Genesis	*Revelation*
The sun is created	The sun is not needed
Satan is victorious	Satan is defeated
Sin enters the human race	Sin is banished
People run and hide from God	People are invited to live with God forever
People are cursed	The curse is removed
Tears are shed, with sorrow for sin	No more sin, no more tears or sorrow
The garden and earth are cursed	God's city is glorified, the earth is made new
The fruit from the tree of life is not to be eaten	God's people may eat from the tree of life
Paradise is lost	Paradise is regained
People are doomed to death	Death is defeated, believers live forever with God

19:11 The name "Faithful and True" contrasts with the faithless and deceitful Babylon described in chapter 18.

19:11–21 John's vision shifts again. Heaven opens and Jesus appears, this time not as a Lamb, but as a warrior on a white horse (symbolizing victory). Jesus came first as a Lamb to be a sacrifice for sin, but he will return as a Conqueror and King to execute judgment (2 Thessalonians 1:7–10). Jesus' first coming brought forgiveness; his second will bring judgment. The battle lines have been drawn between God and evil, and the world is waiting for the King to ride onto the field.

19:12 Although Jesus is called "Faithful and True" (19:11), "The Word of God" (19:13), and "King of kings, and Lord of lords" (19:16), this verse implies that no name can do him justice. He is greater than any description or expression the human mind can devise.

19:13 For more about the symbolism of Jesus' clothes being dipped in blood, see the second note on 7:14.

19:16 This title indicates our God's sovereignty. Most of the world is worshiping the beast, the antichrist, whom they believe has all power and authority. Then suddenly out of heaven rides Christ and his army of angels—the "King of kings, and Lord of lords." His entrance signals the end of the false powers.

19:17 This "great supper of God" is a grim contrast to the wedding supper of the Lamb (19:9). One is a celebration; the other is devastation.

19:19 The beast is identified in the note on 13:1.

19:19–21 The battle lines have been drawn, and the greatest confrontation in the history of the world is about to begin. The beast (the antichrist) and the false prophet have gathered the governments and armies of the earth under the antichrist's rule. The enemy armies believe they have come of their own volition; in reality, God has summoned them to battle in order to defeat them. That they would even presume to fight against God shows how their pride and rebellion have perverted their thinking. There really is no fight, however, because the victory was won when Jesus died on the cross for sin and rose from the dead. Thus the evil leaders are immediately captured and sent to their punishment, and the forces of evil are annihilated.

Doom of the Beast and False Prophet

20 And the beast was seized, and with him the false prophet who performed the signs
in his presence, by which he deceived those who had received the mark of the beast and
those who worshiped his image; these two were thrown alive into the lake of fire which
burns with brimstone.
21 And the rest were killed with the sword which came from the mouth of Him who sat
on the horse, and all the birds were filled with their flesh.

Satan Bound

20 Then I saw an angel coming down from heaven, holding the key of the abyss and
a great chain in his hand.
2 And he laid hold of the dragon, the serpent of old, who is the devil and Satan, and
bound him for a thousand years;
3 and he threw him into the abyss, and shut *it* and sealed *it* over him, so that he would
not deceive the nations any longer, until the thousand years were completed; after these
things he must be released for a short time.
4 Then I saw thrones, and they sat on them, and judgment was given to them. And I
saw the souls of those who had been beheaded because of their testimony of Jesus and
because of the word of God, and those who had not worshiped the beast or his image,
and had not received the mark on their forehead and on their hand; and they came to
life and reigned with Christ for a thousand years.
5 The rest of the dead did not come to life until the thousand years were completed.
This is the first resurrection.
6 Blessed and holy is the one who has a part in the first resurrection; over these the
second death has no power, but they will be priests of God and of Christ and will reign
with Him for a thousand years.

Satan Freed, Doomed

7 When the thousand years are completed, Satan will be released from his prison,
8 and will come out to deceive the nations which are in the four corners of the earth,
Gog and Magog, to gather them together for the war; the number of them is like the
sand of the seashore.

19:20 Rev 16:13; Rev 13:13; Rev 13:14; Rev 13:16f; Rev 13:12, 15; Rev 20:10, 14f; 21:8; Is 30:33; Dan 7:11; Rev 14:10

19:21 Rev 19:15; Rev 19:11, 19; Rev 19:17

20:1 Rev 10:1; Rev 1:18; 9:1

20:2 Gen 3:1; Rev 12:9; Is 24:22; 2 Pet 2:4; Jude 6

20:3 Rev 20:1; Dan 6:17; Matt 27:66; Rev 12:9; 20:8, 10

20:4 Dan 7:9; Matt 19:28; Rev 3:21; Dan 7:22; 1 Cor 6:2; Rev 6:9; Rev 1:9; Rev 13:12, 15; Rev 13:16f; John 14:19; Rev 3:21; 5:10; 20:6; 22:5

20:5 Luke 14:14; Phil 3:11; 1 Thess 4:16

20:6 Rev 14:13; Rev 2:11; 20:14; Rev 1:6; Rev 3:21; 5:10; 20:4; 22:5

20:7 Rev 20:2f

19:20 The lake of fire which burns with brimstone is the final destination of the wicked. This lake is different from the abyss (bottomless pit) referred to in 9:1. The antichrist and the false prophet are thrown into the lake of fire. Then their leader, Satan himself, will be thrown into that lake (20:10), and finally death and Hades (20:14). Afterward, everyone whose name is not recorded in the book of life will be thrown into the lake of fire (20:15).

20:1 The angel and the abyss (bottomless pit) are explained in the notes on 9:1 and 19:20.

20:2 The dragon, Satan, is discussed in more detail in the notes on 12:3–4 and 12:9. The dragon is not bound as punishment—that occurs in 20:10—but so that he cannot deceive the nations.

20:2–4 The 1,000 years are often referred to as the *Millennium* (Latin for 1,000). Just how and when this 1,000 years takes place is understood differently among Christian scholars. The three major positions on this issue are called postmillennialism, premillennialism, and amillennialism.

(1) *Postmillennialism* looks for a literal 1,000-year period of peace on earth ushered in by the church. At the end of the 1,000 years, Satan will be unleashed once more, but then Christ will return to defeat him and reign forever. Christ's second coming will not occur until after the 1,000-year period.

(2) *Premillennialism* also views the 1,000 years as a literal time period, but holds that Christ's second coming initiates his 1,000-year reign and that this reign occurs before the final removal of Satan.

(3) *Amillennialism* understands the 1,000-year period to be symbolic of the time between Christ's ascension and his return. This Millennium is the reign of Christ in the hearts of believers and in his church; thus it is another way of referring to the church age. This period will end with the second coming of Christ.

These different views about the Millennium need not cause division and controversy in the church, because each view acknowledges what is most crucial to Christianity—Christ will return, defeat Satan, and reign forever! Whatever and whenever the Millennium is, Jesus Christ will unite all believers; therefore, we should not let this issue divide us.

20:3 John doesn't say why God once again sets Satan free, but it is part of God's plan for judging the world. Perhaps it is to expose those who rebel against God in their hearts and confirm those who are truly faithful to God. Whatever the reason, Satan's release results in the final destruction of all evil (20:12–15).

20:4 The beast's mark is explained in the note on 13:16–18.

20:5–6 Christians hold two basic views concerning this first resurrection. (1) Some believe that the first resurrection is spiritual (in our hearts at salvation), and that the Millennium is our spiritual reign with Christ between his first and second comings. During this time, we are priests of God because Christ reigns in our hearts. In this view, the second resurrection is the bodily resurrection of all people for judgment. (2) Others believe that the first resurrection occurs after Satan has been set aside. It is a physical resurrection of believers who then reign with Christ on the earth for a literal 1,000 years. The second resurrection occurs at the end of this Millennium in order to judge unbelievers who have died.

20:6 The second death is spiritual death—everlasting separation from God (see 21:8).

20:7–9 Gog and Magog symbolize all the forces of evil that band together to battle God. Noah's son, Japheth, had a son named Magog (Genesis 10:2). Ezekiel presents Gog as a leader of forces against Israel (Ezekiel 38; 39).

20:10
Rev 20:2f; Rev 19:20; 20:14, 15; Rev 16:13; Rev 14:10f

20:11
Rev 4:2; Rev 6:14; 21:1; Dan 2:35; Rev 12:8

20:12
Rev 11:18; Dan 7:10; Rev 3:5; 20:15; Matt 16:27; Rev 2:23; 20:13

20:13
1 Cor 15:26; Rev 1:18; 6:8; 21:4; Is 26:19; Matt 16:27; Rev 2:23; 20:12

20:14
1 Cor 15:26; Rev 1:18; 6:8; 21:4; Rev 19:20; 20:10, 15; Rev 20:6

20:15
Rev 3:5; 20:12

21:1
Is 65:17; 66:22; 2 Pet 3:13; 2 Pet 3:10; Rev 20:11

21:3
Lev 26:11f; Ezek 37:27; 48:35; Heb 8:2; Rev 7:15; John 14:23; 2 Cor 6:16

21:4
Is 25:8; Rev 7:17; 1 Cor 15:26; Rev 20:14; Is 35:10; 51:11; 65:19; 2 Cor 5:17; Heb 12:27

9 And they came up on the broad plain of the earth and surrounded the camp of the
saints and the beloved city, and fire came down from heaven and devoured them.
10 And the devil who deceived them was thrown into the lake of fire and brimstone,
where the beast and the false prophet are also; and they will be tormented day and night
forever and ever.

Judgment at the Throne of God

11 Then I saw a great white throne and Him who sat upon it, from whose presence
earth and heaven fled away, and no place was found for them.
12 And I saw the dead, the great and the small, standing before the throne, and books
were opened; and another book was opened, which is *the book* of life; and the dead were
judged from the things which were written in the books, according to their deeds.
13 And the sea gave up the dead which were in it, and death and Hades gave up the
dead which were in them; and they were judged, every one *of them* according to their
deeds.
14 Then death and Hades were thrown into the lake of fire. This is the second death,
the lake of fire.
15 And if anyone's name was not found written in the book of life, he was thrown into
the lake of fire.

7. Making all things new

The New Heaven and Earth

21 Then I saw a new heaven and a new earth; for the first heaven and the first earth
passed away, and there is no longer *any* sea.
2 And I saw the holy city, new Jerusalem, coming down out of heaven from God, made
ready as a bride adorned for her husband.
3 And I heard a loud voice from the throne, saying, "Behold, the tabernacle of God is
among men, and He will dwell among them, and they shall be His people, and God Himself will be among them,[32]
4 and He will wipe away every tear from their eyes; and there will no longer be *any*

32 One early ms reads, and be *their God*

20:9 This is not a typical battle where the outcome is in doubt during the heat of the conflict. Here there is no contest. Two mighty forces of evil—those of the beast (19:19) and of Satan (20:8)—unite to do battle against God. The Bible uses just two verses to describe each battle—the evil beast and his forces are captured and thrown into the lake of fire (19:20–21), and fire from heaven devours Satan and his attacking armies (20:9–10). For God, it is as easy as that. There will be no doubt, no worry, no second thoughts for believers about whether they have chosen the right side. If you are with God, you will experience this tremendous victory with Christ.

20:10 Satan's power is not eternal—he will meet his doom. He began his evil work in humankind at the beginning (Genesis 3:1–6) and continues it today, but he will be destroyed when he is thrown into the lake of fire and brimstone. The devil will be released from the abyss ("his prison," 20:7), but he will never be released from the lake of fire. He will never be a threat to anyone again.

20:12–15 At the judgment, the books are opened. They represent God's judgment, and in them are recorded the deeds of everyone, good or evil. We are not saved by deeds, but deeds are seen as clear evidence of a person's actual relationship with God. The book of life contains the names of those who have put their trust in Christ to save them.

20:14 Death and Hades are thrown into the lake of fire. God's judgment is finished. The lake of fire is the ultimate destination of everything wicked—Satan, the beast, the false prophet, the demons, death, Hades, and all those whose names are not recorded in the book of life because they did not place their faith in Jesus Christ. John's vision does not permit any gray areas in God's judgment. If by faith we have not identified with Christ, confessing him as Lord, there will be no hope, no second chance, no other appeal.

21:1 The earth as we know it will not last forever, but after God's great judgment he will create a new earth (see Romans 8:18–21; 2 Peter 3:7–13). God had also promised Isaiah that he would create a new and eternal earth (Isaiah 65:17; 66:22). The sea in John's time was viewed as dangerous and changeable. It was also the source of the beast (13:1). We don't know how the new earth will look or where it will be, but God and his followers—those whose names are written in the book of life—will be united to live there forever. Will you be there?

21:2–3 The new Jerusalem is where God lives among his people. Instead of our going up to meet him, he comes down to be with us, just as God became man in Jesus Christ and lived among us (John 1:14). Wherever God reigns, there is peace, security, and love.

21:3–4 Have you ever wondered what eternity will be like? The "holy city, new Jerusalem" is described as the place where God will "wipe away every tear from their eyes." Forevermore, there will be no death, mourning, crying, or pain. What a wonderful truth! No matter what you are going through, it's not the last word—God has written the final chapter, and it is about true fulfillment and eternal joy for those who love him. We do not know as much as we would like, but it is enough to know that eternity with God will be more wonderful than we could ever imagine.

death; there will no longer be *any* mourning, or crying, or pain; the first things have passed away."

5 And He who sits on the throne said, "Behold, I am making all things new." And He ☆said, "Write, for these words are faithful and true."

6 Then He said to me, "It is done. I am the Alpha and the Omega, the beginning and the end. I will give to the one who thirsts from the spring of the water of life without cost.

7 "He who overcomes will inherit these things, and I will be his God and he will be My son.

8 "But for the cowardly and unbelieving and abominable and murderers and immoral persons and sorcerers and idolaters and all liars, their part *will be* in the lake that burns with fire and brimstone, which is the second death."

9 Then one of the seven angels who had the seven bowls full of the seven last plagues came and spoke with me, saying, "Come here, I will show you the bride, the wife of the Lamb."

The New Jerusalem

10 And he carried me away [33]in the Spirit to a great and high mountain, and showed me the holy city, Jerusalem, coming down out of heaven from God,

11 having the glory of God. Her brilliance was like a very costly stone, as a stone of crystal-clear jasper.

12 It had a great and high wall, with twelve gates, and at the gates twelve angels; and names *were* written on them, which are *the names* of the twelve tribes of the sons of Israel.

13 *There were* three gates on the east and three gates on the north and three gates on the south and three gates on the west.

14 And the wall of the city had twelve foundation stones, and on them *were* the twelve names of the twelve apostles of the Lamb.

15 The one who spoke with me had a gold measuring rod to measure the city, and its gates and its wall.

16 The city is laid out as a square, and its length is as great as the width; and he measured the city with the rod, [34]fifteen hundred miles; its length and width and height are equal.

17 And he measured its wall, [35]seventy-two yards, *according to* human measurements, which are *also* angelic *measurements.*

21:5 Rev 4:9; 20:11; 2 Cor 5:17; Heb 12:27; Rev 19:9; 22:6
21:6 Rev 10:6; 16:17; Rev 1:8; 22:13; Is 55:1; John 4:10; Rev 7:17; 22:17; Rev 7:17
21:7 Rev 2:7; 2 Sam 7:14; Ps 89:26f; 2 Cor 6:16, 18; Rev 21:3
21:8 1 Cor 6:9; Gal 5:19-21; Rev 9:21; 21:27; 22:15; Rev 19:20; Rev 2:11
21:9 Rev 17:1; Rev 15:7; Rev 15:1; Rev 19:7; 21:2
21:10 Ezek 40:2; Rev 17:3; Rev 1:10; Rev 21:2
21:11 Is 60:1f; Ezek 43:2; Rev 15:8; 21:23; 22:5; Rev 4:3; 21:18, 19; Rev 4:6
21:12 Ezek 48:31-34; Rev 21:15, 21, 25; 22:14
21:17 Deut 3:11; Rev 13:18; Rev 21:9

33 Or *in spirit* **34** Lit *twelve thousand stadia;* a stadion was approx 600 ft **35** Lit *one hundred forty-four cubits*

21:5 God is the Creator. The Bible begins with the majestic story of his creation of the universe, and it concludes with his creation of a new heaven and a new earth. This is a tremendous hope and encouragement for the believer. When we are with God, with our sins forgiven and our future secure, we will be like Christ. We will be made perfect like him.

21:6 Just as God finished the work of creation (Genesis 2:1–3) and Jesus finished the work of redemption (John 19:30), so the Trinity will finish the entire plan of salvation by inviting the redeemed into a new creation.

21:6 For more about the water of life, see the note on 22:1.

21:7–8 The "cowardly" are not those who are fainthearted in their faith or who sometimes doubt or question, but those who turn back from following God. They are not brave enough to stand up for Christ; they are not humble enough to accept his authority over their lives. They are put in the same list as the unbelieving, the vile, the murderers, the liars, the idolaters, the sexually immoral, and those practicing magic arts.

People who overcome endure "to the end" (Mark 13:13). They will receive the blessings that God promised: (1) eating from the tree of life (2:7), (2) escaping from the lake of fire (the "second death," 2:11), (3) receiving a special name (2:17), (4) having authority over the nations (2:26), (5) being included in the book of life (3:5), (6) being a pillar in God's spiritual temple (3:12), and (7) sitting with Christ on his throne (3:21). Those who can endure the testing of evil and remain faithful will be rewarded by God.

21:8 The lake is explained in the notes on 19:20 and 20:14. The second death is spiritual death, meaning either eternal torment or destruction. In either case, it is permanent separation from God.

21:10ff The rest of the chapter is a stunning description of the new city of God. The vision is symbolic and shows us that our new home with God will defy description. We will not be disappointed by it in any way.

21:12–14 The new Jerusalem is a picture of God's future home for his people. The 12 tribes of Israel (21:12) probably represent all the faithful in the Old Testament; the twelve apostles (21:14) represent the church. Thus, both believing Gentiles and Jews who have been faithful to God will live together in the new earth.

21:15–17 The city's measurements are symbolic of a place that will hold all God's people. Given in cubits, these measurements are all multiples of 12, the number for God's people: There were 12 tribes in Israel and 12 apostles who started the church. The walls are 144 (12 x 12) cubits (200 feet) thick; there are 12 layers in the walls, and 12 gates in the city; and the height, length, and breadth are all the same, 12,000 stadia (1,400 miles). The new Jerusalem is a perfect cube, the same shape as the holy of holies in the temple (1 Kings 6:20). These measurements illustrate that this new home will be perfect for us.

21:18 Rev 21:11
21:19 Ex 28.17-20, Is 54:11f; Ezek 28:13
21:21 Rev 21:12, 15, 25
21:22 Matt 24:2; John 4:21; Rev 1:8
21:23 Is 24:23; 60:19, 20; Rev 21:25; 22:5; Rev 21:11
21:24 Is 60:3, 5; Ps 72:10f; Is 49:23; 60:16
21:25 Zech 14:7;
21:26 Ps 72:10f; Is 49:23; 60:16
21:27 Is 52:1; Ezek 44:9; Zech 14:21; Rev 22:14f; Rev 3:5
22:2 Rev 2:7; Eze 47:12

18 The material of the wall was jasper; and the city was pure gold, like clear glass.
19 The foundation stones of the city wall were adorned with every kind of precious stone.
The first foundation stone was jasper; the second, sapphire; the third, chalcedony; the
fourth, emerald;
20 the fifth, sardonyx; the sixth, sardius; the seventh, chrysolite; the eighth, beryl; the
ninth, topaz; the tenth, chrysoprase; the eleventh, jacinth; the twelfth, amethyst.
21 And the twelve gates were twelve pearls; each one of the gates was a single pearl.
And the street of the city was pure gold, like transparent glass.
22 I saw no temple in it, for the Lord God the Almighty and the Lamb are its temple.
23 And the city has no need of the sun or of the moon to shine on it, for the glory of
God has illumined it, and its lamp *is* the Lamb.
24 The nations will walk by its light, and the kings of the earth will bring their glory
into it.
25 In the daytime (for there will be no night there) its gates will never be closed;
26 and they will bring the glory and the honor of the nations into it;
27 and nothing unclean, and no one who practices abomination and lying, shall ever
come into it, but only those whose names are written in the Lamb's book of life.

The River and the Tree of Life

22 Then he showed me a river of the water of life, clear as crystal, coming from the
throne of God and of [36]the Lamb,
2 in the middle of its street. On either side of the river was the tree of life, bearing
twelve [37]*kinds of* fruit, yielding its fruit every month; and the leaves of the tree were for
the healing of the nations.

36 Or *the Lamb. In the middle of its street, and on either side of the river, was* **37** Or crops of *fruit*

WHAT WE KNOW ABOUT ETERNITY

Description	*Reference*
A place prepared for us	John 14:2–3
Unlimited by physical properties (1 Corinthians 15:35–49)	John 20:19–26
We will be like Jesus	1 John 3:2
We will have new bodies	1 Corinthians 15
Our experience will be wonderful	1 Corinthians 2:9
A new environment	Revelation 21:1
A new experience of God's presence (1 Corinthians 13:12)	Revelation 21:3
New emotions	Revelation 21:4
There will be no more death	Revelation 21:4

The Bible devotes much less space to describing eternity than it does to convincing people that eternal life is available as a free gift from God. Most of the brief descriptions of eternity would be more accurately called hints, since they use terms and ideas from present experience to describe what we cannot fully grasp until we are there ourselves. These references hint at aspects of what our future will be like if we have accepted Christ's gift of eternal life.

21:18–21 The picture of walls made of jewels reveals that the new Jerusalem will be a place of purity and durability—it will last forever.

21:22–24 The temple, the center of God's presence among his people, was the primary place of worship. No temple is needed in the new city, however, because God's presence will be everywhere. He will be worshiped throughout the city, and nothing will hinder us from being with him.

21:25–27 Not everyone will be allowed into the new Jerusalem, but "only those whose names are written in the Lamb's book of life." (The book of life is explained in the notes on 3:5 and 20:12–15.) Don't think that you will get in because of your background, personality, or good behavior. Eternal life is available to you only because of what Jesus, the Lamb, has done. Trust him today to secure your citizenship in his new creation.

22:1 The water of life is a symbol of eternal life. Jesus used this same image with the Samaritan woman (John 4:7–14). It pictures the fullness of life with God and the eternal blessings that come when we believe in him and allow him to satisfy our spiritual thirst (see 22:17).

22:2 This tree of life is like the tree of life in the Garden of Eden (Genesis 2:9). After Adam and Eve sinned, they were forbidden to eat from the tree of life because they could not have eternal life as long as they were under sin's control. But because of the forgiveness of sin through the blood of Jesus, there will be no evil or sin in this city. We will be able to eat freely from the tree of life when sin's control over us is destroyed and our eternity with God is secure.

22:2 Why would the nations need to be healed if all evil is gone? John is quoting from Ezekiel 47:12, where water flowing from the temple produces trees with healing leaves. He is not implying that there will be illness in the new earth; he is emphasizing that the water of life produces health and strength wherever it goes.

3 There will no longer be any curse; and the throne of God and of the Lamb will be in **22:3**
it, and His bond-servants will serve Him; Zec 14:11
4 they will see His face, and His name *will be* on their foreheads. **22:4**
5 And there will no longer be *any* night; and they will not have need of the light of a Mt 5:8
lamp nor the light of the sun, because the Lord God will illumine them; and they will **22:5**
reign forever and ever. Rev 21:23
6 And he said to me, "These words are faithful and true"; and the Lord, the God of **22:6**
the spirits of the prophets, sent His angel to show to His bond-servants the things which Rev 1:1
must soon take place.
7 "And behold, I am coming quickly. Blessed is he who heeds the words of the proph- **22:7**
ecy of this book." Rev1:3
8 I, John, am the one who heard and saw these things. And when I heard and saw, I **22:8**
fell down to worship at the feet of the angel who showed me these things. Rev 19:10
9 But he ☆said to me, "Do not do that. I am a fellow servant of yours and of your breth- **22:9**
ren the prophets and of those who heed the words of this book. Worship God." Rev 19:10

The Final Message

10 And he ☆said to me, "Do not seal up the words of the prophecy of this book, for the **22:10**
time is near. Da 8:26
11 "Let the one who does wrong, still do wrong; and the one who is filthy, still be filthy; **22:11**
and let the one who is righteous, still practice righteousness; and the one who is holy, Eze 3:27
still keep himself holy."
12 "Behold, I am coming quickly, and My reward *is* with Me, to render to every man **22:12**
according to what he has done. Isa 40:10
13 "I am the Alpha and the Omega, the first and the last, the beginning and the end."
14 Blessed are those who wash their robes, so that they may have the right to the tree
of life, and may enter by the gates into the city.
15 Outside are the dogs and the sorcerers and the immoral persons and the murderers **22:15**
and the idolaters, and everyone who loves and practices lying. Gal 5:9-21; Php 3:2
16 "I, Jesus, have sent My angel to testify to you these things for the churches. I am the **22:16**
root and the descendant of David, the bright morning star." Rev 1:1; Rev 5:5
17 The Spirit and the bride say, "Come." And let the one who hears say, "Come." And

---

22:3 "There will no longer be any curse" means that nothing accursed will be in God's presence. This fulfills Zechariah's prophecy (see Zechariah 14:11).

22:8–9 Hearing or reading an eyewitness account is the next best thing to seeing the event yourself. John witnessed the events reported in Revelation and wrote them down so we could see and believe as he did. If you have read this far, you have seen. Have you also believed?

22:8–9 The first of the Ten Commandments is "You shall have no other gods before Me" (Exodus 20:3). Jesus said that the greatest command of Moses' laws was "You shall love the Lord your God with all your heart, and with all your soul, and with all your mind" (Matthew 22:37). Here, at the end of the Bible, this truth is reiterated. The angel instructs John to "worship God." God alone is worthy of our worship and adoration. He is above all creation, even the angels. Are there people, ideas, goals, or possessions that occupy the central place in your life, crowding God out? Worship *only* God by allowing nothing to distract you from your devotion to him.

22:10–11 The angel tells John what to do after his vision is over. Instead of sealing up what he has written, as Daniel was commanded to do (Daniel 12:4–12), the book is to be left open so that all can read and understand. Daniel's message was sealed because it was not a message for Daniel's time. But the book of Revelation was a message for John's time, and it is relevant today. As Christ's return gets closer, there is a greater polarization between God's followers and Satan's followers. We must read the book of Revelation, hear its message, and be prepared for Christ's imminent return.

22:12–14 Those who wash their robes are those who seek to purify themselves from a sinful way of life. They strive daily to remain faithful and ready for Christ's return. This concept is also explained in the second note on 7:14.

22:14 In Eden, Adam and Eve were barred from any access to the tree of life because of their sin (Genesis 3:22–24). In the new earth, God's people will eat from the tree of life because their sins have been removed by Christ's death and resurrection. Those who eat the fruit of this tree will live forever. If Jesus has forgiven your sins, you will have the right to eat from this tree. For more on this concept, see the first note on 22:2.

22:15 The exact location of these sinners is not known, nor is it relevant. They are outside. They were judged and condemned in 21:7–8. The emphasis is that nothing evil and no sinner will be in God's presence to corrupt or harm any of the faithful.

22:16 Jesus is both David's "root" and "descendant." As the Creator of all, Jesus existed long before David. As a human, however, he was one of David's direct descendants (see Isaiah 11:1–5; Matthew 1:1–17). As the Messiah, he is the "bright morning star," the light of salvation to all.

22:17 Both the Holy Spirit and the bride, the church, extend the invitation to all the world to come to Jesus and experience the joys of salvation in Christ.

22:17 When Jesus met the Samaritan woman at the well, he told her of the living water that he could supply (John 4:10–15). This image is used again as Christ invites anyone to come and drink of the water of life. The gospel is unlimited in scope—all people everywhere may come. Salvation cannot be earned, but God gives it freely. We live in a world desperately thirsty for living water, and many are dying of thirst. But it's still not too late. Let us invite everyone to come and drink.

let the one who is thirsty come; let the one who wishes take the water of life without
cost.

22:18 Dt 4:2; Pr 30:6

18 I testify to everyone who hears the words of the prophecy of this book: if anyone
adds to them, God will add to him the plagues which are written in this book;
19 and if anyone takes away from the words of the book of this prophecy, God will take
away his part from the tree of life and from the holy city, which are written in this book.
20 He who testifies to these things says, "Yes, I am coming quickly." Amen. Come, Lord
Jesus.

22:21 Ro 16:20

21 The grace of the Lord Jesus be with [38]all. Amen.

38 One early ms reads *the saints*

22:18–19 This warning is given to those who might purposefully distort the message in this book. Moses gave a similar warning in Deuteronomy 4:1–4. We too must handle the Bible with care and great respect so that we do not distort its message, even unintentionally. We should be quick to put its principles into practice in our lives. No human explanation or interpretation of God's Word should be elevated to the same authority as the text itself.

22:20 We don't know the day or the hour, but Jesus is coming soon and unexpectedly. This is good news to those who trust him, but a terrible message for those who have rejected him and stand under judgment. *Quickly* means at any moment, and we must be ready for him, always prepared for his return. Would Jesus' sudden appearance catch you off guard?

22:21 Revelation closes human history as Genesis opened it—in paradise. But there is one distinct difference in Revelation—evil is gone forever. Genesis describes Adam and Eve walking and talking with God; Revelation describes people worshiping God face-to-face. Genesis describes a garden with an evil serpent; Revelation describes a perfect city with no evil. The Garden of Eden was destroyed by sin; but paradise is re-created in the new Jerusalem.

The book of Revelation ends with an urgent request: "Come, Lord Jesus." In a world of problems, persecution, evil, and immorality, Christ calls us to endure in our faith. Our efforts to better our world are important, but their results cannot compare with the transformation that Jesus will bring about when he returns. He alone controls human history, forgives sin, and will re-create the earth and bring lasting peace.

Revelation is, above all, a book of hope. It shows that no matter what happens on earth, God is in control. It promises that evil will not last forever. And it depicts the wonderful reward that is waiting for all those who believe in Jesus Christ as Savior and Lord.

BIBLICAL UNIT		APPROXIMATE AMERICAN EQUIVALENT		APPROXIMATE METRIC EQUIVALENT	
		WEIGHTS			
talent	(60 minas)	75	pounds	34	kilograms
mina	(50 shekels)	1 1/4	pounds	0.6	kilogram
shekel	(2 bekas)	2/5	ounce	11.5	grams
pim	(2/3 shekel)	1/3	ounce	7.6	grams
beka	(10 gerahs)	1/5	ounce	5.5	grams
gerah		1/50	ounce	0.6	gram
		LENGTH			
cubit		18	inches	0.5	meter
span		9	inches	23	centimeters
handbreadth		3	inches	8	centimeters
		CAPACITY			
		Dry Measure			
cor [homer]	(10 ephahs)	6	bushels	220	liters
lethek	(5 ephahs)	3	bushels	110	liters
ephah	(10 omers)	3/5	bushel	22	liters
seah	(1/3 ephah)	7	quarts	7.3	liters
omer	(1/10 ephah)	2	quarts	2	liters
cab	(1/18 ephah)	1	quart	1	liter
		Liquid Measure			
bath	(1 ephah)	6	gallons	22	liters
hin	(1/6 bath)	4	quarts	4	liters
log	(1/72 bath)	1/3	quart	0.3	liter

The figures of the table are calculated on the basis of a shekel equaling 11.5 grams, a cubit equaling 18 inches and an ephah equaling 22 liters. The quart referred to is either a dry quart (slightly larger than a liter) or a liquid quart (slightly smaller than a liter), whichever is applicable. The ton referred to in the footnotes is the American ton of 2,000 pounds.

This table is based upon the best available information, but it is not intended to be mathematically precise; like the measurement equivalents in the footnotes, it merely gives the approximate amounts and distances. Weights and measures differed somewhat at various times and places in the ancient world. There is uncertainty particularly about the ephah and the bath; further discoveries may shed more light on these units of capacity.

ABBREVIATIONS IN THE INDEX TO NOTES

Following is a list of abbreviations in the Index to Notes:

BOOKS OF THE BIBLE

Genesis	Gn	Isaiah	Is	Romans	Rom
Exodus	Ex	Jeremiah	Jer	1 Corinthians	1 Cor
Leviticus	Lv	Lamentations	Lam	2 Corinthians	2 Cor
Numbers	Nm	Ezekiel	Ez	Galatians	Gal
Deuteronomy	Dt	Daniel	Dn	Ephesians	Eph
Joshua	Jos	Hosea	Hos	Philippians	Phil
Judges	Jgs	Joel	Jl	Colossians	Col
Ruth	Ru	Amos	Am	1 Thessalonians	1 Thes
1 Samuel	1 Sm	Obadiah	Ob	2 Thessalonians	2 Thes
2 Samuel	2 Sm	Jonah	Jon	1 Timothy	1 Tm
1 Kings	1 Kgs	Micah	Mi	2 Timothy	2 Tm
2 Kings	2 Kgs	Nahum	Na	Titus	Ti
1 Chronicles	1 Chr	Habakkuk	Hb	Philemon	Phlm
2 Chronicles	2 Chr	Zephaniah	Zep	Hebrews	Heb
Ezra	Ezr	Haggai	Hg	James	Jas
Nehemiah	Neh	Zechariah	Zec	1 Peter	1 Pt
Esther	Est	Malachi	Mal	2 Peter	2 Pt
Job	Jb	Matthew	Mt	1 John	1 Jn
Psalms	Ps	Mark	Mk	2 John	2 Jn
Proverbs	Prv	Luke	Lk	3 John	3 Jn
Ecclesiastes	Eccl	John	Jn	Jude	Jude
Song of Solomon	Song	Acts	Acts	Revelation	Rv

INDEX TO NOTES

This is an index to the notes, charts, maps, and personality profiles in the *Life Application Study Bible*. Every entry concerning a note has a Bible reference and a page number; every entry concerning a chart, map, or personality profile has a page number. In some instances, a Bible reference is followed by a number in parentheses to indicate that there is more than one note on that particular Scripture. For example, Rv 1:1(2) means that the reader should look up the second note with the heading of 1:1 in Revelation. In most cases, the entries follow in Biblical/canonical order (i.e., from Genesis to Revelation). In some cases, however, the entries follow a chronological order—this is especially true with important people in the Bible. Following the general index are special indexes: Index to Charts, Index to Maps, and Index to Personality Profiles. Because of the emphasis on application in the *Life Application Study Bible*, these indexes are helpful guides for personal and group Bible study, sermon preparation, or teaching.

FAITHFULNESS

FALSE PROPHET, THE

FALSE TEACHERS, TEACHINGS & PROPHETS

FAME

FAMILY, FAMILIES

FAMILY TREE

GOD, KINGDOM OF

GODLINESS

GODS/GODDESSES

GOD'S LAW

GOD'S WILL

GOD'S WORD

GOG

GOLD

GOLDEN CALF

GOLDEN RULE

GOLGOTHA

GOLIATH

SIN, DESERT OF

SINAI, MOUNT

SINCERITY

SINGING, SONGS

SINGLE-MINDEDNESS

SINGLENESS

SINLESSNESS

SIN OFFERING

SISERA

SKEPTICISM

INDEX TO CHARTS

INDEX TO MAPS

Note: maps concerning Jesus' ministry are given in chronological order—see Harmony of the Gospels.

INDEX TO PERSONALITY PROFILES

DICTIONARY–CONCORDANCE–THESAURUS

to the New American Standard Bible

Main entries usually are followed by explanatory notes or by synonyms or related words, which are intended to assist the reader in locating a verse. In the notes, the root meaning of the entry, if known, is first given in parentheses. The abbreviation "unc" is added if the root meaning is uncertain. The meaning itself is in italic typeface, and any additional information is in roman. Unless otherwise indicated, the meaning is from Greek or Hebrew. Roman typeface is used when part of the meaning is implied, but technically is not part of the root meaning (see SAUL). In the explanation, if a word or phrase is cited from the NASB, italic is used (see ADAM). Foreign words and titles of works of literature are also in italic, following standard practice. The concordance portion provides excerpts of Scripture containing the main entry or related descriptions with references. Contributors: W. Don Wilkins, Th.M., Ph.D., General Editor; Duane Wetzler, Ph.D.; Alfred S. Fox, M.A., M.Div.; Robert G. Lambeth, LL.D.; Samuel P. Molina, M.Div., of The Lockman Foundation.

A

AARON (unc, *enlightenment, bright*). *The older brother of Moses and his spokesman. He was the head of the hereditary priesthood in Israel and its first high priest.*
brother of Moses ... Ex 4:14
spokesman for Moses ... Ex 4:28;7:1-2
as priest ... Ex 28:1;29:44
rod of ... Num 17:8; Heb 9:4
critical of Moses ... *Num 12:1*
death ... Deut 10:6

ABADDON *(destruction)*. 1) With the meaning of destruction or ruin it refers to: a) the place of the dead, i.e. the grave; b) the place of ruin in Sheol; c) death. 2) A satanic angel (Gr *Apollyon*, Rev 9:11).
1 *region of dead* ... Job 26:6; Prov 15:11
2 *angel of bottomless pit* ... Rev 9:11

ABANDON *leave*
LORD has *a-ed* us ... Judg 6:13
not *a* His people ... 1 Sam 12:22
a the remnant ... 2 Kin 21:14
not *a* my soul to ... Ps 16:10
not *a* His people ... Ps 94:14
a-ed My inheritance ... Jer 12:7
a my soul to Hades ... Acts 2:27

ABASE *humble*
man will be *a-d* ... Is 2:11
lofty will be *a-d* ... Is 10:33
a the haughtiness ... Is 13:11
a-d before all ... Mal 2:9

ABATED *decreased*
water was *a* ... Gen 8:8
his vigor *a* ... Deut 34:7

ABBA *father* (Aram, *my father*). Jesus addressed God with this word in a time of most intense suffering, just before the cross. Believers are given the privilege of addressing God the Father with the same word.
A! Father ... Mark 14:36
we cry out, *A!* ... Rom 8:15

ABED-NEGO *(servant of Nego)*. The name given to Azariah, Daniel's companion, by the Babylonians when he was chosen to serve in the royal court. He was thrown into a fiery furnace for not worshiping their idol, but was miraculously delivered by God.
Hebrew name Azariah ... Dan 1:6,7
friend of Daniel ... Dan 2:17
faithful to God ... Dan 3:16,17
cast into furnace ... Dan 3:20

ABEL *(vapor, breath)*. The second son of Adam and Eve, a shepherd by occupation. He was killed by his older brother Cain because God honored Abel's sacrifice and not Cain's.
son of Adam ... Gen 4:2
shepherd ... Gen 4:2
favored by God ... Gen 4:4
slain by Cain ... Gen 4:8
called righteous ... Matt 23:35

ABHOR *despise, detest*
associates *a* me ... Job 19:19
greatly *a-red* Israel ... Ps 78:59
nations will *a* him ... Prov 24:24
To the One *a-red* ... Is 49:7
A what is evil ... Rom 12:9

ABIATHAR *(the father is preeminent)*. A priest who escaped when Saul massacred 84 other priests at Nob. He joined David, but later supported Adonijah in his rebellion against David (1 Sam 30:7).

ABIB
early name of first month of Hebrew calendar ... Ex 34:18
month of Passover and Unleavened Bread ... Deut 16:1

ABIDE *remain, stay* Often describes the believer's continuance in Christ as in John 15 and 1 John.
LORD *a-s* forever ... Ps 9:7
a in Your tent ... Ps 15:1
a in the shadow ... Ps 91:1
wrath of God *a-s* ... John 3:36
If you *a* in Me ... John 15:7
a in My love ... John 15:9
now faith...*a* ... 1 Cor 13:13
love of God *a* ... 1 John 3:17
God *a-s* in us ... 1 John 4:12

ABIGAIL (unc, *my father is joy*). Wife of Nabal. After his death, she became David's second wife and bore him a son. A very beautiful and wise woman.
1 *wife of Nabal* ... 1 Sam 25:3
kind to David ... 1 Sam 25:18ff
wife of David ... 1 Sam 25:42
2 *daughter of Nahash* ... 2 Sam 17:25

ABIHU *(he is my father)*. The second son of Aaron to be consecrated as priest. On one occasion he briefly saw God. He lost his life for making an inappropriate offering of incense to God.
son of Aaron ... Ex 6:23
priest ... Ex 28:1
disobeyed God ... Lev 10:1
judged by God ... Lev 10:2

ABIJAH *(my father is Yahweh)*.
1 *son of Samuel* ... 1 Sam 8:2
2 *son of Jeroboam I, king of Israel* ... 1 Kin 14:1
3 *son of Becher* ... 1 Chr 7:8
4 *line of Eleazar* ... 1 Chr 24:10
5 *king of Judah* ... 2 Chr 12:16
6 *Hezekiah's mother* ... 2 Chr 29:1
7 *priest who sealed a covenant of repentance and confession in the days of Nehemiah* ... Neh 10:7;12:4

ABILITY *power, strength*
According to their *a* ... Ezra 2:69
a for serving ... Dan 1:4
a to conceive ... Heb 11:11

ABIMELECH *(father of a king)*. Two kings of Gerar and Philistia respectively, to whom

Abraham and later Isaac tried to present their wives as their sisters, in order to protect themselves.
1 *king of Gerar* ... Gen 20:1-18
2 *king of Gerar* ... Gen 26:1ff
3 *king of Shechem* ... Judg 9:1ff
4 *priest* ... 1 Chr 18:16
5 *Psalm title* ... Ps 34

ABIRAM
opposed Moses ... Num 16:1ff
judged by God ... Num 16:25ff

ABISHAI
brother of Joab ... 1 Sam 26:6
warrior of David ... 1 Chr 18:12
aided Abner's assassination ... 2 Sam 3:30

ABLE *qualified*
a to judge ... 1 Kin 3:9
from these stones God...*a* ... Matt 3:9
I am *a* to do ... Matt 9:28
Him who is *a* ... Matt 10:28
a to separate us ... Rom 8:39
what you are *a* ... 1 Cor 10:13
a to comprehend ... Eph 3:18
be *a* to teach ... 2 Tim 2:2
a to save Him ... Heb 5:7
One who is *a* ... James 4:12
a to open ... Rev 5:3

ABNER *(my father is a lamp).* Uncle of King Saul and a high ranking officer in his army.
Saul's commander ... 1 Sam 17:55
loyal to David ... 2 Sam 3:12ff
killed by Joab ... 2 Sam 3:27
mourned by David ... 2 Sam 3:32

ABODE *habitation*
a of righteousness ... Jer 31:23
Our *a* with him ... John 14:23
their proper *a* ... Jude 6

ABOLISH
not come to *a* ... Matt 5:17
a-ing in His flesh ... Eph 2:15
who *a-ed* death ... 2 Tim 1:10

ABOMINABLE *detestable*
committed *a* deeds ... Ps 14:1
your beauty *a* ... Ezek 16:25
a idolatries ... 1 Pet 4:3
unbelieving and *a* ... Rev 21:8

ABOMINATION *hated thing* Something detestable. Specifically, idolatry is an abomination to God.
see also **ABOMINATION OF DESOLATION**
a to the Egyptians ... Ex 8:26
a into your house ... Deut 7:26
seen their *a-s* ... Deut 29:17
a to the LORD ... Prov 3:32
all their *a-s* ... Ezek 33:29
a-s of the earth ... Rev 17:5

ABOMINATION OF DESOLATION
A prophetic reference to the Antichrist or to an idol that he will set up in the temple in Jerusalem along with pagan sacrifices during the Great Tribulation. The term is used by Daniel and by Jesus.
a of desolation ... Dan 11:31
a of desolation ... Matt 24:15

ABOUND *excel, be plentiful*
faithful man will *a* ... Prov 28:20
May your peace *a* ... Dan 4:1
a in hope ... Rom 15:13
a-ing in the work ... 1 Cor 15:58
affection *a-s* ... 2 Cor 7:15
all grace *a* ... 2 Cor 9:8

ABOVE *over*
exalted *a* the heavens ... Ps 57:5
disciple is not *a* ... Matt 10:24
I am from *a* ... John 8:23
a every name ... Phil 2:9
exalts himself *a* ... 2 Thess 2:4
gift is from *a* ... James 1:17

ABRAHAM *(father of multitudes).* First of the biblical patriarchs, and the father of the nation of Israel. He had great faith in God, for which he was called "friend of God."
covenant ... Gen 17:1-8
promise of Isaac ... Gen 17:19
asked the Lord ... Gen 18:22ff
offers Isaac ... Gen 22:9,10
death ... Gen 25:8
righteousness of ... Rom 4:3-9

ABRAHAM'S BOSOM
see **PARADISE**
rabbinic terminology for Paradise ... Luke 16:22

ABRAM
called of God ... Gen 12:1-3
rescued Lot ... Gen 14:14-16
covenant with God ... Gen 15:18
name changed ... Gen 17:5

ABSALOM *(father of peace).* Son of King David who rebelled against his father and distanced himself from him. Later he tried to usurp the throne, but in an ensuing battle lost his life.
son of David ... 2 Sam 13:1
his revolt ... 2 Sam 15:1,2
popular ... 2 Sam 15:6
slain by Joab ... 2 Sam 18:15

ABSENT *being away*
we are *a* one from ... Gen 31:49
a in body ... 1 Cor 5:3
a from the Lord ... 2 Cor 5:6
a from the body ... 2 Cor 5:8

ABSTAIN *refrain from*
a from wine ... Num 6:3
a-ing from foods ... 1 Tim 4:3
a from wickedness ... 2 Tim 2:19
a from fleshly lusts ... 1 Pet 2:11

ABUNDANCE *plenty, surplus*
seven years of *a* ... Gen 41:34
a of all things ... Deut 28:47
a of Your house ... Ps 36:8
a of peace ... Ps 72:7
a of counselors ... Prov 24:6
he who loves *a* ... Eccl 5:10
delight yourself in *a* ... Is 55:2
one has an *a* ... Luke 12:15
the *a* of grace ... Rom 5:17

ABUNDANT *enough, plenteous*
come...find *a* water ... 2 Chr 32:4
a righteousness ... Job 37:23
a in lovingkindness ... Ps 86:5
comfort is *a* ... 2 Cor 1:5

ABUNDANTLY
they may breed *a* ... Gen 8:17
Populate the earth *a* ... Gen 9:7
will prosper you *a* ... Deut 30:9
drip upon man *a* ... Job 36:28

ABUSE (n) *insulting speech*
hurling *a* at Him ... Matt 27:39
was hurling *a* ... Luke 23:39

ABUSE (v) *hurt, molest*
a-d her all night ... Judg 19:25
uncircumcised...*a* me ... 1 Chr 10:4

ABUSIVE *filthy, vulgar*
a speech from your ... Col 3:8
strife, *a* language ... 1 Tim 6:4

ABYSS *deep, depth (bottomless).* In Rom 10:7, probably the abode of the dead. Elsewhere, the abode and future prison of demons, the Antichrist and Satan.
go away into the *a* ... Luke 8:31
descend into the *a* ... Rom 10:7
angel of the *a* ... Rev 9:11
key of the *a* ... Rev 20:1

ACACIA A small tree whose wood is valued for its durability. Several pieces of furniture for the temple, including the ark of the covenant and the altars of incense and burnt offering were constructed from acacia (Ex 25:23; 27:1).

ACCEPT *receive*
a the work of ... Deut 33:11
a good from God ... Job 2:10
the LORD *a-ed* Job ... Job 42:9
a-ed no chastening ... Jer 2:30
hear the word and *a* ... Mark 4:20
God has *a-ed* him ... Rom 14:3
a one another ... Rom 15:7

ACCEPTABLE *pleasing*
my heart Be *a* ... Ps 19:14
sacrifice, *a* to God ... Rom 12:1
a to the saints ... Rom 15:31
now is the *a* time ... 2 Cor 6:2
to God an *a* service ... Heb 12:28
sacrifices *a* to God ... 1 Pet 2:5

ACCESS *approach, entry* Freedom to approach an important person or a restricted area. In the NT, specifically the privilege to communicate with God the Father in prayer.
grant you free *a* ... Zech 3:7
our *a* in one Spirit ... Eph 2:18

ACCOMPANY *attach to, follow*
who *a* my lord ... 1 Sam 25:27
a-ied the king ... 2 Sam 19:40
a-ied by trumpets ... 2 Chr 5:13
allowed no one to *a* ... Mark 5:37
that *a* salvation ... Heb 6:9

ACCOMPLISH *perform, realize*
a-ed deliverance ... 1 Sam 11:13
shall *a* my desire ... 1 Kin 5:9
God...*a-es all things* ... Ps 57:2
has *a-ed* His wrath ... Lam 4:11
a-ed redemption ... Luke 1:68
a His work ... John 4:34
I am *a-ing* a work ... Acts 13:41
when sin is *a-ed* ... James 1:15
man can *a* much ... James 5:16

ACCORD *agreement, union*
one *a* to fight ... Josh 9:2
voices...with one *a* ... Acts 4:24
one *a* in Solomon's ... Acts 5:12

crowds with one *a* ... Acts 8:6
one *a* they came ... Acts 12:20

ACCORDING
a to your word ... Gen 30:34
Moses did; *a* to all ... Ex 40:16
a to our sins ... Ps 103:10
a to his deeds ... Matt 16:27
a to the revelation ... Rom 16:25
heirs *a* to promise ... Gal 3:29
a to His riches ... Phil 4:19

ACCOUNT (n) *reckoning* A report of various kinds, e.g. 1) a historical record of events, as in Gen 2:4 and Luke 1:1; and 2) a report and explanation of one's actions stated to superiors. The latter includes a report given to God concerning the use of one's gifts and opportunities day by day and, ultimately, at the judgment seat of Christ, as in Rom 14:12.
the *a* of the heavens ... Gen 2:4
On whose *a has* this ... Jon 1:8
settled *a-s* with ... Matt 25:19
who will give an *a* ... Heb 13:17

ACCOUNT (v) *reckon*
do not *a this* sin ... Num 12:11
I am *a-ed* wicked ... Job 9:29
You have taken *a* of ... Ps 56:8
are *a-ed* as nothing ... Dan 4:35

ACCURATELY *correctly*
teaching *a*...things ... Acts 18:25
a handling...word ... 2 Tim 2:15

ACCURSED *damned*
camp of Israel *a* ... Josh 6:18
be *thought a* ... Is 65:20
Depart...*a* ones ... Matt 25:41
he is to be *a* ... Gal 1:8
in greed, *a* children ... 2 Pet 2:14

ACCUSATION *charge of wrong*
wrote an *a* against ... Ezra 4:6
find a ground of *a* ... Dan 6:4
What *a* do you ... John 18:29
a against my nation ... Acts 28:19
Do not receive an *a* ... 1 Tim 5:19

ACCUSE *testify against*
a-d his brother ... Deut 19:18
a-s you in judgment ... Is 54:17
He was being *a-d* ... Matt 27:12
a-ing...vehemently ... Luke 23:10
a you before the ... John 5:45
alternately *a-ing* ... Rom 2:15
not *a-d* of dissipation ... Titus 1:6
unjustly *a-ing* us ... 3 John 10

ACCUSER *complainant*
see **ADVERSARY**
they act as my *a-s* ... Ps 109:4
instructing his *a-s* ... Acts 23:30
when the *a-s* stood ... Acts 25:18
a of our brethren ... Rev 12:10

ACHAIA The southern part of ancient Greece including the Peloponnesus, where Corinth is located. In Roman times it referred to all of Greece south of Thessaly.
province of Greece ... Acts 18:12; Rom 15:26; 1 Cor 16:15

ACHAN *(troubler).* A man from the tribe of Judah who, against the divinely imposed ban, took spoils from the conquest of Jericho. This resulted in a military defeat for the Israelites. He was stoned to death for the offense.
stole from Jericho ... Josh 7:1
executed by people ... Josh 7:25

ACHISH A Philistine king from whom David sought protection while fleeing from Saul (1 Sam 27:3).

ACKNOWLEDGE *confess*
I *a-d* my sin ... Ps 32:5
all your ways *a* Him ... Prov 3:6
Pharisees *a* them all ... Acts 23:8
see fit to *a* God ... Rom 1:28

ACQUAINTED *familiar with*
a with all my ways ... Ps 139:3
a with grief ... Is 53:3

ACQUAINTANCE *friend*
a-s are...estranged ... Job 19:13
dread to my *a-s* ... Ps 31:11
removed my *a-s* far ... Ps 88:8
relatives and *a-s* ... Luke 2:44
And all His *a-s* ... Luke 23:49

ACQUIRE *get, purchase*
a property in it ... Gen 34:10
have *a-d* Ruth ... Ruth 4:10
a wise counsel ... Prov 1:5
You have *a-d* riches ... Ezek 28:4
Do not *a* gold ... Matt 10:9

ACQUIT *declare innocent*
not *a* me of my guilt ... Job 10:14
A me of hidden *faults* ... Ps 19:12
You will not be *a-ted* ... Jer 49:12

ACT (n) *deed, work*
a detestable *a* ... Lev 20:13
mighty *a-s* as Yours ... Deut 3:24
every abominable *a* ... Deut 12:31
the *a-s* of Solomon ... 1 Kin 11:41
over the rebellious *a* ... Mic 7:18

ACT (v) *behave*
they refuse to *a* ... Prov 21:7
I *a-ed* ignorantly ... 1 Tim 1:13
So speak and so *a* ... James 2:12
are *a-ing* faithfully ... 3 John 5

ACTION *behavior, work*
a-s are weighed ... 1 Sam 2:3
a-s of a...harlot ... Ezek 16:30
plan or *a* is ... Acts 5:38
prepare your minds for *a* ... 1 Pet 1:13

ADAM *(man, mankind).* The first man, created by God in His own image. Through Adam's sin the whole of mankind is under condemnation. In 1 Cor 15:45 the name is applied to Christ as *the last Adam* as compared to the first Adam. Also a site in the Jordan Valley.
1 *first man* ... Gen 2:20
fall of man ... Gen 3:6,7
type of Christ ... Rom 5:14
compared to Jesus ... 1 Cor 15:22
2 *site in Jordan Valley* ... Josh 3:16

ADAR
twelfth month of Heb calendar ... Ezra 6:15
Purim observed ... Esth 3:7; 9:19ff

ADD
a to your yoke ... 1 Kin 12:11
a-ing to the wrath ... Neh 13:18
not *a* to His words ... Prov 30:6
if anyone *a-s* to them ... Rev 22:18

ADDER A type of venomous snake.
I am sending...*A-s* ... Jer 8:17

ADJURE *charge solemnly*
many times...I *a* ... 1 Kin 22:16
I *a* you, O daughters ... Song 3:5
I *a* you by Jesus ... Acts 19:13

ADMAH A city near the Dead Sea that was destroyed by God along with Sodom and Gomorrah (Gen 10:19).

ADMINISTRATION In the NT, 1) a spiritual gift given to some believers, enabling them to lead the local church effectively; from the Gr word for "government." 2) God's plan and timing to bring about salvation.
a of the province ... Dan 3:12
healings, helps, *a-s* ... 1 Cor 12:28
in our *a* of this ... 2 Cor 8:20
a of the mystery ... Eph 3:9

ADMONISH *warn*
prophets...had *a-ed* ... Neh 9:26
How shall I *a* you ... Lam 2:13
not cease to *a* each ... Acts 20:31
able also to *a* one ... Rom 15:14
a-ing one another ... Col 3:16
a the unruly ... 1 Thess 5:14
a him as a brother ... 2 Thess 3:15

ADONIJAH *(Yahweh is my Lord).* Son of David; rebelled against Solomon. Name of several others.
1 *son of David* ... 2 Sam 3:4
aspired to throne ... 1 Kin 1:5ff
pardoned ... 1 Kin 1:52ff
executed ... 1 Kin 2:25
2 *Levite* ... 2 Chr 17:8
3 *of the restoration* ... Neh 10:16

ADOPTION *acceptance* In the NT, an aspect of salvation in which God accepts a repentant sinner as His own and makes him a child in His family, a fellow-heir with Christ.
spirit of *a* as sons ... Rom 8:15
to whom belongs...*a* ... Rom 9:4
receive the *a* as sons ... Gal 4:5
predestined us to *a* ... Eph 1:5

ADORN *array, clothe*
A yourself with ... Job 40:10
as a bride *a-s* herself ... Is 61:10
a-ed with beautiful ... Luke 21:5
women to *a* ... 1 Tim 2:9
a the doctrine of God ... Titus 2:10
a-ed with gold ... Rev 17:4
as a bride *a-ed* ... Rev 21:2

ADULLAM *(refuge).* One of the royal cities in Canaan. Known for a cave nearby where David lived for a time. Several of his relatives and the poor and afflicted people of the land came to him there (Josh 12:15).

ADULTERER
a and the adulteress ... Lev 20:10
eye of the *a* waits ... Job 24:15
associate with *a-s* ... Ps 50:18
a-s, nor effeminate ... 1 Cor 6:9
a-s God will judge ... Heb 13:4

ADULTERESS A woman who is unfaithful to her marriage vows. In the Bible, the word is sometimes used in reference to idolatrous Israel.
a shall surely be ... Lev 20:10

a who flatters with ... Prov 2:16
mouth of an *a* ... Prov 22:14
You *a* wife, who ... Ezek 16:32
they are *a-es* ... Ezek 23:45
shall be called an *a* ... Rom 7:3

ADULTERY The unfaithfulness of someone to his or her marriage vows. Expressly forbidden by the seventh commandment and by Jesus.
shall not commit *a* ... Ex 20:14
man who commits *a* ... Lev 20:10
a-ies of faithless ... Jer 3:8
worn out by *a-ies* ... Ezek 23:43
committed *a* with her ... Matt 5:28
woman commits *a* ... Matt 5:32
Do not commit *a* ... Luke 18:20
eyes full of *a* ... 2 Pet 2:14

ADVANCE *ahead, beyond*
old, *a-d* in age ... Gen 24:1
a-d in years ... 1 Sam 17:12
have told you in *a* ... Matt 24:25
both *a-d* in years ... Luke 1:7
a-ing in Judaism ... Gal 1:14

ADVANTAGE *benefit, profit*
lead surely to *a* ... Prov 21:5
What *a* does man ... Eccl 1:3
Wisdom has the *a* ... Eccl 10:10
a that I go away ... John 16:7
what *a* has the Jew ... Rom 3:1
no *a* would be taken of us ... 2 Cor 2:11
sake of *gaining an a* ... Jude 16

ADVERSARY *foe, opponent* One who is antagonistic toward another; an opponent or enemy. Satan is the adversary of God and the accuser of His people.
an *a* to your *a-ies* ... Ex 23:22
an *a* to Solomon ... 1 Kin 11:14
And my *a-ies* will rejoice ... Ps 13:4
a-ies and my enemies ... Ps 27:2
redeemed...from the *a* ... Ps 78:42
crush his *a-ies* ... Ps 89:23
there are many *a-ies* ... 1 Cor 16:9
consume the *a-ies* ... Heb 10:27
Your *a*, the devil ... 1 Pet 5:8

ADVERSITY *distress, misfortune*
death and *a* ... Deut 30:15
not accept *a* ... Job 2:10
relief from...*a* ... Ps 94:13
falls into *a* ... Prov 13:17
A pursues sinners ... Prov 13:21

ADVICE *counsel*
forsook the *a* ... 1 Kin 12:13
a of the young ... 2 Chr 10:14
a of the cunning ... Job 5:13
they took his *a* ... Acts 5:40
have followed my *a* ... Acts 27:21

ADVISER *counselor*
with his *a* Ahuzzath ... Gen 26:26
Pharaoh's wisest *a-s* ... Is 19:11

ADVOCATE *defender, witness* To plead in behalf of something or someone. One who defends another. Jesus Christ is the Christian's advocate with the Father.
my *a* is on high ... Job 16:19
A with the Father ... 1 John 2:1

AFFECTION *devotion, love*
set His *a* to love ... Deut 10:15
in your own *a-s* ... 2 Cor 6:12
a of Christ Jesus ... Phil 1:8
fond an *a* for you ... 1 Thess 2:8

AFFLICT (v) *oppress, trouble*
a them with hard labor ... Ex 1:11
not *a* any widow ... Ex 22:22
Egyptians...*a-ed* us ... Deut 26:6
bind him to *a* him ... Judg 16:5
the wicked *a* them ... 2 Sam 7:10
They *a-ed* his feet ... Ps 105:18
He was *a-ed* ... Is 63:9
will *a* you no longer ... Nah 1:12
were sick or *a-ed* ... Acts 5:16
are a-ed in every ... 2 Cor 4:8
those who *a* you ... 2 Thess 1:6
a-ed, ill-treated ... Heb 11:37

AFFLICTED (n) *troubled*
save an *a* people ... 2 Sam 22:28
to catch the *a* ... Ps 10:9
justice to the *a* ... Ps 82:3
LORD supports the *a* ... Ps 147:6
days of the *a* ... Prov 15:15
O *a* one ... Is 54:11
good news to the *a* ... Is 61:1

AFFLICTION *oppression*
my *a* and the toil ... Gen 31:42
the land of my *a* ... Gen 41:52
the bread of *a* ... Deut 16:3
LORD saw the *a* ... 2 Kin 14:26
You saw the *a* ... Neh 9:9
afflicted in their *a* ... Job 36:15
Look upon my *a* ... Ps 25:18
a severe *a* ... Eccl 6:2
a or persecution ... Mark 4:17
healed of her *a* ... Mark 5:29
a-s await me ... Acts 20:23
out of much *a* ... 2 Cor 2:4
great ordeal of *a* ... 2 Cor 8:2
to suffer *a* ... 1 Thess 3:4

AFRAID *dreading, fearful*
a because...naked ... Gen 3:10
a to look at God ... Ex 3:6
a and fainthearted ... Deut 20:8
Whoever is *a* ... Judg 7:3
a of the terror ... Ps 91:5
not *a* of the snow ... Prov 31:21
a to swear ... Eccl 9:2
a of man who dies ... Is 51:12
a to take Mary ... Matt 1:20
were *a* of Him ... Mark 11:18
Do not be *a*, Mary ... Luke 1:30
a of those who kill ... Luke 12:4
a of the people ... Luke 22:2
a that, as the serpent ... 2 Cor 11:3
Do not be *a* ... Rev 1:17

AGABUS *prophet* ... Acts 11:28;21:10

AGE *period, year*
David reached old *a* ... 1 Chr 23:1
a should speak ... Job 32:7
either in this *a* ... Matt 12:32
the end of the *a* ... Matt 13:40
sons of this *a* are ... Luke 16:8
in the *a-s* to come ... Eph 2:7
hidden...*past a-s* ... Col 1:26
in the present *a* ... Titus 2:12

AGED *old*
Wisdom is...*a* men ... Job 12:12
a are among us ... Job 15:10
refined, *a* wine ... Is 25:6
Paul, the *a* ... Philem 9

AGONY *anguish*
a has seized me ... 2 Sam 1:9
A like...childbirth ... Jer 50:43
in *a* in this flame ... Luke 16:24
in *a* He was praying ... Luke 22:44
the *a* of death ... Acts 2:24

AGREE *consent*
if two of you *a* ... Matt 18:19
did you not *a* ... Matt 20:13
Jews had already *a-d* ... John 9:22
have *a-d* together ... Acts 5:9
words...Prophets *a* ... Acts 15:15
a with sound words ... 1 Tim 6:3

AGREEMENT *accord*
an *a* in writing ... Neh 9:38
Saul was in hearty *a* ... Acts 8:1
a has the temple ... 2 Cor 6:16
three are in *a* ... 1 John 5:8

AGRIPPA Grandson and great-grandson (Agrippa I and II) of Herod the Great, rulers of Palestine under Rome from A.D. 37-44 and 50-100, respectively.
1 *Herod Agrippa I see* ***HEROD***
2 *Herod Agrippa II see* ***HEROD***

AHAB *(the father is my brother)*. An Israelite king who married Jezebel, an idolater from Tyre, under whose influence he introduced the idolatry of Baal and Ashtaroth to Israel and persecuted the prophets of God.
1 *king of Israel* ... 1 Kin 16:28
son of Omri ... 1 Kin 16:29
married Jezebel ... 1 Kin 16:31
idolater ... 1 Kin 16:33
2 *false prophet* ... Jer 29:21,22

AHASUERUS A Persian sovereign who married Esther. Known in Greek history as Xerxes. Also the name of certain other monarchs.
1 *Persian king, Xerxes I* ... Ezra 4:6; Book of Esther
2 *father of Darius the Mede* ... Dan 9:1

AHAZ *(he has grasped)*. King of Judah who began to reign at age 22 and reigned 16 years. He worshiped false gods, rejected the counsel of Isaiah and relied on human wisdom. Among other things, he followed pagan rituals in burning some of his sons.
son of Jotham ... 2 Kin 15:38
king of Judah ... 2 Kin 16:2

AHAZIAH *(Yahweh has sustained)*. Name of two kings, one in Israel and the other in Judah; both engaged in pagan idolatry (1 Kin 22:51; 2 Kin 8:25).

AHIJAH / AHIAH
1 *prophet of Shiloh* ... 1 Kin 14:2
2 *of Issachar* ... 1 Kin 15:27
3 *son of Jerahmeel* ... 1 Chr 2:25
4 *the Pelonite* ... 1 Chr 11:36
5 *under Nehemiah* ... Neh 10:26

AHIKAM *(my brother has risen up)*. Prince of Judah who protected Jeremiah and saved him from being put to death. Sent by King Josiah to a prophetess when the Book of the Law was found in the temple (Jer 26:24).

AHIMELECH
1 *high priest* ... 1 Sam 22:16
gave bread and sword to David ... 1 Sam 21:1-9
2 *Hittite* ... 1 Sam 26:6,7

AHINOAM *(my brother is pleasantness).* One of David's wives who gave birth to Amnon (his firstborn) in Hebron, where the king ascended to the throne (1 Sam 25:43).

AHITHOPHEL *(brother of folly).* One of the valiant men of David and a very wise counselor to the king. His word was taken as being from God. However, he sided with Absalom in the latter's insurrection against David, and when he saw his doom coming, went home and hanged himself.
counselor of David ... 2 Sam 15:12; 1 Chr 27:33

AHOHITE A term derived from an unknown place and applied to certain military heroes of the time of David and Solomon (2 Sam 23:9).

AI *(the heap, ruin).* City-state in Canaan, near Bethel. It was destroyed by Joshua soon after the Israelites were defeated there due to the sin of Achan.
place near Bethel ... Gen 12:8
defeat of Israelites ... Josh 7:5
captured ... Josh 8:23, 29

AIJALON *(deerfield)*
see also **GIBEON**
1 *valley near Jerusalem* ... Josh 10:12
Levitical city ... Josh 21:24
2 *valley* ... Josh 19:42
3 *Zebulunite town* ... Judg 12:12

AIR *breeze, sky*
no *a* can come ... Job 41:16
They pant for *a* ... Jer 14:6
birds of the *a* ... Matt 6:26
not beating the *a* ... 1 Cor 9:26
speaking into the *a* ... 1 Cor 14:9
power of the *a* ... Eph 2:2
the Lord in the *a* ... 1 Thess 4:17

ALABASTER *whitish stone* Fine-grained gypsum that is white and translucent. The perfume with which Jesus was anointed at Bethany was contained in an alabaster vial.
stones and *a* ... 1 Chr 29:2
pillars of *a* ... Song 5:15
brought an *a* vial ... Luke 7:37

ALARM (n) *danger, warning*
when you blow an *a* ... Num 10:5
The *a* of war ... Jer 4:19
shout of *a* at noon ... Jer 20:16
a on My...mountain ... Joel 2:1

ALARM (v) *frighten, warn*
he is not *a-ed* ... Job 40:23
interpretation *a* you ... Dan 4:19
thoughts *a-ed* him ... Dan 5:6
being much *a-ed* ... Acts 10:4
in no way *a-ed* by ... Phil 1:28

ALERT (n) *watch*
be on the *a* ... Matt 24:42

ALERT (v) *be watchful*
keeping *a* in it ... Col 4:2
let us be *a* ... 1 Thess 5:6

ALEXANDER *(defender of man).* A defender of the Christians during the tumult at Ephesus. Also the name of several other individuals.
1 *son of Simon of Cyrene* ... Mark 15:21
2 *of priestly family* ... Acts 4:6
3 *Ephesian Jew* ... Acts 19:33
4 *apostate teacher* ... 1 Tim 1:20
5 *enemy of Paul* ... 2 Tim 4:14

ALEXANDRIAN
1 *of Alexandria* ... Acts 6:9
2 *ship* ... Acts 27:6;28:11
3 *Apollos* ... Acts 18:24

ALIEN *foreigner, stranger*
love for the *a* ... Deut 10:19
give it to the *a* ... Deut 14:21
Our houses to *a-s* ... Lam 5:2
a-s in a foreign land ... Acts 7:6
no longer...*a-s* ... Eph 2:19
he lived as an *a* ... Heb 11:9
I urge you as *a-s* ... 1 Pet 2:11

ALIENATE *estrange*
Or I shall be *a-d* ... Jer 6:8
a this choice *portion* ... Ezek 48:14
were formerly *a-d* ... Col 1:21

ALIVE
Is your father still *a* ... Gen 43:7
down *a* to Sheol ... Num 16:33
go down *a* to Sheol ... Ps 55:15
may keep *a* a heifer ... Is 7:21
when He was...*a* ... Matt 27:63
heard...He was *a* ... Mark 16:11
presented Himself *a* ... Acts 1:3
yet the spirit is *a* ... Rom 8:10
all will be made *a* ... 1 Cor 15:22
made us *a* together ... Eph 2:5
a in the spirit ... 1 Pet 3:18
I am *a* forevermore ... Rev 1:18

ALLEGIANCE *loyalty*
pledged *a* to King ... 1 Chr 29:24
he pledged his *a* ... Ezek 17:18

ALLEGORY A description of something by the use of symbolic or figurative language to portray human conduct and to teach a moral truth (Gal 4:24).

ALLIANCE *agreement*
formed a marriage *a* ... 1 Kin 3:1
after an *a* is made ... Dan 11:23

ALLIED *joined*
a...by marriage ... 2 Chr 18:1
throne of...*a* ... Ps 94:20

ALLOT *apportion, divide*
only *a* it to Israel ... Josh 13:6
a Him a portion ... Is 53:12
a-ted to each...faith ... Rom 12:3

ALLOTMENT *portion*
an *a* from Pharaoh ... Gen 47:22
as a perpetual *a* ... Num 18:19
Jacob is the *a* ... Deut 32:9
set apart the...*a* ... Ezek 48:20

ALLOW *permit*
not *a* the destroyer ... Ex 12:23
whether his body *a-s* ... Lev 15:3
a Your Holy One ... Ps 16:10
Nor *a* Your Holy One ... Acts 2:27
not be *a-ed* to live ... Acts 22:22
a you to be tempted ... 1 Cor 10:13
not *a* a woman ... 1 Tim 2:12

ALMIGHTY *all-powerful* A designation for God as having absolute power over everything. "The Almighty" is a translation of the Heb *Shaddai* and the Gr *pantokrator*.
I am God *A* ... Gen 17:1
vision of the *A* ... Num 24:4
A has afflicted me ... Ruth 1:21
limits of the *A* ... Job 11:7
A was yet with me ... Job 29:5
destruction from...*A* ... Joel 1:15
Lord God, the *A* ... Rev 4:8
the *A*, reigns ... Rev 19:6

ALMOND
a and plane trees ... Gen 30:37
shaped like *a blossoms* ... Ex 37:19
and it bore ripe *a-s* ... Num 17:8

ALMS *charity* A charitable gift, usually money, to alleviate the needs of the poor.
a to the *Jewish* ... Acts 10:2
bring *a* to my nation ... Acts 24:17

ALOES Dried aromatic sap from the *Aquilaria* tree, usually mixed with myrrh (Ps 45:8).

ALONE
So He let him *a* ... Ex 4:26
Leave me *a*, for my ... Job 7:16
not live on bread *a* ... Matt 4:4
He was praying *a* ... Luke 9:18
I am not *a in it* ... John 8:16
receiving but you *a* ... Phil 4:15
and not by faith *a* ... James 2:24

ALOUD *joyful, piercing*
crying *a* as she ... 2 Sam 13:19
read *a* from the book ... Neh 13:1
I will cry *a* ... Ps 77:1
Sing *a* with gladness ... Jer 31:7
The king called *a* ... Dan 5:7
began to weep *a* ... Acts 20:37

ALPHA First letter of the Gr alphabet. Christ is called the Alpha and Omega in reference to His eternal existence and to the fact that, together with the Father, He is the source of all creation.
see also **OMEGA**
first letter of Gr. alphabet ... Rev 1:8
title of Jesus Christ ... Rev 21:6
expresses eternalness of God ... Rev 22:13

ALPHAEUS (unc, *of renewal).* 1) The father of Matthew (Mark 2:14). 2) The father of James the Lesser (Luke 6:15).

ALTAR *place of sacrifice* A raised structure made of various kinds of material on which sacrifices are offered for religious purposes.
offerings on the *a* ... Gen 8:20
Moses built an *a* ... Ex 17:15
fire on the *a* ... Lev 6:9
Gideon built an *a* ... Judg 6:24
erect an *a* to ... 2 Sam 24:18
go to the *a* of God ... Ps 43:4
a-s may become waste ... Ezek 6:6
offering at the *a* ... Matt 5:23
a that sanctifies ... Matt 23:19
golden *a* of incense ... Heb 9:4
we have an *a* ... Heb 13:10
horns of the golden *a* ... Rev 9:13

ALWAYS *ever, forever*
fear the LORD...*a* ... Deut 14:23
He will not *a* strive ... Ps 103:9
fear of the LORD *a* ... Prov 23:17
a loses his temper ... Prov 29:11
will I *a* be angry ... Is 57:16
I am with you *a* ... Matt 28:20
you *a* have...poor ... Mark 14:7
Rejoice in the Lord *a* ... Phil 4:4
a be with...Lord ... 1 Thess 4:17
I will *a* be ready ... 2 Pet 1:12

AMALEK Grandson of Esau (Gen 36:12).

AMALEKITES A nomadic people who were in perennial conflict with Israel and usually allied themselves with Israel's enemies. At one time they were marked for destruction by God. Saul and David partially destroyed them.
descendants of Esau ... Gen 36:12
tribe in Negev and Sinai ... Ex 17:8,9; Num 14:25; 1 Sam 15:7; 1 Chr 4:43

AMASA Nephew of King David, joined forces with Absalom against the king. Later was reinstated to a high ranking position in the army of Israel. Also the name of other officers.
son of Abigail ... 1 Chr 2:17
Absalom's commander ... 2 Sam 17:25
pardoned ... 2 Sam 19:13
an Ephraimite ... 2 Chr 28:12

AMAZED *astonished, astounded*
are *a* at His rebuke ... Job 26:11
a at His teaching ... Mark 1:22
heard Him were *a* ... Luke 2:47
Do not be *a* that I said ... John 3:7
were *a* and astonished ... Acts 2:7
whole earth was *a* ... Rev 13:3

AMAZEMENT *astonishment*
a came upon them ... Luke 4:36
with wonder and *a* ... Acts 3:10

AMAZIAH *(Yahweh is mighty).* A king in Judah who began his reign well, but later committed idolatry. He was the son of Joash, whom he succeeded on the throne. Also the name of other individuals.
1 *king of Judah* ... 2 Kin 12:21
son of Joash ... 2 Kin 14:1
2 *a Simeonite* ... 1 Chr 4:34
3 *son of Hilkiah* ... 1 Chr 6:45
4 *a priest of Bethel* ... Amos 7:10

AMBASSADOR *envoy*
a-s of peace weep ... Is 33:7
a-s for Christ ... 2 Cor 5:20
an *a* in chains ... Eph 6:20

AMBITION *design, intention*
out of selfish *a* ... Phil 1:17
a to lead a quiet ... 1 Thess 4:11
jealousy...selfish *a* ... James 3:14

AMBUSH (n) *cover, hiding place*
a for the city ... Josh 8:2
rise from *your a* ... Josh 8:7
Israel set men in *a* ... Judg 20:29
a...behind them ... 2 Chr 13:13
Place men in *a* ... Jer 51:12

AMBUSH (v) *lie in wait*
going to *a* the city ... Josh 8:4
a the innocent ... Prov 1:11
a their own lives ... Prov 1:18

AMEN *so be it* Heb adverb meaning "truly." A title for Christ as the true One.
people shall say, *A* ... Deut 27:16
the LORD forever! *A* ... Ps 89:52
glory forever...*A* ... Phil 4:20
the *A*, the faithful ... Rev 3:14
A. Come, Lord Jesus ... Rev 22:20

AMMON Another form of the name Ben-ammi *(son of my* kinsman), a son of Lot by his younger daughter (Gen 19:38).

AMMONITES The Semitic nation descended from Ben-Ammi, Lot's son. The Israelites often fought with them.
tribes E of Jordan ... Gen 19:38
defeated Israel ... Judg 3:13
hired Arameans ... 2 Sam 10:6
fought against Judah ... 2 Kin 24:2

AMNON *(faithful).* The son of David, murdered by Absalom because he defiled his half-sister Tamar. He was a man of very weak character, as evidenced by his scandalous treatment of Tamar.
eldest son of David ... 2 Sam 3:2
raped his sister ... 2 Sam 13:2ff
ordered killed ... 2 Sam 13:28

AMON *(trustworthy).*
1 *Ahab's governor* ... 1 Kin 22:26
2 *idolatrous king of Judah* ... 2 Kin 21:18-26
3 *of the Nethinims* ... Neh 7:59
4 *Egyptian deity* ... Jer 46:25

AMORITES *(high ones).* A very ancient Semitic empire, older than the Egyptians, Babylonians and Hittites. They inhabited Palestine and Syria long before other nations.
tribe on both sides of Jordan ... Gen 15:16; Ex 34:11; Deut 1:27; Judg 11:23; Amos 2:9

AMOS *(burdenbearer).* A herdsman and a tender of sycamore trees by trade. He was the first of the writing prophets and he prophesied against the northern kingdom (Israel).
prophet to Israel ... Book of Amos

AMOUNT *measure*
daily *a* of bricks ... Ex 5:19
a of your valuation ... Lev 27:23
large *a* of bronze ... 1 Chr 18:8

AMRAM *(people exalted).* Grandson of Levi and the father of Moses, Aaron, and Miriam. He was the founder of a patriarchal household.
father of Moses ... Ex 6:18-20; 1 Chr 23:13

AMULET An ornament carried or worn on a person as a protection against accidents, sickness, or evil spirits (Isa 3:20).

ANAK / ANAKIM *(longnecks).* Very tall people who inhabited Canaan during the conquest of the Promised Land. Probably the giant Goliath descended from them.
pre-Israelite tribe of Palestine ... Num 13:22-33
giants ... Deut 2:10; Josh 14:15

ANANIAS *(Yahweh has been gracious).* 1) He and his wife were struck dead for putting the Holy Spirit to the test. 2) A disciple from Damascus who prayed for Paul to be filled with the Holy Spirit and to regain his sight. 3) A high priest and president of the Sanhedrin.
1 *deceived Jerusalem church* ... Acts 5:1-5
2 *Damascus Christian* ... Acts 9:10,17
3 *high priest* ... Acts 23:2

ANATHOTH (unc, *answers).* A priestly city in Benjamin (Josh 1:18). Abiathar lived there and it was the birthplace of the prophet Jeremiah, who was persecuted by its inhabitants. Also the name of two individuals (1 Chr 7:8; Neh 10:19).

ANCESTORS *forefathers*
blessings of my *a* ... Gen 49:26
the *a* have set ... Deut 19:14
iniquities of their *a* ... Jer 11:10

ANCHOR
they weighed *a* ... Acts 27:13
they cast four *a-s* ... Acts 27:29
an *a* of the soul ... Heb 6:19

ANCIENT *aged, old*
of the *a* mountains ... Deut 33:15
the records are *a* ... 1 Chr 4:22
keep to the *a* path ... Job 22:15
O *a* doors ... Ps 24:9
the *a-s* were told ... Matt 5:21
from *a* generations ... Acts 15:21
not spare the *a* world ... 2 Pet 2:5

ANCIENT OF DAYS Title used by Daniel for God, in reference to His eternal existence.
A took His seat ... Dan 7:9

ANDREW *(manly).* One of the twelve apostles, he brought his brother Peter to Jesus.
fisherman ... Matt 4:18
brother of Peter ... Matt 4:18
apostle ... Luke 6:14
receives Jesus ... John 1:40-42

ANDRONICUS *(man of victory).* A Jewish Christian and fellow prisoner of Paul (Rom 16:7).

ANGEL *divine messenger (messenger).* Holy angels are special, superhuman beings who serve God and are sometimes sent by Him to deliver messages to people. Fallen angels are demons. All angels, with the exception of the *angel of the* LORD (q.v.), are created beings and are not to be worshiped.
send His *a* before ... Gen 24:7
a-s...were ascending ... Gen 28:12
an *a* to Jerusalem ... 1 Chr 21:15
bread of *a-s* ... Ps 78:25
Praise Him, all His *a-s* ... Ps 148:2
a of His presence ... Is 63:9
a who was speaking ... Zech 4:4
command His *a-s* ... Matt 4:6
a Gabriel was sent ... Luke 1:26
they are like *a-s* ... Luke 20:36
two *a-s* in white ... John 20:12
like the face of an *a* ... Acts 6:15
as an *a* of light ... 2 Cor 11:14
worship of the *a-s* ... Col 2:18
entertained *a-s* ... Heb 13:2

God did not spare *a-s* ... 2 Pet 2:4
a of the church ... Rev 2:1

ANGEL OF THE LORD An angel sent by God to humans. Some believe that in certain OT contexts this angel is actually the Son of God appearing in angelic form.
a called to Abraham ... Gen 22:15
a took his stand ... Num 22:22
I have seen the *a* ... Judg 6:22
a said to Elijah ... 2 Kin 1:3
a destroying ... 1 Chr 21:12
a encamps around those ... Ps 34:7
a admonished Joshua ... Zech 3:6
a commanded him ... Matt 1:24
a appeared to Joseph ... Matt 2:13
a...opened the gates ... Acts 5:19

ANGER *indignation, wrath*
My *a* will be kindled ... Ex 22:24
Moses' *a* burned ... Ex 32:19
from His burning *a* ... Deut 13:17
a with their idols ... 1 Kin 16:13
not turn back His *a* ... Job 9:13
not rebuke me in Your *a* ... Ps 6:1
a is but for a moment ... Ps 30:5
He who is slow to *a* ... Prov 14:29
a man *given* to *a* ... Prov 22:24
a of the LORD ... Is 5:25
sun go down...*a* ... Eph 4:26
put...aside: *a* ... Col 3:8
slow to *a* ... James 1:19

ANGRY *enraged, indignant*
Why are you *a* ... Gen 4:6
king became very *a* ... Esth 1:12
that He not become *a* ... Ps 2:12
a man stirs up strife ... Prov 29:22
a beyond measure ... Is 64:9
and *a* no more ... Ezek 16:42
a with his brother ... Matt 5:22
Be *a*...do not sin ... Eph 4:26
a with this generation ... Heb 3:10

ANGUISH *distress, pain*
writhed in great *a* ... Esth 4:4
My heart is in *a* ... Ps 55:4
land of distress and *a* ... Is 30:6
A has seized us ... Jer 6:24
and *a* of heart ... 2 Cor 2:4

ANIMAL *beast, creature*
from man to *a-s* ... Gen 6:7
lies with an *a* ... Ex 22:19
the fat of the *a* ... Lev 7:25
wild *a-s* of the field ... Jer 27:6
a blemished *a* ... Mal 1:14
four-footed *a-s* ... Acts 10:12
like unreasoning *a-s* ... 2 Pet 2:12

ANNA
prophetess ... Luke 2:36

ANNAS *(merciful, gracious).* A contracted form of *Ananias.* The high priest during John the Baptist's ministry. Jesus was brought before him for interrogation after His arrest.
high priest ... Luke 3:2; John 18:13ff

ANNIHILATE *destroy*
to *a* all the Jews ... Esth 3:13
My enemy *a-d* them ... Lam 2:22
to destroy and *a* ... Dan 11:44
let it be *a-d* ... Zech 11:9

ANNOUNCE *proclaim*
Who *a-s* peace ... Is 52:7
I will *a* My words ... Jer 18:2
a-ing to...disciples ... John 20:18
a-d...the Righteous ... Acts 7:52

ANNUL *dismiss, make void*
he shall *a* her vow ... Num 30:8
husband has *a-led* ... Num 30:12
not *a* Your covenant ... Jer 14:21
a-s one of the least ... Matt 5:19

ANOINT (v) *sprinkle oil upon* In ceremonies, to pour or apply olive oil upon the head as a symbol for the empowering of the Holy Spirit. Jesus underwent a miraculous anointing at His baptism, during which the Holy Spirit came down upon Him in the form of a dove. Anointing with oil was also done for medicinal purposes to parts of the body that had suffered injury, as in the story of the good Samaritan.
a them and ordain ... Ex 28:41
a Aaron and his sons ... Ex 30:30
LORD *a-ed* you king ... 1 Sam 15:17
a-ed my head with oil ... Ps 23:5
a the most holy *place* ... Dan 9:24
has *a-ed* My body ... Mark 14:8
did not *a* My head ... Luke 7:46
and *a-ed* my eyes ... John 9:11
a-ed...feet of Jesus ... John 12:3
a-ed Him...Holy Spirit ... Acts 10:38
a-ing him with oil ... James 5:14

ANOINTED (adj) *consecrated*
if the *a* priest sins ... Lev 4:3
not touch My *a* ... 1 Chr 16:22
a cherub who ... Ezek 28:14
the two *a* ones ... Zech 4:14

ANOINTED (n) *consecrated one*
walk before My *a* ... 1 Sam 2:35
he is the LORD's *a* ... 1 Sam 24:10
against His *A* ... Ps 2:2

ANOINTING (adj) *consecration*
spices for the *a* oil ... Ex 25:6
shall be a holy *a* oil ... Ex 30:31
for the LORD's *a* oil ... Lev 10:7

ANOINTING (n) *consecration*
a will qualify them ... Ex 40:15
a from the Holy ... 1 John 2:20
His *a* teaches you ... 1 John 2:27

ANSWER (n) *response*
consider what *a* I ... 1 Chr 21:12
the king sent an *a* ... Ezra 4:17
Who gives a right *a* ... Prov 24:26
amazed at...His *a-s* ... Luke 2:47

ANSWER (v) *respond*
anyone who will *a* you ... Job 5:1
The LORD *a-ed* me ... Ps 118:5
Jesus *a-ing* said ... Matt 3:15
who *a-s* back to God ... Rom 9:20

ANT *insect*
to the *a,* O sluggard ... Prov 6:6
a-s are not a strong ... Prov 30:25

ANTELOPE *animal*
Like an *a* in a net ... Is 51:20

ANTICHRIST *foe of Christ (against Christ).* The last of many who oppose Christ, he will be His greatest opponent and will be empowered by Satan. After a brief but very destructive career, he will be defeated by Christ at His second coming. Also a title for other enemies of Christ.
a-s have appeared ... 1 John 2:18
This is the *a* ... 1 John 2:22
the *spirit* of the *a* ... 1 John 4:3
deceiver and the *a* ... 2 John 7

ANTIOCH 1) A city in Syria where the followers of Christ were for the first time called Christians. 2) A Greek city in Pisidia, between Ephesus and Cilicia.
1 *city in Syria* ... Acts 6:5;11:19,26
2 *city in Pisidia* ... Acts 13:14; 14:19

ANTIPAS Contraction of Antipater, which means "instead of (his) father." 1) The name of a Christian martyr in Pergamum (Rev 2:13). 2) One of the Herods.
1 *Pergamum martyr* ... Rev 2:13
2 *Herod Antipas*
see **HEROD**

ANXIETY *sorrow*
a because of my sin ... Ps 38:18
There is *a* by the sea ... Jer 49:23
casting all your *a* ... 1 Pet 5:7

ANXIOUS *concerned, worried*
and will become *a* for us ... 1 Sam 9:5
not be *a* in...drought ... Jer 17:8
my spirit is *a* to ... Dan 2:3
Be *a* for nothing ... Phil 4:6

APART *separate*
So they set *a* Kedesh ... Josh 20:7
tear their fetters *a* ... Ps 2:3
a from your Father ... Matt 10:29
a from Him nothing ... John 1:3
a from Me you can ... John 15:5
faith *a* from works ... Rom 3:28

APOLLOS An eloquent Jew from Alexandria who only knew John the Baptist's message, but received instruction in Christian doctrine from Aquila and Priscilla.
Alexandrian Jew ... Acts 18:24
taught at Ephesus ... Acts 18:24
taught at Corinth ... 1 Cor 3:4,6

APOLLYON *(destroyer).* Gr for Abaddon, the Heb name for the angel of the abyss (Rev 9:11).
see **ABADDON** *and* **ABYSS**

APOSTASY *faithlessness (desertion, falling away).* The deliberate act of renunciation of a religious faith.
a-ies are numerous ... Jer 5:6
Turned away in...*a* ... Jer 8:5
I will heal their *a* ... Hos 14:4
unless the *a* comes ... 2 Thess 2:3

APOSTLE *sent with authority (messenger, ambassador).* One who has been commissioned and sent with a message by Jesus Christ as His representative. Originally there were twelve apostles, all of whom had followed Jesus from the time of John the Baptist's ministry until Jesus' ascension to heaven. Paul and others were recognized later. All apostles were eyewitnesses of the resurrected Christ before or after His ascension.
the twelve *a-s* ... Matt 10:2
named as *a-s* ... Luke 6:13
called *as* an *a* ... Rom 1:1
an *a* of Gentiles ... Rom 11:13

not fit to be called an *a* ... 1 Cor 15:9
men are false *a-s* ... 2 Cor 11:13
He gave some *as a-s* ... Eph 4:11
Jesus, the *A* and ... Heb 3:1
a-s of the Lamb ... Rev 21:14

APOSTLESHIP *office of apostle*
received grace and *a* ... Rom 1:5
seal of my *a* ... 1 Cor 9:2
Peter in *his a* to ... Gal 2:8

APPAREL *clothing, garment*
of gold on your *a* ... 2 Sam 1:24
majestic in His *a* ... Is 63:1
put on his royal *a* ... Acts 12:21

APPEAL *ask, entreat*
standing and *a-ing* ... Acts 16:9
I *a* to Caesar ... Acts 25:11
Paul *a-ed* to be held ... Acts 25:21
a-ed to...Emperor ... Acts 25:25
a to *him* as a father ... 1 Tim 5:1
love's sake I...*a* ... Philem 9

APPEAR *become visible*
LORD *a-ed* to Abram ... Gen 12:7
glory of the LORD *a-ed* ... Ex 16:10
a-ed on the wings ... 2 Sam 22:11
and *a-ed* to many ... Matt 27:53
first *a-ed* to Mary ... Mark 16:9
who, *a-ing* in glory ... Luke 9:31
a-ed to them tongues ... Acts 2:3
we must all *a* before ... 2 Cor 5:10
a-ing of the glory ... Titus 2:13
will *a* a second time ... Heb 9:28
Chief Shepherd *a-s* ... 1 Pet 5:4
not *a-ed* as yet ... 1 John 3:2

APPEARANCE *countenance*
handsome in...*a* ... Gen 39:6
the *a* of the angel ... Judg 13:6
at the outward *a* ... 1 Sam 16:7
a is blacker than soot ... Lam 4:8
lapis lazuli in *a* ... Ezek 1:26
they neglect their *a* ... Matt 6:16
judge according to *a* ... John 7:24
a of His coming ... 2 Thess 2:8
a of the locusts ... Rev 9:7

APPEASE *moderate, mollify*
I will *a* him ... Gen 32:20
wise man will *a* it ... Prov 16:14
have *a-d* My wrath ... Zech 6:8

APPETITE *desire, hunger*
our *a* is gone ... Num 11:6
a of the young lions ... Job 38:39
man of *great a* ... Prov 23:2
a is not satisfied ... Eccl 6:7
enlarges his *a* like ... Hab 2:5
whose god is *their a* ... Phil 3:19

APPLE *fruit*
as the *a* of the eye ... Ps 17:8
Like a-s of gold ... Prov 25:11
Refresh me with *a-s* ... Song 2:5
touches the *a* of His ... Zech 2:8

APPOINT *assign, commission*
shall *a as a penalty* ... Ex 21:23
I will *a* over you ... Lev 26:16
who *a-ed* Moses ... 1 Sam 12:6
to *a* their relatives ... 1 Chr 15:16
a magistrates and ... Ezra 7:25
there is a harvest *a-ed* ... Hos 6:11
a-ed elders for them ... Acts 14:23
a-ed a preacher and ... 1 Tim 2:7

For the Law *a-s* men ... Heb 7:28

APPORTION *distribute*
a the inheritance ... Num 34:29
a this land ... Josh 13:7
He *a-s* our fields ... Mic 2:4

APPROPRIATE *suitable*
blessing *a* to him ... Gen 49:28
eat at the *a* time ... Eccl 10:17
a to repentance ... Acts 26:20

APPROVAL *consent*
loved the *a* of men ... John 12:43
give hearty *a* to ... Rom 1:32
men of old gained *a* ... Heb 11:2

APPROVE *accept, attest*
the Lord does not *a* ... Lam 3:36
too pure to *a* evil ... Hab 1:13
standing by *a-ing* ... Acts 22:20
and *a-d* by men ... Rom 14:18
present yourself *a-d* ... 2 Tim 2:15

AQUILA *(eagle).* A tent-maker by trade who, with his wife Priscilla, accompanied Paul on some of his missionary journeys.
a native of Pontus ... Acts 18:2
Corinthian Christian ... Acts 18:18
co-worker with Paul ... Rom 16:3

ARAB
1 *town in Judah* ... Josh 15:52
2 *ethnic identity* ... 1 Kin 10:15; Neh 2:19; Is 13:20

ARABAH *(desert plain).* A geological depression running from north to south in Palestine. Also the name of the lowland along the Jordan River, and another name for the Dead Sea.
1 *desert steppe* ... Is 35:1,6; Jer 52:7
2 *Jordan rift valley* ... Deut 1:1; Josh 3:17
3 *Dead Sea* ... Josh 3:16; 2 Kin 14:25

ARABIA
land SE of Israel / Judah ... Is 21:13; Ezek 30:5; Gal 1:17;4:25

ARAM The land of an ethnic Semitic family, the Arameans, who inhabited territory from Syria in the south to the Euphrates River in the northeast. Also the name of three individuals.
1 *son of Shem* ... Gen 10:22,23
2 *line of Asher* ... 1 Chr 7:34
3 *ancestor of Jesus, shortened to Ram* ... Ruth 4:19; Matt 1:3; Luke 3:33
4 *Syria and N Mesopotamia* ... Num 23:7; 1 Kin 11:25; 2 Kin 13:19; Is 7:8

ARAMAIC A Semitic family of languages, spoken by the Arameans. Similar to Heb and Phoenician. A significant portion of the book of Daniel is written in Aramaic, and it was the first language of most Palestinians, including Jesus.
Semitic language ... 2 Kin 18:26; Ezra 4:7; Is 36:11; Dan 2:4

ARAMEANS
tribes of Aram ... 2 Sam 8:5; 1 Kin 20:20; 2 Kin 24:2

ARARAT A mountainous country in eastern Turkey. Noah's Ark eventually came to rest on one of its mountains.
kingdom and mountain range in Armenia ... Gen 8:4; 2 Kin 19:37; Jer 51:27

ARAUNAH
Jebusite owner of threshing floor on Mt. Moriah ... 2 Sam 24:16,18
David purchases threshing floor for altar and later temple ... 2 Sam 24:23,24
see also **ORNAN**

ARBA *(four).* Father of Anak, and part of the name of a city which later was named Hebron (Josh 15:13).

ARCHANGEL *(chief angel).* Angel(s) of the highest rank. Only Michael is identified specifically as an archangel.
voice of *the a* ... 1 Thess 4:16
But Michael the *a* ... Jude 9

ARCHELAUS *see* **HEROD**

ARCHER *bowman*
the *a-s* hit him ... 1 Sam 31:3
a-s shot King Josiah ... 2 Chr 35:23
a-s equipped with bows ... Ps 78:9
an *a* who wounds ... Prov 26:10

ARCHIPPUS *(horse ruler).* A Christian and the recipient of greetings from Paul. Possibly the son of Philemon and Apphia.
Colossian Christian ... Col 4:17
co-worker with Paul ... Philem 2

AREOPAGUS Hill in Athens where Paul preached to the Athenians about God as being their unknown god. There are two traditional meanings of the name: a) Hill of Ares (Greek god of war, equivalent to Mars in Roman mythology); b) Hill of Curses, i.e. the Furies of Greek mythology. In ancient Greece, court was held on the Areopagus to try homicide cases.
hill and council in Athens ... Acts 17:19,22

ARGUE *dispute, question*
I will *a* my ways ... Job 13:15
hastily to *a your case* ... Prov 25:8
Pharisees...*a* with ... Mark 8:11
scribes *a-ing* with ... Mark 9:14
a-ing with the...*Jews* ... Acts 9:29

ARGUMENT *disagreement*
Please hear my *a* ... Job 13:6
mouth are no *a-s* ... Ps 38:14
a started among them ... Luke 9:46

ARIEL
1 *a Moabite* ... 2 Sam 23:20; 1 Chr 11:22
2 *applied to Jerusalem* ... Is 29:1ff
3 *sent by Ezra* ... Ezra 8:16

ARISE *rise, stand*
A, walk about the ... Gen 13:17
Abraham *arose* early ... Gen 19:27
will *a* and play ... Deut 31:16
you have *a-n* early ... 1 Sam 29:10
arose and tore his robe ... Job 1:20
when God *a-s* ... Job 31:14
A, O LORD; save me ... Ps 3:7
Though war *a* ... Ps 27:3
A, my darling ... Song 2:13
a-n anyone greater ... Matt 11:11
false prophets will *a* ... Matt 24:11
arose from the dead ... Acts 10:41
a from the dead ... Eph 5:14

ARISTARCHUS *(best ruler).* A Christian from Thessalonica who traveled with Paul.
Thessalonian Christian ... Acts 20:4; 27:2

co-worker with Paul ... Col 4:10; Philem 24

ARK *chest, vessel* 1) The vessel in which Noah and his family were saved from the flood. 2) The ark of the testimony: a chest covered with gold and topped with the cherubim. It contained the two tables of the law given by God to Moses and was housed in the most holy place in the tabernacle.
a of gopher wood ... Gen 6:14
into the *a* to Noah ... Gen 7:9
a of acacia wood ... Ex 37:1
a of the covenant ... Josh 4:7
Noah entered the *a* ... Matt 24:38
a of His covenant ... Rev 11:19

ARM (n) *part of body*
the everlasting *a-s* ... Deut 33:27
a without strength ... Job 26:2
a-s of the wicked ... Ps 37:17
His holy *a* have gained ... Ps 98:1
a seal on your *a* ... Song 8:6
be carried in the *a-s* ... Is 60:4
took...in His *a-s* ... Mark 10:16
with an uplifted *a* ... Acts 13:17

ARM (v) *mobilize*
A men from among ... Num 31:3
a-ed for battle ... Num 32:29
a-ed with iron ... 2 Sam 23:7
a yourselves also ... 1 Pet 4:1

ARMAGEDDON *see* **HAR-MAGEDON**

ARMED (adj) *mobilized*
the *a* men went ... Josh 6:13
their *a* camps ... 1 Sam 28:1
So the *a* men left ... 2 Chr 28:14
like an *a* man ... Prov 6:11

ARMOR *protective device*
a joint of the *a* ... 1 Kin 22:34
strip off his outer *a* ... Job 41:13
all his *a* on which ... Luke 11:22
put on...*a* of light ... Rom 13:12
full *a* of God ... Eph 6:11

ARMY *host, war*
not go out with the *a* ... Deut 24:5
like the *a* of God ... 1 Chr 12:22
a ready for battle ... 2 Chr 26:11
officers of the *a* ... Neh 2:9
forth with our *a-ies* ... Ps 60:10
exceedingly great *a* ... Ezek 37:10
a-ies...in heaven ... Rev 19:14
and against His *a* ... Rev 19:19

ARNON *(rushing* or *roaring).* A wadi (water course) that in ancient times served as the boundary between the Amorites and the Moabites. Later, it marked the division between the tribe of Reuben in the north and Moab in the south.
river and border ... Num 21:13
valley in Moab ... Deut 2:24

AROER (unc, *juniper).* Name of three towns in OT times. The two most important are the one by the north bank of the Arnon (Deut 2:36), and a town in the Negev in Judah where David sent spoils after defeating the Amalekites (1 Sam 30:28).

AROMA *odor*
the soothing *a* ... Gen 8:21
his *a* has not changed ... Jer 48:11
through us...sweet *a* ... 2 Cor 2:14
a from life to life ... 2 Cor 2:16
as a fragrant *a* ... Eph 5:2

AROUSE *raise, stir*
A Yourself to help me ... Ps 59:4
a-s for you the spirits ... Is 14:9
a-d one from the north ... Is 41:25
He will *a His* zeal ... Is 42:13
LORD has *a-d* the spirit ... Jer 51:11

ARPAD *(support).* A fortified city near Hamath in Assyria. It could be the same as Arvad (2 Kin 18:34).

ARRANGE *set in order*
a what belongs on it ... Ex 40:4
shall *a* the pieces ... Lev 1:8
he *a-d* the wood ... 1 Kin 18:33
for so he had *a-d* it ... Acts 20:13

ARRAY (n) *arrangement, order*
went up in martial *a* ... Ex 13:18
in battle *a* ... Josh 4:12
Worship...in holy *a* ... 1 Chr 16:29
holy *a,* from the womb ... Ps 110:3

ARRAY (v) *adorn, clothe*
Israel *a-ed* for battle ... Judg 20:20
let them *a* the man ... Esth 6:9
A yourselves before ... Job 33:5

ARREST *restrain*
he *a-ed* Jeremiah ... Jer 37:13
Herod had John *a-ed* ... Matt 14:3
and clubs to *a* Me ... Matt 26:55
proceeded to *a* Peter ... Acts 12:3

ARROGANCE *pride*
your *a* has come ... 2 Kin 19:28
Pride and *a* and ... Prov 8:13
a of the proud ... Is 13:11
a, pride, and fury ... Is 16:6
a of your heart ... Jer 49:16
you boast in your *a* ... James 4:16

ARROGANT *proud*
a men have risen up ... Ps 86:14
But a fool is *a* ... Prov 14:16
a toward the LORD ... Jer 48:26
Knowledge makes *a* ... 1 Cor 8:1
boastful, *a,* revilers ... 2 Tim 3:2
speaking...*a words* ... 2 Pet 2:18

ARROW *dart, missile*
shot an *a* past him ... 1 Sam 20:36
a-s of the Almighty ... Job 6:4
a cannot make him ... Job 41:28
make ready their *a* ... Ps 11:2
broke the flaming *a-s* ... Ps 76:3
sword and a sharp *a* ... Prov 25:18
tongue is a deadly *a* ... Jer 9:8
target for the *a* ... Lam 3:12
deadly *a-s* of famine ... Ezek 5:16
a-s of the evil *one* ... Eph 6:16

ART *craft*
with their secret *a-s* ... Ex 7:22
the perfumers' *a* ... 2 Chr 16:14

ARTAXERXES Name of several Persian kings. One of them allowed Ezra, and later Nehemiah, to go to Jerusalem to take care of religious and civil business regarding Israel and its laws. This Artaxerxes was a benefactor to the Jewish people.
Persian king ... Ezra 4:7,8;7:1,12; Neh 2:1;5:14

ARTEMIS
Greek goddess ... Acts 19:24ff

ARTICLE *object, vessel*
a-s of silver ... Gen 24:53
any wooden *a* ... Lev 11:32
of every precious *a* ... Hos 13:15
every *a* of ivory ... Rev 18:12

ASA *(healer).* A king of Judah who encouraged the worship of God instead of idol worship. Also a Levite.
1 *king of Judah* ... 1 Kin 15:8-24; 2 Chr 14:8-15
2 *a Levite* ... 1 Chr 9:16

ASAHEL *(God has made).* One of David's heroes, known for his swiftness of foot (2 Sam 2:18). Joab and Abishai were his brothers. Name of two other individuals.

ASAPH *(gatherer).* A Levite, a skilled musician mentioned in connection with some of the psalms. The father of a clan who served as musicians in the temple (1 Chr 15:19).

ASCEND *go up*
a into the hill ... Ps 24:3
If I *a* to heaven ... Ps 139:8
Who has *a-ed* into ... Prov 30:4
breath of man *a-s* ... Eccl 3:21
has *a-ed* into heaven ... John 3:13
Son of Man *a-ing* ... John 6:62
a-ed to the Father ... John 20:17
who *a-ed* far above ... Eph 4:10

ASCENT *hill, rise*
by the *a* of Heres ... Judg 8:13
a of the...Olives ... 2 Sam 15:30
Song of *A-s* ... Ps 120-134

ASCRIBE *attribute*
have *a-d* to David ... 1 Sam 18:8
A to the LORD ... 1 Chr 16:28
a righteousness to ... Job 36:3

ASH
but dust and *a-es* ... Gen 18:27
from the *a* heap ... 1 Sam 2:8
a-es on her head ... 2 Sam 13:19
a-es were poured ... 1 Kin 13:5
proverbs of *a-es* ... Job 13:12
repent in dust and *a-es* ... Job 42:6
garland instead of *a-es* ... Is 61:3
roll in *a-es* ... Jer 6:26
sackcloth and *a-es* ... Luke 10:13
a-es of a heifer ... Heb 9:13

ASHAMED *embarrassed*
naked and were not *a* ... Gen 2:25
Let me never be *a* ... Ps 71:1
a of Me...My words ... Mark 8:38
a...when He comes ... Luke 9:26
not *a* of the gospel ... Rom 1:16
a of the testimony ... 2 Tim 1:8
God is not *a* ... Heb 11:16
he is not to be *a* ... 1 Pet 4:16

ASHDOD *(stronghold, fortress).* A city-state in Philistia. The ark of Israel was seized and kept in the sanctuary of their god Dagon for a short time. Philip the evangelist preached at Ashdod.
Philistine city ... Josh 15:47; 1 Sam 5:1,6; Amos 1:8

ASHER *(happy).*
1 *eighth son of Jacob* ... Gen 35:26;49:20
2 *tribe of Israel* ... Num 1:41;13:13; Rev 7:6
3 *town in hill country of Israel* ... Josh 17:7

ASHERAH (unc, *gracious).* The Canaanite goddess of fertility, represented by a wooden object.
Canaanite goddess and symbol ... Deut 16:21; Judg 6:25
Asherim *(pl)* ... 1 Kin 14:15; Mic 5:14
Asheroth *(pl)* ... Judg 3:7; 2 Chr 19:3

ASHKELON A Philistine city not conquered by the Israelites.
Philistine city ... Judg 1:18; 2 Sam 1:20; Jer 47:5; Zeph 2:4

ASHTORETH, ASHTAROTH The name of various goddesses, including a Sidonian goddess whom Solomon worshiped. The plural *Ashtaroth* was a city in Bashan, east of the Jordan River.
1 *Near Eastern goddess* ... 1 Kin 11:5,33; 2 Kin 23:13
Ashtaroth (pl) ... Judg 2:13; 1 Sam 7:4; 31:10
2 *town of Bashan in E Manasseh* ... Deut 1:4; Josh 13:12

ASIA A Roman province in the time of the NT, comprising most of the western part of Asia Minor (western Turkey) and some of its islands.
Roman province of Asia Minor ... Acts 6:9; Rom 16:5; Rev 1:4

ASK *appeal, beg, inquire*
whatever you *a* ... Ruth 3:11
Two things I *a-ed* ... Prov 30:7
A a sign for yourself ... Is 7:11
a for the ancient paths ... Jer 6:16
A rain from the LORD ... Zech 10:1
Give to him who *a-s* ... Matt 5:42
A, and it will be ... Matt 7:7
a...believing ... Matt 21:22
pray and *a,* believe ... Mark 11:24
Jews *a* for signs ... 1 Cor 1:22
let him *a* of God ... James 1:5

ASLEEP *dead, resting*
sound *a*...exhausted ... Judg 4:21
they fall *a* ... Ps 90:5
not died, but is *a* ... Matt 9:24
in the stern, *a* ... Mark 4:38
Lazarus...fallen *a* ... John 11:11
said this, he fell *a* ... Acts 7:60
fallen *a* in Jesus ... 1 Thess 4:14

ASSAIL *attack*
will you *a* a man ... Ps 62:3
Whoever *a-s* you ... Is 54:15
storm was *a-ing us* ... Acts 27:20

ASSEMBLE *gather*
a all the congregation ... Lev 8:3
A the people to Me ... Deut 4:10
David *a-d* all Israel ... 1 Chr 13:5
peoples may be *a-d* ... Is 43:9
A...on the mountains ... Amos 3:9
I will...*a* all of you ... Mic 2:12
whole city *a-d* to ... Acts 13:44
a-d to make war ... Rev 19:19

ASSEMBLY *congregation*
holy *a* on the seventh ... Ex 12:16
the people of the *a* ... Lev 16:33
a before the rock ... Num 20:10
Or calls an *a* ... Job 11:10
a of the righteous ... Ps 1:5
hate the *a* of evildoers ... Ps 26:5
proclaim a solemn *a* ... Joel 2:15
I delight in...*a-ies* ... Amos 5:21
the *a* was divided ... Acts 23:7
general *a* and church ... Heb 12:23
comes into your *a* ... James 2:2

ASSOCIATE (n) *colleague*
All my *a-s* abhor me ... Job 19:19
high priest and...*a-s* ... Acts 5:21

ASSOCIATE (v) *identify with*
shall they *a* with ... 1 Kin 11:2
a with adulterers ... Ps 50:18
not *a* with a man ... Prov 22:24
dared to *a* with them ... Acts 5:13
but *a* with the lowly ... Rom 12:16
not *a* with him ... 2 Thess 3:14

ASSURANCE *confirmation* In the NT, certainty about the outcome of salvation, based on the resurrection of Christ.
no one has *a* of life ... Job 24:22
a of understanding ... Col 2:2
full *a* of hope ... Heb 6:11
full *a* of faith ... Heb 10:22
a of *things* hoped for ... Heb 11:1

ASSURE *confirm*
kingdom will be *a-d* ... Dan 4:26
I *a* you before God ... Gal 1:20
will *a* our heart ... 1 John 3:19

ASSYRIA An ancient world empire which developed in western Asia in the upper region of the Tigris River. It was conquered by Babylonia.
kingdom name from Asshur ... Gen 10:22; 1 Chr 1:17
empire in upper Mesopotamia ... 2 Kin 19:17; Is 19:24; Jer 2:36

ASTONISHED *amazed*
will be *a* and hiss ... 1 Kin 9:8
a at His teaching ... Matt 22:33
listeners were *a* ... Mark 6:2
were utterly *a* ... Mark 7:37
they were all *a* ... Luke 1:63

ASTOUNDED *astonished*
prophets will be *a* ... Jer 4:9
a at the vision ... Dan 8:27
were completely *a* ... Mark 5:42

ASTRAY *erring, wandering*
a like a lost sheep ... Ps 119:176
leading *them a* ... Is 9:16
like sheep have gone *a* ... Is 53:6
led My people *a* ... Jer 23:32
lead *a*...the elect ... Mark 13:22
a from the faith ... 1 Tim 6:21
go *a* in their heart ... Heb 3:10
My bond-servants *a* ... Rev 2:20

ATHALIAH *(Yahweh is exalted).* Daughter of Ahab and wife of Jehoram, king of Judah. Introduced the worship of Baal to the royal court and ruled for six years. Also the name of two other people.
1 *wicked* ... 2 Kin 11:1
daughter of Ahab ... 2 Chr 21:6
wife of Jehoram
2 *a Benjamite* ... 1 Chr 8:26
3 *returned exile* ... Ezra 8:7

ATHENS The principal city of Greece. There Paul preached about God being their unknown god.
leading Greek city ... Acts 17:15ff

ATONEMENT *expiation* Making amends for wrongs against God. In the OT, atonement was accomplished by the priests' offering sacrifices to God for sins. These sacrifices anticipated and represented the future death of Christ in various ways. His death was the actual payment for all sins, including those for which the OT sacrifices were offered.
by which *a* was made ... Ex 29:33
shall make *a* for him ... Lev 4:35
a before the LORD ... Lev 14:31
how can I make *a* ... 2 Sam 21:3
make *a* for iniquity ... Dan 9:24

ATONEMENT, DAY OF *see* **DAY OF ATONEMENT**

ATTACK (n) *assault*
at the first *a* ... 2 Sam 17:9
king ready for the *a* ... Job 15:24
joined in the *a* ... Acts 24:9

ATTACK (v) *assault, fall upon*
that he will come and *a* ... Gen 32:11
adversary who *a-s* ... Num 10:9
and *a-ed* the camp ... Judg 8:11
a the Philistines ... 1 Sam 23:2
it *a-ed* the plant ... Jon 4:7
no man will *a* you ... Acts 18:10

ATTAIN *acquire*
I cannot *a* to it ... Ps 139:6
woman *a-s* honor ... Prov 11:16
worthy to *a* to that ... Luke 20:35
a-ed righteousness ... Rom 9:30
a to the resurrection ... Phil 3:11

ATTEND *pay attention to*
a to your priesthood ... Num 18:7
thousands were *a-ing* ... Dan 7:10
who *a* regularly ... 1 Cor 9:13
a to...business ... 1 Thess 4:11
ears *a* to their prayer ... 1 Pet 3:12

ATTENDANT *helper, servant*
the *a* of Moses ... Num 11:28
king's *a-s,* who served ... Esth 2:2
a-s of...bridegroom ... Mark 2:19

ATTENTION *heed, regard*
no *a* to false words ... Ex 5:9
gives *a* to the word ... Prov 16:20
pays *a* to falsehood ... Prov 29:12
they do not pay *a* ... Is 5:12
pay *a* to myths ... 1 Tim 1:4
a to the...reading ... 1 Tim 4:13

ATTIRE *covering, dress*
in his military *a* ... 2 Sam 20:8
cupbearers...*a* ... 2 Chr 9:4
Him in holy *a* ... 2 Chr 20:21

ATTITUDE *frame of mind*
see your father's *a* ... Gen 31:5
a of the righteous ... Luke 1:17
Have this *a* in ... Phil 2:5
have a different *a* ... Phil 3:15

AUGUSTUS *(exalted, sacred).* The title taken by the Roman Emperor Octavian, successor of Julius Caesar.

name of Caesar Octavianus ... Luke 2:1
see **CAESAR**

AUTHOR *source*
a of their salvation ... Heb 2:10
a...perfecter of faith ... Heb 12:2

AUTHORITY *power, right*
submit...to her *a* ... Gen 16:9
put...your *a* on him ... Num 27:20
Who gave Him *a* ... Job 34:13
a over...day of death ... Eccl 8:8
entrust him with your *a* ... Is 22:21
as *one* having *a* ... Matt 7:29
a on earth to forgive ... Matt 9:6
a over unclean spirits ... Matt 10:1
All *a*...given to Me ... Matt 28:18
Son of Man has *a* ... Luke 5:24
no *a* except from God ... Rom 13:1
majesty, dominion...*a* ... Jude 25
give *a* over...nations ... Rev 2:26

AVENGE *revenge*
He will *a* the blood ... Deut 32:43
the LORD *a* me ... 1 Sam 24:12
Shall I not *a* Myself ... Jer 5:9
I will *a* their blood ... Joel 3:21
a-ing our blood ... Rev 6:10

AVENGER *revenger* In the OT, the avenger of blood was the next of kin to a murder victim. According to the law of Moses, the avenger had the right to kill the murderer. However, there were provisions to protect someone who had killed another person by accident.
The blood *a* himself ... Num 35:19
otherwise the *a* of blood ... Deut 19:6
a of their *evil* deeds ... Ps 99:8
God, an *a* who brings ... Rom 13:4
Lord is *the a* ... 1 Thess 4:6

AVOID *refuse*
A it, do not pass by ... Prov 4:15
a-ing...empty chatter ... 1 Tim 6:20

AWAIT *wait*
afflictions *a* me ... Acts 20:23
a-ing...the revelation ... 1 Cor 1:7
who eagerly *a* Him ... Heb 9:28

AWAKE *be attentive, watch*
awoke from his sleep ... Gen 28:16
A, a, Deborah ... Judg 5:12
Your likeness when I *a* ... Ps 17:15
dream when one *a-s* ... Ps 73:20
arouse or *a-n my* love ... Song 2:7
He *a-ns* My ear ... Is 50:4
A, a, put on strength ... Is 51:9
A, drunkards...weep ... Joel 1:5
that I may *a-n* him ... John 11:11
hour for you to *a-n* ... Rom 13:11

AWARE *know, understand*
the lad was not *a* ... 1 Sam 20:39
Will you not be *a* ... Is 43:19
But Jesus, *a* of *this* ... Matt 12:15
I was *a* that power ... Luke 8:46

AWE *fear, reverence*
stand in *a* of Him ... Ps 33:8
in *a* of Your words ... Ps 119:161
in *a* of My name ... Mal 2:5
feeling a sense of *a* ... Acts 2:43

AWESOME *fearful*
How *a* is this place ... Gen 28:17
angel of God, very *a* ... Judg 13:6
great and *a* God ... Neh 1:5
God is *a* majesty ... Job 37:22
As *a* as an army ... Song 6:4
a day of the LORD ... Joel 2:31

AXE *cutting tool*
his *a,* and his hoe ... 1 Sam 13:20
hammer nor *a* ... 1 Kin 6:7
a head fell into ... 2 Kin 6:5
a is already laid ... Luke 3:9

AZARIAH *(Yahweh has helped).*
1 *ancestor of Samuel* ... 1 Chr 6:36
2 *official of Solomon* ... 1 Kin 4:2
3 *son of Nathan* ... 1 Kin 4:5
4 *prophet who encouraged Asa to destroy the idols in* the land ... 2 Chr 15:1-8
5 *two sons of king Jehoshaphat* ... 2 Chr 21:2
6 *king of Judah, also* ***Uzziah*** ... 2 Kin 15:1; 2 Chr 26:1
7 *high priest* ... 1 Chr 6:10
8 *family of Merari* ... 2 Chr 29:12
9 *son of Hilkiah* ... 1 Chr 6:13,14
10 *original name of Abed-nego* ... Dan 1:7
the name of twelve other individuals in the OT

B

BAAL *(lord).* A common name for Phoenician gods including the chief male god, occasionally worshiped by the Israelites. Baal is also the prefix in the names of a number of places and people.
1 *Canaanite god(s)* ... Num 22:41; Judg 6:25; 1 Kin 18:40
2 *line of Reuben* ... 1 Chr 5:5
3 *personal name* ... 1 Chr 8:30
4 *place name* ... 1 Chr 4:33

BAAL-HANAN
1 *king of Edom* ... Gen 36:38
2 *servant of David* ... 1 Chr 27:28

BAAL-HAZOR
mountain in central Palestine ... 2 Sam 13:23

BAAL-HERMON
part of Mt. Hermon ... Judg 3:3; 1 Chr 5:23

BAAL-ZEBUB
god of Ekron ... 2 Kin 1:2,16
see also **BEELZEBUL**

BAASHA The son of Ahijah who killed the wicked King Nadab, the son of Jeroboam, and all his family; and then ruled in his place. By doing so Baasha fulfilled a prophecy, but he followed Jeroboam's false worship and suffered a similar fate.
king of Israel ... 1 Kin 15:16,32

BABEL *a city* This city and tower seem to have been an effort by man to observe and worship the heavens, besides being a unifying religious center in open challenge to God. At this time all the inhabitants spoke the same language. God knew their wicked intentions and He confused their communication by miraculously causing them to speak in different languages.
founded by Nimrod ... Gen 10:10;11:9
later called Babylon

BABES *infants*
From the mouth of...*b* ... Ps 8:2
abundance to their *b* ... Ps 17:14

BABY *infant*
woe...who are nursing *b-ies* ... Matt 24:19
b leaped...her womb ... Luke 1:41
b wrapped in cloths ... Luke 2:12
b as He lay ... Luke 2:16
like newborn *b-ies* ... 1 Pet 2:2

BABYLON *city (gate of god).* Capital of the ancient empire of Babylonia. In NT times, the name Babylon was sometimes symbolic for opposition to God.
1 *on the Euphrates* ... 2 Kin 17:24; Jer 20:4; Ezek 29:18; Dan 4:29
2 *symbolic of godlessness* ... Rev 14:8;17:5

BACK *part of body*
you shall see My *b* ... Ex 33:23
turned his *b* to leave ... 1 Sam 10:9
law behind their *b-s* ... Neh 9:26
my sins behind Your *b* ... Is 38:17

BAD *evil, wrong*
b report of the land ... Num 13:32
basket had very *b* figs ... Jer 24:2
if your eye is *b* ... Matt 6:23
b tree bears *b* fruit ... Matt 7:17
B company corrupts ... 1 Cor 15:33

BAG *sack*
fill their *b-s* ... Gen 42:25
in the shepherd's *b* ... 1 Sam 17:40
silver in two *b-s* ... 2 Kin 5:23
carrying *his b* of seed ... Ps 126:6
b of...weights ... Mic 6:11
b for *your* journey ... Matt 10:10
Carry no money belt, no *b* ... Luke 10:4

BAGGAGE *bags, supplies*
stayed with the *b* ... 1 Sam 25:13
prepare...yourself *b* ... Ezek 12:3

BAHURIM *(young men).* A town near the Mount of Olives on the road from Jerusalem to the Jordan River (2 Sam 3:16).

BAKE *cook*
b-d unleavened bread ... Gen 19:3
b-d food for Pharaoh ... Gen 40:17
they *b-d* the dough ... Ex 12:39
B what you will *b* ... Ex 16:23
grain offering *b-d* ... Lev 2:4
b twelve cakes ... Lev 24:5
taste of cakes *b-d* ... Num 11:8
fire to *b* bread ... Is 44:15

BAKER *cook*
b for the king ... Gen 40:1
cooks and *b-s* ... 1 Sam 8:13
from the *b-s'* street ... Jer 37:21
oven heated by the *b* ... Hos 7:4

BALAAM (unc, *devourer).* A Midianite prophet hired by the king of Moab to curse the Israelites. God prompted him to bless them instead. He was resisted by the angel of the Lord and was rebuked by his donkey. In the NT Balaam is a symbol of wickedness and apostasy because he seduced Israel into idolatry and fornication.
diviner ... Num 22:5-31;23:5; Josh 13:22; Rev 2:14

BALAK *(devastator).* The Moabite king who hired Balaam to hinder the Israelites from entering the Promised Land.
king of Moab ... Num 22:4; Mic 6:5

BALANCE *scale*
shall have just *b-s* ... Lev 19:36
b-s...with my calamity ... Job 6:2
A false *b* is an ... Prov 11:1
mountains in a *b* ... Is 40:12

BALD *hairless*
If...head becomes *b* ... Lev 13:41
every head is *b* ... Jer 48:37
head was made *b* ... Ezek 29:18

BALDHEAD *hairless*
mocked him...you *b* ... 2 Kin 2:23

BALM *aromatic ointment* A tree, grown mainly in Gilead, from which a medicinal resin is extracted. Merchants exported the resin to Egypt and other places. Sometimes used as a symbol for spiritual or psychological healing.
b and myrrh ... Gen 37:25
a present, a little *b* ... Gen 43:11
no *b* in Gilead ... Jer 8:22
Gilead and obtain *b* ... Jer 46:11
Bring *b* for her pain ... Jer 51:8
honey, oil and *b* ... Ezek 27:17

BALSAM *aromatic gum*
tops of the *b* trees ... 2 Sam 5:24
like a bed of *b* ... Song 5:13

BAN *set apart to God*
city...under the *b* ... Josh 6:17
destroy...under the *b* ... Josh 7:12
who violated the *b* ... 1 Chr 2:7
consign Jacob to the *b* ... Is 43:28

BAND *bond* or *group*
b-s shall be of silver ... Ex 27:10
skillfully woven *b* ... Ex 28:8
saw a marauding *b* ... 2 Kin 13:21
b of destroying angels ... Ps 78:49
b-s of the yoke ... Is 58:6

BANISH *exile*
b-ed one will not ... 2 Sam 14:14
assemble the *b-ed* ... Is 11:12
gaiety...is *b-ed* ... Is 24:11
where I will *b* them ... Ezek 4:13

BANK *slope*
b of the Nile ... Gen 41:3
reeds by the *b* ... Ex 2:3
b of the river ... Ezek 47:7
herd rushed down...*b* ... Luke 8:33

BANNER *flag, standard*
set up our *b-s* ... Ps 20:5
b to those who fear ... Ps 60:4
b over me is love ... Song 2:4
as an army with *b-s* ... Song 6:4

BANQUET *dinner, feast*
b lasting seven days ... Esth 1:5
brought me to *his b* ... Song 2:4
lavish *b* for all ... Is 25:6
place of honor at *b-s* ... Matt 23:6
Herod...gave a *b* ... Mark 6:21

BAPTISM *symbolic washing (immersion).* 1) A spiritual change by which a believer is placed into the body of Christ by the Holy Spirit as the agent or means (1 Cor 12:13). 2) A religious ceremony consisting of immersing someone in water. In the NT, the ceremony was first performed or presided over by John the Baptist as a sign of repentance, and later by the apostles in the name of Jesus for new converts. The ceremony symbolizes spiritual cleansing, or rescue from divine judgment (1 Pet 3:20-21). Many view immersion specifically as a symbol of identification with Christ in His death, burial, and resurrection, based on Rom 6:3-5. 3) A symbolic reference to suffering (Mark 10:38).
Sadducees coming...*b* ... Matt 3:7
b of repentance ... Mark 1:4
b with which I am ... Mark 10:38
with the *b* of John ... Luke 7:29
a *b* to undergo ... Luke 12:50
through *b* into death ... Rom 6:4
one faith, one *b* ... Eph 4:5
buried with Him in *b* ... Col 2:12

BAPTIZE *symbolic washing*
b...Holy Spirit ... Matt 3:11
tax collectors...*b-d* ... Luke 3:12
Jesus was also *b-d* ... Luke 3:21
sent me to *b* in water ... John 1:33
b-ing more disciples ... John 4:1
b-d with the Holy ... Acts 1:5
each of you be *b-d* ... Acts 2:38
he got up and was *b-d* ... Acts 9:18
household...been *b-d* ... Acts 16:15
John *b-d* with the ... Acts 19:4
b-d into Christ Jesus ... Rom 6:3
b-d into Moses ... 1 Cor 10:2
b-d into one body ... 1 Cor 12:13
b-d for the dead ... 1 Cor 15:29

BAR *metal* or *block*
b-s of your yoke ... Lev 26:13
a *b* of gold ... Josh 7:21
like *b-s* of iron ... Job 40:18
earth with its *b-s* ... Jon 2:6

BARABBAS *(son of the father).* This murderer and famous prisoner was freed in order to deliver Jesus to be crucified. Referring to this man, Peter said, *But you disowned the Holy and Righteous One and asked for a murderer....* (Acts 3:14).
robber ... Matt 27:16; Luke 23:18
released by Pilate ... Matt 27:26

BARAK
Deborah's commander ... Judg 4:6

BARBARIAN *non-Hellenic* The literal meaning is, "one who speaks an unintelligible language." Used somewhat derisively by Greeks to refer to non-Greeks, it gradually became a technical term for non-Greeks.
obligation...to *b-s* ... Rom 1:14
who speaks a *b* ... 1 Cor 14:11
b, Scythian, slave ... Col 3:11

BARE (adj) *barren, uncovered*
to cover *their b* flesh ... Ex 28:42
he went to a *b* hill ... Num 23:3
strips the forests *b* ... Ps 29:9
were naked and *b* ... Ezek 16:7

BARE (v) *expose, uncover*
foundations...laid *b* ... Ps 18:15
b-d His holy arm ... Is 52:10
foundation is laid *b* ... Ezek 13:14
open and laid *b* ... Heb 4:13

BAREFOOT *without sandals*
priests walk *b* ... Job 12:19
gone naked and *b* ... Is 20:3

BAR-JESUS
magician ... Acts 13:6
see also **ELYMAS**

BARLEY *grain*
land of wheat and *b* ... Deut 8:8
beginning...*b* harvest ... Ruth 1:22
stinkweed instead...*b* ... Job 31:40
has five *b* loaves ... John 6:9

BARN *farm building*
b-s are torn down ... Joel 1:17
seed still in the *b* ... Hag 2:19
wheat into the *b* ... Matt 3:12
nor gather into *b-s* ... Matt 6:26
tear down my *b-s* ... Luke 12:18

BARNABAS An apostle and a Levite from Cyprus whose original name was Joseph. The apostles surnamed him Barnabas, explained by Luke as "son of encouragement." He set an example of liberality when he sold a piece of property and brought the proceeds to the apostles for the benefit of the church. It was through him that Paul was accepted by the other apostles and was sent by them to investigate the spreading of the good news in Antioch. Barnabas accompanied Paul on his first missionary trip.
Cyprian by birth ... Acts 4:36
introduced Paul ... Acts 9:27
co-worker with Paul ... Acts 13:2,7
separated from Paul ... Acts 15:39

BARREN *childless, sterile*
Sarai was *b* ... Gen 11:30
but Rachel was *b* ... Gen 29:31
wrongs the *b* woman ... Job 24:21
Shout...O *b* one ... Is 54:1
Blessed are the *b* ... Luke 23:29

BARSABBAS
1 *Apostolic candidate, also called Joseph and Justus* ... Acts 1:23
2 *colleague of Paul, also called Judas* ... Acts 15:22

BARTHOLOMEW *(son of Talmai).* One of the twelve apostles, he may be the same man as the Nathanael of John 1:45-51. Nothing else is known about him.
apostle ... Matt 10:3; Luke 6:14; Acts 1:13

BARTIMAEUS
healed by Jesus ... Mark 10:46

BARUCH *(blessed).* A trusted friend and secretary of Jeremiah. Name of two other individuals.
1 *scribe* ... Jer 36:26;43:6
2 *priest* ... Neh 3:20
3 *a Judean* ... Neh 11:5

BASE *dishonorable*
no *b* thought ... Deut 15:9
b things of...world ... 1 Cor 1:28

BASEMATH *(balsam, fragrance).* One of Esau's wives. Also a daughter of Solomon.
1 *Esau's wife* ... Gen 26:34
2 *daughter of Solomon* ... 1 Kin 4:15

BASHAN *(fruitful).* A very fertile area in the northernmost part of Israel, east of the Jordan and the Sea of Galilee.
land E of Jordan ... Num 21:33; Josh 13:11; Is 2:13

BASIN *bowl, vessel*
blood...in the *b* ... Ex 12:22
b-s...of pure gold ... 1 Chr 28:17
a *sacrificial b* ... Zech 9:15
water into the *b* ... John 13:5

BASKET *container*
got him a wicker *b* ... Ex 2:3
b among the reeds ... Ex 2:5
b of summer fruit ... Amos 8:1
lamp...under a *b* ... Matt 5:15
not...put under a *b* ... Mark 4:21
seven large *b-s* full ... Mark 8:8
twelve *b-s full* ... Luke 9:17
let down in a *b* ... 2 Cor 11:33

BATH *measure of capacity* An ancient liquid measure in OT times of about 37 liters. It corresponds to the ephah of dry measure.
two thousand *b-s* ... 1 Kin 7:26
100 *b-s* of oil ... Ezra 7:22
only one *b of wine* ... Is 5:10
a tenth of a *b* from ... Ezek 45:14

BATHE *wash*
wash his clothes and *b* ... Lev 15:5
b his body in water ... Num 19:7
saw a woman *b-ing* ... 2 Sam 11:2
B-d in milk ... Song 5:12

BATHSHEBA *(daughter of Sheba).* A beautiful woman whom David desired so much for himself that he had her husband Uriah sent to the front line of a battle to ensure his death. Later David took Bathsheba as his wife, and from her Solomon was born.
wife of Uriah ... 2 Sam 11:3
taken by David ... 2 Sam 11:4
wife of David ... 2 Sam 11:27
mother of Solomon ... 2 Sam 12:24

BATTLE (n) *conflict, war*
b is the LORD's ... 1 Sam 17:47
b is...God's ... 2 Chr 20:15
scents the *b* from afar ... Job 39:25
with strength for *b* ... Ps 18:39
noise of *b* is in ... Jer 50:22
another king in *b* ... Luke 14:31
horses prepared for *b* ... Rev 9:7

BATTLE (v) *fight*
b against the sons ... Judg 20:14
drew near to *b* ... 1 Sam 7:10
about to go to *b* ... 1 Chr 12:19
nations...to *b* ... Zech 14:2

BDELLIUM The resin of a tree found in Havilah and parts of Babylonia and Media (Gen 2:12).

BEACH *coast*
crowd...on the *b* ... Matt 13:2
Jesus stood on the *b* ... John 21:4
down on the *b* ... Acts 21:5

BEAM *log*
like a weaver's *b* ... 2 Sam 21:19
one was felling a *b* ... 2 Kin 6:5
b-s, the thresholds ... 2 Chr 3:7
b-s of His...chambers ... Ps 104:3

BEAR (n) *animal*
b came and took ... 1 Sam 17:34
b robbed of...cubs ... Prov 17:12
the *b* will graze ... Is 11:7
resembling a *b* ... Dan 7:5

BEAR (v) *sustain*
too great to *b* ... Gen 4:13
bore you on eagles' ... Ex 19:4
not *b* false witness ... Ex 20:16
Lord...*b-s* our burden ... Ps 68:19
b their iniquities ... Is 53:11
b the penalty ... Ezek 23:49
she will *b* a Son ... Matt 1:21
it *b-s* much fruit ... John 12:24
b-ing His own cross ... John 19:17
b fruit for God ... Rom 7:4
b the image of ... 1 Cor 15:49
B...another's burdens ... Gal 6:2
b the sins of many ... Heb 9:28
bore our sins ... 1 Pet 2:24

BEARD *whiskers*
infection...on the *b* ... Lev 13:29
seized *him* by...*b* ... 1 Sam 17:35
shaved...their *b-s* ... 2 Sam 10:4
until your *b-s* grow ... 1 Chr 19:5

BEARER *carrier*
the *b-s* of the ark ... 2 Sam 6:13
strength of...*b-s* ... Neh 4:10
b of good news ... Is 40:9

BEAST *animal, creature* In Daniel, used prophetically in reference to four world empires that oppose God. In the NT, an evil ruler of the future.
God formed every *b* ... Gen 2:19
Noah and all the *b-s* ... Gen 8:1
eliminate harmful *b-s* ... Lev 26:6
b-s of the field ... Lev 26:22
But now ask the *b-s* ... Job 12:7
b of the forest ... Ps 50:10
b also had four heads ... Dan 7:6
they worshiped the *b* ... Rev 13:4
mark of the *b* ... Rev 16:2

BEAT *hit, strike*
b-ing a Hebrew ... Ex 2:11
b out what she ... Ruth 2:17
b-ing tambourines ... Ps 68:25
B your plowshares ... Joel 3:10
b Him with their ... Matt 26:67
b-ing His head with ... Mark 15:19
b-ing his breast ... Luke 18:13
b-en us in public ... Acts 16:37
stopped *b-ing* Paul ... Acts 21:32
b-en with rods ... 2 Cor 11:25

BEAUTIFUL *lovely, pleasing*
daughters...were *b* ... Gen 6:2
Rachel was *b* ... Gen 29:17
foliage of *b* trees ... Lev 23:40
Most *b* among women ... Song 1:8
Branch...will be *b* ... Is 4:2
Your *b* sheep ... Jer 13:20
enter the *B* Land ... Dan 11:41
How *b* are the feet ... Rom 10:15

BEAUTIFUL GATE *see* **GATES OF JERUSALEM**

BEAUTY
Your *b*...is slain ... 2 Sam 1:19
behold the *b* of the LORD ... Ps 27:4
Zion...perfection of *b* ... Ps 50:2
b is vain ... Prov 31:30
see the King in His *b* ... Is 33:17

BED *pallet*
My *b* will comfort me ... Job 7:13
make my *b* swim ... Ps 6:6
remember...on my *b* ... Ps 63:6
in *b* with a fever ... Matt 8:14
pick up your *b* ... Matt 9:6
lamp...under a *b* ... Mark 4:21

BEDROOM *sleeping area*
and into your *b* ... Ex 8:3
you speak in your *b* ... 2 Kin 6:12
his nurse in the *b* ... 2 Chr 22:11

BEELZEBUL (unc, *lord of the dung heap).* A Philistine god in the OT. In the NT, another name for Satan. Beelzebub *(lord of the flies)* is a variant reading.
NT prince of the demons ... Matt 12:27; Luke 11:15
see also **BAAL-ZEBUB**

BEEROTH Canaanite city given to the tribe of Benjamin (2 Sam 4:2).

BEERSHEBA
well / town in Negev ... Gen 21:31; Judg 20:1
home of Abraham ... Gen 22:19
home of Isaac ... Gen 26:23

BEFOREHAND *prior*
do not worry *b* ... Mark 13:11
anointed My body *b* ... Mark 14:8
God announced *b* ... Acts 3:18
prepared *b* for glory ... Rom 9:23

BEG *appeal, ask*
children wander...*b* ... Ps 109:10
b-s during...harvest ... Prov 20:4
b You to look at ... Luke 9:38
I am ashamed to *b* ... Luke 16:3
who used to sit and *b* ... John 9:8
b-ging them to leave ... Acts 16:39

BEGET *bring into being, sire*
Rock who *begot* ... Deut 32:18
whom you will *b* ... 2 Kin 20:18
begotten the...dew ... Job 38:28
I have *begotten* You ... Ps 2:7
have *begotten* You ... Acts 13:33

BEGINNING *origin, starting*
In the *b* God created ... Gen 1:1
from *b* to end ... 1 Sam 3:12
b was insignificant ... Job 8:7
fear of the LORD...*b* ... Ps 111:10
The *b* of the gospel ... Mark 1:1
In the *b* was the Word ... John 1:1
This *b* of *His* signs ... John 2:11
He is the *b* ... Col 1:18
the *b* and the end ... Rev 21:6

BEGOTTEN (adj) *fathered, born* In the NT, specially applied to Jesus Christ as the *only* begotten, referring to His uniqueness as God's Son.
b from the Father ... John 1:14
the only *b* God ... John 1:18
gave His only *b* Son ... John 3:16
only *b* Son of God ... John 3:18
offering...only *b* ... Heb 11:17
sent His only *b* Son ... 1 John 4:9

BEHALF *sake of*
atonement on his *b* ... Lev 5:6

the Father on your *b* ... John 16:26
I ask on their *b* ... John 17:9
one man to die on *b* ... John 18:14
be sin on our *b* ... 2 Cor 5:21

BEHAVE *act*
David *b-d* himself ... 1 Sam 18:30
b-ing as a madman ... 1 Sam 21:14
b properly as in ... Rom 13:13
blamelessly we *b-d* ... 1 Thess 2:10

BEHAVIOR *conduct*
instruction in wise *b* ... Prov 1:3
reverent in their *b* ... Titus 2:3
holy...in all *your b* ... 1 Pet 1:15
the *b* of their wives ... 1 Pet 3:1

BEHEADED *cut off*
killed him and *b* him ... 2 Sam 4:7
John *b* in the prison ... Matt 14:10
John, whom I *b* ... Mark 6:16
b because of their ... Rev 20:4

BEHEMOTH
hippopotamus ... Job 40:15

BEHOLD *look, see*
upright will *b* His face ... Ps 11:7
b the works of the LORD ... Ps 46:8
b-ing as in a mirror ... 2 Cor 3:18
B, I stand at the door ... Rev 3:20

BEING *existence, life*
man became a living *b* ... Gen 2:7
a...*b* coming up ... 1 Sam 28:13
wisdom in the...*b* ... Job 38:36
truth in the...*b* ... Ps 51:6
four living *b-s* ... Ezek 1:5
resembled a...*b* ... Dan 10:16

BEKA *(half).* An ancient Hebrew unit of weight valued at approx. 5.7 grams of silver, equal to half a shekel (Ex 38:26).

BEL *(lord).* Name of the protector god in Babylon, probably a Babylonian name for Baal.
Babylonian god ... Jer 50:2;51:44

BELA
1 *king of Edom* ... Gen 36:32
2 *son of Bejamin* ... Gen 46:21; 1 Chr 8:1
3 *a Reubenite* ... 1 Chr 5:8
4 *city of the plain near the Dead Sea* ... Gen 14:2,8
see also **ZOAR**

BELIAL *(worthlessness).* A title for Satan as the personification of evil (2 Cor 6:15).

BELIEVE *have faith, trust*
he *b-d* in the LORD ... Gen 15:6
did not *b* in God ... Ps 78:22
naive *b-s* everything ... Prov 14:15
you *b* that I am able ... Matt 9:28
ask in prayer, *b-ing* ... Matt 21:22
repent and *b* ... Mark 1:15
they *b-d*...Scripture ... John 2:22
whoever *b-s* in Him ... John 3:16
will you *b* My words ... John 5:47
who *b-s* has eternal ... John 6:47
men will *b* in Him ... John 11:48
b in the Light ... John 12:36
not see, and *yet b-d* ... John 20:29
b-d were of one heart ... Acts 4:32
B in the Lord Jesus ... Acts 16:31
Abraham *b-d* God ... Rom 4:3
How will they *b* ... Rom 10:14
love...*b-s* all ... 1 Cor 13:7
whom I have *b-d* ... 2 Tim 1:12
comes to God must *b* ... Heb 11:6
demons also *b* ... James 2:19
do not *b* every spirit ... 1 John 4:1

BELIEVERS *faithful ones* In the NT, those who have placed their complete faith and trust in Christ for salvation, realizing that they are unable to meet God's standards of righteousness by their own efforts.
all the circumcised *b* ... Acts 10:45
example to all the *b* ... 1 Thess 1:7
toward you *b* ... 1 Thess 2:10

BELL
a *b*...a pomegranate ... Ex 39:26
b-s of the horses ... Zech 14:20

BELLY *stomach*
On your *b*...you go ... Gen 3:14
crawls on its *b* ... Lev 11:42
b of the sea monster ... Matt 12:40

BELOVED *dearly loved*
b of the LORD dwell ... Deut 33:12
gives to His *b even* ... Ps 127:2
b is like a gazelle ... Song 2:9
This is My *b* Son ... Matt 3:17
your upbuilding, *b* ... 2 Cor 12:19
stand firm...my *b* ... Phil 4:1
faithful and *b* brother ... Col 4:9
Luke, the *b* physician ... Col 4:14
slave, a *b* brother ... Philem 16
This is My *b* Son ... 2 Pet 1:17
the called, *b* in God ... Jude 1

BELSHAZZAR *(may Bel protect the king).* The last king of the Babylonian Empire. He defiled the sacred vessels of the Jerusalem temple and was admonished by Daniel, but did not repent. Therefore, God chastised him through "the handwriting on the wall."
ruler of Babylon ... Dan 5:1; 7:1

BELT *waistband*
the *b* of the strong ... Job 12:21
leather *b* around his ... Matt 3:4
no money in their *b* ... Mark 6:8
Paul's *b* and bound ... Acts 21:11

BELTESHAZZAR *(protect his life).* The name given to Daniel by the Babylonians when he was chosen to serve in their royal court.
Daniel's Babylonian name ... Dan 1:7; 2:26; 5:12; 10:1

BENAIAH *(Yahweh has built).* One of David's mighty men and his bodyguard, he performed several great feats. His father was Jehoiada the priest. Name of several other individuals.
1 *son of Jehoiada* ... 2 Sam 8:18
captain of David ... 2 Sam 23:23
2 *Levitical singer* ... 1 Chr 15:18,20
3 *a priest* ... 1 Chr 15:24;16:5
the name of nine other individuals in the OT

BEN-AMMI see **AMMON**

BENEFIT *blessing, profit*
no return for the *b* ... 2 Chr 32:25
forget none of His *b-s* ... Ps 103:2
His *b-s* toward me ... Ps 116:12
the *b* of circumcision ... Rom 3:1

BEN-HADAD (unc, *son of thunderer).* Name of several Aramean kings. On one occasion the southern kingdom (Judah) allied with Ben-Hadad to fight against the northern kingdom (Israel).
1 *Ben-hadad I* ... 1 Kin 15:18-21
2 *Ben-hadad II* ... 1 Kin 20,22
3 *Ben-hadad III* ... 2 Kin 8:7-15;13:22

BEN-HINNOM A valley immediately south of Jerusalem, also called *valley of Hinnom.* In the time of Ahaz (q.v.) parents made their children walk through fire in worship of Molech. Later, Josiah put an end to pagan worship there and made the valley a place for burning refuse. The name *valley of Hinnom* is transliterated as Gehenna (q.v.) in Gr.
valley S of Jerusalem ... Josh 15:8; Neh 11:30
see also **HINNOM**

BENJAMIN *(son of the right hand).* Last of the sons of Jacob. The tribes of Benjamin and Judah formed the southern kingdom.
1 *son of Jacob* ... Gen 35:18
2 *tribe* ... Num 2:22
3 *of clan of Jediael* ... 1 Chr 7:10
4 *of the restoration* ... Neh 3:23

BENJAMIN GATE see **GATES OF JERUSALEM**

BEREA A Macedonian city near Mt. Olympus. The Jews there were commended for searching the Scriptures to see if Paul's preaching was correct. As a result, many of them were converted.
city in Macedonia visited by Paul ... Acts 17:10,13

BEREAVE *deprive, make sad*
be *b-d* of you both ... Gen 27:45
b...of your children ... Lev 26:22
I will *b them* ... Jer 15:7
longer *b* your nation ... Ezek 36:14

BERNICE
daughter of Herod Agrippa I ... Acts 25:13,23

BERODACH-BALADAN
king of Babylon ... 2 Kin 20:12
see also **MERODACH-BALADAN**

BESEECH *ask earnestly*
LORD, I *b* You ... Ps 116:4
do save, we *b* You ... Ps 118:25
leper came...*b-ing* ... Mark 1:40
b the Lord of the ... Luke 10:2

BESIEGE *assail, surround*
When you *b* a city ... Deut 20:19
enemies *b* them ... 2 Chr 6:28
was *b-ing* Jerusalem ... Jer 32:2
b-d...with bitterness ... Lam 3:5

BESTOWED *granted*
b...royal majesty ... 1 Chr 29:25
that the Spirit was *b* ... Acts 8:18
which He freely *b* ... Eph 1:6
b on Him the name ... Phil 2:9
love the Father has *b* ... 1 John 3:1

BETHANY *(house of dates* or *house of affliction).* 1) A town on the eastern slope of the Mount of Olives and the hometown

of Lazarus, Mary, and Martha. The Lord ascended to heaven from a place nearby. 2) Name of another small village on the eastern side of the Jordan River.
1 *E of Jerusalem* ... Matt 21:17
home of Mary, Martha and Lazarus ... John 11:1,18
2 *where John baptized* ... John 1:28

BETH-AVEN *(house of nothing).* 1) Name given to Bethel after it became a "house of iniquity" (Josh 7:2). 2) A place in the land of Benjamin (Hos 10:5).

BETHEL *(house of God).* A town north of Jerusalem with a rich civil and religious history during OT times. The Canaanites used to call it Luz, but Jacob called it Bethel upon receiving a vision there.
town in Benjamin ... Gen 12:8
N of Jerusalem ... Josh 8:17

BETHESDA
pool in Jerusalem ... John 5:2

BETH-HORON (unc, *place of a hole* or *hollow).* Twin cities in Ephraim with a difference of about 500 feet in elevation, known as "the High Beth-Horon" and "the Low Beth-Horon."
1 *famous battle site*
pass NW of Jerusalem ... Josh 10:10,11
2 *two towns at both ends of mountain pass* ... Josh 16:3,5

BETHLEHEM *(house of bread).* Originally called "Ephratha," then "Ephratah." The place of the birth of Jesus and site of Rachel's tomb. It is related to the development of Ruth's history, which probably means that David was born there too. Located about 5 miles south of Jerusalem.
1 *town S of Jerusalem* ... Gen 35:19
home of Ruth and Boaz ... Ruth 4:11
birthplace of Jesus ... Matt 2:1
2 *Zebulunite village* ... Josh 19:15

BETH-PEOR *(house of the opening).* The town in Moab where Moses reiterated the law to Israel.
Moabite city ... Deut 4:46;34:6

BETHPHAGE
village on the Mount of Olives ... Matt 21:1; Mark 11:1

BETHSAIDA *(house of fishing).* The town of Peter, Andrew, and Philip. Located on the northern shore of the Sea of Galilee near Capernaum.
village on Sea of Galilee ... Mark 8:22; Luke 9:10
home of Philip, Andrew and Peter ... John 1:44

BETH-SHAN/BETH-SHEAN
city at junction of Jezreel and Jordan valleys ... Josh 17:11; 1 Kin 4:12; 1 Chr 7:29

BETH-SHEAN *(house of rest).* A very ancient Canaanite city and strategic stronghold. The Philistines hanged Saul's body there on the city wall (1 Sam 31:10).

BETH-SHEMESH
1 *city of Judah* ... Josh 15:10
2 *Issachar border city* ... Josh 19:22
3 *city of Naphtali* ... Josh 19:38

BETRAY *break faith, be disloyal*
do not *b* the fugitive ... Is 16:3
wine *b-s* the haughty ... Hab 2:5
b Him to you ... Matt 26:15
how to *b* Him ... Mark 14:11
one...will *b* Me ... Mark 14:18
Judas, are you *b-ing* ... Luke 22:48

BETROTH *promise to wed*
You shall *b* a wife ... Deut 28:30
I will *b* you to Me ... Hos 2:19
Mary had been *b-ed* ... Matt 1:18
I *b-ed* you to one ... 2 Cor 11:2

BETROTHAL A binding agreement to wed, it is the first stage of a Jewish marriage and can be invalidated only by divorce.

BEWARE *be careful, watch*
B of practicing ... Matt 6:1
B of the scribes ... Mark 12:38
B of the leaven ... Luke 12:1
b...false circumcision ... Phil 3:2

BEYOND *over and above*
it was *b* measure ... Gen 41:49
remove...*b* Babylon ... Acts 7:43
tempted *b* what ... 1 Cor 10:13
b their ability ... 2 Cor 8:3
b all that we ask ... Eph 3:20
and *b* reproach ... Col 1:22

BEZALEL *(in the shadow of God).* A very skilled craftsman who was the chief builder of the tabernacle. Apparently he learned his trade in Egypt. Also the name of an Israelite.
1 *architect of tabernacle* ... Ex 31:1ff
2 *Israelite* ... Ezra 10:30

BEZER
1 *son of Zophah* ... 1 Chr 7:37
2 *city of refuge* ... Josh 20:8

BIG *large*
on the *b* toes ... Ex 29:20
Pharaoh...a *b* noise ... Jer 46:17
gave a *b* reception ... Luke 5:29

BILDAD *(Bel has loved).* A friend of Job who tried to console him when he was in great distress.
one of Job's friends ... Job 2:11;18:1;42:9

BILHAH Rachel's maid, whom she gave to Jacob as a concubine. Bilhah was the mother of Dan and Naphtali. Also the name of a town.
1 *Rachel's servant* ... Gen 29:29
Jacob's concubine ... Gen 30:3,4
2 *Simeonite town* ... 1 Chr 4:29

BIND *fasten, secure*
bound his son Isaac ... Gen 22:9
were *b-ing* sheaves ... Gen 37:7
b them as a sign ... Deut 6:8
b-s up their wounds ... Ps 147:3
B up the testimony ... Is 8:16
b up the brokenhearted ... Is 61:1
b on earth ... Matt 16:19
and *bound* Him ... John 18:12
bound...a thousand ... Rev 20:2

BIRD *fowl*
let *b-s* fly above ... Gen 1:20
eat any clean *b* ... Deut 14:20
b-s of the heavens ... Ps 8:8
Flee *as* a *b* to ... Ps 11:1
snare of a *b* catcher ... Hos 9:8
b-s...*have* nests ... Luke 9:58

BIRTH *act of being born*
A time to give *b* ... Eccl 3:2
You gave me *b* ... Jer 2:27
b of Jesus Christ ... Matt 1:18
rejoice at his *b* ... Luke 1:14
gave *b* to a son ... Luke 1:57
a man blind from *b* ... John 9:1
in pain to give *b* ... Rev 12:2

BIRTHDAY *day of birth*
was Pharaoh's *b* ... Gen 40:20
Herod's *b* came ... Matt 14:6
his *b*...banquet ... Mark 6:21

BIRTHRIGHT *first-born rights* A special privilege normally enjoyed by the firstborn son to inherit a double portion of his father's estate and to become the head of the family.
First sell me your *b* ... Gen 25:31
He took away my *b* ... Gen 27:36
sold his own *b* ... Heb 12:16

BITE
serpent *bit* any man ... Num 21:9
it *b-s* like a serpent ... Prov 23:32
if you *b*...one another ... Gal 5:15

BITHYNIA
territory on the Bosporus in Asia Minor ... Acts 16:7; 1 Pet 1:1

BITTER *painful, unpleasant*
b with hard labor ... Ex 1:14
waters of Marah...*b* ... Ex 15:23
b speech *as* their arrow ... Ps 64:3
substitute *b* for sweet ... Is 5:20
Strong drink is *b* ... Is 24:9
fresh and *b water* ... James 3:11

BITTERNESS *unpleasantness*
in the *b* of my soul ... Job 10:1
because of the *b* ... Is 38:15
full of cursing and *b* ... Rom 3:14
all *b*...be put away ... Eph 4:31
no root of *b* ... Heb 12:15

BLACK *dark*
sky grew *b* with ... 1 Kin 18:45
darkness and *b* gloom ... Job 3:5
I am *b* but lovely ... Song 1:5
behold, a *b* horse ... Rev 6:5
sun became *b* ... Rev 6:12

BLAME *fault, responsibility*
let me bear the *b* ... Gen 43:9
bear the *b*...forever ... Gen 44:32

BLAMELESS *faultless*
show Yourself *b* ... 2 Sam 22:26
just *and b man* is a ... Job 12:4
His way is *b* ... Ps 18:30
b will inherit good ... Prov 28:10
a *b* conscience ... Acts 24:16
holy and *b* before Him ... Eph 1:4
in the Law, found *b* ... Phil 3:6
spotless and *b* ... 2 Pet 3:14
b with great joy ... Jude 24

BLASPHEME *curse*
enemies...to *b* ... 2 Sam 12:14
name is continually *b-d* ... Is 52:5

This *fellow b-s* ... Matt 9:3
b-s...Holy Spirit ... Mark 3:29
force them to *b* ... Acts 26:11
name of God is *b-d* ... Rom 2:24
taught not to *b* ... 1 Tim 1:20
b-d the God of ... Rev 16:11

BLASPHEMY *cursing, profanity* A statement that is irreverent or disrespectful toward God. The Heb word for blasphemy essentially means "to cut" or "wound," and from this comes the concept of reviling or blaspheming. Blasphemy includes using God's name in inappropriate ways and crediting Him with evil, or giving someone else (e.g. Satan) the credit for good which God alone has done. Punishable by death according to OT law.
b against the Spirit ... Matt 12:31
b-ies they utter ... Mark 3:28
You...heard the *b* ... Mark 14:64
man...speaks *b-ies* ... Luke 5:21
stone You...for *b* ... John 10:33
words and *b-ies* ... Rev 13:5

BLAST *burst*
the *b* of Your nostrils ... Ex 15:8
b with the ram's horn ... Josh 6:5
a trumpet *b* of war ... Jer 49:2

BLAZING *burning*
LORD...a *b* fire ... Ex 3:2
furnace of *b* fire ... Dan 3:6
and to a *b* fire ... Heb 12:18

BLEMISH *imperfection, spot*
there is no *b* in you ... Song 4:7
six lambs without *b* ... Ezek 46:4
Himself without *b* ... Heb 9:14
stains and *b-es* ... 2 Pet 2:13

BLESS (v) *bestow favor* or *praise*
God *b-ed* the...day ... Gen 2:3
I will greatly *b* you ... Gen 22:17
LORD *b-ed* the sabbath ... Ex 20:11
and *b* Your inheritance ... Ps 28:9
LORD will *b* His people ... Ps 29:11
B the LORD ... Ps 103:2
generous will be *b-ed* ... Prov 22:9
who *b-es* his friend ... Prov 27:14
rise up and *b* her ... Prov 31:28
b-ed of My Father ... Matt 25:34
He *b-ed the food* ... Mark 6:41
b...who curse you ... Luke 6:28
while He was *b-ing* ... Luke 24:51
you are *b-ed* if you ... John 13:17
B...who persecute ... Rom 12:14
we *b our* Lord ... James 3:9

BLESSED (adj) *favored, happy*
b be God Most High ... Gen 14:20
B are you, O Israel ... Deut 33:29
B be the name of ... Job 1:21
How *b* is the man ... Ps 127:5
b...who finds wisdom ... Prov 3:13
nations will call you *b* ... Mal 3:12
B are the poor in ... Matt 5:3
B are the gentle ... Matt 5:5
B is the...kingdom ... Mark 11:10
B are you among women ... Luke 1:42
more *b* to give ... Acts 20:35
looking for...*b* hope ... Titus 2:13

BLESSING (n) *God's favor* 1) A bestowal by God of His favor or benefits. 2) A form of adoration of God for His goodness.
you shall be a *b* ... Gen 12:2
taken away your *b* ... Gen 27:35
a *b* and a curse ... Deut 11:26
curse into a *b* ... Neh 13:2
b of the LORD be upon ... Ps 129:8
showers of *b* ... Ezek 34:26
pour out for you a *b* ... Mal 3:10
fullness of the *b* ... Rom 15:29
cup of *b* which we ... 1 Cor 10:16
inherit a *b* ... 1 Pet 3:9
honor and glory and *b* ... Rev 5:12

BLIND (adj) *sightless*
misleads a *b person* ... Deut 27:18
To open *b* eyes ... Is 42:7
b...guides a *b* man ... Matt 15:14
b beggar *named* ... Mark 10:46
b man was sitting ... Luke 18:35
I was *b*, now I see ... John 9:25

BLIND (n) *without sight*
block before the *b* ... Lev 19:14
I was eyes to the *b* ... Job 29:15
the b receive sight ... Matt 11:5
a guide to the *b* ... Rom 2:19

BLIND (v) *make sightless*
b-s the clear-sighted ... Ex 23:8
bribe to *b* my eyes ... 1 Sam 12:3
has *b-ed* the minds ... 2 Cor 4:4
darkness has *b-ed* ... 1 John 2:11

BLINDNESS *sightlessness*
madness and with *b* ... Deut 28:28
struck them with *b* ... 2 Kin 6:18
every horse...with *b* ... Zech 12:4

BLOOD In the Scriptures, often represents life and was an important part of OT sacrifices for sin. The blood of Jesus Christ shed on the cross represents His life, which He freely gave to provide cleansing from sin for all who believe in Him.
Whoever sheds man's *b* ... Gen 9:6
bridegroom of *b* ... Ex 4:25
b shall be a sign ... Ex 12:13
not eat...any *b* ... Lev 3:17
land is filled with *b* ... Ezek 9:9
b did not reveal ... Matt 16:17
covenant in My *b* ... Luke 22:20
sweat...drops of *b* ... Luke 22:44
drinks My *b* abides ... John 6:56
Field of *B* ... Acts 1:19
the moon into *b* ... Acts 2:20
justified by His *b* ... Rom 5:9
sharing in the *b* ... 1 Cor 10:16
redemption...His *b* ... Eph 1:7
cleansed with *b* ... Heb 9:22
b, as of a lamb ... 1 Pet 1:19
the sea became *b* ... Rev 8:8
b of the saints ... Rev 17:6

BLOODGUILTINESS
no *b* on his account ... Ex 22:2
b is upon them ... Lev 20:11
b shall be forgiven ... Deut 21:8
Deliver me from *b* ... Ps 51:14

BLOODSHED *killing, murder*
abhors the man of *b* ... Ps 5:6
Men of *b* hate ... Prov 29:10
the *b* of Jerusalem ... Is 4:4
give you over to *b* ... Ezek 35:6
b follows *b* ... Hos 4:2

BLOSSOM *bloom*
the almond tree *b-s* ... Eccl 12:5
Israel will *b* and sprout ... Is 27:6
arrogance has *b-ed* ... Ezek 7:10
fig tree should not *b* ... Hab 3:17

BLOT *erase*
I will *b* out man ... Gen 6:7
b me...from Your book ... Ex 32:32
b out their name ... Deut 9:14
sin be *b-ted* out ... Neh 4:5
b out all my iniquities ... Ps 51:9
works...be *b-ted* out ... Ezek 6:6

BLUE *color*
tent of *b* and purple ... Ex 26:36
ephod all of *b* ... Ex 28:31
royal robes of *b* ... Esth 8:15

BOANERGES
name of James and John ... Mark 3:17

BOAST (n) *bragging*
soul will make its *b* ... Ps 34:2
the *b* of our hope ... Heb 3:6

BOAST (v) *brag, glory*
B no more so ... 1 Sam 2:3
who *b-s* of his gifts ... Prov 25:14
not *b* about tomorrow ... Prov 27:1
let not a rich man *b* ... Jer 9:23
b in God ... Rom 2:17
who *b* in the Law ... Rom 2:23
b...my weaknesses ... 2 Cor 12:9
it *b-s* of great things ... James 3:5

BOASTFUL *proud*
b shall not stand ... Ps 5:5
insolent, arrogant, *b* ... Rom 1:30
b pride of life ... 1 John 2:16

BOASTING *bragging*
Where is your *b* ... Judg 9:38
Where then is *b* ... Rom 3:27
our *b* about you ... 2 Cor 9:3
all such *b* is evil ... James 4:16

BOAT *watercraft*
slip by like reed *b-s* ... Job 9:26
left the *b* and their ... Matt 4:22
Peter got out of...*b* ... Matt 14:29
filled both of the *b-s* ... Luke 5:7
disciples into the *b* ... John 6:22

BOAZ (unc, *quickness*). Married Ruth after she became a widow. He was a rich nobleman from Bethlehem and was an ancestor of the Lord. Also the name of the left-hand pillar in Solomon's porch.
see **JACHIN**
1 *husband of Ruth* ... Ruth 4:13
grandfather of David ... Ruth 4:17ff
2 *temple pillar* ... 2 Chr 3:17

BODY *corpse, flesh*
b cleaves to the earth ... Ps 44:25
lamp of the *b* ... Matt 6:22
perfume on My *b* ... Matt 26:12
this is My *b* ... Mark 14:22
did not find His *b* ... Luke 24:23
b of sin...done away ... Rom 6:6
redemption of our *b* ... Rom 8:23
present your *b-ies* ... Rom 12:1
b-ies are members ... 1 Cor 6:15
b is a temple ... 1 Cor 6:19
you are Christ's *b* ... 1 Cor 12:27
b to be burned ... 1 Cor 13:3
absent from the *b* ... 2 Cor 5:8
one *b* and one Spirit ... Eph 4:4
building up of the *b* ... Eph 4:12

wives as...own *b-ies* ... Eph 5:28
transform the *b* ... Phil 3:21
b be preserved ... 1 Thess 5:23
bore...sins in His *b* ... 1 Pet 2:24

BODYGUARD *guard, protector*
captain of the *b* put ... Gen 40:4
you my *b* for life ... 1 Sam 28:2

BODY OF CHRIST A term found in Paul's epistles referring to all believers (1 Cor 12:27); the true church as it exists throughout the world. The body is represented on a smaller scale by the local church. Paul uses the term to illustrate the fact that all believers help and serve one another in various capacities determined by their spiritual gifts, just as the individual parts of the human body work together and support each other.

BOIL (n) *sore, swelling*
When...has a *b* ... Lev 13:18
b-s of Egypt ... Deut 28:27
smote Job with sore *b-s* ... Job 2:7

BOIL (v) *cook, heat*
not *b* a young goat in its ... Ex 34:26
we *b-ed* my son ... 2 Kin 6:29
fire causes water to *b* ... Is 64:2
b the guilt offering ... Ezek 46:20

BOISTEROUS *clamorous, loud*
woman of folly is *b* ... Prov 9:13
of noise, You *b* town ... Is 22:2
will drink *and* be *b* ... Zech 9:15

BOLD *brave, fearless*
wicked man...*b* face ... Prov 21:29
righteous are *b* as ... Prov 28:1
I *need* not be *b* ... 2 Cor 10:2

BOLDNESS *confidence*
word of God with *b* ... Acts 4:31
b and...access ... Eph 3:12
with *b* the mystery ... Eph 6:19

BOND *band, restraint*
neither *b* nor free ... 2 Kin 14:26
b of the covenant ... Ezek 20:37
with *b-s* of love ... Hos 11:4
he would break his *b-s* ... Luke 8:29
in the *b* of peace ... Eph 4:3
eternal *b-s* under ... Jude 6

BONDAGE *servitude, slavery*
see **BOND-SERVANT**
Israel sighed...*b* ... Ex 2:23
the *b* of iniquity ... Acts 8:23
sold into *b* to sin ... Rom 7:14

BOND-SERVANT *servant, slave* One bound to service without remuneration, i.e. a slave. In the NT, it is used primarily by the apostles to describe the way they viewed themselves in their ministry for Christ.
b-s of...Most High ... Acts 16:17
Paul, a *b* of Christ ... Rom 1:1
ourselves as your *b-s* ... 2 Cor 4:5
b...be quarrelsome ... 2 Tim 2:24
b of God...apostle ... Titus 1:1
His *b-s*...serve Him ... Rev 22:3

BONDSLAVE *servant, slave*
state of His *b* ... Luke 1:48
a *b* of Jesus Christ ... Col 4:12
Urge b-s to be subject ... Titus 2:9
use it as *b-s* of God ... 1 Pet 2:16

BONE
now *b* of my *b-s* ... Gen 2:23
the *b-s* of Joseph ... Josh 24:32
my *b-s* are dismayed ... Ps 6:2
rottenness in his *b-s* ... Prov 12:4
tongue breaks the *b* ... Prov 25:15
can these *b-s* live ... Ezek 37:3
dead men's *b-s* ... Matt 23:27
Not a *b*...be broken ... John 19:36

BOOK *scroll*
in a *b* as a memorial ... Ex 17:14
blot me...from Your *b* ... Ex 32:32
found the *b* of the ... 2 Kin 22:8
seal up the *b* ... Dan 12:4
not contain the *b-s* ... John 21:25
names are in the *b* ... Phil 4:3
worthy to open the *b* ... Rev 5:2
Lamb's *b* of life ... Rev 21:27

BOOK OF LIFE
God's book with names of righteous ... Ps 69:28; Phil 4:3; Rev 13:8; 17:8; 20:15

BOOTH *shelter*
b-s for his livestock ... Gen 33:17
live in *b-s* for seven ... Lev 23:42
in *b-s* during the feast ... Neh 8:14
sitting in the tax *b* ... Luke 5:27

BOOTHS Temporary shelters built as protection from the weather, for the sale of goods, or for use during the Feast of Booths or Tabernacles.
see **BOOTHS, FEAST OF**

BOOTHS, FEAST OF One of the three main festivals of the Jewish people (the others are Passover and Pentecost), during which the people had to live in temporary shelters. It lasted for eight days in commemoration of the time when the people of Israel lived in tents while wandering in the wilderness. All males were required to come up to Jerusalem and to bring an offering during this feast. Also known as the Feast of Ingathering or Tabernacles.
see **FEASTS**

BOOTY *loot, plunder*
b that remained ... Num 31:32
Swift is the *b* ... Is 8:1
divide the *b* with ... Is 53:12
have his *own* life as *b* ... Jer 38:2

BORDER *boundary*
enlarge your *b-s* ... Ex 34:24
b of...city of refuge ... Num 35:26
the Jordan as *a b* ... Deut 3:17
God extends your *b* ... Deut 12:20
peace in your *b-s* ... Ps 147:14

BORN *brought into life*
man is *b* for trouble ... Job 5:7
mountains were *b* ... Ps 90:2
child will be *b* to us ... Is 9:6
land be *b* in one day ... Is 66:8
b King of the Jews ... Matt 2:2
those *b* of women ... Luke 7:28
b not of blood ... John 1:13
unless one is *b* again ... John 3:3
b of the Spirit ... John 3:6
to one untimely *b* ... 1 Cor 15:8
b...to a living hope ... 1 Pet 1:3
loves is *b* of God ... 1 John 4:7

BORROW *use temporarily*
if a man *b-s anything* ... Ex 22:14
you shall not *b* ... Deut 28:12
b-s and does not pay ... Ps 37:21
wants to *b* from you ... Matt 5:42

BOSOM *breast*
iniquity in my *b* ... Job 31:33
take fire in his *b* ... Prov 6:27
to Abraham's *b* ... Luke 16:22
the *b* of the Father ... John 1:18
reclining on Jesus' *b* ... John 13:23

BOTHER *pester*
conscience *b-ed* ... 1 Sam 24:5
you *b* the woman ... Matt 26:10
worried and *b-ed* ... Luke 10:41
this widow *b-s* me ... Luke 18:5

BOTTOMLESS *without bottom*
key of the *b* pit ... Rev 9:1
he opened the *b* pit ... Rev 9:2

BOUGH *branch*
Joseph is a fruitful *b* ... Gen 49:22
b-s of leafy trees ... Lev 23:40
cedars...with its *b-s* ... Ps 80:10
nested in its *b-s* ... Ezek 31:6

BOUND (adj) *fastened, tied*
Foolishness is *b* up ... Prov 22:15
cast *b* into the...fire ... Dan 3:24
A wife is *b* as long ... 1 Cor 7:39

BOUND (n) *boundary, limit*
utmost *b* of...hills ... Gen 49:26
set *b-s* for the people ... Ex 19:12
b-s...the mountain ... Ex 19:23

BOUNDARY *border, limit*
b-ies of the peoples ... Deut 32:8
b of light and ... Job 26:10
the *b-ies* of the earth ... Ps 74:17
set for the sea its *b* ... Prov 8:29
the *b* of the widow ... Prov 15:25

BOUNTY *generous gift*
to his royal *b* ... 1 Kin 10:13
crowned...with Your *b* ... Ps 65:11
over the *b* of the LORD ... Jer 31:12

BOW (n) *rainbow*
set My *b* in the cloud ... Gen 9:13

BOW (n) *shooting device*
his *b* remained firm ... Gen 49:24
a *b* of bronze ... 2 Sam 22:35
not trust in my *b* ... Ps 44:6
b-s are shattered ... Jer 51:56

BOW (v) *bend, worship*
nations *b* down to ... Gen 27:29
Israel *b-ed in* ... Gen 47:31
to Him you shall *b* ... 2 Kin 17:36
My soul is *b-ed* down ... Ps 57:6
B Your heavens, O LORD ... Ps 144:5
nations will *b* down ... Zeph 2:11
He *b-ed* His head ... John 19:30
every knee shall *b* ... Rom 14:11

BOWELS *entrails, innards*
a disease of your *b* ... 2 Chr 21:15
smote him in his *b* ... 2 Chr 21:18

BOWL *dish, jug*
golden *b* is crushed ... Eccl 12:6
from sacrificial *b-s* ... Amos 6:6
dips with Me in...*b* ... Mark 14:20
b-s full of the wrath ... Rev 15:7

BOX *container*
b with the golden ... 1 Sam 6:11
sashes, perfume *b-es* ... Is 3:20
Judas had the...*b* ... John 13:29

BOX *type of tree*
b tree and the cypress ... Is 41:19

BOY *child, lad*
she left the *b* ... Gen 21:15
let the *b-s* live ... Ex 1:17
b will lead them ... Is 11:6
Traded a *b* for a harlot ... Joel 3:3
b was cured at once ... Matt 17:18

BOZRAH *(sheepfold).* A Levitical city in the land of Manasseh, against whom Jeremiah prophesied (Jer 49:13). Also the name of two other cities.

BRACELETS *armlets*
two *b* for her wrists ... Gen 24:22
armlets and *b* ... Num 31:50
earrings, *b*, veils ... Is 3:19

BRAMBLE *briar*
trees said to the *b* ... Judg 9:14
fire...from the *b* ... Judg 9:15

BRANCH *bough*
David a righteous *B* ... Jer 23:5
b-es fit for scepters ... Ezek 19:11
beautiful *b-es* and ... Ezek 31:3
birds...in its *b-es* ... Luke 13:19
b-es of the palm ... John 12:13
b...not bear fruit ... John 15:2
you are the *b-es* ... John 15:5
is holy, the *b-es* ... Rom 11:16

BREACH *break*
For every *b* of trust ... Ex 22:9
LORD had made a *b* ... Judg 21:15
closed up the *b* ... 1 Kin 11:27
that no *b* remained ... Neh 6:1
Heal its *b-es* ... Ps 60:2

BREAD *food*
eat unleavened *b* ... Ex 12:20
rain *b* from heaven ... Ex 16:4
He will bless your *b* ... Ex 23:25
not live by *b* alone ... Deut 8:3
ravens brought...*b* ... 1 Kin 17:6
b of heaven ... Ps 105:40
satisfy...with *b* ... Ps 132:15
b eaten in secret ... Prov 9:17
eat the *b* of idleness ... Prov 31:27
Cast your *b*...waters ... Eccl 11:1
not live on *b* alone ... Matt 4:4
Give us...daily *b* ... Matt 6:11
gives you the true *b* ... John 6:32
I am the *b* of life ... John 6:35

BREAD OF THE PRESENCE Unleavened loaves of bread which the high priest set before the Lord as a communal meal offering on the golden table in the Holy place. The priests were to eat the bread and replenish it every Sabbath. It symbolized the uninterrupted communion of the Lord with His people.
set the *b* ... Ex 25:30

BREAK *divide, shatter*
b down your pride ... Lev 26:19
never *b* My covenant ... Judg 2:1
broke the pitchers ... Judg 7:20
soft tongue *b-s* the ... Prov 25:15
reed He will not *b* ... Is 42:3
I *broke* your yoke ... Jer 2:20
B...fallow ground ... Hos 10:12
disciples *b* the ... Matt 15:2
waves were *b-ing* ... Mark 4:37
she *broke* the vial ... Mark 14:3
their nets *began* to *b* ... Luke 5:6
b his bonds ... Luke 8:29
b-ing the Sabbath ... John 5:18
did not *b* His legs ... John 19:33
your *b-ing* the Law ... Rom 2:23

BREAST *bosom*
orphan from the *b* ... Job 24:9
upon my mother's *b-s* ... Ps 22:9
b-s are like...fawns ... Song 7:3
b-s...never nursed ... Luke 23:29

BREASTPIECE *breast covering* A special garment worn by the high priest which contained twelve precious stones representing the twelve tribes of Israel. It was made out of the same material as the ephod.
a *b* and an ephod ... Ex 28:4
make a *b* of judgment ... Ex 28:15
they bound the *b* ... Ex 39:21

BREASTPLATE *breast armor* Armor piece that protects the chest.
righteousness like a *b* ... Is 59:17
b of faith and love ... 1 Thess 5:8
like *b-s* of iron ... Rev 9:9

BREATH *air, spirit, wind*
the *b* of life ... Gen 2:7
days are *but* a *b* ... Job 7:16
man is a mere *b* ... Ps 39:11
b came into them ... Ezek 37:10
give *b* to the image ... Rev 13:15

BREATHE *inhale and exhale*
Abraham *b-d* his last ... Gen 25:8
such as *b* out violence ... Ps 27:12
garden *b...fragrance* ... Song 4:16
b on these slain ... Ezek 37:9
He *b-d* His last ... Mark 15:39
He *b-d* on them ... John 20:22

BRETHREN *brothers*
beating...his *b* ... Ex 2:11
b from all the nations ... Is 66:20
His *b* Will return ... Mic 5:3
b, why do you injure ... Acts 7:26
sinning against...*b* ... 1 Cor 8:12
dangers...false *b* ... 2 Cor 11:26
Peace be to the *b* ... Eph 6:23
faithful *b* in Christ ... Col 1:2
the love of the *b* ... 1 Thess 4:9
b...not grow weary ... 2 Thess 3:13
my *b*, do not swear ... James 5:12
our lives for the *b* ... 1 John 3:16
accuser of our *b* ... Rev 12:10

BRIAR *thistle, thorn*
b-s and thorns will come ... Is 5:6
land will be *b-s* ... Is 7:24
grapes from a *b* bush ... Luke 6:44

BRIBE *illegal gift*
b blinds...clear-sighted ... Ex 23:8
nor take a *b* ... Deut 10:17
who hates *b-s* will ... Prov 15:27
b corrupts the heart ... Eccl 7:7
Everyone loves a *b* ... Is 1:23

BRICK *clay block*
they used *b* for stone ... Gen 11:3
straw to make *b* as ... Ex 5:7
deliver...quota of *b-s* ... Ex 5:18
burning incense on *b-s* ... Is 65:3

BRIDE *newlywed*
as a *b* adorns herself ... Is 61:10
the voice of the *b* ... Jer 7:34
b out of her *bridal* ... Joel 2:16
He who has the *b* ... John 3:29
b...of the Lamb ... Rev 21:9

BRIDEGROOM *newlywed*
a *b* of blood to me ... Ex 4:25
As a *b* decks himself ... Is 61:10
voice of the *b* ... Jer 7:34
attendants of the *b* ... Matt 9:15
out to meet the *b* ... Matt 25:1

BRIDLE (n) *head harness*
My *b* in your lips ... 2 Kin 19:28
a *b* for the donkey ... Prov 26:3
up to the horses' *b-s* ... Rev 14:20

BRIDLE (v) *control*
not *b* his tongue ... James 1:26
man, able to *b* ... James 3:2

BRIGHT *shining*
b in the skies ... Job 37:21
night is as *b* as ... Ps 139:12
B eyes gladden ... Prov 15:30
b cloud...them ... Matt 17:5
b light...flashed ... Acts 22:6
the *b* morning star ... Rev 22:16

BRIMSTONE *sulfur* Another word for sulphur, usually burning. Sodom and Gomorrah were destroyed by brimstone as a divine punishment.
b and fire from ... Gen 19:24
b and burning wind ... Ps 11:6
rained fire and *b* ... Luke 17:29
tormented with...*b* ... Rev 14:10
lake of fire and *b* ... Rev 20:10

BRING *carry, lead*
will *b* forth children ... Gen 3:16
Cain *brought*...offering ... Gen 4:3
b two of every *kind* ... Gen 6:19
B the ark of God ... 1 Sam 14:18
Kings will *b* gifts ... Ps 68:29
B water for the thirsty ... Is 21:14
B the whole tithe ... Mal 3:10
brought...a paralytic ... Matt 9:2
not...to *b* peace ... Matt 10:34
I *b* you good news ... Luke 2:10
Law *b-s* about wrath ... Rom 4:15
b-ing salvation ... Titus 2:11

BROAD *wide*
into a *b* place ... 2 Sam 22:20
land was *b* and ... 1 Chr 4:40
the sea, great and *b* ... Ps 104:25
dark in *b* daylight ... Amos 8:9
way is *b* that leads to ... Matt 7:13

BROKEN *crushed, separated*
My spirit is *b* ... Job 17:1
A *b* and a contrite heart ... Ps 51:17
they have *b* Your law ... Ps 119:126
deeps were *b* up ... Prov 3:20
silver cord is *b* ... Eccl 12:6
bind up the *b* ... Ezek 34:16
Scripture...be *b* ... John 10:35
Not a bone...*b* ... John 19:36
Branches were *b* off ... Rom 11:19

BROKENHEARTED *grieving*
LORD is near to the *b* ... Ps 34:18
He heals the *b* ... Ps 147:3
sent me to bind...*b* ... Is 61:1

BRONZE *metal*
implements of *b* ... Gen 4:22
made a *b* serpent ... Num 21:9
bend a bow of *b* ... 2 Sam 22:35
as walls of *b* ... Jer 1:18
third kingdom of *b* ... Dan 2:39
costly wood and *b* ... Rev 18:12

BROOD *group, offspring*
b of sinful men ... Num 32:14
You *b* of vipers ... Matt 3:7
hen *gathers* her *b* ... Luke 13:34

BROOK *stream, wadi*
stones from the *b* ... 1 Sam 17:40
by the *b* Cherith ... 1 Kin 17:5
deer pants for...*b-s* ... Ps 42:1
wisdom...bubbling *b* ... Prov 18:4

BROTHER *male relative* In the Scriptures, often used in reference to a more distant relative, or to a fellow Israelite, or fellow Christian, etc.
Am I my *b-'s* ... Gen 4:9
b-s were jealous ... Gen 37:11
b-s may redeem ... Lev 25:48
b-s to dwell together ... Ps 133:1
b is born for ... Prov 17:17
closer than a *b* ... Prov 18:24
b-s of a poor man ... Prov 19:7
reconciled to your *b* ... Matt 5:24
B will betray *b* ... Matt 10:21
behold, His...*b-s* ... Matt 12:46
not forgive his *b* ... Matt 18:35
My *b* and sister ... Mark 3:35
b of yours was dead ... Luke 15:32
left...wife or *b-s* ... Luke 18:29
not even His *b-s* ... John 7:5
b will rise again ... John 11:23
b goes to law with *b* ... 1 Cor 6:6
my *b* to stumble ... 1 Cor 8:13
yet hates his *b* ... 1 John 2:9

BROTHERHOOD In the NT, a term used collectively of the Christian community of men and women.
the covenant of *b* ... Amos 1:9
love the *b*, fear God ... 1 Pet 2:17

BROTHER-IN-LAW, DUTY OF *see* **LEVIRATE MARRIAGE**

BRUISE (n) *wound*
for wound, *b* for *b* ... Ex 21:25
Only b-s, welts and raw ... Is 1:6
the *b* He has inflicted ... Is 30:26

BRUISE (v) *batter, crush*
b him on the heel ... Gen 3:15
b-s me with a tempest ... Job 9:17

BRUTAL *fierce, vicious*
hand of *b* men ... Ezek 21:31
b, haters of good ... 2 Tim 3:3

BUCKLER A small round shield carried in the hand or worn on the arm for defense (Ps 35:2).

BUD *blossom, a sprout*
flax was in *b* ... Ex 9:31
put forth *b-s* ... Num 17:8
the *b* blossoms ... Is 18:5

BUILD *construct, form*
Noah *built* an altar ... Gen 8:20
let us *b*...a city ... Gen 11:4
b for Me a house ... 1 Chr 17:12
b-ing...house of God ... 2 Chr 3:3
built high places ... 2 Chr 33:19
has *built* up Zion ... Ps 102:16
Unless the LORD *b-s* ... Ps 127:1
a time to *b* up ... Eccl 3:3
built his house on ... Matt 7:24
I will *b* My church ... Matt 16:18
able to *b you* up ... Acts 20:32
being *built* together ... Eph 2:22
stones...being *built* ... 1 Pet 2:5

BUILDER *fashioner, maker*
Solomon's *b-s* ... 1 Kin 5:18
b-s had laid the ... Ezra 3:10
the *b-s* rejected ... Matt 21:42
like a wise master *b* ... 1 Cor 3:10
architect and *b* is ... Heb 11:10

BUILDING *structure*
reconstructing this *b* ... Ezra 5:4
b that *was* in front ... Ezek 41:12
what wonderful *b-s* ... Mark 13:1
you are...God's *b* ... 1 Cor 3:9
have a *b* from God ... 2 Cor 5:1
whole *b*, being fitted ... Eph 2:21

BULB *part of plant*
a *b* and a flower ... Ex 25:33
b-s and their branches ... Ex 25:36

BULL *animal*
b of the sin offering ... Lev 4:20
b without blemish ... Ezek 45:18
blood of *b-s* and ... Heb 10:4

BULRUSH *marsh plant* A marsh plant found in the wetlands along the Nile in Egypt.
b in a single day ... Is 9:14
b-es by the Nile ... Is 19:7
palm branch or *b* ... Is 19:15

BULWARK A wall-like barrier used for defense (Ps 91:4).

BUNDLE *package*
b...*was* in his sack ... Gen 42:35
the *b* of the living ... 1 Sam 25:29
in *b-s* to burn ... Matt 13:30

BURDEN (n) *load, weight*
b-s of the Egyptians ... Ex 6:6
the *b* of the people ... Num 11:17
I am a *b* to myself ... Job 7:20
who daily bears our *b* ... Ps 68:19
My *b* is light ... Matt 11:30
b-s hard to bear ... Luke 11:46
Bear one another's *b-s* ... Gal 6:2

BURDEN (v) *weigh down*
b-ed Me with your sins ... Is 43:24
were *b-ed* excessively ... 2 Cor 1:8
not *b* you myself ... 2 Cor 12:16
the church must not be *b-ed* ... 1 Tim 5:16

BURIAL *interment*
give me a *b* site ... Gen 23:4
even have a *proper b* ... Eccl 6:3
to prepare Me for *b* ... Matt 26:12
b custom of the Jews ... John 19:40

BURN (v) *consume, kindle*
Jacob's anger *b-ed* ... Gen 30:2
bush was *b-ing* ... Ex 3:2
Your anger *b* against ... Ex 32:11
Moses' anger *b-ed* ... Ex 32:19
did not *b* any cities ... Josh 11:13
jealousy *b* like fire ... Ps 79:5
to *b* their sons ... Jer 7:31
not to *b* the scroll ... Jer 36:25
will *b* up the chaff ... Luke 3:17
b-ed in their desire ... Rom 1:27
my body to be *b-ed* ... 1 Cor 13:3
works will be *b-ed* ... 2 Pet 3:10
lake of fire...*b-s* ... Rev 19:20

BURNING (adj)
Your *b* anger ... Ex 15:7
shall bewail the *b* ... Lev 10:6
b lips and a wicked ... Prov 26:23
b heat of famine ... Lam 5:10
b anger of the LORD ... Zeph 2:2

BURNISHED *polished*
gleamed like *b* bronze ... Ezek 1:7
feet...like *b* bronze ... Rev 1:15

BURNT OFFERING An offering described in Lev 1, in which the burning of the sacrifice was to go up as a pleasing odor to the Lord. Usually the one making the offering had to place his hands on the sacrificial animal before it was slaughtered, identifying himself with it. The animal offered had to be totally consumed by the fire, and when properly sacrificed, it brought atonement for the one who offered it.
see also **OFFERINGS**

BURST *break*
great deep *b* open ... Gen 7:11
wine will *b* the skins ... Luke 5:37
he *b* open ... Acts 1:18

BURY *place in earth*
b-ied at...old age ... Gen 15:15
that I may *b* my dead ... Gen 23:4
b-ied the bones of ... Josh 24:32
go and *b* my father ... Matt 8:21
dead to *b* their own ... Matt 8:22
devout...*b-ied* Stephen ... Acts 8:2
that He was *b-ied* ... 1 Cor 15:4
b-ied...in baptism ... Col 2:12

BUSH *shrub*
boy under...the *b-es* ... Gen 21:15
the *b* was burning ... Ex 3:2
who dwelt in the *b* ... Deut 33:16
like a *b* in the desert ... Jer 17:6

BUSINESS *occupation, work*
until I...told my *b* ... Gen 24:33
carry on the *king's b* ... Esth 3:9
another to his *b* ... Matt 22:5
a place of *b* ... John 2:16
attend to your...*b* ... 1 Thess 4:11
engage in *b* ... James 4:13

BUSYBODIES *meddlers*
no work...like *b* ... 2 Thess 3:11
gossips and *b* ... 1 Tim 5:13

BUTTER
steps...bathed in *b* ... Job 29:6
smoother than *b* ... Ps 55:21
milk produces *b* ... Prov 30:33

BUYER *purchaser*
Bad, bad, says the *b* ... Prov 20:14
the *b* like the seller ... Is 24:2
Let not the *b* rejoice ... Ezek 7:12

BYSTANDERS *unlookers*
b...said to Peter ... Matt 26:73
the *b* heard it ... Mark 15:35

BYWORD *contemptible*
b among all peoples ... 1 Kin 9:7
a proverb and a *b* ... 2 Chr 7:20
He has made me a *b* ... Job 17:6
b among the nations ... Ps 44:14

C

CAESAR Originally the family name of Julius Caesar, it was later assumed by his adopted son Octavian (*see* **AUGUSTUS**) who was ruling when Christ was born. Succeeding emperors also took the name, so that it came to be a title. References are made to three of them in the NT: Tiberius, Claudius, and Nero.
1 *Roman emperor* ... Matt 22:17,21; Mark 12:14; John 19:12
2 *Augustus* ... Luke 2:1
3 *Tiberius* ... Luke 3:1; John 19:12
4 *Claudius* ... Acts 11:28; 17:7; 18:2
5 *Nero* ... Acts 25:12; 26:32; Phil 4:22

CAESAREA A city on the coast of Israel, a few miles south of Mt. Carmel. To be distinguished from Caesarea Philippi.
Roman coastal city ... Acts 8:40; 10:1; 21:16; 25:4

CAESAREA PHILIPPI A city located at the base of Mt. Hermon and southwest of it. The tetrarch Philip rebuilt the city and named it in honor of the emperor Augustus and himself.
city at base of Mt. Hermon ... Matt 16:13; Mark 8:27

CAIAPHAS The high priest who presided over the trial of Jesus; his name originally was Joseph.
high priest ... Matt 26:57; Luke 3:2; John 11:49ff; Acts 4:6

CAIN (unc, *obtain, acquire*). The firstborn son of Adam and Eve, a produce farmer by occupation. He murdered his brother Abel because God accepted Abel's offering but not his own.
son of Adam ... Gen 4:1
tiller of the ground ... Gen 4:2
killed his brother ... Gen 4:8
marked by sign ... Gen 4:15

CAKE *type of bread*
and make bread *c-s* ... Gen 18:6
took one unleavened *c* ... Lev 8:26
make me a...*c* ... 1 Kin 17:13

CALAMITY *adversity, trouble*
day of my *c* ... 2 Sam 22:19
sorry over the *c* ... 1 Chr 21:15
palate discern *c-ies* ... Job 6:30
c from God is ... Job 31:23
stumble in *time of c* ... Prov 24:16
beginning to work *c* ... Jer 25:29
relents concerning *c* ... Jon 4:2

CALCULATE *count*
shall *c* from the year ... Lev 25:50
c the cost ... Luke 14:28
c the...beast ... Rev 13:18

CALEB One of the twelve spies sent by Moses to investigate the Promised Land. He encouraged the people of Israel to take the land. Also name of another person.
1 *aide to Moses* ... Num 13:30
son of Jephunneh ... Num 32:12
received Hebron ... Josh 14:13
2 *son of Hezron* ... 1 Chr 2:18

CALENDAR (JEWISH) The Jewish calendar was made up of the following lunar months: Abib or Nisan: roughly equivalent to March/April; Ziv: April/May; Sivan: May/June; Tammuz: June/July; Ab: July/August; Elul: August/September; Tishri or Ethanim: September/October; Bul: October/November; Kislev: November/December; Tebeth: December/January; Shebat: January/February; Adar: February/March. A thirteenth month was added seven times during the course of every 19 years.

CALF *animal*
tender and choice *c* ... Gen 18:7
c and the young lion ... Is 11:6
skip about like *c-ves* ... Mal 4:2
bring the fattened *c* ... Luke 15:23
blood of...*c-ves* ... Heb 9:12

CALF, MOLTEN An idol of a young bull crafted by Aaron from gold rings which the Hebrews provided him, when they rebelled while Moses was receiving the law on Mt. Sinai (Ex 32:4).
into a molten *c* ... Ex 32:4

CALL *address, summon, name*
God *c-ed* the light day ... Gen 1:5
c upon the name ... Gen 4:26
c-s up the dead ... Deut 18:11
LORD was *c-ing*...boy ... 1 Sam 3:8
c-ed fine gold my trust ... Job 31:24
c upon the LORD ... Ps 18:3
those who *c* evil good ... Is 5:20
c His name Immanuel ... Is 7:14
You shall *c* Me ... Jer 3:19
who is *c-ed* the Messiah ... Matt 1:16
to *c* the righteous ... Matt 9:13
c-s his own sheep ... John 10:3
c Me Teacher and ... John 13:13
God has not *c-ed* ... 1 Thess 4:7
c-s...a prophetess ... Rev 2:20

CALLING *summoning*
the *c* of assemblies ... Is 1:13
the *c* of God ... Rom 11:29
For consider your *c* ... 1 Cor 1:26
with a holy *c* ... 2 Tim 1:9
His *c* and choosing ... 2 Pet 1:10

CALM *still*
be *c*, have no fear ... Is 7:4
sea may become *c* ... Jon 1:11
it became perfectly *c* ... Matt 8:26
you ought to keep *c* ... Acts 19:36

CAMEL *animal*
dismounted...the *c* ... Gen 24:64
his wives upon *c-s* ... Gen 31:17
a garment of *c-'s* hair ... Matt 3:4
c...eye of a needle ... Matt 19:24
clothed with *c-'s* hair ... Mark 1:6

CAMP (n) *lodging area*
This is God's *c* ... Gen 32:2
people out of the *c* ... Ex 19:17
outside the *c* seven ... Num 31:19
pitch *c-s*, and place ... Ezek 4:2
the *c* of the saints ... Rev 20:9

CAMP (v) *settle*
you shall *c* in front ... Ex 14:2
they shall also *c* ... Num 1:50
Israel *c-ed* at Gilgal ... Josh 5:10
I will *c* against you ... Is 29:3
c around My house ... Zech 9:8

CANA (unc, *reed*). Name of a town in Galilee near Nazareth. Christ performed His first miracle there. It was the home of His disciple Nathanael.
Galilean town ... John 2:1,11;4:46

CANAAN (unc, *be humble, bow down*). Grandson of Noah. Also an ancient name of the Promised Land.
1 *son of Ham* ... Gen 9:18,25
2 *Syro-Palestine* ... Gen 13:12;42:5; Ex 16:35; Ps 105:11
3 *language (Hebrew)* ... Is 19:18
see also **HEBREW**
see also **JUDEAN**

CANAL *water way*
c-s will emit a stench ... Is 19:6
rivers *and* wide *c-s* ... Is 33:21
the Nile *c-s* dry ... Ezek 30:12
in front of the *c* ... Dan 8:3

CAPERNAUM (*village of comfort*). A city on the northwest shore of the Sea of Galilee where Christ had an extensive ministry. Peter settled there (Matt 17:24).
city on Sea of Galilee ... Matt 4:13; Luke 4:23; John 6:24,59

CAPHTOR
Crete ... Deut 2:23; Jer 47:4; Amos 9:7
see also **CRETE**

CAPITAL *top part of column*
height of the other *c* ... 1 Kin 7:16
c on the top of each ... 2 Chr 3:15
c-s...were on top ... 2 Chr 4:12

CAPPADOCIA
province in Asia Minor ... Acts 2:9; 1 Pet 1:1

CAPTAIN *leader*
c of the bodyguard ... Gen 39:1
the *c-s* of hundreds ... Num 31:14
c of the host of ... Josh 5:14
the *c* of the ship ... Acts 27:11

CAPTIVE *prisoner*
firstborn of the *c* ... Ex 12:29
slain and the *c-s* ... Deut 32:42
restores his *c* people ... Ps 14:7
have led *c Your c-s* ... Ps 68:18
release to the *c-s* ... Luke 4:18
every thought *c* ... 2 Cor 10:5
having been held *c* ... 2 Tim 2:26

CAPTIVITY *imprisonment*
restore you from *c* ... Deut 30:3
land of their *c* ... 2 Chr 6:37
had come from the *c* ... Ezra 8:35
had survived the *c* ... Neh 1:2
destined for *c* ... Rev 13:10

CAPTURE *seize, take*
they *c-d* and looted ... Gen 34:29
c-d all his cities ... Deut 2:34
Can anyone *c* him ... Job 40:24
c...with her eyelids ... Prov 6:25
it *c-s* nothing at all ... Amos 3:5

CARAVAN *expedition*
a *c* of Ishmaelites ... Gen 37:25
The *c-s* of Tema ... Job 6:19
O *c-s* of Dedanites ... Is 21:13

CARCASS *corpse*
down upon the *c-es* ... Gen 15:11
one who touches...*c* ... Lev 11:39
c-es will be food ... Deut 28:26
c of the lion ... Judg 14:8
c-es of their...idols ... Jer 16:18

CARE (n) *concern*
into the *c* of...sons ... Gen 30:35
put him in my *c* ... Gen 42:37
friends and receive *c* ... Acts 27:3
c for one another ... 1 Cor 12:25

CARE (v) *have concern for*
He *c-d* for him ... Deut 32:10
No one *c-s* for...soul ... Ps 142:4
c for My sheep ... Ezek 34:12
and took *c* of him ... Luke 10:34
take *c* of the church ... 1 Tim 3:5
he *c-s* for you ... 1 Pet 5:7

CAREFUL *watchful, on guard*
I not be *c* to speak ... Num 23:12
c to observe all ... Deut 6:25
you shall be *c* to do ... Deut 8:1
be *c* not to drink ... Judg 13:4
be *c* how you walk ... Eph 5:15

CARELESS *thoughtless*
a fool is...*c* ... Prov 14:16
food, and *c* ease ... Ezek 16:49
that every *c* word ... Matt 12:36

CARGO *merchandise*
and they threw the *c* ... Jon 1:5
to unload its *c* ... Acts 21:3
no one buys...*c-es* ... Rev 18:11

CARMEL
1 *range of hills* ... 1 Kin 18:42; 2 Kin 4:25; Jer 46:18
2 *town in Judah* ... 1 Sam 15:12;25:5,40

CARPENTER *craftsman*
c-s and stonemasons ... 2 Sam 5:11
to the masons and *c-s* ... Ezra 3:7
this the *c-'s* son ... Matt 13:55
c, the son of Mary ... Mark 6:3

CARRY *bear*
LORD...*c-ied* you ... Deut 1:31
c an ephod before ... 1 Sam 2:28
Spirit...will *c* you ... 1 Kin 18:12
c them in His bosom ... Is 40:11
our sorrows He *c-ied* ... Is 53:4
c-ied away...diseases ... Matt 8:17
C no money belt, no bag ... Luke 10:4
the cross to *c* ... Luke 23:26
c out the desire of ... Gal 5:16

CART *wagon*
So Moses took the *c-s* ... Num 7:6
the cows to the *c* ... 1 Sam 6:7
sin as if with *c* ropes ... Is 5:18
his c and his horses ... Is 28:28

CARVE (v) *cut, fashion*
he *c-d* all the walls ... 1 Kin 6:29
who *c* a resting place ... Is 22:16
c-d with cherubim ... Ezek 41:18
its maker has *c-d* it ... Hab 2:18

CARVED (adj) *cut, etched*
with *c* engravings ... 1 Kin 6:29
c image of the idol ... 2 Chr 33:7
abdomen is *c* ivory ... Song 5:14

CAST *throw*
one who *c-s* a spell ... Deut 18:11
Joshua *c* lots for ... Josh 18:10
c Your law behind ... Neh 9:26
c lots for the orphans ... Job 6:27
c My words behind ... Ps 50:17
Do not *c* me away ... Ps 51:11
c you out of My sight ... Jer 7:15
will *c* out demons ... Mark 16:17
c fire upon...earth ... Luke 12:49
clothing they *c* lots ... John 19:24
c-ing all your anxiety ... 1 Pet 5:7
but *c* them into hell ... 2 Pet 2:4
c their crowns before ... Rev 4:10

CATCH *seize, trap*
shall *c* his wife ... Judg 21:21
to *c* the afflicted ... Ps 10:9
C the foxes for us ... Song 2:15
caught in My snare ... Ezek 12:13
will be *c-ing* men ... Luke 5:10
unable to *c* Him ... Luke 20:26
caught in adultery ... John 8:3
who *c-es* the wise ... 1 Cor 3:19
if anyone is *caught* ... Gal 6:1
child was *caught* up ... Rev 12:5

CATTLE *domestic animals*
c and creeping things ... Gen 1:24
the firstborn of *c* ... Ex 12:29
defect from the *c* ... Lev 22:19
c on a thousand hills ... Ps 50:10
no *c* in the stalls ... Hab 3:17

CAUSE (n) *purpose, reason*
the *c* of the just ... Ex 23:8
to death without a *c* ... 1 Sam 19:5
place my *c* before God ... Job 5:8
hate me without a *c* ... Ps 69:4
wounds without *c* ... Prov 23:29
hated...without a *c* ... John 15:25

CAUSE (v) *make*
I *c* My name to be ... Ex 20:24
c Israel to inherit ... Deut 1:38
has *c-d* His name ... Ezra 6:12
c His face to shine ... Ps 67:1
speech *c* you to sin ... Eccl 5:6
who *c* dissensions ... Rom 16:17
was *c-ing* the growth ... 1 Cor 3:6

CAVE *shelter*
buried him in the *c* ... Gen 25:9
escaped to the *c* ... 1 Sam 22:1
by fifties in a *c* ... 1 Kin 18:4
mountains and *c-s* ... Heb 11:38
hid...in the *c-s* ... Rev 6:15

CEASE *stop*
you shall *c from labor* ... Ex 23:12
poor will never *c* ... Deut 15:11
He makes wars to *c* ... Ps 46:9
C...consideration ... Prov 23:4
make this proverb *c* ... Ezek 12:23
c-d to kiss My feet ... Luke 7:45
tongues, they will *c* ... 1 Cor 13:8
pray without *c-ing* ... 1 Thess 5:17

CEDAR *tree, wood*
with the *c* wood ... Lev 14:6
c-s beside the waters ... Num 24:6
all the *c-s* of Lebanon ... Is 2:13
the height of *c-s* ... Amos 2:9

CELEBRATE *rejoice*
may *c* a feast to Me ... Ex 5:1
you shall *c* it in ... Lev 23:41
C the Passover ... 2 Kin 23:21
all Israel were *c-ing* ... 1 Chr 13:8
to *c the feast* ... 2 Chr 30:23
David...*c-ing* ... 1 Chr 15:29
c with my friends ... Luke 15:29

CENSER *incense container* A special pan used for burning incense.
c-s for yourselves ... Num 16:6
his *c* in his hand ... Ezek 8:11
holding a golden *c* ... Rev 8:3
angel took the *c* ... Rev 8:5

CENSUS *population roll* An official registration of the inhabitants of a country or empire for various purposes. A census had to be taken in Israel to count those who were required to pay the half-shekel tax (Ex 30:12; *see* **TAX**), and in NT times those living under Roman rule had to be registered by census for tax purposes. The Roman censor or officer in charge of the census could assess a person's property and levy a tax on it at his discretion.
c of...congregation ... Num 1:2
number of the *c* ... 1 Chr 21:5
c which...David ... 2 Chr 2:17
the first *c* taken ... Luke 2:2
in the days of the *c* ... Acts 5:37

CENT *money*
paid up the last *c* ... Matt 5:26
sparrows...for a *c* ... Matt 10:29
amount to a *c* ... Mark 12:42

CENTURION *captain* A Roman army officer who was the commander of about 100 men.
Jesus said to the *c* ... Matt 8:13
summoning the *c* ... Mark 15:44
soldiers and *c-s* ... Acts 21:32
gave orders to the *c* ... Acts 24:23

CEPHAS (Aram, *stone*). The name given by Jesus to Simon in recognition of his confession of faith. The Gr is *Peter.*
apostle Peter ... John 1:42; 1 Cor 1:12; 15:5; Gal 2:11

CERTAINTY *sureness*
know with *c* that ... Josh 23:13
c of the words ... Prov 22:21
you know with *c* ... Eph 5:5

CERTIFICATE *permit, record*
a *c* of divorce ... Deut 24:1
a *c* of divorce ... Matt 5:31
c of debt ... Col 2:14

CHAFF *husk* The husks which separate from the grain during threshing or winnowing. The ungodly are likened to chaff blown by the wind.
consumes them as *c* ... Ex 15:7
c which the wind drives ... Ps 1:4
make the hills like *c* ... Is 41:15
c from the summer ... Dan 2:35
burn up the *c* ... Matt 3:12

CHAIN *band*
bound...bronze *c-s* ... Judg 16:21
he drew *c-s* of gold ... 1 Kin 6:21
whose hands are *c-s* ... Eccl 7:26
was bound with *c-s* ... Luke 8:29

c-s fell off his hands ... Acts 12:7
great *c* in his hand ... Rev 20:1

CHALDEA A region in southern Babylonia. Abraham left the region at God's direction to migrate to Canaan.
S Babylonia ... Jer 50:10; 51:24; Ezek 23:15

CHALDEANS
inhabitants of Chaldea ... Gen 11:28; 2 Kin 24:2; Job 1:17; Jer 24:5; Dan 5:11; Hab 1:6

CHAMBER *room*
entered his *c* ... Gen 43:30
in his cool roof *c* ... Judg 3:20
c-s of the storehouse ... Neh 10:38
bridegroom...his *c* ... Ps 19:5
to the *c-s* of death ... Prov 7:27
out of her *bridal c* ... Joel 2:16
c-s in the heavens ... Amos 9:6

CHAMBERLAIN A civic official close to the top person in government and usually in charge of public funds and works (Acts 12:20).

CHAMPION *fighter*
c, the Philistine ... 1 Sam 17:23
a Savior and a *C* ... Is 19:20
like a dread *c* ... Jer 20:11

CHANGE (n) *alteration*
gave *c-s* of garments ... Gen 45:22
had a *c* of heart ... Ex 14:5
two *c-s* of clothes ... 2 Kin 5:23
Until my *c* comes ... Job 14:14
a *c* of law ... Heb 7:12

CHANGE (v) *alter, transform*
and *c-d* my wages ... Gen 31:7
He *c-s* a wilderness ... Ps 107:35
c-d their glory ... Jer 2:11
Ethiopian *c* his skin ... Jer 13:23
He who *c-s* the times ... Dan 2:21
LORD *c-d* His mind ... Amos 7:6
I, the LORD, do not *c* ... Mal 3:6
will all be *c-d* ... 1 Cor 15:51

CHANNEL *furrow*
Who has cleft a *c* ... Job 38:25
c-s of water appeared ... Ps 18:15
heart is *like c-s* ... Prov 21:1
sent out its *c-s* ... Ezek 31:4

CHANT *sing*
David *c-ed*...this ... 2 Sam 1:17
Jeremiah *c-ed* a ... 2 Chr 35:25
daughters...shall *c* ... Ezek 32:16

CHARACTER
and proven *c*, hope ... Rom 5:4
Make sure...your *c* is free ... Heb 13:5

CHARGE (n) *responsibility*
under Joseph's *c* ... Gen 39:23
keep the *c* of the LORD ... Lev 8:35
c of his household ... Matt 24:45
allotted to your *c* ... 1 Pet 5:3

CHARGE (n) *accusation*
far from a false *c* ... Ex 23:7
bring *c-s* against ... Acts 19:38
c against God's elect ... Rom 8:33

CHARGE (n) *cost*
gospel without *c* ... 1 Cor 9:18

CHARGE (v) *command*
Abimelech *c-d* all ... Gen 26:11
I *c-d* your judges ... Deut 1:16
Moses *c-d* us with a ... Deut 33:4
I solemnly *c* you ... 1 Tim 5:21

CHARGE (v) *exact a price*
not *c* him interest ... Ex 22:25
c that to my account ... Philem 18

CHARIOT *wagon* A horse-drawn vehicle used in war, sport, and for the personal transportation of heads of state.
Joseph prepared...*c* ... Gen 46:29
appeared a *c* of fire ... 2 Kin 2:11
Some *boast* in *c-s* ... Ps 20:7
c-s of God are myriads ... Ps 68:17
Your *c-s* of salvation ... Hab 3:8
I will cut off the *c* ... Zech 9:10
and sitting in his *c* ... Acts 8:28

CHARIOTEERS *warriors*
David killed 700 *c* ... 2 Sam 10:18
7,000 *c* and 40,000 ... 1 Chr 19:18
with horses and *c* ... Ezek 39:20

CHARITY *alms*
give that...as *c* ... Luke 11:41
and give to *c* ... Luke 12:33
deeds of...*c* ... Acts 9:36

CHARM *beauty*
A bribe is a *c* ... Prov 17:8
C is deceitful ... Prov 31:30
with *all* your *c-s* ... Song 7:6

CHASE *drive, pursue*
Egyptians *c-d* after ... Ex 14:9
will *c* your enemies ... Lev 26:7
one *c* a thousand ... Deut 32:30
c-ing...Philistines ... 1 Sam 17:53
be *c-d* like chaff ... Is 17:13

CHASTE *pure* 1) Not indulging in sexual activity. 2) The quality of being virtuous and pure, used once of wives who are faithful to their husbands (1 Pet 3:2).
c...behavior ... 1 Pet 3:2
kept themselves *c* ... Rev 14:4

CHASTEN *discipline*
Man is also *c-ed* ... Job 33:19
Nor *c* me in Your wrath ... Ps 6:1
c-ed every morning ... Ps 73:14
who *c-s* the nations ... Ps 94:10

CHASTISE *punish*
You have *c-d* me ... Jer 31:18
I will *c* all of them ... Hos 5:2

CHATTER *babbling*
worldly...empty *c* ... 1 Tim 6:20
avoid...empty *c* ... 2 Tim 2:16

CHEAT *deceive*
your father has *c-ed* ... Gen 31:7
c with...scales ... Amos 8:5

CHEBAR
river in Babylonia ... Ezek 3:15; 10:15

CHEDORLAOMER
king of Elam ... Gen 14:9,17

CHEEK *part of face*
slapped me on the *c* ... Job 16:10
Your *c-s* are lovely ... Song 1:10
tears are on her *c-s* ... Lam 1:2
hits you on the *c* ... Luke 6:29

CHEERFUL
countenance and be *c* ... Job 9:27
joyful heart...a *c* ... Prov 15:13
c heart...feast ... Prov 15:15
God loves a *c* giver ... 2 Cor 9:7
Is anyone *c* ... James 5:13

CHEMOSH A god of the Moabites who was worshiped through human sacrifices.
god of Moab ... Judg 11:24; 1 Kin 11:7; Jer 48:13

CHERETHITES
1 *tribe on Philistine plain* ... 1 Sam 30:14; Ezek 25:16; Zeph 2:5
2 *David's bodyguards* ... 2 Sam 8:18; 15:18; 1 Kin 1:38; 1 Chr 18:17

CHERISH *love*
or the wife you *c* ... Deut 13:6
the wife he *c-es* ... Deut 28:54
men *c* themselves ... Acts 24:15
c-es it, just as Christ ... Eph 5:29

CHERUB, pl. **CHERUBIM** *celestial being* Angelic beings who guarded the way to the tree of life in Eden. Golden cherubim were crafted for the lid of the ark of the covenant, with their wings outstretched over it. They are also said to be beneath the throne of God.
He stationed the *c* ... Gen 3:24
c had *their* wings ... Ex 37:9
enthroned *above*...*c* ... 2 Sam 6:2
He rode on a *c* ... 2 Sam 22:11
one *c*...ten cubits ... 1 Kin 6:26
c stretched out his ... Ezek 10:7
c appeared to have ... Ezek 10:8

CHEST *box*
the priest took a *c* ... 2 Kin 12:9
money in the *c* ... 2 Kin 12:10
levies...into the *c* ... 2 Chr 24:10

CHEW *eat*
which *c* the cud ... Lev 11:4
before it was *c-ed* ... Num 11:33

CHIEF *head, prominent*
c-s of the sons of ... Gen 36:15
the *c-s* of Edom ... Gen 36:43
of the thirty *c* men ... 2 Sam 23:13
c of the magicians ... Dan 4:9
C Shepherd appears ... 1 Pet 5:4

CHILD
c grew...weaned ... Gen 21:8
Train up a *c* in ... Prov 22:6
discipline from the *c* ... Prov 23:13
c will be born to us ... Is 9:6
with *c* by the Holy ... Matt 1:18
take the *C* and His ... Matt 2:13
He called a *c* to ... Matt 18:2
saying, *C*, arise ... Luke 8:54
a woman with *c* ... 1 Thess 5:3

CHILDBIRTH
multiply...pain in *c* ... Gen 3:16
as of a woman in *c* ... Ps 48:6
pains of *c* come ... Hos 13:13
suffers the pains of *c* ... Rom 8:22

CHILDLESS
I am *c*, and the heir ... Gen 15:2
They will die *c* ... Lev 20:20
c among women ... 1 Sam 15:33
and died *c* ... Luke 20:29

CHILDREN
pain...bring forth *c* ... Gen 3:16
Are these all the *c* ... 1 Sam 16:11
compassion on *his c* ... Ps 103:13
c are a gift ... Ps 127:3
c rise up and bless ... Prov 31:28
c were dashed to ... Nah 3:10
slew all the male *c* ... Matt 2:16
stones...to raise up *c* ... Matt 3:9
c...against parents ... Matt 10:21
and become like *c* ... Matt 18:3
bringing *c* to Him ... Mark 10:13
Being...the *c* of God ... Acts 17:29
if *c*, heirs ... Rom 8:17
C, obey your parents ... Eph 6:1
My little *c* ... 1 John 2:1
kill her *c* with ... Rev 2:23

CHINNERETH / CHINNEROTH
1 *lake* ... Num 34:11; Josh 12:3
also **Sea of Galilee**
also **Lake of Gennesaret**
also **Sea of Tiberias**
2 *city of Naphtali* ... Deut 3:17; Josh 19:35
3 *plain near Galilee* ... Josh 11:2; 1 Kin 15:20

CHISLEV
ninth month of Hebrew calendar ... Neh 1:1; Zech 7:1

CHOICE *option* or *best*
Saul, a *c...man* ... 1 Sam 9:2
c men of Israel ... 2 Sam 10:9
And eat its *c* fruits ... Song 4:16
God made a *c* among ... Acts 15:7
God's gracious *c* ... Rom 11:5
His c of you ... 1 Thess 1:4

CHOIR *chorus*
c proceeded to the ... Neh 12:38
two *c-s* took their ... Neh 12:40

CHOKE *stifle*
wealth *c* the word ... Matt 13:22
began to *c him* ... Matt 18:28
thorns...*c-d* it ... Mark 4:7
c-d with worries ... Luke 8:14

CHOOSE *select, take*
C men for us ... Ex 17:9
whom the LORD *c-s* ... Num 16:7
C wise...discerning ... Deut 1:13
He *c-s* our inheritance ... Ps 47:4
refuse evil and *c* good ... Is 7:15
not God *c* the poor ... James 2:5

CHOP *cut*
who *c-s* your wood ... Deut 29:11
c-ped down...altars ... 2 Chr 34:7
C down the tree ... Dan 4:14

CHORAZIN A city on the northern end of the Sea of Galilee, rebuked by Jesus for its unbelief (Matt 11:21).

CHOSE *selected*
Lot *c* for himself ... Gen 13:11
God has *c-n* you ... Deut 7:6
I *c* David to be ... 1 Kin 8:16
when I *c* Israel ... Ezek 20:5
c twelve of them ... Luke 6:13
has *c-n* the weak ... 1 Cor 1:27
He *c* us in Him ... Eph 1:4

CHOSEN *elected, selected*
Moses His *c* one ... Ps 106:23
My *c one in whom* ... Is 42:1
Israel My *c one* ... Is 45:4
c ones shall inherit ... Is 65:9
My Son, *My C* One ... Luke 9:35
c of God, holy and ... Col 3:12
of *His c* angels ... 1 Tim 5:21
you are a *c* race ... 1 Pet 2:9

CHRIST *Messiah*
see also **JESUS CHRIST**
birth of Jesus *C* was ... Matt 1:18
C would suffer and ... Luke 24:46
both Lord and *C* ... Acts 2:36
fellow heirs with *C* ... Rom 8:17
are one body in *C* ... Rom 12:5
preach *C* crucified ... 1 Cor 1:23
judgment seat of *C* ... 2 Cor 5:10
ambassadors for *C* ... 2 Cor 5:20
faith in *C* Jesus ... Gal 2:16
as sons through Jesus *C* ... Eph 1:5
to live is *C* ... Phil 1:21
C, who is our life ... Col 3:4
dead in *C* will ... 1 Thess 4:16
coming of...*C* ... 2 Thess 2:1
C...high priest ... Heb 9:11
Advocate...Jesus *C* ... 1 John 2:1
with *C* for a thousand ... Rev 20:4

CHRIST, DEITY OF *see* **TRINITY**

CHRISTIAN *follower of Christ* A follower of Christ, one who professes faith in Him for salvation. The name was first given to His followers at Antioch.
first called *C-s* in ... Acts 11:26
me to become a *C* ... Acts 26:28
suffers as a *C* ... 1 Pet 4:16

CHRONICLES *book of register*
1 *of kings of Israel* ... 1 Kin 14:19; 15:31; 2 Kin 14:28; 15:26
2 *of kings of Judah* ... 1 Kin 14:29; 15:23; 2 Kin 15:36; 24:5
3 *of kings of Media / Persia* ... Esth 10:2

CHURCH *a called out assembly (called out, separated from)*. The entire group of believers in Christ, usually recognized as existing since the Day of Pentecost in NT times (Acts 2) until the future rapture (q.v.). Also called the body of Christ. In a more limited sense, it often refers to a local assembly of believers.
I will build my *c* ... Matt 16:18
tell it to the *c* ... Matt 18:17
shepherd the *c* ... Acts 20:28
c-es of the Gentiles ... Rom 16:4
together as a *c* ... 1 Cor 11:18
woman...speak in *c* ... 1 Cor 14:35
to the *c-es* of Judea ... Gal 1:22
Christ...head of the *c* ... Eph 5:23
persecutor of the *c* ... Phil 3:6
c of the living God ... 1 Tim 3:15
Spirit says to the *c-es* ... Rev 2:11

CILICIA A province in Asia Minor, whose principal city is Tarsus Paul's birthplace).
region in SE Asia Minor ... Acts 15:41; 21:39; 27:5

CINNAMON *spice*
and of fragrant *c* ... Ex 30:23
myrrh, aloes and *c* ... Prov 7:17
and *c* and spice ... Rev 18:13

CIRCLE *area*
sleeping inside...*c* ... 1 Sam 26:7
He has inscribed a *c* ... Job 26:10
did not sit in the *c* ... Jer 15:17

CIRCUIT *course*
on *c* to Bethel ... 1 Sam 7:16
its *c* to the other end ... Ps 19:6

CIRCULATE *spread*
proclamation was *c-d* ... Ex 36:6
LORD's people *c-ing* ... 1 Sam 2:24
to *c* a proclamation ... 2 Chr 30:5

CIRCUMCISE *be pure* or *cut off*
every male...be *c-d* ... Gen 17:10
Abraham *c-d* his son ... Gen 21:4
So *c* your heart ... Deut 10:16
God will *c*...heart ... Deut 30:6
C yourselves...LORD ... Jer 4:4
came to *c* the child ... Luke 1:59
c-d the eighth day ... Phil 3:5

CIRCUMCISION *act of purity* The Jewish rite of removing the foreskin of male infants when they are eight days old. God commanded that Abraham and his descendants perform this rite as a sign of His covenant with them.
because of the *c* ... Ex 4:26
c is...of the heart ... Rom 2:29
if you receive *c* ... Gal 5:2
if I still preach *c* ... Gal 5:11
we are the *true c* ... Phil 3:3
c made without hands ... Col 2:11
those of the *c* ... Titus 1:10

CIRCUMSTANCE *condition*
spoken in right *c-s* ... Prov 25:11
may know...my *c-s* ... Eph 6:21
peace in every *c* ... 2 Thess 3:16
of humble *c-s* ... James 1:9

CISTERN *reservoir* A reservoir dug out of earth or soft stone, designed to trap and retain rain or spring water. Essential in the Middle East due to the generally dry weather.
a *c* collecting water ... Lev 11:36
water from your...*c* ... Prov 5:15
wheel at the *c* is ... Eccl 12:6
prophet from the *c* ... Jer 38:10

CITADEL *fortress* A fortress built on a high point for defensive purposes. A place of safety and refuge.
c of the king's ... 1 Kin 16:18
c of Susa ... Esth 2:3
in the *c* of Susa ... Dan 8:2
c-s of Jerusalem ... Amos 2:5
Proclaim on the *c-s* ... Amos 3:9
tramples on our *c-s* ... Mic 5:5

CITIES OF REFUGE *see* **MANSLAYER**
1 *Kedesh in Naphtali* ... Josh 20:7
2 *Shechem in Ephraim* ... Josh 20:7
3 *Hebron (Kiriath-arba)* ... Josh 20:7
4 *Bezer in Reuben* ... Josh 20:8
5 *Ramoth-gilead in Gad* ... Josh 20:8
6 *Golan in Manasseh* ... Josh 20:8

CITIZEN *resident*
your fellow *c-s* ... Ezek 33:12
fellow *c-s* who talk ... Ezek 33:30
c-s hated him ... Luke 19:14
c of no insignificant ... Acts 21:39
fellow *c-s* with the ... Eph 2:19

CITY
build...a *c* ... Gen 11:4
burned...their *c-ies* ... Num 31:10

die in my own *c* ... 2 Sam 19:37
glad the *c* of God ... Ps 46:4
LORD guards the *c* ... Ps 127:1
the *C* of Destruction ... Is 19:18
the *C* of Truth ... Zech 8:3
a *c* called Nazareth ... Matt 2:23
into the holy *c* ... Matt 4:5
the *c* was stirred ... Matt 21:10
c, shake the dust off ... Luke 9:5
He has prepared a *c* ... Heb 11:16
I saw the holy *c* ... Rev 21:2

CLAIM *demand*
Let darkness...*c* it ... Job 3:5
Do not *c* honor in ... Prov 25:6
c-ing to be someone ... Acts 8:9

CLAN *family, tribe*
c of the household ... Judg 9:1
and by your *c-s* ... 1 Sam 10:19
among...*c-s* of Judah ... Mic 5:2
I will make the *c-s* ... Zech 12:6

CLAP *applaud*
c-ped their hands ... 2 Kin 11:12
c-s his hands among ... Job 34:37
rivers *c* their hands ... Ps 98:8
trees...will *c* ... Is 55:12

CLAUDIA
Roman Christian ... 2 Tim 4:21

CLAUDIUS
Roman Emperor ... Acts 11:28;18:2
see **CAESAR**

CLAUDIUS LYSIAS
Roman tribune ... Acts 23:26

CLAY
dwell in houses of *c* ... Job 4:19
Father, We are the *c* ... Is 64:8
c in the potter's hand ... Jer 18:6
the *c* to his eyes ... John 9:6

CLEAN *cleansed, washed* Term used in OT law to designate certain kinds of food as ceremonially fit for consumption, and many other things as fit for use (ceremonial offerings, cooking utensils, etc.). Also used in reference to people who were ritually fit to engage in temple worship and Jewish social life. *See also* **UNCLEAN**
animals that are not *c* ... Gen 7:2
eat in a *c* place ... Lev 10:14
pronounce him *c* ... Lev 13:28
Create in me a *c* heart ... Ps 51:10
make yourselves *c* ... Is 1:16
You can make me *c* ... Matt 8:2
things are *c* for you ... Luke 11:41
c because of the word ... John 15:3

CLEANSE *purify, wash*
To *c* the house then ... Lev 14:49
c the house of the ... 2 Chr 29:15
I have *c-d* my heart ... Prov 20:9
I am willing; be *c-d* ... Matt 8:3
the lepers are *c-d* ... Matt 11:5
not eat unless they *c* ... Mark 7:4
let us *c* ourselves ... 2 Cor 7:1
C...you sinners ... James 4:8
blood...*c-s* us ... 1 John 1:7

CLEAR *make free* or *plain*
c-s away many nations ... Deut 7:1
C the way for the LORD ... Is 40:3
c His threshing floor ... Matt 3:12

Christ has made *c* ... 2 Pet 1:14
river...*c* as crystal ... Rev 22:1

CLEFT *crevice*
in the *c* of the rock ... Judg 15:8
the *c-s* of the cliffs ... Is 2:21
who live in the *c-s* ... Obad 3

CLEOPAS
disciple of Christ ... Luke 24:18

CLEVER *smart*
c in their own sight ... Is 5:21
cleverness of the *c* ... 1 Cor 1:19

CLIFF *crag*
nest is set in the *c* ... Num 24:21
On the *c* he dwells ... Job 39:28
c-s are a refuge ... Ps 104:18

CLIMB *ascend*
I will *c* the palm tree ... Song 7:8
the one who *c-s* ... Jer 48:44
c-ed...a sycamore ... Luke 19:4
c-s up...other way ... John 10:1

CLING *cleave*
and *c* to Him ... Deut 13:4
c to the LORD ... Josh 23:8
My soul *c-s* to You ... Ps 63:8
c to Your testimonies ... Ps 119:31
Stop *c-ing* to Me ... John 20:17
c to what is good ... Rom 12:9

CLOAK *coat, mantle* A loose outer garment. Cloaks were of many forms and had many uses.
Give me the *c* ... Ruth 3:15
neither bread nor *c* ... Is 3:7
fringe of His *c* ... Matt 9:20
Wrap your *c* around ... Acts 12:8

CLOSE *shut, stop*
and the LORD *c-d* ... Gen 7:16
floodgates...were *c-d* ... Gen 8:2
earth *c-d* over them ... Num 16:33
c your door...pray ... Matt 6:6
have *c-d* their eyes ... Acts 28:27
every mouth...*c-d* ... Rom 3:19
c-s his heart ... 1 John 3:17

CLOTH *fabric*
spread over *it* a *c* ... Num 4:6
is wrapped in a *c* ... 1 Sam 21:9
with embroidered *c* ... Ezek 16:10
in the linen *c* ... Mark 15:46

CLOTHE *array, dress*
C me with skin ... Job 10:11
meadows are *c-d* with ... Ps 65:13
O Zion; *C* yourself ... Is 52:1
God so *c-s* the grass ... Matt 6:30
naked...you *c-d* Me ... Matt 25:36
are splendidly *c-d* ... Luke 7:25
c-d with power ... Luke 24:49
c...with humility ... 1 Pet 5:5
c-d in the white robes ... Rev 7:13

CLOTHES *garments*
c of her captivity ... Deut 21:13
your *c* have not worn ... Deut 29:5
and worn-out *c* on ... Josh 9:5
and changed his *c* ... 2 Sam 12:20
without wedding *c* ... Matt 22:12
Tearing his *c* ... Mark 14:63

CLOTHING *clothes, raiment*
reduce...her *c* ... Ex 21:10
c did not wear out ... Deut 8:4

purple are their *c* ... Jer 10:9
and the body more than *c* ... Matt 6:25
in sheep's *c* ... Matt 7:15
c as white as snow ... Matt 28:3
His *c became* white ... Luke 9:29
men...in dazzling *c* ... Luke 24:4
sister is without *c* ... James 2:15

CLOUD *mist*
set My bow in the *c* ... Gen 9:13
c where God *was* ... Ex 20:21
c covered...mountain ... Ex 24:15
c for a covering ... Ps 105:39
voice came out...*c* ... Mark 9:7
Son...coming in *c-s* ... Mark 13:26
in a *c* with power ... Luke 21:27
and a *c* received Him ... Acts 1:9

CLOUD, PILLAR OF A miraculous vertical cloud formation close to the ground that represented God's presence with Israel during their wandering in the wilderness. The cloud led the way for them during the day, and would come down and stand at the entrance to the tabernacle whenever Moses entered it. The same cloud turned into fire at night, leading the way for Israel and providing light.
in a *p* ... Ex 13:21

CLUB *weapon*
went...with a *c* ... 2 Sam 23:21
C-s are...as stubble ... Job 41:29
Like a *c* and a ... Prov 25:18
with swords and *c-s* ... Matt 26:47

CLUSTER *collection*
c-s produced ripe ... Gen 40:10
c-s of raisins ... 1 Sam 25:18
breasts are...*c-s* ... Song 7:7
gather the *c-s* ... Rev 14:18

COAL *charcoal*
breath kindles *c-s* ... Job 41:21
man walk on hot *c-s* ... Prov 6:28
burning *c* in his hand ... Is 6:6
heap burning *c-s* ... Rom 12:20

COAST
c of the Great Sea ... Josh 9:1
along the *c* of Asia ... Acts 27:2

COASTLAND
inhabitants of this *c* ... Is 20:6
to the *c-s* of Kittim ... Jer 2:10
c-s shake at the ... Ezek 26:15
c-s of the nations ... Zeph 2:11

COAT *cloak*
opening...*c* of mail ... Ex 28:32
with his *c* torn ... 2 Sam 15:32
have your *c* also ... Matt 5:40
or even two *c-s* ... Matt 10:10
spread their *c-s* ... Mark 11:8

COBRA *snake*
deadly poison of *c-s* ... Deut 32:33
To the venom of *c-s* ... Job 20:14
tread upon the...*c* ... Ps 91:13

COFFIN *bier*
in a *c* in Egypt ... Gen 50:26
and touched the *c* ... Luke 7:14

COHORT *military unit* A Roman military unit in NT times and earlier. It usually consisted of about 600 soldiers, the tenth part of a legion.

the whole *Roman c* ... Matt 27:27
called the Italian *c* ... Acts 10:1
of the Augustan *c* ... Acts 27:1

COIN *money*
Show Me the *c* ... Matt 22:19
woman...loses one *c* ... Luke 15:8
He poured out...*c-s* ... John 2:15

COLD *cool*
covering against the *c* ... Job 24:7
Like the *c* of snow ... Prov 25:13
cup of *c* water ... Matt 10:42
love will grow *c* ... Matt 24:12
neither *c* nor hot ... Rev 3:15

COLLAPSE *fall*
grass *c-s* into the flame ... Is 5:24
pathways will *c* ... Ezek 38:20
ancient hills *c-d* ... Hab 3:6

COLLEAGUES *co-workers*
the rest of his *c* ... Ezra 4:7
and your *c* ... Ezra 6:6

COLLECT *exact, take*
c-ed his strength ... Gen 48:2
cistern *c-ing* water ... Lev 11:36
c captives like sand ... Hab 1:9
C no more than ... Luke 3:13
c-ed a tenth from ... Heb 7:6

COLLECTION *acquisition*
let your *c of idols* ... Is 57:13
no *c-s* be made ... 1 Cor 16:2

COLOSSAE City of Phrygia in Asia Minor. It was a prosperous commercial center located on the Lycus River near Hierapolis and Laodicea.
city in Asia Minor ... Col 1:2

COLT *foal*
camels and their *c-s* ... Gen 32:15
Even on a *c* ... Zech 9:9
and a *c* with her ... Matt 21:2
on a donkey's *c* ... John 12:15

COLUMN *pillar, text*
in a *c* of smoke ... Judg 20:40
and marble *c-s* ... Esth 1:6
read three...*c-s* ... Jer 36:23

COME
C, let us build ... Gen 11:4
C, let us worship ... Ps 95:6
All *came* from...dust ... Eccl 3:20
your king is *c-ing* ... Zech 9:9
Your kingdom *c* ... Matt 6:10
C to Me, all who ... Matt 11:28
children to *c* to Me ... Mark 10:14
not *c*...temptation ... Mark 14:38
Son of Man *c-ing* ... Luke 21:27
Father...hour has *c* ... John 17:1
His judgment has *c* ... Rev 14:7
I am *c-ing* quickly ... Rev 22:20

COMFORT (n) *consolation*
mourning without *c* ... Job 30:28
c in my affliction ... Ps 119:50
he will give you *c* ... Prov 29:17
c of the Holy Spirit ... Acts 9:31
and God of all *c* ... 2 Cor 1:3
your *c* and salvation ... 2 Cor 1:6

COMFORT (v) *console, cheer*
relatives came to *c* ... 1 Chr 7:22
Your rod...they *c* me ... Ps 23:4
I, am He who *c-s* you ... Is 51:12
To *c* all who mourn ... Is 61:2
he is being *c-ed* ... Luke 16:25
c one another ... 1 Thess 4:18

COMFORTER *consoler*
Sorry *c-s* are you all ... Job 16:2
c-s, but I found none ... Ps 69:20
She has no *c* ... Lam 1:9
Where will I seek *c-s* ... Nah 3:7

COMING (n) *arrival*
Joseph's *c* at noon ... Gen 43:25
the day of His *c* ... Mal 3:2
be the sign of Your *c* ... Matt 24:3
c of the Son of Man ... Matt 24:37
Christ's at His *c* ... 1 Cor 15:23
c of the Lord is ... James 5:8
the promise of His *c* ... 2 Pet 3:4

COMMAND (n) *order*
the *c* of the LORD ... Lev 24:12
disobeyed the *c* ... 1 Kin 13:21
to the king's *c* ... 2 Chr 35:10
no *c* of the Lord ... 1 Cor 7:25
could not bear the *c* ... Heb 12:20

COMMAND (v) *declare, order*
I *c-ed* you not to eat ... Gen 3:11
may *c* his children ... Gen 18:19
speak all that I *c* you ... Ex 7:2
bring all that I *c* ... Deut 12:11
the angel...*c-ed* ... Matt 1:24
c that these stones ... Matt 4:3
c-s even the winds ... Luke 8:25
c-ing the jailer ... Acts 16:23

COMMANDER *captain, general*
the *c-s* of Israel ... Judg 5:9
c of Saul's army ... 2 Sam 2:8
his chariot *c-s* ... 1 Kin 9:22
and Joab was the *c* ... 1 Chr 27:34
c for the peoples ... Is 55:4
the *C* of the host ... Dan 8:11
and the flesh of *c-s* ... Rev 19:18

COMMANDMENT *instruction* In the Scriptures, almost always a law given to man by God, defining behavior that is acceptable to Him. Most commonly recognized are the Ten Commandments, but the term includes many other divine laws or precepts. *See* **LAW**
and keep My *c-s* ... Ex 20:6
the Ten *C-s* ... Ex 34:28
and keep His *c-s* ... Josh 22:5
c of the LORD is pure ... Ps 19:8
the *c* of your father ... Prov 6:20
which is the great *c* ... Matt 22:36
A new *c* I give ... John 13:34
will keep My *c-s* ... John 14:15
I have kept...*c-s* ... John 15:10
not writing a new *c* ... 1 John 2:7
keep the *c-s* of God ... Rev 14:12

COMMEND *praise, present*
So I *c-ed* pleasure ... Eccl 8:15
I *c* you to God ... Acts 20:32
food will not *c* us ... 1 Cor 8:8
to *c* ourselves again ... 2 Cor 3:1

COMMISSION *appoint*
c him in their sight ... Num 27:19
He *c-ed* Joshua ... Deut 31:23
king has *c-ed* me ... 1 Sam 21:2
c it against the people ... Is 10:6

COMMISSIONERS *supervisors*
and over them three *c* ... Dan 6:2
Then the *c* and satraps ... Dan 6:4

COMMIT *entrust, practice*
c-ted to Joseph's ... Gen 39:22
shall not *c* adultery ... Ex 20:14
have *c-ted* incest ... Lev 20:12
I *c* my spirit ... Ps 31:5
C your way to the LORD ... Ps 37:5
weary...*c-ting* iniquity ... Jer 9:5
Do not *c* adultery ... Luke 18:20
I *c* My spirit ... Luke 23:46
everyone who *c-s* sin ... John 8:34
who *c-ted* no sin ... 1 Pet 2:22

COMMON *ordinary, shared*
anyone of...*c* people ... Lev 4:27
place of the *c* people ... Jer 26:23
iron...with *c* clay ... Dan 2:41
had all things in *c* ... Acts 2:44
about our *c* salvation ... Jude 3

COMMONWEALTH *nation*
from the *c* of Israel ... Eph 2:12

COMMOTION *disturbance*
the noise of this *c* ... 1 Sam 4:14
great *c* out of the ... Jer 10:22
Why make a *c* and ... Mark 5:39

COMPANION *comrade, friend*
are you striking your *c* ... Ex 2:13
brought thirty *c-s* ... Judg 14:11
And a *c* of ostriches ... Job 30:29
c of fools will suffer ... Prov 13:20
your *c* and your wife ... Mal 2:14
Paul and his *c-s* ... Acts 13:13

COMPANY *assembly, group*
into three *c-ies* ... Judg 9:43
c of the godless ... Job 15:34
c will stone them ... Ezek 23:47
Bad *c* corrupts ... 1 Cor 15:33

COMPARE *contrast, like*
none to *c* with You ... Ps 40:5
to what shall I *c* ... Matt 11:16
c the kingdom of ... Luke 13:20
be *c-d* with the glory ... Rom 8:18

COMPASS
outlines it with a *c* ... Is 44:13
four points of the *c* ... Dan 11:4

COMPASSION *concern, love*
God...grant you *c* ... Gen 43:14
whom I will show *c* ... Ex 33:19
in Your great *c* ... Neh 9:19
have *c* on the poor ... Ps 72:13
have *c* on Zion ... Ps 102:13
His *c-s* never fail ... Lam 3:22
He felt *c* for them ... Matt 9:36
his father...felt *c* ... Luke 15:20
put on a heart of *c* ... Col 3:12
Lord is full of *c* ... James 5:11

COMPASSIONATE *loving*
your God is a *c* God ... Deut 4:31
c, Slow to anger ... Neh 9:17
He is gracious and *c* ... Joel 2:13
a gracious and *c* God ... Jon 4:2

COMPEL *force, press*
Egyptians *c-led* the ... Ex 1:13
c them to come in ... Luke 14:23
c...to be circumcised ... Gal 6:12

COMPETE *strive*
can you *c* with horses ... Jer 12:5

everyone who *c-s* ... 1 Cor 9:25
c-s as an athlete ... 2 Tim 2:5

COMPLAIN *murmur*
c-ed to Abimelech ... Gen 21:25
c in the bitterness ... Job 7:11
I will *c* and murmur ... Ps 55:17
Do not *c*, brethren ... James 5:9

COMPLAINT *grumbling*
c-s of...Israel ... Num 14:27
couch will ease my *c* ... Job 7:13
today my *c* is rebellion ... Job 23:2
hospitable...without *c* ... 1 Pet 4:9

COMPLETE (adj) *full, total*
a sabbath of *c* rest ... Ex 35:2
be seven *c* sabbaths ... Lev 23:15
not...a *c* destruction ... Jer 5:10
you have been made *c* ... Col 2:10
be perfect and *c* ... James 1:4
joy may be made *c* ... 1 John 1:4

COMPLETE (v) *finish, fulfill*
God *c-d* His work ... Gen 2:2
C the week of this ... Gen 29:27
C your work quota ... Ex 5:13
your days are *c* ... 2 Sam 7:12
house...was *c-d* ... 2 Chr 8:16
thousand years are *c-d* ... Rev 20:7

COMPOSE *write*
c words against you ... Job 16:4
have *c-d* songs for ... Amos 6:5
The first account I *c-d* ... Acts 1:1

COMPOSE *make calm*
c-d and quieted my ... Ps 131:2
I *c-d my soul* ... Is 38:13

COMPREHEND *understand*
which we cannot *c* ... Job 37:5
speech...no one *c-s* ... Is 33:19
and they did not *c* ... Luke 18:34
darkness did not *c* ... John 1:5

COMPULSION *coercion*
under *c*...let them go ... Ex 6:1
in effect, by *c* ... Philem 14
not under *c*, but ... 1 Pet 5:2

CONCEAL *cover, hide*
man *c-s* knowledge ... Prov 12:23
They do not *even c it* ... Is 3:9
Do not *c it but* ... Jer 50:2
was *c-ed* from them ... Luke 9:45

CONCEIT *pride*
selfishness or empty *c* ... Phil 2:3
he is *c-ed* ... 1 Tim 6:4
c-ed, lovers of ... 2 Tim 3:4

CONCEIVE *become pregnant*
Sarah *c-d* and bore a ... Gen 21:2
c-d all this people ... Num 11:12
sin my mother *c-d* me ... Ps 51:5
she *c-d* and gave birth ... Is 8:3
when lust has *c-d* ... James 1:15

CONCERN *have care*
master does not *c* ... Gen 39:8
the LORD was *c-ed* ... Ex 4:31
You are *c-ed* about ... Job 7:17
c-ed about the poor ... John 12:6
is married is *c-ed* ... 1 Cor 7:33
not *c-ed* about oxen ... 1 Cor 9:9

CONCUBINE *secondary wife (to lie down with).* A woman living with a man but not legally married to him. In Biblical times, usually a woman whose purpose was to provide some companionship to the man and bear children.
Ephraim...took a *c* ... Judg 19:1
Now Saul had a *c* ... 2 Sam 3:7
king left ten *c-s* ... 2 Sam 15:16
three hundred *c-s* ... 1 Kin 11:3
in charge of the *c-s* ... Esth 2:14

CONDEMN *discredit, judge*
c-ing the wicked ... 1 Kin 8:32
my mouth will *c* me ... Job 9:20
he who *c-s* Me ... Is 50:9
will *c* Him to death ... Mark 10:33
do not *c*, and you ... Luke 6:37
you *c* yourself ... Rom 2:1
he stood *c-ed* ... Gal 2:11
our heart *c-s* us ... 1 John 3:20

CONDEMNATION *judgment* The judicial act of declaring a defendant guilty and sentencing him to appropriate punishment, often death. In the NT, usually God's judgment of unrepentant sinners to eternal death. Everyone who does not trust in Christ for salvation is automatically under this sentence.
receive greater *c* ... Mark 12:40
same sentence of *c* ... Luke 23:40
Their *c* is just ... Rom 3:8
no *c*...in Christ ... Rom 8:1
c upon themselves ... Rom 13:2
c...by the devil ... 1 Tim 3:6

CONDITION *state, stipulation*
with you on this *c* ... 1 Sam 11:2
c-s were good in ... 2 Chr 12:12
c in which...called ... 1 Cor 7:20
or adds *c-s* to it ... Gal 3:15

CONDUCT (n) *behavior*
queen's *c*...known ... Esth 1:17
turn...*from his c* ... Job 33:17
who are upright in *c* ... Ps 37:14
sensual *c* of...men ... 2 Pet 2:7
holy *c* and godliness ... 2 Pet 3:11

CONDUCT (v) *behave*
c-s himself arrogantly ... Job 15:25
c...same spirit ... 2 Cor 12:18
C...with wisdom ... Col 4:5
c yourselves in fear ... 1 Pet 1:17

CONDUIT *channel*
c of the upper pool ... 2 Kin 18:17
at the end of the *c* ... Is 7:3

CONFESS *acknowledge* Usually, to admit to God that one is guilty of a sin. A believer who confesses any sin to God is assured of receiving forgiveness from Him. Also to give evidence of one's faith.
that he shall *c* ... Lev 5:5
c-ing the sins of ... Neh 1:6
c my transgressions ... Ps 32:5
c-es Me before men ... Matt 10:32
c-ing their sins ... Mark 1:5
c with your mouth ... Rom 10:9
If we *c* our sins ... 1 John 1:9
I will *c* his name ... Rev 3:5

CONFESSION *admission*
praying and making *c* ... Ezra 10:1
your *c* of the gospel ... 2 Cor 9:13
testified the good *c* ... 1 Tim 6:13
the *c* of our hope ... Heb 10:23

CONFIDENCE *boldness, trust*
What is this *c* ... 2 Kin 18:19
they lost their *c* ... Neh 6:16
LORD will be your *c* ... Prov 3:26
proud *c* is this ... 2 Cor 1:12
c in me may abound ... Phil 1:26
no *c* in the flesh ... Phil 3:3

CONFINE *imprison, limit*
who were *c-d* in jail ... Gen 40:5
he does not *c* it ... Ex 21:29
be *c-d* in prison ... Is 24:22
c-d in the court ... Jer 33:1

CONFINEMENT *imprisonment*
c in his master's ... Gen 40:7
he put me in *c* ... Gen 41:10

CONFIRM *establish, strengthen*
LORD *c* His word ... 1 Sam 1:23
c-ed Your inheritance ... Ps 68:9
c the work of our ... Ps 90:17
C-ing the word of His ... Is 44:26
c-ed...by the signs ... Mark 16:20
who will also *c* you ... 1 Cor 1:8

CONFIRMATION *verification*
and *c* of the gospel ... Phil 1:7
an oath *given* as *c* ... Heb 6:16

CONFLICT *contention*
one of great *c* ... Dan 10:1
in *c* with the LORD ... Jer 50:24
experiencing...*c* ... Phil 1:30
source of...*c-s* ... James 4:1

CONFORMED *being like*
c...image of His Son ... Rom 8:29
not be *c* to...world ... Rom 12:2
being *c* to His death ... Phil 3:10

CONFOUND *confuse*
LORD *c-ed* them ... Josh 10:10
c their strategy ... Is 19:3
c-ing the Jews ... Acts 9:22

CONFRONT *challenge, face*
snares of death *c-ed* ... 2 Sam 22:6
Days of affliction *c* ... Job 30:27
Arise, O LORD, *c* him ... Ps 17:13
the elders *c-ed Him* ... Luke 20:1

CONFUSE *perplex*
c their language ... Gen 11:7
Send...and *c* them ... Ps 144:6
They are *c-d* by wine ... Is 28:7

CONFUSION *disorder*
into great *c* ... Deut 7:23
Jerusalem was in *c* ... Acts 21:31
not *a God* of *c* ... 1 Cor 14:33

CONGREGATION *assembly*
all the *c* of Israel ... Ex 12:3
c shall stone him ... Num 15:35
strife of the *c* ... Num 27:14
Bless God in the *c-s* ... Ps 68:26
c of the godly ones ... Ps 149:1
the *c* of the disciples ... Acts 6:2
In the midst of the *c* ... Heb 2:12

CONJURER *magician*
magician, *c* or ... Dan 2:10
wise men *and* the *c-s* ... Dan 5:15

CONQUER *be victorious*
c-ed all the country ... Gen 14:7
but could not *c* it ... Is 7:1
c through Him ... Rom 8:37

out *c-ing,* and to *c* … Rev 6:2

CONSCIENCE *moral obligation* The human awareness that evaluates an action, thought or word as right or wrong in relation to an objective standard.
David's *c* bothered … 1 Sam 24:5
always a blameless *c* … Acts 24:16
also for *c'* sake … Rom 13:5
their *c* being weak is … 1 Cor 8:7
faith with a clear *c* … 1 Tim 3:9
seared in their own *c* … 1 Tim 4:2
keep a good *c* … 1 Pet 3:16

CONSECRATE (v) *sanctify*
sons of Israel *c* … Ex 28:38
garments shall be *c-d* … Ex 29:21
c it and all its … Ex 40:9
C yourselves … Lev 11:44
c the fiftieth year … Lev 25:10
c-s his house as holy … Lev 27:14
he shall *c* his head … Num 6:11
C yourselves … Josh 3:5
have *c-d* this house … 1 Kin 9:3

CONSECRATED (adj) *sanctified*
touch any *c* thing … Lev 12:4
c people...LORD … Deut 26:19
there is *c* bread … 1 Sam 21:4
c ones were purer … Lam 4:7
ate the *c* bread … Matt 12:4

CONSECRATION Act by which a person or thing is dedicated or set apart by another for the service of the Lord. For example, the priests had to be consecrated to serve God in the temple ministry (Ex 29:33).

CONSENT *agree*
Do not listen or *c* … 1 Kin 20:8
entice you, Do not *c* … Prov 1:10
If you *c* and obey … Is 1:19
c-s to live with him … 1 Cor 7:12

CONSIDER *observe, think*
were *c-ed* unclean … Neh 7:64
C my groaning … Ps 5:1
he who *c-s* the helpless … Ps 41:1
We are *c-ed* as sheep … Ps 44:22
day of adversity *c* … Eccl 7:14
c the work of His hands … Is 5:12
C the ravens, for … Luke 12:24
c your calling … 1 Cor 1:26
He *c-ed* me faithful … 1 Tim 1:12
c how to stimulate … Heb 10:24
c-ed...God is able … Heb 11:19

CONSIST *be composed of*
reverence for Me *c-s* … Is 29:13
life *c* of his … Luke 12:15
does not *c* in words … 1 Cor 4:20
c-ing of decrees … Col 2:14

CONSOLATION *comfort*
c-s of God too small … Job 15:11
Your *c-s* delight my … Ps 94:19
is any *c* of love … Phil 2:1

CONSOLE *soothe*
Esau is *c-ing* himself … Gen 27:42
servants to *c* him … 2 Sam 10:2
c-d...comforted … Job 42:11
c them concerning … John 11:19

CONSPIRACY *plot, scheme*
the *c* was strong … 2 Sam 15:12
found *c* in Hoshea … 2 Kin 17:4
from the *c-ies* of man … Ps 31:20

CONSPIRE *plot against*
have *c-d* against me … 1 Sam 22:8
c-d against my … 2 Kin 10:9
c together against … Ps 83:3
Amos...*c-d* against … Amos 7:10

CONSTELLATION *stars*
a *c* in its season … Job 38:32
c-s Will not flash … Is 13:10

CONSTRUCT *build*
c a sanctuary for Me … Ex 25:8
c siegeworks … Deut 20:20

CONSTRUCTION *structure*
c of the sanctuary … Ex 36:3
it has been under *c* … Ezra 5:16
the *c* of the ark … 1 Pet 3:20

CONSULT *confer*
c-ed with the elders … 1 Kin 12:6
C the mediums … Is 8:19
Without *c-ing* Me … Is 30:2
people *c* their wooden … Hos 4:12
not...*c* with flesh … Gal 1:16

CONSUME *destroy, devour*
c-d...purchase price … Gen 31:15
the bush was not *c-d* … Ex 3:2
c-d the burnt offering … Lev 9:24
great fire will *c* us … Deut 5:25
c the cedars … Judg 9:15
You *c* as a moth … Ps 39:11
c-d by Your anger … Ps 90:7
c-s his own flesh … Eccl 4:5
fire *c-ing* the stubble … Joel 2:5
Zeal...will *c* … John 2:17
c your flesh like fire … James 5:3

CONSUMING (adj) *destroying*
glory...like a *c* fire … Ex 24:17
the flame of a *c* fire … Is 29:6
our God is a *c* fire … Heb 12:29

CONTAIN *hold*
cannot *c* You … 1 Kin 8:27
c the burnt offering … 2 Chr 7:7
not *c* the books … John 21:25
is *c-ed* in Scripture … 1 Pet 2:6

CONTEMPT *scorn*
He pours *c* on nobles … Job 12:21
With pride and *c* … Ps 31:18
treating Him with *c* … Luke 23:11
your brother with *c* … Rom 14:10

CONTEND *strive*
c with him in battle … Deut 2:24
c-ed...vigorously … Judg 8:1
c with the Almighty … Job 40:2
not *c*...without cause … Prov 3:30
Who will *c* with me … Is 50:8
I will not *c* forever … Is 57:16
he *c-ed* with God … Hos 12:3
c...for the faith … Jude 3

CONTENT *satisfied*
c with your wages … Luke 3:14
c with weaknesses … 2 Cor 12:10
have learned to be *c* … Phil 4:11
c with what you have … Heb 13:5

CONTENTION *strife*
object of *c* to our … Ps 80:6
the *c-s* of a wife … Prov 19:13
Strife exists and *c* … Hab 1:3

CONTENTIOUS *quarrelsome*
a *c*...woman … Prov 21:19
with a *c* woman … Prov 25:24
inclined to be *c* … 1 Cor 11:16

CONTINUE *persevere, persist*
My covenant may *c* … Mal 2:4
c in My word … John 8:31
c in the grace of … Acts 13:43
Are we to *c* in sin … Rom 6:1
you *c* in the faith … Col 1:23
love of the brethren *c* … Heb 13:1

CONTRARY *against*
c to the command … Num 24:13
for the wind was *c* … Matt 14:24
grafted *c* to nature … Rom 11:24
c to the teaching … Rom 16:17
a gospel *c* to what … Gal 1:8
c to sound teaching … 1 Tim 1:10

CONTRIBUTE *give*
Josiah *c-d* to the … 2 Chr 35:7
c yearly one third … Neh 10:32
c-ing to their support … Luke 8:3
c-ing to...the saints … Rom 12:13

CONTRIBUTION *gift, offering*
to raise a *c* for Me … Ex 25:2
as a *c* to the LORD … Lev 7:14
c-s, the first fruits … Neh 12:44
a *c* for the poor … Rom 15:26
liberality of your *c* … 2 Cor 9:13

CONTRITE *sorrowful*
broken and a *c* heart … Ps 51:17
humble and *c* of spirit … Is 66:2

CONTROL (n) *order, rule*
people were out of *c* … Ex 32:25
was it not under...*c* … Acts 5:4
children under *c* … 1 Tim 3:4

CONTROL (v) *rule, subdue*
he *c-led* himself and … Gen 43:31
Joseph could not *c* … Gen 45:1
Haman *c-led* himself … Esth 5:10

CONTROVERSY *dispute*
wise man has a *c* … Prov 29:9
LORD has a *c* with the … Jer 25:31
avoid foolish *c-ies* … Titus 3:9

CONVERSE *discuss*
Stoic...were *c-ing* … Acts 17:18
and *c* with him … Acts 24:26

CONVERSION *change* Becoming a believer in Christ, i.e. committing oneself to Him for salvation.
c of the Gentiles … Acts 15:3

CONVERTED *changed*
sinners will be *c* … Ps 51:13
unless you are *c* … Matt 18:3
perceive...and be *c* … John 12:40

CONVICT *condemn, judge*
one of you *c-s* Me … John 8:46
c...concerning sin … John 16:8
he is *c-ed* by all … 1 Cor 14:24
to *c* all the ungodly … Jude 15

CONVICTION 1) Certainty about matters of faith (Rom 14:22). 2) Awareness of guilt (John 16:8).

CONVINCED *persuaded*
c that John was a … Luke 20:6
c that neither death … Rom 8:38
c in the Lord Jesus … Rom 14:14
c of better things … Heb 6:9

CONVOCATION *conclave*
sabbath...a holy *c* ... Lev 23:3
shall have a holy *c* ... Num 29:7

CONVULSION *paroxysm*
threw him into a *c* ... Mark 9:20
a *c* with foaming ... Luke 9:39

COOK *prepare food*
Jacob had *c-ed* stew ... Gen 25:29
you shall *c* and eat ... Deut 16:7

COOL *cold*
in the *c* of the day ... Gen 3:8
in his *c* roof chamber ... Judg 3:20
who has a *c* spirit ... Prov 17:27

COPPER *metal*
you can dig *c* ... Deut 8:9
not acquire...*c* ... Matt 10:9
widow...*c* coins ... Luke 21:2

COPY *facsimile*
c of this law on a ... Deut 17:18
c of...law of Moses ... Josh 8:32
c of the edict ... Esth 8:13
mere c of the true ... Heb 9:24

CORBAN *offering* A Heb word transliterated in Mark 7:11; translated "given" in Matt 15:5. The word refers to a sacrifice or offering, but it was also taken out of that context and used in precise formulas for vows. Such vows could be, and often were, worded as strong warnings or as refusals of assistance to others. Jesus rightly condemns the Jewish religious leaders for enforcing a vow against a person's own parents, because by doing so they were allowing a much greater evil—that of dishonoring parents—while upholding the sanctity of a vow, in this case one which should never have been permitted.
C (that is...) ... Mark 7:11

CORD *band, rope*
c-s of Sheol ... 2 Sam 22:6
c-s of affliction ... Job 36:8
c-s of death ... Ps 18:4
silver *c* is broken ... Eccl 12:6
the *c-s* of falsehood ... Is 5:18
a scourge of *c-s* ... John 2:15

CORIANDER An herb of the carrot family, the seeds of which were used to flavor or garnish food (Ex 16:31).

CORINTH A city on the northern shore of the Peloponnesus (the Greek peninsula). An important trade center that was strategically located on the commercial route between Europe and Asia. Many of its population were wealthy but notoriously immoral.
city in Greece ... Acts 18:1
NT church site ... 1 Cor 1:1,2

CORNELIUS A Roman centurion from Caesarea who was converted to Christ through the testimony of Peter.
centurion, believer ... Acts 10:1ff

CORNER *angle, intersection*
the chief *c stone* ... Ps 118:22
lurks by every *c* ... Prov 7:12
on the street *c-s* ... Matt 6:5
the chief *c stone* ... Mark 12:10
four *c-s* of the earth ... Rev 7:1

CORNER GATE *see* **GATES OF JERUSALEM**

CORNERSTONE *support stone*
Sometimes a prophetic title applied to Jesus Christ by Himself (Matt 21:42) and others. It refers to the fact that He is the true Messiah (q.v.), but was rejected as such by the nation of Israel. He is also the cornerstone of the church.
who laid its *c* ... Job 38:6
the *c* of her tribes ... Is 19:13
costly *c for* the ... Is 28:16
From them...the *c* ... Zech 10:4

CORPSE *dead body*
made unclean by a *c* ... Lev 22:4
Their *c-s* will rise ... Is 26:19
a mass of *c-s* ... Nah 3:3
boy...like a *c* ... Mark 9:26

CORRECT *reprove*
c him with the rod ... 2 Sam 7:14
He who *c-s* a scoffer ... Prov 9:7
C your son, and he ... Prov 29:17
C me, O LORD ... Jer 10:24
gentleness *c-ing* ... 2 Tim 2:25

CORRECTION *improvement*
Whether for *c*, or ... Job 37:13
refused to take *c* ... Jer 5:3
for reproof, for *c* ... 2 Tim 3:16

CORRUPT (adj) *evil, rotten*
the earth was *c* ... Gen 6:11
detestable and *c* ... Job 15:16
They are *c* ... Ps 14:1
all of them, are *c* ... Jer 6:28

CORRUPT (v) *make evil*
a bribe *c-s* the heart ... Eccl 7:7
c-ed your wisdom ... Ezek 28:17
have *c-ed* the covenant ... Mal 2:8
Bad company *c-s* ... 1 Cor 15:33
harlot who was *c-ing* ... Rev 19:2

CORRUPTION *decay, evil*
their *c* is in them ... Lev 22:25
no negligence or *c* ... Dan 6:4
from the flesh reap *c* ... Gal 6:8
c that is in the world ... 2 Pet 1:4
slaves of *c* ... 2 Pet 2:19

COSMETICS *beautifying aids*
provided her with...*c* ... Esth 2:9
the *c* for women ... Esth 2:12

COST *expense, price*
c of their lives ... Num 16:38
let the *c* be paid ... Ezra 6:4
calculate the *c* ... Luke 14:28
water...without *c* ... Rev 21:6

COSTLY *expensive*
redemption...is *c* ... Ps 49:8
gold, silver, *c* stones ... Dan 11:38
vial of...*c* perfume ... Mark 14:3
pearls or *c* garments ... 1 Tim 2:9

COUCH *bed, pallet*
he went up to my *c* ... Gen 49:4
falling on the *c* ... Esth 7:8
dissolve my *c* with my ... Ps 6:6
sprawl on their *c-es* ... Amos 6:4

COUNCIL *assembly*
not enter into their *c* ... Gen 49:6
the *c* of the holy ones ... Ps 89:7
the *c* of My people ... Ezek 13:9
conferred with his *c* ... Acts 25:12

COUNCIL A governing body, in the NT usually the high Jewish council called the Sanhedrin (q.v.).
Sanhedrin ... Matt 26:59
Jewish governing body ... Mark 15:1,43; Luke 22:66; 23:50

COUNSEL (n) *advice, opinion*
I will give you *c* ... Ex 18:19
Take *c* and speak up ... Judg 19:30
To Him belong *c* ... Job 12:13
not walk in the *c* ... Ps 1:1
Listen to *c* and ... Prov 19:20
the *c* of His will ... Eph 1:11

COUNSEL (v) *advise*
he has *c-ed* rebellion ... Deut 13:5
I *c* that all Israel ... 2 Sam 17:11
How do you *c me* ... 1 Kin 12:6
c you with My eye ... Ps 32:8

COUNSELOR *adviser*
the king and his *c-s* ... Ezra 7:15
c-s walk barefoot ... Job 12:17
abundance of *c-s* ... Prov 11:14
Wonderful *C*, Mighty ... Is 9:6
who became His *c* ... Rom 11:34

COUNT *consider, number*
c the stars, if you ... Gen 15:5
could not be *c-ed* ... 1 Kin 8:5
If I should *c* them ... Ps 139:18
my prayer be *c-ed* ... Ps 141:2
was *c-ed* among us ... Acts 1:17
I *c* all...loss ... Phil 3:8
as some *c* slowness ... 2 Pet 3:9

COUNTENANCE *appearance*
why has your *c* fallen ... Gen 4:6
LORD lift up His *c* ... Num 6:26
light of Your *c* ... Ps 4:6
an angry *c* ... Prov 25:23

COUNTRY *land, region*
Go forth from your *c* ... Gen 12:1
up into the hill *c* ... Deut 1:24
go out into the *c* ... Song 7:11
them from the *c-ies* ... Ezek 34:13
they are seeking a *c* ... Heb 11:14

COUNTRYMAN
not hate...fellow *c* ... Lev 19:17
among your *c-men* ... Deut 17:15
a man and his *c* ... Deut 25:11
my fellow *c-men* and ... Rom 11:14

COURAGE *heart, valor*
he lost *c* ... 2 Sam 4:1
and do not lose *c* ... 2 Chr 15:7
let your heart take *c* ... Ps 27:14
with justice and *c* ... Mic 3:8
Take *c*, son ... Matt 9:2
Take *c*, it is I ... Matt 14:27
c; I have overcome ... John 16:33
we are of good *c* ... 2 Cor 5:8

COURAGEOUS *brave*
Be strong and *c* ... Deut 31:6
be strong and very *c* ... Josh 1:7
I propose to be *c* ... 2 Cor 10:2

COURIER *messenger*
c-s went throughout ... 2 Chr 30:6

Letters...by *c-s* … Esth 3:13
One *c* runs to meet … Jer 51:31

COURSE *area, extent, way*
strong man to run his *c* … Ps 19:5
on its circular *c-s* … Eccl 1:6
I have finished the *c* … 2 Tim 4:7
the *c* of *our* life … James 3:6

COURT *area, hall, tribunal*
c of the tabernacle … Ex 27:9
c of the harem … Esth 2:11
a day in Your *c-s* … Ps 84:10
c of the LORD's house … Jer 26:2
c of the guardhouse … Jer 39:15
if you have law *c-s* … 1 Cor 6:4
drag you into *c* … James 2:6

COURTYARD *compound*
a well in his *c* … 2 Sam 17:18
c of the high priest … Matt 26:58
Peter...in the *c* … Mark 14:66

COVENANT *agreement* A binding agreement between two people. God's covenants with man are reminders of His gracious promises.
establish My *c* … Gen 6:18
for a sign of a *c* … Gen 9:13
for an everlasting *c* … Gen 17:13
ark of the *c* … Num 10:33
My *c* of peace … Num 25:12
book of the *c* … 2 Kin 23:2
Remember His *c* … 1 Chr 16:15
who keep His *c* … Ps 103:18
I will make a new *c* … Jer 31:31
forsake the holy *c* … Dan 11:30
a *c* with Assyria … Hos 12:1
the blood of *My c* … Zech 9:11
cup...is the new *c* … Luke 22:20
c which God made … Acts 3:25
this is My *c* with … Rom 11:27
servants of a new *c* … 2 Cor 3:6
strangers to the *c-s* … Eph 2:12
guarantee...better *c* … Heb 7:22
blood of the...*c* … Heb 13:20
ark of His *c* … Rev 11:19

COVER (n)
c of porpoise skin … Num 4:14
the c of a couch … Amos 3:12

COVER (v) *hide*
and *c* up his blood … Gen 37:26
basket and *c-ed* it … Ex 2:3
Whose sin is *c-ed* … Ps 32:1
He will *c* you with … Ps 91:4
love *c-s* all … Prov 10:12
not *c* My face … Is 50:6
c-ed...with sackcloth … Jon 3:6
to the hills, *C* us … Luke 23:30
c a multitude of sins … James 5:20
love *c-s* a multitude … 1 Pet 4:8

COVERING *canopy*
made...loin *c-s* … Gen 3:7
spread a cloud for a *c* … Ps 105:39
she makes *c-s* for … Prov 31:22
sackcloth their *c* … Is 50:3
given to her for a *c* … 1 Cor 11:15
freedom as a *c* … 1 Pet 2:16

COVET *crave, desire*
not *c* your neighbor's … Ex 20:17
You shall not *c* … Deut 5:21
I *c-ed* them and took … Josh 7:21
They *c* fields and then … Mic 2:2

c-ed no one's silver … Acts 20:33

COVETOUS *desirous*
the *c* and swindlers … 1 Cor 5:10
c, nor drunkards … 1 Cor 6:10

COW *animal*
came up seven *c-s* … Gen 41:2
c calves and does not … Job 21:10
c and the bear will … Is 11:7
you *c-s* of Bashan … Amos 4:1

CRAFTINESS *shrewdness*
the wise in their *c* … 1 Cor 3:19
not walking in *c* … 2 Cor 4:2
by *c* in deceitful … Eph 4:14

CRAFTSMAN *artisan*
the hands of the *c* … Deut 27:15
all the *c-men* and … 2 Kin 24:14
idol, a *c* casts it … Is 40:19
business to...*c-men* … Acts 19:24
c of any craft will … Rev 18:22

CRAG *protrusion, rock*
sharp *c* on the one … 1 Sam 14:4
Upon the rocky *c* … Job 39:28
clefts of the *c-s* … Is 57:5

CRAVE *covet, desire*
day long he is *c-ing* … Prov 21:26
fig *which* I *c* … Mic 7:1
generation *c-s* for … Matt 12:39
would not *c* evil … 1 Cor 10:6

CRAWLING *creeping*
venom of *c* things … Deut 32:24
beasts and the *c* … Acts 11:6
and *c* creatures … Rom 1:23

CREATE *form, make*
c-d the heavens … Gen 1:1
c-d man in His … Gen 1:27
C in me a clean … Ps 51:10
C-ing the praise of … Is 57:19
c new heavens … Is 65:17
one God *c-d* us … Mal 2:10
c-d...for good works … Eph 2:10
c-d in righteousness … Eph 4:24
You *c-d* all … Rev 4:11

CREATION The mighty act of God in which, by His word alone, He brought into existence the universe and everything in it; sometimes called creation *ex nihilo* (Lat, "out of nothing"). Also refers to all that was created.
beginning of *c* … Mark 10:6
preach...to all *c* … Mark 16:15
whole *c* groans … Rom 8:22
beginning of *c* … 2 Pet 3:4

CREATOR *Maker*
Remember...your *C* … Eccl 12:1
The *C* of Israel … Is 43:15
rather than the *C* … Rom 1:25
to a faithful *C* … 1 Pet 4:19

CREATURE *created being*
every living *c* that … Gen 1:21
winged *c* will make … Eccl 10:20
and crawling *c-s* … Rom 1:23
in Christ...new *c* … 2 Cor 5:17
as *c-s* of instinct … 2 Pet 2:12

CREDITOR *lender*
not to act as a *c* to … Ex 22:25
every *c* shall release … Deut 15:2
Let the *c* seize all … Ps 109:11

My *c-s* did I sell you … Is 50:1

CREEP *crawl*
everything that *c-s* … Gen 1:25
that *c* on the earth … Ezek 38:20

CREEPING *crawling*
cattle and *c* things … Gen 1:24
c things and fish … 1 Kin 4:33
c locust has eaten … Joel 1:4
c locust strips and … Nah 3:16

CRETANS
inhabitants of Crete … Acts 2:11; Titus 1:12

CRETE Greek island in the eastern Mediterranean, south of the Aegean Sea.
Mediterranean island … Acts 27:7,21; Titus 1:5
see also **CAPHTOR**

CRIME *vice*
be a lustful *c* … Job 31:11
committed no *c* … Dan 6:22
full of bloody *c-s* … Ezek 7:23
not of such *c-s* … Acts 25:18

CRIMINAL *lawbreaker*
crucified...the *c-s* … Luke 23:33
imprisonment as a *c* … 2 Tim 2:9

CRIMSON *deep red*
purple, *c* and violet … 2 Chr 2:7
like *c*...be like wool … Is 1:18

CRIPPLED *lame*
a son *c* in his feet … 2 Sam 4:4
enter life *c* or lame … Matt 18:8
bring...*c* and blind … Luke 14:21

CRISPUS
Corinthian Christian … Acts 18:8; 1 Cor 1:14

CROOKED *evil, twisted*
and *c* generation … Deut 32:5
to their *c* ways … Ps 125:5
What is *c* cannot be … Eccl 1:15
make *c* the straight … Acts 13:10
c and perverse … Phil 2:15

CROP *yield of produce*
old things from the *c* … Lev 25:22
c-s to the grasshopper … Ps 78:46
c began to sprout … Amos 7:1
share of the *c-s* … 2 Tim 2:6

CROSS (n) *execution device See* **CRUCIFIXION** In the NT, the cross becomes a symbol for Christ's work of redemption (q.v.), and for an attitude of self-sacrifice and devotion to Christ on the part of believers.
take his *c* and … Matt 10:38
down from the *c* … Matt 27:40
to bear His *c* … Mark 15:21
take up his *c* daily … Luke 9:23
standing by the *c* … John 19:25
hanging Him on a *c* … Acts 5:30
c of Christ would … 1 Cor 1:17
word of the *c* is … 1 Cor 1:18
boast, except in the *c* … Gal 6:14
even death on a *c* … Phil 2:8
enemies of the *c* … Phil 3:18
blood of His *c* … Col 1:20
endured the *c* … Heb 12:2

CROSS (v) *pass over*
you *c* the Jordan ... Deut 12:10
c-ed opposite Jericho ... Josh 3:16
kept *c-ing* the ford ... 2 Sam 19:18
Jesus had *c-ed* over ... Mark 5:21
c-ing over to ... Acts 21:2

CROUCH *bow, stoop*
sin is *c-ing* at the ... Gen 4:7
Beneath Him *c* the ... Job 9:13
Nothing...but to *c* ... Is 10:4

CROWD *multitude*
send the *c-s* away ... Matt 14:15
because of the *c* ... Mark 2:4
He summoned the *c* ... Mark 8:34
c of tax collectors ... Luke 5:29
Him...a large *c* ... Luke 23:27
they stirred up the *c* ... Acts 17:8

CROWN (n) *royal emblem* or *top*
on the *c* of the head ... Gen 49:26
the *c* of their king ... 2 Sam 12:30
he set the royal *c* ... Esth 2:17
wife is the *c* of ... Prov 12:4
gray head is a *c* ... Prov 16:31
c of the drunkards ... Is 28:3
a *c* of thorns ... Matt 27:29
receive the *c* of life ... James 1:12
c-s before the throne ... Rev 4:10
golden *c* on His head ... Rev 14:14

CROWN (v) *to place crown on*
c him with glory ... Ps 8:5
Who *c-s* you with ... Ps 103:4
head *c-s* you like ... Song 7:5
c-ed him with glory ... Heb 2:7

CRUCIFIXION From the Lat for "cross" (*crux*). The cross could be in the shape of a small or capital 'T', i.e. with the cross beam attached at the top of a vertical post or down a foot or so, to allow room for a sign. The victim's wrists (the Gr for "hand" can include the wrist and forearm) were nailed to the cross beam, which was then attached to the vertical post. His feet were bent together so that they could be fixed to the post by a single nail driven through both of them. The victim rested some of his weight on a small wooden projection attached to the post, which provided him minimal assistance in breathing but also served to prolong his suffering. Breaking the victim's legs would end the process, because he could no longer push himself up to breathe.

CRUCIFY *to execute on a cross*
scourge and *c Him* ... Matt 20:19
C Him ... Matt 27:22
Jesus...been *c-ied* ... Matt 28:5
c your King ... John 19:15
Paul was not *c-ied* ... 1 Cor 1:13
preach Christ *c-ied* ... 1 Cor 1:23
not have *c-ied* the ... 1 Cor 2:8
c-ied with Christ ... Gal 2:20
world...*c-ied* to me ... Gal 6:14
their Lord was *c-ied* ... Rev 11:8

CRUEL *fierce, harsh*
their...c bondage ... Ex 6:9
c man does...harm ... Prov 11:17
compassion...is *c* ... Prov 12:10
c and have no mercy ... Jer 6:23
people has become *c* ... Lam 4:3

CRUMBS *morsels*
dogs feed on the *c* ... Matt 15:27
on the children's *c* ... Mark 7:28

CRUSH *demolish, destroy*
a foot may *c* them ... Job 39:15
saves...*c-ed* in spirit ... Ps 34:18
lying tongue...*c-es* ... Prov 26:28
by *c-ing* My people ... Is 3:15
c-ed for our iniquities ... Is 53:5
LORD was pleased To *c* ... Is 53:10
who *c* the needy ... Amos 4:1
c Satan under...feet ... Rom 16:20

CRY (n) *scream, sob*
great and bitter *c* ... Gen 27:34
the *c* of triumph ... Ex 32:18
c has come to Me ... 1 Sam 9:16
Hear my *c*, O God ... Ps 61:1
the *c* of Jerusalem ... Jer 14:2
Jesus uttered a...*c* ... Mark 15:37

CRY (v)
do not *c* for help ... Job 36:13
c aloud in the night ... Lam 2:19
His elect, who *c* ... Luke 18:7
stones will *c* out ... Luke 19:40
Jesus stood and *c-ied* ... John 7:37

CRYSTAL *glass*
awesome gleam of *c* ... Ezek 1:22
sea of glass, like *c* ... Rev 4:6
water...clear as *c* ... Rev 22:1

CUB *whelp, young*
robbed of her *c-s* ... 2 Sam 17:8
She reared her *c-s* ... Ezek 19:2
lioness, and lion's *c* ... Nah 2:11

CUBIT *linear measure* A standard linear unit of measurement among the Jews, based on the length of a man's forearm, about 18 inches.
ark three hundred *c-s* ... Gen 6:15
length was nine *c-s* ... Deut 3:11
gallows fifty *c-s* high ... Esth 5:14
the altar by *c-s* ... Ezek 43:13

CUD *previously swallowed food*
chews the *c* ... Lev 11:3
not chew *c*, it is ... Lev 11:7
chews the *c* ... Deut 14:6

CULT *religious ritual*
be a *c* prostitute ... Deut 23:17
male *c* prostitutes ... 1 Kin 14:24
male c prostitutes ... 2 Kin 23:7

CULTIVATE *till*
no man to *c* the ... Gen 2:5
Eden to *c* it ... Gen 2:15
and *c* vineyards ... Deut 28:39
servants shall *c* ... 2 Sam 9:10
and *c* faithfulness ... Ps 37:3

CUMMIN *plant for seasoning* An herb of the carrot family, mentioned with dill. A food flavoring.
driven over *c* ... Is 28:27
mint and dill and *c* ... Matt 23:23

CUNNING *crafty*
he is very *c* ... 1 Sam 23:22
advice of the *c* ... Job 5:13
harlot and *c* of heart ... Prov 7:10

CUP *container*
into Pharaoh's *c* ... Gen 40:11
My *c* overflows ... Ps 23:5
the *c* of salvation ... Ps 116:13
a *c* of consolation ... Jer 16:7
c of cold water ... Matt 10:42
let this *c* pass ... Matt 26:39
washing of *c-s* and ... Mark 7:4
gives you a *c* of ... Mark 9:41
c...new covenant ... Luke 22:20
c of blessing ... 1 Cor 10:16
eat...drink the *c* ... 1 Cor 11:26
c full of abominations ... Rev 17:4

CUPBEARER *royal official* An important official in the government of ancient oriental countries who served wine to the king and enjoyed his confidence. He was selected for his loyalty and he ensured that the wine was not poisoned, sometimes by drinking some of it himself. Nehemiah was a cupbearer.
c spoke to Pharaoh ... Gen 41:9
his *c-s*, and his ... 1 Kin 10:5
c-s and their attire ... 2 Chr 9:4
c to the king ... Neh 1:11

CURDS *butter, cheese*
he took *c* and milk ... Gen 18:8
she brought him *c* ... Judg 5:25
with honey and *c* ... Job 20:17

CURE *heal*
c him of his leprosy ... 2 Kin 5:3
c you of your wound ... Hos 5:13
they could not *c* him ... Matt 17:16
that...time He *c-d* ... Luke 7:21

CURSE (n) *condemning oath*
upon myself a *c* ... Gen 27:12
c on Mount Ebal ... Deut 11:29
c to My chosen ones ... Is 65:15
they will become a *c* ... Jer 44:12
will no longer be a *c* ... Zech 14:11
become a *c* for us ... Gal 3:13

CURSE (v) *verbally condemn*
who *c-s* you I will *c* ... Gen 12:3
You shall not *c* God ... Ex 22:28
not *c* a deaf man ... Lev 19:14
c-d the...anointed ... 2 Sam 19:21
c-d the day of his *birth* ... Job 3:1
began to *c* and ... Mark 14:71
bless and do not *c* ... Rom 12:14
with it we *c* men ... James 3:9

CURSED (adj) *under a curse*
C is the ground ... Gen 3:17
C be Canaan ... Gen 9:25
C is the man who ... Deut 27:15
C...who trusts ... Jer 17:5
C...who hangs ... Gal 3:13

CURTAIN *covering, drape*
on the edge of the *c* ... Ex 26:4
heaven like a *tent c* ... Ps 104:2
c-s of your dwellings ... Is 54:2
c-s of the land of ... Hab 3:7

CUSH Firstborn of Ham and father of Nimrod, his descendants established cities in Nubia and possibly in Mesopotamia.
area of W Asia ... Gen 2:13
patriarch ... Gen 10:6,8
region S of Egypt ... 2 Kin 19:9; Is 20:3

CUSTODY *prison, protection*
they put him in *c* ... Num 15:34
into the *c* of Hegai ... Esth 2:3
John...taken into *c* ... Matt 4:12

holding Jesus in *c* ... Luke 22:63

CUSTOM *manner* or *tax*
it became a *c* in ... Judg 11:39
not pay tribute, *c* ... Ezra 4:13
c, He entered the ... Luke 4:16
burial *c* of the Jews ... John 19:40
c-s...not lawful ... Acts 16:21
c-s of our fathers ... Acts 28:17
whom tax *is due; c* ... Rom 13:7

CUT *destroy, divide*
did not *c* the birds ... Gen 15:10
c off from the earth ... Ex 9:15
c down their Asherim ... Ex 34:13
LORD *c* off...lips ... Ps 12:3
tongue will be *c* ... Prov 10:31
C off your hair and ... Jer 7:29
were *c-ting* branches ... Matt 21:8
and *c* off his ear ... Matt 26:51
were *c* to the quick ... Acts 7:54
you...will be *c* off ... Rom 11:22

CYMBAL *musical instrument*
castanets and *c-s* ... 2 Sam 6:5
loud-sounding *c-s* ... 1 Chr 15:16
with loud *c-s* ... Ps 150:5
or a clanging *c* ... 1 Cor 13:1

CYPRESS *tree*
cedar and *c* timber ... 1 Kin 5:10
c and algum timber ... 2 Chr 2:8
Our rafters, *c-es* ... Song 1:17
Wail, O *c*, for the ... Zech 11:2

CYPRUS
Mediterranean island ... Is 23:1; Acts 11:19; 15:39; 21:16
see also **KITTIM**

CYRENE Situated in northern Africa on a bluff overlooking the Mediterranean, Cyrene was an important city with a large Greek colony. The Simon who carried Jesus' cross was a resident of Cyrene.
NW African port ... Mark 15:21; Luke 23:26; Acts 2:10; 11:20

CYRUS He conquered Babylon in 539 B.C. and founded the Persian empire. In 536 B.C. he released the captive Jews so that they could return to Jerusalem and rebuild the temple (Isa 41:25; 44:28; 45; 1-13).
king of Persia ... 2 Chr 36:22; Is 45:1
decreed to rebuild Temple ... Ezra 1:1; 5:13

D

DAGON The principal god of the Philistines, which was depicted as having the body of a fish and the head of a man. Samson died in one of his temples.
god of Philistines ... Judg 16:23; 1 Sam 5:4; 1 Chr 10:10

DAMAGE (n) *destruction*
any *d* may be found ... 2 Kin 12:5
the *d-s* of the house ... 2 Kin 12:6
d and great loss ... Acts 27:10
incurred this *d* and ... Acts 27:21

DAMAGE (v) *destroy, hurt*
it will *d* the revenue ... Ezra 4:13
and *d-ing* to kings ... Ezra 4:15
enemy has *d-d* ... Ps 74:3
So that no one...*d* it ... Is 27:3

DAMASCUS Said to be the oldest continuously inhabited city in the world, it is located in Syria on a plain watered by the rivers Abanah and Pharpar. It had a large Jewish colony, and it was during a journey to Damascas that Saul, who became the apostle Paul, was converted.
city of Aram (Syria) ... Gen 14:15; 2 Kin 5:12; Acts 9:3, 27; 26:20

DAN *(judge)*. The fifth son of Jacob by Bilhah and the name of a territory occupied by the tribe of Dan in the division of the Promised Land. Also the name of a city in northern Israel.
1 *son of Jacob* ... Gen 30:6;49:16
2 *tribal area* ... Josh 19:40; Judg 18:2
3 *city in N Palestine* ... Josh 19:47

DANCE (n) *rhythmic movement*
timbrels...with *d-ing* ... Ex 15:20
they sing in the *d-s* ... 1 Sam 29:5
will rejoice in the *d* ... Jer 31:13
music and *d-ing* ... Luke 15:25

DANCE (v) *move rhythmically*
from those who *d-d* ... Judg 21:23
David was *d-ing* ... 2 Sam 6:14
and a time to *d* ... Eccl 3:4
Herodias *d-d* before ... Matt 14:6

DANGER *peril*
not only is there *d* ... Acts 19:27
often in *d* of death ... 2 Cor 11:23
d-s from...Gentiles ... 2 Cor 11:26

DANIEL *(God is my judge)*. One of the four major OT prophetic books. Daniel was a man of impeccable integrity despite living and serving in a corrupt royal court; no sin of any kind is ascribed to him. He was taken into captivity to Babylon at a young age, never to return to his homeland.
son of David and Abigail ... 1 Chr 3:1
prophet ... Ezek 14:14; Dan 1:6
see also **BELTESHAZZAR**

DARE *presume, risk*
who *d-s* rouse him up ... Gen 49:9
who would *d* to risk ... Jer 30:21
d from that day ... Matt 22:46
did not *d* pronounce ... Jude 9

DARIUS Popular name among Persian kings. Darius the Mede assigned Daniel as one of three officials who had authority over 120 satraps, who in turn oversaw their respective provinces. Darius also decreed that his kingdom would fear the God of Daniel. Another Darius confirmed Cyrus's decree to rebuild the temple in Jerusalem.
1 *Darius the Mede* ... Dan 5:31
2 *Darius I* ... Ezra 4:5; Hag 1:1
3 *Darius II* ... Neh 12:22

DARK *dim, shadow*
not in *d* sayings ... Num 12:8
d places of the land ... Ps 74:20
live in a *d* land ... Is 9:2
it was still *d* ... John 20:1
shining in a *d* place ... 2 Pet 1:19

DARKEN *obscure*
the land was *d-ed* ... Ex 10:15
this that *d-s* counsel ... Job 38:2
the stars are *d-ed* ... Eccl 12:2
sun will be *d-ed* ... Mark 13:24
their eyes be *d-ed* ... Rom 11:10

DARKNESS *gloom, shadow* A biblical term symbolizing death as opposed to life, man's fallen state after the original sin of Adam and Eve, and the influence of evil.
blind...gropes in *d* ... Deut 28:29
are silenced in *d* ... 1 Sam 2:9
illumines my *d* ... 2 Sam 22:29
that stalks in *d* ... Ps 91:6
those who dwelt in *d* ... Ps 107:10
as light excels *d* ... Eccl 2:13
people who walk in *d* ... Is 9:2
light will rise in *d* ... Is 58:10
into the outer *d* ... Matt 22:13
those who sit in *d* ... Luke 1:79
men loved the *d* ... John 3:19
turn from *d* to light ... Acts 26:18
has light with *d* ... 2 Cor 6:14
unfruitful deeds of *d* ... Eph 5:11
in Him there is no *d* ... 1 John 1:5
brother is in the *d* ... 1 John 2:9

DARLING *love*
you are, my *d* ... Song 1:15
Arise, my *d* ... Song 2:13
my *d*, My dove ... Song 5:2

DATHAN *(strong)*. A Reubenite who joined in the conspiracy of Korah and was buried alive when the earth parted.
rebelled against Moses ... Num 16:12; Ps 106:17

DAUGHTER
d-s were born to them ... Gen 6:1
if a man sells his *d* ... Ex 21:7
inheritance to his *d* ... Num 27:8
Kings' *d-s* are among ... Ps 45:9
d-s of song ... Eccl 12:4
destruction of the *d* ... Is 22:4
the *d* of my people ... Jer 9:1
D rises up against ... Mic 7:6
mother against *d* ... Luke 12:53

DAUGHTER-IN-LAW
said to his *d* Tamar ... Gen 38:11
nakedness of your *d* ... Lev 18:15
said to Ruth her *d* ... Ruth 2:22
D against her ... Mic 7:6

DAVID *(beloved)*. The second and greatest king of Israel, who reigned 40 years. David was called by God while a young shepherd, and was an ancestor of Christ. One of his greatest acts of faith and valor before becoming king was killing the Philistine giant Goliath. Known as the *sweet psalmist* of Israel, he is the author of many of the Psalms.
anointed ... 1 Sam 16:13
killed Goliath ... 1 Sam 17:50
fled from Saul ... 1 Sam 19:18
spared Saul ... 1 Sam 26:9
king of Judah and Israel ... 2 Sam 2:4;5:3
covenant with God ... 2 Sam 7:8
death ... 1 Kin 2:10

DAWN (n) *daylight*
at the approach of *d* ... Judg 19:25
caused the *d* to know ... Job 38:12
rise before *d* and ... Ps 119:147
wings of the *d* ... Ps 139:9
As the *d* is spread ... Joel 2:2

DAWN (v) *become light*
the day began to *d* ... Judg 19:26
when morning *d-s* ... Ps 46:5

a Light *d-ed* … Matt 4:16
d toward the first … Matt 28:1
until the day *d-s* … 2 Pet 1:19

DAY *light* 1) Any or all of a twenty-four hour period. 2) An important calendar event, such as the Day of Atonement. 3) An extended period of time, such as the *day of the Lord.* 4) An experience described metaphorically, e.g. *a day of trouble.*
God called the light *d* … Gen 1:5
come on a festive *d* … 1 Sam 25:8
d...LORD has made … Ps 118:24
what a *d* may bring … Prov 27:1
d-s of your youth … Eccl 12:1
a *d* of reckoning … Is 2:12
has despised the *d* … Zech 4:10
the *d* of His coming … Mal 3:2
Give us this *d* … Matt 6:11
raise...the last *d* … John 6:39
judge...the last *d* … John 12:48
the *d* of salvation … 2 Cor 6:2
perfect it until the *d* … Phil 1:6
d is like a thousand … 2 Pet 3:8
tormented *d*...night … Rev 20:10

DAY OF ATONEMENT This annual observation of the Jewish people was a national day of fasting and repentance. It was held on the tenth day of the seventh month in the Jewish calendar (Tishri). The high priest entered into the Holy of Holies only on this day.
month is the *d* … Lev 23:27
for it is a *d* … Lev 23:28

DAY OF THE LORD A major theme of prophecy, this is a period of time beginning with the seven-year tribulation and extending through the millennium during which Christ will judge and rule in righteousness. It is also described as *the great and terrible day* and *the great day of God,* the Almighty.
d is near … Is 13:6
d will come … 1 Thess 5:2

DAZZLING *blinding, bright*
My beloved is *d* … Song 5:10
Like *d* heat … Is 18:4
near...in *d* clothing … Luke 24:4

DEACON *officer, server* One who helps in ministering to the social and material needs of the church.
overseers and *d-s* … Phil 1:1
D-s likewise *must be* … 1 Tim 3:8
let them serve as *d-s* … 1 Tim 3:10
D-s must be husbands … 1 Tim 3:12
served well as *d-s* … 1 Tim 3:13

DEAD *without life*
you are a *d* man … Gen 20:3
near to a *d* person … Num 6:6
dealt with the *d* … Ruth 1:8
forgotten as a *d* man … Ps 31:12
d do not praise … Ps 115:17
better than a *d* lion … Eccl 9:4
Your *d* will live … Is 26:19
not weep for the *d* … Jer 22:10
rising from the *d* … Mark 9:10
d will hear the … John 5:25
resurrection of the *d* … Acts 23:6
d in your trespasses … Eph 2:1
firstborn from the *d* … Col 1:18
living and the *d* … 2 Tim 4:1
repentance...*d* works … Heb 6:1
to those who are *d* … 1 Pet 4:6
I was *d*...I am alive … Rev 1:18
Hades gave up the *d* … Rev 20:13

DEAF *without hearing*
makes *him* mute or *d* … Ex 4:11
not curse a *d* man … Lev 19:14
Like a *d* cobra … Ps 58:4
the *d* will hear … Is 29:18
and *the d* hear … Matt 11:5
the *d* to hear … Mark 7:37
d and mute spirit … Mark 9:25

DEAL *allot, barter, treat*
let us *d* wisely … Ex 1:10
have you *d-t* with us … Ex 14:11
nor *d* falsely … Lev 19:11
d-t with mediums … 2 Kin 21:6
who *d* treacherously … Ps 25:3
has *d-t* bountifully … Ps 116:7
who *d* faithfully … Prov 12:22
Everyone *d-s* falsely … Jer 6:13
when I have *d-t* … Ezek 20:44
has *d-t* with me … Luke 1:25

DEALINGS *actions, relations*
no *d* with anyone … Judg 18:7
no *d* with Samaritans … John 4:9
of the Lord's *d* … James 5:11

DEAR *beloved*
Is Ephraim My *d* son … Jer 31:20
my life...as *d* to … Acts 20:24
had become very *d* … 1 Thess 2:8

DEATH *cessation of life*
d of the upright … Num 23:10
d encompassed me … 2 Sam 22:5
d for his own sin … 2 Chr 25:4
D rather than my pains … Job 7:15
no mention of You in *d* … Ps 6:5
cords of *d* encompassed … Ps 18:4
the shadow of *d* … Ps 23:4
escapes from *d* … Ps 68:20
doomed to *d* … Ps 102:20
d of His godly ones … Ps 116:15
who hate me love *d* … Prov 8:36
love is as strong as *d* … Song 8:6
He will swallow up *d* … Is 25:8
D cannot praise You … Is 38:18
no pleasure in the *d* … Ezek 18:32
d is better to me … Jon 4:3
is to be put to *d* … Matt 15:4
will not taste *d* … Matt 16:28
to the point of *d* … Mark 14:34
passed out of *d* … John 5:24
he will never see *d* … John 8:51
sickness is not to end in *d* … John 11:4
the agony of *d* … Acts 2:24
d by hanging Him … Acts 10:39
d reigned from Adam … Rom 5:14
wages of sin is *d* … Rom 6:23
the law of sin and of *d* … Rom 8:2
proclaim...Lord's *d* … 1 Cor 11:26
d, where...victory … 1 Cor 15:55
even *d* on a cross … Phil 2:8
He might taste *d* … Heb 2:9
it brings forth *d* … James 1:15
passed out of *d* … 1 John 3:14
Be faithful until *d* … Rev 2:10
had the name *D* … Rev 6:8

DEATH, SECOND The future, eternal destiny of Satan and all his followers, including those who reject Christ; also identified as the lake of fire and brimstone (q.v.).
s...no power … Rev 20:6

DEATH, SPIRITUAL The state of being separated from God (Ezek 18:4). This can only be avoided by accepting Christ as Savior and Lord. Those who do not will eventually suffer the second death (see above).

DEBATE *dispute*
d-d...themselves … Mark 1:27
dissension and *d* … Acts 15:2
had been much *d* … Acts 15:7

DEBORAH *(bee).* A prophetess and the fourth judge of Israel. She encouraged Barak to fight Sisera's Canaanite army. Also the name of Rebekah's nurse.
1 *nurse of Rebekah* … Gen 35:8
2 *prophetess, judge* … Judg 4:4ff

DEBT *obligation*
and pay your *d* … 2 Kin 4:7
exaction of every *d* … Neh 10:31
guarantors for *d-s* … Prov 22:26
forgive us our *d-s* … Matt 6:12

DEBTOR *borrower*
restores to the *d* … Ezek 18:7
forgiven our *d-s* … Matt 6:12
had two *d-s* … Luke 7:41
his master's *d-s* … Luke 16:5

DECAPOLIS *(ten-city).* A confederation of ten important cities, of which all but one were located in a large district east of the Jordan, from Damascus to the Dead Sea (Matt 4:25). Their inhabitants were mostly Gentiles who followed Hellenistic (Greek) culture.

DECAY *corruption*
own eyes see his *d* … Job 21:20
Holy One to...*d* … Acts 2:27
did not undergo *d* … Acts 13:37

DECEASED *dead*
wife of the *d* shall … Deut 25:5
the widow of the *d* … Ruth 4:5
the name of the *d* … Ruth 4:10
the sister of the *d* … John 11:39

DECEIT *deception, falsehood, guile*
full of curses and *d* … Ps 10:7
in whose spirit...no *d* … Ps 32:2
your tongue frames *d* … Ps 50:19
D is in the heart … Prov 12:20
he lays up *d* … Prov 26:24
Offspring of *d* … Is 57:4
houses are full of *d* … Jer 5:27
house of Israel...*d* … Hos 11:12
d, sensuality, envy … Mark 7:22
in whom...is no *d* … John 1:47
full of envy...*d* … Rom 1:29
the lusts of *d* … Eph 4:22
all malice and all *d* … 1 Pet 2:1
nor was any *d* found … 1 Pet 2:22
lips from speaking *d* … 1 Pet 3:10

DECEITFUL *false*
From a *d* tongue … Ps 120:2
the wicked are *d* … Prov 12:5
d are the kisses of … Prov 27:6
Charm is *d* and … Prov 31:30
The heart is more *d* … Jer 17:9
false apostles, *d* … 2 Cor 11:13

DECEIVE *cheat, mislead*
have you *d-d* me ... Gen 29:25
Jacob *d-d* Laban ... Gen 31:20
d-s his companion ... Lev 6:2
both stolen and *d-d* ... Josh 7:11
Do not *d* me ... 2 Kin 4:28
who *d-s* his neighbor ... Prov 26:19
Do not *d* yourselves ... Jer 37:9
your heart has *d-d* you ... Obad 3
they keep *d-ing* ... Rom 3:13
Let no one *d* you ... Eph 5:6
d-ing and being *d-d* ... 2 Tim 3:13

DECEIVER *liar*
as a *d* in his sight ... Gen 27:12
as *d-s* and yet true ... 2 Cor 6:8
d and the antichrist ... 2 John 7

DECEPTION *falsehood*
their mind prepares *d* ... Job 15:35
the hills are a *d* ... Jer 3:23
last *d* will be worse ... Matt 27:64
philosophy and empty *d* ... Col 2:8
reveling in their *d-s* ... 2 Pet 2:13

DECEPTIVE *misleading*
wicked...*d* wages ... Prov 11:18
Do not trust in *d* words ... Jer 7:4
d stream With water ... Jer 15:18

DECISION *judgment, resolution*
d is from the LORD ... Prov 16:33
in the valley of *d* ... Joel 3:14
My *d* is to gather ... Zeph 3:8
majority reached a *d* ... Acts 27:12

DECLARE *explain, proclaim*
Moses *d-d* to...sons ... Lev 23:44
d to Him the number ... Job 31:37
d Your faithfulness ... Ps 30:9
mouth...*d* Your praise ... Ps 51:15
d Your lovingkindness ... Ps 92:2
Who has *d-d this* ... Is 41:26
d-s the LORD ... Amos 4:11
He will *d* all things ... John 4:25
d-d the Son of God ... Rom 1:4

DECLINE *decrease*
for the shadow to *d* ... 2 Kin 20:10
our days have *d-d* ... Ps 90:9
for the day *d-s* ... Jer 6:4

DECREASE *abate, subside*
the water *d-d* steadily ... Gen 8:5
not let their cattle *d* ... Ps 107:38
increase...I must *d* ... John 3:30

DECREE (n) *judgment, order* An order or declaration from one having supreme authority. Royal decrees were made public by couriers and heralds sent throughout the land.
issued a *d* to rebuild ... Ezra 5:13
and *d* of the king ... Esth 2:8
devises mischief by *d* ... Ps 94:20
only one *d* for you ... Dan 2:9
delivering the *d-s* ... Acts 16:4
to the *d-s* of Caesar ... Acts 17:7

DECREE (v) *decide, determine*
been *d-d* against her ... Esth 2:1
will also *d* a thing ... Job 22:28
And rulers *d* justice ... Prov 8:15
Seventy weeks...*d-d* ... Dan 9:24

DEDICATE *consecrate, devote*
D yourselves today ... Ex 32:29
I wholly *d* the silver ... Judg 17:3
d-d by...David ... 1 Kin 7:51
David...*d-d* these ... 1 Chr 18:11
d-d part...the spoil ... 1 Chr 26:27
d-ing it to Him ... 2 Chr 2:4

DEDICATION *consecration* In the OT, ceremonies performed to make sacred objects such as the altar and temple fit for service to the Lord. The ceremonies typically involved animal sacrifices. Also, various voluntary submissions of persons or property to service for God (see Nazirite).
the *d* of the altar ... 2 Chr 7:9
celebrated the *d* of ... Ezra 6:16
d of the wall ... Neh 12:27
d of the image ... Dan 3:2
assembled for the *d* ... Dan 3:3

DEDICATION, FEAST OF *see* **FEAST OF DEDICATION** *and* **FEASTS**

DEED *action* or *document*
What is this *d* ... Gen 44:15
for our evil *d-s* ... Ezra 9:13
blot out...loyal *d-s* ... Neh 13:14
abominable *d-s* ... Ps 14:1
I...sealed the *d* ... Jer 32:10
prophet mighty in *d* ... Luke 24:19
their *d-s* were evil ... John 3:19
d-s of the flesh are ... Gal 5:19
for every good *d* ... Titus 3:1
I know your *d-s* ... Rev 2:2

DEEP (adj) *far ranging*
d sleep falls on men ... Job 4:13
Your judgments are...*d* ... Ps 36:6
casts into a *d* sleep ... Prov 19:15
into *d* darkness ... Jer 13:16
the well is *d* ... John 4:11

DEEP (n) *abyss, depth*
fountains of the...*d* ... Gen 7:11
the *d* lying beneath ... Deut 33:13
surface of the *d* is ... Job 38:30
D calls to *d* ... Ps 42:7
The *d-s* also trembled ... Ps 77:16
His wonders in the *d* ... Ps 107:24
the springs of the *d* ... Prov 8:28

DEER *animal*
besides *d*, gazelles ... 1 Kin 4:23
d pants for the water ... Ps 42:1
lame will leap like a *d* ... Is 35:6

DEFEAT *conquer, overthrow*
d-ed...and pursued ... Gen 14:15
able to *d* them ... Num 22:6
sons of Israel *d-ed* ... Josh 12:7
d the Arameans ... 2 Kin 13:17
d-ed the Philistines ... 1 Chr 18:1
d-ed the entire army ... Jer 37:10

DEFECT (n) *blemish, spot*
No one who has a *d* ... Lev 21:18
one ram without *d* ... Num 6:14
if it has any *d* ... Deut 15:21
no *d* in him ... 2 Sam 14:25
in whom was no *d* ... Dan 1:4

DEFECT (v) *rebel, disobey*
d to his master ... 1 Chr 12:19
many *d-ed* to him ... 2 Chr 15:9
you have deeply *d-ed* ... Is 31:6

DEFEND *protect*
LORD of hosts will *d* ... Zech 9:15
d-ed him and took ... Acts 7:24
or else *d-ing* them ... Rom 2:15
are *d-ing* ourselves ... 2 Cor 12:19

DEFENSE *protection*
d-s are *d-s* of clay ... Job 13:12
the *d* of my life ... Ps 27:1
You have been a *d* ... Is 25:4
the *d*...of the gospel ... Phil 1:7

DEFILE *pollute, profane*
astray...*d-s* herself ... Num 5:29
d-d the high places ... 2 Kin 23:8
d-d the priesthood ... Neh 13:29
d-d Your holy temple ... Ps 79:1
your hands are *d-d* ... Is 59:3
those *d* the man ... Matt 15:18
is what *d-s* the man ... Mark 7:20
conscience...is *d-d* ... 1 Cor 8:7
d-s the entire body ... James 3:6

DEFILEMENT *filth* In OT law, generally contact with anything ceremonially unclean (e.g. a corpse), which in turn renders one unclean and requires a purification ritual before one can again participate in society and religious observances. Also used frequently in reference to improper sexual behavior.
her *interest,* for *d* ... Ezek 22:3
from all *d* of flesh ... 2 Cor 7:1

DEFRAUD *deprive, wrong* To take away or hold back property and rights from others by deceit or treachery.
whom have I *d-ed* ... 1 Sam 12:3
To *d* a man ... Lam 3:36
Do not *d* ... Mark 10:19
no one keep *d-ing* ... Col 2:18

DEITY *God, gods* The essential nature of the triune God which was fully present in Christ (Col 2:9). In the plural it refers to gods foreign to one's own theological framework (Acts 17:18).
see also **TRINITY**
of strange *d-ies* ... Acts 17:18
fullness of *D* dwells ... Col 2:9

DELAY *hinder, linger, stall*
Do not *d* me ... Gen 24:56
Moses *d-ed* to come ... Ex 32:1
shall not *d* to pay ... Deut 23:21
bridegroom...*d-ing* ... Matt 25:5
Do not *d* in coming ... Acts 9:38
now why do you *d* ... Acts 22:16
in case I am *d-ed* ... 1 Tim 3:15

DELICACIES *fancy foods*
eat of their *d* ... Ps 141:4
Do not desire his *d* ... Prov 23:3
Those who ate *d* ... Lam 4:5

DELIGHT (n) *pleasure*
I have no *d* in you ... 2 Sam 15:26
Will he take *d* ... Job 27:10
his *d* is in the law ... Ps 1:2
commandments...*d* ... Ps 119:143
my *d* in the sons of ... Prov 8:31
a just weight is His *d* ... Prov 11:1
the *d* of kings ... Prov 16:13
I took great *d* ... Song 2:3
call the sabbath a *d* ... Is 58:13
My *d* is in her ... Is 62:4

DELIGHT (v) *desire*
LORD *d-ed* over you ... Deut 28:63
d in...offerings ... 1 Sam 15:22

d to revere Your name ... Neh 1:11
d in the Almighty ... Job 22:26
D yourself in the LORD ... Ps 37:4
not *d* in sacrifice ... Ps 51:16
Who *d* in doing evil ... Prov 2:14
d in my ways ... Prov 23:26
takes no *d* in fools ... Eccl 5:4
I *d* in loyalty ... Hos 6:6
d-s...unchanging love ... Mic 7:18
d-ing...self-abasement ... Col 2:18

DELIGHTFUL *pleasant*
d is a timely word ... Prov 15:23
to find *d* words ... Eccl 12:10
and how *d* you are ... Song 7:6
Is he a *d* child ... Jer 31:20

DELILAH A very beautiful Philistine woman who married Samson and eventually aided Philistine leaders by enticing him to tell the secret that his strength came from his uncut hair.
Philistine woman ... Judg 16:4
enticed Samson ... Judg 16:6-20

DELIVER *give, rescue, save*
come down to *d* them ... Ex 3:8
d the manslayer ... Num 35:25
My...power has *d-ed* ... Judg 7:2
can this one *d* ... 1 Sam 10:27
He will *d* you ... Job 5:19
d-ed my soul from ... Ps 56:13
none who can *d* ... Is 43:13
mind on *d-ing* Daniel ... Dan 6:14
d us from evil ... Matt 6:13
d-ed over to death ... 2 Cor 4:11

DELIVERANCE *salvation* The act of rescuing someone. To save from the penalty, power, and ultimately the presence of sin and eternal death.
by a great *d* ... Gen 45:7
given this great *d* ... Judg 15:18
with songs of *d* ... Ps 32:7
a God of *d-s* ... Ps 68:20
d through...prayers ... Phil 1:19

DELIVERER *savior*
the LORD raised up a *d* ... Judg 3:9
gave them *d-s* ... Neh 9:27
my fortress and my *d* ... Ps 18:2
d-s...ascend Mount ... Obad 21
D...come from Zion ... Rom 11:26

DELUDE *lead astray*
they have *d-d* you ... Is 47:10
no one will *d* you ... Col 2:4
who *d* themselves ... James 1:22

DEMAND *order, require*
husband may *d* of him ... Ex 21:22
but I *d* one thing ... 2 Sam 3:13
captors *d-ed* of us ... Ps 137:3
do not *d* it back ... Luke 6:30
d-ing of Him a sign ... Luke 11:16

DEMAS A companion of Paul during his Roman imprisonment. He later deserted Paul (2 Tim 4:10).

DEMETRIUS
1 *Ephesian smith* ... Acts 19:24,38
2 *a Christian* ... 3 John 12

DEMOLISH *destroy*
d all...high places ... Num 33:52
he *d-ed* its stones ... 2 Kin 23:15
to *d* its strongholds ... Is 23:11

DEMON *devil* An evil spirit who has continually opposed God since the rebellion and fall of Satan. The term also is used of heathen gods to whom sacrifices were offered.
sacrificed to *d-s* ... Deut 32:17
daughters to the *d-s* ... Ps 106:37
after the *d* was cast ... Matt 9:33
sacrifice to *d-s* ... 1 Cor 10:20
d-s also believe ... James 2:19
not to worship *d-s* ... Rev 9:20

DEMONIACS *possessed ones*
d, epileptics ... Matt 4:24
what had happened to the *d* ... Matt 8:33

DEMON-POSSESSED
many who were *d* ... Matt 8:16
a mute, *d* man ... Matt 9:32
to the *d* man ... Mark 5:16
sayings of one *d* ... John 10:21

DEMONSTRATE *show*
God *d-s* His own love ... Rom 5:8
to *d* His wrath ... Rom 9:22
d-d yourselves to be ... 2 Cor 7:11
d His...patience ... 1 Tim 1:16

DEMONSTRATION *a showing*
for the *d, I say* ... Rom 3:26
in *d* of the Spirit ... 1 Cor 2:4

DEN *abode*
remains in its *d* ... Job 37:8
From the *d-s* of lions ... Song 4:8
the viper's *d* ... Is 11:8
cast into the lions' *d* ... Dan 6:7
it a robbers' *d* ... Mark 11:17

DENARIUS A Roman silver coin in the NT period that was equal to a day's wage for a common laborer.
Roman silver coin ... Matt 20:2,9
a day's wage ... Luke 20:24
Denarii *(pl)* ... John 6:7;12:5

DENOUNCE *accuse, slander*
And come, *d* Israel ... Num 23:7
the LORD has not *d-d* ... Num 23:8
let us *d* him ... Jer 20:10
He...to *d* the cities ... Matt 11:20

DENY *conceal, refuse*
Sarah *d-ied it* ... Gen 18:15
so that you do not *d* your God ... Josh 24:27
not *d-ied* the words ... Job 6:10
and *d-ing* the LORD ... Is 59:13
whoever *d-ies* Me ... Matt 10:33
has *d-ied* the faith ... 1 Tim 5:8
deeds they *d Him* ... Titus 1:16
us to *d* ungodliness ... Titus 2:12
d-ies the Son ... 1 John 2:23

DEPART *leave*
scepter shall not *d* ... Gen 49:10
sword...never *d* ... 2 Sam 12:10
to *d* from evil is ... Job 28:28
His spirit *d-s* ... Ps 146:4
his foolishness will not *d* ... Prov 27:22
turned aside and *d-ed* ... Jer 5:23
I never knew you; *d* ... Matt 7:23
d from Me, all you ... Luke 13:27
d and be with Christ ... Phil 1:23

DEPARTURE *death* or *leaving*
after their *d* from ... Ex 16:1
speaking of His *d* ... Luke 9:31
time of my *d* has ... 2 Tim 4:6
any time after my *d* ... 2 Pet 1:15

DEPEND *rely, rest upon*
d-ed on the weapons ... Is 22:8
you did not *d* on Him ... Is 22:11
d the whole Law ... Matt 22:40

DEPORTATION *exile*
after the *d* to ... Matt 1:12
to the *d* to Babylon ... Matt 1:17

DEPORTED *exiled*
d...to Babylon ... Ezra 5:12
d...entire population ... Amos 1:6

DEPOSE *release*
d you from your office ... Is 22:19
d-d from his royal ... Dan 5:20

DEPOSIT (n) *security*
in regard to a *d* ... Lev 6:2
d which was entrusted ... Lev 6:4

DEPOSIT (v) *place, put*
d them in the tent ... Num 17:4
d it in your town ... Deut 14:28
d...in the temple ... Ezra 5:15
had *d-ed* the scroll ... Jer 36:20

DEPRAVED *degenerate*
over to a *d* mind ... Rom 1:28
men of *d* mind ... 2 Tim 3:8

DEPRAVITY Absolute moral corruption, the state of all humans due to the sin of Adam (cf. Hos 5:2). The result of depravity is separation from God.

DEPRIVE *take away*
d the needy of justice ... Is 10:2
d-d of...my years ... Is 38:10
d-ing one another ... 1 Cor 7:5
d-d of the truth ... 1 Tim 6:5

DEPTH *abyss, deep*
d-s boil like a pot ... Job 41:31
hand are the *d-s* ... Ps 95:4
went down to the *d-s* ... Ps 107:26
sins Into the *d-s* ... Mic 7:19
drowned in the *d* ... Matt 18:6
it had no *d* of soil ... Mark 4:5
nor height, nor *d* ... Rom 8:39
the *d* of the riches ... Rom 11:33
even the *d-s* of God ... 1 Cor 2:10

DEPUTY *proconsul*
he was the only *d* ... 1 Kin 4:19
Solomon's...*d-ies* ... 1 Kin 5:16
a *d* was king ... 1 Kin 22:47

DERISION *laughingstock*
d among...enemies ... Ex 32:25
d to those around us ... Ps 44:13
reproach and *d* all ... Jer 20:8
d to the rest of the ... Ezek 36:4

DESCEND *go down*
angels of God...*d-ing* ... Gen 28:12
His glory will not *d* ... Ps 49:17
breath of...*d-s* ... Eccl 3:21
will *d* to Hades ... Matt 11:23
Spirit *d-ing*...dove ... John 1:32
d into the abyss ... Rom 10:7
who *d-ed*...ascended ... Eph 4:10

DESCENDANT *seed, offspring*
your *d-s* I will give ... Gen 12:7
will raise up your *d* ... 2 Sam 7:12
His *d-s* shall endure ... Ps 89:36

So shall your *d-s* be ... Rom 4:18
you are Abraham's *d-s* ... Gal 3:29
to the *d* of Abraham ... Heb 2:16
and the *d* of David ... Rev 22:16

DESCENT *hill* or *heritage*
of Median *d* ... Dan 9:1
the *d* of the Mount ... Luke 19:37
were of high-priestly *d* ... Acts 4:6

DESCRIBE *explain*
you shall *d* the land ... Josh 18:6
man, *d* the temple ... Ezek 43:10
who had seen it *d-d* ... Mark 5:16

DESECRATE *defile*
d the sanctuary ... Dan 11:31
tried to *d* the temple ... Acts 24:6

DESERT (n) *wilderness*
d plains of Jericho ... Josh 5:10
grieved Him in the *d* ... Ps 78:40
better to live in a *d* ... Prov 21:19
in the *d* a highway ... Is 40:3
Rivers in the *d* ... Is 43:19
like a bush in the *d* ... Jer 17:6
he lived in the *d-s* ... Luke 1:80

DESERT (v) *abandon, forsake*
d-ed to the king ... 2 Kin 25:11
who had *d-ed* them ... Acts 15:38
so quickly *d-ing* Him ... Gal 1:6
but all *d-ed* me ... 2 Tim 4:16
I will never *d* you ... Heb 13:5

DESERTERS *changers of loyalty*
d who had deserted ... 2 Kin 25:11
d who had gone over ... Jer 39:9

DESERVE *earn, merit*
with him as he *d-d* ... Judg 9:16
done this *d-s* to die ... 2 Sam 12:5
He *d-s* death ... Matt 26:66
receiving what we *d* ... Luke 23:41

DESIGN *creation, plan*
d-s for work in gold ... Ex 31:4
makers of *d-s* ... Ex 35:35
execute any *d* which ... 2 Chr 2:14
All their deadly *d-s* ... Jer 18:23

DESIGNATE *appoint*
if he *d-s* her for ... Ex 21:9
one whom I *d* to ... 1 Sam 16:3
were *d-d* by name ... 1 Chr 16:41
being *d-d* by God ... Heb 5:10

DESIRABLE *attractive*
the tree was *d* ... Gen 3:6
d in your eyes ... 1 Kin 20:6
more *d* than gold ... Ps 19:10
What is *d* in a man ... Prov 19:22
every kind of *d* object ... Nah 2:9

DESIRE (n) *appetite, craving*
d...for your husband ... Gen 3:16
poor from *their d* ... Job 31:16
the *d-s* of your heart ... Ps 37:4
d of the wicked will ... Ps 112:10
d of the righteous ... Prov 10:24
d of your eyes ... Ezek 24:16
great man speaks the *d* ... Mic 7:3
d and my prayer ... Rom 10:1
d-s of the flesh ... Eph 2:3
d to depart and be ... Phil 1:23
evil *d*, and greed ... Col 3:5

DESIRE (v) *crave, wish*
your heart *d-s* ... Deut 14:26
as much as you *d* ... 1 Sam 2:16
I *d* to argue with God ... Job 13:3
You *d* truth ... Ps 51:6
not *d* his delicacies ... Prov 23:3
all that my eyes *d-d* ... Eccl 2:10
righteous men *d-d* ... Matt 13:17
d the greater gifts ... 1 Cor 12:31
d...a good showing ... Gal 6:12
d a better *country* ... Heb 11:16

DESOLATE *lonely, waste*
your sanctuaries *d* ... Lev 26:31
sons of the *d* one ... Is 54:1
high places will be *d* ... Ezek 6:6
d wilderness behind ... Joel 2:3
loaves in *this d* place ... Matt 15:33
homestead be made *d* ... Acts 1:20
children of the *d* ... Gal 4:27

DESOLATION *ruin, waste*
a *d* and a curse ... 2 Kin 22:19
a heap forever, a *d* ... Josh 8:28
D is left in the city ... Is 24:12
d-s of many generations ... Is 61:4
an everlasting *d* ... Ezek 35:9
the abomination of *d* ... Dan 11:31
day of...*d* ... Zeph 1:15
her *d* is near ... Luke 21:20

DESPAIR (n) *grief*
words of one in *d* ... Job 6:26
my soul is in *d* ... Ps 42:6
Why are you in *d* ... Ps 43:5

DESPAIR (v) *grieve*
Saul then will *d* ... 1 Sam 27:1
I...*d-ed* of all ... Eccl 2:20
we *d-ed* even of life ... 2 Cor 1:8
but not *d-ing* ... 2 Cor 4:8

DESPISE *reject, scorn*
d-d his birthright ... Gen 25:34
those who *d* Me ... 1 Sam 2:30
d-d...in her heart ... 2 Sam 6:16
not *d* the discipline ... Job 5:17
hate and *d* falsehood ... Ps 119:163
Fools *d* wisdom and ... Prov 1:7
wisdom...is *d-d* ... Eccl 9:16
has *d-d* the day of ... Zech 4:10
have we *d-d* Your name ... Mal 1:6
not *d* one of these ... Matt 18:10
be devoted to one and *d* ... Luke 16:13
do you *d*...church ... 1 Cor 11:22

DESPOIL *injure, lay waste*
d-ed all the cities ... 2 Chr 14:14
the wicked who *d* me ... Ps 17:9
plundered and *d-ed* ... Is 42:22

DESTINE *appoint*
is *d-d* for the sword ... Job 15:22
d you for the sword ... Is 65:12
things *d-d* to perish ... Col 2:22
not *d-d* us for wrath ... 1 Thess 5:9

DESTITUTE *deprived, in need*
prayer of the *d* ... Ps 102:17
the land is *d* ... Ezek 32:15
being *d*, afflicted ... Heb 11:37

DESTROY *abolish, ruin, waste*
to *d* all flesh ... Gen 6:17
so that I do not *d* you ... 1 Sam 15:6
would You *d* me ... Job 10:8
seek my life to *d* it ... Ps 40:14
the wicked, He will *d* ... Ps 145:20
that which *d-s* kings ... Prov 31:3
one sinner *d-s* much ... Eccl 9:18
stronghold is *d-ed* ... Is 23:14
shepherds...are *d-ing* ... Jer 23:1
He will *d* mighty men ... Dan 8:24
moth and rust *d* ... Matt 6:19
who is able to *d* ... Matt 10:28
You come to *d* us ... Mark 1:24
seeking...to *d* Him ... Mark 11:18
d the temple and ... Mark 15:29
flood...*d-ed* them ... Luke 17:27
D this temple, and ... John 2:19
not for *d-ing* you ... 2 Cor 10:8
to save and to *d* ... James 4:12
heavens will be *d-ed* ... 2 Pet 3:12
d the works of the ... 1 John 3:8

DESTROYER *devastator*
d of our country ... Judg 16:24
of the *d-s* prosper ... Job 12:6
d comes upon him ... Job 15:21
d-s and devastators ... Is 49:17
I will set apart *d-s* ... Jer 22:7

DESTRUCTION *calamity, ruin*
the *d* of my kindred ... Esth 8:6
God apportion *d* ... Job 21:17
Your tongue devises *d* ... Ps 52:2
Pride *goes* before *d* ... Prov 16:18
foolish son is *d* to ... Prov 19:13
called the City of *D* ... Is 19:18
d of the daughter of ... Lam 2:11
broad that leads to *d* ... Matt 7:13
whose end is *d* ... Phil 3:19
d will come ... 1 Thess 5:3
penalty of eternal *d* ... 2 Thess 1:9
bringing swift *d* upon ... 2 Pet 2:1

DETERMINE *decide*
to d whether he laid ... Ex 22:8
his days are *d-d* ... Job 14:5
d-d their appointed ... Acts 17:26
but rather *d* this ... Rom 14:13
d-d to know nothing ... 1 Cor 2:2

DETEST *despise, loathe*
carcasses you shall *d* ... Lev 11:11
not *d* an Egyptian ... Deut 23:7
d his citadels ... Amos 6:8

DETESTABLE *abominable*
not eat any *d* thing ... Deut 14:3
who is *d* and corrupt ... Job 15:16
swine's flesh, *d* ... Is 66:17
their *d* idols ... Jer 16:18
remove all its *d* ... Ezek 11:18
d...sight of God ... Luke 16:15

DEVASTATE *destroy, lay waste*
d-d the nations ... 2 Kin 19:17
Until cities are *d-d* ... Is 6:11
the LORD...*d-s* it ... Is 24:1
my tents are *d-d* ... Jer 4:20
d...pride of Egypt ... Ezek 32:12

DEVASTATION *destruction*
d of the afflicted ... Ps 12:5
Nor *d* or destruction ... Is 60:18
raise up the former *d-s* ... Is 61:4
d in their citadels ... Amos 3:10

DEVICE *plan, scheme*
By their own *d-s* ... Ps 5:10
not promote his *evil d* ... Ps 140:8
a man of evil *d-s* ... Prov 14:17
in their *d-s* you walk ... Mic 6:16

DEVIL *demon, Satan (slanderer).* Another name for Satan (q.v.), based on the fact that he is the accuser of God's people. He is the prince and ruler of the evil spirits.
tempted by the *d* ... Matt 4:1
one of you is a *d* ... John 6:70
you son of the *d* ... Acts 13:10
firm against...the *d* ... Eph 6:11
render powerless...*d* ... Heb 2:14
serpent...the *d* ... Rev 12:9
d...into the lake ... Rev 20:10

DEVISE *design, scheme, plot*
d-d against the Jews ... Esth 9:25
d-ing a vain thing ... Ps 2:1
d-s mischief by decree ... Ps 94:20
continually *d-s* evil ... Prov 6:14
man who *d-s* evil ... Prov 12:2
He *d-s* wicked schemes ... Is 32:7
do not *d* evil in ... Zech 7:10
d futile things ... Acts 4:25

DEVOTE *commit, dedicate*
shall *d* to the LORD ... Ex 13:12
d...to the law ... 2 Chr 31:4
d-d to one and despise ... Matt 6:24
d-ing...to prayer ... Acts 1:14
d-d to one another ... Rom 12:10
D yourselves to prayer ... Col 4:2

DEVOTED *set apart (to God)*
d to destruction ... Lev 27:28
Every *d* thing in ... Num 18:14
d to destruction ... 1 Sam 15:21
d thing in Israel ... Ezek 44:29

DEVOTION *consecration*
his deeds of *d* ... 2 Chr 32:32
excessive *d to books* ... Eccl 12:12
the *d* of your youth ... Jer 2:2

DEVOUR *consume, swallow*
wild beast *d-ed* him ... Gen 37:20
the sword *d* forever ... 2 Sam 2:26
is *d-ed* by disease ... Job 18:13
fire from...*d-ed* ... Ps 18:8
love all words that *d* ... Ps 52:4
To *d* the afflicted ... Prov 30:14
has *d-ed* your prophets ... Jer 2:30
caterpillar was *d-ing* ... Amos 4:9
d widows' houses ... Mark 12:40
bite...*d* one another ... Gal 5:15

DEVOUT *God-fearing*
d men are taken away ... Is 57:1
was righteous and *d* ... Luke 2:25
d men, from every ... Acts 2:5
the *d* women ... Acts 13:50

DEW *drops of moisture*
God give...the *d* ... Gen 27:28
d fell on the camp ... Num 11:9
d on the fleece only ... Judg 6:37
on him as the *d* ... 2 Sam 17:12
neither *d* nor rain ... 1 Kin 17:1
the *d* of Hermon ... Ps 133:3
skies drip with *d* ... Prov 3:20
Like a cloud of *d* ... Is 18:4
drenched with the *d* ... Dan 4:15
sky has withheld its *d* ... Hag 1:10

DIADEM A golden band worn around the head royalty (Isa 28:5).

DIALECT *language*
in the Hebrew *d* ... Acts 21:40
the Hebrew *d* ... Acts 22:2

DIAMOND *jewel*
a sapphire and a *d* ... Ex 28:18
With a *d* point ... Jer 17:1

DIBON 1) A city in southern Judea (Neh 11:25). 2) A city in Moab, east of the Dead Sea (Num 21:30).

DICTATION *spoken words*
at the *d* of Jeremiah ... Jer 36:4
written at the *d* of ... Jer 36:27
book at Jeremiah's *d* ... Jer 45:1

DIDYMUS
see **THOMAS**

DIE *decease, expire*
you will surely *d* ... Gen 2:17
not eat...which *d-s* ... Deut 14:21
Where you *d*, I will *d* ... Ruth 1:17
Curse God and *d* ... Job 2:9
even wise men *d* ... Ps 49:10
fools *d* for lack of ... Prov 10:21
and the fool alike *d* ... Eccl 2:16
soul who sins will *d* ... Ezek 18:4
to *d* with You ... Matt 26:35
child has not *d-d* ... Mark 5:39
live even if he *d-s* ... John 11:25
grain of wheat...*d-s* ... John 12:24
she fell sick and *d-d* ... Acts 9:37
d-d for the ungodly ... Rom 5:6
we who *d-d* to sin ... Rom 6:2
for whom Christ *d-d* ... Rom 14:15
I *d* daily ... 1 Cor 15:31
I *d-d* to the Law ... Gal 2:19
to *d* is gain ... Phil 1:21
Jesus *d-d* and rose ... 1 Thess 4:14
to *d* once and after ... Heb 9:27
these *d-d* in faith ... Heb 11:13
who *d* in the Lord ... Rev 14:13

DIFFICULT *hard*
too *d* for the LORD ... Gen 18:14
test Solomon with *d* ... 2 Chr 9:1
anything too *d* for Me ... Jer 32:27
speech or *d* language ... Ezek 3:5
solving of *d* problems ... Dan 5:12
last days *d* times ... 2 Tim 3:1

DIG *excavate, till*
opens a pit, or *d-s* ... Ex 21:33
you can *d* copper ... Deut 8:9
they *d* into houses ... Job 24:16
He has *dug* a pit ... Ps 7:15
dug through the wall ... Ezek 8:8
dug a wine press ... Matt 21:33
until I *d* around it ... Luke 13:8

DIGNITY *majesty*
Preeminent in *d* ... Gen 49:3
What honor or *d* has ... Esth 6:3
all godliness and *d* ... 1 Tim 2:2
must be men of *d* ... 1 Tim 3:8

DILIGENCE *effort*
carried out with all *d* ... Ezra 6:12
Watch...with all *d* ... Prov 4:23
lagging behind in *d* ... Rom 12:11
show the same *d* ... Heb 6:11

DILIGENT *persistent*
hand of the *d* makes ... Prov 10:4
plans of the *d lead* ... Prov 21:5
d to present ... 2 Tim 2:15
d to enter that rest ... Heb 4:11
I will also be *d* ... 2 Pet 1:15

DIM *cloudy, dark*
eye was not *d* ... Deut 34:7
eyesight...to grow *d* ... 1 Sam 3:2
d because of grief ... Job 17:7
windows grow *d* ... Eccl 12:3

DIMINISH *dwindle, reduce*
you shall *d* its price ... Lev 25:16
d their inheritance ... Num 26:54
are *d-ed* and bowed ... Ps 107:39

DINAH (unc, *justice*). A daughter of Jacob by Leah; sister of Simeon and Levi.
daughter of Jacob ... Gen 34:1,3
raped by Shechem ... Gen 34:2,5

DINE *eat*
men are to *d* with ... Gen 43:16
to *d* with a ruler ... Prov 23:1
came and were *d-ing* ... Matt 9:10

DINNER *meal*
I have prepared...*d* ... Matt 22:4
because of...*d* guests ... Mark 6:26
was giving a big *d* ... Luke 14:16

DIONYSIUS *(of Dionysus,* Greek god of wine*).* Called *the Areopagite* (i.e. member of the Areopagus; q.v.) in Acts 17:34. A convert to Christ through the preaching of Paul in Athens.

DIOTREPHES *(nourished by Zeus).* A lover of prominence and persecutor of believers who was condemned by John in his third letter (3 John 9).

DIP *plunge*
d-ped the tunic in ... Gen 37:31
priest shall *d* his ... Lev 4:6
d your piece of bread ... Ruth 2:14
d-ped...seven times ... 2 Kin 5:14
d-ped...with Me ... Matt 26:23
who *d-s* with Me ... Mark 14:20
robe *d-ped* in blood ... Rev 19:13

DIRECT *arrange, guide, order*
LORD *d-s* his steps ... Prov 16:9
d your heart in the ... Prov 23:19
has *d-ed* the Spirit ... Is 40:13
walks to *d* his steps ... Jer 10:23
I *d-ed* the churches ... 1 Cor 16:1
d their entire body ... James 3:3

DIRECTION *path* or *order*
which turned every *d* ... Gen 3:24
It changes *d* ... Job 37:12
d of the daughter ... Jer 4:11
of their four *d-s* ... Ezek 1:17

DIRGE *lament* A hymn or song of sorrow, normally sung at funerals.
for you as a *d* ... Amos 5:1
we sang a *d* ... Luke 7:32

DISAPPEAR *vanish*
For the faithful *d* ... Ps 12:1
When the grass *d-s* ... Prov 27:25
old is ready to *d* ... Heb 8:13

DISAPPOINT *frustrate*
and were not *d-ed* ... Ps 22:5
hope does not *d* ... Rom 5:5

DISASTER *calamity*
d was close to them ... Judg 20:34
d on this people ... Jer 6:19
because of all its *d-s* ... Jer 19:8
In the day of their *d* ... Obad 13

DISBELIEVE *doubt*
Jews who *d-d* stirred ... Acts 14:2

for those who *d* ... 1 Pet 2:7

DISCERN *understand, recognize*
would *d*...future ... Deut 32:29
king to *d* good ... 2 Sam 14:17
not *d* its appearance ... Job 4:16
d-ed...the youths ... Prov 7:7
d the...sky ... Matt 16:3

DISCERNMENT *judgment* The ability to grasp the nature and meaning of things. In the Bible, often the ability to distinguish good from evil.
blessed be your *d* ... 1 Sam 25:33
asked for yourself *d* ... 1 Kin 3:11
not a people of *d* ... Is 27:11
knowledge and all *d* ... Phil 1:9

DISCHARGE *emission* A secretion of fluids from the body, many of which were covered by hygienic standards set forth in the law of Moses.
a *d* from his body ... Lev 15:2
leper or who has a *d* ... Lev 22:4
everyone having a *d* ... Num 5:2
d, or who is a leper ... 2 Sam 3:29
the *d* of your blood ... Ezek 32:6

DISCIPLE *learner (student).* One who is being mentored by another, with a view to assimilating and propagating what is learned. In Jewish society of the NT and before, rabbis (*see* **RABBI**) usually had younger disciples who studied OT law and tradition under them, and who generally learned about life from them. The disciples in turn followed a code of respectful behavior toward their rabbis which included greeting protocols, going on errands for them, never turning their backs toward them (a sign of disrespect), etc. In the NT, disciples are found chiefly in three categories: a) the twelve disciples chosen by Jesus; b) other disciples of Jesus who are not among the twelve; c) disciples of John the Baptist.
to listen as a *d* ... Is 50:4
His twelve *d-s* ... Matt 10:1
d is not above his ... Matt 10:24
d-s rebuked them ... Matt 19:13
d-s left Him...fled ... Matt 26:56
make *d-s* of all ... Matt 28:19
Your *d-s* do not fast ... Mark 2:18
Passover...My *d-s* ... Mark 14:14
gaze toward His *d-s* ... Luke 6:20
he cannot be My *d* ... Luke 14:26
d-s believed in Him ... John 2:11
His *d-s* withdrew ... John 6:66
wash the *d-s'* feet ... John 13:5
d whom He loved ... John 19:26
d-s were first called ... Acts 11:26

DISCIPLINE (n) *chastisement* In the Bible, usually correction given by God the Father to all His children. Discipline often takes the form of difficulties allowed or caused by God to bring about improvement and maturity in their lives.
the *d* of the LORD ... Deut 11:2
d of the Almighty ... Job 5:17
The rod of *d* ... Prov 22:15
to see your good *d* ... Col 2:5
d...of little profit ... 1 Tim 4:8

DISCIPLINE (v) *chastise*
as a man *d-s* his son ... Deut 8:5
d-d you with whips ... 1 Kin 12:11
D your son while ... Prov 19:18
I *d* my body ... 1 Cor 9:27
d-d by the Lord ... 1 Cor 11:32
father does not *d* ... Heb 12:7

DISCLOSE *reveal*
without *d-ing* it to ... 1 Sam 20:2
Esther had *d-d* what ... Esth 8:1
will *d* Myself to him ... John 14:21
d the motives of ... 1 Cor 4:5
secrets...are *d-d* ... 1 Cor 14:25

DISCOURAGE *dishearten*
d-ing the sons of ... Num 32:7
people of the land *d-d* ... Ezra 4:4
d-d with the work ... Neh 6:9

DISCOVER *find, uncover*
strength was not *d-ed* ... Judg 16:9
d the depths of God ... Job 11:7
man will not *d* ... Eccl 7:14
shamed...he is *d-ed* ... Jer 2:26

DISCRETION *understanding*
LORD give you *d* ... 1 Chr 22:12
sound wisdom and *d* ... Prov 3:21
woman who lacks *d* ... Prov 11:22
Daniel replied with *d* ... Dan 2:14

DISCUSS *converse, reason*
d matters of justice ... Jer 12:1
d...among themselves ... Matt 16:7
What were you *d-ing* ... Mark 9:33
d-ed together what ... Luke 6:11

DISEASE *sickness*
none of the *d-s* on you ... Ex 15:26
harmful *d-s* of Egypt ... Deut 7:15
d-d in his feet ... 2 Chr 16:12
d-d...not healed ... Ezek 34:4
heals all your *d-s* ... Ps 103:3
various *d-s* and pains ... Matt 4:24
power...to heal *d-s* ... Luke 9:1

DISGRACE *reproach, shame*
a *d* to us ... Gen 34:14
nakedness, it is a *d* ... Lev 20:17
sin is a *d* to ... Prov 14:34
not *d* the throne ... Jer 14:21
and bear your *d* ... Ezek 16:52

DISGRACEFUL *shameful*
d thing in Israel ... Gen 34:7
shameful and *d* son ... Prov 19:26
d for a woman to ... 1 Cor 11:6

DISGUISE *pretend*
d-d his sanity ... 1 Sam 21:13
Arise now, and *d* ... 1 Kin 14:2
king of Israel *d-d* ... 1 Kin 22:30
he *d-s* his face ... Job 24:15
d-ing...as apostles ... 2 Cor 11:13

DISH *bowl, plate*
prepare a savory *d* ... Gen 27:7
was one silver *d* ... Num 7:43
as one wipes a *d* ... 2 Kin 21:13
30 gold *d-es* ... Ezra 1:9

DISHEARTENED *discouraged*
not be *d* or crushed ... Is 42:4
you *d* the righteous ... Ezek 13:22

DISHONEST *untruthful*
those who hate *d* gain ... Ex 18:21
order to get *d* gain ... Ezek 22:27
cheat with *d* scales ... Amos 8:5

DISHONOR (n) *disgrace, shame*
to see the king's *d* ... Ezra 4:14
Fill their faces with *d* ... Ps 83:16
man conceals *d* ... Prov 12:16

DISHONOR (v) *disgrace, shame*
who *d-s* his father ... Deut 27:16
be ashamed and *d-ed* ... Ps 35:4
and you *d* Me ... John 8:49
bodies would be *d-ed* ... Rom 1:24
do you *d* God ... Rom 2:23

DISMAY *be troubled, fear*
d-ed at his presence ... Gen 45:3
not tremble or be *d-ed* ... Josh 1:9
d-ed and...afraid ... 1 Sam 17:11
or I will *d* you ... Jer 1:17
are *d-ed* and caught ... Jer 8:9
mighty men...be *d-ed* ... Obad 9

DISMISS *release, send away*
d-ed the people ... Josh 24:28
Solomon *d-ed* ... 1 Kin 2:27
priest did not *d any* ... 2 Chr 23:8
he *d-ed* the assembly ... Acts 19:41

DISOBEDIENCE *rebellion*
the one man's *d* ... Rom 5:19
in the sons of *d* ... Eph 2:2
d received a just ... Heb 2:2
same example of *d* ... Heb 4:11

DISOBEDIENT *rebellious*
d and rebelled ... Neh 9:26
hardened and *d* ... Acts 19:9
d to parents ... Rom 1:30
d...obstinate people ... Rom 10:21

DISPERSE *spread*
d them in Jacob ... Gen 49:7
d-d...the peoples ... Esth 3:8
d them among the ... Ezek 20:23
who are *d-d* abroad ... James 1:1

DISPLAY *declare, show*
to *d* her beauty ... Esth 1:11
d-ed Your splendor ... Ps 8:1
d their sin like ... Is 3:9
works of God...*d-ed* ... John 9:3

DISPLEASE *annoy, trouble*
if it is *d-ing* to you ... Num 22:34
d-ing in the sight ... 1 Sam 8:6
may not *d* the lords ... 1 Sam 29:7
d-ing in His sight ... Is 59:15
it greatly *d-d* Jonah ... Jon 4:1

DISPOSSESS *remove*
d-ed the Amorites ... Num 21:32
Esau *d-ed* them ... Deut 2:12
He will assuredly *d* ... Josh 3:10
d-ing the nations ... Acts 7:45

DISPUTE (n) *controversy*
When they have a *d* ... Ex 18:16
bring the *d-s* to God ... Ex 18:19
d in your courts ... Deut 17:8
a great *d* among ... Acts 28:29

DISPUTE (v) *contend, debate*
wished to *d* with Him ... Job 9:3
with Israel he will *d* ... Mic 6:2
without...*d-ing* ... Phil 2:14
He *d-d* with the devil ... Jude 9

DISSENSION *division*
great *d* and debate ... Acts 15:2
d between the ... Acts 23:7

those who cause *d-s* ... Rom 16:17
without wrath and *d* ... 1 Tim 2:8

DISSIPATION *intemperance* A useless waste of potential or resources; debauchery. Sometimes associated with drunkenness.
weighted...with *d* ... Luke 21:34
wine, for that is *d* ... Eph 5:18
not accused of *d* ... Titus 1:6

DISSOLVE *melt*
d me in a storm ... Job 30:22
I *d* my couch with ... Ps 6:6
d-d in tears ... Is 15:3
And the hills *d* ... Nah 1:5

DISTANCE *far away*
sister stood at a *d* ... Ex 2:4
some *d* from the ... Judg 18:22
following...at a *d* ... Matt 26:58
welcomed...from a *d* ... Heb 11:13

DISTINCTION *difference*
the LORD makes a *d* ... Ex 11:7
d between the holy ... Lev 10:10
have made no *d* ... Ezek 22:26
He made no *d* ... Acts 15:9
for there is no *d* ... Rom 3:22
d-s among yourselves ... James 2:4

DISTINGUISH *discern*
I *d* between good ... 2 Sam 19:35
not *d* the sound ... Ezra 3:13
d...the righteous ... Mal 3:18
d-ing of spirits ... 1 Cor 12:10

DISTINGUISHING (adj)
became your *d* mark ... Ezek 27:7
this is a *d* mark ... 2 Thess 3:17

DISTORT *pervert*
who *d-s* the justice ... Deut 27:19
my garment is *d-ed* ... Job 30:18
they *d* my words ... Ps 56:5
d the gospel of Christ ... Gal 1:7

DISTRESS *adversity, trouble*
day of my *d* ... Gen 35:3
When you are in *d* ... Deut 4:30
deliver me...*d* ... 1 Sam 26:24
I am in great *d* ... 2 Sam 24:14
cry to You in our *d* ... 2 Chr 20:9
refuge in the day of *d* ... Jer 16:19
I am in *d* ... Lam 1:20
d upon the land ... Luke 21:23
d for every soul ... Rom 2:9
assisted those in *d* ... 1 Tim 5:10
widows in their *d* ... James 1:27

DISTRIBUTE *apportion*
d-d by lot in Shiloh ... Josh 19:51
to *d* to their kinsmen ... Neh 13:13
d it to the poor ... Luke 18:22
d-ing to each one ... 1 Cor 12:11

DISTRICT *area, province*
the *d* of Jerusalem ... Neh 3:12
d around the Jordan ... Matt 3:5
d of Galilee ... Mark 1:28
the *d-s* of Libya ... Acts 2:10

DISTURB *annoy, bother*
Why...*d-ed* me ... 1 Sam 28:15
no one *d* his bones ... 2 Kin 23:18
d them and destroy ... Esth 9:24
being greatly *d-ed* ... Acts 4:2
one who is *d-ing* you ... Gal 5:10

DISTURBANCE *turmoil*
to cause a *d* in it ... Neh 4:8
hear of wars and *d-s* ... Luke 21:9
d among the soldiers ... Acts 12:18
arrogance, *d-s* ... 2 Cor 12:20

DIVIDE *apportion, separate*
that *d-s* the hoof ... Deut 14:6
D the living child ... 1 Kin 3:25
d my garments among ... Ps 22:18
He will *d* the booty ... Is 53:12
d-d up His garments ... Matt 27:35
d-d his wealth ... Luke 15:12

DIVINATION *witchcraft* The pagan practice of foretelling or foreseeing the future, either by omens or with the aid of the supernatural. Forbidden by OT law.
nor practice *d* or ... Lev 19:26
witchcraft, used *d* ... 2 Chr 33:6
false vision, *d* ... Jer 14:14
falsehood and lying *d* ... Ezek 13:6
a spirit of *d* met us ... Acts 16:16

DIVINE (adj) *pertaining to deity*
in whom...*d* spirit ... Gen 41:38
I see a *d* being ... 1 Sam 28:13
D Nature...gold ... Acts 17:29
power and *d* nature ... Rom 1:20
is the *d* response ... Rom 11:4

DIVINE (v) *practice divination*
d-d that the LORD ... Gen 30:27
they *d* lies for you ... Ezek 21:29
d-ing lies for them ... Ezek 22:28
prophets *d* for money ... Mic 3:11

DIVINER *seer*
called for the...*d-s* ... 1 Sam 6:2
The *d* and the elder ... Is 3:2
your *d-s* deceive you ... Jer 29:8
d-s will be embarrassed ... Mic 3:7
d-s see lying visions ... Zech 10:2

DIVISION *dissension, segment*
d between My people ... Ex 8:23
divided...into *d-s* ... 1 Chr 23:6
d...in the crowd ... John 7:43
no *d-s* among you ... 1 Cor 1:10
d of soul and spirit ... Heb 4:12

DIVORCE (n) *separation* The termination of the bond between a man and woman during betrothal (Jewish law) or marriage by use of some formal means. In NT times, the rabbis differed over what constituted grounds for divorce according to Deut 24:1. The stricter school (Shammai) limited the grounds to sexual misconduct, while the more liberal school (Hillel) argued that divorce was permissible even if the wife were merely a bad cook.
a certificate of *d* ... Deut 24:1
given her a writ of *d* ... Jer 3:8
For I hate *d* ... Mal 2:16

DIVORCE (v) *separate*
he cannot *d* her ... Deut 22:19
husband *d-s* his wife ... Jer 3:1
man to *d* his wife ... Matt 19:3
Whoever *d-s* his ... Mark 10:11

DIVORCED (adj) *separated*
woman *d* from her ... Lev 21:7
or of a *d* woman ... Num 30:9
marries a *d* woman ... Matt 5:32
marries...who is *d* ... Luke 16:18

DOCTRINE *teaching* Teaching that is accepted as authoritative, sometimes codified in an official statement. May be true and Biblical (orthodox), or false (unorthodox, heretical).
Teaching as *d-s* the ... Matt 15:9
every wind of *d* ... Eph 4:14
to teach strange *d-s* ... 1 Tim 1:3
to exhort in sound *d* ... Titus 1:9

DOCUMENT *manuscript*
the *d* which you sent ... Ezra 4:18
And on the sealed *d* ... Neh 9:38
Darius signed the *d* ... Dan 6:9

DOEG One of Saul's servants who, at his word, slayed the priests of Nob. He was an Edomite (descendant of Esau; 1 Sam 21:7).

DOER *workman*
recompenses the...*d* ... Ps 31:23
d-s of the Law will ... Rom 2:13
d-s of the word ... James 1:22
not a *d* of the law ... James 4:11

DOG *animal, scavenger*
Am I a *d* ... 1 Sam 17:43
d-s have surrounded ... Ps 22:16
they howl like a *d* ... Ps 59:6
live *d* is better than ... Eccl 9:4
Beware of the *d-s* ... Phil 3:2
d-s and the sorcerers ... Rev 22:15

DOMAIN *estate*
give You all this *d* ... Luke 4:6
the *d* of darkness ... Col 1:13
keep their own *d* ... Jude 6

DOMINION *authority, rule*
Yours is the *d* ... 1 Chr 29:11
places of His *d* ... Ps 103:22
d will be from sea ... Zech 9:10
and power and *d* ... Eph 1:21
thrones or *d-s* or ... Col 1:16
glory and the *d* forever ... Rev 1:6

DONKEY *ass*
a wild *d* of a man ... Gen 16:12
Balaam...to the *d* ... Num 22:29
the foal of a *d* ... Zech 9:9
you will find a *d* ... Matt 21:2
and mounted on a *d* ... Matt 21:5
a mute *d*, speaking ... 2 Pet 2:16

DOOR *entrance, opening*
crouching at the *d* ... Gen 4:7
set the *d* of the ark ... Gen 6:16
Uriah slept at the *d* ... 2 Sam 11:9
over the *d* of my lips ... Ps 141:3
d turns on its ... Prov 26:14
each had a double *d* ... Ezek 41:23
close your *d*...pray ... Matt 6:6
I am the *d* ... John 10:9
right at the *d* ... James 5:9
before you an open *d* ... Rev 3:8
I stand at the *d* ... Rev 3:20

DOORKEEPER *guard* One who guarded a door or gate to the home of a superior, or the palace of a king.
d-s have gathered ... 2 Kin 22:4
the Levites, the *d-s* ... 2 Chr 34:9
eunuchs who were *d-s* ... Esth 6:2
commanded the *d* ... Mark 13:34
To him the *d* opens ... John 10:3

DOORPOST The side of a typical door frame. Doorposts played a key role in Jewish history and religious life. During the plague of the death of the firstborn in Egypt, Jewish families were told by Moses to slaughter a lamb and put some of the blood on their doorposts and lintel (the upper part of the door frame), because the angel of death would *pass over* their homes when he saw the blood and not harm them (*see also* **PASSOVER**). Later, the Israelites were commanded to write the words of Deut 6:4ff. on their doorposts. In later Judaism, it became tradition to write Deut 6:4-9 on a piece of parchment (called a *mezuzah*, for "doorpost") which was attached to the outside of the right doorpost.
put it on the two *d-s* ... Ex 12:7
write them on the *d-s* ... Deut 6:9
on the seat by the *d* ... 1 Sam 1:9
Waiting at my *d-s* ... Prov 8:34

DOORWAY *entrance, opening*
the *d* of the tent ... Judg 4:20
d-s and doorposts ... 1 Kin 7:5
at my neighbor's *d* ... Job 31:9
chamber with its *d* ... Ezek 40:38

DORCAS *(gazelle)*. A Christian woman in Joppa whom the Apostle Peter brought back to life after she had succumbed to a fatal illness. Also called *Tabitha*, probably the Aram. equivalent of *Dorcas*.
Tabitha (Dorcas), a Joppa Christian ... Acts 9:36-43

DOTHAN *(two wells)*. A grassy plain north of Samaria, on the road from Syria to Egypt, where Joseph was sold into slavery (Gen 37:17).

DOUBT (n) *unbelief*
life shall hang in *d* ... Deut 28:66
why do *d-s* arise ... Luke 24:38

DOUBT (v) *disbelieve*
why did you *d* ... Matt 14:31
not *d* in his heart ... Mark 11:23
d-s is condemned ... Rom 14:23
who *d-s* is like the ... James 1:6

DOUGH *flour mixture*
people took their *d* ... Ex 12:34
the first of your *d* ... Num 15:20
took *d*, kneaded *it* ... 2 Sam 13:8
knead *d* to make cakes ... Jer 7:18

DOVE *bird*
he sent out a *d* ... Gen 8:8
had wings like a *d* ... Ps 55:6
eyes are *like d-s* ... Song 1:15
descending as a *d* ... Matt 3:16
descending as a *d* ... John 1:32
selling the *d-s* ... John 2:16

DOWNFALL *collapse*
became the *d* of ... 2 Chr 28:23
noise of their *d* ... Jer 49:21

DOWNPOUR *rain*
the *d* and the rain ... Job 37:6
d of waters swept ... Hab 3:10

DOWRY *bequest*
must pay a *d* for her ... Ex 22:16
to the *d* for virgins ... Ex 22:17
d to his daughter ... 1 Kin 9:16

DRACHMA 1) An ancient Greek weight of various values. 2) An ancient gold or silver coin weighing one drachma. 3) The coinage of modern Greece, destabilized since 1932.
Greek gold coin ... Neh 7:70-72
Greek silver coin ... Matt 17:24

DRAG *draw, pull*
grasshopper *d-s* ... Eccl 12:5
D them off like sheep ... Jer 12:3
the dogs to *d* off ... Jer 15:3
Paul and *d-ged* ... Acts 14:19
d you into court ... James 2:6

DRAGON *monster, serpent* A term used to designate various land and sea creatures. In Revelation it is used figuratively of Satan.
d who *lives* in the sea ... Is 27:1
Who pierced the *d* ... Is 51:9
d stood before the ... Rev 12:4
he laid hold of the *d* ... Rev 20:2

DRAIN *empty*
blood is to be *d-ed* ... Lev 1:15
he *d-ed* the dew ... Judg 6:38
must *d and* drink down ... Ps 75:8

DRAW *haul, pull*
out to *d* water ... Gen 24:13
drew him out of the ... Ex 2:10
but are *d-n* away ... Deut 30:17
He *d-s* up the drops ... Job 36:27
d near to my soul ... Ps 69:18
They are *d-ing* back ... Jer 46:5
redemption is *d-ing* ... Luke 21:28
d all men to Myself ... John 12:32
D near to God ... James 4:8

DRAWERS *servants*
wood and *d* of water ... Josh 9:21

DREAD (n) *fear*
in *d*...of Israel ... Ex 1:12
in *d* night and day ... Deut 28:66
d of the Jews ... Esth 8:17
they are in great *d* ... Ps 14:5
d comes like a storm ... Prov 1:27

DREAD (v) *fear*
what I *d* befalls me ... Job 3:25
Whom shall I *d* ... Ps 27:1
whose two kings you *d* ... Is 7:16
are *d-ed* and feared ... Hab 1:7

DREAM (n) *vision*
had a *d*, and behold ... Gen 28:12
man was relating a *d* ... Judg 7:13
flies away like a *d* ... Job 20:8
like a *d*, a vision ... Is 29:7
visions and *d-s* ... Dan 1:17
to Joseph in a *d* ... Matt 2:13

DREAM (v) *see a vision*
asleep and *d-ed* ... Gen 41:5
like those who *d* ... Ps 126:1
when a hungry man *d-s* ... Is 29:8
Your old men will *d* ... Joel 2:28

DREAMER *visionary*
Here comes this *d* ... Gen 37:19
If a prophet or a *d* ... Deut 13:1
your diviners, your *d-s* ... Jer 27:9

DRENCH *soak, wet*
d you with my tears ... Is 16:9
head is *d-ed* with dew ... Song 5:2
d-ed with the dew ... Dan 4:33

DRESS (n) *clothing*
have taken off my *d* ... Song 5:3
d was of fine linen ... Ezek 16:13
or putting on *d-es* ... 1 Pet 3:3

DRESS (v) *array, clothe*
d-ed in his military ... 2 Sam 20:8
D-ed as a harlot ... Prov 7:10
you *d* in scarlet ... Jer 4:30
d-ed Him...purple ... Mark 15:17

DRINK (n) *refreshment*
gave the lad a *d* ... Gen 21:19
or wine, or strong *d* ... Deut 14:26
to desire strong *d* ... Prov 31:4
gave Me *something* to *d* ... Matt 25:35
My blood is true *d* ... John 6:55
thirsty, give him a *d* ... Rom 12:20

DRINK (v)
he *drank* of the wine ... Gen 9:21
Do not *d* wine ... Lev 10:9
d from the brook ... 1 Kin 17:6
they all *drank* from ... Mark 14:23
after *d-ing* old *wine* ... Luke 5:39
who eats and *d-s* ... 1 Cor 11:29
ground that *d-s* the ... Heb 6:7

DRIP *drop*
clouds...They *d* ... Job 36:28
lips...*d* honey ... Song 4:11
d-ped with myrrh ... Song 5:5
D down, O heavens ... Is 45:8

DRIVE *chase, defeat*
You have *d-n* me ... Gen 4:14
and *drove* them away ... Ex 2:17
angel...*d-ing them* on ... Ps 35:5
d hard all your workers ... Is 58:3
drove Him out of...city ... Luke 4:29
drove them all out ... John 2:15
to *d* the ship ... Acts 27:39

DROP (n) *drip*
the *d-s* of water ... Job 36:27
a *d* from a bucket ... Is 40:15
like *d-s* of blood ... Luke 22:44

DROP (v) *fall*
olives will *d* off ... Deut 28:40
his bonds *d-ped* ... Judg 15:14
d off his unripe grape ... Job 15:33
d-ped their wings ... Ezek 1:24

DROSS *metallic waste* The impurities separated from raw ore during the smelting of metal.
of the earth *like d* ... Ps 119:119
Take away the *d* ... Prov 25:4
silver has become *d* ... Is 1:22
Israel has become *d* ... Ezek 22:18

DROUGHT *dryness*
Like heat in *d* ... Is 25:5
in regard to the *d* ... Jer 14:1
I called for a *d* ... Hag 1:11

DROWNED *suffocated*
d in the Red Sea ... Ex 15:4
to be *d* in the depth ... Matt 18:6
were *d* in the sea ... Mark 5:13

DRUNK *intoxicated*
arrows *d* with blood ... Deut 32:42
d, but not with wine ... Is 29:9
made...*d* in My wrath ... Is 63:6
not get *d* with wine ... Eph 5:18
I saw the woman *d* ... Rev 17:6

DRUNKARD *intoxicated person*
a glutton and a *d* ... Deut 21:20
song of the *d-s* ... Ps 69:12
Awake, *d-s,* and weep ... Joel 1:5
a reviler, or a *d* ... 1 Cor 5:11

DRUNKEN *intoxicated*
stagger like a *d* man ... Job 12:25
become like a *d* man ... Jer 23:9

DRUNKENNESS *intoxication*
and not for *d* ... Eccl 10:17
weighted down...*d* ... Luke 21:34
in carousing and *d* ... Rom 13:13
envying, *d,* carousing ... Gal 5:21

DRY (adj) *parched, scorched*
let the *d* land appear ... Gen 1:9
In a *d* and weary land ... Ps 63:1
Better is a *d* morsel ... Prov 17:1
O *d* bones, hear ... Ezek 37:4

DRY (v) *scorch, wither*
My strength is *dried* ... Ps 22:15
dried up...streams ... Ps 74:15
I *d* up the sea ... Is 50:2
new wine *dries* up ... Joel 1:10
dries up...rivers ... Nah 1:4

DUE (adj) *proper, right*
In *d* time their foot ... Deut 32:35
food in *d* season ... Ps 104:27
d penalty of their ... Rom 1:27

DUE (n) *what is owed*
as *their d* forever ... Lev 7:34
be the priests' *d* ... Deut 18:3
Indeed it is Your *d* ... Jer 10:7

DULL *heavy, stupid*
eyes are *d* from wine ... Gen 49:12
Their ears *d* ... Is 6:10
people...become *d* ... Matt 13:15
become *d* of hearing ... Heb 5:11

DUNG *waste*
sweeps away *d* ... 1 Kin 14:10
dove's *d* for five ... 2 Kin 6:25
give you cow's *d* ... Ezek 4:15
their flesh like *d* ... Zeph 1:17

DUNGEON *prison*
put me into the *d* ... Gen 40:15
captive...in the *d* ... Ex 12:29
prisoners from the *d* ... Is 42:7
Jeremiah...into the *d* ... Jer 37:16

DUST *dirt, earth*
God formed man of *d* ... Gen 2:7
And *d* you will eat ... Gen 3:14
the poor from the *d* ... 1 Sam 2:8
repent in *d* and ashes ... Job 42:6
d before the wind ... Ps 18:42
Will the *d* praise You ... Ps 30:9
You who lie in the *d* ... Is 26:19
shake the *d* off ... Matt 10:14
the *d* of your city ... Luke 10:11
d on their heads ... Rev 18:19

DUTY *responsibility*
perform your *d* ... Gen 38:8
charged with any *d* ... Deut 24:5
the *d* of a husband's ... Deut 25:7
his *d* to his wife ... 1 Cor 7:3

DWELL *abide, live*
father of those who *d* ... Gen 4:20
Behold, I am *d-ing* ... 1 Chr 17:1
No evil *d-s* with You ... Ps 5:4
d on Your holy hill ... Ps 15:1
I will *d* in the house ... Ps 23:6
d among the wise ... Prov 15:31
have *d-t* in Jerusalem ... Jer 35:11
flesh, and *d-t* among ... John 1:14
His Spirit who *d-s* in you ... Rom 8:11
of God *d-s* in you ... 1 Cor 3:16
Christ may *d* in your ... Eph 3:17
d on these things ... Phil 4:8

DWELLING *habitation*
earth shall be your *d* ... Gen 27:39
name there for His *d* ... Deut 12:5
place for Your *d* ... 1 Kin 8:13
into the eternal *d-s* ... Luke 16:9
might find a *d* place ... Acts 7:46

DYED *colored*
rams' skins *d* red ... Ex 25:5
A spoil of *d* work ... Judg 5:30

E

EAGLE *bird*
bore you on *e-s'* wings ... Ex 19:4
the *e* swoops down ... Deut 28:49
swifter than *e-s* ... 2 Sam 1:23
with wings like *e-s* ... Is 40:31
the face of an *e* ... Ezek 1:10
was like a flying *e* ... Rev 4:7

EAR *hearing*
heard with our *e-s* ... 2 Sam 7:22
the *e* test words ... Job 12:11
And His *e-s* are *open* ... Ps 34:15
and incline your *e* ... Ps 45:10
He whose *e* listens ... Prov 15:31
e of the wise seeks ... Prov 18:15
e has not been open ... Is 48:8
let your *e* receive ... Jer 9:20
He who has *e-s* to ... Matt 11:15
and cut off his *e* ... Matt 26:51
fingers into his *e-s* ... Mark 7:33
if the *e* says ... 1 Cor 12:16
their *e-s* tickled ... 2 Tim 4:3
He who has an *e* ... Rev 2:7

EARLY *beforetime, soon*
they arose *e* and ... Gen 26:31
Let us rise *e* ... Song 7:12
dew which goes away *e* ... Hos 6:4
e on the first day ... Mark 16:2
at the tomb *e* ... Luke 24:22
the *e* and late rains ... James 5:7

EARNINGS *gain, wages*
her *e* she plants ... Prov 31:16
the *e* of a harlot ... Mic 1:7

EARRING *ornament*
brought...*e-s* ... Ex 35:22
e-s and necklaces ... Num 31:50
Like an *e* of gold ... Prov 25:12
her *e-s* and jewelry ... Hos 2:13

EARTH *land, world*
God created the...*e* ... Gen 1:1
Judge of all the *e* ... Gen 18:25
the *e* is the LORD'S ... Ex 9:29
way of all the *e* ... Josh 23:14
His stand on the *e* ... Job 19:25
foundation of the *e* ... Job 38:4
saints...in the *e* ... Ps 16:3
the shields of the *e* ... Ps 47:9
gave birth to the *e* ... Ps 90:2
He established the *e* ... Ps 104:5
wisdom founded...*e* ... Prov 3:19
the *e* remains forever ... Eccl 1:4
made the *e* tremble ... Is 14:16
the circle of the *e* ... Is 40:22
the ends of the *e* ... Is 45:22
the *e* is My footstool ... Is 66:1
e shone with His ... Ezek 43:2
make the *e* dark ... Amos 8:9
e will be devoured ... Zeph 3:8
shall inherit the *e* ... Matt 5:5
you bind on *e* ... Matt 16:19
on *e* peace among ... Luke 2:14
glorified...on the *e* ... John 17:4
man is from the *e* ... 1 Cor 15:47
heavens and a new *e* ... 2 Pet 3:13
e and heaven fled ... Rev 20:11

EARTHENWARE *pottery*
bird in an *e* vessel ... Lev 14:5
holy water in an *e* ... Num 5:17
shatter them like *e* ... Ps 2:9
buy a potter's *e* jar ... Jer 19:1
vessels of...*e* ... 2 Tim 2:20

EARTHQUAKE *temblor*
LORD *was* not...*e* ... 1 Kin 19:11
punished with...*e* ... Is 29:6
be famines and *e-s* ... Matt 24:7
will be great *e-s* ... Luke 21:11
there was a great *e* ... Rev 6:12
killed in the *e* ... Rev 11:13

EARTHY *mortal*
man is...*e* ... 1 Cor 15:47
those who are *e* ... 1 Cor 15:48

EASE *free from difficulty, pain*
He who is at *e* ... Job 12:5
at *e* and satisfied ... Job 21:23
women who are at *e* ... Is 32:9
Woe to those...at *e* ... Amos 6:1
nations who are at *e* ... Zech 1:15

EAST *direction of compass*
spread out...to the *e* ... Gen 28:14
directed an *e* wind ... Ex 10:13
sons of the *e* were ... Judg 7:12
men of the *e* ... Job 1:3
With the *e* wind You ... Ps 48:7
offspring from the *e* ... Is 43:5
faces toward the *e* ... Ezek 8:16
Jerusalem on the *e* ... Zech 14:4
saw His star in the *e* ... Matt 2:2
lightning...the *e* ... Matt 24:27
kings from the *e* ... Rev 16:12

EAST GATE *see* **GATES OF JERUSALEM**

EASY *without difficulty*
knowledge is *e* to one ... Prov 14:6
My yoke is *e* and ... Matt 11:30

EAT *consume, dine, feast*
shall not *e* from it ... Gen 3:17
they *ate* every plant ... Ex 10:15
not *e*...blood ... Lev 19:26
that we may *e* him ... 2 Kin 6:28
e and be satisfied ... Ps 22:26
not *e* the bread of ... Prov 31:27
will *e* curds and honey ... Is 7:15
words...I *ate* them ... Jer 15:16
e this scroll ... Ezek 3:1
e-ing grass like cattle ... Dan 4:33
what you will *e* ... Matt 6:25
e with unwashed ... Matt 15:20
Take, *e;* this is My ... Matt 26:26
sinners and *e-s* with ... Luke 15:2
e...at My table ... Luke 22:30

He took it and *ate* ... Luke 24:43
e the flesh of...Son ... John 6:53
Peter, kill and *e* ... Acts 10:13
kingdom...not *e-ing* ... Rom 14:17
ate...spiritual food ... 1 Cor 10:3
e-s...judgment ... 1 Cor 11:29

EBAL *(bare).* The name of several people of Edomite ancestry. Also a mountain in Ephraim.
1 *son of Shobal* ... Gen 36:23
2 *son of Joktan* ... 1 Chr 1:22
also *Obal* ... Gen 10:28
3 *mountain near Shechem* ... Deut 11:29

EBENEZER *(stone of help).* A stone memorial set up by Samuel to celebrate the Lord's help in defeating the Philistines.
a memorial stone ... 1 Sam 7:12

EBER
1 *line of Shem* ... Gen 10:21-24
progenitor of Jocktanide Arabs ... Gen 10:25-30
progenitor of Hebrews ... Gen 11:16ff
2 *a Gadite* ... 1 Chr 5:13
3 *son of Elpaal* ... 1 Chr 8:12
4 *son of Shashak* ... 1 Chr 8:22
5 *priest* ... Neh 12:20
see also **HEBER**

EDEN The original garden where Adam and Eve were placed when created. The location is not known. Also the name of another place and of a person.
1 *garden of God* ... Gen 2:15; Is 51:3
2 *city area* ... 2 Kin 19:12; Ezek 27:23
3 *son of Joah* ... 2 Chr 29:12

EDICT *decree*
the king's *e-s* ... Ezra 8:36
a royal *e* be issued ... Esth 1:19
king's command and *e* ... Esth 9:1
afraid of the king's *e* ... Heb 11:23

EDIFICATION *building up* Teaching or encouragement that results in moral or spiritual growth.
his good, to his *e* ... Rom 15:2
speaks to men for *e* ... 1 Cor 14:3
all things...for *e* ... 1 Cor 14:26

EDIFY *build up*
but love *e-ies* ... 1 Cor 8:1
not all things *e* ... 1 Cor 10:23
person is not *e-ied* ... 1 Cor 14:17

EDOM *(red).* Another name of Esau. Also the land where his descendants lived.
1 *name of Esau* ... Gen 25:30
2 *Edomites* ... Num 20:18,20
3 *region or country* ... Gen 32:3; Judg 11:17
see also **SEIR**

EDUCATED *taught*
be *e* three years ... Dan 1:5
Moses was *e* in all ... Acts 7:22
e under Gamaliel ... Acts 22:3

EFFEMINATE *womanlike*
e, nor homosexuals ... 1 Cor 6:9

EGG
in the white of an *e* ... Job 6:6
gathers abandoned *e-s* ... Is 10:14
hatch adders' *e-s* and ... Is 59:5
is asked for an *e* ... Luke 11:12

EGLON *(circle).* Name of a town in Judah, and of a king of Moab whom the Lord used in correcting disobedient Israel.
1 *town in Judah* ... Josh 10:34-37;15:39
2 *Moabite king* ... Judg 3:12-30

EGYPT One of the historic countries of the world, located in northeast Africa. It was the birthplace of Moses and Jesus lived there briefly as a very young child.
country in NE Africa ... Gen 12:10;37:25
source of food ... Gen 42:1,2
on the Nile ... Ex 4:19;7:5
conflict with Moses ... Ex 7:8ff
scene of Passover ... Ex 12:1-36

EHUD *(united, strong).* A judge who delivered Israel from the oppression of Moab. Also the name of two other individuals.
1 *left-handed Benjamite judge of Israel* ... Judg 3:15,21
2 *son of Bilhan* ... 1 Chr 7:10
3 *progenitor of clan* ... 1 Chr 8:6

EKRON (unc, *deep-rooted).* One of the five main Philistine cities.
Philistine city ... Josh 13:3; 1 Sam 5:10; Jer 25:20

ELAH *(oak).* The name of several individuals, one of whom was the father of Hoshea, the last king of Israel. Also a valley in Judah where David killed Goliath.
1 *Edomite* ... Gen 36:41
2 *valley SW of Jerusalem* ... 1 Sam 17:2
3 *father of Shimei* ... 1 Kin 4:18
4 *king of Israel* ... 1 Kin 16:8-10
5 *father of Hoshea* ... 2 Kin 15:30
6 *son of Caleb* ... 1 Chr 4:15
7 *son of Uzzi* ... 1 Chr 9:8

ELAM The name of several people. The land between the Tigris and Euphrates rivers; its ancient capital was Susa.
1 *son of Shem* ... Gen 10:22
2 *son of Shashak* ... 1 Chr 8:24
3 *Korahite Levite* ... 1 Chr 26:3
4 *head of restoration family* ... Ezra 2:7; Neh 7:12
5 *head of restoration family* ... Ezra 2:31; Neh 7:34
6 *chief of people* ... Neh 10:14
7 *priest* ... Neh 12:42
8 *region E of Babylonia* ... Is 21:2; Dan 8:2

ELATH / ELOTH *city*
at Gulf of Aqabah ... 2 Kin 14:22
near Ezion-geber

EL-BETHEL
altar ... Gen 35:7

ELDER *aged, older* In the Bible, often a title of leadership, e.g. a leader of ancient Israel. Also a leader in the church, synonymous with *overseer*. A church elder must meet certain qualifications (e.g. being above reproach) and has spiritual oversight of the church's ministries.
words of her *e* son ... Gen 27:42
the *e-s* of Israel ... Ex 17:6
sits among the *e-s* ... Prov 31:23
Assemble the *e-s* ... Joel 2:16
tradition of the *e-s* ... Matt 15:2
chief priests and *e-s* ... Matt 27:12
scribes...*e-s* came ... Mark 11:27
Council of *e-s* of ... Luke 22:66
e-s of the church ... Acts 20:17
I saw twenty-four *e-s* ... Rev 4:4

ELEAZAR *(God has helped).* The name of several men in the Bible; principally the third son of Aaron who succeeded him as high priest after the deaths of Nadab and Abihu who were childless.
1 *son of Aaron* ... Ex 6:23
high priest ... Num 20:25-28
2 *son of Abinadab* ... 1 Sam 7:1
3 *son of Dodo* ... 2 Sam 23:9
4 *a Levite* ... 1 Chr 23:22
5 *son of Phinehas* ... Ezra 8:33
6 *son of Parosh* ... Ezra 10:18-25
7 *priest* ... Neh 12:27
8 *ancestor of Jesus* ... Matt 1:15

ELECT *chosen*
sake of the *e* ... Matt 24:22
to lead astray...the *e* ... Mark 13:22
justice for His *e* ... Luke 18:7
against God's *e* ... Rom 8:33

ELEMENTARY *basic*
e principles of the ... Col 2:8
e principles of the ... Heb 5:12
e teaching about the ... Heb 6:1

ELEMENTS *physical matter*
e will be destroyed ... 2 Pet 3:10
the *e* will melt with ... 2 Pet 3:12

ELI High priest and judge of Israel. He was the custodian and mentor of the boy Samuel.
high priest ... 1 Sam 1:9;2:12;3:6;4:18

ELIAKIM *(God raises up).* The name of several men, including a son of Hilkiah and prominent official in the palace of King Hezekiah.
1 *son of Hilkiah* ... 2 Kin 18:18;19:2
2 *son of Josiah* ... 2 Kin 23:34
3 *priest* ... Neh 12:41
4 *ancestor of Jesus* ... Matt 1:13
5 *ancestor of Jesus* ... Luke 3:30,31

ELIEZER *(my God is help).* Name of eleven people in Scripture, including a chief household servant of Abraham and his potential heir; the second son of Moses and Zipporah.
1 *Abraham's servant* ... Gen 15:2
2 *son of Moses* ... 1 Chr 23:15
3 *son of Becher* ... 1 Chr 7:8
4 *priest* ... 1 Chr 15:24
5 *son of Zichri* ... 1 Chr 27:16
6 *a prophet* ... 2 Chr 20:37
7 *served under Ezra* ... Ezra 8:16
8 *son of Jeshua* ... Ezra 10:18
9 *Levite* ... Ezra 10:10,23
10 *son Harim* ... Ezra 10:10,31
11 *ancestor of Jesus* ... Luke 3:29

ELIHU *(he is my God).* One of five who bear this name in Scripture, including a descendent of Nahor, Abraham's brother. He was a friend of Job.
1 *son of Tohu* ... 1 Sam 1:1
2 *Manassite captain* ... 1 Chr 12:20
3 *temple gatekeeper* ... 1 Chr 26:1
4 *officer of Judah* ... 1 Chr 27:18
5 *one of Job's friends* ... Job 32:17

ELIJAH *(Yahweh is God).* An OT prophet to Israel during the reigns of Ahab and Ahaziah with one of the most extensive and fruitful ministries.
1 *prophet* ... 1 Kin 17:1
aided by widow ... 1 Kin 17:8ff
revived child ... 1 Kin 17:23
defeats prophets ... 1 Kin 18:20ff
flees Jezebel ... 1 Kin 19:4-8
chooses Elisha ... 1 Kin 19:19-21
taken up ... 2 Kin 2:1-11
2 *Benjamite* ... 1 Chr 8:27
3 *son of Harim* ... Ezra 10:21
4 *son of Elam* ... Ezra 10:26

ELIMELECH *(God is king).* A man of the tribe of Judah who lived in the time of the judges. Because of famine, he went with His wife Naomi and their sons to Moab, where he died (Ruth 1:1-3).

ELIMINATE *remove*
e harmful beasts ... Lev 26:6
I am going to *e* ... Jer 16:9
stomach, and is *e-d* ... Mark 7:19

ELIPHAZ (unc, *God is fine gold).* A friend of Job who tried to console him when he was in great pain. Also a son of Esau by Adah.
1 *son of Esau* ... Gen 36:4
2 *one of Job's friends* ... Job 2:11; 4:1; 42:7,9

ELISHA *(God is salvation).* A prophet from the northern kingdom, Israel, and the successor of Elijah.
prophet ... 2 Kin 6:12
called ... 1 Kin 19:19-21
Elijah's successor ... 2 Kin 2:1ff
miracle of oil ... 2 Kin 4:1-7
revived child ... 2 Kin 4:8-37
death ... 2 Kin 13:20

ELIZABETH (unc, *God is an oath).* A relative of the virgin Mary and mother of John the Baptist, to whom she gave birth despite her advanced age and barrenness.
mother of John the Baptist ... Luke 1:7,13,41,57

ELKANAH *(God has possessed).* The name of several men, including the husband of Hannah and father of Samuel (1 Sam 1:19).

ELOQUENT *persuasive*
I have never been *e* ... Ex 4:10
Apollos...an *e* man ... Acts 18:24

ELUL
sixth month of Heb calendar ... Neh 6:15

ELYMAS
magician ... Acts 13:8
see also **BAR-JESUS**

EMBALM *preserve*
to *e* his father ... Gen 50:2
he was *e-ed* and ... Gen 50:26

EMBARRASSED *ashamed*
e to lift up my face ... Ezra 9:6
e at the gardens ... Is 1:29
diviners will be *e* ... Mic 3:7

EMBITTERED *resentful*
the people were *e* ... 1 Sam 30:6
e them against the ... Acts 14:2

EMBRACE *clasp, hug*
Esau ran...and *e-d* ... Gen 33:4
e...a foreigner ... Prov 5:20
A time to *e* ... Eccl 3:5
ran and *e-d* him ... Luke 15:20

EMBROIDERED *woven*
spoil of dyed work *e* ... Judg 5:30
be led...in *e* work ... Ps 45:14
silk, and *e* cloth ... Ezek 16:13
purple, *e* work ... Ezek 27:16

EMERALD *precious stone*
ruby, topaz and *e* ... Ex 28:17
throne, like an *e* ... Rev 4:3

EMINENT *renowned*
nor anything *e* ... Ezek 7:11
the most *e* apostles ... 2 Cor 11:5
inferior to...*e* ... 2 Cor 12:11

EMISSION *issuance*
man has a seminal *e* ... Lev 15:16
nocturnal *e* ... Deut 23:10

EMMAUS (unc, *warm springs).* A village near Jerusalem where the risen Christ revealed his identity to two travelers.
village near Jerusalem ... Luke 24:13

EMPOWERED *authorized*
e him to eat from ... Eccl 5:19
God has not *e* him ... Eccl 6:2

EMPTY (adj) *containing nothing*
Now the pit was *e* ... Gen 37:24
did not return *e* ... 2 Sam 1:22
sent widows away *e* ... Job 22:9
deceive you with *e* ... Eph 5:6
avoid...*e* chatter ... 2 Tim 2:16

EMPTY (v) *remove contents*
e-ing their sacks ... Gen 42:35
they *e* the house ... Lev 14:36
I *e-ied* them out as ... Ps 18:42
therefore *e* their net ... Hab 1:17
e the golden *oil* ... Zech 4:12
but *e-ied* Himself ... Phil 2:7

ENCAMP *abide, lodge*
the tabernacle *e-s* ... Num 1:51
and *e-ed* together ... Josh 11:5
a host *e* against me ... Ps 27:3
angel of the LORD *e-s* ... Ps 34:7

ENCIRCLE *go around*
entirely *e-ing* the sea ... 2 Chr 4:3
he *e-d* the Ophel ... 2 Chr 33:14
cords...have *e-d* me ... Ps 119:61
Who *e* yourselves with ... Is 50:11

ENCOMPASS *surround*
waves of death *e* ... 2 Sam 22:5
e-ing the walls of ... 1 Kin 6:5
e-ed...with bitterness ... Lam 3:5
Water *e-ed* me to the ... Jon 2:5

ENCOURAGE *strengthen*
charge Joshua and *e* ... Deut 3:28
e-d him in God ... 1 Sam 23:16
e them in the work ... Ezra 6:22
Paul was *e-ing* them ... Acts 27:33
e one another ... 1 Thess 5:11
e the young women ... Titus 2:4

ENCOURAGEMENT *support*
I arose to be an *e* ... Dan 11:1
God who gives...*e* ... Rom 15:5
is any *e* in Christ ... Phil 2:1

we...would have strong *e* ... Heb 6:18

END (n) *extremity, goal, result*
e of all flesh has ... Gen 6:13
one *e* of the heavens ... Deut 4:32
from beginning to *e* ... 1 Sam 3:12
what is my *e* ... Job 6:11
very e-s of the earth ... Ps 2:8
wicked come to an *e* ... Ps 7:9
e is the way of death ... Prov 14:12
no *e* to all his labor ... Eccl 4:8
summer is *e-ed* ... Jer 8:20
The *e* is coming ... Ezek 7:2
who endures to...*e* ... Matt 24:13
to the *e* of the age ... Matt 28:20
kingdom...no *e* ... Luke 1:33
He loved...to the *e* ... John 13:1
Christ...*e* of the law ... Rom 10:4
beginning and the *e* ... Rev 21:6

END (v) *complete, stop*
border *e-ed* at the sea ... Josh 15:4
words of Job are *e-ed* ... Job 31:40
days there were *e-ed* ... Acts 21:5
it *e-s* up being burned ... Heb 6:8

ENDLESS *limitless*
writing...is *e* ... Eccl 12:12
and *e* genealogies ... 1 Tim 1:4

ENDOR *(fountain of dwelling).* A town near the foot of Mt. Tabor and the residence of the medium whom King Saul consulted (1 Sam 28:7).

ENDOW *provide a gift*
God has *e-ed* me ... Gen 30:20
e-ed with discretion ... 2 Chr 2:12
to *e* those who love ... Prov 8:21
e-ed with salvation ... Zech 9:9

ENDURANCE *patience*
in much *e*, in ... 2 Cor 6:4
you have need of *e* ... Heb 10:36
let us run with *e* ... Heb 12:1
of the *e* of Job ... James 5:11

ENDURE *persevere*
will be able to *e* ... Ex 18:23
that I should *e* ... Job 6:11
while the sun *e-s* ... Ps 72:5
May his name *e* ... Ps 72:17
and your name will *e* ... Is 66:22
Can your heart *e* ... Ezek 22:14
the one who has *e-d* ... Matt 10:22
who *e-s* to the end ... Mark 13:13
e-s all things ... 1 Cor 13:7
discipline that you *e* ... Heb 12:7
blessed who *e-d* ... James 5:11
word...LORD *e-s* ... 1 Pet 1:25

ENEMY *foe*
delivered your *e-ies* ... Gen 14:20
Your *e-ies* perish ... Judg 5:31
a man finds his *e* ... 1 Sam 24:19
consider me Your *e* ... Job 13:24
make the *e*...cease ... Ps 8:2
presence of my *e-ies* ... Ps 23:5
e has persecuted my ... Ps 143:3
If your *e* is hungry ... Prov 25:21
kisses of an *e* ... Prov 27:6
love your *e-ies*, and ... Matt 5:44
e-ies with each other ... Luke 23:12
e of all righteousness ... Acts 13:10
e is hungry, feed ... Rom 12:20
e...be abolished ... 1 Cor 15:26
an *e* of God ... James 4:4

ENGAGE *be involved, betroth*
virgin who is not *e-d* ... Ex 22:16
the girl who is *e-d* ... Deut 22:25
e-d in their work ... 1 Chr 9:33
e-d to...Joseph ... Luke 1:27
to *e* in good deeds ... Titus 3:8

ENGEDI
spring and town near Dead Sea ... 1 Sam 23:29; 24:1; Song 1:14

ENGRAVE *inscribe*
shall *e* the two stones ... Ex 28:11
e-d on the tablets ... Ex 32:16
e an inscription ... Zech 3:9
letters *e-d* on stones ... 2 Cor 3:7

ENGRAVINGS *carvings*
like the *e* of a seal ... Ex 28:36
the *e* of a signet ... Ex 39:30
carved *e* of cherubim ... 1 Kin 6:29

ENGULF *overwhelm, swallow*
water...to *e* them ... Deut 11:4
sea *e-ed* their enemies ... Ps 78:53
She has been *e-ed* ... Jer 51:42
great deep *e-ed* me ... Jon 2:5

ENLARGE *extend, increase*
May God *e* Japheth ... Gen 9:27
You will *e* my heart ... Ps 119:32
Sheol has *e-d* its ... Is 5:14
He *e-s* his appetite ... Hab 2:5

ENLIGHTEN *illumine*
e-ing the eyes ... Ps 19:8
eyes...may be *e-ed* ... Eph 1:18
who have...been *e-ed* ... Heb 6:4

ENMITY *hostility*
e Between you and ... Gen 3:15
had everlasting *e* ... Ezek 35:5
sorcery, *e-ies*, strife ... Gal 5:20
abolishing...the *e* ... Eph 2:15

ENOCH *(initiated)*
1 *eldest son of Cain* ... Gen 4:17
2 *city* ... Gen 4:17
3 *Methuselah's father* ... Gen 5:22
walked with God ... Gen 5:24

ENRAGE *anger*
e-d and curse their ... Is 8:21
jealousy *e-s* a man ... Prov 6:34
he became very *e-d* ... Matt 2:16
dragon was *e-d* with ... Rev 12:17

ENRICH *make wealthy*
king will *e* the ... 1 Sam 17:25
You greatly *e* ... Ps 65:9
You *e-ed* the kings ... Ezek 27:33

ENROLLED *recorded*
were *e* by genealogy ... 1 Chr 7:9
people to be *e* by ... Neh 7:5
e in heaven ... Heb 12:23

ENSLAVE *subjugate*
you have been *e-d* ... Is 14:3
e-d and mistreated ... Acts 7:6
anyone *e-s* you ... 2 Cor 11:20
e-d to various lusts ... Titus 3:3

ENSNARE *catch*
An evil man is *e-d* ... Prov 12:13
e him who adjudicates ... Is 29:21

ENTANGLE *ensnare*
camel *e-ing* her ways ... Jer 2:23
No soldier...*e-s* ... 2 Tim 2:4
sin which...*e-s* us ... Heb 12:1

ENTER *go in*
you shall *e* the ark ... Gen 6:18
He *e-s* into judgment ... Job 22:4
E His gates with ... Ps 100:4
E the rock and hide ... Is 2:10
He *e-s* into peace ... Is 57:2
Spirit *e-ed* me and ... Ezek 2:2
not *e* the kingdom ... Matt 5:20
E through the narrow gate ... Matt 7:13
to *e* life crippled ... Matt 18:8
afraid as they *e-ed* ... Luke 9:34
e into the kingdom ... John 3:5
not *e* by the door ... John 10:1
shall not *e* My rest ... Heb 3:11

ENTHRONED *exalted, made king*
e above the cherubim ... 2 Sam 6:2
LORD who is *e above* ... 1 Chr 13:6
e upon the praises of ... Ps 22:3
who sits *e* from of old ... Ps 55:19
Who is *e* on high ... Ps 113:5

ENTICE *deceive, seduce*
E your husband ... Judg 14:15
Who will *e* Ahab ... 2 Chr 18:19
if sinners *e* you ... Prov 1:10
e-d by his own lust ... James 1:14
e-ing unstable souls ... 2 Pet 2:14

ENTRAILS *inner organs* In the OT, the internal organs of the sacrificial animal that were to be treated by the priest according to specific instructions.
fat that covers the *e* ... Ex 29:13
e and the lobe ... Lev 8:16
also washed the *e* ... Lev 9:14

ENTRANCE *doorway*
cloud...at the *e* ... Ex 33:10
mark well the *e* of ... Ezek 44:5
stone against the *e* ... Matt 27:60
e into the eternal ... 2 Pet 1:11

ENTREAT *appeal, ask* To plead with someone to grant a request.
E the LORD that he ... Ex 8:8
Moses *e-ed* the LORD ... Ex 32:11
Please *e* the LORD ... 1 Kin 13:6
gain if we *e* Him ... Job 21:15
demons *began* to *e* ... Matt 8:31

ENTREATY The act of entreating; a plea (Ezra 8:32).

ENTRUST *assign, commit*
security *e-ed to him* ... Lev 6:2
He *e-ed* the vineyard ... Song 8:11
to whom they *e-ed* ... Luke 12:48
not *e-ing* Himself to ... John 2:24

ENVIOUS *covetous*
e of the arrogant ... Ps 73:3
not be *e* of evil men ... Prov 24:1
is your eye *e* ... Matt 20:15
You are *e* ... James 4:2

ENVIRONS *outskirts, suburbs*
the *e* of Jerusalem ... Jer 32:44
devour all his *e* ... Jer 50:32

ENVOY *agent, messenger* A messenger entrusted with official business by his superior.
e-s of the rulers ... 2 Chr 32:31
faithful *e brings* ... Prov 13:17
sent your *e-s* a great ... Is 57:9
his *e-s* to Egypt ... Ezek 17:15

ENVY (n) *jealousy*
full of *e*, murder ... Rom 1:29
preaching...from *e* ... Phil 1:15
out of which arise *e* ... 1 Tim 6:4
life in malice and *e* ... Titus 3:3
e and all slander ... 1 Pet 2:1

ENVY (v) *be discontent, jealous*
Philistines *e-ied* him ... Gen 26:14
e a man of violence ... Prov 3:31
not let your heart *e* ... Prov 23:17
e-ing one another ... Gal 5:26

EPAPHRAS (probably short form of *Epaphroditus*). A teacher in the Colossian church, commended by Paul as "our beloved fellow bond-servant."
Colossian Christian ... Col 1:7;4:12
colleague of Paul ... Philem 23

EPAPHRODITUS *(for Aphrodite)*. A messenger from the Philippian church who carried a gift to Paul during his Roman imprisonment. Paul called him "my brother and fellow worker and fellow soldier."
Philippian Christian ... Phil 2:25
colleague of Paul ... Phil 4:18

EPHAH An Egyptian measure of weight or volume for grain, in use among the Hebrews and equal to about one bushel. *see* **BATH**
Also the name of several persons.
1 *bushel, measure of capacity* ... Lev 5:11; Num 5:15
2 *son of Midian* ... Gen 25:4; 1 Chr 1:33
3 *Caleb's concubine* ... 1 Chr 2:46
4 *son of Jahdai* ... 1 Chr 2:47

EPHESUS *(desirable)*. A very important city of Lydia on the west coast of Asia Minor. Its inhabitants were very idolatrous, worshiping mainly the Greek goddess Artemis (the Roman Diana).
city of Asia Minor ... Acts 18:19; 1 Cor 16:8; Rev 1:11; 2:1

EPHOD The high priest's special garment which had two shoulder pieces and held a pouch where the Urim and Thummim were placed. It was made of material in gold, blue, purple, and scarlet, and of fine twisted linen. Also the name of a person.
1 *priestly garment* ... Ex 28:6; 1 Sam 23:9; 2 Sam 6:14
2 *father of Hanniel* ... Num 34:23

EPHRAIM (unc, *made fruitful*). The younger son of Joseph. Also one of the twelve tribes of Israel, and the name of a city. Sometimes this name is used in reference to the northern kingdom (Israel).
1 *son of Joseph* ... Gen 41:52; 48:17
2 *tribe* ... Josh 16:5; Judg 7:24
3 *northern kingdom* ... Is 7:2-17; Hos 4:17; 9:3-17
4 *city* ... 2 Sam 13:23; John 11:54

EPHRAIM GATE *see* **GATES OF JERUSALEM**

EPHRATH(AH)
1 *Bethlehem* ... Gen 35:19;48:7; Ruth 4:11; Mic 5:2
2 *wife of Caleb* ... 1 Chr 2:19,50
3 *territory* ... Ps 132:6

EPHRON
1 *a Hittite* ... Gen 23:8;50:13
2 *mountain ridge* ... Josh 15:9
3 *city* ... 2 Chr 13:19

EPICUREAN A follower of the philosophy of Epicurus who in the late fourth century B.C. founded his principal school in Lampsacus, located near the mouth of the Marmara Sea (northern coast of Turkey), and later moved to Athens. The best exposition of his system is *On the Nature of Things,* written by the Roman philosopher Lucretius in the first century B.C. The motto "Eat, drink, and be merry for tomorrow you die" is an oversimplification of the philosophy. The main points were that there is no afterlife and therefore no reason to fear eternal punishment from the gods, and that the chief purpose of man is the pursuit of pleasure and the avoidance of pain. This meant that moderate pleasures are good, but excess and debauchery are to be avoided because they lead to poor health and suffering. *Cf.* **STOIC**
a Greek philosophy ... Acts 17:18

EPISTLE *(letter).* The New Testament contains 21 epistles, or letters. Like the other books of the Bible, the epistles were fully inspired by the Holy Spirit.

EPOCHS *ages, seasons*
the times and the *e* ... Dan 2:21
to know times or *e* ... Acts 1:7

EQUAL *same*
shall eat *e* portions ... Deut 18:8
a man my *e* ... Ps 55:13
That I would be *his e* ... Is 40:25
have made them *e* ... Matt 20:12
Himself *e* with God ... John 5:18

EQUIP *furnish, provide*
e-ped for war ... Josh 4:13
e-ped for...work ... 2 Tim 3:17
e you in every good ... Heb 13:21

EQUIPMENT *implements*
the *e* for the service ... Ex 39:40
e for his chariots ... 1 Sam 8:12
e of a foolish ... Zech 11:15

EQUITY *equality, fairness*
eyes look with *e* ... Ps 17:2
have established *e* ... Ps 99:4
justice and *e* ... Prov 1:3
e and every good ... Prov 2:9

ERASTUS
Corinthian Christian ... Acts 19:22; Rom 16:23; 2 Tim 4:20

ERROR *mistake, sin*
can discern *his e-s* ... Ps 19:12
like an *e* which goes ... Eccl 10:5
e against the LORD ... Is 32:6
e of unprincipled ... 2 Pet 3:17
the spirit of *e* ... 1 John 4:6
rushed...into the *e* ... Jude 11

ESARHADDON
Assyrian king ... 2 Kin 19:37; Ezra 4:2; Is 37:38

ESAU (unc, *hairy).* Eldest son of Isaac. He traded his birthright and the blessings that came with it for a plate of stew from his brother Jacob. The Edomites descended from Esau.
son of Isaac ... Gen 25:25
twin of Jacob ... Gen 25:26
skillful hunter ... Gen 25:27
sold birthright ... Gen 25:34
despised Jacob ... Gen 27:41
reconciled with Jacob ... Gen 33:4

ESCAPE (n) *deliverance, refuge*
there will be no *e* ... Job 11:20
is no *e* for me ... Ps 142:4
Let there be no *e* ... Jer 50:29
provide...*e* ... 1 Cor 10:13

ESCAPE (v) *elude*
slave who has *e-d* ... Deut 23:15
let no one *e or* ... 2 Kin 9:15
Our soul has *e-d* ... Ps 124:7
tells lies will not *e* ... Prov 19:5
how shall we *e* ... Is 20:6
nothing at all *e-s* ... Joel 2:3
had not *e-d* notice ... Luke 8:47
how will we *e* if ... Heb 2:3
it *e-s* their notice ... 2 Pet 3:5

ESTABLISH *confirm, found*
I will *e* My covenant ... Gen 17:19
how God *e-es* them ... Job 37:15
e-es the mountains ... Ps 65:6
my ways may be *e-ed* ... Ps 119:5
e-ed in lovingkindness ... Is 16:5
to *e* the heavens ... Is 51:16
we *e* the Law ... Rom 3:31
may *e* your hearts ... 1 Thess 3:13
e-ed in the truth ... 2 Pet 1:12

ESTATE *domain* or *standard*
restore your...*e* ... Job 8:6
us in our low *e* ... Ps 136:23
squandered his *e* ... Luke 15:13

ESTEEM (n) *honor*
man of high *e* ... Dan 10:11
held them in high *e* ... Acts 5:13

ESTEEM (v) *have high regard*
I *e* right all *Your* ... Ps 119:128
e-ed Him stricken ... Is 53:4
e-ed among men ... Luke 16:15
e them...in love ... 1 Thess 5:13

ESTHER *(star).* A very beautiful Jewish woman who, as queen of Persia, saved the lives of her people from an impending massacre.
Hebrew name Hadassah
cousin of Mordecai ... Esth 2:7
Persian queen ... Esth 2:16-18

ESTRANGED *separated*
completely *e* from me ... Job 19:13
e from my brothers ... Ps 69:8

ETAM 1) A place in western Judea where Samson took refuge (Judg 15:8). 2) Name of a town near Bethlehem (2 Chr 11:6).

ETERNAL *everlasting* Without beginning or end, infinite in duration. Sometimes used interchangeably with "everlasting."
e God is a dwelling ... Deut 33:27
E Father, Prince of ... Is 9:6
An *e* decree ... Jer 5:22
cast into the *e* fire ... Matt 18:8
guilty of an *e* sin ... Mark 3:29
e weight of glory ... 2 Cor 4:17
with the *e* purpose ... Eph 3:11
Now to the King *e* ... 1 Tim 1:17
source of *e* salvation ... Heb 5:9
through the *e* Spirit ... Heb 9:14
kept in *e* bonds ... Jude 6
an *e* gospel to preach ... Rev 14:6

ETERNITY *perpetuity* Time without beginning or end. In the Bible, sometimes applied specifically to the past without beginning, or to the unending future.
set *e* in their heart ... Eccl 3:11
from *e* I am He ... Is 43:13
Jesus from all *e* ... 2 Tim 1:9
to the day of *e* ... 2 Pet 3:18

ETHIOPIA *(burnt face).* Also known as Cush in the Bible, its location corresponds approximately to present-day Sudan in northeast Africa, and its inhabitants were supposedly tall and of dark skin color.
NE African country ... Esth 1:1; Ps 68:31; Nah 3:9; Zeph 3:10

EUNICE
mother of Timothy ... 2 Tim 1:5

EUNUCH *chamberlain official (bed keeper).* A castrated man who served as the guard of a harem and as a royal attendant.
seven *e-s* who served ... Esth 1:10
Nor let the *e* say ... Is 56:3
children, and *the e-s* ... Jer 41:16
made *e-s* by men ... Matt 19:12
an Ethiopian *e* ... Acts 8:27

EUPHRATES A river which was a border of Mesopotamia in Biblical times. It is one of the four waterways mentioned in connection with Eden.
river of Mesopotamia ... Gen 2:14; Jer 13:5; 46:10; Rev 9:14; 16:12

EVANGELIST *proclaimer (a bringer of good news).* One who tells the message of salvation in Christ and leads others to faith in Him.
house of Philip the *e* ... Acts 21:8
and some *as e-s* ... Eph 4:11
do the work of an *e* ... 2 Tim 4:5

EVE *(life).* Wife of Adam. God created her from one of Adam's ribs.
first woman ... Gen 2:22
wife of Adam ... Gen 2:23
deceived by serpent ... Gen 3:1-7
named by Adam ... Gen 3:20

EVENING *dusk, darkness*
cloud...from *e* ... Num 9:21
eats food before *e* ... 1 Sam 14:24
as the *e* offering ... Ps 141:2
not be idle in the *e* ... Eccl 11:6
When *e* came ... Matt 8:16

EVENT *happening*
the *e-s* of the war ... 2 Sam 11:18
e became sin to the ... 1 Kin 13:34
recorded these *e-s* ... Esth 9:20
time for every *e* ... Eccl 3:1

EVERLASTING *eternal* Beginning at some point in time and continuing endlessly. Sometimes used interchangeably with "eternal."
e covenant between ... Gen 9:16
the LORD, the *E* God ... Gen 21:33
are the *e* arms ... Deut 33:27

e to e, You are God ... Ps 90:2
lovingkindness is e ... Ps 106:1
From c I was ... Prov 8:23
The E God, the LORD ... Is 40:28
e name which will ... Is 56:5
LORD for an e light ... Is 60:20
loved you with an e ... Jer 31:3

EVIDENCE *facts, testimony*
the e of witnesses ... Num 35:30
on the e of two ... Deut 19:15
not able to give e ... Ezra 2:59
and giving e ... Acts 17:3

EVIDENT *obvious, plain*
the tares became e ... Matt 13:26
for God made it e ... Rom 1:19
work will become e ... 1 Cor 3:13
Law before God is e ... Gal 3:11
it is e that our Lord ... Heb 7:14

EVIL *bad, wicked, wrong*
man's heart is e ... Gen 8:21
keep...from every e ... Deut 23:9
discern good and e ... 2 Sam 14:17
rebellious and e city ... Ezra 4:12
I fear no e ... Ps 23:4
repay me e for good ... Ps 35:12
turn away from e ... Prov 3:7
run rapidly to e ... Prov 6:18
returns e for good ... Prov 17:13
taken away from e ... Is 57:1
committed two *e-s* ... Jer 2:13
deliver us from e ... Matt 6:13
what e has He ... Matt 27:23
If you then, being e ... Luke 11:13
who does e hates the ... John 3:20
Never...e for e ... Rom 12:17
love of money is...e ... 1 Tim 6:10
tongue...restless e ... James 3:8

EVILDOER *wicked one*
LORD repay the e ... 2 Sam 3:39
e-s will be cut off ... Ps 37:9
e listens to wicked ... Prov 17:4
Offspring of *e-s* ... Is 1:4
is godless and an e ... Is 9:17
depart...you *e-s* ... Luke 13:27
punishment of *e-s* ... 1 Pet 2:14

EVIL-MERODACH
king of Babylon ... 2 Kin 25:27; Jer 52:31

EWE *female sheep*
seven e lambs ... Gen 21:28
e lamb without ... Lev 14:10
poor man's e lamb ... 2 Sam 12:4
e-s with suckling ... Ps 78:71
like a flock of *e-s* ... Song 6:6

EXACT (adj) *certain, correct*
e amount of money ... Esth 4:7
e meaning of all this ... Dan 7:16
know the e truth ... Luke 1:4
a more e knowledge ... Acts 24:22

EXACT (v) *collect*
let him e a fifth ... Gen 41:34
he shall not e it ... Deut 15:2
He *e-ed* the silver ... 2 Kin 23:35
You are *e-ing* usury ... Neh 5:7
e a tribute of grain ... Amos 5:11

EXALT *extol, honor, lift*
He is highly *e-ed* ... Ex 15:1
e-ed be God ... 2 Sam 22:47
He is *e-ed* in power ... Job 37:23
let us e His name ... Ps 34:3
e-ed far above all gods ... Ps 97:9
city is *e-ed* ... Prov 11:11
my God; I will e You ... Is 25:1
E that which is low ... Ezek 21:26
humbles...be *e-ed* ... Matt 23:12
e-ed to...right hand ... Acts 2:33
be *e-ed* in my body ... Phil 1:20
He will e you ... James 4:10

EXAMINE *investigate, search*
That You e him every ... Job 7:18
E me, O LORD, and try ... Ps 26:2
e my heart's *attitude* ... Jer 12:3
e-ing the Scriptures ... Acts 17:11
e-d by scourging ... Acts 22:24
a man must e himself ... 1 Cor 11:28

EXAMPLE *model, pattern*
the e of his father ... 2 Chr 17:3
I gave you an e ... John 13:15
e of those who ... 1 Tim 4:12
e of disobedience ... Heb 4:11
be *e-s* to the flock ... 1 Pet 5:3
made them an e ... 2 Pet 2:6

EXCEL *be superior*
e in...wickedness ... Jer 5:28
wisdom *e-s* folly ... Eccl 2:13
you e...more ... 1 Thess 4:1

EXCELLENCE *perfection*
greatness of Your e ... Ex 15:7
are a woman of e ... Ruth 3:11
if there is any e ... Phil 4:8
proclaim the *e-ies* of ... 1 Pet 2:9

EXCELLENT *outstanding*
e wife is the crown ... Prov 12:4
E speech is not ... Prov 17:7
He has done e things ... Is 12:5
e governor Felix ... Acts 23:26
a still more e way ... 1 Cor 12:31
a more e name ... Heb 1:4

EXCESS *too much*
he...had no e ... Ex 16:18
are in e among them ... Num 3:48
same *e-es* of dissipation ... 1 Pet 4:4

EXCHANGE *trade, transfer*
shall e *it* for money ... Deut 14:25
they *e-d* their glory ... Ps 106:20
shall not sell or e ... Ezek 48:14
e-d the truth of God ... Rom 1:25

EXCLUDE *refuse to admit*
e-d from...assembly ... Ezra 10:8
e-d all foreigners ... Neh 13:3
e you for My name's ... Is 66:5
e-d from the life of ... Eph 4:18

EXCUSE (n) *justification*
began to make *e-s* ... Luke 14:18
no e for their sin ... John 15:22
they are without e ... Rom 1:20

EXECUTE *carry out*
e-d the justice of ... Deut 33:21
He has *e-d* judgment ... Ps 9:16
e vengeance on the ... Ps 149:7
Lord will e His word ... Rom 9:28
e judgment upon all ... Jude 15

EXERCISE *perform*
man has *e-d* authority ... Eccl 8:9
e-s lovingkindness ... Jer 9:24
e authority over ... Matt 20:25
e-s self-control in all ... 1 Cor 9:25

EXHAUSTED *used up, wearied*
sound asleep and e ... Judg 4:21
too e to follow ... 1 Sam 30:21
of flour was not e ... 1 Kin 17:16
Their strength is e ... Jer 51:30

EXHORT *admonish, urge*
and kept on *e-ing* ... Acts 2:40
e, with...patience ... 2 Tim 4:2
e in sound doctrine ... Titus 1:9
e and reprove ... Titus 2:15
e-ing and testifying ... 1 Pet 5:12

EXHORTATION *urging* The act of persuading or encouraging someone to do something, usually to improve behavior. Exhortation is one of the gifts of the Holy Spirit.
with many other *e-s* ... Luke 3:18
given them much e ... Acts 20:2
who exhorts, in his e ... Rom 12:8
this word of e ... Heb 13:22

EXILE *banishment* or *capture* The banishing of someone from his own land, usually as a legal penalty or as the result of conquest by an enemy. The best-known example from the Bible is the exile of the nation of Israel in Babylon, i.e. the Babylonian exile or captivity.
Israel away into e ... 2 Kin 17:6
people of the e were ... Ezra 4:1
captivity of the *e-s* ... Neh 7:6
into e from Jerusalem ... Esth 2:6
e will soon be set free ... Is 51:14
Israel went into e ... Ezek 39:23

EXIST *be, live, occur*
they had never *e-ed* ... Obad 16
Strife *e-s* and ... Hab 1:3
live and move and e ... Acts 17:28
authority...which e ... Rom 13:1

EXODUS *departure*
e of...Israel ... Heb 11:22

EXORCISM The expulsion of evil spirits or demons, usually from a demon-possessed person. In the NT, most often referred to as "casting out" demons (Mark 6:13; cf. Acts 19:13).

EXPANSE *firmament, vastness*
e of the heavens ... Gen 1:20
e of the waters ... Job 37:10
in His mighty e ... Ps 150:1
from above the e ... Ezek 1:25

EXPECT *await*
never *e-ed* to see ... Gen 48:11
e-ed good, then evil ... Job 30:26
which we did not e ... Is 64:3
lend, *e-ing* nothing ... Luke 6:35

EXPECTATION *anticipation*
your e is false ... Job 41:9
e of the wicked ... Prov 10:28
to my earnest e ... Phil 1:20
e of judgment ... Heb 10:27

EXPECTED *awaited*
Are You the E One ... Matt 11:3
Are You the E One ... Luke 7:20

EXPERIENCE *undergo*
all who had not *e-d* ... Judg 3:1
Your people e hardship ... Ps 60:3

e-s Your judgments ... Is 26:9
e-d mockings and ... Heb 11:36

EXPERT *very skillful*
an *e* in warfare ... 2 Sam 17:8
be like an *e* warrior ... Jer 50:9
an *e* in all customs ... Acts 26:3

EXPLAIN *make clear*
no one who could *e* ... Gen 41:24
he did not *e* to her ... 2 Chr 9:2
e its interpretation ... Dan 5:7
E the parable to us ... Matt 15:15
e-ing the Scriptures ... Luke 24:32
e-ed to him the way ... Acts 18:26

EXPOSE *disclose, reveal*
shame...be *e-d* ... Is 47:3
He will *e* your sins ... Lam 4:22
deeds will be *e-d* ... John 3:20
would *e* their infants ... Acts 7:19
are *e-d* by the light ... Eph 5:13

EXTEND *enlarge, stretch out*
God *e-s*...border ... Deut 12:20
e-ed lovingkindness ... Ezra 7:28
e-s her hand to the ... Prov 31:20
I *e* peace to her ... Is 66:12
boundary shall *e* ... Ezek 47:17

EXTENT *amount* or *degree*
the *e* of my days ... Ps 39:4
e that you did it to ... Matt 25:40
such an *e* that Jesus ... Mark 1:45

EXTERMINATE *destroy*
planned to *e* us ... 2 Sam 21:5
He will *e* its sinners ... Is 13:9

EXTERNAL *outward*
not with *e* service ... Col 3:22
adornment must not be...*e* ... 1 Pet 3:3

EXTINGUISH *put out*
they will *e* my coal ... 2 Sam 14:7
not *e* the lamp of ... 2 Sam 21:17
my days are *e-ed* ... Job 17:1
when *I e* you ... Ezek 32:7
e all the flaming ... Eph 6:16

EXTOL *praise*
God, and I will *e* Him ... Ex 15:2
I will *e* You, O LORD ... Ps 30:1
I will *e* You, my God ... Ps 145:1
We will *e* your love ... Song 1:4

EXTORTION *stealing*
practicing...*e* ... Jer 22:17
practiced *e*, robbed ... Ezek 18:18

EXTRAORDINARY *exceptional*
will bring *e* plagues ... Deut 28:59
His *e* work ... Is 28:21
insight, and *e* wisdom ... Dan 5:14
e miracles by ... Acts 19:11
showed us *e* kindness ... Acts 28:2

EXULT *rejoice*
heart *e-s* in the LORD ... 1 Sam 2:1
Let the field *e* ... 1 Chr 16:32
e-ed when evil befell ... Job 31:29
let them *e* before God ... Ps 68:3
I will *e* in the LORD ... Hab 3:18
e in our tribulations ... Rom 5:3

EXULTATION *jubilation*
e like the nations ... Hos 9:1
joy or crown of *e* ... 1 Thess 2:19
may rejoice with *e* ... 1 Pet 4:13

EYE *sight*
e-s are dull from ... Gen 49:12
e for *e*, tooth for ... Ex 21:24
be as *e-s* for us ... Num 10:31
his *e* was not dim ... Deut 34:7
right in his own *e-s* ... Judg 17:6
open his *e-s* that he ... 2 Kin 6:17
e-s of the LORD ... 2 Chr 16:9
was *e-s* to the blind ... Job 29:15
e-s...look to You ... Ps 145:15
Haughty *e-s*, a lying ... Prov 6:17
e...mocks a father ... Prov 30:17
e is not satisfied ... Eccl 1:8
To open blind *e-s* ... Is 42:7
e-s will bitterly weep ... Jer 13:17
have *e-s* to see but ... Ezek 12:2
I lifted my *e-s* and ... Dan 8:3
Your e-s...too pure ... Hab 1:13
e for an *e*, and a ... Matt 5:38
e...you to stumble ... Matt 18:9
e is the lamp ... Luke 11:34
the clay to his *e-s* ... John 9:6
which *e* has not seen ... 1 Cor 2:9
e-s of your heart may ... Eph 1:18
e-s full of adultery ... 2 Pet 2:14
the lust of the *e-s* ... 1 John 2:16
God, who has *e-s* like ... Rev 2:18
His *e-s are* a flame ... Rev 19:12

EYEWITNESSES *observers*
e...of the word ... Luke 1:2
e of His majesty ... 2 Pet 1:16

EZEKIEL

(God strengthens). One of the four major prophetic books in the OT. The writer, Ezekiel, was a priest by birth and a prophet during the Babylonian exile, with a ministry that spanned over 20 years.
Hebrew prophet ... Ezek 1:1
called by God ... Ezek 1:1,3
spoke to Israel ... Ezek 14:1ff
taken captive ... Ezek 33:21
spoke to false prophets ... Ezek 34:2ff
spoke to nations ... Ezek 35:2ff
restored temple ... Ezek 40:1ff

EZION-GEBER
on Gulf of Aqabah ... 1 Kin 9:26; 22:48
near Elath / Eloth ... Deut 2:8; 2 Chr 8:17

EZRA (unc, *Yahweh helps).* A priest and scribe who, by putting into practice the Law of Moses, brought about a revival for those Israelites returning from the Babylonian exile.
priest ... Ezra 7:1-5
scribe ... Ezra 7:6
sent by king ... Ezra 7:14,21
brought exiles ... Ezra 8:1-14
Nehemiah's colleague ... Neh 8:2-6

F

FACE *countenance*
sweat of your *f* You ... Gen 3:19
Abram fell on his *f* ... Gen 17:3
speak to Moses *f* to *f* ... Ex 33:11
skin of his *f* shone ... Ex 34:30
make His *f* shine ... Num 6:25
hide Your *f* from me ... Ps 13:1
Who seek Your *f* ... Ps 24:6
His *f* to shine upon us ... Ps 67:1
f of Your anointed ... Ps 84:9
makes a cheerful *f* ... Prov 15:13
set My *f* against you ... Jer 44:11
had the *f* of an eagle ... Ezek 1:10
Each...had four *f-s* ... Ezek 10:21
fast...wash your *f* ... Matt 6:17
they spat in His *f* ... Matt 26:67
like the *f* of an angel ... Acts 6:15
natural *f* in a mirror ... James 1:23
His *f* was like the sun ... Rev 1:16

FACT *truth*
f may be confirmed ... Matt 18:16
are undeniable *f-s* ... Acts 19:36
f is to be confirmed ... 2 Cor 13:1

FACTIONS *divisions*
be *f* among you ... 1 Cor 11:19
dissensions, *f* ... Gal 5:20

FADE *wither*
it *f-s*, and withers ... Ps 90:6
people...*f* away ... Is 24:4
rich man...will *f* ... James 1:11
will not *f* away ... 1 Pet 1:4

FAIL *be spent* or *fall short*
He will not *f* you ... Deut 4:31
none of his words *f* ... 1 Sam 3:19
no man's heart *f* ... 1 Sam 17:32
not one word...*f-ed* ... 1 Kin 8:56
my strength *f-s* me ... Ps 38:10
the olive should *f* ... Hab 3:17
faith may not *f* ... Luke 22:32
Love never *f-s* ... 1 Cor 13:8

FAINT *languish, swoon*
has made my heart *f* ... Job 23:16
soul *f-ed* within ... Ps 107:5
grow *f* before Me ... Is 57:16
I was *f-ing* away ... Jon 2:7
men *f-ing* from fear ... Luke 21:26
f when...reproved ... Heb 12:5

FAINTHEARTED *weak*
Do not be *f* ... Deut 20:3
encourage the *f* ... 1 Thess 5:14

FAIR HAVENS
harbor in Crete ... Acts 27:8

FAITH *believe, trust* In the Bible, frequently belief and reliance upon God. In the NT specifically, often belief and confidence in Jesus Christ, which leads to salvation.
because you broke *f* ... Deut 32:51
Will you have *f* ... Job 39:12
Who keeps *f* forever ... Ps 146:6
will live by his *f* ... Hab 2:4
Seeing their *f*, Jesus ... Matt 9:2
f the size of a mustard seed ... Matt 17:20
Your *f* has saved you ... Luke 7:50
Increase our *f* ... Luke 17:5
your *f* may not fail ... Luke 22:32
man full of *f* ... Acts 6:5
of *f* to the Gentiles ... Acts 14:27
sanctified by *f* in Me ... Acts 26:18
justified by *f* ... Rom 5:1
f...from hearing ... Rom 10:17
if I have all *f* ... 1 Cor 13:2
your *f* also is vain ... 1 Cor 15:14
we walk by *f* ... 2 Cor 5:7
live by *f* in the Son ... Gal 2:20
saved through *f* ... Eph 2:8
one Lord, one *f* ... Eph 4:5
joy in the *f* ... Phil 1:25
stability of your *f* ... Col 2:5

breastplate of *f* ... 1 Thess 5:8
for not all have *f* ... 2 Thess 3:2
fall away from the *f* ... 1 Tim 4:1
conduct, love, *f* ... 1 Tim 4:12
they upset the *f* ... 2 Tim 2:18
sound in the *f* ... Titus 1:13
showing all good *f* ... Titus 2:10
full assurance of *f* ... Heb 10:22
By *f* Enoch was taken ... Heb 11:5
perfecter of *f* ... Heb 12:2
ask in *f* ... James 1:6
prayer offered in *f* ... James 5:15
power of God...*f* ... 1 Pet 1:5
the *f* of the saints ... Rev 13:10

FAITHFUL *loyal, trustworthy*
the *f* God, who keeps ... Deut 7:9
raise...a *f* priest ... 1 Sam 2:35
heart *f* before You ... Neh 9:8
LORD preserves the *f* ... Ps 31:23
commandments...*f* ... Ps 119:86
the LORD who is *f* ... Is 49:7
Well done...*f* ... Matt 25:23
God is *f* ... 1 Cor 1:9
F is He who calls ... 1 Thess 5:24
He considered me *f* ... 1 Tim 1:12
entrust...to *f* men ... 2 Tim 2:2
souls to a *f* Creator ... 1 Pet 4:19
He is *f*...to forgive ... 1 John 1:9
Be *f* until death ... Rev 2:10
called *F* and True ... Rev 19:11

FAITHFULNESS *loyalty* Synonym of truthfulness, fidelity, and dependability.
kindness and *f* ... Gen 47:29
A God of *f* ... Deut 32:4
make known Your *f* ... Ps 89:1
f to all generations ... Ps 100:5
and mercy and *f* ... Matt 23:23
nullify the *f* of God ... Rom 3:3
kindness, goodness, *f* ... Gal 5:22

FAITHLESS *unbelieving*
what *f* Israel did ... Jer 3:6
O *f* daughter ... Jer 31:22
Their heart is *f* ... Hos 10:2
If we are *f* ... 2 Tim 2:13

FALL (n) In theology, a technical term referring to the first sin committed by Adam and Eve (i.e. the original sin) and its widespread consequences, which include the condemnation of all mankind to eternal death. The remedy is salvation through faith in Christ.

FALL (v) *descend* or *fail*
deep sleep to *f* upon ... Gen 2:21
devices let them *f* ... Ps 5:10
I am ready to *f* ... Ps 38:17
dread...had *f-en* ... Ps 105:38
wicked will *f* ... Prov 11:5
a righteous man *f-s* ... Prov 24:16
whether a tree *f-s* ... Eccl 11:3
Assyrian will *f* ... Is 31:8
Babylon has *f-en* ... Jer 51:8
f down and worship ... Dan 3:5
will *f* into a pit ... Matt 15:14
f-ing on his knees ... Mark 1:40
all may *f*...I will ... Mark 14:29
appointed for the *f* ... Luke 2:34
watching Satan *f* ... Luke 10:18
house *divided*...*f-s* ... Luke 11:17
f-ing headlong ... Acts 1:18
sinned and *f* short ... Rom 3:23
have *f-en* asleep ... 1 Cor 15:6
f-en from grace ... Gal 5:4
rich *f* into temptation ... 1 Tim 6:9
rocks, *F* on us ... Rev 6:16

FALLOW *unproductive*
rest and lie *f* ... Ex 23:11
f ground of the poor ... Prov 13:23

FALSE *deceitful, dishonest*
not bear a *f* report ... Ex 23:1
I hate every *f* way ... Ps 119:104
But a *f* witness ... Prov 12:17
f witness will not go ... Prov 19:5
f scale is not good ... Prov 20:23
F and foolish *visions* ... Lam 2:14
And tell *f* dreams ... Zech 10:2
not bear *f* witness ... Matt 19:18
f Christs and *f* ... Matt 24:24
men are *f* apostles ... 2 Cor 11:13
the *f* circumcision ... Phil 3:2
and the *f* prophet ... Rev 20:10

FALSEHOOD *deception*
lifted up his soul to *f* ... Ps 24:4
delight in *f* ... Ps 62:4
I hate and despise *f* ... Ps 119:163
Bread obtained by *f* ... Prov 20:17
trusted in *f* ... Jer 13:25
prophesying *f* in My ... Jer 14:14
laying aside *f* ... Eph 4:25

FAME *greatness*
heard of Your *f* ... Num 14:15
Joshua, and his *f* ... Josh 6:27
the *f* of Solomon ... 1 Kin 10:1
heard My *f* ... Is 66:19
f in *the things of* ... 2 Cor 8:18

FAMILY *household, relatives*
f-ies from the ark ... Gen 8:19
all the *f-ies* of ... Gen 12:3
f may redeem him ... Lev 25:49
f-ies of the Levites ... Num 3:20
my *f* is the least ... Judg 6:15
f-ies like a flock ... Ps 107:41
God of all the *f-ies* ... Jer 31:1
f-ies of the earth ... Amos 3:2
every *f* in heaven ... Eph 3:15
upsetting whole *f-ies* ... Titus 1:11

FAMINE *shortage of food*
a *f* in the land ... Gen 12:10
seven years of *f* ... Gen 41:27
If there is *f* ... 2 Chr 6:28
In *f* He will redeem ... Job 5:20
keep them alive in *f* ... Ps 33:19
f and pestilence ... Jer 14:12
f and wild beasts ... Ezek 5:17
f-s and earthquakes ... Matt 24:7
plagues and *f-s* ... Luke 21:11
Now a *f* came ... Acts 7:11
mourning and *f* ... Rev 18:8

FAMISHED *hungry, parched*
for I am *f* ... Gen 25:30
strength is *f* ... Job 18:12
honorable men are *f* ... Is 5:13

FAMOUS *well-known*
f in Bethlehem ... Ruth 4:11
men of valor, *f* men ... 1 Chr 5:24

FAR *distant*
f from a false charge ... Ex 23:7
come from a *f* country ... Josh 9:6
Be not *f* from me ... Ps 22:11
f above all gods ... Ps 97:9
As *f* as the east ... Ps 103:12
LORD is *f* from the ... Prov 15:29
a God *f* off ... Jer 23:23
heart is *f* away from ... Matt 15:8
f from the kingdom ... Mark 12:34
glory *f* beyond all ... 2 Cor 4:17
f above all rule ... Eph 1:21

FARM *agricultural land*
consume the *f* land ... Amos 7:4
one to his own *f* ... Matt 22:5
or *f-s*, for My sake ... Mark 10:29

FARMER *husbandman*
Does the *f* plow ... Is 28:24
will be your *f-s* ... Is 61:5
f-s...put to shame ... Jer 14:4
the *f* to mourning ... Amos 5:16

FASHION *create, form*
f-ed into a woman ... Gen 2:22
f us in the womb ... Job 31:15
He who *f-s* the hearts ... Ps 33:15
f a graven image ... Is 44:9
I am *f-ing* calamity ... Jer 18:11

FAST (n) *food abstinence*
Proclaim a *f* ... 1 Kin 21:9
you call this a *f* ... Is 58:5
Consecrate a *f* ... Joel 1:14
f was already over ... Acts 27:9

FAST (v) *abstain from food*
and David *f-ed* ... 2 Sam 12:16
maidens also will *f* ... Esth 4:16
you *f* for contention ... Is 58:4
had *f-ed* forty days ... Matt 4:2
whenever you *f* ... Matt 6:16
disciples do not *f* ... Mark 2:18
I *f* twice a week ... Luke 18:12
had *f-ed* and prayed ... Acts 13:3

FASTING *food abstinence* The deliberate act of abstaining from eating (and sometimes, drinking) for a period of time as a sign of repentance or sorrow.
times of *f* ... Esth 9:31
weak from *f* ... Ps 109:24
noticed...when they are *f* ... Matt 6:16
by prayer and *f* ... Matt 17:21
Pharisees were *f* ... Mark 2:18

FAT *animal fat* or *obese*
f of the land ... Gen 45:18
shall not eat any *f* ... Lev 7:23
Go, eat of the *f* ... Neh 8:10
their body is *f* ... Ps 73:4
Good news puts *f* ... Prov 15:30

FATE *destiny*
appalled at his *f* ... Job 18:20
one *f* befalls them ... Eccl 2:14
f for the righteous ... Eccl 9:2
one *f* for all men ... Eccl 9:3

FATHER *God* or *parent* Frequently used in the Bible to refer to God as the Father, the first person of the Trinity.
leave his *f*...mother ... Gen 2:24
f of a multitude ... Gen 17:4
Honor your *f* ... Ex 20:12
who strikes his *f* ... Ex 21:15
iniquity of the *f-s* ... Deut 5:9
Is not He your *F* ... Deut 32:6
your *f-'s* instruction ... Prov 1:8
son makes a *f* glad ... Prov 10:1

Eternal *F*, Prince of ... Is 9:6
all have one *f* ... Mal 2:10
F who sees...in secret ... Matt 6:4
Our *F* who is in ... Matt 6:9
does the will of My *F* ... Matt 7:21
in My *F-'s* kingdom ... Matt 26:29
in the glory of His *F* ... Mark 8:38
be in my *F-'s house* ... Luke 2:49
F, hallowed be Your ... Luke 11:2
F, forgive them ... Luke 23:34
begotten from the *F* ... John 1:14
my *F-'s* house a ... John 2:16
F...testifies ... John 8:18
the *f* of lies ... John 8:44
I and the *F* are one ... John 10:30
In my *F-'s* house are ... John 14:2
F is the vinedresser ... John 15:1
ask the *F* for ... John 16:23
I ascend to My *F* ... John 20:17
one God and *F* of all ... Eph 4:6

FATHER-IN-LAW
she sent to her *f* ... Gen 38:25
returned to Jethro his *f* ... Ex 4:18
his *f*, the girl's ... Judg 19:4
f of Caiaphas ... John 18:13

FATHERLESS *orphan*
father of the *f* ... Ps 68:5
He supports the *f* ... Ps 146:9
fields of the *f* ... Prov 23:10
f and the widow ... Ezek 22:7

FATLING *young lamb* or *kid*
sacrificed...a *f* ... 2 Sam 6:13
f-s...in abundance ... 1 Kin 1:19
f-s of Bashan ... Ezek 39:18

FATNESS *abundance*
f of the earth ... Gen 27:28
Shall I leave my *f* ... Judg 9:9
satisfied as with...*f* ... Ps 63:5
eye bulges from *f* ... Ps 73:7

FAULT *error, offense*
found no *f* in him ... 1 Sam 29:3
let no one find *f* ... Hos 4:4
does He still find *f* ... Rom 9:19
grumblers, finding *f* ... Jude 16

FAVOR *kind regard*
Noah found *f* ... Gen 6:8
I will grant...*f* ... Ex 3:21
show no *f* to them ... Deut 7:2
Why have I found *f* ... Ruth 2:10
surround him with *f* ... Ps 5:12
showed *f* to Your land ... Ps 85:1
obtains *f*...LORD ... Prov 8:35
f is like a cloud ... Prov 16:15
found *f* with God ... Luke 1:30
in *f* with God and ... Luke 2:52
seeking the *f* of men ... Gal 1:10

FEAR (n) *awe, dread, reverence*
no *f* of God in ... Gen 20:11
f of the LORD is clean ... Ps 19:9
f...is the beginning ... Ps 111:10
afraid of sudden *f* ... Prov 3:25
f...prolongs life ... Prov 10:27
f of man brings a ... Prov 29:25
they cried out in *f* ... Matt 14:26
guards shook for *f* ... Matt 28:4
men fainting from *f* ... Luke 21:26
for *f* of the Jews ... John 7:13
no *f* of God before ... Rom 3:18
in weakness and in *f* ... 1 Cor 2:3
knowing the *f* of the ... 2 Cor 5:11
with *f* and trembling ... Eph 6:5
through *f* of death ... Heb 2:15
love casts out *f* ... 1 John 4:18

FEAR (v) *be afraid, revere*
the midwives *f-ed* God ... Ex 1:21
Moses said...Do not *f* ... Ex 14:13
may learn to *f* Me ... Deut 4:10
not *f* other gods ... 2 Kin 17:37
I *f* no evil ... Ps 23:4
Whom shall I *f* ... Ps 27:1
not *f* evil tidings ... Ps 112:7
who *f-s* the LORD ... Prov 31:30
Rather, *f* God ... Eccl 5:7
Take courage, *f* not ... Is 35:4
Do not *f*, for I am ... Is 41:10
will *f* and tremble ... Jer 33:9
do not *f* them ... Matt 10:26
f-ed the crowd ... Matt 14:5
who did not *f* God ... Luke 18:2
slavery leading to *f* ... Rom 8:15
I *f* for you ... Gal 4:11
let us *f* if ... Heb 4:1

FEAR OF GOD A profound reverence for God. Also to dread His punishment.

FEARFUL *terrifying*
it is a *f* thing ... Ex 34:10
were *f* and amazed ... Luke 8:25
will be *f of sinning* ... 1 Tim 5:20

FEAST *celebration*
a *f* to the LORD ... Ex 12:14
godless jesters at a *f* ... Ps 35:16
hate...appointed *f-s* ... Is 1:14
and cheerful *f-s* ... Zech 8:19
refuse of your *f-s* ... Mal 2:3
a wedding *f* ... Matt 22:2
seeking Him at the *f* ... John 7:11
celebrate the *f* ... 1 Cor 5:8
f with you without ... Jude 12

FEAST OF BOOTHS *see* **BOOTHS, FEAST OF** *and* **FEASTS**

FEAST OF DEDICATION Also known as Hanukkah (Heb for "dedication" or "inauguration"). A celebration instituted ca. 165 B.C., commemorating the rededication of the temple and the miracle of the lamp after the Hasmoneans defeated the Greeks, who had desecrated the temple. Only one usable container of lamp oil remained after the desecration, with enough oil to fuel a single lamp for one day, but the lamp miraculously gave light for eight days.
f took place ... John 10:22

FEAST OF PASSOVER *see* **PASSOVER**

FEAST OF WEEKS *see* **PENTECOST**

FEASTS
1 ***Feast of Booths*** ... Lev 23:24; Deut 16:16; 2 Chr 8:13
also **Feast of Ingathering**
2 ***Feast of Dedication*** ... John 10:22
3 ***Feast of Harvest*** ... Ex 23:16
also **Feast of Weeks**
also **Feast of Pentecost**
4 ***Feast of Ingathering*** ... Ex 23:16
also **Feast of Booths**
5 ***Feast of Passover*** ... Ex 34:25; Luke 2:41
6 ***Feast of Unleavened Bread*** ... Ex 23:15; Luke 22:1
7 ***Feast of Weeks*** ... Ex 34:22; Deut 16:10,16
also **Feast of Harvest**
also **Feast of Pentecost**
8 ***Feast of Pentecost*** ... Acts 2:1; 20:16; 1 Cor 16:8
also **Feast of Harvest**
also **Feast of Weeks**

FEEBLE *weak*
when the flock was *f* ... Gen 30:42
What are these *f* Jews ... Neh 4:2
strengthen the *f* ... Is 35:3
knees that are *f* ... Heb 12:12

FEED *eat, supply*
fed you with manna ... Deut 8:3
f him sparingly ... 1 Kin 22:27
F me with the food ... Prov 30:8
He *f-s* on ashes ... Is 44:20
f you on knowledge ... Jer 3:15
He *fed* me this scroll ... Ezek 3:2
I will *f* My flock ... Ezek 34:15
dogs *f* on the ... Matt 15:27
hungry, and *f* You ... Matt 25:37
fed...the *crumbs* ... Luke 16:21
enemy is hungry, *f* ... Rom 12:20

FEEL *sense, touch*
I may *f* you, my son ... Gen 27:21
Isaac...*felt* him and ... Gen 27:22
Let me *f* the pillars ... Judg 16:26
He *felt* compassion ... Matt 9:36
she *felt*...was healed ... Mark 5:29
Jesus *felt* a love for ... Mark 10:21
f-ing a sense of awe ... Acts 2:43
f sensual desires ... 1 Tim 5:11

FELIX (Lat, *happy*). The Roman official before whom Paul was arraigned.
Roman procurator ... Acts 23:26; 24:25; 25:14

FELL *collapse, come upon*
wall *f* down flat ... Josh 6:20
fire of the LORD *f* ... 1 Kin 18:38
the lot *f* on Jonah ... Jon 1:7
seeds f beside the ... Matt 13:4
He *f* asleep ... Luke 8:23
he *f* to the ground ... Acts 9:4
Holy Spirit *f* upon ... Acts 10:44
star *f* from heaven ... Rev 8:10

FELLOW *companion*
oil of joy above Your *f-s* ... Ps 45:7
your *f* exiles ... Ezek 11:15
beat his *f* slaves ... Matt 24:49
f heirs with Christ ... Rom 8:17
f citizens with the ... Eph 2:19
Gentiles are *f* heirs ... Eph 3:6
brother and *f* worker ... Phil 2:25
f worker in the ... 1 Thess 3:2
I am a *f* servant of ... Rev 22:9

FELLOWSHIP Companionship between people of the same background, goals, etc. A community in which people share whatever is held in common.
had sweet *f* together ... Ps 55:14
f...Holy Spirit ... 2 Cor 13:14
right hand of *f* ... Gal 2:9
f of His sufferings ... Phil 3:10
f is with the Father ... 1 John 1:3
f with one another ... 1 John 1:7

FEMALE *girl, woman*
and *f* He created ... Gen 1:27
a *f* slave ... Ex 21:7
f from the flock ... Lev 5:6
likeness of male or *f* ... Deut 4:16
neither male nor *f* ... Gal 3:28

FERTILE *productive*
a *f* land ... Neh 9:25
the *f* valley ... Is 28:4
in *f* soil ... Ezek 17:5

FERVENT *ardent*
being *f* in spirit ... Acts 18:25
f in spirit, serving ... Rom 12:11
keep *f* in your love ... 1 Pet 4:8

FESTIVAL *celebration* In the Bible, any of several assemblies mandated by the Law of Moses. They were of two types: annual, such as Passover, and in intervals of seven, such as every seventh day (Sabbath), month, or year.
celebrate a great *f* ... Neh 8:12
I reject your *f-s* ... Amos 5:21
turn your *f-s* into ... Amos 8:10
during the *f*, otherwise ... Matt 26:5

FESTUS, PORCIUS The procurator of Judea who succeeded Felix.
Roman procurator of Judea ... Acts 24:27; 25:14,23; 26:25

FETTERS *chains* A set of chains with which the feet of prisoners were held to a post.
your feet put in *f* ... 2 Sam 3:34
they are bound in *f* ... Job 36:8
tear their *f* apart ... Ps 2:3
with *f* of iron ... Ps 149:8

FEVER *inflammation*
bones burn with *f* ... Job 30:30
in bed with a *f* ... Matt 8:14
from a high *f* ... Luke 4:38
He rebuked the *f* ... Luke 4:39
the *f* left him ... John 4:52

FIELD *productive land*
hail struck...the *f* ... Ex 9:25
let me go to the *f* ... Ruth 2:2
glean in another *f* ... Ruth 2:8
f of the sluggard ... Prov 24:30
Zion...plowed *as* a *f* ... Jer 26:18
the lilies of the *f* ... Matt 6:28
the *f* is the world ... Matt 13:38
shepherds...in the *f-s* ... Luke 2:8
Two men...in the *f* ... Luke 17:36
f-s...white for ... John 4:35
F of Blood ... Acts 1:19

FIERCE *violent*
anger, for it is *f* ... Gen 49:7
Wrath is *f* ... Prov 27:4
see a *f* people ... Is 33:19
a *f* gale of wind ... Mark 4:37
scorched with *f* heat ... Rev 16:9
f wrath of God ... Rev 19:15

FIERCENESS *intensity*
f of His anger ... Josh 7:26
the *f* of battle ... Is 42:25

FIERY *burning*
LORD sent *f* serpents ... Num 21:6
with *f* heat ... Deut 28:22
His arrows *f* shafts ... Ps 7:13
f ordeal among you ... 1 Pet 4:12

FIG *fruit*
they sewed *f* leaves ... Gen 3:7
But the *f* tree said ... Judg 9:11
a piece of *f* cake ... 1 Sam 30:12
nor *f-s* from thistles ... Matt 7:16
the *f* tree withered ... Matt 21:19
f-s from thorns ... Luke 6:44
under the *f* tree ... John 1:48
Can a *f* tree ... James 3:12

FIGHT *struggle*
Hebrews were *f-ing* ... Ex 2:13
LORD will *f* for you ... Ex 14:14
fought for Israel ... Josh 10:14
stars *fought* from ... Judg 5:20
and *f* our battles ... 1 Sam 8:20
f for your brothers ... Neh 4:14
f-ing against God ... Acts 5:39
fought the good *f* ... 2 Tim 4:7
so you *f* and quarrel ... James 4:2

FIGURATIVE *metaphorical*
in *f* language ... John 16:25

FIGURE *shape, type*
f-s resembling four ... Ezek 1:5
f...of a man ... Ezek 1:26
using a *f* of speech ... John 16:29

FILIGREE *ornamental work* A setting of metal or fabric with a checkered or interwoven pattern.
f settings of gold ... Ex 28:13
cords on the two *f* ... Ex 28:25

FILL (n) *satisfaction*
eat your *f* ... Lev 25:19
They drink their *f* ... Ps 36:8
drink our *f* of love ... Prov 7:18
its *f* of their blood ... Jer 46:10

FILL (v) *make full*
and *f* the earth ... Gen 1:28
f-ed with violence ... Gen 6:11
Can you *f* his skin ... Job 41:7
was *f-ing* with smoke ... Is 6:4
I am *f-ed* with power ... Mic 3:8
hall was *f-ed* ... Matt 22:10
God of hope *f* you ... Rom 15:13

FILTHY *offensive*
are full of *f* vomit ... Is 28:8
like a *f* garment ... Is 64:6
clothed...*f* garments ... Zech 3:3
Let...the one who is *f* ... Rev 22:11

FILTHINESS *disgustingly foul*
not washed...his *f* ... Prov 30:12
your *f* is lewdness ... Ezek 24:13
no f and silly talk ... Eph 5:4
putting aside all *f* ... James 1:21

FIND *discover, uncover*
not *found* a helper ... Gen 2:20
But Noah *found* favor ... Gen 6:8
sin will *f* you out ... Num 32:23
that you may *f* rest ... Ruth 1:9
he who *f-s* me *f-s* life ... Prov 8:35
who *f-s* a wife *f-s* ... Prov 18:22
f gladness and joy ... Is 35:10
few who *f* it ... Matt 7:14
has *found* his life ... Matt 10:39
f rest for your souls ... Matt 11:29
f-ing one pearl ... Matt 13:46
f a colt tied ... Mark 11:2
found...sleeping ... Mark 14:40
seek, and you will *f* ... Luke 11:9
found the Messiah ... John 1:41
was *found* worthy ... Rev 5:4

FINGER *part of hand*
the *f* of God ... Ex 8:19
dip his *f* in the blood ... Lev 4:6
six *f-s* on each ... 2 Sam 21:20
twenty-four *f-s* and ... 1 Chr 20:6
tip of his *f* in water ... Luke 16:24
with His *f* wrote ... John 8:6
Reach here with your *f* ... John 20:27

FINISH *complete*
Moses *f-ed* the work ... Ex 40:33
Solomon *f-ed* the ... 2 Chr 7:11
It is *f-ed* ... John 19:30
I may *f* my course ... Acts 20:24
f doing it also ... 2 Cor 8:11
wrath of God is *f-ed* ... Rev 15:1

FINS *part of fish*
that have *f* and scales ... Lev 11:9
anything that has *f* ... Deut 14:9

FIR *tree, wood*
instruments...of f ... 2 Sam 6:5
He plants a *f* ... Is 44:14

FIRE *burning* or *flame*
the *f* and the knife ... Gen 22:6
bush...burning with *f* ... Ex 3:2
pillar of *f* by night ... Ex 13:21
offered strange *f* ... Num 3:4
f of the LORD fell ... 1 Kin 18:38
a chariot of *f* ... 2 Kin 2:11
jealousy burn like *f* ... Ps 79:5
Israel will become a *f* ... Is 10:17
Is not My word like *f* ... Jer 23:29
the Holy Spirit and *f* ... Matt 3:11
with unquenchable *f* ... Matt 3:12
tongues as of *f* ... Acts 2:3
lake that burns with *f* ... Rev 21:8

FIRE, PILLAR OF *see* **CLOUD, PILLAR OF**

FIREBRAND *burning wood*
who throws *F-s* ... Prov 26:18
you were like a *f* ... Amos 4:11

FIREPAN *used in worship*
a *f* full of coals ... Lev 16:12
the *f-s* of pure gold ... 2 Chr 4:22

FIRM *establish, steadfast*
his bow remained *f* ... Gen 49:24
stood *f* on dry ground ... Josh 3:17
making my footsteps *f* ... Ps 40:2
He made *f* the skies ... Prov 8:28
stand *f* in the faith ... 1 Cor 16:13
f foundation of God ... 2 Tim 2:19
hope *f* until the end ... Heb 3:6

FIRST *number*
f of all your produce ... Prov 3:9
seek *f* His kingdom ... Matt 6:33
f take the log out ... Matt 7:5
f will be last ... Matt 19:30
f called Christians ... Acts 11:26
to the Jew *f* ... Rom 2:10
f fruits of the Spirit ... Rom 8:23
He *f* loved us ... 1 John 4:19
I am the *f* and the ... Rev 1:17
left your *f* love ... Rev 2:4
f things have passed ... Rev 21:4

FIRST FRUITS The first grains or fruits harvested in the year. There were two official feasts in Israel during which the first

fruits were presented as offerings: the Feast of Weeks, celebrating the (spring) wheat harvest; and the Feast of Ingathering (during the Feast of Booths), which celebrated the general harvest (summer). The term is also used metaphorically of Christ, in reference to His resurrection (1 Cor 15:20, 23).
f of your labors ... Ex 23:16

FIRSTBORN *oldest* In OT law firstborn males, whether man or animal, were counted as belonging to God. The firstborn of animals was either to be given to the priests for sacrifice or to be redeemed with another animal (e.g. a lamb) if it was needed by its owner. Firstborn men, however, were always to be redeemed. To accomplish this, God declared that all the Levites would be His to serve in the temple and each man would count for a firstborn male from another tribe. When a count was taken, it was found that there were 22,273 firstborn males and only 22,000 Levites. God told Moses that the additional 273 firstborn males were each to be redeemed with five shekels given to the priests. According to the Talmud, Moses anticipated that every firstborn male might claim to be redeemed by a Levite, so Moses wrote "Levite" on 22,000 slips and "five shekels" on 273 more, and had each firstborn male draw one of the slips from an urn.
Sidon, his *f* ... Gen 10:15
the *f* bore a son ... Gen 19:37
I am Esau your *f* ... Gen 27:19
LORD killed every *f* ... Ex 13:15
birth to her *f* son ... Luke 2:7
church of the *f* ... Heb 12:23
f of the dead ... Rev 1:5

FIRST GATE *see* **GATES OF JERUSALEM**

FISH
rule over the *f* ... Gen 1:26
Their *f* stink ... Is 50:2
a great *f* to swallow ... Jon 1:17
loaves and two *f* ... Matt 14:17
snake instead of a *f* ... Luke 11:11
net *full* of *f* ... John 21:8

FISH GATE *see* **GATES OF JERUSALEM**

FISHERMEN *fishers*
f will lament ... Is 19:8
for they were *f* ... Matt 4:18
the *f* had gotten out ... Luke 5:2

FISHERS *fishermen*
make you *f* of men ... Matt 4:19
become *f* of men ... Mark 1:17

FIT *be suitable, worthy*
f to remove His ... Matt 3:11
f for the kingdom ... Luke 9:62
not *f* to be...apostle ... 1 Cor 15:9
body, being *f-ted* ... Eph 4:16
f-ting in the Lord ... Col 3:18

FIX *make firm, secure*
I will *f* your boundary ... Ex 23:31
f-ed her hope on God ... 1 Tim 5:5
f-ing...eyes on Jesus ... Heb 12:2
f your hope ... 1 Pet 1:13

FIXED *established*
the *f* festivals ... 1 Chr 23:31
f order of the moon ... Jer 31:35
is a great chasm *f* ... Luke 16:26

FLAME *fire*
ascended in the *f* ... Judg 13:20
f...the wicked ... Ps 106:18
f of the LORD ... Song 8:6
his Holy One a *f* ... Is 10:17
crackling of a *f* ... Joel 2:5
f of a burning thorn ... Acts 7:30
eyes *are* a *f* of fire ... Rev 19:12

FLAMING *burning*
the *f* sword ... Gen 3:24
f fire by night ... Is 4:5
eyes were like *f* ... Dan 10:6
angels in *f* fire ... 2 Thess 1:7

FLASH *reflect, sparkle*
why do your eyes *f* ... Job 15:12
lightning was *f-ing* ... Ezek 1:13
Polished to *f* like ... Ezek 21:10
He who *f-es* forth ... Amos 5:9
light suddenly *f-ed* ... Acts 22:6

FLASK *utensil*
take this *f* of oil ... 2 Kin 9:1
took oil in *f-s* ... Matt 25:4

FLATTER
Nor *f any* man ... Job 32:21
f with their tongue ... Ps 5:9
adulteress who *f-s* ... Prov 2:16
who *f-s* his neighbor ... Prov 29:5

FLAX *plant*
the *f* was in bud ... Ex 9:31
looks for wool and *f* ... Prov 31:13
made from combed *f* ... Is 19:9

FLEE *escape, run away*
arise, *f* to Haran ... Gen 27:43
F as a bird ... Ps 11:1
f from Your presence ... Ps 139:7
rulers have *fled* ... Is 22:3
f to Egypt ... Matt 2:13
left Him and *fled* ... Matt 26:56
fled from the tomb ... Mark 16:8
f from idolatry ... 1 Cor 10:14
f from youthful lusts ... 2 Tim 2:22
and heaven *fled* ... Rev 20:11

FLEECE *wool*
put a *f* of wool ... Judg 6:37
dry only on the *f* ... Judg 6:39
warmed with the *f* ... Job 31:20

FLEET *group of ships*
Solomon...built a *f* ... 1 Kin 9:26
sent...with the *f* ... 1 Kin 9:27

FLESH *body, meat* In the NT, flesh can refer to the physical body, and also to man's sinful tendencies as opposed to spiritual qualities. The sinful tendencies (e.g. lust) are a source of temptation, which is to be resisted.
f of my *f* ... Gen 2:23
shall become one *f* ... Gen 2:24
from my *f* I shall see ... Job 19:26
heart and my *f* sing ... Ps 84:2
All *f* is grass ... Is 40:6
the *f* is weak ... Matt 26:41
spirit...not have *f* ... Luke 24:39
the Word became *f* ... John 1:14
born of the *f* is *f* ... John 3:6
who eats My *f* ... John 6:56
children of the *f* ... Rom 9:8
thorn in the *f* ... 2 Cor 12:7
desires of the *f* ... Eph 2:3
polluted by the *f* ... Jude 23
filled with their *f* ... Rev 19:21

FLESHLY *carnal*
not in *f* wisdom ... 2 Cor 1:12
His *f* body ... Col 1:22
abstain from *f* lusts ... 1 Pet 2:11

FLIES *insects*
sent...swarms of *f* ... Ps 78:45
swarm of *f And* gnats ... Ps 105:31
Dead *f* make a ... Eccl 10:1

FLIGHT *departure*
F will perish from ... Amos 2:14
f will not be in ... Matt 24:20
foreign armies to *f* ... Heb 11:34

FLINT *stone*
Zipporah took a *f* ... Ex 4:25
f into a fountain ... Ps 114:8
hoofs...seem like *f* ... Is 5:28
emery harder than *f* ... Ezek 3:9
hearts *like f* ... Zech 7:12

FLOCK *goats, sheep*
a keeper of *f-s* ... Gen 4:2
water their father's *f* ... Ex 2:16
Your people like a *f* ... Ps 77:20
He will tend His *f* ... Is 40:11
scattered My *f* ... Jer 23:2
over their *f* by night ... Luke 2:8
will become one *f* ... John 10:16
f of God among you ... 1 Pet 5:2

FLOOD *overflowing of water* In the Scriptures, often refers to the flood with which God covered the earth in Noah's days, to judge the extreme wickedness of its inhabitants.
I am bringing the *f* ... Gen 6:17
f came upon the earth ... Gen 7:17
end...with a *f* ... Dan 9:26
the *f-s* came ... Matt 7:25
f...destroyed ... Luke 17:27

FLOOR *ground, level*
threshing *f* of Atad ... Gen 50:11
go down to the...*f* ... Ruth 3:3
the *f*...with gold ... 1 Kin 6:30
f-s...full of grain ... Joel 2:24
His threshing *f* ... Matt 3:12
fell...from the third *f* ... Acts 20:9

FLOUR *ground grain*
measures of fine *f* ... Gen 18:6
only a handful of *f* ... 1 Kin 17:12
f...not exhausted ... 1 Kin 17:16

FLOURISH *blossom, thrive*
may the righteous *f* ... Ps 72:7
who did iniquity *f-ed* ... Ps 92:7
your bones will *f* ... Is 66:14
make the dry tree *f* ... Ezek 17:24

FLOW *pour forth*
river *f-ed* out of Eden ... Gen 2:10
f-ing with milk and ... Ex 3:8
eyelids *f* with water ... Jer 9:18
hills will *f* with milk ... Joel 3:18
f of her blood ... Mark 5:29
f...living water ... John 7:38

FLOWER *blossom*
As a *f* of the field ... Ps 103:15
f-s have *already* ... Song 2:12
to the fading *f* ... Is 28:1
glory like the *f* ... 1 Pet 1:24

FLUTE *musical instrument*
tambourine, *f*, and ... 1 Sam 10:5
playing on *f-s* ... 1 Kin 1:40
the *f* or on the harp ... 1 Cor 14:7
musicians...*f-players* ... Rev 18:22

FLY *soar*
let birds *f* above ... Gen 1:20
a raven, and it *flew* ... Gen 8:7
As sparks *f* upward ... Job 5:7
f-ies away like a dream ... Job 20:8
glory will *f* away ... Hos 9:11
heard an eagle *f-ing* ... Rev 8:13
the birds which *f* ... Rev 19:17

FOAL *colt* In the Bible, the young offspring of a donkey.
ties *his f* to the vine ... Gen 49:11
f of a wild donkey ... Job 11:12
f of a beast of burden ... Matt 21:5

FODDER *animal food* Food for domestic animals, usually comprised of a mix of grains.
give his donkey *f* ... Gen 42:27
eat salted *f* ... Is 30:24

FOE *enemy*
before your *f-s* ... 1 Chr 21:12
A *f* and an enemy ... Esth 7:6
iniquity of my *f-s* ... Ps 49:5
the evil to my *f-s* ... Ps 54:5
avenge...His *f-s* ... Jer 46:10

FOLD *animal pen*
goats out of your *f-s* ... Ps 50:9
the peaceful *f-s* ... Jer 25:37
cut off from the *f* ... Hab 3:17
not of this *f* ... John 10:16

FOLLOW *imitate, pursue*
not *f* other gods ... Deut 6:14
turn back from *f-ing* ... Ruth 1:16
f the LORD your God ... 1 Sam 12:14
who *f*...wickedness ... Ps 119:150
bloodshed *f-s* ... Hos 4:2
He said to them, *F* ... Matt 4:19
left...and *f-ed* ... Matt 4:20
his cross, and *f* Me ... Matt 16:24
crowd was *f-ing* ... Mark 5:24
and they *f* Me ... John 10:27
Peter...*f-ing* Jesus ... John 18:15
f-ing after...lusts ... Jude 16
ones who *f* the Lamb ... Rev 14:4

FOLLOWERS *disciples*
His *f*...*began* asking ... Mark 4:10

FOLLY *foolishness*
this act of *f* ... Judg 19:23
of fools spouts *f* ... Prov 15:2
F is joy to him ... Prov 15:21
devising of *f* is sin ... Prov 24:9

FOOD *bread, meat*
shall be *f* for you ... Gen 1:29
tree was good for *f* ... Gen 3:6
in giving them *f* ... Ruth 1:6
tears have been my *f* ... Ps 42:3
it is deceptive *f* ... Prov 23:3
his *f* was locusts ... Matt 3:4
life more than *f* ... Matt 6:25
f is to do the will ... John 4:34
My flesh is true *f* ... John 6:55
milk...not solid *f* ... 1 Cor 3:2

FOOL *unwise person*
The *f* has said in his ... Ps 14:1
F-s despise wisdom ... Prov 1:7
too exalted for a *f* ... Prov 24:7
f multiplies words ... Eccl 10:14
The prophet is a *f* ... Hos 9:7
says, You *f* ... Matt 5:22
f-s and blind men ... Matt 23:17
wise, they became *f-s* ... Rom 1:22
f-s for Christ's sake ... 1 Cor 4:10

FOOLISH *silly, unwise*
O *f* and unwise ... Deut 32:6
a *f* son is a grief ... Prov 10:1
False and *f visions* ... Lam 2:14
Woe to the *f* ... Ezek 13:3
f took their lamps ... Matt 25:3
O *f* men and slow ... Luke 24:25
he must become *f* ... 1 Cor 3:18
You *f* Galatians ... Gal 3:1
do not be *f* ... Eph 5:17

FOOLISHNESS *folly*
The naive inherit *f* ... Prov 14:18
folly of fools is *f* ... Prov 14:24
mouth is speaking *f* ... Is 9:17
f of God is wiser ... 1 Cor 1:25
is *f* before God ... 1 Cor 3:19

FOOT *part of body*
she lay at his *feet* ... Ruth 3:14
six toes on each *f* ... 2 Sam 21:20
pierced...my *feet* ... Ps 22:16
the *f* of pride ... Ps 36:11
lamp to my *feet* ... Ps 119:105
their *feet* run to evil ... Prov 1:16
signals with his *feet* ... Prov 6:13
beautiful...your *feet* ... Song 7:1
feet of the afflicted ... Is 26:6
feet...polished bronze ... Dan 10:6
dust off your *feet* ... Matt 10:14
Bind...hand and *f* ... Matt 22:13
f causes you to ... Mark 9:45
kissing His *feet* ... Luke 7:38
anointed the *feet* ... John 12:3
the disciples' *feet* ... John 13:5
beautiful...the *feet* ... Rom 10:15
Satan under...*feet* ... Rom 16:20
worship at the *feet* ... Rev 22:8

FOOTSTEPS *path*
make His *f* into a way ... Ps 85:13
f of Your anointed ... Ps 89:51
my *f* in Your word ... Ps 119:133

FOOTSTOOL *foot support*
the *f* of our God ... 1 Chr 28:2
worship at His *f* ... Ps 99:5
Your enemies a *f* ... Ps 110:1
the earth is My *f* ... Is 66:1
sit down by my *f* ... James 2:3

FORBEARANCE *restraint*
By *f*...be persuaded ... Prov 25:15
in the *f* of God ... Rom 3:25

FORBID *prohibit*
if her father should *f* ... Num 30:5
f-ding to pay taxes ... Luke 23:2
do not *f* to speak ... 1 Cor 14:39
men who *f* marriage ... 1 Tim 4:3
he *f-s* those who ... 3 John 10

FORCE (n) *power, strength*
with a heavy *f* ... Num 20:20
captains of the *f-s* ... 2 Kin 25:23
use *f* against you ... Neh 13:21
commanders of the *f-s* ... Jer 43:5
with *f* and with ... Ezek 34:4

FORCE (v) *compel*
are *f-d* into bondage ... Neh 5:5
man *f-d* to labor ... Job 7:1
f-s you to go one mile ... Matt 5:41
not take...by *f* ... Luke 3:14
f them to blaspheme ... Acts 26:11
f-d to appeal to ... Acts 28:19

FORCED LABOR *work as tax*
Canaanites to *f* ... Josh 17:13
was over the *f* ... 2 Sam 20:24
will be put to *f* ... Prov 12:24

FORCED LABORERS
Solomon levied *f* ... 1 Kin 5:13
Solomon raised as *f* ... 2 Chr 8:8
men will become *f* ... Is 31:8

FORD *shallow place*
the *f* of the Jabbok ... Gen 32:22
the *f-s* of the Jordan ... Judg 12:5
f-s...been seized ... Jer 51:32

FOREFATHER *ancestor*
iniquity of their *f-s* ... Lev 26:40
Your first *f* sinned ... Is 43:27
I swore to your *f-s* ... Jer 11:5
Abraham, our *f* ... Rom 4:1
the way my *f-s* did ... 2 Tim 1:3

FOREHEAD *brow*
on his bald *f* ... Lev 13:42
stone...into his *f* ... 1 Sam 17:49
put a mark on the *f-s* ... Ezek 9:4
seal of God on their *f-s* ... Rev 9:4
on her *f* a name ... Rev 17:5

FOREIGN *alien, strange*
Put away the *f* gods ... Gen 35:2
sojourner in a *f* land ... Ex 2:22
sell her to a *f* people ... Ex 21:8
drank *f* waters ... 2 Kin 19:24
married *f* women ... Ezra 10:2
f armies to flight ... Heb 11:34

FOREIGNER *alien, stranger*
no *f* is to eat of it ... Ex 12:43
sell it to a *f* ... Deut 14:21
charge...a *f* ... Deut 23:20
since I am a *f* ... Ruth 2:10
a *f* in their sight ... Job 19:15
f-s entered his gate ... Obad 11

FOREKNEW *know beforehand*
whom He *f*, He also ... Rom 8:29
people whom he *f* ... Rom 11:2
He was *foreknown* ... 1 Pet 1:20

FOREKNOWLEDGE The power to know what will happen in the future. It is an attribute of God, and He has communicated some future events to His prophets. In regard to predestination (q.v.), foreknowledge is defined in different ways: 1) God's intimate knowledge of human beings in eternity past before He created them. 2) God's knowledge of what each person will do during the course of his life.
plan and *f* of God ... Acts 2:23
f of God the Father ... 1 Pet 1:2

FOREMOST *first*
f commandment ... Matt 22:38
among whom I am *f* ... 1 Tim 1:15

FORERUNNER *goes before* One who precedes another and prepares the way for him. Used of John the Baptist, who prepared the way for the coming of Jesus; and used of Jesus, who prepares the way for believers to communicate with the Father in prayer.
Jesus...as a *f* for ... Heb 6:20

FORESKIN
the flesh of your *f* ... Gen 17:11
cut off her son's *f* ... Ex 4:25
a hundred *f-s* ... 1 Sam 18:25
the *f-s* of your heart ... Jer 4:4

FOREST *woods*
f devoured more ... 2 Sam 18:8
the *f* of Lebanon ... 1 Kin 7:2
f will sing for joy ... 1 Chr 16:33
every beast of the *f* ... Ps 50:10
the glory of his *f* ... Is 10:18
beasts in the *f*, Come ... Is 56:9
a *f* is set aflame ... James 3:5

FORETOLD *predicted*
the Holy Spirit *f* ... Acts 1:16
just as Isaiah *f* ... Rom 9:29

FOREVER *always, eternal*
eat, and live *f* ... Gen 3:22
not strive with man *f* ... Gen 6:3
throne shall be...*f* ... 1 Chr 17:14
the LORD abides *f* ... Ps 9:7
LORD sits as King *f* ... Ps 29:10
glorify Your name *f* ... Ps 86:12
riches are not *f* ... Prov 27:24
One Who lives *f* ... Is 57:15
Christ is to remain *f* ... John 12:34
He...with you *f* ... John 14:16
He is able...to save *f* ... Heb 7:25
Son, made perfect *f* ... Heb 7:28
they will reign *f* ... Rev 22:5

FORFEIT *lose*
possessions...*f-ed* ... Ezra 10:8
f-s his own life ... Prov 20:2
f my head to the king ... Dan 1:10
and *f-s* his soul ... Matt 16:26

FORGET *forsake, neglect*
God has made me *f* ... Gen 41:51
that you do not *f* the LORD ... Deut 6:12
f-got the God who ... Deut 32:18
God *f-s*...iniquity ... Job 11:6
nations who *f* God ... Ps 9:17
needy...be *f-gotten* ... Ps 9:18
Do not *f* the afflicted ... Ps 10:12
They *f-got* His deeds ... Ps 78:11
do not *f* my teaching ... Prov 3:1
you will *f* the shame ... Is 54:4
My people *f* My name ... Jer 23:27
f-ting what *lies* behind ... Phil 3:13
f your work and ... Heb 6:10

FORGIVE *pardon*
f the transgression ... Gen 50:17
f their sin ... Ex 32:32
f our sins ... Ps 79:9
not *f* their iniquity ... Jer 18:23
f us our debts ... Matt 6:12
authority...to *f* sins ... Matt 9:6
f-gave him the debt ... Matt 18:27
can *f* sins but God ... Mark 2:7
he who is *f-n* little ... Luke 7:47
Father, *f* them ... Luke 23:34
whom you *f* ... 2 Cor 2:10
f-ing each other ... Eph 4:32
f-n us all our ... Col 2:13
righteous to *f* us ... 1 John 1:9

FORGIVENESS *pardon* God's withholding the penalty for sin when a believer confesses, because of the work of Christ on the cross and His present intercession with the Father in heaven.
a God of *f* ... Neh 9:17
there is *f* with You ... Ps 130:4
poured out...for *f* ... Matt 26:28
repentance for *f* ... Luke 24:47
receives *f* of sins ... Acts 10:43
f of our trespasses ... Eph 1:7
the *f* of sins ... Col 1:14
there is no *f* ... Heb 9:22

FORK *instrument*
a three-pronged *f* ... 1 Sam 2:13
His winnowing *f* ... Matt 3:12

FORM (n) *appearance, shape*
beautiful of *f* and ... Gen 29:17
the *f* of the LORD ... Num 12:8
image in the *f* ... Deut 4:23
like the *f* of a man ... Is 44:13
in a different *f* ... Mark 16:12
bodily *f* like a dove ... Luke 3:22
f of corruptible man ... Rom 1:23
existed in the *f* of God ... Phil 2:6

FORM (v) *fashion, shape*
f-ed man of dust ... Gen 2:7
f-ed the dry land ... Ps 95:5
f-ed my inward parts ... Ps 139:13
One *f-ing* light ... Is 45:7
who *f-s* mountains ... Amos 4:13
f-s the spirit of man ... Zech 12:1
plot was *f-ed* against ... Acts 20:3
Christ is *f-ed* in you ... Gal 4:19

FORMATION *rank*
in *f* against ... 1 Chr 19:17
battle *f* in the ... 2 Chr 14:10

FORMLESS *without form*
earth was *f* and void ... Gen 1:2
behold, *it was f* ... Jer 4:23

FORNICATION Any sexual intercourse other than that between husband and wife.
f-s, thefts, false ... Matt 15:19
were not born of *f* ... John 8:41
strangled and from *f* ... Acts 15:29

FORNICATORS
neither *f*, nor ... 1 Cor 6:9
f...God will judge ... Heb 13:4

FORSAKE
Then he *f-sook* God ... Deut 32:15
not fail you or *f* you ... Josh 1:5
f-sook the law of the ... 2 Chr 12:1
f Him, He will *f* you ... 2 Chr 15:2
God has not *f-n* us ... Ezra 9:9
why have You *f-n* me ... Ps 22:1
not *f* your mother's ... Prov 1:8
wicked *f* his way ... Is 55:7
Your sons have *f-n* Me ... Jer 5:7
f the idols of Egypt ... Ezek 20:8
have You *f-n* Me ... Matt 27:46
persecuted...not *f-n* ... 2 Cor 4:9
f-ing...assembling ... Heb 10:25
nor will I ever *f* you ... Heb 13:5

FORTIFICATIONS *stronghold*
the unassailable *f* ... Is 25:12
your *f* are fig trees ... Nah 3:12

FORTIFIED *walled*
live in the *f* cities ... Num 32:17
f with high walls ... Deut 3:5
strike every *f* city ... 2 Kin 3:19
f cities into ... Is 37:26

FORTRESS *stronghold*
God is my strong *f* ... 2 Sam 22:33
my rock and my *f* ... Ps 18:2
My refuge and my *f* ... Ps 91:2
wealth is his *f* ... Prov 10:15
f-es will be destroyed ... Hos 10:14

FORTUNE *one's lot*
and the *f-s* of Israel ... Jer 33:7
f-s of My people ... Hos 6:11
restore their *f* ... Zeph 2:7

FORTY *number*
f days and *f* nights ... Gen 7:4
flood...for *f* days ... Gen 7:17
ate the manna *f* years ... Ex 16:35
with the LORD *f* days ... Ex 34:28
fasted *f* days and *f* ... Matt 4:2
f days being tempted ... Mark 1:13

FOUL *putrid, rotten*
Nile will become *f* ... Ex 7:18
My wounds grow *f* ... Ps 38:5
f with your feet ... Ezek 34:19

FOUNDATION *establishment*
f-s of heaven were ... 2 Sam 22:8
I laid the *f* of the ... Job 38:4
the *f* of His throne ... Ps 97:2
the earth upon its *f-s* ... Ps 104:5
an everlasting *f* ... Prov 10:25
cornerstone *for* the *f* ... Is 28:16
a *f* on the rock ... Luke 6:48
the firm *f* of God ... 2 Tim 2:19
laid the *f* ... Heb 1:10
a *f* of repentance ... Heb 6:1

FOUNDATION GATE *see* **GATES OF JERUSALEM**

FOUNDED *established*
the day it was *f* ... Ex 9:18
f it upon the seas ... Ps 24:2
by wisdom *f* the earth ... Prov 3:19
f His vaulted dome ... Amos 9:6
f on the rock ... Matt 7:25

FOUNTAIN *spring, well*
f-s of the great deep ... Gen 7:11
is the *f* of life ... Ps 36:9
The *f* of wisdom ... Prov 18:4
f of living waters ... Jer 2:13

FOUNTAIN GATE *see* **GATES OF JERUSALEM**

FOWL *bird*
and fattened *f* ... 1 Kin 4:23
things and winged *f* ... Ps 148:10

FOX *small animal*
three hundred *f-es* ... Judg 15:4
f-es that are ruining ... Song 2:15
like *f-es* among ruins ... Ezek 13:4
The *f-es* have holes ... Matt 8:20
Go and tell that *f* ... Luke 13:32

FRAGMENTS *pieces*
forth His ice as *f* ... Ps 147:17

Gather up the...*f* ... John 6:12
twelve baskets with *f* ... John 6:13

FRAGRANCE *pleasant aroma*
oils have a pleasing *f* ... Song 1:3
given forth *their f* ... Song 2:13
f like *the cedars* ... Hos 14:6
we are a *f* of Christ ... 2 Cor 2:15

FRAME *structure*
f-s of the tabernacle ... Num 3:36
with *artistic f-s* ... 1 Kin 6:4
He...knows our *f* ... Ps 103:14
My *f* was not hidden ... Ps 139:15

FRANKINCENSE *spice* A fragrant gum resin obtained from certain trees, frequently associated with myrrh. It was used in the making of perfume and in sacrifices and fumigation.
spices with pure *f* ... Ex 30:34
f and the spices ... 1 Chr 9:29
trees of *f* ... Song 4:14
gold, *f*, and myrrh ... Matt 2:11

FREE *at liberty*
she is not to go *f* ... Ex 21:7
be *f* from the oath ... Josh 2:20
let the oppressed go *f* ... Is 58:6
will make you *f* ... John 8:32
who has died is *f-d* ... Rom 6:7
the *f* gift of God ... Rom 6:23
f from the law ... Rom 8:2
Christ set us *f* ... Gal 5:1
whether slave or *f* ... Eph 6:8

FREEDOM *liberty* In the NT, often of two kinds: 1) power over the sin nature, i.e. the ability to resist temptation and do what is right instead; 2) freedom from the obligation to follow OT law and Jewish religious tradition. The latter is not a license to sin—rather, the believer is to be guided in his behavior by the Holy Spirit who indwells him.
proclaim...*f* to ... Is 61:1
f of the glory ... Rom 8:21
you were called to *f* ... Gal 5:13
do not use your *f* as ... 1 Pet 2:16

FREEWILL The capacity of humans as moral agents to exercise choice.

FREEWILL OFFERINGS *see* **OFFERINGS**

FRESH *new, recently prepared*
found a *f* jawbone ... Judg 15:15
anointed with *f* oil ... Ps 92:10
f water from your ... Prov 5:15
new wine into *f* ... Mark 2:22
f and bitter *water* ... James 3:11

FRIEND *companion, comrade*
man speaks to his *f* ... Ex 33:11
f-s are my scoffers ... Job 16:20
loved ones and my *f-s* ... Ps 38:11
my familiar *f* ... Ps 55:13
A *f* loves at all ... Prov 17:17
Wealth adds...*f-s* ... Prov 19:4
who blesses his *f* ... Prov 27:14
confidence in a *f* ... Mic 7:5
f of tax collectors ... Matt 11:19
F, your sins are ... Luke 5:20
f of the bridegroom ... John 3:29
his life for his *f-s* ... John 15:13
You are My *f-s*, if ... John 15:14

FRIENDSHIP
the *f* of God ... Job 29:4
f with the world ... James 4:4

FRIGHTEN *terrify*
to *f them* away ... Deut 28:26
You *f* me ... Job 7:14
I was *f-ed* and fell ... Dan 8:17
wars, do not be *f-ed* ... Mark 13:7

FRINGE *edge*
the *f-s* of His ways ... Job 26:14
touched the *f* of His ... Matt 9:20

FROGS
smite...with *f* ... Ex 8:2
f which destroyed ... Ps 78:45
land swarmed with *f* ... Ps 105:30
unclean spirits like *f* ... Rev 16:13

FRONTALS *prayer bands*
they shall be as *f* ... Deut 6:8
f on your forehead ... Deut 11:18
see also **PHYLACTERIES**

FROST *freezing*
and the *f* by night ... Gen 31:40
fine as the *f* ... Ex 16:14
sycamore trees with *f* ... Ps 78:47

FRUIT *growth, produce* Metaphorically, good or bad behavior, which serves as evidence of one's intentions and claims. The *fruit* of the Spirit (Gal 5:22) refers specifically to qualities possessed by a Christian.
f trees...bearing *f* ... Gen 1:11
she took from its *f* ... Gen 3:6
the *f* of the womb ... Gen 30:2
offering of first *f-s* ... Lev 2:12
its *f* in its season ... Ps 1:3
yield *f* in old age ... Ps 92:14
eat its choice *f-s* ... Song 4:16
eaten the *f* of lies ... Hos 10:13
know...by their *f-s* ... Matt 7:16
bad tree bears bad *f* ... Matt 7:17
f for life eternal ... John 4:36
the *f* of the Spirit ... Gal 5:22
f in every good work ... Col 1:10

FRUITFUL *productive*
be *f* and multiply ... Gen 9:7
were *f* and increased ... Ex 1:7
gather a *f* harvest ... Ps 107:37
into the *f* land ... Jer 2:7
f labor for me ... Phil 1:22

FRUSTRATE *counteract*
to *f* their counsel ... Ezra 4:5
He *f-s* the plotting ... Job 5:12
plans are *f-d* ... Prov 15:22

FUEL *that which burns*
people are like *f* ... Is 9:19
You will be *f* ... Ezek 21:32

FUGITIVE *one who flees*
do not betray the *f* ... Is 16:3
Meet the *f* with bread ... Is 21:14
gather the *f-s* ... Jer 49:5

FULFILL *complete*
to *f* the word ... 2 Chr 36:21
May the LORD *f* all ... Ps 20:5
f-ing His word ... Ps 148:8
to *f* the vision ... Dan 11:14
the prophet was *f-ed* ... Matt 2:17
to abolish, but to *f* ... Matt 5:17
The time is *f-ed* ... Mark 1:15
f-ed in the kingdom ... Luke 22:16
Scripture...be *f-ed* ... John 13:18
husband must *f* his duty ... 1 Cor 7:3
f the law of Christ ... Gal 6:2
f your ministry ... 2 Tim 4:5

FULFILLMENT *completion*
the *f* of every vision ... Ezek 12:23
f of what had been ... Luke 1:45
f of *the* law ... Rom 13:10

FULL *complete, whole*
I went out *f* ... Ruth 1:21
The earth is *f* of ... Ps 33:5
until the *f* day ... Prov 4:18
twelve *f* baskets ... Matt 14:20
f of dead...bones ... Matt 23:27
f of the Holy Spirit ... Luke 4:1
also is *f* of light ... Luke 11:34
f of grace and truth ... John 1:14
f of the Spirit ... Acts 6:3
f armor of God ... Eph 6:11
f of compassion ... James 5:11

FULLER *one who bleaches cloth* 1) A field located somewhere outside Jerusalem. 2) A person who shrinks or thickens cloth, especially wool.
of the *f-'s* field ... 2 Kin 18:17
like *f-s'* soap ... Mal 3:2

FULLNESS *completeness*
Your presence is *f* of ... Ps 16:11
His *f* we...received ... John 1:16
the *f* of the Gentiles ... Rom 11:25
f of the time came ... Gal 4:4
all the *f* of God ... Eph 3:19
f to dwell in Him ... Col 1:19
the *f* of Deity dwells ... Col 2:9

FURIOUS *angry*
Pharaoh was *f* ... Gen 41:10
became *f* and very ... Neh 4:1
king became...*f* ... Dan 2:12

FURNACE *oven*
As silver tried in a *f* ... Ps 12:6
the *f* of affliction ... Is 48:10
into the midst of a *f* ... Dan 3:6
throw them into the *f* ... Matt 13:42
to glow in a *f* ... Rev 1:15

FURNISH *supply*
f-ed with silver bands ... Ex 38:17
shall *f* him liberally ... Deut 15:14
f-ing every kind ... Ps 144:13
upper room *f-ed* ... Mark 14:15

FURROWS *trench* Grooves made in the soil by a plow; used for irrigation.
its *f* weep together ... Job 31:38
water its *f* ... Ps 65:10
weeds in the *f* ... Hos 10:4

FURY *anger*
brother's *f* subsides ... Gen 27:44
terrify them in His *f* ... Ps 2:5
plucked up in *f* ... Ezek 19:12
the *f* of a fire ... Heb 10:27

FUTILE *useless, vain*
go after *f* things ... 1 Sam 12:21
devise *f* things ... Acts 4:25
f in...speculations ... Rom 1:21

FUTURE *that which is ahead*
discern their *f* ... Deut 32:29
no *f* for the evil ... Prov 24:20

is hope for your *f* ... Jer 31:17
foundation for the *f* ... 1 Tim 6:19

G

GABRIEL *(God is powerful).* The angel who had the special ministry to deliver messages to Daniel, Zacharias, and Mary.
angel of high rank ... Dan 8:16;9:21; Luke 1:19,26

GAD *(fortune).* 1) One of the twelve sons of Jacob; his descendants and a territory in the Promised Land. 2) A prophet in the time of David.
1 *son of Jacob* ... Gen 30:11;35:26
2 *tribe of* ... Num 1:25;2:14
3 *valley* ... 2 Sam 24:5
4 *seer, prophet* ... 2 Sam 24:11,18

GAIETY *cheerfulness*
g...is banished ... Is 24:11
an end to all her *g* ... Hos 2:11

GAIN (n) *profit, increase*
hate dishonest *g* ... Ex 18:21
Ill-gotten *g-s* do not ... Prov 10:2
who rejects unjust *g* ... Is 33:15
greedy for *g* ... Jer 6:13
to die is *g* ... Phil 1:21
fond of sordid *g* ... 1 Tim 3:8

GAIN (v) *acquire*
they might *g* insight ... Neh 8:13
have *g-ed* the victory ... Ps 98:1
he will *g* knowledge ... Prov 19:25
will *g* ascendancy ... Dan 11:5
g-s the whole world ... Matt 16:26
that I may *g* Christ ... Phil 3:8
may *g* the glory ... 2 Thess 2:14

GAIUS 1) Name of associates of Paul. 2) The person to whom the apostle John addressed his third letter.
1 *Macedonian* ... Acts 19:29
2 *companion of Paul* ... Acts 20:4
3 *Corinthian believer* ... 1 Cor 1:14
4 *addressee of 3 John* ... 3 John 1

GALATIA A Roman province in central Asia Minor. Several churches in Galatia were the recipients of Paul's Galatians letter.
province in Asia Minor ... 1 Cor 16:1; 2 Tim 4:10

GALE *storm*
dust before a *g* ... Is 17:13
a fierce *g* of wind ... Mark 4:37

GALILEE *(circuit, district).* The territory west of the Sea of Galilee and extending north and south of it, sometimes referred to as "Galilee of the Gentiles." It had been possessed by the Jewish tribes of Zebulun and Naphtali in OT times, but was conquered by Assyria in the eighth century B.C. and remained Gentile until the Maccabean revolt in the second century B.C. At that time the inhabitants were forced to convert to Judaism, and many did so only as a formality to escape execution.
district in N Palestine ... Josh 21:32; 1 Kin 9:11; Matt 2:22; Acts 10:37

GALILEE, SEA OF A fresh-water lake fed by the Jordan River. Also known as the Sea of Chinnereth, Lake of Gennesaret, and Sea of Tiberias. Some of the disciples fished there for a living; Jesus miraculously calmed it during a storm and walked on the water.
Sea of Galilee ... Matt 4:18; Mark 7:31

GALL *bitter herb, bitterness* That which is distasteful, specifically the bitter secretion of the liver (bile). Also a reference to the myrrh in the wine offered to Christ on the cross, probably because of its bitterness.
gave me *g* for my food ... Ps 69:21
drink...with *g* ... Matt 27:34
the *g* of bitterness ... Acts 8:23

GALLIO A government official in Achaia, a province of Greece.
governor of Achaia ... Acts 18:12,17

GALLOWS *for hanging* An instrument of capital punishment used in hanging.
Have a *g*...made ... Esth 5:14
hanged...on the *g* ... Esth 7:10
his sons...on the *g* ... Esth 9:25

GAMALIEL *(God is my reward).* 1) One of the heads in the tribe of Manasseh who assisted in the census. 2) A prominent member of the Sanhedrin and a Pharisee. He was a respected teacher of the Law under whom Paul was a student.
1 *head of tribe* ... Num 2:20;7:54
2 *Pharisee* ... Acts 5:34;22:3

GARDEN *planted area*
God walking in the *g* ... Gen 3:8
from the *g* of Eden ... Gen 3:23
Make my *g* breathe ... Song 4:16
plant *g-s*, and eat ... Jer 29:5
tabernacle like a *g* ... Lam 2:6
in the *g* with Him ... John 18:26
the *g* a new tomb ... John 19:41

GARLAND *ornament*
a *g* instead of ashes ... Is 61:3
brought...*g-s* to the ... Acts 14:13

GARMENT *clothing, dress*
God made *g-s* of skin ... Gen 3:21
caught him by his *g* ... Gen 39:12
in *g-s* of fine linen ... Gen 41:42
holy *g-s* for Aaron ... Ex 28:2
divide my *g-s* among ... Ps 22:18
on *g-s* of vengeance ... Is 59:17
g-s of glowing colors ... Is 63:1
g of camel's hair ... Matt 3:4
I just touch His *g-s* ... Mark 5:28
dividing up His *g-s* ... Luke 23:34
put his outer *g* on ... John 21:7
become old like a *g* ... Heb 1:11
clothed in white *g-s* ... Rev 3:5

GARRISON *defense* A post or fort used by the military.
g of the Philistines ... 1 Sam 13:4
the *g*...trembled ... 1 Sam 14:15
set *g-s* in the land ... 2 Chr 17:2

GATE *entry way* In ancient times, often a large opening or passageway in a wall protecting an enclosed grounds, building or city, e.g. the Sheep Gate in Jerusalem. City gates were also used often for commerce and the assembly of people.
is the *g* of heaven ... Gen 28:17
oppressed in the *g* ... Job 5:4
g-s with thanksgiving ... Ps 100:4
enter the *g-s* of Sheol ... Is 38:10
justice in the *g* ... Amos 5:15
Enter...narrow *g* ... Matt 7:13
g-s of Hades will ... Matt 16:18
did not open the *g* ... Acts 12:14

GATEKEEPERS *guards*
g for the camp ... 1 Chr 9:18
divisions of the *g* ... 1 Chr 26:12
The sons of the *g* ... Ezra 2:42
g, and the singers ... Neh 10:39

GATES OF JERUSALEM
alternate names in italics
1 **Beautiful Gate** ... Acts 3:10
East Gate
2 **Benjamin Gate** ... Jer 20:2; Zech 14:10
Gate of the Guard
Inspection Gate
Sheep Gate
3 **Corner Gate** ... 2 Kin 14:13; 2 Chr 26:9
4 **East Gate** ... Neh 3:29; Ezek 10:19; 44:1
Beautiful Gate
5 **Ephraim Gate** ... 2 Kin 14:13; Neh 8:16
Middle Gate
Old Gate
6 **First Gate** ... Zech 14:10
7 **Fish Gate** ... 2 Chr 33:14; Neh 3:3
8 **Foundation Gate** ... 2 Chr 23:5
Gate of Sur
9 **Fountain Gate** ... Neh 2:14; 12:37
gate between two walls ... 2 Kin 25:4; Jer 39:4
10 **Guard, Gate of the** ... Neh 12:39
Benjamin Gate
Inspection Gate
Sheep Gate
11 **Horse Gate** ... 2 Chr 23:15; Neh 3:28
12 **Inspection Gate** ... Neh 3:31
Benjamin Gate
Gate of the Guard
Sheep Gate
13 **Middle Gate** ... Jer 39:3
Ephraim Gate
Old Gate
14 **Old Gate** ... Neh 3:6; 12:39
Ephraim Gate
Middle Gate
15 **Refuse Gate** ... Neh 2:13; 12:31
16 **Sheep Gate** ... Neh 3:1
Benjamin Gate
Gate of the Guard
Inspection Gate
17 **Sur, Gate of** ... 2 Kin 11:6
Foundation Gate
18 **Valley Gate** ... 2 Chr 26:9; Neh 3:13
19 **Water Gate** ... Neh 3:26; 8:1,3,16

GATEWAY *entrance*
the *g* of the court ... Ex 40:8
the *g* of the peoples ... Ezek 26:2

GATH *(winepress).* One of the five principal Philistine cities, noted for being the home of the Anakim (giants).
Philistine city ... Josh 11:22; 1 Sam 17:23; 1 Chr 20:8

GATHER *assemble, collect*
g-ed to his people ... Gen 25:8
g stubble for straw ... Ex 5:12
He *g-s* the waters ... Ps 33:7
G My godly ones ... Ps 50:5
g all nations and ... Is 66:18
hen *g-s* her chicks ... Matt 23:37

elders...were *g-ed* ... Matt 26:3
g...His elect ... Mark 13:27
G up the leftover ... John 6:12

GAZA (unc, *stronghold).* An ancient city and one of the five principal Philistine cities, serving as the capital.
Philistine city ... Gen 10:19; Judg 16:1; Jer 47:5

GAZE (n) *view, glance*
Turn Your *g* away from ... Ps 39:13
let your *g* be fixed ... Prov 4:25
turning His *g* toward His ... Luke 6:20

GAZE (v) *look, stare*
man...*g-ing* at her ... Gen 24:21
and *g* after Moses ... Ex 33:8
eye *g-s* on their ... Job 17:2
LORD *g-d* upon the ... Ps 102:19
g-ing...into the sky ... Acts 1:10

GAZELLE *animal* (unc, *the one seeing clearly).* The smallest of the antelope found in the wilderness areas of Israel, noted for its grace and speed.
swift as the *g-s* ... 1 Chr 12:8
a *g* Or a young stag ... Song 2:17
like a hunted *g* ... Is 13:14

GEDALIAH *(Yahweh is great).* Friend and protector of Jeremiah whom the Babylonians appointed as governor over the poor who were left in the land of Judah. Also the name of several other individuals.
entrusted him to G ... Jer 39:14

GEDERAH
1 *town of Judah* ... Josh 15:36
2 *town of Benjamin* ... 1 Chr 12:4

GEHAZI *(valley of vision).* The young man who served the prophet Elisha.
servant of Elisha ... 2 Kin 4:12;5:20;8:4

GEHENNA *(valley of Hinnom).* Originally referred to a valley outside the southern boundary of old Jerusalem where children were once tortured and sacrificed in ritual worship of Moloch. Later, the valley served as a disposal area for burning refuse and became a symbol for the place of everlasting punishment, because its fires were always burning. In the NT it becomes a metaphor referring to the actual place of eternal punishment. It is almost always translated as "hell," which is otherwise known as the Lake of Fire (Matt 5:22; cf. Rev 19:20).

GEMARA *(tradition).* The part of the Talmud that constitutes commentary on the Mishnah (q.v.). It is made up of discussions and decisions of the rabbis regarding specific statements in the Mishnah.

GENEALOGY *family record* Official documents which detail a person's ancestry. These were of utmost importance in Jewish life because they determined an individual's status in society. Jesus' genealogies take on the additional importance of proving that He is a descendant of King David and a legitimate heir to the throne of Israel.
found the book of...*g* ... Neh 7:5
g of Jesus the Messiah ... Matt 1:1
and endless *g-ies* ... 1 Tim 1:4
whose *g* is not traced ... Heb 7:6

GENERATION *age, period* 1) The offspring of an individual. 2) A period of time, whether definite or indefinite. 3) Persons constituting a specific period as representing its traits. 4) People of a particular racial or ethnic identity.
this evil *g* ... Deut 1:35
the righteous *g* ... Ps 14:5
faithfulness to all *g-s* ... Ps 100:5
salvation to all *g-s* ... Is 51:8
this *g* seek for a sign ... Mark 8:12
g-s...not made known ... Eph 3:5
and perverse *g* ... Phil 2:15

GENEROUS *bountiful*
g will be blessed ... Prov 22:9
because I am *g* ... Matt 20:15
g...ready to share ... 1 Tim 6:18

GENNESARET
1 *lake* ... Luke 5:1
also **Sea of Chinnereth**
also **Sea of Galilee**
also **Sea of Tiberias**
2 *land or district* ... Matt 14:34; Mark 6:53

GENTILES *foreigners, non-Jews* Those who were not born as Jews and have not converted to Judaism through the rites and procedures required of a proselyte (convert).
Galilee of the *G* ... Matt 4:15
hand Him over to the *G* ... Matt 20:19
revelation to the *G* ... Luke 2:32
Why did the *G* rage ... Acts 4:25
salvation...to the *G* ... Rom 11:11
preach...among the *G* ... Gal 1:16

GENTLE *compassionate, mild*
g answer turns away ... Prov 15:1
I was like a *g* lamb ... Jer 11:19
Blessed are the *g* ... Matt 5:5
G, and mounted on ... Matt 21:5
a *g* and quiet spirit ... 1 Pet 3:4

GENTLENESS *kindness*
and a spirit of *g* ... 1 Cor 4:21
and *g* of Christ ... 2 Cor 10:1
g, self-control ... Gal 5:23
humility and *g,* with ... Eph 4:2

GERAR
Philistine city ... Gen 20:2;26:6

GERIZIM
mountain near Shechem ... Deut 11:29; Josh 8:33

GERSHOM *(be a sojourner).* The first son of Moses, who so named him because he was a sojourner in Midian. Also the name of two other men.
1 *son of Moses* ... Ex 2:22;18:3
2 *son of Levi* ... 1 Chr 6:16,43
3 *line of Phinehas* ... Ezra 8:2

GERSHON Eldest son of Levi; the sons of Gershon had charge of the fabrics of the tabernacle. The family of Asaph, renowned musicians in David's days, descended from Gershon.
son of Levi ... Gen 46:11; Ex 6:16

GETHSEMANE (Aram, *oil press*). The garden where Jesus prayed before His arrest. It was located on the slope of the Mount of Olives.
garden on Mount of Olives ... Matt 26:36; Mark 14:32

GEZER
Canaanite city of Ephraim ... Josh 10:33; 1 Kin 9:17

GHOST *spirit*
resort to idols and *g-s* ... Is 19:3
and said, It is a *g* ... Matt 14:26
it was a *g* ... Mark 6:49

GIANT
were born to the *g* ... 2 Sam 21:22
from the *g-s* ... 1 Chr 20:6

GIBEAH *(hill).* The name of several places, including a village in Judah where Habakkuk is said to be buried.
1 *village in Judah* ... Josh 15:57
2 *in Ephraim* ... Josh 24:33
3 *town of Benjamin* ... 1 Sam 10:26;13:2; 2 Sam 23:29

GIBEON Along with Aijalon, a place where miracles took place during a battle for the conquest of the Promised Land. At Joshua's command the sun stood still at Gibeon, and the moon in the valley of Aijalon.
town in Benjamin ... Josh 9:3,17; 1 Kin 3:5; 1 Chr 8:29

GIDEON *(cutter down).* One of the judges in Israel, also known as Jerubbaal. One of his many notable feats was defeating the Midianites, a victory which brought peace to the land for 40 years.
son of Joash ... Judg 6:11,36
judge ... Judg 8:4-21

GIFT *present* Sometimes refers to offerings. Gifts from God are undeserved blessings.
see also **CORBAN**
the sacred *g-s* ... Num 18:32
children are a *g* ... Ps 127:3
to Him *g-s* ... Matt 2:11
g of the Holy Spirit ... Acts 2:38
impart...spiritual *g* ... Rom 1:11
g of God is eternal ... Rom 6:23
desire...greater *g-s* ... 1 Cor 12:31
perfect *g* is from ... James 1:17

GIFT, SPIRITUAL A specific ability which God gives to every Christian miraculously by the Holy Spirit, for the benefit of other Christians in the church (1 Cor 12:4, 7).

GIHON *(stream).* A spring near Jerusalem where Solomon was anointed king and Hezekiah built his famous aqueduct. Also one of the four waterways in Eden.
1 *river of Eden* ... Gen 2:13
2 *Jerusalem spring* ... 2 Chr 32:30

GILBOA
mountain ... 2 Sam 1:6
where Saul died ... 2 Sam 21:12

GILEAD (unc, *mound of stones).* The name of three individuals. Also a region east of the Jordan River, known as Perea in NT times, and two other places.
1 *son of Machir* ... Num 36:1
2 *descendant of Gad* ... 1 Chr 5:14

3 *father of Jephthah* ... Judg 11:1
4 *land E of Jordan* ... Num 32:29
5 *mountain* ... Judg 7:3
6 *city* ... Hos 6:8

GILGAL *(circle of stones)*. The site where the Israelites first encamped in the Promised Land. Also the name of other places of uncertain location.
1 *in Arabah* ... Deut 11:30
2 *encampment in Jordan Valley* ... Josh 5:9; 1 Sam 7:16
near Jericho ... Josh 5:8,10
3 *in N Judah* ... Josh 15:7
4 *in Galilee* ... Josh 12:23
5 *village near Bethel* ... 2 Kin 2:1

GIRD *bind*
g him with the...band ... Ex 29:5
g up your loins like ... Job 38:3
g-ed me with gladness ... Ps 30:11
g-s herself with ... Prov 31:17
g-ed...with truth ... Eph 6:14
g-ed across His chest ... Rev 1:13

GIRDLE *belt, waistband*
man with a leather *g* ... 2 Kin 1:8
binds...with a *g* ... Job 12:18

GIRGASHITE(S)
Canaanite tribe ... Gen 10:16; Deut 7:1; Josh 24:11; Neh 9:8

GIRL *maiden*
the *g* and consult ... Gen 24:57
sold a *g* for wine ... Joel 3:3
boys and *g-s* playing ... Zech 8:5
the *g* has not died ... Matt 9:24

GIVE *bestow, yield*
g light on the earth ... Gen 1:17
g-n you every plant ... Gen 1:29
gave me from...tree ... Gen 3:12
in the land...God *g-s* ... Ex 20:12
I will *g* you rest ... Ex 33:14
g him to the LORD ... 1 Sam 1:11
G ear to my prayer ... Ps 17:1
gave me vinegar ... Ps 69:21
G me neither poverty ... Prov 30:8
a son will be *g-n* ... Is 9:6
gave birth to a Son ... Matt 1:25
G us this day ... Matt 6:11
g-ing thanks, He ... Matt 15:36
g you the keys ... Matt 16:19
authority...been *g-n* ... Matt 28:18
what will a man *g* ... Mark 8:37
body which is *g-n* ... Luke 22:19
gave His only...Son ... John 3:16
not as the world *g-s* ... John 14:27
gave up His spirit ... John 19:30
what I do have I *g* ... Acts 3:6
g-n among men ... Acts 4:12
more blessed to *g* ... Acts 20:35
was *g-n* me a thorn ... 2 Cor 12:7
always *g-ing* thanks ... Eph 5:20
who *gave* Himself ... 1 Tim 2:6
Every good thing *g-n* ... James 1:17
g-s a greater grace ... James 4:6
g-n us eternal life ... 1 John 5:11
to be *g-n* a mark ... Rev 13:16

GLAD *pleased*
g in his heart ... Ex 4:14
joy and a *g* heart ... Deut 28:47
righteous see...are *g* ... Job 22:19
Be *g* in the LORD ... Ps 32:11
g when they said ... Ps 122:1
son makes a father *g* ... Prov 10:1
Rejoice, and be *g* ... Matt 5:12
Be *g* in that day ... Luke 6:23

GLADNESS *joy*
celebrate...with *g* ... Neh 12:27
g...for the Jews ... Esth 8:17
Serve the LORD with *g* ... Ps 100:2
g and sincerity of ... Acts 2:46
With the oil of *g* ... Heb 1:9

GLASS *crystal*
or *g* cannot equal ... Job 28:17
sea of *g*, like crystal ... Rev 4:6

GLEAM *brilliance*
awesome *g* of crystal ... Ezek 1:22
g of a Tarshish stone ... Ezek 10:9
g of polished bronze ... Dan 10:6

GLEAN *gather, pick* The right of the poor and needy to gather grain or grapes remaining after a harvest. By OT law, farmers were not to harvest the extreme corners of their fields, but to leave them for gleaning.
Nor shall you *g* ... Lev 19:10
Do not go to *g* ... Ruth 2:8
she *g-ed* in the field ... Ruth 2:17
g the vineyard ... Job 24:6
g-ing ears of grain ... Is 17:5

GLOOM *darkness*
cloud and thick *g* ... Deut 4:11
The land of utter *g* ... Job 10:22
darkness and *g* and ... Heb 12:18
and your joy to *g* ... James 4:9

GLORIFY *honor, worship*
g Your name forever ... Ps 86:12
Let the LORD be *g-ied* ... Is 66:5
g your Father ... Matt 5:16
shepherds...*g-ing* ... Luke 2:20
Jesus...not yet *g-ied* ... John 7:39
Father, *g* Your name ... John 12:28
God is *g-ied* in Him ... John 13:31
were all *g-ing* God ... Acts 4:21
Gentiles to *g* God ... Rom 15:9
g God in your body ... 1 Cor 6:20
did not *g* Himself ... Heb 5:5

GLORIOUS *exalted, great*
g name be blessed ... Neh 9:5
G things are spoken ... Ps 87:3
resting place will be *g* ... Is 11:10
the law great and *g* ... Is 42:21
g gospel of...God ... 1 Tim 1:11

GLORY (n) *honor, splendor* The Heb word has the idea of "weight" or 'honor." The glory of God appeared visibly to Israel in the form of a pillar of cloud or fire. In the NT, glory may be either physical or spiritual.
show me Your *g* ... Ex 33:18
while My *g* is passing ... Ex 33:22
Tell of His *g* ... 1 Chr 16:24
King of *g* may come ... Ps 24:7
exchanged their *g* ... Ps 106:20
earth is full of His *g* ... Is 6:3
their *g* into shame ... Hos 4:7
Solomon in all his *g* ... Matt 6:29
g of the Lord shone ... Luke 2:9
G...in the highest ... Luke 2:14
He comes in His *g* ... Luke 9:26
do not seek My *g* ... John 8:50
short of the *g* of God ... Rom 3:23
all to the *g* of God ... 1 Cor 10:31
eternal weight of *g* ... 2 Cor 4:17
body of His *g* ... Phil 3:21
crowned Him with *g* ... Heb 2:7
unfading crown of *g* ... 1 Pet 5:4

GLORY (v) *exalt*
And *g* in Your praise ... 1 Chr 16:35
G in His holy name ... Ps 105:3
in Him they will *g* ... Jer 4:2
I...have reason to *g* ... Phil 2:16

GLUTTON *excessive eater*
g...come to poverty ... Prov 23:21
a companion of *g-s* ... Prov 28:7
evil beasts, lazy *g-s* ... Titus 1:12

GNASH *grind*
They *g-ed* at me ... Ps 35:16
He will *g* his teeth ... Ps 112:10
They hiss and *g* ... Lam 2:16
g-ing their teeth ... Acts 7:54

GNASHING The grinding together of the teeth to express extreme anger or anguish.

GNAT *insect*
dust...became *g-s* ... Ex 8:17
swarm of flies...*g-s* ... Ps 105:31
strain out a *g* and ... Matt 23:24

GNOSTICISM A word not found in the Bible, referring to a cult that was prominent in the second century A.D. and probably earlier in less developed forms. Many believe that John had this cult partly in mind when he wrote the first few verses of 1 John and that other passages in scripture also address the cult directly or indirectly. It was a very complicated and loosely organized set of beliefs with thirty or so variant forms, but two of the key doctrines were: 1) physical matter is inherently evil and spirit is good; therefore Christ did not really assume human form, which would have polluted Him, but only appeared to do so. 2) The creator god of the OT is not the same as the god of the NT, but a lesser deity who is incapable of creating a perfect world and has fits of anger, vindictiveness, etc.

GO *move, proceed*
Let My people *g* ... Ex 7:16
God who *g-es* before ... Deut 1:30
where you *g*, I will *g* ... Ruth 1:16
the way he should *g* ... Prov 22:6
g one mile, *g*...two ... Matt 5:41
G into all...world ... Mark 16:15
I *g* to prepare a ... John 14:2
night is almost *gone* ... Rom 13:12

GOADS *inducements* Sticks with points on one end to drive or guide oxen.
wise men are like *g* ... Eccl 12:11
kick against the *g* ... Acts 26:14

GOAL *end, object*
press on toward the *g* ... Phil 3:14
g...is love ... 1 Tim 1:5

GOAT *animal*
a young *g* from the flock ... Gen 38:17
curtains of *g-s' hair* ... Ex 26:7
not boil a young *g*...milk ... Ex 34:26
g for a sin offering ... Num 15:27
prepare a young *g* for you ... Judg 13:15

quilt of *g-s' hair* ... 1 Sam 19:13
g had a...horn ... Dan 8:5
shaggy *g represents* ... Dan 8:21
sheep from the *g-s* ... Matt 25:32
never given me a young *g* ... Luke 15:29
blood of *g-s*...bulls ... Heb 9:13

GOD *Deity, Eternal One* The uncreated and supreme triune Being (*see* **TRINITY**), Creator and Sustainer of all things, who is infinite and eternal in all aspects of His person.
In the beginning *G* ... Gen 1:1
G formed man of dust ... Gen 2:7
G sent him out ... Gen 3:23
G gave to Abraham ... Gen 28:4
tablets were *G-'s* work ... Ex 32:16
G is my...fortress ... 2 Sam 22:33
G of my salvation ... Ps 18:46
In *G*...put my trust ... Ps 56:4
Search me, O *G* ... Ps 139:23
word of *G* is tested ... Prov 30:5
servant of the living *G* ... Dan 6:20
I am *G* and not man ... Hos 11:9
Will a man rob *G* ... Mal 3:8
G descending...dove ... Matt 3:16
they shall see *G* ... Matt 5:8
What...*G* has joined ... Matt 19:6
kingdom of *G* is at ... Mark 1:15
My *G*, why have ... Mark 15:34
You the Son of *G* ... Luke 22:70
the Word was *G* ... John 1:1
No one has seen *G* ... John 1:18
the Lamb of *G* ... John 1:29
G so loved the world ... John 3:16
G is spirit ... John 4:24
voice of...Son of *G* ... John 5:25
obey *G* rather than ... Acts 5:29
judgment of *G* ... Rom 2:2
bear fruit for *G* ... Rom 7:4
we are children of *G* ... Rom 8:16
are a temple of *G* ... 1 Cor 3:16
full armor of *G* ... Eph 6:11
one *G*...one mediator ... 1 Tim 2:5
is inspired by *G* ... 2 Tim 3:16
word of *G* is...sharper ... Heb 4:12
impossible...*G* to lie ... Heb 6:18
G is love ... 1 John 4:8
great supper of *G* ... Rev 19:17

GOD *false deity, idols*
no other *g-s* before Me ... Ex 20:3
New *g-s* were chosen ... Judg 5:8
cast their *g-s* into ... Is 37:19
bowed...to other *g-s* ... Jer 22:9
no other *g* who is ... Dan 3:29
The voice of a *g* ... Acts 12:22
g-s...become like ... Acts 14:11
the *g* of this world ... 2 Cor 4:4

GOD, SON OF *see* **SON OF GOD**

GODDESS *female deity*
Ashtoreth the *g* of ... 1 Kin 11:5
great *g* Artemis ... Acts 19:27
blasphemers of...*g* ... Acts 19:37

GODLESS *pagan, without God*
hope of the *g* will ... Job 8:13
joy of...*g* momentary ... Job 20:5
g man destroys his ... Prov 11:9
hands of *g* men ... Acts 2:23
become of the *g* ... 1 Pet 4:18

GODLINESS *holiness*
in all *g* and dignity ... 1 Tim 2:2
the mystery of *g* ... 1 Tim 3:16
g is profitable ... 1 Tim 4:8
to a form of *g* ... 2 Tim 3:5
g, brotherly kindness ... 2 Pet 1:7

GODLY *holy*
keeps...His *g* ones ... 1 Sam 2:9
g man ceases to be ... Ps 12:1
not forsake His *g* ones ... Ps 37:28
and *g* sincerity ... 2 Cor 1:12
to live *g* in Christ ... 2 Tim 3:12
rescue the *g* from ... 2 Pet 2:9

GOG The ruler of Magog and chief prince of Meshech and Tubal, prophetically described as invading Israel in the last days. Also a son of Shemaiah the Reubenite.
1 *a Reubenite* ... 1 Chr 5:4
2 *prince of Meshech and Tubal* ... Ezek 38:2
3 *symbol of godless nations* ... Rev 20:8
see also **MAGOG**

GOLAN
city of refuge ... Josh 21:27
a Levitical city ... 1 Chr 6:71

GOLD *precious metal*
g of that land is good ... Gen 2:12
mercy seat of pure *g* ... Ex 25:17
Almighty...be your *g* ... Job 22:25
more desirable than *g* ... Ps 19:10
refine them like *g* ... Mal 3:3
to Him gifts of *g* ... Matt 2:11
Do not acquire *g* ... Matt 10:9
Divine Nature...*g* ... Acts 17:29
coveted no...*g* ... Acts 20:33
city was pure *g* ... Rev 21:18

GOLDSMITH *gold craftsman*
g-s and...merchants ... Neh 3:32
g, and he makes it ... Is 46:6

GOLGOTHA (Aram, *skull*) Name for the place where Jesus Christ was crucified, also called Calvary (Lat, *skull*).
site of Crucifixion ... Matt 27:33; Mark 15:22; John 19:17

GOLIATH (unc, *conspicuous*). A Philistine giant who for forty days mocked the Israelites. Slain by David.
Philistine giant ... 1 Sam 17:4,23;21:9; 1 Chr 20:5

GOMER (unc, *complete, accomplished*). 1) The firstborn son of Japheth, or grandson of Noah. 2) A people or country to whom Ezekiel refers. 3) The prostitute whom Hosea was instructed by the Lord to marry as a lesson to Israel.
1 *son of Japheth* ... Gen 10:2
2 *group of people* ... Ezek 38:6
3 *wife of Hosea* ... Hos 1:3

GOMORRAH (unc, *tyranny*). A city located near the Dead Sea, and along with several other cities destroyed by God for its wickedness.
city of Jordan plain ... Gen 10:19; 14:10; 19:24
probably S of Dead Sea ... Is 13:19; 2 Pet 2:6

GOOD *complete, right*
God saw that it was *g* ... Gen 1:18
knowledge of *g* and ... Gen 2:9
Proclaim *g* tidings ... 1 Chr 16:23
Do not withhold *g* ... Prov 3:27
joyful heart is *g* ... Prov 17:22
planted in *g* soil ... Ezek 17:8
feed in...*g* pasture ... Ezek 34:18
Seek *g* and not evil ... Amos 5:14
how to give *g* gifts ... Matt 7:11
Well done, *g* and ... Matt 25:23
sown on the *g* soil ... Mark 4:20
Salt is *g* ... Mark 9:50
No one is *g* except ... Luke 18:19
I am the *g* shepherd ... John 10:11
men of *g* reputation ... Acts 6:3
perseverance in...*g* ... Rom 2:7
nothing *g*...in me ... Rom 7:18
work together for *g* ... Rom 8:28
who bring *g* news ... Rom 10:15
overcome evil...*g* ... Rom 12:21
is of *g* repute ... Phil 4:8
g hope by grace ... 2 Thess 2:16
Fight the *g* fight ... 1 Tim 6:12
tasted the *g* word ... Heb 6:5

GOODNESS *excellence, value*
My *g* pass before you ... Ex 33:19
Surely *g*...will follow ... Ps 23:6
How great is Your *g* ... Ps 31:19
kindness, *g* ... Gal 5:22
every desire for *g* ... 2 Thess 1:11

GOODS *possessions, supplies*
the *g* for yourself ... Gen 14:21
have acquired...*g* ... Ezek 38:12

GORE *stab*
if an ox *g-s* a man ... Ex 21:28
g the Arameans ... 1 Kin 22:11

GOSHEN The northeast portion of the Nile delta where the Israelites settled and thrived when Joseph was prime minister of Egypt. Also a region or town in Judah.
1 *district of Egypt in Nile Delta* ... Gen 45:10; 47:6,27
2 *S Judah region* ... Josh 10:41
3 *town in Judah* ... Josh 15:51

GOSPEL *(good news)*. The message of salvation in Jesus Christ. Also a name shared by the first four books of the New Testament.
proclaiming the *g* of ... Matt 4:23
preach the *g* to all ... Mark 16:15
not ashamed of the *g* ... Rom 1:16
if our *g* is veiled ... 2 Cor 4:3
or a different *g* ... 2 Cor 11:4
distort the *g* of Christ ... Gal 1:7
g of your salvation ... Eph 1:13
g of peace ... Eph 6:15
defense of the *g* ... Phil 1:16
the hope of the *g* ... Col 1:23
eternal *g* to preach ... Rev 14:6

GOSSIP *babbler*
associate with a *g* ... Prov 20:19
malice; *they are g-s* ... Rom 1:29
g-s and busybodies ... 1 Tim 5:13

GOVERN *rule*
light to *g* the day ... Gen 1:16
light to *g* the night ... Gen 1:16
when the judges *g-ed* ... Ruth 1:1

GOVERNMENT *authority, rule*
g...on His shoulders ... Is 9:6
be no end to...*His g* ... Is 9:7

GOVERNOR *ruler*
not offer it to your *g* ... Mal 1:8
brought before *g-s* ... Matt 10:18
g was quite amazed ... Matt 27:14
Pilate was *g* of Judea ... Luke 3:1
g over Egypt ... Acts 7:10

GRACE *benevolence, favor* God's gift of good things which are not deserved, especially salvation.
G is poured upon Your ... Ps 45:2
g to the afflicted ... Prov 3:34
g of God was upon ... Luke 2:40
full of *g* and truth ... John 1:14
g abounded...more ... Rom 5:20
g of our Lord Jesus ... Rom 16:20
My *g* is sufficient ... 2 Cor 12:9
by *g* you have been ... Eph 2:8
justified by His *g* ... Titus 3:7
to the throne of *g* ... Heb 4:16
g to the humble ... James 4:6

GRACIOUS *kind*
God be *g* to you ... Gen 43:29
g to whom I will be ... Ex 33:19
a *g* and...God ... Neh 9:31
Be *g* to me, O LORD ... Ps 6:2
and *g*, Slow to anger ... Ps 86:15
g to a poor man ... Prov 19:17
be *g* to...remnant ... Amos 5:15

GRAFT *insert, join*
I might be *g-ed* in ... Rom 11:19
God is able to *g* ... Rom 11:23
g-ed into their own ... Rom 11:24

GRAIN
Joseph stored up *g* ... Gen 41:49
glean among the...*g* ... Ruth 2:2
g...for your enemies ... Is 62:8
then the mature *g* ... Mark 4:28
g of wheat falls ... John 12:24

GRAIN OFFERING *see* **OFFERINGS**

GRANDCHILDREN
G are the crown of ... Prov 17:6
widow has...or *g* ... 1 Tim 5:4

GRANDDAUGHTER
g-s, and all his ... Gen 46:7
g of Omri king of ... 2 Kin 8:26

GRANDSON
g might fear the LORD ... Deut 6:2
sons and thirty *g-s* ... Judg 12:14
master's *g* shall eat ... 2 Sam 9:10

GRANT *give, provide*
g this people favor ... Ex 3:21
have *g-ed* me life ... Job 10:12
g us Your salvation ... Ps 85:7
G that we may sit ... Mark 10:37
Father has *g-ed* Me ... Luke 22:29
g repentance to ... Acts 5:31
g-ing...deliverance ... Acts 7:25

GRAPE *fruit*
nor eat...dried *g-s* ... Num 6:3
of *g-s* you drank ... Deut 32:14
when the *g* harvest is ... Is 24:13
G-s are not gathered ... Matt 7:16
g-s from a briar ... Luke 6:44

GRASP *hold, seize*
hands *g* the spindle ... Prov 31:19
He who *g-s* the bow ... Amos 2:15
a thing to be *g-ed* ... Phil 2:6

GRASS *vegetation*
g springs out ... 2 Sam 23:4
his days are like *g* ... Ps 103:15
dry *g* collapses into ... Is 5:24
g withers, the flower ... Is 40:7
was given *g* to eat ... Dan 5:21
if God so clothes...*g* ... Matt 6:30
All flesh is like *g* ... 1 Pet 1:24
not to hurt the *g* ... Rev 9:4

GRASSHOPPER *insect*
the *g* in its kinds ... Lev 11:22
we became like *g-s* ... Num 13:33
inhabitants are like *g-s* ... Is 40:22

GRATITUDE *thankfulness*
overflowing with *g* ... Col 2:7
is received with *g* ... 1 Tim 4:4
let us show *g* ... Heb 12:28

GRAVE *sepulchre, tomb*
pillar of Rachel's *g* ... Gen 35:20
throat is an open *g* ... Ps 5:9
I will open your *g-s* ... Ezek 37:12
I will prepare your *g* ... Nah 1:14
made the *g* secure ... Matt 27:66

GRAVEN IMAGE *sculptured* An image or idol of various materials crafted by man to serve as an object of worship. One of the more infamous examples was the golden calf made during the exodus.
make...a *g* ... Deut 4:23
ashamed who serve *g* ... Ps 97:7
praise to *g* ... Is 42:8

GRAY *color*
g hair...in sorrow ... Gen 42:38
with the man of *g* ... Deut 32:25
Both the *g-haired* ... Job 15:10
when *I am* old and *g* ... Ps 71:18
g head is a crown ... Prov 16:31

GRAZE *feed*
cattle...*g-ing* in ... 1 Chr 27:29
wolf...shall *g* ... Is 65:25
he will *g* on Carmel ... Jer 50:19

GREAT *big, excellent, grand*
made...two *g* lights ... Gen 1:16
make you a *g* nation ... Gen 12:2
lovingkindness is *g* ... Ps 57:10
your iniquity is *g* ... Jer 30:15
g day of the LORD ... Zeph 1:14
rejoiced...with *g* joy ... Matt 2:10
woman...faith is *g* ... Matt 15:28
good news of *g* joy ... Luke 2:10
reward is *g* in ... Luke 6:23
because of His *g* love ... Eph 2:4
so *g* a salvation ... Heb 2:3
we have a *g*...priest ... Heb 4:14
so *g* a cloud of ... Heb 12:1
g supper of God ... Rev 19:17
a *g* white throne ... Rev 20:11

GREATEST *most important*
who is the *g* among ... Luke 22:26
g of these is love ... 1 Cor 13:13
least to the *g* ... Heb 8:11

GREATNESS *magnitude*
Yours...is the *g* ... 1 Chr 29:11
g...lovingkindness ... Neh 13:22
g of Your compassion ... Ps 51:1
the *g* of His strength ... Is 63:1
amazed at the *g* of ... Luke 9:43
surpassing *g* of His ... Eph 1:19

GREECE 1) The world power prophesied by Daniel, which succeeded Medo-Persia and preceded Rome. 2) After the conquest of the Greek Empire by the Romans, the region in southeastern Europe that was first exposed to Christianity through the ministry of Paul.
country in SE Europe ... Dan 8:21; 10:20; 11:2; Zech 9:13; Acts 20:2

GREED *excessive desire*
caught by *their*...*g* ... Prov 11:6
every form of *g* ... Luke 12:15
wickedness, *g*, evil ... Rom 1:29
a pretext for *g* ... 1 Thess 2:5
a heart trained in *g* ... 2 Pet 2:14

GREEDY *craving*
had *g* desires ... Num 11:4
g man curses ... Ps 10:3
Everyone is *g* for ... Jer 6:13

GREEK The language of Greece. Greek was subsequently kept by the Romans as a universal language. The New Testament was originally written in this language.
Do you know *G*? ... Acts 21:37

GREEKS
people of Greece ... Joel 3:6; Acts 16:1,3; Rom 1:16; 1 Cor 12:13

GREEN *fertile, fruitful*
every *g* plant for ... Gen 1:30
lie down in *g* pastures ... Ps 23:2
dry up the *g* tree ... Ezek 17:24
nor any *g* thing ... Rev 9:4

GREET *hail, welcome*
g no one on the way ... Luke 10:4
G one another with ... 1 Pet 5:14

GRIEF *heartache, sorrow*
weeps because of *g* ... Ps 119:28
foolish son is a *g* ... Prov 17:25
acquainted with *g* ... Is 53:3
our *g-s* He Himself ... Is 53:4
g...turned into joy ... John 16:20
joy and not with *g* ... Heb 13:17

GRIEVE *distress, sorrow*
was *g-d* in His heart ... Gen 6:6
Do not be *g-d* ... Neh 8:10
g-d Him in the desert ... Ps 78:40
g-d His Holy Spirit ... Is 63:10
g-d at their hardness ... Mark 3:5
Peter was *g-d* ... John 21:17
not *g* the Holy Spirit ... Eph 4:30

GRIND *crush, press*
my wife *g* for another ... Job 31:10
g-ing...the poor ... Is 3:15
millstones and *g* meal ... Is 47:2
women...*be g-ing* ... Matt 24:41
and *g-s* his teeth ... Mark 9:18

GROAN *cry, moan*
From the city men *g* ... Job 24:12
man rules, people *g* ... Prov 29:2
wounded will *g* ... Jer 51:52
whole creation *g-s* ... Rom 8:22

GROANING *crying*
God heard their *g* ... Ex 2:24
O LORD, Consider my *g* ... Ps 5:1
g of the prisoner ... Ps 79:11
g-s of a wounded ... Ezek 30:24
g-s too deep for ... Rom 8:26

GROPE *move about blindly*
you will *g* at noon ... Deut 28:29
They *g* in darkness ... Job 12:25
g...like blind men ... Is 59:10
g for Him and find ... Acts 17:27

GROUND *earth, land, soil*
man of dust from...*g* ... Gen 2:7
Cursed is the *g* ... Gen 3:17
crossed on dry *g* ... Josh 3:17
a spirit from the *g* ... Is 29:4
talent in the *g* ... Matt 25:25
finger wrote on the *g* ... John 8:6
standing is holy *g* ... Acts 7:33
g that drinks the rain ... Heb 6:7

GROUNDED *established*
hope...is firmly *g* ... 2 Cor 1:7
rooted and *g* in love ... Eph 3:17

GROW *develop, increase*
Moses had *g-n* up ... Ex 2:11
You are *g-n* fat ... Deut 32:15
my spirit *g-s* faint ... Ps 77:3
youths *g* weary ... Is 40:30
sun and moon *g* dark ... Joel 3:15
lilies of the field *g* ... Matt 6:28
love will *g* cold ... Matt 24:12
Child continued to *g* ... Luke 2:40
grew strong in faith ... Rom 4:20
as your faith *g-s* ... 2 Cor 10:15
not *g* weary of ... 2 Thess 3:13
g in the grace ... 2 Pet 3:18

GROWTH *increase*
new *g* is seen ... Prov 27:25
God who causes the *g* ... 1 Cor 3:7

GRUDGE *hostile feeling*
Esau bore a *g* ... Gen 27:41
nor bear any *g* ... Lev 19:18
Herodias had a *g* ... Mark 6:19

GRUMBLE *complain*
they *g-d* against Moses ... Ex 17:3
the congregation *g* ... Num 14:36
g-d in their tents ... Ps 106:25
scribes *began* to *g* ... Luke 15:2
g among yourselves ... John 6:43

GRUMBLING *complaint*
for He hears your *g-s* ... Ex 16:7
g-s against Me ... Num 17:10
Do all...without *g* ... Phil 2:14

GUARD (n) *keeper*
set a *g* over me ... Job 7:12
be a *g* for them ... Ezek 38:7
g-s shook for fear ... Matt 28:4
Him away under *g* ... Mark 14:44

GUARD (v) *keep watch*
g the way to the tree ... Gen 3:24
g-ed the threshold ... 2 Kin 12:9
G-ing...justice ... Prov 2:8
Discretion will *g* you ... Prov 2:11
soldier...was *g-ing* ... Acts 28:16
will *g* your hearts ... Phil 4:7
g...from idols ... 1 John 5:21

GUARDHOUSE *prison*
the court of the *g* ... Jer 37:21
the court of the *g* ... Jer 38:28

GUARDIAN *overseer*
g-s of *the children* ... 2 Kin 10:1
under *g-s* and ... Gal 4:2
G of your souls ... 1 Pet 2:25

GUEST *visitor*
Herod and his *g-s* ... Mark 6:22
Where...My *g* room ... Mark 14:14
to the invited *g-s* ... Luke 14:7
g of a...sinner ... Luke 19:7

GUIDANCE *counsel*
no *g*, the people fall ... Prov 11:14
make war by wise *g* ... Prov 20:18

GUIDE (n) *advisor, director*
The righteous is a *g* ... Prov 12:26
Woe to...blind *g-s* ... Matt 23:16
You blind *g-s*, who ... Matt 23:24
are a *g* to the blind ... Rom 2:19

GUIDE (v) *direct, lead*
LORD alone *g-d* him ... Deut 32:12
He *g-s* me in the paths ... Ps 23:3
g us until death ... Ps 48:14
my mind was *g-ing me* ... Eccl 2:3
blind...*g-s* a blind ... Matt 15:14
g you into...truth ... John 16:13
unless someone *g-s* ... Acts 8:31

GUILT *offence*
be free from *g* ... Num 5:31
according to his *g* ... Deut 25:2
charge me with a *g* ... 2 Sam 3:8
our *g* has grown ... Ezra 9:6
land is full of *g* ... Jer 51:5
must bear their *g* ... Hos 10:2
I find no *g* in Him ... John 18:38

GUILT OFFERING *see* **OFFERINGS**

GUILTY *charged* or *condemned*
he sins and becomes *g* ... Lev 6:4
murderer...*g* of ... Num 35:31
as one who is *g* ... 2 Sam 14:13
g by the blood ... Ezek 22:4
g of an eternal sin ... Mark 3:29
has become *g* of all ... James 2:10

GUSHED *burst, flowed*
so that waters *g* out ... Ps 78:20
the rock...water *g* ... Is 48:21
all his intestines *g* out ... Acts 1:18

H

HABAKKUK *(embracer).* One of the minor prophets. In his prophecy he called for the Chaldeans to punish Judah.
prophet ... Hab 1:1;3:1

HABITATION *abode, dwelling*
from Your holy *h* ... Deut 26:15
a rock of *h* ... Ps 71:3
h-s of violence ... Ps 74:20
live in a peaceful *h* ... Is 32:18
holy and glorious *h* ... Is 63:15
laid waste his *h* ... Jer 10:25
a *h* of shepherds ... Jer 33:12

HABOR
river in Mesopotamia ... 2 Kin 17:6; 18:11; 1 Chr 5:26

HADAD
1 *son of Ishmael* ... Gen 25:15; 1 Chr 1:30
2 *king of Edom, son of Bedad* ... Gen 36:35,36; 1 Chr 1:46,47
3 *king of Edom* ... Gen 36:39; 1 Chr 1:50,51
4 *Edomite prince* ... 1 Kin 11:14ff

HADASSAH
Esther's Hebrew name ... Esth 2:7

HADES *hell, place of the dead* Usually corresponds to Sheol in the OT, the place of departed souls. In some passages the term is used to refer more specifically to a place of torment after death. It is not the same as Gehenna (q.v.).
will descend to *H* ... Matt 11:23
in *H* he lifted up ... Luke 16:23
abandoned to *H* ... Acts 2:31
see also **HELL** *and* **SHEOL**

HAGAR *(emigration).* Sarah's maid, whom she gave to Abraham to bear children for her (Sarah was barren). Hagar gave birth to Ishmael.
Sarah's handmaiden ... Gen 16:1
Abraham's slave wife ... Gen 16:3
mother of Ishmael ... Gen 16:15

HAGGAI *(festival).* One of the minor prophets and a contemporary of Zechariah. He urged the Jewish people to continue rebuilding the post-exilic temple.
prophet ... Ezra 5:1; Hag 1:1

HAGGITH
David's wife ... 2 Sam 3:4
mother of Adonijah ... 1 Kin 1:11

HAIL (n) *pieces of ice*
rained *h* on the land ... Ex 9:23
storehouses of the *h* ... Job 38:22
gave them *h* for rain ... Ps 105:32
plague of the *h* ... Rev 16:21

HAIL (v) *greeting*
H, Rabbi ... Matt 26:49
H, King of...Jews ... Matt 27:29

HAILSTONES *pieces of ice*
who died from the *h* ... Josh 10:11
H and coals of fire ... Ps 18:13
you, O *h*, will fall ... Ezek 13:11
h...one hundred ... Rev 16:21

HAIR
gray *h*...to Sheol ... Gen 42:38
locks of his *h* and ... Judg 16:14
h...bristled ... Job 4:15
h...like pure wool ... Dan 7:9
garment of camel's *h* ... Matt 3:4
make one *h* white ... Matt 5:36
h-s...all numbered ... Matt 10:30
His feet with her *h* ... John 11:2
not with braided *h* ... 1 Tim 2:9

HALF-TRIBE One-half of the tribe of Manasseh who, together with the tribes of Reuben and Gad, were given permission to settle in the land east of the Jordan River (Josh 1:12-15). The other half of the tribe settled in the Promised Land.

HALL *corridor*
h of pillars ... 1 Kin 7:6
h of judgment ... 1 Kin 7:7
wedding *h* was ... Matt 22:10

HALLELUJAH *(praise Yahweh).* Exclamation or expression of praise to God. The same as *alleluia*, the Gr transliteration without the initial 'h'.
H! Salvation and ... Rev 19:1
H! Her smoke rises ... Rev 19:3
Amen. *H* ... Rev 19:4
H! For the Lord our ... Rev 19:6

HALLOWED *consecrated, holy*
H be Your name ... Matt 6:9

HAM (unc, *land of Egypt*). Youngest son of Noah, father of the Canaanites. Also the name of a city, and another name for Egypt.
1 *son of Noah* ... Gen 5:32; 9:18
2 *city* ... Gen 14:5
3 *poetic name for Egypt* ... Ps 105:27; 106:22

HAMAN The chief officer of King Ahasuerus of Persia who plotted to kill the Jews of the realm. In the end, he was executed on the same gallows where he had wanted to hang the leader of the Jewish people.
Persian prime minister
son of Hammedatha ... Esth 3:1

HAMATH (*citadel*). An ancient royal city of the Hittites (q.v.) in Syria. The king of Hamath made friendly overtures to David.
city in Syria ... 2 Kin 23:33; 25:21

HAMMER *mallet, tool*
and seized a *h* ... Judg 4:21
neither *h* nor axe ... 1 Kin 6:7
smash with...*h-s* ... Ps 74:6
like a *h* which ... Jer 23:29

HAMON-GOG
valley where army of Gog is defeated ... Ezek 39:11,15

HANANIAH
1 *son of Zerubbabel* ... 1 Chr 3:19
2 *son of Shishak* ... 1 Chr 8:24
3 *musician* ... 1 Chr 25:4,23
4 *in Uzziah's army* ... 2 Chr 26:11
5 *repaired wall* ... Neh 3:30
6 *overseer of palace* ... Neh 7:2
7 *false prophet* ... Jer 28:15
8 *Shadrach* ... Dan 1:6,7
name of six other individuals

HAND *part of body*
cover you with My *h* ... Ex 33:22
for tooth, *h* for *h* ... Deut 19:21
sling was in his *h* ... 1 Sam 17:40
They pierced my *h-s* ... Ps 22:16
buries his *h* ... Prov 19:24
the hollow of His *h* ... Is 40:12
clay in the potter's *h* ... Jer 18:6
not let your left *h* ... Matt 6:3
laying His *h-s* on ... Mark 10:16
the right *h* of God ... Mark 16:19
into the *h-s* of men ... Luke 9:44
into Your *h-s* I ... Luke 23:46
reach here your *h* ... John 20:27
not made with *h-s* ... 2 Cor 5:1
lifting up holy *h-s* ... 1 Tim 2:8
h-s of...God ... Heb 10:31

HANDBREADTH A unit of measurement based on the width of the four fingers pressed together, ranging from two and one-half to four inches (1 Kin 7:26).

HANDMAID *servant, slave*
save the son of Your *h* ... Ps 86:16
the son of Your *h* ... Ps 116:16
her *h-s* are moaning ... Nah 2:7

HANDS, LAYING ON OF *see* **LAYING ON OF HANDS**

HANDSOME *attractive*
a choice and *h man* ... 1 Sam 9:2
ruddy, with a *h* ... 1 Sam 17:42

HANG *attach, suspend*
h you on a tree ... Gen 40:19
h up the veil ... Ex 40:8
h-ed is accursed of ... Deut 21:23
h-ing in an oak ... 2 Sam 18:10
they *h-ed* Haman ... Esth 7:10
he...*h-ed* himself ... Matt 27:5
millstone were *hung* ... Luke 17:2
h-ing Him on a cross ... Acts 5:30
who *h-s* on a tree ... Gal 3:13

HANNAH (*grace, favor*). The mother of the prophet Samuel.
mother of Samuel ... 1 Sam 2:21

HANUN An Ammonite king who mistreated David's ambassadors when they went to console him on the death of his father (1 Chr 19:4).

HAPPINESS *joy*
give *h* to his wife ... Deut 24:5
eat your bread in *h* ... Eccl 9:7
I have forgotten *h* ... Lam 3:17

HAPPY *blessed, joyful*
Leah said, *H* am I ... Gen 30:13
h...man whom God ... Job 5:17
h...who keeps the ... Prov 29:18

HARAN The name of three persons. Also an important city of Mesopotamia, where Abraham, Terah, and Jacob lived.
1 *brother of Abraham* ... Gen 11:27
father of Lot ... Gen 11:31
2 *Gershonite Levite* ... 1 Chr 23:9
3 *Mesopotamian city* ... Gen 11:32;27:43

HARD *difficult, firm*
bitter with *h* labor ... Ex 1:14
case that is too *h* ... Deut 1:17
made our yoke *h* ... 2 Chr 10:4
Water becomes *h* ... Job 38:30
h for a rich man ... Matt 19:23
h it is to enter ... Mark 10:24
worked *h* all night ... Luke 5:5

HARDEN *make hard, callous*
h Pharaoh's heart ... Ex 7:3
dust *h-s* into a mass ... Job 38:38
who *h-s his* neck ... Prov 29:1
h-s whom He ... Rom 9:18
minds were *h-ed* ... 2 Cor 3:14
Do not *h* your hearts ... Heb 3:15

HARDNESS *callousness*
give them *h* of heart ... Lam 3:65
Because of your *h* ... Matt 19:8
grieved at their *h* ... Mark 3:5
unbelief and *h* of ... Mark 16:14

HARDSHIP *difficulty*
H after *h* is with me ... Job 10:17
people experience *h* ... Ps 60:3
afflictions, in *h-s* ... 2 Cor 6:4
our labor and *h* ... 1 Thess 2:9
Suffer *h* with *me* ... 2 Tim 2:3

HAREM *royal wives' quarters*
best place in the *h* ... Esth 2:9
from the *h* to the ... Esth 2:13
to the second *h* ... Esth 2:14

HARLOT Another word for "prostitute". In the Bible, the phrase "playing the harlot" is often used metaphorically as a reference to idol worship.
thought she *was* a *h* ... Gen 38:15
the hire of a *h* ... Deut 23:18
h whose name was ... Josh 2:1
Dressed as a *h* ... Prov 7:10
city has become a *h* ... Is 1:21
also played the *h* ... Ezek 16:26
Traded a boy for a *h* ... Joel 3:3
Mother of *H-s* ... Rev 17:5

HARLOTRY *prostitution*
with child by *h* ... Gen 38:24
profaned by *h* ... Lev 21:7
uncovered her *h-ies* ... Ezek 23:18
children of *h* ... Hos 1:2
spirit of *h* ... Hos 5:4

HARM (n) *evil, hurt*
pillar to me, for *h* ... Gen 31:52
h to this people ... Ex 5:22
keep *me* from *h* ... 1 Chr 4:10
Do not devise *h* ... Prov 3:29
great *h* to yourselves ... Jer 44:7
the fire without *h* ... Dan 3:25
did me much *h* ... 2 Tim 4:14

HARM (v) *damage, hurt*
David seeks to *h* ... 1 Sam 24:9
planning to *h* me ... Neh 6:2
have not *h-ed* me ... Dan 6:22
in order to *h* you ... Acts 18:10
is there to *h* you ... 1 Pet 3:13

HAR-MAGEDON (unc, *hill of Megiddo*). A hill near Mt. Carmel, often called Armageddon from its Gr transliteration. The first part of the name (*Har*) means "hill," while the latter part is probably a form of *Megiddo* (q.v.). It is a noted battleground of many conflicts, and the site of the final war of the great day of God.
hill of Megiddo ... Rev 16:16

HARMONY *agreement*
what *h* has Christ ... 2 Cor 6:15
live in *h* in the ... Phil 4:2

HARP *musical instrument*
my *h* is turned to ... Job 30:31
praises...with a *h* ... Ps 33:2
Awake, *h* and lyre ... Ps 57:8
gaiety of the *h* ceases ... Is 24:8
each one holding a *h* ... Rev 5:8
holding *h-s* of God ... Rev 15:2

HARSH *difficult, hard*
man was *h* and evil ... 1 Sam 25:3
h word stirs up anger ... Prov 15:1
A *h* vision ... Is 21:2
under *h* servitude ... Lam 1:3

HARVEST *reap and gather*
Seedtime and *h* ... Gen 8:22
fruits of the wheat *h* ... Ex 34:22
you reap your *h* ... Deut 24:19
he who sleeps in *h* ... Prov 10:5
snow...time of *h* ... Prov 25:13
like rain in *h* ... Prov 26:1
the gladness of *h* ... Is 9:3
time of *h* will come ... Jer 51:33
Lord of the *h* ... Matt 9:38
h is the end of the ... Matt 13:39
fields...white for *h* ... John 4:35
h of the earth is ... Rev 14:15

HARVEST, FEAST OF *see* **FEASTS**

HASHUM
1 *family of exiles* ... Ezra 2:19
2 *was with Ezra* ... Neh 8:4

HASTEN *hurry*
h-ed after deceit ... Job 31:5
H to me, O God ... Ps 70:5
they *h* to shed blood ... Prov 1:16
bird *h-s* to the snare ... Prov 7:23
eye *h-s* after wealth ... Prov 28:22
h-ing...day of God ... 2 Pet 3:12

HATE *despise, loathe*
you *h* discipline ... Ps 50:17
who *h* the LORD ... Ps 81:15
I *h* every false way ... Ps 119:104
fools *h* knowledge ... Prov 1:22
withholds his rod *h-s* ... Prov 13:24
a time to *h* ... Eccl 3:8
H evil, love good ... Amos 5:15
For I *h* divorce ... Mal 2:16
good to those who *h* ... Luke 6:27
you will be *h-d* ... Luke 21:17
he who *h-s* his life ... John 12:25
the very thing I *h* ... Rom 7:15
Esau I *h-d* ... Rom 9:13
h-ing one another ... Titus 3:3
yet h-s his brother ... 1 John 2:9

HATERS *those who hate*
slanderers, *h* of God ... Rom 1:30
brutal, *h* of good ... 2 Tim 3:3

HATRED *hate, ill will*
h for my love ... Ps 109:5
H stirs up strife ... Prov 10:12
who conceals *h has* ... Prov 10:18

HAUGHTY *proud*
nor my eyes *h* ... Ps 131:1
H eyes, a lying ... Prov 6:17
h spirit before ... Prov 16:18
Proud, *H,* Scoffer ... Prov 21:24
wine betrays the *h* ... Hab 2:5
do not be *h* in mind ... Rom 12:16

HAVEN *harbor, shelter*
be a *h* for ships ... Gen 49:13
to their desired *h* ... Ps 107:30

HAVILAH
1 *second son of Cush* ... Gen 10:7
2 *son of Joktan* ... Gen 10:29; 1 Chr 1:23
3 *region encompassed by one of Eden's rivers* ... Gen 2:11
4 *area in W Arabia* ... Gen 25:18

HAWK *bird*
sea gull, and the *h* ... Deut 14:15
h-s will be gathered ... Is 34:15

HAZAEL An important court official under Ben-hadad, king of Damascus. He killed the king and became a powerful king himself who greatly oppressed Israel.
anointed by Elijah ... 1 Kin 19:15
killed Ben Hadad ... 2 Kin 8:15
Aramaic king ... 2 Kin 8:15;9:14
defeated Israel ... 2 Kin 10:32

HAZOR *(settlement).* The capital of the kingdom of Jabin in the days of Joshua. Also the name of three other places.
1 *Canaanite city in N Palestine* ... Josh 11:11
2 *town of the Negev* ... Josh 15:23
3 *Benjamite city* ... Neh 11:33
4 *desert kingdom* ... Jer 49:33

HEAD *chief* or *part of body*
bruise you on the *h* ... Gen 3:15
anointed my *h* with oil ... Ps 23:5
h a garland of grace ... Prov 4:9
gray *h* is a crown ... Prov 16:31
coals on his *h* ... Prov 25:22
h was made bald ... Ezek 29:18
had four *h-s* ... Dan 7:6
an oath by your *h* ... Matt 5:36
nowhere to lay His *h* ... Matt 8:20
h of John the Baptist ... Matt 14:8
not a hair of your *h* ... Luke 21:18
crown...on His *h* ... John 19:2
God is the *h* of ... 1 Cor 11:3
husband is the *h* ... Eph 5:23

HEADLONG *headfirst*
He rushes *h* at Him ... Job 15:26
falling *h,* he burst ... Acts 1:18
h into the error ... Jude 11

HEAL *make well, restore*
will *h* their land ... 2 Chr 7:14
h-s the brokenhearted ... Ps 147:3
a time to *h* ... Eccl 3:3
H me, O LORD ... Jer 17:14
will *h* their apostasy ... Hos 14:4
h-ed all who were ... Matt 8:16
H the sick, raise ... Matt 10:8
h him on...Sabbath ... Mark 3:2
Physician, *h* yourself ... Luke 4:23
you may be *h-ed* ... James 5:16
fatal wound was *h-ed* ... Rev 13:3

HEALING *health, wholeness*
be *h* to your body ... Prov 3:8
h to the bones ... Prov 16:24
sorrow is beyond *h* ... Jer 8:18
There is no *h* for ... Jer 46:11
their leaves for *h* ... Ezek 47:12
h every kind of ... Matt 4:23
gifts of *h* ... 1 Cor 12:9
h of the nations ... Rev 22:2

HEALTH *soundness, wholeness*
no *h* in my bones ... Ps 38:3
restore you to *h* ... Jer 30:17
and be in good *h* ... 3 John 2

HEAP (n) *mound, pile*
stones and made a *h* ... Gen 31:46
waters stood...like a *h* ... Ex 15:8
made a refuse *h* ... Ezra 6:11
needy from the ash *h* ... Ps 113:7
Jerusalem a *h* of ruins ... Jer 9:11
altars are...*h-s* ... Hos 12:11

HEAP (v) *pile up, place*
h misfortunes on ... Deut 32:23
will *h* burning coals ... Prov 25:22
H on the wood ... Ezek 24:10
h up rubble to ... Hab 1:10

HEAR *listen*
h-d the sound of ... Gen 3:10
God *h-d* their groaning ... Ex 2:24
H, O Israel ... Deut 6:4
h the wisdom of ... 1 Kin 4:34
h in heaven ... 1 Kin 8:30
Will God *h* his cry ... Job 27:9
who *h* prayer ... Ps 65:2
h Your lovingkindness ... Ps 143:8
poor *h-s* no rebuke ... Prov 13:8
deaf will *h* words ... Is 29:18
bones, *h* the word ... Ezek 37:4
ears to *h,* let him *h* ... Matt 11:15
h of wars and ... Mark 13:7
he who *h-s* My word ... John 5:24
does not *h* sinners ... John 9:31
sheep *h* My voice ... John 10:27
we *h-d* of your faith ... Col 1:4
anyone *h-s* My voice ... Rev 3:20

HEARING *listening*
in the LORD'S *h* ... 1 Sam 8:21
in the *h* of a fool ... Prov 23:9
fulfilled in your *h* ... Luke 4:21
I will give you a *h* ... Acts 23:35
become dull of *h* ... Heb 5:11

HEART *mind* or *seat of emotions* In the Bible, the heart often refers metaphorically to a person's rational and moral being, as well as to the physical organ.
intent of man's *h* is ... Gen 8:21
I will harden his *h* ... Ex 4:21
great searchings of *h* ... Judg 5:16
LORD looks at the *h* ... 1 Sam 16:7
fool has said in his *h* ... Ps 14:1
meditation of my *h* ... Ps 19:14
My *h* is like wax ... Ps 22:14
in me a clean *h* ... Ps 51:10
and a contrite *h* ... Ps 51:17
Your word...in my *h* ... Ps 119:11
Deceit is in the *h* ... Prov 12:20
A joyful *h* is good ... Prov 17:22
to a troubled *h* ... Prov 25:20
bribe corrupts the *h* ... Eccl 7:7
a new *h* and a new ... Ezek 18:31
uncircumcised in *h* ... Ezek 44:7
are the pure in *h* ... Matt 5:8
adultery...in his *h* ... Matt 5:28
and humble in *h* ... Matt 11:29
h is far...from Me ... Matt 15:8
pondering...in her *h* ... Luke 2:19
pierced to the *h* ... Acts 2:37
cleansing their *h-s* ... Acts 15:9
who searches the *h-s* ... Rom 8:27
tablets of human *h-s* ... 2 Cor 3:3
not lose *h* in doing ... Gal 6:9
melody with your *h* ... Eph 5:19
intentions of the *h* ... Heb 4:12
deceives his *own h* ... James 1:26

HEAT *hotness, warmth*
the *h* of the day ... Gen 18:1
and *h* consume ... Job 24:19
hidden from its *h* ... Ps 19:6
a shade from the *h* ... Is 25:4
burning *h* of famine ... Lam 5:10
scorching *h* of the ... Matt 20:12
with intense *h* ... 2 Pet 3:10
scorched with fierce *h* ... Rev 16:9

HEAVE OFFERING *see* **OFFERINGS**

HEAVEN *place of God* or *sky* In the Bible, the term has several meanings: 1) the atmosphere above the earth where birds fly. 2) The starry universe. 3) The expanse beyond these where God has His primary abode.
God created the *h-s* ... Gen 1:1
rain bread from *h* ... Ex 16:4
shut up the *h-s* ... Deut 11:17
thunder in the *h-s* ... 1 Sam 2:10
fire came...from *h* ... 2 Kin 1:14
make windows in *h* ... 2 Kin 7:2
walks...vault of *h* ... Job 22:14
I consider Your *h-s* ... Ps 8:3
h and earth praise ... Ps 69:34

fixed patterns of *h* ... Jer 33:25
lights in the *h-s* ... Ezek 32:8
open...windows of *h* ... Mal 3:10
kingdom of *h* is at ... Matt 3:2
voice out of the *h-s* ... Matt 3:17
reward in *h* is great ... Matt 5:12
Father who is in *h* ... Matt 6:9
shall have been loosed in *h* ... Matt 16:19
great signs from *h* ... Luke 21:11
Him go into *h* ... Acts 1:11
no...name under *h* ... Acts 4:12
up to the third *h* ... 2 Cor 12:2
citizenship is in *h* ... Phil 3:20
there was war in *h* ... Rev 12:7
new *h* and a new ... Rev 21:1

HEAVENLY *related to God*
h Father is perfect ... Matt 5:48
h Father knows that ... Matt 6:32
h host praising God ... Luke 2:13
I tell you *h* things ... John 3:12
Him in the *h places* ... Eph 2:6
partakers of a *h* ... Heb 3:1
shadow of the *h* ... Heb 8:5

HEAVY *burdensome, hard to lift*
Moses' hands were *h* ... Ex 17:12
servitude was *h* on ... Neh 5:18
h drinkers of wine ... Prov 23:20
A stone is *h* ... Prov 27:3
Jerusalem a *h* stone ... Zech 12:3
eyes were very *h* ... Mark 14:40

HEBER
1 *son of Beriah* ... Gen 46:17
2 *husband of Jael* ... Judg 4:17
3 *son of Mered* ... 1 Chr 4:18
4 *son of Elpaal* ... 1 Chr 8:17
see also **EBER**

HEBREW The language of the ancient Jews, which was later supplanted for the most part by Aramaic. The OT Scriptures were written mostly in Hebrew, with a few portions in Aramaic.

HEBREW(S) *(those from beyond the river)*. The name of a people from the other side of the river Euphrates who settled in the land of Canaan. Later known as Israelites or the Jewish people, who were among the descendants of Abraham.
1 *people* ... Gen 14:13; Ex 1:15; 9:13; Jon 1:9
2 *language* ... John 19:17; Acts 22:2; 26:14
see also **JUDEAN**
see also **CANAAN**

HEBRON *(league, association)*. An ancient town near Jerusalem where Abraham buried Sarah. Later it was conquered by the Israelites and given to Caleb. Also the name of two people.
1 *site of Sarah's death* ... Gen 23:2
visited by spies ... Num 13:22
destroyed ... Josh 10:37
city of refuge ... Josh 20:7
residence of David ... 2 Sam 2:1
2 *son of Kohath* ... Ex 6:18
3 *son of Mareshah* ... 1 Chr 2:42

HEDGE *border* or *protection*
You not made a *h* ... Job 1:10
as a *h* of thorns ... Prov 15:19
along the *h-s*, and ... Luke 14:23

HEEL *back of foot*
bruise him on the *h* ... Gen 3:15
on to Esau's *h* ... Gen 25:26
his *h* against Me ... John 13:18

HEIFER *young cow*
unblemished red *h* ... Num 19:2
plowed with my *h* ... Judg 14:18
Egypt is a pretty *h* ... Jer 46:20
Like a stubborn *h* ... Hos 4:16

HEIGHT *elevation, heaven, sky*
in the *h* of heaven ... Job 22:12
from His holy *h* ... Ps 102:19
Praise Him in the *h-s* ... Ps 148:1
As the heavens for *h* ... Prov 25:3
ascend above the *h-s* ... Is 14:14
nor *h*, nor depth ... Rom 8:39

HEIR *person who inherits*
in my house is my *h* ... Gen 15:3
has he no *h-s* ... Jer 49:1
h-s also, *h-s* of God ... Rom 8:17
an *h* through God ... Gal 4:7
h-s of the kingdom ... James 2:5

HELIOPOLIS
ancient Egyptian city ... Jer 43:13
see also **ON**

HELL *place of the dead*
see **GEHENNA**
go into the fiery *h* ... Matt 5:22
soul and body in *h* ... Matt 10:28
to be cast into *h* ... Mark 9:47
set on fire by *h* ... James 3:6
cast them into *h* ... 2 Pet 2:4
see also **HADES** *and* **SHEOL**

HELLENIST A term used of Jews who spoke Greek and adopted elements of Greek culture.
Greek speaking Jews ... Acts 6:1; 9:29

HELMET *headpiece*
bronze *h* on his ... 1 Sam 17:5
h of salvation ... Is 59:17
take the *h* of ... Eph 6:17

HELP (n) *assistance, relief*
h is not within me ... Job 6:13
He is our *h* and our ... Ps 33:20
present *h* in trouble ... Ps 46:1
I cried for *h* ... Jon 2:2
gifts of...*h-s* ... 1 Cor 12:28

HELP (v) *aid, assist*
h-ing the Hebrew ... Ex 1:16
the LORD *h-ed* David ... 2 Sam 8:6
whence shall my *h* ... Ps 121:1
I will *h* you ... Is 41:13
Lord, *h* me ... Matt 15:25
h my unbelief ... Mark 9:24
must *h* the weak ... Acts 20:35
Spirit also *h-s* our ... Rom 8:26
earth *h-ed* the ... Rev 12:16

HELPER *one who assists*
h of the orphan ... Ps 10:14
be my *h* ... Ps 30:10
Behold, God is my *h* ... Ps 54:4
give you another *H* ... John 14:16
H, the Holy Spirit ... John 14:26

HELPLESS *weak*
the *h* has hope ... Job 5:16
who considers the *h* ... Ps 41:1
while we were still *h* ... Rom 5:6

HEMAN
1 *sage of Solomon* ... 1 Kin 4:31
2 *line of Samuel* ... 1 Chr 15:19

HEMORRHAGE *bleeding*
suffering from a *h* ... Matt 9:20
a *h* for twelve years ... Mark 5:25
her *h* stopped ... Luke 8:44

HEN *fowl*
h gathers her ... Matt 23:37
as a *h gathers* her ... Luke 13:34

HEPHZIBAH
Manasseh's mother ... 2 Kin 21:1
Hezekiah's wife ... 2 Kin 21:3

HERB *dried plant*
bread and bitter *h-s* ... Ex 12:8
fade like the green *h* ... Ps 37:2
h-s of...mountains ... Prov 27:25
sweet-scented *h-s* ... Song 5:13

HERD *cattle, flock*
firstborn of your *h* ... Deut 12:6
h, or flock taste a ... Jon 3:7
h of many swine ... Matt 8:30

HERDSMEN *keepers of flocks*
h of Abram's livestock ... Gen 13:7
between my *h* and ... Gen 13:8
the *h* ran away ... Matt 8:33

HERESY *(choice, sect)*. A religious opinion which denies a doctrine revealed in the Scriptures.
introduce destructive *h-s* ... 2 Pet 2:1

HERITAGE *what is inherited*
the *h* decreed to him ... Job 20:29
my *h* is beautiful ... Ps 16:6
their land as a *h* ... Ps 136:21
inherit the desolate *h-s* ... Is 49:8
you who pillage My *h* ... Jer 50:11

HERMENEUTICS *see* **INTERPRETATION**

HERMES
1 *Greek god* ... Acts 14:12
2 *Roman Christian* ... Rom 16:14

HERMOGENES
Asian Christian who failed to support Paul ... 2 Tim 1:15

HERMON, MOUNT *(sacred* mountain*)*. A mountain at the northeast boundary of the conquests under Moses and Joshua. It is the source of the Jordan River.
mountain region in N Palestine ... Josh 11:17; Ps 42:6; 133:3
N boundary of Promised Land ... Deut 3:8

HEROD The name of several Jewish officials who ruled over Palestine during the years 37 B.C.–70 A.D. They were appointed by Rome.
1 **Herod the Great**
king of Judea, Samaria, Ituraea and Traconitis ... Matt 2:1
ruled during Jesus' birth ... Matt 2:1ff
2 **Herod Archelaus**
son of Herod the Great ... Matt 2:22
governor of Ituraea and Traconitis
3 **Herod Antipas**
son of Herod the Great ... Matt 14:1
tetrarch of Galilee and Perea ... Luke 3:1
ruled during Jesus' ministry ... Luke 13:31; 23:7,8,11

executed John the Baptist ... Matt 14:10; Mark 6:27
4 **Herod Philip I**
son of Herod the Great ... Mark 6:17
5 **Herod Philip II**
son of Herod the Great ... Luke 3:1
tetrarch of Ituraea and Traconitis
6 **Herod Agrippa I**
grandson of Herod the Great ... Acts 12:1
king of Judea and Samaria
persecuted the early church ... Acts 12:2-23
7 **Herod Agrippa II**
son of Agrippa I ... Acts 25:13
tetrarch of Tiberias, Abila and Traconitis
heard Paul's testimony ... Acts 25:23ff; 26:1ff

HERODIANS
influential Jews favoring Herod ... Matt 22:16; Mark 3:6

HERODIAS
wife of Herod Antipas ... Matt 14:3; Mark 6:17
requested head of John the Baptist ... Matt 14:8; Mark 6:24

HESHBON A very fertile city in Moab which the Israelites conquered (Num 21:26).

HETH A descendant of Noah. His descendants are called Hittites (q.v.).
1 *son of Canaan* ... Gen 10:15
2 *Hebrew eponym for Hittites* ... Gen 23:10

HEW *chop, cut*
h down their Asherim ... Deut 7:5
H-n cisterns, vineyards ... Neh 9:25
h-n out in the rock ... Mark 15:46

HEZEKIAH *(Yahweh strengthens).* One of the kings of Judah. He built an aqueduct which saved Jerusalem during the siege of Sennacherib. The aqueduct still exists today.
king of Judah ... 2 Kin 18:1
reformer ... 2 Kin 18:4
warrior ... 2 Kin 18:7,8
builder ... 2 Kin 20:20

HEZRON *(enclosure).* 1) A descendant of Judah whose name is mentioned in the genealogy of Jesus. 2) A place in Judah. 3) A son of Reuben.
1 *son of Perez* ... Matt 1:3
2 *place in Judah* ... Josh 15:3
3 *son of Reuben* ... Gen 46:9

HIDE *conceal, cover*
man and his wife *hid* ... Gen 3:8
I *h* from Abraham ... Gen 18:17
Moses *hid* his face ... Ex 3:6
h me in Sheol ... Job 14:13
h-ing my iniquity ... Job 31:33
H me in the shadow ... Ps 17:8
Do not *h* Your face ... Ps 27:9
wrongs are not *h-den* ... Ps 69:5
sees evil *and h-s* ... Prov 27:12
hid your talent ... Matt 25:25
nothing is *h-den* ... Mark 4:22
Jesus *hid* Himself ... John 8:59
h us from...Him ... Rev 6:16

HIDDEN *concealed*
Acquit me of *h faults* ... Ps 19:12
h wealth of secret ... Is 45:3
h snares for my feet ... Jer 18:22
profound and *h* ... Dan 2:22
some of the *h* manna ... Rev 2:17

HIDING PLACE
Clouds are a *h* ... Job 22:14
He lurks in a *h* ... Ps 10:9
You are my *h* ... Ps 32:7
uncovered his *h-s* ... Jer 49:10

HIERAPOLIS
city in Asia Minor ... Col 4:13

HIGH *elevated* or *heavenly*
it is still *h* day ... Gen 29:7
the *h* places of Baal ... Num 22:41
h above all nations ... Deut 26:19
h as the heavens ... Job 11:8
my advocate is on *h* ... Job 16:19
set him *securely* on *h* ... Ps 91:14
or *h* as heaven ... Is 7:11
to a very *h* mountain ... Matt 4:8
the *h* priest ... Matt 26:57
Son of the Most *H* ... Mark 5:7
from a *h* fever ... Luke 4:38
He ascended on *h* ... Eph 4:8

HIGH PLACE
worship place of God or idols ... Num 22:41; 1 Sam 9:12-14

HIGH PRIEST The chief of the Jewish priests. In Israel's priesthood Aaron was the first, and after him his descendants.
first in hierarchy ... Ex 27:21
under Aaron ... Ex 28:1,2
enters Holy of Holies ... Ex 28:29,30; Heb 9:7
head of Sanhedrin ... Matt 26:57; Acts 5:21
Jesus as High Priest ... Heb 3:1;5:5-9

HIGHWAY *road*
along the king's *h* ... Num 20:17
h from Egypt to ... Is 19:23
the *H* of Holiness ... Is 35:8
a *h* for our God ... Is 40:3
Go out into the *h-s* ... Luke 14:23

HILKIAH *(Yahweh is my portion).* A priest, the father of the prophet Jeremiah, and another priest who stood by Ezra when he read the law to the people of Israel. Also the name of several other persons.
1 *father of Eliakim* ... 2 Kin 18:18
2 *high priest* ... 2 Kin 22:4-14
3 *Merarite Levite* ... 1 Chr 6:45
4 *son of Hosah* ... 1 Chr 26:11
5 *was with Ezra* ... Neh 8:4
6 *returned from exile* ... Neh 12:7

HILL *mountain*
the everlasting *h-s* ... Gen 49:26
the *h* of God ... 1 Sam 10:5
dwell on Your holy *h* ... Ps 15:1
to Your holy *h* ... Ps 43:3
cattle...thousand *h-s* ... Ps 50:10
h-s, Fall on us ... Hos 10:8
city set on a *h* ... Matt 5:14
h...brought low ... Luke 3:5
the brow of the *h* ... Luke 4:29
h-s, Cover us ... Luke 23:30

HIN A Jewish liquid measure of approximately six quarts.

HINDER *delay, impede, restrain*
h meditation before ... Job 15:4
do not *h* them ... Matt 19:14
do not *h* them ... Luke 18:16
h-ed you from obeying ... Gal 5:7
prayers...not be *h-ed* ... 1 Pet 3:7

HINNOM
person for whom valley of Hinnom was named ... 2 Kin 23:10; Jer 7:31

HINNOM, VALLEY OF *see* **BEN-HIMMON**

HIP *part of body*
the sinew of the *h* ... Gen 32:32
curves of your *h-s* are ... Song 7:1
h joints went slack ... Dan 5:6

HIRAM / HURAM *(my brother is exalted).* A king of Tyre who supplied building materials and workers to help David build his palace, and later to help Solomon build the temple. Also name of a skilled craftsman.
1 *king of Tyre* ... 1 Kin 5:1ff; 2 Chr 2:3,11
2 *skilled craftsman* ... 1 Kin 7:14; 2 Chr 4:11

HIRE (n) *wages*
it came for its *h* ... Ex 22:15
the *h* of a harlot ... Deut 23:18

HIRE (v) *engage for labor*
h...for bread ... 1 Sam 2:5
and *h-d* the Arameans ... 2 Sam 10:6
to *h*...chariots ... 1 Chr 19:6
he who *h-s* a fool ... Prov 26:10
to *h* laborers for ... Matt 20:1

HIRED (adj) *employed*
as a *h* man, as if ... Lev 25:40
oppress a *h* servant ... Deut 24:14
as one of your *h* ... Luke 15:19
h hand...not a shepherd ... John 10:12
because he is a *h* hand ... John 10:13

HISS *to show dislike*
h him from his place ... Job 27:23
object of...h-ing ... Jer 18:16
They *h* and shake ... Lam 2:15
h And wave his hand ... Zeph 2:15

HITTITES Descendants of Heth (q.v.) who became a prominent people in Canaan during patriarchal times. The Israelites frequently intermarried with them.
1 *people in Palestine in patriarchal age* ... Gen 15:20; 49:29
2 *inhabitants of Aram during Israelite monarchy* ... 2 Kin 7:6; 2 Chr 8:7

HIVITES A prominent nation in northern Canaan before the settlement of the Promised Land, mentioned among the nations conquered by Israel.
people dispossessed by the Israelites ... Ex 23:28; Josh 3:10; 2 Sam 24:7

HOGLAH
daughter of Zelophehad ... Num 26:33; 27:1; Josh 17:3

HOLD *grasp, retain*
Moses *held* his hand ... Ex 17:11
h fast to Him ... Deut 11:22
h fast...evil purpose ... Ps 64:5
heart *h* fast my words ... Prov 4:4
Take *h* of instruction ... Prov 4:13
h fast My covenant ... Is 56:4
h to the tradition ... Mark 7:8

h fast the word ... 1 Cor 15:2
h-ing to the mystery ... 1 Tim 3:9
h of the eternal ... 1 Tim 6:12
He *held* seven stars ... Rev 1:16

HOLE *opening*
the *h* of the cobra ... Is 11:8
a *h* in the wall ... Ezek 8:7
a purse with *h-s* ... Hag 1:6
foxes have *h-s* ... Matt 8:20

HOLIDAY *period of leisure*
a feast and a *h* ... Esth 8:17
a *h* for rejoicing ... Esth 9:19
mourning into a *h* ... Esth 9:22

HOLINESS *sacredness*
majestic in *h* ... Ex 15:11
H befits Your house ... Ps 93:5
the Highway of *H* ... Is 35:8
without blame in *h* ... 1 Thess 3:13
we may share His *h* ... Heb 12:10

HOLLOW *empty space*
the *h* of a sling ... 1 Sam 25:29
in the *h* of His hand ... Is 40:12

HOLY *sacred, sanctified (set apart).* Someone or something sacred due to being consecrated to God. Holiness is an attribute of God.
standing is *h* ground ... Ex 3:5
sabbath...keep it *h* ... Ex 20:8
you are a *h* people ... Deut 7:6
ten thousand *h* ones ... Deut 33:2
h like the LORD ... 1 Sam 2:2
Worship...*h* array ... 1 Chr 16:29
His *h* dwelling ... 2 Chr 30:27
Jerusalem, the *h* city ... Neh 11:1
Zion, My *h* mountain ... Ps 2:6
to His *h* land ... Ps 78:54
bless His *h* name ... Ps 145:21
H, H, H, is the LORD ... Is 6:3
the *H* One of Israel ... Is 30:15
what is *h* to dogs ... Matt 7:6
righteous and *h* man ... Mark 6:20
the *H* One of God ... Luke 4:34
in the *h* Scriptures ... Rom 1:2
and *h* sacrifice ... Rom 12:1
with a *h* kiss ... Rom 16:16
h both in body ... 1 Cor 7:34
lifting up *h* hands ... 1 Tim 2:8
with a *h* calling ... 2 Tim 1:9
I saw the *h* city ... Rev 21:2

HOLY OF HOLIES The innermost part of the tabernacle (while Israel was wandering in the desert, and later in the temple in Jerusalem), where the ark of the covenant was located. Also called "the most holy place." The high priest could enter the holy of holies only once a year on the Day of Atonement to perform the prescribed rituals for the sins of Israel.
most holy place in the Tabernacle / Temple ... Ex 26:33,34; 2 Chr 3:8

HOLY SPIRIT The third person of the Trinity, equal in essence to God the Father and God the Son. The H.S. was present when the world was created (Gen 1:2). Jesus Christ and the apostles recognized the H.S. as a person of the Godhead with various divine functions. Through the H.S., God is actively present in believers' lives. *see* **TRINITY**
Third Person of the Godhead ... Matt 28:19; 2 Cor 13:14
Helper ... John 14:16,26
Giver of gifts ... Rom 12:6-8; 1 Cor 12:8-11
fruit of the Spirit ... Gal 5:22

HOMAGE *act of reverence*
my people shall do *h* ... Gen 41:40
did *h* to the LORD ... 1 Chr 29:20
and paid *h* to Haman ... Esth 3:2
did *h* to Daniel ... Dan 2:46

HOME *place of dwelling*
free at *h* one year ... Deut 24:5
God makes a *h* ... Ps 68:6
husband is not at *h* ... Prov 7:19
to his eternal *h* ... Eccl 12:5
Go *h* to your people ... Mark 5:19
let him eat at *h* ... 1 Cor 11:34
at *h* in the body ... 2 Cor 5:6
at *h* with the Lord ... 2 Cor 5:8

HOMER *measure of capacity* A Jewish dry measure equal to about 10 bushels. Also a liquid measure of about 90 gallons.
a *h* of barley ... Lev 27:16
a *h* of seed ... Is 5:10
from a *h* of wheat ... Ezek 45:13

HOMESTEAD *family dwelling*
h forlorn and forsaken ... Is 27:10
h be made desolate ... Acts 1:20

HOMOSEXUALS
effeminate, nor *h* ... 1 Cor 6:9
immoral men and *h* ... 1 Tim 1:10

HONEST *respectable, truthful*
we are *h* men ... Gen 42:11
painful are *h* words ... Job 6:25
an *h* and good heart ... Luke 8:15

HONEY *sweetness*
with milk and *h* ... Ex 3:8
swarm of bees and *h* ... Judg 14:8
is sweeter than *h* ... Judg 14:18
sweet as *h* in my ... Ezek 3:3
locusts and wild *h* ... Matt 3:4

HONEYCOMB *honey storage*
drippings of the *h* ... Ps 19:10
Pleasant words...a *h* ... Prov 16:24

HONOR (n) *glory, great respect*
both riches and *h* ... 1 Kin 3:13
stripped my *h* from ... Job 19:9
wise will inherit *h* ... Prov 3:35
is not without *h* ... Matt 13:57
glory and *h* and ... Rom 2:10
Marriage...*be held* in *h* ... Heb 13:4
blessing and *h* and ... Rev 5:13

HONOR (v) *show respect*
H your father ... Ex 20:12
h the aged ... Lev 19:32
who *h* Me I will *h* ... 1 Sam 2:30
am *h-ed* in the sight ... Is 49:5
A son *h-s his* father ... Mal 1:6
may be *h-ed* by men ... Matt 6:2
h-s Me with...lips ... Matt 15:8
does not *h* the Son ... John 5:23
fear God, *h* the king ... 1 Pet 2:17

HONORABLE *respectable*
the elder and *h* man ... Is 9:15
one vessel for *h* use ... Rom 9:21
whatever is *h* ... Phil 4:8

HOOF *part of animal foot*
which divide the *h* ... Lev 11:4
with horns and *h-s* ... Ps 69:31
h-s of beasts will ... Ezek 32:13
tear off their *h-s* ... Zech 11:16

HOOK *fastener*
into pruning *h-s* ... Is 2:4
My *h* in your nose ... Is 37:29
h-s into your jaws ... Ezek 38:4

HOPE (n) *expectation*
Where now is my *h* ... Job 17:15
h of the afflicted ... Ps 9:18
My *h* is in You ... Ps 39:7
You are my *h* ... Ps 71:5
while there is *h* ... Prov 19:18
the *h* of Israel ... Jer 17:13
our *h* has perished ... Ezek 37:11
on trial for the *h* ... Acts 23:6
h does not disappoint ... Rom 5:5
rejoicing in *h* ... Rom 12:12
may the God of *h* ... Rom 15:13
ought to plow in *h* ... 1 Cor 9:10
now faith, *h*, love, abide ... 1 Cor 13:13
h of righteousness ... Gal 5:5
the *h* of His calling ... Eph 1:18
the *h* of the gospel ... Col 1:23
the *h* of glory ... Col 1:27
the *h* of salvation ... 1 Thess 5:8
h of eternal life ... Titus 3:7
to a living *h* ... 1 Pet 1:3
h that is in you ... 1 Pet 3:15

HOPE (v) *expect with confidence*
I will *h* in Him ... Job 13:15
For I *h* in You ... Ps 38:15
We *h* for justice ... Is 59:11
are *h-ing* for light ... Jer 13:16
Gentiles will *h* ... Matt 12:21
h-s all things ... 1 Cor 13:7
first to *h* in Christ ... Eph 1:12
I *h* in the Lord Jesus ... Phil 2:19
of *things h-d* for ... Heb 11:1
I *h* to come to you ... 2 John 12

HOPHNI One of the sons of Eli, a priest who died in a battle with the Philistines when the ark of the testimony was taken.
son of Eli ... 1 Sam 1:3; 4:11

HOPHRA *see* **PHARAOH**

HOR The mountain on the border of Edom where Aaron died and was buried.
mountain ... Num 20:22,23
place of Aaron's death ... Num 20:28; Deut 32:50

HORDE *throng*
against Babylon A *h* ... Jer 50:9
h-s of grasshoppers ... Nah 3:17

HOREB Another name for Mt. Sinai. The place where the Law was given to Moses.
another name for Mount Sinai ... Ex 3:1; Deut 4:10; Ps 106:19

HORITES
inhabitants of Mount Seir in Edom ... Gen 14:6;36:29

HORN
caught...by his *h-s* ... Gen 22:13
h-s of the altar ... Ex 29:12
you shall sound a *h* ... Lev 25:9
with the ram's *h* ... Josh 6:5

h of my salvation ... 2 Sam 22:3
the *h*, flute, lyre ... Dan 3:5
it had ten *h-s* ... Dan 7:7

HORROR *terror*
h overwhelms me ... Is 21:4
object of *h* ... Jer 49:13
clothed with *h* ... Ezek 7:27
cup of *h* ... Ezek 23:33

HORSE *animal*
bites the *h-'s* heels ... Gen 49:17
h-s and chariots of ... 2 Kin 6:17
A *h* is a false hope ... Ps 33:17
whip is for the *h* ... Prov 26:3
slaves *riding* on *h-s* ... Eccl 10:7
behold, a black *h* ... Rev 6:5

HORSE GATE *see* **GATES OF JERUSALEM**

HORSEMEN *cavalry, horse rider*
Pharaoh, his *h* and ... Ex 14:9
chariots and *h* ... 1 Kin 10:26
h riding on ... Ezek 23:12
H charging, Swords ... Nah 3:3
armies of the *h* ... Rev 9:16

HOSANNA *acclamation of praise (save, we pray).* A cry of adoration and praise to the Messiah.
H to the Son of ... Matt 21:9
H in the highest ... Mark 11:10
H! Blessed is He ... John 12:13

HOSEA
prophet ... Hos 1:1,2

HOSHEA *(salvation).* The name of several individuals, including the last king of Israel who submitted to the Assyrians and was forced to pay them tribute. Later he rebelled and joined the Egyptians against the Assyrians, but nothing is known about his fate.
1 *name of Joshua* ... Num 13:8,16
2 *king of Israel* ... 2 Kin 15:30;17:6
3 *Ephraim's officer* ... 1 Chr 27:20
4 *signer of covenant* ... Neh 10:23

HOSPITABLE *friendly*
h, able to teach ... 1 Tim 3:2
h, loving what is ... Titus 1:8
h to one another ... 1 Pet 4:9

HOSPITALITY *open to guests* To admit a traveler into one's home and provide him with food and lodging for the night, etc. It was very important to do this in the ancient world for the safety and well-being of the traveler. The Gr term is used regularly in the NT for the reception of traveling evangelists, teachers, and prophets. Honoring a representative of God in this way is the same as honoring God Himself.
practicing *h* ... Rom 12:13
show *h* to strangers ... Heb 13:2

HOST *army, multitude*
captain...LORD's *h* ... Josh 5:15
LORD of *h-s,* He is ... Ps 24:10
of the heavenly *h* ... Luke 2:13

HOST OF HEAVEN Host signifies a multitude, and this can refer to the army of angelic beings or to the multitude of stars in the celestial sphere.
all the *h* ... Deut 4:19; 1 Kin 22:19

HOSTILE *antagonistic*
h to...Jesus ... Acts 26:9
set on the flesh is *h* ... Rom 8:7
h to all men ... 1 Thess 2:15

HOT *very warm, violent*
when the sun grew *h* ... Ex 16:21
and *h* displeasure ... Deut 9:19
My heart was *h* within ... Ps 39:3
man walk on *h* coals ... Prov 6:28
neither cold nor *h* ... Rev 3:15

HOUR *time*
add a *single h* to ... Matt 6:27
watch...for one *h* ... Matt 26:40
the *h* is at hand ... Matt 26:45
ninth *h* Jesus cried ... Mark 15:34
save Me from this *h* ... John 12:27
the *h* has come ... John 17:1
the *h* of testing ... Rev 3:10

HOUSE *home* or *temple*
born in my *h* is my ... Gen 15:3
passed over the *h-s* ... Ex 12:27
the *h* of slavery ... Ex 20:2
consecrates his *h* ... Lev 27:14
as for me and my *h* ... Josh 24:15
Set your *h* in order ... 2 Kin 20:1
h of God forsaken ... Neh 13:11
h like the spider's ... Job 27:18
Holiness befits Your *h* ... Ps 93:5
LORD builds the *h* ... Ps 127:1
Wisdom...built her *h* ... Prov 9:1
in My *h* of prayer ... Is 56:7
O *h* of Israel ... Jer 18:6
his *h* on the rock ... Matt 7:24
My *h*...a *h* of ... Matt 21:13
devour widows' *h-s* ... Mark 12:40
guards his own *h* ... Luke 11:21
left *h* or wife or ... Luke 18:29
In My Father's *h* ... John 14:2
h not made...hands ... 2 Cor 5:1
h for a holy ... 1 Pet 2:5

HOUSE OF GOD / LORD *see* **TEMPLE**

HOUSE OF THE LORD *see* **TABERNACLE**

HOUSEHOLD *family, home*
herds and a great *h* ... Gen 26:14
stole the *h* idols ... Gen 31:19
each one with his *h* ... Ex 1:1
to the ways of her *h* ... Prov 31:27
like a head of a *h* ... Matt 13:52
are of God's *h* ... Eph 2:19
manages his own *h* ... 1 Tim 3:4
in the *h* of God ... 1 Tim 3:15

HOUSETOP *roof*
As grass on the *h-s* ... 2 Kin 19:26
lonely bird on a *h* ... Ps 102:7
upon the *h-s* ... Matt 10:27
Peter went...the *h* ... Acts 10:9

HULDAH *(weasel).* A prophetess whom King Josiah sought out for prophecy from the Lord concerning the people of Judah's abuse of OT law.
a Hebrew prophetess ... 2 Kin 22:14; 2 Chr 34:22

HUMAN *mankind, person*
the life of any *h* ... Lev 24:17
guilt of *h* blood ... Prov 28:17
they had *h* form ... Ezek 1:5
tablets of *h* hearts ... 2 Cor 3:3

HUMBLE (adj) *gentle, modest*
Moses was very *h* ... Num 12:3
h will inherit ... Ps 37:11
with the *h* is wisdom ... Prov 11:2
H, and mounted on ... Zech 9:9
gentle and *h* in ... Matt 11:29
along with *h* means ... Phil 4:12
grace to the *h* ... James 4:6

HUMBLE (v) *abase*
refuse to *h* yourself ... Ex 10:3
He might *h* you ... Deut 8:2
h...and pray ... 2 Chr 7:14
h-s...as this child ... Matt 18:4
H yourselves ... 1 Pet 5:6

HUMILIATE *embarrass*
h-d who seek my hurt ... Ps 71:24
do not feel *h-d* ... Is 54:4
His opponents...*h-d* ... Luke 13:17

HUMILIATION *embarrassment*
h has overwhelmed me ... Ps 44:15
go away together in *h* ... Is 45:16
let our *h* cover us ... Jer 3:25
In *h* His judgment ... Acts 8:33

HUMILITY *self-abasement* In the Bible, usually an honest self-appraisal, characterized by the knowledge that one is merely human and by the absence of pride. Also refers to material poverty. In the NT, when Jesus applies the term to Himself (Matt 11:29), it refers to His attitude of service to others and His willingness to forego the rights and exaltation that are properly His as the Son of God.
before honor...*h* ... Prov 15:33
with *h* of mind ... Phil 2:3
clothe...with *h* ... 1 Pet 5:5

HUNDRED *number* or *many*
Adam had lived one *h* ... Gen 5:3
h of you will chase ... Lev 26:8
captains of *h-s* ... Num 31:14
h pieces of money ... Josh 24:32
went out by *h-s* ... 2 Sam 18:4
in groups of *h-s* ... Mark 6:40

HUNGER (n) *craving, starvation*
in *h,* in thirst ... Deut 28:48
lions...suffer *h* ... Ps 34:10
man will suffer *h* ... Prov 19:15
h is not satisfied ... Is 29:8
faint because of *h* ... Lam 2:19
sleeplessness, in *h* ... 2 Cor 6:5

HUNGER (v) *crave, need food*
the righteous to *h* ... Prov 10:3
are those who *h* ... Matt 5:6
to Me will not *h* ... John 6:35
They will *h* no longer ... Rev 7:16

HUNGRY *empty, needing food*
let you be *h* ... Deut 8:3
people are *h* and ... 2 Sam 17:29
h soul He has filled ... Ps 107:9
If your enemy is *h* ... Prov 25:21
when a *h* man dreams ... Is 29:8
He then became *h* ... Matt 4:2
disciples became *h* ... Matt 12:1
For I was *h* ... Matt 25:35
if your enemy is *h* ... Rom 12:20

HUNT *pursue, seek*
to *h* for game ... Gen 27:5
h-s a partridge ... 1 Sam 26:20

evil *h* the violent ... Ps 140:11
H-ed me down like ... Lam 3:52

HUNTER *seeker of game*
Nimrod a mighty *h* ... Gen 10:9
became a skillful *h* ... Gen 25:27

HUR An Israelite who helped Aaron to hold Moses' arms up while a battle was going on, in order to secure the blessing of God over the Israelites. Also the name of several other persons.
1 *helped Moses and Aaron* ... Ex 17:12; 24:14
2 *Bezalel's grandfather* ... Ex 31:2
3 *king of Midian* ... Num 31:8
4 *father of Rephaiah* ... Neh 3:9

HURAM
a Benjamite ... 1 Chr 8:5
see also **HIRAM / HURAM**

HURT (n) *damage, harm, wound*
Who delight in my *h* ... Ps 70:2
hoarded...to his *h* ... Eccl 5:13
your brother is *h* ... Rom 14:15

HURT (v) *cause pain, wound*
not allow him to *h* ... Gen 31:7
may be *h* by them ... Eccl 10:9
will not *h* or destroy ... Is 11:9
their power to *h* men ... Rev 9:10

HUSBAND *family head, spouse*
desire...your *h* ... Gen 3:16
honor to their *h-s* ... Esth 1:20
crown of her *h* ... Prov 12:4
is loved by *her h* ... Hos 3:1
divorces her *h* and ... Mark 10:12
have had five *h-s* ... John 4:18
if her *h* dies ... Rom 7:2
have her own *h* ... 1 Cor 7:2
unbelieving *h* is ... 1 Cor 7:14
h is the head of ... Eph 5:23
H-s, love your wives ... Eph 5:25
h-s of...one wife ... 1 Tim 3:12
adorned for her *h* ... Rev 21:2

HUSHAI A friend and counselor of King David whom the king sent to Jerusalem on a mission to trick Absalom, when the latter was plotting against David.
servant of David ... 2 Sam 15:32;16:17

HYMENAEUS
heretical teacher at Ephesus ... 1 Tim 1:20; 2 Tim 2:17

HYMN A song of praise or worship to God.
h-s of thanksgiving ... Neh 12:46
after singing a *h* ... Matt 26:30
singing *h-s* of praise ... Acts 16:25
psalms and *h-s* and ... Eph 5:19

HYPOCRISY *pretense*
full of *h* and ... Matt 23:28
love be without *h* ... Rom 12:9
without *h* ... James 3:17

HYPOCRITE *a pretender*
as the *h-s* do ... Matt 6:2
and Pharisees, *h-s* ... Matt 23:13
You *h,* first take ... Luke 6:42

HYSSOP *fragrant plant* A plant used in OT purification rites for the sprinkling of blood or water.
bunch of *h* and dip it ... Ex 12:22
scarlet string and *h* ... Lev 14:4
Purify me with *h* ... Ps 51:7
upon *a branch of h* ... John 19:29

I

I AM
related to name of God in Hebrew
I WHO I ... Ex 3:14
I has sent me ... Ex 3:14
I the LORD ... Ex 6:2
I the LORD your God ... Lev 19:3
I the first ... Is 44:6
I the Son of God ... Matt 27:43
Jesus said, *I* ... Mark 14:62
believe that *I He* ... John 8:24
will know that *I He* ... John 8:28
before Abraham...*I* ... John 8:58
believe that *I He* ... John 13:19
I the Alpha and ... Rev 1:8
I the first and ... Rev 1:17

ICE *frost*
turbid because of *i* ... Job 6:16
womb has come...*i* ... Job 38:29
casts forth His *i* ... Ps 147:17

ICHABOD
1 *son of Phinehas* ... 1 Sam 4:19,20
grandson of Eli ... 1 Sam 14:3
2 *name commemorates departed glory from Israel* ... 1 Sam 4:21,22

ICONIUM A city in Asia Minor where Paul suffered persecution.
city of Asia Minor ... Acts 14:1,19; 16:2; 2 Tim 3:11

IDDO A prophet who lived in the time of Jeroboam, Rehoboam, and Abijah (2 Chr 9:29). Also the name of several other persons.

IDLE *unemployed, uninvolved*
i man will suffer ... Prov 19:15
been standing here *i* ... Matt 20:6
this *i* babbler ... Acts 17:18

IDOL *false deity, image* Anything that is worshiped instead of God. In the Bible, normally an object carved or fabricated out of various materials in the form of man or beast.
not make...an *i* ... Ex 20:4
Do not turn to *i-s* ... Lev 19:4
who makes an *i* or ... Deut 27:15
the gods...are *i-s* ... Ps 96:5
who blesses an *i* ... Is 66:3
abstain from...*i-s* ... Acts 15:20
guard...from *i-s* ... 1 John 5:21

IDOLATER *idol worshiper*
covetous, or an *i* ... 1 Cor 5:11
Do not be *i-s* ... 1 Cor 10:7
sorcerers and *i-s* ... Rev 21:8

IDOLATRY *idol worship*
flee from *i* ... 1 Cor 10:14
i, sorcery, enmities ... Gal 5:20
and abominable *i-ies* ... 1 Pet 4:3

IGNORANCE *lack of knowledge*
you worship in *i* ... Acts 17:23
i that is in them ... Eph 4:18
silence the *i* of ... 1 Pet 2:15

IGNORANT *without knowledge*
I was senseless and *i* ... Ps 73:22
not *i* of his schemes ... 2 Cor 2:11
and *i* speculations ... 2 Tim 2:23

ILL *unhealthy, sick*
woman who is *i* ... Lev 15:33
became mortally *i* ... Is 38:1
lunatic and is...*i* ... Matt 17:15
healed many...*i* ... Mark 1:34

ILLEGITIMATE *bastard*
No one of *i* birth ... Deut 23:2
borne *i* children ... Hos 5:7
you are *i* children ... Heb 12:8

ILLNESS *infirmity, sickness*
sick with the *i* ... 2 Kin 13:14
after his *i* and ... Is 38:9
because of a bodily *i* ... Gal 4:13

ILLUMINE *light up*
God *i-s* my darkness ... Ps 18:28
fire to *i* by night ... Ps 105:39
glory of God has *i-d* ... Rev 21:23
God will *i* them ... Rev 22:5

IMAGE *copy, likeness*
make man in Our *i* ... Gen 1:26
i of God He made ... Gen 9:6
burn their graven *i-s* ... Deut 7:5
worshiped a molten *i* ... Ps 106:19
made an *i* of gold ... Dan 3:1
i and glory of God ... 1 Cor 11:7
i of the invisible ... Col 1:15
the *i* of the beast ... Rev 13:15

IMITATORS *followers*
be *i* of me ... 1 Cor 4:16
be *i* of God ... Eph 5:1
i of the churches ... 1 Thess 2:14

IMMANUEL *(with us is God).* One of the names for Jesus Christ. A sign from God to King Ahaz, later realized through the birth of Jesus Christ.
1 *son born to a virgin* ... Is 7:14
a sign to King Ahaz ... Is 8:8
2 *title of Jesus* ... Matt 1:23

IMMORAL *lewd, unchaste*
with *i* people ... 1 Cor 5:9
the *i* man sins ... 1 Cor 6:18
i men...liars ... 1 Tim 1:10
i or godless person ... Heb 12:16
and *i* persons ... Rev 21:8

IMMORALITY *immoral acts* Any evil behavior, but in the Bible usually improper sexual relations.
no *i* in your midst ... Lev 20:14
except for *i* ... Matt 19:9
Flee *i* ... 1 Cor 6:18
abstain from...*i* ... 1 Thess 4:3
the wine of her *i* ... Rev 17:2

IMMORTALITY *everlasting life* In the Scriptures, eternal life, both physical and spiritual, received as a gift of God through salvation. It includes the privilege of being with Christ forever, never to experience separation. Eternal life in the physical sense requires a body not subject to deterioration and death. Such a body will be provided to believers by God at their resurrection (those alive at the rapture will receive new bodies without experiencing death).
see also **LIFE, ETERNAL**
must put on *i* ... 1 Cor 15:53
alone possesses *i* ... 1 Tim 6:16
life and *i* to light ... 2 Tim 1:10

IMPATIENT *restless*
the people became *i* ... Num 21:4
should I not be *i* ... Job 21:4
my soul was *i* with ... Zech 11:8

IMPERISHABLE *indestructible*
wreath, but we an *i* ... 1 Cor 9:25
will be raised *i* ... 1 Cor 15:52
inheritance...*is i* ... 1 Pet 1:4

IMPLEMENTS *tools, utensils*
forger of all *i* of ... Gen 4:22
the *i* of the oxen ... 1 Kin 19:21

IMPLORE *ask, beseech, entreat*
I *i* you, give glory ... Josh 7:19
i-d him to avert ... Esth 8:3
i the compassion of ... Job 8:5
centurion...*i-ing* Him ... Matt 8:5
I *i* You by God ... Mark 5:7
They were *i-ing* Him ... Luke 8:31
I *i-d* the Lord ... 2 Cor 12:8
i you to walk in a ... Eph 4:1

IMPORTED *brought in*
chariot was *i* from ... 1 Kin 10:29
horses were *i* ... 2 Chr 1:16

IMPOSE *force upon*
i-d hard labor on us ... Deut 26:6
whatever you *i* on ... 2 Kin 18:14
you *i* heavy rent ... Amos 5:11
i-d until a time of ... Heb 9:10

IMPOSSIBLE *cannot be done*
nothing...will be *i* ... Gen 11:6
With people this is *i* ... Matt 19:26
i for God to lie ... Heb 6:18
without faith it is *i* ... Heb 11:6

IMPRISON *jail, restrict*
i-ed him at Riblah ... 2 Kin 23:33
i his princes at will ... Ps 105:22
not *i* their survivors ... Obad 14
I used to *i* and beat ... Acts 22:19

IMPRISONMENT *confinement*
in *i-s*, in tumults ... 2 Cor 6:5
Remember my *i* ... Col 4:18
even to *i* as a ... 2 Tim 2:9

IMPURE *unclean*
her *i* discharge ... Lev 15:25
eating...with *i* hands ... Mark 7:2
no immoral or *i* person ... Eph 5:5

IMPURITY *uncleanness*
menstrual *i* for seven ... Lev 15:19
i-ies of the sons of ... Lev 16:19
the *i* of the nations ... Ezra 6:21
as slaves to *i* ... Rom 6:19
of *i* with greediness ... Eph 4:19

INCARNATION *(into flesh)*. The fact that the eternal Son of God set aside the glory that He had with the Father, to be born a human being to a virgin, Himself begotten by the Father through the Holy Spirit. He led a sinless life on earth and was fit to be sacrificed for the sins of the world, which He did voluntarily by suffering physical death in the crucifixion. The incarnation was the only way to pay for the sins of mankind and was the supreme act of love by God for man. *see also* **KENOSIS**

INCENSE *fragrant substance* Material that when burned produces a sweet aroma. It was used in various aspects of Jewish worship and was said to represent prayers rising toward heaven.
burn fragrant *i* on ... Ex 30:7
i as an offering ... Lev 2:16
gold pans, full of *i* ... Num 7:86
My altar, to burn *i* ... 1 Sam 2:28
i on the high places ... 2 Kin 14:4
i before the LORD ... 1 Chr 23:13
golden altar of *i* ... Heb 9:4
the smoke of the *i* ... Rev 8:4

INCEST *illicit sexual relations*
they...committed *i* ... Lev 20:12

INCITE *stir up*
i-d David against ... 2 Sam 24:1
Jezebel...*i-d* him ... 1 Kin 21:25
I will *i* Egyptians ... Is 19:2
who *i-s* the people ... Luke 23:14
Jews *i-d* the devout ... Acts 13:50

INCLINE *bend, lean*
i your hearts to ... Josh 24:23
I my heart to Your ... Ps 119:36
i-s toward wickedness ... Is 32:6
I Your ear, O LORD ... Is 37:17
have not *i-d* your ear ... Jer 35:15

INCOME *wages*
i of the wicked ... Prov 10:16
i with injustice ... Prov 16:8
abundance *with its i* ... Eccl 5:10

INCORRUPTIBLE *not impure*
glory of the *i* God ... Rom 1:23
Christ with *i love* ... Eph 6:24

INCREASE (n) *multiplication*
the *i* of your herd ... Deut 7:13
the *i* of your house ... 1 Sam 2:33
the LORD give you *i* ... Ps 115:14
i of *His* government ... Is 9:7

INCREASE (v) *multiply*
If riches *i*, do not ... Ps 62:10
the righteous *i* ... Prov 28:28
i-ing in wisdom ... Luke 2:52
i-ing in...knowledge ... Col 1:10
Lord cause...to *i* ... 1 Thess 3:12

INCURABLE *fatal, without cure*
with an *i* sickness ... 2 Chr 21:18
sickliness and *i* pain ... Is 17:11
Your wound is *i* ... Jer 30:12

INDIA
lower Indus valley in S Asia ... Esth 1:1;8:9

INDIGNANT *be angry*
i toward His enemies ... Is 66:14
the ten became *i* ... Matt 20:24
Jesus...was *i* ... Mark 10:14
i because Jesus had ... Luke 13:14

INDIGNATION *anger*
God who has *i* ... Ps 7:11
Pour out Your *i* ... Ps 69:24
lips are filled with *i* ... Is 30:27
filled me with *i* ... Jer 15:17
stand before His *i* ... Nah 1:6

INERRANCY One of the chief implications of the doctrine of inspiration (q.v.). Every word of Scripture is God-breathed (Gr *theopneustos;* see 1 Pet 1:21) and there are no errors of any kind. Whenever errors seem to occur, they are in fact only apparent, and the vast majority can be explained as the result of over-simplifications of historical accounts or as commonplace ways of describing natural phenomena, etc. The remaining difficulties are due either to a lack of additional information—e.g. archaeological data—which may be remedied at some time in the future, or simply to the limits of human understanding and logic.

INFANT *child*
carries a nursing *i* ... Num 11:12
an *i who lives* ... Is 65:20
tongue of the *i* ... Lam 4:4
the mouth of *i-s* ... Matt 21:16
as to *i-s* in Christ ... 1 Cor 3:1

INFECTION *disease*
an *i* of leprosy ... Lev 13:2
with the scaly *i* ... Lev 13:31
against an *i* of ... Deut 24:8

INFERIOR *lower in status*
I am not *i* to you ... Job 12:3
i against the honorable ... Is 3:5
i to...apostles ... 2 Cor 12:11

INFINITE *unlimited*
His understanding is *i* ... Ps 147:5

INFLICT *strike, impose*
frogs...He had *i-ed* ... Ex 8:12
i all these curses ... Deut 30:7
i-s pain, and gives ... Job 5:18

INGATHERING, FEAST OF *see* **BOOTHS, FEAST OF** *and* **FEASTS**

INHABIT *dwell*
no one would *i* ... Job 15:28
She shall be *i-ed* ... Is 44:26
build houses and *i* ... Is 65:21
those *i-ing* the desert ... Jer 9:26
who *i* the coastlands ... Ezek 39:6
but not *i them* ... Zeph 1:13

INHABITANT *resident*
i-s of the cities ... Gen 19:25
cities...without *i* ... Is 6:11
ruins Without *i* ... Jer 4:7
i-s of the seacoast ... Zeph 2:5
i-s of Jerusalem ... Zech 12:10

INHERIT *receive a legacy*
shall *i it* forever ... Ex 32:13
humble will *i* the land ... Ps 37:11
wise will *i* honor ... Prov 3:35
The naive *i* foolishness ... Prov 14:18
gentle...*i* the earth ... Matt 5:5
do to *i* eternal life ... Luke 10:25
not *i* the kingdom ... 1 Cor 6:9
might *i* a blessing ... 1 Pet 3:9
who overcomes will *i* ... Rev 21:7

INHERITANCE *bequest, legacy*
Levites for an *i* ... Num 18:24
the LORD is his *i* ... Deut 10:9
the nations as Your *i* ... Ps 2:8
will He forsake His *i* ... Ps 94:14
man leaves an *i* ... Prov 13:22
I...abandoned My *i* ... Jer 12:7
Your *i* a reproach ... Joel 2:17
A man and his *i* ... Mic 2:2
the *i* will be ours ... Mark 12:7
we...obtained an *i* ... Eph 1:11
the *i* of the saints ... Col 1:12
i...imperishable ... 1 Pet 1:4

INIQUITY *injustice, wickedness* Gross injustice or wickedness. An act of sin that demonstrates depravity.
bear...their *i-ies* ... Lev 16:22
the *i* of the fathers ... Deut 5:9
those who plow *i* ... Job 4:8
O LORD, Pardon my *i* ... Ps 25:11
my *i* I did not hide ... Ps 32:5
blot out all my *i-ies* ... Ps 51:9
sows *i* will reap ... Prov 22:8
weighed down with *i* ... Is 1:4
the workers of *i* ... Is 31:2
die for his own *i* ... Jer 31:30
Repent...so that *i* ... Ezek 18:30
the bondage of *i* ... Acts 8:23
the *very* world of *i* ... James 3:6
remembered her *i-ies* ... Rev 18:5

INJUNCTION *decree*
establish the *i* ... Dan 6:8

INJURE *harm, wrong*
who seek to *i* me ... Ps 38:12
i-d your neighbors ... Ezek 22:12
nothing will *i* you ... Luke 10:19
do you *i* one another ... Acts 7:26

INJURY *wound*
there is no *further i* ... Ex 21:22
because of my *i* ... Jer 10:19
no *i*...was found ... Dan 6:23

INJUSTICE *inequity, unfairness*
do no *i* in judgment ... Lev 19:15
A God...without *i* ... Deut 32:4
there *i* on my tongue ... Job 6:30
They devise *i-s* ... Ps 64:6
is no *i* with God ... Rom 9:14

INK *writing liquid*
I wrote them with *i* ... Jer 36:18
with pen and *i* ... 3 John 13

INN *lodge for travelers*
no room...in the *i* ... Luke 2:7
brought him to...*i* ... Luke 10:34

INNKEEPER *traveler's host*
gave them to the *i* ... Luke 10:35

INNOCENCE *blamelessness*
wash my hands in *i* ... Ps 26:6
be incapable of *i* ... Hos 8:5

INNOCENT *blameless*
do not kill the *i* ... Ex 23:7
the blood of the *i* ... Deut 19:13
i before the LORD ... 2 Sam 3:28
the *i* mock them ... Job 22:19
that shed *i* blood ... Prov 6:17
and *i* as doves ... Matt 10:16
betraying *i* blood ... Matt 27:4
i of this Man's ... Matt 27:24
holy, *i*, undefiled ... Heb 7:26

INQUIRE *ask, seek*
to *i* of the LORD ... Gen 25:22
I of God, please ... Judg 18:5
David *i-d* of...LORD ... 1 Sam 23:2
you come to *i* of Me ... Ezek 20:3
i-d...where the Messiah ... Matt 2:4
i-d of them the hour ... John 4:52

INSANE *mad*
a demon and is *i* ... John 10:20
I speak as if *i* ... 2 Cor 11:23

INSCRIBE *carve, write*
were *i-d* in a book ... Job 19:23
i it on a scroll ... Is 30:8
and *i* a city on it ... Ezek 4:1
i it on tablets ... Hab 2:2

INSCRIPTION *writing*
could not read the *i* ... Dan 5:8
I will engrave an *i* ... Zech 3:9
Pilate...wrote an *i* ... John 19:19
i, To An Unknown ... Acts 17:23

INSECTS
swarms of *i* on you ... Ex 8:21
all other winged *i* ... Lev 11:23

INSIGHT *discernment*
a counselor with *i* ... 1 Chr 26:14
according to his *i* ... Prov 12:8
i with understanding ... Dan 9:22
not gained any *i* ... Mark 6:52
In all wisdom and *i* ... Eph 1:8

INSIGNIFICANT *unimportant*
was *i* in Your eyes ... 2 Sam 7:19
your beginning was *i* ... Job 8:7
citizen of no *i* city ... Acts 21:39

INSOLENT *arrogant*
acts with *i* pride ... Prov 21:24
haters of God, *i* ... Rom 1:30

INSPECTION GATE *see* **GATES OF JERUSALEM**

INSPIRATION The process by which the Scriptures were written as stated in 2 Tim 3:16 and 1 Pet 1:21. The human authors were guided directly by the Holy Spirit, and the Scriptures themselves are the words of God. As a Christian doctrine, inspiration guarantees that all the words of Scripture are completely reliable and without error (*see* **INERRANCY**). It does not mean that God simply dictated the words to the human authors, though this undoubtedly happened to some extent. Instead, God guided the authors in such a way that their own personalities are discernible in their writings, while the truth and accuracy of their words is ensured.

INSPIRED
the love we *i* in you ... 2 Cor 8:7
All Scripture is *i* ... 2 Tim 3:16

INSTINCT *natural tendency*
as creatures of *i* ... 2 Pet 2:12
they know by *i* ... Jude 10

INSTRUCT *teach*
Your good Spirit to *i* ... Neh 9:20
I will *i* you ... Ps 32:8
the wise is *i-ed* ... Prov 21:11
i-ed out of the Law ... Rom 2:18
just as you were *i-ed* ... Col 2:7
may *i* certain men ... 1 Tim 1:3

INSTRUCTION *teaching*
will walk in My *i* ... Ex 16:4
Heed *i* and be wise ... Prov 8:33
Get wisdom and *i* ... Prov 23:23
i-s to His twelve ... Matt 11:1
written for our *i* ... Rom 15:4
i of the Lord ... Eph 6:4
goal of our *i* is love ... 1 Tim 1:5
i about washings ... Heb 6:2

INSTRUMENT *object, vessel*
cut...with sharp *i-s* ... 1 Chr 20:3
and *i-s* of music ... 2 Chr 5:13
with stringed *i-s* ... Ps 150:4
he is a chosen *i* ... Acts 9:15
i-s of unrighteousness ... Rom 6:13

INSULT (n) *affront, indignity*
i-s of the nations ... Ezek 34:29
evil, or *i* for *i* ... 1 Pet 3:9

INSULT (v) *treat with scorn*
and do not *i* her ... Ruth 2:15
to *i* the LORD ... 2 Chr 32:17
times you have *i-ed* ... Job 19:3
i-ing...with the same words ... Matt 27:44
and *i* you ... Luke 6:22
i-ed the Spirit of ... Heb 10:29

INSURRECTION A rebellion against civil authority or against any established order. Barabbas, the man whom the mob chose instead of Christ to be liberated by Pilate, was charged with insurrection (Luke 23:18-19).

INTEGRITY *honesty*
In the *i* of my heart ... Gen 20:5
dealt in truth and *i* ... Judg 9:19
holds fast his *i* ... Job 2:3
He who walks with *i* ... Ps 15:2
have walked in my *i* ... Ps 26:1
The *i* of the upright ... Prov 11:3

INTELLIGENCE *mental ability*
He deprives of *i* ... Job 12:24
gave them...*i* ... Dan 1:17
Paulus, a man of *i* ... Acts 13:7

INTELLIGENT *bright, smart*
was *i* and beautiful ... 1 Sam 25:3
mind of the *i* seeks ... Prov 15:14
from *the* wise and *i* ... Matt 11:25

INTEND *purpose*
Are you *i-ing* to kill ... Ex 2:14
I *i* to build a house ... 1 Kin 5:5
i to make My people ... Jer 23:27
i-ing to betray Him ... John 12:4
i-ing...to take Paul ... Acts 20:13

INTENTION *aim, goal*
the *i-s* of the heart ... 1 Chr 29:18
i of your heart ... Acts 8:22
kind *i* of His will ... Eph 1:5

INTERCEDE *plead, mediate*
i-d for the people ... Num 21:7
who can *i* for him ... 1 Sam 2:25
And *i-d* for the ... Is 53:12
do not *i* with Me ... Jer 7:16
Spirit Himself *i-s* ... Rom 8:26

INTERCESSION The act of seeking favor or a benefit for another person from that person's superior, usually by making a request. Examples of intercession are Abraham for Ishmael, and for Sodom and Gomorrah; Boaz for Ruth; Daniel for Israel and Judah; and Christ and the Holy Spirit, for all believers.

INTERCOURSE *copulation*
not have *i* with ... Lev 18:20
not have *i*...animal ... Lev 18:23
husband has had *i* ... Num 5:20

INTEREST *concern* or *usury*
not charge him *i* ... Ex 22:25
not take usurious *i* ... Lev 25:36
i to a foreigner ... Deut 23:20
his money at *i* ... Ps 15:5

mind on God's *i-s* ... Matt 16:23
money...with *i* ... Matt 25:27
he has a morbid *i* ... 1 Tim 6:4

INTERMARRY
I with us ... Gen 34:9
shall not *i* with ... Deut 7:3
i with the peoples ... Ezra 9:14

INTERPRET *explain, translate*
no one who could *i* ... Gen 41:8
one who *i-s* omens ... Deut 18:10
He *i* the message ... Is 28:9
unless he *i-s* ... 1 Cor 14:5
pray that he may *i* ... 1 Cor 14:13

INTERPRETATION *explain* The work of one who explains the meaning of something, e.g. a text, statement, or prophetic dream. The discipline of Biblical interpretation is called "Hermeneutics."
i-s belong to God ... Gen 40:8
the dream and its *i* ... Judg 7:15
make its *i* known ... Dan 5:16
the *i* of tongues ... 1 Cor 12:10
of one's own *i* ... 2 Pet 1:20

INTIMATE *close*
my *i* friends have ... Job 19:14
i with the upright ... Prov 3:32
separates *i* friends ... Prov 16:28

INVADE *attack*
king of Assyria *i-d* ... 2 Kin 17:5
nation has *i-d* my land ... Joel 1:6
Assyrian *i-s* our land ... Mic 5:5

INVALIDATE *nullify*
i-d the word of God ... Matt 15:6
i-ing the word of ... Mark 7:13
does not *i* a covenant ... Gal 3:17

INVESTIGATE *examine*
the judges shall *i* ... Deut 19:18
the plot was *i-d* ... Esth 2:23
i, and to seek wisdom ... Eccl 7:25
having *i-d* everything ... Luke 1:3

INVISIBLE *unseen*
His *i* attributes ... Rom 1:20
image of the *i* God ... Col 1:15
visible and *i* ... Col 1:16
eternal, immortal, *i* ... 1 Tim 1:17

INVITE *request*
i-d us to impoverish ... Judg 14:15
you shall *i* Jesse ... 1 Sam 16:3
i-d all the king's ... 2 Sam 13:23
I am *i-d* by her ... Esth 5:12
did not *i* Me in ... Matt 25:43
i the poor ... Luke 14:13

IRON *metal*
was an *i* bedstead ... Deut 3:11
whose stones are *i* ... Deut 8:9
had *i* chariots ... Judg 1:19
made the *i* float ... 2 Kin 6:6
break them...rod of *i* ... Ps 2:9
from the *i* furnace ... Jer 11:4
as strong as *i* ... Dan 2:40
rule...rod of *i* ... Rev 19:15

ISAAC *(laughing).* The son born according to God's promise to Abraham and Sarah, when it was impossible for them to have children due to their old age.
birth, son of Abraham ... Gen 21:3
offered for sacrifice ... Gen 22:2
took Rebekah as wife ... Gen 24
father of twins ... Gen 25:26
blessed Jacob ... Gen 27:1-40

ISAIAH *(Yahweh is salvation).* One of the four major OT prophetic books. Isaiah ministered under several kings and is sometimes called the evangelistic prophet for his "good news" prophecies.
prophet of Judah ... Is 1:1
son of Amoz ... *2 Kin 19:2*
called ... Is 6:8ff
under four kings ... Is 1:1

ISCARIOT There are several possibilities for the meaning of this name, including "the false one," "the assassin," or "the dyer" (an occupation). The most probable meaning is "man of Kerioth," referring to a village in Judea located 12 miles south of Hebron. The name distinguishes Judas, the betrayer of Christ, from the other apostle named Judas.
geographical identity of Judas ... Mark 3:19; John 12:4; 13:26

ISH-BOSHETH *(man of shame).* One of Saul's sons. He reigned over Israel for two troubled years.
son of Saul ... 2 Sam 2:8; 3:8; 4:8

ISHMAEL *(may God hear).* The son who was born to Abraham and Sarah's maid Hagar when Sarah and Abraham became impatient about God's promise of a son to them, and decided to take matters into their own hands. Also the name of other individuals.
1 *son of Abraham* ... Gen 16:11; 17:18; 25:17
2 *son of Nethaniah* ... 2 Kin 25:23
3 *line of Jonathan* ... 1 Chr 8:38; 9:44
4 *Zebadiah's father* ... 2 Chr 19:11
5 *son of Jehohanan* ... 2 Chr 23:1
6 *son of Pashhur* ... Ezra 10:22

ISLAND *surrounded by water*
the many *i-s* be glad ... Ps 97:1
He lifts up the *i-s* ... Is 40:15
i was called Malta ... Acts 28:1
every *i* fled away ... Rev 16:20

ISOLATE *set apart*
priest shall *i him* ... Lev 13:4
i him for seven days ... Lev 13:21
fortified city is *i-d* ... Is 27:10

ISRAEL (unc, *God perseveres).* The patriarch formerly named Jacob. The twelve tribes of Israel, the chosen people of God, descended from Jacob.
1 *Jacob* ... Gen 32:28-32; 35:10; 37:3
2 *line of Jacob* ... Gen 34:7
tribal nation ... Ex 1:7; 4:22; Num 10:29
3 *united kingdom* ... 1 Sam 15:35; 1 Kin 4:1
4 *northern kingdom* ... 1 Kin 14:19; 15:9; 2 Kin 10:29
5 *under Roman rule* ... Luke 2:32; John 1:49; Rom 9:6

ISSACHAR (unc, *a hired man).* The ninth son of Jacob by Leah, and founder of one of the Israelite tribes. Also one of the territories in the Promised Land, and the name of a Levite.
1 *son of Jacob* ... Gen 30:18; 49:14
2 *tribe* ... Num 1:29; Josh 21:28; Rev 7:7
3 *Levite* ... 1 Chr 26:5

ISSUE (n) *outflow, outgo*
first *i* of the womb ... Num 3:12
offspring and *i* ... Is 22:24
like the *i* of horses ... Ezek 23:20
concerning this *i* ... Acts 15:2

ISSUE (v) *go forth, put forth*
Moses *i-d* a command ... Ex 36:6
shall *i* from you ... 2 Kin 20:18
decree was *i-d* at ... Esth 3:15
i-d a proclamation ... Dan 5:29

ITALY
S European country ... Acts 18:2;27: 1,6; Heb 13:24

ITHAMAR (unc, *oasis of palms).* The youngest son of Aaron. He inventoried the items comprising the tabernacle and oversaw the duties of the Gershonites and Merarites which they performed in it (Num 4:28).

ITURAEA
region N of Palestine ... Luke 3:1
tetrarchy of Herod Philip II

IVORY *elephant tusk*
a great throne of *i* ... 1 Kin 10:18
silver, *i* and apes ... 2 Chr 9:21
Out of *i* palaces ... Ps 45:8
every article of *i* ... Rev 18:12

J

JABAL
son of Lamech ... Gen 4:20
father of herders

JABBOK
tributary of Jordan ... Gen 32:22; Num 21:24; Josh 12:2; Judg 11:13,22

JABESH-GILEAD *(dry place of Gilead).* A town of Gilead where, in the times of the judges, the nation of Israel fought against Benjamin. Some of their people buried Saul and his sons, a kindness for which David sent them his blessings.
town of Gilead ... Judg 21:8ff
E of Jordan River ... 1 Sam 11:1,9; 2 Sam 2:4,5

JABIN *(one who is intelligent).* The name of two kings from Hazor who quarreled against Israel (Josh 11:1; Judg 4:23).

JACHIN *(he will establish).* In Solomon's temple, the name of the pillar to the right side in the porch (2 Chr 3:17; *see* **BOAZ**). Also the name of several individuals.

JACINTH *precious stone*
a *j*, an agate ... Ex 28:19
the eleventh, *j* ... Rev 21:20

JACKALS *wild dogs*
j in their...palaces ... Is 13:22
ruins, A haunt of *j* ... Jer 9:11
a lament like the *j* ... Mic 1:8

JACOB (unc, *God has protected).* The former name of Israel, the younger brother of Esau. He was the favorite of his mother Rebekah.
1 *son of Isaac* ... Gen 25:26

brother of Esau ... Gen 25:27
obtained birthright ... Gen 25:33
fled to Aram ... Gen 28:5,6
marriage ... Gen 29:1ff
wrestled angel ... Gen 32:24ff
name changed ... Gen 35:9,10
went down to Egypt ... Gen 46:4ff
death and burial ... Gen 49:28ff
2 *father of Joseph* ... Matt 1:15,16

JAEL *(wild goat).* She assassinated Sisera, the Canaanite general, when he tried to find protection in the house of Heber, Jael's husband.
wife of Heber ... Judg 4:17
slayer of Sisera ... Judg 4:21
described as blessed ... Judg 5:24

JAHAZ A place in Moab where Israel killed Sihon, king of the Amorites (Judg 11:20-21).

JAIL *place of confinement*
put him into the *j* ... Gen 39:20
in *j* in the house ... Jer 37:15
put them in...*j* ... Acts 5:18

JAILER *warden*
sight of the chief *j* ... Gen 39:21
chief *j* did not ... Gen 39:23
the *j* to guard them ... Acts 16:23

JAIR
1 *judge of Israel* ... Judg 10:3
2 *son of Segub* ... 1 Chr 2:22
3 *father of Elhanan* ... 1 Chr 20:5
4 *Mordecai's father* ... Esth 2:5

JAIRUS
ruler of synagogue ... Mark 5:22; Luke 8:41

JAMES Anglicized form of the name *Jacob.*
1 *son of Zebedee* ... Matt 4:21
brother of John ... Matt 10:2
called as apostle ... Matt 10:2ff
martyred ... Acts 12:2
2 *son of Alphaeus* ... Matt 10:3
called as apostle ... Matt 10:3ff
3 *brother of Jesus* ... Matt 13:55; Mark 6:3
church leader ... Acts 12:17; 15:13
4 *Judas's father* ... Luke 6:16

JAPHETH *(may God enlarge).* One of the sons of Noah. He was careful not to disgrace his father when the latter was inebriated.
son of Noah ... Gen 7:13; 9:23,27

JAPHIA
1 *king of Lachish* ... Josh 10:3
2 *son of David* ... 2 Sam 5:15
3 *town of Zebulun* ... Josh 19:12

JAR *container, jug*
and a *j* of honey ... 1 Kin 14:3
Bring me a new *j* ... 2 Kin 2:20
potter's earthenware *j* ... Jer 19:1
j full of sour wine ... John 19:29

JASHAR
book quoted in Bible ... Josh 10:13; 2 Sam 1:18

JASON
Christian of Thessalonica ... Acts 17:5-9; Rom 16:21

JASPER *precious stone* A type of quartz with any of several colors. The last of the precious stones in the high priest's breastplate and the first in the foundation of the wall in the new Jerusalem.
fourth row...a *j* ... Ex 28:20
the onyx, and the *j* ... Ezek 28:13
was like a *j* stone ... Rev 4:3
of crystal-clear *j* ... Rev 21:11

JAVAN
Hebrew word for Greeks or Greece ... Gen 10:2,4; 1 Chr 1:5,7; Is 66:19; Ezek 27:13,19

JAVELIN *spear* A lightweight spear used in war and hunting.
Stretch out the *j* ... Josh 8:18
j slung between his ... 1 Sam 17:6
flashing spear and *j* ... Job 39:23
seize *their*...*j* ... Jer 50:42

JAW *part of face*
j-s of the wicked ... Job 29:17
cleaves to my *j-s* ... Ps 22:15
j teeth *like* knives ... Prov 30:14
hooks into your *j-s* ... Ezek 38:4

JAWBONE
j of a donkey ... Judg 15:15
threw the *j* from ... Judg 15:17

JAZER An Amorite town which the Israelites captured. Later it was declared a Levite city (Josh 21:39).

JEALOUS *envious, zealous*
brothers were *j* of ... Gen 37:11
your God, am a *j* God ... Ex 20:5
whose name is *J,* is ... Ex 34:14
j with My jealousy ... Num 25:11
He is a *j* God ... Josh 24:19
j and avenging God ... Nah 1:2
j for Jerusalem ... Zech 1:14
Jews, becoming *j* ... Acts 17:5
I will make you *j* ... Rom 10:19
love is kind...not *j* ... 1 Cor 13:4

JEBUS Another name for Jerusalem (Judg 19:10,11; 1 Chr 11:4,5).

JEBUSITES The Jebusites were descendants of Canaan (Gen 10:16). They controlled the city of Jerusalem and its environs in spite of the Israeli conquest, and were not expelled until David captured the city and made it his capital. The remaining Jebusites became servants during Solomon's reign (1 Kin 9:20-21).
clan or tribe ... Gen 10:16
inhabitants of Jebus ... Ex 3:8,17; Josh 15:63; 2 Sam 24:16,18; Ezra 9:1; Zech 9:7

JECONIAH
variant of Jehoiachin's name ... 1 Chr 3:16,17; Esth 2:6

JEHAZIEL
1 *Benjamite warrior* ... 1 Chr 12:4
2 *priest* ... 1 Chr 16:6
3 *son of Hebron* ... 1 Chr 23:19
4 *son of Zechariah* ... 2 Chr 20:14

JEHOAHAZ *(Yahweh has taken hold).* One king of Israel (the northern kingdom) and two kings of Judah had this name: 1) A king of Israel after the division of the kingdom, the son and successor of Jehu (2 Kin 10:35); 2) the son and successor of Josiah as king of Judah (2 Kin 23:30-31); 3) the son and successor of Jehoram as king of Judah (2 Chr 21:17), also known as Ahaziah.
1 *son of Jehu* ... 2 Kin 10:35
king of Israel ... 2 Kin 13:1ff
2 *son of Josiah* ... 2 Kin 23:30-34
king of Judah ... 2 Kin 23:30
see also **SHALLUM** ... 1 Chr 3:15
3 *son of Jehoram* ... 2 Chr 21:17
see also **AHAZIAH** ... 2 Chr 22:1ff

JEHOASH
1 *king of Judah* ... 2 Kin 11:21
son of Ahaziah ... 2 Kin 12:1-18
2 *king of Israel* ... 2 Kin 13:10
son of Jehoahaz ... 2 Kin 13:25;14:13

JEHOIACHIN
son of Jehoiakim ... 2 Kin 24:6
king of Judah ... 2 Kin 24:8-15; 2 Chr 36:8,9; Jer 52:31,33

JEHOIACHIN, JECONIAH, JECHONIAS *(Yahweh will uphold).* The son and successor of Jehoiakim as king of Judah (2 Kin 24:6-8). *Jeconiah* is a modified spelling and *Jechonias* the Gr spelling.

JEHOIADA *(Yahweh knows).* A high priest who saved the life of the infant Joash and later helped him to become the king. He was 130 years old when he died and was buried among the kings in recognition of his faithful service. Also the name of several other persons.
1 *father of Benaiah* ... 2 Sam 8:18
priest ... 1 Chr 27:5
2 *son of Benaiah* ... 1 Chr 27:34
3 *high priest* ... 2 Kin 11:4,9
4 *priest* ... Jer 29:26

JEHOIAKIM *(Yahweh will establish).* Son of Josiah, originally his name was Eliakim. He was not a righteous king as his father was.
son of King Josiah ... 2 Kin 23:34; 2 Chr 36:4
king of Judah ... 2 Kin 23:36; 2 Chr 36:5; Jer 22:18; Dan 1:2
father of Jehoiachin ... 2 Kin 24:6

JEHORAM
1 *son of Ahab* ... 2 Kin 3:1
king of Israel ... 2 Kin 3:6
2 *priest* ... 2 Chr 17:8
3 *Jehoshaphat's son* ... 2 Kin 8:16
king of Judah ... 2 Kin 8:25,29
see also **JORAM**

JEHOSHAPHAT *(Yahweh is salvation).* Name of several persons, including the son and successor of Asa. He was a wise man who pursued peace in his reign. Also the name of a valley where the Lord will gather all nations to be judged, the location being uncertain.
1 *son of Ahilud* ... 2 Sam 8:16
2 *son of Paruah* ... 1 Kin 4:17
3 *son of Asa* ... 1 Kin 15:24
king of Judah ... 1 Kin 22:2-51; 2 Chr 17:1-12
4 *father of Jehu* ... 2 Kin 9:2,14

5 *valley* ... Joel 3:2,12

JEHU *(he is Yahweh).* Name of several people, including a former officer in the service of King Ahab. This Jehu was anointed king in place of Ahab, under the auspices of Elijah. Later he seized the throne of Judah by deceit.
1 *prophet, son of Hanani* ... 1 Kin 16:1,7,12; 2 Chr 19:2
2 *king of Israel* ... 1 Kin 19:16; 2 Kin 9:14,30; 2 Chr 22:7
3 *man of Judah* ... 1 Chr 2:38
4 *Simeonite* ... 1 Chr 4:35
5 *Benjamite* ... 1 Chr 12:3

JEMIMAH
daughter of Job ... Job 42:14

JEPHTHAH *(opener).* A judge who was called upon by the elders of Gilead to be their head and lead them in their fight against the Ammonites. He freed Israel from the Ammonites and is listed in Heb 11 as a man of faith.
a Gileadite ... Judg 11:1
judge of Israel ... Judg 11:2-40

JEREMIAH The "weeping" prophet whose writings became one of the four major prophetic books of the OT. Jeremiah was called to the ministry of prophecy through a vision from God. Also the name of several other individuals.
1 *lived in Libnah* ... 2 Kin 23:31
2 *man of Manasseh* ... 1 Chr 5:24
3 *three individuals who joined David* ... 1 Chr 12:4,10,13
4 *prophet* ... Jer 1:1
called ... Jer 1:2-10
put in stocks ... Jer 20:2,3
life threatened ... Jer 26
put in prison ... Jer 32:2; 37:13ff
taken to Egypt ... Jer 43:1-6
5 *son of Habazziniah* ... Jer 35:3
6 *priest* ... Neh 10:2
7 *priest from Babylon* ... Neh 12:1

JERICHO An important and ancient city in Canaan northeast of Jerusalem, well known for its walls falling miraculously during Joshua's siege. It is called "the city of palm trees."
city in Jordan Valley ... Josh 3:16
N of Dead Sea ... Josh 6:1; 1 Kin 16:34; Luke 18:35

JEROBOAM *(increase the nation).* The founder of the northern kingdom after his rebellion against Rehoboam, the inexperienced son of Solomon. Also the name of another king of Israel.
1 *Solomon's warrior* ... 1 Kin 11:28
first king of N Kingdom ... 1 Kin 12:26,27; 2 Chr 10:13
made golden calves ... 1 Kin 12:28
2 *son of Joash* ... 2 Kin 14:27
king of Israel ... 2 Kin 14:28,29

JERUBBAAL
name of Gideon ... Judg 6:32
judge of Israel ... Judg 7:1

JERUSALEM *(city of peace).* The most important city in Biblical history and one of the oldest continuously inhabited, over 4,500 years. This royal city is located on a high plain in central Israel. Its former name was Jebus, but since David's time it has been known as Jerusalem.
city called Salem ... Gen 14:18
city called Jebus ... Judg 1:21;19:10
David's capital ... 2 Sam 5:5,6
capital of united kingdom ... 1 Kin 2:36; 11:42
site of temple ... 1 Kin 6:2; 8:6,12
destroyed by Babylonians ... Jer 52:12-14
rebuilt by remnant ... Neh 2:11-20; 12:27
city of Roman period ... Matt 2:1,3; 21:1,10; Luke 13:34; Acts 11:2,22
new Jerusalem ... Rev 3:12; 21:2,10

JESHUA *(Yahweh is salvation).* Name of many individuals, including a Levite who helped Ezra explain the law to the people who returned from the Babylonian exile. Also the name of a city in Judah.
1 *line of Aaron* ... 1 Chr 24:11
2 *under Kore* ... 2 Chr 31:15
3 *high priest* ... Ezra 3:2; Neh 7:7
4 *of Pahath-moab* ... Ezra 2:6; Neh 7:11
5 *part of remnant* ... Ezra 2:40; Neh 7:43
6 *aided Ezra* ... Neh 8:7
7 *city in Judah* ... Neh 11:26
see also **JOSHUA**

JESHURUN
poetic name for Israel ... Deut 32:15; 33:5,26; Is 44:2

JESSE The father of David and grandson of Boaz and Ruth.
father of David ... 1 Sam 16:1,8; 2 Sam 20:1; 1 Kin 12:16; 1 Chr 2:12,13

JEST *joke, mock*
appeared...be *j-ing* ... Gen 19:14
Against whom do you *j* ... Is 57:4

JESUS
Jewish Christian called Justus ... Col 4:11

JESUS CHRIST *(Yahweh is salvation; Christ, anointed).* The Son of God, the second person of the Trinity (q.v.). *Jesus* was His given earthly name, equivalent to "Joshua" or "Jeshua," and He was commonly known as Jesus of Nazareth. *Christ* is the anglicized form of the Gr word *Christos,* which is equivalent to the Heb *Messiah* (q.v.). In Jesus Christ, OT prophecies about the Messiah were fulfilled, but the Jewish religious leaders and the nation of Israel as a whole rejected Him and demanded His crucifixion. He was vindicated as the Son of God and Savior by His resurrection from the dead.
name of the Lord ... Matt 1:21; 26:71; Luke 1:31
birth in Bethlehem ... Matt 1:18-25; Luke 2:1-7
youth in Nazareth ... Matt 2:19ff
baptized ... Matt 3:13ff; Mark 1:9ff; Luke 3:21; John 1:31ff
tempted ... Matt 4:1-11; Mark 1:12; Luke 4:1ff
called disciples ... Matt 4:18ff; Mark 1:16ff; Luke 5:1ff
transfigured ... Matt 17:1ff; Mark 9:2ff; Luke 9:28ff
triumphal entry to Jerusalem ... Matt 21:1ff; Mark 11:1ff; Luke 19:29ff
crucified ... Matt 27:31ff; Mark 15:20ff; Luke 23:26ff; John 19:16ff
resurrected Christ ... Matt 28:1ff; Mark 16:1ff; Luke 24:13ff; John 20:11ff
ascended to the Father ... Mark 16:19; Luke 24:50ff; Acts 1:9ff

JETHRO (unc, *preeminence).* Father-in-law of Moses and a priest in Midian, known also as Reuel. He gave advice to Moses about delegating responsibilities to others.
priest of Midian ... Ex 3:1
Moses' father-in-law ... Ex 4:18;18:1-12

JEW(S) Technically, the name refers to a descendant of the tribe of Judah, a Judean (2 Kin 16:6). In a general and more practical sense, a person of Jewish ancestry, or someone who has become a convert to Judaism. A person of Jewish ancestry who does not follow the precepts of Judaism (the Jewish faith) is sometimes called a non-observant Jew.
Judean shortened to Jew during exile ... 2 Kin 25:25
synonym for Hebrew ... Ezra 4:12,23; Neh 4:1,2; Esth 4:3,7; Jer 34:9
later term for all Israelites in the land and in Diaspora ... Matt 27:11; Mark 7:3; Luke 23:51; John 4:9; Acts 22:3; Rom 3:1; Gal 3:28; Rev 2:9

JEWEL *precious stone*
precious than *j-s* ... Prov 3:15
better than *j-s* ... Prov 8:11
adorns...her *j-s* ... Is 61:10
the *J* of *his* kingdom ... Dan 11:20

JEWISH
pertaining to Jews ... Neh 5:1; Esth 6:13; John 2:6; Acts 13:6

JEZEBEL A native of Tyre and wife of Ahab, whom she persuaded to worship Baal; she also tried to impose Baal worship in Israel. She was a very cruel woman and later became a symbol for seduction to idolatry. Also the name or nickname of a woman mentioned in Revelation.
1 *wife of Ahab* ... 1 Kin 21:5ff; 2 Kin 9:7ff
2 *woman at Thyatira* ... Rev 2:20

JEZREEL *(God sows).* A fortified city in Issachar where Elijah's prophecy about Jezebel's death was fulfilled. Also the name of two individuals.
1 *valley and plain* ... Josh 17:16; Judg 6:33; Hos 1:5
2 *fortified town* ... Josh 19:18; 1 Kin 18:45; 2 Kin 8:29;9:30
3 *descendant of Etam* ... 1 Chr 4:3
4 *son of Hosea* ... Hos 1:4

JOAB *(Yahweh is father).* One of the main generals in King David's army who had a very successful military career and was instrumental in the establishment of David's kingdom. Also the name of other men.
1 *son of Zeruiah* ... 2 Sam 8:16
David's nephew ... 2 Sam 17:25
David's commander ... 2 Sam 20:23; 1 Chr 11:6
2 *son of Seraiah* ... 1 Chr 4:14
3 *father of those returning from captivity* ... Ezra 2:6;8:9; Neh 7:11

JOANNA
wife of Chuza ... Luke 8:3
ministered to Jesus ... Luke 24:10

JOASH *(Yahweh has bestowed).* The name of several individuals, including a king who fulfilled the prophecy of Elisha upon recovering the cities of Israel from the king of Aram. Also a king of Judah who as an infant was saved by a high priest from being killed by the wicked Athaliah, his grandmother.
1 *father of Gideon* ... Judg 6:11,31
2 *son of Ahab* ... 1 Kin 22:26; 2 Chr 18:25
3 *son of Ahaziah* ... 2 Kin 11:2
king of Judah ... 2 Chr 24:1-4
4 *son of Jehoahaz* ... 2 Kin 13:9
king of Israel ... 2 Kin 13:25
5 *line of Shelah* ... 1 Chr 4:22
6 *son of Becher* ... 1 Chr 7:8
7 *a Benjamite* ... 1 Chr 12:3
8 *official of David* ... 1 Chr 27:28

JOB A wealthy man who probably lived between the times of Abraham and Moses (Jewish tradition made him a contemporary of Moses). By his sufferings, which are recorded in the book that bears his name, he became a proverbial example of patience and piety for those in distress.
pious man from Uz ... Job 1:1
experienced tragedy ... Job 2:7,8
showed great endurance ... Job 2:9,10; James 5:11

JOB *occupation*
workmen...*j* to *j* ... 2 Chr 34:13

JOCHEBED
mother of Moses ... Ex 6:20; Num 26:59

JOEL *(Yahweh is God).* The name of a number of individuals, including one of the minor prophets, best known for his prophecies concerning the "coming of the terrible day of the Lord."
1 *son of Samuel* ... 1 Sam 8:2
2 *line of Simeon* ... 1 Chr 4:35
3 *line of Reuben* ... 1 Chr 5:4
4 *chief of Gadites* ... 1 Chr 5:12
5 *ancestor of Samuel* ... 1 Chr 6:36
6 *son of Izrahiah* ... 1 Chr 7:3
7 *brother of Nathan* ... 1 Chr 11:38
8 *Gershonite Levite* ... 1 Chr 15:7; 26:22
9 *son of Pedaiah* ... 1 Chr 27:20
10 *Kohathite Levite* ... 2 Chr 29:12
11 *son of Nebo* ... Ezra 10:43
12 *son of Zichri* ... Neh 11:9
13 *prophet* ... Joel 1:1; Acts 2:16

JOHN *(Yahweh has been gracious).*
1 *father of Peter* ... John 1:42
2 *the Baptist, forerunner of Christ* ... Matt 3:1
baptizing ... Matt 3:13
beheaded ... Mark 6:25
birth foretold ... Luke 1:13
son of Zacharias ... Luke 1:57ff
praised by Jesus ... Luke 7:28
preached ... John 1:15
3 *the apostle, writer of five NT books* ... Matt 10:2
called by Jesus ... Matt 4:21
Sons of Thunder ... Mark 3:17
inner circle ... Matt 17:1
request refused ... Mark 10:35ff
assigned the care of Mary ... John 19:26,27
with Peter ... Acts 3:1,3
4 *Jewish leader* ... Acts 4:6
5 *Mark, evangelist* ... Acts 12:12,25

JOIN *bring together, couple*
j-ed to his wife ... Gen 2:24
do not *j* your hand ... Ex 23:1
j field to field ... Is 5:8
j...in hypocrisy ... Dan 11:34
God...*j-ed* together ... Matt 19:6
j-ed him...believed ... Acts 17:34
shall be *j-ed* to his wife ... Eph 5:31
j...*me* in suffering ... 2 Tim 1:8

JOINT *juncture*
bones are out of *j* ... Ps 22:14
together by the *j-s* ... Col 2:19
both *j-s* and marrow ... Heb 4:12

JOKTAN (unc, *younger).* A son of Eber and ancestor of thirteen tribes in Arabia.
person and tribe descended from Shem ... Gen 10:25,26,29; 1 Chr 1:19,20,23

JONADAB *(Yahweh is noble).* 1) A son of Rechab the Kenite, known also as Jehonadab (2 Kin 10:15). 2) A son of Shimeah, nephew of David (2 Sam 13:32).

JONAH *(dove).* An OT prophet who first refused to obey God, but later went to prophesy against Nineveh. Jonah was swallowed by a large fish and after three days was spit up by the fish. Jesus compared Jonah's experience with His own death and resurrection, speaking of "the sign of Jonah."
prophet of Israel ... Jon 1:1
son of Amittai ... 2 Kin 14:25
disobedient ... Jon 1:3
preached to Nineveh ... Jon 3:4

JONATHAN *(Yahweh has given).* Name of a number of individuals, including one of the sons of Saul who by his impressive military accomplishments became well liked by the people of Israel. Through his loyalty, Jonathan developed a close friendship with David and saved David's life when Saul wanted to kill him.
1 *son of Gershom* ... Judg 18:30
2 *son of King Saul* ... 1 Sam 13:16;14:49
friend of David ... 1 Sam 18:1
3 *son of Abiathar* ... 2 Sam 15:36
4 *son of Shimei* ... 2 Sam 21:21
5 *son of Jada* ... 1 Chr 2:32
6 *son of Shagee* ... 1 Chr 11:34
7 *official of David* ... 1 Chr 27:25
8 *David's uncle* ... 1 Chr 27:32

JOPPA *(beautiful).* A very ancient seaport to which cedar trees of a very good quality were shipped. Such trees were used in the building of Solomon's temple and also for the one rebuilt by Ezra. From this harbor Jonah sailed to Tarshish.
seaport W of Jerusalem ... 2 Chr 2:16; Ezra 3:7; Jon 1:3; Acts 9:36

JORAM *(Yahweh is exalted).* The name of several individuals, the more important of whom are the son and successor of Ahab, king of Israel, and the son and successor of Jehoshaphat, king of Judah.
1 *son of Toi* ... 2 Sam 8:10
2 *son of Ahab* ... 2 Kin 8:16
king of Israel ... 2 Kin 8:25
3 *line of Eliezer* ... 1 Chr 26:25
4 *son of Jehoshaphat* ... Matt 1:8
king of Judah
see also **JEHORAM**

JORDAN (unc, *descending).* The longest and most important river in Israel. Jesus Christ was baptized in the Jordan, and in OT times the nation of Israel crossed it to enter the Promised Land. Also the name of the valley through which the river runs.
1 *river in Palestine* ... Gen 32:10; Josh 3:17; Judg 8:4; 2 Kin 5:10; Matt 3:6
2 *valley* ... Gen 13:10,11

JOSEPH *(may he add).* The name of a number of individuals, the more important of whom were: 1) The favorite son of Jacob whom his brothers sold to a caravan going to Egypt, where he became governor. 2) The husband of Mary. 3) The member of the Sanhedrin who claimed the body of Jesus after His crucifixion and put it in his own new tomb.
1 *son of Jacob* ... Gen 30:23,24
sold by brothers ... Gen 37:28
put in prison ... Gen 40:3
prime minister ... Gen 41:41
revealed himself ... Gen 45:4
death ... Gen 50:26
2 *father of spy* ... Num 13:7ff
3 *son of Asaph* ... 1 Chr 25:9
4 *son of Bani* ... Ezra 10:42
5 *son of Shebaniah* ... Neh 12:14
6 *husband of Mary* ... Matt 1:18; 2:13; Luke 2:16; John 6:42
7 *brother of Jesus* ... Matt 13:55
see also **JOSES**
8 *brother of James the Less* ... Matt 27:56
see also **JOSES**
9 *of Arimathea* ... Matt 27:57ff
in Sanhedrin (Council) ... Mark 15:43
disciple of Jesus ... John 19:38
provided tomb ... Matt 27:57
10 *ancestor of Jesus* ... Luke 3:24
11 *ancestor of Jesus* ... Luke 3:30
12 *surname Barsabbas* ... Acts 1:23
13 *Barnabas* ... Acts 4:36

JOSES The Gr form of the name *Joseph.*
1 *brother of James the Less* ... Mark 15:40
see also **JOSEPH**
2 *brother of Jesus* ... Mark 6:3
see also **JOSEPH**

JOSHUA *(Yahweh is salvation).* The name of several men, the best known of whom was the son of Nun from the tribe of Ephraim. His original name was Hoshea. Moses trained him and was with him on Mt. Sinai when the idolatry of the golden calf occurred. He was one of the twelve spies who scouted the Promised Land, and later, as Moses' successor, he led Israel into Canaan.
1 *Moses' successor* ... Deut 31:23
attended Moses ... Num 11:28
chosen by God ... Num 27:18
encouraged by God ... Josh 1:1-9
charged Israel ... Josh 23:1ff
death ... Josh 24:29
2 *of Beth-shemesh* ... 1 Sam 6:14
3 *governor* ... 2 Kin 23:8

4 *high priest* ... Hag 1:1,12; Zech 3:1ff
see also **JESHUA**

JOSIAH *(Yahweh supports).* 1) A son and successor of Amon, king of Judah, who became king at the age of 8 years old; Hilkiah, the high priest, was his mentor. A righteous king who found the book of the OT Law in the house of the Lord, conformed to it, and ordered it to be put into practice. 2) A son of Zephaniah.
1 *son of Amon* ... 2 Kin 21:24
king of Judah ... 2 Kin 21:26
removed false worship ... 2 Kin 23:19,24; 2 Chr 34:33
responded to the Law ... 2 Chr 34:15-28
2 *son of Zephaniah* ... Zech 6:10

JOTHAM *(Yahweh is perfect).* The youngest of the seventy sons of Gideon and the only one who escaped the massacre by Abimelech. Also the son of Uzziah, king of Judah, who was a leper and had Jotham reigning as regent; and a descendant of Caleb.
1 *son of Gideon* ... Judg 9:5ff
2 *king of Judah* ... 2 Kin 15:5
son of Uzziah ... 2 Chr 27:2
3 *line of Caleb* ... 1 Chr 2:47

JOURNEY *traveling, trip*
Let us take our *j* ... Gen 33:12
day's *j* on the other ... Num 11:31
seek...a safe *j* ... Ezra 8:21
a bag for *your j* ... Matt 10:10
nothing for *your j* ... Luke 9:3
Sabbath day's *j* away ... Acts 1:12
on frequent *j-s* ... 2 Cor 11:26

JOURNEYED *traveled*
about as they *j* east ... Gen 11:2
Jacob *j* to Succoth ... Gen 33:17
the sons of Israel *j* ... Num 22:1
j from the river ... Ezra 8:31

JOY *delight, happiness*
raise sounds of *j* ... 1 Chr 15:16
shouted aloud for *j* ... Ezra 3:12
see His face with *j* ... Job 33:26
Restore to me the *j* ... Ps 51:12
j at Your name ... Ps 89:12
godly ones sing for *j* ... Ps 132:9
Everlasting *j* will be ... Is 61:7
their mourning into *j* ... Jer 31:13
with great *j* ... Matt 2:10
enter into the *j* ... Matt 25:21
j in heaven over one ... Luke 15:7
j in the Holy Spirit ... Rom 14:17
love, *j*, peace ... Gal 5:22
make my *j* complete ... Phil 2:2

JOYFUL *feeling gladness*
be altogether *j* ... Deut 16:15
j with gladness ... Ps 21:6
shall reap with *j* ... Ps 126:5
j heart is good ... Prov 17:22

JOYFULLY *full of joy, happy*
go *j* with the king ... Esth 5:14
Shout *j* to God, all ... Ps 66:1
They shout *j* together ... Is 52:8
to praise God *j* ... Luke 19:37

JUBAL
inventor of lyre and pipe ... Gen 4:21

JUBILANT *elated*
no ... *j* shouting ... Is 16:10
Is this your *j city* ... Is 23:7
because you are *j* ... Jer 50:11
they may become *j* ... Jer 51:39

JUBILEE, YEAR OF A year of emancipation during which the ancient Hebrews freed their slaves, forgave debts, and returned any properties they possessed to the original owners. The jubilee was celebrated every fifty years as a time of rest for the land and the people.
return of ancestral possessions every fiftieth year
year of liberty ... Lev 25:8ff

JUDAH (unc, *praised).* One of the twelve sons of Jacob. His descendants, together with the descendants of Benjamin, formed the southern kingdom, known as Judah. Also the name of several other individuals and a city.
1 *son of Jacob* ... Gen 29:35; 37:26; 44:14; 49:8,10
2 *tribe* ... Num 1:27; Judg 1:8; 2 Sam 2:4; 1 Kin 12:20
3 *border city* ... Josh 19:34
4 *S kingdom* ... 1 Kin 14:21; 1 Chr 9:1; Ps 60:7; Jer 20:4
5 *relative of Kadmiel* ... Ezra 2:40
6 *urged by Ezra to put away foreign wife* ... Ezra 10:23
7 *Benjamite* ... Neh 11:9
8 *Levite who returned from captivity* ... Neh 12:8
9 *participant in wall dedication* ... Neh 12:34
10 *musician* ... Neh 12:36

JUDAISM *Jewish way of life*
manner of life in *J* ... Gal 1:13
advancing in *J* ... Gal 1:14

JUDAS
1 *Iscariot* ... Matt 10:4
used by Satan ... Luke 22:3
son of Simon ... John 6:71
treasurer ... John 13:29
betrayed Jesus ... John 18:2
2 *Jesus' brother* ... Matt 13:55; Mark 6:3
3 *apostle* ... Luke 6:16; Acts 1:13
4 *Judas of Galilee* ... Acts 5:37
5 *of Damascus* ... Acts 9:11
6 *Barsabbas* ... Acts 15:22,27

JUDAS ISCARIOT *see* **ISCARIOT**

JUDE Anglicized form of the name *Judas,* found only in Jude 1, identifying him as the writer; elsewhere the name *Judas* is used. A half-brother of Jesus who became His follower after Jesus' resurrection.
brother of Jesus ... Matt 13:55; Mark 6:3
brother of James ... Jude 1

JUDEA The name for the territory of Judah by NT times, when it had become a Roman province.
Roman province in Palestine based on earlier Judah ... Matt 2:1; Mark 1:5; Luke 2:4; John 11:7

JUDEAN
language (Hebrew) ... 2 Kin 18:26,28; Is 36:11,13
see also **CANAAN**
see also **HEBREW**

JUDGE (n) *leader* An officer appointed and authorized to make judgments in solving problems and imparting justice. In the OT, during the time before the period of the kings, judges were the leaders of Israel.
J of all the earth ... Gen 18:25
prince or a *j* over us ... Ex 2:14
LORD was with the *j* ... Judg 2:18
For God Himself is *j* ... Ps 50:6
unrighteous *j* said ... Luke 18:6
one Lawgiver and *J* ... James 4:12

JUDGE (v) *pass judgment*
LORD *j* between you ... Gen 16:5
Moses sat to *j* the ... Ex 18:13
LORD will *j*...earth ... 1 Sam 2:10
coming to *j* the earth ... Ps 98:9
He will *j* the poor ... Is 11:4
Do not *j*...will not be *j-d* ... Matt 7:1
Son...world to *j* ... John 3:17
Law...not *j* a man ... John 7:51
not come to *j* the ... John 12:47
able to *j*...thoughts ... Heb 4:12
adulterers God will *j* ... Heb 13:4

JUDGMENT *condemnation* In the Bible, usually an act of God in which He always renders a fair verdict. The result may be negative (punishment for those who rebel against His will) or positive (rewards to believers for service).
I will execute *j-s* ... Ex 12:12
partiality in *j* ... Deut 1:17
let *j* be executed ... Ezra 7:26
will not stand in the *j* ... Ps 1:5
in the day of *j* ... Matt 10:15
j, that the light ... John 3:19
resurrection of *j* ... John 5:29
My *j* is just ... John 5:30
after this *comes j* ... Heb 9:27
incur a stricter *j* ... James 3:1
not fall under *j* ... James 5:12
kept for the day of *j* ... 2 Pet 3:7
j of the great day ... Jude 6
to execute *j* upon all ... Jude 15
His *j-s* are true ... Rev 19:2

JUMP *leap*
legs with which to *j* ... Lev 11:21
if a fox should *j* ... Neh 4:3
j-ed up, and came ... Mark 10:50

JUNIPER *tree*
slept under a *j* tree ... 1 Kin 19:5
The *j*, the box tree ... Is 60:13
like a *j* in the ... Jer 48:6

JUST *fair, right*
shall have *j* balances ... Lev 19:36
a man be *j* with God ... Job 25:4
Hear a *j* cause, O LORD ... Ps 17:1
He is *j* and endowed ... Zech 9:9
My judgment is *j* ... John 5:30
the j for *the* unjust ... 1 Pet 3:18

JUSTICE *fairness, righteousness* The act of rendering and enforcing a fair verdict whether of condemnation or reward. It is one of the attributes of God, who gives abundant mercy but never does so at the expense of justice.
shall not distort *j* ... Deut 16:19
Does God pervert *j* ... Job 8:3
j to the afflicted ... Job 36:6
Righteousness and *j* ... Ps 89:14
do not understand *j* ... Prov 28:5

j is turned back ... Is 59:14
let *j* roll down ... Amos 5:24
j and mercy and ... Matt 23:23
acknowledged...*j* ... Luke 7:29
grant to your slaves *j* ... Col 4:1

JUSTIFICATION *vindication* A vindication or setting right of a wrong. The act of God by which He declares a believing sinner to be in a righteous position before Him, based on the substitutionary death of Christ and His resurrection.
because of our *j* ... Rom 4:25
j of life to all men ... Rom 5:18

JUSTIFY *declare guiltless*
how...*j* ourselves ... Gen 44:16
they *j* the righteous ... Deut 25:1
he *j-ied* himself ... Job 32:2
wishing to *j* himself ... Luke 10:29
these...He also *j-ied* ... Rom 8:30
God...*j-ies* ... Rom 8:33
seeking to be *j-ied* ... Gal 2:17

JUSTUS
1 *Joseph, apostolic candidate* ... Acts 1:23
also called Barsabbas
2 *Titus, Corinthian disciple* ... Acts 18:7
3 *Jewish Christian* ... Col 4:11

JUTTAH
Levitical city in Judah ... Josh 15:55; 21:16

K

KADESH / KADESH-BARNEA An oasis in the wilderness southwest of the Dead Sea, where the Israelites twice encamped on their way from Egypt to enter the Promised Land.
Kadesh, also known as En-mishpat ... Gen 14:7
Israelite encampment ... Num 13:26;33:37

KEDAR *(black, swarthy).* A son of Ishmael and the name of a nomadic Arabian tribe and one of their settlements.
1 *son of Ishmael* ... Gen 25:13
2 *tribal descendants* ... Is 42:11

KEDEMAH
1 *son of Ishmael* ... Gen 25:15
2 *tribal descendants* ... 1 Chr 1:31

KEDESH
1 *city in S Judah* ... Josh 15:23
2 *city of Issachar* ... 1 Chr 6:72
3 *city of Naphtali* ... Josh 12:22
4 *city of refuge, in Galilee* ... Josh 20:7

KEEP *hold, guide, preserve*
k the way of the LORD ... Gen 18:19
love Me and *k* My ... Ex 20:6
shall *k* your sabbath ... Lev 23:32
LORD bless you, and *k* ... Num 6:24
to k the Passover ... Matt 26:18
if anyone *k-s* My ... John 8:51
he will *k* My word ... John 14:23
k-ing faith and a ... 1 Tim 1:19
k yourself free from ... 1 Tim 5:22
k his tongue...evil ... 1 Pet 3:10

KEEPER *guard, protector*
Am I my brother's *k* ... Gen 4:9
been *k-s* of livestock ... Gen 46:32
The LORD is your *k* ... Ps 121:5
I, the LORD, am its *k* ... Is 27:3

KEILAH
1 *town of Judah* ... Josh 15:44; 1 Sam 23:1ff; Neh 3:17,18
2 *line of Caleb* ... 1 Chr 4:19

KENAZ
1 *Esau's grandson* ... Gen 36:10,11
2 *father of Othniel* ... Josh 15:17
3 *line of Caleb* ... 1 Chr 4:15

KENITE(S) A tribe, some of whom lived in Canaan in the time of Abraham and, by the time of Moses, had allied with the Midianites.
Canaanite tribe ... Gen 15:19; Num 24:21
tribe of metal-workers ... Judg 4:11; 1 Sam 15:6

KENIZZITE
Canaanite tribe in S Palestine and Edom ... Gen 15:19; Num 32:12; Josh 14:14

KENOSIS *(emptying).* A theological doctrine about Christ taken from Phil 2:7. It refers to the fact that when the Son of God became a man (*see* **INCARNATION**), He temporarily gave up the glory which He had with the Father and voluntarily took upon Himself the limitations of being human. It is important to note that in doing so, Christ never gave up His deity, but only refrained from fully displaying it. For example, He could have spared Himself any or all of the human afflictions (e.g. thirst and weariness), but did not.

KEREN-HAPPUCH
daughter of Job ... Job 42:14

KERIOTH
1 *town of Judah* ... Josh 15:25
2 *town in Moab* ... Jer 48:41; Amos 2:2

KETURAH *(incense).* Abraham's second wife. They had six children.
second wife of Abraham ... Gen 25:1,4; 1 Chr 1:32,33

KEY *unlocking tool*
k-s of the kingdom ... Matt 16:19
the *k* of knowledge ... Luke 11:52
k-s of death and of ... Rev 1:18
k of the bottomless pit ... Rev 9:1

KEZIAH
daughter of Job ... Job 42:14

KIBROTH-HATTAAVAH *(graves of greed).* The place where the Israelites lustfully craved for several things while wandering through the desert (Deut 9:22).

KIDNEYS *innards*
two *k* and the fat ... Ex 29:13
remove with the *k* ... Lev 3:15
He splits my *k* open ... Job 16:13

KIDRON, KEDRON A brook and ravine near Jerusalem which separated the city from the Mt. of Olives, and had to be crossed on the way to Jericho. Later known as the Valley of Jehoshaphat (2 Sam 15:23; 2 Kin 23:6; 2 Chr 29:16; John 18:1).

KILL *take life*
for Cain *k-ed* him ... Gen 4:25
k-ed every firstborn ... Ex 13:15
who *k-s* a man shall ... Lev 24:21
LORD *k-s* and makes ... 1 Sam 2:6
Am I God, to *k* ... 2 Kin 5:7
jealousy *k-s* the simple ... Job 5:2
he *k-s* the innocent ... Ps 10:8
A time to *k* ... Eccl 3:3
unable to *k* the ... Matt 10:28
k-ed, and be raised ... Luke 9:22
do you seek to *k* Me ... John 7:19
Get up, Peter, *k* and ... Acts 10:13
the letter *k-s,* but ... 2 Cor 3:6
who *k* their father ... 1 Tim 1:9
k a third of mankind ... Rev 9:15

KIND (adj) *good, tender*
be *k* to this people ... 2 Chr 10:7
He Himself is *k* ... Luke 6:35
love is *k* ... 1 Cor 13:4
be *k* to one another ... Eph 4:32

KIND (n) *group, variety*
fruit after their *k* ... Gen 1:11
plant all *k-s* of trees ... Lev 19:23
all *k-s* of evil ... Matt 5:11
k-s of tongues ... 1 Cor 12:28
every *k* of impurity ... Eph 4:19

KINDLE *cause to burn*
anger...was *k-d* ... Num 11:10
His breath *k-s* coals ... Job 41:21
man to *k* strife ... Prov 26:21
all you who *k* a fire ... Is 50:11
k-d a fire in Zion ... Lam 4:11

KINDNESS *tenderness*
teaching of *k* is on ... Prov 31:26
to love *k,* And to ... Mic 6:8
with deeds of *k* ... Acts 9:36
k and...of God ... Rom 11:22
joy, peace, patience, *k* ... Gal 5:22
compassion, *k* ... Col 3:12
tasted the *k* of the ... 1 Pet 2:3
godliness, brotherly *k* ... 2 Pet 1:7

KINDRED *relative*
her people or her *k* ... Esth 2:10
destruction of my *k* ... Esth 8:6
no one...of *k* spirit ... Phil 2:20

KING *monarch, regent*
the *k-'s* highway ... Num 20:17
no *k* in Israel ... Judg 17:6
appoint a *k* for us ... 1 Sam 8:5
anointed David *k* ... 2 Sam 5:3
my *K* and my God ... Ps 5:2
The LORD is *K* forever ... Ps 10:16
Who is the *k* of glory ... Ps 24:8
will shatter *k-s* ... Ps 110:5
By me *k-s* reign ... Prov 8:15
He will...before *k-s* ... Prov 22:29
The Creator...your *K* ... Is 43:15
O *K* of the nations ... Jer 10:7
born *K* of the Jews ... Matt 2:2
Are You the *K* of ... Matt 27:11
your *K* is coming ... John 12:15
no *k* but Caesar ... John 19:15
K of *k-s* and Lord ... 1 Tim 6:15
God, honor the *k* ... 1 Pet 2:17

KINGDOM *domain, monarchy*
his *k* was Babel ... Gen 10:10
to Me a *k* of priests ... Ex 19:6
tear the *k* from ... 1 Kin 11:11
will establish his *k* ... 1 Chr 28:7
the *k* is the LORD'S ... Ps 22:28
Sing to God, O *k-s* ... Ps 68:32
an everlasting *k* ... Ps 145:13
k against *k* ... Is 19:2

showed Him...*k-s* ... Matt 4:8
Your *k* come ... Matt 6:10
sons of the *k* ... Matt 13:38
keys of the *k* ... Matt 16:19
in My Father's *k* ... Matt 26:29
to give you the *k* ... Luke 12:32
cannot see the *k* of ... John 3:3
preaching the *k* ... Acts 28:31
k of His beloved Son ... Col 1:13
to His heavenly *k* ... 2 Tim 4:18
faith conquered *k-s* ... Heb 11:33
heirs of the *k* ... James 2:5

KINGDOM (OF GOD) The spiritual realm where God reigns sovereignly. It is composed of all beings who are willingly subject to His rule and thus enjoy fellowship with Him. *See* **KINGDOM OF HEAVEN**
enter the *k* ... Mark 10:24

KINGDOM OF HEAVEN The earthly kingdom promised in the OT with the Messiah as King. The Son of God, the Messiah, will come from heaven to establish this kingdom on earth. Sometimes synonymous with "Kingdom of God," but at other times the latter may refer to the present spiritual kingdom composed of believers who worship and serve Christ, the Messiah, as their Lord.
k is at ... Matt 3:2

KINSMAN A relative—often called a kinsman-redeemer—whose responsibility it was in Jewish society to buy back the property of his nearest relative, or to redeem the relative himself from service to another, if the latter had previously sold his property or himself (as a slave) to avoid destitution. The best-known and most important example is that of Ruth and Boaz. Both Ruth and her mother-in-law were widowed and desired to have Boaz take the role of kinsman-redeemer, which resulted in his marrying Ruth.
of my master's *k* ... Gen 24:48
he took his *k-men* ... Gen 31:23
a man has no *k* ... Lev 25:26
Naomi had a *k* of her ... Ruth 2:1
k-men stand afar off ... Ps 38:11
Herodion, my *k* ... Rom 16:11

KIRIATHAIM
1 *Reubenite city* ... Num 32:37; Josh 13:19
2 *Levitical city* ... 1 Chr 6:76

KIRIATH-ARBA (unc, *city of Arba).* The former name for Hebron, which was founded by Arba, the father of Anak. Also a city of refuge.
old name of Hebron ... Gen 23:2; Josh 14:15; 15:13,54; Judg 1:10
city of refuge ... Josh 20:7

KIRIATH-JEARIM *(city of forests).* A Canaanite city near Judah where the ark remained after the Philistines returned it to Israel. This place is also known by other names.
Gibeonite town ... Josh 9:17; Judg 18:12; Jer 26:20
location of ark of covenant ... 1 Sam 6:21; 7:1,2; 2 Chr 1:4

KISH
1 *father of Saul* ... 1 Sam 9:3;10:21
2 *son of Jeiel* ... 1 Chr 8:30
3 *son of Mahli* ... 1 Chr 23:21
4 *son of Abdi* ... 2 Chr 29:12
5 *a Benjamite* ... Esth 2:5

KISHON (unc, *bending, winding).* A river in central Israel, second in importance to the Jordan.
battle scene ... Judg 4:7
river ... Judg 4:13; 5:21
priests of Baal slain on its bank ... 1 Kin 18:40

KISS (n) *expression of affection*
threw a *k* from my ... Job 31:27
the *k-es* of his mouth ... Song 1:2
You gave Me no *k* ... Luke 7:45
betraying...with a *k* ... Luke 22:48
with a holy *k* ... Rom 16:16
with a *k* of love ... 1 Pet 5:14

KISS (v) *express affection*
come close and *k* ... Gen 27:26
let me *k* my father ... 1 Kin 19:20
I would *k* you ... Song 8:1
Whomever I *k* ... Mark 14:44
not...to *k* My feet ... Luke 7:45

KITTIM
1 *grandson of Japheth* ... Gen 10:4; 1 Chr 1:7
2 *island of Cyprus* ... Num 24:24; Jer 2:10; Dan 11:30

KNEAD *work dough, clay*
took flour, *k-ed* it ... 1 Sam 28:24
the women *k* dough ... Jer 7:18

KNEE *part of body*
strengthened feeble *k-s* ... Job 4:4
k-s began knocking ... Dan 5:6
every *k* shall bow ... Rom 14:11
every *k* will bow ... Phil 2:10

KNEEL *bend, rest on knee*
made the camels *k* ... Gen 24:11
people *k-ed* to drink ... Judg 7:6
k before the LORD ... Ps 95:6
knelt...before Him ... Matt 27:29
man ran...*knelt* ... Mark 10:17
He *knelt* down ... Luke 22:41

KNIFE *cutting instrument*
k to slay his son ... Gen 22:10
jaw teeth *like k-ves* ... Prov 30:14
with a scribe's *k* ... Jer 36:23

KNIT *joined together*
Jonathan was *k* to ... 1 Sam 18:1
k me together with ... Job 10:11
his thighs are *k* ... Job 40:17
His hand they are *k* ... Lam 1:14
k together in love ... Col 2:2

KNOCK *smite, strike*
his knees began *k-ing* ... Dan 5:6
k, and it will be ... Matt 7:7
stand outside and *k* ... Luke 13:25
he *k-ed* at the door ... Acts 12:13
at the door and *k* ... Rev 3:20

KNOW *experience, understand*
like one of Us, *k-ing* ... Gen 3:22
make *k-n* the statutes ... Ex 18:16
k that my Redeemer ... Job 19:25
Make me *k* Your ways ... Ps 25:4
He *k-s* the secrets ... Ps 44:21
k that I am God ... Ps 46:10
made *k-n* His salvation ... Ps 98:2
Try me and *k* my ... Ps 139:23
You *k* me ... Jer 12:3
left hand *k* what ... Matt 6:3
k...by their fruits ... Matt 7:20
I never *knew* you ... Matt 7:23
God *k-s* your hearts ... Luke 16:15
you will *k* the truth ... John 8:32
I *k* My own ... John 10:14
k-ing that His hour ... John 13:1
k that I love You ... John 21:15
and *k* all mysteries ... 1 Cor 13:2
who *knew* no sin ... 2 Cor 5:21
k the love of Christ ... Eph 3:19
value of *k-ing* Christ ... Phil 3:8
k...I have believed ... 2 Tim 1:12
k...eternal life ... 1 John 5:13
I *k* your deeds ... Rev 2:2

KNOWLEDGE *information*
tree of the *k* of good ... Gen 2:9
LORD is a God of *k* ... 1 Sam 2:3
anyone teach God *k* ... Job 21:22
k is too wonderful ... Ps 139:6
the beginning of *k* ... Prov 1:7
fools hate *k* ... Prov 1:22
Wise...store up *k* ... Prov 10:14
k increases power ... Prov 24:5
would He teach *k* ... Is 28:9
in accordance with *k* ... Rom 10:2
K makes arrogant ... 1 Cor 8:1
k, it will be done ... 1 Cor 13:8
have no *k* of God ... 1 Cor 15:34
love...surpasses *k* ... Eph 3:19
treasures of...*k* ... Col 2:3
grow in...grace and *k* ... 2 Pet 3:18

KOHATH The middle son of Levi; a priest and the founder of the second order of priests (his brothers were Gershon and Merari). The family of Heman, renowned musicians in David's time, descended from Kohath.
son of Levi ... Gen 46:11; Num 3:17; Josh 21:5

KOHATHITES The descendants of Kohath from whom sprang the most important divisions of the Levites.
line of Kohath ... Num 3:30; 4:34; Josh 21:4

KOR *measure of capacity*
k-s of fine flour ... 1 Kin 4:22
20,000 *k-s* of barley ... 2 Chr 2:10
100 *k-s* of wheat ... Ezra 7:22
a bath from *each k* ... Ezek 45:14

KORAH (unc, *baldness).* Name of several persons, including a Levite who led a rebellion against Moses and Aaron. As a result the Lord punished him by making a large fissure in the earth into which Korah and his followers fell, together with their families. Then the earth closed over them.
1 *son of Esau* ... Gen 36:5
2 *opposed Moses* ... Num 16:8,16
3 *son of Hebron* ... 1 Chr 2:43
4 *a Kohathite* ... 1 Chr 6:37

L

LABAN *(white).* Brother of Rebekah and father of Leah and Rachel. Jacob worked

for his uncle Laban 14 years in order to be given Rachel as his wife. Also name of a place.
1 *Abraham's kinsman* ... Gen 24:29
Rachel's father ... Gen 29:10,16
2 *place in the desert* ... Deut 1:1

LABOR (n) *work, childbirth*
fruits of your *l-s* ... Ex 23:16
their *l* to the locust ... Ps 78:46
bread of painful *l-s* ... Ps 127:2
return for their *l* ... Eccl 4:9
in *l* and hardship ... 2 Cor 11:27
fruitful *l* for me ... Phil 1:22
faith and *l* of love ... 1 Thess 1:3
cried out, being in *l* ... Rev 12:2

LABOR (v) *toil, work*
Six days you shall *l* ... Ex 20:9
l in vain who build ... Ps 127:1
for whom am I *l-ing* ... Eccl 4:8
l-ed over you in vain ... Gal 4:11

LABORER *workman*
l-s for his vineyard ... Matt 20:1
Call the *l-s* and pay ... Matt 20:8
l-s into His harvest ... Luke 10:2
l is worthy of his ... Luke 10:7

LACHISH A fortified city which became the frontier of Judah. Captured by the Assyrians under Sennacherib.
city in Judah ... Josh 10:3; 2 Kin 14:19; 2 Chr 32:9

LACK (n) *deficiency, need*
where there is no *l* ... Judg 18:10
for *l* of instruction ... Prov 5:23
for *l* of a shepherd ... Ezek 34:5
l of self-control ... 1 Cor 7:5

LACK (v) *be deficient, need*
will not *l* anything ... Deut 8:9
l-ing in counsel ... Deut 32:28
man *l-ing* sense ... Prov 7:7
am I still *l-ing* ... Matt 19:20
One thing you *l* ... Mark 10:21
not *l-ing* in any gift ... 1 Cor 1:7
if any...*l-s* wisdom ... James 1:5

LAD *boy*
God heard the *l* ... Gen 21:17
the *l* is not *with us* ... Gen 44:31
the *l* was dead ... 2 Kin 4:32
a *l* here who has five ... John 6:9

LADDER *steps*
l...set on the earth ... Gen 28:12

LADY *woman*
Your noble *l-ies* ... Ps 45:9
elder to the chosen *l* ... 2 John 1

LAISH
1 *a Benjamite* ... 1 Sam 25:44; 2 Sam 3:15
2 *place in N Palestine later called Dan* ... Judg 18:27,29

LAKE *pool, water*
standing by the *l* ... Luke 5:1
wind...on the *l* ... Luke 8:23
into the *l* and was ... Luke 8:33
into the *l* of fire ... Rev 20:10

LAMB *young sheep* A young sheep, less than a year old; a very gentle animal. The Israelites were instructed to use lambs or goats as sacrifices to God for their sins. Christ is called the Lamb of God who takes away the sins of the world.
l for the burnt ... Gen 22:7
shall redeem with a *l* ... Ex 34:20
l without defect ... Lev 14:10
will dwell with the *l* ... Is 11:6
l...led to slaughter ... Is 53:7
wolf and the *l* will ... Is 65:25
send you out as *l-s* ... Luke 10:3
Behold, the *L* of God ... John 1:29
Tend My *l-s* ... John 21:15
l before its shearer ... Acts 8:32
Worthy is the *L* ... Rev 5:12
blood of the *L* ... Rev 12:11

LAME *crippled, disabled*
was *l* in both feet ... 2 Sam 9:13
feet to the *l* ... Job 29:15
Then the *l* will leap ... Is 35:6
the l walk ... Matt 11:5
l from his mother's ... Acts 14:8

LAMECH 1) A descendant of Cain who boasted of killing a man who had wounded him. 2) Son of Methuselah and father of Noah.
1 *in lineage of Cain* ... Gen 4:17,18
2 *father of Noah* ... Gen 5:28,29

LAMENT (n) *dirge, wail*
this *l* over Saul ... 2 Sam 1:17
chanted a *l* ... 2 Chr 35:25
I must make a *l* ... Mic 1:8

LAMENT (v) *mourn, wail*
house of Israel *l-ed* ... 1 Sam 7:2
her gates will *l* ... Is 3:26
fishermen will *l* ... Is 19:8
And *l* over you ... Ezek 27:32
weep and *l* over her ... Rev 18:9

LAMENTATION *weeping*
great...sorrowful *l* ... Gen 50:10
in Ramah, *L and* ... Jer 31:15
your songs into *l* ... Amos 8:10
made loud *l* over him ... Acts 8:2

LAMENTATIONS A book by Jeremiah, written on the occasion of the destruction of Jerusalem by Nebuchadnezzar in 586 B.C., in which he describes a very pitiful situation—materially, physically, morally, and religiously.

LAMP *light*
You are my *l* ... 2 Sam 22:29
l-s of pure gold ... 2 Chr 4:20
his *l* goes out ... Job 18:6
Your word is a *l* ... Ps 119:105
commandment is a *l* ... Prov 6:23
l of the body ... Matt 6:22
l-s are going out ... Matt 25:8
l-s in the upper room ... Acts 20:8
l shining in a dark ... 2 Pet 1:19
seven *l-s* of fire ... Rev 4:5

LAMPSTAND *candlestick* A holder for a receptacle in which oil could be burned to give light. The lampstand in the tabernacle held seven lamps.
l of pure gold ... Ex 25:31
and a chair and a *l* ... 2 Kin 4:10
puts it on a *l* ... Luke 8:16
will remove your *l* ... Rev 2:5

LAND *country, earth*
let the dry *l* appear ... Gen 1:9
famine in the *l* ... Gen 12:10
I have given this *l* ... Gen 15:18
out of the *l* of Egypt ... Ex 6:13
l flowing with milk ... Deut 6:3
in to possess the *l* ... Josh 1:11
l of their captivity ... 2 Chr 6:38
will heal their *l* ... 2 Chr 7:14
the *l* of the living ... Job 28:13
will inherit the *l* ... Ps 37:11
In a dry and weary *l* ... Ps 63:1
l be born in one day ... Is 66:8
again to this *l* ... Jer 24:6
l is filled with blood ... Ezek 9:9
smite the *l* with a ... Mal 4:6
darkness...all the *l* ... Matt 27:45
owned a tract of *l* ... Acts 4:37

LAND OF PROMISE *see* **PROMISED LAND**

LANDOWNER *landlord*
slaves of the *l* ... Matt 13:27
kingdom...like a *l* ... Matt 20:1
l who planted a ... Matt 21:33

LANGUAGE *speech, word*
according to his *l* ... Gen 10:5
earth used the same *l* ... Gen 11:1
speech or difficult *l* ... Ezek 3:5
in figurative *l* ... John 16:25
speak in his own *l* ... Acts 2:6
many kinds of *l-s* ... 1 Cor 14:10

LANGUISH *faint*
l-ed because of the ... Gen 47:13
My soul *l-es* for ... Ps 119:81
never *l* again ... Jer 31:12
refresh...who *l-es* ... Jer 31:25

LAODICEA (unc, *people's justice*). A city in Asia Minor whose church was addressed in the book of Revelation. Paul mentioned it several times in his letters.
city in Asia Minor ... Col 2:1
location of early church ... Col 4:15; Rev 1:11; 3:14

LAODICEANS
people of Laodicea ... Col 4:16

LAPIS LAZULI *precious stone*
polishing *was* like *l* ... Lam 4:7
like *l* in appearance ... Ezek 1:26
the jasper; The *l* ... Ezek 28:13

LARGE *big, great, huge*
tears in *l* measure ... Ps 80:5
a *l* upper room ... Mark 14:15
a *l* crowd ... Luke 7:11
what *l* letters ... Gal 6:11

LAST *final, utmost*
breathed his *l* ... Gen 25:8
first will be *l* ... Matt 19:30
The *l* Adam ... 1 Cor 15:45
at the *l* trumpet ... 1 Cor 15:52
it is the *l* hour ... 1 John 2:18
the first and the *l* ... Rev 1:17

LAST DAYS An expression which has several interpretations, depending on the context. It frequently refers to the end of Biblical history, i.e. the chain of events commencing with the Great Tribulation. In a wider sense, it goes back to the times of the early church (Acts 2:16-17).
In the *l* ... Is 2:2
in these *l* ... Heb 1:2

LATIN
language of the Roman Empire
one of three languages written on Jesus' cross ... John 19:20

LATTICE *trellis*
fell through the *l* ... 2 Kin 1:2
looked out...my *l* ... Prov 7:6
peering through...*l* ... Song 2:9

LAUGH *be amused, mock*
Why did Sarah *l* ... Gen 18:13
will *l* at violence ... Job 5:22
l at your calamity ... Prov 1:26
weep, and a time to *l* ... Eccl 3:4
began l-ing at Him ... Matt 9:24

LAUGHINGSTOCK *derision*
l among the peoples ... Ps 44:14
was not Israel a *l* ... Jer 48:27
I have become a *l* ... Lam 3:14

LAUGHTER *amusement*
God has made *l* for ... Gen 21:6
Even in *l* the heart ... Prov 14:13
Sorrow is better than *l* ... Eccl 7:3

LAVER *wash basin* A basin for water where the priests washed their hands and feet as required when they performed their functions of ministry.
make a *l* of bronze ... Ex 30:18
set the *l* between ... Ex 40:7
anoint the *l* ... Ex 40:11

LAW *scripture, statute* Primarily, the Ten Commandments given by God to Moses on Mt. Sinai for the people of Israel. Also a reference to the first five books of the OT (called the books of Moses), or to all of the OT. The rabbis added some 613 commands and prohibitions in the Mishnah (q.v.), which came to be regarded by the Jews as law with authority virtually equal to that of the OT.
tablets with the *l* ... Ex 24:12
Moses wrote this *l* ... Deut 31:9
found the...*l* ... 2 Kin 22:8
walk in My *l* ... 2 Chr 6:16
l...is perfect ... Ps 19:7
I delight in Your *l* ... Ps 119:70
abolish the *L* or the ... Matt 5:17
Our *L*...not judge ... John 7:51
by that *l* He ought ... John 19:7
by a *l* of faith ... Rom 3:27
L brings...wrath ... Rom 4:15
not under *l* ... Rom 6:14
Is the *L* sin ... Rom 7:7
the *L* is holy ... Rom 7:12
L...become our tutor ... Gal 3:24
thereby fulfill the *l* ... Gal 6:2
L...nothing perfect ... Heb 7:19

LAWFUL *legal, right*
not *l* for him to eat ... Matt 12:4
Is it *l* to heal ... Matt 12:10
l...man to divorce ... Mark 10:2
All things are *l* ... 1 Cor 6:12

LAWGIVER *lawmaker*
The LORD is our *l* ... Is 33:22
one *L* and Judge ... James 4:12

LAWLESS *illegal, without law*
l one will be ... 2 Thess 2:8
are *l* and rebellious ... 1 Tim 1:9
from every *l* deed ... Titus 2:14

LAWYER *interpreter of law*
a *l*, asked Him *a* ... Matt 22:35
One of the *l-s* said ... Luke 11:45
Woe to you *l-s* ... Luke 11:52

LAY *place, put*
laid him on the altar ... Gen 22:9
l My hand on Egypt ... Ex 7:4
laid its cornerstone ... Job 38:6
l my glory in the dust ... Ps 7:5
he *l-s* up deceit ... Prov 26:24
laid Him in a tomb ... Mark 15:46
l-s down His life ... John 10:11
I *l* down My life ... John 10:15
have you *laid* Him ... John 11:34
I *L* in Zion a stone ... Rom 9:33
l-ing aside falsehood ... Eph 4:25

LAYING ON OF HANDS In recognition of a divine calling, this symbolic act gave authority to a person commissioned to carry out a task.

LAYMAN *non-ecclesiastic*
l shall not eat *them* ... Ex 29:33
married to a *l* ... Lev 22:12
l who comes near ... Num 3:10

LAZARUS *(God has helped).* The name of the beggar in the parable of the rich man who died and went to Hades. Also the brother of Mary and Martha from Bethany. Jesus raised him from the dead as a sign to the crowd that He had been sent by God.
1 *beggar* ... Luke 16:20-25
2 *brother of Mary and Martha* ... John 11:1,2,5,11,43

LAZY *idle, slothful*
Because they are *l* ... Ex 5:8
You are *l, very l* ... Ex 5:17
You wicked, *l* slave ... Matt 25:26
beasts, *l* gluttons ... Titus 1:12

LEAD (n) *metal*
They sank like *l* ... Ex 15:10
an iron stylus and *l* ... Job 19:24
l is consumed by ... Jer 6:29
l in the furnace ... Ezek 22:18

LEAD (v) *direct, guide*
God *led* the people ... Ex 13:18
cloud by day to *l* ... Ex 13:21
l-s me beside quiet ... Ps 23:2
L me in Your truth ... Ps 25:5
led captive *Your* ... Ps 68:18
little boy will *l* ... Is 11:6
lamb that is *led* to ... Is 53:7
not *l* us into ... Matt 6:13
l astray...the elect ... Mark 13:22
led Him...crucify ... Mark 15:20
and *l-s* them out ... John 10:3
led by the Spirit ... Rom 8:14
led captive a host ... Eph 4:8
that *l-s* to salvation ... 2 Tim 3:15

LEADER *director, guide*
Let us appoint a *l* ... Num 14:4
one *l* of every tribe ... Num 34:18
l over My people ... 1 Kin 14:7
the *l* like the servant ... Luke 22:26
Obey your *l-s* ... Heb 13:17

LEADING (adj) *chief, noted*
gathered *l* men ... Ezra 7:28
number...*l* women ... Acts 17:4
l men of the Jews ... Acts 28:17

LEAF *foliage*
sewed fig *l-ves* ... Gen 3:7
sound of a driven *l* ... Lev 26:36
its *l* does not wither ... Ps 1:3
puts forth its *l-ves* ... Matt 24:32

LEAH *(wild cow).* Eldest daughter of Laban who deceived Jacob by giving her to him instead of Rachel, for whose hand in marriage Jacob had worked for seven years.
wife of Jacob ... Gen 29:23,30
mother of Reuben, Simeon, Levi and Judah ... Gen 29:32-35

LEAN (adj) *thin*
seven *l*...ugly cows ... Gen 41:27
my flesh has grown *l* ... Ps 109:24
and the *l* sheep ... Ezek 34:20

LEAN (v) *incline, rest*
may *l* against them ... Judg 16:26
l...own understanding ... Prov 3:5
l on the God of Israel ... Is 48:2

LEAP *jump, spring*
l-ing and dancing ... 2 Sam 6:16
I can *l* over a wall ... Ps 18:29
baby *l-ed* in her ... Luke 1:41
and *l for joy* ... Luke 6:23
l-ed up and *began* ... Acts 14:10

LEARN *get knowledge*
l to fear the LORD ... Deut 31:13
I may *l* Your statutes ... Ps 119:71
have I *l-ed* wisdom ... Prov 30:3
will they *l* war ... Is 2:4
l from Me ... Matt 11:29
l-ed to be content ... Phil 4:11
He *l-ed* obedience ... Heb 5:8

LEARNING (n) *knowledge*
increase *his l* ... Prov 9:9
l of the Egyptians ... Acts 7:22
great *l* is driving ... Acts 26:24

LEAST *insignificant*
l of my master's ... 2 Kin 18:24
greatest to the *l* ... 2 Chr 34:30
l in the kingdom ... Matt 5:19
the one who is *l*...is ... Matt 11:11
l of the apostles ... 1 Cor 15:9
very *l* of all saints ... Eph 3:8

LEATHER *animal skin*
man with a *l* girdle ... 2 Kin 1:8
a *l* belt around his ... Matt 3:4
and *wore* a *l* belt ... Mark 1:6

LEAVE *abandon, depart, forsake*
shall *l* his father ... Gen 2:24
arise, *l* this land ... Gen 31:13
not *l* me defenseless ... Ps 141:8
kindness and truth *l* ... Prov 3:3
l the ninety-nine ... Matt 18:12
Peace I *l* with you ... John 14:27
I am *l-ing*...world ... John 16:28
L your country ... Acts 7:3

LEAVEN Yeast, the substance that causes dough to ferment and rise. In ancient times it was usually preserved in pieces of dough. When used metaphorically in the Bible, leaven usually symbolizes corruption. It was strictly forbidden in any sacrifices to God. Also, every Jewish household had to be purged of leaven in

preparation for the Feast of Unleavened Bread. There are a few passages in which leaven has positive connotations.
no *l* found in your ... Ex 12:19
not be baked with *l* ... Lev 6:17
seven days no *l* shall ... Deut 16:4
heaven is like *l* ... Matt 13:33
little *l* leavens the ... 1 Cor 5:6

LEAVENED *raised by yeast*
whoever eats what is *l* ... Ex 12:19
with cakes of *l* bread ... Lev 7:13
not eat *l* bread ... Deut 16:3
until it was all *l* ... Matt 13:33

LEBANON *(very white)*. Territory north of the Promised Land, noted for its cedar trees which furnished lumber for the construction of Solomon's temple and palace.
mountain range N of Israel ... Josh 9:1; Judg 3:3; 1 Kin 5:6
showing God's greatness ... Ps 29:6
symbol of prosperity ... Ps 92:12

LEG *part of body*
l-s are pillars of ... Song 5:15
Uncover the *l* ... Is 47:2
not break His *l-s* ... John 19:33

LEGAL *lawful*
has a *l* matter ... Ex 24:14
Give me *l* protection ... Luke 18:3

LEGION *division, group*
twelve *l-s* of angels ... Matt 26:53
My name is *L* ... Mark 5:9
man who had...*l* ... Mark 5:15
L; for many demons ... Luke 8:30

LEMUEL *(belonging to God)*. Identified only as a royal writer whose mother taught him proverbs.
royal author of section of Proverbs ... Prov 31:1,4

LEND *loan*
l-ing them money ... Neh 5:10
l-s...on interest ... Ezek 18:13
l, expecting nothing ... Luke 6:35
l me three loaves ... Luke 11:5

LENDER *loaner*
becomes the *l-'s* slave ... Prov 22:7
l like the borrower ... Is 24:2

LENGTH
the *l* of the ark ... Gen 6:15
l of days and years ... Prov 3:2
breadth and *l* and ... Eph 3:18
l and width...equal ... Rev 21:16

LEOPARD *animal*
l will lie down with ... Is 11:6
Or the *l* his spots ... Jer 13:23
Like a *l* I will lie ... Hos 13:7
beast...was like a *l* ... Rev 13:2

LEPER *one having leprosy*
As for the *l* ... Lev 13:45
King Uzziah...a *l* ... 2 Chr 26:21
a *l* came to Him ... Matt 8:2
cleanse *the l-s* ... Matt 10:8
home of Simon the *l* ... Mark 14:3

LEPROSY *infectious disease (scaly)*. Refers not only to Hansen's disease but also to various inflammatory skin diseases, e.g. psoriasis. True leprosy was a terrible skin disease which was incurable in Biblical times, and the leper was banned from contact with other people and from worship in the temple. OT examples of leprosy are Miriam, Naaman, and Uzziah. In the NT, Jesus healed ten lepers at one time.
of *l* on the skin ... Lev 13:2
mark of *l* on a ... Lev 14:34
an infection of *l* ... Deut 24:8
cure him of his *l* ... 2 Kin 5:3
his *l* was cleansed ... Matt 8:3

LEPROUS *having leprosy*
hand was *l* like snow ... Ex 4:6
is a *l* malignancy ... Lev 13:51
ten *l*...met Him ... Luke 17:12

LET *allow, permit*
L there be light ... Gen 1:3
L My people go ... Ex 5:1
L the children alone ... Matt 19:14
l this cup pass from ... Matt 26:39
Do not *l* your heart be ... John 14:1

LETTER *epistle* or *symbol*
a *l* sent to Solomon ... 2 Chr 2:11
smallest *l* or stroke ... Matt 5:18
You are our *l* ... 2 Cor 3:2
l caused you sorrow ... 2 Cor 7:8
large *l-s* I am writing ... Gal 6:11

LEVEL *flat, plain*
lead me in a *l* path ... Ps 27:11
path of the righteous *l* ... Is 26:7
stood on a *l* place ... Luke 6:17

LEVI (unc, *attached*). Third son of Jacob, by Leah. Founder and head of the tribe that served in the tabernacle and the temple. Also the name of other individuals.
1 *son of Jacob* ... Gen 34:25
2 *tribe* ... Num 1:49; Rev 7:7
3 *two ancestors of Jesus* ... Luke 3:24,29
4 *apostle* ... Mark 2:14; Luke 5:27,29

LEVIATHAN A giant sea monster poetically described as breathing fire and smoke.
symbolic monster of the deep ... Job 3:8; Ps 104:26; Is 27:1

LEVIRATE MARRIAGE *(levirate* from Lat for *brother-in-law)*. The duty of a brother to his deceased brother to raise up children for him by his widow, so that his brother's lineage would continue in Israel (Deut 25:5-6).

LEVITES The tribe that descended from Levi. The Levites served in the temple of God as priests, and performed other religious duties. They had no territory assigned in the Promised Land because God declared Himself to be their inheritance. This meant, among other things, that the Levites received portions of the sacrifices as their food. They also had certain cities assigned to them throughout the other tribes.
descendants of Levi ... Ex 6:19,25
charged with the care of the sanctuary ... Num 1:50; 3:41

LEVY (n) *payment, tax*
the LORD'S *l* ... Num 31:38
l fixed by Moses ... 2 Chr 24:6

LEVY (v) *impose a tax*
l a tax for the LORD ... Num 31:28
l-ied forced laborers ... 1 Kin 9:21

LEWDNESS *lascivious, lust*
land...full of *l* ... Lev 19:29
not commit this *l* ... Ezek 16:43
I will uncover her *l* ... Hos 2:10

LIAR *one telling lies*
who...prove me a *l* ... Job 24:25
a poor man than a *l* ... Prov 19:22
I will be a *l* like ... John 8:55
hypocrisy of *l-s* ... 1 Tim 4:2
we make Him a *l* ... 1 John 1:10

LIBATION *see* **OFFERINGS**

LIBERTY *freedom see* **FREEDOM**
I will walk at *l* ... Ps 119:45
proclaim *l* to captives ... Is 61:1
spy out our *l* ... Gal 2:4
the *law* of *l* ... James 1:25

LIBNAH An encampment for the Israelites while they were in the wilderness. Also a Levitical city in SW Judah.
1 *place in wilderness* ... Num 33:21
2 *Canaanite city* ... Josh 10:29; 2 Kin 23:31
a Levitical city ... 1 Chr 6:57

LIBYA
country in N Africa ... Ezek 30:5; Acts 2:10

LICK *lap up*
dogs will *l* up your ... 1 Kin 21:19
his enemies *l* the dust ... Ps 72:9
dogs were...*l-ing* ... Luke 16:21

LIE (n) *false statement*
speak *l-s* go astray ... Ps 58:3
tells *l-s* will perish ... Prov 19:9
prophesy a *l* to you ... Jer 27:10
the father of *l-s* ... John 8:44
truth of God for a *l* ... Rom 1:25
no *l* is of the truth ... 1 John 2:21

LIE (v) *make false statement*
nor *l* to one another ... Lev 19:11
l-d to Him with their ... Ps 78:36
l-d about the LORD ... Jer 5:12
l to the Holy Spirit ... Acts 5:3
not *l* to one another ... Col 3:9
impossible...God to *l* ... Heb 6:18

LIE (v) *recline*
when you *l* down ... Deut 11:19
she *lay* at his feet ... Ruth 3:14
Saul *lay* sleeping ... 1 Sam 26:7
makes me *l* down ... Ps 23:2
lying in a manger ... Luke 2:12

LIFE *living* or *salvation*
the breath of *l* ... Gen 2:7
l for *l* ... Ex 21:23
l...is in the blood ... Lev 17:11
Our *l* for yours ... Josh 2:14
my *l* is *but* breath ... Job 7:7
Who redeems your *l* ... Ps 103:4
the springs of *l* ... Prov 4:23
way of *l* and...death ... Jer 21:8
to everlasting *l* ... Dan 12:2
take my *l* from me ... Jon 4:3
worried about your *l* ... Matt 6:25
loses his *l* for My ... Matt 16:25
His *l* a ransom for ... Matt 20:28
l is more than food ... Luke 12:23

out of death into *l* ... John 5:24
I am the bread of *l* ... John 6:35
lays down his *l* ... John 10:11
resurrection and...*l* ... John 11:25
truth, and the *l* ... John 14:6
lay down his *l* for ... John 15:13
walk in newness of *l* ... Rom 6:4
the Spirit gives *l* ... 2 Cor 3:6
Christ, who is our *l* ... Col 3:4
an undisciplined *l* ... 2 Thess 3:11
receive...crown of *l* ... James 1:12
lay down our *l-ves* ... 1 John 3:16
book of *l* of the lamb ... Rev 13:8

LIFE, ETERNAL *see* **IMMORTALITY** Eternal life is the possession of every Christian, both while alive and after death, in that Christ is always present with him and will never leave him. The souls of Christians who have died continue to live in a fully conscious state with Christ in Paradise (q.v.), and eventually will be reunited with their bodies through resurrection.
to inherit *e* ... Mark 10:17; Luke 10:25
but have *e* ... John 3:16
He may give *e* ... John 17:2
gift of God is *e* ... Rom 6:23

LIFEBLOOD
I will require your *l* ... Gen 9:5
poured out their *l* ... Is 63:6
l of the innocent ... Jer 2:34

LIFETIME *length of life*
Throughout his *l* ... 2 Chr 34:33
His favor is for a *l* ... Ps 30:5
my *l* of futility ... Eccl 7:15
as the *l* of a tree ... Is 65:22

LIFT *exalt, raise*
l up your eyes and ... Gen 13:14
l up your staff and ... Ex 14:16
l up your voice ... Job 38:34
One who *l-s* my head ... Ps 3:3
I Will *l* up my eyes ... Ps 121:1
will not *l* up sword ... Is 2:4
Spirit *l-ed* me up ... Ezek 3:14
Son of Man be *l-ed* ... John 3:14
He was *l-ed* up ... Acts 1:9
l-ing up holy hands ... 1 Tim 2:8

LIGHT *brightness, lamp* In the Scriptures light is used frequently as a metaphor for Christ and the Christian's proper lifestyle.
Let there be *l* ... Gen 1:3
Israel had *l* in ... Ex 10:23
l of the wicked ... Job 18:5
LORD is my *l* ... Ps 27:1
And a *l* to my path ... Ps 119:105
like the *l* of dawn ... Prov 4:18
walk in the *l* of the ... Is 2:5
your *l* has come ... Is 60:1
stars for *l* by night ... Jer 31:35
the *l* of the world ... Matt 5:14
body will be full of *l* ... Matt 6:22
L of revelation to ... Luke 2:32
There was the true *l* ... John 1:9
I am the *L* ... John 8:12
while you have...*L* ... John 12:35
l of the gospel ... 2 Cor 4:4
walk as children of *L* ... Eph 5:8
Father of *l-s* ... James 1:17
if we walk in the *L* ... 1 John 1:7

LIGHTNING *flash of light in sky*
thunder and *l* flashes ... Ex 19:16
He spreads His *l* ... Job 36:30
makes *l* for the rain ... Jer 10:13
l...from the east ... Matt 24:27
appearance...like *l* ... Matt 28:3

LIKENESS *similarity*
according to Our *l* ... Gen 1:26
an idol, or any *l* ... Ex 20:4
the *l* of sinful flesh ... Rom 8:3
made in the *l* of men ... Phil 2:7

LILY *flower*
The *l* of the valleys ... Song 2:1
blossom like the *l* ... Hos 14:5
l-ies of the field ... Matt 6:28

LIMIT *end, extent*
there is no *l* ... 1 Chr 22:16
no l to windy words ... Job 16:3
set a *l* for the rain ... Job 28:26
no *l* to the treasure ... Nah 2:9

LINE *boundary* or *cord*
draw your *border l* ... Num 34:7
ran from...battle *l* ... 1 Sam 4:12
a *l* into the Nile ... Is 19:8
plumb *l* in the hand ... Zech 4:10

LINEN *type of cloth*
makes *l* garments ... Prov 31:24
buy...a *l* waistband ... Jer 13:1
pulled free of the *l* sheet ... Mark 14:52
wrapped Him...*l* ... Mark 15:46
saw the *l* wrappings ... John 20:5
clothed in fine *l* ... Rev 19:14

LINTEL *horizontal crosspiece*
see **DOORPOST**
blood on the *l* ... Ex 12:23
l and five-sided ... 1 Kin 6:31

LION *wild animal*
Judah is a *l-'s* whelp ... Gen 49:9
a *l* or a bear ... 1 Sam 17:34
hunt me like a *l* ... Job 10:16
tear my soul like a *l* ... Ps 7:2
are bold as a *l* ... Prov 28:1
cast into the *l-s'* ... Dan 6:16
like a roaring *l* ... 1 Pet 5:8

LIPS *part of mouth*
My *l* will praise ... Ps 63:3
With her flattering *l* ... Prov 7:21
Your *l, my* bride ... Song 4:11
a man of unclean *l* ... Is 6:5
honors Me with...*l* ... Matt 15:8

LIQUOR *alcoholic drink*
concerning wine and *l* ... Mic 2:11
drink no wine or *l* ... Luke 1:15

LISTEN *hear, heed*
Pharaoh does not *l* ... Ex 7:4
l to His voice ... Deut 4:30
l...commandments ... Deut 11:27
scoffer does not *l* ... Prov 13:1
L to your father ... Prov 23:22
draw near to *l* ... Eccl 5:1
L to Me, O Jacob ... Is 48:12
L...another parable ... Matt 21:33
care what you *l* to ... Mark 4:24
l-ing to the word ... Luke 5:1
My Son...*l* to Him ... Luke 9:35

LITERATURE *writings*
teach them the *l* ... Dan 1:4
every *branch of l* ... Dan 1:17

LITTLE *small quantity*
a *l* lower than God ... Ps 8:5
a *l* boy will lead ... Is 11:6
You of *l* faith ... Matt 6:30
forgiven *l*, loves *l* ... Luke 7:47
a *l* leaven leavens ... 1 Cor 5:6
l children, abide ... 1 John 2:28

LIVE (v) *reside* or *be alive*
eat, and *l* forever ... Gen 3:22
does not *l* by bread ... Deut 8:3
my Redeemer *l-s* ... Job 19:25
Let my soul *l* ... Ps 119:175
Listen, that you may *l* ... Is 55:3
can these bones *l* ... Ezek 37:3
righteous will *l* by ... Hab 2:4
l-d in...Nazareth ... Matt 2:23
not *l* on bread alone ... Matt 4:4
l even if he dies ... John 11:25
because I *l* ... John 14:19
shall *l* by faith ... Rom 1:17
Christ died and *l-d* ... Rom 14:9
no longer I who *l* ... Gal 2:20
to *l* is Christ ... Phil 1:21
worship Him who *l-s* ... Rev 4:10

LIVER *internal organ*
the lobe of the *l* ... Ex 29:13
l of the sin offering ... Lev 9:10
pierces through his *l* ... Prov 7:23
he looks at the *l* ... Ezek 21:21

LIVESTOCK *domestic animals*
was very rich in *l* ... Gen 13:2
their *l* to Joseph ... Gen 47:17
l of Egypt died ... Ex 9:6
large number of *l* ... Num 32:1

LIVING (adj) *alive*
man became a *l* being ... Gen 2:7
voice of the *l* god ... Deut 5:26
Divide the *l* child ... 1 Kin 3:25
Son of the *l* God ... Matt 16:16
given you *l* water ... John 4:10
I am the *l* bread ... John 6:51
l and holy sacrifice ... Rom 12:1
became a *l* soul ... 1 Cor 15:45
temple of the *l* God ... 2 Cor 6:16
word of God is *l* ... Heb 4:12

LIVING (n) *what is alive*
mother of all *the l* ... Gen 3:20
land of the *l* ... Job 28:13
that the *l* may know ... Dan 4:17
God...of the *l* ... Matt 22:32
judge the *l* and the ... 1 Pet 4:5

LOAD *burden*
in all their *l-s* ... Num 4:27
I alone bear the *l* ... Deut 1:12

LOAF *portion of bread*
gave him a *l* of bread ... Jer 37:21
asks for a *l* ... Matt 7:9
five *l-ves* and two ... Matt 14:17

LO-AMMI
second son of Hosea ... Hos 1:9

LOAN *something lent*
your neighbor a *l* ... Deut 24:10
rich with *l-s* ... Hab 2:6

LOATHE *despise, detest*
I *l-d that* generation ... Ps 95:10
sated man *l-s* honey ... Prov 27:7
I *l* the arrogance of ... Amos 6:8

LOATHSOME *detestable*
l to the Egyptians ... Gen 46:34
like *l* food to me ... Job 6:7
l and malignant sore ... Rev 16:2

LOCK (n) *tuft of hair*
seven *l-s* of my hair ... Judg 16:13
flowing *l-s* of...head ... Song 7:5
a *l* of my head ... Ezek 8:3

LOCK (v) *secure, shut*
l the door behind ... 2 Sam 13:17
l-ed quite securely ... Acts 5:23
l up...the saints ... Acts 26:10

LOCUST *grasshopper* A very destructive insect. One of the ten Egyptian plagues was a great invasion of locusts. The Mosaic law permitted them to be consumed as food, and John the Baptist ate them as a regular part of his diet.
wind brought the *l-s* ... Ex 10:13
you may eat: the *l* ... Lev 11:22
come in like *l-s* ... Judg 6:5
leap like the *l* ... Job 39:20
l-s have no king ... Prov 30:27
like the swarming *l* ... Nah 3:17
food was *l-s* and wild ... Matt 3:4

LOD / LYDDA
town of Benjamin SE of coastal Jaffa ... 1 Chr 8:12; Neh 11:35; Acts 9:32-38

LODGE *dwell, spend the night*
where you *l*, I will *l* ... Ruth 1:16
drank and *l-d* there ... Judg 19:4
In his neck *l-s* ... Job 41:22
l in the wilderness ... Ps 55:7

LODGING (adj) *dwelling*
fodder at the *l* place ... Gen 42:27
about at the *l* place ... Ex 4:24
A wayfarers' *l* place ... Jer 9:2

LOFTINESS *elevated, haughty*
l of man will be ... Is 2:11
l of your dwelling ... Obad 3

LOFTY *grand, high*
built You a *l* house ... 1 Kin 8:13
high and *l* mountain ... Is 57:7

LOG *beam, wood*
he who splits *l-s* ... Eccl 10:9
l out of your own eye ... Matt 7:5

LOINS *lower back*
with your *l* girded ... Ex 12:11
Gird up your *l* ... 2 Kin 4:29
l are full of anguish ... Is 21:3
having girded your *l* ... Eph 6:14

LOIS
grandmother of Timothy ... 2 Tim 1:5

LONELY *alone, isolated*
I am *l* and afflicted ... Ps 25:16
makes a home for the *l* ... Ps 68:6
How *l* sits the city ... Lam 1:1

LONG (adj) *extended*
there was a *l* war ... 2 Sam 3:1
L life is in her ... Prov 3:16
you make *l* prayers ... Matt 23:14
if a man has *l* hair ... 1 Cor 11:14

LONG (v) *desire, want*
Who *l* for death ... Job 3:21
my soul *l-s* for You ... Is 26:9
l-ing to be fed ... Luke 16:21
I *l* to see you ... Rom 1:11
angels *l* to look ... 1 Pet 1:12
l for the pure milk ... 1 Pet 2:2

LOOK *see, stare*
Do not *l* behind you ... Gen 19:17
afraid to *l* at God ... Ex 3:6
LORD *l-s* at...heart ... 1 Sam 16:7
L upon my affliction ... Ps 25:18
The sea *l-ed* and fled ... Ps 114:3
not *l* on the wine ... Prov 23:31
l eagerly for Him ... Is 8:17
l to the Holy One ... Is 17:7
l on Me...pierced ... Zech 12:10
L at the birds of ... Matt 6:26
l-ing up...heaven ... Matt 14:19
plow and *l-ing* back ... Luke 9:62
l on the fields ... John 4:35
l on Him...pierced ... John 19:37
l-ing for the blessed ... Titus 2:13
l-ing for...heavens ... 2 Pet 3:13

LOOSE *release*
l the cords of Orion ... Job 38:31
have *l-d* my bonds ... Ps 116:16
l on earth shall have been ... Matt 16:19
you *l* on earth ... Matt 18:18

LORD *personal name of God* In the NT the title is often used in OT quotations etc. as a substitute for Yahweh, the sacred name of God (*see* **YAHWEH**).
Old Testament
Different Hebrew words are translated as Lord
LORD *(Yahweh)* ... Gen 4:1; Ex 3:2,15; Ps 23:1; Is 40:31; Ezek 11:23
Lord GOD *(Adonai Yahweh)* ... Gen 15:2; 2 Sam 7:18,19; Is 1:24; Ezek 28:6; Hab 3:19
LORD God *(Yahweh Elohim)* ... Gen 2:4; Ps 59:5; 68:18; Jer 15:16; Jon 1:9
Lord *(Adonai)* ... Gen 18:27; Ex 4:10; Josh 3:11; Ps 68:19; Mic 4:13
LORD GOD *(Yah Yahweh)* ... Is 12:2
New Testament
Different Greek words are translated as Lord
Lord *(Kurios, refers to either the Father or the Son)* ... Matt 1:20; John 11:2; Acts 5:19; 2 Cor 5:6; 1 Thess 4:16
Lord *(Despotēs, refers to the Father)* ... Luke 2:29; Acts 4:24; Rev 6:10
Lord God *(Kurios Theos, refers to either the Father or the Son)* ... Luke 1:32; Rev 1:8;11:17;16:7;18:8
Lord Jesus *(Kurios Iēsous)* ... Mark 16:19; Luke 24:3; Acts 4:33; 7:59
Lord Jesus Christ *(Kurios Iēsous Christos)* ... Acts 15:26; Rom 1:7;5:1; 1 Cor 1:10; Eph 1:2,3; 1 Thess 5:9; James 2:1

LORD *human master, ruler* One who has due power, ownership, control, or authority over others. A term of respect for one's father, rulers and government officials, teachers, et al.
Hear us, my *l* ... Gen 23:6
not my *l* be angry ... Gen 31:35
Moses, my *l* ... Num 11:28
l-s of...Philistines ... Judg 16:27
counsel of my *l* ... Ezra 10:3
l-s of the nations ... Is 16:8
his *l* commanded ... Matt 18:25
write to my *l* ... Acts 25:26

LORD'S DAY The first day of the week (Sunday). It became the day of assembly for the church, commemorating the resurrection of Christ (Acts 20:7). Sometimes viewed as the "Christian Sabbath," but the (Jewish) Sabbath was the seventh day (Saturday) and had a different purpose, with many regulations followed by observant Jews.

LORD'S SUPPER A ceremony observed by Christians to commemorate Christ's death. Christ introduced it at the close of the Passover meal that He and His disciples ate on the night of His betrayal (1 Cor 11:23-27).
eat the *L* ... 1 Cor 11:20

LO-RUHAMAH
daughter of Hosea ... Hos 1:6,8

LOSE *mislay, suffer loss*
do not *l* courage ... 2 Chr 15:7
lost their confidence ... Neh 6:16
stars *l* their ... Joel 2:10
his life will *l* it ... Matt 10:39
that which was *lost* ... Matt 18:11
not *l* his reward ... Mark 9:41
whoever *l-s* his life ... Luke 9:24

LOSS *damage, what is lost*
might not suffer *l* ... Dan 6:2
damage and great *l* ... Acts 27:10
might not suffer *l* ... 2 Cor 7:9
all things to be *l* ... Phil 3:8

LOST (adj) *missing, ruined*
like a *l* sheep ... Ps 119:176
have become *l* sheep ... Jer 50:6
l sheep...of Israel ... Matt 10:6
the wine is *l* ... Mark 2:22

LOST (n) *without God*
I will seek the *l* ... Ezek 34:16
sent only to the *l* ... Matt 15:24

LOT *portion* or *decision process*
1) Abraham's nephew. 2) A metaphor of participation or involvement. 3) An object, e.g. a colored stone, used as a means of determining the will of God or for making other decisions.
nephew of Abraham ... Gen 12:5;19:15,36
one *l* for the LORD ... Lev 16:8
clothing they cast *l-s* ... Ps 22:18
your *l* with us ... Prov 1:14
let us cast *l-s* ... Jon 1:7
tear it, but cast *l-s* ... John 19:24
l fell to Matthias ... Acts 1:26

LOUD *great, noisy*
very *l* trumpet sound ... Ex 19:16
with a *l* shout ... Ezra 3:13
Jesus cried...*l* voice ... Matt 27:50
heard...a *l* voice ... Rev 1:10

LOVE (n) *compassion, devotion* In the NT, usually the Gr word *agapé,* which focuses on benevolent actions toward another person, rather than on feelings for the person. Often described as an unconditional, sacrificial love which does what is in the best interest of another, without expecting anything in return.
l covers all ... Prov 10:12
in unchanging *l* ... Mic 7:18
l will grow cold ... Matt 24:12

abide in My *l* ... John 15:10
Greater *l* has no one ... John 15:13
demonstrates His...*l* ... Rom 5:8
separate us from...*l* ... Rom 8:39
l edifies ... 1 Cor 8:1
l is kind ... 1 Cor 13:4
Pursue *l* ... 1 Cor 14:1
l of Christ controls ... 2 Cor 5:14
through *l* serve one ... Gal 5:13
fruit...is *l* ... Gal 5:22
speaking...truth in *l* ... Eph 4:15
l of money is a root ... 1 Tim 6:10
for *l* is from God ... 1 John 4:7
God is *l* ... 1 John 4:16
l casts out fear ... 1 John 4:18
have left your first *l* ... Rev 2:4

LOVE (v) *see* **LOVE** (n)
who *l* Me and keep My ... Ex 20:6
l your neighbor as ... Lev 19:18
l the LORD your God ... Deut 6:5
the LORD *l-d* Israel ... 1 Kin 10:9
I *l* Your testimonies ... Ps 119:119
LORD *l-s* He reproves ... Prov 3:12
friend *l-s* at all ... Prov 17:17
Do not *l* sleep ... Prov 20:13
A time to *l* ... Eccl 3:8
Hate evil, *l* good ... Amos 5:15
do not *l* perjury ... Zech 8:17
l your enemies ... Matt 5:44
l to stand and pray ... Matt 6:5
God so *l-d* the world ... John 3:16
you *l* one another ... John 13:34
l-s a cheerful giver ... 2 Cor 9:7
Husbands, *l*...wives ... Eph 5:25
Do not *l* the world ... 1 John 2:15
whom I *l*, I reprove ... Rev 3:19

LOVERS *one who desires, loves*
l have been crushed ... Jer 22:20
I called to my *l* ... Lam 1:19
the hands of your *l* ... Ezek 16:39
I will go after my *l* ... Hos 2:5
l of pleasure...*l* of ... 2 Tim 3:4

LOVINGKINDNESS *compassion*
His *l* is upon Israel ... Ezra 3:11
abundant in *l* and ... Ps 86:15
sing of the *l* of the ... Ps 89:1
By *l* and truth ... Prov 16:6
with everlasting *l* ... Is 54:8

LOWLAND *low hills*
country and in the *l* ... Deut 1:7
the Negev and the *l* ... Josh 10:40
sycamores in the *l* ... 2 Chr 1:15
the cities of the *l* ... Jer 32:44
see also **SHEPHELAH**

LOWLY *humble, little*
He sets on high...*l* ... Job 5:11
He regards the *l* ... Ps 138:6
associate with the *l* ... Rom 12:16

LOYALTY *faithfulness*
Is this your *l* ... 2 Sam 16:17
proclaims his own *l* ... Prov 20:6
I delight in *l* ... Hos 6:6

LUKE A Greek physician by profession, and author of the Gospel of Luke and the Acts of the Apostles. He was a faithful friend and traveling companion of Paul.
associate of Paul ... 2 Tim 4:11; Philem 24
author of Luke and Acts ... Luke 1:1; Acts 1:1
physician ... Col 4:14

LUKEWARM *tepid*
because you are *l* ... Rev 3:16

LUST *sexual desire*
looks at...woman with *l* ... Matt 5:28
from youthful *l-s* ... 2 Tim 2:22
You *l* and do not ... James 4:2
l of the eyes ... 1 John 2:16

LUXURIANT *lush, productive*
beneath...*l* tree ... 1 Kin 14:23
Israel is a *l* vine ... Hos 10:1

LUXURY *extravagance*
L is not fitting for ... Prov 19:10
clothed and live in *l* ... Luke 7:25

LUZ
1 *ancient name of Bethel* ... Gen 28:19; 48:3
2 *town in Aram* ... Judg 1:26

LYCAONIA
Roman province in Asia Minor ... Acts 14:6

LYDDA *see* **LOD**

LYDIA A businesswoman from Thyatira living in Philippi, who became Paul's first convert to Christ in Europe. Also an ancient country in Asia Minor.
1 *seller of purple dyes and goods* ... Acts 16:14,40
2 *region on the W coast of Asia Minor* ... Jer 46:9

LYE A strong detergent obtained from the ashes of various burned plants. In the Bible, sometimes symbolic of a powerful cleansing agent (Jer 2:22).

LYING (adj) *false*
with a *l* tongue ... Ps 109:2
hatred *has l* lips ... Prov 10:18
l pen of the scribes ... Jer 8:8
and *l* divination ... Ezek 13:6

LYRE *stringed instrument* A musical instrument of the harp class, widely used in worship in the temple.
play the *l* and pipe ... Gen 4:21
prophesy with *l-s* ... 1 Chr 25:1
Awake, harp and *l* ... Ps 57:8

LYSTRA A city in Lycaonia in Asia Minor, visited several times by Paul. He was once stoned there for healing a man who could not walk.
a Lycaonian town ... Acts 14:6; 16:1,2

M

MACEDONIA The first European country in which the gospel was preached. In NT times it was a Roman province which included successful churches at Thessalonica and Philippi.
Roman province ... Acts 16:9,12
N Greece ... Phil 4:15; 1 Tim 1:3
visited by Paul ... Acts 16:10; 2 Cor 2:13

MACHIR Protector of Mephibosheth, the son of Jonathan, and one who remained faithful to David during the rebellion of Absalom.
1 *grandson of Joseph* ... Josh 17:1
2 *son of Ammiel* ... 2 Sam 9:4,5

MACHPELAH (unc, *double*). A field at Hebron containing a cave purchased by Abraham from the Hittites where he buried Sarah. He, Isaac, Rebekah, Leah, and Jacob were later buried there as well.
cave near Hebron ... Gen 23:17,19
Sarah's burial place ... Gen 23:19
Abraham buried there ... Gen 25:9
burial place of Jacob, Isaac, Rebekah, and Leah ... Gen 49:29ff; 50:13

MAD *insane*
makes a wise man *m* ... Eccl 7:7
nations are going *m* ... Jer 51:7

MADMAN *insane person*
behaving as a *m* ... 1 Sam 21:14
m who prophesies ... Jer 29:26

MADNESS *lunacy*
laughter, It is *m* ... Eccl 2:2
consider...*m* and folly ... Eccl 2:12

MAGADAN
village on the Sea of Galilee ... Matt 15:39

MAGDALENE *see* **MARY MAGDALENE**

MAGI An eastern religious caste who specialized in astrology, medicine, and natural science. The wise men who came to worship the infant Jesus were magi.
wise men from Persia ... Matt 2:1,7,16

MAGIC *sorcery*
practicing *m* ... Acts 8:9
who practiced *m* ... Acts 19:19

MAGICIAN *sorcerer, wizard* A skillful person who, whether with good or bad intentions, does things which seem impossible. The practice of magic to imitate divine power (as performed by Pharaoh's magicians and others) is forbidden in the Bible.
called for...*m-s* ... Gen 41:8
the *m-s* of Egypt ... Ex 7:11
of any *m*, conjurer or ... Dan 2:10
found a *m* ... Acts 13:6

MAGISTRATE
appear before the *m* ... Luke 12:58
to the chief *m-s* ... Acts 16:20

MAGNIFY *extol, praise*
name...be *m-ied* ... 2 Sam 7:26
You *m* him ... Job 7:17
O *m* the LORD with me ... Ps 34:3
have *m-ied* Your word ... Ps 138:2
Jesus was...*m-ied* ... Acts 19:17
I *m* my ministry ... Rom 11:13

MAGOG
1 *son of Japheth* ... 1 Chr 1:5
2 *region in Asia Minor or further N ruled by Gog* ... Ezek 38:2;39:6
see also **GOG**

MAHANAIM *(two camps)*. A place where Jacob met the angels of God. It later became a Levite city east of the Jordan, and David fled there during Absalom's revolt.
city in Trans-Jordan ... Josh 13:26,30
Levitical city ... Josh 21:38; 1 Chr 6:80

MAHER-SHALAL-HASH-BAZ
symbolic name of one of Isaiah's sons ... Is 8:3

MAHLAH
1 *daughter of Zelophehad* ... Num 26:33; 27:1; Josh 17:3
2 *a Manassite* ... 1 Chr 7:18

MAHLON
husband of Ruth ... Ruth 1:5; 4:10

MAID
Hagar, Sarai's *m* ... Gen 16:8
gave my *m* to my ... Gen 30:18
I am Ruth your *m* ... Ruth 3:9
way of a man...a *m* ... Prov 30:19

MAIDENS *young woman*
at the Nile...her *m* ... Ex 2:5
m...tambourines ... Ps 68:25

MAIDSERVANT *female slave*
do...to your *m* ... Deut 15:17
give Your *m* a son ... 1 Sam 1:11
let your *m* speak ... 2 Sam 14:12
while your *m* slept ... 1 Kin 3:20

MAJESTIC *dignified, grand*
Who is like You, *m* ... Ex 15:11
with His *m* voice ... Job 37:4
How *m* is Your name ... Ps 8:1
They are the *m* ones ... Ps 16:3
m is His work ... Ps 111:3
by the *M* Glory ... 2 Pet 1:17

MAJESTY *grandeur*
Around God is...*m* ... Job 37:22
He is clothed with *m* ... Ps 93:1
The *m* of our God ... Is 35:2
right hand of the *M* ... Heb 1:3
revile angelic *m-ies* ... Jude 8

MAKE *cause, create, do*
Let Us *m* man in ... Gen 1:26
not *m* for...an idol ... Ex 20:4
M me know Your ways ... Ps 25:4
M ready the way of ... Matt 3:3
m you fishers of men ... Matt 4:19

MAKER *creator*
Where is God my *M* ... Job 35:10
kneel before...our *M* ... Ps 95:6
M of heaven and ... Ps 115:15
I, the LORD, am the *m* ... Is 44:24

MAKKEDAH One of the royal Canaanite cities completely destroyed by Joshua during Israel's conquest of the Promised Land.
Canaanite city in Judah ... Josh 10:21; 15:41

MALACHI *(my messenger).* One of the minor prophets; the last written prophecy in the OT, which bears his name.
prophet ... Mal 1:1

MALCHUS
servant whose ear was cut off by Peter ... John 18:10

MALE
m and female He ... Gen 1:27
lamb...unblemished *m* ... Ex 12:5
likeness of *m* or ... Deut 4:16
slew...*m* children ... Matt 2:16
made...*m* and female ... Matt 19:4
neither *m* nor female ... Gal 3:28

MALICE *evil, mischief*
perceived their *m* ... Matt 22:18
leaven of *m* and ... 1 Cor 5:8
wrath, *m,* slander ... Col 3:8
putting aside all *m* ... 1 Pet 2:1

MALICIOUS *harmful, spiteful*
to be a *m* witness ... Ex 23:1
m gossips, without ... 2 Tim 3:3

MALTA
island S of Sicily where Paul was shipwrecked ... Acts 28:1

MAMRE *(strength).* A place near Hebron where Abraham lived for a time and once provided hospitality to angels. Also the name of an Amorite.
1 *Abraham's dwelling place near Hebron* ... Gen 13:18
2 *Amorite chieftain* ... Gen 14:24

MAN *male*
make *m* in Our image ... Gen 1:26
God formed *m* of dust ... Gen 2:7
Elisha the *m* of God ... 2 Kin 5:8
m is born for trouble ... Job 5:7
blessed is the *m* ... Ps 1:1
m is a mere breath ... Ps 39:11
righteous *m* hates ... Prov 13:5
Will a *m* rob God ... Mal 3:8
light...before *men* ... Matt 5:16
fishers of *men* ... Mark 1:17
Sabbath...for *m* ... Mark 2:27
rich *m* to enter ... Mark 10:25
what is a *m* profited ... Luke 9:25
a *m,* sent from God ... John 1:6
How can a *m* be born ... John 3:4
a *m* of Macedonia ... Acts 16:9
through one *m* sin ... Rom 5:12
as is common to *m* ... 1 Cor 10:13
when I became a *m* ... 1 Cor 13:11
m...leave his father ... Eph 5:31

MAN, SON OF *see* **SON OF MAN**

MANASSEH (unc, *God has made me to forget).* The first son of Joseph, he was born in Egypt and became head of one of the tribes of Israel. Also the name of several others.
1 *son of Joseph* ... Gen 41:51;46:20
2 *tribe and area* ... Num 13:11; Josh 17:1
3 *king of Judah* ... 2 Kin 21:1,11
4 *Pahath-moab's son* ... Ezra 10:30
5 *son of Hashum* ... Ezra 10:33

MANDRAKES *love fruit* A pleasant-smelling narcotic plant grown in countries in the eastern Mediterranean region. The ancients believed that its fruit helped barren woman to conceive.
found *m* in the field ... Gen 30:14
m...fragrance ... Song 7:13

MANGER *feeding trough* A trough or hollowed-out area in a stable where livestock are fed. The baby Jesus was placed in a manger.
spend...at your *m* ... Job 39:9
the *m* is clean ... Prov 14:4
laid Him in a *m* ... Luke 2:7

MANIFEST *reveal*
I have *m-ed* Your name ... John 17:6
became *m* to those ... Rom 10:20
made *m* to God ... 2 Cor 5:11
m-ed to His saints ... Col 1:26

MANIFOLD *many and varied*
the *m* wisdom of God ... Eph 3:10
stewards...*m* grace ... 1 Pet 4:10

MANKIND *the human race*
God...dwell with *m* ... 2 Chr 6:18
All *m* is stupid ... Jer 51:17
His love for *m* ... Titus 3:4
kill a third of *m* ... Rev 9:15

MANNA *food of the desert* (unc, *what is it?).* The food supernaturally supplied for the Israelites while they were wandering in the wilderness for forty years. The manna ceased after they entered the Promised Land.
Israel named it *m* ... Ex 16:31
m was like coriander ... Num 11:7
m ceased on the day ... Josh 5:12
He rained down *m* ... Ps 78:24
Our fathers ate the *m* ... John 6:31

MANNER *way*
Your *m* with those ... Ps 119:132
spoke in such a *m* ... Acts 14:1
m worthy of...saints ... Rom 16:2
walk in a *m* worthy ... Eph 4:1

MANOAH *(resting place).* The father of Samson; of the tribe of Dan.
father of Samson ... Judg 13:2ff

MANSLAYER One who kills another accidentally, as opposed to a murderer. Six cities in Israel were designated as cities of refuge or asylum to which a manslayer could flee and be safe from an avenger of the person he killed until he stood trial. If acquitted of killing with intent, the manslayer could live in the city of refuge until the death of the high priest. Thereafter, he was permitted to return to his hometown. *see* **MURDER**
for the *m* to flee to ... Num 35:6
m might flee there ... Deut 4:42
the *m* who kills any ... Josh 20:3

MANTLE *cloak, garment* A large nearly square piece of cloth, animal hide, or similar material worn over other clothing. Elijah used one, which was passed on to his disciple and successor Elisha.
threw his *m* on him ... 1 Kin 19:19
the *m* of Elijah ... 2 Kin 2:13
like a *m* You will roll ... Heb 1:12

MARAH
spring of bitter water ... Ex 15:23

MARCH *pace, walk*
m around...seven times ... Josh 6:4
m everyone in his path ... Joel 2:8

MARDUK
chief Babylonian god ... Jer 50:2

MARESHAH
1 *father of Hebron* ... 1 Chr 2:42
2 *son of Laadah* ... 1 Chr 4:21
3 *town in Judah* ... 2 Chr 11:5-8

MARK *sign, spot*
make any tattoo *m-s* ... Lev 19:28
m on the foreheads ... Ezek 9:4
m on his forehead ... Rev 14:9
m of the beast ... Rev 19:20

MARK, JOHN *see entry 5 under* **JOHN**
author of Gospel of Mark
accompanied Paul and Barnabas ... Acts 13:5; 15:37

cousin of Barnabas ... Col 4:10

MARKET *selling* or *trading place*
was the *m* of nations ... Is 23:3
coastlands were...*m* ... Ezek 27:15
idle in the *m* place ... Matt 20:3
sold in the meat *m* ... 1 Cor 10:25

MARRIAGE *wedlock* From God's perspective, a covenant between a man and a woman that binds them together for life. God performed the very first marriage in Eden, and Jesus sanctioned marriage by being present at a wedding in Cana of Galilee. In Jewish law and culture, there were two stages in marriage: 1) betrothal (q.v.) and 2) the ceremony of the husband taking the bride to his home.
a *m* alliance with ... 1 Kin 3:1
nor are given in *m* ... Matt 22:30
M is to be held in honor ... Heb 13:4
m supper of the Lamb ... Rev 19:9

MARRY *join in wedlock*
m-ied foreign wives ... Ezra 10:10
m-ies a divorced ... Matt 5:32
better not to *m* ... Matt 19:10
neither *m* nor are ... Mark 12:25
m-ied woman is bound ... Rom 7:2
better to *m* than to ... 1 Cor 7:9

MARTHA (Aram, *Lady*). She and her sister Mary were residents of Bethany. Jesus was entertained by Martha at her house after the resurrection of her brother Lazarus.
sister of Lazarus and Mary ... John 11:1,5

MARVEL *be amazed, wonder*
Jesus heard...*m-ed* ... Matt 8:10
the crowd *m-ed* ... Matt 15:31
m-ed at the sight ... Acts 7:31

MARVELOUS *extraordinary*
and see this *m* sight ... Ex 3:3
It is *m* in our eyes ... Ps 118:23
into His *m* light ... 1 Pet 2:9
m are Your works ... Rev 15:3

MARY The mother of Jesus whom she conceived by the Holy Spirit while she was still a virgin. Also the name of several other women.
1 *mother of Jesus* ... Matt 1:16
3 *mother of James and Joseph* ... Matt 27:56; Mark 16:1
4 *sister of Martha and Lazarus* ... John 11:1
5 *mother of Mark* ... Acts 12:12
6 *wife of Clopas* ... John 19:25
7 *Roman believer* ... Rom 16:6

MARY MAGDALENE A woman from whom Jesus exorcised seven demons. She later ministered to Him, witnessed the crucifixion, and saw Him soon after the resurrection.
from village of Magdala ... Mark 15:40,47; John 20:1,18
sees Jesus crucified, and after His resurrection ... Matt 27:56; 28:1-8; Mark 15:40

MASSAH *(test, trial).* The place where the people of Israel put God to the test by complaining that there was no water (Ps 95:8). Also called Meribah (q.v.).

MASTER *lord, ruler* In the Bible, includes: 1) one who has servants or slaves. 2) A form of address referring to a king. 3) The head of a household. 4) A highly skilled workman. 5) A title used to address Jesus, usually by his disciples. It recognizes His authority and leadership.
God of...*m* Abraham ... Gen 24:12
m shall pierce his ear ... Ex 21:6
can serve two *m-s* ... Matt 6:24
death no longer is *m* ... Rom 6:9
sin shall not be *m* ... Rom 6:14
obedient to...your *m-s* ... Eph 6:5
a *M* in heaven ... Col 4:1

MATTANIAH *(gift of Yahweh).* This was Zedekiah's original name (2 Kin 24:17). Also the name of several other individuals.

MATTHEW *(gift of Yahweh).* A tax collector who became one of the twelve apostles and the writer of the Gospel that bears his name. He was also called Levi.
tax-gatherer ... Matt 9:9; 10:3
apostle ... Matt 10:3; Luke 6:15; Acts 1:13

MATTHIAS *(gift of Yahweh).* The man chosen as the disciple to replace Judas Iscariot after the latter's suicide. The decision was made by the remaining eleven disciples after they had prayed and cast lots (*see* **LOT**).
replaced Judas ... Acts 1:23,26

MATURE *full grown* or *stable*
then the *m* grain ... Mark 4:28
those who are *m* ... 1 Cor 2:6
your thinking be *m* ... 1 Cor 14:20
food is for the *m* ... Heb 5:14

MATURITY *ripeness, adulthood*
bring no fruit to *m* ... Luke 8:14
let us press on to *m* ... Heb 6:1

MEAL *prepared food*
a *m* for enjoyment ... Eccl 10:19
not even eat a *m* ... Mark 3:20
washed before...*m* ... Luke 11:38
m-s together with ... Acts 2:46
for a *single m* ... Heb 12:16

MEAL OFFERING *see* **OFFERINGS**

MEANINGLESS *senseless*
with *m* arguments ... Is 29:21
not use *m* repetition ... Matt 6:7

MEASURE (n) *amount*
a full and just *m* ... Deut 25:15
good *m*-pressed ... Luke 6:38
to each a *m* of faith ... Rom 12:3
m of Christ's gift ... Eph 4:7

MEASURE (v) *determine extent*
he stopped *m-ing it* ... Gen 41:49
m their former work ... Is 65:7
He *m-d* the gate ... Ezek 40:13
will be *m-d* to you ... Mark 4:24
rod to *m* the city ... Rev 21:15

MEASURING *standard*
justice the *m* line ... Is 28:17
was given me a *m* rod ... Rev 11:1

MEAT *flesh, food*
Who will give us *m* ... Num 11:4
LORD...you *m* ... Num 11:18
you may eat *m* ... Deut 12:20
rained *m* upon them ... Ps 78:27
from *m* sacrificed ... Acts 21:25
good not to eat *m* ... Rom 14:21
I will never eat *m* ... 1 Cor 8:13
m sacrificed...idols ... 1 Cor 10:28

MEDEBA
Moabite town E of Dead Sea ... Josh 13:9; 1 Chr 19:7

MEDIA
country of the Medes ... Ezra 6:2; Esth 1:18; Is 21:2

MEDIA, MEDES An Asian country near Assyria, Armenia, and Persia, whose natives are called Medes. Cyrus the Great of Persia gained the throne of Media in 549 B.C., but Media retained its separate identity because Cyrus respected its government and culture. For that reason, the Medes and Persians together formed the Medo-Persian Empire, represented by the ram in Daniel's vision.
ancient Indo-Europeans of NW Iran ... Dan 5:31;11:1

MEDIATOR *intermediary* One who helps others to resolve differences and work out agreements. In the Bible Jesus Christ is described as the Mediator between God and mankind, and the Mediator of a new and better covenant.
by the agency of a *m* ... Gal 3:19
one *m*...between God ... 1 Tim 2:5
Jesus...*m* of a new ... Heb 12:24

MEDITATE *ponder*
Isaac went out to *m* ... Gen 24:63
His law he *m-s* day ... Ps 1:2
M in your heart ... Ps 4:4
I *m* on You in the ... Ps 63:6

MEDITATION *deep reflection*
m...Be acceptable ... Ps 19:14
m be pleasing to Him ... Ps 104:34
my *m* all the day ... Ps 119:97

MEDIUM *summons spirits*
not turn to *m-s* or ... Lev 19:31
m...be put to death ... Lev 20:27
a *m,* or a spiritist ... Deut 18:11
woman who is a *m* ... 1 Sam 28:7
will resort to...*m-s* ... Is 19:3

MEEKNESS *gentleness*
cause of truth and *m* ... Ps 45:4
m and...of Christ ... 2 Cor 10:1

MEET *encounter*
Esau ran to *m* him ... Gen 33:4
people out...to *m* God ... Ex 19:17
God...will *m* me ... Ps 59:10
Prepare to *m*...God ... Amos 4:12
to *m* the bridegroom ... Matt 25:1
m-s his accusers ... Acts 25:16
m...in the air ... 1 Thess 4:17

MEETING *assembly*
house of *m* for all ... Job 30:23
midst of Your *m* place ... Ps 74:4

MEETING, TENT OF *see* **TABERNACLE**

MEGIDDO An important city in Canaan which was conquered by Joshua and later fortified by Solomon. It is probably the city indicated in the name Har-Magedon (q.v.). It was the scene of two important battles between Israel and her enemies, and it will probably be the place of the final great

battle between God and the nations.
strategic city between Manasseh and Issachar ... Josh 12:21; 2 Kin 9:27
plain in Jezreel Valley ... 2 Chr 35:22; Zech 12:11
see also **HAR-MAGEDON**

MELCHIZEDEK *(king of righteousness).* A priest and king of Salem to whom Abraham gave a tithe of the spoils he had taken in battles, and precursor and symbol (type) of the superior priesthood of Jesus Christ.
1 *king of Salem* ... Gen 14:18,19
priest ... Ps 110:4
2 *type of undying priesthood* ... Heb 5:6,10; 6:20; 7:1ff

MELODY *tune*
lyre...the sound of *m* ... Ps 98:5
singing...making *m* ... Eph 5:19

MELT *dissolve*
people *m* with fear ... Josh 14:8
His voice...earth *m-ed* ... Ps 46:6
mountains *m-ed* like ... Ps 97:5
As silver is *m-ed* ... Ezek 22:22

MEMBER *part of the whole*
m-s of...household ... Matt 10:25
m-s one of another ... Rom 12:5
if one *m* suffers ... 1 Cor 12:26
m-s of His body ... Eph 5:30

MEMORIAL *commemoration*
this is My *m-name* ... Ex 3:15
in a book as a *m* ... Ex 17:14
stones...become a *m* ... Josh 4:7
ascended as a *m* ... Acts 10:4

MEMORY *remembrance*
M of him perishes ... Job 18:17
cut off their *m* ... Ps 109:15
m of the righteous ... Prov 10:7
spoken of in *m* of ... Mark 14:9

MEMPHIS
city in Egypt ... Is 19:13; Jer 46:19; Ezek 30:13

MENAHEM *(comforter).* A king of Israel. He paid tribute to the king of Assyria by taxing the wealthy, and continued in the sins of his predecessors.
king of Israel ... 2 Kin 15:14,17

MENĒ, MENĒ, TEKĒL, UPHARSIN A mysterious sentence in Aramaic which translates as "Numbered, numbered, weighed, and divided" (Dan 5:25). After Belshazzar's wise men and conjurers were unable to explain the meaning of the words, Daniel told the Babylonian king that God had determined to put an end to his kingdom.

MENSTRUAL
m impurity for seven ... Lev 15:19
a woman during...*m* ... Ezek 18:6

MENSTRUATION
in the days of her *m* ... Lev 12:2
like her bed at *m* ... Lev 15:26

MEPHIBOSHETH *(utterance of shame).* Son of Jonathan and grandson of Saul. Mephibosheth had crippled feet and King David showed him favor by restoring his inheritance. Also a son of Saul.
1 *son of Jonathan* ... 2 Sam 4:4
see also **MERIB-BAAL** ... 1 Chr 8:34
2 *son of Saul* ... 2 Sam 21:8

MERAB
Saul's daughter ... 1 Sam 18:17,19

MERARI (unc, *bitterness).* A son of Levi; a priest and the founder of the third order of priests (the other two were Gershon and Kohath). The family of Jeduthun, renowned musicians in David's days, are descendants of Merari.
son of Levi ... Gen 46:11
head of a Levitical family ... Ex 6:19; 2 Chr 34:12

MERCHANT *buyer / seller*
m-s procured *them* ... 1 Kin 10:28
m of the peoples ... Ezek 27:3
A *m,* in whose hands ... Hos 12:7
m seeking...pearls ... Matt 13:45
m-s of the earth ... Rev 18:3

MERCIFUL *compassionate*
God *m* and gracious ... Ps 86:15
The LORD is...and *m* ... Ps 145:8
The *m* man...good ... Prov 11:17
Blessed are the *m* ... Matt 5:7
as your Father is *m* ... Luke 6:36
m to me, the sinner ... Luke 18:13

MERCY *compassion* In the Bible, often the kindness of God in withholding deserved judgment and extending undeserved compassion and forgiveness to man. God can do this without compromising His justice, because of the death and resurrection of Christ (*cf.* **JUSTICE**). Mercy is also a Christian virtue encouraged of believers.
Great are Your *m-ies* ... Ps 119:156
in His *m* He redeemed ... Is 63:9
m to *the* poor ... Dan 4:27
the orphan finds *m* ... Hos 14:3
they shall receive *m* ... Matt 5:7
tender *m* of our God ... Luke 1:78
m on whom I have *m* ... Rom 9:15
by the *m-ies* of God ... Rom 12:1
God, being rich in *m* ... Eph 2:4

MERCY SEAT *covering over the ark* The covering or lid of the ark of the covenant signifying the place of atonement, where once a year on the Day of Atonement the high priest sprinkled the blood of the sacrifice for Israel's sins.
a *m* of pure gold ... Ex 25:17
put the *m* on the ark ... Ex 26:34
in front of the *m* ... Ex 30:6
sprinkle it on the *m* ... Lev 16:15
overshadowing the *m* ... Heb 9:5

MERIBAH *(strife).* A name given to a spring in the Wilderness of Sin. Here Moses disobeyed God by striking the rock twice instead of talking to it as God instructed, in order to get water for the thirsty Israelites. It was for this reason that God did not allow Moses to enter the Promised Land. Also the name of another spring.
spring of Rephidim ... Ex 17:7
spring of Kadesh-Barnea ... Num 27:14

MERODACH-BALADAN
king of Babylon ... Is 39:1
see also **BERODACH-BALADAN**

MERRY *joyful, lively*
wine makes life *m* ... Eccl 10:19
eat, drink *and* be *m* ... Luke 12:19

MESHA
1 *territorial boundary in Arabia* ... Gen 10:30
2 *Moabite king* ... 2 Kin 3:4
3 *man of Judah* ... 1 Chr 2:42
4 *a Benjamite* ... 1 Chr 8:9

MESHACH The name given to Mishael by the Babylonians who took him captive. He was thrown into a fiery furnace for not worshiping their idol, but was miraculously kept safe by God.
one of three Jews thrown into furnace ... Dan 3:19ff
see also **MISHAEL** ... Dan 1:7

MESHECH
1 *son of Japheth* ... Gen 10:2
2 *descendants and nation* ... Is 66:19; Ezek 27:13

MESOPOTAMIA *(between the rivers).* Region to the east of Canaan from which Abraham had migrated and to which he sent his servant to get a wife for his son Isaac. Its boundaries were the Euphrates and Tigris rivers.
land of Tigris and Euphrates Rivers ... Deut 23:4; Judg 3:8; 1 Chr 19:6; Acts 7:2

MESSAGE *communication*
m from God for you ... Judg 3:20
m...with authority ... Luke 4:32
m and my preaching ... 1 Cor 2:4
the *m* of truth ... Eph 1:13
m we have heard ... 1 John 1:5

MESSENGER *one sent*
My *m* whom I send ... Is 42:19
m of the LORD of hosts ... Mal 2:7
I send My *m* ahead ... Matt 11:10
m-s of the churches ... 2 Cor 8:23
m of Satan ... 2 Cor 12:7

MESSIAH *(Anointed One).* This important title, for which *Christ* is the Gr equivalent, refers to the fact that Jesus was specially anointed *(see* **ANOINT***)* by the Father to be the ultimate prophet, priest, and king. As such, Jesus Christ is the Great High Priest who offers His own blood as the infinite sacrifice for all the sins of the world, and He is the King of kings and Lord of lords who will return to earth at the Second Coming (q.v.) to establish His great kingdom on earth. The rabbis of NT times thought of the Messiah as a conquering king, and in the Talmud the title "King Messiah" occurs frequently.
see also **JESUS CHRIST**
anointed one ... Dan 9:25,26; John 1:41; 4:25

METAL
like glowing *m* ... Ezek 1:4
their *m* images ... Dan 11:8

METHUSELAH Son of Enoch, he became the father of Lamech and the grandfather of Noah. He died at 969 years of age, the oldest person recorded in the Bible.
son of Enoch ... Gen 5:21
grandfather of Noah ... Gen 5:25ff

MICAH (unc, *who is like Yahweh).* The name of several individuals, including the author of the minor (i.e. short) prophetic book of the same name. He ministered to Judah during the reigns of Jotham, Ahaz, and Hezekiah.
1 *an Ephraimite* ... Judg 17:1
2 *line of Reuben* ... 1 Chr 5:5
3 *father of Abdon* ... 2 Chr 34:20
4 *prophet* ... Jer 26:18; Mic 1:1
name of several other people

MICAIAH (unc, *who is like Yahweh).* The name of several persons in the OT. One of them was the son of Imlah who predicted disaster for Ahab at Ramoth-Gilead.
1 *prophet* ... 1 Kin 22:8-26
2 *father of Achbor* ... 2 Kin 22:12
3 *wife of Rehoboam* ... 2 Chr 13:2
4 *under Jehoshaphat* ... 2 Chr 17:7
5 *line of Asaph* ... Neh 12:35
6 *under Nehemiah* ... Neh 12:41
7 *son of Gemariah* ... Jer 36:11

MICHAEL (unc, *who is like God).* An archangel, chief among the angels. Also the name of several men.
1 *an archangel* ... Dan 10:21;12:1; Jude 9; Rev 12:7
2 *Jehoshaphat's son* ... 2 Chr 21:2
prince of Judah
3 *army captain* ... 1 Chr 12:20
4 *line of Gershom* ... 1 Chr 6:40
name of seven other people

MICHAL Daughter of Saul, who married David. When her father became fearful of David due to David's exploits, and attempted to have him killed, Michal helped him to escape. Later, she mocked David for dancing before the Lord when the ark was moved to Jerusalem.
daughter of Saul ... 1 Sam 18:20
David's wife ... 1 Sam 19:11

MICHMASH A place where the Philistines camped to fight against Saul, but were thwarted by an action of Jonathan (1 Sam 14:1-15).

MIDDLE *midst*
the *m* of the garden ... Gen 3:3
sun stopped in the *m* ... Josh 10:13
m of the lampstands ... Rev 1:13

MIDDLE GATE *see* **GATES OF JERUSALEM**

MIDHEAVEN *directly overhead*
eagle flying in *m* ... Rev 8:13
angel flying in *m* ... Rev 14:6
birds which fly in *m* ... Rev 19:17

MIDIAN A son of Abraham by Keturah, and father of the Midianites who carried Joseph to Egypt as a slave. Also the region to which Moses fled from the Egyptians.
1 *a son of Abraham* ... Gen 25:1,2
2 *land SE of Canaan in desert* ... Ex 2:15; Num 31:8; Judg 8:28

MIDIANITES
people of Midian ... Gen 37:36; Num 31:2; Judg 7:7

MIDST *middle, within*
God is in the *m* ... Ps 46:5
in the *m* of the fire ... Dan 3:25
Holy One in your *m* ... Hos 11:9
I am...in their *m* ... Matt 18:20

MIDWIFE *aids childbirth*
m...tied a scarlet ... Gen 38:28
before the *m* can get ... Ex 1:19

MIGDOL *(fortress).* An encampment near the Red Sea where the Israelites stayed on their journey from Egypt. Also an Egyptian town.
1 *Israelite camp near Red Sea* ... Ex 14:2; Num 33:7
2 *town in Egypt* ... Jer 44:1

MIGHT *strength*
my firstborn; My *m* ... Gen 49:3
and with all your *m* ... Deut 6:5
With Him are...*m* ... Job 12:13
Not by *m* nor by ... Zech 4:6
strength of His *m* ... Eph 1:19

MIGHTY *powerful*
a *m* hunter before ... Gen 10:9
m...awesome God ... Deut 10:17
The LORD *m* in battle ... Ps 24:8
a *m* king will rule ... Is 19:4
m in the Scriptures ... Acts 18:24
the *m* hand of God ... 1 Pet 5:6

MIGHTY MEN A name given to great warriors in Biblical times, especially the 30 strong men of David who were led by three captains (2 Sam 23:13).
m of valor ... 1 Chr 12:8

MILCAH *(queen).* 1) The wife of Nahor, Abraham's brother and grandmother of Rebekah. 2) One of the daughters of Zelophehad. He had no male heirs, therefore Milcah and her sisters asked for a special but fair arrangement for their inheritance.
1 *wife of Nahor* ... Gen 11:29
2 *daughter of Zelophehad* ... Num 26:33;27:1; Josh 17:3

MILCOM
god of Ammonites ... 1 Kin 11:5,33; 2 Kin 23:13; Zeph 1:5
see also **MOLECH**

MILE *distance, measurement*
one *m,* go with him ... Matt 5:41
m-s from Jerusalem ... Luke 24:13

MILETUS
town in Asia Minor ... Acts 20:15,17; 2 Tim 4:20

MILK
land flowing with *m* ... Ex 3:8
pour me out like *m* ... Job 10:10
m produces butter ... Prov 30:33
m to drink, not ... 1 Cor 3:2
pure *m* of the word ... 1 Pet 2:2

MILL *grinding stones*
sound of the...*m* ... Eccl 12:4
at the grinding *m* ... Lam 5:13
women...at the *m* ... Matt 24:41

MILLENNIUM The thousand-year period which John describes briefly in Rev 20:2ff. During this period Christ will establish and rule over a kingdom on earth. Some theologians believe that the kingdom is represented instead by the present church and that the thousand years symbolizes a substantial but indeterminate length of time.

MILLET A small type of grain from which Ezekiel was ordered to bake bread for himself for 390 days (Ezek 4:9).

MILLO *(mound).* Fort near Shechem and a fortress built by David and Solomon in a district of Jerusalem.
1 *fort near Shechem*
Beth-millo ... Judg 9:6,20
2 *fortress in Jerusalem* ... 2 Sam 5:9; 1 Kin 9:15,24; 1 Chr 11:8; 2 Chr 32:5

MILLSTONE *grinding stone*
upper *m* in pledge ... Deut 24:6
woman threw...*m* ... Judg 9:53
m hung around ... Matt 18:6
stone like a great *m* ... Rev 18:21

MINA
measure of gold or silver coin ... 1 Kin 10:17; Ezra 2:69; Neh 7:71; Luke 19:13ff

MIND *memory, thought*
God tries the...*m-s* ... Ps 7:9
Recall it to *m* ... Is 46:8
I test the *m* ... Jer 17:10
Let his *m* be changed ... Dan 4:16
He opened...*m-s* ... Luke 24:45
with one *m* in the ... Acts 2:46
to a depraved *m* ... Rom 1:28
m set on the flesh ... Rom 8:7
the *m* of Christ ... 1 Cor 2:16
m-s were hardened ... 2 Cor 3:14
with humility of *m* ... Phil 2:3

MINDFUL *aware*
Lord be *m* of me ... Ps 40:17
He is *m* that we are ... Ps 103:14
LORD has been *m* ... Ps 115:12
m of the...faith ... 2 Tim 1:5

MINISTER (n) *one who serves*
m-s before the ark ... 1 Chr 16:4
spoken of as *m-s* ... Is 61:6
a *m* and a witness ... Acts 26:16
a *m* of Christ Jesus ... Rom 15:16
is Christ then a *m* ... Gal 2:17
I was made a *m* ... Eph 3:7
faithful *m* in the ... Eph 6:21
His *m-s* a flame of ... Heb 1:7
a *m* in the sanctuary ... Heb 8:2

MINISTER (v) *give help, serve*
to *m* as priest to Me ... Ex 28:1
the boy *m-ed* to ... 1 Sam 2:11
not stand to *m* ... 1 Kin 8:11
to the LORD, To *m* ... Is 56:6
angels were *m-ing* ... Mark 1:13
follow Him and *m* ... Mark 15:41

MINISTRY *service*
He began His *m* ... Luke 3:23
to the *m* of the word ... Acts 6:4
m of the Spirit ... 2 Cor 3:8
m of reconciliation ... 2 Cor 5:18
fulfill your *m* ... 2 Tim 4:5
a more excellent *m* ... Heb 8:6

MIRACLE *supernatural event* Supernatural intervention by God into the normal and natural course of life. Miracles often served as authentication for prophets, apostles and others, including Jesus as the Messiah and Son of God.
Work a *m* ... Ex 7:9

I will perform *m-s* ... Ex 34:10
m-s had occurred ... Matt 11:21
He could do no *m* ... Mark 6:5
perform a *m* in My ... Mark 9:39
this *m* of healing ... Acts 4:22
works *m-s* among you ... Gal 3:5
wonders and...*m-s* ... Heb 2:4

MIRE *mud*
cast me into the *m* ... Job 30:19
Deliver me from the *m* ... Ps 69:14
wallowing in the *m* ... 2 Pet 2:22

MIRIAM The sister of Moses, noted for a song on the deliverance from Egypt which she taught to Israel. Also name of another woman.
1 *sister of Moses and Aaron* ... Ex 15:20; Num 12:4, 12:9,10; 20:1
2 *line of Ezrah* ... 1 Chr 4:17

MIRROR *image reflector*
see in a *m* dimly ... 1 Cor 13:12
natural face in a *m* ... James 1:23

MISCARRIAGE *aborted fetus*
so that she has a *m* ... Ex 21:22
m-s of a woman ... Ps 58:8

MISERABLE *bad, unhappy*
loathe this *m* food ... Num 21:5
m and chronic ... Deut 28:59
Be *m* and mourn ... James 4:9
m and poor and blind ... Rev 3:17

MISERY *sorrow, suffering*
conscious of my *m* ... Job 10:15
Destruction and *m* ... Rom 3:16

MISFORTUNE *adversity*
M will not come ... Jer 5:12
m which He has ... Jer 26:13
The day of his *m* ... Obad 12

MISHAEL (unc, *who is what God is).* Name of several individuals, including one of Daniel's three companions who were deported with him. The Babylonians promoted him and named him Meshach.
1 *of family of Kohath* ... Ex 6:22; Lev 10:4
2 *associate of Ezra* ... Neh 8:4
3 *Daniel's friend* ... Dan 1:6,7,11,19; 2:17
see also **MESHACH**

MISHNAH *(repetition).* The collection of Jewish oral tradition extending back to OT times, compiled and edited from about 30 B.C. to 200 A.D., and included in the Talmud.

MISLEAD *lead astray*
m-s a blind *person* ... Deut 27:18
m-led My people ... Ezek 13:10
that no one *m-s* you ... Mark 13:5
m-ing our nation ... Luke 23:2

MISTREAT *treat badly, wrong*
not *m*...the stranger ... Jer 22:3
slaves...*m-ed* them ... Matt 22:6
pray for...who *m* ... Luke 6:28
mocked and *m-ed* ... Luke 18:32
m and to stone them ... Acts 14:5

MISTRESS *woman in charge*
her *m* was despised ... Gen 16:4
m of the house ... 1 Kin 17:17
the maid like her *m* ... Is 24:2
the *m* of sorceries ... Nah 3:4

MIZPAH / MIZPEH *(watchtower).* The place where Jacob made peace with Laban after fleeing from him. Both agreed not to pass beyond this point to hurt the other. Also a common name for several places in the OT.
1 *heap of stones* ... Gen 31:49
2 *near Mt. Hermon* ... Josh 11:3
3 *village in Judah* ... Josh 15:38
4 *Benjamite town* ... Josh 18:26
5 *town in Gilead* ... Judg 10:17
6 *Moabite town* ... 1 Sam 22:3

MIZRAIM
1 *son of Ham* ... Gen 10:6
father of nations ... Gen 10:13
2 *Heb. for Egypt* ... 1 Chr 1:8,11

MOAB (unc, *from my father).* The son of Lot born through incest with his older daughter. Father of the Moabites who inhabited the region between the brook of Zered and the river Arnon.
1 *son of Lot* ... Gen 19:37
2 *country E of the Dead Sea* ... Ex 15:15; Josh 24:9; Ruth 1:2; 2 Kin 3:7; Ps 60:8; Jer 48:1

MOCK *ridicule, scorn*
lads...*m-ed* him ... 2 Kin 2:23
Fools *m* at sin ... Prov 14:9
who *m-s* the poor ... Prov 17:5
soldiers also *m-ed* ... Luke 23:36
God is not *m-ed* ... Gal 6:7

MOCKERY *object of ridicule*
a *m* of the Egyptians ... Ex 10:2
made a *m* of me ... Num 22:29
a *m* of justice ... Prov 19:28
m and insinuations ... Hab 2:6

MOLECH The god of the Ammonites who was worshiped with sacrifices of children by fire.
god of the Ammonites ... Lev 18:21; 1 Kin 11:7; Jer 32:35
see also **MILCOM**

MOLTEN *cast metal*
made it into a *m* calf ... Ex 32:4
make...no *m* gods ... Ex 34:17
destroy...*m* images ... Num 33:52
capitals of *m* bronze ... 1 Kin 7:16
his *m* images are ... Jer 10:14

MOLTEN CALF *see* **CALF, MOLTEN**

MONEY *currency*
take double *the m* ... Gen 43:12
not sell her for *m* ... Deut 21:14
time to receive *m* ... 2 Kin 5:26
loves *m* will not be ... Eccl 5:10
no *m* in their belt ... Mark 6:8
m in the bank ... Luke 19:23
love of *m* is a root ... 1 Tim 6:10

MONEYCHANGERS
the tables of the *m* ... Matt 21:12
coins of the *m* ... John 2:15

MONSTER *enormous animal*
created...sea *m-s* ... Gen 1:21
sea, or the sea *m* ... Job 7:12
sea *m-s* in the waters ... Ps 74:13
belly of the sea *m* ... Matt 12:40

MONTH *see* **CALENDAR**

MOON
m and...were bowing ... Gen 37:9
the *m* stopped ... Josh 10:13
m and stars to rule ... Ps 136:9
beautiful as...*m* ... Song 6:10
the *m* into blood ... Joel 2:31
m will not...light ... Matt 24:29
signs in...and *m* ... Luke 21:25

MOON, NEW *see* **NEW MOON**

MORALS *principles*
Bad...good *m* ... 1 Cor 15:33

MORDECAI Name of two individuals, one of whom was the Jew who refused to bow down before Haman, who planned to exterminate the Jews in Persia. In the end, Mordecai was honored and Haman executed.
1 *returned from exile with Zerubbabel* ... Ezra 2:2
2 *Esther's cousin* ... Esth 2:7; 3:2; 9:20;10:3

MORIAH The mountain where Isaac was offered in sacrifice by Abraham (God intervened and Isaac was not actually sacrificed), and the site of Solomon's temple.
land / mountain where Abraham offered Isaac ... Gen 22:2
threshing floor of Araunah (Ornan) ... 2 Sam 24:18
site of Temple ... 2 Chr 3:1

MORNING *dawn*
was *m,* a fifth day ... Gen 1:23
Rise early in the *m* ... Ex 8:20
the *m* stars sang ... Job 38:7
m or evening sowing ... Eccl 11:6
the bright *m* star ... Rev 22:16

MORSEL *piece of bread*
have eaten my *m* ... Job 31:17
Better is a dry *m* ... Prov 17:1
After the *m,* Satan ... John 13:27

MORTAL, MORTALITY *what eventually dies* The condition of mankind due to the Fall (q.v.), i.e. the fact that the body will succumb to death.
not trust...In *m* man ... Ps 146:3
life to your *m* bodies ... Rom 8:11
m...immortality ... 1 Cor 15:53
in our *m* flesh ... 2 Cor 4:11

MOSES (unc, *child, son).* The great Hebrew prophet and lawgiver who led the nation of Israel out of slavery in Egypt. God had conversations with Moses like those between friends.
birth ... Ex 2:1-3
in Pharaoh's care ... Ex 2:5-10
killed an Egyptian ... Ex 2:11,12
exiled ... Ex 2:15
called by God ... Ex 3:1-22
opposed Pharaoh ... Ex 5:11
crossed Red Sea ... Ex 14
Ten Commandments ... Ex 20:1-18
saw Canaan ... Deut 3:23ff; 34:1ff
death ... Deut 31:14; 34:5

MOTH *insect*
crushed before the *m* ... Job 4:19
The *m* will eat them ... Is 50:9
like a *m* to Ephraim ... Hos 5:12
m and rust destroy ... Matt 6:19

MOTHER
leave...and his *m* ... Gen 2:24
m of all *the* living ... Gen 3:20
Honor...and your *m* ... Ex 20:12
a grief to his *m* ... Prov 10:1
Contend with your *m* ... Hos 2:2
When His *m* Mary ... Matt 1:18
Take...and His *m* ... Matt 2:13
Who is My *m* ... Matt 12:48
Honor your...*m* ... Matt 19:19
Behold, your *m* ... John 19:27

MOTHER-IN-LAW
who lies with his *m* ... Deut 27:23
Orpah kissed her *m* ... Ruth 1:14
m lying sick in bed ... Matt 8:14

MOTIVES *attitudes, intentions*
LORD weighs the *m* ... Prov 16:2
disclose the *m* of ... 1 Cor 4:5
than from pure *m* ... Phil 1:17
judges with evil *m* ... James 2:4
ask with wrong *m* ... James 4:3

MOUNT (n) *hill, mountain*
In the *m* of the LORD ... Gen 22:14
Moses on *M* Sinai ... Num 3:1
Israel at *M* Carmel ... 1 Kin 18:19
M Zion which He ... Ps 78:68
M of Olives...split ... Zech 14:4

MOUNT (v) *climb up*
to *m* his chariot ... 2 Chr 10:18
m up *with* wings ... Is 40:31
My fury will *m* up ... Ezek 38:18
m-ed on a donkey ... Zech 9:9
m-ed on a donkey ... Matt 21:5

MOUNT OF OLIVES *see* **OLIVES, MOUNT OF**

MOUNT ZION *see* **ZION**

MOUNTAIN Some important mountains (or mounts) mentioned in the Bible are Ararat, Carmel, Hermon, Horeb or Sinai, Moriah or Zion, Nebo, and Olives. Occasionally used as a symbol of strength and stability.
sacrifice on the *m* ... Gen 31:54
from His holy *m* ... Ps 3:4
lift up...to the *m-s* ... Ps 121:1
lovely on the *m-s* ... Is 52:7
eat at the *m* shrines ... Ezek 18:6
m-s will melt ... Mic 1:4
the *m* will move ... Zech 14:4
m-s, Fall on us ... Luke 23:30
withdrew...to the *m* ... John 6:15
faith...remove *m-s* ... 1 Cor 13:2

MOURN *grieve, lament*
m her father and ... Deut 21:13
David m-ed...son ... 2 Sam 13:37
A time to *m* ... Eccl 3:4
earth *m-s and* withers ... Is 24:4
comfort all who *m* ... Is 61:2
Blessed...who *m* ... Matt 5:4
shall *m* and weep ... Luke 6:25
Be miserable and *m* ... James 4:9

MOUSE *rodent*
the mole, and the *m* ... Lev 11:29
five golden *mice* ... 1 Sam 6:4
mice that ravage ... 1 Sam 6:5

MOUTH
has made man's *m* ... Ex 4:11
m condemns you ... Job 15:6
From the *m* of infants ... Ps 8:2
Let the words of my *m* ... Ps 19:14
fool's *m* is his ruin ... Prov 18:7
your *m* is lovely ... Song 4:3
out of the *m* of God ... Matt 4:4
confess with your *m* ... Rom 10:9

MOVE *change position, stir*
Spirit of God...*m-ing* ... Gen 1:2
pillar of cloud *m-d* ... Ex 14:19
I will not be *m-d* ... Ps 10:6
all the hills *m-d* ... Jer 4:24
m-d with compassion ... Mark 1:41
He was deeply *m-d* ... John 11:33
in Him we live...*m* ... Acts 17:28
m-d by the...Spirit ... 2 Pet 1:21

MULE *animal*
mounted his *m* ... 2 Sam 13:29
Absalom...on *his m* ... 2 Sam 18:9
ride on the king's *m* ... 1 Kin 1:44
war horses and *m-s* ... Ezek 27:14

MULTIPLY *increase*
Be fruitful and *m* ... Gen 1:22
the fool *m-ies* words ... Eccl 10:14
He *m-ies* lies and ... Hos 12:1
and peace be *m-ied* ... 2 Pet 1:2

MULTITUDE *crowd, number*
father of a *m* of ... Gen 17:4
cover a *m* of sins ... James 5:20
love covers a *m* of ... 1 Pet 4:8

MURDER *premeditated killing* The act of deliberately killing a human being without just cause. It is forbidden by the sixth commandment. Jesus extended the application of the commandment to include anger. *see* **MANSLAYER**
You shall not *m* ... Ex 20:13
Whoever commits *m* ... Matt 5:21
m-ed the prophets ... Matt 23:31
full of envy, *m* ... Rom 1:29

MURDERER *killer*
m shall be put to ... Num 35:30
m from...beginning ... John 8:44
this man is a *m* ... Acts 28:4
no *m* has eternal ... 1 John 3:15

MUSIC *harmony, melody*
instruments of *m* ... 1 Chr 15:16
m to the LORD ... 2 Chr 7:6
m upon the lyre ... Ps 92:3
heard *m* and ... Luke 15:25

MUSICIAN *skilled in music*
m, a mighty man ... 1 Sam 16:18
the *m-s* after *them* ... Ps 68:25
harpists and *m-s* ... Rev 18:22

MUSTARD *type of plant*
kingdom...like a *m* ... Matt 13:31
faith the size of a *m* seed ... Matt 17:20
It is like a *m* seed ... Luke 13:19

MUTE *silent*
who makes *him m* ... Ex 4:11
I was *m* and silent ... Ps 39:2
a *m*...man ... Matt 9:32
and the *m* to speak ... Mark 7:37
astray to the *m* idols ... 1 Cor 12:2

MUZZLE *gag*
shall not *m* the ox ... Deut 25:4
guard...as with a *m* ... Ps 39:1

MYRIADS *countless*
chariots...are *m* ... Ps 68:17
m of angels ... Heb 12:22
number...was *m* ... Rev 5:11

MYRRH *spice* Aromatic gum resin from a small shrubby tree that was used as a healing stimulant and as a burial spice.
aromatic gum...*m* ... Gen 43:11
Dripping with...*m* ... Song 5:13
frankincense and *m* ... Matt 2:11
mixture of *m* and ... John 19:39

MYRTLE *type of plant*
the *m,* and the olive ... Is 41:19
among the *m* trees ... Zech 1:11

MYSTERY *hidden truth, secret* In the Bible, a hidden or secret truth not known until revealed by God.
no *m* baffles you ... Dan 4:9
God's wisdom in a *m* ... 1 Cor 2:7
know all *m-ies* ... 1 Cor 13:2
into the *m* of Christ ... Eph 3:4
the *m* of the gospel ... Eph 6:19
the *m* of the faith ... 1 Tim 3:9

MYTHS *fables*
to pay attention to *m* ... 1 Tim 1:4
will turn aside to *m* ... 2 Tim 4:4
attention to Jewish *m* ... Titus 1:14

N

NAAMAH
1 *daughter of Lamech* ... Gen 4:22
2 *wife of Solomon* ... 1 Kin 14:21
3 *town in Judah* ... Josh 15:41

NAAMAN *(pleasantness).* Name of several individuals, including a very influential general in the Syrian army who was a leper, but was healed under the instructions of Elisha.
1 *son, grandson, and great grandson of Benjamin* ... Gen 46:21; Num 26:40; 1 Chr 8:7
2 *Ben-hadad's commander* ... 2 Kin 5:1ff

NABAL *(fool).* A wealthy sheep owner who refused to help David when he was in danger. This so irritated David that he was going to take vengeance until Nabal's wife Abigail intervened. Ten days later Nabal died by an act of God.
husband of Abigail ... 1 Sam 25:3ff
refused to help David

NABOTH (unc, *sprouts).* A man from Jezreel who, after refusing to sell his property to King Ahab, was put to death through a scheme by Ahab's wife Jezebel.
owner of a vineyard taken by Ahab ... 1 Kin 21:1-19

NADAB *(generous, noble).* Eldest son of Aaron who, with his brother Abihu, was consumed by fire for offering "strange fire" (forbidden incense) to the Lord. Also the name of three other individuals.
1 *son of Aaron* ... Ex 6:23
2 *king of Israel* ... 1 Kin 14:20
3 *son of Shammai* ... 1 Chr 2:28
4 *son of Jehiel* ... 1 Chr 8:29,30

NAHOR The grandfather of Abraham. Also a brother of Abraham, and a city.
1 *Abram's grandfather* ... Gen 11:24ff
2 *brother of Abram* ... Gen 11:27; 22:23
3 *city in N Mesopotamia* ... Gen 24:10

NAHUM *(compassionate).* A talented poet and native of Elkosh who wrote the prophetic book that bears his name. He foretold the destruction of Nineveh. Also an ancestor of Christ.
1 *prophet* ... Nah 1:1
2 *ancestor of Christ* ... Luke 3:25

NAILED (v) *attached*
you *n* to a cross ... Acts 2:23
n it to the cross ... Col 2:14

NAILS (n) *finger ends* or *pins*
and trim her *n* ... Deut 21:12
fasten it with *n* ... Jer 10:4
imprint of the *n* ... John 20:25

NAIOTH (unc, *habitations).* One of the places where Samuel the prophet lived. Also a place where King David hid when fleeing from Saul (1 Sam 19:22).

NAIVE *simple, not suspicious*
prudence to the *n* ... Prov 1:4
n believes everything ... Prov 14:15
the *n* becomes wise ... Prov 21:11
goes astray or is *n* ... Ezek 45:20

NAKED *unclothed*
n and...not ashamed ... Gen 2:25
n I shall return there ... Job 1:21
n...you clothed Me ... Matt 25:36

NAKEDNESS *unclothed*
the *n* of his father ... Gen 9:22
n of...father's sister ... Lev 18:12
Your *n*...be uncovered ... Is 47:3
shame of your *n* ... Rev 3:18

NAME *designation, title*
man gave *n-s* to all ... Gen 2:20
takes His *n* in vain ... Ex 20:7
blot out his *n* ... Deut 29:20
How majestic is Your *n* ... Ps 8:1
sing praises to Your *n* ... Ps 18:49
good n...desired ... Prov 22:1
LORD, that is My *n* ... Is 42:8
Hallowed be Your *n* ... Matt 6:9
n-s of the twelve ... Matt 10:2
such child in My *n* ... Matt 18:5
n-s are recorded ... Luke 10:20
will come in My *n* ... Luke 21:8
baptized in the *n* ... Acts 2:38
of faith in His *n* ... Acts 3:16
other *n* under heaven ... Acts 4:12
n-s are in the book ... Phil 4:3

NAOMI (unc, *pleasantness).* The mother-in-law of Ruth and Orpah. While sojourning in Moab the three became widows. Naomi and Ruth returned to Bethlehem.
woman of Bethlehem ... Ruth 1:1
Ruth's mother-in-law ... Ruth 1:4,6

NAPHTALI *(my wrestling).* One of the sons of Jacob by Bilhah. Also the tribe that descended from him and the name of a territory in the Promised Land.
1 *son of Jacob* ... Gen 30:8
2 *tribe / district* ... Num 13:14; 1 Chr 2:2; Rev 7:6

NARD *fragrant ointment* A very expensive and ancient perfume extracted from an east Indian plant. Jesus was anointed with nard on the head and later on His feet.
henna with *n* plants ... Song 4:13
perfume of pure *n* ... John 12:3

NARROW *limited*
stood in a *n* path ... Num 22:24
Enter through the *n* gate ... Matt 7:13
the way is *n* ... Matt 7:14

NATHAN *(gift).* The name of several persons, among whom was the prophet who informed David of God's pact with him. Later he rebuked David for his sin with Bathsheba. Also the name of several other persons.
1 *a son of David* ... 2 Sam 5:14; Luke 3:31
2 *prophet* ... 2 Sam 7:2;12:1ff
3 *son of Attai* ... 1 Chr 2:36
4 *helped Ezra* ... Ezra 8:16,17
name of several other individuals

NATHANAEL *(God has given).* A man of integrity who was introduced to Jesus by Philip; probably the same individual as the apostle Bartholomew.
disciple of Jesus ... John 1:49

NATION *government, people*
make you a great *n* ... Gen 12:2
priests and a holy *n* ... Ex 19:6
scatter...the *n-s* ... Lev 26:33
the *n-s* in an uproar ... Ps 2:1
n-s...fear the name ... Ps 102:15
N will not lift up sword ... Is 2:4
sprinkle many *n-s* ... Is 52:15
glory among the *n-s* ... Is 66:19
n...rise against *n* ... Matt 24:7
n not perish ... John 11:50
men, from every *n* ... Acts 2:5
tongue...people and *n* ... Rev 5:9

NATIVE *indigenous*
or a *n* of the land ... Ex 12:19
Or see his *n* land ... Jer 22:10
the *n-s* showed us ... Acts 28:2
n-s saw the creature ... Acts 28:4

NATURAL *normal*
died a *n* death ... Ezek 44:31
n man...not accept ... 1 Cor 2:14
is sown a *n* body ... 1 Cor 15:44

NATURE *essence*
of the same *n* as you ... Acts 14:15
n itself teach you ... 1 Cor 11:14
We *are* Jews by *n* ... Gal 2:15
of *the* divine *n* ... 2 Pet 1:4

NAVE The main interior space of a building, used in reference to the temple (1 Kin 6:5).

NAZARENE *see* **NAZARETH**
1 *of Nazareth* ... John 18:7
2 *follower of Jesus* ... Acts 24:5

NAZARETH A city in Galilee where Jesus spent his childhood and early manhood. For this reason He was called a Nazarene.
town of Galilee ... Matt 2:23
home of Joseph, Mary, and Jesus ... Luke 4:16; John 1:45

NAZIRITE *(one who is consecrated).* A Jew, male or female, who took a vow of abstinence from wine (or any product of the vine), contact with dead bodies and the cutting of his hair. The vow was regarded as an act of piety and could be taken for any period of time from at least 30 days to the rest of one's life. At the conclusion of the period, the Nazirite was required to offer several sacrifices and shave his hair that was to be burned with a peace offering. Samson, Samuel, and (probably) John the Baptist were Nazirites. Jesus has sometimes been called one erroneously, due to confusion with the term *Nazarene.*
1 *one consecrated to God* ... Num 6:2,19,20
2 *religious vow* ... Judg 13:5,7; Amos 2:11,12

NEBAT The father of Jeroboam (1 Kin 11:26).

NEBO 1) Name of two towns. 2) A peak in the Abarim mountains east of the Jordan (*see* **PISGAH**). 3) A Babylonian god. 4) Name of a person.
1 *Moabite town* ... Num 32:38
2 *mountain where Moses viewed promised land* ... Deut 32:49; 34:1
3 *Babylonian god* ... Is 46:1
4 *town W of Jordan* ... Ezra 2:29; Neh 7:33
5 *Jew whose sons married foreign wives* ... Ezra 10:43

NEBUCHADNEZZAR (unc, *Nebo, protect the boundary).* A noted Babylonian king and a clever military man who often was in battle with the Israelites. He eventually destroyed Jerusalem and in 586 B.C. took the people of Israel into captivity in Babylon (the Babylonian exile).
king of Babylon ... 2 Kin 24:1,10
captured Judah ... 1 Chr 6:15; Ezra 2:1

NEBUZARADAN *(Nabu has given offspring).* A Babylonian captain who led Nebuchadnezzar's troops. They completely destroyed the city of Jerusalem and burned the temple. 2 Kin 25:8ff; Jer 39:9,10

NECK *part of body*
you shall break its *n* ... Ex 13:13
yoke on your *n* ... Deut 28:48
stiffened their *n-s* ... Jer 17:23
risked their own *n-s* ... Rom 16:4

NECKLACE *neck ornament*
n around his neck ... Gen 41:42
earrings and *n-s* ... Num 31:50
pride is their *n* ... Ps 73:6

NECO *see* **PHARAOH**

NEED *necessity, obligation*
sufficient for his *n* ... Deut 15:8
ministered to...*n-s* ... Acts 20:34
n-s of the saints ... 2 Cor 9:12
supply all your *n-s* ... Phil 4:19

NEEDLE
the eye of a *n* ... Matt 19:24
n than for a rich ... Mark 10:25

NEEDY *destitute, poor*
to your *n* and poor ... Deut 15:11
a father to the *n* ... Job 29:16
n will not always be ... Ps 9:18
the LORD hears the *n* ... Ps 69:33
n will lie down in ... Is 14:30

NEGEV (unc, *dry).* The southern desert region of Israel (Gen 12:9; Judg 1:9; Jer 32:44; Zech 7:7).

NEGLECT *disregard, ignore*
You *n-ed* the Rock ... Deut 32:18

who *n-s* discipline ... Prov 15:32
n so great a salvation ... Heb 2:3
n to show hospitality ... Heb 13:2
do not *n* doing good ... Heb 13:16

NEHEMIAH *(Yahweh comforts).* Name of several individuals, including a very zealous and valiant Jew who was deeply grieved over the desolation of Jerusalem which resulted from the Babylonian conquest. His efforts led to the rebuilding of the walls around the city. Nehemiah was a cupbearer for the Persian King Artaxerxes.
1 *Jewish exile* ... Ezra 2:2; Neh 7:7
2 *son of Azbuk* ... Neh 3:16
3 *son of Hacaliah* ... Neh 1:1
rebuilt walls ... Neh 3:1ff
governor of Jerusalem ... Neh 8:9

NEIGHBOR *one living nearby*
not covet...*n-'s* wife ... Ex 20:17
shall love your *n* ... Lev 19:18
make your *n-s* drink ... Hab 2:15
love your *n* and ... Matt 5:43
And who is my *n* ... Luke 10:29
love your *n* as ... Gal 5:14

NEPHEW
and Lot his *n* ... Gen 12:5
Lot, Abram's *n* ... Gen 14:12

NEPHILIM
people of great stature ... Gen 6:4; Num 13:33

NER *(lamp).* The father of Abner and grandfather of Saul (1 Chr 8:33).

NEST
n is set in the cliff ... Num 24:21
n among the stars ... Obad 4
birds...*have n-s* ... Matt 8:20

NET *snare*
a *n* for my steps ... Ps 57:6
an antelope in a *n* ... Is 51:20
casting a *n* into ... Matt 4:18
left their *n-s* and ... Mark 1:18
n full of fish ... John 21:8

NETHANEL *(God has given).* One of the brothers of David (1 Chr 2:14-15). Also the name of several other persons.

NETHANIAH *(Yahweh has given).* A son of Asaph and one of the chief musicians in the temple (1 Chr 25:2). Also the name of three other individuals.

NETHINIM
temple servants ... Ezra 7:24

NEW *fresh, recent*
nothing *n* under the ... Eccl 1:9
Will gain *n* strength ... Is 40:31
a *n* spirit within ... Ezek 11:19
n wine into old ... Mark 2:22
A *n* commandment ... John 13:34
he is a *n* creature ... 2 Cor 5:17
a *n* and living way ... Heb 10:20
making all things *n* ... Rev 21:5

NEWBORN *just born*
like *n* babies, long ... 1 Pet 2:2

NEW EARTH *see* **NEW HEAVEN**

NEW HEAVEN The future universe that will be created by God to replace the present world after the Second Coming (Rev 21:1). It includes a new earth and the new Jerusalem (q.v.).

NEW JERUSALEM An amazing city to be made and revealed by God. Among other things, it has a wall with gates made of individual pearls and its dimensions are about 1500 miles in height, width, and depth. It is the future, eternal home of believers after Christ's millennial reign on earth (Rev 21:2, 10-27).

NEW MOON This marked the beginning of a Hebrew month and was a holy day in which special sacrifices were offered and business put on hold. The Talmud states that new moon sacrifices atoned for defilement related to the temple and holy food.

NEWNESS *freshness*
walk in *n* of life ... Rom 6:4
in *n* of the Spirit ... Rom 7:6

NEWS *report, tidings*
a day of good *n* ... 2 Kin 7:9
Good *n* puts fat on ... Prov 15:30
the *n* about Jesus ... Matt 14:1
n about Him spread ... Mark 1:28
n of great joy ... Luke 2:10
bring good *n* of good ... Rom 10:15
n of your faith ... 1 Thess 3:6

NICODEMUS (unc, *victorious among the people).* A leading Pharisee and expert interpreter of the Heb scriptures who came to believe in Jesus. He defended Jesus against the Pharisees and brought spices to anoint Jesus' body at His burial.
Pharisee ... John 3:1,4,9
in Sanhedrin ... John 7:50; 19:39

NICOLAITANS A sect named after Nicolaus, probably not the person named Nicolas (Eng form of Nicolaus) in Acts 6:5 but another, unknown man. Nothing is known for certain of the heresy, but the Nicolaitans probably were against rules and advocated libertine behavior.
sect in Ephesian and Pergamum church ... Rev 2:6,15

NICOLAS
deacon, servant ... Acts 6:1-6
proselyte from Antioch ... Acts 6:5

NIGHT *darkness*
darkness He called *n* ... Gen 1:5
pillar of fire by *n* ... Ex 13:21
meditate...day and *n* ... Josh 1:8
make *n* into day ... Job 17:12
The terror by *n* ... Ps 91:5
At *n* my soul longs ... Is 26:9
over their flock by *n* ... Luke 2:8
a thief in the *n* ... 1 Thess 5:2
tormented day and *n* ... Rev 20:10

NILE (unc, *river).* The most important river in Egypt whose waters were turned to blood prior to the exodus.
river of Egypt ... Gen 41:1; Ex 1:22; 7:20; Is 23:10

NIMROD A distinguished hunter and builder. Tradition says that he founded Babylon.
son of Cush ... Gen 10:8
a mighty hunter ... Gen 10:9
ruler of Shinar ... Gen 10:10

NINEVEH Capital city of the Assyrian Empire, founded by Nimrod. It was a great, wealthy city to which God sent a reluctant Jonah to warn the people of impending judgment for their wickedness.
capital of Assyria ... 2 Kin 19:36
visited by Jonah ... Jon 1:1ff

NISAN
first month of the Hebrew calendar ... Neh 2:1; Esth 3:7

NOAH (unc, *rest).* The patriarch who built the ark. Only Noah, his family, and birds and animals (in pairs and groups of seven) embarked on the ark and were saved from the deadly flood. Also the name of a woman.
1 *son of Lamech* ... Gen 5:28,29
father of Shem, Ham, Japheth ... Gen 5:32
built an ark ... Gen 6:14-22
saved from Flood ... Gen 6:9; 7:15; 8:1; 8:13
promised by God ... Gen 9:9-17
2 *daughter of Zelophehad* ... Num 26:33; 27:1; 36:11

NO-AMON
Egyptian city of Thebes ... Nah 3:8

NOBLE *lofty* or *renowned one*
king's most *n* princes ... Esth 6:9
speak *n* things ... Prov 8:6
all the *n-s* of Judah ... Jer 39:6

NOBLEMAN *of high rank*
the house of the *n* ... Job 21:28
A *n* went to ... Luke 19:12

NOISE *loud sound*
You who were full of *n* ... Is 22:2
Egypt *is but* a big *n* ... Jer 46:17
from heaven a *n* ... Acts 2:2

NOMADS *desert wanderers*
n of the desert bow ... Ps 72:9

NONSENSE *foolishness*
a fool speaks *n* ... Is 32:6
appeared...as *n* ... Luke 24:11

NORTH *direction of compass*
stretches out the *n* ... Job 26:7
Zion *in* the far *n* ... Ps 48:2
king of the *N* will ... Dan 11:13
three gates on the *n* ... Rev 21:13

NOSE *part of face*
the ring on her *n* ... Gen 24:47
n-s...cannot smell ... Ps 115:6
My hook in your *n* ... Is 37:29

NOSTRILS *nose*
breathed into his *n* ... Gen 2:7
breath of His *n* ... 2 Sam 22:16
breath of God...my *n* ... Job 27:3

NOTICE *attention, seen*
take *n* of me ... Ruth 2:10
not *n* the log ... Matt 7:3
deeds to be *n-d* by ... Matt 23:5

NOURISH *feed, sustain*
n-es and cherishes it ... Eph 5:29
constantly n-ed on ... 1 Tim 4:6
she would be *n-ed* ... Rev 12:6

NULLIFY *annul, make void*
LORD *n-ies* the counsel ... Ps 33:10
unbelief will not *n* ... Rom 3:3
the promise is *n-ied* ... Rom 4:14
n the grace of God ... Gal 2:21

NUMBER (n) *group, total*
their *n* according to ... Num 29:21
the *n* of the stars ... Ps 147:4
increasing in *n* daily ... Acts 16:5
his *n* is six hundred ... Rev 13:18

NUMBER (v) *count, enumerate*
n...by their armies ... Num 1:3
You *n* my steps ... Job 14:16
hairs...all *n-ed* ... Matt 10:30

NUN
father of Joshua ... Ex 33:11; Num 14:6; Josh 1:1

NURSE (n) *attendant*
Deborah, Rebekah's *n* ... Gen 35:8
and call a *n* for you ... Ex 2:7
n carries a nursing ... Num 11:12
n in the bedroom ... 2 Kin 11:2

NURSE (v) *suckle an infant*
Sarah...*n* children ... Gen 21:7
the child and *n-d* him ... Ex 2:9
morning to *n* my son ... 1 Kin 3:21
who are *n-ing* babies in ... Mark 13:17
breasts...never *n-d* ... Luke 23:29

O

OAK *type of tree*
by the *o-s* of Mamre ... Gen 13:18
the diviners' *o* ... Judg 9:37
o-s of righteousness ... Is 61:3
strong as the *o-s* ... Amos 2:9

OAR *pole used in rowing*
no boat with *o-s* will ... Is 33:21
All who handle...*o* ... Ezek 27:29
straining at the *o-s* ... Mark 6:48

OATH *declaration, vow* The act of calling upon God as a witness to what one says, or of making a vow. In Judaism, often a promise to abstain from something, thereby treating it as sacred. Violation of an oath or vow was an offense to God. People who took oaths often abused them, swearing by things over which they had no control, or making them for unacceptable reasons (*see* **CORBAN**), etc. In the NT, Jesus condemns such oaths and says that one should only make strong affirmations and refusals. But it is probably permissible to take solemn oaths in appropriate situations, e.g. marriage ceremonies and court proceedings. *see also* **NAZIRITE**
confirm the *o* which ... Deut 9:5
free from the *o* ... Josh 2:20
make no *o* at all ... Matt 5:34
priests without an *o* ... Heb 7:21

OBADIAH *(servant of Yahweh).* The name of a number of persons, includine one of the minor prophets. The prophecy that bears his name was against Edom and about Israel's restoration.
1 *in Ahab's court* ... 1 Kin 18:3ff
2 *Gadite warrior* ... 1 Chr 12:8,9
3 *sent to teach* ... 2 Chr 17:7
4 *Levite, of Merari* ... 2 Chr 34:12
5 *son of Jehiel* ... Ezra 8:9
6 *signer of covenant* ... Neh 10:1,5
7 *prophet* ... Obad 1
name of five other Old Testament people

OBED *(worshiper).* Born to Ruth and Boaz, he was the father of Jesse, and grandfather of David. Also the name of four other persons.
1 *son of Ruth / Boaz* ... Ruth 4:17
ancestor of Jesus ... Matt 1:5; Luke 3:32
2 *son of Ephlal* ... 1 Chr 2:37
3 *warrior* ... 1 Chr 11:26,47
4 *temple gatekeeper* ... 1 Chr 26:1,7
5 *father of Azariah* ... 2 Chr 23:1

OBED-EDOM *(servant of Edom).* A man from Gath (of Philistia) under whose care the ark of the covenant was left for three months until David brought it to Jerusalem. Also the name of two other individuals.
1 *a Gittite* ... 2 Sam 6:10-12
2 *temple musician* ... 1 Chr 15:21
3 *in charge of Temple vessels* ... 2 Chr 25:24

OBEDIENCE *submission*
the *o* of the peoples ... Gen 49:10
pretend *o* to me ... 2 Sam 22:45
the *o* of the One ... Rom 5:19
leading to *o* of faith ... Rom 16:26
in *o* to the truth ... 1 Pet 1:22

OBEDIENT *willing to obey*
we will be *o* ... Ex 24:7
o from the heart ... Rom 6:17
o to the...death ... Phil 2:8
Children, be *o* to ... Col 3:20

OBEY *follow commands, orders*
have *o-ed* My voice ... Gen 22:18
o My voice and keep ... Ex 19:5
o the LORD your God ... Deut 27:10
to *o* is better than ... 1 Sam 15:22
O-ing...His word ... Ps 103:20
and the sea *o* Him ... Matt 8:27
o God rather than ... Acts 5:29
o your parents ... Eph 6:1
O your leaders ... Heb 13:17
to *o* Jesus Christ ... 1 Pet 1:2

OBJECT *implement* or *goal*
struck...an iron *o* ... Num 35:16
an *o* of loathing to ... Ps 88:8
o like a great sheet ... Acts 10:11
god or *o* of worship ... 2 Thess 2:4

OBLIGATION *duty*
o toward the LORD ... Num 32:22
for his daily *o-s* ... 2 Chr 31:16
under *o,* not to the ... Rom 8:12
o to keep the...Law ... Gal 5:3

OBSERVE *keep* or *notice*
surely *o* My sabbaths ... Ex 31:13
o all My statutes ... Lev 19:37
you may *o* discretion ... Prov 5:2
the ant...*O* her ways ... Prov 6:6
O how the lilies ... Matt 6:28
o-ing the traditions ... Mark 7:3
the word...*o* it ... Luke 11:28
o days and months ... Gal 4:10

OBSTACLE *hindrance*
Remove *every o* out of ... Is 57:14
an *o* or a stumbling ... Rom 14:13

OBSTINATE *stubborn*
you are an *o* people ... Ex 33:3
made his heart *o* ... Deut 2:30
Israel is...*o* ... Ezek 3:7
disobedient and *o* ... Rom 10:21

OBTAIN *get possession of*
o children through ... Gen 16:2
finds a wife...*o-s* ... Prov 18:22
may *o* eternal life ... Matt 19:16
o the gift of God ... Acts 8:20
o-ed an inheritance ... Eph 1:11
for *o-ing* salvation ... 1 Thess 5:9

OCCUR *happen, take place*
this sign will *o* ... Ex 8:23
will *o* at the final ... Dan 8:19
otherwise a riot might *o* ... Matt 26:5
predestined to *o* ... Acts 4:28

ODED *(restorer).* The father of the prophet Azariah. Also a prophet in Samaria.
1 *father of Azariah* ... 2 Chr 15:1,8
2 *prophet* ... 2 Chr 28:9

ODIOUS *offensive*
o in Pharaoh's sight ... Ex 5:21
o to the Philistines ... 1 Sam 13:4

OFFEND *insult* or *violate*
I will not *o anymore* ... Job 34:31
A brother *o-ed is* ... Prov 18:19
Pharisees were *o-ed* ... Matt 15:12

OFFENSE *anger* or *transgression*
of my *own o-s* ... Gen 41:9
they took *o* at Him ... Matt 13:57
of the *o* of Adam ... Rom 5:14
and a rock of *o* ... 1 Pet 2:8

OFFER (v) *give, present*
o him...as a burnt ... Gen 22:2
O to God a sacrifice ... Ps 50:14
my mouth *o-s* praises ... Ps 63:5
o both gifts and ... Heb 5:1
o-ed Himself ... Heb 9:14
prayer *o-ed* in faith ... James 5:15
o...spiritual sacrifices ... 1 Pet 2:5

OFFERING (n) *contribution* The act by which a worshiper presents something to God in order to please Him or to obey His law. In the OT, offerings took many tangible forms, from animals to food. In the NT, the term is sometimes used abstractly in Paul's epistles and is used specifically of Christ's sacrifice on the cross.
freewill *o* to the LORD ... Ex 35:29
o of first fruits ... Lev 2:12
your worthless *o-s* ... Is 1:13
presenting your *o* ... Matt 5:23
any o for sin ... Heb 10:18

OFFERINGS
1 **Burnt Offering** ... Gen 22:13; Lev 1:17
2 **Drink Offering** ... Phil 2:17; 2 Tim 4:6
also **Libation**
3 **Freewill Offering** ... Ex 35:29; Lev 7:16
4 **Grain Offering** ... Lev 9:4; Josh 22:29
also **Meal Offering**
5 **Guilt Offering** ... Lev 5:6; Num 6:12
6 **Heave Offering** ... Ex 29:27,28
7 **Libation Offering** ... Num 6:15,17;28:9,10
also **Drink Offering**
8 **Meal Offering** ... 2 Kin 16:15; Ps 40:6
also **Grain Offering**
9 **Ordination Offering** ... Lev 8:28,31
10 **Peace Offering** ... Lev 4:31; Num 6:14
11 **Sin Offering** ... Ex 29:14; Ezek 46:20

12 **Thank Offering** ... 2 Chr 33:16; Jer 33:11
13 **Votive Offering** ... Deut 12:26;23:18
14 **Wave Offering** ... Lev 14:12; Num 18:18

OFFICE *function* or *position*
wield the staff of *o* ... Judg 5:14
priests in their *o-s* ... 2 Chr 35:2
to the *o* of overseer ... 1 Tim 3:1

OFFICIAL *one in authority*
o-s in the palace ... 2 Kin 20:18
o of the synagogue ... Luke 8:41

OFFSPRING *descendants*
o in place of Abel ... Gen 4:25
bring forth *o* from ... Is 65:9

OG A king of Bashan. Moses obtained a very important victory against him and his territory was incorporated by Israel.
Amorite king ... Num 21:33; Deut 3:4; Josh 12:4

OHOLAH, OHOLIBAH The name of two sisters of ill repute in an allegory in Ezekiel. Oholah represented Samaria, and Oholibah, Jerusalem. Both were rebuked by God for making alliances with heathen nations.
symbolic for Samaria and Jerusalem ... Ezek 23:4

OHOLIAB *(father's tent).* A skilled craftsman who helped Bezalel in making furniture for the tabernacle (Ex 31:6).

OHOLIBAMAH *(tent of the high place).*
1 *wife of Esau, also called Judith* ... Gen 36:2-25
2 *descendant of Esau* ... Gen 36:41

OIL A very important product derived most commonly from the olive and used in ancient times for various purposes, including food, fuel for lamps, anointing ceremonies, and medicinal ointment.
o for lighting ... Ex 25:6
anointed my head...*o* ... Ps 23:5
the *o* of joy ... Ps 45:7
words...softer than *o* ... Ps 55:21
prudent took *o* in ... Matt 25:4
not anoint...with *o* ... Luke 7:46

OINTMENT *salve*
a jar of *o* ... Job 41:31
anointed...with *o* ... John 11:2

OLD *aged, obsolete*
buried at a...*o* age ... Gen 15:15
too *o* to have a ... Ruth 1:12
honor of *o* men ... Prov 20:29
o men will dream ... Joel 2:28
wine into *o* wineskins ... Matt 9:17
be born when he is *o* ... John 3:4
o self was crucified ... Rom 6:6
o things passed away ... 2 Cor 5:17
men of *o* gained ... Heb 11:2
serpent of *o*...devil ... Rev 12:9

OLD GATE *see* **GATES OF JERUSALEM**

OLIVE *tree* or *fruit* The most common fruit tree in Israel. Both oil and timber were obtained from it.
freshly picked *o* leaf ... Gen 8:11
land of *o* oil and ... Deut 8:8
cherubim of *o* wood ... 1 Kin 6:23
children like *o* plants ... Ps 128:3

OLIVES, MOUNT OF A hill to the east of Jerusalem separated from the city by the valley of Kidron. Jesus Christ ascended to heaven from this hill.
hill E of Jerusalem ... 2 Sam 15:30; Zech 14:4; Matt 24:3; Mark 11:1
place where Jesus prayed ... Matt 26:30; Luke 22:39-41

OMEGA Long "o," the last letter of the Gr alphabet. Also one of the titles of Jesus Christ. *see* **ALPHA**
last letter of Gr alphabet ... Rev 1:8
title of Jesus Christ ... Rev 21:6
expresses eternalness of God ... Rev 22:13

OMEN *foretells a future event*
who interprets *o-s* ... Deut 18:10
took this as an *o* ... 1 Kin 20:33

OMER *dry measure* An ancient Hebrew measure equal to the portion of manna prescribed for each person's daily use, or about five pints.
take an *o* apiece ... Ex 16:16
o is a tenth of an ... Ex 16:36

OMNIPOTENCE An attribute of God whereby He exercises absolute power over everything and accomplishes whatever He desires, always consistent with His own nature. His creation of the universe is an example. However, he cannot do anything contrary to his own nature, e.g. commit sin.

OMNIPRESENCE An attribute of God, referring to the fact that He is everywhere at all times. This also allows for the fact that God is specifically present in some places and times; e.g. Jesus Christ as the Son of God is eternally present everywhere, but was specifically present on earth beginning with His incarnation, and is now specifically present in His resurrection body with the Father (see also Trinity).

OMNISCIENCE An attribute of God, whereby He knows everything past, present, and future. His knowledge includes the thoughts of every person. When Jesus, the Son of God, says that He does not know the time of the Second Coming, but only the Father does (Matt 24:36, etc.), it must be understood that this is a limitation which He temporarily places upon Himself, and not an exception to divine omniscience.

OMRI *(live long).* A commander of the Israelite army who became king by seizing the throne. He was the father of King Ahab. Also the name of three other persons.
1 *king of Israel* ... 1 Kin 16:22ff
2 *a Benjamite* ... 1 Chr 7:8
3 *line of Perez* ... 1 Chr 9:4
4 *son of Michael* ... 1 Chr 27:18

ON 1) A very ancient and important city in Egypt. It was the seat of worship of the sun god, so the city was called Heliopolis ("city of the sun") by the Greeks. Joseph's Egyptian wife was the daughter of a priest from On. 2) (Heb, *vigor)* A chief of the tribe of Reuben, one of the individuals who rebelled with Korah against Moses.
1 *Egyptian city* ... Gen 41:45,50; 46:20
see also **HELIOPOLIS**
2 *son of Peleth* ... Num 16:1

ONAN *(vigorous).* A son of Judah who died by divine judgment (Gen 38:10)because he deceitfully refused to perform the duty of levirate marriage (q.v.).

ONE *single unit*
shall become *o* flesh ... Gen 2:24
God, the LORD is *o* ... Deut 6:4
Holy *O* of Israel ... Ps 71:22
His chosen *o-s* ... Ps 105:6
Are You the...*O* ... Matt 11:3
joy...over *o* sinner ... Luke 15:7
I...Father are *o* ... John 10:30
they may all be *o* ... John 17:21
o body in Christ ... Rom 12:5
o died for all ... 2 Cor 5:14
o Lord, *o* faith ... Eph 4:5
o God...*o* mediator ... 1 Tim 2:5
husband of *o* wife ... 1 Tim 3:2

ONESIMUS *(useful).* A runaway slave of Philemon, he was converted while in Rome by the ministry of Paul who was in prison there. Onesimus delivered Paul's letter of appeal on his behalf to Philemon, as well as the letter to the Colossians.
Christian slave of Philemon ... Col 4:9; Philem 10

ONESIPHORUS *(profit-bringing).* An Ephesian Christian and faithful friend of Paul. He ministered to Paul's physical needs, despite great personal risk.
Ephesian Christian ... 2 Tim 1:16; 4:19

ONO A town in Benjamin located near Joppa. Also the name of the plain on which it is located (Neh 11:35).

ONYX *precious stone* A gemstone of considerable variety, often mentioned in the Bible.
bdellium and the *o* ... Gen 2:12
o, and the jasper ... Ezek 28:13

OPEN (adj) *not shut, exposed*
throat is an *o* grave ... Ps 5:9
Better is *o* rebuke ... Prov 27:5
before you an *o* door ... Rev 3:8

OPEN (v) *expose, free, unfasten*
eyes will be *o-ed* ... Gen 3:5
Ezra *o-ed* the book ... Neh 8:5
He *o-s* their ear ... Job 36:10
O Lord, *o* my lips ... Ps 51:15
O my eyes, that I ... Ps 119:18
To *o* blind eyes ... Is 42:7
o...windows of heaven ... Mal 3:10
knock...will be *o-ed* ... Matt 7:7
o-ed a door of faith ... Acts 14:27
and *o-s* the door ... Rev 3:20
worthy to *o* the book ... Rev 5:2

OPHEL *(mound, hill).* Part of Jerusalem on a slope immediately south of the temple site.
citadel in Jerusalem ... 2 Chr 27:3; 33:14; Neh 3:27
home of temple servants (Nethinim) ... Neh 3:26; 11:21

OPHIR A region rich in gold. Its exact site is unknown.
1 *son of Joktan* ... Gen 10:29

2 *gold producing region of SW Arabia* ... 1 Kin 10:11; Job 22:24

OPPONENT *adversary*
friends...with your *o* ... Matt 5:25
protection from my *o* ... Luke 18:3

OPPORTUNITY *occasion*
o to betray Jesus ... Matt 26:16
o for your testimony ... Luke 21:13
an *o* for the flesh ... Gal 5:13
not give...devil an *o* ... Eph 4:27

OPPOSE *contend, resist*
o the Prince of ... Dan 8:25
o-d the ordinance of ... Rom 13:2
men also *o* the truth ... 2 Tim 3:8
God is *o-d* to the ... James 4:6

OPPOSITION *hostility*
you...know My *o* ... Num 14:34
these are in *o* ... Gal 5:17
gospel...much *o* ... 1 Thess 2:2

OPPRESS (v) *trouble, tyrannize*
enslaved and *o-ed* ... Gen 15:13
Egyptians are *o-ing* ... Ex 3:9
not *o* your neighbor ... Lev 19:13
woman *o-ed* in ... 1 Sam 1:15
do not *o* the widow ... Zech 7:10
healing all...*o-ed* ... Acts 10:38
the rich who *o* you ... James 2:6

OPPRESSED (n) *afflicted*
stronghold for the *o* ... Ps 9:9
justice for the *o* ... Ps 146:7
let the *o* go free ... Is 58:6
devour...*o* in secret ... Hab 3:14
vengeance for the *o* ... Acts 7:24

OPPRESSION *affliction*
Do not trust in *o* ... Ps 62:10
o makes a...man mad ... Eccl 7:7
and water of *o* ... Is 30:20
o of My people ... Acts 7:34

OPPRESSOR *one who afflicts*
And crush the *o* ... Ps 72:4
a great *o* lacks ... Prov 28:16
punish all their *o-s* ... Jer 30:20

ORACLE *revelation* In the OT, usually an utterance or declaration of God delivered through a prophet.
The *o* of Balaam ... Num 24:3
o concerning Babylon ... Is 13:1
the *o* of the LORD ... Jer 23:33
and misleading *o-s* ... Lam 2:14
entrusted with the *o-s* ... Rom 3:2

ORDAIN *invest, set apart*
anoint...and *o* them ... Ex 28:41
o Aaron and his sons ... Ex 29:9
o-ed His covenant ... Ps 111:9
law as *o-ed* by angels ... Acts 7:53

ORDEAL *difficulty, trial*
great *o* of affliction ... 2 Cor 8:2
at the fiery *o* ... 1 Pet 4:12

ORDER (n) *arrangement*
Set your house in *o* ... 2 Kin 20:1
fixed *o* of the moon ... Jer 31:35
the *o* of Melchizedek ... Heb 5:6

ORDER (v) *command* or *request*
I will *o my prayer* ... Ps 5:3
o-ed him to tell no ... Luke 5:14
confidence...to *o* you ... Philem 8

ORDINANCE *statute* In the Bible, an authoritative ceremony, decree, or statute, usually given by God.
o of the Passover ... Ex 12:43
they rejected My *o-s* ... Lev 26:43
o-s of the heavens ... Job 38:33
opposed the *o* of God ... Rom 13:2

ORDINATION In the OT, usually a law or procedure dictated by God, sometimes establishing a feast day. Also the appointment of a person to an office of ministry.
Aaron's ram of *o* ... Ex 29:26
and the *o* offering ... Lev 7:37
period of your *o* ... Lev 8:33

ORDINATION OFFERING *see* **OFFERINGS**

OREB *(raven).* A Midianite prince defeated by Gideon and killed on the "rock of Oreb," which was named after him (Judg 7:25).

ORIGIN *beginning, source*
of Jewish *o* ... Esth 6:13
o is from antiquity ... Is 23:7
Your *o* and your ... Ezek 16:3

ORIGINATE *bring into being*
not *o* from woman ... 1 Cor 11:8
all things *o*...God ... 1 Cor 11:12

ORION A celestial constellation.
constellation of stars ... Job 9:9; 38:31; Amos 5:8

ORNAMENT *decoration* In the Bible, jewelry for the decoration of the body.
put off your *o-s* ... Ex 33:5
o of fine gold ... Prov 25:12
beauty of His *o-s* ... Ezek 7:20

ORNAN
Jebusite owner of threshing floor on Mount Moriah ... 1 Chr 21:15,18
sells threshing floor to David for altar and temple ... 1 Chr 21:25,28
see also **ARAUNAH**

ORPAH (unc, *neck).* She and Ruth were Naomi's daughters-in-law.
daughter-in-law of Naomi ... Ruth 1:4,14

ORPHAN *fatherless child*
not afflict any...*o* ... Ex 22:22
justice for the *o* ... Deut 10:18
helper of the *o* ... Ps 10:14
may plunder the *o-s* ... Is 10:2
Leave...*o-s* behind ... Jer 49:11
visit *o-s* and widows ... James 1:27

OSTRICH *bird*
the *o* and the owl ... Lev 11:16
a companion of *o-es* ... Job 30:29
cruel Like *o-es* ... Lam 4:3
mourning like the *o-es* ... Mic 1:8

OTHNIEL *(God is might).* Younger brother of Caleb and one of the judges of Israel. Under his leadership the land was at peace for forty years. Also the name of a son of Kenaz.
son of Kenaz ... Josh 15:17
brother or nephew of Caleb ... Judg 1:13;3:11

OUTBURST *sudden release*
great *o* of anger ... Deut 29:24
o of anger I hid My ... Is 54:8
jealousy, *o-s* of anger ... Gal 5:20

OUTCAST *rejected*
the *o-s* of Israel ... Ps 147:2
Hide the *o-s* ... Is 16:3
called you an *o* ... Jer 30:17
o-s from...synagogue ... John 16:2

OUTCRY *strong cry* or *protest*
no *o* in our streets ... Ps 144:14
o is heard among the ... Jer 50:46
a *single o* arose ... Acts 19:34

OUTSIDER *stranger*
o may not come near ... Num 18:4
toward *o-s* ... 1 Thess 4:12

OUTSTRETCHED *extended*
redeem...with an *o* arm ... Ex 6:6
war...with an *o* hand ... Jer 21:5

OUTWARD *external*
at the *o* appearance ... 1 Sam 16:7
is *o* in the flesh ... Rom 2:28

OVEN *baking, cooking vessel*
appeared a...*o* ... Gen 15:17
make them as a fiery *o* ... Ps 21:9

OVERCOME *conquer, master*
a man *o* with wine ... Jer 23:9
I have *o* the world ... John 16:33
but *o* evil with good ... Rom 12:21
have *o* the evil one ... 1 John 2:13
who *o-s* will inherit ... Rev 21:7

OVERCOMER One who is victorious, a conqueror who prevails in a struggle. In the NT, often refers to believers who are steadfast in their faith, as all true believers are (1 John 5:4).

OVERFLOW *flood, inundate*
My cup *o-s* ... Ps 23:5
waters will *o* the ... Is 28:17
I am *o-ing* with joy ... 2 Cor 7:4
o-ing with gratitude ... Col 2:7

OVERLAID *decorate, spread*
o...with gold ... 1 Kin 6:28
vessel *o* with silver ... Prov 26:23
o with gold...silver ... Hab 2:19

OVERLOOK *ignore* or *view*
o a transgression ... Prov 19:11
widows were...*o-ed* ... Acts 6:1

OVERPOWER *subdue*
deceive you and *o* you ... Obad 7
Hades will not *o* ... Matt 16:18
attacks him and *o-s* ... Luke 11:22

OVERSEER *director, leader* A superintendent or supervisor. In the NT, overseer refers specifically to a leader of the local church and is synonymous with a church *elder.*
o in the house of ... Jer 29:26
the *o-s* and deacons ... Phil 1:1
the office of *o* ... 1 Tim 3:1
o...above reproach ... Titus 1:7

OVERSHADOW *engulf, obscure*
Most High...*o* you ... Luke 1:35
o-ing the mercy seat ... Heb 9:5

OVERSIGHT *supervision*
o of the house of ... 2 Kin 12:11
having *o* at...gates ... Ezek 44:11
exercising *o* not ... 1 Pet 5:2

OVERWHELM *crush, overcome*
humiliation has *o-ed* ... Ps 44:15
darkness will *o* me ... Ps 139:11
my spirit was *o-ed* ... Ps 142:3
o-ed by...sorrow ... 2 Cor 2:7

OWE *be indebted*
Pay...what you *o* ... Matt 18:28
O nothing to anyone ... Rom 13:8
that you *o* to me ... Philem 19

OWL *bird*
the *o,* the sea gull ... Deut 14:15
o of the waste places ... Ps 102:6
houses...full of *o-s* ... Is 13:21

OWN (adj) *belonging to*
man in His *o* image ... Gen 1:27
led...His *o* people ... Ps 78:52
calls his *o* sheep ... John 10:3
in his *o* language ... Acts 2:6

OWN (n) *belonging to*
He came to His *o* ... John 1:11
provide for his *o* ... 1 Tim 5:8

OWNER *possessor*
restitution to its *o* ... Ex 22:12
when the *o*...comes ... Matt 21:40
who were *o-s* of land ... Acts 4:34

OX *bull used as draft animal* Animal domesticated from very ancient times for use mainly in plowing, as food and for religious sacrifices.
oxen and donkeys ... Gen 12:16
servant or his *o* ... Ex 20:17
horns of the wild *oxen* ... Ps 22:21
An *o* knows its owner ... Is 1:3
not muzzle the *o* ... 1 Tim 5:18

P

PACE *step, stride*
the *p* of the cattle ... Gen 33:14
not slow down the *p* ... 2 Kin 4:24

PACT *agreement*
Sheol we...made a *p* ... Is 28:15
p with Sheol will ... Is 28:18

PADDAN-ARAM (unc, *garden in Aram*). A city from which both Isaac and Jacob took their wives.
NW Mesopotamia ... Gen 25:20
home of Laban ... Gen 28:5
birthplace of most of Jacob's sons ... Gen 35:22-26

PAHATH-MOAB
1 *head of Jewish clan* ... Ezra 2:6
2 *Jewish clan* ... Neh 3:11

PAIN *discomfort, hurt*
multiply Your *p* ... Gen 3:16
p-s came upon her ... 1 Sam 4:19
rejoice in unsparing *p* ... Job 6:10
rest from your *p* ... Is 14:3
Your *p* is incurable ... Jer 30:15
bring *p* to my soul ... Lam 3:51
no longer be...*p* ... Rev 21:4

PAINFUL *hurting*
p are honest words ... Job 6:25
the bread of *p* labors ... Ps 127:2

PALACE *royal residence*
build...royal *p* ... 2 Chr 2:12
to the king's *p* ... Esth 2:8
Out of ivory *p-s* ... Ps 45:8
A *p* of strangers ... Is 25:2
luxury...royal *p-s* ... Luke 7:25

PALESTINE The ancient name for what is essentially Israel today. The name came from the Romans, who named it for the Philistines, Israel's ancient enemy. Among the rabbis, Palestine is known as "the land of Israel," or simply as "the land."

PALLET *bed, mat*
they let down the *p* ... Mark 2:4
pick up your *p* and ... Mark 2:9

PALM *type of tree*
the city of *p* trees ... Deut 34:3
flourish like the *p* ... Ps 92:12
branches of the *p* ... John 12:13

PALTI *(delivered).* One of the twelve men sent to spy out Canaan. Also the man to whom King Saul gave his daughter Michal, David's wife, after David fled from the king's presence.
1 *son of Raphu* ... Num 13:9
spy for Israel ... Num 13:2
2 *Michal's husband* ... 1 Sam 25:44

PAMPHYLIA Ancient district and Roman province on the south coast of Asia Minor. Paul visited the region during his first missionary journey.
Roman province in Asia Minor ... Acts 2:10; 13:13; 14:24

PANIC *fear*
P seized them there ... Ps 48:6
P and pitfall have ... Lam 3:47
great *p*...will fall ... Zech 14:13

PANT *breathe rapidly*
deer *p-s* for the water ... Ps 42:1
my soul *p-s* for You ... Ps 42:1
I will both gasp and *p* ... Is 42:14
beasts...*p* for You ... Joel 1:20

PAPHOS The capital city on the southwest coast of the island of Cyprus. The Roman proconsul resided there.
city on Cyprus ... Acts 13:6,13

PAPYRUS *reed plant* Plant that grows at the edge of rivers and lakes. A fairly durable writing material was made from this plant; used by the authors of the NT.
p...without a marsh ... Job 8:11
Even in *p* vessels ... Is 18:2

PARABLE *story for illustration (comparison).* A story, usually from everyday life, used to illustrate a specific point of teaching. In the NT, however, Jesus used parables mainly to reserve the meaning of His teaching as a privilege for His disciples and others who are receptive to Him.
speak a *p* to ... Ezek 17:2
p of the sower ... Matt 13:18
heard His *p-s* ... Matt 21:45
p from the fig tree ... Mark 13:28
spoke by way of a *p* ... Luke 8:4

PARACLETE One who intercedes for another (Gr *paraklḗtos*). The **NASB** translates this as *Helper* in reference to the Holy Spirit and *Advocate* in reference to Jesus Christ (John 14:16; 1 John 2:1).

PARADISE *(park, garden).* Originally the garden of Eden. Jesus used the term in reference to a wonderful place where believers go to be with Him after death. It is synonymous with the *third heaven* (2 Cor 12:2) and it seems to be separate from the new heaven and earth prophesied in Revelation. *Abraham's bosom* is probably the same as Paradise. *see* **HEAVEN**
abode of the righteous dead ... Luke 23:43; 2 Cor 12:4; Rev 2:7
see also **ABRAHAM'S BOSOM**

PARALYTIC
said to the *p,* Get up ... Matt 9:6
p, carried by four ... Mark 2:3

PARAN A wilderness from which Moses sent twelve spies to investigate the Promised Land. Many historical events took place there. Also name of a mountain.
wilderness area in Sinai ... Gen 21:21; Num 13:3
place of Israelite wanderings and encampments ... Num 12:16
mountain in Sinai ... Deut 33:2

PARCHMENT A processed animal skin used as a writing material. It was preferred to papyrus (q.v.) because of its greater durability, but was much more expensive.

PARDON *forgive, release*
he will not *p* your ... Ex 23:21
May the...LORD *p* ... 2 Chr 30:18
O LORD, *P* my iniquity ... Ps 25:11
He will abundantly *p* ... Is 55:7
p, and you will be ... Luke 6:37

PARENTS *father and mother*
rise up against *p* ... Matt 10:21
left house or...*p* ... Luke 18:29
evil, disobedient to *p* ... Rom 1:30
Children, obey your *p* ... Eph 6:1
disobedient to *p* ... 2 Tim 3:2

PART *portion*
God...have no *p* in ... 2 Chr 19:7
formed my inward *p-s* ... Ps 139:13
have no *p* with Me ... John 13:8
no *p* or portion in ... Acts 8:21
prophesy in *p* ... 1 Cor 13:9
now I know in *p* ... 1 Cor 13:12
tongue is a small *p* ... James 3:5

PARTAKERS *participators*
do not be *p* with ... Eph 5:7
become *p* of Christ ... Heb 3:14
p of the Holy Spirit ... Heb 6:4
p of *the* divine nature ... 2 Pet 1:4

PARTHIANS Jewish descendants who lived in Parthia, located south of the Caspian Sea (Acts 2:9).

PARTIAL *favoring*
not be *p* to the poor ... Lev 19:15
you shall not be *p* ... Deut 16:19
now be *p* to no one ... Job 32:21
You are not *p* ... Matt 22:16

PARTIALITY *favoritism*
show *p* in judgment ... Deut 1:17
p is not good ... Prov 28:21
God shows no *p* ... Gal 2:6

PARTICIPATE *take part*
not *p*...deeds of ... Eph 5:11

p-s in his evil deeds ... 2 John 11
will not *p* in her sins ... Rev 18:4

PARTNER *comrade*
is a *p* with a thief ... Prov 29:24
been *p-s* with them ... Matt 23:30
regard me a *p* ... Philem 17

PASS *proceed*
LORD will *p* over the ... Ex 12:23
My glory is *p-ing* by ... Ex 33:22
heaven and earth *p* ... Matt 5:18
words will not *p* ... Matt 24:35
this cup *p* from Me ... Matt 26:39
p-ed out of death ... John 5:24
old things *p-ed* away ... 2 Cor 5:17
first earth *p-ed* away ... Rev 21:1

PASSION *desire, lust*
p is rottenness to ... Prov 14:30
over to degrading *p-s* ... Rom 1:26
flesh with its *p-s* ... Gal 5:24
dead to...*p* ... Col 3:5
not in lustful *p* ... 1 Thess 4:5

PASSION *suffering* In theology, a technical term referring to the suffering of Christ during His final week.

PASSOVER One of three main Jewish festivals (Booths and Pentecost are the other two) beginning on the fourteenth of Nisan (March/April) to commemorate protection from the plague of death against the firstborn in Egypt, and liberation from Egyptian slavery. *See also* **DOORPOST**. In the NT, Passover refers to Christ as the Lamb slain once for all.
Israel's firstborn protected from the plague of death ... Ex 12:1-30
Feast of commemoration ... Ex 12:42,43; Lev 23:5; Num 9:2,12,14; Matt 26:2,18; John 19:14; Acts 12:4
see also **FEASTS**

PASTORAL EPISTLES A reference to 1 and 2 Timothy and Titus. These epistles have special instructions by Paul to leaders of the local church.

PASTORS *shepherds of people* (Lat, *shepherd*). One of the positions of leadership in the local church which the Holy Spirit uses for the edification of the body of Christ. A person so gifted is to lead the members of the body, help them to understand and apply the Scriptures and keep them safe from false teachers and unsound doctrine.
and some *as p* ... Eph 4:11

PASTURE (n) *grazing field*
lie down in green *p-s* ... Ps 23:2
sheep of Your *p* ... Ps 79:13

PASTURE (v) *feed, graze*
Moses...*p-ing* the flock ... Ex 3:1
They will *p* on it ... Zeph 2:7
So I *p-d* the flock ... Zech 11:7

PATCH *mending cloth*
p of unshrunk cloth ... Matt 9:16
p pulls away from it ... Mark 2:21

PATH *way* In the Bible, often used metaphorically to refer to a person's goals or his behavior, e.g. "the path of peace," i.e. the pursuit of peace.
snake in the *p* ... Gen 49:17
the *p* of life ... Ps 16:11
a light to my *p* ... Ps 119:105
p of the upright is ... Prov 15:19
Make His *p-s* straight ... Matt 3:3

PATHROS
upper Egypt ... Is 11:11; Jer 44:1,15; Ezek 29:14; 30:14

PATIENCE *endurance* According to Gal 5:22, one of the nine components of the fruit of the Spirit (*see* **FRUIT**). It involves endurance in suffering, tolerance of others, etc.
try the *p* of men ... Is 7:13
in *p*, in kindness ... 2 Cor 6:6
love, joy, peace, *p* ... Gal 5:22
exhort, with great *p* ... 2 Tim 4:2
endure it with *p* ... 1 Pet 2:20

PATIENT *bearing, enduring*
Love is *p*, love is ... 1 Cor 13:4
p when wronged ... 2 Tim 2:24
Lord...is *p* toward ... 2 Pet 3:9

PATMOS A small island in the Aegean Sea where the apostle John was exiled. While there he received the prophecy and visions which he recorded in the book of Revelation.
Aegean island ... Rev 1:9

PATRIARCH *father of clan (head of a family)*. In the Bible, key men in the OT who were leaders of their families, and the tribes and nations that descended from them. In the NT, those listed as patriarchs include David, the twelve sons of Jacob, and Abraham.
regarding the *p* David ... Acts 2:29
the twelve *p-s* ... Acts 7:8
Abraham, the *p*, gave ... Heb 7:4

PATTERN *model, plan*
fixed *p-s* of heaven ... Jer 33:25
walk according to...*p* ... Phil 3:17

PAUL Born as Saul, a highly educated Jew and Roman citizen by birth who persecuted the Church before his conversion. After that, he was appointed by Christ as an apostle to the Gentiles. He is the author of 13 NT epistles.
heritage ... Acts 21:39; 22:3; Phil 3:5
persecuted believers ... Acts 7:58; 8:1,3; 9:1,2; 1 Cor 15:9
conversion and call ... Acts 9:1-19
name changed ... Acts 13:9
Jerusalem council ... Acts 15:2-6
missionary journeys ... Acts 13:1ff; 15:36ff; 18:23ff
apostolic defense ... Acts 11:5ff; Gal 1:13ff
arrest and imprisonment ... Acts 21:33; 22:24-28:31
defense ... Acts 22:1ff; 24:10ff; 25:10,11; 26:2ff
final journey to Rome ... Acts 27,28
see also **SAUL**

PAULUS, SERGIUS
proconsul of Cyprus ... Acts 13:7

PAVEMENT *paved road*
on a *p* of stone ... 2 Kin 16:17
mosaic *p* of porphyry ... Esth 1:6
place called The *P* ... John 19:13

PAY *give what is due*
thief...*p* double ... Ex 22:7
p You my vows ... Ps 66:13
P back what you ... Matt 18:28
Never *p* back evil ... Rom 12:17
p the penalty ... 2 Thess 1:9

PEACE *calmness, tranquility*
grant *p* in the land ... Lev 26:6
made *p* with David ... 1 Chr 19:19
Seek *p*, and pursue ... Ps 34:14
for the *p* of Jerusalem ... Ps 122:6
all her paths are *p* ... Prov 3:17
a time for *p* ... Eccl 3:8
Prince of *P* ... Is 9:6
p...like a river ... Is 66:12
have withdrawn My *p* ... Jer 16:5
not come to bring *p* ... Matt 10:34
on earth *p* among ... Luke 2:14
P I leave with you ... John 14:27
we have *p* with God ... Rom 5:1
love, joy, *p* ... Gal 5:22
He Himself is our *p* ... Eph 2:14
gospel of *p* ... Eph 6:15
p of God...surpasses ... Phil 4:7
p through the blood ... Col 1:20
take *p* from the earth ... Rev 6:4

PEACEABLE
gentle, *p*, free from ... 1 Tim 3:3
be *p*, gentle ... Titus 3:2

PEACEMAKERS
Blessed are the *p* ... Matt 5:9

PEACE OFFERING *see* **OFFERINGS**

PEARL *precious gem*
wisdom is above...*p-s* ... Job 28:18
p-s before swine ... Matt 7:6
one *p* of great value ... Matt 13:46

PEDAIAH *(Yahweh has redeemed)*.
1) Father of Joel, an important officer in David's army (1 Chr 27:20). 2) A Levite whom Nehemiah appointed in charge of the distribution of food for the Levites (Neh 13:13). 3) Name of other individuals in the OT.

PEKAH *(opening)*. The eighteenth king of Israel who tried to overthrow Judah. He followed the idolatry of Jeroboam.
king of Israel ... 2 Kin 15:25ff

PEKAHIAH
king of Israel ... 2 Kin 15:22,23

PELEG (unc, *division, cleft)*. A man who seems to have been named thus because in his lifetime *the earth was divided* (Gen 10:25), probably referring to the confusion of languages at the Tower of Babel (Gen 11:1-9).
son of Eber ... Gen 10:25
descendant of Shem ... Gen 11:18

PENALTY *punishment*
you will bear the *p* ... Ezek 23:49
pay the *p* of eternal ... 2 Thess 1:9
received a just *p* ... Heb 2:2

PENIEL
where Jacob wrestled with God ... Gen 32:30
see also **PENUEL**

PENTATEUCH *(five scrolls).* A collective name for the first five books of the OT, which are also known as the Law (*Torah* in Heb) or the five books of Moses. The word does not appear in the Bible.

PENTECOST *(fiftieth).* One of the three main Jewish festivals (Booths and Passover are the others). It was observed in the early summer and is also known as the "Feast of Weeks" because it occurred seven weeks after the waving of the sheaf of first fruits (50 days after Passover). The church came into being during the first Pentecost after Christ ascended to heaven.
Jewish feast ... Acts 20:16; 1 Cor 16:8
coming of the Holy Spirit ... Acts 2:1
see also **FEASTS**

PENUEL *(face of God).* An place near which Jacob wrestled all night with an angel, probably the angel of the Lord (q.v.). He then received a blessing from the angel, and as part of the blessing his name was changed to Israel. Also the name of two individuals.
1 *tower destroyed* ... Judg 8:17
rebuilt ... 1 Kin 12:25
see also **PENIEL**
2 *father of Gedor* ... 1 Chr 4:4
3 *son of Shashak* ... 1 Chr 8:25

PEOPLE *group, nation*
they are one *p* ... Gen 11:6
Let My *p* go ... Ex 5:1
You are an obstinate *p* ... Ex 33:5
blessed above all *p-s* ... Deut 7:14
Forgive Your *p* Israel ... Deut 21:8
LORD loves His *p* ... 2 Chr 2:11
p who are called by ... 2 Chr 7:14
restores His captive *p* ... Ps 14:7
We are His *p* ... Ps 100:3
LORD will judge His *p* ... Ps 135:14
p are unrestrained ... Prov 29:18
p whom I formed ... Is 43:21
do *p* say that I am ... Mark 8:27
they feared the *p* ... Luke 20:19
die for the *p* ... John 11:50
not rejected His *p* ... Rom 11:2
every tribe and *p* ... Rev 13:7

PEOR
1 *mountain in Moab* ... Num 23:28
2 *Moabite deity* ... Num 25:3

PERCEIVE *be aware, discern*
p-d all the wisdom ... 1 Kin 10:4
listening, but do not *p* ... Is 6:9
p-ing in Himself ... Mark 5:30
p with their heart ... John 12:40

PERDITION *damnation* The state of being lost or destroyed, often used outside the Bible to refer to the destiny of unbelievers. In the Bible, Jesus calls Judas Iscariot *the son of perdition* (John 17:12), meaning that he was destined for ruin.
the son of *p* ... John 17:12

PEREZ
son of Judah ... Gen 38:29

PERFECT (adj) *flawless*
His work is *p* ... Deut 32:4
law of the LORD is *p* ... Ps 19:7
heavenly Father is *p* ... Matt 5:48
p bond of unity ... Col 3:14
be *p* and complete ... James 1:4
p love casts out ... 1 John 4:18

PERFECTED *completed*
is *p* in weakness ... 2 Cor 12:9
love is *p* with us ... 1 John 4:17

PERFORM *carry out*
I will *p* miracles ... Ex 34:10
p My judgments ... Lev 18:4
p-s righteous deeds ... Ps 103:6
p a miracle in My ... Mark 9:39
John *p-ed* no sign ... John 10:41
p-ing great wonders ... Acts 6:8

PERFUME *fragrant oil*
and *p* make the heart ... Prov 27:9
instead of sweet *p* ... Is 3:24
p on My body ... Matt 26:12
anointed...with *p* ... Luke 7:46
prepared...*p-s* ... Luke 23:56

PERGA
city in Asia Minor ... Acts 13:13

PERGAMUM One of the seven cities with churches in the book of Revelation to whom John was ordered to write. The parchment (q.v.) industry was developed and perfected there.
city in Asia Minor ... Rev 1:11
early church ... Rev 2:12

PERISH *be destroyed*
we *p*, we are dying ... Num 17:12
weapons...*p-ed* ... 2 Sam 1:27
if I *p*, I *p* ... Esth 4:16
hope...will *p* ... Job 8:13
the wicked will *p* ... Ps 1:6
rod of his fury will *p* ... Prov 22:8
our hope has *p-ed* ... Ezek 37:11
little ones *p* ... Matt 18:14
p by the sword ... Matt 26:52
p, but have eternal ... John 3:16
for any to *p* ... 2 Pet 3:9

PERIZZITES
early Canaanite tribe ... Gen 34:30; Ex 23:23; Deut 7:1

PERMANENT *lasting*
it is a *p* ordinance ... Lev 6:18
p right of redemption ... Lev 25:32
use them as *p* slaves ... Lev 25:46
p home for the ark ... 1 Chr 28:2

PERMISSION *consent*
p they had from Cyrus ... Ezra 3:7
Jesus gave them *p* ... Mark 5:13
he had given him *p* ... Acts 21:40

PERMIT *allow*
not *p-ting*...demons ... Mark 1:34
p the children ... Mark 10:14
Spirit...did not *p* ... Acts 16:7
if the Lord *p-s* ... 1 Cor 16:7

PERPETUAL *lasting*
p incense before the ... Ex 30:8
as a *p* covenant ... Ex 31:16
for a *p* priesthood ... Ex 40:15
may sleep a *p* sleep ... Jer 51:39

PERSECUTE *afflict, oppress*
Why do you *p* me ... Job 19:22
has *p-d* my soul ... Ps 143:3
pray for those who *p* ... Matt 5:44
p you in one city ... Matt 10:23
why are you *p-ing* Me ... Acts 9:4
used to *p* the church ... Gal 1:13

PERSECUTION *oppression*
p arises because of ... Mark 4:17
p began against the ... Acts 8:1
a *p* against Paul ... Acts 13:50
distress, or *p*, or ... Rom 8:35

PERSEVERANCE *persistence* In theology, to remain true to one's faith in Christ, despite persecution and suffering. All true believers persevere, though they may have lapses of faith. Synonymous with steadfastness and endurance.
by *p* in doing good ... Rom 2:7
tribulation brings...*p* ... Rom 5:3
for your *p* and faith ... 2 Thess 1:4
p of the saints ... Rev 14:12

PERSIA One of the ancient empires of the world. It is now Iran. *see also* **MEDIA**
ancient Near Eastern empire ... 2 Chr 36:20; Ezra 1:1; Esth 1:3; Ezek 27:10; Dan 8:20

PERSON *human being*
If a *p* sins ... Lev 4:2
hungry *p* unsatisfied ... Is 32:6
p...be in subjection ... Rom 13:1
hidden *p* of the heart ... 1 Pet 3:4

PERSUADE *convince, prevail on*
a ruler may be *p-d* ... Prov 25:15
trying to *p* Jews and ... Acts 18:4
p-s men to worship ... Acts 18:13
you will *p* me ... Acts 26:28

PERSUASIVE *convincing*
p words of wisdom ... 1 Cor 2:4
delude you with *p* ... Col 2:4

PERVERSE *corrupt*
a *p* and crooked ... Deut 32:5
A *p* heart shall depart ... Ps 101:4
mind will utter *p* ... Prov 23:33
and *p* generation ... Phil 2:15

PERVERT *distort, misdirect*
not *p* the justice ... Ex 23:6
Does God *p* justice ... Job 8:3
have *p-ed* their way ... Jer 3:21

PESTILENCE *epidemic, plague* Sometimes mentioned with *sword* and *famine,* it is a life-threatening disease or plague affecting masses of people, and is often seen in the Bible as an act of divine judgment for wickedness. *see also* **PLAGUE**
LORD sent a *p* ... 2 Sam 24:15
sword, famine, and *p* ... Jer 27:13
p and mourning and ... Rev 18:8

PETER *(stone).* One of the twelve apostles. *see also* **CEPHAS**
heritage and occupation ... Matt 4:18; John 1:42,44
called by Jesus ... Matt 1:17; Mark 3:16; Luke 5:1ff
names: Cephas, Simon ... Matt 4:18; Mark 3:16; John 1:42; Acts 15:14
walked on water ... Matt 14:28ff
confessed Jesus as Messiah ... Matt 16:16; Luke 9:20
on mount of Transfiguration ... Matt 17:1ff; Mark 9:2ff
denied Jesus ... Matt 26:70; Mark 14:70; Luke 22:58

at Pentecost ... Acts 2
apostle of Christ ... Gal 2:8; 1 Pet 1:1; 2 Pet 1:1

PETITION *request, supplication*
God...grant your *p* ... 1 Sam 1:17
p to any god or man ... Dan 6:7
p-s...be made ... 1 Tim 2:1

PETRA *(rock).* An ancient city and capital of Edom located in northwest Arabia on the slope of Mt. Hor.

PHARAOH *title of Egyptian kings*
1 **Pharaoh,** *time of Abraham* ... Gen 12:15ff
2 **Pharaoh,** *time of Joseph* ... Gen 37:36; 39:1-50:26
3 **Pharaoh,** *during oppression* ... Ex 1:8-2:23
4 **Pharaoh,** *during the Exodus* ... Ex 5:1-12:41
5 **Pharaoh, *father of Bithiah*** ... 1 Chr 4:17
6 **Pharaoh,** *time of David* ... 1 Kin 11:14ff
7 **Pharaoh,** *whose daughter married Solomon* ... 1 Kin 3:1; 7:8; 9:16
8 **Shishak,** *time of Rehoboam* ... 1 Kin 14:25,26
9 **So,** *time of Hoshea* ... 2 Kin 17:4
10 **Tirhakah,** *time of Hezekiah* ... 2 Kin 19:9; Is 37:9
11 **Neco,** *killed Josiah, defeated by Nebuchadnezzar* ... 2 Kin 23:29,33,34
12 **Hophra,** *subject of prophecy* ... Jer 44:30

PHARISEES A very strict Jewish religious sect often mentioned in the NT who tried to apply the Torah (Jewish Law) and their own oral law and traditions to everyday life. They commanded much respect and exercised a great deal of power over the common people, but were often condemned by Jesus for their hypocrisy in allowing the minutiae (small details) of their traditions to contradict the spirit and letter of OT law.
Jewish religious party ... Matt 3:7; 23:13; Mark 2:18; 7:3; Luke 11:42; 16:14; John 3:1; 11:47

PHARPAR
river of Damascus ... 2 Kin 5:12

PHILADELPHIA *(in honor of Philadelphus, brother-loving).* A city of Lydia in Asia Minor about 25 miles southeast of Sardis. One of the seven churches addressed in Revelation.
city in Asia Minor ... Rev 1:11
early church ... Rev 3:7

PHILEMON *(kindly).* A Christian to whom Paul sent his epistle of the same name appealing for Philemon's slave Onesimus.
owner of Onesimus ... Philem 1
friend of Paul

PHILIP *(horse-loving).* Name of several individuals; among the more important are the apostle, one of the Herods, and the evangelist. The apostle is well known because he brought others to the Lord, and when some Greeks wanted to see Jesus, they came to Philip first.
1 *Herod Philip I, son of Herod the Great* ... Mark 6:17
see also **HEROD**
2 *Herod Philip II, son of Herod the Great* ... Luke 3:1
see also **HEROD**
3 *Philip the apostle* ... Matt 10:3; Mark 3:18; Luke 6:14; John 1:43ff; Acts 1:13
4 *Philip the evangelist* ... Acts 6:5; 8:5,29; 21:8

PHILIPPI A Macedonian city and fortress near Thrace, Thessalonica, and Neapolis. The first city in Europe to receive the gospel. Paul and Silas were imprisoned there.
Macedonian city ... Acts 16:12; 20:6

PHILIPPIANS
people of Philippi ... Phil 4:15

PHILISTIA A very fertile land where the Philistines lived, located between the Mediterranean and the region of Shephelah, extending down to Egypt.
coastal area of SW Palestine ... Ex 15:14; Ps 60:8; 83:7; Joel 3:4

PHILISTINES
people of Philistia ... Gen 10:14; Josh 13:2; Judg 13:1; 1 Sam 4:2

PHINEHAS A high priest. Son of Eleazar, grandson of Aaron. Also the name of two other individuals.
1 *grandson of Aaron* ... Num 25:7; 31:6; Judg 20:28
2 *son of Eli* ... 1 Sam 1:3; 4:4,11
3 *father of a priest* ... Ezra 8:33

PHOEBE *(pure, brilliant).* A prominent woman in the church of Cenchrea, the eastern port of Corinth. She may have been a deaconess.
commended by Paul ... Rom 16:1

PHOENICIA
coastal land N of land of Israel ... Acts 11:19; 21:2
visited by Paul ... Acts 15:3

PHRYGIA
Asia Minor province ... Acts 2:10
visited by Paul ... Acts 16:6; 18:23

PHYGELUS
Asian Christian, deserted Paul ... 2 Tim 1:15

PHYLACTERIES *prayer bands (safeguard).* Small leather receptacles containing scriptures written on parchment and worn on the forehead and left arm by men in obedience to the verses contained in them. The verses were Deut 6:4-9; 11:13-21; and Ex 13:1-10, 11-16.
as *p* on your forehead ... Ex 13:16
they broaden their *p* ... Matt 23:5
see also **FRONTALS**

PHYSICIAN
all worthless *p-s* ... Job 13:4
healthy who need a *p* ... Matt 9:12
P, heal yourself ... Luke 4:23
Luke, the beloved *p* ... Col 4:14

PIECE *part, portion*
dip your *p* of bread ... Ruth 2:14
thirty *p-s* of silver ... Matt 27:3
gave Him a *p*...fish ... Luke 24:42
woven in one *p* ... John 19:23

PIERCE *penetrate*
master shall *p* his ear ... Ex 21:6
They *p-d* my hands ... Ps 22:16
He was *p-d* through ... Is 53:5
whom they have *p-d* ... Zech 12:10
sword will *p*...soul ... Luke 2:35
p-d His side ... John 19:34
p-d to the heart ... Acts 2:37

PIETY *reverence* The quality of being reverent and obedient toward God. Also the respect due to parents and grandparents from children.
learn to practice *p* ... 1 Tim 5:4
because of His *p* ... Heb 5:7

PILATE, PONTIUS
Roman governor of Judea ... Matt 27:2; Luke 3:1
presided at Jesus' trial ... Matt 27:11ff; Mark 15:2ff; Luke 23:1ff; John 18:28-38
warned by his wife ... Matt 27:19
orders Jesus' crucifixion ... Matt 27:24ff; Mark 15:15; Luke 23:24,25; John 19:15,16

PILLAR *column* or *memorial*
see also **CLOUD, PILLAR OF**
became a *p* of salt ... Gen 19:26
p of fire by night ... Ex 13:21
set up...a *p* ... 2 Sam 18:18
hewn...her seven *p-s* ... Prov 9:1
feet like *p-s* of fire ... Rev 10:1

PILOT *steersman*
sailors, and your *p-s* ... Ezek 27:27
the *p* and...captain ... Acts 27:11
inclination of the *p* ... James 3:4

PINION *wing*
p and plumage of ... Job 39:13
cover you with His *p-s* ... Ps 91:4

PINNACLE *highest point*
had Him...on the *p* ... Matt 4:5
p of the temple ... Luke 4:9

PISGAH A mountain range in Moab from which Moses viewed the Promised Land and afterwards died in fulfillment of God's promise to him.
mountain height in Moab ... Num 21:20; Josh 13:20
Moses died there ... Deut 34:1-5

PISHON
river of Eden ... Gen 2:11

PISIDIA / PISIDIAN
district of Asia Minor ... Acts 13:14; 14:24

PIT *deep hole, dungeon*
full of tar *p-s* ... Gen 14:10
Joseph...not in the *p* ... Gen 37:29
redeems...from the *p* ... Ps 103:4
harlot is a deep *p* ... Prov 23:27
silenced me in the *p* ... Lam 3:53
to *p-s* of darkness ... 2 Pet 2:4
the bottomless *p* ... Rev 9:1

PITCH (n) *tar*
inside and out with *p* ... Gen 6:14
covered it over...*p* ... Ex 2:3

PITCH (v) *set up*
p-ed his tent in the ... Gen 31:25

he will *p* the tents … Dan 11:45
tabernacle...Lord *p-ed* … Heb 8:2

PITCHER *container*
torches inside the *p-s* … Judg 7:16
Fill four *p-s* … 1 Kin 18:33
carrying a *p* of … Mark 14:13

PITHOM
Egyptian storage city built by Hebrew slaves … Ex 1:11

PITY (n) *sympathy*
shall not show *p* … Deut 19:21
I will not show *p* … Jer 13:14
No eye looked with *p* … Ezek 16:5

PITY (v) *have compassion*
she had *p* on him … Ex 2:6
eye shall not *p* them … Deut 7:16
P me, *p* me, O you … Job 19:21
take *p* on us … Mark 9:22
most to be *p-ied* … 1 Cor 15:19

PLACE *area, space*
waters...into one *p* … Gen 1:9
he enters the holy *p* … Ex 28:29
God is a dwelling *p* … Deut 33:27
a *p* for My people … 1 Chr 17:9
earth out of its *p* … Job 9:6
You are my hiding *p* … Ps 32:7
love the *p* of honor … Matt 23:6
a *p* called Golgotha … Matt 27:33
I go to prepare a *p* … John 14:2

PLAGUE *contagious disease* In the Bible, an affliction sent by God as a punishment or judgment. Plagues took several forms: they could be disasters on crops, diseases on individuals or animals, etc.
see also **PESTILENCE**
no *p* will befall you … Ex 12:13
Remove Your *p* from … Ps 39:10
p of the hail … Rev 16:21
the seven last *p-s* … Rev 21:9

PLAIN *flat area*
p in...Shinar … Gen 11:2
desert *p-s* of Jericho … Josh 4:13
the *p* of Megiddo … 2 Chr 35:22
broad *p* of the earth … Rev 20:9

PLAN *design, scheme*
tabernacle...its *p* … Ex 26:30
P-s formed long ago … Is 25:1
follow our own *p-s* … Jer 18:12
p and foreknowledge … Acts 2:23

PLANT (n) *growth from soil*
every *p* yielding seed … Gen 1:29
eat the *p-s* of the … Gen 3:18
hail...struck every *p* … Ex 9:25
God appointed a *p* … Jon 4:6

PLANT (v) *put into soil*
God *p-ed* a garden … Gen 2:8
p...trees for food … Lev 19:23
shall *p* a vineyard … Deut 28:30
A time to *p* … Eccl 3:2
her earnings she *p-s* … Prov 31:16
p-ed a vineyard … Mark 12:1
I *p-ed*, Apollos … 1 Cor 3:6

PLATTER *shallow dish*
on a *p* the head of … Matt 14:8
his head on a *p* … Mark 6:28

PLAY *take part*
who *p* the lyre … Gen 4:21
man who can *p* … 1 Sam 16:17
p-ed the fool … 1 Sam 26:21
P skillfully with a … Ps 33:3
nursing child will *p* … Is 11:8
not *p* the harlot … Hos 3:3
We *p-ed* the flute … Matt 11:17

PLEAD *appeal, beseech*
p-ed with the LORD … Deut 3:23
man...*p* with God … Job 16:21
LORD...*p* their case … Prov 22:23
P for the widow … Is 1:17
Elijah...*p-s* with God … Rom 11:2

PLEASANT *pleasing*
despised the *p* land … Ps 106:24
P words are a … Prov 16:24
sleep...is *p* … Eccl 5:12
Speak to us *p* words … Is 30:10

PLEASE *satisfy*
it *p* You to bless … 2 Sam 7:29
You are *p-d* with me … Ps 41:11
sacrifices...not *p* Him … Hos 9:4
how he may *p* his … 1 Cor 7:33
p all men in all … 1 Cor 10:33
striving to *p* men … Gal 1:10
to walk and *p* God … 1 Thess 4:1
impossible to *p* … Heb 11:6

PLEASING *agreeable, gratifying*
tree that is *p* … Gen 2:9
meditation be *p* … Ps 104:34
not as *p* men but … 1 Thess 2:4
p in His sight … 1 John 3:22

PLEASURE *gratification*
old, shall I have *p* … Gen 18:12
p in His people … Ps 149:4
He who loves *p will* … Prov 21:17
work for *His* good *p* … Phil 2:13
lovers of *p* rather … 2 Tim 3:4
passing *p-s* of sin … Heb 11:25

PLEDGE *promise*
cloak as a *p* … Ex 22:26
those who give *p-s* … Prov 22:26
the Spirit as a *p* … 2 Cor 5:5
p of our inheritance … Eph 1:14

PLEIADES A group of seven stars.
constellation of stars … Job 9:9; 38:31; Amos 5:8

PLENTIFUL *abundant*
shed abroad a *p* rain … Ps 68:9
harvest is *p* … Matt 9:37

PLOT *plan, scheme*
wicked *p-s* against … Ps 37:12
you have *p-ted evil* … Prov 30:32
Jews *p-ted* together … Acts 9:23

PLOW *dig the soil*
not *p* with an ox … Deut 22:10
those who *p* iniquity … Job 4:8
sluggard does not *p* … Prov 20:4
his hand to the *p* … Luke 9:62
ought to *p* in hope … 1 Cor 9:10

PLOWSHARE *blade of plow* The metal tip at the end of a plow which cuts into the soil.
their swords into *p-s* … Is 2:4
your *p-s* into swords … Joel 3:10

PLUMB LINE *vertical line*
the *p* of emptiness … Is 34:11
p In the midst of My … Amos 7:8
when they see the *p* … Zech 4:10

PLUNDER (n) *booty, loot*
took no *p* in silver … Judg 5:19
You will become *p* … Hab 2:7
wealth will become *p* … Zeph 1:13

PLUNDER (v) *rob*
will *p* the Egyptians … Ex 3:22
stouthearted were *p-ed* … Ps 76:5
he will *p* his house … Matt 12:29

POINT *particular time*
grieved, to the *p* of … Matt 26:38
obedient to the *p* of … Phil 2:8
to the *p* of shedding … Heb 12:4

POISON *lethal substance*
P...under their lips … Ps 140:3
given us *p-ed* water … Jer 8:14
turned justice into *p* … Amos 6:12

POLL-TAX *income and head tax*
collect customs or *p* … Matt 17:25
give a *p* to Caesar … Matt 22:17

POLLUTE *contaminate*
blood *p-s* the land … Num 35:33
earth is also *p-d* … Is 24:5

POMEGRANATE *fruit* A shrub or small tree, also its fruit. Renditions of pomegranates were sown on the priest's robe and used in the decoration of the temple.
golden bell and a *p* … Ex 28:34
p-s of blue and purple … Ex 39:24
juice of my *p-s* … Song 8:2
the fig tree, the *p* … Hag 2:19

PONDER *think deeply*
not *p* the path of life … Prov 5:6
Or *p* things...past … Is 43:18

PONTIUS PILATE The fifth Roman prefect or governor of Judea, Samaria, and Idumea from A.D. 26-36 who condemned Jesus to crucifixion to appease the demands of the crowds who were incited by the Jewish authorities (Mark 15:15).

PONTUS A large district in northern Asia Minor where a significant Jewish population resided.
region in N Asia Minor … Acts 2:9; 1 Pet 1:1
homeland of Aquila … Acts 18:2

POOL *pond*
of the upper *p* … 2 Kin 18:17
rock into a *p* … Ps 114:8
land will become a *p* … Is 35:7
in the *p* of Siloam … John 9:7

POOR *impoverished, needy*
p will never cease … Deut 15:11
raises the *p* from the … 1 Sam 2:8
or you will become *p* … Prov 20:13
not rob the *p* … Prov 22:22
are the *p* in spirit … Matt 5:3
a *p* widow came … Mark 12:42
you always have the *p* … Mark 14:7
sake He became *p* … 2 Cor 8:9
not God choose the *p* … James 2:5

POPULATE *increase number*
P the earth abundantly … Gen 9:7
whole earth was *p-d* … Gen 9:19

POPULATION *people*
with all *his* great *p* … Is 16:14
deported an entire *p* … Amos 1:6

PORPOISE SKIN
covering of *p-s* above … Ex 26:14

PORTICO *porch*
in the *p* of Solomon … John 10:23
one accord in...*p* … Acts 5:12

PORTION *part, share*
gather a day's *p* … Ex 16:4
LORD'S *p* is...people … Deut 32:9
double *p* of...spirit … 2 Kin 2:9
The LORD is my *p* … Ps 119:57
joy over their *p* … Is 61:7

POSSESS *control, take*
give...this land to *p* … Gen 15:7
are to *p* their land … Lev 20:24
go in and *p* the land … Deut 1:8
p-es all the nations … Ps 82:8
p-ed by Beelzebul … Mark 3:22
sell all you *p* … Mark 10:21
p-ed with demons … Luke 8:27
do not *p* silver and … Acts 3:6

POSSESSION *ownership*
for an everlasting *p* … Gen 17:8
you shall be My own *p* … Ex 19:5
people for His own *p* … Deut 4:20
full of Your *p-s* … Ps 104:24
charge of all his *p-s* … Matt 24:47
selling their...*p-s* … Acts 2:45

POSSIBLE *can be done*
all things are *p* … Matt 19:26
p with God … Luke 18:27

POSTERITY *descendants*
P will serve Him … Ps 22:30
p of the wicked … Ps 37:38

POT *container, vessel*
death in the *p* … 2 Kin 4:40
refining *p* is for … Prov 17:3
I see a boiling *p* … Jer 1:13

POTIPHAR An important official in the Pharaoh's administration. He purchased Joseph as a slave from Midianites traders who had purchased him from his brothers.
Egyptian official who purchased Joseph … Gen 39:1

POTIPHERA
Joseph's father-in-law … Gen 41:45,50; 46:20

POTSHERD *piece of pottery* A piece or fragment of pottery, mentioned in the OT as a symbol of dryness. Potsherds were often used in ancient society as a writing material for short notes, etc.
p to scrape himself … Job 2:8
is dried up like a *p* … Ps 22:15

POTTER *one who molds clay*
clay say to the *p* … Is 45:9
and You our *p* … Is 64:8
as it pleased the *p* … Jer 18:4
Throw it to the *p* … Zech 11:13

POTTER'S FIELD A place to bury very poor people, unknown persons, and criminals. Sometimes also used by potters as a source of clay, from which it received this name.
burial place bought with Judas's money … Matt 27:3ff
also called **FIELD OF BLOOD**

POUR *cause to flow*
p me out like milk … Job 10:10
I *p* out my soul … Ps 42:4
P out your heart … Ps 62:8
I will *p* out My Spirit … Is 44:3
P out Your wrath … Jer 10:25
p out...a blessing … Mal 3:10
p-ed it on His … Matt 26:7
p forth of My Spirit … Acts 2:17

POVERTY *destitution, want*
glutton...come to *p* … Prov 23:21
neither *p* nor riches … Prov 30:8
through His *p* might … 2 Cor 8:9

POWER *authority, strength*
to show you My *p* … Ex 9:16
from the *p* of Sheol … Ps 49:15
the *p* of His works … Ps 111:6
p of the tongue … Prov 18:21
the *p* of the sword … Jer 18:21
Not by might nor...*p* … Zech 4:6
Yours is...the *p* … Matt 6:13
the right hand of *p* … Mark 14:62
clothed with *p* from … Luke 24:49
you will receive *p* … Acts 1:8
gospel...*p* of God … Rom 1:16
the *p* of our Lord … 1 Cor 5:4
p of sin is the law … 1 Cor 15:56
p of Christ...dwell … 2 Cor 12:9
prince of the *p* of … Eph 2:2
p of His resurrection … Phil 3:10
timidity, but of *p* … 2 Tim 1:7
by the word of His *p* … Heb 1:3
quenched the *p* of … Heb 11:34
p-s...been subjected … 1 Pet 3:22

POWERLESS *without strength*
p before this great … 2 Chr 20:12
He might render *p* … Heb 2:14

PRACTICE (n) *custom, habit*
evil of their *p-s* … Ps 28:4
disclosing their *p-s* … Acts 19:18
laid aside...*evil p-s* … Col 3:9

PRACTICE (v) *engage in*
keep...statutes and *p* … Lev 20:8
He who *p-s* deceit … Ps 101:7
Who *p* righteousness … Ps 106:3
p-ing hospitality … Rom 12:13
learn to *p* piety … 1 Tim 5:4
the one who *p-s* sin … 1 John 3:8

PRAETORIAN / PRAETORIUM *guard* or *palace* The guards assigned to the governor of a Roman province, or his official residence.
1 *Imperial palace guards in Rome* … Phil 1:13
2 *Pontius Pilate's palace in Jerusalem* … Matt 27:27; Mark 15:16; John 18:28,33
3 *Herod's palace at Caesarea* … Acts 23:35

PRAISE (n) *acclamation, honor*
offering of *p* … Lev 19:24
sing *p-s* to Him … 1 Chr 16:9
songs of *p*...hymns … Neh 12:46
From You...my *p* … Ps 22:25
sound His *p* abroad … Ps 66:8
makes Jerusalem a *p* … Is 62:7
his *p* is not from men … Rom 2:29
anything worthy of *p* … Phil 4:8
a sacrifice of *p* … Heb 13:15
Give *p* to our God … Rev 19:5

PRAISE (v) *extol, glorify*
I will *p* Him … Ex 15:2
greatly to be *p-d* … 1 Chr 16:25
Will the dust *p* You … Ps 30:9
My lips will *p* You … Ps 63:3
heavens will *p* Your … Ps 89:5
P Him, sun and moon … Ps 148:3
P Him with trumpet … Ps 150:3
Death cannot *p* You … Is 38:18
I *p* You, Father … Matt 11:25
heavenly host *p-ing* … Luke 2:13
disciples began to *p* … Luke 19:37
leaping and *p-ing* God … Acts 3:8

PRAY *ask, worship*
Abraham *p-ed* to … Gen 20:17
For this boy I *p-ed* … 1 Sam 1:27
found *courage* to *p* … 1 Chr 17:25
For to You I *p* … Ps 5:2
P for...Jerusalem … Ps 122:6
p to a god who cannot … Is 45:20
We earnestly *p* … Jon 1:14
p for...persecute … Matt 5:44
by Himself to *p* … Matt 14:23
p and ask, believe … Mark 11:24
until I have *p-ed* … Mark 14:32
Lord, teach us to *p* … Luke 11:1
they ought to *p* … Luke 18:1
I have *p-ed* for you … Luke 22:32
p-ed with fasting … Acts 14:23
if I *p* in a tongue … 1 Cor 14:14
p without ceasing … 1 Thess 5:17
p for one another … James 5:16
p-ing in the...Spirit … Jude 20

PRAYER A petition, supplication or praise addressed to God. Probably the best known from the Bible is the Lord's Prayer, i.e. the prayer which Jesus taught His disciples as an example of how they should pray.
I have heard your *p* … 2 Chr 7:12
And my *p* is pure … Job 16:17
LORD receives my *p* … Ps 6:9
Give ear to my *p* … Ps 55:1
p of the righteous … Prov 15:29
joyful in My house of *p* … Is 56:7
ask in *p*, believing … Matt 21:22
you make long *p-s* … Matt 23:14
whole night in *p* … Luke 6:12
My house...of *p* … Luke 19:46
devoting...to *p* … Acts 1:14
offering *p* with joy … Phil 1:4
but in everything by *p* … Phil 4:6
p-s...not be hindered … 1 Pet 3:7
p-s of the saints … Rev 5:8

PREACH *exhort, proclaim*
Jesus began to *p* … Matt 4:17
as you go, *p* … Matt 10:7
teach and *p* in their … Matt 11:1
p-ing...repentance … Mark 1:4
p the gospel to all … Mark 16:15
p the kingdom of … Luke 4:43
he *p-ed* Jesus to him … Acts 8:35
p...the good news … Acts 13:32
How will they *p* … Rom 10:15
we *p* Christ crucified … 1 Cor 1:23
He...*p-ed* peace … Eph 2:17
p the word … 2 Tim 4:2

PREACHER *one who proclaims*
hear without a *p* ... Rom 10:14
appointed a *p* and an ... 1 Tim 2:7
Noah, a *p* of ... 2 Pet 2:5

PRECEPTS *commandments*
All His *p* are sure ... Ps 111:7
meditate on Your *p* ... Ps 119:15
as doctrines the *p* of ... Matt 15:9

PRECIOUS *beloved* or *costly*
P in the sight of ... Ps 116:15
like the *p* oil upon the ... Ps 133:2
more *p* than jewels ... Prov 3:15
p things...no profit ... Is 44:9
more *p* than gold ... 1 Pet 1:7
with *p* blood ... 1 Pet 1:19

PREDESTINATION The doctrine based primarily on Rom 8:28-30, that God has from eternity past destined certain individuals to come to a saving faith in Christ. The basis for His choice of individuals was His foreknowledge (q.v.).

PREDESTINED *foreordained*
purpose *p* to occur ... Acts 4:28
foreknew, He also *p* ... Rom 8:29
God *p* before the ages ... 1 Cor 2:7
p us to adoption ... Eph 1:5
p according to His ... Eph 1:11

PREDETERMINED
p plan...of God ... Acts 2:23

PREEMINENT *foremost*
P in dignity ... Gen 49:3

PREFECTS *Persian officials*
shatter governors...*p* ... Jer 51:23
the satraps, the *p* ... Dan 3:3

PREGNANT *with child*
And her womb ever *p* ... Jer 20:17
ripped open...*p* ... Amos 1:13
Elizabeth...became *p* ... Luke 1:24

PREPARATION *readiness*
distracted with...*p-s* ... Luke 10:40
Jewish day of *p* ... John 19:42
making *p-s*, he fell ... Acts 10:10
p of the gospel of ... Eph 6:15

PREPARATION DAY The day before the Sabbath, on which the Jews made the necessary preparations to observe the weekly holy day (Mark 15:42; John 19:42). Since it is the Jewish custom to reckon a 24-hour day from sundown to the following sundown, Preparation Day begins at sundown (6 P.M.) Thursday and ends at sundown Friday, when the Sabbath officially begins.

PREPARE *make ready*
p a savory dish ... Gen 27:4
mind *p-s* deception ... Job 15:35
p a table before me ... Ps 23:5
P to meet your God ... Amos 4:12
will *p* Your way ... Matt 11:10
kingdom *p-d* for ... Matt 25:34
to *p* Me for burial ... Matt 26:12
p-d spices and ... Luke 23:56
I go to *p* a place ... John 14:2
worlds were *p-d* by ... Heb 11:3
p your minds for ... 1 Pet 1:13

PRESBYTERY The body or board of elders who placed hands on Timothy as part of their ceremony of ordaining him to ministry (1 Tim 4:14). In modern Protestant churches, governing bodies sometimes go by this same name or may instead be called a board of elders, overseers, deacons, etc.

PRESENCE *appearance*
My *p* shall go *with* ... Ex 33:14
in the *p* of my enemies ... Ps 23:5
the light of Your *p* ... Ps 44:3
tremble at Your *p* ... Is 64:2
the *p* of His glory ... Jude 24
the *p* of the Lamb ... Rev 14:10

PRESENT (n) *gift*
a *p* for his brother ... Gen 32:13
sent a *p* to the king ... 2 Kin 16:8
and a *p* to Hezekiah ... Is 39:1

PRESENT (v) *give, offer*
p you with a crown of ... Prov 4:9
you *p* the blind for ... Mal 1:8
p Him to the Lord ... Luke 2:22
p yourselves to God ... Rom 6:13
p your bodies a ... Rom 12:1
p you before Him holy ... Col 1:22

PRESERVE *protect*
no son to *p* my ... 2 Sam 18:18
P me, O God ... Ps 16:1
P my soul ... Ps 86:2
LORD *p-s* the simple ... Ps 116:6
p-d ones of Israel ... Is 49:6
p the unity of the ... Eph 4:3
be *p-d* complete ... 1 Thess 5:23

PRESS (n) Equipment for extracting oil from olives or juice from grapes. In Revelation the press is used as a metaphor for the wrath of God as seen in battle.
wine *p* of the wrath ... Rev 14:19

PRESS (v) *compel, force*
measure, *p-ed* down ... Luke 6:38
I *p* on toward...goal ... Phil 3:14

PRETEND *deceive, feign*
p to be a mourner ... 2 Sam 14:2
p to be another ... 1 Kin 14:5
p-s to be poor ... Prov 13:7
spies who *p-ed* to ... Luke 20:20

PREVAIL *exist* or *triumph*
water *p-ed*...increased ... Gen 7:18
not by might...man *p* ... 1 Sam 2:9
Iniquities *p* against me ... Ps 65:3
overcome me and *p-ed* ... Jer 20:7

PREY *what is hunted*
birds of *p* came ... Gen 15:11
lion tearing the *p* ... Ezek 22:25
no longer be a *p* to ... Ezek 34:28

PRICE *cost, value*
shall increase its *p* ... Lev 25:16
their redemption *p* ... Num 18:16
p of the pardoning of ... Is 27:9
it is the *p* of blood ... Matt 27:6
p of his wickedness ... Acts 1:18
kept back *some*...*p* ... Acts 5:2
bought with a *p* ... 1 Cor 7:23

PRIDE *exaggerated self-esteem*
P goes before ... Prov 16:18
you an everlasting *p* ... Is 60:15
p of Israel testifies ... Hos 5:5
envy, slander, *p* ... Mark 7:22
boastful *p* of life ... 1 John 2:16

PRIEST *intermediary* A person appointed to perform the sacred rites of a religion; therefore, a mediatory agent between God and mankind. Jesus is the Great High Priest who has replaced the priests who ministered in the tabernacle and temple. Christians individually are priests, enjoying access, by prayer, to God the Father through Christ the Great High Priest; therefore they have no need for human priests.
a *p* of God Most ... Gen 14:18
a kingdom of *p-s* ... Ex 19:6
Aaron's sons, the *p-s* ... Lev 1:5
if the anointed *p* sins ... Lev 4:3
p...make atonement ... Lev 4:31
without a teaching *p* ... 2 Chr 15:3
You are a *p* forever ... Ps 110:4
all the chief *p-s* ... Matt 2:4
show yourself to the *p* ... Matt 8:4
faithful high *p* ... Heb 2:17
have a great high *p* ... Heb 4:14
You are a *p* forever ... Heb 5:6

PRIESTHOOD *office of priest*
for a perpetual *p* ... Ex 40:15
have defiled the *p* ... Neh 13:29
His *p* permanently ... Heb 7:24
royal *p*, a holy nation ... 1 Pet 2:9

PRIME *fully mature period*
die in the *p* of life ... 1 Sam 2:33
p of life...fleeting ... Eccl 11:10

PRINCE *ruler*
Who made you a *p* ... Ex 2:14
p-s of the tribes ... 1 Chr 29:6
contempt upon *p-s* ... Ps 107:40
Do not trust in *p-s* ... Ps 146:3
Father, *P* of Peace ... Is 9:6
p-s will rule justly ... Is 32:1
to death the *P* of life ... Acts 3:15
p of...the air ... Eph 2:2

PRISCA / PRISCILLA (*Priscilla* is diminutive form of *Prisca)* Wife of Aquila, she hosted a church in her home, and assisted Paul in his ministry.
wife of Aquila ... Rom 16:3
co-worker with Paul ... Acts 18:2,18,26; 1 Cor 16:19

PRISON *jail*
Put this man in *p* ... 1 Kin 22:27
my soul out of *p* ... Ps 142:7
beheaded in the *p* ... Matt 14:10
I was in *p*, and ... Matt 25:36
opened...the *p* ... Acts 5:19
spirits *now* in *p* ... 1 Pet 3:19

PRISONER *one who is confined*
sets the *p-s* free ... Ps 146:7
a notorious *p* ... Matt 27:16
p of the law of sin ... Rom 7:23
Paul, a *p* of Christ ... Philem 1

PRIVATE *not public*
show him his fault in *p* ... Matt 18:15
but *I did so* in *p* ... Gal 2:2

PRIZE *reward*
one receives the *p* ... 1 Cor 9:24
p of the upward call ... Phil 3:14

PROCEED *go forth*
p from evil to evil ... Jer 9:3

p-s out of the mouth ... Matt 4:4
p-s from...Father ... John 15:26

PROCLAIM *announce, declare*
p...name of the LORD ... Ex 33:19
P good tidings ... 1 Chr 16:23
appointed...to *p* ... Neh 6:7
p liberty to captives ... Is 61:1
p justice to the ... Matt 12:18
he *began* to *p* Jesus ... Acts 9:20
first to *p* light ... Acts 26:23
faith is being *p-ed* ... Rom 1:8
p...eternal life ... 1 John 1:2

PROCLAMATION *declaration*
a *p* was circulated ... Ex 36:6
made *p* to the spirits ... 1 Pet 3:19

PROCONSUL *Roman governor* A governor or military commander of a Roman province.
the *p*, Sergius Paulus ... Acts 13:7
p-s are *available* ... Acts 19:38

PRODUCE (n) *yield of the soil*
land will yield its *p* ... Lev 25:19
tithe all the *p* ... Deut 14:22
earth has yielded its *p* ... Ps 67:6
precious *p* of...soil ... James 5:7

PRODUCE (v) *bring forth*
milk *p-s* butter ... Prov 30:33
cannot *p* bad fruit ... Matt 7:18
they *p* quarrels ... 2 Tim 2:23
faith *p-s* endurance ... James 1:3

PROFANE *defile, desecrate*
p My holy name ... Lev 20:3
is *p-d* by harlotry ... Lev 21:7
and *p-d* My sabbaths ... Ezek 22:8
p-d your sanctuaries ... Ezek 28:18
to *p* the covenant ... Mal 2:10

PROFESS *confess, declare*
P-ing to be wise ... Rom 1:22
They *p* to know God ... Titus 1:16

PROFIT (n) *benefit, gain*
labor there is *p* ... Prov 14:23
no *p* for the charmer ... Eccl 10:11
not seeking my...*p* ... 1 Cor 10:33
business...make a *p* ... James 4:13

PROFIT (v) *reap an advantage*
p...my destruction ... Job 30:13
what does it *p* a ... Mark 8:36
the flesh *p-s* nothing ... John 6:63
it *p-s* me nothing ... 1 Cor 13:3

PROFITABLE *useful*
not all things are *p* ... 1 Cor 6:12
godliness is *p* ... 1 Tim 4:8
p for teaching ... 2 Tim 3:16

PROMINENT *well-known*
a *p* member of the ... Mark 15:43
of *p* Greek women ... Acts 17:12
p men of the city ... Acts 25:23

PROMISE (n) *agreement, pledge*
p of the Holy Spirit ... Acts 2:33
the *p* made by God ... Acts 26:6
the *p* is nullified ... Rom 4:14
children of the *p* ... Rom 9:8
commandment...a *p* ... Eph 6:2
heirs of the *p* ... Heb 6:17
precious...*p-s* ... 2 Pet 1:4
the *p* of His coming ... 2 Pet 3:4

PROMISED *made an agreement*
land which He had *p* ... Deut 9:28
p to keep Your words ... Ps 119:57
p long ages ago ... Titus 1:2
He who *p* is faithful ... Heb 10:23

PROMISED LAND The land which God promised to give to Abraham's descendants. The boundaries of the land are stated in general terms in Ex 23:31. In the OT, it is described frequently as a land *flowing with milk and* honey.

PRONOUNCE *declare officially*
shall *p* him clean ... Lev 13:23
I will *p* My judgments ... Jer 1:16
Pilate *p-d* sentence ... Luke 23:24
God...*p-d* judgment ... Rev 18:20

PROOF *evidence*
furnished *p* to all ... Acts 17:31
p of your love ... 2 Cor 8:24
p of the Christ ... 2 Cor 13:3

PROPER *suitable*
fulfilled...*p* time ... Luke 1:20
is it *p* for a woman ... 1 Cor 11:13
as is *p* among saints ... Eph 5:3

PROPERTY *goods* or *land*
acquire *p* in it ... Gen 34:10
p...too great ... Gen 36:7
buys a slave as *his p* ... Lev 22:11
who owned much *p* ... Matt 19:22
selling their *p* and ... Acts 2:45
things...common *p* ... Acts 4:32

PROPHECY *proclamation* The words of God spoken or written by a prophet. Prophecy usually communicates what God will do in the future. In the OT, prophecies often were warnings of what would happen if the people failed to correct their sinful behavior. OT prophecies concerning the Messiah are fulfilled by Jesus.
seal up vision and *p* ... Dan 9:24
p...fulfilled ... Matt 13:14
have *the gift of p* ... 1 Cor 13:2
no *p*...of human will ... 2 Pet 1:21
the spirit of *p* ... Rev 19:10

PROPHESY *predict, proclaim* For true prophets, to speak or write by divine command. In the Bible it usually involves foretelling the future; however, many believe that it can also be equivalent to communicating God's word without the predictive element.
to *p* with lyres ... 1 Chr 25:1
he never *p-ies* good ... 2 Chr 18:7
p-ing...false vision ... Jer 14:14
P over these bones ... Ezek 37:4
sons and...will *p* ... Joel 2:28
did we...*p* in Your ... Matt 7:22
P to us...Christ ... Matt 26:68
speaking...*p-ing* ... Acts 19:6
who *p-ies* edifies ... 1 Cor 14:4

PROPHET *spokesman for God* One who conveys messages from God and thus serves as His spokesman. In the Bible, a prophet of God was genuine only if his predictions proved completely true and he urged the people to serve and obey the true God.
Aaron shall be your *p* ... Ex 7:1
a *p* or a dreamer ... Deut 13:1
I will raise up a *p* ... Deut 18:18
p in your place ... 1 Kin 19:16
summon all...*p-s* ... 2 Kin 10:19
vision of...the *p* ... 2 Chr 32:32
Woe...foolish *p-s* ... Ezek 13:3
written by the *p* ... Matt 2:5
persecuted the *p-s* ... Matt 5:12
Beware...false *p-s* ... Matt 7:15
He...receives a *p* ... Matt 10:41
the *p* Jesus ... Matt 21:11
false *p-s*...arise ... Mark 13:22
p of the Most High ... Luke 1:76
great *p* has arisen ... Luke 7:16
Are you the *P* ... John 1:21
reading Isaiah the *p* ... Acts 8:30
a Jewish false *p* ... Acts 13:6
All are not *p-s* ... 1 Cor 12:29
and some *as p-s* ... Eph 4:11
beast and...false *p* ... Rev 20:10

PROPHETESS *speaker for God*
Miriam the *p* ... Ex 15:20
Deborah, a *p* ... Judg 4:4
there was a *p*, Anna ... Luke 2:36
calls herself a *p* ... Rev 2:20

PROPHETIC *predictive*
not...*p* utterances ... 1 Thess 5:20
p word...sure ... 2 Pet 1:19

PROPITIATION *atonement* A sacrifice that satisfies God's demands of judgment for sin. Christ has provided this once for all time by His death on the cross.
a *p* in His blood ... Rom 3:25
p for the sins ... Heb 2:17
He himself is the *p* ... 1 John 2:2
p for our sins ... 1 John 4:10

PROSELYTE *(convert).* In the Bible, a convert to Judaism; formerly a Gentile.
both Jews and *p-s* ... Acts 2:10
a *p* from Antioch ... Acts 6:5
God-fearing *p-s* ... Acts 13:43

PROSPER *flourish, succeed*
I will surely *p* you ... Gen 32:12
David was *p-ing* ... 1 Sam 18:14
they built and *p-ed* ... 2 Chr 14:7
His ways *p* at all ... Ps 10:5
they *p* who love you ... Ps 122:6

PROSPERITY *success, wealth*
my *p* has passed away ... Job 30:15
soul will abide in *p* ... Ps 25:13
saw the *p* of the wicked ... Ps 73:3
know how to live in *p* ... Phil 4:12

PROSPEROUS *successful*
exceedingly *p* ... Gen 30:43
make your way *p* ... Josh 1:8
generous man...be *p* ... Prov 11:25

PROSTITUTE *harlot*
Where...temple *p* ... Gen 38:21
male cult *p-s* in the ... 1 Kin 14:24
an adulterer and a *p* ... Is 57:3
to a *p* is one body ... 1 Cor 6:16

PROSTRATE *fall down flat*
p-d himself before ... 2 Sam 18:28
man dies and lies *p* ... Job 14:10
fell...*p-d* ... Matt 18:26

PROTECT *guard, shield*
The LORD will *p* him ... Ps 41:2
LORD *p-s* the strangers ... Ps 146:9
LORD...*p* Jerusalem ... Is 31:5

He will...*p* you ... 2 Thess 3:3
p-ed by the power of ... 1 Pet 1:5

PROTECTION *safe-keeping*
p has been removed ... Num 14:9
For wisdom is *p* ... Eccl 7:12
p from the storm ... Is 4:6
let him rely on My *p* ... Is 27:5

PROUD *exaggerated self-esteem*
heart will become *p* ... Deut 8:14
recompense to the *p* ... Ps 94:2
eyes and a *p* heart ... Prov 21:4
daughters of Zion are *p* ... Is 3:16
opposed to the *p* ... James 4:6

PROVE *establish, test*
you will be *p-d* a liar ... Prov 30:6
will *p* Myself holy ... Ezek 20:41
p to be My disciples ... John 15:8
p...the will of God ... Rom 12:2
p yourselves doers ... James 1:22

PROVERB *adage, short saying*
become...a *p* ... Deut 28:37
spoke 3,000 *p-s* ... 1 Kin 4:32
Israel...become a *p* ... 1 Kin 9:7
To understand a *p* ... Prov 1:6
quote this *p* to Me ... Luke 4:23
to the true *p* ... 2 Pet 2:22

PROVIDE *furnish, supply*
p for Himself...lamb ... Gen 22:8
p for...redemption ... Lev 25:24
p-d bread from heaven ... Neh 9:15
Who *p-s* rain for the ... Ps 147:8
p...way of escape ... 1 Cor 10:13
not *p* for his own ... 1 Tim 5:8
God had *p-d* ... Heb 11:40

PROVINCE *district* or *territory*
rulers of the *p-s* ... 1 Kin 20:17
holiday for the *p-s* ... Esth 2:18
whole *p* of Babylon ... Dan 2:48
arrived in the *p* ... Acts 25:1

PROVISION *supply, requirement*
bread of their *p* was ... Josh 9:5
bless her *p* ... Ps 132:15
p-s of the law ... Matt 23:23
no *p* for the flesh ... Rom 13:14

PROVOKE *evoke, excite*
images to *p* Me ... 1 Kin 14:9
who *p* God are secure ... Job 12:6
love...is not *p-d* ... 1 Cor 13:4,5
not *p* your children ... Eph 6:4

PROWL *roam in search*
beasts...*p* about ... Ps 104:20
devil, *p-s* around like ... 1 Pet 5:8

PRUDENT *careful, wise*
a *p* man conceals ... Prov 12:16
p wife is from the ... Prov 19:14
the *p* took oil in ... Matt 25:4
you are *p* in Christ ... 1 Cor 4:10

PRUNING *cutting*
spears into *p* hooks ... Is 2:4

PSALMS *sacred songs (songs, instrumental music).* Compositions or songs of praise to God, many of which were written by David.
shout...with *p* ... Ps 95:2
P must be fulfilled ... Luke 24:44
speaking...in *p* ... Eph 5:19

PUBLIC *open*
of his *p* appearance ... Luke 1:80
beaten us in *p* ... Acts 16:37
refuted...Jews in *p* ... Acts 18:28
made a *p* display ... Col 2:15
made a *p* spectacle ... Heb 10:33

PUBLICAN (Lat, *officer of the state*). Old word for a tax collector (q.v.).

PUL
Tiglath-pileser III, king of Assyria ... 2 Kin 15:19; 1 Chr 5:26

PUNISH *chastise, penalize*
p them for their sin ... Ex 32:34
and are *p-ed* for it ... Prov 22:3
p the world for its ... Is 13:11
will *p* your iniquity ... Lam 4:22
p Him and release ... Luke 23:16
I *p-ed* them often ... Acts 26:11
p all disobedience ... 2 Cor 10:6

PUNISHMENT *penalty*
My *p* is too great ... Gen 4:13
p of the sword ... Job 19:29
fear involves *p* ... 1 John 4:18
the *p* of eternal fire ... Jude 7

PUPIL *part of eye* or *student*
as the *p* of His eye ... Deut 32:10
p is not above his ... Luke 6:40

PUR, PURIM *(lots).* The yearly feast commemorating the deliverance of the Jews from Haman during the times of Queen Esther (Est 9:28).

PURCHASE *buy*
p-d with His...blood ... Acts 20:28
p-d for God with Your ... Rev 5:9

PURE *genuine, undefiled*
mercy seat of *p* gold ... Ex 25:17
be *p* before his Maker ... Job 4:17
My teaching is *p* ... Job 11:4
commandment...is *p* ... Ps 19:8
pleasant words are *p* ... Prov 15:26
As *p* as the sun ... Song 6:10
hair...like *p* wool ... Dan 7:9
Blessed are the *p* in ... Matt 5:8
whatever is *p* ... Phil 4:8
love from a *p* heart ... 1 Tim 1:5
p milk of the word ... 1 Pet 2:2
the city was *p* gold ... Rev 21:18

PURGE *remove*
p...evil from among ... Deut 13:5
Many will be *p-d* ... Dan 12:10

PURIFICATION *cleansing* Procedures prescribed by OT law and Jewish tradition for cleansing from some cause of defilement, such as contact with a corpse.
Jewish custom of *p* ... John 2:6
He...made *p* of sins ... Heb 1:3

PURIFY *make clean*
p-ied these waters ... 2 Kin 2:21
P me with hyssop ... Ps 51:7
p...a people ... Titus 2:14
p your hearts ... James 4:8
p-ied your souls ... 1 Pet 1:22

PURIM
Jewish festival ... Esth 9:26ff

PURITY *not corrupted*
who loves *p* of heart ... Prov 22:11
love, faith *and p* ... 1 Tim 4:12
with p in doctrine ... Titus 2:7

PURPLE *color*
a veil of blue and *p* ... Ex 26:31
Those reared in *p* ... Lam 4:5
clothed Daniel with *p* ... Dan 5:29
dressed Him...*p* ... Mark 15:17
a seller of *p* fabrics ... Acts 16:14
clothed in *p* and ... Rev 17:4

PURPOSE *intention, reason*
p of shedding blood ... Ezek 22:9
rejected God's *p* ... Luke 7:30
for this *p* I have ... Acts 26:16
according to *His p* ... Rom 8:28

PURSUE *chase, follow*
p the manslayer ... Deut 19:6
They *p* my honor ... Job 30:15
the enemy *p* my soul ... Ps 7:5
Seek peace, and *p* it ... Ps 34:14
Adversity *p-s* ... Prov 13:21
p-s righteousness ... Prov 21:21
may *p* strong drink ... Is 5:11
p righteousness ... 2 Tim 2:22
P peace with...men ... Heb 12:14

PUT *place*
p enmity Between ... Gen 3:15
He *p* a new song ... Ps 40:3
p a purple robe on Him ... John 19:2
p on the Lord Jesus ... Rom 13:14
p on the new self ... Eph 4:24
P on the full armor ... Eph 6:11

PUT
1 *son of Ham* ... Gen 10:6; 1 Chr 1:8
2 *African country* ... Jer 46:9; Ezek 27:10; 30:5; Nah 3:9

Q

QUAIL *type of bird* A game bird which God miraculously provided to the Israelites for food while they were in the desert wilderness.
q-s came up and ... Ex 16:13
q from the sea ... Num 11:31

QUAKE *shake, tremble*
The mountains *q-d* ... Judg 5:5
made the land *q* ... Ps 60:2
The earth *q-d* ... Ps 68:8
q at Your presence ... Is 64:1

QUALITY *character*
test the *q* of each ... 1 Cor 3:13
imperishable *q* of a ... 1 Pet 3:4

QUANTITY *amount*
large *q-ies* of cedar ... 1 Chr 22:4
a great *q* of fish ... Luke 5:6

QUARANTINE *isolate*
shall *q* the article ... Lev 13:50
q the house for ... Lev 14:38

QUARREL (n) *altercation*
if men have a *q* ... Ex 21:18
So abandon the *q* ... Prov 17:14
are *q-s* among you ... 1 Cor 1:11
the source of *q-s* ... James 4:1

QUARREL (v) *contend, fight*
did not *q* over it ... Gen 26:22
Why do you *q* with me ... Ex 17:2
any fool will *q* ... Prov 20:3
those who *q* with you ... Is 41:12

QUART *measure*
A *q* of wheat for a ... Rev 6:6

QUARTUS (Lat, *fourth*). A Corinthian Christian whose greetings Paul sent to the church at Rome (Rom 16:23).

QUEEN *female sovereign*
when the *q* of Sheba ... 1 Kin 10:1
king saw Esther the *q* ... Esth 5:2
The *q* of kingdoms ... Is 47:5
The Q of *the* South ... Matt 12:42
Candace, *q* of the ... Acts 8:27

QUEEN OF HEAVEN A false divinity whom the Jews worshiped in the days of Jeremiah (Jer 7:18). It could be the same as Ashtoreth.

QUEEN OF SHEBA *see* **SHEBA**

QUENCH *extinguish* In the Bible, 1) to extinguish a fire or put an end to one's thirst. 2) As a metaphor, to reduce the influence or effect of something or someone.
donkeys *q* their thirst ... Ps 104:11
waters cannot *q* love ... Song 8:7
not *q* the Spirit ... 1 Thess 5:19
q-ed...power of fire ... Heb 11:34

QUESTION (n) *inquiry, problem*
Was it not just a *q* ... 1 Sam 17:29
answered all her *q-s* ... 2 Chr 9:2
Jesus asked...a *q* ... Matt 22:41
in controversial *q-s* ... 1 Tim 6:4

QUESTION (v) *ask*
q-ed the priests ... 2 Chr 31:9
Jeremiah and *q-ed* ... Jer 38:27
He *began* to *q* them ... Mark 9:33
to *q* Him closely on ... Luke 11:53
Q those who have ... John 18:21

QUICK (adj) *rapid*
is *q*-tempered exalts ... Prov 14:29
q to hear, slow to ... James 1:19

QUICK (n) *deepest feelings*
cut to the *q* and ... Acts 5:33
were cut to the *q* ... Acts 7:54

QUIET (adj) *calm, still*
he knew no *q* within ... Job 20:20
me beside *q* waters ... Ps 23:2
lead a...*q* life ... 1 Tim 2:2
gentle and *q* spirit ... 1 Pet 3:4

QUIET (v) *become calm, still*
God, do not remain *q* ... Ps 83:1
and *q-ed* my soul ... Ps 131:2
will be *q* in His love ... Zeph 3:17
Be *q*, and come out ... Mark 1:25

QUIRINIUS This Syrian government official's full name was *Publius* Silpicius Quirinius. He is also known as *Cyrenius.* In Luke 2 he is associated with the taking of a Roman census.
Roman governor at time of Judean census ... Luke 2:2

QUIVER *case for holding arrows*
your *q* and your bow ... Gen 27:3
man whose *q* is full ... Ps 127:5
hidden Me in His *q* ... Is 49:2
q is like an open grave ... Jer 5:16
fill the *q-s* ... Jer 51:11

QUOTA *portion assigned*
complete your work *q* ... Ex 5:13
deliver the *q* of bricks ... Ex 5:18

QUOTE *repeat a passage*
who *q-s* proverbs ... Ezek 16:44
will *q* this proverb ... Luke 4:23

R

RAAMSES / RAMESES
where Joseph settled ... Gen 47:11
Egyptian storage city built by Hebrew slaves ... Ex 1:11
origin of exodus ... Ex 12:37; Num 33:3,5

RABBAH *(great).* Main city of the Ammonites, located east of the Jordan River (2 Sam 12:26).

RABBI / RABBONI *(my lord, my master).* A respectful title by which the Jews addressed their spiritual leaders. It was sometimes used synonymously with *teacher.*
respectful form of address ... Matt 23:7; 26:25; Mark 10:51
master, teacher ... John 1:49; 6:25; 11:8; 20:16

RAB-MAG
title of Babylonian official ... Jer 39:3,13

RAB-SARIS
title of Assyrian official ... 2 Kin 18:17; Jer 39:3,13

RABSHAKEH
title of Assyrian official ... 2 Kin 18:17ff; Is 36:2,4,11

RACE (n) *nation, people*
r has intermingled ... Ezra 9:2
mongrel *r* will dwell ... Zech 9:6
advantage of our *r* ... Acts 7:19
you are a chosen *r* ... 1 Pet 2:9

RACE (n) *competition of speed*
r is not to...swift ... Eccl 9:11
in a *r* all run, but ... 1 Cor 9:24
r...set before us ... Heb 12:1

RACHEL *(ewe).* The younger daughter of Laban and second wife of Jacob. Being barren, she gave her maid to her husband and "conceived" through her, following the custom of the land. She later became the mother of Joseph and Benjamin.
Jacob's wife ... Gen 29:18,28
mother of Joseph and Benjamin ... Gen 30:25; 35:24; 46:19

RADIANCE *brightness*
a *r* around Him ... Ezek 1:27
His r is like ... Hab 3:4
r of His glory ... Heb 1:3

RADIANT *shining brightly*
looked to Him...were *r* ... Ps 34:5
you will see and be *r* ... Is 60:5
His garments...*r* ... Mark 9:3

RAFTS *boats*
r to go by sea ... 1 Kin 5:9
bring it to you on *r* ... 2 Chr 2:16

RAGE (n) *violent anger*
Haman was filled...*r* ... Esth 3:5
with *r* as they heard ... Luke 4:28

RAGE (v) *be very angry*
r-s against the LORD ... Prov 19:3
foolish man...*r-s* ... Prov 29:9
Why...Gentiles *r* ... Acts 4:25

RAHAB A prostitute in Jericho who aided two of the twelve spies from Israel. Figuratively, the name also denotes Egypt, suggesting the nature of a sea monster.
1 *prostitute in Jericho* ... Josh 2:1
assisted spies ... Josh 2:4-7
family spared ... Josh 2:13,14; 6:22,23
ancestor of Jesus ... Matt 1:5
example of faith ... Heb 11:31; James 2:25
2 *symbolic for sea monster* ... Job 9:13; 26:12; Ps 89:10
3 *symbolic for Egypt* ... Ps 87:4; Is 30:7

RAID (n) *robbery*
a *r* on the land ... 1 Sam 23:27
a *r* on the camels ... Job 1:17

RAID (v) *make a sudden attack*
r at their heels ... Gen 49:19
Bandits *r* outside ... Hos 7:1

RAIMENT Used in reference to clothing in general, but particularly to outer garments which are easily seen (Isa 63:3).

RAIN (n)
God had not sent *r* ... Gen 2:5
r fell upon the earth ... Gen 7:12
I shall give you *r-s* ... Lev 26:4
LORD sent...*r* ... 1 Sam 12:18
no *r* in the land ... 1 Kin 17:7
the mountain *r-s* ... Job 24:8
shed...a plentiful *r* ... Ps 68:9
r is over *and* gone ... Song 2:11
anger a flooding *r* ... Ezek 13:13
r on *the* righteous ... Matt 5:45
ground...drinks the *r* ... Heb 6:7

RAIN (v) *fall down, pour*
r bread from heaven ... Ex 16:4
the LORD *r-ed* hail ... Ex 9:23
it *r-ed* fire and ... Luke 17:29
not *r*...for three ... James 5:17

RAINBOW *colored arc in sky* In the OT, used by God after the great flood as a sign of His covenant with Noah in which He promised not to destroy mankind and animals again by water.
appearance of the *r* ... Ezek 1:28
a *r* around the throne ... Rev 4:3
r was upon his head ... Rev 10:1

RAISE *elevate, lift*
will *r* up a prophet ... Deut 18:18
LORD *r-d* up judges ... Judg 2:16
r-s the poor from ... 1 Sam 2:8
eyelids are *r-d in* ... Prov 30:13
r up shepherds over ... Jer 23:4
He will *r* us up ... Hos 6:2
Heal...*r the* dead ... Matt 10:8
He will be *r-d* up ... Matt 20:19
three days I will *r* ... John 2:19
Jesus God *r-d* up ... Acts 2:32
r-d a spiritual ... 1 Cor 15:44
r-d us up with Him ... Eph 2:6
God is able to *r people* ... Heb 11:19

RAISIN *dried grapes*
clusters of *r-s* ... 2 Sam 16:1
Sustain me with *r* ... Song 2:5
and love *r* cakes ... Hos 3:1

RAM *male sheep*
Abraham...took the *r* … Gen 22:13
a *r* without defect … Lev 5:15
the *r* of atonement … Num 5:8
r which had two horns … Dan 8:3

RAMAH
1 *city of Naphtali* … Josh 19:36
2 *town of Asher* … Josh 19:29
3 *town of Benjamin* … Josh 18:25; Judg 4:5; 19:13
4 *town in the Negev* … Josh 19:8
5 *town in Gilead* … 2 Kin 8:28,29; 2 Chr 22:5,6

RAMESES Sometimes spelled *Raamses.* 1) A northeastern Egyptian royal city in the region of Goshen. 2) One of two storage cities built by Hebrew slaves while in Egypt.
1 *Egyptian city* … Gen 47:11
2 *storage city* … Ex 1:11

RAMOTH
1 *city in Gilead* … Deut 4:43; Josh 20:8
see **RAMOTH-GILEAD**
2 *city in the Negev* … 1 Sam 30:27
see also **RAMAH OF THE NEGEV**
3 *Gershonite city* … 1 Chr 6:73

RAMOTH-GILEAD *(high places of Gilead).* One of the cities of refuge in the territory of Gad.
Gadite city E of the Jordan … Deut 4:43
city of refuge … Josh 20:8
Ahab killed … 1 Kin 22:29-37

RAMPART *bulwark, siege* A wall or embankment used for defense.
and *r-s* for security … Is 26:1
Whose *r was* the sea … Nah 3:8
station myself on the *r* … Hab 2:1

RAMSES The name of certain Egyptian Pharaohs reigning in ancient times.

RANK *position*
men of *r* are a lie … Ps 62:9
He...has a higher *r* … John 1:15
a Man...higher *r* … John 1:30

RANSOM (n) *payment* A price demanded for the redemption or liberty of a person. In OT law and later Judaism, the basic idea of ransoming was that a condemned man might in some situations escape execution by offering something in place of his life. The concept of the ransom carries over to prophecy, where God speaks of His power to ransom Israel from death. Christ offered His own life as a ransom for all the sins committed by mankind.
give a *r* for himself … Ex 30:12
not take *r* for … Num 35:31
wicked is a *r* for … Prov 21:18
His life a *r* for … Matt 20:28
gave Himself as a *r* … 1 Tim 2:6

RANSOM (v) *redeem*
You have *r-ed* me … Ps 31:5
R me because of my … Ps 69:18
LORD has *r-ed* Jacob … Jer 31:11
Shall I *r* them from … Hos 13:14

RAPTURE (Lat, *seizing and carrying off*). A theological term not found in the Bible. It refers to the future coming of the Lord to take believers, both those who are alive and the dead (who will first be resurrected), from the earth to be with Him forever. The main passage dealing with the rapture is 1 Thess 4:14-17. There are different views of the timing and circumstances of the rapture, but it is expected to occur immediately before, during, or at the end of the Great Tribulation. *see* **TRIBULATION**

RAVAGE *devastate*
famine will *r* the … Gen 41:30
mice that *r* the land … 1 Sam 6:5
r-ing the church … Acts 8:3

RAVEN *type of bird*
he sent out a *r* … Gen 8:7
young *r-s* which cry … Ps 147:9
Consider the *r-s* … Luke 12:24

RAVENOUS *wildly hungry*
Benjamin is a *r* wolf … Gen 49:27
inwardly are *r* wolves … Matt 7:15

RAVINE *gorge*
settle on the steep *r-s* … Is 7:19
smooth *stones* of the *r* … Is 57:6
Every *r* will be filled … Luke 3:5

RAVISH *seize and take*
you may *r* them … Judg 19:24
And their wives *r-ed* … Is 13:16
r-ed...women in Zion … Lam 5:11

RAZOR *instrument for shaving*
no *r* shall pass over … Num 6:5
no *r* shall come upon … Judg 13:5
A *r* has never come … Judg 16:17
Like a sharp *r* … Ps 52:2

READ
you shall *r* this … Deut 31:11
r from the scroll … Jer 36:6
who *r-s* it may run … Hab 2:2
r-ing...Isaiah … Acts 8:28
prophets...are *read* … Acts 13:27
Moses is *read* … 2 Cor 3:15
Blessed is he who *r-s* … Rev 1:3

READY *equipped, prepared*
and *r* to forgive … Ps 86:5
Let Your hand be *r* … Ps 119:173
Make *r* the way … Matt 3:3
you also must be *r* … Matt 24:44
be *r* in season … 2 Tim 4:2
r to make a defense … 1 Pet 3:15

REALIZE *achieve* or *understand*
Desire *r-d* is sweet … Prov 13:19
r-d through Jesus … John 1:17
to *r*...assurance … Heb 6:11

REALM *area, kingdom*
ruler over the *r* of … Dan 4:17
kingdom is not...*r* … John 18:36

REAP *cut, gather*
when you *r*...harvest … Lev 19:9
iniquity will *r* vanity … Prov 22:8
they *r* the whirlwind … Hos 8:7
nor *r* … Matt 6:26
neither sow nor *r* … Luke 12:24
sows...another *r-s* … John 4:37
r eternal life … Gal 6:8
your sickle and *r* … Rev 14:15

REAPER *harvester*
after the *r-s* … Ruth 2:3
will overtake the *r* … Amos 9:13
the *r-s* are angels … Matt 13:39

REASON (n) *explanation*
r a man shall leave … Matt 19:5
this *r* the Father … John 10:17
this *r* I found mercy … 1 Tim 1:16
For this *r*, rejoice … Rev 12:12

REASON (v) *analyze, argue*
upright would *r* with … Job 23:7
let us *r* together … Is 1:18
Pharisees began to *r* … Luke 5:21
r-ing in...synagogue … Acts 17:17
like a child, *r* like a … 1 Cor 13:11

REBEKAH The wife of Isaac and mother of Esau and Jacob. She helped Jacob obtain the privileges of birthright by deceit.
wife of Isaac … Gen 24:67; 26:8
mother of Esau and Jacob … Gen 25:21ff

REBEL (n) *rebellious one*
Your rulers are *r-s* … Is 1:23
called a *r* from birth … Is 48:8
their princes are *r-s* … Hos 9:15

REBEL (v) *revolt*
not *r* against the … Num 14:9
r-led against...words … Ps 107:11
r-led against Me … Ezek 20:21

REBELLION *insurrection*
he has counseled *r* … Deut 13:5
I know your *r* … Deut 31:27
r is as the sin of … 1 Sam 15:23
my *r* and my sin … Job 13:23
children of *r* … Is 57:4

REBELLIOUS *defiant*
r against the LORD … Deut 9:7
r generation … Ps 78:8
A *r* man seeks only … Prov 17:11
stubborn and *r* heart … Jer 5:23
there are many *r* … Titus 1:10

REBUILD *restore*
r the house of the … Ezra 1:3
let us *r* the wall … Neh 2:17
r the ancient ruins … Is 58:12
r it in three days … Matt 26:61
r the tabernacle … Acts 15:16

REBUKE (n) *reprimand*
amazed at His *r* … Job 26:11
At Your *r* they fled … Ps 104:7
the poor hears no *r* … Prov 13:8

REBUKE (v) *scold*
r me not in Your wrath … Ps 38:1
r the arrogant … Ps 119:21
LORD *r* you, Satan … Zech 3:2
r-d the winds … Matt 8:26
Jesus *r-d* him … Matt 17:18
He *r-d* the fever … Luke 4:39
Do not sharply *r* … 1 Tim 5:1
reprove, *r*, exhort … 2 Tim 4:2

RECEIVE *encounter, take*
The LORD *r-s* my prayer … Ps 6:9
r me to glory … Ps 73:24
man *r-s* a bribe … Prov 17:23
Freely you *r-d* … Matt 10:8
who *r-s* you *r-s* Me … Matt 10:40
the blind *r* sight … Matt 11:5
ask...you will *r* … Matt 21:22
r-d up into heaven … Mark 16:19
This man *r-s* sinners … Luke 15:2
as many as *r-d* Him … John 1:12
r you to Myself … John 14:3
R the Holy Spirit … John 20:22

you will *r* power ... Acts 1:8
to give than to *r* ... Acts 20:35
one *r-s* the prize ... 1 Cor 9:24
r the crown of life ... James 1:12
whatever...ask we *r* ... 1 John 3:22
r-d the mark of ... Rev 19:20

RECHABITES
line of Jonadab ... Jer 35:6
strict life style ... Jer 35:1-18

RECKONED *accounted for*
r it to him as ... Gen 15:6
r among the nations ... Num 23:9
r...as righteousness ... James 2:23

RECLINE *lean, lie down* In ancient times, the customary dining position. Usually the diner lay on his left side, propping up his head with his left arm and using his right hand to take food and beverages.
r on beds of ivory ... Amos 6:4
r at the table in ... Luke 13:29
r-ing on Jesus' ... John 13:23

RECOGNIZE *be aware, know*
he did not *r* him ... Gen 27:23
Saul *r-d* David's ... 1 Sam 26:17
r that He is near ... Matt 24:33
I did not *r* Him ... John 1:31

RECOMPENSE (n) *reward*
the *r* of the wicked ... Ps 91:8
r to the proud ... Ps 94:2
r of God will come ... Is 35:4

RECOMPENSE (v) *compensate*
LORD has *r-d* me ... 2 Sam 22:25
He will *r* the evil ... Ps 54:5
But if you do *r* Me ... Joel 3:4

RECONCILE *bring together*
r-d to your brother ... Matt 5:24
be *r-d* to God ... 2 Cor 5:20
r them both in one ... Eph 2:16
r all...to Himself ... Col 1:20

RECONCILIATION Restoring a damaged relationship between two parties. Through the sacrifice of Christ, God reconciled humanity to Himself.
now received the *r* ... Rom 5:11
the *r* of the world ... Rom 11:15
the ministry of *r* ... 2 Cor 5:18
the word of *r* ... 2 Cor 5:19

RECORD (n) *document, register*
the *r-s* are ancient ... 1 Chr 4:22
r-s of the kings ... 2 Chr 33:18
discover in...*r* books ... Ezra 4:15
I found the...*r* ... Neh 7:5

RECORD (v) *register, write*
r-ed their starting ... Num 33:2
R the vision ... Hab 2:2
are *r-ed* in heaven ... Luke 10:20

RECOVER *reclaim, become well*
did you not *r* them ... Judg 11:26
Will I *r* from this ... 2 Kin 8:8
and they will *r* ... Mark 16:18

RED *color*
first came forth *r* ... Gen 25:25
water...*r* as blood ... 2 Kin 3:22
they are *r* like crimson ... Is 1:18
the sky is *r* ... Matt 16:2
a great *r* dragon ... Rev 12:3

RED HEIFER This animal was sacrificed and its ashes were used when necessary for ceremonial purification when one had come into contact with a corpse. An acceptable red heifer was extremely valuable because one which had no defect (Num 19:2) was very hard to find.

RED SEA The sea that the Israelites crossed during the exodus as they fled from the Egyptian army. Also called the Sea of Reeds. The actual body of water crossed was probably an offshoot of that known now as the Red Sea, and its exact location is uncertain.
Hebrew: Sea of Reeds ... Ex 10:19
body of water between Egypt and Sinai ... Ex 13:18; Ps 106:9; Jer 49:21

REDEEM To buy back. To free from captivity by payment or ransom.
I will also *r* you ... Ex 6:6
family may *r* him ... Lev 25:49
wish to *r* the field ... Lev 27:19
I will *r it* ... Ruth 4:4
God will *r* my soul ... Ps 49:15
He will *r* Israel ... Ps 130:8
Christ *r-ed* us ... Gal 3:13
He might *r* those ... Gal 4:5

REDEEMER *one who buys back* Someone who repurchases property or liberates a slave. In the NT, primarily a designation for the Lord Jesus Christ in His role of redeeming from the slave market of sin those who believe in Him.
left you without a *r* ... Ruth 4:14
know that my *R* lives ... Job 19:25
my rock and my *R* ... Ps 19:14
your *R* is the Holy ... Is 41:14
our Father, Our *R* ... Is 63:16
Their *R* is strong ... Jer 50:34

REDEMPTION *deliverance* The act by which an owner recovers what was previously his by a trade or payment. In reference to Christ, redemption is the payment for the sins of the world which He provided by His death on the cross, freeing all those who trust in Him from the condemnation of eternal punishment.
r of the land ... Lev 25:24
have my right of *r* ... Ruth 4:6
r of his soul is ... Ps 49:8
r is drawing near ... Luke 21:28
r...in Christ Jesus ... Rom 3:24
r of our body ... Rom 8:23
r through His blood ... Eph 1:7
in whom we have *r* ... Col 1:14
obtained eternal *r* ... Heb 9:12

REED *tall marsh grass* A tall grass with slender stems that usually grows in wet areas. Often seen in prophecy as a symbol of fragility or flexibility. Also an instrument of linear measurement equal to six cubits or about nine feet.
set *it* among the *r-s* ... Ex 2:3
bruised *r* He will ... Is 42:3
the *r*...to beat Him ... Matt 27:30
and put it on a *r* ... Matt 27:48

REEL *stagger, sway*
earth *r-s* to and fro ... Is 24:20
r with strong drink ... Is 28:7

REFINE *purify*
r-d seven times ... Ps 12:6
in order to *r* ... Dan 11:35
R them as silver ... Zech 13:9
r them like gold ... Mal 3:3
gold *r-d* by fire ... Rev 3:18

REFRAIN *abstain*
not *r* from spitting ... Job 30:10
to *r* from working ... 1 Cor 9:6
r from judging ... Rev 6:10

REFRESH *renew, replenish*
you may *r* yourselves ... Gen 18:5
R me with apples ... Song 2:5
times of *r-ing* may ... Acts 3:19
r my heart in Christ ... Philem 20

REFUGE *protection, shelter*
in whom I take *r* ... 2 Sam 22:3
God is our *r* ... Ps 46:1
r in the LORD ... Ps 118:8
the *r* of lies ... Is 28:17
r in...distress ... Jer 16:19
who have taken *r* ... Heb 6:18

REFUGE, CITIES OF *see* **CITIES OF REFUGE**

REFUSE (n) *waste*
be made a *r* heap ... Ezra 6:11
corpses lay like *r* ... Is 5:25
its waters toss up *r* ... Is 57:20
sell...*r* of the wheat ... Amos 8:6

REFUSE (v) *decline*
r you his grave ... Gen 23:6
r to let My people go ... Ex 10:4
his hands *r* to work ... Prov 21:25
they *r* to know Me ... Jer 9:6
r-d to be comforted ... Matt 2:18
can *r* the water ... Acts 10:47
not *r* Him who is ... Heb 12:25

REFUSE GATE *see* **GATES OF JERUSALEM**

REFUTE *prove wrong*
R me if you can ... Job 33:5
he...*r-d* the Jews ... Acts 18:28
to *r* those who ... Titus 1:9

REGAIN *recover*
r-ed their sight ... Matt 20:34
want to *r* my sight ... Mark 10:51
he might *r* his sight ... Acts 9:12

REGARD (n) *respect*
LORD had *r* for Abel ... Gen 4:4
r to the prayer ... 1 Kin 8:28
have *r* for his Maker ... Is 17:7
r for the humble ... Luke 1:48

REGARD (v) *esteem, respect*
If I *r* wickedness ... Ps 66:18
Yet He *r-s* the lowly ... Ps 138:6
who *r-s* reproof ... Prov 15:5
highly *r-ed* by him ... Luke 7:2
r one another ... Phil 2:3
did not *r* equality ... Phil 2:6

REGENERATION *renewal* In the NT, 1) spiritual renewal, what God does at the moment of salvation when someone accepts Christ as Savior and Lord. The person begins to enjoy the presence of Christ and the Holy Spirit in his life and becomes a member of the body of Christ. 2) A reference to life in the Messiah's

kingdom on earth when all believers will have new immortal bodies.
the washing of *r* ... Titus 3:5
r when the Son ... Matt 19:28

REGION *area*
r of the Jordan ... Josh 22:10
the *r-s* of Galilee ... Matt 2:22
to the *r* of Judea ... Mark 10:1
same *r*...shepherds ... Luke 2:8

REGISTER *enroll, record*
r...people of Israel ... 2 Sam 24:4
to *r* for the census ... Luke 2:3

REHOBOAM *(may the people enlarge).* A son of Solomon and his successor. Due to his lack of wisdom, the land of Israel became divided into the southern kingdom (Judah) and the northern (Israel).
son of Solomon ... 1 Kin 11:43
king of Judah ... 1 Kin 12:16ff; 2 Chr 11:1ff

REIGN *rule*
LORD shall *r* forever ... Ex 15:18
Shall Saul *r* over ... 1 Sam 11:12
David *r-ed* over all ... 2 Sam 8:15
The LORD *r-s* ... Ps 93:1
By me kings *r* ... Prov 8:15
will *r* righteously ... Is 32:1
death *r-ed*...Adam ... Rom 5:14
He must *r* until ... 1 Cor 15:25
also *r* with Him ... 2 Tim 2:12
He will *r* forever ... Rev 11:15
will *r* with Him ... Rev 20:6

REJECT *decline, refuse*
have *r-ed* the LORD ... Num 11:20
will *r* you forever ... 1 Chr 28:9
not *r* the discipline ... Prov 3:11
A fool *r-s* his ... Prov 15:5
have *r-ed* this word ... Is 30:12
He who *r-s* unjust gain ... Is 33:15
r-ed My ordinances ... Ezek 20:13
have *r-ed* knowledge ... Hos 4:6
they *r-ed* the law ... Amos 2:4
the builders *r-ed* ... Matt 21:42
who *r-s* you *r-s* Me ... Luke 10:16
He who *r-s* Me ... John 12:48

REJOICE *be glad*
r before the LORD ... Lev 23:40
R, O nations ... Deut 32:43
I *r* in Your salvation ... 1 Sam 2:1
let the earth *r* ... 1 Chr 16:31
my soul shall *r* ... Ps 35:9
king will *r* in God ... Ps 63:11
Let us *r* and be glad ... Ps 118:24
I *r* at Your word ... Ps 119:162
R, young man ... Eccl 11:9
God will *r* over you ... Is 62:5
r-d exceedingly ... Matt 2:10
r at his birth ... Luke 1:14
crowd was *r-ing* ... Luke 13:17
you would have *r-d* ... John 14:28
r-ing in hope ... Rom 12:12
yet always *r-ing* ... 2 Cor 6:10
R in the Lord ... Phil 4:4
I *r* in my sufferings ... Col 1:24
r, O heavens ... Rev 12:12

REJOICING (n) *delight*
a holiday for *r* ... Esth 9:19
hills gird...with *r* ... Ps 65:12
Jerusalem *for r* ... Is 65:18

RELATIONS *sexual intercourse*
r with his wife Eve ... Gen 4:1
had no *r* with a man ... Judg 11:39
we may have *r* with ... Judg 19:22
had *r* with Hannah ... 1 Sam 1:19

RELATIVE *kinsman*
and to my *r-s* ... Gen 24:4
The man is our *r* ... Ruth 2:20
My *r-s* have failed ... Job 19:14
among his *own r-s* ... Mark 6:4
your *r* Elizabeth has ... Luke 1:36

RELEASE (n) *liberation*
a *r* through the land ... Lev 25:10
r for you the King ... Mark 15:9
r to the captives ... Luke 4:18

RELEASE (v) *set free*
he *r-d* Barabbas ... Matt 27:26
wanting to *r* Jesus ... Luke 23:20
efforts to *r* Him ... John 19:12
you *r-d* from a wife ... 1 Cor 7:27
r-d us from our sins ... Rev 1:5
R the four angels ... Rev 9:14

RELENT *yield*
I am tired of *r-ing* ... Jer 15:6
r...the calamity ... Jer 18:8
whether He will...*r* ... Joel 2:14
God may turn and *r* ... Jon 3:9

RELIEF *lessening of burden*
r and deliverance ... Esth 4:14
my *prayer for r* ... Lam 3:56
r of the brethren ... Acts 11:29

RELIGION *system of belief*
about their own *r* ... Acts 25:19
sect of our *r* ... Acts 26:5
pure and undefiled *r* ... James 1:27

RELIGIOUS *devout, pious*
r in all respects ... Acts 17:22
thinks...to be *r* ... James 1:26

RELY *depend, trust*
r-ied on the LORD ... 2 Chr 16:8
who...*r* on horses ... Is 31:1
r on his God ... Is 50:10
You *r* on your sword ... Ezek 33:26
r upon the Law ... Rom 2:17

REMAIN *abide, be left*
While the earth *r-s* ... Gen 8:22
R...in his place ... Ex 16:29
ark...not *r* with us ... 1 Sam 5:7
r-s yet...youngest ... 1 Sam 16:11
flee to Egypt, and *r* ... Matt 2:13
dove...*r-ed* upon ... John 1:32
not *r* in darkness ... John 12:46
not *r* on the cross ... John 19:31
she must *r* unmarried ... 1 Cor 7:11
gospel would *r* ... Gal 2:5
He *r-s* faithful ... 2 Tim 2:13

REMEMBER *recall, recollect*
God *r-ed* Noah ... Gen 8:1
I will *r* My covenant ... Gen 9:15
R the sabbath day ... Ex 20:8
not *r* the sins of my ... Ps 25:7
R also your Creator ... Eccl 12:1
O LORD, *R* me ... Jer 15:15
sin I will *r* no more ... Jer 31:34
Peter *r-ed* the word ... Matt 26:75
R Lot's wife ... Luke 17:32
r the words of ... Acts 20:35
to *r* the poor ... Gal 2:10

REMEMBRANCE *memory*
Your *r*, O LORD ... Ps 135:13
Put Me in *r* ... Is 43:26
a book of *r* was ... Mal 3:16
do this in *r* of Me ... Luke 22:19
in *r* of Me ... 1 Cor 11:25

REMNANT *remaining part*
preserve for you a *r* ... Gen 45:7
prayer for the *r* ... 2 Kin 19:4
an escaped *r* ... Ezra 9:8
A *r* will return ... Is 10:21
the *r* of Israel ... Jer 6:9
a *r* of the Spirit ... Mal 2:15
r that will be saved ... Rom 9:27

REMOVE *take away* or *off*
r your sandals ... Ex 3:5
r-d all the idols ... 1 Kin 15:12
He *r-d* the high ... 2 Kin 18:4
r the heart of stone ... Ezek 36:26
not fit to *r* His ... Matt 3:11
r this cup from Me ... Luke 22:42
R the stone ... John 11:39
as to *r* mountains ... 1 Cor 13:2

REND *tear*
r the heavens ... Is 64:1
r their garments ... Jer 36:24
r your heart and not ... Joel 2:13

RENDER *inflict, repay*
I will *r* vengeance ... Deut 32:41
R recompense to the ... Ps 94:2
r to Caesar the ... Matt 22:21
R to all what is due ... Rom 13:7

RENEW *make new, revive*
r a steadfast spirit ... Ps 51:10
r-ed like the eagle ... Ps 103:5
R our days as of old ... Lam 5:21
inner man...*r-ed* ... 2 Cor 4:16

RENOWN *fame*
men of *r* ... Gen 6:4
a people, for *r* ... Jer 13:11
shame into...and *r* ... Zeph 3:19

REPAIR *restore*
r the house of ... 1 Chr 26:27
r-ing...foundations ... Ezra 4:12
r of the walls ... Neh 4:7

REPAY *pay back*
you thus *r* the LORD ... Deut 32:6
so God has *repaid* ... Judg 1:7
LORD *r* the evildoer ... 2 Sam 3:39
repaid me evil for ... Ps 109:5
r their iniquity ... Jer 16:18
He will fully *r* ... Jer 51:56
is Mine, I will *r* ... Rom 12:19
no one *r-s*...evil ... 1 Thess 5:15

REPENT *change mind*
that He should *r* ... Num 23:19
r in dust and ashes ... Job 42:6
have refused to *r* ... Jer 5:3
R, for the kingdom ... Matt 3:2
r-ed long ago in ... Matt 11:21
r and believe ... Mark 1:15
one sinner who *r-s* ... Luke 15:7
R...be baptized ... Acts 2:38
all...should *r* ... Acts 17:30
r and turn to God ... Acts 26:20

REPENTANCE *change of mind* To stop living a sinful lifestyle, or to determine to refrain from committing a particular sin.

Usually accompanied by regret and the desire for forgiveness; but the key element is a change of mind and attitude from one's former outlook or way of life. In the OT, regret or repentance on God's part is anthropomorphic (a figure of speech). It is not to be taken literally, but to describe God's ways in human terms, which are necessarily limited.
with water for *r* ... Matt 3:11
baptism of *r* ... Mark 1:4
r for forgiveness ... Luke 24:47
appropriate to *r* ... Acts 26:20
r without regret ... 2 Cor 7:10
r from dead works ... Heb 6:1
to come to *r* ... 2 Pet 3:9

REPHAIM A people tall in stature who descended from the Nephilim (giants) and lived during the time of Abraham. Also a valley southwest of Jerusalem.
1 *pre-Israelite people of Palestine* ... Gen 14:5; 15:20
people of large stature
2 *valley near Jerusalem* ... Josh 15:8; 2 Sam 23:13

REPHIDIM An encampment where the people of Israel complained about lack of water. Moses provided it for them by striking the rock of Horeb.
Israelite campsite in Sinai ... Ex 17:1,8; Num 33:14,15

REPORT *account, statement*
not bear a false *r* ... Ex 23:1
r concerning Him ... Luke 7:17
has believed our *r* ... John 12:38

REPRESENTATION *likeness*
exact *r* of His nature ... Heb 1:3

REPRESENTATIVE *substitute*
people's *r* before God ... Ex 18:19
the king's *r* ... Neh 11:24

REPROACH (n) *dishonor*
taken away my *r* ... Gen 30:23
a *r* on all Israel ... 1 Sam 11:2
I have become a *r* ... Ps 31:11
with dishonor...*r* ... Prov 18:3
not fear the *r* of ... Is 51:7
the *r* of Christ ... Heb 11:26

REPROACH (v) *accuse, rebuke*
to *r* the living God ... 2 Kin 19:4
My heart does not *r* ... Job 27:6
foolish man *r-es* You ... Ps 74:22
enemies have *r-ed* me ... Ps 102:8
He *r-ed* them for ... Mark 16:14

REPROOF *correction, rebuke* In the Bible, constructive censure meant to correct sinful behavior and to enable the offending person to avoid future punishment or harm to himself. As such, reproof is to be appreciated and followed.
spurned all my *r* ... Prov 1:30
regards *r* is sensible ... Prov 15:5
who hates *r* will ... Prov 15:10
and *r* give wisdom ... Prov 29:15
for teaching, for *r* ... 2 Tim 3:16

REPROVE *correct, rebuke*
r your neighbor ... Lev 19:17
LORD loves He *r-s* ... Prov 3:12
Do not *r* a scoffer ... Prov 9:8
R the ruthless ... Is 1:17
r, rebuke, exhort ... 2 Tim 4:2
whom I love, I *r* ... Rev 3:19

REPTILE *snake*
and the sand *r* ... Lev 11:30
r-s of the earth ... Mic 7:17
r-s and creatures ... James 3:7

REPUTATION *character*
seven men of good *r* ... Acts 6:3
a *r* for good works ... 1 Tim 5:10

REQUEST *desire, petition*
my people as my *r* ... Esth 7:3
the *r* of his lips ... Ps 21:2
He gave them their *r* ... Ps 106:15
r-s be made known to ... Phil 4:6

REQUIRE *demand, insist*
r your lifeblood ... Gen 9:5
God *r* from you ... Deut 10:12
as each day *r-d* ... Ezra 3:4
your soul is *r-d* ... Luke 12:20
r-d of stewards ... 1 Cor 4:2

REQUIREMENT *necessity*
r-s of the Lord ... Luke 1:6
r of the Law ... Rom 8:4
law of physical *r* ... Heb 7:16

RESCUE *deliver, redeem*
O LORD, *r* my soul ... Ps 6:4
R the weak and needy ... Ps 82:4
He delivers and *r-s* ... Dan 6:27
The Lord will *r* me ... 2 Tim 4:18
r the godly from ... 2 Pet 2:9

RESERVE *retain, store up*
r-d a blessing for ... Gen 27:36
darkness...in *r* ... Job 20:26
lips may *r* knowledge ... Prov 5:2
r-s wrath for ... Nah 1:2
r-d in heaven ... 1 Pet 1:4
r-d for fire ... 2 Pet 3:7

RESIDE *dwell, live*
stranger who *r-s* ... Lev 19:34
a son of man *r* in it ... Jer 49:18
those who *r* as aliens ... 1 Pet 1:1

RESIST *oppose, withstand*
not *r* an evil person ... Matt 5:39
none...able to *r* ... Luke 21:15
r-ing the Holy Spirit ... Acts 7:51
whoever *r-s* authority ... Rom 13:2
R the devil ... James 4:7

RESPECT (n) *regard*
no *r* for the old ... Deut 28:50
where is My *r* ... Mal 1:6
please *Him* in all *r-s* ... Col 1:10
to your masters...*r* ... 1 Pet 2:18

RESPECT (v) *esteem*
They will *r* my son ... Matt 21:37
not fear God nor *r* ... Luke 18:4
R what is right ... Rom 12:17
wife...*r-s* her husband ... Eph 5:33

RESPOND *answer, reply*
He will *r* to them ... Is 19:22
r to the heavens ... Hos 2:21
how you should *r* ... Col 4:6
Peter *r-ed* to her ... Acts 5:8

REST (n) *remainder*
r turned and fled ... Judg 20:45
the *r* of the exiles ... Ezra 6:16
the *r* of your days ... Prov 19:20
I will slay the *r* ... Amos 9:1
to the *r*...parables ... Luke 8:10

REST (n) *tranquility*
r from our work ... Gen 5:29
sabbath of solemn *r* ... Lev 16:31
God gives you *r* ... Josh 1:13
the weary are at *r* ... Job 3:17
Return to your *r* ... Ps 116:7
whole earth is at *r* ... Is 14:7
there is no *r* ... Lam 5:5
I will give you *r* ... Matt 11:28
no *r* for my spirit ... 2 Cor 2:13
not enter My *r* ... Heb 3:11
no *r* day and night ... Rev 14:11

REST (v) *settled, refresh*
the ark *r-ed* upon ... Gen 8:4
glory...LORD *r-ed* ... Ex 24:16
Spirit *r-ed* upon ... Num 11:25
R in the LORD ... Ps 37:7
Wisdom *r-s* in ... Prov 14:33
government will *r* on ... Is 9:6
iniquity *r-ed* on ... Ezek 32:27
r-ed on the seventh ... Heb 4:4
r from their labors ... Rev 14:13

RESTING PLACE
dove found no *r* ... Gen 8:9
This is My *r* forever ... Ps 132:14
Do not destroy his *r* ... Prov 24:15
r will be glorious ... Is 11:10

RESTITUTION *reparation*
owner...make *r* ... Ex 21:34
make *r* in full ... Num 5:7
r for the lamb ... 2 Sam 12:6

RESTORE *reestablish, replace*
son he had *r-d* to ... 2 Kin 8:1
they *r-d* Jerusalem ... Neh 3:8
r His righteousness ... Job 33:26
He *r-s* my soul ... Ps 23:3
R to me the joy ... Ps 51:12
O God, *r* us ... Ps 80:3
the LORD *r-s* Zion ... Is 52:8
R us to You ... Lam 5:21
his hand was *r-d* ... Mark 3:5
r-ing the kingdom ... Acts 1:6

RESTRAIN *hold back*
the rain...was *r-ed* ... Gen 8:2
who can *r* Him ... Job 11:10
He *r-ed* His anger ... Ps 78:38
who *r-s* his lips ... Prov 10:19
Will You *r* Yourself ... Is 64:12
R your voice from ... Jer 31:16
r-ed the crowds ... Acts 14:18

RESULT (n) *consequence, effect*
a *r* of the anguish ... Is 53:11
not as a *r* of works ... Eph 2:9
have *its* perfect *r* ... James 1:4
as a *r* of the works ... James 2:22

RESULT (v) *follow, happen*
r-ed In reproach ... Jer 20:8
sin *r-ing* in death ... Rom 6:16
proved to *r* in death ... Rom 7:10
r-ing in salvation ... Rom 10:10

RESURRECTION The miracle of a dead person's coming back to life. The resurrection of Christ is the cornerstone of the Christian faith and the proof that all believers who have died will one day be

resurrected as well. The apostle Paul says that if Christ had not been resurrected, Christians would be *of all men most to be pitied* (1 Cor 15:19).
who say...no *r* ... Matt 22:23
r of the righteous ... Luke 14:14
being sons of the *r* ... Luke 20:36
r of judgment ... John 5:29
the *r* and the life ... John 11:25
r of the dead ... Acts 24:21
if there is no *r* ... 1 Cor 15:13
power of His *r* ... Phil 3:10
hope through the *r* ... 1 Pet 1:3
This is the first *r* ... Rev 20:5

RETRIBUTION *punishment*
days of *r* have come ... Hos 9:7
stumbling block...*r* ... Rom 11:9
dealing out *r* to ... 2 Thess 1:8

RETURN *go back* or *repay*
to dust you shall *r* ... Gen 3:19
r-ed me evil for ... 1 Sam 25:21
clouds *r* after the ... Eccl 12:2
a remnant...will *r* ... Is 10:22
ransomed...will *r* ... Is 51:11
r-ed to Galilee ... Luke 4:14
repent and *r* ... Acts 3:19
not *r-ing* evil for ... 1 Pet 3:9

REUBEN, REUBENITES The first son of Jacob by Leah. The tribe formed by his descendants are called Reubenites.
1 *son of Jacob / Leah* ... Gen 29:32
2 *tribe* ... Ex 6:14; Num 1:21

REVEAL *expose, make known*
God had *r-ed* Himself ... Gen 35:7
He *r-s* mysteries ... Job 12:22
will *r* his iniquity ... Job 20:27
do not *r* the secret ... Prov 25:9
glory...will be *r-ed* ... Is 40:5
r this mystery ... Dan 2:47
r-ed them to infants ... Matt 11:25
blood did not *r this* ... Matt 16:17
Son of Man is *r-ed* ... Luke 17:30
glory...to be *r-ed* ... Rom 8:18
r-ed with fire ... 1 Cor 3:13
to *r* His Son in me ... Gal 1:16
lawlessness is *r-ed* ... 2 Thess 2:3
r-ed in the flesh ... 1 Tim 3:16

REVELATION *divine disclosure (unveiling).* Something brought to light or divinely communicated. Specifically, the apocalyptic writings of John addressed to the seven churches of Asia Minor.
a *r* to Your servant ... 2 Sam 7:27
the *r* ended ... Dan 7:28
r to the Gentiles ... Luke 2:32
r of...judgment ... Rom 2:5
the *r* of the mystery ... Rom 16:25
awaiting...the *r* ... 1 Cor 1:7
through a *r* of Jesus ... Gal 1:12
by *r*...made known ... Eph 3:3
The *R* of Jesus ... Rev 1:1

REVENGE *vengeance*
take our *r* on him ... Jer 20:10
Never take...*r* ... Rom 12:19

REVERE *adore, venerate*
r My sanctuary ... Lev 19:30
nations will *r* You ... Is 25:3

REVERENCE *respect, awe* Honor or respect shown those to whom it is due, including God and one's parents. The foundation for it is a healthy fear of one's superiors as taught in the Scriptures.
you do away with *r* ... Job 15:4
Worship...with *r* ... Ps 2:11
bow in *r* for You ... Ps 5:7
in *r* prepared an ark ... Heb 11:7
service with *r* and ... Heb 12:28

REVILE *use abusive language*
Do you *r* God's high ... Acts 23:4
are *r-d,* we bless ... 1 Cor 4:12
r-d for the name of ... 1 Pet 4:14
r angelic majesties ... Jude 8

REVIVE *bring back to life*
they *r* the stones ... Neh 4:2
let your heart *r* ... Ps 69:32
r us again ... Ps 85:6
r me in Your ways ... Ps 119:37
r-d your concern ... Phil 4:10

REVOLT *rebellion*
incited *r* within it ... Ezra 4:15
Speaking...and *r* ... Is 59:13
stirred up a *r* ... Acts 21:38

REWARD *prize* Something given in return for a service or for merit. In the NT, rewards in heaven are promised to believers, not because they truly deserve them, but because of the grace of God.
emptiness...his *r* ... Job 15:31
r for the righteous ... Ps 58:11
The *r* of humility ... Prov 22:4
chases after *r-s* ... Is 1:23
His *r* is with Him ... Is 62:11
your *r* in heaven ... Matt 5:12
not lose his *r* ... Matt 10:42
looking to the *r* ... Heb 11:26
receive a full *r* ... 2 John 8

RHODA *(rose bush)*
Christian servant girl . ... Acts 12:13

RHODES An island off the southwest coast of Asia Minor which had great commercial importance. Its harbor had the Colossus, a statue of the sun god, which was one of the seven wonders of the ancient world. Paul stayed on Rhodes during his journey from Troas to Caesarea.
Mediterranean isle ... Acts 21:1

RIB *bone*
took one of his *r-s* ... Gen 2:21
r-s were in its mouth ... Dan 7:5

RICH (adj) *wealthy*
Abram was very *r* ... Gen 13:2
LORD makes poor...*r* ... 1 Sam 2:7
not a *r* man boast ... Jer 9:23
woe to you who are *r* ... Luke 6:24
a *r* man ... Luke 16:1
being *r* in mercy ... Eph 2:4
r in good works ... 1 Tim 6:18

RICH (n) *wealthy*
r shall not pay more ... Ex 30:15
the *r* above the poor ... Job 34:19
r among the people ... Ps 45:12
The *r* and the poor ... Prov 22:2

RICHES *wealth*
R do not profit ... Prov 11:4
who trusts in his *r* ... Prov 11:28
neither poverty nor *r* ... Prov 30:8
choked with...*r* ... Luke 8:14
abounding in *r* ... Rom 10:12
r of His grace ... Eph 1:7
r of Christ ... Eph 3:8
His *r* in glory ... Phil 4:19
uncertainty of *r* ... 1 Tim 6:17
Your *r* have rotted ... James 5:2

RIDDLE *puzzle*
propound a *r* ... Judg 14:12
my *r* on the harp ... Ps 49:4
wise and their *r-s* ... Prov 1:6
propound a *r* ... Ezek 17:2

RIGHT (adj) *correct* or *direction*
r in the sight of ... Deut 12:25
r in his own eyes ... Judg 17:6
precepts...are *r* ... Ps 19:8
r eye makes you ... Matt 5:29
what your *r* hand is ... Matt 6:3
Sit at My *r* hand ... Matt 22:44
the *r* hand of God ... Mark 16:19
at the *r* time Christ ... Rom 5:6
r hand of fellowship ... Gal 2:9
whatever is *r* ... Phil 4:8
forsaking the *r* way ... 2 Pet 2:15

RIGHT (n) *due, prerogative*
her conjugal *r-s* ... Ex 21:10
r of redemption ... Lev 25:32
r of the firstborn ... Deut 21:17
the *r-s* of the poor ... Prov 29:7
r-s of the afflicted ... Prov 31:9
my *r* in the gospel ... 1 Cor 9:18

RIGHTEOUS (adj) *virtuous*
Noah was a *r* man ... Gen 6:9
LORD is the *r* one ... Ex 9:27
You are more *r* ... 1 Sam 24:17
God is a *r* judge ... Ps 7:11
A *r* man hates ... Prov 13:5
for David a *r* Branch ... Jer 23:5
LORD our God is *r* ... Dan 9:14
ninety-nine *r* ... Luke 15:7
coming of the *R* One ... Acts 7:52
r man shall live by ... Rom 1:17
none *r,* not even one ... Rom 3:10
many will be made *r* ... Rom 5:19
prayer of a *r* man ... James 5:16

RIGHTEOUS (n) *moral one* One who lives according to ethical and moral principles. Also to be declared free of the penalty of one's sins because of faith in Christ's death and resurrection.
assembly of the *r* ... Ps 1:5
LORD tests the *r* ... Ps 11:5
LORD loves the *r* ... Ps 146:8
the paths of the *r* ... Prov 2:20
the *r* will flourish ... Prov 11:28
joy for the *r* ... Prov 21:15
way of the *r* is ... Is 26:7
they sell the *r* for ... Amos 2:6
sends rain on *the r* ... Matt 5:45
r into eternal life ... Matt 25:46

RIGHTEOUSNESS One of the attributes of God, which speaks of His justice. For man, doing what is right, just and good. No one can achieve or obtain true righteousness through his own efforts, but must instead depend upon Christ to be counted as righteous by God (*see* **RIGHTEOUS** [n]) and to live a life of righteousness by His power.
reckoned it...as *r* ... Gen 15:6

will repay...his *r* ... 1 Sam 26:23
I put on *r* ... Job 29:14
in the paths of *r* ... Ps 23:3
judge the world in *r* ... Ps 96:13
declare His *r* ... Ps 97:6
His *r* endures forever ... Ps 111:3
R exalts a nation ... Prov 14:34
clouds pour down *r* ... Is 45:8
wrapped me with...*r* ... Is 61:10
The LORD our *r* ... Jer 23:6
to rain *r* on you ... Hos 10:12
to fulfill all *r* ... Matt 3:15
and thirst for *r* ... Matt 5:6
kingdom and His *r* ... Matt 6:33
you enemy of all *r* ... Acts 13:10
through one act of *r* ... Rom 5:18
breastplate of *r* ... Eph 6:14
pursue *r*, faith ... 2 Tim 2:22
the crown of *r* ... 2 Tim 4:8
peaceful fruit of *r* ... Heb 12:11
not achieve the *r* ... James 1:20
suffer for...*r* ... 1 Pet 3:14

RIMMON
1 *a Benjamite* ... 2 Sam 4:2
2 *Aramean deity* ... 2 Kin 5:18
3 *town in Simeon* ... Josh 19:1,7
4 *city of Zebulun* ... Josh 19:13
5 *rock of* ... Judg 20:45; 21:13

RING *jewelry, ornament*
make four gold *r-s* ... Ex 25:26
took his signet *r* ... Esth 3:10
As a *r* of gold ... Prov 11:22
finger *r-s*, nose *r-s* ... Is 3:21

RIOT *tumult, uprising*
otherwise a *r* might occur ... Matt 26:5
a *r* was starting ... Matt 27:24
accused of a *r* ... Acts 19:40

RIPE *fully developed*
old man of *r* age ... Gen 35:29
produced *r* grapes ... Gen 40:10
the harvest is *r* ... Joel 3:13
harvest...is *r* ... Rev 14:15

RISE *go up, issue forth*
mist used to *r* from ... Gen 2:6
Cain *rose* up against ... Gen 4:8
scepter shall *r* ... Num 24:17
witnesses *r* up ... Ps 35:11
children *r* up ... Prov 31:28
nation will *r* ... Matt 24:7
r-n, just as He said ... Matt 28:6
children will *r* up ... Mark 13:12
Lord has really *r-n* ... Luke 24:34

RIVER
r flowed out of Eden ... Gen 2:10
the *r* Euphrates ... Josh 1:4
r of Your delights ... Ps 36:8
He changes *r-s* into ... Ps 107:33
the *r-s* of Babylon ... Ps 137:1
A place of *r-s* and ... Is 33:21
r-s in the desert ... Is 43:20
peace...like a *r* ... Is 66:12
tears...like a *r* ... Lam 2:18
baptized...Jordan *R* ... Mark 1:5
r-s of living water ... John 7:38
r of the water of life ... Rev 22:1

RIZPAH *(live coal)*. A concubine of Saul whom Abner took as his wife after Saul's death.
concubine of Saul ... 2 Sam 3:7

ROAD *path, way*
a lion in the *r* ... Prov 26:13
the rough *r-s* smooth ... Luke 3:5
coats on the *r* ... Luke 19:36
the Lord on the *r* ... Acts 9:27

ROAR (n) *loud deep sound*
the sound of the *r* ... 1 Kin 18:41
young lions' *r* ... Zech 11:3
pass away with a *r* ... 2 Pet 3:10

ROAR (v) *utter a deep sound*
a voice *r-s* ... Job 37:4
Let the sea *r* ... Ps 96:11
LORD will *r* from ... Jer 25:30
a lion *r* in the ... Amos 3:4

ROAST *cook*
grain *r-ed* in the fire ... Lev 2:14
r-ed the...*animals* ... 2 Chr 35:13
lazy man...*r* ... Prov 12:27

ROB *steal*
bear *r-bed* of her ... Prov 17:12
Do not *r* the poor ... Prov 22:22
Will a man *r* God ... Mal 3:8
do you *r* temples ... Rom 2:22
I *r-bed*...churches ... 2 Cor 11:8

ROBBER *thief*
she lurks as a *r* ... Prov 23:28
become a den of *r-s* ... Jer 7:11
crucified two *r-s* ... Mark 15:27
fell among *r-s* ... Luke 10:30
a thief and a *r* ... John 10:1
r-s of temples ... Acts 19:37

ROBBERY *theft*
not vainly hope in *r* ... Ps 62:10
I hate *r* in the ... Is 61:8
they are full of *r* ... Matt 23:25
you are full of *r* ... Luke 11:39

ROBE *cloak, garment*
cut off...Saul's *r* ... 1 Sam 24:4
justice was like a *r* ... Job 29:14
r of righteousness ... Is 61:10
put a scarlet *r* on ... Matt 27:28
walk...in long *r-s* ... Mark 12:38
wearing a white *r* ... Mark 16:5
bring...the best *r* ... Luke 15:22
washed their *r-s* ... Rev 7:14
a *r* dipped in blood ... Rev 19:13

ROCK Often used figuratively in reference to both God and Christ, emphasizing qualities like strength and security.
the cleft of the *r* ... Ex 33:22
struck the *r* twice ... Num 20:11
R of his salvation ... Deut 32:15
LORD is my *r* ... 2 Sam 22:2
engraved in the *r* ... Job 19:24
my *r* and my fortress ... Ps 18:2
r and my Redeemer ... Ps 19:14
set my feet upon a *r* ... Ps 40:2
a *r* to stumble over ... Is 8:14
an everlasting *R* ... Is 26:4
his house on the *r* ... Matt 7:24
upon this *r* I will ... Matt 16:18
the *r-s* were split ... Matt 27:51
hewn out in the *r* ... Mark 15:46
a *r* of offense ... Rom 9:33

ROD *staff, stick* A stick used in biblical times for measurement and as an instrument of discipline or punishment by shepherds and others.
fresh *r-s* of poplar ... Gen 30:37
r of Aaron ... Num 17:8
break them with a *r* ... Ps 2:9
Your *r* and Your staff ... Ps 23:4
who withholds his *r* ... Prov 13:24
The *r* of discipline ... Prov 22:15
r of My anger ... Is 10:5
rule them with a *r* ... Rev 19:15

ROLL *move*
sky will be *r-ed* up ... Is 34:4
let justice *r* down ... Amos 5:24
r-ed away the stone ... Matt 28:2
Who will *r* away the ... Mark 16:3

ROMANS
citizens of Roman Empire ... John 11:48; Acts 16:21,37

ROME An ancient world empire, also the capital city of the empire. Rome is represented by the fourth beast in Daniel's prophecy (Dan 7:7f.) and by one of the heads of the first beast in Rev 13:1ff. The head suffers a fatal wound which is nevertheless healed, indicating that the Roman Empire would apparently be destroyed but would later be revived.
Italian city ... Acts 2:10
Roman Empire capital ... Acts 18:2
Paul held there ... Acts 28:14,16

ROOF
brought...to the *r* ... Josh 2:6
r...woman bathing ... 2 Sam 11:2
removed the *r* above ... Mark 2:4
r and let him down ... Luke 5:19

ROOM *chamber*
the ark with *r-s* ... Gen 6:14
go into your inner *r* ... Matt 6:6
a large upper *r* ... Mark 14:15
no *r* for them in ... Luke 2:7
r for the wrath ... Rom 12:19

ROOSTER *bird*
The strutting *r* ... Prov 30:31
before a *r* crows ... Matt 26:34
r will not crow ... John 13:38

ROOT (n) *source*
the *r* of Jesse ... Is 11:10
no *r*, it withered ... Mark 4:6
if the *r* is holy ... Rom 11:16
of money is a *r* ... 1 Tim 6:10
no *r* of bitterness ... Heb 12:15
the *R* of David ... Rev 5:5

ROOT (v) *establish* or *tear out*
r out your Asherim ... Mic 5:14
r-ed and grounded in ... Eph 3:17

ROPE *cord*
them down by a *r* ... Josh 2:15
bound...two new *r-s* ... Judg 15:13
he snapped the *r-s* ... Judg 16:12
Instead of a belt, a *r* ... Is 3:24

ROSE (n) *flower*
I am the *r* of Sharon ... Song 2:1

ROSH
1 *son of Benjamin* ... Gen 46:21
2 *place of God* ... Ezek 38:2,3; 39:1

ROT *decay*
their flesh will *r* ... Zech 14:12
riches have *r-ted* ... James 5:2

ROTTENNESS *decay*
passion is *r* to ... Prov 14:30
r to the house of ... Hos 5:12

ROUGH *jagged, uneven*
r ground become a ... Is 40:4
the *r* places smooth ... Is 45:2

ROYAL *kingly*
captured the *r* city ... 2 Sam 12:26
his *r* bounty ... 1 Kin 10:13
all the *r* offspring ... 2 Kin 11:1
put on her *r* robes ... Esth 5:1
And a *r* diadem ... Is 62:3
roof of the *r* palace ... Dan 4:29
a *r* official ... John 4:46
fulfilling the *r* law ... James 2:8
a *r* priesthood ... 1 Pet 2:9

RUDDY *reddish in complexion*
he was *r* ... 1 Sam 16:12
a youth, and *r* ... 1 Sam 17:42
beloved is...and *r* ... Song 5:10

RUHAMAH
symbolic for Israel ... Hos 2:1

RUIN (n) *destruction*
shall be a *r* forever ... Deut 13:16
become a heap of *r-s* ... 1 Kin 9:8
the perpetual *r-s* ... Ps 74:3
Jerusalem in *r-s* ... Ps 79:1
r of the poor is ... Prov 10:15
fool's mouth is his *r* ... Prov 18:7
rebuild its *r-s* ... Acts 15:16

RUIN (v) *destroy*
to *r* him without ... Job 2:3
the grain is *r-ed* ... Joel 1:10
skins will be *r-ed* ... Luke 5:37

RULE (n) *authority, government*
to establish his *r* ... 1 Chr 18:3
against the *r* of ... 2 Chr 21:8
will walk by this *r* ... Gal 6:16
above all *r* and ... Eph 1:21
according to the *r-s* ... 2 Tim 2:5

RULE (v) *govern*
r over the fish ... Gen 1:26
Gideon, *R* over us ... Judg 8:22
godless men...not *r* ... Job 34:30
r-s over the nations ... Ps 22:28
The sun to *r* by day ... Ps 136:8
By me princes *r* ... Prov 8:16
women *r* over them ... Is 3:12
r over the Gentiles ... Rom 15:12
peace of Christ *r* ... Col 3:15
r them with a rod ... Rev 2:27

RULER *king, monarch*
Joseph was the *r* ... Gen 42:6
nor curse a *r* ... Ex 22:28
no chief...or *r* ... Prov 6:7
your *r-s* have fled ... Is 22:3
Most High is *r* ... Dan 4:32
come forth a *R* ... Matt 2:6
r of the demons ... Matt 9:34
r-s of the Gentiles ... Mark 10:42
the *r* of this world ... John 12:31
Who made you a *r* ... Acts 7:27
be subject to *r-s* ... Titus 3:1

RUMOR *gossip, hearsay*
r will be *added* to *r* ... Ezek 7:26
wars and *r-s* of wars ... Matt 24:6

RUN *move rapidly*
to *r* his course ... Ps 19:5
their feet *r* to evil ... Prov 1:16
streams *r-ning* with ... Is 30:25
r and not get tired ... Is 40:31
rivers to *r* like oil ... Ezek 32:14
Peter got up and *ran* ... Luke 24:12
disciple *ran* ahead ... John 20:4
who *r* in a race ... 1 Cor 9:24

RUSH *move quickly*
and *r* upon the city ... Judg 9:33
r-es headlong at Him ... Job 15:26
herd *r-ed* down the ... Matt 8:32
horses *r-ing* to battle ... Rev 9:9

RUSHES *marshy plant*
Can the *r* grow ... Job 8:11
reeds and *r* will rot ... Is 19:6

RUST *corrosion*
in which there is *r* ... Ezek 24:6
moth and *r* destroy ... Matt 6:19
r will be a witness ... James 5:3

RUTH *(companion, friend)*. A widow who by marrying Boaz became the great-grandmother of King David and an ancestor of the Lord Jesus Christ. She and Orpah were Naomi's daughters-in-law.
Moabitess ... Ruth 1:4
Naomi's daughter-in-law ... Ruth 1:14ff
married Boaz ... Ruth 4:13
in Messianic line ... Matt 1:5

RUTHLESS *cruel*
r men attain riches ... Prov 11:16
Reprove the *r* ... Is 1:17
song of the *r* is ... Is 25:5
most *r* of the ... Ezek 28:7

S

SABAOTH *(hosts, armies)*. Term added to the name of God as in *Lord of Sabaoth*, emphasizing His might and power.
Lord of Sabaoth is same as Lord of Hosts ... Rom 9:29; James 5:4
see also **HOST**

SABBATH *day of rest (cessation, rest)*. The seventh day of the week and certain other times of commemoration in Judaism. The weekly Sabbath began at sundown Friday and continued to sundown Saturday. No work was to be done and, in addition to the OT regulations, the rabbis developed many stringent rules designed to avoid violations in questionable situations. In the NT, Jesus criticizes the Pharisees for their gross hypocrisy in enforcing Sabbath laws and tradition, even to the point of forbidding healings and thus prolonging human suffering.
Remember the *s* day ... Ex 20:8
LORD blessed the *s* day ... Ex 20:11
keep My *s-s* and ... Lev 26:2
Observe the *s* day ... Deut 5:12
new moon nor *s* ... 2 Kin 4:23
call the *s* a delight ... Is 58:13
My *s-s* to be a sign ... Ezek 20:12
is Lord of the *S* ... Matt 12:8
S was made for man ... Mark 2:27
to do good...on the *S* ... Mark 3:4
the cross on the *S* ... John 19:31
a *S* day's journey ... Acts 1:12
are read every *S* ... Acts 13:27
S rest for the people ... Heb 4:9

SABBATICAL YEAR
seventh year of rest ... Lev 25:5

SABEANS
people of Sheba in SW Arabia ... Job 1:15; Is 45:14; Joel 3:8

SACKCLOTH *coarse cloth* A coarse material used to make sacks and often worn in times of mourning. It was made of goat or camel hair.
put *s* on his loins ... Gen 37:34
gird on *s* and lament ... 2 Sam 3:31
put on *s* and ashes ... Esth 4:1
sewed *s* over my skin ... Job 16:15
with fasting, *s*, and ... Dan 9:3
sun became black as *s* ... Rev 6:12

SACRAMENT Sometimes used as a synonym for *ordinance* in reference to baptism and the Lord's Supper, but may also include marriage, foot washing, etc., depending upon the beliefs of the church or denomination observing the practice. The term is not found in the Bible.

SACRED *consecrated, holy*
took all the *s* things ... 2 Kin 12:18
perform *s* services ... 1 Cor 9:13
known...*s* writings ... 2 Tim 3:15
table and the *s* bread ... Heb 9:2

SACRIFICE (n) *offering of a life* In the Bible, usually the slaughtering of an animal or bird according to strict OT procedures. Afterwards it was placed on an altar where it was burned as an offering to God.
Jacob offered a *s* ... Gen 31:54
a Passover *s* to ... Ex 12:27
s-s of righteousness ... Ps 4:5
The *s* of the wicked ... Prov 15:8
loyalty rather than *s* ... Hos 6:6
compassion...not *s* ... Matt 9:13
a *s* to the idol ... Acts 7:41
a living and holy *s* ... Rom 12:1
an acceptable *s* ... Phil 4:18
by the *s* of Himself ... Heb 9:26
s-s God is pleased ... Heb 13:16
offer up spiritual *s-s* ... 1 Pet 2:5

SACRIFICE (v) *offer a life*
we may *s* to the Lord ... Ex 5:3
s on it your burnt ... Ex 20:24
when you *s* a sacrifice ... Lev 22:29
they *s-d* to the LORD ... Judg 2:5
even *s-d* their sons ... Ps 106:37
s-ing to the Baals ... Hos 11:2
lamb had to be *s-d* ... Luke 22:7
they *s* to demons ... 1 Cor 10:20

SAD *sorrowful, unhappy*
people heard...*s* word ... Ex 33:4
Why is your face *s* ... Neh 2:2
heart is *s*, the ... Prov 15:13

SADDUCEES A wealthy but relatively small Jewish sect which controlled and maintained the temple. They wielded major religious and political influence within Judaism, particularly in Jerusalem, and were prevalent among the most influential priestly families. Historically, the high priest, chief priests, and elders were Sadducees. They generally opposed the Pharisees. The Sadducees considered only the Pentateuch authoritative and, unlike the Pharisees, they denied the resurrection and

the existence of angels and spirits.
Jewish religious party ... Matt 3:7; 16:11,12; Mark 12:18; Acts 5:17; 23:6-8

SAFE *free from danger*
houses are *s* from fear ... Job 21:9
runs into it and is *s* ... Prov 18:10
back *s* and sound ... Luke 15:27

SAIL (n) *canvas for wind*
Nor spread out the *s* ... Is 33:23
s was...embroidered ... Ezek 27:7

SAIL (v) *proceed by boat*
they *s-ed* to Cyprus ... Acts 13:4
to *s* past Ephesus ... Acts 20:16
set *s* from Crete ... Acts 27:21

SAILOR *mariner, seaman*
s-s...knew the sea ... 1 Kin 9:27
s-s and your pilots ... Ezek 27:27
every passenger and *s* ... Rev 18:17

SAINTS *ones faithful to God (holy, separated from, set apart).* Those who have been set apart by God for Himself.
s...in the earth ... Ps 16:3
the *s* of the Highest ... Dan 7:22
s...fallen asleep ... Matt 27:52
lock up...*s* in prisons ... Acts 26:10
intercedes for the *s* ... Rom 8:27
s will judge the ... 1 Cor 6:2
citizens with the *s* ... Eph 2:19
perseverance of the *s* ... Rev 14:12

SALAMIS
city on Cyprus ... Acts 13:5

SALEM
Jerusalem ... Gen 14:18; Ps 76:2; Heb 7:1,2

SALOME *(peace).* The mother of James and John. One of the women who remained faithful to Jesus until His death and were at the tomb the morning of His resurrection. Also the daughter of Herodias, who danced before Herod.
1 *wife of Zebedee* ... Mark 15:40
mother of James and John at open tomb ... Mark 16:1
2 *daughter of Herodias* ... Matt 14:6ff; Mark 6:22-26

SALT *preservative*
became a pillar of *s* ... Gen 19:26
and sowed it with *s* ... Judg 9:45
be eaten without *s* ... Job 6:6
the *s* of the earth ... Matt 5:13
seasoned with *s* ... Col 4:6
can s water produce ... James 3:12

SALT SEA
the Dead Sea ... Gen 14:3; Num 34:3; Deut 3:17; Josh 15:2

SALT, VALLEY OF
S of Dead Sea ... 2 Sam 8:13; 2 Chr 25:11

SALVATION *deliverance* In general, rescue or deliverance from any danger. The Bible is primarily a historical account of how God has provided mankind with salvation from eternal death, which is the penalty of sin. Salvation has always been bestowed by the grace of God through faith (Eph 2:8). Those of OT times expressed their faith by following the provisions of OT law, or by their obedience to God (Hebrews 11). Since the advent of Christ, those who trust in Him are saved at the moment of their confession of faith and are no longer slaves to sin. They enjoy the benefit of an intimate relationship with God through the presence of Christ and the Holy Spirit in their lives. In the future, all believers will enjoy eternal life in heaven.
For Your *s* I wait ... Gen 49:18
He has become my *s* ... Ex 15:2
scorned...his *s* ... Deut 32:15
S belongs to the LORD ... Ps 3:8
my light and my *s* ... Ps 27:1
lift up the cup of *s* ... Ps 116:13
My *s* will be forever ... Is 51:6
helmet of *s* on His ... Is 59:17
S is from the LORD ... Jon 2:9
eyes have seen Your *s* ... Luke 2:30
s in no one else ... Acts 4:12
power of God for *s* ... Rom 1:16
now is the day of *s* ... 2 Cor 6:2
take the helmet of *s* ... Eph 6:17
work out your *s* with ... Phil 2:12
s through our Lord ... 1 Thess 5:9
that leads to *s* ... 2 Tim 3:15
who will inherit *s* ... Heb 1:14
neglect so great a *s* ... Heb 2:3
S to our God who ... Rev 7:10

SAMARIA A territory in Israel whose borders changed in ancient times, but was generally the region north of the Dead Sea and south of the Sea of Galilee, bordered on the west by the Mediterranean and on the east by the Jordan River. The region had as its center the city of Samaria.
1 *capital of N kingdom* ... 1 Kin 16:24; 2 Chr 18:9
2 *another name for N kingdom* ... 1 Kin 13:32; 2 Kin 17:24; Hos 8:5; Amos 3:9; Obad 19
3 *region of central hill country* ... John 4:4-7; Acts 8:1ff

SAMARITANS A people inhabiting the territory of Samaria who claimed to be descendants of the tribes of Ephraim and Manasseh after the exile of the ten tribes, and who viewed themselves as the keepers of the Jewish faith (based on *Samaritan* as derived from the Heb word for "keep"). The Jewish position is that Samaritans are descendants of the people of 2 Kin 24:17ff., whom Sargon, the ruler of Assyria, had imported mainly from the Babylonian town of Cuth to colonize Samaria, and that the colonists were non-Jews. At some point they converted to Judaism because the Lord sent a plague of lions to punish them for their wickedness (2 Kin 17:25ff.), but the conversion was half-hearted and after the plague ended they continued either in idolatry or in a mix of idolatry and worship of the Lord. Before and during NT times, the Samaritans were observant of some points of OT law and worship but not of others, and their status among the Jews shifted between tolerance and contempt, depending on the relationship between the two peoples at any given time.

SAMOTHRACE
N Aegean island ... Acts 16:11

SAMSON *(little sun).* One of the judges of Israel, he was a person of superhuman strength which was a gift from God, but of weak character. He was tricked by Delilah into revealing the secret of his strength and betrayed by her to the Philistines.
a Hebrew judge ... Judg 13:24
weak in character ... Judg 14:1ff
slave of passion ... Judg 16:1ff
great strength ... Judg 16:5,12

SAMUEL *(name of God).* Considered the last of the judges of Israel and the first of the prophets. He was called by God to his ministry at a very young age and was the one who anointed Saul and David as kings of Israel.
son of Elkanah and Hannah ... 1 Sam 1:20
dedicated to God ... 1 Sam 1:21ff
called by God ... 1 Sam 3:1-18
judge ... 1 Sam 7:15-17
opposed monarchy ... 1 Sam 8:6
anointed Saul ... 1 Sam 10:1
anointed David ... 1 Sam 16:12
death ... 1 Sam 25:1

SANBALLAT (unc, *Sin* [a Babylonian god] *gave life).* An influential person who opposed Nehemiah during the rebuilding of the walls of Jerusalem.
man of Beth-horon ... Neh 2:10
against Nehemiah ... Neh 6:1ff

SANCTIFICATION *holiness See* **SAINT**
Sanctification conveys two ideas: 1) the believer is in the state or position of having been set apart by God and is declared righteous by Him because of Christ's sacrifice. 2) The believer progresses in his sanctification, or godly lifestyle, through daily prayer, study and meditation on the Word of God, acts of Christian love toward others, etc.
resulting in *s* ... Rom 6:22
righteousness and *s* ... 1 Cor 1:30
will of God, your *s* ... 1 Thess 4:3
s by the Spirit ... 2 Thess 2:13
s without which no ... Heb 12:14

SANCTIFY *set apart to God*
S to Me every ... Ex 13:2
the LORD who *s-ies* ... Lev 22:32
They will *s* My name ... Is 29:23
will *s* the Holy One ... Is 29:23
S My sabbaths ... Ezek 20:20
S them in the truth ... John 17:17
s-ied by the...Spirit ... Rom 15:16
husband is *s-ied* ... 1 Cor 7:14
s Christ as Lord ... 1 Pet 3:15

SANCTUARY *place of worship*
construct a *s* for Me ... Ex 25:8
revere My *s* ... Lev 19:30
utensils of the *s* ... 1 Chr 9:29
into the *s* of God ... Ps 73:17
Praise God in His *s* ... Ps 150:1
beautify...My *s* ... Is 60:13
a minister in the *s* ... Heb 8:2

SAND
descendants as the *s* ... Gen 32:12
treasures of the *s* ... Deut 33:19
built...on the *s* ... Matt 7:26
innumerable as the *s* ... Heb 11:12

SANDAL *footwear*
s has not worn out ... Deut 29:5
fit to remove His *s-s* ... Matt 3:11
two coats, or *s-s* ... Matt 10:10

SANHEDRIN *see* **COUNCIL** *(place of those who sit together).* The supreme council and tribunal of the Jewish people in NT times. It had 70 members who were scribes, elders, chief priests, and the high priest who served as president.

SAPPHIRA
wife of Ananias ... Acts 5:1-10
struck dead for lying

SAPPHIRE *precious stone*
a *s* and a diamond ... Ex 28:18
Inlaid with *s-s* ... Song 5:14
foundations...in *s-s* ... Is 54:11

SARAH / SARAI Abraham's wife who in her old age bore him Isaac, the son who was promised to him by God. God Himself changed Sarah's name from Sarai to Sarah *(princess)* (Gen 17:15).
wife of Abraham ... Gen 11:29
barren ... Gen 11:30
beautiful ... Gen 12:11
gave birth to Isaac ... Gen 21:2,3
death ... Gen 23:2

SARDIS A city in the province of Asia. Its church was one of the recipients of John's messages in Revelation.
city in Asia Minor ... Rev 1:11; 3:1,4

SARGON
son of Tiglath-pileser III ... Is 20:1
king of Assyria

SATAN (Heb, *adversary).* The chief adversary of God and the lord of demons and evil. Many believe that Is 14:12ff. refers indirectly to Satan as indicated by Jesus' statement in Luke 10:18.
see also **DEVIL**
Titles:
Abaddon ... Rev 9:11
accuser ... Ps 109:6; Rev 12:10
adversary ... 1 Pet 5:8
Apollyon ... Rev 9:11
Beelzebul ... Matt 10:25; Mark 3:22
Belial ... 2 Cor 6:15
deceiver of the world ... Rev 12:9
devil ... Matt 4:1,5; 25:41; John 6:70; 13:2; Eph 4:27; 6:11; 1 Tim 3:6,7; Heb 2:14; 1 Pet 5:8; Rev 2:10; 20:2,10
dragon ... Rev 12:9
enemy ... Matt 13:28,39
evil one ... Matt 13:19,38; John 17:15; Eph 6:16; 1 John 2:13,14; 5:18,19
father of lies ... John 8:44
god of this world ... 2 Cor 4:4
liar ... John 8:44
murderer ... John 8:44
prince of the power of the air ... Eph 2:2
ruler of the demons ... Matt 9:34; Mark 3:22
ruler of this world ... John 12:31; 14:30; 16:11
serpent of old ... Rev 12:9

SATISFY *be content*
eat and not be *s-ied* ... Lev 26:26
s-ied their desire ... Ps 78:30
steals To *s* himself ... Prov 6:30
Nor will he be *s-ied* ... Prov 6:35
hunger is not *s-ied* ... Is 29:8
to *s* the crowd ... Mark 15:15

SATRAPS *Persian officials* Important officials in the Medo-Persian government during the times of Daniel, Ezra, and Esther.
to the king's *s* ... Ezra 8:36
the *s*, the governors ... Esth 8:9
commissioners and *s* ... Dan 6:4

SAUL *(asked* of Yahweh). 1) The first king of Israel, anointed by Samuel. 2) The original name of the apostle Paul (*see* **PAUL**).
1 *son of Kish* ... 1 Sam 9:1,2
anointed ... 1 Sam 10:1ff
first king ... 1 Sam 11:15
rejected as king ... 1 Sam 15:11ff
jealous of David ... 1 Sam 18:6ff
death ... 1 Sam 31:4ff
2 *apostle Paul, see* **PAUL**

SAVE *deliver, rescue*
s-d by the LORD ... Deut 33:29
S with Your right hand ... Ps 60:5
He will *s* you ... Prov 20:22
Turn to Me, and be *s-d* ... Is 45:22
s you from afar ... Jer 30:10
he will *s* his life ... Ezek 18:27
will *s* His people ... Matt 1:21
wishes to *s* his life ... Matt 16:25
Son...has come to *s* ... Matt 18:11
faith has *s-d* you ... Luke 7:50
world might be *s-d* ... John 3:17
Father, *s* Me from ... John 12:27
by which we...be *s-d* ... Acts 4:12
be *s-d* by His life ... Rom 5:10
will *s* your husband ... 1 Cor 7:16
Jesus came...to *s* ... 1 Tim 1:15
One who is able to *s* ... James 4:12
the righteous is *s-d* ... 1 Pet 4:18

SAVIOR *one who saves* One who saves or rescues others from danger. A title of Jesus Christ who saves those who believe in Him from sin and eternal death.
My *s*, You ... 2 Sam 22:3
forgot God their *S* ... Ps 106:21
send them a *S* and a ... Is 19:20
no *s* besides Me ... Is 43:11
righteous God and a *S* ... Is 45:21
S, who is Christ ... Luke 2:11
the *S* of the world ... John 4:42
as a Prince and a *S* ... Acts 5:31
S of all men ... 1 Tim 4:10
appearing of our *S* ... 2 Tim 1:10
our great God and *S* ... Titus 2:13
kingdom of our...*S* ... 2 Pet 1:11

SAVORY *appetizing*
prepare a *s* dish for ... Gen 27:4
mother made *s* food ... Gen 27:14

SAWS *cutting tools*
set *them* under *s* ... 2 Sam 12:31
cut *them* with *s* ... 1 Chr 20:3

SAY *pronounce, speak*
God blessed...*s-ing* ... Gen 1:22
not *s* in your heart ... Deut 9:4
to the wicked God *s-s* ... Ps 50:16
Do not *s* to your ... Prov 3:28
s-s the Preacher ... Eccl 1:2
He will *s*, Here I am ... Is 58:9
Many will *s* to Me ... Matt 7:22
If we *s*...no sin ... 1 John 1:8

SAYINGS *statements*
utter dark *s* of old ... Ps 78:2
s of understanding ... Prov 1:2
s of the wise ... Prov 24:23
anyone hears my *s* ... John 12:47

SCALE *for measuring weight*
with accurate *s-s* ... Job 31:6
false *s* is not good ... Prov 20:23
been weighed on the *s-s* ... Dan 5:27
with dishonest *s-s* ... Amos 8:5
justify wicked *s-s* ... Mic 6:11
a pair of *s-s* in his ... Rev 6:5

SCAPEGOAT *for removal of sin* The goat which on the Day of Atonement was not to be sacrificed to God, but was a symbol of atonement for the sins of the people. The high priest was to transfer all the sins of Israel symbolically to the goat by placing his hands on its head and confessing those sins. Afterwards someone who was designated for the purpose had the task of leading the goat away into the wilderness and leaving it there to die.
lot for the *s* fell ... Lev 16:10
released the goat...*s* ... Lev 16:26

SCARLET *bright red*
tied a *s thread* ... Gen 38:28
s thread...window ... Josh 2:18
lips are like a *s* ... Song 4:3
sins are as *s* ... Is 1:18
put a *s* robe on Him ... Matt 27:28

SCATTER *spread, sprinkle*
s among the nations ... Lev 26:33
Brimstone is *s-ed* on ... Job 18:15
storm will *s* them ... Is 41:16
s-ing the sheep of ... Jer 23:1
s him like dust ... Matt 21:44
sheep...shall be *s-ed* ... Matt 26:31

SCEPTER *symbol of authority* A staff or baton which a sovereign ruler used as a symbol of his authority.
s shall not depart ... Gen 49:10
s...rise from Israel ... Num 24:17
A *s* of uprightness ... Ps 45:6
The *s* of rulers ... Is 14:5
s of His kingdom ... Heb 1:8

SCHEME *plan, plot*
s...he had devised ... Esth 9:25
s brings him down ... Job 18:7
carries out wicked *s-s* ... Ps 37:7
ignorant of his *s-s* ... 2 Cor 2:11
the *s-s* of the devil ... Eph 6:11

SCOFF *mock, sneer*
s-ed...His prophets ... 2 Chr 36:16
The Lord *s-s* at them ... Ps 2:4
s at all the nations ... Ps 59:8
were *s-ing* at Him ... Luke 16:14

SCOFFER *mocker*
My friends are my *s-s* ... Job 16:20
sit in the seat of *s-s* ... Ps 1:1
He who corrects a *s* ... Prov 9:7
Behold, you *s-s* ... Acts 13:41

SCORCHING *burning*
words are like *s* fire ... Prov 16:27
s heat or sun strike ... Is 49:10
appointed a *s* east wind ... Jon 4:8
s heat of the day ... Matt 20:12

SCORN *treat with contempt*
s-ed...his salvation ... Deut 32:15
and *s-s* a mother ... Prov 30:17

SCORPION *poisonous arachnid*
serpents and *s-s* ... Deut 8:15
discipline...with *s-s* ... 1 Kin 12:11
tread on...*s-s* ... Luke 10:19
not give him a *s* ... Luke 11:12
s-s...have power ... Rev 9:3

SCOURGE (n) *whip* An instrument used for whipping or flogging. The Romans often used a short whip with leather straps in which were imbedded pieces of metal or bone, designed to tear the flesh of the victim.
the *s* of the tongue ... Job 5:21
arouse a *s* against ... Is 10:26
He made a *s* of cords ... John 2:15

SCOURGE (v) *flog, whip*
s and crucify *Him* ... Matt 20:19
having Jesus *s-d* ... Matt 27:26
lawful for you to *s* ... Acts 22:25
He *s-s* every son ... Heb 12:6

SCRAPE *rub, scratch*
plaster that they *s* ... Lev 14:41
s-d the honey into ... Judg 14:9
potsherd to *s* himself ... Job 2:8

SCREEN *conceal, separate*
s the ark with the veil ... Ex 40:3
s-ed off the ark ... Ex 40:21

SCRIBE *copier, writer* This term referred to several occupations in Jewish society, from clerks or lawyers (those drawing up legal documents) to a special class of OT scholars, traditionally beginning with Ezra (Ezra 7:6) and extending to the third century B.C. and perhaps later. Before and during NT times, there were scribes who meticulously copied OT law (Heb "Torah"), and the term was also used more loosely of teachers of the OT who are often linked with the Pharisees.
and Sheva was *s* ... 2 Sam 20:25
then the king's *s* ... 2 Chr 24:11
Ezra the *s* stood ... Neh 8:4
lying pen of the *s-s* ... Jer 8:8
chief priests and *s-s* ... Matt 2:4
and not as the *s-s* ... Mark 1:22
Where is the *s* ... 1 Cor 1:20

SCRIPTURE A term specifically applied to the Word of God, which was given by the inspiration of the Holy Spirit. Christians include both the OT and NT under the term, while Jews refer only to the OT, i.e. the Hebrew Bible.
understanding...*S-s* ... Matt 22:29
fulfill...*S-s* ... Mark 14:49
S has been fulfilled ... Luke 4:21
You search the *S-s* ... John 5:39
S cannot be broken ... John 10:35
mighty in the *S-s* ... Acts 18:24
what does the *S* say ... Rom 4:3
S is inspired by God ... 2 Tim 3:16

SCROLL *parchment* The usual form of "books" in ancient times, i.e. a single rolled-up piece of papyrus or other writing material. The name *Bible* comes from the Gr word for a scroll (*biblos*). For practical purposes the scroll was replaced in the early Christian centuries by the codex, a book with leaves bound at the spine.
these curses on a *s* ... Num 5:23
Take a *s* and write ... Jer 36:2
eat this *s*, and go ... Ezek 3:1
like a *s*...rolled ... Rev 6:14

SCYTHIAN A nomadic people from Scythia (probably around Iran), whom the Greeks viewed as uncivilized (Col 3:11).

SEA *body of salt water*
waters He called *s-s* ... Gen 1:10
s, or the *s* monster ... Job 7:12
founded it upon the *s-s* ... Ps 24:2
to the *s* in ships ... Ps 107:23
the waters cover the *s* ... Is 11:9
rebukes the *s* and ... Nah 1:4
walking on the *s* ... Matt 14:26
s began to be stirred ... John 6:18
dangers on the *s* ... 2 Cor 11:26
s of glass, like crystal ... Rev 4:6

SEA OF GALILEE *see* **GALILEE, SEA OF**

SEACOAST *seashore*
remnant of the *s* ... Ezek 25:16
inhabitants of the *s* ... Zeph 2:5
s will be pastures ... Zeph 2:6

SEAL (n) *mark, stamp* An artifact made out of a hard material, e.g. a metal finger ring, which had engraved upon it something that would identify its owner. It was used for signing documents, sealing up scrolls or marking property, usually by applying molten wax to an item and making an impression in the wax with the seal. Paul uses the term figuratively to describe the Holy Spirit's work in securing the believer.
Your *s* and your cord ... Gen 38:18
the engravings of a *s* ... Ex 28:21
the *s* of perfection ... Ezek 28:12
testimony has set his *s* ... John 3:33
s of God on their ... Rev 9:4

SEAL (v) *mark, secure*
s-ed...his seal ... 1 Kin 21:8
s it...king's signet ... Esth 8:8
a spring *s-ed* up ... Song 4:12
to *s* up vision ... Dan 9:24
s up the book until ... Dan 12:4

SEARCH *examine, inquire*
LORD *s-es* all hearts ... 1 Chr 28:9
S me, O God, and ... Ps 139:23
LORD, *s* the heart ... Jer 17:10
s for the Child ... Matt 2:13
companions *s-ed* for ... Mark 1:36
You *s* the Scriptures ... John 5:39

SEASHORE *sea coast*
sand that is on the *s* ... Josh 11:4
the *s* in abundance ... 1 Kin 4:20
the dragon stood on...*s* ... Rev 13:1

SEASON *time of the year*
rains in their *s* ... Lev 26:4
grain in its *s* ... Job 5:26
its fruit in its *s* ... Ps 1:3
in *s and* out of *s* ... 2 Tim 4:2

SEAT (n) *chair, stool*
mercy *s* of pure gold ... Ex 25:17
sit in the *s* of scoffers ... Ps 1:1
sit in the *s* of gods ... Ezek 28:2
s-s in the synagogues ... Matt 23:6
before...judgment *s* ... Rom 14:10

SEAT (v) *sit*
s-ed at the Lord's feet ... Luke 10:39
coming, *s-ed*...colt ... John 12:15
s-ed at the right hand ... Col 3:1

SEBA, SABEANS First son of Cush (Gen 10:7). His descendants were called Sabeans, an Ethiopian tribe living in a region called Seba, possibly in Africa (Isa 45:14).

SECOND COMING The future coming of Jesus Christ, the Messiah, to end the normal course of history and begin His millennial reign on earth. Theologians differ over the interpretation of various aspects of the second coming and the events which follow.

SECOND DEATH *see* **DEATH, SECOND**

SECRET *what is hidden*
sets *it* up in *s* ... Deut 27:15
the *s-s* of wisdom ... Job 11:6
the *s-s* of the heart ... Ps 44:21
bread *eaten* in *s* ... Prov 9:17
A gift in *s* subdues ... Prov 21:14
have not spoken in *s* ... Is 45:19
giving will be in *s* ... Matt 6:4
Father who sees...in *s* ... Matt 6:4
God will judge the *s-s* ... Rom 2:16

SECT *faction, party* In the NT, a religious party, e.g. the Pharisees, Sadducees, Essenes, Herodians, and Zealots.
s of the Sadducees ... Acts 5:17
s of the Pharisees ... Acts 15:5
s of the Nazarenes ... Acts 24:5

SECURE *safe, stable*
overthrows the *s* ... Job 12:19
be *s* on their land ... Ezek 34:27
s in the mountain ... Amos 6:1
made the grave *s* ... Matt 27:66

SECURITY *certainty, safety*
Israel dwells in *s* ... Deut 33:28
in it living in *s* ... Judg 18:7
provides them with *s* ... Job 24:23
will lie down in *s* ... Is 14:30
will dwell in *s* ... Zech 14:11

SEDUCE *entice, persuade*
if a man *s-s* a virgin ... Ex 22:16
s you from...LORD ... Deut 13:10
s-d them to do evil ... 2 Kin 21:9
lips she *s-s* him ... Prov 7:21

SEE *look, perceive*
I have *s-n* God face ... Gen 32:30
No eye will *s* me ... Job 24:15
s the works of God ... Ps 66:5
the blind will *s* ... Is 29:18
s the glory of the LORD ... Is 35:2
to *s* but do not *s* ... Ezek 12:2
s your good works ... Matt 5:16
and the blind *s-ing* ... Matt 15:31
s the Son of Man ... Matt 16:28
s-ing their faith ... Mark 2:5
s-n Your salvation ... Luke 2:30
we *saw* His glory ... John 1:14
No one has *s-n* God ... John 1:18
s the Son of Man ... John 6:62
you will *s* Me ... John 16:16
may *s* My glory ... John 17:24
s in a mirror dimly ... 1 Cor 13:12
of things not *s-n* ... Heb 11:1
No one has *s-n* ... 1 John 4:12

SEED *descendant* or *plant* A grain of wheat, etc., but also used to denote human offspring, e.g. the seed of Abraham or Israel.
sow your *s* uselessly ... Lev 26:16
establish your *s* ... Ps 89:4
O *s* of Abraham ... Ps 105:6
s to the sower ... Is 55:10
like a mustard *s* ... Matt 13:31
went out to sow his *s* ... Luke 8:5
s is the word of God ... Luke 8:11
s which is perishable ... 1 Pet 1:23
His *s* abides in him ... 1 John 3:9

SEEK *pursue, search for*
s the LORD your God ... Deut 4:29
pray, and *s* My face ... 2 Chr 7:14
S peace, and pursue it ... Ps 34:14
s me will find me ... Prov 8:17
man *s-s* only evil ... Prov 17:11
s wisdom and an ... Eccl 7:25
I will *s* the lost ... Ezek 34:16
time to *s* the LORD ... Hos 10:12
S good and not evil ... Amos 5:14
s first His kingdom ... Matt 6:33
s, and you will find ... Matt 7:7
s for a sign ... Mark 8:12
he who *s-s*, finds ... Luke 11:10
I do not *s* My glory ... John 8:50
s-ing the favor of men ... Gal 1:10
s-ing the things above ... Col 3:1

SEER *prophet* A synonym for "prophet", particularly in the sense of one who sees visions, e.g. the apostle John, the human author of Revelation.
prophets...every *s* ... 2 Kin 17:13
Who say to the *s-s* ... Is 30:10
Go, you *s*, flee away ... Amos 7:12
s-s will be ashamed ... Mic 3:7

SEIR *(hairy).* A range of mountains along the southern end of the Dead Sea and another name for Edom. Also a mountain in Israel and the name of an individual.
1 *land of Edom* ... Gen 32:3; 36:8,9; Num 24:18; Ezek 25:8
2 *mountain range within Edom* ... Gen 14:6; Deut 1:2; 2:4
3 *on boundary of Judah* ... Josh 11:17; 15:10
4 *a Horite* ... Gen 36:20

SEIZE *grasp, take*
mother shall *s* him ... Deut 21:19
Babylon has been *s-d* ... Jer 50:46
and *s* her plunder ... Ezek 29:19
fields and then *s them* ... Mic 2:2
seeking to *s* Him ... John 7:30

SELA
rock city in Edom ... Judg 1:36; Is 16:1; 42:11
also **JOKTHEEL** ... 2 Kin 14:7
later known as Petra

SELAH *(lift up, exalt).* An expression that occurs often in the Psalms. Its exact purpose is uncertain, but it seems to have indicated some kind of pause or interlude in the reading.
musical or liturgical sign ... Ps 3:2,4,8; 20:3; 60:4; 81:7; Hab 3:3,9,13

SELEUCIA
port in N Syria ... Acts 13:4

SELF-CONTROL
s and the judgment ... Acts 24:25
your lack of *s* ... 1 Cor 7:5
gentleness, *s* ... Gal 5:23
without *s*, brutal ... 2 Tim 3:3
in *your* knowledge, *s* ... 2 Pet 1:6

SELFISH *self-centered*
the bread of a *s* man ... Prov 23:6
s ambition in your ... James 3:14

SELL *barter, trade*
s me your birthright ... Gen 25:31
s me food for money ... Deut 2:28
s the oil and pay ... 2 Kin 4:7
sold a girl for wine ... Joel 3:3
sold all that he had ... Matt 13:46
s-ing their property ... Acts 2:45
sold into bondage ... Rom 7:14

SELLER *merchant, trader*
the buyer like the *s* ... Is 24:2
a *s* of purple ... Acts 16:14

SENATE
Sanhedrin ... Acts 5:21
see also **COUNCIL**

SEND *convey, dispatch*
s rain on the earth ... Gen 7:4
he *sent* out a raven ... Gen 8:7
Whom shall I *s* ... Is 6:8
Lord God has *sent* Me ... Is 48:16
s-s rain on *the* ... Matt 5:45
He has *sent* Me ... Luke 4:18
s-ing His own Son ... Rom 8:3
not *s* her husband ... 1 Cor 7:13
s him...in peace ... 1 Cor 16:11
God *sent* forth His Son ... Gal 4:4

SENNACHERIB *(Sin* [a pagan deity] *multiplied brothers).* An Assyrian ruler who threatened the southern kingdom, Judah.
king of Assyria ... 2 Kin 18:13; 19:16,20; 2 Chr 32:1-22; Is 36:1; 37:17

SENSUALITY
deceit, *s*, envy ... Mark 7:22
promiscuity and *s* ... Rom 13:13
themselves over to *s* ... Eph 4:19
the wealth of her *s* ... Rev 18:3

SENTENCE *judgment*
s is by the decree ... Dan 4:17
escape the *s* of hell ... Matt 23:33
Pilate pronounced *s* ... Luke 23:24
to the *s* of death ... Luke 24:20

SEPARATE *divide, set apart*
God *s-d* the light ... Gen 1:4
They *s* with the lip ... Ps 22:7
s-s intimate friends ... Prov 16:28
let no man *s* ... Matt 19:6
Who will *s* us from ... Rom 8:35

SEPARATION *division, isolation*
of his *s* to the LORD ... Num 6:6
his *s* he is holy ... Num 6:8
his *s* was defiled ... Num 6:12
have made a *s* ... Is 59:2

SEPHARAD
place in Assyria for Jerusalem exiles ... Obad 20

SEPHARVAIM
place in Aram; people relocated to Samaria ... 2 Kin 17:31; 18:34; Is 36:19; 37:13

SEPTUAGINT (Lat, *seventy*). A translation into Greek of the Hebrew Scriptures, completed ca. 250 B.C. by a group of 72 Jewish scholars, for the benefit of Jews who knew only Greek. It was held in high esteem and is sometimes quoted in the NT. The quality of translation in the Septuagint varies from the very literal to the paraphrastic, sometimes adding material not found in the original Hebrew.

SERAPHIM Celestial beings who seem to be of a high rank in the angelic hierarchy. They have six wings and appear before the Lord in constant adoration.
celestial beings ... Is 6:2,6

SERGIUS PAULUS *see* **PAULUS, SERGIUS**

SERPENT *snake* Originally an animal through whom Satan spoke to Eve in the Garden of Eden. God punished the serpent afterward by giving it the form of a snake, to which the term usually refers. In the OT, it may also refer to a kind of sea creature and in Revelation used synonymously with *dragon* as a reference to Satan.
s was more crafty ... Gen 3:1
they turned into *s-s* ... Ex 7:12
viper and flying *s* ... Is 30:6
be shrewd as *s-s* ... Matt 10:16
will pick up *s-s* ... Mark 16:18
Moses lifted up the *s* ... John 3:14

SERVANT *helper, slave* Often one who voluntarily serves others, in contrast to a *bond-servant* (q.v.). The Gr word translated *servant* is also the word sometimes rendered as *deacon* (q.v.).
s of *s-s* He shall be ... Gen 9:25
Your *s* is listening ... 1 Sam 3:9
to shine upon Your *s* ... Ps 31:16
s-s of a new covenant ... 2 Cor 3:6
they *s-s* of Christ ... 2 Cor 11:23
s of Christ Jesus ... 1 Tim 4:6

SERVE *help, work for*
shall *s* the LORD ... Ex 23:25
s Him with...heart ... Josh 22:5
s-d as priests ... 1 Chr 24:2
you will *s* strangers ... Jer 5:19
God whom we *s* is ... Dan 3:17
s God and wealth ... Matt 6:24
If anyone *s-s* Me ... John 12:26
s-ing the Lord ... Rom 12:11
through love *s* one ... Gal 5:13

SERVICE *ministry, work*
s of righteous ... Is 32:17
spiritual *s* of worship ... Rom 12:1
for the work of *s* ... Eph 4:12
s with reverence ... Heb 12:28

SETH *(appointed).* Third son of Adam and Eve, whom Eve considered a replacement for Abel, the son murdered by Cain.
son of Adam ... Gen 4:25,26; 5:3-8; 1 Chr 1:1
line of Jesus ... Luke 3:38

SETTLED *arranged* or *inhabited*
Lot *s* in the cities ... Gen 13:12
cloud *s* over the ... Num 9:18
assault shall be *s* ... Deut 21:5
word is *s* in heaven ... Ps 119:89

mountains were *s* ... Prov 8:25
s in the lawful ... Acts 19:39

SEVEN *number*
Jacob served *s* years ... Gen 29:20
For *s* women...one man ... Is 4:1
will be s weeks ... Dan 9:25
s other spirits more ... Matt 12:45
forgive...*s* times ... Matt 18:21
John to the *s* churches ... Rev 1:4
s golden lampstands ... Rev 1:12

SEVERE *difficult, hard*
famine was *s* ... Gen 12:10
a very *s* pestilence ... Ex 9:3
s and lasting plagues ... Deut 28:59
s judgments against ... Ezek 14:21
a *s* earthquake had ... Matt 28:2

SEW *fasten, join*
s-ed fig leaves together ... Gen 3:7
s-ed sackcloth over ... Job 16:15
a time to *s* together ... Eccl 3:7
women who *s magic* ... Ezek 13:18

SEXUAL
not in *s* promiscuity ... Rom 13:13
from *s* immorality ... 1 Thess 4:3

SHACKLES *fetters*
will tear off your *s* ... Nah 1:13
s broken in pieces ... Mark 5:4
with chains and *s* ... Luke 8:29

SHADE *protection*
cover him with *s* ... Job 40:22
The LORD is your *s* ... Ps 121:5
lived under its *s* ... Ezek 31:6
over Jonah to be a *s* ... Jon 4:6
nest under its *s* ... Mark 4:32

SHADOW *image of shade*
days...like a *s* ... 1 Chr 29:15
the *s* of Your wings ... Ps 17:8
in the *s*...Almighty ... Ps 91:1
the *s-s* flee away ... Song 2:17
his *s* might fall on ... Acts 5:15
s of the heavenly ... Heb 8:5

SHADRACH The name given to Hananiah by the Babylonians who took him captive. He was one of the three companions of Daniel, all of whom were thrown into a fiery furnace for not worshiping the golden idol set up by Nebuchadnezzar the king. They were miraculously protected from the fire by God.
Hebrew: Hananiah ... Dan 1:7
friend of Daniel ... Dan 2:49; 3:12-30

SHAKE *quiver, tremble*
made all my bones *s* ... Job 4:14
s my head at you ... Job 16:4
peace will not be *s-n* ... Is 54:10
s the dust off ... Matt 10:14
A reed *s-n* by the ... Matt 11:7
heavens will be *s-n* ... Luke 21:26
he *shook* the creature ... Acts 28:5
voice *shook* the earth ... Heb 12:26

SHALLUM *(payment, recompense).* The name of a number of persons mentioned in the Bible, including the sixteenth king of Israel and the chief of the porters in the time of David.
1 *king of Israel* ... 2 Kin 15:8-15
2 *Huldah's husband* ... 2 Kin 22:14
3 *son of Josiah* ... 1 Chr 3:15
king of Judah ... 2 Kin 23:31-33
called **JEHOAHAZ** ... 2 Kin 23:30
4 *gatekeeper* ... 1 Chr 9:17
5 *son of Zadok* ... 1 Chr 6:12
6 *time of Nehemiah* ... Neh 3:12
name of nine other men

SHALMANESER
king of Assyria ... 2 Kin 17:3;18:9

SHAME *disgrace, dishonor*
wicked be put to *s* ... Ps 31:17
my reproach and my *s* ... Ps 69:19
s to his mother ... Prov 29:15
wise men are put to *s* ... Jer 8:9
unjust knows no *s* ... Zeph 3:5
worthy to suffer *s* ... Acts 5:41
glory is in their *s* ... Phil 3:19
put Him to open *s* ... Heb 6:6

SHAMGAR The name of the third judge of Israel. He is renowned for slaying 600 Philistines, using an oxgoad for a weapon. *see* **GOAD**
judge of Israel ... Judg 3:31; 5:6

SHARE (n) *portion*
them take their *s* ... Gen 14:24
s from My offerings ... Lev 6:17
give me the *s* ... Luke 15:12
I do my *s* ... Col 1:24

SHARE (v) *partake, participate*
stranger does not *s* ... Prov 14:10
s in the inheritance ... Prov 17:2
s it...yourselves ... Luke 22:17
s all good things ... Gal 6:6
may *s* His holiness ... Heb 12:10
s the sufferings of ... 1 Pet 4:13

SHARON A fertile plain along the Mediterranean coast extending from Joppa to the north for about fifty miles. Also a pasture land in Gilead.
coastal plain in central Israel ... Is 33:9; 65:10
pasture land ... 1 Chr 5:16

SHARP *cutting*
their tongue a *s* sword ... Ps 57:4
S...two-edged sword ... Prov 5:4
Put in your *s* sickle ... Rev 14:18

SHATTER *break, burst*
s-ed every tree of the ... Ex 9:25
the mighty are *s-ed* ... 1 Sam 2:4
s them like earthenware ... Ps 2:9
s the doors of bronze ... Is 45:2
iron crushes and *s-s* ... Dan 2:40

SHAUL
1 *king of Edom* ... Gen 36:37,38
2 *son of Simeon* ... Gen 46:10
3 *Kohathite Levite* ... 1 Chr 6:24

SHAVE *cut* or *scrape*
he shall *s* his head ... Lev 14:9
s off the seven ... Judg 16:19
s-d off half of ... 2 Sam 10:4
will *s* with a razor ... Is 7:20

SHEAF *bundle of grain stalks*
s-ves in the field ... Gen 37:7
s of the first fruits ... Lev 23:10
among the *s-ves* ... Ruth 2:15

SHEARER *wool cutter*
silent before its *s-s* ... Is 53:7
lamb before its *s* ... Acts 8:32

SHEAR-JASHUB
son of Isaiah ... Is 7:3
name symbolizes prophecy

SHEBA A famous queen from this place visited Solomon in order to observe his wisdom for herself. The exact location of Sheba is not known, but it may be somewhere on the southwest coast of the Arabian peninsula. Also the name of a town and several other persons.
1 *son of Raamah* ... Gen 10:7
2 *son of Joktan* ... Gen 10:28
3 *grandson of Abraham* ... Gen 25:3
4 *Simeonite town* ... Josh 19:2
5 *a Benjamite* ... 2 Sam 20:1-7
6 *a Gadite* ... 1 Chr 5:13
7 *kingdom* ... Job 6:19; Ps 72:10,15; Jer 6:20
8 *Queen of* ... 2 Chr 9:1ff

SHEBAT
eleventh month of Hebrew calendar ... Zech 1:7

SHECHEM *(shoulder).* An important city in the territory of Ephraim. Jacob lived there and dug the well where Jesus had a conversation with a woman from Samaria. One of the six cities of refuge. Also the name of three individuals.
1 *city in Ephraim hill country* ... Gen 12:6; 33:18; 1 Chr 7:28
city of refuge ... Josh 20:7
2 *son of Hamor* ... Gen 34:2
3 *line of Manasseh* ... Num 26:31
4 *son of Shemida* ... 1 Chr 7:19

SHED *pour out*
Whoever *s-s* man's ... Gen 9:6
s streams of water ... Ps 119:136
hasten to *s* blood ... Prov 1:16
will not *s* its light ... Is 13:10
bribes to *s* blood ... Ezek 22:12
swift to *s* blood ... Rom 3:15
s-ding of blood ... Heb 9:22

SHEEP *animal* In the NT, used metaphorically to represent Jesus' followers for whom He is the Good Shepherd. He sometimes distinguishes them from goats, who represent unbelievers.
Rachel came with...*s* ... Gen 29:9
not be like *s* ... Num 27:17
the fleece of my *s* ... Job 31:20
s of His pasture ... Ps 100:3
All of us like *s* ... Is 53:6
a *s* that is silent ... Is 53:7
will care for My *s* ... Ezek 34:12
lost *s* of...Israel ... Matt 10:6
s from the goats ... Matt 25:32
my *s* which was lost ... Luke 15:6
His life for the *s* ... John 10:11
s hear My voice ... John 10:27
Tend My *s* ... John 21:17
Shepherd of the *s* ... Heb 13:20

SHEEP GATE *see* **GATES OF JERUSALEM**

SHEEPFOLDS *enclosure*
s for the flocks ... 2 Chr 32:28
lie down among the *s* ... Ps 68:13
took him from the *s* ... Ps 78:70

SHEEPSKINS *coverings*
they went about in *s* ... Heb 11:37

SHEET
hammered out gold *s-s* ... Ex 39:3
s over *his* naked ... Mark 14:51
object like a great *s* ... Acts 10:11

SHEKEL A Hebrew and Babylonian unit of weight (half-ounce) which became the name of a silver coin (Ex 30:13; Matt 17:27).

SHELTER *cover, refuge*
under the *s* of my ... Gen 19:8
in the *s* of Your wings ... Ps 61:4
a *s* to *give* shade ... Is 4:6
a *s* from the storm ... Is 32:2
made a *s* for himself ... Jon 4:5

SHEM *(name, fame, renown)*. A son of Noah. Shem is an ancestor of Abraham and the term "Semitic" is derived from his name.
son of Noah ... Gen 5:32; 6:10; 9:27; 11:11

SHEMAIAH *(Yahweh has heard)*. A prophet sent by God to rebuke Rehoboam (1 Kin 12:22). Also the name of several other individuals.

SHEOL In the OT, the underworld or realm of the dead, sometimes equated with Hades (q.v.).
place of the dead ... Gen 37:35; Job 7:9; Ps 49:15; Prov 15:11; Is 38:10; Ezek 32:27; Hab 2:5
see also **HADES** *and* **HELL**

SHEPHELAH
low hill country ... 1 Chr 27:28; Obad 19
see also **LOWLAND**

SHEPHERD (n) A caretaker or tender of sheep and goats. His chief responsibilities were to lead the flock to pasture and to protect them from danger and predators. Metaphorically, used of God the Father, Jesus, and the leaders of a congregation who help the flock to feed on the Word of God, and protect them from false teachers and unsound doctrine.
sheep...have no *s* ... Num 27:17
The LORD is my *s* ... Ps 23:1
Like a *s* He ... Is 40:11
s-s after My own heart ... Jer 3:15
for lack of a *s* ... Ezek 34:5
raise up a *s* ... Zech 11:16
sheep without a *s* ... Matt 9:36
strike down the *s* ... Matt 26:31
s-s...in the fields ... Luke 2:8
I am the good *s* ... John 10:11
the great *S* ... Heb 13:20
the Chief *S* ... 1 Pet 5:4

SHEPHERD (v)
s My people ... 2 Sam 5:2
s My people ... Matt 2:6
S My sheep ... John 21:16
to *s* the church ... Acts 20:28
s the flock of God ... 1 Pet 5:2

SHESHBAZZAR
governor of Judah under Cyprus ... Ezra 5:14,16

SHIBBOLETH
test word for identification ... Judg 12:6

SHIELD *protection*
Abram, I am a *s* ... Gen 15:1
He is a *s* to all ... 2 Sam 22:31
My *s* is with God ... Ps 7:10
faithfulness Is a *s* ... Ps 91:4
the *s* of faith ... Eph 6:16

SHILOH A town in Ephraim that was the place of the central sanctuary for the Israelites in the time of Joshua and later. It was here that the boy Samuel spent his ministry under Eli. In Gen 49:10, Shiloh is linked in some way with the Messiah.
1 *Messianic title* ... Gen 49:10
2 *town N of Bethel* ... Josh 18:1
site of tabernacle ... Judg 18:31

SHINAR An ancient plain in Babylon.
Babylonian plain ... Gen 10:10; Gen 11:2; Josh 7:21; Dan 1:2

SHINE *be radiant, glow*
his face *shone* ... Ex 34:29
His face *s* on you ... Num 6:25
Your face to *s upon us* ... Ps 80:3
light *s* before men ... Matt 5:16
s-s in the darkness ... John 1:5
lamp *s-ing* in a dark ... 2 Pet 1:19
Light is...*s-ing* ... 1 John 2:8

SHIP *boat*
a haven for *s-s* ... Gen 49:13
to the sea in *s-s* ... Ps 107:23
like merchant *s-s* ... Prov 31:14
escape from the *s* ... Acts 27:30

SHISHAK *see* **PHARAOH** An Egyptian king who protected Jeroboam when he was fleeing from Solomon (1 Kin 11:40). Shishak later attacked Jerusalem, looting the temple and the king's palace (2 Chr 12:2).

SHITTIM *(the acacias)*. 1) An encampment for the Israelites during their pilgrimage. From here Joshua sent out two spies to investigate the Promised Land (Num 25:1; Moses had sent out spies from Paran). 2) The dry valley of the Jordan north of the Dead Sea (Joel 3:18).

SHOBAB 1) A son of David (2 Sam 5:14). 2) A descendant of Caleb (1 Chr 2:18).

SHOOT *new growth*
s will spring from ... Is 11:1
like a tender *s* ... Is 53:2
His *s-s* will sprout ... Hos 14:6

SHORT *lacking*
Is My hand so *s* ... Is 50:2
days will be cut *s* ... Matt 24:22
s of the grace ... Heb 12:15

SHOULDER *part of body*
He bowed his *s* ... Gen 49:15
turned a stubborn *s* ... Neh 9:29
relieved his *s* ... Ps 81:6
government...on His *s-s* ... Is 9:6

SHOUT *cry out loudly*
s with a great *s* ... Josh 6:5
the people *s-ed* with ... Ezra 3:11
s for joy ... Ps 35:27
S joyfully to God ... Ps 66:1

SHOW *manifest, reveal*
land...I will *s* you ... Gen 12:1
s me Your glory ... Ex 33:18
s you the secrets ... Job 11:6
s Your lovingkindness ... Ps 17:7
s him his fault in private ... Matt 18:15
S us the Father ... John 14:9
God *s-s* no partiality ... Gal 2:6
s hospitality ... Heb 13:2
if you *s* partiality ... James 2:9

SHOWBREAD The consecrated unleavened bread that the priest placed on a table in the sanctuary every Sabbath.
tables of *s* ... 1 Chr 28:16
s is *set*...table ... 2 Chr 13:11

SHOWER *abundant flow*
roar of a *heavy s* ... 1 Kin 18:41
Like *s-s* that water ... Ps 72:6
be *s-s* of blessing ... Ezek 34:26
A *s* is coming ... Luke 12:54

SHREWD *cunning*
frustrates...the *s* ... Job 5:12
be *s* as serpents ... Matt 10:16

SHRINE *object of worship*
built yourself a *s* ... Ezek 16:24
tear down your *s-s* ... Ezek 16:39
who made silver *s-s* ... Acts 19:24

SHUAH A son of Abraham and Keturah (Gen 25:2). The Shuhites, an Aramean tribe, probably descended from him.

SHULAMMITE
title of young woman ... Song 6:13

SHUNAMMITE from *Shunem*
1 *David's nurse* ... 1 Kin 1:3,15; 2:17,21,22
2 *hostess of Elisha* ... 2 Kin 4:12ff

SHUR *(wall)*. A desert in the land of Egypt. The Amalekites and Ishmaelites lived there.
wilderness in NW Sinai ... Gen 16:7; 20:1; Ex 15:22; 1 Sam 15:7

SHUT *close*
wilderness has *s* them ... Ex 14:3
s the lions' mouths ... Dan 6:22
power to *s* up the sky ... Rev 11:6

SIBBOLETH
test word for identification ... Judg 12:6

SICK *unwell*
strengthen the *s* ... Ezek 34:16
lying *s* with a fever ... Mark 1:30
Lazarus was *s* ... John 11:2
anyone among you *s* ... James 5:14

SICKLE *cutting tool* A metal utensil with a wooden handle used in the reaping of grain. In the Bible, also used in prophecy as a metaphor for divine judgment.
who wields the *s* ... Jer 50:16
sharp *s* in His hand ... Rev 14:14
Put in your *s* ... Rev 14:15

SICKNESS *illness*
remove from you...*s* ... Deut 7:15
every kind of *s* ... Matt 4:23
authority over...*s* ... Matt 10:1
s is not to end in death ... John 11:4

SIDON A son of Canaan, and an ancient Phoenician city near Tyre. One of Joel's prophecies was directed to it. Wood was brought from there for the construction of the second temple.
1 *son of Canaan* ... Gen 10:15; 1 Chr 1:13
2 *Phoenician port* ... Gen 10:19; Is 23:4; Ezek 28:22

SIEGE *encirclement* A military blockade of the entrances of an enemy city designed to force its inhabitants to surrender due to lack of food and supplies.
throw up a *s* ramp ... 2 Kin 19:32
city came under *s* ... 2 Kin 24:10
their *s* towers ... Is 23:13
s against Jerusalem ... Jer 6:6
build a *s* wall ... Ezek 4:2

SIEGEWORKS An implement of war, typically a large structure or movable tower with a battering ram, used to break down the wall to enter a city or fortress (Deut 20:20; Eccl 9:14).

SIGHT *perception, vision*
pleasing to the *s* ... Gen 2:9
acceptable in Your *s* ... Ps 19:14
precious in My *s* ... Is 43:4
blind receive *s* ... Matt 11:5
three days without *s* ... Acts 9:9
by faith, not by *s* ... 2 Cor 5:7

SIGN *indication* or *wonder* In the Bible, often a miracle or significant event indicating the will of God, or verifying the authority of prophets and others.
a *s* for Cain ... Gen 4:15
s of the covenant ... Gen 9:12
this shall be the *s* ... Ex 3:12
blood shall be a *s* ... Ex 12:13
His *s-s* in Egypt ... Ps 78:43
Ask a *s* for yourself ... Is 7:11
an everlasting *s* ... Is 55:13
a *s* from You ... Matt 12:38
s of Your coming ... Matt 24:3
show *s-s* and ... Mark 13:22
s-s in sun and moon ... Luke 21:25
beginning of *His s-s* ... John 2:11
s of circumcision ... Rom 4:11
Jews ask for *s-s* ... 1 Cor 1:22
tongues are for a *s* ... 1 Cor 14:22
s-s...false wonders ... 2 Thess 2:9

SIGNET *seal* A ring used to seal a document. *see* **SEAL**
examine...whose *s* ... Gen 38:25
engravings of a *s* ... Ex 39:14
s rings of his nobles ... Dan 6:17

SIHON An Amorite king defeated by the Israelites during their journey to the Promised Land.

SILAS, SILVANUS (unc, *asked for*). Two forms of the same name. Silas was used among Jews; Silvanus, among Greeks and Hellenists. A member and a prophet of the church at Jerusalem who accompanied Paul on his second missionary journey. Paul mentions him along with Timothy at the beginning of both epistles to the Thessalonians.
co-worker with Paul ... Acts 15:22,32,40; 16:19,25; 17:4,10,14
also **SILVANUS**

SILENCE *quietness*
My soul *waits* in *s* ... Ps 62:1
war will be *s-d* ... Jer 50:30
s the ignorance ... 1 Pet 2:15
s in heaven ... Rev 8:1

SILENT *quiet*
LORD, do not keep *s* ... Ps 35:22
A time to be *s* ... Eccl 3:7
But Jesus kept *s* ... Matt 26:63
women...keep *s* ... 1 Cor 14:34

SILOAM *(sent)*. A tower and an ancient pool in Jerusalem. The pool was so named because its waters were sent to it through a long tunnel.
1 *tower in Jerusalem* ... Luke 13:4
2 *water pool in Jerusalem* ... John 9:7,11

SILVANUS *see* **SILAS**

SILVER *precious metal*
rich in...*s* ... Gen 13:2
took no plunder in *s* ... Judg 5:19
as *s* is refined ... Ps 66:10
in settings of *s* ... Prov 25:11
s has become dross ... Is 1:22
The *s* is Mine ... Hag 2:8
not acquire...*s* ... Matt 10:9
thirty pieces of *s* ... Matt 26:15

SIMEON *(hearing)*. Second son of Jacob by Leah and the name of the tribe that descended from him. Also the name of other persons.
1 *son of Jacob* ... Gen 29:33
2 *tribe* ... Num 1:23; Rev 7:7
3 *devout Jew* ... Luke 2:25
4 *ancestor of Jesus* ... Luke 3:30
5 *Christian prophet* ... Acts 13:1
6 *Simon Peter* ... Acts 15:14

SIMON Another form of the name *Simeon*. Two of the apostles had this name: Simon Peter and Simon the Zealot. Also the name of other men, including a half-brother of Jesus and the man who was ordered to help Jesus carry his cross to Golgotha.
1 *apostle* ... Matt 4:18; Mark 1:16
see also **PETER**
2 *the Zealot* ... Matt 10:4; Mark 3:18; Luke 6:15
3 *brother of Jesus* ... Matt 13:55; Mark 6:3
4 *leper* ... Matt 26:6; Mark 14:3
5 *a Pharisee* ... Luke 7:40,43
6 *of Cyrene* ... Matt 27:32
carried Jesus' cross ... Mark 15:21; Luke 23:26
7 *father of Judas* ... John 6:71;13:2
8 *Magus* ... Acts 8:9,13,18
sorcerer
9 *the tanner* ... Acts 9:43;10:6,32

SIMPLE *innocent* or *humble*
making wise the *s* ... Ps 19:7
LORD preserves the *s* ... Ps 116:6

SIN (n) *transgression* Any action which violates God's law. Before the giving of the Ten Commandments and the many other OT laws found in Exodus, Leviticus, and Deuteronomy, God occasionally spoke directly to individuals about what He required of them (e.g. Gen 2:17). The OT laws later spelled out in great detail what constituted sin, and what one had to do to atone for sin. In the Gospels, Jesus further explains sin as including not only actions but also evil thoughts, such as unfounded anger toward others.
please forgive my *s* ... Ex 10:17
atonement for your *s* ... Ex 32:30
purification from *s* ... Num 19:9
s will find you out ... Num 32:23
s of divination ... 1 Sam 15:23
the *s-s* of my youth ... Ps 25:7
s my mother conceived ... Ps 51:5
Fools mock at *s* ... Prov 14:9
bore the *s* of many ... Is 53:12
s-s of her prophets ... Lam 4:13
an eternal *s* ... Mark 3:29
forgive us our *s-s* ... Luke 11:4
takes away the *s* ... John 1:29
wash away your *s-s* ... Acts 22:16
wages of *s* is death ... Rom 6:23
died for our *s-s* ... 1 Cor 15:3
Him who knew no *s* ... 2 Cor 5:21
pleasures of *s* ... Heb 11:25
confess your *s-s* ... James 5:16
a multitude of *s-s* ... James 5:20
confess our *s-s* ... 1 John 1:9
s is lawlessness ... 1 John 3:4

SIN (v) *transgress*
When a leader *s-s* ... Lev 4:22
s against the LORD ... 1 Sam 14:34
Job did not *s* ... Job 1:22
s against You ... Ps 119:11
Father, I have *s-ned* ... Luke 15:18
s no more ... John 8:11
all have *s-ned* ... Rom 3:23
that you may not *s* ... 1 John 2:1

SIN 1) A wilderness east of the Red Sea. 2) The name of a city in Egypt (perhaps Egyptian for "clay").
1 *wilderness in Sinai* ... Ex 16:1; Num 33:11,12
2 *Egyptian city* ... Ezek 30:15,16

SIN OFFERING *see* **OFFERINGS**

SINAI The triangular peninsula where the Israelites wandered through a wilderness. Also the mountain on which the Law was given to Moses; it is sometimes called Horeb.
1 *mountain* ... Ex 19:11; Lev 26:46; Num 28:6
where Law received ... Ex 31:18; 34:29
see also **HOREB**
2 *desert wilderness* ... Ex 16:1; 19:1; Num 1:19; 9:5

SINCERE *without deceit*
be *s* and blameless ... Phil 1:10
mindful of the *s* faith ... 2 Tim 1:5
s love...brethren ... 1 Pet 1:22

SINEW *strength* or *tendon*
with bones and *s-s* ... Job 10:11
neck is an iron *s* ... Is 48:4
will put *s-s* on you ... Ezek 37:6

SINFUL *wicked*
a brood of *s* men ... Num 32:14
s generation ... Mark 8:38
I am a *s* man ... Luke 5:8
likeness of *s* flesh ... Rom 8:3

SING
s to the LORD ... Ex 15:1
s-ing and dancing ... 1 Sam 18:6
I will *s* praises ... 2 Sam 22:50
morning stars *sang* ... Job 38:7
S to Him a new song ... Ps 33:3
the righteous *s-s* ... Prov 29:6
birds will *s* ... Zeph 2:14
after *s-ing* a hymn ... Mark 14:26
s-ing...thankfulness ... Col 3:16
sang a new song ... Rev 5:9

SINGERS
these are the *s* ... 1 Chr 9:33
male and female *s* ... Eccl 2:8

SINK *descend, fall*
do not let me *s* ... Ps 69:14
so shall Babylon *s* ... Jer 51:64

SINNER *wrongdoer* A person who commits any sin; thus every member of the human race is a sinner, with the exception of Jesus. Also a technical term in first-century Jewish society referring to Jews who had no regard for the Pharisees' directives, or who flagrantly violated the Law of Moses.
He instructs *s-s* ... Ps 25:8
if *s-s* entice you ... Prov 1:10
Adversity...*s-s* ... Prov 13:21
one *s* destroys much ... Eccl 9:18
a friend of...*s-s* ... Matt 11:19
one *s* who repents ... Luke 15:7
merciful to me...*s* ... Luke 18:13
God...not hear *s-s* ... John 9:31
while we were yet *s-s* ... Rom 5:8
came...to save *s-s* ... 1 Tim 1:15

SISERA A Canaanite captain who, when fleeing from Barak, was killed by a woman. Also one of the exiles who returned from captivity in Babylon.
1 *Canaanite warrior* ... Judg 4:2ff
2 *class of Nethinim* ... Ezra 2:53; Neh 7:55

SISTER
She is my *s* ... Gen 12:19
We have a little *s* ... Song 8:8
a *s* called Mary ... Luke 10:39
commend...our *s* ... Rom 16:1
younger women...*s-s* ... 1 Tim 5:2

SIT *recline, rest*
Moses *sat* to judge ... Ex 18:13
Nor *s* in the seat ... Ps 1:1
S at My right hand ... Ps 110:1
lonely *s-s* the city ... Lam 1:1
s down on the grass ... Matt 14:19
who *s* in darkness ... Luke 1:79
dead man *sat* up ... Luke 7:15
where the harlot *s-s* ... Rev 17:15

SIVAN
third month of Hebrew calendar ... Esth 8:9

SKILL *proficiency*
filled them with *s* ... Ex 35:35
the heavens with *s* ... Ps 136:5
work of *s-ed* men ... Jer 10:9
s-ed in destruction ... Ezek 21:31

SKILLFUL *accomplished*
became a *s* hunter ... Gen 25:27
s player on...harp ... 1 Sam 16:16
praises with a *s* psalm ... Ps 47:7

SKIN *covering*
garments of *s* ... Gen 3:21
s of his face shone ... Ex 34:29
Clothe me with *s* ... Job 10:11
My *s* turns black ... Job 30:30
will burst the *s-s* ... Mark 2:22

SKIP *hop, leap*
children *s* about ... Job 21:11
Lebanon *s* like a calf ... Ps 29:6
go forth and *s* ... Mal 4:2

SKULL *bony framework of head*
head, crushing his *s* ... Judg 9:53
the *s* and the feet ... 2 Kin 9:35
Place of a *S* ... Matt 27:33

SKY *heavens*
sun stopped in...*s* ... Josh 10:13
the *s* grew black ... 1 Kin 18:45
witness in the *s* ... Ps 89:37
s will be rolled up ... Is 34:4
for the *s* is red ... Matt 16:2
will appear in the *s* ... Matt 24:30
s was shut up ... Luke 4:25
gazing...into the *s* ... Acts 1:10
s was split apart ... Rev 6:14

SLANDER (n) *defamation*
spreads *s* is a fool ... Prov 10:18
s-s, gossip ... 2 Cor 12:20
and *s* be put away ... Eph 4:31

SLANDER (v) *defame*
He does not *s* ... Ps 15:3
Whoever secretly *s-s* ... Ps 101:5
Do not *s* a slave ... Prov 30:10

SLANDERER *defamer*
s separates...friends ... Prov 16:28
s-s, haters of God ... Rom 1:30

SLAUGHTER (n) *brutal killing*
great *s* at Gibeon ... Josh 10:10
lamb led to the *s* ... Jer 11:19
as a sheep to *s* ... Acts 8:32
in a day of *s* ... James 5:5

SLAUGHTER (v) *kill*
shall *s* the bull ... Ex 29:11
shall *s* the lamb ... Lev 14:25
Who *s* the children ... Is 57:5
s-ed My children ... Ezek 16:21

SLAVE *bond-servant*
The Hebrew *s* ... Gen 39:17
s at forced labor ... Gen 49:15
sold *in* a *s* sale ... Lev 25:42
Is Israel a *s* ... Jer 2:14
S-s rule over us ... Lam 5:8
s above his master ... Matt 10:24
good and faithful *s* ... Matt 25:21
shall be *s* of all ... Mark 10:44
is the *s* of sin ... John 8:34
neither *s* nor free ... Gal 3:28
as *s-s* of Christ ... Eph 6:6

SLAVERY *servitude*
from the house of *s* ... Ex 13:3
ransomed you from...*s* ... Mic 6:4
received a spirit of *s* ... Rom 8:15
to a yoke of *s* ... Gal 5:1

SLAY *destroy, kill*
knife to *s* his son ... Gen 22:10
s-s the foolish ... Job 5:2
Though He *s* me ... Job 13:15
Evil...*s* the wicked ... Ps 34:21
s her with thirst ... Hos 2:3
Lamb that was *slain* ... Rev 5:12

SLEEP (n) *rest*
caused a deep *s* ... Gen 2:21
Do not love *s* ... Prov 20:13
a spirit of deep *s* ... Is 29:10
s fled from him ... Dan 6:18
overcome by *s* ... Acts 20:9

SLEEP (v) *slumber*
why do You *s* ... Ps 44:23
neither slumber nor *s* ... Ps 121:4
who *s-s* in harvest ... Prov 10:5
found them *s-ing* ... Matt 26:43
we will not all *s* ... 1 Cor 15:51

SLOW *not quick*
I am *s* of speech ... Ex 4:10
gracious, *S* to anger ... Ps 103:8
to hear, *s* to speak ... James 1:19
Lord is not *s* ... 2 Pet 3:9

SLUGGARD *lazy one*
to the ant, O *s* ... Prov 6:6
the *s* craves ... Prov 13:4
s buries his hand ... Prov 26:15

SLUMBER *sleep*
s in their beds ... Job 33:15
He...will not *s* ... Ps 121:3
None *s-s* or sleeps ... Is 5:27
Dreamers...love to *s* ... Is 56:10

SMALL *little*
both *s* and great ... 2 Kin 25:26
s among the nations ... Jer 49:15
day of *s* things ... Zech 4:10
For the gate is *s* ... Matt 7:14
a few *s* fish ... Mark 8:7
he was *s* in stature ... Luke 19:3
tongue is a *s* part ... James 3:5

SMILE *grin*
I *s-d* on them ... Job 29:24
that I may *s again* ... Ps 39:13
she *s-s* at the future ... Prov 31:25

SMITE *hit, strike*
s...with frogs ... Ex 8:2
smote Job with sore ... Job 2:7
sun will not *s* you ... Ps 121:6
righteous *s* me ... Ps 141:5

SMITH *worker of metal*
a vessel for the *s* ... Prov 25:4
created the *s* who ... Is 54:16
s-s from Jerusalem ... Jer 24:1

SMOKE *mist, vapor*
s...ascended ... Gen 19:28
Sinai *was* all in *s* ... Ex 19:18
like *s* they vanish ... Ps 37:20
temple was filling with *s* ... Is 6:4
s rises up forever ... Rev 19:3

SMOOTH *no roughness*
I am a *s* man ... Gen 27:11
five *s* stones ... 1 Sam 17:40
Make *s*...a highway ... Is 40:3
the rough roads *s* ... Luke 3:5
s...flattering speech ... Rom 16:18

SMYRNA An ancient city on the west coast of Asia Minor. Its church was one of the seven addressed in Revelation.
city in Asia Minor ... Rev 1:11; 2:8

SNAKE *serpent*
horned *s* in the path ... Gen 49:17
a *s* bites him ... Amos 5:19
s instead of a fish ... Luke 11:11

SNARE *trap*
gods will be a *s* ... Judg 2:3
s-s of death ... 2 Sam 22:6
laid a *s* for me ... Ps 119:110
his lips are the *s* ... Prov 18:7
caught in My *s* ... Ezek 12:13
table become a *s* ... Rom 11:9
s of the devil ... 1 Tim 3:7

SNOW *ice flakes*
storehouses of the *s* ... Job 38:22
be whiter than *s* ... Ps 51:7
He gives *s* like wool ... Ps 147:16
Like *s* in summer ... Prov 26:1
as white as *s* ... Matt 28:3

SNUFFER Artifact used to extinguish the flame of a lamp. Snuffers were included among the sacred utensils of the tabernacle and temple (Ex 25:38).

SOBER *serious, temperate*
words of *s* truth ... Acts 26:25
be alert and *s* ... 1 Thess 5:6
Be of *s spirit* ... 1 Pet 5:8

SODOM The most notorious of five ancient cities in the valley of the Jordan. Due to its wickedness, it was destroyed by God with fire.
city S of Dead Sea ... Gen 10:19
home of Lot ... Gen 19:1,4
destroyed by God ... Gen 19:24

SODOMITE
one guilty of unnatural sexual practices ... 1 Kin 22:46

SOFT *kind*
speak to you *s* words ... Job 41:3
s tongue breaks the ... Prov 25:15

SOIL *earth, ground*
first fruits of your *s* ... Ex 23:19
he loved the *s* ... 2 Chr 26:10
fell into the good *s* ... Mark 4:8
produce of the *s* ... James 5:7

SOJOURN *visit temporarily*
S in this land ... Gen 26:3
stranger *s-s* with you ... Ex 12:48
s...land of Moab ... Ruth 1:1

SOJOURNER
s in a foreign land ... Ex 2:22
are *s-s* before You ... 1 Chr 29:15
oppressed the *s* ... Ezek 22:29

SOLDIER *military man*
s-s took Him away ... Mark 15:16
s-s also mocked ... Luke 23:36
s-s pierced His side ... John 19:34
a devout *s* ... Acts 10:7
good *s* of Christ ... 2 Tim 2:3

SOLEMN *deeply earnest, serious*
sabbath of *s* rest ... Lev 16:31
have a *s* assembly ... Num 29:35
sworn s oaths ... Ezek 21:23
bound...a *s* oath ... Acts 23:14

SOLOMON David's son and successor to the throne and the last king of the united kingdom. He was divinely gifted with great wisdom and his major legacy was the construction of the second temple.
son of David ... 2 Sam 12:24
king of Israel ... 1 Kin 1:43
ruled wisely ... 1 Kin 4:29,34
built the Temple ... 1 Kin 6:2;9:1
international fame ... 1 Kin 10:1
ruled foolishly ... 1 Kin 11:6
death ... 1 Kin 11:43

SON *male descendant*
the *s-s* of Noah ... Gen 9:18
Take...your only *s* ... Gen 22:2
O Absalom, my *s* ... 2 Sam 18:33
to be a *s* to Me ... 1 Chr 28:6
s-s of God shouted ... Job 38:7
You are My *S* ... Ps 2:7
wise *s* makes a ... Prov 10:1
Discipline your *s* ... Prov 19:18
bear a *s*...Immanuel ... Is 7:14
Egypt I called My *s* ... Hos 11:1
she gave birth to a *S* ... Matt 1:25
This is My beloved *S* ... Matt 3:17
the carpenter's *s* ... Matt 13:55
I am the *S* of God ... Matt 27:43
S of Man...suffer ... Mark 8:31
her firstborn *s* ... Luke 2:7
If You are the *S* ... Luke 4:3
man had two *s-s* ... Luke 15:11
only begotten *S* ... John 3:16
S also gives life ... John 5:21
become *s-s* of Light ... John 12:36
sending His own *S* ... Rom 8:3
image of His *S* ... Rom 8:29
not spare His own *S* ... Rom 8:32
fellowship with His *S* ... 1 Cor 1:9
if a *s*, then an heir ... Gal 4:7
shall be a *S* to Me ... Heb 1:5
abide in the *S* ... 1 John 2:24
He who has the *S* ... 1 John 5:12

SON-IN-LAW
the *s* of the Timnite ... Judg 15:6
be the king's *s* ... 1 Sam 18:18
s of Sanballat ... Neh 13:28

SON OF GOD One of the most common titles of Jesus Christ, which speaks of His Messiahship and equality with God the Father. The title also appears in the OT.
Messianic title indicating deity of Jesus Christ ... Matt 4:3; 8:29; 16:16; Mark 1:20; 3:11; 14:61; Luke 1:35; John 3:13; 11:27; Acts 8:37

SON OF MAN Jesus uses this title more than 80 times in the Gospels to refer to Himself as the representative Man who would die for the sins of all mankind. As the Son of Man, He is also the Messiah, the Son of God, who will receive the future earthly kingdom from His Father at His Second Coming and rule over all the nations (Dan 7:13-14).
Messianic title of Jesus Christ ... Matt 8:20; 9:6; Mark 2:10; 10:33; Luke 12:10; 18:31; John 6:27; 13:31

SONG *melody, music*
LORD is my...*s* ... Ex 15:2
ministered with *s* ... 1 Chr 6:32
gives *s-s* in the night ... Job 35:10
s-s of deliverance ... Ps 32:7
Sing to Him a new *s* ... Ps 33:3
A *s* of my beloved ... Is 5:1
Praise the LORD in *s* ... Is 12:5
not drink wine with *s* ... Is 24:9
hymns...spiritual *s-s* ... Eph 5:19

SOOTHSAYER One who claims to foretell the future by magic arts. In the Bible, soothsayers are ranked together with false prophets (Isa 2:6).

SORCERER *witch* A person who practices sorcery and the occult, including alleged contact with the dead.
interprets...or a *s* ... Deut 18:10
witness against the *s-s* ... Mal 3:5
immoral persons...*s-s* ... Rev 21:8

SORCERY *witchcraft* The use of illusion or possibly power gained through the assistance of demonic beings. Prohibited in the Bible.
practiced *s* ... 2 Chr 33:6
idolatry, *s*, enmities ... Gal 5:20
deceived by your *s* ... Rev 18:23

SORDID *filthy*
fond of *s* gain ... 1 Tim 3:8
the sake of *s* gain ... Titus 1:11
not for *s* gain ... 1 Pet 5:2

SOREK
valley SW of Jerusalem ... Judg 16:4

SORROW *grief, sadness*
down to Sheol in *s* ... Gen 42:38
life is spent with *s* ... Ps 31:10
man of *s-s* ... Is 53:3
s is beyond healing ... Jer 8:18
if I cause you *s* ... 2 Cor 2:2

SOSTHENES One of Paul's associates, who seems to be an official of a Jewish synagogue at Corinth.
synagogue leader ... Acts 18:17
Corinthian believer ... 1 Cor 1:27

SOUL *life, spirit* 1) In the plural, often synonymous with "persons" or "people"; in the singular, a living being (Gen 2:7). 2) The seat of feelings, desires, and emotions. 3) The nonmaterial element of man—the most important part of human existence—as seen in the human personality. This element lives on after the death of the body, and will ultimately be joined again with a resurrected body to spend eternity in heaven or in the lake of fire (*hell*, Matt 10:28).
her *s* was departing ... Gen 35:18
humble your *s-s* ... Lev 16:29
poured out my *s* ... 1 Sam 1:15
not abandon my *s* ... Ps 16:10
He restores my *s* ... Ps 23:3
my *s* pants for You ... Ps 42:1
Bless...LORD, O my *s* ... Ps 103:1
who is wise wins *s-s* ... Prov 11:30
s who sins will die ... Ezek 18:4
unable to kill the *s* ... Matt 10:28
exchange for his *s* ... Matt 16:26
My *s* is...grieved ... Matt 26:38
and forfeit his *s* ... Mark 8:36
My *s* exalts the Lord ... Luke 1:46
your *s* is required ... Luke 12:20
one heart and *s* ... Acts 4:32
an anchor of the *s* ... Heb 6:19
able to save your *s-s* ... James 1:21
save his *s* from ... James 5:20
war against the *s* ... 1 Pet 2:11

SOUND (adj) *accurate, stable*
s wisdom...two sides ... Job 11:6
I give you *s* teaching ... Prov 4:2
the *s* doctrine ... 1 Tim 4:6

SOUND (n) *noise*
s of You in...garden ... Gen 3:10
s of war in the camp ... Ex 32:17
s of a great army ... 2 Kin 7:6
s of many waters ... Ezek 43:2

SOUND (v) *express*
s His praise abroad ... Ps 66:8
s an alarm ... Joel 2:1
trumpet will *s* ... 1 Cor 15:52

SOUR *distasteful, tart*
eaten *s* grapes ... Jer 31:29
offering...*s* wine ... Luke 23:36

SOURCE *origin*
the *s* of sapphires ... Job 28:6
s of eternal salvation ... Heb 5:9
s of quarrels ... James 4:1

SOVEREIGNTY *authority*
His *s* rules over all ... Ps 103:19
s from Damascus ... Is 17:3
s will be uprooted ... Dan 11:4

SOW *plant, spread*
you may *s* the land ... Gen 47:23
s your seed uselessly ... Lev 26:16
who *s* in tears ... Ps 126:5
who *s-s* iniquity will ... Prov 22:8
they *s* the wind ... Hos 8:7
birds...do not *s* ... Matt 6:26
s good seed ... Matt 13:27
s-ed spiritual things ... 1 Cor 9:11
whatever a man *s-s* ... Gal 6:7

SOWER *planter*
seed to the *s* ... Is 55:10
s went out to sow ... Matt 13:3
s sows the word ... Mark 4:14

SPAIN
S European land ... Rom 15:24,28

SPARE *save* or *be lenient*
did not *s* their soul ... Ps 78:50
No man *s-s* his brother ... Is 9:19
not *s* His own Son ... Rom 8:32
I will not *s anyone* ... 2 Cor 13:2
God did not *s* angels ... 2 Pet 2:4

SPEAK *proclaim, tell*
God *spoke* to Noah ... Gen 8:15
God *s-s* with man ... Deut 5:24
S of all His wonders ... 1 Chr 16:9
He who *s-s* falsehood ... Ps 101:7
and a time to *s* ... Eccl 3:7
the mute to *s* ... Mark 7:37
s of what we know ... John 3:11
Never has a man *spoken* ... John 7:46
s with other tongues ... Acts 2:4
we *s* God's wisdom ... 1 Cor 2:7
If I *s* with...tongues ... 1 Cor 13:1

SPEAR *weapon*
leaning on his *s* ... 2 Sam 1:6
s-s into pruning hooks ... Is 2:4
pruning hooks into *s-s* ... Joel 3:10
pierced...with a *s* ... John 19:34

SPECK *particle*
regarded as a *s* of ... Is 40:15
s out of your eye ... Matt 7:4

SPEECH *message, word*
I am slow of *s* ... Ex 4:10
His *s* was smoother ... Ps 55:21
in cleverness of *s* ... 1 Cor 1:17
I am unskilled in *s* ... 2 Cor 11:6

SPELL *incantation*
one who casts a *s* ... Deut 18:11
skillful caster of *s-s* ... Ps 58:5
power of your *s-s* ... Is 47:9

SPICE
s and the oil ... Ex 35:28
mix in the *s-s* ... Ezek 24:10
prepared *s-s* and ... Luke 23:56
wrappings with...*s-s* ... John 19:40

SPIES (n) *clandestine persons*
we are not *s* ... Gen 42:31
two men as *s* ... Josh 2:1
David sent out *s* ... 1 Sam 26:4
welcomed the *s* ... Heb 11:31

SPIN *make thread*
nor do they *s* ... Matt 6:28
neither toil nor *s* ... Luke 12:27

SPIRIT 1) The nature of God. 2) A supernatural being or essence, usually evil. 3) A nonmaterial part of man which some believe is the same as the soul (q.v.), while others think that it exists separately with the soul. 4) A pervading attitude, e.g. *a spirit of gentleness* (1 Cor 4:21).
S rested upon them ... Num 11:26
God sent an evil *s* ... Judg 9:23
My *s* is broken ... Job 17:1
renew a steadfast *s* ... Ps 51:10
my *s* grows faint ... Ps 77:3
a haughty *s* before ... Prov 16:18
the *S* lifted me up ... Ezek 3:14
his *s* was troubled ... Dan 2:1
four *s-s* of heaven ... Zech 6:5
are the poor in *s* ... Matt 5:3
authority over...*s-s* ... Matt 10:1
put My *S* upon Him ... Matt 12:18
blasphemy...the *S* ... Matt 12:31
yielded up *His s* ... Matt 27:50
S like a dove ... Mark 1:10
s...not have flesh ... Luke 24:39
born of...the *S* ... John 3:5
worship in *s* and ... John 4:24
gave up His *s* ... John 19:30
pour forth of My *S* ... Acts 2:17
Jesus, receive my *s* ... Acts 7:59
power of the *S* ... Rom 15:19
taught by the *s* ... 1 Cor 2:13
pray with the *s* ... 1 Cor 14:15
walk by the *S* ... Gal 5:16
fruit of the *S* is love ... Gal 5:22
one body and one *S* ... Eph 4:4
be filled with the *S* ... Eph 5:18
sword of the *S* ... Eph 6:17
not quench the *S* ... 1 Thess 5:19
division of soul and *s* ... Heb 4:12
the *s-s now* in prison ... 1 Pet 3:19
S who testifies ... 1 John 5:6
see also **HOLY SPIRIT**

SPIRIT, HOLY *see* **HOLY SPIRIT**

SPIRIT OF GOD
the *S* was moving ... Gen 1:2
S came upon him ... 1 Sam 10:10
a vision by the *S* ... Ezek 11:24
S descending as a ... Matt 3:16
being led by the *S* ... Rom 8:14
S dwells in you ... 1 Cor 3:16
worship in the *S* ... Phil 3:3
see also **HOLY SPIRIT**

SPIRIT OF THE LORD
S came upon him ... Judg 3:10
S departed from ... 1 Sam 16:14
S gave them rest ... Is 63:14
filled with...the *S* ... Mic 3:8
S is upon Me ... Luke 4:18
see also **HOLY SPIRIT**

SPIRITIST *medium*
not turn to...*s-s* ... Lev 19:31
s...be put to death ... Lev 20:27
removed...the *s-s* ... 2 Kin 23:24

SPIRITUAL *of the spirit*
the Law is *s* ... Rom 7:14
s service of worship ... Rom 12:1
raised a *s* body ... 1 Cor 15:44
with every *s* blessing ... Eph 1:3
hymns and *s* songs ... Eph 5:19
offer up *s* sacrifices ... 1 Pet 2:5

SPIRITUAL DEATH *see* **DEATH, SPIRITUAL**

SPIRITUAL GIFT *see* **GIFT, SPIRITUAL**

SPIT
began to *s* at Him ... Mark 14:65
and *s* upon ... Luke 18:32
He *spat* on...ground ... John 9:6
I will *s* you out ... Rev 3:16

SPLENDOR *magnificence*
the moon going in *s* ... Job 31:26
displayed Your *s* ... Ps 8:1
Your *s* and Your majesty ... Ps 45:3
clothed with *s* ... Ps 104:1
s covers the heavens ... Hab 3:3

SPLIT *divide*
He *s* the rock ... Is 48:21
valleys will be *s* ... Mic 1:4
Mount...will be *s* ... Zech 14:4
sky was *s* apart ... Rev 6:14

SPOIL *booty, pillage*
he divides the *s* ... Gen 49:27
the *s* of the cities ... Deut 2:35
divide the *s* with ... Prov 16:19
widows may be their *s* ... Is 10:2
for *s* to the nations ... Ezek 25:7

SPONGE *absorbent matter*
taking a *s*, he filled ... Matt 27:48
a *s* with sour wine ... Mark 15:36

SPOT *speck*
Or the leopard his *s-s* ... Jer 13:23
no *s* or wrinkle ... Eph 5:27

SPOTLESS *no defects*
unblemished and *s* ... 1 Pet 1:19
s and blameless ... 2 Pet 3:14

SPREAD *stretch out*
He *s* His wings ... Deut 32:11
I *s* My skirt over ... Ezek 16:8
death *s* to all men ... Rom 5:12

SPRING (adj) *period, season*
has been no *s* rain ... Jer 3:3
Like the *s* rain ... Hos 6:3
s crop began to sprout ... Amos 7:1

SPRING (n) *water source*
went down to the *s* ... Gen 24:16
twelve *s-s* of water ... Ex 15:27
stop all *s-s* of water ... 2 Kin 3:19
s-s of the deep...fixed ... Prov 8:28
the *s-s* of salvation ... Is 12:3
s of the water of life ... Rev 21:6

SPRING (v) *jump, leap*
S up, O well ... Num 21:17
Truth *s-s* from the ... Ps 85:11
s-ing up to eternal ... John 4:14

SPRINKLE *scatter*
take its blood and *s* ... Ex 29:16
s some of the blood ... Lev 4:6
s it seven times ... Lev 4:17
s some of the oil ... Lev 14:16

SPY (v) *investigate*
Moses sent...to *s* ... Num 13:17
to *s* out Jericho ... Josh 6:25
spied out Bethel ... Judg 1:23
s out our liberty ... Gal 2:4

SQUARE *area* or *shape*
altar shall be *s* ... Ex 27:1
voice in the *s* ... Prov 1:20
city is...a *s* ... Rev 21:16

STAFF *rod* A long stick which served various purposes in ancient times. A simple purpose was that of a walking stick or cane. A man's staff might also be a token of identification which could serve as a pledge, i.e. a symbol of its owner's authority or responsibility. A staff could also be employed as a weapon for protection. Shepherds used staffs to guide and hold back sheep. Certain staffs mentioned in the Bible, e.g. that of Moses, became special instruments used in connection with divine miracles.
s of God in his hand ... Ex 4:20
Your *s*, they comfort ... Ps 23:4
or sandals, or a *s* ... Matt 10:10
a mere *s*; no bread ... Mark 6:8

STAIN *blemish*
s of your iniquity ... Jer 2:22
without *s*...reproach ... 1 Tim 6:14

STAND *maintain position*
s before the LORD ... Deut 10:8
O sun, *s* still ... Josh 10:12
s before kings ... Prov 22:29
word of our God *s-s* ... Is 40:8
will *s* on the Mount ... Zech 14:4
love to *s* and pray ... Matt 6:5
s-ing by the cross ... John 19:25
why do you *s* looking ... Acts 1:11
s by your faith ... Rom 11:20
s before...judgment ... Rom 14:10
s firm in the faith ... 1 Cor 16:13
foundation...*s-s* ... 2 Tim 2:19
I *s* at the door ... Rev 3:20

STANDARD *banner* or *rule*
set up their own *s-s* ... Ps 74:4
set up My *s* ... Is 49:22
s of the Law ... Acts 22:12
s of sound words ... 2 Tim 1:13

STAR *heavenly body*
He made the *s-s* ... Gen 1:16
s shall come forth ... Num 24:17
morning *s-s* sang ... Job 38:7
s of the morning ... Is 14:12
s-s for light by night ... Jer 31:35
His *s* in the east ... Matt 2:2
morning *s* arises ... 2 Pet 1:19
wandering *s-s* ... Jude 13
s fell from heaven ... Rev 8:10
the bright morning *s* ... Rev 22:16

STATE *position*
s of expectation ... Luke 3:15
of our humble *s* ... Phil 3:21
s has become worse ... 2 Pet 2:20

STATEMENT *assertion*
let your *s* be ... Matt 5:37
trap Him in a *s* ... Mark 12:13
catch Him in...*s* ... Luke 20:20
This is a difficult *s* ... John 6:60

STATURE *height*
was growing in *s* ... 1 Sam 2:26
in wisdom and *s* ... Luke 2:52
he was small in *s* ... Luke 19:3
measure of the *s* ... Eph 4:13

STATUTE *law, rule*
My *s-s* and My laws ... Gen 26:5
a perpetual *s* ... Ex 29:9
keep My *s-s* ... Lev 18:5
Teach me Your *s-s* ... Ps 119:26
not walked in My *s-s* ... Ezek 5:7

STEADFAST *established, firm*
be *s* and not fear ... Job 11:15
renew a *s* spirit ... Ps 51:10
My heart is *s* ... Ps 57:7
s in righteousness ... Prov 11:19
be *s*, immovable ... 1 Cor 15:58

STEAL *rob, take*
You shall not *s* ... Ex 20:15
be in want and *s* ... Prov 30:9
thieves break in...*s* ... Matt 6:19
Do not *s* ... Mark 10:19

STEPHANAS
Corinthian Christian ... 1 Cor 1:16; 16:15,17

STEPHEN In the book of Acts, one of seven exemplary men chosen by the apostles to aid in the distribution of items to the Hellenistic widows. A man *full of faith and of the Holy Spirit,* he was the first martyr of the Christian church.
deacon ... Acts 6:5,8
martyred ... Acts 7:59; 8:2

STEPS *distance* or *movements*
number my *s* ... Job 14:16
s...bathed in butter ... Job 29:6
His *s* do not slip ... Ps 37:31
s take hold of Sheol ... Prov 5:5
in the *s* of the faith ... Rom 4:12
follow in His *s* ... 1 Pet 2:21

STEWARD *supervisor*
and sensible *s* ... Luke 12:42
s-s of the mysteries ... 1 Cor 4:1
above reproach...*s* ... Titus 1:7

STEWARDSHIP *responsibility* The delegated responsibility and accountability of wisely managing what belongs to another. The term was used by the apostle Paul to describe his charge to preach the gospel to the Gentiles. By analogy, every Christian has a stewardship to use God-given spiritual gifts as well as time and money for Christian ministry.
a *s* entrusted to me ... 1 Cor 9:17
s of God's grace ... Eph 3:2

STIFFEN *make rigid*
s your neck no longer ... Deut 10:16
do not *s* your neck ... 2 Chr 30:8
have *s-ed* their necks ... Jer 19:15

STILL *motionless* or *quiet*
O sun, stand *s* ... Josh 10:12
the storm to be *s* ... Ps 107:29
Why are we sitting *s* ... Jer 8:14
sea, Hush, be *s* ... Mark 4:39

STIMULATE *excite*
how to *s* my body ... Eccl 2:3
s one another to ... Heb 10:24

STING *pain*
where is your *s* ... 1 Cor 15:55
s of death is sin ... 1 Cor 15:56

STIR *agitate*
S up Yourself ... Ps 35:23
word *s-s* up anger ... Prov 15:1
man *s-s* up strife ... Prov 29:22
s-red up the water ... John 5:4

STOCKS *confinement* A wooden frame with holes used to immobilize a prisoner by securing the ankles, and sometimes the wrists, in the frame. Roman stocks had several holes for the ankles, designed to torture the prisoner by spreading his legs far apart.
put my feet in the *s* ... Job 13:27
Jeremiah from the *s* ... Jer 20:3
their feet in the *s* ... Acts 16:24

STOIC A follower of the philosophy of Zeno, who founded a school in Athens in the late fourth century B.C. The name comes from the Gr word *stoa,* or "porch," referring to the colonnade in the Athenian Agora (marketplace) where Zeno taught his students. Among the precepts of Stoicism were the beliefs that virtue is the only good and is its own reward, and that happiness is to be found within oneself, without regard to external circumstances, whether pleasant or painful. The Stoics also believed that every event in the universe was destined and that a person should accept everything that happens to him as a part of destiny. The austerity of Stoicism and its emphasis on virtue appealed to the Romans. *cf.* **EPICUREAN**
Epicurean and S philosophers ... Acts 17:18

STOMACH *part of body*
s will be satisfied ... Prov 18:20
s of the fish ... Jon 1:17
Food is for the *s* ... 1 Cor 6:13
s was made bitter ... Rev 10:10

STONE (n) *rock*
they used brick for *s* ... Gen 11:3
two *s* tablets ... Ex 34:1
do these *s-s* mean ... Josh 4:6
five smooth *s-s* ... 1 Sam 17:40
there was no *s* seen ... 1 Kin 6:18
Water wears...*s-s* ... Job 14:19
foot against a *s* ... Ps 91:12
in Zion a *s* ... Is 28:16
take the heart of *s* ... Ezek 11:19
serving wood and *s* ... Ezek 20:32
foot against a *s* ... Matt 4:6
will give him a *s* ... Matt 7:9
rolled away the *s* ... Matt 28:2
s-s will cry out ... Luke 19:40
six *s* waterpots ... John 2:6
first to throw a *s* ... John 8:7
Remove the *s* ... John 11:39
s-s, wood, hay ... 1 Cor 3:12
as to a living *s* ... 1 Pet 2:4
A *s* of stumbling ... 1 Pet 2:8

STONE (v) *throw stones*
people will *s* us ... Luke 20:6
seeking to *s* You ... John 11:8
went on *s-ing* Stephen ... Acts 7:59
they *s-d* Paul ... Acts 14:19

STOP *cease*
the sun *s-ped* ... Josh 10:13
And the oil *s-ped* ... 2 Kin 4:6
put a *s* to sacrifice ... Dan 9:27
s weeping for Me ... Luke 23:28
s sinning ... 1 Cor 15:34

STORE *accumulate*
s up the grain ... Gen 41:35
His sin is *s-d* up ... Hos 13:12
s up...treasures ... Matt 6:20
place to *s* my crops ... Luke 12:17
s-d up your treasure ... James 5:3

STOREHOUSE *storage place*
s-s of the snow ... Job 38:22
wind from His *s-s* ... Jer 10:13
tithe into the *s* ... Mal 3:10

STORK *bird*
the *s*, the heron ... Lev 11:19
the *s* in the sky ... Jer 8:7
wings of a *s* ... Zech 5:9

STORM *tempest, whirlwind*
A refuge from the *s* ... Is 25:4
will come like a *s* ... Ezek 38:9
a great *s* on the sea ... Jon 1:4
mists driven by a *s* ... 2 Pet 2:17

STRAIGHT *direct*
Make Your way *s* ... Ps 5:8
make your paths *s* ... Prov 3:6
Make His paths *s* ... Matt 3:3
Make *s* the way ... John 1:23

STRANGE *foreign*
offered *s* fire ... Lev 10:1
no *s* god among you ... Ps 81:9
to teach *s* doctrines ... 1 Tim 1:3
went after *s* flesh ... Jude 7

STRANGER *alien, sojourner*
s-s in a land ... Gen 15:13
a *s* and a sojourner ... Gen 23:4
shall not wrong a *s* ... Ex 22:21
a *s* in the earth ... Ps 119:19
LORD protects the *s-s* ... Ps 146:9
violence to the *s* ... Jer 22:3
I was a *s* ... Matt 25:35
hospitality to *s-s* ... Heb 13:2

STRAW *stalk of grain*
s to make brick ... Ex 5:7
s for the horses ... 1 Kin 4:28
as *s* before the wind ... Job 21:18
wood, hay, *s* ... 1 Cor 3:12

STRAY *wander*
not *s* into her paths ... Prov 7:25
no longer *s* from Me ... Ezek 14:11
s-s from the truth ... James 5:19
s-ing like sheep ... 1 Pet 2:25

STREAM *current, flow*
planted by *s-s* of water ... Ps 1:3
The *s* of God ... Ps 65:9
like a rushing *s* ... Is 59:19

STREET *road, way*
Wisdom shouts in...*s* ... Prov 1:20
race madly in the *s-s* ... Nah 2:4
on the *s* corners ... Matt 6:5
s of the city...gold ... Rev 21:21

STRENGTH *force, power*
no longer yield its *s* ... Gen 4:12
The LORD is my *s* ... Ex 15:2
was no *s* in him ... 1 Sam 28:20
My *s* is dried up ... Ps 22:15
The LORD is my *s* ... Ps 28:7
s in time of trouble ... Ps 37:39
God is our refuge...*s* ... Ps 46:1
s of my salvation ... Ps 140:7
your *s* to women ... Prov 31:3
s to the weary ... Is 40:29
Strangers devour his *s* ... Hos 7:9
with all your *s* ... Mark 12:30
s which God supplies ... 1 Pet 4:11
sun shining in its *s* ... Rev 1:16

STRENGTHEN *make strong*
please *s* me ... Judg 16:28
David *s-ed* himself ... 1 Sam 30:6
s-ed weak hands ... Job 4:3
s the feeble ... Is 35:3
s the sick ... Ezek 34:16
s your brothers ... Luke 22:32
s-ed in the faith ... Acts 16:5
Him who *s-s* me ... Phil 4:13
s-ed with all power ... Col 1:11
s your hearts ... 2 Thess 2:17
who has *s-ed* me ... 1 Tim 1:12

STRETCH *extend*
I will *s* out My hand ... Ex 3:20
He *s-es* out the north ... Job 26:7
S-ing out heaven ... Ps 104:2
I *s-ed* out the heavens ... Is 45:12

STRIFE *discord, quarrel*
s between...herdsmen ... Gen 13:7
the *s* of tongues ... Ps 31:20
Hatred stirs up *s* ... Prov 10:12
fool's lips bring *s* ... Prov 18:6
puts an end to *s* ... Prov 18:18
of envy, murder, *s* ... Rom 1:29
and *s* among you ... 1 Cor 3:3
enmities, *s*, jealousy ... Gal 5:20

STRIKE *hit*
I will *s* the water ... Ex 7:17
you shall *s* the rock ... Ex 17:6
He who *s-s* a man ... Ex 21:12
s the timbrel ... Ps 81:2
you do not *s* your foot ... Ps 91:12
S a scoffer ... Prov 19:25
He will *s* the earth ... Is 11:4
let us *s* at him ... Jer 18:18
S the Shepherd ... Zech 13:7
s...the shepherd ... Matt 26:31
struck Jesus ... John 18:22
struck them with many blows ... Acts 16:23
s the earth ... Rev 11:6

STRIVE *contend, struggle*
not *s* with man forever ... Gen 6:3
He will not always *s* ... Ps 103:9
and *s-ing* after wind ... Eccl 1:14
s together with me ... Rom 15:30
s-ing to please men ... Gal 1:10
we labor and *s* ... 1 Tim 4:10
s-ing against sin ... Heb 12:4

STRONG *powerful, steadfast*
a very *s* west wind ... Ex 10:19
not drink...*s* drink ... Lev 10:9
Be *s* and courageous ... Deut 31:6
Israel became *s* ... Judg 1:28
God is...*s* fortress ... 2 Sam 22:33
The LORD *s* and mighty ... Ps 24:8
s drink a brawler ... Prov 20:1
their Redeemer is *s* ... Prov 23:11
ants are not a *s* people ... Prov 30:25
love is as *s* as death ... Song 8:6
Their Redeemer is *s* ... Jer 50:34
grew *s* in faith ... Rom 4:20
act like men, be *s* ... 1 Cor 16:13
be *s* in the Lord ... Eph 6:10
weakness...made *s* ... Heb 11:34
I saw a *s* angel ... Rev 5:2

STRONGHOLD *fortress, refuge*
David lived in the *s* ... 2 Sam 5:9
s and my refuge ... 2 Sam 22:3
s for the oppressed ... Ps 9:9
For God is my *s* ... Ps 59:9
my salvation, My *s* ... Ps 62:2
a *s* to the upright ... Prov 10:29

STRUGGLE (n) *conflict*
the days of my *s* ... Job 14:14
our *s* is not against ... Eph 6:12
have shared my *s* ... Phil 4:3

STRUGGLE (v) *contend*
children *s-d* together ... Gen 25:22
men *s*...each other ... Ex 21:22

STUBBLE *short stumps*
gather *s* for straw ... Ex 5:12
fire consumes *s* ... Is 5:24
give birth to *s* ... Is 33:11
house of Esau...*s* ... Obad 18

STUBBORN *obstinate*
Pharaoh's heart is *s* ... Ex 7:14
you are a *s* people ... Deut 9:6
s...generation ... Ps 78:8
house of Israel is *s* ... Ezek 3:7

STUBBORNNESS *intractable*
I know your...*s* ... Deut 31:27
s of their heart ... Ps 81:12
s...unrepentant heart ... Rom 2:5

STUMBLE *fall, trip*
your foot will not *s* ... Prov 3:23
a rock to *s* over ... Is 8:14
arrogant one will *s* ... Jer 50:32
eye makes you *s* ... Matt 5:29
a stone of *s-ing* ... Rom 9:33
all *s* in many *ways* ... James 3:2

STUMBLING BLOCK *obstacle* Anything that causes a person to trip or fall. In the Bible, often used as a metaphor for anything that leads someone to sin. Sometimes used of Christ's crucifixion in that the Jews could not accept the idea of a Messiah who would have to suffer and die. This attitude resulted in their rejection of Jesus as the Messiah.
s before the blind ... Lev 19:14
s of iniquity ... Ezek 44:12
You are a *s* to Me ... Matt 16:23
to Jews a *s* ... 1 Cor 1:23
s of the cross ... Gal 5:11

STUMP *part of plant*
s dies in the dry soil ... Job 14:8
The holy seed is its *s* ... Is 6:13
the *s* with the roots ... Dan 4:26

STUPID *foolish, senseless*
s and the senseless ... Ps 49:10
I am more *s* than ... Prov 30:2
they are altogether *s* ... Jer 10:8

STYLUS *marking / writing device*
an iron *s* and lead ... Job 19:24
with an iron *s* ... Jer 17:1

SWEAT *perspiration*
By the *s* of your face ... Gen 3:19
s...like drops of ... Luke 22:44

SWEET *fresh, pleasant*
waters became *s* ... Ex 15:25
s psalmist of Israel ... 2 Sam 23:1
who had *s* fellowship ... Ps 55:14
s are Your words ... Ps 119:103
your sleep will be *s* ... Prov 3:24
Stolen water is *s* ... Prov 9:17
it was *s* as honey ... Ezek 3:3

SWIFT *fast, rapid*
horses and *s* steeds ... 1 Kin 4:28
s as the gazelles ... 1 Chr 12:8
race is not to the *s* ... Eccl 9:11
riding on a *s* cloud ... Is 19:1
s to shed blood ... Rom 3:15

SWINDLER *cheater*
cursed be the *s* ... Mal 1:14
a drunkard, or a *s* ... 1 Cor 5:11
revilers, nor *s-s* ... 1 Cor 6:10

SWINE *pig*
gold in a *s-'s* snout ... Prov 11:22
Who eat *s-'s* flesh ... Is 65:4
your pearls before *s* ... Matt 7:6
Send us into the *s* ... Mark 5:12

SWORD *weapon with blade*
flaming *s*...turned ... Gen 3:24
by your *s* you shall ... Gen 27:40
the *s* will bereave ... Deut 32:25
A *s* for the LORD ... Judg 7:20
s devour forever ... 2 Sam 2:26
fell on his *s* ... 1 Chr 10:5
tongue a sharp *s* ... Ps 57:4
as a two-edged *s* ... Prov 5:4
teeth are *like s-s* ... Prov 30:14
s against nation ... Is 2:4
the power of the *s* ... Jer 18:21
abolish...the *s* ... Hos 2:18
s-s into plowshares ... Mic 4:3
perish by the *s* ... Matt 26:52
s of the Spirit ... Eph 6:17
than any two-edged *s* ... Heb 4:12
s of My mouth ... Rev 2:16

SYCAMORE *tree*
olive and *s* trees ... 1 Chr 27:28
plentiful as *s-s* ... 2 Chr 1:15
grower of *s* figs ... Amos 7:14
climbed up into a *s* ... Luke 19:4

SYCHAR
town in Samaria ... John 4:5
also **SHECHEM**

SYMPATHY *mutual feeling*
I looked for *s* ... Ps 69:20
s to the prisoners ... Heb 10:34

SYNAGOGUE *(assembly).* The local meeting place for a Jewish community of at least ten males who were the heads of their households. It had significant religious, educational, and social functions for Jewish life. Synagogues probably came into being during the Babylonian exile. Jesus preached in synagogues, as did Paul.
pray in the *s-s* ... Matt 6:5
He went into their *s* ... Matt 12:9
flogged in *the s-s* ... Mark 13:9
chief seats in...*s-s* ... Luke 20:46
outcasts from the *s* ... John 16:2
taught in *s-s* ... John 18:20
reasoning in the *s* ... Acts 17:17
but are a *s* of Satan ... Rev 2:9

SYRIA A country extending from the eastern shore of the Mediterranean to the upper Euphrates River and the Tarsus mountains.
NE of Israel ... Matt 4:24; Acts 15:23,41; 20:3
see also **ARAM**

T

TAANACH A royal Canaanite city whose king was defeated by Joshua, who in turn gave the city to the tribe of Manasseh. Later it became a Levite city used by the Kohathites.
Canaanite royal city ... Josh 12:21; 21:25; Judg 5:19

TABERNACLE *assembly and area for sacrificial worship (dwelling place).* The structure that served as a site of worship and the dwelling of God while the Israelites wandered in the wilderness. It was essentially an elaborate tent enclosed by a courtyard.
dwelling place of God among the Israelites ... Ex 25:8
construction directed by God ... Ex 25:9
contained Ark of the Covenant ... Ex 25:10
other descriptive names of the tabernacle:
house of the LORD ... Ex 23:19; 34:26; Deut 23:18
tabernacle of the house of God ... 1 Chr 6:48
tabernacle of the tent of meeting ... Ex 39:40; 40:6,29
tabernacle of the testimony ... Ex 38:21; Num 1:50,53
tent of meeting ... Ex 29:32; 30:26; 38:30; 38:43; 40:2,6,7

TABERNACLES, FEAST OF *see* **BOOTHS, FEAST OF**

TABITHA *see* **DORCAS**

TABLE *furniture*
gold t before the LORD ... Lev 24:6
You prepare a *t* ... Ps 23:5
crumbs...masters' *t* ... Matt 15:27
t-s...moneychangers ... Matt 21:12
dogs under the *t* ... Mark 7:28
drink at My *t* ... Luke 22:30
in order to serve *t-s* ... Acts 6:2
t of the Lord ... 1 Cor 10:21

TABLET *writing surface*
give you the stone *t-s* ... Ex 24:12
t-s of the testimony ... Ex 31:18
the *t* of their heart ... Jer 17:1
t-s of human hearts ... 2 Cor 3:3

TABOR
1 *mountain* ... Judg 4:6,12
2 *city in Zebulun* ... 1 Chr 6:77
3 *oak in Benjamin* ... 1 Sam 10:3

TAHPANHES A city in Egypt to which Jeremiah and others fled from Babylonian captivity.
Egyptian city ... Jer 2:16
place where Jeremiah escaped ... Jer 43:7-9; 44:1

TAHPENES An Egyptian wife of the Pharaoh who sheltered Hadad, an Edomite prince, when he fled to Egypt from Edom.
queen of Egypt ... 1 Kin 11:19,20

TAIL
grasp *it* by its *t* ... Ex 4:4
the foxes t to *t* ... Judg 15:4
cuts off head and *t* ... Is 9:14
t-s like scorpions ... Rev 9:10

TAKE *get, grasp*
t...the tree of life ... Gen 3:22
T My yoke upon ... Matt 11:29
T, eat; this is My ... Matt 26:26
t-s away the sin ... John 1:29
day that He was *t-n* ... Acts 1:22
to *t* hold of...hope ... Heb 6:18

TALENT The largest of the Hebrew measures of weight, about 75 pounds (3,000 shekels), used in quantifying metals, including silver and gold (a very large sum of money). Jesus used the measure in describing the money entrusted to three slaves in the parable of the talents. In English usage, the term gradually came to be applied abstractly to one's natural, God-given abilities.
measure of weight ... Ex 38:27; 2 Sam 12:30; 1 Chr 20:2
measure of money ... 1 Kin 20:39; Matt 18:24; 25:15,25

TALK (n) *conversation, speech*
argue with useless *t* ... Job 15:3
no...silly *t* ... Eph 5:4
their *t* will spread ... 2 Tim 2:17

TALK (v) *converse, speak*
God *t-ed* with him ... Gen 17:3
lips *t* of trouble ... Prov 24:2
who *t* about you ... Ezek 33:30
they were *t-ing* ... Luke 24:15
Paul kept on *t-ing* ... Acts 20:9

TALL *high*
cut...its *t* cedars ... 2 Kin 19:23
a nation *t* and smooth ... Is 18:2
grew up, became *t* ... Ezek 16:7

TALMUD *(teaching, study).* Specifically the Babylonian Talmud, the authoritative body of Jewish tradition (oral and written) made up of the Mishnah and the Gemara, compiled in written form ca. 200-500 A.D.

TAMAR *(date palm).* Name of three women, among whom was a daughter of David who was violated by Amnon, her half-brother. Also the name of a city in Judah.
1 *Judah's daughter-in-law* ... Gen 38:6ff
2 *daughter of David* ... 2 Sam 13:1
3 *daughter of Absalom* ... 2 Sam 14:27
4 *town near the Dead Sea* ... 1 Kin 9:18; Ezek 47:19; 48:28

TAMARISK *tree*
a *t* tree at Beersheba ... Gen 21:33
under the *t* tree ... 1 Sam 22:6

TAMBOURINE
accompanied by...*t* ... Is 5:12
gaiety of *t-s* ceases ... Is 24:8

TAMMUZ
Mesopotamian god ... Ezek 8:14

TANNER The occupation of processing animal hides for various uses. In the Talmud, the rabbis acknowledge the need for tanners, but pronounce woe upon anyone who takes up the occupation, due undoubtedly to the odor emitted from a tannery. Tanners usually had to live outside the cities, and it was while staying at the house of Simon the tanner by the sea that Peter had his vision of the animals on a sheet descending from the sky (Acts 9:43).

TARES *weeds*
t among the wheat ... Matt 13:25
gather up the *t* ... Matt 13:30
parable of the *t* ... Matt 13:36

TARSHISH *(brightness).* 1) The name of three people in Scripture. 2) A term designating ships that carried smelted or refined ores. 3) The name of the place to which Jonah attempted to flee, perhaps as far west as Spain.
1 *lineage of Japheth* ... Gen 10:4
2 *ships of* ... 1 Kin 10:22; 22:48; 2 Chr 9:21; Ps 48:7
3 *line of Benjamin* ... 1 Chr 7:6-10
4 *Persian official* ... Esth 1:14
5 *city* ... Is 66:19; Jon 1:3

TARSUS A city in the southeast part of Asia Minor, capital of Cilicia and the birthplace of the apostle Paul. Its inhabitants loved Greek philosophy.
birthplace of Paul ... Acts 21:39
capital of Cilicia ... Acts 22:3

TASKMASTERS *overseers* Superintendents of forced labor.
appointed *t* over them ... Ex 1:11
Pharaoh commanded...*t* ... Ex 5:6

TASTE *test flavor*
As the palate *t-s* ... Job 34:3
O *t* and see ... Ps 34:8
will not *t* death ... Matt 16:28
t death for everyone ... Heb 2:9
t-d...heavenly gift ... Heb 6:4

TASTELESS *without taste*
Can something *t* be ... Job 6:6
salt has become *t* ... Matt 5:13

TAUNT *object of ridicule*
a *t* among all ... Deut 28:37
I have become their *t* ... Job 30:9

TAX *charge, tribute* A monetary charge imposed by the government on persons or property. In ancient times countries or empires that conquered other countries typically imposed tribute taxes on them. The Romans registered the inhabitants of the empire by census (q.v.) to collect a poll-tax or "head" tax, i.e. a per-person tax. Also, Jewish males aged 20 or older were required by OT law to pay a half-shekel temple tax.
a *t* for the LORD ... Num 31:28
money for the king's *t* ... Neh 5:4
sitting in the *t* collector's booth ... Matt 9:9
pay *t-es* to Caesar ... Luke 20:22
t to whom *t is due* ... Rom 13:7

TAX COLLECTOR *tax gatherer* In NT times, the Roman government accepted bids from private individuals, some of whom were Jews, to serve as tax collectors or "tax farmers." These people were then permitted to collect as much money as they could, turning over the required amount to Rome and keeping the rest for themselves. For this reason they were considered swindlers by the people who were taxed, and the occupation was especially despised among the Jews because it involved cooperation with Rome and defilement through contact with Gentiles and pagan coins. The Jews who took these positions often were banned from the synagogues and rejected by their families and friends. This was the original occupation of the apostle Matthew (Levi).
see also **TAX** *and* **CENSUS**
t-s do the same ... Matt 5:46
many *t-s* and sinners ... Matt 9:10
Matthew the *t* ... Matt 10:3
a friend of *t-s* ... Matt 11:19
he was a chief *t* ... Luke 19:2

TEACH *instruct*
t you what...to say ... Ex 4:12
t them the good way ... 1 Kin 8:36
Can anyone *t* God ... Job 21:22
T me Your paths ... Ps 25:4
T me to do Your will ... Ps 143:10
would He *t* knowledge ... Is 28:9
He...*began* to *t* them ... Matt 5:2
t-ing...in parables ... Mark 4:2
Lord, *t* us to pray ... Luke 11:1
Spirit will *t* you ... Luke 12:12
He will *t* you all ... John 14:26
t strange doctrines ... 1 Tim 1:3
allow a woman to *t* ... 1 Tim 2:12
she *t-es* and leads ... Rev 2:20

TEACHER *instructor*
will behold your *T* ... Is 30:20
T, I will follow You ... Matt 8:19
not above his *t* ... Matt 10:24
why trouble the *T* ... Mark 5:35
the *t* of Israel ... John 3:10
call Me *T* and Lord ... John 13:13
t of the immature ... Rom 2:20
as pastors and *t-s* ... Eph 4:11
t of the Gentiles ... 1 Tim 2:7
false *t-s* among you ... 2 Pet 2:1

TEACHING (n) *instruction*
t drop as the rain ... Deut 32:2
your mother's *t* ... Prov 1:8
amazed at His *t* ... Matt 7:28
My *t* is not Mine ... John 7:16
contrary to sound *t* ... 1 Tim 1:10

TEAR *crying*
have seen your *t-s* ... 2 Kin 20:5
my *t-s* in Your bottle ... Ps 56:8
sow in *t-s* shall reap ... Ps 126:5
drench you with my *t-s* ... Is 16:9
eyes a fountain of *t-s* ... Jer 9:1
His feet with her *t-s* ... Luke 7:38
God...wipe every *t* ... Rev 7:17

TEBETH
name of the tenth month in Hebrew calendar ... Esth 2:16

TEKOA The city which was the birthplace of the prophet Amos, and was located six miles south of Bethlehem (Amos 1:1). Also the name of an individual (1 Chr 2:24).

TEL-ABIB
place in Babylonia ... Ezek 3:15
Jewish exiles located there

TELL *relate, speak*
not *t* the riddle ... Judg 14:14
T of His glory ... 1 Chr 16:24
t of Your righteousness ... Ps 71:15
t-s lies will perish ... Prov 19:9
t you great and mighty ... Jer 33:3
See that you *t* no one ... Matt 8:4
t you about Me ... John 18:34
t you the mystery ... Rev 17:7

TEMA
1 *son of Ishmael* ... Gen 25:15
2 *town in Arabia* ... Job 6:19; Is 21:14

TEMAN Grandson of Esau, and the region his descendants inhabited (Gen 36:10-11).

TEMPER *anger*
always loses his *t* ... Prov 29:11
the ruler's *t* rises ... Eccl 10:4

TEMPEST *storm*
bruises me with a *t* ... Job 9:17
stormy wind *and t* ... Ps 55:8
t of destruction ... Is 28:2
on the day of *t* ... Amos 1:14

TEMPLE *structure for worship* 1) A building dedicated for the worship of God, therefore the house of God. Specifically, it refers to the three buildings constructed from the time of Solomon to that of Herod. The last one, Herod's temple, was destroyed in 70 A.D. by Titus, the Roman general and (later) emperor. Of Herod's temple it was said, "He who has not seen the Temple of Herod has never seen a beautiful building." The "Wailing Wall" is the western wall of that temple complex left standing by Titus as a reminder to the Jews of Roman might. 2) The physical body of Jesus or a believer. 3) All believers corporately. 4) God and the Lamb in the new Jerusalem.
doorpost of the *t* ... 1 Sam 1:9
t is not for man ... 1 Chr 29:1
LORD is in His holy *t* ... Ps 11:4
meditate in His *t* ... Ps 27:4
t of the LORD ... Jer 7:4
pinnacle of the *t* ... Matt 4:5
will destroy this *t* ... Mark 14:58
veil of the *t* ... Luke 23:45
Destroy this *t*, and ... John 2:19
you are a *t* of God ... 1 Cor 3:16
t of the Holy Spirit ... 1 Cor 6:19
his seat in the *t* ... 2 Thess 2:4
the Lamb, are its *t* ... Rev 21:22

TEMPT *test, try*
And *t-ed* God in the ... Ps 106:14
being *t-ed* by Satan ... Mark 1:13
so that Satan will not *t* you ... 1 Cor 7:5
t-ed beyond what ... 1 Cor 10:13
Himself does not *t* ... James 1:13

TEMPTATION *testing, trial* Being enticed to do wrong or enticing someone to do wrong. The Bible firmly states that God cannot be tempted by evil and that He Himself does not tempt anyone (Jam 1:13).
not lead us into *t* ... Matt 6:13
not enter into *t* ... Matt 26:41

time of *t* fall away ... Luke 8:13
t has overtaken you ... 1 Cor 10:13
the godly from *t* ... 2 Pet 2:9

TEN *number*
it had *t* horns ... Dan 7:7
has the *t* talents ... Matt 25:28

TEN COMMANDMENTS The commandments miraculously engraved on two stone tablets and given by God to Moses on Mt. Sinai (Ex 20). When he came down from the mountain and saw the idolatry and immoral celebrations of the people of Israel, Moses threw the tablets down to the ground, where they shattered. He later was told by God to make two more tablets and God repeated the commandments on them. Also known as the Decalogue, the ten commandments were placed in the ark of the testimony.
T which the Lord had spoken ... Deut 10:4

TEND *take care of*
t his father's flock ... 1 Sam 17:15
He will *t* His flock ... Is 40:11
T My lambs ... John 21:15
T My sheep ... John 21:17

TENDER *gentle, young*
t and choice calf ... Gen 18:7
your heart was *t* ... 2 Kin 22:19
like a *t* shoot ... Is 53:2
t mercy of our God ... Luke 1:78

TENT *mobile shelter*
Abram moved his *t* ... Gen 13:18
man, living in *t-s* ... Gen 25:27
your *t-s*, O Israel ... 1 Kin 12:16
t-s of the destroyers ... Job 12:6
dwell in Your *t* forever ... Ps 61:4
grumbled in their *t-s* ... Ps 106:25
Like a shepherd's *t* ... Is 38:12

TENT OF MEETING
perhaps the same as the Tabernacle or at certain periods a separate meeting place ... Ex 33:7; Lev 1:1; Num 7:5; Josh 18:1
see also **TABERNACLE**

TENT OF TESTIMONY *see* **TABERNACLE**

TERAH The father of Abraham, Nahor, and Haran. Also a place where the Israelites encamped in the wilderness.
father of Abraham ... Gen 11:24; Luke 3:34
place in wilderness ... Num 33:27

TERAPHIM A kind of idol, some of which are small, designed to be kept at home. They are condemned in the Bible.
household gods, idols ... 2 Kin 23:24; Zech 10:2

TEREBINTH A tree that is similar in appearance to an oak (Isa 6:13; Hos 4:13). Abraham probably entertained his angelic guests under a terebinth.

TERRIBLE *dreadful*
and *t* wilderness ... Deut 8:15
t day of the LORD ... Mal 4:5
into *t* convulsions ... Mark 9:26

TERRIFY *frighten*
t-ied by the sword ... 1 Chr 21:30
t me by visions ... Job 7:14
t them with Your storm ... Ps 83:15
Him and were *t-ied* ... Mark 6:50
t you by my letters ... 2 Cor 10:9

TERRITORY *country, land*
smite your whole *t* ... Ex 8:2
God enlarges your *t* ... Deut 19:8
t of...inheritance ... Josh 19:10
possess the *t* ... Obad 19

TERROR *intense fear*
Sounds of *t* are in ... Job 15:21
t-s of thick darkness ... Job 24:17
t-s of Sheol came ... Ps 116:3
meditate on *t* ... Is 33:18
t-s and great signs ... Luke 21:11

TERTIUS (Lat, *third*). Paul's secretary, or amanuensis, when he wrote his epistle to the Romans.
Paul's scribe ... Rom 16:22

TERTULLUS (diminutive form of *Tertius*). A Roman lawyer whom the Jewish authorities used in the prosecution of Paul before Felix (Acts 24:1).

TEST (n) *trial*
put God to the *t* ... Ps 78:18
put Him to the *t* ... Luke 10:25
you fail the *t* ... 2 Cor 13:5

TEST (v) *try* 1) A challenge or difficult situation imposed by God for the purpose of strengthening faith; not to be confused with temptation to evil (Jam 1:13). 2) The act of putting God to the test, demanding that He prove Himself and His power in some way, as Satan attempted to persuade Jesus to do. 3) The act of one person's challenging another to prove himself by answering difficult questions, etc.
God *t-ed* Abraham ... Gen 22:1
Why do you *t* the LORD ... Ex 17:2
she came to *t* him ... 1 Kin 10:1
T my mind and my ... Ps 26:2
word of God is *t-ed* ... Prov 30:5
Spirit...to the *t* ... Acts 5:9
fire itself will *t* ... 1 Cor 3:13
t the spirits to see ... 1 John 4:1

TESTAMENT A covenant, a formal agreement between two parties, conveying the idea of a will (Heb 9:15-17).

TESTIFY *bear witness*
nor shall you *t* ... Ex 23:2
them *t* against him ... 1 Kin 21:10
I will *t* against you ... Ps 50:7
our sins *t* against us ... Is 59:12
John *t-ied* ... John 1:15
John *t-ied* ... John 1:32
Jesus Himself *t-ied* ... John 4:44
If I *alone t* ... John 5:31
t about Me ... John 15:26
you *will t* ... John 15:27
Spirit...*t-ies* ... Rom 8:16
three that *t* ... 1 John 5:7

TESTIMONY *witness*
into the ark the *t* ... Ex 25:16
two tablets of the *t* ... Ex 31:18
t of the LORD is sure ... Ps 19:7
t-ies are righteous ... Ps 119:144
Bind up the *t* ... Is 8:16
t to all the nations ... Matt 24:14
t against Jesus ... Matt 26:59
My *t* is true ... John 8:14
t of two men is true ... John 8:17
t concerning Christ ... 1 Cor 1:6
ashamed of the *t* ... 2 Tim 1:8
This *t* is true ... Titus 1:13
t of God is greater ... 1 John 5:9

TETRARCH (*four* and *ruler*). Originally the ruler of a fourth part of a region, but later a minor ruler, inferior to a king. Herod Antipas, the son of Herod the Great, was tetrarch over Galilee and Perea from 4 B.C.–39 A.D.
governor of a region ... Matt 14:1; Luke 3:1,19; Acts 13:1

THADDAEUS (unc, *breast*). One of the twelve apostles who also was named Judas (not Iscariot).
apostle ... Matt 10:3; Mark 3:18

THANK (v) *express gratitude*
my song I shall *t* Him ... Ps 28:7
God, I *t* You ... Luke 18:11
I *t* my God always ... 1 Cor 1:4

THANKS (n) *gratitude*
give *t* to the LORD ... 1 Chr 16:7
It is good to give *t* ... Ps 92:1
giving *t*, He broke ... Matt 15:36
a cup and given *t* ... Matt 26:27
But *t* be to God ... Rom 6:17
not cease giving *t* ... Eph 1:16
always to give *t* ... 2 Thess 1:3

THANKSGIVING *gratitude* The giving of thanks to God, acknowledging Him as the source of all blessings.
the sacrifice of *t* ... Lev 7:12
with the voice of *t* ... Ps 26:7
His presence with *t* ... Ps 95:2
supplication with *t* ... Phil 4:6
t and honor and ... Rev 7:12

THEBES (*city of Amon* [an Egyptian god]). The Gr name of an Egyptian city near Memphis.
Egyptian city ... Jer 46:25; Ezek 30:14-16

THEFT *robbery*
be sold for his *t* ... Ex 22:3
t-s, murders ... Mark 7:21

THEOPHANY (*God revealed*). A manifestation of God in a visible form, such as the burning bush seen by Moses or the pillar of cloud and fire that led Israel in the wilderness. The term is not found in the Bible.

THEOPHILUS (*loved of God*). The person to whom Luke addressed his Gospel and Acts. He may have been an influential member of the Roman government.
addressee of Luke's gospel and Acts ... Luke 1:3; Acts 1:1

THESSALONICA A city in Macedonia which had a large Jewish community and a synagogue during NT times. Paul and Silas organized a church there and wrote two letters to it.
Macedonian city ... Acts 27:2; Phil 4:16
visited by Paul ... Acts 17:1,11,13

THICKET *underbrush*
ram caught in the *t* ... Gen 22:13
the *t* of the Jordan ... Jer 50:44

THIEF *robber*
that *t* shall die ... Deut 24:7
partner with a *t* ... Prov 29:24
companions of *t-ves* ... Is 1:23
enter...like a *t* ... Joel 2:9
t comes...to steal ... John 10:10
a *t* in the night ... 1 Thess 5:2

THIGH *part of leg*
hand under my *t* ... Gen 24:2
socket of Jacob's *t* ... Gen 32:25
Your sword on *Your t* ... Ps 45:3
on His *t*...a name ... Rev 19:16

THIN *lean*
t ears scorched ... Gen 41:27
t yellowish hair ... Lev 13:30
streams...will *t* out ... Is 19:6

THINK *ponder, reflect*
as he *t-s*...so he is ... Prov 23:7
not *t*...to abolish ... Matt 5:17
not to *t* more highly ... Rom 12:3
t like a child ... 1 Cor 13:11
t-s he is something ... Gal 6:3
beyond all that we...*t* ... Eph 3:20

THIRD *number*
morning, a *t* day ... Gen 1:13
raised...the *t* day ... Matt 16:21
raised on the *t* day ... 1 Cor 15:4
to the *t* heaven ... 2 Cor 12:2

THIRST (n) *craving, dryness*
for my *t*...vinegar ... Ps 69:21
donkeys quench...*t* ... Ps 104:11
not hunger or *t* ... Is 49:10
in Me will never *t* ... John 6:35
no longer...nor *t* ... Rev 7:16

THIRST (v) *have a craving*
My soul *t-s* for God ... Ps 42:2
Every one who *t-s*, come ... Is 55:1
t for righteousness ... Matt 5:6

THIRSTY *lacking water*
satisfied the *t* soul ... Ps 107:9
In a dry and *t* land ... Ezek 19:13
I was *t*, and you ... Matt 25:35
If anyone is *t* ... John 7:37
one who is *t* come ... Rev 22:17

THOMAS (Aram, *twin*). One of the twelve apostles, also called *Didymus* (Gr for "twin"). He was the inquisitive, skeptical apostle who said that he would not believe that Jesus had arisen unless he could see and touch the wounds Jesus suffered on the cross. He is known proverbially as Doubting Thomas." He later saw Jesus and believed.
apostle ... Matt 10:3; Mark 3:18; Luke 6:15
doubted Jesus' resurrection ... John 20:24-28

THORN *sharp point*
Both *t-s* and thistles ... Gen 3:18
as *t-s* in your sides ... Num 33:55
as a hedge of *t-s* ... Prov 15:19
lily among the *t-s* ... Song 2:2
have reaped *t-s* ... Jer 12:13
fell among the *t-s* ... Matt 13:7
a crown of *t-s* ... Matt 27:29
a burning *t* bush ... Acts 7:30
t in the flesh ... 2 Cor 12:7

THOUGHT *concept, idea*
t-s of his heart ... Gen 6:5
knows the *t-s* of man ... Ps 94:11
My *t-s* are not your *t-s* ... Is 55:8
Jesus knowing...*t-s* ... Matt 9:4
heart come evil *t-s* ... Matt 15:19
every *t* captive ... 2 Cor 10:5

THREAD *string*
cord of scarlet *t* ... Josh 2:18
lips...a scarlet *t* ... Song 4:3

THREE *number*
Job's *t* friends ... Job 2:11
or *t* have gathered ... Matt 18:20
deny Me *t* times ... Matt 26:34
t days I will raise ... John 2:19

THRESH *beat out*
ox while he is *t-ing* ... Deut 25:4
like the dust at *t-ing* ... 2 Kin 13:7
will *t* the mountains ... Is 41:15
Arise and *t* ... Mic 4:13

THRESHING FLOOR
winnows...at the *t* ... Ruth 3:2
David bought...*t* ... 2 Sam 24:24
clear His *t* ... Matt 3:12

THROAT *part of neck*
t is an open grave ... Ps 5:9
my *t* is parched ... Ps 69:3
has enlarged its *t* ... Is 5:14
t is an open grave ... Rom 3:13

THRONE *seat of sovereign*
sitting on His *t* ... 1 Kin 22:19
LORD'S *t* is in heaven ... Ps 11:4
Your *t* is established ... Ps 93:2
it is the *t* of God ... Matt 5:34
sit upon twelve *t-s* ... Matt 19:28
Your *t*...is forever ... Heb 1:8
to the *t* of grace ... Heb 4:16
a great white *t* ... Rev 20:11

THRUST *cast, push*
He will *t* them out ... Josh 23:5
t away like thorns ... 2 Sam 23:6
Nor to *t* aside ... Prov 18:5
LORD has *t*...down ... Jer 46:15

THUMMIM This and the Urim were parts of the breastpiece worn by the high priest, and were somehow used to seek God's will. What they actually were and how they were used is not known, but they may have been special stones or gems.
kept in high priest's breastplate for determining will of God ... Ex 28:30; Lev 8:8; Deut 33:8; Ezra 2:63; Neh 7:65

THUNDER (n)
LORD sent *t* ... Ex 9:23
But His mighty *t* ... Job 26:14
the hiding place of *t* ... Ps 81:7
be punished with *t* ... Is 29:6
sound of loud *t* ... Rev 14:2

THUNDER (v)
t in the heavens ... 1 Sam 2:10
you *t* with a voice ... Job 40:9
LORD also *t-ed* ... Ps 18:13

THYATIRA A city in Asia Minor known for its numerous trade guilds. Lydia, a well known merchant of dyed material, lived there. One of the seven churches addressed in the book of Revelation was located there.
city in Asia minor
home of Lydia ... Acts 16:14
early church ... Rev 1:11;2:18,24

TIBERIAS A city on the Sea of Galilee (also called the Sea of Tiberias) built and named in honor of the emperor Tiberius (q.v.) by Herod Antipas.
city on W shore of Sea of Galilee ... John 6:23

TIBERIUS The third Roman emperor; he is the "Caesar" mentioned in the book of Luke.
Roman emperor ... Luke 3:1
see also **CAESAR**

TIDINGS *information, news*
t of His salvation ... 1 Chr 16:23
not fear evil *t* ... Ps 112:7

TIGLATH-PILESER An Assyrian king who carried away many Palestinians into exile and to whom Pekah, king of Israel, paid tribute.
Assyrian king ... 2 Kin 15:29;16:7,10
see also **PUL** *and* **TILGATH-PILNESER**

TIGRIS Together with the Euphrates, this river served as the border of Mesopotamia in ancient times. One of the four waterways springing out of Eden.
Mesopotamian river ... Gen 2:14; Dan 10:4

TILGATH-PILNESER
Assyrian king ... 1 Chr 5:6,26; 2 Chr 28:20
see also **PUL**
see also **TIGLATH-PILESER**

TILLER *cultivator*
Cain was a *t* ... Gen 4:2
a *t* of the ground ... Zech 13:5

TIMBER *wood*
cedar and cypress *t* ... 1 Kin 9:11
whatever *t* you need ... 2 Chr 2:16
t of Lebanon ... Song 3:9

TIMBREL *musical instrument*
with songs, with *t* ... Gen 31:27
strike the *t* ... Ps 81:2
Praise Him with *t* ... Ps 150:4

TIME *day, period, season*
in *t-s* of trouble ... Ps 9:9
t-s are in Your hand ... Ps 31:15
for a *t*, *t-s*, and half ... Dan 12:7
t to seek the LORD ... Hos 10:12
signs of the *t-s* ... Matt 16:3
My *t* is near ... Matt 26:18
deny Me three *t-s* ... Luke 22:61
My *t* is not yet ... John 7:6
not...you to know *t-s* ... Acts 1:7
is the acceptable *t* ... 2 Cor 6:2
grace...in *t* of need ... Heb 4:16
for the *t* is near ... Rev 1:3

TIMNAH *(allotted portion)*. Name of two cities, one about 15 miles south of Jerusalem in the territory of Judah, assigned to the tribe of Dan; the other is in the hill country of Judah (Gen 38:12; 2 Chr 28:18).

TIMOTHY *(one who honors God)*. A convert of Paul whose mother and

grandmother were Jewish, and his father Greek. A frequent companion of Paul, he was physically weak but strong in the spirit. Paul wrote two letters to him.
companion of Paul ... Acts 17:15; 18:5; Phil 1:1; Col 1:1; Heb 13:23

TIRED *weary*
I am *t* of living ... Gen 27:46
run and not get *t* ... Is 40:31

TIRZAH
1 *daughter of Zelophehad* ... Num 26:33; 27:1; 36:11
2 *royal Canaanite city* ... 1 Kin 14:17; 2 Kin 15:14

TISHBITE
town identity of Elijah ... 1 Kin 17:1; 21:17; 2 Kin 1:3,8

TITHE (n) *tenth* A tenth portion of one's produce or income to be given as an offering of thanksgiving to God in recognition of the fact that He is the source of every good thing that one receives. OT law prescribed a number of required tithes, and Jewish tradition (the Talmud) goes into great detail regarding tithing requirements, e.g. which items of farm produce are subject to tithes and under what conditions.
all the *t* of the land ... Lev 27:30
a *t* of the *t* ... Num 18:26
the *t* of your grain ... Deut 12:17
t into the storehouse ... Mal 3:10
t-s of all that I get ... Luke 18:12
mortal men receive *t-s* ... Heb 7:8

TITHE (v) *pay a tithe*
shall surely *t* all ... Deut 14:22
you *t* mint and dill ... Matt 23:23

TITUS A trusted companion of Paul. He was a former Greek pagan who was converted and had a very successful ministry.
co-worker with Paul ... 2 Cor 2:13; 8:23; Gal 2:1

TODAY *present time*
t you...be with Me ... Luke 23:43
same yesterday and *t* ... Heb 13:8

TOGARMAH
grandson of Japheth ... Gen 10:1-3; 1 Chr 1:6

TOIL (n) *labor, work*
the *t* of our hands ... Gen 5:29
t is not *in* vain ... 1 Cor 15:58

TOIL (v) *work hard*
I have *t-ed* in vain ... Is 49:4
they do not *t* nor ... Matt 6:28

TOMB *grave, sepulchre*
from womb to *t* ... Job 10:19
you have hewn a *t* ... Is 22:16
like whitewashed *t-s* ... Matt 23:27
laid Him in a *t* ... Mark 15:46
Lazarus out of the *t* ... John 12:17
outside the *t* ... John 20:11

TOMORROW *future time*
not boast about *t* ... Prov 27:1
for *t* we may die ... Is 22:13
not worry about *t* ... Matt 6:34

TONGUE *speech, talk*
speech and slow of *t* ... Ex 4:10
flatter with their *t* ... Ps 5:9
their *t* a sharp sword ... Ps 57:4
a lying *t* ... Prov 6:17
t of the wise ... Prov 12:18
soft *t* breaks...bone ... Prov 25:15
His *t* is like...fire ... Is 30:27
t is a deadly arrow ... Jer 9:8
impediment of his *t* ... Mark 7:35
and his *t loosed* ... Luke 1:64
no one...tame the *t* ... James 3:8

TONGUE *language*
speak with new *t-s* ... Mark 16:17
speak with other *t-s* ... Acts 2:4
t-s of men...angels ... 1 Cor 13:1
if I pray in a *t* ... 1 Cor 14:14
every tribe and *t* ... Rev 5:9

TOOL *work instrument*
among your *t-s* ... Deut 23:13
nor any iron *t* ... 1 Kin 6:7
iron into a cutting *t* ... Is 44:12

TOOTH
teeth white from ... Gen 49:12
eye for eye, *t* for *t* ... Ex 21:24
and a *t* for a *t* ... Matt 5:38

TOPAZ *precious stone* A semi-precious stone mentioned several times in the Bible.
ruby, *t*, and emerald ... Ex 39:10
t of Ethiopia ... Job 28:19
the ninth, *t* ... Rev 21:20

TOPHETH *(place of burning).* A high place in the Valley of Hinnom where many people sacrificed their children by fire to the god Molech. King Josiah terminated these sacrifices.
site of pagan worship ... 2 Kin 23:10; Jer 7:31,32; 19:6,12,14

TORMENT (n) *pain, torture*
this place of *t* ... Luke 16:28
their *t* was like ... Rev 9:5
the fear of her *t* ... Rev 18:15

TORMENT (v) *annoy, harass*
long will you *t* me ... Job 19:2
t us before the time ... Matt 8:29
do not *t* me ... Luke 8:28
Satan to *t* me ... 2 Cor 12:7

TORRENT *flood*
The ancient *t* ... Judg 5:21
t-s of destruction ... 2 Sam 22:5
t-s of ungodliness ... Ps 18:4
like an overflowing *t* ... Is 30:28

TOUCH *feel, handle*
not eat...or *t* it ... Gen 3:3
an angel *t-ing* him ... 1 Kin 19:5
evil will not *t* you ... Job 5:19
not *t* My anointed ... Ps 105:15
T nothing unclean ... Is 52:11
t the fringe of His ... Matt 14:36
not to *t* a woman ... 1 Cor 7:1

TOWER *fortress structure*
t whose top *will reach* ... Gen 11:4
Count her *t-s* ... Ps 48:12
name...strong *t* ... Prov 18:10
and built a *t* ... Matt 21:33

TOWN *city, village*
many unwalled *t-s* ... Deut 3:5
founds a *t* with ... Hab 2:12
except in his home *t* ... Matt 13:57

TRADE (n) *business, occupation*
abundance of your *t* ... Ezek 28:16
of the same *t* ... Acts 18:3

TRADE (v) *buy* or *sell*
may *t* in the land ... Gen 42:34
t-d with them ... Matt 25:16

TRADERS *merchants*
Midianite *t* passed ... Gen 37:28
king's *t* procured ... 2 Chr 1:16
in a city of *t* ... Ezek 17:4
increased your *t* ... Nah 3:16

TRADITION *custom*
sake of your *t* ... Matt 15:3
hold to the *t* of men ... Mark 7:8
hold...to the *t-s* ... 1 Cor 11:2
my ancestral *t-s* ... Gal 1:14

TRAIN *guide, instruct*
T up a child ... Prov 22:6
will they *t* for war ... Mic 4:3
t-ed to discern good ... Heb 5:14
heart *t-ed* in greed ... 2 Pet 2:14

TRAMPLE *crush, hurt*
t-s down the waves ... Job 9:8
let him *t* my life ... Ps 7:5
t-d the nations ... Hab 3:12
Jerusalem...*t-d* ... Luke 21:24

TRANCE *daze, dream*
he fell into a *t* ... Acts 10:10
in a *t* I saw a vision ... Acts 11:5
fell into a *t* ... Acts 22:17

TRANSFIGURATION A supernatural change of the appearance of Jesus while He was on a mountain with Peter, James, and John. During this time He was seen speaking with Moses and Elijah. The transfiguration served as a special preview of the glory Jesus will have in His kingdom.

TRANSFIGURED *changed*
He was *t* before them ... Matt 17:2
See also **TRANSFIGURATION**

TRANSFORM *change*
t-ed by the renewing ... Rom 12:2
t-ed into the same ... 2 Cor 3:18
who will *t* the body ... Phil 3:21

TRANSGRESS *break, overstep*
you *t* the covenant ... Josh 23:16
rulers also *t-ed* ... Jer 2:8
they *t-ed* laws ... Is 24:5

TRANSGRESSION *trespass, sin (an overstepping, false step).* A violation of human or divine law. Several words are used in the Bible to define various aspects of transgression, the most common of which is "sin."
forgives iniquity, *t* ... Ex 34:7
I am pure, without *t* ... Job 33:9
I know my *t-s* ... Ps 51:3
removed our *t-s* from ... Ps 103:12
love covers all *t-s* ... Prov 10:12
pierced...for our *t-s* ... Is 53:5
not forgive your *t-s* ... Matt 6:15
dead in our *t-s* ... Eph 2:5

TRANSGRESSOR *sinner*
teach *t-s* Your ways ... Ps 51:13

numbered with the *t-s* ... Is 53:12
a *t* of the law ... James 2:11

TRANSLATED
t and read before me ... Ezra 4:18
Immanuel...*t* means ... Matt 1:23
Golgotha, which is *t* ... Mark 15:22
Messiah...*t* means ... John 1:41

TRAP (n) *snare*
a snare and a *t* ... Josh 23:13
hidden a *t* for me ... Ps 142:3
table become...a *t* ... Rom 11:9

TRAP (v) *catch*
they might *t* Him ... Matt 22:15
in order to *t* Him ... Mark 12:13

TRAVAIL *intense pain*
t-ed nor given birth ... Is 23:4

TRAVEL *journey*
t by day and by night ... Ex 13:21
who *t* on the road ... Judg 5:10
Jesus...*began t-ing* ... Luke 24:15

TREACHEROUS *traitorous*
I behold the *t* ... Ps 119:158
t will be uprooted ... Prov 2:22
way of the *t* is hard ... Prov 13:15

TREAD *walk on*
They *t* wine presses ... Job 24:11
as the potter *t-s* clay ... Is 41:25
t on serpents ... Luke 10:19
t-s the wine press ... Rev 19:15

TREASURE (n) *valuable thing*
t-s of the sand ... Deut 33:19
the LORD is his *t* ... Is 33:6
opening their *t-s* ... Matt 2:11
for where your *t* is ... Matt 6:21
have *t* in heaven ... Matt 19:21
t in earthen vessels ... 2 Cor 4:7
stored up your *t* ... James 5:3

TREASURE (v) *value greatly*
I have *t-d* the words ... Job 23:12
Your word I have *t-d* ... Ps 119:11
t my commandments ... Prov 7:1

TREASURY *place of valuables*
t of the LORD ... Josh 6:19
paid from the royal *t* ... Ezra 6:4
fill their *t-ies* ... Prov 8:21
into the temple *t* ... Matt 27:6

TREATY *agreement, contract*
Let there be a *t* ... 1 Kin 15:19
go, break your *t* ... 2 Chr 16:3

TREE *woody plant*
fruit *t-s*...bearing ... Gen 1:11
t of life ... Gen 2:9
gave me from the *t* ... Gen 3:12
hang him on a *t* ... Deut 21:22
said to the olive *t* ... Judg 9:8
t firmly planted ... Ps 1:3
she is a *t* of life ... Prov 3:18
Beneath the apple *t* ... Song 8:5
like a *t* planted by ... Jer 17:8
under his fig *t* ... Mic 4:4
good *t* bears good ... Matt 7:17
the fig *t* withered ... Matt 21:19
a sycamore *t* ... Luke 19:4
autumn *t-s* without ... Jude 12
eat of the *t* of life ... Rev 2:7

TREMBLE *shake*
T before Him ... 1 Chr 16:30
pillars of heaven *t* ... Job 26:11
T, and do not sin ... Ps 4:4
make the heavens *t* ... Is 13:13
His soul *t-s* ... Is 15:4
my inward parts *t-d* ... Hab 3:16

TREMBLING (n) *fear, reverence*
rejoice with *t* ... Ps 2:11
eat...with *t* ... Ezek 12:18
with fear and *t* ... Phil 2:12

TRESPASS *fault, sin* See Sin.
Saul died for his *t* ... 1 Chr 10:13
caught in any *t* ... Gal 6:1
dead in your *t-es* ... Eph 2:1

TRIAL *testing* 1) A judicial trial for wrongdoing; in the NT, usually held before the Jewish Sanhedrin or a Roman official, depending upon the nature of the charges and the penalties sought. 2) Times of great difficulty or persecution which Christians must endure. Such trials are allowed by God for the purpose of strengthening faith and character.
if we are on *t* today ... Acts 4:9
which was a *t* to you ... Gal 4:14
perseveres under *t* ... James 1:12

TRIBE *common ancestry*
twelve *t-s* of Israel ... Gen 49:28
a man of each *t* ... Num 1:4
t-s of the LORD ... Ps 122:4
judging...twelve *t-s* ... Luke 22:30
men from every *t* ... Rev 5:9

TRIBULATION *affliction* In general, an extended time of suffering or persecution. Specifically, the great tribulation, a period of seven years of catastrophic divine judgments preceding the second coming of Christ. *see also* **RAPTURE**
will be a great *t* ... Matt 24:21
world you have *t* ... John 16:33
exult in our *t-s* ... Rom 5:3
my *t-s* on your behalf ... Eph 3:13
out of the great *t* ... Rev 7:14

TRIBUNAL *court*
before Caesar's *t* ... Acts 25:10

TRIBUTE *tax* This term describes several kinds of taxes (*see* **TAX**), but can also include forced labor.
sons of Israel sent *t* ... Judg 3:15
impose...*t* or toll ... Ezra 7:24
exact a *t* of grain ... Amos 5:11

TRIGON *musical instrument*
sound of...lyre, *t* ... Dan 3:5

TRINITY *(triad)*. The fact that God is one essence existing in three distinct persons: the Father, the Son, and the Holy Spirit. All three persons are absolutely equal in their essence and deity (q.v.); but the Son voluntarily submits to the will of the Father, and the Holy Spirit submits to the Son, being sent by Him to believers. Because He was incarnate (see Incarnation), the Son, Jesus Christ, was completely man and completely God, and now has a special resurrection body. All three persons of the Trinity have existed and will continue to exist eternally. The word "Trinity" does not occur in the Bible, but there are ample Bible passages teaching the doctrine.

TRIUMPH *victory*
the righteous *t* ... Prov 28:12
t in Christ ... 2 Cor 2:14
mercy *t-s* over ... James 2:13

TROAS A seaport in Asia Minor where Paul received the vision of a man asking Paul to go to Macedonia.
city in Asia Minor ... Acts 16:8,11
visited by Paul ... Acts 20:5; 2 Cor 2:12

TROPHIMUS *(foster child)*. An Ephesian convert of Paul who accompanied him to Jerusalem. While there, Paul was accused of bringing him into the temple and thus polluting it, since Trophimus was a Gentile.
companion of Paul ... Acts 20:4; 2 Tim 4:20
Ephesian Christian ... Acts 21:29

TROUBLE (n) *affliction*
forget all my *t* ... Gen 41:51
man is born for *t* ... Job 5:7
Look upon...my *t* ... Ps 25:18
very present help in *t* ... Ps 46:1
remember his *t* no ... Prov 31:7
t is heavy upon him ... Eccl 8:6
day has enough *t* ... Matt 6:34

TROUBLE (v) *bother, disturb*
t you in the land ... Num 33:55
t-s his own house ... Prov 11:29
also *t* the hearts ... Ezek 32:9
Herod...was *t-d* ... Matt 2:3
why *t* the Teacher ... Mark 5:35
your heart be *t-d* ... John 14:1

TROUBLED (adj) *disturbed*
songs to a *t* heart ... Prov 25:20
soul has become *t* ... John 12:27

TRUE *actual, real, reliable*
gets a *t* reward ... Prov 11:18
There was the *t* light ... John 1:9
gives you...*t* bread ... John 6:32
let God be found *t* ... Rom 3:4
signs of a *t* apostle ... 2 Cor 12:12
This testimony is *t* ... Titus 1:13
t grace of God ... 1 Pet 5:12
faithful and *t* Witness ... Rev 3:14

TRUMPET *wind instrument*
t-s of rams' horns ... Josh 6:6
t-s...empty pitchers ... Judg 7:16
Praise Him with *t* ... Ps 150:3
do not sound a *t* ... Matt 6:2
at the last *t* ... 1 Cor 15:52
voice like...a *t* ... Rev 1:10

TRUST (n) *confidence, hope See* **FAITH**
whose *t* a spider's web ... Job 8:14
In God...put my *t* ... Ps 56:11
put My *t* in Him ... Heb 2:13

TRUST (v) *commit to See* **FAITH**
t in the LORD ... Ps 4:5
Than to *t* in man ... Ps 118:8
t-s in his riches ... Prov 11:28
not *t* in a neighbor ... Mic 7:5
not *t* in ourselves ... 2 Cor 1:9

TRUSTWORTHY *reliable*
t witness will not lie ... Prov 14:5
who can find a *t* ... Prov 20:6
It is a *t* statement ... 1 Tim 3:1

TRUTH *genuineness, honesty*
walk before Me in *t* ... 1 Kin 2:4
speaks *t* in his heart ... Ps 15:2
Your word is *t* ... Ps 119:160
Buy *t*, and do not ... Prov 23:23
judge with *t* ... Zech 8:16
full of grace and *t* ... John 1:14
worship in...*t* ... John 4:24
t will make you free ... John 8:32
the way, and the *t* ... John 14:6
exchanged the *t* of ... Rom 1:25
t of the gospel ... Gal 2:5
speaking the *t* in love ... Eph 4:15
the word of *t* ... 2 Tim 2:15
the *t* is not in us ... 1 John 1:8

TUBAL
1 *son of Japheth* ... Gen 10:2
2 *land ruled by Gog* ... Ezek 38:3; 39:1

TUBAL-CAIN
son of Zillah ... Gen 4:22
inventor of cutting tools

TUMULT *disturbance*
t of the peoples ... Ps 65:7
A sound of *t* ... Is 13:4
t of waters ... Jer 51:16

TUNIC *cloak, garment*
a varicolored *t* ... Gen 37:3
the holy linen *t* ... Lev 16:4

TURBAN *headdress*
a *t* of fine linen ... Ex 28:39
justice was like...a *t* ... Job 29:14
Remove the *t* ... Ezek 21:26

TURMOIL *tumult*
treasure and *t* with ... Prov 15:16
rest from your...*t* ... Is 14:3
ill repute, full of *t* ... Ezek 22:5

TURN *change* or *move*
not *t* to mediums ... Lev 19:31
leave you *or t* back ... Ruth 1:16
T from your evil ... 2 Kin 17:13
forget, nor *t* away ... Prov 4:5
T to Me, and be saved ... Is 45:22
t-ed to his own way ... Is 53:6
t their mourning into ... Jer 31:13
t...shame into praise ... Zeph 3:19
t from darkness to ... Acts 26:18
he who *t-s* a sinner ... James 5:20
t away from evil ... 1 Pet 3:11

TURTLEDOVE *bird*
t for a sin offering ... Lev 12:6
the voice of the *t* ... Song 2:12

TUTOR *teacher*
t-s in Christ ... 1 Cor 4:15
Law...become our *t* ... Gal 3:24

TWELVE *number*
t tribes of Israel ... Gen 49:28
summoned His *t* ... Matt 10:1
t legions of angels ... Matt 26:53
when He became *t* ... Luke 2:42
a crown of *t* stars ... Rev 12:1

TWELVE, THE The disciples whom Jesus chose and later commissioned as *apostles* (Matt 10:1-2).

TWILIGHT *darkness, dusk*
lamb...offer at *t* ... Ex 29:39
waits for the *t* ... Job 24:15
midday as in the *t* ... Is 59:10

TWINKLING *flicker*
in the *t* of an eye ... 1 Cor 15:52

TWINS *pair, two*
t in her womb ... Gen 25:24
T of a gazelle ... Song 4:5

TWO-EDGED *with two edges*
than any *t* sword ... Heb 4:12
His mouth...*t* sword ... Rev 1:16

TYCHICUS *(fortunate).* A Christian from the province of Asia. He delivered Paul's epistles to Ephesus and to Colossae (Eph 6:21; Col 4:7).

TYRE A very ancient city in Phoenicia. One of its kings, Hiram, was a friend of David and Solomon.
Phoenician seaport ... Josh 19:29; Ezek 27:3; Matt 15:21; Acts 21:3

U

UGLY *unsightly*
u and gaunt cows ... Gen 41:4
seven lean...*u* cows ... Gen 41:27

UNBELIEF *lack of faith*
wondered at their *u* ... Mark 6:6
help my *u* ... Mark 9:24
continue in their *u* ... Rom 11:23

UNBELIEVER *non-believer*
a place with the *u-s* ... Luke 12:46
wife who is an *u* ... 1 Cor 7:12
ungifted men or *u-s* ... 1 Cor 14:23
bound...with *u-s* ... 2 Cor 6:14
worse than an *u* ... 1 Tim 5:8

UNBELIEVING *doubting*
O *u* generation ... Mark 9:19
u husband is ... 1 Cor 7:14
blinded the...*u* ... 2 Cor 4:4
evil, *u* heart ... Heb 3:12

UNBLEMISHED *without defect*
shall be an *u* male ... Ex 12:5
u and spotless ... 1 Pet 1:19

UNCEASING *continuous*
u complaint in his ... Job 33:19
sorrow and *u* grief ... Rom 9:2

UNCHANGEABLENESS
the *u* of His purpose ... Heb 6:17

UNCIRCUMCISED
But an *u* male ... Gen 17:14
u heart...humbled ... Lev 26:41
the nations are *u* ... Jer 9:26
who is physically *u* ... Rom 2:27
the gospel to the *u* ... Gal 2:7

UNCIRCUMCISION
has become *u* ... Rom 2:25
who are called *U* ... Eph 2:11
the *u* of your flesh ... Col 2:13

UNCLEAN *not clean* or *not holy* A distinction in Jewish law applied to various kinds of foods and utensils and to people who for any of a number of reasons may become ritually defiled. Things designated unclean could not be used, and people so designated were banned from participation in certain aspects of Jewish society and worship. Perhaps the best known unclean food was pork. Women who were menstruating and anyone who came into contact with a corpse are examples of people who were rendered temporarily unclean. Various purification rites were prescribed to remove temporary uncleanness, many of which involved cemonial immersion in water.
see also **CLEAN**
touches any *u* thing ... Lev 5:2
u in their practices ... Ps 106:39
man of *u* lips ... Is 6:5
authority over *u* ... Matt 10:1
u spirits entered ... Mark 5:13
eaten anything...*u* ... Acts 10:14
nothing is *u* in itself ... Rom 14:14

UNCOVER *expose*
to *u* her nakedness ... Lev 18:7
u his feet and ... Ruth 3:4
head *u-ed* while ... 1 Cor 11:5

UNDEFILED *uncorrupted*
holy, innocent, *u* ... Heb 7:26
marriage bed...*be u* ... Heb 13:4
pure and *u* religion ... James 1:27
imperishable and *u* ... 1 Pet 1:4

UNDERGARMENTS
u next to his flesh ... Lev 6:10
linen *u* shall be on ... Ezek 44:18

UNDERGO *experience*
Holy One to *u* decay ... Ps 16:10
should not *u* decay ... Ps 49:9
did not *u* decay ... Acts 13:37

UNDERSTAND *comprehend*
u-s every intent ... 1 Chr 28:9
To *u* a proverb ... Prov 1:6
O fools, *u* wisdom ... Prov 8:5
do not *u* justice ... Prov 28:5
Who can *u* it ... Jer 17:9
u that the vision ... Dan 8:17
Hear, and *u* ... Matt 15:10
to *u* the Scriptures ... Luke 24:45
Why do you not *u* ... John 8:43
none who *u-s* ... Rom 3:11
things hard to *u* ... 2 Pet 3:16

UNDERSTANDING
a wise and *u* people ... Deut 4:6
servant an *u* heart ... 1 Kin 3:9
Holy One is *u* ... Prov 9:10

UNDISCIPLINED
in an *u* manner ... 2 Thess 3:7
leading an *u* life ... 2 Thess 3:11

UNDISTURBED *peaceful*
land was *u* for forty ... Judg 8:28
an *u* habitation ... Is 33:20

UNFADING *lasting*
u crown of glory ... 1 Pet 5:4

UNFAITHFUL
u to her husband ... Num 5:27
very *u* to the LORD ... 2 Chr 28:19
u to our God ... Ezra 10:2

UNFAITHFULNESS *faithless*
u...they committed ... Lev 26:40
to Babylon for their *u* ... 1 Chr 9:1
the *u* of the exiles ... Ezra 9:4

UNFATHOMABLE
How...*u* His ways ... Rom 11:33
u riches of Christ ... Eph 3:8

UNFRUITFUL *not productive*
the land is *u* ... 2 Kin 2:19
my mind is *u* ... 1 Cor 14:14
u deeds of darkness ... Eph 5:11

UNGODLINESS *sinfulness*
torrents of *u* terrified ... Ps 18:4
remove *u*...Jacob ... Rom 11:26
lead to further *u* ... 2 Tim 2:16

UNGODLY *sinful, wicked*
who justifies the *u* ... Rom 4:5
Christ died for the *u* ... Rom 5:6
destruction of *u* men ... 2 Pet 3:7
their own *u* lusts ... Jude 18

UNHOLY *not holy*
no *longer* consider *u* ... Acts 10:15
for the *u* and profane ... 1 Tim 1:9

UNINTENTIONALLY
If a person sins *u* ... Lev 4:2
who kills a person *u* ... Num 35:15

UNITED *joined, union*
u as one man ... Judg 20:11
become *u* with *Him* ... Rom 6:5
love, *u* in spirit ... Phil 2:2
not *u* by faith ... Heb 4:2

UNITY *united, union*
dwell together in *u* ... Ps 133:1
perfected in *u* ... John 17:23
all attain to the *u* ... Eph 4:13
perfect bond of *u* ... Col 3:14

UNJUST *unfair*
u man is abominable ... Prov 29:27
For God is not *u* ... Heb 6:10
the just for *the u* ... 1 Pet 3:18

UNKNOWN *not known*
To An *U* God ... Acts 17:23
as *u* yet well-known ... 2 Cor 6:9

UNLEAVENED (BREAD) *non-fermented*
Bread made from unfermented dough, required by OT law for certain religious feasts.
and baked *u* bread ... Gen 19:3
you shall eat *u* bread ... Ex 12:15
first day of *U* Bread ... Matt 26:17
you are *in fact u* ... 1 Cor 5:7

UNLEAVENED BREAD, FEAST OF *see* **FEASTS**

UNLOVED *not loved*
that Leah was *u* ... Gen 29:31
loved and the *u* ... Deut 21:15
Under an *u* woman ... Prov 30:23

UNMARRIED *single*
I say to the *u* ... 1 Cor 7:8
she must remain *u* ... 1 Cor 7:11

UNPRINCIPLED *unscrupulous*
conduct of *u* men ... 2 Pet 2:7
error of *u* men ... 2 Pet 3:17

UNPROFITABLE *without value*
u and worthless ... Titus 3:9
grief...*u* for you ... Heb 13:17

UNPUNISHED *not punished*
not leave him *u* ... Ex 20:7
shall go *u* ... Ex 21:19
not let him go *u* ... 1 Kin 2:9

UNQUENCHABLE
burn...with *u* fire ... Matt 3:12
into the *u* fire ... Mark 9:43

UNRESTRAINED *uncontrolled*
the people are *u* ... Prov 29:18
with *u* persecution ... Is 14:6

UNRIGHTEOUS *evil, wicked*
u man his thoughts ... Is 55:7
rain on...*the u* ... Matt 5:45
u in a...little thing ... Luke 16:10
God...is not *u* ... Rom 3:5
u will not inherit ... 1 Cor 6:9
u under punishment ... 2 Pet 2:9

UNRIGHTEOUSNESS *evil*
have no part in *u* ... 2 Chr 19:7
no *u* in Him ... Ps 92:15
not rejoice in *u* ... 1 Cor 13:6
cleanse us from all *u* ... 1 John 1:9
All *u* is sin ... 1 John 5:17

UNRULY *disorderly*
admonish the *u* ... 1 Thess 5:14
who leads an *u* life ... 2 Thess 3:6

UNSEARCHABLE *inscrutable*
His greatness is *u* ... Ps 145:3
u are His judgments ... Rom 11:33

UNSKILLED *lack of training*
I am *u* in speech ... Ex 6:12
u in speech, yet I ... 2 Cor 11:6

UNSTABLE *unreliable*
Her ways are *u* ... Prov 5:6
u in all his ways ... James 1:8
enticing *u* souls ... 2 Pet 2:14

UNWILLING *reluctant*
u to move the ark ... 2 Sam 6:10
they were *u* to come ... Matt 22:3
He was *u* to drink ... Matt 27:34
u to be obedient ... Acts 7:39

UNWISE *foolish*
foolish and *u* people ... Deut 32:6
walk, not as *u* men ... Eph 5:15

UNWORTHY *not deserving*
u of...lovingkindness ... Gen 32:10
We are *u* slaves ... Luke 17:10
u of eternal life ... Acts 13:46

UPRIGHT *honest, just*
the death of the *u* ... Num 23:10
blameless and *u* man ... Job 1:8
u will behold His face ... Ps 11:7
led you in *u* paths ... Prov 4:11
God made men *u* ... Eccl 7:29
no *u*...among men ... Mic 7:2
Stand *u* on your feet ... Acts 14:10

UPROAR *loud noise*
Why...such an *u* ... 1 Kin 1:41
nations in an *u* ... Ps 2:1
there occurred a great *u* ... Acts 23:9

UPROOT *tear out*
He will *u* Israel ... 1 Kin 14:15
He has *u-ed* my hope ... Job 19:10
u-ed and be planted ... Luke 17:6

UR An ancient city in Mesopotamia from which God called Abraham. Also the father of one of David's mighty men.
1 *city in S Mesopotamia* ... Gen 11:31; 15:7
original home of Abraham ... Gen 11:28; Neh 9:7
2 *father of Eliphal* ... 1 Chr 11:35

URBANUS
Roman Christian ... Rom 16:9

URGE *entreat*
Do not *u* me to leave ... Ruth 1:16
hunger *u-s* him *on* ... Prov 16:26
Therefore I *u* you ... Rom 12:1

URIAH
1 *husband of Bathsheba* ... 2 Sam 11:3;12:9
2 priest under Ezra ... Neh 8:4
3 *priest under Ahaz* ... Is 8:2
also **Urijah** ... 2 Kin 16:10ff
4 *time of Jeremiah* ... Jer 26:20

URIM *see* **THUMMIM**
kept in high priest's breastplate for determining the will of God ... Ex 28:30; Lev 8:8; Num 27:21

USE *utilization*
be of *u* to God ... Job 22:2
for common *u* ... Ezek 48:15
for honorable *u* ... Rom 9:21
not make full *u* of ... 1 Cor 7:31

USEFUL *beneficial*
man be *u* to himself ... Job 22:2
u to me for service ... 2 Tim 4:11

USELESS *worthless*
they have become *u* ... Rom 3:12
without works is *u* ... James 2:20

USURY *interest*
leave off this *u* ... Neh 5:10
by interest and *u* ... Prov 28:8

UTENSILS *vessels*
table also and its *u* ... Ex 31:8
u of the sanctuary ... 1 Chr 9:29

UTTER *express*
righteous *u-s* wisdom ... Ps 37:30
Let my lips *u* praise ... Ps 119:171
He *u-s* His voice ... Jer 10:13
u words of...truth ... Acts 26:25

UTTERANCE *expression*
was giving them *u* ... Acts 2:4
in faith and *u* ... 2 Cor 8:7
u may be given ... Eph 6:19
through prophetic *u* ... 1 Tim 4:14

UZ (unc, *counsel).* 1) Name of several individuals. 2) The area where Job lived.
1 *grandson of Shem* ... Gen 10:23
2 *son of Nahor* ... Gen 22:21
3 *son of Dishan* ... Gen 36:28
4 *home of Job* ... Job 1:1
land of Uz ... Jer 25:20; Lam 4:21

V

VAIN *empty* or *profane*
name of...God in *v* ... Ex 20:7
devising a *v* thing ... Ps 2:1
labor in *v* who build ... Ps 127:1
our preaching is *v* ... 1 Cor 15:14

VALIANT *brave, strong*
these...*v* warriors ... Judg 20:46
be a *v* man for me ... 1 Sam 18:17
even all the *v* men ... 1 Chr 28:1
He drags off the *v* ... Job 24:22

VALLEY *ravine*
v of the Jordan ... Gen 13:10
the *v* of Aijalon ... Josh 10:12

v of the shadow of ... Ps 23:4
The lily of the *v-s* ... Song 2:1
v of the dead bodies ... Jer 31:40
v...full of bones ... Ezek 37:1
the *v* of decision ... Joel 3:14

VALLEY GATE This gate is located in the southwest part of the wall of Jerusalem; it leads to the Valley of Hinnom.
see **GATES OF JERUSALEM**

VALOR *bravery*
mighty man of *v* ... 1 Sam 16:18
mighty men of *v* ... 1 Chr 12:8

VALUE *worth*
one pearl of great *v* ... Matt 13:46
v of knowing Christ ... Phil 3:8

VANISH *disappear*
When a cloud *v-es* ... Job 7:9
sky will *v* like smoke ... Is 51:6
v-ed from...sight ... Luke 24:31

VANITY *futility, pride*
will reap *v* ... Prov 22:8
V of *v-ies!* All is *v* ... Eccl 1:2
arrogant *words* of *v* ... 2 Pet 2:18

VAPOR *smoke*
causes the *v-s* to ... Ps 135:7
Is a fleeting *v* ... Prov 21:6
You are *just* a *v* ... James 4:14

VARICOLORED *multicolored*
made him a *v* tunic ... Gen 37:3

VARIOUS *different*
v diseases and pains ... Matt 4:24
led on by *v* impulses ... 2 Tim 3:6
encounter *v* trials ... James 1:2
distressed by *v* trials ... 1 Pet 1:6

VASHTI The Persian queen who refused the order of King Ahasuerus to come into his presence so that his guests could see her beauty. She was replaced by Esther.
deposed queen of Ahasuerus ... Esth 1:19; 2:4

VEGETABLE *plant*
like a *v* garden ... Deut 11:10
Better...dish of *v-s* ... Prov 15:17
weak eats *v-s only* ... Rom 14:2

VEGETATION *plant life*
earth brought forth *v* ... Gen 1:12
ate up all *v* ... Ps 105:35
wither all their *v* ... Is 42:15

VEIL *cover, curtain* 1) A head and face covering worn by Hebrew women of Bible times as a sign of modesty and submission. The veil is worn by many women in the Middle East today. Also worn by Moses when he spoke to the people after meeting with God. 2) A tapestry hung between the two inner rooms of the tabernacle and temple, also symbolic of being in the Father's presence in heaven. 3) A term used to describe Jesus' body. 4) A symbol of spiritual blindness.
a *v* over his face ... Ex 34:33
v of the sanctuary ... Lev 4:6
Remove your *v* ... Is 47:2
v of the temple ... Matt 27:51
v remains unlifted ... 2 Cor 3:14
enters within the *v* ... Heb 6:19
the *v,* that is, His flesh ... Heb 10:20

VENGEANCE *revenge*
not take *v* ... Lev 19:18
V is Mine ... Deut 32:35
God...executes *v* ... 2 Sam 22:48
LORD takes *v* on His ... Nah 1:2
V is Mine, I will ... Heb 10:30

VESSEL *utensil*
Go, borrow *v-s* ... 2 Kin 4:3
I am like a broken *v* ... Ps 31:12
v-s of wrath ... Rom 9:22
treasure in...*v-s* ... 2 Cor 4:7
be a *v* for honor ... 2 Tim 2:21
v-s of the potter ... Rev 2:27

VESTURE *apparel*
v was like...snow ... Dan 7:9

VIAL *small container*
alabaster *v* of ... Matt 26:7
she broke the *v* ... Mark 14:3

VICTORIOUS *triumphant*
A *v* warrior ... Zeph 3:17
v over the beast ... Rev 15:2

VICTORY *triumph*
LORD brought...*v* ... 2 Sam 23:10
had given *v* to Aram ... 2 Kin 5:1
the glory and the *v* ... 1 Chr 29:11
gained the *v* for Him ... Ps 98:1
v belongs to...LORD ... Prov 21:31
He leads justice to *v* ... Matt 12:20
swallowed up in *v* ... 1 Cor 15:54
v that has overcome ... 1 John 5:4

VIGOR *vitality*
nor his *v* abated ... Deut 34:7
grave in full *v* ... Job 5:26
his youthful *v* ... Job 20:11

VILLAGE *small town*
land of unwalled *v-s* ... Ezek 38:11
Go into the *v* ... Matt 21:2
entered a *v* ... Luke 10:38

VINDICATE *justify*
will *v* His people ... Deut 32:36
V the weak ... Ps 82:3
wisdom is *v-d* by ... Matt 11:19

VINE *stem of plant*
trees said to the *v* ... Judg 9:12
every man...his *v* ... 1 Kin 4:25
like a fruitful *v* ... Ps 128:3
the *v-s* in blossom ... Song 2:13
mother was like a *v* ... Ezek 19:10
Israel is a luxuriant *v* ... Hos 10:1
The *v* dries up ... Joel 1:12
fruit of the *v* ... Matt 26:29
I am the true *v* ... John 15:1

VINEDRESSER *gardener*
v-s and plowmen ... 2 Kin 25:12
My Father is the *v* ... John 15:1

VINEGAR *sour liquid*
he shall drink no *v* ... Num 6:3
bread in the *v* ... Ruth 2:14
gave me *v* to drink ... Ps 69:21
Like *v* to the teeth ... Prov 10:26

VINE-GROWERS
rented it out to *v* ... Matt 21:33
and destroy the *v* ... Mark 12:9

VINEYARD *grapevines*
Noah...planted a *v* ... Gen 9:20
Nor...glean your *v* ... Lev 19:10
Hewn cisterns, *v-s* ... Neh 9:25
shelter in a *v* ... Is 1:8
ruined My *v* ... Jer 12:10
laborers for his *v* ... Matt 20:1
Who plants a *v* ... 1 Cor 9:7

VIOLATE *assault* or *break*
shall not *v* his word ... Num 30:2
do not *v* me ... 2 Sam 13:12
who *v-d* the ban ... 1 Chr 2:7
If they *v* My statutes ... Ps 89:31

VIOLENCE *destructive action*
earth was filled with *v* ... Gen 6:11
implements of *v* ... Gen 49:5
such as breathe out *v* ... Ps 27:12
drink the wine of *v* ... Prov 4:17
He had done no *v* ... Is 53:9
not mistreat *or* do *v* ... Jer 22:3

VIOLENT *destructive*
a wicked, *v* man ... Ps 37:35
a *v*, rushing wind ... Acts 2:2

VIPER *snake*
v-'s tongue slays him ... Job 20:16
hand on the *v-'s* den ... Is 11:8
v and flying serpent ... Is 30:6
You brood of *v-s* ... Matt 3:7

VIRGIN *unmarried maiden*
very beautiful, a *v* ... Gen 24:16
if a man seduces a *v* ... Ex 22:16
could I gaze at a *v* ... Job 31:1
the *v* will rejoice ... Jer 31:13
v shall be with child ... Matt 1:23
kept her a *v* ... Matt 1:25
comparable to ten *v-s* ... Matt 25:1
v-'s name was Mary ... Luke 1:27
if a *v* marries ... 1 Cor 7:28

VIRGIN BIRTH The birth of Jesus to Mary, who was married to Joseph but was still a virgin (Matt 1:23, 25). She conceived by the Holy Spirit, therefore Jesus was born without sin.

VISIBLE *manifest, seen*
He become *v* ... Acts 10:40
becomes *v* is light ... Eph 5:13
things which are *v* ... Heb 11:3

VISION *dream, foresight* A supernatural view of an event or a messenger, etc. given by God to someone whom He momentarily puts into a trance-like state. Unlike dreaming, the person receiving the vision is awake. Examples include Paul's vision of a Macedonian man (Acts 16:9), and the visions John recorded in Revelation.
to Abram in a *v* ... Gen 15:1
v-s were infrequent ... 1 Sam 3:1
Where there is no *v* ... Prov 29:18
prophets find No *v* ... Lam 2:9
I saw *v-s* of God ... Ezek 1:1
in a night *v* ... Dan 2:19
young men...see *v-s* ... Joel 2:28
Tell the *v* to no one ... Matt 17:9
young men...see *v-s* ... Acts 2:17

VISIT *come* or *go to see*
v-ing the iniquity of ... Ex 20:5
You *v* the earth ... Ps 65:9
you did not *v* Me ... Matt 25:43
For He has *v-ed* us ... Luke 1:68
v orphans...widows ... James 1:27

VOICE *sound, speech*
have obeyed My *v* ... Gen 22:18
listen to His *v* ... Deut 4:30
v of singing men ... 2 Sam 19:35
You will hear my *v* ... Ps 5:3
the *v* of my teachers ... Prov 5:13
v of the turtledove ... Song 2:12
Give ear...hear my *v* ... Is 28:23
A *v* is calling ... Is 40:3
v came from heaven ... Dan 4:31
v...heard in Ramah ... Matt 2:18
v...out of the cloud ... Mark 9:7
v of one crying in ... Luke 3:4
v of the Son of God ... John 5:25
v has gone out ... Rom 10:18
v of *the* archangel ... 1 Thess 4:16
His *v* shook...earth ... Heb 12:26
if anyone hears My *v* ... Rev 3:20
with a *v* of thunder ... Rev 6:1

VOID *empty, invalid*
was formless and *v* ... Gen 1:2
make *v* the counsel ... Jer 19:7
faith is made *v* ... Rom 4:14
cross...be made *v* ... 1 Cor 1:17

VOMIT *throw up*
will *v* them up ... Job 20:15
returns to its *v* ... Prov 26:11
staggers in his *v* ... Is 19:14
and it *v-ed* Jonah ... Jon 2:10
returns to its own *v* ... 2 Pet 2:22

VOTIVE *dedicated*
his offering is a *v* ... Lev 7:16
choice *v* offerings ... Deut 12:11

VOW *solemn promise* Akin to an oath, a voluntary promise made to God to perform some specific act or service, or to abstain from something. *see* **OATH** *and* **NAZIRITE**
Jacob made a *v* ... Gen 28:20
v of a Nazirite ... Num 6:2
I shall pay my *v-s* ... Ps 22:25
not make false *v-s* ... Matt 5:33
he was keeping a *v* ... Acts 18:18

VOYAGE *journey*
v was now dangerous ... Acts 27:9

VULTURE *bird*
not eat...the *v* ... Deut 14:12
the *v-s* will gather ... Matt 24:28

W

WAFER *thin cake of bread*
w-s with honey ... Ex 16:31
one unleavened *w* ... Num 6:19

WAGE *salary*
God has given...*w-s* ... Gen 30:18
w-s of the righteous ... Prov 10:16
w is not credited ... Rom 4:4
the *w-s* of sin ... Rom 6:23
worthy of his *w-s* ... 1 Tim 5:18

WAIL *lament, mourn*
w with a broken spirit ... Is 65:14
w, son of man ... Ezek 21:12
I must lament and *w* ... Mic 1:8
W, O inhabitants of ... Zeph 1:11
weeping and *w-ing* ... Mark 5:38

WAIT *expect*
For You I *w* ... Ps 25:5
I *w* for Your word ... Ps 119:81
who *w* for the LORD ... Is 40:31
creation *w-s* eagerly ... Rom 8:19
w-ing for the hope ... Gal 5:5

WALK *follow, go along*
w-ing in the garden ... Gen 3:8
W before Me ... Gen 17:1
w in My instruction ... Ex 16:4
w in My statutes ... Lev 26:3
w-ed forty years ... Josh 5:6
w before Me in truth ... 1 Kin 2:4
W about Zion ... Ps 48:12
I will *w* at liberty ... Ps 119:45
fool *w-s* in darkness ... Eccl 2:14
w in the light ... Is 2:5
w and not...weary ... Is 40:31
w-ed with Me in peace ... Mal 2:6
Get up, and *w* ... Matt 9:5
w-ed on the water ... Matt 14:29
w in newness of life ... Rom 6:4
we *w* by faith ... 2 Cor 5:7
w by the Spirit ... Gal 5:16
w in love ... Eph 5:2
w as children of Light ... Eph 5:8
if we *w* in the Light ... 1 John 1:7
w by its light ... Rev 21:24

WALL *structure*
living on the *w* ... Josh 2:15
So we built the *w* ... Neh 4:6
I can leap over a *w* ... Ps 18:29
w-s of Jerusalem ... Jer 39:8
built a siege *w* ... Jer 52:4
you whitewashed *w* ... Acts 23:3
w-s of Jericho fell ... Heb 11:30
a great and high *w* ... Rev 21:12

WANDER *roam*
w in the wilderness ... Num 32:13
I would *w* far away ... Ps 55:7
w...Your statutes ... Ps 119:118
people w like sheep ... Zech 10:2
w-ed...the faith ... 1 Tim 6:10
w-ing stars, for whom ... Jude 13

WANDERER *roamer*
a *w* on the earth ... Gen 4:12
an exile and a *w* ... Is 49:21
w-s among...nations ... Hos 9:17

WAR *battle, conflict*
when they see *w* ... Ex 13:17
sound of *w* in...camp ... Ex 32:17
land...rest from *w* ... Josh 11:23
He makes *w-s* to cease ... Ps 46:9
the weapons of *w* ... Ps 76:3
A time for *w* ... Eccl 3:8
will they learn *w* ... Is 2:4
w-s...rumors of *w-s* ... Matt 24:6
w against the law ... Rom 7:23
w in your members ... James 4:1
w against the soul ... 1 Pet 2:11
judges and wages *w* ... Rev 19:11

WARS OF THE LORD, BOOK OF THE
ancient Hebrew literature ... Num 21:14

WARM *heat*
could not keep *w* ... 1 Kin 1:1
the child became *w* ... 2 Kin 4:34
can one be *w alone* ... Eccl 4:11
no one is *w enough* ... Hag 1:6

WARN *give notice*
w the people ... Ex 19:21
not...*w* the wicked ... Ezek 33:8
w-ed...in a dream ... Matt 2:12
w you whom to fear ... Luke 12:5
Moses was *w-ed* ... Heb 8:5

WARRIOR *soldier*
The LORD is a *w* ... Ex 15:3
O valiant *w* ... Judg 6:12
w from his youth ... 1 Sam 17:33
w-s will flee naked ... Amos 2:16

WASH *bathe, clean*
w your feet, and rest ... Gen 18:4
w in the Jordan ... 2 Kin 5:10
w...in innocence ... Ps 26:6
W...from my iniquity ... Ps 51:2
w-ed off your blood ... Ezek 16:9
do not *w* their hands ... Matt 15:2
ceremonially *w-ed* ... Luke 11:38
w in the pool of ... John 9:7
w the disciples' feet ... John 13:5
w away your sins ... Acts 22:16
w-ed...saints' feet ... 1 Tim 5:10
w-ed with pure ... Heb 10:22
who *w* their robes ... Rev 22:14

WASTE (n) *wilderness*
land was laid *w* ... Ex 8:24
land into a salt *w* ... Ps 107:34
lay *w* the mountains ... Is 42:15
laid *w* like a desert ... Jer 9:12
altars may become *w* ... Ezek 6:6
Egypt...become a *w* ... Joel 3:19

WASTE (v) *destroy, use up*
he *w-d* his seed ... Gen 38:9
w away the eyes ... Lev 26:16
sick man *w-s* away ... Is 10:18
perfume been *w-d* ... Mark 14:4

WASTE PLACE *barren*
w-s of the wealthy ... Is 5:17
Seek Me in a *w* ... Is 45:19
like the ancient *w-s* ... Ezek 26:20
w-s will be rebuilt ... Ezek 36:10

WATCH (n) *guard* 1) A prescribed duration of time for which a guard would be on duty. Among the Jews, a watch lasted for four hours; for the Romans, it was three hours. 2) A term used in reference to such a guard.
at the morning *w* ... Ex 14:24
posted the *w* ... Judg 7:19
in the night *w-es* ... Ps 63:6
His eyes keep *w* ... Ps 66:7
keep *w* with Me ... Matt 26:38
w over their flock ... Luke 2:8
w over your souls ... Heb 13:17

WATCH (v) *observe* To stay awake and be alert.
LORD *w* between you ... Gen 31:49
w all my paths ... Job 13:27
W over your heart ... Prov 4:23
who *w-es* the wind ... Eccl 11:4
w...for the LORD ... Mic 7:7

WATCHMAN *one who guards*
w keeps awake in vain ... Ps 127:1
w-men for...morning ... Ps 130:6
W, how far gone is ... Is 21:11
I set *w-men* over you ... Jer 6:17
Ephraim *was* a *w* ... Hos 9:8

WATER (n) *flood, liquid*
moving over...the *w-s* ... Gen 1:2
flood of *w* came ... Gen 7:6
w-s were like a wall ... Ex 14:22
w of bitterness ... Num 5:18

WHITEWASHED *wall covering*
like *w* tombs ... Matt 23:27
you *w* wall ... Acts 23:3

WHOLE *entire*
water the *w* surface ... Gen 2:6
w earth...populated ... Gen 9:19
leavens the *w* lump ... 1 Cor 5:6
keeps the *w* law ... James 2:10

WICK *candle thread*
extinguished like a *w* ... Is 43:17
a smoldering *w* ... Matt 12:20

WICKED *evil, ungodly*
condemn the *w* ... Deut 25:1
w ones are silenced ... 1 Sam 2:9
counsel of the *w* ... Ps 1:1
the *w* spurned God ... Ps 10:13
The *w* strut about ... Ps 12:8
devises *w* plans ... Prov 6:18
When a *w* man dies ... Prov 11:7
no peace for the *w* ... Is 48:22
turn from his *w* way ... Jon 3:8
taking...some *w* men ... Acts 17:5
righteous and the *w* ... Acts 24:15

WICKEDNESS *evil*
w of man was great ... Gen 6:5
If I regard *w* ... Ps 66:18
eat the bread of *w* ... Prov 4:17
inclines toward *w* ... Is 32:6
w of My people ... Jer 7:12
You have plowed *w* ... Hos 10:13
repent of this *w* ... Acts 8:22
spiritual *forces* of *w* ... Eph 6:12

WIDOW *husband dead*
Remain a *w* ... Gen 38:11
not afflict any *w* ... Ex 22:22
sent *w-s* away empty ... Job 22:9
judge for the *w-s* ... Ps 68:5
Plead for the *w* ... Is 1:17
devour *w-s'* houses ... Matt 23:14
w put in more ... Mark 12:43
Honor *w-s* ... 1 Tim 5:3
visit orphans...*w-s* ... James 1:27

WIFE *married woman*
joined to his *w* ... Gen 2:24
man and his *w* hid ... Gen 3:8
shall not covet...*w* ... Ex 20:17
w of your youth ... Prov 5:18
An excellent *w* ... Prov 31:10
who divorces his *w* ... Matt 5:32
Remember Lot's *w* ... Luke 17:32
have his own *w* ... 1 Cor 7:2
head of the *w* ... Eph 5:23
husband of one *w* ... 1 Tim 3:2
w-ves, be submissive ... 1 Pet 3:1
w of the Lamb ... Rev 21:9

WILD *untamed*
w donkey of a man ... Gen 16:12
horns of the *w* ox ... Num 23:22
locusts and *w* honey ... Mark 1:6
being a *w* olive ... Rom 11:17

WILDERNESS *barren area*
water in the *w* ... Gen 16:7
journey into the *w* ... Ex 5:3
to die in the *w* ... Ex 14:11
forty years in the *w* ... Deut 29:5
pastures of the *w* ... Ps 65:12
roadway in the *w* ... Is 43:19
Have I been a *w* ... Jer 2:31
preaching in the *w* ... Matt 3:1
into the *w*...tempted ... Matt 4:1
crying in the *w* ... Mark 1:3
manna in the *w* ... John 6:31

WILL *attitude, purpose*
delight to do Your *w* ... Ps 40:8
Your *w* be done ... Matt 6:10
the *w* of My Father ... Matt 7:21
not My *w*, but ... Luke 22:42
nor of the *w* of man ... John 1:13
who resists His *w* ... Rom 9:19
what the *w* of God ... Rom 12:2
knowledge of His *w* ... Col 1:9
come to do Your *w* ... Heb 10:9
an act of human *w* ... 2 Pet 1:21

WIN *succeed*
wise *w-s* souls ... Prov 11:30
we will *w* him over ... Matt 28:14
that I might *w* Jews ... 1 Cor 9:20
won without a word ... 1 Pet 3:1

WIND
caused a *w* to pass ... Gen 8:1
scorched by...*w* ... Gen 41:27
will inherit *w* ... Prov 11:29
prophets are *as w* ... Jer 5:13
they sow the *w* ... Hos 8:7
reed shaken by...*w* ... Matt 11:7
w and the sea obey ... Mark 4:41
He...rebuked the *w* ... Luke 8:24
violent, rushing *w* ... Acts 2:2
every *w* of doctrine ... Eph 4:14
driven by strong *w-s* ... James 3:4

WINDOW *opening*
enter through the *w-s* ... Joel 2:9
open...*w-s* of heaven ... Mal 3:10
sitting on the *w* sill ... Acts 20:9
basket through a *w* ... 2 Cor 11:33

WINE *strong drink*
eyes...dull from *w* ... Gen 49:12
Do not drink *w* ... Lev 10:9
overflow with new *w* ... Prov 3:10
W is a mocker ... Prov 20:1
love is better than *w* ... Song 1:2
new *w* into old ... Matt 9:17
gave Him *w* to ... Matt 27:34
made the water *w* ... John 4:46
full of sweet *w* ... Acts 2:13
not get drunk with *w* ... Eph 5:18
not addicted to *w* ... 1 Tim 3:3

WINEPRESS *see* **PRESS**

WINESKINS *animal skin bag*
These *w*...were new ... Josh 9:13
Like new *w* ... Job 32:19
wine into fresh *w* ... Matt 9:17

WINGS
bore you on eagles' *w* ... Ex 19:4
He spread His *w* ... Deut 32:11
under whose *w* ... Ruth 2:12
under His *w*...refuge ... Ps 91:4
with w like eagles ... Is 40:31
healing in its *w* ... Mal 4:2
chicks under her *w* ... Matt 23:37

WINK *blink*
w maliciously ... Ps 35:19
w-s with his eyes ... Prov 6:13

WINNOW *scatter* A step in the process of threshing in which the grain and chaff are tossed into the air and the breeze or wind is allowed to blow away the chaff, letting the heavier grain fall to the floor.
king *w-s* the wicked ... Prov 20:26
You will *w* them ... Is 41:16
His *w-ing* fork ... Matt 3:12

WINNOWING FORK An implement resembling a pitchfork but with thicker, wooden tines used for tossing harvested grain in the air during the winnowing process (Jer 15:7; Matt 3:12).

WINTER *season*
And summer and *w* ... Gen 8:22
the *w* is past ... Song 2:11
even spend the *w* ... 1 Cor 16:6

WIPE *pass over, rub*
GOD will *w* tears ... Is 25:8
w-d His feet ... John 11:2
sins...*w-d* away ... Acts 3:19
w away every tear ... Rev 21:4

WISDOM *discernment*
the spirit of *w* ... Ex 28:3
w has two sides ... Job 11:6
the beginning of *w* ... Ps 111:10
Fools despise *w* ... Prov 1:7
w to fear Your name ... Mic 6:9
w given to Him ... Mark 6:2
kept increasing in *w* ... Luke 2:52
made foolish the *w* ... 1 Cor 1:20
any of you lacks *w* ... James 1:5

WISE *judicious, prudent*
not find a *w* man ... Job 17:10
making *w* the simple ... Ps 19:7
w in your own eyes ... Prov 3:7
the words of the *w* ... Prov 22:17
He is not a *w* son ... Hos 13:13
Who...you is *w* ... James 3:13

WITCHCRAFT *magic, sorcery* A very ancient practice of the occult condemned in the Bible.
who practices *w* ... Deut 18:10
practiced *w* and ... 2 Kin 21:6

WITHER *dry up*
its leaf does not *w* ... Ps 1:3
w...like the grass ... Ps 37:2
earth mourns *and w-s* ... Is 24:4
the leaf will *w* ... Jer 8:13
whose hand was *w-ed* ... Mark 3:1
the fig tree *w-ed* ... Mark 11:20

WITNESS (n) *testimony* A person who may be called to give testimony concerning an agreement or event that has been observed. In the Bible, an animal or object, such as a mound, may also be designated as a witness in the sense that it is personified as an observer of the agreement or event, or viewed as a symbol of it. In less common English usage, *witness* is also used to refer to testimony which has been or can be given.
This heap is a *w* ... Gen 31:48
is *w* between us ... Judg 11:10
my *w* is in heaven ... Job 16:19
a *w* to the LORD ... Is 19:20
He came as a *w* ... John 1:7
you shall be My *w-es* ... Acts 1:8
For God is my *w* ... Phil 1:8
Christ, the faithful *w* ... Rev 1:5

WITNESS (v) *testify*
not bear false *w* ... Ex 20:16

w against you today ... Deut 4:26

WOLF *animal*
w will dwell with ... Is 11:6
the midst of *w-ves* ... Matt 10:16
w snatches them ... John 10:12

WOMAN *female, lady*
She shall be called *W* ... Gen 2:23
w...not wear man's ... Deut 22:5
a *w* of excellence ... Ruth 3:11
Man...born of *w* ... Job 14:1
gracious *w* attains ... Prov 11:16
a contentious *w* ... Prov 25:24
like a *w* in labor ... Is 42:14
looks at a *w* with lust ... Matt 5:28
w-en...grinding ... Matt 24:41
Blessed...among *w-en* ... Luke 1:42
W, behold, your son ... John 19:26
not to touch a *w* ... 1 Cor 7:1
w is the glory of ... 1 Cor 11:7
w to speak in ... 1 Cor 14:35
His Son, born of a *w* ... Gal 4:4
w clothed with...sun ... Rev 12:1

WOMB
nations...in your *w* ... Gen 25:23
LORD...closed her *w* ... 1 Sam 1:5
from *w* to tomb ... Job 10:19
formed you from the *w* ... Is 44:2
baby leaped in...*w* ... Luke 1:41

WONDER *marvel, sign* A miraculous event which usually takes place on a large scale and provokes fear or awe. Frequently used in conjunction with *signs* (q.v.) as evidence demanded by the Jews of God's presence or activity.
consider the *w-s* of ... Job 37:14
tell of all Your *w-s* ... Ps 9:1
His *w-s* in the deep ... Ps 107:24
w-s in the sky ... Joel 2:30
were filled with *w* ... Acts 3:10

WONDERFUL *marvelous*
His *w* deeds ... 1 Chr 16:12
name will be called *W* ... Is 9:6

WOOD *cut tree*
ark of gopher *w* ... Gen 6:14
other gods, *w* and ... Deut 28:36
children gather *w* ... Jer 7:18
stones, *w*, hay ... 1 Cor 3:12

WOOL *cloth* or *hair*
of *w* and linen ... Deut 22:11
put a fleece of *w* on ... Judg 6:37
They will be like *w* ... Is 1:18
hair...like pure *w* ... Dan 7:9
white like white *w* ... Rev 1:14

WORD *message, speech* In the phrase *word of God,* often a reference to the Bible, or to preaching or to a prophecy given to or delivered by a prophet. When applied to the Son of God, as in John 1:1, it refers in part to the fact that the Father is revealed to mankind through the Son, Jesus Christ.
to the *w* of Moses ... Lev 10:7
declare to you the *w* ... Deut 5:5
Joshua wrote...*w-s* ... Josh 24:26
proclaim the *w* of ... 1 Sam 9:27
Your *w*...confirmed ... 2 Chr 6:17
no limit to windy *w-s* ... Job 16:3
w-s of my mouth ... Ps 19:14
Your *w* is a lamp ... Ps 119:105
harsh *w* stirs up ... Prov 15:1
w of God is tested ... Prov 30:5
despised the *w* ... Is 5:24
w-s of a sealed book ... Is 29:11
speak My *w* in truth ... Jer 23:28
conceal these *w-s* ... Dan 12:4
every *w* that proceeds ... Matt 4:4
these *w-s* of Mine ... Matt 7:24
sower sows the *w* ... Mark 4:14
the *W* was God ... John 1:1
the *W* became flesh ... John 1:14
w-s of eternal life ... John 6:68
continue in My *w* ... John 8:31
glorifying the *w* ... Acts 13:48
too deep for *w-s* ... Rom 8:26
hearing by the *w* ... Rom 10:17
the *w* of the cross ... 1 Cor 1:18
fulfilled in one *w* ... Gal 5:14
no unwholesome *w* ... Eph 4:29
sanctified by...*w* ... 1 Tim 4:5
the *w* of truth ... 2 Tim 2:15
the faithful *w* ... Titus 1:9
w of God is living ... Heb 4:12
doers of the *w* ... James 1:22
pure milk of the *w* ... 1 Pet 2:2
the *W* of Life ... 1 John 1:1
The *W* of God ... Rev 19:13

WORK (n) *act, deed, labor*
God completed His *w* ... Gen 2:2
You shall *w* six days ... Ex 34:21
His *w* is perfect ... Deut 32:4
the *w* of His hands ... Ps 19:1
see the *w-s* of God ... Ps 66:5
Commit your *w-s* to ... Prov 16:3
let Him hasten His *w* ... Is 5:19
His *w* on Mount Zion ... Is 10:12
see your good *w-s* ... Matt 5:16
the *w-s* of Christ ... Matt 11:2
the *w* of the Law ... Rom 2:15
faith apart from *w-s* ... Rom 3:28
not...a result of *w-s* ... Eph 2:9
for the *w* of service ... Eph 4:12
began a good *w* ... Phil 1:6
fruit in...good *w* ... Col 1:10
rich in good *w-s* ... 1 Tim 6:18
faith without *w-s* ... James 2:20

WORK (v) *perform, produce*
has *w-ed* with God ... 1 Sam 14:45
those who *w* iniquity ... Ps 28:3
Who...*w-s* wonders ... Ps 72:18
not *w* for the food ... John 6:27
w together for good ... Rom 8:28
So death *w-s* in us ... 2 Cor 4:12
w out your salvation ... Phil 2:12
anyone is not willing to *w* ... 2 Thess 3:10

WORKER *laborer*
O *w* of deceit ... Ps 52:2
w-s of iniquity ... Prov 10:29
w is worthy of his ... Matt 10:10
God's fellow *w-s* ... 1 Cor 3:9
beware...evil *w-s* ... Phil 3:2
pure, *w-s* at home ... Titus 2:5

WORKMAN *craftsman*
a skillful *w* ... Ex 38:23
approved...as a *w* ... 2 Tim 2:15

WORKMANSHIP *craftsmanship*
we are His *w* ... Eph 2:10

WORLD *earth, humanity* 1) The physical earth; 2) all the people who inhabit the earth; 3) the physical universe; 4) the system of sin in the world under the control of Satan and the attitudes and lifestyles of those who have not yet trusted in Christ for salvation, or are opposed to Him.
foundations of...*w* ... 2 Sam 22:16
He will judge the *w* ... Ps 9:8
first dust of the *w* ... Prov 8:26
the light of the *w* ... Matt 5:14
the field is the *w* ... Matt 13:38
Go into all the *w* ... Mark 16:15
gains the whole *w* ... Luke 9:25
God so loved the *w* ... John 3:16
Savior of the *w* ... John 4:42
w cannot hate you ... John 7:7
the Light of the *w* ... John 8:12
overcome the *w* ... John 16:33
have upset the *w* ... Acts 17:6
sin entered...the *w* ... Rom 5:12
reconciling the *w* ... 2 Cor 5:19
unstained by the *w* ... James 1:27
flood upon the *w* ... 2 Pet 2:5
Do not love the *w* ... 1 John 2:15

WORLDLY *earthly*
w fables fit only ... 1 Tim 4:7
avoid *w*...chatter ... 2 Tim 2:16

WORM *creeping animal*
But I am a *w* ... Ps 22:6
w-s are your covering ... Is 14:11
God appointed a *w* ... Jon 4:7
their *w* does not die ... Mark 9:48
he was eaten by *w-s* ... Acts 12:23

WORMWOOD A bitter, green liqueur—also known as absinthe—that is highly toxic to the nervous system. In Revelation, also the name given to a star which falls into a third of the earth's rivers and poisons them.
1 *a bitter plant* ... Deut 29:18
2 *used figuratively* ... Prov 5:4; Amos 6:12; Rev 8:11

WORRY *anxious*
not be *w-ied* about your life ... Matt 6:25
not *w* about tomorrow ... Matt 6:34
do not *w* beforehand ... Mark 13:11
w-ing can add a *single* ... Luke 12:25

WORSHIP *bow, revere* Adoration, praise to God or (in idolatry) to false gods. The OT tabernacle and the temple were the places to worship the living God until Christ came. In the NT, worship can be done anywhere because the believer can communicate with God directly through prayer. Much of the worship recorded in the NT takes place in homes or other meeting places, wherever believers may be gathered together.
not *w* any other god ... Ex 34:14
you shall *w* Him ... Deut 6:13
W the LORD ... Ps 2:11
earth will *w* You ... Ps 66:4
in vain do they *w* ... Matt 15:9
w in spirit and truth ... John 4:24
w in the Spirit ... Phil 3:3
w Him who lives ... Rev 4:10
who *w* the beast ... Rev 14:11

WORTHLESS *useless*
all *w* physicians ... Job 13:4
w man digs up evil ... Prov 16:27
your *w* offerings ... Is 1:13
your faith is *w* ... 1 Cor 15:17
w for any good ... Titus 1:16
man's religion is *w* ... James 1:26

WORTHY *having merit*
sin *w* of death ... Deut 21:22
w of his support ... Matt 10:10
is not *w* of Me ... Matt 10:37
is *w* of his wages ... Luke 10:7
manner *w* of the ... Rom 16:2
w of the gospel ... Phil 1:27
world was not *w* ... Heb 11:38
W is the Lamb ... Rev 5:12

WOUND *injury*
My *w* is incurable ... Job 34:6
binds up their *w-s* ... Ps 147:3
Your *w* is incurable ... Jer 30:12
bandaged...his *w-s* ... Luke 10:34
by His *w-s* you were ... 1 Pet 2:24
fatal *w* was healed ... Rev 13:3

WRAPPINGS *cloth coverings*
bound...with *w* ... John 11:44
linen *w* lying *there* ... John 20:5

WRATH *anger, indignation* Similar to anger but usually more intense. In the OT, translated from a word with a basic meaning of "heat" or "rage"; in the NT, *anger* and *wrath* usually represent the same Gr word *(orgé).* Wrath often refers to the righteous judgment of God upon evil or wicked behavior.
and in great *w* ... Deut 29:28
Nor chasten...in Your *w* ... Ps 6:1
Pour out Your *w* ... Ps 79:6
turns away *w* ... Prov 15:1
Or else My *w* will go forth ... Jer 4:4
spent My *w* upon ... Ezek 5:13
from the *w* to come ... Matt 3:7
w of God abides on ... John 3:36
God who inflicts *w* ... Rom 3:5
children of *w* ... Eph 2:3
w of God will come ... Col 3:6
the *w* of the Lamb ... Rev 6:16

WRETCHED *miserable*
in to this *w* place ... Num 20:5
W man that I am ... Rom 7:24

WRITE *inscribe*
Moses, *W* this in a ... Ex 17:14
W them on the tablet ... Prov 3:3
he *wrote* the dream ... Dan 7:1
w a certificate ... Mark 10:4
with His finger *wrote* ... John 8:6
w...King of the Jews ... John 19:21
W in a book ... Rev 1:11

WRITINGS *literary work*
not believe his *w* ... John 5:47
known the sacred *w* ... 2 Tim 3:15

WRITTEN *inscribed*
w by...God ... Ex 31:18
w in the law ... 2 Chr 23:18
remembrance was *w* ... Mal 3:16
w by the prophet ... Matt 2:5
about whom it is *w* ... Matt 11:10
Law *w* in...hearts ... Rom 2:15
name has not been *w* ... Rev 13:8
w in the Lamb's ... Rev 21:27

WRONG *do evil, harm*
not *w* a stranger ... Ex 22:21
not *w* one another ... Lev 25:14
I...have done *w* ... 2 Sam 24:17
Love does no *w* ... Rom 13:10

WROUGHT *accomplished*
He *w* wonders ... Ps 78:12
been *w* in God ... John 3:21

X

XERXES Though the name is not found in the Bible, it is the Gr equivalent of *Ahasuerus*, the king who married Esther and ruled the Persian Empire during the fifth century B.C. (Est 1:1).

Y

YAHWEH The name of God in Hebrew as He revealed it to godly men of the OT. It is known as the tetragrammaton (Gr for "four letters") because ancient Hebrew was written only in consonants, and the actual letters of the divine name are "YHWH" (the vowels "a" and "e" are the most probable choices based on research). It probably is derived from a Hebrew verb meaning "to be." Recognizing that the name is sacred and fearing to use it improperly, the Jews began the practice of substituting "my Lord" (Heb *Adonai)* as a reference to it. This practice was maintained throughout NT times and beyond (the Gr word for "Lord" is *kurios).* A similar practice is followed in the NASB, partly in honor of the tradition, but also in recognition of the fact that "Yahweh" is not a familiar name to most readers, and that the spelling is uncertain, due to the absence of vowels in ancient Hebrew. The traditional English rendering "Jehovah" is a misunderstanding of the Heb spelling, due not only to the absence of vowels, but also to the mistaken insertion of "o" between the "h" and the "v".
see also **LORD**

YEAR *period, time*
atonement...every *y* ... Lev 16:34
fiftieth *y*...jubilee ... Lev 25:11
the *y* of remission ... Deut 15:9
crowned the *y* with ... Ps 65:11
length of...*y-s* ... Prov 3:2
favorable *y* of the LORD ... Is 61:2
thirty *y-s* of age ... Luke 3:23
y of the LORD ... Luke 4:19
priest *enters,* once a *y* ... Heb 9:7
sacrifices...*y* by *y* ... Heb 10:1
y-s like one day ... 2 Pet 3:8
reign...thousand *y-s* ... Rev 20:6

YEARLING *one year old*
a *y* ewe lamb ... Lev 14:10
With *y* calves ... Mic 6:6

YEARNS *deeply moved*
my flesh *y* for You ... Ps 63:1
My heart *y* for him ... Jer 31:20

YEAR OF JUBILEE *see* **JUBILEE, YEAR OF**

YESTERDAY *past*
we are *only* of *y* ... Job 8:9
thousand years...*y* ... Ps 90:4
same *y* and today ... Heb 13:8

YHWH *see* **YAHWEH** *and* **LORD**
See also **INTRODUCTORY MATERIAL TO NASB**

YIELD *produce*
no longer *y* its ... Gen 4:12
land...*y* its produce ... Lev 25:19
Which *y-s* its fruit ... Ps 1:3
y-ed up *His* spirit ... Matt 27:50
not *y* in subjection ... Gal 2:5
y-s the peaceful ... Heb 12:11

YOKE *wooden bar* A wooden apparatus placed over the necks of oxen and other pulling animals which connects them and enables them to pull carts, plows, etc. In the Bible it is used as a metaphor for unions between people, and for labor or service.
break his *y* from ... Gen 27:40
iron *y* on...neck ... Deut 28:48
made our *y* hard ... 1 Kin 12:4
the *y* of their burden ... Is 9:4
Take My *y* upon ... Matt 11:29
to a *y* of slavery ... Gal 5:1

YOUNG *early age, youth*
he sent *y* men ... Ex 24:5
or two *y* pigeons ... Lev 15:29
glory of *y* men is ... Prov 20:29
y men stumble ... Is 40:30
like a *y* lion ... Hos 5:14
finding a *y* donkey ... John 12:14
y men...visions ... Acts 2:17
urge the *y* men ... Titus 2:6

YOUTH *young*
evil from his *y* ... Gen 8:21
fresher than in *y* ... Job 33:25
the sins of my *y* ... Ps 25:7
confidence from my *y* ... Ps 71:5
your *y* is renewed ... Ps 103:5
the wife of your *y* ... Prov 5:18
y-s grow weary ... Is 40:30
the reproach of my *y* ... Jer 31:19
life from my *y* up ... Acts 26:4

Z

ZACCHEUS *(pure, righteous).* A wealthy tax collector who once climbed a tree to see Jesus and later had the privilege of Jesus' visit to his home.
tax collector who followed Jesus ... Luke 19:2,5,8

ZACHARIAS A priest in the temple, to whom God promised a son. The son, John the Baptist, was destined to be the forerunner for Jesus the Messiah, i.e. to prepare the people of Israel for His coming.
father of John the Baptist ... Luke 1:5,12,18; 3:2

ZADOK *(righteous).* A priest closely associated with David and Solomon (1 Kin 1:32, 39). Also the name of several other individuals.

ZALMUNNA *(protection refused).* A Midianite king, pursued and killed by Gideon (Jud 8:21).

ZAREPHATH A seacoast town between Tyre and Sidon. Elijah was sent there to a widow who provided for him.
scene of miracle by Elijah ... 1 Kin 17:9,10
Phoenician town ... Obad 20; Luke 4:26

ZARETHAN A place by the junction of the Jabbok and Jordan rivers (Josh 3:16). It is very near the point of passage where the Israelites crossed into the Promised Land.

ZEAL *fervor, passion*
kill them in his *z* ... 2 Sam 21:2
my *z* for the LORD ... 2 Kin 10:16
z has consumed me ... Ps 119:139
Your z for the people ... Is 26:11
have a *z* for God ... Rom 10:2
your *z* for me ... 2 Cor 7:7

ZEALOT A Jewish sect (q.v.) that strongly opposed foreign domination of Israel, especially by Rome. Also, Jews who were recognized for their righteous indignation against those who violated OT or Jewish law, and were allowed some latitude to punish offenders.
member of radical Jewish nationalist party ... Matt 10:4; Mark 3:18; Luke 6:15; Acts 1:13

ZEALOUS *fervent*
z for the LORD ... 1 Kin 19:10
all *z* for the Law ... Acts 21:20
z of...*gifts* ... 1 Cor 14:12
z for good deeds ... Titus 2:14
be *z* and repent ... Rev 3:19

ZEBADIAH *(Yahweh has given).* The name of nine men in the OT, including a Levite teacher of the law in the reign of Jehoshaphat (2 Chr 19:11).

ZEBAH *(sacrifice).* A Midianite king pursued and killed by Gideon (Judg 8:21).

ZEBEDEE *(gift of Yahweh).* A fisherman and the father of two of the Twelve Apostles: James and John.
father of James and John ... Matt 4:21; 27:56; Mark 1:19; 10:35; Luke 5:10; John 21:2

ZEBOIIM A town in the region of Sodom and Gomorrah which was destroyed when they were (Deut 29:23).

ZEBULUN *(dwelling).* One of Jacob's twelve sons born to Leah. His descendants became the tribe that carried his name.
1 *son of Jacob* ... Gen 30:20
2 *tribe* ... Num 34:25; Josh 21:34
3 *territory of the tribe, located in N Palestine* ... Josh 19:27; Judg 12:12; Is 9:1; Ezek 48:27

ZECHARIAH *(Yahweh remembers).* The name of many individuals, including the writer of one of the minor prophetic books and a contemporary of the prophet Haggai.
1 *son of Jeiel* ... 1 Chr 9:35-37
2 *priest with ark* ... 1 Chr 15:24
3 *son of Isshiah* ... 1 Chr 24:25
4 *father of Iddo* ... 1 Chr 27:21
5 *son of Benaiah* ... 2 Chr 20:14
6 *son of Jehoshaphat* ... 2 Chr 21:2
7 *son of Jehoida* ... 2 Chr 24:20
8 *prophet* ... 2 Chr 26:5
9 *priest under Ezra* ... Neh 12:41
10 *minor prophet* ... Zech 1:1

ZEDEKIAH *(Yahweh is my righteousness).* The last king of Judah (2 Kin 24:18; Jer 52:11). Also the name of several other individuals.

ZEEB *(wolf).* A prince of Midian killed by Gideon's troops (Judg 7:25).

ZELOPHEHAD (unc, *shadow from terror).* A man from the tribe of Manasseh. He left only female heirs, who were given an inheritance in the Promised Land.
Manassite, son of Hepher ... Num 26:33
daughters became his heirs ... Num 27:1; 36:2

ZEPHANIAH *(Yahweh has treasured).* The name of four individuals, including one of the minor prophets. He ministered in the days of King Josiah.
1 *priest* ... 2 Kin 25:18
2 *Kohathite Levite* ... 1 Chr 6:36
3 *minor prophet* ... Zeph 1:1
4 *father of Josiah* ... Zech 6:10

ZERED A brook which the people of Israel crossed on their journey to the Promised Land (Deut 2:13). Its valley separates Edom and Moab.

ZERUBBABEL (unc, *seed of Babylon).* A leader who returned to Israel with the exiles from Babylon. He helped in the rebuilding of the temple and was appointed by Cyrus as governor of a province.
line of David ... 1 Chr 3:1-19
helped rebuild temple ... Ezra 3:8

ZERUIAH *(perfumed with mastic).* David's sister or half-sister and the mother of three important men in his army: Joab, Abishai, and Asahel.
mother of Joab, Abishai, and Asahel ... 2 Sam 2:18
David's (half-) sister ... 1 Chr 2:16; 2 Sam 17:25

ZICHRI (unc, *remembrance).* A priest in the time of Nehemiah (Neh 12:17). Also the name of several other individuals.

ZIKLAG A city which Achish, a Philistine king, gave to David when David was fleeing from Saul.
town in S Judah ... Josh 15:31; 1 Sam 27:6; 1 Chr 12:1

ZILPAH One of Leah's female slaves who, as Jacob's concubine, gave birth to Gad and Asher.
concubine of Jacob ... Gen 29:24; 30:10; 46:18

ZIN A wilderness region which the people of Israel passed by during their journey to Canaan.
wilderness in Negev ... Num 13:21; Deut 32:51; Josh 15:1,3

ZION Originally a fortified hill which later became Jerusalem, the chief city of Israel. Thereafter the name came to refer to the temple area "temple mount"), and to Jerusalem in general or its inhabitants. Also a prophetic reference to the heavenly Jerusalem.
1 *hill / City of David which is Jerusalem* ... 2 Sam 5:7; 1 Chr 11:5
2 *after Temple built, name extended to top of hill, Mount Zion* ... Is 8:18; 18:7; Mic 4:7
3 *applied to all of Jerusalem as city spreads* ... 2 Kin 19:21; Ps 69:35; Is 1:8
4 *used in the corporate sense for the people and land* ... Ps 97:8; 149:2; Is 3:16; 8:14; 59:20; Joel 2:23; Zech 9:9; Rom 9:33; 1 Pet 2:3
5 *used eschatologically for heavenly Jerusalem* ... Is 60:14; Heb 12:22; Rev 14:1

ZIPPORAH *(sparrow).* Daughter of Jethro, wife of Moses, and the mother of Gershom and Eliezer.
wife of Moses ... Ex 2:21; 4:25

ZIV
name of the second month in Hebrew calendar ... 1 Kin 6:1,37

ZOAN
Egyptian delta city ... Num 13:22; Ps 78:12; Is 19:11; Ezek 30:14

ZOAR *(little).* The only one of the Cities of the Valley which was not destroyed by fire from God. Lot fled there from Sodom.
city of the plain near the Dead Sea ... Gen 13:10; 14:2; 19:23,30; Deut 34:3; Jer 48:34
see also **BELA**

ZOBAH A kingdom near Hamath against which Saul and David fought (1 Sam 14:47; 2 Sam 8:3).

ZOPHAR A friend of Job who tried to console Job during his suffering.
one of Job's friends ... Job 2:11; 11:1; 20:1; 42:9

ZUZIM
pre-Israelite tribe in Palestine ... Gen 14:5

Map 1: **WORLD OF THE PATRIARCHS**

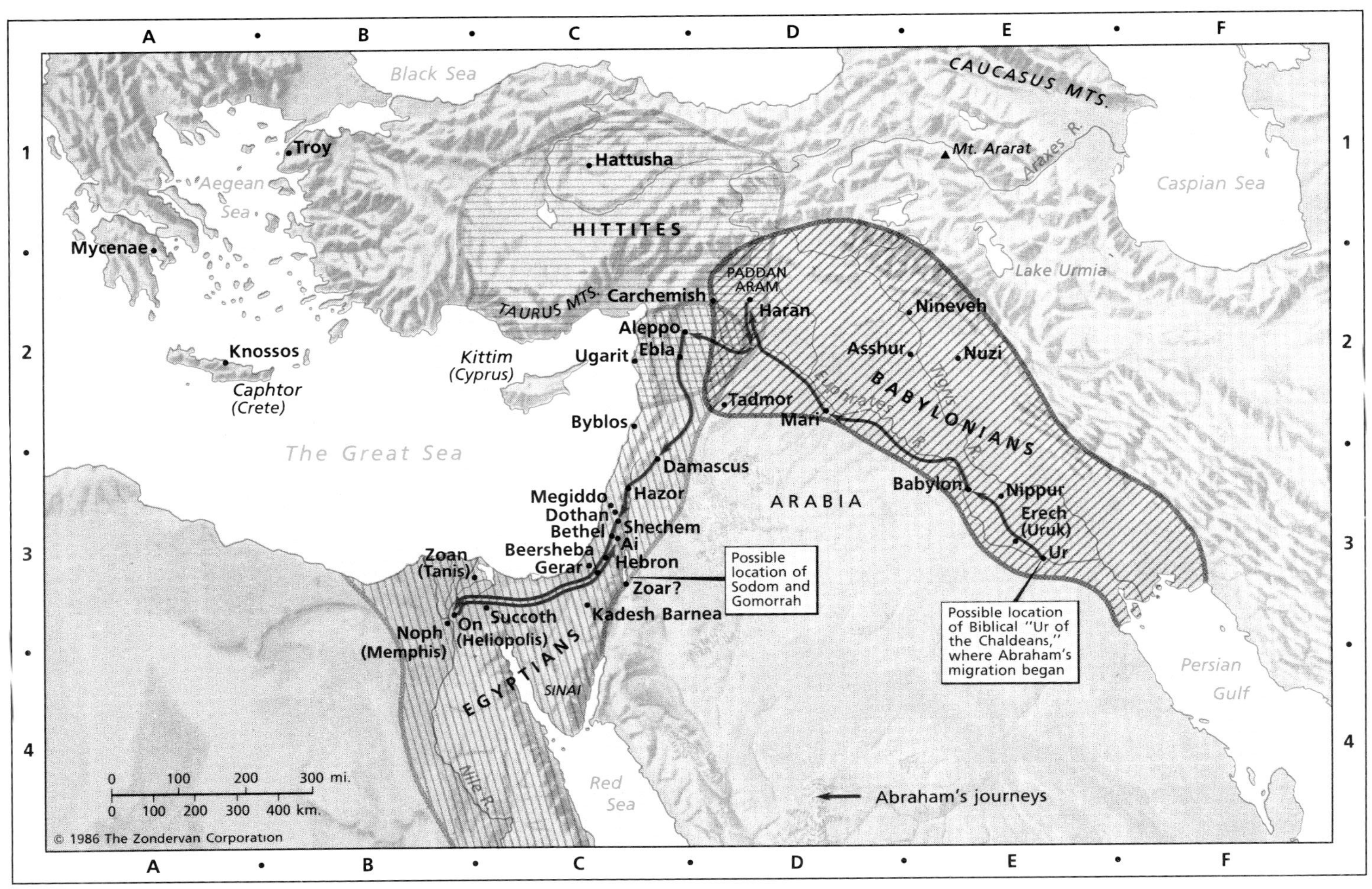

Map 2: **PALESTINE AND SINAI**

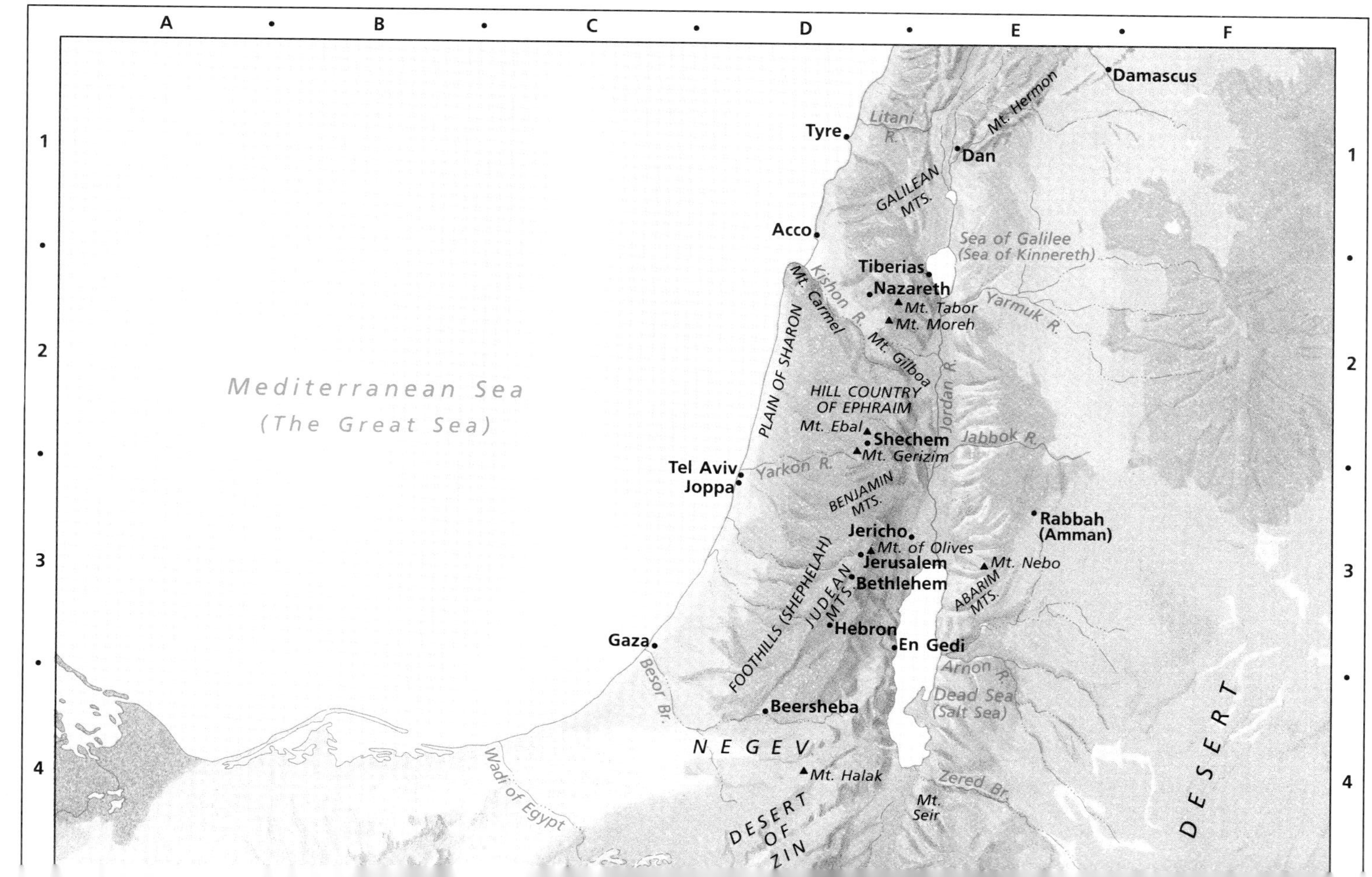

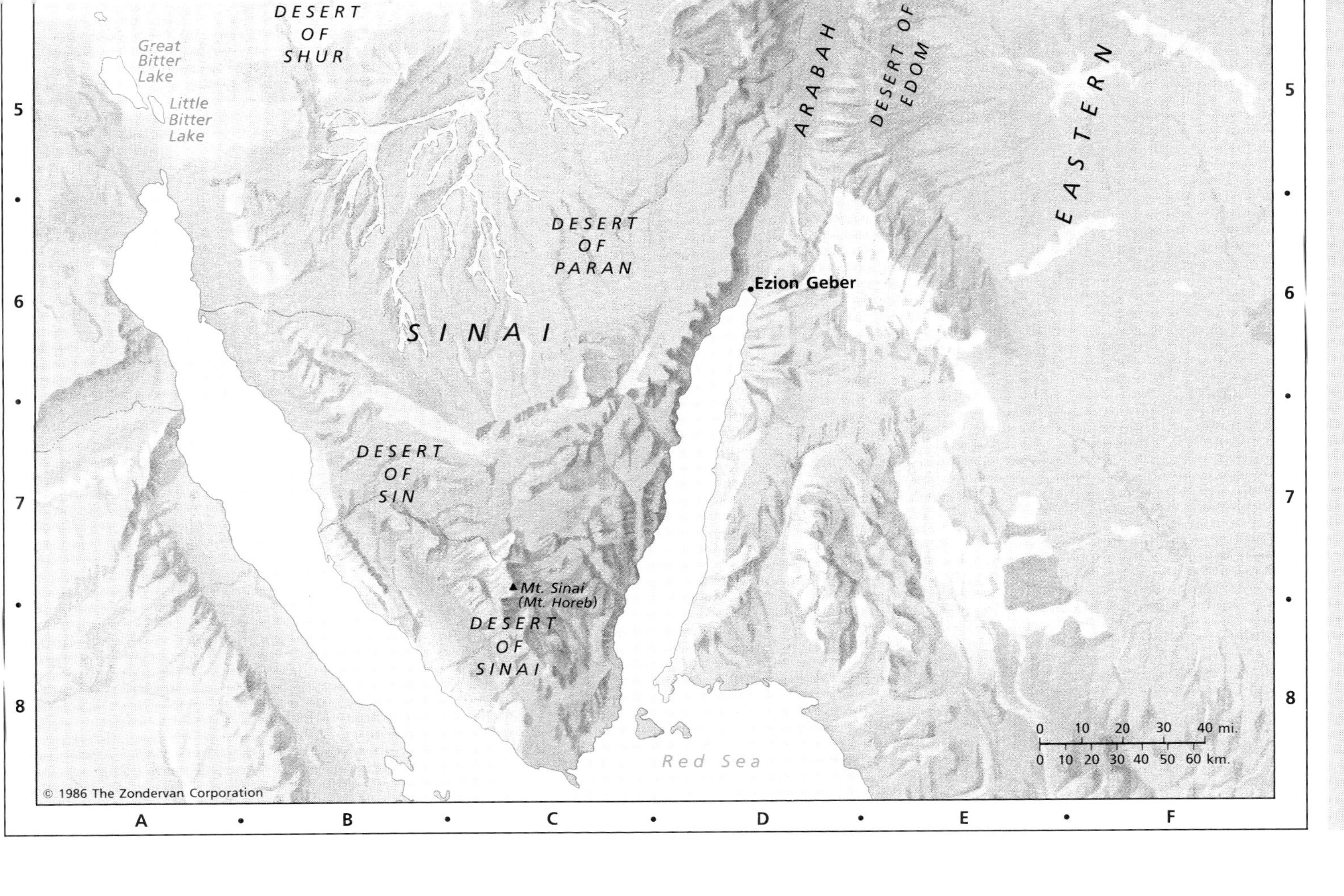
DESERT OF SHUR
Great Bitter Lake
Little Bitter Lake
ARABAH
DESERT OF EDOM
EASTERN
DESERT OF PARAN
Ezion Geber
SINAI
DESERT OF SIN
Mt. Sinai (Mt. Horeb)
DESERT OF SINAI
Red Sea
0 10 20 30 40 mi.
0 10 20 30 40 50 60 km.
A B C D E F
5 6 7 8
© 1986 The Zondervan Corporation

Map 3: **EXODUS AND CONQUEST OF CANAAN**

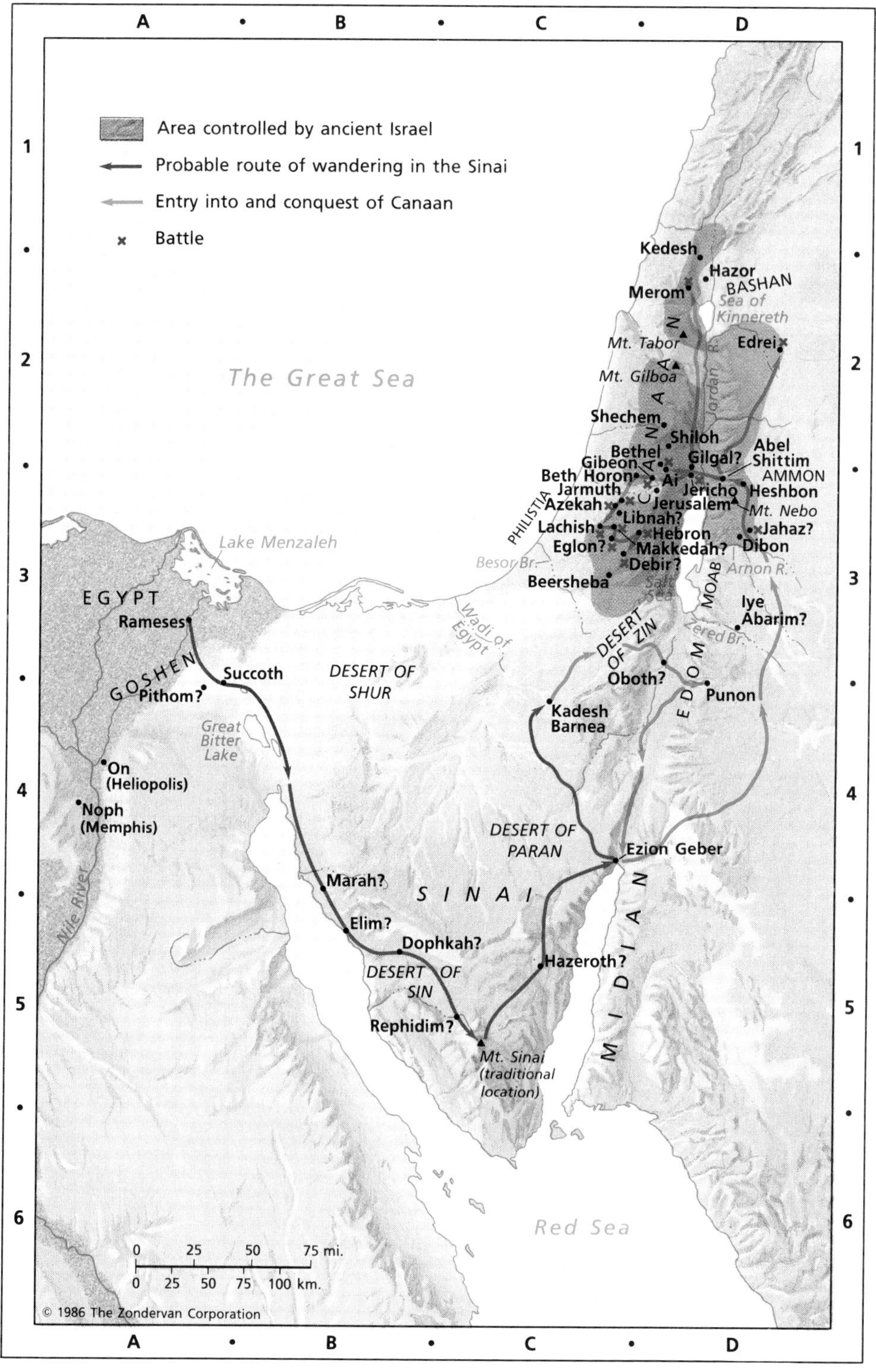

A
B
C
D
1
2
3
4
5
6
Area controlled by ancient Israel
Probable route of wandering in the Sinai
Entry into and conquest of Canaan
Battle
The Great Sea
Kedesh
Hazor
BASHAN
Merom
Sea of Kinnereth
Mt. Tabor
Edrei
Mt. Gilboa
Jordan R.
CANAAN
Shechem
Shiloh
Bethel
Abel Shittim
Gilgal?
Gibeon
Beth Horon
AMMON
Ai
Jarmuth
Jericho
Heshbon
Azekah
Jerusalem
Mt. Nebo
PHILISTIA
Libnah?
Lachish
Hebron
Jahaz?
Eglon?
Makkedah?
Dibon
Lake Menzaleh
Besor Br.
Debir?
Arnon R.
Beersheba
Salt Sea
MOAB
EGYPT
Iye Abarim?
Rameses
Wadi of Egypt
DESERT OF ZIN
Zered Br.
GOSHEN
Succoth
DESERT OF SHUR
Oboth?
EDOM
Pithom?
Punon
Kadesh Barnea
Great Bitter Lake
On (Heliopolis)
Noph (Memphis)
DESERT OF PARAN
Ezion Geber
Marah?
SINAI
Nile River
Elim?
MIDIAN
Dophkah?
Hazeroth?
DESERT OF SIN
Rephidim?
Mt. Sinai (traditional location)
Red Sea
0 25 50 75 mi.
0 25 50 75 100 km.
© 1986 The Zondervan Corporation

Map 4: **LAND OF THE TWELVE TRIBES**

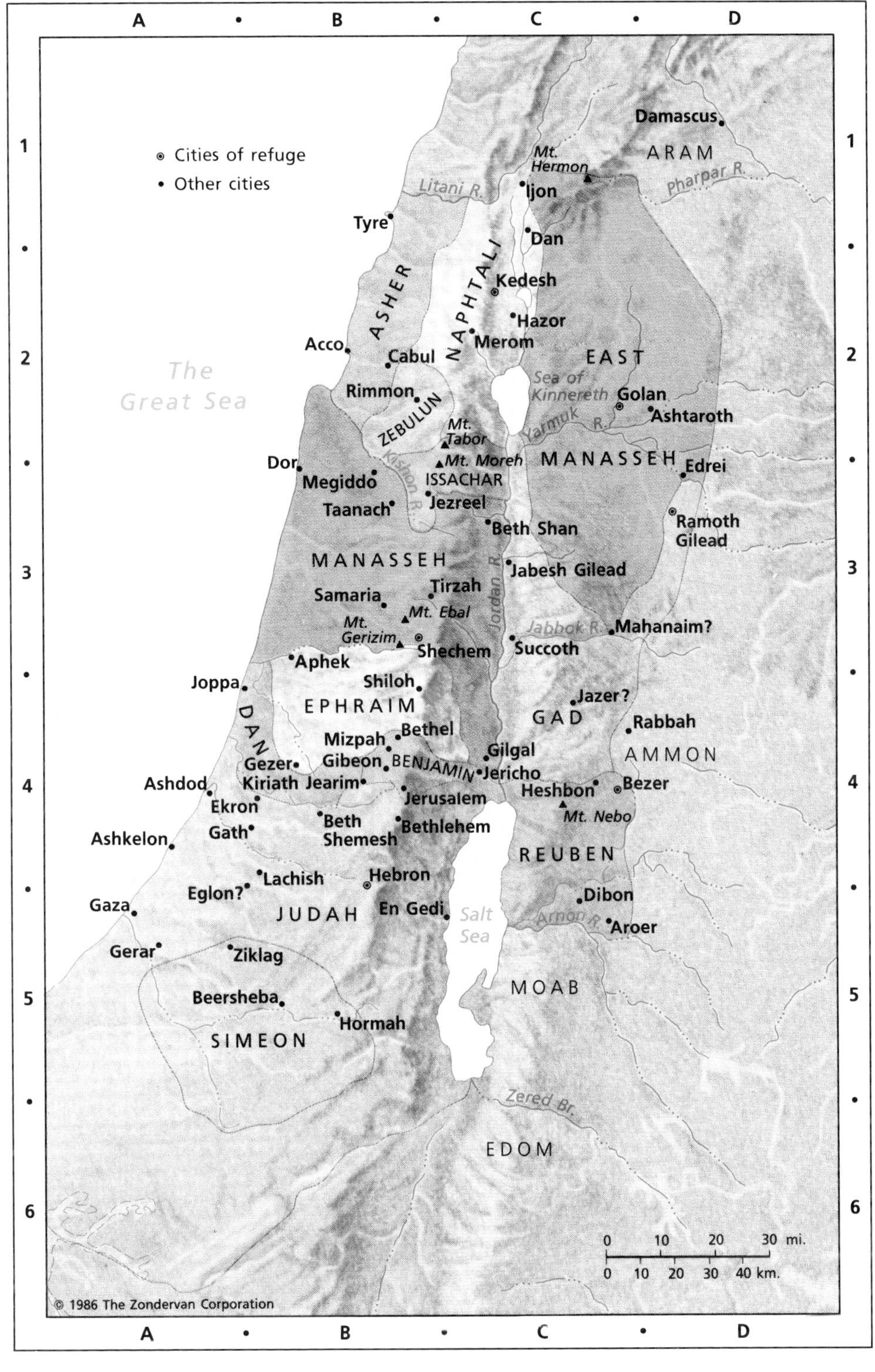

A
B
C
D
1
2
3
4
5
6
Cities of refuge
Other cities
The Great Sea
Damascus
ARAM
Mt. Hermon
Pharpar R.
Litani R.
Ijon
Tyre
Dan
ASHER
NAPHTALI
Kedesh
Hazor
Acco
Merom
Cabul
EAST
Sea of Kinnereth
Rimmon
Golan
Ashtaroth
ZEBULUN
Yarmuk R.
Mt. Tabor
Dor
Mt. Moreh
MANASSEH
Edrei
Megiddo
ISSACHAR
Kishon R.
Jezreel
Taanach
Ramoth Gilead
Beth Shan
MANASSEH
Jabesh Gilead
Tirzah
Samaria
Jordan R.
Mt. Ebal
Mt. Gerizim
Jabbok R.
Mahanaim?
Shechem
Succoth
Aphek
Joppa
Shiloh
Jazer?
EPHRAIM
GAD
DAN
Rabbah
Bethel
Mizpah
Gilgal
AMMON
Gezer
Gibeon
BENJAMIN
Jericho
Ashdod
Kiriath Jearim
Heshbon
Bezer
Ekron
Jerusalem
Mt. Nebo
Gath
Beth Shemesh
Bethlehem
Ashkelon
REUBEN
Lachish
Hebron
Dibon
Eglon?
Gaza
JUDAH
En Gedi
Salt Sea
Arnon R.
Aroer
Gerar
Ziklag
MOAB
Beersheba
Hormah
SIMEON
Zered Br.
EDOM
0 10 20 30 mi.
0 10 20 30 40 km.
© 1986 The Zondervan Corporation

Map 5: **KINGDOM OF DAVID AND SOLOMON**

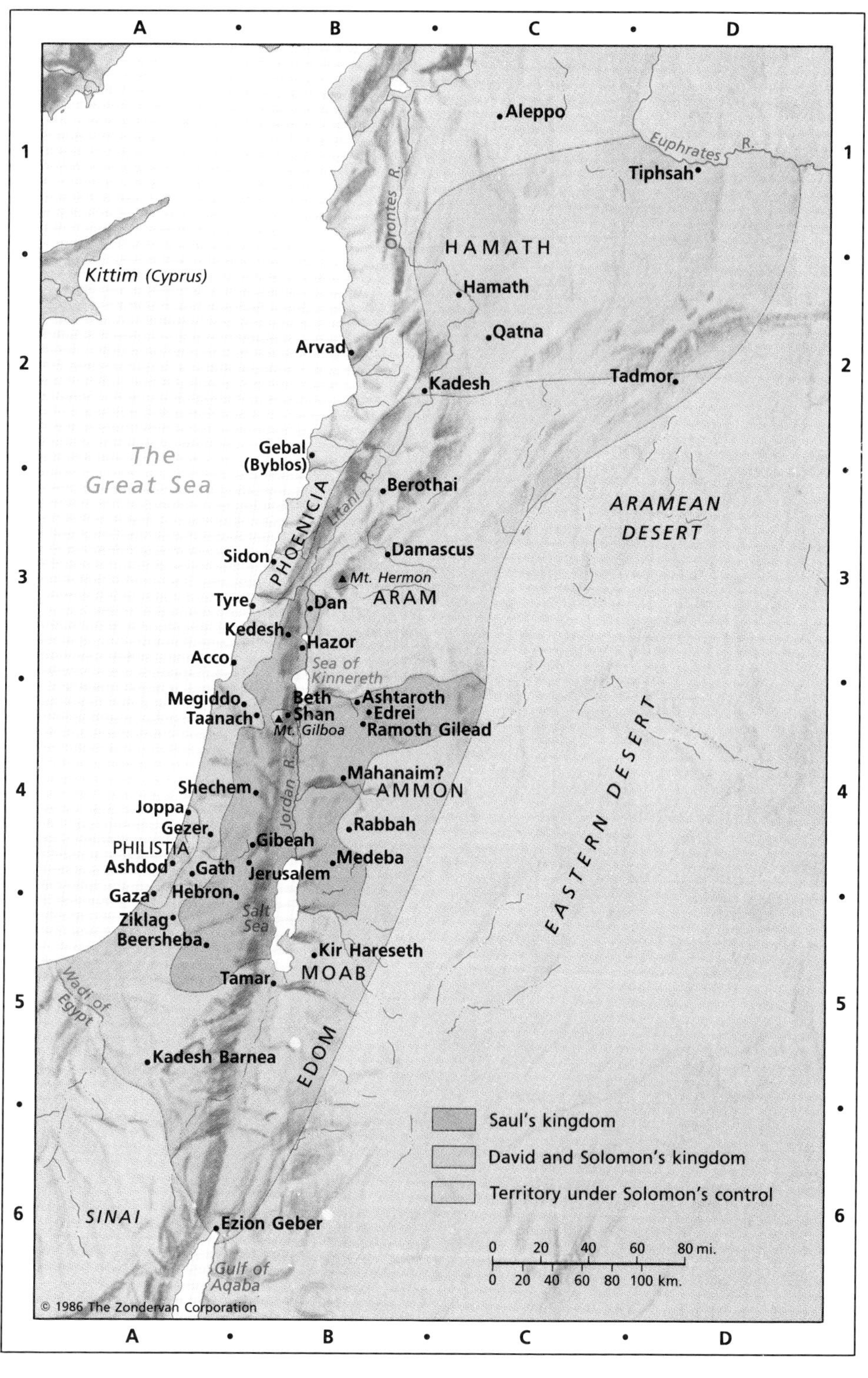

Map 6: **PROPHETS IN ISRAEL AND JUDAH**

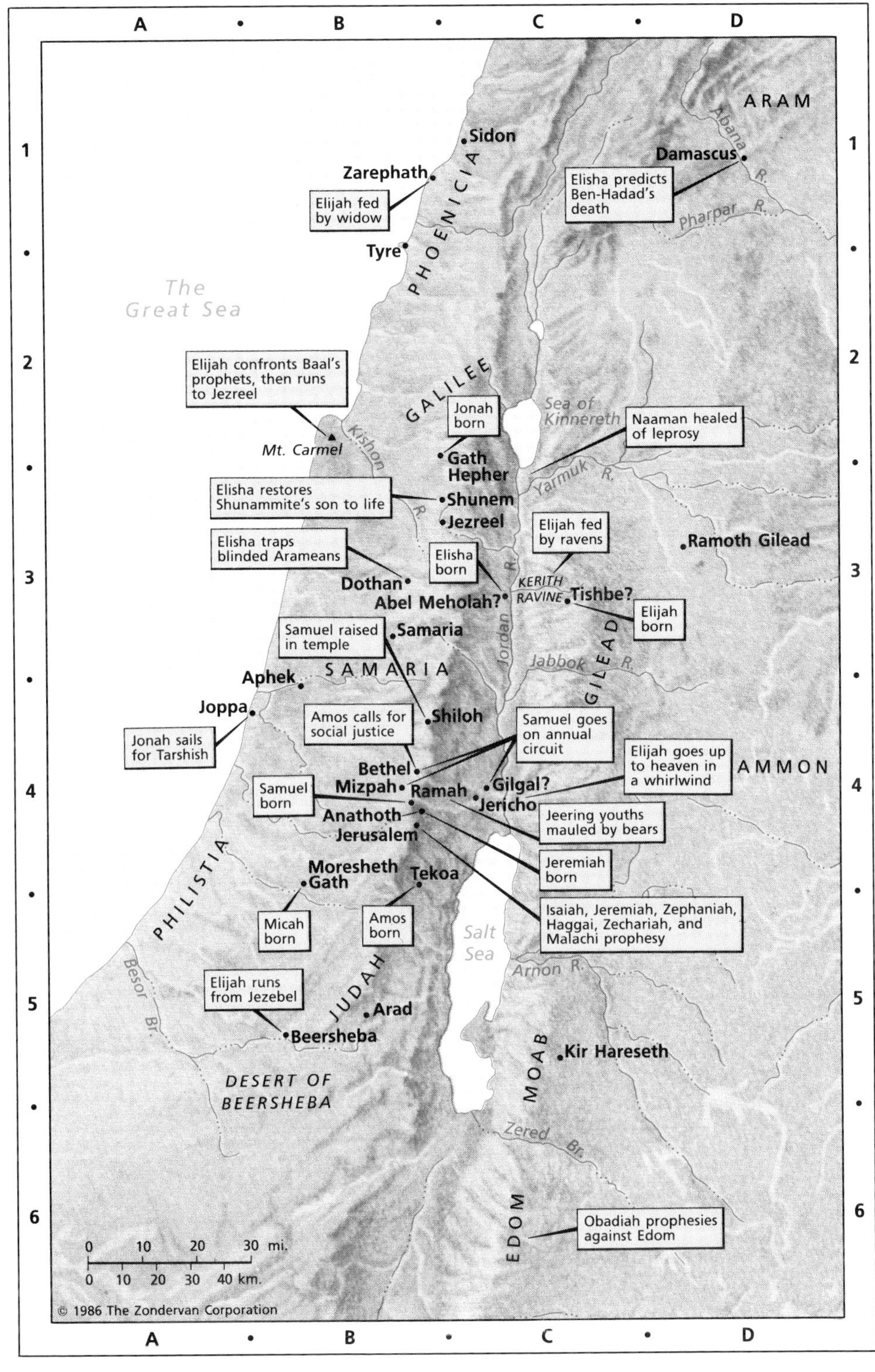

A
B
C
D
1
2
3
4
5
6
ARAM
Abana R.
Pharpar R.
Sidon
Damascus
Zarephath
Elijah fed by widow
Elisha predicts Ben-Hadad's death
PHOENICIA
Tyre
The Great Sea
Elijah confronts Baal's prophets, then runs to Jezreel
GALILEE
Jonah born
Sea of Kinnereth
Naaman healed of leprosy
Mt. Carmel
Kishon R.
Gath Hepher
Yarmuk R.
Elisha restores Shunammite's son to life
Shunem
Jezreel
Elijah fed by ravens
Ramoth Gilead
Elisha traps blinded Arameans
Elisha born
Dothan
KERITH RAVINE
Abel Meholah?
Tishbe?
Elijah born
Samuel raised in temple
Samaria
Jordan R.
GILEAD
Jabbok R.
Aphek
SAMARIA
Joppa
Shiloh
Amos calls for social justice
Samuel goes on annual circuit
Jonah sails for Tarshish
Elijah goes up to heaven in a whirlwind
AMMON
Bethel
Mizpah
Ramah
Gilgal?
Samuel born
Jericho
Anathoth
Jeering youths mauled by bears
Jerusalem
Jeremiah born
Moresheth Gath
Tekoa
PHILISTIA
Isaiah, Jeremiah, Zephaniah, Haggai, Zechariah, and Malachi prophesy
Micah born
Amos born
Salt Sea
Arnon R.
Besor Br.
Elijah runs from Jezebel
JUDAH
Arad
Beersheba
MOAB
Kir Hareseth
DESERT OF BEERSHEBA
Zered Br.
EDOM
Obadiah prophesies against Edom
0 10 20 30 mi.
0 10 20 30 40 km.

Map 7: ASSYRIAN AND BABYLONIAN EMPIRES

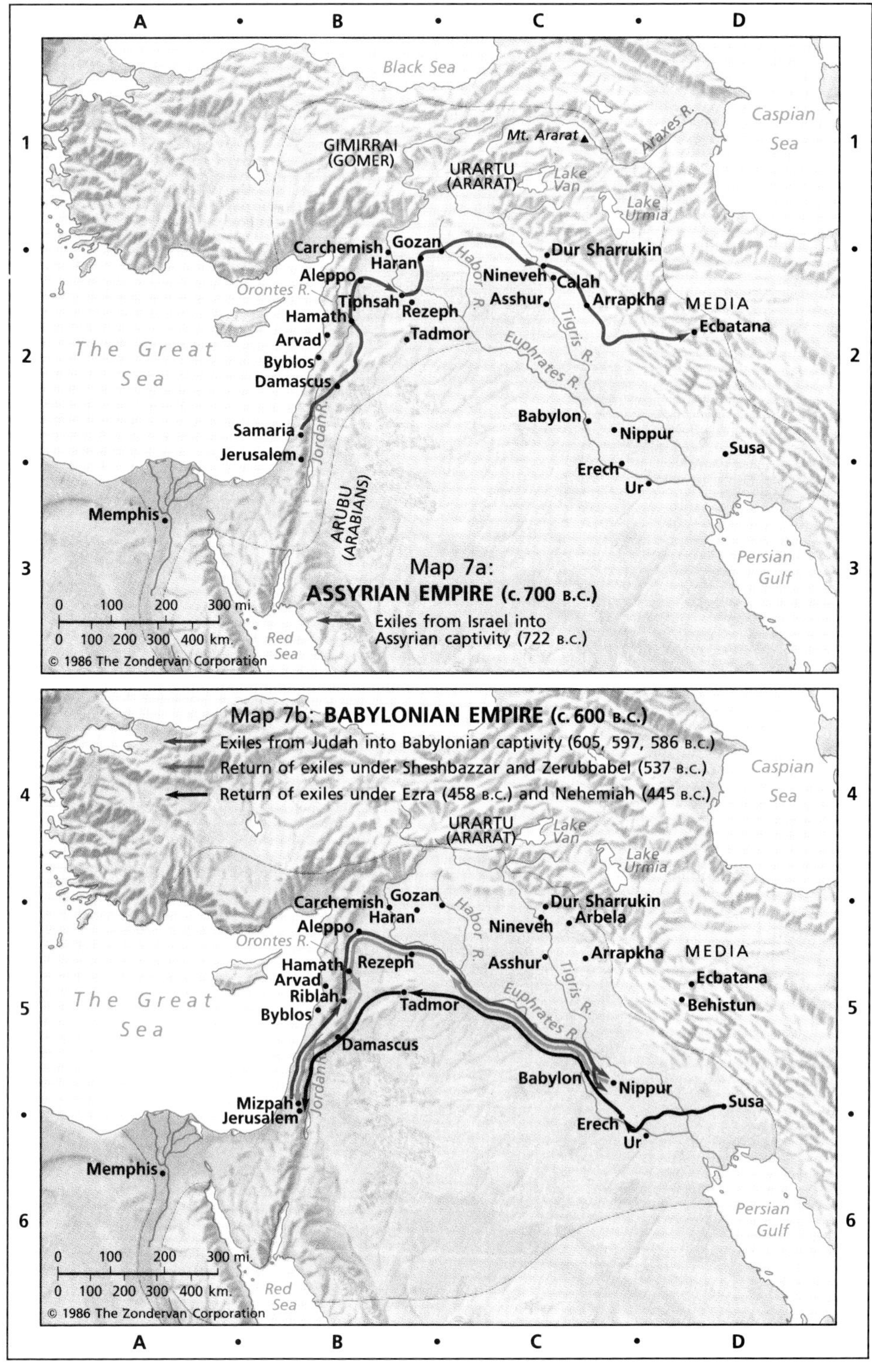

Map 8: **JERUSALEM IN JESUS' TIME**

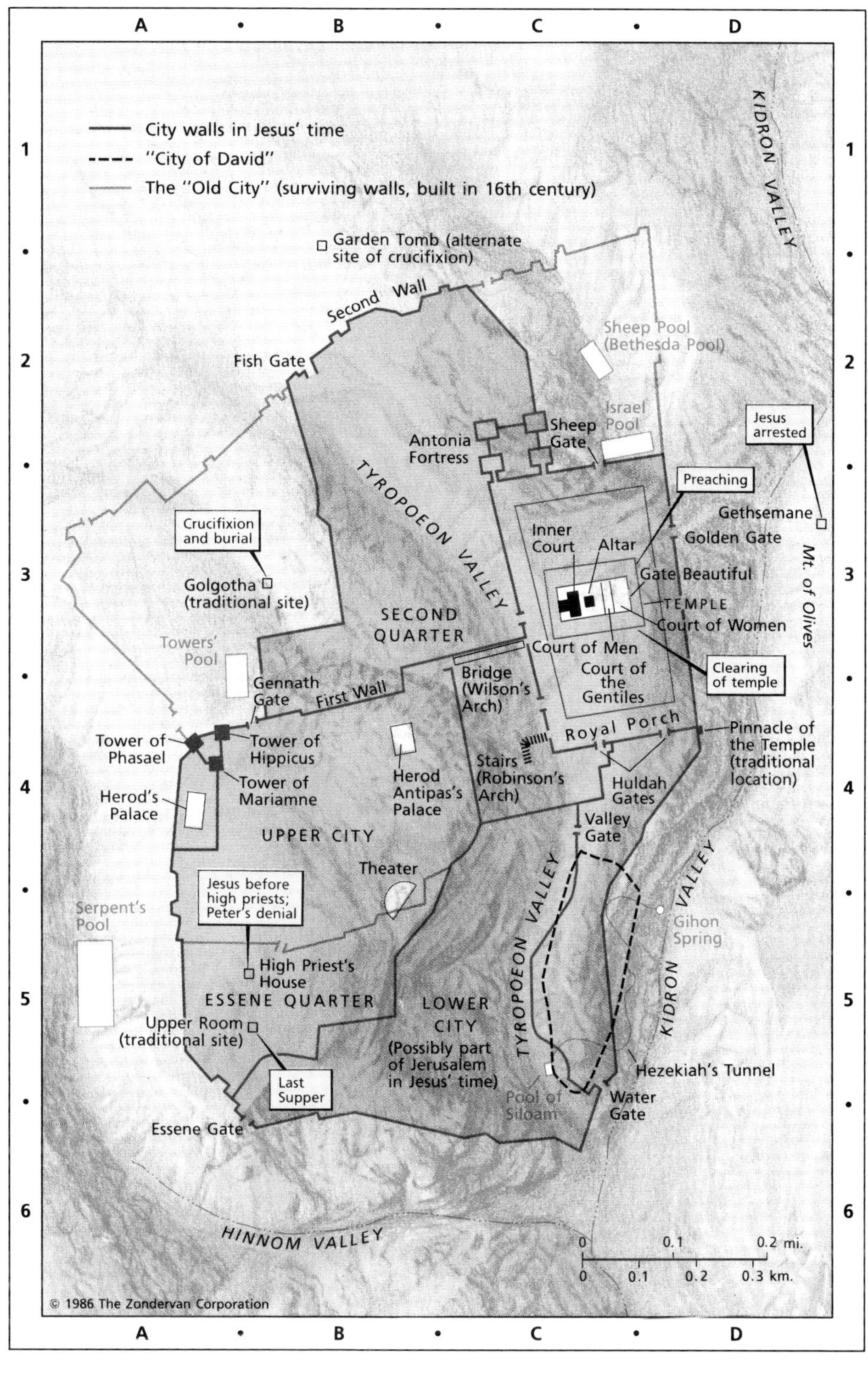
A
B
C
D
1
2
3
4
5
6
City walls in Jesus' time
"City of David"
The "Old City" (surviving walls, built in 16th century)
KIDRON VALLEY
Garden Tomb (alternate site of crucifixion)
Second Wall
Sheep Pool (Bethesda Pool)
Fish Gate
Israel Pool
Jesus arrested
Antonia Fortress
Sheep Gate
Preaching
TYROPOEON VALLEY
Gethsemane
Golden Gate
Crucifixion and burial
Inner Court
Altar
Mt. of Olives
Gate Beautiful
Golgotha (traditional site)
TEMPLE
SECOND QUARTER
Court of Women
Towers' Pool
Court of Men
Court of the Gentiles
Clearing of temple
Bridge (Wilson's Arch)
Gennath Gate
First Wall
Royal Porch
Pinnacle of the Temple (traditional location)
Tower of Phasael
Tower of Hippicus
Stairs (Robinson's Arch)
Tower of Mariamne
Herod Antipas's Palace
Huldah Gates
Herod's Palace
Valley Gate
UPPER CITY
Theater
Jesus before high priests; Peter's denial
Serpent's Pool
Gihon Spring
KIDRON VALLEY
High Priest's House
ESSENE QUARTER
LOWER CITY
(Possibly part of Jerusalem in Jesus' time)
TYROPOEON VALLEY
Upper Room (traditional site)
Last Supper
Hezekiah's Tunnel
Pool of Siloam
Water Gate
Essene Gate
HINNOM VALLEY
0 0.1 0.2 mi.
0 0.1 0.2 0.3 km.
© 1986 The Zondervan Corporation

Map 9: **JESUS' MINISTRY**

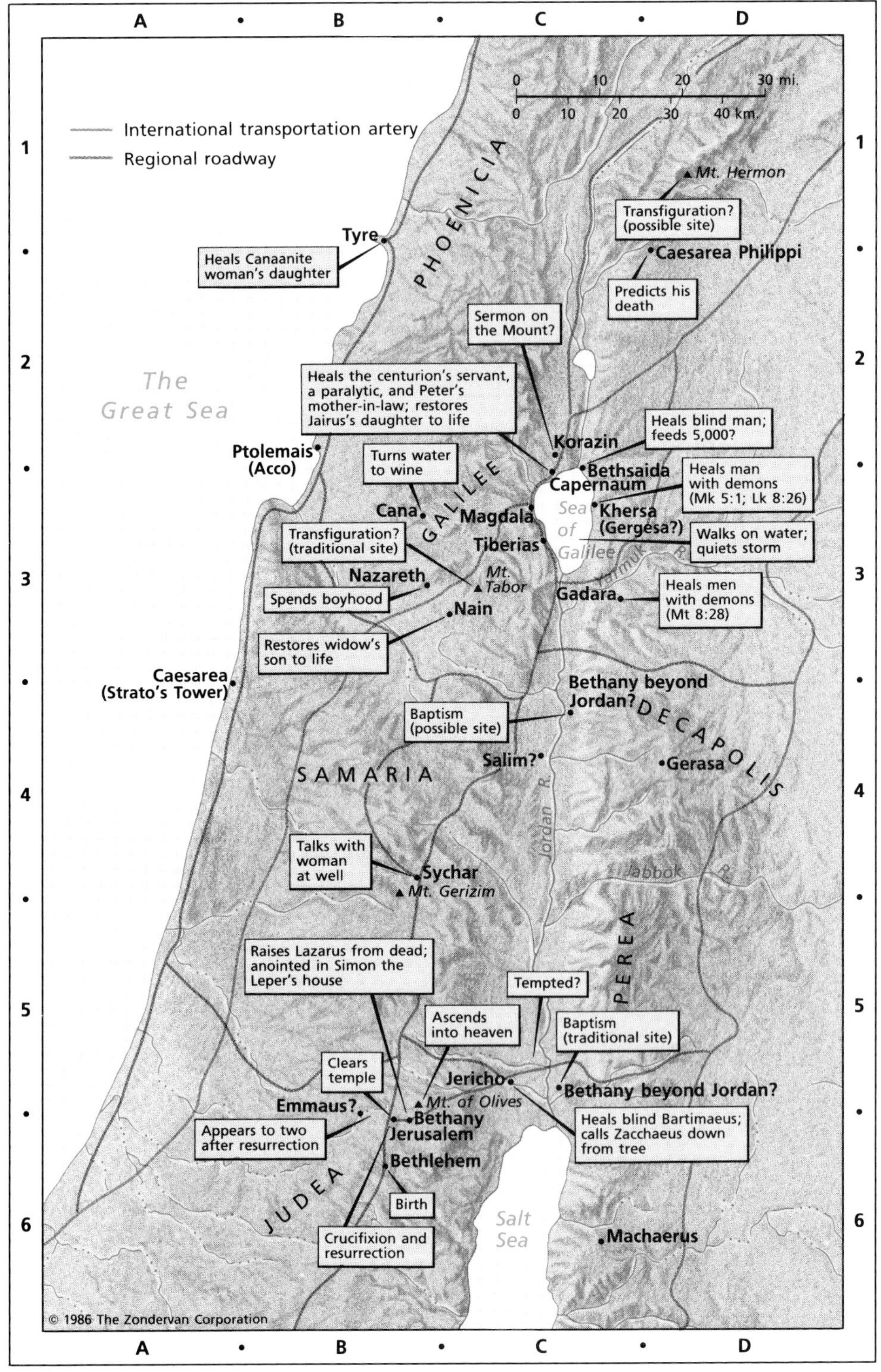

A
B
C
D
1
2
3
4
5
6
0
10
20
30 mi.
0
10
20
30
40 km.
International transportation artery
Regional roadway
Mt. Hermon
Transfiguration? (possible site)
Caesarea Philippi
Predicts his death
PHOENICIA
Tyre
Heals Canaanite woman's daughter
Sermon on the Mount?
The Great Sea
Heals the centurion's servant, a paralytic, and Peter's mother-in-law; restores Jairus's daughter to life
Korazin
Heals blind man; feeds 5,000?
Ptolemais (Acco)
Turns water to wine
Bethsaida
Capernaum
Heals man with demons (Mk 5:1; Lk 8:26)
GALILEE
Cana
Magdala
Sea of Galilee
Khersa (Gergesa?)
Walks on water; quiets storm
Transfiguration? (traditional site)
Tiberias
Yarmuk R.
Nazareth
Mt. Tabor
Spends boyhood
Gadara
Heals men with demons (Mt 8:28)
Nain
Restores widow's son to life
Caesarea (Strato's Tower)
Bethany beyond Jordan?
DECAPOLIS
Baptism (possible site)
Salim?
Gerasa
SAMARIA
Jordan R.
Talks with woman at well
Sychar
Mt. Gerizim
Jabbok R.
PEREA
Raises Lazarus from dead; anointed in Simon the Leper's house
Tempted?
Ascends into heaven
Baptism (traditional site)
Clears temple
Jericho
Bethany beyond Jordan?
Mt. of Olives
Emmaus?
Bethany
Appears to two after resurrection
Jerusalem
Heals blind Bartimaeus; calls Zacchaeus down from tree
Bethlehem
JUDEA
Birth
Salt Sea
Machaerus
Crucifixion and resurrection

Map 10: **APOSTLES' EARLY TRAVELS**

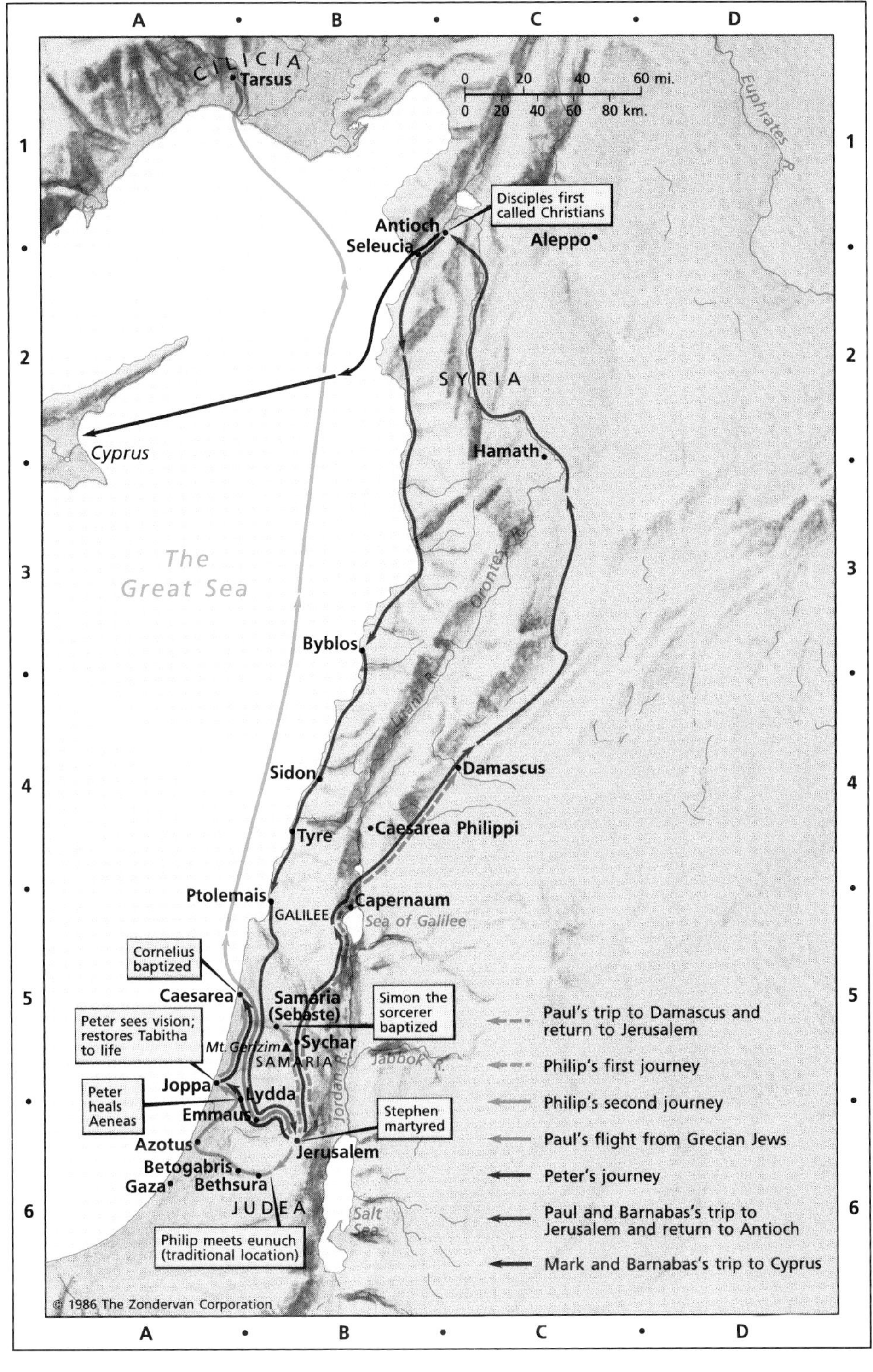

A
B
C
D
1
2
3
4
5
6
CILICIA
Tarsus
0 20 40 60 mi.
0 20 40 60 80 km.
Euphrates R.
Disciples first called Christians
Antioch
Seleucia
Aleppo
SYRIA
Cyprus
Hamath
The Great Sea
Orontes R.
Byblos
Litani R.
Sidon
Damascus
Tyre
Caesarea Philippi
Ptolemais
Capernaum
GALILEE
Sea of Galilee
Cornelius baptized
Caesarea
Samaria (Sebaste)
Simon the sorcerer baptized
Peter sees vision; restores Tabitha to life
Mt. Gerizim
Sychar
SAMARIA
Jabbok R.
Joppa
Lydda
Peter heals Aeneas
Emmaus
Jordan R.
Stephen martyred
Azotus
Jerusalem
Betogabris
Gaza
Bethsura
JUDEA
Salt Sea
Philip meets eunuch (traditional location)
Paul's trip to Damascus and return to Jerusalem
Philip's first journey
Philip's second journey
Paul's flight from Grecian Jews
Peter's journey
Paul and Barnabas's trip to Jerusalem and return to Antioch
Mark and Barnabas's trip to Cyprus
© 1986 The Zondervan Corporation

Map 11: **PAUL'S MISSIONARY JOURNEYS**

A
B
C
D
1
2
3
4
5
6
GERMANIA
GALLIA
DALMATIA
Adriatic Sea
ITALY
Corsica
Rome
Forum of Appius
Three Taverns
Puteoli
Sardinia
MACED
Berea
Tyrrhenian Sea
EPIRUS
Rhegium
Ionian Sea
ACH
Sicily
Syracuse
NUMIDIA
Malta
AFRICA
The
TRIPOLITANIA
First Missionary Journey (A.D. 46–48)
Second Missionary Journey (A.D. 49–52)
Third Missionary Journey (A.D. 53–57)
Trip to Rome (A.D. 59–60)
© 1986 The Zondervan Corporation

E
F
G
H
1
2
3
4
5
6
DACIA
Black Sea
MOESIA
THRACE
BITHYNIA AND PONTUS
GALATIA
Philippi
Neapolis
Amphipolis
Apollonia
Samothrace
Thessalonica
Mt. Olympus
Troas
Assos
Mitylene
Aegean Sea
MYSIA
Pergamum
ASIA
Thyatira
Sardis
Philadelphia
Kios
Smyrna
LYDIA
Delphi
Corinth
Athens
Samos
Ephesus
Laodicea
Colosse
PHRYGIA
Cenchrea
Miletus
Patmos
Sparta
Cos
Cnidus
LYCIA
Patara
Myra
Rhodes
Pisidian Antioch
LYCAONIA
PISIDIA
PAMPHYLIA
Attalia
Perga
Iconium
Lystra
Derbe
CAPPADOCIA
COMMAGENE
CILICIA
Tarsus
Issus
Euphrates R.
Antioch
Aleppo
Seleucia
SYRIA
Cyprus
Salamis
Paphos
Phoenix
Crete
Lasea
Fair Havens
Salmone
Sidon
PHOENICIA
ABILENE
Damascus
Tyre
Ptolemais
Caesarea
JUDEA
Jordan R.
Jerusalem
Salt Sea
ARABIA
Great Sea
CYRENAICA
EGYPT
Nile R.
Red Sea
0 100 200 mi.
0 100 200 300 km.

Map 12: THE WORLD TODAY

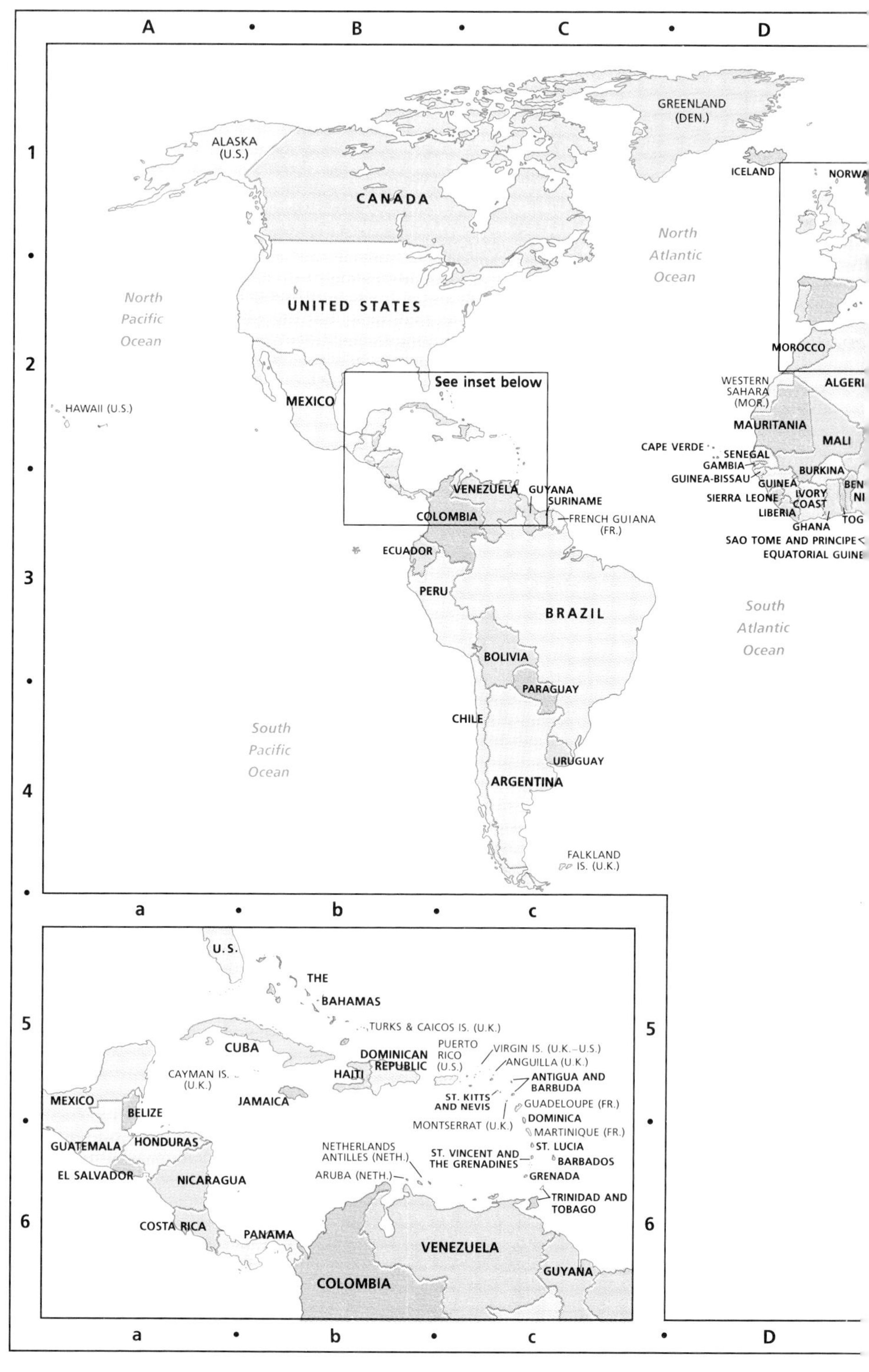

A
B
C
D
1
2
3
4
5
6
a
b
c
GREENLAND
(DEN.)
ALASKA
(U.S.)
ICELAND
CANADA
North
Atlantic
Ocean
North
Pacific
Ocean
UNITED STATES
MOROCCO
See inset below
WESTERN
SAHARA
(MOR.)
ALGERI
HAWAII (U.S.)
MEXICO
MAURITANIA
MALI
CAPE VERDE
SENEGAL
GAMBIA
GUINEA-BISSAU
BURKINA
GUINEA
VENEZUELA
GUYANA
SURINAME
SIERRA LEONE
IVORY
COAST
LIBERIA
COLOMBIA
FRENCH GUIANA
(FR.)
GHANA
SAO TOME AND PRINCIPE
EQUATORIAL GUINE
ECUADOR
PERU
BRAZIL
South
Atlantic
Ocean
BOLIVIA
PARAGUAY
CHILE
South
Pacific
Ocean
URUGUAY
ARGENTINA
FALKLAND
IS. (U.K.)
U.S.
THE
BAHAMAS
TURKS & CAICOS IS. (U.K.)
CUBA
PUERTO
RICO
(U.S.)
VIRGIN IS. (U.K.–U.S.)
ANGUILLA (U.K.)
DOMINICAN
REPUBLIC
CAYMAN IS.
(U.K.)
HAITI
ANTIGUA AND
BARBUDA
ST. KITTS
AND NEVIS
MEXICO
JAMAICA
GUADELOUPE (FR.)
BELIZE
DOMINICA
MONTSERRAT (U.K.)
MARTINIQUE (FR.)
GUATEMALA
HONDURAS
NETHERLANDS
ANTILLES (NETH.)
ST. VINCENT AND
THE GRENADINES
ST. LUCIA
BARBADOS
EL SALVADOR
NICARAGUA
ARUBA (NETH.)
GRENADA
TRINIDAD AND
TOBAGO
COSTA RICA
PANAMA
VENEZUELA
GUYANA
COLOMBIA

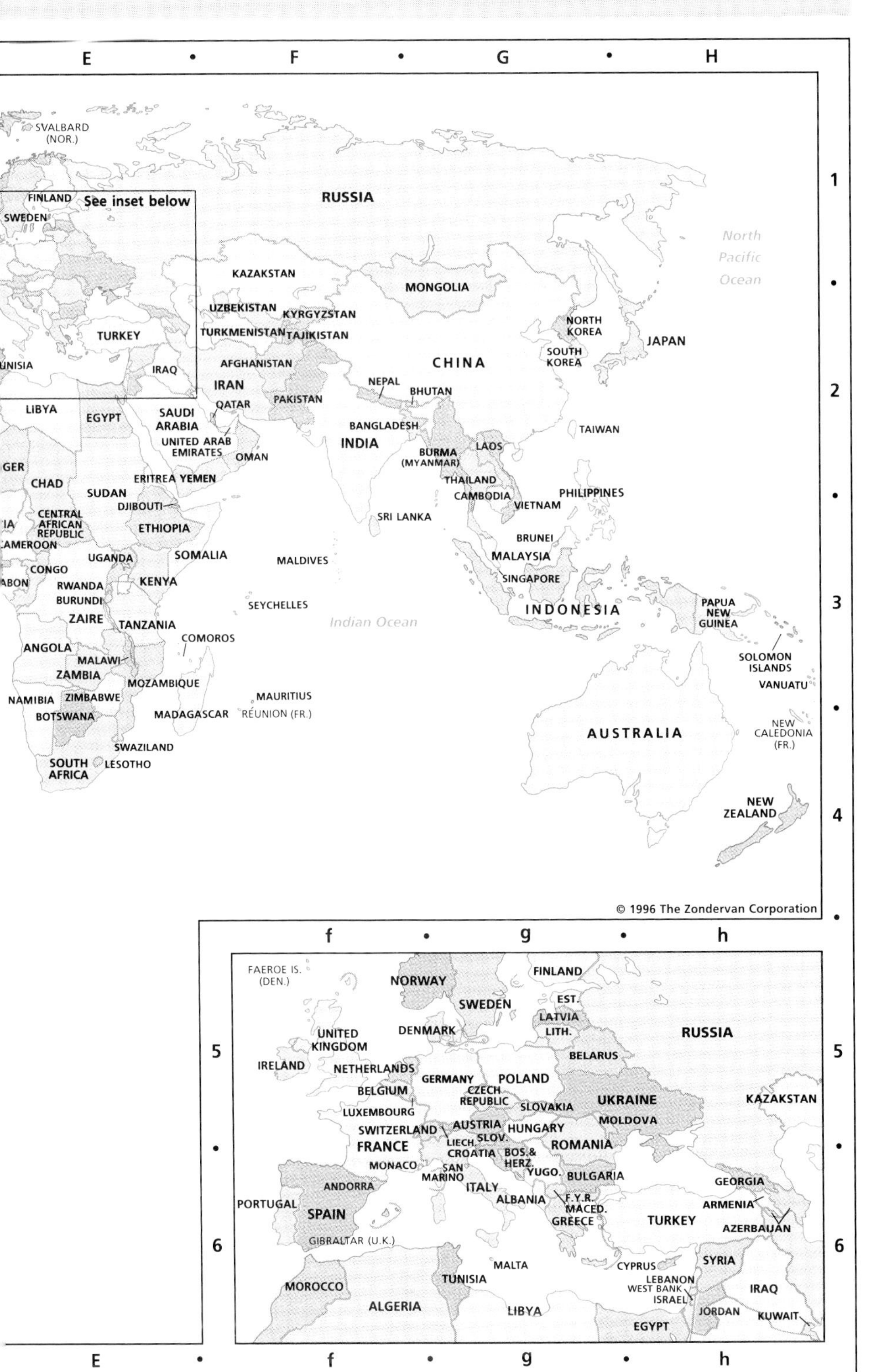
E
F
G
H
1
2
3
4
5
6
SVALBARD (NOR.)
FINLAND
See inset below
SWEDEN
RUSSIA
North Pacific Ocean
KAZAKSTAN
MONGOLIA
UZBEKISTAN
KYRGYZSTAN
TURKMENISTAN
TAJIKISTAN
TURKEY
NORTH KOREA
JAPAN
SOUTH KOREA
UNISIA
IRAQ
AFGHANISTAN
CHINA
IRAN
NEPAL
BHUTAN
QATAR
PAKISTAN
LIBYA
EGYPT
SAUDI ARABIA
BANGLADESH
TAIWAN
UNITED ARAB EMIRATES
INDIA
LAOS
OMAN
BURMA (MYANMAR)
GER
CHAD
ERITREA
YEMEN
THAILAND
SUDAN
CAMBODIA
PHILIPPINES
DJIBOUTI
VIETNAM
CENTRAL AFRICAN REPUBLIC
SRI LANKA
ETHIOPIA
CAMEROON
BRUNEI
UGANDA
SOMALIA
MALAYSIA
CONGO
MALDIVES
ABON
KENYA
SINGAPORE
RWANDA
BURUNDI
SEYCHELLES
INDONESIA
PAPUA NEW GUINEA
ZAIRE
TANZANIA
Indian Ocean
ANGOLA
COMOROS
SOLOMON ISLANDS
MALAWI
ZAMBIA
MOZAMBIQUE
VANUATU
NAMIBIA
ZIMBABWE
MAURITIUS
BOTSWANA
MADAGASCAR
RÉUNION (FR.)
NEW CALEDONIA (FR.)
AUSTRALIA
SWAZILAND
SOUTH AFRICA
LESOTHO
NEW ZEALAND
f
g
h
FAEROE IS. (DEN.)
NORWAY
FINLAND
SWEDEN
EST.
LATVIA
UNITED KINGDOM
DENMARK
LITH.
RUSSIA
IRELAND
BELARUS
NETHERLANDS
GERMANY
POLAND
BELGIUM
CZECH REPUBLIC
UKRAINE
KAZAKSTAN
LUXEMBOURG
SLOVAKIA
MOLDOVA
SWITZERLAND
AUSTRIA
HUNGARY
LIECH.
SLOV.
FRANCE
CROATIA
BOS.& HERZ.
ROMANIA
MONACO
SAN MARINO
YUGO.
BULGARIA
ANDORRA
ITALY
GEORGIA
PORTUGAL
ALBANIA
F.Y.R. MACED.
ARMENIA
SPAIN
GREECE
TURKEY
AZERBAIJAN
GIBRALTAR (U.K.)
MALTA
CYPRUS
SYRIA
TUNISIA
LEBANON
WEST BANK
MOROCCO
ISRAEL
IRAQ
ALGERIA
LIBYA
JORDAN
KUWAIT
EGYPT

Map 13: **ROMAN EMPIRE**

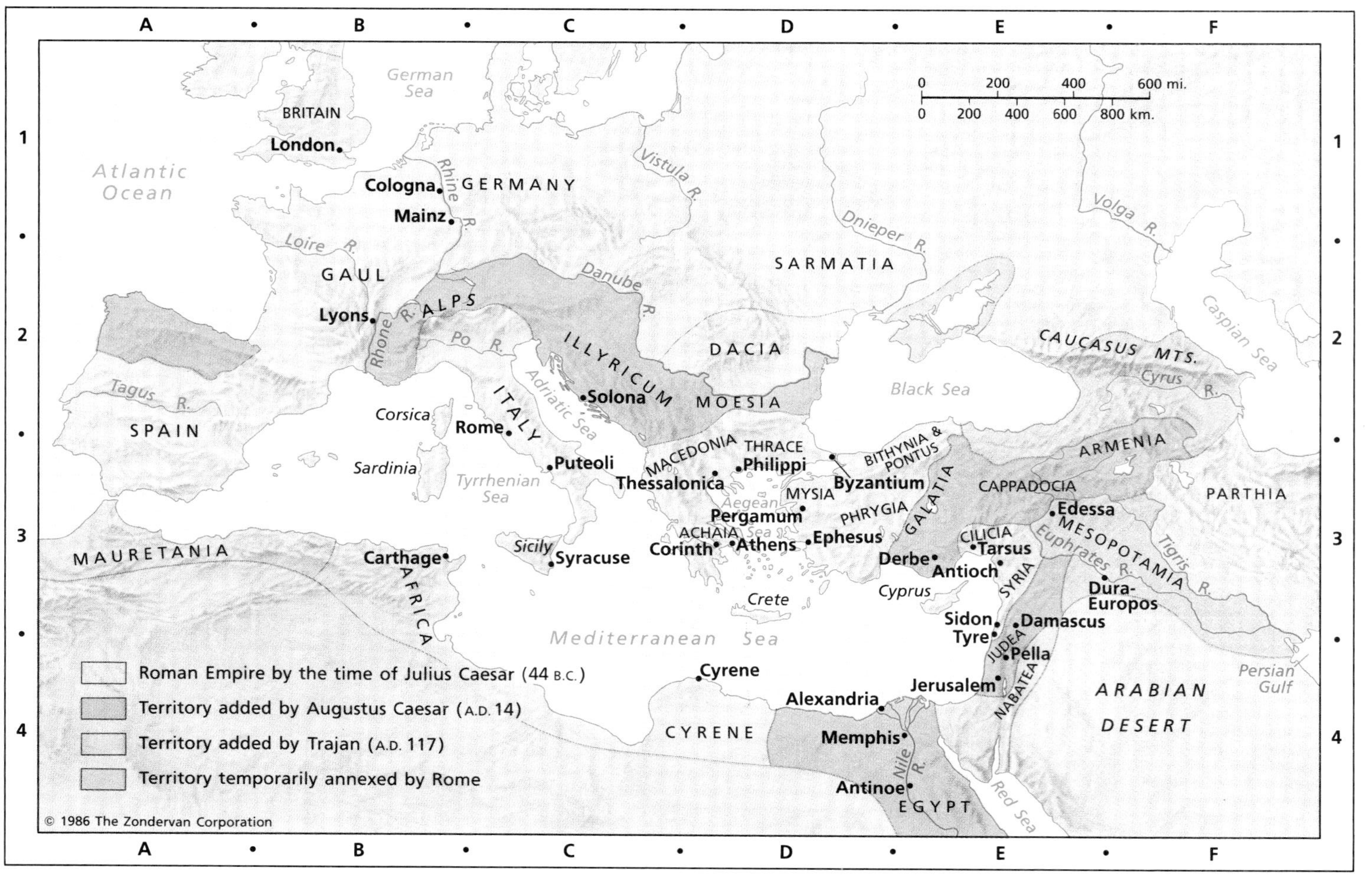

A
B
C
D
E
F
1
2
3
4
0
200
400
600 mi.
0
200
400
600
800 km.
Atlantic Ocean
German Sea
BRITAIN
London
GAUL
Loire R.
Lyons
Rhone R.
Cologna
Mainz
Rhine R.
GERMANY
ALPS
Po R.
SPAIN
Tagus R.
MAURETANIA
Corsica
Sardinia
Carthage
AFRICA
Sicily
Syracuse
ITALY
Rome
Tyrrhenian Sea
Puteoli
Adriatic Sea
ILLYRICUM
Solona
Danube R.
Vistula R.
DACIA
MOESIA
SARMATIA
Dnieper R.
Volga R.
Caspian Sea
CAUCASUS MTS.
Cyrus R.
ARMENIA
PARTHIA
Black Sea
BITHYNIA & PONTUS
Byzantium
THRACE
MACEDONIA
Thessalonica
Philippi
MYSIA
Pergamum
Aegean Sea
ACHAIA
Corinth
Athens
Ephesus
PHRYGIA
GALATIA
CAPPADOCIA
Derbe
CILICIA
Tarsus
Antioch
SYRIA
Edessa
MESOPOTAMIA
Euphrates R.
Tigris R.
Dura-Europos
Persian Gulf
ARABIAN DESERT
Damascus
Sidon
Tyre
Pella
JUDEA
NABATEA
Jerusalem
Cyprus
Crete
Mediterranean Sea
Cyrene
CYRENE
Alexandria
Memphis
Nile R.
Antinoe
EGYPT
Red Sea
Roman Empire by the time of Julius Caesar (44 B.C.)
Territory added by Augustus Caesar (A.D. 14)
Territory added by Trajan (A.D. 117)
Territory temporarily annexed by Rome

(c) a court to which an application is made shall vary the settlement to such extent (if any) as appears appropriate to reflect the effect of section 3.

(6) Where legal proceedings are determined on or after that date and before the date on which this Act is passed, a party to the proceedings may apply to the court to vary the determination; and—

(a) "the court" means the court which determined the proceedings,
(b) the application shall be treated as an application in the proceedings, and
(c) the court shall vary the determination to such extent (if any) as appears appropriate to reflect the effect of section 3.

NOTES

Orders: the Compensation Act 2006 (Commencement No 1) Order 2006; the Compensation Act 2006 (Commencement No 2) Order 2007, SI 2007/94; the Compensation Act 2006 (Commencement No 3) Order 2007, SI 2007/922.

[1.1433]
17 Extent

(1) This Act shall extend to England and Wales only.

(2) But section 3 (and section 16(3) to (6)) shall extend to—

(a) England and Wales,
(b) Scotland, and
(c) Northern Ireland.

[1.1434]
18 Short title

This Act may be cited as the Compensation Act 2006.

SCHEDULE
CLAIMS MANAGEMENT REGULATIONS

Section 9

Introduction

[1.1435]
1. In this Schedule "regulations" means regulations under section 9.

2. Regulations made by virtue of a provision of this Schedule may confer a discretion on the Regulator.

Waiver of requirement for authorisation

3. (1) Regulations may permit the Regulator to waive the requirement for authorisation, as mentioned in section 4(1)(c), in specified cases or circumstances.

(2) Regulations by virtue of this sub-paragraph may permit waiver in relation to a person only—

(a) if the Secretary of State intends to exempt the person under section 6, and
(b) for a single period not exceeding six months.

(3) The regulations may, in particular, permit or require the Regulator to provide for waiver to be subject to a condition of a kind specified in the regulations.

Grant of authorisations

4. (1) Regulations shall prescribe the procedure for applying to the Regulator for authorisation.

(2) Regulations may, in particular, require the provision of information or documents relating to the applicant or to any person who appears to the Regulator to be connected with the applicant.

5. (1) Regulations shall require the Regulator not to grant an application for authorisation unless satisfied of the applicant's competence and suitability to provide regulated claims management services of the kind to which the application relates.

(2) For that purpose the Regulator shall apply such criteria, and have regard to such matters, as the regulations shall specify.

(3) Regulations by virtue of sub-paragraph (2) may, in particular—

(a) refer to a provision of directions, *guidance or a code given or issued* under section 5(4);
(b) relate to persons who are or are expected to be employed or engaged by, or otherwise connected with, the applicant;
(c) relate to—
 (i) criminal records;
 (ii) proceedings in any court or tribunal;
 (iii) proceedings of a body exercising functions in relation to a trade or profession;
 (iv) financial circumstances;
 (v) management structure;
 (vi) actual or proposed connections or arrangements with other persons;
 (vii) qualifications;

(viii) actual or proposed arrangements for training;
(ix) arrangements for accounting;
(x) practice or proposed practice in relation to the provision of information about fees;
(xi) arrangements or proposed arrangements for holding clients' money;
(xii) arrangements or proposed arrangements for insurance.

6. Regulations may—
(a) provide for authorisation to be on specified terms or subject to compliance with specified conditions;
(b) permit the Regulator to grant authorisation on terms or subject to conditions;
(c) permit the Regulator to grant an application for authorisation only to a specified extent or only in relation to specified matters, cases or circumstances.

7. Regulations may—
(a) enable the Regulator to charge—
(i) fees in connection with applications for, or the grant of, authorisation;
(ii) periodic fees for authorised persons;
(b) specify the consequences of failure to pay fees;
(c) permit the charging of different fees for different cases or circumstances (which may, in particular, be defined wholly or partly by reference to turnover or other criteria relating to an authorised person's business);
(d) permit the waiver, reduction or repayment of fees in specified circumstances;
(e) provide for the amount of fees to be prescribed or controlled by the *Secretary of State*;
(f) make provision for the manner in which fees are to be accounted for;
(g) make provision for the application of income from fees (which may, in respect of a time when the Secretary of State is exercising functions of the Regulator under section 5(9) or (10), include provision permitting or requiring payment into the Consolidated Fund [after consultation with the Secretary of State]).

Conduct of authorised persons

8. (1) Regulations shall require the Regulator to prescribe rules for the professional conduct of authorised persons.
(2) Regulations under sub-paragraph (1) shall include provision—
(a) about the manner in which rules are to be prepared and published (which may, in particular, include provision requiring—
(i) consultation;
(ii) the submission of a draft to the *Secretary of State* for approval);
(b) about the consequences of failure to comply with the rules (which may, in particular, include—
(i) provision for rules to be treated as conditions of authorisations;
(ii) provision enabling the Regulator to impose conditions on, suspend or cancel authorisations).

9. (1) Regulations shall enable the Regulator to issue one or more codes of practice about the professional conduct of authorised persons.
(2) Regulations under sub-paragraph (1) shall include provision—
(a) about the manner in which a code is to be prepared and published (which may, in particular, include provision requiring—
(i) consultation;
(ii) the submission of a draft to the *Secretary of State* for approval);
(b) about the consequences of failure to comply with a code (which may, in particular—
(i) provide for compliance with a code to be treated as a condition of authorisations;
(ii) enable the Regulator to impose conditions on, suspend or cancel authorisations).

10. (1) Regulations shall provide for the Regulator to investigate complaints about the professional conduct of an authorised person.
(2) Regulations under sub-paragraph (1) shall enable the Regulator to—
(a) impose conditions on a person's authorisation;
(b) suspend a person's authorisation;
(c) cancel a person's authorisation.

11. (1) Regulations may require, or permit the Regulator to require, an authorised person to take out a policy of professional indemnity insurance in respect of his actions in the course of providing or purporting to provide regulated claims management services.
(2) Regulations under sub-paragraph (1) may, in particular—
(a) make provision about the level or nature of insurance cover to be provided by the policy;

(b) include provision about failure to comply (which may, in particular, provide for compliance to be treated as a condition of authorisations or enable the Regulator to impose conditions on, suspend or cancel authorisations).

12. (1) Regulations may require the Regulator to establish a scheme to compensate a client of an authorised person where—

(a) money is paid to the authorised person in complete or partial satisfaction of the client's claim, and

(b) the client is unable to obtain all or part of the money because the authorised person becomes insolvent or is otherwise unable or unwilling to pay.

(2) In particular, regulations may make provision—

(a) about the purchase of bonds or other forms of insurance or indemnity;

(b) about the funding of the scheme (which may include the application of part of fees charged in accordance with paragraph 7 and may not include payments, or other financial assistance, by a Minister of the Crown);

(c) about procedure in connection with compensation (including criteria to be applied);

(d) about the amount of compensation.

Enforcement

13. Regulations may permit or require the Regulator to take action of a specified kind for the purpose of assessing compliance with terms or conditions of authorisations.

14. (1) Regulations may enable the Regulator, for the purpose of investigating a complaint about the activities of an authorised person or for the purpose of assessing compliance with terms and conditions of an authorisation, to require the provision of information or documents.

(2) The Regulations may provide that on an application by the Regulator a judge of the High Court, Circuit judge or justice of the peace may issue a warrant authorising the Regulator—

[(a) to enter and search premises on which a person conducts or is alleged to conduct regulated claims management business, for the purposes of—

(i) investigating a complaint about the activities of an authorised person, or

(ii) assessing compliance with terms and conditions of an authorisation, and

(b) to take possession of written or electronic records found on the search for the purposes of taking copies in accordance with regulations under sub-paragraph (3).]

(3) Regulations may enable the Regulator to take copies of written or electronic records found on a search by virtue of sub-paragraph (2) for a purpose specified in that subsection.

(4) Regulations may enable the Regulator to impose conditions on, suspend or cancel a person's authorisation if—

(a) a requirement imposed by virtue of sub-paragraph (1) is not complied with, or

(b) an attempt to exercise a power by virtue of sub-paragraph (2) or (3) is obstructed.

(5) In this paragraph a reference to the Regulator includes a reference to a person authorised by him in writing.

(6) Regulations shall—

(a) specify matters of which a judge or justice of the peace must be satisfied, or to which he must have regard, before issuing a warrant under sub-paragraph (2),

(b) regulate the exercise of a power under or by virtue of sub-paragraph (1), (2) or (3) (whether by restricting the circumstances in which a power may be exercised, by specifying conditions to be complied with in the exercise of a power, or otherwise).

15. Regulations may make provision about the exercise by the Regulator of a power under section 8.

NOTES

Para 5: for the words in italics in sub-para (3)(a) there are substituted the words "or guidance given" by the Legal Services Act 2007, s 187, Sch 19, paras 1, 11(1), (2), as from a day to be appointed.

Para 7: for the words in italics in sub-paras (e) and (g) there are substituted the words "Legal Services Board", and the words in square brackets in sub-para (g) are inserted, by the Legal Services Act 2007, s 187, Sch 19, paras 1, 11(1), (3), as from a day to be appointed.

Paras 8, 9: for the words in italics in sub-para (2)(a) there are substituted the words "Legal Services Board" by the Legal Services Act 2007, s 187, Sch 19, paras 1, 11(1), (4), (5), as from a day to be appointed.

Para 14: words in square brackets substituted by the Legal Services Act 2007, s 187, Sch 19, paras 1, 11(1), (6), as from 30 June 2008.

COMPANIES ACT 2006

(2006 c 46)

ARRANGEMENT OF SECTIONS

PART 10
A COMPANY'S DIRECTORS

CHAPTER 1
APPOINTMENT AND REMOVAL OF DIRECTORS

Requirement to have directors

Appointment

Removal

CHAPTER 2
GENERAL DUTIES OF DIRECTORS

Introductory

The general duties

Supplementary provisions

CHAPTER 3
DECLARATION OF INTEREST IN EXISTING TRANSACTION OR ARRANGEMENT

CHAPTER 4
TRANSACTIONS WITH DIRECTORS REQUIRING APPROVAL OF MEMBERS

Service contracts

Payments for loss of office

An Act to reform company law and restate the greater part of the enactments relating to companies; to make other provision relating to companies and other forms of business organisation; to make

Part 1 Statutes

provision about directors' disqualification, business names, auditors and actuaries; to amend Part 9 of the Enterprise Act 2002; and for connected purposes

[8 November 2006]

NOTES

Only certain sections of this Act are directly relevant to employment law, and accordingly, only those sections of most relevance have been included in this work. For reasons of space, the subject matter of the sections and Schedules omitted is not annotated.

Interpretation of provisions in this Act: the Companies Act 2006 (Commencement No 1, Transitional Provisions and Savings) Order 2006, SI 2006/3428, art 6 provides as set out below. Note that a similar provision is also made by each of the Companies Act 2006 (Commencement No 2, Consequential Amendments, Transitional Provisions and Savings) Order 2007, SI 2007/1093, art 4, the Companies Act 2006 (Commencement No 3, Consequential Amendments, Transitional Provisions and Savings) Order 2007, SI 2007/2194, art 7, the Companies Act 2006 (Commencement No 4 and Commencement No 3 (Amendment)) Order 2007, SI 2007/2607, art 3, the Companies Act 2006 (Commencement No 5, Transitional Provisions and Savings) Order 2007, SI 2007/3495, art 7, and the Companies Act 2006 (Commencement No 7, Transitional Provisions and Savings) Order 2008, SI 2008/1886, art 6—

"6 Interpretation of provisions brought into force

Where an expression in a provision brought into force by this Order (or in an adaptation made by this Order of such a provision)—

(a) is defined in the 1985 Act or the 1986 Order ("the old definition"); and

(b) is defined in the Companies Act 2006 by another provision that is not yet in force for the purposes of the provision brought into force ("the new definition"),

the expression has, for the purposes of the provision brought into force (or the adaptation), the meaning given by the old definition until the new definition is brought into force for the purposes of that provision.".

Offences: see the Companies Act 2006 (Commencement No 8, Transitional Provisions and Savings) Order 2008, art 7 (prosecution of offences in transitional cases). In relation to offences under the Companies Act 1985, see also Sch 2, para 116 to that Order (savings for provisions relating to offences).

Application to other bodies, etc: various provisions of this Act are applied with modifications to specified types of other bodies, etc; these include the following: (i) the Limited Liability Partnerships (Accounts and Audit) (Application of Companies Act 2006) Regulations 2008, SI 2008/1911 (application to LLPs); (ii) the Unregistered Companies Regulations 2009, SI 2009/2436 (application to unregistered companies); (iii) the Insurance Accounts Directive (Miscellaneous Insurance Undertakings) Regulations 2008, SI 2008/565 and the Insurance Accounts Directive (Lloyd's Syndicate and Aggregate Accounts) Regulations 2008, SI 2008/1950 (application to insurance undertakings); (iv) the Bank Accounts Directive (Miscellaneous Banks) Regulations 2008, SI 2008/567 (application to banks; as to the application of certain provisions of this Act to particular banks, see also the Banking (Special Provisions) Act 2008 and the Banking Act 2009, and the Orders made under those Acts); (v) the Partnerships (Accounts) Regulations 2008, SI 2008/569 (application to partnerships); (vi) the Overseas Companies Regulations 2009, SI 2009/1801 (application to overseas companies).

Civil Procedure Rules: the Civil Procedure Rules 1998, SI 1998/3132, rule 49 (as amended), states that those Rules apply to proceedings under this Act subject to the provisions of the relevant practice direction which applies to those proceedings.

PART 10
A COMPANY'S DIRECTORS

CHAPTER 1
APPOINTMENT AND REMOVAL OF DIRECTORS

Requirement to have directors

[1.1436]

154 Companies required to have directors

(1) A private company must have at least one director.

(2) A public company must have at least two directors.

[1.1437]

155 Companies required to have at least one director who is a natural person

(1) A company must have at least one director who is a natural person.

(2) This requirement is met if the office of director is held by a natural person as a corporation sole or otherwise by virtue of an office.

NOTES

Commencement: 1 October 2008.

Transitional provisions: Sch 4, Pt 3, para 46 to the Companies Act 2006 (Commencement No 5, Transitional Provisions and Savings) Order 2007, SI 2007/3495 provides as follows—

"Requirement to have at least one director who is a natural person (s 155)

46. If on 8th November 2006—

(a) none of a company's directors were natural persons, and

(b) section 282 of the 1985 Act or Article 290 of the 1986 Order (requirement as to number of directors) was complied with in relation to the company,

section 155 of the Companies Act 2006 (companies required to have at least one director who is a natural person) does not apply to the company until 1st October 2010.".

Appointment

[1.1438]

160 Appointment of directors of public company to be voted on individually

(1) At a general meeting of a public company a motion for the appointment of two or more persons as directors of the company by a single resolution must not be made unless a resolution that it should be so made has first been agreed to by the meeting without any vote being given against it.
(2) A resolution moved in contravention of this section is void, whether or not its being so moved was objected to at the time.

But where a resolution so moved is passed, no provision for the automatic reappointment of retiring directors in default of another appointment applies.
(3) For the purposes of this section a motion for approving a person's appointment, or for nominating a person for appointment, is treated as a motion for his appointment.
(4) Nothing in this section applies to a resolution amending the company's articles.

[1.1439]

161 Validity of acts of directors

(1) The acts of a person acting as a director are valid notwithstanding that it is afterwards discovered—

- (a) that there was a defect in his appointment;
- (b) that he was disqualified from holding office;
- (c) that he had ceased to hold office;
- (d) that he was not entitled to vote on the matter in question.

(2) This applies even if the resolution for his appointment is void under section 160 (appointment of directors of public company to be voted on individually).

Removal

[1.1440]

168 Resolution to remove director

(1) A company may by ordinary resolution at a meeting remove a director before the expiration of his period of office, notwithstanding anything in any agreement between it and him.
(2) Special notice is required of a resolution to remove a director under this section or to appoint somebody instead of a director so removed at the meeting at which he is removed.
(3) A vacancy created by the removal of a director under this section, if not filled at the meeting at which he is removed, may be filled as a casual vacancy.
(4) A person appointed director in place of a person removed under this section is treated, for the purpose of determining the time at which he or any other director is to retire, as if he had become director on the day on which the person in whose place he is appointed was last appointed a director.
(5) This section is not to be taken—

- (a) as depriving a person removed under it of compensation or damages payable to him in respect of the termination of his appointment as director or of any appointment terminating with that as director, or
- (b) as derogating from any power to remove a director that may exist apart from this section.

[1.1441]

169 Director's right to protest against removal

(1) On receipt of notice of an intended resolution to remove a director under section 168, the company must forthwith send a copy of the notice to the director concerned.
(2) The director (whether or not a member of the company) is entitled to be heard on the resolution at the meeting.
(3) Where notice is given of an intended resolution to remove a director under that section, and the director concerned makes with respect to it representations in writing to the company (not exceeding a reasonable length) and requests their notification to members of the company, the company shall, unless the representations are received by it too late for it to do so—

- (a) in any notice of the resolution given to members of the company state the fact of the representations having been made; and
- (b) send a copy of the representations to every member of the company to whom notice of the meeting is sent (whether before or after receipt of the representations by the company).

(4) If a copy of the representations is not sent as required by subsection (3) because received too late or because of the company's default, the director may (without prejudice to his right to be heard orally) require that the representations shall be read out at the meeting.
(5) Copies of the representations need not be sent out and the representations need not be read out at the meeting if, on the application either of the company or of any other person who claims to be aggrieved, the court is satisfied that the rights conferred by this section are being abused.
(6) The court may order the company's costs (in Scotland, expenses) on an application under subsection (5) to be paid in whole or in part by the director, notwithstanding that he is not a party to the application.

CHAPTER 2
GENERAL DUTIES OF DIRECTORS

Introductory

[1.1442]
170 Scope and nature of general duties

(1) The general duties specified in sections 171 to 177 are owed by a director of a company to the company.

(2) A person who ceases to be a director continues to be subject—

(a) to the duty in section 175 (duty to avoid conflicts of interest) as regards the exploitation of any property, information or opportunity of which he became aware at a time when he was a director, and

(b) to the duty in section 176 (duty not to accept benefits from third parties) as regards things done or omitted by him before he ceased to be a director.

To that extent those duties apply to a former director as to a director, subject to any necessary adaptations.

(3) The general duties are based on certain common law rules and equitable principles as they apply in relation to directors and have effect in place of those rules and principles as regards the duties owed to a company by a director.

(4) The general duties shall be interpreted and applied in the same way as common law rules or equitable principles, and regard shall be had to the corresponding common law rules and equitable principles in interpreting and applying the general duties.

(5) The general duties apply to shadow directors where, and to the extent that, the corresponding common law rules or equitable principles so apply.

The general duties

[1.1443]
171 Duty to act within powers

A director of a company must—

(a) act in accordance with the company's constitution, and

(b) only exercise powers for the purposes for which they are conferred.

[1.1444]
172 Duty to promote the success of the company

(1) A director of a company must act in the way he considers, in good faith, would be most likely to promote the success of the company for the benefit of its members as a whole, and in doing so have regard (amongst other matters) to—

(a) the likely consequences of any decision in the long term,

(b) the interests of the company's employees,

(c) the need to foster the company's business relationships with suppliers, customers and others,

(d) the impact of the company's operations on the community and the environment,

(e) the desirability of the company maintaining a reputation for high standards of business conduct, and

(f) the need to act fairly as between members of the company.

(2) Where or to the extent that the purposes of the company consist of or include purposes other than the benefit of its members, subsection (1) has effect as if the reference to promoting the success of the company for the benefit of its members were to achieving those purposes.

(3) The duty imposed by this section has effect subject to any enactment or rule of law requiring directors, in certain circumstances, to consider or act in the interests of creditors of the company.

[1.1445]
173 Duty to exercise independent judgment

(1) A director of a company must exercise independent judgment.

(2) This duty is not infringed by his acting—

(a) in accordance with an agreement duly entered into by the company that restricts the future exercise of discretion by its directors, or

(b) in a way authorised by the company's constitution.

[1.1446]
174 Duty to exercise reasonable care, skill and diligence

(1) A director of a company must exercise reasonable care, skill and diligence.

(2) This means the care, skill and diligence that would be exercised by a reasonably diligent person with—

(a) the general knowledge, skill and experience that may reasonably be expected of a person carrying out the functions carried out by the director in relation to the company, and

(b) the general knowledge, skill and experience that the director has.

[1.1447]

175 Duty to avoid conflicts of interest

(1) A director of a company must avoid a situation in which he has, or can have, a direct or indirect interest that conflicts, or possibly may conflict, with the interests of the company.

(2) This applies in particular to the exploitation of any property, information or opportunity (and it is immaterial whether the company could take advantage of the property, information or opportunity).

(3) This duty does not apply to a conflict of interest arising in relation to a transaction or arrangement with the company.

(4) This duty is not infringed—

(a) if the situation cannot reasonably be regarded as likely to give rise to a conflict of interest; or

(b) if the matter has been authorised by the directors.

(5) Authorisation may be given by the directors—

(a) where the company is a private company and nothing in the company's constitution invalidates such authorisation, by the matter being proposed to and authorised by the directors; or

(b) where the company is a public company and its constitution includes provision enabling the directors to authorise the matter, by the matter being proposed to and authorised by them in accordance with the constitution.

(6) The authorisation is effective only if—

(a) any requirement as to the quorum at the meeting at which the matter is considered is met without counting the director in question or any other interested director, and

(b) the matter was agreed to without their voting or would have been agreed to if their votes had not been counted.

(7) Any reference in this section to a conflict of interest includes a conflict of interest and duty and a conflict of duties.

NOTES

Commencement: 1 October 2008.

Transitional provisions: Sch 4, Pt 3, para 47 to the Companies Act 2006 (Commencement No 5, Transitional Provisions and Savings) Order 2007, SI 2007/3495 provides as follows—

"*Duty of directors to avoid conflicts of interest (s 175)*

47.—(1) Section 175 of the Companies Act 2006 (duty to avoid conflicts of interest) applies where the situation described in subsection (1) of that section arises on or after 1st October 2008.

(2) The law that applied before that date continues to apply to such a situation that arose before that date.

(3) Section 175(5)(a) of that Act (private companies: authorisation by directors) applies—

(a) to companies incorporated on or after 1st October 2008, and

(b) to companies incorporated before that date where the members of the company have resolved (before, on or after 1st October 2008) that authorisation may be given in accordance with that provision.

(4) Chapter 3 of Part 3 of the Companies Act 2006 (resolutions and agreements affecting a company's constitution) applies to any such resolution.

(5) For the purposes of section 30 of that Act (copies of resolutions to be forwarded to registrar) such a resolution passed before 1st October 2008 is treated as if passed on that date.".

[1.1448]

176 Duty not to accept benefits from third parties

(1) A director of a company must not accept a benefit from a third party conferred by reason of—

(a) his being a director, or

(b) his doing (or not doing) anything as director.

(2) A "third party" means a person other than the company, an associated body corporate or a person acting on behalf of the company or an associated body corporate.

(3) Benefits received by a director from a person by whom his services (as a director or otherwise) are provided to the company are not regarded as conferred by a third party.

(4) This duty is not infringed if the acceptance of the benefit cannot reasonably be regarded as likely to give rise to a conflict of interest.

(5) Any reference in this section to a conflict of interest includes a conflict of interest and duty and a conflict of duties.

NOTES

Commencement: 1 October 2008.

[1.1449]

177 Duty to declare interest in proposed transaction or arrangement

(1) If a director of a company is in any way, directly or indirectly, interested in a proposed transaction or arrangement with the company, he must declare the nature and extent of that interest to the other directors.

(2) The declaration may (but need not) be made—

(a) at a meeting of the directors, or

(b) by notice to the directors in accordance with—
  (i) section 184 (notice in writing), or
  (ii) section 185 (general notice).

(3) If a declaration of interest under this section proves to be, or becomes, inaccurate or incomplete, a further declaration must be made.

(4) Any declaration required by this section must be made before the company enters into the transaction or arrangement.

(5) This section does not require a declaration of an interest of which the director is not aware or where the director is not aware of the transaction or arrangement in question.

For this purpose a director is treated as being aware of matters of which he ought reasonably to be aware.

(6) A director need not declare an interest—
  (a) if it cannot reasonably be regarded as likely to give rise to a conflict of interest;
  (b) if, or to the extent that, the other directors are already aware of it (and for this purpose the other directors are treated as aware of anything of which they ought reasonably to be aware); or
  (c) if, or to the extent that, it concerns terms of his service contract that have been or are to be considered—
    (i) by a meeting of the directors, or
    (ii) by a committee of the directors appointed for the purpose under the company's constitution.

NOTES

Commencement: 1 October 2008.

Transitional provisions: Sch 4, Pt 3, para 48 to the Companies Act 2006 (Commencement No 5, Transitional Provisions and Savings) Order 2007, SI 2007/3495 provides as follows—

"Declaration by directors of interest in proposed transaction or arrangement (s 177)

48.—(1) Section 177(1) of the Companies Act 2006 (duty of director to declare interest in proposed transaction or arrangement) applies where the duty to declare an interest arises on or after 1st October 2008.

(2) Section 317 of the 1985 Act or Article 325 of the 1986 Order continues to apply in relation to a duty arising before that date.

(3) For the purposes of section 177(3) of the Companies Act 2006 (previous declaration under that section proving or becoming inadequate), a declaration of interest in relation to a proposed transaction or arrangement made before 1st October 2008 under section 317 of the 1985 Act or Article 325 of the 1986 Order is treated on and after that date as if made under section 177 of the Companies Act 2006.".

Supplementary provisions

[1.1450]

178 Civil consequences of breach of general duties

(1) The consequences of breach (or threatened breach) of sections 171 to 177 are the same as would apply if the corresponding common law rule or equitable principle applied.

(2) The duties in those sections (with the exception of section 174 (duty to exercise reasonable care, skill and diligence)) are, accordingly, enforceable in the same way as any other fiduciary duty owed to a company by its directors.

[1.1451]

179 Cases within more than one of the general duties

Except as otherwise provided, more than one of the general duties may apply in any given case.

[1.1452]

180 Consent, approval or authorisation by members

(1) In a case where—
  (a) section 175 (duty to avoid conflicts of interest) is complied with by authorisation by the directors, or
  (b) section 177 (duty to declare interest in proposed transaction or arrangement) is complied with,

the transaction or arrangement is not liable to be set aside by virtue of any common law rule or equitable principle requiring the consent or approval of the members of the company.

This is without prejudice to any enactment, or provision of the company's constitution, requiring such consent or approval.

(2) The application of the general duties is not affected by the fact that the case also falls within Chapter 4 (transactions requiring approval of members) [or 4A], except that where *that Chapter* applies and—
  (a) approval is given under *that Chapter*, or
  (b) the matter is one as to which it is provided that approval is not needed,

it is not necessary also to comply with section 175 (duty to avoid conflicts of interest) or section 176 (duty not to accept benefits from third parties).

(3) Compliance with the general duties does not remove the need for approval under any applicable provision of Chapter 4 (transactions requiring approval of members) [or 4A].

(4) The general duties—

(a) have effect subject to any rule of law enabling the company to give authority, specifically or generally, for anything to be done (or omitted) by the directors, or any of them, that would otherwise be a breach of duty, and

(b) where the company's articles contain provisions for dealing with conflicts of interest, are not infringed by anything done (or omitted) by the directors, or any of them, in accordance with those provisions.

(5) Otherwise, the general duties have effect (except as otherwise provided or the context otherwise requires) notwithstanding any enactment or rule of law.

NOTES

Sub-s (2): words in square brackets inserted, for the first words in italics there are substituted the words "either of those Chapters", and for the words in italics in para (a) there are substituted the words "the Chapter concerned", by the Enterprise and Regulatory Reform Act 2013, s 81(1), (2)(a), (b), as from a day to be appointed.

Sub-s (3): words in square brackets added by the Enterprise and Regulatory Reform Act 2013, s 81(1), (2)(c), as from a day to be appointed.

[1.1453]

181 Modification of provisions in relation to charitable companies

(1) In their application to a company that is a charity, the provisions of this Chapter have effect subject to this section.

(2) Section 175 (duty to avoid conflicts of interest) has effect as if—

(a) for subsection (3) (which disapplies the duty to avoid conflicts of interest in the case of a transaction or arrangement with the company) there were substituted—

"(3) This duty does not apply to a conflict of interest arising in relation to a transaction or arrangement with the company if or to the extent that the company's articles allow that duty to be so disapplied, which they may do only in relation to descriptions of transaction or arrangement specified in the company's articles.";

(b) for subsection (5) (which specifies how directors of a company may give authority under that section for a transaction or arrangement) there were substituted—

"(5) Authorisation may be given by the directors where the company's constitution includes provision enabling them to authorise the matter, by the matter being proposed to and authorised by them in accordance with the constitution.".

(3) Section 180(2)(b) (which disapplies certain duties under this Chapter in relation to cases excepted from requirement to obtain approval by members under Chapter 4) applies only if or to the extent that the company's articles allow those duties to be so disapplied, which they may do only in relation to descriptions of transaction or arrangement specified in the company's articles.

(4) *(Inserted the Charities Act 1993, s 26(5A) and was repealed by the Charities Act 2011, s 354, Sch 10, as from 14 March 2012.)*

(5) This section does not extend to Scotland.

CHAPTER 3
DECLARATION OF INTEREST IN EXISTING TRANSACTION OR ARRANGEMENT

[1.1454]

182 Declaration of interest in existing transaction or arrangement

(1) Where a director of a company is in any way, directly or indirectly, interested in a transaction or arrangement that has been entered into by the company, he must declare the nature and extent of the interest to the other directors in accordance with this section.

This section does not apply if or to the extent that the interest has been declared under section 177 (duty to declare interest in proposed transaction or arrangement).

(2) The declaration must be made—

(a) at a meeting of the directors, or

(b) by notice in writing (see section 184), or

(c) by general notice (see section 185).

(3) If a declaration of interest under this section proves to be, or becomes, inaccurate or incomplete, a further declaration must be made.

(4) Any declaration required by this section must be made as soon as is reasonably practicable.

Failure to comply with this requirement does not affect the underlying duty to make the declaration.

(5) This section does not require a declaration of an interest of which the director is not aware or where the director is not aware of the transaction or arrangement in question.

For this purpose a director is treated as being aware of matters of which he ought reasonably to be aware.

(6) A director need not declare an interest under this section—
 (a) if it cannot reasonably be regarded as likely to give rise to a conflict of interest;
 (b) if, or to the extent that, the other directors are already aware of it (and for this purpose the other directors are treated as aware of anything of which they ought reasonably to be aware); or
 (c) if, or to the extent that, it concerns terms of his service contract that have been or are to be considered—
  (i) by a meeting of the directors, or
  (ii) by a committee of the directors appointed for the purpose under the company's constitution.

NOTES

Commencement: 1 October 2008.

Transitional provisions: Sch 4, Pt 3, para 50 to the Companies Act 2006 (Commencement No 5, Transitional Provisions and Savings) Order 2007, SI 2007/3495 provides as follows—

"Declaration of interest in existing transaction or arrangement (ss 182 to 187)

50.—(1) Sections 182 to 187 of the Companies Act 2006 (declaration by director of interest in existing transaction or arrangement) apply in relation to transactions or arrangements entered into by a company on or after 1st October 2008.

(2) Section 317 of the 1985 Act or Article 325 of the 1986 Order continues to apply in relation to transactions or arrangements entered into before that date.

(3) For the purposes of section 182(1) of the Companies Act 2006 (declaration of interest in existing transaction not previously declared under section 177), a declaration of interest made before 1st October 2008 under section 317 of the 1985 Act or Article 325 of the 1986 Order is treated on and after that date as if made under section 177.

(4) For the purposes of section 182(3) of the Companies Act 2006 (previous declaration under that section proving or becoming inadequate), a declaration of interest made before 1st October 2008 under section 317 of the 1985 Act or Article 325 of the 1986 Order is treated on and after that date as if made under section 182.".

[1.1455]

183 Offence of failure to declare interest

(1) A director who fails to comply with the requirements of section 182 (declaration of interest in existing transaction or arrangement) commits an offence.

(2) A person guilty of an offence under this section is liable—
 (a) on conviction on indictment, to a fine;
 (b) on summary conviction, to a fine not exceeding the statutory maximum.

NOTES

Commencement: 1 October 2008.

Transitional provisions: see the note to s 182 at **[1.1454]**.

[1.1456]

184 Declaration made by notice in writing

(1) This section applies to a declaration of interest made by notice in writing.

(2) The director must send the notice to the other directors.

(3) The notice may be sent in hard copy form or, if the recipient has agreed to receive it in electronic form, in an agreed electronic form.

(4) The notice may be sent—
 (a) by hand or by post, or
 (b) if the recipient has agreed to receive it by electronic means, by agreed electronic means.

(5) Where a director declares an interest by notice in writing in accordance with this section—
 (a) the making of the declaration is deemed to form part of the proceedings at the next meeting of the directors after the notice is given, and
 (b) the provisions of section 248 (minutes of meetings of directors) apply as if the declaration had been made at that meeting.

NOTES

Commencement: 1 October 2008.

Transitional provisions: see the note to s 182 at **[1.1454]**.

[1.1457]

185 General notice treated as sufficient declaration

(1) General notice in accordance with this section is a sufficient declaration of interest in relation to the matters to which it relates.

(2) General notice is notice given to the directors of a company to the effect that the director—
 (a) has an interest (as member, officer, employee or otherwise) in a specified body corporate or firm and is to be regarded as interested in any transaction or arrangement that may, after the date of the notice, be made with that body corporate or firm, or
 (b) is connected with a specified person (other than a body corporate or firm) and is to be regarded as interested in any transaction or arrangement that may, after the date of the notice, be made with that person.

(3) The notice must state the nature and extent of the director's interest in the body corporate or firm or, as the case may be, the nature of his connection with the person.

(4) General notice is not effective unless—

(a) it is given at a meeting of the directors, or

(b) the director takes reasonable steps to secure that it is brought up and read at the next meeting of the directors after it is given.

NOTES

Commencement: 1 October 2008.

Transitional provisions: see the note to s 182 at **[1.1454]**.

CHAPTER 4
TRANSACTIONS WITH DIRECTORS REQUIRING APPROVAL OF MEMBERS

Service contracts

[1.1458]

188 Directors' long-term service contracts: requirement of members' approval

(1) This section applies to provision under which the guaranteed term of a director's employment—

(a) with the company of which he is a director, or

(b) where he is the director of a holding company, within the group consisting of that company and its subsidiaries,

is, or may be, longer than two years.

(2) A company may not agree to such provision unless it has been approved—

(a) by resolution of the members of the company, and

(b) in the case of a director of a holding company, by resolution of the members of that company.

(3) The guaranteed term of a director's employment is—

(a) the period (if any) during which the director's employment—

(i) is to continue, or may be continued otherwise than at the instance of the company (whether under the original agreement or under a new agreement entered into in pursuance of it), and

(ii) cannot be terminated by the company by notice, or can be so terminated only in specified circumstances, or

(b) in the case of employment terminable by the company by notice, the period of notice required to be given,

or, in the case of employment having a period within paragraph (a) and a period within paragraph (b), the aggregate of those periods.

(4) If more than six months before the end of the guaranteed term of a director's employment the company enters into a further service contract (otherwise than in pursuance of a right conferred, by or under the original contract, on the other party to it), this section applies as if there were added to the guaranteed term of the new contract the unexpired period of the guaranteed term of the original contract.

(5) A resolution approving provision to which this section applies must not be passed unless a memorandum setting out the proposed contract incorporating the provision is made available to members—

(a) in the case of a written resolution, by being sent or submitted to every eligible member at or before the time at which the proposed resolution is sent or submitted to him;

(b) in the case of a resolution at a meeting, by being made available for inspection by members of the company both—

(i) at the company's registered office for not less than 15 days ending with the date of the meeting, and

(ii) at the meeting itself.

(6) No approval is required under this section on the part of the members of a body corporate that—

(a) is not a UK-registered company, or

(b) is a wholly-owned subsidiary of another body corporate.

(7) In this section "employment" means any employment under a director's service contract.

[1.1459]

189 Directors' long-term service contracts: civil consequences of contravention

If a company agrees to provision in contravention of section 188 (directors' long-term service contracts: requirement of members' approval)

(a) the provision is void, to the extent of the contravention, and

(b) the contract is deemed to contain a term entitling the company to terminate it at any time by the giving of reasonable notice.

Payments for loss of office

[1.1460]

215 Payments for loss of office

(1) In this Chapter a "payment for loss of office" means a payment made to a director or past director of a company—

(a) by way of compensation for loss of office as director of the company,

(b) by way of compensation for loss, while director of the company or in connection with his ceasing to be a director of it, of—

(i) any other office or employment in connection with the management of the affairs of the company, or

(ii) any office (as director or otherwise) or employment in connection with the management of the affairs of any subsidiary undertaking of the company,

(c) as consideration for or in connection with his retirement from his office as director of the company, or

(d) as consideration for or in connection with his retirement, while director of the company or in connection with his ceasing to be a director of it, from—

(i) any other office or employment in connection with the management of the affairs of the company, or

(ii) any office (as director or otherwise) or employment in connection with the management of the affairs of any subsidiary undertaking of the company.

(2) The references to compensation and consideration include benefits otherwise than in cash and references in this Chapter to payment have a corresponding meaning.

(3) For the purposes of sections 217 to 221 (payments requiring members' approval)—

(a) payment to a person connected with a director, or

(b) payment to any person at the direction of, or for the benefit of, a director or a person connected with him,

is treated as payment to the director.

(4) References in those sections to payment by a person include payment by another person at the direction of, or on behalf of, the person referred to.

[(5) Nothing in this section or sections 216 to 222 applies in relation to a payment for loss of office to a director of a quoted company other than a payment to which section 226C does not apply by virtue of section 226D(6).]

NOTES

Sub-s (5): added by the Enterprise and Regulatory Reform Act 2013, s 81(1), (4), as from a day to be appointed and subject to transitional provisions in s 82(5) thereof at **[1.1859]**.

[1.1461]

216 Amounts taken to be payments for loss of office

(1) This section applies where in connection with any such transfer as is mentioned in section 218 or 219 (payment in connection with transfer of undertaking, property or shares) a director of the company—

(a) is to cease to hold office, or

(b) is to cease to be the holder of—

(i) any other office or employment in connection with the management of the affairs of the company, or

(ii) any office (as director or otherwise) or employment in connection with the management of the affairs of any subsidiary undertaking of the company.

(2) If in connection with any such transfer—

(a) the price to be paid to the director for any shares in the company held by him is in excess of the price which could at the time have been obtained by other holders of like shares, or

(b) any valuable consideration is given to the director by a person other than the company,

the excess or, as the case may be, the money value of the consideration is taken for the purposes of those sections to have been a payment for loss of office.

[1.1462]

217 Payment by company: requirement of members' approval

(1) A company may not make a payment for loss of office to a director of the company unless the payment has been approved by a resolution of the members of the company.

(2) A company may not make a payment for loss of office to a director of its holding company unless the payment has been approved by a resolution of the members of each of those companies.

(3) A resolution approving a payment to which this section applies must not be passed unless a memorandum setting out particulars of the proposed payment (including its amount) is made available to the members of the company whose approval is sought—

(a) in the case of a written resolution, by being sent or submitted to every eligible member at or before the time at which the proposed resolution is sent or submitted to him;

(b) in the case of a resolution at a meeting, by being made available for inspection by the members both—
   (i) at the company's registered office for not less than 15 days ending with the date of the meeting, and
   (ii) at the meeting itself.

(4) No approval is required under this section on the part of the members of a body corporate that—
   (a) is not a UK-registered company, or
   (b) is a wholly-owned subsidiary of another body corporate.

[1.1463]

218 Payment in connection with transfer of undertaking etc: requirement of members' approval

(1) No payment for loss of office may be made by any person to a director of a company in connection with the transfer of the whole or any part of the undertaking or property of the company unless the payment has been approved by a resolution of the members of the company.

(2) No payment for loss of office may be made by any person to a director of a company in connection with the transfer of the whole or any part of the undertaking or property of a subsidiary of the company unless the payment has been approved by a resolution of the members of each of the companies.

(3) A resolution approving a payment to which this section applies must not be passed unless a memorandum setting out particulars of the proposed payment (including its amount) is made available to the members of the company whose approval is sought—
   (a) in the case of a written resolution, by being sent or submitted to every eligible member at or before the time at which the proposed resolution is sent or submitted to him;
   (b) in the case of a resolution at a meeting, by being made available for inspection by the members both—
      (i) at the company's registered office for not less than 15 days ending with the date of the meeting, and
      (ii) at the meeting itself.

(4) No approval is required under this section on the part of the members of a body corporate that—
   (a) is not a UK-registered company, or
   (b) is a wholly-owned subsidiary of another body corporate.

(5) A payment made in pursuance of an arrangement—
   (a) entered into as part of the agreement for the transfer in question, or within one year before or two years after that agreement, and
   (b) to which the company whose undertaking or property is transferred, or any person to whom the transfer is made, is privy,

is presumed, except in so far as the contrary is shown, to be a payment to which this section applies.

[1.1464]

219 Payment in connection with share transfer: requirement of members' approval

(1) No payment for loss of office may be made by any person to a director of a company in connection with a transfer of shares in the company, or in a subsidiary of the company, resulting from a takeover bid unless the payment has been approved by a resolution of the relevant shareholders.

(2) The relevant shareholders are the holders of the shares to which the bid relates and any holders of shares of the same class as any of those shares.

(3) A resolution approving a payment to which this section applies must not be passed unless a memorandum setting out particulars of the proposed payment (including its amount) is made available to the members of the company whose approval is sought—
   (a) in the case of a written resolution, by being sent or submitted to every eligible member at or before the time at which the proposed resolution is sent or submitted to him;
   (b) in the case of a resolution at a meeting, by being made available for inspection by the members both—
      (i) at the company's registered office for not less than 15 days ending with the date of the meeting, and
      (ii) at the meeting itself.

(4) Neither the person making the offer, nor any associate of his (as defined in section 988), is entitled to vote on the resolution, but—
   (a) where the resolution is proposed as a written resolution, they are entitled (if they would otherwise be so entitled) to be sent a copy of it, and
   (b) at any meeting to consider the resolution they are entitled (if they would otherwise be so entitled) to be given notice of the meeting, to attend and speak and if present (in person or by proxy) to count towards the quorum.

(5) If at a meeting to consider the resolution a quorum is not present, and after the meeting has been adjourned to a later date a quorum is again not present, the payment is (for the purposes of this section) deemed to have been approved.

(6) No approval is required under this section on the part of shareholders in a body corporate that—

(a) is not a UK-registered company, or

(b) is a wholly-owned subsidiary of another body corporate.

(7) A payment made in pursuance of an arrangement—

(a) entered into as part of the agreement for the transfer in question, or within one year before or two years after that agreement, and

(b) to which the company whose shares are the subject of the bid, or any person to whom the transfer is made, is privy,

is presumed, except in so far as the contrary is shown, to be a payment to which this section applies.

[1.1465]

220 Exception for payments in discharge of legal obligations etc

(1) Approval is not required under section 217, 218 or 219 (payments requiring members' approval) for a payment made in good faith—

(a) in discharge of an existing legal obligation (as defined below),

(b) by way of damages for breach of such an obligation,

(c) by way of settlement or compromise of any claim arising in connection with the termination of a person's office or employment, or

(d) by way of pension in respect of past services.

(2) In relation to a payment within section 217 (payment by company) an existing legal obligation means an obligation of the company, or any body corporate associated with it, that was not entered into in connection with, or in consequence of, the event giving rise to the payment for loss of office.

(3) In relation to a payment within section 218 or 219 (payment in connection with transfer of undertaking, property or shares) an existing legal obligation means an obligation of the person making the payment that was not entered into for the purposes of, in connection with or in consequence of, the transfer in question.

(4) In the case of a payment within both section 217 and section 218, or within both section 217 and section 219, subsection (2) above applies and not subsection (3).

(5) A payment part of which falls within subsection (1) above and part of which does not is treated as if the parts were separate payments.

[1.1466]

221 Exception for small payments

(1) Approval is not required under section 217, 218 or 219 (payments requiring members' approval) if—

(a) the payment in question is made by the company or any of its subsidiaries, and

(b) the amount or value of the payment, together with the amount or value of any other relevant payments, does not exceed £200.

(2) For this purpose "other relevant payments" are payments for loss of office in relation to which the following conditions are met.

(3) Where the payment in question is one to which section 217 (payment by company) applies, the conditions are that the other payment was or is paid—

(a) by the company making the payment in question or any of its subsidiaries,

(b) to the director to whom that payment is made, and

(c) in connection with the same event.

(4) Where the payment in question is one to which section 218 or 219 applies (payment in connection with transfer of undertaking, property or shares), the conditions are that the other payment was (or is) paid in connection with the same transfer—

(a) to the director to whom the payment in question was made, and

(b) by the company making the payment or any of its subsidiaries.

[1.1467]

222 Payments made without approval: civil consequences

(1) If a payment is made in contravention of section 217 (payment by company)—

(a) it is held by the recipient on trust for the company making the payment, and

(b) any director who authorised the payment is jointly and severally liable to indemnify the company that made the payment for any loss resulting from it.

(2) If a payment is made in contravention of section 218 (payment in connection with transfer of undertaking etc), it is held by the recipient on trust for the company whose undertaking or property is or is proposed to be transferred.

(3) If a payment is made in contravention of section 219 (payment in connection with share transfer)—

(a) it is held by the recipient on trust for persons who have sold their shares as a result of the offer made, and

(b) the expenses incurred by the recipient in distributing that sum amongst those persons shall be borne by him and not retained out of that sum.

(4) If a payment is in contravention of section 217 and section 218, subsection (2) of this section applies rather than subsection (1).

(5) If a payment is in contravention of section 217 and section 219, subsection (3) of this section applies rather than subsection (1), unless the court directs otherwise.

Supplementary

[1.1468]

223 Transactions requiring members' approval: application of provisions to shadow directors

(1) For the purposes of—

(a) sections 188 and 189 (directors' service contracts),

(b) sections 190 to 196 (property transactions),

(c) sections 197 to 214 (loans etc), and

(d) sections 215 to 222 (payments for loss of office),

a shadow director is treated as a director.

(2) Any reference in those provisions to loss of office as a director does not apply in relation to loss of a person's status as a shadow director.

[CHAPTER 4A
DIRECTORS OF QUOTED COMPANIES: SPECIAL PROVISION

Interpretation

[1.1469]

226A Key definitions

(1) In this Chapter—

"directors' remuneration policy" means the policy of a quoted company with respect to the making of remuneration payments and payments for loss of office;

"quoted company" has the same meaning as in Part 15 of this Act;

"remuneration payment" means any form of payment or other benefit made to or otherwise conferred on a person as consideration for the person—

(a) holding, agreeing to hold or having held office as director of a company, or

(b) holding, agreeing to hold or having held, during a period when the person is or was such a director—

(i) any other office or employment in connection with the management of the affairs of the company, or

(ii) any office (as director or otherwise) or employment in connection with the management of the affairs of any subsidiary undertaking of the company,

other than a payment for loss of office;

"payment for loss of office" has the same meaning as in Chapter 4 of this Part.

(2) Subsection (3) applies where, in connection with a relevant transfer, a director of a quoted company is—

(a) to cease to hold office as director, or

(b) to cease to be the holder of—

(i) any other office or employment in connection with the management of the affairs of the company, or

(ii) any office (as director or otherwise) or employment in connection with the management of the affairs of any subsidiary undertaking of the company.

(3) If in connection with the transfer—

(a) the price to be paid to the director for any shares in the company held by the director is in excess of the price which could at the time have been obtained by other holders of like shares, or

(b) any valuable consideration is given to the director by a person other than the company,

the excess or, as the case may be, the money value of the consideration is taken for the purposes of section 226C to have been a payment for loss of office.

(4) In subsection (2), "relevant transfer" means—

(a) a transfer of the whole or any part of the undertaking or property of the company or a subsidiary of the company;

(b) a transfer of shares in the company, or in a subsidiary of the company, resulting from a takeover bid.

(5) References in this Chapter to the making of a remuneration payment or to the making of a payment for loss of office are to be read in accordance with this section.

(6) References in this Chapter to a payment by a company include a payment by another person at the direction of, or on behalf of, the company.

(7) References in this Chapter to a payment to a person ("B") who is, has been or is to be a director of a company include—

(a) a payment to a person connected with B, or
(b) a payment to a person at the direction of, or for the benefit of, B or a person connected with B.

(8) Section 252 applies for the purposes of determining whether a person is connected with a person who has been, or is to be, a director of a company as it applies for the purposes of determining whether a person is connected with a director.

(9) References in this Chapter to a director include a shadow director but references to loss of office as a director do not include loss of a person's status as a shadow director.]

NOTES

Commencement: to be appointed.

This section and ss 226B–226F (Chapter 4A) are inserted by the Enterprise and Regulatory Reform Act 2013, s 80, as from a day to be appointed.

[Restrictions relating to remuneration or loss of office payments

[1.1470]

226B Remuneration payments

(1) A quoted company may not make a remuneration payment to a person who is, or is to be or has been, a director of the company unless—
(a) the payment is consistent with the approved directors' remuneration policy, or
(b) the payment is approved by resolution of the members of the company.

(2) The approved directors' remuneration policy is the most recent remuneration policy to have been approved by a resolution passed by the members of the company in general meeting.]

NOTES

Commencement: to be appointed.

Inserted as noted to s 226A at **[1.1469]**.

[1.1471]

[226C Loss of office payments

(1) No payment for loss of office may be made by any person to a person who is, or has been, a director of a quoted company unless—
(a) the payment is consistent with the approved directors' remuneration policy, or
(b) the payment is approved by resolution of the members of the company.

(2) The approved directors' remuneration policy is the most recent remuneration policy to have been approved by a resolution passed by the members of the company in general meeting.]

NOTES

Commencement: to be appointed.

Inserted as noted to s 226A at **[1.1469]**.

[1.1472]

[226D Sections 226B and 226C: supplementary

(1) A resolution approving a payment for the purposes of section 226B(1)(b) or 226C(1)(b) must not be passed unless a memorandum setting out particulars of the proposed payment (including its amount) is made available for inspection by the members of the company—
(a) at the company's registered office for not less than 15 days ending with the date of the meeting at which the resolution is to be considered, and
(b) at that meeting itself.

(2) The memorandum must explain the ways in which the payment is inconsistent with the approved directors' remuneration policy (within the meaning of the section in question).

(3) The company must ensure that the memorandum is made available on the company's website from the first day on which the memorandum is made available for inspection under subsection (1) until its next accounts meeting.

(4) Failure to comply with subsection (3) does not affect the validity of the meeting at which a resolution is passed approving a payment to which the memorandum relates or the validity of anything done at the meeting.

(5) Nothing in section 226B or 226C authorises the making of a remuneration payment or (as the case may be) a payment for loss of office in contravention of the articles of the company concerned.

(6) Nothing in section 226B or 226C applies in relation to a remuneration payment or (as the case may be) a payment for loss of office made to a person who is, or is to be or has been, a director of a quoted company before the earlier of—
(a) the end of the first financial year of the company to begin on or after the day on which it becomes a quoted company, and
(b) the date from which the company's first directors' remuneration policy to be approved under section 439A takes effect.

(7) In this section the "company's website" is the website on which the company makes material available under section 430.]

NOTES

Commencement: to be appointed.
Inserted as noted to s 226A at **[1.1469]**.
Transitional provisions: see the Enterprise and Regulatory Reform Act 2013, s 82 at **[1.1859]**.

[Supplementary

[1.1473]
226E Payments made without approval: civil consequences

(1) An obligation (however arising) to make a payment which would be in contravention of section 226B or 226C has no effect.

(2) If a payment is made in contravention of section 226B or 226C—

(a) it is held by the recipient on trust for the company or other person making the payment, and
(b) in the case of a payment by a company, any director who authorised the payment is jointly and severally liable to indemnify the company that made the payment for any loss resulting from it.

(3) If a payment for loss of office is made in contravention of section 226C to a director of a quoted company in connection with the transfer of the whole or any part of the undertaking or property of the company or a subsidiary of the company—

(a) subsection (2) does not apply, and
(b) the payment is held by the recipient on trust for the company whose undertaking or property is or is proposed to be transferred.

(4) If a payment for loss of office is made in contravention of section 226C to a director of a quoted company in connection with a transfer of shares in the company, or in a subsidiary of the company, resulting from a takeover bid—

(a) subsection (2) does not apply,
(b) the payment is held by the recipient on trust for persons who have sold their shares as a result of the offer made, and
(c) the expenses incurred by the recipient in distributing that sum amongst those persons shall be borne by the recipient and not retained out of that sum.

(5) If in proceedings against a director for the enforcement of a liability under subsection (2)(b)—

(a) the director shows that he or she has acted honestly and reasonably, and
(b) the court considers that, having regard to all the circumstances of the case, the director ought to be relieved of liability,

the court may relieve the director, either wholly or in part, from liability on such terms as the court thinks fit.]

NOTES

Commencement: to be appointed.
Inserted as noted to s 226A at **[1.1469]**.

[1.1474]
[226F Relationship with requirements under Chapter 4

(1) This Chapter does not affect any requirement for approval by a resolution of the members of a company which applies in relation to the company under Chapter 4.

(2) Where the making of a payment to which section 226B or 226C applies requires approval by a resolution of the members of the company concerned under Chapter 4, approval obtained for the purposes of that Chapter is to be treated as satisfying the requirements of section 226B(1)(b) or (as the case may be) 226C(1)(b).]

NOTES

Commencement: to be appointed.
Inserted as noted to s 226A at **[1.1469]**.

CHAPTER 5
DIRECTORS' SERVICE CONTRACTS

[1.1475]
227 Directors' service contracts

(1) For the purposes of this Part a director's "service contract", in relation to a company, means a contract under which—

(a) a director of the company undertakes personally to perform services (as director or otherwise) for the company, or for a subsidiary of the company, or
(b) services (as director or otherwise) that a director of the company undertakes personally to perform are made available by a third party to the company, or to a subsidiary of the company.

(2) The provisions of this Part relating to directors' service contracts apply to the terms of a person's appointment as a director of a company.

They are not restricted to contracts for the performance of services outside the scope of the ordinary duties of a director.

[1.1476]

228 Copy of contract or memorandum of terms to be available for inspection

(1) A company must keep available for inspection—

(a) a copy of every director's service contract with the company or with a subsidiary of the company, or

(b) if the contract is not in writing, a written memorandum setting out the terms of the contract.

(2) All the copies and memoranda must be kept available for inspection at—

(a) the company's registered office, or

(b) a place specified in regulations under section 1136.

(3) The copies and memoranda must be retained by the company for at least one year from the date of termination or expiry of the contract and must be kept available for inspection during that time.

(4) The company must give notice to the registrar—

(a) of the place at which the copies and memoranda are kept available for inspection, and

(b) of any change in that place,

unless they have at all times been kept at the company's registered office.

(5) If default is made in complying with subsection (1), (2) or (3), or default is made for 14 days in complying with subsection (4), an offence is committed by every officer of the company who is in default.

(6) A person guilty of an offence under this section is liable on summary conviction to a fine not exceeding level 3 on the standard scale and, for continued contravention, a daily default fine not exceeding one-tenth of level 3 on the standard scale.

(7) The provisions of this section apply to a variation of a director's service contract as they apply to the original contract.

NOTES

As of 6 April 2013 no Regulations has been made under s 1136 of the 2006 Act specifying a place for the purposes of section 228(2)(b). Note also that s 1068 of that Act came into force for all remaining purposes on 1 October 2009.

[1.1477]

229 Right of member to inspect and request copy

(1) Every copy or memorandum required to be kept under section 228 must be open to inspection by any member of the company without charge.

(2) Any member of the company is entitled, on request and on payment of such fee as may be prescribed, to be provided with a copy of any such copy or memorandum.

The copy must be provided within seven days after the request is received by the company.

(3) If an inspection required under subsection (1) is refused, or default is made in complying with subsection (2), an offence is committed by every officer of the company who is in default.

(4) A person guilty of an offence under this section is liable on summary conviction to a fine not exceeding level 3 on the standard scale and, for continued contravention, a daily default fine not exceeding one-tenth of level 3 on the standard scale.

(5) In the case of any such refusal or default the court may by order compel an immediate inspection or, as the case may be, direct that the copy required be sent to the person requiring it.

NOTES

Regulations: the Companies (Fees for Inspection and Copying of Company Records) Regulations 2007, SI 2007/2612.

[1.1478]

230 Directors' service contracts: application of provisions to shadow directors

A shadow director is treated as a director for the purposes of the provisions of this Chapter.

CHAPTER 7
DIRECTORS' LIABILITIES

Provision protecting directors from liability

[1.1479]

232 Provisions protecting directors from liability

(1) Any provision that purports to exempt a director of a company (to any extent) from any liability that would otherwise attach to him in connection with any negligence, default, breach of duty or breach of trust in relation to the company is void.

(2) Any provision by which a company directly or indirectly provides an indemnity (to any extent) for a director of the company, or of an associated company, against any liability attaching to him in connection with any negligence, default, breach of duty or breach of trust in relation to the company of which he is a director is void, except as permitted by—

(a) section 233 (provision of insurance),

(b) section 234 (qualifying third party indemnity provision), or
(c) section 235 (qualifying pension scheme indemnity provision).

(3) This section applies to any provision, whether contained in a company's articles or in any contract with the company or otherwise.

(4) Nothing in this section prevents a company's articles from making such provision as has previously been lawful for dealing with conflicts of interest.

[1.1480]
233 Provision of insurance

Section 232(2) (voidness of provisions for indemnifying directors) does not prevent a company from purchasing and maintaining for a director of the company, or of an associated company, insurance against any such liability as is mentioned in that subsection.

[1.1481]
234 Qualifying third party indemnity provision

(1) Section 232(2) (voidness of provisions for indemnifying directors) does not apply to qualifying third party indemnity provision.

(2) Third party indemnity provision means provision for indemnity against liability incurred by the director to a person other than the company or an associated company.

Such provision is qualifying third party indemnity provision if the following requirements are met.

(3) The provision must not provide any indemnity against—
(a) any liability of the director to pay—
(i) a fine imposed in criminal proceedings, or
(ii) a sum payable to a regulatory authority by way of a penalty in respect of non-compliance with any requirement of a regulatory nature (however arising); or
(b) any liability incurred by the director—
(i) in defending criminal proceedings in which he is convicted, or
(ii) in defending civil proceedings brought by the company, or an associated company, in which judgment is given against him, or
(iii) in connection with an application for relief (see subsection (6)) in which the court refuses to grant him relief.

(4) The references in subsection (3)(b) to a conviction, judgment or refusal of relief are to the final decision in the proceedings.

(5) For this purpose—
(a) a conviction, judgment or refusal of relief becomes final—
(i) if not appealed against, at the end of the period for bringing an appeal, or
(ii) if appealed against, at the time when the appeal (or any further appeal) is disposed of; and
(b) an appeal is disposed of—
(i) if it is determined and the period for bringing any further appeal has ended, or
(ii) if it is abandoned or otherwise ceases to have effect.

(6) The reference in subsection (3)(b)(iii) to an application for relief is to an application for relief under—

section 661(3) or (4) (power of court to grant relief in case of acquisition of shares by innocent nominee), or

section 1157 (general power of court to grant relief in case of honest and reasonable conduct).

[1.1482]
235 Qualifying pension scheme indemnity provision

(1) Section 232(2) (voidness of provisions for indemnifying directors) does not apply to qualifying pension scheme indemnity provision.

(2) Pension scheme indemnity provision means provision indemnifying a director of a company that is a trustee of an occupational pension scheme against liability incurred in connection with the company's activities as trustee of the scheme.

Such provision is qualifying pension scheme indemnity provision if the following requirements are met.

(3) The provision must not provide any indemnity against—
(a) any liability of the director to pay—
(i) a fine imposed in criminal proceedings, or
(ii) a sum payable to a regulatory authority by way of a penalty in respect of non-compliance with any requirement of a regulatory nature (however arising); or
(b) any liability incurred by the director in defending criminal proceedings in which he is convicted.

(4) The reference in subsection (3)(b) to a conviction is to the final decision in the proceedings.

(5) For this purpose—
(a) a conviction becomes final—
(i) if not appealed against, at the end of the period for bringing an appeal, or

(ii) if appealed against, at the time when the appeal (or any further appeal) is disposed of; and
(b) an appeal is disposed of—
(i) if it is determined and the period for bringing any further appeal has ended, or
(ii) if it is abandoned or otherwise ceases to have effect.

(6) In this section "occupational pension scheme" means an occupational pension scheme as defined in section 150(5) of the Finance Act 2004 (c 12) that is established under a trust.

[1.1483]
236 Qualifying indemnity provision to be disclosed in directors' report
(1) This section requires disclosure in the directors' report of—
(a) qualifying third party indemnity provision, and
(b) qualifying pension scheme indemnity provision.

Such provision is referred to in this section as "qualifying indemnity provision".

(2) If when a directors' report is approved any qualifying indemnity provision (whether made by the company or otherwise) is in force for the benefit of one or more directors of the company, the report must state that such provision is in force.

(3) If at any time during the financial year to which a directors' report relates any such provision was in force for the benefit of one or more persons who were then directors of the company, the report must state that such provision was in force.

(4) If when a directors' report is approved qualifying indemnity provision made by the company is in force for the benefit of one or more directors of an associated company, the report must state that such provision is in force.

(5) If at any time during the financial year to which a directors' report relates any such provision was in force for the benefit of one or more persons who were then directors of an associated company, the report must state that such provision was in force.

CHAPTER 9
SUPPLEMENTARY PROVISIONS

Provision for employees on cessation or transfer of business

[1.1484]
247 Power to make provision for employees on cessation or transfer of business
(1) The powers of the directors of a company include (if they would not otherwise do so) power to make provision for the benefit of persons employed or formerly employed by the company, or any of its subsidiaries, in connection with the cessation or the transfer to any person of the whole or part of the undertaking of the company or that subsidiary.

(2) This power is exercisable notwithstanding the general duty imposed by section 172 (duty to promote the success of the company).

(3) In the case of a company that is a charity it is exercisable notwithstanding any restrictions on the directors' powers (or the company's capacity) flowing from the objects of the company.

(4) The power may only be exercised if sanctioned—
(a) by a resolution of the company, or
(b) by a resolution of the directors,

in accordance with the following provisions.

(5) A resolution of the directors—
(a) must be authorised by the company's articles, and
(b) is not sufficient sanction for payments to or for the benefit of directors, former directors or shadow directors.

(6) Any other requirements of the company's articles as to the exercise of the power conferred by this section must be complied with.

(7) Any payment under this section must be made—
(a) before the commencement of any winding up of the company, and
(b) out of profits of the company that are available for dividend.

NOTES

Commencement: 1 October 2009.

Transitional provisions: Sch 2, para 40 to the Companies Act 2006 (Commencement No 8, Transitional Provisions and Savings) Order 2008, SI 2008/2860 provides as follows—

> **"Power to make provision for employees on cessation or transfer of business (s 247)**
> 40.—(1) Section 247 of the Companies Act 2006 (power to make provision for employees on cessation or transfer of business) applies to provision made on or after 1st October 2009 (subject to sub-paragraph (2)(b)).
> (2) Section 719 of the 1985 Act or Article 668 of the 1986 Order continues to apply—
> (a) to provision made before that date, and
> (b) to anything sanctioned in accordance with subsection (3) of that section or paragraph (3) of that Article before that date.".

Note: the Companies Act 2006 (Commencement No 3, Consequential Amendments, Transitional Provisions and Savings) Order 2007, SI 2007/2194, art 2(1)(d) originally provided that this section would come into force on 1 October 2007 (subject to transitional provisions in Sch 3, para 18 to that Order). Article 2(1)(d) was subsequently amended by the Companies Act 2006 (Commencement No 4 and Commencement No 3 (Amendment)) Order 2007, SI 2007/2607, art 4(1) (with effect from 30 September 2007) so that the commencement of this section on 1 October 2007 was reversed. The transitional provisions in Sch 3, para 18 were revoked at the same time.

PART 15
ACCOUNTS AND REPORTS

CHAPTER 5
DIRECTORS' REPORT

Directors' report

[1.1485]

416 Contents of directors' report: general

(1) The directors' report for a financial year must state—

(a) the names of the persons who, at any time during the financial year, were directors of the company, and

(b) the principal activities of the company in the course of the year.

(2) In relation to a group directors' report subsection (1)(b) has effect as if the reference to the company was to the undertakings included in the consolidation.

(3) Except in the case of a company [entitled to the small companies exemption], the report must state the amount (if any) that the directors recommend should be paid by way of dividend.

(4) The Secretary of State may make provision by regulations as to other matters that must be disclosed in a directors' report.

Without prejudice to the generality of this power, the regulations may make any such provision as was formerly made by Schedule 7 to the Companies Act 1985.

NOTES

Sub-s (3): words in square brackets substituted by the Companies Act 2006 (Amendment) (Accounts and Reports) Regulations 2008, SI 2008/393, reg 6(3).

Regulations: the Small Companies and Groups (Accounts and Directors' Report) Regulations 2008, SI 2008/409; the Large and Medium-sized Companies and Groups (Accounts and Reports) Regulations 2008, SI 2008/410.

CHAPTER 6
QUOTED COMPANIES: DIRECTORS' REMUNERATION REPORT

[1.1486]

420 Duty to prepare directors' remuneration report

(1) The directors of a quoted company must prepare a directors' remuneration report for each financial year of the company.

(2) In the case of failure to comply with the requirement to prepare a directors' remuneration report, every person who—

(a) was a director of the company immediately before the end of the period for filing accounts and reports for the financial year in question, and

(b) failed to take all reasonable steps for securing compliance with that requirement,

commits an offence.

(3) A person guilty of an offence under this section is liable—

(a) on conviction on indictment, to a fine;

(b) on summary conviction, to a fine not exceeding the statutory maximum.

[1.1487]

421 Contents of directors' remuneration report

(1) The Secretary of State may make provision by regulations as to—

(a) the information that must be contained in a directors' remuneration report,

(b) how information is to be set out in the report, and

(c) what is to be the auditable part of the report.

(2) Without prejudice to the generality of this power, the regulations may make any such provision as was made, immediately before the commencement of this Part, by Schedule 7A to the Companies Act 1985 (c 6).

[(2A) The regulations must provide that any information required to be included in the report as to the policy of the company with respect to the making of remuneration payments and payments for loss of office (within the meaning of Chapter 4A of Part 10) is to be set out in a separate part of the report.]

(3) It is the duty of—

(a) any director of a company, and

(b) any person who is or has at any time in the preceding five years been a director of the company,

to give notice to the company of such matters relating to himself as may be necessary for the purposes of regulations under this section.
(4) A person who makes default in complying with subsection (3) commits an offence and is liable on summary conviction to a fine not exceeding level 3 on the standard scale.

NOTES

Sub-s (2A): inserted by the Enterprise and Regulatory Reform Act 2013, s 79(1), as from 25 April 2013 (so far as is necessary for enabling the exercise of any power to make regulations) and as from a day to be appointed (otherwise).

Regulations: the Large and Medium-sized Companies and Groups (Accounts and Reports) Regulations 2008, SI 2008/410.

[1.1488]
422 Approval and signing of directors' remuneration report
(1) The directors' remuneration report must be approved by the board of directors and signed on behalf of the board by a director or the secretary of the company.
(2) If a directors' remuneration report is approved that does not comply with the requirements of this Act, every director of the company who—
(a) knew that it did not comply, or was reckless as to whether it complied, and
(b) failed to take reasonable steps to secure compliance with those requirements or, as the case may be, to prevent the report from being approved,

commits an offence.
(3) A person guilty of an offence under this section is liable—
(a) on conviction on indictment, to a fine;
(b) on summary conviction, to a fine not exceeding the statutory maximum.

[1.1489]
[422A Revisions to directors' remuneration policy
(1) The directors' remuneration policy contained in a company's directors' remuneration report may be revised.
(2) Any such revision must be approved by the board of directors.
(3) The policy as so revised must be set out in a document signed on behalf of the board by a director or the secretary of the company.
(4) Regulations under section 421(1) may make provision as to—
(a) the information that must be contained in a document setting out a revised directors' remuneration policy, and
(b) how information is to be set out in the document.
(5) Sections 422(2) and (3), 454, 456 and 463 apply in relation to such a document as they apply in relation to a directors' remuneration report.
(6) In this section, "directors' remuneration policy" means the policy of a company with respect to the matters mentioned in section 421(2A).]

NOTES

Commencement: 25 April 2013 (so far as is necessary for enabling the exercise of any power to make regulations); to be appointed (otherwise).

Inserted by the Enterprise and Regulatory Reform Act 2013, s 79(2), as from 25 April 2013 (so far as is necessary for enabling the exercise of any power to make regulations) and as from a day to be appointed (otherwise).

CHAPTER 9
QUOTED COMPANIES: MEMBERS' APPROVAL OF DIRECTORS' REMUNERATION REPORT

[1.1490]
439 Quoted companies: members' approval of directors' remuneration report
(1) A quoted company must, prior to the accounts meeting, give to the members of the company entitled to be sent notice of the meeting notice of the intention to move at the meeting, as an ordinary resolution, a resolution approving the directors' remuneration report for the financial year [other than the part containing the directors' remuneration policy (as to which see section 439A)].
(2) The notice may be given in any manner permitted for the service on the member of notice of the meeting.
(3) The business that may be dealt with at the accounts meeting includes the resolution.
This is so notwithstanding any default in complying with subsection (1) or (2).
(4) The existing directors must ensure that the resolution is put to the vote of the meeting.
(5) No entitlement of a person to remuneration is made conditional on the resolution being passed by reason only of the provision made by this section.
(6) In this section—
"the accounts meeting" means the general meeting of the company before which the company's annual accounts for the financial year are to be laid; and
"existing director" means a person who is a director of the company immediately before that meeting.

NOTES

Sub-s (1): words in square brackets added by the Enterprise and Regulatory Reform Act 2013, s 79(3), as from a day to be appointed.

[1.1491]

[439A Quoted companies: members' approval of directors' remuneration policy

(1) A quoted company must give notice of the intention to move, as an ordinary resolution, a resolution approving the relevant directors' remuneration policy—

- (a) at the accounts meeting held in the first financial year which begins on or after the day on which the company becomes a quoted company, and
- (b) at an accounts or other general meeting held no later than the end of the period of three financial years beginning with the first financial year after the last accounts or other general meeting in relation to which notice is given under this subsection.

(2) A quoted company must give notice of the intention to move at an accounts meeting, as an ordinary resolution, a resolution approving the relevant directors' remuneration policy if—

- (a) a resolution required to be put to the vote under section 439 was not passed at the last accounts meeting of the company, and
- (b) no notice under this section was given in relation to that meeting or any other general meeting held before the next accounts meeting.

(3) Subsection (2) does not apply in relation to a quoted company before the first meeting in relation to which it gives notice under subsection (1).

(4) A notice given under subsection (2) is to be treated as given under subsection (1) for the purpose of determining the period within which the next notice under subsection (1) must be given.

(5) Notice of the intention to move a resolution to which this section applies must be given, prior to the meeting in question, to the members of the company entitled to be sent notice of the meeting.

(6) Subsections (2) to (4) of section 439 apply for the purposes of a resolution to which this section applies as they apply for the purposes of a resolution to which section 439 applies, with the modification that, for the purposes of a resolution relating to a general meeting other than an accounts meeting, subsection (3) applies as if for "accounts meeting" there were substituted "general meeting".

(7) For the purposes of this section, the relevant directors' remuneration policy is—

- (a) in a case where notice is given in relation to an accounts meeting, the remuneration policy contained in the directors' remuneration report in respect of which a resolution under section 439 is required to be put to the vote at that accounts meeting;
- (b) in a case where notice is given in relation to a general meeting other than an accounts meeting—
  - (i) the remuneration policy contained in the directors' remuneration report in respect of which such a resolution was required to be put to the vote at the last accounts meeting to be held before that other general meeting, or
  - (ii) where that policy has been revised in accordance with section 422A, the policy as so revised.

(8) In this section—

- (a) "accounts meeting" means a general meeting of the company before which the company's annual accounts for a financial year are to be laid;
- (b) "directors' remuneration policy" means the policy of the company with respect to the matters mentioned in section 421(2A).]

NOTES

Commencement: to be appointed.

Inserted by the Enterprise and Regulatory Reform Act 2013, s 79(4), as from a day to be appointed.

Transitional provisions: see the Enterprise and Regulatory Reform Act 2013, s 82 at **[1.1859]**.

PART 47
FINAL PROVISIONS

[1.1492]

1298 Short title

The short title of this Act is the Companies Act 2006.

[1.1493]

1299 Extent

Except as otherwise provided (or the context otherwise requires), the provisions of this Act extend to the whole of the United Kingdom.

[1.1494]

1300 Commencement

(1) The following provisions come into force on the day this Act is passed—

(a) Part 43 (transparency obligations and related matters), except the amendment in paragraph 11(2) of Schedule 15 of the definition of "regulated market" in Part 6 of the Financial Services and Markets Act 2000 (c 8),
(b) in Part 44 (miscellaneous provisions)—
section 1274 (grants to bodies concerned with actuarial standards etc), and
section 1276 (application of provisions to Scotland and Northern Ireland),
(c) Part 46 (general supplementary provisions), except section 1295 and Schedule 16 (repeals), and
(d) this Part.

(2) The other provisions of this Act come into force on such day as may be appointed by order of the Secretary of State or the Treasury.

NOTES

Orders: the Companies Act 2006 (Commencement No 1, Transitional Provisions and Savings) Order 2006, SI 2006/3428; the Companies Act 2006 (Commencement No 2, Consequential Amendments, Transitional Provisions and Savings) Order 2007, SI 2007/1093; the Companies Act 2006 (Commencement No 3, Consequential Amendments, Transitional Provisions and Savings) Order 2007, SI 2007/2194; the Companies Act 2006 (Commencement No 4 and Commencement No 3 (Amendment)) Order 2007, SI 2007/2607; the Companies Act 2006 (Commencement No 5, Transitional Provisions and Savings) Order 2007, SI 2007/3495; the Companies Act 2006 (Commencement No 6, Saving and Commencement Nos 3 and 5 (Amendment)) Order 2008, SI 2008/674; the Companies Act 2006 (Commencement No 7, Transitional Provisions and Savings) Order 2008, SI 2008/1886; the Companies Act 2006 (Commencement No 8, Transitional Provisions and Savings) Order 2008, SI 2008/2860; the Companies Act 2006 (Consequential Amendments, Transitional Provisions and Savings) Order 2009, SI 2009/1941; the Companies Act 2006 and Limited Liability Partnerships (Transitional Provisions and Savings) (Amendment) Regulations 2009, SI 2009/2476.

LEGISLATIVE AND REGULATORY REFORM ACT 2006

(2006 c 51)

An Act to enable provision to be made for the purpose of removing or reducing burdens resulting from legislation and promoting regulatory principles; to make provision about the exercise of regulatory functions; to make provision about the interpretation of legislation relating to the European Communities and the European Economic Area; to make provision relating to section 2(2) of the European Communities Act 1972; and for connected purposes

[8 November 2006]

NOTES

Only those provisions of this Act relevant to employment law are reproduced. Provisions not reproduced are not annotated. The provisions reproduced here extend to the whole of the United Kingdom (s 34) and the entire Act came into force on 8 January 2007 (s 33).

PART 2
REGULATORS

Exercise of regulatory functions

[1.1495]
21 Principles

(1) Any person exercising a regulatory function to which this section applies must have regard to the principles in subsection (2) in the exercise of the function.

(2) Those principles are that—
(a) regulatory activities should be carried out in a way which is transparent, accountable, proportionate and consistent;
(b) regulatory activities should be targeted only at cases in which action is needed.

(3) The duty in subsection (1) is subject to any other requirement affecting the exercise of the regulatory function.

[1.1496]
22 Code of practice

(1) A Minister of the Crown may issue and from time to time revise a code of practice in relation to the exercise of regulatory functions.

(2) Any person exercising a regulatory function to which this section applies must, except in a case where subsection (3) applies, have regard to the code in determining any general policy or principles by reference to which the person exercises the function.

(3) Any person exercising a regulatory function to which this section applies which is a function of setting standards or giving guidance generally in relation to the exercise of other regulatory functions must have regard to the code in the exercise of the function.

(4) The duties in subsections (2) and (3) are subject to any other requirement affecting the exercise of the regulatory function.

NOTES

Note: the Statutory Code of Practice for Regulators was issued by the Department for Business, Enterprise and Regulatory Reform (now the Department for Business, Innovation and Skills) on 17 December 2007. It is available on the BIS website.

[1.1497]

23 Code of practice: procedure

(1) Where a Minister of the Crown proposes to issue or revise a code of practice under section 22, he shall prepare a draft of the code (or revised code).

(2) The Minister shall, in preparing the draft, seek to secure that it is consistent with the principles specified in section 21(2).

(3) The Minister shall consult the following about the draft—

(a) persons appearing to him to be representative of persons exercising regulatory functions;

(b) such other persons as he considers appropriate.

(4) If the Minister determines to proceed with the draft (either in its original form or with modifications) he shall lay the draft before Parliament.

(5) Where the draft laid before Parliament under subsection (4) is approved by resolution of each House of Parliament, the Minister may issue the code (or revised code).

(6) A code (or revised code) issued under subsection (5) shall come into force on such date as the Minister may by order made by statutory instrument appoint.

NOTES

Orders: the Legislative and Regulatory Reform Code of Practice (Appointed Day) Order 2007, SI 2007/3548. This Order appoints 6 April 2008 for the coming into force of the Regulators' Compliance Code (as to which, see s 22 *ante*).

[1.1498]

24 Functions to which sections 21 and 22 apply

(1) Sections 21 and 22 apply to regulatory functions specified under this section.

(2) A Minister of the Crown may by order in accordance with this section specify regulatory functions as functions to which sections 21 and 22 apply.

(3) A Minister may not under subsection (2) specify—

(a) a regulatory function so far as exercisable in Scotland, if or to the extent that the function relates to matters which are not reserved matters;

(b) a regulatory function so far as exercisable in Northern Ireland, if or to the extent that the function relates to matters which are transferred matters; or

(c) a regulatory function exercisable only in or as regards Wales.

(4) [The Welsh Ministers] may by order in accordance with this section specify regulatory functions exercisable only in or as regards Wales as functions to which sections 21 and 22 apply.

(5) An order under this section may not specify regulatory functions conferred on or exercisable by any of the following—

(a) the Gas and Electricity Markets Authority;

(b) the Office of Communications;

(c) the Office of Rail Regulation;

(d) . . .

(e) the Water Services Regulation Authority.

(6) Before making an order under this section, the authority making the order must consult the following—

(a) any person (other than the authority) whose functions are to be specified in the order;

(b) such other persons as the authority considers appropriate.

(7) An order under this section may make such consequential, supplementary, incidental, or transitional provision (including provision amending any enactment) as the authority making it considers appropriate; and may make different provision for different purposes.

(8) An order under this section must be made by statutory instrument.

(9) A Minister of the Crown may not make a statutory instrument containing an order under this section unless a draft has been laid before, and approved by resolution of, each House of Parliament.

[(9A) The Welsh Ministers may not make a statutory instrument containing an order under this section unless a draft has been laid before, and approved by resolution of, the Assembly.]

(10) In this section—

"reserved matter" and "Scotland" have the same meanings as in the Scotland Act 1998 (c 46);

"transferred matter" and "Northern Ireland" have the same meanings as in the Northern Ireland Act 1998 (c 47);

"Wales" has the same meaning as in the [Government of Wales Act 2006].

NOTES

Sub-ss (4), (10): words in square brackets substituted by the Government of Wales Act 2006 (Consequential Modifications and Transitional Provisions) Order 2007, SI 2007/1388, art 3, Sch 1, paras 143, 148(a), (c).

Sub-s (5): para (d) repealed by the Postal Services Act 2011, s 91(1), (2), Sch 12, Pt 3, para 174, as from 1 October 2011.

Sub-s (9A): inserted by SI 2007/1388, art 3, Sch 1, paras 143, 148(b).

Orders: the Legislative and Regulatory Reform (Regulatory Functions) Order 2007, SI 2007/3544; the Legislative and Regulatory Reform (Regulatory Functions) (Amendment) Order 2009, SI 2009/2981; the Legislative and Regulatory Reform (Regulatory Functions) (Amendment) Order 2010, SI 2010/3028. The 2007 Order, which came into force on 6 April 2008, specifies the regulatory functions to which the duties in ss 21 and 22 of this Act apply.

CORPORATE MANSLAUGHTER AND CORPORATE HOMICIDE ACT 2007

(2007 c 19)

ARRANGEMENT OF SECTIONS

An Act to create a new offence that, in England and Wales or Northern Ireland, is to be called corporate manslaughter and, in Scotland, is to be called corporate homicide; and to make provision in connection with that offence

[26 July 2007]

Corporate manslaughter and corporate homicide

[1.1499]

1 The offence

(1) An organisation to which this section applies is guilty of an offence if the way in which its activities are managed or organised—

(a) causes a person's death, and

(b) amounts to a gross breach of a relevant duty of care owed by the organisation to the deceased.

(2) The organisations to which this section applies are—

(a) a corporation;

(b) a department or other body listed in Schedule 1;

(c) a police force;

(d) a partnership, or a trade union or employers' association, that is an employer.

(3) An organisation is guilty of an offence under this section only if the way in which its activities are managed or organised by its senior management is a substantial element in the breach referred to in subsection (1).

(4) For the purposes of this Act—

(a) "relevant duty of care" has the meaning given by section 2, read with sections 3 to 7;

(b) a breach of a duty of care by an organisation is a "gross" breach if the conduct alleged to amount to a breach of that duty falls far below what can reasonably be expected of the organisation in the circumstances;

(c) "senior management", in relation to an organisation, means the persons who play significant roles in—

(i) the making of decisions about how the whole or a substantial part of its activities are to be managed or organised, or

(ii) the actual managing or organising of the whole or a substantial part of those activities.

(5) The offence under this section is called—

(a) corporate manslaughter, in so far as it is an offence under the law of England and Wales or Northern Ireland;

(b) corporate homicide, in so far as it is an offence under the law of Scotland.

(6) An organisation that is guilty of corporate manslaughter or corporate homicide is liable on conviction on indictment to a fine.

(7) The offence of corporate homicide is indictable only in the High Court of Justiciary.

Relevant duty of care

[1.1500]

2 Meaning of "relevant duty of care"

(1) A "relevant duty of care", in relation to an organisation, means any of the following duties owed by it under the law of negligence—

(a) a duty owed to its employees or to other persons working for the organisation or performing services for it;

(b) a duty owed as occupier of premises;

(c) a duty owed in connection with—

(i) the supply by the organisation of goods or services (whether for consideration or not),

(ii) the carrying on by the organisation of any construction or maintenance operations,

(iii) the carrying on by the organisation of any other activity on a commercial basis, or

(iv) the use or keeping by the organisation of any plant, vehicle or other thing;

(d) a duty owed to a person who, by reason of being a person within subsection (2), is someone for whose safety the organisation is responsible.

(2) A person is within this subsection if—

(a) he is detained at a custodial institution or in a custody area at a court[, a police station or customs premises];

[(aa) he is detained in service custody premises;]

(b) he is detained at a removal centre or short-term holding facility;

(c) he is being transported in a vehicle, or being held in any premises, in pursuance of prison escort arrangements or immigration escort arrangements;

(d) he is living in secure accommodation in which he has been placed;

(e) he is a detained patient.

(3) Subsection (1) is subject to sections 3 to 7.

(4) A reference in subsection (1) to a duty owed under the law of negligence includes a reference to a duty that would be owed under the law of negligence but for any statutory provision under which liability is imposed in place of liability under that law.

(5) For the purposes of this Act, whether a particular organisation owes a duty of care to a particular individual is a question of law.

The judge must make any findings of fact necessary to decide that question.

(6) For the purposes of this Act there is to be disregarded—

(a) any rule of the common law that has the effect of preventing a duty of care from being owed by one person to another by reason of the fact that they are jointly engaged in unlawful conduct;

(b) any such rule that has the effect of preventing a duty of care from being owed to a person by reason of his acceptance of a risk of harm.

(7) In this section—

"construction or maintenance operations" means operations of any of the following descriptions—

(a) construction, installation, alteration, extension, improvement, repair, maintenance, decoration, cleaning, demolition or dismantling of—

(i) any building or structure,

(ii) anything else that forms, or is to form, part of the land, or

(iii) any plant, vehicle or other thing;

(b) operations that form an integral part of, or are preparatory to, or are for rendering complete, any operations within paragraph (a);

"custodial institution" means a prison, a young offender institution, a secure training centre, a young offenders institution, a young offenders centre, a juvenile justice centre or a remand centre;

["customs premises" means premises wholly or partly occupied by persons designated under section 3 (general customs officials) or 11 (customs revenue officials) of the Borders, Citizenship and Immigration Act 2009;]

"detained patient" means—

(a) a person who is detained in any premises under—

(i) Part 2 or 3 of the Mental Health Act 1983 (c 20) ("the 1983 Act"), or

(ii) Part 2 or 3 of the Mental Health (Northern Ireland) Order 1986 (SI 1986/595 (NI 4)) ("the 1986 Order");

(b) a person who (otherwise than by reason of being detained as mentioned in paragraph (a)) is deemed to be in legal custody by—

(i) section 137 of the 1983 Act,

(ii) Article 131 of the 1986 Order, or

(iii) article 11 of the Mental Health (Care and Treatment) (Scotland) Act 2003 (Consequential Provisions) Order 2005 (SI 2005/2078);

(c) a person who is detained in any premises, or is otherwise in custody, under the Mental Health (Care and Treatment) (Scotland) Act 2003 (asp 13) or Part 6 of the Criminal Procedure (Scotland) Act 1995 (c 46) or who is detained in a hospital under section 200 of that Act of 1995;

"immigration escort arrangements" means arrangements made under section 156 of the Immigration and Asylum Act 1999 (c 33);

"the law of negligence" includes—

(a) in relation to England and Wales, the Occupiers' Liability Act 1957 (c 31), the Defective Premises Act 1972 (c 35) and the Occupiers' Liability Act 1984 (c 3);

(b) in relation to Scotland, the Occupiers' Liability (Scotland) Act 1960 (c 30);

(c) in relation to Northern Ireland, the Occupiers' Liability Act (Northern Ireland) 1957 (c 25), the Defective Premises (Northern Ireland) Order 1975 (SI 1975/1039 (NI 9)), the Occupiers' Liability (Northern Ireland) Order 1987 (SI 1987/1280 (NI 15)) and the Defective Premises (Landlord's Liability) Act (Northern Ireland) 2001 (c 10);

"prison escort arrangements" means arrangements made under section 80 of the Criminal Justice Act 1991 (c 53) or under section 102 or 118 of the Criminal Justice and Public Order Act 1994 (c 33);

"removal centre" and "short-term holding facility" have the meaning given by section 147 of the Immigration and Asylum Act 1999;

"secure accommodation" means accommodation, not consisting of or forming part of a custodial institution, provided for the purpose of restricting the liberty of persons under the age of 18;

["service custody premises" has the meaning given by section 300(7) of the Armed Forces Act 2006]

NOTES

Commencement: 6 April 2008 (sub-ss (1)(a)–(c), (2)–(7)); 1 September 2011 (otherwise).

The words in square brackets in sub-s (2)(a) were substituted, sub-s (2)(aa) was inserted, and the definitions "customs premises" and "service custody premises" in sub-s (7) were inserted, by the Corporate Manslaughter and Corporate Homicide Act 2007 (Amendment) Order 2011, SI 2011/1868, art 2, as from 1 September 2011.

[1.1501]

3 Public policy decisions, exclusively public functions and statutory inspections

(1) Any duty of care owed by a public authority in respect of a decision as to matters of public policy (including in particular the allocation of public resources or the weighing of competing public interests) is not a "relevant duty of care".

(2) Any duty of care owed in respect of things done in the exercise of an exclusively public function is not a "relevant duty of care" unless it falls within section 2(1)(a), (b) or (d).

(3) Any duty of care owed by a public authority in respect of inspections carried out in the exercise of a statutory function is not a "relevant duty of care" unless it falls within section 2(1)(a) or (b).

(4) In this section—

"exclusively public function" means a function that falls within the prerogative of the Crown or is, by its nature, exercisable only with authority conferred—

(a) by the exercise of that prerogative, or

(b) by or under a statutory provision;

"statutory function" means a function conferred by or under a statutory provision.

[1.1502]

4 Military activities

(1) Any duty of care owed by the Ministry of Defence in respect of—

(a) operations within subsection (2),

(b) activities carried on in preparation for, or directly in support of, such operations, or

(c) training of a hazardous nature, or training carried out in a hazardous way, which it is considered needs to be carried out, or carried out in that way, in order to improve or maintain the effectiveness of the armed forces with respect to such operations,

is not a "relevant duty of care".

(2) The operations within this subsection are operations, including peacekeeping operations and operations for dealing with terrorism, civil unrest or serious public disorder, in the course of which members of the armed forces come under attack or face the threat of attack or violent resistance.

(3) Any duty of care owed by the Ministry of Defence in respect of activities carried on by members of the special forces is not a "relevant duty of care".

(4) In this section "the special forces" means those units of the armed forces the maintenance of whose capabilities is the responsibility of the Director of Special Forces or which are for the time being subject to the operational command of that Director.

[1.1503]

5 Policing and law enforcement

(1) Any duty of care owed by a public authority in respect of—

(a) operations within subsection (2),

(b) activities carried on in preparation for, or directly in support of, such operations, or

(c) training of a hazardous nature, or training carried out in a hazardous way, which it is considered needs to be carried out, or carried out in that way, in order to improve or maintain the effectiveness of officers or employees of the public authority with respect to such operations,

is not a "relevant duty of care".

(2) Operations are within this subsection if—

(a) they are operations for dealing with terrorism, civil unrest or serious disorder,

(b) they involve the carrying on of policing or law-enforcement activities, and

(c) officers or employees of the public authority in question come under attack, or face the threat of attack or violent resistance, in the course of the operations.

(3) Any duty of care owed by a public authority in respect of other policing or law-enforcement activities is not a "relevant duty of care" unless it falls within section 2(1)(a), (b) or (d).

(4) In this section "policing or law-enforcement activities" includes—

(a) activities carried on in the exercise of functions that are—

(i) functions of police forces, or

(ii) functions of the same or a similar nature exercisable by public authorities other than police forces;

(b) activities carried on in the exercise of functions of constables employed by a public authority;

(c) activities carried on in the exercise of functions exercisable under Chapter 4 of Part 2 of the Serious Organised Crime and Police Act 2005 (c 15) (protection of witnesses and other persons);

(d) activities carried on to enforce any provision contained in or made under the Immigration Acts.

[1.1504]

6 Emergencies

(1) Any duty of care owed by an organisation within subsection (2) in respect of the way in which it responds to emergency circumstances is not a "relevant duty of care" unless it falls within section 2(1)(a) or (b).

(2) The organisations within this subsection are—

(a) a fire and rescue authority in England and Wales;

[(b) the Scottish Fire and Rescue Service;]

(c) the Northern Ireland Fire and Rescue Service Board;

(d) any other organisation providing a service of responding to emergency circumstances either—

(i) in pursuance of arrangements made with an organisation within paragraph (a), (b) or (c), or

(ii) (if not in pursuance of such arrangements) otherwise than on a commercial basis;

(e) a relevant NHS body;

(f) an organisation providing ambulance services in pursuance of arrangements—

(i) made by, or at the request of, a relevant NHS body, or

(ii) made with the Secretary of State or with the Welsh Ministers;

(g) an organisation providing services for the transport of organs, blood, equipment or personnel in pursuance of arrangements of the kind mentioned in paragraph (f);

(h) an organisation providing a rescue service;

(i) the armed forces.

(3) For the purposes of subsection (1), the way in which an organisation responds to emergency circumstances does not include the way in which—

(a) medical treatment is carried out, or

(b) decisions within subsection (4) are made.

(4) The decisions within this subsection are decisions as to the carrying out of medical treatment, other than decisions as to the order in which persons are to be given such treatment.

(5) Any duty of care owed in respect of the carrying out, or attempted carrying out, of a rescue operation at sea in emergency circumstances is not a "relevant duty of care" unless it falls within section 2(1)(a) or (b).

(6) Any duty of care owed in respect of action taken—

(a) in order to comply with a direction under Schedule 3A to the Merchant Shipping Act 1995 (c 21) (safety directions), or

(b) by virtue of paragraph 4 of that Schedule (action in lieu of direction),

is not a "relevant duty of care" unless it falls within section 2(1)(a) or (b).

(7) In this section—

"emergency circumstances" means circumstances that are present or imminent and—

(a) are causing, or are likely to cause, serious harm or a worsening of such harm, or

(b) are likely to cause the death of a person;

"medical treatment" includes any treatment or procedure of a medical or similar nature;

"relevant NHS body" means—

[(za) the National Health Service Commissioning Board;]

(a) [a clinical commissioning group,] . . . *NHS trust,* Special Health Authority or NHS foundation trust in England;

(b) a Local Health Board, NHS trust or Special Health Authority in Wales;

(c) a Health Board or Special Health Board in Scotland, or the Common Services Agency for the Scottish Health Service;

(d) a Health and Social Services trust or Health and Social Services Board in Northern Ireland;

"serious harm" means—

(a) serious injury to or the serious illness (including mental illness) of a person;

(b) serious harm to the environment (including the life and health of plants and animals);

(c) serious harm to any building or other property.

(8) A reference in this section to emergency circumstances includes a reference to circumstances that are believed to be emergency circumstances.

NOTES

Sub-s (2): para (b) substituted by the Police and Fire Reform (Scotland) Act 2012, s 128(1), Sch 7, Pt 2, para 71, as from 1 April 2013.

Sub-s (7): in the definition of "relevant NHS body", para (za) and the words in square brackets in para (a) are inserted (as from 1 October 2012), words omitted from para (a) repealed (as from 1 April 2013), and the words in italics in para (a) are repealed (as from a day to be appointed), by the Health and Social Care Act 2012, ss 55(2), 179, Sch 5, para 147, Sch 14, para 102.

[1.1505]

7 Child-protection and probation functions

(1) A duty of care to which this section applies is not a "relevant duty of care" unless it falls within section 2(1)(a), (b) or (d).

(2) This section applies to any duty of care that a local authority or other public authority owes in respect of the exercise by it of functions conferred by or under—

(a) Parts 4 and 5 of the Children Act 1989 (c 41),

(b) Part 2 of the Children (Scotland) Act 1995 (c 36), or

(c) Parts 5 and 6 of the Children (Northern Ireland) Order 1995 (SI 1995/755 (NI 2)).

(3) This section also applies to any duty of care that a local probation board[, a provider of probation services] or other public authority owes in respect of the exercise by it of functions conferred by or under—

(a) Chapter 1 of Part 1 of the Criminal Justice and Court Services Act 2000 (c 43),

[(aa) section 13 of the Offender Management Act 2007 (c 21),]

(b) section 27 of the Social Work (Scotland) Act 1968 (c 49), or

(c) Article 4 of the Probation Board (Northern Ireland) Order 1982 (SI 1982/713 (NI 10)).

[(4) This section also applies to any duty of care that a provider of probation services owes in respect of the carrying out by it of activities in pursuance of arrangements under section 3 of the Offender Management Act 2007.]

NOTES

Sub-s (3): words in first pair of square brackets, and para (aa), inserted by the Offender Management Act 2007 (Consequential Amendments) Order 2008, SI 2008/912, art 3, Sch 1, Pt 1, para 25(1), (2)(a).

Sub-s (4): added by SI 2008/912, art 3, Sch 1, Pt 1, para 25(1), (2)(b).

Gross breach

[1.1506]

8 Factors for jury

(1) This section applies where—

(a) it is established that an organisation owed a relevant duty of care to a person, and

(b) it falls to the jury to decide whether there was a gross breach of that duty.

(2) The jury must consider whether the evidence shows that the organisation failed to comply with any health and safety legislation that relates to the alleged breach, and if so—

(a) how serious that failure was;

(b) how much of a risk of death it posed.

(3) The jury may also—

(a) consider the extent to which the evidence shows that there were attitudes, policies, systems or accepted practices within the organisation that were likely to have encouraged any such failure as is mentioned in subsection (2), or to have produced tolerance of it;

(b) have regard to any health and safety guidance that relates to the alleged breach.

(4) This section does not prevent the jury from having regard to any other matters they consider relevant.

(5) In this section "health and safety guidance" means any code, guidance, manual or similar publication that is concerned with health and safety matters and is made or issued (under a statutory provision or otherwise) by an authority responsible for the enforcement of any health and safety legislation.

Remedial orders and publicity orders

[1.1507]

9 Power to order breach etc to be remedied

(1) A court before which an organisation is convicted of corporate manslaughter or corporate homicide may make an order (a "remedial order") requiring the organisation to take specified steps to remedy—

(a) the breach mentioned in section 1(1) ("the relevant breach");

(b) any matter that appears to the court to have resulted from the relevant breach and to have been a cause of the death;

(c) any deficiency, as regards health and safety matters, in the organisation's policies, systems or practices of which the relevant breach appears to the court to be an indication.

(2) A remedial order may be made only on an application by the prosecution specifying the terms of the proposed order.

Any such order must be on such terms (whether those proposed or others) as the court considers appropriate having regard to any representations made, and any evidence adduced, in relation to that matter by the prosecution or on behalf of the organisation.

(3) Before making an application for a remedial order the prosecution must consult such enforcement authority or authorities as it considers appropriate having regard to the nature of the relevant breach.

(4) A remedial order—

(a) must specify a period within which the steps referred to in subsection (1) are to be taken;

(b) may require the organisation to supply to an enforcement authority consulted under subsection (3), within a specified period, evidence that those steps have been taken.

A period specified under this subsection may be extended or further extended by order of the court on an application made before the end of that period or extended period.

(5) An organisation that fails to comply with a remedial order is guilty of an offence, and liable on conviction on indictment to a fine.

[1.1508]

10 Power to order conviction etc to be publicised

(1) A court before which an organisation is convicted of corporate manslaughter or corporate homicide may make an order (a "publicity order") requiring the organisation to publicise in a specified manner—

(a) the fact that it has been convicted of the offence;

(b) specified particulars of the offence;

(c) the amount of any fine imposed;

(d) the terms of any remedial order made.

(2) In deciding on the terms of a publicity order that it is proposing to make, the court must—

(a) ascertain the views of such enforcement authority or authorities (if any) as it considers appropriate, and

(b) have regard to any representations made by the prosecution or on behalf of the organisation.

(3) A publicity order—

(a) must specify a period within which the requirements referred to in subsection (1) are to be complied with;

(b) may require the organisation to supply to any enforcement authority whose views have been ascertained under subsection (2), within a specified period, evidence that those requirements have been complied with.

(4) An organisation that fails to comply with a publicity order is guilty of an offence, and liable on conviction on indictment to a fine.

NOTES

Commencement: 15 February 2010 (except in relation to an offence of corporate manslaughter or corporate homicide committed before that date).

Application to particular categories of organisation

[1.1509]

11 Application to Crown bodies

(1) An organisation that is a servant or agent of the Crown is not immune from prosecution under this Act for that reason.

(2) For the purposes of this Act—

(a) a department or other body listed in Schedule 1, or

(b) a corporation that is a servant or agent of the Crown,

is to be treated as owing whatever duties of care it would owe if it were a corporation that was not a servant or agent of the Crown.

(3) For the purposes of section 2—

(a) a person who is—

(i) employed by or under the Crown for the purposes of a department or other body listed in Schedule 1, or

(ii) employed by a person whose staff constitute a body listed in that Schedule,

is to be treated as employed by that department or body;

(b) any premises occupied for the purposes of—

(i) a department or other body listed in Schedule 1, or

(ii) a person whose staff constitute a body listed in that Schedule,

are to be treated as occupied by that department or body.

(4) For the purposes of sections 2 to 7 anything done purportedly by a department or other body listed in Schedule 1, although in law by the Crown or by the holder of a particular office, is to be treated as done by the department or other body itself.

(5) Subsections (3)(a)(i), (3)(b)(i) and (4) apply in relation to a Northern Ireland department as they apply in relation to a department or other body listed in Schedule 1.

[1.1510]

12 Application to armed forces

(1) In this Act "the armed forces" means any of the naval, military or air forces of the Crown raised under the law of the United Kingdom.

(2) For the purposes of section 2 a person who is a member of the armed forces is to be treated as employed by the Ministry of Defence.

(3) A reference in this Act to members of the armed forces includes a reference to—

(a) members of the reserve forces (within the meaning given by section 1(2) of the Reserve Forces Act 1996 (c 14)) when in service or undertaking training or duties;

(b) persons serving on Her Majesty's vessels (within the meaning given by section 132(1) of the Naval Discipline Act 1957 (c 53)).

[1.1511]

13 Application to police forces

(1) In this Act "police force" means—

(a) a police force within the meaning of—

(i) the Police Act 1996 (c 16), or

(ii) the Police (Scotland) Act 1967 (c 77);

(b) the Police Service of Northern Ireland;

(c) the Police Service of Northern Ireland Reserve;

(d) the British Transport Police Force;

(e) the Civil Nuclear Constabulary;

(f) the Ministry of Defence Police.

(2) For the purposes of this Act a police force is to be treated as owing whatever duties of care it would owe if it were a body corporate.

(3) For the purposes of section 2—

(a) a member of a police force is to be treated as employed by that force;

(b) a special constable appointed for a police area in England and Wales is to be treated as employed by the police force maintained by the [local policing body] for that area;

(c) a special constable appointed for a police force mentioned in paragraph (d) or (f) of subsection (1) is to be treated as employed by that force;

(d) a police cadet undergoing training with a view to becoming a member of a police force mentioned in paragraph (a) or (d) of subsection (1) is to be treated as employed by that force;

(e) a police trainee appointed under section 39 of the Police (Northern Ireland) Act 2000 (c 32) or a police cadet appointed under section 42 of that Act is to be treated as employed by the Police Service of Northern Ireland;

(f) a police reserve trainee appointed under section 40 of that Act is to be treated as employed by the Police Service of Northern Ireland Reserve;

(g) a member of a police force *seconded to the Serious Organised Crime Agency or the National Policing Improvement Agency to serve as a member of its staff is to be treated* as employed by that Agency.

(4) A reference in subsection (3) to a member of a police force is to be read, in the case of a force mentioned in paragraph (a)(ii) of subsection (1), as a reference to a constable of that force.

(5) For the purposes of section 2 any premises occupied for the purposes of a police force are to be treated as occupied by that force.

(6) For the purposes of sections 2 to 7 anything that would be regarded as done by a police force if the force were a body corporate is to be so regarded.

(7) Where—

(a) by virtue of subsection (3) a person is treated for the purposes of section 2 as employed by a police force, and

(b) by virtue of any other statutory provision (whenever made) he is, or is treated as, employed by another organisation,

the person is to be treated for those purposes as employed by both the force and the other organisation.

NOTES

Sub-s (3): words in square brackets in para (b) substituted by the Police Reform and Social Responsibility Act 2011, s 99, Sch 16, Pt 3, para 365, as from 16 January 2012 (for general transitional provisions relating to police reform and the abolition of existing police authorities, see Sch 15 to the 2011 Act, and the Police Reform and Social Responsibility Act 2011 (Commencement No 3 and Transitional Provisions) Order 2011, SI 2011/3019); for the words in italics in para (g) there are substituted the words "seconded to the National Crime Agency to serve as a National Crime Agency officer is to be treated" by the Crime and Courts Act 2013, s 15(3), Sch 8, Pt 2, paras 173, 174, as from a day to be appointed.

[1.1512]

14 Application to partnerships

(1) For the purposes of this Act a partnership is to be treated as owing whatever duties of care it would owe if it were a body corporate.

(2) Proceedings for an offence under this Act alleged to have been committed by a partnership are to be brought in the name of the partnership (and not in that of any of its members).

(3) A fine imposed on a partnership on its conviction of an offence under this Act is to be paid out of the funds of the partnership.

(4) This section does not apply to a partnership that is a legal person under the law by which it is governed.

Miscellaneous

15 *((Procedure, evidence and sentencing) outside the scope of this work.)*

[1.1513]
16 Transfer of functions

(1) This section applies where—
  (a) a person's death has occurred, or is alleged to have occurred, in connection with the carrying out of functions by a relevant public organisation, and
  (b) subsequently there is a transfer of those functions, with the result that they are still carried out but no longer by that organisation.

(2) In this section "relevant public organisation" means—
  (a) a department or other body listed in Schedule 1;
  (b) a corporation that is a servant or agent of the Crown;
  (c) a police force.

(3) Any proceedings instituted against a relevant public organisation after the transfer for an offence under this Act in respect of the person's death are to be instituted against—
  (a) the relevant public organisation, if any, by which the functions mentioned in subsection (1) are currently carried out;
  (b) if no such organisation currently carries out the functions, the relevant public organisation by which the functions were last carried out.

This is subject to subsection (4).

(4) If an order made by the Secretary of State so provides in relation to a particular transfer of functions, the proceedings referred to in subsection (3) may be instituted, or (if they have already been instituted) may be continued, against—
  (a) the organisation mentioned in subsection (1), or
  (b) such relevant public organisation (other than the one mentioned in subsection (1) or the one mentioned in subsection (3)(a) or (b)) as may be specified in the order.

(5) If the transfer occurs while proceedings for an offence under this Act in respect of the person's death are in progress against a relevant public organisation, the proceedings are to be continued against—
  (a) the relevant public organisation, if any, by which the functions mentioned in subsection (1) are carried out as a result of the transfer;
  (b) if as a result of the transfer no such organisation carries out the functions, the same organisation as before.

This is subject to subsection (6).

(6) If an order made by the Secretary of State so provides in relation to a particular transfer of functions, the proceedings referred to in subsection (5) may be continued against—
  (a) the organisation mentioned in subsection (1), or
  (b) such relevant public organisation (other than the one mentioned in subsection (1) or the one mentioned in subsection (5)(a) or (b)) as may be specified in the order.

(7) An order under subsection (4) or (6) is subject to negative resolution procedure.

[1.1514]
17 DPP's consent required for proceedings

Proceedings for an offence of corporate manslaughter—
  (a) may not be instituted in England and Wales without the consent of the Director of Public Prosecutions;
  (b) may not be instituted in Northern Ireland without the consent of the Director of Public Prosecutions for Northern Ireland.

[1.1515]
18 No individual liability

(1) An individual cannot be guilty of aiding, abetting, counselling or procuring the commission of an offence of corporate manslaughter.

[(1A) An individual cannot be guilty of an offence under Part 2 of the Serious Crime Act 2007 (encouraging or assisting crime) by reference to an offence of corporate manslaughter.]

(2) An individual cannot be guilty of aiding, abetting, counselling or procuring, or being art and part in, the commission of an offence of corporate homicide.

NOTES

Sub-s (1A): inserted, in relation to England, Wales and Northern Ireland, by the Serious Crime Act 2007, s 62, as from 1 October 2008.

[1.1516]
19 Convictions under this Act and under health and safety legislation

(1) Where in the same proceedings there is—
  (a) a charge of corporate manslaughter or corporate homicide arising out of a particular set of circumstances, and

(b) a charge against the same defendant of a health and safety offence arising out of some or all of those circumstances,

the jury may, if the interests of justice so require, be invited to return a verdict on each charge.

(2) An organisation that has been convicted of corporate manslaughter or corporate homicide arising out of a particular set of circumstances may, if the interests of justice so require, be charged with a health and safety offence arising out of some or all of those circumstances.

(3) In this section "health and safety offence" means an offence under any health and safety legislation.

[1.1517]

20 Abolition of liability of corporations for manslaughter at common law

The common law offence of manslaughter by gross negligence is abolished in its application to corporations, and in any application it has to other organisations to which section 1 applies.

General and supplemental

[1.1518]

21 Power to extend section 1 to other organisations

(1) The Secretary of State may by order amend section 1 so as to extend the categories of organisation to which that section applies.

(2) An order under this section may make any amendment to this Act that is incidental or supplemental to, or consequential on, an amendment made by virtue of subsection (1).

(3) An order under this section is subject to affirmative resolution procedure.

[1.1519]

22 Power to amend Schedule 1

(1) The Secretary of State may amend Schedule 1 by order.

(2) A statutory instrument containing an order under this section is subject to affirmative resolution procedure, unless the only amendments to Schedule 1 that it makes are amendments within subsection (3).

In that case the instrument is subject to negative resolution procedure.

(3) An amendment is within this subsection if—

(a) it is consequential on a department or other body listed in Schedule 1 changing its name,

(b) in the case of an amendment adding a department or other body to Schedule 1, it is consequential on the transfer to the department or other body of functions all of which were previously exercisable by one or more organisations to which section 1 applies, or

(c) in the case of an amendment removing a department or other body from Schedule 1, it is consequential on—

(i) the abolition of the department or other body, or

(ii) the transfer of all the functions of the department or other body to one or more organisations to which section 1 applies.

NOTES

Orders: the Corporate Manslaughter and Corporate Homicide Act 2007 (Amendment of Schedule 1) Order 2008, SI 2008/396.

23, 23A, 24 *(S 23 (Power to extend section 2(2)), s 23A (Powers of Department of Justice in Northern Ireland), s 24 (Orders) outside the scope of this work.)*

[1.1520]

25 Interpretation

In this Act—

"armed forces" has the meaning given by section 12(1);

"corporation" does not include a corporation sole but includes any body corporate wherever incorporated;

"employee" means an individual who works under a contract of employment or apprenticeship (whether express or implied and, if express, whether oral or in writing), and related expressions are to be construed accordingly; see also sections 11(3)(a), 12(2) and 13(3) (which apply for the purposes of section 2);

"employers' association" has the meaning given by section 122 of the Trade Union and Labour Relations (Consolidation) Act 1992 (c 52) or Article 4 of the Industrial Relations (Northern Ireland) Order 1992 (SI 1992/807 (NI 5));

"enforcement authority" means an authority responsible for the enforcement of any health and safety legislation;

"health and safety legislation" means any statutory provision dealing with health and safety matters, including in particular provision contained in the Health and Safety at Work etc Act 1974 (c 37) or the Health and Safety at Work (Northern Ireland) Order 1978 (SI 1978/1039 (NI 9));

"member", in relation to the armed forces, is to be read in accordance with section 12(3);

"partnership" means—

(a) a partnership within the Partnership Act 1890 (c 39), or

(b) a limited partnership registered under the Limited Partnerships Act 1907 (c 24),

or a firm or entity of a similar character formed under the law of a country or territory outside the United Kingdom;

"police force" has the meaning given by section 13(1);

"premises" includes land, buildings and moveable structures;

"public authority" has the same meaning as in section 6 of the Human Rights Act 1998 (c 42) (disregarding subsections (3)(a) and (4) of that section);

"publicity order" means an order under section 10(1);

"remedial order" means an order under section 9(1);

"statutory provision", except in section 15, means provision contained in, or in an instrument made under, any Act, any Act of the Scottish Parliament or any Northern Ireland legislation;

"trade union" has the meaning given by section 1 of the Trade Union and Labour Relations (Consolidation) Act 1992 (c 52) or Article 3 of the Industrial Relations (Northern Ireland) Order 1992 (SI 1992/807 (NI 5)).

26 *(Introduces Sch 2 (Minor and consequential amendments).)*

[1.1521]
27 Commencement and savings

(1) The preceding provisions of this Act come into force in accordance with provision made by order by the Secretary of State [(subject to subsection (1A))].

[(1A) The power in subsection (1) is exercisable by the Department of Justice in Northern Ireland (and not by the Secretary of State) for the purposes of the law of Northern Ireland.]

(2) An order [of the Secretary of State] bringing into force paragraph (d) of section 2(1) is subject to affirmative resolution procedure.

(3) Section 1 does not apply in relation to anything done or omitted before the commencement of that section.

(4) Section 20 does not affect any liability, investigation, legal proceeding or penalty for or in respect of an offence committed wholly or partly before the commencement of that section.

(5) For the purposes of subsection (4) an offence is committed wholly or partly before the commencement of section 20 if any of the conduct or events alleged to constitute the offence occurred before that commencement.

NOTES

The words in square brackets in sub-ss (1), (2) were inserted, and sub-s (1A) was inserted, by the Northern Ireland Act 1998 (Devolution of Policing and Justice Functions) Order 2010, SI 2010/976, art 7, Sch 9, paras 1, 5, as from 12 April 2010.

Orders: the Corporate Manslaughter and Corporate Homicide Act 2007 (Commencement No 1) Order 2008, SI 2008/401; the Corporate Manslaughter and Corporate Homicide Act 2007 (Commencement No 2) Order 2010, SI 2010/276; the Corporate Manslaughter and Corporate Homicide Act 2007 (Commencement No 3) Order 2011, SI 2011/1867 (made under sub-s (1))..

[1.1522]
28 Extent and territorial application

(1) Subject to subsection (2), this Act extends to England and Wales, Scotland and Northern Ireland.

(2) An amendment made by this Act extends to the same part or parts of the United Kingdom as the provision to which it relates.

(3) Section 1 applies if the harm resulting in death is sustained in the United Kingdom or—

(a) within the seaward limits of the territorial sea adjacent to the United Kingdom;

(b) on a ship registered under Part 2 of the Merchant Shipping Act 1995 (c 21);

(c) on a British-controlled aircraft as defined in section 92 of the Civil Aviation Act 1982 (c 16);

(d) on a British-controlled hovercraft within the meaning of that section as applied in relation to hovercraft by virtue of provision made under the Hovercraft Act 1968 (c 59);

(e) in any place to which an Order in Council under section 10(1) of the Petroleum Act 1998 (c 17) applies (criminal jurisdiction in relation to offshore activities).

(4) For the purposes of subsection (3)(b) to (d) harm sustained on a ship, aircraft or hovercraft includes harm sustained by a person who—

(a) is then no longer on board the ship, aircraft or hovercraft in consequence of the wrecking of it or of some other mishap affecting it or occurring on it, and

(b) sustains the harm in consequence of that event.

[1.1523]
29 Short title

This Act may be cited as the Corporate Manslaughter and Corporate Homicide Act 2007.

SCHEDULES

SCHEDULE 1
LIST OF GOVERNMENT DEPARTMENTS ETC

Section 1

[1.1524]

. . .
Attorney General's Office
Cabinet Office
Central Office of Information
Crown Office and Procurator Fiscal Service
Crown Prosecution Service
[. . .]
[Department for Business, Innovation and Skills]
[. . .]
Department for Communities and Local Government
. . .
Department for Culture, Media and Sport
. . .
[Department for Education]
[Department of Energy and Climate Change]
Department for Environment, Food and Rural Affairs
[. . .]
Department for International Development
Department for Transport
Department for Work and Pensions
Department of Health
. . .
Export Credits Guarantee Department
Foreign and Commonwealth Office
Forestry Commission
General Register Office for Scotland
Government Actuary's Department
Her Majesty's Land Registry
Her Majesty's Revenue and Customs
Her Majesty's Treasury
Home Office
Ministry of Defence
[Ministry of Justice (including the Scotland Office and the Wales Office)]
National Archives
National Archives of Scotland
[National Crime Agency]
. . .
National Savings and Investments
National School of Government
Northern Ireland Audit Office
Northern Ireland Court Service
Northern Ireland Office
Office for National Statistics
. . .
Office of Her Majesty's Chief Inspector of Education and Training in Wales
Ordnance Survey
. . .
Public Prosecution Service for Northern Ireland
Registers of Scotland Executive Agency
Revenue and Customs Prosecutions Office
Royal Mint
Scottish Executive
Serious Fraud Office
Treasury Solicitor's Department
UK Trade and Investment
Welsh Assembly Government

NOTES

Entry "Assets Recovery Agency" (omitted) repealed by the Serious Crime Act 2007, s 74(2)(g), Sch 8, Pt 7, para 178.

Part 1 Statutes

Entry "Department for Business, Enterprise and Regulatory Reform" (omitted) originally inserted by the Corporate Manslaughter and Corporate Homicide Act 2007 (Amendment of Schedule 1) Order 2008, SI 2008/396, art 2(1), (2), and repealed by the Secretary of State for Business, Innovation and Skills Order 2009, SI 2009/2748, art 8, Schedule, Pt 1, para 8(b), as from 13 November 2009.

Entry "Department for Business, Innovation and Skills" inserted by SI 2009/2748, art 8, Schedule, Pt 1, para 8(a), as from 13 November 2009.

Entry "Department for Children, Schools and Families" (omitted) originally inserted by SI 2008/396, art 2(1), (2), and repealed by the Secretary of State for Education Order 2010, SI 2010/1836, art 6, Schedule, Pt 1, para 4(a), as from 18 August 2010.

Entry "Department for Constitutional Affairs (including the Scotland Office and the Wales Office)" (omitted) repealed by SI 2008/396, art 2(1), (3).

Entry "Department for Education and Skills" (omitted) repealed by SI 2008/396, art 2(1), (3).

Entry "Department for Education" inserted by SI 2010/1836, art 6, Schedule, Pt 1, para 4(b), as from 18 August 2010.

Entry "Department of Energy and Climate Change" inserted by SI 2009/229, art 9, Sch 2, Pt 1, para 5, as from 5 March 2009.

Entry "Department for Innovation, Universities and Skills" (omitted) originally inserted by SI 2008/396, art 2(1), (2), and repealed by SI 2009/2748, art 8, Schedule, Pt 1, para 8(c), as from 13 November 2009.

Entry "Department of Trade and Industry" (omitted) repealed by SI 2008/396, art 2(1), (3).

Entry "Ministry of Justice (including the Scotland Office and the Wales Office)" inserted by SI 2008/396, art 2(1), (2).

Entry "National Audit Office" (omitted) repealed by Budget Responsibility and National Audit Act 2011, s 26, Sch 5, Pt 2, para 32(1), as from 1 April 2012. Note that Sch 5, Pt 2, para 32(2) provides that in relation to any offence alleged to have been committed by old NAO before the coming into force of sub-para (1), proceedings may be brought or continued against NAO as if anything done by, on behalf of or in relation to old NAO had been done by, on behalf of or in relation to NAO. By virtue of Sch 5, Pt 1, para 1 "old NAO" means the National Audit Office established by section 3 of the National Audit Act 1983.

Entry "National Crime Agency" inserted by the Crime and Courts Act 2013, s 15(3), Sch 8, Pt 2, paras 173, 175, as from a day to be appointed.

Entry "Office of the Deputy Prime Minister" (omitted) repealed by SI 2008/396, art 2(1), (3).

Entry "Privy Council Office" (omitted) repealed by SI 2008/396, art 2(1), (3).

SCHEDULE 2

(Sch 2 (Minor and Consequential Amendments) contains amendments to enactments that are outside the scope of this work.)

TRIBUNALS, COURTS AND ENFORCEMENT ACT 2007

(2007 c 15)

ARRANGEMENT OF SECTIONS

PART 1
TRIBUNALS AND INQUIRIES

CHAPTER 1
TRIBUNAL JUDICIARY: INDEPENDENCE AND SENIOR PRESIDENT

CHAPTER 2
FIRST-TIER TRIBUNAL AND UPPER TRIBUNAL

Establishment

CHAPTER 4
ADMINISTRATIVE MATTERS IN RESPECT OF CERTAIN TRIBUNALS

CHAPTER 6
SUPPLEMENTARY

An Act to make provision about tribunals and inquiries; to establish an Administrative Justice and Tribunals Council; to amend the law relating to judicial appointments and appointments to the Law Commission; to amend the law relating to the enforcement of judgments and debts; to make further provision about the management and relief of debt; to make provision protecting cultural objects from seizure or forfeiture in certain circumstances; to amend the law relating to the taking of possession of land affected by compulsory purchase; to alter the powers of the High Court in judicial review applications; and for connected purposes

[19 July 2007]

NOTES

Only those provisions of this Act relevant to employment law are reproduced. Provisions not reproduced are not annotated. The provisions reproduced here extend to the whole of the United Kingdom (s 147).

See *Harvey* PI.

PART 1
TRIBUNALS AND INQUIRIES

CHAPTER 1
TRIBUNAL JUDICIARY: INDEPENDENCE AND SENIOR PRESIDENT

[1.1525]

1 Independence of tribunal judiciary

In section 3 of the Constitutional Reform Act 2005 (c 4) (guarantee of continued judicial independence), after subsection (7) insert—

"(7A) In this section "the judiciary" also includes every person who—
- (a) holds an office listed in Schedule 14 or holds an office listed in subsection (7B), and
- (b) but for this subsection would not be a member of the judiciary for the purposes of this section.

(7B) The offices are those of—
- (a) Senior President of Tribunals;
- (b) President of Employment Tribunals (Scotland);
- (c) Vice President of Employment Tribunals (Scotland);
- (d) member of a panel of chairmen of Employment Tribunals (Scotland);
- (e) member of a panel of members of employment tribunals that is not a panel of chairmen;
- (f) adjudicator appointed under section 5 of the Criminal Injuries Compensation Act 1995."

[1.1526]

2 Senior President of Tribunals

(1) Her Majesty may, on the recommendation of the Lord Chancellor, appoint a person to the office of Senior President of Tribunals.

(2) Schedule 1 makes further provision about the Senior President of Tribunals and about recommendations for appointment under subsection (1).

(3) A holder of the office of Senior President of Tribunals must, in carrying out the functions of that office, have regard to—
- (a) the need for tribunals to be accessible,
- (b) the need for proceedings before tribunals—
  - (i) to be fair, and
  - (ii) to be handled quickly and efficiently,
- (c) the need for members of tribunals to be experts in the subject-matter of, or the law to be applied in, cases in which they decide matters, and
- (d) the need to develop innovative methods of resolving disputes that are of a type that may be brought before tribunals.

(4) In subsection (3) "tribunals" means—
- (a) the First-tier Tribunal,
- (b) the Upper Tribunal,
- (c) employment tribunals, [and]
- (d) the Employment Appeal Tribunal, . . .
- (e) . . .

NOTES

Sub-s (4): word "and" in square brackets at the end of para (c) inserted, and para (e) (and the word immediately preceding it) repealed, by the Transfer of Functions of the Asylum and Immigration Tribunal Order 2010, SI 2010/21, art 5(1), Sch 1, paras 36, 37, as from 15 February 2010 (for general savings and transitional provisions in relation to existing cases before the Asylum and Immigration Tribunal, etc, see Sch 4 to the 2010 Order).

CHAPTER 2
FIRST-TIER TRIBUNAL AND UPPER TRIBUNAL

Establishment

[1.1527]

3 The First-tier Tribunal and the Upper Tribunal

(1) There is to be a tribunal, known as the First-tier Tribunal, for the purpose of exercising the functions conferred on it under or by virtue of this Act or any other Act.
(2) There is to be a tribunal, known as the Upper Tribunal, for the purpose of exercising the functions conferred on it under or by virtue of this Act or any other Act.
(3) Each of the First-tier Tribunal, and the Upper Tribunal, is to consist of its judges and other members.
(4) The Senior President of Tribunals is to preside over both of the First-tier Tribunal and the Upper Tribunal.
(5) The Upper Tribunal is to be a superior court of record.

NOTES

Commencement: 3 November 2008.

CHAPTER 4
ADMINISTRATIVE MATTERS IN RESPECT OF CERTAIN TRIBUNALS

[1.1528]

39 The general duty

(1) The Lord Chancellor is under a duty to ensure that there is an efficient and effective system to support the carrying on of the business of—
- (a) the First-tier Tribunal,
- (b) the Upper Tribunal,
- (c) employment tribunals, [and]
- (d) the Employment Appeal Tribunal, . . .
- (e) . . .

and that appropriate services are provided for those tribunals (referred to in this section and in sections 40 and 41 as "the tribunals").
(2) Any reference in this section, or in section 40 or 41, to the Lord Chancellor's general duty in relation to the tribunals is to his duty under subsection (1).
(3) The Lord Chancellor must annually prepare and lay before each House of Parliament a report as to the way in which he has discharged his general duty in relation to the tribunals.

NOTES

Sub-s (1): word "and" in square brackets at the end of para (c) inserted, and para (e) (and the word immediately preceding it) repealed, by the Transfer of Functions of the Asylum and Immigration Tribunal Order 2010, SI 2010/21, art 5(1), Sch 1, paras 36, 40, as from 15 February 2010 (for general savings and transitional provisions in relation to existing cases before the Asylum and Immigration Tribunal, etc, see Sch 4 to the 2010 Order).

[1.1529]

40 Tribunal staff and services

(1) The Lord Chancellor may appoint such staff as appear to him appropriate for the purpose of discharging his general duty in relation to the tribunals.
(2) Subject to subsections (3) and (4), the Lord Chancellor may enter into such contracts with other persons for the provision, by them or their sub-contractors, of staff or services as appear to him appropriate for the purpose of discharging his general duty in relation to the tribunals.
(3) The Lord Chancellor may not enter into contracts for the provision of staff to discharge functions which involve making judicial decisions or exercising any judicial discretion.
(4) The Lord Chancellor may not enter into contracts for the provision of staff to carry out the administrative work of the tribunals unless an order made by the Lord Chancellor authorises him to do so.
(5) Before making an order under subsection (4) the Lord Chancellor must consult the Senior President of Tribunals as to what effect (if any) the order might have on the proper and efficient administration of justice.
(6) An order under subsection (4) may authorise the Lord Chancellor to enter into contracts for the provision of staff to discharge functions—
- (a) wholly or to the extent specified in the order,
- (b) generally or in cases or areas specified in the order, and
- (c) unconditionally or subject to the fulfilment of conditions specified in the order.

NOTES

Orders: the Contracting Out (Administrative Work of Tribunals) Order 2009, SI 2009/121. This Order (as amended), which came into force on 2 March 2009, enables the Lord Chancellor to enter into contracts with other persons for the provision of staff for carrying out the administrative work of the tribunals listed in art 2 of the Order. These tribunals are: (a) the First-tier Tribunal, (b) the Upper Tribunal, (c) employment tribunals, and (d) the Employment Appeal Tribunal.

[1.1530]

41 Provision of accommodation

(1) The Lord Chancellor may provide, equip, maintain and manage such tribunal buildings, offices and other accommodation as appear to him appropriate for the purpose of discharging his general duty in relation to the tribunals.

(2) The Lord Chancellor may enter into such arrangements for the provision, equipment, maintenance or management of tribunal buildings, offices or other accommodation as appear to him appropriate for the purpose of discharging his general duty in relation to the tribunals.

(3) The powers under—

(a) section 2 of the Commissioners of Works Act 1852 (c 28) (acquisition by agreement), and

(b) section 228(1) of the Town and Country Planning Act 1990 (c 8) (compulsory acquisition),

to acquire land necessary for the public service are to be treated as including power to acquire land for the purpose of its provision under arrangements entered into under subsection (2).

(4) In this section "tribunal building" means any place where any of the tribunals sits, including the precincts of any building in which it sits.

[1.1531]

42 Fees

(1) The Lord Chancellor may by order prescribe fees payable in respect of—

(a) anything dealt with by the First-tier Tribunal,

(b) anything dealt with by the Upper Tribunal,

(c) . . .

(d) anything dealt with by an added tribunal, and

(e) mediation conducted by staff appointed under section 40(1).

(2) An order under subsection (1) may, in particular, contain provision as to—

(a) scales or rates of fees;

(b) exemptions from or reductions in fees;

(c) remission of fees in whole or in part.

(3) In subsection (1)(d) "added tribunal" means a tribunal specified in an order made by the Lord Chancellor.

(4) A tribunal may be specified in an order under subsection (3) only if—

(a) it is established by or under an enactment, whenever passed or made, and

(b) is not an ordinary court of law.

(5) Before making an order under this section, the Lord Chancellor must consult—

(a) the Senior President of Tribunals, and

(b) the Administrative Justice and Tribunals Council.

(6) The making of an order under subsection (1) requires the consent of the Treasury except where the order contains provision only for the purpose of altering amounts payable by way of fees already prescribed under that subsection.

(7) The Lord Chancellor must take such steps as are reasonably practicable to bring information about fees under subsection (1) to the attention of persons likely to have to pay them.

(8) Fees payable under subsection (1) are recoverable summarily as a civil debt.

(9) Subsection (8) does not apply to the recovery in Scotland of fees payable under this section.

(10) Until the Administrative Justice and Tribunals Council first has ten members appointed under paragraph 1(2) of Schedule 7, the reference to that council in subsection (5) is to be read as a reference to the Council on Tribunals.

NOTES

Sub-s (1): para (c) repealed by the Transfer of Functions of the Asylum and Immigration Tribunal Order 2010, SI 2010/21, art 5(1), Sch 1, paras 36, 41, as from 15 February 2010 (for general savings and transitional provisions in relation to existing cases before the Asylum and Immigration Tribunal, etc, see Sch 4 to the 2010 Order).

Orders: the Upper Tribunal (Lands Chamber) Fees Order 2009, SI 2009/1114; the First-tier Tribunal (Gambling) Fees Order 2010, SI 2010/42; the First-tier Tribunal (Gambling) Fees (Amendment) Order 2010, SI 2010/633; the Upper Tribunal (Lands Chamber) Fees (Amendment) Order 2010, SI 2010/2601; the Upper Tribunal (Immigration and Asylum Chamber) (Judicial Review) (England and Wales) Fees Order 2011, SI 2011/2344; the First-tier Tribunal (Immigration and Asylum Chamber) Fees Order 2011, SI 2011/2841.

Draft Orders: see the Employment Tribunals and the Employment Appeal Tribunal Fees Order 2013 at **[2.1707]** and the Added Tribunals (Employment Tribunals and Employment Appeal Tribunal) Order 2013 at **[2.1708]**. The Government has announced that the date for implementation of these draft Orders will be 29 July 2013 (subject to Parliamentary approval of the two draft Orders).

[1.1532]

43 Report by Senior President of Tribunals

(1) Each year the Senior President of Tribunals must give the Lord Chancellor a report covering, in relation to relevant tribunal cases—

(a) matters that the Senior President of Tribunals wishes to bring to the attention of the Lord Chancellor, and
(b) matters that the Lord Chancellor has asked the Senior President of Tribunals to cover in the report.

(2) The Lord Chancellor must publish each report given to him under subsection (1).

(3) In this section "relevant tribunal cases" means—
(a) cases coming before the First-tier Tribunal,
(b) cases coming before the Upper Tribunal,
(c) cases coming before the Employment Appeal Tribunal, . . . [and]
(d) cases coming before employment tribunals[, . . .
(e) . . .].

NOTES

Commencement: 3 November 2008.

Sub-s (3) is amended as follows:

The original word "and" omitted from para (c) was repealed, and para (e) (and the word immediately preceding it) was originally inserted, by the UK Borders Act 2007, ss 56(1), 58, Schedule.

The word "and" in square brackets at the end of para (c) was reinserted, and para (e) (and the word immediately preceding it) was repealed, by the Transfer of Functions of the Asylum and Immigration Tribunal Order 2010, SI 2010/21, art 5(1), Sch 1, paras 36, 42, as from 15 February 2010 (for general savings and transitional provisions in relation to existing cases before the Asylum and Immigration Tribunal, etc, see Sch 4 to the 2010 Order).

CHAPTER 6
SUPPLEMENTARY

[1.1533]

49 Orders and regulations under Part 1: supplemental and procedural provisions

(1) Power—
(a) of the Lord Chancellor to make an order, or regulations, under this Part,
(b) of the Senior President of Tribunals to make an order under section 7(9), or
(c) of the Scottish Ministers, or the Welsh Ministers, to make an order under paragraph 25(2) of Schedule 7,

is exercisable by statutory instrument.

(2) The Statutory Instruments Act 1946 (c 36) shall apply in relation to the power to make orders conferred on the Senior President of Tribunals by section 7(9) as if the Senior President of Tribunals were a Minister of the Crown.

(3) Any power mentioned in subsection (1) includes power to make different provision for different purposes.

(4) Without prejudice to the generality of subsection (3), power to make an order under section 30 or 31 includes power to make different provision in relation to England, Scotland, Wales and Northern Ireland respectively.

(5) No order mentioned in subsection (6) is to be made unless a draft of the statutory instrument containing it (whether alone or with other provision) has been laid before, and approved by a resolution of, each House of Parliament.

(6) Those orders are—
(a) an order under section 11(8), 13(6) or (14), 30, 31(1), 32, 33, 34, 35, 36, 37 or 42(3);
(b) an order under paragraph 15 of Schedule 4;
(c) an order under section 42(1)(a) to (d) that provides for fees to be payable in respect of things for which fees have never been payable;
(d) an order under section 31(2), (7) or (9), or paragraph 30(1) of Schedule 5, that contains provision taking the form of an amendment or repeal of an enactment comprised in an Act.

(7) A statutory instrument that—
(a) contains—
(i) an order mentioned in subsection (8), or
(ii) regulations under Part 3 of Schedule 9, and
(b) is not subject to any requirement that a draft of the instrument be laid before, and approved by a resolution of, each House of Parliament,

is subject to annulment in pursuance of a resolution of either House of Parliament.

(8) Those orders are—
(a) an order made by the Lord Chancellor under this Part;
(b) an order made by the Senior President of Tribunals under section 7(9).

(9) A statutory instrument that contains an order made by the Scottish Ministers under paragraph 25(2) of Schedule 7 is subject to annulment in pursuance of a resolution of the Scottish Parliament.

(10) A statutory instrument that contains an order made by the Welsh Ministers under paragraph 25(2) of Schedule 7 is subject to annulment in pursuance of a resolution of the National Assembly for Wales.

NOTES

Draft Orders: see the Employment Tribunals and the Employment Appeal Tribunal Fees Order 2013 at **[2.1707]** and the Added Tribunals (Employment Tribunals and Employment Appeal Tribunal) Order 2013 at **[2.1708]**. The Government has announced that the date for implementation of these draft Orders will be 29 July 2013 (subject to Parliamentary approval of the two draft Orders).

EMPLOYMENT ACT 2008

(2008 c 24)

An Act to make provision about the procedure for the resolution of employment disputes; to provide for compensation for financial loss in cases of unlawful underpayment or non-payment; to make provision about the enforcement of minimum wages legislation and the application of the national minimum wage to Cadet Force Adult Volunteers and voluntary workers; to make provision about the enforcement of offences under the Employment Agencies Act 1973; to make provision about the right of trade unions to expel or exclude members on the grounds of membership of a political party; and for connected purposes

[13 November 2008]

[1.1534]

NOTES

This Act received Royal assent on 13 November 2008 and is, to a large extent, amending only. A brief summary of the effect of each section and Schedule is given below (with the exception of ss 22, 23 which are reproduced in full). As to the commencement of this Act, see s 22 below, the Employment Act 2008 (Commencement No 1, Transitional Provisions and Savings) Order 2008, SI 2008/3232, and the Employment Act 2008 (Commencement No 2, Transitional Provisions and Savings) Order 2009, SI 2009/603. All amendments made by this Act have been incorporated at the appropriate place. Amendments to the Employment Act 2002 are at **[1.1225]** et seq; amendments to the Employment Rights Act 1996 are at **[1.743]** et seq; amendments to the Trade Union and Labour Relations (Consolidation) Act 1992 are at **[1.241]** et seq; amendments to the Employment Tribunals Act 1996 are at **[1.720]** et seq; amendments to the National Minimum Wage Act 1998 are at **[1.1119]** et seq; and amendments to the Employment Agencies Act 1973 are at **[1.20]** et seq. Transitional provisions and savings have also been noted where relevant.

See *Harvey* AII(7), BI(4).

Dispute resolution

1 Statutory dispute resolution procedures

(Repeals the Employment Act 2002, ss 29–33 and Schs 2–4.)

2 Procedural fairness

(Repeals the Employment Rights Act 1996, s 98A.)

3 Non-compliance with statutory Codes of Practice

(Inserts the Trade Union and Labour Relations (Consolidation) Act 1992, s 207A, Sch A2, and amends the Employment Rights Act 1996, s 124A.)

4 Determination of proceedings without hearing

(Amends the Employment Tribunals Act 1996, s 7.)

5 Conciliation before bringing of proceedings

(Amends the Employment Tribunals Act 1996, s 18 and is repealed by the Enterprise and Regulatory Reform Act 2013, s 7(2), Sch 1, para 12, as from a day to be appointed.)

6 Conciliation after bringing of proceedings

(Repeals the Employment Tribunals Act 1996, ss 18(2A), 19(2).)

7 Compensation for financial loss

(Amends the Employment Rights Act 1996, ss 24, 163.)

National minimum wage etc

8 Arrears payable in cases of non-compliance

(Amends the National Minimum Wage Act 1998, s 17 and the Agricultural Wages Act 1948, s 3A. It also provides that: (i) the amendments to s 17 of the 1998 Act do not affect that section as it has effect for the purposes of the Agricultural Wages (Scotland) Act 1949, or the Agricultural Wages (Regulation) (Northern Ireland) Order 1977 (SI 1977/2151), and (ii) the amendments made by this section apply in relation to a pay reference period (within the meaning of the National Minimum Wage Act 1998) ending before, as well as after, this section comes into force. Repealed in part by the Enterprise and Regulatory Reform Act 2013, s 72(4), Sch 20, as from a day to be appointed.)

9 Notices of underpayment
(Section 9(1) substitutes the National Minimum Wage Act 1998, ss 19, 19A–19H for the existing ss 19–22F. Section 9(2) provides that in any period after the coming into force of sub-s (1) above and before the coming into force of s 62 of the Tribunals, Courts and Enforcement Act 2007, s 19E(a) of the National Minimum Wage Act 1998 (as substituted by sub-s (1)), shall have effect as if for "under section 85 of the County Courts Act 1984" there were substituted "by execution issued from the county court". Section 9(3)–(6) amend the National Minimum Wage Act 1998, s 51, the Employment Tribunals Act 1996, s 4, the Commissioners for Revenue and Customs Act 2005, s 44, and the Agricultural Wages Act 1948, s 3A. Section 9(7) provides that nothing in this section (or Part 2 of the Schedule) affects any provision of the National Minimum Wage Act 1998 as that provision has effect for the purposes of the Agricultural Wages (Scotland) Act 1949, or the Agricultural Wages (Regulation) (Northern Ireland) Order 1977 (SI 1977/2151). Repealed in part by the Enterprise and Regulatory Reform Act 2013, s 72(4), Sch 20, as from a day to be appointed.)

10 Powers of officers to take copies of records
(Section 10(1)–(3) amend the National Minimum Wage Act 1998, s 14. Section 10(4) provides that nothing in this section (or Part 3 of the Schedule) affects s 14 of the 1998 Act as that provision has effect for the purposes of the Agricultural Wages (Scotland) Act 1949, or the Agricultural Wages (Regulation) (Northern Ireland) Order 1977 (SI 1977/2151).)

11 Offences: mode of trial and penalties
(Amends the National Minimum Wage Act 1998, ss 31, 33 and further provides that nothing in this section or Part 4 of the Schedule) affects ss 31 or 33 of the 1998 Act as they have effect for the purposes of the Agricultural Wages (Scotland) Act 1949, or the Agricultural Wages (Regulation) (Northern Ireland) Order 1977 (SI 1977/2151).)

12 Powers to investigate criminal offences
(Amends the Finance Act 2007, s 84 and the Criminal Law (Consolidation) (Scotland) Act 1995, s 23A.)

13 Cadet Force Adult Volunteers
(Inserts the National Minimum Wage Act 1998, s 37A.)

14 Voluntary workers
(Inserts the National Minimum Wage Act 1998, s 44(1A).)

Employment agencies

15 Offences: mode of trial and penalties
(Amends the Employment Agencies Act 1973, ss 3B, 5, 6.)

16 Enforcement powers
(Amends the Employment Agencies Act 1973, s 9.)

17 Offences by partnerships in Scotland
(Amends the Employment Agencies Act 1973, s 11.)

Miscellaneous

18 Employment agencies and national minimum wage legislation: information
(Inserts the National Minimum Wage Act 1998, s 15(5A) and amends the Employment Agencies Act 1973, s 9.)

19 Exclusion or expulsion from trade union for membership of political party
(Inserts the Trade Union and Labour Relations (Consolidation) Act 1992, s 174(4C)–(4H) and amends s 176 of that Act.)

General

20 Repeals
(Introduces the Schedule to this Act (repeals).)

21 Extent
(Provides only that an amendment or repeal effected by this Act has the same extent as the enactment (or the relevant part of the enactment) to which it relates.)

[1.1535]
22 Commencement
(1) The provisions of this Act come into force as follows—
- (a) sections 1 to 9 and Parts 1 and 2 of the Schedule come into force on such day as the Secretary of State may by order appoint;
- (b) section 10 and Part 3 of the Schedule come into force at the end of the period of two months beginning with the day on which this Act is passed;
- (c) sections 11 and 12 and Part 4 of the Schedule come into force on such day as the Secretary of State may by order appoint;
- (d) sections 13 and 14 come into force at the end of the period of two months beginning with the day on which this Act is passed;

(e) sections 15 to 17 and Part 5 of the Schedule come into force on 6 April 2009;
(f) sections 18 and 19 come into force on such day as the Secretary of State may by order appoint;
(g) the remaining provisions of this Act come into force on the day on which this Act is passed.

(2) An order under subsection (1) is to be made by statutory instrument.

(3) An order under subsection (1) may—
(a) appoint different days for different purposes;
(b) contain transitional provision, or savings.

NOTES

Commencement: 13 November 2008.

Orders: the Employment Act 2008 (Commencement No 1, Transitional Provisions and Savings) Order 2008, SI 2008/3232; the Employment Act 2008 (Commencement No 2, Transitional Provisions and Savings) Order 2009, SI 2009/603.

[1.1536]
23 Short title

This Act may be cited as the Employment Act 2008.

NOTES

Commencement: 13 November 2008.

Schedule

(Contains various repeals which are noted at the appropriate place where they are within the scope of this work.)

EDUCATION AND SKILLS ACT 2008 (NOTE)

(2008 c 25)

[1.1537]

NOTES

Part 1 of this Act was reproduced in previous editions along with certain ancillary provisions. That Part (Duty to Participate in Education or Training: England) places a duty on young people to participate in education or training until the age of 18 (or until attaining a level 3 qualification if earlier). Section 173(4) of the Act provides that the Act will come into force in accordance with provision made by the Secretary of State by Order.

As of 6 April 2013 Part 1 had not been brought into force and no proposals to bring it into force had been announced. This Act has therefore been omitted from this edition.

PENSIONS ACT 2008

(2008 c 30)

ARRANGEMENT OF SECTIONS

PART 1
PENSION SCHEME MEMBERSHIP FOR JOBHOLDERS

CHAPTER 1
EMPLOYERS' DUTIES

CHAPTER 8
APPLICATION AND INTERPRETATION

Workers

General

PART 6
GENERAL

An Act to make provision relating to pensions; and for connected purposes

[26 November 2008]

NOTES

Only certain parts of this Act most relevant to employment law are reproduced. Provisions omitted are not annotated. Duties of employers to enrol employees are being brought into effect in stages from 1 October 2012 (see the Employers' Duties (Implementation) Regulations 2010, SI 2010/4, reg 4 at **[2.1273]**, as amended.

Employment Appeal Tribunal: an appeal lies to the Employment Appeal Tribunal on any question of law arising from any decision of, or in any proceedings before, an employment tribunal under or by virtue of this Act; see the Employment Tribunals Act 1996, s 21(1)(gd) at **[1.713]**.

See *Harvey* BI(8).

PART 1
PENSION SCHEME MEMBERSHIP FOR JOBHOLDERS

CHAPTER 1
EMPLOYERS' DUTIES

Jobholders

[1.1538]

1 Jobholders

(1) For the purposes of this Part a jobholder is a worker—

- (a) who is working or ordinarily works in Great Britain under the worker's contract,
- (b) who is aged at least 16 and under 75, and
- (c) to whom qualifying earnings are payable by the employer in the relevant pay reference period (see sections 13 and 15).

(2) Where a jobholder has more than one employer, or a succession of employers, this Chapter applies separately in relation to each employment.

(3) Accordingly—

- (a) references to the employer are references to the employer concerned;
- (b) references to membership of a pension scheme are references to membership in relation to the employment concerned.

NOTES

Commencement: 30 June 2012.

Employers' duties

[1.1539]

2 Continuity of scheme membership

(1) If a jobholder is an active member of a qualifying scheme, the employer must not take any action, or make any omission, by which (without the jobholder ceasing to be employed by the employer)—

(a) the jobholder ceases to be an active member of the scheme, or

(b) the scheme ceases to be a qualifying scheme.

(2) Subsection (1) is not contravened if the jobholder remains an active member of another qualifying scheme.

[(3) Subsection (1) is not contravened if by virtue of section 5 the jobholder becomes an active member of an automatic enrolment scheme with effect from—

(a) the day after the cessation referred to in paragraph (a) or (b) of subsection (1), or

(b) a day within the prescribed period (if a period is prescribed).]

(4) Subsection (1) is not contravened if the action or omission is at the jobholder's request.

(5) In this Part as it applies in the case of any jobholder, references to a qualifying scheme are references to a pension scheme which is a qualifying scheme in relation to that jobholder (see section 16).

NOTES

Commencement: 30 June 2012.

Sub-s (3): substituted by the Pensions Act 2011, s 4(1), as from 30 June 2012.

Regulations: the Occupational and Personal Pension Schemes (Automatic Enrolment) Regulations 2010, SI 2010/772 at **[2.1362]**; the Automatic Enrolment (Miscellaneous Amendments) Regulations 2012, SI 2012/215; the Occupational and Personal Pension Schemes (Automatic Enrolment) (Amendment) Regulations 2012, SI 2012/1257.

[1.1540]

3 Automatic enrolment

[(1) This section applies to a jobholder—

(a) who is aged at least 22,

(b) who has not reached pensionable age, and

(c) to whom earnings of more than [£9,440] are payable by the employer in the relevant pay reference period (see section 15).]

(2) The employer must make prescribed arrangements by which the jobholder becomes an active member of an automatic enrolment scheme with effect from the automatic enrolment date.

(3) Subsection (2) does not apply if the jobholder was an active member of a qualifying scheme on the automatic enrolment date.

(4) Subsection (2) does not apply if, within the prescribed period before the automatic enrolment date, the jobholder ceased to be an active member of a qualifying scheme because of any action or omission by the jobholder.

(5) For the purposes of arrangements under subsection (2) regulations may require information to be provided to any person by the employer or—

(a) where the arrangements relate to an occupational pension scheme, the trustees or managers of the scheme;

(b) where the arrangements relate to a personal pension scheme, the provider of the scheme.

(6) For the purposes of arrangements made under subsection (2) in relation to a personal pension scheme, regulations may deem an agreement to exist (subject to section 8) between the jobholder and the provider of the scheme for the jobholder to be an active member of the scheme on terms and conditions determined in accordance with the regulations.

[(6A) In this section "earnings" has the meaning given in section 13(3).

(6B) In the case of a pay reference period of less or more than 12 months, subsection (1) applies as if the amount in paragraph (c) were proportionately less or more.]

(7) The automatic enrolment date, in relation to any person, is the first day on which this section applies to the person as a jobholder of the employer. [This is subject to section 4.]

(8) In this Part as it applies in the case of any jobholder, references to an automatic enrolment scheme are references to a pension scheme which is an automatic enrolment scheme in relation to that jobholder (see section 17).

NOTES

Commencement: 26 November 2008 (in so far as it confers any power to make Regulations); 30 June 2012 (otherwise).

Sub-s (1): substituted by the Pensions Act 2011, s 5(1), as from 30 June 2012; sum in square brackets in para (c) substituted by the Automatic Enrolment (Earnings Trigger and Qualifying Earnings Band) Order 2013, SI 2013/667, art 2(1), as from 6 April 2013. (Note the previous sum was £8,105, as substituted for the original sum of £7,475, by SI 2012/1506.)

Sub-ss (6A), (6B): inserted by the Pensions Act 2011, s 5(2), as from 30 June 2012.

Sub-s (7): words in square brackets inserted by the Pensions Act 2011, s 6(1), as from 30 June 2012.

See further: for rounded figures for the purposes of sub-s (6B) above in respect of specified pay reference periods, the Automatic Enrolment (Earnings Trigger and Qualifying Earnings Band) Order 2013, SI 2013/667, art 3 at **[2.1670]**.

Regulations: the Occupational and Personal Pension Schemes (Automatic Enrolment) Regulations 2010, SI 2010/772 at **[2.1362]**; the Automatic Enrolment (Miscellaneous Amendments) Regulations 2012, SI 2012/215; the Occupational and Personal Pension Schemes (Automatic Enrolment) (Amendment) Regulations 2012, SI 2012/1257.

[1.1541]

[4 Postponement or disapplication of automatic enrolment

(1) Where—

(a) an employer (E) gives to a person employed by E on E's staging date ("the worker") notice that E intends to defer automatic enrolment for the worker until a date specified in the notice ("the deferral date"), and

(b) any prescribed requirements in relation to the notice are met,

the worker's automatic enrolment date is the deferral date if on that date section 3 applies to the worker as a jobholder of E; if not, subsection (4) applies.

(2) Where—

(a) a person ("the worker") begins to be employed by an employer (E) after E's staging date,

(b) E gives the worker notice that E intends to defer automatic enrolment until a date specified in the notice ("the deferral date"), and

(c) any prescribed requirements in relation to the notice are met,

the worker's automatic enrolment date is the deferral date if on that date section 3 applies to the worker as a jobholder of E; if not, subsection (4) applies.

(3) Where—

(a) a person ("the worker") employed by an employer (E) becomes, after E's staging date, a jobholder to whom section 3 applies,

(b) E gives the worker notice that E intends to defer automatic enrolment until a date specified in the notice ("the deferral date"), and

(c) any prescribed requirements in relation to the notice are met,

the worker's automatic enrolment date is the deferral date if on that date section 3 applies to the worker as a jobholder of E; if not, subsection (4) applies.

(4) Where this subsection applies, section 3(2) does not apply in relation to any employment of the worker by E in the period beginning with the starting day and ending with the deferral date.

(5) A notice under this section may be given on or before the starting day or within a prescribed period after that day.

(6) The deferral date may be any date in the period of three months after the starting day.

(7) An employer who gives a worker a notice under subsection (1) or (2) may not give the worker a notice under subsection (3) in relation to any occasion on or before the deferral date specified in the notice on which the worker becomes a jobholder to whom section 3 applies.

(8) In this section—

"staging date", in relation to an employer of a particular description, means the date prescribed under section 12 in relation to employers of that description;

"starting day" means—

(a) E's staging date, in the case of a notice under subsection (1);

(b) the day on which the worker begins to be employed by E, in the case of a notice under subsection (2);

(c) the day on which the worker becomes a jobholder to whom section 3 applies, in the case of a notice under subsection (3).]

NOTES

Commencement: 30 June 2012.

Substituted by the Pensions Act 2011, s 6(2), as from 30 June 2012.

[1.1542]

5 Automatic re-enrolment

[(1) This section applies to a jobholder—

(a) who is aged at least 22,

(b) who has not reached pensionable age, and

(c) to whom earnings of more than [£9,440] are payable by the employer in the relevant pay reference period (see section 15).]

[(1A) This section also applies to a jobholder who—

(a) is aged at least 22,

(b) has not reached pensionable age, and

(c) is not an active member of a qualifying scheme because there has been a period beginning at any time after the jobholder's automatic enrolment date during which the requirements of section 1(1)(a) or (c) were not met (so that the person was not a jobholder for that period).

(1B) This section also applies to a jobholder who has ceased to be an active member of a qualifying scheme because of something other than an action or omission by the jobholder.]

(2) The employer must make prescribed arrangements by which the jobholder becomes an active member of an automatic enrolment scheme with effect from the automatic re-enrolment date.

(3) Subsection (2) does not apply if the jobholder was an active member of a qualifying scheme on the automatic re-enrolment date.

[(4) Regulations may provide for subsection (2) not to apply in relation to a jobholder who in prescribed circumstances—

(a) has ceased to be an active member of a qualifying scheme because of any action or omission by the jobholder, or by the employer at the jobholder's request, or

(b) is treated as not being an active member of a qualifying scheme because the jobholder has given notice under section 8.]

(5) . . .

(6) For the purposes of arrangements under subsection (2) regulations may require information to be provided to any person by the employer or—

(a) where the arrangements relate to an occupational pension scheme, the trustees or managers of the scheme;

(b) where the arrangements relate to a personal pension scheme, the provider of the scheme.

(7) For the purposes of arrangements made under subsection (2) in relation to a personal pension scheme, regulations may deem an agreement to exist (subject to section 8) between the jobholder and the provider of the scheme for the jobholder to be an active member of the scheme on terms and conditions determined in accordance with the regulations.

[(7A) In this section "earnings" has the meaning given in section 13(3).

(7B) In the case of a pay reference period of less or more than 12 months, subsection (1) applies as if the amount in paragraph (c) were proportionately less or more.]

(8) Automatic re-enrolment dates are dates . . . that are to be determined in accordance with regulations.

NOTES

Commencement: 26 November 2008 (in so far as it confers any power to make Regulations); 30 June 2012 (otherwise).

Sub-s (1): substituted by the Pensions Act 2011, s 5(3), as from 30 June 2012; sum in square brackets in para (c) substituted by the Automatic Enrolment (Earnings Trigger and Qualifying Earnings Band) Order 2013, SI 2013/667, art 2(1), as from 6 April 2013. (Note the previous sum was £8,105, as substituted for the original sum of £7,475, by SI 2012/1506.)

Sub-ss (1A), (1B): inserted by the Pensions Act 2011, s 4(2), as from 30 June 2012.

Sub-s (4): substituted by the Pensions Act 2011, s 4(3), as from 3 November 2011.

Sub-s (5): repealed by the Pensions Act 2011, s 6(3), as from 30 June 2012.

Sub-ss (7A), (7B): inserted by the Pensions Act 2011, s 5(4), as from 30 June 2012.

Sub-s (8): words omitted repealed by the Pensions Act 2011, s 4(4), as from 30 June 2012.

See further: for rounded figures for the purposes of sub-s (7B) above in respect of specified pay reference periods, the Automatic Enrolment (Earnings Trigger and Qualifying Earnings Band) Order 2013, SI 2013/667, art 3 at **[2.1670]**.

Regulations: the Occupational and Personal Pension Schemes (Automatic Enrolment) Regulations 2010, SI 2010/772 at **[2.1362]**; the Automatic Enrolment (Miscellaneous Amendments) Regulations 2012, SI 2012/215; the Occupational and Personal Pension Schemes (Automatic Enrolment) (Amendment) Regulations 2012, SI 2012/1257.

[1.1543]

6 Timing of automatic re-enrolment

(1) Regulations under section 5(8) must either—

(a) secure that for any jobholder there is no automatic re-enrolment date less than three years after the jobholder's automatic enrolment date, and that there is not more than one automatic re-enrolment date in any period of three years, or

(b) secure that for any employer there is not more than one automatic re-enrolment date in any period of [2 years and 9 months].

(2) Subsection (1) does not restrict the provision that regulations may make about the timing of a jobholder's automatic re-enrolment date ("the relevant date") in the following cases.

(3) . . .

(4) The [first case] is where—

(a) . . . the jobholder ceases to be an active member of a qualifying scheme . . . ,

(b) that event is not the effect of any action or omission by the jobholder . . . , and

(c) the relevant date is the jobholder's first automatic re-enrolment date after that [event].

(5) The [second case] is where—

(a) there is a period beginning at any time after the jobholder's automatic enrolment date during which the requirements of section 1(1)(a) or (c) are not met (so that the person is not a jobholder for that period), and

(b) the relevant date is the jobholder's first automatic re-enrolment date after that period.

(6) . . .

NOTES

Commencement: 26 November 2008 (in so far as it confers any power to make Regulations); 30 June 2012 (otherwise).

Sub-s (1): words in square brackets substituted by the Pensions Act 2011, s 7, as from 3 November 2011.

Sub-ss (3), (6): repealed by the Pensions Act 2011, s 6(4)(a), as from 30 June 2012.

Sub-s (4): words in square brackets substituted and words omitted repealed by the Pensions Act 2011, ss 4(5), 6(4)(b).

Sub-s (5): words in square brackets substituted by the Pensions Act 2011, s 6(4)(c), as from 30 June 2012.

Regulations: the Occupational and Personal Pension Schemes (Automatic Enrolment) Regulations 2010, SI 2010/772 at **[2.1362]**; the Automatic Enrolment (Miscellaneous Amendments) Regulations 2012, SI 2012/215; the Occupational and Personal Pension Schemes (Automatic Enrolment) (Amendment) Regulations 2012, SI 2012/1257.

[1.1544]

7 Jobholder's right to opt in

(1) This section applies to a jobholder who is not an active member of a qualifying scheme.

(2) But it does not apply at a time when—

(a) arrangements are required to be made under section 3 or 5 in respect of the jobholder, . . .

(b) . . .

(3) The jobholder may by notice require the employer to arrange for the jobholder to become an active member of an automatic enrolment scheme.

(4) The Secretary of State may by regulations make provision—

(a) about the form and content of the notice;

(b) about the arrangements that the employer is required to make;

(c) for determining the date with effect from which the jobholder is to become an active member under the arrangements.

(5) For the purposes of arrangements under subsection (3) regulations may require information to be provided to any person by the employer or—

(a) where the arrangements relate to an occupational pension scheme, the trustees or managers of the scheme;

(b) where the arrangements relate to a personal pension scheme, the provider of the scheme.

(6) For the purposes of arrangements made under subsection (3) in relation to a personal pension scheme, regulations may deem an agreement to exist (subject to section 8) between the jobholder and the provider of the scheme for the jobholder to be an active member of the scheme on terms and conditions determined in accordance with the regulations.

(7) Subsections (8) and (9) apply where a jobholder becomes an active member of an automatic enrolment scheme in pursuance of a notice under this section and, within the period of 12 months beginning with the day on which that notice was given—

(a) ceases to be an active member of that scheme, and

(b) gives the employer a further notice under this section.

(8) The further notice does not have effect to require the employer to arrange for the jobholder to become an active member of an automatic enrolment scheme.

(9) But any arrangements the employer makes for the jobholder to become, within that period, an active member of such a scheme must be made in accordance with regulations under this section.

NOTES

Commencement: 26 November 2008 (in so far as it confers any power to make Regulations); 30 June 2012 (otherwise).

Sub-s (2): para (b) and word immediately preceding it repealed by the Pensions Act 2011, s 6(5), as from 30 June 2012.

Regulations: the Occupational and Personal Pension Schemes (Automatic Enrolment) Regulations 2010, SI 2010/772 at **[2.1362]**; the Automatic Enrolment (Miscellaneous Amendments) Regulations 2012, SI 2012/215; the Occupational and Personal Pension Schemes (Automatic Enrolment) (Amendment) Regulations 2012, SI 2012/1257.

[1.1545]

8 Jobholder's right to opt out

(1) This section applies on any occasion when arrangements under section 3(2), 5(2) or 7(3) apply to a jobholder (arrangements for the jobholder to become an active member of an automatic enrolment scheme).

(2) If the jobholder gives notice under this section—

(a) the jobholder is to be treated for all purposes as not having become an active member of the scheme on that occasion;

(b) any contributions paid by the jobholder, or by the employer on behalf or in respect of the jobholder, on the basis that the jobholder has become an active member of the scheme on that occasion must be refunded in accordance with prescribed requirements.

(3) Regulations under subsection (2)(b) may, in particular, make provision about—

(a) the time within which contributions must be refunded;

(b) how the amount to be refunded is calculated;

(c) the procedure for refunding contributions.

(4) The Secretary of State may by regulations make further provision in relation to notices under this section.

(5) The regulations may in particular make provision—

(a) as to the form and content of a notice;

(b) as to the period within which a notice must be given;

(c) as to the person to whom a notice must be given;

(d) requiring any person to make prescribed arrangements for enabling notices to be given;

(e) requiring any person to take prescribed action in consequence of a notice (in addition to any action prescribed under subsection (2)(b)).

(6) The regulations must provide for the notice—
  (a) to include information about the effect in relation to jobholders of giving notice under this section, and
  (b) to be signed or otherwise authorised by the jobholder.

NOTES

Commencement: 26 November 2008 (in so far as it confers any power to make Regulations); 30 June 2012 (otherwise).

Regulations: the Occupational and Personal Pension Schemes (Automatic Enrolment) Regulations 2010, SI 2010/772 at **[2.1362]**; the Occupational and Personal Pension Schemes (Automatic Enrolment) (Amendment) Regulations 2012, SI 2012/1257.

Duty in relation to workers without qualifying earnings

[1.1546]

9 Workers without qualifying earnings

(1) This section applies to a worker—
  (a) to whom paragraphs (a) and (b) of section 1(1) apply (working in Great Britain and aged between 16 and 75),
  (b) to whom paragraph (c) of section 1(1) does not apply (qualifying earnings), and
  (c) who is not an active member of a pension scheme that satisfies the requirements of this section.

(2) The worker may by notice require the employer to arrange for the worker to become an active member of a pension scheme that satisfies the requirements of this section.

(3) The Secretary of State may by regulations make provision—
  (a) about the form and content of the notice;
  (b) about the arrangements that the employer is required to make;
  (c) for determining the date with effect from which the worker is (subject to compliance with any requirements of the scheme) to become an active member under the arrangements.

(4) Subsections (5) and (6) apply where a worker becomes an active member of a pension scheme in pursuance of a notice under this section and, within the period of 12 months beginning with the day on which that notice was given—
  (a) ceases to be an active member of that scheme because of any action or omission by the worker, and
  (b) gives the employer a further notice under this section.

(5) The further notice does not have effect to require the employer to arrange for the worker to become an active member of a pension scheme.

(6) But any arrangements the employer makes for the worker to become, within that period, an active member of a pension scheme that satisfies the requirements of this section must be made in accordance with regulations under this section.

(7) A pension scheme satisfies the requirements of this section if—
  (a) it is registered under Chapter 2 of Part 4 of the Finance Act 2004 (c 12), and
  (b) in the case of a personal pension scheme, there are, in relation to the worker concerned, direct payment arrangements (within the meaning of section 111A of the Pension Schemes Act 1993 (c 48)) between the worker and the employer.

NOTES

Commencement: 26 November 2008 (in so far as it confers any power to make Regulations); 30 June 2012 (otherwise).

Regulations: the Occupational and Personal Pension Schemes (Automatic Enrolment) Regulations 2010, SI 2010/772 at **[2.1362]**; the Occupational and Personal Pension Schemes (Automatic Enrolment) (Amendment) Regulations 2012, SI 2012/1257.

Supplementary provision about the duties

[1.1547]

10 Information to be given to workers

(1) The Secretary of State must make provision by regulations—
  (a) for all jobholders to be given information about the effect of sections 2 to 8 in relation to them;
  (b) for all workers to whom section 9 applies to be given information about the effect of that section in relation to them;
  (c) for a prescribed person to be required to provide the information.

(2) Regulations under this section must state—
  (a) what information must be given;
  (b) in what circumstances it must be given;
  (c) how and when it must be given.

NOTES

Commencement: 26 November 2008 (in so far as it confers any power to make Regulations); 30 June 2012 (otherwise).

Regulations: the Occupational and Personal Pension Schemes (Automatic Enrolment) Regulations 2010, SI 2010/772 at **[2.1362]**; the Automatic Enrolment (Miscellaneous Amendments) Regulations 2012, SI 2012/215; the Occupational and Personal Pension Schemes (Automatic Enrolment) (Amendment) Regulations 2012, SI 2012/1257.

[1.1548]
11 Information to be given to the Pensions Regulator

(1) The Secretary of State may make regulations requiring employers to provide the Pensions Regulator ("the Regulator") with information about action they have taken or intend to take for the purposes of any provision of, or of regulations under, sections 2 to 10.

(2) The regulations may in particular—

- (a) require an employer to provide information about pension schemes to which any action relates;
- (b) require an employer to identify which of any prescribed descriptions a scheme falls within;
- (c) require an employer to provide information that appears to the Secretary of State to be required for the performance by the Regulator of its functions under Chapter 2 of this Part;
- (d) make provision about how and in what form any information is to be provided.

NOTES

Commencement: 26 November 2008 (in so far as it confers any power to make Regulations); to be appointed (otherwise).

Regulations: the Employers' Duties (Registration and Compliance) Regulations 2010, SI 2010/5; the Automatic Enrolment (Miscellaneous Amendments) Regulations 2012, SI 2012/215.

[1.1549]
12 Introduction of employers' duties

The Secretary of State may by regulations provide that sections 2 to 9 do not apply in the case of an employer of any description until such date after the commencement of those sections as is prescribed in relation to employers of that description.

NOTES

Commencement: 26 November 2008 (in so far as it confers any power to make Regulations); to be appointed (otherwise).

Regulations: the Employers' Duties (Implementation) Regulations 2010, SI 2010/4 at **[2.1270]**; the Automatic Enrolment (Miscellaneous Amendments) Regulations 2012, SI 2012/215; Employers' Duties (Implementation) (Amendment) Regulations 2012, SI 2012/1813.

[Qualifying earnings and earnings trigger]

[1.1550]
13 Qualifying earnings

(1) A person's qualifying earnings in a pay reference period of 12 months are the part (if any) of the gross earnings payable to that person in that period that is—

- (a) more than [£5,668], and
- (b) not more than [£41,450].

(2) In the case of a pay reference period of less or more than 12 months, subsection (1) applies as if the amounts in paragraphs (a) and (b) were proportionately less or more.

(3) In this section, "earnings", in relation to a person, means sums of any of the following descriptions that are payable to the person in connection with the person's employment—

- (a) salary, wages, commission, bonuses and overtime;
- (b) statutory sick pay under Part 11 of the Social Security Contributions and Benefits Act 1992 (c 4);
- (c) statutory maternity pay under Part 12 of that Act;
- (d) ordinary statutory paternity pay or additional statutory paternity pay under Part 12ZA of that Act;
- (e) statutory adoption pay under Part 12ZB of that Act;
- (f) sums prescribed for the purposes of this section.

NOTES

Commencement: 30 June 2012.

Words in square brackets in the cross-heading preceding this section substituted by the Pensions Act 2011, s 8(2), as from 3 January 2012.

Sub-s (1): sums in square brackets substituted by the Automatic Enrolment (Earnings Trigger and Qualifying Earnings Band) Order 2013, SI 2013/667, art 2(2), as from 6 April 2013. (Note the previous sums were £5,564 and £42,475 respectively, as substituted for the original sums of £5,035 and £33,540, by SI 2012/1506.)

See further: for rounded figures for the purposes of sub-s (2) above in respect of specified pay reference periods, the Automatic Enrolment (Earnings Trigger and Qualifying Earnings Band) Order 2013, SI 2013/667, art 3 at **[2.1670]**.

Regulations: as of 6 April 2013 no Regulations had been made under this section.

[1.1551]

[14 Review of earnings trigger and qualifying earnings band

(1) The Secretary of State must in each tax year consider whether any of the amounts in sections 3(1)(c), 5(1)(c) and 13(1)(a) and (b) should be increased or decreased.

(2) If the Secretary of State considers that any of those amounts should be increased or decreased, the Secretary of State may make an order substituting in the provisions in question the amounts that the Secretary of State thinks appropriate.

(3) For the purposes of subsection (1) the Secretary of State may take into account any of the factors specified in subsection (4) (as well as any others that the Secretary of State thinks relevant).

(4) The factors are—

(a) the amounts for the time being specified in Chapter 2 of Part 3 (personal allowances) of the Income Tax Act 2007;

(b) the amounts for the time being specified in regulations under section 5 of the Social Security Contributions and Benefits Act 1992 (earnings limits and thresholds for Class 1 national insurance contributions);

(c) the amount for the time being specified in section 44(4) of that Act (rate of basic state pension);

(d) the general level of prices in Great Britain, and the general level of earnings there, estimated in such manner as the Secretary of State thinks fit.]

NOTES

Commencement: as to the commencement of this section, see the note below.

Substituted by the Pensions Act 2011, s 8(1) (as to the commencement of this amendment, see the note below).

Note: by virtue of s 149(2)(k) of this Act (*post*) this section as originally enacted came into force on 26 November 2008 (in so far as it conferred any power to make an Order), and as from a day to be appointed (otherwise). The section was subsequently substituted by the Pensions Act 2011, s 8(1), as from 3 November 2011 in so far as it modifies or confers any power to make an Order or Regulations (see s 38(1), (4) of that Act)). The Pensions Act 2011 (Commencement No 1) Order 2011, SI 2011/3034, art 3 brought s 8 of the 2011 Act into force on 3 January 2012 (in so far as that section was not already in force). Subsequently, the Pensions Act 2008 (Commencement No 12) Order 2012, SI 2012/683, art 2 brought this section into force on 6 March 2012 (in so far as it was not already in force). It is believed that the effect of the Pensions Act 2011 (Commencement No 1) Order 2011 was merely to bring into force the substitution by the 2011 Act, but that this section was not actually in force when that substitution was commenced (as there has been no Pensions Act 2008 commencement order bringing it into force at that date). Accordingly, it is further believed that this section came fully into force on 6 March 2012 by virtue of the Pensions Act 2008 (Commencement No 12) Order 2012.

Orders: the Automatic Enrolment (Earnings Trigger and Qualifying Earnings Band) Order 2013, SI 2013/667 at **[2.1669]**.

[1.1552]

15 Pay reference period

(1) In relation to any person a pay reference period is the period prescribed.

(2) The Secretary of State may by regulations—

(a) make provision for determining a person's earnings in any pay reference period;

(b) make provision for determining the first date of each pay reference period in relation to a person.

(3) A reference in any provision to the relevant pay reference period is a reference to the period determined in accordance with regulations under this section, as they apply for the purposes of that provision in the case concerned.

NOTES

Commencement: 26 November 2008 (in so far as it confers any power to make Regulations); 30 June 2012 (otherwise).

Regulations: the Occupational and Personal Pension Schemes (Automatic Enrolment) Regulations 2010, SI 2010/772 at **[2.1362]**; the Automatic Enrolment (Miscellaneous Amendments) Regulations 2012, SI 2012/215; the Occupational and Personal Pension Schemes (Automatic Enrolment) (Amendment) Regulations 2012, SI 2012/1257.

[1.1553]

[15A Power to specify rounded figures

[(1) The Secretary of State may by order specify rounded figures for the purposes of section 3(6B), 5(7B) or 13(2) in the case of pay reference periods of any length specified in the order.

(2) A rounded figure so specified applies in place of the amount that would otherwise apply ("the exact amount").

(3) The Secretary of State must decide in relation to any particular amount whether to specify—

(a) a figure that is a whole number of pounds, or

(b) a figure that is divisible by 10 pence, or

(c) a figure that includes a whole number of pennies.

(4) It is for the Secretary of State to decide whether to round any particular amount up or down. Accordingly, a figure specified under this section may be the figure within paragraph (a) or (b) or (c) of subsection (3) that is closest to the exact amount or the one that is next closest to it (or, if two figures are joint closest, it may be either of those).]

NOTES

Commencement: as to the commencement of this section, see the note below.

Inserted by the Pensions Act 2011, s 9, as from 3 November 2011 in so far as it modifies or confers any power to make an Order or Regulations (see s 38(1), (4) of that Act)).The Pensions Act 2011 (Commencement No 2) Order 2012, SI 2012/682, art 2 brought s 9 of the 2011 Act into force on 6 March 2012 (in so far as that section was not already in force). Subsequently, the Pensions Act 2008 (Commencement No 12) Order 2012, SI 2012/683, art 2 brought this section into force on 7 March 2012 (in so far as it was not already in force). It is believed that the effect of the Pensions Act 2011 (Commencement No 2) Order 2012 was merely to bring into force the amendment made by the 2011 Act but that, as at 6 March 2012, this section was not in force. Accordingly, it is further believed that this section came fully into force on 7 March 2012 by virtue of the Pensions Act 2008 (Commencement No 12) Order 2012.

Orders: the Automatic Enrolment (Earnings Trigger and Qualifying Earnings Band) Order 2013, SI 2013/667 at **[2.1669]**.

Qualifying schemes and automatic enrolment schemes

[1.1554]

16 Qualifying schemes

(1) A pension scheme is a qualifying scheme in relation to a jobholder (J) if—

(a) the scheme is an occupational pension scheme or a personal pension scheme,

(b) the scheme is registered under Chapter 2 of Part 4 of the Finance Act 2004 (c 12), and

(c) while J is an active member, the scheme satisfies the quality requirement in relation to J.

(2) The Secretary of State may by regulations provide that subsection (1)(b) does not apply in relation to a scheme to which section 25 or 27 applies, if prescribed requirements are satisfied.

(3) The Secretary of State may by regulations provide that a scheme is not a qualifying scheme in relation to J if—

(a) while J is an active member, the payments that must be made to the scheme by, or on behalf or in respect of, J for purposes other than the provision of benefits exceed a prescribed amount,

(b) while J is an active member, the contributions that must be paid to the scheme by, or on behalf or in respect of, J exceed a prescribed amount, or

(c) the scheme provides for average salary benefits to be provided to or in respect of J and contains prescribed features.

[(4) For the purposes of subsection (3) administration charges are due from a person to the extent that—

(a) any payments made to the scheme by, or on behalf or in respect of, the person,

(b) any income or capital gain arising from the investment of such payments, or

(c) the value of the person's rights under the scheme,

may be used to defray the administrative expenses of the scheme, to pay commission or in any other way that does not result in the provision of pension benefits for or in respect of members.

(5) In subsection (3)(aa) "former active member" means a person who at some time after the automatic enrolment date was both a jobholder and an active member but is no longer an active member.]

NOTES

Commencement: 26 November 2008 (in so far as it confers any power to make Regulations); 30 June 2012 (otherwise).

Sub-s (3): para (a) substituted by the Pensions Act 2011, s 10(1), (2), as from 3 November 2011 in so far as it modifies or confers any power to make an Order or Regulations, and as from a day to be appointed for all other purposes (see s 38(1), (4) of that Act)), as follows—

"(a) administration charges due from J while J is an active member exceed a prescribed amount,

(aa) administration charges due from former active members while J is an active member exceed a prescribed amount,

(ab) while J is an active member, the scheme contains provision under which administration charges that will be due from J when J is no longer an active member will exceed a prescribed amount, or will do so in particular circumstances,".

Sub-ss (4), (5): inserted by the Pensions Act 2011, s 10(1), (3) (as to the commencement of this amendment, see the note above).

Regulations: the Occupational and Personal Pension Schemes (Automatic Enrolment) Regulations 2010, SI 2010/772 at **[2.1362]**; the Automatic Enrolment (Miscellaneous Amendments) Regulations 2012, SI 2012/215; the Occupational and Personal Pension Schemes (Automatic Enrolment) (Amendment) Regulations 2012, SI 2012/1257; the Occupational and Personal Pension Schemes (Automatic Enrolment) (Amendment) (No 3) Regulations 2012, SI 2012/2691.

[1.1555]

17 Automatic enrolment schemes

(1) A pension scheme is an automatic enrolment scheme in relation to a jobholder (J) if—

(a) it is a qualifying scheme in relation to J,

(b) it satisfies the conditions in subsection (2), and

(c) it satisfies any further conditions prescribed.

(2) The conditions mentioned in subsection (1)(b) are that—

(a) no provision of the scheme prevents the employer from making arrangements prescribed by regulations under section 3(2), 5(2) or 7(4) for J to become an active member of the scheme;

(b) no provision of the scheme requires J to express a choice in relation to any matter, or to provide any information, in order to remain an active member.

NOTES

Commencement: 26 November 2008 (in so far as it confers any power to make Regulations); 30 June 2012 (otherwise).

Regulations: the Occupational and Personal Pension Schemes (Automatic Enrolment) (Amendment) Regulations 2012, SI 2012/1257.

[1.1556]

18 Occupational pension schemes

For the purposes of this Part, each of these is an occupational pension scheme—

(a) an occupational pension scheme within the meaning of section 1(1) of the Pension Schemes Act 1993 (c 48) that has its main administration in the United Kingdom;

(b) an institution for occupational retirement provision within the meaning of Article 6(a) of the IORP Directive, that has its main administration in an EEA State other than the United Kingdom;

(c) a pension scheme that is prescribed or is of a prescribed description and that has its main administration elsewhere than in an EEA State.

NOTES

Commencement: 26 November 2008 (in so far as it confers any power to make Regulations); 30 June 2012 (otherwise).

Regulations: the Occupational and Personal Pension Schemes (Automatic Enrolment) Regulations 2010, SI 2010/772 at **[2.1362]**; the Occupational and Personal Pension Schemes (Automatic Enrolment) (Amendment) Regulations 2012, SI 2012/1257.

[1.1557]

19 Personal pension schemes

For the purposes of this Part, a personal pension scheme is a pension scheme that is not an occupational pension scheme.

NOTES

Commencement: 30 June 2012.

Quality requirements

[1.1558]

20 Quality requirement: UK money purchase schemes

(1) A money purchase scheme that has its main administration in the United Kingdom satisfies the quality requirement in relation to a jobholder if under the scheme—

(a) the jobholder's employer must pay contributions in respect of the jobholder;

(b) the employer's contribution, however calculated, must be equal to or more than 3% of the amount of the jobholder's qualifying earnings in the relevant pay reference period;

(c) the total amount of contributions paid by the jobholder and the employer, however calculated, must be equal to or more than 8% of the amount of the jobholder's qualifying earnings in the relevant pay reference period.

(2) . . .

(3) A scheme does not fail to satisfy the quality requirement under this section merely because the trustees or managers of the scheme may on any occasion refuse to accept a contribution below an amount prescribed for the purposes of this section on the grounds that it is below that amount.

NOTES

Commencement: 26 November 2008 (in so far as it confers any power to make Regulations); 30 June 2012 (otherwise).

Sub-s (2): repealed by the Pensions Act 2007 (Abolition of Contracting-out for Defined Contribution Pension Schemes) (Consequential Amendments) (No 2) Regulations 2011, SI 2011/1724, reg 3, as from 6 April 2012.

See further, in relation to the application of sub-s (1) above, with modifications, for the purposes of non-UK occupational pension schemes: the Occupational and Personal Pension Schemes (Automatic Enrolment) Regulations 2010, SI 2010/772, reg 45(2).

[1.1559]

21 Quality requirement: UK defined benefits schemes

(1) Subject to subsection (3), a defined benefits scheme that has its main administration in the United Kingdom satisfies the quality requirement in relation to a jobholder if the jobholder is in contracted-out employment.

(2) A defined benefits scheme that has its main administration in the United Kingdom satisfies the quality requirement in relation to a jobholder who is not in contracted-out employment if it satisfies the test scheme standard in relation to that jobholder.

(3) The Secretary of State may by order provide that a scheme does not satisfy the quality requirement in relation to a jobholder who is in contracted-out employment unless it satisfies the test scheme standard in relation to that jobholder, with the substitution of a higher fraction, not exceeding 1/80th, for the fraction of 1/120th in section 23(4)(a).

(4) In relation to any scheme, a jobholder is in contracted-out employment for the purposes of this section and section 22 if a certificate has been issued in respect of the jobholder under section 7(1) of the Pension Schemes Act 1993 (c 48) stating that the employment of the jobholder is contracted-out employment by reference to the scheme.

NOTES

Commencement: 26 November 2008 (in so far as it confers any power to make an Order); 30 June 2012 (otherwise).

See further, in relation to the application of this section, with modifications, for the purposes of non-UK occupational pension schemes: the Occupational and Personal Pension Schemes (Automatic Enrolment) Regulations 2010, SI 2010/772, reg 45(4).

Miscellaneous

[1.1560]

32 Power of trustees [or managers] to modify by resolution

(1) The trustees [or managers] of an occupational pension scheme may by resolution modify the scheme—

(a) with a view to enabling the scheme to comply with the conditions in section 17(2), or

(b) by increasing the amount required to be paid in contributions, in order for the scheme [to satisfy—

(i) the requirements contained in section 20(1),

(ii) those requirements as modified under section 24(1)(a), or

(iii) a requirement prescribed under section 28(2)(b)].

(2) An increase under subsection (1)(b) may be made only—

(a) by increasing the amount of any contribution, directly or by modifying the basis on which it is calculated, or

(b) by increasing the frequency of any contributions.

(3) No modification may be made by virtue of subsection (1) without the consent of the employer in relation to the scheme.

(4) In the application of subsection (3) to a scheme in relation to which there is more than one employer, references to the employer have effect as if they were references to a person nominated by the employers, or by the scheme, to act as the employers' representative for the purposes of this section or, if no such nomination is made, to all of the employers.

(5) Regulations may provide that this section does not apply to occupational pension schemes within a prescribed class or description.

NOTES

Commencement: 26 November 2008 (in so far as it confers any power to make Regulations); 30 June 2012 (otherwise).

Words in square brackets in the section heading and words in first pair of square brackets in sub-s (1) inserted by the Pensions Act 2011, s 16, as from 30 June 2012; words in second pair of square brackets in sub-s (1) substituted by the Pensions Act 2011, s 12(8), as from 6 March 2012.

Regulations: as of 6 April 2013 no Regulations had been made under this section.

[1.1561]

33 Deduction of contributions

(1) An employer who arranges for a person to become a member of a scheme in accordance with section 3(2), 5(2) or 7(3), or of an occupational pension scheme in accordance with section 9(2), may deduct the person's contributions to the scheme from the person's remuneration and pay them to the trustees or managers of the scheme (in the case of an occupational pension scheme) or the provider of the scheme (in the case of a personal pension scheme).

(2) Regulations prescribing arrangements for the purposes of section 3(2), 5(2), 7(3) or 9(2), may require the employer to make such a deduction or payment at any time on or after the date with effect from which the jobholder is to become an active member of a scheme under the arrangements.

NOTES

Commencement: 26 November 2008 (in so far as it confers any power to make Regulations); 30 June 2012 (otherwise).

Regulations: the Occupational and Personal Pension Schemes (Automatic Enrolment) Regulations 2010, SI 2010/772 at **[2.1362]**; the Occupational and Personal Pension Schemes (Automatic Enrolment) (Amendment) Regulations 2012, SI 2012/1257.

CHAPTER 2
COMPLIANCE

Effect of failure to comply

[1.1562]

34 Effect of failure to comply

(1) Contravention of any of the employer duty provisions does not give rise to a right of action for breach of statutory duty.

(2) But nothing in the employer duty provisions or this Chapter affects any right of action arising apart from those provisions.

(3) In this Chapter, references to the employer duty provisions are references to any provision of sections 2 to 11 or of regulations under those sections.

NOTES

Commencement: 30 June 2012.

Compliance notices and unpaid contributions notices

[1.1563]

35 Compliance notices

(1) The Regulator may issue a compliance notice to a person if the Regulator is of the opinion that the person has contravened one or more of the employer duty provisions.

(2) A compliance notice is a notice directing the person to whom it is issued to take, or refrain from taking, the steps specified in the notice in order to remedy the contravention.

(3) A compliance notice may, in particular—

(a) state the period within which any step must be taken or must cease to be taken;

(b) require the person to whom it is issued to provide within a specified period specified information relating to the contravention;

(c) require the person to inform the Regulator, within a specified period, how the person has complied or is complying with the notice;

(d) state that, if the person fails to comply with the requirements of the notice, the Regulator may issue a fixed penalty notice under section 40.

(4) The steps specified in the notice may, in particular, include such steps as the Regulator thinks appropriate for placing the worker in the same position (as nearly as possible) as if the contravention had not occurred.

(5) If the compliance notice is issued in respect of a failure to comply with an enrolment duty and the specified steps relate to membership of a defined benefits scheme or a hybrid scheme, the notice may, in particular, require the employer to ensure that the worker is entitled to the same benefits under the scheme as if the employer had complied with that duty.

NOTES

Commencement: 30 June 2012.

[1.1564]

36 Third party compliance notices

(1) The Regulator may issue a third party compliance notice if it is of the opinion that—

(a) a person has contravened one or more of the employer duty provisions,

(b) the contravention is or was, wholly or partly, a result of a failure of another person (the "third party") to do any thing, and

(c) that failure is not itself a contravention of any of the employer duty provisions.

(2) A third party compliance notice is a notice directing the third party to take, or refrain from taking, the steps specified in the notice in order to remedy or prevent a recurrence of the failure.

(3) A third party notice may, in particular—

(a) state the period within which any step must be taken or must cease to be taken;

(b) require the third party to inform the Regulator, within a specified period, how the third party has complied or is complying with the notice;

(c) state that, if the third party fails to comply with the requirements of the notice, the Regulator may issue a fixed penalty notice under section 40.

(4) A third party notice may give the third party a choice between different ways of remedying or preventing the recurrence of the third party's failure.

NOTES

Commencement: 30 June 2012.

[1.1565]

37 Unpaid contributions notices

(1) The Regulator may issue an unpaid contributions notice to an employer if it is of the opinion that relevant contributions have not been paid on or before the due date.

(2) An unpaid contributions notice is a notice requiring an employer to pay into a pension scheme by a specified date an amount in respect of relevant contributions that have not been paid.

(3) "Due date" has the meaning prescribed.

(4) An unpaid contributions notice may, in particular—

(a) specify the scheme to which the contributions are due;

(b) specify the workers, or category of workers, in respect of whom the contributions are due;

(c) state the period in respect of which the contributions are due;

(d) state the due date in respect of the contributions;

(e) require the employer to take such other steps in relation to remedying the failure to pay the contributions as the Regulator considers appropriate;

(f) state that if the employer fails to comply with the notice, the Regulator may issue a fixed penalty notice under section 40.

(5) In this section, "employer" in relation to a worker means the person by whom the worker is or, if the employment has ceased, was employed.

NOTES

Commencement: 26 November 2008 (in so far as it confers any power to make Regulations); 30 June 2012 (otherwise).

Regulations: the Occupational and Personal Pension Schemes (Automatic Enrolment) Regulations 2010, SI 2010/772 at **[2.1362]**; the Automatic Enrolment (Miscellaneous Amendments) Regulations 2012, SI 2012/215; the Occupational and Personal Pension Schemes (Automatic Enrolment) (Amendment) Regulations 2012, SI 2012/1257.

Penalty notices

[1.1566]

40 Fixed penalty notices

(1) The Regulator may issue a fixed penalty notice to a person if it is of the opinion that the person has failed to comply with—

(a) a compliance notice under section 35,
(b) a third party compliance notice under section 36,
(c) an unpaid contributions notice under section 37, or
(d) a notice issued under section 72 of the Pensions Act 2004 (c 35) (provision of information).

(2) The Regulator may issue a fixed penalty notice to a person if it is of the opinion that the person has contravened—

(a) any provision of regulations under section 3(2) or 5(2) (prescribed arrangements for automatic enrolment or re-enrolment),
(b) any provision of regulations under section 7(4) (prescribed arrangements: jobholder's right to opt in),
(c) section 8(2)(b) (refund of contributions if jobholder opts out of scheme membership), and any provision of regulations under that provision,
(d) section 10 (requirement to give information to workers), and any provision of regulations under that section, or
(e) any provision of regulations under section 60 (requirement to keep records).

(3) A fixed penalty notice is a notice requiring the person to whom it is issued to pay a penalty within the period specified in the notice.

(4) The penalty—

(a) is to be determined in accordance with regulations, and
(b) must not exceed £50,000.

(5) A fixed penalty notice must—

(a) state the amount of the penalty;
(b) state the date, which must be at least 4 weeks after the date on which the notice is issued, by which the penalty must be paid;
(c) state the period to which the penalty relates;
(d) if the notice is issued under subsection (1), specify the failure to which the notice relates;
(e) if the notice is issued under subsection (2), specify the provision or provisions that have been contravened;
(f) if the notice is issued under subsection (1), state that, if the failure to comply continues, the Regulator may issue an escalating penalty notice under section 41;
(g) notify the person to whom the notice is issued of the review process under section 43 and the right of referral to the [a tribunal] under section 44.

NOTES

Commencement: 26 November 2008 (in so far as it confers any power to make Regulations); 30 June 2012 (sub-ss (1)(a)–(c), (2)–(5) (for remaining purposes) and sub-s (1)(d) (for the purposes of the exercise of the Regulator's functions under or by virtue of Part 1 of this Act)); to be appointed (sub-s (1)(d) for remaining purposes).

Sub-s (5): words in square brackets in para (g) substituted by the Transfer of Tribunal Functions Order 2010, SI 2010/22, art 5(1), Sch 2, paras 146, 147, as from 6 April 2010 (for general savings and transitional provisions in relation to existing cases before the Pensions Regulator Tribunal, see Sch 5 to the 2010 Order).

Regulations: the Employers' Duties (Registration and Compliance) Regulations 2010, SI 2010/5; the Automatic Enrolment (Miscellaneous Amendments) Regulations 2012, SI 2012/215.

[1.1567]

41 Escalating penalty notices

(1) The Regulator may issue an escalating penalty notice to a person if it is of the opinion that the person has failed to comply with—

(a) a compliance notice under section 35,
(b) a third party compliance notice under section 36,
(c) an unpaid contributions notice under section 37, or
(d) a notice under section 72 of the Pensions Act 2004 (c 35) (provision of information).

(2) But the Regulator may not issue an escalating penalty notice if—

(a) it relates to failure to comply with a notice within subsection (1)(a), (b) or (c), the person to whom that notice was issued has applied for a review of it under section 43, and any review has not been completed;

(b) it relates to failure to comply with any notice within subsection (1), the person has exercised the right of referral to [a tribunal] under section 44 in respect of a fixed penalty notice issued in relation to that notice, and the reference has not been determined.

(3) An escalating penalty notice is a notice requiring a person to pay an escalating penalty if the person fails to comply with a notice referred to in subsection (1) before a specified date.

(4) An escalating penalty is a penalty which is calculated by reference to a prescribed daily rate.

(5) The prescribed daily rate—

(a) is to be determined in accordance with regulations, and

(b) must not exceed £10,000.

(6) An escalating penalty notice must—

(a) specify the failure to which the notice relates;

(b) state that, if the person fails to comply with the notice referred to in subsection (1) before a specified date, the person will be liable to pay an escalating penalty;

(c) state the daily rate of the escalating penalty and the way in which the penalty is calculated;

(d) state the date from which the escalating penalty will be payable, which must not be earlier than the date specified in the fixed penalty notice under section 40(5)(b);

(e) state that the escalating penalty will continue to be payable at the daily rate until the date on which the person complies with the notice referred to in subsection (1) or such earlier date as the Regulator may determine;

(f) notify the person of the review process under section 43 and the right of referral to [a tribunal] under section 44.

NOTES

Commencement: 26 November 2008 (in so far as it confers any power to make Regulations); 30 June 2012 (sub-ss (1)(a)–(c), (2)–(6) (for remaining purposes) and sub-s (1)(d) (for the purposes of the exercise of the Regulator's functions under or by virtue of Part 1 of this Act)); to be appointed (sub-s (1)(d) for remaining purposes).

Sub-ss (2), (6): words in square brackets substituted by the Transfer of Tribunal Functions Order 2010, SI 2010/22, art 5(1), Sch 2, paras 146, 148, as from 6 April 2010 (for general savings and transitional provisions in relation to existing cases before the Pensions Regulator Tribunal, see Sch 5 to the 2010 Order).

Regulations: the Employers' Duties (Registration and Compliance) Regulations 2010, SI 2010/5; the Automatic Enrolment (Miscellaneous Amendments) Regulations 2012, SI 2012/215.

[1.1568]

42 Penalty notices: recovery

(1) Any penalty payable under section 40 or section 41 is recoverable by the Regulator.

(2) In England and Wales, any such penalty is, if *a county court* so orders, recoverable under section 85 of the County Courts Act 1984 (c 28) or otherwise as if it were payable under an order of that court.

(3) In Scotland, a fixed penalty notice or escalating penalty notice is enforceable as if it were an extract registered decree arbitral bearing a warrant for execution issued by the sheriff court of any sheriffdom in Scotland.

(4) The Regulator must pay into the Consolidated Fund any penalty recovered under this section.

NOTES

Commencement: 30 June 2012.

Sub-s (2): for the words in italics there are substituted the words "the county court" by the Crime and Courts Act 2013, s 17(5), Sch 9, Pt 3, para 52, as from a day to be appointed.

Reviews and references

[1.1569]

43 Review of notices

(1) The Regulator may review a notice to which this section applies—

(a) on the written application of the person to whom the notice was issued, or

(b) if the Regulator otherwise considers it appropriate.

(2) This section applies to—

(a) a compliance notice issued under section 35;

(b) a third party compliance notice issued under section 36;

(c) an unpaid contributions notice issued under section 37;

(d) a fixed penalty notice issued under section 40;

(e) an escalating penalty notice issued under section 41.

(3) Regulations may prescribe the period within which—

(a) an application to review a notice may be made under subsection (1)(a);

(b) a notice may be reviewed under subsection (1)(b).

(4) On a review of a notice, the effect of the notice is suspended for the period beginning when the Regulator determines to carry out the review and ending when the review is completed.

(5) In carrying out a review, the Regulator must consider any representations made by the person to whom the notice was issued.

(6) The Regulator's powers on a review include power to—

(a) confirm, vary or revoke the notice;

(b) substitute a different notice.

NOTES

Commencement: 26 November 2008 (in so far as it confers any power to make Regulations); 30 June 2012 (otherwise).

Regulations: the Employers' Duties (Registration and Compliance) Regulations 2010, SI 2010/5; the Automatic Enrolment (Miscellaneous Amendments) Regulations 2012, SI 2012/215.

[1.1570]

44 References to [First-tier Tribunal or upper Tribunal]

(1) A person to whom a notice is issued under section 40 or 41 may, if one of the conditions in subsection (2) is satisfied, make a reference to [the Tribunal] in respect of—

(a) the issue of the notice;

(b) the amount of the penalty payable under the notice.

(2) The conditions are—

(a) that the Regulator has completed a review of the notice under section 43;

(b) that the person to whom the notice was issued has made an application for the review of the notice under section 43(1)(a) and the Regulator has determined not to carry out such a review.

(3) On a reference to [the Tribunal] in respect of a notice, the effect of the notice is suspended for the period beginning when the Tribunal receives notice of the reference and ending—

(a) when the reference is withdrawn or completed, or

(b) if the reference is made out of time, on the Tribunal determining not to allow the reference to proceed.

(4) For the purposes of subsection (3), a reference is completed when—

(a) the reference has been determined,

(b) the Tribunal has remitted the matter to the Regulator, and

(c) any directions of the Tribunal for giving effect to its determination have been complied with.

[(4A) In this section "the Tribunal", in relation to a reference under this section, means—

(a) the Upper Tribunal, in any case where it is determined by or under Tribunal Procedure Rules that the Upper Tribunal is to hear the reference;

(b) the First-tier Tribunal, in any other case.]

(5)–(9) . . .

NOTES

Commencement: 30 June 2012.

Sub-s (4A) was inserted, and the words in square brackets in the section heading and in sub-ss (1), (3) were substituted, by the Transfer of Tribunal Functions Order 2010, SI 2010/22, art 5(1), Sch 2, paras 146, 149, as from 6 April 2010 (for general savings and transitional provisions in relation to existing cases before the Pensions Regulator Tribunal, see Sch 5 to the 2010 Order).

Sub-ss (5)–(9): repealed by SI 2010/22, art 5(3), Sch 4, Pt 2, as from 6 April 2010 (for general savings and transitional provisions in relation to existing cases before the Pensions Regulator Tribunal, see Sch 5 to the 2010 Order).

Offences and monitoring

[1.1571]

45 Offences of failing to comply

(1) An offence is committed by an employer who wilfully fails to comply with—

(a) the duty under section 3(2) (automatic enrolment),

(b) the duty under section 5(2) (automatic re-enrolment), or

(c) the duty under section 7(3) (jobholder's right to opt in).

(2) A person guilty of an offence under this section is liable—

(a) on conviction on indictment, to imprisonment for a term not exceeding two years, or to a fine, or both;

(b) on summary conviction to a fine not exceeding the statutory maximum.

NOTES

Commencement: 30 June 2012.

[1.1572]

46 Offences by bodies corporate

(1) Subsection (2) applies where an offence under section 45 committed by a body corporate is proved—

(a) to have been committed with the consent or connivance of an officer of the body corporate, or

(b) to be attributable to any neglect on the part of an officer of the body corporate.

(2) The officer, as well as the body corporate, is guilty of the offence and is liable to be proceeded against and punished accordingly.

(3) "Officer" in this section means—

(a) a director, manager, secretary or other similar officer, or

(b) a person purporting to act in such a capacity.

(4) Where the affairs of a body corporate are managed by its members, this section applies in relation to the acts and defaults of a member in connection with the member's functions of management as if the member were an officer of the body corporate.

NOTES

Commencement: 30 June 2012.

[1.1573]

47 Offences by partnerships and unincorporated associations

(1) Proceedings for an offence under section 45 alleged to have been committed by a partnership or an unincorporated association may be brought in the name of the partnership or association.

(2) For the purposes of such proceedings—

(a) rules of court relating to the service of documents are to have effect as if the partnership or association were a body corporate;

(b) the following provisions apply in relation to the partnership or association as they apply in relation to a body corporate—

(i) section 33 of the Criminal Justice Act 1925 (c 86) and Schedule 3 to the Magistrates' Courts Act 1980 (c 43);

(ii) section 70 of the Criminal Procedure (Scotland) Act 1995 (c 46).

(3) A fine imposed on a partnership or association on its conviction of an offence under section 45 is to be paid out of the funds of the partnership or association.

(4) Subsection (5) applies where an offence under section 45 committed by a partnership is proved—

(a) to have been committed with the consent or connivance of a partner, or

(b) to be attributable to any neglect on the part of a partner.

(5) The partner, as well as the partnership, is guilty of the offence and is liable to be proceeded against and punished accordingly.

(6) Subsection (7) applies where an offence under section 45 committed by an unincorporated association is proved—

(a) to have been committed with the consent or connivance of an officer of the association, or

(b) to be attributable to any neglect on the part of an officer of the association.

(7) The officer, as well as the association, is guilty of the offence and is liable to be proceeded against and punished accordingly.

(8) "Officer" in this section means—

(a) an officer of the association or a member of its governing body, or

(b) a person purporting to act in such capacity.

(9) "Partner" in this section includes a person purporting to act as a partner.

NOTES

Commencement: 30 June 2012.

CHAPTER 3
SAFEGUARDS: EMPLOYMENT AND PRE-EMPLOYMENT

Prohibited recruitment conduct

[1.1574]

50 Prohibited recruitment conduct

(1) An employer contravenes this section if any statement made or question asked by or on behalf of the employer for the purposes of recruitment indicates (expressly or impliedly) that an application for employment with the employer may be determined by reference to whether or not an applicant might opt out of automatic enrolment.

(2) The reference in subsection (1) to a statement made or a question asked for the purposes of recruitment is a reference to one made or asked in the course of any of the following—

(a) inviting applications for employment;

(b) requesting information from an applicant, referee or other person in connection with an application for employment;

(c) providing information about employment;

(d) proposing terms or conditions of employment.

(3) The reference in subsection (1) to an applicant opting out of automatic enrolment is a reference to the applicant, if becoming at any time in the course of the employment a jobholder to whom section 3 or 5 applies, giving notice in accordance with section 8 in relation to arrangements made by the employer under the relevant section.

(4) In this section and sections 51 and 52, "employer" means the prospective employer in relation to any employment.

NOTES

Commencement: 30 June 2012.

[1.1575]

51 Compliance notices

(1) The Regulator may issue a compliance notice to an employer if the Regulator is of the opinion that the employer has contravened section 50.

(2) A compliance notice is a notice directing the employer to take, or refrain from taking, the steps specified in the notice in order to—

- (a) remedy the contravention, or
- (b) prevent the contravention being repeated.

(3) A compliance notice may, in particular—

- (a) state the period within which any step must be taken or must cease to be taken;
- (b) require the employer to provide within a specified period specified information relating to the contravention;
- (c) require the employer to inform the Regulator, within a specified period, how the employer has complied or is complying with the notice;
- (d) state that, if the employer fails to comply with the requirements of the notice, the Regulator may issue a penalty notice under section 52.

(4) A compliance notice must specify the contravention to which the notice relates.

NOTES

Commencement: 30 June 2012.

[1.1576]

52 Penalty notices

(1) The Regulator may issue a penalty notice to an employer if the Regulator is of the opinion that the employer—

- (a) has contravened section 50, or
- (b) has failed to comply with a compliance notice under section 51.

(2) A penalty notice is a notice requiring the person to whom it is issued to pay a penalty within the period specified in the notice.

(3) The penalty—

- (a) is to be determined in accordance with regulations, and
- (b) must not exceed £50,000.

(4) A penalty notice must—

- (a) state the amount of the penalty;
- (b) state the date, which must be at least 4 weeks after the date on which the notice is issued, by which the penalty must be paid;
- (c) specify the contravention or failure to which the notice relates;
- (d) notify the employer of the review process under section 43 and the right to make a reference under section 44 (as applied by section 53).

(5) Section 42 (penalty notices: recovery) applies to a penalty payable under this section, and to a notice under this section, as it applies to a penalty payable under section 40, and to a notice under that section.

NOTES

Commencement: 26 November 2008 (in so far as it confers any power to make Regulations); 30 June 2012 (otherwise).

Regulations: the Employers' Duties (Registration and Compliance) Regulations 2010, SI 2010/5; the Automatic Enrolment (Miscellaneous Amendments) Regulations 2012, SI 2012/215.

[1.1577]

53 Review of notices and references to Pensions Regulator Tribunal

(1) Section 43 (review of notices) also applies to a compliance notice issued under section 51 and to a penalty notice issued under section 52.

(2) Section 44 (references to the [First-tier Tribunal or Upper Tribunal]) applies in relation to a penalty notice issued under section 52 as it applies in relation to a notice issued under section 40 or 41.

NOTES

Commencement: 30 June 2012.

Sub-s (2): words in square brackets substituted by the Transfer of Tribunal Functions Order 2010, SI 2010/22, art 5(1), Sch 2, paras 146, 150, as from 6 April 2010 (for general savings and transitional provisions in relation to existing cases before the Pensions Regulator Tribunal, see Sch 5 to the 2010 Order).

Inducements

[1.1578]

54 Inducements

(1) An employer contravenes this section if the employer takes any action for the sole or main purpose of—

(a) inducing a worker to give up membership of a relevant scheme without becoming an active member of another relevant scheme [with effect from—

(i) the day after the membership is given up, or

(ii) a day within the prescribed period (if a period is prescribed)], or

(b) inducing a jobholder to give a notice under section 8 without becoming an active member of a qualifying scheme [with effect from—

(i) the day on which the jobholder became an active member of the scheme to which the notice relates, or

(ii) a day within the prescribed period (if a period is prescribed)].

(2) Section 35 applies in relation to a contravention of this section as it applies in relation to a contravention of section 2(1), and sections 38 to 44 apply accordingly.

(3) But the Regulator may not issue a compliance notice in respect of a contravention of this section unless the contravention occurred within the prescribed period before—

(a) the time when a complaint was made to the Regulator about the contravention, or

(b) the time when the Regulator informed the employer of an investigation of the contravention, if no complaint was made before that time.

(4) A compliance notice in respect of a contravention of this section may direct the employer to take or refrain from taking specified steps in order to prevent the contravention being repeated.

(5) For the purposes of this section a worker gives up membership of a relevant scheme if the worker—

(a) takes action or makes an omission by which the worker, without ceasing to be employed by the employer, ceases to be an active member of the scheme, or

(b) requests or authorises the employer to take such action or to make such an omission.

(6) In this section, "relevant scheme" means—

(a) in relation to a jobholder, a qualifying scheme;

(b) in relation to a worker to whom section 9 applies, a scheme which satisfies the requirements of that section.

NOTES

Commencement: 30 June 2012.

Sub-s (1): words in square brackets substituted by the Pensions Act 2011, s 4(6), as from 30 June 2012.

Regulations: the Employers' Duties (Registration and Compliance) Regulations 2010, SI 2010/5; the Automatic Enrolment (Miscellaneous Amendments) Regulations 2012, SI 2012/215.

Protection of employment rights

[1.1579]

55 The right not to suffer detriment

(1) A worker has the right not to be subjected to any detriment by an act, or a deliberate failure to act, by the worker's employer, done on the ground that—

(a) any action was taken, or was proposed to be taken, with a view to enforcing in favour of the worker a requirement to which this section applies,

(b) the employer was prosecuted for an offence under section 45 as a result of action taken for the purpose of enforcing in favour of the worker a requirement to which this section applies, or

(c) any provision of Chapter 1 of this Part applies to the worker, or will or might apply.

(2) It is immaterial for the purposes of paragraph (a) or (b) of subsection (1)—

(a) whether or not the requirement applies in favour of the worker, or

(b) whether or not the requirement has been contravened,

but, for that subsection to apply, the claim that the requirement applies and, if applicable, the claim that it has been contravened must be made in good faith.

(3) This section applies to any requirement imposed on the employer by or under any provision of Chapter 1 of this Part.

(4) This section does not apply where the detriment in question amounts to dismissal within the meaning of Part 10 of the Employment Rights Act 1996 (c 18) (unfair dismissal).

(5) In this section references to enforcing a requirement include references to securing its benefit in any way.

NOTES

Commencement: 30 June 2012.

[1.1580]

56 Enforcement of the right

(1) A worker may present a complaint to an employment tribunal that the worker has been subjected to a detriment in contravention of section 55.

(2) Subject to the following provisions of this section, the provisions of *sections 48(2) to (4)* and 49 of the Employment Rights Act 1996 (complaints to employment tribunals and remedies), apply in relation to a complaint under this section as they apply in relation to a complaint under section 48 of that Act, but taking references in those provisions to the employer as references to the employer within the meaning of section 55(1).

(3) Where—

(a) the detriment to which the worker is subjected is the termination of the worker's contract, but

(b) that contract is not a contract of employment,

any compensation awarded under section 49 of the Employment Rights Act 1996 by virtue of subsection (2) must not exceed the limit specified in subsection (4).

(4) The limit is the total of—

(a) the sum which would be the basic award for unfair dismissal, calculated in accordance with section 119 of the Employment Rights Act 1996, if the worker had been an employee within the meaning of that Act and the contract terminated had been a contract of employment, and

(b) the sum for the time being specified in section 124(1) of that Act which is the limit for a compensatory award to a person calculated in accordance with section 123 of that Act.

(5) Where the worker has been working under arrangements which do not fall to be regarded as a worker's contract for the purposes of the Employment Rights Act 1996, the worker is to be treated for the purposes of subsections (3) and (4) as if any arrangements under which the worker has been working constituted a worker's contract falling within section 230(3)(b) of that Act.

(6) *(Amends the Employment Tribunals Act 1996, s 18 at* **[1.706]**.*)*

NOTES

Commencement: 30 June 2012.

Sub-s (2): for the words in italics there are substituted the words "sections 48(2) to (4A)" by the Enterprise and Regulatory Reform Act 2013, s 8, Sch 2, para 41, as from a day to be appointed.

Conciliation: employment tribunal proceedings and claims which could be the subject of employment tribunal proceedings under this section are proceedings to which the Employment Tribunals Act 1996, s 18 applies; see s 18(1)(v) of that Act at **[1.706]**.

57 *(Inserts the Employment Rights Act 1996, s 104D at* **[1.911]**, *and amends ss 105, 108 of the 1996 Act at* **[1.915]**, **[1.918]**, *and the Trade Union and Labour Relations (Consolidation) Act 1992, ss 237, 238 at* **[1.517]**, **[1.518]**.*)*

[1.1581]

58 Restrictions on agreements to limit operation of this Part

(1) Any provision in any agreement (whether a worker's contract or not) is void in so far as it purports—

(a) to exclude or limit the operation of any provision of this Part, or

(b) to preclude a person from bringing proceedings under section 56 before an employment tribunal.

(2) The fact that an agreement is to any extent void under subsection (1) does not entitle the employer to recover any property transferred, or the value of any benefit conferred, as an inducement to enter into, or otherwise in connection with, the agreement.

(3) Subsection (1) does not apply to any agreement to refrain from instituting or continuing proceedings where a conciliation officer has taken action under *section 18* of the Employment Tribunals Act 1996 (c 17) (conciliation).

(4) Subsection (1) does not apply to any agreement to refrain from instituting or continuing before an employment tribunal any proceedings within section 18(1)(v) of the Employment Tribunals Act 1996 (proceedings under this Act where conciliation is available) if the conditions regulating *compromise* agreements under this Act are satisfied in relation to the agreement.

(5) For the purposes of subsection (4) the conditions regulating *compromise* agreements under this Act are that—

(a) the agreement must be in writing,

(b) the agreement must relate to the particular proceedings,

(c) the worker must have received advice from a relevant independent adviser as to the terms and effect of the proposed agreement and, in particular, its effect on his ability to pursue his rights before an employment tribunal,

(d) there must be in force, when the adviser gives the advice, a contract of insurance, or an indemnity provided for members of a profession or a professional body, covering the risk of a claim by the worker in respect of loss arising in consequence of the advice,

(e) the agreement must identify the adviser, and

(f) the agreement must state that the conditions regulating *compromise* agreements under this Act are satisfied.

(6) A person is a relevant independent adviser for the purposes of subsection (5)(c) if that person—

(a) is a qualified lawyer,

(b) is an officer, official, employee or member of an independent trade union who has been certified in writing by the trade union as competent to give advice and as authorised to do so on behalf of the trade union,

(c) works at an advice centre (whether as an employee or a volunteer) and has been certified in writing by the centre as competent to give advice and as authorised to do so on behalf of the centre, or

(d) is a person of a description specified in an order made by the Secretary of State.

(7) But a person is not a relevant independent adviser for the purposes of subsection (5)(c) in relation to the worker—

(a) if the person is employed by, or is acting in the matter for, the employer or an associated employer,

(b) in the case of a person within subsection (6)(b) or (c), if the trade union or advice centre is the employer or an associated employer,

(c) in the case of a person within subsection (6)(c), if the worker makes a payment for the advice received from the person, or

(d) in the case of a person of a description specified in an order under subsection (6)(d), if any condition specified in the order in relation to the giving of advice by persons of that description is not satisfied.

(8) In this section "qualified lawyer" means—

(a) as respects England and Wales—

(i) a barrister (whether in practice as such or employed to give legal advice),

(ii) a solicitor who holds a practising certificate, or

(iii) a person other than a barrister or solicitor who is an authorised advocate or authorised litigator (within the meaning of the Courts and Legal Services Act 1990);

(b) as respects Scotland—

(i) an advocate (whether in practice as such or employed to give legal advice), or

(ii) a solicitor who holds a practising certificate.

(9) For the purposes of this section any two employers are associated if—

(a) one is a company of which the other (directly or indirectly) has control, or

(b) both are companies of which a third person (directly or indirectly) has control;

and "associated employer" is to be read accordingly.

NOTES

Commencement: 26 November 2008 (in so far as it confers any power to make an Order); 30 June 2012 (otherwise).

Sub-s (3): for the words in italics there are substituted the words "any of sections 18A to 18C" by the Enterprise and Regulatory Reform Act 2013, s 7(2), Sch 1, para 13, as from a day to be appointed.

Sub-ss (4), (5): for the word "compromise" in each place it appears there is substituted the word "settlement" by the Enterprise and Regulatory Reform Act 2013, s 23(1)(c), a day to be appointed.

Orders: the Compromise Agreements (Automatic Enrolment) (Description of Person) Order 2012, SI 2012/212. This Order (which came into force on 1 July 2012) specifies that, for the purposes of sub-s (5)(c) above, a legal executive is a "relevant independent adviser" for the purposes of being able to give advice in relation to compromise agreements under this Act.

59 *(Amends the Employment Tribunals Act 1996, s 21 at* **[1.713]***.)*

CHAPTER 8
APPLICATION AND INTERPRETATION

Workers

[1.1582]

88 "Employer", "worker" and related expressions

(1) This section applies for the purposes of this Part.

(2) "Contract of employment" means a contract of service or apprenticeship, whether express or implied, and (if it is express) whether oral or in writing.

(3) "Worker" means an individual who has entered into or works under—

(a) a contract of employment, or

(b) any other contract by which the individual undertakes to do work or perform services personally for another party to the contract.

(4) But a contract is not within subsection (3)(b) if the status of the other party is by virtue of the contract that of a client or customer of a profession or business undertaking carried on by the individual concerned.

(5) For the purposes of subsection (3)(b), it does not matter whether the contract is express or implied or (if it is express) whether it is oral or in writing.

(6) Any reference to a worker's contract is to be read in accordance with subsections (3) to (5).

(7) "Employer", in relation to a worker, means the person by whom the worker is employed (subject to sections 37(5) and 38(6)).
(8) "Employment" in relation to a worker, means employment under the worker's contract, and related expressions are to be read accordingly.

NOTES
Commencement: 30 June 2012.

[1.1583]
89 Agency workers
(1) This section applies to an individual ("the agency worker")—
(a) who is supplied by a person ("the agent") to do work for another person ("the principal") under a contract or other arrangements made between the agent and the principal,
(b) who is not, as respects that work, a worker, because of the absence of a worker's contract between the individual and the agent or the principal, and
(c) who is not a party to a contract under which the agency worker undertakes to do the work for another party to the contract whose status is, by virtue of the contract, that of a client or customer of a profession or business undertaking carried on by the individual.
(2) Where this section applies, the other provisions of this Part have effect—
(a) as if there were a worker's contract for the doing of the work by the agency worker, made between the agency worker and the relevant person under subsection (3), and
(b) as if that person were the agency worker's employer.
(3) The relevant person is—
(a) whichever of the agent and the principal is responsible for paying the agency worker in respect of the work, or
(b) if neither the agent nor the principal is responsible for doing so, whichever of them pays the agency worker in respect of the work.

NOTES
Commencement: 30 June 2012.

[1.1584]
90 Directors
(1) A person who holds office as a director of a company is not, by virtue of that office or of any employment by the company, a worker for the purposes of this Part, unless—
(a) the person is employed by the company under a contract of employment, and
(b) there is at least one other person who is employed by the company under a contract of employment.
(2) In this section, "company" includes any body corporate.

NOTES
Commencement: 30 June 2012.

[1.1585]
91 Crown employment
(1) This Part has effect in relation to employment by or under the Crown as it has effect in relation to other employment.
(2) For the purposes of the application of the provisions of this Part in accordance with subsection (1)—
(a) references to a worker are to be construed as references to a person employed by or under the Crown;
(b) references to a worker's contract are to be construed as references to the terms of employment of a person employed by or under the Crown.
(3) This section does not impose criminal liability on the Crown.
(4) But on the application of the Regulator the High Court or the Court of Session may declare unlawful a failure by the Crown to comply with any of the duties mentioned in section 45(1).

NOTES
Commencement: 30 June 2012.

[1.1586]
92 Armed forces
(1) A person serving as a member of the naval, military or air forces of the Crown is not, by virtue of that service, a worker for the purposes of this Part.
(2) A member of any of the forces specified in subsection (3) who assists the activities of any of those forces is not, by virtue of anything done in assisting those activities, a worker for the purposes of this Part.
(3) The forces are—

(a) the Combined Cadet Force;
(b) the Sea Cadet Corps;
(c) the Army Cadet Force;
(d) the Air Training Corps.

NOTES

Commencement: 30 June 2012.

[1.1587]
93 House of Lords staff

(1) This Part has effect in relation to employment as a relevant member of the House of Lords staff as it has effect in relation to other employment.

(2) In this section, "relevant member of the House of Lords staff" means any person who is employed under a worker's contract with the Corporate Officer of the House of Lords.

NOTES

Commencement: 30 June 2012.

[1.1588]
94 House of Commons staff

(1) This Part has effect in relation to employment as a relevant member of the House of Commons staff as it has effect in relation to other employment.

(2) In this section, "relevant member of the House of Commons staff" means any person—
(a) who was appointed by the House of Commons Commission, or
(b) who is a member of the Speaker's personal staff.

(3) For the purposes of the application of the provisions of this Part in relation to a relevant member of the House of Commons staff—
(a) references to a worker are to be read as references to a relevant member of the House of Commons staff, and
(b) references to a worker's contract are to be read as references to the terms of employment of a relevant member of the House of Commons staff.

NOTES

Commencement: 30 June 2012.

[1.1589]
95 Police

(1) This Part has effect in relation to a person who—
(a) holds the office of constable or an appointment as a police cadet, and
(b) does not hold that office or appointment under a contract of employment,

as if the person were employed by the [relevant local policing body or] relevant police authority under a worker's contract.

(2) A [local policing body, or a] police authority that maintains a police force is the relevant [local policing body, or relevant] police authority—
(a) in relation to a constable, if the constable is a member of that police force;
(b) in relation to a police cadet, if the cadet is undergoing training with a view to becoming a member of that police force.

NOTES

Commencement: 30 June 2012.

Words in square brackets inserted by the Police Reform and Social Responsibility Act 2011, s 99, Sch 16, Pt 3, para 371, as from 16 January 2012 (for general transitional provisions relating to police reform and the abolition of existing police authorities, see Sch 15 to the 2011 Act, and the Police Reform and Social Responsibility Act 2011 (Commencement No 3 and Transitional Provisions) Order 2011, SI 2011/3019).

[1.1590]
96 Persons working on vessels

(1) Subject to regulations under this section, a person employed or engaged in any capacity on board a ship is not, by virtue of that employment or engagement, a worker for the purposes of this Part.

(2) The Secretary of State may by regulations provide that, to the extent and for the purposes specified in the regulations, the relevant provisions apply, with or without modification, in relation to a person employed or engaged in any capacity on board a ship (whether or not that person is working or ordinarily works in any part of the United Kingdom).

(3) For the purposes of this section, the relevant provisions are—
(a) this Part (and any enactment as amended by this Part), and
(b) any provision in force in Northern Ireland corresponding to any provision of this Part (and any enactment as amended by such a provision).

(4) Regulations under this section—

(a) may provide for a provision to apply in relation to individuals whether or not they are British subjects;
(b) may provide for a provision to apply in relation to bodies corporate whether or not they are incorporated under the law of a part of the United Kingdom;
(c) may do so even where the application may affect the individual's or body's activities outside the United Kingdom.

(5) Regulations under this section—
(a) may provide for a court or tribunal on which jurisdiction is conferred by the relevant provisions to have jurisdiction, in respect of offences or other matters, for the purposes of any provision as it applies by virtue of the regulations;
(b) may exclude from the operation of section 3 of the Territorial Waters Jurisdiction Act 1878 (c 73) (consents required for prosecutions) proceedings for offences under any provision as it applies by virtue of the regulations;
(c) may provide that such proceedings may not be brought without such consent as may be required by the regulations.

(6) Any jurisdiction conferred on a court or tribunal under this section is without prejudice to jurisdiction exercisable apart from this section by that or any other court or tribunal.

(7) In this section, "ship" includes—
(a) a hovercraft within the meaning of the Hovercraft Act 1968 (c 59), and
(b) every description of vessel used in navigation.

NOTES

Commencement: 26 November 2008 (in so far as it confers any power to make Regulations); 30 June 2012 (otherwise).

Regulations: the Occupational and Personal Pension Schemes (Automatic Enrolment) (Amendment) Regulations 2012, SI 2012/1257.

[1.1591]

97 Persons in offshore employment

(1) Her Majesty may by Order in Council provide that, to the extent and for the purposes specified in the Order, the relevant provisions apply, with or without modification, in relation to a person in offshore employment.

(2) For the purposes of this section, the relevant provisions are—
(a) this Part (and any enactment as amended by this Part), and
(b) any provision in force in Northern Ireland corresponding to any provision of this Part (and any enactment as amended by such a provision).

(3) In this section, "offshore employment" has the same meaning as in section 201(1) of the Employment Rights Act 1996 (c 18).

(4) An Order in Council under this section—
(a) may provide for a provision to apply in relation to individuals whether or not they are British subjects;
(b) may provide for a provision to apply in relation to bodies corporate whether or not they are incorporated under the law of a part of the United Kingdom;
(c) may do so even where the application may affect the individual's or body's activities outside the United Kingdom.

(5) An Order in Council under this section—
(a) may make different provision for different cases;
(b) may provide for a court or tribunal on which jurisdiction is conferred by the relevant provisions to have jurisdiction, in respect of offences or other matters, for the purposes of any provision as it applies by virtue of the Order;
(c) may (without prejudice to subsection (1) and paragraph (a)) provide for a provision to apply in relation to any person in employment in a part of the areas referred to in section 201(1)(a) and (b) of the Employment Rights Act 1996 (c 18);
(d) may exclude from the operation of section 3 of the Territorial Waters Jurisdiction Act 1878 (c 73) (consents required for prosecutions) proceedings for offences under any provision as it applies by virtue of the Order;
(e) may provide that such proceedings may not be brought without such consent as may be required by the Order.

(6) Any jurisdiction conferred on a court or tribunal under this section is without prejudice to jurisdiction exercisable apart from this section by that or any other court or tribunal.

(7) No Order in Council may be made under this section unless a draft of the Order has been laid before and approved by a resolution of each House of Parliament.

NOTES

Commencement: 26 November 2008 (in so far as it confers any power to make an Order); 30 June 2012 (otherwise).

Orders: as of 6 April 2013 no Orders had been made under this section.

[1.1592]

98 Extension of definition of worker

The Secretary of State may by regulations make provision for this Part to apply with or without modifications—

(a) as if any individual of a prescribed description (who would not otherwise be a worker) were a worker,

(b) as if there were in the case of any such individual a worker's contract of a prescribed description under which the individual works, and

(c) as if a person of a prescribed description were the employer under that contract.

NOTES

Commencement: 26 November 2008 (in so far as it confers any power to make Regulations); to be appointed (otherwise).

Regulations: the Occupational and Personal Pension Schemes (Automatic Enrolment) (Amendment) Regulations 2012, SI 2012/1257.

General

[1.1593]

99 Interpretation of Part

In this Part—

"active member"—

(a) in relation to an occupational pension scheme, means a person who is in pensionable service under the scheme;

(b) in relation to a personal pension scheme, means a jobholder in relation to whom there is an agreement within section 26(4) between the provider of the scheme and the employer or (where section 9 applies) a worker in relation to whom there are direct payment arrangements (within the meaning of section 111A of the Pension Schemes Act 1993 (c 48)) between the worker and the employer;

"automatic enrolment scheme" is to be read in accordance with section 3(8);

"average salary benefits" means benefits the rate or amount of which is calculated by reference to the average salary of a member over the period of service on which the benefits are based;

"contract of employment" has the meaning given by section 88;

"defined benefits", in relation to a member of an occupational pension scheme, means benefits which are not money purchase benefits (but the rate or amount of which is calculated by reference to earnings or service of the member or any other factor other than an amount available for their provision);

"defined benefits scheme" means an occupational pension scheme under which all the benefits that may be provided are defined benefits;

"employer", "employment" and related expressions have the meaning given by section 88;

"enrolment duty" means a duty under section 3(2), 5(2), 7(3) or 9(2);

"hybrid scheme" means an occupational pension scheme which is neither a defined benefits scheme nor a money purchase scheme;

the "IORP Directive" means Directive 2003/41/EC of the European Parliament and of the Council on the activities and supervision of institutions for occupational retirement provision;

"jobholder" has the meaning given by section 1(1);

"money purchase benefits", in relation to a member of a pension scheme, means benefits the rate or amount of which is calculated by reference to a payment or payments made by the member or by any other person in respect of the member and [which fall within section 99A];

"money purchase scheme" means an occupational pension scheme under which all the benefits that may be provided are money purchase benefits;

"occupational pension scheme" has the meaning given by section 18;

"pension scheme" has the meaning given by section 1(5) of the Pension Schemes Act 1993 (c 48);

"pensionable age" has the meaning given by the rules in paragraph 1 of Schedule 4 to the Pensions Act 1995 (c 26);

"pensionable service", in relation to a member of an occupational pension scheme, means service in any description of employment to which the scheme relates which qualifies the member (on the assumption that it continues for the appropriate period) for pension or other benefits under the scheme;

"personal pension scheme" has the meaning given by section 19;

"prescribed" means prescribed by regulations;

"provider"—

(a) in relation to a personal pension scheme to which section 26 applies, means the person referred to in subsection (1)(b) of that section;

(b) in relation to any other personal pension scheme, has the meaning prescribed;

"qualifying earnings" has the meaning given by section 13;
"qualifying scheme" is to be read in accordance with section 2(5);
"regulations" means regulations made by the Secretary of State;
"the Regulator" means the Pensions Regulator;
"tax year" means the 12 months beginning with 6th April in any year;
"trustee or manager"—

(a) in relation to England and Wales or Scotland, is to be construed in accordance with section 178 of the Pension Schemes Act 1993 (c 48) (trustees and managers of schemes: interpretation);

(b) in relation to Northern Ireland, is to be construed in accordance with section 173 of the Pension Schemes (Northern Ireland) Act 1993 (c 49) (trustees or managers of schemes);

"worker" has the meaning given by section 88.

NOTES

Commencement: 5 July 2010.

Words in square brackets in the definition "money purchase benefits" substituted by the Pensions Act 2011, s 29(3), with retrospective effect.

PART 6
GENERAL

[1.1594]

143 Orders and regulations

(1) Any power conferred on the Secretary of State to make an order or regulations under this Act is exercisable by statutory instrument.

(2) A statutory instrument containing such an order or regulations is subject to annulment in pursuance of a resolution of either House of Parliament.

(3) Subsection (2) does not apply to a statutory instrument containing an order under section 149 or to a statutory instrument to which subsection (4) applies.

(4) A statutory instrument to which this subsection applies may not be made unless a draft of the instrument has been laid before and approved by a resolution of each House of Parliament.

(5) Subsection (4) applies to a statutory instrument containing (alone or with other provision)—

(a) regulations under section 16(3)(c), 17(1)(c), 28, 96, 98 or 142;
(b) the first regulations under section 3(2) or (6), 5(2) or (7), 7(4)(b) or (6) or 9(3)(b);
(c) an order under section [14(2),] 28(9), 67 or 70(4);
(d) an order under section 145 amending or repealing any provision of an Act;
(e) an order under paragraph 9(7) of Schedule 5.

NOTES

Commencement: 26 November 2008.

Sub-s (5): figure in square brackets in para (c) inserted by the Pensions Act 2011, s 8(3), as from 3 November 2011.

[1.1595]

144 Orders and regulations: supplementary

(1) This section applies to an order or regulations made by the Secretary of State under this Act.

(2) An order or regulations may include—

(a) such incidental, supplemental, consequential or transitional provision as appears to the Secretary of State to be expedient;
(b) provision conferring a discretion on any person.

(3) An order under section 67 may include provision for anything that may be prescribed by the order to be determined under it, and for anything falling to be so determined to be determined by such persons, in accordance with such procedure and by reference to such matters, and to the opinion of such persons, as may be prescribed.

(4) The power to make an order or regulations may be exercised—

(a) either in relation to all cases to which the power extends, or in relation to those cases subject to specified exceptions, or in relation to any specified cases or classes of case,
(b) so as to make, as respects the cases in relation to which it is exercised—
    (i) the full provision to which the power extends or any less provision (whether by way of exception or otherwise),
    (ii) the same provision for all cases in relation to which the power is exercised, or different provision for different cases or different classes of case or different provision as respects the same case or class of case for different purposes of this Act, or
    (iii) any such provision either unconditionally or subject to any specified condition.

NOTES

Commencement: 26 November 2008.

[1.1596]

145 Power to make further provision

(1) The Secretary of State may by order make—

(a) such supplemental, incidental or consequential provision, or

(b) such transitory, transitional or saving provision,

as the Secretary of State thinks appropriate for the general purposes, or any particular purpose, of this Act or in consequence of any provision made by or under this Act or for giving full effect to this Act or any such provision.

(2) An order under this section may, for purposes of or in consequence of or for giving full effect to any provision of or made under Chapter 5 of Part 1 or section 106, make provision for applying (with or without modifications) or amending, repealing or revoking any provision of or made under an Act passed before this Act or in the same Session.

(3) Amendments made under this section are in addition, and without prejudice, to those made by or under any other provision of this Act.

(4) No other provision of this Act restricts the powers conferred by this section.

NOTES

Commencement: 26 November 2008.

Orders: the Pensions Act 2008 (Abolition of Safeguarded Rights) (Consequential) Order 2009, SI 2009/598; the National Employment Savings Trust (Consequential Provisions) Order 2010, SI 2010/9; the Pensions Act 2008 (Abolition of Protected Rights) (Consequential Amendments) Order 2011, SI 2011/1246; the Pensions Act 2008 (Abolition of Protected Rights) (Consequential Amendments) (No 2) Order 2011, SI 2011/1730; the Pensions Act 2008 (Abolition of Protected Rights) (Consequential Amendments) (No 2) (Amendment) Order 2012, SI 2012/709.

[1.1597]

146 Pre-consolidation amendments

(1) The Secretary of State may by order make such modifications of enactments within subsection (2) as in the Secretary of State's opinion facilitate, or are otherwise desirable in connection with, the consolidation of any of those enactments.

(2) The enactments are—

(a) the Pension Schemes Act 1993 (c 48);

(b) the Pensions Act 1995 (c 26);

(c) Parts 1 to 4 of the Welfare Reform and Pensions Act 1999 (c 30);

(d) Chapter 2 of Part 2 of the Child Support, Pensions and Social Security Act 2000 (c 19);

(e) the Pensions Act 2004 (c 35);

(f) the Pensions Act 2007 (c 22);

(g) this Act;

(h) enactments referring to any enactment within paragraphs (a) to (g).

(3) No order may be made under this section unless a Bill for consolidating the enactments modified by the order (with or without other enactments) has been presented to either House of Parliament.

(4) An order under this section, so far as it modifies any enactment, is not to come into force except in accordance with provision made for the purpose by the Act resulting from that Bill.

(5) An order under this section must not make any provision which would, if it were included in an Act of the Scottish Parliament, be within the legislative competence of that Parliament.

NOTES

Commencement: 26 November 2008.

[1.1598]

147 General financial provisions

There is to be paid out of money provided by Parliament—

(a) any expenditure incurred by the Secretary of State or a government department in consequence of this Act, and

(b) any increase attributable to this Act in the sums payable out of money so provided under any other enactment.

NOTES

Commencement: 26 November 2008.

[1.1599]

149 Commencement

(1) Subject to the following provisions, this Act comes into force in accordance with provision made by order by the Secretary of State.

(2) Subsection (1) does not apply to—

(a)–(h) (*outside the scope of this work*);

(i) this Part, except section 148 and Schedule 11 (subject to paragraph (j));

(j) (*outside the scope of this work*);

(k) any other provision of this Act so far as it confers any power to make regulations, rules, an Order in Council or an order under this Act.

(3)–(5) (*Outside the scope of this work*).

(6) An order under subsection (1) may appoint different days for different purposes.

NOTES

Commencement: 26 November 2008.

Orders: many commencement orders have been made under this section. in so far as relevant their effect is noted *ante*.

[1.1600]

150 Extent

(1) Subject to the following provisions, this Act extends to England and Wales and Scotland.

(2) The following provisions extend also to Northern Ireland—

(a) Chapters 5 and 6 of Part 1 and section 99 so far as it relates to those Chapters;

(b) section 96(2) to (7);

(c) section 97;

(d), (e) (*outside the scope of this work*);

(f) sections [143, 144, 145 and 146];

(g) section 149, this section and section 151.

(3) An amendment or repeal by this Act has the same extent as the enactment amended or repealed (subject to the provision made by section 63(3), section 64(2) and paragraph 9 of Schedule 10).

NOTES

Commencement: 26 November 2008.

Sub-s (2): words in brackets in para (f) substituted by the Pensions Act 2011, s 36(3), as from 30 June 2012.

[1.1601]

151 Short title

This Act may be cited as the Pensions Act 2008.

NOTES

Commencement: 26 November 2008.

APPRENTICESHIPS, SKILLS, CHILDREN AND LEARNING ACT 2009

(2009 c 22)

ARRANGEMENT OF SECTIONS

PART 1
APPRENTICESHIPS, STUDY AND TRAINING

CHAPTER 1
APPRENTICESHIPS

Completing an apprenticeship

Apprenticeship agreements: England and Wales

General

PART 13
GENERAL

An Act to make provision about apprenticeships, education, training and children's services; to amend the Employment Rights Act 1996; to establish the Young People's Learning Agency for England, the office of Chief Executive of Skills Funding, the Office of Qualifications and Examinations Regulation and the School Support Staff Negotiating Body and to make provision about those bodies and that office; to make provision about the Qualifications and Curriculum Authority; to make provision about schools and institutions within the further education sector; to make provision about student loans; and for connected purposes

[12 November 2009]

NOTES

Only certain parts of this Act most relevant to employment law are reproduced. Provisions omitted are not annotated.

PART 1
APPRENTICESHIPS, STUDY AND TRAINING

CHAPTER 1
APPRENTICESHIPS

Completing an apprenticeship

[1.1602]

1 Meaning of "completing an English apprenticeship"

(1) This section applies for the purposes of this Chapter.

(2) A person completes an English apprenticeship in relation to an apprenticeship framework if—

(a) the standard English completion conditions are met, or

(b) the alternative English completion conditions are met.

(3) The standard English completion conditions are—

(a) that the person has entered into an apprenticeship agreement in connection with the apprenticeship framework,

(b) that at the date of that agreement the framework was a recognised English framework,

(c) that the person has completed a course of training for the competencies qualification identified in the framework,

(d) that, throughout the duration of the course, the person was working under the apprenticeship agreement, and

(e) that the person meets the requirements specified in the framework for the purpose of the issue of an apprenticeship certificate.

(4) In subsection (3)(d)—

(a) the reference to the apprenticeship agreement mentioned in subsection (3)(a) includes a reference to any apprenticeship agreement which the person subsequently entered into in connection with the same apprenticeship framework;

(b) the reference to the course of training for the competencies qualification is to be read, in a case where the person has followed two or more courses of training for the competencies qualification, as a reference to both or all of them.

(5) The alternative English completion conditions are conditions which—

(a) apply in cases where a person works otherwise than under an apprenticeship agreement, and

(b) are specified in regulations.

(6) The kinds of working in relation to which provision may be made under subsection (5) include—

(a) working as a self-employed person;

(b) working otherwise than for reward.

NOTES

Commencement: 6 April 2011.

Regulations: the Apprenticeships (Alternative English Completion Conditions) Regulations 2012, SI 2012/1199.

[1.1603]

2 Meaning of "completing a Welsh apprenticeship"

(1) This section applies for the purposes of this Chapter.

(2) A person completes a Welsh apprenticeship in relation to an apprenticeship framework if—

(a) the standard Welsh completion conditions are met, or

(b) the alternative Welsh completion conditions are met.

(3) The standard Welsh completion conditions are—

(a) that the person has entered into an apprenticeship agreement in connection with the apprenticeship framework,
(b) that at the date of that agreement the framework was a recognised Welsh framework,
(c) that the person has completed a course of training for the competencies qualification identified in the framework,
(d) that, throughout the duration of the course, the person was working under the apprenticeship agreement, and
(e) that the person meets the requirements specified in the framework for the purpose of the issue of an apprenticeship certificate.

(4) In subsection (3)(d)—
(a) the reference to the apprenticeship agreement mentioned in subsection (3)(a) includes a reference to any apprenticeship agreement which the person subsequently entered into in connection with the same apprenticeship framework;
(b) the reference to the course of training for the competencies qualification is to be read, in a case where the person has followed two or more courses of training for the competencies qualification, as a reference to both or all of them.

(5) The alternative Welsh completion conditions are conditions which—
(a) apply in cases where a person works otherwise than under an apprenticeship agreement, and
(b) are specified in regulations made by the Welsh Ministers.

(6) The kinds of working in relation to which provision may be made under subsection (5) include—
(a) working as a self-employed person;
(b) working otherwise than for reward.

NOTES

Commencement: to be appointed.

Apprenticeship agreements: England and Wales

[1.1604]

32 Meaning of "apprenticeship agreement"

(1) In this Chapter, "apprenticeship agreement" means an agreement in relation to which each of the conditions in subsection (2) is satisfied.

(2) The conditions are—
(a) that a person (the "apprentice") undertakes to work for another (the "employer") under the agreement;
(b) that the agreement is in the prescribed form;
(c) that the agreement states that it is governed by the law of England and Wales;
(d) that the agreement states that it is entered into in connection with a qualifying apprenticeship framework.

(3) The power conferred by subsection (2)(b) may be exercised, in particular—
(a) to specify provisions that must be included in an apprenticeship agreement;
(b) to specify provisions that must not be included in an apprenticeship agreement;
(c) to specify all or part of the wording of provisions that must be included in an apprenticeship agreement.

(4) Where an agreement states that it is entered into in connection with an apprenticeship framework ("the relevant framework") that is not a qualifying apprenticeship framework, subsection (2)(d) is to be taken to be satisfied in relation to the agreement if—
(a) at a time within the period of three years ending with the date of the agreement, the relevant framework was a qualifying apprenticeship framework;
(b) at the date of the agreement, the apprentice has not completed the whole of a course of training for the competencies qualification identified in the relevant framework,
(c) before the date of the agreement, the apprentice entered into an apprenticeship agreement ("the earlier agreement") which stated that it was entered into in connection with the relevant framework, and
(d) at the date of the earlier agreement, the relevant framework was a qualifying apprenticeship framework.

(5) In subsection (4)(b), the reference to a course of training for the competencies qualification is to be read, in a case where the person follows two or more courses of training for the competencies qualification, as a reference to both or all of them.

(6) An apprenticeship framework is a "qualifying apprenticeship framework", for the purposes of this section, if it is—
(a) a recognised English framework, or
(b) a recognised Welsh framework.

NOTES

Commencement: 6 April 2011 (in relation to England); 1 August 2011 (in relation to Wales).

Regulations: the Apprenticeships (Form of Apprenticeship Agreement) Regulations 2012, SI 2012/844 at **[2.1624]**.

[1.1605]

33 Ineffective provisions

(1) To the extent that provision included in an apprenticeship agreement conflicts with the prescribed apprenticeship provisions, it has no effect.

(2) In this section, the "prescribed apprenticeship provisions", in relation to an apprenticeship agreement, means those provisions—

(a) that are included in the agreement, and

(b) without the inclusion of which the agreement would not satisfy section 32(2)(b).

NOTES

Commencement: 6 April 2011 (in relation to England); 1 August 2011 (in relation to Wales).

[1.1606]

34 Variation

(1) If a variation to an apprenticeship agreement is within subsection (2), it has effect only if, before it was made, the employer complied with the requirement in subsection (3).

(2) A variation to an apprenticeship agreement is within this subsection if its nature is such that, were it to take effect, the agreement would cease to be an apprenticeship agreement.

(3) The employer must give the apprentice written notice stating that, if the variation takes effect, the agreement will cease to be an apprenticeship agreement.

NOTES

Commencement: 6 April 2011 (in relation to England); 1 August 2011 (in relation to Wales).

[1.1607]

35 Status

(1) To the extent that it would otherwise be treated as being a contract of apprenticeship, an apprenticeship agreement is to be treated as not being a contract of apprenticeship.

(2) To the extent that it would not otherwise be treated as being a contract of service, an apprenticeship agreement is to be treated as being a contract of service.

(3) This section applies for the purposes of any enactment or rule of law.

NOTES

Commencement: 6 April 2011 (in relation to England); 1 August 2011 (in relation to Wales).

[1.1608]

36 Crown servants and Parliamentary staff

(1) Sections 32 to 35 apply in relation to—

(a) an agreement under which a person undertakes Crown employment,

(b) an agreement under which a person undertakes service as a member of the naval, military or air forces of the Crown, and

(c) an agreement under which a person undertakes employment as—

(i) a relevant member of the House of Lords staff, or

(ii) a relevant member of the House of Commons staff,

as they apply in relation to any other agreement under which a person undertakes to work for another.

(2) Subsection (1) is subject to subsection (3) and to any modifications which may be prescribed under subsection (5).

(3) Section 35(2) does not apply in relation to an apprenticeship agreement that is an agreement within paragraph (a), (b) or (c) of subsection (1).

(4) Without prejudice to section 262(3), the power conferred by section 32(2)(b) may be exercised, in particular, to make provision in relation to an apprenticeship agreement which is an agreement within any of paragraphs (a), (b) and (c) of subsection (1) that differs from provision made in relation to other apprenticeship agreements.

(5) Regulations may provide for any provision of this Chapter . . . to apply with modifications in relation to—

(a) an agreement within paragraph (a), (b) or (c) of subsection (1), or

(b) a person working, or proposing to work, under such an agreement.

(6) In subsection (1)—

"Crown employment" means employment under or for the purposes of a government department or any officer or body exercising on behalf of the Crown functions conferred by a statutory provision (but does not include service as a member of the naval, military or air forces of the Crown);

"relevant member of the House of Commons staff" has the meaning given by section 195(5) of the Employment Rights Act 1996 (c 18);

"relevant member of the House of Lords staff" has the meaning given by section 194(6) of that Act.

NOTES

Commencement: 6 April 2011 (in relation to England); 1 August 2011 (in relation to Wales).

Sub-s (5): words omitted repealed by the Education Act 2011, s 69(3), Sch 18, paras 1, 3, as from 1 September 2012.

Regulations: the Apprenticeships (Form of Apprenticeship Agreement) Regulations 2012, SI 2012/844 at **[2.1624]**.

General

[1.1609]

39 Interpretation of Chapter

(1) In this Chapter—

"apprenticeship agreement" has the meaning given by section 32(1);

"apprenticeship certificate" means a certificate issued under section 3, 4, 7 or 8;

"apprenticeship framework" has the meaning given by section 12(1);

"apprenticeship sector" means a sector specified under section 38;

"the competencies qualification", in relation to an apprenticeship framework, means the qualification identified in the framework as being the competencies qualification;

["English certifying authority", in relation to an apprenticeship certificate of any description, has the meaning given by section 6(1);]

"English issuing authority", in relation to an apprenticeship framework, has the meaning given by section 13(5);

"recognised English framework" has the meaning given by section 12(3);

"recognised Welsh framework" has the meaning given by section 12(4);

"the specification of apprenticeship standards for England" means the specification of apprenticeship standards having effect for the time being by virtue of an order made by the Secretary of State under section 24 or 25;

"the specification of apprenticeship standards for Wales" means the specification of apprenticeship standards having effect for the time being by virtue of an order made by the Welsh Ministers under section 28 or 29;

"Welsh certifying authority", in relation to an apprenticeship certificate of any description, has the meaning given by section 10(1);

"Welsh issuing authority", in relation to an apprenticeship framework, has the meaning given by section 18(5).

(2) References in this Chapter—

(a) to the level of an apprenticeship framework, or

(b) to the apprenticeship sector to which an apprenticeship framework relates,

are to be construed in accordance with section 12(5).

(3) References in this Chapter to an employer and an apprentice, in relation to an apprenticeship agreement, are to be construed in accordance with section 32.

NOTES

Commencement: 6 April 2011 (in relation to England); to be appointed (in relation to Wales).

Sub-s (1): definition "English certifying authority" substituted by the Education Act 2011, s 71(1), (4), as from 1 April 2012.

CHAPTER 2
STUDY AND TRAINING

40 *(Inserts the Employment Rights Act 1996, Pt 6A (ss 63D–63K) at* **[1.840]** *et seq, adds ss 47F and 104E of that Act at* **[1.812]** *and* **[1.912]**, *and introduces Sch 1 to this Act (Employee Study and Training: Minor and Consequential Amendments).)*

PART 10
SCHOOLS

227–241 *(Ss 227–241 (Chapter 4–School Support Staff Pay and Conditions: England) together with Sch 15 (the School Support Staff Negotiating Body) were repealed by the Education Act 2011, s 18, as from 1 February 2012.)*

PART 13
GENERAL

[1.1610]

262 Orders and regulations

(1) A power to make an order or regulations under Chapter 1 of Part 1, or Part 3 or 4—

(a) so far as exercisable by the Secretary of State, the Welsh Ministers or the Scottish Ministers, is exercisable by statutory instrument;

(b) so far as exercisable by the Department for Employment and Learning in Northern Ireland, is exercisable by statutory rule for the purposes of the Statutory Rules (Northern Ireland) Order 1979 (SI 1979/1573 (NI 12)).

(2) Any other power of the Secretary of State to make an order or regulations under this Act is exercisable by statutory instrument.

(3) A power of the Secretary of State or the Welsh Ministers to make an order or regulations under this Act (except a power conferred by section 17, 22 or 269) includes power—

(a) to make different provision for different purposes (including different areas);

(b) to make provision generally or in relation to specific cases;

(c) to make incidental, consequential, supplementary, transitional, transitory or saving provision.

[(3A)], (4) *(Outside the scope of this work.)*

(5) Subject to subsections (6) to (8), a statutory instrument containing an order or regulations made by the Secretary of State under any provision of this Act (other than an order under section 269) is subject to annulment in pursuance of a resolution of either House of Parliament.

(6) A statutory instrument which contains (whether alone or with other provision) any of the following may not be made unless a draft of the instrument has been laid before, and approved by a resolution of, each House of Parliament—

(aa) regulations under section 1(5);

[(ab)]–(h) *(outside the scope of this work.)*

(7), (8) *(Outside the scope of this work.)*

(9) Subject to subsection (10), a statutory instrument containing an order or regulations made by the Welsh Ministers under Chapter 1 of Part 1 (other than an order under section 10) or under section 68 or 107 is subject to annulment in pursuance of a resolution of the National Assembly for Wales.

(10) A statutory instrument which contains (whether alone or with other provision) regulations under section 2(5) may not be made unless a draft of the instrument has been laid before, and approved by a resolution of, the National Assembly for Wales.

(11)–(13) *(Outside the scope of this work.)*

NOTES

Commencement: 12 November 2009.

Note that sub-s (6)(aa) is an original paragraph; it was not inserted by a subsequent amending enactment.

Regulations: the Young People's Learning Agency for England (Specified Charges) Regulations 2010, SI 2010/598; the Apprenticeships (Form of Apprenticeship Agreement) Regulations 2012, SI 2012/844 at **[2.1624]**; the Apprenticeships (Alternative English Completion Conditions) Regulations 2012, SI 2012/1199; the Apprenticeships (the Apprenticeship Offer) (Prescribed Persons) Regulations 2013, SI 2013/560.

Orders: the Apprenticeships, Skills, Children and Learning Act 2009 (Commencement No 1) (Wales) Order 2009, SI 2009/3341; the Apprenticeships, Skills, Children and Learning Act 2009 (Consequential Amendments) (England and Wales) Order 2010, SI 2010/1080.

[1.1611]

263 Directions

A direction given under this Act—

(a) may be amended or revoked by the person or body by whom it is given;

(b) may make different provision for different purposes.

NOTES

Commencement: 12 November 2009.

[1.1612]

264 General interpretation of Act

(1) In this Act, unless the context otherwise requires—

"prescribed" means prescribed by regulations;

"regulations" means regulations made by the Secretary of State.

(2)–(6) *(Outside the scope of this work.)*

NOTES

Commencement: 12 November 2009.

[1.1613]

265 Power to make consequential and transitional provision etc

(1) The Secretary of State may by order make—

(a) such supplementary, incidental or consequential provision, or

(b) such transitory, transitional or saving provision,

as the Secretary of State thinks appropriate for the general purposes, or any particular purpose, of this Act or in consequence of, or for giving full effect to, any provision made by this Act.

(2) An order under this section may in particular—

(a) provide for any provision of this Act which comes into force before another provision made by or under this or any other Act has come into force to have effect, until that other provision has come into force, with specified modifications;
(b) amend, repeal, revoke or otherwise modify any provision of—
  (i) an Act passed before or in the same Session as this Act, or
  (ii) an instrument made under an Act before the passing of this Act.

(3) Nothing in this section limits the powers conferred by section 262(3)(c) or 269(8)(b).
(4) The amendments that may be made by virtue of subsection (2)(b) are in addition to those that are made by any other provision of this Act.

NOTES

Commencement: 12 November 2009.

Orders: the Apprenticeships, Skills, Children and Learning Act 2009, Parts 7 and 8 (Consequential Amendments) Order 2010, SI 2010/677; the Apprenticeships, Skills, Children and Learning Act 2009 (Consequential Amendments) (England and Wales) Order 2010, SI 2010/1080; the Apprenticeships, Skills, Children and Learning Act 2009 (Consequential Amendments to Subordinate Legislation) (England) Order 2010, SI 2010/1941; the Apprenticeships, Skills, Children and Learning Act 2009 (Consequential Amendments to Subordinate Legislation) (England and Wales) Order 2012, SI 2012/3112.

[1.1614]
268 Extent

(1) This Act extends to England and Wales only, subject to subsections (2) to (4).
(2), (3) *(Application of Act to Scotland and Northern Ireland; outside the scope of this work.)*
(4) An amendment, repeal or revocation made by this Act has the same extent as the provision to which it relates.

NOTES

Commencement: 12 November 2009.

[1.1615]
269 Commencement

(1) This Part (except section 266) comes into force on the day on which this Act is passed.
(2) *(Outside the scope of this work.)*
(3) The following provisions of this Act come into force on such day as the Welsh Ministers may by order appoint—
  (a) sections 2 and 7 to 10;
  (b)–(d) *(outside the scope of this work)*;
  (e) section 39, so far as relating to Wales;
  (f)–(n) *(outside the scope of this work).*
(4) The other provisions of this Act come into force on such day as the Secretary of State may by order appoint.
(5), (6) *(Outside the scope of this work.)*
(7) The powers conferred by this section are exercisable by statutory instrument.
(8) An order under this section may—
  (a) appoint different days for different purposes (including different areas);
  (b) contain transitional, transitory or saving provision in connection with the coming into force of this Act.

NOTES

Commencement: 12 November 2009.

Orders: the Apprenticeships, Skills, Children and Learning Act 2009 (Commencement No 1 and Saving Provision) Order 2009, SI 2009/3317; the Apprenticeships, Skills, Children and Learning Act 2009 (Commencement No 2 and Transitional and Saving Provisions) Order 2010, SI 2010/303; the Apprenticeships, Skills, Children and Learning Act 2009 (Commencement No 3 and Transitional and Transitory Provisions) and (Commencement No 2 (Amendment)) Order 2010, SI 2010/1151; the Apprenticeships, Skills, Children and Learning Act 2009 (Commencement No 3 (Amendment)) Order 2010, SI 2010/1702; the Apprenticeships, Skills, Children and Learning Act 2009 (Commencement No 2 (Amendment) and Transitional Provision) Order 2010, SI 2010/1891; the Apprenticeships, Skills, Children and Learning Act 2009 (Commencement No 4) Order 2010, SI 2010/2374; the Apprenticeships, Skills, Children and Learning Act 2009 (Commencement No 2 and Transitional Provisions) (Wales) Order 2010, SI 2010/2413; the Apprenticeships, Skills, Children and Learning Act 2009 (Commencement No 5) Order 2011, SI 2011/200; the Apprenticeships, Skills, Children and Learning Act 2009 (Commencement No 2 and Transitional and Saving Provisions) Order 2010 (Amendment) Order 2011, SI 2011/882.

[1.1616]
270 Short title

(1) This Act may be cited as the Apprenticeships, Skills, Children and Learning Act 2009.
(2) This Act is to be included in the list of Education Acts set out in section 578 of the Education Act 1996 (c 56).

NOTES

Commencement: 12 November 2009.

CORONERS AND JUSTICE ACT 2009

(2009 c 25)

An Act to amend the law relating to coroners, to investigation of deaths and to certification and registration of deaths; to amend the criminal law; to make provision about criminal justice and about dealing with offenders; to make provision about the Commissioner for Victims and Witnesses; to make provision relating to the security of court and other buildings; to make provision about legal aid and about payments for legal services provided in connection with employment matters; to make provision for payments to be made by offenders in respect of benefits derived from the exploitation of material pertaining to offences; to amend the Data Protection Act 1998; and for connected purposes

[12 November 2009]

NOTES

Most of this Act covers matters outside the scope of this work, and only s 71 below is directly relevant to employment law. For reasons of space, the subject matter of sections not printed is not annotated. Section 71 applies to England, Wales and Northern Ireland only (see s 181).

PART 2
CRIMINAL OFFENCES

CHAPTER 3
OTHER OFFENCES

[1.1617]

71 Slavery, servitude and forced or compulsory labour

(1) A person (D) commits an offence if—

(a) D holds another person in slavery or servitude and the circumstances are such that D knows or ought to know that the person is so held, or

(b) D requires another person to perform forced or compulsory labour and the circumstances are such that D knows or ought to know that the person is being required to perform such labour.

(2) In subsection (1) the references to holding a person in slavery or servitude or requiring a person to perform forced or compulsory labour are to be construed in accordance with Article 4 of the Human Rights Convention (which prohibits a person from being held in slavery or servitude or being required to perform forced or compulsory labour).

(3) A person guilty of an offence under this section is liable—

(a) on summary conviction, to imprisonment for a term not exceeding the relevant period or a fine not exceeding the statutory maximum, or both;

(b) on conviction on indictment, to imprisonment for a term not exceeding 14 years or a fine, or both.

(4) In this section—

"Human Rights Convention" means the Convention for the Protection of Human Rights and Fundamental Freedoms agreed by the Council of Europe at Rome on 4 November 1950;

"the relevant period" means—

(a) in relation to England and Wales, 12 months;

(b) in relation to Northern Ireland, 6 months.

NOTES

Commencement: 6 April 2010.

EQUALITY ACT 2010

(2010 c 15)

ARRANGEMENT OF SECTIONS

PART 1
SOCIO-ECONOMIC INEQUALITIES

PART 2
EQUALITY: KEY CONCEPTS

CHAPTER 1
PROTECTED CHARACTERISTICS

CHAPTER 2
PROHIBITED CONDUCT

Discrimination

Adjustments for disabled persons

Discrimination: supplementary

Other prohibited conduct

PART 5
WORK

CHAPTER 1
EMPLOYMENT, ETC

Employees

Police officers

Partners

PART 6
EDUCATION

CHAPTER 3
GENERAL QUALIFICATIONS BODIES

PART 8
PROHIBITED CONDUCT: ANCILLARY

PART 9
ENFORCEMENT

CHAPTER 1
INTRODUCTORY

CHAPTER 2
CIVIL COURTS

CHAPTER 3
EMPLOYMENT TRIBUNALS

CHAPTER 4
EQUALITY OF TERMS

CHAPTER 5
MISCELLANEOUS

PART 10
CONTRACTS, ETC

Contracts and other agreements

Final provisions

SCHEDULES

An Act to make provision to require Ministers of the Crown and others when making strategic decisions about the exercise of their functions to have regard to the desirability of reducing socio-economic inequalities; to reform and harmonise equality law and restate the greater part of the enactments relating to discrimination and harassment related to certain personal characteristics; to enable certain employers to be required to publish information about the differences in pay between male and female employees; to prohibit victimisation in certain circumstances; to require the exercise of certain functions to be with regard to the need to eliminate discrimination and other prohibited conduct; to enable duties to be imposed in relation to the exercise of public procurement functions; to increase equality of opportunity; to amend the law relating to rights and responsibilities in family relationships; and for connected purposes

[8 April 2010]

NOTES

This Act covers unlawful discrimination both in the employment and related fields and in relation to goods, facilities, services, transport and certain public services. Only those Parts of the Act which deal with employment and related areas, and the provisions of general application, such as definitions and provisions relating to enforcement and remedies, are reproduced. Other provisions are omitted for reasons of space and/or as outside the scope of this work.

The Act is largely a re-enactment in a more accessible and coherent form of the many and disparate provisions of previous legislation on unlawful discrimination, but also effects significant changes in the law. Details may be found in commentaries on the Act; see in particular the Explanatory Notes to the Act, available alongside the Act itself on the official government legislation website at (www.legislation.gov.uk).

As of 6 April 2013, a total of ten commencement orders have been made under s 216 bringing various provisions into force on various dates (see **[1.1766]** for details). The main one for the purposes of the provisions reproduced here is the Equality Act 2010 (Commencement No 4, Savings, Consequential, Transitional, Transitory and Incidental Provisions and Revocation) Order 2010, SI 2010/2317 at **[2.1558]** which contains a variety of transitional provisions affecting the commencement of this Act, and savings with regard to the repeal and revocation of the previous discrimination legislation. Note that the government has announced that it does not intend to bring into force ss 1–3 or s 78 of this Act.

Note also that this Act was amended by the Equality Act 2010 (Consequential Amendments, Saving and Supplementary Provisions) Order 2010, SI 2010/2279 (as noted below where relevant). In particular, note that the original Schs 26 and 27 (Amendments and Repeals & revocations) were heavily renumbered and amended. The new paragraph number is given for all amendments to other material elsewhere in this Handbook.

Employment Appeal Tribunal: an appeal lies to the Employment Appeal Tribunal on any question of law arising from any decision of, or in any proceedings before, an employment tribunal under or by virtue of this Act; see the Employment Tribunals Act 1996, s 21(1)(ge) at **[1.713]**.

PART 1
SOCIO-ECONOMIC INEQUALITIES

[1.1618]

1 Public sector duty regarding socio-economic inequalities

(1) An authority to which this section applies must, when making decisions of a strategic nature about how to exercise its functions, have due regard to the desirability of exercising them in a way that is designed to reduce the inequalities of outcome which result from socio-economic disadvantage.

(2) In deciding how to fulfil a duty to which it is subject under subsection (1), an authority must take into account any guidance issued by a Minister of the Crown.

(3) The authorities to which this section applies are—

(a) a Minister of the Crown;

(b) a government department other than the Security Service, the Secret Intelligence Service or the Government Communications Head-quarters;

(c) a county council or district council in England;

(d) the Greater London Authority;

(e) a London borough council;

(f) the Common Council of the City of London in its capacity as a local authority;

(g) the Council of the Isles of Scilly;

(h) . . .

(i) . . .

(j) . . .

(k) a [police and crime commissioner] established for an area in England.

(4) This section also applies to an authority that—

(a) is a partner authority in relation to a responsible local authority, and

(b) does not fall within subsection (3),

but only in relation to its participation in the preparation or modification of a sustainable community strategy.

(5) In subsection (4)—

"partner authority" has the meaning given by section 104 of the Local Government and Public Involvement in Health Act 2007;

"responsible local authority" has the meaning given by section 103 of that Act;

"sustainable community strategy" means a strategy prepared under section 4 of the Local Government Act 2000.

(6) The reference to inequalities in subsection (1) does not include any inequalities experienced by a person as a result of being a person subject to immigration control within the meaning given by section 115(9) of the Immigration and Asylum Act 1999.

NOTES

Commencement: to be appointed.

Sub-s (3) is amended as follows:

Paras (h), (i) repealed by the Health and Social Care Act 2012, s 55(2), Sch 5, paras 180, 181, as from 1 April 2013.

Para (j) repealed by the Public Bodies Act 2011, s 30(3), Sch 6, as from 1 July 2012.

Words in square brackets in para (k) substituted by the Police Reform and Social Responsibility Act 2011, s 99, Sch 16, Pt 3, paras 380, 381, as from 22 November 2012 (for general transitional provisions relating to police reform and the abolition of existing police authorities, see Sch 15 to the 2011 Act)

[1.1619]

2 Power to amend section 1

(1) A Minister of the Crown may by regulations amend section 1 so as to—

(a) add a public authority to the authorities that are subject to the duty under subsection (1) of that section;

(b) remove an authority from those that are subject to the duty;

(c) make the duty apply, in the case of a particular authority, only in relation to certain functions that it has;

(d) in the case of an authority to which the application of the duty is already restricted to certain functions, remove or alter the restriction.

(2) In subsection (1) "public authority" means an authority that has functions of a public nature.

(3) Provision made under subsection (1) may not impose a duty on an authority in relation to any devolved Scottish functions or devolved Welsh functions.

(4) The Scottish Ministers or the Welsh Ministers may by regulations amend section 1 so as to—

(a) add a relevant authority to the authorities that are subject to the duty under subsection (1) of that section;
(b) remove a relevant authority from those that are subject to the duty;
(c) make the duty apply, in the case of a particular relevant authority, only in relation to certain functions that it has;
(d) in the case of a relevant authority to which the application of the duty is already restricted to certain functions, remove or alter the restriction.

(5) For the purposes of the power conferred by subsection (4) on the Scottish Ministers, "relevant authority" means an authority whose functions—
(a) are exercisable only in or as regards Scotland,
(b) are wholly or mainly devolved Scottish functions, and
(c) correspond or are similar to those of an authority for the time being specified in section 1(3).

(6) For the purposes of the power conferred by subsection (4) on the Welsh Ministers, "relevant authority" means an authority whose functions—
(a) are exercisable only in or as regards Wales,
(b) are wholly or mainly devolved Welsh functions, and
(c) correspond or are similar to those of an authority for the time being specified in subsection (3) of section 1 or referred to in subsection (4) of that section.

(7) Before making regulations under this section, the Scottish Ministers or the Welsh Ministers must consult a Minister of the Crown.

(8) Regulations under this section may make any amendments of section 1 that appear to the Minister or Ministers to be necessary or expedient in consequence of provision made under subsection (1) or (as the case may be) subsection (4).

(9) Provision made by the Scottish Ministers or the Welsh Ministers in reliance on subsection (8) may, in particular, amend section 1 so as to—
(a) confer on the Ministers a power to issue guidance;
(b) require a relevant authority to take into account any guidance issued under a power conferred by virtue of paragraph (a);
(c) disapply section 1(2) in consequence of the imposition of a requirement by virtue of paragraph (b).

(10) Before issuing guidance under a power conferred by virtue of subsection (9)(a), the Ministers must—
(a) take into account any guidance issued by a Minister of the Crown under section 1;
(b) consult a Minister of the Crown.

(11) For the purposes of this section—
(a) a function is a devolved Scottish function if it is exercisable in or as regards Scotland and it does not relate to reserved matters (within the meaning of the Scotland Act 1998);
(b) a function is a devolved Welsh function if it relates to a matter in respect of which functions are exercisable by the Welsh Ministers, the First Minister for Wales or the Counsel General to the Welsh Assembly Government, or to a matter within the legislative competence of the National Assembly for Wales.

NOTES

Commencement: to be appointed.

[1.1620]

3 Enforcement

A failure in respect of a performance of a duty under section 1 does not confer a cause of action at private law.

NOTES

Commencement: to be appointed.

PART 2
EQUALITY: KEY CONCEPTS

CHAPTER 1
PROTECTED CHARACTERISTICS

[1.1621]

4 The protected characteristics

The following characteristics are protected characteristics—

age;
disability;
gender reassignment;
marriage and civil partnership;
pregnancy and maternity;

race;
religion or belief;
sex;
sexual orientation.

NOTES

Commencement: 1 October 2010.

[1.1622]

5 Age

(1) In relation to the protected characteristic of age—

(a) a reference to a person who has a particular protected characteristic is a reference to a person of a particular age group;

(b) a reference to persons who share a protected characteristic is a reference to persons of the same age group.

(2) A reference to an age group is a reference to a group of persons defined by reference to age, whether by reference to a particular age or to a range of ages.

NOTES

Commencement: 1 October 2010.

[1.1623]

6 Disability

(1) A person (P) has a disability if—

(a) P has a physical or mental impairment, and

(b) the impairment has a substantial and long-term adverse effect on P's ability to carry out normal day-to-day activities.

(2) A reference to a disabled person is a reference to a person who has a disability.

(3) In relation to the protected characteristic of disability—

(a) a reference to a person who has a particular protected characteristic is a reference to a person who has a particular disability;

(b) a reference to persons who share a protected characteristic is a reference to persons who have the same disability.

(4) This Act (except Part 12 and section 190) applies in relation to a person who has had a disability as it applies in relation to a person who has the disability; accordingly (except in that Part and that section)—

(a) a reference (however expressed) to a person who has a disability includes a reference to a person who has had the disability, and

(b) a reference (however expressed) to a person who does not have a disability includes a reference to a person who has not had the disability.

(5) A Minister of the Crown may issue guidance about matters to be taken into account in deciding any question for the purposes of subsection (1).

(6) Schedule 1 (disability: supplementary provision) has effect.

NOTES

Commencement: 6 July 2010 (sub-s (5) for the purpose of enabling subordinate legislation or guidance to be made, and sub-s (6) (in so far as relating to Sch 1, paras 1–5, 7, 8, 10, 11, 13–16) for the same purpose); 1 October 2010 (otherwise).

Transitional provisions: see the Equality Act 2010 (Commencement No 4, Savings, Consequential, Transitional, Transitory and Incidental Provisions and Revocation) Order 2010, SI 2010/2317, art 13 at **[2.1566]**.

Guidance under sub-s (5): see the Guidance on matters to be taken into account in determining questions relating to the definition of disability (April 2011) at **[4.238]**. See also the Equality Act 2010 (Guidance on the Definition of Disability) Appointed Day Order 2011, SI 2011/1159 at **[2.1608]** which was made under this section and which commences the Guidance from 1 May 2011 and, in art 3, provides for transitional provisions with regard to the continued operation of the 1996 Guidance.

[1.1624]

7 Gender reassignment

(1) A person has the protected characteristic of gender reassignment if the person is proposing to undergo, is undergoing or has undergone a process (or part of a process) for the purpose of reassigning the person's sex by changing physiological or other attributes of sex.

(2) A reference to a transsexual person is a reference to a person who has the protected characteristic of gender reassignment.

(3) In relation to the protected characteristic of gender reassignment—

(a) a reference to a person who has a particular protected characteristic is a reference to a transsexual person;

(b) a reference to persons who share a protected characteristic is a reference to transsexual persons.

NOTES

Commencement: 1 October 2010.

[1.1625]
8 Marriage and civil partnership

(1) A person has the protected characteristic of marriage and civil partnership if the person is married or is a civil partner.

(2) In relation to the protected characteristic of marriage and civil partnership—

(a) a reference to a person who has a particular protected characteristic is a reference to a person who is married or is a civil partner;

(b) a reference to persons who share a protected characteristic is a reference to persons who are married or are civil partners.

NOTES

Commencement: 1 October 2010.

[1.1626]
9 Race

(1) Race includes—

(a) colour;

(b) nationality;

(c) ethnic or national origins.

(2) In relation to the protected characteristic of race—

(a) a reference to a person who has a particular protected characteristic is a reference to a person of a particular racial group;

(b) a reference to persons who share a protected characteristic is a reference to persons of the same racial group.

(3) A racial group is a group of persons defined by reference to race; and a reference to a person's racial group is a reference to a racial group into which the person falls.

(4) The fact that a racial group comprises two or more distinct racial groups does not prevent it from constituting a particular racial group.

(5) A Minister of the Crown *may by order*—

(a) [must by order] amend this section so as to provide for caste to be an aspect of race;

(b) [may by order] amend this Act so as to provide for an exception to a provision of this Act to apply, or not to apply, to caste or to apply, or not to apply, to caste in specified circumstances.

(6) The power under section 207(4)(b), in its application to subsection (5), includes power to amend this Act.

NOTES

Commencement: 1 October 2010.

Sub-s (5): words in italics repealed and words in square brackets in paras (a), (b) inserted, by the Enterprise and Regulatory Reform Act 2013, s 97(1)–(4), as from 25 April 2013 (so far as is necessary for enabling the exercise of any power to make orders) and as from 25 June 2013 (otherwise).

See further: the Enterprise and Regulatory Reform Act 2013, s 97(5)–(10) at **[1.1860]**.

[1.1627]
10 Religion or belief

(1) Religion means any religion and a reference to religion includes a reference to a lack of religion.

(2) Belief means any religious or philosophical belief and a reference to belief includes a reference to a lack of belief.

(3) In relation to the protected characteristic of religion or belief—

(a) a reference to a person who has a particular protected characteristic is a reference to a person of a particular religion or belief;

(b) a reference to persons who share a protected characteristic is a reference to persons who are of the same religion or belief.

NOTES

Commencement: 1 October 2010.

[1.1628]
11 Sex

In relation to the protected characteristic of sex—

(a) a reference to a person who has a particular protected characteristic is a reference to a man or to a woman;

(b) a reference to persons who share a protected characteristic is a reference to persons of the same sex.

NOTES

Commencement: 1 October 2010.

[1.1629]
12 Sexual orientation

(1) Sexual orientation means a person's sexual orientation towards—
- (a) persons of the same sex,
- (b) persons of the opposite sex, or
- (c) persons of either sex.

(2) In relation to the protected characteristic of sexual orientation—
- (a) a reference to a person who has a particular protected characteristic is a reference to a person who is of a particular sexual orientation;
- (b) a reference to persons who share a protected characteristic is a reference to persons who are of the same sexual orientation.

NOTES
Commencement: 1 October 2010.

CHAPTER 2
PROHIBITED CONDUCT

Discrimination

[1.1630]
13 Direct discrimination

(1) A person (A) discriminates against another (B) if, because of a protected characteristic, A treats B less favourably than A treats or would treat others.
(2) If the protected characteristic is age, A does not discriminate against B if A can show A's treatment of B to be a proportionate means of achieving a legitimate aim.
(3) If the protected characteristic is disability, and B is not a disabled person, A does not discriminate against B only because A treats or would treat disabled persons more favourably than A treats B.
(4) If the protected characteristic is marriage and civil partnership, this section applies to a contravention of Part 5 (work) only if the treatment is because it is B who is married or a civil partner.
(5) If the protected characteristic is race, less favourable treatment includes segregating B from others.
(6) If the protected characteristic is sex—
- (a) less favourable treatment of a woman includes less favourable treatment of her because she is breast-feeding;
- (b) in a case where B is a man, no account is to be taken of special treatment afforded to a woman in connection with pregnancy or childbirth.

(7) Subsection (6)(a) does not apply for the purposes of Part 5 (work).
(8) This section is subject to sections 17(6) and 18(7).

NOTES
Commencement: 1 October 2010.

[1.1631]
14 Combined discrimination: dual characteristics

(1) A person (A) discriminates against another (B) if, because of a combination of two relevant protected characteristics, A treats B less favourably than A treats or would treat a person who does not share either of those characteristics.
(2) The relevant protected characteristics are—
- (a) age;
- (b) disability;
- (c) gender reassignment;
- (d) race
- (e) religion or belief;
- (f) sex;
- (g) sexual orientation.

(3) For the purposes of establishing a contravention of this Act by virtue of subsection (1), B need not show that A's treatment of B is direct discrimination because of each of the characteristics in the combination (taken separately).
(4) But B cannot establish a contravention of this Act by virtue of subsection (1) if, in reliance on another provision of this Act or any other enactment, A shows that A's treatment of B is not direct discrimination because of either or both of the characteristics in the combination.
(5) Subsection (1) does not apply to a combination of characteristics that includes disability in circumstances where, if a claim of direct discrimination because of disability were to be brought, it would come within section 116 (special educational needs).
(6) A Minister of the Crown may by order amend this section so as to—

(a) make further provision about circumstances in which B can, or in which B cannot, establish a contravention of this Act by virtue of subsection (1);
(b) specify other circumstances in which subsection (1) does not apply.

(7) The references to direct discrimination are to a contravention of this Act by virtue of section 13.

NOTES

Commencement: to be appointed.

[1.1632]

15 Discrimination arising from disability

(1) A person (A) discriminates against a disabled person (B) if—
(a) A treats B unfavourably because of something arising in consequence of B's disability, and
(b) A cannot show that the treatment is a proportionate means of achieving a legitimate aim.

(2) Subsection (1) does not apply if A shows that A did not know, and could not reasonably have been expected to know, that B had the disability.

NOTES

Commencement: 1 October 2010.

[1.1633]

16 Gender reassignment discrimination: cases of absence from work

(1) This section has effect for the purposes of the application of Part 5 (work) to the protected characteristic of gender reassignment.

(2) A person (A) discriminates against a transsexual person (B) if, in relation to an absence of B's that is because of gender reassignment, A treats B less favourably than A would treat B if—
(a) B's absence was because of sickness or injury, or
(b) B's absence was for some other reason and it is not reasonable for B to be treated less favourably.

(3) A person's absence is because of gender reassignment if it is because the person is proposing to undergo, is undergoing or has undergone the process (or part of the process) mentioned in section 7(1).

NOTES

Commencement: 1 October 2010.

[1.1634]

17 Pregnancy and maternity discrimination: non-work cases

(1) This section has effect for the purposes of the application to the protected characteristic of pregnancy and maternity of—
(a) Part 3 (services and public functions);
(b) Part 4 (premises);
(c) Part 6 (education);
(d) Part 7 (associations).

(2) A person (A) discriminates against a woman if A treats her unfavourably because of a pregnancy of hers.

(3) A person (A) discriminates against a woman if, in the period of 26 weeks beginning with the day on which she gives birth, A treats her unfavourably because she has given birth.

(4) The reference in subsection (3) to treating a woman unfavourably because she has given birth includes, in particular, a reference to treating her unfavourably because she is breast-feeding.

(5) For the purposes of this section, the day on which a woman gives birth is the day on which—
(a) she gives birth to a living child, or
(b) she gives birth to a dead child (more than 24 weeks of the pregnancy having passed).

(6) Section 13, so far as relating to sex discrimination, does not apply to anything done in relation to a woman in so far as—
(a) it is for the reason mentioned in subsection (2), or
(b) it is in the period, and for the reason, mentioned in subsection (3).

NOTES

Commencement: 1 October 2010.

[1.1635]

18 Pregnancy and maternity discrimination: work cases

(1) This section has effect for the purposes of the application of Part 5 (work) to the protected characteristic of pregnancy and maternity.

(2) A person (A) discriminates against a woman if, in the protected period in relation to a pregnancy of hers, A treats her unfavourably—
(a) because of the pregnancy, or

(b) because of illness suffered by her as a result of it.

(3) A person (A) discriminates against a woman if A treats her unfavourably because she is on compulsory maternity leave.

(4) A person (A) discriminates against a woman if A treats her unfavourably because she is exercising or seeking to exercise, or has exercised or sought to exercise, the right to ordinary or additional maternity leave.

(5) For the purposes of subsection (2), if the treatment of a woman is in implementation of a decision taken in the protected period, the treatment is to be regarded as occurring in that period (even if the implementation is not until after the end of that period).

(6) The protected period, in relation to a woman's pregnancy, begins when the pregnancy begins, and ends—

(a) if she has the right to ordinary and additional maternity leave, at the end of the additional maternity leave period or (if earlier) when she returns to work after the pregnancy;

(b) if she does not have that right, at the end of the period of 2 weeks beginning with the end of the pregnancy.

(7) Section 13, so far as relating to sex discrimination, does not apply to treatment of a woman in so far as—

(a) it is in the protected period in relation to her and is for a reason mentioned in paragraph (a) or (b) of subsection (2), or

(b) it is for a reason mentioned in subsection (3) or (4).

NOTES

Commencement: 1 October 2010.

[1.1636]

19 Indirect discrimination

(1) A person (A) discriminates against another (B) if A applies to B a provision, criterion or practice which is discriminatory in relation to a relevant protected characteristic of B's.

(2) For the purposes of subsection (1), a provision, criterion or practice is discriminatory in relation to a relevant protected characteristic of B's if—

(a) A applies, or would apply, it to persons with whom B does not share the characteristic,

(b) it puts, or would put, persons with whom B shares the characteristic at a particular disadvantage when compared with persons with whom B does not share it,

(c) it puts, or would put, B at that disadvantage, and

(d) A cannot show it to be a proportionate means of achieving a legitimate aim.

(3) The relevant protected characteristics are—

age;
disability;
gender reassignment;
marriage and civil partnership;
race;
religion or belief;
sex;
sexual orientation.

NOTES

Commencement: 1 October 2010.

Adjustments for disabled persons

[1.1637]

20 Duty to make adjustments

(1) Where this Act imposes a duty to make reasonable adjustments on a person, this section, sections 21 and 22 and the applicable Schedule apply; and for those purposes, a person on whom the duty is imposed is referred to as A.

(2) The duty comprises the following three requirements.

(3) The first requirement is a requirement, where a provision, criterion or practice of A's puts a disabled person at a substantial disadvantage in relation to a relevant matter in comparison with persons who are not disabled, to take such steps as it is reasonable to have to take to avoid the disadvantage.

(4) The second requirement is a requirement, where a physical feature puts a disabled person at a substantial disadvantage in relation to a relevant matter in comparison with persons who are not disabled, to take such steps as it is reasonable to have to take to avoid the disadvantage.

(5) The third requirement is a requirement, where a disabled person would, but for the provision of an auxiliary aid, be put at a substantial disadvantage in relation to a relevant matter in comparison with persons who are not disabled, to take such steps as it is reasonable to have to take to provide the auxiliary aid.

(6) Where the first or third requirement relates to the provision of information, the steps which it is reasonable for A to have to take include steps for ensuring that in the circumstances concerned the information is provided in an accessible format.

(7) A person (A) who is subject to a duty to make reasonable adjustments is not (subject to express provision to the contrary) entitled to require a disabled person, in relation to whom A is required to comply with the duty, to pay to any extent A's costs of complying with the duty.

(8) A reference in section 21 or 22 or an applicable Schedule to the first, second or third requirement is to be construed in accordance with this section.

(9) In relation to the second requirement, a reference in this section or an applicable Schedule to avoiding a substantial disadvantage includes a reference to—
- (a) removing the physical feature in question,
- (b) altering it, or
- (c) providing a reasonable means of avoiding it.

(10) A reference in this section, section 21 or 22 or an applicable Schedule (apart from paragraphs 2 to 4 of Schedule 4) to a physical feature is a reference to—
- (a) a feature arising from the design or construction of a building,
- (b) a feature of an approach to, exit from or access to a building,
- (c) a fixture or fitting, or furniture, furnishings, materials, equipment or other chattels, in or on premises, or
- (d) any other physical element or quality.

(11) A reference in this section, section 21 or 22 or an applicable Schedule to an auxiliary aid includes a reference to an auxiliary service.

(12) A reference in this section or an applicable Schedule to chattels is to be read, in relation to Scotland, as a reference to moveable property.

(13) The applicable Schedule is, in relation to the Part of this Act specified in the first column of the Table, the Schedule specified in the second column.

Part of this Act	Applicable Schedule
Part 3 (services and public functions)	Schedule 2
Part 4 (premises)	Schedule 4
Part 5 (work)	Schedule 8
Part 6 (education)	Schedule 13
Part 7 (associations)	Schedule 15
Each of the Parts mentioned above	Schedule 21

NOTES

Commencement: 1 October 2010.

[1.1638]

21 Failure to comply with duty

(1) A failure to comply with the first, second or third requirement is a failure to comply with a duty to make reasonable adjustments.

(2) A discriminates against a disabled person if A fails to comply with that duty in relation to that person.

(3) A provision of an applicable Schedule which imposes a duty to comply with the first, second or third requirement applies only for the purpose of establishing whether A has contravened this Act by virtue of subsection (2); a failure to comply is, accordingly, not actionable by virtue of another provision of this Act or otherwise.

NOTES

Commencement: 1 October 2010.

[1.1639]

22 Regulations

(1) Regulations may prescribe—
- (a) matters to be taken into account in deciding whether it is reasonable for A to take a step for the purposes of a prescribed provision of an applicable Schedule;
- (b) descriptions of persons to whom the first, second or third requirement does not apply.

(2) Regulations may make provision as to—
- (a) circumstances in which it is, or in which it is not, reasonable for a person of a prescribed description to have to take steps of a prescribed description;
- (b) what is, or what is not, a provision, criterion or practice;
- (c) things which are, or which are not, to be treated as physical features;
- (d) things which are, or which are not, to be treated as alterations of physical features;
- (e) things which are, or which are not, to be treated as auxiliary aids.

(3) Provision made by virtue of this section may amend an applicable Schedule.

NOTES

Commencement: 6 July 2010 (for the purpose of enabling subordinate legislation or guidance to be made); 1 October 2010 (otherwise).

Regulations: the Equality Act 2010 (Disability) Regulations 2010, SI 2010/2128 at **[2.1506]**.

Discrimination: supplementary

[1.1640]

23 Comparison by reference to circumstances

(1) On a comparison of cases for the purposes of section 13, 14, or 19 there must be no material difference between the circumstances relating to each case.

(2) The circumstances relating to a case include a person's abilities if—

(a) on a comparison for the purposes of section 13, the protected characteristic is disability;

(b) on a comparison for the purposes of section 14, one of the protected characteristics in the combination is disability.

(3) If the protected characteristic is sexual orientation, the fact that one person (whether or not the person referred to as B) is a civil partner while another is married is not a material difference between the circumstances relating to each case.

NOTES

Commencement: 1 October 2010.

[1.1641]

24 Irrelevance of alleged discriminator's characteristics

(1) For the purpose of establishing a contravention of this Act by virtue of section 13(1), it does not matter whether A has the protected characteristic.

(2) For the purpose of establishing a contravention of this Act by virtue of section 14(1), it does not matter—

(a) whether A has one of the protected characteristics in the combination;

(b) whether A has both.

NOTES

Commencement: 1 October 2010.

[1.1642]

25 References to particular strands of discrimination

(1) Age discrimination is—

(a) discrimination within section 13 because of age;

(b) discrimination within section 19 where the relevant protected characteristic is age.

(2) Disability discrimination is—

(a) discrimination within section 13 because of disability;

(b) discrimination within section 15;

(c) discrimination within section 19 where the relevant protected characteristic is disability;

(d) discrimination within section 21.

(3) Gender reassignment discrimination is—

(a) discrimination within section 13 because of gender reassignment;

(b) discrimination within section 16;

(c) discrimination within section 19 where the relevant protected characteristic is gender reassignment.

(4) Marriage and civil partnership discrimination is—

(a) discrimination within section 13 because of marriage and civil partnership;

(b) discrimination within section 19 where the relevant protected characteristic is marriage and civil partnership.

(5) Pregnancy and maternity discrimination is discrimination within section 17 or 18.

(6) Race discrimination is—

(a) discrimination within section 13 because of race;

(b) discrimination within section 19 where the relevant protected characteristic is race.

(7) Religious or belief-related discrimination is—

(a) discrimination within section 13 because of religion or belief;

(b) discrimination within section 19 where the relevant protected characteristic is religion or belief.

(8) Sex discrimination is—

(a) discrimination within section 13 because of sex;

(b) discrimination within section 19 where the relevant protected characteristic is sex.

(9) Sexual orientation discrimination is—

(a) discrimination within section 13 because of sexual orientation;

(b) discrimination within section 19 where the relevant protected characteristic is sexual orientation.

NOTES

Commencement: 1 October 2010.

Other prohibited conduct

[1.1643]

26 Harassment

(1) A person (A) harasses another (B) if—

(a) A engages in unwanted conduct related to a relevant protected characteristic, and

(b) the conduct has the purpose or effect of—

(i) violating B's dignity, or

(ii) creating an intimidating, hostile, degrading, humiliating or offensive environment for B.

(2) A also harasses B if—

(a) A engages in unwanted conduct of a sexual nature, and

(b) the conduct has the purpose or effect referred to in subsection (1)(b).

(3) A also harasses B if—

(a) A or another person engages in unwanted conduct of a sexual nature or that is related to gender reassignment or sex,

(b) the conduct has the purpose or effect referred to in subsection (1)(b), and

(c) because of B's rejection of or submission to the conduct, A treats B less favourably than A would treat B if B had not rejected or submitted to the conduct.

(4) In deciding whether conduct has the effect referred to in subsection (1)(b), each of the following must be taken into account—

(a) the perception of B;

(b) the other circumstances of the case;

(c) whether it is reasonable for the conduct to have that effect.

(5) The relevant protected characteristics are—

age;
disability;
gender reassignment;
race;
religion or belief;
sex;
sexual orientation.

NOTES

Commencement: 1 October 2010.

[1.1644]

27 Victimisation

(1) A person (A) victimises another person (B) if A subjects B to a detriment because—

(a) B does a protected act, or

(b) A believes that B has done, or may do, a protected act.

(2) Each of the following is a protected act—

(a) bringing proceedings under this Act;

(b) giving evidence or information in connection with proceedings under this Act;

(c) doing any other thing for the purposes of or in connection with this Act;

(d) making an allegation (whether or not express) that A or another person has contravened this Act.

(3) Giving false evidence or information, or making a false allegation, is not a protected act if the evidence or information is given, or the allegation is made, in bad faith.

(4) This section applies only where the person subjected to a detriment is an individual.

(5) The reference to contravening this Act includes a reference to committing a breach of an equality clause or rule.

NOTES

Commencement: 1 October 2010.

Transitional provisions: see the Equality Act 2010 (Commencement No 4, Savings, Consequential, Transitional, Transitory and Incidental Provisions and Revocation) Order 2010, SI 2010/2317, art 8 at **[2.1561]**.

28–38 *(Ss 28–31 (Part 3: Services and Public Functions) and ss 32–38 (Part 4: Premises) are outside the scope of this work.)*

PART 5
WORK

NOTES

Offshore work: as to the application of this Part to offshore work, see the Equality Act 2010 (Offshore Work) Order 2010, SI 2010/1835 at **[2.1499]**.

Work on hovercraft and ships: as to the application of this Part to seafarers working on UK ships and hovercraft, or on ships and hovercraft from other EEA States, see the Equality Act 2010 (Work on Ships and Hovercraft) Regulations 2011, SI 2011/1771 at **[2.1611]**.

CHAPTER 1
EMPLOYMENT, ETC

Employees

[1.1645]

39 Employees and applicants

(1) An employer (A) must not discriminate against a person (B)—

(a) in the arrangements A makes for deciding to whom to offer employment;

(b) as to the terms on which A offers B employment;

(c) by not offering B employment.

(2) An employer (A) must not discriminate against an employee of A's (B)—

(a) as to B's terms of employment;

(b) in the way A affords B access, or by not affording B access, to opportunities for promotion, transfer or training or for receiving any other benefit, facility or service;

(c) by dismissing B;

(d) by subjecting B to any other detriment.

(3) An employer (A) must not victimise a person (B)—

(a) in the arrangements A makes for deciding to whom to offer employment;

(b) as to the terms on which A offers B employment;

(c) by not offering B employment.

(4) An employer (A) must not victimise an employee of A's (B)—

(a) as to B's terms of employment;

(b) in the way A affords B access, or by not affording B access, to opportunities for promotion, transfer or training or for any other benefit, facility or service;

(c) by dismissing B;

(d) by subjecting B to any other detriment.

(5) A duty to make reasonable adjustments applies to an employer.

(6) Subsection (1)(b), so far as relating to sex or pregnancy and maternity, does not apply to a term that relates to pay—

(a) unless, were B to accept the offer, an equality clause or rule would have effect in relation to the term, or

(b) if paragraph (a) does not apply, except in so far as making an offer on terms including that term amounts to a contravention of subsection (1)(b) by virtue of section 13, 14 or 18.

(7) In subsections (2)(c) and (4)(c), the reference to dismissing B includes a reference to the termination of B's employment—

(a) by the expiry of a period (including a period expiring by reference to an event or circumstance);

(b) by an act of B's (including giving notice) in circumstances such that B is entitled, because of A's conduct, to terminate the employment without notice.

(8) Subsection (7)(a) does not apply if, immediately after the termination, the employment is renewed on the same terms.

NOTES

Commencement: 1 October 2010.

[1.1646]

40 Employees and applicants: harassment

(1) An employer (A) must not, in relation to employment by A, harass a person (B)—

(a) who is an employee of A's;

(b) who has applied to A for employment.

(2) The circumstances in which A is to be treated as harassing B under subsection (1) include those where—

(a) a third party harasses B in the course of B's employment, and

(b) A failed to take such steps as would have been reasonably practicable to prevent the third party from doing so.

(3) Subsection (2) does not apply unless A knows that B has been harassed in the course of B's employment on at least two other occasions by a third party; and it does not matter whether the third party is the same or a different person on each occasion.

(4) A third party is a person other than—

(a) A, or

(b) an employee of A's.

NOTES

Commencement: 1 October 2010.

Sub-ss (2)–(4): repealed by the Enterprise and Regulatory Reform Act 2013, s 65, as from a day to be appointed.

[1.1647]

41 Contract workers

(1) A principal must not discriminate against a contract worker—

(a) as to the terms on which the principal allows the worker to do the work;

(b) by not allowing the worker to do, or to continue to do, the work;

(c) in the way the principal affords the worker access, or by not affording the worker access, to opportunities for receiving a benefit, facility or service;

(d) by subjecting the worker to any other detriment.

(2) A principal must not, in relation to contract work, harass a contract worker.

(3) A principal must not victimise a contract worker—

(a) as to the terms on which the principal allows the worker to do the work;

(b) by not allowing the worker to do, or to continue to do, the work;

(c) in the way the principal affords the worker access, or by not affording the worker access, to opportunities for receiving a benefit, facility or service;

(d) by subjecting the worker to any other detriment.

(4) A duty to make reasonable adjustments applies to a principal (as well as to the employer of a contract worker).

(5) A "principal" is a person who makes work available for an individual who is—

(a) employed by another person, and

(b) supplied by that other person in furtherance of a contract to which the principal is a party (whether or not that other person is a party to it).

(6) "Contract work" is work such as is mentioned in subsection (5).

(7) A "contract worker" is an individual supplied to a principal in furtherance of a contract such as is mentioned in subsection (5)(b).

NOTES

Commencement: 1 October 2010.

Police officers

[1.1648]

42 Identity of employer

(1) For the purposes of this Part, holding the office of constable is to be treated as employment—

(a) by the chief officer, in respect of any act done by the chief officer in relation to a constable or appointment to the office of constable;

(b) by the responsible authority, in respect of any act done by the authority in relation to a constable or appointment to the office of constable.

(2) For the purposes of this Part, holding an appointment as a police cadet is to be treated as employment—

(a) by the chief officer, in respect of any act done by the chief officer in relation to a police cadet or appointment as one;

(b) by the responsible authority, in respect of any act done by the authority in relation to a police cadet or appointment as one.

(3) Subsection (1) does not apply to service with the Civil Nuclear Constabulary (as to which, see section 55(2) of the Energy Act 2004).

(4) Subsection (1) does not apply to a constable at *SOCA*, SPSA or SCDEA.

(5) A constable at *SOCA* or SPSA is to be treated as employed by it, in respect of any act done by it in relation to the constable.

(6) A constable at SCDEA is to be treated as employed by the Director General of SCDEA, in respect of any act done by the Director General in relation to the constable.

NOTES

Commencement: 1 October 2010.

Sub-ss (4), (5): for the references in italics there is substituted "NCA" by the Crime and Courts Act 2013, s 15(3), Sch 8, Pt 2, paras 180, 181, as from a day to be appointed.

[1.1649]

43 Interpretation

(1) This section applies for the purposes of section 42.

(2) "Chief officer" means—

(a) in relation to an appointment under a relevant Act, the chief officer of police for the police force to which the appointment relates;
(b) in relation to any other appointment, the person under whose direction and control the body of constables or other persons to which the appointment relates is;
(c) in relation to a constable or other person under the direction and control of a chief officer of police, that chief officer of police;
(d) in relation to any other constable or any other person, the person under whose direction and control the constable or other person is.

(3) "Responsible authority" means—
(a) in relation to an appointment under a relevant Act, the [local policing body or police authority] that maintains the police force to which the appointment relates;
(b) in relation to any other appointment, the person by whom a person would (if appointed) be paid;
(c) in relation to a constable or other person under the direction and control of a chief officer of police, the [local policing body or police authority] that maintains the police force for which that chief officer is the chief officer of police;
(d) in relation to any other constable or any other person, the person by whom the constable or other person is paid.

(4) "Police cadet" means a person appointed to undergo training with a view to becoming a constable.

(5) "SOCA" means the Serious Organised Crime Agency; and a reference to a constable at SOCA is a reference to a constable seconded to it to serve as a member of its staff.

(6) "SPSA" means the Scottish Police Services Authority; and a reference to a constable at SPSA is a reference to a constable—
(a) seconded to it to serve as a member of its staff, and
(b) not at SCDEA.

(7) "SCDEA" means the Scottish Crime and Drugs Enforcement Agency; and a reference to a constable at SCDEA is a reference to a constable who is a police member of it by virtue of paragraph 7(2)(a) or (b) of Schedule 2 to the Police, Public Order and Criminal Justice (Scotland) Act 2006 (asp 10) (secondment).

(8) For the purposes of this section, the relevant Acts are—
(a) the Metropolitan Police Act 1829;
(b) the City of London Police Act 1839;
(c) the Police (Scotland) Act 1967;
[(d) the Police Reform and Social Responsibility Act 2011]

(9) A reference in subsection (2) or (3) to a chief officer of police includes, in relation to Scotland, a reference to a chief constable.

NOTES

Commencement: 1 October 2010.

Sub-ss (3), (8): words in square brackets substituted by the Police Reform and Social Responsibility Act 2011, s 99, Sch 16, Pt 3, paras 380, 382, as from 16 January 2012 (for general transitional provisions relating to police reform and the abolition of existing police authorities, see Sch 15 to the 2011 Act, and the Police Reform and Social Responsibility Act 2011 (Commencement No 3 and Transitional Provisions) Order 2011, SI 2011/3019).

Sub-s (5): substituted by the Crime and Courts Act 2013, s 15(3), Sch 8, Pt 2, paras 180, 182, as from a day to be appointed, as follows:

> "(5) "NCA" means the National Crime Agency; and a reference to a constable at NCA is a reference to a constable seconded to it to serve as an NCA officer.".

Partners

[1.1650]

44 Partnerships

(1) A firm or proposed firm must not discriminate against a person—
(a) in the arrangements it makes for deciding to whom to offer a position as a partner;
(b) as to the terms on which it offers the person a position as a partner;
(c) by not offering the person a position as a partner.

(2) A firm (A) must not discriminate against a partner (B)—
(a) as to the terms on which B is a partner;
(b) in the way A affords B access, or by not affording B access, to opportunities for promotion, transfer or training or for receiving any other benefit, facility or service;
(c) by expelling B;
(d) by subjecting B to any other detriment.

(3) A firm must not, in relation to a position as a partner, harass—
(a) a partner;
(b) a person who has applied for the position.

(4) A proposed firm must not, in relation to a position as a partner, harass a person who has applied for the position.

(5) A firm or proposed firm must not victimise a person—
  (a) in the arrangements it makes for deciding to whom to offer a position as a partner;
  (b) as to the terms on which it offers the person a position as a partner;
  (c) by not offering the person a position as a partner.
(6) A firm (A) must not victimise a partner (B)—
  (a) as to the terms on which B is a partner;
  (b) in the way A affords B access, or by not affording B access, to opportunities for promotion, transfer or training or for receiving any other benefit, facility or service;
  (c) by expelling B;
  (d) by subjecting B to any other detriment.
(7) A duty to make reasonable adjustments applies to—
  (a) a firm;
  (b) a proposed firm.
(8) In the application of this section to a limited partnership within the meaning of the Limited Partnerships Act 1907, "partner" means a general partner within the meaning of that Act.

NOTES

Commencement: 1 October 2010.

[1.1651]

45 Limited liability partnerships

(1) An LLP or proposed LLP must not discriminate against a person—
  (a) in the arrangements it makes for deciding to whom to offer a position as a member;
  (b) as to the terms on which it offers the person a position as a member;
  (c) by not offering the person a position as a member.
(2) An LLP (A) must not discriminate against a member (B)—
  (a) as to the terms on which B is a member;
  (b) in the way A affords B access, or by not affording B access, to opportunities for promotion, transfer or training or for receiving any other benefit, facility or service;
  (c) by expelling B;
  (d) by subjecting B to any other detriment.
(3) An LLP must not, in relation to a position as a member, harass—
  (a) a member;
  (b) a person who has applied for the position.
(4) A proposed LLP must not, in relation to a position as a member, harass a person who has applied for the position.
(5) An LLP or proposed LLP must not victimise a person—
  (a) in the arrangements it makes for deciding to whom to offer a position as a member;
  (b) as to the terms on which it offers the person a position as a member;
  (c) by not offering the person a position as a member.
(6) An LLP (A) must not victimise a member (B)—
  (a) as to the terms on which B is a member;
  (b) in the way A affords B access, or by not affording B access, to opportunities for promotion, transfer or training or for receiving any other benefit, facility or service;
  (c) by expelling B;
  (d) by subjecting B to any other detriment.
(7) A duty to make reasonable adjustments applies to—
  (a) an LLP;
  (b) a proposed LLP.

NOTES

Commencement: 1 October 2010.

[1.1652]

46 Interpretation

(1) This section applies for the purposes of sections 44 and 45.
(2) "Partnership" and "firm" have the same meaning as in the Partnership Act 1890.
(3) "Proposed firm" means persons proposing to form themselves into a partnership.
(4) "LLP" means a limited liability partnership (within the meaning of the Limited Liability Partnerships Act 2000).
(5) "Proposed LLP" means persons proposing to incorporate an LLP with themselves as members.
(6) A reference to expelling a partner of a firm or a member of an LLP includes a reference to the termination of the person's position as such—
  (a) by the expiry of a period (including a period expiring by reference to an event or circumstance);

(b) by an act of the person (including giving notice) in circumstances such that the person is entitled, because of the conduct of other partners or members, to terminate the position without notice;
(c) (in the case of a partner of a firm) as a result of the dissolution of the partnership.
(7) Subsection (6)(a) and (c) does not apply if, immediately after the termination, the position is renewed on the same terms.

NOTES
Commencement: 1 October 2010.

The Bar

[1.1653]
47 Barristers
(1) A barrister (A) must not discriminate against a person (B)—
(a) in the arrangements A makes for deciding to whom to offer a pupillage or tenancy;
(b) as to the terms on which A offers B a pupillage or tenancy;
(c) by not offering B a pupillage or tenancy.
(2) A barrister (A) must not discriminate against a person (B) who is a pupil or tenant—
(a) as to the terms on which B is a pupil or tenant;
(b) in the way A affords B access, or by not affording B access, to opportunities for training or gaining experience or for receiving any other benefit, facility or service;
(c) by terminating the pupillage;
(d) by subjecting B to pressure to leave chambers;
(e) by subjecting B to any other detriment.
(3) A barrister must not, in relation to a pupillage or tenancy, harass—
(a) the pupil or tenant;
(b) a person who has applied for the pupillage or tenancy.
(4) A barrister (A) must not victimise a person (B)—
(a) in the arrangements A makes for deciding to whom to offer a pupillage or tenancy;
(b) as to the terms on which A offers B a pupillage or tenancy;
(c) by not offering B a pupillage or tenancy.
(5) A barrister (A) must not victimise a person (B) who is a pupil or tenant—
(a) as to the terms on which B is a pupil or tenant;
(b) in the way A affords B access, or by not affording B access, to opportunities for training or gaining experience or for receiving any other benefit, facility or service;
(c) by terminating the pupillage;
(d) by subjecting B to pressure to leave chambers;
(e) by subjecting B to any other detriment.
(6) A person must not, in relation to instructing a barrister—
(a) discriminate against a barrister by subjecting the barrister to a detriment;
(b) harass the barrister;
(c) victimise the barrister.
(7) A duty to make reasonable adjustments applies to a barrister.
(8) The preceding provisions of this section (apart from subsection (6)) apply in relation to a barrister's clerk as they apply in relation to a barrister; and for that purpose the reference to a barrister's clerk includes a reference to a person who carries out the functions of a barrister's clerk.
(9) A reference to a tenant includes a reference to a barrister who is permitted to work in chambers (including as a squatter or door tenant); and a reference to a tenancy is to be construed accordingly.

NOTES
Commencement: 1 October 2010.

[1.1654]
48 Advocates
(1) An advocate (A) must not discriminate against a person (B)—
(a) in the arrangements A makes for deciding who to take as A's devil or to whom to offer membership of a stable;
(b) as to the terms on which A offers to take B as A's devil or offers B membership of a stable;
(c) by not offering to take B as A's devil or not offering B membership of a stable.
(2) An advocate (A) must not discriminate against a person (B) who is a devil or a member of a stable—
(a) as to the terms on which B is a devil or a member of the stable;
(b) in the way A affords B access, or by not affording B access, to opportunities for training or gaining experience or for receiving any other benefit, facility or service;
(c) by terminating A's relationship with B (where B is a devil);
(d) by subjecting B to pressure to leave the stable;

(e) by subjecting B to any other detriment.

(3) An advocate must not, in relation to a relationship with a devil or membership of a stable, harass—

(a) a devil or member;

(b) a person who has applied to be taken as the advocate's devil or to become a member of the stable.

(4) An advocate (A) must not victimise a person (B)—

(a) in the arrangements A makes for deciding who to take as A's devil or to whom to offer membership of a stable;

(b) as to the terms on which A offers to take B as A's devil or offers B membership of a stable;

(c) by not offering to take B as A's devil or not offering B membership of a stable.

(5) An advocate (A) must not victimise a person (B) who is a devil or a member of a stable—

(a) as to the terms on which B is a devil or a member of the stable;

(b) in the way A affords B access, or by not affording B access, to opportunities for training or gaining experience or for receiving any other benefit, facility or service;

(c) by terminating A's relationship with B (where B is a devil);

(d) by subjecting B to pressure to leave the stable;

(e) by subjecting B to any other detriment.

(6) A person must not, in relation to instructing an advocate—

(a) discriminate against the advocate by subjecting the advocate to a detriment;

(b) harass the advocate;

(c) victimise the advocate.

(7) A duty to make reasonable adjustments applies to an advocate.

(8) This section (apart from subsection (6)) applies in relation to an advocate's clerk as it applies in relation to an advocate; and for that purpose the reference to an advocate's clerk includes a reference to a person who carries out the functions of an advocate's clerk.

(9) "Advocate" means a practising member of the Faculty of Advocates.

NOTES

Commencement: 1 October 2010.

Office-holders

[1.1655]

49 Personal offices: appointments, etc

(1) This section applies in relation to personal offices.

(2) A personal office is an office or post—

(a) to which a person is appointed to discharge a function personally under the direction of another person, and

(b) in respect of which an appointed person is entitled to remuneration.

(3) A person (A) who has the power to make an appointment to a personal office must not discriminate against a person (B)—

(a) in the arrangements A makes for deciding to whom to offer the appointment;

(b) as to the terms on which A offers B the appointment;

(c) by not offering B the appointment.

(4) A person who has the power to make an appointment to a personal office must not, in relation to the office, harass a person seeking, or being considered for, the appointment.

(5) A person (A) who has the power to make an appointment to a personal office must not victimise a person (B)—

(a) in the arrangements A makes for deciding to whom to offer the appointment;

(b) as to the terms on which A offers B the appointment;

(c) by not offering B the appointment.

(6) A person (A) who is a relevant person in relation to a personal office must not discriminate against a person (B) appointed to the office—

(a) as to the terms of B's appointment;

(b) in the way A affords B access, or by not affording B access, to opportunities for promotion, transfer or training or for receiving any other benefit, facility or service;

(c) by terminating B's appointment;

(d) by subjecting B to any other detriment.

(7) A relevant person in relation to a personal office must not, in relation to that office, harass a person appointed to it.

(8) A person (A) who is a relevant person in relation to a personal office must not victimise a person (B) appointed to the office—

(a) as to the terms of B's appointment;

(b) in the way A affords B access, or by not affording B access, to opportunities for promotion, transfer or training or for receiving any other benefit, facility or service;

(c) by terminating B's appointment;

(d) by subjecting B to any other detriment.

(9) A duty to make reasonable adjustments applies to—

(a) a person who has the power to make an appointment to a personal office;

(b) a relevant person in relation to a personal office.

(10) For the purposes of subsection (2)(a), a person is to be regarded as discharging functions personally under the direction of another person if that other person is entitled to direct the person as to when and where to discharge the functions.

(11) For the purposes of subsection (2)(b), a person is not to be regarded as entitled to remuneration merely because the person is entitled to payments—

(a) in respect of expenses incurred by the person in discharging the functions of the office or post, or

(b) by way of compensation for the loss of income or benefits the person would or might have received had the person not been discharging the functions of the office or post.

(12) Subsection (3)(b), so far as relating to sex or pregnancy and maternity, does not apply to a term that relates to pay—

(a) unless, were B to accept the offer, an equality clause or rule would have effect in relation to the term, or

(b) if paragraph (a) does not apply, except in so far as making an offer on terms including that term amounts to a contravention of subsection (3)(b) by virtue of section 13, 14 or 18.

NOTES

Commencement: 1 October 2010.

[1.1656]

50 Public offices: appointments, etc

(1) This section and section 51 apply in relation to public offices.

(2) A public office is—

(a) an office or post, appointment to which is made by a member of the executive;

(b) an office or post, appointment to which is made on the recommendation of, or subject to the approval of, a member of the executive;

(c) an office or post, appointment to which is made on the recommendation of, or subject to the approval of, the House of Commons, the House of Lords, the National Assembly for Wales or the Scottish Parliament[

[(d) an office or post, appointment to which is made by the Lord Chief Justice or the Senior President of Tribunals.]

(3) A person (A) who has the power to make an appointment to a public office within subsection (2)(a) *or (b)* must not discriminate against a person (B)—

(a) in the arrangements A makes for deciding to whom to offer the appointment;

(b) as to the terms on which A offers B the appointment;

(c) by not offering B the appointment.

(4) A person who has the power to make an appointment to a public office within subsection (2)(a) *or (b)* must not, in relation to the office, harass a person seeking, or being considered for, the appointment.

(5) A person (A) who has the power to make an appointment to a public office within subsection (2)(a) *or (b)* must not victimise a person (B)—

(a) in the arrangements A makes for deciding to whom to offer the appointment;

(b) as to the terms on which A offers B the appointment;

(c) by not offering B the appointment.

(6) A person (A) who is a relevant person in relation to a public office within subsection (2)(a) *or (b)* must not discriminate against a person (B) appointed to the office—

(a) as to B's terms of appointment;

(b) in the way A affords B access, or by not affording B access, to opportunities for promotion, transfer or training or for receiving any other benefit, facility or service;

(c) by terminating the appointment;

(d) by subjecting B to any other detriment.

(7) A person (A) who is a relevant person in relation to a public office within subsection (2)(c) must not discriminate against a person (B) appointed to the office—

(a) as to B's terms of appointment;

(b) in the way A affords B access, or by not affording B access, to opportunities for promotion, transfer or training or for receiving any other benefit, facility or service;

(c) by subjecting B to any other detriment (other than by terminating the appointment).

(8) A relevant person in relation to a public office must not, in relation to that office, harass a person appointed to it.

(9) A person (A) who is a relevant person in relation to a public office within subsection (2)(a) *or (b)* must not victimise a person (B) appointed to the office—

(a) as to B's terms of appointment;

(b) in the way A affords B access, or by not affording B access, to opportunities for promotion, transfer or training or for receiving any other benefit, facility or service;

(c) by terminating the appointment;
(d) by subjecting B to any other detriment.

(10) A person (A) who is a relevant person in relation to a public office within subsection (2)(c) must not victimise a person (B) appointed to the office—

(a) as to B's terms of appointment;
(b) in the way A affords B access, or by not affording B access, to opportunities for promotion, transfer or training or for receiving any other benefit, facility or service;
(c) by subjecting B to any other detriment (other than by terminating the appointment).

(11) A duty to make reasonable adjustments applies to—

(a) a relevant person in relation to a public office;
(b) a person who has the power to make an appointment to a public office within subsection (2)(a) *or (b)*.

(12) Subsection (3)(b), so far as relating to sex or pregnancy and maternity, does not apply to a term that relates to pay—

(a) unless, were B to accept the offer, an equality clause or rule would have effect in relation to the term, or
(b) if paragraph (a) does not apply, except in so far as making an offer on terms including that term amounts to a contravention of subsection (3)(b) by virtue of section 13, 14 or 18.

NOTES

Commencement: 1 October 2010.

Sub-s (2): para (d) inserted by the Crime and Courts Act 2013, s 20, Sch 13, Pt 4, para 50(1), (2), as from a day to be appointed.

Sub-ss (3)–(6), (9), (11): for the words in italics in each place they appear, there are substituted the words ", (b) or (d)", by the Crime and Courts Act 2013, s 20, Sch 13, Pt 4, para 50(1), (3), as from a day to be appointed.

[1.1657]

51 Public offices: recommendations for appointments, etc

(1) A person (A) who has the power to make a recommendation for or give approval to an appointment to a public office within section 50(2)(a) *or (b)*, must not discriminate against a person (B)—

(a) in the arrangements A makes for deciding who to recommend for appointment or to whose appointment to give approval;
(b) by not recommending B for appointment to the office;
(c) by making a negative recommendation of B for appointment to the office;
(d) by not giving approval to the appointment of B to the office.

(2) A person who has the power to make a recommendation for or give approval to an appointment to a public office within section 50(2)(a) *or (b)* must not, in relation to the office, harass a person seeking or being considered for the recommendation or approval.

(3) A person (A) who has the power to make a recommendation for or give approval to an appointment to a public office within section 50(2)(a) *or (b)*, must not victimise a person (B)—

(a) in the arrangements A makes for deciding who to recommend for appointment or to whose appointment to give approval;
(b) by not recommending B for appointment to the office;
(c) by making a negative recommendation of B for appointment to the office;
(d) by not giving approval to the appointment of B to the office.

(4) A duty to make reasonable adjustments applies to a person who has the power to make a recommendation for or give approval to an appointment to a public office within section 50(2)(a) *or (b)*.

(5) A reference in this section to a person who has the power to make a recommendation for or give approval to an appointment to a public office within section 50(2)(a) [or (d)] is a reference only to a relevant body which has that power; and for that purpose "relevant body" means a body established—

(a) by or in pursuance of an enactment, or
(b) by a member of the executive.

NOTES

Commencement: 1 October 2010.

Sub-ss (1)–(4): for the words in italics in each place they appear, there are substituted the words ", (b) or (d)", by the Crime and Courts Act 2013, s 20, Sch 13, Pt 4, para 51(1), (2), as from a day to be appointed.

Sub-s (5): words in square brackets inserted by the Crime and Courts Act 2013, s 20, Sch 13, Pt 4, para 51(1), (3), as from a day to be appointed.

[1.1658]

52 Interpretation and exceptions

(1) This section applies for the purposes of sections 49 to 51.
(2) "Personal office" has the meaning given in section 49.
(3) "Public office" has the meaning given in section 50.

(4) An office or post which is both a personal office and a public office is to be treated as being a public office only.
(5) Appointment to an office or post does not include election to it.
(6) "Relevant person", in relation to an office, means the person who, in relation to a matter specified in the first column of the table, is specified in the second column (but a reference to a relevant person does not in any case include the House of Commons, the House of Lords, the National Assembly for Wales or the Scottish Parliament).

Matter	Relevant person
A term of appointment	The person who has the power to set the term.
Access to an opportunity	The person who has the power to afford access to the opportunity (or, if there is no such person, the person who has the power to make the appointment).
Terminating an appointment	The person who has the power to terminate the appointment.
Subjecting an appointee to any other detriment	The person who has the power in relation to the matter to which the conduct in question relates (or, if there is no such person, the person who has the power to make the appointment).
Harassing an appointee	The person who has the power in relation to the matter to which the conduct in question relates.

(7) A reference to terminating a person's appointment includes a reference to termination of the appointment—
(a) by the expiry of a period (including a period expiring by reference to an event or circumstance);
(b) by an act of the person (including giving notice) in circumstances such that the person is entitled, because of the relevant person's conduct, to terminate the appointment without notice.
(8) Subsection (7)(a) does not apply if, immediately after the termination, the appointment is renewed on the same terms.
(9) Schedule 6 (excluded offices) has effect.

NOTES
Commencement: 1 October 2010.

Qualifications

[1.1659]
53 Qualifications bodies
(1) A qualifications body (A) must not discriminate against a person (B)—
(a) in the arrangements A makes for deciding upon whom to confer a relevant qualification;
(b) as to the terms on which it is prepared to confer a relevant qualification on B;
(c) by not conferring a relevant qualification on B.
(2) A qualifications body (A) must not discriminate against a person (B) upon whom A has conferred a relevant qualification—
(a) by withdrawing the qualification from B;
(b) by varying the terms on which B holds the qualification;
(c) by subjecting B to any other detriment.
(3) A qualifications body must not, in relation to conferment by it of a relevant qualification, harass—
(a) a person who holds the qualification, or
(b) a person who applies for it.
(4) A qualifications body (A) must not victimise a person (B)—
(a) in the arrangements A makes for deciding upon whom to confer a relevant qualification;
(b) as to the terms on which it is prepared to confer a relevant qualification on B;
(c) by not conferring a relevant qualification on B.
(5) A qualifications body (A) must not victimise a person (B) upon whom A has conferred a relevant qualification—
(a) by withdrawing the qualification from B;
(b) by varying the terms on which B holds the qualification;
(c) by subjecting B to any other detriment.
(6) A duty to make reasonable adjustments applies to a qualifications body.
(7) The application by a qualifications body of a competence standard to a disabled person is not disability discrimination unless it is discrimination by virtue of section 19.

NOTES

Commencement: 1 October 2010.

[1.1660]

54 Interpretation

(1) This section applies for the purposes of section 53.

(2) A qualifications body is an authority or body which can confer a relevant qualification.

(3) A relevant qualification is an authorisation, qualification, recognition, registration, enrolment, approval or certification which is needed for, or facilitates engagement in, a particular trade or profession.

(4) An authority or body is not a qualifications body in so far as—

(a) it can confer a qualification to which section 96 applies,

(b) it is the responsible body of a school to which section 85 applies,

(c) it is the governing body of an institution to which section 91 applies,

(d) it exercises functions under the Education Acts, or

(e) it exercises functions under the Education (Scotland) Act 1980.

(5) A reference to conferring a relevant qualification includes a reference to renewing or extending the conferment of a relevant qualification.

(6) A competence standard is an academic, medical or other standard applied for the purpose of determining whether or not a person has a particular level of competence or ability.

NOTES

Commencement: 1 October 2010.

Employment services

[1.1661]

55 Employment service-providers

(1) A person (an "employment service-provider") concerned with the provision of an employment service must not discriminate against a person—

(a) in the arrangements the service-provider makes for selecting persons to whom to provide, or to whom to offer to provide, the service;

(b) as to the terms on which the service-provider offers to provide the service to the person;

(c) by not offering to provide the service to the person.

(2) An employment service-provider (A) must not, in relation to the provision of an employment service, discriminate against a person (B)—

(a) as to the terms on which A provides the service to B;

(b) by not providing the service to B;

(c) by terminating the provision of the service to B;

(d) by subjecting B to any other detriment.

(3) An employment service-provider must not, in relation to the provision of an employment service, harass—

(a) a person who asks the service-provider to provide the service;

(b) a person for whom the service-provider provides the service.

(4) An employment service-provider (A) must not victimise a person (B)—

(a) in the arrangements A makes for selecting persons to whom to provide, or to whom to offer to provide, the service;

(b) as to the terms on which A offers to provide the service to B;

(c) by not offering to provide the service to B.

(5) An employment service-provider (A) must not, in relation to the provision of an employment service, victimise a person (B)—

(a) as to the terms on which A provides the service to B;

(b) by not providing the service to B;

(c) by terminating the provision of the service to B;

(d) by subjecting B to any other detriment.

(6) A duty to make reasonable adjustments applies to an employment service-provider, except in relation to the provision of a vocational service.

(7) The duty imposed by section 29(7)(a) applies to a person concerned with the provision of a vocational service; but a failure to comply with that duty in relation to the provision of a vocational service is a contravention of this Part for the purposes of Part 9 (enforcement).

NOTES

Commencement: 1 October 2010.

[1.1662]

56 Interpretation

(1) This section applies for the purposes of section 55.

(2) The provision of an employment service includes—

- (a) the provision of vocational training;
- (b) the provision of vocational guidance;
- (c) making arrangements for the provision of vocational training or vocational guidance;
- (d) the provision of a service for finding employment for persons;
- (e) the provision of a service for supplying employers with persons to do work;
- (f) the provision of a service in pursuance of arrangements made under section 2 of the Employment and Training Act 1973 (functions of the Secretary of State relating to employment);
- (g) the provision of a service in pursuance of arrangements made or a direction given under section 10 of that Act (careers services);
- (h) the exercise of a function in pursuance of arrangements made under section 2(3) of the Enterprise and New Towns (Scotland) Act 1990 (functions of Scottish Enterprise, etc relating to employment);
- (i) an assessment related to the conferment of a relevant qualification within the meaning of section 53 above (except in so far as the assessment is by the qualifications body which confers the qualification).

(3) This section does not apply in relation to training or guidance in so far as it is training or guidance in relation to which another provision of this Part applies.

(4) This section does not apply in relation to training or guidance for pupils of a school to which section 85 applies in so far as it is training or guidance to which the responsible body of the school has power to afford access (whether as the responsible body of that school or as the responsible body of any other school at which the training or guidance is provided).

(5) This section does not apply in relation to training or guidance for students of an institution to which section 91 applies in so far as it is training or guidance to which the governing body of the institution has power to afford access.

(6) "Vocational training" means—

- (a) training for employment, or
- (b) work experience (including work experience the duration of which is not agreed until after it begins).

(7) A reference to the provision of a vocational service is a reference to the provision of an employment service within subsection (2)(a) to (d) (or an employment service within subsection (2)(f) or (g) in so far as it is also an employment service within subsection (2)(a) to (d)); and for that purpose—

- (a) the references to an employment service within subsection (2)(a) do not include a reference to vocational training within the meaning given by subsection (6)(b), and
- (b) the references to an employment service within subsection (2)(d) also include a reference to a service for assisting persons to retain employment.

(8) A reference to training includes a reference to facilities for training.

NOTES

Commencement: 1 October 2010.

Trade organisations

[1.1663]

57 Trade organisations

(1) A trade organisation (A) must not discriminate against a person (B)—

- (a) in the arrangements A makes for deciding to whom to offer membership of the organisation;
- (b) as to the terms on which it is prepared to admit B as a member;
- (c) by not accepting B's application for membership.

(2) A trade organisation (A) must not discriminate against a member (B)—

- (a) in the way it affords B access, or by not affording B access, to opportunities for receiving a benefit, facility or service;
- (b) by depriving B of membership;
- (c) by varying the terms on which B is a member;
- (d) by subjecting B to any other detriment.

(3) A trade organisation must not, in relation to membership of it, harass—

- (a) a member, or
- (b) an applicant for membership.

(4) A trade organisation (A) must not victimise a person (B)—

- (a) in the arrangements A makes for deciding to whom to offer membership of the organisation;
- (b) as to the terms on which it is prepared to admit B as a member;

(c) by not accepting B's application for membership.

(5) A trade organisation (A) must not victimise a member (B)—

(a) in the way it affords B access, or by not affording B access, to opportunities for receiving a benefit, facility or service;

(b) by depriving B of membership;

(c) by varying the terms on which B is a member;

(d) by subjecting B to any other detriment.

(6) A duty to make reasonable adjustments applies to a trade organisation.

(7) A trade organisation is—

(a) an organisation of workers,

(b) an organisation of employers, or

(c) any other organisation whose members carry on a particular trade or profession for the purposes of which the organisation exists.

NOTES

Commencement: 1 October 2010.

Local authority members

[1.1664]

58 Official business of members

(1) A local authority must not discriminate against a member of the authority in relation to the member's carrying out of official business—

(a) in the way the authority affords the member access, or by not affording the member access, to opportunities for training or for receiving any other facility;

(b) by subjecting the member to any other detriment.

(2) A local authority must not, in relation to a member's carrying out of official business, harass the member.

(3) A local authority must not victimise a member of the authority in relation to the member's carrying out of official business—

(a) in the way the authority affords the member access, or by not affording the member access, to opportunities for training or for receiving any other facility;

(b) by subjecting the member to any other detriment.

(4) A member of a local authority is not subjected to a detriment for the purposes of subsection (1)(b) or (3)(b) only because the member is—

(a) not appointed or elected to an office of the authority,

(b) not appointed or elected to, or to an office of, a committee or sub-committee of the authority, or

(c) not appointed or nominated in exercise of an appointment power of the authority.

(5) In subsection (4)(c), an appointment power of a local authority is a power of the authority, or of a group of bodies including the authority, to make—

(a) appointments to a body;

(b) nominations for appointment to a body.

(6) A duty to make reasonable adjustments applies to a local authority.

NOTES

Commencement: 1 October 2010.

[1.1665]

59 Interpretation

(1) This section applies for the purposes of section 58.

(2) "Local authority" means—

(a) a county council in England;

(b) a district council in England;

(c) the Greater London Authority;

(d) a London borough council;

(e) the Common Council of the City of London;

(f) the Council of the Isles of Scilly;

(g) a parish council in England;

(h) a county council in Wales;

(i) a community council in Wales;

(j) a county borough council in Wales;

(k) a council constituted under section 2 of the Local Government etc (Scotland) Act 1994;

(l) a community council in Scotland.

(3) A Minister of the Crown may by order amend subsection (2) so as to add, vary or omit a reference to a body which exercises functions that have been conferred on a local authority within paragraph (a) to (l).

(4) A reference to the carrying-out of official business by a person who is a member of a local authority is a reference to the doing of anything by the person—

- (a) as a member of the authority,
- (b) as a member of a body to which the person is appointed by, or appointed following nomination by, the authority or a group of bodies including the authority, or
- (c) as a member of any other public body.

(5) "Member", in relation to the Greater London Authority, means—

- (a) the Mayor of London;
- (b) a member of the London Assembly.

NOTES

Commencement: 1 October 2010.

Recruitment

[1.1666]

60 Enquiries about disability and health

(1) A person (A) to whom an application for work is made must not ask about the health of the applicant (B)—

- (a) before offering work to B, or
- (b) where A is not in a position to offer work to B, before including B in a pool of applicants from whom A intends (when in a position to do so) to select a person to whom to offer work.

(2) A contravention of subsection (1) (or a contravention of section 111 or 112 that relates to a contravention of subsection (1)) is enforceable as an unlawful act under Part 1 of the Equality Act 2006 (and, by virtue of section 120(8), is enforceable only by the Commission under that Part).

(3) A does not contravene a relevant disability provision merely by asking about B's health; but A's conduct in reliance on information given in response may be a contravention of a relevant disability provision.

(4) Subsection (5) applies if B brings proceedings before an employment tribunal on a complaint that A's conduct in reliance on information given in response to a question about B's health is a contravention of a relevant disability provision.

(5) In the application of section 136 to the proceedings, the particulars of the complaint are to be treated for the purposes of subsection (2) of that section as facts from which the tribunal could decide that A contravened the provision.

(6) This section does not apply to a question that A asks in so far as asking the question is necessary for the purpose of—

- (a) establishing whether B will be able to comply with a requirement to undergo an assessment or establishing whether a duty to make reasonable adjustments is or will be imposed on A in relation to B in connection with a requirement to undergo an assessment,
- (b) establishing whether B will be able to carry out a function that is intrinsic to the work concerned,
- (c) monitoring diversity in the range of persons applying to A for work,
- (d) taking action to which section 158 would apply if references in that section to persons who share (or do not share) a protected characteristic were references to disabled persons (or persons who are not disabled) and the reference to the characteristic were a reference to disability, or
- (e) if A applies in relation to the work a requirement to have a particular disability, establishing whether B has that disability.

(7) In subsection (6)(b), where A reasonably believes that a duty to make reasonable adjustments would be imposed on A in relation to B in connection with the work, the reference to a function that is intrinsic to the work is to be read as a reference to a function that would be intrinsic to the work once A complied with the duty.

(8) Subsection (6)(e) applies only if A shows that, having regard to the nature or context of the work—

- (a) the requirement is an occupational requirement, and
- (b) the application of the requirement is a proportionate means of achieving a legitimate aim.

(9) "Work" means employment, contract work, a position as a partner, a position as a member of an LLP, a pupillage or tenancy, being taken as a devil, membership of a stable, an appointment to a personal or public office, or the provision of an employment service; and the references in subsection (1) to offering a person work are, in relation to contract work, to be read as references to allowing a person to do the work.

(10) A reference to offering work is a reference to making a conditional or unconditional offer of work (and, in relation to contract work, is a reference to allowing a person to do the work subject to fulfilment of one or more conditions).

(11) The following, so far as relating to discrimination within section 13 because of disability, are relevant disability provisions—

- (a) section 39(1)(a) or (c);

(b) section 41(1)(b);
(c) section 44(1)(a) or (c);
(d) section 45(1)(a) or (c);
(e) section 47(1)(a) or (c);
(f) section 48(1)(a) or (c);
(g) section 49(3)(a) or (c);
(h) section 50(3)(a) or (c);
(i) section 51(1);
(j) section 55(1)(a) or (c).

(12) An assessment is an interview or other process designed to give an indication of a person's suitability for the work concerned.

(13) For the purposes of this section, whether or not a person has a disability is to be regarded as an aspect of that person's health.

(14) This section does not apply to anything done for the purpose of vetting applicants for work for reasons of national security.

NOTES

Commencement: 1 October 2010.

CHAPTER 2
OCCUPATIONAL PENSION SCHEMES

[1.1667]

61 Non-discrimination rule

(1) An occupational pension scheme must be taken to include a non-discrimination rule.

(2) A non-discrimination rule is a provision by virtue of which a responsible person (A)—
(a) must not discriminate against another person (B) in carrying out any of A's functions in relation to the scheme;
(b) must not, in relation to the scheme, harass B;
(c) must not, in relation to the scheme, victimise B.

(3) The provisions of an occupational pension scheme have effect subject to the non-discrimination rule.

(4) The following are responsible persons—
(a) the trustees or managers of the scheme;
(b) an employer whose employees are, or may be, members of the scheme;
(c) a person exercising an appointing function in relation to an office the holder of which is, or may be, a member of the scheme.

(5) A non-discrimination rule does not apply in relation to a person who is a pension credit member of a scheme.

(6) An appointing function is any of the following—
(a) the function of appointing a person;
(b) the function of terminating a person's appointment;
(c) the function of recommending a person for appointment;
(d) the function of approving an appointment.

(7) A breach of a non-discrimination rule is a contravention of this Part for the purposes of Part 9 (enforcement).

(8) It is not a breach of a non-discrimination rule for the employer or the trustees or managers of a scheme to maintain or use in relation to the scheme rules, practices, actions or decisions relating to age which are of a description specified by order by a Minister of the Crown.

(9) An order authorising the use of rules, practices, actions or decisions which are not in use before the order comes into force must not be made unless the Minister consults such persons as the Minister thinks appropriate.

(10) A non-discrimination rule does not have effect in relation to an occupational pension scheme in so far as an equality rule has effect in relation to it (or would have effect in relation to it but for Part 2 of Schedule 7).

(11) A duty to make reasonable adjustments applies to a responsible person.

NOTES

Commencement: 6 July 2010 (sub-ss (8), (9) for the purpose of enabling subordinate legislation or guidance to be made); 1 October 2010 (otherwise).

Orders: the Equality Act (Age Exceptions for Pension Schemes) Order 2010, SI 2010/2133 at **[2.1526]**; the Equality Act (Age Exceptions for Pension Schemes) (Amendment) Order 2010, SI 2010/2285.

[1.1668]

62 Non-discrimination alterations

(1) This section applies if the trustees or managers of an occupational pension scheme do not have power to make non-discrimination alterations to the scheme.

(2) This section also applies if the trustees or managers of an occupational pension scheme have power to make non-discrimination alterations to the scheme but the procedure for doing so—

(a) is liable to be unduly complex or protracted, or
(b) involves obtaining consents which cannot be obtained or which can be obtained only with undue delay or difficulty.

(3) The trustees or managers may by resolution make non-discrimination alterations to the scheme.

(4) Non-discrimination alterations may have effect in relation to a period before the date on which they are made.

(5) Non-discrimination alterations to an occupational pension scheme are such alterations to the scheme as may be required for the provisions of the scheme to have the effect that they have in consequence of section 61(3).

NOTES

Commencement: 1 October 2010.

[1.1669]

63 Communications

(1) In their application to communications the following provisions apply in relation to a disabled person who is a pension credit member of an occupational pension scheme as they apply in relation to a disabled person who is a deferred member or pensioner member of the scheme—

(a) section 61;
(b) section 120;
(c) section 126;
(d) paragraph 19 of Schedule 8 (and such other provisions of that Schedule as apply for the purposes of that paragraph).

(2) Communications include—

(a) the provision of information;
(b) the operation of a dispute resolution procedure.

NOTES

Commencement: 1 October 2010.

CHAPTER 3
EQUALITY OF TERMS

Sex equality

[1.1670]

64 Relevant types of work

(1) Sections 66 to 70 apply where—

(a) a person (A) is employed on work that is equal to the work that a comparator of the opposite sex (B) does;
(b) a person (A) holding a personal or public office does work that is equal to the work that a comparator of the opposite sex (B) does.

(2) The references in subsection (1) to the work that B does are not restricted to work done contemporaneously with the work done by A.

NOTES

Commencement: 1 October 2010.

[1.1671]

65 Equal work

(1) For the purposes of this Chapter, A's work is equal to that of B if it is—

(a) like B's work,
(b) rated as equivalent to B's work, or
(c) of equal value to B's work.

(2) A's work is like B's work if—

(a) A's work and B's work are the same or broadly similar, and
(b) such differences as there are between their work are not of practical importance in relation to the terms of their work.

(3) So on a comparison of one person's work with another's for the purposes of subsection (2), it is necessary to have regard to—

(a) the frequency with which differences between their work occur in practice, and
(b) the nature and extent of the differences.

(4) A's work is rated as equivalent to B's work if a job evaluation study—

(a) gives an equal value to A's job and B's job in terms of the demands made on a worker, or
(b) would give an equal value to A's job and B's job in those terms were the evaluation not made on a sex-specific system.

(5) A system is sex-specific if, for the purposes of one or more of the demands made on a worker, it sets values for men different from those it sets for women.

(6) A's work is of equal value to B's work if it is—

(a) neither like B's work nor rated as equivalent to B's work, but

(b) nevertheless equal to B's work in terms of the demands made on A by reference to factors such as effort, skill and decision-making.

NOTES

Commencement: 1 October 2010.

[1.1672]

66 Sex equality clause

(1) If the terms of A's work do not (by whatever means) include a sex equality clause, they are to be treated as including one.

(2) A sex equality clause is a provision that has the following effect—

(a) if a term of A's is less favourable to A than a corresponding term of B's is to B, A's term is modified so as not to be less favourable;

(b) if A does not have a term which corresponds to a term of B's that benefits B, A's terms are modified so as to include such a term.

(3) Subsection (2)(a) applies to a term of A's relating to membership of or rights under an occupational pension scheme only in so far as a sex equality rule would have effect in relation to the term.

(4) In the case of work within section 65(1)(b), a reference in subsection (2) above to a term includes a reference to such terms (if any) as have not been determined by the rating of the work (as well as those that have).

NOTES

Commencement: 1 October 2010.

[1.1673]

67 Sex equality rule

(1) If an occupational pension scheme does not include a sex equality rule, it is to be treated as including one.

(2) A sex equality rule is a provision that has the following effect—

(a) if a relevant term is less favourable to A than it is to B, the term is modified so as not to be less favourable;

(b) if a term confers a relevant discretion capable of being exercised in a way that would be less favourable to A than to B, the term is modified so as to prevent the exercise of the discretion in that way.

(3) A term is relevant if it is—

(a) a term on which persons become members of the scheme, or

(b) a term on which members of the scheme are treated.

(4) A discretion is relevant if its exercise in relation to the scheme is capable of affecting—

(a) the way in which persons become members of the scheme, or

(b) the way in which members of the scheme are treated.

(5) The reference in subsection (3)(b) to a term on which members of a scheme are treated includes a reference to the term as it has effect for the benefit of dependants of members.

(6) The reference in subsection (4)(b) to the way in which members of a scheme are treated includes a reference to the way in which they are treated as the scheme has effect for the benefit of dependants of members.

(7) If the effect of a relevant matter on persons of the same sex differs according to their family, marital or civil partnership status, a comparison for the purposes of this section of the effect of that matter on persons of the opposite sex must be with persons who have the same status.

(8) A relevant matter is—

(a) a relevant term;

(b) a term conferring a relevant discretion;

(c) the exercise of a relevant discretion in relation to an occupational pension scheme.

(9) This section, so far as relating to the terms on which persons become members of an occupational pension scheme, does not have effect in relation to pensionable service before 8 April 1976.

(10) This section, so far as relating to the terms on which members of an occupational pension scheme are treated, does not have effect in relation to pensionable service before 17 May 1990.

NOTES

Commencement: 1 October 2010.

[1.1674]

68 Sex equality rule: consequential alteration of schemes

(1) This section applies if the trustees or managers of an occupational pension scheme do not have power to make sex equality alterations to the scheme.

(2) This section also applies if the trustees or managers of an occupational pension scheme have power to make sex equality alterations to the scheme but the procedure for doing so—

(a) is liable to be unduly complex or protracted, or

(b) involves obtaining consents which cannot be obtained or which can be obtained only with undue delay or difficulty.

(3) The trustees or managers may by resolution make sex equality alterations to the scheme.

(4) Sex equality alterations may have effect in relation to a period before the date on which they are made.

(5) Sex equality alterations to an occupational pension scheme are such alterations to the scheme as may be required to secure conformity with a sex equality rule.

NOTES

Commencement: 1 October 2010.

[1.1675]

69 Defence of material factor

(1) The sex equality clause in A's terms has no effect in relation to a difference between A's terms and B's terms if the responsible person shows that the difference is because of a material factor reliance on which—

(a) does not involve treating A less favourably because of A's sex than the responsible person treats B, and

(b) if the factor is within subsection (2), is a proportionate means of achieving a legitimate aim.

(2) A factor is within this subsection if A shows that, as a result of the factor, A and persons of the same sex doing work equal to A's are put at a particular disadvantage when compared with persons of the opposite sex doing work equal to A's.

(3) For the purposes of subsection (1), the long-term objective of reducing inequality between men's and women's terms of work is always to be regarded as a legitimate aim.

(4) A sex equality rule has no effect in relation to a difference between A and B in the effect of a relevant matter if the trustees or managers of the scheme in question show that the difference is because of a material factor which is not the difference of sex.

(5) "Relevant matter" has the meaning given in section 67.

(6) For the purposes of this section, a factor is not material unless it is a material difference between A's case and B's.

NOTES

Commencement: 1 October 2010.

[1.1676]

70 Exclusion of sex discrimination provisions

(1) The relevant sex discrimination provision has no effect in relation to a term of A's that—

(a) is modified by, or included by virtue of, a sex equality clause or rule, or

(b) would be so modified or included but for section 69 or Part 2 of Schedule 7.

(2) Neither of the following is sex discrimination for the purposes of the relevant sex discrimination provision—

(a) the inclusion in A's terms of a term that is less favourable as referred to in section 66(2)(a);

(b) the failure to include in A's terms a corresponding term as referred to in section 66(2)(b).

(3) The relevant sex discrimination provision is, in relation to work of a description given in the first column of the table, the provision referred to in the second column so far as relating to sex.

Description of work	Provision
Employment	Section 39(2)
Appointment to a personal office	Section 49(6)
Appointment to a public office	Section 50(6)

NOTES

Commencement: 1 October 2010.

[1.1677]

71 Sex discrimination in relation to contractual pay

(1) This section applies in relation to a term of a person's work—

(a) that relates to pay, but

(b) in relation to which a sex equality clause or rule has no effect.

(2) The relevant sex discrimination provision (as defined by section 70) has no effect in relation to the term except in so far as treatment of the person amounts to a contravention of the provision by virtue of section 13 or 14.

NOTES

Commencement: 1 October 2010.

Pregnancy and maternity equality

[1.1678]

72 Relevant types of work

Sections 73 to 76 apply where a woman—

(a) is employed, or

(b) holds a personal or public office.

NOTES

Commencement: 1 October 2010.

[1.1679]

73 Maternity equality clause

(1) If the terms of the woman's work do not (by whatever means) include a maternity equality clause, they are to be treated as including one.

(2) A maternity equality clause is a provision that, in relation to the terms of the woman's work, has the effect referred to in section 74(1), (6) and (8).

(3) In the case of a term relating to membership of or rights under an occupational pension scheme, a maternity equality clause has only such effect as a maternity equality rule would have.

NOTES

Commencement: 1 October 2010.

[1.1680]

74 Maternity equality clause: pay

(1) A term of the woman's work that provides for maternity-related pay to be calculated by reference to her pay at a particular time is, if each of the following three conditions is satisfied, modified as mentioned in subsection (5).

(2) The first condition is that, after the time referred to in subsection (1) but before the end of the protected period—

(a) her pay increases, or

(b) it would have increased had she not been on maternity leave.

(3) The second condition is that the maternity-related pay is not—

(a) what her pay would have been had she not been on maternity leave, or

(b) the difference between the amount of statutory maternity pay to which she is entitled and what her pay would have been had she not been on maternity leave.

(4) The third condition is that the terms of her work do not provide for the maternity-related pay to be subject to—

(a) an increase as mentioned in subsection (2)(a), or

(b) an increase that would have occurred as mentioned in subsection (2)(b).

(5) The modification referred to in subsection (1) is a modification to provide for the maternity-related pay to be subject to—

(a) any increase as mentioned in subsection (2)(a), or

(b) any increase that would have occurred as mentioned in subsection (2)(b).

(6) A term of her work that—

(a) provides for pay within subsection (7), but

(b) does not provide for her to be given the pay in circumstances in which she would have been given it had she not been on maternity leave,

is modified so as to provide for her to be given it in circumstances in which it would normally be given.

(7) Pay is within this subsection if it is—

(a) pay (including pay by way of bonus) in respect of times before the woman is on maternity leave,

(b) pay by way of bonus in respect of times when she is on compulsory maternity leave, or

(c) pay by way of bonus in respect of times after the end of the protected period.

(8) A term of the woman's work that—

(a) provides for pay after the end of the protected period, but

(b) does not provide for it to be subject to an increase to which it would have been subject had she not been on maternity leave,

is modified so as to provide for it to be subject to the increase.

(9) Maternity-related pay is pay (other than statutory maternity pay) to which a woman is entitled—

(a) as a result of being pregnant, or

(b) in respect of times when she is on maternity leave.

(10) A reference to the protected period is to be construed in accordance with section 18.

NOTES

Commencement: 1 October 2010.

[1.1681]

75 Maternity equality rule

(1) If an occupational pension scheme does not include a maternity equality rule, it is to be treated as including one.

(2) A maternity equality rule is a provision that has the effect set out in subsections (3) and (4).

(3) If a relevant term does not treat time when the woman is on maternity leave as it treats time when she is not, the term is modified so as to treat time when she is on maternity leave as time when she is not.

(4) If a term confers a relevant discretion capable of being exercised so that time when she is on maternity leave is treated differently from time when she is not, the term is modified so as not to allow the discretion to be exercised in that way.

(5) A term is relevant if it is—

(a) a term relating to membership of the scheme,

(b) a term relating to the accrual of rights under the scheme, or

(c) a term providing for the determination of the amount of a benefit payable under the scheme.

(6) A discretion is relevant if its exercise is capable of affecting—

(a) membership of the scheme,

(b) the accrual of rights under the scheme, or

(c) the determination of the amount of a benefit payable under the scheme.

(7) This section does not require the woman's contributions to the scheme in respect of time when she is on maternity leave to be determined otherwise than by reference to the amount she is paid in respect of that time.

(8) This section, so far as relating to time when she is on ordinary maternity leave but is not being paid by her employer, applies only in a case where the expected week of childbirth began on or after 6 April 2003.

(9) This section, so far as relating to time when she is on additional maternity leave but is not being paid by her employer—

(a) does not apply to the accrual of rights under the scheme in any case;

(b) applies for other purposes only in a case where the expected week of childbirth began on or after 5 October 2008.

(10) In this section—

(a) a reference to being on maternity leave includes a reference to having been on maternity leave, and

(b) a reference to being paid by the employer includes a reference to receiving statutory maternity pay from the employer.

NOTES

Commencement: 1 October 2010.

[1.1682]

76 Exclusion of pregnancy and maternity discrimination provisions

(1) The relevant pregnancy and maternity discrimination provision has no effect in relation to a term of the woman's work that is modified by a maternity equality clause or rule.

[(1A) The relevant pregnancy and maternity discrimination provision has no effect in relation to a term of the woman's work—

(a) that relates to pay, but

(b) in relation to which a maternity equality clause or rule has no effect.]

(2) The inclusion in the woman's terms of a term that requires modification by virtue of section 73(2) or (3) is not pregnancy and maternity discrimination for the purposes of the relevant pregnancy and maternity discrimination provision.

(3) The relevant pregnancy and maternity discrimination provision is, in relation to a description of work given in the first column of the table, the provision referred to in the second column so far as relating to pregnancy and maternity.

Description of work	*Provision*
Employment	Section 39(2)
Appointment to a personal office	Section 49(6)
Appointment to a public office	Section 50(6)

NOTES

Commencement: 1 October 2010.

Sub-s (1A): inserted by the Equality Act 2010 (Amendment) Order 2010, SI 2010/2622, art 2, as from 30 October 2010.

Disclosure of information

[1.1683]

77 Discussions about pay

(1) A term of a person's work that purports to prevent or restrict the person (P) from disclosing or seeking to disclose information about the terms of P's work is unenforceable against P in so far as P makes or seeks to make a relevant pay disclosure.

(2) A term of a person's work that purports to prevent or restrict the person (P) from seeking disclosure of information from a colleague about the terms of the colleague's work is unenforceable against P in so far as P seeks a relevant pay disclosure from the colleague; and "colleague" includes a former colleague in relation to the work in question.

(3) A disclosure is a relevant pay disclosure if made for the purpose of enabling the person who makes it, or the person to whom it is made, to find out whether or to what extent there is, in relation to the work in question, a connection between pay and having (or not having) a particular protected characteristic.

(4) The following are to be treated as protected acts for the purposes of the relevant victimisation provision—

(a) seeking a disclosure that would be a relevant pay disclosure;

(b) making or seeking to make a relevant pay disclosure;

(c) receiving information disclosed in a relevant pay disclosure.

(5) The relevant victimisation provision is, in relation to a description of work specified in the first column of the table, section 27 so far as it applies for the purposes of a provision mentioned in the second column.

Description of work	*Provision by virtue of which section 27 has effect*
Employment	Section 39(3) or (4)
Appointment to a personal office	Section 49(5) or (8)
Appointment to a public office	Section 50(5) or (9)

NOTES

Commencement: 1 October 2010.

[1.1684]

78 Gender pay gap information

(1) Regulations may require employers to publish information relating to the pay of employees for the purpose of showing whether, by reference to factors of such description as is prescribed, there are differences in the pay of male and female employees.

(2) This section does not apply to—

(a) an employer who has fewer than 250 employees;

(b) a person specified in Schedule 19;

(c) a government department or part of the armed forces not specified in that Schedule.

(3) The regulations may prescribe—

(a) descriptions of employer;

(b) descriptions of employee;

(c) how to calculate the number of employees that an employer has;

(d) descriptions of information;

(e) the time at which information is to be published;

(f) the form and manner in which it is to be published.

(4) Regulations under subsection (3)(e) may not require an employer, after the first publication of information, to publish information more frequently than at intervals of 12 months.

(5) The regulations may make provision for a failure to comply with the regulations—

(a) to be an offence punishable on summary conviction by a fine not exceeding level 5 on the standard scale;

(b) to be enforced, otherwise than as an offence, by such means as are prescribed.

(6) The reference to a failure to comply with the regulations includes a reference to a failure by a person acting on behalf of an employer.

NOTES

Commencement: to be appointed.

Supplementary

[1.1685]

79 Comparators

(1) This section applies for the purposes of this Chapter.

(2) If A is employed, B is a comparator if subsection (3) or (4) applies.

(3) This subsection applies if—

(a) B is employed by A's employer or by an associate of A's employer, and

(b) A and B work at the same establishment.

(4) This subsection applies if—

(a) B is employed by A's employer or an associate of A's employer,

(b) B works at an establishment other than the one at which A works, and

(c) common terms apply at the establishments (either generally or as between A and B).

(5) If A holds a personal or public office, B is a comparator if—

(a) B holds a personal or public office, and

(b) the person responsible for paying A is also responsible for paying B.

(6) If A is a relevant member of the House of Commons staff, B is a comparator if—

(a) B is employed by the person who is A's employer under subsection (6) of section 195 of the Employment Rights Act 1996, or

(b) if subsection (7) of that section applies in A's case, B is employed by the person who is A's employer under that subsection.

(7) If A is a relevant member of the House of Lords staff, B is a comparator if B is also a relevant member of the House of Lords staff.

(8) Section 42 does not apply to this Chapter; accordingly, for the purposes of this Chapter only, holding the office of constable is to be treated as holding a personal office.

(9) For the purposes of this section, employers are associated if—

(a) one is a company of which the other (directly or indirectly) has control, or

(b) both are companies of which a third person (directly or indirectly) has control.

NOTES

Commencement: 1 October 2010.

[1.1686]

80 Interpretation and exceptions

(1) This section applies for the purposes of this Chapter.

(2) The terms of a person's work are—

(a) if the person is employed, the terms of the person's employment that are in the person's contract of employment, contract of apprenticeship or contract to do work personally;

(b) if the person holds a personal or public office, the terms of the person's appointment to the office.

(3) If work is not done at an establishment, it is to be treated as done at the establishment with which it has the closest connection.

(4) A person (P) is the responsible person in relation to another person if—

(a) P is the other's employer;

(b) P is responsible for paying remuneration in respect of a personal or public office that the other holds.

(5) A job evaluation study is a study undertaken with a view to evaluating, in terms of the demands made on a person by reference to factors such as effort, skill and decision-making, the jobs to be done—

(a) by some or all of the workers in an undertaking or group of undertakings, or

(b) in the case of the armed forces, by some or all of the members of the armed forces.

(6) In the case of Crown employment, the reference in subsection (5)(a) to an undertaking is to be construed in accordance with section 191(4) of the Employment Rights Act 1996.

(7) "Civil partnership status" has the meaning given in section 124(1) of the Pensions Act 1995.

(8) Schedule 7 (exceptions) has effect.

NOTES

Commencement: 4 August 2010 (sub-s (8) in so far as it relates to Sch 7, paras 4–6, for the purpose of enabling subordinate legislation or guidance to be made); 1 October 2010 (otherwise).

CHAPTER 4
SUPPLEMENTARY

[1.1687]

81 Ships and hovercraft

(1) This Part applies in relation to—

(a) work on ships,

(b) work on hovercraft, and

(c) seafarers,

only in such circumstances as are prescribed.

(2) For the purposes of this section, it does not matter whether employment arises or work is carried out within or outside the United Kingdom.

(3) "Ship" has the same meaning as in the Merchant Shipping Act 1995.

(4) "Hovercraft" has the same meaning as in the Hovercraft Act 1968.

(5) "Seafarer" means a person employed or engaged in any capacity on board a ship or hovercraft.

(6) Nothing in this section affects the application of any other provision of this Act to conduct outside England and Wales or Scotland.

NOTES

Commencement: 6 July 2010 (for the purpose of enabling subordinate legislation or guidance to be made); 1 October 2010 (otherwise).

Transitional provisions: see the Equality Act 2010 (Commencement No 4, Savings, Consequential, Transitional, Transitory and Incidental Provisions and Revocation) Order 2010, SI 2010/2317, arts 10, 11 at **[2.1563]** et seq.

Regulations: the Equality Act 2010 (Work on Ships and Hovercraft) Regulations 2011, SI 2011/1771 at **[2.1611]**.

[1.1688]

82 Offshore work

(1) Her Majesty may by Order in Council provide that in the case of persons in offshore work—

(a) specified provisions of this Part apply (with or without modification);

(b) Northern Ireland legislation making provision for purposes corresponding to any of the purposes of this Part applies (with or without modification).

(2) The Order may—

(a) provide for these provisions, as applied by the Order, to apply to individuals (whether or not British citizens) and bodies corporate (whether or not incorporated under the law of a part of the United Kingdom), whether or not such application affects activities outside the United Kingdom;

(b) make provision for conferring jurisdiction on a specified court or class of court or on employment tribunals in respect of offences, causes of action or other matters arising in connection with offshore work;

(c) exclude from the operation of section 3 of the Territorial Waters Jurisdiction Act 1878 (consents required for prosecutions) proceedings for offences under the provisions mentioned in subsection (1) in connection with offshore work;

(d) provide that such proceedings must not be brought without such consent as may be required by the Order.

(3) "Offshore work" is work for the purposes of—

(a) activities in the territorial sea adjacent to the United Kingdom,

(b) activities such as are mentioned in subsection (2) of section 11 of the Petroleum Act 1998 in waters within subsection (8)(b) or (c) of that section, or

(c) activities mentioned in paragraphs (a) and (b) of section 87(1) of the Energy Act 2004 in waters to which that section applies.

(4) Work includes employment, contract work, a position as a partner or as a member of an LLP, or an appointment to a personal or public office.

(5) Northern Ireland legislation includes an enactment contained in, or in an instrument under, an Act that forms part of the law of Northern Ireland.

(6) In the application to Northern Ireland of subsection (2)(b), the reference to employment tribunals is to be read as a reference to industrial tribunals.

(7) Nothing in this section affects the application of any other provision of this Act to conduct outside England and Wales or Scotland.

NOTES

Commencement: 6 July 2010 (for the purpose of enabling subordinate legislation or guidance to be made); 1 October 2010 (otherwise).

Orders: the Equality Act 2010 (Offshore Work) Order 2010, SI 2010/1835 at **[2.1499]**.

[1.1689]

83 Interpretation and exceptions

(1) This section applies for the purposes of this Part.

(2) "Employment" means—

(a) employment under a contract of employment, a contract of apprenticeship or a contract personally to do work;
(b) Crown employment;
(c) employment as a relevant member of the House of Commons staff;
(d) employment as a relevant member of the House of Lords staff.

(3) This Part applies to service in the armed forces as it applies to employment by a private person; and for that purpose—
(a) references to terms of employment, or to a contract of employment, are to be read as including references to terms of service;
(b) references to associated employers are to be ignored.

(4) A reference to an employer or an employee, or to employing or being employed, is (subject to section 212(11)) to be read with subsections (2) and (3); and a reference to an employer also includes a reference to a person who has no employees but is seeking to employ one or more other persons.

(5) "Relevant member of the House of Commons staff" has the meaning given in section 195 of the Employment Rights Act 1996; and such a member of staff is an employee of—
(a) the person who is the employer of that member under subsection (6) of that section, or
(b) if subsection (7) of that section applies in the case of that member, the person who is the employer of that member under that subsection.

(6) "Relevant member of the House of Lords staff" has the meaning given in section 194 of that Act (which provides that such a member of staff is an employee of the Corporate Officer of the House of Lords).

(7) In the case of a person in Crown employment, or in employment as a relevant member of the House of Commons staff, a reference to the person's dismissal is a reference to the termination of the person's employment.

(8) A reference to a personal or public office, or to an appointment to a personal or public office, is to be construed in accordance with section 52.

(9) "Crown employment" has the meaning given in section 191 of the Employment Rights Act 1996.

(10) Schedule 8 (reasonable adjustments) has effect.

(11) Schedule 9 (exceptions) has effect.

NOTES

Commencement: 4 August 2010 (sub-s (11) in so far as it relates to Sch 9, para 16, for the purpose of enabling subordinate legislation or guidance to be made); 1 October 2010 (otherwise).

PART 6
EDUCATION

84–94 *(Ss 84–89 (Chapter 1: Schools) and ss 90–94 (Chapter 2: Further and Higher Education) are outside the scope of this work.)*

CHAPTER 3
GENERAL QUALIFICATIONS BODIES

[1.1690]
95 Application of this Chapter

This Chapter does not apply to the protected characteristic of marriage and civil partnership.

NOTES

Commencement: 1 October 2010.

[1.1691]
96 Qualifications bodies

(1) A qualifications body (A) must not discriminate against a person (B)—
(a) in the arrangements A makes for deciding upon whom to confer a relevant qualification;
(b) as to the terms on which it is prepared to confer a relevant qualification on B;
(c) by not conferring a relevant qualification on B.

(2) A qualifications body (A) must not discriminate against a person (B) upon whom A has conferred a relevant qualification—
(a) by withdrawing the qualification from B;
(b) by varying the terms on which B holds the qualification;
(c) by subjecting B to any other detriment.

(3) A qualifications body must not, in relation to conferment by it of a relevant qualification, harass—
(a) a person who holds the qualification, or
(b) a person who applies for it.

(4) A qualifications body (A) must not victimise a person (B)—

(a) in the arrangements A makes for deciding upon whom to confer a relevant qualification;
(b) as to the terms on which it is prepared to confer a relevant qualification on B;
(c) by not conferring a relevant qualification on B.

(5) A qualifications body (A) must not victimise a person (B) upon whom A has conferred a relevant qualification—
(a) by withdrawing the qualification from B;
(b) by varying the terms on which B holds the qualification;
(c) by subjecting B to any other detriment.

(6) A duty to make reasonable adjustments applies to a qualifications body.

(7) Subsection (6) does not apply to the body in so far as the appropriate regulator specifies provisions, criteria or practices in relation to which the body—
(a) is not subject to a duty to make reasonable adjustments;
(b) is subject to a duty to make reasonable adjustments, but in relation to which such adjustments as the regulator specifies should not be made.

(8) For the purposes of subsection (7) the appropriate regulator must have regard to—
(a) the need to minimise the extent to which disabled persons are disadvantaged in attaining the qualification because of their disabilities;
(b) the need to secure that the qualification gives a reliable indication of the knowledge, skills and understanding of a person upon whom it is conferred;
(c) the need to maintain public confidence in the qualification.

(9) The appropriate regulator—
(a) must not specify any matter for the purposes of subsection (7) unless it has consulted such persons as it thinks appropriate;
(b) must publish matters so specified (including the date from which they are to have effect) in such manner as is prescribed.

(10) The appropriate regulator is—
(a) in relation to a qualifications body that confers qualifications in England, a person prescribed by a Minister of the Crown;
(b) in relation to a qualifications body that confers qualifications in Wales, a person prescribed by the Welsh Ministers;
(c) in relation to a qualifications body that confers qualifications in Scotland, a person prescribed by the Scottish Ministers.

(11) For the purposes of subsection (10), a qualification is conferred in a part of Great Britain if there are, or may reasonably be expected to be, persons seeking to obtain the qualification who are or will be assessed for those purposes wholly or mainly in that part.

NOTES

Commencement: 6 July 2010 (sub-ss (10), (11) for the purpose of enabling subordinate legislation or guidance to be made); 3 September 2010 (sub-s (9)(b) for the purpose of enabling subordinate legislation or guidance to be made); 1 October 2010 (otherwise).

Regulations: the Equality Act 2010 (General Qualifications Bodies Regulator and Relevant Qualifications) (Wales) Regulations 2010, SI 2010/2217 at **[2.1546]**; the Equality Act 2010 (General Qualifications Bodies) (Appropriate Regulator and Relevant Qualifications) Regulations 2010, SI 2010/2245 at **[2.1550]**; the Equality Act 2010 (Qualifications Body Regulator and Relevant Qualifications) (Scotland) Regulations 2010, SSI 2010/315 at **[2.1555]**.

[1.1692]

97 Interpretation

(1) This section applies for the purposes of section 96.

(2) A qualifications body is an authority or body which can confer a relevant qualification.

(3) A relevant qualification is an authorisation, qualification, approval or certification of such description as may be prescribed—
(a) in relation to conferments in England, by a Minister of the Crown;
(b) in relation to conferments in Wales, by the Welsh Ministers;
(c) in relation to conferments in Scotland, by the Scottish Ministers.

(4) An authority or body is not a qualifications body in so far as—
(a) it is the responsible body of a school to which section 85 applies,
(b) it is the governing body of an institution to which section 91 applies,
(c) it exercises functions under the Education Acts, or
(d) it exercises functions under the Education (Scotland) Act 1980.

(5) A qualifications body does not include an authority or body of such description, or in such circumstances, as may be prescribed.

(6) A reference to conferring a relevant qualification includes a reference—
(a) to renewing or extending the conferment of a relevant qualification;
(b) to authenticating a relevant qualification conferred by another person.

(7) A reference in section 96(8), (10) or (11) to a qualification is a reference to a relevant qualification.

(8) Subsection (11) of section 96 applies for the purposes of subsection (3) of this section as it applies for the purposes of subsection (10) of that section.

NOTES

Commencement: 6 July 2010 (for the purpose of enabling subordinate legislation or guidance to be made); 1 October 2010 (otherwise).

Regulations: see the note to s 96 *ante*.

98–107 *(Ss 98, 99 (Chapter 4: Miscellaneous) and ss 100–107 (Part 7: Associations) are outside the scope of this work.)*

PART 8
PROHIBITED CONDUCT: ANCILLARY

[1.1693]

108 Relationships that have ended

(1) A person (A) must not discriminate against another (B) if—

(a) the discrimination arises out of and is closely connected to a relationship which used to exist between them, and

(b) conduct of a description constituting the discrimination would, if it occurred during the relationship, contravene this Act.

(2) A person (A) must not harass another (B) if—

(a) the harassment arises out of and is closely connected to a relationship which used to exist between them, and

(b) conduct of a description constituting the harassment would, if it occurred during the relationship, contravene this Act.

(3) It does not matter whether the relationship ends before or after the commencement of this section.

(4) A duty to make reasonable adjustments applies to A [if B is] placed at a substantial disadvantage as mentioned in section 20.

(5) For the purposes of subsection (4), sections 20, 21 and 22 and the applicable Schedules are to be construed as if the relationship had not ended.

(6) For the purposes of Part 9 (enforcement), a contravention of this section relates to the Part of this Act that would have been contravened if the relationship had not ended.

(7) But conduct is not a contravention of this section in so far as it also amounts to victimisation of B by A.

NOTES

Commencement: 1 October 2010.

Sub-s (4): words in square brackets substituted by the Equality Act 2010 (Consequential Amendments, Saving and Supplementary Provisions) Order 2010, SI 2010/2279, arts 2, 5, as from 1 October 2010.

[1.1694]

109 Liability of employers and principals

(1) Anything done by a person (A) in the course of A's employment must be treated as also done by the employer.

(2) Anything done by an agent for a principal, with the authority of the principal, must be treated as also done by the principal.

(3) It does not matter whether that thing is done with the employer's or principal's knowledge or approval.

(4) In proceedings against A's employer (B) in respect of anything alleged to have been done by A in the course of A's employment it is a defence for B to show that B took all reasonable steps to prevent A—

(a) from doing that thing, or

(b) from doing anything of that description.

(5) This section does not apply to offences under this Act (other than offences under Part 12 (disabled persons: transport)).

NOTES

Commencement: 1 October 2010.

[1.1695]

110 Liability of employees and agents

(1) A person (A) contravenes this section if—

(a) A is an employee or agent,

(b) A does something which, by virtue of section 109(1) or (2), is treated as having been done by A's employer or principal (as the case may be), and

(c) the doing of that thing by A amounts to a contravention of this Act by the employer or principal (as the case may be).

(2) It does not matter whether, in any proceedings, the employer is found not to have contravened this Act by virtue of section 109(4).
(3) A does not contravene this section if—
 (a) A relies on a statement by the employer or principal that doing that thing is not a contravention of this Act, and
 (b) it is reasonable for A to do so.
(4) A person (B) commits an offence if B knowingly or recklessly makes a statement mentioned in subsection (3)(a) which is false or misleading in a material respect.
(5) A person guilty of an offence under subsection (4) is liable on summary conviction to a fine not exceeding level 5 on the standard scale.
(6) Part 9 (enforcement) applies to a contravention of this section by A as if it were the contravention mentioned in subsection (1)(c).
(7) The reference in subsection (1)(c) to a contravention of this Act does not include a reference to disability discrimination in contravention of Chapter 1 of Part 6 (schools).

NOTES
Commencement: 1 October 2010.

[1.1696]
111 Instructing, causing or inducing contraventions
(1) A person (A) must not instruct another (B) to do in relation to a third person (C) anything which contravenes Part 3, 4, 5, 6 or 7 or section 108(1) or (2) or 112(1) (a basic contravention).
(2) A person (A) must not cause another (B) to do in relation to a third person (C) anything which is a basic contravention.
(3) A person (A) must not induce another (B) to do in relation to a third person (C) anything which is a basic contravention.
(4) For the purposes of subsection (3), inducement may be direct or indirect.
(5) Proceedings for a contravention of this section may be brought—
 (a) by B, if B is subjected to a detriment as a result of A's conduct;
 (b) by C, if C is subjected to a detriment as a result of A's conduct;
 (c) by the Commission.
(6) For the purposes of subsection (5), it does not matter whether—
 (a) the basic contravention occurs;
 (b) any other proceedings are, or may be, brought in relation to A's conduct.
(7) This section does not apply unless the relationship between A and B is such that A is in a position to commit a basic contravention in relation to B.
(8) A reference in this section to causing or inducing a person to do something includes a reference to attempting to cause or induce the person to do it.
(9) For the purposes of Part 9 (enforcement), a contravention of this section is to be treated as relating—
 (a) in a case within subsection (5)(a), to the Part of this Act which, because of the relationship between A and B, A is in a position to contravene in relation to B;
 (b) in a case within subsection (5)(b), to the Part of this Act which, because of the relationship between B and C, B is in a position to contravene in relation to C.

NOTES
Commencement: 1 October 2010.

[1.1697]
112 Aiding contraventions
(1) A person (A) must not knowingly help another (B) to do anything which contravenes Part 3, 4, 5, 6 or 7 or section 108(1) or (2) or 111 (a basic contravention).
(2) It is not a contravention of subsection (1) if—
 (a) A relies on a statement by B that the act for which the help is given does not contravene this Act, and
 (b) it is reasonable for A to do so.
(3) B commits an offence if B knowingly or recklessly makes a statement mentioned in subsection (2)(a) which is false or misleading in a material respect.
(4) A person guilty of an offence under subsection (3) is liable on summary conviction to a fine not exceeding level 5 on the standard scale.
(5) For the purposes of Part 9 (enforcement), a contravention of this section is to be treated as relating to the provision of this Act to which the basic contravention relates.
(6) The reference in subsection (1) to a basic contravention does not include a reference to disability discrimination in contravention of Chapter 1 of Part 6 (schools).

NOTES
Commencement: 1 October 2010.

PART 9
ENFORCEMENT

CHAPTER 1
INTRODUCTORY

[1.1698]

113 Proceedings

(1) Proceedings relating to a contravention of this Act must be brought in accordance with this Part.

(2) Subsection (1) does not apply to proceedings under Part 1 of the Equality Act 2006.

(3) Subsection (1) does not prevent—

  (a) a claim for judicial review;

  (b) proceedings under the Immigration Acts;

  (c) proceedings under the Special Immigration Appeals Commission Act 1997;

  (d) in Scotland, an application to the supervisory jurisdiction of the Court of Session.

(4) This section is subject to any express provision of this Act conferring jurisdiction on a court or tribunal.

(5) The reference to a contravention of this Act includes a reference to a breach of an equality clause or rule.

(6) Chapters 2 and 3 do not apply to proceedings relating to an equality clause or rule except in so far as Chapter 4 provides for that.

(7) This section does not apply to—

  (a) proceedings for an offence under this Act;

  (b) proceedings relating to a penalty under Part 12 (disabled persons: transport).

NOTES

Commencement: 1 October 2010.

Transitional provisions: see the Equality Act 2010 (Commencement No 4, Savings, Consequential, Transitional, Transitory and Incidental Provisions and Revocation) Order 2010, SI 2010/2317, art 7 at **[2.1560]**.

CHAPTER 2
CIVIL COURTS

[1.1699]

114 Jurisdiction

(1) *A county court* or, in Scotland, the sheriff has jurisdiction to determine a claim relating to—

  (a) a contravention of Part 3 (services and public functions);

  (b) a contravention of Part 4 (premises);

  (c) a contravention of Part 6 (education);

  (d) a contravention of Part 7 (associations);

  (e) a contravention of section 108, 111 or 112 that relates to Part 3, 4, 6 or 7.

(2) Subsection (1)(a) does not apply to a claim within section 115.

(3) Subsection (1)(c) does not apply to a claim within section 116.

(4) Subsection (1)(d) does not apply to a contravention of section 106.

(5) For the purposes of proceedings on a claim within subsection (1)(a)—

  (a) a decision in proceedings on a claim mentioned in section 115(1) that an act is a contravention of Part 3 is binding;

  (b) it does not matter whether the act occurs outside the United Kingdom.

(6) The county court or sheriff—

  (a) must not grant an interim injunction or interdict unless satisfied that no criminal matter would be prejudiced by doing so;

  (b) must grant an application to stay or sist proceedings under subsection (1) on grounds of prejudice to a criminal matter unless satisfied the matter will not be prejudiced.

(7) In proceedings in England and Wales on a claim within subsection (1), the power under section 63(1) of the County Courts Act 1984 (appointment of assessors) must be exercised unless the judge is satisfied that there are good reasons for not doing so.

(8) In proceedings in Scotland on a claim within subsection (1), the power under rule 44.3 of Schedule 1 to the Sheriff Court (Scotland) Act 1907 (appointment of assessors) must be exercised unless the sheriff is satisfied that there are good reasons for not doing so.

(9) The remuneration of an assessor appointed by virtue of subsection (8) is to be at a rate determined by the Lord President of the Court of Session.

NOTES

Commencement: 1 October 2010.

Sub-s (1): for the words in italics there are substituted the words "The county court" by the Crime and Courts Act 2013, s 17(5), Sch 9, Pt 3, para 52, as from a day to be appointed.

Transitional provisions: see the Equality Act 2010 (Commencement No 4, Savings, Consequential, Transitional, Transitory and Incidental Provisions and Revocation) Order 2010, SI 2010/2317, art 7 at **[2.1560]**.

115, 116 *(S 115 (Immigration cases) and s 116 (Education cases) are outside the scope of this work.)*

[1.1700]
117 National security

(1) Rules of court may, in relation to proceedings on a claim within section 114, confer power as mentioned in subsections (2) to (4); but a power so conferred is exercisable only if the court thinks it expedient to do so in the interests of national security.

(2) The rules may confer power to exclude from all or part of the proceedings—

(a) the claimant or pursuer;

(b) a representative of the claimant or pursuer;

(c) an assessor.

(3) The rules may confer power to permit a claimant, pursuer or representative who has been excluded to make a statement to the court before the commencement of the proceedings, or part of the proceedings, to which the exclusion relates.

(4) The rules may confer power to take steps to keep secret all or part of the reasons for the court's decision.

(5) The Attorney General or, in Scotland, the Advocate General for Scotland may appoint a person to represent the interests of a claimant or pursuer in, or in any part of, proceedings to which an exclusion by virtue of subsection (2)(a) or (b) relates.

(6) A person (P) may be appointed under subsection (5) only if—

(a) in relation to proceedings in England and Wales, P is a person who, for the purposes of the Legal Services Act 2007, is an authorised person in relation to an activity which constitutes the exercise of a right of audience or the conduct of litigation;

(b) in relation to proceedings in Scotland, P is an advocate or qualified to practice as a solicitor in Scotland.

(7) P is not responsible to the person whose interests P is appointed to represent.

NOTES

6 July 2010 (sub-ss (1)–(4) for the purpose of enabling subordinate legislation or guidance to be made); 1 October 2010 (otherwise).

Transitional provisions: see the Equality Act 2010 (Commencement No 4, Savings, Consequential, Transitional, Transitory and Incidental Provisions and Revocation) Order 2010, SI 2010/2317, art 7 at **[2.1560]**.

Subordinate Legislation: the Act of Sederunt (Sheriff Court Rules) (Equality Act 2010) 2010, SSI 2010/340.

[1.1701]
118 Time limits

(1) [Subject to section 140A] Proceedings on a claim within section 114 may not be brought after the end of—

(a) the period of 6 months starting with the date of the act to which the claim relates, or

(b) such other period as the county court or sheriff thinks just and equitable.

(2) If subsection (3) *or (4)* applies, subsection (1)(a) has effect as if for "6 months" there were substituted "9 months".

(3) This subsection applies if—

(a) the claim relates to the act of a qualifying institution, and

(b) a complaint relating to the act is referred under the student complaints scheme before the end of the period of 6 months starting with the date of the act.

(4) This subsection applies if—

(a) the claim relates to a dispute referred for conciliation in pursuance of arrangements under section 27 of the Equality Act 2006, and

(b) subsection (3) does not apply.

(5) If it has been decided under the immigration provisions that the act of an immigration authority in taking a relevant decision is a contravention of Part 3 (services and public functions), subsection (1) has effect as if for paragraph (a) there were substituted—

> "(a) the period of 6 months starting with the day after the expiry of the period during which, as a result of section 114(2), proceedings could not be brought in reliance on section 114(1)(a);".

(6) For the purposes of this section—

(a) conduct extending over a period is to be treated as done at the end of the period;

(b) failure to do something is to be treated as occurring when the person in question decided on it.

(7) In the absence of evidence to the contrary, a person (P) is to be taken to decide on failure to do something—

(a) when P does an act inconsistent with doing it, or

(b) if P does no inconsistent act, on the expiry of the period in which P might reasonably have been expected to do it.

(8) In this section—

"immigration authority", "immigration provisions" and "relevant decision" each have the meaning given in section 115;

"qualifying institution" has the meaning given in section 11 of the Higher Education Act 2004;

"the student complaints scheme" means a scheme for the review of qualifying complaints (within the meaning of section 12 of that Act) that is provided by the designated operator (within the meaning of section 13(5)(b) of that Act).

NOTES

Commencement: 1 October 2010.

Sub-s (1): words in square brackets inserted by the Cross-Border Mediation (EU Directive) Regulations 2011, SI 2011/1133, regs 54, 55, as from 20 May 2011.

Sub-s (2): words in italics repealed by the Enterprise and Regulatory Reform Act 2013, s 64(12), (13)(a), as from 25 June 2013.

Sub-s (4): repealed by the Enterprise and Regulatory Reform Act 2013, s 64(12), (13)(b), as from 25 June 2013.

Transitional provisions: see the Equality Act 2010 (Commencement No 4, Savings, Consequential, Transitional, Transitory and Incidental Provisions and Revocation) Order 2010, SI 2010/2317, art 7 at **[2.1560]**.

[1.1702]

119 Remedies

(1) This section applies if *a county court* or the sheriff finds that there has been a contravention of a provision referred to in section 114(1).

(2) The county court has power to grant any remedy which could be granted by the High Court—

(a) in proceedings in tort;

(b) on a claim for judicial review.

(3) The sheriff has power to make any order which could be made by the Court of Session—

(a) in proceedings for reparation;

(b) on a petition for judicial review.

(4) An award of damages may include compensation for injured feelings (whether or not it includes compensation on any other basis).

(5) Subsection (6) applies if the county court or sheriff—

(a) finds that a contravention of a provision referred to in section 114(1) is established by virtue of section 19, but

(b) is satisfied that the provision, criterion or practice was not applied with the intention of discriminating against the claimant or pursuer.

(6) The county court or sheriff must not make an award of damages unless it first considers whether to make any other disposal.

(7) The county court or sheriff must not grant a remedy other than an award of damages or the making of a declaration unless satisfied that no criminal matter would be prejudiced by doing so.

NOTES

Commencement: 1 October 2010.

Sub-s (1): for the words in italics there are substituted the words "the county court" by the Crime and Courts Act 2013, s 17(5), Sch 9, Pt 3, para 52, as from a day to be appointed.

Transitional provisions: see the Equality Act 2010 (Commencement No 4, Savings, Consequential, Transitional, Transitory and Incidental Provisions and Revocation) Order 2010, SI 2010/2317, art 7 at **[2.1560]**.

CHAPTER 3
EMPLOYMENT TRIBUNALS

[1.1703]

120 Jurisdiction

(1) An employment tribunal has, subject to section 121, jurisdiction to determine a complaint relating to—

(a) a contravention of Part 5 (work);

(b) a contravention of section 108, 111 or 112 that relates to Part 5.

(2) An employment tribunal has jurisdiction to determine an application by a responsible person (as defined by section 61) for a declaration as to the rights of that person and a worker in relation to a dispute about the effect of a non-discrimination rule.

(3) An employment tribunal also has jurisdiction to determine an application by the trustees or managers of an occupational pension scheme for a declaration as to their rights and those of a member in relation to a dispute about the effect of a non-discrimination rule.

(4) An employment tribunal also has jurisdiction to determine a question that—

(a) relates to a non-discrimination rule, and

(b) is referred to the tribunal by virtue of section 122.

(5) In proceedings before an employment tribunal on a complaint relating to a breach of a non-discrimination rule, the employer—

(a) is to be treated as a party, and
(b) is accordingly entitled to appear and be heard.

(6) Nothing in this section affects such jurisdiction as the High Court, *a county court*, the Court of Session or the sheriff has in relation to a non-discrimination rule.

(7) Subsection (1)(a) does not apply to a contravention of section 53 in so far as the act complained of may, by virtue of an enactment, be subject to an appeal or proceedings in the nature of an appeal.

(8) In subsection (1), the references to Part 5 do not include a reference to section 60(1).

NOTES

Commencement: 1 October 2010.

Sub-s (6): for the words in italics there are substituted the words "the county court" by the Crime and Courts Act 2013, s 17(5), Sch 9, Pt 3, para 52, as from a day to be appointed.

Transitional provisions: see the Equality Act 2010 (Commencement No 4, Savings, Consequential, Transitional, Transitory and Incidental Provisions and Revocation) Order 2010, SI 2010/2317, art 7 at **[2.1560]**.

Tribunal jurisdiction: the Employment Act 2002, s 38 applies to proceedings before the employment tribunal relating to a claim under this section; see s 38(1) of, and Sch 5 to, the 2002 Act at **[1.1228]**, **[1.1236]**. See also the Trade Union and Labour Relations (Consolidation) Act 1992, s 207A at **[1.474]** (as inserted by the Employment Act 2008). That section provides that in proceedings before an employment tribunal relating to a claim by an employee under any of the jurisdictions listed in Sch A2 to the 1992 Act at **[1.648]** (which includes this section) the tribunal may adjust any award given if the employer or the employee has unreasonably failed to comply with the relevant Code of Practice as defined by s 207A(4). See also the revised Acas Code of Practice 1 – Disciplinary and Grievance Procedures (2009) at **[4.1]**.

Conciliation: employment tribunal proceedings and claims which could be the subject of employment tribunal proceedings under this section are proceedings to which the Employment Tribunals Act 1996, s 18 applies; see s 18(1)(a) of that Act at **[1.706]**.

[1.1704]

121 Armed forces cases

(1) Section 120(1) does not apply to a complaint relating to an act done when the complainant was serving as a member of the armed forces unless—
(a) the complainant has made a service complaint about the matter, and
(b) the complaint has not been withdrawn.

(2) If the complaint is made under the service complaint procedures, it is to be treated for the purposes of subsection (1)(b) as withdrawn if—
(a) neither the officer to whom it is made nor a superior officer refers it to the Defence Council, and
(b) the complainant does not apply for it to be referred to the Defence Council.

(3) If the complaint is made under the old service redress procedures, it is to be treated for the purposes of subsection (1)(b) as withdrawn if the complainant does not submit it to the Defence Council under those procedures.

(4) The reference in subsection (3) to the old service redress procedures is a reference to the procedures (other than those relating to the making of a report on a complaint to Her Majesty) referred to in—
(a) section 180 of the Army Act 1955,
(b) section 180 of the Air Force Act 1955, or
(c) section 130 of the Naval Discipline Act 1957.

(5) The making of a complaint to an employment tribunal in reliance on subsection (1) does not affect the continuation of the service complaint procedures or (as the case may be) the old service redress procedures.

NOTES

Commencement: 1 October 2010.

Transitional provisions: see the Equality Act 2010 (Commencement No 4, Savings, Consequential, Transitional, Transitory and Incidental Provisions and Revocation) Order 2010, SI 2010/2317, art 7 at **[2.1560]**.

[1.1705]

122 References by court to tribunal, etc

(1) If it appears to a court in which proceedings are pending that a claim or counter-claim relating to a non-discrimination rule could more conveniently be determined by an employment tribunal, the court may strike out the claim or counter-claim.

(2) If in proceedings before a court a question arises about a non-discrimination rule, the court may (whether or not on an application by a party to the proceedings)—
(a) refer the question, or direct that it be referred by a party to the proceedings, to an employment tribunal for determination, and
(b) stay or sist the proceedings in the meantime.

NOTES

Commencement: 1 October 2010.

Transitional provisions: see the Equality Act 2010 (Commencement No 4, Savings, Consequential, Transitional, Transitory and Incidental Provisions and Revocation) Order 2010, SI 2010/2317, art 7 at **[2.1560]**.

[1.1706]

123 Time limits

(1) [Subject to *section 140A*] Proceedings on a complaint within section 120 may not be brought after the end of—

(a) the period of 3 months starting with the date of the act to which the complaint relates, or

(b) such other period as the employment tribunal thinks just and equitable.

(2) Proceedings may not be brought in reliance on section 121(1) after the end of—

(a) the period of 6 months starting with the date of the act to which the proceedings relate, or

(b) such other period as the employment tribunal thinks just and equitable.

(3) For the purposes of this section—

(a) conduct extending over a period is to be treated as done at the end of the period;

(b) failure to do something is to be treated as occurring when the person in question decided on it.

(4) In the absence of evidence to the contrary, a person (P) is to be taken to decide on failure to do something—

(a) when P does an act inconsistent with doing it, or

(b) if P does no inconsistent act, on the expiry of the period in which P might reasonably have been expected to do it.

NOTES

Commencement: 1 October 2010.

Sub-s (1): words in square brackets inserted by the Cross-Border Mediation (EU Directive) Regulations 2011, SI 2011/1133, regs 54, 56; as from 20 May 2011; for the words in italics there are substituted the words "sections 140A and 140B" by the Enterprise and Regulatory Reform Act 2013, s 8, Sch 2, paras 42, 43, as from a day to be appointed.

Transitional provisions: see the Equality Act 2010 (Commencement No 4, Savings, Consequential, Transitional, Transitory and Incidental Provisions and Revocation) Order 2010, SI 2010/2317, art 7 at **[2.1560]**.

[1.1707]

124 Remedies: general

(1) This section applies if an employment tribunal finds that there has been a contravention of a provision referred to in section 120(1).

(2) The tribunal may—

(a) make a declaration as to the rights of the complainant and the respondent in relation to the matters to which the proceedings relate;

(b) order the respondent to pay compensation to the complainant;

(c) make an appropriate recommendation.

(3) An appropriate recommendation is a recommendation that within a specified period the respondent takes specified steps for the purpose of obviating or reducing the adverse effect of any matter to which the proceedings relate—

(a) on the complainant;

(b) on any other person.

(4) Subsection (5) applies if the tribunal—

(a) finds that a contravention is established by virtue of section 19, but

(b) is satisfied that the provision, criterion or practice was not applied with the intention of discriminating against the complainant.

(5) It must not make an order under subsection (2)(b) unless it first considers whether to act under subsection (2)(a) or (c).

(6) The amount of compensation which may be awarded under subsection (2)(b) corresponds to the amount which could be awarded by *a county court* or the sheriff under section 119.

(7) If a respondent fails, without reasonable excuse, to comply with an appropriate recommendation in so far as it relates to the complainant, the tribunal may—

(a) if an order was made under subsection (2)(b), increase the amount of compensation to be paid;

(b) if no such order was made, make one.

NOTES

Commencement: 1 October 2010.

Sub-s (6): for the words in italics there are substituted the words "the county court" by the Crime and Courts Act 2013, s 17(5), Sch 9, Pt 3, para 52, as from a day to be appointed.

Transitional provisions: see the Equality Act 2010 (Commencement No 4, Savings, Consequential, Transitional, Transitory and Incidental Provisions and Revocation) Order 2010, SI 2010/2317, art 7 at **[2.1560]**.

[1.1708]

125 Remedies: national security

(1) In national security proceedings, an appropriate recommendation (as defined by section 124) must not be made in relation to a person other than the complainant if the recommendation would affect anything done by—

(a) the Security Service,

(b) the Secret Intelligence Service,

(c) the Government Communications Headquarters, or

(d) a part of the armed forces which is, in accordance with a requirement of the Secretary of State, assisting the Government Communications Headquarters.

(2) National security proceedings are—

(a) proceedings to which a direction under section 10(3) of the Employment Tribunals Act 1996 (national security) relates;

(b) proceedings to which an order under section 10(4) of that Act relates;

(c) proceedings (or the part of proceedings) to which a direction pursuant to regulations made under section 10(5) of that Act relates;

(d) proceedings (or the part of proceedings) in relation to which an employment tribunal acts pursuant to regulations made under section 10(6) of that Act.

NOTES

Commencement: 1 October 2010.

Transitional provisions: see the Equality Act 2010 (Commencement No 4, Savings, Consequential, Transitional, Transitory and Incidental Provisions and Revocation) Order 2010, SI 2010/2317, art 7 at **[2.1560]**.

[1.1709]

126 Remedies: occupational pension schemes

(1) This section applies if an employment tribunal finds that there has been a contravention of a provision referred to in section 120(1) in relation to—

(a) the terms on which persons become members of an occupational pension scheme, or

(b) the terms on which members of an occupational pension scheme are treated.

(2) In addition to anything which may be done by the tribunal under section 124 the tribunal may also by order declare—

(a) if the complaint relates to the terms on which persons become members of a scheme, that the complainant has a right to be admitted to the scheme;

(b) if the complaint relates to the terms on which members of the scheme are treated, that the complainant has a right to membership of the scheme without discrimination.

(3) The tribunal may not make an order under subsection (2)(b) of section 124 unless—

(a) the compensation is for injured feelings, or

(b) the order is made by virtue of subsection (7) of that section.

(4) An order under subsection (2)—

(a) may make provision as to the terms on which or the capacity in which the claimant is to enjoy the admission or membership;

(b) may have effect in relation to a period before the order is made.

NOTES

Commencement: 1 October 2010.

Transitional provisions: see the Equality Act 2010 (Commencement No 4, Savings, Consequential, Transitional, Transitory and Incidental Provisions and Revocation) Order 2010, SI 2010/2317, art 7 at **[2.1560]**.

CHAPTER 4
EQUALITY OF TERMS

[1.1710]

127 Jurisdiction

(1) An employment tribunal has, subject to subsection (6), jurisdiction to determine a complaint relating to a breach of an equality clause or rule.

(2) The jurisdiction conferred by subsection (1) includes jurisdiction to determine a complaint arising out of a breach of an equality clause or rule; and a reference in this Chapter to a complaint relating to such a breach is to be read accordingly.

(3) An employment tribunal also has jurisdiction to determine an application by a responsible person for a declaration as to the rights of that person and a worker in relation to a dispute about the effect of an equality clause or rule.

(4) An employment tribunal also has jurisdiction to determine an application by the trustees or managers of an occupational pension scheme for a declaration as to their rights and those of a member in relation to a dispute about the effect of an equality rule.

(5) An employment tribunal also has jurisdiction to determine a question that—

(a) relates to an equality clause or rule, and

(b) is referred to the tribunal by virtue of section 128(2).

(6) This section does not apply to a complaint relating to an act done when the complainant was serving as a member of the armed forces unless—

(a) the complainant has made a service complaint about the matter, and

(b) the complaint has not been withdrawn.

(7) Subsections (2) to (5) of section 121 apply for the purposes of subsection (6) of this section as they apply for the purposes of subsection (1) of that section.

(8) In proceedings before an employment tribunal on a complaint relating to a breach of an equality rule, the employer—

(a) is to be treated as a party, and

(b) is accordingly entitled to appear and be heard.

(9) Nothing in this section affects such jurisdiction as the High Court, *a county court*, the Court of Session or the sheriff has in relation to an equality clause or rule.

NOTES

Commencement: 1 October 2010.

Sub-s (9): for the words in italics there are substituted the words "the county court" by the Crime and Courts Act 2013, s 17(5), Sch 9, Pt 3, para 52, as from a day to be appointed.

Transitional provisions: see the Equality Act 2010 (Commencement No 4, Savings, Consequential, Transitional, Transitory and Incidental Provisions and Revocation) Order 2010, SI 2010/2317, art 7 at **[2.1560]**.

Tribunal jurisdiction: the Employment Act 2002, s 38 applies to proceedings before the employment tribunal relating to a claim under this section; see s 38(1) of, and Sch 5 to, the 2002 Act at **[1.1228]**, **[1.1236]**. See also the Trade Union and Labour Relations (Consolidation) Act 1992, s 207A at **[1.474]** (as inserted by the Employment Act 2008). That section provides that in proceedings before an employment tribunal relating to a claim by an employee under any of the jurisdictions listed in Sch A2 to the 1992 Act at **[1.648]** (which includes this section) the tribunal may adjust any award given if the employer or the employee has unreasonably failed to comply with the relevant Code of Practice as defined by s 207A(4). See also the revised Acas Code of Practice 1 – Disciplinary and Grievance Procedures (2009) at **[4.1]**.

Conciliation: employment tribunal proceedings and claims which could be the subject of employment tribunal proceedings under this section are proceedings to which the Employment Tribunals Act 1996, s 18 applies; see s 18(1)(a) of that Act at **[1.706]**.

[1.1711]

128 References by court to tribunal, etc

(1) If it appears to a court in which proceedings are pending that a claim or counter-claim relating to an equality clause or rule could more conveniently be determined by an employment tribunal, the court may strike out the claim or counter-claim.

(2) If in proceedings before a court a question arises about an equality clause or rule, the court may (whether or not on an application by a party to the proceedings)—

(a) refer the question, or direct that it be referred by a party to the proceedings, to an employment tribunal for determination, and

(b) stay or sist the proceedings in the meantime.

NOTES

Commencement: 1 October 2010.

Transitional provisions: see the Equality Act 2010 (Commencement No 4, Savings, Consequential, Transitional, Transitory and Incidental Provisions and Revocation) Order 2010, SI 2010/2317, art 7 at **[2.1560]**.

[1.1712]

129 Time limits

(1) This section applies to—

(a) a complaint relating to a breach of an equality clause or rule;

(b) an application for a declaration referred to in section 127(3) or (4).

(2) Proceedings on the complaint or application may not be brought in an employment tribunal after the end of the qualifying period.

(3) If the complaint or application relates to terms of work other than terms of service in the armed forces, the qualifying period is, in a case mentioned in the first column of the table, the period mentioned in the second column[, subject to *section 140A*].

Case	Qualifying period
A standard case	The period of 6 months beginning with the last day of the employment or appointment.
A stable work case (but not if it is also a concealment or incapacity case (or both))	The period of 6 months beginning with the day on which the stable working relationship ended.
A concealment case (but not if it is also an incapacity case)	The period of 6 months beginning with the day on which the worker discovered (or could with reasonable diligence have discovered) the qualifying fact.

Case	Qualifying period
An incapacity case (but not if it is also a concealment case)	The period of 6 months beginning with the day on which the worker ceased to have the incapacity.
A case which is a concealment case and an incapacity case.	The period of 6 months beginning with the later of the days on which the period would begin if the case were merely a concealment or incapacity case.

(4) If the complaint or application relates to terms of service in the armed forces, the qualifying period is, in a case mentioned in the first column of the table, the period mentioned in the second column[, subject to section 140B].

Case	Qualifying period
A standard case	The period of 9 months beginning with the last day of the period of service during which the complaint arose.
A concealment case (but not if it is also an incapacity case)	The period of 9 months beginning with the day on which the worker discovered (or could with reasonable diligence have discovered) the qualifying fact.
An incapacity case (but not if it is also a concealment case)	The period of 9 months beginning with the day on which the worker ceased to have the incapacity.
A case which is a concealment case and an incapacity case.	The period of 9 months beginning with the later of the days on which the period would begin if the case were merely a concealment or incapacity case.

NOTES

Commencement: 1 October 2010.

Sub-s (3): words in square brackets inserted by the Cross-Border Mediation (EU Directive) Regulations 2011, SI 2011/1133, regs 54, 57, as from 20 May 2011; for the words in italics there are substituted the words "sections 140A and 140B", by the Enterprise and Regulatory Reform Act 2013, s 8, Sch 2, paras 42, 44(a), as from a day to be appointed.

Sub-s (4): words in square brackets inserted by the Enterprise and Regulatory Reform Act 2013, s 8, Sch 2, paras 42, 44(b), as from a day to be appointed.

Transitional provisions: see the Equality Act 2010 (Commencement No 4, Savings, Consequential, Transitional, Transitory and Incidental Provisions and Revocation) Order 2010, SI 2010/2317, art 7 at **[2.1560]**.

[1.1713]

130 Section 129: supplementary

(1) This section applies for the purposes of section 129.

(2) A standard case is a case which is not—

- (a) a stable work case,
- (b) a concealment case,
- (c) an incapacity case, or
- (d) a concealment case and an incapacity case.

(3) A stable work case is a case where the proceedings relate to a period during which there was a stable working relationship between the worker and the responsible person (including any time after the terms of work had expired).

(4) A concealment case in proceedings relating to an equality clause is a case where—

- (a) the responsible person deliberately concealed a qualifying fact from the worker, and
- (b) the worker did not discover (or could not with reasonable diligence have discovered) the qualifying fact until after the relevant day.

(5) A concealment case in proceedings relating to an equality rule is a case where—

- (a) the employer or the trustees or managers of the occupational pension scheme in question deliberately concealed a qualifying fact from the member, and
- (b) the member did not discover (or could not with reasonable diligence have discovered) the qualifying fact until after the relevant day.

(6) A qualifying fact for the purposes of subsection (4) or (5) is a fact—

- (a) which is relevant to the complaint, and
- (b) without knowledge of which the worker or member could not reasonably have been expected to bring the proceedings.

(7) An incapacity case in proceedings relating to an equality clause with respect to terms of work other than terms of service in the armed forces is a case where the worker had an incapacity during the period of 6 months beginning with the later of—

(a) the relevant day, or
(b) the day on which the worker discovered (or could with reasonable diligence have discovered) the qualifying fact deliberately concealed from the worker by the responsible person.

(8) An incapacity case in proceedings relating to an equality clause with respect to terms of service in the armed forces is a case where the worker had an incapacity during the period of 9 months beginning with the later of—

(a) the last day of the period of service during which the complaint arose, or
(b) the day on which the worker discovered (or could with reasonable diligence have discovered) the qualifying fact deliberately concealed from the worker by the responsible person.

(9) An incapacity case in proceedings relating to an equality rule is a case where the member of the occupational pension scheme in question had an incapacity during the period of 6 months beginning with the later of—

(a) the relevant day, or
(b) the day on which the member discovered (or could with reasonable diligence have discovered) the qualifying fact deliberately concealed from the member by the employer or the trustees or managers of the scheme.

(10) The relevant day for the purposes of this section is—

(a) the last day of the employment or appointment, or
(b) the day on which the stable working relationship between the worker and the responsible person ended.

NOTES

Commencement: 1 October 2010.

Transitional provisions: see the Equality Act 2010 (Commencement No 4, Savings, Consequential, Transitional, Transitory and Incidental Provisions and Revocation) Order 2010, SI 2010/2317, art 7 at **[2.1560]**.

[1.1714]

131 Assessment of whether work is of equal value

(1) This section applies to proceedings before an employment tribunal on—

(a) a complaint relating to a breach of an equality clause or rule, or
(b) a question referred to the tribunal by virtue of section 128(2).

(2) Where a question arises in the proceedings as to whether one person's work is of equal value to another's, the tribunal may, before determining the question, require a member of the panel of independent experts to prepare a report on the question.

(3) The tribunal may withdraw a requirement that it makes under subsection (2); and, if it does so, it may—

(a) request the panel member to provide it with specified documentation;
(b) make such other requests to that member as are connected with the withdrawal of the requirement.

(4) If the tribunal requires the preparation of a report under subsection (2) (and does not withdraw the requirement), it must not determine the question unless it has received the report.

(5) Subsection (6) applies where—

(a) a question arises in the proceedings as to whether the work of one person (A) is of equal value to the work of another (B), and
(b) A's work and B's work have been given different values by a job evaluation study.

(6) The tribunal must determine that A's work is not of equal value to B's work unless it has reasonable grounds for suspecting that the evaluation contained in the study—

(a) was based on a system that discriminates because of sex, or
(b) is otherwise unreliable.

(7) For the purposes of subsection (6)(a), a system discriminates because of sex if a difference (or coincidence) between values that the system sets on different demands is not justifiable regardless of the sex of the person on whom the demands are made.

(8) A reference to a member of the panel of independent experts is a reference to a person—

(a) who is for the time being designated as such by the Advisory, Conciliation and Arbitration Service (ACAS) for the purposes of this section, and
(b) who is neither a member of the Council of ACAS nor one of its officers or members of staff.

(9) "Job evaluation study" has the meaning given in section 80(5).

NOTES

Commencement: 1 October 2010.

Transitional provisions: see the Equality Act 2010 (Commencement No 4, Savings, Consequential, Transitional, Transitory and Incidental Provisions and Revocation) Order 2010, SI 2010/2317, art 7 at **[2.1560]**.

[1.1715]

132 Remedies in non-pensions cases

(1) This section applies to proceedings before a court or employment tribunal on a complaint relating to a breach of an equality clause, other than a breach with respect to membership of or rights under an occupational pension scheme.

(2) If the court or tribunal finds that there has been a breach of the equality clause, it may—

(a) make a declaration as to the rights of the parties in relation to the matters to which the proceedings relate;

(b) order an award by way of arrears of pay or damages in relation to the complainant.

(3) The court or tribunal may not order a payment under subsection (2)(b) in respect of a time before the arrears day.

(4) In relation to proceedings in England and Wales, the arrears day is, in a case mentioned in the first column of the table, the day mentioned in the second column.

Case	Arrears day
A standard case	The day falling 6 years before the day on which the proceedings were instituted.
A concealment case or an incapacity case (or a case which is both).	The day on which the breach first occurred.

(5) In relation to proceedings in Scotland, the arrears day is the first day of—

(a) the period of 5 years ending with the day on which the proceedings were commenced, or

(b) if the case involves a relevant incapacity, or a relevant fraud or error, [the period determined in accordance with section 135(6) and (7)].

NOTES

Commencement: 1 October 2010.

Sub-s (5): words in square brackets in para (b) substituted by the Equality Act 2010 (Consequential Amendments, Saving and Supplementary Provisions) Order 2010, SI 2010/2279, arts 2, 6, as from 1 October 2010.

Transitional provisions: see the Equality Act 2010 (Commencement No 4, Savings, Consequential, Transitional, Transitory and Incidental Provisions and Revocation) Order 2010, SI 2010/2317, art 7 at **[2.1560]**.

[1.1716]

133 Remedies in pensions cases

(1) This section applies to proceedings before a court or employment tribunal on a complaint relating to—

(a) a breach of an equality rule, or

(b) a breach of an equality clause with respect to membership of, or rights under, an occupational pension scheme.

(2) If the court or tribunal finds that there has been a breach as referred to in subsection (1)—

(a) it may make a declaration as to the rights of the parties in relation to the matters to which the proceedings relate;

(b) it must not order arrears of benefits or damages or any other amount to be paid to the complainant.

(3) Subsection (2)(b) does not apply if the proceedings are proceedings to which section 134 applies.

(4) If the breach relates to a term on which persons become members of the scheme, the court or tribunal may declare that the complainant is entitled to be admitted to the scheme with effect from a specified date.

(5) A date specified for the purposes of subsection (4) must not be before 8 April 1976.

(6) If the breach relates to a term on which members of the scheme are treated, the court or tribunal may declare that the complainant is, in respect of a specified period, entitled to secure the rights that would have accrued if the breach had not occurred.

(7) A period specified for the purposes of subsection (6) must not begin before 17 May 1990.

(8) If the court or tribunal makes a declaration under subsection (6), the employer must provide such resources to the scheme as are necessary to secure for the complainant (without contribution or further contribution by the complainant or other members) the rights referred to in that subsection.

NOTES

Commencement: 1 October 2010.

Transitional provisions: see the Equality Act 2010 (Commencement No 4, Savings, Consequential, Transitional, Transitory and Incidental Provisions and Revocation) Order 2010, SI 2010/2317, art 7 at **[2.1560]**.

[1.1717]
134 Remedies in claims for arrears brought by pensioner members

(1) This section applies to proceedings before a court or employment tribunal on a complaint by a pensioner member of an occupational pension scheme relating to a breach of an equality clause or rule with respect to a term on which the member is treated.

(2) If the court or tribunal finds that there has been a breach referred to in subsection (1), it may—

(a) make a declaration as to the rights of the complainant and the respondent in relation to the matters to which the proceedings relate;

(b) order an award by way of arrears of benefits or damages or of any other amount in relation to the complainant.

(3) The court or tribunal must not order an award under subsection (2)(b) in respect of a time before the arrears day.

(4) If the court or tribunal orders an award under subsection (2)(b), the employer must provide such resources to the scheme as are necessary to secure for the complainant (without contribution or further contribution by the complainant or other members) the amount of the award.

(5) In relation to proceedings in England and Wales, the arrears day is, in a case mentioned in the first column of the table, the day mentioned in the second column.

Case	Arrears day
A standard case	The day falling 6 years before the day on which the proceedings were commenced.
A concealment case or an incapacity case (or a case which is both).	The day on which the breach first occurred.

(6) In relation to proceedings in Scotland, the arrears day is the first day of—

(a) the period of 5 years ending with the day on which the proceedings were commenced, or

(b) if the case involves a relevant incapacity, or a relevant fraud or error, [the period determined in accordance with section 135(6) and (7)].

NOTES

Commencement: 1 October 2010.

Sub-s (6): words in square brackets in para (b) substituted by the Equality Act 2010 (Consequential Amendments, Saving and Supplementary Provisions) Order 2010, SI 2010/2279, arts 2, 6, as from 1 October 2010.

Transitional provisions: see the Equality Act 2010 (Commencement No 4, Savings, Consequential, Transitional, Transitory and Incidental Provisions and Revocation) Order 2010, SI 2010/2317, art 7 at **[2.1560]**.

[1.1718]
135 Supplementary

(1) This section applies for the purposes of sections 132 to 134.

(2) A standard case is a case which is not—

(a) a concealment case,

(b) an incapacity case, or

(c) a concealment case and an incapacity case.

(3) A concealment case in relation to an equality clause is a case where—

(a) the responsible person deliberately concealed a qualifying fact (as defined by section 130) from the worker, and

(b) the worker commenced the proceedings before the end of the period of 6 years beginning with the day on which the worker discovered (or could with reasonable diligence have discovered) the qualifying fact.

(4) A concealment case in relation to an equality rule is a case where—

(a) the employer or the trustees or managers of the occupational pension scheme in question deliberately concealed a qualifying fact (as defined by section 130) from the member, and

(b) the member commenced the proceedings before the end of the period of 6 years beginning with the day on which the member discovered (or could with reasonable diligence have discovered) the qualifying fact.

(5) An incapacity case is a case where the worker or member—

(a) had an incapacity when the breach first occurred, and

(b) commenced the proceedings before the end of the period of 6 years beginning with the day on which the worker or member ceased to have the incapacity.

(6) A case involves a relevant incapacity or a relevant fraud or error if the period of 5 years referred to in section 132(5)(a) [or 134(6)(a)] is, as a result of subsection (7) below, reckoned as a period of more than [5 years; and—

(a) if, as a result of subsection (7), that period is reckoned as a period of more than 5 years but no more than 20 years, the period for the purposes of section 132(5)(b) or (as the case may be) section 134(6)(b) is that extended period;

(b) if, as a result of subsection (7), that period is reckoned as a period of more than 20 years, the period for the purposes of section 132(5)(b) or (as the case may be) section 134(6)(b) is a period of 20 years].

(7) For the purposes of the reckoning referred to in subsection (6), no account is to be taken of time when the worker or member—

(a) had an incapacity, or

(b) was induced by a relevant fraud or error to refrain from commencing proceedings (not being a time after the worker or member could with reasonable diligence have discovered the fraud or error).

(8) For the purposes of subsection (7)—

(a) a fraud is relevant in relation to an equality clause if it is a fraud on the part of the responsible person;

(b) an error is relevant in relation to an equality clause if it is induced by the words or conduct of the responsible person;

(c) a fraud is relevant in relation to an equality rule if it is a fraud on the part of the employer or the trustees or managers of the scheme;

(d) an error is relevant in relation to an equality rule if it is induced by the words or conduct of the employer or the trustees or managers of the scheme.

(9) A reference in subsection (8) to the responsible person, the employer or the trustees or managers includes a reference to a person acting on behalf of the person or persons concerned.

(10) In relation to terms of service, a reference in section 132(5) or subsection (3) or (5)(b) of this section to commencing proceedings is to be read as a reference to making a service complaint.

(11) A reference to a pensioner member of a scheme includes a reference to a person who is entitled to the present payment of pension or other benefits derived through a member.

(12) In relation to proceedings before a court—

(a) a reference to a complaint is to be read as a reference to a claim, and

(b) a reference to a complainant is to be read as a reference to a claimant.

NOTES

Commencement: 1 October 2010.

Sub-s (6): words in first pair of square brackets inserted, and words in second pair of square brackets substituted, by the Equality Act 2010 (Consequential Amendments, Saving and Supplementary Provisions) Order 2010, SI 2010/2279, arts 2, 7, as from 1 October 2010.

Transitional provisions: see the Equality Act 2010 (Commencement No 4, Savings, Consequential, Transitional, Transitory and Incidental Provisions and Revocation) Order 2010, SI 2010/2317, art 7 at **[2.1560]**.

CHAPTER 5
MISCELLANEOUS

[1.1719]

136 Burden of proof

(1) This section applies to any proceedings relating to a contravention of this Act.

(2) If there are facts from which the court could decide, in the absence of any other explanation, that a person (A) contravened the provision concerned, the court must hold that the contravention occurred.

(3) But subsection (2) does not apply if A shows that A did not contravene the provision.

(4) The reference to a contravention of this Act includes a reference to a breach of an equality clause or rule.

(5) This section does not apply to proceedings for an offence under this Act.

(6) A reference to the court includes a reference to—

(a) an employment tribunal;

(b) the Asylum and Immigration Tribunal;

(c) the Special Immigration Appeals Commission;

(d) the First-tier Tribunal;

(e) the Special Educational Needs Tribunal for Wales;

(f) an Additional Support Needs Tribunal for Scotland.

NOTES

Commencement: 1 October 2010 (except sub-s (6)(f)); 18 March 2011 (sub-s (6)(f)).

Transitional provisions: see the Equality Act 2010 (Commencement No 4, Savings, Consequential, Transitional, Transitory and Incidental Provisions and Revocation) Order 2010, SI 2010/2317, art 7 at **[2.1560]**.

[1.1720]

137 Previous findings

(1) A finding in relevant proceedings in respect of an act which has become final is to be treated as conclusive in proceedings under this Act.

(2) Relevant proceedings are proceedings before a court or employment tribunal under any of the following—

(a) section 19 or 20 of the Race Relations Act 1968;

(b) the Equal Pay Act 1970;

(c) the Sex Discrimination Act 1975;

(d) the Race Relations Act 1976;
(e) section 6(4A) of the Sex Discrimination Act 1986;
(f) the Disability Discrimination Act 1995;
(g) Part 2 of the Equality Act 2006;
(h) the Employment Equality (Religion and Belief) Regulations 2003 (SI 2003/1660);
(i) the Employment Equality (Sexual Orientation) Regulations 2003 (SI 2003/1661);
(j) the Employment Equality (Age) Regulations 2006 (SI 2006/1031);
(k) the Equality Act (Sexual Orientation) Regulations 2007 (SI 2007/1263).

(3) A finding becomes final—
(a) when an appeal against the finding is dismissed, withdrawn or abandoned, or
(b) when the time for appealing expires without an appeal having been brought.

NOTES

Commencement: 1 October 2010.

Transitional provisions: see the Equality Act 2010 (Commencement No 4, Savings, Consequential, Transitional, Transitory and Incidental Provisions and Revocation) Order 2010, SI 2010/2317, art 7 at **[2.1560]**.

[1.1721]
138 Obtaining information, etc

(1) In this section—
(a) P is a person who thinks that a contravention of this Act has occurred in relation to P;
(b) R is a person who P thinks has contravened this Act.

(2) A Minister of the Crown must by order prescribe—
(a) forms by which P may question R on any matter which is or may be relevant;
(b) forms by which R may answer questions by P.

(3) A question by P or an answer by R is admissible as evidence in proceedings under this Act (whether or not the question or answer is contained in a prescribed form).

(4) A court or tribunal may draw an inference from—
(a) a failure by R to answer a question by P before the end of the period of 8 weeks beginning with the day on which the question is served;
(b) an evasive or equivocal answer.

(5) Subsection (4) does not apply if—
(a) R reasonably asserts that to have answered differently or at all might have prejudiced a criminal matter;
(b) R reasonably asserts that to have answered differently or at all would have revealed the reason for not commencing or not continuing criminal proceedings;
(c) R's answer is of a kind specified for the purposes of this paragraph by order of a Minister of the Crown;
(d) R's answer is given in circumstances specified for the purposes of this paragraph by order of a Minister of the Crown;
(e) R's failure to answer occurs in circumstances specified for the purposes of this paragraph by order of a Minister of the Crown.

(6) The reference to a contravention of this Act includes a reference to a breach of an equality clause or rule.

(7) A Minister of the Crown may by order—
(a) prescribe the period within which a question must be served to be admissible under subsection (3);
(b) prescribe the manner in which a question by P, or an answer by R, may be served.

(8) This section—
(a) does not affect any other enactment or rule of law relating to interim or preliminary matters in proceedings before a county court, the sheriff or an employment tribunal, and
(b) has effect subject to any enactment or rule of law regulating the admissibility of evidence in such proceedings.

NOTES

Commencement: 6 July 2010 (sub-ss (1), (2), (5)–(7) for the purpose of enabling subordinate legislation or guidance to be made); 1 October 2010 (otherwise).

Repealed by the Enterprise and Regulatory Reform Act 2013, s 66(1), as from a day to be appointed, except in relation to proceedings that relate to a contravention occurring before this repeal comes into force (see s 66(2) of the 2013 Act at **[1.1856]**.

Sub-s (8): for the words "a county court" there are substituted the words "the county court" by the Crime and Courts Act 2013, s 17(5), Sch 9, Pt 3, para 52, as from a day to be appointed.

Transitional provisions: see the Equality Act 2010 (Commencement No 4, Savings, Consequential, Transitional, Transitory and Incidental Provisions and Revocation) Order 2010, SI 2010/2317, art 7 at **[2.1560]**.

Orders: the Equality Act 2010 (Obtaining Information) Order 2010, SI 2010/2194 at **[2.1536]**.

[1.1722]
139 Interest

(1) Regulations may make provision—

(a) for enabling an employment tribunal to include interest on an amount awarded by it in proceedings under this Act;
(b) specifying the manner in which, and the periods and rate by reference to which, the interest is to be determined.

(2) Regulations may modify the operation of an order made under section 14 of the Employment Tribunals Act 1996 (power to make provision as to interest on awards) in so far as it relates to an award in proceedings under this Act.

NOTES

Commencement: 1 October 2010.

Transitional provisions: see the Equality Act 2010 (Commencement No 4, Savings, Consequential, Transitional, Transitory and Incidental Provisions and Revocation) Order 2010, SI 2010/2317, art 7 at **[2.1560]**.

As of 6 April 2013 no Regulations had been made under this section. However, the Employment Tribunals (Interest on Awards in Discrimination Cases) Regulations 1996, SI 1996/2803 at **[2.257]** have effect as if made under this section by virtue of the Equality Act 2010 (Commencement No 4, Savings, Consequential, Transitional, Transitory and Incidental Provisions and Revocation) Order 2010, SI 2010/2317, art 21, Sch 7.

[1.1723]

[139A Equal pay audits

(1) Regulations may make provision requiring an employment tribunal to order the respondent to carry out an equal pay audit in any case where the tribunal finds that there has been an equal pay breach.

(2) An equal pay breach is—
(a) a breach of an equality clause, or
(b) a contravention in relation to pay of section 39(2), 49(6) or 50(6), so far as relating to sex discrimination.

(3) An equal pay audit is an audit designed to identify action to be taken to avoid equal pay breaches occurring or continuing.

(4) The regulations may make further provision about equal pay audits, including provision about—
(a) the content of an audit;
(b) the powers and duties of a tribunal for deciding whether its order has been complied with;
(c) any circumstances in which an audit may be required to be published or may be disclosed to any person.

(5) The regulations must provide for an equal pay audit not to be ordered where the tribunal considers that—
(a) an audit completed by the respondent in the previous 3 years meets requirements prescribed for this purpose,
(b) it is clear without an audit whether any action is required to avoid equal pay breaches occurring or continuing,
(c) the breach the tribunal has found gives no reason to think that there may be other breaches, or
(d) the disadvantages of an equal pay audit would outweigh its benefits.

(6) The regulations may provide for an employment tribunal to have power, where a person fails to comply with an order to carry out an equal pay audit, to order that person to pay a penalty to the Secretary of State of not more than an amount specified in the regulations.

(7) The regulations may provide for that power—
(a) to be exercisable in prescribed circumstances;
(b) to be exercisable more than once, if the failure to comply continues.

(8) The first regulations made by virtue of subsection (6) must not specify an amount of more than £5,000.

(9) Sums received by the Secretary of State under the regulations must be paid into the Consolidated Fund.

(10) The first regulations under this section must specify an exemption period during which the requirement to order an equal pay audit does not apply in the case of a business that—
(a) had fewer than 10 employees immediately before a specified time, or
(b) was begun as a new business in a specified period.

(11) For the purposes of subsection (10)—
(a) "specified" means specified in the regulations, and
(b) the number of employees a business had or the time when a business was begun as a new business is to be determined in accordance with the regulations.

(12) Before making regulations under this section, a Minister of the Crown must consult any other Minister of the Crown with responsibility for employment tribunals.]

NOTES

Commencement: 25 April 2013.

Inserted by the Enterprise and Regulatory Reform Act 2013, s 98(1), (2), as from 25 April 2013.

[1.1724]

140 Conduct giving rise to separate proceedings

(1) This section applies in relation to conduct which has given rise to two or more separate proceedings under this Act, with at least one being for a contravention of section 111 (instructing, causing or inducing contraventions).

(2) A court may transfer proceedings to an employment tribunal.

(3) An employment tribunal may transfer proceedings to a court.

(4) A court or employment tribunal is to be taken for the purposes of this Part to have jurisdiction to determine a claim or complaint transferred to it under this section; accordingly—

(a) a reference to a claim within section 114(1) includes a reference to a claim transferred to a court under this section, and

(b) a reference to a complaint within section 120(1) includes a reference to a complaint transferred to an employment tribunal under this section.

(5) A court or employment tribunal may not make a decision that is inconsistent with an earlier decision in proceedings arising out of the conduct.

(6) "Court" means—

(a) in relation to proceedings in England and Wales, *a county court*;

(b) in relation to proceedings in Scotland, the sheriff.

NOTES

Commencement: 1 October 2010.

Sub-s (6): for the words in italics there are substituted the words "the county court" by the Crime and Courts Act 2013, s 17(5), Sch 9, Pt 3, para 52, as from a day to be appointed.

Transitional provisions: see the Equality Act 2010 (Commencement No 4, Savings, Consequential, Transitional, Transitory and Incidental Provisions and Revocation) Order 2010, SI 2010/2317, art 7 at **[2.1560]**.

[1.1725]

[140A Extension of time limits because of mediation in certain cross-border disputes

(1) In this section—

(a) "Mediation Directive" means Directive 2008/52/EC of the European Parliament and of the Council of 21 May 2008 on certain aspects of mediation in civil and commercial matters,

(b) "mediation" has the meaning given by article 3(a) of the Mediation Directive,

(c) "mediator" has the meaning given by article 3(b) of the Mediation Directive, and

(d) "relevant dispute" means a dispute to which article 8(1) of the Mediation Directive applies (certain cross-border disputes).

(2) Subsection (3) applies where—

(a) a time limit is set by section 118(1)(a), 118(2) or 129(3) in relation to the whole or part of a relevant dispute,

(b) a mediation in relation to the relevant dispute starts before the time limit expires, and

(c) if not extended by this section, the time limit would expire before the mediation ends or less than eight weeks after it ends.

(3) The time limit expires instead at the end of eight weeks after the mediation ends (subject to subsection (4)).

(4) If a time limit mentioned in subsection (2)(a) has been extended by this section, subsections (2) and (3) apply to the extended time limit as they apply to a time limit mentioned in subsection (2)(a).

(5) Subsection (6) applies where—

(a) a time limit is set by section 123(1)(a) in relation to the whole or part of a relevant dispute,

(b) a mediation in relation to the relevant dispute starts before the time limit expires, and

(c) if not extended by this section the time limit would expire before the mediation ends or less than four weeks after it ends.

(6) The time limit expires instead at the end of four weeks after the mediation ends (subject to subsection (7)).

(7) If a time limit mentioned in subsection (5)(a) has been extended by this section, subsections (5) and (6) apply to the extended time limit as they apply to a time limit mentioned in subsection (5)(a).

(8) Where more than one time limit applies in relation to a relevant dispute, the extension by subsection (3) or (6) of one of those time limits does not affect the others.

(9) For the purposes of this section, a mediation starts on the date of the agreement to mediate that is entered into by the parties and the mediator.

(10) For the purposes of this section, a mediation ends on the date of the first of these to occur—

(a) the parties reach an agreement in resolution of the relevant dispute,

(b) a party completes the notification of the other parties that it has withdrawn from the mediation,

(c) a party to whom a qualifying request is made fails to give a response reaching the other parties within 14 days of the request,

(d) the parties, after being notified that the mediator's appointment has ended (by death, resignation or otherwise), fail to agree within 14 days to seek to appoint a replacement mediator,

(e) the mediation otherwise comes to an end pursuant to the terms of the agreement to mediate.

(11) For the purpose of subsection (10), a qualifying request is a request by a party that another (A) confirm to all parties that A is continuing with the mediation.

(12) In the case of any relevant dispute, references in this section to a mediation are references to the mediation so far as it relates to that dispute, and references to a party are to be read accordingly.

(13) Where a court or tribunal has power under section 118(1)(b) or 123(1)(b) to extend a period of limitation, the power is exercisable in relation to the period of limitation as extended by this section.]

NOTES

Commencement: 20 May 2011.

Inserted by the Cross-Border Mediation (EU Directive) Regulations 2011, SI 2011/1133, regs 54, 58, as from 20 May 2011.

[1.1726]

[140B Extension of time limits to facilitate conciliation before institution of proceedings

(1) This section applies where a time limit is set by section 123(1)(a) or 129(3) or (4).

But it does not apply to a dispute that is (or so much of a dispute as is) a relevant dispute for the purposes of section 140A.

(2) In this section—

(a) Day A is the day on which the complainant or applicant concerned complies with the requirement in subsection (1) of section 18A of the Employment Tribunals Act 1996 (requirement to contact ACAS before instituting proceedings) in relation to the matter in respect of which the proceedings are brought, and

(b) Day B is the day on which the complainant or applicant concerned receives or, if earlier, is treated as receiving (by virtue of regulations made under subsection (11) of that section) the certificate issued under subsection (4) of that section.

(3) In working out when the time limit set by section 123(1)(a) or 129(3) or (4) expires the period beginning with the day after Day A and ending with Day B is not to be counted.

(4) If the time limit set by section 123(1)(a) or 129(3) or (4) would (if not extended by this subsection) expire during the period beginning with Day A and ending one month after Day B, the time limit expires instead at the end of that period.

(5) The power conferred on the employment tribunal by subsection (1)(b) of section 123 to extend the time limit set by subsection (1)(a) of that section is exercisable in relation to that time limit as extended by this section.]

NOTES

Commencement: to be appointed.

Inserted by the Enterprise and Regulatory Reform Act 2013, s 8, Sch 2, paras 42, 45, as from a day to be appointed.

[1.1727]

141 Interpretation, etc

(1) This section applies for the purposes of this Part.

(2) A reference to the responsible person, in relation to an equality clause or rule, is to be construed in accordance with Chapter 3 of Part 5.

(3) A reference to a worker is a reference to the person to the terms of whose work the proceedings in question relate; and, for the purposes of proceedings relating to an equality rule or a non-discrimination rule, a reference to a worker includes a reference to a member of the occupational pension scheme in question.

(4) A reference to the terms of a person's work is to be construed in accordance with Chapter 3 of Part 5.

(5) A reference to a member of an occupational pension scheme includes a reference to a prospective member.

(6) In relation to proceedings in England and Wales, a person has an incapacity if the person—

(a) has not attained the age of 18, or

(b) lacks capacity (within the meaning of the Mental Capacity Act 2005).

(7) In relation to proceedings in Scotland, a person has an incapacity if the person—

(a) has not attained the age of 16, or

(b) is incapable (within the meaning of the Adults with Incapacity (Scotland) Act 2000 (asp 4)).

(8) "Service complaint" means a complaint under section 334 of the Armed Forces Act 2006; and "service complaint procedures" means the procedures prescribed by regulations under that section (except in so far as relating to references under section 337 of that Act).

(9) "Criminal matter" means—

(a) an investigation into the commission of an alleged offence;

(b) a decision whether to commence criminal proceedings;

(c) criminal proceedings.

NOTES

Commencement: 1 October 2010.

Transitional provisions: see the Equality Act 2010 (Commencement No 4, Savings, Consequential, Transitional, Transitory and Incidental Provisions and Revocation) Order 2010, SI 2010/2317, art 7 at **[2.1560]**.

PART 10
CONTRACTS, ETC

Contracts and other agreements

[1.1728]

142 Unenforceable terms

(1) A term of a contract is unenforceable against a person in so far as it constitutes, promotes or provides for treatment of that or another person that is of a description prohibited by this Act.

(2) A relevant non-contractual term is unenforceable against a person in so far as it constitutes, promotes or provides for treatment of that or another person that is of a description prohibited by this Act, in so far as this Act relates to disability.

(3) A relevant non-contractual term is a term which—

(a) is a term of an agreement that is not a contract, and

(b) relates to the provision of an employment service within section 56(2)(a) to (e) or to the provision under a group insurance arrangement of facilities by way of insurance.

(4) A reference in subsection (1) or (2) to treatment of a description prohibited by this Act does not include—

(a) a reference to the inclusion of a term in a contract referred to in section 70(2)(a) or 76(2), or

(b) a reference to the failure to include a term in a contract as referred to in section 70(2)(b).

(5) Subsection (4) does not affect the application of section 148(2) to this section.

NOTES

Commencement: 1 October 2010.

[1.1729]

143 Removal or modification of unenforceable terms

(1) *A county court* or the sheriff may, on an application by a person who has an interest in a contract or other agreement which includes a term that is unenforceable as a result of section 142, make an order for the term to be removed or modified.

(2) An order under this section must not be made unless every person who would be affected by it—

(a) has been given notice of the application (except where notice is dispensed with in accordance with rules of court), and

(b) has been afforded an opportunity to make representations to the county court or sheriff.

(3) An order under this section may include provision in respect of a period before the making of the order.

NOTES

Commencement: 1 October 2010.

Sub-s (1): for the words in italics there are substituted the words "The county court" by the Crime and Courts Act 2013, s 17(5), Sch 9, Pt 3, para 52, as from a day to be appointed.

[1.1730]

144 Contracting out

(1) A term of a contract is unenforceable by a person in whose favour it would operate in so far as it purports to exclude or limit a provision of or made under this Act.

(2) A relevant non-contractual term (as defined by section 142) is unenforceable by a person in whose favour it would operate in so far as it purports to exclude or limit a provision of or made under this Act, in so far as the provision relates to disability.

(3) This section does not apply to a contract which settles a claim within section 114.

(4) This section does not apply to a contract which settles a complaint within section 120 if the contract—

(a) is made with the assistance of a conciliation officer, or

(b) is a qualifying *compromise contract*.

(5) A contract within subsection (4) includes a contract which settles a complaint relating to a breach of an equality clause or rule or of a non-discrimination rule.

(6) A contract within subsection (4) includes an agreement by the parties to a dispute to submit the dispute to arbitration if—

(a) the dispute is covered by a scheme having effect by virtue of an order under section 212A of the Trade Union and Labour Relations (Consolidation) Act 1992, and

(b) the agreement is to submit the dispute to arbitration in accordance with the scheme.

NOTES

Commencement: 1 October 2010.

Sub-s (4): for the words in italics there are substituted the words "settlement agreement" by the Enterprise and Regulatory Reform Act 2013, s 23(5), as from a day to be appointed.

Collective agreements and rules of undertakings

[1.1731]

145 Void and unenforceable terms

(1) A term of a collective agreement is void in so far as it constitutes, promotes or provides for treatment of a description prohibited by this Act.

(2) A rule of an undertaking is unenforceable against a person in so far as it constitutes, promotes or provides for treatment of the person that is of a description prohibited by this Act.

NOTES

Commencement: 1 October 2010.

[1.1732]

146 Declaration in respect of void term, etc

(1) A qualifying person (P) may make a complaint to an employment tribunal that a term is void, or that a rule is unenforceable, as a result of section 145.

(2) But subsection (1) applies only if—

(a) the term or rule may in the future have effect in relation to P, and

(b) where the complaint alleges that the term or rule provides for treatment of a description prohibited by this Act, P may in the future be subjected to treatment that would (if P were subjected to it in present circumstances) be of that description.

(3) If the tribunal finds that the complaint is well-founded, it must make an order declaring that the term is void or the rule is unenforceable.

(4) An order under this section may include provision in respect of a period before the making of the order.

(5) In the case of a complaint about a term of a collective agreement, where the term is one made by or on behalf of a person of a description specified in the first column of the table, a qualifying person is a person of a description specified in the second column.

Description of person who made collective agreement	**Qualifying person**
Employer	A person who is, or is seeking to be, an employee of that employer
Organisation of employers	A person who is, or is seeking to be, an employee of an employer who is a member of that organisation
Association of organisations of employers	A person who is, or is seeking to be, an employee of an employer who is a member of an organisation in that association

(6) In the case of a complaint about a rule of an undertaking, where the rule is one made by or on behalf of a person of a description specified in the first column of the table, a qualifying person is a person of a description specified in the second column.

Description of person who made rule of undertaking	**Qualifying person**
Employer	A person who is, or is seeking to be, an employee of that employer
Trade organisation or qualifications body	A person who is, or is seeking to be, a member of the organisation or body
	A person upon whom the body has conferred a relevant qualification
	A person seeking conferment by the body of a relevant qualification

NOTES

Commencement: 1 October 2010.

Supplementary

[1.1733]

147 Meaning of "qualifying *compromise contract*"

(1) This section applies for the purposes of this Part.

(2) A qualifying *compromise contract* is a contract in relation to which each of the conditions in subsection (3) is met.

(3) Those conditions are that—

(a) the contract is in writing,

(b) the contract relates to the particular complaint,

(c) the complainant has, before entering into the contract, received advice from an independent adviser about its terms and effect (including, in particular, its effect on the complainant's ability to pursue the complaint before an employment tribunal),

(d) on the date of the giving of the advice, there is in force a contract of insurance, or an indemnity provided for members of a profession or professional body, covering the risk of a claim by the complainant in respect of loss arising from the advice,

(e) the contract identifies the adviser, and

(f) the contract states that the conditions in paragraphs (c) and (d) are met.

(4) Each of the following is an independent adviser—

(a) a qualified lawyer;

(b) an officer, official, employee or member of an independent trade union certified in writing by the trade union as competent to give advice and as authorised to do so on its behalf;

(c) a worker at an advice centre (whether as an employee or a volunteer) certified in writing by the centre as competent to give advice and as authorised to do so on its behalf;

(d) a person of such description as may be specified by order.

(5) Despite subsection (4), none of the following is an independent adviser [to the complainant] in relation to a qualifying *compromise contract*—

(a) a person [(other than the complainant)] who is a party to the contract or the complaint;

(b) a person who is connected to a person within paragraph (a);

(c) a person who is employed by a person within paragraph (a) or (b);

(d) a person who is acting for a person within paragraph (a) or (b) in relation to the contract or the complaint;

(e) a person within subsection (4)(b) or (c), if the trade union or advice centre is a person within paragraph (a) or (b);

(f) a person within subsection (4)(c) to whom the complainant makes a payment for the advice.

(6) A "qualified lawyer", for the purposes of subsection (4)(a), is—

(a) in relation to England and Wales, a person who, for the purposes of the Legal Services Act 2007, is an authorised person in relation to an activity which constitutes the exercise of a right of audience or the conduct of litigation;

(b) in relation to Scotland, an advocate (whether in practice as such or employed to give legal advice) or a solicitor who holds a practising certificate.

(7) "Independent trade union" has the meaning given in section 5 of the Trade Union and Labour Relations (Consolidation) Act 1992.

(8) Two persons are connected for the purposes of subsection (5) if—

(a) one is a company of which the other (directly or indirectly) has control, or

(b) both are companies of which a third person (directly or indirectly) has control.

(9) Two persons are also connected for the purposes of subsection (5) in so far as a connection between them gives rise to a conflict of interest in relation to the contract or the complaint.

NOTES

Commencement: 6 July 2010 (sub-s (4) for the purpose of enabling subordinate legislation or guidance to be made); 1 October 2010 (otherwise).

Section heading, sub-s (2): for the words in italics there are substituted the words "settlement agreement" by the Enterprise and Regulatory Reform Act 2013, s 23(6), as from a day to be appointed.

Sub-s (5): words in square brackets inserted by the Equality Act 2010 (Amendment) Order 2012, SI 2012/334, art 2, as from 6 April 2012; for the words in italics there are substituted the words "settlement agreement" by the Enterprise and Regulatory Reform Act 2013, s 23(6), as from a day to be appointed.

Orders: the Equality Act 2010 (Qualifying Compromise Contract Specified Person) Order 2010, SI 2010/2192 at **[2.1534]**.

[1.1734]

148 Interpretation

(1) This section applies for the purposes of this Part.

(2) A reference to treatment of a description prohibited by this Act does not include treatment in so far as it is treatment that would contravene—

(a) Part 1 (public sector duty regarding socio-economic inequalities), or

(b) Chapter 1 of Part 11 (public sector equality duty).

(3) "Group insurance arrangement" means an arrangement between an employer and another person for the provision by that other person of facilities by way of insurance to the employer's employees (or a class of those employees).
(4) "Collective agreement" has the meaning given in section 178 of the Trade Union and Labour Relations (Consolidation) Act 1992.
(5) A rule of an undertaking is a rule within subsection (6) or (7).
(6) A rule within this subsection is a rule made by a trade organisation or a qualifications body for application to—
 (a) its members or prospective members,
 (b) persons on whom it has conferred a relevant qualification, or
 (c) persons seeking conferment by it of a relevant qualification.
(7) A rule within this subsection is a rule made by an employer for application to—
 (a) employees,
 (b) persons who apply for employment, or
 (c) persons the employer considers for employment.
(8) "Trade organisation", "qualifications body" and "relevant qualification" each have the meaning given in Part 5 (work).

NOTES
Commencement: 1 October 2010.

PART 11
ADVANCEMENT OF EQUALITY

CHAPTER 1
PUBLIC SECTOR EQUALITY DUTY

[1.1735]
149 Public sector equality duty
(1) A public authority must, in the exercise of its functions, have due regard to the need to—
 (a) eliminate discrimination, harassment, victimisation and any other conduct that is prohibited by or under this Act;
 (b) advance equality of opportunity between persons who share a relevant protected characteristic and persons who do not share it;
 (c) foster good relations between persons who share a relevant protected characteristic and persons who do not share it.
(2) A person who is not a public authority but who exercises public functions must, in the exercise of those functions, have due regard to the matters mentioned in subsection (1).
(3) Having due regard to the need to advance equality of opportunity between persons who share a relevant protected characteristic and persons who do not share it involves having due regard, in particular, to the need to—
 (a) remove or minimise disadvantages suffered by persons who share a relevant protected characteristic that are connected to that characteristic;
 (b) take steps to meet the needs of persons who share a relevant protected characteristic that are different from the needs of persons who do not share it;
 (c) encourage persons who share a relevant protected characteristic to participate in public life or in any other activity in which participation by such persons is disproportionately low.
(4) The steps involved in meeting the needs of disabled persons that are different from the needs of persons who are not disabled include, in particular, steps to take account of disabled persons' disabilities.
(5) Having due regard to the need to foster good relations between persons who share a relevant protected characteristic and persons who do not share it involves having due regard, in particular, to the need to—
 (a) tackle prejudice, and
 (b) promote understanding.
(6) Compliance with the duties in this section may involve treating some persons more favourably than others; but that is not to be taken as permitting conduct that would otherwise be prohibited by or under this Act.
(7) The relevant protected characteristics are—
 age;
 disability;
 gender reassignment;
 pregnancy and maternity;
 race;
 religion or belief;
 sex;
 sexual orientation.

(8) A reference to conduct that is prohibited by or under this Act includes a reference to—
(a) a breach of an equality clause or rule;
(b) a breach of a non-discrimination rule.
(9) Schedule 18 (exceptions) has effect.

NOTES
Commencement: 5 April 2011.

[1.1736]
150 Public authorities and public functions
(1) A public authority is a person who is specified in Schedule 19.
(2) In that Schedule—
Part 1 specifies public authorities generally;
Part 2 specifies relevant Welsh authorities;
Part 3 specifies relevant Scottish authorities.
(3) A public authority specified in Schedule 19 is subject to the duty imposed by section 149(1) in relation to the exercise of all of its functions unless subsection (4) applies.
(4) A public authority specified in that Schedule in respect of certain specified functions is subject to that duty only in respect of the exercise of those functions.
(5) A public function is a function that is a function of a public nature for the purposes of the Human Rights Act 1998.

NOTES
Commencement: 18 January 2011 (for the purposes of ss 151–155, 157, Sch 19); 5 April 2011 (otherwise).

[1.1737]
151 Power to specify public authorities
(1) A Minister of the Crown may by order amend Part 1, 2 or 3 of Schedule 19.
(2) The Welsh Ministers may by order amend Part 2 of Schedule 19.
(3) The Scottish Ministers may by order amend Part 3 of Schedule 19.
(4) The power under subsection (1), (2) or (3) may not be exercised so as to—
(a) add an entry to Part 1 relating to a relevant Welsh or Scottish authority or a cross-border Welsh or Scottish authority;
(b) add an entry to Part 2 relating to a person who is not a relevant Welsh authority;
(c) add an entry to Part 3 relating to a person who is not a relevant Scottish authority.
(5) A Minister of the Crown may by order amend Schedule 19 so as to make provision relating to a cross-border Welsh or Scottish authority.
(6) On the first exercise of the power under subsection (5) to add an entry relating to a cross-border Welsh or Scottish authority to Schedule 19, a Minister of the Crown must—
(a) add a Part 4 to the Schedule for cross-border authorities, and
(b) add the cross-border Welsh or Scottish authority to that Part.
(7) Any subsequent exercise of the power under subsection (5) to add an entry relating to a cross-border Welsh or Scottish authority to Schedule 19 must add that entry to Part 4 of the Schedule.
(8) An order may not be made under this section so as to extend the application of section 149 unless the person making it considers that the extension relates to a person by whom a public function is exercisable.
(9) An order may not be made under this section so as to extend the application of section 149 to—
(a) the exercise of a function referred to in paragraph 3 of Schedule 18 (judicial functions, etc);
(b) a person listed in paragraph 4(2)(a) to (e) of that Schedule (Parliament, devolved legislatures and General Synod);
(c) the exercise of a function listed in paragraph 4(3) of that Schedule (proceedings in Parliament or devolved legislatures).

NOTES
Commencement: 18 January 2011.
Orders: the Equality Act 2010 (Specification of Public Authorities) (Scotland) Order 2011, SSI 2011/233; the Equality Act 2010 (Public Authorities and Consequential and Supplementary Amendments) Order 2011, SI 2011/1060; the Equality Act 2010 (Specification of Relevant Welsh Authorities) Order 2011, SI 2011/1063; the Equality Act 2010 (Specification of Public Authorities) (Scotland) Order 2012, SSI 2012/55.

[1.1738]
152 Power to specify public authorities: consultation and consent
(1) Before making an order under a provision specified in the first column of the Table, a Minister of the Crown must consult the person or persons specified in the second column.

Provision	Consultees
Section 151(1)	The Commission
Section 151(1), so far as relating to a relevant Welsh authority	The Welsh Ministers
Section 151(1), so far as relating to a relevant Scottish authority	The Scottish Ministers
Section 151(5)	The Commission
Section 151(5), so far as relating to a cross-border Welsh authority	The Welsh Ministers
Section 151(5), so far as relating to a cross-border Scottish authority	The Scottish Ministers

(2) Before making an order under section 151(2), the Welsh Ministers must—

(a) obtain the consent of a Minister of the Crown, and

(b) consult the Commission.

(3) Before making an order under section 151(3), the Scottish Ministers must—

(a) obtain the consent of a Minister of the Crown, and

(b) consult the Commission.

NOTES

Commencement: 18 January 2011.

[1.1739]

153 Power to impose specific duties

(1) A Minister of the Crown may by regulations impose duties on a public authority specified in Part 1 of Schedule 19 for the purpose of enabling the better performance by the authority of the duty imposed by section 149(1).

(2) The Welsh Ministers may by regulations impose duties on a public authority specified in Part 2 of Schedule 19 for that purpose.

(3) The Scottish Ministers may by regulations impose duties on a public authority specified in Part 3 of Schedule 19 for that purpose.

(4) Before making regulations under this section, the person making them must consult the Commission.

NOTES

Commencement: 18 January 2011.

Regulations: the Equality Act 2010 (Statutory Duties) (Wales) Regulations 2011, SI 2011/1064 at **[2.1579]**; the Equality Act 2010 (Specific Duties) Regulations 2011, SI 2011/2260 at **[2.1617]**; the Equality Act 2010 (Specific Duties) (Scotland) Regulations 2012, SSI 2012/162 at **[2.1638]**.

[1.1740]

154 Power to impose specific duties: cross-border authorities

(1) If a Minister of the Crown exercises the power in section 151(5) to add an entry for a public authority to Part 4 of Schedule 19, the Minister must include after the entry a letter specified in the first column of the Table in subsection (3).

(2) Where a letter specified in the first column of the Table in subsection (3) is included after an entry for a public authority in Part 4 of Schedule 19, the person specified in the second column of the Table—

(a) may by regulations impose duties on the authority for the purpose of enabling the better performance by the authority of the duty imposed by section 149(1), subject to such limitations as are specified in that column;

(b) must in making the regulations comply with the procedural requirement specified in that column.

(3) This is the Table—

Letter	Person by whom regulations may be made and procedural requirements
A	Regulations may be made by a Minister of the Crown in relation to the authority's functions that are not devolved Welsh functions. The Minister of the Crown must consult the Welsh Ministers before making the regulations. Regulations may be made by the Welsh Ministers in relation to the authority's devolved Welsh functions. The Welsh Ministers must consult a Minister of the Crown before making the regulations.
B	Regulations may be made by a Minister of the Crown in relation to the authority's functions that are not devolved Scottish functions.

Letter	Person by whom regulations may be made and procedural requirements
	The Minister of the Crown must consult the Scottish Ministers before making the regulations.
	Regulations may be made by the Scottish Ministers in relation to the authority's devolved Scottish functions.
	The Scottish Ministers must consult a Minister of the Crown before making the regulations.
C	Regulations may be made by a Minister of the Crown in relation to the authority's functions that are neither devolved Welsh functions nor devolved Scottish functions.
	The Minister of the Crown must consult the Welsh Ministers and the Scottish Ministers before making the regulations.
	Regulations may be made by the Welsh Ministers in relation to the authority's devolved Welsh functions.
	The Welsh Ministers must consult a Minister of the Crown before making the regulations.
	Regulations may be made by the Scottish Ministers in relation to the authority's devolved Scottish functions.
	The Scottish Ministers must consult a Minister of the Crown before making the regulations.
D	The regulations may be made by a Minister of the Crown.
	The Minister of the Crown must consult the Welsh Ministers before making the regulations.

(4) Before making regulations under subsection (2), the person making them must consult the Commission.

NOTES

Commencement: 18 January 2011.

Regulations: the Equality Act 2010 (Specific Duties) Regulations 2011, SI 2011/2260 at **[2.1617]**.

[1.1741]

155 Power to impose specific duties: supplementary

(1) Regulations under section 153 or 154 may require a public authority to consider such matters as may be specified from time to time by—

(a) a Minister of the Crown, where the regulations are made by a Minister of the Crown;
(b) the Welsh Ministers, where the regulations are made by the Welsh Ministers;
(c) the Scottish Ministers, where the regulations are made by the Scottish Ministers.

(2) Regulations under section 153 or 154 may impose duties on a public authority that is a contracting authority within the meaning of the Public Sector Directive in connection with its public procurement functions.

(3) In subsection (2)—

"public procurement functions" means functions the exercise of which is regulated by the Public Sector Directive;

"the Public Sector Directive" means Directive 2004/18/EC of the European Parliament and of the Council of 31 March 2004 on the coordination of procedures for the award of public works contracts, public supply contracts and public service contracts, as amended from time to time.

(4) Subsections (1) and (2) do not affect the generality of section 153 or 154(2)(a).

(5) A duty imposed on a public authority under section 153 or 154 may be modified or removed by regulations made by—

(a) a Minister of the Crown, where the original duty was imposed by regulations made by a Minister of the Crown;
(b) the Welsh Ministers, where the original duty was imposed by regulations made by the Welsh Ministers;
(c) the Scottish Ministers, where the original duty was imposed by regulations made by the Scottish Ministers.

NOTES

Commencement: 18 January 2011.

Regulations: the Equality Act 2010 (Specific Duties) (Scotland) Regulations 2012, SSI 2012/162 at **[2.1638]**.

[1.1742]
156 Enforcement
A failure in respect of a performance of a duty imposed by or under this Chapter does not confer a cause of action at private law.

NOTES
Commencement: 5 April 2011.

[1.1743]
157 Interpretation
(1) This section applies for the purposes of this Chapter.
(2) A relevant Welsh authority is a person (other than the Assembly Commission) whose functions—
(a) are exercisable only in or as regards Wales, and
(b) are wholly or mainly devolved Welsh functions.
(3) A cross-border Welsh authority is a person other than a relevant Welsh authority (or the Assembly Commission) who has any function that—
(a) is exercisable in or as regards Wales, and
(b) is a devolved Welsh function.
(4) The Assembly Commission has the same meaning as in the Government of Wales Act 2006.
(5) A function is a devolved Welsh function if it relates to—
(a) a matter in respect of which functions are exercisable by the Welsh Ministers, the First Minister for Wales or the Counsel General to the Welsh Assembly Government, or
(b) a matter within the legislative competence of the National Assembly for Wales.
(6) A relevant Scottish authority is a public body, public office or holder of a public office—
(a) which is not a cross-border Scottish authority or the Scottish Parliamentary Corporate Body,
(b) whose functions are exercisable only in or as regards Scotland, and
(c) at least some of whose functions do not relate to reserved matters.
(7) A cross-border Scottish authority is a cross-border public authority within the meaning given by section 88(5) of the Scotland Act 1998.
(8) A function is a devolved Scottish function if it—
(a) is exercisable in or as regards Scotland, and
(b) does not relate to reserved matters.
(9) Reserved matters has the same meaning as in the Scotland Act 1998.

NOTES
Commencement: 18 January 2011.

CHAPTER 2
POSITIVE ACTION

[1.1744]
158 Positive action: general
(1) This section applies if a person (P) reasonably thinks that—
(a) persons who share a protected characteristic suffer a disadvantage connected to the characteristic,
(b) persons who share a protected characteristic have needs that are different from the needs of persons who do not share it, or
(c) participation in an activity by persons who share a protected characteristic is disproportionately low.
(2) This Act does not prohibit P from taking any action which is a proportionate means of achieving the aim of—
(a) enabling or encouraging persons who share the protected characteristic to overcome or minimise that disadvantage,
(b) meeting those needs, or
(c) enabling or encouraging persons who share the protected characteristic to participate in that activity.
(3) Regulations may specify action, or descriptions of action, to which subsection (2) does not apply.
(4) This section does not apply to—
(a) action within section 159(3), or
(b) anything that is permitted by virtue of section 104.
(5) If section 104(7) is repealed by virtue of section 105, this section will not apply to anything that would have been so permitted but for the repeal.
(6) This section does not enable P to do anything that is prohibited by or under an enactment other than this Act.

NOTES

Commencement: 1 October 2010.

[1.1745]

159 Positive action: recruitment and promotion

(1) This section applies if a person (P) reasonably thinks that—

(a) persons who share a protected characteristic suffer a disadvantage connected to the characteristic, or

(b) participation in an activity by persons who share a protected characteristic is disproportionately low.

(2) Part 5 (work) does not prohibit P from taking action within subsection (3) with the aim of enabling or encouraging persons who share the protected characteristic to—

(a) overcome or minimise that disadvantage, or

(b) participate in that activity.

(3) That action is treating a person (A) more favourably in connection with recruitment or promotion than another person (B) because A has the protected characteristic but B does not.

(4) But subsection (2) applies only if—

(a) A is as qualified as B to be recruited or promoted,

(b) P does not have a policy of treating persons who share the protected characteristic more favourably in connection with recruitment or promotion than persons who do not share it, and

(c) taking the action in question is a proportionate means of achieving the aim referred to in subsection (2).

(5) "Recruitment" means a process for deciding whether to—

(a) offer employment to a person,

(b) make contract work available to a contract worker,

(c) offer a person a position as a partner in a firm or proposed firm,

(d) offer a person a position as a member of an LLP or proposed LLP,

(e) offer a person a pupillage or tenancy in barristers' chambers,

(f) take a person as an advocate's devil or offer a person membership of an advocate's stable,

(g) offer a person an appointment to a personal office,

(h) offer a person an appointment to a public office, recommend a person for such an appointment or approve a person's appointment to a public office, or

(i) offer a person a service for finding employment.

(6) This section does not enable P to do anything that is prohibited by or under an enactment other than this Act.

NOTES

Commencement: 1 October 2010 (sub-s (3) for the purposes of s 158(4)); 6 April 2011 (otherwise).

160–188 *(Ss 160–188 (Part 12—Disabled Persons: Transport) outside the scope of this work.)*

PART 13
DISABILITY: MISCELLANEOUS

[1.1746]

189 Reasonable adjustments

Schedule 21 (reasonable adjustments: supplementary) has effect.

NOTES

Commencement: 4 August 2010 (in so far as it relates to Sch 21, para 6, for the purpose of enabling subordinate legislation or guidance to be made); 1 October 2010 (otherwise).

190 *(S 190 (Improvements to let dwelling houses) outside the scope of this work.)*

PART 14
GENERAL EXCEPTIONS

[1.1747]

191 Statutory provisions

Schedule 22 (statutory provisions) has effect.

NOTES

Commencement: 1 October 2010 (except in so far as it applies to the protected characteristic of age in Parts 3 and 7 of this Act); 1 October 2012 (otherwise).

[1.1748]

192 National security

A person does not contravene this Act only by doing, for the purpose of safeguarding national security, anything it is proportionate to do for that purpose.

NOTES

Commencement: 1 October 2010.

[1.1749]

193 Charities

(1) A person does not contravene this Act only by restricting the provision of benefits to persons who share a protected characteristic if—

(a) the person acts in pursuance of a charitable instrument, and
(b) the provision of the benefits is within subsection (2).

(2) The provision of benefits is within this subsection if it is—

(a) a proportionate means of achieving a legitimate aim, or
(b) for the purpose of preventing or compensating for a disadvantage linked to the protected characteristic.

(3) It is not a contravention of this Act for—

(a) a person who provides supported employment to treat persons who have the same disability or a disability of a prescribed description more favourably than those who do not have that disability or a disability of such a description in providing such employment;
(b) a Minister of the Crown to agree to arrangements for the provision of supported employment which will, or may, have that effect.

(4) If a charitable instrument enables the provision of benefits to persons of a class defined by reference to colour, it has effect for all purposes as if it enabled the provision of such benefits—

(a) to persons of the class which results if the reference to colour is ignored, or
(b) if the original class is defined by reference only to colour, to persons generally.

(5) It is not a contravention of this Act for a charity to require members, or persons wishing to become members, to make a statement which asserts or implies membership or acceptance of a religion or belief; and for this purpose restricting the access by members to a benefit, facility or service to those who make such a statement is to be treated as imposing such a requirement.

(6) Subsection (5) applies only if—

(a) the charity, or an organisation of which it is part, first imposed such a requirement before 18 May 2005, and
(b) the charity or organisation has not ceased since that date to impose such a requirement.

(7) It is not a contravention of section 29 for a person, in relation to an activity which is carried on for the purpose of promoting or supporting a charity, to restrict participation in the activity to persons of one sex.

(8) A charity regulator does not contravene this Act only by exercising a function in relation to a charity in a manner which the regulator thinks is expedient in the interests of the charity, having regard to the charitable instrument.

(9) Subsection (1) does not apply to a contravention of—

(a) section 39;
(b) section 40;
(c) section 41;
(d) section 55, so far as relating to the provision of vocational training.

(10) Subsection (9) does not apply in relation to disability.

NOTES

Commencement: 1 October 2010.

[1.1750]

194 Charities: supplementary

(1) This section applies for the purposes of section 193.

(2) That section does not apply to race, so far as relating to colour.

(3) "Charity"—

(a) in relation to England and Wales, has the meaning given by [section 1(1) of the Charities Act 2011];
(b) in relation to Scotland, means a body entered in the Scottish Charity Register.

(4) "Charitable instrument" means an instrument establishing or governing a charity (including an instrument made or having effect before the commencement of this section).

(5) The charity regulators are—

(a) the Charity Commission for England and Wales;
(b) the Scottish Charity Regulator.

(6) Section 107(5) applies to references in subsection (5) of section 193 to members, or persons wishing to become members, of a charity.

(7) "Supported employment" means facilities provided, or in respect of which payments are made, under section 15 of the Disabled Persons (Employment) Act 1944.

NOTES

Commencement: 1 October 2010.

Sub-s (3): words in square brackets in para (a) substituted by the Charities Act 2011, s 354(1), Sch 7, Pt 2, para 144, as from 14 March 2012 (for general transitional provisions and savings (including those relating to the continuity of law etc) see Sch 8 to the 2011 Act).

[1.1751]

195 Sport

(1) A person does not contravene this Act, so far as relating to sex, only by doing anything in relation to the participation of another as a competitor in a gender-affected activity.

(2) A person does not contravene section 29, 33, 34 or 35, so far as relating to gender reassignment, only by doing anything in relation to the participation of a transsexual person as a competitor in a gender-affected activity if it is necessary to do so to secure in relation to the activity—

(a) fair competition, or

(b) the safety of competitors.

(3) A gender-affected activity is a sport, game or other activity of a competitive nature in circumstances in which the physical strength, stamina or physique of average persons of one sex would put them at a disadvantage compared to average persons of the other sex as competitors in events involving the activity.

(4) In considering whether a sport, game or other activity is gender-affected in relation to children, it is appropriate to take account of the age and stage of development of children who are likely to be competitors.

(5) A person who does anything to which subsection (6) applies does not contravene this Act only because of the nationality or place of birth of another or because of the length of time the other has been resident in a particular area or place.

(6) This subsection applies to—

(a) selecting one or more persons to represent a country, place or area or a related association, in a sport or game or other activity of a competitive nature;

(b) doing anything in pursuance of the rules of a competition so far as relating to eligibility to compete in a sport or game or other such activity.

[(7) A person does not contravene this Act, so far as relating to age discrimination, only by doing anything in relation to the participation of another as a competitor in an age-banded activity if it is necessary to do so—

(a) to secure in relation to the activity fair competition or the safety of competitors,

(b) to comply with the rules of a national or international competition, or

(c) to increase participation in that activity.

(8) For the purposes of subsection (7), an age-banded activity is a sport, game or other activity of a competitive nature in circumstances in which the physical or mental strength, agility, stamina, physique, mobility, maturity or manual dexterity of average persons of a particular age group would put them at a disadvantage compared to average persons of another age group as competitors in events involving the activity.]

NOTES

Commencement: 1 October 2010.

Sub-ss (7), (8): added by the Equality Act 2010 (Age Exceptions) Order 2012, SI 2012/2466, art 9, as from 1 October 2012.

[1.1752]

196 General

Schedule 23 (general exceptions) has effect.

NOTES

Commencement: 1 October 2010 (except in so far as it applies to the protected characteristic of age in Parts 3 and 7 of this Act); 1 October 2012 (otherwise).

[1.1753]

197 Age

(1) A Minister of the Crown may by order amend this Act to provide that any of the following does not contravene this Act so far as relating to age—

(a) specified conduct;

(b) anything done for a specified purpose;

(c) anything done in pursuance of arrangements of a specified description.

(2) Specified conduct is conduct—

(a) of a specified description,

(b) carried out in specified circumstances, or

(c) by or in relation to a person of a specified description.

(3) An order under this section may—

(a) confer on a Minister of the Crown or the Treasury a power to issue guidance about the operation of the order (including, in particular, guidance about the steps that may be taken by persons wishing to rely on an exception provided for by the order);

(b) require the Minister or the Treasury to carry out consultation before issuing guidance under a power conferred by virtue of paragraph (a);

(c) make provision (including provision to impose a requirement) that refers to guidance issued under a power conferred by virtue of paragraph (a).

(4) Guidance given by a Minister of the Crown or the Treasury in anticipation of the making of an order under this section is, on the making of the order, to be treated as if it has been issued in accordance with the order.

(5) For the purposes of satisfying a requirement imposed by virtue of subsection (3)(b), the Minister or the Treasury may rely on consultation carried out before the making of the order that imposes the requirement (including consultation carried out before the commencement of this section).

(6) Provision by virtue of subsection (3)(c) may, in particular, refer to provisions of the guidance that themselves refer to a document specified in the guidance.

(7) Guidance issued (or treated as issued) under a power conferred by virtue of subsection (3)(a) comes into force on such day as the person who issues the guidance may by order appoint; and an order under this subsection may include the text of the guidance or of extracts from it.

(8) This section is not affected by any provision of this Act which makes special provision in relation to age.

(9) The references to this Act in subsection (1) do not include references to—

(a) Part 5 (work);

(b) Chapter 2 of Part 6 (further and higher education).

NOTES

Commencement: 19 June 2012.

Orders: the Equality Act 2010 (Age Exceptions) Order 2012, SI 2012/2466.

198–201 *(Ss 198–201 (Part 15: Family Property) outside the scope of this work.)*

PART 16
GENERAL AND MISCELLANEOUS

202 *(S 202 (Civil partnerships on religious premises) outside the scope of this work.)*

EU obligations

[1.1754]

203 Harmonisation

(1) This section applies if—

(a) there is [an EU] obligation of the United Kingdom which a Minister of the Crown thinks relates to the subject matter of the Equality Acts,

(b) the obligation is to be implemented by the exercise of the power under section 2(2) of the European Communities Act 1972 (the implementing power), and

(c) the Minister thinks that it is appropriate to make harmonising provision in the Equality Acts.

(2) The Minister may by order make the harmonising provision.

(3) If the Minister proposes to make an order under this section, the Minister must consult persons and organisations the Minister thinks are likely to be affected by the harmonising provision.

(4) If, as a result of the consultation under subsection (3), the Minister thinks it appropriate to change the whole or part of the proposal, the Minister must carry out such further consultation with respect to the changes as the Minister thinks appropriate.

(5) The Equality Acts are the Equality Act 2006 and this Act.

(6) Harmonising provision is provision made in relation to relevant subject matter of the Equality Acts—

(a) which corresponds to the implementing provision, or

(b) which the Minister thinks is necessary or expedient in consequence of or related to provision made in pursuance of paragraph (a) or the implementing provision.

(7) The implementing provision is provision made or to be made in exercise of the implementing power in relation to so much of the subject matter of the Equality Acts as implements [an EU] obligation.

(8) Relevant subject matter of the Equality Acts is so much of the subject matter of those Acts as does not implement [an EU] obligation.

(9) A harmonising provision may amend a provision of the Equality Acts.

(10) The reference to this Act does not include a reference to this section or Schedule 24 or to a provision specified in that Schedule.

(11) A Minister of the Crown must report to Parliament on the exercise of the power under subsection (2)—

(a) at the end of the period of 2 years starting on the day this section comes into force;

(b) at the end of each succeeding period of 2 years.

NOTES

Commencement: 8 April 2010.

Sub-ss (1), (7), (8): words in square brackets substituted by the Treaty of Lisbon (Changes in Terminology) Order 2011, SI 2011/1043, art 6(1)(e), (3), as from 22 April 2011.

[1.1755]

204 Harmonisation: procedure

(1) If, after the conclusion of the consultation required under section 203, the Minister thinks it appropriate to proceed with the making of an order under that section, the Minister must lay before Parliament—

(a) a draft of a statutory instrument containing the order, together with

(b) an explanatory document.

(2) The explanatory document must—

(a) introduce and give reasons for the harmonising provision;

(b) explain why the Minister thinks that the conditions in subsection (1) of section 203 are satisfied;

(c) give details of the consultation carried out under that section;

(d) give details of the representations received as a result of the consultation;

(e) give details of such changes as were made as a result of the representations.

(3) Where a person making representations in response to the consultation has requested the Minister not to disclose them, the Minister must not disclose them under subsection (2)(d) if, or to the extent that, to do so would (disregarding any connection with proceedings in Parliament) constitute an actionable breach of confidence.

(4) If information in representations made by a person in response to consultation under section 203 relates to another person, the Minister need not disclose the information under subsection (2)(d) if or to the extent that—

(a) the Minister thinks that the disclosure of information could adversely affect the interests of that other person, and

(b) the Minister has been unable to obtain the consent of that other person to the disclosure.

(5) The Minister may not act under subsection (1) before the end of the period of 12 weeks beginning with the day on which the consultation under section 203(3) begins.

(6) Laying a draft of a statutory instrument in accordance with subsection (1) satisfies the condition as to laying imposed by subsection (8) of section 208, in so far as that subsection applies in relation to orders under section 203.

NOTES

Commencement: 8 April 2010.

Application

[1.1756]

205 Crown application

(1) The following provisions of this Act bind the Crown—

(a) Part 1 (public sector duty regarding socio-economic inequalities);

(b) Part 3 (services and public functions), so far as relating to the exercise of public functions;

(c) Chapter 1 of Part 11 (public sector equality duty).

(2) Part 5 (work) binds the Crown as provided for by that Part.

(3) The remainder of this Act applies to Crown acts as it applies to acts done by a private person.

(4) For the purposes of subsection (3), an act is a Crown act if (and only if) it is done—

(a) by or on behalf of a member of the executive,

(b) by a statutory body acting on behalf of the Crown, or

(c) by or on behalf of the holder of a statutory office acting on behalf of the Crown.

(5) A statutory body or office is a body or office established by an enactment.

(6) The provisions of Parts 2 to 4 of the Crown Proceedings Act 1947 apply to proceedings against the Crown under this Act as they apply to proceedings in England and Wales which, as a result of section 23 of that Act, are treated for the purposes of Part 2 of that Act as civil proceedings by or against the Crown.

(7) The provisions of Part 5 of that Act apply to proceedings against the Crown under this Act as they apply to proceedings in Scotland which, as a result of that Part, are treated as civil proceedings by or against the Crown.

(8) But the proviso to section 44 of that Act (removal of proceedings from the sheriff to the Court of Session) does not apply to proceedings under this Act.

NOTES

Commencement: 8 April 2010.

[1.1757]

206 Information society services

Schedule 25 (information society services) has effect.

NOTES

Commencement: 1 October 2010.

Subordinate legislation

[1.1758]

207 Exercise of power

(1) A power to make an order or regulations under this Act is exercisable by a Minister of the Crown, unless there is express provision to the contrary.

(2) Orders, regulations or rules under this Act must be made by statutory instrument.

(3) Subsection (2) does not apply to—

(a) a transitional exemption order under Part 1 of Schedule 11,

(b) a transitional exemption order under Part 1 of Schedule 12, or

(c) an order under paragraph 1(3) of Schedule 14 that does not modify an enactment.

(4) Orders or regulations under this Act—

(a) may make different provision for different purposes;

(b) may include consequential, incidental, supplementary, transitional, transitory or saving provision.

(5) Nothing in section 163(4), 174(4) or 182(3) affects the generality of the power under subsection (4)(a).

(6) The power under subsection (4)(b), in its application to section 37, [139A,] 153, 154(2), 155(5), 197 or 216 or to paragraph 7(1) of Schedule 11 or paragraph 1(3) or 2(3) of Schedule 14, includes power to amend an enactment (including, in the case of section [139A,] 197 or 216, this Act).

(7) In the case of section 216 (commencement), provision by virtue of subsection (4)(b) may be included in a separate order from the order that provides for the commencement to which the provision relates; and, for that purpose, it does not matter—

(a) whether the order providing for the commencement includes provision by virtue of subsection (4)(b);

(b) whether the commencement has taken place.

(8) A statutory instrument containing an Order in Council under section 82 (offshore work) is subject to annulment in pursuance of a resolution of either House of Parliament.

NOTES

Commencement: 8 April 2010.

Sub-s (6): references in square brackets inserted by the Enterprise and Regulatory Reform Act 2013, s 98(1), (3), as from 25 April 2013.

[1.1759]

208 Ministers of the Crown, etc

(1) This section applies where the power to make an order or regulations under this Act is exercisable by a Minister of the Crown or the Treasury.

(2) A statutory instrument containing (whether alone or with other provision) an order or regulations that amend this Act or another Act of Parliament, or an Act of the Scottish Parliament or an Act or Measure of the National Assembly for Wales, is subject to the affirmative procedure.

(3) But a statutory instrument is not subject to the affirmative procedure by virtue of subsection (2) merely because it contains—

(a) an order under section 59 (local authority functions);

(b) an order under section 151 (power to amend list of public authorities for the purposes of the public sector equality duty) that provides for the omission of an entry where the authority concerned has ceased to exist or the variation of an entry where the authority concerned has changed its name;

(c) an order under paragraph 1(3) of Schedule 14 (educational charities and endowments) that modifies an enactment.

(4) A statutory instrument containing (whether alone or with other provision) an order or regulations mentioned in subsection (5) is subject to the affirmative procedure.

(5) The orders and regulations referred to in subsection (4) are—

(a) regulations under section 30 (services: ships and hovercraft);

(b) regulations under section 78 (gender pay gap information);

(c) regulations under section 81 (work: ships and hovercraft);

(d) an order under section 105 (election candidates: expiry of provision);

(e) regulations under section 106 (election candidates: diversity information);
[(ea) regulations under section 139A (equal pay audits);]
(f) regulations under section 153 or 154(2) (public sector equality duty: powers to impose specific duties);
(g) regulations under section 184(4) (rail vehicle accessibility: procedure for exemption orders);
(h) an order under section 203 (EU obligations: harmonisation);
(i) regulations under paragraph 9(3) of Schedule 20 (rail vehicle accessibility: determination of turnover for purposes of penalties).

(6) A statutory instrument that is not subject to the affirmative procedure by virtue of subsection (2) or (4) is subject to the negative procedure.

(7) But a statutory instrument is not subject to the negative procedure by virtue of subsection (6) merely because it contains—
(a) an order under section 183(1) (rail vehicle accessibility: exemptions);
(b) an order under section 216 (commencement) that—
(i) does not amend an Act of Parliament, an Act of the Scottish Parliament or an Act or Measure of the National Assembly for Wales, and
(ii) is not made in reliance on section 207(7).

(8) If a statutory instrument is subject to the affirmative procedure, the order or regulations contained in it must not be made unless a draft of the instrument is laid before and approved by a resolution of each House of Parliament.

(9) If a statutory instrument is subject to the negative procedure, it is subject to annulment in pursuance of a resolution of either House of Parliament.

(10) If a draft of a statutory instrument containing an order or regulations under section 2, 151, 153, 154(2) or 155(5) would, apart from this subsection, be treated for the purposes of the Standing Orders of either House of Parliament as a hybrid instrument, it is to proceed in that House as if it were not a hybrid instrument.

NOTES

Commencement: 8 April 2010.
Sub-s (5): para (ea) inserted by the Enterprise and Regulatory Reform Act 2013, s 98(1), (4), as from 25 April 2013.

[1.1760]
209 The Welsh Ministers

(1) This section applies where the power to make an order or regulations under this Act is exercisable by the Welsh Ministers.

(2) A statutory instrument containing (whether alone or with other provision) an order or regulations mentioned in subsection (3) is subject to the affirmative procedure.

(3) The orders and regulations referred to in subsection (2) are—
(a) regulations under section 2 (socio-economic inequalities);
(b) an order under section 151 (power to amend list of public authorities for the purposes of the public sector equality duty);
(c) regulations under section 153 or 154(2) (public sector equality duty: powers to impose specific duties);
(d) regulations under section 155(5) that amend an Act of Parliament or an Act or Measure of the National Assembly for Wales (public sector equality duty: power to modify or remove specific duties).

(4) But a statutory instrument is not subject to the affirmative procedure by virtue of subsection (2) merely because it contains an order under section 151 that provides for—
(a) the omission of an entry where the authority concerned has ceased to exist, or
(b) the variation of an entry where the authority concerned has changed its name.

(5) A statutory instrument that is not subject to the affirmative procedure by virtue of subsection (2) is subject to the negative procedure.

(6) If a statutory instrument is subject to the affirmative procedure, the order or regulations contained in it must not be made unless a draft of the instrument is laid before and approved by a resolution of the National Assembly for Wales.

(7) If a statutory instrument is subject to the negative procedure, it is subject to annulment in pursuance of a resolution of the National Assembly for Wales.

NOTES

Commencement: 8 April 2010.

[1.1761]
210 The Scottish Ministers

(1) This section applies where the power to make an order, regulations or rules under this Act is exercisable by the Scottish Ministers.

(2) A statutory instrument containing (whether alone or with other provision) an order or regulations mentioned in subsection (3) is subject to the affirmative procedure.

(3) The orders and regulations referred to in subsection (2) are—

(a) regulations under section 2 (socio-economic inequalities);

(b) regulations under section 37 (power to make provision about adjustments to common parts in Scotland);

(c) an order under section 151 (power to amend list of public authorities for the purposes of the public sector equality duty);

(d) regulations under section 153 or 154(2) (public sector equality duty: powers to impose specific duties);

(e) regulations under section 155(5) that amend an Act of Parliament or an Act of the Scottish Parliament (public sector equality duty: power to modify or remove specific duties).

(4) But a statutory instrument is not subject to the affirmative procedure by virtue of subsection (2) merely because it contains an order under section 151 that provides for—

(a) the omission of an entry where the authority concerned has ceased to exist, or

(b) the variation of an entry where the authority concerned has changed its name.

(5) A statutory instrument that is not subject to the affirmative procedure by virtue of subsection (2) is subject to the negative procedure.

(6) If a statutory instrument is subject to the affirmative procedure, the order or regulations contained in it must not be made unless a draft of the instrument is laid before and approved by a resolution of the Scottish Parliament.

(7) If a statutory instrument is subject to the negative procedure, it is subject to annulment in pursuance of a resolution of the Scottish Parliament.

NOTES

Commencement: 8 April 2010.

Amendments, etc

211 *(Introduces Sch 26 (Amendments) and Sch 27 (Repeals and Revocations.)*

Interpretation

[1.1762]

212 General interpretation

(1) In this Act—

"armed forces" means any of the naval, military or air forces of the Crown;

"the Commission" means the Commission for Equality and Human Rights;

"detriment" does not, subject to subsection (5), include conduct which amounts to harassment;

"the Education Acts" has the meaning given in section 578 of the Education Act 1996;

"employment" and related expressions are (subject to subsection (11)) to be read with section 83;

"enactment" means an enactment contained in—

(a) an Act of Parliament,

(b) an Act of the Scottish Parliament,

(c) an Act or Measure of the National Assembly for Wales, or

(d) subordinate legislation;

"equality clause" means a sex equality clause or maternity equality clause;

"equality rule" means a sex equality rule or maternity equality rule;

"man" means a male of any age;

"maternity equality clause" has the meaning given in section 73;

"maternity equality rule" has the meaning given in section 75;

"non-discrimination rule" has the meaning given in section 61;

"occupational pension scheme" has the meaning given in section 1 of the Pension Schemes Act 1993;

"parent" has the same meaning as in—

(a) the Education Act 1996 (in relation to England and Wales);

(b) the Education (Scotland) Act 1980 (in relation to Scotland);

"prescribed" means prescribed by regulations;

"profession" includes a vocation or occupation;

"sex equality clause" has the meaning given in section 66;

"sex equality rule" has the meaning given in section 67;

"subordinate legislation" means—

(a) subordinate legislation within the meaning of the Interpretation Act 1978, or

(b) an instrument made under an Act of the Scottish Parliament or an Act or Measure of the National Assembly for Wales;

"substantial" means more than minor or trivial;

"trade" includes any business;

"woman" means a female of any age.

(2) A reference (however expressed) to an act includes a reference to an omission.

(3) A reference (however expressed) to an omission includes (unless there is express provision to the contrary) a reference to—

(a) a deliberate omission to do something;
(b) a refusal to do it;
(c) a failure to do it.

(4) A reference (however expressed) to providing or affording access to a benefit, facility or service includes a reference to facilitating access to the benefit, facility or service.

(5) Where this Act disapplies a prohibition on harassment in relation to a specified protected characteristic, the disapplication does not prevent conduct relating to that characteristic from amounting to a detriment for the purposes of discrimination within section 13 because of that characteristic.

(6) A reference to occupation, in relation to premises, is a reference to lawful occupation.

(7) The following are members of the executive—
(a) a Minister of the Crown;
(b) a government department;
(c) the Welsh Ministers, the First Minister for Wales or the Counsel General to the Welsh Assembly Government;
(d) any part of the Scottish Administration.

(8) A reference to a breach of an equality clause or rule is a reference to a breach of a term modified by, or included by virtue of, an equality clause or rule.

(9) A reference to a contravention of this Act does not include a reference to a breach of an equality clause or rule, unless there is express provision to the contrary.

(10) "Member", in relation to an occupational pension scheme, means an active member, a deferred member or a pensioner member (within the meaning, in each case, given by section 124 of the Pensions Act 1995).

(11) "Employer", "deferred member", "pension credit member", "pensionable service", "pensioner member" and "trustees or managers" each have, in relation to an occupational pension scheme, the meaning given by section 124 of the Pensions Act 1995.

(12) A reference to the accrual of rights under an occupational pension scheme is to be construed in accordance with that section.

(13) Nothing in section 28, 32, 84, 90, 95 or 100 is to be regarded as an express exception.

NOTES

Commencement: 8 April 2010.

[1.1763]

213 References to maternity leave, etc

(1) This section applies for the purposes of this Act.

(2) A reference to a woman on maternity leave is a reference to a woman on—
(a) compulsory maternity leave,
(b) ordinary maternity leave, or
(c) additional maternity leave.

(3) A reference to a woman on compulsory maternity leave is a reference to a woman absent from work because she satisfies the conditions prescribed for the purposes of section 72(1) of the Employment Rights Act 1996.

(4) A reference to a woman on ordinary maternity leave is a reference to a woman absent from work because she is exercising the right to ordinary maternity leave.

(5) A reference to the right to ordinary maternity leave is a reference to the right conferred by section 71(1) of the Employment Rights Act 1996.

(6) A reference to a woman on additional maternity leave is a reference to a woman absent from work because she is exercising the right to additional maternity leave.

(7) A reference to the right to additional maternity leave is a reference to the right conferred by section 73(1) of the Employment Rights Act 1996.

(8) "Additional maternity leave period" has the meaning given in section 73(2) of that Act.

NOTES

Commencement: 8 April 2010.

[1.1764]

214 Index of defined expressions

Schedule 28 lists the places where expressions used in this Act are defined or otherwise explained.

NOTES

Commencement: 8 April 2010.

Final provisions

[1.1765]

215 Money

There is to be paid out of money provided by Parliament any increase attributable to this Act in the expenses of a Minister of the Crown.

NOTES

Commencement: 8 April 2010.

[1.1766]

216 Commencement

(1) The following provisions come into force on the day on which this Act is passed—

(a) section 186(2) (rail vehicle accessibility: compliance);

(b) this Part (except sections 202 (civil partnerships on religious premises), 206 (information society services) and 211 (amendments, etc)).

(2) Part 15 (family property) comes into force on such day as the Lord Chancellor may by order appoint.

(3) The other provisions of this Act come into force on such day as a Minister of the Crown may by order appoint.

NOTES

Commencement: 8 April 2010.

Orders: the Equality Act 2010 (Commencement No 1) Order 2010, SI 2010/1736; the Equality Act 2010 (Commencement No 2) Order 2010, SI 2010/1966; the Equality Act 2010 (Commencement No 3) Order 2010, SI 2010/2191; the Equality Act 2010 (Consequential Amendments, Saving and Supplementary Provisions) Order 2010, SI 2010/2279; the Equality Act 2010 (Commencement No 4, Savings, Consequential, Transitional, Transitory and Incidental Provisions and Revocation) Order 2010, SI 2010/2317 at **[2.1558]**; the Equality Act 2010 (Commencement No 4, Savings, Consequential, Transitional, Transitory and Incidental Provisions and Revocation) Order 2010 (Amendment) Order 2010, SI 2010/2337; the Equality Act 2010 (Commencement No 5) Order 2011, SI 2011/96; the Equality Act 2010 (Commencement No 6) Order 2011, SI 2011/1066; the Equality Act 2010 (Commencement No 7) Order 2011, SI 2011/1636; the Equality Act 2010 (Commencement No 8) Order 2011, SI 2011/2646; the Equality Act 2010 (Commencement No 9) Order 2012, SI 2012/1569; the Equality Act 2010 (Commencement No 10) Order 2012, SI 2012/2184.

[1.1767]

217 Extent

(1) This Act forms part of the law of England and Wales.

(2) This Act, apart from section 190 (improvements to let dwelling houses) and Part 15 (family property), forms part of the law of Scotland.

(3) Each of the following also forms part of the law of Northern Ireland—

(a) section 82 (offshore work);

(b) section 105(3) and (4) (expiry of Sex Discrimination (Election Candidates) Act 2002);

(c) section 199 (abolition of presumption of advancement).

NOTES

Commencement: 8 April 2010.

[1.1768]

218 Short title

This Act may be cited as the Equality Act 2010.

NOTES

Commencement: 8 April 2010.

SCHEDULES

SCHEDULE 1
DISABILITY: SUPPLEMENTARY PROVISION

Section 6

PART 1
DETERMINATION OF DISABILITY

[1.1769]

1. Impairment

Regulations may make provision for a condition of a prescribed description to be, or not to be, an impairment.

2. Long-term effects

(1) The effect of an impairment is long-term if—

(a) it has lasted for at least 12 months,

(b) it is likely to last for at least 12 months, or

(c) it is likely to last for the rest of the life of the person affected.

(2) If an impairment ceases to have a substantial adverse effect on a person's ability to carry out normal day-to-day activities, it is to be treated as continuing to have that effect if that effect is likely to recur.

(3) For the purposes of sub-paragraph (2), the likelihood of an effect recurring is to be disregarded in such circumstances as may be prescribed.

(4) Regulations may prescribe circumstances in which, despite sub-paragraph (1), an effect is to be treated as being, or as not being, long-term.

3. Severe disfigurement

(1) An impairment which consists of a severe disfigurement is to be treated as having a substantial adverse effect on the ability of the person concerned to carry out normal day-to-day activities.

(2) Regulations may provide that in prescribed circumstances a severe disfigurement is not to be treated as having that effect.

(3) The regulations may, in particular, make provision in relation to deliberately acquired disfigurement.

4. Substantial adverse effects

Regulations may make provision for an effect of a prescribed description on the ability of a person to carry out normal day-to-day activities to be treated as being, or as not being, a substantial adverse effect.

5. Effect of medical treatment

(1) An impairment is to be treated as having a substantial adverse effect on the ability of the person concerned to carry out normal day-to-day activities if—
  (a) measures are being taken to treat or correct it, and
  (b) but for that, it would be likely to have that effect.

(2) "Measures" includes, in particular, medical treatment and the use of a prosthesis or other aid.

(3) Sub-paragraph (1) does not apply—
  (a) in relation to the impairment of a person's sight, to the extent that the impairment is, in the person's case, correctable by spectacles or contact lenses or in such other ways as may be prescribed;
  (b) in relation to such other impairments as may be prescribed, in such circumstances as are prescribed.

6. Certain medical conditions

(1) Cancer, HIV infection and multiple sclerosis are each a disability.

(2) HIV infection is infection by a virus capable of causing the Acquired Immune Deficiency Syndrome.

7. Deemed disability

(1) Regulations may provide for persons of prescribed descriptions to be treated as having disabilities.

(2) The regulations may prescribe circumstances in which a person who has a disability is to be treated as no longer having the disability.

(3) This paragraph does not affect the other provisions of this Schedule.

8. Progressive conditions

(1) This paragraph applies to a person (P) if—
  (a) P has a progressive condition,
  (b) as a result of that condition P has an impairment which has (or had) an effect on P's ability to carry out normal day-to-day activities, but
  (c) the effect is not (or was not) a substantial adverse effect.

(2) P is to be taken to have an impairment which has a substantial adverse effect if the condition is likely to result in P having such an impairment.

(3) Regulations may make provision for a condition of a prescribed description to be treated as being, or as not being, progressive.

9. Past disabilities

(1) A question as to whether a person had a disability at a particular time ("the relevant time") is to be determined, for the purposes of section 6, as if the provisions of, or made under, this Act were in force when the act complained of was done had been in force at the relevant time.

(2) The relevant time may be a time before the coming into force of the provision of this Act to which the question relates.

NOTES

Commencement: 6 July 2010 (paras 1–5, 7, 8 for the purpose of enabling subordinate legislation or guidance to be made); 1 October 2010 (otherwise).

Regulations: the Equality Act 2010 (Disability) Regulations 2010, SI 2010/2128 at **[2.1506]**.

PART 2
GUIDANCE

[1.1770]

10. Preliminary

This Part of this Schedule applies in relation to guidance referred to in section 6(5).

11. Examples

The guidance may give examples of—

(a) effects which it would, or would not, be reasonable, in relation to particular activities, to regard as substantial adverse effects;

(b) substantial adverse effects which it would, or would not, be reasonable to regard as long-term.

12. Adjudicating bodies

(1) In determining whether a person is a disabled person, an adjudicating body must take account of such guidance as it thinks is relevant.

(2) An adjudicating body is—

(a) a court;

(b) a tribunal;

(c) a person (other than a court or tribunal) who may decide a claim relating to a contravention of Part 6 (education).

13. Representations

Before issuing the guidance, the Minister must—

(a) publish a draft of it;

(b) consider any representations made to the Minister about the draft;

(c) make such modifications as the Minister thinks appropriate in the light of the representations.

14. Parliamentary procedure

(1) If the Minister decides to proceed with proposed guidance, a draft of it must be laid before Parliament.

(2) If, before the end of the 40-day period, either House resolves not to approve the draft, the Minister must take no further steps in relation to the proposed guidance.

(3) If no such resolution is made before the end of that period, the Minister must issue the guidance in the form of the draft.

(4) Sub-paragraph (2) does not prevent a new draft of proposed guidance being laid before Parliament.

(5) The 40-day period—

(a) begins on the date on which the draft is laid before both Houses (or, if laid before each House on a different date, on the later date);

(b) does not include a period during which Parliament is prorogued or dissolved;

(c) does not include a period during which both Houses are adjourned for more than 4 days.

15. Commencement

The guidance comes into force on the day appointed by order by the Minister.

16. Revision and revocation

(1) The Minister may—

(a) revise the whole or part of guidance and re-issue it;

(b) by order revoke guidance.

(2) A reference to guidance includes a reference to guidance which has been revised and re-issued.

NOTES

Commencement: 6 July 2010 (paras 10, 11, 13–16 for the purpose of enabling subordinate legislation or guidance to be made); 1 October 2010 (otherwise).

Orders: the Equality Act 2010 (Guidance on the Definition of Disability) Appointed Day Order 2011, SI 2011/1159 at **[2.1608]**. The Guidance introduced by this order is at **[4.238]**.

SCHEDULES 2–5

(Sch 2 (Services and Public Functions: Reasonable Adjustments), Sch 3 (Services and Public Functions: Exceptions), Sch 4 (Premises: Reasonable Adjustments), Sch 5 (Premises: Exceptions) outside the scope of this work.)

SCHEDULE 6
OFFICE-HOLDERS: EXCLUDED OFFICES

Section 52

[1.1771]

1. Work to which other provisions apply

(1) An office or post is not a personal or public office in so far as one or more of the provisions mentioned in sub-paragraph (2)—

(a) applies in relation to the office or post, or

(b) would apply in relation to the office or post but for the operation of some other provision of this Act.

(2) Those provisions are—

(a) section 39 (employment);

(b) section 41 (contract work);

(c) section 44 (partnerships).

(d) section 45 (LLPs);

(e) section 47 (barristers);

(f) section 48 (advocates);

(g) section 55 (employment services) so far as applying to the provision of work experience within section 56(2)(a) or arrangements within section 56(2)(c) for such provision.

2. Political offices

(1) An office or post is not a personal or public office if it is a political office.

(2) A political office is an office or post set out in the second column of the following Table—

Political setting	Office or post
Houses of Parliament	An office of the House of Commons held by a member of that House
	An office of the House of Lords held by a member of that House
	A Ministerial office within the meaning of section 2 of the House of Commons Disqualification Act 1975
	The office of the Leader of the Opposition within the meaning of the Ministerial and other Salaries Act 1975
	The office of the Chief Opposition Whip, or of an Assistant Opposition Whip, within the meaning of that Act
Scottish Parliament	An office of the Scottish Parliament held by a member of the Parliament
	The office of a member of the Scottish Executive
	The office of a junior Scottish Minister
National Assembly for Wales	An office of the National Assembly for Wales held by a member of the Assembly
	The office of a member of the Welsh Assembly Government
Local government in England (outside London)	An office of a county council, district council or parish council in England held by a member of the council
	An office of the Council of the Isles of Scilly held by a member of the Council
Local government in London	An office of the Greater London Authority held by the Mayor of London or a member of the London Assembly
	An office of a London borough council held by a member of the council
	An office of the Common Council of the City of London held by a member of the Council
Local government in Wales	An office of a county council, county borough council or community council in Wales held by a member of the council

Political setting	Office or post
Local government in Scotland	An office of a council constituted under section 2 of the Local Government etc (Scotland) Act 1994 held by a member of the council An office of a council established under section 51 of the Local Government (Scotland) Act 1973 held by a member of the council
Political parties	An office of a registered political party

(3) The reference to a registered political party is a reference to a party registered in the Great Britain register under Part 2 of the Political Parties, Elections and Referendums Act 2000.

3. Honours etc

A life peerage (within the meaning of the Life Peerages Act 1958), or any other dignity or honour conferred by the Crown, is not a personal or public office.

NOTES

Commencement: 1 October 2010.

SCHEDULE 7
EQUALITY OF TERMS: EXCEPTIONS

Section 80

PART 1
TERMS OF WORK

[1.1772]

1. Compliance with laws regulating employment of women, etc

Neither a sex equality clause nor a maternity equality clause has effect in relation to terms of work affected by compliance with laws regulating—

(a) the employment of women;
(b) the appointment of women to personal or public offices.

2. Pregnancy, etc

A sex equality clause does not have effect in relation to terms of work affording special treatment to women in connection with pregnancy or childbirth.

NOTES

Commencement: 1 October 2010.

PART 2
OCCUPATIONAL PENSION SCHEMES

Preliminary

[1.1773]

3. (1) A sex equality rule does not have effect in relation to a difference as between men and women in the effect of a relevant matter if the difference is permitted by or by virtue of this Part of this Schedule.

(2) "Relevant matter" has the meaning given in section 67.

4. State retirement pensions

(1) This paragraph applies where a man and a woman are eligible, in such circumstances as may be prescribed, to receive different amounts by way of pension.

(2) The difference is permitted if, in prescribed circumstances, it is attributable only to differences between men and women in the retirement benefits to which, in prescribed circumstances, the man and woman are or would be entitled.

(3) "Retirement benefits" are benefits under sections 43 to 55 of the Social Security Contributions and Benefits Act 1992 (state retirement pensions).

5. Actuarial factors

(1) A difference as between men and women is permitted if it consists of applying to the calculation of the employer's contributions to an occupational pension scheme actuarial factors which—

(a) differ for men and women, and
(b) are of such description as may be prescribed.

(2) A difference as between men and women is permitted if it consists of applying to the determination of benefits of such description as may be prescribed actuarial factors which differ for men and women.

6. Power to amend

(1) Regulations may amend this Part of this Schedule so as to add, vary or omit provision about cases where a difference as between men and women in the effect of a relevant matter is permitted.

(2) The regulations may make provision about pensionable service before the date on which they come into force (but not about pensionable service before 17 May 1990).

NOTES

Commencement: 6 July 2010 (paras 4–6 for the purpose of enabling subordinate legislation or guidance to be made); 1 October 2010 (otherwise).

Regulations: the Equality Act 2010 (Sex Equality Rule) (Exceptions) Regulations 2010, SI 2010/2132 at **[2.1522]**.

SCHEDULE 8
WORK: REASONABLE ADJUSTMENTS

Section 83

PART 1
INTRODUCTORY

[1.1774]

1. Preliminary

This Schedule applies where a duty to make reasonable adjustments is imposed on A by this Part of this Act.

2. The duty

(1) A must comply with the first, second and third requirements.

(2) For the purposes of this paragraph—

- (a) the reference in section 20(3) to a provision, criterion or practice is a reference to a provision, criterion or practice applied by or on behalf of A;
- (b) the reference in section 20(4) to a physical feature is a reference to a physical feature of premises occupied by A;
- (c) the reference in section 20(3), (4) or (5) to a disabled person is to an interested disabled person.

(3) In relation to the first and third requirements, a relevant matter is any matter specified in the first column of the applicable table in Part 2 of this Schedule.

(4) In relation to the second requirement, a relevant matter is—

- (a) a matter specified in the second entry of the first column of the applicable table in Part 2 of this Schedule, or
- (b) where there is only one entry in a column, a matter specified there.

(5) If two or more persons are subject to a duty to make reasonable adjustments in relation to the same interested disabled person, each of them must comply with the duty so far as it is reasonable for each of them to do so.

3. (1) This paragraph applies if a duty to make reasonable adjustments is imposed on A by section 55 (except where the employment service which A provides is the provision of vocational training within the meaning given by section 56(6)(b)).

(2) The reference in section 20(3), (4) and (5) to a disabled person is a reference to an interested disabled person.

(3) In relation to each requirement, the relevant matter is the employment service which A provides.

(4) Sub-paragraph (5) of paragraph 2 applies for the purposes of this paragraph as it applies for the purposes of that paragraph.

NOTES

Commencement: 1 October 2010.

PART 2
INTERESTED DISABLED PERSON

[1.1775]
4. Preliminary

An interested disabled person is a disabled person who, in relation to a relevant matter, is of a description specified in the second column of the applicable table in this Part of this Schedule.

5. Employers (see section 39)

(1) This paragraph applies where A is an employer.

Relevant matter	Description of disabled person
Deciding to whom to offer employment.	A person who is, or has notified A that the person may be, an applicant for the employment.
Employment by A.	An applicant for employment by A.
	An employee of A's.

(2) Where A is the employer of a disabled contract worker (B), A must comply with the first, second and third requirements on each occasion when B is supplied to a principal to do contract work.

(3) In relation to the first requirement (as it applies for the purposes of sub-paragraph (2))—
- (a) the reference in section 20(3) to a provision, criterion or practice is a reference to a provision, criterion or practice applied by or on behalf of all or most of the principals to whom B is or might be supplied,
- (b) the reference to being put at a substantial disadvantage is a reference to being likely to be put at a substantial disadvantage that is the same or similar in the case of each of the principals referred to in paragraph (a), and
- (c) the requirement imposed on A is a requirement to take such steps as it would be reasonable for A to have to take if the provision, criterion or practice were applied by or on behalf of A.

(4) In relation to the second requirement (as it applies for the purposes of sub-paragraph (2))—
- (a) the reference in section 20(4) to a physical feature is a reference to a physical feature of premises occupied by each of the principals referred to in sub-paragraph (3)(a),
- (b) the reference to being put at a substantial disadvantage is a reference to being likely to be put at a substantial disadvantage that is the same or similar in the case of each of those principals, and
- (c) the requirement imposed on A is a requirement to take such steps as it would be reasonable for A to have to take if the premises were occupied by A.

(5) In relation to the third requirement (as it applies for the purposes of sub-paragraph (2))—
- (a) the reference in section 20(5) to being put at a substantial disadvantage is a reference to being likely to be put at a substantial disadvantage that is the same or similar in the case of each of the principals referred to in sub-paragraph (3)(a), and
- (b) the requirement imposed on A is a requirement to take such steps as it would be reasonable for A to have to take if A were the person to whom B was supplied.

6. Principals in contract work (see section 41)

(1) This paragraph applies where A is a principal.

Relevant matter	Description of disabled person
Contract work that A may make available.	A person who is, or has notified A that the person may be, an applicant to do the work.
Contract work that A makes available.	A person who is supplied to do the work.

(2) A is not required to do anything that a disabled person's employer is required to do by virtue of paragraph 5.

7. Partnerships (see section 44)

(1) This paragraph applies where A is a firm or a proposed firm.

Relevant matter	Description of disabled person
Deciding to whom to offer a position as a partner.	A person who is, or has notified A that the person may be, a candidate for the position.
A position as a partner.	A candidate for the position.
	The partner who holds the position.

(2) Where a firm or proposed firm (A) is required by this Schedule to take a step in relation to an interested disabled person (B)—

(a) the cost of taking the step is to be treated as an expense of A;

(b) the extent to which B should (if B is or becomes a partner) bear the cost is not to exceed such amount as is reasonable (having regard in particular to B's entitlement to share in A's profits).

8. LLPs (see section 45)

(1) This paragraph applies where A is an LLP or a proposed LLP.

Relevant matter	Description of disabled person
Deciding to whom to offer a position as a member.	A person who is, or has notified A that the person may be, a candidate for the position.
A position as a member.	A candidate for the position.
	The member who holds the position.

(2) Where an LLP or proposed LLP (A) is required by this Schedule to take a step in relation to an interested disabled person (B)—

(a) the cost of taking the step is to be treated as an expense of A;

(b) the extent to which B should (if B is or becomes a member) bear the cost is not to exceed such amount as is reasonable (having regard in particular to B's entitlement to share in A's profits).

9. Barristers and their clerks (see section 47)

This paragraph applies where A is a barrister or barrister's clerk.

Relevant matter	Description of disabled person
Deciding to whom to offer a pupillage or tenancy.	A person who is, or has notified A that the person may be, an applicant for the pupillage or tenancy.
A pupillage or tenancy.	An applicant for the pupillage or tenancy.
	The pupil or tenant.

10. Advocates and their clerks (see section 48)

This paragraph applies where A is an advocate or advocate's clerk.

Relevant matter	Description of disabled person
Deciding who to offer to take as a devil or to whom to offer membership of a stable.	A person who applies, or has notified A that the person may apply, to be taken as a devil or to become a member of the stable.
The relationship with a devil or membership of a stable.	An applicant to be taken as a devil or to become a member of the stable.
	The devil or member.

11. Persons making appointments to offices etc (see sections 49 to 51)

This paragraph applies where A is a person who has the power to make an appointment to a personal or public office.

Relevant matter	Description of disabled person
Deciding to whom to offer the appointment.	A person who is, or has notified A that the person may be, seeking the appointment.
	A person who is being considered for the appointment.
Appointment to the office.	A person who is seeking, or being considered for, appointment to the office.

12. This paragraph applies where A is a relevant person in relation to a personal or public office.

Relevant matter	Description of disabled person
Appointment to the office.	A person appointed to the office.

13. This paragraph applies where A is a person who has the power to make a recommendation for, or give approval to, an appointment to a public office.

Relevant matter	Description of disabled person
Deciding who to recommend or approve for appointment to the office.	A person who is, or has notified A that the person may be, seeking recommendation or approval for appointment to the office.
	A person who is being considered for recommendation or approval for appointment to the office.
An appointment to the office.	A person who is seeking, or being considered for, appointment to the office in question.

14. In relation to the second requirement in a case within paragraph 11, 12 or 13, the reference in paragraph 2(2)(b) to premises occupied by A is to be read as a reference to premises—
- (a) under the control of A, and
- (b) at or from which the functions of the office concerned are performed.

15. Qualifications bodies (see section 53)

(1) This paragraph applies where A is a qualifications body.

Relevant matter	Description of disabled person
Deciding upon whom to confer a relevant qualification.	A person who is, or has notified A that the person may be, an applicant for the conferment of the qualification.
Conferment by the body of a relevant qualification.	An applicant for the conferment of the qualification.
	A person who holds the qualification.

(2) A provision, criterion or practice does not include the application of a competence standard.

16. Employment service-providers (see section 55)

This paragraph applies where—
- (a) A is an employment service-provider, and
- (b) the employment service which A provides is vocational training within the meaning given by section 56(6)(b).

Relevant matter	Description of disabled person
Deciding to whom to offer to provide the service.	A person who is, or has notified A that the person may be, an applicant for the provision of the service.
Provision by A of the service.	A person who applies to A for the provision of the service.
	A person to whom A provides the service.

17. Trade organisations (see section 57)

This paragraph applies where A is a trade organisation.

Relevant matter	Description of disabled person
Deciding to whom to offer membership of the organisation.	A person who is, or has notified A that the person may be, an applicant for membership.
Membership of the organisation.	An applicant for membership.
	A member.

18. Local authorities (see section 58)

(1) This paragraph applies where A is a local authority.

Relevant matter	Description of disabled person
A member's carrying-out of official business.	The member.

(2) Regulations may, for the purposes of a case within this paragraph, make provision—
- (a) as to circumstances in which a provision, criterion or practice is, or is not, to be taken to put a disabled person at the disadvantage referred to in the first requirement;
- (b) as to circumstances in which a physical feature is, or is not, to be taken to put a disabled person at the disadvantage referred to in the second requirement;

(c) as to circumstances in which it is, or in which it is not, reasonable for a local authority to be required to take steps of a prescribed description;
(d) as to steps which it is always, or which it is never, reasonable for a local authority to take.

19. Occupational pensions (see section 61)

This paragraph applies where A is, in relation to an occupational pension scheme, a responsible person within the meaning of section 61.

Relevant matter	Description of disabled person
Carrying out A's functions in relation to the scheme.	A person who is or may be a member of the scheme.

NOTES

Commencement: 1 October 2010.

PART 3
LIMITATIONS ON THE DUTY

[1.1776]

20. Lack of knowledge of disability, etc

(1) A is not subject to a duty to make reasonable adjustments if A does not know, and could not reasonably be expected to know—

(a) in the case of an applicant or potential applicant, that an interested disabled person is or may be an applicant for the work in question;
(b) [in any case referred to in Part 2 of this Schedule], that an interested disabled person has a disability and is likely to be placed at the disadvantage referred to in the first, second or third requirement.

(2) An applicant is, in relation to the description of A specified in the first column of the table, a person of a description specified in the second column (and the reference to a potential applicant is to be construed accordingly).

Description of A	Applicant
An employer	An applicant for employment
A firm or proposed firm	A candidate for a position as a partner
An LLP or proposed LLP	A candidate for a position as a member
A barrister or barrister's clerk	An applicant for a pupillage or tenancy
An advocate or advocate's clerk	An applicant for being taken as an advocate's devil or for becoming a member of a stable
A relevant person in relation to a personal or public office	A person who is seeking appointment to, or recommendation or approval for appointment to, the office
A qualifications body	An applicant for the conferment of a relevant qualification
An employment service-provider	An applicant for the provision of an employment service
A trade organisation	An applicant for membership

(3) If the duty to make reasonable adjustments is imposed on A by section 55, this paragraph applies only in so far as the employment service which A provides is vocational training within the meaning given by section 56(6)(b).

NOTES

Commencement: 1 October 2010.

Para 20: words in square brackets in sub-para (1)(b) substituted by Equality Act 2010 (Public Authorities and Consequential and Supplementary Amendments) Order, SI 2011/1060, art 6(1), (2), as from 4 April 2011.

SCHEDULE 9
WORK: EXCEPTIONS

Section 83

PART 1
OCCUPATIONAL REQUIREMENTS

[1.1777]

1. General

(1) A person (A) does not contravene a provision mentioned in sub-paragraph (2) by applying in relation to work a requirement to have a particular protected characteristic, if A shows that, having regard to the nature or context of the work—

(a) it is an occupational requirement,

(b) the application of the requirement is a proportionate means of achieving a legitimate aim, and

(c) the person to whom A applies the requirement does not meet it (or A has reasonable grounds for not being satisfied that the person meets it).

(2) The provisions are—

(a) section 39(1)(a) or (c) or (2)(b) or (c);

(b) section 41(1)(b);

(c) section 44(1)(a) or (c) or (2)(b) or (c);

(d) section 45(1)(a) or (c) or (2)(b) or (c);

(e) section 49(3)(a) or (c) or (6)(b) or (c);

(f) section 50(3)(a) or (c) or (6)(b) or (c);

(g) section 51(1).

(3) The references in sub-paragraph (1) to a requirement to have a protected characteristic are to be read—

(a) in the case of gender reassignment, as references to a requirement not to be a transsexual person (and section 7(3) is accordingly to be ignored);

(b) in the case of marriage and civil partnership, as references to a requirement not to be married or a civil partner (and section 8(2) is accordingly to be ignored).

(4) In the case of a requirement to be of a particular sex, sub-paragraph (1) has effect as if in paragraph (c), the words from "(or" to the end were omitted.

2. Religious requirements relating to sex, marriage etc, sexual orientation

(1) A person (A) does not contravene a provision mentioned in sub-paragraph (2) by applying in relation to employment a requirement to which sub-paragraph (4) applies if A shows that—

(a) the employment is for the purposes of an organised religion,

(b) the application of the requirement engages the compliance or non-conflict principle, and

(c) the person to whom A applies the requirement does not meet it (or A has reasonable grounds for not being satisfied that the person meets it).

(2) The provisions are—

(a) section 39(1)(a) or (c) or (2)(b) or (c);

(b) section 49(3)(a) or (c) or (6)(b) or (c);

(c) section 50(3)(a) or (c) or (6)(b) or (c);

(d) section 51(1).

(3) A person does not contravene section 53(1) or (2)(a) or (b) by applying in relation to a relevant qualification (within the meaning of that section) a requirement to which sub-paragraph (4) applies if the person shows that—

(a) the qualification is for the purposes of employment mentioned in sub-paragraph (1)(a), and

(b) the application of the requirement engages the compliance or non-conflict principle.

(4) This sub-paragraph applies to—

(a) a requirement to be of a particular sex;

(b) a requirement not to be a transsexual person;

(c) a requirement not to be married or a civil partner;

(d) a requirement not to be married to, or the civil partner of, a person who has a living former spouse or civil partner;

(e) a requirement relating to circumstances in which a marriage or civil partnership came to an end;

(f) a requirement related to sexual orientation.

(5) The application of a requirement engages the compliance principle if the requirement is applied so as to comply with the doctrines of the religion.

(6) The application of a requirement engages the non-conflict principle if, because of the nature or context of the employment, the requirement is applied so as to avoid conflicting with the strongly held religious convictions of a significant number of the religion's followers.

(7) A reference to employment includes a reference to an appointment to a personal or public office.

(8) In the case of a requirement within sub-paragraph (4)(a), sub-paragraph (1) has effect as if in paragraph (c) the words from "(or" to the end were omitted.

3. Other requirements relating to religion or belief

A person (A) with an ethos based on religion or belief does not contravene a provision mentioned in paragraph 1(2) by applying in relation to work a requirement to be of a particular religion or belief if A shows that, having regard to that ethos and to the nature or context of the work—

(a) it is an occupational requirement,

(b) the application of the requirement is a proportionate means of achieving a legitimate aim, and

(c) the person to whom A applies the requirement does not meet it (or A has reasonable grounds for not being satisfied that the person meets it).

4. Armed forces

(1) A person does not contravene section 39(1)(a) or (c) or (2)(b) by applying in relation to service in the armed forces a relevant requirement if the person shows that the application is a proportionate means of ensuring the combat effectiveness of the armed forces.

(2) A relevant requirement is—

(a) a requirement to be a man;

(b) a requirement not to be a transsexual person.

(3) This Part of this Act, so far as relating to age or disability, does not apply to service in the armed forces; and section 55, so far as relating to disability, does not apply to work experience in the armed forces.

5. Employment services

(1) A person (A) does not contravene section 55(1) or (2) if A shows that A's treatment of another person relates only to work the offer of which could be refused to that other person in reliance on paragraph 1, 2, 3 or 4.

(2) A person (A) does not contravene section 55(1) or (2) if A shows that A's treatment of another person relates only to training for work of a description mentioned in sub-paragraph (1).

(3) A person (A) does not contravene section 55(1) or (2) if A shows that—

(a) A acted in reliance on a statement made to A by a person with the power to offer the work in question to the effect that, by virtue of sub-paragraph (1) or (2), A's action would be lawful, and

(b) it was reasonable for A to rely on the statement.

(4) A person commits an offence by knowingly or recklessly making a statement such as is mentioned in sub-paragraph (3)(a) which in a material respect is false or misleading.

(5) A person guilty of an offence under sub-paragraph (4) is liable on summary conviction to a fine not exceeding level 5 on the standard scale.

6. Interpretation

(1) This paragraph applies for the purposes of this Part of this Schedule.

(2) A reference to contravening a provision of this Act is a reference to contravening that provision by virtue of section 13.

(3) A reference to work is a reference to employment, contract work, a position as a partner or as a member of an LLP, or an appointment to a personal or public office.

(4) A reference to a person includes a reference to an organisation.

(5) A reference to section 39(2)(b), 44(2)(b), 45(2)(b), 49(6)(b) or 50(6)(b) is to be read as a reference to that provision with the omission of the words "or for receiving any other benefit, facility or service".

(6) A reference to section 39(2)(c), 44(2)(c), 45(2)(c), 49(6)(c), 50(6)(c), 53(2)(a) or 55(2)(c) (dismissal, etc) does not include a reference to that provision so far as relating to sex.

(7) The reference to paragraph (b) of section 41(1), so far as relating to sex, is to be read as if that paragraph read—

"(b) by not allowing the worker to do the work."

NOTES

Commencement: 1 October 2010.

PART 2
EXCEPTIONS RELATING TO AGE

[1.1778]
7. Preliminary

For the purposes of this Part of this Schedule, a reference to an age contravention is a reference to a contravention of this Part of this Act, so far as relating to age.

8, 9. . . .

10. Benefits based on length of service

(1) It is not an age contravention for a person (A) to put a person (B) at a disadvantage when compared with another (C), in relation to the provision of a benefit, facility or service in so far as the disadvantage is because B has a shorter period of service than C.

(2) If B's period of service exceeds 5 years, A may rely on sub-paragraph (1) only if A reasonably believes that doing so fulfils a business need.

(3) A person's period of service is whichever of the following A chooses—
- (a) the period for which the person has been working for A at or above a level (assessed by reference to the demands made on the person) that A reasonably regards as appropriate for the purposes of this paragraph, or
- (b) the period for which the person has been working for A at any level.

(4) The period for which a person has been working for A must be based on the number of weeks during the whole or part of which the person has worked for A.

(5) But for that purpose A may, so far as is reasonable, discount—
- (a) periods of absence;
- (b) periods that A reasonably regards as related to periods of absence.

(6) For the purposes of sub-paragraph (3)(b), a person is to be treated as having worked for A during any period in which the person worked for a person other than A if—
- (a) that period counts as a period of employment with A as a result of section 218 of the Employment Rights Act 1996, or
- (b) if sub-paragraph (a) does not apply, that period is treated as a period of employment by an enactment pursuant to which the person's employment was transferred to A.

(7) For the purposes of this paragraph, the reference to a benefit, facility or service does not include a reference to a benefit, facility or service which may be provided only by virtue of a person's ceasing to work.

11. The national minimum wage: young workers

(1) It is not an age contravention for a person to pay a young worker (A) at a lower rate than that at which the person pays an older worker (B) if—
- (a) the hourly rate for the national minimum wage for a person of A's age is lower than that for a person of B's age, and
- (b) the rate at which A is paid is below the single hourly rate.

(2) A young worker is a person who qualifies for the national minimum wage at a lower rate than the single hourly rate; and an older worker is a person who qualifies for the national minimum wage at a higher rate than that at which the young worker qualifies for it.

(3) The single hourly rate is the rate prescribed under section 1(3) of the National Minimum Wage Act 1998.

12. The national minimum wage: apprentices

(1) It is not an age contravention for a person to pay an apprentice who does not qualify for the national minimum wage at a lower rate than the person pays an apprentice who does.

(2) An apprentice is a person who—
- (a) is employed under a contract of apprenticeship, or
- (b) as a result of provision made by virtue of section 3(2)(a) of the National Minimum Wage Act 1998 (persons not qualifying), is treated as employed under a contract of apprenticeship.

13. Redundancy

(1) It is not an age contravention for a person to give a qualifying employee an enhanced redundancy payment of an amount less than that of an enhanced redundancy payment which the person gives to another qualifying employee, if each amount is calculated on the same basis.

(2) It is not an age contravention to give enhanced redundancy payments only to those who are qualifying employees by virtue of sub-paragraph (3)(a) or (b).

(3) A person is a qualifying employee if the person—
- (a) is entitled to a redundancy payment as a result of section 135 of the Employment Rights Act 1996,

(b) agrees to the termination of the employment in circumstances where the person would, if dismissed, have been so entitled,
(c) would have been so entitled but for section 155 of that Act (requirement for two years' continuous employment), or
(d) agrees to the termination of the employment in circumstances where the person would, if dismissed, have been so entitled but for that section.

(4) An enhanced redundancy payment is a payment the amount of which is, subject to sub-paragraphs (5) and (6), calculated in accordance with section 162(1) to (3) of the Employment Rights Act 1996.

(5) A person making a calculation for the purposes of sub-paragraph (4)—
(a) may treat a week's pay as not being subject to a maximum amount;
(b) may treat a week's pay as being subject to a maximum amount above that for the time being specified in section 227(1) of the Employment Rights Act 1996;
(c) may multiply the appropriate amount for each year of employment by a figure of more than one.

(6) Having made a calculation for the purposes of sub-paragraph (4) (whether or not in reliance on sub-paragraph (5)), a person may multiply the amount calculated by a figure of more than one.

(7) In sub-paragraph (5), "the appropriate amount" has the meaning given in section 162 of the Employment Rights Act 1996, and "a week's pay" is to be read with Chapter 2 of Part 14 of that Act.

(8) For the purposes of sub-paragraphs (4) to (6), the reference to "the relevant date" in subsection (1)(a) of section 162 of that Act is, in the case of a person who is a qualifying employee by virtue of sub-paragraph (3)(b) or (d), to be read as reference to the date of the termination of the employment.

[14. Insurance etc

(1) It is not an age contravention for an employer to make arrangements for, or afford access to, the provision of insurance or a related financial service to or in respect of an employee for a period ending when the employee attains whichever is the greater of—
(a) the age of 65, and
(b) the state pensionable age.

(2) It is not an age contravention for an employer to make arrangements for, or afford access to, the provision of insurance or a related financial service to or in respect of only such employees as have not attained whichever is the greater of—
(a) the age of 65, and
(b) the state pensionable age.

(3) Sub-paragraphs (1) and (2) apply only where the insurance or related financial service is, or is to be, provided to the employer's employees or a class of those employees—
(a) in pursuance of an arrangement between the employer and another person, or
(b) where the employer's business includes the provision of insurance or financial services of the description in question, by the employer.

(4) The state pensionable age is the pensionable age determined in accordance with the rules in paragraph 1 of Schedule 4 to the Pensions Act 1995.]

15. Child care

(1) A person does not contravene a relevant provision, so far as relating to age, only by providing, or making arrangements for or facilitating the provision of, care for children of a particular age group.

(2) The relevant provisions are—
(a) section 39(2)(b);
(b) section 41(1)(c);
(c) section 44(2)(b);
(d) section 45(2)(b);
(e) section 47(2)(b);
(f) section 48(2)(b);
(g) section 49(6)(b);
(h) section 50(6)(b);
(i) section 57(2)(a);
(j) section 58(3)(a).

(3) Facilitating the provision of care for a child includes—
(a) paying for some or all of the cost of the provision;
(b) helping a parent of the child to find a suitable person to provide care for the child;
(c) enabling a parent of the child to spend more time providing care for the child or otherwise assisting the parent with respect to the care that the parent provides for the child.

(4) A child is a person who has not attained the age of 17.

(5) A reference to care includes a reference to supervision.

16. Contributions to personal pension schemes

(1) A Minister of the Crown may by order provide that it is not an age contravention for an employer to maintain or use, with respect to contributions to personal pension schemes, practices, actions or decisions relating to age which are of a specified description.

(2) An order authorising the use of practices, actions or decisions which are not in use before the order comes into force must not be made unless the Minister consults such persons as the Minister thinks appropriate.

(3) "Personal pension scheme" has the meaning given in section 1 of the Pension Schemes Act 1993; and "employer", in relation to a personal pension scheme, has the meaning given in section 318(1) of the Pensions Act 2004.

NOTES

Commencement: 6 July 2010 (para 16 for the purpose of enabling subordinate legislation or guidance to be made); 1 October 2010 (otherwise).

Paras 8, 9 repealed, and para 14 substituted, by the Employment Equality (Repeal of Retirement Age Provisions) Regulations 2011, SI 2011/1069, reg 2, as from 6 April 2011; for savings in relation to para 8, see reg 5 of the 2011 Regulations at **[2.1603]**.

Orders: the Equality Act (Age Exceptions for Pension Schemes) Order 2010, SI 2010/2133 at **[2.1526]**; the Equality Act (Age Exceptions for Pension Schemes) (Amendment) Order 2010, SI 2010/2285.

PART 3
OTHER EXCEPTIONS

[1.1779]

17. Non-contractual payments to women on maternity leave

(1) A person does not contravene section 39(1)(b) or (2), so far as relating to pregnancy and maternity, by depriving a woman who is on maternity leave of any benefit from the terms of her employment relating to pay.

(2) The reference in sub-paragraph (1) to benefit from the terms of a woman's employment relating to pay does not include a reference to—

- (a) maternity-related pay (including maternity-related pay that is increase-related),
- (b) pay (including increase-related pay) in respect of times when she is not on maternity leave, or
- (c) pay by way of bonus in respect of times when she is on compulsory maternity leave.

(3) For the purposes of sub-paragraph (2), pay is increase-related in so far as it is to be calculated by reference to increases in pay that the woman would have received had she not been on maternity leave.

(4) A reference to terms of her employment is a reference to terms of her employment that are not in her contract of employment, her contract of apprenticeship or her contract to do work personally.

(5) "Pay" means benefits—

- (a) that consist of the payment of money to an employee by way of wages or salary, and
- (b) that are not benefits whose provision is regulated by the contract referred to in sub-paragraph (4).

(6) "Maternity-related pay" means pay to which a woman is entitled—

- (a) as a result of being pregnant, or
- (b) in respect of times when she is on maternity leave.

18. Benefits dependent on marital status, etc

(1) A person does not contravene this Part of this Act, so far as relating to sexual orientation, by doing anything which prevents or restricts a person who is not married from having access to a benefit, facility or service—

- (a) the right to which accrued before 5 December 2005 (the day on which section 1 of the Civil Partnership Act 2004 came into force), or
- (b) which is payable in respect of periods of service before that date.

(2) A person does not contravene this Part of this Act, so far as relating to sexual orientation, by providing married persons and civil partners (to the exclusion of all other persons) with access to a benefit, facility or service.

19. Provision of services etc to the public

(1) A does not contravene a provision mentioned in sub-paragraph (2) in relation to the provision of a benefit, facility or service to B if A is concerned with the provision (for payment or not) of a benefit, facility or service of the same description to the public.

(2) The provisions are—

- (a) section 39(2) and (4);
- (b) section 41(1) and (3);

(c) sections 44(2) and (6) and 45(2) and (6);
(d) sections 49(6) and (8) and 50(6), (7), (9) and (10).

(3) Sub-paragraph (1) does not apply if—
(a) the provision by A to the public differs in a material respect from the provision by A to comparable persons,
(b) the provision to B is regulated by B's terms, or
(c) the benefit, facility or service relates to training.

(4) "Comparable persons" means—
(a) in relation to section 39(2) or (4), the other employees;
(b) in relation to section 41(1) or (3), the other contract workers supplied to the principal;
(c) in relation to section 44(2) or (6), the other partners of the firm;
(d) in relation to section 45(2) or (6), the other members of the LLP;
(e) in relation to section 49(6) or (8) or 50(6), (7), (9) or (10), persons holding offices or posts not materially different from that held by B.

(5) "B's terms" means—
(a) the terms of B's employment,
(b) the terms on which the principal allows B to do the contract work,
(c) the terms on which B has the position as a partner or member, or
(d) the terms of B's appointment to the office.

(6) A reference to the public includes a reference to a section of the public which includes B.

20. Insurance contracts, etc

(1) It is not a contravention of this Part of this Act, so far as relating to relevant discrimination, to do anything in relation to an annuity, life insurance policy, accident insurance policy or similar matter involving the assessment of risk if—
(a) that thing is done by reference to actuarial or other data from a source on which it is reasonable to rely, and
(b) it is reasonable to do it.

(2) "Relevant discrimination" is—
(a) gender reassignment discrimination;
(b) marriage and civil partnership discrimination;
(c) pregnancy and maternity discrimination;
(d) sex discrimination.

NOTES

Commencement: 1 October 2010.

SCHEDULES 10–17

(Sch 10 (Accessibility for Disabled Pupils), Sch 11 (Schools: Exceptions), Sch 12 (Further and Higher Education Exceptions), Sch 13 (Education: Reasonable Adjustments), Sch 14 (Educational Charities and Endowments), Sch 15 (Associations: Reasonable Adjustments), Sch 16 (Associations: Exceptions), Sch 17 (Disabled Pupils: Enforcement) are outside the scope of this work.)

SCHEDULE 18
PUBLIC SECTOR EQUALITY DUTY: EXCEPTIONS

Section 149

[1.1780]

1. Children

(1) Section 149, so far as relating to age, does not apply to the exercise of a function relating to—
(a) the provision of education to pupils in schools;
(b) the provision of benefits, facilities or services to pupils in schools;
(c) the provision of accommodation, benefits, facilities or services in community homes pursuant to section 53(1) of the Children Act 1989;
(d) the provision of accommodation, benefits, facilities or services pursuant to arrangements under section 82(5) of that Act (arrangements by the Secretary of State relating to the accommodation of children);
(e) the provision of accommodation, benefits, facilities or services in residential establishments pursuant to section 26(1)(b) of the Children (Scotland) Act 1995.

(2) "Pupil" and "school" each have the same meaning as in Chapter 1 of Part 6.

2. Immigration

(1) In relation to the exercise of immigration and nationality functions, section 149 has effect as if subsection (1)(b) did not apply to the protected characteristics of age, race or religion or belief; but for that purpose "race" means race so far as relating to—

(a) nationality, or
(b) ethnic or national origins.

(2) "Immigration and nationality functions" means functions exercisable by virtue of—
(a) the Immigration Acts (excluding sections 28A to 28K of the Immigration Act 1971 so far as they relate to criminal offences),
(b) the British Nationality Act 1981,
(c) the British Nationality (Falkland Islands) Act 1983,
(d) the British Nationality (Hong Kong) Act 1990,
(e) the Hong Kong (War Wives and Widows) Act 1996,
(f) the British Nationality (Hong Kong) Act 1997,
(g) the Special Immigration Appeals Commission Act 1997, or
(h) a provision made under section 2(2) of the European Communities Act 1972, or of [EU law], which relates to the subject matter of an enactment within paragraphs (a) to (g).

3. Judicial functions, etc

(1) Section 149 does not apply to the exercise of—
(a) a judicial function;
(b) a function exercised on behalf of, or on the instructions of, a person exercising a judicial function.

(2) The references to a judicial function include a reference to a judicial function conferred on a person other than a court or tribunal.

4. Exceptions that are specific to section 149(2)

(1) Section 149(2) (application of section 149(1) to persons who are not public authorities but by whom public functions are exercisable) does not apply to—
(a) a person listed in sub-paragraph (2);
(b) the exercise of a function listed in sub-paragraph (3).

(2) Those persons are—
(a) the House of Commons;
(b) the House of Lords;
(c) the Scottish Parliament;
(d) the National Assembly for Wales;
(e) the General Synod of the Church of England;
(f) the Security Service;
(g) the Secret Intelligence Service;
(h) the Government Communications Headquarters;
(i) a part of the armed forces which is, in accordance with a requirement of the Secretary of State, assisting the Government Communications Headquarters.

(3) Those functions are—
(a) a function in connection with proceedings in the House of Commons or the House of Lords;
(b) a function in connection with proceedings in the Scottish Parliament (other than a function of the Scottish Parliamentary Corporate Body);
(c) a function in connection with proceedings in the National Assembly for Wales (other than a function of the Assembly Commission).

5. Power to amend Schedule

(1) A Minister of the Crown may by order amend this Schedule so as to add, vary or omit an exception to section 149.

(2) But provision by virtue of sub-paragraph (1) may not amend this Schedule—
(a) so as to omit an exception in paragraph 3;
(b) so as to omit an exception in paragraph 4(1) so far as applying for the purposes of paragraph 4(2)(a) to (e) or (3);
(c) so as to reduce the extent to which an exception referred to in paragraph (a) or (b) applies.

NOTES

Commencement: 5 April 2011.

Para 2: words in square brackets in sub-para (2)(h) substituted by the Equality Act 2010 (Consequential Amendments, Saving and Supplementary Provisions) Order 2010, SI 2010/2279, arts 2, 11, as from 1 October 2010.

SCHEDULE 19
PUBLIC AUTHORITIES

Section 150

PART 1
PUBLIC AUTHORITIES: GENERAL

Ministers of the Crown and government departments

[1.1781]
A Minister of the Crown.

A government department other than the Security Service, the Secret Intelligence Service or the Government Communications Headquarters.

[Broadcasting

The British Broadcasting Corporation ("BBC"), except in respect of functions relating to the provision of a content service (within the meaning given by section 32(7) of the Communications Act 2003); and the reference to the BBC includes a reference to a body corporate which—
- (a) is a wholly owned subsidiary of the BBC,
- (b) is not operated with a view to generating a profit, and
- (c) undertakes activities primarily in order to promote the BBC's public purposes.

The Channel Four Television Corporation, except in respect of—
- (a) functions relating to the provision of a content service (within the meaning given by section 32(7) of the Communications Act 2003), and
- (b) the function of carrying on the activities referred to in section 199 of that Act.

The Welsh Authority (as defined by section 56(1) of the Broadcasting Act 1990), except in respect of functions relating to the provision of a content service (within the meaning given by section 32(7) of the Communications Act 2003).]

[Civil liberties

The Commission for Equality and Human Rights.

The Information Commissioner.]

[Court services and legal services

The Children and Family Court Advisory and Support Service.

The Judicial Appointments Commission.

The Legal Services Board.

. . .]

[Criminal justice

Her Majesty's Chief Inspector of Constabulary.

Her Majesty's Chief Inspector of the Crown Prosecution Service.

Her Majesty's Chief Inspector of Prisons.

Her Majesty's Chief Inspector of Probation for England and Wales.

The Parole Board for England and Wales.

A probation trust established by an order made under section 5(1) of the Offender Management Act 2007.

The Youth Justice Board for England and Wales.]

[Environment, housing and development

The Homes and Communities Agency.

Natural England.

. . . .

The Olympic Delivery Authority.]

Armed forces

Any of the armed forces other than any part of the armed forces which is, in accordance with a requirement of the Secretary of State, assisting the Government Communications Headquarters.

[Health, social care and social security

[The National Health Service Commissioning Board.

A clinical commissioning group established under section 14D of the National Health Service Act 2006.]

The Care Quality Commission.

. . .

The Health Service Commissioner for England, in respect of—

(a) the Commissioner's functions set out in paragraph 11 of Schedule 1 to the Health Service Commissioners Act 1993; and
(b) the Commissioner's public procurement functions (as defined in section 155(3) of this Act).

[Monitor].

An NHS foundation trust within the meaning given by section 30 of the National Health Service Act 2006.

An NHS trust established under section 25 of [the National Health Service Act 2006].

. . .

A Special Health Authority established under section 28 of that Act other than NHS Blood and Transplant and the NHS Business Services Authority.

. . .

[The National Institute for Health and Care Excellence.]
[The Health and Social Care Information Centre.]]

[Industry, business, finance etc

The Advisory, Conciliation and Arbitration Service.

The Bank of England, in respect of its public functions.

The Civil Aviation Authority.

The Competition Commission.

[The Competition and Markets Authority.]

[The Comptroller and Auditor General.]

[The Financial Conduct Authority.]

The National Audit Office.

The Office of Communications.

[The Office for Budget Responsibility.]

[The Prudential Regulation Authority.]]

Local government

A county council, district council or parish council in England.

A parish meeting constituted under section 13 of the Local Government Act 1972.

Charter trustees constituted under section 246 of that Act for an area in England.

The Greater London Authority.

A London borough council.

The Common Council of the City of London in its capacity as a local authority or port health authority.

The Sub-Treasurer of the Inner Temple or the Under-Treasurer of the Middle Temple, in that person's capacity as a local authority.

. . .

The London Fire and Emergency Planning Authority.

Transport for London.

[a Mayoral development corporation.]

The Council of the Isles of Scilly.

The Broads Authority established by section 1 of the Norfolk and Suffolk Broads Act 1988.

. . .

A fire and rescue authority constituted by a scheme under section 2 of the Fire and Rescue Services Act 2004, or a scheme to which section 4 of that Act applies, for an area in England.

An internal drainage board which is continued in being by virtue of section 1 of the Land Drainage Act 1991 for an area in England.

A National Park authority established by an order under section 63 of the Environment Act 1995 for an area in England.

A Passenger Transport Executive for an integrated transport area in England (within the meaning of Part 2 of the Transport Act 1968).

A port health authority constituted by an order under section 2 of the Public Health (Control of Disease) Act 1984 for an area in England.

A waste disposal authority established by virtue of an order under section 10(1) of the Local Government Act 1985.

A joint authority established under Part 4 of that Act for an area in England (including, by virtue of section 77(9) of the Local Transport Act 2008, an Integrated Transport Authority established under Part 5 of that Act of 2008).

A body corporate established pursuant to an order under section 67 of the Local Government Act 1985.

A joint committee constituted in accordance with section 102(1)(b) of the Local Government Act 1972 for an area in England.

A joint board which is continued in being by virtue of section 263(1) of that Act for an area in England.

[The Audit Commission for Local Authorities and the National Health Service in England.

A Local Commissioner in England as defined by section 23(3) of the Local Government Act 1974, in respect of—

(a) the Commissioner's functions under sections 29(6A) and 34G(6) of that Act, and section 210(5) of the Apprenticeships, Skills, Children and Learning Act 2009; and
(b) the Commissioner's public procurement functions (as defined in section 155(3) of this Act).

The Standards Board for England.]

Other educational bodies

The governing body of an educational establishment maintained by an English local authority (within the meaning of section 162 of the Education and Inspections Act 2006).

The governing body of an institution in England within the further education sector (within the meaning of section 91(3) of the Further and Higher Education Act 1992).

The governing body of an institution in England within the higher education sector (within the meaning of section 91(5) of that Act).

[The Higher Education Funding Council for England.

A local authority with respect to the pupil referral units it establishes and maintains by virtue of section 19 of the Education Act 1996.

The proprietor of a City Technology College, a City College for Technology or the Arts, or an Academy.]

[Parliamentary and devolved bodies

The National Assembly for Wales Commission (Comisiwn Cynulliad Cenedlaethol Cymru).

The Parliamentary Commissioner for Administration, in respect of—
(a) the Commissioner's functions set out in section 3(1) and (1A) of the Parliamentary Commissioner Act 1967; and
(b) the Commissioner's public procurement functions (as defined in section 155(3) of this Act).

The Scottish Parliamentary Corporate Body.]

[Police

The British Transport Police Force.

A chief constable of a police force maintained under section 2 of the Police Act 1996.

The Chief Inspector of the UK Border Agency.

The Civil Nuclear Police Authority.

The Commissioner of Police for the City of London.

The Commissioner of Police of the Metropolis.

The Common Council of the City of London in its capacity as a police authority.

The Independent Police Complaints Commission.

[A police and crime commissioner established under section 1 of the Police Reform and Social Responsibility Act 2011.]

[The Mayor's Office for Policing and Crime established under section 3 of that Act.]

A Port Police Force established under an order made under section 14 of the Harbours Act 1964.

The Port Police Force established under Part 10 of the Port of London Act 1968.

A Port Police Force established under section 79 of the Harbours, Docks and Piers Clauses Act 1847.

The Serious Organised Crime Agency.]

[Regulators

The Association of Authorised Public Accountants, in respect of its public functions.

The Association of Certified Chartered Accountants, in respect of its public functions.

The Association of International Accountants, in respect of its public functions.

The Chartered Institute of Patent Attorneys, in respect of its public functions.

The Council for Licensed Conveyancers, in respect of its public functions.

The General Chiropractic Council, in respect of its public functions.

The General Council of the Bar, in respect of its public functions.

The General Dental Council, in respect of its public functions.

The General Medical Council, in respect of its public functions.

The Health and Safety Executive.

The Insolvency Practitioners Association, in respect of its public functions.

The Institute of Chartered Accountants in England and Wales, in respect of its public functions.

The Institute of Legal Executives, in respect of its public functions.

The Institute of Trade Mark Attorneys, in respect of its public functions.

The Law Society of England and Wales, in respect of its public functions.

The Nursing and Midwifery Council, in respect of its public functions.

The Office of the Immigration Services Commissioner.]

NOTES

Commencement: 18 January 2011.

Heading "Broadcasting" and related entries inserted by the Equality Act 2010 (Public Authorities and Consequential and Supplementary Amendments) Order 2011, SI 2011/1060, art 2(1), (2), Sch 1, paras 1, 2, as from 4 April 2011.

Heading "Civil liberties" and related entries inserted by SI 2011/1060, art 2(1), (2), Sch 1, paras 1, 2, as from 4 April 2011.

Heading "Court services and legal services" and related entries inserted by SI 2011/1060, art 2(1), (2), Sch 1, paras 1, 2, as from 4 April 2011; entry "The Legal Services Commission" (omitted) repealed by the Legal Aid, Sentencing and Punishment of Offenders Act 2012, s 39, Sch 5, Pt 1, para 70, as from 1 April 2013.

Heading "Criminal justice" and related entries inserted by SI 2011/1060, art 2(1), (2), Sch 1, paras 1, 2, as from 4 April 2011.

Heading "Environment, housing and development" and related entries inserted by SI 2011/1060, art 2(1), (2), Sch 1, paras 1, 2, as from 4 April 2011.

Heading "Health, social care and social security" and related entries substituted, for heading "National Health Service" and related entries as originally enacted, by SI 2011/1060, art 2(1), (2), Sch 1, paras 1, 3, as from 4 April 2011, and the entries under this heading are subsequently amended as follows:

entries "The National Health Service Commissioning Board" and "A clinical commissioning group" inserted by the Health and Social Care Act 2012, s 55(2), Sch 5, para 182(a), as from 1 October 2012;

entry "The Child Maintenance and Enforcement Commission" (omitted) repealed by the Public Bodies (Child Maintenance and Enforcement Commission: Abolition and Transfer of Functions) Order 2012, SI 2012/2007, art 3(2), Schedule, Pt 1, para 109(e), as from 1 August 2012;

entry "Monitor" substituted, for entry "The Independent Regulator of NHS Foundation Trusts" as originally enacted, by the Health and Social Care Act 2012, s 150(5), Sch 13, para 19, as from 1 July 2012;

in entry relating to "An NHS trust" words in square brackets substituted by the Health and Social Care Act 2012, s 55(2), Sch 5, para 182(b), as from 1 April 2013, and the entry is repealed by the Health and Social Care Act 2012, s 179(6), Sch 14, Pt 2, para 116, as from a day to be appointed;

entries relating to "A Primary Care Trust" and "A Strategic Health Authority" (omitted) repealed by the Health and Social Care Act 2012, s 55(2), Sch 5, para 182(c), (d), as from 1 April 2013;

entries "The Health and Social Care Information Centre" and "The National Institute for Health and Care Excellence" inserted by the Health and Social Care Act 2012, ss 249(1), 277, Sch 17, para 14, Sch 19, para 13, as from 1 April 2013.

Heading "Industry, business, finance etc" and related entries inserted by SI 2011/1060, art 2(1), (2), Sch 1, paras 1, 4, as from 4 April 2011; entry "The Comptroller and Auditor General" inserted (as from 1 April 2012) and entry "The Office for Budget Responsibility" inserted (as from 4 April 2012) by the Budget Responsibility and National Audit Act 2011, ss 3, 26, Sch 1, para 28, Sch 5, Pt 2, para 34; entry "The Competition and Markets Authority" inserted by the Enterprise and Regulatory Reform Act 2013, s 25(4), Sch 4, Pt 1, para 26, as from a day to be appointed; entry "The Financial Conduct Authority" substituted for original entry "The Financial Services Authority" and entry "The Prudential Regulation Authority" inserted, by the Financial Services Act 2012, s 114(1), Sch 18, Pt 2, para 131, as from 1 April 2013.

Under the heading "Local government", entries beginning "The Audit Commission", "A Local Commissioner" and "The Standards Board" inserted by SI 2011/1060, art 2(1), (2), Sch 1, paras 1, 5, as from 4 April 2011; entries "The Office for Tenants and Social Landlords" (omitted) and "The London Development Agency" (omitted) repealed, and entry "A Mayoral development corporation" inserted, by the Localism Act 2011, ss 178, 222, 237, Sch 16, Pt 2, para 62, Sch 22, para 62, Sch 25, Pts 26, 32. Note that the repeals came into force on 1 April 2012 and 31 March 2012 respectively, and the insertion is as from a day to be appointed; entry "A regional development agency" (omitted) repealed by the Public Bodies Act 2011, s 30(3), Sch 6, as from 1 July 2012.

Under the heading "Other educational bodies", entries beginning "The Higher Education", "A local authority" and "The proprietor of a City Technology College" inserted by SI 2011/1060, art 2(1), (2), Sch 1, paras 1, 6, as from 4 April 2011.

Heading "Parliamentary and devolved bodies" and related entries inserted by SI 2011/1060, art 2(1), (2), Sch 1, paras 1, 7, as from 4 April 2011.

Heading "Police" and related entries substituted by SI 2011/1060, art 2(1), (2), Sch 1, paras 1, 8, as from 4 April 2011; entries "A police and crime commissioner established under section 1 of the Police Reform and Social Responsibility Act 2011" and "The Mayor's Office for Policing and Crime established under section 3 of that Act" substituted by the Police Reform and Social Responsibility Act 2011, s 99, Sch 16, Pt 3, paras 380, 383, as from 16 January 2012 (for general transitional provisions relating to police reform and the abolition of existing police authorities, see Sch 15 to the 2011 Act, and the Police Reform and Social Responsibility Act 2011 (Commencement No 3 and Transitional Provisions) Order 2011, SI 2011/3019); entry "The Serious Organised Crime Agency" repealed by the Crime and Courts Act 2013, s 15(3), Sch 8, Pt 2, paras 180, 183, as from a day to be appointed.

Heading "Regulators" and related entries inserted by SI 2011/1060, art 2(1), (2), Sch 1, paras 1, 9, as from 4 April 2011.

PART 2
PUBLIC AUTHORITIES: RELEVANT WELSH AUTHORITIES

Welsh Assembly Government, etc

[1.1782]

The Welsh Ministers.

The First Minister for Wales.

The Counsel General to the Welsh Assembly Government.

A subsidiary of the Welsh Ministers (within the meaning given by section 134(4) of the Government of Wales Act 2006).

National Health Service

A Local Health Board established under section 11 of the National Health Service (Wales) Act 2006.

An NHS trust established under section 18 of that Act.

. . .

A Community Health Council in Wales.

[The Board of Community Health Councils in Wales or Bwrdd Cynghorau Iechyd Cymuned Cymru.]

Local government

[A county council or county borough council in Wales.]

. . .

A fire and rescue authority constituted by a scheme under section 2 of the Fire and Rescue Services Act 2004, or a scheme to which section 4 of that Act applies, for an area in Wales.

. . .

A National Park authority established by an order under section 63 of the Environment Act 1995 for an area in Wales.

. . .

. . .

. . .

. . .

Other educational bodies

The governing body of an educational establishment maintained by a Welsh local authority (within the meaning of section 162 of the Education and Inspections Act 2006).

The governing body of an institution in Wales within the further education sector (within the meaning of section 91(3) of the Further and Higher Education Act 1992).

The governing body of an institution in Wales within the higher education sector (within the meaning of section 91(5) of that Act).

[The Higher Education Funding Council for Wales or Cyngor Cyllido Addysg Uwch Cymru.

The General Teaching Council for Wales or Cyngor Addysgu Cyffredinol Cymru.

Her Majesty's Chief Inspector of Education and Training in Wales or Prif Arolygydd Ei Mawrhydi dros Addysg a Hyfforddiant yng Nghymru.

Other public authorities

The Auditor General for Wales or Archwilydd Cyffredinol Cymru.

The Public Services Ombudsman for Wales or Ombwdsmon Gwasanaethau Cyhoeddus Cymru.

The Care Council for Wales or Cyngor Gofal Cymru.

The Arts Council for Wales or Cyngor Celfyddydau Cymru.

The National Museum of Wales or Amgueddfa Genedlaethol Cymru.

The National Library of Wales or Llyfrgell Genedlaethol Cymru.

The Sports Council for Wales or Cyngor Chwaraeon Cymru.

[Comisiynydd y Gymraeg (The Welsh Language Commissioner).]

. . .

The Commissioner for Older People in Wales or Comisiynydd Pobl Hyn Cymru.

The Children's Commissioner for Wales or Comisiynydd Plant Cymru.]

NOTES

Commencement: 18 January 2011.

Entry "Comisiynydd y Gymraeg (The Welsh Language Commissioner)" substituted (for the original entry "The Welsh Language Board or Bwrdd yr Iaith Gymraeg") by the Welsh Language (Wales) Measure 2011 (Transfer of functions, Transitional and Consequential Provisions) Order 2012, SI 2012/990, art 11, as from 1 April 2012.

Entry "The Countryside Council for Wales or Cyngor Cefn Gwlad Cymru" (omitted) repealed by the Natural Resources Body for Wales (Functions) Order 2013, SI 2013/755, art 4(1), Sch 2, para 450(1), (2), as from 1 April 2013.

All other amendments to this Part were made by the Equality Act 2010 (Specification of Relevant Welsh Authorities) Order 2011, SI 2011/1063, art 2, as from 4 April 2011.

PART 3
PUBLIC AUTHORITIES: RELEVANT SCOTTISH AUTHORITIES

Scottish Administration

[1.1783]
An office-holder in the Scottish Administration (within the meaning given by section 126(7)(a) of the Scotland Act 1998).

National Health Service

A Health Board constituted under section 2 of the National Health Service (Scotland) Act 1978.

A Special Health Board constituted under that section.

Local government

A council constituted under section 2 of the Local Government etc (Scotland) Act 1994.

A community council established under section 51 of the Local Government (Scotland) Act 1973.

A joint board within the meaning of section 235(1) of that Act.

A joint fire and rescue board constituted by a scheme under section 2(1) of the Fire (Scotland) Act 2005.

A licensing board established under section 5 of the Licensing (Scotland) Act 2005, or continued in being by virtue of that section.

A National Park authority established by a designation order made under section 6 of the National Parks (Scotland) Act 2000.

Scottish Enterprise and Highlands and Islands Enterprise, established under the Enterprise and New Towns (Scotland) Act 1990.

Other educational bodies

An education authority in Scotland (within the meaning of section 135(1) of the Education (Scotland) Act 1980).

The managers of a grant-aided school (within the meaning of that section).

The board of management of a college of further education (within the meaning of section 36(1) of the Further and Higher Education (Scotland) Act 1992).

In the case of such a college of further education not under the management of a board of management, the board of governors of the college or any person responsible for the management of the college, whether or not formally constituted as a governing body or board of governors.

The governing body of an institution within the higher education sector (within the meaning of Part 2 of the Further and Higher Education (Scotland) Act 1992).

Police

A police authority established under section 2 of the Police (Scotland) Act 1967.

[Other bodies and offices added on 6th April 2011

Accounts Commission for Scotland.

Audit Scotland.

Board of Trustees of the National Galleries of Scotland.

Board of Trustees of the National Museums of Scotland.

Board of Trustees of the Royal Botanic Garden, Edinburgh.

Bòrd na Gàidhlig.

A Chief Constable of a police force maintained under section 1 of the Police (Scotland) Act 1967.

A chief officer of a community justice authority.

A Chief Officer of a relevant authority appointed under section 7 of the Fire (Scotland) Act 2005.

Commissioner for Children and Young People in Scotland.

Commission for Ethical Standards in Public Life in Scotland.

The Common Services Agency for the Scottish Health Service.

A community justice authority.

Creative Scotland.

The Crofters Commission.

The General Teaching Council for Scotland.

Healthcare Improvement Scotland

Learning and Teaching Scotland.

The Mental Welfare Commission for Scotland.

[The Police Investigations and Review Commissioner.]

Quality Meat Scotland.

A regional Transport Partnership created by an order under section 1(1) of the Transport (Scotland) Act 2005.

Risk Management Authority.

Royal Commission on the Ancient and Historical Monuments of Scotland.

Scottish Children's Reporter Administration.

Scottish Commission for Human Rights.

The Scottish Criminal Cases Review Commission.

Scottish Environment Protection Agency.

Scottish Further and Higher Education Funding Council.

Scottish Futures Trust Ltd.

Scottish Information Commissioner.

The Scottish Legal Aid Board.

The Scottish Legal Complaints Commission.

Scottish Natural Heritage.

The Scottish Police Services Authority.

Scottish Public Services Ombudsman.

Scottish Qualifications Authority.

The Scottish Road Works Commissioner.

The Scottish Social Services Council.

The Scottish Sports Council.

Scottish Water.

Skills Development Scotland.

Social Care and Social Work Improvement Scotland.

The Standards Commission for Scotland.

The Trustees of the National Library of Scotland.

VisitScotland.

A Water Customer Consultation Panel.

The Water Industry Commission for Scotland.]

[Other bodies and offices added on 5th March 2012

Children's Hearings Scotland.

The National Convener of Children's Hearings Scotland.]

NOTES

Commencement: 18 January 2011.

Heading "Other bodies and offices added on 6th April 2011" and associated entries added by the Equality Act 2010 (Specification of Public Authorities) (Scotland) Order 2011, SSI 2011/233, as from 6 April 2011; entry "The Police Investigations and Review Commissioner" in square brackets substituted for original entry "The Police Complaints Commissioner for Scotland", by the Police and Fire Reform (Scotland) Act 2012, s 61(3), as from 1 April 2013.

Heading "Other bodies and offices added on 5th March 2012" and associated entries added by the Equality Act 2010 (Specification of Public Authorities) (Scotland) Order 2012, SSI 2012/55, as from 6 March 2012.

[PART 4
PUBLIC AUTHORITIES: CROSS-BORDER AUTHORITIES

Cross-border Welsh authorities

[1.1784]
The Environment Agency—D

[The Natural Resources Body for Wales—A]

NHS Blood and Transplant—D

The NHS Business Services Authority—D

The Student Loans Company Limited—D]

NOTES

Commencement: 4 April 2011.

Inserted by the Equality Act 2010 (Public Authorities and Consequential and Supplementary Amendments) Order 2011, SI 2011/1060, art 2(1), (3), Sch 2, as from 4 April 2011.

Entry in square brackets inserted by the Natural Resources Body for Wales (Functions) Order 2013, SI 2013/755, art 4(1), Sch 2, para 450(1), (3), as from 1 April 2013.

SCHEDULE 20

(Sch 20 (Rail Vehicle Accessibility: Compliance) outside the scope of this work.)

SCHEDULE 21
REASONABLE ADJUSTMENTS: SUPPLEMENTARY

Section 189

[1.1785]
1. Preliminary

This Schedule applies for the purposes of Schedules 2, 4, 8, 13 and 15.

2. Binding obligations, etc

(1) This paragraph applies if—
  (a) a binding obligation requires A to obtain the consent of another person to an alteration of premises which A occupies,
  (b) where A is a controller of let premises, a binding obligation requires A to obtain the consent of another person to a variation of a term of the tenancy, or
  (c) where A is a responsible person in relation to common parts, a binding obligation requires A to obtain the consent of another person to an alteration of the common parts.

(2) For the purpose of discharging a duty to make reasonable adjustments—
  (a) it is always reasonable for A to have to take steps to obtain the consent, but
  (b) it is never reasonable for A to have to make the alteration before the consent is obtained.

(3) In this Schedule, a binding obligation is a legally binding obligation in relation to premises, however arising; but the reference to a binding obligation in sub-paragraph (1)(a) or (c) does not include a reference to an obligation imposed by a tenancy.

(4) The steps referred to in sub-paragraph (2)(a) do not include applying to a court or tribunal.

3. Landlord's consent

(1) This paragraph applies if—

(a) A occupies premises under a tenancy,

(b) A is proposing to make an alteration to the premises so as to comply with a duty to make reasonable adjustments, and

(c) but for this paragraph, A would not be entitled to make the alteration.

(2) This paragraph also applies if—

(a) A is a responsible person in relation to common parts,

(b) A is proposing to make an alteration to the common parts so as to comply with a duty to make reasonable adjustments,

(c) A is the tenant of property which includes the common parts, and

(d) but for this paragraph, A would not be entitled to make the alteration.

(3) The tenancy has effect as if it provided—

(a) for A to be entitled to make the alteration with the written consent of the landlord,

(b) for A to have to make a written application for that consent,

(c) for the landlord not to withhold the consent unreasonably, and

(d) for the landlord to be able to give the consent subject to reasonable conditions.

(4) If a question arises as to whether A has made the alteration (and, accordingly, complied with a duty to make reasonable adjustments), any constraint attributable to the tenancy must be ignored unless A has applied to the landlord in writing for consent to the alteration.

(5) For the purposes of sub-paragraph (1) or (2), A must be treated as not entitled to make the alteration if the tenancy—

(a) imposes conditions which are to apply if A makes an alteration, or

(b) entitles the landlord to attach conditions to a consent to the alteration.

4. Proceedings before county court or sheriff

(1) This paragraph applies if, in a case within Part 3, 4, 6 or 7 of this Act—

(a) A has applied in writing to the landlord for consent to the alteration, and

(b) the landlord has refused to give consent or has given consent subject to a condition.

(2) A (or a disabled person with an interest in the alteration being made) may refer the matter to *a county court* or, in Scotland, the sheriff.

(3) The county court or sheriff must determine whether the refusal or condition is unreasonable.

(4) If the county court or sheriff finds that the refusal or condition is unreasonable, the county court or sheriff—

(a) may make such declaration as it thinks appropriate;

(b) may make an order authorising A to make the alteration specified in the order (and requiring A to comply with such conditions as are so specified).

5. Joining landlord as party to proceedings

(1) This paragraph applies to proceedings relating to a contravention of this Act by virtue of section 20.

(2) A party to the proceedings may request the employment tribunal, county court or sheriff ("the judicial authority") to direct that the landlord is joined or sisted as a party to the proceedings.

(3) The judicial authority—

(a) must grant the request if it is made before the hearing of the complaint or claim begins;

(b) may refuse the request if it is made after the hearing begins;

(c) must refuse the request if it is made after the complaint or claim has been determined.

(4) If the landlord is joined or sisted as a party to the proceedings, the judicial authority may determine whether—

(a) the landlord has refused to consent to the alteration;

(b) the landlord has consented subject to a condition;

(c) the refusal or condition was unreasonable.

(5) If the judicial authority finds that the refusal or condition was unreasonable, it—

(a) may make such declaration as it thinks appropriate;

(b) may make an order authorising A to make the alteration specified in the order (and requiring A to comply with such conditions as are so specified);

(c) may order the landlord to pay compensation to the complainant or claimant.

(6) An employment tribunal may act in reliance on sub-paragraph (5)(c) instead of, or in addition to, acting in reliance on section 124(2); but if it orders the landlord to pay compensation it must not do so in reliance on section 124(2).

(7) If *a county court* or the sheriff orders the landlord to pay compensation, it may not order A to do so.

6. Regulations

(1) Regulations may make provision as to circumstances in which a landlord is taken for the purposes of this Schedule to have—
  (a) withheld consent;
  (b) withheld consent reasonably;
  (c) withheld consent unreasonably.

(2) Regulations may make provision as to circumstances in which a condition subject to which a landlord gives consent is taken—
  (a) to be reasonable;
  (b) to be unreasonable.

(3) Regulations may make provision supplementing or modifying the preceding paragraphs of this Schedule, or provision made under this paragraph, in relation to a case where A's tenancy is a sub-tenancy.

(4) Provision made by virtue of this paragraph may amend the preceding paragraphs of this Schedule.

7. Interpretation

An expression used in this Schedule and in Schedule 2, 4, 8, 13 or 15 has the same meaning in this Schedule as in that Schedule.

NOTES

Commencement: 6 July 2010 (para 6 for the purpose of enabling subordinate legislation or guidance to be made); 1 October 2010 (otherwise).

Paras 4, 5: for the words in italics there are substituted the words "the county court" by the Crime and Courts Act 2013, s 17(5), Sch 9, Pt 3, para 52, as from a day to be appointed.

Regulations : the Equality Act 2010 (Disability) Regulations 2010, SI 2010/2128 at **[2.1506]**. See further reg 14 of those Regulations at **[2.1519]** (modification of this Schedule in relation to any case where the occupier occupies premises under a sub-tenancy).

SCHEDULE 22
STATUTORY PROVISIONS

Section 191

[1.1786]

1. Statutory authority

(1) A person (P) does not contravene a provision specified in the first column of the table, so far as relating to the protected characteristic specified in the second column in respect of that provision, if P does anything P must do pursuant to a requirement specified in the third column.

Specified provision	Protected characteristic	Requirement
Parts 3 to 7	Age	A requirement of an enactment
Parts 3 to 7 and 12	Disability	A requirement of an enactment
		A relevant requirement or condition imposed by virtue of an enactment
Parts 3 to 7	Religion or belief	A requirement of an enactment
		A relevant requirement or condition imposed by virtue of an enactment
Section 29(6) and Parts 6 and 7	Sex	A requirement of an enactment
Parts 3, 4, 6 and 7	Sexual orientation	A requirement of an enactment
		A relevant requirement or condition imposed by virtue of an enactment

(2) A reference in the table to Part 6 does not include a reference to that Part so far as relating to vocational training.

(3) In this paragraph a reference to an enactment includes a reference to—
  (a) a Measure of the General Synod of the Church of England;
  (b) an enactment passed or made on or after the date on which this Act is passed.

(4) In the table, a relevant requirement or condition is a requirement or condition imposed (whether before or after the passing of this Act) by—
  (a) a Minister of the Crown;
  (b) a member of the Scottish Executive;

(c) the National Assembly for Wales (constituted by the Government of Wales Act 1998);
(d) the Welsh Ministers, the First Minister for Wales or the Counsel General to the Welsh Assembly Government.

2. Protection of women

(1) A person (P) does not contravene a specified provision only by doing in relation to a woman (W) anything P is required to do to comply with—
(a) a pre-1975 Act enactment concerning the protection of women;
(b) a relevant statutory provision (within the meaning of Part 1 of the Health and Safety at Work etc Act 1974) if it is done for the purpose of the protection of W (or a description of women which includes W);
(c) a requirement of a provision specified in Schedule 1 to the Employment Act 1989 (provisions concerned with protection of women at work).

(2) The references to the protection of women are references to protecting women in relation to—
(a) pregnancy or maternity, or
(b) any other circumstances giving rise to risks specifically affecting women.

(3) It does not matter whether the protection is restricted to women.

(4) These are the specified provisions—
(a) Part 5 (work);
(b) Part 6 (education), so far as relating to vocational training.

(5) A pre-1975 Act enactment is an enactment contained in—
(a) an Act passed before the Sex Discrimination Act 1975;
(b) an instrument approved or made by or under such an Act (including one approved or made after the passing of the 1975 Act).

(6) If an Act repeals and re-enacts (with or without modification) a pre-1975 enactment then the provision re-enacted must be treated as being in a pre-1975 enactment.

(7) For the purposes of sub-paragraph (1)(c), a reference to a provision in Schedule 1 to the Employment Act 1989 includes a reference to a provision for the time being having effect in place of it.

(8) This paragraph applies only to the following protected characteristics—
(a) pregnancy and maternity;
(b) sex.

3. Educational appointments, etc: religious belief

(1) A person does not contravene Part 5 (work) only by doing a relevant act in connection with the employment of another in a relevant position.

(2) A relevant position is—
(a) the head teacher or principal of an educational establishment;
(b) the head, a fellow or other member of the academic staff of a college, or institution in the nature of a college, in a university;
(c) a professorship of a university which is a canon professorship or one to which a canonry is annexed.

(3) A relevant act is anything it is necessary to do to comply with—
(a) a requirement of an instrument relating to the establishment that the head teacher or principal must be a member of a particular religious order;
(b) a requirement of an instrument relating to the college or institution that the holder of the position must be a woman;
(c) an Act or instrument in accordance with which the professorship is a canon professorship or one to which a canonry is annexed.

(4) Sub-paragraph (3)(b) does not apply to an instrument taking effect on or after 16 January 1990 (the day on which section 5(3) of the Employment Act 1989 came into force).

(5) A Minister of the Crown may by order provide that anything in sub-paragraphs (1) to (3) does not have effect in relation to—
(a) a specified educational establishment or university;
(b) a specified description of educational establishments.

(6) An educational establishment is—
(a) a school within the meaning of the Education Act 1996 or the Education (Scotland) Act 1980;
(b) a college, or institution in the nature of a college, in a university;
(c) an institution designated by order made, or having effect as if made, under section 129 of the Education Reform Act 1988;
(d) a college of further education within the meaning of section 36 of the Further and Higher Education (Scotland) Act 1992;
(e) a university in Scotland;

(f) an institution designated by order under section 28 of the Further and Higher Education Act 1992 or section 44 of the Further and Higher Education (Scotland) Act 1992.

(7) This paragraph does not affect paragraph 2 of Schedule 9.

4. A person does not contravene this Act only by doing anything which is permitted for the purposes of—

(a) section 58(6) or (7) of the School Standards and Framework Act 1998 (dismissal of teachers because of failure to give religious education efficiently);
(b) section 60(4) and (5) of that Act (religious considerations relating to certain appointments);
(c) section 124A of that Act (preference for certain teachers at independent schools of a religious character);
[(d) section 124AA(5) to (7) of that Act (religious considerations relating to certain teachers at Academies with religious character)].

5. Crown employment, etc

(1) A person does not contravene this Act—

(a) by making or continuing in force rules mentioned in sub-paragraph (2);
(b) by publishing, displaying or implementing such rules;
(c) by publishing the gist of such rules.

(2) The rules are rules restricting to persons of particular birth, nationality, descent or residence—

(a) employment in the service of the Crown;
(b) employment by a prescribed public body;
(c) holding a public office (within the meaning of section 50).

(3) The power to make regulations for the purpose of sub-paragraph (2)(b) is exercisable by the Minister for the Civil Service.

(4) In this paragraph "public body" means a body (whether corporate or unincorporated) exercising public functions (within the meaning given by section 31(4)).

NOTES

Commencement: 1 October 2010 (except in so far as it applies to the protected characteristic of age in Parts 3 and 7 of this Act); 1 October 2012 (otherwise).

Para 4: sub-para (d) inserted by the Education Act 2011, s 62(1), (4)(c), as from 1 February 2012.

SCHEDULE 23
GENERAL EXCEPTIONS

Section 196

[1.1787]

1. Acts authorised by statute or the executive

(1) This paragraph applies to anything done—

(a) in pursuance of an enactment;
(b) in pursuance of an instrument made by a member of the executive under an enactment;
(c) to comply with a requirement imposed (whether before or after the passing of this Act) by a member of the executive by virtue of an enactment;
(d) in pursuance of arrangements made (whether before or after the passing of this Act) by or with the approval of, or for the time being approved by, a Minister of the Crown;
(e) to comply with a condition imposed (whether before or after the passing of this Act) by a Minister of the Crown.

(2) A person does not contravene Part 3, 4, 5 or 6 by doing anything to which this paragraph applies which discriminates against another because of the other's nationality.

(3) A person (A) does not contravene Part 3, 4, 5 or 6 if, by doing anything to which this paragraph applies, A discriminates against another (B) by applying to B a provision, criterion or practice which relates to—

(a) B's place of ordinary residence;
(b) the length of time B has been present or resident in or outside the United Kingdom or an area within it.

2. Organisations relating to religion or belief

(1) This paragraph applies to an organisation the purpose of which is—

(a) to practise a religion or belief,
(b) to advance a religion or belief,
(c) to teach the practice or principles of a religion or belief,
(d) to enable persons of a religion or belief to receive any benefit, or to engage in any activity, within the framework of that religion or belief, or
(e) to foster or maintain good relations between persons of different religions or beliefs.

(2) This paragraph does not apply to an organisation whose sole or main purpose is commercial.

(3) The organisation does not contravene Part 3, 4 or 7, so far as relating to religion or belief or sexual orientation, only by restricting—

(a) membership of the organisation;

(b) participation in activities undertaken by the organisation or on its behalf or under its auspices;

(c) the provision of goods, facilities or services in the course of activities undertaken by the organisation or on its behalf or under its auspices;

(d) the use or disposal of premises owned or controlled by the organisation.

(4) A person does not contravene Part 3, 4 or 7, so far as relating to religion or belief or sexual orientation, only by doing anything mentioned in sub-paragraph (3) on behalf of or under the auspices of the organisation.

(5) A minister does not contravene Part 3, 4 or 7, so far as relating to religion or belief or sexual orientation, only by restricting—

(a) participation in activities carried on in the performance of the minister's functions in connection with or in respect of the organisation;

(b) the provision of goods, facilities or services in the course of activities carried on in the performance of the minister's functions in connection with or in respect of the organisation.

(6) Sub-paragraphs (3) to (5) permit a restriction relating to religion or belief only if it is imposed—

(a) because of the purpose of the organisation, or

(b) to avoid causing offence, on grounds of the religion or belief to which the organisation relates, to persons of that religion or belief.

(7) Sub-paragraphs (3) to (5) permit a restriction relating to sexual orientation only if it is imposed—

(a) because it is necessary to comply with the doctrine of the organisation, or

(b) to avoid conflict with strongly held convictions within sub-paragraph (9).

(8) In sub-paragraph (5), the reference to a minister is a reference to a minister of religion, or other person, who—

(a) performs functions in connection with a religion or belief to which the organisation relates, and

(b) holds an office or appointment in, or is accredited, approved or recognised for the purposes of the organisation.

(9) The strongly held convictions are—

(a) in the case of a religion, the strongly held religious convictions of a significant number of the religion's followers;

(b) in the case of a belief, the strongly held convictions relating to the belief of a significant number of the belief's followers.

(10) This paragraph does not permit anything which is prohibited by section 29, so far as relating to sexual orientation, if it is done—

(a) on behalf of a public authority, and

(b) under the terms of a contract between the organisation and the public authority.

(11) In the application of this paragraph in relation to sexual orientation, sub-paragraph (1)(e) must be ignored.

(12) In the application of this paragraph in relation to sexual orientation, in sub-paragraph (3)(d), "disposal" does not include disposal of an interest in premises by way of sale if the interest being disposed of is—

(a) the entirety of the organisation's interest in the premises, or

(b) the entirety of the interest in respect of which the organisation has power of disposal.

(13) In this paragraph—

(a) "disposal" is to be construed in accordance with section 38;

(b) "public authority" has the meaning given in section 150(1).

3. Communal accommodation

(1) A person does not contravene this Act, so far as relating to sex discrimination or gender reassignment discrimination, only because of anything done in relation to—

(a) the admission of persons to communal accommodation;

(b) the provision of a benefit, facility or service linked to the accommodation.

(2) Sub-paragraph (1)(a) does not apply unless the accommodation is managed in a way which is as fair as possible to both men and women.

(3) In applying sub-paragraph (1)(a), account must be taken of—

(a) whether and how far it is reasonable to expect that the accommodation should be altered or extended or that further accommodation should be provided, and

(b) the frequency of the demand or need for use of the accommodation by persons of one sex as compared with those of the other.

(4) In applying sub-paragraph (1)(a) in relation to gender reassignment, account must also be taken of whether and how far the conduct in question is a proportionate means of achieving a legitimate aim.

(5) Communal accommodation is residential accommodation which includes dormitories or other shared sleeping accommodation which for reasons of privacy should be used only by persons of the same sex.

(6) Communal accommodation may include—

(a) shared sleeping accommodation for men and for women;

(b) ordinary sleeping accommodation;

(c) residential accommodation all or part of which should be used only by persons of the same sex because of the nature of the sanitary facilities serving the accommodation.

(7) A benefit, facility or service is linked to communal accommodation if—

(a) it cannot properly and effectively be provided except for those using the accommodation, and

(b) a person could be refused use of the accommodation in reliance on sub-paragraph (1)(a).

(8) This paragraph does not apply for the purposes of Part 5 (work) unless such arrangements as are reasonably practicable are made to compensate for—

(a) in a case where sub-paragraph (1)(a) applies, the refusal of use of the accommodation;

(b) in a case where sub-paragraph (1)(b) applies, the refusal of provision of the benefit, facility or service.

4. Training provided to non-EEA residents, etc

(1) A person (A) does not contravene this Act, so far as relating to nationality, only by providing a non-resident (B) with training, if A thinks that B does not intend to exercise in Great Britain skills B obtains as a result.

(2) A non-resident is a person who is not ordinarily resident in an EEA state.

(3) The reference to providing B with training is—

(a) if A employs B in relevant employment, a reference to doing anything in or in connection with the employment;

(b) if A as a principal allows B to do relevant contract work, a reference to doing anything in or in connection with allowing B to do the work;

(c) in a case within paragraph (a) or (b) or any other case, a reference to affording B access to facilities for education or training or ancillary benefits.

(4) Employment or contract work is relevant if its sole or main purpose is the provision of training in skills.

(5) In the case of training provided by the armed forces or Secretary of State for purposes relating to defence, sub-paragraph (1) has effect as if—

(a) the reference in sub-paragraph (2) to an EEA state were a reference to Great Britain, and

(b) in sub-paragraph (4), for "its sole or main purpose is" there were substituted "it is for purposes including".

(6) "Contract work" and "principal" each have the meaning given in section 41.

NOTES

Commencement: 1 October 2010 (except in so far as it applies to the protected characteristic of age in Parts 3 and 7 of this Act); 1 October 2012 (otherwise).

SCHEDULE 24
HARMONISATION: EXCEPTIONS

Section 203

[1.1788]

Part 1 (public sector duty regarding socio-economic inequalities)

Chapter 2 of Part 5 (occupational pensions)

Section 78 (gender pay gap)

Section 106 (election candidates: diversity information)

Chapters 1 to 3 and 5 of Part 9 (enforcement), except section 136

Sections 142 and 146 (unenforceable terms, declaration in respect of void terms)

Chapter 1 of Part 11 (public sector equality duty)

Part 12 (disabled persons: transport)

Part 13 (disability: miscellaneous)

Section 197 (power to specify age exceptions)

Part 15 (family property)

Part 16 (general and miscellaneous)

Schedule 1 (disability: supplementary provision)

In Schedule 3 (services and public functions: exceptions)—
- (a) in Part 3 (health and care), paragraphs 13 and 14;
- (b) Part 4 (immigration);
- (c) Part 5 (insurance);
- (d) Part 6 (marriage);
- (e) Part 7 (separate and single services), except paragraph 30;
- (f) Part 8 (television, radio and on-line broadcasting and distribution);
- (g) Part 9 (transport);
- (h) Part 10 (supplementary)

Schedule 4 (premises: reasonable adjustments)

Schedule 5 (premises: exceptions), except paragraph 1

Schedule 6 (office-holders: excluded offices), except so far as relating to colour or nationality or marriage and civil partnership

Schedule 8 (work: reasonable adjustments)

In Schedule 9 (work: exceptions)—
- (a) Part 1 (general), except so far as relating to colour or nationality;
- (b) Part 2 (exceptions relating to age);
- (c) Part 3 (other exceptions), except paragraph 19 so far as relating to colour or nationality

Schedule 10 (education: accessibility for disabled pupils)

Schedule 13 (education: reasonable adjustments), except paragraphs 2, 5, 6 and 9

Schedule 17 (education: disabled pupils: enforcement)

Schedule 18 (public sector equality duty: exceptions)

Schedule 19 (list of public authorities)

Schedule 20 (rail vehicle accessibility: compliance)

Schedule 21 (reasonable adjustments: supplementary)

In Schedule 22 (exceptions: statutory provisions), paragraphs 2 and 5

Schedule 23 (general exceptions), except paragraph 2

Schedule 25 (information society services)

NOTES

Commencement: 8 April 2010.

SCHEDULE 25
INFORMATION SOCIETY SERVICES

Section 206

[1.1789]

1. Service providers

(1) This paragraph applies where a person concerned with the provision of an information society service (an "information society service provider") is established in Great Britain.

(2) This Act applies to anything done by the person in an EEA state (other than the United Kingdom) in providing the service as this Act would apply if the act in question were done by the person in Great Britain.

2. (1) This paragraph applies where an information society service provider is established in an EEA state (other than the United Kingdom).

(2) This Act does not apply to anything done by the person in providing the service.

3. Exceptions for mere conduits

(1) An information society service provider does not contravene this Act only by providing so much of an information society service as consists in—

(a) the provision of access to a communication network, or
(b) the transmission in a communication network of information provided by the recipient of the service.

(2) But sub-paragraph (1) applies only if the service provider does not—
(a) initiate the transmission,
(b) select the recipient of the transmission, or
(c) select or modify the information contained in the transmission.

(3) For the purposes of sub-paragraph (1), the provision of access to a communication network, and the transmission of information in a communication network, includes the automatic, intermediate and transient storage of the information transmitted so far as the storage is solely for the purpose of carrying out the transmission in the network.

(4) Sub-paragraph (3) does not apply if the information is stored for longer than is reasonably necessary for the transmission.

4. Exception for caching

(1) This paragraph applies where an information society service consists in the transmission in a communication network of information provided by a recipient of the service.

(2) The information society service provider does not contravene this Act only by doing anything in connection with the automatic, intermediate and temporary storage of information so provided if—
(a) the storage of the information is solely for the purpose of making more efficient the onward transmission of the information to other recipients of the service at their request, and
(b) the condition in sub-paragraph (3) is satisfied.

(3) The condition is that the service-provider—
(a) does not modify the information,
(b) complies with such conditions as are attached to having access to the information, and
(c) (where sub-paragraph (4) applies) expeditiously removes the information or disables access to it.

(4) This sub-paragraph applies if the service-provider obtains actual knowledge that—
(a) the information at the initial source of the transmission has been removed from the network,
(b) access to it has been disabled, or
(c) a court or administrative authority has required the removal from the network of, or the disablement of access to, the information.

5. Exception for hosting

(1) An information society service provider does not contravene this Act only by doing anything in providing so much of an information society service as consists in the storage of information provided by a recipient of the service, if—
(a) the service provider had no actual knowledge when the information was provided that its provision amounted to a contravention of this Act, or
(b) on obtaining actual knowledge that the provision of the information amounted to a contravention of that section, the service provider expeditiously removed the information or disabled access to it.

(2) Sub-paragraph (1) does not apply if the recipient of the service is acting under the authority of the control of the service provider.

6. Monitoring obligations

An injunction or interdict under Part 1 of the Equality Act 2006 may not impose on a person concerned with the provision of a service of a description given in paragraph 3(1), 4(1) or 5(1)—
(a) a liability the imposition of which would contravene Article 12, 13 or 14 of the E-Commerce Directive;
(b) a general obligation of the description given in Article 15 of that Directive.

7. Interpretation

(1) This paragraph applies for the purposes of this Schedule.

(2) "Information society service"—
(a) has the meaning given in Article 2(a) of the E-Commerce Directive (which refers to Article 1(2) of Directive 98/34/EC of the European Parliament and of the Council of 22 June 1998 laying down a procedure for the provision of information in the field of technical standards and regulations), and
(b) is summarised in recital 17 of the E-Commerce Directive as covering "any service normally provided for remuneration, at a distance, by means of electronic equipment for the processing (including digital compression) and storage of data, and at the individual request of a recipient of a service".

(3) "The E-Commerce Directive" means Directive 2000/31/EC of the European Parliament and of the Council of 8 June 2000 on certain legal aspects of information society services, in particular electronic commerce, in the Internal Market (Directive on electronic commerce).

(4) "Recipient" means a person who (whether for professional purposes or not) uses an information society service, in particular for seeking information or making it accessible.

(5) An information society service-provider is "established" in a country or territory if the service-provider—

(a) effectively pursues an economic activity using a fixed establishment in that country or territory for an indefinite period, and

(b) is a national of an EEA state or a body mentioned in [Article 54 of the Treaty on the Functioning of the European Union].

(6) The presence or use in a particular place of equipment or other technical means of providing an information society service is not itself sufficient to constitute the establishment of a service-provider.

(7) Where it cannot be decided from which of a number of establishments an information society service is provided, the service is to be regarded as provided from the establishment at the centre of the information society service provider's activities relating to that service.

(8) Section 212(4) does not apply to references to providing a service.

NOTES

Commencement: 1 October 2010.

Para 7: words in square brackets in sub-para (5)(b) substituted by the Treaty of Lisbon (Changes in Terminology or Numbering) Order 2012, SI 2012/1809, art 3(1), Schedule, Pt 1, as from 1 August 2012.

SCHEDULES 26 AND 27

(Sch 26 (Amendments) contains various amendments which, in so far as relevant to this work, are incorporated in the appropriate place (see further the introductory notes to this Act); Sch 27 (Repeals and Revocations) contains various repeals and revocations, including the following: the Equal Pay Act 1970, the Sex Discrimination Act 1975, the Race Relations Act 1976, the Sex Discrimination Act 1986, the Employment Act 1989, ss 1–7, 9, the Social Security Act 1989, Sch 5, para 5, the Disability Discrimination Act 1995 , the Pensions Act 1995, ss 62–65, the Equality Act 2006, ss 25, 26, 33, 43–81, 83–90, 94 (in part), Sch 3, paras 6–35, 41–56, the Occupational Pension Schemes (Equal Treatment) Regulations 1995 (SI 1995/3183), the Employment Equality (Religion or Belief) Regulations 2003 (SI 2003/1660), the Employment Equality (Sexual Orientation) Regulations 2003 (SI 2003/1661), the Disability Discrimination Act 1995 (Pensions) Regulations 2003 (SI 2003/2770), the Occupational Pension Schemes (Equal Treatment) (Amendment) Regulations 2005 (SI 2005/1923), the Employment Equality (Age) Regulations 2006 (SI 2006/1031) (the whole Regulations other than Schs 6 and 8), the Equality Act (Sexual Orientation) Regulations 2007 (SI 2007/1263), and the Sex Discrimination (Amendment of Legislation) Regulations 2008 (SI 2008/963).)

SCHEDULE 28
INDEX OF DEFINED EXPRESSIONS

Section 214

[1.1790]

Expression	Provision
Accrual of rights, in relation to an occupational pension scheme	Section 212(12)
Additional maternity leave	Section 213(6) and (7)
Additional maternity leave period	Section 213(8)
Age discrimination	Section 25(1)
Age group	Section 5(2)
Armed forces	Section 212(1)
Association	Section 107(2)
Auxiliary aid	Section 20(11)
Belief	Section 10(2)
Breach of an equality clause or rule	Section 212(8)
The Commission	Section 212(1)
Commonhold	Section 38(7)
Compulsory maternity leave	Section 213(3)

Expression	Provision
Contract work	Section 41(6)
Contract worker	Section 41(7)
Contravention of this Act	Section 212(9)
Crown employment	Section 83(9)
Detriment	Section 212(1) and (5)
Disability	Section 6(1)
Disability discrimination	Section 25(2)
Disabled person	Section 6(2) and (4)
Discrimination	Sections 13 to 19, 21 and 108
Disposal, in relation to premises	Section 38(3) to (5)
Education Acts	Section 212(1)
Employer, in relation to an occupational pension scheme	Section 212(11)
Employment	Section 212(1)
Enactment	Section 212(1)
Equality clause	Section 212(1)
Equality rule	Section 212(1)
Firm	Section 46(2)
Gender reassignment	Section 7(1)
Gender reassignment discrimination	Section 25(3)
Harassment	Section 26(1)
Independent educational institution	Section 89(7)
LLP	Section 46(4)
Man	Section 212(1)
Marriage and civil partnership	Section 8
Marriage and civil partnership discrimination	Section 25(4)
Maternity equality clause	Section 212(1)
Maternity equality rule	Section 212(1)
Maternity leave	Section 213(2)
Member, in relation to an occupational pension scheme	Section 212(10)
Member of the executive	Section 212(7)
Non-discrimination rule	Section 212(1)
Occupation, in relation to premises	Section 212(6)
Occupational pension scheme	Section 212(1)
Offshore work	Section 82(3)
Ordinary maternity leave	Section 213(4) and (5)
Parent	Section 212(1)
Pension credit member	Section 212(11)
Pensionable service	Section 212(11)
Pensioner member	Section 212(11)
Personal office	Section 49(2)
Physical feature	Section 20(10)
Pregnancy and maternity discrimination	Section 25(5)
Premises	Section 38(2)
Prescribed	Section 212(1)
Profession	Section 212(1)
Proposed firm	Section 46(3)
Proposed LLP	Section 46(5)
Proprietor, in relation to a school	Section 89(4)
Protected characteristics	Section 4

Expression	**Provision**
Protected period, in relation to pregnancy	Section 18(6)
Provision of a service	Sections 31 and 212(4)
Public function	Sections 31(4) and 150(5)
Public office	Sections 50(2) and 52(4)
Pupil	Section 89(3)
Race	Section 9(1)
Race discrimination	Section 25(6)
Reasonable adjustments, duty to make	Section 20
Relevant member of the House of Commons staff	Section 83(5)
Relevant member of the House of Lords staff	Section 83(6)
Relevant person, in relation to a personal or public office	Section 52(6)
Religion	Section 10(1)
Religious or belief-related discrimination	Section 25(7)
Requirement, the first, second or third	Section 20
Responsible body, in relation to a further or higher education institution	Section 91(12)
Responsible body, in relation to a school	Section 85(9)
School	Section 89(5) and (6)
Service-provider	Section 29(1)
Sex	Section 11
Sex discrimination	Section 25(8)
Sex equality clause	Section 212(1)
Sex equality rule	Section 212(1)
Sexual orientation	Section 12(1)
Sexual orientation discrimination	Section 25(9)
Student	Section 94(3)
Subordinate legislation	Section 212(1)
Substantial	Section 212(1)
Taxi, for the purposes of Part 3 (services and public functions)	Schedule 2, paragraph 4
Taxi, for the purposes of Chapter 1 of Part 12 (disabled persons: transport)	Section 173(1)
Tenancy	Section 38(6)
Trade	Section 212(1)
Transsexual person	Section 7(2)
Trustees or managers, in relation to an occupational pension scheme	Section 212(11)
University	Section 94(4)
Victimisation	Section 27(1)
Vocational training	Section 56(6)
Woman	Section 212(1)

NOTES

Commencement: 8 April 2010.

APPENDIX: TABLE OF COMMENCEMENTS FOR THE EQUALITY ACT 2010

[1.1791]

NOTES

This table sets out the commencement dates for the provisions of this Act included above. Provisions not included are omitted from this table. Commencement is provided for in s 216 of the Act (at **[1.1766]**) and by the following commencement orders made under that section: the Equality Act 2010 (Commencement No 1) Order 2010, SI 2010/1736; the Equality Act 2010 (Commencement No 2) Order 2010, SI 2010/1966; the Equality Act 2010 (Commencement No 3) Order 2010, SI 2010/2191; the Equality Act 2010 (Commencement No 4, Savings, Consequential, Transitional, Transitory and Incidental Provisions and Revocation) Order 2010, SI 2010/2317 at **[2.1558]**; the Equality Act 2010 (Commencement No 5) Order 2011, SI 2011/96; the Equality Act 2010 (Commencement No 6) Order 2011, SI 2011/1066; the Equality Act 2010 (Commencement No 7) Order 2011, SI 2011/1636; the Equality Act 2010 (Commencement No 8) Order 2011, SI 2011/2646; the Equality Act 2010 (Commencement No 9) Order 2012, SI 2012/1569; the Equality Act 2010 (Commencement No 10) Order 2012, SI 2012/2184.

Note that the second commencement order brought into force ss 6(6), 38(8), 80(8), 83(11), 94(12), 116(3), and 189 on 4 August 2010 in so far as they relate to the provisions listed in Table 2 of the Schedule to the first commencement order and in so far as necessary for the purpose of making subordinate legislation or guidance under the provisions so listed. Table 2 of the Schedule to the first commencement order brought into force certain paragraphs in Schs 1, 4, 7, 9, 12, 17, and 21 in so far as necessary for the purpose of making subordinate legislation or guidance. The sections listed *ante* are the enabling provisions for the Schedules listed *ante* and, therefore, the purpose of the second commencement order is merely to correct an oversight in the first commencement order which did not commence the relevant enabling provisions when commencing the Schedules for certain purposes.

Note also that seventh, eighth and tenth commencement orders only bring into force provisions that are outside the scope of this work and which have not been reproduced *ante*.

Provision of Act		**Commencement**
1–3		*Not yet in force*
4, 5		1 Oct 2010 (SI 2010/2317)
6	(1)–(4)	1 Oct 2010 (SI 2010/2317)
	(5)	6 Jul 2010 (for the purpose of enabling subordinate legislation or guidance to be made) (SI 2010/1736)
		1 Oct 2010 (otherwise) (SI 2010/2317)[1]
	(6)	See Sch 1 below
7–13		1 Oct 2010 (SI 2010/2317)
14		*Not yet in force*
15–21		1 Oct 2010 (SI 2010/2317)
22		6 Jul 2010 (for the purpose of enabling subordinate legislation or guidance to be made) (SI 2010/1736)
		1 Oct 2010 (otherwise) (SI 2010/2317)
23–27		1 Oct 2010 (SI 2010/2317)[1]
39–60		1 Oct 2010 (SI 2010/2317)
61	(1)–(7)	1 Oct 2010 (SI 2010/2317)
	(8), (9)	6 Jul 2010 (for the purpose of enabling subordinate legislation or guidance to be made) (SI 2010/1736)
		1 Oct 2010 (otherwise) (SI 2010/2317)
	(10), (11)	1 Oct 2010 (SI 2010/2317)
62–77		1 Oct 2010 (SI 2010/2317)
78		*Not yet in force*
79		1 Oct 2010 (SI 2010/2317)
80	(1)–(7)	1 Oct 2010 (SI 2010/2317)
	(8)	See Sch 7 below
81, 82		6 Jul 2010 (for the purpose of enabling subordinate legislation or guidance to be made) (SI 2010/1736)
		1 Oct 2010 (otherwise) (SI 2010/2317)
83	(1)–(9)	1 Oct 2010 (SI 2010/2317)
	(10)	See Sch 8 below
	(11)	See Sch 9 below
95		1 Oct 2010 (SI 2010/2317)
96	(1)–(8)	1 Oct 2010 (SI 2010/2317)
	(9)(a)	1 Oct 2010 (SI 2010/2317)
	(9)(b)	3 Sep 2010 (for the purpose of enabling regulations to be made) (SI 2010/2191)

Provision of Act		**Commencement**
		1 Oct 2010 (otherwise) (SI 2010/2317)
	(10), (11)	6 Jul 2010 (for the purpose of enabling subordinate legislation or guidance to be made) (SI 2010/1736)
		1 Oct 2010 (otherwise) (SI 2010/2317)
97		6 Jul 2010 (for the purpose of enabling subordinate legislation or guidance to be made) (SI 2010/1736)
		1 Oct 2010 (otherwise) (SI 2010/2317)
108–114		1 Oct 2010 (SI 2010/2317)[1]
117	(1)–(4)	6 Jul 2010 (for the purpose of enabling subordinate legislation or guidance to be made) (SI 2010/1736)
		1 Oct 2010 (otherwise) (SI 2010/2317)[1]
	(5)–(7)	1 Oct 2010 (SI 2010/2317)[1]
118–135		1 Oct 2010 (SI 2010/2317)[1]
136	(1)–(5)	1 Oct 2010 (SI 2010/2317)[1]
	(6)(a)–(e)	1 Oct 2010 (SI 2010/2317)[1]
	(6)(f)	18 Mar 2011 (SI 2010/2317)[1]
137		1 Oct 2010 (SI 2010/2317)[1]
138	(1), (2)	6 Jul 2010 (for the purpose of enabling subordinate legislation or guidance to be made) (SI 2010/1736)
		1 Oct 2010 (otherwise) (SI 2010/2317)[1]
	(3), (4)	1 Oct 2010 (SI 2010/2317)[1]
	(5)–(7)	6 Jul 2010 (for the purpose of enabling subordinate legislation or guidance to be made) (SI 2010/1736)
		1 Oct 2010 (otherwise) (SI 2010/2317)[1]
	(8)	1 Oct 2010 (SI 2010/2317)[1]
139–146		1 Oct 2010 (SI 2010/2317)[1]
147	(1)–(3)	1 Oct 2010 (SI 2010/2317)
	(4)	6 Jul 2010 (for the purpose of enabling subordinate legislation or guidance to be made) (SI 2010/1736)
		1 Oct 2010 (otherwise) (SI 2010/2317)
	(5)–(9)	1 Oct 2010 (SI 2010/2317)
148		1 Oct 2010 (SI 2010/2317)
149	(1)–(8)	5 Apr 2011 (SI 2011/1066)
	(9)	See Sch 18 below
150		18 Jan 2011 (for the purposes of ss 151–155, 157, Sch 19) (SI 2011/96)
		5 Apr 2011 (otherwise) (SI 2011/1066)
151–155		18 Jan 2011 (SI 2011/96)
156		5 Apr 2011 (SI 2011/1066)
157		18 Jan 2011 (SI 2011/96)
158		1 Oct 2010 (SI 2010/2317)
159	(1), (2)	6 April 2011 (SI 2011/96)
	(3)	1 Oct 2010 (for the purposes of s 158(4)) (SI 2010/2317)
		6 April 2011 (otherwise) (SI 2011/96)
	(4)–(6)	6 April 2011 (SI 2011/96)
189		See Sch 21 below
191		See Sch 22 below
192–195		1 Oct 2010 (SI 2010/2317)
196		See Sch 23 below
197		19 Jun 2012 (SI 2012/1569)
203–205		8 Apr 2010 (s 216(1)(b))
206		See Sch 25 below
207–210		8 Apr 2010 (s 216(1)(b))
212–218		8 Apr 2010 (s 216(1)(b))

Provision of Act		Commencement
Sch 1	paras 1–5	6 Jul 2010 (for the purpose of enabling subordinate legislation or guidance to be made) (SI 2010/1736)
		1 Oct 2010 (otherwise) (SI 2010/2317)
	para 6	1 Oct 2010 (SI 2010/2317)
	paras 7, 8	6 Jul 2010 (for the purpose of enabling subordinate legislation or guidance to be made) (SI 2010/1736)
		1 Oct 2010 (otherwise) (SI 2010/2317)
	para 9	1 Oct 2010 (SI 2010/2317)
	paras 10, 11	6 Jul 2010 (for the purpose of enabling subordinate legislation or guidance to be made) (SI 2010/1736)
		1 Oct 2010 (otherwise) (SI 2010/2317)
	para 12	1 Oct 2010 (SI 2010/2317)
	paras 13–16	6 Jul 2010 (for the purpose of enabling subordinate legislation or guidance to be made) (SI 2010/1736)
		1 Oct 2010 (otherwise) (SI 2010/2317)
Sch 6		1 Oct 2010 (SI 2010/2317)
Sch 7	paras 1–3	1 Oct 2010 (SI 2010/2317)
	paras 4–6	6 Jul 2010 (for the purpose of enabling subordinate legislation or guidance to be made) (SI 2010/1736)
		1 Oct 2010 (otherwise) (SI 2010/2317)
Sch 8		1 Oct 2010 (SI 2010/2317)
Sch 9	paras 1–15	1 Oct 2010 (SI 2010/2317)
	para 16	6 Jul 2010 (for the purpose of enabling subordinate legislation or guidance to be made) (SI 2010/1736)
		1 Oct 2010 (otherwise) (SI 2010/2317)
	paras 17–20	1 Oct 2010 (SI 2010/2317)
Sch 17	para 1	6 Jul 2010 (for the purpose of enabling subordinate legislation or guidance to be made) (SI 2010/1736)
		1 Oct 2010 (otherwise) (SI 2010/2317)[1]
	paras 2–5	1 Oct 2010 (SI 2010/2317)[1]
	para 6(1)–(7)	6 Jul 2010 (for the purpose of enabling subordinate legislation or guidance to be made) (SI 2010/1736)
		1 Oct 2010 (otherwise) (SI 2010/2317)[1]
	para 6(8), (9)	1 Oct 2010 (SI 2010/2317)[1]
	paras 7–12	1 Oct 2010 (in so far as confers or relates to the power to make rules under para 10) (SI 2010/2317)
		18 Mar 2011 (otherwise) (SI 2010/2317)[1]
	paras 13, 14	1 Oct 2010 (SI 2010/2317)[1]
Sch 18		5 Apr 2011 (SI 2011/1066)
Sch 19		18 Jan 2011 (SI 2011/96)
Sch 21	paras 1–5	1 Oct 2010 (SI 2010/2317)
	para 6	6 Jul 2010 (for the purpose of enabling subordinate legislation or guidance to be made) (SI 2010/1736)
		1 Oct 2010 (otherwise) (SI 2010/2317)
	para 7	1 Oct 2010 (SI 2010/2317)
Schs 22, 23		1 Oct 2010 (except in so far as it applies to the protected characteristic of age in Pts 3, 7 of this Act) (SI 2010/2317)
		1 Oct 2012 (exception noted above) (SI 2012/1569)
Sch 24		8 Apr 2010 (s 216(1)(b))
Sch 25		1 Oct 2010 (SI 2010/2317)
Sch 28		8 Apr 2010 (s 216(1)(b))

[1] For savings, transitional, transitory and incidental provisions, see the Equality Act 2010 (Commencement No 4, Savings, Consequential, Transitional, Transitory and Incidental Provisions and Revocation) Order 2010, SI 2010/2317 at **[2.1558]** et seq.

BRIBERY ACT 2010

(2010 c 23)

ARRANGEMENT OF SECTIONS

An Act to make provision about offences relating to bribery; and for connected purposes

[8 April 2010]

General bribery offences

[1.1792]

1 Offences of bribing another person

(1) A person ("P") is guilty of an offence if either of the following cases applies.

(2) Case 1 is where—

(a) P offers, promises or gives a financial or other advantage to another person, and

(b) P intends the advantage—

(i) to induce a person to perform improperly a relevant function or activity, or

(ii) to reward a person for the improper performance of such a function or activity.

(3) Case 2 is where—

(a) P offers, promises or gives a financial or other advantage to another person, and

(b) P knows or believes that the acceptance of the advantage would itself constitute the improper performance of a relevant function or activity.

(4) In case 1 it does not matter whether the person to whom the advantage is offered, promised or given is the same person as the person who is to perform, or has performed, the function or activity concerned.

(5) In cases 1 and 2 it does not matter whether the advantage is offered, promised or given by P directly or through a third party.

NOTES

Commencement: 1 July 2011.

[1.1793]

2 Offences relating to being bribed

(1) A person ("R") is guilty of an offence if any of the following cases applies.

(2) Case 3 is where R requests, agrees to receive or accepts a financial or other advantage intending that, in consequence, a relevant function or activity should be performed improperly (whether by R or another person).

(3) Case 4 is where—

(a) R requests, agrees to receive or accepts a financial or other advantage, and

(b) the request, agreement or acceptance itself constitutes the improper performance by R of a relevant function or activity.

(4) Case 5 is where R requests, agrees to receive or accepts a financial or other advantage as a reward for the improper performance (whether by R or another person) of a relevant function or activity.

(5) Case 6 is where, in anticipation of or in consequence of R requesting, agreeing to receive or accepting a financial or other advantage, a relevant function or activity is performed improperly—

(a) by R, or

(b) by another person at R's request or with R's assent or acquiescence.

(6) In cases 3 to 6 it does not matter—

(a) whether R requests, agrees to receive or accepts (or is to request, agree to receive or accept) the advantage directly or through a third party,

(b) whether the advantage is (or is to be) for the benefit of R or another person.

(7) In cases 4 to 6 it does not matter whether R knows or believes that the performance of the function or activity is improper.

(8) In case 6, where a person other than R is performing the function or activity, it also does not matter whether that person knows or believes that the performance of the function or activity is improper.

NOTES

Commencement: 1 July 2011.

[1.1794]

3 Function or activity to which bribe relates

(1) For the purposes of this Act a function or activity is a relevant function or activity if—

(a) it falls within subsection (2), and

(b) meets one or more of conditions A to C.

(2) The following functions and activities fall within this subsection—

(a) any function of a public nature,

(b) any activity connected with a business,

(c) any activity performed in the course of a person's employment,

(d) any activity performed by or on behalf of a body of persons (whether corporate or unincorporate).

(3) Condition A is that a person performing the function or activity is expected to perform it in good faith.

(4) Condition B is that a person performing the function or activity is expected to perform it impartially.

(5) Condition C is that a person performing the function or activity is in a position of trust by virtue of performing it.

(6) A function or activity is a relevant function or activity even if it—

(a) has no connection with the United Kingdom, and

(b) is performed in a country or territory outside the United Kingdom.

(7) In this section "business" includes trade or profession.

NOTES

Commencement: 1 July 2011.

[1.1795]

4 Improper performance to which bribe relates

(1) For the purposes of this Act a relevant function or activity—

(a) is performed improperly if it is performed in breach of a relevant expectation, and

(b) is to be treated as being performed improperly if there is a failure to perform the function or activity and that failure is itself a breach of a relevant expectation.

(2) In subsection (1) "relevant expectation"—

(a) in relation to a function or activity which meets condition A or B, means the expectation mentioned in the condition concerned, and

(b) in relation to a function or activity which meets condition C, means any expectation as to the manner in which, or the reasons for which, the function or activity will be performed that arises from the position of trust mentioned in that condition.

(3) Anything that a person does (or omits to do) arising from or in connection with that person's past performance of a relevant function or activity is to be treated for the purposes of this Act as being done (or omitted) by that person in the performance of that function or activity.

NOTES

Commencement: 1 July 2011.

[1.1796]

5 Expectation test

(1) For the purposes of sections 3 and 4, the test of what is expected is a test of what a reasonable person in the United Kingdom would expect in relation to the performance of the type of function or activity concerned.

(2) In deciding what such a person would expect in relation to the performance of a function or activity where the performance is not subject to the law of any part of the United Kingdom, any local custom or practice is to be disregarded unless it is permitted or required by the written law applicable to the country or territory concerned.

(3) In subsection (2) "written law" means law contained in—

(a) any written constitution, or provision made by or under legislation, applicable to the country or territory concerned, or

(b) any judicial decision which is so applicable and is evidenced in published written sources.

NOTES

Commencement: 1 July 2011.

Bribery of foreign public officials

[1.1797]

6 Bribery of foreign public officials

(1) A person ("P") who bribes a foreign public official ("F") is guilty of an offence if P's intention is to influence F in F's capacity as a foreign public official.

(2) P must also intend to obtain or retain—

(a) business, or

(b) an advantage in the conduct of business.

(3) P bribes F if, and only if—

(a) directly or through a third party, P offers, promises or gives any financial or other advantage—

(i) to F, or

(ii) to another person at F's request or with F's assent or acquiescence, and

(b) F is neither permitted nor required by the written law applicable to F to be influenced in F's capacity as a foreign public official by the offer, promise or gift.

(4) References in this section to influencing F in F's capacity as a foreign public official mean influencing F in the performance of F's functions as such an official, which includes—

(a) any omission to exercise those functions, and

(b) any use of F's position as such an official, even if not within F's authority.

(5) "Foreign public official" means an individual who—

(a) holds a legislative, administrative or judicial position of any kind, whether appointed or elected, of a country or territory outside the United Kingdom (or any subdivision of such a country or territory),

(b) exercises a public function—

(i) for or on behalf of a country or territory outside the United Kingdom (or any subdivision of such a country or territory), or

(ii) for any public agency or public enterprise of that country or territory (or subdivision), or

(c) is an official or agent of a public international organisation.

(6) "Public international organisation" means an organisation whose members are any of the following—

(a) countries or territories,

(b) governments of countries or territories,

(c) other public international organisations,

(d) a mixture of any of the above.

(7) For the purposes of subsection (3)(b), the written law applicable to F is—

(a) where the performance of the functions of F which P intends to influence would be subject to the law of any part of the United Kingdom, the law of that part of the United Kingdom,

(b) where paragraph (a) does not apply and F is an official or agent of a public international organisation, the applicable written rules of that organisation,

(c) where paragraphs (a) and (b) do not apply, the law of the country or territory in relation to which F is a foreign public official so far as that law is contained in—

(i) any written constitution, or provision made by or under legislation, applicable to the country or territory concerned, or

(ii) any judicial decision which is so applicable and is evidenced in published written sources.

(8) For the purposes of this section, a trade or profession is a business.

NOTES

Commencement: 1 July 2011.

Failure of commercial organisations to prevent bribery

[1.1798]

7 Failure of commercial organisations to prevent bribery

(1) A relevant commercial organisation ("C") is guilty of an offence under this section if a person ("A") associated with C bribes another person intending—

(a) to obtain or retain business for C, or

(b) to obtain or retain an advantage in the conduct of business for C.

(2) But it is a defence for C to prove that C had in place adequate procedures designed to prevent persons associated with C from undertaking such conduct.

(3) For the purposes of this section, A bribes another person if, and only if, A—

(a) is, or would be, guilty of an offence under section 1 or 6 (whether or not A has been prosecuted for such an offence), or

(b) would be guilty of such an offence if section 12(2)(c) and (4) were omitted.

(4) See section 8 for the meaning of a person associated with C and see section 9 for a duty on the Secretary of State to publish guidance.

(5) In this section—

"partnership" means—

(a) a partnership within the Partnership Act 1890, or

(b) a limited partnership registered under the Limited Partnerships Act 1907,

or a firm or entity of a similar character formed under the law of a country or territory outside the United Kingdom,

"relevant commercial organisation" means—

(a) a body which is incorporated under the law of any part of the United Kingdom and which carries on a business (whether there or elsewhere),

(b) any other body corporate (wherever incorporated) which carries on a business, or part of a business, in any part of the United Kingdom,

(c) a partnership which is formed under the law of any part of the United Kingdom and which carries on a business (whether there or elsewhere), or

(d) any other partnership (wherever formed) which carries on a business, or part of a business, in any part of the United Kingdom,

and, for the purposes of this section, a trade or profession is a business.

NOTES

Commencement: 1 July 2011.

[1.1799]

8 Meaning of associated person

(1) For the purposes of section 7, a person ("A") is associated with C if (disregarding any bribe under consideration) A is a person who performs services for or on behalf of C.

(2) The capacity in which A performs services for or on behalf of C does not matter.

(3) Accordingly A may (for example) be C's employee, agent or subsidiary.

(4) Whether or not A is a person who performs services for or on behalf of C is to be determined by reference to all the relevant circumstances and not merely by reference to the nature of the relationship between A and C.

(5) But if A is an employee of C, it is to be presumed unless the contrary is shown that A is a person who performs services for or on behalf of C.

NOTES

Commencement: 1 July 2011.

[1.1800]

9 Guidance about commercial organisations preventing bribery

(1) The Secretary of State must publish guidance about procedures that relevant commercial organisations can put in place to prevent persons associated with them from bribing as mentioned in section 7(1).

(2) The Secretary of State may, from time to time, publish revisions to guidance under this section or revised guidance.

(3) The Secretary of State must consult the Scottish Ministers [and the Department of Justice in Northern Ireland] before publishing anything under this section.

(4) Publication under this section is to be in such manner as the Secretary of State considers appropriate.

(5) Expressions used in this section have the same meaning as in section 7.

NOTES

Commencement: 1 July 2011.

Sub-s (3): words in square brackets inserted by the Northern Ireland Act 1998 (Devolution of Policing and Justice Functions) Order 2012, SI 2012/2595, art 19(1), (2), as from 18 October 2012.

Prosecution and penalties

[1.1801]

10 Consent to prosecution

(1) No proceedings for an offence under this Act may be instituted in England and Wales except by or with the consent of—

(a) the Director of Public Prosecutions,

(b) the Director of the Serious Fraud Office, or

(c) the Director of Revenue and Customs Prosecutions.

(2) No proceedings for an offence under this Act may be instituted in Northern Ireland except by or with the consent of—

(a) the Director of Public Prosecutions for Northern Ireland, or

(b) the Director of the Serious Fraud Office.

(3) No proceedings for an offence under this Act may be instituted in England and Wales or Northern Ireland by a person—

(a) who is acting—

(i) under the direction or instruction of the Director of Public Prosecutions, the Director of the Serious Fraud Office or the Director of Revenue and Customs Prosecutions, or

(ii) on behalf of such a Director, or

(b) to whom such a function has been assigned by such a Director,

except with the consent of the Director concerned to the institution of the proceedings.

(4) The Director of Public Prosecutions, the Director of the Serious Fraud Office and the Director of Revenue and Customs Prosecutions must exercise personally any function under subsection (1), (2) or (3) of giving consent.

(5) The only exception is if—

(a) the Director concerned is unavailable, and

(b) there is another person who is designated in writing by the Director acting personally as the person who is authorised to exercise any such function when the Director is unavailable.

(6) In that case, the other person may exercise the function but must do so personally.

(7) Subsections (4) to (6) apply instead of any other provisions which would otherwise have enabled any function of the Director of Public Prosecutions, the Director of the Serious Fraud Office or the Director of Revenue and Customs Prosecutions under subsection (1), (2) or (3) of giving consent to be exercised by a person other than the Director concerned.

(8) No proceedings for an offence under this Act may be instituted in Northern Ireland by virtue of section 36 of the Justice (Northern Ireland) Act 2002 (delegation of the functions of the Director of Public Prosecutions for Northern Ireland to persons other than the Deputy Director) except with the consent of the Director of Public Prosecutions for Northern Ireland to the institution of the proceedings.

(9) The Director of Public Prosecutions for Northern Ireland must exercise personally any function under subsection (2) or (8) of giving consent unless the function is exercised personally by the Deputy Director of Public Prosecutions for Northern Ireland by virtue of section 30(4) or (7) of the Act of 2002 (powers of Deputy Director to exercise functions of Director).

(10) Subsection (9) applies instead of section 36 of the Act of 2002 in relation to the functions of the Director of Public Prosecutions for Northern Ireland and the Deputy Director of Public Prosecutions for Northern Ireland under, or (as the case may be) by virtue of, subsections (2) and (8) above of giving consent.

NOTES

Commencement: 1 July 2011.

[1.1802]

11 Penalties

(1) An individual guilty of an offence under section 1, 2 or 6 is liable—

(a) on summary conviction, to imprisonment for a term not exceeding 12 months, or to a fine not exceeding the statutory maximum, or to both,

(b) on conviction on indictment, to imprisonment for a term not exceeding 10 years, or to a fine, or to both.

(2) Any other person guilty of an offence under section 1, 2 or 6 is liable—

(a) on summary conviction, to a fine not exceeding the statutory maximum,

(b) on conviction on indictment, to a fine.

(3) A person guilty of an offence under section 7 is liable on conviction on indictment to a fine.

(4) The reference in subsection (1)(a) to 12 months is to be read—

(a) in its application to England and Wales in relation to an offence committed before the commencement of section 154(1) of the Criminal Justice Act 2003, and
(b) in its application to Northern Ireland,
as a reference to 6 months.

NOTES
Commencement: 1 July 2011.

Other provisions about offences

[1.1803]
12 Offences under this Act: territorial application
(1) An offence is committed under section 1, 2 or 6 in England and Wales, Scotland or Northern Ireland if any act or omission which forms part of the offence takes place in that part of the United Kingdom.
(2) Subsection (3) applies if—
(a) no act or omission which forms part of an offence under section 1, 2 or 6 takes place in the United Kingdom,
(b) a person's acts or omissions done or made outside the United Kingdom would form part of such an offence if done or made in the United Kingdom, and
(c) that person has a close connection with the United Kingdom.
(3) In such a case—
(a) the acts or omissions form part of the offence referred to in subsection (2)(a), and
(b) proceedings for the offence may be taken at any place in the United Kingdom.
(4) For the purposes of subsection (2)(c) a person has a close connection with the United Kingdom if, and only if, the person was one of the following at the time the acts or omissions concerned were done or made—
(a) a British citizen,
(b) a British overseas territories citizen,
(c) a British National (Overseas),
(d) a British Overseas citizen,
(e) a person who under the British Nationality Act 1981 was a British subject,
(f) a British protected person within the meaning of that Act,
(g) an individual ordinarily resident in the United Kingdom,
(h) a body incorporated under the law of any part of the United Kingdom,
(i) a Scottish partnership.
(5) An offence is committed under section 7 irrespective of whether the acts or omissions which form part of the offence take place in the United Kingdom or elsewhere.
(6) Where no act or omission which forms part of an offence under section 7 takes place in the United Kingdom, proceedings for the offence may be taken at any place in the United Kingdom.
(7) Subsection (8) applies if, by virtue of this section, proceedings for an offence are to be taken in Scotland against a person.
(8) Such proceedings may be taken—
(a) in any sheriff court district in which the person is apprehended or in custody, or
(b) in such sheriff court district as the Lord Advocate may determine.
(9) In subsection (8) "sheriff court district" is to be read in accordance with section 307(1) of the Criminal Procedure (Scotland) Act 1995.

NOTES
Commencement: 1 July 2011.

[1.1804]
13 Defence for certain bribery offences etc
(1) It is a defence for a person charged with a relevant bribery offence to prove that the person's conduct was necessary for—
(a) the proper exercise of any function of an intelligence service, or
(b) the proper exercise of any function of the armed forces when engaged on active service.
(2) The head of each intelligence service must ensure that the service has in place arrangements designed to ensure that any conduct of a member of the service which would otherwise be a relevant bribery offence is necessary for a purpose falling within subsection (1)(a).
(3) The Defence Council must ensure that the armed forces have in place arrangements designed to ensure that any conduct of—
(a) a member of the armed forces who is engaged on active service, or
(b) a civilian subject to service discipline when working in support of any person falling within paragraph (a),
which would otherwise be a relevant bribery offence is necessary for a purpose falling within subsection (1)(b).
(4) The arrangements which are in place by virtue of subsection (2) or (3) must be arrangements which the Secretary of State considers to be satisfactory.

(5) For the purposes of this section, the circumstances in which a person's conduct is necessary for a purpose falling within subsection (1)(a) or (b) are to be treated as including any circumstances in which the person's conduct—

(a) would otherwise be an offence under section 2, and

(b) involves conduct by another person which, but for subsection (1)(a) or (b), would be an offence under section 1.

(6) In this section—

"active service" means service in—

(a) an action or operation against an enemy,

(b) an operation outside the British Islands for the protection of life or property, or

(c) the military occupation of a foreign country or territory,

"armed forces" means Her Majesty's forces (within the meaning of the Armed Forces Act 2006),

"civilian subject to service discipline" and "enemy" have the same meaning as in the Act of 2006,

"GCHQ" has the meaning given by section 3(3) of the Intelligence Services Act 1994,

"head" means—

(a) in relation to the Security Service, the Director General of the Security Service,

(b) in relation to the Secret Intelligence Service, the Chief of the Secret Intelligence Service, and

(c) in relation to GCHQ, the Director of GCHQ,

"intelligence service" means the Security Service, the Secret Intelligence Service or GCHQ,

"relevant bribery offence" means—

(a) an offence under section 1 which would not also be an offence under section 6,

(b) an offence under section 2,

(c) an offence committed by aiding, abetting, counselling or procuring the commission of an offence falling within paragraph (a) or (b),

(d) an offence of attempting or conspiring to commit, or of inciting the commission of, an offence falling within paragraph (a) or (b), or

(e) an offence under Part 2 of the Serious Crime Act 2007 (encouraging or assisting crime) in relation to an offence falling within paragraph (a) or (b).

NOTES

Commencement: 1 July 2011.

[1.1805]

14 Offences under sections 1, 2 and 6 by bodies corporate etc

(1) This section applies if an offence under section 1, 2 or 6 is committed by a body corporate or a Scottish partnership.

(2) If the offence is proved to have been committed with the consent or connivance of—

(a) a senior officer of the body corporate or Scottish partnership, or

(b) a person purporting to act in such a capacity,

the senior officer or person (as well as the body corporate or partnership) is guilty of the offence and liable to be proceeded against and punished accordingly.

(3) But subsection (2) does not apply, in the case of an offence which is committed under section 1, 2 or 6 by virtue of section 12(2) to (4), to a senior officer or person purporting to act in such a capacity unless the senior officer or person has a close connection with the United Kingdom (within the meaning given by section 12(4)).

(4) In this section—

"director", in relation to a body corporate whose affairs are managed by its members, means a member of the body corporate,

"senior officer" means—

(a) in relation to a body corporate, a director, manager, secretary or other similar officer of the body corporate, and

(b) in relation to a Scottish partnership, a partner in the partnership.

NOTES

Commencement: 1 July 2011.

[1.1806]

15 Offences under section 7 by partnerships

(1) Proceedings for an offence under section 7 alleged to have been committed by a partnership must be brought in the name of the partnership (and not in that of any of the partners).

(2) For the purposes of such proceedings—

(a) rules of court relating to the service of documents have effect as if the partnership were a body corporate, and

(b) the following provisions apply as they apply in relation to a body corporate—

(i) section 33 of the Criminal Justice Act 1925 and Schedule 3 to the Magistrates' Courts Act 1980,

(ii) section 18 of the Criminal Justice Act (Northern Ireland) 1945 (c 15 (NI)) and Schedule 4 to the Magistrates' Courts (Northern Ireland) Order 1981 (SI 1981/1675 (NI 26)),

(iii) section 70 of the Criminal Procedure (Scotland) Act 1995.

(3) A fine imposed on the partnership on its conviction for an offence under section 7 is to be paid out of the partnership assets.

(4) In this section "partnership" has the same meaning as in section 7.

NOTES

Commencement: 1 July 2011.

Supplementary and final provisions

[1.1807]

16 Application to Crown

This Act applies to individuals in the public service of the Crown as it applies to other individuals.

NOTES

Commencement: 8 April 2010.

[1.1808]

17 Consequential provision

(1) The following common law offences are abolished—

(a) the offences under the law of England and Wales and Northern Ireland of bribery and embracery,

(b) the offences under the law of Scotland of bribery and accepting a bribe.

(2) Schedule 1 (which contains consequential amendments) has effect.

(3) Schedule 2 (which contains repeals and revocations) has effect.

(4) The relevant national authority may by order make such supplementary, incidental or consequential provision as the relevant national authority considers appropriate for the purposes of this Act or in consequence of this Act.

(5) The power to make an order under this section—

(a) is exercisable by statutory instrument [(subject to subsection (9A))],

(b) includes power to make transitional, transitory or saving provision,

(c) may, in particular, be exercised by amending, repealing, revoking or otherwise modifying any provision made by or under an enactment (including any Act passed in the same Session as this Act).

(6) Subject to subsection (7), a statutory instrument containing an order of the Secretary of State under this section may not be made unless a draft of the instrument has been laid before, and approved by a resolution of, each House of Parliament.

(7) A statutory instrument containing an order of the Secretary of State under this section which does not amend or repeal a provision of a public general Act or of devolved legislation is subject to annulment in pursuance of a resolution of either House of Parliament.

(8) Subject to subsection (9), a statutory instrument containing an order of the Scottish Ministers under this section may not be made unless a draft of the instrument has been laid before, and approved by a resolution of, the Scottish Parliament.

(9) A statutory instrument containing an order of the Scottish Ministers under this section which does not amend or repeal a provision of an Act of the Scottish Parliament or of a public general Act is subject to annulment in pursuance of a resolution of the Scottish Parliament.

[(9A) The power of the Department of Justice in Northern Ireland to make an order under this section is exercisable by statutory rule for the purposes of the Statutory Rules (Northern Ireland) Order 1979 (and not by statutory instrument).

(9B) Subject to subsection (9C), an order of the Department of Justice in Northern Ireland made under this section is subject to affirmative resolution (within the meaning of section 41(4) of the Interpretation Act (Northern Ireland) 1954).

(9C) An order of the Department of Justice in Northern Ireland made under this section which does not amend or repeal a provision of an Act of the Northern Ireland Assembly or of a public general Act is subject to negative resolution (within the meaning of section 41(6) of the Interpretation Act (Northern Ireland) 1954).]

(10) In this section—

"devolved legislation" means an Act of the Scottish Parliament, a Measure of the National Assembly for Wales or an Act of the Northern Ireland Assembly,

"enactment" includes an Act of the Scottish Parliament and Northern Ireland legislation,

"relevant national authority" means—

(a) in the case of provision which would be within the legislative competence of the Scottish Parliament if it were contained in an Act of that Parliament, the Scottish Ministers, . . .

[(aa) in the case of provision which could be made by an Act of the Northern Ireland Assembly without the consent of the Secretary of State (see sections 6 to 8 of the Northern Ireland Act 1998), the Department of Justice in Northern Ireland, and]

(b) in any other case, the Secretary of State.

NOTES

Commencement: 8 April 2010 (sub-ss (4)–(10)); 1 July 2011 (otherwise).

Sub-s (5): words in square brackets inserted by the Northern Ireland Act 1998 (Devolution of Policing and Justice Functions) Order 2012, SI 2012/2595, art 19(1), (3)(a), as from 18 October 2012.

Sub-ss (9A)–(9C): inserted by SI 2012/2595, art 19(1), (3)(b), as from 18 October 2012.

Sub-s (10): in definition "relevant national authority", word omitted repealed and para (aa) inserted, by SI 2012/2595, art 19(1), (3)(c), as from 18 October 2012.

Orders: the Bribery Act 2010 (Consequential Amendments) Order 2011, SI 2011/1441.

[1.1809]

18 Extent

(1) Subject as follows, this Act extends to England and Wales, Scotland and Northern Ireland.

(2) Subject to subsections (3) to (5), any amendment, repeal or revocation made by Schedule 1 or 2 has the same extent as the provision amended, repealed or revoked.

(3) The amendment of, and repeals in, the Armed Forces Act 2006 do not extend to the Channel Islands.

(4) The amendments of the International Criminal Court Act 2001 extend to England and Wales and Northern Ireland only.

(5) Subsection (2) does not apply to the repeal in the Civil Aviation Act 1982.

NOTES

Commencement: 8 April 2010.

[1.1810]

19 Commencement and transitional provision etc

(1) Subject to subsection (2), this Act comes into force on such day as the Secretary of State may by order made by statutory instrument appoint.

(2) Sections 16, 17(4) to (10) and 18, this section (other than subsections (5) to (7)) and section 20 come into force on the day on which this Act is passed.

(3) An order under subsection (1) may—

(a) appoint different days for different purposes,

(b) make such transitional, transitory or saving provision as the Secretary of State considers appropriate in connection with the coming into force of any provision of this Act.

(4) The Secretary of State must consult the Scottish Ministers before making an order under this section in connection with any provision of this Act which would be within the legislative competence of the Scottish Parliament if it were contained in an Act of that Parliament.

(5) This Act does not affect any liability, investigation, legal proceeding or penalty for or in respect of—

(a) a common law offence mentioned in subsection (1) of section 17 which is committed wholly or partly before the coming into force of that subsection in relation to such an offence, or

(b) an offence under the Public Bodies Corrupt Practices Act 1889 or the Prevention of Corruption Act 1906 committed wholly or partly before the coming into force of the repeal of the Act by Schedule 2 to this Act.

(6) For the purposes of subsection (5) an offence is partly committed before a particular time if any act or omission which forms part of the offence takes place before that time.

(7) Subsections (5) and (6) are without prejudice to section 16 of the Interpretation Act 1978 (general savings on repeal).

NOTES

Commencement: 8 April 2010 (sub-ss (1)–(4)); 1 July 2011 (otherwise).

Orders: the Bribery Act 2010 (Commencement) Order 2011, SI 2011/1418.

[1.1811]

20 Short title

This Act may be cited as the Bribery Act 2010.

NOTES

Commencement: 8 April 2010.

SCHEDULES 1 AND 2

(Sch 1 (Consequential Amendments) and Sch 2 (Repeals and Revocations) contain various

amendments, repeals and revocations of enactments that are outside the scope of this work.)

SUPERANNUATION ACT 2010

(2010 c 37)

An Act to make provision for and in connection with limiting the value of the benefits which may be provided under so much of any scheme under section 1 of the Superannuation Act 1972 as provides by virtue of section 2(2) of that Act for benefits to be provided by way of compensation to or in respect of persons who suffer loss of office or employment; and to make provision about the procedure for modifying such a scheme.

[16 December 2010]

[1.1812]

1 Consents required for civil service compensation scheme modifications

(1)–(3) *(Amend the Superannuation Act 1972, s 2 at* **[1.8]***).*

(4) The amendments made by this section apply in relation to reductions to which effect is given by a scheme made under section 1 of the 1972 Act after the coming into force of this section.

(5) Subsection (6) applies if—

- (a) a scheme under section 1 of the 1972 Act is made after this section comes into force, and
- (b) consultation on the proposed scheme took place to any extent before this section came into force.

(6) The fact that the amendments made by this section were not in force when that consultation took place does not affect the question whether the consultation satisfied the requirements of section 1(3) of the 1972 Act.

NOTES

Commencement: 16 December 2010.

[1.1813]

2 Consultation in relation to civil service compensation scheme modifications

(1)–(3) *(Amend the Superannuation Act 1972, s 2 at* **[1.8]***).*

(4) The amendments made by this section apply in relation to reductions to which effect is given by a scheme made under section 1 of the 1972 Act after the coming into force of this section.

NOTES

Commencement: 16 February 2011.

3 *(Repealed by the Superannuation Act 2010 (Repeal of Limits on Compensation) Order 2010, SI 2010/2996, art 2, as from 21 December 2010 (except in relation to any provision of a scheme made under the Superannuation Act 1972, s 1 before the time at which this section came into force except in so far as the provision has effect by virtue of a scheme made after that time).)*

[1.1814]

4 Final provisions

(1) This Act may be cited as the Superannuation Act 2010.

(2) Subject to subsection (3), this Act comes into force on the day it is passed.

(3) Section 2 comes into force at the end of the period of 2 months beginning with that day.

(4) Except so far as otherwise provided under this section, section 3 expires at the end of the period of 12 months beginning with the day on which that section comes into force.

(5) The Minister may by order—

- (a) repeal section 3;
- (b) provide that that section—
  - (i) is not to expire at the time when it would otherwise expire under subsection (4) or in accordance with the most recent order under this subsection, but
  - (ii) is to continue in force after that time for a period not exceeding 6 months;
- (c) (subject to subsection (6)) at any time revive that section (following its expiry or repeal) for a period not exceeding 6 months.

(6) An order under subsection (5)(c) may not be made after the end of the period of 3 years beginning with the day on which this Act is passed.

(7) The expiry or repeal of section 3 does not affect the application of that section in relation to compensation benefits provided to or in respect of a person in connection with a loss of office or employment occurring before its expiry or repeal.

(8) An order made by the Minister under this Act—

- (a) is to be made by statutory instrument;
- (b) may include supplementary, incidental, transitional or saving provision.

(9) A statutory instrument containing an order under section 3(11) or subsection (5)(b) or (c) of this section may not be made unless a draft of the instrument has been laid before and approved by a resolution of the House of Commons.
(10) Any other statutory instrument containing an order under this Act is subject to annulment in pursuance of a resolution of the House of Commons.
(11) In this Act "the Minister" means the Minister for the Civil Service.

NOTES

Commencement: 16 December 2010.
Orders: the Superannuation Act 2010 (Repeal of Limits on Compensation) Order 2010, SI 2010/2996.

POSTAL SERVICES ACT 2011

(2011 c 5)

An Act to make provision for the restructuring of the Royal Mail group and about the Royal Mail Pension Plan; to make new provision about the regulation of postal services, including provision for a special administration regime; and for connected purposes

[13 June 2011]

NOTES

Most of this Act covers matters outside the scope of this work, and only s 9 below is directly relevant to employment law. For reasons of space, the subject matter of sections not printed is not annotated. This Act applies to the whole of the United Kingdom (see s 93). Section 9 came into force on 1 October 2011 by virtue of the Postal Services Act 2011 (Commencement No 1 and Transitional Provisions) Order 2011, SI 2011/2329.

PART 1
RESTRUCTURING OF ROYAL MAIL GROUP

Transfer of property etc

[1.1815]

9 Transfer of employees otherwise than under transfer scheme

(1) This section applies if an agreement between companies within subsection (3) provides for the transfer from one to the other of rights and liabilities under contracts of employment.
(2) This section also applies if—
- (a) employees of a company within subsection (3) ("company A") are provided to another company within that subsection ("company B"),
- (b) an agreement between the companies provides for the employees to cease to be provided to company B, and
- (c) company B intends to employ the employees.

(3) A company is within this subsection if—
- (a) it is the original holding company or a subsidiary of that company, and
- (b) it is wholly owned by the Crown.

(4) At any time before the agreement comes into force, the Secretary of State may—
- (a) in a case within subsection (1), designate any contract of employment the rights and liabilities under which are to be transferred under the agreement, and
- (b) in a case within subsection (2), designate any employee of company A who is provided as mentioned in subsection (2)(a).

(5) The designation may specify or describe the contracts of employment or employees.
(6) On the coming into force of the agreement, the Transfer of Undertakings (Protection of Employment) Regulations 2006 apply in relation to—
- (a) the transfer of designated contracts of employment, and
- (b) the cessation of the provision of designated employees to company B,

whether or not the agreement would otherwise be regarded for the purposes of those regulations as giving rise to a relevant transfer.
(7) Where by virtue of the agreement a designated employee of a company within subsection (3) ("the transferor") becomes an employee of another company within that subsection ("the transferee")—
- (a) a period of employment with the transferor is to be treated as a period of employment with the transferee, and
- (b) the transfer to the transferee is not to be treated as a break in service.

NOTES

Commencement: 1 October 2011.

EUROPEAN UNION ACT 2011

(2011 c 12)

An Act to make provision about treaties relating to the European Union and decisions made under them, including provision implementing the Protocol signed at Brussels on 23 June 2010 amending the Protocol (No 36) on transitional provisions annexed to the Treaty on European Union, to the Treaty on the Functioning of the European Union and to the Treaty establishing the European Atomic Energy Community; and to make provision about the means by which directly applicable or directly effective European Union law has effect in the United Kingdom

[19 July 2011]

NOTES

Most of this Act covers matters outside the scope of this work. Section 15 amends the European Communities Act 1972, s 1 at **[1.14]**. Only s 18 below is directly relevant to employment law. For reasons of space, the subject matter of sections not printed is not annotated. This Act applies to the whole of the United Kingdom (see s 20). Sections 15 and 18 came into force on 19 July 2011 (ie, the date of Royal assent) by virtue of s 21 of this Act.

PART 3
GENERAL

Status of EU law

[1.1816]

18 Status of EU law dependent on continuing statutory basis

Directly applicable or directly effective EU law (that is, the rights, powers, liabilities, obligations, restrictions, remedies and procedures referred to in section 2(1) of the European Communities Act 1972) falls to be recognised and available in law in the United Kingdom only by virtue of that Act or where it is required to be recognised and available in law by virtue of any other Act.

NOTES

Commencement: 19 July 2011.

LOCALISM ACT 2011

(2011 c 20)

ARRANGEMENT OF SECTIONS

PART I
LOCAL GOVERNMENT

CHAPTER 8
PAY ACCOUNTABILITY

An Act to make provision about the functions and procedures of local and certain other authorities; to make provision about the functions of the Commission for Local Administration in England; to enable the recovery of financial sanctions imposed by the Court of Justice of the European Union on the United Kingdom from local and public authorities; to make provision about local government finance; to make provision about town and country planning, the Community Infrastructure Levy and the authorisation of nationally significant infrastructure projects; to make provision about social and other housing; to make provision about regeneration in London; and for connected purposes

[15 November 2011]

NOTES

Most of this Act covers matters outside the scope of this work and, for reasons of space, the subject matter of sections not printed is not annotated. Sections 38–43 came into force on 15 January 2012 in relation to England (by virtue of s 240(1)(b) of this Act), and on 31 January 2012 in relation to Wales (by virtue of the Localism Act 2011 (Commencement No 1) (Wales)

Order 2012, SI 2012/193 which was made under s 240(3)). The provisions of the Act reproduced here apply to England and Wales only (see s 239).

PART 1
LOCAL GOVERNMENT

CHAPTER 8
PAY ACCOUNTABILITY

[1.1817]

38 Pay policy statements

(1) A relevant authority must prepare a pay policy statement for the financial year 2012-2013 and each subsequent financial year.

(2) A pay policy statement for a financial year must set out the authority's policies for the financial year relating to—

- (a) the remuneration of its chief officers,
- (b) the remuneration of its lowest-paid employees, and
- (c) the relationship between—
  - (i) the remuneration of its chief officers, and
  - (ii) the remuneration of its employees who are not chief officers.

(3) The statement must state—

- (a) the definition of "lowest-paid employees" adopted by the authority for the purposes of the statement, and
- (b) the authority's reasons for adopting that definition.

(4) The statement must include the authority's policies relating to—

- (a) the level and elements of remuneration for each chief officer,
- (b) remuneration of chief officers on recruitment,
- (c) increases and additions to remuneration for each chief officer,
- (d) the use of performance-related pay for chief officers,
- (e) the use of bonuses for chief officers,
- (f) the approach to the payment of chief officers on their ceasing to hold office under or to be employed by the authority, and
- (g) the publication of and access to information relating to remuneration of chief officers.

(5) A pay policy statement for a financial year may also set out the authority's policies for the financial year relating to the other terms and conditions applying to the authority's chief officers.

NOTES

Commencement: 15 January 2012 (in relation to England); 31 January 2012 (in relation to Wales).

[1.1818]

39 Supplementary provisions relating to statements

(1) A relevant authority's pay policy statement must be approved by a resolution of the authority before it comes into force.

(2) The first statement must be prepared and approved before the end of 31 March 2012.

(3) Each subsequent statement must be prepared and approved before the end of the 31 March immediately preceding the financial year to which it relates.

(4) A relevant authority may by resolution amend its pay policy statement (including after the beginning of the financial year to which it relates).

(5) As soon as is reasonably practicable after approving or amending a pay policy statement, the authority must publish the statement or the amended statement in such manner as it thinks fit (which must include publication on the authority's website).

NOTES

Commencement: 15 January 2012 (in relation to England); 31 January 2012 (in relation to Wales).

[1.1819]

40 Guidance

(1) A relevant authority in England must, in performing its functions under section 38 or 39, have regard to any guidance issued or approved by the Secretary of State.

(2) A relevant authority in Wales must, in performing its functions under section 38 or 39, have regard to any guidance issued or approved by the Welsh Ministers.

NOTES

Commencement: 15 January 2012 (in relation to England); 31 January 2012 (in relation to Wales).

[1.1820]

41 Determinations relating to remuneration etc

(1) This section applies to a determination that—

(a) is made by a relevant authority in a financial year beginning on or after 1 April 2012 and

(b) relates to the remuneration of or other terms and conditions applying to a chief officer of the authority.

(2) The relevant authority must comply with its pay policy statement for the financial year in making the determination.

(3) Any power of a fire and rescue authority within section 43(1)(i) to appoint officers and employees is subject to the requirement in subsection (2).

(4) *(Amends the Local Government Act 1972, s 112.)*

NOTES

Commencement: 15 January 2012 (in relation to England); 31 January 2012 (in relation to Wales).

[1.1821]

42 Exercise of functions

(1) The functions conferred on a relevant authority by this Chapter are not to be the responsibility of an executive of the authority under executive arrangements.

(2) Section 101 of the Local Government Act 1972 (arrangements for discharge of functions by local authorities) does not apply to the function of passing a resolution under this Chapter.

(3) The function of a fire and rescue authority within section 43(1)(i) of passing a resolution under this Chapter may not be delegated by the authority.

NOTES

Commencement: 15 January 2012 (in relation to England); 31 January 2012 (in relation to Wales).

[1.1822]

43 Interpretation

(1) In this Chapter "relevant authority" means—

(a) a county council,

(b) a county borough council,

(c) a district council,

(d) a London borough council,

(e) the Common Council of the City of London in its capacity as a local authority,

(f) the Council of the Isles of Scilly,

(g) the London Fire and Emergency Planning Authority,

(h) a metropolitan county fire and rescue authority, or

(i) a fire and rescue authority constituted by a scheme under section 2 of the Fire and Rescue Services Act 2004 or a scheme to which section 4 of that Act applies.

(2) In this Chapter "chief officer", in relation to a relevant authority, means each of the following—

(a) the head of its paid service designated under section 4(1) of the Local Government and Housing Act 1989;

(b) its monitoring officer designated under section 5(1) of that Act;

(c) a statutory chief officer mentioned in section 2(6) of that Act;

(d) a non-statutory chief officer mentioned in section 2(7) of that Act;

(e) a deputy chief officer mentioned in section 2(8) of that Act.

(3) In this Chapter "remuneration", in relation to a chief officer and a relevant authority, means—

(a) the chief officer's salary or, in the case of a chief officer engaged by the authority under a contract for services, payments made by the authority to the chief officer for those services,

(b) any bonuses payable by the authority to the chief officer,

(c) any charges, fees or allowances payable by the authority to the chief officer,

(d) any benefits in kind to which the chief officer is entitled as a result of the chief officer's office or employment,

(e) any increase in or enhancement of the chief officer's pension entitlement where the increase or enhancement is as a result of a resolution of the authority, and

(f) any amounts payable by the authority to the chief officer on the chief officer ceasing to hold office under or be employed by the authority, other than amounts that may be payable by virtue of any enactment.

(4) In this Chapter "terms and conditions", in relation to a chief officer and a relevant authority, means the terms and conditions on which the chief officer holds office under or is employed by the authority.

(5) References in this Chapter to the remuneration of, or the other terms and conditions applying to, a chief officer include—

(a) the remuneration that may be provided to, or the terms and conditions that may apply to, that chief officer in the future, and

(b) the remuneration that is to be provided to, or the terms and conditions that are to apply to, chief officers of that kind that the authority may appoint in the future.

(6) In this Chapter "remuneration", in relation to a relevant authority and an employee of its who is not a chief officer, means—

(a) the employee's salary,
(b) any bonuses payable by the authority to the employee,
(c) any allowances payable by the authority to the employee,
(d) any benefits in kind to which the employee is entitled as a result of the employee's employment,
(e) any increase in or enhancement of the employee's pension entitlement where the increase or enhancement is as a result of a resolution of the authority, and
(f) any amounts payable by the authority to the employee on the employee ceasing to be employed by the authority, other than any amounts that may be payable by virtue of any enactment.

(7) References in this Chapter to the remuneration of an employee who is not a chief officer include—

(a) the remuneration that may be provided to that employee in the future, and
(b) the remuneration that is to be provided to employees of the same kind that the authority may employ in the future.

(8) In this Chapter—

"enactment" includes an enactment comprised in subordinate legislation (within the meaning of the Interpretation Act 1978);

"financial year" means the period of 12 months ending with 31 March in any year.

NOTES

Commencement: 15 January 2012 (in relation to England); 31 January 2012 (in relation to Wales).

PUBLIC BODIES ACT 2011

(2011 c 24)

ARRANGEMENT OF SECTIONS

PART 1
GENERAL ORDER-MAKING POWERS

Powers of Ministers

Powers of Ministers: supplementary

Restrictions on powers of Ministers and Welsh Ministers

Transfer of property, rights and liabilities

PART 3
FINAL

SCHEDULES

An Act to confer powers on Ministers of the Crown in relation to certain public bodies and offices; to confer powers on Welsh Ministers in relation to environmental and other public bodies; to make provision about delegation and shared services in relation to persons exercising environmental functions; to abolish regional development agencies; to make provision about the funding of Sianel Pedwar Cymru; to make provision about the powers of bodies established under the National Heritage Act 1983 to form companies; to repeal provisions of the Coroners and Justice Act 2009 relating to appeals to the Chief Coroner; to make provision about amendment of Schedule 1 to the Superannuation Act 1972; and for connected purposes

[14 December 2011]

PART 1
GENERAL ORDER-MAKING POWERS

Powers of Ministers

[1.1823]

1 Power to abolish

(1) A Minister may by order abolish a body or office specified in Schedule 1.

(2) An order under subsection (1) may include provision transferring functions from the body or office being abolished to an eligible person.

(3) In this Act, "eligible person" means—

(a) a Minister, the Scottish Ministers, a Northern Ireland department or the Welsh Ministers,

(b) any other person exercising public functions,

(c) a company limited by guarantee,

(d) a community interest company,

(e) a co-operative society,

(f) a community benefit society,

(g) a charitable incorporated organisation, or

(h) a body of trustees or other unincorporated body of persons.

NOTES

Commencement: 14 February 2012.

Orders: the Public Bodies (Abolition of the National Endowment for Science, Technology and the Arts) Order 2012, SI 2012/964; the Public Bodies (Abolition of Courts Boards) Order 2012, SI 2012/1206; the Inland Waterways Advisory Council (Abolition) Order 2012, SI 2012/1658; the Advisory Committee on Hazardous Substances (Abolition) Order 2012, SI 2012/1923; the Public Bodies (Child Maintenance and Enforcement Commission: Abolition and Transfer of Functions) Order 2012, SI 2012/2007; the Public Bodies (Abolition of Crown Court Rule Committee and Magistrates' Courts Rule Committee) Order 2012, SI 2012/2398; the Public Bodies (Abolition of Her Majesty's Inspectorate of Courts Administration and the Public Guardian Board) Order 2012, SI 2012/2401; the Public Bodies (Abolition of Regional and Local Fisheries Advisory Committees) Order 2012, SI 2012/2406; the Public Bodies (Abolition of Environment Protection Advisory Committees) Order 2012, SI 2012/2407; the Public Bodies (Abolition of the Commission for Rural Communities) Order 2012, SI 2012/2654; the Public Bodies (Abolition of the Railway Heritage Committee) Order 2013, SI 2013/64; the Public Bodies (Abolition of the Disability Living Allowance Advisory Board) Order 2013, SI 2013/252; the Public Bodies (Abolition of the Aircraft and Shipbuilding Industries Arbitration Tribunal) Order 2013, SI 2013/686; the Public Bodies (Abolition of British Shipbuilders) Order 2013, SI 2013/687.

[1.1824]

2 Power to merge

(1) A Minister may by order merge any group of bodies or offices specified in Schedule 2.

(2) In this section, to "merge" a group means—

(a) to abolish all the bodies or offices in the group, create a new body corporate or office and transfer some or all of the functions of the abolished bodies or offices to the new one, or

(b) to abolish all but one of the bodies or offices in the group and to transfer some or all of the functions of the abolished bodies or offices to the remaining one.

(3) An order under subsection (1) may include provision to transfer a function from a body or office being abolished to an eligible person not included in the group.

NOTES

Commencement: 14 February 2012.

[1.1825]
3 Power to modify constitutional arrangements
(1) A Minister may by order modify the constitutional arrangements of a body or office specified in Schedule 3.
(2) In this Act, references to the constitutional arrangements of a body include matters relating to—
(a) the name of the body;
(b) the chair of the body (including qualifications and procedures for appointment and functions);
(c) members of the body (including the number of members, qualifications and procedures for appointment and functions);
(d) employees of the body exercising functions on its behalf (including qualifications and procedures for appointment and functions);
(e) the body's powers to employ staff;
(f) governing procedures and arrangements (including the role and membership of committees and sub-committees);
(g) reports and accounts;
(h) the extent to which the body is accountable to Ministers;
(i) the extent to which the body exercises functions on behalf of the Crown.
(3) In this Act, references to the constitutional arrangements of an office include matters relating to—
(a) the name of the office;
(b) appointment of the office-holder (including qualifications and procedures for appointment);
(c) the office-holder's powers to employ staff;
(d) reports and accounts;
(e) the extent to which the office-holder is accountable to Ministers;
(f) the extent to which the office-holder exercises functions on behalf of the Crown.

NOTES
Commencement: 14 February 2012.

[1.1826]
4 Power to modify funding arrangements
(1) A Minister may by order modify the funding arrangements of a body or office specified in Schedule 4.
(2) The consent of the Treasury is required to make an order under this section.
(3) In this Act, references to modifying the funding arrangements of a body or office include—
(a) modifying the extent to which it is funded by a Minister;
(b) conferring power on the body, or the office-holder, to charge fees for the exercise of a function (and to determine their amount).

NOTES
Commencement: 14 February 2012.
Orders: the Public Bodies (Water Supply and Water Quality Fees) Order 2013, SI 2013/277.

[1.1827]
5 Power to modify or transfer functions
(1) A Minister may by order—
(a) modify the functions of a body, or the holder of an office, specified in Schedule 5, or
(b) transfer a function of such a person to an eligible person.
(2) In this Act, references to modifying the functions of a person include—
(a) conferring a function on the person;
(b) abolishing a function of the person;
(c) changing the purpose or objective for which the person exercises a function;
(d) changing the conditions under which the person exercises a function.

NOTES
Commencement: 14 February 2012.
Orders: the British Waterways Board (Transfer of Functions) Order 2012, SI 2012/1659; the Public Bodies (The Office of Fair Trading Transfer of Consumer Advice Scheme Function and Modification of Enforcement Functions) Order 2013, SI 2013/783.

[1.1828]
6 Consequential provision etc
(1) An order under sections 1 to 5 may make consequential, supplementary, incidental or transitional provision, or savings.
(2) Where an order under section 1, 2 or 5(1)(b) transfers functions, the power in subsection (1) includes power to make consequential or supplementary provision—

(a) to modify functions of the transferor or transferee;
(b) to modify the constitutional or funding arrangements of the transferor or transferee.

(3) Where an order under section 5(1)(a) modifies functions of a body or office-holder, the power in subsection (1) includes power to make consequential or supplementary provision to modify the constitutional or funding arrangements of the body or office.

(4) The consent of the Treasury is required to make provision by virtue of subsection (2)(b) or (3) modifying funding arrangements.

(5) An order under sections 1 to 5 may include provision repealing the entry in the Schedule by virtue of which the order was made.

NOTES

Commencement: 14 February 2012.

Orders: the Public Bodies (Abolition of Courts Boards) Order 2012, SI 2012/1206; the Inland Waterways Advisory Council (Abolition) Order 2012, SI 2012/1658; the British Waterways Board (Transfer of Functions) Order 2012, SI 2012/1659; the Public Bodies (Child Maintenance and Enforcement Commission: Abolition and Transfer of Functions) Order 2012, SI 2012/2007; the Public Bodies (Abolition of Crown Court Rule Committee and Magistrates' Courts Rule Committee) Order 2012, SI 2012/2398; the Public Bodies (Abolition of Her Majesty's Inspectorate of Courts Administration and the Public Guardian Board) Order 2012, SI 2012/2401; the Public Bodies (Abolition of Regional and Local Fisheries Advisory Committees) Order 2012, SI 2012/2406; the Public Bodies (Abolition of Environment Protection Advisory Committees) Order 2012, SI 2012/2407; the Public Bodies (Abolition of the Commission for Rural Communities) Order 2012, SI 2012/2654; the Public Bodies (Abolition of the Railway Heritage Committee) Order 2013, SI 2013/64; the Public Bodies (Abolition of the Disability Living Allowance Advisory Board) Order 2013, SI 2013/252; the Public Bodies (Water Supply and Water Quality Fees) Order 2013, SI 2013/277; the Public Bodies (Abolition of the Aircraft and Shipbuilding Industries Arbitration Tribunal) Order 2013, SI 2013/686; the Public Bodies (Abolition of British Shipbuilders) Order 2013, SI 2013/687; the Public Bodies (The Office of Fair Trading Transfer of Consumer Advice Scheme Function and Modification of Enforcement Functions) Order 2013, SI 2013/783.

Powers of Ministers: supplementary

[1.1829]

7 Restrictions on Ministerial powers

(1) The modification or transfer of a function by an order under sections 1 to 5 must not prevent it (to the extent that it continues to be exercisable) from being exercised independently of Ministers in any of the following cases.

(2) Those cases are—
(a) where the function is a judicial function (whether or not exercised by a court or a tribunal);
(b) where the function's exercise involves enforcement activities in relation to obligations imposed on a Minister;
(c) where the function's exercise otherwise constitutes the exercise of oversight or scrutiny of the actions of a Minister.

(3) Provision made by an order under sections 1 to 5 must be proportionate to the reasons for the order.

(4) In this section "enforcement activities" means—
(a) the bringing of legal proceedings or the provision of assistance with the bringing of legal proceedings,
(b) the carrying out of an investigation with a view to bringing legal proceedings or to providing such assistance, or
(c) the taking of steps preparatory to any of those things.

NOTES

Commencement: 14 February 2012.

[1.1830]

8 Purpose and conditions

(1) A Minister may make an order under sections 1 to 5 only if the Minister considers that the order serves the purpose of improving the exercise of public functions, having regard to—
(a) efficiency,
(b) effectiveness,
(c) economy, and
(d) securing appropriate accountability to Ministers.

(2) A Minister may make an order under those sections only if the Minister considers that—
(a) the order does not remove any necessary protection, and
(b) the order does not prevent any person from continuing to exercise any right or freedom which that person might reasonably expect to continue to exercise.

NOTES

Commencement: 14 February 2012.

[1.1831]

9 Devolution

(1) An order under sections 1 to 5 requires the consent of the Scottish Parliament to make provision—

(a) which would be within the legislative competence of the Scottish Parliament if it were contained in an Act of that Parliament, or

(b) which modifies the functions of the Scottish Ministers.

(2) Consent is not required under subsection (1)(b) in relation to provision abolishing a function of the Scottish Ministers which relates to a body abolished under section 1 or 2.

(3) An order under sections 1 to 5 requires the consent of the Northern Ireland Assembly to make provision—

(a) which would be within the legislative competence of the Northern Ireland Assembly if it were contained in an Act of the Assembly, or

(b) which modifies the functions of a person within subsection (4).

(4) The persons referred to in subsection (3)(b) are—

(a) the First Minister and deputy First Minister of Northern Ireland;

(b) a Northern Ireland Minister;

(c) the Attorney General for Northern Ireland;

(d) a Northern Ireland department;

(e) a person exercising public functions in relation to a transferred matter (within the meaning of the Northern Ireland Act 1998).

(5) Consent is not required under subsection (3)(a) in relation to any provision if—

(a) a Bill for an Act of the Northern Ireland Assembly containing the provision would require the consent of the Secretary of State under section 8 of the Northern Ireland Act 1998, and

(b) the provision does not affect, other than incidentally, a transferred matter (within the meaning of that Act).

(6) An order under sections 1 to 5 requires the consent of the National Assembly for Wales to make provision which would be within the legislative competence of the Assembly if it were contained in an Act of the Assembly.

(7) An order under sections 1 to 5 requires the consent of the Welsh Ministers to make provision not falling within subsection (6)—

(a) which modifies the functions of the Welsh Ministers, the First Minister for Wales or the Counsel General to the Welsh Assembly Government, or

(b) which could be made by any of those persons.

(8) In subsection (7), references to a function do not include—

(a) a function of giving consent to, or being consulted about, the exercise of a function by a Minister, or

(b) a function relating to the constitutional arrangements of a body or office.

NOTES

Commencement: 14 February 2012.

[1.1832]

10 Consultation

(1) A Minister proposing to make an order under sections 1 to 5 must consult—

(a) the body or the holder of the office to which the proposal relates,

(b) such other persons as appear to the Minister to be representative of interests substantially affected by the proposal,

(c) the Scottish Ministers, if the proposal relates to any matter, so far as applying in or as regards Scotland, in relation to which the Scottish Ministers exercise functions (and where the consent of the Scottish Parliament is not required under section 9),

(d) a Northern Ireland department, if the proposal relates to any matter, so far as applying in or as regards Northern Ireland, in relation to which the department exercises functions (and where the consent of the Northern Ireland Assembly is not required under section 9),

(e) the Welsh Ministers, if the proposal relates to any matter, so far as applying in or as regards Wales, in relation to which the Welsh Ministers exercise functions (and where the consent of the National Assembly for Wales or the Welsh Ministers is not required under section 9),

(f) where the functions affected by the proposal relate to the administration of justice, the Lord Chief Justice, and

(g) such other persons as the Minister considers appropriate.

(2) If, as a result of consultation under subsection (1), it appears to the Minister appropriate to change the whole or part of the proposal, the Minister must carry out such further consultation with respect to the changes as seems appropriate.

(3) It is immaterial for the purposes of this section whether consultation is carried out before or after the commencement of this section.

(4) Subsection (1)(a) does not apply to a body with no members or an office which is vacant; and, where a body is consulted under that provision, any vacancy in its membership is immaterial.

NOTES

Commencement: 14 December 2011.

[1.1833]

11 Procedure

(1) If after consultation under section 10 the Minister considers it appropriate to proceed with the making of an order under sections 1 to 5, the Minister may lay before Parliament—

(a) a draft order, and

(b) an explanatory document.

(2) The explanatory document must—

(a) introduce and give reasons for the order,

(b) explain why the Minister considers that—

(i) the order serves the purpose in section 8(1), and

(ii) the conditions in section 8(2)(a) and (b) are satisfied,

(c) if the order contains provision made by virtue of more than one entry in Schedules 1 to 5, explain why the Minister considers it appropriate for it to do so, and

(d) contain a summary of representations received in the consultation.

(3) The Minister may not act under subsection (1) before the end of the period of twelve weeks beginning with the day on which the consultation began.

(4) Subject as follows, if after the expiry of the 40-day period the draft order laid under subsection (1) is approved by a resolution of each House of Parliament, the Minister may make an order in the terms of the draft order.

(5) The procedure in subsections (6) to (9) shall apply to the draft order instead of the procedure in subsection (4) if—

(a) either House of Parliament so resolves within the 30-day period, or

(b) a committee of either House charged with reporting on the draft order so recommends within the 30-day period and the House to which the recommendation is made does not by resolution reject the recommendation within that period.

(6) The Minister must have regard to—

(a) any representations,

(b) any resolution of either House of Parliament, and

(c) any recommendations of a committee of either House of Parliament charged with reporting on the draft order,

made during the 60-day period with regard to the draft order.

(7) If after the expiry of the 60-day period the draft order is approved by a resolution of each House of Parliament, the Minister may make an order in the terms of the draft order.

(8) If after the expiry of the 60-day period the Minister wishes to proceed with the draft order but with material changes, the Minister may lay before Parliament—

(a) a revised draft order, and

(b) a statement giving a summary of the changes proposed.

(9) If the revised draft order is approved by a resolution of each House of Parliament, the Minister may make an order in the terms of the revised draft order.

(10) For the purposes of this section an order is made in the terms of a draft order or revised draft order if it contains no material changes to its provisions.

(11) In this section, references to the "30-day", "40-day" and "60-day" periods in relation to any draft order are to the periods of 30, 40 and 60 days beginning with the day on which the draft order was laid before Parliament.

(12) For the purposes of subsection (11) no account is to be taken of any time during which Parliament is dissolved or prorogued or during which either House is adjourned for more than four days.

NOTES

Commencement: 14 December 2011.

[1.1834]

12 Time limits

Any entry in Schedules 1 to 5 ceases to have effect at the end of the period of five years beginning with the day on which it came into force (without affecting any order already made by virtue of that entry).

NOTES

Commencement: 14 February 2012.

13–19 *(Ss 13–19 (Powers of Welsh Ministers, etc) outside the scope of this work.)*

Restrictions on powers of Ministers and Welsh Ministers

[1.1835]

20 Restriction on creation of functions

(1) An order under the preceding provisions of this Act may not create—

(a) a power to make subordinate legislation,

(b) a power of forcible entry, search or seizure, or

(c) a power to compel the giving of evidence.

(2) Subsection (1) does not prevent an order from repealing and re-enacting a power.

NOTES

Commencement: 14 February 2012.

[1.1836]

21 Restriction on transfer and delegation of functions

(1) An order under the preceding provisions of this Act may not transfer any function to—

(a) a charity, or

(b) a person not otherwise exercising public functions who is not a charity,

unless the charity or person has consented.

(2) An order under the preceding provisions of this Act may not transfer an excluded function to a person not otherwise exercising public functions.

(3) In subsection (2) "excluded function" means—

(a) a function of a tribunal exercising the judicial power of the State,

(b) a power to make subordinate legislation,

(c) a power of forcible entry, search or seizure,

(d) a power to compel the giving of evidence, or

(e) any other function the exercise or non-exercise of which would necessarily interfere with, or otherwise affect, the liberty of an individual.

NOTES

Commencement: 14 February 2012.

[1.1837]

22 Restriction on creation of criminal offences

(1) An order under the preceding provisions of this Act may not, in relation to any transfer or modification of functions, create a criminal offence that is punishable—

(a) on indictment, with imprisonment for a term exceeding two years, or

(b) on summary conviction, with—

(i) imprisonment for a term exceeding the normal maximum term, or

(ii) a fine exceeding level 5 on the standard scale.

(2) In subsection (1)(b)(i) "the normal maximum term" means—

(a) in relation to England and Wales—

(i) in the case of a summary offence, 51 weeks, and

(ii) in the case of an offence triable either way, twelve months;

(b) in relation to Scotland—

(i) in the case of an offence triable only summarily, six months, and

(ii) in the case of an offence triable either summarily or on indictment, twelve months;

(c) in relation to Northern Ireland, six months.

(3) In Scotland, in the case of an offence which, if committed by an adult, is triable either on indictment or summarily and is not an offence triable on indictment only by virtue of—

(a) Part 5 of the Criminal Justice Act 1988, or

(b) section 292(6) and (7) of the Criminal Procedure (Scotland) Act 1995,

the reference in subsection (1)(b)(ii) to a fine exceeding level 5 on the standard scale is to be construed as a reference to the statutory maximum.

(4) In England and Wales—

(a) in the case of a summary offence committed before the coming into force of section 281(5) of the Criminal Justice Act 2003, the reference in subsection (2)(a)(i) to 51 weeks is to be read as a reference to six months, and

(b) in the case of an offence triable either way which is committed before the coming into force of section 154(1) of that Act, the reference in subsection (2)(a)(ii) to twelve months is to be read as a reference to six months.

(5) Subsection (1) does not prevent an order from repealing and re-enacting a criminal offence.

NOTES

Commencement: 14 February 2012.

Transfer of property, rights and liabilities

[1.1838]
23 Transfer schemes

(1) A scheme for the transfer of property, rights and liabilities (a "transfer scheme") may be made by—

(a) a Minister, in connection with an order under sections 1 to 5;
(b) the Welsh Ministers, in connection with an order under section 13 or 14.

(2) In the case of a transfer scheme under subsection (1)(a), property, rights and liabilities must be transferred to—

(a) a Minister, where the scheme is made in connection with an order under section 3 or 4 (modification of constitutional or funding arrangements), or
(b) an eligible person or a body corporate, in any other case.

(3) In the case of a transfer scheme under subsection (1)(b), property, rights and liabilities must be transferred to—

(a) the Welsh Ministers,
(b) a person exercising Welsh devolved functions, or
(c) a body corporate.

(4) A transfer scheme may not transfer anything to a charity unless it has consented.

(5) The things that may be transferred under a transfer scheme include—

(a) property, rights and liabilities that could not otherwise be transferred;
(b) property acquired, and rights and liabilities arising, after the making of the scheme.

(6) A transfer scheme may make consequential, supplementary, incidental or transitional provision and may in particular—

(a) create rights, or impose liabilities, in relation to property or rights transferred;
(b) make provision about the continuing effect of things done by the transferor in respect of anything transferred;
(c) make provision about the continuation of things (including legal proceedings) in the process of being done by, on behalf of or in relation to the transferor in respect of anything transferred;
(d) make provision for references to the transferor in an instrument or other document in respect of anything transferred to be treated as references to the transferee;
(e) make provision for the shared ownership or use of property;
(f) if the TUPE regulations do not apply in relation to the transfer, make provision which is the same or similar.

(7) A transfer scheme may provide—

(a) for modification by agreement;
(b) for modifications to have effect from the date when the original scheme came into effect.

(8) For the purposes of this section—

(a) an individual who holds employment in the civil service is to be treated as employed by virtue of a contract of employment, and
(b) the terms of the individual's employment in the civil service are to be regarded as constituting the terms of the contract of employment.

(9) In this section—

"civil service" means the civil service of the State;
"TUPE regulations" means the Transfer of Undertakings (Protection of Employment) Regulations 2006 (SI 2006/246);
references to rights and liabilities include rights and liabilities relating to a contract of employment;
references to the transfer of property include the grant of a lease.

NOTES

Commencement: 14 February 2012.
Orders: the Public Bodies (Child Maintenance and Enforcement Commission: Abolition and Transfer of Functions) Order 2012, SI 2012/2007; the Public Bodies (Abolition of British Shipbuilders) Order 2013, SI 2013/687.

[1.1839]
24 Transfer schemes: procedure

(1) A transfer scheme made by a Minister under section 23(1)(a) may be included in an order under sections 1 to 5; but if not so included must be laid before Parliament after being made.

(2) A transfer scheme made by the Welsh Ministers under section 23(1)(b) may be included in an order under section 13 or 14; but if not so included must be laid before the National Assembly for Wales after being made.

(3) The Secretary of State's consent is required for a transfer scheme under section 23(1)(b) transferring anything from or to the Environment Agency, the Forestry Commissioners or a cross-border operator.

NOTES

Commencement: 14 February 2012.

25–34 *(S 25 (Transfer schemes: taxation) and ss 26–34 (Part 2 Other Provisions Relating to Public Bodies) outside the scope of this work.)*

PART 3
FINAL

[1.1840]

35 Orders: supplementary

(1) An order under this Act must be made by statutory instrument.

(2) The provision which may be made by an order under this Act, other than an order under sections 26 to 29, may be made by repealing, revoking or amending an enactment (whenever passed or made).

(3) The powers conferred by this Act are without prejudice to any other power conferred on a Minister or the Welsh Ministers.

(4) If the draft of an instrument containing an order under this Act (alone or with other provision) would, apart from this section, be a hybrid instrument for the purposes of the standing orders of either House of Parliament, it is to proceed in that House as if it were not such an instrument.

NOTES

Commencement: 14 December 2011.

[1.1841]

36 Interpretation

(1) In this Act—

"charity" has the meaning given in section 1(1) of the Charities Act 2006;

"community benefit society" means—

(a) a society registered as a community benefit society under the Co-operative and Community Benefit Societies and Credit Unions Act 1965,

(b) a pre-2010 Act society (as defined by section 4A(1) of that Act) which meets the condition in section 1(3) of that Act, or

(c) a society registered or deemed to be registered under the Industrial and Provident Societies Act (Northern Ireland) 1969 which meets the condition in section 1(2)(b) of that Act;

"constitutional arrangements" is to be construed in accordance with section 3(2) and (3);

"co-operative society" means—

(a) a society registered as a co-operative society under the Co-operative and Community Benefit Societies and Credit Unions Act 1965,

(b) a pre-2010 Act society (as defined by section 4A(1) of that Act) which meets the condition in section 1(2) of that Act, or

(c) a society registered or deemed to be registered under the Industrial and Provident Societies Act (Northern Ireland) 1969 which meets the condition in section 1(2)(a) of that Act;

"cross-border operator" means a person exercising functions or carrying on activities in or with respect to Wales (or any part of it) and England (or any part of it), but does not include—

(a) an internal drainage board, or

(b) a Regional Flood and Coastal Committee established under section 22(1)(c) of the Flood and Water Management Act 2010;

"eligible person" has the meaning given in section 1(3);

"enactment" means any primary or subordinate legislation;

"Minister" means—

(a) a Minister of the Crown (as defined by section 8 of the Ministers of the Crown Act 1975), or

(b) the Commissioners for Her Majesty's Revenue and Customs;

"modify", in relation to functions, is to be construed in accordance with section 5(2);

"modify", in relation to funding arrangements, is to be construed in accordance with section 4(3);

"non-devolved function" means a function that is not a Welsh devolved function;

"primary legislation" means any Act, Act of the Scottish Parliament, Northern Ireland legislation or Measure or Act of the National Assembly for Wales;

"public function" means a function conferred under an enactment or royal charter;

"subordinate legislation" means an instrument made under primary legislation;

"Wales" has the same meaning as in the Government of Wales Act 2006;

"Welsh devolved function" means—

(a) a function conferred under an Act or Measure of the National Assembly for Wales,

(b) a function which is exercisable in or as regards Wales and could be conferred by an Act of the Assembly, or
(c) a function in relation to which a function (other than a function of being consulted) is exercisable by the Welsh Ministers, the First Minister or the Counsel General to the Welsh Assembly Government,

and references to a person exercising a Welsh devolved function do not include a person exercising such a function by virtue of arrangements under section 27;

"Welsh environmental function" means a Welsh devolved function relating to the environment.

(2) Until the coming into force of section 1 of the Co-operative and Benefit Societies and Credit Unions Act 2010—

(a) the definition of "community benefit society" in subsection (1) above has effect as if for paragraphs (a) and (b) there were substituted—

"(a) a society registered or deemed to be registered under the Industrial and Provident Societies Act 1965 which meets the condition in section 1(2)(b) of that Act, or";

(b) the definition of "co-operative society" in subsection (1) above has effect as if for paragraphs (a) and (b) there were substituted—

"(a) a society registered or deemed to be registered under the Industrial and Provident Societies Act 1965 which meets the condition in section 1(2)(a) of that Act, or".

(3) Subsection (2) ceases to have effect on the coming into force of section 1 of the Co-operative and Community Benefit Societies and Credit Unions Act 2010.

NOTES

Commencement: 14 December 2011.

[1.1842]
37 Extent

(1) This Act extends to England and Wales, Scotland and Northern Ireland, subject as follows.
(2) The amendments made by section 32 (V & A, Science Museum, Kew and English Heritage) have the same extent as the enactments which they amend.
(3) The repeals in section 33 (Chief Coroner) have the same extent as the enactments to which they relate.
(4) The repeals in Schedule 6 (regional development agencies: consequential repeals) have the same extent as the enactments to which they relate.
(5) An order under this Act which repeals, revokes or amends an enactment extending to any other jurisdiction may also extend there.

NOTES

Commencement: 14 December 2011.

[1.1843]
38 Commencement

(1) This Act comes into force at the end of the period of two months beginning with the day on which it is passed, subject as follows.
(2) Sections 10 and 11 (consultation and procedure) and 35 to 39 (final) come into force on the day on which this Act is passed.
(3) Section 30 and Schedule 6 (regional development agencies) come into force on such day as the Secretary of State may by order appoint (and different days may be appointed for different purposes, including the purposes of different regional development agencies).

NOTES

Commencement: 14 December 2011.
Orders: the Public Bodies Act 2011 (Commencement No 1) Order 2011, SI 2011/3043; the Public Bodies Act 2011 (Commencement No 2) Order 2012, SI 2012/1662.

[1.1844]
39 Short title

This Act may be cited as the Public Bodies Act 2011.

NOTES

Commencement: 14 December 2011.

SCHEDULES

SCHEDULE 1
POWER TO ABOLISH: BODIES AND OFFICES

Section 1

[1.1845]
Administrative Justice and Tribunals Council.

. . .

Advisory Committee on Pesticides and Advisory Committee on Pesticides for Northern Ireland (bodies established under section 16(7) of the Food and Environment Protection Act 1985).

Agricultural dwelling-house advisory committees for areas in England.

Agricultural Wages Board for England and Wales.

Agricultural wages committees for areas in England.

. . .

. . .

BRB (Residuary) Limited.

. . .

. . .

Committee on Agricultural Valuation (the body established under section 92 of the Agricultural Holdings Act 1986).

Competition Service.

. . .

. . .

. . .

Disabled Persons Transport Advisory Committee.

. . .

Food from Britain.

Home Grown Timber Advisory Committee.

Inland Waterways Advisory Council.

. . .

Library Advisory Council for England.

. . .

National Consumer Council ("Consumer Focus").

. . .

Plant Varieties and Seeds Tribunal.

Public Guardian Board.

. . .

. . .

Registrar of Public Lending Right.

Sports Grounds Safety Authority.

Valuation Tribunal Service.

Victims' Advisory Panel.

. . .

NOTES

Commencement: 14 February 2012.

Entry "Advisory Committee on Hazardous Substances" (omitted) repealed by the Advisory Committee on Hazardous Substances (Abolition) Order 2012, SI 2012/1923, art 3, Schedule, as from 23 July 2012.

Entry "Aircraft and Shipbuilding Industries Arbitration Tribunal" (omitted) repealed by the Public Bodies (Abolition of the Aircraft and Shipbuilding Industries Arbitration Tribunal) Order 2013, SI 2013/686, art 3, Sch 1, para 10, as from 22 March 2013.

Entry relating to British Shipbuilders (omitted) repealed by the Public Bodies (Abolition of British Shipbuilders) Order 2013, SI 2013/687, art 5, Sch 1, para 15(1), (2)(a), as from 22 March 2013.

Entry "Child Maintenance and Enforcement Commission" (omitted) repealed by the Public Bodies (Child Maintenance and Enforcement Commission: Abolition and Transfer of Functions) Order 2012, SI 2012/2007, art 3(2), Schedule, Pt 1, para 109(f), as from 2 August 2012.

Entry "Commission for Rural Communities" (omitted) repealed by the Public Bodies (Abolition of the Commission for Rural Communities) Order 2012, SI 2012/2654, art 4, Schedule, as from 2 April 2013.

Entry "Courts boards" (omitted) repealed by the Public Bodies (Abolition of Courts Boards) Order 2012, SI 2012/1206, art 3, as from 3 May 2012.

Entries "Crown Court Rule Committee" and "Magistrates' Courts Rule Committee" (both omitted) repealed by the Public Bodies (Abolition of Crown Court Rule Committee and Magistrates' Courts Rule Committee) Order 2012, SI 2012/2398, arts 2(4), 3(3), as from 19 September 2012.

Entry "Disability Living Allowance Advisory Board" (omitted) repealed by the Public Bodies (Abolition of the Disability Living Allowance Advisory Board) Order 2013, SI 2013/252, art 6, as from 8 February 2013.

Entry "Environment Protection Advisory Committees" (omitted) repealed by the Public Bodies (Abolition of Environment Protection Advisory Committees) Order 2012, SI 2012/2407, art 3, as from 20 September 2012.

Entry "Her Majesty's Inspectorate of Court Administration" (omitted) repealed by the Public Bodies (Abolition of Her Majesty's Inspectorate of Courts Administration and the Public Guardian Board) Order 2012, SI 2012/2401, art 2(6), Sch 1, paras 36, 37, as from 19 September 2012.

Entry "National Endowment for Science, Technology and the Arts" (omitted) repealed by the Public Bodies (Abolition of the National Endowment for Science, Technology and the Arts) Order 2012, SI 2012/964, art 3(2), as from 2 April 2012.

Entry "Railway Heritage Committee" (omitted) repealed by the Public Bodies (Abolition of the Railway Heritage Committee) Order 2013, SI 2013/64, art 5, as from 2 April 2013.

Entry "Regional and local fisheries advisory committees" (omitted) repealed by the Public Bodies (Abolition of Regional and Local Fisheries Advisory Committees) Order 2012, SI 2012/2406, art 3, as from 20 September 2012.

Final words omitted repealed by SI 2013/687, art 5, Sch 1, para 15(1), (2)(b), as from 22 March 2013.

SCHEDULE 2
POWER TO MERGE: BODIES AND OFFICES

Section 2

[1.1846]

Group 1

Central Arbitration Committee.
Certification Officer.

Group 2

Gambling Commission.
National Lottery Commission.

Group 3

Pensions Ombudsman.
Ombudsman for the Board of the Pension Protection Fund.

Group 4

Director of Public Prosecutions.
Director of Revenue and Customs Prosecutions.

Group 5

Competition Commission.
Office of Fair Trading ("OFT").

NOTES

Commencement: 14 February 2012.

SCHEDULE 3
POWER TO MODIFY CONSTITUTIONAL ARRANGEMENTS: BODIES AND OFFICES

Section 3

[1.1847]

Administrative Justice and Tribunals Council.

British Hallmarking Council.

Broads Authority.

Commission for Equality and Human Rights.

English Tourist Board.

Internal drainage boards for areas wholly or mainly in England.

Joint Nature Conservation Committee.

National Park authorities in England.

Passengers' Council ("Passenger Focus").

Sianel Pedwar Cymru ("S4C").

Theatres Trust.

NOTES

Commencement: 14 February 2012.

SCHEDULE 4
POWER TO MODIFY FUNDING ARRANGEMENTS: BODIES AND OFFICES

Section 4

[1.1848]

Administrative Justice and Tribunals Council.

Commission for Equality and Human Rights.

Inspectors appointed by the Secretary of State under section 86 of the Water Industry Act 1991.

Marine Management Organisation.

Natural England.

Office of Communications ("Ofcom").

NOTES

Commencement: 14 February 2012.

SCHEDULES 5 AND 6

(Sch 5 (Power to Modify or Transfer Functions: Bodies and Offices) and Sch 6 (Regional Development Agencies: Consequential Repeals) outside the scope of this work.)

HEALTH AND SOCIAL CARE ACT 2012

(2012 c 7)

An Act to establish and make provision about a National Health Service Commissioning Board and clinical commissioning groups and to make other provision about the National Health Service in England; to make provision about public health in the United Kingdom; to make provision about regulating health and adult social care services; to make provision about public involvement in health and social care matters, scrutiny of health matters by local authorities and co-operation between local authorities and commissioners of health care services; to make provision about regulating health and social care workers; to establish and make provision about a National Institute for Health and Care Excellence; to establish and make provision about a Health and Social Care Information Centre and to make other provision about information relating to health or social care matters; to abolish certain public bodies involved in health or social care; to make other provision about health care; and for connected purposes

[27 March 2012]

NOTES

Only the three provisions of this Act most relevant to employment law are reproduced. Provisions omitted are not annotated. Sections 300, 301 and Sch 23 apply to England and Wales, and also apply to Scotland and Northern Ireland insofar as they confer powers in connection with the abolition of the Health Protection Agency (see s 308(1), (3)(i)). Certain specified provisions of this Act (which are outside the scope of this work) came into force on the date of Royal assent (27 March 2012). This Act also came into force on 27 March 2012 so far as necessary for enabling the exercise on or after that day of any power to make an Order or Regulations or to give directions. For all other purposes, this Act comes into force in accordance with Orders made under s 306.

PART 11
MISCELLANEOUS

Transfer schemes

[1.1849]

300 Transfer schemes

(1) The Secretary of State may make a property transfer scheme or a staff transfer scheme in connection with—

(a) the establishment or abolition of a body by this Act, or

(b) the modification of the functions of a body or other person by or under this Act.

(2) A property transfer scheme is a scheme for the transfer from a body or other person mentioned in the first column of the Table in Schedule 22 of any property, rights or liabilities, other than rights or liabilities under or in connection with a contract of employment, to a body or other person mentioned in the corresponding entry in the second column.

(3) A staff transfer scheme is a scheme for the transfer from a body or other person mentioned in the first column of the Table in Schedule 23 of any rights or liabilities under or in connection with a contract of employment to a body or other person mentioned in the corresponding entry in the second column.

(4) The Secretary of State may direct the Board or a qualifying company to exercise the functions of the Secretary of State in relation to the making of a property transfer scheme or a staff transfer scheme in connection with the abolition of—

(a) one or more Primary Care Trusts specified in the direction, or

(b) one or more Strategic Health Authorities so specified.

(5) Where the Secretary of State gives a direction under subsection (4), the Secretary of State may give directions to the Board or (as the case may be) the company about its exercise of the functions.

(6) For the purposes of this section and section 301—

(a) an individual who holds employment in the civil service is to be treated as employed by virtue of a contract of employment, and

(b) the terms of the individual's employment in the civil service are to be regarded as constituting the terms of the contract of employment.

(7) In this section and sections 301 and 302 references to the transfer of property include references to the grant of a lease.

(8) In this section and Schedules 22 and 23, "qualifying company" means—

(a) a company which is formed under section 223 of the National Health Service Act 2006 and wholly or partly owned by the Secretary of State or the Board, or

(b) a subsidiary of a company which is formed under that section and wholly owned by the Secretary of State.

(9) In section 301 and Schedules 22 and 23—

"local authority" means—

(a) a county council in England;

(b) a district council in England, other than a council for a district in a county for which there is a county council;

(c) a London borough council;

(d) the Council of the Isles of Scilly;

(e) the Common Council of the City of London;

"public authority" means any body or other person which has functions conferred by or under an Act or by royal charter.

NOTES

Commencement: 27 March 2012 (in so far as is necessary for enabling the exercise on or after that date of any power to give directions); 1 July 2012 (except insofar as relates to (a) the National Health Service Commissioning Board, (b) a clinical commissioning group, (c) any person with whom the Secretary of State has made, or has decided to make, an agreement under section 12ZA(1) of the Mental Health Act 1983, (d) the National Institute for Health and Care Excellence and (e) the Health and Social Care Information Centre); 1 October 2012 (insofar as relates to the Board and a clinical commissioning group); 1 April 2013 (otherwise).

Regulations: the National Health Service and Public Health (Functions and Miscellaneous Provisions) Regulations 2013, SI 2013/261.

[1.1850]

301 Transfer schemes: supplemental

(1) The things that may be transferred under a property transfer scheme or a staff transfer scheme include—

(a) property, rights and liabilities that could not otherwise be transferred;

(b) property acquired, and rights and liabilities arising, after the making of the scheme;

(c) criminal liabilities but only where the transfer is to a person mentioned in subsection (2).

(2) Those persons are—

(a) the National Health Service Commissioning Board;

(b) a clinical commissioning group;

(c) a local authority;
(d) the Care Quality Commission;
(e) Monitor;
(f) the National Institute for Health and Care Excellence;
(g) the Health and Social Care Information Centre;
(h) the Health and Care Professions Council;
(i) a public authority other than a Minister of the Crown.

(3) A property transfer scheme or a staff transfer scheme may make supplementary, incidental, transitional and consequential provision and may in particular—

(a) create rights, or impose liabilities, in relation to property or rights transferred;
(b) make provision about the continuing effect of things done by the transferor in respect of anything transferred;
(c) make provision about the continuation of things (including legal proceedings) in the process of being done by, on behalf of or in relation to the transferor in respect of anything transferred;
(d) make provision for references to the transferor in an instrument or other document in respect of anything transferred to be treated as references to the transferee.

(4) A property transfer scheme may make provision for the shared ownership or use of property.

(5) A staff transfer scheme may make provision which is the same or similar to the TUPE regulations.

(6) A property transfer scheme or a staff transfer scheme may provide—

(a) for the scheme to be modified by agreement after it comes into effect, and
(b) for any such modifications to have effect from the date when the original scheme comes into effect.

(7) Where a Primary Care Trust, a Strategic Health Authority or a Special Health Authority is abolished by this Act, the Secretary of State must exercise the powers conferred by section 300 and this section so as to secure that all the body's liabilities (other than criminal liabilities) are dealt with.

(8) In this section, "TUPE regulations" means the Transfer of Undertakings (Protection of Employment) Regulations 2006 (SI 2006/246).

NOTES

Commencement: 1 July 2012 (except insofar as relates to (a) the National Health Service Commissioning Board, (b) a clinical commissioning group, (c) any person with whom the Secretary of State has made, or has decided to make, an agreement under section 12ZA(1) of the Mental Health Act 1983, (d) the National Institute for Health and Care Excellence and (e) the Health and Social Care Information Centre); 1 October 2012 (insofar as relates to the Board and a clinical commissioning group); 1 April 2013 (otherwise).

SCHEDULES

SCHEDULE 23
STAFF TRANSFER SCHEMES

Section 300(3)

[1.1851]

Transferor	**Permitted transferees**
Any Primary Care Trust	The Secretary of State
	The National Health Service Commissioning Board
	A clinical commissioning group
	A local authority
	The Care Quality Commission
	A Special Health Authority
	Any public authority which exercises functions in relation to health and is prescribed in regulations
	A qualifying company
	Any person with whom the Secretary of State has made, or has decided to make, an agreement under section 12ZA(1) of the Mental Health Act 1983
Any Strategic Health Authority	The Secretary of State
	The National Health Service Commissioning Board

Transferor	Permitted transferees
	A clinical commissioning group
	The Care Quality Commission
	Monitor
	A Special Health Authority
	Any public authority which exercises functions in relation to health and is prescribed in regulations
	A qualifying company
	Any person with whom the Secretary of State has made, or has decided to make, an agreement under section 12ZA(1) of the Mental Health Act 1983
The Special Health Authority known as National Institute for Health and Clinical Excellence	The National Institute for Health and Care Excellence (established under section 232)
The Special Health Authority known as the Health and Social Care Information Centre	The Health and Social Care Information Centre (established under section 252)
The Special Health Authority known as the NHS Institute for Innovation and Improvement	The National Health Service Commissioning Board
The Special Health Authority known as the National Patient Safety Agency	The National Health Service Commissioning Board
	The Health and Social Care Information Centre
The Special Health Authority known as the NHS Business Services Authority	The Health and Social Care Information Centre
The Appointments Commission	A Minister of the Crown
	A Special Health Authority
The General Social Care Council	The Secretary of State
	The Health and Care Professions Council
	A person authorised by the Secretary of State under subsection (5)(b) of section 67 of the Care Standards Act 2000 to exercise functions of the Secretary of State under that section
	Any other person who carries on activities in connection with social work or social care work
The Health Protection Agency	The Secretary of State
The Secretary of State	The National Health Service Commissioning Board
	The Care Quality Commission
	Monitor
	The Health and Social Care Information Centre

NOTES

Commencement: 1 July 2012 (except insofar as relates to (a) the National Health Service Commissioning Board, (b) a clinical commissioning group, (c) any person with whom the Secretary of State has made, or has decided to make, an agreement under section 12ZA(1) of the Mental Health Act 1983, (d) the National Institute for Health and Care Excellence and (e) the Health and Social Care Information Centre); 1 October 2012 (insofar as relates to the Board and a clinical commissioning group); 1 April 2013 (otherwise).

Regulations: the National Health Service and Public Health (Functions and Miscellaneous Provisions) Regulations 2013, SI 2013/261.

LEGAL AID, SENTENCING AND PUNISHMENT OF OFFENDERS ACT 2012

(2012 c 10)

An Act to make provision about legal aid; to make further provision about funding legal services; to make provision about costs and other amounts awarded in civil and criminal proceedings; to make provision about referral fees in connection with the provision of legal services; to make provision about sentencing offenders, including provision about release on licence or otherwise; to make provision about the collection of fines and other sums; to make provision about bail and about remand otherwise than on bail; to make provision about the employment, payment and transfer of persons detained in prisons and other institutions; to make provision about penalty notices for disorderly behaviour and cautions; to make provision about the rehabilitation of offenders; to create new offences of threatening with a weapon in public or on school premises and of causing serious injury by dangerous driving; to create a new offence relating to squatting; to increase penalties for offences relating to scrap metal dealing and to create a new offence relating to payment for scrap metal; and to amend section 76 of the Criminal Justice and Immigration Act 2008.

[1 May 2012]

NOTES

Only Sch 4, Pt 1 to this Act, which is of most relevance to employment law, is reproduced. Provisions omitted are not annotated. Certain specified provisions of the Act came into force on the date of Royal Assent (1 May 2012); the remainder comes into force in accordance with orders made under s 151 (Commencement).

SCHEDULE 4
TRANSFER OF EMPLOYEES AND PROPERTY ETC OF LEGAL SERVICES COMMISSION

Section 38

PART 1
TRANSFER OF EMPLOYEES ETC

[1.1852]

Transfer

1 (1) An individual who is an employee of the Legal Services Commission ("the LSC") immediately before the transfer day becomes employed in the civil service of the State on that day.

(2) The terms and conditions of the individual's contract of employment immediately before the transfer day have effect, on and after that day, as if they were terms and conditions of the individual's employment in the civil service of the State, subject to paragraph 4(1) and (2).

(3) All of the rights, powers, duties and liabilities of the LSC in connection with the individual's employment are transferred to the Crown on the transfer day, subject to paragraph 4(1) and (2).

(4) Anything done (or having effect as if done) before the transfer day—

(a) by or in relation to the LSC, and

(b) for the purposes of, or in connection with, anything transferred by virtue of sub-paragraphs (1) to (3),

is to have effect, so far as necessary for continuing its effect on and after that day, as if done by or in relation to the Crown.

(5) Anything which is in the process of being done immediately before the transfer day—

(a) by or in relation to the LSC, and

(b) for the purposes of, or in connection with, anything transferred by virtue of sub-paragraphs (1) to (3),

may be continued by or in relation to the Crown.

(6) A reference to the LSC in a document, including an enactment, constituting or relating to anything transferred by virtue of sub-paragraphs (1) to (3) is to have effect, so far as is necessary for giving effect to those sub-paragraphs, as a reference to the Crown.

Continuity of employment

2 A transfer under paragraph 1 does not break the continuity of the individual's employment and accordingly—

(a) the individual is not to be regarded for the purposes of Part 11 of the Employment Rights Act 1996 (redundancy) as having been dismissed by reason of that transfer, and

(b) the individual's period of employment with the LSC counts as a period of employment in the civil service of the State for the purposes of that Act.

Right to object to transfer

3 (1) This paragraph has effect where, before the transfer day, an individual who is an employee of the LSC informs the LSC or the Lord Chancellor that the individual objects to becoming employed in the civil service of the State by virtue of paragraph 1(1).

(2) Where this paragraph has effect—

(a) the individual does not become employed in the civil service of the State by virtue of paragraph 1(1),

(b) the rights, powers, duties and liabilities under the individual's contract of employment do not transfer by virtue of paragraph 1(3),

(c) the individual's contract of employment terminates immediately before the transfer day, and

(d) the individual is not to be treated, for any purpose, as having been dismissed by the LSC by reason of the termination of the contract under this paragraph.

Pension schemes and compensation schemes

4 (1) On and after the transfer day, the terms and conditions of employment of an individual who is employed in the civil service of the State by virtue of paragraph 1(1) do not include any term or condition that was part of the individual's contract of employment immediately before the transfer day and that relates to—

(a) an occupational pension scheme,

(b) a compensation scheme, or

(c) rights, powers, duties or liabilities under or in connection with such a scheme.

(2) Accordingly, paragraph 1(3) does not apply in relation to rights, powers, duties or liabilities under or in connection with an occupational pension scheme or a compensation scheme.

(3) The Lord Chancellor may make one or more schemes providing for the transfer to the Lord Chancellor or the Secretary of State of the LSC's rights, powers, duties and liabilities under or in connection with—

(a) an occupational pension scheme, or

(b) a compensation scheme,

whether the rights, powers, duties and liabilities arise under the occupational pension scheme or compensation scheme, under an enactment, under a contract of employment or otherwise.

(4) A transfer scheme may provide that anything done (or having effect as if done) before the day on which the transfer scheme takes effect—

(a) by or in relation to the LSC, and

(b) for the purposes of, or in connection with, anything transferred by virtue of the transfer scheme,

is to have effect, so far as is necessary for continuing its effect on and after that day, as if done by or in relation to the transferee.

(5) A transfer scheme may provide that anything which is in the process of being done immediately before the day on which the transfer scheme takes effect—

(a) by or in relation to the LSC, and

(b) for the purposes of, or in connection with, anything transferred by virtue of the transfer scheme,

may be continued by or in relation to the transferee.

(6) A transfer scheme may provide that a reference to the LSC in a document, including an enactment, constituting or relating to anything transferred by virtue of the scheme is to have effect, so far as is necessary for giving effect to that scheme, as a reference to the transferee.

(7) A transfer scheme may, so far as is necessary for giving effect to that scheme, provide that an enactment that applies in relation to compensation schemes or occupational pension schemes applies to a compensation scheme or occupational pension scheme that is the subject of the transfer scheme, the members of such a scheme or the transferee with modifications specified in the transfer scheme.

(8) A transfer scheme may—

(a) amend or otherwise modify a compensation scheme that is the subject of the transfer scheme, and

(b) create, modify or remove rights, powers, duties or liabilities under or in connection with such a scheme.

(9) The powers under sub-paragraph (8) include power to amend or otherwise modify any instrument relating to the constitution, management or operation of a compensation scheme.

(10) Transfer schemes amending or otherwise modifying a compensation scheme have effect in spite of any provision (of any nature) which would otherwise prevent or restrict the amendment or modification.

(11) A transfer scheme may include consequential, incidental, supplementary, transitional, transitory and saving provision.

[(11A) Where an individual—

(a) was a member of a relevant LSC scheme immediately before the transfer day,

(b) had been a member of that scheme immediately before 1 April 2012, and

(c) becomes, on or after the transfer day, a member of a civil service scheme by virtue of employment in the civil service of the State,

the individual is to be regarded, for the purposes of section 18(5) of the Public Service Pensions Act 2013 (transitional protection under existing schemes), as having been a member of the civil service scheme immediately before 1 April 2012.

(11B) In sub-paragraph (11A)—

(a) "relevant LSC scheme" means a scheme made or treated as made under paragraph 10(1) of Schedule 1 to the Access to Justice Act 1999;

(b) "civil service scheme" means a scheme under section 1 of the Superannuation Act 1972.]

(12) In this paragraph—

"compensation scheme" means so much of any scheme as makes provision for payment by way of compensation on or in respect of termination of employment;

"occupational pension scheme" has the same meaning as in the Pension Schemes Act 1993;

"transfer scheme" means a scheme made under sub-paragraph (3).

Power to merge LSC occupational pension schemes

5 (1) The Lord Chancellor may make a scheme providing for the merger of LSC occupational pension schemes.

(2) A scheme under this paragraph may in particular—

(a) provide for the assets and liabilities of one LSC occupational pension scheme to become assets and liabilities of another,

(b) create, modify or remove rights, powers, duties or liabilities under or in connection with an LSC occupational pension scheme,

(c) provide for the winding up of an LSC occupational pension scheme,

(d) provide for references to one LSC occupational pension scheme in a document, including an enactment, to have effect as references to another, and

(e) include consequential, incidental, supplementary, transitional, transitory and saving provision.

(3) A scheme under this paragraph may in particular amend or otherwise modify—

(a) the trust deed of an LSC occupational pension scheme,

(b) rules of an LSC occupational pension scheme, and

(c) any other instrument relating to the constitution, management or operation of an LSC occupational pension scheme.

(4) A scheme under this paragraph must ensure that the merger of the LSC occupational pension schemes does not, to any extent, deprive members of the LSC occupational pension schemes, or other beneficiaries under those schemes, of rights that accrue to them under those schemes before the merger takes effect.

(5) Subject to sub-paragraph (4), a scheme under this paragraph has effect in spite of any provision (of any nature) which would otherwise prevent the merger of the LSC occupational pension schemes.

(6) In this paragraph—

"LSC occupational pension scheme" means an occupational pension scheme under which—

(a) the LSC has rights, powers, duties or liabilities, or

(b) the Lord Chancellor or the Secretary of State has rights, powers, duties or liabilities by virtue of a scheme under paragraph 4(3);

"occupational pension scheme" has the same meaning as in the Pension Schemes Act 1993.

NOTES

Commencement: 4 March 2013.

Para 4: sub-paras (11A), (11B) inserted by the Public Service Pensions Act 2013, s 27, Sch 8, para 31, as from a day to be appointed.

ENTERPRISE AND REGULATORY REFORM ACT 2013

(2013 c 24)

ARRANGEMENT OF SECTIONS

PART 2
EMPLOYMENT

An Act to make provision about the UK Green Investment Bank; to make provision about employment law; to establish and make provision about the Competition and Markets Authority and to abolish the Competition Commission and the Office of Fair Trading; to amend the Competition Act 1998 and the Enterprise Act 2002; to make provision for the reduction of legislative burdens; to make provision about copyright and rights in performances; to make provision about payments to company directors; to make provision about redress schemes relating to lettings agency work and property management work; to make provision about the supply of customer data; to make provision for the protection of essential supplies in cases of insolvency; to make provision about certain bodies established by Royal Charter; to amend section 9(5) of the Equality Act 2010; and for connected purposes.

[25 April 2013]

1–6 (*(Pt 1) Outside the scope of this work.*)

PART 2
EMPLOYMENT

7–12 (*S 7 inserts the Employment Tribunals Act 1996, ss 18A, 18B at* **[1.707]**, **[1.708]** *and introduces Sch 1 (conciliation: minor and consequential amendments) to the Act; s 8 introduces Sch 2 (extension of limitation periods to allow for conciliation) to the Act; ss 9, 11, 12 amend various provisions in the Employment Tribunals Act 1996 at* **[1.678]** *et seq; s 10 inserts the Trade Union and Labour Relations (Consolidation) Act 1992, 251B at* **[1.535]**.)

Unfair dismissal

13, 14 (*S 13 amends the Employment Rights Act 1996, s 108 at* **[1.918]**; *s 14 inserts s 111A thereof at* **[1.921]**.)

[1.1853]

15 Power by order to increase or decrease limit of compensatory award

(1) The Secretary of State may by order made by statutory instrument amend section 124 of the Employment Rights Act 1996 (limit of compensatory award etc) so as to vary the limit imposed for the time being by subsection (1) of that section.

(2) The limit as so varied may be—

(a) a specified amount, or

(b) the lower of—

(i) a specified amount, and

(ii) a specified number multiplied by a week's pay of the individual concerned.

(3) Different amounts may be specified by virtue of subsection (2)(a) or (b)(i) in relation to employers of different descriptions.

(4) An amount specified by virtue of subsection (2)(a) or (b)(i)—

(a) may not be less than median annual earnings;

(b) may not be more than three times median annual earnings.

(5) A number specified by virtue of subsection (2)(b)(ii) may not be less than 52.

(6) An order under this section may make consequential, supplemental, transitional, transitory or saving provision.

(7) The consequential provision that may be made under subsection (6) includes provision inserting a reference to section 124 of the Employment Rights Act 1996 in section 226(3) of that Act (week's pay: calculation date in unfair dismissal cases).

(8) A statutory instrument containing an order under this section is not to be made unless a draft of the instrument has been laid before each House of Parliament and approved by a resolution of each House.

(9) In this section "median annual earnings" means—

(a) the latest figure for median gross annual earnings of full-time employees in the United Kingdom published by the Statistics Board (disregarding any provisional figures), or

(b) if that figure was published by the Statistics Board more than two years before the laying of the draft of the statutory instrument in question, an estimate of the current amount of such earnings worked out in whatever way the Secretary of State thinks fit.

(10) . . .

NOTES

Commencement: 25 April 2013 (so far as is necessary for enabling the exercise of any power to make orders); 25 June 2013 (otherwise).

Sub-s (10): amends the Employment Relations Act 1999, s 34 at **[1.1202]**.

16 (*Inserts the Employment Tribunals Act 1996, s 12A at* **[1.699]** *and introduces Sch 3 (financial penalties: minor and consequential amendments) to this Act.*)

Protected disclosures

17–19 (*Amend various provisions of the Employment Rights Act 1996 at* **[1.743]** *et seq.*)

[1.1854]

20 Extension of meaning of "worker"

(1)–(9) . . .

(10) Until the coming into force of the repeal (made by Schedule 3 to the Smoking, Health and Social Care (Scotland) Act 2005 (asp 13)) of sections 27 to 28 of the National Health Service (Scotland) Act 1978 ("the 1978 Act"), section 43K(1)(c)(ii) of the Employment Rights Act 1996 has effect as if it included a reference to section 27A of the 1978 Act.

NOTES

Commencement: 25 June 2013.

Sub-ss (1)–(8): amend the Employment Rights Act 1996, ss 43K, 236 at **[1.797]**, **[1.1043]**.

Sub-s (9): outside the scope of this work.

21–23 (*Amend various provisions which, in so far as relevant to this work, have been incorporated at the appropriate place.*)

General

[1.1855]

24 Transitional provision

(1) Section 10 does not apply in relation to a disclosure, or a request for information, made before that section comes into force.

(2) Section 12 does not apply in relation to proceedings that are in the process of being heard by the Employment Appeal Tribunal when that section comes into force.
(3) Section 13 does not apply where the effective date of termination of the contract of employment in question is earlier than the date on which that section comes into force.
"Effective date of termination" here has the meaning given by section 97(1) of the Employment Rights Act 1996.
(4) Section 14 does not apply to any offer made or discussions held before the commencement of that section.
(5) Section 16 does not apply in relation to any claim presented before the end of the sixth month after the day on which this Act is passed (or before the commencement of that section).
(6) Section 17, 18, 19 or 20 does not apply to a qualifying disclosure made before the section comes into force.
"Qualifying disclosure" here has the meaning given by section 43B of the Employment Rights Act 1996.

NOTES
Commencement: 25 April 2013.

25–58 (*Pt 3 (ss 25–28: The Competition and Markets Authority) and Pt 4 (ss 29–58: Competition Reform) outside the scope of this work.*)

PART 5
REDUCTION OF LEGISLATIVE BURDENS

59–63 (*Outside the scope of this work.*)

Equality Acts

64, 65 (*Amend various provisions in the Equality Act 2006 at* **[1.1350]** *et seq and the Equality Act 2010 at* **[1.1618]** *et seq.*)

[1.1856]
66 Equality Act 2010: obtaining information for proceedings
(1) . . .
(2) That does not affect section 138 for the purposes of proceedings that relate to a contravention occurring before this section comes into force.

NOTES
Commencement: to be appointed.
Sub-s (1): repeals the Equality Act 2010, s 138 at **[1.1721]**.

67, 68 (*Outside the scope of this work.*)

Miscellaneous

[1.1857]
69 Civil liability for breach of health and safety duties
(1)–(7) . . .
(8) Where, on the commencement of this section, there is in force an Order in Council made under section 84(3) of the Health and Safety at Work etc Act 1974 that applies to matters outside Great Britain any of the provisions of that Act that are amended by this section, that Order is to be taken as applying those provisions as so amended.
(9) The amendments made by this section do not apply in relation to breach of a duty which it would be within the legislative competence of the Scottish Parliament to impose by an Act of that Parliament.
(10) The amendments made by this section do not apply in relation to breach of a duty where that breach occurs before the commencement of this section.

NOTES
Commencement: to be appointed.
Sub-ss (1)–(7): amend the Health and Safety at Work etc Act 1974, s 47 at **[1.70]**.

70, 71 (*Outside the scope of this work.*)

[1.1858]
72 Abolition of Agricultural Wages Board and related English bodies
(1) The Agricultural Wages Board for England and Wales is abolished.
(2) Every agricultural wages committee for an area in England is abolished.
(3) Every agricultural dwelling-house advisory committee for an area in England is abolished.
(4) Schedule 20 (abolition of Agricultural Wages Board and related English bodies: consequential provision) has effect.

NOTES

Commencement: to be appointed.

73 (*Outside the scope of this work.*)

PART 6
MISCELLANEOUS AND GENERAL

74–78 (*Outside the scope of this work.*)

Payments to directors of quoted companies

79–81 (*Amend the Companies Act 2006 at* **[1.1436]** *et seq; these amendments have been incorporated at the appropriate place.*)

[1.1859]

82 Payments to directors: transitional provision

(1) In relation to a company that is a quoted company immediately before the day on which section 79 of this Act comes into force, section 439A(1)(a) of the Companies Act 2006 (as inserted by section 79(4) of this Act) applies as if—

(a) the reference to the day on which the company becomes a quoted company were a reference to the day on which section 79 of this Act comes into force, and

(b) at the end of the paragraph (but before the ", and") there were inserted "or at an earlier general meeting".

(2) In relation to a company that is a quoted company immediately before the day on which section 79 of this Act comes into force, section 226D(6)(a) of the Companies Act 2006 (as inserted by section 80 of this Act) applies as if the reference to the day on which the company becomes a quoted company were a reference to the day on which section 79 of this Act comes into force.

(3) Chapter 4A of Part 10 of the Companies Act 2006 does not apply in relation to remuneration payments or payments for loss of office that are required to be made under an agreement entered into before 27 June 2012 or in consequence of any other obligation arising before that date.

(4) An agreement entered into, or any other obligation arising, before 27 June 2012 that is modified or renewed on or after that date is to be treated for the purposes of subsection (3) as having been entered into or (as the case may be) as having arisen on the date on which it was modified or renewed.

(5) The amendment made by section 81(4) does not apply in relation to a payment for loss of office to which subsection (3) of this section applies.

NOTES

Commencement: to be appointed.

83–96 (*Outside the scope of this work.*)

Caste as an aspect of race

[1.1860]

97 Equality Act 2010: caste as an aspect of race

(1)–(4) . . .

(5) A Minister of the Crown—

(a) may carry out a review of the effect of section 9(5) of the Equality Act 2010 (and orders made under it) and whether it remains appropriate, and

(b) must publish a report on the outcome of any such review.

(6) The power under subsection (5)(a) may not be exercised before the end of the period of 5 years beginning with the day on which this Act is passed (but may be exercised on more than one occasion after that).

(7) If a Minister of the Crown considers it appropriate in the light of the outcome of a review under subsection (5), the Minister may by order repeal or otherwise amend section 9(5) of the Equality Act 2010.

(8) The power to make an order under subsection (7) includes power to make incidental, supplementary, consequential, transitional or saving provision, including doing so by amending an Act or subordinate legislation (within the meaning of the Interpretation Act 1978).

(9) An order under subsection (7) must be made by statutory instrument.

(10) A statutory instrument containing an order under subsection (7) may not be made unless a draft of the instrument has been laid before, and approved by a resolution of, each House of Parliament.

NOTES

Commencement: 25 April 2013 (so far as is necessary for enabling the exercise of any power to make orders); 25 June 2013 (otherwise).

Sub-ss (1)–(4): amend the Equality Act 2010, s 9 at **[1.1626]**.

98 (*Inserts the Equality Act 2010, s 139A at* **[1.1723]** *and amends ss 207, 208 thereof at* **[1.1758]**, **[1.1759]**.)

General

[1.1861]

99 Consequential amendments, repeals and revocations

(1) The Secretary of State may by order made by statutory instrument make such provision as the Secretary of State considers appropriate in consequence of this Act.

(2) The power conferred by subsection (1) includes power—

(a) to make transitional, transitory or saving provision;

(b) to amend, repeal, revoke or otherwise modify any provision made by or under an enactment (including any enactment passed or made in the same Session as this Act).

(3) An order under subsection (1) which makes provision for the transfer of a function from the Competition Commission or the Office of Fair Trading to the Competition and Markets Authority in consequence of Part 3 of this Act may make such modifications to the function as the Secretary of State considers appropriate in consequence of the transfer.

(4) The modifications mentioned in subsection (3) may, in particular, alter the circumstances in which, or the conditions under which, the function is exercisable.

(5) A statutory instrument containing (whether alone or with other provision) an order under this section which amends, repeals or revokes any provision of primary legislation is not to be made unless a draft of the instrument has been laid before, and approved by a resolution of, each House of Parliament.

(6) A statutory instrument containing an order under this section which does not amend, repeal or revoke any provision of primary legislation is subject to annulment in pursuance of a resolution of either House of Parliament.

(7) In this section—

"enactment" includes an Act of the Scottish Parliament, a Measure or Act of the National Assembly for Wales and Northern Ireland legislation;

"primary legislation" means—

(a) an Act of Parliament,

(b) an Act of the Scottish Parliament,

(c) a Measure or Act of the National Assembly for Wales, and

(d) Northern Ireland legislation.

NOTES

Commencement: 25 April 2013.

[1.1862]

100 Transitional, transitory or saving provision

The Secretary of State may by order made by statutory instrument make such transitional, transitory or saving provision as the Secretary of State considers appropriate in connection with the coming into force of any provision of this Act.

NOTES

Commencement: 25 April 2013.

[1.1863]

101 Financial provision

There is to be paid out of money provided by Parliament—

(a) any expenditure incurred under or by virtue of this Act by the Secretary of State or the Competition and Markets Authority, and

(b) any increase attributable to this Act in the sums payable under any other Act out of money so provided.

NOTES

Commencement: 25 April 2013.

[1.1864]

102 Extent

(1) Part 1 extends to England and Wales, Scotland and Northern Ireland.

(2) Part 2 extends only to England and Wales and Scotland, except that the following provisions of that Part extend also to Northern Ireland—

(a) section 23(3);

(b) paragraph 11 of Schedule 1;

(c) paragraphs 36 to 39 of Schedule 2.

(3), (4) . . .

(5) Part 5 extends as follows—

(a) sections 59, 62, 67, 68 and 70 and Part 1 of Schedule 21 extend to England and Wales, Scotland and Northern Ireland,
(b) section 69 extends only to England and Wales and Scotland except that it also extends to Northern Ireland so far as Parts 1 and 4 of the Health and Safety at Work etc Act 1974 extend there,
(c) sections 64, 65 and 66 and paragraphs 1, 56 to 58, 60 and 66 of Schedule 19 (and section 71(3) so far as it relates to those paragraphs) extend only to England and Wales and Scotland,
(d) sections 60, 61, 63, 71(1) and (2) and 72(1) to (3), Schedules 16, 17 and 18, paragraphs 2 to 55, 59, 61 to 65 of Schedule 19 (and section 71(3) so far as it relates to those paragraphs) and Parts 2 and 3 of Schedule 21 extend only to England and Wales, and
(e) an amendment, repeal or revocation made by Schedule 20 has the same extent as the provision amended, repealed or revoked, subject to subsection (6).

(6), (7) . . .
(8) This Part extends to England and Wales, Scotland and Northern Ireland except that—
(a) sections 92, 93, 95, 97 and 98 extend only to England and Wales and Scotland;
(b) sections 83 to 88, 94 and 96 extend only to England and Wales.

NOTES
Commencement: 25 April 2013.
Sub-ss (3), (4), (6), (7): outside the scope of this work.

[1.1865]
103 Commencement

(1) The following provisions come into force on the day on which this Act is passed—
(a) section 10;
(b) section 24;
(c)–(g) *(outside the scope of this work)*
(h) sections 98 to 104;
(i) any other provision so far as is necessary for enabling the exercise on or after the day on which this Act is passed of any power (arising under or by virtue of that provision) to make provision by regulations, rules or order made by statutory instrument.

(2) The following provisions (so far as not already in force by virtue of subsection (1)(i)) come into force at the end of the period of 2 months beginning with the day on which this Act is passed—
(a) Part 1;
(b) sections 12, 13, 15, 17, 18, 20, 21 and 22;
(c) *outside the scope of this work.*
(d) section 64;
(e) section 97;
(f), (g) *(outside the scope of this work.)*

(3) Except as provided by subsections (1) and (2), the provisions of this Act come into force on such day as the Secretary of State may by order made by statutory instrument appoint.
(4) An order under subsection (3) may appoint different days for different purposes.

NOTES
Commencement: 25 April 2013.

[1.1866]
104 Short title

This Act may be cited as the Enterprise and Regulatory Reform Act 2013.

NOTES
Commencement: 25 April 2013.

SCHEDULES 1–21

(Schs 1–3, 20 contain amendments, repeals and revocations which, in so far as relevant to this work, have been incorporated at the appropriate place; Schs 4–18, 21 outside the scope of this work; Sch 19 amends the Insolvency Act 1986, s 285 at **[1.144]** *and other provisions of that Act which are outside the scope of this work.)*

PUBLIC SERVICE PENSIONS ACT 2013

(2013 c 25)

ARRANGEMENT OF SECTIONS

SCHEDULES

An Act to make provision for public service pension schemes; and for connected purposes.

[25 April 2013]

Establishment of new schemes

[1.1867]

1 Schemes for persons in public service

(1) Regulations may establish schemes for the payment of pensions and other benefits to or in respect of persons specified in subsection (2).

(2) Those persons are—

(a) civil servants;
(b) the judiciary;
(c) local government workers for England, Wales and Scotland;
(d) teachers for England, Wales and Scotland;
(e) health service workers for England, Wales and Scotland;
(f) fire and rescue workers for England, Wales and Scotland;
(g) members of police forces for England, Wales and Scotland;
(h) the armed forces.

(3) These terms are defined in Schedule 1.

(4) In this Act, regulations under this section are called "scheme regulations".

NOTES

Commencement: to be appointed.

[1.1868]

2 Responsible authority for schemes

(1) The persons who may make scheme regulations are set out in Schedule 2.

(2) In this Act, the person who may make scheme regulations for any description of persons specified in section 1(2) is called the "responsible authority" for the scheme for those persons.

NOTES

Commencement: to be appointed.

[1.1869]

3 Scheme regulations

(1) Scheme regulations may, subject to this Act, make such provision in relation to a scheme under section 1 as the responsible authority considers appropriate.

(2) That includes in particular—

(a) provision as to any of the matters specified in Schedule 3;
(b) consequential, supplementary, incidental or transitional provision in relation to the scheme or any provision of this Act.

(3) Scheme regulations may—

(a) make different provision for different purposes or cases (including different provision for different descriptions of persons);
(b) make retrospective provision (but see section 23);
(c) allow any person to exercise a discretion.

(4) The consequential provision referred to in subsection (2)(b) includes consequential provision amending any primary legislation passed before or in the same session as this Act (as well as consequential provision amending any secondary legislation).

(5) Scheme regulations require the consent of the Treasury before being made, unless one of the following exceptions applies.

(6) The exceptions are—

(a) scheme regulations of the Scottish Ministers relating to local government workers, fire and rescue workers and members of a police force;
(b) scheme regulations of the Welsh Ministers relating to fire and rescue workers.

NOTES

Commencement: to be appointed.

Governance

[1.1870]

4 Scheme manager

(1) Scheme regulations for a scheme under section 1 must provide for a person to be responsible for managing or administering—

(a) the scheme, and

(b) any statutory pension scheme that is connected with it.

(2) In this Act, that person is called the "scheme manager" for the scheme (or schemes).

(3) The scheme manager may in particular be the responsible authority.

(4) Subsection (1) does not apply to a scheme under section 1 which is an injury or compensation scheme.

(5) Scheme regulations may comply with the requirement in subsection (1)(a) or (b) by providing for different persons to be responsible for managing or administering different parts of a scheme (and references in this Act to the "scheme manager", in such a case, are to be construed accordingly).

(6) For the purposes of this Act, a scheme under section 1 and another statutory pension scheme are connected if and to the extent that the schemes make provision in relation to persons of the same description.

(7) Scheme regulations may specify exceptions to subsection (6).

NOTES

Commencement: to be appointed.

[1.1871]

5 Pension board

(1) Scheme regulations for a scheme under section 1 must provide for the establishment of a board with responsibility for assisting the scheme manager (or each scheme manager) in relation to the following matters.

(2) Those matters are—

(a) securing compliance with the scheme regulations and other legislation relating to the governance and administration of the scheme and any statutory pension scheme that is connected with it;

(b) securing compliance with requirements imposed in relation to the scheme and any connected scheme by the Pensions Regulator;

(c) such other matters as the scheme regulations may specify.

(3) In making the regulations the responsible authority must have regard to the desirability of securing the effective and efficient governance and administration of the scheme and any connected scheme.

(4) The regulations must include provision—

(a) requiring the scheme manager—

(i) to be satisfied that a person to be appointed as a member of the board does not have a conflict of interest, and

(ii) to be satisfied from time to time that none of the members of the board has a conflict of interest;

(b) requiring a member of the board, or a person proposed to be appointed as a member of the board, to provide the scheme manager with such information as the scheme manager reasonably requires for the purposes of provision under paragraph (a);

(c) requiring the board to include employer representatives and member representatives in equal numbers.

(5) In subsection (4)(a) "conflict of interest", in relation to a person, means a financial or other interest which is likely to prejudice the person's exercise of functions as a member of the board (but does not include a financial or other interest arising merely by virtue of membership of the scheme or any connected scheme).

(6) In subsection (4)(c)—

(a) "employer representatives" means persons appointed to the board for the purpose of representing employers for the scheme and any connected scheme;

(b) "member representatives" means persons appointed to the board for the purpose of representing members of the scheme and any connected scheme.

(7) Where the scheme manager of a scheme under section 1 is a committee of a local authority, the scheme regulations may provide for that committee also to be the board for the purposes of this section.

(8) In this Act, a board established under this section is called a "pension board".

(9) This section does not apply to a scheme under section 1 which is an injury or compensation scheme.

NOTES

Commencement: to be appointed.

[1.1872]

6 Pension board: information

(1) The scheme manager for a scheme under section 1 and any statutory pension scheme that is connected with it must publish information about the pension board for the scheme or schemes (and keep that information up-to-date).

(2) That information must include information about—

- (a) who the members of the board are,
- (b) representation on the board of members of the scheme or schemes, and
- (c) the matters falling within the board's responsibility.

(3) This section does not apply to a scheme under section 1 which is an injury or compensation scheme.

NOTES

Commencement: to be appointed.

[1.1873]

7 Scheme advisory board

(1) Scheme regulations for a scheme under section 1 which is a defined benefits scheme must provide for the establishment of a board with responsibility for providing advice to the responsible authority, at the authority's request, on the desirability of changes to the scheme.

(2) Where, by virtue of section 4(5), there is more than one scheme manager for a scheme mentioned in subsection (1) (and accordingly there is more than one pension board for the scheme), the regulations may also provide for the board to provide advice (on request or otherwise) to the scheme managers or the scheme's pension boards in relation to the effective and efficient administration and management of—

- (a) the scheme and any statutory pension scheme that is connected with it, or
- (b) any pension fund of the scheme and any connected scheme.

(3) A person to whom advice is given by virtue of subsection (1) or (2) must have regard to the advice.

(4) The regulations must include provision—

- (a) requiring the responsible authority—
  - (i) to be satisfied that a person to be appointed as a member of the board does not have a conflict of interest, and
  - (ii) to be satisfied from time to time that none of the members of the board has a conflict of interest;
- (b) requiring a member of the board, or a person proposed to be appointed as a member of the board, to provide the responsible authority with such information as the authority reasonably requires for the purposes of provision under paragraph (a).

(5) In subsection (4)(a) "conflict of interest", in relation to a person, means a financial or other interest which is likely to prejudice the person's exercise of functions as a member of the board (but does not include a financial or other interest arising merely by virtue of membership of the scheme or any connected scheme).

(6) In this Act, a board established under this section is called a "scheme advisory board".

NOTES

Commencement: to be appointed.

Design

[1.1874]

8 Types of scheme

(1) Scheme regulations may establish a scheme under section 1 as—

- (a) a defined benefits scheme,
- (b) a defined contributions scheme, or
- (c) a scheme of any other description.

(2) A scheme under section 1 which is a defined benefits scheme must be—

- (a) a career average revalued earnings scheme, or
- (b) a defined benefits scheme of such other description as Treasury regulations may specify.

(3) Treasury regulations may not specify a final salary scheme under subsection (2)(b).

(4) A scheme under section 1 is a "career average revalued earnings scheme" if—

- (a) the pension payable to or in respect of a person, so far as it is based on the person's pensionable service, is determined by reference to the person's pensionable earnings in each year of pensionable service, and
- (b) those earnings, or a proportion of those earnings accrued as a pension, are under the scheme revalued each year until the person leaves pensionable service.

(5) Treasury regulations under this section are subject to the negative Commons procedure.

NOTES

Commencement: to be appointed.

[1.1875]

9 Revaluation

(1) This section applies in relation to a scheme under section 1 which—
- (a) requires a revaluation of pensionable earnings of a person, or a proportion of those earnings accrued as a pension, until the person leaves pensionable service, and
- (b) requires such a revaluation to be by reference to a change in prices or earnings (or both) in a given period.

(2) The change in prices or earnings to be applied for the purposes of such a revaluation is to be such percentage increase or decrease as a Treasury order may specify in relation to the period.

(3) For the purposes of making such an order the Treasury may determine the change in prices or earnings in any period by reference to the general level of prices or earnings estimated in such manner as the Treasury consider appropriate.

(4) A Treasury order under this section—
- (a) must be made in each year;
- (b) may make different provision for different purposes.

(5) A Treasury order under this section is subject to—
- (a) the affirmative Commons procedure, if the order specifies a percentage decrease for the purposes of subsection (2), and
- (b) the negative Commons procedure, in any other case.

(6) For the purposes of subsection (1) any gap in the person's pensionable service which does not exceed five years is to be disregarded.

NOTES

Commencement: to be appointed.

[1.1876]

10 Pension age

(1) The normal pension age of a person under a scheme under section 1 must be—
- (a) the same as the person's state pension age, or
- (b) 65, if that is higher.

(2) Subsection (1) does not apply in relation to—
- (a) fire and rescue workers who are firefighters,
- (b) members of a police force, and
- (c) members of the armed forces.

The normal pension age of such persons under a scheme under section 1 must be 60.

(3) The deferred pension age of a person under a scheme under section 1 must be—
- (a) the same as the person's state pension age, or
- (b) 65, if that is higher.

(4) Where—
- (a) a person's state pension age changes, and
- (b) the person's normal or deferred pension age under a scheme under section 1 changes as a result of subsection (1) or (3),

the change to the person's normal or deferred pension age must under the scheme apply in relation to all the benefits (including benefits already accrued under the scheme) which may be paid to or in respect of the person under the scheme and to which the normal or deferred pension age is relevant.

(5) In this Act—
- (a) "normal pension age", in relation to a person and a scheme, means the earliest age at which the person is entitled to receive benefits under the scheme (without actuarial adjustment) on leaving the service to which the scheme relates (and disregarding any special provision as to early payment of benefits on the grounds of ill-health or otherwise);
- (b) "deferred pension age", in relation to a person and a scheme, means the earliest age at which the person is entitled to receive benefits under the scheme (without actuarial adjustment) after leaving the service to which the scheme relates at a time before normal pension age (and disregarding any special provision as to early payment of benefits on the grounds of ill-health or otherwise);
- (c) "state pension age", in relation to a person, means the pensionable age of the person as specified from time to time in Part 1 of Schedule 4 to the Pensions Act 1995.

NOTES

Commencement: to be appointed.

Cost control

[1.1877]

11 Valuations

(1) Scheme regulations for a scheme under section 1 which is a defined benefits scheme must provide for actuarial valuations to be made of—
 (a) the scheme, and
 (b) any statutory pension scheme that is connected with it.
(2) Such a valuation is to be carried out in accordance with Treasury directions.
(3) Treasury directions under subsection (2) may in particular specify—
 (a) how and when a valuation is to be carried out;
 (b) the time in relation to which a valuation is to be carried out;
 (c) the data, methodology and assumptions to be used in a valuation;
 (d) the matters to be covered by a valuation;
 (e) where a scheme under section 1 and another statutory pension scheme are connected, whether the schemes are to be valued separately or together (and if together, how);
 (f) the period within which any changes to the employer contribution rate under a scheme under section 1 must take effect following a valuation.
(4) Treasury directions under subsection (2), and variations and revocations of such directions, may only be made after the Treasury has consulted the Government Actuary.
(5) Scheme regulations for a scheme under section 1 which is not a defined benefits scheme may provide for actuarial valuations to be made of the scheme and any statutory pension scheme that is connected with it; and if they do, subsections (2) to (4) apply.

NOTES

Commencement: to be appointed.

[1.1878]

12 Employer cost cap

(1) Scheme regulations for a scheme under section 1 which is a defined benefits scheme must set a rate, expressed as a percentage of pensionable earnings of members of the scheme, to be used for the purpose of measuring changes in the cost of the scheme.
(2) In this section, the rate set under subsection (1) is called the "employer cost cap".
(3) The employer cost cap is to be set in accordance with Treasury directions.
(4) Treasury directions may in particular specify—
 (a) how the first valuation under section 11 of a scheme under section 1 is to be taken into account in setting the cap;
 (b) the costs, or changes in costs, that are to be taken into account on subsequent valuations of a scheme under section 1 for the purposes of measuring changes in the cost of the scheme against the cap;
 (c) the extent to which costs or changes in the costs of any statutory pension scheme which is connected with a scheme under section 1 are to be taken into account for the purposes of this section.
(5) Treasury regulations must make—
 (a) provision requiring the cost of a scheme (and any connected scheme) to remain within specified margins either side of the employer cost cap, and
 (b) for cases where the cost of a scheme would otherwise go beyond either of those margins, provision specifying a target cost within the margins.
(6) For cases where the cost of the scheme would otherwise go beyond the margins, scheme regulations may provide for—
 (a) a procedure for the responsible authority, the scheme manager (if different), employers and members (or representatives of employers and members) to reach agreement on the steps required to achieve the target cost for the scheme, and
 (b) the steps to be taken for that purpose if agreement is not reached under that procedure.
(7) The steps referred to in subsection (6) may include the increase or decrease of members' benefits or contributions.
(8) Treasury regulations under this section may—
 (a) include consequential or supplementary provision;
 (b) make different provision for different schemes.
(9) Treasury regulations under this section are subject to the negative Commons procedure.

NOTES

Commencement: to be appointed.

[1.1879]

13 Employer contributions in funded schemes

(1) This section applies in relation to a scheme under section 1 which is a defined benefits scheme with a pension fund.

(2) Scheme regulations must provide for the rate of employer contributions to be set at an appropriate level to ensure—

(a) the solvency of the pension fund, and

(b) the long-term cost-efficiency of the scheme, so far as relating to the pension fund.

(3) For that purpose, scheme regulations must require actuarial valuations of the pension fund.

(4) Where an actuarial valuation under subsection (3) has taken place, a person appointed by the responsible authority is to report on whether the following aims are achieved—

(a) the valuation is in accordance with the scheme regulations;

(b) the valuation has been carried out in a way which is not inconsistent with other valuations under subsection (3);

(c) the rate of employer contributions is set as specified in subsection (2).

(5) A report under subsection (4) must be published; and a copy must be sent to the scheme manager and (if different) the responsible authority.

(6) If a report under subsection (4) states that, in the view of the person making the report, any of the aims in that subsection has not been achieved—

(a) the report may recommend remedial steps;

(b) the scheme manager must—

(i) take such remedial steps as the scheme manager considers appropriate, and

(ii) publish details of those steps and the reasons for taking them;

(c) the responsible authority may—

(i) require the scheme manager to report on progress in taking remedial steps;

(ii) direct the scheme manager to take such remedial steps as the responsible authority considers appropriate.

(7) The person appointed under subsection (4) must, in the view of the responsible authority, be appropriately qualified.

NOTES

Commencement: to be appointed.

Administration

[1.1880]

14 Information about benefits

(1) Scheme regulations must require the scheme manager for a scheme under section 1 which is a defined benefits scheme to provide benefit information statements to each person in pensionable service under the scheme in accordance with this section.

(2) A benefit information statement must include—

(a) a description of the benefits earned by the person in respect of his or her pensionable service, and

(b) such other information as Treasury directions may specify.

(3) The information included in a benefit information statement must comply with such requirements as Treasury directions may specify.

(4) A benefit information statement must be provided—

(a) no later than the relevant date, and

(b) at least once in each year ending with the anniversary of that date.

(5) The relevant date is the last day of the period of 17 months beginning with the day on which scheme regulations establishing the scheme come into force.

(6) A benefit information statement must be provided in such manner as Treasury directions may specify.

NOTES

Commencement: to be appointed.

[1.1881]

15 Information about schemes

(1) Treasury directions may require the scheme manager or responsible authority of a scheme under section 1 to—

(a) publish scheme information, or

(b) provide scheme information to the Treasury.

(2) In subsection (1), "scheme information" means information about the scheme and any statutory pension scheme that is connected with it.

(3) The information to which Treasury directions under this section may relate includes in particular—

(a) scheme accounts;

(b) information about any scheme funding, assets and liabilities;

(c) information about scheme membership;

(d) information about employer and member contributions;

(e) information about scheme administration and governance.

(4) Treasury directions under this section may specify how and when information is to be published or provided.
(5) Treasury directions under this section may not require publication or provision of anything that the scheme manager or responsible authority could not otherwise lawfully publish or provide.

NOTES

Commencement: to be appointed.

[1.1882]
16 Records
(1) The scheme manager for a scheme under section 1 and any statutory pension scheme that is connected with it must keep such records as may be specified in regulations made by the Secretary of State.
(2) Regulations under this section are subject to the negative procedure.

NOTES

Commencement: to be appointed.

17 (*Outside the scope of this work.*)

Transitional

[1.1883]
18 Restriction of existing pension schemes
(1) No benefits are to be provided under an existing scheme to or in respect of a person in relation to the person's service after the closing date.
(2) In this Act "existing scheme" means a scheme listed in Schedule 5 (whether made before or after this section comes into force).
(3) Subsection (1) does not apply—
 (a) in relation to an existing scheme which is a defined contributions scheme;
 (b) to benefits excepted by Schedule 5.
(4) The closing date is—
 (a) 31 March 2014 for an existing scheme which is a relevant local government scheme, and
 (b) 31 March 2015 in any other case.
This is subject to subsection (7).
(5) Scheme regulations may provide for exceptions to subsection (1) in the case of—
 (a) persons who were members of an existing scheme, or who were eligible to be members of such a scheme, immediately before 1 April 2012, and
 (b) such other persons as the regulations may specify, being persons who before that date had ceased to be members of an existing scheme or to be eligible for membership of such a scheme.
(6) Exceptions under subsection (5) may, in particular, be framed by reference to the satisfaction of a specified condition (for example, the attainment of normal pension age under the existing scheme or another specified age) before a specified date.
(7) Where an exception to subsection (1) is framed by reference to the satisfaction of a specified condition before a specified date, scheme regulations may also provide for a different closing date for persons in whose case the condition—
 (a) is not satisfied before the specified date, but
 (b) is satisfied no more than 4 years after that date.
(8) Provision made under subsection (5) or (7) may in particular be made by amending the relevant existing scheme.
(9) In subsection (1), the reference to benefits in relation to a person's service includes benefits relating to the person's death in service.
(10) In subsection (4), "relevant local government scheme" means regulations under section 7 of the Superannuation Act 1972 which relate to persons in England and Wales.

NOTES

Commencement: to be appointed.

[1.1884]
19 Closure of existing injury and compensation schemes
(1) Scheme regulations for a scheme under section 1 may secure that no benefits are to be provided under a scheme listed in Schedule 6 that is connected with it.
(2) Where Schedule 6 specifies particular benefits in relation to a scheme, the power under subsection (1) is exercisable only in relation to those benefits.
(3) Scheme regulations may provide for exceptions to subsection (1).
(4) Provision made under this section may in particular be made by amending the connected scheme.

NOTES

Commencement: to be appointed.

[1.1885]

20 Final salary link

Schedule 7 contains provision for a "final salary link" in relation to schemes to which section 18(1) applies (and see section 31(14)).

NOTES

Commencement: to be appointed.

Procedure for scheme regulations

[1.1886]

21 Consultation

(1) Before making scheme regulations the responsible authority must consult such persons (or representatives of such persons) as appear to the authority likely to be affected by them.
(2) The responsible authority must publish a statement indicating the persons that the authority would normally expect to consult under subsection (1) (and keep the statement up-to-date).
(3) Subsection (1) may be satisfied by consultation before, as well as by consultation after, the coming into force of this section.

NOTES

Commencement: to be appointed.

[1.1887]

22 Procedure for protected elements

(1) This section applies where, after the coming into force of scheme regulations establishing a scheme under section 1, the responsible authority proposes to make further scheme regulations containing provision changing the protected elements of the scheme within the protected period.
(2) The responsible authority must—
  (a) consult the persons specified in subsection (3) with a view to reaching agreement with them, and
  (b) lay a report before the appropriate legislature.
(3) The persons referred to in subsection (2)(a) are the persons (or representatives of the persons) who appear to the responsible authority to be likely to be affected by the regulations if they were made.
(4) The report under subsection (2)(b) must set out why the responsible authority proposes to make the regulations, having regard to the desirability of not making a change to the protected elements of a scheme under section 1 within the protected period.
(5) In this section—
"the appropriate legislature" means—
  (a) Parliament, where the responsible authority is the Secretary of State, the Minister for the Civil Service or the Lord Chancellor;
  (b) the Scottish Parliament, where the responsible authority is the Scottish Ministers;
  (c) the National Assembly for Wales, where the responsible authority is the Welsh Ministers;
"protected period" means the period beginning with the coming into force of this section and ending with 31 March 2040;
"protected elements", in relation to a scheme under section 1, means—
  (a) the extent to which the scheme is a career average revalued earnings scheme;
  (b) members' contribution rates under the scheme;
  (c) benefit accrual rates under the scheme.
(6) In this section, references to a change to the protected elements do not include a change appearing to the responsible authority to be required by or consequential upon section 12 (employer cost cap).
(7) In a case where this section applies, there is no requirement to consult under section 21(1).

NOTES

Commencement: to be appointed.

[1.1888]

23 Procedure for retrospective provision

(1) Where the responsible authority proposes to make scheme regulations containing retrospective provision which appears to the authority to have significant adverse effects in relation to the pension payable to or in respect of members of the scheme, the authority must first obtain the consent of the persons referred to in subsection (3).

(2) Where the responsible authority proposes to make scheme regulations containing retrospective provision which appears to the authority—

(a) not to have significant adverse effects as specified in subsection (1), but

(b) to have significant adverse effects in any other way in relation to members of the scheme (for example, in relation to injury or compensation benefits),

the authority must first consult the persons specified in subsection (3) with a view to reaching agreement with them.

(3) The persons referred to in subsections (1) and (2) are the persons (or representatives of the persons) who appear to the responsible authority to be likely to be affected by the provision if it were made.

(4) The responsible authority must, in a case falling within subsection (1) or (2), lay a report before the appropriate legislature (as defined in section 22).

(5) In a case falling within subsection (1) or (2) there is no requirement to consult under section 21(1).

NOTES

Commencement: to be appointed.

[1.1889]

24 Other procedure

(1) Scheme regulations are subject to the affirmative procedure if—

(a) they amend primary legislation,

(b) section 23(1) or (2) (procedure for retrospective provision having significant adverse effects) applies, or

(c) they are scheme regulations for a scheme relating to the judiciary, unless the pension board for that scheme has stated that it considers the regulations to be minor or wholly beneficial.

(2) Scheme regulations are subject to the negative procedure in any other case.

(3) If scheme regulations otherwise subject to the negative procedure are combined with scheme regulations subject to the affirmative procedure, the combined regulations are subject to the affirmative procedure.

NOTES

Commencement: to be appointed.

New schemes: supplementary

[1.1890]

25 Extension of schemes

(1) Scheme regulations for a scheme under section 1 may make provision for the payment of pensions and other benefits to or in respect of—

(a) persons who are specified in section 1(2), but

(b) in relation to whom the responsible authority could not otherwise make a scheme under section 1.

(2) Scheme regulations for a scheme under section 1 may make provision to deem persons of any description to fall within a given description of persons specified in section 1(2).

(3) Scheme regulations for a scheme under section 1 may specify persons, not being persons specified in section 1(2), as persons to whom the scheme may potentially relate.

(4) The persons specified under subsection (3) may be any persons (other than persons specified in section 1(2)) that the responsible authority considers appropriate.

(5) The responsible authority may then at any time determine that the scheme is to relate to some or all of those persons.

(6) By virtue of a determination under subsection (5) the scheme regulations then apply to the persons to whom the determination relates as they apply to other persons to or in respect of whom pensions and other benefits are provided under the scheme (or such class of other persons as may be specified in the determination).

(7) Subsection (6) is subject to—

(a) any special provision made in the scheme regulations, and

(b) a direction under subsection (8).

(8) Scheme regulations made under subsection (2) or (3) in relation to any persons may include provision authorising the responsible authority by direction to modify provisions of the regulations in their application to those persons for the purpose of—

(a) securing appropriate protection against additional costs to the scheme that might result from the application of the scheme regulations to those persons,

(b) obtaining information about those persons, their employers and other relevant persons, or

(c) taking appropriate account of—

(i) the arrangements under which those persons are employed, and

(ii) the organisational structures of their employers.

(9) The responsible authority for a scheme under section 1 must publish a list of the persons to whom the scheme relates by virtue of determinations under subsection (5) (and keep the published list up-to-date).
(10) A determination under subsection (5) may have retrospective effect.
(11) Where, by virtue of section 4(5), there is more than one scheme manager for a scheme under section 1, the responsible authority may delegate its functions under subsection (5) or (9) to the scheme managers, subject to such conditions as the responsible authority considers appropriate.

NOTES
Commencement: to be appointed.

[1.1891]
26 Non-scheme benefits
(1) The scheme manager or employer for a scheme under section 1 may make such payments as the scheme manager or employer considers appropriate towards the provision, otherwise than by virtue of the scheme, of pensions and other benefits to or in respect of—
(a) persons within the description of persons specified in section 1(2) for which the responsible authority may make the scheme, and
(b) any other persons to whom the scheme relates by virtue of section 25.
(2) Subsection (1) is subject to any provision made in the scheme regulations for the scheme that restricts or otherwise affects the power to make payments under that subsection.

NOTES
Commencement: to be appointed.

27 *(Introduces Sch 8 to the Act (consequential and minor amendments).)*

Existing schemes: supplementary

[1.1892]
28 Existing local government schemes
(1) This section applies in relation to regulations under section 7 of the Superannuation Act 1972 which relate to persons in England and Wales which are in force immediately before the coming into force of this section.
(2) To the extent that—
(a) such regulations make provision for the payment of pensions and other benefits to or in respect of a person in relation to the person's service on or after 1 April 2014, and
(b) that provision could be made under scheme regulations,
the regulations are to have effect as if they were scheme regulations relating to local government workers in England and Wales.
(3) Accordingly, to that extent a scheme under such regulations is to have effect as a scheme under section 1.

NOTES
Commencement: to be appointed.

29 *(Introduces Sch 9 to the Act (amendments to the Superannuation Act 1972).)*

Public body pension schemes

[1.1893]
30 New public body pension schemes
(1) The following provisions of this Act apply in relation to a new public body pension scheme (and any statutory pension scheme that is connected with it) as to a scheme under section 1 (and any connected scheme)—
(a) section 3(1) and (2) and Schedule 3 (scheme regulations);
(b) section 4 (scheme manager);
(c) sections 5 and 6 (pension board), if the scheme has more than one member;
(d) sections 8 to 10 (scheme design);
(e) sections 11 and 12 (cost control);
(f) sections 14 to 16 (information and records).
(2) For the purposes of subsection (1), the provisions referred to in that subsection are to be read with the following modifications—
(a) references to scheme regulations are to be read as references to the rules of the scheme;
(b) references to the responsible authority are to be read as references to the public authority which established the scheme.
(3) A new public body pension scheme, and any variation to the rules of the scheme, requires the consent of the Treasury.
(4) This section does not apply to a new public body pension scheme which relates to a devolved body or office.

(5) In this Act—

"public body pension scheme" means a scheme (other than an existing scheme) established by a public authority for the payment of pensions and other benefits to or in respect of members or staff of a statutory body or the holder of a statutory office;

"new public body pension scheme" means a public body pension scheme established after the coming into force of this section.

NOTES

Commencement: to be appointed.

[1.1894]

31 Restriction of certain existing public body pension schemes

(1) This section applies to a public body pension scheme which relates to members or staff of a body, or the holder of an office, listed in Schedule 10.

(2) The public authority responsible for the scheme must make provision to secure that no benefits are provided under the scheme to or in respect of a person in relation to the person's service after a date determined by the authority.

(3) Subsection (2) does not apply—

(a) in relation to a public body pension scheme which is a defined contributions scheme, or

(b) to injury or compensation benefits.

(4) The public authority responsible for a scheme to which subsection (2) applies may provide for exceptions to the provision made under subsection (2), and section 18(6) and (7) apply in relation to any such exceptions (reading references to scheme regulations as references to rules of the scheme).

(5) Provision made under subsection (2) or (4) may in particular be made by amending the public body pension scheme.

(6) In subsection (2), the reference to benefits in relation to a person's service includes benefits relating to the person's death in service.

(7) If any of the persons to whom a scheme to which subsection (2) applies relates are not eligible for membership of a scheme under section 1, the public authority responsible for the scheme may establish a new scheme for the payment of pensions or other benefits to or in respect of those persons (and see section 30).

(8) Where a scheme to which subsection (2) applies was established in exercise of a statutory function or other power, the function or power may not be exercised again so as to establish a new defined benefits scheme in relation to the body or office.

(9) In the case of a scheme established by deed of trust, subsections (2) and (4) apply irrespective of the provisions of the deed or the law relating to trusts.

(10) A Treasury order may amend Schedule 10 so as to—

(a) remove any body or office specified there;

(b) add any body or office to it (by name or description),

but may not add a devolved body or office.

(11) A Treasury order under subsection (10) may make consequential or supplementary provision, including in particular provision made by amending any legislation.

(12) A Treasury order under subsection (10) is subject to the negative procedure.

(13) It is immaterial for the purposes of subsection (1) whether a scheme is made before or after the coming into force of this section.

(14) Schedule 7 contains provision for a "final salary link" in relation to schemes to which subsection (2) applies.

NOTES

Commencement: to be appointed.

[1.1895]

32 Existing public body pension schemes: pension age

(1) A public body pension scheme established before the coming into force of this section may include—

(a) provision securing that the normal and deferred pension age of a person under the scheme is—

(i) the same as the person's state pension age, or

(ii) 65, if that is higher, and

(b) provision securing that changes in the person's normal or deferred pension age occurring in consequence of provision under paragraph (a) apply in relation to relevant accrued benefits (as well as other benefits).

(2) In subsection (1)(b) "relevant accrued benefits", in relation to a person and a scheme, means benefits accrued after the coming into force of the provision under subsection (1) which may be paid to or in respect of the person under the scheme and to which the normal or deferred pension age is relevant.

(3) This section does not apply to a public body pension scheme which relates to a devolved body or office.

NOTES

Commencement: to be appointed.

Parliamentary and other pension schemes

[1.1896]

33 Great offices of state

Schedule 11 makes provision about pension arrangements for the offices of—

(a) Prime Minister and First Lord of the Treasury,
(b) Lord Chancellor, and
(c) Speaker of the House of Commons.

NOTES

Commencement: to be appointed.

34–36 *(Outside the scope of this work.)*

General

[1.1897]

37 General interpretation

In this Act—

"the affirmative procedure" and "the affirmative Commons procedure" have the meanings given in section 38;

"armed forces" has the meaning given in Schedule 1;

"body" includes an unincorporated body or organisation of persons (for example, a committee or board of trustees);

"career average revalued earnings scheme" has the meaning given in section 8(4);

"civil servants" has the meaning given in Schedule 1;

"compensation benefits" means benefits by way of compensation for loss of office or employment;

"connected", in relation to a scheme under section 1 and another statutory pension scheme, or a new public body pension scheme and another statutory pension scheme, has the meaning given by section 4(6);

"defined benefits scheme": a pension scheme is a "defined benefits scheme" if or to the extent that the benefits that may be provided under the scheme are not money purchase benefits (within the meaning of the Pension Schemes Act 1993) or injury and compensation benefits;

"defined contributions scheme": a pension scheme is a "defined contributions scheme" if or to the extent that the benefits that may be provided under the scheme are money purchase benefits (within the meaning of the Pension Schemes Act 1993);

"deferred pension age" has the meaning given in section 10(5);

"devolved": a body or office is "devolved" if or to the extent that provision about pensions payable to or in respect of members or staff of the body, or a holder of the office—

(a) would be within the legislative competence of the Northern Ireland Assembly were that provision contained in an Act of the Assembly, or
(b) is not a reserved matter within the meaning of the Scotland Act 1998;

"earnings" includes any remuneration or profit derived from an employment;

"employer", in relation to a pension scheme, means—

(a) any employer of persons to whom the scheme relates,
(b) the person responsible for the remuneration of an office-holder to whom the scheme relates, or
(c) such other persons (in addition to, or instead of, any person falling within paragraph (a) or (b)) as scheme regulations or (in the case of a public body pension scheme) the rules of the scheme may provide;

"existing scheme" has the meaning given in section 18(2);

"final salary", in relation to a person to or in respect of whom a pension under a pension scheme is payable, means the person's pensionable earnings, or highest, average or representative pensionable earnings, in a specified period ending at, or defined by reference to, the time when the person's pensionable service in relation to that scheme terminates;

"final salary scheme": a pension scheme is a "final salary scheme" if entitlement to the pension payable to or in respect of a person which is based on the pensionable service of that person is or may be determined to any extent by reference to the person's final salary;

"fire and rescue workers" has the meaning given in Schedule 1;

"injury benefits" means benefits by way of compensation for incapacity or death as a result of injury or illness;

"injury or compensation scheme": a pension scheme is an "injury or compensation scheme" if it provides only for injury or compensation benefits (or both);

"judiciary" has the meaning given in Schedule 1;
"health service workers" has the meaning given in Schedule 1;
"legislation" means primary or secondary legislation;
"local authority" means—
- (a) a local authority in England and Wales within the meaning of Part 1 of the Local Government and Housing Act 1989, or
- (b) a council constituted under section 2 of the Local Government etc (Scotland) Act 1994;

"local government workers" has the meaning given in Schedule 1;
"members of a police force" has the meaning given in Schedule 1;
"the negative procedure" and "the negative Commons procedure" have the meanings given in section 38;
"normal pension age" has the meaning given in section 10(5);
"pension board" has the meaning given by section 5(8);
"pension scheme" means a scheme for the payment of pensions or other benefits to or in respect of persons with service of a particular description;
"pensionable earnings", in relation to a pension scheme and a member of it, means earnings by reference to which a pension or other benefits under the scheme are calculated;
"pensionable service", in relation to a pension scheme, means service which qualifies a person to a pension or other benefits under that scheme;
"primary legislation" means an Act, Act of the Scottish Parliament, Act or Measure of the National Assembly for Wales or Northern Ireland legislation;
"public authority" means—
- (a) a Minister of the Crown (as defined by section 8 of the Ministers of the Crown Act 1975),
- (b) a statutory body or the holder of a statutory office, or
- (c) a person exercising a statutory function;

"public body pension scheme" and "new public body pension scheme" have the meanings given in section 30(5);
"responsible authority", in relation to a scheme under section 1, has the meaning given by section 2(2);
"scheme" includes arrangements of any description;
"scheme advisory board" has the meaning given by section 7(6);
"scheme manager", in relation to a scheme under section 1, has the meaning given in section 4(2);
"scheme regulations" has the meaning given in section 1(4);
"secondary legislation" means an instrument made under primary legislation;
"staff", in relation to a body, includes any employee or officer of the body;
"state pension age" has the meaning given in section 10(5);
"statutory body" and "statutory office" mean a body or office established under any legislation;
"statutory function" means a function conferred by any legislation;
"statutory pension scheme" means—
- (a) a pension scheme which is established by or under any legislation, and
- (b) a public body pension scheme which is not so established;

"teachers" has the meaning given in Schedule 1;
"Treasury directions" means directions given by the Treasury;
"Treasury order" means an order made by the Treasury;
"Treasury regulations" means regulations made by the Treasury.

NOTES

Commencement: 25 April 2013.

[1.1898]

38 Regulations, orders and directions

(1) For the purposes of this Act any power of the Secretary of State, the Minister for the Civil Service, the Treasury, the Lord Chancellor or the Welsh Ministers to make regulations or an order is exercisable by statutory instrument.

(2) In this Act, the "affirmative procedure" means—
- (a) in the case of regulations or an order of the Secretary of State, the Minister for the Civil Service or the Lord Chancellor, that the regulations or order may not be made unless a draft of the instrument containing them or it has been laid before, and approved by resolution of, each House of Parliament;
- (b) in the case of regulations of the Welsh Ministers, that the regulations may not be made unless a draft of the instrument containing them has been laid before, and approved by resolution of, the National Assembly for Wales.

(3) In this Act, the "negative procedure" means—

(a) in the case of regulations or an order of the Secretary of State, the Minister for the Civil Service, the Lord Chancellor or the Treasury, that the instrument containing them or it is subject to annulment in pursuance of a resolution of either House of Parliament;

(b) in the case of regulations or an order of the Welsh Ministers, that the instrument containing them or it is subject to annulment in pursuance of a resolution of the National Assembly for Wales.

(4) In this Act, the "affirmative Commons procedure", in relation to a Treasury order, means that the order may not be made unless a draft of the instrument containing it has been laid before, and approved by resolution of, the House of Commons.

(5) In this Act, the "negative Commons procedure", in relation to Treasury regulations or a Treasury order, means that the instrument containing them or it is subject to annulment in pursuance of a resolution of the House of Commons.

(6) For regulations and orders of the Scottish Ministers, see Part 2 of the Interpretation and Legislative Reform (Scotland) Act 2010 (asp 10).

(7) Treasury directions under this Act may be varied or revoked.

NOTES

Commencement: 25 April 2013.

Final

[1.1899]

39 Financial provision

(1) Scheme regulations may provide for any pension or other sum payable under the regulations to or in respect of a person who has held an office specified in Part 1 of Schedule 1 to the Judicial Pensions and Retirement Act 1993 to be charged on, and paid out of, the Consolidated Fund.

(2) There shall be paid out of money provided by Parliament—

(a) any expenditure incurred under or by virtue of this Act by a Minister of the Crown, and

(b) any increase attributable to this Act in the sums payable under or by virtue of any other Act out of money so provided.

NOTES

Commencement: 25 April 2013.

[1.1900]

40 Extent

(1) An amendment or repeal in this Act has the same extent as the provision amended or repealed.

(2) That aside, this Act extends to England and Wales, Scotland and Northern Ireland.

NOTES

Commencement: 25 April 2013.

[1.1901]

41 Commencement

(1) The following provisions of this Act come into force on the day on which this Act is passed—

(a) section 29 and Schedule 9 (existing schemes for civil servants: extension of access);

(b) section 33 and Schedule 11 (great offices of state);

(c) sections 37 to 40, this section and section 42.

(2) The other provisions of this Act come into force on such day or days as may be appointed by Treasury order.

(3) An order under subsection (2) may—

(a) appoint different days for different purposes;

(b) make transitional, transitory or saving provision.

NOTES

Commencement: 25 April 2013.

[1.1902]

42 Short title

This Act may be cited as the Public Service Pensions Act 2013.

NOTES

Commencement: 25 April 2013.

SCHEDULE 1
PERSONS IN PUBLIC SERVICE: DEFINITIONS

Section 1(3)

Civil servants

[1.1903]

1 In this Act, "civil servants" means persons employed in the civil service of the State (not including the civil service of Northern Ireland).

Judiciary

2 (1) In this Act, "the judiciary" means holders of an office specified in an order made by—

(a) the Secretary of State, in relation to an office with a jurisdiction exercised exclusively in relation to Scotland, or

(b) the Lord Chancellor, in any other case.

(2) An order under sub-paragraph (1) may only specify an office in or as regards Scotland or Northern Ireland if the office is not a devolved office.

(3) An order under this paragraph is subject to the negative procedure.

Local government workers

3 (1) In this Act, "local government workers" means persons employed in local government service and specified in scheme regulations.

(2) In this paragraph, "local government service" means service specified in scheme regulations.

Teachers

4 In this Act, "teachers" includes persons who are employed otherwise than as teachers—

(a) in a capacity connected with education which to a substantial extent involves the control or supervision of teachers, or

(b) in employment which involves the performance of duties in connection with the provision of education or services ancillary to education, and

who are specified in scheme regulations.

Health service workers

5 (1) In this Act, "health service workers" means persons engaged in health services and specified in scheme regulations.

(2) In this paragraph, "health services" means services specified in scheme regulations.

Fire and rescue workers

6 In this Act, "fire and rescue workers" means persons employed by—

(a) a fire and rescue authority in England or Wales, or

(b) the Scottish Fire and Rescue Service.

Police forces

7 In this Act "members of a police force"—

(a) in relation to England and Wales, includes special constables and police cadets;

(b) in relation to Scotland, means members of the Police Service of Scotland and police cadets.

Armed forces

8 In this Act, "the armed forces" means the naval, military and air forces of the Crown.

Transitional provision

9 In relation to a time before the coming into force of section 101 of the Police and Fire Reform (Scotland) Act 2012 (asp 8), the reference in paragraph 6(b) to the Scottish Fire and Rescue Service is to be read as a reference to a relevant authority (as defined in section 6 of the Fire (Scotland) Act 2005 (asp 5)).

10 In relation to a time before the coming into force of section 6 of the Police and Fire Reform (Scotland) Act 2012, the reference in paragraph 7(b) to the Police Service of Scotland is to be read as a reference to a police force within the meaning of the Police (Scotland) Act 1967.

NOTES

Commencement: to be appointed.

SCHEDULE 2
RESPONSIBLE AUTHORITIES

Section 2(1)

Civil servants and judiciary

[1.1904]

1 Scheme regulations for civil servants may be made by the Minister for the Civil Service.

2 (1) Scheme regulations for the judiciary may be made by the Lord Chancellor.

(2) Before making scheme regulations in relation to an office with a jurisdiction exercised exclusively in relation to Scotland, the Lord Chancellor must consult the Secretary of State.

Local government workers

3 Scheme regulations for local government workers may be made by—
- (a) the Secretary of State, in or as regards England and Wales;
- (b) the Scottish Ministers, in or as regards Scotland.

Teachers

4 Scheme regulations for teachers may be made by—
- (a) the Secretary of State, in or as regards England and Wales;
- (b) the Scottish Ministers, in or as regards Scotland.

Health service workers

5 Scheme regulations for health service workers may be made by—
- (a) the Secretary of State, in or as regards England and Wales;
- (b) the Scottish Ministers, in or as regards Scotland.

Fire and rescue workers

6 Scheme regulations for fire and rescue workers may be made by—
- (a) the Secretary of State, in or as regards England;
- (b) the Welsh Ministers, in or as regards Wales;
- (c) the Scottish Ministers, in or as regards Scotland.

Police forces

7 Scheme regulations for members of a police force may be made by—
- (a) the Secretary of State, in or as regards England and Wales;
- (b) the Scottish Ministers, in or as regards Scotland.

Armed forces

8 Scheme regulations for the armed forces may be made by the Secretary of State.

NOTES

Commencement: to be appointed.

SCHEDULE 3
SCOPE OF SCHEME REGULATIONS: SUPPLEMENTARY MATTERS

Section 3(2)(a)

[1.1905]

1 Eligibility and admission to membership.

This includes—
- (a) specifying who, of the persons in relation to whom the scheme regulations may be made, is eligible for membership;
- (b) conditions of eligibility.

2 The benefits which must or may be paid under the scheme.

Those benefits may include—
- (a) pensions and other benefits on leaving service to which the scheme relates (whether before, at or after normal pension age);
- (b) benefits payable on death (in service or otherwise);
- (c) compensation payments (including for death, injury or redundancy);
- (d) discretionary payments and concessions.

3 The persons to whom benefits under the scheme are payable.

Those persons may include—
- (a) active, deferred and pensioner members of the scheme;
- (b) pension credit members of the scheme;

(c) widows, widowers, surviving civil partners and surviving dependants.

4 The conditions subject to which benefits are payable.

5 The assignment of benefits, including restrictions on assignment.

6 The forfeiture or suspension of benefits.

7 The recovery of overpaid benefits.

8 The exclusion of double recovery of compensation or damages.

This includes—

(a) exclusion or modification of rights to compensation or damages in respect of any matter in a case where benefits are paid under the scheme in respect of the same matter;

(b) exclusion or modification of rights to benefits under the scheme where compensation or damages are received in respect of the same matter from another source.

9 Contributions, including—

(a) the making of contributions by employers and members;

(b) contribution rates;

(c) interest on late payment of contributions;

(d) the return of contributions (with or without interest).

10 The payment or receipt of transfer values or other lump sum payments for the purpose of creating or restoring rights to benefits (under the scheme or otherwise).

11 Pension funds (for schemes which have them).

This includes the administration, management and winding-up of any pension funds.

12 The administration and management of the scheme, including—

(a) the giving of guidance or directions by the responsible authority to the scheme manager (where those persons are different);

(b) the person by whom benefits under the scheme are to be provided;

(c) the provision or publication of information about the scheme.

13 The delegation of functions under scheme regulations, including—

(a) delegation of functions by the scheme manager or responsible authority;

(b) further delegation of functions by any delegatee.

14 The payment by an employer of—

(a) any costs relating to the administration of the scheme;

(b) any costs incurred because of a failure by the employer to comply with the employer's obligations under the scheme;

(c) interest relating to payments to be made by virtue of this paragraph.

15 The resolution of disputes and appeals (including the referral to a court of law of questions of law which under the scheme fall to be determined by the responsible authority).

NOTES

Commencement: to be appointed.

SCHEDULE 4

(Sch 4 amends provisions of the Pensions Act 2004 that are outside the scope of this work.)

SCHEDULE 5
EXISTING PENSION SCHEMES

Section 18

Civil servants

[1.1906]

1 A scheme under section 1 of the Superannuation Act 1972.

Exception: injury benefits and compensation benefits

Judiciary

2 A scheme constituted by section 20 of the Sheriff Courts (Scotland) Act 1907.

3 A scheme constituted by paragraph 23 of Schedule 9 to the Agriculture Act 1947, so far as relating to payment of pension benefits.

4 A scheme constituted by or made under any provision of Part XIII of the County Courts Act (Northern Ireland) 1959 (c 25 (NI)).

5 A scheme constituted by or made under any provision of the District Judges (Magistrates' Courts) Pensions Act (Northern Ireland) 1960 (c 2 (NI)).

6 A scheme constituted by or made under any provision of the Sheriffs' Pensions (Scotland) Act 1961.

7 A scheme under paragraph 7A of Schedule 10 to the Rent Act 1977.
Exception: injury benefits and compensation benefits

8 A scheme constituted by or made under any provision of the Judicial Pensions Act 1981.
Exception: injury benefits under a scheme constituted by or made under Part 3 of Schedule 1 to that Act

9 A scheme constituted by paragraph 9 of Schedule 4 to the Rent (Scotland) Act 1984.

10 A scheme constituted by or made under any provision of Part 1 or section 19 of the Judicial Pensions and Retirement Act 1993.
Exception: benefits payable to or in respect of a holder of a devolved office

11 A scheme constituted by paragraph 4(1) of Schedule 1 to the Scottish Land Court Act 1993.

12 A scheme constituted by or made under paragraph 6 of Schedule 2 to the Mental Health (Care and Treatment) (Scotland) Act 2003 (asp 13).

13 A scheme constituted by or made under paragraph 9 of Schedule 1 to the Education (Additional Support for Learning) (Scotland) Act 2004 (asp 4).

14 A scheme constituted by paragraph 2(1)(b) of Schedule 2 to the Charities and Trustee Investment (Scotland) Act 2005 (asp 10), so far as relating to payment of pension benefits.

15 A scheme constituted by paragraph 6(3) of Schedule 11 to the Welsh Language (Wales) Measure 2011 (nawm 1).

Local government workers

16 A scheme constituted by paragraph 2 of Schedule 1 to the Coroners Act 1988.

17 Regulations under section 7 of the Superannuation Act 1972.
Exception: injury benefits

Teachers

18 Regulations under section 9 of the Superannuation Act 1972.
Exception: injury benefits

Health service workers

19 Regulations under section 10 of the Superannuation Act 1972.
Exception: injury benefits

Fire and rescue workers

20 A scheme under section 26 of the Fire Services Act 1947.

21 A scheme under section 34 of the Fire and Rescue Services Act 2004.
Exception: injury benefits and compensation benefits

Members of police forces

22 Regulations under section 1 of the Police Pensions Act 1976.
Exception: injury benefits

23 A scheme under section 48 of the Police and Fire Reform (Scotland) Act 2012 (asp 8).
Exception: injury benefits and compensation benefits

Armed forces

24 The scheme constituted by the Royal Warrant of 19 December 1949 (see Army Order 151 of 1949).
Exception: injury benefits

25 An Order in Council under section 3 of the Naval and Marine Pay and Pensions Act 1865.
Exception: injury benefits

26 An order under section 2 of the Pensions and Yeomanry Pay Act 1884.
Exception: injury benefits

27 An order under section 2 of the Air Force (Constitution) Act 1917.
Exception: injury benefits

28 Orders or regulations under section 4 of the Reserve Forces Act 1996 containing provision made under section 8 of that Act.

Exception: injury benefits and compensation benefits

29 (1) A scheme under section 1(1) of the Armed Forces (Pensions and Compensation) Act 2004.
Exception: injury benefits and compensation benefits

(2) For the purposes of sub-paragraph (1), "compensation benefits" includes benefits by way of payments for resettlement or retraining.

NOTES

Commencement: to be appointed.

SCHEDULE 6
EXISTING INJURY AND COMPENSATION SCHEMES

Section 19

Civil servants

[1.1907]

1 A scheme under section 1 of the Superannuation Act 1972.
Specified benefits: injury benefits and compensation benefits

Judiciary

2 A scheme under paragraph 7A of Schedule 10 to the Rent Act 1977.
Specified benefits: injury benefits and compensation benefits

3 A scheme constituted by or made under Part 3 of Schedule 1 to the Judicial Pensions Act 1981.

4 A scheme constituted by section 11(b) of the Judicial Pensions Act 1981.

Local government workers

5 Regulations under section 7 of the Superannuation Act 1972.
Specified benefits: injury benefits

Teachers

6 Regulations under section 9 of the Superannuation Act 1972.
Specified benefits: injury benefits

Health service workers

7 Regulations under section 10 of the Superannuation Act 1972.
Specified benefits: injury benefits

Fire and rescue workers

8 A scheme under section 34 of the Fire and Rescue Services Act 2004.
Specified benefits: injury benefits and compensation benefits

Members of police forces

9 Regulations under section 1 of the Police Pensions Act 1976.
Specified benefits: injury benefits

10 A scheme under section 48 of the Police and Fire Reform (Scotland) Act 2012 (asp 8).
Specified benefits: injury benefits and compensation benefits

Armed forces

11 The scheme constituted by the Royal Warrant of 19 December 1949 (see Army Order 151 of 1949).
Specified benefits: injury benefits

12 An Order in Council under section 3 of the Naval and Marine Pay and Pensions Act 1865.
Specified benefits: injury benefits

13 An order under section 2 of the Pensions and Yeomanry Pay Act 1884.
Specified benefits: injury benefits

14 An order under section 2 of the Air Force (Constitution) Act 1917.
Specified benefits: injury benefits

15 An order or regulations under section 4 of the Reserve Forces Act 1996 containing provision made under section 8 of that Act.
Specified benefits: injury benefits and compensation benefits

16 (1) A scheme under section 1(1) of the Armed Forces (Pensions and Compensation) Act 2004.
Specified benefits: injury benefits and compensation benefits
(2) For the purposes of sub-paragraph (1), "compensation benefits" includes benefits by way of payments for resettlement or retraining.

17 A scheme under section 1(2) of the Armed Forces (Pensions and Compensation) Act 2004.

Compensation schemes for loss of office etc

18 Regulations under section 24 of the Superannuation Act 1972.

NOTES
Commencement: to be appointed.

SCHEDULE 7
FINAL SALARY LINK

Sections 20 and 31

Persons who remain in an old scheme for past service

[1.1908]
1 (1) This paragraph applies in a case where—
(a) a person is a member of an existing scheme to which section 18(1) applies or a scheme to which section 31(2) applies ("the old scheme") by virtue of his or her pensionable service for that scheme ("the old scheme service"), and
(b) the person is also a member of a scheme under section 1 or a new public body pension scheme ("the new scheme") by virtue of his or her pensionable service for that scheme ("the new scheme service").

(2) If, in a case where this paragraph applies—
(a) the old scheme service and the new scheme service are continuous, and
(b) the person's employer in relation to the old scheme service is the person's employer in relation to the new scheme service (or any other employer in relation to the new scheme),

then, in determining the person's final salary for any purpose of the old scheme—
(i) the old scheme service is to be regarded as having ended when the new scheme service ended, and
(ii) such earnings as scheme regulations for the new scheme may specify, being earnings derived by the person from the new scheme service, are to be regarded as derived from the old scheme service (subject to sub-paragraph (3)).

(3) The amount of the earnings that are to be regarded as derived from the old scheme service must not be materially less than the amount of the earnings that would have been the person's pensionable earnings derived from that service had the new scheme service been old scheme service.

Persons whose benefits under an old scheme are transferred to another closed scheme

2 (1) This paragraph applies in a case where—
(a) a person has been a member of an existing scheme to which section 18(1) applies or a scheme to which section 31(2) applies ("the old scheme") by virtue of his or her pensionable service for that scheme ("the old scheme service"),
(b) the person is also a member of a scheme under section 1 or a new public body pension scheme ("the new scheme") by virtue of his or her pensionable service for that scheme ("the new scheme service"),
(c) the person's rights to benefit under the old scheme have been transferred after the date referred to in section 18(1) or 31(2) to an existing scheme to which section 18(1) applies or a scheme to which section 31(2) applies ("the transfer scheme"), and
(d) the old scheme service is treated, by virtue of that transfer, as pensionable service of the person for the transfer scheme ("the deemed transfer scheme service").

(2) If, in a case where this paragraph applies—
(a) the deemed transfer scheme service and the new scheme service are continuous, and
(b) the person's employer in relation to the new scheme service is an employer in relation to the transfer scheme,

then, in determining the person's final salary for any purpose of the transfer scheme—
(i) the deemed transfer scheme service is to be regarded as having ended when the new scheme service ended, and
(ii) such earnings as scheme regulations for the new scheme may specify, being earnings derived by the person from the new scheme service, are to be regarded as derived from the deemed transfer scheme service (subject to sub-paragraph (3)).

(3) The amount of the earnings that are to be regarded as derived from the deemed transfer scheme service must not be materially less than the amount of the earnings that would have been the person's pensionable earnings derived from that service had the new scheme service been deemed transfer scheme service.

(4) In sub-paragraph (1)(c), the reference to a transfer of rights to benefit includes the making of a transfer payment in respect of such rights.

Continuity of employment

3 (1) For the purposes of paragraphs 1(2)(a) and 2(2)(a), there are to be disregarded—
(a) any gap in service where the person was in pensionable public service;
(b) a single gap of service where the person was not in pensionable public service, if that gap does not exceed five years;
(c) two or more gaps in service where the person was not in pensionable public service, if none of the gaps exceeds five years.

(2) In this paragraph, "pensionable public service" means service which is pensionable service in relation to—
(a) a scheme under section 1, or
(b) a new public body pension scheme.

Movement between new schemes

4 Where the condition in sub-paragraph (1)(b) of paragraph 1 or 2 applies by virtue of periods of pensionable service for two or more different schemes—
(a) identify the last period of pensionable service by virtue of which that paragraph applies and the scheme to which that service relates, and
(b) disregard, for the purposes of that sub-paragraph, periods of pensionable service relating to other schemes.

Final salary link not to apply again to a pension in payment

5 (1) Scheme regulations may provide that where a pension in payment under a scheme to which section 18(1) or 31(2) applies has been calculated by reference to this Schedule, the pension cannot be recalculated by reference to this Schedule where there is a subsequent period of pensionable public service (within the meaning of paragraph 3).

(2) Provision made under sub-paragraph (1) may in particular be made by amending the scheme under which the pension is in payment.

NOTES

Commencement: to be appointed.

SCHEDULES 8, 9

(Sch 8 contains consequential and minor amendments which, in so far as relevant to this work, have been incorporated at the appropriate place; Sch 9 amends the Superannuation Act 1972, s 1 at **[1.6]** *and inserts s 1A thereof at* **[1.7]**.)

SCHEDULE 10
PUBLIC BODIES WHOSE PENSION SCHEMES MUST BE RESTRICTED

Section 31(1)

[1.1909]

1 Arts and Humanities Research Council.

2 Biotechnology and Biological Sciences Research Council.

3 Civil Nuclear Police Authority.

4 Commissioners of Irish Lights.

5 Economic and Social Research Council.

6 Engineering and Physical Sciences Research Council.

7 Natural Environment Research Council.

8 Commissioners of Northern Lighthouses.

9 Science and Technology Facilities Council.

10 Secret Intelligence Service.

11 Security Service.

12 Technology Strategy Board.

13 Trinity House Lighthouse Service.

14 United Kingdom Atomic Energy Authority.

NOTES

Commencement: to be appointed.

SCHEDULE 11

(Sch 11 amends legislation outside the scope of this work.)

GROWTH AND INFRASTRUCTURE ACT 2013

(2013 c 27)

An Act to make provision in connection with facilitating or controlling the following, namely, the provision or use of infrastructure, the carrying-out of development, and the compulsory acquisition of land; to make provision about when rating lists are to be compiled; to make provision about the rights of employees of companies who agree to be employee shareholders; and for connected purposes.

[25 April 2013]

NOTES

Most of this Act covers matters outside the scope of this work and the subject matter of provisions not printed is not annotated. The Act comes into force in accordance with s 35 *post* and Orders made thereunder.

Economic measures

31 (*Inserts the Employment Rights Act 1996, ss 47G, 104G, 205A at* **[1.813]**, **[1.914]**, **[1.1011]** *and amends ss 48, 108, 236 thereof at* **[1.814]**, **[1.918]**, **[1.1043]**.)

General provisions

[1.1910]

32 Orders

(1) Any power of the Secretary of State to make an order under this Act—

(a) is exercisable by statutory instrument, and

(b) includes—

(i) power to make different provision for different purposes, and

(ii) power to make incidental, supplementary, consequential, transitional or transitory provision or savings.

(2) The Secretary of State may not make an order to which subsection (3) applies unless a draft of the statutory instrument containing the order (whether alone or with other provisions) has been laid before, and approved by a resolution of, each House of Parliament.

(3) This subsection applies to—

(a) an order under section 7(5);

(b) an order under section 33 which amends or repeals any provision of an Act of Parliament, an Act of the Scottish Parliament or an Act or Measure of the National Assembly for Wales.

(4) A statutory instrument that—

(a) contains an order made by the Secretary of State under this Act, and

(b) is not subject to any requirement that a draft of the instrument be laid before, and approved by a resolution of, each House of Parliament,

is subject to annulment in pursuance of a resolution of either House of Parliament.

(5) Subsection (4) does not apply to an order under section 7(6).

(6) Subsections (1)(b) and (4) do not apply to an order under section 35.

NOTES

Commencement: 25 April 2013.

[1.1911]

33 Consequential amendments

(1) The Secretary of State may by order make such provision as the Secretary of State considers appropriate in consequence of this Act.

(2) The power to make an order under this section may, in particular, be exercised by amending, repealing, revoking or otherwise modifying any provision made by or under an enactment.

(3) In this section "enactment" means an enactment whenever passed or made, and includes an Act of the Scottish Parliament or an Act or Measure of the National Assembly for Wales.

NOTES

Commencement: 25 April 2013.

[1.1912]

34 Financial provisions

There is to be paid out of money provided by Parliament any increase attributable to this Act in the sums payable under any other Act out of money so provided.

NOTES

Commencement: to be appointed.

[1.1913]

35 Commencement

(1) Subject as follows, this Act comes into force on such day as the Secretary of State may by order appoint; and different days may be appointed for different purposes.

(2) Section 1(1) so far as it inserts the new section 62B, sections 4, 7, 9, 16, 19, 26, 32 and 33, this section and section 36, and Schedules 2 and 4, come into force on the day on which this Act is passed.

(3), (4) . . .

(5) The Scottish Ministers may by order make such transitional, transitory or saving provision as the Scottish Ministers consider appropriate in connection with the coming into force of section 21(4) to (6).

(6) The Secretary of State may by order make such transitional, transitory or saving provision as the Secretary of State considers appropriate in connection with the coming into force of any other provision of this Act.

(7) Power to make an order under subsection (5) or (6) includes power to make different provision for different purposes.

NOTES

Commencement: 25 April 2013.

Sub-ss (3), (4): outside the scope of this work.

Orders: the Growth and Infrastructure (Commencement No 1 and Transitional and Saving Provisions) Order 2013, SI 2013/1124 (which brings into force provisions outside the scope of this work).

[1.1914]

36 Short title and extent

(1) This Act may be cited as the Growth and Infrastructure Act 2013.

(2) Subject as follows, this Act extends to England and Wales only.

(3) Sections 9(4) and 32 to 35, and this section, extend also to Scotland and Northern Ireland.

(4) Any amendment or repeal made by this Act has the same extent as the provision to which it relates, subject to subsection (5).

(5), (6) . . .

NOTES

Commencement: 25 April 2013.

Sub-ss (5), (6): outside the scope of this work.

PART 2
STATUTORY INSTRUMENTS

TRADE UNIONS AND EMPLOYERS' ASSOCIATIONS (AMALGAMATIONS, ETC) REGULATIONS 1975

(SI 1975/536)

NOTES

Made: 26 March 1975.

Authority: originally made under the Trade Union (Amalgamations, etc) Act 1964, s 7 (repealed); now have effect under the Trade Union and Labour Relations (Consolidation) Act 1992, s 108.

Commencement: 12 May 1975.

See *Harvey* M8.

ARRANGEMENT OF REGULATIONS

SCHEDULES

[2.1]

1 Citation, commencement and revocation

(1) These Regulations may be cited as the Trade Unions and Employers' Associations (Amalgamations, etc) Regulations 1975 and shall come into operation on 12th May 1975.

(2) . . .

NOTES

Para (2): revokes the Employers' and Workers' Organisations (Amalgamations, etc) Regulations 1971, SI 1971/1542.

[2.2]

2 Interpretation

(1) The Interpretation Act 1889 shall apply to these Regulations as it applies to an Act of Parliament.

(2) For the purposes of these Regulations, unless the context otherwise requires, the following expressions shall have the meanings hereby assigned to them respectively, that is to say—

"the 1964 Act" means the Trade Union (Amalgamations, etc) Act 1964;

"the 1974 Act" means the Trade Union and Labour Relations Act 1974;

["the Certification Officer" means the officer appointed under section 7(1) of the Employment Protection Act 1975 or any assistant certification officer appointed under section 7(4) of the said Act to whom, in accordance with section 7(5) of the said Act, functions have been delegated in relation to any matter authorised or required to be dealt with under these Regulations];

"duly authenticated" means bearing the signature of [the Certification Officer] and the date of the signature;

"organisation" means any trade union as defined in section 28(1) of the 1974 Act, or any employers' association as defined in section 28(2) of the 1974 Act which is not a corporate body;

"Northern Ireland union" has the meaning assigned to it by section 10(5) of the 1964 Act.

NOTES

Para (2): definition "the Certification Officer" substituted by the Trade Unions and Employers' Associations (Amalgamations, etc) (Amendment) Regulations 1978, SI 1978/1344. As to the appointment of the Certification Officer, see now the Trade Union and Labour Relations (Consolidation) Act 1992, s 254.

Interpretation Act 1889: see now the Interpretation Act 1978.

Trade Union (Amalgamations, etc) Act 1964; Trade Union and Labour Relations Act 1974: repealed and replaced by the Trade Union and Labour Relations (Consolidation) Act 1992.

[2.3]
3 Approval of proposed instruments and notices

(1) An application pursuant to section 1(4) of the 1964 Act for approval of a proposed instrument of amalgamation or transfer shall be submitted to [the Certification Officer]—

(a) in the case of a proposed instrument of amalgamation, by one of the amalgamating organisations; and

(b) in the case of a proposed instrument of transfer, by the transferor organisation, and

the application shall be accompanied by two copies of the proposed instrument both of which shall be signed as required by paragraph 6 of Schedule 1 or, as the case may be, paragraph 4 of Schedule 2 to these Regulations [by the fee prescribed by Regulation 11(1)], and by copies of the current rules of the organisations which are parties to the instrument.

(2) An application pursuant to section 1(4) of the 1964 Act for approval of a proposed notice to be supplied to members of an organisation in accordance with section 1(2)(d) of that Act shall be accompanied by two copies of the proposed notice.

(3) [The Certification Officer] shall signify his approval of such instrument or notice by returning to the applicant organisation one of the copies endorsed with the word "Approved" and duly authenticated.

NOTES

Para (1): words in first pair of square brackets substituted by the Trade Unions and Employers' Associations (Amalgamations, etc) (Amendment) Regulations 1978, SI 1978/1344; words in second pair of square brackets substituted by the Certification Officer (Amendment of Fees) Regulations 1988, SI 1988/310, reg 2.

Para (3): words in square brackets substituted by SI 1978/1344.

[2.4]
4 Contents of instrument of amalgamation or transfer

(1) Subject to Regulation 5 an instrument of amalgamation shall contain the particulars and information specified in Schedule 1 to these Regulations.

(2) Subject to Regulation 5 an instrument of transfer shall contain the particulars and information specified in Schedule 2 to these Regulations.

[2.5]
5

Regulation 4 shall not apply to any instrument of amalgamation or instrument of transfer which, before the coming into operation of these Regulations, has been approved by the Chief [Certification Officer] of Trade Unions and Employers' Associations or by any assistant registrar appointed by him for the purpose of section 8 of the 1964 Act.

NOTES

Words in square brackets substituted by the Trade Unions and Employers' Associations (Amalgamations, etc) (Amendment) Regulations 1978, SI 1978/1344.

[2.6]
6 Application for registration of instruments

(1) An application pursuant to section 1(5) of the 1964 Act for registration of an instrument of amalgamation shall be signed by three members of the committee of management or other governing body and the secretary of each of the amalgamating organisations and shall be submitted to [the Certification Officer] in the form to be provided by him for that purpose. The application shall be accompanied by two copies of the instrument and two copies of the proposed rules of the amalgamated organisation and by a statutory declaration from each of the amalgamating organisations in the form to be provided by [the Certification Officer] for that purpose. Each copy of the proposed rules shall be signed by the secretary of each of the amalgamating organisations.

(2) An application pursuant to section 1(5) of the 1964 Act for registration of an instrument of transfer shall be signed by three members of the committee of management or other governing body and the secretary of each of the organisations concerned and shall be submitted to [the Certification Officer] by the transferee organisation in the form to be provided by him for that purpose. The application shall be accompanied by two copies of the instrument and by statutory declarations made by the secretary of the transferor organisation and the secretary of the transferee organisation in the forms to be provided by [the Certification Officer] for that purpose. The application shall also be accompanied by two copies of any amendments to the rules of the transferee organisation made since the date of the application for approval of the proposed instrument of transfer under Regulation 3(1).

(3) In any case where he considers it desirable with a view to ensuring that adequate publicity is given to the date by which complaints must be made to him, under section 4 of the 1964 Act, as to the validity of a resolution approving an instrument of amalgamation or transfer, [the Certification

Officer] may, not later than seven days after the date on which he receives the application for registration of the instrument, require notice to be given or published in such manner, in such form, and on or before such date, as he may direct of the fact that the application for registration has been or is to be made to him.

NOTES

Words in square brackets substituted by the Trade Unions and Employers' Associations (Amalgamations, etc) (Amendment) Regulations 1978, SI 1978/1344.

[2.7]

7 Registration of instruments

(1) Before registering an instrument of amalgamation, [the Certification Officer] shall satisfy himself that the proposed rules of the amalgamated organisation are in no way inconsistent with the terms of the said instrument.

(2) Upon registering the instrument [the Certification Officer] shall send to the address specified for that purpose on the form of application for registration one copy of the instrument endorsed with the word "Registered" and duly authenticated.

NOTES

Words in square brackets substituted by the Trade Unions and Employers' Associations (Amalgamations, etc) (Amendment) Regulations 1978, SI 1978/1344.

[2.8]

8

(1) Before registering an instrument of transfer [the Certification Officer] shall satisfy himself that the rules of the transferee organisation are in no way inconsistent with the terms of the said instrument.

(2) Upon registering the instrument [the Certification Officer] shall send to the transferee organisation one copy of the instrument endorsed with the word "Registered" and duly authenticated.

NOTES

Words in square brackets substituted by the Trade Unions and Employers' Associations (Amalgamations, etc) (Amendment) Regulations 1978, SI 1978/1344.

[2.9]

9 Approval of change of name

(1) An application by an organisation pursuant to section 6(2) of the 1964 Act for the approval of a change of name shall be signed by three members of the committee of management or other governing body and the secretary of the organisation and shall be submitted to [the Certification Officer] in duplicate in the form to be provided by him for that purpose.

(2) The application shall be accompanied by a statutory declaration as to the manner in which the change of name was effected by the secretary of the organisation in the form to be provided by [the Certification Officer] for the purpose.

(3) Upon approving the change of name [the Certification Officer] shall return to the organisation one copy of the application endorsed with the word "Approved" and duly authenticated.

NOTES

Words in square brackets substituted by the Trade Unions and Employers' Associations (Amalgamations, etc) (Amendment) Regulations 1978, SI 1978/1344.

[2.10]

10 Amalgamations of transfers involving Northern Ireland Unions

Where a Northern Ireland union is a party to an amalgamation or transfer of engagements, these Regulations shall have effect subject to the following modifications, that is to say:—

(a) Regulations 3 and 6(3) shall not apply to a Northern Ireland union;

(b) Regulation 4(2) shall not apply to an instrument of transferor if the transfer organisation is a Northern Ireland union;

(c) Regulation 6 shall not require any statutory declaration from a Northern Ireland union;

(d) the application to the Certification Officer under Regulation 6(2) for the registration of an instrument of transfer shall be submitted by the transferor organisation of the transferee organisation is a Northern Ireland union.

[2.11]

[11 Fees

(1) The fee referred to in Regulation 3(1) (fee to accompany an application for approval of a proposed instrument of amalgamation or transfer) shall be [£1850].

Part 2 Statutory Instruments

(2) The following fees shall be payable in advance—

For approval of a change of name	[£96]
For every inspection on the same day of documents kept by the Certification Officer under the 1964 Act relating to one and the same organisation	[£19].]

NOTES

Substituted by the Certification Officer (Amendment of Fees) Regulations 1988, SI 1988/310, reg 2.

Sums in square brackets substituted by the Certification Officer (Amendment of Fees) Regulations 2005, SI 2005/713, regs 2, 3.

[2.12]
[12

A fee of [£41] shall be payable for the entry of an amalgamated organisation on the list of trade unions or employers' associations maintained by the Certification Officer under section 8 of the 1974 Act where each of the amalgamating organisations is already entered on the list.]

NOTES

Substituted by the Trade Unions and Employers' Associations (Amalgamations, etc) (Amendment) Regulations 1978, SI 1978/1344.

Sum in square brackets substituted by the Certification Officer (Amendment of Fees) Regulations 2005, SI 2005/713, reg 4.

SCHEDULES

SCHEDULE 1
CONTENTS OF INSTRUMENT OF AMALGAMATION

Regulation 4(1)

[2.13]

1. The instrument shall state that it is an instrument of amalgamation between the organisations named therein as the amalgamating organisations, and that upon the coming into operation of the instrument the members of the amalgamating organisations will become members of the amalgamated organisation and be subject to that organisation's rules.

2. The instrument shall either set out the proposed rules of the amalgamated organisation or state who are the persons authorised to draw up those rules.

3. If the instrument does not set out the proposed rules it shall contain a summary of what those rules will provide with regard to the following matters:—

(i) the name and principal purposes of the amalgamated organisation;
(ii) the conditions of admission to membership;
(iii) the structure of the amalgamated organisation;
(iv) the method of appointing and removing its governing body and principal officials and of altering its rules;
(v) the contributions and benefits applicable to members of the amalgamating organisations.

4. The instrument shall specify property held for the benefit of any of the amalgamating organisations or for the benefit of a branch of any of those organisations which is not to be vested in the appropriate trustees as defined in section 5(3) of the 1964 Act, and shall state the proposed disposition of any such property.

5. Without prejudice to section 1(5) of the 1964 Act, the instrument shall state the date on which it is to take effect.

6. The instrument shall be signed by three members of the committee of management or other governing body and the secretary of each of the amalgamating organisations.

SCHEDULE 2
CONTENTS OF INSTRUMENT OF TRANSFER

Regulation 4(2)

[2.14]

1. The instrument shall state that it is an instrument of transfer of the engagements of the organisation named therein as the transferor organisation to the organisation named therein as the transferee organisation, and that upon the coming into operation of the instrument the members of the transferor organisation will become members of the transferee organisation and be subject to that organisation's rules.

2. The instrument shall:—

(i) state what contributions and benefits will be applicable to members of the transferor organisation under the transferee organisation's rules;
(ii) if members of the transferor organisation are to be allocated to a branch or section or to branches or sections of the transferee organisation, give particulars of such allocation or the method by which it is to be decided;
(iii) state whether before registration of the instrument the transferee organisation's rules are to be altered in their application to members of the transferor organisation and, if so, the effect of any alterations;
(iv) without prejudice to section 1(5) of the 1964 Act, state the date on which the instrument is to take effect.

3. The instrument shall specify any property held for the benefit of the transferor organisation or for the benefit of a branch of the transferor organisation which is not to be vested in the appropriate trustees as defined in section 5(3) of the 1964 Act, and shall state the proposed disposition of any such property.

4. The instrument shall be signed by three members of the committee of management or other governing body and the secretary of each of the organisations.

REHABILITATION OF OFFENDERS ACT 1974 (EXCEPTIONS) ORDER 1975

(SI 1975/1023)

NOTES

Made: 24 June 1975.
Authority: Rehabilitation of Offenders Act 1974, ss 4(4), 7(4).
Commencement: 1 July 1975.
Note: this Order was revoked in relation to Scotland by the Rehabilitation of Offenders Act 1974 (Exclusions and Exceptions) (Scotland) Order 2003, SSI 2003/231, art 6(a), as from 29 March 2003. This Order remains in force for England and Wales only. Amendments made to this Order before 29 March 2003 which applied to Scotland only have now been omitted from the Order as reproduced here. The current Order relating to Scotland is the Rehabilitation of Offenders Act 1974 (Exclusions and Exceptions) (Scotland) Order 2013, SSI 2013/50 at **[2.1679]**.
See *Harvey* DI(9), (13).

ARRANGEMENT OF ARTICLES

SCHEDULES

[2.15]
1
This Order may be cited as the Rehabilitation of Offenders Act 1974 (Exceptions) Order 1975 and shall come into operation on 1st July 1975.

NOTES

Revoked in relation to Scotland as noted at the beginning of this Order.

[2.16]
2
[(1) In this Order, except where the context otherwise requires—
["the 2000 Act" means the Financial Services and Markets Act 2000;]
["the 2006 Act" means the Safeguarding Vulnerable Groups Act 2006;]

"the Act" means the Rehabilitation of Offenders Act 1974;
["administration of justice offence" means—
(a) the offence of perverting the course of justice,
(b) any offence under section 51 of the Criminal Justice and Public Order Act 1994 (intimidation etc of witnesses, jurors and others),
(c) an offence under section 1, 2, 6 or 7 of the Perjury Act 1911 (perjury),
or any offence committed under the law of any part of the United Kingdom (other than England or Wales) or of any other country where the conduct which constitutes the offence would, if it all took place in England or Wales, constitute one or more of the offences specified by paragraph (a) to (c);]
["adoption agency" has the meaning given to it by section 1 of the Adoption Act 1976;]
["associate", in relation to a person ("A"), means someone who is a controller, director or manager of A or, where A is a partnership, any partner of A;]
["authorised payment institution" has the meaning given by regulation 2(1) of the Payment Services Regulations 2009;]
. . .
["child minding" means—
[(a) child minding within the meaning of section 79A of the Children Act 1989; and
(b) early years childminding within the meaning of section 96(4) of the Childcare Act 2006, or later years childminding within the meaning of section 96(8) of that Act;]]
["collective investment scheme" has the meaning given by section 235 of the 2000 Act;]
[. . .]
["contracting authority" means a contracting authority within the meaning of Article 1(9) of Directive 2004/18/EC;]
["contracting entity" means a contracting entity within the meaning of Article 2(2) of Directive 2004/17/EC;]
["controller" has the meaning given by section 422 of the 2000 Act;]
[. . .]
["Council of Lloyd's" means the council constituted by section 3 of Lloyd's Act 1982;]
["day care" means—
[(a) day care for which registration is required by section 79D(5) of the Children Act 1989; and
(b) early years provision within the meaning of section 96(2) of the Childcare Act 2006 (other than early years childminding), or later years provision within the meaning of section 96(6) of that Act (other than later years childminding), for which registration is required, or permitted, under Part 3 of that Act;]]
["day care premises" means any premises on which day care is provided, but does not include any part of the premises where children are not looked after;]
["Directive 2004/17/EC" means Directive 2004/17/EC of the European Parliament and of the Council of 31 March 2004;]
["Directive 2004/18/EC" means Directive 2004/18/EC of the European Parliament and of the Council of 31 March 2004;]
["director" has the meaning given by section 417 of the 2000 Act;]
["electronic money institution" has the meaning given by regulation 2(1) of the Electronic Money Regulations 2011;]
["the FCA" means the Financial Conduct Authority;]
["key worker" means—
(a) any individual who is likely, in the course of exercising the duties of that individual's office or employment, to play a significant role in the decision making process of the FCA, the PRA or the Bank of England in relation to the exercise of its public functions (within the meaning of section 349(5) of the 2000 Act); or
(b) any individual who is likely, in the course of exercising the duties of that individual's office or employment, to support directly an individual mentioned in paragraph (a);]
["manager" has the meaning given by section 423 of the 2000 Act;]
["open-ended investment company" has the meaning given by section 236 of the 2000 Act]
["Part 4A permission" has the meaning given by section 55A(5) of the 2000 Act;]
["payment services" has the meaning given by regulation 2(1) of the Payment Services Regulations 2009;]
["the PRA" means the Prudential Regulation Authority;]
["recognised clearing house" means a recognised clearing house as defined in section 285 of the 2000 Act;]
["relevant collective investment scheme" means a collective investment scheme which is recognised under section 264 (schemes constituted in other EEA States), 270 (schemes authorised in designated countries or territories) or 272 (individually recognised overseas schemes) of the 2000 Act;]
. . .

["small payment institution" has the meaning given by regulation 2(1) of the Payment Services Regulations 2009;]

["taxi driver licence" means a licence granted under—

[(i) section 46 of the Town Police Clauses Act 1847;]

(ii) section 8 of the Metropolitan Public Carriage Act 1869;

(iii) section 9 of the Plymouth City Council Act 1975;

(iv) section 51 of the Local Government (Miscellaneous Provisions) Act 1976; or

(v) section 13 of the Private Hire Vehicles (London) Act 1998;]

["trustee", in relation to a unit trust scheme, has the meaning given by section 237 of the 2000 Act;]

[. . .]

["UK recognised investment exchange" means an investment exchange in relation to which a recognition order under section 290 of the 2000 Act, otherwise than by virtue of section 292(2) of that Act (overseas investment exchanges), is in force;]

["work" includes—

(a) work of any kind, whether paid or unpaid, and whether under a contract of service or apprenticeship, under a contract for services, or otherwise than under a contract; and

(b) an office established by or by virtue of an enactment;]

["work with children" means work of the kind described in paragraph 14 [or 14A] of [Part 2 of] Schedule 1 to this Order;]

. . .

(2) Where, by virtue of this Order, the operation of any of the provisions of the Act is excluded in relation to spent convictions the exclusion shall be taken to extend to spent convictions for offences of every description . . .].

(3) Part IV of Schedule 1 to this Order shall have effect for the interpretation of expressions used in that Schedule.

(4) In this Order a reference to any enactment shall be construed as a reference to that enactment as amended, extended or applied by or under any other enactment.

[(4A) In this Order any reference to a conviction shall where relevant include a reference to a caution, and any reference to spent convictions shall be construed accordingly.]

(5) The Interpretation Act 1889 shall apply to the interpretation of this Order as it applies to the interpretation of an Act of Parliament.

NOTES

Revoked in relation to Scotland as noted at the beginning of this Order.

Para (1) is amended as follows:

Substituted, together with para (2), by the Rehabilitation of Offenders Act 1974 (Exceptions) (Amendment No 2) Order 1986, SI 1986/2268, art 2(1), Schedule, para 1.

Definitions "the 2000 Act", "administration of justice offence", "associate", "collective investment scheme", "the competent authority for listing", "controller", "Council of Lloyd's", "director", "key worker", "manager", "open-ended investment company", "relevant collective investment scheme", "trustee", and "UK recognised investment exchange" inserted by the Rehabilitation of Offenders Act 1974 (Exceptions) (Amendment) (No 2) Order 2001, SI 2001/3816, arts 2, 3(1).

Definition "the 2006 Act" inserted by the Rehabilitation of Offenders Act 1974 (Exceptions) (Amendment) (England and Wales) Order 2009, SI 2009/1818, arts 2, 3, as from 7 July 2009.

Definitions "adoption agency", "child minding", "day care", "day care premises", "work", and "work with children" inserted by the Rehabilitation of Offenders Act 1974 (Exceptions) (Amendment) Order 2001, SI 2001/1192, arts 2, 3. Paras (a), (b) of definitions "child minding" and "day care" subsequently substituted, and words in second pair of square brackets in definition "work with children" inserted, by the Rehabilitation of Offenders Act 1974 (Exceptions) (Amendment) (England and Wales) Order 2008, SI 2008/3259, arts 2, 3(1), as from 18 December 2008. Definition "child minding" further amended in relation to Wales by the Children and Families (Wales) Measure 2010 (Commencement No 2, Savings and Transitional Provisions) Order 2010, SI 2010/2582, art 5, Sch 4, para 1(1), (2)(a), as from 1 April 2011, as follows: in para (a) for "section 79A of the Children Act 1989" substitute "section 19 of the Children and Families (Wales) Measure 2010". Definition "day care" also amended in relation to Wales by SI 2010/2582, art 5, Sch 4, para 1(1), (2)(b), as from 1 April 2011, as follows: in para (a) for "section 79D(5) of the Children Act 1989" substitute "section 23(1) of the Children and Families (Wales) Measure 2010". Words in first pair of square brackets in definition "work with children" inserted by the Rehabilitation of Offenders Act 1974 (Exceptions) (Amendment) (England and Wales) Order 2012, SI 2012/1957, arts 2, 7, as from 25 July 2012.

Definitions "authorised payment institution", payment services" and "small payment institution" inserted by the Rehabilitation of Offenders Act 1974 (Exceptions) (Amendment) (England and Wales) Order 2011, SI 2011/1800, art 2(1), (2), as from 21 July 2011.

Definition "the Building Societies Commission" (omitted) revoked by SI 2001/3816, arts 2, 3(3).

Definition "the competent authority for listing" (omitted) revoked, definitions "the FCA" and "the PRA" inserted, definition "key worker" substituted and definition "Part 4A permission" substituted for definition "Part IV permission" (as originally inserted by SI 2001/3816, arts 2, 3(1)), by the Financial Services Act 2012 (Consequential Amendments and Transitional Provisions) Order 2013, SI 2013/472, art 3, Sch 2, para 1(1), (2), as from 1 April 2013.

Definitions "contracting authority", "contracting entity", "Directive 2004/17/EC", and "Directive 2004/18/EC" inserted by the Rehabilitation of Offenders Act 1974 (Exceptions) (Amendment) (England and Wales) Order 2006, SI 2006/2143, arts 2, 3(b).

Definition "Council" (omitted) inserted by the Rehabilitation of Offenders Act 1974 (Exceptions) (Amendment) (England and Wales) Order 2003, SI 2003/965, arts 2, 3(a) and revoked by the Rehabilitation of Offenders Act 1974 (Exceptions) (Amendment) (England and Wales) Order 2012, SI 2012/1957, arts 2, 4, as from 1 August 2012.

Definition "electronic money institution" inserted by the Electronic Money Regulations 2011, SI 2011/99, reg 79, Sch 4, Pt 2, para 7(a), as from 30 April 2011.

Definition "recognised clearing house" inserted by the Financial Services and Markets Act 2000 (Over the Counter Derivatives, Central Counterparties and Trade Repositories) Regulations 2013, SI 2013/504, reg 28(1), (2)(b), as from 1 April 2013.

Definition "relevant offence" (omitted) revoked by the Rehabilitation of Offenders Act 1974 (Exceptions) (Amendment) (England and Wales) Order 2007, SI 2007/2149, arts 2, 3(1).

Definition "taxi driver licence" inserted by SI 2003/965, arts 2, 3(a); para (i) substituted by SI 2006/2143, arts 2, 3(a).

Definition "UK recognised clearing house" (omitted) originally inserted by SI 2001/3816, arts 2, 3(1); revoked by SI 2013/504, reg 28(1), (2)(a), as from 1 April 2013.

Final words omitted revoked by SI 2001/3816, arts 2, 3(3).

Para (2): substituted as noted above; words omitted revoked by SI 2007/2149, arts 2, 3(2).

Para (4A): inserted by SI 2008/3259, arts 2, 3(2), as from 18 December 2008.

Adoption Act 1976, s 1: repealed by the Adoption and Children Act 2002, s 139(3), Sch 5. As to the meaning of "adoption agency", see now s 2(1) of the 2002 Act.

Children Act 1989, ss 79A, 79D: repealed, in relation to Wales, by the Children and Families (Wales) Measure 2010, s 73, Sch 2; as to the meaning of "child minding" in the 2010 Measure see s 19 thereof, and as to the registration of day care providers, see s 23.

Interpretation Act 1889: repealed and replaced by the Interpretation Act 1978.

[2.17]
3

[Neither section 4(2) of, nor paragraph 3(3) of Schedule 2 to,] the Act shall apply in relation to—

(a) any question asked by or on behalf of any person, in the course of the duties of his office or employment, in order to assess the suitability—
- (i) of the person to whom the question relates for admission to any of the professions specified in Part I of Schedule 1 to this Order; or
- [(ii) of the person to whom the question relates for any office or employment specified in Part II of the said Schedule 1 or for any other work specified in paragraph [12A, 13, 14, 14A, 20, 21, 35, 36, . . . [38, 40 or 43]] of Part II of the said Schedule 1; or]
- (iii) of the person to whom the question relates or of any other person to pursue any occupation specified in Part III of the said Schedule 1 or to pursue it subject to a particular condition or restriction; or
- (iv) of the person to whom the question relates or of any other person to hold a licence, certificate or permit of a kind specified in Schedule 2 to this Order or to hold it subject to a particular condition or restriction,

where the person questioned is informed at the time the question is asked that, by virtue of this Order, spent convictions are to be disclosed;

[(aa) any question asked by or on behalf of any person, in the course of the duties of his work, in order to assess the suitability of a person to work with children, where—
- (i) the question relates to the person whose suitability is being assessed;
- (ii) the person whose suitability is being assessed lives on the premises where his work with children would normally take place and the question relates to a person living in the same household as him;
- (iii) the person whose suitability is being assessed lives on the premises where his work with children would normally take place and the question relates to a person who regularly works on those premises at a time when the work with children usually takes place; or
- (iv) the work for which the person's suitability is being assessed is child minding which would normally take place on premises other than premises where that person lives and the question relates to a person who lives on those other premises or to a person who regularly works on them at a time when the child minding takes place,

and where the person to whom the question relates is informed at the time the question is asked that, by virtue of this Order, spent convictions are to be disclosed;]

[(ab) . . .]

(b) any question asked by or on behalf of any person, in the course of his duties as a person employed in the service of the Crown, the United Kingdom Atomic Energy Authority, [the FCA or the PRA] in order to assess, for the purpose of safeguarding national security, the suitability of the person to whom the question relates or of any other person for any office or employment where the person questioned is informed at the time the question is asked that, by virtue of this Order, spent convictions are to be disclosed for the purpose of safeguarding national security;

[(bb) any question asked by or on behalf of
- (i) the Civil Aviation Authority,
- (ii) any other person authorised to provide air traffic services under section 4 or section 5 of the Transport Act 2000 (in any case where such person is a company, an "authorised company"),

(iii) any company which is a subsidiary (within the meaning given by section 736(1) of the Companies Act 1985) of an authorised company, or

(iv) any company of which an authorised company is a subsidiary,

where, in the case of sub-paragraphs (iii) and (iv) of this paragraph the question is put in relation to the provision of air traffic services, and in all cases, where the question is put in order to assess, for the purpose of safeguarding national security, the suitability of the person to whom the question relates or of any other person for any office or employment where the person questioned is informed at the time the question is asked that, by virtue of this Order, spent convictions are to be disclosed for the purpose of safeguarding national security;]

[(e) any question asked by or on behalf of any person in the course of his duties as a person employed by an adoption agency for the purpose of assessing the suitability of any person to adopt children in general or a child in particular where—

(i) the question relates to the person whose suitability is being assessed; or

(ii) the question relates to a person over the age of 18 living in the same household as the person whose suitability is being assessed,

and where the person to whom the question relates is informed at the time the question is asked that, by virtue of this Order, spent convictions are to be disclosed;

(f) any question asked by or on behalf of any person, in the course of the duties of his work, in order to assess the suitability of a person to provide day care where—

(i) the question relates to the person whose suitability is being assessed; or

(ii) the question relates to a person who lives on the premises which are or are proposed to be day care premises,

and where the person to whom the question relates is informed at the time the question is asked that, by virtue of this Order, spent convictions are to be disclosed];

[(g) any question asked by, or on behalf of, the person listed in the second column of any entry in the table below to the extent that it relates to a conviction . . . (or any circumstances ancillary to . . . a conviction) of any individual, but only if—

(i) the person questioned is informed at the time the question is asked that, by virtue of this Order, spent convictions . . . are to be disclosed; and

(ii) the question is asked in order to assess the suitability of the individual to whom the question relates to have the status specified in the first column of that entry.

[Status		*Questioner*
1	A person with Part 4A permission.	The FCA, the PRA or the Bank of England.
2	(a) A person in relation to whom an approval is given under section 59 of the 2000 Act (approval for particular arrangements). An associate of the person (whether or not an individual) mentioned in sub-paragraph (a).	The FCA, the PRA or the authorised person (within the meaning of section 31(2) of the 2000 Act) or the applicant for Part 4A permission who made the application for the approval of the appropriate regulator (within the meaning of section 59(4) of the 2000 Act) under section 59 of the 2000 Act in relation to the person mentioned in sub-paragraph (a) of the first column.
3	(a) The manager or trustee of an authorised unit trust scheme (within the meaning of section 237 of the 2000 Act). An associate of the person (whether or not an individual) mentioned in sub-paragraph (a).	The FCA or the unit trust scheme mentioned in the first column.
4	(a) A director of an open-ended investment company. (b) An associate of that person (whether or not an individual) mentioned in sub-paragraph (a).	The FCA, the PRA or the open-ended investment company mentioned in the first column.
5	An associate of the operator or trustee of a relevant collective investment scheme.	The FCA, the PRA or the collective investment scheme mentioned in the first column.
[6	An associate of a UK recognised investment exchange or recognised clearing house.	The FCA, the PRA, or the Bank of England or the investment exchange or clearing house mentioned in the first column.]

Part 2 Statutory Instruments

[Status		Questioner
7	A controller of a person with Part 4A permission.	The FCA, the PRA or the person with Part 4A permission mentioned in the first column.
8	(a) A person who carries on a regulated activity (within the meaning of section 22 of the 2000 Act) but to whom the general prohibition does not apply by virtue of section 327 of the 2000 Act (exemption from the general prohibition for members of a designated professional body).	The FCA or the PRA.
	(b) An associate of the person (whether or not an individual) mentioned in sub-paragraph (a).	In the case of a person mentioned in sub-paragraph (b) of the first column, the person mentioned in sub-paragraph (a) of that column.
9	A key worker of the FCA, the PRA or the Bank of England.	The FCA, the PRA or the Bank of England.
10	An ombudsman (within the meaning of Schedule 17 to the 2000 Act) of the Financial Ombudsman Service.	The scheme operator (within the meaning of section 225 of the 2000 Act) of the Financial Ombudsman Service.
11	An associate of the issuer of securities which have been admitted to the official list maintained by the FCA for listing under section 74 of the 2000 Act.	The FCA.
12	A sponsor (within the meaning of section 88(2) of the 2000 Act).	The FCA.
13	(a) A Primary information provider (within the meaning of section 89P of the 2000 Act).	The FCA or the PRA.
	(b) An associate of the person (whether or not an individual) mentioned in sub-paragraph (a).	In the case of a person mentioned in sub-paragraph (2) of the first column, the person mentioned in sub-paragraph (1) of that column.
14	An associate of a person who has a Part 4A permission and who is admitted to Lloyd's as an underwriting agent (within the meaning of section 2 of Lloyd's Act 1982).	(a) The Council of Lloyd's. (b) The person with Part 4A permission specified in the first column (or a person applying for such permission).
15	An associate of the Council of Lloyd's.	The Council of Lloyd's.
16	[(a) Any member of a UK recognised investment exchange or recognised clearing house.	The UK recognised investment exchange or recognised clearing house specified in the first column.]
	(b) An associate of the person (whether or not an individual) mentioned in sub-paragraph (a).	In the case of a person mentioned in sub-paragraph (b) of the first column, the person mentioned in sub-paragraph (a) of that column.
17	A director or person responsible for the management of the electronic money or payment services business of an electronic money institution.	The FCA.
18	A controller of an electronic money institution.	The FCA.
19	A director or a person responsible for the management of an authorised payment institution or a small payment institution.	The FCA.
20	A person responsible for the management of payment services provided, or to be provided, by an authorised payment institution or a small payment institution.	The FCA.
21	A controller of an authorised payment institution or a small payment institution.	The FCA.]]

[(h) any question asked by or on behalf of the National Lottery Commission for the purpose of determining whether to grant or revoke a licence under Part I of the National Lottery etc Act 1993 where the question relates to an individual—

(i) who manages the business or any part of the business carried on under the licence (or who is likely to do so if the licence is granted), or

(ii) for whose benefit that business is carried on (or is likely to be carried on if the licence is granted),

and where the person to whom the question relates is informed at the time that the question is asked that, by virtue of this Order, spent convictions are to be disclosed];

[(i) any question asked by or on behalf of the [Care Council for Wales] for the purpose of determining whether or not to grant an application for registration under Part IV of the Care Standards Act 2000, where the person questioned is informed at the time the question is asked that, by virtue of this Order, spent convictions are to be disclosed];

[(j) any question asked by or on behalf of a contracting authority or contracting entity in relation to a conviction within the meaning of Article 45(1) of Directive 2004/18/EC which is a spent conviction (or any circumstances ancillary to such a conviction) for the purpose of determining whether or not to treat a person as ineligible:

(i) for the purposes of regulation 23 of the Public Contracts Regulations 2006 or regulation 23 of the Utilities Contracts Regulations 2006; or

(ii) to participate in a design contest for the purposes of regulation 33 of the Public Contracts Regulations 2006 or regulation 34 of the Utilities Contracts Regulations 2006,

where the person questioned is informed at the time the question is asked that, by virtue of this Order, convictions within the meaning of Article 45(1) of Directive 2004/18/EC which are spent convictions are to be disclosed;

(k) any question asked, by or on behalf of the Football Association[, Football League] or Football Association Premier League in order to assess the suitability of the person to whom the question relates or of any other person to be approved as able to undertake, in the course of acting as a steward at a sports ground at which football matches are played or as a supervisor or manager of such a person, licensable conduct within the meaning of the Private Security Industry Act 2001 without a licence issued under that Act, in accordance with . . . section 4 of that Act];

[(l) any question asked by the Secretary of State for the purpose of considering the suitability of an individual to have access to information released under sections 113A and 113B of the Police Act 1997].

[(m) any question asked by or on behalf of the Master Locksmiths Association for the purposes of assessing the suitability of any person who has applied to be granted membership of that Association;

(n) any question asked by or on behalf of the Secretary of State for the purpose of assessing the suitability of any person or body to obtain or retain a licence under regulation 5 of the Misuse of Drugs Regulations 2001 or under Article 3(2) of Regulation 2004/273/EC or under article 6(1) of Regulation 2005/111/EC where—

(i) the question relates to the holder of, or an applicant for, such a licence or any person who as a result of his role in the company or other body concerned is required to be named in the application for such a licence (or would have been so required if that person had had that role at the time the application was made), and

(ii) any person to whom the question relates is informed at the time the question is asked that by virtue of this Order, spent convictions are to be disclosed.]

NOTES

Revoked in relation to Scotland as noted at the beginning of this Order.

Words in first pair of square brackets substituted by the Rehabilitation of Offenders Act 1974 (Exceptions) (Amendment) (England and Wales) Order 2008, SI 2008/3259, arts 2, 4, as from 18 December 2008.

Para (a): sub-para (ii) substituted by the Rehabilitation of Offenders Act 1974 (Exceptions) (Amendment) Order 2001, SI 2001/1192, arts 2, 4(1); words in first (outer) pair square brackets in sub-para (ii) substituted by the Rehabilitation of Offenders Act 1974 (Exceptions) (Amendment) (England and Wales) Order 2009, SI 2009/1818, arts 2, 4(1), as from 7 July 2009; words in second (inner) pair of square brackets in sub-para (ii) substituted by the Protection of Freedoms Act 2012 (Disclosure and Barring Service Transfer of Functions) Order 2012, SI 2012/3006, arts 18, 19, as from 1 December 2012; figure omitted from sub-para (ii) revoked by the Rehabilitation of Offenders Act 1974 (Exceptions) (Amendment) (England and Wales) Order 2012, SI 2012/1957, arts 2, 8, as from 25 July 2012.

Para (aa): inserted by the Rehabilitation of Offenders Act 1974 (Exceptions) (Amendment) Order 1986, SI 1986/1249, art 2, Schedule; substituted by SI 2001/1192, arts 2, 4(2).

Para (ab): inserted by the Rehabilitation of Offenders Act 1974 (Exceptions) (Amendment No 2) Order 1986, SI 1986/2268, art 2(1), Schedule, para 2; revoked by the Rehabilitation of Offenders Act 1974 (Exceptions) (Amendment) (No 2) Order 2001, SI 2001/3816, arts 2, 4(1), (2).

Para (b): words in square brackets substituted by the Financial Services Act 2012 (Consequential Amendments and Transitional Provisions) Order 2013, SI 2013/472, art 3, Sch 2, para 1(1), (3)(a), as from 1 April 2013.

Para (bb): inserted by SI 2002/441, arts 2, 3(3), as from a day to be appointed (ie, the day on which the Police Act 1997, s 133(d) comes into force in England and Wales).

Paras (e), (f): added by SI 2001/1192, arts 2, 4(3). Note that SI 2001/1192 purports to insert these paragraphs after para (d) but it is believed that this is a drafting error as this article does not contain a para (d).

Para (g): added by SI 2001/3816, arts 2, 4(1), (4); words omitted revoked by SI 2007/2149, arts 2, 4(2), (3); table substituted by SI 2013/472, art 3, Sch 2, para 1(1), (3)(b), as from 1 April 2013; paras 6, 16(a) of the table substituted by the Financial Services and Markets Act 2000 (Over the Counter Derivatives, Central Counterparties and Trade Repositories) Regulations 2013, SI 2013/504, reg 28(1), (3), as from 1 April 2013.

Para (h): added by SI 2002/441, arts 2, 3(4).

Para (i): added by SI 2003/965, arts 2, 5; words in square brackets substituted by SI 2012/1957, arts 2, 5, as from 1 August 2012.

Para (j): added, together with para (k), by the Rehabilitation of Offenders Act 1974 (Exceptions) (Amendment) (England and Wales) Order 2006, SI 2006/2143, arts 2, 4.

Para (k): added as noted above; words in square brackets inserted, and words omitted revoked, by the Rehabilitation of Offenders Act 1974 (Exceptions) (Amendment No 2) (England and Wales) Order 2006, SI 2006/3290, art 2.

Para (l): added by SI 2007/2149, arts 2, 4(4).

Paras (m), (n): added by SI 2009/1818, arts 2, 4(2), as from 7 July 2009.

Companies Act 1985, s 736(1): repealed by the Companies Act 2006 (the equivalent provision is in s 1159(1) of the 2006 Act).

[2.18]
[3A

(1) Neither section 4(2) of, nor paragraph 3(3) of Schedule 2 to, the Act applies to a question to which paragraph (2) or (3) applies.

(2) This paragraph applies to any question asked by or on behalf of any person ("A"), in the course of the duties of A's office or employment, in order to assess the suitability of the person to whom the question relates ("B") for any work which is a controlled activity relating to children within the meaning of section 21 of the 2006 Act [as it had effect immediately before the coming into force of section 68 of the Protection of Freedoms Act 2012], where the person questioned is told at the time the question is asked, that by virtue of this Order, spent convictions are to be disclosed but only if that person knows that B—

(a) is a person barred from regulated activity relating to children within the meaning of section 3(2) of the 2006 Act;
(b) is included in the list kept under section 1 of the Protection of Children Act 1999; or
(c) is subject to a direction made under section 142 of the Education Act 2002.

(3) This paragraph applies to any question asked by or on behalf of any person ("A"), in the course of the duties of A's office or employment, in order to assess the suitability of the person to whom the question relates ("B") for any work which is a controlled activity relating to vulnerable adults within the meaning of section 22 of the 2006 Act [as it had effect immediately before the coming into force of section 68 of the Protection of Freedoms Act 2012], where the person questioned is told at the time the question is asked, that by virtue of this Order, spent convictions are to be disclosed but only if that person knows that B—

(a) is a person barred from regulated activity relating to vulnerable adults within the meaning of section 3(3) of the 2006 Act; or
(b) is included in the list kept under section 81 of the Care Standards Act 2000.]

NOTES

Commencement: 31 March 2010.

Inserted by the Rehabilitation of Offenders Act 1974 (Exceptions) (Amendment) (England and Wales) Order 2010, SI 2010/1153, arts 2, 3, as from 31 March 2010.

Paras (2), (3): words in square brackets inserted by the Rehabilitation of Offenders Act 1974 (Exceptions) (Amendment) (England and Wales) Order 2012, SI 2012/1957, arts 2, 9, as from 10 September 2012.

Protection of Children Act 1999, s 1; Care Standards Act 2000, s 81; Education Act 2002, s 142: repealed by the Safeguarding Vulnerable Groups Act 2006, s 63, Sch 9, Pt 1, paras 8(1), (2), 9, Sch 10, as from 12 October 2009, subject to transitional provisions and savings (see SI 2009/2611), but partly as from a day to be appointed in the case of the repeal of s 142 of the 2002 Act.

[2.19]
4

[Neither paragraph (b) of section 4(3) of, nor paragraph 3(5) of Schedule 2 to, the Act shall apply] in relation to—

(a) the dismissal or exclusion of any person from any profession specified in Part I of Schedule 1 to this Order;
[(b) any office, employment or occupation specified in Part II or Part III of the said Schedule 1 or any other work specified in paragraph [12A, 13, 14, 14A, 20, 21, 35, 36, . . . 40, 43 or 44] of Part II of the said Schedule 1;]
(c) any action taken for the purpose of safeguarding national security;
[(d) [any decision by the FCA, the PRA or the Bank of England]—
  (i) to refuse an application for [Part 4A permission] under the 2000 Act,
  (ii) to vary or to cancel such permission (or to refuse to vary or cancel such permission) or to impose a requirement under [section 55L, 55M or 55O] of that Act or,

(iii) to make, or to refuse to vary or revoke, an order under section 56 of that Act (prohibition orders),
(iv) to refuse an application for . . . approval under section 59 of that Act or to withdraw such approval,
(v) to refuse to make, or to revoke, an order declaring a unit trust scheme to be an authorised unit trust scheme under section 243 of the 2000 Act or to refuse to give its approval under section 251 of the 2000 Act to a proposal to replace the manager or trustee of such a scheme,
(vi) to give a direction under section 257 of the 2000 Act (authorised unit trust schemes), or to vary (or to refuse to vary or revoke) such a direction,
(vii) to refuse to make, or to revoke, an authorisation order under regulation 14 of the Open-Ended Investment Companies Regulations 2001 or to refuse to give its approval under regulation 21 of those Regulations to a proposal to replace a director or to appoint an additional director of an open-ended investment company,
(viii) to give a direction to an open-ended investment company under regulation 25 of those Regulations or to vary (or refuse to vary or revoke) such a direction,
(ix) to refuse to give its approval to a collective investment scheme being recognised under section 270 of the 2000 Act or to direct that such a scheme cease to be recognised by virtue of that section or to refuse to make, or to revoke, an order declaring a collective investment scheme to be a recognised scheme under section 272 of that Act,
(x) to refuse to make, or to revoke, a recognition order under section 290 of the 2000 Act, otherwise than by virtue of section 292(2) of that Act [to refuse to vary a recognition order under section 290ZA(1) of the 2000 Act, to vary a recognition order under section 290ZA(2) of the 2000 Act,], or to give a direction to a UK recognised investment exchange or [recognised clearing house] under section 296 [or 296A] of the 2000 Act,
(xi) to make, or to refuse to vary or to revoke, an order under section 329 (orders in respect of members of a designated professional body in relation to the general prohibition), . . .
(xii) to dismiss, fail to promote or exclude a person from being a key worker of [the FCA or the PRA],
[(xiii) to refuse an application for registration as an authorised electronic money institution or a small electronic money institution under the Electronic Money Regulations 2011, . . .
(xiv) to vary or cancel such registration (or to refuse to vary or cancel such registration) or to impose a requirement under regulation 7 of those Regulations,]
[(xv) to refuse an application for registration as an authorised payment institution or a small payment institution under the Payment Services Regulations 2009, . . .]
(xvi) to vary or cancel such registration (or to refuse to vary or cancel such registration) or to impose a requirement under regulation 7 of those Regulations,]
[(xvii) in a case requiring any decision referred to in paragraphs (i) to (xvi), where the FCA, the PRA or the Bank of England has the function of deciding whether to give consent or conditional consent in relation to the decision which is proposed in that case, to give or refuse to give consent or to give conditional consent, or
(xviii) in a case requiring any decision referred to in paragraphs (i) to (xvi), where the FCA, the PRA or the Bank of England has the power under the 2000 Act to direct another regulator as to the decision to be taken in that case, to decide whether to give a direction and, if a direction is to be given, what direction to give,]

by reason of, or partly by reason of, a spent conviction of an individual . . . , or of any circumstances ancillary to such a conviction or of a failure (whether or not by that individual) to disclose such a conviction or any such circumstances;

(e) any decision by the scheme operator (within the meaning of section 225 of the 2000 Act) of the Financial Ombudsman Service to dismiss, or not to appoint, an individual as, an ombudsman (within the meaning of Schedule 17 to the 2000 Act) of the Financial Ombudsman Service by reason of, or partly by reason of, his spent conviction . . . , or of any circumstances ancillary to such a conviction or of a failure (whether or not by that individual) to disclose such a conviction or any such circumstances;

(f) [any decision of the FCA]—
(i) to refuse an application for listing under Part VI of the 2000 Act or to discontinue or suspend the listing of any securities under section 77 of that Act,
(ii) to refuse to grant a person's application for approval as a sponsor under section 88 of the 2000 Act or to cancel such approval, . . .
(iii) to dismiss, fail to promote or exclude a person from being a key worker of [the FCA in relation to the exercise of its functions under Part 6 of the 2000 Act, or],
[(iv) to refuse to grant a person's application under information provider rules (within the meaning of section 89P(9) of the 2000 Act) for approval as a Primary information

provider, to impose limitations or other restrictions on the giving of information to which such an approval relates or to cancel such an approval,]

by reason of, or partly by reason of, a spent conviction of an individual . . . , or of any circumstances ancillary to such a conviction or of a failure (whether or not by that individual) to disclose such a conviction or any such circumstances;

(g) any decision of anyone who is specified in any of sub-paragraphs 2 to 4 or 5 to 7 of the second column of the table in article 3(g), other than [the FCA or the PRA], to dismiss an individual who has, or to fail to promote or exclude an individual who is seeking to obtain, the status specified in the corresponding entry in the first column of that table (but not, where applicable, the status of being an associate of another person), by reason of, or partly by reason of, a spent conviction of that individual or of his associate . . . , or of any circumstances ancillary to such a conviction or of a failure (whether or not by that individual) to disclose such a conviction or any such circumstances;

(h) any decision of anyone who is specified in sub-paragraph 8(a), 14(a) or 16(a) of the second column of the table in article 3(g) to dismiss an individual who has, or to fail to promote or exclude an individual who is seeking to obtain, the status specified in the corresponding entry in sub-paragraph (b) of the first column of that table (associate), by reason of, or partly by reason of, a spent conviction of that individual . . . , or of any circumstances ancillary to such a conviction or of a failure (whether or not by that individual) to disclose such a conviction or any such circumstances;

(i) any decision of the Council of Lloyd's—

(i) to refuse to admit any person as, or to exclude, an underwriting agent (within the meaning of section 2 of Lloyd's Act 1982), where that person has, or who has applied for, [Part 4A permission], or

(ii) to dismiss, or to exclude a person from being, an associate of the Council of Lloyd's,

by reason of, or partly by reason of, a spent conviction of an individual . . . , or of any circumstances ancillary to such a conviction or of a failure (whether or not by that individual) to disclose such a conviction or any such circumstances;

(j) any decision of a UK recognised investment exchange or [recognised clearing house] to refuse to admit any person as, or to exclude, a member by reason of, or partly by reason of, a spent conviction of an individual . . . , or of any circumstances ancillary to such a conviction or of a failure (whether or not by that individual) to disclose such a conviction or any such circumstances;]

[(k) any decision by the [Care Council for Wales] to refuse to grant an application for registration under Part IV of the Care Standards Act 2000 or to suspend, remove or refuse to restore a person's registration under that Part;

(l) any decision to refuse to grant a taxi driver licence, to grant such a licence subject to conditions or to suspend, revoke or refuse to renew such a licence;

(m) any decision by the Security Industry Authority to refuse to grant a licence under section 8 of the Private Security Industry Act 2001, to grant such a licence subject to conditions, to modify such a licence (including any of the conditions of that licence) or to revoke such a licence];

[(n) any decision by the Football Association[, Football League] or Football Association Premier League to refuse to approve a person as able to undertake, in the course of acting as a steward at a sports ground at which football matches are played or as a supervisor or manager of such a person, licensable conduct within the meaning of the Private Security Industry Act 2001 without a licence issued under that Act, in accordance with . . . section 4 of that Act].

NOTES

Revoked in relation to Scotland as noted at the beginning of this Order.

Words in first pair of square brackets substituted by the Rehabilitation of Offenders Act 1974 (Exceptions) (Amendment) (England and Wales) Order 2008, SI 2008/3259, arts 2, 5, as from 18 December 2008.

Para (b): substituted by the Rehabilitation of Offenders Act 1974 (Exceptions) (Amendment) Order 2001, SI 2001/1192, arts 2, 5; words in square brackets in para (b) substituted by the Rehabilitation of Offenders Act 1974 (Exceptions) (Amendment) (England and Wales) Order 2009, SI 2009/1818, arts 2, 5, as from 7 July 2009; figure omitted therefrom revoked by the Rehabilitation of Offenders Act 1974 (Exceptions) (Amendment) (England and Wales) Order 2012, SI 2012/1957, arts 2, 8, as from 25 July 2012.

Para (d): inserted by the Rehabilitation of Offenders Act 1974 (Exceptions) (Amendment No 2) Order 1986, SI 1986/2268, art 2(1), Schedule, para 3, and substituted (by new paras (d)–(j)) by the Rehabilitation of Offenders Act 1974 (Exceptions) (Amendment) (No 2) Order 2001, SI 2001/3816, arts 2, 5; words in first pair of square brackets substituted, words in square brackets in sub-paras (i), (ii), (xii) substituted, words omitted from sub-paras (iv), (xv) revoked, words in third pair of square brackets in sub-para (x) inserted, and sub-paras (xvii), (xviii) added, by the Financial Services Act 2012 (Consequential Amendments and Transitional Provisions) Order 2013, SI 2013/472, art 3, Sch 2, para 1(1), (4)(a), as from 1 April 2013; words in first pair of square brackets in sub-para (x) inserted, and words in second pair of square brackets substituted, by the Financial Services and Markets Act 2000 (Over the Counter Derivatives, Central Counterparties and Trade Repositories) Regulations 2013, SI 2013/504, reg 28(1), (4)(a), as from 1 April 2013; the word omitted from sub-para (xi) was revoked, and sub-paras (xiii), (xiv) were added, by the Electronic Money Regulations 2011, SI 2011/99, reg 79, Sch 4, Pt 2, para 7(c), as from 30 April 2011; the word omitted from sub-para (xiii) was revoked, and sub-paras (xv), (xvi) were added, by the Rehabilitation of Offenders Act 1974 (Exceptions) (Amendment) (England and Wales) Order 2011, SI 2011/1800, art 2(1), (4), as from 21 July 2011; other words omitted revoked by SI 2007/2149, arts 2, 5(1).

Para (e): substituted as noted above; words omitted revoked by SI 2007/2149, arts 2, 5(1).

Para (f): substituted as noted above; words in first pair of square brackets and words in square brackets in sub-para (iii) substituted, word omitted from sub-para (ii) revoked, and sub-para (iv) inserted, by SI 2013/472, art 3, Sch 2, para 1(1), (4)(b), as from 1 April 2013; final words omitted revoked by SI 2007/2149, arts 2, 5(1).

Para (g): substituted as noted above; words in square brackets substituted by SI 2013/472, art 3, Sch 2, para 1(1), (4)(c), as from 1 April 2013; words omitted revoked by SI 2007/2149, arts 2, 5(1).

Para (h): substituted as noted above; words omitted revoked by SI 2007/2149, arts 2, 5(1).

Para (i): substituted as noted above; words in square brackets substituted by SI 2013/472, art 3, Sch 2, para 1(1), (4)(d), as from 1 April 2013; words omitted revoked by SI 2007/2149, arts 2, 5(1).

Para (j): substituted as noted above; words omitted revoked by SI 2007/2149, arts 2, 5(1); words in square brackets substituted by SI 2013/504, reg 28(1), (4)(b), as from 1 April 2013.

Paras (k)–(m): added by SI 2003/965, arts 2, 7; words in square brackets in para (k) substituted by SI 2012/1957, arts 2, 5, as from 1 August 2012.

Para (n): added by the Rehabilitation of Offenders Act 1974 (Exceptions) (Amendment) (England and Wales) Order 2006, SI 2006/2143, arts 2, 5; words in square brackets inserted, and words omitted revoked, by the Rehabilitation of Offenders Act 1974 (Exceptions) (Amendment No 2) (England and Wales) Order 2006, SI 2006/3290, art 2.

[2.20]
[4A

(1) Section 4(2) of the Act shall not apply to a question asked by or on behalf of any person, in the course of the duties of the person's office or employment, in order to assess whether the person to whom the question relates is disqualified by reason of section 66(3)(c) of the 2011 Act from being elected as, or being, a police and crime commissioner.

(2) Section 4(3)(a) of the Act shall not apply in relation to any obligation to disclose any matter if the obligation is imposed in order to assess whether a person is disqualified by reason of section 66(3)(c) of the 2011 Act from being elected as, or being, a police and crime commissioner.

(3) Section 4(3)(b) of the Act shall not apply in relation to the disqualification of a person from being elected as, or being, a police and crime commissioner under section 66(3)(c) of the 2011 Act.

(4) In this article—

"the 2011 Act" means the Police Reform and Social Responsibility Act 2011; and

"police and crime commissioner" means a police and crime commissioner established under section 1 of the 2011 Act.]

NOTES

Commencement: 25 July 2012.

Inserted by the Rehabilitation of Offenders Act 1974 (Exceptions) (Amendment) (England and Wales) Order 2012, SI 2012/1957, arts 2, 3, as from 25 July 2012.

[2.21]
[5

(1) [Neither section 4(1) of, nor paragraph 3(1) of Schedule 2 to, the Act shall]—

(a) apply in relation to any proceedings specified in Schedule 3 to this Order;

(b) apply in relation to any proceedings specified in paragraph (2) below to the extent that there falls to be determined therein any issue relating to a person's spent conviction . . . or to circumstances ancillary thereto;

(c) prevent, in any proceedings specified in paragraph (2) below, the admission or requirement of any evidence relating to a person's spent conviction . . . or to circumstances ancillary thereto.

[(2) The proceedings referred to in paragraph (1) above are any proceedings with respect to a decision or proposed decision of the kind specified in article 4(d) to [(n)].]]

NOTES

Revoked in relation to Scotland as noted at the beginning of this Order.

Substituted by the Rehabilitation of Offenders Act 1974 (Exceptions) (Amendment No 2) Order 1986, SI 1986/2268, art 2(1), Schedule, para 4.

Para (1): words in square brackets substituted by the Rehabilitation of Offenders Act 1974 (Exceptions) (Amendment) (England and Wales) Order 2008, SI 2008/3259, arts 2, 6(1), as from 18 December 2008; words omitted revoked by the Rehabilitation of Offenders Act 1974 (Exceptions) (Amendment) (England and Wales) Order 2007, SI 2007/2149, arts 2, 6.

Para (2): substituted by the Rehabilitation of Offenders Act 1974 (Exceptions) (Amendment) (No 2) Order 2001, SI 2001/3816, arts 2, 6; reference to "(n)" in square brackets substituted by SI 2008/3259, arts 2, 6(2), as from 18 December 2008.

[2.22]
[6

(1) Neither section 4(2) of, nor paragraph 3(3) of Schedule 2 to, the Act applies to a question to which paragraph (2) applies.

(2) This paragraph applies to a question asked by or on behalf of any person in the course of that person's office or employment in the Channel Islands or the Isle of Man in order to assess the suitability of the person to whom the question relates for any purposes referred to in article 3 or 3A, where—

(a) the person asking the question states that a corresponding question and purpose are also provided for in—
   (i) the Rehabilitation of Offenders (Exceptions) (Jersey) Regulations 2002 ("the Jersey Regulations");
   (ii) the Rehabilitation of Offenders (Bailiwick of Guernsey) Law 2002 (Commencement, Exclusions and Exceptions) Ordinance 2006 ("the Guernsey Ordinance"); or
   (iii) the Rehabilitation of Offenders Act 2001 (Exceptions) Order 2001 ("the Isle of Man Exceptions Order"), and

(b) the person questioned is one to whom article 3 or 3A would apply and is informed at the time the question is asked that spent convictions are to be disclosed.

(3) Neither subsection (1) or (3) of section 4 of, nor paragraph 3(1) or (5) of Schedule 2 to, the Act apply to a question to which paragraph (4) applies.

(4) This paragraph applies to a question asked by or on behalf of any person in the course of that person's office or employment in the Channel Islands or the Isle of Man in respect of a case or class of case and conviction specified in article 4 or for a purpose mentioned in article 5, where the person asking the question states that the Jersey Regulations or the Guernsey Ordinance or the Isle of Man Exceptions Order provides for a corresponding case or class of case and conviction or a corresponding purpose, and the person questioned is a person to whom article 4 or 5 would apply.]

NOTES

Commencement: 31 March 2010.

Added by the Rehabilitation of Offenders Act 1974 (Exceptions) (Amendment) (England and Wales) Order 2009, SI 2009/1818, arts 2, 6, and substituted by the Rehabilitation of Offenders Act 1974 (Exceptions) (Amendment) (England and Wales) Order 2010, SI 2010/1153, arts 2, 4, as from 31 March 2010.

SCHEDULES

SCHEDULE 1
[EXCEPTED PROFESSIONS, OFFICES, EMPLOYMENTS, WORK AND OCCUPATIONS]

Article 2(3), 3, 4

PART I
PROFESSIONS

[2.23]
[**1.** Health care professional.]

2. Barrister (in England and Wales), advocate (in Scotland), solicitor.

3. Chartered accountant, certified accountant.

[**4.** . . .]

5. Veterinary surgeon.

6. . . .

7. . . .

[**8.** . . .

8A. . . .]

9. Registered teacher (in Scotland).

10. . . .

[**11.** . . .]

[**12.** . . .]

[**13.** . . .

14. Actuary.

15. Registered foreign lawyer.

16. Legal executive.

17. Receiver appointed by the Court of Protection.]

[**18.** Home inspector.]

NOTES

Revoked in relation to Scotland as noted at the beginning of this Order.

Schedule heading: substituted by the Rehabilitation of Offenders Act 1974 (Exceptions) (Amendment) Order 2001, SI 2001/1192, arts 2, 6(1).

Para 1: substituted by the Rehabilitation of Offenders Act 1974 (Exceptions) (Amendment) (England and Wales) Order 2012, SI 2012/1957, arts 2, 6(1), (2)(a), as from 25 July 2012.

Para 4: substituted by the Health Care and Associated Professions (Miscellaneous Amendments and Practitioner Psychologists) Order 2009, SI 2009/1182, art 4(1), Sch 4, Pt 6, para 37(a), as from 14 May 2009 and revoked by SI 2012/1957, arts 2, 6(1), (2)(b), as from 25 July 2012.

Paras 6, 7: revoked by SI 2012/1957, arts 2, 6(1), (2)(b), as from 25 July 2012.

Paras 8, 8A: substituted, for the original para 8, by the Pharmacists and Pharmacy Technicians Order 2007, SI 2007/289, art 67, Sch 1, Pt 2, para 12(a), and revoked by SI 2012/1957, arts 2, 6(1), (2)(b), as from 25 July 2012.

Para 10: revoked by SI 2012/1957, arts 2, 6(1), (2)(b), as from 25 July 2012.

Para 11: added by the Osteopaths Act 1993, s 39(2) and revoked by SI 2012/1957, arts 2, 6(1), (2)(b), as from 25 July 2012.

Para 12: added by the Chiropractors Act 1994, s 40(2) and revoked by SI 2012/1957, arts 2, 6(1), (2)(b), as from 25 July 2012.

Paras 13: added, together with paras 14–17, by the Rehabilitation of Offenders Act 1974 (Exceptions) (Amendment) Order 2002, SI 2002/441, arts 2, 5(1); revoked by SI 2009/1182, art 4(1), Sch 4, Pt 1, para 1(a), as from 1 July 2009.

Paras 14-17: added as noted above.

Para 18: added by the Rehabilitation of Offenders Act 1974 (Exceptions) (Amendment) (England and Wales) Order 2006, SI 2006/2143, arts 2, 6.

Solicitor: the reference to a solicitor should now be read as including a reference to a registered European lawyer, see the European Communities (Lawyer's Practice) Regulations 2000, SI 2000/1119, reg 37(3), Sch 4, para 19.

PART II
[OFFICES, EMPLOYMENTS AND WORK]

[2.24]

1. Judicial appointments.

[**2.** The Director of Public Prosecutions and any office or employment in the Crown Prosecution Service.]

3. . . .

[**4.** [Designated officers for magistrates' courts, for justices of the peace or for local justice areas], justices' clerks [and assistants to justices' clerks].]

5. Clerks (including depute and assistant clerks) and officers of the High Court of Justiciary, the Court of Session and the district court, sheriff clerks (including sheriff clerks depute) and their clerks and assistants.

6. Constables, persons appointed as police cadets to undergo training with a view to becoming constables and persons employed for the purposes of, or to assist the constables of, a police force established under any enactment; naval, military and air force police.

7. Any employment which is concerned with the administration of, or is otherwise normally carried out wholly or partly within the precincts of, a prison, remand centre, [removal centre, short-term holding facility,] [young offender institution] or young offenders institution, and members of boards of visitors appointed under section 6 of the Prison Act 1952 or of visiting committees appointed under section 7 of the Prisons (Scotland) Act 1952.

8. Traffic wardens appointed under section 81 of the Road Traffic Regulation Act 1967 or section 9 of the Police (Scotland) Act 1967.

9. Probation officers appointed under Schedule 3 to the Powers of Criminal Courts Act 1973.

10, 11. . . .

[**12.** Any office or employment which is concerned with:
(a) the provision of care services to vulnerable adults; or
(b) the representation of, or advocacy services for, vulnerable adults by a service that has been approved by the Secretary of State or created under any enactment;
and which is of such a kind as to enable a person, in the course of his normal duties, to have access to vulnerable adults in receipt of such services.]

[**12A.** Any work which is regulated activity relating to vulnerable adults within the meaning of Part 2 of Schedule 4 to the 2006 Act [as it had effect immediately before the coming into force of section 66 of the Protection of Freedoms Act 2012].]

[**13.** Any employment or other work which is concerned with the provision of health services and which is of such a kind as to enable the holder of that employment or the person engaged in that work to have access to persons in receipt of such services in the course of his normal duties.]

[**14.** Any work which is—
(a) work in a regulated position; or
(b) work in a further education institution [or 16 to 19 Academy] where the normal duties of that work involve regular contact with persons aged under 18.]

[**14A.** Any work which is regulated activity relating to children within the meaning of Part 1 of Schedule 4 to the 2006 Act [as it had effect immediately before the coming into force of section 64 of the Protection of Freedoms Act 2012].]

[**15.** Any employment in the Royal Society for the Prevention of Cruelty to Animals where the person employed or working, as part of his duties, may carry out the [humane] killing of animals.

16. Any office or employment in the Serious Fraud Office.

17. Any office or employment in the [Serious Organised Crime Agency].

[**18.** The Commissioners for Her Majesty's Revenue and Customs and any office or employment in their service.

18A. The Director and any office or employment in the Revenue and Customs Prosecutions Office.]

19. Any employment which is concerned with the monitoring, for the purposes of child protection, of communications by means of the internet.]

[**20.** Any employment or other work which is normally carried out in premises approved under section 9 of the Criminal Justice and Court Services Act 2000.

21. Any employment or other work which is normally carried out in a hospital used only for the provision of high security psychiatric services.]

[**22.** An individual designated under section 2 of the Traffic Management Act 2004.

23. Judges' clerks, secretaries and legal secretaries within the meaning of section 98 of the Supreme Court Act 1981.

24. Court officers and court contractors, who in the course of their work, have face to face contact with judges of the Supreme Court, or access to such judges' lodgings.

25. Persons who in the course of their work have regular access to personal information relating to an identified or identifiable member of the judiciary.

26. Court officers and court contractors, who, in the course of their work, attend either the Royal Courts of Justice or the Central Criminal Court.

27. Court security officers, and tribunal security officers.

28. Court contractors, who, in the course of their work, have unsupervised access to court-houses, offices and other accommodation used in relation to the courts.

29. Contractors, sub-contractors, and any person acting under the authority of such a contractor or sub-contractor, who, in the course of their work, have unsupervised access to tribunal buildings, offices and other accommodation used in relation to tribunals.

30. The following persons—
(a) Court officers who execute county court warrants;
(b) High Court enforcement officers;
(c) sheriffs and under-sheriffs;
(d) tipstaffs;
(e) any other persons who execute High Court writs or warrants who act under the authority of a person listed at (a) to (d);
(f) persons who execute writs of sequestration;
(g) civilian enforcement officers as defined in section 125A of the Magistrates' Courts Act 1980;
(h) persons who are authorised to execute warrants under section 125B(1) of the Magistrates' Courts Act 1980, and any other person, (other than a constable), who is authorised to execute a warrant under section 125(2) of the 1980 Act;
(i) persons who execute clamping orders, as defined in paragraph 38(2) of Schedule 5 to the Courts Act 2003.

31. The Official Solicitor and his deputy.

32. Persons appointed to the office of Public Trustee or deputy Public Trustee, and officers of the Public Trustee.

33. Court officers and court contractors who exercise functions in connection with the administration and management of funds in court including the deposit, payment, delivery and transfer in, into and out of any court of funds in court and regulating the evidence of such deposit, payment, delivery or transfer and court officers and court contractors, who receive payments in pursuance of a conviction or order of a magistrates' court.]

[**34.** People working in [the Department for Education], the Office for Standards in Education, Children's Services and Skills . . . with access to sensitive or personal information about children . . .

35. Any office, employment or other work which is concerned with the establishment or operation of a database under section 12 of the Children Act 2004, and which is of such a kind as to enable the holder of that office or employment, or the person engaged in that work, to have access to information included in the database.

36. Any office, employment or other work which is of such a kind that the person is or may be permitted or required to be given access to a database under section 12 of the Children Act 2004.

37. . . .

38. The chairman, other members, and members of staff (including any person seconded to serve as a member of staff) of the [Disclosure and Barring Service][, and any other work in the Disclosure and Barring Service].

39. Staff working within the Public Guardianship Office, (to be known as the Office of the Public Guardian from October 2007), with access to data relating to children and vulnerable adults.

40. The Commissioner for Older People in Wales, and his deputy, and any person appointed by the Commissioner to assist him in the discharge of his functions or authorised to discharge his functions on his behalf.

41. The Commissioners for the Gambling Commission and any office or employment in their service.

42. Individuals seeking authorisation from the Secretary of State for the Home Department to become authorised search officers.

43. Any employment or other work where the normal duties

(a) involve caring for, training, supervising, or being solely in charge of, persons aged under 18 serving in the naval, military or air forces of the Crown; or

(b) include supervising or managing a person employed or working in a capacity referred to in paragraph (a).]

[**44.** . . .]

NOTES

Revoked in relation to Scotland as noted at the beginning of this Order.

Part heading: substituted by the Rehabilitation of Offenders Act 1974 (Exceptions) (Amendment) Order 2001, SI 2001/1192, arts 2, 6(2).

Para 2: substituted by the Rehabilitation of Offenders Act 1974 (Exceptions) (Amendment) Order 2002, SI 2002/441, arts 2, 5(2)(a), (b).

Para 3: revoked by the Rehabilitation of Offenders Act 1974 (Exceptions) (Amendment) (England and Wales) Order 2006, SI 2006/2143, arts 2, 7(a).

Para 4: substituted by SI 2001/1192, arts 2, 6(3); words in first pair of square brackets substituted by the Courts Act 2003 (Consequential Provisions) (No 2) Order 2005, SI 2005/617, art 2, Schedule, para 55; words in second pair of square brackets substituted by SI 2006/2143, arts 2, 7(b)(i).

Para 7: words in first pair of square brackets inserted by SI 2006/2143, arts 2, 7(b)(ii); words in second pair of square brackets substituted by virtue of the Criminal Justice Act 1988, s 123(6), Sch 8, paras 1, 3.

Paras 10, 11: revoked by the Rehabilitation of Offenders Act 1974 (Exceptions) (Amendment) Order 1986, SI 1986/1249, art 2, Schedule.

Para 12: substituted by SI 2006/2143, arts 2, 7(c).

Paras 12A, 14A: inserted by the Rehabilitation of Offenders Act 1974 (Exceptions) (Amendment) (England and Wales) Order 2009, SI 2009/1818, arts 2, 7(1)(a), (b), as from 12 October 2009; words in square brackets inserted by the Rehabilitation of Offenders Act 1974 (Exceptions) (Amendment) (England and Wales) Order 2012, SI 2012/1957, arts 2, 10(1)–(3), as from 10 September 2012.

Para 13: substituted by SI 2001/1192, arts 2, 6(4).

Para 14: substituted, for the original paras 14, 15, by SI 1986/1249, art 2, Schedule; further substituted by SI 2001/1192, arts 2, 6(5); words in square brackets in sub-para (b) inserted by the Alternative Provision Academies and 16 to 19 Academies

(Consequential Amendments to Subordinate Legislation) (England) Order 2012, SI 2012/979, art 2, Schedule, para 2, as from 1 May 2012, in relation to England only.

Para 15: added (together with paras 16, 17, 18, 19) by SI 2002/441, arts 2, 5(2)(c); word in square brackets inserted by SI 2006/2143, arts 2, 7(b)(iii).

Paras 16, 19: added as noted above.

Para 17: added as noted above; words in square brackets substituted by the Serious Organised Crime and Police Act 2005 (Consequential and Supplementary Amendments to Secondary Legislation) Order 2006, SI 2006/594, art 2, Schedule, para 2.

Paras 18, 18A: para 18 originally added as noted above; subsequently substituted by new paras 18, 18A by SI 2006/2143, arts 2, 7(d).

Paras 20, 21: added by the Rehabilitation of Offenders Act 1974 (Exceptions) (Amendment) (England and Wales) Order 2003, SI 2003/965, arts 2, 8.

Paras 22–33: added by SI 2006/2143, arts 2, 7(e).

Paras 34–43: added by the Rehabilitation of Offenders Act 1974 (Exceptions) (Amendment) (England and Wales) Order 2007, SI 2007/2149, arts 2, 7; words in square brackets in para 34 substituted by the Secretary of State for Education Order 2010, SI 2010/1836, art 6, Schedule, Pt 2, para 11(a), as from 18 August 2010; words omitted from para 34 and the whole of para 37 revoked by SI 2012/1957, arts 2, 10(1), (4), (5), as from 25 July 2012; in para 38, words in first pair of square brackets substituted and words in second pair of square brackets inserted by the Protection of Freedoms Act 2012 (Disclosure and Barring Service Transfer of Functions) Order 2012, SI 2012/3006, arts 18, 20(1), (2), as from 1 December 2012.

Para 44: added by SI 2009/1818, arts 2, 7(1)(c), as from 7 July 2009 and revoked by SI 2012/3006, arts 18, 20(1), (3), as from 1 December 2012.

Road Traffic Regulation Act 1967, s 81: repealed by the Road Traffic Regulation Act 1984, and replaced by s 95 thereof.

Prison Act 1952, s 6: Boards of visitors appointed under the Prison Act 1952, s 6 have been renamed as independent monitoring boards by the Offender Management Act 2007, s 26(1) (and s 6 of the 1952 Act has been amended accordingly by s 26(2) of the 2007 Act).

Powers of Criminal Courts Act 1973, Sch 3: repealed by the Probation Service Act 1993, and replaced by s 4 thereof; s 4 was in turn repealed by the Criminal Justice and Court Services Act 2000, s 75, Sch 8. As to the provision of probation services, see now the Offender Management Act 2007, Pt 1.

PART III
REGULATED OCCUPATIONS

[2.25]

1. Firearms dealer.

2. Any occupation in respect of which an application to the Gaming Board for Great Britain for a licence, certificate or registration is required by or under any enactment.

3. . . .

4. Dealer in securities.

5. Manager or trustee under a unit trust scheme.

6. Any occupation which is concerned with—

(a) the management of a place in respect of which the approval of the Secretary of State is required by section 1 of the Abortion Act 1967; or

(b) in England and Wales, carrying on a nursing home in respect of which registration is required by section 187 of the Public Health Act 1936 or section 14 of the Mental Health Act 1959; or

(c) in Scotland, carrying on a nursing home in respect of which registration is required under section 1 of the Nursing Homes Registration (Scotland) Act 1938 or a private hospital in respect of which registration is required under section 15 of the Mental Health (Scotland) Act 1960.

7. Any occupation which is concerned with carrying on an establishment in respect of which registration is required by section 37 of the National Assistance Act 1948 or section 61 of the Social Work (Scotland) Act 1968.

8. Any occupation in respect of which the holder, as occupier of premises on which explosives are kept, is required [pursuant to regulations 4 and 7 of the Control of Explosives Regulations 1991 to obtain from the chief officer of police a valid explosives certificate certifying him to be a fit person to acquire or acquire and keep explosives].

[**9.** . . .]

[**10.** Approved legal services body manager.]

[**11.** A regulated immigration adviser.]

[**12.** A head of finance and administration of a licensed body.

[**13.** A head of legal practice of a licensed body.]

NOTES

Revoked in relation to Scotland as noted at the beginning of this Order.

Para 3: revoked by the Rehabilitation of Offenders Act 1974 (Exceptions) (Amendment) (No 2) Order 2001, SI 2001/3816, arts 2, 7(a).

Paras 4, 5: revoked by the Rehabilitation of Offenders Act 1974 (Exceptions) (Amendment No 2) Order 1986, SI 1986/2268, art 2(2)(a), as from the date on which the Financial Services Act 1986, s 189, Sch 14 is brought into force for the purposes of this revocation. Note, however, that the 1986 Act was repealed by the Financial Services and Markets Act 2000 (Consequential Amendments and Repeals) Order 2001, SI 2001/3649, art 3(1)(c), as from 1 December 2001, without ever having been brought into force for these purposes.

Para 8: words in square brackets substituted by the Manufacture and Storage of Explosives Regulations 2005, SI 2005/1082, reg 28(1), Sch 5, Pt 2, para 27(1), (2).

Para 9: added by the Rehabilitation of Offenders Act 1974 (Exceptions) (Amendment) Order 2002, SI 2002/441, arts 2, 5(3)(a); revoked by the Rehabilitation of Offenders Act 1974 (Exceptions) (Amendment) (England and Wales) Order 2003, SI 2003/965, arts 2, 9.

Para 10: added by the Rehabilitation of Offenders Act 1974 (Exceptions) (Amendment) (England and Wales) Order 2008, SI 2008/3259, arts 2, 7(1), as from 18 December 2008.

Para 11: added by the Rehabilitation of Offenders Act 1974 (Exceptions) (Amendment) (England and Wales) Order 2009, SI 2009/1818, arts 2, 7(2), as from 7 July 2009.

Paras 12, 13: added by the Rehabilitation of Offenders Act 1974 (Exceptions) (Amendment) (England and Wales) Order 2011, SI 2011/1800, art 2(1), (5), as from 21 July 2011.

Gaming Board for Great Britain: functions, etc, transferred to the Gambling Commission by the Gambling Act 2005, s 21, Sch 5.

Public Health Act 1936, s 187; Mental Health Act 1959, s 14 (both repealed): in England the registration of health and adult social care is now under the Health and Social Care Act 2008, Pt 1, Chapter 2, and the registration of all children's services is under the Care Standards Act 2000, Pt II. In Wales the registration of health and all social care is under Pt II of the 2000 Act.

National Assistance Act 1948, s 37 (repealed): that section made provision for the registration of disabled persons' and old persons' homes; see now the note above.

PART IV
INTERPRETATION

[2.26]

In this Schedule—

["actuary" means a member of [the Institute and Faculty of Actuaries];

["approved legal services body manager" means a person who must be approved by the Law Society under section 9A(2)(e) of the Administration of Justice Act 1985;]

["assistants to justices' clerks" has the meaning given by section 27(5) of the Courts Act 2003;]

["authorised search officer" means a person authorised to carry out searches in accordance with sections 40 and 41 of the Immigration, Asylum and Nationality Act 2006;]

"care services" means

(i) accommodation and nursing or personal care in a care home (where "care home" has the same meaning as in the Care Standards Act 2000);

(ii) personal care or nursing or support for a person to live independently in his own home;

(iii) social care services; or

(iv) any services provided in an establishment catering for a person with learning difficulties;]

"certified accountant" means a member of the Association of Certified Accountants;

"chartered accountant" means a member of the Institute of Chartered Accountants in England and Wales or of the Institute of Chartered Accountants of Scotland;

[. . .]

["child" means a person under the age of eighteen (and "children" is to be construed accordingly);]

["court contractor" means a person who has entered into a contract with the Lord Chancellor under section 2(4) of the Courts Act 2003, such a person's sub-contractor, and persons acting under the authority of such a contractor or sub-contractor for the purpose of discharging the Lord Chancellor's general duty in relation to the courts;]

["court officer" means a person appointed by the Lord Chancellor under section 2(1) of the Courts Act 2003;]

["court security officers" has the meaning given by section 51 of the Courts Act 2003;]

"dealer in securities" means a person dealing in securities within the meaning of section 26(1) of the Prevention of Fraud (Investments) Act 1958;

"firearms dealer" has the meaning assigned to that expression by section 57(4) of the Firearms Act 1968;

["funds in court" has the meaning given by section 47 of the Administration of Justice Act 1982;]

"further education" has the meaning assigned to that expression by section 41 of the Education Act 1944 or, in Scotland, section 4 of the Education (Scotland) Act 1962;

["further education institution" has the meaning given to it by paragraph 3 of the Education (Restriction of Employment) Regulations 2000;]

["head of finance and administration of a licensed body" means an individual who is designated as head of finance and administration and whose designation is approved in accordance with licensing rules made under section 83 of, and paragraphs 13 and 14 of Schedule 11 to, the Legal Services Act 2007;

"head of legal practice of a licensed body" means an individual who is designated as head of legal practice and whose designation is approved in accordance with licensing rules made under section 83 of, and paragraphs 11 and 12 of Schedule 11 to, the Legal Services Act 2007;]

["health care professional" means a person who is a member of a profession regulated by a body mentioned in subsection (3) of section 25 of the National Health Service Reform and Health Care Professions Act 2002 (and for the purposes of this definition subsection (3A) of that section is to be ignored);]

"health services" means services provided under the National Health Service Acts 1946 to 1973 or the National Health Service (Scotland) Acts 1947 to 1973 and similar services provided otherwise than under the National Health Service;

["high security psychiatric services" has the meaning given by section 4 of the National Health Service Act 1977;]

["home inspector" means a person who is a member of a certification scheme approved by the Secretary of State in accordance with section 164(3) of the Housing Act 2004;]

. . .

["judges of the Supreme Court" means the Lord Chief Justice, the Master of the Rolls, the President of the Queen's Bench Division, the President of the Family Division, the Chancellor of the High Court, the Lords Justices of Appeal and the puisne judges of the High Court;]

"judicial appointment" means an appointment to any office by virtue of which the holder has power (whether alone or with others) under any enactment or rule of law to determine any question affecting the rights, privileges, obligations or liabilities of any person;

["legal executive" means a fellow of the Institute of Legal Executives;]

["members of the judiciary" means persons appointed to any office by virtue of which the holder has power (whether alone or with others) under any enactment or rule of law to determine any question affecting the rights, privileges, obligations or liabilities of any person;]

["personal information" means any information which is of a personal or confidential nature and is not in the public domain and it includes information in any form but excludes anything disclosed for the purposes of proceedings in a particular cause or matter;]

"proprietor" and "independent school" have the meanings assigned to those expressions by section 114(1) of the Education Act 1944 or, in Scotland, section 145 of the Education (Scotland) Act 1962;

[. . .]

[. . .]

["registered foreign lawyer" has the meaning given by section 89 of the Courts and Legal Services Act 1990;]

[. . .]

[. . .]

[. . .]

"registered teacher" means a teacher registered under the Teaching Council (Scotland) Act 1965 and includes a provisionally registered teacher;

["regulated immigration adviser" means any person who provides immigration advice or immigration services as defined in section 82(1) of the Immigration and Asylum Act 1999 and is—

(i) a registered person under Part 5 of that Act, or

(ii) a person who acts on behalf of and under the supervision of such a registered person, or

(iii) a person who falls within section 84(4)(a), (b) or (c) of that Act.]

["regulated position" means a position which is a regulated position for the purposes of Part II of the Criminal Justice and Court Services Act 2000 [other than a position which would not be a regulated position if in section 36(4) of that Act "employment" included unpaid employment];]

["removal centre" and "short-term holding facility" have the meaning given by section 147 of the Immigration and Asylum Act 1999;]

"school" has the meaning assigned to that expression by section 114(1) of the Education Act 1944 or, in Scotland, section 145 of the Education (Scotland) Act 1962;

. . .

[. . .]

"teacher" includes a warden of a community centre, leader of a youth club or similar institution, youth worker and, in Scotland, youth and community worker;

["tribunal security officers" means persons who, in the course of their work, guard tribunal buildings, offices and other accommodation used in relation to tribunals against unauthorised access or occupation, against outbreaks of disorder or against damage;]

["tribunals" means any person exercising the judicial power of the State, that is not a court listed in section 1(1) of the Courts Act 2003;]

"unit trust scheme" has the meaning assigned to that expression by section 26(1) of the Prevention of Fraud (Investments) Act 1958 and, in relation thereto, "manager" and "trustee" shall be construed in accordance with section 26(3) of that Act

["vulnerable adult" has the meaning given by section 59 of the 2006 Act as it had effect immediately before the coming into force of section 65 of the Protection of Freedoms Act 2012.]

NOTES

Revoked in relation to Scotland as noted at the beginning of this Order.

Definitions "actuary", "care services", "legal executive" and "registered foreign lawyer" inserted by the Rehabilitation of Offenders Act 1974 (Exceptions) (Amendment) Order 2002, SI 2002/441, arts 2, 5(4)(a), (c), (d).

Words in square brackets in definition "actuary" substituted by the Rehabilitation of Offenders Act 1974 (Exceptions) (Amendment) (England and Wales) Order 2011, SI 2011/1800, art 2(1), (6)(a), as from 21 July 2011.

Definition "approved legal services body manager" inserted by the Rehabilitation of Offenders Act 1974 (Exceptions) (Amendment) (England and Wales) Order 2008, SI 2008/3259, arts 2, 7(2), as from 18 December 2008.

Definitions "assistants to justices' clerks", "court contractor", "court officer", "court security officers", "funds in court", "home inspector", "judges of the Supreme Court", "members of the judiciary", "personal information", "removal centre", "short-term holding facility", "tribunal security officers", and "tribunals" inserted by the Rehabilitation of Offenders Act 1974 (Exceptions) (Amendment) (England and Wales) Order 2006, SI 2006/2143, arts 2, 8.

Definitions "authorised search officer" and "child" inserted by the Rehabilitation of Offenders Act 1974 (Exceptions) (Amendment) (England and Wales) Order 2007, SI 2007/2149, arts 2, 8.

Definition "chartered psychologist" (omitted) originally inserted by SI 2002/441, arts 2, 5(4)(b), and revoked by the Health Care and Associated Professions (Miscellaneous Amendments and Practitioner Psychologists) Order 2009, SI 2009/1182, art 4(1), Sch 4, Pt 1, para 1(b), as from 1 July 2009.

Definitions "dealer in securities" and "unit trust scheme" revoked by the Rehabilitation of Offenders Act 1974 (Exceptions) (Amendment No 2) Order 1986, SI 1986/2268, art 2(2)(a), as from the date on which the Financial Services Act 1986, s 189, Sch 14 is brought into force for the purposes of this revocation (note, however, that the 1986 Act was repealed by the Financial Services and Markets Act 2000 (Consequential Amendments and Repeals) Order 2001, SI 2001/3649, art 3(1)(c), as from 1 December 2001, without ever having been brought into force for these purposes).

Definition "further education institution" inserted by the Rehabilitation of Offenders Act 1974 (Exceptions) (Amendment) Order 2001, SI 2001/1192, arts 2, 6(6)(a).

Definitions "head of finance and administration of a licensed body" and "head of legal practice of a licensed body" inserted by SI 2011/1800, art 2(1), (6)(b), as from 21 July 2011.

Definition "health care professional" inserted by the Rehabilitation of Offenders Act 1974 (Exceptions) (Amendment) (England and Wales) Order 2012, SI 2012/1957, arts 2, 6(1), (3)(a), as from 25 July 2012.

Definition "high security psychiatric services" inserted by the Rehabilitation of Offenders Act 1974 (Exceptions) (Amendment) (England and Wales) Order 2003, SI 2003/965, arts 2, 10(a).

Definition "insurance company" (omitted) revoked by the Rehabilitation of Offenders Act 1974 (Exceptions) (Amendment) (No 2) Order 2001, SI 2001/3816, arts 2, 7(b).

Definition "registered chiropractor" (omitted) inserted by the Chiropractors Act 1994, s 40(4) and revoked by SI 2012/1957, arts 2, 6(1), (3)(b), as from 25 July 2012.

Definition "registered dental care professional" (omitted) inserted by SI 2009/1182, art 4(1), Sch 4, Pt 6, para 37(b), as from 14 May 2009 and revoked by SI 2012/1957, arts 2, 6(1), (3)(b), as from 25 July 2012.

Definition "registered osteopath" (omitted) inserted by the Osteopaths Act 1993, s 39(4) and revoked by SI 2012/1957, arts 2, 6(1), (3)(b), as from 25 July 2012.

Definitions "registered pharmacist" and "registered pharmacy technician" (both omitted) originally inserted by the Pharmacists and Pharmacy Technicians Order 2007, SI 2007/289, art 67, Sch 1, Pt 2, para 12(b), substituted by the Pharmacy Order 2010, SI 2010/231, art 68, Sch 4, Pt 2, para 18, as from 27 September 2010 and revoked by SI 2012/1957, arts 2, 6(1), (3)(b), as from 25 July 2012.

Definition "regulated immigration adviser" inserted by the Rehabilitation of Offenders Act 1974 (Exceptions) (Amendment) (England and Wales) Order 2009, SI 2009/1818, arts 2, 7(3), as from 7 July 2009.

Definition "regulated position" inserted by SI 2001/1192, arts 2, 6(6)(b); words in square brackets inserted by SI 2012/1957, arts 2, 11(1), (3), as from 25 July 2012.

Definition "social services" (omitted) revoked by SI 2002/441, arts 2, 5(4)(e).

Definition "taxi driver" (omitted) originally inserted by SI 2002/441, arts 2, 5(4)(e), and revoked by SI 2003/965, arts 2, 10(b).

Definition "vulnerable adult" inserted by SI 2002/441, arts 2, 5(4)(f), and substituted by SI 2012/1957, arts 2, 11(1), (2), as from 10 September 2012.

Education Act 1944, ss 41, 114(1): repealed by the Education Act 1996, s 582(2), Sch 38, Pt I.

Prevention of Fraud (Investments) Act 1958: repealed by the Financial Services Act 1986, s 212, Sch 17 (now itself repealed).

National Health Service Acts 1946 to 1973: repealed and consolidated in the National Health Service Act 1977. The 1977 Act has either been repealed, or is prospectively repealed, by the National Health Service (Consequential Provisions) Act 2006. See now, generally, the National Health Service Act 2006 and the National Health Service (Wales) Act 2006.

Education (Restriction of Employment) Regulations 2000: revoked by the Education (Prohibition from Teaching or Working with Children) Regulations 2003, SI 2003/1184.

SCHEDULES 2 AND 3

(Sch 2 (Excepted Licences, Certificates and Permits) and Sch 3 (Excepted Proceedings) are outside the scope of this work.)

SAFETY REPRESENTATIVES AND SAFETY COMMITTEES REGULATIONS 1977

(SI 1977/500)

NOTES

Made: 16 March 1997.

Authority: Health and Safety at Work etc Act 1974, ss 2(4), (7), 15(1), (3)(b), (5)(b), 80(1), (4), 82(3)(a).

Commencement: 1 October 1978.

See also the Health and Safety Commission Codes of Practice 'Safety Representatives and Safety Committees' (1978) and 'Time off for the Training of Safety Representatives' (1978) at **[4.167]** and **[4.169]** respectively.

See *Harvey* NI(13), NIII(7)(D).

ARRANGEMENT OF REGULATIONS

SCHEDULES

[2.27]

1 Citation and commencement

These Regulations may be cited as the Safety Representatives and Safety Committees Regulations 1977 and shall come into operation on 1st October 1978.

[2.28]

2 Interpretation

(1) In these Regulations, unless the context otherwise requires—

"the 1974 Act" means the Health and Safety at Work etc Act 1974 as amended by the 1975 Act;

"the 1975 Act" means the Employment Protection Act 1975;

"employee" has the meaning assigned by section 53(1) of the 1974 Act and "employer" shall be construed accordingly;

"recognised trade union" [. . .] means an independent trade union as defined in section 30(1) of the Trade Union and Labour Relations Act 1974 which the employer concerned recognises for the purpose of negotiations relating to or connected with one or more of the matters specified in section 29(1) of that Act in relation to persons employed by him or as to which the Advisory, Conciliation and Arbitration Service has made a recommendation for recognition under the 1975 Act which is operative within the meaning of section 15 of that Act;

"safety representative" means a person appointed under Regulation 3(1) of these Regulations to be a safety representative;

"welfare at work" means those aspects of welfare at work which are the subject of health and safety regulations or of any of the existing statutory provisions within the meaning of section 53(1) of the 1974 Act;

"workplace" in relation to a safety representative means any place or places where the group or groups of employees he is appointed to represent are likely to work or which they are likely to frequent in the course of their employment or incidentally to it.

(2) The Interpretation Act 1889 shall apply to the interpretation of these Regulations as it applies to the interpretation of an Act of Parliament.

(3) These Regulations shall not be construed as giving any person a right to inspect any place, article, substance or document which is the subject of restrictions on the grounds of national security unless he satisfies any test or requirement imposed on those grounds by or on behalf of the Crown.

NOTES

Para (1): in definition "recognised trade union" words omitted originally inserted by the Police (Health and Safety) Regulations 1999, SI 1999/860, reg 3(1), (2), and revoked by the Serious Organised Crime and Police Act 2005 (Consequential and Supplementary Amendments to Secondary Legislation) Order 2006, SI 2006/594, art 2, Schedule, para 3(1), (2)(a). Note that the Queen's Printer's copy of SI 2006/594 actually provides that the words be omitted from the definition "regional trade union".

Employment Protection Act 1975: largely repealed and consolidated in the Trade Union and Labour Relations (Consolidation) Act 1992.

Trade Union and Labour Relations Act 1974: see now the Trade Union and Labour Relations (Consolidation) Act 1992. As to s 29(1) of the 1974 Act, see s 218 of the 1992 Act, and as to s 30(1) of the 1974 Act, see s 5 of the 1992 Act.

The reference in the definition of "recognised trade union" to the 1975 Act is now otiose, the relevant provisions of the 1975 Act having been repealed by the Employment Act 1980.

Interpretation Act 1889: see now the Interpretation Act 1978.

2A *(Inserted by the Police (Health and Safety) Regulations 1999, SI 1999/860, reg 3(1), (3); revoked by the Serious Organised Crime and Police Act 2005 (Consequential and Supplementary Amendments to Secondary Legislation) Order 2006, SI 2006/594, art 2, Schedule, para 3(1), (2)(a).)*

[2.29]

3 Appointment of safety representatives

(1) For the purposes of section 2(4) of the 1974 Act, a recognised trade union may appoint safety representatives from amongst the employees in all cases where one or more employees are employed by an employer by whom it is recognised, . . .

(2) Where the employer has been notified in writing by or on behalf of a trade union of the names of the persons appointed as safety representatives under this Regulation and the group or groups of employees they represent, each such safety representative shall have the functions set out in Regulation 4 below.

(3) A person shall cease to be a safety representative for the purposes of these Regulations when—

(a) the trade union which appointed him notifies the employer in writing that his appointment has been terminated; or

(b) he ceases to be employed at the workplace but if he was appointed to represent employees at more than one workplace he shall not cease by virtue of this sub-paragraph to be a safety representative so long as he continues to be employed at any one of them; or

(c) he resigns.

(4) A person appointed under paragraph (1) above as a safety representative shall so far as is reasonably practicable either have been employed by his employer throughout the preceding two years or have had at least two years experience in similar employment.

NOTES

Para (1): words omitted revoked by the Health and Safety (Consultation with Employees) Regulations 1996, SI 1996/1513, reg 13.

[2.30]

4 Functions of safety representatives

(1) In addition to his function under section 2(4) of the 1974 Act to represent the employees in consultations with the employer under section 2(6) of the 1974 Act (which requires every employer to consult safety representatives with a view to the making and maintenance of arrangements which will enable him and his employees to cooperate effectively in promoting and developing measures to ensure the health and safety at work of the employees and in checking the effectiveness of such measures), each safety representative shall have the following functions—

(a) to investigate potential hazards and dangerous occurrences at the workplace (whether or not they are drawn to his attention by the employees he represents) and to examine the causes of accidents at the workplace;

(b) to investigate complaints by any employee he represents relating to that employee's health, safety or welfare at work;

(c) to make representations to the employer on matters arising out of sub-paragraphs (a) and (b) above;

(d) to make representations to the employer on general matters affecting the health, safety or welfare at work of the employees at the workplace;

(e) to carry out inspections in accordance with Regulations 5, 6 and 7 below;

(f) to represent the employees he was appointed to represent in consultations at the workplace with inspectors of the Health and Safety Executive and of any other enforcing authority;

(g) to receive information from inspectors in accordance with section 28(8) of the 1974 Act; and

(h) to attend meetings of safety committees where he attends in his capacity as a safety representative in connection with any of the above functions;

but, without prejudice to sections 7 and 8 of the 1974 Act, no function given to a safety representative by this paragraph shall be construed as imposing any duty on him.

(2) An employer shall permit a safety representative to take such time off with pay during the employee's working hours as shall be necessary for the purposes of—

(a) performing his functions under section 2(4) of the 1974 Act and paragraph (1)(a) to (h) above;

(b) undergoing such training in aspects of those functions as may be reasonable in all the circumstances having regard to any relevant provisions of a code of practice relating to time off for training approved for the time being by the [the Health and Safety Executive] under section 16 of the 1974 Act.

In this paragraph "with pay" means with pay in accordance with [Schedule 2] to these Regulations.

NOTES

Para (2): words in first pair of square brackets substituted by the Legislative Reform (Health and Safety Executive) Order 2008, SI 2008/960, art 22, Sch 3; words in second pair of square brackets substituted by the Police (Health and Safety) Regulations 1999, SI 1999/860, reg 3(1), (4).

[2.31]

[4A Employer's duty to consult and provide facilities and assistance

(1) Without prejudice to the generality of section 2(6) of the Health and Safety at Work etc Act 1974, every employer shall consult safety representatives in good time with regard to—

(a) the introduction of any measure at the workplace which may substantially affect the health and safety of the employees the safety representatives concerned represent;

(b) his arrangements for appointing or, as the case may be, nominating persons in accordance with [regulations 7(1) and 8(1)(b) of the Management of Health and Safety at Work Regulations 1999] [or article 13(3)(b) of the Regulatory Reform (Fire Safety) Order 2005];

(c) any health and safety information he is required to provide to the employees the safety representatives concerned represent by or under the relevant statutory provisions;

(d) the planning and organisation of any health and safety training he is required to provide to the employees the safety representatives concerned represent by or under the relevant statutory provisions; and

(e) the health and safety consequences for the employees the safety representatives concerned represent of the introduction (including the planning thereof) of new technologies into the workplace.

(2) Without prejudice to regulations 5 and 6 of these Regulations, every employer shall provide such facilities and assistance as safety representatives may reasonably require for the purpose of carrying out their functions under section 2(4) of the 1974 Act and under these Regulations.]

NOTES

Inserted by the Management of Health and Safety at Work Regulations 1992, SI 1992/2051, reg 17, Schedule.

Para (1): words in first pair of square brackets in sub-para (b) substituted by the Management of Health and Safety at Work Regulations 1999, SI 1999/3242, reg 29(2), Sch 2; words in second pair of square brackets in sub-para (b) originally inserted by the Fire Precautions (Workplace) Regulations 1997, SI 1997/1840, reg 21(1), and substituted by the Regulatory Reform (Fire Safety) Order 2005, SI 2005/1541, art 41(1), in relation to England and Wales only. A corresponding amendment has been made in relation to Scotland by the Fire (Scotland) Act 2005 (Consequential Modifications and Savings) (No 2) Order 2006, SSI 2006/457, which provides that the words should now read "or regulation 12(3)(b) of the Fire Safety (Scotland) Regulations 2006".

[2.32]

5 Inspections of the workplace

(1) Safety representatives shall be entitled to inspect the workplace or a part of it if they have given the employer or his representative reasonable notice in writing of their intention to do so and have not inspected it, or that part of it, as the case may be, in the previous three months; and may carry out more frequent inspections by agreement with the employer.

(2) Where there has been a substantial change in the conditions of work (whether because of the introduction of new machinery or otherwise) or new information has been published by . . . the Health and Safety Executive relevant to the hazards of the workplace since the last inspection under this Regulation, the safety representatives after consultation with the employer shall be entitled to carry out a further inspection of the part of the workplace concerned notwithstanding that three months have not elapsed since the last inspection.

(3) The employer shall provide such facilities and assistance as the safety representatives may reasonably require (including facilities for independent investigation by them and private discussion with the employees) for the purpose of carrying out an inspection under this Regulation, but nothing in this paragraph shall preclude the employer or his representative from being present in the workplace during the inspection.

(4) An inspection carried out under section 123 of the Mines and Quarries Act 1954 [or regulation 40 of the Quarries Regulations 1999] shall count as an inspection under this Regulation.

NOTES

Para (2): words omitted revoked by the Legislative Reform (Health and Safety Executive) Order 2008, SI 2008/960, art 22, Sch 3.

Para (4): words in square brackets inserted by the Quarries Regulations 1999, SI 1999/2024, reg 48(1), Sch 5, Pt II.

[2.33]

6 Inspections following notifiable accidents, occurrences and diseases

(1) Where there has been [an over three day injury,] notifiable accident or dangerous occurrence in a workplace or a notifiable disease has been contracted there and—

(a) it is safe for an inspection to be carried out; and

(b) the interests of employees in the group or groups which safety representatives are appointed to represent might be involved,

those safety representatives may carry out an inspection of the part of the workplace concerned and so far as is necessary for the purpose of determining the cause they may inspect any other part of the workplace; where it is reasonably practicable to do so they shall notify the employer or his representative of their intention to carry out the inspection.

(2) The employer shall provide such facilities and assistance as the safety representatives may reasonably require (including facilities for independent investigation by them and private discussion with the employees) for the purpose of carrying out an inspection under this Regulation; but nothing in this paragraph shall preclude the employer or his representative from being present in the workplace during the inspection.

[(3) In this regulation—

"notifiable accident or dangerous occurrence" and "notifiable disease" mean any accident, dangerous occurrence or disease, as the case may be, notice of which is required to be given by virtue of any of the relevant statutory provisions within the meaning of section 53(1) of the 1974 Act; and

"over three day injury" means an injury required to be recorded in accordance with regulation 7(1)(aa) of the Reporting of Injuries, Diseases and Dangerous Occurrences Regulations 1995.]

NOTES

Para (1): words in square brackets substituted by the Reporting of Injuries, Diseases and Dangerous Occurrences (Amendment) Regulations 2012, SI 2012/199, reg 6(1), (2)(a), as from 6 April 2012.

Para (3): substituted by SI 2012/199, reg 6(1), (2)(b), as from 6 April 2012.

[2.34]

7 Inspection of documents and provision of information

(1) Safety representatives shall for the performance of their functions under section 2(4) of the 1974 Act and under Regulations, if they have given the employer reasonable notice, be entitled to inspect and take copies of any document relevant to the workplace or to the employees the safety representatives represent which the employer is required to keep by virtue of any relevant statutory provision within the meaning of section 53(1) of the 1974 Act except a document consisting of or relating to any health record of an identifiable individual.

(2) An employer shall make available to safety representatives the information, within the employer's knowledge, necessary to enable them to fulfil their functions except—

(a) any information the disclosure of which would be against the interests of national security; or

(b) any information which he could not disclose without contravening a prohibition imposed by or under an enactment; or

(c) any information relating specifically to an individual, unless he has consented to its being disclosed; or

(d) any information the disclosure of which would, for reasons other than its effect on health, safety or welfare at work, cause substantial injury to the employer's undertaking or, where the information was supplied to him by some other person, to the undertaking of that other person; or

(e) any information obtained by the employer for the purpose of bringing, prosecuting or defending any legal proceedings.

(3) Paragraph (2) above does not require an employer to produce or allow inspection of any document or part of a document which is not related to health, safety or welfare.

[2.35]
8 Cases where safety representatives need not be employees

(1) In the cases mentioned in paragraph (2) below safety representatives appointed under Regulation 3(1) of these Regulations need not be employees of the employer concerned; and section 2(4) of the 1974 Act shall be modified accordingly.

(2) The said cases are those in which the employees in the group or groups the safety representatives are appointed to represent are members of the British Actors' Equity Association or of the Musicians' Union.

(3) Regulations 3(3)(b) and (4) and 4(2) of these Regulations shall not apply to safety representatives appointed by virtue of this Regulation and in the case of safety representatives to be so appointed Regulation 3(1) shall have effect as if the words "from amongst the employees" were omitted.

[2.36]
9 Safety committees

(1) For the purposes of section 2(7) of the 1974 Act (which requires an employer in prescribed cases to establish a safety committee if requested to do so by safety representatives) the prescribed cases shall be any cases in which at least two safety representatives request the employer in writing to establish a safety committee.

(2) Where an employer is requested to establish a safety committee in a case prescribed in paragraph (1) above, he shall establish it in accordance with the following provisions—

(a) he shall consult with the safety representatives who made the request and with the representatives of recognised trade unions whose members work in any workplace in respect of which he proposes that the committee should function;

(b) the employer shall post a notice stating the composition of the committee and the workplace or workplaces to be covered by it in a place where it may be easily read by the employees;

(c) the committee shall be established not later than three months after the request for it.

[2.37]
10 Power of [the Health and Safety Executive] to grant exemptions

The [the Health and Safety Executive] may grant exemptions from any requirement imposed by these Regulations and any such exemption may be unconditional or subject to such conditions as [the Executive] may impose and may be with or without a limit of time.

NOTES

Words in square brackets substituted by the Legislative Reform (Health and Safety Executive) Order 2008, SI 2008/960, art 22, Sch 3.

[2.38]
11 Provisions as to [employment tribunals]

(1) A safety representative may, in accordance with the jurisdiction conferred on [employment tribunals] by paragraph 16(2) of Schedule 1 to the Trade Union and Labour Relations Act 1974, present a complaint to an [employment tribunal] that—

(a) the employer has failed to permit him to take time off in accordance with Regulation 4(2) of these Regulations; or

(b) the employer has failed to pay him in accordance with Regulation 4(2) of and the Schedule to these Regulations.

(2) An [employment tribunal] shall not consider a complaint under paragraph (1) above unless it is presented within three months of the date when the failure occurred or within such further period as the tribunal considers reasonable in a case where it is satisfied that it was not reasonably practicable for the complaint to be presented within the period of three months.

(3) Where an [employment tribunal] finds a complaint under paragraph (1)(a) above well-founded the tribunal shall make a declaration to that effect and may make an award of compensation to be paid by the employer to the employee which shall be of such amount as the tribunal considers just and equitable in all the circumstances having regard to the employer's default in failing to permit time off to be taken by the employee and to any loss sustained by the employee which is attributable to the matters complained of.

(4) Where on a complaint under paragraph (1)(b) above an [employment tribunal] finds that the employer has failed to pay the employee the whole or part of the amount required to be paid under paragraph (1)(b), the tribunal shall order the employer to pay the employee the amount which it finds due to him.

(5) . . .

NOTES

Words in square brackets substituted by the Employment Rights (Dispute Resolution) Act 1998, s 1(2)(a), (b).

Para (5): amended the Trade Union and Labour Relations Act 1974, Sch 1, para 16 (and is now spent).

1974 Act: the references to the 1974 Act in para (1) have been superseded; the jurisdiction of employment tribunals is now conferred by the Employment Tribunals Act 1996, s 2.

SCHEDULES

SCHEDULE 1

(Sch 1 inserted by the Police (Health and Safety) Regulations 1999, SI 1999/860, reg 3(1), (5); revoked by the Serious Organised Crime and Police Act 2005 (Consequential and Supplementary Amendments to Secondary Legislation) Order 2006, SI 2006/594, art 2, Schedule, para 3(1), (2)(a).)

[SCHEDULE 2]
PAY FOR TIME OFF ALLOWED TO SAFETY REPRESENTATIVES

Regulation 4(2)

[2.39]

1. Subject to paragraph 3 below, where a safety representative is permitted to take time off in accordance with Regulation 4(2) of these Regulations, his employer shall pay him—

(a) where the safety representative's remuneration for the work he would ordinarily have been doing during that time does not vary with the amount of work done, as if he had worked at that work for the whole of that time;

(b) where the safety representative's remuneration for that work varies with the amount of work done, an amount calculated by reference to the average hourly earnings for that work (ascertained in accordance with paragraph 2 below).

2. The average hourly earnings referred to in paragraph 1(b) above are the average hourly earnings of the safety representative concerned or, if no fair estimate can be made of those earnings, the average hourly earnings for work of that description of persons in comparable employment with the same employer or, if there are no such persons, a figure of average hourly earnings which is reasonable in the circumstances.

3. Any payment to a safety representative by an employer in respect of a period of time off—

(a) if it is a payment which discharges any liability which the employer may have under section 57 of the 1975 Act in respect of that period, shall also discharge his liability in respect of the same period under Regulation 4(2) of these Regulations;

(b) if it is a payment under any contractual obligation, shall go towards discharging the employer's liability in respect of the same period under Regulation 4(2) of these Regulations;

(c) if it is a payment under Regulation 4(2) of these Regulations shall go towards discharging any liability of the employer to pay contractual remuneration in respect of the same period.

NOTES

Original Schedule renumbered as Schedule 2 by the Police (Health and Safety) Regulations 1999, SI 1999/860, reg 3(1), (6).

"Section 57": see now the Trade Union and Labour Relations (Consolidation) Act 1992, s 169.

STATUTORY SICK PAY (GENERAL) REGULATIONS 1982

(SI 1982/894)

NOTES

Made: 30 June 1982.

Authority: Social Security and Housing Benefits Act 1982, ss 1(3), (4), 3(5), (7), 4(2), 5(5), 6(1), 8(1)–(3), 17(4), 18(1), 20, 26(1), (3)–(5), Sch 1, para 1, Sch 2, paras 2(3), 3(2) (repealed). These Regulations now have effect as if made under the Social Security Contributions and Benefits Act 1992, ss 151(4)–(6), 153(5), (6), (10), 154(2), 155(5), 156(1), 163(1), (3)–(5), Sch 12, paras 2(3), 3(2), and the Social Security Administration Act 1992, ss 5, 130(1), (2), (3)(c)(i), (4), by virtue of the Social Security (Consequential Provisions) Act 1992, s 2(2).

Commencement: 6 April 1983.

Transfer of functions: the functions of the Secretary of State conferred by regs 9A–9C, 10, 14 were transferred to the Commissioners of Inland Revenue by the Social Security Contributions (Transfer of Functions, etc) Act 1999, s 1(2), Sch 2. Note also that a reference to the Commissioners of Inland Revenue is now to be taken as a reference to the Commissioners for Her Majesty's Revenue and Customs; see the Commissioners for Revenue and Customs Act 2005, s 50(1), (7).

See *Harvey* BI(2)(B).

ARRANGEMENT OF REGULATIONS

[2.40]
1 Citation, commencement and interpretation

(1) These regulations may be cited as the Statutory Sick Pay (General) Regulations 1982, and shall come into operation on 6th April 1983.

(2) In these regulations—

"the Act" means the Social Security and Housing Benefits Act 1982;

["the Contributions and Benefits Act" means the Social Security Contributions and Benefits Act 1992;]

["income tax month" means the period beginning on the 6th day of any calendar month and ending on the 5th day of the following calendar month;]

"Part I" means Part I of the Act;

and other expressions, unless the context otherwise requires, have the same meanings as in Part I.

(3) Unless the context otherwise requires, any reference—

(a) in these regulations to a numbered section or Schedule is a reference to the section or Schedule, as the case may be, of or to the Act bearing that number;

(b) in these regulations to a numbered regulation is a reference to the regulation bearing that number in these regulations; and

(c) in any of these regulations to a numbered paragraph is a reference to the paragraph bearing that number in that regulation.

NOTES

Para (2): definition "the Contributions and Benefits Act" inserted by the Social Security (Miscellaneous Provisions) Amendment Regulations 1992, SI 1992/2595, reg 14; definition "income tax month" inserted by the Social Security Contributions, Statutory Maternity Pay and Statutory Sick Pay (Miscellaneous Amendments) Regulations 1996, SI 1996/777, reg 2(1), (2).

Social Security and Housing Benefits Act 1982: largely repealed by the Social Security (Consequential Provisions) Act 1992; see now the Social Security Administration Act 1992 and the Social Security Contributions and Benefits Act 1992.

[2.41]
2 Persons deemed incapable of work

(1) A person who is not incapable of work of which he can reasonably be expected to do under a particular contract of service may be deemed to be incapable of work of such a kind by reason of some specific disease or bodily or mental disablement for any day on which either—

(a)

(i) he is under medical care in respect of a disease or disablement as aforesaid,

(ii) it is stated by a registered medical practitioner that for precautionary or convalescent reasons consequential on such disease or disablement he should abstain from work, or from work of such a kind, and

(iii) he does not work under that contract of service, or

[(b) he is—

(i) excluded or abstains from work, or from work of such a kind, pursuant to a request or notice in writing lawfully made under an enactment; or

(ii) otherwise prevented from working pursuant to an enactment,

[by reason of it being known or reasonably suspected that he is infected or contaminated by, or has been in contact with a case of, a relevant infection or contamination]].

(2) A person who at the commencement of any day is, or thereafter on that day becomes, incapable of work of such a kind by reason of some specific disease or bodily or mental disablement, and

(a) on that day, under that contract of service, does no work, or no work except during a shift which ends on that day having begun on the previous day; and

(b) does no work under that contract of service during a shift which begins on that day and ends on the next,

shall be deemed to be incapable of work of such a kind by reason of that disease or bodily or mental disablement throughout that day.

[(3) For the purposes of paragraph (1)(b)—

"enactment" includes an enactment comprised in, or in an instrument made under—

(a) an Act; or

(b) an Act of the Scottish Parliament; and

["relevant infection or contamination" means—

(a) in England and Wales—

(i) any incidence or spread of infection or contamination, within the meaning of section 45A(3) of the Public Health (Control of Disease) Act 1984 in respect of which regulations are made under Part 2A of that Act (public health protection) for the purpose of preventing, protecting against, controlling or providing a public health response to, such incidence or spread, or

(ii) any disease, food poisoning, infection, infectious disease or notifiable disease to which regulation 9 (powers in respect of persons leaving aircraft) of the Public Health (Aircraft) Regulations 1979 applies or to which regulation 10 (powers in respect of certain persons on ships) of the Public Health (Ships) Regulations 1979 applies; and

(b) in Scotland, any—

(i) infectious disease within the meaning of section 1(5) of the Public Health etc (Scotland) Act 2008, or exposure to an organism causing that disease, or

(ii) contamination within the meaning of section 1(5) of that Act, or exposure to a contaminant,

to which sections 56 to 58 of that Act (compensation) apply.]]

NOTES

Para (1): sub-para (b) substituted by the Statutory Sick Pay (General) Amendment Regulations 2006, SI 2006/799, reg 2(1), (2); words in square brackets in sub-para (b) substituted by the Social Security (Miscellaneous Amendments) (No 3) Regulations 2011, SI 2011/2425, reg 6(a), as from 6 April 2012.

Para (3): added by SI 2006/799, reg 2(1), (3); definition "relevant infection or contamination" substituted (for the original definition "relevant disease") by SI 2011/2425, reg 6(b), as from 6 April 2012.

2A (*Spent; this regulation was inserted by the Statutory Sick Pay (General) Amendment Regulations 1986, SI 1986/477, reg 2, and amended the Social Security and Housing Benefits Act 1982, s 2(3), which was repealed by the Social Security (Consequential Provisions) Act 1992, s 3(1), Sch 1.*)

[2.42]

3 Period of entitlement ending or not arising

(1) In a case where an employee is detained in legal custody or sentenced to a term of imprisonment (except where the sentence is suspended) on a day which in relation to him falls within a period of entitlement, that period shall end with that day.

(2) A period of entitlement shall not arise in relation to a period of incapacity for work where at any time on the first day of that period of incapacity for work the employee in question is in legal custody or sentenced to or undergoing a term of imprisonment (except where the sentence is suspended).

[(2A) A period of entitlement in respect of an employee who was entitled to incapacity benefit, maternity allowance or severe disablement allowance shall not arise in relation to any day within a period of incapacity for work beginning with the first day on which paragraph 2(d) of Schedule 11 to the Contributions and Benefits Act ceases to have effect where the employee in question is a person to whom regulation 13A of the Social Security (Incapacity for Work) (General) Regulations 1995 (welfare to work beneficiary) applies.]

[(2B) Paragraph (2A) shall not apply, in the case of an employee who was entitled to incapacity benefit, where paragraph 2(d)(i) of Schedule 11 to the Contributions and Benefits Act ceases to have effect by virtue of paragraph 5A of that Schedule.]

[(2C) A period of entitlement in respect of an employee who was entitled to employment and support allowance shall not arise in relation to any day within a period of limited capability for work beginning with the first day on which paragraph 2(dd) of Schedule 11 to the Contributions and Benefits Act ceases to have effect where the employee in question is a person to whom regulation 148 of the Employment and Support Allowance Regulations 2008 (work and training beneficiaries) applies.]

[(3) A period of entitlement as between an employee and his employer shall end after 3 years if it has not otherwise ended in accordance with [section 153(2) of the Contributions and Benefits Act] or with regulations (other than this paragraph) made under [section 153(6) of the Contributions and Benefits Act.]

[[(4) Where a period of entitlement is current as between an employee and her employer and the employee—

(a) is pregnant or has been confined; and
(b) is incapable of work wholly or partly because of pregnancy or confinement on any day which falls on or after the beginning of the [4th week] before the expected week of confinement; and
(c) is not by virtue of that pregnancy or confinement entitled to statutory maternity pay under Part XII of the Contributions and Benefits Act or to maternity allowance under section 35 of that Act;

the period of entitlement shall end on that day or, if earlier, on the day she was confined.

(5) Where an employee—

(a) is pregnant or has been confined; and
(b) is incapable of work wholly or partly because of pregnancy or confinement on any day which falls on or after the beginning of the [4th week] before the expected week of confinement; and
(c) is not by virtue of that pregnancy or confinement entitled to statutory maternity pay under Part XII of the Contributions and Benefits Act or to maternity allowance under section 35 of that Act;

a period of entitlement as between her and her employer shall not arise in relation to a period of incapacity for work where the first day in that period falls within 18 weeks of the beginning of the week containing the day referred to at (b) above or, if earlier, of the week in which she was confined.]

(6) In paragraphs (4) and (5) "confinement" and "confined" have the same meanings as in [section 171 of the Contributions and Benefits Act.]]

NOTES

Para (2A): inserted by the Social Security (Welfare to Work) Regulations 1998, SI 1998/2231, reg 6.

Para (2B): inserted by the Employment Equality (Age) (Consequential Amendments) Regulations 2007, SI 2007/825, reg 5(1), (2).

Para (2C): inserted by the Employment and Support Allowance (Consequential Provisions) (No 2) Regulations 2008, SI 2008/1554, reg 45, as from 27 October 2008.

Para (3): added by the Statutory Sick Pay (General) Amendment Regulations 1986, SI 1986/477, reg 3; words in square brackets substituted by the Social Security Maternity Benefits and Statutory Sick Pay (Amendment) Regulations 1994, SI 1994/1367, reg 9(1), (2).

Paras (4), (5): added by the Statutory Sick Pay (General) Amendment (No 2) Regulations 1987, SI 1987/868, reg 2, and substituted by SI 1994/1367, reg 9(1), (3), (4); words in square brackets substituted by the Social Security, Statutory Maternity Pay and Statutory Sick Pay (Miscellaneous Amendments) Regulations 2002, SI 2002/2690, reg 13.

Para (6): added by SI 1987/868, reg 2; words in square brackets substituted by SI 1994/1367, reg 9(1), (5).

3A *(Inserted by the Statutory Sick Pay (General) Amendment Regulations 1986, SI 1986/477, reg 4; revoked by the Statutory Sick Pay (General) (Amendment) Regulations 2008, SI 2008/1735, reg 3, as from 27 October 2008.)*

[2.43]

4 Contract of service ended for the purpose of avoiding liability for statutory sick pay

(1) The provisions of this regulation apply in any case where an employer's contract of service with an employee is brought to an end by the employer solely or mainly for the purpose of avoiding liability for statutory sick pay.

(2) Where a period of entitlement is current on the day on which the contract is brought to an end, the employer shall be liable to pay statutory sick pay to the employee until the occurrence of an event which, if the contract had still been current, would have caused the period of entitlement to

come to an end under section 3(2)(a), (b) or (d) or regulation 3(1) [of these regulations or regulation 10(2) of the Statutory Sick Pay (Mariners, Airmen and Persons Abroad) Regulations 1982], or (if earlier) until the date on which the contract would have expired.

NOTES

Para (2): words in square brackets inserted by the Statutory Sick Pay (Mariners, Airmen and Persons Abroad) Regulations 1982, SI 1982/1349, reg 10(3).

[2.44]

5 Qualifying days

(1) In this regulation "week" means a period of 7 consecutive days beginning with Sunday.

(2) Where an employee and an employer of his have not agreed which day or days in any week are or were qualifying days [or where in any week the only day or days are or were such as are referred to in paragraph (3)], the qualifying day or days in that week shall be—

- (a) the day or days on which it is agreed between the employer and the employee that the employee is or was required to work (if not incapable) for that employer or, if it is so agreed that there is or was no such day,
- (b) the Wednesday, or, if there is no such agreement between the employer and employee as mentioned in sub-paragraph (a),
- (c) every day, except that or those (if any) on which it is agreed between the employer and the employee that none of that employer's employees are or were required to work (any agreement that all days are or were such days being ignored).

[(3) No effect shall be given to any agreement between an employee and his employer to treat as qualifying days—

- (a) any day where the day is identified, whether expressly or otherwise, by reference to that or another day being a day of incapacity for work in relation to the employee's contract of service with an employer;
- (b) any day identified, whether expressly or otherwise, by reference to a period of entitlement or to a period of incapacity for work.]

NOTES

Para (2): words in square brackets inserted by the Statutory Sick Pay (General) Amendment Regulations 1985, SI 1985/126, reg 2.

Para (3): added by SI 1985/126, reg 2.

[2.45]

6 Calculation of entitlement limit

(1) Where an employee's entitlement to statutory sick pay is calculated by reference to different weekly rates in the same period of entitlement . . . , the entitlement limit shall be calculated in the manner described in paragraphs (2) and (3), or, as the case may be, (4) and (5); and where a number referred to in paragraph (2)(b) or (d) or (4)(a)(ii) or (d)(ii) is not a whole number [of thousandths, it shall be rounded up to the next thousandth].

(2) For the purpose of determining whether an employee has reached his maximum entitlement to statutory sick pay in respect of a period of entitlement, there shall be calculated—

- (a) the amount of statutory sick pay to which the employee became entitled during the part of the period of entitlement before the change in the weekly rate;
- (b) the number by which the weekly rate (before the change) must be multiplied in order to produce the amount mentioned in sub-paragraph (a);
- (c) the amount of statutory sick pay to which the employee has so far become entitled during the part of the period of entitlement after the change in the weekly rate; and
- (d) the number by which the weekly rate (after the change) must be multiplied in order to produce the amount mentioned in sub-paragraph (c);
- (e) the sum of the amounts mentioned in sub-paragraphs (a) and (c); and
- (f) the sum of the numbers mentioned in sub-paragraphs (b) and (d).

(3) When the sum mentioned in paragraph (2)(f) reaches [28], the sum mentioned in paragraph (2)(e) reaches the entitlement limit.

(4), (5) . . .

NOTES

Para (1): words omitted revoked by the Statutory Sick Pay (General) Amendment Regulations 1986, SI 1986/477, reg 9; words in square brackets substituted by the Statutory Sick Pay (General) Amendment Regulations 1984, SI 1984/385, reg 2.

Para (3): number in square brackets substituted by SI 1986/477, reg 9.

Paras (4), (5): revoked by SI 1986/477, reg 9.

[2.46]
7 Time and manner of notification of incapacity for work

(1) Subject to paragraph (2), notice of any day of incapacity for work shall be given by or on behalf of an employee to his employer—

(a) in a case where the employer has decided on a time limit (not being one which requires the notice to be given earlier than . . . the first qualifying day in the period of incapacity for work which includes that day of incapacity for work [or by a specified time during that qualifying day]) and taken reasonable steps to make it known to the employee, within that time limit; and

(b) in any other case, on or before the seventh day after that day of incapacity for work.

(2) Notice of any day of incapacity for work may be given [one month] later than as provided by paragraph (1) where there is good cause for giving it later [or if in the particular circumstances that is not practicable, as soon as it is reasonably practicable thereafter], so however that it shall in any event be given on or before the 91st day after that day.

(3) A notice contained in a letter which is properly addressed and sent by prepaid post shall be deemed to have been given on the day on which it was posted.

(4) Notice of any day of incapacity for work shall be given by or on behalf of an employee to his employer—

(a) in a case where the employer has decided on a manner in which it is to be given (not being a manner which imposes a requirement such as is specified in paragraph (5)) and taken reasonable steps to make it known to the employee, in that manner; and

(b) in any other case, in any manner, so however that unless otherwise agreed between the employer and employee it shall be given in writing.

(5) The requirements mentioned in paragraph (4)(a) are that notice shall be given—

(a) personally;
(b) in the form of medical evidence;
(c) more than one in every 7 days during a period of entitlement;
(d) on a document supplied by the employer; or
(e) on a printed form.

NOTES

Para (1): words omitted revoked, and words in square brackets inserted, by the Statutory Sick Pay (General) Amendment Regulations 1984, SI 1984/385, reg 2.

Para (2): words in square brackets inserted by the Social Security Contributions, Statutory Maternity Pay and Statutory Sick Pay (Miscellaneous Amendments) Regulations 1996, SI 1996/777, reg 2(1), (3).

[2.47]
8 Manner in which statutory sick pay may not be paid

Statutory sick pay may not be paid in kind or by way of the provision of board or lodging or of services or other facilities.

[2.48]
9 Time limits for paying statutory sick pay

(1) In this regulation, "pay day" means a day on which it has been agreed, or it is the normal practice, between an employer and an employee of his, that payments by way of remuneration are to be made, or, where there is no such agreement or normal practice, the last day of a calendar month.

(2) In any case where—

(a) a decision has been made by an [adjudication officer], [social security appeal tribunal] or Commissioner in proceedings under Part I that an employee is entitled to an amount of statutory sick pay; and

(b) the time for bringing an appeal against the decision has expired and either—

(i) no such appeal has been brought; or
(ii) such an appeal has been brought and has been finally disposed of,

that amount of statutory sick pay is to be paid within the time specified in paragraph (3).

(3) Subject to paragraphs (4) and (5), the employer is required to pay the amount not later than the first pay day after—

(a) where an appeal has been brought, the day on which the employer receives notification that it has been finally disposed of;

(b) where leave to appeal has been refused and there remains no further opportunity to apply for leave, the day on which the employer receives notification of the refusal; and

(c) in any other case, the day on which the time for bringing an appeal expires.

(4) Subject to paragraph (5), where it is impracticable, in view of the employer's methods of accounting for and paying remuneration, for the requirement of payment referred to in paragraph (3) to be met by the pay day referred to in that paragraph, it shall be met not later than the next following pay day.

(5) Where the employer would not have remunerated the employee for his work on the day of incapacity for work in question (if it had not been a day of incapacity for work) as early as the pay day specified in paragraph (3) or (if it applies) paragraph (4), the requirement of payment shall be met on the first day on which the employee would have been remunerated for his work on that day.

NOTES

Para (2): words in square brackets substituted by virtue of the Health and Social Services and Social Security Adjudications Act 1983, s 25, Sch 8, Pt I, para 1(1), (3)(a).

[2.49]

[9A Liability of the [Commissioners of Inland Revenue] for payments of statutory sick pay

(1) Notwithstanding the provisions of section 1 of the Act and subject to paragraph (4), where—

(a) an adjudicating authority has determined that an employer is liable to make payments of statutory sick pay to an employee, and

(b) the time for appealing against that determination has expired, and

(c) no appeal against the determination has been lodged or leave to appeal against the determination is required and has been refused,

then for any day of incapacity for work in respect of which it was determined the employer was liable to make those payments, and for any further days of incapacity for work which fall within the same spell of incapacity for work and in respect of which the employer was liable to make payments of statutory sick pay to that employee, the liability to make payments of statutory sick pay in respect of those days shall, to the extent that payment has not been made by the employer, be that of the [Commissioners of Inland Revenue] and not the employer.

(2) For the purposes of this regulation a spell of incapacity for work consists of consecutive days of incapacity for work with no day of the week disregarded.

(3) In paragraph (1) above "adjudicating authority" means, as the case may be, the Chief or other adjudication officer, [the First-tier Tribunal or the Upper Tribunal].

(4) This regulation shall not apply to any liability of an employer to make a payment of statutory sick pay where the day of incapacity for work in respect of which the liability arose falls within a period of entitlement which commenced before 6th April 1987.]

NOTES

Inserted by the Statutory Sick Pay (General) Amendment Regulations 1987, SI 1987/372, reg 2.

Regulation heading, para (1): words in square brackets substituted by virtue of the Social Security Contributions (Transfer of Functions, etc) Act 1999, s 1(2), Sch 2.

Para (3): words in square brackets substituted by the Tribunals, Courts and Enforcement Act 2007 (Transitional and Consequential Provisions) Order 2008, SI 2008/2683, art 6(1), Sch 1, para 18, as from 3 November 2008.

Commissioners of Inland Revenue: a reference to the Commissioners of Inland Revenue is now to be taken as a reference to the Commissioners for Her Majesty's Revenue and Customs; see the Commissioners for Revenue and Customs Act 2005, s 50(1), (7).

[2.50]

[9B Insolvency of employer

(1) Notwithstanding the provisions of section 1 of the Act and subject to paragraph (3), any liability arising under Part I of the Act to make a payment of statutory sick pay in respect of a day of incapacity for work in relation to an employee's contract of service with his employer shall be that of the [Commissioners of Inland Revenue] and not that of the employer where the employer is insolvent on that day.

(2) For the purposes of paragraph (1) an employer shall be taken to be insolvent if, and only if—

(a) in England and Wales—

(i) he has been adjudged bankrupt or has made a composition or arrangement with his creditors;

(ii) he has died and his estate falls to be administered in accordance with an order under section 421 of the Insolvency Act 1986; or

(iii) where an employer is a company, a winding-up order . . . is made or a resolution for voluntary winding-up is passed with respect to it [or it enters administration], or a receiver or manager of its undertaking is duly appointed, or possession is taken by or on behalf of the holders of any debentures secured by a floating charge, or any property of the company comprised in or subject to the charge or a voluntary arrangement proposed for the purposes of Part I of the Insolvency Act 1986 is approved under that Part;

(b) in Scotland—

(i) an award of sequestration is made on his estate or he executes a trust deed for his creditors or enters into a composition contract;

(ii) he has died and a judicial factor appointed under section 11A of the Judicial Factors (Scotland) Act 1889 is required by that section to divide his insolvent estate among his creditors; or

(iii) where the employer is a company, a winding-up order . . . . is made or a resolution for voluntary winding-up is passed with respect to it [or it enters administration] or a receiver of its undertaking is duly appointed or a voluntary arrangement proposed for the purposes of Part I of the Insolvency Act 1986 is approved under that Part.

(3) This regulation shall not apply where the employer became insolvent before 6th April 1987].

NOTES

Inserted by the Statutory Sick Pay (General) Amendment Regulations 1987, SI 1987/372, reg 2.

Para (1): words in square brackets substituted by virtue of the Social Security Contributions (Transfer of Functions, etc) Act 1999, s 1(2), Sch 2.

Para (2): words omitted revoked, and words in square brackets inserted, by the Enterprise Act 2002 (Insolvency) Order 2003, SI 2003/2096, art 5, Schedule, Pt 2, para 42, except in relation to any case where a petition for an administration order was presented before 15 September 2003.

Commissioners of Inland Revenue: a reference to the Commissioners of Inland Revenue is now to be taken as a reference to the Commissioners for Her Majesty's Revenue and Customs; see the Commissioners for Revenue and Customs Act 2005, s 50(1), (7).

[2.51]

[9C Payments by the [Commissioners of Inland Revenue]

Where the [Commissioners of Inland Revenue became] liable in accordance with regulation 9A or 9B to make payments of statutory sick pay to a person, the first payment shall be made as soon as reasonably practicable after he becomes so liable, and payments thereafter shall be made at weekly intervals, by means of an instrument of payment[, instrument for benefit payment] or by such other means as appears to the [Commissioners of Inland Revenue] to be appropriate in the circumstances of the particular case.]

NOTES

Inserted by the Statutory Sick Pay (General) Amendment Regulations 1987, SI 1987/372, reg 2.

Words "Commissioners of Inland Revenue" and "Commissioners of Inland Revenue became" in square brackets substituted by virtue of the Social Security Contributions (Transfer of Functions, etc) Act 1999, s 1(2), Sch 2; other words in square brackets inserted by the Social Security (Claims and Payments Etc) Amendment Regulations 1996, SI 1996/672, reg 3.

Commissioners of Inland Revenue: a reference to the Commissioners of Inland Revenue is now to be taken as a reference to the Commissioners for Her Majesty's Revenue and Customs; see the Commissioners for Revenue and Customs Act 2005, s 50(1), (7).

[2.52]

10 Persons unable to act

(1) Where in the case of any employee—

(a) statutory sick pay is payable to him or he is alleged to be entitled to it;

(b) he is unable for the time being to act; and

(c) either—

(i) no receiver has been appointed by the Court of Protection with power to receive statutory sick pay on his behalf, or

(ii) in Scotland, his estate is not being administered by any tutor, curator or other guardian acting or appointed in terms of law,

the [Commissioners of Inland Revenue] may, upon written application to [them] by a person who, if a natural person, is over the age of 18, appoint that person to exercise, on behalf of the employee, any right to which he may be entitled under Part I and to deal on his behalf with any sums payable to him.

(2) Where the [Commissioners of Inland Revenue have] made an appointment under paragraph (1)—

(a) [they] may at any time in [their] absolute discretion revoke it;

(b) the person appointed may resign his office after having given one month's notice in writing to the [Commissioners of Inland Revenue] of his intention to do so; and

(c) the appointment shall terminate when the [Commissioners of Inland Revenue are] notified that a receiver or other person to whom paragraph (1)(c) applies has been appointed.

(3) Anything required by Part I to be done by or to any employee who is unable to act may be done by or to the person appointed under this regulation to act on his behalf, and the receipt of the person so appointed shall be a good discharge to the employee's employer for any sum paid.

NOTES

Words in square brackets substituted by virtue of the Social Security Contributions (Transfer of Functions, etc) Act 1999, s 1(2), Sch 2.

Commissioners of Inland Revenue: a reference to the Commissioners of Inland Revenue is now to be taken as a reference to the Commissioners for Her Majesty's Revenue and Customs; see the Commissioners for Revenue and Customs Act 2005, s 50(1), (7).

[2.53]

11 Rounding to avoid fractional amounts

Where any payment of statutory sick pay is made and the statutory sick pay due for the period for which the payment purports to be made includes a fraction of a penny, the payment shall be rounded up to the next whole number of pence.

[2.54]

12 Days not to be treated as, or as parts of, periods of interruption of employment

In a case to which paragraph 3 of Schedule 2 applies, the day of incapacity for work mentioned in sub-paragraph (1)(b) of that paragraph shall not be, or form part of, a period of interruption of employment where it is a day which, by virtue of section 17(1) or (2) of the Social Security Act 1975 or any regulations made thereunder, is not to be treated as a day of incapacity for work.

NOTES

"Section 17(1) or (2) of the Social Security Act 1975": repealed.

[2.55]

13 Records to be maintained by employers

[(1)] Every employer shall maintain for 3 years after the end of each tax year a record, in relation to each employee of his, of—

(a) any day in that tax year which was one of 4 or more consecutive days on which, according to information supplied by or on behalf of the employee, the employee was incapable by reason of some specific disease or bodily or mental disablement of doing work which he could reasonably be expected to do under any contract of service between him and the employer, whether or not he would normally have been expected to work on that day; [and

(b) any payment of statutory sick pay made in respect of any day recorded under sub-paragraph (a).]

[(1A) For the purposes of paragraph (1)(b) only, the employer is not to be regarded as having made a payment of statutory sick pay where, in respect of any day recorded under paragraph (1)(a), the employee is entitled to receive, and does in fact receive, a payment or payments by way of contractual remuneration from his employer which, in aggregate, equal or exceed the amount of statutory sick pay payable in respect of that day.]

[(2)–(5) . . .]

NOTES

Para (1): numbered as such by the Statutory Sick Pay (General) Amendment Regulations 1986, SI 1986/477, reg 5; sub-para (b) and the word immediately preceding it substituted, for the original sub-paras (b)–(d), by the Social Security Contributions, Statutory Maternity Pay and Statutory Sick Pay (Miscellaneous Amendments) Regulations 1996, SI 1996/777, reg 2(1), (4)(a).

Para (1A): inserted by the Statutory Sick Pay (General) Amendment Regulations 1996, SI 1996/3042, reg 2.

Paras (2)–(5): added by SI 1986/477, reg 5, and revoked by SI 1996/777, reg 2(1), (4)(b).

[2.56]

[13A Production of employer's records

(1) An authorised officer of the Commissioners of Inland Revenue may by notice require an employer to produce to him at the place of keeping such records as are in the employer's possession or power and as (in the officer's reasonable opinion) contain, or may contain, information relevant to satisfy him that statutory sick pay has been paid and is being paid in accordance with these regulations to employees or former employees who are entitled to it.

(2) A notice referred to in paragraph (1) shall be in writing and the employer shall produce the records referred to in that paragraph within 30 days after the date of such a notice.

(3) The production of records in pursuance of this regulation shall be without prejudice to any lien which a third party may have in respect of those records.

(4) References in this regulation to "records" means—

(a) any wage sheet or deductions working sheet; or

(b) any other document which relates to the calculation or payment of statutory sick pay to his employees or former employees,

whether kept in written form, electronically, or otherwise.

(5) In paragraph (1), "place of keeping" means such place in Great Britain that an employer and an authorised officer may agree upon, or, in the absence of such agreement—

(a) any place in Great Britain where records referred to in paragraph (1) are normally kept; or

(b) if there is no such place, the employer's principal place of business in Great Britain.]

NOTES

Inserted by the Statutory Maternity Pay (General) and Statutory Sick Pay (General) (Amendment) Regulations 2005, SI 2005/989, reg 3(1), (2).

Commissioners of Inland Revenue: a reference to the Commissioners of Inland Revenue is now to be taken as a reference to the Commissioners for Her Majesty's Revenue and Customs; see the Commissioners for Revenue and Customs Act 2005, s 50(1), (7).

[2.57]

14 Provision of information in connection with determination of questions

Any person claiming to be entitled to statutory sick pay, or any other person who is a party to proceedings arising under Part I, shall, if he receives notification from the [Commissioners of Inland Revenue] that any information is required from him for the determination of any question arising in connection therewith, furnish that information to the [Commissioners of Inland Revenue] within 10 days of receiving that notification.

NOTES

Words in square brackets substituted by virtue of the Social Security Contributions (Transfer of Functions, etc) Act 1999, s 1(2), Sch 2.

Commissioners of Inland Revenue: a reference to the Commissioners of Inland Revenue is now to be taken as a reference to the Commissioners for Her Majesty's Revenue and Customs; see the Commissioners for Revenue and Customs Act 2005, s 50(1), (7).

[2.58]

15 Provision of information by employers to employees

(1) [Subject to paragraph (1A),] in a case which falls within paragraph (a), (b) or (c) of section 18(3) (provision of information by employers in connection with the making of claims for [short-term incapacity] and other benefits), the employer shall furnish to his employee, in writing on a form approved by the Secretary of State for the purpose [or in a form in which it can be processed by equipment operating automatically in response to instructions given for that purpose], the information specified in paragraph (2), (3) or (4) below respectively within the time specified in the appropriate one of those paragraphs.

[(1A) For the purposes of paragraph (1), where, in the particular circumstances of a case, it is not practicable for the employer to furnish the information within the specified time mentioned in paragraph (2), (3), (4)(b)(ii) or (5), he shall, not later than the first pay day within the meaning of regulation 9(1) immediately following the relevant specified time, furnish the information to his employee.]

(2) In a case which falls within paragraph (a) (no period of entitlement arising in relation to a period of incapacity for work) of section 18(3)—

- (a) the information mentioned in paragraph (1) is a statement of all the reasons why, under the provisions of paragraph 1 of Schedule 1 and regulations made thereunder, a period of entitlement does not arise; and
- (b) it shall be furnished not more than 7 days after the day on which the employer is notified by or on behalf of the employee of the employee's incapacity for work on the fourth day of the period of incapacity for work.

(3) In a case which falls within paragraph (b) (period of entitlement ending but period of incapacity for work continuing) of section 18(3)—

- [[(a) the information mentioned in paragraph (1) above is a statement informing the employee of—
  - (i) the reason why the period of entitlement ended;
  - (ii) the date of the last day in respect of which the employer is or was liable to make a payment of statutory sick pay to him]; and
- (b) the statement shall be furnished not more than 7 days after the day on which the period of entitlement ended, or if earlier, on the day on which it is already required to be furnished under paragraph (4).]

(4) In a case which falls within paragraph (c) (period of entitlement expected to end before period of incapacity for work ends, on certain assumptions) of section 18(3)—

- [[(a) the information mentioned in paragraph (1) above is a statement informing the employee of—
  - (i) the reason why the period of entitlement is expected to end;
  - (ii) the date of the last day in respect of which the employer is or was expected to be liable to make a payment of statutory sick pay to him]; and
- (b) the statement shall be furnished—
  - (i) in a case where the period of entitlement is expected to end in accordance with section 3(2)(b) of the Act (maximum entitled to statutory sick pay), on or before the 42nd day before the period of entitlement is expected to end, or
  - (ii) in any other case, on or before the seventh day before the period of entitlement is expected to end,

  . . .]

(5) For the purposes of section 18(3)(c)(i) (period for which the period of incapacity for work is to be assumed to continue to run) the prescribed period shall be 14 days.

NOTES

Para (1): words in first and third pairs of square brackets inserted by the Social Security Contributions, Statutory Maternity Pay and Statutory Sick Pay (Miscellaneous Amendments) Regulations 1996, SI 1996/777, reg 2(1), (5)(a); words in second pair of square brackets substituted by the Social Security (Incapacity Benefit) (Consequential and Transitional Amendments and Savings) Regulations 1995, SI 1995/829, reg 15.

Para (1A): inserted by SI 1996/777, reg 2(1), (5)(b).

Para (3): sub-paras (a), (b) substituted by the Statutory Sick Pay (General) Amendment Regulations 1986, SI 1986/477, reg 6; sub-para (a) further substituted by the Statutory Sick Pay (General) (Amendment) Regulations 2008, SI 2008/1735, reg 2(1), (2)(a), as from 27 October 2008.

Para (4): sub-paras (a), (b) substituted by SI 1986/477, reg 6; sub-para (a) further substituted by SI 2008/1735, reg 2(1), (2)(b), as from 27 October 2008; words omitted from sub-para (b) revoked by SI 1996/777, reg 2(1), (5)(c).

"Section 18(3)": see now the Social Security Administration Act 1992, s 130(2), (3).

15A *(Inserted by the Statutory Sick Pay (General) Amendment Regulations 1986, SI 1986/477, reg 7; revoked by the Statutory Sick Pay (General) (Amendment) Regulations 2008, SI 2008/1735, reg 3, as from 27 October 2008.)*

[2.59]

16 Meaning of "employee"

(1) [Subject to paragraph (1ZA),] in a case where, and in so far as, a person . . . is treated as an employed earner by virtue of the Social Security (Categorisation of Earners) Regulations 1978, he shall be treated as an employee for the purposes of Part I and in a case where, and in so far as, such a person is treated otherwise than as an employed earner by virtue of those regulations, he shall not be treated as an employee for the purposes of Part I.

[(1ZA) Paragraph (1) shall have effect in relation to a person who—

- (a) is under the age of 16; and
- (b) would or, as the case may be, would not have been treated as an employed earner by virtue of the Social Security (Categorisation of Earners) Regulations 1978 had he been over that age,

as it has effect in relation to a person who is or, as the case may be, is not so treated.]

[(1A) Any person who is in employed earner's employment within the meaning of the Social Security Act 1975 under a contract of apprenticeship shall be treated as an employee for the purposes of Part I.]

(2) A person who is in employed earner's employment within the meaning of the Social Security Act 1975 but whose employer—

- (a) does not fulfil the conditions prescribed in regulation 119(1)(b) of the Social Security (Contributions) Regulations 1979 as to residence or presence in Great Britain, or
- (b) is a person who, by reason of any international treaty to which the United Kingdom is a party or of any international convention binding the United Kingdom—
  - (i) is exempt from the provisions of the Social Security Act 1975, or
  - (ii) is a person against whom the provisions of that Act are not enforceable,

shall not be treated as an employee for the purposes of Part I.

NOTES

Para (1): words in square brackets inserted, and words omitted revoked, by the Employment Equality (Age) Regulations 2006, SI 2006/1031, reg 49(1), Sch 8, Pt 2, paras 49, 50(1), (2).

Para (1ZA): inserted by SI 2006/1031, reg 49(1), Sch 8, Pt 2, paras 49, 50(1), (3); substituted by the Employment Equality (Age) (Consequential Amendments) Regulations 2007, SI 2007/825, reg 5(1), (3).

Para (1A): inserted by the Statutory Sick Pay (Compensation of Employers) and Miscellaneous Provisions Regulations 1983, SI 1983/376, reg 5(2).

Social Security Act 1975: see now the Social Security Contributions and Benefits Act 1992.

[2.60]

17 Meaning of "earnings"

(1) . . .

[(2) For the purposes of section 163(2) of the Contributions and Benefits Act, the expression "earnings" refers to gross earnings and includes any remuneration or profit derived from a person's employment except any payment or amount which is—

- (a) excluded [or disregarded in the calculation of a person's earnings under regulation 25, 27 or 123 of, or Schedule 3 to, the Social Security (Contributions) Regulations 2001] [(or would have been so excluded had he not been under the age of 16)];
- (b) a chargeable emolument under section 10A of the Social Security Contributions and Benefits Act 1992, except where, in consequence of such a chargeable emolument being

excluded from earnings, a person would not be entitled to statutory sick pay [(or where such a payment or amount would have been so excluded and in consequence he would not have been entitled to statutory sick pay had he not been under the age of 16)].]

[(2A) . . .]

(3) For the purposes of [section 163(2) of the Contributions and Benefits Act] the expression "earnings" includes also—

[(za) any amount retrospectively treated as earnings by regulations made by virtue of section 4B(2) of the Contributions and Benefits Act;]

(a) any sum payable by way of maternity pay or payable by the Secretary of State in pursuance of section 40 of the Employment Protection (Consolidation) Act 1978 in respect of maternity pay;

(b) any sum which is payable by the Secretary of State by virtue of section 122(3)(a) of that Act in respect of arrears of pay and which by virtue of section 42(1) of that Act is to go towards discharging a liability to pay maternity pay;

(c) any sum payable in respect of arrears of pay in pursuance of an order for re-instatement or re-engagement under that Act;

(d) any sum payable by way of pay in pursuance of an order under the Act for the continuation of a contract of employment;

(e) any sum payable by way of remuneration in pursuance of a protective award under the Employment Protection Act 1975;

(f) any sum payable to any employee under the Temporary Short-time Working Compensation Scheme administered under powers conferred by the Employment Subsidies Act 1978;

(g) any sum paid in satisfaction of any entitlement to statutory sick pay;

[(h) any sum payable by way of statutory maternity pay under Part V of the Social Security Act 1986, including sums payable in accordance with regulations made under section 46(8)(b) of that Act];

[(i) any sum payable by way of statutory paternity pay, including any sums payable in accordance with regulations made under section 171ZD(3) of the Contributions and Benefits Act;

(j) any sum payable by way of statutory adoption pay, including any sums payable in accordance with regulations made under section 171ZM(3) of the Contributions and Benefits Act].

(4), (5) . . .

NOTES

Paras (1), (4), (5): revoked by the Social Security (Miscellaneous Provisions) Amendment Regulations 1992, SI 1992/2595, reg 15.

Para (2): substituted by the Social Security Contributions, Statutory Maternity Pay and Statutory Sick Pay (Miscellaneous Amendments) Regulations 1999, SI 1999/567, reg 13; words in first pair of square brackets in sub-para (a) substituted by the Social Security, Occupational Pension Schemes and Statutory Payments (Consequential Provisions) Regulations 2007, SI 2007/1154, reg 5(1), (2); words in second pair of square brackets in sub-para (a) and words in square brackets in sub-para (b) inserted by the Employment Equality (Age) Regulations 2006, SI 2006/1031, reg 49(1), Sch 8, Pt 2, para 51.

Para (2A): inserted by the Statutory Sick Pay (Compensation of Employers) and Miscellaneous Provisions Regulations 1983, SI 1983/376, reg 5(3); revoked by SI 1992/2595, reg 15.

Para (3): words in first pair of square brackets substituted by the Social Security, Statutory Maternity Pay and Statutory Sick Pay (Miscellaneous Amendments) Regulations 2002, SI 2002/2690, reg 14(a); sub-para (za) inserted by SI 2007/1154, reg 5(1), (3); sub-para (h) added by the Statutory Sick Pay (General) Amendment (No 2) Regulations 1987, SI 1987/868, reg 4(b); sub-paras (i), (j) added by SI 2002/2690, reg 14(b).

Statutory paternity pay: the Work and Families Act 2006, s 11(2) at **[1.1411]** provides that any reference to statutory paternity pay in any instrument or document made before the commencement of paras 12 and 13 of Sch 1 to that Act (which came into force on 6 April 2010) is to be read, in relation to any time after the commencement of these provisions, as a reference to ordinary statutory paternity pay.

"Section 40 of the Employment Protection (Consolidation) Act 1978": s 40 as then in force was repealed by the Social Security Act 1986: see now the Social Security Contributions and Benefits Act 1992, Pt XII.

"Section 122(3)(a) of that Act": see now the Employment Rights Act 1996, s 184(1).

"Employment Protection Act 1975": relevant provisions are now contained in the Trade Union and Labour Relations (Consolidation) Act 1992, s 188 et seq.

"Part V of the Social Security Act 1986": see now the Social Security Contributions and Benefits Act 1992, Pt XII.

[2.61]

18 Payments to be treated or not to be treated as contractual remuneration

For the purposes of paragraph 2(1) and (2) of Schedule 2 to the Act, those things which are included within the expression "earnings" by regulation 17 (except paragraph (3)(g) thereof) shall be, and those things which are excluded from that expression by that regulation shall not be, treated as contractual remuneration.

[2.62]

19 Normal weekly earnings

(1) For the purposes of section 26(2) and (4), an employee's normal weekly earnings shall be determined in accordance with the provisions of this regulation.

(2) In this regulation—

"the critical date" means the first day of the period of entitlement in relation to which a person's normal weekly earnings fall to be determined, or, in a case to which paragraph 2(c) of Schedule 1 applies, the relevant date within the meaning of Schedule 1;

"normal pay day" means a day on which the terms of an employee's contract of service require him to be paid, or the practice in his employment is for him to be paid, if any payment is due to him; and

"day of payment" means a day on which the employee was paid.

(3) Subject to paragraph (4), the relevant period (referred to in section 26(2)) is the period between—

(a) the last normal pay day to fall before the critical date; and

(b) the last normal pay day to fall at least 8 weeks earlier than the normal pay day mentioned in sub-paragraph (a),

including the normal pay day mentioned in sub-paragraph (a) but excluding that first mentioned in sub-paragraph (b).

(4) In a case where an employee has no identifiable normal pay day, paragraph (3) shall have effect as if the words "day of payment" were substituted for the words "normal pay day" in each place where they occur.

(5) In a case where an employee has normal pay days at intervals of or approximating to one or more calendar months (including intervals of or approximating to a year) his normal weekly earnings shall be calculated by dividing his earnings in the relevant period by the number of calendar months in that period (or, if it is not a whole number, the nearest whole number), multiplying the result by 12 and dividing by 52.

(6) In a case to which paragraph (5) does not apply and the relevant period is not an exact number of weeks, the employee's normal weekly earnings shall be calculated by dividing his earnings in the relevant period by the number of days in the relevant period and multiplying the result by 7.

(7) In a case where the normal pay day mentioned in sub-paragraph (a) of paragraph (3) exists but that first mentioned in sub-paragraph (b) of that paragraph does not yet exist, the employee's normal weekly earnings shall be calculated as if the period for which all the earnings under his contract of service received by him before the critical date represented payment were the relevant period.

(8) In a case where neither of the normal pay days mentioned in paragraph (3) yet exists, the employee's normal weekly earnings shall be the remuneration to which he is entitled, in accordance with the terms of his contract of service, for, as the case may be—

(a) a week's work; or

(b) a number of calendar months' work, divided by that number of months, multiplied by 12 and divided by 52.

[2.63]

20 Treatment of one or more employers as one

(1) In a case where the earnings paid to an employee in respect of 2 or more employments are aggregated and treated as a single payment of earnings under regulation 12(1) of the Social Security (Contributions) Regulations 1979, the employers of the employee in respect of those employments shall be treated as one for all purposes of Part I.

(2) Where 2 or more employers are treated as one under the provisions of paragraph (1), liability for the statutory sick pay payable by them to the employee shall be apportioned between them in such proportions as they may agree or, in default of agreement, in the proportions which the employee's earnings from each employment bear to the amount of the aggregated earnings.

(3) [Subject to paragraphs (4) and (5)] where a contract of service ("the current contract") was preceded by a contract of service entered into between the same employer and employee ("the previous contract"), and the interval between the date on which the previous contract ceased to have effect and that on which the current contract came into force was not more than 8 weeks, then for the purposes of establishing the employee's maximum entitlement within the meaning of section 5 (limitation on entitlement to statutory sick pay in any one period of entitlement or tax year), the provisions of Part I shall not have effect as if the employer were a different employer in relation to each of those contracts of service.

[(4) Where a contract of service ("the current contract") was preceded by two or more contracts of service entered into between the same employer and employee ("the previous contracts") and the previous contracts—

(a) existed concurrently for at least part of their length, and

(b) the intervals between the dates on which each of the previous contracts ceased to have effect and that on which the current contract came into force was not more than 8 weeks,

then for the purposes of establishing the employee's maximum entitlement within the meaning of section 5 the provisions of Part I shall not have effect as if the employer were a different employer in relation to the current contract and whichever of the previous contracts was the contract by virtue of which the employer had become liable to pay the greatest proportion of statutory sick pay in respect of any tax year or period of entitlement.

(5) If, in any case to which paragraph (4) applies, the same proportion of the employer's liability for statutory sick pay becomes due under each of the previous contracts, then for the purpose of establishing the employee's maximum entitlement within the meaning of section 5, the provisions of Part I shall have effect in relation to only one of the previous contracts.]

NOTES

Words in square brackets in para (3) inserted, and paras (4), (5) added, by the Statutory Sick Pay (Compensation of Employers) and Miscellaneous Provisions Regulations 1983, SI 1983/376, reg 3(4).

[2.64]

21 Treatment of more than one contract of service as one

Where 2 or more contracts of service exist concurrently between one employer and one employee, they shall be treated as one for all purposes of Part I except where, by virtue of regulation 11 of the Social Security (Contributions) Regulations 1979, the earnings from those contracts of service are not aggregated for the purposes of earnings-related contributions.

[2.65]

[21A Election to be treated as different employers not to apply to recovery of statutory sick pay

(1) Paragraph (2) below applies for the purposes of section 159A of the Contributions and Benefits Act (power to provide for recovery by employers of sums paid by way of statutory sick pay) and of any order made under that section.

(2) Where an employer has made 2 or more elections under regulation 3 of the Income Tax (Employments) Regulations 1993 to be treated as a different employer in respect of each of the groups of employees specified in the election, the different employers covered by each of those elections shall be treated as one employer.]

NOTES

Inserted by the Statutory Sick Pay Percentage Threshold Order 1995, SI 1995/513, art 3.

22 (*Revoked by the Statutory Maternity Pay (General) and Statutory Sick Pay (General) (Amendment) Regulations 2005, SI 2005/989, reg 3(1), (3).*)

STATUTORY SICK PAY (MEDICAL EVIDENCE) REGULATIONS 1985

(SI 1985/1604)

NOTES

Made: 22 October 1985.

Authority: Social Security and Housing Benefits Act 1982, s 17(2A), as inserted by the Social Security Act 1985, s 20 (repealed). By virtue of the Social Security (Consequential Provisions) Act 1992, s 2(2), these Regulations now have effect as if made under the Social Security Administration Act 1992, s 14(2).

Commencement: 6 April 1986.

See *Harvey* BI(2)(B).

[2.66]

1 Citation, commencement and interpretation

(1) These regulations may be cited as the Statutory Sick Pay (Medical Evidence) Regulations 1985 and shall come into operation on 6th April 1986.

(2) In these regulations, unless the context otherwise requires—

["the 1992 Act" means the Social Security Administration Act 1992;

"signature" means, in relation to a statement given in accordance with these regulations, the name by which the person giving that statement is usually known (any name other than the surname being either in full or otherwise indicated) written by that person in his own handwriting; and "signed" shall be construed accordingly.

(3) . . .

NOTES

Para (2): definition "the 1992 Act" substituted for original definition "the 1982 Act" by the Social Security (Medical Evidence) and Statutory Sick Pay (Medical Evidence) (Amendment) Regulations 2010, SI 2010/137, reg 3(1), (2), as from 6 April 2010.

Para (3): revoked by the Social Security (Miscellaneous Provisions) Amendment Regulations 1992, SI 1992/247, reg 6(1), (2).

[2.67]

2 Medical information

[(1) Medical information required under section 14(1) of the 1992 Act relating to incapacity for work shall be provided either—

(a) in the form of a statement given by a doctor in accordance with the rules set out in Part 1 of Schedule 1 to these Regulations; or

(b) by such other means as may be sufficient in the circumstances of any particular case.]

(2) An employee shall not be required under [section 14(1) of the 1992 Act] to provide medical information in respect of the first 7 days in any spell of incapacity for work; and for this purpose "spell of incapacity" means a continuous period of incapacity for work which is immediately preceded by a day on which the claimant either worked or was not incapable of work.

NOTES

Para (1): substituted by the Social Security (Medical Evidence) and Statutory Sick Pay (Medical Evidence) (Amendment) Regulations 2010, SI 2010/137, reg 3(1), (3)(a), as from 6 April 2010.

Para (2): words in square brackets substituted by SI 2010/137, reg 3(1), (3)(b), as from 6 April 2010.

[SCHEDULE 1

Regulation 2(1)(a)

PART I
RULES

[2.68]

1. In these rules, unless the context otherwise requires—

"assessment" means either a consultation between a patient and a doctor which takes place in person or by telephone or a consideration by a doctor of a written report by another doctor or other health care professional;

"condition" means a specific disease or bodily or mental disability;

"doctor" means a registered medical practitioner not being the patient;

"other health care professional" means a person (other than a registered medical practitioner and not being the patient) who is a registered nurse, a registered midwife, an occupational therapist or physiotherapist registered with a regulatory body established by an Order in Council under section 60 of the Health Act 1999, or a member of any profession regulated by a body mentioned in section 25(3) of the National Health Service Reform and Health Care Professions Act 2002;

"patient" means the person in respect of whom a statement is given in accordance with these rules.

2. Where a doctor issues a statement to a patient in accordance with an obligation arising under a contract, agreement or arrangement under Part 4 of the National Health Service Act 2006 or Part 4 of the National Health Service (Wales) Act 2006 or Part 1 of the National Health Service (Scotland) Act 1978 the doctor's statement shall be in a form set out at Part 2 of this Schedule and shall be signed by that doctor.

3. Where a doctor issues a statement in any case other than in accordance with rule 2, the doctor's statement shall be in the form set out in Part 2 of this Schedule or in a form to like effect and shall be signed by the doctor attending the patient.

4. A doctor's statement must be based on an assessment made by that doctor.

5. A doctor's statement shall be completed in ink or other indelible substance and shall contain the following particulars—

(a) the patient's name;

(b) the date of the assessment (whether by consultation or consideration of a report as the case may be) on which the doctor's statement is based;

(c) the condition in respect of which the doctor advises the patient they are not fit for work;

(d) a statement, where the doctor considers it appropriate, that the patient may be fit for work;

(e) a statement that the doctor will or, as the case may be will not, need to assess the patient's fitness for work again;

(f) the date on which the doctor's statement is given;

(g) the address of the doctor,

and shall bear, opposite the words "Doctor's signature", the signature in ink of the doctor making the statement.

6. Subject to rule 8, the condition in respect of which the doctor is advising the patient is not fit for work or, as the case may be, which has caused the patient's absence from work shall be specified as precisely as the doctor's knowledge of the patient's condition at the time of the assessment permits.

7. Where a doctor considers that a patient may be fit for work the doctor shall state the reasons for that advice and where this is considered appropriate, the arrangements which the patient might make, with their employer's agreement, to return to work.

8. The condition may be specified less precisely where, in the doctor's opinion, disclosure of the precise condition would be prejudicial to the patient's well-being, or to the patient's position with their employer.

9. A doctor's statement may be given on a date after the date of the assessment on which it is based, however no further statement shall be furnished in respect of that assessment other than a doctor's statement by way of replacement of an original which has been lost, in which case it shall be clearly marked "duplicate".

10. Where, in the doctor's opinion, the patient will become fit for work on a day not later than 14 days after the date of the assessment on which the doctor's statement is based, the doctor's statement shall specify that day.

11. Subject to rules 12 and 13, the doctor's statement shall specify the minimum period for which, in the doctor's opinion, the patient will not be fit for work or, as the case may be, for which they may be fit for work.

12. The period specified shall begin on the date of the assessment on which the doctor's statement is based and shall not exceed 3 months unless the patient has, on the advice of a doctor, refrained from work for at least 6 months immediately preceding that date.

13. Where—

(a) the patient has been advised by a doctor that they are not fit for work and, in consequence, has refrained from work for at least 6 months immediately preceding the date of the assessment on which the doctor's statement is based; and

(b) in the doctor's opinion, the patient will not be fit for work for the foreseeable future,

instead of specifying a period, the doctor may, having regard to the circumstances of the particular case, enter, after the words "case for", the words "an indefinite period".]

NOTES

Commencement: 6 April 2010.

Original Schedule numbered as Sch 1 by the Social Security (Miscellaneous Provisions) Amendment Regulations 1992, SI 1992/247, reg 6(1), (4); Sch 1 subsequently substituted by the Social Security (Medical Evidence) and Statutory Sick Pay (Medical Evidence) (Amendment) Regulations 2010, SI 2010/137, reg 3(1), (4), as from 6 April 2010.

[PART II
FORM OF DOCTOR'S STATEMENT

STATEMENT OF FITNESS FOR WORK FOR SOCIAL SECURITY OR STATUTORY SICK PAY

[2.69]

Patient's name — Mr, Mrs, Miss, Ms ....

I assessed your case on: ..../..../....

and, because of the following condition(s): ....

I advise you that: ☐ you are not fit for work.

☐ you may be fit for work taking account of the following advice:

If available, and with your employer's agreement, you may benefit from:

☐ a phased return to work
☐ altered hours
☐ amended duties
☐ workplace adaptations

Comments, including functional effects of your condition(s):

....
....

This will be the case for ....

or from ..../..../.... to ..../..../....

I will/will not need to assess your fitness for work again at the end of this period.
(Please delete as applicable)

Doctor's signature ....

Date of statement ..../..../....

Doctor's address ....]

NOTES

Commencement: 6 April 2010.

Substituted as noted to Pt I of this Schedule at **[2.68]**.

SCHEDULE 1A

(Sch 1A added by the Social Security (Miscellaneous Provisions) Amendment Regulations 1992, SI 1992/247, reg 6(1), (5), Sch 2; revoked by the Social Security (Medical Evidence) and Statutory Sick Pay (Medical Evidence) (Amendment) Regulations 2010, SI 2010/137, reg 3(1), (5), as from 6 April 2010.)

Part 2 Statutory Instruments

STATUTORY MATERNITY PAY (GENERAL) REGULATIONS 1986

(SI 1986/1960)

NOTES

Made: 17 November 1986.

Authority: Social Security Act 1986, ss 46(4), (7), (8), 47(1), (3), (6), (7), 48(3), (6), 50(1), (2), (4), (5), 51(1)(g), (k), (n), (r), (4), 54(1), 83(1), 84(1), Sch 4, paras 6, 8, 12(3) (repealed apart from ss 54(1), 83(1), 84(1)). By virtue of the Social Security (Consequential Provisions) Act 1992, s 2(2), these Regulations now have effect as if made under the Social Security Contributions and Benefits Act 1992, ss 164(4), (8), (9), 165(1), (3), (7), 166(3), 171(1), (2), (5), (6), Sch 13, and the Social Security Administration Act 1992, ss 5, 132.

Commencement: 6 April 1987.

Transfer of functions: the functions of the Secretary of State conferred by regs 7, 25, 30, 31 have been transferred to the Commissioners of Inland Revenue by the Social Security Contributions (Transfer of Functions, etc) Act 1999, s 1(2), Sch 2. Note also that a reference to the Commissioners of Inland Revenue is now to be taken as a reference to the Commissioners for Her Majesty's Revenue and Customs; see the Commissioners for Revenue and Customs Act 2005, s 50(1), (7).

See *Harvey* J(2).

ARRANGEMENT OF REGULATIONS

PART I
INTRODUCTION

[2.70]

1 Citation, commencement and interpretation

(1) These regulations may be cited as the Statutory Maternity Pay (General) Regulations 1986 and shall come into operation in the case of regulations 1, 22 and 23 on 15th March 1987, and in the case of the remainder of the regulations on 6th April 1987.

(2) In these regulations, unless the context otherwise requires—

"the 1975 Act" means the Social Security Act 1975;

"the 1978 Act" means the Employment Protection (Consolidation) Act 1978;

"the 1986 Act" means the Social Security Act 1986;

["the Contributions and Benefits Act" means the Social Security Contributions and Benefits Act 1992];

["statutory maternity leave" means ordinary maternity leave and any additional maternity leave under, respectively, sections 71 and 73 of the Employment Rights Act 1996].

(3) Unless the context otherwise requires, any references in these regulations to—

(a) a numbered regulation is a reference to the regulation bearing that number in these regulations and any reference in a regulation to a numbered paragraph is a reference to the paragraph of that regulation bearing that number;

(b) any provision made by or contained in an enactment or instrument shall be construed as a reference to that provision as amended or extended by any enactment or instrument and as including a reference to any provision which it re-enacts or replaces, or which may re-enact or replace it, with or without modifications.

NOTES

Para (2): definition "the Contributions and Benefits Act" added by the Social Security (Miscellaneous Provisions) Amendment (No 2) Regulations 1992, SI 1992/2595, reg 12; definition "statutory maternity leave" added by the Statutory Maternity Pay (General) (Amendment) Regulations 2005, SI 2005/729, reg 2.

Social Security Act 1975, Social Security Act 1986: largely repealed and consolidated in the Social Security Contributions and Benefits Act 1992 and the Social Security Administration Act 1992.

Employment Protection (Consolidation) Act 1978: repealed and largely consolidated in the Trade Union and Labour Relations (Consolidation) Act 1992, the Employment Rights Act 1996 and the Employment Tribunals Act 1996.

PART II
ENTITLEMENT

[2.71]

[2 The Maternity Pay Period

(1) Subject to paragraphs (3) to (5), where—

(a) a woman gives notice to her employer of the date from which she expects his liability to pay her statutory maternity pay to begin; and

(b) in conformity with that notice ceases to work for him in a week which is later than the 12th week before the expected week of confinement,

the first day of the maternity pay period shall be the day on which she expects his liability to pay her statutory maternity pay to begin in conformity with that notice provided that day is not later than the day immediately following the day on which she is confined.

(2) The maternity pay period shall be a period of 39 consecutive weeks.

(3) In a case where a woman is confined—

(a) before the 11th week before the expected week of confinement; or

(b) after the 12th week before the expected week of confinement and the confinement occurs on a day which precedes that mentioned in a notice given to her employer as being the day on which she expects his liability to pay her statutory maternity pay to begin,

section 165 of the Contributions and Benefits Act shall have effect so that the first day of the maternity pay period shall be the day following the day on which she is so confined.

(4) In a case where a woman is absent from work wholly or partly because of pregnancy or confinement on any day—

(a) which falls on or after the beginning of the 4th week before the expected week of confinement; but

(b) not later than the day immediately following the day on which she is confined,

the first day of the maternity pay period shall be the day following the day on which she is so absent.

(5) In a case where a woman leaves her employment—

(a) at any time falling after the beginning of the 11th week before the expected week of confinement and before the start of the maternity pay period, but

(b) not later than the day on which she is confined,

the first day of the maternity pay period shall be the day following the day on which she leaves her employment.]

NOTES

Substituted by the Statutory Maternity Pay, Social Security (Maternity Allowance) and Social Security (Overlapping Benefits) (Amendment) Regulations 2006, SI 2006/2379, reg 3(1), (2).

[2.72]

3 Contract of service ended for the purpose of avoiding liability for statutory maternity pay

(1) A former employer shall be liable to make payments of statutory maternity pay to any woman who was employed by him for a continuous period of at least 8 weeks and whose contract of service with him was brought to an end by the former employer solely or mainly for the purpose of avoiding liability for statutory maternity pay.

(2) In order to determine the amount payable by the former employer—

(a) the woman shall be deemed for the purposes of Part V of the 1986 Act to have been employed by him from the date her employment with him ended until the end of the week immediately preceding the 14th week before the expected week of confinement on the same terms and conditions of employment as those subsisting immediately before her employment ended, and

(b) her normal weekly earnings for the period of 8 weeks immediately preceding the 14th week before the expected week of confinement shall for those purposes be calculated by reference to her normal weekly earnings for the period of 8 weeks ending with the last day in respect of which she was paid under her former contract of service.

NOTES

"Part V of the 1986 Act": see now the Social Security Contributions and Benefits Act 1992, Pt XII.

[2.73]

4 Modification of entitlement provisions

(1) . . .

(2) In relation to a woman in employed earner's employment who was confined before the 14th week before the expected week of confinement [section 164(2)(a) and (b) of the Contributions and Benefits Act] shall have effect as if for the conditions there set out, there was substituted the conditions that—

(a) she would but for her confinement have been in employed earner's employment with an employer for a continuous period of at least 26 weeks ending with the week immediately preceding the 14th week before the expected week of confinement, and

(b) her normal weekly earnings for the period of 8 weeks ending with the week immediately preceding the week of her confinement are not less than the lower earnings limit in force under [section 5(1)(a) of the Contributions and Benefits Act] immediately before the commencement of the week of her confinement.

[(3) In relation to a woman to whom paragraph (2) applies, section 166 of the Contributions and Benefits Act shall be modified so that subsection (2) has effect as if the reference to the period of 8 weeks immediately preceding the 14th week before the expected week of confinement was a reference to the period of 8 weeks immediately preceding the week in which her confinement occurred.]

NOTES

Para (1): revoked by the Social Security Maternity Benefits and Statutory Sick Pay (Amendment) Regulations 1994, SI 1994/1367, reg 3(1), (2).

Para (2): words in square brackets substituted by SI 1994/1367, reg 3(1), (3).

Para (3): added by the Statutory Maternity Pay (General) Amendment Regulations 1988, SI 1988/532, reg 2; substituted by SI 1994/1367, reg 3(1), (4).

"Lower earnings limit": this is currently £109 per week, as from 6 April 2013: see the Social Security (Contributions) Regulations 2001, SI 2001/1004, reg 10(a) (as amended by the Social Security (Contributions) (Limits and Thresholds) (Amendment) Regulations 2013, SI 2013/558, regs 2, 3(b)). The previous sums were: £107 (as from 6 April 2012: see the Social Security (Contributions) (Limits and Thresholds) (Amendment) Regulations 2012, SI 2012/804, regs 2, 3(b)); £102 (as from 6 April 2011; see the Social Security (Contributions) (Amendment No 2) Regulations 2011, SI 2011/940, regs 2, 3(b)).

[2.74]

5 Treatment of more than one contract of service as one

Where 2 or more contracts of service exist concurrently between one employer and one employee, they shall be treated as one for the purposes of Part V of the 1986 Act, except where, by virtue of regulation 11 of the Social Security (Contributions) Regulations 1979 the earnings from those contracts of service are not aggregated for the purposes of earnings-related contributions.

NOTES

"Part V of the 1986 Act": see now the Social Security Contributions and Benefits Act 1992, Pt XII.

[2.75]

[6 Prescribed rate of statutory maternity pay

The rate of statutory maternity pay prescribed under section 166(1)(b) of the Contributions and Benefits Act is a weekly rate of [£136.78].]

NOTES

Substituted by the Social Security, Statutory Maternity Pay and Statutory Sick Pay (Miscellaneous Amendments) Regulations 2002, SI 2002/2690, reg 3.

Sum in square brackets substituted by the Social Security Benefits Up-rating Order 2013, SI 2013/574, art 9, as from 7 April 2013 (except for the purpose of determining the rate of maternity allowance in accordance with Social Security Contributions and Benefits Act 1992, s 35A(1), for which purpose it came into force on 8 April 2013).
The previous amount was £135.45, as from 1 April 2012 and 9 April 2012 respectively (see the Social Security Benefits Up-rating Order 2012, SI 2012/780, art 10). Prior to those dates the amounts were £128.73 (see SI 2011/821, art 10), £124.88 (see SI 2010/793, art 10), £123.06 (see SI 2009/947, art 10), £117.18 (see SI 2008/632, art 10), £112.75 (see SI 2007/688, art 10) and £108.80 (see SI 2006/645, art 10).

[2.76]

7 Liability of [Commissioners of Inland Revenue] to pay statutory maternity pay

(1) Where—
- (a) an adjudicating authority has determined that an employer is liable to make payments of statutory maternity pay to a woman, and
- (b) the time for appealing against that determination has expired, and
- (c) no appeal against the determination has been lodged or leave to appeal against the determination is required and has been refused,

then for any week in respect of which the employer was liable to make payments of statutory maternity pay but did not do so, and for any subsequent weeks in the maternity pay period the liability to make those payments shall, notwithstanding section 46(3) of the 1986 Act, be that of the [Commissioners of Inland Revenue] and not the employer.

(2) In paragraph (1) adjudicating authority means, as the case may be, the Chief or any other adjudication officer, [the First-tier Tribunal or the Upper Tribunal].

(3) Liability to make payments of statutory maternity pay shall, notwithstanding section 46(3) of the 1986 Act, be a liability of the [Commissioners of Inland Revenue] and not the employer as from the week in which the employer first becomes insolvent until the end of the maternity pay period.

(4) For the purposes of paragraph (3) an employer shall be taken to be insolvent if, and only if—
- (a) in England and Wales—
  - (i) he has been adjudged bankrupt or has made a composition or arrangement with his creditors;
  - (ii) he has died and his estate falls to be administered in accordance with an order under section 421 of the Insolvency Act 1986; or
  - (iii) where an employer is a company, a winding-up order . . . is made or a resolution for voluntary winding-up is passed with respect to it [or it enters administration], or a receiver or manager of its undertaking is duly appointed, or possession is taken by or on behalf of the holders of any debentures secured by a floating charge, of any property of the company comprised in or subject to the charge or a voluntary arrangement proposed for the purposes of Part I of the Insolvency Act 1986 is approved under that Part;
- (b) in Scotland—
  - (i) an award of sequestration is made on his estate or he executes a trust deed for his creditors or enters into a composition contract;
  - (ii) he has died and a judicial factor appointed under section 11A of the Judicial Factors (Scotland) Act 1889 is required by that section to divide his insolvent estate among his creditors; or
  - (iii) where the employer is a company, a winding-up order . . . is made or a resolution for voluntary winding-up is passed with respect to it [or it enters administration] or a receiver of its undertaking is duly appointed or a voluntary arrangement proposed for the purposes of Part I of the Insolvency Act 1986 is approved under that Part.

NOTES

Regulation heading, paras (1), (3): words in square brackets substituted by virtue of the Social Security Contributions (Transfer of Functions, etc) Act 1999, s 1(2), Sch 2.

Para (2): words in square brackets substituted by the Tribunals, Courts and Enforcement Act 2007 (Transitional and Consequential Provisions) Order 2008, SI 2008/2683, art 6(1), Sch 1, para 42, as from 3 November 2008.

Para (4): words omitted revoked, and words in square brackets inserted, by the Enterprise Act 2002 (Insolvency) Order 2003, SI 2003/2096, art 5, Schedule, Pt 2, para 44, except in relation to any case where a petition for an administration order was presented before 15 September 2003.

Commissioners of Inland Revenue: a reference to the Commissioners of Inland Revenue is now to be taken as a reference to the Commissioners for Her Majesty's Revenue and Customs; see the Commissioners for Revenue and Customs Act 2005, s 50(1), (7).

"Section 46(3) of the 1986 Act": see now the Social Security Contributions and Benefits Act 1992, s 164(3).

[2.77]

8 Work after confinement

(1) Where in the week immediately preceding the 14th week before the expected week of confinement a woman had 2 or more employers but one or more of them were not liable to make payments to her of statutory maternity pay ("non-liable employer"), section 47(6) of the 1986 Act shall not apply in respect of any week after the week of confinement but within the maternity pay period in which she works only for a non-liable employer.

(2) Where after her confinement a woman—

(a) works for an employer who is not liable to pay her statutory maternity pay and is not a non-liable employer, but

(b) before the end of her maternity pay period ceases to work for that employer,

the person who before she commenced work was liable to make payments of statutory maternity pay to her shall, notwithstanding section 46 of the 1986 Act, not be liable to make such payments to her for any weeks in the maternity pay period after she ceases work.

NOTES

"Section 47(6) of the 1986 Act": see now the Social Security Contributions and Benefits Act 1992, s 165(6); as to s 46 of the 1986 Act, see now s 164 of the 1992 Act.

[2.78]

9 No liability to pay statutory maternity pay

Notwithstanding the provisions of section 46(1) of the 1986 Act, no liability to make payments of statutory maternity pay to a woman shall arise in respect of a week within the maternity pay period for any part of which she is detained in legal custody or sentenced to a term of imprisonment (except where the sentence is suspended), or of any subsequent week within that period.

NOTES

"Section 46(1) of the 1986 Act": see now the Social Security Contributions and Benefits Act 1992, s 164(1).

[2.79]

[9A Working for not more than 10 days in the Maternity Pay Period

In a case where a woman does any work under a contract of service with her employer on any day, but for not more than 10 days (whether consecutive or not), during her maternity pay period, statutory maternity pay shall continue to be payable to the employee by the employer.]

NOTES

Inserted by the Statutory Maternity Pay, Social Security (Maternity Allowance) and Social Security (Overlapping Benefits) (Amendment) Regulations 2006, SI 2006/2379, reg 3(1), (3).

[2.80]

10 Death of woman

An employer shall not be liable to make payments of statutory maternity pay in respect of a woman for any week within the maternity pay period which falls after the week in which she dies.

PART III
CONTINUOUS EMPLOYMENT AND NORMAL WORKING HOURS

[2.81]

11 Continuous employment

(1) Subject to the following provisions of this regulation, where in any week a woman is, for the whole or part of the week,—

(a) incapable of work in consequence of sickness or injury, or

(b) absent from work on account of a temporary cessation of work, or

(c) absent from work in circumstances such that, by arrangement or custom, she is regarded as continuing in the employment of her employer for all or any purpose, or

(d) absent from work wholly or partly because of pregnancy or confinement, [or]

[(e) absent from work in consequence of taking paternity leave, adoption leave or parental leave under Part 8 of the Employment Rights Act 1996,]

and returns to work for her employer after the incapacity for or absence from work, that week shall be treated for the purposes of Part V of the 1986 Act as part of a continuous period of employment with that employer, notwithstanding that no contract of service exists with that employer in respect of that week.

(2) Incapacity for work which lasts for more than 26 consecutive weeks shall not count for the purposes of paragraph (1)(a).

(3) Paragraph (1)(d) shall only apply to a woman who—

(a) has a contract of service with the same employer both before and after the confinement but not during any period of absence from work due to her confinement and the period between those contracts does not exceed 26 weeks, or

(b) returns to work in accordance with section 45(1) of the 1978 Act or in pursuance of an offer made in circumstances described in section 56A(2) of that Act after a period of absence from work wholly or partly occasioned by pregnancy or confinement.

[(3A) Where a woman who is pregnant—

(a) is an employee in an employed earner's employment in which the custom is for the employer—

(i) to offer work for a fixed period of not more than 26 consecutive weeks;

(ii) to offer work for such period on 2 or more occasions in a year for periods which do not overlap; and

(iii) to offer the work available to those persons who had worked for him during the last or a recent such period, but

(b) is absent from work—

(i) wholly or partly because of the pregnancy or her confinement, or

(ii) because of incapacity arising from some specific disease or bodily or mental disablement,

then in her case paragraph (1) shall apply as if the words "and returns to work for an employer after the incapacity for or absence from work" were omitted and paragraph (4) shall not apply.]

(4) Where a woman is employed under a contract of service for part only of the week immediately preceding the 14th week before the expected week of confinement, the whole of that week shall count in computing any period of continuous employment for the purposes of Part V of the 1986 Act.

NOTES

Para (1): word in square brackets in sub-para (d) added, and para (e) added by the Social Security, Statutory Maternity Pay and Statutory Sick Pay (Miscellaneous Amendments) Regulations 2002, SI 2002/2690, reg 4.

Para (3A): inserted by the Statutory Maternity Pay (General) Amendment Regulations 1990, SI 1990/622, reg 2.

"Part V of the 1986 Act": see now the Social Security Contributions and Benefits Act 1992, Pt XII.

"Section 45(1) of the 1978 Act": see now the Employment Rights Act 1996, s 79.

"Section 56A(2) of that Act": replaced by the Employment Rights Act 1996, s 96(3) (repealed).

[2.82]

12 Continuous employment and unfair dismissal

(1) This regulation applies to a woman in relation to whose dismissal an action is commenced which consists—

(a) of the presentation by her of a complaint under section 67(1) of the 1978 Act; or

(b) of her making a claim in accordance with a dismissals procedure agreement designated by an order under section 65 of that Act; or

(c) of any action taken by a conciliation officer under section 134(3) of that Act; [or

(d) of a decision arising out of the use of a statutory dispute resolution procedure contained in Schedule 2 to the Employment Act 2002 in a case where, in accordance with the Employment Act 2002 (Dispute Resolution) Regulations 2004, such a procedure applies].

(2) If in consequence of an action of the kind specified in paragraph (1) a woman is reinstated or re-engaged by her employer or by a successor or associated employer of that employer the continuity of her employment shall be preserved for the purposes of Part V of the 1986 Act and any week which falls within the interval beginning with the effective date of termination and ending with the date of reinstatement or re-engagement, as the case may be, shall count in the computation of her period of continuous employment.

(3) In this regulation—

"successor" and "dismissals procedure agreement" have the same meanings as in section 30(3) and (4) of the Trade Union and Labour Relations Act 1974, and

"associated employer" shall be construed in accordance with section 153(4) of the 1978 Act.

NOTES

Para (1): sub-para (d) and the word immediately preceding it inserted by the Statutory Maternity Pay (General) and Statutory Paternity Pay and Statutory Adoption Pay (General) (Amendment) Regulations 2005, SI 2005/358, reg 3.

"Section 67(1) of the 1978 Act": see now the Employment Rights Act 1996, s 111(1).

"Section 65 of that Act": see now the Employment Rights Act 1996, s 110.

"Section 134(3) of that Act": see now the Employment Tribunals Act 1996, s 18(5).

"Part V of the 1986 Act": see now the Social Security Contributions and Benefits Act 1992, Pt XII.

"Section 30(3) and (4) of the Trade Union and Labour Relations Act 1974": see now the Employment Rights Act 1996, s 235.

"Section 153(4) of the 1978 Act": see now the Employment Rights Act 1996, s 231 and the Employment Tribunals Act 1996, s 42(3).

[2.83]

13 Continuous employment and stoppages of work

(1) Where for any week or part of a week a woman does no work because there is, within the meaning of section 19 of the 1975 Act a stoppage of work due to a trade dispute at her place of employment the continuity of her employment shall, subject to paragraph (2), be treated as continuing throughout the stoppage but, subject to paragraph (3), no such week shall count in the computation of her period of employment.

(2) Subject to paragraph (3), where during the stoppage of work a woman is dismissed from her employment, the continuity of her employment shall not be treated in accordance with paragraph (1) as continuing beyond the commencement of the day she stopped work.

(3) The provisions of paragraph (1) to the extent that they provide that a week in which a stoppage of work occurred shall not count in the computation of a period of employment, and paragraph (2) shall not apply to a woman who proves that at no time did she have a direct interest in the trade dispute in question.

NOTES

"Section 19 of the 1975 Act": replaced by the Social Security Contributions and Benefits Act 1992, s 27 (repealed); see now the Jobseekers Act 1995, s 14.

[2.84]

14 Change of employer

A woman's employment shall, notwithstanding the change of employer, be treated as continuous employment with the second employer where—

(a) the employer's trade or business or an undertaking (whether or not it is an undertaking established by or under an Act of Parliament) is transferred from one person to another;

(b) by or under an Act of Parliament, whether public or local and whenever passed, a contract of employment between any body corporate and the woman is modified and some other body corporate is substituted as her employer;

(c) on the death of her employer, the woman is taken into the employment of the personal representatives or trustees of the deceased;

(d) the woman is employed by partners, personal representatives or trustees and there is a change in the partners, or, as the case may be, personal representatives or trustees;

(e) the woman is taken into the employment of an employer who is, at the time she entered his employment, an associated employer of her previous employer, and for this purpose "associated employer" shall be construed in accordance with section 153(4) of the 1978 Act;

(f) on the termination of her employment with an employer she is taken into the employment of another employer and [those employers are the governors of a school maintained by a [local authority (within the meaning of the Education Act 1996)] and that authority].

NOTES

Para (f): words in first (outer) pair of square brackets substituted by the Statutory Maternity Pay (General) Amendment Regulations 1990, SI 1990/622, reg 3; words in second (inner) pair of square brackets substituted by the Local Education Authorities and Children's Services Authorities (Integration of Functions) (Local and Subordinate Legislation) Order 2010, SI 2010/1172, art 5, Sch 3, para 11, as from 5 May 2010.

"Section 153(4) of the 1978 Act": see now the Employment Rights Act 1996, s 231 and the Employment Tribunals Act 1996, s 42(3).

[2.85]

15 Reinstatement after service with the armed forces etc

If a woman who is entitled to apply to her former employer under the Reserve Forces (Safeguard of Employment) Act 1985 enters the employment of that employer not later than the 6 month period mentioned in section 1(4)(b) of that Act, her previous period of employment with that employer (or if there was more than one such period, the last of those periods) and the period of employment beginning in the said period of 6 months shall be treated as continuous.

[2.86]

16 Normal working weeks

(1) For the purposes of section 48(5) of the 1986 Act, a woman's contract of service shall be treated as not normally involving or having involved employment for less than 16 hours weekly where she is normally employed for 16 hours or more weekly.

(2) Where a woman's relations with her employer were governed for a continuous period of at least 2 years by a contract of service which normally involved employment for not less than 16 hours weekly and this period was followed by a further period, ending with the week immediately preceding the 14th week before the expected week of confinement, in which her relations with that employer were governed by a contract of service which normally involved employment for less than 16 hours, but not less than 8 hours weekly, then her contract of service shall be treated for the purpose of section 48(5) of the 1986 Act as not normally involving or having involved employment for less than 16 hours weekly.

(3) Where a woman's relations with her employer are or were governed for a continuous period of at least 2 years by a contract of service which involved

(a) for not more than 26 weeks in that period, employment for 8 hours or more but less than 16 hours weekly, and

(b) for the whole of the remainder of that period employment for not less than 16 hours weekly,

the contract of service shall be treated for the purposes of section 48(5) of the 1986 Act as not normally involving or having involved employment for less than 16 hours weekly.

NOTES

"Section 48(5) of the 1986 Act": replaced by the Social Security Contributions and Benefits Act 1992, s 166(5) (subsequently repealed by the Maternity Allowance and Statutory Maternity Pay Regulations 1994, SI 1994/1230, reg 4(4)).

[2.87]

[16A Meaning of "week"

Where a woman has been in employed earner's employment with the same employer in each of 26 consecutive weeks (but no more than 26 weeks) ending with the week immediately preceding the 14th week before the expected week of confinement then for the purpose of determining whether that employment amounts to a continuous period of at least 26 weeks, the first of those 26 weeks shall be a period commencing on the first day of her employment with the employer and ending at midnight on the first Saturday thereafter or on that day where her first day is a Saturday.]

NOTES

Inserted by the Statutory Maternity Pay (General) Amendment Regulations 1990, SI 1990/622, reg 4.

PART IV
GENERAL PROVISIONS

[2.88]

17 Meaning of "employee"

(1) [Subject to paragraph (1A),] in a case where, and in so far as, a woman . . . is treated as an employed earner by virtue of the Social Security (Categorisation of Earners) Regulations 1978 she shall be treated as an employee for the purposes of Part V of the 1986 Act and in a case where, and in so far as, such a woman is treated otherwise than as an employed earner by virtue of those regulations, she shall not be treated as an employee for the purposes of Part V.

[(1A) Paragraph (1) shall have effect in relation to a woman who—

(a) is under the age of 16; and

(b) would or, as the case may be, would not have been treated as an employed earner by virtue of the Social Security (Categorisation of Earners) Regulations 1978 had she been over that age,

as it has effect in relation to a woman who is, or, as the case may be, is not so treated.]

(2) Any woman who is in employed earner's employment within the meaning of the 1975 Act under a contract of apprenticeship shall be treated as an employee for the purposes of Part V.

(3) A woman who is in employed earner's employment within the meaning of the 1975 Act but whose employer—

(a) does not fulfil the conditions prescribed in regulation 119(1)(b) of the Social Security (Contributions) Regulations 1979 as to residence or presence in Great Britain, or

(b) is a woman who, by reason of any international treaty to which the United Kingdom is a party or of any international convention binding the United Kingdom—

(i) is exempt from the provisions of the 1975 Act, or

(ii) is a woman against whom the provisions of that Act are not enforceable,

shall not be treated as an employee for the purposes of Part V of the 1986 Act.

NOTES

Para (1): words in square brackets inserted, and words omitted revoked, by the Employment Equality (Age) Regulations 2006, SI 2006/1031, reg 49(1), Sch 8, Pt 2, paras 52, 53(1), (2).

Para (1A): inserted by SI 2006/1031, reg 49(1), Sch 8, Pt 2, paras 52, 53(1), (3); substituted by the Employment Equality (Age) (Consequential Amendments) Regulations 2007, SI 2007/825, reg 6.

"Part V of the 1986 Act": see now the Social Security Contributions and Benefits Act 1992, Pt XII.

[2.89]

18 Treatment of two or more employers as one

(1) In a case where the earnings paid to a woman in respect of 2 or more employments are aggregated and treated as a single payment of earnings under regulation 12(1) of the Social Security (Contributions) Regulations 1979, the employers of the woman in respect of those employments shall be treated as one for all purposes of Part V of the 1986 Act.

(2) Where 2 or more employers are treated as one under the provisions of paragraph (1), liability for statutory maternity pay payable by them to a woman shall be apportioned between them in such proportions as they may agree or, in default of agreement, in the proportions which the woman's earnings from each employment bear to the amount of the aggregated earnings.

NOTES

"Part V of the 1986 Act": see now the Social Security Contributions and Benefits Act 1992, Pt XII.

[2.90]

19 Payments to be treated as contractual remuneration

For the purposes of paragraph 12(1) and (2) of Schedule 4 to the 1986 Act, the payments which are to be treated as contractual remuneration are sums payable under the contract of service—

(a) by way of remuneration;
(b) for incapacity for work due to sickness or injury, and
(c) by reason of pregnancy or confinement.

NOTES

"1986 Act, Sch 4, para 12": see now the Social Security Contributions and Benefits Act 1992, Sch 13, para 3.

[2.91]

20 Meaning of "earnings"

(1) . . .

[(2) For the purposes of section 171(4) of the Contributions and Benefits Act, the expression "earnings" refers to gross earnings and includes any remuneration or profit derived from a woman's employment except any payment or amount which is—

(a) excluded [or disregarded in the calculation of a person's earnings under regulation 25, 27 or 123 of, or Schedule 3 to, the Social Security (Contributions) Regulations 2001] (payments to be disregarded and payments to directors to be disregarded respectively) [(or would have been so excluded had she not been under the age of 16)];
(b) a chargeable emolument under section 10A of the Social Security Contributions and Benefits Act 1992, except where, in consequence of such a chargeable emolument being excluded from earnings, a woman would not be entitled to statutory maternity pay [(or where such a payment or amount would have been so excluded and in consequence she would not have been entitled to statutory maternity pay had she not been under the age of 16)].]

(3) . . .

(4) For the purposes of [section 171(4) of the Contributions and Benefits Act] the expression "earnings" includes also—

[(za) any amount retrospectively treated as earnings by regulations made by virtue of section 4B(2) of the Contributions and Benefits Act;]
(a) any sum payable in respect of arrears of pay in pursuance of an order for reinstatement or re-engagement under the 1978 Act;
(b) any sum payable by way of pay in pursuance of an order under the 1978 Act for the continuation of a contract of employment;
(c) any sum payable by way of remuneration in pursuance of a protective award under the Employment Protection Act 1975;
(d) any sum payable by way of statutory sick pay, including sums payable in accordance with regulations made under section 1(5) of the Social Security and Housing Benefits Act 1982;
[(e) any sum payable by way of statutory maternity pay, including sums payable in accordance with regulations made under section 164(9)(b) of the Contributions and Benefits Act;
(f) any sum payable by way of statutory paternity pay, including sums payable in accordance with regulations made under section 171ZD(3) of the Contributions and Benefits Act;

(g) any sum payable by way of statutory adoption pay, including sums payable in accordance with regulations made under section 171ZM(3) of the Contributions and Benefits Act].

(5), (6) . . .

NOTES

Paras (1), (3), (5), (6): revoked by the Social Security (Miscellaneous Provisions) Amendment (No 2) Regulations 1992, SI 1992/2595, reg 13(1), (2), (4).

Para (2): substituted by the Social Security Contributions, Statutory Maternity Pay and Statutory Sick Pay (Miscellaneous Amendments) Regulations 1999, SI 1999/567, reg 12; words in first pair of square brackets in sub-para (a) substituted by the Social Security, Occupational Pension Schemes and Statutory Payments (Consequential Provisions) Regulations 2007, SI 2007/1154, reg 4(1), (2); words in second pair of square brackets in sub-para (a) and words in square brackets in sub-para (b) inserted by the Employment Equality (Age) Regulations 2006, SI 2006/1031, reg 49(1), Sch 8, Pt 2, paras 52, 54.

Para (4): words in first pair of square brackets substituted by the Social Security, Statutory Maternity Pay and Statutory Sick Pay (Miscellaneous Amendments) Regulations 2002, SI 2002/2690, reg 5(a); sub-para (za) inserted by SI 2007/1154, reg 4(1), (3); paras (e)–(g) added by reg 5(b) of the 2002 Regulations.

Statutory paternity pay: the Work and Families Act 2006, s 11(2) at **[1.1411]** provides that any reference to statutory paternity pay in any instrument or document made before the commencement of paras 12 and 13 of Sch 1 to that Act (which came into force on 6 April 2010) is to be read, in relation to any time after the commencement of these provisions, as a reference to ordinary statutory paternity pay.

"Protective award under the Employment Protection Act 1975": see now the Trade Union and Labour Relations (Consolidation) Act 1992, ss 189–191.

"Section 1(5) of the Social Security and Housing Benefits Act 1982": see now the Social Security Contributions and Benefits Act 1992, s 151(4)–(6).

[2.92]

21 Normal weekly earnings

(1) For the purposes of [Part XII of the Contributions and Benefits Act], a woman's normal weekly earnings shall be calculated in accordance with the following provisions of this regulation.

(2) In this regulation—

"the appropriate date" means the first day of the 14th week before the expected week of confinement, or the first day in the week in which the woman is confined, whichever is the earlier, . . .

"normal pay day" means a day on which the terms of a woman's contract of service require her to be paid, or the practice in her employment is for her to be paid, if any payment is due to her; and

"day of payment" means a day on which the woman was paid.

(3) Subject to paragraph (4), the relevant period for the purposes of [section 171(4) of the Contributions and Benefits Act] is the period between—

(a) the last normal pay day to fall before the appropriate date; and

(b) the last normal pay day to fall at least 8 weeks earlier than the normal pay day mentioned in sub-paragraph (a),

including the normal pay day mentioned in sub-paragraph (a) but excluding that first mentioned in sub-paragraph (b).

(4) In a case where a woman has no identifiable normal pay day, paragraph (3) shall have effect as if the words "day of payment" were substituted for the words "normal pay day" in each place where they occur.

(5) In a case where a woman has normal pay days at intervals of or approximating to one or more calendar months (including intervals of or approximating to a year) her normal weekly earnings shall be calculated by dividing her earnings in the relevant period by the number of calendar months in that period (or, if it is not a whole number, the nearest whole number), multiplying the result by 12 and dividing by 52.

(6) In a case to which paragraph (5) does not apply and the relevant period is not an exact number of weeks, the woman's normal weekly earnings shall be calculated by dividing her earnings in the relevant period by the number of days in the relevant period and multiplying the result by 7.

[(7) In any case where—

(a) a woman is awarded a pay increase (or would have been awarded such an increase had she not then been absent on statutory maternity leave); and

(b) that pay increase applies to the whole or any part of the period between the beginning of the relevant period and the end of her period of statutory maternity leave,

her normal weekly earnings shall be calculated as if such an increase applied in each week of the relevant period.]

NOTES

Paras (1), (3): words in square brackets substituted by the Social Security Maternity Benefits and Statutory Sick Pay (Amendment) Regulations 1994, SI 1994/1367, reg 5(1), (2), (4).

Para (2): words omitted revoked by SI 1994/1367, reg 5(1), (3).

Para (7): added by the Statutory Maternity Pay (General) Amendment Regulations 1996, SI 1996/1335, reg 2, and substituted by the Statutory Maternity Pay (General) (Amendment) Regulations 2005, SI 2005/729, reg 3.

21A *(Inserted by the Statutory Maternity Pay (General) Amendment Regulations 1988, SI 1988/532, reg 3; revoked by the Social Security, Statutory Maternity Pay and Statutory Sick Pay (Miscellaneous Amendments) Regulations 2002, SI 2002/2690, reg 6.)*

[2.93]
[21B Effect of maternity allowance on statutory maternity pay
Where a woman, in any week which falls within the maternity pay period, is—
(a) in receipt of maternity allowance pursuant to the provisions of sections 35 and 35A of the Contributions and Benefits Act; and
(b) entitled to receive statutory maternity pay in consequence of[—
(i) receiving a pay increase referred to in regulation 21(7), or
(ii) being treated as having been paid retrospective earnings under regulation 20(4)(za)],
the employer shall not be liable to make payments of statutory maternity pay in respect of such a week unless, and to the extent by which, the rate of statutory maternity pay exceeds the rate of maternity allowance received by her in that week.]

NOTES
Inserted by the Statutory Maternity Pay (General) Amendment Regulations 1996, SI 1996/1335, reg 3, and substituted by the Statutory Maternity Pay (General) (Amendment) Regulations 2005, SI 2005/729, reg 4.
Sub-paras (b)(i), (ii) substituted by the Social Security, Occupational Pension Schemes and Statutory Payments (Consequential Provisions) Regulations 2007, SI 2007/1154, reg 4(1), (4).

PART V
ADMINISTRATION

[2.94]
22 Evidence of expected week of confinement or of confinement
(1) A woman shall in accordance with the following provisions of this regulation, provide the person who is liable to pay her statutory maternity pay with evidence as to—
(a) the week in which the expected date of confinement occurs, and
(b) where her entitlement to statutory maternity pay depends upon the fact of her confinement, the week in which she was confined.
(2) For the purpose of paragraph (1)(b) a certificate of birth shall be sufficient evidence that the woman was confined in the week in which the birth occurred.
(3) The evidence shall be submitted to the person who will be liable to make payments of statutory maternity pay not later than the end of the third week of the maternity pay period so however that where the woman has good cause the evidence may be submitted later than that date but not later than the end of the 13th week of the maternity pay period.
(4) For the purposes of paragraph (3) evidence contained in an envelope which is properly addressed and sent by prepaid post shall be deemed to have been submitted on the day on which it was posted.

[2.95]
23 Notice of absence from work
(1) Where a woman is confined before the beginning of the 14th week before the expected week of confinement, she shall be entitled to payments of statutory maternity pay only if—
(a) she gives notice to the person who will be liable to pay it [of the date on which she was confined], and
(b) that notice is given within [28 days] of the date she was confined or if in the particular circumstances that is not practicable, as soon as is reasonably practicable thereafter; and
(c) where the person so requests, the notice is in writing.
(2) Where a woman is confined before the date stated in a notice provided in accordance with [section 164(4) of the Contributions and Benefits Act] as being the date her absence from work is due to begin, she shall be entitled to payments of statutory maternity pay only if—
(a) she gives a further notice to the person who will be liable to pay it specifying the date she was confined and the date her absence from work . . . began, and
(b) that further notice is given within [28 days] of the date she was confined or if in the particular circumstances that is not practicable, as soon as is reasonably practicable thereafter; and
(c) where the person so requests, the notice is in writing.
(3) For the purposes of this regulation, a notice contained in an envelope which is properly addressed and sent by prepaid post shall be deemed to be given on the date on which it is posted.

[(4) Subject to paragraph (5), section 164(4) of the Contributions and Benefits Act (statutory maternity pay-entitlement and liability to pay) shall not have effect in the case of a woman who leaves her employment with the person who will be liable to pay her statutory maternity pay after the beginning of the week immediately preceding the 14th week before the expected week of confinement.]

[(5) A woman who is exempted from section 164(4) of the Contributions and Benefits Act by paragraph (4) but who is confined before the 11th week before the expected week of confinement shall only be entitled to statutory maternity pay if she gives the person who will be liable to pay it notice specifying the date she was confined.]

NOTES

Para (1): words in square brackets substituted by the Social Security, Statutory Maternity Pay and Statutory Sick Pay (Miscellaneous Amendments) Regulations 2002, SI 2002/2690, reg 6(1), (2).

Para (2): words in first pair of square brackets substituted by the Social Security Maternity Benefits and Statutory Sick Pay (Amendment) Regulations 1994, SI 1994/1367, reg 6(1), (2); words omitted revoked, and words in second pair of square brackets substituted, by SI 2002/2690, reg 6(1), (3).

Para (4): substituted by SI 2002/2690, reg 6(1), (4).

Para (5): substituted by SI 1994/1367, reg 6(1), (3).

[2.96]

24 Notification of employment after confinement

A woman who after the date of confinement but within the maternity pay period commences work in employed earner's employment with a person who is not liable to make payments of statutory maternity pay to her and is not a non-liable employer for the purposes of regulation 8(1), shall within 7 days of the day she commenced work inform any person who is so liable of the date she commenced work.

[2.97]

25 Provision of information in connection with determination of questions

Any woman claiming to be entitled to statutory maternity pay, or any other person who is a party to proceedings arising under the 1986 Act relating to statutory maternity pay, shall, if she receives notification from the [Commissioners of Inland Revenue] that any information is required from her for the determination of any question arising in connection therewith, furnish that information to the [Commissioners of Inland Revenue] within 10 days of receiving that notification.

NOTES

Words in square brackets substituted by virtue of the Social Security Contributions (Transfer of Functions, etc) Act 1999, s 1(2), Sch 2.

Commissioners of Inland Revenue: a reference to the Commissioners of Inland Revenue is now to be taken as a reference to the Commissioners for Her Majesty's Revenue and Customs; see the Commissioners for Revenue and Customs Act 2005, s 50(1), (7).

[2.98]

[25A Provision of information relating to claims for certain other benefits

(1) Where an employer who has been given notice in accordance with [section 164(4)(a) or (9)(ea) of the Contributions and Benefits Act] or regulation 23 by a woman who is or has been an employee—

(a) decides that he has no liability to make payments of statutory maternity pay to her, or

(b) has made one or more payments of statutory maternity pay to her but decides, before the end of the maternity pay period and for a reason specified in paragraph (3), that he has no liability to make further payments to her,

then, in connection with the making of a claim by the woman for a maternity allowance[, incapacity benefit or an employment and support allowance], he shall furnish her with the information specified in the following provisions of this regulation.

(2) Where the employer decides he has no liability to make payments of statutory maternity pay to the woman, he shall furnish her with details of the decision and the reasons for it.

(3) Where the employer decides he has no liability to make further payments of statutory maternity pay to the woman because . . . she has within the maternity pay period been detained in legal custody or sentenced to a term of imprisonment which was not suspended, . . . he shall furnish her with—

(a) details of his decision and the reasons for it; and

(b) details of the last week in respect of which a liability to pay statutory maternity pay arose and the total number of weeks within the maternity pay period in which such a liability arose.

(4) The employer shall—

(a) return to the woman any maternity certificate provided by her in support of the notice referred to in paragraph (1); and

Part 2 Statutory Instruments

(b) comply with any requirements imposed by the preceding provisions of this regulation—
 (i) in a case to which paragraph (2) applies, within 7 days of the decision being made, or, if earlier, within [28 days] of the day the woman gave notice of her intended absence or of her confinement if that had occurred; or
 (ii) in a case to which paragraph (3) refers, within 7 days of being notified of the woman's detention or sentence . . .

(5) In this regulation, "incapacity benefit" means [incapacity benefit] or a severe disablement allowance.]

NOTES

Inserted by the Statutory Maternity Pay (General) Amendment Regulations 1990, SI 1990/622, reg 7.

Para (1): words in first pair of square brackets substituted by the Social Security, Statutory Maternity Pay and Statutory Sick Pay (Miscellaneous Amendments) Regulations 2002, SI 2002/2690, reg 8(1), (2); words in second pair of square brackets substituted by the Employment and Support Allowance (Consequential Provisions) (No 2) Regulations 2008, SI 2008/1554, reg 46, as from 27 October 2008.

Para (3): words omitted revoked by SI 2002/2690, reg 8(1), (3).

Para (4): words in square brackets substituted, and words omitted revoked, by SI 2002/2690, reg 8(1), (4).

Para (5): words in square brackets substituted by the Social Security (Incapacity Benefit) (Consequential and Transitional Amendments and Savings) Regulations 1995, SI 1995/829, reg 18(1), (3).

[2.99]

26 Records to be maintained by employers

(1) Every employer shall maintain for 3 years after the end of the tax year in which the maternity pay period ends a record in relation to any woman who is or was an employee of his of—
 (a) the date of the first day of absence from work wholly or partly because of pregnancy or confinement as notified by her and, if different, the date of the first day when such absence commenced;
 (b) the weeks in that tax year in which statutory maternity pay was paid and the amount paid in each week; and
 (c) any week in that tax year which was within her maternity pay period but for which no payment of statutory maternity pay was made to her and the reasons no payment was made.

(2) Except where he was not liable to make a payment of statutory maternity pay and subject to paragraphs (3) and (4), every employer shall retain for 3 years after the end of the tax year in which the maternity pay period ends any medical certificate or other evidence relating to the expected week of confinement, or as the case may be, the confinement which was provided to him by a woman who is or was an employee of his.

(3) Where an employer returns a medical certificate to an employee of his for the purpose of enabling her to make a claim for benefit under the 1975 Act, it shall be sufficient for the purposes of paragraph (2) if he retains a copy of that certificate.

(4) An employer shall not retain any certificate of birth provided to him as evidence of confinement by a woman who is or was an employee of his, but shall retain a record of the date of birth.

[2.100]

[26A Production of employer's records

(1) An authorised officer of the Commissioners of Inland Revenue may by notice require an employer to produce to him at the place of keeping such records as are in the employer's possession or power and as (in the officer's reasonable opinion) contain, or may contain, information relevant to satisfy him that statutory maternity pay has been paid and is being paid in accordance with these regulations to employees or former employees who are entitled to it.

(2) A notice referred to in paragraph (1) shall be in writing and the employer shall produce the records referred to in that paragraph within 30 days after the date of such a notice.

(3) The production of records in pursuance of this regulation shall be without prejudice to any lien which a third party may have in respect of those records.

(4) References in this regulation to "records" means—
 (a) any wage sheet or deductions working sheet; or
 (b) any other document which relates to the calculation or payment of statutory maternity pay to his employees or former employees,

whether kept in written form, electronically, or otherwise.

(5) In paragraph (1), "place of keeping" means such place in Great Britain that an employer and an authorised officer may agree upon, or, in the absence of such agreement—
 (a) any place in Great Britain where records referred to in paragraph (1) are normally kept; or
 (b) if there is no such place, the employer's principal place of business in Great Britain.]

NOTES

Inserted by the Statutory Maternity Pay (General) and Statutory Sick Pay (General) (Amendment) Regulations 2005, SI 2005/989, reg 2(1), (2).

Commissioners of Inland Revenue: a reference to the Commissioners of Inland Revenue is now to be taken as a reference to the Commissioners for Her Majesty's Revenue and Customs; see the Commissioners for Revenue and Customs Act 2005, s 50(1), (7).

PART VI
PAYMENT

[2.101]
27 Payment of statutory maternity pay

Payment of statutory maternity pay may be made in a like manner to payments of remuneration but shall not include payments in kind or by way of the provision of board or lodgings or of services or other facilities.

[2.102]
[28 Rounding to avoid fractional amounts

Where any payment of statutory maternity pay is paid for any week or part of a week and the amount due includes a fraction of a penny, the payment shall be rounded up to the next whole number of pence.]

NOTES

Substituted by the Statutory Maternity Pay, Social Security (Maternity Allowance) and Social Security (Overlapping Benefits) (Amendment) Regulations 2006, SI 2006/2379, reg 3(1), (4).

[2.103]
29 Time when statutory maternity pay is to be paid

(1) In this regulation, "pay day" means a day on which it has been agreed, or it is the normal practice between an employer or former employer and a woman who is or was an employee of his, that payments by way of remuneration are to be made, or, where there is no such agreement or normal practice, the last day of a calendar month.

(2) In any case where—
- (a) a decision has been made by an adjudication officer, appeal tribunal or Commissioner in proceedings under Part III of the 1975 Act as a result of which a woman is entitled to an amount of statutory maternity pay; and
- (b) the time for bringing an appeal against the decision has expired and either—
  - (i) no such appeal has been brought; or
  - (ii) such an appeal has been brought and has been finally disposed of,

that amount of statutory maternity pay shall be paid within the time specified in paragraph (3).

(3) Subject to paragraphs (4) and (5), the employer or former employer shall pay the amount not later than the first pay day after—
- (a) where an appeal has been brought, the day on which the employer or former employer receives notification that it has been finally disposed of;
- (b) where leave to appeal has been refused and there remains no further opportunity to apply for leave, the day on which the employer or former employer receives notification of the refusal; and
- (c) in any other case, the day on which the time for bringing an appeal expires.

(4) Subject to paragraph (5), where it is impracticable, in view of the employer's or former employer's methods of accounting for and paying remuneration, for the requirement of payment referred to in paragraph (3) to be met by the pay day referred to in that paragraph, it shall be met not later than the next following pay day.

(5) Where the employer or former employer would not have remunerated the woman for her work in the week in question as early as the pay day specified in paragraph (3) or (if it applies) paragraph (4), the requirement of payment shall be met on the first day on which the woman would have been remunerated for her work in that week.

[2.104]
30 Payments by the [Commissioners of Inland Revenue]

Where the [Commissioners of Inland Revenue become] liable in accordance with regulation 7 to make payments of statutory maternity pay to a woman, the first payment shall be made as soon as reasonably practicable after he becomes so liable, and payments thereafter shall be made at weekly intervals, by means of an instrument of payment or by such other means as appears to the [Commissioners of Inland Revenue] to be appropriate in the circumstances of any particular case.

NOTES

Words in square brackets substituted by virtue of the Social Security Contributions (Transfer of Functions, etc) Act 1999, s 1(2), Sch 2.

Commissioners of Inland Revenue: a reference to the Commissioners of Inland Revenue is now to be taken as a reference to the Commissioners for Her Majesty's Revenue and Customs; see the Commissioners for Revenue and Customs Act 2005, s 50(1), (7).

[2.105]

31 Persons unable to act

(1) Where in the case of any woman—

(a) statutory maternity pay is payable to her or she is alleged to be entitled to it;

(b) she is unable for the time being to act; and

(c) either—

(i) no receiver has been appointed by the Court of Protection with power to receive statutory maternity pay on her behalf, or

(ii) in Scotland, her estate is not being administered by any tutor, curator or other guardian acting or appointed in terms of law,

the [Commissioners of Inland Revenue] may, upon written application to him by a person who, if a natural person, is over the age of 18, appoint that person to exercise, on behalf of the woman any right to which she may be entitled under Part V of the 1986 Act and to deal on her behalf with any sums payable to her.

(2) Where the [Commissioners of Inland Revenue have] made an appointment under paragraph (1)—

(a) [they] may at any time in [their] absolute discretion revoke it;

(b) the person appointed may resign his office after having given one month's notice in writing to the [Commissioners of Inland Revenue] of his intention to do so; and

(c) the appointment shall terminate when the [Commissioners of Inland Revenue are] notified that a receiver or other person to whom paragraph (1)(c) applies has been appointed.

(3) Anything required by Part V of the 1986 Act to be done by or to any woman who is unable to act may be done by or to the person appointed under this regulation to act on her behalf, and the receipt of the person so appointed shall be a good discharge to the woman's employer or former employer for any sum paid.

NOTES

Paras (1), (2): words in square brackets substituted by virtue of the Social Security Contributions (Transfer of Functions, etc) Act 1999, s 1(2), Sch 2.

Commissioners of Inland Revenue: a reference to the Commissioners of Inland Revenue is now to be taken as a reference to the Commissioners for Her Majesty's Revenue and Customs; see the Commissioners for Revenue and Customs Act 2005, s 50(1), (7).

"Part V of the 1986 Act": see now the Social Security Contributions and Benefits Act 1992, Pt XII.

32 *(Reg 32 (Pt V) revoked by the Statutory Maternity Pay (General) and Statutory Sick Pay (General) (Amendment) Regulations 2005, SI 2005/989, reg 2(1), (3).)*

STATUTORY MATERNITY PAY (MEDICAL EVIDENCE) REGULATIONS 1987

(SI 1987/235)

NOTES

Made: 19 February 1987.

Authority: Social Security Act 1986, ss 49 (repealed), 84(1), Sch 4, para 6 (repealed). These Regulations now have effect as if made under the Social Security Administration Act 1992, s 15(1), by virtue of the Social Security (Consequential Provisions) Act 1992, s 2(2).

Commencement: 15 March 1987.

See *Harvey* J(2).

[2.106]

1 Citation, commencement and interpretation

(1) These regulations may be cited as the Statutory Maternity Pay (Medical Evidence) Regulations 1987 and shall come into force on 15th March 1987.

(2) In these regulations, unless the context otherwise requires—

"the Act" means the Social Security Act 1986;

["registered midwife" means a midwife who is registered as a midwife with the Nursing and Midwifery Council under the Nursing and Midwifery Order 2001;]

"doctor" means a registered medical practitioner;

[. . .]

"signature" means, in relation to any statement or certificate given in accordance with these regulations, the name by which the person giving that statement or certificate, as the case may be, is usually known (any name other than the surname being either in full or otherwise indicated) written by that person in his own handwriting; and "signed" shall be construed accordingly.

NOTES

Para (2): definition "registered midwife" substituted by the Nursing and Midwifery Order 2001 (Consequential Amendments) Order 2002, SI 2002/881, art 2, Schedule, para 2; definition "Primary Care Trust" inserted by the National Health Service Reform and Health Care Professions Act 2002 (Supplementary, Consequential etc Provisions) Regulations 2002, SI 2002/2469, reg 11, Sch 8 and revoked by the National Treatment Agency (Abolition) and the Health and Social Care Act 2012 (Consequential, Transitional and Saving Provisions) Order 2013, SI 2013/235, art 11, Sch 2, Pt 1, para 9(1), (2), as from 1 April 2013.

Social Security Act 1986: largely repealed and consolidated in the Social Security Contributions and Benefits Act 1992 and the Social Security Administration Act 1992.

[2.107]

2 Evidence of pregnancy and confinement

The evidence as to pregnancy and the expected date of confinement which a woman is required to provide to a person who is liable to pay her statutory maternity pay shall be furnished in the form of a maternity certificate given by a doctor or by a registered midwife, not earlier than the beginning of the [20th week] before the expected week of confinement, in accordance with the rules set out in Part I of the Schedule to these regulations—

(a) in the appropriate form as set out in Part II of that Schedule, or
(b) in a form substantially to the like effect with such variations as the circumstances may require.

NOTES

Words in square brackets substituted by the Social Security (Medical Evidence) and Statutory Maternity Pay (Medical Evidence) (Amendment) Regulations 2001, SI 2001/2931, reg 3(1), (2).

SCHEDULE

Regulation 2

PART I
RULES

[2.108]

1. In these rules any reference to a woman is a reference to the woman in respect of whom a maternity certificate is given in accordance with these rules.

2. A maternity certificate shall be given by a doctor or registered midwife attending the woman and shall not be given by the woman herself.

3. The maternity certificate shall be on a form provided by the Secretary of State for the purpose and the wording shall be that set out in the appropriate part of the form specified in Part II of this Schedule.

4. Every maternity certificate shall be completed in ink or other indelible substance and shall contain the following particulars—

(a) the woman's name;
(b) the week in which the woman is expected to be confined or, if the maternity certificate is given after confinement, the date of that confinement and the date the confinement was expected to take place . . . ;
(c) the date of the examination on which the maternity certificate is based;
(d) the date on which the maternity certificate is signed; and
[(e) the address of the doctor or where the maternity certificate is signed by a registered midwife the personal identification number given to her on her registration in . . . the register maintained by the Nursing and Midwifery Council [("NMC") under article 5 of] the Nursing and Midwifery Order 2001 and the expiry date of that registration,]

and shall bear opposite the word "Signature", the signature of the person giving the maternity certificate written after there has been entered on the maternity certificate the woman's name and the expected date or, as the case may be, the date of the confinement.

5. After a maternity certificate has been given, no further maternity certificate based on the same examination shall be furnished other than a maternity certificate by way of replacement of an original which has been lost or mislaid, in which case it shall be clearly marked "duplicate".

NOTES

Para 4: words omitted from sub-para (b) revoked by the Social Security (Miscellaneous Provisions) Amendment Regulations 1991, SI 1991/2284, reg 23; sub-para (e) substituted by the Nursing and Midwifery Order 2001 (Consequential Amendments) Order 2002, SI 2002/881, art 2, Schedule, para 3; words omitted from sub-para (e) revoked, and words in square brackets in that paragraph substituted, by the Health Act 1999 (Consequential Amendments) (Nursing and Midwifery) Order 2004, SI 2004/1771, art 3, Schedule, Pt 2, para 51(a).

[PART II
FORM OF CERTIFICATE

MATERNITY CERTIFICATE

[2.109]

Please fill in this form in ink

Name of patient . . . .

Fill in this part if you are giving the certificate before the confinement. *Do not fill this in more [than 20 weeks] before the week the baby is expected.*	*Fill in this part if you are giving the certificate after the confinement.*
I certify that I examined you on the date given below. In my opinion you can expect to have your baby in the week that includes . . . ./. . . . ./ . . . . *Weeks means a period of 7 days starting on a Sunday and ending on a Saturday*	I certify that I attended you in connection with the birth which took place on . . . . /. . . . . / . . . . when you were delivered of a child [ ] children. In my opinion your baby was expected in the week that includes. . . . . / . . . ./. . . . .
Date of examination. . . . . / . . . ./.	Registered midwives
Date of signing. . . . . / . . . ./.	Please give your [NMC] Personal Identification Number and the expiry date of your registration with the [NMC].
Signature.	. . . .
	Doctors
	Please stamp your name and address here [(unless the form has been stamped, in Wales, by the Local Health Board in whose medical performers list you are included or, in Scotland,] [by the Health Board in whose primary medical services performers list you are included)]
	. . . .

NOTES

Substituted by the Social Security (Miscellaneous Provisions) Amendment Regulations 1991, SI 1991/2284, reg 24.

Words in square brackets in the left column substituted by the Social Security (Medical Evidence) and Statutory Maternity Pay (Medical Evidence) (Amendment) Regulations 2001, SI 2001/2931, reg 3(1), (3); "NMC" in square brackets in both places it occurs in the right column substituted by the Health Act 1999 (Consequential Amendments) (Nursing and Midwifery) Order 2004, SI 2004/1771, art 3, Schedule, Pt 2, para 51(b); words in penultimate pair of square brackets in the right hand column substituted by the National Treatment Agency (Abolition) and the Health and Social Care Act 2012 (Consequential, Transitional and Saving Provisions) Order 2013, SI 2013/235, art 11, Sch 2, Pt 1, para 9(1), (3), as from 1 April 2013; final words in square brackets in the right column substituted, in relation to England and Scotland, by the General Medical Services and Personal Medical Services Transitional and Consequential Provisions Order 2004, SI 2004/865, art 119, Sch 1, para 5, and in relation to Wales by the General Medical Services Transitional and Consequential Provisions (Wales) (No 2) Order 2004, SI 2004/1016, art 95, Sch 1, para 5.

HEALTH AND SAFETY INFORMATION FOR EMPLOYEES REGULATIONS 1989

(SI 1989/682)

NOTES

Made: 18 April 1989.

Authority: Health and Safety at Work etc Act 1974, s 15(1), (2), (3)(a), (4)(a), (5)(b), (6)(b), Sch 3, para 15(1).

Commencement: 18 October 1989.

See *Harvey* NI(13).

ARRANGEMENT OF REGULATIONS

[2.110]

1 Citation and commencement

These Regulations may be cited as the Health and Safety Information for Employees Regulations 1989 and shall come into force on 18th October 1989.

[2.111]

2 Interpretation and application

(1) In these Regulations, unless the context otherwise requires—

"the 1974" Act means the Health and Safety at Work etc Act 1974;

["the 1995 Order" means the Health and Safety at Work etc Act 1974 (Application outside Great Britain) Order 1995;]

"the approved poster" and "the approved leaflet" have the meanings assigned by regulation 3;

"employment medical advisory service" means the employment medical advisory service referred to in section 55 of the 1974 Act;

"ship" has the meaning assigned to it by section 742 of the Merchant Shipping Act 1894.

(2) Any reference in these Regulations to the enforcing authority for premises is a reference to the enforcing authority which has responsibility for the enforcement of section 2 of the 1974 Act in relation to the main activity carried on in those premises.

(3) Any reference in these Regulations to—

(a) a numbered regulation is a reference to the regulation so numbered in these Regulations;

(b) a numbered paragraph is a reference to the paragraph so numbered in the regulation in which the reference appears.

(4) These Regulations shall have effect for the purpose of providing information to employees relating to health, safety and welfare but they shall not apply in relation to the master and crew of a sea going ship [(except to the extent that the master and crew are engaging in activities falling within articles 4, 5 and 6 of the 1995 Order)].

[(5) These Regulations shall, subject to paragraph (4) apply to and in relation to the premises and activities outside Great Britain to which sections 1 to 59 and 80 and 82 of the Health and Safety at Work etc Act 1974 apply by virtue of the 1995 Order as they apply to premises and activities within Great Britain.]

NOTES

Para (1): definition "the 1995 Order" inserted by the Health and Safety Information for Employees (Modifications and Repeals) Regulations 1995, SI 1995/2923, reg 2(a)(i).

Para (4): words in square brackets added by SI 1995/2923, reg 2(a)(ii).

Para (5): added by SI 1995/2923, reg 2(a)(iii).

The Health and Safety at Work etc Act 1974 (Application outside Great Britain) Order 1995, SI 1995/263: revoked and replaced by the Health and Safety at Work etc Act 1974 (Application outside Great Britain) Order 2001, SI 2001/2127.

[2.112]

3 Meaning of and revisions to the approved poster and leaflet

(1) In these Regulations "the approved poster" or "the approved leaflet" means, respectively, a poster or leaflet in the form approved and published for the purposes of these Regulations by the Health and Safety Executive, as revised from time to time in accordance with paragraph (2).

(2) The Health and Safety Executive may approve a revision (in whole or in part) to the form of poster or leaflet; and where it does so it shall publish the revised form of poster or leaflet and issue a notice in writing specifying the date the revision was approved.

(3) Such a revision shall not take effect until [five years] after the date of its approval, but during that time the employer may use the approved poster or the approved leaflet incorporating that revision for the purposes of regulation 4(1).

[(4) The Health and Safety Executive may approve a particular form of poster or leaflet for use in relation to a particular employment or class of employment and where any such form has been approved the Executive shall publish it and issue a notice in writing specifying the date that form was approved and the particular employment or class of employment in respect of which it is approved.

(5) Where a particular form of poster or leaflet has been approved under paragraph (4) then paragraphs (2) and (3) shall apply to the revision of that particular form as they apply to the revision of an approved poster or an approved leaflet save that the notice in writing issued under paragraph (2) in respect of the revised form shall also specify the employment or class of employment in respect of which the revised form is approved.

(6) An employer may, in respect of employment for which a particular poster or leaflet has been approved under paragraph (4), comply with the requirements of regulation 4(1) by displaying that particular form of poster or giving that particular form of leaflet and in connection with any such compliance regulation 4 shall be construed as if the references to the approved poster and the approved leaflet in that regulation were references to the particular form of poster and the particular form of leaflet approved under paragraph (4) and as if the reference in regulation 4(3) to revision pursuant to regulation 3(2) were a reference to a revision pursuant to regulation 3(5).]

NOTES

Para (3): words in square brackets substituted by the Health and Safety Information for Employees (Amendment) Regulations 2009, SI 2009/606, reg 2(1), (2), as from 6 April 2009.

Paras (4)–(6): added by the Health and Safety Information for Employees (Modifications and Repeals) Regulations 1995, SI 1995/2923, reg 2(b).

[2.113]

4 Provision of poster or leaflet

(1) An employer shall, in relation to each of his employees—

- (a) ensure that the approved poster is kept displayed in a readable condition—
  - (i) at a place which is reasonably accessible to the employee while he is at work, and
  - (ii) in such a position in that place as to be easily seen and read by that employee; or
- (b) give to the employee the approved leaflet.

(2) An employer shall be treated as having complied with paragraph (1)(b) from the date these Regulations come into force or the date the employee commences employment with him (if later) if he gives to the employee the approved leaflet as soon as is reasonably practicable after that date.

(3) Where the form of poster or leaflet is revised pursuant to regulation 3(2), then on or before the date the revision takes effect—

- (a) an employer relying on compliance with paragraph (1)(a) shall ensure that the approved poster displayed is the one as revised;
- (b) an employer relying on compliance with paragraph (1)(b) shall either give to the employees concerned fresh approved leaflets (as so revised) or bring the revision to their notice in writing.

[2.114]

5 Provision of further information

(1) An employer relying on compliance with regulation 4(1)(a) shall, subject to paragraph (2), ensure that the following information is clearly and indelibly written on the poster in the appropriate space—

- (a) the name of the enforcing authority for the premises where the poster is displayed and the address of the office of that authority for the area in which those premises are situated; and
- (b) the address of the office of the employment medical advisory service for the area in which those premises are situated[; or
- (c) information as to how any of his employees may obtain the information referred to in (a) and (b) above].

(2) Where there is a change in any of the matters referred to in paragraph (1) it shall be sufficient compliance with that paragraph for the corresponding amendment to the poster to be made within six months from the date thereof.

(3) An employer who gives to his employee a leaflet pursuant to regulation 4(1)(b) shall give with the leaflet a written notice containing—

- (a) the name of the enforcing authority for the premises where the employee works, and the address of the office of that authority for the area in which those premises are situated; and

(b) the address of the office of the employment medical advisory service for the area in which those premises are situated[; or

(c) information as to how any of his employees may obtain the information referred to in (a) and (b) above].

(4) Where the employee works in more than one location he shall, for the purposes of paragraph (3), be treated as working at the premises from which his work is administered, and if his work is administered from two or more premises, the employer may choose any one of them for the purpose of complying with that paragraph.

(5) Where an employer relies on compliance with regulation 4(1)(b) and there is a change in any of the matters referred to in paragraph (3) the employer shall within six months of the date thereof give to the employee a written notice specifying the change.

NOTES

Paras (1), (3): sub-para (c) and the word immediately preceding it inserted by the Health and Safety Information for Employees (Amendment) Regulations 2009, SI 2009/606, reg 2(1), (3), (4), as from 6 April 2009.

[2.115]
6 Exemption certificates

(1) Subject to paragraph (2) the Health and Safety Executive may, by a certificate in writing, exempt any person or class of persons from all or any of the requirements imposed by these Regulations and any such exemption may be granted subject to conditions and to a limit of time and may be revoked in writing at any time.

(2) The Executive shall not grant any such exemption unless, having regard to the circumstances of the case, and in particular to—

(a) the conditions if any, which it proposes to attach to the exemption; and

(b) any other requirements imposed by or under any enactment which apply to the case;

it is satisfied that the health, safety and welfare of persons who are likely to be affected by the exemption will not be prejudiced in consequence of it.

[2.116]
7 Defence

In any proceedings for an offence for a contravention of these Regulations it shall be a defence for the accused to prove that he took all reasonable precautions and exercised all due diligence to avoid the commission of that offence.

8 *(Introduces the repeals, revocations and modifications set out in the Schedule.)*

SCHEDULE

(Schedule (Repeals, revocations and modifications) outside the scope of this work.)

SEX DISCRIMINATION ACT 1975 (EXEMPTION OF SPECIAL TREATMENT FOR LONE PARENTS) ORDER 1989

(SI 1989/2140)

NOTES

Made: 17 November 1989.
Authority: Employment Act 1989, ss 8, 28.
Commencement: 19 December 1989.

[2.117]
1 Citation and commencement

This Order may be cited as the Sex Discrimination Act 1975 (Exemption of Special Treatment for Lone Parents) Order 1989 and shall come into force on 19th December 1989.

[2.118]
2 Interpretation

In this Order—

"child of that lone parent" means a person who for the purposes of any regulations made in pursuance of section 20(1)(a) of the Social Security Act 1986 is—

(a) a child or young person for whom that lone parent is responsible, and

(b) a member of the same household as that lone parent; and

"Employment Training" means the arrangements known by that name made under section 2 of the Employment and Training Act 1973 [or section 2 of the Enterprise and New Towns (Scotland) Act 1990].

NOTES

In definition "Employment Training" words in square brackets added by the Enterprise (Scotland) Consequential Amendments Order 1991, SI 1991/387, art 2, Schedule.

Social Security Act 1986: largely repealed and consolidated in the Social Security Contributions and Benefits Act 1992 and the Social Security Administration Act 1992. As to s 20(1)(a) of the 1986 Act, see now the Social Security Contributions and Benefits Act 1992, s 123(1).

[2.119]

3 Exemption of Special Treatment

With respect to Employment Training, section 8 of the Employment Act 1989 shall apply to any special treatment afforded—

(a) by the making of any payment, in connection with the participation of a lone parent in Employment Training, to a person having the care of a child of that lone parent, or

(b) by the fixing of any special condition for the participation of lone parents in Employment Training.

[EMPLOYMENT TRIBUNALS] (INTEREST) ORDER 1990

(SI 1990/479)

NOTES

Made: 6 March 1990.

Authority: Employment Protection (Consolidation) Act 1978, Sch 9, paras 1, 6A (repealed). These Regulations now have effect as if made under the Employment Tribunals Act 1996, s 14.

Commencement: 1 April 1990.

Title: words in square brackets substituted by the Employment Rights (Dispute Resolution) Act 1998, s 1(2)(b).

By virtue of the Employment Tribunals (Interest on Awards in Discrimination Cases) Regulations 1996, SI 1996/2803 at **[2.257]** (as amended), this Order applies to (i) an award, under the Equal Pay Act 1970, of arrears of remuneration or damages, or (ii) an Order under the Sex Discrimination Act 1975, s 65(1)(b), the Race Relations Act 1976, s 56(1)(b), the Disability Discrimination Act 1995, s 8(2)(b), the Employment Equality (Sexual Orientation) Regulations 2003, reg 30(1)(b), the Employment Equality (Religion or Belief) Regulations 2003, reg 30(1)(b), and the Employment Equality (Age) Regulations 2006, reg 38(1)(b), for payment of compensation as if (a) references to the calculation day were references to the day immediately following the relevant decision day (as defined in art 2(3) of this Order) and accordingly (subject to (b) below) interest is to accrue under this Order from that day onwards (including that day) and (b) (notwithstanding (a) above) no interest is to be payable by virtue of this Order if payment of the full amount of the award (including any interest awarded under reg 2 of SI 1996/2803) is made within 14 days after the relevant decision day. The 1970, 1975, 1976 and 1995 Acts and both 2003 Regulations and the 2006 Regulations were repealed or revoked by the Equality Act 2010, s 211, Sch 27, as from 1 October 2010, subject to a variety of transitional provisions and savings in the the Equality Act 2010 (Commencement No 4, Savings, Consequential, Transitional, Transitory and Incidental Provisions and Revocation) Order 2010, SI 2010/2317 at **[2.1558]** et seq.

Note that the Disability Discrimination Act 1995, s 8(2)(b) became s 17A(2)(b) following the amendments made to that Act by the Disability Discrimination Act 1995 (Amendment) Regulations 2003, SI 2003/1673. However, no consequential amendment has been made to SI 1996/2803 to take account of this.

See *Harvey* PI(1), (2A).

ARRANGEMENT OF ARTICLES

[2.120]

1 Citation, commencement and transitional provisions

(1) This Order may be cited as the [Employment Tribunals] (Interest) Order 1990 and shall come into force on 1st April 1990.

(2) Where a relevant decision day or a day to be treated as if it were a relevant decision day would, but for this paragraph of this Article, fall on a day before 1st April 1990, the relevant decision day or day to be treated as if it were that day shall be 1st April 1990.

NOTES

Para (1): words in square brackets substituted by the Employment Rights (Dispute Resolution) Act 1998, s 1(2)(b).

[2.121]

2 Interpretation

(1) In this Order, except in so far as the context otherwise requires—

"appellate court" means the Employment Appeal Tribunal, the High Court, the Court of Appeal, the Court of Session or the House of Lords as the case may be;

"the calculation day" in relation to a relevant decision means the day immediately following the expiry of the period of 42 days beginning with the relevant decision day;

"interest" means simple interest which accrues from day to day;

"relevant decision" in relation to a tribunal means any award or other determination of the tribunal by virtue of which one party to proceedings before the tribunal is required to pay a sum of money, excluding a sum representing costs or expenses, to another party to those proceedings;

"Rules of Procedure" means rules having effect in relation to proceedings before a tribunal by virtue of any regulations or order made pursuant to an enactment;

"the stipulated rate of interest" has the meaning assigned to it in Article 4 below;

"tribunal" means in England and Wales an [employment tribunal] (England and Wales) established in pursuance of the Industrial Tribunals (England and Wales) Regulations 1965 and in Scotland an [employment tribunal] (Scotland) established in pursuance of the Industrial Tribunals (Scotland) Regulations 1965.

(2) For the purposes of this Order a sum of money is required to be paid by one party to proceedings to another such party if, and only if, an amount of money required to be so paid is—

(a) specified in an award or other determination of a tribunal or, as the case may be, in an order or decision of an appellate court; or

(b) otherwise ascertainable solely by reference to the terms of such an award or determination or, as the case may be, solely by reference to the terms of such an order or decision,

but where a tribunal or, as the case may be, appellate court has made a declaration as to entitlement under a contract nothing in this Order shall be taken to provide for interest to be payable on any payment under that contract in respect of which no obligation to make the payment has arisen under that contract before the declaration was made.

(3) In this Order, except in so far as the context otherwise requires, "decision day" means the day signified by the date recording the sending of the document which is sent to the parties recording an award or other determination of a tribunal and "relevant decision day", subject to Article 5, 6 and 7 below, means the day so signified in relation to a relevant decision.

(4) In this Order "party" includes the Secretary of State where he has elected to appear as if he were a party in accordance with a Rule of Procedure entitling him so to elect.

NOTES

Para (1): in definition "tribunal" words in square brackets substituted by the Employment Rights (Dispute Resolution) Act 1998, s 1(2)(a).

Industrial Tribunals (England and Wales) Regulations 1965, Industrial Tribunals (Scotland) Regulations 1965: see now the Employment Tribunals (Constitution and Rules of Procedure) Regulations 2004, SI 2004/1861 at **[2.809]**.

[2.122]

3 Computation of interest

(1) Subject to paragraphs (2) and (3) of this Article and to Article 11 below, where the whole or any part of a sum of money payable by virtue of a relevant decision of a tribunal remains unpaid on the calculation day the sum of money remaining unpaid on the calculation day shall carry interest at the stipulated rate of interest from the calculation day (including that day).

(2) Where, after the calculation day, a party pays to another party some but not all of such a sum of money remaining unpaid on the calculation day, then beginning with the day on which the payment is made interest shall continue to accrue only on that part of the sum of money which then remains unpaid.

(3) For the purposes of the computation of interest under this Order, there shall be disregarded—

(a) any part of a sum of money which pursuant to the Employment Protection (Recoupment of Unemployment Benefit and Supplementary Benefit) Regulations 1977 has been claimed by the Secretary of State in a recoupment notice; and

(b) any part of a sum of money which the party required to pay the sum of money is required, by virtue of any provision contained in or having effect under any enactment, to deduct and pay over to a public authority in respect of income tax or contributions under Part I of the Social Security Act 1975.

NOTES

Employment Protection (Recoupment of Unemployment Benefit and Supplementary Benefit) Regulations 1977 (SI 1977/674): revoked and replaced by the Employment Protection (Recoupment of Jobseeker's Allowance and Income Support) Regulations 1996, SI 1996/2349 at **[2.246]**.

Social Security Act 1975, Pt I: repealed by the Social Security (Consequential Provisions) Act 1992, and replaced by the Social Security Contributions and Benefits Act 1992, Pt I.

[2.123]
4 Rate of interest

The stipulated rate of interest shall be the rate of interest specified in section 17 of the Judgments Act 1838 on the relevant decision day.

NOTES

The specified rate is (as of 6 April 2013) 8% per annum. This has been the rate since 1 April 1993 (see SI 1993/564 which amends the Judgments Act 1838, s 17).

[2.124]
5 Reviews

Where a tribunal reviews its decision pursuant to the Rules of Procedure and the effect of the review, or of any re-hearing which takes place as a result of the review, is that a sum of money payable by one party to another party is confirmed or varied the relevant decision day shall be the decision day of the decision which is the subject of the review.

[2.125]
6 Decisions on remission to a tribunal

Where an appellate court remits a matter to a tribunal for re-assessment of the sum of money which would have been payable by virtue of a previous relevant decision or by virtue of an order of another appellate court, the relevant decision day shall be the decision day of that previous relevant decision or the day on which the other appellate court promulgated its order, as the case may be.

[2.126]
7 Appeals from relevant decisions

Where, on an appeal from a relevant decision, or on a further appeal arising from a relevant decision an appellate court makes an order which confirms or varies the sum of money which would have been payable by virtue of that relevant decision if there had been no appeal, the relevant decision day shall be the decision day of that relevant decision.

[2.127]
8 Other appeals

(1) This Article applies in relation to any order made by an appellate court on an appeal from a determination of any issue by a tribunal which is not a relevant decision, or on any further appeal arising from such a determination, where the effect of the order is that for the first time in relation to that issue one party to the proceedings is required to pay a sum of money, other than a sum representing costs or expenses, to another party to the proceedings.

(2) Where this Article applies in relation to an order, Articles 3 and 4 above shall apply to the sum of money payable by virtue of the order as if it was a sum of money payable by virtue of a relevant decision and as if the day on which the appellate court promulgated the order was the relevant decision day.

[2.128]
9

Where, on an appeal from an order in relation to which Article 8 applies or on a further appeal arising from such an order, an appellate court makes an order which confirms or varies the sum of money which would have been payable by virtue of the order in relation to which Article 8 applies if there had been no appeal, the day to be treated as the relevant decision day shall be the day on which the order in relation to which Article 8 applies was promulgated.

[2.129]
10 Reviews by the Employment Appeal Tribunal

Where the Employment Appeal Tribunal reviews an order to which Article 8 above applies, the day to be treated as the relevant decision day shall be the day on which the order reviewed was promulgated.

[2.130]
11 Variations of the sum of money on appeal etc

Where a sum of money payable by virtue of a relevant decision is varied under one of the procedures referred to in Articles 5, 6 and 7 above, or a sum of money treated as being so payable by virtue of Article 8 above is varied under one of the procedures referred to in Articles 6, 9 and 10 above, the reference in paragraph (1) of Article 3 above, to a sum of money payable by virtue of a relevant decision shall be treated as if it were a reference to that sum as so varied.

[2.131]
12 Notices

(1) Where a decision of a tribunal is a relevant decision and a copy of a document recording that decision is sent to all parties entitled to receive that decision, it shall be the duty of the Secretary of the Central Office of the [Employment Tribunals] (England and Wales) or the Secretary of the Central Office of the [Employment Tribunals] (Scotland), as the case may be, to cause a notice containing the matters detailed in paragraph (2) below to accompany that document.

(2) The notice referred to in paragraph (1) above shall specify the decision day, the stipulated rate of interest and the calculation day in respect of the decision concerned.

(3) The failure to discharge the duty under paragraph (1) above correctly or at all shall have no effect on the liability of one party to pay to another party any sum of money which is payable by virtue of this Order.

NOTES

Para (1): words in square brackets substituted by virtue of the Employment Rights (Dispute Resolution) Act 1998, s 1.

SEX DISCRIMINATION ACT 1975 (EXEMPTION OF SPECIAL TREATMENT FOR LONE PARENTS) ORDER 1991

(SI 1991/2813)

NOTES

Made: 12 December 1991.
Authority: Employment Act 1989, ss 8, 28.
Commencement: 14 January 1992.

[2.132]
1 Citation and commencement

This Order may be cited as the Sex Discrimination Act 1975 (Exemption of Special Treatment for Lone Parents) Order 1991 and shall come into force on 14th January 1992.

[2.133]
2 Interpretation

In this Order—

"the Council" means the National Council for One Parent Families;

"the Return to Work Programme" means arrangements known by that name made under section 2 of the Employment and Training Act 1973 for the provision by or on behalf of the Council of training and other assistance to persons wishing to obtain employment.

[2.134]
3 Exemption of special treatment

With respect to the Return to Work Programme, section 8 of the Employment Act 1989 shall apply to any special treatment afforded to or in respect of lone parents—

(a) by the fixing of any special condition for participation in the Programme, or

(b) by the making of any payment in respect of the care of a child of a lone parent while that lone parent is participating in the Programme.

TRADE UNION BALLOTS AND ELECTIONS (INDEPENDENT SCRUTINEER QUALIFICATIONS) ORDER 1993

(SI 1993/1909)

NOTES

Made: 27 July 1993.
Authority: Trade Union and Labour Relations (Consolidation) Act 1992, ss 49(2), 75(2), 100A(2), 226B(2).
Commencement: 30 August 1993.
See *Harvey* M(5).

ARRANGEMENT OF ARTICLES

[2.135]

1 Citation, commencement and interpretation

(1) This Order may be cited as the Trade Union Ballots and Elections (Independent Scrutineer Qualifications) Order 1993 and shall come into force on 30 August 1993.

(2) In this Order, unless the context otherwise requires—

"an individual potentially qualified to be a scrutineer" means an individual who satisfies the requirement specified in either paragraph (a) of article 3 or paragraph (a) of article 4;

"the 1992 Act" means the Trade Union and Labour Relations (Consolidation) Act 1992;

"the relevant provisions" means the provisions of sections 49(2)(a), 75(2)(a), 100A(2)(a) and 226B(2)(a) of the 1992 Act.

[2.136]

2 Qualifications

An individual satisfies the condition specified for the purposes of the relevant provisions in relation to a ballot or election, (as the case may be), if he satisfies the condition specified in article 3 or 4.

[2.137]

3

An individual satisfies this condition if—

(a) he has in force a practising certificate issued by the Law Society of England and Wales or the Law Society of Scotland; and

(b) he is not disqualified from satisfying this condition by virtue of article 5.

[2.138]

4

An individual satisfies this condition if—

(a) he is qualified to be an auditor of a trade union by virtue of section 34(1) of the 1992 Act; and

(b) he is not disqualified from satisfying this condition by virtue of article 5.

[2.139]

5

(1) An individual potentially qualified to be a scrutineer does not satisfy the condition specified in article 3 or 4 if he or any existing partner of his has—

(a) during the preceding 12 months, been a member, an officer or an employee of the trade union proposing to hold the ballot or election; or

(b) in acting at any time as a scrutineer for any trade union, knowingly permitted any member, officer or employee of the trade union to assist him in carrying out any of the functions referred to in sections 49(3), 75(3), 100A(3) and 226B(1) of the 1992 Act.

(2) References in this article to an officer shall be construed as not including an auditor.

[2.140]
6

A partnership satisfies the condition specified for the purposes of the relevant provisions in relation to a ballot or election, (as the case may be), if—

(a) every member of the partnership is an individual potentially qualified to be a scrutineer; and

(b) no member of the partnership is disqualified from being a scrutineer by virtue of article 5.

[2.141]
[7

The following persons are specified for the purpose of the relevant provisions—

Association of Electoral Administrators;
DRS Data Services Limited;
Electoral Reform Services Limited;
Involvement and Participation Association;
Opt2Vote Limited; and
Popularis Limited.]

NOTES

Commencement: 6 April 2010.

Substituted by the Trade Union Ballots and Elections (Independent Scrutineer Qualifications) (Amendment) Order 2010, SI 2010/436, art 2, as from 6 April 2010.

8 *(Revokes the Trade Union Ballots and Elections (Independent Scrutineer Qualifications) Order 1988, SI 1988/2117.)*

EMPLOYMENT APPEAL TRIBUNAL RULES 1993

(SI 1993/2854)

NOTES

Made: 23 November 1993.

Authority: Employment Protection (Consolidation) Act 1978, s 154(3), Sch 11, paras 17(1), 18, 18A(1), 19(1) (repealed). These rules have effect as if made under the Employment Tribunals Act 1996, ss 30(1), (2), 31, 34, 41(4).

Commencement: 16 December 1993.

The rules were extensively amended by the Employment Appeal Tribunal (Amendment) Rules 2001, SI 2001/1128, as amended by SI 2001/1476, and were further amended by the Employment Appeal Tribunal (Amendment) Rules 2004, SI 2004/2526 (for transitional provisions see the notes to the individual rules subject to such transitional provisions) and by the Employment Appeal Tribunal (Amendment) Rules 2005, SI 2005/1871. Further amendments are noted below.

See also the Employment Appeal Tribunal Practice Direction 2008 at **[5.28]**.

See *Harvey* PI(2), U3.

ARRANGEMENT OF RULES

[2.142]

1 Citation and commencement

(1) These Rules may be cited as the Employment Appeal Tribunal Rules 1993 and shall come into force on 16th December 1993.

(2) As from that date the Employment Appeal Tribunal Rules 1980, the Employment Appeal Tribunal (Amendment) Rules 1985 and the Employment Appeal Tribunal (Amendment) Rules 1988 shall be revoked.

[2.143]

[2 Interpretation

(1) In these rules—

"the 1992 Act" means the Trade Union and Labour Relations (Consolidation) Act 1992;

"the 1996 Act" means the Employment Tribunals Act 1996;

"the 1999 Regulations" means the Transnational Information and Consultation of Employees Regulations 1999;

["the 2004 Regulations" means the European and Public Limited-Liability Company Regulations 2004;]

["the Information and Consultation Regulations" means the Information and Consultation of Employees Regulations 2004;]

["the 2007 Regulations" means the Companies (Cross-Border Mergers) Regulations 2007;]

"the Appeal Tribunal" means the Employment Appeal Tribunal established under section 87 of the Employment Protection Act 1975 and continued in existence under section 20(1) of the 1996 Act and includes the President, a judge, a member or the Registrar acting on behalf of the Tribunal;

"the CAC" means the Central Arbitration Committee;

"the Certification Officer" means the person appointed to be the Certification Officer under section 254(2) of the 1992 Act;

"costs officer" means any officer of the Appeal Tribunal authorised by the President to assess costs or expenses;

"Crown employment proceedings" has the meaning given by section 10(8) of the 1996 Act;

["document" includes a document delivered by way of electronic communication;]

["electronic communication" shall have the meaning given to it by section 15(1) of the Electronic Communications Act 2000;]

"excluded person" means, in relation to any proceedings, a person who has been excluded from all or part of the proceedings by virtue of—

(a) a direction of a Minister of the Crown under rule 30A(1)(b) or (c); or

(b) an order of the Appeal Tribunal under rule 30A(2)(a) read with rule 30A(1)(b) or (c);

"judge" means a judge of the Appeal Tribunal nominated under section 22(1)(a) or (b) of the 1996 Act and includes a judge nominated under section 23(2) of, or a judge appointed under section 24(1) of, the 1996 Act to be a temporary additional judge of the Appeal Tribunal;

["legal representative" shall mean a person, including a person who is a party's employee, who—

(a) has a general qualification within the meaning of the Courts and Legal Services Act 1990;

(b) is an advocate or solicitor in Scotland; or

(c) is a member of the Bar of Northern Ireland or a [Solicitor of the Court of Judicature of Northern Ireland];]

"member" means a member of the Appeal Tribunal appointed under section 22(1)(c) of the 1996 Act and includes a member appointed under section 23(3) of the 1996 Act to act temporarily in the place of a member appointed under that section;

["national security proceedings" shall have the meaning given to it in regulation 2 of the Employment Tribunals (Constitution and Rules of Procedure) Regulations 2004;]

"the President" means the judge appointed under section 22(3) of the 1996 Act to be President of the Appeal Tribunal and includes a judge nominated under section 23(1) of the 1996 Act to act temporarily in his place;

"the Registrar" means the person appointed to be Registrar of the Appeal Tribunal and includes any officer of the Tribunal authorised by the President to act on behalf of the Registrar;

"the Secretary of Employment Tribunals" means the person acting for the time being as the Secretary of the Central Office of the Employment Tribunals (England and Wales) or, as may be appropriate, of the Central Office of the Employment Tribunals (Scotland);

"special advocate" means a person appointed pursuant to rule 30A(4);

["writing" includes writing delivered by means of electronic communication].

(2) . . .

(3) Any reference in these Rules to a person who was the [claimant] or, as the case may be, the respondent in the proceedings before an employment tribunal includes, where those proceedings are still continuing, a reference to a person who is the [claimant] or, as the case may be, is the respondent in those proceedings.]

NOTES

Substituted by the Employment Appeal Tribunal (Amendment) Rules 2001, SI 2001/1128, r 2.

Para (1): definitions "the 2004 Regulations", "document", "electronic communication", "legal representative", "national security proceedings", and "writing" inserted by the Employment Appeal Tribunal (Amendment) Rules 2004, SI 2004/2526, r 2(1); definition "the Information and Consultation Regulations" inserted by the Information and Consultation of Employees Regulations 2004, SI 2004/3426, reg 41(a); definition "the 2007 Regulations" inserted by the Companies (Cross-Border Mergers) Regulations 2007, SI 2007/2974, reg 64(1); in definition "legal representative" words in square brackets substituted by the Constitutional Reform Act 2005, s 59(5), Sch 11, Pt 3, para 5, as from 1 October 2009.

Para (2): revoked by SI 2004/2526, r 2(2).

Para (3): words in square brackets substituted by SI 2004/2526, r 2(3).

[2.144]
[2A

(1) The overriding objective of these Rules is to enable the Appeal Tribunal to deal with cases justly.

(2) Dealing with a case justly includes, so far as practicable —

(a) ensuring that the parties are on an equal footing;

(b) dealing with the case in ways which are proportionate to the importance and complexity of the issues;

(c) ensuring that it is dealt with expeditiously and fairly; and

(d) saving expense.

(3) The parties shall assist the Appeal Tribunal to further the overriding objective.]

NOTES

Inserted by the Employment Appeal Tribunal (Amendment) Rules 2004, SI 2004/2526, r 3.

[2.145]

[3 Institution of Appeal

(1) Every appeal to the Appeal Tribunal shall, subject to paragraphs (2) and (4), be instituted by serving on the Tribunal the following documents—

(a) a notice of appeal in, or substantially in, accordance with Form 1, 1A or 2 in the Schedule to these rules;

[(b) in the case of an appeal from a judgment of an employment tribunal a copy of any claim and response in the proceedings before the employment tribunal or an explanation as to why either is not included; and]

[(c) in the case of an appeal from a judgment of an employment tribunal a copy of the written record of the judgment of the employment tribunal which is subject to appeal and the written reasons for the judgment, or an explanation as to why written reasons are not included;] and

(d) in the case of an appeal made pursuant to regulation 38(8) of the 1999 Regulations [or regulation 47(6) of the 2004 Regulations] [or regulation 35(6) of the Information and Consultation Regulations] [or regulation 57(6) of the 2007 Regulations] from a declaration or order of the CAC, a copy of that declaration or order[; and]

[(e) in the case of an appeal from an order of an employment tribunal a copy of the written record of the order of the employment tribunal which is subject to appeal and (if available) the written reasons for the order;

(f) in the case of an appeal from a decision or order of the Certification Officer a copy of the decision or order of the Certification Officer which is subject to appeal and the written reasons for that decision or order.]

[(2) In an appeal from a judgment or order of the employment tribunal in relation to national security proceedings where the appellant was the claimant—

(i) the appellant shall not be required by virtue of paragraph (1)(b) to serve on the Appeal Tribunal a copy of the response if the response was not disclosed to the appellant; and

(ii) the appellant shall not be required by virtue of paragraph (1)(c) or (e) to serve on the Appeal Tribunal a copy of the written reasons for the judgment or order if the written reasons were not sent to the appellant but if a document containing edited reasons was sent to the appellant, he shall serve a copy of that document on the Appeal Tribunal.]

(3) The period within which an appeal to the Appeal Tribunal may be instituted is—

[(a) in the case of an appeal from a judgment of the employment tribunal—

(i) where the written reasons for the judgment subject to appeal—

(aa) were requested orally at the hearing before the employment tribunal or in writing within 14 days of the date on which the written record of the judgment was sent to the parties; or

(bb) were reserved and given in writing by the employment tribunal

42 days from the date on which the written reasons were sent to the parties;

(ii) in an appeal from a judgment given in relation to national security proceedings, where there is a document containing edited reasons for the judgment subject to appeal, 42 days from the date on which that document was sent to the parties; or

(iii) where the written reasons for the judgment subject to appeal—

(aa) were not requested orally at the hearing before the employment tribunal or in writing within 14 days of the date on which the written record of the judgment was sent to the parties; and

(bb) were not reserved and given in writing by the employment tribunal

42 days from the date on which the written record of the judgment was sent to the parties;]

[(b) in the case of an appeal from an order of an employment tribunal, 42 days from the date of the order;]

(c) in the case of an appeal from a decision of the Certification Officer, 42 days from the date on which the written record of that decision was sent to the appellant;

(d) in the case of an appeal from a declaration or order of the CAC under regulation 38(8) of the 1999 Regulations [or regulation 47(6) of the 2004 Regulations] [or regulation 35(6) of the Information and Consultation Regulations] [or regulation 57(6) of the 2007 Regulations], 42 days from the date on which the written notification of that declaration or order was sent to the appellant.

(4) In the case of [an appeal from a judgment or order of the employment tribunal in relation to national security proceedings], the appellant shall not set out the grounds of appeal in his notice of appeal and shall not append to his notice of appeal the [written reasons for the judgment] of the tribunal.

(5) In [an appeal from the employment tribunal in relation to national security proceedings] in relation to which the appellant was the respondent in the proceedings before the employment tribunal, the appellant shall, within the period described in paragraph (3)(a), provide to the Appeal Tribunal a document setting out the grounds on which the appeal is brought.

(6) In [an appeal from the employment tribunal in relation to national security proceedings] in relation to which the appellant was the [claimant] in the proceedings before the employment tribunal—

(a) the appellant may, within the period described in [paragraph 3(a)(ii) or (iii) or paragraph 3(b), whichever is applicable,] provide to the Appeal Tribunal a document setting out the grounds on which the appeal is brought; and

(b) a special advocate appointed in respect of the appellant may, within the period described in [paragraph 3(a)(ii) or (iii) or paragraph 3(b), whichever is applicable,] or within 21 days of his appointment, whichever is later, provide to the Appeal Tribunal a document setting out the grounds on which the appeal is brought or providing supplementary grounds of appeal.

[(7) Where it appears to a judge or the Registrar that a notice of appeal or a document provided under paragraph (5) or (6)—

(a) discloses no reasonable grounds for bringing the appeal; or

(b) is an abuse of the Appeal Tribunal's process or is otherwise likely to obstruct the just disposal of proceedings,

he shall notify the Appellant or special advocate accordingly informing him of the reasons for his opinion and, subject to paragraphs (8) and (10), no further action shall be taken on the notice of appeal or document provided under paragraph (5) or (6).]

[(7A) In paragraphs (7) and (10) reference to a notice of appeal or a document provided under paragraph (5) or (6) includes reference to part of a notice of appeal or document provided under paragraph (5) or (6).]

(8) Where notification has been given under paragraph (7), the appellant or the special advocate, as the case may be, may serve a fresh notice of appeal, or a fresh document under paragraph (5) or (6), within the time remaining under paragraph (3) or (6) or within 28 days from the date on which [the notification given under paragraph (7)] was sent to him, whichever is the longer period.

(9) Where the appellant or the special advocate serves a fresh notice of appeal or a fresh document under paragraph (8), [a judge or the Registrar] shall consider such fresh notice of appeal or document with regard to jurisdiction as though it were an original notice of appeal lodged pursuant to paragraphs (1) and (3), or as though it were an original document provided pursuant to paragraph (5) or (6), as the case may be.]

[(10) Where notification has been given under paragraph (7) and within 28 days of the date the notification was sent, an appellant or special advocate expresses dissatisfaction in writing with the reasons given by the judge or Registrar for his opinion, he is entitled to have the matter heard before a judge who shall make a direction as to whether any further action should be taken on the notice of appeal or document under paragraph (5) or (6).]

NOTES

Substituted by the Employment Appeal Tribunal (Amendment) Rules 2001, SI 2001/1128, r 3.

Para (1): sub-paras (b), (c) substituted, words in first pair of square brackets in sub-para (d) inserted, word in final pair of square brackets in that paragraph substituted, and sub-paras (e), (f) inserted, by the Employment Appeal Tribunal (Amendment) Rules 2004, SI 2004/2526, r 4(1) (subject to transitional provisions, in r 26(1) of those Rules, in relation to any proceedings commenced in an employment tribunal prior to 1 October 2004); words in second pair of square brackets in sub-para (d) inserted by the Information and Consultation of Employees Regulations 2004, SI 2004/3426, reg 41(b); words in third pair of square brackets in sub-para (d) inserted by the Companies (Cross-Border Mergers) Regulations 2007, SI 2007/2974, reg 64(2).

Paras (2), (7), (10): substituted by SI 2004/2526, r 4(2), (6), (11) (subject to transitional provisions as noted above).

Para (3): sub-paras (a), (b) substituted, and words in first pair of square brackets in sub-para (d) inserted, by SI 2004/2526, r 4(3) (subject to transitional provisions as noted above); words in second pair of square brackets in sub-para (d) inserted by SI 2004/3426, reg 41(b); words in third pair of square brackets in sub-para (d) inserted by SI 2007/2974, reg 64(2).

Paras (4)–(6), (8), (9): words in square brackets substituted by SI 2004/2526, r 4(4)–(6), (9), (10) (subject to transitional provisions as noted above).

Para (7A): inserted by SI 2004/2526, r 4(8) (subject to transitional provisions as noted above).

[2.146]

4 Service of notice of appeal

[(1)] On receipt of notice under rule 3, the Registrar shall seal the notice with the Appeal Tribunal's seal and shall serve a sealed copy on the appellant and on—

(a) every person who, in accordance with rule 5, is a respondent to the appeal; and

(b) the Secretary of [Employment Tribunals] in the case of an appeal from an [employment tribunal]; or

(c) the Certification Officer in the case of an appeal from any of his decisions; or

(d) the Secretary of State in the case of an appeal under . . . Chapter II of Part IV of the 1992 Act [or Part XI of the Employment Rights Act 1996] to which he is not a respondent[; or

Part 2 Statutory Instruments

(e) the Chairman of the CAC in the case of an appeal from the CAC under regulation 38(8) of the 1999 Regulations [or regulation 47(6) of the 2004 Regulations] [or regulation 35(6) of the Information and Consultation Regulations] [or regulation 57(6) of the 2007 Regulations]].

[(2) On receipt of a document provided under rule 3(5)—

(a) the Registrar shall not send the document to a person in respect of whom a Minister of the Crown has informed the Registrar that he wishes to address the Appeal Tribunal in accordance with rule 30A(3) with a view to the Appeal Tribunal making an order applicable to this stage of the proceedings under rule 30A(2)(a) read with 30A(1)(b) or (c) (exclusion of a party or his representative), at any time before the Appeal Tribunal decides whether or not to make such an order; but if it decides not to make such an order, the Registrar shall, subject to sub-paragraph (b), send the document to such a person 14 days after the Appeal Tribunal's decision not to make the order; and

(b) the Registrar shall not send a copy of the document to an excluded person, but if a special advocate is appointed in respect of such a person, the Registrar shall send a copy of the document to the special advocate.

(3) On receipt of a document provided under rule 3(6)(a) or (b), the Registrar shall not send a copy of the document to an excluded person, but shall send a copy of the document to the respondent.]

NOTES

Para (1): numbered as such, words omitted from sub-para (d) revoked, words in square brackets in that paragraph inserted, and para (e) and the word immediately preceding it added, by the Employment Appeal Tribunal (Amendment) Rules 2001, SI 2001/1128, r 4(a)–(d); words in square brackets in sub-para (b) substituted by the Employment Rights (Dispute Resolution) Act 1998, s 1(2)(a), (b); words in first pair of square brackets in sub-para (e) inserted by the Employment Appeal Tribunal (Amendment) Rules 2004, SI 2004/2526, r 5; words in second pair of square brackets in sub-para (e) inserted by the Information and Consultation of Employees Regulations 2004, SI 2004/3426, reg 41(b); words in third pair of square brackets in sub-para (e) inserted by the Companies (Cross-Border Mergers) Regulations 2007, SI 2007/2974, reg 64(2).

Paras (2), (3): added by SI 2001/1128, r 4(d).

[2.147]

5 Respondents to appeals

The respondents to an appeal shall be—

(a) in the case of an appeal from an [employment tribunal] or of an appeal made pursuant to [section 45D, 56A, 95, 104 or 108C] of the 1992 Act from a decision of the Certification Officer, the parties (other than the appellant) to the proceedings before the [employment tribunal] or the Certification Officer;

(b) in the case of an appeal made pursuant to [section 9 or 126] of the 1992 Act from a decision of the Certification Officer, that Officer;

[(c) in the case of an appeal made pursuant to regulation 38(8) of the 1999 Regulations [or regulation 47(6) of the 2004 Regulations] [or regulation 35(6) of the Information and Consultation Regulations] [or regulation 57(6) of the 2007 Regulations] from a declaration or order of the CAC, the parties (other than the appellant) to the proceedings before the CAC].

NOTES

Words in first and third pairs of square brackets substituted by the Employment Rights (Dispute Resolution) Act 1998, s 1(2)(a); words in second and fourth pairs of square brackets substituted, and para (c) added, by the Employment Appeal Tribunal (Amendment) Rules 2001, SI 2001/1128, r 5; words in first pair of square brackets in sub-para (c) inserted by the Employment Appeal Tribunal (Amendment) Rules 2004, SI 2004/2526, r 6; words in second pair of square brackets in sub-para (c) inserted by the Information and Consultation of Employees Regulations 2004, SI 2004/3426, reg 41(b); words in third pair of square brackets in sub-para (c) inserted by the Companies (Cross-Border Mergers) Regulations 2007, SI 2007/2974, reg 64(2).

[2.148]

6 Respondent's answer and notice of cross-appeal

(1) The Registrar shall, as soon as practicable, notify every respondent of the date appointed by the Appeal Tribunal by which any answer under this rule must be delivered.

(2) A respondent who wishes to resist an appeal shall, [subject to paragraph (6), and] within the time appointed under paragraph (1) of this rule, deliver to the Appeal Tribunal an answer in writing in, or substantially in, accordance with Form 3 in the Schedule to these Rules, setting out the grounds on which he relies, so, however, that it shall be sufficient for a respondent to an appeal referred to in rule 5(a) [or 5(c)] who wishes to rely on any ground which is the same as a ground relied on by the [employment tribunal][, the Certification Officer or the CAC] for making the [judgment,] decision[, declaration] or order appealed from to state that fact in his answer.

(3) A respondent who wishes to cross-appeal may [subject to paragraph (6),] do so by including in his answer a statement of the grounds of his cross-appeal, and in that event an appellant who wishes to resist the cross-appeal shall, within a time to be appointed by the Appeal Tribunal, deliver to the Tribunal a reply in writing setting out the grounds on which he relies.

(4) The Registrar shall serve a copy of every answer and reply to a cross-appeal on every party other than the party by whom it was delivered.

(5) Where the respondent does not wish to resist an appeal, the parties may deliver to the Appeal Tribunal an agreed draft of an order allowing the appeal and the Tribunal may, if it thinks it right to do so, make an order allowing the appeal in the terms agreed.

[(6) In [an appeal from the employment tribunal in relation to national security proceedings], the respondent shall not set out the grounds on which he relies in his answer to an appeal, nor include in his answer a statement of the grounds of any cross-appeal.

(7) In [an appeal from the employment tribunal in relation to national security proceedings] in relation to which the respondent was not the [claimant] in the proceedings before the employment tribunal, the respondent shall, within the time appointed under paragraph (1), provide to the Registrar a document, setting out the grounds on which he intends to resist the appeal, and may include in that document a statement of the grounds of any cross-appeal.

(8) In [an appeal from the employment tribunal in relation to national security proceedings] in relation to which the respondent was the [claimant] in the proceedings before the employment tribunal—

(a) the respondent may, within the time appointed under paragraph (1) provide to the Registrar a document, setting out the grounds on which he intends to resist the appeal, and may include in that document a statement of the grounds of any cross-appeal; and

(b) a special advocate appointed in respect of the respondent may, within the time appointed under paragraph (1), or within 21 days of his appointment, whichever is the later, provide to the Registrar a document, setting out the grounds, or the supplementary grounds, on which the respondent intends to resist the appeal, and may include in that document a statement of the grounds, or the supplementary grounds, of any cross-appeal.

(9) In [an appeal from the employment tribunal in relation to national security proceedings], if the respondent, or any special advocate appointed in respect of a respondent, provides in the document containing grounds for resisting an appeal a statement of grounds of cross-appeal and the appellant wishes to resist the cross-appeal—

(a) where the appellant was not the [claimant] in the proceedings before the employment tribunal, the appellant shall within a time to be appointed by the Appeal Tribunal deliver to the Tribunal a reply in writing setting out the grounds on which he relies; and

(b) where the appellant was the [claimant] in the proceedings before the employment tribunal, the appellant, or any special advocate appointed in respect of him, may within a time to be appointed by the Appeal Tribunal deliver to the Tribunal a reply in writing setting out the grounds on which the appellant relies.

(10) Any document provided under paragraph (7) or (9)(a) shall be treated by the Registrar in accordance with rule 4(2), as though it were a document received under rule 3(5).

(11) Any document provided under paragraph (8) or (9)(b) shall be treated by the Registrar in accordance with rule 4(3), as though it were a document received under rule 3(6)(a) or (b).]

[(12) Where it appears to a judge or the Registrar that a statement of grounds of cross-appeal contained in respondent's answer or document provided under paragraph (7) or (8)—

(a) discloses no reasonable grounds for bringing the cross-appeal; or

(b) is an abuse of the Appeal Tribunal's process or is otherwise likely to obstruct the just disposal of proceedings,

he shall notify the appellant or special advocate accordingly informing him of the reasons for his opinion and, subject to paragraphs (14) and (16), no further action shall be taken on the statement of grounds of cross-appeal.

(13) In paragraphs (12) and (16) reference to a statement of grounds of cross-appeal includes reference to part of a statement of grounds of cross-appeal.

(14) Where notification has been given under paragraph (12), the respondent or special advocate, as the case may be, may serve a fresh statement of grounds of cross-appeal before the time appointed under paragraph (1) or within 28 days from the date on which the notification given under paragraph (12) was sent to him, whichever is the longer.

(15) Where the respondent or special advocate serves a fresh statement of grounds of cross-appeal, a judge or the Registrar shall consider such statement with regard to jurisdiction as though it was contained in the original Respondent's answer or document provided under (7) or (8).

(16) Where notification has been given under paragraph (12) and within 28 days of the date the notification was sent, a respondent or special advocate expresses dissatisfaction in writing with the reasons given by the judge or Registrar for his opinion, he is entitled to have the matter heard before a judge who shall make a direction as to whether any further action should be taken on the statement of grounds of cross-appeal.]

NOTES

Para (2): words in first, second and sixth pairs of square brackets inserted, and words in fourth pair of square brackets substituted, by the Employment Appeal Tribunal (Amendment) Rules 2001, SI 2001/1128, r 6(a), (b); words in third pair of square brackets substituted by the Employment Rights (Dispute Resolution) Act 1998, s 1(2)(a); word in fifth pair of square brackets inserted by the Employment Appeal Tribunal (Amendment) Rules 2004, SI 2004/2526, r 7(1)(a).

Para (3): words in square brackets substituted by SI 2001/1128, r 6(b).

Paras (6)–(11): added by SI 2001/1128, r 6(c); words in square brackets in paras (6)–(9) substituted by SI 2004/2526, r 7(1)(b), (c).

Paras (12)–(16): added by SI 2004/2526, r 7(2).

[2.149]
7 Disposal of appeal

(1) The Registrar shall, as soon as practicable, give notice of the arrangements made by the Appeal Tribunal for hearing the appeal to—

(a) every party to the proceedings; and
(b) the Secretary of [Employment Tribunals] in the case of an appeal from an [employment tribunal]; or
(c) the Certification Officer in the case of an appeal from one of his decisions; or
(d) the Secretary of State in the case of an appeal under [Part XI of the Employment Rights Act 1996] or Chapter II of Part IV of the 1992 Act to which he is not a respondent[; or
(e) the Chairman of the CAC in the case of an appeal from a declaration or order of, or arising in any proceedings before, the CAC under regulation 38(8) of the 1999 Regulations [or regulation 47(6) of the 2004 Regulations] [or regulation 35(6) of the Information and Consultation Regulations] [or regulation 57(6) of the 2007 Regulations]].

(2) Any such notice shall state the date appointed by the Appeal Tribunal by which any [interim] application must be made.

NOTES

Para (1): words in square brackets in sub-para (b) substituted by the Employment Rights (Dispute Resolution) Act 1998, s 1(2)(a), (b); words in square brackets in sub-para (d) substituted, and sub-para (e) and word immediately preceding it added, by the Employment Appeal Tribunal (Amendment) Rules 2001, SI 2001/1128, r 7; words in first pair of square brackets in sub-para (e) inserted by the Employment Appeal Tribunal (Amendment) Rules 2004, SI 2004/2526, r 8(1); words in second pair of square brackets in sub-para (e) inserted by the Information and Consultation of Employees Regulations 2004, SI 2004/3426, reg 41(b); words in third pair of square brackets in sub-para (e) inserted by the Companies (Cross-Border Mergers) Regulations 2007, SI 2007/2974, reg 64(2).

Para (2): word in square brackets substituted by SI 2004/2526, r 8(2).

[2.150]
8 Application in respect of exclusion or expulsion from, or unjustifiable discipline by, a trade union

Every application under section 67 or 176 of the 1992 Act to the Appeal Tribunal for—

(a) an award of compensation for exclusion or expulsion from a trade union; or
(b) one or both of the following, that is to say—
   (i) an award of compensation for unjustifiable discipline;
   (ii) an order that the union pay to the applicant an amount equal to any sum which he has paid in pursuance of any such determination as is mentioned in section 64(2)(b) of the 1992 Act;

shall be made in writing in, or substantially in, accordance with Form 4 in the Schedule to these Rules and shall be served on the Appeal Tribunal together with a copy of the decision or order declaring that the applicant's complaint against the trade union was well-founded.

[2.151]
9

If on receipt of an application under rule 8(a) it becomes clear that at the time the application was made the applicant had been admitted or re-admitted to membership of the union against which the complaint was made, the Registrar shall forward the application to the Central Office of [Employment Tribunals].

NOTES

Words in square brackets substituted by the Employment Rights (Dispute Resolution) Act 1998, s 1(2)(b).

[2.152]
10 Service of application under rule 8

On receipt of an application under rule 8, the Registrar shall seal it with the Appeal Tribunal's seal and shall serve a sealed copy on the applicant and on the respondent trade union and the Secretary of [Employment Tribunals].

NOTES

Words in square brackets substituted by the Employment Rights (Dispute Resolution) Act 1998, s 1(2)(b).

[2.153]
11 Appearance by respondent trade union

(1) Subject to paragraph (2) of this rule, a respondent trade union wishing to resist an application under rule 8 shall within 14 days of receiving the sealed copy of the application enter an appearance in, or substantially in, accordance with Form 5 in the Schedule to these Rules and setting out the grounds on which the union relies.

(2) Paragraph (1) above shall not require a respondent trade union to enter an appearance where the application is before the Appeal Tribunal by virtue of having been transferred there by an [employment tribunal] and, prior to that transfer, the respondent had entered an appearance to the proceedings before the [employment tribunal].

NOTES

Para (2): words in square brackets substituted by the Employment Rights (Dispute Resolution) Act 1998, s 1(2)(a).

[2.154]
12

On receipt of the notice of appearance under rule 11 the Registrar shall serve a copy of it on the applicant.

[2.155]
13 Application for restriction of proceedings order

Every application to the Appeal Tribunal by the Attorney General or the Lord Advocate under [section 33 of the 1996 Act] for a restriction of proceedings order shall be made in writing in, or substantially in, accordance with Form 6 in the Schedule to these Rules, accompanied by an affidavit in support, and shall be served on the Tribunal.

NOTES

Words in square brackets substituted by the Employment Appeal Tribunal (Amendment) Rules 2001, SI 2001/1128, r 8.

[2.156]
14 Service of application under rule 13

On receipt of an application under rule 13, the Registrar shall seal it with the Appeal Tribunal's seal and shall serve a sealed copy on the Attorney General or the Lord Advocate, as the case may be, on the Secretary of [Employment Tribunals] and on the person named in the application.

NOTES

Words in square brackets substituted by the Employment Rights (Dispute Resolution) Act 1998, s 1(2)(b).

[2.157]
15 Appearance by person named in application under rule 13

A person named in an application under rule 13 who wishes to resist the application shall within 14 days of receiving the sealed copy of the application enter an appearance in, or substantially in, accordance with Form 7 in the Schedule to these Rules, accompanied by an affidavit in support.

[2.158]
16

On receipt of the notice of appearance under rule 15 the Registrar shall serve a copy of it on the Attorney General or the Lord Advocate, as the case may be.

16A *(This rule was originally inserted (together with rr 16B–16D) by the Employment Appeal Tribunal (Amendment) Rules 2001, SI 2001/1128, r 9; it was revoked by the Transnational Information and Consultation of Employees (Amendment) Regulations 2010, SI 2010/1088, reg 30(1), (2), as from 5 June 2011.)*

[2.159]
[16AA Applications under regulation 33(6) of the 2004 Regulations

Every application under regulation 33(6) of the 2004 Regulations [or regulation 22(6) of the Information and Consultation Regulations] [or regulation 53(6) of the 2007 Regulations] [or

Part 2 Statutory Instruments

regulation 20(7), 21(6) or 21A(5) of the 1999 Regulations] shall be made by way of application in writing in, or substantially in, accordance with Form 4B in the Schedule to these Rules and shall be served on the Appeal Tribunal together with a copy of the declaration referred to in regulation 33(4) of [the 2004 Regulations or regulation 22(4) of the Information and Consultation Regulations] [or regulation 53(4) of the 2007 Regulations] [or the decision referred to in regulation 20(4), 21(4) or 21A(3) of the 1999 Regulations], or an explanation as to why none is included.]

NOTES

Inserted by the Employment Appeal Tribunal (Amendment) Rules 2004, SI 2004/2526, r 9.

Words in first pair of square brackets inserted, and words in fourth pair of square brackets substituted, by the Information and Consultation of Employees Regulations 2004, SI 2004/3426, reg 41(c); words in second and fifth pairs of square brackets inserted by the Companies (Cross-Border Mergers) Regulations 2007, SI 2007/2974, reg 64(3); words in third and sixth pairs of square brackets inserted by the Transnational Information and Consultation of Employees (Amendment) Regulations 2010, SI 2010/1088, reg 30(1), (3), as from 5 June 2011.

[2.160]
[16B Service of application under rule 16AA

On receipt of an application under rule 16AA, the Registrar shall seal it with the Appeal Tribunal's seal and shall serve a sealed copy on the applicant and on the respondent.]

NOTES

Inserted (together with rr 16A (now revoked) and rr 16C, 16D) by the Employment Appeal Tribunal (Amendment) Rules 2001, SI 2001/1128, r 9

Substituted by the Transnational Information and Consultation of Employees (Amendment) Regulations 2010, SI 2010/1088, reg 30(1), (4), as from 5 June 2011.

[2.161]
[16C Appearance by respondent

A respondent wishing to resist an application under rule . . . [16AA] shall within 14 days of receiving the sealed copy of the application enter an appearance in, or substantially in, accordance with Form 5A in the Schedule to these Rules and setting out the grounds on which the respondent relies.]

NOTES

Inserted as noted to r 16B at **[2.160]**.

Words omitted revoked by the Transnational Information and Consultation of Employees (Amendment) Regulations 2010, SI 2010/1088, reg 30(1), (5), as from 5 June 2011; figure in square brackets inserted by the Employment Appeal Tribunal (Amendment) Rules 2004, SI 2004/2526, r 10.

[2.162]
[16D

On receipt of the notice of appearance under rule 16C the Registrar shall serve a copy of it on the applicant.]

NOTES

Inserted as noted to r 16B at **[2.160]**.

[2.163]
17 Disposal of application

(1) The Registrar shall, as soon as practicable, give notice to the parties to an application under rule 8[, 13[, . . . or 16AA]] of the arrangements made by the Appeal Tribunal for hearing the application.

(2) Any such notice shall state the date appointed by the Appeal Tribunal by which any [interim] application must be made.

NOTES

Para (1): words in first (outer) pair of square brackets substituted by the Employment Appeal Tribunal (Amendment) Rules 2001, SI 2001/1128, r 10; words in second (inner) pair of square brackets substituted by the Employment Appeal Tribunal (Amendment) Rules 2004, SI 2004/2526, r 11; figure omitted revoked by the Transnational Information and Consultation of Employees (Amendment) Regulations 2010, SI 2010/1088, reg 30(1), (6), as from 5 June 2011.

Para (2): word in square brackets substituted by SI 2004/2526, r 12.

[2.164]
18 Joinder of parties

The Appeal Tribunal may, on the application of any person or of its own motion, direct that any person not already a party to the proceedings be added as a party, or that any party to proceedings shall cease to be a party, and in either case may give such consequential directions as it considers necessary.

[2.165]
19 [Interim] applications

(1) An [interim] application may be made to the Appeal Tribunal by giving notice in writing specifying the direction or order sought.

(2) On receipt of a notice under paragraph (1) of this rule, the Registrar shall serve a copy on every other party to the proceedings who appears to him to be concerned in the matter to which the notice relates and shall notify the applicant and every such party of the arrangements made by the Appeal Tribunal for disposing of the application.

NOTES

Words in square brackets substituted by the Employment Appeal Tribunal (Amendment) Rules 2004, SI 2004/2526, r 12.

[2.166]
[20 Disposal of interim applications

(1) Every interim application made to the Appeal Tribunal shall be considered in the first place by the Registrar who shall have regard to rule 2A (the overriding objective) and, where applicable, to rule 23(5).

(2) Subject to sub-paragraphs (3) and (4), every interim application shall be disposed of by the Registrar except that any matter which he thinks should properly be decided by the President or a judge shall be referred by him to the President or judge who may dispose of it himself or refer it in whole or part to the Appeal Tribunal as required to be constituted by section 28 of the 1996 Act or refer it back to the Registrar with such directions as he thinks fit.

(3) Every interim application for a restricted reporting order shall be disposed of by the President or a judge or, if he so directs, the application shall be referred to the Appeal Tribunal as required to be constituted by section 28 of the 1996 Act who shall dispose of it.

(4) Every interim application for permission to institute or continue or to make a claim or application in any proceedings before an employment tribunal or the Appeal Tribunal, pursuant to section 33(4) of the 1996 Act, shall be disposed of by the President or a judge, or, if he so directs, the application shall be referred to the Appeal Tribunal as required to be constituted by section 28 of the 1996 Act who shall dispose of it.]

NOTES

Substituted by the Employment Appeal Tribunal (Amendment) Rules 2004, SI 2004/2526, r 13.

[2.167]
21 Appeals from Registrar

(1) Where an application is disposed of by the Registrar in pursuance of rule 20(2) any party aggrieved by his decision may appeal to a judge and in that case . . . the judge may determine the appeal himself or refer it in whole or in part to the Appeal Tribunal as required to be constituted by [section 28 of the 1996 Act].

(2) Notice of appeal under paragraph (1) of this rule may be given to the Appeal Tribunal, either orally or in writing, within five days of the decision appealed from and the Registrar shall notify every other party who appears to him to be concerned in the appeal and shall inform every such party and the appellant of the arrangements made by the Tribunal for disposing of the appeal.

NOTES

Para (1): words omitted revoked, and words in square brackets substituted, by the Employment Appeal Tribunal (Amendment) Rules 2001, SI 2001/1128, r 12.

[2.168]
22 Hearing of interlocutory applications

(1) The Appeal Tribunal may, subject to [any direction of a Minister of the Crown under rule 30A(1) or order of the Appeal Tribunal under rule 30A(2)(a) read with rule 30A(1),] and, where applicable, to rule 23(6), sit either in private or in public for the hearing of any [interim] application.

(2) . . .

NOTES

Para (1): words in first pair of square brackets substituted by the Employment Appeal Tribunal (Amendment) Rules 2001, SI 2001/1128, r 13(a); word in second pair of square brackets substituted by the Employment Appeal Tribunal (Amendment) Rules 2004, SI 2004/2526, r 14.

Para (2): revoked by SI 2001/1128, r 13(b).

[2.169]
23 Cases involving allegations of sexual misconduct or the commission of sexual offences

(1) This rule applies to any proceedings to which [section 31 of the 1996 Act] applies.

(2) In any such proceedings where the appeal appears to involve allegations of the commission of a sexual offence, the Registrar shall omit from any register kept by the Appeal Tribunal, which is available to the public, or delete from any order, judgment or other document, which is available to the public, any identifying matter which is likely to lead members of the public to identify any person affected by or making such an allegation.

(3) In any proceedings to which this rule applies where the appeal involves allegations of sexual misconduct the Appeal Tribunal may at any time before promulgation of its decision either on the application of a party or of its own motion make a restricted reporting order having effect, if not revoked earlier by the Appeal Tribunal, until the promulgation of its decision.

(4) A restricted reporting order shall specify the persons who may not be identified.

[(5) Subject to paragraph (5A) the Appeal Tribunal shall not make a full restricted reporting order unless it has given each party to the proceedings an opportunity to advance oral argument at a hearing, if they so wish.]

[(5A) The Appeal Tribunal may make a temporary restricted reporting order without a hearing.

(5B) Where a temporary restricted reporting order has been made the Registrar shall inform the parties to the proceedings in writing as soon as possible of:

(a) the fact that the order has been made; and

(b) their right to apply to have the temporary restricted reporting order revoked or converted into a full restricted reporting order within 14 days of the temporary order being made.

(5C) If no such application is made under subparagraph (5B)(b) within the 14 days, the temporary restricted reporting order shall lapse and cease to have any effect on the fifteenth day after it was made. When such an application is made the temporary restricted reporting order shall continue to have effect until the Hearing at which the application is considered.]

(6) Any . . . hearing shall, subject to [any direction of a Minister of the Crown under rule 30A(1) or order of the Appeal Tribunal under rule 30A(2)(a) read with rule 30A(1),] or unless the Appeal Tribunal decides for any of the reasons mentioned in rule 29(2) to sit in private to hear evidence, be held in public.

(7) The Appeal Tribunal may revoke a restricted reporting order at any time where it thinks fit.

(8) Where the Appeal Tribunal makes a restricted reporting order, the Registrar shall ensure that a notice of that fact is displayed on the notice board of the Appeal Tribunal at the office in which the proceedings in question are being dealt with, on the door of the room in which those proceedings are taking place and with any list of the proceedings taking place before the Appeal Tribunal.

(9) In this rule, "promulgation of its decision" means the date recorded as being the date on which the Appeal Tribunal's order finally disposing of the appeal is sent to the parties.

NOTES

Para (1): words in square brackets substituted by the Employment Appeal Tribunal (Amendment) Rules 2001, SI 2001/1128, r 14(a).

Para (5): substituted by the Employment Appeal Tribunal (Amendment) Rules 2004, SI 2004/2526, r 15(1).

Paras (5A)–(5C): inserted by SI 2004/2526, r 15(2).

Para (6): word omitted revoked by SI 2004/2526, r 15(3); words in square brackets substituted by SI 2001/1128, r 14(b).

[2.170]

[23A Restricted reporting orders in disability cases

(1) This rule applies to proceedings to which section 32(1) of [the [1996 Act]] applies.

(2) In proceedings to which this rule applies the Appeal Tribunal may, on the application of the complainant or of its own motion, make a restricted reporting order having effect, if not revoked earlier by the Appeal Tribunal, until the promulgation of its decision.

(3) Where the Appeal Tribunal makes a restricted reporting order under paragraph (2) of this rule in relation to an appeal which is being dealt with by the Appeal Tribunal together with any other proceedings, the Appeal Tribunal may direct that the order is to apply also in relation to those other proceedings or such part of them as it may direct.

(4) Paragraphs (5) to (9) of rule 23 apply in relation to the making of a restricted reporting order under this rule as they apply in relation to the making of a restricted reporting order under that rule.]

NOTES

Inserted by the Employment Appeal Tribunal (Amendment) Rules 1996, SI 1996/3216, r 2.

Para (1): word in first (outer) pair of square brackets substituted by the Employment Rights (Dispute Resolution) Act 1998, s 1(2)(c); words in second (inner) pair of square brackets substituted by the Employment Appeal Tribunal (Amendment) Rules 2001, SI 2001/1128, r 15.

[2.171]

24 Appointment for direction

(1) Where it appears to the Appeal Tribunal that the future conduct of any proceedings would thereby be facilitated, the Tribunal may (either of its own motion or on application) at any stage in the proceedings appoint a date for a meeting for directions as to their future conduct and thereupon the following provisions of this rule shall apply.

(2) The Registrar shall give to every party in the proceedings notice of the date appointed under paragraph (1) of this rule and any party applying for directions shall, if practicable, before that date give to the Appeal Tribunal particulars of any direction for which he asks.

(3) The Registrar shall take such steps as may be practicable to inform every party of any directions applied for by any other party.

(4) On the date appointed under paragraph (1) of this rule, the Appeal Tribunal shall consider every application for directions made by any party and any written representations relating to the application submitted to the Tribunal and shall give such directions as it thinks fit for the purpose of securing the just, expeditious and economical disposal of the proceedings, including, where appropriate, directions in pursuance of rule 36, for the purpose of ensuring that the parties are enabled to avail themselves of opportunities for conciliation.

(5) Without prejudice to the generality of paragraph (4) of this rule, the Appeal Tribunal may give such directions as it thinks fit as to—

- (a) the amendment of any notice, answer or other document;
- (b) the admission of any facts or documents;
- (c) the admission in evidence of any documents;
- (d) the mode in which evidence is to be given at the hearing;
- (e) the consolidation of the proceedings with any other proceedings pending before the Tribunal;
- (f) the place and date of the hearing.

(6) An application for further directions or for the variation of any directions already given may be made in accordance with rule 19.

[2.172]

25 Appeal Tribunal's power to give directions

The Appeal Tribunal may either of its own motion or on application, at any stage of the proceedings, give any party directions as to any steps to be taken by him in relation to the proceedings.

[2.173]

26 Default by parties

If a respondent to any proceedings fails to deliver an answer or, in the case of an application made under section 67 or 176 of the 1992 Act[, section 33 of the 1996 Act[,] [regulation 20, 21 or 21A of the 1999 Regulations]], [. . . regulation 33 of the 2004 Regulations] [. . . regulation 22 of the Information and Consultation Regulations] [or regulation 53 the 2007 Regulations], a notice of appearance within the time appointed under these Rules, or if any party fails to comply with an order or direction of the Appeal Tribunal, the Tribunal may order that he be debarred from taking any further part in the proceedings, or may make such other order as it thinks just.

NOTES

Words in first (outer) pair of square brackets substituted by the Employment Appeal Tribunal (Amendment) Rules 2001, SI 2001/1128, r 16.

The comma in second (inner) pair of square brackets was substituted (for the original word "or") by the Employment Appeal Tribunal (Amendment) Rules 2004, SI 2004/2526, r 17(1).

Words in third (inner) pair of square brackets substituted by the Transnational Information and Consultation of Employees (Amendment) Regulations 2010, SI 2010/1088, reg 30(1), (7), as from 5 June 2011.

Words in fourth pair of square brackets inserted by SI 2004/2526, r 17(2), and the words omitted therefrom were revoked by the Information and Consultation of Employees Regulations 2004, SI 2004/3426, reg 41(d)(i).

Words in the penultimate pair of square brackets inserted by SI 2004/3426, reg 41(d)(ii), and the words omitted therefrom were revoked by the Companies (Cross-Border Mergers) Regulations 2007, SI 2007/2974, reg 64(4).

Words in final pair of square brackets inserted by SI 2007/2974, reg 64(4).

[2.174]

27 Attendance of witnesses and production of documents

(1) The Appeal Tribunal may, on the application of any party, order any person to attend before the Tribunal as a witness or to produce any document.

[(1A) Where—

- (a) a Minister has at any stage issued a direction under rule 30A(1)(b) or (c) (exclusion of a party or his representative), or the Appeal Tribunal has at any stage made an order under rule 30A(2)(a) read with rule 30A(1)(b) or (c); and

(b) the Appeal Tribunal is considering whether to impose, or has imposed, a requirement under paragraph (1) on any person,

the Minister (whether or not he is a party to the proceedings) may make an application to the Appeal Tribunal objecting to the imposition of a requirement under paragraph (1) or, where a requirement has been imposed, an application to vary or set aside the requirement, as the case may be. The Appeal Tribunal shall hear and determine the Minister's application in private and the Minister shall be entitled to address the Appeal Tribunal thereon. The application shall be made by notice to the Registrar and the Registrar shall give notice of the application to each party.]

(2) No person to whom an order is directed under paragraph (1) of this rule shall be treated as having failed to obey that order unless at the time at which the order was served on him there was tendered to him a sufficient sum of money to cover his costs of attending before the Appeal Tribunal.

NOTES

Para (1A): inserted by the Employment Appeal Tribunal (Amendment) Rules 2001, SI 2001/1128, r 17.

[2.175]
28 Oaths

The Appeal Tribunal may, either of its own motion or on application, require any evidence to be given on oath.

[2.176]
29 Oral hearings

(1) Subject to paragraph (2) of this rule and to [any direction of a Minister of the Crown under rule 30A(1)(a) or order of the Appeal Tribunal under rule 30A(2)(a) read with rule 30A(1)(a),] an oral hearing at which any proceedings before the Appeal Tribunal are finally disposed of shall take place in public before, where applicable, such members of the Tribunal as (subject to [section 28 of the 1996 Act]) the President may nominate for the purpose.

[(2) Notwithstanding paragraph (1), the Appeal Tribunal may sit in private for the purpose of hearing evidence from any person which in the opinion of the Tribunal is likely to consist of—

(a) information which he could not disclose without contravening a prohibition imposed by or by virtue of any enactment;

(b) information which has been communicated to him in confidence or which he has otherwise obtained in consequence of the confidence reposed in him by another person; or

(c) information the disclosure of which would, for reasons other than its effect on negotiations with respect to any of the matters mentioned in section 178(2) of the 1992 Act, cause substantial injury to any undertaking of his or in which he works.]

NOTES

Para (1): words in square brackets substituted by the Employment Appeal Tribunal (Amendment) Rules 2001, SI 2001/1128, r 18(a).

Para (2): substituted by SI 2001/1128, r 18(b).

[2.177]
[30 Duty of Appeal Tribunal concerning disclosure of information

When exercising its functions, the Appeal Tribunal shall ensure that information is not disclosed contrary to the interests of national security.]

NOTES

Substituted, together with r 30A, for the original r 30, by the Employment Appeal Tribunal (Amendment) Rules 2001, SI 2001/1128, r 19.

[2.178]
[30A Proceedings in cases concerning national security

(1) A Minister of the Crown (whether or not he is a party to the proceedings) may, if he considers it expedient in the interests of national security, direct the Appeal Tribunal by notice to the Registrar to—

(a) sit in private for all or part of particular Crown employment proceedings;

(b) exclude any party who was the [claimant] in the proceedings before the employment tribunal from all or part of particular Crown employment proceedings;

(c) exclude the representatives of any party who was the [claimant] in the proceedings before the employment tribunal from all or part of particular Crown employment proceedings;

(d) take steps to conceal the identity of a particular witness in particular Crown employment proceedings.

(2) The Appeal Tribunal may, if it considers it expedient in the interests of national security, by order—

(a) do [in relation to particular proceedings before it] anything of a kind which the Appeal Tribunal can be required to do [in relation to particular Crown employment proceedings] by direction under paragraph (1) of this rule;

(b) direct any person to whom any document (including any decision or record of the proceedings) has been provided for the purposes of the proceedings not to disclose any such document or the content thereof—

(i) to any excluded person;

(ii) in any case in which a direction has been given under paragraph (1)(a) or an order has been made under paragraph (2)(a) read with paragraph (1)(a), to any person excluded from all or part of the proceedings by virtue of such direction or order; or

(iii) in any case in which a Minister of the Crown has informed the Registrar in accordance with paragraph (3) that he wishes to address the Appeal Tribunal with a view to the Tribunal making an order under paragraph (2)(a) read with paragraph (1)(b) or (c), to any person who may be excluded from all or part of the proceedings by virtue of such an order, if an order is made, at any time before the Appeal Tribunal decides whether or not to make such an order;

(c) take steps to keep secret all or part of the reasons for any order it makes.

The Appeal Tribunal shall keep under review any order it makes under this paragraph.

(3) In any proceedings in which a Minister of the Crown considers that it would be appropriate for the Appeal Tribunal to make an order as referred to in paragraph (2), he shall (whether or not he is a party to the proceedings) be entitled to appear before and to address the Appeal Tribunal thereon. The Minister shall inform the Registrar by notice that he wishes to address the Appeal Tribunal and the Registrar shall copy the notice to the parties.

(4) In any proceedings in which there is an excluded person, the Appeal Tribunal shall inform the Attorney General or, in the case of an appeal from an employment tribunal in Scotland, the Advocate General for Scotland, of the proceedings before it with a view to the Attorney General (or, as the case may be, the Advocate General), if he thinks it fit to do so, appointing a special advocate to represent the interests of the person who was the [claimant] in the proceedings before the employment tribunal in respect of those parts of the proceedings from which—

(a) any representative of his is excluded;

(b) both he and his representative are excluded; or

(c) he is excluded, where he does not have a representative.

(5) A special advocate shall have a general qualification within the meaning of section 71 of the Courts and Legal Services Act 1990, or, in the case of an appeal from an employment tribunal in Scotland, shall be—

(a) an advocate; or

(b) a solicitor who has by virtue of section 25A of the Solicitors (Scotland) Act 1980 rights of audience in the Court of Session or the High Court of Justiciary.

(6) Where the excluded person is a party to the proceedings, he shall be permitted to make a statement to the Appeal Tribunal before the commencement of the proceedings, or the part of the proceedings, from which he is excluded.

(7) Except in accordance with paragraphs (8) to (10), the special advocate may not communicate directly or indirectly with any person (including an excluded person)—

(a) (except in the case of the Appeal Tribunal or the party who was the respondent in the proceedings before the employment tribunal) on any matter contained in the documents referred to in rule 3(5), 3(6), 6(7) or 6(8)(b); or

(b) (except in the case of a person who was present) on any matter discussed or referred to during any part of the proceedings in which the Appeal Tribunal sat in private pursuant to a direction of the Minister under paragraph (1)(a) or an order of the Appeal Tribunal under paragraph (2)(a) read with paragraph (1)(a).

(8) The special advocate may apply for directions from the Appeal Tribunal authorising him to seek instructions from, or otherwise to communicate with, an excluded person—

(a) on any matter contained in the documents referred to in rule 3(5), 3(6), 6(7) or 6(8)(b); or

(b) on any matter discussed or referred to during any part of the proceedings in which the Appeal Tribunal sat in private as referred to in paragraph (7)(b).

(9) An application under paragraph (8) shall be made by presenting to the Registrar a notice of application, which shall state the title of the proceedings and set out the grounds of the application.

(10) The Registrar shall notify the Minister of an application for directions under paragraph (8) and the Minister shall be entitled to address the Appeal Tribunal on the application.

(11) In these rules, in any case in which a special advocate has been appointed in respect of a party, any reference to a party shall (save in those references specified in paragraph (12)) include the special advocate.

(12) The references mentioned in paragraph (11) are those in rules 5 and 18, the first and second references in rule 27(1A), paragraphs (1) and (6) of this rule, the first reference in paragraph (3) of this rule, rule 34(1), the reference in item 4 of Form 1, and in item 4 of Form 1A, in the Schedule to these Rules.]

NOTES

Substituted as noted to r 30 at **[2.177]**.

Paras (1), (4): words in square brackets substituted by the Employment Appeal Tribunal (Amendment) Rules 2004, SI 2004/2526, r 16.

Para (2): words in square brackets in sub-para (a) inserted by the Employment Appeal Tribunal (Amendment) Rules 2005, SI 2005/1871, r 2.

[2.179]

31 Drawing up, reasons for, and enforcement of orders

(1) Every order of the Appeal Tribunal shall be drawn up by the Registrar and a copy, sealed with the seal of the Tribunal, shall be served by the Registrar on every party to the proceedings to which it relates and—

(a) in the case of an order disposing of an appeal from an [employment tribunal] or of an order under [section 33 of the 1996 Act] on the Secretary of the [Employment Tribunals]; . . .

(b) in the case of an order disposing of an appeal from the Certification Officer, on that Officer.

[(c) in the case of an order imposing a penalty notice [regulation 20, 21 or 21A of the 1999 Regulations], [. . . regulation 33 of the 2004 Regulations] [or regulation 22 of the Information and Consultation Regulations] [. . . regulation 53 the 2007 Regulations], on the Secretary of State; or

(d) in the case of an order disposing of an appeal from the CAC made under regulation 38(8) of the 1999 Regulations, on the Chairman of the CAC.]

(2) [Subject to rule 31A,] the Appeal Tribunal shall, on the application of any party made within 14 days after the making of an order finally disposing of any proceedings, give its reasons in writing for the order unless it was made after the delivery of a reasoned judgment.

(3) Subject to any order made by the Court of Appeal or Court of Session and to any directions given by the Appeal Tribunal, an appeal from the Tribunal shall not suspend the enforcement of any order made by it.

NOTES

Para (1) is amended as follows:

Words in first and third pairs of square brackets in sub-para (a) substituted by the Employment Rights (Dispute Resolution) Act 1998, s 1(2)(a), (b).

Words in second pair of square brackets in sub-para (a) substituted, word omitted from the end of that paragraph revoked, and sub-paras (c), (d) added, by the Employment Appeal Tribunal (Amendment) Rules 2001, SI 2001/1128, r 20(a)–(c).

Words in first pair of square brackets in sub-para (c) substituted by the Transnational Information and Consultation of Employees (Amendment) Regulations 2010, SI 2010/1088, reg 30(1), (8), as from 5 June 2011.

Words in second pair of square brackets in sub-para (c) inserted by the Employment Appeal Tribunal (Amendment) Rules 2004, SI 2004/2526, r 18.

First word omitted from sub-para (c) revoked, and words in third pair of square brackets in that paragraph inserted, by the Information and Consultation of Employees Regulations 2004, SI 2004/3426, reg 41(d)(ii).

Second word omitted from sub-para (c) revoked, and words in final pair of square brackets in that paragraph inserted, by the Companies (Cross-Border Mergers) Regulations 2007, SI 2007/2974, reg 64(4).

Para (2): words in square brackets inserted by SI 2001/1128, r 20(d).

[2.180]

[31A Reasons for orders in cases concerning national security

(1) Paragraphs (1) to (5) of this rule apply to the document setting out the reasons for the Appeal Tribunal's order prepared under rule 31(2) or any reasoned judgment of the Appeal Tribunal as referred to in rule 31(2), in any particular Crown employment proceedings in which a direction of a Minister of the Crown has been given under rule 30A(1)(a), (b) or (c) or an order of the Appeal Tribunal has been made under rule 30A(2)(a) read with rule 30A(1)(a), (b) or (c).

(2) Before the Appeal Tribunal gives its reasons in writing for any order or delivers any reasoned judgment, the Registrar shall send a copy of the reasons or judgment to the Minister.

(3) If the Minister considers it expedient in the interests of national security, he may—

(a) direct the Appeal Tribunal that the document containing its reasons for any order or its reasoned judgment shall not be disclosed to any person who was excluded from all or part of the proceedings and to prepare a further document setting out the reasons for its order, or a further reasoned judgment, but with the omission of such reasons as are specified in the direction; or

(b) direct the Appeal Tribunal that the document containing its reasons for any order or its reasoned judgment shall not be disclosed to any person who was excluded from all or part of the proceedings, but that no further document setting out the Appeal Tribunal's reasons for its order or further reasoned judgment should be prepared.

(4) Where the Minister has directed the Appeal Tribunal in accordance with paragraph (3)(a), the document prepared pursuant to that direction shall be marked in each place where an omission has been made. The document may then be given by the Registrar to the parties.

(5) The Registrar shall send the document prepared pursuant to a direction of the Minister in accordance with paragraph (3)(a) and the full document without the omissions made pursuant to that direction—

(a) to whichever of the appellant and the respondent was not the [claimant] in the proceedings before the employment tribunal;

(b) if he was not an excluded person, to the person who was the [claimant] in the proceedings before the employment tribunal and, if he was not an excluded person, to his representative;

(c) if applicable, to the special advocate; and

(d) where there are proceedings before a superior court relating to the order in question, to that court.

(6) Where the Appeal Tribunal intends to take steps under rule 30A(2)(c) to keep secret all or part of the reasons for any order it makes, it shall send the full reasons for its order to the persons listed in sub-paragraphs (a) to (d) of paragraph (5), as appropriate.]

NOTES

Inserted by the Employment Appeal Tribunal (Amendment) Rules 2001, SI 2001/1128, r 21.

Para (5): words in square brackets in sub-paras (a), (b) substituted by the Employment Appeal Tribunal (Amendment) Rules 2004, SI 2004/2526, r 16.

[2.181]

32 Registration and proof of awards in respect of exclusion or expulsion from, or unjustifiable discipline by, a trade union

(1) This rule applies where an application has been made to the Appeal Tribunal under section 67 or 176 of the 1992 Act.

(2) Without prejudice to rule 31, where the Appeal Tribunal makes an order in respect of an application to which this rule applies, and that order—

(a) makes an award of compensation, or

(b) is or includes an order of the kind referred to in rule 8(b)(ii),

or both, the Registrar shall as soon as may be enter a copy of the order, sealed with the seal of the Tribunal, into a register kept by the Tribunal (in this rule referred to as "the Register").

(3) The production in any proceedings in any court of a document, purporting to be certified by the Registrar to be a true copy of an entry in the Register of an order to which this rule applies shall, unless the contrary is proved, be sufficient evidence of the document and of the facts stated therein.

[2.182]

33 Review of decisions and correction of errors

(1) The Appeal Tribunal may, either of its own motion or on application, review any order made by it and may, on such review, revoke or vary that order on the grounds that—

(a) the order was wrongly made as the result of an error on the part of the Tribunal or its staff;

(b) a party did not receive proper notice of the proceedings leading to the order; or

(c) the interests of justice require such review.

(2) An application under paragraph (1) above shall be made within 14 days of the date of the order.

(3) A clerical mistake in any order arising from an accidental slip or omission may at any time be corrected by, or on the authority of, a judge or member.

[(4) The decision to grant or refuse an application for review may be made by a judge.]

NOTES

Para (4): added by the Employment Appeal Tribunal (Amendment) Rules 2004, SI 2004/2526, r 19.

[2.183]

[34 General power to make costs or expenses orders

(1) In the circumstances listed in rule 34A the Appeal Tribunal may make an order ("a costs order") that a party or a special advocate, ("the paying party") make a payment in respect of the costs incurred by another party or a special advocate ("the receiving party").

(2) For the purposes of these Rules "costs" includes fees, charges, disbursements and expenses incurred by or on behalf of a party or special advocate in relation to the proceedings, including the reimbursement allowed to a litigant in person under rule 34D. In Scotland, all references to costs or costs orders (except in the expression "wasted costs") shall be read as references to expenses or orders for expenses.

(3) A costs order may be made against or in favour of a respondent who has not had an answer accepted in the proceedings in relation to the conduct of any part which he has taken in the proceedings.

(4) A party or special advocate may apply to the Appeal Tribunal for a costs order to be made at any time during the proceedings. An application may also be made at the end of a hearing, or in writing to the Registrar within 14 days of the date on which the order of the Appeal Tribunal finally disposing of the proceedings was sent to the parties.

(5) No costs order shall be made unless the Registrar has sent notice to the party or special advocate against whom the order may be made giving him the opportunity to give reasons why the order should not be made. This paragraph shall not be taken to require the Registrar to send notice to the party or special advocate if the party or special advocate has been given an opportunity to give reasons orally to the Appeal Tribunal as to why the order should not be made.

(6) Where the Appeal Tribunal makes a costs order it shall provide written reasons for doing so if a request for written reasons is made within 21 days of the date of the costs order. The Registrar shall send a copy of the written reasons to all the parties to the proceedings.]

NOTES

Substituted by the Employment Appeal Tribunal (Amendment) Rules 2004, SI 2004/2526, r 20.

[2.184]

[34A When a costs or expenses order may be made

(1) Where it appears to the Appeal Tribunal that any proceedings brought by the paying party were unnecessary, improper, vexatious or misconceived or that there has been unreasonable delay or other unreasonable conduct in the bringing or conducting of proceedings by the paying party, the Appeal Tribunal may make a costs order against the paying party.

(2) The Appeal Tribunal may in particular make a costs order against the paying party when—

- (a) he has not complied with a direction of the Appeal Tribunal;
- (b) he has amended its notice of appeal, document provided under rule 3 sub- paragraphs (5) or (6), Respondent's answer or statement of grounds of cross-appeal, or document provided under rule 6 sub-paragraphs (7) or (8); or
- (c) he has caused an adjournment of proceedings.

(3) Nothing in paragraph (2) shall restrict the Appeal Tribunal's discretion to award costs under paragraph (1).]

NOTES

Inserted, together with rr 34B–34D, by the Employment Appeal Tribunal (Amendment) Rules 2004, SI 2004/2526, r 21.

[2.185]

[34B The amount of a costs or expenses order

(1) Subject to sub-paragraphs (2) and (3) the amount of a costs order against the paying party can be determined in the following ways:

- (a) the Appeal Tribunal may specify the sum which the paying party must pay to the receiving party;
- (b) the parties may agree on a sum to be paid by the paying party to the receiving party and if they do so the costs order shall be for the sum agreed; or
- (c) the Appeal Tribunal may order the paying party to pay the receiving party the whole or a specified part of the costs of the receiving party with the amount to be paid being determined by way of detailed assessment in the High Court in accordance with the Civil Procedure Rules 1998 or in Scotland the Appeal Tribunal may direct that it be taxed by the Auditor of the Court of Session, from whose decision an appeal shall lie to a judge.

(2) The Appeal Tribunal may have regard to the paying party's ability to pay when considering the amount of a costs order.

(3) The costs of an assisted person in England and Wales shall be determined by detailed assessment in accordance with the Civil Procedure Rules.]

NOTES

Inserted as noted to r 34A at **[2.184]**.

[2.186]

[34C Personal liability of representatives for costs

(1) The Appeal Tribunal may make a wasted costs order against a party's representative.

(2) In a wasted costs order the Appeal Tribunal may disallow or order the representative of a party to meet the whole or part of any wasted costs of any party, including an order that the representative repay to his client any costs which have already been paid.

(3) "Wasted costs" means any costs incurred by a party (including the representative's own client and any party who does not have a legal representative):

(a) as a result of any improper, unreasonable or negligent act or omission on the part of any representative; or

(b) which, in the light of any such act or omission occurring after they were incurred, the Appeal Tribunal considers it reasonable to expect that party to pay.

(4) In this rule "representative" means a party's legal or other representative or any employee of such representative, but it does not include a representative who is not acting in pursuit of profit with regard to the proceedings. A person is considered to be acting in pursuit of profit if he is acting on a conditional fee arrangement.

(5) Before making a wasted costs order, the Appeal Tribunal shall give the representative a reasonable opportunity to make oral or written representations as to reasons why such an order should not be made. The Appeal Tribunal may also have regard to the representative's ability to pay when considering whether it shall make a wasted costs order or how much that order should be.

(6) When the Appeal Tribunal makes a wasted costs order, it must specify in the order the amount to be disallowed or paid.

(7) The Registrar shall inform the representative's client in writing—

(a) of any proceedings under this rule; or

(b) of any order made under this rule against the party's representative.

(8) Where the Appeal Tribunal makes a wasted costs order it shall provide written reasons for doing so if a request is made for written reasons within 21 days of the date of the wasted costs order. The Registrar shall send a copy of the written reasons to all parties to the proceedings.]

NOTES

Inserted as noted to r 34A at **[2.184]**. This rule does not apply to proceedings in the Appeal Tribunal which were commenced before 1 October 2004 (see SI 2004/2526, r 26(2)).

[2.187]

[34D Litigants in person and party litigants

(1) This rule applies where the Appeal Tribunal makes a costs order in favour of a party who is a litigant in person.

(2) The costs allowed under this rule must not exceed, except in the case of a disbursement, two-thirds of the amount which would have been allowed if the litigant in person had been represented by a legal representative.

(3) The litigant in person shall be allowed—

(a) costs for the same categories of—

(i) work; and

(ii) disbursements,

which would have been allowed if the work had been done or the disbursements had been made by a legal representative on the litigant in person's behalf;

(b) the payments reasonably made by him for legal services relating to the conduct of the proceedings;

(c) the costs of obtaining expert assistance in assessing the costs claim; and

(d) other expenses incurred by him in relation to the proceedings.

(4) The amount of costs to be allowed to the litigant in person for any item of work claimed shall be—

(a) where the litigant in person can prove financial loss, the amount that he can prove he had lost for the time reasonably spent on doing the work; or

(b) where the litigant in person cannot prove financial loss, an amount for the time which the Tribunal considers reasonably spent on doing the work at the rate of £25.00 per hour;

(5) For the year commencing 6th April 2006 the hourly rate of £25.00 shall be increased by the sum of £1.00 and for each subsequent year commencing on 6 April, the hourly rate for the previous year shall also be increased by the sum of £1.00.

(6) A litigant in person who is allowed costs for attending at court to conduct his case is not entitled to a witness allowance in respect of such attendance in addition to those costs.

(7) For the purpose of this rule, a litigant in person includes—

(a) a company or other corporation which is acting without a legal representative; and

(b) in England and Wales a barrister, solicitor, solicitor's employee or other authorised litigator (as defined in the Courts and Legal Services Act), who is acting for himself; and
(c) in Scotland, an advocate or solicitor (within the meaning of the Solicitors (Scotland) Act 1980) who is acting for himself.

(8) In the application of this rule to Scotland, references to a litigant in person shall be read as references to a party litigant.]

NOTES

Inserted as noted to r 34A at **[2.184]**.

[2.188]

35 Service of documents

(1) Any notice or other document required or authorised by these Rules to be served on, or delivered to, any person may be sent to him by post to his address for service or, where no address for service has been given, to his registered office, principal place of business, head or main office or last known address, as the case may be, and any notice or other document required or authorised to be served on, or delivered to, the Appeal Tribunal may be sent by post or delivered to the Registrar—
(a) in the case of a notice instituting proceedings, at the central office or any other office of the Tribunal; or
(b) in any other case, at the office of the Tribunal in which the proceedings in question are being dealt with in accordance with rule 38(2).

(2) Any notice or other document required or authorised to be served on, or delivered to, an unincorporated body may be sent to its secretary, manager or other similar officer.

(3) Every document served by post shall be assumed, in the absence of evidence to the contrary, to have been delivered in the normal course of post.

(4) The Appeal Tribunal may inform itself in such manner as it thinks fit of the posting of any document by an officer of the Tribunal.

(5) The Appeal Tribunal may direct that service of any document be dispensed with or be effected otherwise than in the manner prescribed by these Rules.

[2.189]

36 Conciliation

Where at any stage of any proceedings it appears to the Appeal Tribunal that there is a reasonable prospect of agreement being reached between the parties [or of disposal of the appeal or a part of it by consensual means], the Tribunal may take such steps as it thinks fit to enable the parties to avail themselves of any opportunities for conciliation, whether by adjourning any proceedings or otherwise.

NOTES

Words in square brackets inserted by the Employment Appeal Tribunal (Amendment) Rules 2004, SI 2004/2526, r 22.

[2.190]

37 Time

(1) The time prescribed by these Rules or by order of the Appeal Tribunal for doing any act may be extended (whether it has already expired or not) or abridged, and the date appointed for any purpose may be altered, by order of the Tribunal.

[(1A) Where an act is required to be done on or before a particular day it shall be done by 4 pm on that day.]

(2) Where the last day for the doing of any act falls on a day on which the appropriate office of the Tribunal is closed and by reason thereof the act cannot be done on that day, it may be done on the next day on which that office is open.

(3) An application for an extension of the time prescribed for the doing of an act, including the institution of an appeal under rule 3, shall be heard and determined as an [interim] application under rule 20.

[(4) An application for an extension of the time prescribed for the institution of an appeal under rule3 shall not be heard until the notice of the appeal has been served on the Appeal Tribunal.]

NOTES

Para (1A): inserted by the Employment Appeal Tribunal (Amendment) Rules 2004, SI 2004/2526, r 23(1).
Para (3): word in square brackets substituted by SI 2004/2526, r 23(2).
Para (4): added by the Employment Appeal Tribunal (Amendment) Rules 2001, SI 2001/1128, r 23.

[2.191]

38 Tribunal offices and allocation of business

(1) The central office and any other office of the Appeal Tribunal shall be open at such times as the President may direct.

(2) Any proceedings before the Tribunal may be dealt with at the central office or at such other office as the President may direct.

[2.192]

39 Non-compliance with, and waiver of, rules

(1) Failure to comply with any requirements of these Rules shall not invalidate any proceedings unless the Appeal Tribunal otherwise directs.

(2) The Tribunal may, if it considers that to do so would lead to the more expeditious or economical disposal of any proceedings or would otherwise be desirable in the interests of justice, dispense with the taking of any step required or authorised by these Rules, or may direct that any such steps be taken in some manner other than that prescribed by these Rules.

(3) The powers of the Tribunal under paragraph (2) extend to authorising the institution of an appeal notwithstanding that the period prescribed in rule 3(2) may not have commenced.

[2.193]

40 Transitional provisions

(1) Where, prior to 16th December 1993, an [employment tribunal] has given full written reasons for its decision or order, those reasons shall be treated as extended written reasons for the purposes of rule 3(1)(c) and rule 3(2) and for the purposes of Form 1 in the Schedule to these Rules.

(2) Anything validly done under or pursuant to the Employment Appeal Tribunal Rules 1980 shall be treated as having been done validly for the purposes of these Rules, whether or not what was done could have been done under or pursuant to these Rules.

NOTES

Para (1): words in square brackets substituted by the Employment Rights (Dispute Resolution) Act 1998, s 1(2)(a).
Employment Appeal Tribunal Rules 1980, SI 1980/2035: revoked by r 1(2) of these Rules.

SCHEDULE

[FORM 1

Rule 3

Notice of Appeal from Decision of Employment Tribunal

[2.194]

1. The appellant is (*name and address of appellant*).

2. Any communication relating to this appeal may be sent to the appellant at (*appellant's address for service, including telephone number if any*).

3. The appellant appeals from (*here give particulars of the judgment, decision or order of the employment tribunal from which the appeal is brought including the location of the employment tribunal and the date*).

4. The parties to the proceedings before the employment tribunal, other than the appellant, were (*name and addresses of other parties to the proceedings resulting in judgment, decision or order appealed from*).

5. Copies of—
- (a) the written record of the employment tribunal's judgment, decision or order and the written reasons of the employment tribunal;
- (b) the claim (ET1);
- (c) the response (ET3); and/or (*where relevant*)
- (d) an explanation as to why any of these documents are not included;

are attached to this notice.

6. If the appellant has made an application to the employment tribunal for a review of its judgment or decision, copies of—
- (a) the review application;
- (b) the judgment;
- (c) the written reasons of the employment tribunal in respect of that review application; and /or;
- (d) a statement by or on behalf of the appellant, if such be the case, that a judgment is awaited

are attached to this Notice. If any of these documents exist but cannot be included, then a written explanation must be given.

Part 2 Statutory Instruments

7. The grounds upon which this appeal is brought are that the employment tribunal erred in law in that (*here set out in paragraphs the various grounds of appeal*).

Date . . . .

Signed . . . .

NB. The details entered on your Notice of Appeal must be legible and suitable for photocopying or electronic scanning. The use of black ink or typescript is recommended.]

NOTES

Substituted by the Employment Appeal Tribunal (Amendment) Rules 2005, SI 2005/1871, r 3(a).

[FORM 1A

Rule 3

Notice of Appeal from the CAC Made Pursuant to Regulation 38(8) of the Transnational Information and Consultation of Employees Regulations 1999, [. . . regulation 47(6) of the European Public Limited-Liability Company Regulations 2004] [. . . regulation 35(6) of the Information and Consultation of Employees Regulations 2004] [or regulation 57(6) of the Companies (Cross-Border Mergers) Regulations 2007]

[2.195]

1. The appellant is *(name and address of appellant)*.

2. Any communication relating to this appeal may be sent to the appellant at *(appellant's address for service, including telephone number if any)*.

3. The appellant appeals from *(here give particulars of the decision, declaration or order of the CAC from which the appeal is brought including the date)*.

4. The parties to the proceedings before the CAC, other than the appellant, were *(names and addresses of other parties to the proceedings resulting in decision appealed from)*.

5. A copy of the CAC's decision, declaration or order appealed from is attached to this notice.

6. The grounds upon which this appeal is brought are that the CAC erred in law in that *(here set out in paragraphs the various grounds of appeal)*.

Date. . . . .

Signed. . . . .]

NOTES

Inserted by the Employment Appeal Tribunal (Amendment) Rules 2001, SI 2001/1128, r 24.

Words in first pair of square brackets in the heading inserted by the Employment Appeal Tribunal (Amendment) Rules 2004, SI 2004/2526, r 25(1); first word omitted from the heading revoked, and words in second pair of square brackets inserted, by the Information and Consultation of Employees Regulations 2004, SI 2004/3426, reg 41(e); second word omitted revoked, and words in final pair of square brackets added, by the Companies (Cross-Border Mergers) Regulations 2007, SI 2007/2974, reg 64(5).

FORM 2

Rule 3

Notice of Appeal from Decision of Certification Officer

[2.196]

1. The appellant is *(name and address of appellant)*.

2. Any communication relating to this appeal may be sent to the appellant at *(appellant's address for service, including telephone number if any)*.

3. The appellant appeals from

(here give particulars of the order or decision of the Certification Officer from which the appeal is brought).

4. The appellant's grounds of appeal are:

(here state the grounds of appeal).

5. A copy of the Certification Officer's decision is attached to this notice.

Date. . . . .

Signed. . . . .

FORM 3

Rule 6

Respondent's Answer

[2.197]

1. The respondent is *(name and address of respondent).*

2. Any communication relating to this appeal may be sent to the respondent at *(respondent's address for service, including telephone number if any).*

3. The respondent intends to resist the appeal of (here give the name of appellant). The grounds on which the respondent will rely are (the grounds relied upon by the [employment tribunal]/Certification Officer for making the [judgment,] decision or order appealed from) (and) (the following grounds):

(here set out any grounds which differ from those relied upon by the [employment tribunal] or Certification Officer, as the case may be).

4. The respondent cross-appeals from

(here give particulars of the decision appealed from).

5. The respondent's grounds of appeal are:

(here state the grounds of appeal).

Date. . . . .

Signed. . . . .

NOTES

Para 3: words in first and third pairs of square brackets substituted by the Employment Rights (Dispute Resolution) Act 1998, s 1(2)(a); word in second pair of square brackets inserted by the Employment Appeal Tribunal (Amendment) Rules 2005, SI 2005/1871, r 3(b)(ii).

FORM 4

Rule 8

Application to the Employment Appeal Tribunal for Compensation for Exclusion or Expulsion from a Trade Union or for Compensation or an Order in respect of Unjustifiable Discipline

[2.198]

1. My name is

My address is

2. Any communication relating to this application may be sent to me at

(state address for service, including telephone number, if any).

3. My complaint against *(state the name and address of the trade union)* was declared to be well-founded by *(state tribunal)* on *(give date of decision or order).*

4. *(Where the application relates to exclusion or expulsion from a trade union)* I have not been admitted/re-admitted* to membership of the above-named trade union and hereby apply for compensation on the following grounds.

(Where the application relates to unjustifiable discipline) The determination infringing my right not to be unjustifiably disciplined has not been revoked./ The trade union has failed to take all the steps necessary for securing the reversal of things done for the purpose of giving effect to the determination.*

(*Delete as appropriate)

Date. . . . .

Signed. . . . .

NB.—A copy of the decision or order declaring the complaint against the trade union to be well-founded must be enclosed with this application.

FORM 4A

. . .

NOTES

Inserted by the Employment Appeal Tribunal (Amendment) Rules 2001, SI 2001/1128, r 25.

Revoked by the Transnational Information and Consultation of Employees (Amendment) Regulations 2010, SI 2010/1088, reg 30(1), (9)(a), as from 5 June 2011.

[FORM 4B

Rule 16AA

Applications under Regulation 33 of the European Public Limited–Liability Company Regulations 2004 [or regulation 22 of the Information and Consultation of Employees Regulations 2004] [or regulation 53 of the Companies (Cross-Border Mergers) Regulations 2007][or regulation 20, 21 or 21A of the 1999 Regulations]

[2.199]

1. The applicant's name is *(name and address of applicant)*

2. Any communication relating to this application may be sent to the applicant at *(applicant's address for service, including telephone number if any).*

3. The application is made against *(state identity of respondent)*

4. The address of the respondent is

5. The Central Arbitration Committee made a declaration [or decision *(delete which does not apply)*] in my favour on [] *(insert date)* and I request the Employment Tribunal to issue a penalty notice in accordance with regulation 33 of the European Public Limited-Liability Company Regulations 2004 [or regulation 22 of the Information and Consultation of Employees Regulations 2004 [or regulation 53 of the Companies (Cross-Border Mergers) Regulations 2007] [or regulation 20, 21 or 21A of the Transnational Information and Consultation of Employees Regulations 1999] *(delete which does not apply)*].

Date. . . . .

Signed. . . . .]

NOTES

Inserted by the Employment Appeal Tribunal (Amendment) Rules 2004, SI 2004/2526, r 25(2).

Words in first pair of square brackets in the heading, and second (outer) pair of square brackets in para 5, inserted by the Information and Consultation of Employees Regulations 2004, SI 2004/3426, reg 41(f); words in second pair of square brackets in the heading, and third (inner) pair of square brackets in para 5, inserted by the Companies (Cross-Border Mergers) Regulations 2007, SI 2007/2974, reg 64(6); words in third pair of square brackets in the heading, and words in first and fourth (inner) pairs of square brackets in para 5 inserted by the Transnational Information and Consultation of Employees (Amendment) Regulations 2010, SI 2010/1088, reg 30(1), (9)(b), (c), as from 5 June 2011.

FORM 5

Rule 11

Notice of appearance to Application to Employment Appeal Tribunal for Compensation for Exclusion or Expulsion from a Trade Union or for Compensation or an Order in respect of Unjustifiable Discipline

[2.200]

1. The respondent trade union is *(name and address of union).*

2. Any communication relating to this application may be sent to the respondent at *(respondent's address for service, including telephone number, if any).*

3. The respondent intends to resist the application of *(here give name of the applicant).*

The grounds on which the respondent will rely are as follows:

4. *(Where the application relates to exclusion or expulsion from the trade union, state whether or not the applicant had been admitted or re-admitted to membership on or before the date of application.)*

(Where the application relates to unjustifiable discipline, state whether—

(a) the determination infringing the applicant's right not to be unjustifiably disciplined has been revoked; and

(b) the trade union has taken all the steps necessary for securing the reversal of anything done for the purpose of giving effect to the determination.)

Date. . . . .

Signed. . . . .

Position in union. . . . .

[FORM 5A

Rule 16C

Notice of Appearance to the Employment Appeal Tribunal under [Regulation 20, 21 or 21A of the Transnational Information and Consultation of Employees Regulations 1999 or Regulation 20(6) of the European Public Limited-Liability Company (Employee Involvement) (Great Britain) Regulations 2009 or Regulation 22(6) of the Information and Consultation of Employees Regulations 2004 or Regulation 53(6) of the Companies (Cross-Border Mergers) Regulations 2007]

[2.201]
1. The respondent is *(name and address of respondent).*

2. Any communication relating to this application may be sent to the respondent at *(respondent's address for service, including telephone number, if any).*

3. The respondent intends to resist the application of *(here give the name or description of the applicant).*

The grounds on which the respondent will rely are as follows: *(give particulars, set out in paragraphs and making reference to the specific provisions in the Transnational Information and Consultation of Employees Regulations 1999* [*or European Public Limited-Liability Company (Employee Involvement) (Great Britain) Regulations 2009 or Information and Consultation of Employees Regulations 2004 or Companies (Cross-Border Mergers) Regulations 2007*] *alleged to have been breached*).

Date. . . . .

Signed. . . . .

Position in respondent company or undertaking:. . . . .

(Where appropriate give position in respondent central or local management or position held in relation to respondent Works Council).]

NOTES

Inserted by the Employment Appeal Tribunal (Amendment) Rules 2001, SI 2001/1128, r 26.

Words in square brackets in the heading substituted, and words in square brackets in para 3 inserted, by the Transnational Information and Consultation of Employees (Amendment) Regulations 2010, SI 2010/1088, reg 30(1), (9)(d), (e), as from 5 June 2011.

FORM 6

Rule 13

Application to the Employment Appeal Tribunal Under [section 33 of the 1996 Act] for a Restriction of Proceedings Order

[2.202]
1. The applicant is *(the Attorney General/Lord Advocate).*

2. Any communication relating to this application may be sent to the applicant at *(state address for service, including telephone number).*

3. The application is for a restriction of proceedings order to be made against *(state the name and address of the person against whom the order is sought).*

4. An affidavit in support of the application is attached.

Date. . . . .

Signed. . . . .

NOTES

Words in square brackets substituted by the Employment Appeal Tribunal (Amendment) Rules 2001, SI 2001/1128, r 27.

FORM 7

Rule 15

Notice of appearance to Application to the Employment Appeal Tribunal under [section 33 of the 1996 Act] for a Restriction of Proceedings Order

[2.203]
1. The respondent is *(state name and address of respondent).*

2. Any communication relating to this application may be sent to the respondent at *(respondent's address for service, including telephone number, if any).*

3. The respondent intends to resist the application. An affidavit in support is attached to this notice.

Date. . . . .

Signed. . . . .

NOTES

Words in square brackets substituted by the Employment Appeal Tribunal (Amendment) Rules 2001, SI 2001/1128, r 27.

REDUNDANCY PAYMENTS (NATIONAL HEALTH SERVICE) (MODIFICATION) ORDER 1993

(SI 1993/3167)

NOTES

Made: 16 December 1993.

Authority: Employment Protection (Consolidation) Act 1978, ss 149(1)(b), 154(3) (repealed). This Order now has effect as if made under the Employment Rights Act 1996, ss 209(1)(b), 236(5).

Commencement: 13 January 1994.

See *Harvey* E(3)(H)

ARRANGEMENT OF ARTICLES

SCHEDULES

[2.204]

1 Citation, commencement and interpretation

(1) This Order may be cited as the Redundancy Payments (National Health Service) (Modification) Order 1993 and shall come into force on 13th January 1994.

(2) In this Order, unless the context otherwise requires—

(a) "relevant event" means any event occurring on or after the coming into force of this Order on the happening of which an employee may become entitled to a redundancy payment in accordance with the provisions of the 1978 Act;

(b) "the 1978 Act" means the Employment Protection (Consolidation) Act 1978.

NOTES

Employment Protection (Consolidation) Act 1978: repealed and largely consolidated in the Trade Union and Labour Relations (Consolidation) Act 1992, the Employment Rights Act 1996 and the Employment Tribunals Act 1996.

[2.205]

2 Application of order

This Order applies to any person who immediately before the occurrence of the relevant event is employed by an employer described in Schedule 1 to this Order, for the purposes of determining that person's entitlement to a redundancy payment under the 1978 Act and the amount of such payment.

NOTES

"The 1978 Act": as to redundancy payments, etc see now the Employment Rights Act 1996, Pt XI (ss 135–181).

[2.206]

3 Application of certain redundancy payments provisions with modifications

In relation to any person to whom this Order applies the provisions of the 1978 Act mentioned in Schedule 2 to this Order shall have effect subject to the modifications specified in that Schedule.

[2.207]

4 Transitional, supplementary and incidental provisions

(1) Any reference to the 1978 Act in any enactment shall have effect as a reference to that Act as modified by this Order in relation to persons to whom this Order applies.

(2) Any document which refers, whether specifically or by means of a general description, to an enactment which is modified by any provision of this Order shall, except so far as the context otherwise requires, be construed as referring, or as including a reference, to that provision.

(3) Where a period of employment of a person to whom this Order applies falls to be computed in accordance with the provisions of the 1978 Act as modified by this Order, the provisions of this Order shall have effect in relation to any period whether falling wholly or partly before or after the coming into force of this Order.

SCHEDULES

SCHEDULE 1
EMPLOYMENT TO WHICH THIS ORDER APPLIES: EMPLOYERS IMMEDIATELY BEFORE THE RELEVANT EVENT

Article 2

[2.208]

[**1.** a Strategic Health Authority or Health Authority established under section 8 of the National Health Service Act 1977 ("the 1977 Act");

1A. a Special Health Authority established under section 11 of the 1977 Act;]

2. a National Health Service trust established by an order made under section 5(1) of the National Health Service and Community Care Act 1990;

[**2ZA.** an NHS foundation trust within the meaning of section 1(1) of the Health and Social Care (Community Health and Standards) Act 2003;]

[**2A.** a Primary Care Trust established under section 16A of the 1977 Act;]

[**2B.** a clinical commissioning group established under section 14D of the National Health Service Act 2006;

2C. the National Health Service Commissioning Board;

2D. the National Institute for Health and Care Excellence;

2E. the Health and Social Care Information Centre;]

3. a Family Health Services Authority (formerly called a Family Practitioner Committee) established by an order made under section 10(1) of the 1977 Act;

4. the Dental Practice Board (formerly called the Dental Estimates Board) constituted by regulations made under section 37(1) of the 1977 Act;

5. . . .

6. a Health Board or a special Health Board constituted under section 2(1)(a) or section 2(1)(b) respectively of the National Health Service (Scotland) Act 1978 (hereinafter in this Schedule referred to as "the 1978 Act");

7. . . .

8. the Common Services Agency for the Scottish Health Service established under section 10 of the 1978 Act;

9. a National Health Service trust established under section 12A(1) of the 1978 Act;

10. the Scottish Dental Practice Board (formerly called the Scottish Dental Estimates Board) constituted by regulations made under section 4 of the 1978 Act.

NOTES

Paras 1, 1A: substituted, for the original para 1, by the National Health Service Reform and Health Care Professions Act 2002 (Supplementary, Consequential etc Provisions) Regulations 2002, SI 2002/2469, reg 4, Sch 1, Pt 2, para 61.

Para 2ZA: inserted by the Health and Social Care (Community Health and Standards) Act 2003 (Supplementary and Consequential Provision) (NHS Foundation Trusts) Order 2004, SI 2004/696, art 3(1), Sch 1, para 14.

Para 2A: inserted by the Health Act 1999 (Supplementary, Consequential etc Provisions) (No 2) Order 2000, SI 2000/694, art 3, Schedule, Pt II, para 6.

Paras 2B–2E: inserted by the National Treatment Agency (Abolition) and the Health and Social Care Act 2012 (Consequential, Transitional and Saving Provisions) Order 2013, SI 2013/235, art 11, Sch 2, Pt 1, para 24, as from 1 April 2013.

Para 5: revoked by the Health and Social Care (Community Health and Standards) Act 2003 (Public Health Laboratory Service Board) (Consequential Provisions) Order 2005, SI 2005/1622, art 3, Schedule.

Para 7: revoked by the Mental Health (Care and Treatment) (Scotland) Act 2003 (Consequential Provisions) Order 2005, SI 2005/2078, art 15, Sch 2, para 16 (in relation to England and Wales), and by the Mental Health (Care and Treatment)

(Scotland) Act 2003 (Modification of Subordinate Legislation) Order 2005, SSI 2005/445, art 2, Schedule, para 20 (in relation to Scotland).

SCHEDULE 2
MODIFICATIONS TO CERTAIN REDUNDANCY PAYMENTS PROVISIONS OF THE 1978 ACT

Article 3

[2.209]

1. Section 81 of the 1978 Act shall have effect as if:—

(a) in subsection (1) for the words "has been continuously employed for the requisite period" there were substituted the words "has been employed in relevant health service for the requisite period" and for the words "Schedules 4, 13 and 14" there were substituted the words "Schedule 4, as modified by the Redundancy Payments (National Health Service) (Modification) Order 1993, and Schedules 13 and 14";

(b) after subsection (4) there were inserted the following subsection:—

"(5) In this section and Schedule 4—

(a) "relevant health service" means—

(i) continuous employment by an employer referred to in the Appendix to Schedule 2 to the Redundancy Payments (National Health Service) (Modification) Order 1993, or

(ii) where immediately before the relevant event a person has been successively employed by two or more employers referred to in the Appendix to Schedule 2 to the said Order, such aggregate period of service with such employers as would be continuous employment if they were a single employer;

(b) "relevant event" means any event occurring on or after the coming into force of the Redundancy Payments (National Health Service) (Modification) Order 1993 on the happening of which an employee may become entitled to a redundancy payment in accordance with this Act.".

2. Section 82 of the 1978 Act shall have effect as if immediately after subsection (7) there were inserted—

"(7A) Any reference in this section to re-engagement by the employer shall be construed as including a reference to re-engagement by any employer referred to in the Appendix to Schedule 2 to the Redundancy Payments (National Health Service) (Modification) Order 1993 and any reference in this section to an offer by the employer shall be construed as including a reference to an offer made by any such employer."

3. Section 84 of the 1978 Act shall have effect as if immediately after subsection (7) thereof there were inserted the following subsection—

"(7A) Any reference in this section to re-engagement by the employer shall be construed as including a reference to re-engagement by any employer referred to in the Appendix to Schedule 2 to the Redundancy Payments (National Health Service) (Modification) Order 1993 and any reference in this section to an offer made by the employer shall be construed as including a reference to an offer made by any such employer."

4. Schedule 4 to the 1978 Act shall have effect as if for paragraph 1 there were substituted the following paragraph—

"1. The amount of a redundancy payment to which an employee is entitled in any case to which the Redundancy Payments (National Health Service) (Modification) Order 1993 applies shall, subject to the following provisions of this Schedule, be calculated by reference to the period ending with the relevant date during which he has been employed in relevant health service."

5. Schedule 6 to the 1978 Act shall have effect as if in paragraph 1 for the words "Schedule 4" there were substituted the words "Schedule 4 as modified by the Redundancy Payments (National Health Service) (Modification) Order 1993".

NOTES

"The 1978 Act": for provisions as to redundancy payments, etc see now the Employment Rights Act 1996, Pt XI (ss 135–181).

APPENDIX
EMPLOYERS WITH WHICH EMPLOYMENT MAY CONSTITUTE RELEVANT HEALTH SERVICE

[2.210]
Any employer described in Schedule 1 whether or not in existence at the time of the relevant event.

[EMPLOYMENT TRIBUNALS] EXTENSION OF JURISDICTION (ENGLAND AND WALES) ORDER 1994

(SI 1994/1623)

NOTES

Made: 11 July 1994.

Authority: Employment Protection (Consolidation) Act 1978, ss 131(1), (4A), (5), (5A), 154(3) (repealed). This Order now has effect as if made under the Employment Tribunals Act 1996, ss 3(1), 8(2)–(4), 41(4).

Commencement: 12 July 1994.

Title: words in square brackets substituted by the Employment Rights (Dispute Resolution) Act 1998, s 1(2)(b).

This Order applies only to England and Wales. For the equivalent Scottish Order, see the Employment Tribunals Extension of Jurisdiction (Scotland) Order 1994, SI 1994/1624 at **[2.222]**.

Tribunal jurisdiction: the Employment Act 2002, s 38 applies to proceedings before the employment tribunal relating to a claim under this Order; see s 38(1) of, and Sch 5 to, the 2002 Act at **[1.1228]**, **[1.1236]**. See also the Trade Union and Labour Relations (Consolidation) Act 1992, s 207A at **[1.474]** (as inserted by the Employment Act 2008). That section provides that in proceedings before an employment tribunal relating to a claim by an employee under any of the jurisdictions listed in Sch A2 to the 1992 Act at **[1.648]** (which includes this Order) the tribunal may adjust any award given if the employer or the employee has unreasonably failed to comply with the relevant Code of Practice as defined by s 207A(4). See also the revised Acas Code of Practice 1 – Disciplinary and Grievance Procedures (2009) at **[4.1]**.

Conciliation: proceedings in respect of which an employment tribunal has jurisdiction by virtue of the Employment Tribunals Act 1996, s 3 are proceedings to which s 18 of that Act applies; see s 18(1)(e) at **[1.706]**.

See *Harvey* PI(1), U2.

ARRANGEMENT OF ARTICLES

[2.211]
1 Citation, commencement and interpretation

(1) This Order may be cited as the [Employment Tribunals] Extension of Jurisdiction (England and Wales) Order 1994 and comes into force on the first day after it is made.

(2) In this Order—
"contract claim" means a claim in respect of which proceedings may be brought before an [employment tribunal] by virtue of article 3 or 4; and
"the 1978 Act" means the Employment Protection (Consolidation) Act 1978.

NOTES

Words in square brackets substituted by the Employment Rights (Dispute Resolution) Act 1998, s 1(2)(a), (b).

Employment Protection (Consolidation) Act 1978: repealed and largely consolidated in the Trade Union and Labour Relations (Consolidation) Act 1992, the Employment Rights Act 1996 and the Employment Tribunals Act 1996.

[2.212]
2 Transitional provision

This Order does not enable proceedings in respect of a contract claim to be brought before an [employment tribunal] unless—
(a) the effective date of termination (as defined in section 55(4) of the 1978 Act) in respect of the contract giving rise to the claim, or
(b) where there is no effective date of termination, the last day upon which the employee works in the employment which has terminated,

occurs on or after the day on which the Order comes into force.

Part 2 Statutory Instruments

NOTES

Words in square brackets substituted by the Employment Rights (Dispute Resolution) Act 1998, s 1(2)(a).
"Section 55(4) of the 1978 Act": see now the Employment Rights Act 1996, s 97(1).

[2.213]
3 Extension of jurisdiction

Proceedings may be brought before an [employment tribunal] in respect of a claim of an employee for the recovery of damages or any other sum (other than a claim for damages, or for a sum due, in respect of personal injuries) if—

(a) the claim is one to which section 131(2) of the 1978 Act applies and which a court in England and Wales would under the law for the time being in force have jurisdiction to hear and determine;
(b) the claim is not one to which article 5 applies; and
(c) the claim arises or is outstanding on the termination of the employee's employment.

NOTES

Words in square brackets substituted by the Employment Rights (Dispute Resolution) Act 1998, s 1(2)(a).
"Section 131(2) of the 1978 Act": see now the Employment Tribunals Act 1996, s 3(2).

[2.214]
4

Proceedings may be brought before an [employment tribunal] in respect of a claim of an employer for the recovery of damages or any other sum (other than a claim for damages, or for a sum due, in respect of personal injuries) if—

(a) the claim is one to which section 131(2) of the 1978 Act applies and which a court in England and Wales would under the law for the time being in force have jurisdiction to hear and determine;
(b) the claim is not one to which article 5 applies;
(c) the claim arises or is outstanding on the termination of the employment of the employee against whom it is made; and
(d) proceedings in respect of a claim of that employee have been brought before an [employment tribunal] by virtue of this Order.

NOTES

Words in square brackets substituted by the Employment Rights (Dispute Resolution) Act 1998, s 1(2)(a).
"Section 131(2) of the 1978 Act": see now the Employment Tribunals Act 1996, s 3(2).

[2.215]
5

This article applies to a claim for breach of a contractual term of any of the following descriptions—

(a) a term requiring the employer to provide living accommodation for the employee;
(b) a term imposing an obligation on the employer or the employee in connection with the provision of living accommodation;
(c) a term relating to intellectual property;
(d) a term imposing an obligation of confidence;
(e) a term which is a covenant in restraint of trade.

In this article, "intellectual property" includes copyright, rights in performances, moral rights, design right, registered designs, patents and trade marks.

[2.216]
6 Manner in which proceedings may be brought

Proceedings on a contract claim may be brought before an [employment tribunal] by presenting a complaint to an [employment tribunal].

NOTES

Words in square brackets substituted by the Employment Rights (Dispute Resolution) Act 1998, s 1(2)(a).

[2.217]
7 Time within which proceedings may be brought

[Subject to article 8A, an employment tribunal] shall not entertain a complaint in respect of an employee's contract claim unless it is presented—

(a) within the period of three months beginning with the effective date of termination of the contract giving rise to the claim, or

(b) where there is no effective date of termination, within the period of three months beginning with the last day upon which the employee worked in the employment which has terminated, or

[(ba) where the period within which a complaint must be presented in accordance with paragraph (a) or (b) is extended by regulation 15 of the Employment Act 2002 (Dispute Resolution) Regulations 2004, the period within which the complaint must be presented shall be the extended period rather than the period in paragraph (a) or (b)],

(c) where the tribunal is satisfied that it was not reasonably practicable for the complaint to be presented within whichever of those periods is applicable, within such further period as the tribunal considers reasonable.

NOTES

Words in first pair of square brackets substituted by the Cross-Border Mediation (EU Directive) Regulations 2011, SI 2011/1133, regs 59, 60, as from 20 May 2011.

Para (ba) inserted by the Employment Act 2002 (Dispute Resolution) Regulations 2004, SI 2004/752, reg 17(c).

Note: the text of this provision has been changed following the comments of Underhill J in *HM Prison Service v Barua* [2007] IRLR 4. In setting out this article in the text of his judgment, Underhill J commented—

"I have reproduced this as it appears in Butterworths Employment Law Handbook, but it is in fact unclear whether the "or" at the end of para (ba) should not appear at the end of para (b) instead; reg 17(c) of the 2004 Regulations, which inserts para (ba) into the 1994 Order, is arguably ambiguous on this point. Either way, however, although the lay-out is clumsy it is clear that para (ba) is intended as a qualification to paras (a) and (b)".

Accordingly, the "or" that followed para (ba) of this article in the fourteenth edition of this work has been moved to the end of para (b).

[2.218]
8

[Subject to article 8A, an employment tribunal] shall not entertain a complaint in respect of an employer's contract claim unless—

(a) it is presented at a time when there is before the tribunal a complaint in respect of a contract claim of a particular employee which has not been settled or withdrawn;

(b) it arises out of a contract with that employee; and

(c) it is presented—

  (i) within the period of six weeks beginning with the day, or if more than one the last of the days, on which the employer (or other person who is the respondent party to the employee's contract claim) received from the tribunal a copy of an originating application in respect of a contract claim of that employee; or

  (ii) where the tribunal is satisfied that it was not reasonably practicable for the complaint to be presented within that period, within such further period as the tribunal considers reasonable.

NOTES

Words in square brackets substituted by the Cross-Border Mediation (EU Directive) Regulations 2011, SI 2011/1133, regs 59, 61, as from 20 May 2011.

[2.219]
[8A Extension of time limits because of mediation in certain cross-border disputes

(1) In this article—

(a) "Mediation Directive" means Directive 2008/52/EC of the European Parliament and of the Council of 21 May 2008 on certain aspects of mediation in civil and commercial matters;

(b) "mediation" has the meaning given by article 3(a) of the Mediation Directive;

(c) "mediator" has the meaning given by article 3(b) of the Mediation Directive; and

(d) "relevant dispute" means a dispute to which article 8(1) of the Mediation Directive applies (certain cross-border disputes).

(2) Paragraph (3) applies where—

(a) a time limit is set by article 7(a) or (b) in relation to the whole or part of a relevant dispute;

(b) a mediation in relation to the relevant dispute starts before the period expires; and

(c) if not extended by this article, the time limit would expire before the mediation ends or less than four weeks after it ends.

(3) The time limit expires instead at the end of four weeks after the mediation ends (subject to paragraph (4)).

(4) If a time limit mentioned in paragraph (2)(a) has been extended by this article, paragraphs (2) and (3) apply to the extended time limit as they apply to a time limit mentioned in paragraph (2)(a).

(5) Paragraph (6) applies where—

(a) a time limit is set by article 8(c)(i) in relation to the whole or part of a relevant dispute;

(b) a mediation in relation to the relevant dispute starts before the time limit expires; and

(c) if not extended by this article the time limit would expire before the mediation ends or less than two weeks after it ends.

(6) The time limit expires instead at the end of two weeks after the mediation ends (subject to paragraph (7)).

(7) If a time limit mentioned in paragraph (5)(a) has been extended by this article, paragraphs (5) and (6) apply to the extended time limit as they apply to a time limit mentioned in paragraph (5)(a).

(8) Where more than one time limit applies in relation to a relevant dispute, the extension by paragraph (3) or (6) of one of those time limits does not affect the others.

(9) For the purposes of this article, a mediation starts on the date of the agreement to mediate that is entered into by the parties and the mediator.

(10) For the purposes of this article, a mediation ends on the date of the first of these to occur—

(a) the parties reach an agreement in resolution of the relevant dispute;

(b) a party completes the notification of the other parties that it has withdrawn from the mediation;

(c) a party to whom a qualifying request is made fails to give a response reaching the other parties within 14 days of the request;

(d) the parties, after being notified that the mediator's appointment has ended (by death, resignation or otherwise), fail to agree within 14 days to seek to appoint a replacement mediator; or

(e) the mediation otherwise comes to an end pursuant to the terms of the agreement to mediate.

(11) For the purpose of paragraph (10), a qualifying request is a request by a party that another (A) confirm to all parties that A is continuing with the mediation.

(12) In the case of any relevant dispute, references in this article to a mediation are references to the mediation so far as it relates to that dispute, and references to a party are to be read accordingly.

(13) Where the tribunal has the power under article 7(c) or 8(c)(ii) to extend a period of limitation, the power is exercisable in relation to the period of limitation as extended by this article.]

NOTES

Commencement: 20 May 2011.

Inserted by the Cross-Border Mediation (EU Directive) Regulations 2011, SI 2011/1133, regs 59, 62, as from 20 May 2011.

[2.220]

9 Death and bankruptcy

(1) Where proceedings in respect of a contract claim have been brought before an [employment tribunal] and an employee or employer party to them dies before their conclusion, the proceedings shall not abate by reason of the death and the tribunal may, if it thinks it necessary in order to ensure that all matters in dispute may be effectually and completely determined and adjudicated upon, order the personal representatives of the deceased party, or other persons whom the tribunal considers appropriate, to be made parties and the proceedings to be carried on as if they had been substituted for the deceased party.

(2) Where proceedings in respect of a contract claim have been brought before an [employment tribunal] and the employee or employer who is the applicant party to them becomes bankrupt before their conclusion, the proceedings shall not abate by reason of the bankruptcy and the tribunal may, if it thinks it necessary in order to ensure that all matters in dispute may be effectually and completely adjudicated upon, order the person in whom the interest of the bankrupt party has vested to be made a party and the proceedings to be carried on as if he had been substituted for the bankrupt party.

NOTES

Words in square brackets substituted by the Employment Rights (Dispute Resolution) Act 1998, s 1(2)(a).

[2.221]

10 Limit on payment to be ordered

An [employment tribunal] shall not in proceedings in respect of a contract claim, or in respect of a number of contract claims relating to the same contract, order the payment of an amount exceeding £25,000.

NOTES

Words in square brackets substituted by the Employment Rights (Dispute Resolution) Act 1998, s 1(2)(a).

[EMPLOYMENT TRIBUNALS] EXTENSION OF JURISDICTION (SCOTLAND) ORDER 1994

(SI 1994/1624)

NOTES

Made: 11 July 1994.

Authority: Employment Protection (Consolidation) Act 1978, ss 131(1), (4A), (5), (5A), 154(3) (repealed). This Order now has effect as if made under the Employment Tribunals Act 1996, ss 3(1), 8(2)–(4), 41(4).

Commencement: 12 July 1994.

Title: words in square brackets substituted by the Employment Rights (Dispute Resolution) Act 1998, s 1(2)(b).

This Order applies only to Scotland. For the equivalent Order applying to England and Wales, see the Employment Tribunals Extension of Jurisdiction (England and Wales) Order 1994, SI 1994/1623 at **[2.211]**.

Tribunal jurisdiction: the Employment Act 2002, s 38 applies to proceedings before the employment tribunal relating to a claim under this Order; see s 38(1) of, and Sch 5 to, the 2002 Act at **[1.1228]**, **[1.1236]**. See also the Trade Union and Labour Relations (Consolidation) Act 1992, s 207A at **[1.474]** (as inserted by the Employment Act 2008). That section provides that in proceedings before an employment tribunal relating to a claim by an employee under any of the jurisdictions listed in Sch A2 to the 1992 Act at **[1.648]** (which includes this Order) the tribunal may adjust any award given if the employer or the employee has unreasonably failed to comply with the relevant Code of Practice as defined by s 207A(4). See also the revised Acas Code of Practice 1 – Disciplinary and Grievance Procedures (2009) at **[4.1]**.

Conciliation: proceedings in respect of which an employment tribunal has jurisdiction by virtue of the Employment Tribunals Act 1996, s 3 are proceedings to which s 18 of that Act applies; see s 18(1)(e) at **[1.706]**.

See *Harvey* PI(1), U2.

ARRANGEMENT OF ARTICLES

Part 2 Statutory Instruments

[2.222]

1 Citation, commencement and interpretation

(1) This Order may be cited as the [Employment Tribunals] Extension of Jurisdiction (Scotland) Order 1994 and comes into force on the first day after it is made.

(2) In this Order—

"contract claim" means a claim in respect of which proceedings may be brought before an [employment tribunal] by virtue of article 3 or 4; and

"the 1978 Act" means the Employment Protection (Consolidation) Act 1978.

NOTES

Words in square brackets substituted by the Employment Rights (Dispute Resolution) Act 1998, s 1(2)(a), (b).

Employment Protection (Consolidation) Act 1978: repealed and largely consolidated in the Trade Union and Labour Relations (Consolidation) Act 1992, the Employment Rights Act 1996 and the Employment Tribunals Act 1996.

[2.223]

2 Transitional provision

This Order does not enable proceedings in respect of a contract claim to be brought before an [employment tribunal] unless—

(a) the effective date of termination (as defined in section 55(4) of the 1978 Act) in respect of the contract giving rise to the claim, or

(b) where there is no effective date of termination, the last day upon which the employee works in the employment which has terminated,

occurs on or after the day on which the Order comes into force.

NOTES

Words in square brackets substituted by the Employment Rights (Dispute Resolution) Act 1998, s 1(2)(a).

"Section 55(4) of the 1978 Act": see now the Employment Rights Act 1996, s 97(1).

[2.224]

3 Extension of jurisdiction

Proceedings may be brought before an [employment tribunal] in respect of a claim of an employee for the recovery of damages or any other sum (other than a claim for damages, or for a sum due, in respect of personal injuries) if—

(a) the claim is one to which section 131(2) of the 1978 Act applies and which a court in Scotland would under the law for the time being in force have jurisdiction to hear and determine;
(b) the claim is not one to which article 5 applies; and
(c) the claim arises or is outstanding on the termination of the employee's employment.

NOTES
Words in square brackets substituted by the Employment Rights (Dispute Resolution) Act 1998, s 1(2)(a).
"Section 131(2) of the 1978 Act": see now the Employment Tribunals Act 1996, s 3(2).

[2.225]
4
Proceedings may be brought before an [employment tribunal] in respect of a claim of an employer for the recovery of damages or any other sum (other than a claim for damages, or for a sum due, in respect of personal injuries) if—
(a) the claim is one to which section 131(2) of the 1978 Act applies and which a court in Scotland would under the law for the time being in force have jurisdiction to hear and determine;
(b) the claim is not one to which article 5 applies;
(c) the claim arises or is outstanding on the termination of the employment of the employee against whom it is made; and
(d) proceedings in respect of a claim of that employee have been brought before an [employment tribunal] by virtue of this Order.

NOTES
Words in square brackets substituted by the Employment Rights (Dispute Resolution) Act 1998, s 1(2)(a).
"Section 131(2) of the 1978 Act": see now the Employment Tribunals Act 1996, s 3(2).

[2.226]
5
This article applies to a claim for breach of a contractual term of any of the following descriptions—
(a) a term requiring the employer to provide living accommodation for the employee;
(b) a term imposing an obligation on the employer or the employee in connection with the provision of living accommodation;
(c) a term relating to intellectual property;
(d) a term imposing an obligation of confidence;
(e) a term which is a covenant in restraint of trade.

In this article, "intellectual property" includes copyright, rights in performances, moral rights, design right, registered designs, patents and trade marks.

[2.227]
6 Manner in which proceedings may be brought
Proceedings on a contract claim may be brought before an [employment tribunal] by presenting a complaint to an [employment tribunal].

NOTES
Words in square brackets substituted by the Employment Rights (Dispute Resolution) Act 1998, s 1(2)(a).

[2.228]
7 Time within which proceedings may be brought
An [employment tribunal] shall not entertain a complaint in respect of an employee's contract claim unless it is presented—
(a) within the period of three months beginning with the effective date of termination of the contract giving rise to the claim, or
(b) where there is no effective date of termination, within the period of three months beginning with the last day upon which the employee worked in the employment which has terminated, or
[(ba) where the period within which a complaint must be presented in accordance with paragraph (a) or (b) is extended by regulation 15 of the Employment Act 2002 (Dispute Resolution) Regulations 2004, the period within which the complaint must be presented shall be the extended period rather than the period in paragraph (a) or (b),]
(c) where the tribunal is satisfied that it was not reasonably practicable for the complaint to be presented within whichever of those periods is applicable, within such further period as the tribunal considers reasonable.

NOTES

Words in first pair of square brackets substituted by the Employment Rights (Dispute Resolution) Act 1998, s 1(2)(a).

Para (ba) inserted by the Employment Act 2002 (Dispute Resolution) Regulations 2004, SI 2004/752, reg 17(d).

See also the comments of Underhill J as set out in the notes to art 7 of the English equivalent of this article at **[2.217]**. Those comments are equally applicable here and the word "or" has been moved accordingly.

[2.229]
8

An [employment tribunal] shall not entertain a complaint in respect of an employer's contract claim unless—

(a) it is presented at a time when there is before the tribunal a complaint in respect of a contract claim of a particular employee which has not been settled or withdrawn;
(b) it arises out of a contract with that employee; and
(c) it is presented—
   (i) within the period of six weeks beginning with the day, or if more than one the last of the days, on which the employer (or other person who is the respondent party to the employee's contract claim) received from the tribunal a copy of an originating application in respect of a contract claim of that employee; or
   (ii) where the tribunal is satisfied that it was not reasonably practicable for the complaint to be presented within that period, within such further period as the tribunal considers reasonable.

NOTES

Words in square brackets substituted by the Employment Rights (Dispute Resolution) Act 1998, s 1(2)(a).

[2.230]
9 Death and legal incapacity

Where proceedings in respect of a contract claim have been brought before an [employment tribunal] and an employee or employer party to them dies or comes under legal incapacity before the conclusion of the proceedings, the tribunal may order any person who represents that party or his estate to be made a party to the proceedings in place of the party who has died or come under legal incapacity and the proceedings to be carried on accordingly.

NOTES

Words in square brackets substituted by the Employment Rights (Dispute Resolution) Act 1998, s 1(2)(a).

[2.231]
10 Limit on payment to be ordered

An [employment tribunal] shall not in proceedings in respect of a contract claim, or in respect of a number of contract claims relating to the same contract, order the payment of an amount exceeding £25,000.

NOTES

Words in square brackets substituted by the Employment Rights (Dispute Resolution) Act 1998, s 1(2)(a).

OCCUPATIONAL PENSION SCHEMES (EQUAL TREATMENT) REGULATIONS 1995 (NOTE)

(SI 1995/3183)

[2.232]

NOTES

These Regulations supplemented the requirements for equal treatment relating to occupational pension schemes provided for in the Pensions Act 1995, ss 62–66 (repealed). They did so by applying and modifying the Equal Pay Act 1970. These Regulations were revoked by the Equality Act 2010, s 211(2), Sch 27, Pt 2, as from 1 October 2010. The Equality Act 2010 (Commencement No 4, Savings, Consequential, Transitional, Transitory and Incidental Provisions and Revocation) Order 2010, SI 2010/2317 (at **[2.1558]** et seq) provides for various transitional provisions and savings in connection with the commencement of the 2010 Act and the repeal of previous legislation. See, in particular, art 15 (savings for various enactments (including the Equal Pay Act 1970) in cases where the act complained of occurs wholly before 1 October 2010). There are no specific transitional provisions in the 2010 Order relating to these Regulations but, in so far as they apply to the 1970 Act, the transitional provisions relating to the repeal of that Act would apply to the modification thereof by these Regulations.

HEALTH AND SAFETY (CONSULTATION WITH EMPLOYEES) REGULATIONS 1996

(SI 1996/1513)

NOTES

Made: 10 June 1996.
Authority: European Communities Act 1972, s 2(2).
Commencement: 1 October 1996.
See *Harvey* NI(13), NIII(7).

ARRANGEMENT OF REGULATIONS

SCHEDULES

[2.233]

1 Citation, extent and commencement

These Regulations, which extend to Great Britain, may be cited as the Health and Safety (Consultation with Employees) Regulations 1996 and shall come into force on 1st October 1996.

[2.234]

2 Interpretation

(1) In these Regulations, unless the context otherwise requires—

"the 1974 Act" means the Health and Safety at Work etc Act 1974;

"the 1977 Regulations" means the Safety Representatives and Safety Committees Regulations 1977;

"employee" has the meaning assigned to it by section 53(1) of the 1974 Act but shall not include a person employed as a domestic servant in a private household; and "employer" shall be construed accordingly;

"the relevant statutory provisions" has the meaning assigned to it by section 53(1) of the 1974 Act;

"representatives of employee safety" shall be construed in accordance with regulation 4(1)(b);

"safety representative" has the meaning assigned to it by regulation 2(1) of the 1977 Regulations;

"workplace" means, in relation to an employee, any place or places where that employee is likely to work or which he is likely to frequent in the course of his employment or incidentally to it and, in relation to a representative of employee safety, any place or places where the employees he represents are likely so to work or frequent.

(2) Any reference in these Regulations to consulting employees directly or consulting representatives of employee safety is a reference to consulting them pursuant to regulation 3 and regulation 4(1)(a) or (b), as the case may be.

(3) Unless the context otherwise requires, any reference in these Regulations to—

(a) a numbered regulation or schedule is a reference to the regulation or schedule in these Regulations so numbered; and

(b) a numbered paragraph is a reference to the paragraph so numbered in the regulation or schedule in which the reference appears.

[2.235]

3 Duty of employer to consult

Where there are employees who are not represented by safety representatives under the 1977 Regulations, the employer shall consult those employees in good time on matters relating to their health and safety at work and, in particular, with regard to—

(a) the introduction of any measure at the workplace which may substantially affect the health and safety of those employees;

(b) his arrangements for appointing or, as the case may be, nominating persons in accordance with [regulations 7(1) and 8(1)(b) of the Management of Health and Safety at Work Regulations 1999] [or article 13(3)(b) of the Regulatory Reform (Fire Safety) Order 2005]];

(c) any health and safety information he is required to provide to those employees by or under the relevant statutory provisions;

(d) the planning and organisation of any health and safety training he is required to provide to those employees by or under the relevant statutory provisions; and

(e) the health and safety consequences for those employees of the introduction (including the planning thereof) of new technologies into the workplace.

NOTES

Para (b): words in first pair of square brackets substituted by the Management of Health and Safety at Work Regulations 1999, SI 1999/3242, reg 29(2), Sch 2; words in second pair of square brackets originally inserted by the Fire Precautions (Workplace) Regulations 1997, SI 1997/1840, reg 21(1), and substituted by the Regulatory Reform (Fire Safety) Order 2005, SI 2005/1541, art 41(2), in relation to England and Wales only. A corresponding amendment has been made in relation to Scotland by the Fire (Scotland) Act 2005 (Consequential Modifications and Savings) (No 2) Order 2006, SSI 2006/457, which provides that the words should now read "or regulation 12(3)(b) of the Fire Safety (Scotland) Regulations 2006".

[2.236]

4 Persons to be consulted

(1) The consultation required by regulation 3 is consultation with either—

(a) the employees directly; or

(b) in respect of any group of employees, one or more persons in that group who were elected, by the employees in that group at the time of the election, to represent that group for the purposes of such consultation (and any such persons are in these Regulations referred to as "representatives of employee safety").

(2) Where an employer consults representatives of employee safety he shall inform the employees represented by those representatives of—

(a) the names of those representatives; and

(b) the group of employees represented by those representatives.

(3) An employer shall not consult a person as a representative of employee safety if—

(a) that person has notified the employer that he does not intend to represent the group of employees for the purposes of such consultation;

(b) that person has ceased to be employed in the group of employees which he represents;

(c) the period for which that person was elected has expired without that person being re-elected; or

(d) that person has become incapacitated from carrying out his functions under these regulations;

and where pursuant to this paragraph an employer discontinues consultation with that person he shall inform the employees in the group concerned of that fact.

(4) Where an employer who has been consulting representatives of employee safety decides to consult employees directly he shall inform the employees and the representatives of that fact.

[2.237]

5 Duty of employer to provide information

(1) Where an employer consults employees directly he shall, subject to paragraph (3), make available to those employees such information, within the employer's knowledge, as is necessary to enable them to participate fully and effectively in the consultation.

(2) Where an employer consults representatives of employee safety he shall, subject to paragraph (3), make available to those representatives such information, within the employer's knowledge, as is—

(a) necessary to enable them to participate fully and effectively in the consultation and in the carrying out of their functions under these Regulations;

(b) contained in any record which he is required to keep by regulation 7 of the Reporting of Injuries, Diseases and Dangerous Occurrences Regulations 1995 and which relates to the workplace or the group of employees represented by those representatives.

(3) Nothing in paragraph (1) or (2) shall require an employer to make available any information—

(a) the disclosure of which would be against the interests of national security;

(b) which he could not disclose without contravening a prohibition imposed by or under any enactment;

(c) relating specifically to an individual, unless he has consented to its being disclosed;

(d) the disclosure of which would, for reasons other than its effect on health or safety, cause substantial injury to the employer's undertaking or, where the information was supplied to him by some other person, to the undertaking of that other person; or

(e) obtained by the employer for the purpose of bringing, prosecuting or defending any legal proceedings;

or to provide or allow the inspection of any document or part of a document which is not related to health or safety.

[2.238]

6 Functions of representatives of employee safety

Where an employer consults representatives of employee safety each of those representatives shall, for the period for which that representative is so consulted, have the following functions—

(a) to make representations to the employer on potential hazards and dangerous occurrences at the workplace which affect, or could affect, the group of employees he represents;

(b) to make representations to the employer on general matters affecting the health and safety at work of the group of employees he represents and, in particular, on such matters as he is consulted about by the employer under regulation 3; and

(c) to represent the group of employees he represents in consultations at the workplace with inspectors appointed under section 19(1) of the 1974 Act.

[2.239]

7 Training, time off and facilities for representatives of employee safety and time off for candidates

(1) Where an employer consults representatives of employee safety, he shall—

(a) ensure that each of those representatives is provided with such training in respect of that representative's functions under these Regulations as is reasonable in all the circumstances and the employer shall meet any reasonable costs associated with such training including travel and subsistence costs; and

(b) permit each of those representatives to take such time off with pay during that representative's working hours as shall be necessary for the purpose of that representative performing his functions under these Regulations or undergoing any training pursuant to paragraph (1)(a).

(2) An employer shall permit a candidate standing for election as a representative of employee safety reasonable time off with pay during that person's working hours in order to perform his functions as such a candidate.

(3) Schedule 1 (pay for time off) and Schedule 2 (provisions as to [employment tribunals]) shall have effect.

(4) An employer shall provide such other facilities and assistance as a representative of employee safety may reasonably require for the purpose of carrying out his functions under these Regulations.

NOTES

Para (3): words in square brackets substituted by the Employment Rights (Dispute Resolution) Act 1998, s 1(2)(b).

8 *(Amends the Employment Rights Act 1996, ss 44, 100 at* **[1.801]**, **[1.900]**.*)*

[2.240]

9 Exclusion of civil liability

Breach of a duty imposed by these Regulations shall, subject to regulation 7(3) and Schedule 2, not confer any right of action in any civil proceedings.

[2.241]

10 Application of health and safety legislation

Sections 16 to 21, 23, 24, 26, 28, 33, 34, 36 to 39, 42(1) to (3) and 46 of the 1974 Act, the Health and Safety (Enforcing Authority) Regulations 1989 and the Health and Safety (Training for Employment) Regulations 1990 shall apply as if any references therein to health and safety regulations or to the relevant statutory provisions included references to these Regulations.

NOTES

Health and Safety (Enforcing Authority) Regulations 1989: revoked and replaced by the Health and Safety (Enforcing Authority) Regulations 1998, SI 1998/494.

[2.242]

11 Application to the Crown and armed forces

(1) Section 48 of the 1974 Act shall, subject to paragraph (2), apply in respect of these Regulations as it applies in respect of regulations made under Part I of that Act.

(2) These Regulations shall apply in respect of members of the armed forces of the Crown subject to the following—

(a) references to "representatives of employee safety" (in regulation 4(1)(b) and elsewhere) shall, in respect of any group of employees, be references to one or more persons in that group who were appointed by the employer to represent that group for the purposes of such consultation;
(b) references to "elected" and "re-elected" in regulation 4(3)(c) shall be, respectively, references to "appointed" and "re-appointed"; and
(c) regulation 7(l)(b), (2) and (3) shall not apply.

[2.243]
12 Disapplication to sea-going ships

These Regulations shall not apply to or in relation to the master or crew of a seagoing ship or to the employer of such persons in respect of the normal ship-board activities of a ship's crew under the direction of the master.

13 *(Amends the Safety Representatives and Safety Committees Regulations 1977, SI 1977/500, reg 3 at* **[2.29]***.)*

SCHEDULES

SCHEDULE 1
PAY FOR TIME OFF

Regulation 7(3)

[2.244]
1. Subject to paragraph 3 below, where a person is permitted to take time off in accordance with regulation 7(l)(b) or 7(2), his employer shall pay him—
(a) where the person's remuneration for the work he would ordinarily have been doing during that time does not vary with the amount of work done, as if he had worked at that work for the whole of that time;
(b) where the person's remuneration for that work varies with the amount of work done, an amount calculated by reference to the average hourly earnings for that work (ascertained in accordance with paragraph 2).

2. The average hourly earnings referred to in paragraph 1(b) are the average hourly earnings of the person concerned or, if no fair estimate can be made of those earnings, the average hourly earnings for work of that description of persons in comparable employment with the same employer or, if there are no such persons, a figure of average hourly earnings which is reasonable in all the circumstances.

3. Any payment to a person by an employer in respect of a period of time off—
(a) if it is a payment which discharges any liability which the employer may have under sections 168 or 169 of the Trade Union and Labour Relations (Consolidation) Act 1992, in respect of that period, shall also discharge his liability in respect of the same period under regulation 7(l)(b) or 7(2);
(b) if it is a payment under any contractual obligation, shall go towards discharging the employer's liability in respect of the same period under regulation 7(l)(b) or 7(2);
(c) if it is a payment under regulation 7(l)(b) or 7(2), shall go towards discharging any liability of the employer to pay contractual remuneration in respect of the same period.

SCHEDULE 2
PROVISIONS AS TO [EMPLOYMENT TRIBUNALS]

Regulation 7(3)

[2.245]
1. An [employment tribunal] shall have jurisdiction to determine complaints in accordance with the following provisions of this Schedule.

2. A person (referred to in this Schedule as the "complainant") may present a complaint to an [employment tribunal] that—
(a) his employer has failed to permit him to take time off in accordance with regulation 7(1)(b) or 7(2); or
(b) his employer has failed to pay him in accordance with regulation 7(1)(b) or 7(2) and Schedule 1.

3. An [employment tribunal] shall not consider a complaint under paragraph 2 unless it is presented within three months of the date when the failure occurred or within such further period as the tribunal considers reasonable in a case where it is satisfied that it was not reasonably practicable for the complaint to be presented within the period of three months.

4. Where an [employment tribunal] finds a complaint under paragraph 2(a) well-founded the tribunal shall make a declaration to that effect and may make an award of compensation to be paid by the employer to the complainant which shall be of such amount as the tribunal considers just and equitable in all the circumstances having regard to the employer's default in failing to permit time off to be taken by the complainant and to any loss sustained by the complainant which is attributable to the matters complained of.

5. Where on a complaint under paragraph 2(b) an [employment tribunal] finds that the employer has failed to pay the complainant the whole or part of the amount required to be paid in accordance with regulation 7(1)(b) or 7(2) and Schedule 1, the tribunal shall order the employer to pay the complainant the amount which it finds due to him.

NOTES

Words in square brackets substituted by the Employment Rights (Dispute Resolution) Act 1998, s 1(2)(a), (b).

EMPLOYMENT PROTECTION (RECOUPMENT OF *JOBSEEKER'S ALLOWANCE AND INCOME SUPPORT*) REGULATIONS 1996

(SI 1996/2349)

NOTES

Title: for the words "Jobseeker's Allowance and Income Support" in italics there is substituted the word "Benefits" by the Universal Credit (Consequential, Supplementary, Incidental and Miscellaneous Provisions) Regulations 2013, SI 2013/630, reg 50(1), (2), as from 29 April 2013.

Made: 10 September 1996.

Authority: Employment Tribunals Act 1996, ss 16, 41(4); Social Security Administration Act 1992, s 58(1) (repealed subject to certain exceptions). Now have effect wholly under the Employment Tribunals Act 1996, ss 16, 41(4) (as amended by the Social Security Act 1998, s 86, Sch 7, para 147, Sch 8).

Commencement: 7 October 1996.

See also the Employment and Support Allowance (Transitional Provisions, Housing Benefit and Council Tax Benefit) (Existing Awards) (No 2) Regulations 2010, SI 2010/1907. The 2010 Regulations make transitional provision in relation to the introduction of employment and support allowance and apply to persons entitled to any existing award (which is defined in the Welfare Reform Act 2007, Sch 4, in terms of incapacity benefit, severe disablement allowance and income support on grounds of disability). The 2010 Regulations set out the process for determining whether existing awards are to be converted into awards of an employment and support allowance.

See *Harvey* DI(19)(D5).

ARRANGEMENT OF REGULATIONS

PART I
INTRODUCTORY

[2.246]

1 Citation and Commencement

These Regulations may be cited as the Employment Protection (Recoupment of *Jobseeker's Allowance and Income Support*) Regulations 1996 and shall come into force on 7th October 1996.

NOTES

For the words in italics there is substituted the word "Benefits" by the Universal Credit (Consequential, Supplementary, Incidental and Miscellaneous Provisions) Regulations 2013, SI 2013/630, reg 50(1), (3), as from 29 April 2013.

[2.247]

2 Interpretation

(1) In these Regulations, unless the context otherwise requires, the following expressions have the meanings hereby assigned to them respectively, that is to say—

"the 1992 Act" means the Trade Union and Labour Relations (Consolidation) Act 1992;

"the 1996 Act" means the Employment Rights Act 1996;

"prescribed element" has the meaning assigned to it in Regulation 3 below and the Schedule to these Regulations;

"protected period" has the same meaning as in section 189(5) of the 1992 Act;

"protective award" has the same meaning as in section 189(3) of the 1992 Act;

"recoupable benefit" means any jobseeker's allowance[, income-related employment and support allowance][, universal credit] or income support as the case may be, which is recoupable under these Regulations;

"recoupment notice" means a notice under these Regulations;

"Secretary of the Tribunals" means the Secretary of the Central Office of the [Employment Tribunals] (England and Wales) or, as the case may require, the Secretary of the Central Office of the [Employment Tribunals] (Scotland) for the time being;

["universal credit" means universal credit under Part 1 of the Welfare Reform Act 2012].

(2) In the Schedule to these Regulations references to sections are references to sections of the 1996 Act unless otherwise indicated and references in column 3 of the table to the conclusion of the tribunal proceedings are references to the conclusion of the proceedings mentioned in the corresponding entry in column 2.

(3) For the purposes of these Regulations (and in particular for the purposes of any calculations to be made by an [employment tribunal] as respects the prescribed element) the conclusion of the tribunal proceedings shall be taken to occur—

(a) where the [employment tribunal] at the hearing announces the effect of its decision to the parties, on the date on which that announcement is made;

(b) in any other case, on the date on which the decision of the tribunal is sent to the parties.

(4) References to parties in relevant [employment tribunal] proceedings shall be taken to include references to persons appearing on behalf of parties in a representative capacity.

(5) References in these Regulations to anything done, or to be done, in, or in consequence of, any tribunal proceedings include references to anything done, or to be done, in, or in consequence of any such proceedings as are in the nature of a review, or re-hearing or a further hearing consequent on an appeal.

NOTES

Words in first pair of square brackets in the definition "recoupable benefit" inserted by the Social Security (Miscellaneous Amendments) (No 5) Regulations 2010, SI 2010/2429, reg 5(a), as from 1 November 2010; words in second pair of square brackets in the definition "recoupable benefit" inserted and definition "universal credit" inserted by the Universal Credit (Consequential, Supplementary, Incidental and Miscellaneous Provisions) Regulations 2013, SI 2013/630, reg 50(1), (4), as from 29 April 2013; all other words in square brackets substituted by the Employment Rights (Dispute Resolution) Act 1998, s 1(2)(a), (b).

Note that "protected period" is actually defined in s 189(4) of the 1992 Act, and not s 189(5) as stated in para (1) above.

PART II
[EMPLOYMENT TRIBUNAL] PROCEEDINGS

[2.248]

3 Application to payments and proceedings

(1) Subject to paragraph (2) below these Regulations apply—

(a) to the payments described in column 1 of the table contained in the Schedule to these Regulations, being, in each case, payments which are the subject of [employment tribunal] proceedings of the kind described in the corresponding entry in column 2 and the prescribed element in relation to each such payment is so much of the relevant monetary award as is attributable to the matter described in the corresponding entry in column 3; and

(b) to payments of remuneration in pursuance of a protective award.

(2) The payments to which these Regulations apply by virtue of paragraph (1)(a) above include payments in proceedings under section 192 of the 1992 Act and, accordingly, where an order is made on an employee's complaint under that section, the relevant protective award shall, as respects that employee and to the appropriate extent, be taken to be subsumed in the order made under section 192 so that the provisions of these Regulations relating to monetary awards shall apply to payments under that order to the exclusion of the provisions relating to protective awards, but without prejudice to anything done under the latter in connection with the relevant protective award before the making of the order under section 192.

NOTES

Words in square brackets in para (1) and in the heading preceding this regulation substituted by the Employment Rights (Dispute Resolution) Act 1998, s 1(2)(a).

[2.249]

4 Duties of the [employment tribunals] and of the Secretary of the Tribunals in respect of monetary awards

(1) Where these Regulations apply, no regard shall be had, in assessing the amount of a monetary award, to the amount of any jobseeker's allowance[, income-related employment and support allowance][, universal credit] or any income support which may have been paid to or claimed by the employee for a period which coincides with any part of a period to which the prescribed element is attributable.

(2) Where the [employment tribunal] in arriving at a monetary award makes a reduction on account of the employee's contributory fault or on account of any limit imposed by or under the 1992 Act or 1996 Act, a proportionate reduction shall be made in arriving at the amount of the prescribed element.

(3) Subject to the following provisions of this Regulation it shall be the duty of the [employment tribunal] to set out in any decision which includes a monetary award the following particulars—

(a) the monetary award;

(b) the amount of the prescribed element, if any;

(c) the dates of the period to which the prescribed element is attributable;

(d) the amount, if any, by which the monetary award exceeds the prescribed element.

(4) Where the [employment tribunal] at the hearing announces to the parties the effect of a decision which includes a monetary award it shall inform those parties at the same time of the amount of any prescribed element included in the monetary award and shall explain the effect of Regulations 7 and 8 below in relation to the prescribed element.

(5) Where the [employment tribunal] has made such an announcement as is described in paragraph (4) above the Secretary of the Tribunals shall forthwith notify the Secretary of State that the tribunal has decided to make a monetary award including a prescribed element and shall notify him of the particulars set out in paragraph (3) above.

(6) As soon as reasonably practicable after the Secretary of the Tribunals has sent a copy of a decision containing the particulars set out in paragraph (3) above to the parties he shall send a copy of that decision to the Secretary of State.

(7) In addition to containing the particulars required under paragraph (3) above, any such decision as is mentioned in that paragraph shall contain a statement explaining the effect of Regulations 7 and 8 below in relation to the prescribed element.

(8) The requirements of paragraphs (3) to (7) above do not apply where the tribunal is satisfied that in respect of each day falling within the period to which the prescribed element relates the employee has neither received nor claimed jobseeker's allowance[, income-related employment and support allowance][, universal credit] or income support.

NOTES

Words in first pair of square brackets in paras (1), (8) inserted by the Social Security (Miscellaneous Amendments) (No 5) Regulations 2010, SI 2010/2429, reg 5(b), as from 1 November 2010; words in second pair of square brackets in paras (1), (8) inserted by the Universal Credit (Consequential, Supplementary, Incidental and Miscellaneous Provisions) Regulations 2013, SI 2013/630, reg 50(1), (5), as from 29 April 2013; all other words in square brackets substituted by the Employment Rights (Dispute Resolution) Act 1998, s 1(2)(a), (b).

[2.250]

5 Duties of the [employment tribunals] and of the Secretary of the Tribunals in respect of protective awards

(1) Where, on a complaint under section 189 of the 1992 Act, an [employment tribunal]—

(a) at the hearing announces to the parties the effect of a decision to make a protective award; or

(b) (where it has made no such announcement) sends a decision to make such an award to the parties;

the Secretary of the Tribunals shall forthwith notify the Secretary of State of the following particulars relating to the award—

(i) where the [employment tribunal] has made such an announcement as is described in paragraph (1)(a) above, the date of the hearing or where it has made no such announcement, the date on which the decision was sent to the parties;

(ii) the location of the tribunal;

(iii) the name and address of the employer;

(iv) the description of the employees to whom the award relates; and

(v) the dates of the protected period.

(2)

(a) Where an [employment tribunal] makes such an announcement as is described in paragraph (1)(a) above in the presence of the employer or his representative it shall advise him of his duties under Regulation 6 below and shall explain the effect of Regulations 7 and 8 below in relation to remuneration under the protective award.

(b) Without prejudice to (a) above any decision of an [employment tribunal] to make a protective award under section 189 of the 1992 Act shall contain a statement advising the employer of his duties under Regulation 6 below and an explanation of the effect of Regulations 7 and 8 below in relation to remuneration under the protective award.

NOTES

Words in square brackets substituted by the Employment Rights (Dispute Resolution) Act 1998, s 1(2)(a), (b).

[2.251]

6 Duties of the employer to give information about protective awards

(1) Where an [employment tribunal] makes a protective award under section 189 of the 1992 Act against an employer, the employer shall give to the Secretary of State the following information in writing—

(a) the name, address and national insurance number of every employee to whom the award relates; and

(b) the date of termination (or proposed termination) of the employment of each such employee.

(2) Subject to paragraph (3) below the employer shall comply with paragraph (1) above within the period of ten days commencing on the day on which the [employment tribunal] at the hearing announces to the parties the effect of a decision to make a protective award or (in the case where no such announcement is made) on the day on which the relevant decision is sent to the parties.

(3) Where, in any case, it is not reasonably practicable for the employer to comply with paragraph (1) above within the period applicable under paragraph (2) above he shall comply as soon as reasonably practicable after the expiration of that period.

NOTES

Words in square brackets substituted by the Employment Rights (Dispute Resolution) Act 1998, s 1(2)(a).

PART III
RECOUPMENT OF BENEFIT

[2.252]

7 Postponement of Awards

(1) This Regulation shall have effect for the purpose of postponing relevant awards in order to enable the Secretary of State to initiate recoupment under Regulation 8 below.

(2) Accordingly—

(a) so much of the monetary award as consists of the prescribed element;

(b) payment of any remuneration to which an employee would otherwise be entitled under a protective award,

shall be treated as stayed (in Scotland, sisted) as respects the relevant employee until—

(i) the Secretary of State has served a recoupment notice on the employer; or

(ii) the Secretary of State has notified the employer in writing that he does not intend to serve a recoupment notice.

(3) The stay or sist under paragraph (2) above is without prejudice to the right of an employee under section 192 of the 1992 Act to present a complaint to an [employment tribunal] of his employer's failure to pay remuneration under a protective award and Regulation 3(2) above has effect as respects any such complaint and as respects any order made under section 192(3) of that Act.

NOTES

Para (3): words in square brackets substituted by the Employment Rights (Dispute Resolution) Act 1998, s 1(2)(a).

[2.253]

8 Recoupment of Benefit

(1) Recoupment shall be initiated by the Secretary of State serving on the employer a recoupment notice claiming by way of total or partial recoupment of jobseeker's allowance[, income-related employment and support allowance][, universal credit] or income support the appropriate amount, computed, as the case may require, under paragraph (2) or (3) below.

(2) In the case of monetary awards the appropriate amount shall be whichever is the less of the following two sums—

(a) the amount of the prescribed element (less any tax or social security contributions which fall to be deducted therefrom by the employer); or

(b)

[(i)] the amount paid by way of or paid as on account of jobseeker's allowance[, income-related employment and support allowance] or income support to the employee for any period which coincides with any part of the period to which the prescribed element is attributable[; or

(ii) in the case of an employee entitled to an award of universal credit for any period ("the UC period") which coincides with any part of the period to which the prescribed element is attributable, any amount paid by way of or on account of universal credit for the UC period that would not have been paid if the person's earned income for that period was the same as immediately before the period to which the prescribed element is attributable].

(3) In the case of remuneration under a protective award the appropriate amount shall be whichever is the less of the following two sums—

(a) the amount (less any tax or social security contributions which fall to be deducted therefrom by the employer) accrued due to the employee in respect of so much of the protected period as falls before the date on which the Secretary of State receives from the employer the information required under Regulation 6 above; or

(b)

[(i)] the amount paid by way of or paid as on account of jobseeker's allowance[, income-related employment and support allowance] or income support to the employee for any period which coincides with any part of the protected period falling before the date described in (a) above[; or

(ii) in the case of an employee entitled to an award of universal credit for any period ("the UC period") which coincides with any part of the protected period falling before the date described in (a) above, any amount paid by way of or on account of universal credit for the UC period that would not have been paid if the person's earned income for that period was the same as immediately before the protected period].

(4) A recoupment notice shall be served on the employer by post or otherwise and copies shall likewise be sent to the employee and, if requested, to the Secretary of the Tribunals.

(5) The Secretary of State shall serve a recoupment notice on the employer, or notify the employer that he does not intend to serve such a notice, within the period applicable, as the case may require, under paragraph (6) or (7) below, or as soon as practicable thereafter.

(6) In the case of a monetary award the period shall be—

(a) in any case in which the tribunal at the hearing announces to the parties the effect of its decision as described in Regulation 4(4) above, the period ending 21 days after the conclusion of the hearing or the period ending 9 days after the decision has been sent to the parties, whichever is the later; or

(b) in any other case, the period ending 21 days after the decision has been sent to the parties.

(7) In the case of a protective award the period shall be the period ending 21 days after the Secretary of State has received from the employer the information required under Regulation 6 above.

(8) A recoupment notice served on an employer shall operate as an instruction to the employer to pay, by way of deduction out of the sum due under the award, the recoupable amount to the Secretary of State and it shall be the duty of the employer to comply with the notice. The employer's duty under this paragraph shall not affect his obligation to pay any balance that may be due to the employee under the relevant award.

(9) The duty imposed on the employer by service of the recoupment notice shall not be discharged by payment of the recoupable amount to the employee during the postponement period or thereafter if a recoupment notice is served on the employer during the said period.

(10) Payment by the employer to the Secretary of State under this Regulation shall be a complete discharge in favour of the employer as against the employee in respect of any sum so paid but without prejudice to any rights of the employee under Regulation 10 below.

(11) The recoupable amount shall be recoverable by the Secretary of State from the employer as a debt.

[(12) For the purposes of paragraphs (2)(b)(ii) and (3)(b)(ii), "earned income" has the meaning given in regulation 52 of the Universal Credit Regulations 2013.]

NOTES

Para (1): words in first pair of square brackets inserted by the Social Security (Miscellaneous Amendments) (No 5) Regulations 2010, SI 2010/2429, reg 5(c), as from 1 November 2010; words in second pair of square brackets inserted by the Universal Credit (Consequential, Supplementary, Incidental and Miscellaneous Provisions) Regulations 2013, SI 2013/630, reg 50(1), (6)(a), as from 29 April 2013.

Para (2): sub-para (b)(i) numbered as such and sub-para (b)(ii) inserted together with word immediately preceding it, by SI 2013/630, reg 50(1), (6)(b), as from 29 April 2013; words in square brackets in sub-para (b)(i) inserted by SI 2010/2429, reg 5(c), as from 1 November 2010.

Para (3): sub-para (b)(i) numbered as such and sub-para (b)(ii) inserted together with word immediately preceding it, by SI 2013/630, reg 50(1), (6)(c), as from 29 April 2013; words in square brackets in sub-para (b)(i) inserted by SI 2010/2429, reg 5(c), as from 1 November 2010.

Para (12): added by SI 2013/630, reg 50(1), (6)(d), as from 29 April 2013.

[2.254]

9 Order made in secondary proceedings

(1) In the application of any of the above provisions in the case of—

- (a) proceedings for an award under section 192 of the 1992 Act; or
- (b) proceedings in the nature of a review, a re-hearing or a further hearing consequent on an appeal,

it shall be the duty of the [employment tribunal] or, as the case may require, the Secretary of State, to take the appropriate account of anything done under or in consequence of these Regulations in relation to any award made in the original proceedings.

(2) For the purposes of this Regulation the original proceedings are—

- (a) where paragraph (1)(a) above applies the proceedings under section 189 of the 1992 Act; or
- (b) where paragraph (1)(b) above applies the proceedings in respect of which the re-hearing, the review or the further hearing consequent on an appeal takes place.

NOTES

Para (1): words in square brackets substituted by the Employment Rights (Dispute Resolution) Act 1998, s 1(2)(a).

PART IV
DETERMINATION . . . OF BENEFIT RECOUPED

[2.255]

10 Provisions relating to determination of amount paid by way of or paid as on account of benefit

(1) Without prejudice to the right of the Secretary of State to recover from an employer the recoupable benefit, an employee on whom a copy of a recoupment notice has been served in accordance with Regulation 8 above may, within 21 days of the date on which such notice was served on him or within such further time as the Secretary of State may for special reasons allow, give notice in writing to the Secretary of State that he does not accept that the amount specified in the recoupment notice in respect of jobseeker's allowance[, income-related employment and support allowance][, universal credit] or income support is correct.

[(2) Where an employee has given notice in writing to the Secretary of State under paragraph (1) above that he does not accept that an amount specified in the recoupment notice is correct, the Secretary of State shall make a decision as to the amount of jobseeker's allowance[, income-related employment and support allowance][, universal credit] or, as the case may be, income support paid in respect of the period to which the prescribed element is attributable or, as appropriate, in respect of so much of the protected period as falls before the date on which the employer complies with Regulation 6 above.

(2A) The Secretary of State may revise either upon application made for the purpose or on his own initiative a decision under paragraph (2) above.

(2B) The employee shall have a right of appeal to [the First-tier Tribunal] against a decision of the Secretary of State whether as originally made under paragraph (2) or as revised under paragraph (2A) above.

Part 2 Statutory Instruments

(2C) The Social Security and Child Support (Decisions and Appeals) Regulations 1999 shall apply for the purposes of paragraphs (2A) and (2B) above as though a decision of the Secretary of State under paragraph (2A) above were made under section 9 of the 1998 Act and any appeal from such a decision were made under section 12 of that Act.

(2D) In this Regulation "the 1998 Act" means the Social Security Act 1998.

(3) Where the Secretary of State recovers too much money from an employer under these Regulations the Secretary of State shall pay to the employee an amount equal to the excess.]

(4) In any case where, after the Secretary of State has recovered from an employer any amount by way of recoupment of benefit, the decision given by the [employment tribunal] in consequence of which such recoupment took place is set aside or varied on appeal or on a re-hearing by the [employment tribunal], the Secretary of State shall make such repayment to the employer or payment to the employee of the whole or part of the amount recovered as he is satisfied should properly be made having regard to the decision given on appeal or re-hearing.

NOTES

The words omitted from the heading preceding this regulation were revoked, and paras (2), (2A)–(2D), (3), were substituted for the original paras (2), (3), by the Social Security Act 1998 (Commencement No 12 and Consequential and Transitional Provisions) Order 1999, SI 1999/3178, art 3(1), (14), Sch 14.

The words in first pair of square brackets in paras (1), (2) were inserted by the Social Security (Miscellaneous Amendments) (No 5) Regulations 2010, SI 2010/2429, reg 5(d), as from 1 November 2010, and words in second pair of square brackets in paras (1), (2) were inserted by the Universal Credit (Consequential, Supplementary, Incidental and Miscellaneous Provisions) Regulations 2013, SI 2013/630, reg 50(1), (7), as from 29 April 2013.

The words in square brackets in para (2B) were substituted by the Tribunals, Courts and Enforcement Act 2007 (Transitional and Consequential Provisions) Order 2008, SI 2008/2683, art 6(1), Sch 1, para 73, as from 3 November 2008.

The words in square brackets in para (4) were substituted by the Employment Rights (Dispute Resolution) Act 1998, s 1(2)(a).

11 *(Revokes the Employment Protection (Recoupment of Unemployment Benefit and Supplementary Benefit) Regulations 1977, SI 1977/674.)*

SCHEDULE
TABLE RELATING TO MONETARY AWARDS

Regulation 3

[2.256]

Column 1	*Column 2*	*Column 3*
Payment	*Proceedings*	*Matter to which prescribed element is attributable*
1. Guarantee payments under section 28.	1. Complaint under section 34.	1. Any amount found to be due to the employee and ordered to be paid under section 34(3) for a period before the conclusion of the tribunal proceedings.
2. Payments under any collective agreement having regard to which the appropriate Minister has made an exemption order under section 35.	2. Complaint under section 35(4).	2. Any amount found to be due to the employee and ordered to be paid under section 34(3), as applied by section 35(4), for a period before the conclusion of the tribunal proceedings.
3. Payments of remuneration in respect of a period of suspension on medical grounds under section 64 and section 108(2).	3. Complaint under section 70.	3. Any amount found to be due to the employee and ordered to be paid under section 70(3) for a period before the conclusion of the tribunal proceedings.
4. Payments of remuneration in respect of a period of suspension on maternity grounds under section 68.	4. Complaint under section 70.	4. Any amount found to be due to the employee and ordered to be paid under section 70(3) for a period before the conclusion of the tribunal proceedings.
5. Payments under an order for reinstatement under section 114(1).	5. Complaint of unfair dismissal under section 111(1).	5. Any amount ordered to be paid under section 114(2)(a) in respect of arrears of pay for a period before the conclusion of the tribunal proceedings.

Column 1	*Column 2*	*Column 3*
6. Payments under an order for re-engagement under section 117(8).	6. Complaint of unfair dismissal under section 111(1).	6. Any amount ordered to be paid under section 115(2)(d) in respect of arrears of pay for a period before the conclusion of the tribunal proceedings.
7. Payments under an award of compensation for unfair dismissal in cases falling under section 112(4) (cases where no order for reinstatement or re-engagement has been made).	7. Complaint of unfair dismissal under section 111(1).	7. Any amount ordered to be paid and calculated under section 123 in respect of compensation for loss of wages for a period before the conclusion of the tribunal proceedings.
8. Payments under an award of compensation for unfair dismissal under section 117(3) where reinstatement order not complied with.	8. Proceedings in respect of non-compliance with order.	8. Any amount ordered to be paid and calculated under section 123 in respect of compensation for loss of wages for a period before the conclusion of the tribunal proceedings.
9. Payments under an award of compensation for unfair dismissal under section 117(3) where re-engagement order not complied with.	9. Proceedings in respect of non-compliance with order.	9. Any amount ordered to be paid and calculated under section 123 in respect of compensation for loss of wages for a period before the conclusion of the tribunal proceedings.
10. Payments under an interim order for reinstatement under section 163(4) of the 1992 Act.	10. Proceedings on an application for an order for interim relief under section 161(1) of the 1992 Act.	10. Any amount found to be due to the complainant and ordered to be paid in respect of arrears of pay for the period between the date of termination of employment and the conclusion of the tribunal proceedings.
11. Payments under an interim order for re-engagement under section 163(5)(a) of the 1992 Act.	11. Proceedings on an application for an order for interim relief under section 161(1) of the 1992 Act.	11. Any amount found to be due to the complainant and ordered to be paid in respect of arrears of pay for the period between the date of termination of employment and the conclusion of the tribunal proceedings.
12. Payments under an order for the continuation of a contract of employment under section 163(5)(b) of the 1992 Act where employee reasonably refuses re-engagement.	12. Proceedings on an application for an order for interim relief under section 161(1) of the 1992 Act.	12. Any amount found to be due to the complainant and ordered to be paid in respect of arrears of pay for the period between the date of termination of employment and the conclusion of the tribunal proceedings.
13. Payments under an order for the continuation of a contract of employment under section 163(6) of the 1992 Act where employer fails to attend or is unwilling to reinstate or re-engage.	13. Proceedings on an application for an order for interim relief under section 161(1) of the 1992 Act.	13. Any amount found to be due to the complainant and ordered to be paid in respect of arrears of pay for the period between the date of termination of employment and the conclusion of the tribunal proceedings.
14. Payments under an order for the continuation of a contract of employment under sections 166(1) and (2) of the 1992 Act where reinstatement or re-engagement order not complied with.	14. Proceedings in respect of non-compliance with order.	14. Any amount ordered to be paid to the employee by way of compensation under section 166(1)(b) of the 1992 Act for loss of wages for the period between the date of termination of employment and the conclusion of the tribunal proceedings.

Column 1	Column 2	Column 3
15. Payments under an order for compensation under sections 166(3)(5) of the 1992 Act where order for the continuation of contract of employment not complied with.	15. Proceedings in respect of non-compliance with order.	15. Any amount ordered to be paid to the employee by way of compensation under section 166(3)(4) of the 1992 Act for loss of wages for the period between the date of termination of employment and the conclusion of the tribunal proceedings.
16. Payments under an order under section 192(3) of the 1992 Act on employer's default in respect of remuneration due to employee under protective award.	16. Complaint under section 192(1) of the 1992 Act.	16. Any amount ordered to be paid to the employee in respect of so much of the relevant protected period as falls before the date of the conclusion of the tribunal proceedings.

[EMPLOYMENT TRIBUNALS] (INTEREST ON AWARDS IN DISCRIMINATION CASES) REGULATIONS 1996

(SI 1996/2803)

NOTES

Made: 5 November 1996.

Authority: European Communities Act 1972, s 2(2); Race Relations Act 1976, s 56(5), (6); Disability Discrimination Act 1995, s 17A(6), (7). In so far as these Regulations were made under provisions of the 1976 and 1995 Acts (which were repealed by the Equality Act 2010, s 211(2), Sch 27, Pt 1, as from 1 October 2010), they now have effect under the Equality Act 2010, s 139 (see the Equality Act 2010 (Commencement No 4, Savings, Consequential, Transitional, Transitory and Incidental Provisions and Revocation) Order 2010, SI 2010/2317, art 21, Sch 7). See also Sch 4 to that Order at **[2.1578]** (Savings of subordinate legislation in relation to work on ships, work on hovercraft and seafarers).

Commencement: 2 December 1996.

Title: words in square brackets substituted by the Employment Rights (Dispute Resolution) Act 1998, s 1(2)(b).

See *Harvey* PI(1)(ZA).

ARRANGEMENT OF REGULATIONS

[2.257]

1 Citation, commencement, interpretation and revocation

(1) These Regulations may be cited as the [Employment Tribunals] (Interest on Awards in Discrimination Cases) Regulations 1996 and shall come into force on 2nd December 1996.

(2) In these Regulations—

"the 1970 Act" means the Equal Pay Act 1970;

"the 1975 Act" means the Sex Discrimination Act 1975;

"the 1976 Act" means the Race Relations Act 1976;

"the 1995 Act" means the Disability Discrimination Act 1995 and;

"an award under the relevant legislation" means—

(a) an award under the 1970 Act of arrears of remuneration or damages, or

(b) an order under section 65(1)(b) of the 1975 Act, section 56(1)(b) of the 1976 Act . . . section 8(2)(b) of the 1995 Act [. . . regulation 30(1)(b) of the Employment Equality (Sexual Orientation) Regulations 2003] [. . . regulation 30(1)(b) of the Employment Equality (Religion or Belief) Regulations 2003] [or regulation 38(1)(b) of the Employment Equality (Age) Regulations 2006] for payment of compensation,

but does not include an award of costs under rule 12 in Schedule 1 to the [Employment Tribunals] (Constitution and Rules of Procedure) Regulations 1993, or of expenses under rule 12 in Schedule 1 to the [Employment Tribunals] (Constitution and Rules of Procedure)

(Scotland) Regulations 1993, even if the award of costs or expenses is made in the same proceedings as an award under the 1970 Act or such an order.

(3) . . .

NOTES

Para (1): words in square brackets substituted by the Employment Rights (Dispute Resolution) Act 1998, s 1(2)(b).

Para (2): in definition "an award under the relevant legislation" first words omitted from para (b) revoked, and words in first pair of square brackets in that paragraph inserted, by the Employment Equality (Sexual Orientation) Regulations 2003, SI 2003/1661, reg 39, Sch 5, para 3; second words omitted from para (b) of that definition revoked, and words in second pair of square brackets in that paragraph inserted, by the Employment Equality (Religion or Belief) Regulations 2003, SI 2003/1660, reg 39(2), Sch 5, para 3; final words omitted from para (b) of that definition revoked, and words in final pair of square brackets in that paragraph inserted, by the Employment Equality (Age) Regulations 2006, SI 2006/1031, reg 49(1), Sch 8, Pt 2, para 56(1), (2)(a); other words in square brackets in that definition substituted by the Employment Rights (Dispute Resolution) Act 1998, s 1(2)(b).

Para (3): revokes the Sex Discrimination and Equal Pay (Remedies) Regulations 1993, SI 1993/2978, and the Race Relations (Interest on Awards) Regulations 1994, SI 1994/1748.

Employment Tribunals (Constitution and Rules of Procedure) Regulations 1993, SI 1993/2867; Employment Tribunals (Constitution and Rules of Procedure) (Scotland) Regulations 1993, SI 1993/2688: revoked and replaced; see now, the Employment Tribunals (Constitution and Rules of Procedure) Regulations 2004, SI 2004/1861 at **[2.809]**.

Note that the Equal Pay Act 1970, the Sex Discrimination Act 1975, the Race Relations Act 1976, the Disability Discrimination Act 1995, the Employment Equality (Sexual Orientation) Regulations 2003, reg 30, the Employment Equality (Religion or Belief) Regulations 2003, reg 30, and the Employment Equality (Age) Regulations 2006, reg 38 were all repealed or revoked by the Equality Act 2010, s 211(2), Sch 27. However, these Regulations have not been amended to insert a reference to awards made under the 2010 Act (as of 6 April 2013). Note also that the Disability Discrimination Act 1995, s 8(2)(b) became s 17A(2)(b) following the amendments made to the 1995 Act by the Disability Discrimination Act 1995 (Amendment) Regulations 2003, SI 2003/1673.

[2.258]

2 Interest on awards

(1) Where, at any time after the commencement of these Regulations, an [employment tribunal] makes an award under the relevant legislation—

(a) it may, subject to the following provisions of these Regulations, include interest on the sums awarded; and

(b) it shall consider whether to do so, without the need for any application by a party in the proceedings.

(2) Nothing in paragraph (1) shall prevent the tribunal from making an award or decision, with regard to interest, in terms which have been agreed between the parties.

NOTES

Para (1): words in square brackets substituted by the Employment Rights (Dispute Resolution) Act 1998, s 1(2)(a).

[2.259]

3 Rate of interest

(1) Interest shall be calculated as simple interest which accrues from day to day.

(2) Subject to paragraph (3), the rate of interest to be applied shall be, in England and Wales, the rate from time to time prescribed for the Special Investment Account under rule 27(1) of the Court Funds Rules 1987 and, in Scotland, the rate fixed, for the time being, by the Act of Sederunt (Interest in Sheriff Court Decrees or Extracts) 1975.

(3) Where the rate of interest in paragraph (2) has varied during a period for which interest is to be calculated, the tribunal may, if it so desires in the interests of simplicity, apply such median or average of those rates as seems to it appropriate.

NOTES

Rate of interest: the rate of interest currently prescribed for England and Wales is 0.5% (as from 1 July 2009). Previous rates were 6% (from 1 February 2002), 3% (from 1 February 2009), and 1.5% (from 1 June 2009)

Court Funds Rules 1987: revoked and replaced by the Court Funds Rules 2011, SI 2011/1734. The relevant provision is now r 13 of the 2011 Rules (Accrual of interest).

[2.260]

4 Calculation of interest

(1) In this regulation and regulations 5 and 6, "day of calculation" means the day on which the amount of interest is calculated by the tribunal.

(2) In regulation 6, "mid-point date" means the day which falls half-way through the period mentioned in paragraph (3) or, where the number of days in that period is even, the first day of the second half of the period.

(3) The period referred to in paragraph (2) is the period beginning on the date, in the case of an award under the 1970 Act, of the contravention and, in other cases, of the act of discrimination complained of, and ending on the day of calculation.

[2.261]
5

No interest shall be included in respect of any sum awarded for a loss or matter which will occur after the day of calculation or in respect of any time before the contravention or act of discrimination complained of.

[2.262]
6

(1) Subject to the following paragraphs of this regulation—

(a) in the case of any sum for injury to feelings, interest shall be for the period beginning on the date of the contravention or act of discrimination complained of and ending on the day of calculation;

(b) in the case of all other sums of damages or compensation (other than any sum referred to in regulation 5) and all arrears of remuneration, interest shall be for the period beginning on the mid-point date and ending on the day of calculation.

(2) Where any payment has been made before the day of calculation to the complainant by or on behalf of the respondent in respect of the subject matter of the award, interest in respect of that part of the award covered by the payment shall be calculated as if the references in paragraph (1), and in the definition of "mid-point date" in regulation 4, to the day of calculation were to the date on which the payment was made.

(3) Where the tribunal considers that in the circumstances, whether relating to the case as a whole or to a particular sum in an award, serious injustice would be caused if interest were to be awarded in respect of the period or periods in paragraphs (1) or (2), it may—

(a) calculate interest, or as the case may be interest on the particular sum, for such different period, or

(b) calculate interest for such different periods in respect of various sums in the award,

as it considers appropriate in the circumstances, having regard to the provisions of these Regulations.

[2.263]
7 Decision in writing

(1) The tribunal's written statement of reasons for its decision shall contain a statement of the total amount of any interest awarded under regulation 2 and, unless this amount has been agreed between the parties, either a table showing how it has been calculated or a description of the manner in which it has been calculated.

(2) The tribunal's written statement of reasons shall include reasons for any decision not to award interest under regulation 2.

[2.264]
8 Interest for period after award

(1) The [Employment Tribunals] (Interest) Order 1990 shall apply in relation to an award under the relevant legislation (whether or not including interest under regulation 2) as if references in that Order to the calculation day were references to the day immediately following the relevant decision day (as defined in Article 2(3) of the Order) and accordingly interest shall accrue under the Order from that day onwards (including that day).

(2) Notwithstanding paragraph (1), no interest shall be payable by virtue of that Order if payment of the full amount of the award (including any interest under regulation 2) is made within 14 days after the relevant decision day.

NOTES

Para (1): words in square brackets substituted by the Employment Rights (Dispute Resolution) Act 1998, s 1(2)(b).

EMPLOYMENT PROTECTION (CONTINUITY OF EMPLOYMENT) REGULATIONS 1996

(SI 1996/3147)

NOTES

Made: 16 December 1996.
Authority: Employment Rights Act 1996, s 219.
Commencement: 13 January 1997.
See *Harvey* H(1).

[2.265]

1 Citation, commencement and revocation

(1) These Regulations may be cited as the Employment Protection (Continuity of Employment) Regulations 1996 and shall come into force on 13th January 1997.

(2) The Employment Protection (Continuity of Employment) Regulations 1993 are revoked.

[2.266]

2 Application

These Regulations apply to any action taken in relation to the dismissal of an employee which consists of—

(a) his making a claim in accordance with a dismissal procedures agreement designated by an order under section 110 of the Employment Rights Act 1996,

(b) the presentation by him of a relevant complaint of dismissal,

(c) any action taken by a conciliation officer under section 18 of [the Employment Tribunals Act 1996], . . .

(d) the making of a relevant compromise contract[, . . .

(e) the making of an agreement to submit a dispute to arbitration in accordance with a scheme having effect by virtue of an order under section 212A of the Trade Union and Labour Relations (Consolidation) Act 1992,][. . .

(f) a decision taken arising out of the use of a statutory dispute resolution procedure contained in Schedule 2 to the Employment Act 2002 in a case where, in accordance with the Employment Act 2002 (Dispute Resolution) Regulations 2004, such a procedure applies][, or

(g) a decision taken arising out of the use of the statutory duty to consider procedure contained in Schedule 6 to the Employment Equality (Age) Regulations 2006].

NOTES

Words in square brackets in para (c) substituted by the Employment Rights (Dispute Resolution) Act 1998, s 1(2)(c).

Word omitted from para (c) revoked, and para (e) and the word immediately preceding it added, by the Employment Protection (Continuity of Employment) (Amendment) Regulations 2001, SI 2001/1188, reg 2.

Word omitted from para (d) revoked, and para (f) and the word immediately preceding it added, by the Employment Act 2002 (Dispute Resolution) Regulations 2004, SI 2004/752, reg 17(e).

Word omitted from para (e) revoked, and para (g) and the word immediately preceding it added, by the Employment Equality (Age) Regulations 2006, SI 2006/1031, reg 49(1), Sch 8, Pt 2, para 57.

Relevant complaint of dismissal; relevant compromise contract: these were defined in the Employment Rights Act 1996, s 219(3), (4) (repealed by the Employment Rights (Dispute Resolution) Act 1998, s 15, Sch 1, para 25, Sch 2).

Employment Act 2002 (Dispute Resolution) Regulations 2004; Employment Equality (Age) Regulations 2006: lapsed and revoked respectively (both subject to transitional provisions).

[2.267]

3 Continuity of employment where employee re-engaged

(1) The provisions of this regulation shall have effect to preserve the continuity of a person's period of employment for the purposes of—

(a) Chapter I of Part XIV of the Employment Rights Act 1996 (continuous employment), and

(b) that Chapter as applied by subsection (2) of section 282 of the Trade Union and Labour Relations (Consolidation) Act 1992 for the purposes of that section.

(2) If in consequence of any action to which these Regulations apply a dismissed employee is reinstated or re-employed by his employer or by a successor or associated employer of the employer—

(a) the continuity of that employee's period of employment shall be preserved, and

(b) the period beginning with the date on which the dismissal takes effect and ending with the date of reinstatement or re-engagement shall count in the computation of the employee's period of continuous employment.

[2.268]

4 Exclusion of operation of section 214 of the Employment Rights Act 1996 where redundancy or equivalent payment repaid

(1) Section 214 of the Employment Rights Act 1996 (continuity broken where employee re-employed after the making of a redundancy payment or equivalent payment) shall not apply where—

(a) in consequence of any action to which these Regulations apply a dismissed employee is reinstated or re-employed by his employer or by a successor or associated employer of the employer,

(b) the terms upon which he is so reinstated or re-engaged include provision for him to repay the amount of a redundancy payment or an equivalent payment paid in respect of the relevant dismissal, and

(c) that provision is complied with.

(2) For the purposes of this regulation the cases in which a redundancy payment shall be treated as having been paid are the cases mentioned in section 214(5) of the Employment Rights Act 1996.

WORKING TIME REGULATIONS 1998

(SI 1998/1833)

NOTES

Made: 30 July 1998.

Authority: European Communities Act 1972, s 2(2).

Commencement: 1 October 1998.

These Regulations are the domestic implementation of Council Directive 93/104/EC on working time, and (in part) of Council Directive 94/33/EC on the protection of young people at work at **[3.181]**. The 1993 Directive was repealed by Council Directive 2003/88/EC concerning certain aspects of the organisation of working time at **[3.418]**, which consolidates the 1993 Directive and a subsequent amending Directive, as from 2 August 2004.

Conciliation: employment tribunal proceedings and claims which could be the subject of employment tribunal proceedings under reg 30 of these Regulations are proceedings to which the Employment Tribunals Act 1996, s 18 applies; see s 18(1)(ff) of that Act, at **[1.706]**.

Employment Appeal Tribunal: an appeal lies to the Employment Appeal Tribunal on any question of law arising from any decision of, or in any proceedings before, an employment tribunal under or by virtue of these Regulations; see the Employment Tribunals Act 1996, s 21(1)(h) at **[1.713]**.

The rights conferred by these Regulations are "relevant statutory rights" for the purposes of the Employment Rights Act 1996, s 104 (dismissal on grounds of assertion of statutory right); see s 104(4)(d) of that Act at **[1.907]**.

See *Harvey* CI(1).

ARRANGEMENT OF REGULATIONS

PART I
GENERAL

PART II
RIGHTS AND OBLIGATIONS CONCERNING WORKING TIME

PART III
EXCEPTIONS

PART IV
MISCELLANEOUS

PART V
SPECIAL CLASSES OF PERSON

SCHEDULES

Part 2 Statutory Instruments

PART I
GENERAL

[2.269]

1 Citation, commencement and extent

(1) These Regulations may be cited as the Working Time Regulations 1998 and shall come into force on 1st October 1998.

(2) These Regulations extend to Great Britain only.

[2.270]

2 Interpretation

(1) In these Regulations—

"the 1996 Act" means the Employment Rights Act 1996;

"adult worker" means a worker who has attained the age of 18;

"the armed forces" means any of the naval, military and air forces of the Crown;

"calendar year" means the period of twelve months beginning with 1st January in any year;

"the civil protection services" includes the police, fire brigades and ambulance services, the security and intelligence services, customs and immigration officers, the prison service, the coastguard, and lifeboat crew and other voluntary rescue services;

"collective agreement" means a collective agreement within the meaning of section 178 of the Trade Union and Labour Relations (Consolidation) Act 1992, the trade union parties to which are independent trade unions within the meaning of section 5 of that Act;

"day" means a period of 24 hours beginning at midnight;

"employer", in relation to a worker, means the person by whom the worker is (or, where the employment has ceased, was) employed;

"employment", in relation to a worker, means employment under his contract, and "employed" shall be construed accordingly;

["fishing vessel" has the same meaning as in section 313 of the Merchant Shipping Act 1995;

"mobile worker" means any worker employed as a member of travelling or flying personnel by an undertaking which operates transport services for passengers or goods by road or air;]

"night time", in relation to a worker, means a period—

(a) the duration of which is not less than seven hours, and

(b) which includes the period between midnight and 5 am,

which is determined for the purposes of these Regulations by a relevant agreement, or, in default of such a determination, the period between 11 pm and 6 am;

"night work" means work during night time;

"night worker" means a worker—

(a) who, as a normal course, works at least three hours of his daily working time during night time, or

(b) who is likely, during night time, to work at least such proportion of his annual working time as may be specified for the purposes of these Regulations in a collective agreement or a workforce agreement;

and, for the purpose of paragraph (a) of this definition, a person works hours as a normal course (without prejudice to the generality of that expression) if he works such hours on the majority of days on which he works;

["offshore work" means work performed mainly on or from offshore installations (including drilling rigs), directly or indirectly in connection with the exploration, extraction or exploitation of mineral resources, including hydrocarbons, and diving in connection with such activities, whether performed from an offshore installation or a vessel[, including any such work performed in the territorial waters of the United Kingdom adjacent to Great Britain or in any area (except one or part of one in which the law of Northern Ireland applies) designated under section 1(7) of the Continental Shelf Act 1964];]

"relevant agreement", in relation to a worker, means a workforce agreement which applies to him, any provision of a collective agreement which forms part of a contract between him and his employer, or any other agreement in writing which is legally enforceable as between the worker and his employer;

"relevant training" means work experience provided pursuant to a training course or programme, training for employment, or both, other than work experience or training—

(a) the immediate provider of which is an educational institution or a person whose main business is the provision of training, and

(b) which is provided on a course run by that institution or person;

"rest period", in relation to a worker, means a period which is not working time, other than a rest break or leave to which the worker is entitled under these Regulations;

["the restricted period", in relation to a worker, means the period between 10 pm and 6 am or, where the worker's contract provides for him to work after 10 pm, the period between 11 pm and 7 am;]

["ship" has the same meaning as in section 313 of the Merchant Shipping Act 1995;]

"worker" means an individual who has entered into or works under (or, where the employment has ceased, worked under)—

(a) a contract of employment; or

(b) any other contract, whether express or implied and (if it is express) whether oral or in writing, whereby the individual undertakes to do or perform personally any work or services for another party to the contract whose status is not by virtue of the contract that of a client or customer of any profession or business undertaking carried on by the individual;

and any reference to a worker's contract shall be construed accordingly;

"worker employed in agriculture" has the same meaning as in the Agricultural Wages Act 1948 or the Agricultural Wages (Scotland) Act 1949, and a reference to a worker partly employed in agriculture is to a worker employed in agriculture whose employer also employs him for non-agricultural purposes;

"workforce agreement" means an agreement between an employer and workers employed by him or their representatives in respect of which the conditions set out in Schedule 1 to these Regulations are satisfied;

"working time", in relation to a worker, means—

(a) any period during which he is working, at his employer's disposal and carrying out his activity or duties,

(b) any period during which he is receiving relevant training, and

(c) any additional period which is to be treated as working time for the purpose of these Regulations under a relevant agreement;

and "work" shall be construed accordingly;

"Working Time Directive" means Council Directive 93/104/EC of 23rd November 1993 concerning certain aspects of the organization of working time;

"young worker" means a worker who has attained the age of 15 but not the age of 18 and who, as respects England and Wales, is over compulsory school age (construed in accordance with section 8 of the Education Act 1996) and, as respects Scotland, is over school age (construed in accordance with section 31 of the Education (Scotland) Act 1980), and

"Young Workers Directive" means Council Directive 94/33/EC of 22nd June 1994 on the protection of young people at work.

(2) In the absence of a definition in these Regulations, words and expressions used in particular provisions which are also used in corresponding provisions of the Working Time Directive or the Young Workers Directive have the same meaning as they have in those corresponding provisions.

(3) In these Regulations—

(a) a reference to a numbered regulation is to the regulation in these Regulations bearing that number;

(b) a reference in a regulation to a numbered paragraph is to the paragraph in that regulation bearing that number; and

(c) a reference in a paragraph to a lettered sub-paragraph is to the sub-paragraph in that paragraph bearing that letter.

NOTES

Para (1): definitions "fishing vessel", "mobile worker", "offshore work", and "ship" inserted by the Working Time (Amendment) Regulations 2003, SI 2003/1684, regs 2, 3; words in square brackets in definition "offshore work" inserted by the Working Time (Amendment) (No 2) Regulations 2006, SI 2006/2389, reg 2; definition "the restricted period" inserted by the Working Time (Amendment) Regulations 2002, SI 2002/3128, regs 2, 3.

PART II
RIGHTS AND OBLIGATIONS CONCERNING WORKING TIME

[2.271]

3 General

[(1)] The provisions of this Part have effect subject to the exceptions provided for in Part III of these Regulations.

[(2) Where, in this Part, separate provision is made as respects the same matter in relation to workers generally and to young workers, the provision relating to workers generally applies only to adult workers and those young workers to whom, by virtue of any exception in Part 3, the provision relating to young workers does not apply.]

NOTES

Para (1) numbered as such, and para (2) added, by the Working Time (Amendment) Regulations 2002, SI 2002/3128, regs 2, 4.

[2.272]

4 Maximum weekly working time

(1) [Unless his employer has first obtained the worker's agreement in writing to perform such work], a worker's working time, including overtime, in any reference period which is applicable in his case shall not exceed an average of 48 hours for each seven days.

(2) An employer shall take all reasonable steps, in keeping with the need to protect the health and safety of workers, to ensure that the limit specified in paragraph (1) is complied with in the case of each worker employed by him in relation to whom it applies [and shall keep up-to-date records of all workers who carry out work to which it does not apply by reason of the fact that the employer has obtained the worker's agreement as mentioned in paragraph (1)].

(3) Subject to paragraphs (4) and (5) and any agreement under regulation 23(b), the reference periods which apply in the case of a worker are—

(a) where a relevant agreement provides for the application of this regulation in relation to successive periods of 17 weeks, each such period, or

(b) in any other case, any period of 17 weeks in the course of his employment.

(4) Where a worker has worked for his employer for less than 17 weeks, the reference period applicable in his case is the period that has elapsed since he started work for his employer.

(5) Paragraphs (3) and (4) shall apply to a worker who is excluded from the scope of certain provisions of these Regulations by regulation 21 as if for each reference to 17 weeks there were substituted a reference to 26 weeks.

(6) For the purposes of this regulation, a worker's average working time for each seven days during a reference period shall be determined according to the formula—

$$A + B / C$$

where—

A is the aggregate number of hours comprised in the worker's working time during the course of the reference period;

B is the aggregate number of hours comprised in his working time during the course of the period beginning immediately after the end of the reference period and ending when the number of days in that subsequent period on which he has worked equals the number of excluded days during the reference period; and

C is the number of weeks in the reference period.

(7) In paragraph (6), "excluded days" means days comprised in—

(a) any period of annual leave taken by the worker in exercise of his entitlement under regulation 13;

(b) any period of sick leave taken by the worker;

(c) any period of maternity [paternity, adoption or parental] leave taken by the worker; and

(d) any period in respect of which the limit specified in paragraph (1) did not apply in relation to the worker [by reason of the fact that the employer has obtained the worker's agreement as mentioned in paragraph (1)].

NOTES

Para (1): words in square brackets substituted by the Working Time Regulations 1999, SI 1999/3372, regs 1(1), 3(1)(a).

Para (2): words in square brackets added by SI 1999/3372, regs 1(1), 3(1)(b).

Para (7): words in first pair of square brackets inserted by the Working Time (Amendment) Regulations 2002, SI 2002/3128, regs 2, 5; words in second pair of square brackets substituted by the Working Time Regulations 1999, SI 1999/3372, regs 1(1), 3(1)(a), (c).

[2.273]

5 Agreement to exclude the maximum

(1) . . .

(2) An agreement for the purposes of [regulation 4]—

(a) may either relate to a specified period or apply indefinitely; and

(b) subject to any provision in the agreement for a different period of notice, shall be terminable by the worker by giving not less than seven days' notice to his employer in writing.

(3) Where an agreement for the purposes of [regulation 4] makes provision for the termination of the agreement after a period of notice, the notice period provided for shall not exceed three months.

(4) . . .

NOTES

Paras (1), (4): revoked by the Working Time Regulations 1999, SI 1999/3372, regs 1(1), 3(2)(a).

Paras (2), (3): words in square brackets substituted by SI 1999/3372, regs 1(1), 3(2)(b).

[2.274]

[5A Maximum working time for young workers

(1) A young worker's working time shall not exceed—

(a) eight hours a day, or

(b) 40 hours a week.

(2) If, on any day, or, as the case may be, during any week, a young worker is employed by more than one employer, his working time shall be determined for the purpose of paragraph (1) by aggregating the number of hours worked by him for each employer.

(3) For the purposes of paragraphs (1) and (2), a week starts at midnight between Sunday and Monday.

(4) An employer shall take all reasonable steps, in keeping with the need to protect the health and safety of workers, to ensure that the limits specified in paragraph (1) are complied with in the case of each worker employed by him in relation to whom they apply.]

NOTES

Inserted by the Working Time (Amendment) Regulations 2002, SI 2002/3128, regs 2, 6.

[2.275]

6 Length of night work

(1) A night worker's normal hours of work in any reference period which is applicable in his case shall not exceed an average of eight hours for each 24 hours.

(2) An employer shall take all reasonable steps, in keeping with the need to protect the health and safety of workers, to ensure that the limit specified in paragraph (1) is complied with in the case of each night worker employed by him.

(3) The reference periods which apply in the case of a night worker are—

(a) where a relevant agreement provides for the application of this regulation in relation to successive periods of 17 weeks, each such period, or

(b) in any other case, any period of 17 weeks in the course of his employment.

(4) Where a worker has worked for his employer for less than 17 weeks, the reference period applicable in his case is the period that has elapsed since he started work for his employer.

(5) For the purposes of this regulation, a night worker's average normal hours of work for each 24 hours during a reference period shall be determined according to the formula—

$$A / B - C$$

where—

A is the number of hours during the reference period which are normal working hours for that worker;

B is the number of days during the reference period, and

C is the total number of hours during the reference period comprised in rest periods spent by the worker in pursuance of his entitlement under regulation 11, divided by 24.

(6) . . .

(7) An employer shall ensure that no night worker employed by him whose work involves special hazards or heavy physical or mental strain works for more than eight hours in any 24-hour period during which the night worker performs night work.

(8) For the purposes of paragraph (7), the work of a night worker shall be regarded as involving special hazards or heavy physical or mental strain if—

(a) it is identified as such in—

(i) a collective agreement, or

(ii) a workforce agreement,

which takes account of the specific effects and hazards of night work, or

(b) it is recognised in a risk assessment made by the employer under [regulation 3 of the Management of Health and Safety at Work Regulations 1999] as involving a significant risk to the health or safety of workers employed by him.

NOTES

Para (6): revoked by the Working Time (Amendment) Regulations 2002, SI 2002/3128, regs 2, 7.

Para (8): words in square brackets substituted by the Management of Health and Safety at Work Regulations 1999, SI 1999/3242, reg 29(2), Sch 2.

[2.276]

[6A Night work by young workers

An employer shall ensure that no young worker employed by him works during the restricted period.]

NOTES

Inserted by the Working Time (Amendment) Regulations 2002, SI 2002/3128, regs 2, 8.

[2.277]

7 Health assessment and transfer of night workers to day work

(1) An employer—

(a) shall not assign an adult worker to work which is to be undertaken during periods such that the worker will become a night worker unless—

(i) the employer has ensured that the worker will have the opportunity of a free health assessment before he takes up the assignment; or

(ii) the worker had a health assessment before being assigned to work to be undertaken during such periods on an earlier occasion, and the employer has no reason to believe that that assessment is no longer valid, and

(b) shall ensure that each night worker employed by him has the opportunity of a free health assessment at regular intervals of whatever duration may be appropriate in his case.

(2) Subject to paragraph (4), an employer—

(a) shall not assign a young worker to work during [the restricted period] unless—

(i) the employer has ensured that the young worker will have the opportunity of a free assessment of his health and capacities before he takes up the assignment; or

(ii) the young worker had an assessment of his health and capacities before being assigned to work during the restricted period on an earlier occasion, and the employer has no reason to believe that that assessment is no longer valid; and

(b) shall ensure that each young worker employed by him and assigned to work during the restricted period has the opportunity of a free assessment of his health and capacities at regular intervals of whatever duration may be appropriate in his case.

(3) For the purposes of paragraphs (1) and (2), an assessment is free if it is at no cost to the worker to whom it relates.

(4) The requirements in paragraph (2) do not apply in a case where the work a young worker is assigned to do is of an exceptional nature.

(5) No person shall disclose an assessment made for the purposes of this regulation to any person other than the worker to whom it relates, unless—

(a) the worker has given his consent in writing to the disclosure, or

(b) the disclosure is confined to a statement that the assessment shows the worker to be fit—

(i) in a case where paragraph (1)(a)(i) or (2)(a)(i) applies, to take up an assignment, or

(ii) in a case where paragraph (1)(b) or (2)(b) applies, to continue to undertake an assignment.

(6) Where—

(a) a registered medical practitioner has advised an employer that a worker employed by the employer is suffering from health problems which the practitioner considers to be connected with the fact that the worker performs night work, and

(b) it is possible for the employer to transfer the worker to work—

(i) to which the worker is suited, and

(ii) which is to be undertaken during periods such that the worker will cease to be a night worker,

the employer shall transfer the worker accordingly.

NOTES

Para (2): words in square brackets substituted by the Working Time (Amendment) Regulations 2002, SI 2002/3128, regs 2, 9.

[2.278]

8 Pattern of work

Where the pattern according to which an employer organizes work is such as to put the health and safety of a worker employed by him at risk, in particular because the work is monotonous or the work-rate is predetermined, the employer shall ensure that the worker is given adequate rest breaks.

[2.279]

9 Records

An employer shall—

(a) keep records which are adequate to show whether the limits specified in regulations 4(1)[, 5A(1)] and 6(1) and (7) and the requirements in regulations [6A and] 7(1) and (2) are being complied with in the case of each worker employed by him in relation to whom they apply; and

(b) retain such records for two years from the date on which they were made.

NOTES

Words in square brackets inserted by the Working Time (Amendment) Regulations 2002, SI 2002/3128, regs 2, 10.

[2.280]

10 Daily rest

(1) [A worker] is entitled to a rest period of not less than eleven consecutive hours in each 24-hour period during which he works for his employer.

(2) Subject to paragraph (3), a young worker is entitled to a rest period of not less than twelve consecutive hours in each 24-hour period during which he works for his employer.

(3) The minimum rest period provided for in paragraph (2) may be interrupted in the case of activities involving periods of work that are split up over the day or of short duration.

NOTES

Para (1): words in square brackets substituted by the Working Time (Amendment) Regulations 2002, SI 2002/3128, regs 2, 11.

[2.281]

11 Weekly rest period

(1) Subject to paragraph (2), [a worker] is entitled to an uninterrupted rest period of not less than 24 hours in each seven-day period during which he works for his employer.

(2) If his employer so determines, [a worker] shall be entitled to either—

(a) two uninterrupted rest periods each of not less than 24 hours in each 14-day period during which he works for his employer; or

(b) one uninterrupted rest period of not less than 48 hours in each such 14-day period, in place of the entitlement provided for in paragraph (1).

(3) Subject to paragraph (8), a young worker is entitled to a rest period of not less than 48 hours in each seven-day period during which he works for his employer.

(4) For the purpose of paragraphs (1) to (3), a seven-day period or (as the case may be) 14-day period shall be taken to begin—

(a) at such times on such days as may be provided for the purposes of this regulation in a relevant agreement; or

(b) where there are no provisions of a relevant agreement which apply, at the start of each week or (as the case may be) every other week.

(5) In a case where, in accordance with paragraph (4), 14-day periods are to be taken to begin at the start of every other week, the first such period applicable in the case of a particular worker shall be taken to begin—

(a) if the worker's employment began on or before the date on which these Regulations come into force, on 5th October 1998; or

(b) if the worker's employment begins after the date on which these Regulations come into force, at the start of the week in which that employment begins.

(6) For the purposes of paragraphs (4) and (5), a week starts at midnight between Sunday and Monday.

(7) The minimum rest period to which [a worker] is entitled under paragraph (1) or (2) shall not include any part of a rest period to which the worker is entitled under regulation 10(1), except where this is justified by objective or technical reasons or reasons concerning the organization of work.

(8) The minimum rest period to which a young worker is entitled under paragraph (3)—

(a) may be interrupted in the case of activities involving periods of work that are split up over the day or are of short duration; and

(b) may be reduced where this is justified by technical or organization reasons, but not to less than 36 consecutive hours.

NOTES

Paras (1), (2), (7): words in square brackets substituted by the Working Time (Amendment) Regulations 2002, SI 2002/3128, regs 2, 12.

[2.282]

12 Rest breaks

(1) Where [a worker's] daily working time is more than six hours, he is entitled to a rest break.

(2) The details of the rest break to which [a worker] is entitled under paragraph (1), including its duration and the terms on which it is granted, shall be in accordance with any provisions for the purposes of this regulation which are contained in a collective agreement or a workforce agreement.

(3) Subject to the provisions of any applicable collective agreement or workforce agreement, the rest break provided for in paragraph (1) is an uninterrupted period of not less than 20 minutes, and the worker is entitled to spend it away from his workstation if he has one.

(4) Where a young worker's daily working time is more than four and a half hours, he is entitled to a rest break of at least 30 minutes, which shall be consecutive if possible, and he is entitled to spend it away from his workstation if he has one.

(5) If, on any day, a young worker is employed by more than one employer, his daily working time shall be determined for the purpose of paragraph (4) by aggregating the number of hours worked by him for each employer.

NOTES

Paras (1), (2): words in square brackets substituted by the Working Time (Amendment) Regulations 2002, SI 2002/3128, regs 2, 13.

[2.283]

13 Entitlement to annual leave

[(1) Subject to paragraph (5), a worker is entitled to four weeks' annual leave in each leave year.]

(2) . . .

(3) A worker's leave year, for the purposes of this regulation, begins—
- (a) on such date during the calendar year as may be provided for in a relevant agreement; or
- (b) where there are no provisions of a relevant agreement which apply—
  - (i) if the worker's employment began on or before 1st October 1998, on that date and each subsequent anniversary of that date; or
  - (ii) if the worker's employment begins after 1st October 1998, on the date on which that employment begins and each subsequent anniversary of that date.

(4) Paragraph (3) does not apply to a worker to whom Schedule 2 applies (workers employed in agriculture) except where, in the case of a worker partly employed in agriculture, a relevant agreement so provides.

(5) Where the date on which a worker's employment begins is later than the date on which (by virtue of a relevant agreement) his first leave year begins, the leave to which he is entitled in that leave year is a proportion of the period applicable under [paragraph (1)] equal to the proportion of that leave year remaining on the date on which his employment begins.

(6)–(8) . . .

(9) Leave to which a worker is entitled under this regulation may be taken in instalments, but—
- (a) it may only be taken in the leave year in respect of which it is due, and
- (b) it may not be replaced by a payment in lieu except where the worker's employment is terminated.

NOTES

Para (1): substituted by the Working Time (Amendment) Regulations 2001, SI 2001/3256, art 2(1), (2).
Paras (2), (7), (8): revoked by SI 2001/3256, art 2(1), (3), (6).
Para (5): words in square brackets substituted by SI 2001/3256, art 2(1), (4).
Para (6): revoked by the Working Time (Amendment) Regulations 2007, SI 2007/2079, reg 2(1), (4).
Para (6): words omitted revoked by SI 2001/3256, art 2(1), (5).

[2.284]
[13A Entitlement to additional annual leave

(1) Subject to regulation 26A and paragraphs (3) and (5), a worker is entitled in each leave year to a period of additional leave determined in accordance with paragraph (2).

(2) The period of additional leave to which a worker is entitled under paragraph (1) is—
- (a) in any leave year beginning on or after 1st October 2007 but before 1st April 2008, 0.8 weeks;
- (b) in any leave year beginning before 1st October 2007, a proportion of 0.8 weeks equivalent to the proportion of the year beginning on 1st October 2007 which would have elapsed at the end of that leave year;
- (c) in any leave year beginning on 1st April 2008, 0.8 weeks;
- (d) in any leave year beginning after 1st April 2008 but before 1st April 2009, 0.8 weeks and a proportion of another 0.8 weeks equivalent to the proportion of the year beginning on 1st April 2009 which would have elapsed at the end of that leave year;
- (e) in any leave year beginning on or after 1st April 2009, 1.6 weeks.

(3) The aggregate entitlement provided for in paragraph (2) and regulation 13(1) is subject to a maximum of 28 days.

(4) A worker's leave year begins for the purposes of this regulation on the same date as the worker's leave year begins for the purposes of regulation 13.

(5) Where the date on which a worker's employment begins is later than the date on which his first leave year begins, the additional leave to which he is entitled in that leave year is a proportion of the period applicable under paragraph (2) equal to the proportion of that leave year remaining on the date on which his employment begins.

(6) Leave to which a worker is entitled under this regulation may be taken in instalments, but it may not be replaced by a payment in lieu except where—
- (a) the worker's employment is terminated; or
- (b) the leave is an entitlement that arises under paragraph (2)(a), (b) or (c); or
- (c) the leave is an entitlement to 0.8 weeks that arises under paragraph (2)(d) in respect of that part of the leave year which would have elapsed before 1st April 2009.

(7) A relevant agreement may provide for any leave to which a worker is entitled under this regulation to be carried forward into the leave year immediately following the leave year in respect of which it is due.

(8) This regulation does not apply to workers to whom the Agricultural Wages (Scotland) Act 1949 applies (as that Act had effect on 1 July 1999).]

NOTES

Inserted by the Working Time (Amendment) Regulations 2007, SI 2007/2079, reg 2(1), (2).

[2.285]

14 Compensation related to entitlement to leave

(1) This regulation applies where—

(a) a worker's employment is terminated during the course of his leave year, and

(b) on the date on which the termination takes effect ("the termination date"), the proportion he has taken of the leave to which he is entitled in the leave year under [regulation 13] [and regulation 13A] differs from the proportion of the leave year which has expired.

(2) Where the proportion of leave taken by the worker is less than the proportion of the leave year which has expired, his employer shall make him a payment in lieu of leave in accordance with paragraph (3).

(3) The payment due under paragraph (2) shall be—

(a) such sum as may be provided for the purposes of this regulation in a relevant agreement, or

(b) where there are no provisions of a relevant agreement which apply, a sum equal to the amount that would be due to the worker under regulation 16 in respect of a period of leave determined according to the formula—

$$(A \times B) - C$$

where—

A is the period of leave to which the worker is entitled under [regulation 13] [and regulation 13A];

B is the proportion of the worker's leave year which expired before the termination date, and

C is the period of leave taken by the worker between the start of the leave year and the termination date.

(4) A relevant agreement may provide that, where the proportion of leave taken by the worker exceeds the proportion of the leave year which has expired, he shall compensate his employer, whether by a payment, by undertaking additional work or otherwise.

Part 2 Statutory Instruments

NOTES

Paras (1), (3): words in first pair of square brackets substituted by the Working Time (Amendment) Regulations 2001, SI 2001/3256, art 3; words in second pair of square brackets inserted by the Working Time (Amendment) Regulations 2007, SI 2007/2079, reg 2(1), (5).

[2.286]

15 Dates on which leave is taken

(1) A worker may take leave to which he is entitled under [regulation 13] [and regulation 13A] on such days as he may elect by giving notice to his employer in accordance with paragraph (3), subject to any requirement imposed on him by his employer under paragraph (2).

(2) A worker's employer may require the worker—

(a) to take leave to which the worker is entitled under [regulation 13] [or regulation 13A]; or

(b) not to take such leave,

on particular days, by giving notice to the worker in accordance with paragraph (3).

(3) A notice under paragraph (1) or (2)—

(a) may relate to all or part of the leave to which a worker is entitled in a leave year;

(b) shall specify the days on which leave is or (as the case may be) is not to be taken and, where the leave on a particular day is to be in respect of only part of the day, its duration; and

(c) shall be given to the employer or, as the case may be, the worker before the relevant date.

(4) The relevant date, for the purposes of paragraph (3), is the date—

(a) in the case of a notice under paragraph (1) or (2)(a), twice as many days in advance of the earliest day specified in the notice as the number of days or part-days to which the notice relates, and

(b) in the case of a notice under paragraph (2)(b), as many days in advance of the earliest day so specified as the number of days or part-days to which the notice relates.

(5) Any right or obligation under paragraphs (1) to (4) may be varied or excluded by a relevant agreement.

(6) This regulation does not apply to a worker to whom Schedule 2 applies (workers employed in agriculture) except where, in the case of a worker partly employed in agriculture, a relevant agreement so provides.

NOTES

Paras (1), (2): words in first pair of square brackets substituted by the Working Time (Amendment) Regulations 2001, SI 2001/3256, art 3; words in second pair of square brackets inserted by the Working Time (Amendment) Regulations 2007,

SI 2007/2079, reg 2(1), (5), (6).

[2.287]

[15A Leave during the first year of employment

(1) During the first year of his employment, the amount of leave a worker may take at any time in exercise of his entitlement under regulation 13 [or regulation 13A] is limited to the amount which is deemed to have accrued in his case at that time under paragraph (2) [or (2A)], as modified under paragraph (3) in a case where that paragraph applies, less the amount of leave (if any) that he has already taken during that year.

(2) For the purposes of paragraph (1), [in the case of workers to whom the Agricultural Wages (Scotland) Act 1949 applies,] leave is deemed to accrue over the course of the worker's first year of employment, at the rate of one-twelfth of the amount specified in regulation 13(1) on the first day of each month of that year.

[(2A) Except where paragraph (2) applies, for the purposes of paragraph (1), leave is deemed to accrue over the course of the worker's first year of employment, at the rate of one-twelfth of the amount specified in regulation 13(1) and regulation 13A(2), subject to the limit contained in regulation 13A(3), on the first day of each month of that year.]

(3) Where the amount of leave that has accrued in a particular case includes a fraction of a day other than a half-day, the fraction shall be treated as a half-day if it is less than a half-day and as a whole day if it is more than a half-day.

(4) This regulation does not apply to a worker whose employment began on or before 25th October 2001.]

NOTES

Inserted by the Working Time (Amendment) Regulations 2001, SI 2001/3256, art 4.

Paras (1), (2): words in square brackets inserted by the Working Time (Amendment) Regulations 2007, SI 2007/2079, reg 2(1), (6)–(8).

Para (2A): inserted by SI 2007/2079, reg 2(1), (9).

[2.288]

16 Payment in respect of periods of leave

(1) A worker is entitled to be paid in respect of any period of annual leave to which he is entitled under regulation 13 [and regulation 13A], at the rate of a week's pay in respect of each week of leave.

(2) Sections 221 to 224 of the 1996 Act shall apply for the purpose of determining the amount of a week's pay for the purposes of this regulation, subject to the modifications set out in paragraph (3).

(3) The provisions referred to in paragraph (2) shall apply—

(a) as if references to the employee were references to the worker;

(b) as if references to the employee's contract of employment were references to the worker's contract;

(c) as if the calculation date were the first day of the period of leave in question; and

(d) as if the references to sections 227 and 228 did not apply.

(4) A right to payment under paragraph (1) does not affect any right of a worker to remuneration under his contract ("contractual remuneration").

(5) Any contractual remuneration paid to a worker in respect of a period of leave goes towards discharging any liability of the employer to make payments under this regulation in respect of that period; and, conversely, any payment of remuneration under this regulation in respect of a period goes towards discharging any liability of the employer to pay contractual remuneration in respect of that period.

NOTES

Para (1): words in square brackets inserted by the Working Time (Amendment) Regulations 2007, SI 2007/2079, reg 2(1), (5).

[2.289]

17 Entitlements under other provisions

Where during any period a worker is entitled to a rest period, rest break or annual leave both under a provision of these Regulations and under a separate provision (including a provision of his contract), he may not exercise the two rights separately, but may, in taking a rest period, break or leave during that period, take advantage of whichever right is, in any particular respect, the more favourable.

PART III
EXCEPTIONS

[2.290]

[18 Excluded sectors

[(1) These Regulations do not apply—

(a) to workers to whom the European Agreement on the organisation of working time of seafarers dated 30th September 1998 and put into effect by Council Directive 1999/63/EC of 21st June 1999 applies;

[(b) to workers to whom the Fishing Vessels (Working Time: Sea-fishermen) Regulations 2004 apply;] or

[(c) to workers to whom the Merchant Shipping (Working Time: Inland Waterways) Regulations 2003 apply].

(2) Regulations 4(1) and (2), 6(1), (2) and (7), 7(1) and (6), 8, 10(1), 11(1) and (2), 12(1), 13[, 13A] and 16 do not apply—

(a) where characteristics peculiar to certain specific services such as the armed forces or the police, or to certain specific activities in the civil protection services, inevitably conflict with the provisions of these Regulations;

(b) to workers to whom the European Agreement on the organisation of working time of mobile staff in civil aviation concluded on 22nd March 2000 and implemented by Council Directive 2000/79/EC of 27th November 2000 applies; or

(c) to the activities of workers who are doctors in training.

(3) Paragraph (2)(c) has effect only until 31st July 2004.

(4) Regulations 4(1) and (2), 6(1), (2) and (7), 8, 10(1), 11(1) and (2) and 12(1) do not apply to workers to whom Directive 2002/15/EC of the European Parliament and of the Council on the organisation of the working time of persons performing mobile road transport activities, dated 11th March 2002 applies.]

[(5) Regulation 24 does not apply to workers to whom the Cross-border Railways Services (Working Time) Regulations 2008 apply.]]

NOTES

Substituted by the Working Time (Amendment) Regulations 2003, SI 2003/1684, regs 2, 4.

Para (1): sub-para (b) substituted by the Fishing Vessels (Working Time: Sea-fishermen) Regulations 2004, SI 2004/1713, reg 21, Sch 2, para 5; sub-para (c) substituted by the Merchant Shipping (Working Time: Inland Waterways) Regulations 2003, SI 2003/3049, reg 20, Sch 2, para 6.

Para (2): figure in square brackets inserted by the Working Time (Amendment) Regulations 2007, SI 2007/2079, reg 2(1), (10).

Para (5): added by the Cross-border Railway Services (Working Time) Regulations 2008, SI 2008/1660, reg 19, Sch 3, para 4, as from 27 July 2008.

[2.291]

19 Domestic service

Regulations 4(1) and (2), [5A(1) and (4),] 6(1), (2) and (7), [6A,] 7(1), (2) and (6) and 8 do not apply in relation to a worker employed as a domestic servant in a private household.

NOTES

Words in square brackets inserted by the Working Time (Amendment) Regulations 2002, SI 2002/3128, regs 2, 14.

[2.292]

20 Unmeasured working time

[(1)] Regulations 4(1) and (2), 6(1), (2) and (7), 10(1), 11(1) and (2) and 12(1) do not apply in relation to a worker where, on account of the specific characteristics of the activity in which he is engaged, the duration of his working time is not measured or predetermined or can be determined by the worker himself, as may be the case for—

(a) managing executives or other persons with autonomous decision-taking powers;

(b) family workers; or

(c) workers officiating at religious ceremonies in churches and religious communities.

[(2) . . .]

NOTES

Para (1): numbered as such by the Working Time Regulations 1999, SI 1999/3372, regs 1(1), 4.

Para (2): added by SI 1999/3372, regs 1(1), 4, and revoked by the Working Time (Amendment) Regulations 2006, SI 2006/99, reg 2.

[2.293]
21 Other special cases

Subject to regulation 24, regulations 6(1), (2) and (7), 10(1), 11(1) and (2) and 12(1) do not apply in relation to a worker—

(a) where the worker's activities are such that his place of work and place of residence are distant from one another[, including cases where the worker is employed in offshore work,] or his different places of work are distant from one another;
(b) where the worker is engaged in security and surveillance activities requiring a permanent presence in order to protect property and persons, as may be the case for security guards and caretakers or security firms;
(c) where the worker's activities involve the need for continuity of service or production, as may be the case in relation to—
 (i) services relating to the reception, treatment or care provided by hospitals or similar establishments [(including the activities of doctors in training)], residential institutions and prisons;
 (ii) work at docks or airports;
 (iii) press, radio, television, cinematographic production, postal and telecommunications services and civil protection services;
 (iv) gas, water and electricity production, transmission and distribution, household refuse collection and incineration;
 (v) industries in which work cannot be interrupted on technical grounds;
 (vi) research and development activities;
 (vii) agriculture;
 [(viii) the carriage of passengers on regular urban transport services;]
(d) where there is a foreseeable surge of activity, as may be the case in relation to—
 (i) agriculture;
 (ii) tourism; and
 (iii) postal services;
(e) where the worker's activities are affected by—
 (i) an occurrence due to unusual and unforeseeable circumstances, beyond the control of the worker's employer;
 (ii) exceptional events, the consequences of which could not have been avoided despite the exercise of all due care by the employer; or
 (iii) an accident or the imminent risk of an accident;
[(f) where the worker works in railway transport and—
 (i) his activities are intermittent;
 (ii) he spends his working time on board trains; or
 (iii) his activities are linked to transport timetables and to ensuring the continuity and regularity of traffic].

NOTES

Words in square brackets in paras (a), (c)(i) inserted, and paras (c)(viii), (f) added, by the Working Time (Amendment) Regulations 2003, SI 2003/1684, regs 2, 5.

[2.294]
22 Shift workers

(1) Subject to regulation 24—
(a) regulation 10(1) does not apply in relation to a shift worker when he changes shift and cannot take a daily rest period between the end of one shift and the start of the next one;
(b) paragraphs (1) and (2) of regulation 11 do not apply in relation to a shift worker when he changes shift and cannot take a weekly rest period between the end of one shift and the start of the next one; and
(c) neither regulation 10(1) nor paragraphs (1) and (2) of regulation 11 apply to workers engaged in activities involving periods of work split up over the day, as may be the case for cleaning staff.

(2) For the purposes of this regulation—

"shift worker" means any worker whose work schedule is part of shift work; and

"shift work" means any method of organizing work in shifts whereby workers succeed each other at the same workstations according to a certain pattern, including a rotating pattern, and which may be continuous or discontinuous, entailing the need for workers to work at different times over a given period of days or weeks.

[2.295]
23 Collective and workforce agreements

A collective agreement or a workforce agreement may—

(a) modify or exclude the application of regulations 6(1) to (3) and (7), 10(1), 11(1) and (2) and 12(1), and

(b) for objective or technical reasons or reasons concerning the organization of work, modify the application of regulation 4(3) and (4) by the substitution, for each reference to 17 weeks, of a different period, being a period not exceeding 52 weeks,

in relation to particular workers or groups of workers.

[2.296]

24 Compensatory rest

Where the application of any provision of these Regulations is excluded by regulation 21 or 22, or is modified or excluded by means of a collective agreement or a workforce agreement under regulation 23(a), and a worker is accordingly required by his employer to work during a period which would otherwise be a rest period or rest break—

(a) his employer shall wherever possible allow him to take an equivalent period of compensatory rest, and

(b) in exceptional cases in which it is not possible, for objective reasons, to grant such a period of rest, his employer shall afford him such protection as may be appropriate in order to safeguard the worker's health and safety.

[2.297]

[24A Mobile workers

(1) Regulations 6(1), (2) and (7), 10(1), 11(1) and (2) and 12(1) do not apply to a mobile worker in relation to whom the application of those regulations is not excluded by any provision of regulation 18.

(2) A mobile worker, to whom paragraph (1) applies, is entitled to adequate rest, except where the worker's activities are affected by any of the matters referred to in regulation 21(e).

(3) For the purposes of this regulation, "adequate rest" means that a worker has regular rest periods, the duration of which are expressed in units of time and which are sufficiently long and continuous to ensure that, as a result of fatigue or other irregular working patterns, he does not cause injury to himself, to fellow workers or to others and that he does not damage his health, either in the short term or in the longer term.]

NOTES

Inserted by the Working Time (Amendment) Regulations 2003, SI 2003/1684, regs 2, 6.

[2.298]

25 Workers in the armed forces

(1) Regulation 9 does not apply in relation to a worker serving as a member of the armed forces.

(2) Regulations [5A, 6A,] 10(2) and 11(3) do not apply in relation to a young worker serving as a member of the armed forces.

(3) In a case where a young worker is accordingly required to work during [the restricted period, or is not permitted the minimum rest period provided for in regulation 10(2) or 11(3),] he shall be allowed an appropriate period of compensatory rest.

NOTES

Para (2): figures in square brackets inserted by the Working Time (Amendment) Regulations 2002, SI 2002/3128, regs 2, 15(a).

Para (3): words in square brackets substituted by SI 2002/3128, regs 2, 15(b).

[2.299]

[25A Doctors in training

[[(1) Paragraph (1) of regulation 4 is modified in its application to workers to whom this paragraph applies by substituting for the reference to 48 hours a reference to 52 hours—

(a) in the case of doctors in training who are employed in an employment falling within Table 1 of Schedule 2A, with effect from 1st August 2009 until 31st July 2011; and

(b) in the case of doctors in training who are employed in an employment falling within Table 2 of Schedule 2A, with effect from 2nd November 2009 until 31st July 2011.]

(1A) Paragraph (1) applies to workers who are doctors in training who are employed—

(a) by an employer who is listed in column 1 of [Table 1 or Table 2] contained in Schedule 2A,

(b) at a place listed in column 2 of [the applicable table] in respect of that employer,

(c) to provide at that place one of the specialist services listed in column 3 of [the applicable table] in respect of that place, and

(d) in one of the grades listed in column 4 of [the applicable table] in respect of that specialist service and, where applicable, working as part of a rota referred to in that column in respect of that grade, or those grades.]

(2) In the case of workers who are doctors in training, paragraphs (3)–(5) of regulation 4 shall not apply and paragraphs (3) and (4) of this regulation shall apply in their place.

(3) Subject to paragraph (4), the reference period which applies in the case of a worker who is a doctor in training is, with effect from 1st August 2004—

(a) where a relevant agreement provides for the application of this regulation in relation to successive periods of 26 weeks, each such period; and

(b) in any other case, any period of 26 weeks in the course of his employment.

(4) Where a doctor in training has worked for his employer for less than 26 weeks, the reference period applicable in his case is the period that has elapsed since he started work for his employer.]

NOTES

Inserted by the Working Time (Amendment) Regulations 2003, SI 2003/1684, regs 2, 7.

Para (1): substituted, together with para (1A) for original para (1), by the Working Time (Amendment) Regulations 2009, SI 2009/1567, reg 2, as from 1 August 2009; further substituted by the Working Time (Amendment) (No 2) Regulations 2009, SI 2009/2766, reg 2(a), as from 2 November 2009.

Para (1A): substituted, together with para (1) for original para (1), by SI 2009/1567, reg 2, as from 1 August 2009; words in square brackets substituted by SI 2009/2766, reg 2(b), as from 2 November 2009.

Schedule 2A: this lists the hospitals, and categories of doctors, to whom para (1) applied (until 31 July 2011), and is now spent.

[2.300]

[25B Workers employed in offshore work

(1) In the case of workers employed in offshore work, paragraphs (3)–(5) of regulation 4 shall not apply and paragraphs (2) and (3) of this regulation shall apply in their place.

(2) Subject to paragraph (3), the reference period which applies in the case of workers employed in offshore work is—

(a) where a relevant agreement provides for the application of this regulation in relation to successive periods of 52 weeks, each such period; and

(b) in any other case, any period of 52 weeks in the course of his employment.

(3) Where a worker employed in offshore work has worked for his employer for less than 52 weeks, the reference period applicable in his case is the period that has elapsed since he started work for his employer.]

NOTES

Inserted by the Working Time (Amendment) Regulations 2003, SI 2003/1684, regs 2, 8.

26 (*Revoked by the Working Time (Amendment) Regulations 2003, SI 2003/1684, regs 2, 9.*)

[2.301]

[26A Entitlement to additional annual leave under a relevant agreement

(1) Regulation 13A does not apply in relation to a worker whose employer, as at 1st October 2007 and by virtue of a relevant agreement, provides each worker employed by him with an annual leave entitlement of 1.6 weeks or 8 days (whichever is the lesser) in addition to each worker's entitlement under regulation 13, provided that such additional annual leave—

(a) may not be replaced by a payment in lieu except in relation to a worker whose employment is terminated;

(b) may not be carried forward into a leave year other than that which immediately follows the leave year in respect of which the leave is due; and

(c) is leave for which the worker is entitled to be paid at not less than the rate of a week's pay in respect of each week of leave, calculated in accordance with sections 221 to 224 of the 1996 Act, modified such that—

(i) references to the employee are references to the worker;

(ii) references to the employee's contract of employment are references to the worker's contract;

(iii) the calculation date is the first day of the period of leave in question; and

(iv) the references to sections 227 and 228 do not apply.

(2) Notwithstanding paragraph (1), any additional annual leave in excess of 1.6 weeks or 8 days (whichever is the lesser) to which a worker is entitled, shall not be subject to the conditions of that paragraph.

(3) This regulation shall cease to apply to a worker from the day when an employer ceases to provide additional annual leave in accordance with the conditions in paragraph (1).

(4) This regulation does not apply to workers to whom the Agricultural Wages (Scotland) Act 1949 applies (as that Act had effect on 1 July 1999).]

NOTES

Inserted by the Working Time (Amendment) Regulations 2007, SI 2007/2079, reg 2(1), (3).

[2.302]
27 Young workers: force majeure

(1) Regulations [5A, 6A,] 10(2) and 12(4) do not apply in relation to a young worker where his employer requires him to undertake work which no adult worker is available to perform and which—

(a) is occasioned by either—
  (i) an occurrence due to unusual and unforeseeable circumstances, beyond the employer's control, or
  (ii) exceptional events, the consequences of which could not have been avoided despite the exercise of all due care by the employer;
(b) is of a temporary nature; and
(c) must be performed immediately.

(2) Where the application of regulation [5A, 6A,] 10(2) or 12(4) is excluded by paragraph (1), and a young worker is accordingly required to work during a period which would otherwise be a rest period or rest break, his employer shall allow him to take an equivalent period of compensatory rest within the following three weeks.

NOTES

Figures in square brackets inserted by the Working Time (Amendment) Regulations 2002, SI 2002/3128, regs 2, 18.

[2.303]
[27A Other exceptions relating to young workers

(1) Regulation 5A does not apply in relation to a young worker where—
(a) the young worker's employer requires him to undertake work which is necessary either to maintain continuity of service or production or to respond to a surge in demand for a service or product;
(b) no adult worker is available to perform the work, and
(c) performing the work would not adversely affect the young worker's education or training.

(2) Regulation 6A does not apply in relation to a young worker employed—
(a) in a hospital or similar establishment, or
(b) in connection with cultural, artistic, sporting or advertising activities,

in the circumstances referred to in paragraph (1).

(3) Regulation 6A does not apply, except in so far as it prohibits work between midnight and 4 am, in relation to a young worker employed in—
(a) agriculture;
(b) retail trading;
(c) postal or newspaper deliveries;
(d) a catering business;
(e) a hotel, public house, restaurant, bar or similar establishment, or
(f) a bakery,

in the circumstances referred to in paragraph (1).

(4) Where the application of regulation 6A is excluded by paragraph (2) or (3), and a young worker is accordingly required to work during a period which would otherwise be a rest period or rest break—
(a) he shall be supervised by an adult worker where such supervision is necessary for the young worker's protection, and
(b) he shall be allowed an equivalent period of compensatory rest.]

NOTES

Inserted by the Working Time (Amendment) Regulations 2002, SI 2002/3128, regs 2, 17.

PART IV
MISCELLANEOUS

[2.304]
[28 Enforcement

(1) In this regulation, regulations 29–29E and Schedule 3—

"the 1974 Act" means the Health and Safety at Work etc Act 1974;

"the Civil Aviation Authority" means the authority referred to in section 2(1) of the Civil Aviation Act 1982;

"code of practice" includes a standard, a specification and any other documentary form of practical guidance;

. . .

"enforcement authority" means the Executive, a local authority, the Civil Aviation Authority[, VOSA or the Office of Rail Regulation];

"the Executive" means the Health and Safety Executive referred to in [section 10(1)] of the 1974 Act;

"local authority" means—

(a) in relation to England, a county council so far as they are the council for an area for which there are no district councils, a district council, a London borough council, the Common Council of the City of London, the Sub-Treasurer of the Inner Temple or the Under-Treasurer of the Middle Temple;

(b) in relation to Wales, a county council or a county borough council;

(c) in relation to Scotland, a council constituted under section 2 of the Local Government etc (Scotland) Act 1994;

"premises" includes any place and, in particular, includes—

(a) any vehicle, vessel, aircraft or hovercraft;

(b) any installation on land (including the foreshore and other land intermittently covered by water), any offshore installation, and any other installation (whether floating, or resting on the seabed or the subsoil thereof, or resting on other land covered with water or the subsoil thereof) and

(c) any tent or movable structure;

"relevant civil aviation worker" means a mobile worker who works mainly on board civil aircraft, excluding any worker to whom regulation 18(2)(b) applies;

"the relevant requirements" means the following provisions—

(a) regulations 4(2), 5A(4), 6(2) and (7), 6A, 7(1), (2) and (6), 8, 9 and 27A(4)(a);

(b) regulation 24, in so far as it applies where regulation 6(1), (2) or (7) is modified or excluded, and

(c) regulation 24A(2), in so far as it applies where regulations 6(1), (2) or (7) is excluded;

"relevant road transport worker" means a mobile worker to whom one or more of the following applies—

(a) Council Regulation (EEC) 3820/85,

(b) the European Agreement concerning the Work of Crews of Vehicles engaged in International Road Transport (AETR) of 1st July 1970, and

(c) the United Kingdom domestic driver's hours code, which is set out in Part VI of the Transport Act 1968;

"the relevant statutory provisions" means—

(a) the provisions of the 1974 Act and of any regulations made under powers contained in that Act; and

(b) while and to the extent that they remain in force, the provisions of the Acts mentioned in Schedule 1 to the 1974 Act and which are specified in the third column of that Schedule and the regulations, orders or other instruments of a legislative character made or having effect under a provision so specified; and

"VOSA" means the Vehicle and Operator Services Agency.

(2) It shall be the duty of the Executive to make adequate arrangements for the enforcement of the relevant requirements except to the extent that—

(a) a local authority is made responsible for their enforcement by paragraph (3);

(b) the Civil Aviation Authority is made responsible for their enforcement by paragraph (5); . . .

(c) VOSA is made responsible for their enforcement by paragraph (6);

[(d) the Office of Rail Regulation is made responsible for their enforcement by paragraph (3A)].

(3) Where the relevant requirements apply in relation to workers employed in premises in respect of which a local authority is responsible, under the Health and Safety (Enforcing Authority) Regulations 1998, for enforcing any of the relevant statutory provisions, it shall be the duty of that authority to enforce those requirements.

[(3A) Where the relevant requirements apply in relation to workers employed in the carrying out of any of the activities specified in regulation 3(2) of the Health and Safety (Enforcing Authority for Railways and Other Guided Transport Systems) Regulations 2006 it shall be the duty of the Office of Rail Regulation to enforce those requirements.]

(4) The duty imposed on local authorities by paragraph (3) shall be performed in accordance with such guidance as may be given to them by [the Executive].

(5) It shall be the duty of the Civil Aviation Authority to enforce the relevant requirements in relation to relevant civil aviation workers.

(6) It shall be the duty of VOSA to enforce the relevant requirements in relation to relevant road transport workers.

(7) The provisions of Schedule 3 shall apply in relation to the enforcement of the relevant requirements.

(8) . . .]

NOTES

Substituted by the Working Time (Amendment) Regulations 2003, SI 2003/1684, regs 2, 10.

Para (1) is amended as follows:

Definition "the Commission" (omitted) revoked by the Legislative Reform (Health and Safety Executive) Order 2008, SI 2008/960, art 22, Sch 3.

Words in square brackets in definition "enforcement authority" substituted by the Health and Safety (Enforcing Authority for Railways and Other Guided Transport Systems) Regulations 2006, SI 2006/557, reg 6, Schedule, para 7(a).

Words in square brackets in definition "the Executive" substituted by SI 2008/960, art 22, Sch 3.

Para (2): word omitted from sub-para (b) revoked, and sub-para (d) added, by SI 2006/557, reg 6, Schedule, para 7(b)(ii).

Para (3A): inserted by SI 2006/557, reg 6, Schedule, para 7(c).

Para (4): words in square brackets substituted by SI 2008/960, art 22, Sch 3.

Para (8): revoked by SI 2008/960, art 22, Sch 3.

[2.305]

[29 Offences

[(1) An employer who fails to comply with any of the relevant requirements shall be guilty of an offence.

(2) The provisions of paragraph (3) shall apply where an inspector is exercising or has exercised any power conferred by Schedule 3.

(3) It is an offence for a person—

- (a) to contravene any requirement imposed by the inspector under paragraph 2 of Schedule 3;
- (b) to prevent or attempt to prevent any other person from appearing before the inspector or from answering any question to which the inspector may by virtue of paragraph 2(2)(e) of Schedule 3 require an answer;
- (c) to contravene any requirement or prohibition imposed by an improvement notice or a prohibition notice (including any such notice as is modified on appeal);
- (d) intentionally to obstruct the inspector in the exercise or performance of his powers or duties;
- (e) to use or disclose any information in contravention of paragraph 8 of Schedule 3;
- (f) to make a statement which he knows to be false or recklessly to make a statement which is false, where the statement is made in purported compliance with a requirement to furnish any information imposed by or under these Regulations.

(4) An employer guilty of an offence under paragraph (1) shall be liable—

- (a) on summary conviction, to a fine not exceeding the statutory maximum;
- (b) on conviction on indictment, to a fine.

(5) A person guilty of an offence under paragraph (3) shall be liable to the penalty prescribed in relation to that provision by paragraphs (6), (7) or (8) as the case may be.

(6) A person guilty of an offence under sub-paragraph (3)(a), (b) or (d) shall be liable on summary conviction to a fine not exceeding level 5 on the standard scale.

(7) A person guilty of an offence under sub-paragraph (3)(c) shall be liable—

- (a) on summary conviction, to imprisonment for a term not exceeding three months, or a fine not exceeding the statutory maximum;
- (b) on conviction on indictment, to imprisonment for a term not exceeding two years, or a fine, or both.

(8) A person guilty of an offence under any of the sub-paragraphs of paragraph (3) not falling within paragraphs (6) or (7) above, shall be liable—

- (a) on summary conviction, to a fine not exceeding the statutory maximum;
- (b) on conviction on indictment—
  - (i) if the offence is under sub-paragraph (3)(e), to imprisonment for a term not exceeding two years or a fine or both;
  - (ii) if the offence is not one to which the preceding sub-paragraph applies, to a fine.

(9) The provisions set out in regulations 29A–29E below shall apply in relation to the offences provided for in paragraphs (1) and (3).]

NOTES

Substituted, together with regs 29A–29E for the original reg 29, by the Working Time (Amendment) Regulations 2003, SI 2003/1684, regs 2, 10.

[2.306]

[29A Offences due to fault of other person

Where the commission by any person of an offence is due to the act or default of some other person, that other person shall be guilty of the offence, and a person may be charged with and convicted of the offence by virtue of this paragraph whether or not proceedings are taken against the first-mentioned person.]

NOTES

Substituted as noted to reg 29 at **[2.305]**.

[2.307]

[29B Offences by bodies corporate

(1) Where an offence committed by a body corporate is proved to have been committed with the consent or connivance of, or to have been attributable to any neglect on the part of, any director, manager, secretary or other similar officer of the body corporate or a person who was purporting to act in any such capacity, he as well as the body corporate shall be guilty of that offence and shall be liable to be proceeded against and punished accordingly.

(2) Where the affairs of a body corporate are managed by its members, the preceding paragraph shall apply in relation to the acts and defaults of a member in connection with his functions of management as if he were a director of the body corporate.]

NOTES

Substituted as noted to reg 29 at **[2.305]**.

[2.308]

[29C Restriction on institution of proceedings in England and Wales

Proceedings for an offence shall not, in England and Wales, be instituted except by an inspector or by or with the consent of the Director of Public Prosecutions.]

NOTES

Substituted as noted to reg 29 at **[2.305]**.

[2.309]

[29D Prosecutions by inspectors

(1) An inspector, if authorised in that behalf by an enforcement authority, may, although not of counsel or a solicitor, prosecute before a magistrate's court proceedings for an offence under these Regulations.

(2) This regulation shall not apply to Scotland.]

NOTES

Substituted as noted to reg 29 at **[2.305]**.

[2.310]

[29E Power of court to order cause of offence to be remedied

(1) Where a person is convicted of an offence in respect of any matters which appear to the court to be matters which it is in his power to remedy, the court may, in addition to or instead of imposing any punishment, order him, within such time as may be fixed by the order, to take such steps as may be specified in the order for remedying the said matters.

(2) The time fixed by an order under paragraph (1) may be extended or further extended by order of the court on an application made before the end of that time as originally fixed or as extended under this paragraph, as the case may be.

(3) Where a person is ordered under paragraph (1) to remedy any matters, that person shall not be liable under these Regulations in respect of those matters in so far as they continue during the time fixed by the order or any further time allowed under paragraph (2).]

NOTES

Substituted as noted to reg 29 at **[2.305]**.

[2.311]

30 Remedies

(1) A worker may present a complaint to an employment tribunal that his employer—
- (a) has refused to permit him to exercise any right he has under—
  - [(i) regulation 10(1) or (2), 11(1), (2) or (3), 12(1) or (4), 13 or 13A;]
  - (ii) regulation 24, in so far as it applies where regulation 10(1), 11(1) or (2) or 12(1) is modified or excluded; . . .
  - [(iii) regulation 24A, in so far as it applies where regulation 10(1), 11(1) or (2) or 12(1) is excluded; or
  - (iv) regulation 25(3), 27A(4)(b) or 27(2); or]
- (b) has failed to pay him the whole or any part of any amount due to him under regulation 14(2) or 16(1).

(2) [Subject to article 30A, an employment tribunal] shall not consider a complaint under this regulation unless it is presented—

(a) before the end of the period of three months (or, in a case to which regulation 38(2) applies, six months) beginning with the date on which it is alleged that the exercise of the right should have been permitted (or in the case of a rest period or leave extending over more than one day, the date on which it should have been permitted to begin) or, as the case may be, the payment should have been made;

(b) within such further period as the tribunal considers reasonable in a case where it is satisfied that it was not reasonably practicable for the complaint to be presented before the end of that period of three or, as the case may be, six months.

[(2A) Where the period within which a complaint must be presented in accordance with paragraph (2) is extended by regulation 15 of the Employment Act 2002 (Dispute Resolution) Regulations 2004, the period within which the complaint must be presented shall be the extended period rather than the period in paragraph (2).]

(3) Where an employment tribunal finds a complaint under paragraph (1)(a) well-founded, the tribunal—

(a) shall make a declaration to that effect, and

(b) may make an award of compensation to be paid by the employer to the worker.

(4) The amount of the compensation shall be such as the tribunal considers just and equitable in all the circumstances having regard to—

(a) the employer's default in refusing to permit the worker to exercise his right, and

(b) any loss sustained by the worker which is attributable to the matters complained of.

(5) Where on a complaint under paragraph (1)(b) an employment tribunal finds that an employer has failed to pay a worker in accordance with regulation 14(2) or 16(1), it shall order the employer to pay to the worker the amount which it finds to be due to him.

NOTES

Para (1): sub-para (a)(i) substituted by the Working Time (Amendment) Regulations 2007, SI 2007/2079, reg 2(1), (11); word omitted from sub-para (a)(ii) revoked, and sub-paras (a)(iii), (iv) substituted for the original sub-para (a)(iii), by the Working Time (Amendment) Regulations 2003, SI 2003/1684, regs 2, 11.

Para (2): words in square brackets substituted by the Cross-Border Mediation (EU Directive) Regulations 2011, SI 2011/1133, regs 67, 68, as from 20 May 2011.

Para (2A): inserted by the Employment Act 2002 (Dispute Resolution) Regulations 2004, SI 2004/752, reg 17(f). Note that this paragraph has not been revoked despite the 2004 Regulations lapsing on 6 April 2009.

Conciliation: employment tribunal proceedings and claims which could be the subject of employment tribunal proceedings under this regulation are proceedings to which the Employment Tribunals Act 1996, s 18 applies; see s 18(1)(ff) of that Act, at **[1.706]**.

Tribunal jurisdiction: the Employment Act 2002, s 38 applies to proceedings before the employment tribunal relating to a claim under this regulation; see s 38(1) of, and Sch 5 to, the 2002 Act at **[1.1228]**, **[1.1236]**. See also the Trade Union and Labour Relations (Consolidation) Act 1992, s 207A at **[1.474]** (as inserted by the Employment Act 2008). That section provides that in proceedings before an employment tribunal relating to a claim by an employee under any of the jurisdictions listed in Sch A2 to the 1992 Act at **[1.648]** (which includes this regulation) the tribunal may adjust any award given if the employer or the employee has unreasonably failed to comply with the relevant Code of Practice as defined by s 207A(4). See also the revised Acas Code of Practice 1 – Disciplinary and Grievance Procedures (2009) at **[4.1]**.

[2.312]

[30A Extension of time limits because of mediation in certain cross-border disputes

(1) In this regulation—

(a) "Mediation Directive" means Directive 2008/52/EC of the European Parliament and of the Council of 21 May 2008 on certain aspects of mediation in civil and commercial matters;

(b) "mediation" has the meaning given by article 3(a) of the Mediation Directive;

(c) "mediator" has the meaning given by article 3(b) of the Mediation Directive; and

(d) "relevant dispute" means a dispute to which article 8(1) of the Mediation Directive applies (certain cross-border disputes).

(2) Paragraph (3) applies where—

(a) a three month time limit is set by regulation 30(2) in relation to the whole or part of a relevant dispute;

(b) a mediation in relation to the relevant dispute starts before the period expires; and

(c) if not extended by this regulation, the time limit would expire before the mediation ends or less than four weeks after it ends.

(3) The time limit expires instead at the end of four weeks after the mediation ends (subject to paragraph (4)).

(4) If a time limit mentioned in paragraph (2)(a) has been extended by this article, paragraphs (2) and (3) apply to the extended time limit as they apply to a time limit mentioned in paragraph (2)(a).

(5) Where more than one time limit applies in relation to a relevant dispute, the extension by paragraph (3) of one of those time limits does not affect the others.

(6) For the purposes of this regulation, a mediation starts on the date of the agreement to mediate that is entered into by the parties and the mediator.

(7) For the purposes of this regulation, a mediation ends on the date of the first of these to occur—

(a) the parties reach an agreement in resolution of the relevant dispute;

(b) a party completes the notification of the other parties that it has withdrawn from the mediation;

(c) a party to whom a qualifying request is made fails to give a response reaching the other parties within 14 days of the request;

(d) the parties, after being notified that the mediator's appointment has ended (by death, resignation or otherwise), fail to agree within 14 days to seek to appoint a replacement mediator; or

(e) the mediation otherwise comes to an end pursuant to the terms of the agreement to mediate.

(8) For the purpose of paragraph (7), a qualifying request is a request by a party that another (A) confirm to all parties that A is continuing with the mediation.

(9) In the case of any relevant dispute, references in this regulation to a mediation are references to the mediation so far as it relates to that dispute, and references to a party are to be read accordingly.

(10) Where the tribunal has the power under regulation 30(2)(b) to extend a period of limitation, the power is exercisable in relation to the period of limitation as extended by this regulation.]

NOTES

Commencement: 20 May 2011.

Inserted by the Cross-Border Mediation (EU Directive) Regulations 2011, SI 2011/1133, regs 67, 69, as from 20 May 2011.

31–34 (*Regs 31, 32 contain various amendments to the Employment Rights Act 1996 which have been incorporated at the appropriate place (see that Act at* **[1.743]** *et seq); regs 33, 34 amend the Employment Tribunals Act 1996, ss 18 and 21 at* **[1.706]** *and* **[1.713]**.)

[2.313]

35 Restrictions on contracting out

(1) Any provision in an agreement (whether a contract of employment or not) is void in so far as it purports—

(a) to exclude or limit the operation of any provision of these Regulations, save in so far as these Regulations provide for an agreement to have that effect, or

(b) to preclude a person from bringing proceedings under these Regulations before an employment tribunal.

(2) Paragraph (1) does not apply to—

(a) any agreement to refrain from instituting or continuing proceedings where a conciliation officer has taken action under section 18 of the Employment Tribunals Act 1996 (conciliation); or

(b) any agreement to refrain from instituting or continuing proceedings within section 18(1)(ff) of the Employment Tribunals Act 1996 (proceedings under these Regulations where conciliation is available), if the conditions regulating compromise agreements under these Regulations are satisfied in relation to the agreement.

(3) For the purposes of paragraph (2)(b) the conditions regulating compromise agreements under these Regulations are that—

(a) the agreement must be in writing,

(b) the agreement must relate to the particular complaint,

(c) the worker must have received advice from a relevant independent adviser as to the terms and effect of the proposed agreement and, in particular, its effect on his ability to pursue his rights before an employment tribunal,

(d) there must be in force, when the adviser gives the advice, a contract of insurance, or an indemnity provided for members of a profession or professional body, covering the risk of a claim by the worker in respect of loss arising in consequence of the advice,

(e) the agreement must identify the adviser, and

(f) the agreement must state that the conditions regulating compromise agreements under these Regulations are satisfied.

(4) A person is a relevant independent adviser for the purposes of paragraph (3)(c)—

(a) if he is a qualified lawyer,

(b) if he is an officer, official, employee or member of an independent trade union who has been certified in writing by the trade union as competent to give advice and as authorised to do so on behalf of the trade union, or

(c) if he works at an advice centre (whether as an employee or as a volunteer) and has been certified in writing by the centre as competent to give advice and as authorised to do so on behalf of the centre.

(5) But a person is not a relevant independent adviser for the purposes of paragraph (3)(c) in relation to the worker—

(a) if he, is employed by or is acting in the matter for the employer or an associated employer,

(b) in the case of a person within paragraph (4)(b) or (c), if the trade union or advice centre is the employer or an associated employer, or

(c) in the case of a person within paragraph (4)(c), if the worker makes a payment for the advice received from him.

(6) In paragraph (4)(a), "qualified lawyer" means—

(a) as respects England and Wales, [a person who, for the purposes of the Legal Services Act 2007), is an authorised person in relation to an activity which constitutes the exercise of a right of audience or the conduct of litigation (within the meaning of that Act)]; and

(b) as respects Scotland, an advocate (whether in practice as such or employed to give legal advice), or a solicitor who holds a practising certificate.

[(6A) A person shall be treated as being a qualified lawyer within paragraph (6)(a) if he is a Fellow of the Institute of Legal Executives [practising in a solicitor's practice (including a body recognised under section 9 of the Administration of Justice Act 1985)].]

(7) For the purposes of paragraph (5) any two employers shall be treated as associated if—

(a) one is a company of which the other (directly or indirectly) has control; or

(b) both are companies of which a third person (directly or indirectly) has control; and "associated employer" shall be construed accordingly.

NOTES

Para (6): words in square brackets substituted by the Legal Services Act 2007 (Consequential Amendments) Order 2009, SI 2009/3348, art 23, Sch 2, as from 1 January 2010.

Para (6A): inserted by the Working Time Regulations 1998 (Amendment) Regulations 2004, SI 2004/2516, reg 2; words in square brackets substituted by SI 2009/3348, art 22, Sch 1, as from 16 December 2009.

[2.314]

[35A

(1) The Secretary of State shall, after consulting persons appearing to him to represent the two sides of industry, arrange for the publication, in such form and manner as he considers appropriate, of information and advice concerning the operation of these Regulations.

(2) The information and advice shall be such as appear to him best calculated to enable employers and workers affected by these Regulations to understand their respective rights and obligations under them.]

NOTES

Inserted by the Working Time Regulations 1999, SI 1999/3372, regs 1(1), 5.

PART V
SPECIAL CLASSES OF PERSON

[2.315]

36 Agency workers not otherwise "workers"

(1) This regulation applies in any case where an individual ("the agency worker")—

(a) is supplied by a person ("the agent") to do work for another ("the principal") under a contract or other arrangements made between the agent and the principal; but

(b) is not, as respects that work, a worker, because of the absence of a worker's contract between the individual and the agent or the principal; and

(c) is not a party to a contract under which he undertakes to do the work for another party to the contract whose status is, by virtue of the contract, that of a client or customer of any profession or business undertaking carried on by the individual.

(2) In a case where this regulation applies, the other provisions of these Regulations shall have effect as if there were a worker's contract for the doing of the work by the agency worker made between the agency worker and—

(a) whichever of the agent and the principal is responsible for paying the agency worker in respect of the work; or

(b) if neither the agent nor the principal is so responsible, whichever of them pays the agency worker in respect of the work,

and as if that person were the agency worker's employer.

[2.316]

37 Crown employment

(1) Subject to paragraph (4) and regulation 38, these Regulations have effect in relation to Crown employment and persons in Crown employment as they have effect in relation to other employment and other workers.

(2) In paragraph (1) "Crown employment" means employment under or for the purposes of a government department or any officer or body exercising on behalf of the Crown functions conferred by a statutory provision.

(3) For the purposes of the application of the provisions of these Regulations in relation to Crown employment in accordance with paragraph (1)—

(a) references to a worker shall be construed as references to a person in Crown employment; and

(b) references to a worker's contract shall be construed as references to the terms of employment of a person in Crown employment.

(4) No act or omission by the Crown which is an offence under regulation 29 shall make the Crown criminally liable, but the High Court or, in Scotland, the Court of Session may, on the application of a person appearing to the Court to have an interest, declare any such act or omission unlawful.

[2.317]
38 Armed forces

(1) Regulation 37 applies—

(a) subject to paragraph (2), to service as a member of the armed forces, and

(b) to employment by an association established for the purposes of Part XI of the Reserve Forces Act 1996.

(2) No complaint concerning the service of any person as a member of the armed forces may be presented to an employment tribunal under regulation 30 unless—

(a) that person has made a complaint in respect of the same matter to an officer under the service redress procedures, and

(b) that complaint has not been withdrawn.

[(3) For the purpose of paragraph (2)(b), a person shall be treated as having withdrawn his complaint if, having made a complaint to an officer under the service redress procedures—

(a) where the service redress procedures are those referred to in section 334 of the Armed Forces Act 2006, neither that officer nor a superior officer has decided to refer the complaint to the Defence Council, and the person who made the complaint fails to apply for such a reference to be made;

(b) in any other case, the person who made the complaint fails to submit the complaint to the Defence Council under the service redress procedures.]

(4) Where a complaint of the kind referred to in paragraph (2) is presented to an employment tribunal, the service redress procedures may continue after the complaint is presented.

(5) In this regulation, "the service redress procedures" means the procedures, excluding those which relate to the making of a report on a complaint to Her Majesty, referred to in section 180 of the Army Act 1955, section 180 of the Air Force Act 1955[, section 130 of the Naval Discipline Act 1957 or section 334 of the Armed Forces Act 2006].

NOTES

Para (3): substituted by the Armed Forces (Service Complaints) (Consequential Amendments) Order 2008, SI 2008/1696, art 2(1), (2), as from 28 June 2008.

Para (5): words in square brackets substituted by SI 2008/1696, art 2(1), (3), as from 28 June 2008.

[2.318]
39 House of Lords staff

(1) These Regulations have effect in relation to employment as a relevant member of the House of Lords staff as they have effect in relation to other employment.

(2) Nothing in any rule of law or the law or practice of Parliament prevents a relevant member of the House of Lords staff from presenting a complaint to an employment tribunal under regulation 30.

(3) In this regulation "relevant member of the House of Lords staff" means any person who is employed under a worker's contract with the Corporate Officer of the House of Lords.

[2.319]
40 House of Commons staff

(1) These Regulations have effect in relation to employment as a relevant member of the House of Commons staff as they have effect in relation to other employment.

(2) For the purposes of the application of the provisions of these Regulations in relation to a relevant member of the House of Commons staff—

(a) references to a worker shall be construed as references to a relevant member of the House of Commons staff; and

(b) references to a worker's contract shall be construed as references to the terms of employment of a relevant member of the House of Commons staff.

(3) Nothing in any rule of law or the law or practice of Parliament prevents a relevant member of the House of Commons staff from presenting a complaint to an employment tribunal under regulation 30.

(4) In this regulation "relevant member of the House of Commons staff" means any person—
(a) who was appointed by the House of Commons Commission; or
(b) who is a member of the Speaker's personal staff.

[2.320]
41 Police service

(1) [Subject to paragraph (1A),] for the purposes of these Regulations, the holding, otherwise than under a contract of employment, of the office of constable or an appointment as a police cadet shall be treated as employment, under a worker's contract, by the relevant officer.

[(1A) For the purposes of these Regulations, any constable who has been seconded to the Serious Organised Crime Agency to serve as a member of its staff shall be treated as employed by the Serious Organised Crime Agency.]

(2) Any matter relating to the employment of a worker which may be provided for the purposes of these Regulations in a workforce agreement may be provided for the same purposes in relation to the service of a person holding the office of constable or an appointment as a police cadet by an agreement between the relevant officer and a joint branch board.

(3) In this regulation—
"a joint branch board" means a joint branch board constituted in accordance with regulation 7(3) of the Police Federation Regulations 1969 or regulation 7(3) of the Police Federation (Scotland) Regulations 1985, and
"the relevant officer" means—
(a) in relation to a member of a police force or a special constable or police cadet appointed for a police area, the chief officer of police (or, in Scotland, the chief constable);
(b) . . .
(c) in relation to any other person holding the office of constable or an appointment as a police cadet, the person who has the direction and control of the body of constables or cadets in question.

[(4) For the purposes of these Regulations the relevant officer, as defined by paragraph (3), shall be treated as a corporation sole.

(5) Where, in a case in which the relevant officer, as so defined, is guilty of an offence under these Regulations, it is proved—
(a) that the office-holder personally consented to the commission of the offence;
(b) that he personally connived in its commission; or
(c) that the commission of the offence was attributable to personal neglect on his part,
the office-holder (as well as the corporation sole) shall be guilty of an offence and shall be liable to be proceeded against and punished accordingly.

(6) In paragraph (5) above "the office-holder", in relation to the relevant officer, means an individual who, at the time of the consent, connivance or neglect—
(a) held the office or other position mentioned in paragraph (3) above as the office or position of that officer; or
(b) was for the time being responsible for exercising and performing the powers and duties of that office or position.

(7) In the application of this regulation to Scotland—
(a) paragraph (4) shall have effect as if for the words "corporation sole" there were substituted "distinct juristic person (that is to say, as a juristic person distinct from the individual who for the time being is the office-holder)";
(b) paragraph (5) shall have effect as if for the words "corporation sole" there were substituted "juristic person"; and
(c) paragraph (6) shall have effect as if for the words "paragraph (5)" there were substituted "paragraphs (4) and (5)".]

NOTES

Para (1): words in square brackets inserted by the Serious Organised Crime and Police Act 2005 (Consequential and Supplementary Amendments to Secondary Legislation) Order 2006, SI 2006/594, art 2, Schedule, para 16(1), (2).
Para (1A): inserted by SI 2006/594, art 2, Schedule, para 16(1), (3).
Para (3): para (b) of definition "the relevant officer" revoked by SI 2006/594, art 2, Schedule, para 16(1), (4).
Paras (4)–(7): added by the Working Time Regulations 1998 (Amendment) Order 2005, SI 2005/2241, art 2.

[2.321]
42 Non-employed trainees

For the purposes of these Regulations, a person receiving relevant training, otherwise than under a contract of employment, shall be regarded as a worker, and the person whose undertaking is providing the training shall be regarded as his employer.

[2.322]

43 Agricultural workers

The provisions of Schedule 2 have effect in relation to workers employed in agriculture.

SCHEDULES

SCHEDULE 1
WORKFORCE AGREEMENTS

Regulation 2

[2.323]

1. An agreement is a workforce agreement for the purposes of these Regulations if the following conditions are satisfied—

- (a) the agreement is in writing;
- (b) it has effect for a specified period not exceeding five years;
- (c) it applies either—
  - (i) to all of the relevant members of the workforce, or
  - (ii) to all of the relevant members of the workforce who belong to a particular group;
- (d) the agreement is signed—
  - (i) in the case of an agreement of the kind referred to in sub-paragraph (c)(i), by the representatives of the workforce, and in the case of an agreement of the kind referred to in sub-paragraph (c)(ii) by the representatives of the group to which the agreement applies (excluding, in either case, any representative not a relevant member of the workforce on the date on which the agreement was first made available for signature), or
  - (ii) if the employer employed 20 or fewer workers on the date referred to in sub-paragraph (d)(i), either by the appropriate representatives in accordance with that sub-paragraph or by the majority of the workers employed by him;
- (e) before the agreement was made available for signature, the employer provided all the workers to whom it was intended to apply on the date on which it came into effect with copies of the text of the agreement and such guidance as those workers might reasonably require in order to understand it fully.

2. For the purposes of this Schedule—

"a particular group" is a group of the relevant members of a workforce who undertake a particular function, work at a particular workplace or belong to a particular department or unit within their employer's business;

"relevant members of the workforce" are all of the workers employed by a particular employer, excluding any worker whose terms and conditions of employment are provided for, wholly or in part, in a collective agreement;

"representatives of the workforce" are workers duly elected to represent the relevant members of the workforce, "representatives of the group" are workers duly elected to represent the members of a particular group, and representatives are "duly elected" if the election at which they were elected satisfied the requirements of paragraph 3 of this Schedule.

3. The requirements concerning elections referred to in paragraph 2 are that—

- (a) the number of representatives to be elected is determined by the employer;
- (b) the candidates for election as representatives of the workforce are relevant members of the workforce, and the candidates for election as representatives of a group are members of the group;
- (c) no worker who is eligible to be a candidate is unreasonably excluded from standing for election;
- (d) all the relevant members of the workforce are entitled to vote for representatives of the workforce, and all the members of a particular group are entitled to vote for representatives of the group;
- (e) the workers entitled to vote may vote for as many candidates as there are representatives to be elected;
- (f) the election is conducted so as to secure that—
  - (i) so far as is reasonably practicable, those voting do so in secret, and
  - (ii) the votes given at the election are fairly and accurately counted.

SCHEDULE 2
WORKERS EMPLOYED IN AGRICULTURE

Regulations 13(4), 15(6) and 43

[2.324]

1. Except where, in the case of a worker partly employed in agriculture, different provision is made by a relevant agreement—

(a) for the purposes of regulation 13 [and regulation 13A], the leave year of a worker employed in agriculture begins on 6th April each year or such other date as may be specified in an agricultural wages order which applies to him; and
(b) the dates on which leave is taken by a worker employed in agriculture shall be determined in accordance with an agricultural wages order which applies to him.

2. Where, in the case referred to in paragraph 1 above, a relevant agreement makes provision different from sub-paragraph (a) or (b) of that paragraph—
(a) neither section 11 of the Agricultural Wages Act 1948 nor section 11 of the Agricultural Wages (Scotland) Act 1949 shall apply to that provision; and
(b) an employer giving effect to that provision shall not thereby be taken to have failed to comply with the requirements of an agricultural wages order.

3. In this Schedule, "an agricultural wages order" means an order under section 3 of the Agricultural Wages Act 1948 or section 3 of the Agricultural Wages (Scotland) Act 1949.

NOTES

Para 1: words in square brackets in sub-para (a) inserted by the Working Time (Amendment) Regulations 2007, SI 2007/2079, reg 2(1), (5).

SCHEDULE 2A

(Sch 2A, which listed those categories of doctors in training to whom the 52 hour working time limit provided for by reg 25A(1) ante applied as inserted by the Working Time (Amendment) Regulations 2009, SI 2009/1567, reg 3, as from 1 August 2009 and subsequently amended by the Working Time (Amendment) (No 2) Regulations 2009, SI 2009/2766, reg 3, as from 2 November 2009, in both cases until 31 July 2011. It is now spent and is omitted for that reason.)

[SCHEDULE 3
ENFORCEMENT

Regulation 28(7)

[2.325]

1 Appointment of inspectors

(1) Each enforcement authority may appoint as inspectors (under whatever title it may from time to time determine) such persons having suitable qualifications as it thinks necessary for carrying into effect these Regulations within its field of responsibility, and may terminate any appointment made under this paragraph.

(2) Every appointment of a person as an inspector under this paragraph shall be made by an instrument in writing specifying which of the powers conferred on inspectors by these Regulations are to be exercisable by the person appointed; and an inspector shall in right of his appointment under this paragraph—
(a) be entitled to exercise only such of those powers as are so specified; and
(b) be entitled to exercise the powers so specified only within the field of responsibility of the authority which appointed him.

(3) So much of an inspector's instrument of appointment as specifies the powers which he is entitled to exercise may be varied by the enforcement authority which appointed him.

(4) An inspector shall, if so required when exercising or seeking to exercise any power conferred on him by these Regulations, produce his instrument of appointment or a duly authenticated copy thereof.

2 Powers of inspectors

(1) Subject to the provisions of paragraph 1 and this sub-paragraph, an inspector may, for the purpose of carrying into effect these Regulations within the field of responsibility of the enforcement authority which appointed him, exercise the powers set out in sub-paragraph (2) below.

(2) The powers of an inspector referred to in the preceding sub-paragraph are the following, namely—
(a) at any reasonable time (or, in a situation which in his opinion is or may be dangerous, at any time) to enter any premises which he has reason to believe it is necessary for him to enter for the purpose mentioned in sub-paragraph (1) above;
(b) to take with him a constable if he has reasonable cause to apprehend any serious obstruction in the execution of his duty;
(c) without prejudice to the preceding sub-paragraph, on entering any premises by virtue of paragraph (a) above to take with him—
(i) any other person duly authorised by the inspector's enforcement authority; and

Part 2 Statutory Instruments

(ii) any equipment or materials required for any purpose for which the power of entry is being exercised;

(d) to make such examination and investigation as may in any circumstances be necessary for the purpose mentioned in sub-paragraph (1) above;

(e) to require any person whom he has reasonable cause to believe to be able to give any information relevant to any examination or investigation under paragraph (d) above to answer (in the absence of persons other than a person nominated by him to be present and any persons whom the inspector may allow to be present) such questions as the inspector thinks fit to ask and to sign a declaration of the truth of his answers;

(f) to require the production of, inspect, and take copies of or of any entry in—

(i) any records which by virtue of these Regulations are required to be kept, and

(ii) any other books, records or documents which it is necessary for him to see for the purposes of any examination or investigation under paragraph (d) above;

(g) to require any person to afford him such facilities and assistance with respect to any matters or things within that person's control or in relation to which that person has responsibilities as are necessary to enable the inspector to exercise any of the powers conferred on him by this paragraph;

(h) any other power which is necessary for the purpose mentioned in sub-paragraph (1) above.

(3) No answer given by a person in pursuance of a requirement imposed under sub-paragraph (2)(e) above shall be admissible in evidence against that person or the husband or wife of that person in any proceedings.

(4) Nothing in this paragraph shall be taken to compel the production by any person of a document of which he would on grounds of legal professional privilege be entitled to withhold production on an order for discovery in an action in the High Court or, as the case may be, on an order for the production of documents in an action in the Court of Session.

3 Improvement notices

If an inspector is of the opinion that a person—

(a) is contravening one or more of these Regulations; or

(b) has contravened one or more of these Regulations in circumstances that make it likely that the contravention will continue or be repeated,

he may serve on him a notice (in this Schedule referred to as "an improvement notice") stating that he is of that opinion, specifying the provision or provisions as to which he is of that opinion, giving particulars of the reasons why he is of that opinion, and requiring that person to remedy the contravention or, as the case may be, the matters occasioning it within such period (ending not earlier than the period within which an appeal against the notice can be brought under paragraph 6) as may be specified in the notice.

4 Prohibition notices

(1) This paragraph applies to any activities which are being or are likely to be carried on by or under the control of any person, being activities to or in relation to which any of these Regulations apply or will, if the activities are so carried on, apply.

(2) If as regards any activities to which this paragraph applies an inspector is of the opinion that, as carried on or likely to be carried on by or under the control of the person in question, the activities involve or, as the case may be, will involve a risk of serious personal injury, the inspector may serve on that person a notice (in this Schedule referred to as "a prohibition notice").

(3) A prohibition notice shall—

(a) state that the inspector is of the said opinion;

(b) specify the matters which in his opinion give or, as the case may be, will give rise to the said risk;

(c) where in his opinion any of those matters involves or, as the case may be, will involve a contravention of any of these Regulations, state that he is of that opinion, specify the regulation or regulations as to which he is of that opinion, and give particulars of the reasons why he is of that opinion; and

(d) direct that the activities to which the notice relates shall not be carried on by or under the control of the person on whom the notice is served unless the matters specified in the notice in pursuance of paragraph (b) above and any associated contraventions of provisions so specified in pursuance of paragraph (c) above have been remedied.

(4) A direction contained in a prohibition notice in pursuance of sub-paragraph (3)(d) above shall take effect—

(a) at the end of the period specified in the notice; or

(b) if the notice so declares, immediately.

5 Provisions supplementary to paragraphs 3 and 4

(1) In this paragraph "a notice" means an improvement notice or a prohibition notice.

(2) A notice may (but need not) include directions as to the measures to be taken to remedy any contravention or matter to which the notice relates; and any such directions—

(a) may be framed to any extent by reference to any approved code of practice; and
(b) may be framed so as to afford the person on whom the notice is served a choice between different ways of remedying the contravention or matter.

(3) Where an improvement notice or a prohibition notice which is not to take immediate effect has been served—

(a) the notice may be withdrawn by an inspector at any time before the end of the period specified therein in pursuance of paragraph 3 or paragraph 4(4) as the case may be; and
(b) the period so specified may be extended or further extended by an inspector at any time when an appeal against the notice is not pending.

6 Appeal against improvement or prohibition notice

(1) In this paragraph "a notice" means an improvement or a prohibition notice.

(2) A person on whom a notice is served may within 21 days from the date of its service appeal to an employment tribunal; and on such an appeal the tribunal may either cancel or affirm the notice and, if it affirms it, may do so either in its original form or with such modifications as the tribunal may in the circumstances think fit.

(3) Where an appeal under this paragraph is brought against a notice within the period allowed under the preceding sub-paragraph, then—

(a) in the case of an improvement notice, the bringing of the appeal shall have the effect of suspending the operation of the notice until the appeal is finally disposed of or, if the appeal is withdrawn, until the withdrawal of the appeal;
(b) in the case of a prohibition notice, the bringing of the appeal shall have the like effect if, but only if, on the application of the appellant the tribunal so directs (and then only from the giving of the direction).

(4) One or more assessors may be appointed for the purposes of any proceedings brought before an employment tribunal under this paragraph.

7 Power of enforcement authority to indemnify inspectors

Where an action has been brought against an inspector in respect of an act done in the execution or purported execution of these Regulations and the circumstances are such that he is not legally entitled to require the enforcement authority to indemnify him, that authority may, nevertheless, indemnify him against the whole or part of any damages and costs or expenses which he may have been ordered to pay or may have incurred, if the authority is satisfied that the inspector honestly believed that the act complained of was within his powers and that his duty as an inspector required or entitled him to do it.

8 Restrictions on disclosure of information

(1) In this and the two following sub-paragraphs—

(a) "relevant information" means information obtained by an inspector in pursuance of a requirement imposed under paragraph 2(2)(e) or (f); and
(b) "the recipient", in relation to any relevant information, means the person by whom that information was so obtained or to whom that information was so furnished, as the case may be.

(2) Subject to the following sub-paragraph, no relevant information shall be disclosed without the consent of the person by whom it was furnished.

(3) The preceding sub-paragraph shall not apply to—

(a) disclosure of information to the Commission, a government department or any enforcement authority;
(b) without prejudice to paragraph (a) above, disclosure by the recipient of information to any person for the purpose of any function conferred on the recipient by or under any of the relevant statutory provisions or under these Regulations;
(c) without prejudice to paragraph (a) above, disclosure by the recipient of information to—
    (i) an officer of a local authority who is authorised by that authority to receive it; or
    (ii) a constable authorised by a chief officer of police to receive it; or
(d) disclosure by the recipient of information in a form calculated to prevent it from being identified as relating to a particular person or case.

(4) In the preceding sub-paragraph any reference to the Commission, a government department or an enforcement authority includes respectively a reference to an officer of that body or authority (including in the case of an enforcement authority, any inspector appointed by it), and also, in the case of a reference to the Commission, includes a reference to—

(a) a person performing any functions of the Commission or the Executive on its behalf by virtue of section 13(1)(a) of the 1974 Act;
(b) an officer of a body which is so performing any such functions; and
(c) an adviser appointed in pursuance of section 13(1)(d) of the 1974 Act.

(5) A person to whom information is disclosed in pursuance of sub-paragraph (3) above shall not use the information for a purpose other than—

(a) in a case falling within sub-paragraph (3)(a), a purpose of the Commission, of the government department, or of the enforcement authority in question in connection with these Regulations or with the relevant statutory provisions, as the case may be;

(b) in the case of information given to an officer of a body which is a local authority, the purposes of the body in connection with the relevant statutory provisions or any enactment whatsoever relating to working time, public health, public safety or the protection of the environment;

(c) in the case of information given to a constable, the purposes of the police in connection with these Regulations, the relevant statutory provisions or any enactment whatsoever relating to working time, public health, public safety or the safety of the State.

(6) A person shall not disclose any information obtained by him as a result of the exercise of any power conferred by paragraph 2 of this Schedule (including in particular any information with respect to any trade secret obtained by him in any premises entered by him by virtue of any such power) except—

(a) for the purposes of his functions;

(b) for the purposes of any legal proceedings; or

(c) with the relevant consent.

In this sub-paragraph "the relevant consent" means the consent of the person who furnished it, and, in any other case, the consent of a person having responsibilities in relation to the premises where the information was obtained.

(7) Notwithstanding anything in the preceding sub-paragraph an inspector shall, in circumstances in which it is necessary to do so for the purpose of assisting in keeping persons (or the representatives of persons) employed at any premises adequately informed about matters affecting their health, safety and welfare or working time, give to such persons or their representatives the following descriptions of information, that is to say—

(a) factual information obtained by him as mentioned in that sub-paragraph which relates to those premises or anything which was or is therein or was or is being done therein; and

(b) information with respect to any action which he has taken or proposes to take in or in connection with those premises in the performance of his functions;

and, where an inspector does as aforesaid, he shall give the like information to the employer of the first-mentioned persons.

(8) Notwithstanding anything in sub-paragraph (6) above, a person who has obtained such information as is referred to in that sub-paragraph may furnish to a person who appears to him to be likely to be a party to any civil proceedings arising out of any accident, occurrence, situation or other matter, a written statement of the relevant facts observed by him in the course of exercising any of the powers referred to in that sub-paragraph.]

NOTES

Added by the Working Time (Amendment) Regulations 2003, SI 2003/1684, regs 2, 12.

CIVIL PROCEDURE RULES 1998

(SI 1998/3132)

NOTES

Made: 10 December 1998.

Authority: Civil Procedure Act 1997, ss 1, 2.

Commencement: 26 April 1999.

Most of these Rules cover matters outside the scope of this work, and only those provisions most directly relevant to employment law are printed. For reasons of space, the subject matter of rules not printed is not annotated.

ARRANGEMENT OF RULES

PART 1
OVERRIDING OBJECTIVE

PART 2
APPLICATION AND INTERPRETATION OF THE RULES

PART 3
THE COURT'S CASE AND COSTS MANAGEMENT POWERS

Section I—Case Management

PART 18
FURTHER INFORMATION

PART 24
SUMMARY JUDGMENT

PART 31
DISCLOSURE AND INSPECTION OF DOCUMENTS

PART 35
EXPERTS AND ASSESSORS

PART 36
OFFERS TO SETTLE

SECTION I
PART 36 OFFERS TO SETTLE

PART 1
OVERRIDING OBJECTIVE

[2.326]
1.1 The overriding objective

(1) These Rules are a new procedural code with the overriding objective of enabling the court to deal with cases justly [and at proportionate cost].

(2) Dealing with a case justly [and at proportionate cost] includes, so far as is practicable—
- (a) ensuring that the parties are on an equal footing;
- (b) saving expense;
- (c) dealing with the case in ways which are proportionate—
  - (i) to the amount of money involved;
  - (ii) to the importance of the case;
  - (iii) to the complexity of the issues; and
  - (iv) to the financial position of each party;
- (d) ensuring that it is dealt with expeditiously and fairly; . . .
- (e) allotting to it an appropriate share of the court's resources, while taking into account the need to allot resources to other cases[; and]
- [(f) enforcing compliance with rules, practice directions and orders.]

NOTES

Para (1): words in square brackets added by the Civil Procedure (Amendment) Rules 2013, SI 2013/262, r 4(a), as from 1 April 2013.

Para (2): words in square brackets inserted and word omitted revoked, by SI 2013/262, r 4(b), as from 1 April 2013.

[2.327]
1.2 Application by the court of the overriding objective

The court must seek to give effect to the overriding objective when it—
- (a) exercises any power given to it by the Rules; or
- (b) interprets any rule[, subject to [rules 76.2, 79.2 and 80.2]].

NOTES

Words in first (outer) pair of square brackets in para (b) inserted by the Civil Procedure (Amendment No 2) Rules 2005 SI 2005/656, r 3; words in second (inner) pair of square brackets in that paragraph substituted by the Civil Procedure (Amendment No 3) Rules 2011, SI 2011/2970, r 3, as from 15 December 2011.

[2.328]
1.3 Duty of the parties

The parties are required to help the court to further the overriding objective.

[2.329]

1.4 Court's duty to manage cases

(1) The court must further the overriding objective by actively managing cases.

(2) Active case management includes—

- (a) encouraging the parties to co-operate with each other in the conduct of the proceedings;
- (b) identifying the issues at an early stage;
- (c) deciding promptly which issues need full investigation and trial and accordingly disposing summarily of the others;
- (d) deciding the order in which issues are to be resolved;
- (e) encouraging the parties to use an alternative dispute resolution procedure if the court considers that appropriate and facilitating the use of such procedure;
- (f) helping the parties to settle the whole or part of the case;
- (g) fixing timetables or otherwise controlling the progress of the case;
- (h) considering whether the likely benefits of taking a particular step justify the cost of taking it;
- (i) dealing with as many aspects of the case as it can on the same occasion;
- (j) dealing with the case without the parties needing to attend at court;
- (k) making use of technology; and
- (l) giving directions to ensure that the trial of a case proceeds quickly and efficiently.

PART 2
APPLICATION AND INTERPRETATION OF THE RULES

[2.330]

2.8 Time

(1) This rule shows how to calculate any period of time for doing any act which is specified—

- (a) by these Rules;
- (b) by a practice direction; or
- (c) by a judgment or order of the court.

(2) A period of time expressed as a number of days shall be computed as clear days.

(3) In this rule "clear days" means that in computing the number of days—

- (a) the day on which the period begins; and
- (b) if the end of the period is defined by reference to an event, the day on which that event occurs,

are not included.

Examples

(i) Notice of an application must be served at least 3 days before the hearing.
An application is to be heard on Friday 20 October.
The last date for service is Monday 16 October.

(ii) The court is to fix a date for a hearing.
The hearing must be at least 28 days after the date of notice.
If the court gives notice of the date of the hearing on 1 October, the earliest date for the hearing is 30 October.

(iii) Particulars of claim must be served within 14 days of service of the claim form.
The claim form is served on 2 October.
The last day for service of the particulars of claim is 16 October.

(4) Where the specified period—

- (a) is 5 days or less; and
- (b) includes—
  - (i) a Saturday or Sunday; or
  - (ii) a Bank Holiday, Christmas Day or Good Friday,

that day does not count.

Example

Notice of an application must be served at least 3 days before the hearing.
An application is to be heard on Monday 20 October.
The last date for service is Tuesday 14 October.

(5) [Subject to the provisions of Practice Direction 5C, when the period specified—]

- (a) by these Rules or a practice direction; or
- (b) by any judgment or court order,

for doing any act at the court office ends on a day on which the office is closed, that act shall be in time if done on the next day on which the court office is open.

NOTES

Para (5): words in square brackets substituted by the Civil Procedure (Amendment No 2) Rules 2009, SI 2009/3390, r 3(b), as from 1 April 2010.

[2.331]
2.9 Dates for compliance to be calendar dates and to include time of day

(1) Where the court gives a judgment, order or direction which imposes a time limit for doing any act, the last date for compliance must, wherever practicable—

(a) be expressed as a calendar date; and

(b) include the time of day by which the act must be done.

(2) Where the date by which an act must be done is inserted in any document, the date must, wherever practicable, be expressed as a calendar date.

[2.332]
2.10 Meaning of "month" in judgments, etc

Where "month" occurs in any judgment, order, direction or other document, it means a calendar month.

[2.333]
2.11 Time limits may be varied by parties

Unless these Rules or a practice direction provide otherwise or the court orders otherwise, the time specified by a rule or by the court for a person to do any act may be varied by the written agreement of the parties.

(Rules 3.8 (sanctions have effect unless defaulting party obtains relief), 28.4 (variation of case management timetable—fast track) and 29.5 (variation of case management timetable—multi-track) provide for time limits that cannot be varied by agreement between the parties).

PART 3
THE COURT'S CASE [AND COSTS] MANAGEMENT POWERS

NOTES

Part heading: words in square brackets inserted by the Civil Procedure (Amendment) Rules 2013, SI 2013/262, r 5(a), as from 1 April 2013.

[SECTION I
CASE MANAGEMENT]

NOTES

Section heading: inserted by the Civil Procedure (Amendment) Rules 2013, SI 2013/262, r 5(c), as from 1 April 2013.

[2.334]
3.1 The court's general powers of management

(1) The list of powers in this rule is in addition to any powers given to the court by any other rule or practice direction or by any other enactment or any powers it may otherwise have.

(2) Except where these Rules provide otherwise, the court may—

(a) extend or shorten the time for compliance with any rule, practice direction or court order (even if an application for extension is made after the time for compliance has expired);

(b) adjourn or bring forward a hearing;

(c) require a party or a party's legal representative to attend the court;

(d) hold a hearing and receive evidence by telephone or by using any other method of direct oral communication;

(e) direct that part of any proceedings (such as a counterclaim) be dealt with as separate proceedings;

(f) stay the whole or part of any proceedings or judgment either generally or until a specified date or event;

(g) consolidate proceedings;

(h) try two or more claims on the same occasion;

(i) direct a separate trial of any issue;

(j) decide the order in which issues are to be tried;

(k) exclude an issue from consideration;

(l) dismiss or give judgment on a claim after a decision on a preliminary issue;

[(ll) order any party to file and serve an estimate of costs;]

(m) take any other step or make any other order for the purpose of managing the case and furthering the overriding objective.

(3) When the court makes an order, it may—

(a) make it subject to conditions, including a condition to pay a sum of money into court; and

(b) specify the consequence of failure to comply with the order or a condition.

(4) Where the court gives directions it [will] take into account whether or not a party has complied with [the Practice Direction (Pre-Action Conduct) and] any relevant pre-action protocol.

(5) The court may order a party to pay a sum of money into court if that party has, without good reason, failed to comply with a rule, practice direction or a relevant pre-action protocol.

(6) When exercising its power under paragraph (5) the court must have regard to—

(a) the amount in dispute; and

(b) the costs which the parties have incurred or which they may incur.

[(6A) Where a party pays money into court following an order under paragraph (3) or (5), the money shall be security for any sum payable by that party to any other party in the proceedings . . .].

(7) A power of the court under these Rules to make an order includes a power to vary or revoke the order.

[(8) The court may contact the parties from time to time in order to monitor compliance with directions. The parties must respond promptly to any such enquiries from the court.]

NOTES

Para (2): sub-para (ll) inserted by the Civil Procedure (Amendment No 3) Rules 2005, SI 2005/2292, r 3.

Para (4): word in first pair of square brackets substituted, and words in second pair of square brackets inserted, by the Civil Procedure (Amendment No 3) Rules 2008, SI 2008/3327, r 3, as from 6 April 2009.

Para (6A): inserted by the Civil Procedure (Amendment) Rules 1999, SI 1999/1008, r 4; words omitted revoked by the Civil Procedure (Amendment No 3) Rules 2006, SI 2006/3435, r 3.

Para (8): added by the Civil Procedure (Amendment) Rules 2013, SI 2013/262, r 5(d), as from 1 April 2013.

[2.335]

3.2 Court officer's power to refer to a judge

Where a step is to be taken by a court officer—

(a) the court officer may consult a judge before taking that step;

(b) the step may be taken by a judge instead of the court officer.

[2.336]

3.3 Court's power to make order of its own initiative

(1) Except where a rule or some other enactment provides otherwise, the court may exercise its powers on an application or of its own initiative.

(Part 23 sets out the procedure for making an application).

(2) Where the court proposes to make an order of its own initiative—

(a) it may give any person likely to be affected by the order an opportunity to make representations; and

(b) where it does so it must specify the time by and the manner in which the representations must be made.

(3) Where the court proposes—

(a) to make an order of its own initiative; and

(b) to hold a hearing to decide whether to make the order,

it must give each party likely to be affected by the order at least 3 days' notice of the hearing.

(4) The court may make an order of its own initiative without hearing the parties or giving them an opportunity to make representations.

(5) Where the court has made an order under paragraph (4)—

(a) a party affected by the order may apply to have it set aside, varied or stayed; and

(b) the order must contain a statement of the right to make such an application.

(6) An application under paragraph (5)(a) must be made—

(a) within such period as may be specified by the court; or

(b) if the court does not specify a period, not more than 7 days after the date on which the order was served on the party making the application.

[(7) If the court of its own initiative strikes out a statement of case or dismisses an application [(including an application for permission to appeal or for permission to apply for judicial review)], and it considers that the claim or application is totally without merit—

(a) the court's order must record that fact; and

(b) the court must at the same time consider whether it is appropriate to make a civil restraint order.]

NOTES

Para (7): added by the Civil Procedure (Amendment No 2) Rules 2004, SI 2004/2072, r 4; words in square brackets inserted by the Civil Procedure (Amendment No 3) Rules 2005, SI 2005/2292, r 4.

[2.337]

3.4 Power to strike out a statement of case

(1) In this rule and rule 3.5, reference to a statement of case includes reference to part of a statement of case.

(2) The court may strike out a statement of case if it appears to the court—

(a) that the statement of case discloses no reasonable grounds for bringing or defending the claim;

(b) that the statement of case is an abuse of the court's process or is otherwise likely to obstruct the just disposal of the proceedings; or

(c) that there has been a failure to comply with a rule, practice direction or court order.

(3) When the court strikes out a statement of case it may make any consequential order it considers appropriate.

(4) Where—

(a) the court has struck out a claimant's statement of case;

(b) the claimant has been ordered to pay costs to the defendant; and

(c) before the claimant pays those costs, he starts another claim against the same defendant, arising out of facts which are the same or substantially the same as those relating to the claim in which the statement of case was struck out,

the court may, on the application of the defendant, stay that other claim until the costs of the first claim have been paid.

(5) Paragraph (2) does not limit any other power of the court to strike out a statement of case.

[(6) If the court strikes out a claimant's statement of case and it considers that the claim is totally without merit—

(a) the court's order must record that fact; and

(b) the court must at the same time consider whether it is appropriate to make a civil restraint order.]

NOTES

Para (6): added by the Civil Procedure (Amendment No 2) Rules 2004, SI 2004/2072, r 5.

[2.338]

3.8 Sanctions have effect unless defaulting party obtains relief

(1) Where a party has failed to comply with a rule, practice direction or court order, any sanction for failure to comply imposed by the rule, practice direction or court order has effect unless the party in default applies for and obtains relief from the sanction.

(Rule 3.9 sets out the circumstances which the court [will] consider on an application to grant relief from a sanction).

(2) Where the sanction is the payment of costs, the party in default may only obtain relief by appealing against the order for costs.

(3) Where a rule, practice direction or court order—

(a) requires a party to do something within a specified time, and

(b) specifies the consequence of failure to comply,

the time for doing the act in question may not be extended by agreement between the parties.

NOTES

Para (1): word in square brackets substituted by the Civil Procedure (Amendment) Rules 2013, SI 2013/262, r 5(f), as from 1 April 2013.

[2.339]

3.9 Relief from sanctions

[(1) On an application for relief from any sanction imposed for a failure to comply with any rule, practice direction or court order, the court will consider all the circumstances of the case, so as to enable it to deal justly with the application, including the need—

(a) for litigation to be conducted efficiently and at proportionate cost; and

(b) to enforce compliance with rules, practice directions and orders.]

(2) An application for relief must be supported by evidence.

NOTES

Para (1): substituted by the Civil Procedure (Amendment) Rules 2013, SI 2013/262, r 5(g), as from 1 April 2013.

PART 18
FURTHER INFORMATION

[2.340]

18.1 Obtaining further information

(1) The court may at any time order a party to—

(a) clarify any matter which is in dispute in the proceedings; or

(b) give additional information in relation to any such matter,

whether or not the matter is contained or referred to in a statement of case.

(2) Paragraph (1) is subject to any rule of law to the contrary.

(3) Where the court makes an order under paragraph (1), the party against whom it is made must—

(a) file his response; and
(b) serve it on the other parties,

within the time specified by the court.

(Part 22 requires a response to be verified by a statement of truth).

[(Part 53 (defamation) restricts requirements for providing further information about sources of information in defamation claims).]

NOTES

Words in square brackets inserted by the Civil Procedure (Amendment) Rules 2000, SI 2000/221, r 8.

[2.341]
18.2 Restriction on the use of further information

The court may direct that information provided by a party to another party (whether given voluntarily or following an order made under rule 18.1) must not be used for any purpose except for that of the proceedings in which it is given.

PART 24
SUMMARY JUDGMENT

[2.342]
24.1 Scope of this Part

This Part sets out a procedure by which the court may decide a claim or a particular issue without a trial.

[(Part 53 makes special provision about summary disposal of defamation claims in accordance with the Defamation Act 1996).]

NOTES

Words in square brackets inserted by the Civil Procedure (Amendment) Rules 2000, SI 2000/221, r 12(a).

[2.343]
24.2 Grounds for summary judgment

The court may give summary judgment against a claimant or defendant on the whole of a claim or on a particular issue if—

(a) it considers that—
  (i) that claimant has no real prospect of succeeding on the claim or issue; or
  (ii) that defendant has no real prospect of successfully defending the claim or issue; and
(b) there is no other [compelling] reason why the case or issue should be disposed of at a trial.

(Rule 3.4 makes provision for the court to strike out a statement of case or part of a statement of case if it appears that it discloses no reasonable grounds for bringing or defending a claim).

NOTES

Word in square brackets in para (b) inserted by the Civil Procedure (Amendment No 3) Rules 2000, SI 2000/1317, r 9.

[2.344]
24.5 Evidence for the purposes of a summary judgment hearing

(1) If the respondent to an application for summary judgment wishes to rely on written evidence at the hearing, he must—

(a) file the written evidence; and
(b) serve copies on every other party to the application, at least 7 days before the summary judgment hearing.

(2) If the applicant wishes to rely on written evidence in reply, he must—

(a) file the written evidence; and
(b) serve a copy on the respondent,

at least 3 days before the summary judgment hearing.

(3) Where a summary judgment hearing is fixed by the court of its own initiative—

(a) any party who wishes to rely on written evidence at the hearing must—
  (i) file the written evidence; and
  (ii) unless the court orders otherwise, serve copies on every other party to the proceedings,

  at least 7 days before the date of the hearing;
(b) any party who wishes to rely on written evidence at the hearing in reply to any other party's written evidence must—
  (i) file the written evidence in reply; and

Part 2 Statutory Instruments

(ii) unless the court orders otherwise serve copies on every other party to the proceedings,

at least 3 days before the date of the hearing.

(4) This rule does not require written evidence—

(a) to be filed if it has already been filed; or

(b) to be served on a party on whom it has already been served.

[2.345]

24.6 Court's powers when it determines a summary judgment application

When the court determines a summary judgment application it may—

(a) give directions as to the filing and service of a defence;

(b) give further directions about the management of the case.

(Rule 3.1(3) provides that the court may attach conditions when it makes an order).

PART 31
DISCLOSURE AND INSPECTION OF DOCUMENTS

[2.346]

31.1 Scope of this Part

(1) This Part sets out rules about the disclosure and inspection of documents.

(2) This Part applies to all claims except a claim on the small claims track.

[2.347]

31.2 Meaning of disclosure

A party discloses a document by stating that the document exists or has existed.

[2.348]

31.3 Right of inspection of a disclosed document

(1) A party to whom a document has been disclosed has a right to inspect that document except where—

(a) the document is no longer in the control of the party who disclosed it;

(b) the party disclosing the document has a right or a duty to withhold inspection of it; . . .

(c) paragraph (2) applies[; or

(d) rule 78.26 applies].

(Rule 31.8 sets out when a document is in the control of a party).

(Rule 31.19 sets out the procedure for claiming a right or duty to withhold inspection).

[(Rule 78.26 contains rules in relation to the disclosure and inspection of evidence arising out of mediation of certain cross-border disputes.)]

(2) Where a party considers that it would be disproportionate to the issues in the case to permit inspection of documents within a category or class of document disclosed under rule 31.6(b)—

(a) he is not required to permit inspection of documents within that category or class; but

(b) he must state in his disclosure statement that inspection of those documents will not be permitted on the grounds that to do so would be disproportionate.

(Rule 31.6 provides for standard disclosure).

(Rule 31.10 makes provision for a disclosure statement).

(Rule 31.12 provides for a party to apply for an order for specific inspection of documents).

NOTES

Word omitted revoked, and words in square brackets inserted, by the Civil Procedure (Amendment) Rules 2011, SI 2011/88, r 9(a), (b), as from 6 April 2011.

[2.349]

31.4 Meaning of document

In this Part—

"document" means anything in which information of any description is recorded; and

"copy", in relation to a document, means anything onto which information recorded in the document has been copied, by whatever means and whether directly or indirectly.

[2.350]

[31.5 Disclosure limited to standard disclosure

(1) In all claims to which rule 31.5(2) does not apply—

(a) an order to give disclosure is an order to give standard disclosure unless the court directs otherwise;

(b) the court may dispense with or limit standard disclosure; and

(c) the parties may agree in writing to dispense with or to limit standard disclosure.

(2) Unless the court otherwise orders, paragraphs (3) to (8) apply to all multi-track claims, other than those which include a claim for personal injuries.

(3) Not less than 14 days before the first case management conference each party must file and serve a report verified by a statement of truth, which—

- (a) describes briefly what documents exist or may exist that are or may be relevant to the matters in issue in the case;
- (b) describes where and with whom those documents are or may be located;
- (c) in the case of electronic documents, describes how those documents are stored;
- (d) estimates the broad range of costs that could be involved in giving standard disclosure in the case, including the costs of searching for and disclosing any electronically stored documents; and
- (e) states which of the directions under paragraphs (7) or (8) are to be sought.

(4) In cases where the Electronic Documents Questionnaire has been exchanged, the Questionnaire should be filed with the report required by paragraph (3).

(5) Not less than seven days before the first case management conference, and on any other occasion as the court may direct, the parties must, at a meeting or by telephone, discuss and seek to agree a proposal in relation to disclosure that meets the overriding objective.

(6) If—

- (a) the parties agree proposals for the scope of disclosure; and
- (b) the court considers that the proposals are appropriate in all the circumstances,

the court may approve them without a hearing and give directions in the terms proposed.

(7) At the first or any subsequent case management conference, the court will decide, having regard to the overriding objective and the need to limit disclosure to that which is necessary to deal with the case justly, which of the following orders to make in relation to disclosure—

- (a) an order dispensing with disclosure;
- (b) an order that a party disclose the documents on which it relies, and at the same time request any specific disclosure it requires from any other party;
- (c) an order that directs, where practicable, the disclosure to be given by each party on an issue by issue basis;
- (d) an order that each party disclose any documents which it is reasonable to suppose may contain information which enables that party to advance its own case or to damage that of any other party, or which leads to an enquiry which has either of those consequences;
- (e) an order that a party give standard disclosure;
- (f) any other order in relation to disclosure that the court considers appropriate.

(8) The court may at any point give directions as to how disclosure is to be given, and in particular—

- (a) what searches are to be undertaken, of where, for what, in respect of which time periods and by whom and the extent of any search for electronically stored documents;
- (b) whether lists of documents are required;
- (c) how and when the disclosure statement is to be given;
- (d) in what format documents are to be disclosed (and whether any identification is required);
- (e) what is required in relation to documents that once existed but no longer exist; and
- (f) whether disclosure shall take place in stages.

(9) To the extent that the documents to be disclosed are electronic, the provisions of Practice Direction 31B—Disclosure of Electronic Documents will apply in addition to paragraphs (3) to (8).]

NOTES

Commencement: 1 April 2013.

Substituted by the Civil Procedure (Amendment) Rules 2013, SI 2013/262, r 11, as from 1 April 2013.

[2.351]

31.6 Standard disclosure—what documents are to be disclosed

Standard disclosure requires a party to disclose only—

- (a) the documents on which he relies; and
- (b) the documents which—
  - (i) adversely affect his own case;
  - (ii) adversely affect another party's case; or
  - (iii) support another party's case; and
- (c) the documents which he is required to disclose by a relevant practice direction.

[2.352]

31.7 Duty of search

(1) When giving standard disclosure, a party is required to make a reasonable search for documents falling within rule 31.6(b) or (c).

(2) The factors relevant in deciding the reasonableness of a search include the following—

(a) the number of documents involved;
(b) the nature and complexity of the proceedings;
(c) the ease and expense of retrieval of any particular document; and
(d) the significance of any document which is likely to be located during the search.

(3) Where a party has not searched for a category or class of document on the grounds that to do so would be unreasonable, he must state this in his disclosure statement and identify the category or class of document.

(Rule 31.10 makes provision for a disclosure statement).

[2.353]
31.8 Duty of disclosure limited to documents which are or have been in party's control

(1) A party's duty to disclose documents is limited to documents which are or have been in his control.

(2) For this purpose a party has or has had a document in his control if—
(a) it is or was in his physical possession;
(b) he has or has had a right to possession of it; or
(c) he has or has had a right to inspect or take copies of it.

[2.354]
31.9 Disclosure of copies

(1) A party need not disclose more than one copy of a document.

(2) A copy of a document that contains a modification, obliteration or other marking or feature—
(a) on which a party intends to rely; or
(b) which adversely affects his own case or another party's case or supports another party's case;

shall be treated as a separate document.

(Rule 31.4 sets out the meaning of a copy of a document).

[2.355]
31.10 Procedure for standard disclosure

(1) The procedure for standard disclosure is as follows.

(2) Each party must make and serve on every other party, a list of documents in the relevant practice form.

(3) The list must identify the documents in a convenient order and manner and as concisely as possible.

(4) The list must indicate—
(a) those documents in respect of which the party claims a right or duty to withhold inspection; and
(b)
  (i) those documents which are no longer in the party's control; and
  (ii) what has happened to those documents.

(Rule 31.19(3) and (4) require a statement in the list of documents relating to any documents inspection of which a person claims he has a right or duty to withhold).

(5) The list must include a disclosure statement.

(6) A disclosure statement is a statement made by the party disclosing the documents—
(a) setting out the extent of the search that has been made to locate documents which he is required to disclose;
(b) certifying that he understands the duty to disclose documents; and
(c) certifying that to the best of his knowledge he has carried out that duty.

(7) Where the party making the disclosure statement is a company, firm, association or other organisation, the statement must also—
(a) identify the person making the statement; and
(b) explain why he is considered an appropriate person to make the statement.

(8) The parties may agree in writing—
(a) to disclose documents without making a list; and
(b) to disclose documents without the disclosing party making a disclosure statement.

(9) A disclosure statement may be made by a person who is not a party where this is permitted by a relevant practice direction.

[2.356]
31.11 Duty of disclosure continues during proceedings

(1) Any duty of disclosure continues until the proceedings are concluded.

(2) If documents to which that duty extends come to a party's notice at any time during the proceedings, he must immediately notify every other party.

[2.357]

31.12 Specific disclosure or inspection

(1) The court may make an order for specific disclosure or specific inspection.

(2) An order for specific disclosure is an order that a party must do one or more of the following things—

(a) disclose documents or classes of documents specified in the order;
(b) carry out a search to the extent stated in the order;
(c) disclose any documents located as a result of that search.

(3) An order for specific inspection is an order that a party permit inspection of a document referred to in rule 31.3(2).

(Rule 31.3(2) allows a party to state in his disclosure statement that he will not permit inspection of a document on the grounds that it would be disproportionate to do so).

[(Rule 78.26 contains rules in relation to the disclosure and inspection of evidence arising out of mediation of certain cross-border disputes.)]

NOTES

Words in square brackets inserted by the Civil Procedure (Amendment) Rules 2011, SI 2011/88, r 9(c), as from 6 April 2011.

[2.358]

31.13 Disclosure in stages

The parties may agree in writing, or the court may direct, that disclosure or inspection or both shall take place in stages.

[2.359]

31.14 Documents referred to in statements of case etc

[(1)] A party may inspect a document mentioned in—

(a) a statement of case;
(b) a witness statement;
(c) a witness summary; [or]
(d) an affidavit[.]
(e) . . .

[(2) Subject to rule 35.10(4), a party may apply for an order for inspection of any document mentioned in an expert's report which has not already been disclosed in the proceedings.]

(Rule 35.10(4) makes provision in relation to instructions referred to in an expert's report).

NOTES

Para (1) was numbered as such, para (2) was added, and all amendments to para (1) were made, by the Civil Procedure (Amendment No 5) Rules 2001, SI 2001/4015, r 20.

[2.360]

31.15 Inspection and copying of documents

Where a party has a right to inspect a document—

(a) that party must give the party who disclosed the document written notice of his wish to inspect it;
(b) the party who disclosed the document must permit inspection not more than 7 days after the date on which he received the notice; and
(c) that party may request a copy of the document and, if he also undertakes to pay reasonable copying costs, the party who disclosed the document must supply him with a copy not more than 7 days after the date on which he received the request.

(Rule 31.3 and 31.14 deal with the right of a party to inspect a document).

[2.361]

31.16 Disclosure before proceedings start

(1) This rule applies where an application is made to the court under any Act for disclosure before proceedings have started.

(2) The application must be supported by evidence.

(3) The court may make an order under this rule only where—

(a) the respondent is likely to be a party to subsequent proceedings;
(b) the applicant is also likely to be a party to those proceedings;
(c) if proceedings had started, the respondent's duty by way of standard disclosure, set out in rule 31.6, would extend to the documents or classes of documents of which the applicant seeks disclosure; and
(d) disclosure before proceedings have started is desirable in order to—
    (i) dispose fairly of the anticipated proceedings;
    (ii) assist the dispute to be resolved without proceedings; or

(iii) save costs.

(4) An order under this rule must—

(a) specify the documents or the classes of documents which the respondent must disclose; and

(b) require him, when making disclosure, to specify any of those documents—

(i) which are no longer in his control; or

(ii) in respect of which he claims a right or duty to withhold inspection.

(5) Such an order may—

(a) require the respondent to indicate what has happened to any documents which are no longer in his control; and

(b) specify the time and place for disclosure and inspection.

[(Rule 78.26 contains rules in relation to the disclosure and inspection of evidence arising out of mediation of certain cross-border disputes.)]

NOTES

Words in square brackets inserted by the Civil Procedure (Amendment) Rules 2011, SI 2011/88, r 9(d), as from 6 April 2011.

[2.362]

31.17 Orders for disclosure against a person not a party

(1) This rule applies where an application is made to the court under any Act for disclosure by a person who is not a party to the proceedings.

(2) The application must be supported by evidence.

(3) The court may make an order under this rule only where—

(a) the documents of which disclosure is sought are likely to support the case of the applicant or adversely affect the case of one of the other parties to the proceedings; and

(b) disclosure is necessary in order to dispose fairly of the claim or to save costs.

(4) An order under this rule must—

(a) specify the documents or the classes of documents which the respondent must disclose; and

(b) require the respondent, when making disclosure, to specify any of those documents—

(i) which are no longer in his control; or

(ii) in respect of which he claims a right or duty to withhold inspection.

(5) Such an order may—

(a) require the respondent to indicate what has happened to any documents which are no longer in his control; and

(b) specify the time and place for disclosure and inspection.

[(Rule 78.26 contains rules in relation to the disclosure and inspection of evidence arising out of mediation of certain cross-border disputes.)]

NOTES

Words in square brackets inserted by the Civil Procedure (Amendment) Rules 2011, SI 2011/88, r 9(e), as from 6 April 2011.

[2.363]

31.18 Rules not to limit other powers of the court to order disclosure

Rules 31.16 and 31.17 do not limit any other power which the court may have to order—

(a) disclosure before proceedings have started; and

(b) disclosure against a person who is not a party to proceedings.

[2.364]

31.19 Claim to withhold inspection or disclosure of a document

(1) A person may apply, without notice, for an order permitting him to withhold disclosure of a document on the ground that disclosure would damage the public interest.

(2) Unless the court orders otherwise, an order of the court under paragraph (1)—

(a) must not be served on any other person; and

(b) must not be open to inspection by any person.

(3) A person who wishes to claim that he has a right or a duty to withhold inspection of a document, or part of a document, must state in writing—

(a) that he has such a right or duty; and

(b) the grounds on which he claims that right or duty.

(4) The statement referred to in paragraph (3) must be made—

(a) in the list in which the document is disclosed; or

(b) if there is no list, to the person wishing to inspect the document.

(5) A party may apply to the court to decide whether a claim made under paragraph (3) should be upheld.

(6) For the purpose of deciding an application under paragraph (1) (application to withhold disclosure) or paragraph (3) (claim to withhold inspection) the court may—

(a) require the person seeking to withhold disclosure or inspection of a document to produce that document to the court; and

(b) invite any person, whether or not a party, to make representations.

(7) An application under paragraph (1) or paragraph (5) must be supported by evidence.

(8) This Part does not affect any rule of law which permits or requires a document to be withheld from disclosure or inspection on the ground that its disclosure or inspection would damage the public interest.

[2.365]
31.20 Restriction on use of a privileged document inspection of which has been inadvertently allowed

Where a party inadvertently allows a privileged document to be inspected, the party who has inspected the document may use it or its contents only with the permission of the court.

[2.366]
31.21 Consequence of failure to disclose documents or permit inspection

A party may not rely on any document which he fails to disclose or in respect of which he fails to permit inspection unless the court gives permission.

[2.367]
31.22 Subsequent use of disclosed documents [and completed Electronic document Questionnaires]

(1) A party to whom a document has been disclosed may use the document only for the purpose of the proceedings in which it is disclosed, except where—

(a) the document has been read to or by the court, or referred to, at a hearing which has been held in public;

(b) the court gives permission; or

(c) the party who disclosed the document and the person to whom the document belongs agree.

(2) The court may make an order restricting or prohibiting the use of a document which has been disclosed, even where the document has been read to or by the court, or referred to, at a hearing which has been held in public.

(3) An application for such an order may be made—

(a) by a party; or

(b) by any person to whom the document belongs.

[(4) For the purpose of this rule, an Electronic Documents Questionnaire which has been completed and served by another party pursuant to Practice Direction 31B is to be treated as if it is a document which has been disclosed.]

NOTES

Words in square brackets in the rule heading added, and para (4) added, by the Civil Procedure (Amendment No 2) Rules 2010, SI 2010/1953, r 4, as from 1 October 2010.

[2.368]
[31.23 False disclosure statements

(1) Proceedings for contempt of court may be brought against a person if he makes, or causes to be made, a false disclosure statement, without an honest belief in its truth.

[(Section 6 of Part 81 contains provisions in relation to committal for making a false disclosure statement.)]

(2) . . .]

NOTES

Added by the Civil Procedure (Amendment) Rules 2000, SI 2000/221, r 16.

Para (1): words in square brackets added by the Civil Procedure (Amendment No 2) Rules 2012, SI 2012/2208, r 5(a), as from 1 October 2012, subject to transitional provisions in r 20 thereof.

Para (2): revoked by SI 2012/2208, r 5(b), as from 1 October 2012, subject to transitional provisions in r 20 thereof.

PART 35
EXPERTS AND ASSESSORS

[2.369]
35.1 Duty to restrict expert evidence

Expert evidence shall be restricted to that which is reasonably required to resolve the proceedings.

[2.370]

[35.2 Interpretation and definitions

(1) A reference to an 'expert' in this Part is a reference to a person who has been instructed to give or prepare expert evidence for the purpose of proceedings.

(2) 'Single joint expert' means an expert instructed to prepare a report for the court on behalf of two or more of the parties (including the claimant) to the proceedings.]

NOTES

Commencement: 1 October 2009.

Substituted by the Civil Procedure (Amendment) Rules 2009, SI 2009/2092, r 5(b), as from 1 October 2009.

[2.371]

35.3 Experts—overriding duty to the court

(1) [It is the duty of experts to help the court on matters within their expertise].

(2) This duty overrides any obligation to the person from whom [experts have received instructions or by whom they are paid].

NOTES

Words in square brackets substituted by the Civil Procedure (Amendment) Rules 2009, SI 2009/2092, r 5(c), (d), as from 1 October 2009.

[2.372]

35.4 Court's power to restrict expert evidence—

(1) No party may call an expert or put in evidence an expert's report without the court's permission.

[(2) When parties apply for permission they must [provide an estimate of the costs of the proposed expert evidence and] identify—

(a) the field in which expert evidence is required [and the issues which the expert evidence will address]; and

(b) where practicable, the name of the proposed expert.]

(3) If permission is granted . . . it shall be in relation only to the expert named or the field identified under paragraph (2). [The order granting permission may specify the issues which the expert evidence should address.]

[(3A) Where a claim has been allocated to the small claims track or the fast track, if permission is given for expert evidence, it will normally be given for evidence from only one expert on a particular issue.

(Paragraph 7 of [Practice Direction] 35 sets out some of the circumstances the court will consider when deciding whether expert evidence should be given by a single joint expert.)]

[(4) The court may limit the amount of a party's expert's fees and expenses that may be recovered from any other party.]

NOTES

Para (2): substituted by the Civil Procedure (Amendment) Rules 2009, SI 2009/2092, r 5(e), as from 1 October 2009; words in square brackets inserted by the Civil Procedure (Amendment) Rules 2013, SI 2013/262, r 13(a), (b), as from 1 April 2013.

Para (3): words omitted revoked by SI 2009/2092, r 5(f), as from 1 October 2009; words in square brackets added by SI 2013/262, r 13(c), as from 1 April 2013

Para (3A): inserted by SI 2009/2092, r 5(g), as from 1 October 2009; words in square brackets substituted by the Civil Procedure (Amendment No 2) Rules 2009, SI 2009/3390, r 18(a), as from 6 April 2010.

Para (4): substituted by SI 2009/2092, r 5(h), as from 1 October 2009.

[2.373]

35.5 General requirement for expert evidence to be given in a written report

(1) Expert evidence is to be given in a written report unless the court directs otherwise.

(2) If a claim is on the [small claims track or the] fast track, the court will not direct an expert to attend a hearing unless it is necessary to do so in the interests of justice.

NOTES

Para (2): words in square brackets inserted by the Civil Procedure (Amendment) Rules 2009, SI 2009/2092, r 5(i), as from 1 October 2009.

[2.374]

35.6 Written questions to experts

[(1) A party may put written questions about an expert's report (which must be proportionate) to—

(a) an expert instructed by another party; or

(b) a single joint expert appointed under rule 35.7.]

(2) Written questions under paragraph (1)—
(a) may be put once only;
(b) must be put within 28 days of service of the expert's report; and
(c) must be for the purpose only of clarification of the report,
unless in any case,
(i) the court gives permission; or
(ii) the other party agrees.

(3) An expert's answers to questions put in accordance with paragraph (1) shall be treated as part of the expert's report.

(4) Where—
(a) a party has put a written question to an expert instructed by another party . . . ; and
(b) the expert does not answer that question,
the court may make one or both of the following orders in relation to the party who instructed the expert—
(i) that the party may not rely on the evidence of that expert; or
(ii) that the party may not recover the fees and expenses of that expert from any other party.

NOTES

Para (1): substituted by the Civil Procedure (Amendment) Rules 2009, SI 2009/2092, r 5(j)(i), as from 1 October 2009.
Para (4): words omitted from sub-para (a) revoked by SI 2009/2092, r 5(j)(ii), as from 1 October 2009.

[2.375]
[35.7 Court's power to direct that evidence is to be given by a single joint expert

(1) Where two or more parties wish to submit expert evidence on a particular issue, the court may direct that the evidence on that issue is to be given by a single joint expert.

(2) Where the parties who wish to submit the evidence ("the relevant parties") cannot agree who should be the single joint expert, the court may—
(a) select the expert from a list prepared or identified by the relevant parties; or
(b) direct that the expert be selected in such other manner as the court may direct.]

NOTES

Commencement: 1 October 2009.
Substituted by the Civil Procedure (Amendment) Rules 2009, SI 2009/2092, r 5(k), as from 1 October 2009.

[2.376]
35.8 Instructions to a single joint expert

(1) Where the court gives a direction under rule 35.7 for a single joint expert to be used, [any relevant] party may give instructions to the expert.

[(2) When a party gives instructions to the expert that party must, at the same time, send a copy to the other relevant parties.]

(3) The court may give directions about—
(a) the payment of the expert's fees and expenses; and
(b) any inspection, examination or experiments which the expert wishes to carry out.

(4) The court may, before an expert is instructed—
(a) limit the amount that can be paid by way of fees and expenses to the expert; and
(b) direct that [some or all of the relevant] parties pay that amount into court.

(5) Unless the court otherwise directs, the [relevant] parties are jointly and severally liable for the payment of the expert's fees and expenses.

NOTES

Paras (1), (4), (5): words in square brackets substituted by the Civil Procedure (Amendment) Rules 2009, SI 2009/2092, r 5(l), (n), (o), as from 1 October 2009.
Para (2): substituted by SI 2009/2092, r 5(m), as from 1 October 2009.

[2.377]
35.9 Power of court to direct a party to provide information

Where a party has access to information which is not reasonably [available to another party], the court may direct the party who has access to the information to—
(a) prepare and file a document recording the information; and
(b) serve a copy of that document on the other party.

NOTES

Words in square brackets substituted by the Civil Procedure (Amendment) Rules 2009, SI 2009/2092, r 5(p), as from 1 October 2009.

[2.378]
35.10 Contents of report

(1) An expert's report must comply with the requirements set out in [[Practice Direction] 35].

[(2) At the end of an expert's report there must be a statement that the expert understands and has complied with their duty to the court.]

(3) The expert's report must state the substance of all material instructions, whether written or oral, on the basis of which the report was written.

(4) The instructions referred to in paragraph (3) shall not be privileged against disclosure but the court will not, in relation to those instructions—

(a) order disclosure of any specific document; or

(b) permit any questioning in court, other than by the party who instructed the expert,

unless it is satisfied that there are reasonable grounds to consider the statement of instructions given under paragraph (3) to be inaccurate or incomplete.

NOTES

Para (1): words in first (outer) pair of square brackets substituted by the Civil Procedure (Amendment) Rules 2009, SI 2009/2092, r 5(q)(i), as from 1 October 2009; words in second (inner) pair of square brackets substituted by the Civil Procedure (Amendment No 2) Rules 2009, SI 2009/3390, r 18(b), as from 6 April 2010.

Para (2): substituted by SI 2009/2092, r 5(q)(ii), as from 1 October 2009.

[2.379]
35.11 Use by one party of expert's report disclosed by another

Where a party has disclosed an expert's report, any party may use that expert's report as evidence at the trial.

[2.380]
35.12 Discussions between experts

(1) The court may, at any stage, direct a discussion between experts for the purpose of requiring the experts to—

[(a) identify and discuss the expert issues in the proceedings; and

(b) where possible, reach an agreed opinion on those issues].

(2) The court may specify the issues which the experts must discuss.

[(3) The court may direct that following a discussion between the experts they must prepare a statement for the court setting out those issues on which—

(a) they agree; and

(b) they disagree, with a summary of their reasons for disagreeing.]

(4) The content of the discussion between the experts shall not be referred to at the trial unless the parties agree.

(5) Where experts reach agreement on an issue during their discussions, the agreement shall not bind the parties unless the parties expressly agree to be bound by the agreement.

NOTES

Para (1): sub-paras (a), (b) substituted by the Civil Procedure (Amendment No 5) Rules 2001, SI 2001/4015, r 21.

Para (3): substituted by the Civil Procedure (Amendment) Rules 2009, SI 2009/2092, r 5(r), as from 1 October 2009.

[2.381]
35.13 Consequence of failure to disclose expert's report

A party who fails to disclose an expert's report may not use the report at the trial or call the expert to give evidence orally unless the court gives permission.

[PART 36
OFFERS TO SETTLE]

NOTES

Rules 36.1–36.15 (Section I of this Part) were substituted for the original Part 36 (rr 36.1–36.23) by the Civil Procedure (Amendment No 3) Rules 2006, SI 2006/3435, r 7(1), Sch 1.

Section II of this Part (which was added by the Civil Procedure (Amendment) Rules 2010, SI 2010/621), ie, rr 36.16–36.22: RTA Protocol offers to settle, is omitted as outside the scope of this work.

[2.382]
[36.A1 Scope of this Part

(1) This Part contains rules about—

(a) offers to settle; and

(b) the consequences where an offer to settle is made in accordance with this Part.

(2) Section I of this Part contains rules about offers to settle other than where Section II applies.

(3) Section II of this Part contains rules about offers to settle where the parties have followed the Pre-Action Protocol for Low Value Personal Injury Claims in Road Traffic Accidents ("the RTA Protocol") and have started proceedings under Part 8 in accordance with Practice Direction 8B.]

NOTES

Commencement: 30 April 2010.

Inserted by the Civil Procedure (Amendment) Rules 2010, SI 2010/621, r 6(b), as from 30 April 2010.

[SECTION I
PART 36 OFFERS TO SETTLE]

[2.383]

[36.1 Scope of this Section

(1) This Section does not apply to an offer to settle to which Section II of this Part applies.]

(2) Nothing in this [Section] prevents a party making an offer to settle in whatever way he chooses, but if the offer is not made in accordance with rule 36.2, it will not have the consequences specified in rules 36.10, 36.11 and 36.14.

(Rule 44.3 requires the court to consider an offer to settle that does not have the costs consequences set out in this [Section] in deciding what order to make about costs)]

NOTES

Rules 36.1–36.15 were substituted as noted in the notes following the Part 36 heading *ante*.

The provision name and para (1) were subsequently substituted, and the heading preceding this rule was inserted, by the Civil Procedure (Amendment) Rules 2010, SI 2010/621, r 6(b), as from 30 April 2010.

The words in square brackets in para (2) were substituted by SI 2010/621, r 6(c), (d), as from 30 April 2010.

[2.384]

[36.2 Form and content of a Part 36 offer

(1) An offer to settle which is made in accordance with this rule is called a Part 36 offer.

(2) A Part 36 offer must—
- (a) be in writing;
- (b) state on its face that it is intended to have the consequences of [Section I of] Part 36;
- (c) specify a period of not less than 21 days within which the defendant will be liable for the claimant's costs in accordance with rule 36.10 if the offer is accepted;
- (d) state whether it relates to the whole of the claim or to part of it or to an issue that arises in it and if so to which part or issue; and
- (e) state whether it takes into account any counterclaim.

(Rule 36.7 makes provision for when a Part 36 offer is made)

(3) Rule 36.2(2)(c) does not apply if the offer is made less than 21 days before the start of the trial.

(4) In appropriate cases, a Part 36 offer must contain such further information as is required by rule 36.5 (Personal injury claims for future pecuniary loss), rule 36.6 (Offer to settle a claim for provisional damages), and rule 36.15 (Deduction of benefits).

(5) An offeror may make a Part 36 offer solely in relation to liability.]

NOTES

Rules 36.1–36.15 were substituted as noted in the notes following the Part 36 heading *ante*.

Para (2): words in square brackets inserted by the Civil Procedure (Amendment) Rules 2010, SI 2010/621, r 6(e), as from 30 April 2010.

[2.385]

[36.3 Part 36 offers—general provisions

(1) In this Part—
- (a) the party who makes an offer is the "offeror";
- (b) the party to whom an offer is made is the "offeree"; and
- (c) "the relevant period" means—
  - (i) in the case of an offer made not less than 21 days before trial, the period stated under rule 36.2(2)(c) or such longer period as the parties agree;
  - (ii) otherwise, the period up to end of the trial or such other period as the court has determined.

(2) A Part 36 offer—
- (a) may be made at any time, including before the commencement of proceedings; and
- (b) may be made in appeal proceedings.

(3) A Part 36 offer which offers to pay or offers to accept a sum of money will be treated as inclusive of all interest until—
- (a) the date on which the period stated under rule 36.2(2)(c) expires; or

(b) if rule 36.2(3) applies, a date 21 days after the date the offer was made.

(4) A Part 36 offer shall have the consequences set out [in this Section] only in relation to the costs of the proceedings in respect of which it is made, and not in relation to the costs of any appeal from the final decision in those proceedings.

(5) Before expiry of the relevant period, a Part 36 offer may be withdrawn or its terms changed to be less advantageous to the offeree, only if the court gives permission.

(6) After expiry of the relevant period and provided that the offeree has not previously served notice of acceptance, the offeror may withdraw the offer or change its terms to be less advantageous to the offeree without the permission of the court.

(7) The offeror does so by serving written notice of the withdrawal or change of terms on the offeree.

(Rule 36.14(6) deals with the costs consequences following judgment of an offer that is withdrawn)]

NOTES

Rules 36.1–36.15 were substituted as noted in the notes following the Part 36 heading *ante*.

Para (4): words in square brackets substituted by the Civil Procedure (Amendment) Rules 2010, SI 2010/621, r 6(f), as from 30 April 2010.

[2.386]

[36.4 Part 36 offers—defendants' offers

(1) Subject to rule 36.5(3) and rule 36.6(1), a Part 36 offer by a defendant to pay a sum of money in settlement of a claim must be an offer to pay a single sum of money.

(2) But, an offer that includes an offer to pay all or part of the sum, if accepted, at a date later than 14 days following the date of acceptance will not be treated as a Part 36 offer unless the offeree accepts the offer.]

NOTES

Rules 36.1–36.15 were substituted as noted in the notes following the Part 36 heading *ante*.

[2.387]

[36.5 Personal injury claims for future pecuniary loss

(1) This rule applies to a claim for damages for personal injury which is or includes a claim for future pecuniary loss.

(2) An offer to settle such a claim will not have the consequences set out in rules 36.10, 36.11 and 36.14 unless it is made by way of a Part 36 offer under this rule.

(3) A Part 36 offer to which this rule applies may contain an offer to pay, or an offer to accept—
- (a) the whole or part of the damages for future pecuniary loss in the form of—
  - (i) a lump sum; or
  - (ii) periodical payments; or
  - (iii) both a lump sum and periodical payments;
- (b) the whole or part of any other damages in the form of a lump sum.

(4) A Part 36 offer to which this rule applies—
- (a) must state the amount of any offer to pay the whole or part of any damages in the form of a lump sum;
- (b) may state—
  - (i) what part of the lump sum, if any, relates to damages for future pecuniary loss; and
  - (ii) what part relates to other damages to be accepted in the form of a lump sum;
- (c) must state what part of the offer relates to damages for future pecuniary loss to be paid or accepted in the form of periodical payments and must specify—
  - (i) the amount and duration of the periodical payments;
  - (ii) the amount of any payments for substantial capital purchases and when they are to be made; and
  - (iii) that each amount is to vary by reference to the retail prices index (or to some other named index, or that it is not to vary by reference to any index); and
- (d) must state either that any damages which take the form of periodical payments will be funded in a way which ensures that the continuity of payment is reasonably secure in accordance with section 2(4) of the Damages Act 1996 or how such damages are to be paid and how the continuity of their payment is to be secured.

(5) Rule 36.4 applies to the extent that a Part 36 offer by a defendant under this rule includes an offer to pay all or part of any damages in the form of a lump sum.

(6) Where the offeror makes a Part 36 offer to which this rule applies and which offers to pay or to accept damages in the form of both a lump sum and periodical payments, the offeree may only give notice of acceptance of the offer as a whole.

(7) If the offeree accepts a Part 36 offer which includes payment of any part of the damages in the form of periodical payments, the claimant must, within 7 days of the date of acceptance, apply to the court for an order for an award of damages in the form of periodical payments under rule 41.8.

([Practice Direction 41B] contains information about periodical payments under the Damages Act 1996).]

NOTES

Rules 36.1–36.15 were substituted as noted in the notes following the Part 36 heading *ante*.

Words in square brackets substituted by the Civil Procedure (Amendment No 2) Rules 2009, SI 2009/3390, r 19, as from 6 April 2010.

[2.388]

[36.6 Offer to settle a claim for provisional damages

(1) An offeror may make a Part 36 offer in respect of a claim which includes a claim for provisional damages.

(2) Where he does so, the Part 36 offer must specify whether or not the offeror is proposing that the settlement shall include an award of provisional damages.

(3) Where the offeror is offering to agree to the making of an award of provisional damages the Part 36 offer must also state—

- (a) that the sum offered is in satisfaction of the claim for damages on the assumption that the injured person will not develop the disease or suffer the type of deterioration specified in the offer;
- (b) that the offer is subject to the condition that the claimant must make any claim for further damages within a limited period; and
- (c) what that period is.

(4) Rule 36.4 applies to the extent that a Part 36 offer by a defendant includes an offer to agree to the making of an award of provisional damages.

(5) If the offeree accepts the Part 36 offer, the claimant must, within 7 days of the date of acceptance, apply to the court for an order for an award of provisional damages under rule 41.2.]

NOTES

Rules 36.1–36.15 were substituted as noted in the notes following the Part 36 heading *ante*.

[2.389]

[36.7 Time when a Part 36 offer is made

(1) A Part 36 offer is made when it is served on the offeree.

(2) A change in the terms of a Part 36 offer will be effective when notice of the change is served on the offeree.

(Rule 36.3 makes provision about when permission is required to change the terms of an offer to make it less advantageous to the offeree)]

NOTES

Rules 36.1–36.15 were substituted as noted in the notes following the Part 36 heading *ante*.

[2.390]

[36.8 Clarification of a Part 36 offer

(1) The offeree may, within 7 days of a Part 36 offer being made, request the offeror to clarify the offer.

(2) If the offeror does not give the clarification requested under paragraph (1) within 7 days of receiving the request, the offeree may, unless the trial has started, apply for an order that he does so.

(Part 23 contains provisions about making an application to the court)

(3) If the court makes an order under paragraph (2), it must specify the date when the Part 36 offer is to be treated as having been made.]

NOTES

Rules 36.1–36.15 were substituted as noted in the notes following the Part 36 heading *ante*.

[2.391]

[36.9 Acceptance of a Part 36 offer

(1) A Part 36 offer is accepted by serving written notice of the acceptance on the offeror.

(2) Subject to rule 36.9(3), a Part 36 offer may be accepted at any time (whether or not the offeree has subsequently made a different offer) unless the offeror serves notice of withdrawal on the offeree.

[(Rule 21.10 deals with compromise etc by or on behalf of a child or protected party).]

(3) The court's permission is required to accept a Part 36 offer where—

- (a) rule 36.12(4) applies;
- (b) rule 36.15(3)(b) applies, the relevant period has expired and further deductible [amounts] have been paid to the claimant since the date of the offer;
- (c) an apportionment is required under rule 41.3A; or
- (d) the trial has started.

(Rule 36.12 deals with offers by some but not all of multiple defendants)

[(Rule 36.15 defines "deductible amounts".)]

(Rule 41.3A requires an apportionment in proceedings under the Fatal Accidents Act 1976 and Law Reform (Miscellaneous Provisions) Act 1934)

(4) Where the court gives permission under paragraph (3), unless all the parties have agreed costs, the court will make an order dealing with costs, and may order that the costs consequences set out in rule 36.10 will apply.

(5) Unless the parties agree, a Part 36 offer may not be accepted after the end of the trial but before judgment is handed down.]

NOTES

Rules 36.1–36.15 were substituted as noted in the notes following the Part 36 heading *ante*.

Para (2): words in square brackets substituted by the Civil Procedure (Amendment) Rules 2007, SI 2007/2204, r 11.

Para (3): words in square brackets substituted by the Civil Procedure (Amendment) Rules 2008, SI 2008/2178, r 17(b), as from 1 October 2008.

[2.392]

[36.10 Costs consequences of acceptance of a Part 36 offer

(1) Subject to paragraph (2) and paragraph (4)(a), where a Part 36 offer is accepted within the relevant period the claimant will be entitled to [the] costs of the proceedings up to the date on which notice of acceptance was served on the offeror.

(2) Where—

- (a) a defendant's Part 36 offer relates to part only of the claim; and
- (b) at the time of serving notice of acceptance within the relevant period the claimant abandons the balance of the claim,

the claimant will be entitled to [the] costs of the proceedings up to the date of serving notice of acceptance unless the court orders otherwise.

(3) Costs under paragraphs (1) and (2) of this rule will be assessed on the standard basis if the amount of costs is not agreed.

(Rule 44.4(2) explains the standard basis for assessment of costs)

[(Rule 44.12 contains provisions about when a costs order is deemed to have been made and applying for an order under section 194(3) of the Legal Services Act 2007.)]

(4) Where—

- (a) a Part 36 offer that was made less than 21 days before the start of trial is accepted; or
- (b) a Part 36 offer is accepted after expiry of the relevant period,

if the parties do not agree the liability for costs, the court will make an order as to costs.

(5) Where paragraph (4)(b) applies, unless the court orders otherwise—

- (a) the claimant will be entitled to [the] costs of the proceedings up to the date on which the relevant period expired; and
- (b) the offeree will be liable for the offeror's costs for the period from the date of expiry of the relevant period to the date of acceptance.

(6) The claimant's costs include any costs incurred in dealing with the defendant's counterclaim if the Part 36 offer states that it takes into account the counterclaim.]

NOTES

Rules 36.1–36.15 were substituted as noted in the notes following the Part 36 heading *ante*.

All words in square brackets in this rule were substituted or inserted by the Civil Procedure (Amendment) Rules 2008, SI 2008/2178, r 17(c), as from 1 October 2008.

[2.393]

[36.11 The effect of acceptance of a Part 36 offer

(1) If a Part 36 offer is accepted, the claim will be stayed.

(2) In the case of acceptance of a Part 36 offer which relates to the whole claim the stay will be upon the terms of the offer.

(3) If a Part 36 offer which relates to part only of the claim is accepted—

- (a) the claim will be stayed as to that part upon the terms of the offer; and
- (b) subject to rule 36.10(2), unless the parties have agreed costs, the liability for costs shall be decided by the court.

(4) If the approval of the court is required before a settlement can be binding, any stay which would otherwise arise on the acceptance of a Part 36 offer will take effect only when that approval has been given.

(5) Any stay arising under this rule will not affect the power of the court—
  (a) to enforce the terms of a Part 36 offer;
  (b) to deal with any question of costs (including interest on costs) relating to the proceedings.

(6) Unless the parties agree otherwise in writing, where a Part 36 offer by a defendant that is or that includes an offer to pay a single sum of money is accepted, that sum must be paid to the offeree within 14 days of the date of—
  (a) acceptance; or
  (b) the order when the court makes an order under rule 41.2 (order for an award of provisional damages) or rule 41.8 (order for an award of periodical payments), unless the court orders otherwise.

(7) If the accepted sum is not paid within 14 days or such other period as has been agreed the offeree may enter judgment for the unpaid sum.

(8) Where—
  (a) a Part 36 offer (or part of a Part 36 offer) which is not an offer to which paragraph (6) applies is accepted; and
  (b) a party alleges that the other party has not honoured the terms of the offer,

that party may apply to enforce the terms of the offer without the need for a new claim.]

NOTES

Rules 36.1–36.15 were substituted as noted in the notes following the Part 36 heading *ante*.

[2.394]

[36.12 Acceptance of a Part 36 offer made by one or more, but not all, defendants

(1) This rule applies where the claimant wishes to accept a Part 36 offer made by one or more, but not all, of a number of defendants.

(2) If the defendants are sued jointly or in the alternative, the claimant may accept the offer if—
  (a) he discontinues his claim against those defendants who have not made the offer; and
  (b) those defendants give written consent to the acceptance of the offer.

(3) If the claimant alleges that the defendants have a several liability to him, the claimant may—
  (a) accept the offer; and
  (b) continue with his claims against the other defendants if he is entitled to do so.

(4) In all other cases the claimant must apply to the court for an order permitting him to accept the Part 36 offer.]

NOTES

Rules 36.1–36.15 were substituted as noted in the notes following the Part 36 heading *ante*.

[2.395]

[36.13 Restriction on disclosure of a Part 36 offer

(1) A Part 36 offer will be treated as "without prejudice except as to costs".

(2) The fact that a Part 36 offer has been made must not be communicated to the trial judge or to the judge (if any) allocated in advance to conduct the trial until the case has been decided.

(3) Paragraph (2) does not apply—
  (a) where the defence of tender before claim has been raised;
  (b) where the proceedings have been stayed under rule 36.11 following acceptance of a Part 36 offer; or
  (c) where the offeror and the offeree agree in writing that it should not apply.]

NOTES

Rules 36.1–36.15 were substituted as noted in the notes following the Part 36 heading *ante*.

[2.396]

[36.14 Costs consequences following judgment

(1) This rule applies where upon judgment being entered—
  (a) a claimant fails to obtain a judgment more advantageous than a defendant's Part 36 offer; or
  (b) judgment against the defendant is at least as advantageous to the claimant as the proposals contained in a claimant's Part 36 offer.

[(1A) For the purposes of paragraph (1), in relation to any money claim or money element of a claim, "more advantageous" means better in money terms by any amount, however small, and "at least as advantageous" shall be construed accordingly.]

(2) Subject to paragraph (6), where rule 36.14(1)(a) applies, the court will, unless it considers it unjust to do so, order that the defendant is entitled to—
- (a) his costs from the date on which the relevant period expired; and
- (b) interest on those costs.

(3) Subject to paragraph (6), where rule 36.14(1)(b) applies, the court will, unless it considers it unjust to do so, order that the claimant is entitled to—
- (a) interest on the whole or part of any sum of money (excluding interest) awarded at a rate not exceeding 10% above base rate for some or all of the period starting with the date on which the relevant period expired;
- (b) . . . costs on the indemnity basis from the date on which the relevant period expired; . . .
- (c) interest on those costs at a rate not exceeding 10% above base rate[; and]
- [(d) an additional amount, which shall not exceed £75,000, calculated by applying the prescribed percentage set out below to an amount which is—
  - (i) where the claim is or includes a money claim, the sum awarded to the claimant by the court; or
  - (ii) where the claim is only a non-monetary claim, the sum awarded to the claimant by the court in respect of costs—

Amount awarded by the court	*Prescribed percentage*
Up to £500,000	10% of the amount awarded.
Above £500,000 up to £1,000,000	10% of the first £500,000 and 5% of the amount awarded above that figure.]

(4) In considering whether it would be unjust to make the orders referred to in paragraphs (2) and (3) above, the court will take into account all the circumstances of the case including—
- (a) the terms of any Part 36 offer;
- (b) the stage in the proceedings when any Part 36 offer was made, including in particular how long before the trial started the offer was made;
- (c) the information available to the parties at the time when the Part 36 offer was made; and
- (d) the conduct of the parties with regard to the giving or refusing to give information for the purposes of enabling the offer to be made or evaluated.

(5) Where the court awards interest under this rule and also awards interest on the same sum and for the same period under any other power, the total rate of interest may not exceed 10% above base rate.

(6) Paragraphs (2) and (3) of this rule do not apply to a Part 36 offer—
- (a) that has been withdrawn;
- (b) that has been changed so that its terms are less advantageous to the offeree, and the offeree has beaten the less advantageous offer;
- (c) made less than 21 days before trial, unless the court has abridged the relevant period.

(Rule 44.3 requires the court to consider an offer to settle that does not have the costs consequences set out in this [Section] in deciding what order to make about costs).]

NOTES

Rules 36.1–36.15 were substituted as noted in the notes following the Part 36 heading *ante*.

Para (3): words omitted from sub-para (b) revoked, word in square brackets in sub-para (c) inserted, and sub-para (d) added by the Civil Procedure (Amendment) Rules 2013, SI 2013/262, r 14, as from 1 April 2013.

Para (1A): inserted by the Civil Procedure (Amendment No 2) Rules 2011, SI 2011/1979, r 4, in relation to offers to settle made in accordance with r 36.2 on or after 1 October 2011.

Para (6): word in square brackets substituted by the Civil Procedure (Amendment) Rules 2010, SI 2010/621, r 6(g), as from 30 April 2010.

[2.397]
[36.15 [Deduction of benefits and lump sum payments]

[(1) In this rule and rule 36.9—
- (a) "the 1997 Act" means the Social Security (Recovery of Benefits) Act 1997;
- (b) "the 2008 Regulations" means the Social Security (Recovery of Benefits) (Lump Sum Payments) Regulations 2008;
- (c) "recoverable amount" means—
  - (i) "recoverable benefits" as defined in section 1(4)(c) of the 1997 Act; and
  - (ii) "recoverable lump sum payments" as defined in regulation 4 of the 2008 Regulations;

(d) "deductible amount" means—
   (i) any benefits by the amount of which damages are to be reduced in accordance with section 8 of, and Schedule 2 to the 1997 Act ("deductible benefits"); and
   (ii) any lump sum payment by the amount of which damages are to be reduced in accordance with regulation 12 of the 2008 Regulations ("deductible lump sum payments"); and
(e) "certificate"—
   (i) in relation to recoverable benefits is construed in accordance with the provisions of the 1997 Act; and
   (ii) in relation to recoverable lump sum payments has the meaning given in section 29 of the 1997 Act as applied by regulation 2 of, and modified by Schedule 1 to the 2008 Regulations.

(2) This rule applies where a payment to a claimant following acceptance of a Part 36 offer would be a compensation payment as defined in section 1(4)(b) or 1A(5)(b) of the 1997 Act.]

(3) A defendant who makes a Part 36 offer should state either—
   (a) that the offer is made without regard to any liability for recoverable [amounts]; or
   (b) that it is intended to include any deductible [amounts].

(4) Where paragraph (3)(b) applies, paragraphs (5) to (9) of this rule will apply to the Part 36 offer.

(5) Before making the Part 36 offer, the offeror must apply for a certificate . . .

(6) Subject to paragraph (7), the Part 36 offer must state—
   (a) the amount of gross compensation;
   (b) the name and amount of any deductible [amount] by which [the] gross amount is reduced; and
   (c) the net amount [of compensation].

[(7) If at the time the offeror makes the Part 36 offer, the offeror has applied for, but has not received a certificate, the offeror must clarify the offer by stating the matters referred to in paragraphs (6)(b) and (6)(c) not more than 7 days after receipt of the certificate.]

(8) For the purposes of rule 36.14(1)(a), a claimant fails to recover more than any sum offered (including a lump sum offered under rule 36.5) if [the claimant] fails upon judgment being entered to recover a sum, once deductible [amounts] identified in the judgment have been deducted, greater than the net amount stated under paragraph (6)(c).

[(Section 15(2) of the 1997 Act provides that the court must specify the compensation payment attributable to each head of damage. Schedule 1 to the 2008 Regulations modifies section 15 of the 1997 Act in relation to lump sum payments and provides that the court must specify the compensation payment attributable to each or any dependant who has received a lump sum payment.)]

(9) Where—
   (a) further deductible [amounts] have accrued since the Part 36 offer was made; and
   (b) the court gives permission to accept the Part 36 offer,

the court may direct that the amount of the offer payable to the offeree shall be reduced by a sum equivalent to the deductible [amounts] paid to the claimant since the date of the offer.

(Rule 36.9(3)(b) states that permission is required to accept an offer where the relevant period has expired and further deductible [amounts] have been paid to the claimant).]

NOTES

Rules 36.1–36.15 were substituted as noted in the notes following the Part 36 heading *ante*.

All words in square brackets in this rule were substituted (including those in the provision heading), and the words omitted from para (5) were revoked, by the Civil Procedure (Amendment) Rules 2008, SI 2008/2178, r 17(d), as from 1 October 2008.

36.16–36.22 *(Rules 36.16–36.22 (Section II: RTA Protocol offers to settle) outside the scope of this work.)*

Part 2 Statutory Instruments

NATIONAL MINIMUM WAGE REGULATIONS 1999

(SI 1999/584)

NOTES

Made: 6 March 1999.
Authority: National Minimum Wage Act 1998, ss 1(3), (4), 2, 3, 9, 51.
Commencement: 1 April 1999.
See Harvey BI(4).

ARRANGEMENT OF REGULATIONS

PART I
GENERAL AND INTERPRETATION

PART II
THE RATE OF THE NATIONAL MINIMUM WAGE

PART III
WORKING TIME FOR THE PURPOSES OF THE NATIONAL MINIMUM WAGE

PART IV
REMUNERATION COUNTING TOWARDS THE NATIONAL MINIMUM WAGE

PART I
GENERAL AND INTERPRETATION

[2.398]

1 Citation and commencement

These Regulations may be cited as the National Minimum Wage Regulations 1999 and shall come into force on 1st April 1999.

Interpretation

[2.399]

2 General interpretative provisions

(1) In these Regulations—

"the Act" means the National Minimum Wage Act 1998;

"allowance", other than in regulation 8(b), means any payment paid by the employer to a worker attributable to a particular aspect of his working arrangements or to his working or personal circumstances that is not consolidated into his standard pay, but does not include an allowance designed to refund a worker in respect of expenses incurred by him in connection with his employment;

"[Government arrangements]" means—

(a) in England and Wales, arrangements made by the Secretary of State under section 2 of the Employment and Training Act 1973 [or section 17B of the Jobseekers Act 1995],

(b) in Scotland, arrangements made by the Secretary of State [or the Scottish Ministers] under section 2 of the Employment and Training Act 1973 or by Scottish Enterprise or Highlands and Islands Enterprise under section 2 of the Enterprise and New Towns (Scotland) Act 1990,

(c) in Northern Ireland, arrangements made by the Department of Economic Development under section 1 of the Employment and Training Act (Northern Ireland) 1950;

["compulsory school age" has the meaning given to it by section 8 of the Education Act 1996;]

"employer" has the meaning given to it by section 54(4) of the Act but, in relation to a worker (as defined in section 54(3) of the Act), includes in addition, except in paragraph (6) of regulation 12—

(a) an agent or principal in relation to whom, by virtue of section 34(2) of the Act, the provisions of the Act have effect as if there were a worker's contract between him and an agency worker for the doing of work by the agency worker, and

(b) an employer of a home worker who is a worker by virtue of section 35 of the Act;

["further education course" means—

(a) in England, a course of education that is suitable to the requirements of persons who are over compulsory school age and that—

(i) is funded by the [Secretary of State under section 14 of the Education Act 2002],

(ii) is funded by the Chief Executive of Skills Funding,

(iii) is funded by a local authority,

(iv) leads to a qualification to which Part 7 of the Apprenticeships, Skills, Children and Learning Act 2009 applies which is awarded or authenticated by a body which is recognised by the Office of Qualifications and Examinations Regulation under section 132 of that Act in respect of the qualification, or

(v) leads to a qualification that is approved pursuant to section 98 of the Learning and Skills Act 2000,

except that it does not include a higher education course;

(b) in Wales, a course of education that is suitable to the requirements of persons who are over compulsory school age and that—
   (i) is funded by the Welsh Ministers,
   (ii) is funded by a local authority,
   (iii) leads to a qualification that is accredited by the Welsh Ministers pursuant to section 30 of the Education Act 1997, or
   (iv) leads to a qualification that is approved pursuant to section 99 of the Learning and Skills Act 2000,

   except that it does not include a higher education course;

(c) in Scotland, a course of "fundable further education" as defined in section 5(1) and (2) of the Further and Higher Education (Scotland) Act 2005;

(d) in Northern Ireland, a course of education or training as defined in article 3(1) and (2) of the Further Education (Northern Ireland) Order 1997;

"Further Education Institution" refers to an institution within the further education sector as defined by section 91(3) of the Further and Higher Education Act 1992;

"higher education course" means—

(a) in England and Wales, a course of a description referred to in Schedule 6 to the Education Reform Act 1988;

(b) in Scotland, a course of "fundable higher education" as defined in section 5(3), (4) and (5) of the Further and Higher Education (Scotland) Act 2005;

(c) in Northern Ireland, a course of a description referred to in Schedule 1 to the Further Education (Northern Ireland) Order 1997;

"Higher Education Institution" refers to an institution within the higher education sector as defined by section 91(5) of the Further and Higher Education Act 1992;]

"performance bonus" means a performance bonus or other merit payment attributable to the quality or amount of work done in the course of more than one pay reference period, and not therefore payable directly in respect of work done in specific hours;

"the total of reductions" means the total of reductions determined in accordance with regulations 31 to 37;

"the total of remuneration" means the total of money payments determined in accordance with regulation 30;

"pay reference period" has the meaning assigned to it by regulation 10;

"worker" has the same meaning as in section 54(3) of the Act but, except in [paragraphs (5) and (6) of regulation 12], includes in addition—

(a) an agency worker in relation to whom, by virtue of section 34(2) of the Act, the provisions of the Act have effect as if there were a worker's contract for the doing of his work between him and an agent or principal; and

(b) a home worker who is a worker by virtue of section 35 of the Act.

(2) In these Regulations "work" does not include work (of whatever description) relating to the employer's family household done by a worker where the conditions in sub-paragraphs (a) or (b) are satisfied.

(a) The conditions to be satisfied under this sub-paragraph are—
   (i) that the worker resides in the family home of the employer for whom he works,
   (ii) that the worker is not a member of that family, but is treated as such, in particular as regards to the provision of accommodation and meals and the sharing of tasks and leisure activities;
   (iii) that the worker is neither liable to any deduction, nor to make any payment to the employer, or any other person, in respect of the provision of the living accommodation or meals; and
   (iv) that, had the work been done by a member of the employer's family, it would not be treated as being performed under a worker's contract or as being work because the conditions in sub-paragraph (b) would be satisfied.

(b) The conditions to be satisfied under this sub-paragraph are—
   (i) that the worker is a member of the employer's family,
   (ii) that the worker resides in the family home of the employer,
   (iii) that the worker shares in the tasks and activities of the family,

   and that the work is done in that context.

(3) In these Regulations "work" does not include work (of whatever description) relating to an employer's family business, done by a worker who satisfies the conditions in paragraph (4).

(4) The conditions to be satisfied under this paragraph are—
   (i) that the worker is a member of the employer's family,
   (ii) that the worker resides in the family home of the employer,
   (iii) that the worker participates in the running of the family business,

and that the work is done in that context.

NOTES

Para (1) is amended as follows:

In definition "Government arrangements" (previously "arrangements made by the Government") words in first pair of square brackets substituted, and words in third pair of square brackets inserted, by the National Minimum Wage Regulations 1999 (Amendment) Regulations 2008, SI 2008/1894, reg 2, as from 1 October 2008; words in second pair of square brackets inserted by the National Minimum Wage (Amendment) Regulations 2011, SI 2011/2345, reg 2, as from 1 October 2011.

Definition "compulsory school age" inserted by the National Minimum Wage (Amendment) (No 2) Regulations 2011, SI 2011/2347, reg 2(a), as from 1 October 2011.

Definitions "further education course", "Further Education Institution", "higher education course" and "Higher Education Institution" inserted by SI 2011/2347, reg 2(b), as from 1 October 2011.

Words in square brackets in sub-para (a)(i) of the definition "further education course" substituted by the Young People's Learning Agency Abolition (Consequential Amendments to Subordinate Legislation) (England) Order 2012, SI 2012/956, art 7, as from 1 May 2012.

Words in square brackets in definition "worker" substituted by the National Minimum Wage Regulations 1999 (Amendment) Regulations 2010, SI 2010/1901, reg 2, as from 1 October 2010.

[2.400]

3 The meaning of time work

In these Regulations "time work" means—

(a) work that is paid for under a worker's contract by reference to the time for which a worker works and is not salaried hours work;

(b) work that is paid for under a worker's contract by reference to a measure of the output of the worker per hour or other period of time during the whole of which the worker is required to work, and is not salaried hours work; and

(c) work that would fall within paragraph (b) but for the fact that the worker is paid by reference to the length of the period of time alone when his output does not exceed a particular level.

[2.401]

4 The meaning of salaried hours work

(1) In these Regulations "salaried hours work" means work—

(a) that is done under a contract to do salaried hours work; and

(b) that falls within paragraph (6) below.

(2) A contract to do salaried hours work is a contract under which a worker—

(a) is entitled to be paid for an ascertainable basic number of hours in a year (referred to in this regulation as "the basic hours"); and

(b) is entitled, in respect of hours that consist of or include the basic hours, to be paid an annual salary—

(i) by equal weekly or monthly instalments of wages, or

(ii) by monthly instalments of wages that vary but have the result that the worker is entitled to be paid an equal amount in each quarter,

regardless of the number of hours in respect of which the worker is entitled to the annual salary that are actually worked by him (if any) in any particular week or month; and

(c) has, in respect of those hours, no entitlement to any payment other than his annual salary or no such entitlement other than an entitlement to a performance bonus.

(3) A contract that satisfies the conditions in paragraph (2) does so—

(a) whether or not all the basic hours are working hours;

(b) whether or not the worker can be required under his contract to work, or does in fact work, any hours in addition to the total of hours in respect of which he is entitled to his annual salary, and regardless of any payments made in respect of those additional hours.

(4) Circumstances having the result that in practice a worker may not be or is not paid by equal instalments of wages, or by an equal amount in each quarter, for hours in respect of which he is entitled under his contract only to his annual salary do not prevent the contract from being a contract for salaried hours work, for example—

(a) that a worker may be awarded a performance bonus,

(b) that the amount of a worker's annual salary may be varied,

(c) that by virtue of regulation 22 or 23 the worker is entitled to the national minimum wage in respect of hours in addition to his basic hours when, under his contract, there is no entitlement to any payment in addition to his annual salary for those additional hours (or to no payment in addition other than a performance bonus), and

(d) that the worker's employment may start or terminate during a week or month with the result that the worker is paid a proportionate amount of his annual salary for the week or month in question.

(5) The fact that, by reason of an absence from work for hours in respect of which his annual salary is normally payable, a worker is entitled under his contract, in respect of those hours, to be paid less than he would be but for the absence or to no payment does not prevent the worker's contract from being a contract for salaried hours work.

(6) The work done under a contract to do salaried hours work that falls within this paragraph, and is therefore salaried hours work, is work in respect of which the worker is entitled to no payment in addition to his annual salary, or to no payment in addition to his annual salary other than a performance bonus.

(7) References in regulation 22 to work or hours of work in respect of which a worker is entitled to no payment other than his annual salary refer also to work or hours of work in respect of which the only payment to which the worker is entitled other than his annual salary is payment of a performance bonus.

[2.402]

5 The meaning of output work

In these Regulations "output work" means work that is paid for under a worker's contract that is not time work and, but for the effect of the Act and these Regulations or anything done pursuant to these Regulations, would be paid for under that contract wholly by reference to the number of pieces made or processed by the worker, or wholly by reference to some other measure of output such as the number or value of sales made or transactions completed by the worker or as a result of his work.

[2.403]

6 The meaning of unmeasured work

In these Regulations "unmeasured work" means any other work that is not time work, salaried hours work or output work including, in particular, work in respect of which there are no specified hours and the worker is required to work when needed or when work is available.

[2.404]

7 Travelling

A worker is to be treated as travelling for the purposes of regulations 15(2), 16(2) and (5)(b), 17(1), 18(1) and 19(1)(b) if—

(a) he is in the course of a journey by a mode of transport or is making a journey on foot;
(b) he is waiting at a place of departure to begin his journey by a mode of transport;
(c) where his journey is broken, he is waiting at a place of departure for his journey to re-commence either by the same or another mode of transport, except for any time during such a period he spends in taking a rest break; or
(d) he is waiting at the end of a journey, in the case of regulations 15(2), 16(2), 17(1) and 18(1), for the purpose of carrying out his duties, or, in the case of regulations 16(5)(b) and 19(1)(b), to receive training, except for any time before he is due to carry out his duties or receive training which he spends in taking a rest break.

[2.405]

8 The meaning of payments

References in these Regulations to payments paid by the employer to the worker are references to payments paid by the employer to the worker in his capacity as a worker before any deductions are made, excluding—

(a) any payment by way of an advance under an agreement for a loan or by way of an advance of wages;
(b) any payment by way of a pension, by way of an allowance or gratuity in connection with the worker's retirement or as compensation for loss of office;
(c) any payment of an award made by a court or tribunal or to settle proceedings which have been or might be brought before a court or tribunal, other than the payment of an amount due under the worker's contract;
(d) any payment referable to the worker's redundancy;
(e) any payment by way of an award under a suggestions scheme.

[2.406]

9 Benefits in kind not to count as payments

For the purposes of these Regulations the following shall not be treated as payments by the employer to the worker—

(a) any benefit in kind provided to the worker, whether or not a monetary value is attached to the benefit, other than living accommodation;
(b) any voucher, stamp or similar document capable of being exchanged for money, goods or services (or for any combination of those things) provided by the employer to the worker.

[2.407]

10 The pay reference period

(1) The pay reference period is a month or, in the case of a worker who is paid wages by reference to a period shorter than a month, that period.

(2) When a worker's contract terminates regulations 14 and 30 to 37 shall be applied in relation to payments made in the period of a month beginning with the day immediately following the last day on which the worker worked under the contract as if such payments had been made in the worker's final pay reference period.

PART II
THE RATE OF THE NATIONAL MINIMUM WAGE

The rate and exclusions

[2.408]

11 The rate of the national minimum wage

The single hourly rate of the national minimum wage is [£6.19].

NOTES

Sum in square brackets substituted by the National Minimum Wage (Amendment) Regulations 2012, SI 2012/2397, regs 2(1), (2), 4, as from 1 October 2012 (except in relation to any pay reference period beginning before that date). The previous sum was £6.08 (from 1 October 2011: see SI 2011/2345). Prior to that date, the sums were: £5.93 (from 1 October 2010: see SI 2010/1901), £5.80 (from 1 October 2009: see SI 2009/1902), £5.73 (from 1 October 2008: see SI 2008/1894), £5.52 (from 1 October 2007: see SI 2007/2318), £5.35 (from 1 October 2006: see SI 2006/2001), £5.05 (from 1 October 2005: see SI 2005/2019), £4.85 (from 1 October 2004: see SI 2004/1930), £4.50 (from 1 October 2003: see SI 2003/1923), £4.20 (from 1 October 2002: see SI 2002/1999), £4.10 (from 1 October 2001: see SI 2001/2673), £3.70 (from 1 October 2000: see SI 2000/1989), and £3.60 (from 1 April 1999).

The Government has announced that the rate will increase from 1 October 2013 to £6.31, but the relevant Regulations had not, as at 6 April 2013, been made.

[2.409]

12 Workers who do not qualify for the national minimum wage

(1)–(4) . . .

[(4A) A worker who is participating in a scheme provided to that worker—
- (a) in England, under the Government arrangements known, at 1st October 2010, as Programme Led Apprenticeships,
- (b) in Scotland, under the Government arrangements known, at 1st October 2010, as Get Ready for Work or Skillseekers,
- (c) in Northern Ireland, under the Government arrangements known, at 1st October 2010, as Programme Led Apprenticeships or Training for Success,
- (d) in Wales, under the Government arrangements known, at 1st October 2010, as Skill Build, [or known, at 1st August 2011, as Traineeships or Steps to Employment,]

does not qualify for the national minimum wage in respect of work done for the employer as part of the scheme.]

[(5) A worker who is participating in a scheme designed to provide training, work experience or temporary work, or to assist in seeking or obtaining work, which is—
- (a) a scheme provided under Government arrangements that are not specified in paragraph (4A) or (5A), or
- (b) a scheme, not being one provided under Government arrangements, funded in whole or in part under the European Social Fund,

does not qualify for the national minimum wage in respect of work done for the employer as part of that scheme except to the extent that paragraph (6) or (7) otherwise provides.]

[(5A) For the purposes of paragraph (5), the Government arrangements specified are—
- (a) in England, Government arrangements known, at 1st October 2010, as Apprenticeships or Advanced Apprenticeships[, or known as Intermediate Level Apprenticeships or Advanced Level Apprenticeships];
- (b) in Scotland, Government arrangements known, at 1st October 2010, as Modern Apprenticeships;
- (c) in Northern Ireland, Government arrangements known, at 1st October 2010, as Apprenticeships NI or Modern Apprenticeships;
- (d) in Wales, Government arrangements known, at 1st October 2010, as Foundation Modern Apprenticeships, Modern Apprenticeships, Foundation Apprenticeships or Apprenticeships.]

[(6) Paragraph (5) does not apply to a person who—
- (a) is a worker within the meaning given by section 54(3) of the Act,
- (b) is participating in a scheme falling within sub-paragraph (a) of paragraph (5),
- (c) is employed by the employer for whom he works under the scheme, and
- (d) is—

(i) remunerated by the employer in respect of that employment, or
(ii) entitled to remuneration from the employer under his contract with the employer, or
(iii) participating in a trial period of work with a prospective employer under Government arrangements for a period in excess of six weeks.

(6A) For the purposes of paragraph (6)(d)(i) and (6)(d)(ii), remuneration does not include a payment by an employer to a person in respect of expenses—
(a) actually incurred in the performance of that person's duties, or
(b) reasonably estimated as likely to be or to have been so incurred.

(6B) For the purposes of paragraph (6A), expenses which—
(a) are incurred in order to enable the person to perform his duties, and
(b) are reasonably so incurred,
are to be regarded as actually incurred in the performance of his duties.]

(7) Paragraph (5) does not apply to an employee who is participating in a scheme falling within sub-paragraph [(b)] of paragraph (5) if he is employed by the employer for whom he works under the scheme, unless the employee is engaged, for a period not exceeding [six] weeks, in a trial period of work with a prospective employer under [Government arrangements].

[(8) A worker who is [undertaking] a higher education course, and before the course ends is required, as part of that course, to attend a period of work experience not exceeding one year, does not qualify for the national minimum wage in respect of work done for his employer as part of that course.]

(9) . . .

[(9A) A worker who is undertaking a further education course and before the course ends is required, as part of that course, to attend a period of work experience not exceeding one year, does not qualify for the national minimum wage in respect of work done for his employer as part of that course.

(9B), (9C) . . .]

(10) A worker who satisfies the condition set out in paragraph (11) and is participating in a scheme which satisfies the conditions set out in paragraph (12), under which he is provided with shelter and other benefits (which may include money benefits) in return for performing work, does not qualify for the national minimum wage in respect of work performed for his employer under that scheme.

(11) A worker satisfies the condition referred to in paragraph (10) if, immediately before his entry into the scheme—
(a) he was either homeless or residing in a hostel for homeless persons; and
(b) he—
(i) was in receipt of, or entitled to, [universal credit under Part 1 of the Welfare Reform Act 2012,] income support[, income-based jobseeker's allowance or income-related employment and support allowance payable under Part 1 of the Welfare Reform Act 2007] [or, as the case may be, Part 1 of the Welfare Reform Act (Northern Ireland) 2007], or
(ii) was not entitled to receive *either* of those benefits only because he was not habitually resident in the United Kingdom.

(12) A scheme satisfies this paragraph if—
(a) the arrangements under which the scheme operates prevent the person operating the scheme or any other person from making a profit out of the provision of the scheme, other than one which may only be applied in running the scheme or other schemes satisfying the requirements of this paragraph or, where the person operating the scheme is a charity, for a purpose, being a purpose of the charity, relating to the alleviation of poverty;
(b) every person participating in the scheme satisfies the condition set out in paragraph (11), or would satisfy it if he were a worker;
(c) the accommodation available under the scheme is provided by the person operating the scheme or under arrangements made between that person and another person; and
(d) the work done under the scheme is both provided by, and performed for, the person operating the scheme.

[(13) A worker who is participating in the second phase of the European Community Leonardo da Vinci programme (established pursuant to Council Decision 99/382/EC), does not qualify for the national minimum wage in respect of work done for his employer as part of that scheme.]

[(14) A worker who is participating in the European Community Leonardo da Vinci programme (established pursuant to Decision No 1720/2006/EC of the European Parliament and the Council of the European Union establishing an action programme in the field of lifelong learning), does not qualify for the national minimum wage in respect of work done for his employer as part of that scheme.

(15) A worker who is participating in the European Community Youth in Action Programme (established pursuant to Decision No 1719/2006/EC of the European Parliament and the Council of the European Union, does not qualify for the national minimum wage in respect of work done for his employer as part of that programme.]

[(16) A worker who is participating in the European Community Erasmus Programme or Comenius Programme (both established pursuant to Decision No 1720/2006/EC of the European Parliament and the Council of the European Union establishing an action programme in the field of lifelong learning), does not qualify for the national minimum wage in respect of work done for his employer as part of that scheme.]

NOTES

Para (1): revoked by the National Minimum Wage Regulations 1999 (Amendment) (No 2) Regulations 2004, SI 2004/1930, regs 3(a), 7.

Paras (2)–(4): revoked by the National Minimum Wage Regulations 1999 (Amendment) Regulations 2010, SI 2010/1901, regs 4(a), 9, as from 1 October 2010 (except in relation to any pay reference period beginning before that date).

Para (4A): inserted by SI 2004/1930, reg 3(c); substituted by SI 2010/1901, regs 4(b), 9, as from 1 October 2010 (except in relation to any pay reference period beginning before that date); words in square brackets in sub-para (d) inserted by the National Minimum Wage (Amendment) Regulations 2011, SI 2011/2345, reg 4, as from 1 August 2011.

Para (5): substituted by SI 2010/1901, regs 4(c), 9, as from 1 October 2010 (except in relation to any pay reference period beginning before that date).

Para (5A): inserted by SI 2010/1901, regs 4(d), 9, as from 1 October 2010 (except in relation to any pay reference period beginning before that date); words in square brackets in sub-para (a) inserted by the National Minimum Wage (Amendment) Regulations 2012, SI 2012/2397, reg 2(1), (3), as from 1 October 2012.

Paras (6), (6A), (6B): substituted, for the original para (6), by the National Minimum Wage Regulations 1999 (Amendment) Regulations 2008, SI 2008/1894, regs 4(1), (2), 7, as from 1 October 2008 (except in relation to any work trial commencing before 17 July 2008).

Para (7): reference to "(b)" in square brackets substituted by SI 2010/1901, reg 4(e), as from 1 October 2010 (except in relation to any pay reference period beginning before that date); word "six" in square brackets substituted by SI 2008/1894, regs 4(1), (3), 7, as from 1 October 2008 (except in relation to any work trial commencing before 17 July 2008); final words in square brackets substituted by SI 2001/1108, reg 6.

Para (8): substituted by SI 2000/1989, reg 4(3); word in square brackets substituted by SI 2007/2318, regs 3(1), (3), 9.

Para (9): revoked by the National Minimum Wage (Amendment) (No 2) Regulations 2011, SI 2011/2347, reg 3, as from 1 October 2011.

Paras (9A)–(9C): inserted by SI 2007/2318, regs 3(1), (5), 9; paras (9B), (9C) revoked by SI 2011/2347, reg 3, as from 1 October 2011.

Para (11): words in first pair of brackets in sub-para (b)(i) inserted and for the word in italics in sub-para (b)(ii) there is substituted the word "any", by the Universal Credit (Consequential, Supplementary, Incidental and Miscellaneous Provisions) Regulations 2013, SI 2013/630, reg 52, as from 29 April 2013; words in second pair of square brackets in sub-para (b)(i) substituted by the Employment and Support Allowance (Consequential Provisions) (No 3) Regulations 2008, SI 2008/1879, reg 3, as from 27 October 2008; words in third pair of square brackets in sub-para (b)(i) inserted by the Employment and Support Allowance (Consequential Provisions No 2) Regulations (Northern Ireland) 2008, SR 2008/412, reg 7, as from 27 October 2008.

Para (13): added by the National Minimum Wage Regulations 1999 (Amendment) Regulations 2005, SI 2005/2019, reg 3.

Paras (14), (15): added by SI 2007/2318, regs 3(1), (6), 9.

Para (16): added by the National Minimum Wage Regulations 1999 (Amendment) Regulations 2009, SI 2009/1902, regs 3, 7, as from 1 October 2009 (except in relation to any pay reference period beginning before that date).

[2.410]

[13 Workers who qualify for the national minimum wage at a different rate

(1) Subject to paragraph (3), the hourly rate of the national minimum wage is [£4.98] for a worker who has attained the age of 18 but not the age of 21.

(2) Subject to paragraph (3), the hourly rate of the national minimum wage is [£3.68] for a worker who has not attained the age of 18.

(3) The hourly rate of the national minimum wage is [£2.65] for a worker who—

- (a) is employed under a contract of apprenticeship or, in accordance with paragraph (6), is to be treated as employed under a contract of apprenticeship, and
- (b) is within the first 12 months after the commencement of that employment or has not attained the age of 19.

(4) Paragraphs (1) to (3) do not apply in relation to a worker who, by virtue of regulation 12, does not qualify for the national minimum wage.

(5) For the purposes of paragraph (3)(b) a person does not commence employment with an employer where that person has previously been employed by another employer and continuity of employment is preserved between the two employments by or under any enactment.

(6) A person is to be treated for the purposes of paragraph (3)(a) as a worker who is employed under a contract of apprenticeship, if, and only if, that person is—

- (a) a worker within the meaning given by section 54(3) of the Act; and
- (b) engaged—

(i) in England, under the Government arrangements known, at 1st October 2010, as Apprenticeships or Advanced Apprenticeships[, or known as Intermediate Level Apprenticeships or Advanced Level Apprenticeships];

(ii) in Scotland, under the Government arrangements known, at 1st October 2010, as Modern Apprenticeships;

(iii) in Northern Ireland, under the Government arrangements known, at 1st October 2010, as Apprenticeships NI or Modern Apprenticeships; or

(iv) in Wales, under the Government arrangements known, at 1st October 2010, as Foundation Modern Apprenticeships, Modern Apprenticeships, Foundation Apprenticeships or Apprenticeships.]

NOTES

Commencement: 1 October 2010.

Substituted by National Minimum Wage Regulations 1999 (Amendment) Regulations 2010, SI 2010/1901, regs 5, 9, as from 1 October 2010 (except in relation to any pay reference period beginning before that date).

Paras (1), (2): sums in square brackets substituted by the National Minimum Wage (Amendment) Regulations 2011, SI 2011/2345, regs 5(a), (b), 8, as from 1 October 2011 (except in relation to any pay reference period beginning before that date). The previous sums were £4.92 and £3.64 respectively (see further the note below). Note that these sums were not further increased when the rates specified in reg 11, and in para (3) of this regulation, were increased in 2012.

Para (3): sum in square brackets substituted by the National Minimum Wage (Amendment) Regulations 2012, SI 2012/2397, regs 2(1), (4)(a), 4, as from 1 October 2012 (except in relation to any pay reference period beginning before that date). The previous sums were £2.60 (as from 1 October 2011: see SI 2011/2345), and £2.50 (as from 1 October 2010: see SI 2010/1901) (see further the note below).

Para (6): words in square brackets in sub-para (b) inserted by SI 2012/2397, reg 2(1), (4)(b), as from 1 October 2012.

Prior to its substitution as noted above, para (1) of this regulation provided that the hourly rate of the national minimum wage was £4.83 for a worker who had attained the age of 18 but not the age of 22 (from 1 October 2009, see SI 2009/1902, reg 4(a)) and para (1A) provided that the hourly rate was £3.57 for a worker who had not attained the age of 18 (from 1 October 2009, see SI 2009/1902, reg 4(b)). Paras (2)–(6) had been revoked, but para (7) provided that paras (1), (1A) did not apply in relation to a worker who, by virtue of reg 12, did not qualify for the national minimum wage.

The Government has announced that the rates specified in paras (1), (2) and (3) respectively will be increased to £5.03, £3.72 and £2.68 from 1 October 2013, but the Regulations to give effect to this had not been made as at 6 April 2013.

[2.411]

[13A Workers working under an apprenticeship agreement

For the purposes of these Regulations, the expression "a worker who is employed under a contract of apprenticeship" includes a worker who is working under an apprenticeship agreement (within the meaning of section 32 of the Apprenticeships, Skills, Children and Learning Act 2009).]

NOTES

Commencement: 9 January 2013.

Inserted by the Apprenticeships, Skills, Children and Learning Act 2009 (Consequential Amendments to Subordinate Legislation) (England and Wales) Order 2012, SI 2012/3112, art 2, as from 9 January 2013.

Calculation of the hourly rate

[2.412]

14 Method of determining whether the national minimum wage has been paid

(1) The hourly rate paid to a worker in a pay reference period shall be determined by dividing the total calculated in accordance with paragraph (2) by the number of hours specified in paragraph (3).

(2) The total referred to in paragraph (1) shall be calculated by subtracting from the total of remuneration in the pay reference period determined under regulation 30, the total of reductions determined under regulations 31 to 37.

(3) The hours referred to in paragraph (1) are the total number of hours of time work, salaried hours work, output work and unmeasured work worked by the worker in the pay reference period that have been ascertained in accordance with regulations 20 to [29A].

NOTES

Para (3): figure in square brackets substituted by the National Minimum Wage Regulations 1999 (Amendment) Regulations 2000, SI 2000/1989, regs 5, 10(1).

[2.413]

[14A Determining the applicable national minimum rate

The hourly rate at which a worker is entitled to be remunerated in respect of his work in any pay reference period is the rate, prescribed by regulations, that is in force on the first day of that period.]

NOTES

Inserted by the National Minimum Wage Regulations 1999 (Amendment) Regulations 2002, SI 2002/1999, reg 2.

PART III
WORKING TIME FOR THE PURPOSES OF THE NATIONAL MINIMUM WAGE

Provisions in relation to working time

[2.414]
15 Provisions in relation to time work

[(1) Subject to paragraph (1A), time work includes time when a worker is available at or near a place of work for the purpose of doing time work and is required to be available for such work except where—

(a) the worker's home is at or near the place of work; and

(b) the time is time the worker is entitled to spend at home.

(1A) In relation to a worker who by arrangement sleeps at or near a place of work and is provided with suitable facilities for sleeping, time during the hours he is permitted to use those facilities for the purpose of sleeping shall only be treated as being time work when the worker is awake for the purpose of working.

(2) Time when a worker is travelling for the purpose of duties carried out by him in the course of time work shall be treated as being time work except where—

(a) the travelling is incidental to the duties carried out in the course of time work, the time work is not assignment work and the time is time when the worker would not otherwise be working; or

(b) the travelling is between the worker's home, or an address where he is temporarily residing other than for the purposes of performing work, and his place of work or a place where an assignment is carried out.

(3) For the purposes of paragraph (2)(a)—

(a) travelling is incidental to the duties carried out by a worker unless duties involved in his work are necessarily carried out in the course of the travelling, as in the case of a worker driving a bus, serving in a bar on a train or whose main duty is to transport items from one place to another, and

(b) time work is assignment work if it consists of assignments of work to be carried out at a different places between which the worker is obliged to travel that are not places occupied by the worker's employer.]

(4) Where a worker's hours of work vary either as to their length or in respect of the time at which they are performed and, as a result, it is uncertain in relation to particular time when the worker is travelling whether he would otherwise be working, that time shall be treated, for the purposes of paragraph (2)(a), as time when he would otherwise be working.

(5) Except as mentioned in paragraph (2) and regulation 19, time work does not include time when a worker is absent from work.

(6) A worker engaged in taking industrial action in the course of time work shall be treated as being absent from work for the time during which he is so engaged.

(7) Where a worker is entitled to a rest break in the course of time work, the period of the break shall be treated as time when the worker is absent from work; but a worker shall not be treated as being entitled to any rest breaks during time which is required to be treated as time work by paragraph (2).

NOTES

Paras (1), (1A), (2), (3): substituted, for the original paras (1)–(3), by the National Minimum Wage Regulations 1999 (Amendment) Regulations 2000, SI 2000/1989, regs 6, 10(1).

[2.415]
16 Provisions in relation to salaried hours work

[(1) Subject to paragraph (1A), time when a worker is available at or near a place of work for the purpose of doing salaried hours work and is required to be available for such work shall be treated as being working hours for the purpose of and to the extent mentioned in regulation 22(3)(d) and (4)(b) except where—

(a) the worker's home is at or near the place or work; and

(b) the time is time the worker is entitled to spend at home.

(1A) In relation to a worker who by arrangement sleeps at or near a place of work and is provided with suitable facilities for sleeping, time during the hours he is permitted to use those facilities for the purpose of sleeping shall only be treated as being salaried hours work when the worker is awake for the purpose of working.

(2) Time when a worker is travelling for the purpose of duties carried out by him in the course of salaried hours work shall be treated as being working hours for the purpose of and to the extent mentioned in regulation 22(3)(d) and (4)(b) except where—

Part 2 Statutory Instruments

(a) the travelling is incidental to the duties carried out in the course of salaried hours work, the salaried hours work is not assignment work and the time is time when the worker would not otherwise be working; or

(b) the travelling is between the worker's home, or an address where he is temporarily residing other than for the purposes of performing work, and his place of work or a place where an assignment is carried out.

(3) For the purposes of paragraph (2)(a)—

(a) travelling is incidental to the duties carried out by a worker unless duties involved in his work are necessarily carried out in the course of the travelling, as in the case of a worker driving a bus, serving in a bar on a train or whose main duty is to transport items from one place to another, and

(b) salaried hours work is assignment work if it consists of assignments of work to be carried out at different places between which the worker is obliged to travel that are not places occupied by the worker's employer.]

(4) Where a worker's hours of work vary either as to their length or in respect of the time at which they are performed and, as a result, it is uncertain in relation to particular time when the worker is travelling whether he would otherwise be working, that time shall be treated, for the purposes of paragraph (2)(a), as time when he would otherwise be working.

(5) Time when a worker is—

(a) attending at a place other than his normal place of work, when he would otherwise be working, for the purpose of receiving training wholly or mainly in connection with salaried hours work that has been approved by his employer,

(b) travelling, when he would otherwise be working, between a place of work and a place where he is receiving such training, or

(c) receiving such training at his normal place of work,

shall be treated as working hours for the purpose of and to the extent mentioned in regulation 22(3)(d) and (4)(b).

NOTES

Paras (1), (1A), (2), (3): substituted, for the original paras (1)–(3), by the National Minimum Wage Regulations 1999 (Amendment) Regulations 2000, SI 2000/1989, regs 7, 10(1).

[2.416]

17 Provisions in relation to output work

(1) Time spent by a worker in travelling for the purposes of doing output work shall be treated as time spent doing output work except for time spent travelling between his home, or a place where he is temporarily residing, and—

(a) premises from which he works; or

(b) except in the case of a worker whose work consists in producing tangible items at his home, premises to which he reports.

(2) A worker shall not be treated as doing output work, for the purpose of regulation 24, during time when he is engaged in taking industrial action nor as having worked, for the purpose of regulation 26, during such time.

[2.417]

18 Provisions in relation to unmeasured work

(1) Time when a worker is travelling for the purpose of unmeasured work shall be treated as being unmeasured work.

(2) A worker shall not be treated as carrying out his contractual duties to do unmeasured work, for the purpose of regulation 27, during time when he is engaged in taking industrial action, nor as being available to carry out those duties, for the purpose of regulation 29, during such time.

[2.418]

19 Time spent on training to be time work

(1) Time when a worker is—

(a) attending at a place other than his normal place of work, when he would otherwise be working, for the purpose of receiving training that has been approved by his employer,

(b) travelling, when he would otherwise be working, between a place of work and a place where he is receiving such training, or

(c) receiving such training at his normal place of work,

shall be treated as time work.

(2) Where a worker's hours of work vary either as to their length or in respect of the time at which they are performed and, as a result, it is uncertain in relation to particular time when the worker is attending at a place or travelling, whether he would otherwise be working, that time shall be treated for the purposes of paragraph (1)(a) or, as the case may be, (1)(b) as time when he would otherwise be working.

(3) Paragraph (1) does not apply in relation to training wholly or mainly in connection with salaried hours work.

The hours worked in a pay reference period

[2.419]

20 Time work

The time work worked by a worker in a pay reference period shall be the total number of hours of time work done by him in the pay reference period.

[2.420]

21 Salaried hours work

(1) In this regulation, "the basic hours" means the basic number of hours in a year in respect of which a worker is entitled under his contract to his annual salary as ascertained in accordance with his contract on the first day of the pay reference period in question.

(2) Except as mentioned in paragraph (3) and regulations 22 and 23, the salaried hours work worked by a worker in a pay reference period shall be the basic hours divided by—

- (a) where the pay reference period is a week, 52;
- (b) where the pay reference period is a month, 12; and
- (c) where the pay reference period is any other period, by the figure obtained by dividing 365 by the number of days in the pay reference period (including non-working days).

(3) Where in a pay reference period—

- (a) a worker is absent from work for a number of hours in respect of which his annual salary is payable, and
- (b) is, for that reason, entitled to be paid less and is paid less than the normal proportion of his annual salary in respect of the pay reference period,

the salaried hours work worked by the worker in the pay reference period shall be the number of hours determined under paragraph (2) in relation to the pay reference period reduced by the number of hours referred to in sub-paragraph (a) of this paragraph.

(4) Hours in a pay reference period during which a worker is engaged in taking industrial action and in respect of which his annual salary is or, but for his engagement in the action, would be payable, shall be regarded as satisfying the requirements in sub-paragraphs (a) and (b) of paragraph (3) whether or not the worker's entitlement to the normal proportion of his annual salary is affected by his engagement in the action and whether or not he is paid any amount in respect of those hours.

[2.421]

22 Determining the hours of salaried hours work where the basic hours have been exceeded

(1) Where in any calculation year the total of the hours referred to in paragraph (3) exceeds the basic hours, this regulation, and not regulation 21, applies for the purpose of determining the salaried hours work worked by a worker in the pay reference period during which the basic hours are exceeded and in the subsequent pay reference periods (if any) in the calculation year.

(2) In this regulation and regulation 23—

"the basic hours" means—

- (a) in a calculation year when the basic number of hours in respect of which the worker is entitled under his contract to his annual salary is not varied, that basic number;
- (b) in a calculation year when that basic number of hours is varied—
  - (i) where the basic hours are determined in respect of the calculation year before the only or first variation takes effect, the basic number of hours ignoring the effect of the variation,
  - (ii) where the basic hours are determined after a variation has taken effect, the sum of the following numbers of hours—
    - (aa) for the period beginning with the day on which the variation in question takes effect until the end of the year, the proportion of the basic number of hours in respect of which the worker would be entitled to his annual salary, in accordance with that variation, in a year of 365 days, which the number of days in the period bears to 365,
    - (bb) for the period starting with the beginning of the year and ending with the day before the day on which the only or first variation took effect, the proportion of the basic number of hours in respect of which the worker would be entitled to his annual salary, before the variation, in a year of 365 days, which the number of days in the period bears to 365, and
    - (cc) where there has been more than one variation, for each period beginning with the day on which a particular variation took effect and ending on the last day before the next variation took effect, the proportion of the basic number of hours in respect of which the

Part 2 Statutory Instruments

worker would be entitled to his annual salary, in accordance with the earlier variation, in a year of 365 days, which the number of days in the period bears to 365,

but in applying [regulation 21] for the purposes of paragraphs (5)(a) and (b)(i) and (6)(a) the definition of "the basic hours" in regulation 21(1) shall be used;

"calculation year" means—

(a) in the case of a worker employed by an employer when these Regulations come into force, for so long as he continues in that employment, the year beginning on the day these Regulations come into force, and each subsequent year beginning on the anniversary of that day;

(b) in the case of a worker whose annual salary is payable monthly and who becomes employed by an employer after these Regulations come into force, for so long as he continues in the same employment—

(i) where the worker becomes employed on the first day of a month, the year beginning with the first day of that month and each subsequent year beginning on the anniversary of that day,

(ii) where the worker becomes employed on any other day of a month, the period beginning with that day and ending with the day before the first anniversary of the first day of the next month, and each year beginning on that anniversary or on a subsequent anniversary of the first day of that month;

(c) in the case of a worker whose annual salary is payable weekly and who becomes employed by an employer after these Regulations come into force, for so long as he continues in the same employment, the year beginning with the first day of his employment and each subsequent year beginning on the anniversary of that day.

(3) In determining for the purposes of paragraph (1) whether the basic hours have been exceeded by a worker in any calculation year and, if so, when they were exceeded, the following hours in that year shall be taken into account—

(a) the number of the worker's working hours that fell within the basic hours,

(b) the number of hours for which the worker has been absent from work that fell within the basic hours,

(c) any hours worked by the worker outside the basic hours in respect of which the worker had no entitlement under his contract to any payment other than his annual salary,

(d) time required to be treated as working hours by regulation 16, to the extent that such time consisted of hours in respect of which the worker had no entitlement under his contract to his annual salary or to any other payment,

but excluding the number of hours, if any, during which the worker was engaged in taking industrial action.

(4) In that part of the pay reference period during which the basic hours are exceeded which is referred to in paragraph (5)(b) and in each subsequent pay reference period (if any) in the calculation year, a worker shall be treated as working for the sum of the following—

(a) the number of hours in the pay reference period that would have fallen to be taken into account under paragraph (3)(a) if the basic hours had not been exceeded, but excluding any time during those hours in which the worker was engaged in taking industrial action, and

(b) time required to be treated as working hours by regulation 16, to the extent that such time consists of hours in respect of which the worker is not entitled under his contract to his annual salary or to any other payment,

and the number of hours determined under this paragraph is referred to in paragraphs (5) and (6) and in regulation 23(3) as "the actual working hours".

(5) The salaried hours work worked by a worker in the pay reference period during which the basic hours are exceeded shall be the sum of the following—

(a) in relation to the part of the pay reference period before the day on which the basic hours are exceeded, the number of hours that result from applying regulation 21 to the part as if it were a pay reference period containing the number of days in the part; and

(b) in relation to the part of the pay reference period beginning with the day on which the basic hours are exceeded, the sum of—

(i) the number of hours that result from applying regulation 21(2) to the part as if it were a pay reference period containing the number of days in the part, but ignoring any reduction required by regulation 21(3), and

(ii) the actual working hours in that part.

(6) The salaried hours work worked by a worker in each subsequent pay reference period until the end of the calculation year shall be the sum of—

(a) the number of hours that result from applying regulation 21(2) in relation to the pay reference period, but ignoring any reduction required by regulation 21(3); and

(b) the actual working hours in the pay reference period.

NOTES

Para (2): words in square brackets in definition "basic hours" substituted by the National Minimum Wage Regulations 1999 (Amendment) Regulations 2000, SI 2000/1989, reg 8.

[2.422]

23 Determining the hours of salaried hours work in certain cases where the employment terminates

(1) This regulation applies, in the circumstances specified in paragraphs (2) and (3), to the final pay reference period of a worker whose employment terminates in the course of a calculation year and in cases where the employment of a worker is treated as being terminated by virtue of paragraph (4).

(2) Where the basic hours have not been exceeded at the end of the final pay reference period but, at the end of that pay reference period, the total of the hours to be taken into account under regulation 22(3) since the beginning of the calculation year (the "A" hours) exceeds the total of the number of hours determined in accordance with regulation 21 in relation to all of the pay reference periods (including the final pay reference period) since the beginning of the calculation year (the "B" hours), the salaried hours work worked by the worker in that pay reference period shall be regarded as including (in addition to the number of hours determined in relation to the pay reference period in accordance with regulation 21) the number of hours by which the "A" hours exceed the "B" hours.

(3) Where the basic hours have been exceeded at any time during the calculation year before the end of the final pay reference period, the salaried hours work worked by the worker in that pay reference period shall be regarded as including (in addition to the number of hours determined in relation to the pay reference period in accordance with regulation 22(5) or, as the case may be, (6)) the number of hours that result from applying regulation 21(2) in relation to the period beginning with the day immediately following the last day of the worker's final pay reference period and ending at the end of the calculation year ("the subsequent period"), as if—

- (a) the whole of the subsequent period was a single pay reference period (containing the number of days in it), and
- (b) the worker had continued to be employed under his contract to do salaried hours work for the whole of the subsequent period and had not been absent from work during it for any hours in respect of which regulation 21(3) requires a reduction.

(4) Where a worker's contract is varied so that any salaried hours work required to be done under the contract becomes work that is not salaried hours work, this regulation shall apply as if—

- (a) the employment of the worker had been terminated; and
- (b) the last day of the worker's final pay reference period had fallen on the day before the day on which the variation took effect.

[2.423]

[24 Output work

[(1) The output work of a worker in a pay reference period relating to a type of piece produced or a type of task performed shall be the number of hours spent by the worker during the pay reference period in producing that type of piece, or performing that type of task, except where the output work relating to that type of piece or task is rated output work.

(2) Output work is rated output work if—

- (a) it satisfies the conditions in paragraph (1) of regulation 25, and
- (b) it is work in respect of which the employer has given the worker a notice that satisfies the requirements of paragraph (2) of regulation 25.]

NOTES

Substituted, together with regs 25, 26, 26A for the original regs 24–26, by the National Minimum Wage Regulations 1999 (Amendment) Regulations 2004, SI 2004/1161, reg 2.

[2.424]

[25 Rated output work: conditions and notice

(1) The conditions referred to in regulation 24(2)(a) are—

- (a) that the output work relating to the type of piece in question ("the subject piece") or the type of task in question ("the subject task") is work in respect of which the worker's contract does not set any normal, minimum or maximum working hours;
- (b) that the employer does not in practice determine or control the hours worked by the worker in relation to the subject piece or the subject task; and
- (c) that the employer has determined the mean hourly output rate, as defined in paragraph (3) of regulation 26, for the subject piece or the subject task.

(2) A notice satisfies the requirements of this paragraph if—

(a) it was given in writing to the worker at any time before the beginning of the pay reference period (whether or not it was given before the beginning of, and had effect in relation to, any earlier pay reference periods); and

(b) it contains statements conveying the following information—

(i) that it is being given to inform the worker that, for the purpose of securing compliance with the national minimum wage legislation, he will be treated, in respect of, as appropriate, his production of the subject piece or his performance of the subject task during the pay reference period, as working for a certain period of time;

(ii) that, for the purpose of determining the period of time the worker will be treated as working, the employer has conducted a test or, where applicable, made an estimate of the average speed at which workers employed by the employer produce the subject piece or perform the subject task, as appropriate;

(iii) what the mean hourly output rate for the subject piece or the subject task is;

(iv) the rate to be paid to the worker for the production of a single subject piece or the performance of a single subject task, as appropriate; and

(v) the telephone number of the national minimum wage helpline, which number is identified as being the national minimum wage helpline number.]

NOTES

Substituted as noted to reg 24 at **[2.423]**.

[2.425]

[26 Rated output work: determination of hours worked

(1) Where output work is rated output work consisting of the production of subject pieces, the number of hours of output work spent by the worker in producing subject pieces during the pay reference period shall be treated as being [120 per cent of] the number of hours that a worker producing the subject pieces at the mean hourly output rate would have taken to produce the number of subject pieces produced by the worker in the pay reference period.

(2) Where output work is rated output work consisting of the performance of subject tasks, the number of hours of output work spent by the worker in performing subject tasks during the pay reference period shall be treated as being [120 per cent of] the number of hours that a worker performing at the mean hourly output rate would have taken to perform the number of subject tasks performed by the worker in the pay reference period.

(3) In this regulation and in regulations 25 and 26A, "mean hourly output rate" means the average number (including any fraction) of—

(a) subject pieces, or fraction of a subject piece, produced in an hour by workers of the employer producing the subject piece, or

(b) subject tasks, or fraction of a subject task, performed in an hour by workers of the employer performing the subject task,

as determined in accordance with regulation 26A.]

NOTES

Substituted as noted to reg 24 at **[2.423]**.

Paras (1), (2): words in square brackets inserted by the National Minimum Wage Regulations 1999 (Amendment) Regulations 2004, SI 2004/1161, reg 3.

[2.426]

[26A Rated output work: determining the mean hourly output rate

(1) To determine the mean hourly output rate for a subject piece or a subject task, the employer must—

(a) conduct a satisfactory test, in accordance with paragraph (2), of the speed at which every worker in one of the groups specified in that paragraph produces the subject piece or performs the subject task, and then divide the total number of subject pieces or subject tasks (or the fraction of a subject piece or subject task) that all the workers in the group tested have produced or performed per hour during the period of the test by the number of workers in the group tested, or

(b) make a satisfactory estimate, in accordance with paragraph (3), of the average speed, in terms of pieces or tasks per hour, at which the workers producing the subject piece or performing the subject task are likely to produce that piece or perform that task.

(2) The permitted groups for the purposes of the test mentioned in paragraph (1)(a) are—

(a) all of the workers of the employer who produce the subject piece or perform the subject task, or

(b) a sample of those workers of the employer that, in respect of the speed at which the workers in the sample work, is representative of all those workers, and a test is satisfactory only if all the workers in the group are tested in working circumstances similar to those in which the worker is or will be producing the subject piece or performing the subject task.

(3) Subject to paragraph (4), an estimate is satisfactory for the purposes of paragraph (1)(b) if the employer has—

(a) tested the average speed, in terms of pieces or tasks per hour, at which a sample of workers of the employer working in similar working circumstances to the worker produce a piece or perform a task that is reasonably similar to the subject piece or subject task and, in making the estimate, has fairly adjusted that average speed to take account of the increased or decreased time involved in production of the subject piece or performance of the subject task, or

(b) tested the average speed, in terms of pieces or tasks per hour, at which a sample of workers of the employer working in different working circumstances from the worker produce the subject piece or perform the subject task and, in making the estimate, has fairly adjusted that average speed to take account of the increased or decreased time involved in producing the subject piece or performing the subject task in the same working circumstances as the worker,

and if the sample of workers tested is, so far as reasonably practicable, representative, in respect of the speed at which they work, of the speed at which the workers who produce the subject piece or perform the subject task work.

(4) Where a satisfactory test has been conducted or a satisfactory estimate has been made, subsequent changes in the number or identity of the workers of the employer who produce the subject piece or perform the subject task do not require the employer to conduct a further satisfactory test or make a further satisfactory estimate unless the employer has reason to believe that the changes materially affect the mean hourly output rate.]

NOTES

Substituted as noted to reg 24 at **[2.423]**.

[2.427]

27 Unmeasured work

Unless the condition in regulation 28(1) is satisfied, the unmeasured work worked by a worker in a pay reference period shall be the total of the number of hours spent by him during the pay reference period in carrying out the contractual duties required of him under his contract to do such work.

[2.428]

28 "Daily average" agreements for unmeasured work

(1) The condition referred to in regulation 27 is that there is an agreement in writing between the worker and his employer, made at any time before the beginning of the pay reference period, determining the average daily number of hours the worker is likely to spend in carrying out the duties required of him under his contract to do unmeasured work on days when he is available to carry out those duties for the full amount of time contemplated by the contract.

(2) The condition in paragraph (1) is not satisfied if the employer cannot show that the average daily number of hours determined is a realistic average.

(3) Unless otherwise agreed the agreement referred to in paragraph (1) has effect solely for the purpose of determining the amount of unmeasured work the worker is to be treated as having worked for the purpose of these Regulations and does not vary the worker's contract.

[2.429]

29 Determining the hours of unmeasured work where there is a "daily average" agreement

(1) In paragraph (2) the term "ascertained hours" means the number of hours of unmeasured work that would have been worked by the worker in a pay reference period if he had worked—

(a) on each day worked by him in the pay reference period on which he was available to carry out his duties for at least the full amount of time contemplated by the contract, for the average daily number of hours specified in the agreement referred to in regulation 28(1); and

(b) on each day worked by him in the pay reference period on which he was available to carry out his duties for only part of that amount of time, for the proportion of that average number of hours which the part bears to the full amount of time contemplated by the contract.

(2) Where the condition in regulation 28(1) is satisfied the hours of unmeasured work worked by a worker in the pay reference period shall be treated as being the ascertained hours.

[2.430]

[29A Special provision where payment for work due only on submission of record

Where at the time of the making of a determination under regulation 14 any work done by a worker in the pay reference period in question is work in respect of which—

(a) the worker is not entitled to payment until a record of the work has been submitted to the employer, and

(b) no such record has been submitted to the employer,

the number of hours attributable to that work shall be excluded from the total number of hours referred to in paragraph (3) of regulation 14 in making the determination.]

NOTES

Inserted by the National Minimum Wage Regulations 1999 (Amendment) Regulations 2000, SI 2000/1989, regs 9, 10(1).

PART IV
REMUNERATION COUNTING TOWARDS THE NATIONAL MINIMUM WAGE

[2.431]

30 Payments to the worker to be taken into account

The total of remuneration in a pay reference period shall be calculated by adding together—

(a) all money payments paid by the employer to the worker in the pay reference period;

(b) any money payments paid by the employer to the worker in the following pay reference period in respect of the pay reference period (whether in respect of work or not);

(c) any money payment paid by the employer to the worker later than the end of the following pay reference period in respect of work done in the pay reference period, being work in respect of which—

(i) the worker is under an obligation to complete a record of the amount of work done,

(ii) the worker is not entitled to payment until the completed record has been submitted by him to the employer, and

(iii) the worker has failed to submit a record before the fourth working day before the end of that following pay reference period,

provided that the payment is paid in either the pay reference period in which the record is submitted to the employer or the pay reference period after that;

(d) where the employer has provided the worker with living accommodation during the pay reference period, but in respect of that provision is neither entitled to make any deduction from the wages of the worker nor to receive any payment from him, the amount determined in accordance with regulation 36.

[2.432]

31 Reductions from payments to be taken into account

(1) The total of reductions required to be subtracted from the total of remuneration shall be calculated by adding together—

(a) any money payments paid by the employer to the worker in the pay reference period that, by virtue of regulation 30(b) or (c), are required to be included in the total of remuneration for an earlier pay reference period;

(b) in the case of—

(i) work other than salaried hours work, any money payments paid by the employer to the worker in respect of periods when the worker was absent from work or engaged in taking industrial action;

(ii) salaried hours work, any money payment paid by the employer to the worker attributable to the hours (if any) by which the number of hours determined under regulation 21(2) is required to be reduced under regulation 21(3) (worker entitled to less than normal proportion of annual salary because of absence from work), whether under the direct application of those regulations or the application of them required by regulation 22(5)(a);

(c) any money payments paid by the employer to the worker in respect of—

(i) time work worked by him in the pay reference period involving particular duties that is paid for at a higher rate per hour than the lowest rate per hour payable to the worker in respect of time work worked by him involving those duties during the pay reference period, to the extent that the total of those payments exceeds the total of the money payments that would have been payable in respect of the work if that lowest rate per hour had been applicable to the work;

(ii) particular output work worked by him in the pay reference period that is paid for at a higher rate than the normal rate applicable to that work by reason of the work being done at a particular time or in particular circumstances, to the extent that the total of those payments exceeds the total of the money payments that would have been payable in respect of the work if the normal rate had been applicable to the work;

(d) any money payment paid by the employer to the worker by way of an allowance other than an allowance attributable to the performance of the worker in carrying out his work;

(e) any money payment paid by the employer to the worker representing amounts paid by customers by way of a service charge, tip, gratuity or cover charge . . . ;

(f) any money payment paid by the employer to the worker to meet a payment by the worker that would fall within regulation 34(1)(b) (payments by workers on account of expenditure in connection with their employment to persons other than their employer) but for the worker's payment being met or designed to be met by the employer;

(g) any deduction falling within regulation 32;

(h) any payment made by or due from the worker in the pay reference period falling within regulation 34;

(i) the amount of any deduction the employer is entitled to make, or payment he is entitled to receive from the worker, in respect of the provision of living accommodation by him to the worker in the pay reference period, as adjusted, where applicable, in accordance with regulation 37, to the extent that it exceeds the amount determined in accordance with regulation 36;

[(j) any money payments paid by the employer to the worker in the pay reference period in respect of travelling expenses that are allowed as deductions from earnings under section 338 of the Income Tax (Earnings and Pensions) Act 2003].

(2) To the extent that any payment or deduction is required to be subtracted from the total of remuneration by virtue of more than one sub-paragraph of paragraph (1), it shall be subtracted only once.

[(3) Any payment made to or deduction by a local housing authority or a registered social landlord in respect of the provision of living accommodation shall be exempted from the operation of sub-paragraph (i) of paragraph (1), except where the living accommodation is provided to the worker in connection with his employment with the local housing authority or registered social landlord.

(4) For the purposes of paragraph (3), "local housing authority" means—

(a) in England and Wales, a local housing authority as defined in Part 1 of the Housing Act 1985 and shall in addition include county councils;

(b) in Scotland, a local authority landlord as defined in section 11(3) of the Housing (Scotland) Act 2001;

(c) in Northern Ireland, the Northern Ireland Housing Executive.

(5) For the purposes of paragraph (3), "registered social landlord" means—

(a) in England and Wales . . . [—

(i) a private registered provider of social housing, and shall in addition include subsidiaries or associates as defined in Part 2 of the Housing and Regeneration Act 2008, or

(ii)] a social landlord registered under Part 1 of the Housing Act 1996 and shall in addition include subsidiaries or associates as defined in that Act;

(b) in Scotland, a body registered in the register maintained under [section 20(1) of the Housing (Scotland) Act 2010];

(c) in Northern Ireland, a housing association registered under Chapter II of Part II of the Housing (Northern Ireland) Order 1992.]

[(6) Any payment made to or deduction by a Higher Education Institution[, Further Education Institution or a 16 to 19 Academy] in respect of the provision of living accommodation shall be exempted from the operation of sub-paragraph (i) of paragraph (1) where the living accommodation is provided to a worker who is enrolled on a full-time higher education course or a full-time further education course at that Higher Education Institution or Further Education Institution [or on a full-time course provided by a 16 to 19 Academy].]

NOTES

Para (1): words omitted from sub-para (e) revoked by the National Minimum Wage Regulations 1999 (Amendment) Regulations 2009, SI 2009/1902, regs 5, 7, as from 1 October 2009 (except in relation to any pay reference period beginning before that date); sub-para (j) added by the National Minimum Wage (Amendment) (No 2) Regulations 2010, SI 2010/3001, regs 2, 3, as from 1 January 2011 (except in relation to any pay reference period beginning before that date).

Paras (3)–(5): added by the National Minimum Wage Regulations 1999 (Amendment) Regulations 2007, SI 2007/2318, regs 5, 9; the comma omitted from sub-para (5)(a) was revoked, and the words in square brackets in that paragraph were inserted, by the Housing and Regeneration Act 2008 (Consequential Provisions) (No 2) Order 2010, SI 2010/671, art 4, Sch 1, para 23, as from 1 April 2010; words in square brackets in sub-para (5)(b) substituted by the Housing (Scotland) Act 2010 (Consequential Provisions and Modifications) Order 2012, SI 2012/700, art 4, Schedule, Pt 2, para 11, as from 1 April 2012.

Para (6): added by the National Minimum Wage (Amendment) (No 2) Regulations 2011, SI 2011/2347, reg 4, as from 1 October 2011; words in first pair of square brackets substituted for original words "or Further Education Institution" and words in second pair of square brackets inserted, by the Alternative Provision Academies and 16 to 19 Academies (Consequential Amendments to Subordinate Legislation) (England) Order 2012, SI 2012/979, art 2, Schedule, para 5, as from 1 May 2012, in relation to England only.

[2.433]
32 Deductions to be subtracted under regulation 31(1)(g)

(1) The deductions required to be subtracted from the total of remuneration by regulation 31(1)(g) are—

(a) any deduction in respect of the worker's expenditure in connection with his employment;
(b) any deduction made by the employer for his own use and benefit (and accordingly not attributable to any amount paid or payable by the employer to any other person on behalf of the worker), except one specified in regulation 33.

(2) To the extent that any deduction is required to be subtracted by virtue of both sub-paragraphs of paragraph (1), it shall be subtracted only once.

[2.434]
33 Deductions not to be subtracted under regulation 31(1)(g)

The deductions excepted from the operation of regulation 32(1)(b) are—

(a) any deduction in respect of conduct of the worker, or any other event, in respect of which he (whether together with any other workers or not) is contractually liable;
(b) any deduction on account of an advance under an agreement for a loan or an advance of wages;
(c) any deduction made to recover an accidental overpayment of wages made to the worker;
(d) any deduction in respect of the purchase by the worker of any shares, other securities or share option, or of any share in a partnership[; or
(e) any deduction in respect of the provision of living accommodation which is exempted from regulation 31(1)(i) by regulation 31(3) [or (6)]].

NOTES

Para (e) and the word immediately preceding it inserted by the National Minimum Wage Regulations 1999 (Amendment) Regulations 2007, SI 2007/2318, reg 6; words in square brackets therein inserted by the National Minimum Wage (Amendment) Regulations 2012, SI 2012/2397, reg 2(1), (5), as from 1 October 2012.

[2.435]
34 Payments made by or due from a worker to be subtracted under regulation 31(1)(h)

(1) The payments made by or due from the worker required to be subtracted from the total of remuneration by regulation 31(1)(h) are—

(a) any payment due from the worker to the employer in the pay reference period on account of the worker's expenditure in connection with his employment;
(b) any payment paid in the pay reference period on account of the worker's expenditure in connection with his employment to the extent that the expenditure consists of a payment to a person other than the employer and is not met, or designed to be met, by a payment paid to him by the employer;
(c) any other payment due from the worker to the employer in the pay reference period that the employer retains or is entitled to retain for his own use and benefit except for a payment required to be left out of account by regulation 35.

(2) To the extent that any payment is required to be subtracted by virtue of more than one sub-paragraph of paragraph (1), it shall be subtracted only once.

[2.436]
35 Payments not to be subtracted under regulation 31(1)(h)

The payments excepted from the operation of regulation 34(1)(c) are—

(a) any payment in respect of conduct of the worker, or any other event, in respect of which he (whether together with any other workers or not) is contractually liable;
(b) any payment on account of an advance under an agreement for a loan or an advance of wages;
(c) any payment made to refund the employer in respect of an accidental overpayment of wages made by the employer to the worker;
(d) any payment in respect of the purchase by the worker of any shares, other securities or share option, or of any share in a partnership;
(e) any payment in respect of the purchase by the worker of any goods or services from the employer, unless the purchase is made in order to comply with a requirement in the worker's contract or any other requirement imposed on him by the employer in connection with his employment[; or
(f) any payment in respect of the provision of living accommodation which is exempted from regulation 31(1)(i) by regulation 31(3) [or (6)]].

NOTES

Para (f) and the word immediately preceding it inserted by the National Minimum Wage Regulations 1999 (Amendment) Regulations 2007, SI 2007/2318, reg 7; words in square brackets therein inserted by the National Minimum Wage (Amendment) Regulations 2012, SI 2012/2397, reg 2(1), (5), as from 1 October 2012.

[2.437]

36 Amount permitted to be taken into account where living accommodation is provided

[(1) The amount referred to in regulations 30(d) and 31(1)(i) is the amount resulting from multiplying the number of days in the pay reference period for which accommodation was provided by [£4.82].]

(2) For the purposes of paragraph (1), living accommodation is provided for a day only if it is provided for the whole of a day from midnight to midnight.

NOTES

Para (1): substituted by the National Minimum Wage Regulations 1999 (Amendment) Regulations 2003, SI 2003/1923, reg 4.

Sum in square brackets in para (1) substituted by the National Minimum Wage (Amendment) Regulations 2012, SI 2012/2397, regs 2(1), (6), 4, as from 1 October 2012 (except in relation to any pay reference period beginning before that date). The previous daily rate, as from 1 October 2011, was £4.73 (see SI 2011/2345). Prior to that date, the sums were £4.61 (as from 1 October 2010: see SI 2010/1901); £4.51 (as from 1 October 2009: see SI 2009/1902); £4.46 (as from 1 October 2008: see SI 2008/1894); £4.30 (as from 1 October 2007: see SI 2007/2318); £4.15 (as from 1 October 2006: see SI 2006/2001); £3.90 (as from 1 October 2005: see SI 2005/2019); £3.75 (as from 1 October 2004: see SI 2004/1930); £3.50 (from 1 October 2003: see SI 2003/1923); £3.25 (from 1 October 2002: see SI 2001/2763); £2.85 (from 1 April 1999).

The Government has announced that the amount specified in this regulation is to be increased to £4.91 as from 1 October 2013, but the Regulations to give effect to this had not been made, as at 6 April 2013.

[2.438]

[36A Determining the applicable living accommodation amount

Any amounts required to be determined for the purpose of regulations 30(d) or 31(1)(i) of these regulations in respect of any pay reference period shall be determined in accordance with the regulations as they are in force on the first day of the pay reference period.]

NOTES

Inserted by the National Minimum Wage Regulations 1999 (Amendment) Regulations 2003, SI 2003/1923, reg 5.

[2.439]

37 Adjusted deductions and payments in respect of living accommodation

(1) Where an employer is entitled to make deductions or receive payments in respect of the provision of living accommodation to a worker and in a pay reference period—

(a) a worker is absent from work for a day or more when, but for his absence, he would be expected to perform time work (for example because he is sick or taking a holiday),

(b) during that period of absence he is paid, for the hours of time work for which he is absent, an amount not less than the amount to which he would have been entitled under these Regulations, but for his absence,

(c) the hours of time work worked by the worker in the pay reference period are, by reason of his absence, less than they would be in a pay reference period containing the same number of working days in which the worker worked for the normal number of working hours (and for no additional hours), and

(d) the amount of the deduction the employer is entitled to make or payment he is entitled to receive in respect of the provision of living accommodation to the worker during the pay reference period does not increase by reason of the worker's absence from work,

the provisions of paragraph (2) shall apply.

(2) For the purposes of regulation 31(1)(i), the amount of the deduction the employer is entitled to make or payment he is entitled to receive in respect of the provision of living accommodation shall be adjusted by multiplying that amount by the number of hours of time work actually worked by the worker in the pay reference period (as determined in accordance with regulation 20) and dividing the figure so obtained by the total number of hours of time work the worker would have worked in the pay reference period (including the hours of time work actually worked) but for his absence.

PART V
RECORDS

[2.440]

38 Records to be kept by an employer

(1) The employer of a worker who qualifies for the national minimum wage shall keep in respect of that worker records sufficient to establish that he is remunerating the worker at a rate at least equal to the national minimum wage.

(2) The records required to be kept under paragraph (1) shall be in a form which enables the information kept about a worker in respect of a pay reference period to be produced in a single document.

(3) The employer of a worker who qualifies for the national minimum wage who has entered into any agreement with the worker referred to in [regulation] 28(1) (unmeasured work), shall keep a copy of that agreement.

[(3A) The employer of a worker who qualifies for the national minimum wage who has given the worker a notice in accordance with regulation 24(2)(b), shall keep a copy of that notice and a copy of such data as is necessary to show how he has determined the rates referred to in paragraphs (iii) and (iv) of regulation 25(2)(b).]

((4) The employer of a worker who qualifies for an agricultural minimum rate of wages shall, in addition to the records he is required to keep under [paragraphs (1), (3), and (3A),] keep in respect of that worker records sufficient to establish that he is remunerating the worker at a rate at least equal to any agricultural minimum rate of wages applicable to the worker.

(5) In paragraph (4), "agricultural minimum rate of wages" means—

(a) in England and Wales, a minimum rate of wages fixed under section 3(1)(a) of the Agricultural Wages Act 1948;

(b) in Scotland, a minimum rate of wages fixed under section 3(1)(a) of the Agricultural Wages (Scotland) Act 1949;

(c) in Northern Ireland, a minimum rate of wages fixed under Article 4(1) of the Agricultural Wages (Regulation) (Northern Ireland) Order 1977.

(6) Where under paragraph (4) an employer is required to keep records in respect of a worker in addition to those he is required to keep under paragraph (1), those additional records shall be in a form which enables the information kept under paragraph (4) about a worker in respect of a pay reference period to be produced in a single document.

(7) The records required to be kept by this regulation shall be kept by the employer for a period of three years beginning with the day upon which the pay reference period immediately following that to which they relate ends.

(8) The records required to be kept by this regulation may be kept by means of a computer.

NOTES

Para (3): word in square brackets substituted by National Minimum Wage Regulations 1999 (Amendment) Regulations 2010, SI 2010/1901, reg 7, as from 1 October 2010.

Para (3A): inserted by SI 2004/1930, reg 6(b).

Para (4): words in square brackets substituted by SI 2004/1930, reg 6(c).

Para (5): sub-para (a) revoked by the Enterprise and Regulatory Reform Act 2013, s 72(4), Sch 20, as from a day to be appointed.

POLICE (HEALTH AND SAFETY) REGULATIONS 1999

(SI 1999/860)

NOTES

Made: 17 March 1999.

Authority: Health and Safety at Work etc Act 1974, ss 2(4), 15(1), (2), (8), 51A(4), 82(3)(a), Sch 3, paras 1(1)(a), (2), 11.

Commencement: 14 April 1999.

[2.441]

1 Citation and commencement

These Regulations may be cited as the Police (Health and Safety) Regulations 1999 and shall come into force on 14th April 1999.

[2.442]

2 Amendment to the meaning of "employee" and "at work" in regulations made under Part I of the Health and Safety at Work etc Act 1974

For the purposes of regulations made under Part I of the 1974 Act before the coming into force of the Police (Health and Safety) Act 1997—

(a) a person who, otherwise than under a contract of employment, holds the office of constable or an appointment as police cadet shall be treated as an employee of the relevant officer referred to in section 51A of the 1974 Act; and

(b) a person holding the office of constable shall be treated as at work throughout the time when he is on duty but not otherwise,

and any reference to an "employee" and "at work" in those regulations shall have effect accordingly.

3–5 *(Reg 3 amended the Safety Representatives and Safety Committees Regulations 1977, SI 1977/500, reg 2(1), and inserted reg 2A (revoked) and is now spent; regs 4, 5 amend the Personal*

Protective Equipment at Work Regulations 1992, SI 1992/2966, and the Provision and Use of Work Equipment Regulations 1998, SI 1998/2306.)

SCHEDULE

(The Schedule set out the Safety Representatives and Safety Committees Regulations 1977, SI 1977/500, Sch 1 (revoked) and is now spent.)

PUBLIC INTEREST DISCLOSURE (PRESCRIBED PERSONS) ORDER 1999

(SI 1999/1549)

NOTES

Made: 5 June 1999.

Authority: Employment Rights Act 1996, s 43F.

Commencement: 2 July 1999.

The principal provision of this Order, the Schedule, was substituted in its entirety by the Public Interest Disclosure (Prescribed Persons) (Amendment) Order 2003, SI 2003/1993, art 2. It is printed as so substituted (and subsequently amended).

See Harvey CIII.

[2.443]

1 Citation and commencement

This Order may be cited as the Public Interest Disclosure (Prescribed Persons) Order 1999 and shall come into force on 2nd July 1999.

[2.444]

2 Prescribed Persons

(1) The persons and descriptions of persons prescribed for the purposes of section 43F of the Employment Rights Act 1996 are the persons and descriptions of persons specified in the first column of the Schedule.

(2) The descriptions of matters in respect of which each person, or persons of each description, specified in the first column of the Schedule is or are prescribed are the descriptions of matters respectively specified opposite them in the second column of the Schedule.

[SCHEDULE

Article 2

[2.445]

First Column	*Second Column*
Persons and descriptions of people	*Descriptions of matters*
Accounts Commission for Scotland and auditors appointed by the Commission to audit the accounts of local government bodies.	The proper conduct of public business, value for money, fraud and corruption in local government bodies.
Audit Commission for England and Wales and auditors appointed by the Commission to audit the accounts of local government, and health service, bodies.	The proper conduct of public business, value for money, fraud and corruption in local government, and health service, bodies.
Certification Officer.	Fraud, and other irregularities, relating to the financial affairs of trade unions and employers' associations.
Charity Commissioners for England and Wales.	The proper administration of charities and of funds given or held for charitable purposes.
The Scottish Ministers.	The proper administration of charities and of funds given or held for charitable purposes.
Chief Executive of the Criminal Cases Review Commission.	Actual or potential miscarriages of justice.
Chief Executive of the Scottish Criminal Cases Review Commission.	Actual or potential miscarriages of justice.
Civil Aviation Authority.	Compliance with the requirements of civil aviation legislation, including aviation safety.

Part 2 Statutory Instruments

First Column	***Second Column***
[Office of Communications.	Matters relating to— (a) the provision of electronic communications networks and services and the use of the electro-magnetic spectrum; (b) broadcasting and the provision of television and radio services; (c) media ownership and control; and (d) competition in communications markets.]
. . .	. . .
Commissioners of Customs and Excise.	Value added tax, insurance premium tax, excise duties and landfill tax. The import and export of prohibited or restricted goods.
Commissioners of the Inland Revenue.	Income tax, corporation tax, capital gains tax, petroleum revenue tax, inheritance tax, stamp duties, national insurance contributions, statutory maternity pay, statutory sick pay, tax credits, child benefits, collection of student loans and the enforcement of the national minimum wage.
[Comptroller and Auditor General.]	The proper conduct of public business, value for money, fraud and corruption in relation to the provision of centrally-funded public services.
Auditor General for Wales.	The proper conduct of public business, value for money, fraud and corruption in relation to the provision of public services.
Auditor General for Scotland and persons appointed by or on his behalf under the Public Finance and Accountability (Scotland) Act 2000 to act as auditors or examiners for the purposes of sections 21 to 24 of that Act.	The proper conduct of public business, value for money, fraud and corruption in relation to the provision of public services.
Audit Scotland.	The proper conduct of public business, value for money, fraud and corruption in public bodies.
[Gas and Electricity Markets Authority.	The generation, transmission, distribution and supply of electricity, participation in the operation of an electricity interconnector (as defined in section 4(3E) of the Electricity Act 1989) [or providing a smart meter communication service (as defined in section 4(3G) of that Act)] and activities ancillary to these matters. The transportation, shipping and supply of gas through pipes, participation in the operation of a gas interconnector (as defined in section 5(8) of the Gas Act 1986) [or providing a smart meter communication service (as defined in section 5(11) of that Act)] and activities ancillary to these matters.]
. . .	. . .
. . .	. . .
. . .	. . .
[Water Services Regulation Authority].	The supply of water and the provision of sewerage services.
[Convener of the Water Customer Consultation Panels and any member of those Panels.	The supply of water and the provision of sewerage services.
Water Industry Commission for Scotland.	The supply of water and the provision of sewerage services.]
Water Industry Commissioner for Scotland.	The supply of water and the provision of sewerage services.
Director of the Serious Fraud Office.	Serious or complex fraud.

First Column	*Second Column*
Lord Advocate, Scotland.	Serious or complex fraud.
Environment Agency.	Acts or omissions which have an actual or potential effect on the environment or the management or regulation of the environment, including those relating to pollution, abstraction of water, flooding, the flow in rivers, inland fisheries and migratory salmon or trout.
Scottish Environment Protection Agency.	Acts or omissions which have an actual or potential effect on the environment or the management or regulation of the environment, including those relating to flood warning systems and pollution.
Food Standards Agency.	Matters which may affect the health of any member of the public in relation to the consumption of food and other matters concerning the protection of the interests of consumers in relation to food.
[Financial Conduct Authority.	The listing of securities on a stock exchange; prospectuses on offers of transferable securities to the public; the carrying on of investment business or of insurance business; the operation of banks and building societies, deposit-taking businesses and wholesale money market regimes; the operation of friendly societies, benevolent societies, working men's clubs, specially authorised societies, and industrial and provident societies; the functioning of financial markets and investment exchanges; money laundering, financial crime, and other serious financial misconduct, in connection with activities regulated by the Financial Conduct Authority.
Prudential Regulation Authority.	The carrying on of investment business or of insurance business; the operation of banks and building societies, deposit-taking businesses and wholesale money market regimes; the operation of friendly societies, benevolent societies, working men's clubs, specially authorised societies, and industrial and provident societies.
The Bank of England.	The functioning of clearing houses.]
[The Financial Reporting Council Limited and its operating bodies the Professional Oversight Board, the Financial Reporting Review Panel and the Accountancy and Actuarial Discipline Board	Matters relating to— (a) the independent oversight of the regulation of the accountancy, auditing and actuarial professions; (b) the independent supervision of Auditors General (as defined in section 1226 of the Companies Act 2006); (c) the monitoring of major audits (as defined in section 525 of that Act for the purposes of that section or section 522, or paragraph 13(10) of Schedule 10 to that Act for the purposes of that paragraph); (d) the registration of third country auditors (as defined in section 1261 of that Act); (e) compliance with the requirements of legislation relating to accounting and reporting; and (f) the investigation of the conduct of auditors, accountants and actuaries and the holding of disciplinary hearings in public interest cases (as defined in paragraph 24 of Schedule 10 to that Act).]
. . .	. . .
Care Council for Wales.	Matters relating to the registration of social care workers under the Care Standards Act 2000.
Scottish Social Services Council.	Matters relating to the registration of the social services workforce by the Scottish Social Services Council.
[Children's Commissioner	Matters relating to the views and interests of children.

First Column	*Second Column*
Commissioner for Children and Young People in Scotland	Matters relating to promoting and safeguarding the rights of children and young people.]
Children's Commissioner for Wales.	Matters relating to the rights and welfare of children.
Health and Safety Executive.	Matters which may affect the health or safety of any individual at work; matters, which may affect the health and safety of any member of the public, arising out of or in connection with the activities of persons at work.
[Regulator of Social Housing.]	The registration and operation of [private registered providers of social housing], including their administration of public and private funds and management of their housing stock.
Local authorities which are responsible for the enforcement of health and safety legislation.	Matters which may affect the health or safety of any individual at work; matters, which may affect the health and safety of any member of the public, arising out of or in connection with the activities of persons at work.
[Independent Police Complaints Commission.	Matters relating to the conduct of a person serving with the police (as defined in section 12(7) of the Police Reform Act 2002) or of any other person in relation to whose conduct the Independent Police Complaints Commission exercises functions in or under any legislation.]
Information Commissioner.	Compliance with the requirements of legislation relating to data protection and to freedom of information.
Scottish Information Commissioner.	Compliance with the requirements of legislation relating to freedom of information.
[. . .	. . .]
[Care Quality Commission.	Matters relating to— (a) the registration and provision of a regulated activity as defined in section 8 of the Health and Social Care Act 2008 and the carrying out of any reviews and investigations under Part 1 of that Act; or (b) any activities not covered by (a) in relation to which the Care Quality Commission exercises its functions.]
[The [Monitor]	Matters relating to— (a) the regulation and performance of NHS foundation trusts; and (b) any activities not covered by (a) in relation to which the [Monitor] exercises its functions . . .]
[National Assembly for Wales.	Matters relating to the provision of Part II services as defined in section 8 of the Care Standards Act 2000 and the Children Act 1989. Matters relating to the inspection and performance assessment of Welsh local authority social services as defined in section 148 of the Health and Social Care (Community Heath and Standards) Act 2003. Matters relating to the review of, and investigation into, the provision of health care by and for Welsh NHS bodies as defined under the Health and Social Care (Community Health and Standards) Act 2003. The registration and operation of registered social landlords, including their administration of public and private funds and management of their housing stock.]
[Social Care and Social Work Improvement Scotland.	Matters relating to the provision of care services, as defined in the Public Services Reform (Scotland) Act 2010.

First Column	*Second Column*
Healthcare Improvement Scotland.	Matters relating to the provision of independent health care services, as defined in the National Health Service (Scotland) Act 1978.]
[Pensions Regulator].	Matters relating to occupational pension schemes and other private pension arrangements [including matters relating to the Regulator's objective of maximising compliance with the duties under Chapter 1 of Part 1 (and the safeguards in sections 50 and 54) of the Pensions Act 2008].
Office of Fair Trading.	Matters concerning the sale of goods or the supply of services, which adversely affect the interests of consumers.
	Competition affecting markets in the United Kingdom.
[Office of Qualifications and Examinations Regulation	Matters in relation to which the Office of Qualifications and Examinations Regulation exercises functions under the Apprenticeships, Skills, Children and Learning Act 2009]
[Office of Rail Regulation.]	The provision and supply of railway services.
Standards Board for England.	Breaches by a member or co-opted member of a relevant authority (as defined in section 49(6) of the Local Government Act 2000) of that authority's code of conduct.
Local Commissioner in Wales.	Breaches by a member or co-opted member of a relevant authority (as defined in section 49(6) of the Local Government Act 2000) of that authority's code of conduct.
Standards Commission for Scotland and the Chief Investigating Officer.	Breaches by a councillor or a member of a devolved public body (as defined in section 28 of the Ethical Standards in Public Life etc (Scotland) Act 2000) of the code of conduct applicable to that councillor or member under that Act.
Treasury.	The carrying on of insurance business.
[Secretary of State for Business, Innovation and Skills].	Fraud, and other misconduct, in relation to companies, investment business, insurance business, or multi-level marketing schemes (and similar trading schemes); insider dealing.
	Consumer safety.
Secretary of State for Transport.	Compliance with merchant shipping law, including maritime safety.
Local authorities which are responsible for the enforcement of consumer protection legislation.	Compliance with the requirements of consumer protection legislation.
Local authorities which are responsible for the enforcement of food standards.	Compliance with the requirements of food safety legislation.
A person ("person A") carrying out functions, by virtue of legislation, relating to relevant failures falling within one or more matters within a description of matters in respect of which another person ("person B") is prescribed by this Order, where person B was previously responsible for carrying out the same or substantially similar functions and has ceased to be so responsible.	Matters falling within the description of matters in respect of which person B is prescribed by this Order, to the extent that those matters relate to functions currently carried out by person A.]

NOTES

Substituted by the Public Interest Disclosure (Prescribed Persons) (Amendment) Order 2003, SI 2003/1993, art 2, Schedule.

Entry relating to "The competent authority under Part IV of the Financial Services and Markets Act 2000" (omitted) revoked, and entries "Financial Conduct Authority", "Prudential Regulation Authority" and "The Bank of England" substituted for original entry "Financial Services Authority", by the Financial Services Act 2012 (Consequential Amendments and Transitional Provisions) Order 2013, SI 2013/472, art 3, Sch 2, para 25, as from 1 April 2013.

Entry relating to the "Office of Communications" inserted by the Public Interest Disclosure (Prescribed Persons) (Amendment) Order 2005, SI 2005/2464, arts 2, 3(1), Schedule.

Entry relating to the "Comptroller and Auditor General" substituted (for original entry "Comptroller and Auditor General of the National Audit Office") by the Budget Responsibility and National Audit Act 2011 (Consequential Amendments) Order 2012, SI 2012/725, art 2(4), as from 1 April 2012.

Entries relating to the "Director General of Electricity Supply", "Director General of Gas Supply", and "Director General of Telecommunications" (all omitted) revoked by SI 2005/2464, arts 2, 3(2), (4).

Entry relating to the "Gas and Electricity Markets Authority" inserted by SI 2005/2464, arts 2, 3(3), Schedule; words in square brackets therein inserted by the Electricity and Gas (Smart Meters Licensable Activity) Order 2012, SI 2012/2400, art 34, as from 19 September 2012.

Entry "Water Services Regulation Authority" in Column 1 substituted (for the original entry "Director General of Water Services") by the Water Act 2003 (Consequential and Supplementary Provisions) Regulations 2005, SI 2005/2035, reg 17.

Entry relating to the "Convener of the Water Customer Consultation Panels" (omitted) originally inserted by the Water Services etc (Scotland) Act 2005 (Consequential Provisions and Modifications) Order 2005, SI 2005/3172, art 11, Schedule, Pt 2, para 5, and revoked by the Public Services Reform (Scotland) Act 2010 (Consequential Modifications of Enactments) Order 2011, SI 2011/2581, art 2, Sch 3, Pt 2, para 3, as from 28 October 2011.

Entry relating to the "Water Industry Commission for Scotland" inserted by SI 2005/3172, art 11, Schedule, Pt 2, para 5.

Entry relating to "The Financial Reporting Council Limited" inserted by the Public Interest Disclosure (Prescribed Persons) (Amendment) Order 2009, SI 2009/2457, arts 2, 4, Schedule, as from 1 October 2009.

Entry relating to the "General Social Care Council" (omitted) revoked by the Health and Social Care Act 2012 (Consequential Provision—Social Workers) Order 2012, SI 2012/1479, art 11, Schedule, Pt 2, para 71, as from 1 August 2012.

Entries relating to the "Children's Commissioner" and the "Commissioner for Children and Young People in Scotland" inserted by the Public Interest Disclosure (Prescribed Persons) (Amendment) Order 2008, SI 2008/531, arts 2, 3, Schedule, as from 6 April 2008.

In entry relating to the "Regulator of Social Housing" (formerly "Housing Corporation") words in square brackets in Column 1 substituted by the Housing and Regeneration Act 2008 (Consequential Provisions) (No 2) Order 2008, SI 2008/2831, art 4, Sch 2, para 2, as from 1 December 2008; words in square brackets in Column 2 substituted by the Housing and Regeneration Act 2008 (Commencement No 7 and Transitional and Saving Provisions) Order 2010, SI 2010/671, art 4, Sch 1, para 25, as from 1 April 2010.

Entry relating to the "Independent Police Complaints Commission" inserted by the Public Interest Disclosure (Prescribed Persons) (Amendment) Order 2004, SI 2004/3265, art 2, Schedule.

Entry relating to the "Commission for Healthcare Audit and Inspection" (as substituted by SI 2005/2464, arts 2, 3(5), Schedule) (omitted) revoked by the Health and Social Care Act 2008 (Commencement No 9, Consequential Amendments and Transitory, Transitional and Saving Provisions) Order 2009, SI 2009/462, art 12, Sch 5, para 5, as from 1 April 2009.

Entry relating to the "Care Quality Commission" substituted (for entry relating to the "Commission for Social Care Inspection" as substituted by SI 2005/2464, arts 2, 3(5), Schedule) by SI 2009/462, art 12, Sch 5, para 5, as from 1 April 2009.

Entry relating to "The Monitor" (entry relating to "The Independent Regulator of NHS Foundation Trusts" as enacted) inserted by SI 2009/2457, arts 2, 3, Schedule, as from 1 October 2009; words in square brackets substituted and words omitted revoked by the NHS Commissioning Board Authority (Abolition and Transfer of Staff, Property and Liabilities) and the Health and Social Care Act 2012 (Consequential Amendments) Order 2012, SI 2012/1641, art 10, Sch 4, para 5, as from 1 October 2012.

Entry relating to the "National Assembly for Wales" substituted by SI 2005/2464, arts 2, 3(6), Schedule.

Entries relating to the "Social Care and Social Work Improvement Scotland" and the "Healthcare Improvement Scotland" substituted (for original entry relating to the "Scottish Commission for the Regulation of Care") by SI 2011/2581, art 2, Sch 2, Pt 2, para 26, as from 28 October 2011.

Entry "Pensions Regulator" in Column 1 substituted (for the original entry "Occupational Pensions Regulatory Authority") by SI 2005/2464, arts 2, 3(7); words in square brackets in Column 2 inserted by the Public Interest Disclosure (Prescribed Persons) (Amendment) Order 2010, SI 2010/7, art 2, as from 1 October 2012.

Entry relating to the "Office of Qualifications and Examinations Regulation" inserted by Public Interest Disclosure (Prescribed Persons) (Amendment) Order 2012, SI 2012/462, art 2, Schedule, as from 22 March 2012.

Entry "Office of Rail Regulation" in Column 1 substituted (for the original entry "Rail Regulator") by the Railways and Transport Safety Act 2003, s 16(4), (5), Sch 3, para 4.

Words "Secretary of State for Business, Innovation and Skills" substituted for words "Secretary of State for Business, Enterprise and Regulatory Reform" by the Secretary of State for Business, Innovation and Skills Order 2009, SI 2009/2748, art 8, Schedule, Pt 2, para 20, as from 13 November 2009.

Commissioners of Inland Revenue; Commissioners of Customs and Excise: references to the Commissioners of Inland Revenue and the Commissioners of Customs and Excise are now to be taken as a reference to the Commissioners for Her Majesty's Revenue and Customs; see the Commissioners for Revenue and Customs Act 2005, s 50(1), (7).

Charity Commissioners: the office of Charity Commissioner for England and Wales is abolished and replaced by the Charity Commission for England and Wales (as to which, see the Charities Act 2011, Pt 2).

REDUNDANCY PAYMENTS (CONTINUITY OF EMPLOYMENT IN LOCAL GOVERNMENT, ETC) (MODIFICATION) ORDER 1999

(SI 1999/2277)

NOTES

Made: 11 August 1999.
Authority: Employment Rights Act 1996, ss 209(1)(b), 236.
Commencement: 1 September 1999.

ARRANGEMENT OF ARTICLES

SCHEDULES

[2.446]
1 Citation, commencement and interpretation

(1) This Order may be cited as the Redundancy Payments (Continuity of Employment in Local Government, etc) (Modification) Order 1999 and shall come into force on 1st September 1999.

(2) In this Order—
- (a) "the 1983 Order" means the Redundancy Payments (Local Government) (Modification) Order 1983;
- (b) "the 1972 Act" means the Local Government Act 1972;
- (c) "the 1978 Act" means the Employment Protection (Consolidation) Act 1978;
- (d) "the 1980 Act" means the Education (Scotland) Act 1980;
- (e) "the 1985 Act" means the Local Government Act 1985;
- (f) "the 1988 Act" means the Education Reform Act 1988;
- (g) "the 1992 Act" means the Further and Higher Education Act 1992;
- (h) "the 1994 Act" means the Local Government etc (Scotland) Act 1994;
- (i) "the 1996 Act" means the Employment Rights Act 1996;
- (j) "the 1998 Act" means the School Standards and Framework Act 1998;
- (k) "the Education Act" means the Education Act 1996.

(3) Subject to paragraph (4) below, in this Order "relevant event" in relation to a person means any event occurring on or after the day on which this Order comes into force on the happening of which that person may become entitled to a redundancy payment in accordance with the 1996 Act.

(4) Where an event has occurred on or after 21st June 1998 but before the day on which this Order comes into force, on the happening of which a person employed immediately before that event by the English Sports Council may have become entitled to a redundancy payment in accordance with the 1996 Act, "relevant event" in this Order includes that event in relation to that person.

[2.447]
2 Application of this Order

(1) This Order applies to any person who immediately before the occurrence of a relevant event is employed by an employer specified in Schedule 1 to this Order.

(2) Where a person commenced employment with a Further Education Funding Council established by section 1 of the 1992 Act before 1st April 1996 and left that employment either—
- (a) before that date, or
- (b) by reason of a relevant event after the date on which this Order comes into force,

this Order applies to that person as if that Council were specified in Schedule 1 to this Order.

Part 2 Statutory Instruments

[2.448]

3 Modification of certain redundancy payments provisions

In relation to any person to whom this Order applies, the provisions of the 1996 Act mentioned in Part I of Schedule 2 to this Order shall, for the purposes of determining that person's entitlement to a redundancy payment under the 1996 Act and the amount of such payment, have effect subject to the modifications specified in that Part.

[2.449]

4 Revocation

The Orders specified in Schedule 3 to this Order are revoked.

[2.450]

5 Transitional, supplementary and incidental provisions

(1) In relation to a person to whom this Order applies—

(a) any reference to the 1996 Act in any enactment shall have effect as a reference to that Act as modified by this Order; and

(b) any document which refers, whether specifically or by means of a general description, to the 1996 Act shall, except so far as the context otherwise requires, be construed as referring to that Act as modified by this Order.

(2) Where a period of employment of a person to whom this Order applies falls to be calculated in accordance with the provisions of the 1996 Act as modified by this Order, the provisions of this Order shall have effect in relation to that calculation whether the period in question falls wholly or partly before or wholly after this Order comes into force.

(3) Notwithstanding the revocation by article 4 above of the Orders specified in Schedule 3 to this Order, in relation to determining any person's entitlement to a redundancy payment following an event which occurred before the date on which this Order comes into force (or, in the case of a person such as is referred to in paragraph (4) of article 1, before the date referred to in that paragraph), and which would have been a relevant event if it had occurred on or after that date, the 1983 Order shall continue to have effect as it had effect on the date of that event.

SCHEDULES

SCHEDULE 1
EMPLOYMENT TO WHICH THIS ORDER APPLIES: EMPLOYERS IMMEDIATELY BEFORE THE RELEVANT EVENT

Article 2

Section 1—Local Government

[2.451]

1. In relation to England, a county council, a district council, a London borough council, the Common Council of the City of London, the Council of the Isles of Scilly; in relation to Wales, a county council or a county borough council, established under section 20 of the 1972 Act.

2. A council constituted under section 2 of the 1994 Act.

3. In relation to England, a parish council, a common parish council, a parish meeting; in relation to Wales, a community council, a common community council.

4. Any authority established by an order under section 10 of the 1985 Act.

5. A joint board or joint body constituted by or under any enactment for the purposes of exercising the functions of two or more bodies described in any of paragraphs 1 to 4 above.

6. Any other authority or body, not specified in any of paragraphs 1 to 4 above, established by or under any enactment for the purpose of exercising the functions of, or advising, one or more of the bodies specified in paragraphs 1 to 4 above.

[6A. The Greater London Authority.

6B. Transport for London.]

[6C. A functional body as defined in section 424 of the Greater London Authority Act 1999 but excluding Transport for London.

6D. The London Transport Users' Committee established under section 247 of the 1999 Act.

6E. The Cultural Strategy Group for London established under section 375 of that Act.]

7. Any committee (including a joint committee) established by or under any enactment for the purpose of exercising the functions of, or advising, one or more of the bodies specified in any of paragraphs 1 to 6 above.

8. Any two or more bodies described in any of paragraphs 1 to 7 above acting jointly or as a combined authority.

9. Any association which is representative of any two or more authorities described in any of paragraphs 1 to 4 above.

10. Any committee established by one or more of the associations described in paragraph 9 above for the purpose of exercising the functions of, or advising, one or more of such associations.

11. An association which is representative of one or more of the associations described in paragraph 9 above and of another body or other bodies, and included in whose objects is the assembling and dissemination of information and advising with regard to conditions of service in local government service and generally.

12. An organisation which is representative of an association or associations described in paragraph 9 above and employees' organisations and among whose objects is the negotiation of pay and conditions of service in local government service.

13. A National Park authority established under section 63 of the Environment Act 1995.

[**13A.** A National Park Authority established under sections 6 to 8 of the National Parks (Scotland) Act 2000.]

14. A residuary body established by section 57(1)(b) of the 1985 Act.

15. The Residuary Body for Wales (Corff Gweddilliol Cymru).

[**16.** Audit Scotland.]

17. The Commission for Local Administration in England.

18. The Commission for Local Administration in Wales.

19. The Commission for Local Administration in Scotland.

20. The Local Government Management Board.

21. Employers Organisation for Local Government.

22. Improvement and Development Agency for Local Government.

[**23.** Improvement Service Company.]

Section 2—Planning and development

1. One North East.

2. Yorkshire Forward.

3. North West Development Agency (NWDA).

4. Advantage West Midlands.

[**4A.** Dewsbury Partnership Limited.]

5. East Midlands Development Agency (EMDA).

6. East of England Development Agency (EEDA).

7. South East of England Development Agency (SEEDA).

[**7A.** SEERA Limited.]

8. South West of England Development Agency (SWERDA).

9. A development corporation within the meaning of the New Towns Act 1981.

[**9A.** A Mayoral development corporation within the meaning of section 198 of the Localism Act 2011.]

10. An Urban Development Corporation established under section 135 of the Local Government Planning and Land Act 1980.

11. A housing action trust established under Part III of the Housing Act 1988.

12. The Broads Authority, established under the Norfolk and Suffolk Broads Act 1988.

[**13.** . . .]

14. The Countryside Commission for Scotland.

15. The Development Board for Rural Wales.

16. The Edinburgh New Town Conservation Committee.

[**17.** The Regulator of Social Housing.]

18. Huddersfield Pride Limited.

19. Scottish Enterprise, established under the Enterprise and New Towns (Scotland) Act 1990.

20. Scottish Homes, established under the Housing (Scotland) Act 1988.

21. Springfield Horseshoe Housing Management Co-operative Limited.

22. Housing for Wales (Tai Cymru).

23. . . .

24. Batley Action Limited.

25. Bethnal Green City Challenge Company Limited.

26. The Blackburn City Challenge Partnership Board.

27. Bolton City Challenge Partnership Limited.

28. Bradford City Challenge Limited.

29. Brixton Challenge Company Limited.

30. Community North (Sunderland) Limited.

31. Dalston City Partnership Limited.

32. Deptford City Challenge Limited.

33. Derby Pride Limited.

34. Douglas Valley Partnership Limited.

35. Harlesden City Challenge Limited.

36. Hulme Regeneration Limited.

37. Leicester City Challenge Limited.

[**37A.** Manchester Investment and Development Agency Service Limited (MIDAS).]

38. Newcastle West End Partnership Limited.

39. Newtown South Aston City Challenge Limited.

40. North Kensington City Challenge Company Limited.

41. North Tyneside City Challenge Partnership Limited.

[**41A.** . . .]

42. Stratford Development Partnership Limited.

43. Wolverhampton City Challenge Limited.

44. . . .

[**45.** Pennine Housing 2000 Limited.

46. Twin Valley Homes Limited.

47. Urban Futures London Limited.]

[**48.** Aire-Wharfe Community Housing Trust Limited.

49. Bradford Building Services Limited.

50. Bradford Community Housing Trust Limited.

51. Bradford West City Community Housing Trust Limited.

[**51A.** City Building (Glasgow) LLP.]

52. Coast & County Housing Limited.

53. Dumfries and Galloway Housing Partnership Limited.

54. East Bradford Community Housing Trust Limited.

55. Knowsley Housing Trust.

56. North Bradford Community Housing Trust Limited.

57. Northern Housing Consortium Limited.

58. Shipley Community Housing Trust Limited.

59. South Bradford Community Housing Trust Limited.

60. Sunderland Housing Group.]

Section 3—Education

1. The governing body of a further education establishment for the time being mainly dependent for its maintenance on assistance from [local authorities (within the meaning of the Education Act)], or grants under section 485 of the Education Act or on such assistance and grants taken together.

2. The governing body of an aided school within the meaning of the Education Act.

3. The governing body of a foundation school, voluntary aided school or foundation special school within the meaning of the 1998 Act.

4. The managers of a grant-aided school as defined in section 135(1) of the 1980 Act.

5. The governing body of a central institution as defined in section 135(1) of the 1980 Act other than a college of agriculture.

6. The governing body of a College of Education as defined in section 135(1) of the 1980 Act.

7. The managers, other than a local authority, of a school which before any direction made by the Secretary of State under paragraph 2(1) of Schedule 7 to the Social Work (Scotland) Act 1968 was a school which immediately before the commencement of Part III of that Act was approved under section 83 of the Children and Young Persons (Scotland) Act 1937 if the employee was employed by those managers at the date the direction became effective.

8. A person carrying on a city technology college[, a city college for the technology of the arts or [an Academy]] established under an agreement with the Secretary of State under section 482 of the Education Act.

9. A company formed to manage a college of further education by virtue of section 65(1) of the Self-Governing Schools etc (Scotland) Act 1989.

10. The board of management of a self-governing school as defined in section 80(1) of the Self-Governing Schools etc (Scotland) Act 1989.

11. A further education corporation established under section 15 or 16 of the 1992 Act or in respect of which an order has been made under section 47 of that Act.

12. The governing body of an institution which is a designated institution for the purposes of Part I of the 1992 Act or, in the case of such an institution conducted by a company, that company.

13. The board of management of a college of further education, established under Part I of the Further and Higher Education (Scotland) Act 1992.

14. The governing body of a designated institution within the meaning of section 44(2) of the Further and Higher Education (Scotland) Act 1992.

15. A higher education corporation established under section 121 or 122 of the 1988 Act or in respect of which an order has been made under section 122A of that Act.

16. The governing body of an institution designated under section 129 of the 1988 Act or, in the case of such an institution conducted by a company, that company.

17. An Education Action Forum established under sections 10 and 11 of the 1998 Act.

18. The governing body of a grant-maintained school.

19. The governing body of a grant-maintained special school.

20. The Central Council for Education and Training in Social Work.

21. The Centre for Information on Language Teaching and Research.

[**21A.** The Centre for Literacy in Primary Education.

21B. Connexions Lancashire Limited.]

22. Cwmni Cynnal.

23. The General Teaching Council for Scotland, established under the [Public Services Reform (General Teaching Council for Scotland) Order 2011].

24. The National Institute of Adult Continuing Education (England and Wales).

25. Newbattle Abbey College.

26. The Scottish Community Education Council.

27. Scottish Consultative Council on the Curriculum.

28. The Scottish Council for Educational Technology.

29. The Scottish Council for Research in Education.

30. The Scottish Examination Board.

31. The Scottish Vocational Education Council.

[[**32.** Shetland Arts Development Agency.]

33. VT Four S Limited.]

Section 4—Careers guidance

1. Argyll & Bute Careers Partnership Limited.

2. Calderdale and Kirklees Careers Service Partnership Limited.

3. Cambridgeshire Careers Guidance Limited.

4. Capital Careers Limited.

5. Career Connections Limited.

6. Career Decisions Limited.

7. Career Development Edinburgh and Lothians.

8. Career Path (Northamptonshire) Limited.

9. Careerpaths (Cardiff and Vale) Limited.

10. Careers and Education Business Partnership.

11. Careers Central Limited.

[**11A.** Careers Enterprise (Futures) Limited.]

12. Careers Partnership Limited.

13. Careers Service Lancashire Area West Limited.

14. Central Careers Limited.

15. Cornwall and Devon Careers Limited.

[**15A.** Coventry, Solihull and Warwickshire Partnership Limited.]

16. Derbyshire Careers Service Limited.

17. East Lancashire Careers Services Limited.

18. Education Business Partnership (Wigan) Limited.

19. Essex Careers and Business Partnership Limited.

20. Future Steps Limited.

21. Futures Careers Limited.

22. Grampian Careers.

23. Guidance Enterprises Group Limited.

24. GuideLine Career Services Limited.

25. Gwent Careers Service Partnership Limited.

26. Hereford and Worcester Careers Service Limited.

27. Hertfordshire Careers Services Limited.

28. Highland Careers Services Limited.

29. The Humberside Partnership.

30. Learning Partnership West.

31. Leeds Careers Guidance.

32. Leicestershire Careers and Guidance Services Limited.

33. Lifetime Careers Barnsley, Doncaster and Rotherham Limited.

34. Lifetime Careers Bolton, Bury and Rochdale Limited.

35. Lifetime Careers Brent and Harrow Limited.

36. Lifetime Careers Stockport and High Peak Limited.

37. Lifetime Careers Wiltshire Limited.

38. Lincolnshire Careers and Guidance Services Limited.

[**38A.** London South Bank Careers.]

39. Mid Glamorgan Careers Limited.

40. Norfolk Careers Services Limited.

41. North East Wales Careers Service Company Limited.

[**41A.** Oldham Education Business and Guidance Services.]

42. Orkney Opportunities Centre.

43. Prospects Careers Services Limited.

44. Quality Careers Services Limited.

45. St Helens Careers Service Limited.

46. Sheffield Careers Guidance Services.

47. Shropshire Careers Service Limited.

48. Suffolk Careers Limited.

49. Tayside Careers Limited.

50. West Glamorgan Careers and Education Business Company Limited.

Section 5—Public transport

1. A Passenger Transport Executive established under section 9(1) of the Transport Act 1968.

2. A metropolitan county passenger transport authority established by section 28 of the 1985 Act.

3. The Forth Road Bridge Joint Board.

4. The Tay Road Bridge Joint Board.

Section 6—Police, fire and civil defence

1. A fire authority constituted by a combination scheme made under the Fire Services Act 1947.

[**1A.** A fire and rescue authority constituted by a scheme under section 2 of the Fire and Rescue Services Act 2004 or a scheme to which section 4 of that Act applies.]

[**2.** A police and crime commissioner established under section 1 of the Police Reform and Social Responsibility Act 2011.

2A. A chief constable established under section 2 of the Police Reform and Social Responsibility Act 2011.

2B. The Commissioner of Police of the Metropolis established under section 4 of the Police Reform and Social Responsibility Act 2011.]

3. A [metropolitan county fire and rescue authority] established by section 26 of the 1985 Act.

[**4.** A company the members of which comprise fire and rescue authorities in England and whose objects include the operation of a regional fire control centre.]

Section 7—Sports Councils

1. The English Sports Council.

2. The Scottish Sports Council.

3. The Sports Council for Wales.

4. The United Kingdom Sports Council.

Section 8—Social services

1. Coverage Care Limited.

[**1ZA.** Essex Cares Limited.

1ZB. Essex Community Support Limited.

1ZC. Essex Employment and Inclusion Limited.

1ZD. Essex Equipment Services Limited.]

[**1A.** Forfarshire Society for the Blind.

1B. Harlow Welfare Rights & Advice.]

2. The Humberside Independent Care Association.

[**2A.** New Charter Building Company Limited.

2B. New Charter Housing Trust Limited.]

3. Quantum Care Limited.

4. Sandwell Community Caring Trust Limited.

[[**4ZA.** Social Care and Social Work Improvement Scotland.]

4ZB. The Scottish Social Services Council.

4ZC. Shetland Council of Social Services.]

[**4A.** Shetland Welfare Trust.

4AA. Tynedale Housing Company Limited.]

5. Waltham Forest Specialist Housing Consortium Limited.

6. The Wrekin Housing Trust Limited.

Section 9—Museums

1. The Board of Governors of the Museum of London.

2. The Board of Trustees of The National Museums and Galleries on Merseyside.

3. Coventry Museum of British Road Transport.

4. The Geffrye Museum Trust.

5. The Horniman Public Museum and Public Park Trust.

6. National Coal Mining Museum for England Trust Limited.

7. The Scottish Museums Council.

[**8.** Woodhorn Charitable Trust.]

Section 10—Miscellaneous bodies

[**1.** A valuation tribunal in Wales established under the Local Government Finance Act 1988.]

2. . . .

3. An area tourist board established by virtue of an order made under section 172, 173 or 174 of the 1994 Act.

4. A probation committee within the meaning of the Probation Service Act 1993.

[**4A.** A local probation board within the meaning of the Criminal Justice and Court Services Act 2000.]

[**4B.** a probation trust.]

5. A magistrates' courts committee or the Committee of Magistrates for the Inner London Area, within the meaning of the Justices of the Peace Act 1979.

[**5A.** A body designated as a Care Trust under section 45 of the Health and Social Care Act 2001.]

[**5B.** A community justice authority under section 3 of the Management of Offenders (Scotland) Act 2005.

5C. Active Stirling Limited.

5D. Ardroy Outdoor Learning Trust.

5E. Arts and Theatres Trust Fife Limited.]

[**6.** Blyth Valley Arts and Leisure Limited.

6A. The Business Shop—Angus Limited.

6AA. The Care Quality Commission.]

6B. The Care Standards Inspectorate for Wales.

6C. The Children and Family Court Advisory and Support Service.]

[**6D.** City Markets (Glasgow) LLP.

6E. City Parking (Glasgow) LLP.

6F. City Property (Glasgow) LLP.]

7. CIP (Hounslow) Limited.

[**7A.** Clackmannanshire Leisure.]

8. Community Initiative Partnerships.

[**8AA.** Cordia (Services) LLP.]

[**8A.** Coventry Sports Trust Limited.]

[**8B.** CV One Limited.]

[**8C.** Culture and Sport Glasgow.

8D. Culture and Sport Glasgow (Trading) CIC.]

9. Derwentside Leisure Limited.

[**9ZA.** East End Partnership Limited.]

[**9A.** Edinburgh Leisure.

9AA. Enfield Leisure Centres Limited.]

[**9B.** Enjoy East Lothian Limited.]

10. The Environment Agency.

[**10A.** Fife Coast and Countryside Trust.

10B. Fife Sports and Leisure Trust Limited.

10C. Forth Valley GIS Limited.

10D. Glasgow Community and Safety Services Limited.]

11. Greenwich Leisure Limited.

[**11A.** Herefordshire Community Leisure Trust.]

12. Hounslow Cultural and Community Services.

13. Hounslow Sports and Recreation Services.

[**13A.** The Islesburgh Trust.

13B. Kirklees Active Leisure Trust.]

14. The Land Authority for Wales.

15. Leisure Tynedale.

16. The Lee Valley Regional Park Authority.

17. The London Pensions Fund Authority.

[**17A.** The National Care Standards Commission.]

[**17B, 17C.** . . .]

18. National Mobility Services Trust Limited.

19. New Park Village TMC Limited.

[**19ZA.** North Lanarkshire Leisure Limited.

19ZB. Nuneaton and Bedworth Leisure Trust.]

[**19A.** Oldham Community Leisure Limited.

[**19AA.** Pendle Leisure Limited.]

19B. Renfrewshire Leisure Limited.

19C. Salford Community Leisure Limited.

[**19CA.** Sandwell Arts Trust.]

19D. Sandwell Sport and Leisure Trust.]

20. The Scottish Children's Reporter Administration established under section 128 of the 1994 Act.

21. The Scottish Environment Protection Agency.

[**22.** Scottish Water.]

[**22A.** Shetland Recreational Trust.]

[**22B.** Somerset Leisure Limited.]

23. The South Yorkshire Pensions Authority.

[**23A.** Sport Aberdeen.]

24. Strathclyde European Partnerships Limited.

[**24A.** Tameside Sports Trust.

24B. Tees Active Limited.

24C. The Valuation Tribunal Service.

24D. The Water Industry Commissioner for Scotland.]

25. West Lothian Leisure Limited.

[**26.** Wigan Leisure and Culture Trust.]

NOTES

Section 1: paras 6A–6E inserted by the London Government (Continuity of Employment) Order 2000, SI 2000/1042, art 4(1)–(3); paras 13A, 23 inserted, and para 16 substituted, by the Redundancy Payments (Continuity of Employment in Local Government, etc) (Modification) Order (Amendment) Order 2010, SI 2010/903, arts 2, 3, as from 15 April 2010.

Section 2: paras 4A, 37A, 48–60 inserted and added respectively by the Redundancy Payments (Continuity of Employment in Local Government, etc) (Modification) (Amendment) Order 2004, SI 2004/1682, art 2(1), (2); para 7A inserted by the

Redundancy Payments (Continuity of Employment in Local Government, etc) (Modification) (Amendment) Order 2001, SI 2001/866, art 2(1), (2); para 9A inserted by the Localism Act 2011 (Housing and Regeneration Functions in Greater London) (Consequential, Transitory, Transitional and Saving Provisions) Order 2012, SI 2012/666, art 8(1), Sch 1, para 2(1), (2)(a), as from 1 April 2012; paras 13, 17 substituted by the Housing and Regeneration Act 2008 (Consequential Provisions) (No 2) Order 2008, SI 2008/2831, arts 3, 4, Sch 1, para 10, Sch 2, para 3, as from 1 December 2008; para 13 subsequently revoked by the Localism Act 2011 (Regulation of Social Housing) (Consequential Provisions) Order 2012, SI 2012/641, art 2(4), as from 1 April 2012; para 23 revoked by the Welsh Development Agency (Transfer of Functions to the National Assembly for Wales and Abolition) Order 2005, SI 2005/3226, art 7(1)(b), Sch 2, Pt 1, para 4; paras 41A, 51A inserted by SI 2010/903, arts 2, 4, as from 15 April 2010; para 41A subsequently revoked by SI 2012/666, art 8(1), Sch 1, para 2(1), (2)(b), as from 1 April 2012; para 44 revoked by the Abolition of the Commission for the New Towns and the Urban Regeneration Agency (Appointed Day and Consequential Amendments) Order 2009, SI 2009/801, reg 3(1), as from 1 April 2009; paras 45–47 added by the Redundancy Payments (Continuity of Employment in Local Government, etc) (Modification) (Amendment) Order 2002, SI 2002/532, art 2(1), (2)(a).

Section 3: words in square brackets in para 1 substituted by the Local Education Authorities and Children's Services Authorities (Integration of Functions) (Local and Subordinate Legislation) Order 2010, SI 2010/1172, art 4, Sch 3, para 33(1), (2), as from 5 May 2010; words in first (outer) pair of square brackets in para 8 substituted by SI 2001/866, art 2(1), (3); words in second (inner) pair of square brackets in para 8 substituted, and paras 21A, 21B, 32, 33 inserted and added respectively, by SI 2004/1682, art 2(1), (3); words in square brackets in para 23 substituted by the Public Services Reform (General Teaching Council for Scotland) Order 2011, SSI 2011/215, art 33(1), Sch 6, para 4, as from 2 April 2012; para 32 substituted by SI 2010/903, arts 2, 5, as from 15 April 2010.

Section 4: para 11A inserted by SI 2001/866, art 2(1), (7); paras 15A, 41A inserted by SI 2004/1682, art 2(1), (4); para 38A inserted by SI 2002/532, art 2(1), (3).

Section 6: para 1A inserted by the Fire and Rescue Services Act 2004 (Consequential Amendments) (England) Order 2004, SI 2004/3168, art 50, in relation to England, and by the Fire and Rescue Services Act 2004 (Consequential Amendments) (Wales) Order 2005, SI 2005/2929, art 50, in relation to Wales; paras 2, 2A, 2B substituted for original para 2, by the Local Policing Bodies (Consequential Amendments and Transitional Provision) Order 2012, SI 2012/2733, art 2, as from 22 November 2012; words in square brackets in para 3 substituted by the Civil Contingencies Act 2004, s 32(1), Sch 2, Pt 1, para 10(1), (2); original para 4 revoked by SI 2000/1042, art 4(1), (4)(b) and new para 4 added by SI 2010/903, arts 2, 6, as from 15 April 2010.

Section 8: paras 1ZA–1ZD inserted by SI 2010/903, arts 2, 7, as from 15 April 2010; paras 1A, 1B, 4ZA–4ZC inserted by SI 2004/1682, art 2(1), (5); paras 2A, 2B inserted by SI 2001/866, art 2(1), (5); paras 4A, 4AA substituted, for para 4A (as inserted by SI 2001/866, art 2(1), (5)), by SI 2002/532, art 2(1), (4)(a); para 4ZA substituted by SI 2011/2581, art 2, Sch 2, Pt 2, para 27, as from 28 October 2011.

Section 9: para 8 added by SI 2010/903, arts 2, 8, as from 15 April 2010.

Section 10: paras 1, 22 substituted, para 2 revoked, paras 4A, 8B, 9ZA, 11A, 13A, 13B, 19A–19D, 22A, 24A–24D, 26 inserted, and paras 6, 6A, 6B, 6C substituted, for para 6 (as originally enacted), para 6A (as inserted by SI 2001/866, art 2(1), (6)(a)), and original para 6AA (as inserted by SI 2002/532, art 2(1), (5)(b)), by SI 2004/1682, art 2(1), (6); para 4B inserted by the Offender Management Act 2007 (Consequential Amendments) Order 2008, SI 2008/912, art 3, Sch 2, para 1, as from 1 April 2008; paras 5A, 7A, 8A, 17A inserted, and paras 9A, 9AA substituted, for para 9A (as inserted by SI 2001/866, art 2(1), (6)(b)), by SI 2002/532, art 2(1), (5); paras 5B–5E, 6D–6F, 8AA, 8C, 8D, 9B, 10A–10D, 19ZA, 19ZB, 19AA, 19CA, 22B, 23A inserted by SI 2010/903, arts 2, 9, as from 15 April 2010; new para 6AA inserted by the Health and Social Care Act 2008 (Consequential Amendments and Transitory Provisions) Order 2008, SI 2008/2250, art 2(1), (3), as from 1 October 2008; paras 17B, 17C (as inserted by SI 2004/664, art 2, Sch 1, para 2) (omitted) revoked by the Health and Social Care Act 2008 (Commencement No 9, Consequential Amendments and Transitory, Transitional and Saving Provisions) Order 2009, SI 2009/462, art 12, Sch 5, para 6, as from 1 April 2009.

The Commission for Local Administration in Wales was abolished by the Public Services Ombudsman (Wales) Act 2005, s 36(1) on 1 April 2006.

The reference to a metropolitan county passenger transport authority in Section 5, para 2 above is to be read as a reference to an Integrated Transport Authority: see the Local Transport Act 2008, s 77(2), (4)(a).

SCHEDULE 2

PART I
MODIFICATIONS TO CERTAIN REDUNDANCY PAYMENTS PROVISIONS OF THE 1996 ACT

Article 3

[2.452]

1. Section 146 of the 1996 Act shall have effect as if immediately after subsection (1) there were inserted—

SI 1999/2277

"(1A) The reference in subsection (1) to re-engagement by the employer includes a reference to re-engagement by any employer specified in Part II of Schedule 2 to the Redundancy Payments (Continuity of Employment in Local Government, etc) (Modification) Order 1999 and the reference in subsection (1) to an offer made by the employer includes a reference to an offer made by any employer so specified."

2. Section 155 of the 1996 Act shall have effect as if—

for the words "continuously employed" there were substituted the words "employed in relevant service";

the provisions of that section modified as provided in sub-paragraph (a) were subsection (1) of that section; and

Part 2 Statutory Instruments

after that subsection there were inserted the following subsections—

SI 1999/2277 "(2) In subsection (1) "relevant service" means

(a) continuous employment by an employer specified in Part II of Schedule 2 to the Redundancy Payments (Continuity of Employment in Local Government, etc) (Modification) Order 1999 ("the 1999 Order"), or

(b) where immediately before the relevant event a person has been successively employed by two or more employers specified in Part II of that Schedule, such aggregate period of service with such employers as would be continuous employment if they were a single employer.

(3) In subsection (2)(b) "relevant event" has the same meaning as in the 1999 Order."

3. Section 162 of the 1996 Act shall have effect as if—

for the words "continuously employed" in subsection (1)(a) there were substituted the words "employed in relevant service"; and

after subsection (1) there were inserted the following subsections—

SI 1999/2277 "(1A) In subsection (1)(a) "relevant service" means—

(a) continuous employment by an employer specified in Part II of Schedule 2 to the Redundancy Payments (Continuity of Employment in Local Government, etc) (Modification) Order 1999 ("the 1999 Order"), or

(b) where immediately before the relevant event a person has been successively employed by two or more employers specified in Part II of that Schedule, such aggregate period of service with such employers as would be continuous employment if they were a single employer.

(1B) In subsection (1A)(b) "relevant event" has the same meaning as in the 1999 Order."

PART II
EMPLOYERS WITH WHOM EMPLOYMENT MAY CONSTITUTE RELEVANT SERVICE

Section 1

Any employer specified in Schedule 1 to this Order whether or not in existence at the time of the relevant event.

Section 2—Local government

[2.453]

1. The Greater London Council.

2. The London Residuary Body established by section 57(1)(a) of the 1985 Act.

3. The council of an administrative county, county borough (other than one established under section 20 of the 1972 Act), metropolitan borough or county district.

4. A regional council, islands council or district council established by or under the Local Government (Scotland) Act 1973.

5. The council of a county, county of a city, large burgh, small burgh or district ceasing to exist after 15th May 1975.

6. Any joint board or joint body constituted by or under any enactment for the purpose of exercising the functions of two or more of the bodies described in any of paragraphs 1 to 5 above, and any special planning board within the meaning of paragraph 3 of Schedule 17 to the 1972 Act.

7. Any other body, not specified in any of paragraphs 1 to 6 above, established by or under any enactment for the purpose of exercising the functions of, or advising, one or more of the bodies specified in any of paragraphs 1 to 6 above.

8. Any committee (including a joint committee) established by or under any enactment for the purpose of exercising the functions of, or advising, one or more of the bodies described in any of paragraphs 1 to 6 above.

9. Any two or more bodies described in any of paragraphs 1 to 8 above acting jointly or as a combined authority.

10. Any association which was representative of any two or more bodies described in any of paragraphs 1 to 5 above.

11. Any committee established by one or more of the associations described in paragraph 10 above for the purpose of exercising the functions of, or advising, one or more of such associations.

12. An organisation which was representative of an association or associations described in paragraph 10 above and employees' organisations and among whose objects was to negotiate pay and conditions of service in local government service.

13. The council of a county or district in Wales ceasing to exist after 31st March 1996.

14. The Local Government Training Board.

[**15.** The Accounts Commission for Scotland.]

Section 3—Planning and development

1. A development corporation within the meaning of the New Towns Act 1946 or the New Towns Act 1965.

2. A development corporation established under section 2 of the New Towns (Scotland) Act 1968.

[**2A.** Olympic Park Legacy Company Limited.]

3. The Scottish Development Agency.

4. The Scottish Special Housing Association.

5. The English Industrial Estates Corporation established by the Local Employment Act 1960.

Section 4—Education

1. The governing body of an aided school within the meaning of the Education Act.

2. The governing body of a grant-maintained school.

3. The governing body of a grant-maintained special school.

4. The proprietor (within the meaning of section 579(1) of the Education Act) of a school for the time being recognised as a grammar school for the purposes of regulation 4(1) of the Direct Grant Schools Regulations 1959, being a school in relation to which, before 1st January 1976, the Secretary of State was satisfied as mentioned in regulation 3(1) of the Direct Grant Grammar Schools (Cessation of Grant) Regulations 1975.

5. The proprietor (within the meaning of section 114(1) of the Education Act 1944) of a school not falling within paragraph 1 of this section which throughout the period of employment was recognised as a grammar school or, as the case may be, as a direct grant grammar school for the purposes of regulation 4(1) of the Direct Grant Schools Regulations 1959, of Part IV of the Schools Grant Regulations 1951 or of Part IV of the Primary and Secondary Schools (Grant Conditions) Regulations 1945.

6. The managers of a school which during the period of employment was approved under section 83 of the Children and Young Persons (Scotland) Act 1937.

7. The managers of a school which during the period of employment was a grant-aided school within the meaning of section 143(1) of the Education (Scotland) Act 1946, section 145(22) of the Education (Scotland) Act 1962 or section 135(1) of the 1980 Act.

8. The managers of a school which during the period of employment was a school which, immediately before the commencement of Part III of the Social Work (Scotland) Act 1968, was approved under section 83 of the Children and Young Persons (Scotland) Act 1937.

9. An institution within the PCFC funding sector, within the meaning of section 132(6) of the 1988 Act.

10. The Further Education Staff College.

11. The Inner London Education Authority, known as the Inner London Interim Education Authority for a period prior to the abolition date as defined in section 1(2) of the 1985 Act.

12. The National Advisory Body for Public Sector Higher Education.

13. The Polytechnics and College Funding Council as established by section 132 of the 1988 Act.

14. The Scottish Association for National Certificates and Diplomas.

15. The Scottish Business Education Council.

16. The Scottish Council for Commercial, Administrative and Professional Education.

17. The Scottish Technical Education Council.

18. The Secretary of State for Defence in relation only to employees in schools administered by the Service Children's Education Authority.

19. The Secretary of State for Education and Employment[, the Secretary of State for Education and Skills] [the Secretary of State for Children, Schools and Families or the Secretary of State for Education], in relation only to teachers employed under contract in the European School established under Article 1 of the Statute of the European School and in schools designated as European Schools under Article 1 of the Protocol to that Statute.

[**19A.** Shetland Arts Trust.]

[**20.** A person who during the period of employment performed an education function of a local authority pursuant to a direction given by the Secretary of State under section 497A(4) of the Education Act, and in this paragraph "education function" and "local authority" have the same meanings as in the Education Act.]

Section 5—Careers guidance

1. Black Country Careers Services Limited.

2. Buckinghamshire Careers Service Limited.

3. Kent Careers and Guidance Service Limited.

Section 6—[Police, fire and civil defence]

[**1.**] A previous police authority in relation to which Schedule 11 to the Police Act 1964 had effect or which was the police authority for an area or district which was before 1st April 1947 or after 31st March 1946 a separate police area or, in Scotland, a previous police authority for an area which was before 16th May 1975 a separate or combined police area.

[**2.** The London Fire and Civil Defence Authority.]

Section 7—Sports Councils

The Sports Council.

Section 8—Social services

A person or body of persons responsible for the management of an assisted community home within the meaning of section 36 of the Children and Young Persons Act 1969 or of an approved institution within the meaning of section 46 of that Act.

Section 9—Miscellaneous

1. A regional water board established under section 5 of the Water (Scotland) Act 1967.

2. A river purification board established under section 2 of the Rivers (Prevention of Pollution) (Scotland) Act 1951.

3. A river purification board established under section 135 of the Local Government (Scotland) Act 1973.

4. A local valuation panel constituted under the Local Government Act 1948 or established under the General Rate Act 1967.

[**4A.** A valuation tribunal in England established under the Local Government Finance Act 1988.]

5. The Central Scotland Water Development Board.

6. The Scottish Industrial Estates Corporation (formerly the Industrial Estates Management Corporation for Scotland) established by section 8 of the Local Employment Act 1960.

7. The Small Industries Council for Rural Areas of Scotland, being a company which was dissolved by section 15(5) of the Scottish Development Agency Act 1975 and was until then registered under the Companies Acts from time to time in force.

[**7A.** The Traffic Director for London.]

8. The Welsh Industrial Estates Corporation (formerly the Industrial Estates Management Corporation for Wales) established by section 8 of the Local Employment Act 1960.

NOTES

Section 2: para 15 added by the Redundancy Payments (Continuity of Employment in Local Government, etc) (Modification) Order (Amendment) Order 2010, SI 2010/903, arts 10, 11, as from 15 April 2010.

Section 3: para 2A inserted by the Localism Act 2011 (Housing and Regeneration Functions in Greater London) (Consequential, Transitory, Transitional and Saving Provisions) Order 2012, SI 2012/666, art 8(1), Sch 1, para 2(1), (3), as from 1 April 2012.

Section 4: words in first pair of square brackets in para 19 substituted by the Secretaries of State for Children, Schools and Families, for Innovation, Universities and Skills and for Business, Enterprise and Regulatory Reform Order 2007, SI 2007/3224, art 15, Schedule, Pt 2, para 26, as from 12 December 2007; words in second pair of square brackets in para 19 substituted by the Secretary of State for Education Order 2010, SI 2010/1836, art 6, Schedule, Pt 2, para 5, as from 18 August 2010; para 19A inserted by SI 2010/903, arts 10, 12, as from 15 April 2010; para 20 added by the Redundancy Payments (Continuity of Employment in Local Government, etc) (Modification) (Amendment) Order 2001, SI 2001/866, art 2(1), (7), and substituted by the Local Education Authorities and Children's Services Authorities (Integration of Functions) (Local and Subordinate Legislation) Order 2010, SI 2010/1172, art 4, Sch 3, para 33(1), (3), as from 5 May 2010.

Section 6: words in square brackets in the heading substituted, para 1 numbered as such, and para 2 added, by the London Government (Continuity of Employment) Order 2000, SI 2000/1042, art 4(1), (5).

Section 9: para 4A inserted by the Redundancy Payments (Continuity of Employment in Local Government, etc) (Modification) (Amendment) Order 2004, SI 2004/1682, art 2(1), (7); para 7A inserted by SI 2010/903, arts 10, 13, as from 15 April 2010.

SCHEDULE 3

(Sch 3 revokes the Redundancy Payments (Local Government) (Modification) Order 1983, SI 1983/1160 (and the various Orders that amended the 1983 Order).)

MANAGEMENT OF HEALTH AND SAFETY AT WORK REGULATIONS 1999

(SI 1999/3242)

NOTES

Made: 3 December 1999.

Authority: European Communities Act 1972, s 2(2), Health and Safety at Work etc Act 1974, ss 15(1), (2), (3)(a), (5), (9), 47(2), 52(2), (3), 80(1), 82(3)(a), Sch 3, paras 6(1), 7, 8(1), 10, 14, 15, 16.

Commencement: 29 December 1999.

These Regulations revoke and replace the Management of Health and Safety at Work Regulations 1992, SI 1992/2051, and are the continuing domestic implementation of Council Directive 89/391 at **[3.115]** and, in part, Council Directive 92/85 at **[3.163]**.

See also the Code of Practice "Management of Health and Safety at Work" (not printed in this work) issued in conjunction with the 1992 Regulations by the Health and Safety Commission under the Health and Safety at Work, etc Act 1974, s 16.

See *Harvey* J(6).

ARRANGEMENT OF REGULATIONS

Part 2 Statutory Instruments

[2.454]
1 Citation, commencement and interpretation

(1) These Regulations may be cited as the Management of Health and Safety at Work Regulations 1999 and shall come into force on 29th December 1999.

(2) In these Regulations—

"the 1996 Act" means the Employment Rights Act 1996;

"the assessment" means, in the case of an employer or self-employed person, the assessment made or changed by him in accordance with regulation 3;

"child"—

(a) as respects England and Wales, means a person who is not over compulsory school age, construed in accordance with section 8 of the Education Act 1996; and

(b) as respects Scotland, means a person who is not over school age, construed in accordance with section 31 of the Education (Scotland) Act 1980;

"employment business" means a business (whether or not carried on with a view to profit and whether or not carried on in conjunction with any other business) which supplies persons (other than seafarers) who are employed in it to work for and under the control of other persons in any capacity;

"fixed-term contract of employment" means a contract of employment for a specific term which is fixed in advance or which can be ascertained in advance by reference to some relevant circumstance;

"given birth" means delivered a living child or, after twenty-four weeks of pregnancy, a stillborn child;

"new or expectant mother" means an employee who is pregnant; who has given birth within the previous six months; or who is breastfeeding;

"the preventive and protective measures" means the measures which have been identified by the employer or by the self-employed person in consequence of the assessment as the measures he needs to take to comply with the requirements and prohibitions imposed upon him by or under the relevant statutory provisions . . . ;

"young person" means any person who has not attained the age of eighteen.

(3) Any reference in these Regulations to—

(a) a numbered regulation or Schedule is a reference to the regulation or Schedule in these Regulations so numbered; or

(b) a numbered paragraph is a reference to the paragraph so numbered in the regulation in which the reference appears.

NOTES

Para (2): words omitted from the definition "the preventive and protective measures" revoked by the Regulatory Reform (Fire Safety) Order 2005, SI 2005/1541, art 53(2), Sch 5 (in relation to England and Wales), and by the Fire (Scotland) Act 2005 (Consequential Modifications and Savings) (No 2) Order 2006, SSI 2006/457, art 2(2), Sch 2 (in relation to Scotland).

[2.455]
[2 Disapplication of these Regulations

(1) These Regulations shall not apply to or in relation to the master or crew of a ship, or to the employer of such persons, in respect of the normal ship-board activities of a ship's crew which are carried out solely by the crew under the direction of the master.

(2) Regulations 3(4), (5), 10(2) and 19 shall not apply to occasional work or short-term work involving work regarded as not being harmful, damaging or dangerous to young people in a family undertaking.

(3) In this regulation—

"normal ship-board activities" include—

(a) the construction, reconstruction or conversion of a ship outside, but not inside, Great Britain; and

(b) the repair of a ship save repair when carried out in dry dock;

"ship" includes every description of vessel used in navigation, other than a ship belonging to Her Majesty which forms part of Her Majesty's Navy.]

NOTES

Substituted by the Management of Health and Safety at Work and Fire Precautions (Workplace) (Amendment) Regulations 2003, SI 2003/2457, regs 2, 3.

[2.456]

3 Risk assessment

(1) Every employer shall make a suitable and sufficient assessment of—

(a) the risks to the health and safety of his employees to which they are exposed whilst they are at work; and

(b) the risks to the health and safety of persons not in his employment arising out of or in connection with the conduct by him of his undertaking,

for the purpose of identifying the measures he needs to take to comply with the requirements and prohibitions imposed upon him by or under the relevant statutory provisions . . . .

(2) Every self-employed person shall make a suitable and sufficient assessment of—

(a) the risks to his own health and safety to which he is exposed whilst he is at work; and

(b) the risks to the health and safety of persons not in his employment arising out of or in connection with the conduct by him of his undertaking,

for the purpose of identifying the measures he needs to take to comply with the requirements and prohibitions imposed upon him by or under the relevant statutory provisions.

(3) Any assessment such as is referred to in paragraph (1) or (2) shall be reviewed by the employer or self-employed person who made it if—

(a) there is reason to suspect that it is no longer valid; or

(b) there has been a significant change in the matters to which it relates;

and where as a result of any such review changes to an assessment are required, the employer or self-employed person concerned shall make them.

(4) An employer shall not employ a young person unless he has, in relation to risks to the health and safety of young persons, made or reviewed an assessment in accordance with paragraphs (1) and (5).

(5) In making or reviewing the assessment, an employer who employs or is to employ a young person shall take particular account of—

(a) the inexperience, lack of awareness of risks and immaturity of young persons;

(b) the fitting-out and layout of the workplace and the workstation;

(c) the nature, degree and duration of exposure to physical, biological and chemical agents;

(d) the form, range, and use of work equipment and the way in which it is handled;

(e) the organisation of processes and activities;

(f) the extent of the health and safety training provided or to be provided to young persons; and

(g) risks from agents, processes and work listed in the Annex to Council Directive 94/33/EC on the protection of young people at work.

(6) Where the employer employs five or more employees, he shall record—

(a) the significant findings of the assessment; and

(b) any group of his employees identified by it as being especially at risk.

NOTES

Para (1): words omitted revoked by the Regulatory Reform (Fire Safety) Order 2005, SI 2005/1541, art 53(2), Sch 5 (in relation to England and Wales), and by the Fire (Scotland) Act 2005 (Consequential Modifications and Savings) (No 2) Order 2006, SSI 2006/457, art 2(2), Sch 2 (in relation to Scotland).

As to the layout of this regulation, see the Management of Health and Safety at Work and Fire Precautions (Workplace) (Amendment) Regulations 2003, SI 2003/2457, reg 4 which provides as follows—

"In regulation 3(3) the words "and where" to the end shall follow and not appear in sub-paragraph (b).".

[2.457]

4 Principles of prevention to be applied

Where an employer implements any preventive and protective measures he shall do so on the basis of the principles specified in Schedule 1 to these Regulations.

[2.458]

5 Health and safety arrangements

(1) Every employer shall make and give effect to such arrangements as are appropriate, having regard to the nature of his activities and the size of his undertaking, for the effective planning, organisation, control, monitoring and review of the preventive and protective measures.

(2) Where the employer employs five or more employees, he shall record the arrangements referred to in paragraph (1).

[2.459]
6 Health surveillance

Every employer shall ensure that his employees are provided with such health surveillance as is appropriate having regard to the risks to their health and safety which are identified by the assessment.

[2.460]
7 Health and safety assistance

(1) Every employer shall, subject to paragraphs (6) and (7), appoint one or more competent persons to assist him in undertaking the measures he needs to take to comply with the requirements and prohibitions imposed upon him by or under the relevant statutory provisions . . .

(2) Where an employer appoints persons in accordance with paragraph (1), he shall make arrangements for ensuring adequate co-operation between them.

(3) The employer shall ensure that the number of persons appointed under paragraph (1), the time available for them to fulfil their functions and the means at their disposal are adequate having regard to the size of his undertaking, the risks to which his employees are exposed and the distribution of those risks throughout the undertaking.

(4) The employer shall ensure that—

- (a) any person appointed by him in accordance with paragraph (1) who is not in his employment—
  - (i) is informed of the factors known by him to affect, or suspected by him of affecting, the health and safety of any other person who may be affected by the conduct of his undertaking, and
  - (ii) has access to the information referred to in regulation 10; and
- (b) any person appointed by him in accordance with paragraph (1) is given such information about any person working in his undertaking who is—
  - (i) employed by him under a fixed-term contract of employment, or
  - (ii) employed in an employment business,

  as is necessary to enable that person properly to carry out the function specified in that paragraph.

(5) A person shall be regarded as competent for the purposes of paragraphs (1) and (8) where he has sufficient training and experience or knowledge and other qualities to enable him properly to assist in undertaking the measures referred to in paragraph (1).

(6) Paragraph (1) shall not apply to a self-employed employer who is not in partnership with any other person where he has sufficient training and experience or knowledge and other qualities properly to undertake the measures referred to in that paragraph himself.

(7) Paragraph (1) shall not apply to individuals who are employers and who are together carrying on business in partnership where at least one of the individuals concerned has sufficient training and experience or knowledge and other qualities—

- (a) properly to undertake the measures he needs to take to comply with the requirements and prohibitions imposed upon him by or under the relevant statutory provisions; and
- (b) properly to assist his fellow partners in undertaking the measures they need to take to comply with the requirements and prohibitions imposed upon them by or under the relevant statutory provisions.

(8) Where there is a competent person in the employer's employment, that person shall be appointed for the purposes of paragraph (1) in preference to a competent person not in his employment.

NOTES

Para (1): words omitted revoked by the Regulatory Reform (Fire Safety) Order 2005, SI 2005/1541, art 53(2), Sch 5 (in relation to England and Wales), and by the Fire (Scotland) Act 2005 (Consequential Modifications and Savings) (No 2) Order 2006, SSI 2006/457, art 2(2), Sch 2 (in relation to Scotland).

[2.461]
8 Procedures for serious and imminent danger and for danger areas

(1) Every employer shall—

- (a) establish and where necessary give effect to appropriate procedures to be followed in the event of serious and imminent danger to persons at work in his undertaking;
- (b) nominate a sufficient number of competent persons to implement those procedures in so far as they relate to the evacuation from premises of persons at work in his undertaking; and
- (c) ensure that none of his employees has access to any area occupied by him to which it is necessary to restrict access on grounds of health and safety unless the employee concerned has received adequate health and safety instruction.

(2) Without prejudice to the generality of paragraph (1)(a), the procedures referred to in that sub-paragraph shall—

(a) so far as is practicable, require any persons at work who are exposed to serious and imminent danger to be informed of the nature of the hazard and of the steps taken or to be taken to protect them from it;

(b) enable the persons concerned (if necessary by taking appropriate steps in the absence of guidance or instruction and in the light of their knowledge and the technical means at their disposal) to stop work and immediately proceed to a place of safety in the event of their being exposed to serious, imminent and unavoidable danger; and

(c) save in exceptional cases for reasons duly substantiated (which cases and reasons shall be specified in those procedures), require the persons concerned to be prevented from resuming work in any situation where there is still a serious and imminent danger.

(3) A person shall be regarded as competent for the purposes of paragraph (1)(b) where he has sufficient training and experience or knowledge and other qualities to enable him properly to implement the evacuation procedures referred to in that sub-paragraph.

[2.462]
9 Contacts with external services

Every employer shall ensure that any necessary contacts with external services are arranged, particularly as regards first-aid, emergency medical care and rescue work.

[2.463]
10 Information for employees

(1) Every employer shall provide his employees with comprehensible and relevant information on—

(a) the risks to their health and safety identified by the assessment;

(b) the preventive and protective measures;

(c) the procedures referred to in regulation 8(1)(a) . . . ;

(d) the identity of those persons nominated by him in accordance with regulation 8(1)(b) . . . ; and

(e) the risks notified to him in accordance with regulation 11(1)(c).

(2) Every employer shall, before employing a child, provide a parent of the child with comprehensible and relevant information on—

(a) the risks to his health and safety identified by the assessment;

(b) the preventive and protective measures; and

(c) the risks notified to him in accordance with regulation 11(1)(c).

(3) The reference in paragraph (2) to a parent of the child includes—

(a) in England and Wales, a person who has parental responsibility, within the meaning of section 3 of the Children Act 1989, for him; and

(b) in Scotland, a person who has parental rights, within the meaning of section 8 of the Law Reform (Parent and Child) (Scotland) Act 1986 for him.

NOTES

Para (1): words omitted from sub-paras (c), (d) revoked by the Regulatory Reform (Fire Safety) Order 2005, SI 2005/1541, art 53(2), Sch 5 (in relation to England and Wales), and by the Fire (Scotland) Act 2005 (Consequential Modifications and Savings) (No 2) Order 2006, SSI 2006/457, art 2(2), Sch 2 (in relation to Scotland).

[2.464]
11 Co-operation and co-ordination

(1) Where two or more employers share a workplace (whether on a temporary or a permanent basis) each such employer shall—

(a) co-operate with the other employers concerned so far as is necessary to enable them to comply with the requirements and prohibitions imposed upon them by or under the relevant statutory provisions . . . ;

(b) (taking into account the nature of his activities) take all reasonable steps to co-ordinate the measures he takes to comply with the requirements and prohibitions imposed upon him by or under the relevant statutory provisions . . . with the measures the other employers concerned are taking to comply with the requirements and prohibitions imposed upon them by that legislation; and

(c) take all reasonable steps to inform the other employers concerned of the risks to their employees' health and safety arising out of or in connection with the conduct by him of his undertaking.

(2) Paragraph (1) . . . shall apply to employers sharing a workplace with self-employed persons and to self-employed persons sharing a workplace with other self-employed persons as it applies to employers sharing a workplace with other employers; and the references in that paragraph to employers and the reference in the said paragraph to their employees shall be construed accordingly.

NOTES

Paras (1), (2): words omitted revoked by the Regulatory Reform (Fire Safety) Order 2005, SI 2005/1541, art 53(2), Sch 5 (in relation to England and Wales), and by the Fire (Scotland) Act 2005 (Consequential Modifications and Savings) (No 2) Order 2006, SSI 2006/457, art 2(2), Sch 2 (in relation to Scotland).

[2.465]

12 Persons working in host employers' or self-employed persons' undertakings

(1) Every employer and every self-employed person shall ensure that the employer of any employees from an outside undertaking who are working in his undertaking is provided with comprehensible information on—

- (a) the risks to those employees' health and safety arising out of or in connection with the conduct by that first-mentioned employer or by that self-employed person of his undertaking; and
- (b) the measures taken by that first-mentioned employer or by that self-employed person in compliance with the requirements and prohibitions imposed upon him by or under the relevant statutory provisions . . . in so far as the said requirements and prohibitions relate to those employees.

(2) Paragraph (1) . . . shall apply to a self-employed person who is working in the undertaking of an employer or a self-employed person as it applies to employees from an outside undertaking who are working therein; and the reference in that paragraph to the employer of any employees from an outside undertaking who are working in the undertaking of an employer or a self-employed person and the references in the said paragraph to employees from an outside undertaking who are working in the undertaking of an employer or a self-employed person shall be construed accordingly.

(3) Every employer shall ensure that any person working in his undertaking who is not his employee and every self-employed person (not being an employer) shall ensure that any person working in his undertaking is provided with appropriate instructions and comprehensible information regarding any risks to that person's health and safety which arise out of the conduct by that employer or self-employed person of his undertaking.

(4) Every employer shall—

- (a) ensure that the employer of any employees from an outside undertaking who are working in his undertaking is provided with sufficient information to enable that second-mentioned employer to identify any person nominated by that first mentioned employer in accordance with regulation 8(1)(b) to implement evacuation procedures as far as those employees are concerned; and
- (b) take all reasonable steps to ensure that any employees from an outside undertaking who are working in his undertaking receive sufficient information to enable them to identify any person nominated by him in accordance with regulation 8(1)(b) to implement evacuation procedures as far as they are concerned.

(5) Paragraph (4) shall apply to a self-employed person who is working in an employer's undertaking as it applies to employees from an outside undertaking who are working therein; and the reference in that paragraph to the employer of any employees from an outside undertaking who are working in an employer's undertaking and the references in the said paragraph to employees from an outside undertaking who are working in an employer's undertaking shall be construed accordingly.

NOTES

Paras (1), (2): words omitted revoked by the Regulatory Reform (Fire Safety) Order 2005, SI 2005/1541, art 53(2), Sch 5 (in relation to England and Wales), and by the Fire (Scotland) Act 2005 (Consequential Modifications and Savings) (No 2) Order 2006, SSI 2006/457, art 2(2), Sch 2 (in relation to Scotland).

[2.466]

13 Capabilities and training

(1) Every employer shall, in entrusting tasks to his employees, take into account their capabilities as regards health and safety.

(2) Every employer shall ensure that his employees are provided with adequate health and safety training—

- (a) on their being recruited into the employer's undertaking; and
- (b) on their being exposed to new or increased risks because of—
  - (i) their being transferred or given a change of responsibilities within the employer's undertaking,
  - (ii) the introduction of new work equipment into or a change respecting work equipment already in use within the employer's undertaking,
  - (iii) the introduction of new technology into the employer's undertaking, or

(iv) the introduction of a new system of work into or a change respecting a system of work already in use within the employer's undertaking.

(3) The training referred to in paragraph (2) shall—

(a) be repeated periodically where appropriate;

(b) be adapted to take account of any new or changed risks to the health and safety of the employees concerned; and

(c) take place during working hours.

[2.467]

14 Employees' duties

(1) Every employee shall use any machinery, equipment, dangerous substance, transport equipment, means of production or safety device provided to him by his employer in accordance both with any training in the use of the equipment concerned which has been received by him and the instructions respecting that use which have been provided to him by the said employer in compliance with the requirements and prohibitions imposed upon that employer by or under the relevant statutory provisions.

(2) Every employee shall inform his employer or any other employee of that employer with specific responsibility for the health and safety of his fellow employees—

(a) of any work situation which a person with the first-mentioned employee's training and instruction would reasonably consider represented a serious and immediate danger to health and safety; and

(b) of any matter which a person with the first-mentioned employee's training and instruction would reasonably consider represented a shortcoming in the employer's protection arrangements for health and safety,

in so far as that situation or matter either affects the health and safety of that first mentioned employee or arises out of or in connection with his own activities at work, and has not previously been reported to his employer or to any other employee of that employer in accordance with this paragraph.

[2.468]

15 Temporary workers

(1) Every employer shall provide any person whom he has employed under a fixed-term contract of employment with comprehensible information on—

(a) any special occupational qualifications or skills required to be held by that employee if he is to carry out his work safely; and

(b) any health surveillance required to be provided to that employee by or under any of the relevant statutory provisions,

and shall provide the said information before the employee concerned commences his duties.

(2) Every employer and every self-employed person shall provide any person employed in an employment business who is to carry out work in his undertaking with comprehensible information on—

(a) any special occupational qualifications or skills required to be held by that employee if he is to carry out his work safely; and

(b) health surveillance required to be provided to that employee by or under any of the relevant statutory provisions.

(3) Every employer and every self-employed person shall ensure that every person carrying on an employment business whose employees are to carry out work in his undertaking is provided with comprehensible information on—

(a) any special occupational qualifications or skills required to be held by those employees if they are to carry out their work safely; and

(b) the specific features of the jobs to be filled by those employees (in so far as those features are likely to affect their health and safety);

and the person carrying on the employment business concerned shall ensure that the information so provided is given to the said employees.

[2.469]

16 Risk assessment in respect of new or expectant mothers

(1) Where—

(a) the persons working in an undertaking include women of child-bearing age; and

(b) the work is of a kind which could involve risk, by reason of her condition, to the health and safety of a new or expectant mother, or to that of her baby, from any processes or working conditions, or physical, biological or chemical agents, including those specified in Annexes I and II of Council Directive 92/85/EEC on the introduction of measures to encourage improvements in the safety and health at work of pregnant workers and workers who have recently given birth or are breastfeeding,

the assessment required by regulation 3(1) shall also include an assessment of such risk.

(2) Where, in the case of an individual employee, the taking of any other action the employer is required to take under the relevant statutory provisions would not avoid the risk referred to in paragraph (1) the employer shall, if it is reasonable to do so, and would avoid such risks, alter her working conditions or hours of work.

(3) If it is not reasonable to alter the working conditions or hours of work, or if it would not avoid such risk, the employer shall, subject to section 67 of the 1996 Act suspend the employee from work for so long as is necessary to avoid such risk.

(4) In paragraphs (1) to (3) references to risk, in relation to risk from any infectious or contagious disease, are references to a level of risk at work which is in addition to the level to which a new or expectant mother may be expected to be exposed outside the workplace.

[2.470]
[16A Alteration of working conditions in respect of new or expectant mothers (agency workers)

(1) Where, in the case of an individual agency worker, the taking of any other action the hirer is required to take under the relevant statutory provisions would not avoid the risk referred to in regulation 16(1) the hirer shall, if it is reasonable to do so, and would avoid such risks, alter her working conditions or hours of work.

(2) If it is not reasonable to alter the working conditions or hours of work, or if it would not avoid such risk, the hirer shall without delay inform the temporary work agency, who shall then end the supply of that agency worker to the hirer.

(3) In paragraphs (1) and (2) references to risk, in relation to risk from any infectious or contagious disease, are references to a level of risk at work which is in addition to the level to which a new or expectant mother may be expected to be exposed outside the workplace.]

NOTES

Commencement: 1 October 2011.

Inserted by the Agency Workers Regulations 2010, SI 2010/93, reg 25, Sch 2, Pt 2, para 17, as from 1 October 2011.

[2.471]
17 Certificate from registered medical practitioner in respect of new or expectant mothers

Where—

(a) a new or expectant mother works at night; and

(b) a certificate from a registered medical practitioner or a registered midwife shows that it is necessary for her health or safety that she should not be at work for any period of such work identified in the certificate,

the employer shall, subject to section 67 of the 1996 Act, suspend her from work for so long as is necessary for her health or safety.

[2.472]
[17A Certificate from registered medical practitioner in respect of new or expectant mothers (agency workers)

Where—

(a) a new or expectant mother works at night; and

(b) a certificate from a registered medical practitioner or a registered midwife shows that it is necessary for her health or safety that she should not be at work for any period of such work identified in the certificate,

the hirer shall without delay inform the temporary work agency, who shall then end the supply of that agency worker to the hirer.]

NOTES

Commencement: 1 October 2011.

Inserted by the Agency Workers Regulations 2010, SI 2010/93, reg 25, Sch 2, Pt 2, paras 17(1), 18, as from 1 October 2011.

[2.473]
18 Notification by new or expectant mothers

(1) Nothing in paragraph (2) or (3) of regulation 16 shall require the employer to take any action in relation to an employee until she has notified the employer in writing that she is pregnant, has given birth within the previous six months, or is breastfeeding.

(2) Nothing in paragraph (2) or (3) of regulation 16 or in regulation 17 shall require the employer to maintain action taken in relation to an employee—

(a) in a case—

 (i) to which regulation 16(2) or (3) relates; and

 (ii) where the employee has notified her employer that she is pregnant, where she has failed, within a reasonable time of being requested to do so in writing by her employer, to produce for the employer's inspection a certificate from a registered medical practitioner or a registered midwife showing that she is pregnant;

(b) once the employer knows that she is no longer a new or expectant mother; or

(c) if the employer cannot establish whether she remains a new or expectant mother.

[2.474]

[18A Notification by new or expectant mothers (agency workers)

(1) Nothing in regulation 16A(1) or (2) shall require the hirer to take any action in relation to an agency worker until she has notified the hirer in writing that she is pregnant, has given birth within the previous six months, or is breastfeeding.

(2) Nothing in regulation 16A(2) shall require the temporary work agency to end the supply of the agency worker until she has notified the temporary work agency in writing that she is pregnant, has given birth within the previous six months, or is breastfeeding.

(3) Nothing in regulation 16A(1) shall require the hirer to maintain action taken in relation to an agency worker—

(a) in a case—

(i) to which regulation 16A(1) relates; and

(ii) where the agency worker has notified the hirer, that she is pregnant, where she has failed, within a reasonable time of being requested to do so in writing by the hirer, to produce for the hirer's inspection a certificate from a registered medical practitioner or a registered midwife showing that she is pregnant; or

(b) once the hirer knows that she is no longer a new or expectant mother; or

(c) if the hirer cannot establish whether she remains a new or expectant mother.]

NOTES

Commencement: 1 October 2011.

Inserted, together with reg 18AB, by the Agency Workers Regulations 2010, SI 2010/93, reg 25, Sch 2, Pt 2, paras 17(1), 19, as from 1 October 2011.

[2.475]

[18AB Agency workers: general provisions

(1) Without prejudice to any other duties of the hirer or temporary work agency under any enactment or rule of law in relation to health and safety at work, regulation 16A, 17A and 18A shall not apply where the agency worker—

(a) has not completed the qualifying period, or

(b) is no longer entitled to the rights conferred by regulation 5 of the Agency Workers Regulations 2010 pursuant to regulation 8(a) or (b) of those Regulations.

(2) Nothing in regulations 16A or 17A imposes a duty on the hirer or temporary work agency beyond the original intended duration, or likely duration of the assignment, whichever is the longer.

(3) This regulation, and regulations 16A, 17A and 18A do not apply in circumstances where regulations 16, 17 and 18 apply.

(4) For the purposes of this regulation and regulations 16A, 17A or 18A the following have the same meaning as in the Agency Workers Regulations 2010—

"agency worker";

"assignment";

"hirer";

"qualifying period";

"temporary work agency".]

NOTES

Commencement: 1 October 2011.

Inserted as noted to reg 18A at **[2.474]**.

[2.476]

19 Protection of young persons

(1) Every employer shall ensure that young persons employed by him are protected at work from any risks to their health or safety which are a consequence of their lack of experience, or absence of awareness of existing or potential risks or the fact that young persons have not yet fully matured.

(2) Subject to paragraph (3), no employer shall employ a young person for work—

(a) which is beyond his physical or psychological capacity;

(b) involving harmful exposure to agents which are toxic or carcinogenic, cause heritable genetic damage or harm to the unborn child or which in any other way chronically affect human health;

(c) involving harmful exposure to radiation;

(d) involving the risk of accidents which it may reasonably be assumed cannot be recognised or avoided by young persons owing to their insufficient attention to safety or lack of experience or training; or
(e) in which there is a risk to health from—
(i) extreme cold or heat;
(ii) noise; or
(iii) vibration,

and in determining whether work will involve harm or risks for the purposes of this paragraph, regard shall be had to the results of the assessment.

(3) Nothing in paragraph (2) shall prevent the employment of a young person who is no longer a child for work—
(a) where it is necessary for his training;
(b) where the young person will be supervised by a competent person; and
(c) where any risk will be reduced to the lowest level that is reasonably practicable.

(4) . . .

NOTES

Para (4): revoked by the Management of Health and Safety at Work and Fire Precautions (Workplace) (Amendment) Regulations 2003, SI 2003/2457, regs 2, 5.

[2.477]
20 Exemption certificates

(1) The Secretary of State for Defence may, in the interests of national security, by a certificate in writing exempt—
(a) any of the home forces, any visiting force or any headquarters from those requirements of these Regulations which impose obligations other than those in [regulations 16–18AB] on employers; or
(b) any member of the home forces, any member of a visiting force or any member of a headquarters from the requirements imposed by regulation 14;

and any exemption such as is specified in sub-paragraph (a) or (b) of this paragraph may be granted subject to conditions and to a limit of time and may be revoked by the said Secretary of State by a further certificate in writing at any time.

(2) In this regulation—
(a) "the home forces" has the same meaning as in section 12(1) of the Visiting Forces Act 1952;
(b) "headquarters" means a headquarters for the time being specified in Schedule 2 to the Visiting Forces and International Headquarters (Application of Law) Order 1999;
(c) "member of a headquarters" has the same meaning as in paragraph 1(1) of the Schedule to the International Headquarters and Defence Organisations Act 1964; and
(d) "visiting force" has the same meaning as it does for the purposes of any provision of Part I of the Visiting Forces Act 1952.

NOTES

Para (1): words in square brackets substituted by the Agency Workers Regulations 2010, SI 2010/93, reg 25, Sch 2, Pt 2, paras 17(1), 20, as from 1 October 2011.

[2.478]
21 Provisions as to liability

Nothing in the relevant statutory provisions shall operate so as to afford an employer a defence in any criminal proceedings for a contravention of those provisions by reason of any act or default of—
(a) an employee of his, or
(b) a person appointed by him under regulation 7.

[2.479]
[22 Restriction of civil liability for breach of statutory duty

(1) Breach of a duty imposed on an employer by these Regulations shall not confer a right of action in any civil proceedings insofar as that duty applies for the protection of a third party.

(2) Breach of a duty imposed on an employee by regulation 14 shall not confer a right of action in any civil proceedings insofar as that duty applies for the protection of a third party.

(3) In this regulation, "third party", in relation to the undertaking, means any person who may be affected by that undertaking other than the employer whose undertaking it is and persons in his employment.]

NOTES

Substituted by the Management of Health and Safety at Work (Amendment) Regulations 2006, SI 2006/438, reg 2.

[2.480]

23 Extension outside Great Britain

(1) These Regulations shall, subject to regulation 2, apply to and in relation to the premises and activities outside Great Britain to which sections 1 to 59 and 80 to 82 of the Health and Safety at Work etc Act 1974 apply by virtue of the Health and Safety at Work etc Act 1974 (Application Outside Great Britain) Order 1995 as they apply within Great Britain.

(2) For the purposes of Part I of the 1974 Act, the meaning of "at work" shall be extended so that an employee or a self-employed person shall be treated as being at work throughout the time that he is present at the premises to and in relation to which these Regulations apply by virtue of paragraph (1); and, in that connection, these Regulations shall have effect subject to the extension effected by this paragraph.

NOTES

The Health and Safety at Work etc Act 1974 (Application outside Great Britain) Order 1995, SI 1995/263 was revoked and replaced by the Health and Safety at Work etc Act 1974 (Application outside Great Britain) Order 2001, SI 2001/2127.

24–28 *Reg 24 revokes the Health and Safety (First-Aid) Regulations 1981, SI 1981/917, reg 6; reg 25 amends the Offshore Installations and Pipeline Works (First-Aid) Regulations 1989, SI 1989/1671, reg 7; reg 26 amends the Mines Miscellaneous Health and Safety Provisions Regulations 1995, SI 1995/2005, reg 4; reg 27 revoked by the Construction (Design and Management) Regulations 2007, SI 2007/320, reg 48(1), Sch 4; reg 28 revoked by the Regulatory Reform (Fire Safety) Order 2005, SI 2005/1541, art 53(2), Sch 5 (in relation to England and Wales), and by the Fire (Scotland) Act 2005 (Consequential Modifications and Savings) (No 2) Order 2006, SSI 2006/457, art 2(2), Sch 2 (in relation to Scotland).)*

[2.481]

29 Revocations and consequential amendments

(1) The Management of Health and Safety at Work Regulations 1992, the Management of Health and Safety at Work (Amendment) Regulations 1994, the Health and Safety (Young Persons) Regulations 1997 and Part III of the Fire Precautions (Workplace) Regulations 1997 are hereby revoked.

(2) The instruments specified in column 1 of Schedule 2 shall be amended in accordance with the corresponding provisions in column 3 of that Schedule.

[2.482]

30 Transitional provision

The substitution of provisions in these Regulations for provisions of the Management of Health and Safety at Work Regulations 1992 shall not affect the continuity of the law; and accordingly anything done under or for the purposes of such provision of the 1992 Regulations shall have effect as if done under or for the purposes of any corresponding provision of these Regulations.

SCHEDULES

SCHEDULE 1
GENERAL PRINCIPLES OF PREVENTION

Regulation 4

[2.483]

(This Schedule specifies the general principles of prevention set out in Article 6(2) of Council Directive 89/391/EEC)

(a) avoiding risks;
(b) evaluating the risks which cannot be avoided;
(c) combating the risks at source;
(d) adapting the work to the individual, especially as regards the design of workplaces, the choice of work equipment and the choice of working and production methods, with a view, in particular, to alleviating monotonous work and work at a predetermined work-rate and to reducing their effect on health;
(e) adapting to technical progress;
(f) replacing the dangerous by the non-dangerous or the less dangerous;
(g) developing a coherent overall prevention policy which covers technology, organisation of work, working conditions, social relationships and the influence of factors relating to the working environment;
(h) giving collective protective measures priority over individual protective measures; and
(i) giving appropriate instructions to employees.

SCHEDULE 2

(Sch 2 (consequential amendments) in so far as these are within the scope of this work, they have been incorporated at the appropriate place.)

MATERNITY AND PARENTAL LEAVE ETC REGULATIONS 1999

(SI 1999/3312)

NOTES

Made: 10 December 1999.

Authority: Employment Rights Act 1996, ss 47C(2), (3), 71(1)–(3), (6), 72(1), (2), 73(1), (2), (4), (7), 74(1), (3), (4), 75(1), 76(1), (2), (5), 77(1), (4), 78(1), (2), (7), 79(1), (2), 99(1).

Commencement: 15 December 1999. For transitional provisions affecting Pt II, Pt III, and regs 19 and 20, see reg 3 (further transitional provisions in reg 13(3) have subsequently been revoked by SI 2001/4010, as noted to that regulation).

These Regulations, so far as relating to parental leave, are the domestic implementation of Directive 96/34/EC at **[3.238]**, as extended to the UK by Directive 97/75/EC. Note that Directive 96/34/EC is repealed and replaced by Directive 2010/18/EU at **[3.625]** et seq, with effect from 8 March 2012 (see Art 4 thereof at **[3.629]**).

See *Harvey* DII, J(3), (7), (8).

ARRANGEMENT OF REGULATIONS

PART I
GENERAL

PART II
MATERNITY LEAVE

PART III
PARENTAL LEAVE

PART IV
PROVISIONS APPLICABLE IN RELATION TO MORE THAN ONE KIND OF ABSENCE

SCHEDULES

PART I
GENERAL

[2.484]

1 Citation and commencement

These Regulations may be cited as the Maternity and Parental Leave etc Regulations 1999 and shall come into force on 15th December 1999.

[2.485]

2 Interpretation

(1) In these Regulations—

"the 1996 Act" means the Employment Rights Act 1996;

["additional adoption leave" means leave under section 75B of the 1996 Act;]

"additional maternity leave" means leave under section 73 of the 1996 Act;

["armed forces independence payment" means armed forces independence payment under the Armed Forces and Reserve Forces (Compensation Scheme) Order 2011;]

"business" includes a trade or profession and includes any activity carried on by a body of persons (whether corporate or unincorporated);

"child" means a person under the age of eighteen;

"childbirth" means the birth of a living child or the birth of a child whether living or dead after 24 weeks of pregnancy;

"collective agreement" means a collective agreement within the meaning of section 178 of the Trade Union and Labour Relations (Consolidation) Act 1992, the trade union parties to which are independent trade unions within the meaning of section 5 of that Act;

"contract of employment" means a contract of service or apprenticeship, whether express or implied, and (if it is express) whether oral or in writing;

"disability living allowance" means the disability living allowance provided for in Part III of the Social Security Contributions and Benefits Act 1992;

"employee" means an individual who has entered into or works under (or, where the employment has ceased, worked under) a contract of employment;

"employer" means the person by whom an employee is (or, where the employment has ceased, was) employed;

"expected week of childbirth" means the week, beginning with midnight between Saturday and Sunday, in which it is expected that childbirth will occur, and "week of childbirth" means the week, beginning with midnight between Saturday and Sunday, in which childbirth occurs;

"job", in relation to an employee returning after . . . maternity leave or parental leave, means the nature of the work which she is employed to do in accordance with her contract and the capacity and place in which she is so employed;

"ordinary maternity leave" means leave under section 71 of the 1996 Act;

"parental leave" means leave under regulation 13(1);

"parental responsibility" has the meaning given by section 3 of the Children Act 1989, and "parental responsibilities" has the meaning given by section 1(3) of the Children (Scotland) Act 1995;

["personal independence payment" means personal independence payment under Part 4 of the Welfare Reform Act 2012;]

["statutory leave" means leave provided for in Part 8 of the 1996 Act;]

["statutory maternity leave" means ordinary maternity leave and additional maternity leave;

"statutory maternity leave period" means the period during which the employee is on statutory maternity leave;]

"workforce agreement" means an agreement between an employer and his employees or their representatives in respect of which the conditions set out in Schedule 1 to these Regulations are satisfied.

(2) A reference in any provision of these Regulations to a period of continuous employment is to a period computed in accordance with Chapter I of Part XIV of the 1996 Act, as if that provision were a provision of that Act.

(3) For the purposes of these Regulations any two employers shall be treated as associated if—

(a) one is a company of which the other (directly or indirectly) has control; or

(b) both are companies of which a third person (directly or indirectly) has control;

and "associated employer" shall be construed accordingly.

(4) In these Regulations, unless the context otherwise requires,—

(a) a reference to a numbered regulation or schedule is to the regulation or schedule in these Regulations bearing that number;

(b) a reference in a regulation or schedule to a numbered paragraph is to the paragraph in that regulation or schedule bearing that number, and

(c) a reference in a paragraph to a lettered sub-paragraph is to the sub-paragraph in that paragraph bearing that letter.

NOTES

Para (1): definitions "additional adoption leave" and "statutory leave" inserted, and word omitted from definition "job" revoked, by the Maternity and Parental Leave (Amendment) Regulations 2002, SI 2002/2789, regs 3, 4; definition "armed forces independence payment" inserted by the Armed Forces and Reserve Forces Compensation Scheme (Consequential Provisions: Subordinate Legislation) Order 2013, SI 2013/591, art 7, Schedule, para 16(1), (2), as from 8 April 2013; definition "personal independence payment" inserted by the Personal Independence Payment (Supplementary Provisions and Consequential Amendments) Regulations 2013, SI 2013/388, reg 8, Schedule, Pt 2, para 22(1), (2), as from 8 April 2013; definitions "statutory maternity leave" and "statutory maternity leave period" inserted by the Maternity and Parental Leave etc and the Paternity and Adoption Leave (Amendment) Regulations 2006, SI 2006/2014, regs 3, 4.

[2.486]

3 Application

(1) The provisions of Part II of these Regulations have effect only in relation to employees whose expected week of childbirth begins on or after 30th April 2000.

(2) Regulation 19 (protection from detriment) has effect only in relation to an act or failure to act which takes place on or after 15th December 1999.

(3) For the purposes of paragraph (2)—

(a) where an act extends over a period, the reference to the date of the act is a reference to the last day of that period, and

(b) a failure to act is to be treated as done when it was decided on.

(4) For the purposes of paragraph (3), in the absence of evidence establishing the contrary an employer shall be taken to decide on a failure to act—

(a) when he does an act inconsistent with doing the failed act, or

(b) if he has done no such inconsistent act, when the period expires within which he might reasonably have been expected to do the failed act if it was to be done.

(5) Regulation 20 (unfair dismissal) has effect only in relation to dismissals where the effective date of termination (within the meaning of section 97 of the 1996 Act) falls on or after 15th December 1999.

PART II
MATERNITY LEAVE

[2.487]

4 Entitlement to ordinary maternity leave [and to additional maternity leave]

(1) An employee is entitled to ordinary maternity leave [and to additional maternity leave] provided that she satisfies the following conditions—

(a) [no later than the end of the fifteenth week before her expected week of childbirth], or, if that is not reasonably practicable, as soon as is reasonably practicable, she notifies her employer of—

  (i) her pregnancy;

  (ii) the expected week of childbirth, and

  (iii) the date on which she intends her ordinary maternity leave period to start,

and

(b) if requested to do so by her employer, she produces for his inspection a certificate from—

  (i) a registered medical practitioner, or

  (ii) a registered midwife,

stating the expected week of childbirth.

[(1A) An employee who has notified her employer under paragraph (1)(a)(iii) of the date on which she intends her ordinary maternity leave period to start may subsequently vary that date, provided that she notifies her employer of the variation at least—

(a) 28 days before the date varied, or

(b) 28 days before the new date,

whichever is the earlier, or, if that is not reasonably practicable, as soon as is reasonably practicable.]

(2) [Notification under paragraph (1)(a)(iii) or (1A)]—

(a) shall be given in writing, if the employer so requests, and

(b) shall not specify a date earlier than the beginning of the eleventh week before the expected week of childbirth.

(3) Where, by virtue of regulation 6(1)(b), an employee's ordinary maternity leave period commences with [the day which follows] the first day after the beginning of [the fourth week] before the expected week of childbirth on which she is absent from work wholly or partly because of pregnancy—

(a) paragraph (1) does not require her to notify her employer of the date specified in that paragraph, but
(b) (whether or not she has notified him of that date) she is not entitled to ordinary maternity leave [or to additional maternity leave] unless she notifies him as soon as is reasonably practicable that she is absent from work wholly or partly because of pregnancy [and of the date on which her absence on that account began].

(4) Where, by virtue of regulation 6(2), an employee's ordinary maternity leave period commences [on the day which follows] the day on which childbirth occurs—
(a) paragraph (1) does not require her to notify her employer of the date specified in that paragraph, but
(b) (whether or not she has notified him of that date) she is not entitled to ordinary maternity leave [or to additional maternity leave] unless she notifies him as soon as is reasonably practicable after the birth that she has given birth [and of the date on which the birth occurred].

(5) The notification provided for in paragraphs (3)(b) and (4)(b) shall be given in writing, if the employer so requests.

NOTES

Regulation heading: words in square brackets added by the Maternity and Parental Leave etc and the Paternity and Adoption Leave (Amendment) Regulations 2006, SI 2006/2014, regs 3, 5(a).

Para (1): words in first pair of square brackets inserted by SI 2006/2014, regs 3, 5(a); words in second pair of square brackets substituted by the Maternity and Parental Leave (Amendment) Regulations 2002, SI 2002/2789, regs 3, 5(a).

Para (1A): inserted by SI 2002/2789, regs 3, 5(b).

Para (2): words in square brackets substituted by SI 2002/2789, regs 3, 5(c).

Para (3): words in first and final pairs of square brackets inserted, and words in second pair of square brackets substituted, by SI 2002/2789, regs 3, 5(d); words in third pair of square brackets inserted by SI 2006/2014, regs 3, 5(b).

Para (4): words in first pair of square brackets substituted, and words in third pair of square brackets inserted, by SI 2002/2789, regs 3, 5(e); words in second pair of square brackets inserted by SI 2006/2014, regs 3, 5(b).

5 *(Revoked by the Maternity and Parental Leave etc and the Paternity and Adoption Leave (Amendment) Regulations 2006, SI 2006/2014, regs 3, 6.)*

[2.488]

6 Commencement of maternity leave periods

(1) Subject to paragraph (2), an employee's ordinary maternity leave period commences with the earlier of—
(a) the date which . . . she notifies to her employer[, in accordance with regulation 4,] as the date on which she intends her ordinary maternity leave period to start, [or, if by virtue of the provision for variation in that regulation she has notified more than one such date, the last date she notifies,] and
(b) [the day which follows] the first day after the beginning of [the fourth week] before the expected week of childbirth on which she is absent from work wholly or partly because of pregnancy.

(2) Where the employee's ordinary maternity leave period has not commenced by virtue of paragraph (1) when childbirth occurs, her ordinary maternity leave period commences [on the day which follows] the day on which childbirth occurs.

(3) An employee's additional maternity leave period commences on the day after the last day of her ordinary maternity leave period.

NOTES

Para (1): words omitted revoked, words in first, second and third pairs of square brackets inserted, and words in fourth pair of square brackets substituted, by the Maternity and Parental Leave (Amendment) Regulations 2002, SI 2002/2789, regs 3, 7(a), (b).

Para (2): words in square brackets substituted by SI 2002/2789, regs 3, 7(c).

[2.489]

7 Duration of maternity leave periods

(1) Subject to paragraphs (2) and (5), an employee's ordinary maternity leave period continues for the period of [26 weeks] from its commencement, or until the end of the compulsory maternity leave period provided for in regulation 8 if later.

(2) Subject to paragraph (5), where any requirement imposed by or under any relevant statutory provision prohibits the employee from working for any period after the end of the period determined under paragraph (1) by reason of her having recently given birth, her ordinary maternity leave period continues until the end of that later period.

(3) In paragraph (2), "relevant statutory provision" means a provision of—
(a) an enactment, or
(b) an instrument under an enactment,

other than a provision for the time being specified in an order under section 66(2) of the 1996 Act.

(4) Subject to paragraph (5), where an employee is entitled to additional maternity leave her additional maternity leave period continues until the end of the period of [26 weeks from the day on which it commenced].

(5) Where the employee is dismissed after the commencement of an ordinary or additional maternity leave period but before the time when (apart from this paragraph) that period would end, the period ends at the time of the dismissal.

[(6) An employer who is notified under any provision of regulation 4 of the date on which, by virtue of any provision of regulation 6, an employee's ordinary maternity leave period will commence or has commenced shall notify the employee of the date on which [her additional maternity leave period shall end]—

(a), (b) . . .

(7) The notification provided for in paragraph (6) shall be given to the employee—

(a) where the employer is notified under regulation 4(1)(a)(iii), (3)(b) or (4)(b), within 28 days of the date on which he received the notification;

(b) where the employer is notified under regulation 4(1A), within 28 days of the date on which the employee's ordinary maternity leave period commenced.]

NOTES

Paras (1), (4): words in square brackets substituted by the Maternity and Parental Leave (Amendment) Regulations 2002, SI 2002/2789, regs 3, 8(a), (b).

Para (6): added, together with para (7), by SI 2002/2789, regs 3, 8(c); words in square brackets inserted, and paras (a), (b) revoked, by the Maternity and Parental Leave etc and the Paternity and Adoption Leave (Amendment) Regulations 2006, SI 2006/2014, regs 3, 7.

Para (7): added as noted above.

[2.490]

8 Compulsory maternity leave

The prohibition in section 72 of the 1996 Act, against permitting an employee who satisfies prescribed conditions to work during a particular period (referred to as a "compulsory maternity leave period"), applies—

(a) in relation to an employee who is entitled to ordinary maternity leave, and

(b) in respect of the period of two weeks which commences with the day on which childbirth occurs.

[2.491]

[9 Application of terms and conditions during ordinary maternity leave [and additional maternity leave]

(1) An employee who takes ordinary maternity leave [or additional maternity leave]—

(a) is entitled, during the period of leave, to the benefit of all of the terms and conditions of employment which would have applied if she had not been absent, and

(b) is bound, during that period, by any obligations arising under those terms and conditions, subject only to [the exceptions in sections 71(4)(b) and 73(4)(b)] of the 1996 Act.

(2) In paragraph (1)(a), "terms and conditions" has the meaning given by [sections 71(5) and 73(5)] of the 1996 Act, and accordingly does not include terms and conditions about remuneration.

(3) For the purposes of [sections 71 and 73] of the 1996 Act, only sums payable to an employee by way of wages or salary are to be treated as remuneration.

[(4) In the case of accrual of rights under an employment-related benefit scheme within the meaning given by Schedule 5 to the Social Security Act 1989, nothing in paragraph (1)(a) concerning the treatment of additional maternity leave shall be taken to impose a requirement which exceeds the requirements of paragraph 5 of that Schedule.]]

NOTES

Substituted by the Maternity and Parental Leave (Amendment) Regulations 2002, SI 2002/2789, regs 3, 9.

Regulation heading: words in square brackets inserted by the Maternity and Parental Leave etc and the Paternity and Adoption Leave (Amendment) Regulations 2008, SI 2008/1966, regs 2(1), 3, 4(1)(a), as from 23 July 2008 (with effect in relation to employees whose expected week of childbirth begins on or after 5 October 2008).

Para (1): words in first pair of square brackets inserted, and words in second pair of square brackets substituted, by SI 2008/1966, regs 2(1), 3, 4(1)(b), (c), as from 23 July 2008 (with effect in relation to employees whose expected week of childbirth begins on or after 5 October 2008).

Paras (2), (3): words in square brackets substituted by SI 2008/1966, regs 2(1), 3, 4(1)(d), (e), as from 23 July 2008 (with effect in relation to employees whose expected week of childbirth begins on or after 5 October 2008).

Para (4): added by SI 2008/1966, regs 2(1), 3, 4(1)(f), as from 23 July 2008 (with effect in relation to employees whose expected week of childbirth begins on or after 5 October 2008).

[2.492]

10 Redundancy during maternity leave

(1) This regulation applies where, during an employee's ordinary or additional maternity leave period, it is not practicable by reason of redundancy for her employer to continue to employ her under her existing contract of employment.

(2) Where there is a suitable available vacancy, the employee is entitled to be offered (before the end of her employment under her existing contract) alternative employment with her employer or his successor, or an associated employer, under a new contract of employment which complies with paragraph (3) (and takes effect immediately on the ending of her employment under the previous contract).

(3) The new contract of employment must be such that—

(a) the work to be done under it is of a kind which is both suitable in relation to the employee and appropriate for her to do in the circumstances, and

(b) its provisions as to the capacity and place in which she is to be employed, and as to the other terms and conditions of her employment, are not substantially less favourable to her than if she had continued to be employed under the previous contract.

[2.493]

11 Requirement to notify intention to return during a maternity leave period

[(1) An employee who intends to return to work earlier than the end of her additional maternity leave period, shall give to her employer not less than 8 weeks' notice of the date on which she intends to return.]

(2) If an employee attempts to return to work earlier than the end of [her additional maternity leave period] without complying with paragraph (1), her employer is entitled to postpone her return to a date such as will secure, subject to paragraph (3), that he has [8 weeks'] notice of her return.

[(2A) An employee who complies with her obligations in paragraph (1) or whose employer has postponed her return in the circumstances described in paragraph (2), and who then decides to return to work—

(a) earlier than the original return date, must give her employer not less than 8 weeks' notice of the date on which she now intends to return;

(b) later than the original return date, must give her employer not less than 8 weeks' notice ending with the original return date.

(2B) In paragraph (2A) the "original return date" means the date which the employee notified to her employer as the date of her return to work under paragraph (1), or the date to which her return was postponed by her employer under paragraph (2).]

(3) An employer is not entitled under paragraph (2) to postpone an employee's return to work to a date after the end of the relevant maternity leave period.

(4) If an employee whose return to work has been postponed under paragraph (2) has been notified that she is not to return to work before the date to which her return was postponed, the employer is under no contractual obligation to pay her remuneration until the date to which her return was postponed if she returns to work before that date.

[(5) This regulation does not apply in a case where the employer did not notify the employee in accordance with regulation 7(6) and (7) of the date on which [her additional maternity leave period] would end.]

NOTES

Para (1): substituted by the Maternity and Parental Leave etc and the Paternity and Adoption Leave (Amendment) Regulations 2006, SI 2006/2014, regs 3, 8(a).

Para (2): words in square brackets substituted by SI 2006/2014, regs 3, 8(b).

Paras (2A), (2B): inserted by SI 2006/2014, regs 3, 8(c).

Para (5): added by SI 2002/2789, regs 3, 10(c); words in square brackets substituted by SI 2006/2014, regs 3, 8(d).

12 *(Revoked by the Maternity and Parental Leave (Amendment) Regulations 2002, SI 2002/2789, regs 3, 11.)*

[2.494]

[12A Work during maternity leave period

[(1) Subject to paragraph (5), an employee may carry out up to 10 days' work for her employer during her statutory maternity leave period without bringing her maternity leave to an end.

(2) For the purposes of this regulation, any work carried out on any day shall constitute a day's work.

(3) Subject to paragraph (4), for the purposes of this regulation, work means any work done under the contract of employment and may include training or any activity undertaken for the purposes of keeping in touch with the workplace.

Part 2 Statutory Instruments

(4) Reasonable contact from time to time between an employee and her employer which either party is entitled to make during a maternity leave period (for example to discuss an employee's return to work) shall not bring that period to an end.

(5) Paragraph (1) shall not apply in relation to any work carried out by the employee at any time from childbirth to the end of the period of two weeks which commences with the day on which childbirth occurs.

(6) This regulation does not confer any right on an employer to require that any work be carried out during the statutory maternity leave period, nor any right on an employee to work during the statutory maternity leave period.

(7) Any days' work carried out under this regulation shall not have the effect of extending the total duration of the statutory maternity leave period.]

NOTES

Inserted by the Maternity and Parental Leave etc and the Paternity and Adoption Leave (Amendment) Regulations 2006, SI 2006/2014, regs 3, 9.

PART III
PARENTAL LEAVE

[2.495]

13 Entitlement to parental leave

(1) An employee who—

(a) has been continuously employed for a period of not less than a year [or is to be treated as having been so employed by virtue of paragraph (1A)]; and

(b) has, or expects to have, responsibility for a child,

is entitled, in accordance with these Regulations, to be absent from work on parental leave for the purpose of caring for that child.

[(1A) If, in a case where regulation 15(2) or (3) applies—

(a) the employee was employed, during the period between 15th December 1998 and 9th January 2002, by a person other than the person who was his employer on 9th January 2002, and

(b) the period of his employment by that person (or, if he was employed by more than one person during that period, any such person) was not less than a year,

then, for the purposes of paragraph (1), he shall be treated as having been continuously employed for a period of not less than a year.]

(2) An employee has responsibility for a child, for the purposes of paragraph (1), if—

(a) he has parental responsibility or, in Scotland, parental responsibilities for the child; or

(b) he has been registered as the child's father under any provision of section 10(1) or 10A(1) of the Births and Deaths Registration Act 1953 or of section 18(1) or (2) of the Registration of Births, Deaths and Marriages (Scotland) Act 1965.

(3) . . .

NOTES

Para (1): words in square brackets in sub-para (a) inserted by the Maternity and Parental Leave (Amendment) Regulations 2001, SI 2001/4010, regs 2, 3(a).

Para (1A): inserted by SI 2001/4010, regs 2, 3(b).

Para (3): revoked by SI 2001/4010, regs 2, 3(c).

[2.496]

14 Extent of entitlement

[(1) An employee is entitled to eighteen weeks' leave in respect of any individual child.]

[(1A) . . .]

(2) Where the period for which an employee is normally required, under his contract of employment, to work in the course of a week does not vary, a week's leave for the employee is a period of absence from work which is equal in duration to the period for which he is normally required to work.

(3) Where the period for which an employee is normally required, under his contract of employment, to work in the course of a week varies from week to week or over a longer period, or where he is normally required under his contract to work in some weeks but not in others, a week's leave for the employee is a period of absence from work which is equal in duration to the period calculated by dividing the total of the periods for which he is normally required to work in a year by 52.

(4) Where an employee takes leave in periods shorter than the period which constitutes, for him, a week's leave under whichever of paragraphs (2) and (3) is applicable in his case, he completes a week's leave when the aggregate of the periods of leave he has taken equals the period constituting a week's leave for him under the applicable paragraph.

NOTES

Para (1): substituted by the Parental Leave (EU Directive) Regulations 2013, SI 2013/283, reg 3(1), (2)(a), as from 8 March 2013.

Para (1A): inserted by the Maternity and Parental Leave (Amendment) Regulations 2001, SI 2001/4010, regs 2, 4(b) and revoked by SI 2013/283, reg 3(1), (2)(b), as from 8 March 2013.

[2.497]

[15 When parental leave may be taken

(1) Except in the cases referred to in paragraphs (2)–(4), an employee may not exercise any entitlement to parental leave in respect of a child after the date of the child's fifth birthday or, in the case of a child placed with the employee for adoption by him, on or after—

(a) the fifth anniversary of the date on which the placement began, or

(b) the date of the child's eighteenth birthday,

whichever is the earlier.

(2) In the case of child—

(a) born before 15th December 1999, whose fifth birthday was or is on or after that date, or

(b) placed with the employee for adoption by him before 15th December 1999, the fifth anniversary of whose placement was or is on or after that date,

not being a case to which paragraph (3) or (4) applies, any entitlement to parental leave may not be exercised after 31st March 2005.

(3) In the case of a child who is entitled to a disability living allowance[, armed forces independence payment] [or personal independence payment], any entitlement to parental leave may not be exercised on or after the date of the child's eighteenth birthday.

(4) In a case where—

(a) the provisions set out in Schedule 2 apply, and

(b) the employee was unable to take leave in respect of a child within the time permitted in the case of that child under paragraphs(1) or (2) because the employer postponed the period of leave under paragraph 6 of that Schedule,

the entitlement to leave is exercisable until the end of the period to which the leave was postponed.]

NOTES

Substituted by the Maternity and Parental Leave (Amendment) Regulations 2001, SI 2001/4010, regs 2, 5.

Para (3): words in first pair of square brackets inserted by the Armed Forces and Reserve Forces Compensation Scheme (Consequential Provisions: Subordinate Legislation) Order 2013, SI 2013/591, art 7, Schedule, para 16(1), (4), as from 8 April 2013; words in second pair of square brackets inserted by the Personal Independence Payment (Supplementary Provisions and Consequential Amendments) Regulations 2013, SI 2013/388, reg 8, Schedule, Pt 2, para 22(1), (4), as from 8 April 2013.

[2.498]

16 Default provisions in respect of parental leave

The provisions set out in Schedule 2 apply in relation to parental leave in the case of an employee whose contract of employment does not include a provision which—

(a) confers an entitlement to absence from work for the purpose of caring for a child, and

(b) incorporates or operates by reference to all or part of a collective agreement or workforce agreement.

[2.499]

[16A Review

(1) The Secretary of State must from time to time—

(a) carry out a review of regulations 13 to 16 and Schedule 2,

(b) set out the conclusions of the review in a report, and

(c) publish the report.

(2) In carrying out the review the Secretary of State must, so far as is reasonable, have regard to how Council Directive 2010/18/EU of 8 March 2010 implementing the revised framework agreement on parental leave (which is implemented by means of regulations 13 to 16 and Schedule 2) is implemented in other member States.

(3) The report must in particular—

(a) set out the objectives intended to be achieved by the regulatory system established by those regulations,

(b) assess the extent to which those objectives are achieved, and

(c) assess whether those objectives remain appropriate and, if so, the extent to which they could be achieved with a system that imposes less regulation.

(4) The first report under this regulation must be published before the end of the period of five years beginning with the day on which this regulation comes into force.

(5) Reports under this regulation are afterwards to be published at intervals not exceeding five years.]

NOTES

Commencement: 8 March 2013.

Inserted by the Parental Leave (EU Directive) Regulations 2013, SI 2013/283, reg 3(1), (3), as from 8 March 2013.

PART IV
PROVISIONS APPLICABLE IN RELATION TO MORE THAN ONE KIND OF ABSENCE

[2.500]

17 Application of terms and conditions during periods of leave

An employee who takes . . . parental leave—

(a) is entitled, during the period of leave, to the benefit of her employer's implied obligation to her of trust and confidence and any terms and conditions of her employment relating to—
   (i) notice of the termination of the employment contract by her employer;
   (ii) compensation in the event of redundancy, or
   (iii) disciplinary or grievance procedures;

(b) is bound, during that period, by her implied obligation to her employer of good faith and any terms and conditions of her employment relating to—
   (i) notice of the termination of the employment contract by her;
   (ii) the disclosure of confidential information;
   (iii) the acceptance of gifts or other benefits, or
   (iv) the employee's participation in any other business.

NOTES

Words omitted revoked by the Maternity and Parental Leave etc and the Paternity and Adoption Leave (Amendment) Regulations 2008, SI 2008/1966, regs 2(1), 3, 4(2), as from 23 July 2008 (with effect in relation to employees whose expected week of childbirth begins on or after 5 October 2008).

[2.501]

[18 Right to return after maternity or parental leave

(1) An employee who returns to work after a period of ordinary maternity leave, or a period of parental leave of four weeks or less, which was—

(a) an isolated period of leave, or

(b) the last of two or more consecutive periods of statutory leave which did not include any period of additional maternity leave or additional adoption leave, or a period of parental leave of more than four weeks,

is entitled to return to the job in which she was employed before her absence.

(2) An employee who returns to work after—

(a) a period of additional maternity leave, or a period of parental leave of more than four weeks, whether or not preceded by another period of statutory leave, or

(b) a period of ordinary maternity leave, or a period of parental leave of four weeks or less, not falling within the description in paragraph (1)(a) or (b) above,

is entitled to return from leave to the job in which she was employed before her absence or, if it is not reasonably practicable for the employer to permit her to return to that job, to another job which is both suitable for her and appropriate for her to do in the circumstances.

(3) The reference in paragraphs (1) and (2) to the job in which an employee was employed before her absence is a reference to the job in which she was employed—

(a) if her return is from an isolated period of statutory leave, immediately before that period began;

(b) if her return is from consecutive periods of statutory leave, immediately before the first such period.

(4) This regulation does not apply where regulation 10 applies.]

NOTES

Substituted, together with reg 18A, for the original reg 18, by the Maternity and Parental Leave (Amendment) Regulations 2002, SI 2002/2789, regs 3, 12.

[2.502]

[18A Incidents of the right to return

(1) An employee's right to return under regulation 18(1) or (2) is a right to return—

[(a) with her seniority, pension rights and similar rights as they would have been if she had not been absent, and]

(b) on terms and conditions not less favourable than those which would have applied if she had not been absent.

[(2) In the case of accrual of rights under an employment-related benefit scheme within the meaning given by Schedule 5 to the Social Security Act 1989, nothing in paragraph (1)(a) concerning the treatment of additional maternity leave shall be taken to impose a requirement which exceeds the requirements of paragraphs 5 and 6 of that Schedule.]

(3) The provisions [in paragraph (1)] for an employee to be treated as if she had not been absent refer to her absence—

(a) if her return is from an isolated period of statutory leave, since the beginning of that period;

(b) if her return is from consecutive periods of statutory leave, since the beginning of the first such period.]

NOTES

Substituted as noted to reg 18 at **[2.501]**.

Para (1): sub-para (a) substituted by the Maternity and Parental Leave etc and the Paternity and Adoption Leave (Amendment) Regulations 2008, SI 2008/1966, regs 2(1), 3, 5(a), as from 23 July 2008 (with effect in relation to employees whose expected week of childbirth begins on or after 5 October 2008).

Para (2): substituted by SI 2008/1966, regs 2(1), 3, 5(b), as from 23 July 2008 (with effect as noted above).

Para (3): words in square brackets substituted by SI 2008/1966, regs 2(1), 3, 5(c), as from 23 July 2008 (with effect as noted above).

[2.503]

19 Protection from detriment

(1) An employee is entitled under section 47C of the 1996 Act not to be subjected to any detriment by any act, or any deliberate failure to act, by her employer done for any of the reasons specified in paragraph (2).

(2) The reasons referred to in paragraph (1) are that the employee—

(a) is pregnant;

(b) has given birth to a child;

(c) is the subject of a relevant requirement, or a relevant recommendation, as defined by section 66(2) of the 1996 Act;

(d) took, sought to take or availed herself of the benefits of, ordinary maternity leave [or additional maternity leave];

(e) took or sought to take—

(i) . . .

(ii) parental leave, or

(iii) time off under section 57A of the 1996 Act;

[(ee) failed to return after a period of ordinary or additional maternity leave in a case where—

(i) the employer did not notify her, in accordance with regulation 7(6) and (7) or otherwise, of the date on which the period in question would end, and she reasonably believed that that period had not ended, or

(ii) the employer gave her less than 28 days' notice of the date on which the period in question would end, and it was not reasonably practicable for her to return on that date;]

[(eee) undertook, considered undertaking or refused to undertake work in accordance with regulation 12A;]

(f) declined to sign a workforce agreement for the purpose of these Regulations, or

(g) being—

(i) a representative of members of the workforce for the purposes of Schedule 1, or

(ii) a candidate in an election in which any person elected will, on being elected, become such a representative,

performed (or proposed to perform) any functions or activities as such a representative or candidate.

(3) For the purposes of paragraph (2)(d), a woman avails herself of the benefits of ordinary maternity leave if, during her ordinary maternity leave period, she avails herself of the benefit of any of the terms and conditions of her employment preserved by section 71 of the 1996 Act [and regulation 9] during that period.

[(3A) For the purposes of paragraph (2)(d), a woman avails herself of the benefits of additional maternity leave if, during her additional maternity leave period, she avails herself of the benefit of any of the terms and conditions of her employment preserved by section 73 of the 1996 Act and regulation 9 during that period.]

(4) Paragraph (1) does not apply in a case where the detriment in question amounts to dismissal within the meaning of Part X of the 1996 Act.

(5) Paragraph (2)(b) only applies where the act or failure to act takes place during the employee's ordinary or additional maternity leave period.

(6) For the purposes of paragraph (5)—

(a) where an act extends over a period, the reference to the date of the act is a reference to the last day of that period, and

(b) a failure to act is to be treated as done when it was decided on.

(7) For the purposes of paragraph (6), in the absence of evidence establishing the contrary an employer shall be taken to decide on a failure to act—

(a) when he does an act inconsistent with doing the failed act, or

(b) if he has done no such inconsistent act, when the period expires within which he might reasonably have been expected to do the failed act if it were to be done.

NOTES

Para (2) is amended as follows:

Words in square brackets in sub-para (d) inserted, and sub-para (e)(i) revoked, by the Maternity and Parental Leave etc and the Paternity and Adoption Leave (Amendment) Regulations 2008, SI 2008/1966, regs 2(1), 3, 6(a), (b), as from 23 July 2008 (with effect in relation to employees whose expected week of childbirth begins on or after 5 October 2008).

Sub-para (ee) inserted by the Maternity and Parental Leave (Amendment) Regulations 2002, SI 2002/2789, regs 3, 13(a).

Sub-para (eee) inserted by the Maternity and Parental Leave etc and the Paternity and Adoption Leave (Amendment) Regulations 2006, SI 2006/2014, regs 3, 10.

Para (3): words in square brackets inserted by SI 2002/2789, regs 3, 13(b).

Para (3A): inserted by SI 2008/1966, regs 2(1), 3, 6(c), as from 23 July 2008 (with effect in relation to employees whose expected week of childbirth begins on or after 5 October 2008).

[2.504]

20 Unfair dismissal

(1) An employee who is dismissed is entitled under section 99 of the 1996 Act to be regarded for the purposes of Part X of that Act as unfairly dismissed if—

(a) the reason or principal reason for the dismissal is of a kind specified in paragraph (3), or

(b) the reason or principal reason for the dismissal is that the employee is redundant, and regulation 10 has not been complied with.

(2) An employee who is dismissed shall also be regarded for the purposes of Part X of the 1996 Act as unfairly dismissed if—

(a) the reason (or, if more than one, the principal reason) for the dismissal is that the employee was redundant;

(b) it is shown that the circumstances constituting the redundancy applied equally to one or more employees in the same undertaking who held positions similar to that held by the employee and who have not been dismissed by the employer, and

(c) it is shown that the reason (or, if more than one, the principal reason) for which the employee was selected for dismissal was a reason of a kind specified in paragraph (3).

(3) The kinds of reason referred to in paragraphs (1) and (2) are reasons connected with—

(a) the pregnancy of the employee;

(b) the fact that the employee has given birth to a child;

(c) the application of a relevant requirement, or a relevant recommendation, as defined by section 66(2) of the 1996 Act;

(d) the fact that she took, sought to take or availed herself of the benefits of, ordinary maternity leave [or additional maternity leave];

(e) the fact that she took or sought to take—

(i) . . .

(ii) parental leave, or

(iii) time off under section 57A of the 1996 Act;

[(ee) the fact that she failed to return after a period of ordinary or additional maternity leave in a case where—

(i) the employer did not notify her, in accordance with regulation 7(6) and (7) or otherwise, of the date on which the period in question would end, and she reasonably believed that that period had not ended, or

(ii) the employer gave her less than 28 days' notice of the date on which the period in question would end, and it was not reasonably practicable for her to return on that date;]

[(eee) the fact that she undertook, considered undertaking or refused to undertake work in accordance with regulation 12A;]

(f) the fact that she declined to sign a workforce agreement for the purposes of these Regulations, or

(g) the fact that the employee, being—

(i) a representative of members of the workforce for the purposes of Schedule 1, or

(ii) a candidate in an election in which any person elected will, on being elected, become such a representative,

performed (or proposed to perform) any functions or activities as such a representative or candidate.

(4) Paragraphs (1)(b) and (3)(b) only apply where the dismissal ends the employee's ordinary or additional maternity leave period.

[(5) Paragraphs (3) and (3A) of regulation 19 apply for the purposes of paragraph (3)(d) as they apply for the purposes of paragraph (2)(d) of that regulation.]

(6) . . .

(7) Paragraph (1) does not apply in relation to an employee if—

(a) it is not reasonably practicable for a reason other than redundancy for the employer (who may be the same employer or a successor of his) to permit her to return to a job which is both suitable for her and appropriate for her to do in the circumstances;

(b) an associated employer offers her a job of that kind, and

(c) she accepts or unreasonably refuses that offer.

(8) Where on a complaint of unfair dismissal any question arises as to whether the operation of paragraph (1) is excluded by the provisions of paragraph . . . (7), it is for the employer to show that the provisions in question were satisfied in relation to the complainant.

NOTES

Para (3) is amended as follows:

Words in square brackets in sub-para (d) inserted, and sub-para (e)(i) revoked, by the Maternity and Parental Leave etc and the Paternity and Adoption Leave (Amendment) Regulations 2008, SI 2008/1966, regs 2(1), 3, 7(a), (b), as from 23 July 2008 (with effect in relation to employees whose expected week of childbirth begins on or after 5 October 2008).

Sub-para (ee) inserted by the Maternity and Parental Leave (Amendment) Regulations 2002, SI 2002/2789, regs 3, 14.

Sub-para (eee) inserted by the Maternity and Parental Leave etc and the Paternity and Adoption Leave (Amendment) Regulations 2006, SI 2006/2014, regs 3, 11(a).

Para (5): substituted by SI 2008/1966, regs 2(1), 3, 7(c), as from 23 July 2008 (with effect in relation to employees whose expected week of childbirth begins on or after 5 October 2008).

Para (6): revoked by SI 2006/2014, regs 3, 11(b).

Para (8): words omitted revoked by SI 2006/2014, regs 3, 11(c).

[2.505]

21 Contractual rights to maternity or parental leave

(1) This regulation applies where an employee is entitled to—

(a) ordinary maternity leave;

(b) additional maternity leave, or

(c) parental leave,

(referred to in paragraph (2) as a "statutory right") and also to a right which corresponds to that right and which arises under the employee's contract of employment or otherwise.

(2) In a case where this regulation applies—

(a) the employee may not exercise the statutory right and the corresponding right separately but may, in taking the leave for which the two rights provide, take advantage of whichever right is, in any particular respect, the more favourable, and

(b) the provisions of the 1996 Act and of these Regulations relating to the statutory right apply, subject to any modifications necessary to give effect to any more favourable contractual terms, to the exercise of the composite right described in sub-paragraph (a) as they apply to the exercise of the statutory right.

[2.506]

22 Calculation of a week's pay

Where—

(a) under Chapter II of Part XIV of the 1996 Act, the amount of a week's pay of an employee falls to be calculated by reference to the average rate of remuneration, or the average amount of remuneration, payable to the employee in respect of a period of twelve weeks ending on a particular date (referred to as "the calculation date");

(b) during a week in that period, the employee was absent from work on ordinary or additional maternity leave or parental leave, and

(c) remuneration is payable to the employee in respect of that week under her contract of employment, but the amount payable is less than the amount that would be payable if she were working,

that week shall be disregarded for the purpose of the calculation and account shall be taken of remuneration in earlier weeks so as to bring up to twelve the number of weeks of which account is taken.

SCHEDULES

SCHEDULE 1
WORKFORCE AGREEMENTS

Regulation 2(1)

[2.507]

1. An agreement is a workforce agreement for the purposes of these Regulations if the following conditions are satisfied—

(a) the agreement is in writing;
(b) it has effect for a specified period not exceeding five years;
(c) it applies either—
 (i) to all of the relevant members of the workforce, or
 (ii) to all of the relevant members of the workforce who belong to a particular group;
(d) the agreement is signed—
 (i) in the case of an agreement of the kind referred to in sub-paragraph (c)(i), by the representatives of the workforce, and in the case of an agreement of the kind referred to in sub-paragraph (c)(ii), by the representatives of the group to which the agreement applies (excluding, in either case, any representative not a relevant member of the workforce on the date on which the agreement was first made available for signature), or
 (ii) if the employer employed 20 or fewer employees on the date referred to in sub-paragraph (d)(i), either by the appropriate representatives in accordance with that sub-paragraph or by the majority of the employees employed by him;

and
(e) before the agreement was made available for signature, the employer provided all the employees to whom it was intended to apply on the date on which it came into effect with copies of the text of the agreement and such guidance as those employees might reasonably require in order to understand it in full.

2. For the purposes of this Schedule—

"a particular group" is a group of the relevant members of a workforce who undertake a particular function, work at a particular workplace or belong to a particular department or unit within their employer's business;

"relevant members of the workforce" are all of the employees employed by a particular employer, excluding any employee whose terms and conditions of employment are provided for, wholly or in part, in a collective agreement;

"representatives of the workforce" are employees duly elected to represent the relevant members of the workforce, "representatives of the group" are employees duly elected to represent the members of a particular group, and representatives are "duly elected" if the election at which they were elected satisfied the requirements of paragraph 3 of this Schedule.

3. The requirements concerning elections referred to in paragraph 2 are that—
(a) the number of representatives to be elected is determined by the employer;
(b) the candidates for election as representatives of the workforce are relevant members of the workforce, and the candidates for election as representatives of a group are members of the group;
(c) no employee who is eligible to be a candidate is unreasonably excluded from standing for election;
(d) all the relevant members of the workforce are entitled to vote for representatives of the workforce, and all the members of a particular group are entitled to vote for representatives of the group;
(e) the employees entitled to vote may vote for as many candidates as there are representatives to be elected, and
(f) the election is conducted so as to secure that—
 (i) so far as is reasonably practicable, those voting do so in secret, and
 (ii) the votes given at the election are fairly and accurately counted.

SCHEDULE 2
DEFAULT PROVISIONS IN RESPECT OF PARENTAL LEAVE

Regulation 16

Conditions of entitlement

[2.508]

1. An employee may not exercise any entitlement to parental leave unless—
(a) he has complied with any request made by his employer to produce for the employer's inspection evidence of his entitlement, of the kind described in paragraph 2;
(b) he has given his employer notice, in accordance with whichever of paragraphs 3 to 5 is applicable, of the period of leave he proposes to take, and
(c) in a case where paragraph 6 applies, his employer has not postponed the period of leave in accordance with that paragraph.

2. The evidence to be produced for the purpose of paragraph 1(a) is such evidence as may reasonably be required of—
(a) the employee's responsibility or expected responsibility for the child in respect of whom the employee proposes to take parental leave;

(b) the child's date of birth or, in the case of a child who was placed with the employee for adoption, the date on which the placement began, and
(c) in a case where the employee's right to exercise an entitlement to parental leave under regulation 15, or to take a particular period of leave under paragraph 7, depends upon whether the child is entitled to a disability living allowance[, armed forces independence payment] [or personal independence payment], the child's entitlement to that allowance [or payment].

[2A. Where regulation 13(1A) applies, and the employee's entitlement to parental leave arises out of a period of employment by a person other than the person who was his employer on 9th January 2002, the employee may not exercise the entitlement unless he has given his employer notice of that period of employment, and provided him with such evidence of it as the employer may reasonably require.]

Notice to be given to employer

3. Except in a case where paragraph 4 or 5 applies, the notice required for the purpose of paragraph 1(b) is notice which—
(a) specifies the dates on which the period of leave is to begin and end, and
(b) is given to the employer at least 21 days before the date on which that period is to begin.

4. Where the employee is the father of the child in respect of whom the leave is to be taken, and the period of leave is to begin on the date on which the child is born, the notice required for the purpose of paragraph 1(b) is notice which—
(a) specifies the expected week of childbirth and the duration of the period of leave, and
(b) is given to the employer at least 21 days before the beginning of the expected week of childbirth.

5. Where the child in respect of whom the leave is to be taken is to be placed with the employee for adoption by him and the leave is to begin on the date of the placement, the notice required for the purpose of paragraph 1(b) is notice which—
(a) specifies the week in which the placement is expected to occur and the duration of the period of leave, and
(b) is given to the employer at least 21 days before the beginning of that week, or, if that is not reasonably practicable, as soon as is reasonably practicable.

Postponement of leave

6. An employer may postpone a period of parental leave where—
(a) neither paragraph 4 nor paragraph 5 applies, and the employee has accordingly given the employer notice in accordance with paragraph 3;
(b) the employer considers that the operation of his business would be unduly disrupted if the employee took leave during the period identified in his notice;
(c) the employer agrees to permit the employee to take a period of leave—
(i) of the same duration as the period identified in the employee's notice, . . .
(ii) beginning on a date determined by the employer after consulting the employee, which is no later than six months after the commencement of that period; [and
(iii) ending before the date of the child's eighteenth birthday.]
(d) the employer gives the employee notice in writing of the postponement which—
(i) states the reason for it, and
(ii) specifies the dates on which the period of leave the employer agrees to permit the employee to take will begin and end,
and
(e) that notice is given to the employee not more than seven days after the employee's notice was given to the employer.

Minimum periods of leave

7. An employee may not take parental leave in a period other than the period which constitutes a week's leave for him under regulation 14 or a multiple of that period, except in a case where the child in respect of whom leave is taken is entitled to a disability living allowance[, armed forces independence payment] [or personal independence payment].

Maximum annual leave allowance

8. An employee may not take more than four weeks' leave in respect of any individual child during a particular year.

9. For the purposes of paragraph 8, a year is the period of twelve months beginning—
(a) except where sub-paragraph (b) applies, on the date on which the employee first became entitled to take parental leave in respect of the child in question, or

(b) in a case where the employee's entitlement has been interrupted at the end of a period of continuous employment, on the date on which the employee most recently became entitled to take parental leave in respect of that child,

and each successive period of twelve months beginning on the anniversary of that date.

NOTES

Para 2: words in first pair of square brackets inserted by the Armed Forces and Reserve Forces Compensation Scheme (Consequential Provisions: Subordinate Legislation) Order 2013, SI 2013/591, art 7, Schedule, para 16(1), (5)(a), as from 8 April 2013; words in second and third pairs of square brackets inserted by the Personal Independence Payment (Supplementary Provisions and Consequential Amendments) Regulations 2013, SI 2013/388, reg 8, Schedule, Pt 2, para 22(1), (5)(a), as from 8 April 2013.

Para 2A: inserted by the Maternity and Parental Leave (Amendment) Regulations 2001, SI 2001/4010, regs 2, 6(a).

Para 6: word omitted from sub-para (c)(i) revoked, and sub-para (c)(ii) and word immediately preceding it added, by SI 2001/4010, regs 2, 6(b).

Para 7: words in first pair of square brackets inserted by SI 2013/591, art 7, Schedule, para 16(1), (5)(b), as from 8 April 2013; words in second pair of square brackets inserted by SI 2013/388, reg 8, Schedule, Pt 2, para 22(1), (5)(b), as from 8 April 2013.

TRANSNATIONAL INFORMATION AND CONSULTATION OF EMPLOYEES REGULATIONS 1999

(SI 1999/3323)

NOTES

Made: 12 December 1999.

Authority: European Communities Act 1972, s 2(2).

Commencement: 15 January 2000.

These Regulations are the domestic implementation for the UK of Directive 94/45/EC at **[3.202]**, as extended to the UK by Directive 97/74/EC. Note that Directive 94/45/EC was repealed and replaced by Directive 2009/38/EC at **[3.601]** et seq, with effect from 6 June 2011 (see Art 17 thereof at **[3.618]**). Amendments to these Regulations to give effect to Directive 2009/38/EC were made by the Transnational Information and Consultation of Employees (Amendment) Regulations 2010, SI 2010/1088, as noted below.

Employment Appeal Tribunal: an appeal lies to the Employment Appeal Tribunal on any question of law arising from any decision of, or in any proceedings before, an employment tribunal under or by virtue of these Regulations; see the Employment Tribunals Act 1996, s 21(1)(i) at **[1.713]**.

Conciliation: employment tribunal proceedings and claims which could be the subject of employment tribunal proceedings under regs 27, 32 are proceedings to which the Employment Tribunals Act 1996, s 18 applies; see s 18(1)(g) of that Act at **[1.706]**.

See *Harvey* NIII(3).

ARRANGEMENT OF REGULATIONS

PART I
GENERAL

PART II
EMPLOYEE NUMBERS & REQUEST TO NEGOTIATE ESTABLISHMENT OF A EUROPEAN WORKS COUNCIL OR INFORMATION AND CONSULTATION PROCEDURE

PART III
SPECIAL NEGOTIATING BODY

PART IV
EUROPEAN WORKS COUNCIL AND INFORMATION AND CONSULTATION PROCEDURE

PART V
COMPLIANCE AND ENFORCEMENT

PART VI
CONFIDENTIAL INFORMATION

PART VII
PROTECTIONS FOR MEMBERS OF A EUROPEAN WORKS COUNCIL, ETC

PART VIII
MISCELLANEOUS

The Appeal Tribunal, Industrial Court, CAC, ACAS and the Labour Relations Agency

Restrictions on contracting out

PART IX
EXCEPTIONS

PART X
TRANSITIONALS

Part 2 Statutory Instruments

PART I
GENERAL

[2.509]

1 Citation, commencement and extent

(1) These Regulations may be cited as the Transnational Information and Consultation of Employees Regulations 1999 and shall come into force on 15th January 2000.

(2) These Regulations extend to Northern Ireland.

[2.510]

2 Interpretation

(1) In these Regulations—

"the 1996 Act" means the Employment Rights Act 1996;

"the 1996 Order" means the Employment Rights (Northern Ireland) Order 1996;

"ACAS" means the Advisory, Conciliation and Arbitration Service;

["agency worker" has the meaning provided for in regulation 3 of the Agency Workers Regulations 2010;]

"Appeal Tribunal" means the Employment Appeal Tribunal;

"CAC" means the Central Arbitration Committee;

"central management" means—

(a) the central management of a Community-scale undertaking, or

(b) in the case of a Community-scale group of undertakings, the central management of the controlling undertaking,

or, where appropriate, the central management of an undertaking or group of undertakings that could be or is claimed to be a Community-scale undertaking or Community-scale group of undertakings;

"Community-scale undertaking" means an undertaking with at least 1000 employees within the Member States and at least 150 employees in each of at least two Member States;

"Community-scale group of undertakings" means a group of undertakings which has—

(a) at least 1000 employees within the Member States,

(b) at least two group undertakings in different Member States, and

(c) at least one group undertaking with at least 150 employees in one Member State and at least one other group undertaking with at least 150 employees in another Member State;

"consultation" means the exchange of views and establishment of dialogue between members of a European Works Council in the context of a European Works Council, or information and consultation representatives in the context of an information and consultation procedure, and central management or any more appropriate level of management;

"contract of employment" means a contract of service or apprenticeship, whether express or implied, and (if it is express) whether oral or in writing;

"controlled undertaking" has the meaning assigned to it by regulation 3;

"controlling undertaking" has the meaning assigned to it by regulation 3;

"employee" means an individual who has entered into or works under a contract of employment and in Part VII and regulation 41 includes, where the employment has ceased, an individual who worked under a contract of employment;

"employees' representatives" means—

(a) if the employees are of a description in respect of which an independent trade union is recognised by their employer for the purpose of collective bargaining, representatives of the trade union who normally take part as negotiators in the collective bargaining process, and

(b) any other employee representatives elected or appointed by employees to positions in which they are expected to receive, on behalf of the employees, information—

(i) which is relevant to the terms and conditions of employment of the employees, or

(ii) about the activities of the undertaking which may significantly affect the interests of the employees,

but excluding representatives who are expected to receive information relevant only to a specific aspect of the terms and conditions or interests of the employees, such as health and safety or collective redundancies;

"European Works Council" means the council, established under and in accordance with—

(a) regulation 17, or regulation 18 and the provisions of the Schedule, or

(b) where appropriate, the provisions of the law or practice of a Member State other than the United Kingdom which are designed to give effect to Article 6 of, or Article 7 of and the Annex to, the Transnational Information and Consultation Directive,

with the purpose of informing and consulting employees;

"Extension Directive" means Council Directive 97/74/EC of 15 December 1997 extending, to the United Kingdom, the Transnational Information and Consultation Directive;

"group of undertakings" means a controlling undertaking and its controlled undertakings;

"group undertaking" means an undertaking which is part of a Community-scale group of undertakings;

["hirer" has the meaning provided for in regulation 2 of the Agency Workers Regulations 2010;]

"independent trade union" has the same meaning as in the Trade Union and Labour Relations (Consolidation) Act 1992, or in Northern Ireland the 1996 Order;

"information and consultation procedure" means one or more information and consultation procedures agreed under—

(a) regulation 17, or

(b) where appropriate, the provisions of the law or practice of a Member State other than the United Kingdom which are designed to give effect to Article 6(3) of the Transnational Information and Consultation Directive;

"information and consultation representative" means a person who represents employees in the context of an information and consultation procedure;

"local management" means the management of one or more establishments in a Community-scale undertaking or of one or more undertakings in a Community-scale group of undertakings which is not the central management;

"Member State" means a state which is a Contracting Party to the Agreement on the European Economic Area signed at Oporto on 2nd May 1992 as adjusted by the Protocol signed at Brussels on 17th March 1993;

["national employee representation body" means—

(a) where the employees are of a description in respect of which an independent trade union is recognised by their employer for the purpose of collective bargaining, that trade union, and

(b) a body which has not been established with information and consultation on transnational matters as its main purpose, to which any employee representatives are elected or appointed by employees, as a result of which they hold positions in which they are expected to receive, on behalf of the employees, information—

(i) which is relevant to the terms and conditions of employment of the employees, or

(ii) about the activities of the undertaking which may significantly affect the interests of the employees,

(including information relevant only to a specific aspect of the terms and conditions or interests of the employees, such as health and safety or collective redundancies);

"relevant date" has the meaning given to it in regulation 6(4);]

"special negotiating body" means the body established for the purposes of negotiating with central management an agreement for a European Works Council or an information and consultation procedure;

["suitable information relating to the use of agency workers" means—

(a) the number of agency workers working temporarily for and under the supervision and direction of the undertaking;

(b) the parts of the undertaking in which those agency workers are working; and

(c) the type of work those agency workers are carrying out;

"temporary work agency" has the meaning provided for in regulation 4 of the Agency Workers Regulations 2010;]

"Transnational Information and Consultation Directive" means Council Directive 94/45/EC of 22 September 1994 on the establishment of a European Works Council or a procedure in Community-scale undertakings and Community-scale groups of undertakings for the purposes of informing and consulting employees;

"UK management" means the management which is, or would be, subject to the obligation in regulation 13(2) or paragraph 4(1) of the Schedule, being either the central management in the United Kingdom or the local management in the United Kingdom;

"UK member of the special negotiating body" means a member of the special negotiating body who represents UK employees for the purposes of negotiating with central management an agreement for a European Works Council or an information and consultation procedure.

(2) To the extent that the Transnational Information and Consultation Directive and the Extension Directive permit the establishment of more than one European Works Council in a Community-scale undertaking or Community-scale group of undertakings, these Regulations shall be construed accordingly.

(3) In paragraphs (1) and (4) of this regulation and in regulations 6, 13 to 15 and paragraphs 3 to 5 of the Schedule, references to "UK employees" are references to employees who are employed in the United Kingdom by a Community-scale undertaking or Community-scale group of undertakings.

(4) In regulations 13 and 15 and paragraphs 3 and 4 of the Schedule, references to "UK employees' representatives" are references to employees' representatives who represent UK employees.

[(4A) In paragraph (1) in the definition of "national employee representation body" and in regulation 18A, matters are transnational where they concern—

(a) the Community-scale undertaking or Community-scale group of undertakings as a whole, or

(b) at least two undertakings or establishments of the Community-scale undertaking or Community-scale group of undertakings situated in two different Member States.

(4B) The arrangements to link information and consultation of a European Works Council with information and consultation of the national employee representation bodies—

(a) in regulation 17(4)(c) may relate to any matters including, as the case may be—

(i) the content of the information, the time when, or manner in which it is given, or

(ii) the content of the consultation, the time when, or manner in which it takes place;

(b) in regulations 17(4)(c) and 19E are subject to the limitation in regulation 18A(7); and

(c) in regulations 17(4)(c) and 19E shall not affect the main purpose for which a national employee representation body was established.

(4C) An agency worker who has a contract within regulation 3(1)(b) of the Agency Workers Regulations 2010 (contract with the temporary work agency) with a temporary work agency which is a Community-scale undertaking or Community-scale group of undertakings at the relevant date, which is not a contract of employment, shall be treated as being employed by that agency for the duration of their assignment with a hirer for the purposes of—

(a) calculating the number of employees within the definitions of "Community-scale undertaking" and "Community-scale group of undertakings" in this regulation; and

(b) the means of calculating the number of employees in regulation 6.]

(5) In the absence of a definition in these Regulations, words and expressions used in particular regulations and particular paragraphs of the Schedule to these Regulations which are also used in the provisions of the Transnational Information and Consultation Directive or the Extension Directive to which they are designed to give effect have the same meaning as they have in those provisions.

NOTES

Para (1): definitions "national employee representation body" and "relevant date" inserted as from 5 June 2011, and definitions "agency worker", "hirer", "suitable information relating to the use of agency workers" and "temporary work agency" inserted as from 1 October 2011, by the Transnational Information and Consultation of Employees (Amendment) Regulations 2010, SI 2010/1088, regs 2, 3(a).

Paras (4A)–(4C): inserted by SI 2010/1088, regs 2, 3(b), as from 5 June 2011 (in relation to paras (4A), (4B)) and as from 1 October 2011 (in relation to para (4C)).

[2.511]

3 Controlled and Controlling Undertaking

(1) In these Regulations "controlling undertaking" means an undertaking which can exercise a dominant influence over another undertaking by virtue, for example, of ownership, financial participation or the rules which govern it and "controlled undertaking" means an undertaking over which such a dominant influence can be exercised.

(2) The ability of an undertaking to exercise a dominant influence over another undertaking shall be presumed, unless the contrary is proved, when in relation to another undertaking it directly or indirectly—

(a) can appoint more than half of the members of that undertaking's administrative, management or supervisory body;

(b) controls a majority of the votes attached to that undertaking's issued share capital; or

(c) holds a majority of that undertaking's subscribed capital.

(3) In applying the criteria in paragraph (2), a controlling undertaking's rights as regards voting and appointment shall include—

(a) the rights of its other controlled undertakings; and

(b) the rights of any person or body acting in his or its own name but on behalf of the controlling undertaking or of any other of the controlling undertaking's controlled undertakings.

(4) Notwithstanding paragraphs (1) and (2) an undertaking shall not be a controlling undertaking of another undertaking in which it has holdings where the first undertaking is a company referred to in Article 3(5)(a) or (c) of Council Regulation [(EC) No 139/2004 of 20 January 2004] on the control of concentrations between undertakings.

(5) A dominant influence shall not be presumed to be exercised solely by virtue of the fact that an office holder is exercising functions, according to the law of a Member State, relating to liquidation, winding-up, insolvency, cessation of payments, compositions of creditors or analogous proceedings.

(6) Where the law governing an undertaking is the law of a Member State, the law applicable in order to determine whether an undertaking is a controlling undertaking shall be the law of that Member State.

(7) Where the law governing an undertaking is not that of a Member State the law applicable shall be the law of the Member State within whose territory—

(a) the representative of the undertaking is situated; or

(b) in the absence of such a representative, the management of the group undertaking which employs the greatest number of employees is situated.

(8) If two or more undertakings (whether situated in the same or in different Member States) meet one or more of the criteria in paragraph (2) in relation to another undertaking, the criteria shall be applied in the order listed in relation to each of the first-mentioned undertakings and that which meets the criterion that is highest in the order listed shall be presumed, unless the contrary is proved, to exercise a dominant influence over the undertaking in question.

NOTES

Para (4): words in square brackets substituted by the EC Merger Control (Consequential Amendments) Regulations 2004, SI 2004/1079, reg 2, Schedule, para 4.

[2.512]

4 Circumstances in which provisions of these Regulations apply

(1) Subject to paragraph (2) the provisions of regulations 7 to 41 and of regulation 46 shall apply in relation to a Community-scale undertaking or Community-scale group of undertakings only where, in accordance with regulation 5, the central management is situated in the United Kingdom.

(2) The following regulations shall apply in relation to a Community-scale undertaking or Community-scale group of undertakings whether or not the central management is situated in the United Kingdom—

(a) regulations 7 and 8(1), (2) and (4) (provision of information on employee numbers);

(b) regulations 13 to 15 (UK members of the special negotiating body);

(c) regulation 18 to the extent it applies paragraphs 3 to 5 of the Schedule (UK members of the European Works Council);

(d) regulations 23(1) to (5) (breach of statutory duty);

(e) regulations 25 to 33 (protections for members of a European Works Council, etc);

(f) regulations 34 to 39 (enforcement bodies) to the extent they relate to applications made or complaints presented under any of the other regulations referred to in this paragraph;

(g) regulations 40 and 41 (restrictions on contracting out).

[2.513]

5 The central management

(1) The central management shall be responsible for creating the conditions and means necessary for the setting up of a European Works Council or an information and consultation procedure in a Community-scale undertaking or Community-scale group of undertakings where—

(a) the central management is situated in the United Kingdom;

(b) the central management is not situated in a Member State and the representative agent of the central management (to be designated if necessary) is situated in the United Kingdom; or

(c) neither the central management nor the representative agent (whether or not as a result of being designated) is situated in a Member State and—

(i) in the case of a Community-scale undertaking, there are employed in an establishment, which is situated in the United Kingdom, more employees than are employed in any other establishment which is situated in a Member State, or

(ii) in the case of a Community-scale group of undertakings, there are employed in a group undertaking, which is situated in the United Kingdom, more employees than are employed in any other group undertaking which is situated in a Member State,

and the central management initiates, or by virtue of regulation 9(1) is required to initiate, negotiations for a European Works Council or information and consultation procedure.

(2) Where the circumstances described in paragraph (1)(b) or (1)(c) apply, the central management shall be treated, for the purposes of these Regulations, as being situated in the United Kingdom and—

(a) the representative agent referred to in paragraph (1)(b); or

(b) the management of the establishment referred to in paragraph (1)(c)(i) or of the group undertaking, referred to in paragraph (1)(c)(ii),

shall be treated, respectively, as being the central management.

PART II
EMPLOYEE NUMBERS & REQUEST TO NEGOTIATE ESTABLISHMENT OF A EUROPEAN WORKS COUNCIL OR INFORMATION AND CONSULTATION PROCEDURE

[2.514]

6 Calculation of numbers of employees

(1) For the purposes of determining whether an undertaking is a Community-scale undertaking or a group of undertakings is a Community-scale group of undertakings, the number of employees employed by the undertaking, or group of undertakings, shall be determined—

- (a) in the case of UK employees, by ascertaining the average number of employees employed during a two year period, calculated in accordance with paragraph (2) below;
- (b) in the case of employees in another Member State, by ascertaining the average number of employees employed during a two year period, calculated in accordance with the provisions of the law or practice of that Member State which is designed to give effect to the Transnational Information and Consultation Directive.

(2) Subject to paragraph (3), the average number of UK employees is to be ascertained by—

- (a) determining the number of UK employees in each month in the two year period preceding the relevant date (whether they were employed throughout the month or not);
- (b) adding together all of the monthly numbers, and

dividing the number so determined by 24.

(3) For the purposes of the calculation in paragraph 2(a) if for the whole of a month within the two year period an employee works under a contract by virtue of which he would have worked for 75 hours or less in that month—

- (a) were the month to have contained 21 working days;
- (b) were the employee to have had no absences from work; and
- (c) were the employee to have worked no overtime,

the employee may be counted as half a person for the month in question, if the UK management so decides.

(4) For the purposes of this regulation, [regulations 2(4C), 7 to 10, 19F and 20] "relevant date" means—

- (a) where a request under regulation 7 is made and no valid request under regulation 9 has been made, the last day of the month preceding the month in which the request under regulation 7 is made; and
- (b) where a valid request under regulation 9 is made (whether or not a request under regulation 7 has been made), the last day of the month preceding the month in which the request under regulation 9 is made.

(5) Where appropriate, the references in paragraph (4) to regulations 7 and 9 shall be read, instead, as references to the provisions of the law or practice of a Member State other than the United Kingdom which are designed to give effect to, respectively, Article 11(2) and Article 5(1) of the Transnational Information and Consultation Directive.

NOTES

Para (4): words in square brackets substituted by the Transnational Information and Consultation of Employees (Amendment) Regulations 2010, SI 2010/1088, regs 2, 4, as from 5 June 2011.

[2.515]

7 Entitlement to information

(1) An employee or an employees' representative may request information from the management of an establishment, or of an undertaking, in the United Kingdom for the purpose of determining whether, in the case of an establishment, it is part of a Community-scale undertaking or Community-scale group of undertakings or, in the case of an undertaking, it is a Community-scale undertaking or is part of a Community-scale group of undertakings.

(2) In this regulation and regulation 8, the management of an establishment or undertaking to which a request under paragraph (1) is made is referred to as the "recipient".

[(3) The recipient must obtain and provide the employee or employees' representative who has made the request with information—

- (a) on the average number of employees employed by the undertaking, or as the case may be the group of undertakings, in the United Kingdom and in each of the other Member States in the last two years; and
- (b) relating to the structure of—
  - (i) the undertaking, or as the case may be the group of undertakings, and
  - (ii) its workforce,

  in the United Kingdom and in each of the other Member States in the last two years.

(4) Where information disclosed under paragraph (3) includes information as to the employment situation in the undertaking, or as the case may be the group of undertakings, this shall include suitable information relating to the use of agency workers (if any).]

NOTES

Paras (3), (4): substituted (for the original para (3)) by the Transnational Information and Consultation of Employees (Amendment) Regulations 2010, SI 2010/1088, regs 2, 5, as from 5 June 2011 (in relation to para (3)), and as from 1 October 2011 (in relation to para (4)).

[2.516]

8 Complaint of failure to provide information

(1) An employee or employees' representative who has requested information under regulation 7 may present a complaint to the CAC that—

[(a) the recipient has failed to provide, or as the case may be obtain and provide, the information referred to in regulation 7(3); or]

(b) the information which has been provided by the recipient is false or incomplete in a material particular.

[(2) Where the CAC finds the complaint well-founded it shall make an order requiring the recipient to disclose information to the complainant which order shall specify—

(a) the information in respect of which the CAC finds that the complaint is well-founded and which is to be disclosed, or as the case may be obtained and disclosed, to the complainant;

(b) the date (or if more than one, the earliest date) on which the recipient refused or failed to disclose, or as the case may be obtain and disclose, information, or disclosed false or incomplete information; and

(c) a date (not less than one week from the date of the order) by which the recipient must disclose, or as the case may be obtain and disclose, the information specified in the order.]

(3) If the CAC considers that, from the information it has obtained in considering the complaint, it is beyond doubt that the undertaking is, or that the establishment is part of, a Community-scale undertaking or that the establishment or undertaking is part of a Community-scale group of undertakings, it may make a declaration to that effect.

(4) The CAC shall not consider a complaint presented under this regulation unless it is made after the expiry of a period of one month beginning on the date on which the complainant made his request for information under regulation 7.

NOTES

Para (1)(a) and para (2) substituted by the Transnational Information and Consultation of Employees (Amendment) Regulations 2010, SI 2010/1088, regs 2, 6, as from 5 June 2011.

[2.517]

9 Request to negotiate an agreement for a European Works Council or information and consultation procedure

(1) The central management shall initiate negotiations for the establishment of a European Works Council or an information and consultation procedure where—

(a) a valid request has been made by employees or employees' representatives; and

(b) on the relevant date the undertaking is a Community-scale undertaking or the group of undertakings is a Community-scale group of undertakings.

(2) A valid request may consist of—

(a) a single request made by at least 100 employees, or employees' representatives who represent at least that number, in at least two undertakings or establishments in at least two different Member States; or

(b) a number of separate requests made on the same or different days by employees, or by employees' representatives, which when taken together mean that at least 100 employees, or employees' representatives who represent at least that number, in at least two undertakings or establishments in at least two different Member States have made requests.

(3) To amount to a valid request the single request referred to in paragraph (2)(a) or each separate request referred to in paragraph (2)(b) must—

(a) be in writing;

(b) be sent to—

(i) the central management, or

(ii) the local management;

(c) specify the date on which it was sent; and

(d) where appropriate, be made after the expiry of a period of two years, commencing on the date of a decision under regulation 16(3) (unless the special negotiating body and central management have otherwise agreed).

(4) The date on which a valid request is made is—

(a) where it consists of a single request satisfying paragraph 2(a) or of separate requests made on the same day satisfying paragraph 2(b), the date on which the request is or requests are sent; and

(b) where it consists of separate requests made on different days satisfying paragraph 2(b), the date of the sending of the request which resulted in that paragraph being satisfied.

(5) The central management may initiate the negotiations referred to in paragraph (1) on its own initiative.

[2.518]

10 Dispute as to whether valid request made or whether obligation in regulation 9(1) applies

(1) If the central management considers that a request (or separate request) did not satisfy any requirement of regulation 9(2) or (3) it may apply to the CAC for a declaration as to whether the request satisfied the requirement.

(2) The CAC shall only consider an application for a declaration made under paragraph (1) if—

(a) the application is made within a three month period beginning on the date when a request, or if more than one the first request, was made for the purposes of regulation 9, whether or not that request satisfied the requirements of regulations 9(2) and (3);

(b) the application is made before the central management takes any step to initiate negotiations for the establishment of a European Works Council or an information and consultation procedure; and

(c) at the time when the application is made, there has been no application by the central management for a declaration under paragraph (3).

(3) If the central management considers for any reason that the obligation in regulation 9(1) did not apply to it on the relevant date, it may, within a period of three months commencing on the date on which the valid request was made, apply to the CAC for a declaration as to whether that obligation applied to it on the relevant date.

(4) Where the date on which the valid request was made is a date falling before the date of any declaration made pursuant to an application made under this regulation the operation of the periods of time specified in paragraphs (1)(b) and (1)(c) of regulation 18 shall be suspended for a period of time—

(a) commencing on the date of the application; and

(b) ending on the date of the declaration.

(5) If on an application for a declaration under this regulation the CAC does not make any declaration in favour of the central management and considers that the central management has, in making the application or conducting the proceedings, acted frivolously, vexatiously, or otherwise unreasonably, the CAC shall make a declaration to the effect that paragraph (4) does not apply.

PART III
SPECIAL NEGOTIATING BODY

[2.519]

11 Functions of the special negotiating body

The special negotiating body shall have the task of determining, with the central management, by written agreement, the scope, composition, functions, and term of office of a European Works Council or the arrangements for implementing an information and consultation procedure.

[2.520]

[12 Composition of the special negotiating body

(1) Subject to paragraph (3), the special negotiating body shall be constituted in accordance with paragraph (2).

(2) In each Member State in which employees of a Community-scale undertaking or Community-scale group of undertakings are employed to work, those employees shall elect or appoint one member of the special negotiating body for each 10% (or fraction of 10%) which those employees represent of the total number of employees of the Community-scale undertaking or Community-scale group of undertakings employed in those Member States.

(3) Paragraph (1) does not apply to a special negotiating body constituted before 5th June 2011.

(4) The special negotiating body shall inform the central management, local managements and the European social partner organisations of the composition of the special negotiating body and of the date they propose to start the negotiations.]

NOTES

Commencement: 5 June 2011.

Substituted by the Transnational Information and Consultation of Employees (Amendment) Regulations 2010, SI 2010/1088, regs 2, 7, as from 5 June 2011.

[2.521]

13 Ballot arrangements

(1) Subject to regulation 15, the UK members of the special negotiating body shall be elected by a ballot of the UK employees.

(2) The UK management must arrange for the holding of a ballot of employees referred to in paragraph (1), which satisfies the requirements specified in paragraph (3).

(3) The requirements referred to in paragraph (2) are that—

(a) the ballot of the UK employees must comprise a single ballot but may instead, if the UK management so decides, comprise separate ballots of employees in such constituencies as the UK management may determine where—

(i) the number of UK members of the special negotiating body to be elected is more than one, and

(ii) the UK management considers that if separate ballots were held for those constituencies, the UK members of the special negotiating body to be elected would better reflect the interests of the UK employees as a whole than if a single ballot were held;

(b) a UK employee who is an employee of the Community-scale undertaking or the Community-scale group of undertakings on the day on which votes may be cast in the ballot, or if the votes may be cast on more than one day, on the first day of those days, is entitled to vote in the ballot of the UK employees;

(c) any UK employee, or UK employees' representative, who is an employee of, or an employees' representative in, the Community-scale undertaking or Community scale group of undertakings immediately before the latest time at which a person may become a candidate in the ballot, is entitled to stand in the ballot of the UK employees as a candidate for election as a UK member of the special negotiating body;

(d) the UK management must, in accordance with paragraph (7), appoint an independent ballot supervisor to supervise the conduct of the ballot of the UK employees but may instead, where there are to be separate ballots, appoint more than one independent ballot supervisor in accordance with that paragraph, each of whom is to supervise such of the separate ballots as the UK management may determine, provided that each separate ballot is supervised by a supervisor;

(e) after the UK management has formulated proposals as to the arrangements for the ballot of the UK employees and before it has published the final arrangements under sub-paragraph (f) it must, so far as reasonably practicable, consult with the UK employees' representatives on the proposed arrangements for the ballot of the UK employees;

(f) the UK management must publish the final arrangements for the ballot of the UK employees in such manner as to bring them to the attention of, so far as reasonably practicable, the UK employees and the UK employees' representatives.

(4) Any UK employee or UK employees' representative who believes that the arrangements for the ballot of the UK employees are defective may, within a period of 21 days beginning on the date on which the UK management published the final arrangements under sub-paragraph (f), present a complaint to the CAC.

(5) Where the CAC finds the complaint well-founded it shall make a declaration to that effect and may make an order requiring the UK management to modify the arrangements it has made for the ballot of the UK employees or to satisfy the requirements in sub-paragraph (e) or (f) of paragraph (3).

(6) An order under paragraph (5) shall specify the modifications to the arrangements which the UK management is required to make and the requirements which it must satisfy.

(7) A person is an independent ballot supervisor for the purposes of paragraph (3)(d) if the UK management reasonably believes that he will carry out any functions conferred on him in relation to the ballot competently and has no reasonable grounds for believing that his independence in relation to the ballot might reasonably be called into question.

(8) For the purposes of paragraph (4) the arrangements for the ballot of the UK employees are defective if—

(a) any of the requirements specified in sub-paragraphs (b) to (f) of paragraph (3) is not satisfied; or

(b) in a case where the ballot is to comprise separate ballots, the constituencies determined by the UK management do not reflect adequately the interests of the UK employees as a whole.

[2.522]

14 Conduct of ballot

(1) The UK management must—

(a) ensure that a ballot supervisor appointed under regulation 13(3)(d) carries out his functions under this regulation and that there is no interference with his carrying out of those functions from the UK management, or the central management (where it is not also the UK management); and

(b) comply with all reasonable requests made by a ballot supervisor for the purposes of, or in connection with, the carrying out of those functions.

(2) A ballot supervisor's appointment shall require that he—

(a) supervises the conduct of the ballot, or the separate ballots he is being appointed to supervise, in accordance with the arrangements for the ballot of the UK employees published by the UK management under regulation 13(3)(f) or, where appropriate, in accordance with the arrangements as required to be modified by an order made as a result of a complaint presented under regulation 13(4);

(b) does not conduct the ballot or any of the separate ballots before the UK management has satisfied the requirement specified in regulation 13(3)(e) and—

(i) where no complaint has been presented under regulation 13(4), before the expiry of a period of 21 days beginning on the date on which the UK management published its arrangements under regulation 13(3)(f); or

(ii) where a complaint has been presented under regulation 13(4), before the complaint has been determined and, where appropriate, the arrangements have been modified as required by an order made as a result of the complaint;

(c) conducts the ballot, or each separate ballot, so as to secure that—

(i) so far as reasonably practicable, those entitled to vote are given the opportunity to vote,

(ii) so far as reasonably practicable, those entitled to stand as candidates are given the opportunity to stand,

(iii) so far as is reasonably practicable, those voting are able to do so in secret, and

(iv) the votes given in the ballot are fairly and accurately counted.

(3) As soon as reasonably practicable after the holding of the ballot, the ballot supervisor must publish the results of the ballot in such manner as to make them available to the UK management and, so far as reasonably practicable, the UK employees entitled to vote in the ballot and the persons who stood as candidates in the ballot.

(4) A ballot supervisor shall publish a report ("an ineffective ballot report") where he considers (whether or not on the basis of representations made to him by another person) that—

(a) any of the requirements referred to in paragraph (2) was not satisfied with the result that the outcome of the ballot would have been different; or

(b) there was interference with the carrying out of his functions or a failure by management to comply with all reasonable requests made by him with the result that he was unable to form a proper judgment as to whether each of the requirements referred to in paragraph (2) was satisfied in relation to the ballot.

(5) Where a ballot supervisor publishes an ineffective ballot report the report must be published within a period of one month commencing on the date on which the ballot supervisor publishes the results of the ballot under paragraph (3).

(6) A ballot supervisor shall publish an ineffective ballot report in such manner as to make it available to the UK management and, so far as reasonably practicable, the UK employees entitled to vote in the ballot and the persons who stood as candidates in the ballot.

(7) Where a ballot supervisor publishes an ineffective ballot report then—

(a) if there has been a single ballot or an ineffective ballot report has been published in respect of every separate ballot, the outcome of the ballot or ballots shall have no effect and the UK management shall again be under the obligation in regulation 13(2);

(b) if there have been separate ballots and sub-paragraph (a) does not apply—

(i) the UK management shall arrange for the separate ballot or ballots in respect of which an ineffective ballot report was issued to be reheld in accordance with regulation 13 and this regulation, and

(ii) no such ballot shall have effect until it has been reheld and no ineffective ballot report has been published in respect of it.

(8) All costs relating to the holding of a ballot, including payments made to a ballot supervisor for supervising the conduct of the ballot, shall be borne by the central management (whether or not an ineffective ballot report has been made).

[2.523]

15 Consultative Committee

(1) Where a consultative committee exists—

(a) no UK member of the special negotiating body shall be elected by a ballot of the UK employees, except in the circumstances specified in paragraphs (2), (3) or (9) below; and

(b) the committee shall be entitled to nominate from its number the UK members of the special negotiating body.

(2) Where the consultative committee fails to nominate any UK members of the special negotiating body, all of the UK members of the special negotiating body shall be elected by a ballot of the UK employees in accordance with regulations 13 and 14.

(3) Where the consultative committee nominates such number of persons to be a UK member, or UK members, of the special negotiating body, which number is less or more than the number of UK members of the special negotiating body required, the consultative committee shall be treated as having failed to have nominated any UK members of the special negotiating body.

(4) In this regulation, "a consultative committee" means a body of persons—

- (a) whose normal functions include or comprise the carrying out of an information and consultation function;
- (b) which is able to carry out its information and consultation function without interference from the UK management, or from the central management (where it is not also the UK management);
- (c) which, in carrying out its information and consultation function, represents all the UK employees; and
- (d) which consists wholly of persons who were elected by a ballot (which may have consisted of a number of separate ballots) in which all the employees who, at the time, were UK employees were entitled to vote.

(5) In paragraph (4) "information and consultation function" means the function of—

- (a) receiving, on behalf of all the UK employees, information which may significantly affect the interests of the UK employees, but excluding information which is relevant only to a specific aspect of the interests of the employees, such as health and safety or collective redundancies; and
- (b) being consulted by the UK management or the central management (where it is not also the UK management) on the information referred to in sub-paragraph (a) above.

(6) The consultative committee must publish the names of the persons whom it has nominated to be UK members of the special negotiating body in such manner as to bring them to the attention of the UK management and, so far as reasonably practicable, the UK employees and UK employees' representatives.

(7) Where the UK management, a UK employee or a UK employees' representative believes that—

- (a) the consultative committee does not satisfy the requirements in paragraph (4) above; or
- (b) any of the persons nominated by the consultative committee is not entitled to be nominated,

it, or as the case may be he, may, within a period of 21 days beginning on the date on which the consultative committee published under paragraph (6) the names of persons nominated, present a complaint to the CAC.

(8) Where the CAC finds the complaint well-founded it shall make a declaration to that effect.

(9) Where the CAC has made a declaration under paragraph (8)—

- (a) no nomination made by the consultative committee shall have effect; and
- (b) all of the UK members of the special negotiating body shall be elected by a ballot of the UK employees in accordance with regulations 13 and 14.

(10) Where the consultative committee nominates any person to be a UK member of the special negotiating body, that nomination shall have effect after—

- (a) where no complaint has been presented under paragraph (7), the expiry of a period of 21 days beginning on the date on which the consultative committee published under paragraph (6) the names of persons nominated; or
- (b) where a complaint has been presented under paragraph (7), the complaint has been determined without a declaration under paragraph (8) having been made.

PART IV
EUROPEAN WORKS COUNCIL AND INFORMATION AND CONSULTATION PROCEDURE

[2.524]

16 Negotiation procedure

(1) With a view to concluding an agreement referred to in regulation 17 the central management must convene a meeting with the special negotiating body and must inform local managements accordingly.

[(1A) Within a reasonable time both before and after any meeting with the central management, the members of the special negotiating body are entitled to meet without the central management or its representatives being present, using any means necessary for communication at those meetings.]

(2) Subject to paragraph (3), the special negotiating body shall take decisions by a majority of the votes cast by its members and each member of the special negotiating body is to have one vote.

(3) The special negotiating body may decide not to open negotiations with central management or to terminate negotiations. Any such decision must be taken by at least two thirds of the votes cast by its members.

(4) Any decision made under paragraph (3) shall have the following effects—

(a) the procedure to negotiate and conclude the agreement referred to in regulation 17 shall cease from the date of the decision; and

(b) a purported request made under regulation 9 less than two years after the date of the decision shall not be treated as such a request, unless the special negotiating body and the central management otherwise agree.

(5) For the purpose of the negotiations, the special negotiating body may be assisted by experts of its choice [(which may include representatives of European trade union organisations) who may, at the request of the special negotiating body, attend in an advisory capacity any meeting convened in accordance with paragraph (1)].

(6) The central management shall pay for any reasonable expenses relating to the negotiations that are necessary to enable the special negotiating body to carry out its functions in an appropriate manner; but where the special negotiating body is assisted by more than one expert the central management is not required to pay such expenses in respect of more than one of them.

NOTES

Para (1A): inserted by the Transnational Information and Consultation of Employees (Amendment) Regulations 2010, SI 2010/1088, regs 2, 8(a), as from 5 June 2011.

Para (5): words in square brackets inserted by SI 2010/1088, regs 2, 8(b), as from 5 June 2011.

[2.525]

17 Content and scope of a European Works Council agreement and information and consultation procedure

(1) The central management and the special negotiating body are under a duty to negotiate in a spirit of cooperation with a view to reaching a written agreement on the detailed arrangements for the information and consultation of employees in a Community-scale undertaking or Community-scale group of undertakings.

(2) In this regulation and regulations 18 and 20, the central management and the special negotiating body are referred to as "the parties".

(3) The parties may decide in writing to establish an information and consultation procedure instead of a European Works Council.

(4) Without prejudice to the autonomy of the parties, where the parties decide to proceed with the establishment of a European Works Council, the agreement establishing it shall determine—

(a) the undertakings of the Community-scale group of undertakings or the establishments of the Community-scale undertaking which are covered by the agreement;

(b) the composition of the European Works Council, the number of members, the allocation of seats and the term of office of the members;

(c) the functions and the procedure for information and consultation of the European Works Council [and arrangements to link information and consultation of the European Works Council with information and consultation of national employee representation bodies];

(d) the venue, frequency and duration of meetings of the European Works Council;

[(dd) where the parties decide that it is necessary to establish a select committee, the composition of the select committee, the procedure for appointing its members, the functions and the procedural rules;]

(e) the financial and material resources to be allocated to the European Works Council; and

[(f) the date of entry into force of the agreement and its duration, the arrangements for amending or terminating the agreement, the circumstances in which the agreement is to be renegotiated including where the structure of the Community-scale undertaking or Community-scale group of undertakings changes and the procedure for renegotiation of the agreement.]

[(4A) In determining the allocation of seats under paragraph (4)(b), an agreement shall, so far as reasonably practicable, take into account the need for balanced representation of employees with regard to their role and gender and the sector in which they work.]

[(5) If the parties decide to establish an information and consultation procedure instead of a European Works Council, the agreement establishing the procedure must specify a method by which the information and consultation representatives are to enjoy the right to meet to discuss the information conveyed to them.]

(6) An agreement referred to in paragraph (4) or (5) is not to be subject to the provisions of the Schedule, except to the extent that the parties provide in the agreement that any of those requirements are to apply.

(7) Where a Community-scale group of undertakings comprises one or more undertakings or groups of undertakings which are themselves Community-scale undertakings or Community-scale groups of undertakings, the European Works Council shall be established at the level of the first-mentioned Community-scale group of undertakings, unless an agreement referred to in paragraph (4) provides otherwise.

(8) Unless a wider scope is provided for in an agreement referred to in paragraph (1), the powers and competence of a European Works Council and the scope of an information and consultation procedure shall, in the case of a Community-scale undertaking, cover all the establishments located within the Member States and, in the case of a Community-scale group of undertakings, all group undertakings located within the Member States.

[(9) Where information disclosed under a European Works Council agreement or an information and consultation procedure includes information as to the employment situation in the Community-scale undertaking or, as the case may be, the Community-scale group of undertakings, this shall include suitable information relating to the use of agency workers (if any).]

NOTES

Para (4): words in square brackets in sub-para (c) inserted, sub-para (dd) inserted, and sub-para (f) substituted, by the Transnational Information and Consultation of Employees (Amendment) Regulations 2010, SI 2010/1088, regs 2, 9(a)–(c), as from 5 June 2011.

Para (4A): inserted by SI 2010/1088, regs 2, 9(d), as from 5 June 2011.

Para (5): substituted by SI 2010/1088, regs 2, 9(e), as from 5 June 2011.

Para (9): added by SI 2010/1088, regs 2, 9(f), as from 1 October 2011.

[2.526]

18 Subsidiary requirements

(1) The provisions of the Schedule shall apply if—

(a) the parties so agree;

(b) within the period of six months beginning on the date on which a valid request referred to in regulation 9 was made, the central management refuses to commence negotiations; or

(c) after the expiry of a period of three years beginning on the date on which a valid request referred to in regulation 9 was made, the parties have failed to conclude an agreement under regulation 17 and the special negotiating body has not taken the decision under regulation 16(3).

[2.527]

[18A Information and consultation

(1) This regulation applies where—

(a) a European Works Council or information and consultation procedure has been established under regulation 17; or

(b) a European Works Council has been established by virtue of regulation 18.

(2) The central management, or any more appropriate level of management, shall give information to—

(a) members of a European Works Council; or

(b) information and consultation representatives,

as the case may be, in accordance with paragraph (3).

(3) The content of the information, the time when, and manner in which it is given, must be such as to enable the recipients to—

(a) acquaint themselves with and examine its subject matter;

(b) undertake a detailed assessment of its possible impact; and

(c) where appropriate, prepare for consultation.

(4) The central management, or any more appropriate level of management, shall consult with—

(a) members of a European Works Council; or

(b) information and consultation representatives,

as the case may be, in accordance with paragraph (5).

(5) The content of the consultation, the time when, and manner in which it takes place, must be such as to enable a European Works Council or information and consultation representatives to express an opinion on the basis of the information provided to them.

(6) The opinion referred to in paragraph (5) shall be provided within a reasonable time after the information is provided to the European Works Council or the information and consultation representatives and, having regard to the responsibilities of management to take decisions effectively, may be taken into account by the central management or any more appropriate level of management.

(7) The information provided to the members of a European Works Council or information and consultation representatives, and the consultation of the members of a European Works Council or information and consultation representatives shall be limited to transnational matters.

(8) Where information as to the employment situation in the Community-scale undertaking or, as the case may be, the Community-scale group of undertakings, is disclosed by the central management or any more appropriate level of management, this shall include suitable information relating to the use of agency workers (if any).]

NOTES

Commencement: 5 June 2011 (paras (1)–(7)); 1 October 2011 (para (8)).

Inserted by the Transnational Information and Consultation of Employees (Amendment) Regulations 2010, SI 2010/1088, regs 2, 10, as from 5 June 2011 (in relation to paras (1)–(7)) and 1 October 2011 (in relation to para (8)).

[2.528]

19 Cooperation

(1) The central management and the European Works Council are under a duty to work in a spirit of cooperation with due regard to their reciprocal rights and obligations.

(2) The duty in paragraph (1) shall apply also to the central management and information and consultation representatives.

[2.529]

[19A Means required

(1) Subject to paragraph (2), the central management shall provide the members of a European Works Council with the means required to fulfil their duty to represent collectively the interests of the employees of the Community-scale undertaking or Community-scale group of undertakings under these Regulations.

(2) The obligation on central management in paragraph (1) does not include an obligation to provide a member of a European Works Council with—

(a) time off during working hours to perform functions as such a member, or remuneration for such time off (as required by regulations 25 and 26);

(b) the means required to undertake training (as required by regulation 19B); or

(c) time off during working hours to undertake training, or remuneration for such time off (as required by regulations 25 and 26).]

NOTES

Commencement: 5 June 2011.

Inserted, together with regs 19B–19F by the Transnational Information and Consultation of Employees (Amendment) Regulations 2010, SI 2010/1088, regs 2, 11, as from 5 June 2011 (except in relation to reg 19F(7)) and as from 1 October 2011 (in relation to reg 19F(7)).

[2.530]

[19B Right to training for members of a European Works Council, etc

(1) Subject to paragraph (2), the central management shall provide an employee who is—

(a) a member of a special negotiating body; or

(b) a member of a European Works Council,

with the means required to undertaking training to the extent necessary for the exercise of the employee's representative duties.

(2) The obligation on central management referred to in paragraph (1) does not include an obligation to provide time off during working hours to undertaking training, or remuneration for such time off (as required by regulations 25 and 26).]

NOTES

Commencement: 5 June 2011.

Inserted as noted to reg 19A at **[2.529]**.

[2.531]

[19C European Works Council to inform, etc

Subject to regulation 23, a European Works Council shall inform—

(a) the employees' representatives in the establishments of a Community-scale undertaking or in the undertakings of a Community-scale group of undertakings; or

(b) to the extent that any employees are not represented by employees' representatives, the employees themselves,

of the content and outcome of the information and consultation procedure carried out in accordance with these Regulations.]

NOTES

Commencement: 5 June 2011.

Inserted as noted to reg 19A at **[2.529]**.

[2.532]

[19D Complaint of failure to inform

(1) An employee or employees' representative may present a complaint to the CAC that—

(a) the European Works Council has failed to inform them under regulation 19C of the content or outcome of the information and consultation procedure; or

(b) the information which has been provided by the European Works Council is false or incomplete in a material particular.

(2) Where the CAC finds the complaint well-founded it shall make an order requiring the European Works Council to disclose information to the complainant which order shall specify—

(a) the information in respect of which the CAC finds that the complaint is well-founded and which is to be disclosed to the complainant;

(b) the date (or if more than one, the earliest date) on which the European Works Council refused or failed to disclose information, or disclosed false or incomplete information; and

(c) a date (not less than one week from the date of the order) by which the European Works Council must disclose the information specified in the order.

(3) The CAC shall not find a complaint under this regulation well-founded where it considers that the failure to inform, or the provision of false or incomplete information, resulted from a failure by the central management to provide the members of the European Works Council with the means required to fulfil their duty to represent collectively the interests of the employees of the Community-scale undertaking or Community-scale group of undertakings (as required by regulation 19A).

(4) A complaint brought under paragraph (1) must be brought within a period of six months beginning with the date of the alleged failure to inform, or the provision of false or incomplete information.]

NOTES

Commencement: 5 June 2011.

Inserted as noted to reg 19A at **[2.529]**.

[2.533]

[19E Links between information and consultation of European Works Council and national employee representation bodies

(1) Paragraph (2) applies where—

(a) no arrangements to link information and consultation of a European Works Council with information and consultation of national employee representation bodies have been made under regulation 17(4)(c), and

(b) there are circumstances likely to lead to substantial changes in work organisation or contractual relations.

(2) Subject to regulation 2(4B), the—

(a) management of every undertaking belonging to the Community-scale group of undertakings;

(b) central management; or

(c) representative agent or the management treated as the central management of the Community-scale undertaking or Community-scale group of undertakings within the meaning of regulation 5(2),

as the case may be, shall ensure that the procedures for informing and consulting the European Works Council and the national employee representation bodies in relation to the substantial changes in work organisation or contractual relations referred to in sub-paragraph (b) of paragraph (1) are linked so as to begin within a reasonable time of each other.

(3) The national employee representation bodies referred to in paragraph (2) are those bodies which are entitled, whether by law, agreement or custom and practice, to be informed and consulted on the substantial changes in work organisation or contractual relations referred to in sub-paragraph (b) of paragraph (1).]

NOTES

Commencement: 5 June 2011.

Inserted as noted to reg 19A at **[2.529]**.

[2.534]

[19F Adaptation

(1) The central management shall initiate negotiations for the establishment of a European Works Council or an information and consultation procedure where the structure of a Community-scale undertaking or Community-scale group of undertakings changes significantly and paragraphs (2) and (3) apply.

(2) This paragraph applies where there is—

(a) one European Works Council agreement, or one agreement for an information and consultation procedure;
(b) more than one European Works Council agreement;
(c) more than one agreement for an information and consultation procedure;
(d) at least one European Works Council agreement and at least one agreement for an information and consultation procedure,

in force and there are no provisions for the continuance of the European Works Council or information and consultation procedure, as the case may be, where there are significant changes in the structure of the Community-scale undertaking or Community-scale group of undertakings or there are such provisions, but there is a conflict between them.

(3) This paragraph applies where a valid request within the meaning of regulation 9(2) and (3) has been made by employees or employees' representatives and on the relevant date the undertaking is a Community-scale undertaking or the group of undertakings is a Community-scale group of undertakings.

(4) Notwithstanding paragraph (1), the central management may initiate the negotiations referred to in paragraph (1) on its own initiative.

(5) Where the central management has initiated negotiations under paragraph (1) or (4), there shall be on the special negotiating body at least three members of every existing European Works Council in addition to the members elected or appointed in accordance with regulation 12(2).

(6) Before the establishment of a European Works Council or an information and consultation procedure under paragraph (1) or (4), any agreement establishing an existing European Works Council or information and consultation procedure—
(a) shall continue to operate in accordance with its terms, and
(b) may be adapted by agreement between the members of the European Works Council and the central management, or the information and consultation representatives and the central management, as the case may be, as a result of the change in structured referred to in paragraph (1).

(7) Where information is to be disclosed under a European Works Council agreement or an information and consultation procedure which includes information as to the employment situation in the Community-scale undertaking or, as the case may be, the Community-scale group of undertakings, this shall include suitable information relating to the use of agency workers (if any).]

NOTES

Commencement: 5 June 2011 (paras (1)–(6)); 1 October 2011 (para (7)).
Inserted as noted to reg 19A at **[2.529]**.

PART V
COMPLIANCE AND ENFORCEMENT

[2.535]

20 Failure to establish European Works Council or information and consultation procedure

(1) A complaint may be presented to the [CAC] by a relevant applicant who considers—
(a) that the parties have reached agreement on the establishment of a European Works Council or an information and consultation procedure, or that regulation 18 applies; and
(b) that, because of a failure of the central management, the European Works Council or information and consultation procedure has not been established at all, or has not been established fully in accordance with the terms of the agreement under regulation 17 or, as the case may be, in accordance with the provisions of the Schedule.

(2) In this regulation "failure" means an act or omission and a failure by the local management shall be treated as a failure by the central management.

(3) In this regulation "relevant applicant" means—
(a) in a case where a special negotiating body exists, the special negotiating body; or
(b) in a case where a special negotiating body does not exist, an employee, employees' representative, or person who was a member of the special negotiating body (if that body existed previously).

(4) Where the [CAC] finds the complaint well-founded it shall make a decision to that effect and may make an order requiring the central management to take such steps as are necessary to establish the European Works Council or information and consultation procedure in accordance with the terms of the agreement under regulation 17 or, as the case may be, to establish a European Works Council in accordance with the provisions of the Schedule.

(5) The [CAC] shall not find a complaint under this regulation to be well-founded where—
(a) the central management made no application in relation to the request under regulation 10(1), or where the request consisted of separate requests was unable by reason

of the time limit in sub-paragraph (a) of that regulation to make an application under the regulation in relation to a particular request, and shows that the request was not a valid request because a requirement of regulation 9(2) or (3) was not satisfied; or

(b) the central management made no application under regulation 10(3) but shows that the obligation in regulation 9(1) did not, for any reason, apply to it on the relevant date.

(6) An order under paragraph (4) shall specify—

(a) the steps which the central management is required to take;

(b) the date of the failure of the central management; and

(c) the period within which the order must be complied with.

[(7) If the Appeal Tribunal makes a decision under paragraph (4) the relevant applicant may, within the period of three months beginning with the date on which the decision is made, make an application to the Appeal Tribunal for a penalty notice to be issued.]

[(7A) Where such an application is made, the Appeal Tribunal shall issue a written penalty notice to the central management requiring it to pay a penalty to the Secretary of State in respect of the failure.]

(8) Paragraph [(7A)] shall not apply if the Appeal Tribunal is satisfied, on hearing the representations of the central management, that the failure resulted from a reason beyond the central management's control or that it has some other reasonable excuse for its failure.

(9) Regulation 22 shall apply in respect of a penalty notice issued under this regulation.

(10) No order of the [CAC] under this regulation shall have the effect of suspending or altering the effect of any act done or of any agreement made by the central management or the local management.

NOTES

Paras (1), (4), (5), (10): words in square brackets substituted by the Transnational Information and Consultation of Employees (Amendment) Regulations 2010, SI 2010/1088, regs 2, 12(a), as from 5 June 2011.

Para (7): substituted by SI 2010/1088, regs 2, 12(b), as from 5 June 2011.

Para (7A): inserted by SI 2010/1088, regs 2, 12(c), as from 5 June 2011.

Para (8): figure in square brackets substituted by SI 2010/1088, regs 2, 12(d), as from 5 June 2011.

[2.536]

21 Disputes about operation of European Works Council or information and consultation procedure

[(1) Where—

(a) a European Works Council or information and consultation procedure has been established under regulation 17; or

(b) a European Works Council has been established by virtue of regulation 18,

a complaint may be presented to the CAC by a relevant applicant where paragraph (1A) applies.]

[(1A) This paragraph applies where a relevant applicant considers that, because of the failure of a defaulter—

(a) the terms of the agreement under regulation 17 or, as the case may be, the provisions of the Schedule, have not been complied with; or

(b) regulation 18A has not been complied with, or the information which has been provided by the management under regulation 18A is false or incomplete in a material particular.

(1B) A complaint brought under paragraph (1) must be brought within a period of six months beginning with the date of the alleged failure or non-compliance.]

(2) In this regulation, "failure" means an act or omission and a failure by the local management shall be treated as a failure by the central management.

(3) In this regulation "relevant applicant" means—

(a) in the case of a failure concerning a European Works Council, either the central management or the European Works Council; or

(b) in the case of a failure concerning an information and consultation procedure, either the central management or any one or more of the information and consultation representatives,

and "defaulter" means the persons mentioned in sub-paragraph (a) or (b) against whom the complaint is presented.

(4) Where the [CAC] finds the complaint well-founded it shall make a decision to that effect and may make an order requiring the defaulter to take such steps as are necessary to comply with the terms of the agreement under regulation 17 or, as the case may be, the provisions of the Schedule.

(5) An order made under paragraph (4) shall specify—

(a) the steps which the defaulter is required to take;

(b) the date of the failure; and

(c) the period within which the order must be complied with.

(6) If the [CAC] makes a decision under paragraph (4) and the defaulter in question is the central management [the relevant applicant may, within the period of three months beginning with the date on which the decision is made, make an application to the Appeal Tribunal for a penalty notice to be issued].

[(6A) Where such an application is made, the Appeal Tribunal shall issue a written penalty notice to the central management requiring it to pay a penalty to the Secretary of State in respect of the failure.]

(7) Paragraph [(6A)] shall not apply if the Appeal Tribunal is satisfied, on hearing the representations of the central management, that the failure resulted from a reason beyond the central management's control or that it has some other reasonable excuse for its failure.

(8) Regulation 22 shall apply in respect of a penalty notice issued under this regulation.

(9) No order of the [CAC] under this regulation shall have the effect of suspending or altering the effect of any act done or of any agreement made by the central management or the local management.

NOTES

Para (1): substituted by the Transnational Information and Consultation of Employees (Amendment) Regulations 2010, SI 2010/1088, regs 2, 13(a), as from 5 June 2011.

Paras (1A), (1B), (6A): inserted by SI 2010/1088, regs 2, 13(b), (e), as from 5 June 2011.

Paras (4), (6), (9): words in square brackets substituted by SI 2010/1088, regs 2, 13(c), (d), as from 5 June 2011.

Para (7): figure in square brackets substituted by SI 2010/1088, regs 2, 13(f), as from 5 June 2011.

[2.537]

[21A Disputes about failures of management

(1) A complaint may be presented to the CAC by a relevant applicant who considers that—

- (a) because of the failure of a defaulter, the members of the special negotiating body have been unable to meet in accordance with regulation 16(1A);
- (b) because of the failure of a defaulter, the members of the European Works Council have not been provided with the means required to fulfil their duty to represent collectively the interests of the employees of the Community-scale undertaking or Community-scale group of undertakings in accordance with regulation 19A;
- (c) because of the failure of a defaulter, a member of a special negotiating body or a member of the European Works Council has not been provided with the means required to undertake the training referred to in regulation 19B; or
- (d) regulation 19E(2) applies and that, because of the failure of a defaulter, the European Works Council and the national employee representation bodies have not been informed and consulted in accordance with that regulation.

(2) A complaint brought under paragraph (1) must be brought within a period of six months beginning with the date of the alleged failure.

(3) Where the CAC finds the complaint well-founded it shall make a decision to that effect and may make an order requiring the defaulter to take such steps as are necessary to comply with regulation 16(1A), 19A, 19B or 19E(2), as the case may be.

(4) An order made under paragraph (3) shall specify—

- (a) the steps which the defaulter is required to take;
- (b) the date of the failure; and
- (c) the period within which the order must be complied with.

(5) If the CAC makes a decision under paragraph (3), the relevant applicant may, within the period of three months beginning with the date on which the decision is made, make an application to the Appeal Tribunal for a penalty notice to be issued.

(6) Where such an application is made, the Appeal Tribunal shall issue a written penalty notice to the defaulter requiring it to pay a penalty to the Secretary of State in respect of the failure.

(7) Paragraph (6) shall not apply if the Appeal Tribunal is satisfied, on hearing the representations of the defaulter, that the failure resulted from a reason beyond the defaulter's control or that it has some other reasonable excuse for its failure.

(8) Regulation 22 shall apply to a penalty notice issued under this regulation.

(9) No order of the CAC under this regulation shall have the effect of suspending or altering the effect of any act done or of any agreement made by the central management or the local management.

(10) In this regulation—

- (a) "defaulter" means, as the case may be—
  - (i) the management of any undertaking belonging to the Community-scale group of undertakings;
  - (ii) the central management; or

(iii) the representative agent or the management treated as the central management of the Community-scale undertaking or Community-scale group of undertakings within the meaning of regulation 5(2);

(b) "failure" means an act or omission and a failure by the local management shall be treated as a failure by the central management;

(c) "relevant applicant" means—

(i) for a complaint in relation to regulation 16(1A), a member of the special negotiating body;

(ii) for a complaint in relation to regulation 19A, a member of the European Works Council;

(iii) for a complaint in relation to regulation 19B, a member of the special negotiating body or a member of the European Works Council;

(iv) for a complaint in relation to regulation 19E(2), a member of the European Works Council, a national employee representation body, an employee, or an employees' representative.]

NOTES

Commencement: 5 June 2011.

Inserted by the Transnational Information and Consultation of Employees (Amendment) Regulations 2010, SI 2010/1088, regs 2, 14, as from 5 June 2011.

[2.538]

22 Penalties

(1) A penalty notice issued under [regulation 20, 21 or 21A] shall specify—

(a) the amount of the penalty which is payable;

(b) the date before which the penalty must be paid; and

(c) the failure and period to which the penalty relates.

(2) No penalty set by the Appeal Tribunal under this regulation may exceed [£100,000].

(3) When setting the amount of the penalty, the Appeal Tribunal shall take into account—

(a) the gravity of the failure;

(b) the period of time over which the failure occurred;

(c) the reason for the failure;

(d) the number of employees affected by the failure; and

(e) the number of employees of the Community-scale undertaking or Community-scale group of undertakings in the Member States.

(4) The date specified under paragraph (1)(b) above must not be earlier than the end of the period within which an appeal against a decision or order made by the [CAC] under [regulation 20, 21 or 21A] may be made.

(5) If the specified date in a penalty notice has passed and—

(a) the period during which an appeal may be made has expired without an appeal having been made; or

(b) such an appeal has been made and determined,

the Secretary of State may recover from the central management, as a civil debt due to him, any amount payable under the penalty notice which remains outstanding.

(6) The making of an appeal suspends the effect of a penalty notice.

[(7) Any sums received by the Secretary of State, or in Northern Ireland the Department for Employment and Learning, under regulation 20, 21 or 21A or this regulation shall be paid into, respectively, the Consolidated Fund or the Consolidated Fund of Northern Ireland.]

NOTES

The words in square brackets in paras (1), (2), (4) were substituted, and para (7) was substituted, by the Transnational Information and Consultation of Employees (Amendment) Regulations 2010, SI 2010/1088, regs 2, 15, as from 5 June 2011.

PART VI
CONFIDENTIAL INFORMATION

[2.539]

23 Breach of statutory duty

(1) A person who is or at any time was—

(a) a member of a special negotiating body or a European Works Council;

(b) an information and consultation representative; or

(c) an expert assisting a special negotiating body, a European Works Council or its select committee, or information and consultation representatives,

shall not disclose any information or document which is or has been in his possession by virtue of his position as described in sub-paragraph (a), (b) or (c) of this paragraph, which the central management has entrusted to him on terms requiring it to be held in confidence.

(2) In this regulation and in regulation 24, a person specified in paragraph (1)(a), (b) or (c) of this regulation is referred to as a "recipient".

(3) The obligation to comply with paragraph (1) is a duty owed to the central management, and a breach of the duty is actionable accordingly (subject to the defences and other incidents applying to actions for breach of statutory duty).

(4) Paragraph (3) shall not affect the liability which any person may incur, nor affect any right which any person may have, apart from paragraph (3).

(5) No action shall lie under paragraph (3) where the recipient reasonably believed the disclosure to be a "protected disclosure" within the meaning given to that expression by section 43A of the 1996 Act or, as the case may be, Article 67A of the 1996 Order.

(6) A recipient whom the central management (which is situated in the United Kingdom) has entrusted with any information or document on terms requiring it to be held in confidence may apply to the CAC for a declaration as to whether it was reasonable for the central management to impose such a requirement.

(7) If the CAC considers that the disclosure of the information or document by the recipient would not, or would not be likely to, prejudice or cause serious harm to the undertaking, it shall make a declaration that it was not reasonable for the central management to require the recipient to hold the information or document in confidence.

(8) If a declaration is made under paragraph (7), the information or document shall not at any time thereafter be regarded as having been entrusted to the recipient who made the application under paragraph (6), or to any other recipient, on terms requiring it to be held in confidence.

[2.540]

24 Withholding of information by central management

(1) The central management is not required to disclose any information or document to a recipient when the nature of the information or document is such that, according to objective criteria, the disclosure of the information or document would seriously harm the functioning of, or would be prejudicial to, the undertaking or group of undertakings concerned.

(2) Where there is a dispute between the central management and a recipient as to whether the nature of the information or document which the central management has failed to provide is such as is described in paragraph (1), the central management or a recipient may apply to the CAC for a declaration as to whether the information or document is of such a nature.

(3) If the CAC makes a declaration that the disclosure of the information or document in question would not, according to objective criteria, seriously harm the functioning of, or be prejudicial to, the undertaking or group of undertakings concerned, the CAC shall order the central management to disclose the information or document.

(4) An order under paragraph (3) above shall specify—

(a) the information or document to be disclosed;

(b) the recipient or recipients to whom the information or document is to be disclosed;

(c) any terms on which the information or document is to be disclosed; and

(d) the date before which the information or document is to be disclosed.

PART VII
PROTECTIONS FOR MEMBERS OF A EUROPEAN WORKS COUNCIL, ETC

[2.541]

25 Right to time off for members of a European Works Council, etc

(1) An employee who is—

(a) a member of a special negotiating body;

(b) a member of a European Works Council;

(c) an information and consultation representative; or

(d) a candidate in an election in which any person elected will, on being elected, be such a member or representative,

is entitled to be permitted by his employer to take reasonable time off during the employee's working hours in order to perform his functions as such a member, representative or candidate.

[(1A) An employer shall permit an employee who is—

(a) a member of a special negotiating body; or

(b) a member of a European Works Council,

to take reasonable time off during the employee's working hours in order to undertake the training referred to in regulation 19B.]

(2) For the purposes of this regulation the working hours of an employee shall be taken to be any time when, in accordance with his contract of employment, the employee is required to be at work.

NOTES

Para (1A): inserted by the Transnational Information and Consultation of Employees (Amendment) Regulations 2010, SI 2010/1088, regs 2, 16, as from 5 June 2011.

[2.542]

26 Right to remuneration for time off under regulation 25

(1) An employee who is permitted to take time off under regulation 25 is entitled to be paid remuneration by his employer for the time taken off at the appropriate hourly rate.

(2) Chapter II of Part XIV of the 1996 Act (a week's pay) and, in relation to Northern Ireland, Chapter IV of Part I of the 1996 Order shall apply in relation to this regulation as they apply, respectively, in relation to section 62 of the 1996 Act and Article 90 of the 1996 Order.

(3) The appropriate hourly rate, in relation to an employee, is the amount of one week's pay divided by the number of normal working hours in a week for that employee when employed under the contract of employment in force on the day when the time is taken.

(4) But where the number of normal working hours differs from week to week or over a longer period, the amount of one week's pay shall be divided instead by—

- (a) the average number of normal working hours calculated by dividing by twelve the total number of the employee's normal working hours during the period of twelve weeks ending with the last complete week before the day on which the time off is taken; or
- (b) where the employee has not been employed for a sufficient period to enable the calculation to be made under sub-paragraph (a), a number which fairly represents the number of normal working hours in a week having regard to such of the considerations specified in paragraph (5) as are appropriate in the circumstances.

(5) The considerations referred to in paragraph (4)(b) are—

- (a) the average number of normal working hours in a week which the employee could expect in accordance with the terms of his contract; and
- (b) the average number of normal working hours of other employees engaged in relevant comparable employment with the same employer.

(6) A right to any amount under paragraph (1) does not affect any right of an employee in relation to remuneration under his contract of employment ("contractual remuneration").

(7) Any contractual remuneration paid to an employee in respect of a period of time off under regulation 25 goes towards discharging any liability of the employer to pay remuneration under paragraph (1) in respect of that period, and, conversely, any payment of remuneration under paragraph (1) in respect of a period goes towards discharging any liability of the employer to pay contractual remuneration in respect of that period.

[2.543]

27 Right to time off: complaints to tribunals

(1) An employee may present a complaint, in Great Britain to an employment tribunal and in Northern Ireland to an industrial tribunal, that his employer—

- (a) has unreasonably refused to permit him to take time off as required by regulation 25; or
- (b) has failed to pay the whole or any part of any amount to which the employee is entitled under regulation 26.

(2) A tribunal shall not consider a complaint under this regulation unless it is presented—

- (a) before the end of the period of three months beginning with the day on which the time off was taken or on which it is alleged the time off should have been permitted; or
- (b) within such further period as the tribunal considers reasonable in a case where it is satisfied that it was not reasonably practicable for the complaint to be presented before the end of that period of three months.

(3) Where a tribunal finds a complaint under this regulation well-founded, the tribunal shall make a declaration to that effect.

(4) If the complaint is that the employer has unreasonably refused to permit the employee to take time off, the tribunal shall also order the employer to pay to the employee an amount equal to the remuneration to which he would have been entitled under regulation 26 if the employer had not refused.

(5) If the complaint is that the employer has failed to pay the employee the whole or part of any amount to which he is entitled under regulation 26, the tribunal shall also order the employer to pay to the employee the amount which it finds due to him.

NOTES

Conciliation: employment tribunal proceedings and claims which could be the subject of employment tribunal proceedings under this regulation are proceedings to which the Employment Tribunals Act 1996, s 18 applies; see s 18(1)(g) of that Act at **[1.706]**.

[2.544]

28 Unfair dismissal

(1) An employee who is dismissed and to whom paragraph (2) or (5) applies shall be regarded, if the reason (or, if more than one, the principal reason) for the dismissal is a reason specified in, respectively, paragraph (3) or (6), as unfairly dismissed for the purposes of Part X of the 1996 Act and of Part XI of the 1996 Order.

(2) This paragraph applies to an employee who is—

(a) a member of a special negotiating body;

(b) a member of a European Works Council;

(c) an information and consultation representative; or

(d) a candidate in an election in which any person elected will, on being elected, be such a member or representative.

(3) The reason is that—

(a) the employee performed any functions or activities as such a member, representative or candidate; or

(b) the employee or a person acting on his behalf made a request to exercise an entitlement conferred on the employee by regulation 25 or 6;

or proposed to do so.

(4) The reason in paragraph (3)(a) does not apply where the reason (or principal reason) for the dismissal is that in the performance, or purported performance, of the employee's functions or activities he has disclosed any information or document in breach of the duty in regulation 23(1), unless the employee reasonably believed the disclosure to be a "protected disclosure" within the meaning given to that expression by section 43A of the 1996 Act or, as the case may be, by Article 67A of the 1996 Order.

(5) This paragraph applies to any employee whether or not he is an employee to whom paragraph (2) applies.

(6) The reasons are that the employee—

(a) took, or proposed to take, any proceedings before an employment tribunal or industrial tribunal to enforce a right or secure an entitlement conferred on him by these Regulations;

(b) exercised, or proposed to exercise, any entitlement to apply or complain to the Appeal Tribunal or the CAC, or in Northern Ireland [the High Court or] the Industrial Court, conferred by these Regulations;

(c) requested, or proposed to request, information in accordance with regulation 7;

(d) acted with a view to securing that a special negotiating body, a European Works Council or an information and consultation procedure did or did not come into existence;

(e) indicated that he supported or did not support the coming into existence of a special negotiating body, a European Works Council or an information and consultation procedure;

(f) stood as a candidate in an election in which any person elected would, on being elected, be a member of a special negotiating body or of a European Works Council or an information and consultation representative;

(g) influenced or sought to influence the way in which votes were to be cast by other employees in a ballot arranged under these Regulations;

(h) voted in such a ballot;

(i) expressed doubts, whether to a ballot supervisor or otherwise, as to whether such a ballot had been properly conducted; or

(j) proposed to do, failed to do, or proposed to decline to do, any of the things mentioned in sub-paragraphs (d) to (i).

(7) It is immaterial for the purposes of paragraph (6)(a)—

(a) whether or not the employee has the right; or

(b) whether or not the right has been infringed;

but for that paragraph to apply, the claim to the right and, if applicable, the claim that it has been infringed must be made in good faith.

NOTES

Para (6): words in square brackets in sub-para (b) inserted by the Transnational Information and Consultation of Employees (Amendment) Regulations 2010, SI 2010/1088, regs 2, 17, as from 5 June 2011.

29, 30 *(Reg 29 amends the Employment Rights Act 1996, ss 105, 108, and amended s 109 (repealed); reg 30 applies to Northern Ireland and is outside the scope of this work.)*

[2.545]

31 Detriment

(1) An employee to whom paragraph (2) or (5) applies has the right not to be subjected to any detriment by any act, or deliberate failure to act, by his employer, done on a ground specified in, respectively, paragraph (3) or (6).

(2) This paragraph applies to an employee who is—

(a) a member of a special negotiating body;
(b) a member of a European Works Council;
(c) an information and consultation representative; or
(d) a candidate in an election in which any person elected will, on being elected, be such a member or representative.

(3) The ground is that—
(a) the employee performed any functions or activities as such a member, representative or candidate; or
(b) the employee or a person acting on his behalf made a request to exercise an entitlement conferred on the employee by regulation 25 or 26;

or proposed to do so.

(4) The ground in paragraph (3)(a) does not apply where the ground for the subjection to detriment is that in the performance, or purported performance, of the employee's functions or activities he has disclosed any information or document in breach of the duty in regulation 23(1), unless the employee reasonably believed the disclosure to be a "protected disclosure" within the meaning given to that expression by section 43A of the 1996 Act or, as the case may be, Article 67A of the 1996 Order.

(5) This paragraph applies to any employee, whether or not he is an employee to whom paragraph (2) applies.

(6) The grounds are that the employee—
(a) took, or proposed to take, any proceedings before an employment tribunal or industrial tribunal to enforce a right or secure an entitlement conferred on him by these Regulations;
(b) exercised, or proposed to exercise, any entitlement to apply or complain to the Appeal Tribunal, the CAC, or in Northern Ireland [the High Court or] the Industrial Court, conferred by these Regulations;
(c) requested, or proposed to request, information in accordance with regulation 7;
(d) acted with a view to securing that a special negotiating body, a European Works Council or an information and consultation procedure did or did not come into existence;
(e) indicated that he supported or did not support the coming into existence of a special negotiating body, a European Works Council or an information and consultation procedure;
(f) stood as a candidate in an election in which any person elected would, on being elected, be a member of a special negotiating body or of a European Works Council or an information and consultation representative;
(g) influenced or sought to influence the way in which votes were to be cast by other employees in a ballot arranged under these Regulations;
(h) voted in such a ballot;
(i) expressed doubts, whether to a ballot supervisor or otherwise, as to whether such a ballot had been properly conducted; or
(j) proposed to do, failed to do, or proposed to decline to do, any of the things mentioned in sub-paragraphs (d) to (i).

(7) It is immaterial for the purposes of paragraph (6)(a)—
(a) whether or not the employee has the right; or
(b) whether or not the right has been infringed;

but for that paragraph to apply, the claim to the right and, if applicable, the claim that it has been infringed must be made in good faith.

NOTES

Para (6): words in square brackets in sub-para (b) inserted by the Transnational Information and Consultation of Employees (Amendment) Regulations 2010, SI 2010/1088, regs 2, 18, as from 5 June 2011.

[2.546]

32 Detriment: enforcement and subsidiary provisions

(1) An employee may present a complaint, in Great Britain to an employment tribunal and in Northern Ireland to an industrial tribunal, that he has been subjected to a detriment in contravention of regulation 31.

(2) The provisions of—
(a) sections 48(2) to (4) and 49 of the 1996 Act (complaints to employment tribunals and remedies); or
(b) in relation to Northern Ireland, Articles 71(2) to (4) and 72 of the 1996 Order (complaints to industrial tribunals and remedies);

shall apply in relation to a complaint under this regulation as they apply in relation to a complaint under section 48 of that Act or Article 71 of that Order (as the case may be), but taking references in those provisions to the employer as references to the employer within the meaning of regulation 31(1) above.

(3) Regulation 31 does not apply where the detriment in question amounts to dismissal.

NOTES

Conciliation: employment tribunal proceedings and claims which could be the subject of employment tribunal proceedings under this regulation are proceedings to which the Employment Tribunals Act 1996, s 18 applies; see s 18(1)(g) of that Act at **[1.706]**.

Tribunal jurisdiction: the Employment Act 2002, s 38 applies to proceedings before the employment tribunal relating to a claim under this regulation; see s 38(1) of, and Sch 5 to, the 2002 Act at **[1.1228]**, **[1.1236]**. See also the Trade Union and Labour Relations (Consolidation) Act 1992, s 207A at **[1.474]** (as inserted by the Employment Act 2008). That section provides that in proceedings before an employment tribunal relating to a claim by an employee under any of the jurisdictions listed in Sch A2 to the 1992 Act at **[1.648]** (which includes this regulation) the tribunal may adjust any award given if the employer or the employee has unreasonably failed to comply with the relevant Code of Practice as defined by s 207A(4). See also the revised Acas Code of Practice 1 – Disciplinary and Grievance Procedures (2009) at **[4.1]**.

33 *(Para (1) amends the Employment Tribunals Act 1996, s 18 at* **[1.706]**; *para (2) applies to Northern Ireland and is outside the scope of this work.)*

PART VIII
MISCELLANEOUS

The Appeal Tribunal, Industrial Court, CAC, ACAS and the Labour Relations Agency

[2.547]

34 Appeal Tribunal: jurisdiction

(1) Any proceedings before the Appeal Tribunal arising under these Regulations, other than proceedings before the Appeal Tribunal under paragraph (i) of section 21(1) of the Employment Tribunals Act 1996, shall—

(a) where the central management is situated in England and Wales, be in England and Wales;
(b) where the central management is situated in Scotland, be in Scotland.

(2) Paragraph (1) shall apply to proceedings before the Appeal Tribunal arising under regulation 8 as if for the words "central management" there were substituted the words "recipient (within the meaning given to that term by regulation 7)".

(3) Paragraph (1) shall apply to proceedings before the Appeal Tribunal arising under regulation 13 or 15 or paragraph 4 of the Schedule as if for the words "central management" there were substituted the words "UK management".

35–37 (*Reg 35 amends the Employment Tribunals Act 1996, ss 20, 21, 30 at* **[1.712]**, **[1.713]**, **[1.724]**; *regs 36, 37 apply to Northern Ireland and are outside the scope of this work.*)

[2.548]

38 CAC: proceedings

(1) Where under these Regulations a person presents a complaint or makes an application to the CAC the complaint or application must be in writing and in such form as the CAC may require.

(2) In its consideration of an application or complaint under these Regulations, the CAC shall make such enquiries as it sees fit and give any person whom it considers has a proper interest in the application or complaint an opportunity to be heard.

(3) Where the central management is situated in England and Wales—

(a) a declaration or order made by the CAC under these Regulations may be relied on as if it were a declaration or order made by the High Court in England and Wales; and
(b) an order made by the CAC under these Regulations may be enforced in the same way as an order of the High Court in England and Wales.

(4) Where the central management is situated in Scotland—

(a) a declaration or order made by the CAC under these Regulations may be relied on as if it were a declaration or order made by the Court of Session; and
(b) an order made by the CAC under these Regulations may be enforced in the same way as an order of the Court of Session.

(5) Paragraphs (3) and (4) shall apply to an order made under regulation 8 as if for the words "central management" there were substituted the word "recipient".

(6) Paragraphs (3) and (4) shall apply, as appropriate, to a declaration or order made under regulation 13 or 15 or paragraph 4 of the Schedule as if for the words "central management" there were substituted the words "UK management".

(7) A declaration or order made by the CAC under these Regulations must be in writing and state the reasons for the CAC's findings.

(8) An appeal lies to the Appeal Tribunal on any question of law arising from any declaration or order of, or arising in any proceedings before, the CAC under these Regulations.

[2.549]

39 ACAS and the Labour Relations Agency

(1) If on receipt of an application or complaint under these Regulations the CAC, . . . or as the case may be the Industrial Court, is of the opinion that it is reasonably likely to be settled by conciliation, it shall refer the application or complaint to ACAS or to the Labour Relations Agency and shall notify the applicant or complainant and any persons whom it considers have a proper interest in the application or complaint accordingly, whereupon ACAS, or as the case may be the Labour Relations Agency, shall seek to promote a settlement of the matter.

(2) If an application or complaint so referred is not settled or withdrawn and ACAS, or as the case may be the Labour Relations Agency, is of the opinion that further attempts at conciliation are unlikely to result in a settlement, it shall inform the CAC, . . . or as the case may be the Industrial Court, of its opinion.

(3) If the application or complaint is not referred to ACAS or to the Labour Relations Agency, or if it is so referred, on ACAS, or as the case may be the Labour Relations Agency, informing the CAC, . . . or as the case may be the Industrial Court, of its opinion that further attempts at conciliation are unlikely to result in a settlement, the CAC, . . . or as the case may be the Industrial Court, shall proceed to hear and determine the application or complaint.

NOTES

Words omitted revoked by the Transnational Information and Consultation of Employees (Amendment) Regulations 2010, SI 2010/1088, regs 2, 21, as from 5 June 2011.

Restrictions on contracting out

[2.550]

40 Restrictions on contracting out: general

(1) Any provision in any agreement (whether an employee's contract or not) is void in so far as it purports—

(a) to exclude or limit the operation of any provision of these Regulations other than a provision of Part VII; or

(b) to preclude a person from bringing any proceedings before the Appeal Tribunal or the CAC, or in Northern Ireland [the High Court or] the Industrial Court, under any provision of these Regulations other than a provision of Part VII.

(2) Paragraph (1) does not apply to any agreement to refrain from continuing any proceedings referred to in sub-paragraph (b) of that paragraph made after the proceedings have been instituted.

NOTES

Para (1): words in square brackets in sub-para (b) inserted by the Transnational Information and Consultation of Employees (Amendment) Regulations 2010, SI 2010/1088, regs 2, 22, as from 5 June 2011.

[2.551]

41 Restrictions on contracting out: Part VII

(1) Any provision in any agreement (whether an employee's contract or not) is void in so far as it purports—

(a) to exclude or limit the operation of any provision of Part VII of these Regulations; or

(b) to preclude a person from bringing any proceedings before an employment tribunal, or in Northern Ireland an industrial tribunal, under that Part.

(2) Paragraph (1) does not apply to any agreement to refrain from instituting or continuing proceedings before an employment tribunal or, in Northern Ireland, an industrial tribunal where—

(a) a conciliation officer has taken action under section 18 of the Employment Tribunals Act 1996 (conciliation); or

(b) in relation to Northern Ireland, the Labour Relations Agency has taken action under Article 20 of the Industrial Tribunals (Northern Ireland) Order 1996 (conciliation).

(3) Paragraph (1) does not apply to any agreement to refrain from instituting or continuing before an employment tribunal, or in Northern Ireland an industrial tribunal, proceedings within—

(a) section 18(1)(g) of the Employment Tribunals Act 1996 (proceedings under these Regulations where conciliation is available); or

(b) in relation to Northern Ireland, Article 20(1)(g) of the Industrial Tribunals (Northern Ireland) Order 1996,

if the conditions regulating compromise agreements under these Regulations are satisfied in relation to the agreement.

(4) For the purposes of paragraph (3) the conditions regulating compromise agreements are that—

(a) the agreement must be in writing;

(b) the agreement must relate to the particular proceedings;

(c) the employee must have received advice from a relevant independent adviser as to the terms and effect of the proposed agreement and, in particular, its effect on his ability to pursue his rights before an employment tribunal or, in Northern Ireland, an industrial tribunal;

(d) there must be in force, when the adviser gives the advice, a contract of insurance, or an indemnity provided for members of a profession or professional body, covering the risk of a claim by the employee in respect of loss arising in consequence of the advice;

(e) the agreement must identify the adviser; and

(f) the agreement must state that the conditions in sub-paragraphs (a) to (e) are satisfied.

(5) A person is a relevant independent adviser for the purposes of paragraph (4)(c)—

(a) if he is a qualified lawyer;

(b) if he is an officer, official, employee or member of an independent trade union who has been certified in writing by the trade union as competent to give advice and as authorised to do so on behalf of the trade union; or

(c) if he works at an advice centre (whether as an employee or as a volunteer) and has been certified in writing by the centre as competent to give advice and as authorised to do so on behalf of the centre.

(6) But a person is not a relevant independent adviser for the purposes of paragraph (4)(c) in relation to the employee—

(a) if he is, is employed by or is acting in the matter for the employer or an associated employer;

(b) in the case of a person within paragraph (5)(b) or (c), if the trade union or advice centre is the employer or an associated employer; or

(c) in the case of a person within paragraph (5)(c), if the employee makes a payment for the advice received from him.

(7) In paragraph (5)(a), "qualified lawyer" means—

(a) as respects England and Wales, [a person who, for the purposes of the Legal Services Act 2007), is an authorised person in relation to an activity which constitutes the exercise of a right of audience or the conduct of litigation (within the meaning of that Act)];

(b) as respects Scotland, an advocate (whether in practice as such or employed to give legal advice) or a solicitor who holds a practising certificate; and

(c) as respects Northern Ireland, a barrister (whether in practice as such or employed to give legal advice) or a solicitor who holds a practising certificate.

[(7A) A person shall be treated as being a qualified lawyer within paragraph (7)(a) if he is a Fellow of the Institute of Legal Executives [practising in a solicitor's practice (including a body recognised under section 9 of the Administration of Justice Act 1985)].]

(8) For the purposes of paragraph (6) any two employers shall be treated as associated if—

(a) one is a company of which the other (directly or indirectly) has control; or

(b) both are companies of which a third person (directly or indirectly) has control;

and "associated employer" shall be construed accordingly.

NOTES

Para (7): words in square brackets substituted by the Legal Services Act 2007 (Consequential Amendments) Order 2009, SI 2009/3348, art 23, Sch 2, as from 1 January 2010.

Para (7A): inserted by the Transnational Information and Consultation of Employees Regulations 1999 (Amendment) Regulations 2004, SI 2004/2518, reg 2; words in square brackets substituted by SI 2009/3348, art 22, Sch 1, as from 16 December 2009.

PART IX
EXCEPTIONS

[2.552]

42 Article 6 agreements

(1) Where, in accordance with regulation 5, the central management is situated in the United Kingdom and, immediately before the date on which these Regulations come into force an Article 6 agreement is in force, those provisions referred to in regulation 4(1) which apply only where the central management is situated in the United Kingdom shall only apply if—

(a) the parties to the Article 6 agreement agree or have agreed (whether before or after these Regulations come into force) to the effect that the provisions of these Regulations which would have applied in respect of the agreement had it been made under regulation 17 should apply in respect of the Article 6 agreement; or

(b) the Article 6 agreement ceases to have effect.

(2) In paragraph (1) and regulation 47 "Article 6 agreement" means an agreement for the establishment of a European Works Council or information and consultation procedure made under the provisions of the law or practice of a Member State other than the United Kingdom which are designed to give effect to Article 6 of the Transnational Information and Consultation Directive.

(3) Where paragraph (1)(a) applies these Regulations shall apply as if the Article 6 agreement had been made under regulation 17.

[2.553]

43 Article 7 European Works Councils

(1) Where, in accordance with regulation 5, the central management is situated in the United Kingdom, and immediately before the date these Regulations come into force an Article 7 European Works Council exists, those provisions referred to in regulation 4(1) which apply only where the central management is situated in the United Kingdom shall only apply if—

(a) the central management and European Works Council agree or have agreed (whether before or after these Regulations come into force) to the effect that the provisions of these Regulations which would have applied in respect of the European Works Council had it been made, by virtue of regulation 18, under these Regulations should apply in respect of the Article 7 European Works Council; or

(b) the European Works Council decides, under the provisions of the law or practice of a Member State other than the United Kingdom which are designed to give effect to paragraph 1(f) of the Annex to the Transnational Information and Consultation Directive, to negotiate an agreement for a European Works Council or an information and consultation procedure.

(2) In paragraph (1) and regulations 47 and 48 "Article 7 European Works Council" means a European Works Council established under the provisions of the law or practice of a Member State other than the United Kingdom which are designed to give effect to Article 7 of, and the Annex to, the Transnational Information and Consultation Directive.

(3) Where paragraph (1)(a) or (b) applies these Regulations shall apply, subject to the modifications referred to in paragraphs (4) to (6) of regulation 48, as if the Article 7 European Works Council had been established, by virtue of regulation 18, under these Regulations and, in a case where paragraph (1)(b) applies, as if a decision had been taken under paragraph 10(2) of the Schedule.

[2.554]

[44 Article 3 agreements

(1) Subject to paragraphs (4) and (5), none of the obligations in these Regulations, except those in regulation 19F, applies to a Community-scale undertaking or Community-scale group of undertakings where the conditions specified in Article 3 of the Extension Directive are satisfied.

(2) The conditions referred to in paragraph (1) are that—

(a) an agreement is in force which—

(i) was in force immediately before 16th December 1999;

(ii) covers the entire workforce in the Member States; and

(iii) provides for the transnational information and consultation of employees, and

(b) the obligation (whether arising under these Regulations or under the national law or practice of any other Member State) to initiate negotiations for the establishment of a European Works Council or information and consultation procedure would, but for this paragraph, have applied to the Community-scale undertaking or Community-scale group of undertakings solely as a result of the Extension Directive.

(3) If an agreement when taken together with one or more other agreements satisfies the requirements specified in paragraph (2)(a), that agreement, when taken together with such other agreements, shall be treated as an agreement for the purposes of that paragraph.

(4) Regulations 9 to 18 apply where the structure of a Community-scale undertaking or Community-scale group of undertakings changes significantly and there is—

(a) one European Works Council agreement, or one agreement for an information and consultation procedure;

(b) more than one European Works Council agreement;

(c) more than one agreement for an information and consultation procedure; or

(d) at least one European Works Council agreement and at least one agreement for an information and consultation procedure,

in force and there are no provisions for the continuance of the European Works Council or information and consultation procedure, as the case may be, where there are significant changes in the structure of the Community-scale undertaking or Community-scale group of undertakings or there are such provisions, but there is a conflict between them.

(5) Regulations 25(1) and (2), 26 to 28, 31 and 32 apply to an employee who is a member of a special negotiating body or a candidate in an election in which any person elected will, on being elected, be such a member, where the structure of a Community-scale undertaking or Community-scale group of undertakings changes significantly and paragraphs (6) and (7) apply.

(6) This paragraph applies where there is—

(a) one European Works Council agreement, or one agreement for an information and consultation procedure;

(b) more than one European Works Council agreement;
(c) more than one agreement for an information and consultation procedure; or
(d) at least one European Works Council agreement and at least one agreement for an information and consultation procedure,

in force and there are no provisions for the continuance of the European Works Council or information and consultation procedure, as the case may be, where there are significant changes in the structure of the Community-scale undertaking or Community-scale group of undertakings or there are such provisions, but there is a conflict between them.

(7) This paragraph applies where the central management has initiated negotiations for the establishment of a European Works Council or an information and consultation procedure under regulation 19F(1) or (3).]

NOTES

Commencement: 5 June 2011.

Regulations 44, 45, 45A substituted (for the original regs 44, 45), by the Transnational Information and Consultation of Employees (Amendment) Regulations 2010, SI 2010/1088, regs 2, 23, as from 5 June 2011.

[2.555]

[45 Article 13 agreements

(1) Subject to paragraphs (4) and (5), none of the obligations in these Regulations, except those in regulation 19F, applies to a Community-scale undertaking or Community-scale group of undertakings where the conditions specified in Article 13 of the Transnational Information and Consultation Directive are satisfied.

(2) The conditions referred to in paragraph (1) are that an agreement is in force which—
(a) was in force immediately before whichever is the earlier of 23rd September 1996 and the day after the date on which the national law or practice giving effect to the Transnational Information and Consultation Directive came into force in the Member State (other than the United Kingdom) whose national law governs the agreement;
(b) covers the entire workforce in the Member States; and
(c) provides for the transnational information and consultation of employees.

(3) If an agreement when taken together with one or more other agreements satisfies the requirements specified in paragraph (2), that agreement, when taken together with such other agreements, shall be treated as an agreement for the purposes of that paragraph.

(4) Regulations 9 to 18 apply where the structure of a Community-scale undertaking or Community-scale group of undertakings changes significantly and there is—
(a) one European Works Council agreement or one agreement for an information and consultation procedure;
(b) more than one European Works Council agreement;
(c) more than one agreement for an information and consultation procedure; or
(d) at least one European Works Council agreement and at least one agreement for an information and consultation procedure,

in force and there are no provisions for the continuance of the European Works Council or information and consultation procedure, as the case may be, where there are significant changes in the structure of the Community-scale undertaking or Community-scale group of undertakings or there are such provisions, but there is a conflict between them.

(5) Regulations 25(1) and (2), 26 to 28, 31 and 32 apply to an employee who is a member of a special negotiating body or a candidate in an election in which any person elected will, on being elected, be such a member, where the structure of a Community-scale undertaking or Community-scale group of undertakings changes significantly and paragraphs (6) and (7) apply.

(6) This paragraph applies where there is—
(a) one European Works Council agreement, or one agreement for an information and consultation procedure;
(b) more than one European Works Council agreement;
(c) more than one agreement for an information and consultation procedure; or
(d) at least one European Works Council agreement and at least one agreement for an information and consultation procedure,

in force and there are no provisions for the continuance of the European Works Council or information and consultation procedure, as the case may be, where there are significant changes in the structure of the Community-scale undertaking or Community-scale group of undertakings or there are such provisions, but there is a conflict between them.

(7) This paragraph applies where the central management has initiated negotiations for the establishment of a European Works Council or an information and consultation procedure under regulation 19F(1) or (3).]

NOTES

Commencement: 5 June 2011.

Substituted as noted to reg 44 at **[2.554]**.

[2.556]

[45A Agreements signed or revised on or after 5th June 2009 and before 5th June 2011

(1) Subject to paragraph (4), where the conditions specified in paragraph (2) are satisfied, these Regulations shall apply to a Community-scale undertaking or Community-scale group of undertakings as if the amendments listed in paragraph (3) had not been made.

(2) The conditions referred to in paragraph (1) are that an agreement is in force which—

- (a) establishes a European Works Council or information and consultation procedure under regulation 17 of these Regulations; and
- (b) is signed or revised on or after 5th June 2009 and before 5th June 2011.

(3) The amendments referred to in paragraph (1) are those made by the following provisions of the 2010 Regulations—

- (a) regulation 3, in so far as it inserts the definition of "national employee representation bodies" and paragraphs (4A) and (4B) into regulation 2 of these Regulations;
- (b) regulations 5 to 10;
- (c) regulation 11, in so far as it inserts regulations 19A, 19B, 19C, 19D and 19E into these Regulations;
- (d) regulation 13, in so far as it inserts paragraph (1A)(b) into regulation 21 of these Regulations;
- (e) regulation 14, in so far as it inserts regulation 21A(1)(b), (c) and (d) into these Regulations and makes provision for the resolution of complaints in relation to regulations 19A, 19B and 19E(2);
- (f) regulation 16;
- (g) regulation 23, in so far as it amends regulations 44 and 45 of these Regulations; and
- (h) regulations 24 to 29.

(4) Regulations 9 to 18 apply where the structure of a Community-scale undertaking or Community-scale group of undertakings changes significantly and there is—

- (a) one European Works Council agreement, or one agreement for an information and consultation procedure;
- (b) more than one European Works Council agreement;
- (c) more than one agreement for an information and consultation procedure; or
- (d) at least one European Works Council agreement and at least one agreement for an information and consultation procedure,

in force and there are no provisions for the continuance of the European Works Council or information and consultation procedure, as the case may be, where there are significant changes in the structure of the Community-scale undertaking or Community-scale group of undertakings or there are such provisions, but there is a conflict between them.

(5) In this regulation "the 2010 Regulations" means the Transnational Information and Consultation of Employees (Amendment) Regulations 2010.]

NOTES

Commencement: 5 June 2011.
Substituted as noted to reg 44 at **[2.554]**.

[2.557]

46 Merchant Navy

(1) Subject to paragraph (3), no long haul crew member shall be—

- (a) a member of a special negotiating body;
- (b) a member of a European Works Council; or
- (c) an information and consultation representative.

(2) In paragraph (1), a "long haul crew member" means a person who is a member of a merchant navy crew other than—

- (a) a ferry worker; or
- (b) a person who normally works on voyages the duration of which is less than 48 hours.

(3) Paragraph (1) shall not apply where the central management decides that the long haul crew member in question shall be permitted to be, as the case may be, a member of a special negotiating body or of a European Works Council, or an information and consultation representative.

(4) Where paragraph (1) applies, no long haul crew member shall—

- (a) stand as a candidate for election as a member of a special negotiating body or of a European Works Council, or as an information and consultation representative; or
- (b) be appointed or nominated to be a member of a special negotiating body or of a European Works Council, or an information and consultation representative.

[2.558]
[46A

(1) These regulations do not apply to an SE that is—
- (a) a Community-scale undertaking, or
- (b) a controlling undertaking of a Community-scale group of undertakings,

except where the special negotiating body has taken the decision referred to in regulation 17 of the European Public Limited-Liability Company (Employee Involvement) (Great Britain) Regulations 2009 (decision not to open, or to terminate, negotiations) (SI 2009/2401) or, as the case may be, regulation 17 of the European Public Limited-Liability Company (Employee Involvement) (Northern Ireland) Regulations 2009 (SI 2009/2402).

(2) In this regulation an "SE" means a company established in accordance with the European Public Limited-Liability Company Regulations 2004 (SI 2004/2326).]

NOTES

Commencement: 1 October 2009.

Inserted by the European Public Limited-Liability Company Regulations 2004, SI 2004/2326, reg 53, and substituted by the European Public Limited-Liability Company (Employee Involvement) (Great Britain) Regulations 2009, SI 2009/2401, reg 40, as from 1 October 2009.

[2.559]
[46B

[(1) These regulations do not apply to an SCE that is—
- (a) a Community-scale undertaking, or
- (b) a controlling undertaking of a Community-scale group of undertakings,

except where the special negotiating body has taken the decision referred to in regulation 19 of, or paragraph 13 of Schedule 1 to, the European Cooperative Society (Involvement of Employees) Regulations 2006 (decision not to open, or to terminate, negotiations).

(2) In this regulation an "SCE" means a European Cooperative Society established in accordance with the European Cooperative Society Regulations 2006.]

NOTES

Inserted by the European Cooperative Society (Involvement of Employees) Regulations 2006, SI 2006/2059, reg 42.

PART X
TRANSITIONALS

[2.560]
47 Transitionals: special negotiating body

(1) Where immediately before the date on which these Regulations come into force—
- (a) a special negotiating body has been validly requested or established under the provisions of the law or practice of a Member State other than the United Kingdom which is designed to give effect to the Transnational Information and Consultation Directive;
- (b) no Article 6 agreement is in force; and
- (c) no Article 7 European Works Council has been established—

paragraphs (2) and (3) shall apply.

(2) Where the central management is situated in the United Kingdom these Regulations shall apply, with the modifications specified in paragraphs (4) to (6), as if a valid request had been made under regulation 9 and, where appropriate, as if the special negotiating body had been established under these Regulations.

(3) Where the central management is not situated in the United Kingdom the regulations referred to in regulation 4(2) shall apply with the modifications specified in paragraphs (5) and (6) of this regulation.

(4) Regulation 12 shall apply in respect of the composition of the special negotiating body only to the extent that it determines the number of UK members on the special negotiating body but shall not affect in any way the number of non-UK members on the special negotiating body.

(5) Where, as a result of the implementation of the Extension Directive by a Member State (including the United Kingdom) there are required to be UK members on the special negotiating body and immediately before the date on which these Regulations come into force—
- (a) no person has been designated to attend meetings of the special negotiating body as a representative of employees in the United Kingdom; or
- (b) one or more persons have been designated to attend meetings of the special negotiating body as a representative of employees in the United Kingdom,

then in the case mentioned in sub-paragraph (a), the UK members of the special negotiating body shall be elected or appointed in accordance with regulations 13 to 15, and in the case mentioned in sub-paragraph (b), the person or persons shall be treated as from the date on which these Regulations come into force as a UK member of the special negotiating body who has been elected or appointed in accordance with regulations 13 to 15.

(6) Where the number of persons referred to in paragraph (5)(b) is—

(a) in a case where regulation 12 applies, less than the number of UK members of the special negotiating body required by that regulation, or

(b) in a case where regulation 12 does not apply, less than the number of UK members of the special negotiating body required by the provisions of the law or practice of the Member State under which the special negotiating body was established,

the additional number of UK members of the special negotiating body needed to secure compliance with regulation 12 or, as the case may be, the law or practice of the Member State referred to in sub-paragraph (b) of this paragraph shall be elected or appointed in accordance with regulations 13 to 15.

[2.561]

48 Transitionals: Article 7 European Works Councils

(1) Where, immediately before the date on which these Regulations come into force, a European Works Council has been established under the provisions of the law or practice of a Member State other than the United Kingdom, which are designed to give effect to Article 7 of, and the Annex to, the Transnational Information and Consultation Directive, paragraphs (2) and (3) shall apply.

(2) Where the central management is situated in the United Kingdom and regulation 43(1) (a) or 43(1)(b) applies these Regulations shall apply with the modifications specified in paragraphs (4) to (6) as if the European Works Council had been established under these Regulations.

(3) Where the central management is not situated in the United Kingdom, or is situated in the United Kingdom but neither regulation 43(1)(a) nor 43(1)(b) applies, the regulations referred to in regulation 4(2) shall apply with the modifications specified in paragraphs (5) and (6) of this regulation.

(4) Paragraph 2 of the Schedule shall apply in respect of the composition of the European Works Council only to the extent that it determines the number of UK members on the European Works Council but shall not affect in any way the number of non-UK members on the European Works Council.

(5) Where, as a result of the implementation of the Extension Directive by a Member State (including the United Kingdom), there are required to be UK members on the European Works Council and immediately before the date on which these Regulations come into force—

(a) no person has been designated to attend meetings of the European Works Council as a representative of employees in the United Kingdom; or

(b) one or more persons have been designated to attend meetings of the European Works Council as a representative of employees in the United Kingdom,

then in the case mentioned in sub-paragraph (a), the UK members of the European Works Council shall be appointed or elected in accordance with paragraphs 3 to 5 of the Schedule, and in the case mentioned in sub-paragraph (b), the person or persons shall be treated as from the date on which these Regulations come into force as a UK member of the European Works Council who has been elected or appointed in accordance with paragraphs 3 to 5 of the Schedule.

(6) Where the number of persons referred to in paragraph (5)(b) is—

(a) in a case where paragraph 2 of the Schedule applies, less than the number of UK members of the European Works Council required by that paragraph; or

(b) in a case where paragraph 2 of the Schedule does not apply, less than the number of UK members of the European Works Council required by the law or practice of the Member State under which the European Works Council was established,

the additional number of UK members needed to secure compliance with paragraph 2 or, as the case may be, the law or practice of the Member State referred to in sub-paragraph (b) of this paragraph shall be elected or appointed in accordance with paragraphs 3 to 5 of the Schedule.

SCHEDULE
SUBSIDIARY REQUIREMENTS

Regulation 18

[2.562]

1 Establishment of European Works Council

A European Works Council shall be established in the Community-scale undertaking or Community-scale group of undertakings in accordance with the provisions in this Schedule.

[2 Composition of the European Works Council

(1) The European Works Council shall be constituted in accordance with sub-paragraph (2).

(2) In each Member State in which employees of a Community-scale undertaking or Community-scale group of undertakings are employed to work, those employees shall elect or appoint one member of the European Works Council for each 10% (or fraction of 10%) which those employees represent of the total number of employees of the Community-scale undertaking or Community-scale group of undertakings employed in those Member States.

(3) The European Works Council shall inform the central management and any more appropriate level of management of the composition of the European Works Council.

(4) To ensure that it can co-ordinate its activities, the European Works Council shall elect from among its members a select committee comprising no more than five members who are to act on behalf of the European Works Council.]

3 Appointment or election of UK members of the European Works Council

(1) The UK members of the European Works Council must be UK employees and—

(a) in a case where all of those employees are represented by UK employees' representatives, shall be elected or appointed by such employees' representatives;

(b) in a case where not all of those employees are represented by UK employees' representatives, shall be elected by ballot.

(2) For the purposes of this paragraph all of the UK employees are represented by UK employees' representatives if each of the employees referred to in sub-paragraph (1) is a UK employee—

(a) in respect of which an independent trade union is recognised by his employer for the purpose of collective bargaining; or

(b) who has elected or appointed an employees' representative for the purpose of receiving, on the employee's behalf, information—

(i) which is relevant to the employee's terms and conditions of employment; or

(ii) about the activities of the undertaking which may significantly affect the employee's interests

but excluding representatives who are expected to receive information relevant only to a specific aspect of the terms and conditions or interests of the employee, such as health and safety or collective redundancies.

(3) Where sub-paragraph (1)(a) above applies, the election or appointment of members of the European Works Council shall be carried out by whatever method the UK employees' representatives decide.

(4) Where sub-paragraph (1)(b) applies, the UK members of the European Works Council are to be elected by a ballot of the UK employees in accordance with paragraphs 4 and 5.

4 Ballot arrangements

(1) The UK management must arrange for the holding of a ballot of employees referred to in paragraph 3(4), which satisfies the requirements specified in sub-paragraph (2).

(2) The requirements referred to in sub-paragraph (1) are that—

(a) the ballot of the UK employees must comprise a single ballot, but may instead, if the UK management so decides, comprise separate ballots of employees in such constituencies as the UK management may determine where—

(i) the number of UK members of the European Works Council to be elected is more than one, and

(ii) the UK management considers that if separate ballots were held for those constituencies, the UK members of the European Works Council to be elected would better reflect the interests of the UK employees as a whole than if a single ballot were held;

(b) a UK employee who is an employee of the Community-scale undertaking or the Community-scale group of undertakings on the day on which votes may be cast in the ballot or, if the votes may be cast on more than one day, on the first day of those days is entitled to vote in a ballot of the UK employees;

(c) any UK employee who is an employee of the Community-scale undertaking or Community-scale group of undertakings immediately before the latest time at which a person may become a candidate in the ballot, is entitled to stand in the ballot of the UK employees as a candidate for election as a UK member of the European Works Council;

(d) the UK management must, in accordance with sub-paragraph (6), appoint an independent ballot supervisor to supervise the conduct of the ballot of the UK employees but may instead, where there are to be separate ballots, appoint more than one independent ballot supervisor in accordance with that sub-paragraph, each of whom is to supervise such of the separate ballots as the UK management may determine, provided that each separate ballot is supervised by a supervisor;

(e) after the UK management has formulated proposals as to the arrangements for the ballot of the UK employees and before it has published the final arrangements under paragraph (f) it must, so far as reasonably practicable, consult with the UK employees' representatives on the proposed arrangements for the ballot of the UK employees;

(f) the UK management must publish the final arrangements for the ballot of the UK employees in such manner as to bring them to the attention of, so far as reasonably practicable, the UK employees and the UK employees' representatives.

(3) Any UK employee or UK employees' representative who believes that the arrangements for the ballot of the UK employees are defective may, within a period of 21 days beginning on the date the UK management published the final arrangements under paragraph (f), present a complaint to the CAC.

(4) Where the CAC finds the complaint well-founded it shall make a declaration to that effect and may make an order requiring the UK management to modify the arrangements it has made for the ballot of the UK employees or to satisfy the requirements in paragraph (e) or (f) of sub-paragraph (2).

(5) An order under sub-paragraph (4) shall specify the modifications to the arrangements which the UK management is required to make and the requirements which it must satisfy.

(6) A person is an independent ballot supervisor for the purposes of sub-paragraph (2)(d) if the UK management reasonably believes that he will carry out any functions conferred on him in relation to the ballot competently and has no reasonable grounds for believing that his independence in relation to the ballot might reasonably be called into question.

(7) For the purposes of sub-paragraph (3), the arrangements for the ballot of the UK employees are defective if—

(a) any of the requirements specified in paragraphs (b) to (f) of sub-paragraph (2) is not satisfied; or

(b) in a case where the ballot is to comprise separate ballots, the constituencies determined by the UK management do not reflect adequately the interests of the UK employees as a whole.

5 Conduct of ballot

(1) The UK management must—

(a) ensure that a ballot supervisor appointed under paragraph 4(2)(d) carries out his functions under this paragraph and that there is no interference with his carrying out of those functions from the UK management, or the central management (where it is not also the UK management); and

(b) comply with all reasonable requests made by a ballot supervisor for the purposes of, or in connection with, the carrying out of those functions.

(2) A ballot supervisor's appointment shall require that he—

(a) supervises the conduct of the ballot, or the separate ballots he is being appointed to supervise, in accordance with the arrangements for the ballot of the UK employees published by the UK management under paragraph 4(2)(f) or, where appropriate, in accordance with the arrangements as required to be modified by an order made as a result of a complaint presented under paragraph 4(3);

(b) does not conduct the ballot or any of the separate ballots before the UK management has satisfied the requirement specified in paragraph 4(2)(e) and—

(i) where no complaint has been presented under paragraph 4(3), before the expiry of a period of 21 days beginning on the date on which the UK management published its arrangements under paragraph 4(2)(f); or

(ii) where a complaint has been presented under paragraph 4(3), before the complaint has been determined and, where appropriate, the arrangements have been modified as required by an order made as a result of the complaint;

(c) conducts the ballot, or each separate ballot, so as to secure that—

(i) so far as reasonably practicable, those entitled to vote are given the opportunity to vote,

(ii) so far as reasonably practicable, those entitled to stand as candidates are given the opportunity to stand,

(iii) so far as is reasonably practicable, those voting are able to do so in secret, and

(iv) the votes given in the ballot are fairly and accurately counted.

(3) As soon as reasonably practicable after the holding of the ballot, or each separate ballot, the ballot supervisor must publish the results of the ballot in such manner as to make them available to the UK management and, so far as reasonably practicable, the UK employees entitled to vote in the ballot or who stood as candidates in the ballot.

(4) A ballot supervisor shall publish an ineffective ballot report where he considers (whether or not on the basis of representations made to him by another person) that—

(a) any of the requirements referred to in sub-paragraph (2) was not satisfied with the result that the outcome of the ballot would have been different; or

(b) there was interference with the carrying out of his functions or a failure by management to comply with all reasonable requests made by him with the result that he was unable to form a proper judgment as to whether each of the requirements referred to in sub-paragraph (2) was satisfied in relation to the ballot.

(5) Where a ballot supervisor publishes an ineffective ballot report the report must be published within a period of one month commencing on the date on which the ballot supervisor publishes the results of the ballot under sub-paragraph (3).

(6) A ballot supervisor shall publish an ineffective ballot report in such manner as to make it available to the UK management and, so far as reasonably practicable, the UK employees entitled to vote in the ballot or who stood as candidates in the ballot.

(7) Where a ballot supervisor publishes an ineffective ballot report then—

(a) if there has been a single ballot or an ineffective ballot report has been published in respect of every separate ballot, the outcome of the ballot or ballots shall have no effect and the UK management shall again be under the obligation in paragraph 4(1);

(b) if there have been separate ballots and paragraph (a) does not apply—

(i) the UK management shall arrange for the separate ballot or ballots in respect of which an ineffective ballot report was issued to be reheld in accordance with paragraph 4 and this paragraph, and

(ii) no such ballot shall have effect until it has been so reheld and no ineffective ballot report has been published in respect of it.

(8) All costs relating to the holding of a ballot, including payments made to a ballot supervisor for supervising the conduct of the ballot, shall be borne by the central management (whether or not an ineffective ballot report has been made).

6 Competence of the European Works Council

(1) The competence of the European Works Council shall be limited to information and consultation on the matters which concern the Community-scale undertaking or Community-scale group of undertakings as a whole or at least two of its establishments or group undertakings situated in different Member States.

(2) In the case of a Community-scale undertaking or Community-scale group of undertakings falling within regulation 5(1)(b) or 5(1)(c), the competence of the European Works Council shall be limited to those matters concerning all of its establishments or group undertakings situated within the Member States or concerning at least two of its establishments or group undertakings situated in different Member States.

[(3) Information and consultation of employees shall take place between members of a European Works Council and the most appropriate level of management according to the matters under discussion.]

7 Information and consultation meetings

(1) Subject to paragraph 8, the European Works Council shall have the right to meet with the central management once a year in an information and consultation meeting, to be informed and consulted, on the basis of a report drawn up by the central management, on the progress of the business of the Community-scale undertaking or Community-scale group of undertakings and its prospects.

(2) The central management shall inform the local managements accordingly.

[(3) The information provided to the European Works Council shall relate in particular to the structure, economic and financial situation, the probable development of the business and of production and sales of the Community-scale undertaking or Community-scale group of undertakings.

(4) The information and consultation meeting shall relate in particular to the situation and probable trend of employment, investments, and substantial changes concerning organisation, introduction of new working methods or production processes, transfers of production, mergers, cut-backs or closures of undertakings, establishments or important parts of such undertakings or establishments, and collective redundancies.]

8 Exceptional information and consultation meetings

(1) Where there are exceptional circumstances affecting the employees' interests to a considerable extent, particularly in the event of relocations, the closure of establishments or undertakings or collective redundancies, the select committee or, where no such committee exists, the European Works Council shall have the right to be informed. It shall have the right to meet in an exceptional information and consultation meeting, at its request, the central management, or any other more appropriate level of management within the Community-scale undertaking or group of undertakings having its own powers of decision, so as to be informed and consulted . . .

(2) Those members of the European Works Council who have been elected or appointed by the establishments or undertakings which are directly concerned by the [circumstances] in question shall also have the right to participate in an exceptional information and consultation meeting referred to in sub-paragraph (1) of this paragraph organised with the select committee elected under sub-paragraph (6) of paragraph 2.

(3) The exceptional information and consultation meeting referred to in sub-paragraph (1) of this paragraph shall take place as soon as possible on the basis of a report drawn up by the central management or any other appropriate level of management of the Community-scale undertaking or Community-scale group of undertakings, on which an opinion may be delivered at the end of the meeting or within a reasonable time.

(4) The exceptional information and consultation meeting referred to in sub-paragraph (1) of this paragraph shall not affect the prerogatives of the central management.

[8A Use of agency workers

Where information is to be disclosed under paragraph 7 or 8 which includes information as to the employment situation in the Community-scale undertaking or, as the case may be, the Community-scale group of undertakings, this shall include suitable information relating to the use of agency workers (if any).]

9 Procedures

(1) Before an information and consultation meeting or exceptional information and consultation meeting with the central management, the European Works Council or the select committee, where necessary enlarged in accordance with sub-paragraph (2) of paragraph 8, shall be entitled to meet without the management concerned being present.

(2) Subject to regulation 23, the members of the European Works Council shall inform—

- (a) the employees' representatives of the employees in the establishments of a Community-scale undertaking or in the undertakings of a Community-scale group of undertakings; or
- (b) to the extent that any employees are not represented by employees' representatives, the employees themselves

of the content and outcome of the information and consultation procedure carried out in accordance with the provisions of this Schedule.

(3) The European Works Council shall adopt its own rules of procedure.

(4) The European Works Council or the select committee may be assisted by experts of its choice, in so far as this is necessary for it to carry out its tasks.

(5) The operating expenses of the European Works Council shall be borne by the central management; but where the European Works Council is assisted by more than one expert the central management is not required to pay such expenses in respect of more than one of them.

(6) The central management shall provide the members of the European Works Council [and its select committee] with such financial and material resources as enable them to perform their duties in an appropriate manner. In particular, the cost of organising meetings and arranging for interpretation facilities and the accommodation and travelling expenses of members of the European Works Council and its select committee shall be met by the central management unless the central management and European Works Council, or select committee, otherwise agree.

[(7) The employer must ensure that the consultation referred to in paragraphs 7(1) and 8(1) is conducted in such a way that the members of the European Works Council can, if they so request—

- (a) meet with the central management; and
- (b) obtain a reasoned response from the central management to any opinion expressed by those representatives on the reports referred to in paragraphs 7(1) and 8(3).

(8) Information and consultation carried out in accordance with this Schedule shall be carried out subject to regulation 23.]

10 The continuing application of the subsidiary requirements

(1) Four years after the European Works Council is established it shall examine whether to open negotiations for the conclusion of an agreement referred to in regulation 17 or to continue to apply the subsidiary requirements adopted in accordance with the provisions of this Schedule.

(2) If the European Works Council decides to negotiate an agreement in accordance with regulation 17, it shall notify the central management in writing to that effect, and

- (a) such notification shall be treated as a valid request made under regulation 9; and
- (b) regulations 16, 17 and 18 shall apply in respect of the negotiations for an agreement as if references in those regulations to the special negotiating body were references to the European Works Council.

NOTES

Para 2: substituted by the Transnational Information and Consultation of Employees (Amendment) Regulations 2010, SI 2010/1088, regs 2, 24, as from 5 June 2011.

Para 6: sub-para (3) added by SI 2010/1088, regs 2, 25, as from 5 June 2011.

Para 7: sub-paras (3), (4) substituted (for the original sub-para (3)) by SI 2010/1088, regs 2, 26, as from 5 June 2011.
Para 8: word omitted revoked, and word in square brackets substituted, by SI 2010/1088, regs 2, 27, as from 5 June 2011.
Para 8A: added by SI 2010/1088, regs 2, 28, as from 1 October 2011.
Para 9: words in square brackets in sub-para (6) inserted, and sub-paras (7), (8) added, by SI 2010/1088, regs 2, 29, as from 5 June 2011.

DATA PROTECTION (PROCESSING OF SENSITIVE PERSONAL DATA) ORDER 2000

(SI 2000/417)

NOTES

Made: 17 February 2000.
Authority: Data Protection Act 1998, s 67(2), Sch 3, para 10.
Commencement: 1 March 2000.

[2.563]
1

(1) This Order may be cited as the Data Protection (Processing of Sensitive Personal Data) Order 2000 and shall come into force on 1st March 2000.

(2) In this Order, "the Act" means the Data Protection Act 1998.

[2.564]
2

For the purposes of paragraph 10 of Schedule 3 to the Act, the circumstances specified in any of the paragraphs in the Schedule to this Order are circumstances in which sensitive personal data may be processed.

SCHEDULE
CIRCUMSTANCES IN WHICH SENSITIVE PERSONAL DATA MAY BE PROCESSED

Article 2

[2.565]

1. (1) The processing—
(a) is in the substantial public interest;
(b) is necessary for the purposes of the prevention or detection of any unlawful act; and
(c) must necessarily be carried out without the explicit consent of the data subject being sought so as not to prejudice those purposes.

(2) In this paragraph, "act" includes a failure to act.

2. The processing—
(a) is in the substantial public interest;
(b) is necessary for the discharge of any function which is designed for protecting members of the public against—
(i) dishonesty, malpractice, or other seriously improper conduct by, or the unfitness or incompetence of, any person, or
(ii) mismanagement in the administration of, or failures in services provided by, any body or association; and
(c) must necessarily be carried out without the explicit consent of the data subject being sought so as not to prejudice the discharge of that function.

3. (1) The disclosure of personal data—
(a) is in the substantial public interest;
(b) is in connection with—
(i) the commission by any person of any unlawful act (whether alleged or established),
(ii) dishonesty, malpractice, or other seriously improper conduct by, or the unfitness or incompetence of, any person (whether alleged or established), or
(iii) mismanagement in the administration of, or failures in services provided by, any body or association (whether alleged or established);
(c) is for the special purposes as defined in section 3 of the Act; and
(d) is made with a view to the publication of those data by any person and the data controller reasonably believes that such publication would be in the public interest.

(2) In this paragraph, "act" includes a failure to act.

4. The processing—
(a) is in the substantial public interest;

(b) is necessary for the discharge of any function which is designed for the provision of confidential counselling, advice, support or any other service; and
(c) is carried out without the explicit consent of the data subject because the processing—
(i) is necessary in a case where consent cannot be given by the data subject,
(ii) is necessary in a case where the data controller cannot reasonably be expected to obtain the explicit consent of the data subject, or
(iii) must necessarily be carried out without the explicit consent of the data subject being sought so as not to prejudice the provision of that counselling, advice, support or other service.

5. (1) The processing—
(a) is necessary for the purpose of—
(i) carrying on insurance business, or
(ii) making determinations in connection with eligibility for, and benefits payable under, an occupational pension scheme as defined in section 1 of the Pension Schemes Act 1993;
(b) is of sensitive personal data consisting of information falling within section 2(e) of the Act relating to a data subject who is the parent, grandparent, great grandparent or sibling of—
(i) in the case of paragraph (a)(i), the insured person, or
(ii) in the case of paragraph (a)(ii), the member of the scheme;
(c) is necessary in a case where the data controller cannot reasonably be expected to obtain the explicit consent of that data subject and the data controller is not aware of the data subject withholding his consent; and
(d) does not support measures or decisions with respect to that data subject.

(2) In this paragraph—
[(a) insurance business" means business which consists of effecting or carrying out contracts of insurance of the following kind—
(i) life and annuity,
(ii) linked long term,
(iii) permanent health,
(iv) accident, or
(v) sickness; and]
(b) "insured" and "member" includes an individual who is seeking to become an insured person or member of the scheme respectively.

[(2A) The definition of "insurance business" in sub-paragraph (2) above must be read with—
(a) section 22 of the Financial Services and Markets Act 2000;
(b) any relevant order under that section; and
(c) Schedule 2 to that Act.]

6. The processing—
(a) is of sensitive personal data in relation to any particular data subject that are subject to processing which was already under way immediately before the coming into force of this Order;
(b) is necessary for the purpose of—
[(i) effecting or carrying out contracts of long-term insurance of the kind mentioned in sub-paragraph (2)(a)(i), (ii) or (iii) of paragraph 5 above;] or
(ii) establishing or administering an occupational pension scheme as defined in section 1 of the Pension Schemes Act 1993; and
(c) either—
(i) is necessary in a case where the data controller cannot reasonably be expected to obtain the explicit consent of the data subject and that data subject has not informed the data controller that he does not so consent, or
(ii) must necessarily be carried out even without the explicit consent of the data subject so as not to prejudice those purposes.

7. (1) Subject to the provisions of sub-paragraph (2), the processing—
(a) is of sensitive personal data consisting of information falling within section 2(c) or (e) of the Act;
(b) is necessary for the purpose of identifying or keeping under review the existence or absence of equality of opportunity or treatment between persons—
(i) holding different beliefs as described in section 2(c) of the Act, or
(ii) of different states of physical or mental health or different physical or mental conditions as described in section 2(e) of the Act,

with a view to enabling such equality to be promoted or maintained;
(c) does not support measures or decisions with respect to any particular data subject otherwise than with the explicit consent of that data subject; and
(d) does not cause, nor is likely to cause, substantial damage or substantial distress to the data subject or any other person.

(2) Where any individual has given notice in writing to any data controller who is processing personal data under the provisions of sub-paragraph (1) requiring that data controller to cease processing personal data in respect of which that individual is the data subject at the end of such period as is reasonable in the circumstances, that data controller must have ceased processing those personal data at the end of that period.

8. (1) Subject to the provisions of sub-paragraph (2), the processing—

(a) is of sensitive personal data consisting of information falling within section 2(b) of the Act;

(b) is carried out by any person or organisation included in the register maintained pursuant to section 1 of the Registration of Political Parties Act 1998 in the course of his or its legitimate political activities; and

(c) does not cause, nor is likely to cause, substantial damage or substantial distress to the data subject or any other person.

(2) Where any individual has given notice in writing to any data controller who is processing personal data under the provisions of sub-paragraph (1) requiring that data controller to cease processing personal data in respect of which that individual is the data subject at the end of such period as is reasonable in the circumstances, that data controller must have ceased processing those personal data at the end of that period.

9. The processing—

(a) is in the substantial public interest;

(b) is necessary for research purposes (which expression shall have the same meaning as in section 33 of the Act);

(c) does not support measures or decisions with respect to any particular data subject otherwise than with the explicit consent of that data subject; and

(d) does not cause, nor is likely to cause, substantial damage or substantial distress to the data subject or any other person.

10. The processing is necessary for the exercise of any functions conferred on a constable by any rule of law.

NOTES

Para 5: sub-para (2)(a) substituted, and sub-para (2A) inserted, by the Financial Services and Markets Act 2000 (Consequential Amendments and Repeals) Order 2001, SI 2001/3649, art 587(1)–(3).

Para 6: sub-para (b)(i) substituted by SI 2001/3649, art 587(1), (4).

TRADE UNION RECOGNITION (METHOD OF COLLECTIVE BARGAINING) ORDER 2000

(SI 2000/1300)

NOTES

Made: 11 May 2000.
Authority: Trade Union and Labour Relations (Consolidation) Act 1992, Sch A1, para 168(1).
Commencement: 6 June 2000.
See *Harvey* NI(7).

[2.566]

1 Citation and commencement

This Order may be cited as the Trade Union Recognition (Method of Collective Bargaining) Order 2000 and comes into force on 6th June 2000.

[2.567]

2 Specification of method

The method specified for the purposes of paragraphs 31(3) and 63(2) of Schedule A1 to the Trade Union and Labour Relations (Consolidation) Act 1992 is the method set out under the heading "the specified method" in the Schedule to this Order.

SCHEDULE

[2.568]

PREAMBLE

The method specified below ("the specified method") is one by which collective bargaining might be conducted in the particular, and possibly rare, circumstances discussed in the following paragraph. The specified method is not designed to be applied as a model for voluntary procedural agreements between employers and unions. Because most voluntary agreements are not legally binding and are usually concluded in a climate of trust and co-operation, they do not need to be as prescriptive as the specified method. However, the Central Arbitration Committee ("CAC") must take the specified method into account when exercising its powers to impose a method of collective bargaining under paragraphs 31(3) and 63(2) of Schedule A1 to the Trade Union and Labour Relations (Consolidation) Act 1992. In exercising those powers the CAC may depart from the specified method to such extent as it thinks appropriate in the circumstances of individual cases.

Paragraph 31(3) provides for the CAC to impose a method of collective bargaining in cases where a union (or unions, where two or more unions act jointly) has been recognised by an employer by means of an award of the CAC under Part I of Schedule A1, but the employer and union(s) have been unable to agree a method of bargaining between themselves, or have failed to follow an agreed method. Paragraph 63(2) provides for the CAC to impose a bargaining method in cases where an employer and a union (or unions) have entered an agreement for recognition, as defined by paragraph 52 of Part II of Schedule A1, but cannot agree a method of bargaining, or have failed to follow the agreed method.

The bargaining method imposed by the CAC has effect as if it were a legally binding contract between the employer and the union(s). If one party believes the other is failing to respect the method, the first party may apply to the court for an order of specific performance, ordering the other party to comply with the method. Failure to comply with such an order could constitute contempt of court.

Once the CAC has imposed a bargaining method, the parties can vary it, including the fact that it is legally binding, by agreement provided that they do so in writing.

The fact that the CAC has imposed a method does not affect the rights of individual workers under either statute or their contracts of employment. For example, it does not prevent or limit the rights of individual workers to discuss, negotiate or agree with their employer terms of their contract of employment, which differ from the terms of any collective agreement into which the employer and the union may enter as a result of collective bargaining conducted by this method. Nor does the imposed method affect an individual's statutory entitlement to time off for trade union activities or duties.

In cases where the CAC imposes a bargaining method on the parties, the employer is separately obliged, in accordance with Section 70B of the Trade Union and Labour Relations (Consolidation) Act 1992 (as inserted by section 5 of the Employment Relations Act 1999), to consult union representatives periodically on his policy, actions and plans on training. The specified method does not discuss how such consultations should be organised.

The law confers certain entitlements on independent trade unions which are recognised for collective bargaining purposes. For example, employers must disclose, on request, certain types of information to the representatives of the recognised unions. The fact that the CAC has imposed a bargaining method does not affect these existing statutory entitlements.

THE SPECIFIED METHOD

The Parties

1. The method shall apply in each case to two parties, who are referred to here as the "employer" and the "union". Unless the text specifies otherwise, the term "union" should be read to mean "unions" in cases where two or more unions are jointly recognised.

The Purpose

2. The purpose is to specify a method by which the employer and the union conduct collective bargaining concerning the pay, hours and holidays of the workers comprising the bargaining unit.

3. The employer shall not grant the right to negotiate pay, hours and holidays to any other union in respect of the workers covered by this method.

The Joint Negotiating Body

4. The employer and the union shall establish a Joint Negotiating Body (JNB) to discuss and negotiate the pay, hours and holidays of the workers comprising the bargaining unit. No other body or group shall undertake collective bargaining on the pay, hours and holidays of these workers, unless the employer and the union so agree.

JNB Membership

5. The membership of the JNB shall usually comprise three employer representatives (who together shall constitute the Employer Side of the JNB) and three union representatives (who together shall constitute the Union Side of the JNB). Each union recognised by the employer in respect of the bargaining unit shall be entitled to one seat at least. To meet this requirement, the Union Side may need to be larger than three and in this eventuality the employer shall be entitled to increase his representation on the JNB by the same number, if he wishes.

6. The employer shall select those individuals who comprise the Employer Side. The individuals must either be those who take the final decisions within the employer's organisation in respect of the pay, hours and holidays of the workers in the bargaining unit or who are expressly authorised by the employer to make recommendations directly to those who take such final decisions. Unless it would be unreasonable to do so, the employer shall select as a representative the most senior person responsible for employment relations in the bargaining unit.

7. The union shall select those individuals who comprise the Union Side in accordance with its own rules and procedures. The representatives must either be individuals employed by the employer or individuals employed by the union who are officials of the union within the meaning of sections 1 and 119 of the Trade Union and Labour Relations (Consolidation) Act 1992 ("the 1992 Act").

8. The JNB shall determine their own rules in respect of the attendance at JNB meetings of observers and substitutes who deputise for JNB members.

Officers

9. The Employer Side shall select one of its members to act as its Chairman and one to act as its Secretary. The Union Side shall select one of its members to act as its Chairman and one to act as its Secretary. The same person may perform the roles of Chairman and Secretary of a Side.

10. For the twelve months from the date of the JNB's first meeting, meetings of the JNB shall be chaired by the Chairman of the Employer Side. The Chairman of the Union Side shall chair the JNB's meetings for the following twelve months. The chairmanship of JNB meetings will alternate in the same way thereafter at intervals of twelve months. In the absence of the person who should chair JNB meetings, a JNB meeting shall be chaired by another member of that person's Side.

11. The Secretary of the Employer Side shall act as Secretary to the JNB. He shall circulate documentation and agendas in advance of JNB meetings, arrange suitable accommodation for meetings, notify members of meetings and draft the written record of JNB meetings. The Secretary of the Employer Side shall work closely with the Secretary of the Union Side in the discharge of these duties, disclosing full information about his performance of these tasks.

JNB Organisation

12. Draft agendas shall be circulated at least three working days in advance of JNB meetings. The draft record of JNB meetings shall be circulated within ten working days of the holding of meetings for approval at the next JNB meeting. The record does not need to be a verbatim account, but should fully describe the conclusions reached and the actions to be taken.

13. Subject to the timetable of meetings stipulated in paragraphs 15, 17, 20 and 28 below, the date, timing and location of meetings shall be arranged by the JNB's Secretary, in full consultation with the Secretary of the Union Side, to ensure maximum attendance at meetings. A meeting of the JNB shall be quorate if 50% or more of each Side's members (or, where applicable, their substitutes) are in attendance.

Bargaining Procedure

14 The union's proposals for adjustments to pay, hours and holidays shall be dealt with on an annual basis, unless the two Sides agree a different bargaining period.

15. The JNB shall conduct these negotiations for each bargaining round according to the following staged procedure.

Step 1—The union shall set out in writing, and send to the employer, its proposals (the "claim") to vary the pay, hours and holidays, specifying which aspects it wants to change. In its claim, the union shall set out the reasons for its proposals, together with the main supporting evidence at its disposal at the time. In cases where there is no established annual date when the employer reviews the pay, hours and holidays of all the workers in the bargaining unit, the union shall put forward its first claim within three months of this method being imposed (and by the same date in subsequent rounds). Where such a common review date is established, the union shall submit its first claim at least a month in advance of that date (and by the same date in subsequent rounds). In either case, the employer and the union may agree a different date by which the claim should be submitted each year. If the union fails to submit its claim by this date, then the procedure shall be ended for the bargaining round in question. Exceptionally, the union may submit a late claim without this penalty if its work on the claim was delayed while the Central Arbitration Committee considered a relevant complaint by the union of failure by the employer to disclose information for collective bargaining purposes.

Step 2—Within ten working days of the Employer Side's receipt of the union's letter, a quorate meeting of the JNB shall be held to discuss the claim. At this meeting, the Union Side shall explain its claim and answer any reasonable questions arising to the best of its ability.

Step 3—

(a) Within fifteen working days immediately following the Step 2 meeting, the employer shall either accept the claim in full or write to the union responding to its claim. If the Employer Side requests it, a quorate meeting of the JNB shall be held within the fifteen day period to enable the employer to present this written response directly to the Union Side. In explaining the basis of his response, the employer shall set out in this written communication all relevant information in his possession. In particular, the written communication shall contain information costing each element of the claim and describing the business consequences, particularly any staffing implications, unless the employer is not required to disclose such information for any of the reasons specified in section 182(1) of the 1992 Act. The basis of these estimated costs and effects, including the main assumptions that the employer has used, shall be set out in the communication. In determining what information is disclosed as relevant, the employer shall be under no greater obligation that he is under the general duty imposed on him by sections 181 and 182 of the 1992 Act to disclose information for the purposes of collective bargaining.

(b) If the response contains any counter-proposals, the written communication shall set out the reasons for making them, together with the supporting evidence. The letter shall provide information estimating the costs and staffing consequences of implementing each element of the counter-proposals, unless the employer is not required to disclose such information for any of the reasons specified in section 182(1) of the 1992 Act.

Step 4—Within ten working days of the Union Side's receipt of the employer's written communication, a further quorate meeting of the JNB shall be held to discuss the employer's response. At this meeting, the Employer Side shall explain its response and answer any reasonable questions arising to the best of its ability.

Step 5—If no agreement is reached at the Step 4 meeting (or the last of such meetings if more than one is held at that stage in the procedure), another quorate meeting of the JNB shall be held within ten working days. The union may bring to this meeting a maximum of two other individuals employed by the union who are officials within the meaning of the sections 1 and 119 of the 1992 Act. The employer may bring to the meeting a maximum of two other individuals who are employees or officials of an employer's organisation to which the employer belongs. These additional persons shall be allowed to contribute to the meeting, as if they were JNB members.

Step 6—If no agreement is reached at the Step 5 meeting (or the last of such meetings if more than one meeting is held at that stage in the procedure), within five working days the employer and the union shall consider, separately or jointly, consulting ACAS about the prospect of ACAS helping them to find a settlement of their differences through conciliation. In the event that both parties agree to invite ACAS to conciliate, both parties shall give such assistance to ACAS as is necessary to enable it to carry out the conciliation efficiently and effectively.

16. The parties shall set aside half a working day for each JNB meeting, unless the Employer Side Chairman and the Union Side Chairman agree a different length of time for the meeting. Unless it is essential to do otherwise, meetings shall be held during the normal working time of most union members of the JNB. Meetings may be adjourned, if both Sides agree. Additional meetings at any point in the procedure may be arranged, if both Sides agree. In addition, if the Employer Side requests it, a meeting of the JNB shall be held before the union has submitted its claim or before the employer is required to respond, enabling the Employer Side to explain the business context within which the employer shall assess the claim.

17. The employer shall not vary the contractual terms affecting the pay, hours or holidays of workers in the bargaining unit, unless he has first discussed his proposals with the union. Such proposals shall normally be made by the employer in the context of his consideration of the union's claim at Steps 3 or 4. If, however, the employer has not tabled his proposals during that process and he wishes to make proposals before the next bargaining round commences, he must write to the union setting out his proposals and the reasons for making them, together with the supporting evidence. The letter shall provide information estimating the costs and staffing consequences of implementing each element of the proposals, unless the employer is not required to disclose such information for any of the reasons specified in section 182(1) of the 1992 Act. A quorate meeting of the JNB shall be held within five working days of the Union Side's receipt of the letter. If there is a failure to resolve the issue at that meeting, then meetings shall be arranged, and steps shall be taken, in accordance with Steps 5 and 6 of the above procedure.

18. Paragraph 17 does not apply to terms in the contract of an individual worker where that worker has agreed that the terms may be altered only by direct negotiation between the worker and the employer.

Collective Agreements

19. Any agreements affecting the pay, hours and holidays of workers in the bargaining unit, which the employer and the union enter following negotiations, shall be set down in writing and signed by the Chairman of the Employer Side and by the Chairman of the Union Side or, in their absence, by another JNB member on their respective Sides.

20. If either the employer or union consider that there has been a failure to implement the agreement, then that party can request in writing a meeting of the JNB to discuss the alleged failure. A quorate meeting shall be held within five working days of the receipt of the request by the JNB Secretary. If there is a failure to resolve the issue at that meeting, then meetings shall be arranged, and steps shall be taken, in accordance with Steps 5 and 6 of the above procedure.

Facilities and Time Off

21. If they are employed by the employer, union members of the JNB:

— shall be given paid time off by the employer to attend JNB meetings;

— shall be given paid time off by the employer to attend a two hour pre-meeting of the Union Side before each JNB meeting; and

— shall be given paid time off by the employer to hold a day-long meeting to prepare the claim at Step 1 in the bargaining procedure.

The union members of the JNB shall schedule such meetings at times which minimise the effect on production and services. In arranging these meetings, the union members of the JNB shall provide the employer and their line management with as much notice as possible and give details of the purpose of the time off, the intended location of the meeting and the timing and duration of the time off. The employer shall provide adequate heating and lighting for these meetings, and ensure that they are held in private.

22. If they are not employed by the employer, union members of the JNB or other union officials attending JNB meetings shall be given sufficient access to the employer's premises to allow them to attend Union Side pre-meetings, JNB meetings and meetings of the bargaining unit as specified in paragraph 23.

23. The employer shall agree to the union's reasonable request to hold meetings with members of the bargaining unit on company premises to discuss the Step 1 claim, the employer's offer or revisions to either. The request shall be made at least three working days in advance of the proposed meeting. However, the employer is not required to provide such facilities, if the employer does not possess available premises which can be used for meetings on the scale suggested by the union. The employer shall provide adequate heating and lighting for meetings, and ensure that the meeting is held in private. Where such meetings are held in working time, the employer is under no obligation to pay individuals for the time off. Where meetings take place outside normal working hours, they should be arranged at a time which is otherwise convenient for the workers.

24. Where resources permit, the employer shall make available to the Union Side of the JNB such typing, copying and word-processing facilities as it needs to conduct its business in private.

25. Where resources permit, the employer shall set aside a room for the exclusive use of the Union Side of the JNB. The room shall possess a secure cabinet and a telephone.

26. In respect of issues which are not otherwise specified in this method, the employer and the union shall have regard to the guidance issued in the ACAS Code of Practice on Time Off for Trade Union Duties and Activities and ensure that there is no unwarranted or unjustified failure to abide by it.

Disclosure of Information

27. The employer and the union shall have regard to the ACAS Code of Practice on the Disclosure of Information to Trade Unions for Collective Bargaining Purposes and ensure that there is no unwarranted or unjustified failure to abide by it in relation to the bargaining arrangements specified by this method.

Revision of the Method

28. The employer or the union may request in writing a meeting of the JNB to discuss revising any element of this method, including its status as a legally binding contract. A quorate meeting of the JNB shall be held within ten working days of the receipt of the request by the JNB Secretary. This meeting shall be held in accordance with the same arrangements for the holding of other JNB meetings.

General

29. The employer and the union shall take all reasonable steps to ensure that this method to conduct collective bargaining is applied efficiently and effectively.

30. The definition of a "working day" used in this method is any day other than a Saturday or a Sunday, Christmas Day or Good Friday, or a day which is a bank holiday.

31. All time limits mentioned in this method may be varied on any occasion, if both the employer and the union agree.

RECOGNITION AND DERECOGNITION BALLOTS (QUALIFIED PERSONS) ORDER 2000

(SI 2000/1306)

NOTES

Made: 11 May 2000.

Authority: Trade Union and Labour Relations (Consolidation) Act 1992, Sch A1, paras 25(7)(a), 117(9)(a).

Commencement: 6 June 2000.

[2.569]

1 Citation, commencement and interpretation

(1) This Order may be cited as the Recognition and Derecognition Ballots (Qualified Persons) Order 2000 and shall come into force on 6th June 2000.

(2) In this Order "the relevant provisions" means paragraphs 25(7)(a) and 117(9)(a) of Schedule A1 to the Trade Union and Labour Relations (Consolidation) Act 1992.

[2.570]

2 Qualifications

In relation to an individual, the condition specified for the purposes of the relevant provisions is that he—

(a) has in force a practising certificate issued by the Law Society of England and Wales or the Law Society of Scotland; or

[(b) is eligible for appointment as a statutory auditor under Part 42 of the Companies Act 2006].

NOTES

Para (b): substituted by the Recognition and Derecognition Ballots (Qualified Persons) (Amendment) Order 2010, SI 2010/437, art 2(a), as from 6 April 2010.

[2.571]

3

In relation to a partnership, the condition specified for the purposes of the relevant provisions is that every member of the partnership is an individual who satisfies the condition specified in Article 2.

[2.572]

[4 Persons specified by name

The following persons are specified for the purpose of the relevant provisions—

Association of Electoral Administrators;
DRS Data Services Limited;
Electoral Reform Services Limited;
Involvement and Participation Association;
Opt2Vote Limited; and
Popularis Limited.]

NOTES

Commencement: 6 April 2010.

Substituted by the Recognition and Derecognition Ballots (Qualified Persons) (Amendment) Order 2010, SI 2010/437, art 2(b), as from 6 April 2010.

EMPLOYMENT TRIBUNALS ACT 1996 (APPLICATION OF CONCILIATION PROVISIONS) ORDER 2000

(SI 2000/1337)

NOTES

Made: 16 May 2000.

Authority: Employment Tribunals Act 1996, s 18(8)(a), (b).

Commencement: 6 June 2000.

[2.573]

1 Citation and commencement

This Order may be cited as the Employment Tribunals Act 1996 (Application of Conciliation Provisions) Order 2000 and comes into force on 6th June 2000.

2 *(Amends the Employment Tribunals Act 1996, s 18(1) at* **[1.706]**.*)*

Part 2 Statutory Instruments

[2.574]

3 Application of provisions

The Secretary of State specifies section 70B of, and paragraph 156 of Schedule A1 to, the Trade Union and Labour Relations (Consolidation) Act 1992 as provisions to which section 18(1)(f) of the Employment Tribunals Act 1996 applies.

PART-TIME WORKERS (PREVENTION OF LESS FAVOURABLE TREATMENT) REGULATIONS 2000

(SI 2000/1551)

NOTES

Made: 8 June 2000.

Authority: Employment Relations Act 1999, s 19.

Commencement: 1 July 2000.

These Regulations implement Council Directive 97/81/EC at **[3.250]**, as extended to the United Kingdom by Council Directive 98/23/EC.

Employment Appeal Tribunal: an appeal lies to the Employment Appeal Tribunal on any question of law arising from any decision of, or in any proceedings before, an employment tribunal under or by virtue of these Regulations; see the Employment Tribunals Act 1996, s 21(1)(j) at **[1.713]**.

Conciliation: employment tribunal proceedings and claims which could be the subject of employment tribunal proceedings arising out of a contravention, or alleged contravention, of reg 5(1) or reg 7(2) are proceedings to which the Employment Tribunals Act 1996, s 18 applies; see s 18(1)(h) of that Act at **[1.706]**.

See *Harvey* AI(2), DII.

ARRANGEMENT OF REGULATIONS

PART I
GENERAL AND INTERPRETATION

[2.575]

1 Citation, commencement and interpretation

(1) These Regulations may be cited as the Part-time Workers (Prevention of Less Favourable Treatment) Regulations 2000 and shall come into force on 1st July 2000.

(2) In these Regulations—

"the 1996 Act" means the Employment Rights Act 1996;

"contract of employment" means a contract of service or of apprenticeship, whether express or implied, and (if it is express) whether oral or in writing;

"employee" means an individual who has entered into or works under or (except where a provision of these Regulations otherwise requires) where the employment has ceased, worked under a contract of employment;

"employer", in relation to any employee or worker, means the person by whom the employee or worker is or (except where a provision of these Regulations otherwise requires) where the employment has ceased, was employed;

"pro rata principle" means that where a comparable full-time worker receives or is entitled to receive pay or any other benefit, a part-time worker is to receive or be entitled to receive not less than the proportion of that pay or other benefit that the number of his weekly hours bears to the number of weekly hours of the comparable full-time worker;

"worker" means an individual who has entered into or works under or (except where a provision of these Regulations otherwise requires) where the employment has ceased, worked under—

(a) a contract of employment; or

(b) any other contract, whether express or implied and (if it is express) whether oral or in writing, whereby the individual undertakes to do or perform personally any work or services for another party to the contract whose status is not by virtue of the contract that of a client or customer of any profession or business undertaking carried on by the individual.

(3) In the definition of the pro rata principle and in regulations 3 and 4 "weekly hours" means the number of hours a worker is required to work under his contract of employment in a week in which he has no absences from work and does not work any overtime or, where the number of such hours varies according to a cycle, the average number of such hours.

[2.576]

2 Meaning of full-time worker, part-time worker and comparable full-time worker

(1) A worker is a full-time worker for the purpose of these Regulations if he is paid wholly or in part by reference to the time he works and, having regard to the custom and practice of the employer in relation to workers employed by the worker's employer under the same type of contract, is identifiable as a full-time worker.

(2) A worker is a part-time worker for the purpose of these Regulations if he is paid wholly or in part by reference to the time he works and, having regard to the custom and practice of the employer in relation to workers employed by the worker's employer under the same type of contract, is not identifiable as a full-time worker.

[(3) For the purposes of paragraphs (1), (2) and (4), the following shall be regarded as being employed under different types of contract—

(a) employees employed under a contract that is not a contract of apprenticeship;

(b) employees employed under a contract of apprenticeship;

(c) workers who are not employees;

(d) any other description of worker that it is reasonable for the employer to treat differently from other workers on the ground that workers of that description have a different type of contract.]

(4) A full-time worker is a comparable full-time worker in relation to a part-time worker if, at the time when the treatment that is alleged to be less favourable to the part-time worker takes place—

(a) both workers are—

  (i) employed by the same employer under the same type of contract, and

  (ii) engaged in the same or broadly similar work having regard, where relevant, to whether they have a similar level of qualification, skills and experience; and

(b) the full-time worker works or is based at the same establishment as the part-time worker or, where there is no full-time worker working or based at that establishment who satisfies the requirements of sub-paragraph (a), works or is based at a different establishment and satisfies those requirements.

NOTES

Para (3): substituted by the Part-time Workers (Prevention of Less Favourable Treatment) Regulations 2000 (Amendment) Regulations 2002, SI 2002/2035, reg 2(a).

[2.577]

3 Workers becoming part-time

(1) This regulation applies to a worker who—

(a) was identifiable as a full-time worker in accordance with regulation 2(1); and

(b) following a termination or variation of his contract, continues to work under a new or varied contract, whether of the same type or not, that requires him to work for a number of weekly hours that is lower than the number he was required to work immediately before the termination or variation.

(2) Notwithstanding regulation 2(4), regulation 5 shall apply to a worker to whom this regulation applies as if he were a part-time worker and as if there were a comparable full-time worker employed under the terms that applied to him immediately before the variation or termination.

(3) The fact that this regulation applies to a worker does not affect any right he may have under these Regulations by virtue of regulation 2(4).

[2.578]
4 Workers returning part-time after absence

(1) This regulation applies to a worker who—

(a) was identifiable as a full-time worker in accordance with regulation 2(1) immediately before a period of absence (whether the absence followed a termination of the worker's contract or not);

(b) returns to work for the same employer within a period of less than twelve months beginning with the day on which the period of absence started;

(c) returns to the same job or to a job at the same level under a contract, whether it is a different contract or a varied contract and regardless of whether it is of the same type, under which he is required to work for a number of weekly hours that is lower than the number he was required to work immediately before the period of absence.

(2) Notwithstanding regulation 2(4), regulation 5 shall apply to a worker to whom this regulation applies ("the returning worker") as if he were a part-time worker and as if there were a comparable full-time worker employed under—

(a) the contract under which the returning worker was employed immediately before the period of absence; or

(b) where it is shown that, had the returning worker continued to work under the contract mentioned in sub-paragraph (a) a variation would have been made to its term during the period of absence, the contract mentioned in that sub-paragraph including that variation.

(3) The fact that this regulation applies to a worker does not affect any right he may have under these Regulations by virtue of regulation 2(4).

PART II
RIGHTS AND REMEDIES

[2.579]
5 Less favourable treatment of part-time workers

(1) A part-time worker has the right not to be treated by his employer less favourably than the employer treats a comparable full-time worker—

(a) as regards the terms of his contract; or

(b) by being subjected to any other detriment by any act, or deliberate failure to act, of his employer.

(2) The right conferred by paragraph (1) applies only if—

(a) the treatment is on the ground that the worker is a part-time worker, and

(b) the treatment is not justified on objective grounds.

(3) In determining whether a part-time worker has been treated less favourably than a comparable full-time worker the pro rata principle shall be applied unless it is inappropriate.

(4) A part-time worker paid at a lower rate for overtime worked by him in a period than a comparable full-time worker is or would be paid for overtime worked by him in the same period shall not, for that reason, be regarded as treated less favourably than the comparable full-time worker where, or to the extent that, the total number of hours worked by the part-time worker in the period, including overtime, does not exceed the number of hours the comparable full-time worker is required to work in the period, disregarding absences from work and overtime.

NOTES

Conciliation: employment tribunal proceedings and claims which could be the subject of employment tribunal proceedings arising out of a contravention, or alleged contravention, of reg 5(1) or reg 7(2) are proceedings to which the Employment Tribunals Act 1996, s 18 applies; see s 18(1)(h) of that Act at **[1.706]**.

[2.580]
6 Right to receive a written statement of reasons for less favourable treatment

(1) If a worker who considers that his employer may have treated him in a manner which infringes a right conferred on him by regulation 5 requests in writing from his employer a written statement giving particulars of the reasons for the treatment, the worker is entitled to be provided with such a statement within twenty-one days of his request.

(2) A written statement under this regulation is admissible as evidence in any proceedings under these Regulations.

(3) If it appears to the tribunal in any proceedings under these Regulations—

(a) that the employer deliberately, and without reasonable excuse, omitted to provide a written statement, or

(b) that the written statement is evasive or equivocal,

it may draw any inference which it considers it just and equitable to draw, including an inference that the employer has infringed the right in question.

(4) This regulation does not apply where the treatment in question consists of the dismissal of an employee, and the employee is entitled to a written statement of reasons for his dismissal under section 92 of the 1996 Act.

[2.581]

7 Unfair dismissal and the right not to be subjected to detriment

(1) An employee who is dismissed shall be regarded as unfairly dismissed for the purposes of Part X of the 1996 Act if the reason (or, if more than one, the principal reason) for the dismissal is a reason specified in paragraph (3).

(2) A worker has the right not to be subjected to any detriment by any act, or any deliberate failure to act, by his employer done on a ground specified in paragraph (3).

(3) The reasons or, as the case may be, grounds are—

(a) that the worker has—

(i) brought proceedings against the employer under these Regulations;

(ii) requested from his employer a written statement of reasons under regulation 6;

(iii) given evidence or information in connection with such proceedings brought by any worker;

(iv) otherwise done anything under these Regulations in relation to the employer or any other person;

(v) alleged that the employer had infringed these Regulations; or

(vi) refused (or proposed to refuse) to forgo a right conferred on him by these Regulations, or

(b) that the employer believes or suspects that the worker has done or intends to do any of the things mentioned in sub-paragraph (a).

(4) Where the reason or principal reason for dismissal or, as the case may be, ground for subjection to any act or deliberate failure to act, is that mentioned in paragraph (3)(a)(v), or (b) so far as it relates thereto, neither paragraph (1) nor paragraph (2) applies if the allegation made by the worker is false and not made in good faith.

(5) Paragraph (2) does not apply where the detriment in question amounts to the dismissal of an employee within the meaning of Part X of the 1996 Act.

NOTES

Conciliation: see the note to reg 5 at **[2.579]**.

[2.582]

8 Complaints to employment tribunals etc

(1) Subject to regulation 7(5), a worker may present a complaint to an employment tribunal that his employer has infringed a right conferred on him by regulation 5 or 7(2).

(2) Subject to paragraph (3), an employment tribunal shall not consider a complaint under this regulation unless it is presented before the end of the period of three months (or, in a case to which regulation 13 applies, six months) beginning with the date of the less favourable treatment or detriment to which the complaint relates or, where an act or failure to act is part of a series of similar acts or failures comprising the less favourable treatment or detriment, the last of them.

(3) A tribunal may consider any such complaint which is out of time if, in all the circumstances of the case, it considers that it is just and equitable to do so.

(4) For the purposes of calculating the date of the less favourable treatment or detriment under paragraph (2)—

(a) where a term in a contract is less favourable, that treatment shall be treated, subject to paragraph (b), as taking place on each day of the period during which the term is less favourable;

(b) where an application relies on regulation 3 or 4 the less favourable treatment shall be treated as occurring on, and only on, in the case of regulation 3, the first day on which the applicant worked under the new or varied contract and, in the case of regulation 4, the day on which the applicant returned; and

(c) a deliberate failure to act contrary to regulation 5 or 7(2) shall be treated as done when it was decided on.

(5) In the absence of evidence establishing the contrary, a person shall be taken for the purposes of paragraph (4)(c) to decide not to act—

(a) when he does an act inconsistent with doing the failed act; or

(b) if he has done no such inconsistent act, when the period expires within which he might reasonably have been expected to have done the failed act if it was to be done.

(6) Where a worker presents a complaint under this regulation it is for the employer to identify the ground for the less favourable treatment or detriment.

(7) Where an employment tribunal finds that a complaint presented to it under this regulation is well founded, it shall take such of the following steps as it considers just and equitable—

(a) making a declaration as to the rights of the complainant and the employer in relation to the matters to which the complaint relates;

(b) ordering the employer to pay compensation to the complainant;

(c) recommending that the employer take, within a specified period, action appearing to the tribunal to be reasonable, in all the circumstances of the case, for the purpose of obviating or reducing the adverse effect on the complainant of any matter to which the complaint relates.

(8) . . .

(9) Where a tribunal orders compensation under paragraph (7)(b), the amount of the compensation awarded shall be such as the tribunal considers just and equitable in all the circumstances . . . having regard to—

(a) the infringement to which the complaint relates, and

(b) any loss which is attributable to the infringement having regard, in the case of an infringement of the right conferred by regulation 5, to the pro rata principle except where it is inappropriate to do so.

(10) The loss shall be taken to include—

(a) any expenses reasonably incurred by the complainant in consequence of the infringement, and

(b) loss of any benefit which he might reasonably be expected to have had but for the infringement.

(11) Compensation in respect of treating a worker in a manner which infringes the right conferred on him by regulation 5 shall not include compensation for injury to feelings.

(12) In ascertaining the loss the tribunal shall apply the same rule concerning the duty of a person to mitigate his loss as applies to damages recoverable under the common law of England and Wales or (as the case may be) Scotland.

(13) Where the tribunal finds that the act, or failure to act, to which the complaint relates was to any extent caused or contributed to by action of the complainant, it shall reduce the amount of the compensation by such proportion as it considers just and equitable having regard to that finding.

(14) If the employer fails, without reasonable justification, to comply with a recommendation made by an employment tribunal under paragraph (7)(c) the tribunal may, if it thinks it just and equitable to do so—

(a) increase the amount of compensation required to be paid to the complainant in respect of the complaint, where an order was made under paragraph (7)(b); or

(b) make an order under paragraph (7)(b).

NOTES

Para (8): revoked by the Part-time Workers (Prevention of Less Favourable Treatment) Regulations 2000 (Amendment) Regulations 2002, SI 2002/2035, reg 2(b)(i).

Para (9): words omitted revoked by SI 2002/2035, reg 2(b)(ii).

[2.583]

9 Restrictions on contracting out

Section 203 of the 1996 Act (restrictions on contracting out) shall apply in relation to these Regulations as if they were contained in that Act.

PART III
MISCELLANEOUS

[2.584]

10 Amendments to primary legislation

The amendments in the Schedule to these Regulations shall have effect.

[2.585]

11 Liability of employers and principals

(1) Anything done by a person in the course of his employment shall be treated for the purposes of these Regulations as also done by his employer, whether or not it was done with the employer's knowledge or approval.

(2) Anything done by a person as agent for the employer with the authority of the employer shall be treated for the purposes of these Regulations as also done by the employer.

(3) In proceedings under these Regulations against any person in respect of an act alleged to have been done by a worker of his, it shall be a defence for that person to prove that he took such steps as were reasonably practicable to prevent the worker from—

- (a) doing that act; or
- (b) doing, in the course of his employment, acts of that description.

PART IV
SPECIAL CLASSES OF PERSON

[2.586]

12 Crown employment

(1) Subject to regulation 13, these Regulations have effect in relation to Crown employment and persons in Crown employment as they have effect in relation to other employment and other employees and workers.

(2) In paragraph (1) "Crown employment" means employment under or for the purposes of a government department or any officer or body exercising on behalf of the Crown functions conferred by a statutory provision.

(3) For the purposes of the application of the provisions of these Regulations in relation to Crown employment in accordance with paragraph (1)—

- (a) references to an employee and references to a worker shall be construed as references to a person in Crown employment to whom the definition of employee or, as the case may be, worker is appropriate; and
- (b) references to a contract in relation to an employee and references to a contract in relation to a worker shall be construed as references to the terms of employment of a person in Crown employment to whom the definition of employee or, as the case may be, worker is appropriate.

[2.587]

13 Armed forces

(1) These Regulations, shall have effect in relation—

- (a) subject to paragraphs (2) and (3) and apart from regulation 7(1), to service as a member of the armed forces, and
- (b) to employment by an association established for the purposes of Part XI of the Reserve Forces Act 1996.

(2) These Regulations shall not have effect in relation to service as a member of the reserve forces in so far as that service consists in undertaking training obligations—

- (a) under section 38, 40 or 41 of the Reserve Forces Act 1980,
- (b) under section 22 of the Reserve Forces Act 1996,
- (c) pursuant to regulations made under section 4 of the Reserve Forces Act 1996,

or consists in undertaking voluntary training or duties under section 27 of the Reserve Forces Act 1996.

(3) No complaint concerning the service of any person as a member of the armed forces may be presented to an employment tribunal under regulation 8 unless—

- (a) that person has made a complaint in respect of the same matter to an officer under the service redress procedures, and
- (b) that complaint has not been withdrawn.

[(4) For the purpose of paragraph (3)(b), a person shall be treated as having withdrawn his complaint if, having made a complaint to an officer under the service redress procedures—

- (a) where the service redress procedures are those referred to in section 334 of the Armed Forces Act 2006, neither that officer nor a superior officer has decided to refer the complaint to the Defence Council, and the person who made the complaint fails to apply for such a reference to be made;
- (b) in any other case, the person who made the complaint fails to submit the complaint to the Defence Council under the service redress procedures.]

(5) Where a complaint of the kind referred to in paragraph (3) is presented to an employment tribunal, the service redress procedures may continue after the complaint is presented.

(6) In this regulation, "the service redress procedures" means the procedures, excluding those which relate to the making of a report to Her Majesty, referred to in section 180 of the Army Act 1955, section 180 of the Air Force Act 1955[, section 130 of the Naval Discipline Act 1957 or section 334 of the Armed Forces Act 2006].

NOTES

Para (4): substituted by the Armed Forces (Service Complaints) (Consequential Amendments) Order 2008, SI 2008/1696, art 3(1), (2), as from 28 June 2008.

Para (6): words in square brackets substituted by SI 2008/1696, art 3(1), (3), as from 28 June 2008.

[2.588]

14 House of Lords staff

(1) These Regulations have effect in relation to employment as a relevant member of the House of Lords staff as they have effect in relation to other employment.

(2) In this regulation "relevant member of the House of Lords staff" means any person who is employed under a contract with the Corporate Officer of the House of Lords by virtue of which he is a worker.

[2.589]

15 House of Commons staff

(1) These Regulations have effect in relation to employment as a relevant member of the House of Commons staff as they have effect in relation to other employment.

(2) In this regulation "relevant member of the House of Commons staff" means any person—
- (a) who was appointed by the House of Commons Commission; or
- (b) who is a member of the Speaker's personal staff.

[2.590]

16 Police service

(1) For the purposes of these Regulations, the holding, otherwise than under a contract of employment, of the office of constable or an appointment as a police cadet shall be treated as employment, under a contract of employment, by the relevant officer.

[(1A) For the purposes of these Regulations, any constable who has been seconded to SOCA to serve as a member of its staff shall be treated as employed by SOCA, in respect of actions taken by, or on behalf of, SOCA.

(1B) For the purposes of regulation 11 (liability of employers and principals),—
- (a) the secondment of any constable to SOCA to serve as a member of its staff shall be treated as employment by SOCA (and not as being employment by any other person); and
- (b) anything done by a constable so seconded in the performance, or purported performance, of his functions shall be treated as done in the course of that employment.]

(2) In this regulation "the relevant officer" means—
- (a) in relation to a member of a police force or a special constable or police cadet appointed for a police area, the chief officer of police (or, in Scotland, the chief constable);
- (b) . . . ; and
- (c) in relation to any other person holding the office of constable or an appointment as a police cadet, the person who has the direction and control of the body of constables or cadets in question.

[(4) For the purposes of these Regulations the relevant officer, as defined by paragraph (3), shall be treated as a corporation sole.

(5) In the application of this regulation to Scotland paragraph (4) shall have effect as if for the words "corporation sole" there were substituted "distinct juristic person (that is to say, as a juristic person distinct from the individual who for the time being is the office-holder)".]

[(6) In this regulation "SOCA" means the Serious Organised Crime Agency.]

NOTES

Paras (1A), (1B), (6): inserted and added respectively by the Serious Organised Crime and Police Act 2005 (Consequential and Supplementary Amendments to Secondary Legislation) Order 2006, SI 2006/594, art 2, Schedule, para 21(1), (2), (4).

Para (2): sub-para (b) revoked by SI 2006/594, art 2, Schedule, para 21(1), (3).

Paras (4), (5): added by the Part-time Workers (Prevention of Less Favourable Treatment) Regulations 2000 (Amendment) Order 2005, SI 2005/2240, art 2. Note that art 2 provides that these paragraphs should be inserted "after paragraph (3)"; this appears to be an error, as does the reference in para (4) to "paragraph (3)".

[2.591]

17 Holders of judicial offices

These Regulations do not apply to any individual in his capacity as the holder of a judicial office if he is remunerated on a daily fee-paid basis.

SCHEDULE

(The Schedule amends the Employment Tribunals Act 1996, ss 18, 21 at **[1.706]**, **[1.713]**, *the Employment Rights Act 1996, ss 105, 108 at* **[1.915]**, **[1.918]** *and amended s 109 of that Act (repealed).)*

TELECOMMUNICATIONS (LAWFUL BUSINESS PRACTICE) (INTERCEPTION OF COMMUNICATIONS) REGULATIONS 2000

(SI 2000/2699)

NOTES

Made: 2 October 2000.
Authority: Regulation of Investigatory Powers Act 2000, ss 4(2), 78(5).
Commencement: 24 October 2000.

[2.592]

1 Citation and commencement

These Regulations may be cited as the Telecommunications (Lawful Business Practice) (Interception of Communications) Regulations 2000 and shall come into force on 24th October 2000.

[2.593]

2 Interpretation

In these Regulations—

(a) references to a business include references to activities of a government department, of any public authority or of any person or office holder on whom functions are conferred by or under any enactment;

(b) a reference to a communication as relevant to a business is a reference to—

(i) a communication—

(aa) by means of which a transaction is entered into in the course of that business, or

(bb) which otherwise relates to that business, or

(ii) a communication which otherwise takes place in the course of the carrying on of that business;

(c) "regulatory or self-regulatory practices or procedures" means practices or procedures—

(i) compliance with which is required or recommended by, under or by virtue of—

(aa) any provision of the law of a member state or other state within the European Economic Area, or

(bb) any standard or code of practice published by or on behalf of a body established in a member state or other state within the European Economic Area which includes amongst its objectives the publication of standards or codes of practice for the conduct of business, or

(ii) which are otherwise applied for the purpose of ensuring compliance with anything so required or recommended;

(d) "system controller" means, in relation to a particular telecommunication system, a person with a right to control its operation or use.

[2.594]

3 Lawful interception of a communication

(1) For the purpose of section 1(5)(a) of the Act, conduct is authorised, subject to paragraphs (2) and (3) below, if it consists of interception of a communication, in the course of its transmission by means of a telecommunication system, which is effected by or with the express . . . consent of the system controller for the purpose of—

(a) monitoring or keeping a record of communications—

(i) in order to—

(aa) establish the existence of facts, or

(bb) ascertain compliance with regulatory or self-regulatory practices or procedures which are—

— applicable to the system controller in the carrying on of his business or

— applicable to another person in the carrying on of his business where that person is supervised by the system controller in respect of those practices or procedures, or (cc) ascertain or demonstrate the standards which are achieved or ought to be achieved by persons using the system in the course of their duties, or

(ii) in the interests of national security, or

(iii) for the purpose of preventing or detecting crime, or

(iv) for the purpose of investigating or detecting the unauthorised use of that or any other telecommunication system, or

(v) where that is undertaken—

(aa) in order to secure, or

(bb) as an inherent part of,

the effective operation of the system (including any monitoring or keeping of a record which would be authorised by section 3(3) of the Act if the conditions in paragraphs (a) and (b) thereof were satisfied); or

(b) monitoring communications for the purpose of determining whether they are communications relevant to the system controller's business which fall within regulation 2(b)(i) above; or

(c) monitoring communications made to a confidential voice-telephony counselling or support service which is free of charge (other than the cost, if any, of making a telephone call) and operated in such a way that users may remain anonymous if they so choose.

(2) Conduct is authorised by paragraph (1) of this regulation only if—

(a) the interception in question is effected solely for the purpose of monitoring or (where appropriate) keeping a record of communications relevant to the system controller's business;

(b) the telecommunication system in question is provided for use wholly or partly in connection with that business;

(c) the system controller has made all reasonable efforts to inform every person who may use the telecommunication system in question that communications transmitted by means thereof may be intercepted; and

(d) in a case falling within—

(i) paragraph (1)(a)(ii) above, the person by or on whose behalf the interception is effected is a person specified in section 6(2)(a) to (i) of the Act;

(ii) paragraph (1)(b) above, the communication is one which is intended to be received (whether or not it has been actually received) by a person using the telecommunication system in question.

[(3) Conduct falling within paragraph (1)(a)(i) above is authorised only to the extent that Article 5 of Directive 2002/58/EC of the European Parliament and of the Council of 12 July 2002 concerning the processing of personal data and the protection of privacy in the electronic communications sector so permits [as amended by Directive 2009/136/EC of the European Parliament and of the Council of 25 November 2009 amending Directive 2002/22/EC on universal service and users' rights relating to electronic communications networks and services, Directive 2002/58/EC concerning the processing of personal data and the protection of privacy in the electronic communications sector and Regulation (EC) No 2006/2004 on cooperation between national authorities responsible for the enforcement of consumer protection laws].]

NOTES

Para (1): words omitted revoked by the Privacy and Electronic Communications (EC Directive) (Amendment) Regulations 2011, SI 2011/1208, reg 15(a), as from 26 May 2011.

Para (3): substituted by the Privacy and Electronic Communications (EC Directive) Regulations 2003, SI 2003/2426, reg 34; words in square brackets inserted by SI 2011/1208, reg 15(b), as from 26 May 2011.

RACE RELATIONS ACT 1976 (STATUTORY DUTIES) ORDER 2001 (NOTE)

(SI 2001/3458)

[2.595]

NOTES

This Order was made on 23 October 2001 under the powers conferred by the Race Relations Act 1976, s 71(2), (3). It came into force on 3 December 2001. This Order imposed certain duties on certain bodies and other persons who were subject to the general duty under s 71(1) of the 1976 Act to have due regard, when exercising their functions, to the need to eliminate unlawful racial discrimination and to promote equality of opportunity and good relations between persons of different racial groups. The duties were imposed for the purpose of ensuring the better performance of the general duty. Section 71 of the 1976 Act was repealed on 5 April 2011 by the Equality Act 2010, s 211(2), Sch 27, Pt 1 and, accordingly, this Order lapsed on that date.

RACE RELATIONS ACT 1976 (STATUTORY DUTIES) (SCOTLAND) ORDER 2002 (NOTE)

(SSI 2002/62)

[2.596]

NOTES

This Order was made by the Scottish Ministers on 14 February 2002 under the powers conferred by the Race Relations Act 1976, s 71(2), (3). It came into force on 13 March 2002. It applied only within Scotland and to such bodies and persons as were specified in the Schedule. The equivalent Order, applying to non-devolved bodies within Scotland, as well as to England and Wales, was the Race Relations Act 1976 (Statutory Duties) Order 2001, SI 2001/3458. This Order imposed specific duties which corresponded to those in the English Order on such bodies. Section 71 of the 1976 Act was repealed on 5 April 2011 and, accordingly, this Order lapsed on that date.

FIXED-TERM EMPLOYEES (PREVENTION OF LESS FAVOURABLE TREATMENT) REGULATIONS 2002

(SI 2002/2034)

NOTES

Made: 30 July 2002.

Authority: Employment Act 2002, ss 45, 51(1).

Commencement: 1 October 2002.

These Regulations are the domestic implementation of Council Directive 99/70, and the framework agreement on fixed-term work embodied therein, at **[3.272]**.

Conciliation: employment tribunal proceedings and claims which could be the subject of employment tribunal proceedings arising out of a contravention, or alleged contravention, of regs 3, 6(2), or under reg 9, are proceedings to which the Employment Tribunals Act 1996, s 18 applies; see s 18(1)(i), (j) of that Act at **[1.706]**.

Employment Appeal Tribunal: an appeal lies to the Employment Appeal Tribunal on any question of law arising from any decision of, or in any proceedings before, an employment tribunal under or by virtue of these Regulations; see the Employment Tribunals Act 1996, s 21(1)(k) at **[1.713]**.

See *Harvey* AI(3).

ARRANGEMENT OF REGULATIONS

SCHEDULES

PART 1
GENERAL AND INTERPRETATION

[2.597]

1 Citation, commencement and interpretation

(1) These Regulations may be cited as the Fixed-term Employees (Prevention of Less Favourable Treatment) Regulations 2002 and shall come into force on 1st October 2002.

(2) In these Regulations—

"the 1996 Act" means the Employment Rights Act 1996;

"collective agreement" means a collective agreement within the meaning of section 178 of the Trade Union and Labour Relations (Consolidation) Act 1992; the trade union parties to which are independent trade unions within the meaning of section 5 of that Act;

"employer", in relation to any employee, means the person by whom the employee is (or, where the employment has ceased, was) employed;

"fixed-term contract" means a contract of employment that, under its provisions determining how it will terminate in the normal course, will terminate—

(a) on the expiry of a specific term,

(b) on the completion of a particular task, or

(c) on the occurrence or non-occurrence of any other specific event other than the attainment by the employee of any normal and bona fide retiring age in the establishment for an employee holding the position held by him,

and any reference to "fixed-term" shall be construed accordingly;

"fixed-term employee" means an employee who is employed under a fixed-term contract;

"permanent employee" means an employee who is not employed under a fixed-term contract, and any reference to "permanent employment" shall be construed accordingly;

"pro rata principle" means that where a comparable permanent employee receives or is entitled to pay or any other benefit, a fixed-term employee is to receive or be entitled to such proportion of that pay or other benefit as is reasonable in the circumstances having regard to the length of his contract of employment and to the terms on which the pay or other benefit is offered;

"renewal" includes extension and references to renewing a contract shall be construed accordingly;

"workforce agreement" means an agreement between an employer and his employees or their representatives in respect of which the conditions set out in Schedule 1 to these Regulations are satisfied.

[2.598]

2 Comparable employees

(1) For the purposes of these Regulations, an employee is a comparable permanent employee in relation to a fixed-term employee if, at the time when the treatment that is alleged to be less favourable to the fixed-term employee takes place,

(a) both employees are—

(i) employed by the same employer, and

(ii) engaged in the same or broadly similar work having regard, where relevant, to whether they have a similar level of qualification and skills; and

(b) the permanent employee works or is based at the same establishment as the fixed-term employee or, where there is no comparable permanent employee working or based at that establishment who satisfies the requirements of sub-paragraph (a), works or is based at a different establishment and satisfies those requirements.

(2) For the purposes of paragraph (1), an employee is not a comparable permanent employee if his employment has ceased.

PART 2
RIGHTS AND REMEDIES

[2.599]

3 Less favourable treatment of fixed-term employees

(1) A fixed-term employee has the right not to be treated by his employer less favourably than the employer treats a comparable permanent employee—

(a) as regards the terms of his contract; or

(b) by being subjected to any other detriment by any act, or deliberate failure to act, of his employer.

(2) Subject to paragraphs (3) and (4), the right conferred by paragraph (1) includes in particular the right of the fixed-term employee in question not to be treated less favourably than the employer treats a comparable permanent employee in relation to—

(a) any period of service qualification relating to any particular condition of service,

(b) the opportunity to receive training, or

(c) the opportunity to secure any permanent position in the establishment.

(3) The right conferred by paragraph (1) applies only if—

(a) the treatment is on the ground that the employee is a fixed-term employee, and

(b) the treatment is not justified on objective grounds.

(4) Paragraph (3)(b) is subject to regulation 4.

(5) In determining whether a fixed-term employee has been treated less favourably than a comparable permanent employee, the pro rata principle shall be applied unless it is inappropriate.

(6) In order to ensure that an employee is able to exercise the right conferred by paragraph (1) as described in paragraph (2)(c) the employee has the right to be informed by his employer of available vacancies in the establishment.

(7) For the purposes of paragraph (6) an employee is "informed by his employer" only if the vacancy is contained in an advertisement which the employee has a reasonable opportunity of reading in the course of his employment or the employee is given reasonable notification of the vacancy in some other way.

NOTES

Conciliation: employment tribunal proceedings and claims which could be the subject of employment tribunal proceedings arising out of a contravention, or alleged contravention, of this regulation are proceedings to which the Employment Tribunals Act 1996, s 18 applies; see s 18(1)(i) of that Act at **[1.706]**.

[2.600]

4 Objective justification

(1) Where a fixed-term employee is treated by his employer less favourably than the employer treats a comparable permanent employee as regards any term of his contract, the treatment in question shall be regarded for the purposes of regulation 3(3)(b) as justified on objective grounds if the terms of the fixed-term employee's contract of employment, taken as a whole, are at least as favourable as the terms of the comparable permanent employee's contract of employment.

(2) Paragraph (1) is without prejudice to the generality of regulation 3(3)(b).

[2.601]

5 Right to receive a written statement of reasons for less favourable treatment

(1) If an employee who considers that his employer may have treated him in a manner which infringes a right conferred on him by regulation 3 requests in writing from his employer a written statement giving particulars of the reasons for the treatment, the employee is entitled to be provided with such a statement within twenty-one days of his request.

(2) A written statement under this regulation is admissible as evidence in any proceedings under these Regulations.

(3) If it appears to the tribunal in any proceedings under these Regulations—

(a) that the employer deliberately, and without reasonable excuse, omitted to provide a written statement, or

(b) that the written statement is evasive or equivocal,

it may draw any inference which it considers it just and equitable to draw, including an inference that the employer has infringed the right in question.

(4) This regulation does not apply where the treatment in question consists of the dismissal of an employee, and the employee is entitled to a written statement of reasons for his dismissal under section 92 of the 1996 Act.

[2.602]

6 Unfair dismissal and the right not to be subjected to detriment

(1) An employee who is dismissed shall be regarded as unfairly dismissed for the purposes of Part 10 of the 1996 Act if the reason (or, if more than one, the principal reason) for the dismissal is a reason specified in paragraph (3).

(2) An employee has the right not to be subjected to any detriment by any act, or any deliberate failure to act, of his employer done on a ground specified in paragraph (3).

(3) The reasons or, as the case may be, grounds are—
- (a) that the employee—
  - (i) brought proceedings against the employer under these Regulations;
  - (ii) requested from his employer a written statement under regulation 5 or regulation 9;
  - (iii) gave evidence or information in connection with such proceedings brought by any employee;
  - (iv) otherwise did anything under these Regulations in relation to the employer or any other person;
  - (v) alleged that the employer had infringed these Regulations;
  - (vi) refused (or proposed to refuse) to forgo a right conferred on him by these Regulations;
  - (vii) declined to sign a workforce agreement for the purposes of these Regulations, or
  - (viii) being—
    - (aa) a representative of members of the workforce for the purposes of Schedule 1, or
    - (bb) a candidate in an election in which any person elected will, on being elected, become such a representative,

    performed (or proposed to perform) any functions or activities as such a representative or candidate, or
- (b) that the employer believes or suspects that the employee has done or intends to do any of the things mentioned in sub-paragraph (a).

(4) Where the reason or principal reason for dismissal or, as the case may be, ground for subjection to any act or deliberate failure to act, is that mentioned in paragraph (3)(a)(v), or (b) so far as it relates thereto, neither paragraph (1) nor paragraph (2) applies if the allegation made by the employee is false and not made in good faith.

(5) Paragraph (2) does not apply where the detriment in question amounts to dismissal within the meaning of Part 10 of the 1996 Act.

NOTES

Conciliation: employment tribunal proceedings and claims which could be the subject of employment tribunal proceedings arising out of a contravention, or alleged contravention, of para (2) of this regulation are proceedings to which the Employment Tribunals Act 1996, s 18 applies; see s 18(1)(i) of that Act at **[1.706]**.

[2.603]

7 Complaints to employment tribunals etc

(1) An employee may present a complaint to an employment tribunal that his employer has infringed a right conferred on him by regulation 3, or (subject to regulation 6(5)), regulation 6(2).

(2) Subject to paragraph (3), an employment tribunal shall not consider a complaint under this regulation unless it is presented before the end of the period of three months beginning—
- (a) in the case of an alleged infringement of a right conferred by regulation 3(1) or 6(2), with the date of the less favourable treatment or detriment to which the complaint relates or, where an act or failure to act is part of a series of similar acts or failures comprising the less favourable treatment or detriment, the last of them;
- (b) in the case of an alleged infringement of the right conferred by regulation 3(6), with the date, or if more than one the last date, on which other individuals, whether or not employees of the employer, were informed of the vacancy.

(3) A tribunal may consider any such complaint which is out of time if, in all the circumstances of the case, it considers that it is just and equitable to do so.

(4) For the purposes of calculating the date of the less favourable treatment or detriment under paragraph (2)(a)—
- (a) where a term in a contract is less favourable, that treatment shall be treated, subject to paragraph (b), as taking place on each day of the period during which the term is less favourable;
- (b) a deliberate failure to act contrary to regulation 3 or 6(2) shall be treated as done when it was decided on.

(5) In the absence of evidence establishing the contrary, a person shall be taken for the purposes of paragraph (4)(b) to decide not to act—
- (a) when he does an act inconsistent with doing the failed act; or

(b) if he has done no such inconsistent act, when the period expires within which he might reasonably have been expected to have done the failed act if it was to be done.

(6) Where an employee presents a complaint under this regulation in relation to a right conferred on him by regulation 3 or 6(2) it is for the employer to identify the ground for the less favourable treatment or detriment.

(7) Where an employment tribunal finds that a complaint presented to it under this regulation is well founded, it shall take such of the following steps as it considers just and equitable—

(a) making a declaration as to the rights of the complainant and the employer in relation to the matters to which the complaint relates;

(b) ordering the employer to pay compensation to the complainant;

(c) recommending that the employer take, within a specified period, action appearing to the tribunal to be reasonable, in all the circumstances of the case, for the purpose of obviating or reducing the adverse effect on the complainant of any matter to which the complaint relates.

(8) Where a tribunal orders compensation under paragraph (7)(b), the amount of the compensation awarded shall be such as the tribunal considers just and equitable in all the circumstances having regard to—

(a) the infringement to which the complaint relates, and

(b) any loss which is attributable to the infringement.

(9) The loss shall be taken to include—

(a) any expenses reasonably incurred by the complainant in consequence of the infringement, and

(b) loss of any benefit which he might reasonably be expected to have had but for the infringement.

(10) Compensation in respect of treating an employee in a manner which infringes the right conferred on him by regulation 3 shall not include compensation for injury to feelings.

(11) In ascertaining the loss the tribunal shall apply the same rule concerning the duty of a person to mitigate his loss as applies to damages recoverable under the common law of England and Wales or (as the case may be) the law of Scotland.

(12) Where the tribunal finds that the act, or failure to act, to which the complaint relates was to any extent caused or contributed to by action of the complainant, it shall reduce the amount of the compensation by such proportion as it considers just and equitable having regard to that finding.

(13) If the employer fails, without reasonable justification, to comply with a recommendation made by an employment tribunal under paragraph (7)(c) the tribunal may, if it thinks it just and equitable to do so—

(a) increase the amount of compensation required to be paid to the complainant in respect of the complaint, where an order was made under paragraph (7)(b); or

(b) make an order under paragraph (7)(b).

[2.604]

8 Successive fixed-term contracts

(1) This regulation applies where—

(a) an employee is employed under a contract purporting to be a fixed-term contract, and

(b) the contract mentioned in sub-paragraph (a) has previously been renewed, or the employee has previously been employed on a fixed-term contract before the start of the contract mentioned in sub-paragraph (a).

(2) Where this regulation applies then, with effect from the date specified in paragraph (3), the provision of the contract mentioned in paragraph (1)(a) that restricts the duration of the contract shall be of no effect, and the employee shall be a permanent employee, if—

(a) the employee has been continuously employed under the contract mentioned in paragraph 1(a), or under that contract taken with a previous fixed-term contract, for a period of four years or more, and

(b) the employment of the employee under a fixed-term contract was not justified on objective grounds—

(i) where the contract mentioned in paragraph (1)(a) has been renewed, at the time when it was last renewed;

(ii) where that contract has not been renewed, at the time when it was entered into.

(3) The date referred to in paragraph (2) is whichever is the later of—

(a) the date on which the contract mentioned in paragraph (1)(a) was entered into or last renewed, and

(b) the date on which the employee acquired four years' continuous employment.

(4) For the purposes of this regulation Chapter 1 of Part 14 of the 1996 Act shall apply in determining whether an employee has been continuously employed, and any period of continuous employment falling before the 10th July 2002 shall be disregarded.

(5) A collective agreement or a workforce agreement may modify the application of paragraphs (1) to (3) of this regulation in relation to any employee or specified description of employees, by substituting for the provisions of paragraph (2) or paragraph (3), or for the provisions of both of those paragraphs, one or more different provisions which, in order to prevent abuse arising from the use of successive fixed-term contracts, specify one or more of the following—

(a) the maximum total period for which the employee or employees of that description may be continuously employed on a fixed-term contract or on successive fixed-term contracts;

(b) the maximum number of successive fixed-term contracts and renewals of such contracts under which the employee or employees of that description may be employed; or

(c) objective grounds justifying the renewal of fixed-term contracts, or the engagement of the employee or employees of that description under successive fixed-term contracts,

and those provisions shall have effect in relation to that employee or an employee of that description as if they were contained in paragraphs (2) and (3).

[2.605]
9 Right to receive written statement of variation

(1) If an employee who considers that, by virtue of regulation 8, he is a permanent employee requests in writing from his employer a written statement confirming that his contract is no longer fixed-term or that he is now a permanent employee, he is entitled to be provided, within twenty-one days of his request, with either—

(a) such a statement, or

(b) a statement giving reasons why his contract remains fixed-term.

(2) If the reasons stated under paragraph (1)(b) include an assertion that there were objective grounds for the engagement of the employee under a fixed-term contract, or the renewal of such a contract, the statement shall include a statement of those grounds.

(3) A written statement under this regulation is admissible as evidence in any proceedings before a court, an employment tribunal and the Commissioners of the Inland Revenue.

(4) If it appears to the court or tribunal in any proceedings—

(a) that the employer deliberately, and without reasonable excuse, omitted to provide a written statement, or

(b) that the written statement is evasive or equivocal,

it may draw any inference which it considers it just and equitable to draw.

(5) An employee who considers that, by virtue of regulation 8, he is a permanent employee may present an application to an employment tribunal for a declaration to that effect.

(6) No application may be made under paragraph (5) unless—

(a) the employee in question has previously requested a statement under paragraph (1) and the employer has either failed to provide a statement or given a statement of reasons under paragraph (1)(b), and

(b) the employee is at the time the application is made employed by the employer.

NOTES

Conciliation: employment tribunal proceedings and claims which could be the subject of employment tribunal proceedings under this regulation are proceedings to which the Employment Tribunals Act 1996, s 18 applies; see s 18(1)(j) of that Act at **[1.706]**.

Commissioners of Inland Revenue: a reference to the Commissioners of Inland Revenue is now to be taken as a reference to the Commissioners for Her Majesty's Revenue and Customs; see the Commissioners for Revenue and Customs Act 2005, s 50(1), (7).

PART 3
MISCELLANEOUS

[2.606]
10 Restrictions on contracting out

Section 203 of the 1996 Act (restrictions on contracting out) shall apply in relation to these Regulations as if they were contained in that Act.

[2.607]
11 Amendments to primary legislation

The amendments in Part 1 of Schedule 2 to these Regulations shall have effect subject to the transitional provisions in Part 2 of the Schedule.

[2.608]
12 Liability of employers and principals

(1) Anything done by a person in the course of his employment shall be treated for the purposes of these Regulations as also done by his employer, whether or not it was done with the employer's knowledge or approval.

(2) Anything done by a person as agent for the employer with the authority of the employer shall be treated for the purposes of these Regulations as also done by the employer.

(3) In proceedings under these Regulations against any person in respect of an act alleged to have been done by an employee of his, it shall be a defence for that person to prove that he took such steps as were reasonably practicable to prevent the employee from—

(a) doing that act, or
(b) doing, in the course of his employment, acts of that description.

PART 4
SPECIAL CLASSES OF PERSON

[2.609]
13 Crown employment

(1) Subject to regulation 14, these Regulations have effect in relation to Crown employment and persons in Crown employment as they have effect in relation to other employment and other employees.

(2) For the purposes of paragraphs (1) and (3) a person is to be regarded as being in Crown employment only if—

(a) he is in employment under or for the purposes of a government department or any officer or body exercising on behalf of the Crown functions conferred by a statutory provision, and
(b) having regard to the terms and conditions under which he works, he would be an employee if he was not in Crown employment.

(3) For the purposes of the application of the provisions of these Regulations in relation to Crown employment and persons in Crown employment in accordance with paragraph (1)—

(a) references to an employee shall be construed as references to a person in Crown employment;
(b) references to a contract of employment shall be construed, in relation to a person in Crown employment, as references to the terms and conditions mentioned in paragraph (2)(b); and
(c) references to dismissal shall be construed as references to the termination of Crown employment.

[2.610]
14 Armed forces

(1) These Regulations—

(a) do not apply to service as a member of the naval, military or air forces of the Crown, but
(b) do apply to employment by an association established for the purposes of Part 11 of the Reserve Forces Act 1996.

NOTES

Note: this regulation is reproduced as it appears in the Queen's Printer's copy of these Regulations, ie, with no para (2).

[2.611]
15 House of Lords staff

(1) These Regulations have effect in relation to employment as a relevant member of the House of Lords staff as they have effect in relation to other employment.

(2) In this regulation "relevant member of the House of Lords staff" means any person who is employed under a contract with the Corporate Officer of the House of Lords by virtue of which he is an employee.

[2.612]
16 House of Commons staff

(1) These Regulations have effect in relation to employment as a relevant member of the House of Commons staff as they have effect in relation to other employment.

(2) In this regulation "relevant member of the House of Commons staff" means any person—

(a) who was appointed by the House of Commons Commission; or
(b) who is a member of the Speaker's personal staff.

[2.613]
17 Police service

(1) For the purposes of these Regulations, the holding, otherwise than under a contract of employment, of the office of constable or an appointment as a police cadet shall be treated as employment, under a contract of employment, by the relevant officer.

[(1A) For the purposes of these Regulations, any constable or other person who has been seconded to SOCA to serve as a member of its staff shall be treated as employed by SOCA, in respect of actions taken by, or on behalf of, SOCA.

(1B) For the purposes of regulation 12 (liability of employers and principals),—

(a) the secondment of any constable or other person to SOCA to serve as a member of its staff shall be treated as employment by SOCA (and not as being employment by any other person); and

(b) anything done by a person so seconded in the performance, or purported performance, of his functions shall be treated as done in the course of that employment.]

(2) In this regulation "the relevant officer" means—

(a) in relation to a member of a police force or a special constable or police cadet appointed for a police area, the chief officer of police (or, in Scotland, the chief constable);

(b) . . . ; and

(c) in relation to any other person holding the office of constable or an appointment as a police cadet, the person who has the direction and control of the body of constables or cadets in question.

[(3) In this regulation "SOCA" means the Serious Organised Crime Agency.]

NOTES

Paras (1A), (1B), (3): inserted and added respectively by the Serious Organised Crime and Police Act 2005 (Consequential and Supplementary Amendments to Secondary Legislation) Order 2006, SI 2006/594, art 2, Schedule, para 30(1), (2).

Para (2): sub-para (b) revoked by SI 2006/594, art 2, Schedule, para 30(1), (3).

PART 5
EXCLUSIONS

[2.614]
18 Government training schemes etc

(1) These Regulations shall not have effect in relation to a fixed-term employee who is employed on a scheme, designed to provide him with training or work experience for the purpose of assisting him to seek or obtain work, which is either—

(a) provided to him under arrangements made by the Government, or

(b) funded in whole or part by an Institution of the [European Union].

(2) These Regulations shall not have effect in relation to a fixed-term employee whose employment consists in attending a period of work experience not exceeding one year that he is required to attend as part of a higher education course.

(3) For the purpose of paragraph (2) "a higher education course" means—

(a) in England and Wales, a course of a description referred to in Schedule 6 to the Education Reform Act 1988;

(b) in Scotland, a course of a description falling within section 38 of the Further and Higher Education (Scotland) Act 1992; and

(c) in Northern Ireland, a course of a description referred to in Schedule 1 to the Further Education (Northern Ireland) Order 1997.

NOTES

Para (1): words in square brackets substituted by the Treaty of Lisbon (Changes in Terminology) Order 2011, SI 2011/1043, art 4(1), as from 22 April 2011.

[2.615]
19 Agency workers

[(1) Save in respect of paragraph 1 of Part 1 of Schedule 2, these Regulations shall not have effect in relation to employment under a fixed-term contract where the employee is an agency worker.]

(2) In this regulation "agency worker" means any person who is supplied by an employment business to do work for another person under a contract or other arrangements made between the employment business and the other person.

(3) In this regulation "employment business" means the business (whether or not carried on with a view to profit and whether or not carried on in conjunction with any other business) of supplying persons in the employment of the person carrying on the business, to act for, and under the control of, other persons in any capacity.

NOTES

Para (1): substituted by the Fixed-term Employees (Prevention of Less Favourable Treatment) (Amendment) Regulations 2008, SI 2008/2776, reg 2, as from 27 October 2008.

[2.616]
20 Apprentices

These Regulations shall not have effect in relation to employment under a fixed-term contract where the contract is a contract of apprenticeship [or an apprenticeship agreement (within the meaning of section 32 of the Apprenticeships, Skills, Children and Learning Act 2009)].

NOTES

Words in square brackets added by the Apprenticeships, Skills, Children and Learning Act 2009 (Consequential Amendments to Subordinate Legislation) (England and Wales) Order 2012, SI 2012/3112, art 3, as from 9 January 2013.

SCHEDULES

SCHEDULE 1
WORKFORCE AGREEMENTS

Regulations 1 and 8

[2.617]

1. An agreement is a workforce agreement for the purposes of these Regulations if the following conditions are satisfied—

(a) the agreement is in writing;
(b) it has effect for a specified period not exceeding five years;
(c) it applies either—
  (i) to all of the relevant members of the workforce, or
  (ii) to all of the relevant members of the workforce who belong to a particular group;
(d) the agreement is signed—
  (i) in the case of an agreement of the kind referred to in sub-paragraph (c)(i), by the representatives of the workforce, and in the case of an agreement of the kind referred to in sub-paragraph (c)(ii) by the representatives of the group to which the agreement applies (excluding, in either case, any representative not a relevant member of the workforce on the date on which the agreement was first made available for signature), or
  (ii) if the employer employed 20 or fewer employees on the date referred to in sub-paragraph (d)(i), either by the appropriate representatives in accordance with that sub-paragraph or by the majority of the employees employed by him;
(e) before the agreement was made available for signature, the employer provided all the employees to whom it was intended to apply on the date on which it came into effect with copies of the text of the agreement and such guidance as those employees might reasonably require in order to understand it fully.

2. For the purposes of this Schedule—

"a particular group" is a group of the relevant members of a workforce who undertake a particular function, work at a particular workplace or belong to a particular department or unit within their employer's business;

"relevant members of the workforce" are all of the employees employed by a particular employer, excluding any employee whose terms and conditions of employment are provided for, wholly or in part, in a collective agreement;

"representatives of the workforce" are employees duly elected to represent the relevant members of the workforce, "representatives of the group" are employees duly elected to represent the members of a particular group, and representatives are "duly elected" if the election at which they were elected satisfied the requirements of paragraph 3 of this Schedule.

3. The requirements concerning elections referred to in paragraph 2 are that—

(a) the number of representatives to be elected is determined by the employer;
(b) the candidates for election as representatives of the workforce are relevant members of the workforce, and the candidates for election as representatives of a group are members of that group;
(c) no employee who is eligible to be a candidate is unreasonably excluded from standing for election;
(d) all the relevant members of the workforce are entitled to vote for representatives of the workforce, and all the members of a particular group are entitled to vote for representatives of the group;
(e) the employees entitled to vote may vote for as many candidates as there are representatives to be elected;
(f) the election is conducted so as to secure that—
  (i) so far as is reasonably practicable, those voting do so in secret, and
  (ii) the votes given at the election are fairly and accurately counted.

SCHEDULE 2

Regulation 11

(Sch 2, Pt 1 amends the Social Security Contributions and Benefits Act 1992, Sch 11 at **[1.235]** *, the Employment Tribunals Act 1996, ss 18, 21 at* **[1.706]**, **[1.713]** *, the Employment Rights Act 1996, ss 29, 65, 86, 92, 95, 97, 105, 108, 136, 145, 199, 203, 235 at* **[1.743]** *et seq, amended s 109 of that Act (repealed) and repeals s 197 of that Act.)*

PART 2
TRANSITIONAL PROVISIONS

[2.618]
4. Paragraph 1 of this Schedule applies where the relevant date (as defined in paragraph 3 of Schedule 11 to the Social Security Contributions and Benefits Act 1992) falls on or after 1st October 2002.

5. (1) This paragraph applies to the dismissal of an employee employed under a contract for a fixed term of two years or more which consists of the expiry of the term without its being renewed, where the employee has agreed in accordance with section 197 of the 1996 Act to exclude any right to a redundancy payment in that event.

(2) The repeal of sections 197, 199(6) and 203(2)(d) of the 1996 Act provided for by paragraph 3(k) of this Schedule shall have effect in relation to a dismissal to which this paragraph applies where the relevant date (within the meaning of section 145 of the 1996 Act) falls on or after 1st October 2002, unless both the following conditions are satisfied—

(a) that, where there has been no renewal of the contract, the contract was entered into before 1st October 2002 or, where there have been one or more renewals, the only or most recent renewal was agreed before that date, and

(b) that the agreement to exclude any right to a redundancy payment was entered into and took effect before 1st October 2002.

PATERNITY AND ADOPTION LEAVE REGULATIONS 2002

(SI 2002/2788)

NOTES

Made: 11 November 2002.

Authority: Employment Rights Act 1996, ss 47C(2), 75A(1)–(3), (6), (7), 75B(1), (2), (4), (8), 75C(1), (2), 75D(1), 80A(1), (2), (5), 80B(1), (2), (5), 80C(1), (6), 80D(1), 80E, 99(1).

Commencement: 8 December 2002; see reg 3 at **[2.621]** for detailed provision as to the application of particular regulations.

Adoption from overseas: as to the application of these Regulations, with certain modifications, to adoptions from overseas, see the Paternity and Adoption Leave (Adoption from Overseas) Regulations 2003, SI 2003/921. Note that the amendments made by the Maternity and Parental Leave etc and the Paternity and Adoption Leave (Amendment) Regulations 2008, SI 2008/1966 to these Regulations, as applied to adoptions from overseas by SI 2003/921, have effect only where the adopter's child enters Great Britain on or after 5 October 2008 (see SI 2008/1966, reg 2(4)).

See *Harvey* J(8).

ARRANGEMENT OF REGULATIONS

PART 1
GENERAL

PART 2
PATERNITY LEAVE

PART 3
ADOPTION LEAVE

PART 4
PROVISIONS APPLICABLE IN RELATION TO
BOTH PATERNITY AND ADOPTION LEAVE

PART 1
GENERAL

[2.619]
1 Citation and commencement

These Regulations may be cited as the Paternity and Adoption Leave Regulations 2002 and shall come into force on 8th December 2002.

[2.620]
2 Interpretation

(1) In these Regulations—

"the 1996 Act" means the Employment Rights Act 1996;

"additional adoption leave" means leave under section 75B of the 1996 Act;

"additional maternity leave" means leave under section 73 of the 1996 Act;

"adopter", in relation to a child, means a person who has been matched with the child for adoption, or, in a case where two people have been matched jointly, whichever of them has elected to be the child's adopter for the purposes of these Regulations;

"adoption agency" has the meaning given, in relation to England and Wales, by section 1(4) of the Adoption Act 1976 and, in relation to Scotland, by [section 119(1) of the Adoption and Children (Scotland) Act 2007];

"adoption leave" means ordinary or additional adoption leave;

"child" means a person who is, or when placed with an adopter for adoption was, under the age of 18;

"contract of employment" means a contract of service or apprenticeship, whether express or implied, and (if it is express) whether oral or in writing;

"employee" means an individual who has entered into or works under (or, where the employment has ceased, worked under) a contract of employment;

"employer" means the person by whom an employee is (or, where the employment has ceased, was) employed;

"expected week", in relation to the birth of a child, means the week, beginning with midnight between Saturday and Sunday, in which it is expected that the child will be born;

"ordinary adoption leave" means leave under section 75A of the 1996 Act;

"parental leave" means leave under regulation 13(1) of the Maternity and Parental Leave etc Regulations 1999;

"partner", in relation to a child's mother or adopter, means a person (whether of a different sex or the same sex) who lives with the mother or adopter and the child in an enduring family relationship but is not a relative of the mother or adopter of a kind specified in paragraph (2);

"paternity leave" means leave under regulation 4 or regulation 8 of these Regulations;

["statutory adoption leave" means ordinary adoption leave and additional adoption leave;

"statutory adoption leave period" means the period during which the adopter is on statutory adoption leave;]

"statutory leave" means leave provided for in Part 8 of the 1996 Act.

(2) The relatives of a child's mother or adopter referred to in the definition of "partner" in paragraph (1) are the mother's or adopter's parent, grandparent, sister, brother, aunt or uncle.

(3) References to relationships in paragraph (2)—

(a) are to relationships of the full blood or half blood or, in the case of an adopted person, such of those relationships as would exist but for the adoption, and

(b) include the relationship of a child with his adoptive, or former adoptive, parents,

but do not include any other adoptive relationships.

(4) For the purposes of these Regulations—

(a) a person is matched with a child for adoption when an adoption agency decides that that person would be a suitable adoptive parent for the child, either individually or jointly with another person, and

(b) a person is notified of having been matched with a child on the date on which he receives notification of the agency's decision, under regulation 11(2) of the Adoption Agencies Regulations 1983 or [regulation 8(5) of the Adoption Agencies (Scotland) Regulations 2009];

(c) a person elects to be a child's adopter, in a case where the child is matched with him and another person jointly, if he and that person agree, at the time at which they are matched, that he and not the other person will be the adopter.

(5) A reference in any provision of these Regulations to a period of continuous employment is to a period computed in accordance with Chapter 1 of Part 14 of the 1996 Act, as if that provision were a provision of that Act.

(6) For the purposes of these Regulations, any two employers shall be treated as associated if—

(a) one is a company of which the other (directly or indirectly) has control; or

(b) both are companies of which a third person (directly or indirectly) has control;

and "associated employer" shall be construed accordingly.

NOTES

Para (1) is amended as follows:

Words in square brackets in definition "adoption agency" substituted by the Adoption and Children (Scotland) Act 2007 (Consequential Modifications) Order 2011, SI 2011/1740, art 2, Sch 1, Pt 2, para 30(1), (2)(a), as from 15 July 2011.

Definitions "statutory adoption leave" and "statutory adoption leave period" inserted by the Maternity and Parental Leave etc and the Paternity and Adoption Leave (Amendment) Regulations 2006, SI 2006/2014, regs 12, 13.

Para (4): words in square brackets in sub-para (b) substituted by SI 2011/1740, art 2, Sch 1, Pt 2, para 30(1), (2)(b), as from 15 July 2011.

Adoption from overseas: as to the modification of this regulation in relation to adoptions from overseas, see the Paternity and Adoption Leave (Adoption from Overseas) Regulations 2003, SI 2003/921, reg 4.

[2.621]

3 Application

(1) The provisions relating to paternity leave under regulation 4 below have effect only in relation to children—

(a) born on or after 6th April 2003, or

(b) whose expected week of birth begins on or after that date.

(2) The provisions relating to paternity leave under regulation 8 and adoption leave under regulation 15 below have effect only in relation to children—

(a) matched with a person who is notified of having been matched on or after 6th April 2003, or

(b) placed for adoption on or after that date.

(3) Regulation 28 (protection from detriment) has effect only in relation to an act or failure to act which takes place on or after 8th December 2002.

(4) For the purposes of paragraph (3)—

(a) where an act extends over a period, the reference to the date of the act is a reference to the last day of that period, and

(b) a failure to act is to be treated as done when it was decided on.

(5) For the purposes of paragraph (4), in the absence of evidence establishing the contrary an employer shall be taken to decide on a failure to act—

(a) when he does an act inconsistent with doing the failed act, or

(b) if he has done no such inconsistent act, when the period expires within which he might reasonably have been expected to do the failed act if it was to be done.

(6) Regulation 29 (unfair dismissal) has effect only in relation to dismissals where the effective date of termination (within the meaning of section 97 of the 1996 Act) falls on or after 8th December 2002.

NOTES

Adoption from overseas: as to the modification of this regulation in relation to adoptions from overseas, see the Paternity and Adoption Leave (Adoption from Overseas) Regulations 2003, SI 2003/921, reg 5.

PART 2
PATERNITY LEAVE

[2.622]

4 Entitlement to paternity leave: birth

(1) An employee is entitled to be absent from work for the purpose of caring for a child or supporting the child's mother if he—

- (a) satisfies the conditions specified in paragraph (2), and
- (b) has complied with the notice requirements in regulation 6 and, where applicable, the evidential requirements in that regulation.

(2) The conditions referred to in paragraph (1) are that the employee—

- (a) has been continuously employed for a period of not less than 26 weeks ending with the week immediately preceding the 14th week before the expected week of the child's birth;
- (b) is either—
  - (i) the father of the child or;
  - (ii) married to[, the civil partner] or the partner of the child's mother, but not the child's father;
- (c) has, or expects to have—
  - (i) if he is the child's father, responsibility for the upbringing of the child;
  - (ii) if he is the mother's husband[, civil partner] or partner but not the child's father, the main responsibility (apart from any responsibility of the mother) for the upbringing of the child.

(3) An employee shall be treated as having satisfied the condition in paragraph (2)(a) on the date of the child's birth notwithstanding the fact that he has not then been continuously employed for a period of not less than 26 weeks, where—

- (a) the date on which the child is born is earlier than the 14th week before the week in which its birth is expected, and
- (b) the employee would have been continuously employed for such a period if his employment had continued until that 14th week.

(4) An employee shall be treated as having satisfied the condition in paragraph (2)(b)(ii) if he would have satisfied it but for the fact that the child's mother has died.

(5) An employee shall be treated as having satisfied the condition in paragraph (2)(c) if he would have satisfied it but for the fact that the child was stillborn after 24 weeks of pregnancy or has died.

(6) An employee's entitlement to leave under this regulation shall not be affected by the birth, or expected birth, of more than one child as a result of the same pregnancy.

NOTES

Para (2): words in square brackets inserted by the Civil Partnership Act 2004 (Amendments to Subordinate Legislation) Order 2005, SI 2005/2114, art 2(17), Sch 17, para 1(1), (2).

Adoption from overseas: this regulation and regs 5–7 are disapplied in relation to adoptions from overseas, by the Paternity and Adoption Leave (Adoption from Overseas) Regulations 2003, SI 2003/921, reg 6.

[2.623]

5 Options in respect of leave under regulation 4

(1) An employee may choose to take either one week's leave or two consecutive weeks' leave in respect of a child under regulation 4.

(2) The leave may only be taken during the period which begins with the date on which the child is born and ends—

- (a) except in the case referred to in sub-paragraph (b), 56 days after that date;
- (b) in a case where the child is born before the first day of the expected week of its birth, 56 days after that day.

(3) Subject to paragraph (2) and, where applicable, paragraph (4), an employee may choose to begin his period of leave on—

- (a) the date on which the child is born;
- (b) the date falling such number of days after the date on which the child is born as the employee may specify in a notice under regulation 6, or
- (c) a predetermined date, specified in a notice under that regulation, which is later than the first day of the expected week of the child's birth.

(4) In a case where the leave is in respect of a child whose expected week of birth begins before 6th April 2003, an employee may choose to begin a period of leave only on a predetermined date, specified in a notice under regulation 6, which is at least 28 days after the date on which that notice is given.

NOTES

Adoption from overseas: disapplied as noted to reg 4 at **[2.622]**.

[2.624]

6 Notice and evidential requirements for leave under regulation 4

(1) An employee must give his employer notice of his intention to take leave in respect of a child under regulation 4, specifying—

(a) the expected week of the child's birth;

(b) the length of the period of leave that, in accordance with regulation 5(1), the employee has chosen to take, and

(c) the date on which, in accordance with regulation 5(3) or (4), the employee has chosen that his period of leave should begin.

(2) The notice provided for in paragraph (1) must be given to the employer—

(a) in or before the 15th week before the expected week of the child's birth, or

(b) in a case where it was not reasonably practicable for the employee to give the notice in accordance with sub-paragraph (a), as soon as is reasonably practicable.

(3) Where the employer requests it, an employee must also give his employer a declaration, signed by the employee, to the effect that the purpose of his absence from work will be that specified in regulation 4(1) and that he satisfies the conditions of entitlement in regulation 4(2)(b) and (c).

(4) An employee who has given notice under paragraph (1) may vary the date he has chosen as the date on which his period of leave will begin, subject to paragraph (5) and provided that he gives his employer notice of the variation—

(a) where the variation is to provide for the employee's period of leave to begin on the date on which the child is born, at least 28 days before the first day of the expected week of the child's birth;

(b) where the variation is to provide for the employee's period of leave to begin on a date that is a specified number of days (or a different specified number of days) after the date on which the child is born, at least 28 days before the date falling that number of days after the first day of the expected week of the child's birth;

(c) where the variation is to provide for the employee's period of leave to begin on a predetermined date (or a different predetermined date), at least 28 days before that date,

or, if it is not reasonably practicable to give the notice at least 28 days before whichever day or date is relevant, as soon as is reasonably practicable.

(5) In a case where regulation 5(4) applies, an employee may only vary the date which he has chosen as the date on which his period of leave will begin by substituting a different predetermined date.

(6) In a case where—

(a) the employee has chosen to begin his period of leave on a particular predetermined date, and

(b) the child is not born on or before that date,

the employee must vary his choice of date, by substituting a later predetermined date or (except in a case where regulation 5(4) applies) exercising an alternative option under regulation 5(3), and give his employer notice of the variation as soon as is reasonably practicable.

(7) An employee must give his employer a further notice, as soon as is reasonably practicable after the child's birth, of the date on which the child was born.

(8) Notice under paragraph (1), (4), (6) or (7) shall be given in writing, if the employer so requests.

NOTES

Adoption from overseas: disapplied as noted to reg 4 at **[2.622]**.

[2.625]

7 Commencement of leave under regulation 4

(1) Except in the case referred to in paragraph (2), an employee's period of paternity leave under regulation 4 begins on the date specified in his notice under regulation 6(1), or, where he has varied his choice of date under regulation 6(4) or (6), on the date specified in his notice under that provision (or the last such notice if he has varied his choice more than once).

(2) In a case where—

(a) the employee has chosen to begin his period of leave on the date on which the child is born, and

(b) he is at work on that date,

the employee's period of leave begins on the day after that date.

NOTES

Adoption from overseas: disapplied as noted to reg 4 at **[2.622]**.

[2.626]

8 Entitlement to paternity leave: adoption

(1) An employee is entitled to be absent from work for the purpose of caring for a child or supporting the child's adopter if he—

(a) satisfies the conditions specified in paragraph (2), and

(b) has complied with the notice requirements in regulation 10 and, where applicable, the evidential requirements in that regulation.

(2) The conditions referred to in paragraph (1) are that the employee—

(a) has been continuously employed for a period of not less than 26 weeks ending with the week in which the child's adopter is notified of having been matched with the child;

(b) is either married to[, the civil partner] or the partner of the child's adopter, and

(c) has, or expects to have, the main responsibility (apart from the responsibility of the adopter) for the upbringing of the child.

(3) In paragraph (2)(a), "week" means the period of seven days beginning with Sunday.

(4) An employee shall be treated as having satisfied the condition in paragraph (2)(b) if he would have satisfied it but for the fact that the child's adopter died during the child's placement.

(5) An employee shall be treated as having satisfied the condition in paragraph (2)(c) if he would have satisfied it but for the fact that the child's placement with the adopter has ended.

(6) An employee's entitlement to leave under this regulation shall not be affected by the placement for adoption of more than one child as part of the same arrangement.

NOTES

Para (2): words in square brackets in sub-para (b) inserted by the Civil Partnership Act 2004 (Amendments to Subordinate Legislation) Order 2005, SI 2005/2114, art 2(17), Sch 17, para 1(1), (3).

Adoption from overseas: as to the substitution of this regulation in relation to adoptions from overseas, see the Paternity and Adoption Leave (Adoption from Overseas) Regulations 2003, SI 2003/921, reg 7.

[2.627]

9 Options in respect of leave under regulation 8

(1) An employee may choose to take either one week's leave or two consecutive weeks' leave in respect of a child under regulation 8.

(2) The leave may only be taken during the period of 56 days beginning with the date on which the child is placed with the adopter.

(3) Subject to paragraph (2) and, where applicable, paragraph (4), an employee may choose to begin a period of leave under regulation 8 on—

(a) the date on which the child is placed with the adopter;

(b) the date falling such number of days after the date on which the child is placed with the adopter as the employee may specify in a notice under regulation 10, or

(c) a predetermined date, specified in a notice under that regulation, which is later than the date on which the child is expected to be placed with the adopter.

(4) In a case where the adopter was notified of having been matched with the child before 6th April 2003, the employee may choose to begin a period of leave only on a predetermined date, specified in a notice under regulation 10, which is at least 28 days after the date on which that notice is given.

NOTES

Adoption from overseas: as to the substitution of this regulation in relation to adoptions from overseas, see the Paternity and Adoption Leave (Adoption from Overseas) Regulations 2003, SI 2003/921, reg 7.

[2.628]

10 Notice and evidential requirements for leave under regulation 8

(1) An employee must give his employer notice of his intention to take leave in respect of a child under regulation 8, specifying—

(a) the date on which the adopter was notified of having been matched with the child;

(b) the date on which the child is expected to be placed with the adopter;

(c) the length of the period of leave that, in accordance with regulation 9(1), the employee has chosen to take, and

(d) the date on which, in accordance with regulation 9(3) or (4), the employee has chosen that his period of leave should begin.

(2) The notice provided for in paragraph (1) must be given to the employer—

(a) no more than seven days after the date on which the adopter is notified of having been matched with the child, or

(b) in a case where it was not reasonably practicable for the employee to give notice in accordance with sub-paragraph (a), as soon as is reasonably practicable.

(3) Where the employer requests it, an employee must also give his employer a declaration, signed by the employee, to the effect that the purpose of his absence from work will be that specified in regulation 8(1) and that he satisfies the conditions of entitlement in regulation 8(2)(b) and (c).

(4) An employee who has given notice under paragraph (1) may vary the date he has chosen as the date on which his period of leave will begin, subject to paragraph (5) and provided that he gives his employer notice of the variation—

(a) where the variation is to provide for the employee's period of leave to begin on the date on which the child is placed with the adopter, at least 28 days before the date specified in the employee's notice under paragraph (1) as the date on which the child is expected to be placed with the adopter;

(b) where the variation is to provide for the employee's period of leave to begin on a date that is a specified number of days (or a different specified number of days) after the date on which the child is placed with the adopter, at least 28 days before the date falling that number of days after the date specified in the employee's notice under paragraph (1) as the date on which the child is expected to be placed with the adopter;

(c) where the variation is to provide for the employee's period of leave to begin on a predetermined date, at least 28 days before that date,

or, if it is not reasonably practicable to give the notice at least 28 days before whichever date is relevant, as soon as is reasonably practicable.

(5) In a case where regulation 9(4) applies, an employee may only vary the date which he has chosen as the date on which his period of leave will begin by substituting a different predetermined date.

(6) In a case where—

(a) the employee has chosen to begin his period of leave on a particular predetermined date, and

(b) the child is not placed with the adopter on or before that date,

the employee must vary his choice of date, by substituting a later predetermined date or (except in a case where regulation 9(4) applies) exercising an alternative option under regulation 9(3), and give his employer notice of the variation as soon as is reasonably practicable.

(7) An employee must give his employer a further notice, as soon as is reasonably practicable after the child's placement, of the date on which the child was placed.

(8) Notice under paragraph (1), (4), (6) or (7) shall be given in writing, if the employer so requests.

NOTES

Adoption from overseas: as to the substitution of this regulation in relation to adoptions from overseas, see the Paternity and Adoption Leave (Adoption from Overseas) Regulations 2003, SI 2003/921, reg 7.

[2.629]

11 Commencement of leave under regulation 8

(1) Except in the case referred to in paragraph (2), an employee's period of paternity leave under regulation 8 begins on the date specified in his notice under regulation 10(1), or, where he has varied his choice of date under regulation 10(4) or (6), on the date specified in his notice under that provision (or the last such date if he has varied his choice more than once).

(2) In a case where—

(a) the employee has chosen to begin his period of leave on the date on which the child is placed with the adopter, and

(b) he is at work on that date,

the employee's period of leave begins on the day after that date.

NOTES

Adoption from overseas: as to the modification of this regulation in relation to adoptions from overseas, see the Paternity and Adoption Leave (Adoption from Overseas) Regulations 2003, SI 2003/921, reg 8.

[2.630]

12 Application of terms and conditions during paternity leave

(1) An employee who takes paternity leave—

(a) is entitled, during the period of leave, to the benefit of all of the terms and conditions of employment which would have applied if he had not been absent, and

(b) is bound, during that period, by any obligations arising under those terms and conditions, subject only to the exception in section 80C(1)(b) of the 1996 Act.

(2) In paragraph (1)(a), "terms and conditions of employment" has the meaning given by section 80C(5) of the 1996 Act, and accordingly does not include terms and conditions about remuneration.

(3) For the purposes of section 80C of the 1996 Act, only sums payable to an employee by way of wages or salary are to be treated as remuneration.

[2.631]

13 Right to return after paternity leave

(1) An employee who returns to work after a period of paternity leave which was—

(a) an isolated period of leave, or

(b) the last of two or more consecutive periods of statutory leave, which did not include any period of additional maternity leave or additional adoption leave or a period of parental leave of more than four weeks,

is entitled to return from leave to the job in which he was employed before his absence.

(2) An employee who returns to work after a period of paternity leave not falling within the description in paragraph (1)(a) or (b) above is entitled to return from leave to the job in which he was employed before his absence, or, if it is not reasonably practicable for the employer to permit him to return to that job, to another job which is both suitable for him and appropriate for him to do in the circumstances.

(3) The reference in paragraphs (1) and (2) to the job in which an employee was employed before his absence is a reference to the job in which he was employed—

(a) if his return is from an isolated period of paternity leave, immediately before that period began;

(b) if his return is from consecutive periods of statutory leave, immediately before the first such period.

[2.632]

14 Incidents of the right to return after paternity leave

(1) An employee's right to return under regulation 13 is a right to return—

(a) with his seniority, pension rights and similar rights—

(i) in a case where the employee is returning from consecutive periods of statutory leave which included a period of additional adoption leave or additional maternity leave, as they would have been if the period or periods of his employment prior to the additional adoption leave or (as the case may be) additional maternity leave were continuous with the period of employment following it;

(ii) in any other case, as they would have been if he had not been absent, and

(b) on terms and conditions not less favourable than those which would have applied if he had not been absent.

(2) The provision in paragraph (1)(a)(i) concerning the treatment of periods of additional maternity leave or additional adoption leave is subject to the requirements of [paragraphs 5, 5B and 6 of Schedule 5 to the Social Security Act 1989 (equal treatment under pension schemes: maternity absence, adoption leave and family leave)].

(3) The provisions in paragraph (1)(a)(ii) and (b) for an employee to be treated as if he had not been absent refer to his absence—

(a) if his return is from an isolated period of paternity leave, since the beginning of that period;

(b) if his return is from consecutive periods of statutory leave, since the beginning of the first such period.

NOTES

Para (2): words in square brackets substituted by the Pensions Act 2004 (Commencement No 2, Transitional Provisions and Consequential Amendments) Order 2005, SI 2005/275, art 5.

Part 2 Statutory Instruments

PART 3
ADOPTION LEAVE

[2.633]

15 Entitlement to ordinary adoption leave

(1) An employee is entitled to ordinary adoption leave in respect of a child if he—

(a) satisfies the conditions specified in paragraph (2), and

(b) has complied with the notice requirements in regulation 17 and, where applicable, the evidential requirements in that regulation.

(2) The conditions referred to in paragraph (1) are that the employee—

(a) is the child's adopter;

(b) has been continuously employed for a period of not less than 26 weeks ending with the week in which he was notified of having been matched with the child, and

(c) has notified the agency that he agrees that the child should be placed with him and on the date of placement.

(3) In paragraph (2)(b), "week" means the period of seven days beginning with Sunday.

(4) An employee's entitlement to leave under this regulation shall not be affected by the placement for adoption of more than one child as part of the same arrangement.

NOTES

Adoption from overseas: as to the substitution of this regulation in relation to adoptions from overseas, see the Paternity and Adoption Leave (Adoption from Overseas) Regulations 2003, SI 2003/921, reg 9.

[2.634]

16 Options in respect of ordinary adoption leave

(1) Except in the case referred to in paragraph (2), an employee may choose to begin a period of ordinary adoption leave on—

(a) the date on which the child is placed with him for adoption, or

(b) a predetermined date, specified in a notice under regulation 17, which is no more than 14 days before the date on which the child is expected to be placed with the employee and no later than that date.

(2) In a case where the employee was notified of having been matched with the child before 6th April 2003, the employee may choose to begin a period of leave only on a predetermined date, specified in a notice under regulation 17, which is after 6th April 2003 and at least 28 days after the date on which that notice is given.

NOTES

Adoption from overseas: as to the substitution of this regulation in relation to adoptions from overseas, see the Paternity and Adoption Leave (Adoption from Overseas) Regulations 2003, SI 2003/921, reg 9.

[2.635]

17 Notice and evidential requirements for ordinary adoption leave

(1) An employee must give his employer notice of his intention to take ordinary adoption leave in respect of a child, specifying—

(a) the date on which the child is expected to be placed with him for adoption, and

(b) the date on which, in accordance with regulation 16(1) or (2), the employee has chosen that his period of leave should begin.

(2) The notice provided for in paragraph (1) must be given to the employer—

(a) no more than seven days after the date on which the employee is notified of having been matched with the child for the purposes of adoption, or

(b) in a case where it was not reasonably practicable for the employee to give notice in accordance with sub-paragraph (a), as soon as is reasonably practicable.

(3) Where the employer requests it, an employee must also provide his employer with evidence, in the form of one or more documents issued by the adoption agency that matched the employee with the child, of—

(a) the name and address of the agency;

(b) . . .

(c) the date on which the employee was notified that he had been matched with the child, and

(d) the date on which the agency expects to place the child with the employee.

(4) An employee who has given notice under paragraph (1) may vary the date he has chosen as the date on which his period of leave will begin, subject to paragraph (5) and provided that he gives his employer notice of the variation—

(a) where the variation is to provide for the employee's period of leave to begin on the date on which the child is placed with him for adoption, at least 28 days before the date specified in his notice under paragraph (1) as the date on which the child is expected to be placed with him;

(b) where the variation is to provide for the employee's period of leave to begin on a predetermined date (or a different predetermined date), at least 28 days before that date,

or, if it is not reasonably practicable to give the notice 28 days before whichever date is relevant, as soon as is reasonably practicable.

(5) In a case where regulation 16(2) applies, an employee may only vary the date which he has chosen as the date on which his period of leave will begin by substituting a different predetermined date.

(6) Notice under paragraph (1) or (4) shall be given in writing, if the employer so requests.

(7) An employer who is given notice under paragraph (1) or (4) of the date on which an employee has chosen that his period of ordinary adoption leave should begin shall notify the employee, within 28 days of his receipt of the notice, of the date on which the period of additional adoption leave to which the employee will be entitled (if he satisfies the conditions in regulation 20(1)) after his period of ordinary adoption leave ends.

(8) The notification provided for in paragraph (7) shall be given to the employee—

(a) where the employer is given notice under paragraph (1), within 28 days of the date on which he received that notice;

(b) where the employer is given notice under paragraph (4), within 28 days of the date on which the employee's ordinary adoption leave period began.

NOTES

Para (3): sub-para (b) revoked by the Paternity and Adoption Leave (Amendment) Regulations 2004, SI 2004/923, regs 2, 3.

Adoption from overseas: as to the substitution of this regulation in relation to adoptions from overseas, see the Paternity and Adoption Leave (Adoption from Overseas) Regulations 2003, SI 2003/921, reg 9.

[2.636]

18 Duration and commencement of ordinary adoption leave

(1) Subject to regulations 22 and 24, an employee's ordinary adoption leave period is a period of 26 weeks.

(2) Except in the case referred to in paragraph (3), an employee's ordinary adoption leave period begins on the date specified in his notice under regulation 17(1), or, where he has varied his choice of date under regulation 17(4), on the date specified in his notice under that provision (or the last such date if he has varied his choice more than once).

(3) In a case where—

(a) the employee has chosen to begin his period of leave on the date on which the child is placed with him, and

(b) he is at work on that date,

the employee's period of leave begins on the day after that date.

NOTES

Adoption from overseas: as to the modification of this regulation in relation to adoptions from overseas, see the Paternity and Adoption Leave (Adoption from Overseas) Regulations 2003, SI 2003/921, reg 10.

[2.637]

19 Application of terms and conditions during ordinary adoption leave [and additional adoption leave]

(1) An employee who takes ordinary adoption leave [or additional adoption leave]—

(a) is entitled, during the period of leave, to the benefit of all of the terms and conditions of employment which would have applied if he had not been absent, and

(b) is bound, during that period, by any obligations arising under those terms and conditions, subject only to [the exceptions in sections 75A(3)(b) and 75B(4)(b)] of the 1996 Act.

(2) In paragraph (1)(a), "terms and conditions of employment" has the meaning given by [sections 75A(4) and 75B(5)] of the 1996 Act, and accordingly does not include terms and conditions about remuneration.

(3) For the purposes of [sections 75A and 75B] of the 1996 Act, only sums payable to an employee by way of wages or salary are to be treated as remuneration.

NOTES

The words in square brackets in the Regulation heading and the words in first pair of square brackets in para (1) were inserted, and the other words in square brackets in this regulation were substituted, by the Maternity and Parental Leave etc and the Paternity and Adoption Leave (Amendment) Regulations 2008, SI 2008/1966, regs 8, 9(1), as from 23 July 2008 (with effect in relation to an employee with whom a child is expected to be placed for adoption, where the placement is expected to occur on or after 5 October 2008: see SI 2008/1966, reg 2(2), (3)).

[2.638]

20 Additional adoption leave: entitlement, duration and commencement

(1) An employee is entitled to additional adoption leave in respect of a child if—

(a) the child was placed with him for adoption,

(b) he took ordinary adoption leave in respect of the child, and

(c) his ordinary adoption leave period did not end prematurely under regulation 22(2)(a) or 24.

(2) Subject to regulations 22 and 24, an employee's additional adoption leave period is a period of 26 weeks beginning on the day after the last day of his ordinary adoption leave period.

NOTES

Adoption from overseas: as to the modification of this regulation in relation to adoptions from overseas, see the Paternity and Adoption Leave (Adoption from Overseas) Regulations 2003, SI 2003/921, reg 11.

21 *(Revoked by the Maternity and Parental Leave etc and the Paternity and Adoption Leave (Amendment) Regulations 2008, SI 2008/1966, regs 8, 9(1), as from 23 July 2008 (with effect in relation to an employee with whom a child is expected to be placed for adoption, where the placement is expected to occur on or after 5 October 2008: see SI 2008/1966, reg 2(2), (3)).)*

[2.639]

[21A Work during adoption leave period

(1) An employee may carry out up to 10 days' work for his employer during his statutory adoption leave period without bringing his statutory adoption leave to an end.

(2) For the purposes of this regulation, any work carried out on any day shall constitute a day's work.

(3) Subject to paragraph (4), for the purposes of this regulation, work means any work done under the contract of employment and may include training or any activity undertaken for the purposes of keeping in touch with the workplace.

(4) Reasonable contact from time to time between an employee and his employer which either party is entitled to make during an adoption leave period (for example to discuss an employee's return to work) shall not bring that period to an end.

(5) This regulation does not confer any right on an employer to require that any work be carried out during the statutory adoption leave period, nor any right on an employee to work during the statutory adoption leave period.

(6) Any days' work carried out under this regulation shall not have the effect of extending the total duration of the statutory adoption leave period.]

NOTES

Inserted by the Maternity and Parental Leave etc and the Paternity and Adoption Leave (Amendment) Regulations 2006, SI 2006/2014, regs 12, 14.

[2.640]

22 Disrupted placement in the course of adoption leave

(1) This regulation applies where—

(a) an employee has begun a period of adoption leave in respect of a child before the placement of the child with him, and the employee is subsequently notified that the placement will not be made, or

(b) during an employee's period of adoption leave in respect of a child placed with him—

(i) the child dies, or

(ii) the child is returned to the adoption agency under section 30(3) of the Adoption Act 1976 or [in Scotland, the child is returned to the adoption agency, adoption society or nominated person in accordance with section 25(6) of the Adoption and Children (Scotland) Act 2007].

(2) Subject to regulation 24, in a case where this regulation applies—

(a) except in the circumstances referred to in sub-paragraphs (b) and (c), the employee's adoption leave period ends eight weeks after the end of the relevant week specified in paragraph (3);

(b) where the employee is taking ordinary adoption leave and the period of 26 weeks provided for in regulation 18 ends within eight weeks of the end of the relevant week—

(i) the employee's ordinary adoption leave period ends on the expiry of the 26-week period;

(ii) the employee is entitled to additional adoption leave, and

(iii) the employee's additional adoption leave period ends eight weeks after the end of the relevant week;

(c) where the employee is taking additional adoption leave and the period of 26 weeks provided for in regulation 20 ends within eight weeks of the end of the relevant week, the employee's additional adoption leave period ends on the expiry of the 26-week period.

(3) The relevant week referred to in paragraph (2) is—

(a) in a case falling within paragraph (1)(a), the week during which the person with whom the child was to be placed for adoption is notified that the placement will not be made;

(b) in a case falling within paragraph (1)(b)(i), the week during which the child dies;

(c) in a case falling within paragraph (1)(b)(ii), the week during which the child is returned.

(4) In paragraph (3), "week" means the period of seven days beginning with Sunday.

NOTES

Para (1): words in square brackets in sub-para (b)(ii) substituted by SI 2011/1740, art 2, Sch 1, Pt 2, para 30(1), (3), as from 5 July 2011.

Adoption from overseas: as to the modification of this regulation in relation to adoptions from overseas, see the Paternity and Adoption Leave (Adoption from Overseas) Regulations 2003, SI 2003/921, reg 12.

[2.641]

23 Redundancy during adoption leave

(1) This regulation applies where, during an employee's ordinary or additional adoption leave period, it is not practicable by reason of redundancy for his employer to continue to employ him under his existing contract of employment.

(2) Where there is a suitable available vacancy, the employee is entitled to be offered (before the end of his employment under his existing contract) alternative employment with his employer or his employer's successor, or an associated employer, under a new contract of employment which complies with paragraph (3) and takes effect immediately on the ending of his employment under the previous contract.

(3) The new contract of employment must be such that—

(a) the work to be done under it is of a kind which is both suitable in relation to the employee and appropriate for him to do in the circumstances, and

(b) its provisions as to the capacity and place in which he is to be employed, and as to the other terms and conditions of his employment, are not substantially less favourable to him than if he had continued to be employed under the previous contract.

[2.642]

24 Dismissal during adoption leave

Where an employee is dismissed after an ordinary or additional adoption leave period has begun but before the time when (apart from this regulation) that period would end, the period ends at the time of the dismissal.

[2.643]

25 Requirement to notify intention to return during adoption leave period

(1) An employee who intends to return to work earlier than the end of his additional adoption leave period must give his employer at least [8 weeks'] notice of the date on which he intends to return.

(2) If an employee attempts to return to work earlier than the end of his additional adoption leave period without complying with paragraph (1), his employer is entitled to postpone his return to a date such as will secure, subject to paragraph (3), that he has at least [8 weeks'] notice of the employee's return.

[(2A) An employee who complies with his obligations in paragraph (1) or whose employer has postponed his return in the circumstances described in paragraph (2), and who then decides to return to work—

(a) earlier than the original return date, must give his employer not less than 8 weeks' notice of the date on which he now intends to return;

(b) later than the original return date, must give his employer not less than 8 weeks' notice ending with the original return date.

(2B) In paragraph (2A) the "original return date" means the date which the employee notified to his employer as the date of his return to work under paragraph (1), or the date to which his return was postponed by his employer under paragraph (2).]

(3) An employer is not entitled under paragraph (2) to postpone an employee's return to work to a date after the end of the employee's additional adoption leave period.

(4) If an employee whose return has been postponed under paragraph (2) has been notified that he is not to return to work before the date to which his return was postponed, the employer is under no contractual obligation to pay him remuneration until the date to which his return was postponed if he returns to work before that date.

(5) This regulation does not apply in a case where the employer did not notify the employee in accordance with regulation 17(7) and (8) of the date on which the employee's additional adoption leave period would end.

(6) In a case where an employee's adoption leave is curtailed because regulation 22 applies, the references in this regulation to the end of an employee's additional adoption leave period are references to the date on which that period would have ended had that regulation not applied, irrespective of whether it was the employee's ordinary adoption leave period or his additional adoption leave period that was curtailed.

NOTES

Paras (1), (2): words in square brackets substituted by the Maternity and Parental Leave etc and the Paternity and Adoption Leave (Amendment) Regulations 2006, SI 2006/2014, regs 12, 15(a), (b).

Paras (2A), (2B):inserted by SI 2006/2014, regs 12, 15(c).

[2.644]

26 Right to return after adoption leave

(1) An employee who returns to work after a period of ordinary adoption leave which was—

(a) an isolated period of leave, or

(b) the last of two or more consecutive periods of statutory leave, which did not include any period of additional maternity leave or additional adoption leave or a period of parental leave of more than four weeks,

is entitled to return from leave to the job in which he was employed before his absence.

(2) An employee who returns to work after—

(a) a period of additional adoption leave, whether or not preceded by another period of statutory leave, or

(b) a period of ordinary adoption leave not falling within the description in paragraph (1)(a) or (b) above,

is entitled to return from leave to the job in which he was employed before his absence, or, if it is not reasonably practicable for the employer to permit him to return to that job, to another job which is both suitable for him and appropriate for him to do in the circumstances.

(3) The reference in paragraphs (1) and (2) to the job in which an employee was employed before his absence is a reference to the job in which he was employed—

(a) if his return is from an isolated period of adoption leave, immediately before that period began;

(b) if his return is from consecutive periods of statutory leave, immediately before the first such period.

(4) This regulation does not apply where regulation 23 applies.

[2.645]

27 Incidents of the right to return from adoption leave

(1) An employee's right to return under regulation 26 is to return—

[(a) with his seniority, pension rights and similar rights as they would have been if he had not been absent, and]

(b) on terms and conditions . . . not less favourable than those which would have been applied to him if he had not been absent.

[(2) In the case of accrual of rights under an employment-related benefit scheme within the meaning given by Schedule 5 to the Social Security Act 1989, nothing in paragraph (1)(a) concerning the treatment of additional adoption leave shall be taken to impose a requirement which exceeds the requirements of paragraphs 5, 5B and 6 of that Schedule.]

(3) The provisions [in paragraph (1)] for an employee to be treated as if he had not been absent refer to his absence—

(a) if his return is from an isolated period of ordinary adoption leave, since the beginning of that period;

(b) if his return is from consecutive periods of statutory leave, since the beginning of the first such period.

NOTES

Para (1): sub-para (a) substituted by the Maternity and Parental Leave etc and the Paternity and Adoption Leave (Amendment) Regulations 2008, SI 2008/1966, regs 8, 10(a), as from 23 July 2008 (with effect in relation to an employee with whom a child is expected to be placed for adoption, where the placement is expected to occur on or after 5 October 2008: see SI 2008/1966, reg 2(2), (3)); words omitted from sub-para (b) revoked by the Paternity and Adoption Leave (Amendment) Regulations 2004, SI 2004/923, regs 2, 4.

Para (2): substituted by SI 2008/1966, regs 8, 10(b), as from 23 July 2008 (subject to reg 2(2), (3) of those Regulations as noted above).

Para (3): words in square brackets substituted by SI 2008/1966, regs 8, 10(c), as from 23 July 2008 (subject to reg 2(2), (3) of those Regulations as noted above).

PART 4
PROVISIONS APPLICABLE IN RELATION TO BOTH PATERNITY AND ADOPTION LEAVE

[2.646]

28 Protection from detriment

(1) An employee is entitled under section 47C of the 1996 Act not to be subjected to any detriment by any act, or any deliberate failure to act, by his employer because—

(a) the employee took or sought to take paternity leave or ordinary or additional adoption leave;

(b) the employer believed that the employee was likely to take ordinary or additional adoption leave, . . .

[(bb) the employee undertook, considered undertaking or refused to undertake work in accordance with regulation 21A; or]

(c) the employee failed to return after a period of additional adoption leave in a case where—

(i) the employer did not notify him, in accordance with regulation 17(7) and (8) or otherwise, of the date on which that period ended, and he reasonably believed that the period had not ended, or

(ii) the employer gave him less than 28 days' notice of the date on which the period would end, and it was not reasonably practicable for him to return on that date.

(2) Paragraph (1) does not apply where the detriment in question amounts to dismissal within the meaning of Part 10 of the 1996 Act.

NOTES

Para (1): word omitted from sub-para (b) revoked, and sub-para (bb) inserted, by the Maternity and Parental Leave etc and the Paternity and Adoption Leave (Amendment) Regulations 2006, SI 2006/2014, regs 12, 16.

[2.647]
29 Unfair dismissal

(1) An employee who is dismissed is entitled under section 99 of the 1996 Act to be regarded for the purpose of Part 10 of that Act as unfairly dismissed if—

(a) the reason or principal reason for the dismissal is of a kind specified in paragraph (3), or

(b) the reason or principal reason for the dismissal is that the employee is redundant, and regulation 23 has not been complied with.

(2) An employee who is dismissed shall also be regarded for the purposes of Part 10 of the 1996 Act as unfairly dismissed if—

(a) the reason (or, if more than one, the principal reason) for the dismissal is that the employee was redundant;

(b) it is shown that the circumstances constituting the redundancy applied equally to one or more employees in the same undertaking who had positions similar to that held by the employee and who have not been dismissed by the employer, and

(c) it is shown that the reason (or, if more than one, the principal reason) for which the employee was selected for dismissal was a reason of a kind specified in paragraph (3).

(3) The kinds of reason referred to in paragraph (1) and (2) are reasons connected with the fact that—

(a) the employee took, or sought to take, paternity or adoption leave;

(b) the employer believed that the employee was likely to take ordinary or additional adoption leave, . . .

[(bb) the employee undertook, considered undertaking or refused to undertake work in accordance with regulation 21A; or]

(c) the employee failed to return after a period of additional adoption leave in a case where—

(i) the employer did not notify him, in accordance with regulation 17(7) and (8) or otherwise, of the date on which that period would end, and he reasonably believed that the period had not ended, or

(ii) the employer gave him less than 28 days' notice of the date on which the period would end, and it was not reasonably practicable for him to return on that date.

(4) . . .

(5) Paragraph (1) does not apply in relation to an employee if—

(a) it is not reasonably practicable for a reason other than redundancy for the employer (who may be the same employer or a successor of his) to permit the employee to return to a job which is both suitable for the employee and appropriate for him to do in the circumstances;

(b) an associated employer offers the employee a job of that kind, and

(c) the employee accepts or unreasonably refuses that offer.

(6) Where, on a complaint of unfair dismissal, any question arises as to whether the operation of paragraph (1) is excluded by the provisions of paragraph . . . (5), it is for the employer to show that the provisions in question were satisfied in relation to the complainant.

NOTES

Para (3): word omitted from sub-para (b) revoked, and sub-para (bb) inserted, by the Maternity and Parental Leave etc and the Paternity and Adoption Leave (Amendment) Regulations 2006, SI 2006/2014, regs 12, 17(a).

Para (4): revoked by SI 2006/2014, regs 12, 17(b).

Para (6): words omitted revoked by SI 2006/2014, regs 12, 17(c).

[2.648]
30 Contractual rights to paternity or adoption leave

(1) This regulation applies where an employee is entitled to—

(a) paternity leave,

(b) ordinary adoption leave, or

(c) additional adoption leave,

(referred to in paragraph (2) as a "statutory right") and also to a right which corresponds to that right and which arises under the employee's contract of employment or otherwise.

(2) In a case where this regulation applies—

(a) the employee may not exercise the statutory right and the corresponding right separately but may, in taking the leave for which the two rights provide, take advantage of whichever right is, in any particular respect, the more favourable, and

(b) the provisions of the 1996 Act and of these Regulations relating to the statutory right apply, subject to any modifications necessary to give effect to any more favourable contractual terms, to the exercise of the composite right described in sub-paragraph (a) as they apply to the exercise of the statutory right.

[2.649]

31 Calculation of a week's pay

Where—

(a) under Chapter 2 of Part 14 of the 1996 Act, the amount of a week's pay of an employee falls to be calculated by reference to the average rate of remuneration, or the average amount of remuneration, payable to the employee in respect of a period of twelve weeks ending on a particular date (referred to as "the calculation date");

(b) during a week in that period, the employee was absent from work on paternity leave or ordinary or additional adoption leave, and

(c) remuneration is payable to the employee in respect of that week under his contract of employment, but the amount payable is less than the amount that would be payable if he were working,

that week shall be disregarded for the purpose of the calculation and account shall be taken of remuneration in earlier weeks so as to bring up to twelve the number of weeks of which account is taken.

STATUTORY PATERNITY PAY AND STATUTORY ADOPTION PAY (WEEKLY RATES) REGULATIONS 2002

(SI 2002/2818)

NOTES

Made: 11 November 2002.

Authority: Social Security Contributions and Benefits Act 1992, ss 171ZE(1), 171ZN(1); Social Security Administration Act 1992, s 5(1)(l).

Commencement: 8 December 2002.

Statutory paternity pay: the Work and Families Act 2006, s 11(2) at **[1.1411]** provides that any reference to statutory paternity pay in any instrument or document made before the commencement of paras 12 and 13 of Sch 1 to that Act is to be read, in relation to any time after that commencement, as a reference to ordinary statutory paternity pay. Section 11(2), and Sch 1, paras 12, 13, were brought into force on 6 April 2010 (see SI 2010/495).

[2.650]

1 Citation and commencement

These Regulations may be cited as the Statutory Paternity Pay and Statutory Adoption Pay (Weekly Rates) Regulations and shall come into force on 8th December 2002.

[2.651]

[2 Weekly rate of payment of statutory paternity pay

The weekly rate of payment of statutory paternity pay shall be the smaller of the following two amounts—

(a) [£136.78];

(b) 90 per cent of the normal weekly earnings of the person claiming statutory paternity pay, determined in accordance with regulations 39 and 40 of the Statutory Paternity Pay and Statutory Adoption Pay (General) Regulations 2002.]

NOTES

Substituted by the Statutory Paternity Pay and Statutory Adoption Pay (Weekly Rates) (Amendment) Regulations 2004, SI 2004/925, reg 2.

Sum in square brackets in para (a) substituted by the Social Security Benefits Up-rating Order 2013, SI 2013/574, art 10(1)(a), as from 7 April 2013.

The previous amounts were: £75 (where the paternity pay period began before 6 April 2003) and £100 (where the paternity pay period began on or after that date), both sums by virtue of these Regulations as originally enacted; £102.80 (as from 4 April 2004, see the Social Security Benefits Up-rating Order 2004, SI 2004/552); £106.00 (as from 3 April 2005, see the Social Security Benefits Up-rating Order 2005, SI 2005/522, art 11(a)); £108.85 (as from 2 April 2006, see the Social Security Benefits Up-rating Order 2006, SI 2006/645, art 11(a)); £112.75 (as from 1 April 2007, see the Social Security Benefits Up-rating Order 2007, SI 2007/688, art 11(a)); £117.18 (as from 6 April 2008, see the Social Security Benefits Up-rating Order 2008, SI 2008/632, art 11(a)); £123.06 (as from 5 April 2009, see the Social Security Benefits Up-rating Order 2009, SI 2009/497, art 11(a)); £124.88 (as from 4 April 2010, see the Social Security Benefits Up-rating Order 2010, SI 2010/793, art 11(a)); £128.73 (as from 3 April 2011, see the Social Security Benefits Up-rating Order 2011, SI 2011/821, art 11(1)(a)); £135.45 (as from 1 April 2012, see the Social Security Benefits Up-rating Order 2012, SI 2012/780, art 11(1)(a)).

[2.652]
3 Weekly rate of payment of statutory adoption pay

The weekly rate of payment of statutory adoption pay shall be the smaller of the following two amounts—

(a) [£136.78];

(b) 90 per cent of the normal weekly earnings of the person claiming statutory adoption pay, determined in accordance with regulations 39 and 40 of the Statutory Paternity Pay and Statutory Adoption Pay (General) Regulations 2002.

NOTES

Sum in square brackets in para (a) substituted by the Social Security Benefits Up-rating Order 2013, SI 2013/574, art 10(1)(b), as from 7 April 2013.

The previous amounts were as set out in the final note to reg 2 above.

[2.653]
[4 Rounding of fractional amounts

Where any payment of—

(a) statutory paternity pay is made on the basis of a calculation at—
  (i) the weekly rate specified in regulation 2(b); or
  (ii) the daily rate of one-seventh of the weekly rate specified in regulation 2(a) or (b); or

(b) statutory adoption pay is made on the basis of a calculation at—
  (i) the weekly rate specified in regulation 3(b); or
  (ii) the daily rate of one-seventh of the weekly rate specified in regulation 3(a) or (b),

and that amount includes a fraction of a penny, the payment shall be rounded up to the next whole number of pence.]

NOTES

Substituted by the Statutory Paternity Pay and Statutory Adoption Pay (General) and the Statutory Paternity Pay and Statutory Adoption Pay (Weekly Rates) (Amendment) Regulations 2006, SI 2006/2236, regs 6, 7.

STATUTORY PATERNITY PAY AND STATUTORY ADOPTION PAY (ADMINISTRATION) REGULATIONS 2002

(SI 2002/2820)

NOTES

Made: 13 November 2002.

Authority: Employment Act 2002, ss 7(1), (2)(a), (b), (4)(a)–(c), (5), 8(1), (2)(a)–(c), 10(1), (2), 51(1); Social Security Contributions (Transfer of Functions, etc) Act 1999, ss 8(1)(f), (ga), 25.

Commencement: 8 December 2002.

Statutory paternity pay: the Work and Families Act 2006, s 11(2) at **[1.1411]** provides that any reference to statutory paternity pay in any instrument or document made before the commencement of paras 12 and 13 of Sch 1 to that Act is to be read, in relation to any time after that commencement, as a reference to ordinary statutory paternity pay. Section 11(2), and Sch 1, paras 12, 13, were brought into force on 6 April 2010 (see SI 2010/495).

Adoption from overseas: as to the application of these Regulations to adoptions from overseas, see the Statutory Paternity Pay (Adoption) and Statutory Adoption Pay (Adoptions from Overseas) (Administration) Regulations 2003, SI 2003/1192.

See *Harvey* J(8).

ARRANGEMENT OF REGULATIONS

[2.654]

1 Citation and commencement

These Regulations may be cited as the Statutory Paternity Pay and Statutory Adoption Pay (Administration) Regulations 2002 and shall come into force on 8th December 2002.

[2.655]

2 Interpretation

(1) In these Regulations—

"adopter", in relation to a child, means a person with whom the child is matched for adoption;

"adoption leave" means leave under section 75A of the Employment Rights Act 1996;

"adoption pay period" means the period prescribed under section 171ZN(2) of the Contributions and Benefits Act as the period in respect of which statutory adoption pay is payable to a person;

"the Board" means the Commissioners of Inland Revenue;

"the Contributions and Benefits Act" means the Social Security Contributions and Benefits Act 1992;

"contributions payments" has the same meaning as in section 7 of the Employment Act;

"the Contributions Regulations" means the Social Security (Contributions) Regulations 2001;

"the Employment Act" means the Employment Act 2002;

"income tax month" means the period beginning on the 6th day of any calendar month and ending on the 5th day of the following calendar month;

"income tax quarter" means the period beginning on the 6th day of April and ending on the 5th day of July, the period beginning on the 6th day of July and ending on the 5th day of October, the period beginning on the 6th day of October and ending on the 5th day of January or the period beginning on the 6th day of January and ending on the 5th day of April;

"paternity leave" means leave under section 80A or section 80B of the Employment Rights Act 1996;

"paternity pay period" means the period determined in accordance with section 171ZE(2) of the Contributions and Benefits Act as the period in respect of which statutory paternity pay is payable to a person;

"statutory adoption pay" means any payment under section 171ZL of the Contributions and Benefits Act;

"statutory paternity pay" means any payment under section 171ZA or section 171ZB of the Contributions and Benefits Act;

"tax year" means the 12 months beginning with 6th April in any year;

"writing" includes writing delivered by means of electronic communications approved by directions issued by the Board pursuant to regulations under section 132 of the Finance Act 1999.

(2) Any reference in these Regulations to the employees of an employer includes former employees of his.

NOTES

Adoption from overseas: as to the modification of this regulation in relation to adoptions from overseas, see the Statutory Paternity Pay (Adoption) and Statutory Adoption Pay (Adoptions from Overseas) (Administration) Regulations 2003, SI 2003/1192, reg 3(1)–(3).

Commissioners of Inland Revenue: a reference to the Commissioners of Inland Revenue is now to be taken as a reference to the Commissioners for Her Majesty's Revenue and Customs; see the Commissioners for Revenue and Customs Act 2005, s 50(1), (7).

[2.656]

3 Funding of employers' liabilities to make payments of statutory paternity or statutory adoption pay

(1) An employer who has made any payment of statutory paternity pay or statutory adoption pay shall be entitled—

(a) to an amount equal to 92 per cent of such payment; or

(b) if the payment qualifies for small employer's relief by virtue of section 7(3) of the Employment Act—

 (i) to an amount equal to such payment; and

 (ii) to an additional payment equal to the amount to which the employer would have been entitled under section 167(2)(b) of the Contributions and Benefits Act had the payment been a payment of statutory maternity pay.

(2) The employer shall be entitled in either case (a) or case (b) to apply for advance funding in respect of such payment in accordance with regulation 4, or to deduct it in accordance with regulation 5 from amounts otherwise payable by him.

[2.657]

4 Application for funding from the Board

(1) If an employer is entitled to a payment determined in accordance with regulation 3 in respect of statutory paternity pay or statutory adoption pay which he is required to pay to an employee or employees for an income tax month or income tax quarter, and the payment exceeds the aggregate of—

(a) the total amount of tax which the employer is required to pay to the collector of taxes in respect of the deductions from the emoluments of his employees in accordance with the Income Tax (Employments) Regulations 1993 for the same income tax month or income tax quarter,

(b) the total amount of the deductions made by the employer from the emoluments of his employees for the same income tax month or income tax quarter in accordance with regulations under section 22(5) of the Teaching and Higher Education Act 1998 or section 73B of the Education (Scotland) Act 1980 or in accordance with article 3(5) of the Education (Student Support) (Northern Ireland) Order 1998,

(c) the total amount of contributions payments which the employer is required to pay to the collector of taxes in respect of the emoluments of his employees (whether by means of deduction or otherwise) in accordance with the Contributions Regulations for the same income tax month or income tax quarter, and

(d) the total amount of payments which the employer is required to pay to the collector of taxes in respect of the deductions made on account of tax from payments to sub-contractors in accordance with section 559 of the Income and Corporation Taxes Act 1988 for the same income tax month or income tax quarter,

the employer may apply to the Board in accordance with paragraph (2) for funds to pay the statutory paternity pay or statutory adoption pay (or so much of it as remains outstanding) to the employee or employees.

(2) Where—

(a) the condition in paragraph (1) is satisfied, or

(b) the employer considers that the condition in paragraph (1) will be satisfied on the date of any subsequent payment of emoluments to one or more employees who are entitled to payment of statutory paternity pay or statutory adoption pay,

the employer may apply to the Board for funding in a form approved for that purpose by the Board.

(3) An application by an employer under paragraph (2) shall be for an amount up to, but not exceeding, the amount of the payment to which the employer is entitled in accordance with regulation 3 in respect of statutory paternity pay and statutory adoption pay which he is required to pay to an employee or employees for the income tax month or income tax quarter to which the payment of emoluments relates.

[2.658]

5 Deductions from payments to the Board

An employer who is entitled to a payment determined in accordance with regulation 3 may recover such payment by making one or more deductions from the aggregate of the amounts specified in sub-paragraphs (a) to (d) of regulation 4(1) except where and in so far as—

(a) those amounts relate to earnings paid before the beginning of the income tax month or income tax quarter in which the payment of statutory paternity pay or statutory adoption pay was made;

(b) those amounts are paid by him later than six years after the end of the tax year in which the payment of statutory paternity pay or statutory adoption pay was made;

(c) the employer has received payment from the Board under regulation 4; or

(d) the employer has made a request in writing under regulation 4 that the payment to which he is entitled in accordance with regulation 3 be paid to him and he has not received notification by the Board that the request is refused.

[2.659]

6 Payments to employers by the Board

If the total amount which an employer is or would otherwise be entitled to deduct under regulation 5 is less than the payment to which the employer is entitled in accordance with regulation 3 in an income tax month or income tax quarter, and the Board are satisfied that this is so, then provided that the employer has in writing requested them to do so, the Board shall pay the employer such amount as the employer was unable to deduct.

[2.660]

7 Date when certain contributions are to be treated as paid

Where an employer has made a deduction from a contributions payment under regulation 5, the date on which it is to be treated as having been paid for the purposes of section 7(5) of the Employment Act (when amount deducted from contributions payment to be treated as paid and received by the Board) is—

(a) in a case where the deduction did not extinguish the contributions payment, the date on which the remainder of the contributions payment or, as the case may be, the first date on which any part of the remainder of the contributions payment was paid; and

(b) in a case where the deduction extinguished the contributions payment, the 14th day after the end of the income tax month or income tax quarter during which there were paid the earnings in respect of which the contributions payment was payable.

[2.661]

8 Overpayments

(1) This regulation applies where funds have been provided to the employer pursuant to regulation 4 in respect of one or more employees and it appears to an officer of the Board that the employer has not used the whole or part of those funds to pay statutory paternity pay or statutory adoption pay.

(2) An officer of the Board shall decide to the best of his judgement the amount of funds provided pursuant to regulation 4 and not used to pay statutory paternity pay or statutory adoption pay and shall serve notice in writing of his decision on the employer.

(3) A decision under this regulation may cover funds provided pursuant to regulation 4—

(a) for any one income tax month or income tax quarter, or more than one income tax month or income tax quarter, in a tax year, and

(b) in respect of a class or classes of employees specified in the decision notice (without naming the individual employees), or in respect of one or more employees named in the decision notice.

(4) Subject to the following provisions of this regulation, Part 6 of the Taxes Management Act 1970 (collection and recovery) shall apply with any necessary modifications to a decision under this regulation as if it were an assessment and as if the amount of funds determined were income tax charged on the employer.

(5) Where an amount of funds determined under this regulation relates to more than one employee, proceedings may be brought for the recovery of that amount without distinguishing the amounts making up that sum which the employer is liable to repay in respect of each employee and without specifying the employee in question, and the amount determined under this regulation shall be one cause of action or one matter of complaint for the purposes of proceedings under section 65, 66 or 67 of the Taxes Management Act 1970.

(6) Nothing in paragraph (5) prevents the bringing of separate proceedings for the recovery of any amount which the employer is liable to repay in respect of each employee.

[2.662]

9 Records to be maintained by employers

Every employer shall maintain for three years after the end of a tax year in which he made payments of statutory paternity pay or statutory adoption pay to any employee of his a record of—

- (a) if the employee's paternity pay period or adoption pay period began in that year—
  - (i) the date on which that period began, and
  - (ii) the evidence of entitlement to statutory paternity pay or statutory adoption pay provided by the employee pursuant to regulations made under section 171ZC(3)(c) or section 171ZL(8)(c) of the Contributions and Benefits Act;
- (b) the weeks in that tax year in which statutory paternity pay or statutory adoption pay was paid to the employee and the amount paid in each week; and
- (c) any week in that tax year which was within the employee's paternity pay period or adoption pay period but for which no payment of statutory paternity pay or statutory adoption pay was made to him and the reason no payment was made.

[2.663]

10 Inspection of employers' records

(1) Every employer, whenever called upon to do so by any authorised officer of the Board, shall produce the documents and records specified in paragraph (2) to that officer for inspection, at such time as that officer may reasonably require, at the prescribed place.

(2) The documents and records specified in this paragraph are—

- (a) all wages sheets, deductions working sheets, records kept in accordance with regulation 9 and other documents and records whatsoever relating to the calculation or payment of statutory paternity pay or statutory adoption pay to his employees in respect of the years specified by such officer; or
- (b) such of those wages sheets, deductions working sheets, or other documents and records as may be specified by the authorised officer.

(3) The "prescribed place" mentioned in paragraph (1) means—

- (a) such place in Great Britain as the employer and the authorised officer may agree upon; or
- (b) in default of such agreement, the place in Great Britain at which the documents and records referred to in paragraph (2)(a) are normally kept; or
- (c) in default of such agreement and if there is no such place as is referred to in sub-paragraph (b) above, the employer's principal place of business in Great Britain.

(4) The authorised officer may—

- (a) take copies of, or make extracts from, any document or record produced to him for inspection in accordance with paragraph (1);
- (b) remove any document or record so produced if it appears to him to be necessary to do so, at a reasonable time and for a reasonable period.

(5) Where any document or record is removed in accordance with paragraph (4)(b), the authorised officer shall provide—

- (a) a receipt for the document or record so removed; and
- (b) a copy of the document or record, free of charge, within seven days, to the person by whom it was produced or caused to be produced where the document or record is reasonably required for the proper conduct of a business.

(6) Where a lien is claimed on a document produced in accordance with paragraph (1), the removal of the document under paragraph (4)(b) shall not be regarded as breaking the lien.

(7) Where records are maintained by computer, the person required to make them available for inspection shall provide the authorised officer with all facilities necessary for obtaining information from them.

[2.664]

11 Provision of information relating to entitlement to statutory paternity pay or statutory adoption pay

(1) Where an employer who has been given evidence of entitlement to statutory paternity pay or statutory adoption pay pursuant to regulations made under section 171ZC(3)(c) or section 171ZL(8)(c) of the Contributions and Benefits Act by a person who is or has been an

employee decides that he has no liability to make payments of statutory paternity pay or statutory adoption pay to the employee, the employer shall furnish the employee with details of the decision and the reasons for it.

(2) Where an employer who has been given such evidence of entitlement to statutory adoption pay has made one or more payments of statutory adoption pay to the employee but decides, before the end of the adoption pay period, that he has no liability to make further payments to the employee because he has been detained in legal custody or sentenced to a term of imprisonment which was not suspended, the employer shall furnish the employee with—

(a) details of his decision and the reasons for it; and

(b) details of the last week in respect of which a liability to pay statutory adoption pay arose and the total number of weeks within the adoption pay period in which such a liability arose.

(3) The employer shall—

(a) return to the employee any evidence provided by him as referred to in paragraph (1) or (2); and

(b) comply with the requirements imposed by paragraph (1) within 28 days of—

(i) in the case of entitlement to statutory paternity pay under section 171ZA(1) of the Contributions and Benefits Act, the day the employee gave notice of his intended absence or the end of the fifteenth week before the expected week of birth, whichever is the later, or

(ii) in the case of entitlement to statutory paternity pay under section 171ZB(1) or of statutory adoption pay under section 171ZL(1) of the Contributions and Benefits Act, the end of the seven-day period that starts on the date on which the adopter is notified of having been matched with the child;

(c) comply with the requirements imposed by paragraph (2) within seven days of being notified of the employee's detention or sentence.

(4) For the purposes of paragraph (3)(b)(ii), an adopter is notified of having been matched with a child on the date on which he receives notification, under regulation 11(2) of the Adoption Agencies Regulations 1983 or [regulation 8(5) of the Adoption Agencies (Scotland) Regulations 2009] that an adoption agency has decided that he would be a suitable adoptive parent for the child.

NOTES

Para (4): words in square brackets substituted by the Adoption and Children (Scotland) Act 2007 (Consequential Modifications) Order 2011, SI 2011/1740, art 2, Sch 1, Pt 2, para 31, as from 15 July 2011.

Adoption from overseas: as to the modification of this regulation in relation to adoptions from overseas, see the Statutory Paternity Pay (Adoption) and Statutory Adoption Pay (Adoptions from Overseas) (Administration) Regulations 2003, SI 2003/1192, reg 3(1), (4), (5).

[2.665]

12 Application for the determination of any issue arising as to, or in connection with, entitlement to statutory paternity pay or statutory adoption pay

(1) An application for the determination of any issue arising as to, or in connection with, entitlement to statutory paternity pay or statutory adoption pay may be submitted to an officer of the Board by the employee concerned.

(2) Such an issue shall be decided by an officer of the Board only on the basis of such an application or on his own initiative.

[2.666]

13 Applications in connection with statutory paternity pay or statutory adoption pay

(1) An application for the determination of any issue referred to in regulation 12 shall be made in a form approved for the purpose by the Board.

(2) Where such an application is made by an employee, it shall—

(a) be made to an officer of the Board within six months of the earliest day in respect of which entitlement to statutory paternity pay or statutory adoption pay is in issue;

(b) state the period in respect of which entitlement to statutory paternity pay or statutory adoption pay is in issue; and

(c) state the grounds (if any) on which the applicant's employer had denied liability for statutory paternity pay or statutory adoption pay in respect of the period specified in the application.

[2.667]

14 Provision of information

(1) Any person specified in paragraph (2) shall, where information or documents are reasonably required from him to ascertain whether statutory paternity pay or statutory adoption pay is or was payable, furnish that information or those documents within 30 days of receiving a notification from an officer of the Board requesting such information or documents.

(2) The requirement to provide such information or documents applies to—
(a) any person claiming to be entitled to statutory paternity pay or statutory adoption pay;
(b) any person who is, or has been, the spouse[, civil partner] or partner of such a person as is specified in paragraph (a);
(c) any person who is, or has been, an employer of such a person as is specified in paragraph (a);
(d) any person carrying on an agency or other business for the introduction or supply to persons requiring them of persons available to do work or to perform services; and
(e) any person who is a servant or agent of any such person as is specified in paragraphs (a) to (d).

NOTES

Para (2): words in square brackets in sub-para (b) inserted by the Civil Partnership Act 2004 (Amendments to Subordinate Legislation) Order 2005, SI 2005/2114, art 2(17), Sch 17, para 2.

STATUTORY PATERNITY PAY AND STATUTORY ADOPTION PAY (GENERAL) REGULATIONS 2002

(SI 2002/2822)

NOTES

Made: 13 November 2002.

Authority: Social Security Contributions and Benefits Act 1992, ss 171ZA(2)(a), 171ZB(2)(a), 171ZC(3)(a), (c), (d), (f), (g), 171ZD(2), (3), 171ZE(2)(a), (b)(i), (3), (7), (8), 171ZG(3), 171ZJ(1), (3), (4), (7), (8), 171ZL(8)(b)–(d), (f), (g), 171ZM(2), (3), 171ZN(2), (5), (6), 171ZP(6), 171ZS(1), (3), (4), (7), (8), 175(4); Social Security Administration Act 1992, s 5(1)(g), (i), (p).

Commencement: 8 December 2002.

Statutory paternity pay: the Work and Families Act 2006, s 11(2) at **[1.1411]** provides that any reference to statutory paternity pay in any instrument or document made before the commencement of paras 12 and 13 of Sch 1 to that Act is to be read, in relation to any time after that commencement, as a reference to ordinary statutory paternity pay. Section 11(2), and Sch 1, paras 12, 13, were brought into force on 6 April 2010 (see SI 2010/495).

See *Harvey* J(8).

ARRANGEMENT OF REGULATIONS

PART 1
INTRODUCTION

PART 2
STATUTORY PATERNITY PAY (BIRTH)

PART 3
STATUTORY PATERNITY PAY (ADOPTION)

PART 4
STATUTORY PATERNITY PAY: PROVISIONS APPLICABLE TO BOTH STATUTORY PATERNITY PAY (BIRTH) AND STATUTORY PATERNITY PAY (ADOPTION)

PART 1
INTRODUCTION

[2.668]

1 Citation and commencement

These Regulations may be cited as the Statutory Paternity Pay and Statutory Adoption Pay (General) Regulations 2002 and shall come into force on 8th December 2002.

[2.669]

2 Interpretation

(1) In these Regulations—

"the Act" means the Social Security Contributions and Benefits Act 1992;

"adopter", in relation to a child, means a person who has been matched with the child for adoption;

"adoption agency" has the meaning given, in relation to England and Wales, by section 1(4) of the Adoption Act 1976 and in relation to Scotland, by [section 119(1) of the Adoption and Children (Scotland) Act 2007];

"the Board" means the Commissioners of Inland Revenue;

"the Contributions Regulations" means the Social Security (Contributions) Regulations 2001;

"expected week", in relation to the birth of a child, means the week, beginning with midnight between Saturday and Sunday, in which it is expected that the child will be born;

"statutory paternity pay (adoption)" means statutory paternity pay payable in accordance with the provisions of Part 12ZA of the Act where the conditions specified in section 171ZB(2) of the Act are satisfied;

"statutory paternity pay (birth)" means statutory paternity pay payable in accordance with the provisions of Part 12ZA of the Act where the conditions specified in section 171ZA(2) of the Act are satisfied.

(2) For the purposes of these Regulations—
- (a) a person is matched with a child for adoption when an adoption agency decides that that person would be a suitable adoptive parent for the child, either individually or jointly with another person, and
- (b) a person is notified of having been matched with a child on the date on which he receives notification of the agency's decision, under regulation 11(2) of the Adoption Agencies Regulations 1983 or [regulation 8(5) of the Adoption Agencies (Scotland) Regulations 2009].

NOTES

The words in square brackets in the definition "adoption agency" in para (1) were substituted, and the words in square brackets in para (2)(b) were substituted, by the Adoption and Children (Scotland) Act 2007 (Consequential Modifications) Order 2011, SI 2011/1740, art 2, Sch 1, Pt 2, para 32(1), (2), as from 15 July 2011.

Commissioners of Inland Revenue: a reference to the Commissioners of Inland Revenue is now to be taken as a reference to the Commissioners for Her Majesty's Revenue and Customs; see the Commissioners for Revenue and Customs Act 2005, s 50(1), (7).

[2.670]

3 Application

(1) Subject to the provisions of Part 12ZA of the Act (statutory paternity pay) and of these Regulations, there is entitlement to—
- (a) statutory paternity pay (birth) in respect of children—
  - (i) born on or after 6th April 2003; or
  - (ii) whose expected week of birth begins on or after that date;
- (b) statutory paternity pay (adoption) in respect of children—
  - (i) matched with a person who is notified of having been matched on or after 6th April 2003; or
  - (ii) placed for adoption on or after that date.

(2) Subject to the provisions of Part 12ZB of the Act (statutory adoption pay) and of these Regulations, there is entitlement to statutory adoption pay in respect of children—
- (a) matched with a person who is notified of having been matched on or after 6th April 2003; or
- (b) placed for adoption on or after that date.

PART 2
STATUTORY PATERNITY PAY (BIRTH)

[2.671]

4 Conditions of entitlement to statutory paternity pay (birth): relationship with newborn child and child's mother

The conditions prescribed under section 171ZA(2)(a) of the Act are those prescribed in regulation 4(2)(b) and (c) of the Paternity and Adoption Leave Regulations 2002.

[2.672]

5 Modification of entitlement conditions: early birth

Where a person does not meet the conditions specified in section 171ZA(2)(b) to (d) of the Act because the child's birth occurred earlier than the 14th week before the expected week of the birth, it shall have effect as if, for the conditions there set out, there were substituted the conditions that—
- (a) the person would, but for the date on which the birth occurred, have been in employed earner's employment with an employer for a continuous period of at least 26 weeks ending with the week immediately preceding the 14th week before the expected week of the child's birth;
- (b) his normal weekly earnings for the period of 8 weeks ending with the week immediately preceding the week in which the child is born are not less than the lower earnings limit in force under section 5(1)(a) of the Act immediately before the commencement of the week in which the child is born.

[2.673]

6 Period of payment of statutory paternity pay (birth)

(1) Subject to paragraph (2) and regulation 8, a person entitled to statutory paternity pay (birth) may choose the statutory paternity pay period to begin on—
- (a) the date on which the child is born or, where he is at work on that day, the following day;
- (b) the date falling such number of days after the date on which the child is born as the person may specify;
- (c) a predetermined date, specified by the person, which is later than the first day of the expected week of the child's birth.

(2) In a case where statutory paternity pay (birth) is payable in respect of a child whose expected week of birth begins before 6th April 2003, the statutory paternity pay period shall begin on a predetermined date, specified by the person entitled to such pay in a notice under section 171ZC(1) of the Act, which is at least 28 days after the date on which that notice was given, unless the person liable to pay statutory paternity pay (birth) agrees to the period beginning earlier.

(3) A person may choose for statutory paternity pay (birth) to be paid in respect of a period of a week.

(4) A choice made in accordance with paragraph (1) or (2) is not irrevocable, but where a person subsequently makes a different choice in relation to the beginning of the statutory pay period, section 171ZC(1) of the Act shall apply to it.

[2.674]

7 Additional notice requirements for statutory paternity pay (birth)

(1) Where the choice made by a person in accordance with paragraph (1) of regulation 6 and notified in accordance with section 171ZC(1) of the Act is that mentioned in sub-paragraph (a) or (b) of that paragraph, the person shall give further notice to the person liable to pay him statutory paternity pay, as soon as is reasonably practicable after the child's birth, of the date the child was born.

(2) Where the choice made by a person in accordance with paragraph (1) of regulation 6 and notified in accordance with section 171ZC(1) of the Act is that specified in sub-paragraph (c) of that paragraph, and the date of the child's birth is later than the date so specified, the person shall, if he wishes to claim statutory paternity pay (birth), give notice to the person liable to pay it, as soon as is reasonably practicable, that the period in respect of which statutory paternity pay is to be paid shall begin on a date different from that originally chosen by him.

(3) That date may be any date chosen in accordance with paragraph (1) of regulation 6.

[2.675]

8 Qualifying period for statutory paternity pay (birth)

The qualifying period for the purposes of section 171ZE(2) of the Act (period within which the statutory paternity pay period must occur) is a period which begins on the date of the child's birth and ends—

(a) except in the case referred to in paragraph (b), 56 days after that date;
(b) in a case where the child is born before the first day of the expected week of its birth, 56 days after that day.

[2.676]

9 Evidence of entitlement to statutory paternity pay (birth)

(1) A person shall provide evidence of his entitlement to statutory paternity pay (birth) by providing in writing to the person who will be liable to pay him statutory paternity pay (birth)—

(a) the information specified in paragraph (2);
(b) a declaration that he meets the conditions prescribed under section 171ZA(2)(a) of the Act and that it is not the case that statutory paternity pay (birth) is not payable to him by virtue of the provisions of section 171ZE(4) of the Act.

(2) The information referred to in paragraph (1)(a) is as follows—

(a) the name of the person claiming statutory paternity pay (birth);
(b) the expected week of the child's birth and, where the birth has already occurred, the date of birth;
(c) the date from which it is expected that the liability to pay statutory paternity pay (birth) will begin;
(d) whether the period chosen in respect of which statutory paternity pay (birth) is to be payable is a week.

(3) The information and declaration referred to in paragraph (1) shall be provided at least 28 days before the date mentioned in sub-paragraph (c) of paragraph (2) or, if that is not reasonably practicable, as soon as is reasonably practicable thereafter.

(4) Where the person who will be liable to pay statutory paternity pay (birth) so requests, the person entitled to it shall inform him of the date of the child's birth within 28 days, or as soon as is reasonably practicable thereafter.

[2.677]

10 Entitlement to statutory paternity pay (birth) where there is more than one employer

Statutory paternity pay (birth) shall be payable to a person in respect of a statutory pay week during any part of which he works only for an employer—

(a) who is not liable to pay him statutory paternity pay (birth); and
(b) for whom he has worked in the week immediately preceding the 14th week before the expected week of the child's birth.

PART 3
STATUTORY PATERNITY PAY (ADOPTION)

[2.678]

11 Conditions of entitlement to statutory paternity pay (adoption): relationship with child and with person with whom the child is placed for adoption

(1) The conditions prescribed under section 171ZB(2)(a) of the Act are that a person—

(a) is married to[, the civil partner] or the partner of a child's adopter (or in a case where there are two adopters, married to[, the civil partner] or the partner of the other adopter), and

(b) has, or expects to have, the main responsibility (apart from the responsibility of the child's adopter, or in a case where there two adopters, together with the other adopter) for the upbringing of the child.

(2) For the purposes of paragraph (1), "partner" means a person (whether of a different sex or the same sex) who lives with the adopter and the child in an enduring family relationship but is not a relative of the adopter of a kind specified in paragraph [(2A)].

[(2A) The relatives of the adopter referred to in paragraph (2) are the adopter's parent, grandparent, sister, brother, aunt or uncle.]

(3) References to relationships in paragraph [(2A)]—

(a) are to relationships of the full blood or half blood, or, in the case of an adopted person, such of those relationships as would exist but for the adoption, and

(b) include the relationship of a child with his adoptive, or former adoptive parents but do not include any other adoptive relationships.

NOTES

Para (1): words in square brackets in sub-para (a) inserted by the Civil Partnership Act 2004 (Amendments to Subordinate Legislation) Order 2005, SI 2005/2114, art 2(17), Sch 17, para 3.

Paras (2), (3): figures in square brackets substituted by the Statutory Paternity Pay and Statutory Adoption Pay (Amendment) Regulations 2004, SI 2004/488, reg 2(1), (2)(a), (c).

Para (2A): inserted by SI 2004/488, reg 2(1), (2)(b).

[2.679]

12 Period of payment of statutory paternity pay (adoption)

(1) Subject to paragraph (2) and regulation 14, a person entitled to statutory paternity pay (adoption) may choose the statutory paternity pay period to begin on—

(a) the date on which the child is placed with the adopter or, where the person is at work on that day, the following day;

(b) the date falling such number of days after the date on which the child is placed with the adopter as the person may specify;

(c) a predetermined date, specified by the person, which is later than the date on which the child is expected to be placed with the adopter.

(2) In a case where statutory paternity pay (adoption) is payable in respect of a child matched with an adopter who is notified of having been matched before 6th April 2003, the statutory paternity pay period shall begin on a predetermined date, specified by the person entitled to such pay in a notice under section 171ZC(1) of the Act, which is at least 28 days after the date on which that notice was given, unless the person liable to pay statutory paternity pay (birth) agrees to the period beginning earlier.

(3) A person may choose for statutory paternity pay (adoption) to be paid in respect of a period of a week.

(4) A choice made in accordance with paragraph (1) is not irrevocable, but where a person subsequently makes a different choice in relation to the beginning of the statutory paternity pay period, section 171ZC(1) of the Act shall apply to it.

[2.680]

13 Additional notice requirements for statutory paternity pay (adoption)

(1) Where the choice made by a person in accordance with paragraph (1) of regulation 12 and notified in accordance with section 171ZC(1) of the Act is that mentioned in sub-paragraph (a) or (b) of that paragraph, the person shall give further notice to the person liable to pay him statutory paternity pay as soon as is reasonably practicable of the date on which the placement occurred.

(2) Where the choice made by a person in accordance with paragraph (1) of regulation 12 and notified in accordance with section 171ZC(1) of the Act is that mentioned in sub-paragraph (c) of that paragraph, or a date is specified under paragraph (2) of that regulation, and the child is placed for adoption later than the date so specified, the person shall, if he wishes to claim statutory paternity pay (adoption), give notice to the person liable to pay it, as soon as is reasonably practicable, that the period in respect of which statutory paternity pay is to be paid shall begin on a date different from that originally chosen by him.

(3) That date may be any date chosen in accordance with paragraph (1) of regulation 12.

[2.681]
14 Qualifying period for statutory paternity pay (adoption)

The qualifying period for the purposes of section 171ZE(2) of the Act (period within which the statutory pay period must occur) is a period of 56 days beginning with the date of the child's placement for adoption.

[2.682]
15 Evidence of entitlement for statutory paternity pay (adoption)

(1) A person shall provide evidence of his entitlement to statutory paternity pay (adoption) by providing in writing to the person who will be liable to pay him statutory paternity pay (adoption)—

(a) the information specified in paragraph (2);
(b) a declaration that he meets the conditions prescribed under section 171ZB(2)(a) of the Act and that it is not the case that statutory paternity pay (adoption) is not payable to him by virtue of the provisions of section 171ZE(4) of the Act;
(c) a declaration that he has elected to receive statutory paternity pay (adoption), and not statutory adoption pay under Part 12ZB of the Act.

(2) The information referred to in paragraph (1) is as follows—

(a) the name of the person claiming statutory paternity pay (adoption);
(b) the date on which the child is expected to be placed for adoption or, where the child has already been placed for adoption, the date of placement of the child;
(c) the date from which it is expected that the liability to pay statutory paternity pay (adoption) will begin;
(d) whether the period chosen in respect of which statutory paternity pay (adoption) is to be payable is a week;
(e) the date the adopter was notified he had been matched with the child for the purposes of adoption.

(3) The information and declarations referred to in paragraph (1) shall be provided to the person liable to pay statutory paternity pay at least 28 days before the date mentioned in sub-paragraph (c) of paragraph (2) or, if that is not reasonably practicable, as soon as is reasonably practicable thereafter.

(4) Where the person who will be liable to pay statutory paternity pay (adoption) so requests, the person entitled to it shall inform him of the date of the child's placement within 28 days, or as soon as is reasonably practicable thereafter.

[2.683]
16 Entitlement to statutory paternity pay (adoption) where there is more than one employer

Statutory paternity pay (adoption) shall be payable to a person in respect of a statutory pay week during any part of which he works only for an employer—

(a) who is not liable to pay him statutory paternity pay (adoption); and
(b) for whom he has worked in the week in which the adopter is notified of being matched with the child.

PART 4
STATUTORY PATERNITY PAY: PROVISIONS APPLICABLE TO BOTH STATUTORY PATERNITY PAY (BIRTH) AND STATUTORY PATERNITY PAY (ADOPTION)

[2.684]
17 Work during a statutory paternity pay period

(1) Where, in a case where statutory paternity pay is being paid to a person who works during the statutory paternity pay period for an employer who is not liable to pay him statutory paternity pay and who does not fall within paragraph (b) of regulation 10 or, as the case may be, paragraph (b) of regulation 16, there shall be no liability to pay statutory paternity pay in respect of any remaining part of the statutory paternity pay period.

(2) In a case falling within paragraph (1), the person shall notify the person liable to pay statutory paternity pay within 7 days of the first day during which he works during the statutory pay period.

(3) The notification mentioned in paragraph (2) shall be in writing, if the person who has been liable to pay statutory paternity pay so requests.

[2.685]
18 Cases where there is no liability to pay statutory paternity pay

There shall be no liability to pay statutory paternity pay in respect of any week—

(a) during any part of which the person entitled to it is entitled to statutory sick pay under Part 11 of the Act;
(b) following that in which the person claiming it has died; or

(c) during any part of which the person entitled to it is detained in legal custody or sentenced to a term of imprisonment (except where the sentence is suspended), or which is a subsequent week within the same statutory paternity pay period.

[2.686]
19 Statutory paternity pay and contractual remuneration

For the purposes of section 171ZG(1) and (2) of the Act, the payments which are to be treated as contractual remuneration are sums payable under a contract of service—

(a) by way of remuneration;
(b) for incapacity for work due to sickness or injury;
(c) by reason of the birth or adoption of a child.

[2.687]
20 Avoidance of liability for statutory paternity pay

(1) A former employer shall be liable to make payments of statutory paternity pay to a former employee in any case where the employee had been employed for a continuous period of at least 8 weeks and his contract of service was brought to an end by the former employer solely, or mainly, for the purpose of avoiding liability for statutory paternity pay.

(2) In a case falling within paragraph (1)—

(a) the employee shall be treated as if he had been employed for a continuous period ending with the child's birth or, as the case may be, the placement of the child for adoption;
(b) his normal weekly earnings shall be calculated by reference to his normal weekly earnings for the period of 8 weeks ending with the last day in respect of which he was paid under his former contract of service.

PART 5
STATUTORY ADOPTION PAY

[2.688]
21 Adoption pay period

(1) Subject to paragraph (2), a person entitled to statutory adoption pay may choose the adoption pay period to begin—

(a) on the date on which the child is placed with him for adoption or, where he is at work on that day, on the following day;
(b) subject to paragraph (2), on a predetermined date, specified by him, which is no more than 14 days before the date on which the child is expected to be placed with him and no later than that date.

(2) In a case where statutory adoption pay is payable in respect of a child matched with an adopter who is notified of having been matched before 6th April 2003, the statutory adoption pay period shall begin on a predetermined date which is—

(a) on or after 6th April 2003, and
(b) no more than 14 days before the date on which the child is expected to be placed with the adopter.

(3) Subject to paragraph (4), where the choice made is that mentioned in sub-paragraph (b) of paragraph (1) or in a case where paragraph (2) applies, the adoption pay period shall, unless the employer agrees to the adoption pay period beginning earlier, begin no earlier than 28 days after notice under section 171ZL(6) of the Act has been given.

(4) Where the beginning of the adoption pay period determined in accordance with paragraph (3) is later than the date of placement, it shall be the date of placement.

(5) Subject to regulation 22, the duration of any adoption pay period shall be a continuous period of [39] weeks.

(6) A choice made under paragraph (1), or a date specified under paragraph (2), is not irrevocable, but where a person subsequently makes a different choice, section 171ZL(6) of the Act shall apply to it.

NOTES

Para (5): figure in square brackets substituted by the Statutory Paternity Pay and Statutory Adoption Pay (General) and the Statutory Paternity Pay and Statutory Adoption Pay (Weekly Rates) (Amendment) Regulations 2006, SI 2006/2236, regs 3, 4.

[2.689]
22 Adoption pay period in cases where adoption is disrupted

(1) Where—

(a) after a child has been placed for adoption—
(i) the child dies;

(ii) the child is returned to the adoption agency under section 30(3) of the Adoption Act 1976 or [in Scotland, the child is returned to the adoption agency, adoption society or nominated person in accordance with section 25(6) of the Adoption and Children (Scotland) Act 2007], or

(b) the adoption pay period has begun prior to the date the child has been placed for adoption, but the placement does not take place,

the adoption pay period shall terminate in accordance with the provisions of paragraph (2).

(2) The adoption pay period shall, in a case falling within paragraph (1), terminate 8 weeks after the end of the week specified in paragraph (3).

(3) The week referred to in paragraph (2) is—

(a) in a case falling within paragraph (1)(a)(i), the week during which the child dies;

(b) in a case falling within paragraph (1)(a)(ii), the week during which the child is returned;

(c) in a case falling within paragraph (1)(b), the week during which the person with whom the child was to be placed for adoption is notified that the placement will not be made.

(4) For the purposes of paragraph (3), "week" means a period of seven days beginning with Sunday.

NOTES

Para (1): words in square brackets in sub-para (a)(ii) substituted by the Adoption and Children (Scotland) Act 2007 (Consequential Modifications) Order 2011, SI 2011/1740, art 2, Sch 1, Pt 2, para 32(1), (3), as from 15 July 2011.

[2.690]

23 Additional notice requirements for statutory adoption pay

(1) Where a person gives notice under section 171ZL(6) of the Act he shall at the same time give notice of the date on which the child is expected to be placed for adoption.

(2) Where the choice made in accordance with paragraph (1) of regulation 21 and notified in accordance with section 171ZL(6) of the Act is that mentioned in sub-paragraph (a) of that paragraph, the person shall give further notice to the person liable to pay him statutory adoption pay as soon as is reasonably practicable of the date the child is placed for adoption.

[2.691]

24 Evidence of entitlement to statutory adoption pay

(1) A person shall provide evidence of his entitlement to statutory adoption pay by providing to the person who will be liable to pay it—

(a) the information specified in paragraph (2), in the form of one or more documents provided to him by an adoption agency, containing that information;

(b) a declaration that he has elected to receive statutory adoption pay, and not statutory paternity pay (adoption) under Part 12ZA of the Act.

(2) The information referred to in paragraph (1) is—

(a) the name and address of the adoption agency and of the person claiming payment of statutory adoption pay;

(b) the date on which the child is expected to be placed for adoption or, where the child has already been placed for adoption, the date of placement; and

(c) the date on which the person claiming payment of statutory adoption pay was informed by the adoption agency that the child would be placed for adoption with him.

(3) The information and declaration referred to in paragraph (1) shall be provided to the person liable to pay statutory adoption pay at least 28 days before the date chosen as the beginning of the adoption pay period in accordance with paragraph (1) of regulation 21, or, if that is not reasonably practicable, as soon as is reasonably practicable thereafter.

[2.692]

25 Entitlement to statutory adoption pay where there is more than one employer

Statutory adoption pay shall be payable to a person in respect of a week during any part of which he works only for an employer—

(a) who is not liable to pay him statutory adoption pay; and

(b) for whom he has worked in the week in which he is notified of being matched with the child.

[2.693]

26 Work during an adoption pay period

(1) Where, in a case where statutory adoption pay is being paid to a person who works during the adoption pay period for an employer who is not liable to pay him statutory adoption pay and who does not fall within paragraph (b) of regulation 25, there shall be no liability to pay statutory adoption pay in respect of any remaining part of the adoption pay period.

(2) In a case falling within paragraph (1), the person shall notify the person liable to pay statutory adoption pay within 7 days of the first day during which he works during the adoption pay period.

(3) The notification contained in paragraph (2) shall be in writing if the person who has been liable to pay statutory adoption pay so requests.

[2.694]
27 Cases where there is no liability to pay statutory adoption pay

(1) There shall be no liability to pay statutory adoption pay in respect of any week—
- (a) during any part of which the person entitled to it is entitled to statutory sick pay under Part 11 of the Act;
- (b) following that in which the person claiming it has died; or
- (c) subject to paragraph (2), during any part of which the person entitled to it is detained in legal custody or sentenced to a term of imprisonment (except where the sentence is suspended).

(2) There shall be liability to pay statutory adoption pay in respect of any week during any part of which the person entitled to it is detained in legal custody where that person—
- (a) is released subsequently without charge;
- (b) is subsequently found not guilty of any offence and is released; or
- (c) is convicted of an offence but does not receive a custodial sentence.

[2.695]
[27A Working for not more than 10 days during an adoption pay period

In the case where an employee does any work under a contract of service with his employer on any day for not more than 10 such days during his adoption pay period, whether consecutive or not, statutory adoption pay shall continue to be payable to the employee by the employer.]

NOTES

Inserted by the Statutory Paternity Pay and Statutory Adoption Pay (General) and the Statutory Paternity Pay and Statutory Adoption Pay (Weekly Rates) (Amendment) Regulations 2006, SI 2006/2236, regs 3, 5.

[2.696]
28 Statutory adoption pay and contractual remuneration

For the purposes of section 171ZP(4) and (5) of the Act, the payments which are to be treated as contractual remuneration are sums payable under a contract of service—
- (a) by way of remuneration;
- (b) for incapacity for work due to sickness or injury;
- (c) by reason of the adoption of a child.

[2.697]
29 Termination of employment before start of adoption pay period

(1) Where the employment of a person who satisfies the conditions of entitlement to statutory adoption pay terminates for whatever reason (including dismissal) before the adoption pay period chosen in accordance with regulation 21 has begun, the period shall begin 14 days before the expected date of placement or, where the termination occurs on, or within 14 days before, the expected date of placement, on the day immediately following the last day of his employment.

(2) In a case falling within paragraph (1), the notice requirements set out in section 171ZL(6) of the Act and these Regulations shall not apply.

[2.698]
30 Avoidance of liability for statutory adoption pay

(1) A former employer shall be liable to make payments of statutory adoption pay to a former employee in any case where the employee had been employed for a continuous period of at least 8 weeks and his contract of service was brought to an end by the former employer solely, or mainly, for the purpose of avoiding liability for statutory adoption pay.

(2) In a case falling within paragraph (1)—
- (a) the employee shall be treated as if he had been employed for a continuous period ending with the week in which he was notified of having been matched with the child for adoption; and
- (b) his normal weekly earnings shall be calculated by reference to his normal weekly earnings for the period of 8 weeks ending with the last day in respect of which he was paid under his former contract of service.

PART 6
STATUTORY PATERNITY PAY AND STATUTORY ADOPTION PAY: PROVISIONS APPLICABLE TO BOTH STATUTORY PATERNITY PAY AND STATUTORY ADOPTION PAY

[2.699]
31 Introductory

(1) Subject to paragraph (2), the provisions of regulations 32 to 47 below apply to statutory paternity pay payable under Part 12ZA of the Act and to statutory adoption pay payable under 12ZB of the Act.

(2) The provisions of regulation 44 only apply to statutory adoption pay.

[2.700]
32 Treatment of persons as employees

(1) [Subject to paragraph (1A),] in a case where, and in so far as, a person . . . is treated as an employed earner by virtue of the Social Security (Categorisation of Earners) Regulations 1978 he shall be treated as an employee for the purposes of Parts 12ZA and 12ZB of the Act, and in a case where, and in so far as, such a person is treated otherwise than as an employed earner by virtue of those regulations, he shall not be treated as an employee for the purposes of Parts 12ZA and 12ZB of the Act.

[(1A) Paragraph (1) shall have effect in relation to a person who—

(a) is under the age of 16; and

(b) would or, as the case may be, would not have been treated as an employed earner by virtue of the Social Security (Categorisation of Earners) Regulations 1978 had he been over that age,

as it has effect in relation to a person who is or, as the case may be, is not so treated.]

(2) A person who is in employed earner's employment within the meaning of the Act under a contract of apprenticeship shall be treated as an employee for the purposes of Parts 12ZA and 12ZB of the Act.

(3) A person who is in employed earner's employment within the meaning of the Act but whose employer—

(a) does not fulfil the conditions prescribed in regulation 145(1) of the Contributions Regulations in so far as that provision relates to residence or presence in Great Britain; or

(b) is a person who, by reason of any international treaty to which the United Kingdom is a party or of any international convention binding the United Kingdom—

(i) is exempt from the provisions of the Act; or

(ii) is a person against whom the provisions of the Act are not enforceable,

shall not be treated as an employee for the purposes of Parts 12ZA and 12ZB of the Act.

NOTES

Para (1): words in square brackets inserted, and words omitted revoked, by the Employment Equality (Age) Regulations 2006, SI 2006/1031, reg 49(1), Sch 8, Pt 2, paras 59, 60(1), (2).

Para (1A): inserted by SI 2006/1031, reg 49(1), Sch 8, Pt 2, paras 59, 60(1), (3); substituted by the Employment Equality (Age) (Consequential Amendments) Regulations 2007, SI 2007/825, reg 7.

[2.701]
33 Continuous employment

(1) Subject to the following provisions of this regulation, where in any week a person is, for the whole or part of the week—

(a) incapable of work in consequence of sickness or injury;

(b) absent from work on account of a temporary cessation of work;

(c) absent from work in circumstances such that, by arrangement or custom, he is regarded as continuing in the employment of his employer for all or any purposes,

and returns to work for his employer after the incapacity for or absence from work, that week shall be treated for the purposes of sections 171ZA, 171ZB and 171ZL of the Act as part of a continuous period of employment with that employer, notwithstanding that no contract of service exists with that employer in respect of that week.

(2) Incapacity for work which lasts for more than 26 consecutive weeks shall not count for the purposes of paragraph (1)(a).

(3) Where a person—

(a) is an employee in an employed earner's employment in which the custom is for the employer—

(i) to offer work for a fixed period of not more than 26 consecutive weeks;

(ii) to offer work for such period on two or more occasions in a year for periods which do not overlap; and

(iii) to offer the work available to those persons who had worked for him during the last or a recent such period, but

(b) is absent from work because of incapacity arising from some specific disease or bodily or mental disablement,

then in that case paragraph (1) shall apply as if the words "and returns to work for his employer after the incapacity for or absence from work," were omitted and paragraph (4) shall not apply.

(4) Where a person is employed under a contract of service for part only of the relevant week within the meaning of subsection (3) of section 171ZL of the Act (entitlement to statutory adoption pay), the whole of that week shall count in computing a period of continuous employment for the purposes of that section.

[2.702]
34 Continuous employment and unfair dismissal

(1) This regulation applies to a person in relation to whose dismissal an action is commenced which consists—

(a) of the presentation by him of a complaint under section 111(1) of the Employment Rights Act 1996;

(b) of his making a claim in accordance with a dismissals procedure agreement designated by an order under section 110 of that Act; . . .

(c) of any action taken by a conciliation officer under section 18 of the Employment Tribunals Act 1996; [or

(d) of a decision arising out of the use of a statutory dispute resolution procedure contained in Schedule 2 to the Employment Act 2002 in a case where, in accordance with the Employment Act 2002 (Dispute Resolution) Regulations 2004, such a procedure applies].

(2) If, in consequence of an action of the kind specified in paragraph (1), a person is reinstated or re-engaged by his employer or by a successor or associated employer of that employer, the continuity of his employment shall be preserved for the purposes of Part 12ZA or, as the case may be, Part 12ZB of the Act, and any week which falls within the interval beginning with the effective date of termination and ending with the date of reinstatement or re-engagement, as the case may be, shall count in the computation of his period of continuous employment.

(3) In this regulation—

"successor" and "dismissal procedures agreement" have the same meanings as in section 235 of the Employment Rights Act 1996; and

"associated employer" shall be construed in accordance with section 231 of the Employment Rights Act 1996.

NOTES

Para (1): word omitted from sub-para (b) revoked, and sub-para (d) and the word immediately preceding it inserted, by the Statutory Maternity Pay (General) and Statutory Paternity Pay and Statutory Adoption Pay (General) (Amendment) Regulations 2005, SI 2005/358, reg 4.

[2.703]
35 Continuous employment and stoppages of work

(1) Where, for any week or part of a week a person does not work because there is a stoppage of work due to a trade dispute within the meaning of section 35(1) of the Jobseekers Act 1995 at his place of employment, the continuity of his employment shall, subject to paragraph (2), be treated as continuing throughout the stoppage but, subject to paragraph (3), no such week shall count in the computation of his period of employment.

(2) Subject to paragraph (3), where during the stoppage of work a person is dismissed from his employment, the continuity of his employment shall not be treated in accordance with paragraph (1) as continuing beyond the commencement of the day he stopped work.

(3) The provisions of paragraph (1), to the extent that they provide that a week in which the stoppage of work occurred shall not count in the computation of a period of employment, and paragraph (2) shall not apply to a person who proves that at no time did he have a direct interest in the trade dispute in question.

[2.704]
36 Change of employer

A person's employment shall, notwithstanding a change of employer, be treated as continuous employment with the second employer where—

(a) the employer's trade or business or an undertaking (whether or not it is an undertaking established by or under an Act of Parliament) is transferred from one person to another;

(b) by or under an Act of Parliament, whether public or local and whenever passed, a contract of employment between any body corporate and the person is modified and some other body corporate is substituted as his employer;

(c) on the death of his employer, the person is taken into employment of the personal representatives or trustees of the deceased;

(d) the person is employed by partners, personal representatives or trustees and there is a change in the partners, or, as the case may be, personal representatives or trustees;

(e) the person is taken into the employment of an employer who is, at the time he entered his employment, an associated employer of his previous employer, and for this purpose "associated employer" shall be construed in accordance with section 231 of the Employment Rights Act 1996;

(f) on the termination of his employment with an employer he is taken into the employment of another employer and those employers are governors of a school maintained by a [local authority] and that authority.

NOTES

Words in square brackets in para (f) substituted by the Local Education Authorities and Children's Services Authorities (Integration of Functions) (Local and Subordinate Legislation) Order 2010, SI 2010/1172, art 5, Sch 3, para 47, as from 5 May 2010.

[2.705]

37 Reinstatement after service with the armed forces etc

If a person who is entitled to apply to his employer under the Reserve Forces (Safeguard of Employment) Act 1985 enters the employment of that employer within the 6-month period mentioned in section 1(4)(b) of that Act, his previous period of employment with that employer (or if there was more than one such period, the last of those periods) and the period of employment beginning in that 6 month period shall be treated as continuous.

[2.706]

38 Treatment of two or more employers or two or more contracts of service as one

(1) In a case where the earnings paid to a person in respect of two or more employments are aggregated and treated as a single payment of earnings under regulation 15(1) of the Contributions Regulations, the employers of that person in respect of those employments shall be treated as one for the purposes of Part 12ZA or, as the case may be, Part 12ZB of the Act.

(2) Where two or more employers are treated as one under the provisions of paragraph (1), liability for statutory paternity pay or, as the case may be, statutory adoption pay, shall be apportioned between them in such proportions as they may agree or, in default of agreement, in the proportions which the person's earnings from each employment bear to the amount of the aggregated earnings.

(3) Where two or more contracts of service exist concurrently between one employer and one employee, they shall be treated as one for the purposes of Part 12ZA or, as the case may be, Part 12ZB of the Act, except where, by virtue of regulation 14 of the Contributions Regulations, the earnings from those contracts of service are not aggregated for the purposes of earnings-related contributions.

[2.707]

39 Meaning of "earnings"

(1) For the purposes of section 171ZJ(6) (normal weekly earnings for the purposes of Part 12ZA of the Act) and of section 171ZS(6) of the Act (normal weekly earnings for the purposes of Part 12ZB of the Act), the expression "earnings" shall be construed in accordance with the following provisions of this regulation.

(2) The expression "earnings" refers to gross earnings and includes any remuneration or profit derived from a person's employment except any payment or amount which is—

(a) excluded from the computation of a person's earnings under regulation 25 of and Schedule 3 to, and regulation 123 of, the Contributions Regulations (payments to be disregarded) and regulation 27 of those Regulations (payments to directors to be disregarded) [(or would have been so excluded had he not been under the age of 16)];

(b) a chargeable emolument under section 10A of the Act, except where, in consequence of such a chargeable emolument being excluded from earnings, a person would not be entitled to statutory paternity pay or, as the case may be, statutory adoption pay [(or where such a payment or amount would have been so excluded and in consequence he would not have been entitled to statutory paternity pay or, as the case may be, statutory adoption pay had he not been under the age of 16)].

(3) For the avoidance of doubt, "earnings" includes—

[(za) any amount retrospectively treated as earnings by regulations made by virtue of section 4B(2) of the Act;]

(a) any sum payable in respect of arrears of pay in pursuance of an order for reinstatement or re-engagement under the Employment Rights Act 1996;

(b) any sum payable by way of pay in pursuance of an order made under the Employment Rights Act 1996 for the continuation of a contract of employment;

(c) any sum payable by way of remuneration in pursuance of a protective award under section 189 of the Trade Union and Labour Relations (Consolidation) Act 1992;
(d) any sum payable by way of statutory sick pay, including sums payable in accordance with regulations made under section 151(6) of the Act;
(e) any sum payable by way of statutory maternity pay;
(f) any sum payable by way of statutory paternity pay;
(g) any sum payable by way of statutory adoption pay.

NOTES

Para (2): words in square brackets inserted by the Employment Equality (Age) Regulations 2006, SI 2006/1031, reg 49(1), Sch 8, Pt 2, paras 59, 61.

Para (3): sub-para (za) inserted by the Social Security, Occupational Pension Schemes and Statutory Payments (Consequential Provisions) Regulations 2007, SI 2007/1154, reg 6(1), (2).

[2.708]

40 Normal weekly earnings

(1) For the purposes of Part 12ZA and Part 12ZB of the Act, a person's normal weekly earnings shall be calculated in accordance with the following provisions of this regulation.

(2) In this regulation—

"the appropriate date" means—

(a) in relation to statutory paternity pay (birth), the first day of the 14th week before the expected week of the child's birth or the first day in the week in which the child is born, whichever is the earlier;
(b) in relation to statutory paternity pay (adoption) and statutory adoption pay, the first day of the week after the week in which the adopter is notified of being matched with the child for the purposes of adoption;

"normal pay day" means a day on which the terms of a person's contract of service require him to be paid, or the practice in his employment is for him to be paid, if any payment is due to him; and

"day of payment" means a day on which the person was paid.

(3) Subject to paragraph (4), the relevant period for the purposes of section 171ZJ(6) and 171ZS(6) is the period between—

(a) the last normal pay day to fall before the appropriate date; and
(b) the last normal pay day to fall at least 8 weeks earlier than the normal pay day mentioned in sub-paragraph (a),

including the normal pay day mentioned in sub-paragraph (a) but excluding that first mentioned in sub-paragraph (b).

(4) In a case where a person has no identifiable normal pay day, paragraph (3) shall have effect as if the words "day of payment" were substituted for the words "normal pay day" in each place where they occur.

(5) In a case where a person has normal pay days at intervals of or approximating to one or more calendar months (including intervals of or approximating to a year) his normal weekly earnings shall be calculated by dividing his earnings in the relevant period by the number of calendar months in that period (or, if it is not a whole number, the nearest whole number), multiplying the result by 12 and dividing by 52.

(6) In a case to which paragraph (5) does not apply and the relevant period is not an exact number of weeks, the person's normal weekly earnings shall be calculated by dividing his earnings in the relevant period by the number of days in the relevant period and multiplying the result by 7.

(7) In any case where a person receives a back-dated pay increase which includes a sum in respect of a relevant period, normal weekly earnings shall be calculated as if such a sum was paid in that relevant period even though received after that period.

[2.709]

41 Payment of statutory paternity pay and statutory adoption pay

Payments of statutory paternity pay and statutory adoption pay may be made in a like manner to payments of remuneration but shall not include payment in kind or by way of the provision of board or lodgings or of services or other facilities.

[2.710]

42 Time when statutory paternity pay and statutory adoption pay are to be paid

(1) In this regulation, "pay day" means a day on which it has been agreed, or it is the normal practice between an employer or former employer and a person who is or was an employee of his, that payments by way of remuneration are to be made, or, where there is no such agreement or normal practice, the last day of a calendar month.

(2) In any case where—

(a) a decision has been made by an officer of the Board under section 8(1) of the Social Security Contributions (Transfer of Functions, etc) Act 1999 as a result of which a person is entitled to an amount of statutory paternity pay or statutory adoption pay; and
(b) the time for bringing an appeal against the decision has expired and either—
  (i) no such appeal has been brought; or
  (ii) such an appeal has been brought and has been finally disposed of,

that amount of statutory paternity pay or statutory adoption pay shall be paid within the time specified in paragraph (3).

(3) Subject to paragraphs (4) and (5), the employer or former employer shall pay the amount not later than the first pay day after—
(a) where an appeal has been brought, the day on which the employer or former employer receives notification that it has been finally disposed of;
(b) where leave to appeal has been refused and there remains no further opportunity to apply for leave, the day on which the employer or former employer receives notification of the refusal; and
(c) in any other case, the day on which the time for bringing an appeal expires.

(4) Subject to paragraph (5), where it is impracticable, in view of the employer's or former employer's methods of accounting for and paying remuneration, for the requirement of payment referred to in paragraph (3) to be met by the pay day referred to in that paragraph, it shall be met not later than the next following pay day.

(5) Where the employer or former employer would not have remunerated the employee for his work in the week in question as early as the pay day specified in paragraph (3) or (if it applies) paragraph (4), the requirement of payment shall be met on the first day on which the employee would have been remunerated for his work in that week.

[2.711]

43 Liability of the Board to pay statutory paternity pay or statutory adoption pay

(1) Where—
(a) an officer of the Board has decided that an employer is liable to make payments of statutory paternity pay or, as the case may be, statutory adoption pay to a person;
(b) the time for appealing against the decision has expired; and
(c) no appeal against the decision has been lodged or leave to appeal against the decision is required and has been refused,

then for any week in respect of which the employer was liable to make payments of statutory paternity pay or, as the case may be, statutory adoption pay but did not do so, and for any subsequent weeks in the paternity pay period or, as the case may be, adoption pay period, the liability to make those payments shall, notwithstanding sections 171ZD and 171ZM of the Act, be that of the Board and not the employer.

(2) Liability to make payments of statutory paternity pay or, as the case may be, statutory adoption pay shall, notwithstanding sections 171ZD and 171ZM of the Act, be a liability of the Board and not the employer as from the week in which the employer first becomes insolvent until the end of the paternity pay or adoption pay period.

(3) For the purposes of paragraph (2) an employer shall be taken to be insolvent if, and only if—
(a) in England and Wales—
  (i) he has been adjudged bankrupt or has made a composition or arrangement with his creditors;
  (ii) he has died and his estate falls to be administered in accordance with an order made under section 421 of the Insolvency Act 1986; or
  (iii) where an employer is a company or a limited liability partnership, a winding-up order . . . is made or a resolution for a voluntary winding-up is passed (or, in the case of a limited liability partnership, a determination for a voluntary winding-up has been made) with respect to it [or it enters administration], or a receiver or a manager of its undertaking is duly appointed, or possession is taken, by or on behalf of the holders of any debentures secured by a floating charge, of any property of the company or limited liability partnership comprised in or subject to the charge, or a voluntary arrangement proposed for the purposes of Part 1 of the Insolvency Act 1986 is approved under that Part of that Act;
(b) in Scotland—
  (i) an award of sequestration is made on his estate or he executes a trust deed for his creditors or enters into a composition contract;
  (ii) he has died and a judicial factor appointed under section 11A of the Judicial Factors (Scotland) Act 1889 is required by that section to divide his insolvent estate among his creditors; or
  (iii) where the employer is a company or a limited liability partnership, a winding-up order . . . is made or a resolution for voluntary winding-up is passed (or, in the case of a limited liability partnership, a determination for a voluntary winding-up is

made) with respect to it [or it enters administration], or a receiver of its undertaking is duly appointed, or a voluntary arrangement proposed for the purposes of Part 1 of the Insolvency Act 1986 is approved under that Part.

NOTES

Para (3): words omitted revoked, and words in square brackets inserted, by the Enterprise Act 2002 (Insolvency) Order 2003, SI 2003/2096, art 5, Schedule, Pt 2, para 79, except in relation to any case where a petition for an administration order was presented before 15 September 2003.

[2.712]

44 Liability of the Board to pay statutory adoption pay in cases of legal custody or imprisonment

Where—

(a) there is liability to pay statutory adoption pay in respect of a period which is subsequent to the last week falling within paragraph (1)(c) of regulation 27, or

(b) there is liability to pay statutory adoption pay during a period of detention in legal custody by virtue of the provisions of paragraph (2) of that regulation,

that liability shall, notwithstanding section 171ZM of the Act, be that of the Board and not the employer.

[2.713]

45 Payments by the Board

Where the Board become liable in accordance with regulation 43 or 44 to make payments of statutory paternity pay or, as the case may be, statutory adoption pay to a person, the first payment shall be made as soon as reasonably practicable after they become so liable, and payments thereafter shall be made at weekly intervals, by means of an instrument of payment or by such other means as appears to the Board to be appropriate in the circumstance of any particular case.

[2.714]

46 Persons unable to act

(1) Where in the case of any person—

(a) statutory paternity pay or, as the case may be, statutory adoption pay is payable to him or he is alleged to be entitled to it;

(b) he is unable for the time being to act; and

(c) either—

(i) no receiver has been appointed by the Court of Protection with power to receive statutory paternity pay or, as the case may be, statutory adoption pay on his behalf, or

(ii) in Scotland, his estate is not being administered by any tutor, curator or other guardian acting or appointed in terms of law,

the Board may, upon written application to them by a person who, if a natural person, is over the age of 18, appoint that person to exercise, on behalf of the person unable to act, any right to which he may be entitled under Part 12ZA or, as the case may be, Part 12ZB of the Act and to deal on his behalf with any sums payable to him.

(2) Where the Board have made an appointment under paragraph (1)—

(a) they may at any time in their absolute discretion revoke it;

(b) the person appointed may resign his office after having given one month's notice in writing to the Board of his intention to do so; and

(c) the appointment shall terminate when the Board are notified that a receiver or other person to whom paragraph (1)(c) applies has been appointed.

(3) Anything required by Part 12ZA or 12ZB of the Act to be done by or to any person who is unable to act may be done by or to the person appointed under this regulation to act on his behalf, and the receipt of the person so appointed shall be a good discharge to the person's employer or former employer for any sum paid.

[2.715]

47 Service of notices by post

A notice given in accordance with the provisions of these Regulations in writing contained in an envelope which is properly addressed and sent by prepaid post shall be treated as having been given on the day on which it is posted.

FLEXIBLE WORKING (PROCEDURAL REQUIREMENTS) REGULATIONS 2002

(SI 2002/3207)

NOTES

Made: 20 December 2002.
Authority: Employment Rights Act 1996, s 80G(2), (3).
Commencement: 6 April 2003.
See *Harvey* DII(J), J(9).

ARRANGEMENT OF REGULATIONS

[2.716]
1 Citation and commencement

These Regulations may be cited as the Flexible Working (Procedural Requirements) Regulations 2002 and shall come into force on 6th April 2003.

[2.717]
2 Interpretation

(1) In these Regulations—

"the 1996 Act" means the Employment Rights Act 1996;

"application" means an application under section 80F of the 1996 Act (statutory right to request a contract variation);

"contract of employment" means a contract of service or apprenticeship, whether express or implied, and (if it is express) whether oral or in writing;

"contract variation" means a change in the terms and conditions of a contract of employment of a kind specified in section 80F(1)(a) of the 1996 Act;

"electronic communication" means an electronic communication within the meaning of section 15(1) of the Electronic Communications Act 2000;

"employee" means an individual who has entered into or works under (or, where the employment has ceased, worked under) a contract of employment;

"employer" means the person by whom an employee is (or, where the employment has ceased, was) employed;

"worker" means an individual who has entered into or works under (or, where the employment has ceased, worked under)—

(a) a contract of employment, or

(b) any other contract, whether express or implied and (if it is express) whether oral or in writing, whereby the individual undertakes to do or perform personally any work or services for another party to the contract whose status is not by virtue of the contract that of a client or customer of any profession or business undertaking carried on by the individual.

"writing" includes writing delivered by means of electronic communication.

(2) For the purposes of these Regulations, unless the contrary is proved, an application is taken as having been made on the day the application is received.

(3) The reference in paragraph (2) to the day on which an application is received is a reference—

(a) in relation to an application transmitted by electronic communication, to the day on which it is transmitted,

(b) in relation to an application sent by post, to the day on which the application would be delivered in the ordinary course of post.

(4) For the purpose of these Regulations, unless the contrary is proved, a notice is taken as being given—

(a) in relation to a notice transmitted by electronic communication, on the day on which it is transmitted,

(b) in relation to a notice sent by post, the day on which the notice would be delivered in the ordinary course of post.

[2.718]
3 The meeting to discuss an application with an employee

(1) Subject to paragraph (2) and regulation 13, an employer to whom an application for a contract variation is made shall hold a meeting to discuss the application with the employee within 28 days after the date on which the application is made.

(2) Paragraph (1) does not apply where the employer agrees to the application and notifies the employee accordingly in writing within the period referred to in that paragraph.

(3) A notice under paragraph (2) shall specify—
- (a) the contract variation agreed to, and
- (b) the date from which the variation is to take effect.

[2.719]
4

Where a meeting is held to discuss an application the employer shall give the employee notice of his decision on the application within 14 days after the date of the meeting.

[2.720]
5

A notice under regulation 4 shall—
- (a) be in writing,
- (b)
  - (i) where the employer's decision is to agree to the application, specify the contract variation agreed to and state the date on which the variation is to take effect,
  - (ii) where the decision is to refuse the application, state which of the grounds for refusal specified in section 80G(1)(b) of the 1996 Act are considered by the employer to apply, contain a sufficient explanation as to why those grounds apply in relation to the application, and set out the appeal procedure, and
- (c) be dated.

[2.721]
6 Appeals

An employee is entitled to appeal against his employer's decision to refuse an application by giving notice in accordance with regulation 7 within 14 days after the date on which notice of the decision is given.

[2.722]
7

A notice of appeal under regulation 6 shall—
- (a) be in writing,
- (b) set out the grounds of appeal, and
- (c) be dated.

[2.723]
8

(1) Subject to paragraph (2), the employer shall hold a meeting with the employee to discuss the appeal within 14 days after the employee's notice under regulation 6 is given.

(2) Paragraph (1) does not apply where, within 14 days after the date on which notice under regulation 6 is given, the employer—
- (a) upholds the appeal, and
- (b) notifies the employee in writing of his decision, specifying the contract variation agreed to and stating the date from which the contract variation is to take effect.

[2.724]
9

Where a meeting is held to discuss the appeal, the employer shall notify the employee of his decision on the appeal within 14 days after the date of the meeting.

[2.725]
10

Notice under regulation 9 shall—
- (a) be in writing,
- (b)
  - (i) where the employer upholds the appeal, specify the contract variation agreed to and state the date from which the variation is to take effect, or

(ii) where the employer dismisses the appeal, state the grounds for the decision and contain a sufficient explanation as to why those grounds apply, and

(c) be dated.

[2.726]
11

The time and place of a meeting under regulation 3(1) or 8(1) shall be convenient to the employer and the employee.

[2.727]
12 Extension of periods

(1) An employer and an employee may agree to an extension of any of the periods referred to in regulations 3, 4, 6, 8, 9 and 13.

(2) An agreement under paragraph (1) must be recorded in writing by the employer.

(3) The employer's record referred to in paragraph (2) must—

(a) specify what period the extension relates to,
(b) specify the date on which the extension is to end,
(c) be dated, and
(d) be sent to the employee.

[2.728]
13

Where the individual who would ordinarily consider an application is absent from work on annual leave or on sick leave on the day on which the application is made, the period referred to in regulation 3(1) commences on the day the individual returns to work or 28 days after the application is made, whichever is the sooner.

[2.729]
14 Right to be accompanied

(1) This regulation applies where—

(a) a meeting is held under regulation 3(1) or 8(1), and
(b) the employee reasonably requests to be accompanied at the meeting.

(2) Where this regulation applies the employer must permit the employee to be accompanied at the meeting by a single companion who—

(a) is chosen by the employee and is within paragraph (3),
(b) is to be permitted to address the meeting (but not to answer questions on behalf of the employee), and
(c) is to be permitted to confer with the employee during the meeting.

(3) A person comes within this paragraph if he is a worker employed by the same employer as the employee.

(4) If—

(a) an employee has a right under this regulation to be accompanied at a meeting,
(b) his chosen companion will not be available at the time proposed for the meeting by the employer, and
(c) the employee proposes an alternative time which satisfies paragraph (5),

the employer must postpone the meeting to the time proposed by the employee.

(5) An alternative time must—

(a) be convenient for employer, employee and companion, and
(b) fall before the end of the period of seven days beginning with the first day after the day proposed by the employer.

(6) An employer shall permit a worker to take time off during working hours for the purpose of accompanying an employee in accordance with a request under paragraph (1)(b).

(7) Sections 168(3) and (4), 169 and 171 to 173 of the Trade Union and Labour Relations (Consolidation) Act 1992 (time off for carrying out trade union duties) shall apply in relation to paragraph (6) above as they apply in relation to section 168(1) of that Act.

[2.730]
15 Complaint to employment tribunal

(1) An employee may present a complaint to an employment tribunal that his employer has failed, or threatened to fail, to comply with regulation 14(2) or (4).

(2) A tribunal shall not consider a complaint under this regulation in relation to a failure or threat unless the complaint is presented—

(a) before the end of the period of three months beginning with the date of the failure or threat, or

(b) within such further period as the tribunal considers reasonable in a case where it is satisfied that it was not reasonably practicable for the complaint to be presented before the end of that period of three months.

(3) Where a tribunal finds that a complaint under this regulation is well-founded it shall order the employer to pay compensation to the worker of an amount not exceeding two weeks' pay.

(4) Chapter 2 of Part 14 of the 1996 Act (calculation of a week's pay) shall apply for the purposes of paragraph (3); and in applying that Chapter the calculation date shall be taken to be the date on which the relevant meeting took place (or was to have taken place).

(5) The limit in section 227(1) of the Employment Rights Act 1996 (maximum amount of a week's pay) shall apply for the purposes of paragraph (3) above.

NOTES

There is no provision in ss 18 or 21 of the Employment Tribunals Act 1996 respectively for conciliation or complaints under this regulation, or for appeals to the EAT against any determination of an Employment Tribunal of such a complaint.

[2.731]

16 Detriment and dismissal

(1) A person has the right not to be subjected to any detriment by any act, or any deliberate failure to act, by his employer done on the ground that he—

(a) exercised or sought to exercise the right under regulation 14(2) or (4), or

(b) accompanied or sought to accompany an employee pursuant to a request under that regulation.

(2) Section 48 of the 1996 Act shall apply in relation to contraventions of paragraph (1) above as it applies in relation to contraventions of certain sections of that Act.

(3) A person who is dismissed shall be regarded for the purposes of Part 10 of the 1996 Act as unfairly dismissed if the reason (or, if more than one, the principle reason) for the dismissal is that he—

(a) exercised or sought to exercise his right under regulation 14(2) or (4), or

(b) accompanied or sought to accompany an employee pursuant to a request under that regulation.

(4) Sections 108 and 109 of the 1996 Act (qualifying period of employment and upper age limit) shall not apply in relation to paragraph (3) above.

(5) Sections 128 to 132 of the 1996 Act (interim relief) shall apply in relation to dismissal for the reason specified in paragraph 3(a) or (b) above as they apply in relation to dismissal for a reason specified in section 128(1)(b) of that Act.

(6) In the application of Chapter 2 of Part 10 of the 1996 Act in relation to paragraph (3) above, a reference to an employee shall be taken as a reference to a worker.

NOTES

"Sections 108 and 109 of the 1996 Act": section 109 was repealed by the Employment Equality (Age) Regulations 2006, SI 2006/1031, reg 49(1), Sch 8, Pt 1, para 25, but there has been no corresponding amendment to para (4) above.

[2.732]

17 Withdrawal of application by the employee

(1) An employer shall treat an application as withdrawn where the employee has—

(a) notified to him whether orally or in writing that he is withdrawing the application,

(b) without reasonable cause, failed to attend a meeting under regulation 3(1) or 8(1) more than once, or

(c) without reasonable cause, refused to provide the employer with information the employer requires in order to assess whether the contract variation should be agreed to.

(2) An employer shall confirm the withdrawal of the application to the employee in writing unless the employee has provided him with written notice of the withdrawal under paragraph 1(a).

FLEXIBLE WORKING (ELIGIBILITY, COMPLAINTS AND REMEDIES) REGULATIONS 2002

(SI 2002/3236)

NOTES

Made: 31 December 2002.
Authority: Employment Rights Act 1996, ss 80F(1)(b), (5), (8)(a), 80H(3)(b), 80I(3).
Commencement: 6 April 2003.
See *Harvey* DII(J), J(9).

ARRANGEMENT OF REGULATIONS

[2.733]
1 Citation and commencement

These Regulations may be cited as the Flexible Working (Eligibility, Complaints and Remedies) Regulations 2002 and shall come into force on 6th April 2003.

[2.734]
2 Interpretation

(1) In these Regulations—

"the 1996 Act" means the Employment Rights Act 1996;

"the Procedure Regulations" means the Flexible Working (Procedural Requirements) Regulations 2002;

["adopter", in relation to a child, means—

(a) a person with whom an adoption agency has decided the child should be placed for adoption, or

(b) a person who has given notice of his intention to apply for an adoption order as required by section 44 of the Adoption and Children Act 2002 or [section 18 of the Adoption and Children (Scotland) Act 2007];]

["adoption agency" means an adoption agency within the meaning of section 2 of the Adoption and Children Act 2002, Article 3(3) of the Adoption (Northern Ireland) Order 1987 or [section 119(1) of the Adoption and Children (Scotland) Act 2007];]

"application" means an application under section 80F of the 1996 Act (statutory right to request contract variation);

"contract of employment" means a contract of service or apprenticeship, whether express or implied, and (if it is express) whether oral or in writing;

"contract variation", means a change in the terms and conditions of a contract of employment of a kind specified in section 80F(1)(a) of the 1996 Act;

["disabled" means entitled to a disability living allowance within the meaning of section 71 of the Social Security Contributions and Benefits Act 1992 [or armed forces independence payment under the Armed Forces and Reserve Forces (Compensation Scheme) Order 2011] [or personal independence payment under Part 4 of the Welfare Reform Act 2012];]

"electronic communication" means an electronic communication within the meaning of section 15(1) of the Electronic Communications Act 2000;

"employee" means an individual who has entered into or works under (or, where the employment has ceased, worked under) a contract of employment;

"employer" means the person by whom an employee is (or, where the employment has ceased, was) employed;

"foster parent" means a foster parent within the meaning of regulation 2(1) of the Fostering Services Regulations 2002 or a foster carer within the meaning of regulation 2(1) of the Fostering of Children (Scotland) Regulations 1996;

"guardian" means a person appointed as a guardian under section 5 of the Children Act 1989 or section 7 or 11 of the Children (Scotland) Act 1995;

["partner" means the other member of a couple consisting of—

(a) a man and a woman who are not married to each other but are living together as if they were husband and wife, or

(b) two people of the same sex who are not civil partners of each other but are living together as if they were civil partners;]

["private foster carer" means a person fostering a child privately within the meaning of section 66 of the Children Act 1989 or an individual other than a parent of the child who maintains the child as a foster child for the purposes of the Foster Children (Scotland) Act 1984, or otherwise looks after the child in circumstances in which that Act applies by virtue of section 17 of that Act;]

["relative" means a mother, father, adopter, guardian, special guardian, parent-in-law, step-parent, son, step-son, [son-in-law,] daughter, step-daughter, [daughter-in-law,] brother, step-brother, brother-in-law, sister, step-sister, sister-in-law, uncle, aunt or grandparent, and includes adoptive relationships and relationships of the full blood or half blood or, in the case of an adopted person, such of those relationships as would exist but for the adoption;

["residence order" means a residence order as defined by section 8(1) of the Children Act 1989 or section 11(2)(c) of the Children (Scotland) Act 1995;]

"special guardian", means a person appointed as a special guardian under section 14A of the Children Act 1989;]

"writing" includes writing delivered by means of electronic communication.

[(2) A reference in any provision of these Regulations to a period of continuous employment is to a period computed in accordance with Chapter 1 of Part 14 of the 1996 Act, as if the provision were a provision of that Act.]

(3) . . .

NOTES

Para (1) is amended as follows:

Definition "adopter" substituted, and definitions "adoption agency", "private foster carer" and "residence order" inserted, by the Flexible Working (Eligibility, Complaints and Remedies) (Amendment) (No 2) Regulations 2007, SI 2007/2286, regs 2, 3.

Words in square brackets in definitions "adopter" and "adoption agency" substituted by the Adoption and Children (Scotland) Act 2007 (Consequential Modifications) Order 2011, SI 2011/1740, art 2, Sch 1, Pt 2, para 33(1), (2), as from 15 July 2011.

Definitions "disabled", "relative" and "special guardian" inserted, and definition "partner" substituted, by the Flexible Working (Eligibility, Complaints and Remedies) (Amendment) Regulations 2006, SI 2006/3314, regs 2, 3(1), (2).

In definition "disabled", words in first pair of square brackets inserted by the Armed Forces and Reserve Forces Compensation Scheme (Consequential Provisions: Subordinate Legislation) Order 2013, SI 2013/591, art 7, Schedule, para 28, as from 8 April 2013, and words in second pair of square brackets inserted by the Personal Independence Payment (Supplementary Provisions and Consequential Amendments) Regulations 2013, SI 2013/388, reg 8, Schedule, Pt 2, para 32, as from 8 April 2013.

Words in square brackets in definition "relative" inserted by the Flexible Working (Eligibility, Complaints and Remedies) (Amendment) Regulations 2007, SI 2007/1184, regs 2, 3.

Para (2): substituted by SI 2006/3314, regs 2, 3(1), (3).

Para (3): revoked by SI 2006/3314, regs 2, 3(1), (4).

[2.735]

3 Entitlement to request a contract variation [to care for a child]

(1) An employee is entitled to make an application to his employer for a contract variation [to enable him, in accordance with section 80F(1)(b)(i) of the 1996 Act, to care for a child] if he—

(a) has been continuously employed for a period of not less than 26 weeks;

[(b) is either—

(i) the mother, father, adopter, guardian, special guardian, foster parent or private foster carer of, or a person in whose favour a residence order is in force in respect of, the child; or

(ii) married to, the civil partner of or the partner of—

(aa) the child's mother, father, adopter, guardian, special guardian, foster parent or private foster carer, or

(bb) a person in whose favour a residence order is in force in respect of the child;]

(c) has, or expects to have responsibility for the upbringing of the child.

(2) . . .

NOTES

Regulation heading: words in square brackets inserted by the Flexible Working (Eligibility, Complaints and Remedies) (Amendment) Regulations 2006, SI 2006/3314, regs 2, 4(1), (2).

Para (1): first words in square brackets inserted by SI 2006/3314, regs 2, 4(1), (3); sub-para (b) substituted by the Flexible Working (Eligibility, Complaints and Remedies) (Amendment) (No 2) Regulations 2007, SI 2007/2286, regs 2, 4.

Para (2): revoked by SI 2006/3314, regs 2, 4(1), (5).

[2.736]

[3A Age of child

An application under regulation 3 must be made before the day on which the child concerned reaches the age of 17 or, if disabled, 18.]

NOTES

Commencement: 6 April 2009.

Inserted, together with reg 3B, by the Flexible Working (Eligibility, Complaints and Remedies) (Amendment) Regulations 2006, SI 2006/3314, regs 2, 5; substituted by the Flexible Working (Eligibility, Complaints and Remedies) (Amendment) Regulations 2009, SI 2009/595, reg 2, as from 6 April 2009.

[2.737]

[3B Entitlement to request a contract variation to care for an adult

An employee is entitled to make an application to his employer for a contract variation to enable him, in accordance with section 80F(1)(b)(ii) of the 1996 Act, to care for a person aged 18 or over if the employee—

(a) has been continuously employed for a period of not less than 26 weeks;

(b) is or expects to be caring for a person in need of care who is either—

(i) married to or the partner or civil partner of the employee;

(ii) a relative of the employee; or

(iii) living at the same address as the employee.]

NOTES

Inserted, together with reg 3A, by the Flexible Working (Eligibility, Complaints and Remedies) (Amendment) Regulations 2006, SI 2006/3314, regs 2, 5.

[2.738]

4 Form of the application

An application shall—

(a) be made in writing,

(b) state whether a previous application has been made by the employee to the employer and, if so, when, and

(c) be dated.

[2.739]

5 Date when an application is taken as made

(1) Unless the contrary is proved, an application is taken as having been made on the day the application is received.

(2) The reference in paragraph (1) to the day on which an application is received is a reference—

(a) in relation to an application transmitted by electronic communication, to the day on which it is transmitted,

(b) in relation to an application sent by post, to the day on which the application would be delivered in the ordinary course of post.

[2.740]

6 Breaches of the Procedure Regulations by the employer entitling an employee to make a complaint to an employment tribunal

The breaches of the Procedure Regulations which entitle an employee to make a complaint to an employment tribunal under section 80H of the 1996 Act notwithstanding the fact that his application has not been disposed of by agreement or withdrawn are—

(a) failure to hold a meeting in accordance with regulation 3(1) or 8(1),

(b) failure to notify a decision in accordance with regulation 4 or 9.

[2.741]

7 Compensation

The maximum amount of compensation that an employment tribunal may award under section 80I of the 1996 Act where it finds a complaint by an employee under section 80H of the Act well-founded is 8 weeks' pay.

EMPLOYMENT EQUALITY (RELIGION OR BELIEF) REGULATIONS 2003 (NOTE)

(SI 2003/1660)

[2.742]

NOTES

These Regulations were made on 26 June 2003 under the powers conferred by the European Communities Act 1972, s 2(2). They came into force on 2 December 2003. They implemented Council Directive 2000/78/EC of 27 November 2000 establishing a general framework for equal treatment in employment and occupation (at **[3.300]**) so far as it related to discrimination on grounds of religion or belief. The Regulations made it unlawful to discriminate on grounds of religion or belief in employment and vocational training. They prohibited direct discrimination, indirect discrimination, victimisation and harassment.

The whole of these Regulations were revoked by the Equality Act 2010, s 211(2), Sch 27, Pt 2, as from 1 October 2010. The Equality Act 2010 (Commencement No 4, Savings, Consequential, Transitional, Transitory and Incidental Provisions and Revocation) Order 2010, SI 2010/2317 (at **[2.1558]** et seq) provides for various transitional provisions and savings in connection with the commencement of the 2010 Act and the revocation of these Regulations. See, in particular, art 15 (saving where the act complained of occurs wholly before 1 October 2010), and Sch 3 (savings in relation to work on ships, hovercraft and in relation to seafarers).

EMPLOYMENT EQUALITY (SEXUAL ORIENTATION) REGULATIONS 2003 (NOTE)

(SI 2003/1661)

[2.743]

NOTES

These Regulations were made on 26 June 2003 under the powers conferred by the European Communities Act 1972, s 2(2). They came into force on 1 December 2003. They implemented Council Directive 2000/78/EC of 27 November 2000 establishing a general framework for equal treatment in employment and occupation (at **[3.300]**) so far as it related to discrimination on grounds of sexual orientation. The Regulations made it unlawful to discriminate on grounds of sexual orientation in employment and vocational training. They prohibited direct discrimination, indirect discrimination, victimisation and harassment.

The whole of these Regulations were revoked by the Equality Act 2010, s 211(2), Sch 27, Pt 2, as from 1 October 2010. The Equality Act 2010 (Commencement No 4, Savings, Consequential, Transitional, Transitory and Incidental Provisions and Revocation) Order 2010, SI 2010/2317 (at **[2.1558]** et seq) provides for various transitional provisions and savings in connection with the commencement of the 2010 Act and the revocation of these Regulations. See, in particular, art 15 (saving where the act complained of occurs wholly before 1 October 2010), and Sch 3 (savings in relation to work on ships, hovercraft and in relation to seafarers).

EDUCATION (MODIFICATION OF ENACTMENTS RELATING TO EMPLOYMENT) (ENGLAND) ORDER 2003

(SI 2003/1964)

NOTES

Made: 5 August 2003.

Authority: School Standards and Framework Act 1998, ss 81, 138(7).

Commencement: 1 September 2003.

Extent: this Order applies to England. The equivalent provisions for Wales are in the Education (Modification of Enactments Relating to Employment) (Wales) Order 2006, SI 2006/1073 at **[2.1040]**. There is no equivalent provision for Scotland.

ARRANGEMENT OF ARTICLES

[2.744]

1 Citation, commencement, application and revocation

(1) This Order may be cited as the Education (Modification of Enactments Relating to Employment) (England) Order 2003 and shall come into force on 1st September 2003.

(2) These Regulations apply only in relation to England.

(3) The Education (Modification of Enactments Relating to Employment) Order 1999 is revoked, in relation to England.

[2.745]
2 Interpretation

(1) In this Order—

"the 1996 Act" means the Employment Rights Act 1996;

"the 1998 Act" means the School Standards and Framework Act 1998;

"the 2003 Regulations" mean the School Staffing (England) Regulations 2003;

"authority" means the [local authority] by which a maintained school is, or a proposed school is to be, maintained;

"governing body" means the governing body of a school which is maintained by an authority;

"governing body having a right to a delegated budget" and "school having a delegated budget" have the same meaning as in Part 2 of the 1998 Act.

(2) In this Order references to employment powers are references to the powers of appointment, suspension, conduct and discipline, capability and dismissal of staff conferred by the 2003 Regulations.

NOTES

Para (1): words in square brackets in definition "authority" substituted by the Local Education Authorities and Children's Services Authorities (Integration of Functions) (Local and Subordinate Legislation) Order 2010, SI 2010/1172, art 4(3)(a), as from 5 May 2010.

[2.746]
3 General modifications of employment enactments

(1) In their application to a governing body having a right to a delegated budget, the enactments set out in the Schedule have effect as if—

(a) any reference to an employer (however expressed) included a reference to the governing body acting in the exercise of its employment powers and as if that governing body had at all material times been such an employer;

(b) in relation to the exercise of the governing body's employment powers, employment by the authority at a school were employment by the governing body of the school;

(c) references to employees were references to employees at the school in question;

(d) references to dismissal by an employer included references to dismissal by the authority following notification of a determination by a governing body under regulation 18(1) of the 2003 Regulations; and

(e) references to trade unions recognised by an employer were references to trade unions recognised by the authority or the governing body.

(2) Paragraph (1) does not cause the exemption in respect of an employer with fewer employees than is specified in section 7(1) of the Disability Discrimination Act 1995 to apply (without prejudice to whether it applies irrespective of that paragraph).

[2.747]
4

Without prejudice to the generality of article 3, where an employee employed at a school having a delegated budget is dismissed by the authority following notification of such a determination as is mentioned in article 3(1)(d)—

(a) section 92 of the 1996 Act has effect as if the governing body had dismissed him and as if references to the employer's reasons for dismissing the employee were references to the reasons for which the governing body made its determination; and

(b) Part X of the 1996 Act has effect in relation to the dismissal as if the governing body had dismissed him, and the reason or principal reason for which the governing body did so had been the reason or principal reason for which it made its determination.

[2.748]
5 Trade disputes

(1) Subject to paragraph (2), a dispute between staff employed to work at a school having a delegated budget and the school's governing body, which relates wholly or mainly to one of the matters set out in section 244(1) of the Trade Union and Labour Relations (Consolidation) Act 1992 is a trade dispute within the meaning of that Act.

(2) In any case where there is a trade dispute only by virtue of this article, nothing in section 219 of that Act prevents an act from being actionable in tort where the inducement, interference or threat mentioned in that section relates to a contract the performance of which does not affect directly or indirectly the school over which the governing body in question exercises its functions.

[2.749]

6 Applications to Employment Tribunals

(1) Without prejudice to articles 3 and 4, and notwithstanding any provision in the Employment Tribunals Act 1996 and any regulations made under section 1(1) of that Act, this article applies in respect of any application to an employment tribunal, and any proceedings pursuant to such an application, in relation to which by virtue of article 3 or 4 a governing body is to be treated as if it were an employer (however expressed).

(2) The application must be made, and the proceedings must be carried on, against that governing body.

(3) Notwithstanding paragraph (2), any decision, declaration, order, recommendation or award made in the course of such proceedings except in so far as it requires reinstatement or re-engagement has effect as if made against the authority.

(4) Where any application is made against a governing body under paragraph (2)—

(a) the governing body must notify the authority within 14 days of receiving notification; and

(b) the authority, on written application to the employment tribunal, is entitled to be made an additional party to the proceedings and to take part in the proceedings accordingly.

SCHEDULE

Article 3

[2.750]

Sex Discrimination Act 1975
sections 6, 7, 9, 41 and 82(1A)

Race Relations Act 1976
sections 4, 5, 7 and 32

Trade Union and Labour Relations (Consolidation) Act 1992
sections 146, 147, 152–154 and 181–185

Disability Discrimination Act 1995
sections 4–6, 11, 12, 16, 55, 57 and 58

Employment Rights Act 1996
sections 66–68, 70, 71, 92, 93 and Part X

[Employment Act 2002
sections 29–32 and Schedules 2–4].

NOTES

Entry relating to the "Employment Act 2002" inserted by the Education (Modification of Enactments Relating to Employment) (England) (Amendment) Order 2004, SI 2004/2325, art 2. Note that these provisions of the 2002 Act were repealed by the Employment Act 2008, as from 6 April 2009 (for transitional provisions and savings in connection with the repeal, see the Employment Act 2008 (Commencement No 1, Transitional Provisions and Savings) Order 2008, SI 2008/3232, Schedule, Pt 1).

Sex Discrimination Act 1975, Race Relations Act 1976, Disability Discrimination Act 1995: repealed by the Equality Act 2010, s 211(2), Sch 27, Pt 1.

CONDUCT OF EMPLOYMENT AGENCIES AND EMPLOYMENT BUSINESSES REGULATIONS 2003

(SI 2003/3319)

NOTES

Made: 17 December 2003.

Authority: Employment Agencies Act 1973, ss 5(1), 6(1), 12(3).

Commencement: 6 April 2004 (all except regs 26(7), 32); 6 July 2004 (regs 26(7), 32).

Only those provisions of most relevance to this work have been included.

ARRANGEMENT OF REGULATIONS

PART I
GENERAL AND INTERPRETATION

PART II
GENERAL OBLIGATIONS

PART III
REQUIREMENTS TO BE SATISFIED BEFORE SERVICES ARE PROVIDED

PART IV
REQUIREMENTS TO BE SATISFIED IN RELATION TO THE INTRODUCTION OR SUPPLY OF A WORK-SEEKER TO A HIRER

PART VI
CLIENT ACCOUNTS AND CHARGES TO WORK-SEEKERS

PART VII
MISCELLANEOUS

SCHEDULES

PART I
GENERAL AND INTERPRETATION

[2.751]
1 Citation and commencement

(1) These Regulations may be cited as the Conduct of Employment Agencies and Employment Businesses Regulations 2003.

(2) With the exception of regulations 26(7) and 32, the Regulations shall come into force on 6th April 2004.

(3) Regulations 26(7) and 32 shall come into force on 6th July 2004.

[2.752]
2 Interpretation

In these Regulations, unless the context otherwise requires—

"the Act" means the Employment Agencies Act 1973;

"advertisement" includes every form of advertising by whatever means;

"agency" means an employment agency as defined in section 13(1) and (2) of the Act and includes a person carrying on an agency, and in the case of a person who carries on both an agency and an employment business means such a person in his capacity in carrying on the agency;

"business day" means a day other than a Saturday or a Sunday, Christmas Day or Good Friday, or a day which is a bank holiday under or by virtue of the Banking and Financial Dealings Act 1971 in that part of Great Britain;

"company" includes any body corporate (whether incorporated in Great Britain or elsewhere) and references to directors and other officers of a company and to voting power at any general meeting of a company have effect in the case of a company incorporated outside Great Britain with any necessary modifications;

"employment business" means an employment business as defined in section 13(1) and (3) of the Act and includes a person carrying on an employment business, and in the case of a person who carries on both an employment business and an agency means such a person in his capacity in carrying on the employment business;

"hirer" means a person (including an employment business) to whom an agency or employment business introduces or supplies or holds itself out as being capable of introducing or supplying a work-seeker;

"publication" means any publication whether in paper or electronic form other than a programme service within the meaning of the Broadcasting Act 1990;

["vulnerable person" means any person who by reason of age, infirmity, illness, disability or any other circumstance is in need of care or attention, and includes any person under the age of eighteen;]

"work-finding services" means services (whether by the provision of information or otherwise) provided—

(a) by an agency to a person for the purpose of finding that person employment or seeking to find that person employment;

(b) by an employment business to an employee of the employment business for the purpose of finding or seeking to find another person, with a view to the employee acting for and under the control of that other person;

(c) by an employment business to a person (the "first person") for the purpose of finding or seeking to find another person (the "second person"), with a view to the first person becoming employed by the employment business and acting for and under the control of the second person;

"work-seeker" means a person to whom an agency or employment business provides or holds itself out as being capable of providing work-finding services.

NOTES

Definition "vulnerable person" inserted by the Conduct of Employment Agencies and Employment Businesses (Amendment) Regulations 2010, SI 2010/1782, regs 2, 3, as from 1 October 2010.

[2.753]

3 The meaning of "connected"

(1) For the purposes of these Regulations a person is connected with—

(a) his spouse [or civil partner] or minor child or stepchild;

(b) any individual who employs him or is his employee;

(c) any person who is in partnership with him;

(d) any company of which he is a director or other officer and any company connected with that company;

(e) in the case of a company—

(i) any person who is a director or other officer of that company;

(ii) any subsidiary or holding company, both as defined in section 736 of the Companies Act 1985, of that company and any person who is a director or other officer, or an employee of any such subsidiary or holding company;

(iii) any company of which the same person or persons have control; and

(f) in the case of a trustee of a trust, a beneficiary of the trust, and any person to whom the terms of the trust confer a power that may be exercised for that person's benefit.

(2) For the purposes of paragraph (1)(e)(iii) a person is to be taken as having control of a company if—

(a) he or any person with whom he is connected is a director of that company or of another company which has control of it;

(b) the directors of that company or another company which has control of it (or any of them) are accustomed to act in accordance with his directions or instructions; or

(c) he is entitled to exercise, or control the exercise of, one third or more of the voting power at any general meeting of the company or of another company which has control of it.

NOTES

Para (1): words in square brackets in sub-para (a) inserted by the Civil Partnership Act 2004 (Amendments to Subordinate Legislation) Order 2005, SI 2005/2114, art 2(17), Sch 17, para 8.

Stepchild: as to the interpretation of the word "stepchild" in reg 3(1)(a), see the Civil Partnership Act 2004, s 246 and the Civil Partnership Act 2004 (Relationships Arising Through Civil Partnership) Order 2005, SI 2005/3137, art 3(1), Schedule, para 129.

Companies Act 1985, s 736: repealed by the Companies Act 2006, s 1295, Sch 16, as from 1 October 2009. The equivalent section of the 2006 Act is s 1159. There has been no amendment to this section to reflect the change.

[2.754]
4 Transitional and Saving Provisions and Revocation

(1) The transitional and saving provisions in Schedule 1 shall apply.

(2) Subject to the provisions of Schedule 1, the following statutory instruments are hereby revoked—

(a) the Conduct of Employment Agencies and Employment Businesses Regulations 1976;
(b) the Employment Agencies Act 1973 (Charging Fees to Workers) Regulations 1976; and
(c) the Employment Agencies Act 1973 (Charging Fees to Au Pairs) Regulations 1981.

PART II
GENERAL OBLIGATIONS

[2.755]
5 [Restriction on use of additional services]

[(1)] Neither an agency nor an employment business may make the provision to a work-seeker of work-finding services conditional upon the work-seeker—

(a) using other services for which the Act does not prohibit the charging of a fee, or
(b) hiring or purchasing goods,

whether provided by the agency or the employment business or by any person with whom the agency or employment business is connected.

[(2) Where the work-seeker uses services for which the Act does not prohibit the charging of a fee, an agency or employment business providing or making provision for such services shall ensure that the work-seeker is able to cancel or withdraw from those services at any time without incurring any detriment or penalty, subject to the work-seeker giving to the provider of those services in paper form or by electronic means notice of five business days or, for services relating to the provision of living accommodation, notice of ten business days.]

[(3) In addition, where the work-seeker is seeking employment as an actor, background artist, dancer, extra, musician, singer or other performer or as a photographic or fashion model and that work-seeker uses a service, for which the Act does not prohibit the charging of a fee, which includes the production of a photographic image or audio or video recording of the work-seeker, an agency or employment business providing or making provision for such service shall ensure that, for 30 days from the date of the agency or employment business entering into a contract for such a service whether written or oral—

(a) the agency or the employment business shall not charge a fee to a work-seeker for that part of the service which consists of providing or making provision for a photographic image or audio or video recording of the work-seeker; and
(b) the work-seeker shall be entitled without detriment or penalty to cancel or withdraw from any contract with the agency or employment business for such a service with immediate effect by informing the agency or employment business of cancellation or withdrawal and where the work-seeker informs the agency or employment business of cancellation or withdrawal the work-seeker has no obligation to make any payment under the contract.

(4) Paragraphs (2) and (3) do not apply to a service for which a fee may be charged by virtue of regulation 26(1).]

NOTES

Regulation heading substituted, para (1) numbered as such, and para (2) added, by the Conduct of Employment Agencies and Employment Businesses (Amendment) Regulations 2007, SI 2007/3575, regs 2, 3.

Paras (3), (4) added by the Conduct of Employment Agencies and Employment Businesses (Amendment) Regulations 2010, SI 2010/1782, regs 2, 4, as from 1 October 2010.

[2.756]
6 Restriction on detrimental action relating to work-seekers working elsewhere

(1) Neither an agency nor an employment business may (whether by the inclusion of a term in a contract with a relevant work-seeker or otherwise)—

(a) subject or threaten to subject a relevant work-seeker to any detriment on the ground that—
    (i) the relevant work-seeker has terminated or given notice to terminate any contract between the work-seeker and the agency or employment business, or
    (ii) in the case of an employment business, the relevant work-seeker has taken up or proposes to take up employment with any other person; or
(b) require the relevant work-seeker to notify the agency or the employment business, or any person with whom it is connected, of the identity of any future employer of the relevant work-seeker.

(2) For the avoidance of doubt, the following shall not constitute a detriment within the meaning of paragraph (1)(a)—

(a) the loss of any benefits to which the relevant work-seeker might have become entitled had he not terminated the contract;

(b) the recovery of losses incurred by an agency or employment business as a result of the failure of the relevant work-seeker to perform work he has agreed to perform; or

(c) a requirement in a contract with the agency or employment business for the work-seeker to give a period of notice which is reasonable to terminate the contract.

(3) In this regulation, "relevant work-seeker" means any work-seeker other than, in the case of an employment business, a work-seeker who is or will be employed by the employment business under a contract of service or apprenticeship.

[2.757]
7 Restriction on providing work-seekers in industrial disputes

(1) Subject to paragraph (2) an employment business shall not introduce or supply a work-seeker to a hirer to perform—

(a) the duties normally performed by a worker who is taking part in a strike or other industrial action ("the first worker"), or

(b) the duties normally performed by any other worker employed by the hirer and who is assigned by the hirer to perform the duties normally performed by the first worker,

unless in either case the employment business does not know, and has no reasonable grounds for knowing, that the first worker is taking part in a strike or other industrial action.

(2) Paragraph (1) shall not apply if, in relation to the first worker, the strike or other industrial action in question is an unofficial strike or other unofficial industrial action for the purposes of section 237 of the Trade Union and Labour Relations (Consolidation) Act 1992.

[2.758]
8 Restriction on paying work-seekers' remuneration

(1) Subject to paragraph (2), an agency shall not, in respect of a work-seeker whom the agency has introduced or supplied to a hirer—

(a) pay to;

(b) make arrangements for the payment to; or

(c) introduce or refer the hirer to any person with whom the agency is connected with a view to that person paying to, or making arrangements for the payment to,

the work-seeker, his remuneration arising from the employment with the hirer.

(2) Paragraph (1) shall not apply in the case of an introduction or supply of a work-seeker to a hirer where—

(a)

(i) the agency is permitted by regulation 26(1) to charge a fee to that work-seeker in respect of that introduction or supply; and

(ii) the agency complies with the provisions of regulation 25 and Schedule 2; or

(b) the hirer and the agency are connected.

[2.759]
9 Restriction on agencies and employment businesses purporting to act on a different basis

(1) Neither an agency nor an employment business may, in relation to the introduction or supply of a work-seeker to a hirer, purport to the work-seeker to be acting as an agency and purport to the hirer to be acting as an employment business.

(2) Neither an agency nor an employment business may, in relation to the introduction or supply of a work-seeker to a hirer, purport to the work-seeker to be acting as an employment business and purport to the hirer to be acting as an agency.

[2.760]
10 Restriction on charges to hirers

(1) Any term of a contract between an employment business and a hirer which is contingent on a work-seeker taking up employment with the hirer or working for the hirer pursuant to being supplied by another employment business is unenforceable by the employment business in relation to that work-seeker unless the contract provides that instead of a transfer fee the hirer may by notice to the employment business elect for a hire period of such length as is specified in the contract during which the work-seeker will be supplied to the hirer—

(a) in a case where there has been no supply, on the terms specified in the contract; or

(b) in any other case, on terms no less favourable to the hirer than those which applied immediately before the employment business received the notice.

(2) In paragraph (1), "transfer fee" means any payment in connection with the work-seeker taking up employment with the hirer or in connection with the work-seeker working for the hirer pursuant to being supplied by another employment business.

(3) Any term as mentioned in paragraph (1) is unenforceable where the employment business does not supply the work-seeker to the hirer, in accordance with the contract, for the duration of the hire period referred to in paragraph (1) unless the employment business is in no way at fault.

(4) Any term of a contract between an employment business and a hirer which is contingent on any of the following events, namely a work-seeker—

- (a) taking up employment with the hirer;
- (b) taking up employment with any person (other than the hirer) to whom the hirer has introduced him; or
- (c) working for the hirer pursuant to being supplied by another employment business,

is unenforceable by the employment business in relation to the event concerned where the work-seeker begins such employment or begins working for the hirer pursuant to being supplied by another employment business, as the case may be, after the end of the relevant period.

(5) In paragraph (4), "the relevant period" means whichever of the following periods ends later, namely—

- (a) the period of 8 weeks commencing on the day after the day on which the work-seeker last worked for the hirer pursuant to being supplied by the employment business; or
- (b) subject to paragraph (6), the period of 14 weeks commencing on the first day on which the work-seeker worked for the hirer pursuant to the supply of that work-seeker to that hirer by the employment business.

(6) In determining for the purposes of paragraph (5)(b) the first day on which the work-seeker worked for the hirer pursuant to the supply of that work-seeker to that hirer by the employment business, no account shall be taken of any supply that occurred prior to a period of more than 42 days during which that work-seeker did not work for that hirer pursuant to being supplied by that employment business.

(7) An employment business shall not—

- (a) seek to enforce against the hirer, or otherwise seek to give effect to, any term of a contract which is unenforceable by virtue of paragraph (1), (3) or (4); or
- (b) otherwise directly or indirectly request a payment to which by virtue of this regulation the employment business is not entitled.

[2.761]

11 Entering into a contract on behalf of a client

(1) An employment business shall not enter into, nor purport to enter into, a contract—

- (a) on behalf of a work-seeker, with a hirer; or
- (b) on behalf of a hirer, with a work-seeker.

(2) An agency shall not enter into, nor purport to enter into, a contract—

- (a) on behalf of a work-seeker, with a hirer; or
- (b) on behalf of a hirer, with a work-seeker,

unless the requirements in paragraph (3) are satisfied.

(3) The requirements referred to in paragraph (2) are that—

- (a) the person for whom the agency acts has appointed the agency as his agent with authority to enter into the contract on his behalf; and
- (b) where the agency acts for the work-seeker, it is permitted by regulation 26(1) to charge a fee in relation to the introduction or supply to which the contract relates.

(4) Where an agency enters into a contract on behalf of a work-seeker with a hirer, or on behalf of a hirer with a work-seeker, the agency shall ensure that the terms of the contract are notified to the party on whose behalf the agency entered into the contract, as soon as is reasonably practicable and in any event no later than the end of the fifth business day following the day on which the agency entered into the contract.

(5) Where an agency enters into a contract on behalf of a work-seeker with a hirer, or on behalf of a hirer with a work-seeker, the agency shall ensure that the terms of the contract are notified to the party or parties to the contract other than the party on whose behalf the contract was entered into, as soon as is reasonably practicable and in any event no later than the end of the fifth business day following the day on which the agency entered into the contract.

(6) An agency shall not enter into a contract between a work-seeker and a hirer on behalf of both the work-seeker and the hirer.

[2.762]

12 Prohibition on employment businesses withholding payment to work-seekers on certain grounds

An employment business shall not, in respect of a work-seeker whom it supplies to a hirer, withhold or threaten to withhold from the work-seeker (whether by means of the inclusion of a term in a contract with the work-seeker or otherwise) the whole or any part of any payment in respect of any work done by the work-seeker on any of the following grounds—

(a) non-receipt of payment from the hirer in respect of the supply of any service provided by the employment business to the hirer;
(b) the work-seeker's failure to produce documentary evidence authenticated by the hirer of the fact that the work-seeker has worked during a particular period of time, provided that this provision shall not prevent the employment business from satisfying itself by other means that the work-seeker worked for the particular period in question;
(c) the work-seeker not having worked during any period other than that to which the payment relates; or
(d) any matter within the control of the employment business.

PART III
REQUIREMENTS TO BE SATISFIED BEFORE SERVICES ARE PROVIDED

[2.763]
13 Notification of charges and the terms of offers

(1) Subject to paragraph (2), on the first occasion that an agency or employment business offers to provide or arrange the provision of a service to a work-seeker, the agency or employment business shall give notice to the work-seeker stating—

(a) whether that service is a work-finding service for which the Act prohibits the agency or employment business from charging a fee; and
(b) whether any other services or goods which may be provided by the agency or employment business or any other person are services or goods for which the agency or employment business or other person providing them will or may charge a fee, together with details of any such fee including—
  (i) the amount or method of calculation of the fee;
  (ii) the identity of the person to whom the fee is or will be payable;
  (iii) a description of the services or goods to which the fee relates [and a statement of the work-seeker's right to cancel or withdraw from the service [and, as the case may be, of the notice period required under paragraph (2) of regulation 5 or of the period during which the right under paragraph (3) of that regulation can be exercised]]; and
  (iv) the circumstances, if any, in which refunds or rebates are payable to the work-seeker, the scale of such refunds or rebates, and if no refunds or rebates are payable, a statement to that effect.

(2) Paragraph (1) shall apply only where one or more services or goods referred to in paragraph (1)(b) for which the work-seeker will or may be charged a fee may be provided to the work-seeker.

(3) An agency or employment business shall give a further notice to a work-seeker stating the matters referred to in paragraph (1)(b) where, subsequent to the first occasion that it offers to provide or arrange the provision of a service to the work-seeker, the agency or employment business or the person providing to the work-seeker any services or goods referred to in paragraph 1(b), introduces or varies any fees in relation to any services or goods referred to in paragraph 1(b).

(4) Where an agency or employment business offers any gift or makes an offer of any benefit to a work-seeker, in order to induce him to engage the agency or employment business to provide him with services, the agency or employment business shall notify the work-seeker of the terms on which the gift or benefit is offered before the offer is open for acceptance by the work-seeker.

NOTES

Para (1): words in first (outer) pair of square brackets in sub-para (b)(iii) inserted by the Conduct of Employment Agencies and Employment Businesses (Amendment) Regulations 2007, SI 2007/3575, regs 2, 4; words in second (inner) pair of square brackets in that sub-paragraph substituted by the Conduct of Employment Agencies and Employment Businesses (Amendment) Regulations 2010, SI 2010/1782, regs 2, 5, as from 1 October 2010.

[2.764]
[14 Requirement to obtain agreement to terms with work-seekers: Employment Businesses

(1) Before first providing any work-finding services to a work-seeker, an employment business shall obtain the agreement of the work-seeker to the terms which apply or will apply as between the employment business and the work-seeker including—

(a) a statement that the employment business will operate as an employment business in relation to the work-seeker;
(b) the type of work the employment business will find or seek to find for the work-seeker; and
(c) the terms referred to in regulation 15.

(2) Subject to paragraph (3), an employment business shall ensure that—

(a) all terms in respect of which the employment business has obtained the work-seeker's agreement are recorded in a single document or, where this is not possible, in more than one document; and

(b) copies of all such documents are given at the same time as each other by the employment business to the work-seeker before the employment business provides any services to the work-seeker to which the terms contained in such documents relate.

(3) Paragraph (2) shall not apply in the case of an employment business where the work-seeker has been given a written statement of particulars of employment in accordance with Part I of the Employment Rights Act 1996.

(4) An employment business may not vary any terms set out in any document issued in accordance with paragraph (2), unless the work-seeker agrees to the variation.

(5) If the employment business and the work-seeker agree to any variation in the terms set out in any of the documents referred to in paragraph (2), the employment business shall as soon as possible, and in any event no later than the end of the fifth business day following the day on which the employment business and the work-seeker agree to the variation, give to the work-seeker a single document or, where this is not possible, more than one document containing details of the terms as agreed to be varied and stating the date on or after which it is agreed that the varied terms are to take effect.

(6) An employment business may not make the continued provision of any services by it to a work-seeker conditional on the agreement by the work-seeker to any such variation.]

(7) This regulation shall not apply in the case of an agency where the only service provided by the agency to the work-seeker concerned is the provision of information to him in the form of a publication.

NOTES

Commencement: 1 October 2010.

Substituted by the Conduct of Employment Agencies and Employment Businesses (Amendment) Regulations 2010, SI 2010/1782, regs 2, 6, as from 1 October 2010.

[2.765]

15 Content of terms with work-seekers: Employment businesses

In the case of an employment business, the terms to be agreed in accordance with regulation 14 shall include—

(a) whether the work-seeker is or will be employed by the employment business under a contract of service or apprenticeship, or a contract for services, and in either case, the terms and conditions of employment of the work-seeker which apply, or will apply;

(b) an undertaking that the employment business will pay the work-seeker in respect of work done by him, whether or not it is paid by the hirer in respect of that work;

(c) the length of notice of termination which the work-seeker will be required to give the employment business, and which he will be entitled to receive from the employment business, in respect of particular assignments with hirers;

(d) either—

(i) the rate of remuneration payable to the work-seeker; or

(ii) the minimum rate of remuneration the employment business reasonably expects to achieve for the work-seeker;

(e) details of the intervals at which remuneration will be paid; and

(f) details of any entitlement to annual holidays and to payment in respect of such holidays.

[2.766]

[16 Requirement to obtain agreement to terms with work-seekers and content of terms with work-seekers: Agencies

(1) Before first providing any work-finding services to a work-seeker, for which it is permitted by regulation 26(1) to charge a fee, an agency shall obtain the agreement of the work-seeker to the terms which apply or will apply as between the agency and the work-seeker including—

(a) details of the work-finding services to be provided by the agency;

(b) details of the agency's authority, if any, to act on behalf of the work-seeker, including whether, and if so, upon what terms it is (in accordance with regulation 11) authorised to enter into contracts with hirers on behalf of the work-seeker;

(c) a statement as to whether the agency is authorised to receive money on behalf of the work-seeker;

(d) details of any fee which may be payable by the work-seeker to the agency for work-finding services including—

(i) the amount or method of calculation of the fee,

(ii) a description of the particular work-finding service to which the fee relates,

(iii) the circumstances, if any, in which refunds or rebates are payable to the work-seeker, the scale of such refunds or rebates, and if no refunds or rebates are payable, a statement to that effect, and

(iv) the method of payment of the fee and, if the fee is to be deducted from the work-seeker's earnings received by the agency, the circumstances in which it is to be so deducted;

(e) a statement as to whether the work-seeker is required to give notice to terminate the contract between the work-seeker and the agency and, if so, a statement as to the length of the notice required; and

(f) a statement as to whether the work-seeker is entitled to receive notice of termination of the contract between the work-seeker and the agency and, if so, a statement of the length of the notice.

(2) In the case of an agency which is to provide the work-seeker with work-finding services to which regulation 26(5) applies, before first providing any such work-finding services to the work-seeker, the terms to be agreed, in addition to the terms in paragraph (1), are—

(a) that an agency shall not charge a fee permitted under regulation 26(5) to the work-seeker until the period referred to, as the case may be, in sub-paragraph (d) or (e) of regulation 26(5), during which the work-seeker may withdraw or cancel, has elapsed;

(b) that the work-seeker has the right without detriment or penalty to cancel or withdraw from the contract with immediate effect by informing the agency of such cancellation or withdrawal during the period referred to, as the case may be, in sub-paragraph (d) or (e) of regulation 26(5);

(c) that an agency shall not include information about the work-seeker in a publication until—

(i) where sub-paragraph (d) of regulation 26(5) applies, the period referred to in that sub-paragraph has elapsed or,

(ii) where sub-paragraph (f) of regulation 26(5) applies, the later of, the date on which the period referred to in that sub-paragraph has elapsed or, following an objection, the date on which the reasonable requirements of the work-seeker have been addressed;

(d) in relation to a contract with a work-seeker seeking employment as an actor, background artist, dancer, extra, musician, singer or other performer, under which the agency proposes to include information about the work-seeker in a publication, that—

(i) the agency shall make a copy of the information available to the work-seeker;

(ii) at the same time, the agency shall inform the work-seeker of the right to object, its effect and the time limit for exercising that right; and

(iii) for the period referred to in paragraph (5)(f) of regulation 26, the work-seeker is entitled to object to any aspect of the information relating to the work-seeker by informing the agency of the objection;

(e) in a contract to which sub-paragraph (d) applies, that where the work-seeker informs the agency of an objection, the agency shall not charge a fee or include the information in a publication until the work-seeker's reasonable requirements have been addressed (even if addressing the requirements takes longer than the period referred to in paragraph (5)(f) of regulation 26);

(f) in a contract to which sub-paragraph (d) applies, that where an agency makes available to the work-seeker a copy of the information referred to in that sub-paragraph—

(i) during the period referred to in paragraph (5)(e) of regulation 26, where the period referred to in paragraph (5)(f) of regulation 26 has elapsed without an objection or where the reasonable requirements of the work-seeker have been addressed, paragraph (5)(e) of regulation 26 continues to apply; or

(ii) after the period referred to in paragraph (5)(e) of regulation 26 has elapsed, paragraph (5)(f) of regulation 26 applies from the expiry of that period until the later of, the date on which the period referred to in paragraph (5)(f) of regulation 26 has elapsed or, following an objection, the date on which the reasonable requirements of the work-seeker have been addressed; and

(g) that the work-seeker is entitled to receive a full refund of the fees paid if the publication including, or proposed to include, the work-seeker's information is not produced and made available to potential hirers within 60 days from the date on which payment is made by the work-seeker.

(3) Any reference in paragraph (2) to the inclusion of information about a work-seeker in a publication, includes the inclusion of a photographic image or audio or video recording of the work-seeker in a publication.

(4) Paragraph (3) shall not be construed, when read with paragraph (2), as preventing an agency producing a photographic image or audio or video recording for the purpose of providing a copy of the image or recording to the work-seeker.

(5) An agency shall ensure that—

(a) all terms in respect of which the agency has obtained the work-seeker's agreement are recorded in a single document or, where this is not possible, in more than one document; and

(b) copies of all such documents are given at the same time as each other by the agency to the work-seeker before the agency provides any services to the work-seeker to which the terms contained in such documents relate.

(6) An agency may not vary any terms set out in any document issued in accordance with paragraph (5), unless the work-seeker agrees to the variation.

(7) If the agency and the work-seeker agree to any variation in the terms set out in any of the documents referred to in paragraph (5), the agency shall as soon as possible, and in any event no later than the end of the fifth business day following the day on which the agency and the work-seeker agree to the variation, give to the work-seeker a single document or, where this is not possible, more than one document containing details of the terms as agreed to be varied and stating the date on or after which it is agreed that the varied terms are to take effect.

(8) An agency may not make the continued provision of any services by it to a work-seeker conditional on the agreement by the work-seeker to any such variation.]

NOTES

Commencement: 1 October 2010.

Substituted by the Conduct of Employment Agencies and Employment Businesses (Amendment) Regulations 2010, SI 2010/1782, regs 2, 7, as from 1 October 2010.

[2.767]

[17 Requirement for employment businesses to obtain agreement to terms with hirers

(1) Before first providing services to a hirer, an employment business shall agree with the hirer the terms which apply or will apply between the employment business and the hirer, including—

(a) a statement that the employment business will operate as an employment business in relation to the hirer;

(b) details of any fee which may be payable by the hirer to the employment business including—

(i) the amount or method of calculation of such fee, and

(ii) the circumstances, if any, in which refunds or rebates are payable to the hirer, the scale of such refunds or rebates, and if no refunds or rebates are payable, a statement to that effect; and

(c) details of the procedure to be followed if a work-seeker introduced or supplied to the hirer proves unsatisfactory.

(2) The employment business shall ensure that all of the terms are recorded in one or more documents and that, unless the hirer has a copy, a copy is sent to the hirer as soon as is reasonably practicable.

(3) If the employment business and the hirer agree to any variation in the terms set out in the document referred to in paragraph (2), the employment business shall, unless the hirer has a copy of that document, as soon as is reasonably practicable, give to the hirer a document containing details of the variation and stating the date on or after which it is agreed that the varied terms are to take effect.]

NOTES

Commencement: 1 October 2010.

Substituted by the Conduct of Employment Agencies and Employment Businesses (Amendment) Regulations 2010, SI 2010/1782, regs 2, 8, as from 1 October 2010.

PART IV
REQUIREMENTS TO BE SATISFIED IN RELATION TO THE INTRODUCTION OR SUPPLY OF A WORK-SEEKER TO A HIRER

[2.768]

18 Information to be obtained from a hirer

Neither an agency nor an employment business may introduce or supply a work-seeker to a hirer unless the agency or employment business has obtained sufficient information from the hirer to select a suitable work-seeker for the position which the hirer seeks to fill, including the following information—

(a) the identity of the hirer and, if applicable, the nature of the hirer's business;

(b) the date on which the hirer requires a work-seeker to commence work and the duration, or likely duration, of the work;

(c) the position which the hirer seeks to fill, including the type of work a work-seeker in that position would be required to do, the location at which and the hours during which he would be required to work and any risks to health or safety known to the hirer and what steps the hirer has taken to prevent or control such risks;

(d) the experience, training, qualifications and any authorisation which the hirer considers are necessary, or which are required by law, or by any professional body, for a work-seeker to possess in order to work in the position;

(e) any expenses payable by or to the work-seeker; and

(f) in the case of an agency—

(i) the minimum rate of remuneration and any other benefits which the hirer would offer to a person in the position which it seeks to fill, and the intervals at which the person would be paid; and

(ii) where applicable, the length of notice which a work-seeker in such a position would be required to give, and entitled to receive, to terminate the employment with the hirer.

[2.769]

[19 Confirmation to be obtained about a work-seeker

(1) An employment business may not introduce or supply a work-seeker to a hirer unless it has obtained confirmation—

(a) of the identity of the work-seeker, and

(b) that the work-seeker has the experience, training, qualifications and any authorisation which the hirer considers are necessary, or which are required by law or by any professional body, to work in the position which the hirer seeks to fill.

(2) An agency may not introduce or supply a work-seeker to a hirer with a view to the work-seeker taking up a position which involves working with, caring for or attending a vulnerable person, unless it has obtained confirmation—

(a) of the identity of the work-seeker, and

(b) that the work-seeker has the experience, training, qualifications and any authorisation which the hirer considers are necessary, or which are required by law or by any professional body, to work in the position which the hirer seeks to fill.

(3) Neither an agency nor an employment business may introduce or supply a work-seeker to a hirer unless it has obtained confirmation that the work-seeker is willing to work in the position which the hirer seeks to fill.]

NOTES

Commencement: 1 October 2010.

Substituted by the Conduct of Employment Agencies and Employment Businesses (Amendment) Regulations 2010, SI 2010/1782, regs 2, 9, as from 1 October 2010.

[2.770]

20 Steps to be taken for the protection of the work-seeker and the hirer

(1) Neither an agency nor an employment business may introduce or supply a work-seeker to a hirer unless the agency or employment business has—

(a) taken all such steps, as are reasonably practicable, to ensure that the work-seeker and the hirer are each aware of any requirements imposed by law, or by any professional body, which must be satisfied by the hirer or the work-seeker to enable the work-seeker to work for the hirer in the position which the hirer seeks to fill; and

(b) without prejudice to any of its duties under any enactment or rule of law in relation to health and safety at work, made all such enquiries, as are reasonably practicable, to ensure that it would not be detrimental to the interests of the work-seeker or the hirer for the work-seeker to work for the hirer in the position which the hirer seeks to fill.

(2) Where an employment business receives or obtains information, which gives it reasonable grounds to believe that a work-seeker is unsuitable for the position with a hirer for which the work-seeker is being supplied, it shall, without delay—

(a) inform the hirer of that information; and

(b) end the supply of that work-seeker to the hirer.

(3) Where an employment business receives or obtains information which indicates that a work-seeker may be unsuitable for the position with a hirer for which the work-seeker is being supplied, but where that information does not give it reasonable grounds to believe that the work-seeker is unsuitable, it shall, without delay—

(a) inform the hirer of that information; and

(b) commence making such further enquiries as are reasonably practicable as to the suitability of the work-seeker for the position concerned, and inform the hirer of the enquiries made and any further information it receives or obtains.

(4) Where, as a result of the enquiries made under paragraph (3) an employment business has reasonable grounds to believe that the work-seeker is unsuitable for the position concerned, it shall, without delay—

(a) inform the hirer of that information; and

(b) end the supply of that work-seeker to the hirer.

(5) Where an agency, having introduced a work-seeker to a hirer, receives or obtains information, which indicates that the work-seeker is or may be unsuitable for the position in which the work-seeker has been employed with that hirer, it shall inform the hirer of that information without delay.

(6) Paragraph (5) shall apply for a period of 3 months from the date of introduction of a work-seeker by an agency to a hirer.

(7) In this regulation, "without delay" means on the same day, or where that is not reasonably practicable, on the next business day.

[2.771]

21 Provision of information to work-seekers and hirers

(1) Subject to [paragraphs (3), (4) and (5)], an agency or employment business shall ensure that at the same time as—

- (a) it proposes a particular work-seeker to a hirer—
  - (i) it gives to the hirer (whether orally or otherwise) all information it has been provided with about the matters referred to in regulation 19; and
  - (ii) in the case of an employment business, the information it gives to the hirer (whether orally or otherwise) includes whether the work-seeker to be supplied will be employed by it under a contract of service or apprenticeship or a contract for services;
- (b) it offers a work-seeker a position with a hirer—
  - (i) it gives to the work-seeker (whether orally or otherwise) all information it has been provided with about the matters referred to in paragraphs (a) to (e) and, where applicable, paragraph (f) of regulation 18; and
  - (ii) in the case of an employment business that has not agreed a rate of remuneration in accordance with regulation 15(d)(i), it informs the work-seeker (whether orally or otherwise) of the rate of remuneration it will pay him to work in that position.

(2) Where any of the information referred to in paragraph (1) is not given to the work-seeker or hirer, as the case may be, in paper form or by electronic means at the time referred to in paragraph (1), the agency or employment business shall confirm such information in paper form or by electronic means to the work-seeker or hirer, as the case may be, as soon as possible and in any event no later than the end of the third business day following the day on which it was given to the work-seeker or hirer in accordance with paragraph (1).

(3) Paragraph (1) shall not apply where—

- (a) an agency or employment business intends to introduce or supply a work-seeker to a hirer to work in the same position with that hirer as he has worked within the previous five business days; and
- (b) the information which that agency or employment business would be required to give the work-seeker and hirer by virtue of this regulation (other than that required by regulation 18(b)), would be the same as the information which the work-seeker and hirer have already received,

unless the work-seeker or hirer requests otherwise.

[(4) Subject to paragraphs (3) and (5), where an employment business intends to introduce or supply a work-seeker to a hirer for an assignment of five consecutive business days' duration or less—

- (a) paragraph (1)(a)(i) may be satisfied by the employment business giving to the hirer (whether orally or otherwise) the name of the work-seeker to be supplied and a written confirmation by the employment business that it has complied with regulation 19; and
- (b) paragraph (1)(b) may be satisfied, where the employment business has previously provided the work-seeker with the information referred to under that paragraph and that information remains unchanged, by the employment business giving to the work-seeker in paper form or by electronic means the information referred to in regulation 18(a) and (b).

(5) Where, after it has started, an assignment to which paragraph (4) applies is extended beyond a duration of five business days, the information referred to in paragraph (1) which has not already been provided shall be provided in paper form or by electronic means by the end of the eighth business day of the assignment, or by the end of the assignment if sooner.]

NOTES

Para (1): words in square brackets substituted by the Conduct of Employment Agencies and Employment Businesses (Amendment) Regulations 2007, SI 2007/3575, regs 2, 5(a).

Paras (4), (5): added by SI 2007/3575, regs 2, 5(b).

[2.772]

[22 Additional requirements where professional qualifications or authorisation are required or where work-seekers are to work with vulnerable persons

(1) Where the work-seeker is to be supplied or introduced to a hirer with a view to taking up a position which involves working with, caring for or attending a vulnerable person, neither an agency nor an employment business may introduce or supply the work-seeker to a hirer unless, in addition to the requirements in regulations 18 to 21, the requirements in paragraph (2) are satisfied.

(2) The requirements referred to in paragraph (1) are that the agency or employment business has—

(a) subject to paragraph (3), obtained copies of any relevant qualifications or authorisations of the work-seeker and offered to provide copies of those documents to the hirer;

(b) subject to paragraph (3), obtained two references from persons who are not relatives of the work-seeker and who have agreed that the reference provided may be disclosed to the hirer, and the agency or employment business has offered to provide copies of those references to the hirer; and

(c) taken all other reasonably practicable steps to confirm that the work-seeker is suitable for the position concerned.

(3) (3) Where the agency or employment business has taken all reasonably practicable steps to comply with the requirements in paragraph (2) and has been unable to do so fully, it may instead—

(a) comply with those requirements to the extent that it is able to do so;

(b) inform the hirer that it has taken all reasonably practicable steps to comply fully with those requirements and has been unable to do so; and

(c) inform the hirer of the details of the steps that it has taken in order to try and comply fully with those requirements.

(4) Where the work-seeker is required by law, or any professional body, to have any qualifications or authorisation to work in a position for which the work-seeker is to be supplied or introduced to a hirer, an employment business may not introduce or supply the work-seeker to a hirer unless, in addition to the requirements in regulations 18 to 21, the requirements in paragraph (5) are satisfied.

(5) The requirements referred to in paragraph (4) are that the employment business has—

(a) subject to paragraph (6), obtained copies of any relevant qualifications or authorisation of the work-seeker, and offered to provide copies of those documents to the hirer; and

(b) taken all other reasonably practicable steps to confirm that the work-seeker is suitable for the position concerned.

(6) Where the employment business has taken all reasonably practicable steps to comply with the requirements in paragraph (5) and has been unable to do so fully, it may instead—

(a) comply with those requirements to the extent that it is able to do so;

(b) inform the hirer that it has taken all reasonably practicable steps to comply fully with those requirements and has been unable to do so; and

(c) inform the hirer of the details of the steps that it has taken in order to try and comply fully with those requirements.

(7) In this regulation "relative" has the same meaning as it is given in section 63 the Family Law Act 1996.]

NOTES

Commencement: 1 October 2010.

Substituted by the Conduct of Employment Agencies and Employment Businesses (Amendment) Regulations 2010, SI 2010/1782, regs 2, 10, as from 1 October 2010.

23, 24 *((Pt V Special situations) outside the scope of this work.)*

PART VI
CLIENT ACCOUNTS AND CHARGES TO WORK-SEEKERS

25 *((Client accounts) outside the scope of this work.)*

[2.773]

26 Circumstances in which fees may be charged to work-seekers

(1) Subject to paragraphs (3) and (4), the restriction on charging fees to work-seekers contained in section 6(1)(a) of the Act shall not apply in respect of a fee charged by an agency for the service provided by it of finding or seeking to find a work-seeker employment in any of the occupations listed in Schedule 3.

(2) Where paragraph (1) applies, subject to paragraph (5), any fee charged by the agency may consist only of a charge or commission payable out of the work-seeker's earnings in any such employment which the agency has found for him.

(3) Paragraphs (1) and (7) shall not apply where the agency, or any person connected with it, charges a fee to the hirer in respect of the service of supplying or introducing that work-seeker to him.

(4) In any case in which the agency is connected with the hirer, paragraphs (1) and (7) only apply if, prior to the provision of the service in respect of which the fee is to be charged, the agency informs the work-seeker of the fact that it is connected with the hirer.

(5) Paragraph (2) shall not apply to any fee charged to a work-seeker[, who is not a work-seeker seeking employment as a photographic or fashion model,] by an agency in respect of the inclusion of information about the work-seeker in a publication provided that—

- (a) the publication is wholly for one or both of the following purposes, namely the purpose of finding work-seekers employment in, or providing hirers with information about work-seekers in relation to, any of the occupations listed in Schedule 3[, other than photographic or fashion model]; and
- (b) either—
  - (i) the only work-finding service provided by the agency or any person connected with it to the work-seeker is the service described in this paragraph; or
  - (ii) the fee charged to the work-seeker amounts to no more than a reasonable estimate of the cost of production and circulation of the publication attributable to the inclusion of information about that work-seeker in the publication; and
- (c) in addition to the requirements in regulations 13 . . . and 16, in so far as they are applicable, the agency has, before it entered into the contract with the work-seeker by reference to which the fee is to be charged, made available to him a copy of a current edition of the publication (or, where the publication exists only in electronic form, given him access to a current edition of the publication) in which it is offering to include information about him[; and]
- [(d) in relation to a work-seeker who is not seeking employment as an actor, background artist, dancer, extra, musician, singer or other performer, where an agency proposes to include information about the work-seeker in a publication, for 7 days from the date of the agency and the work-seeker entering into a contract for such a service, whether written or oral and whether or not expressly mentioning fees permitted under this paragraph—
  - (i) the agency shall not charge a fee permitted by this paragraph to a work-seeker;
  - (ii) the work-seeker shall be entitled without detriment or penalty to cancel or withdraw from any such contract with immediate effect by informing the agency of such cancellation or withdrawal; and
  - (iii) the agency shall not include the information in the publication,

  and before entering into any such contract the agency shall inform the work-seeker of the right to cancel or withdraw from any such contract and the time limit for exercising that right;]]
- [(e) where an agency proposes to include information about a work-seeker seeking employment as an actor, background artist, dancer, extra, musician, singer or other performer in a publication, for 30 days from the date of the agency and the work-seeker entering into a contract for such a service, whether written or oral and whether or not expressly mentioning fees permitted under this paragraph—
  - (i) the agency shall not charge a fee permitted by this paragraph to a work-seeker; and
  - (ii) the work-seeker shall be entitled without detriment or penalty to cancel or withdraw from any such contract with immediate effect by informing the agency of such cancellation or withdrawal,

  and before entering into any such contract the agency shall inform the work-seeker of the right to cancel or withdraw from any such contract and the time limit for exercising that right;
- (f) where an agency proposes to include information about a work-seeker referred to in sub-paragraph (e) in a publication, after the date of the agency and the work-seeker entering into the contract referred to in that sub-paragraph, the agency shall make available to the work-seeker a copy of the information and at the same time shall inform the work-seeker of the right to object, its effect and the time limit for exercising that right and for 7 days from the date on which the agency first makes available a copy of the information to the work-seeker—
  - (i) the agency shall not charge a fee permitted by this paragraph to a work-seeker;
  - (ii) the agency shall not include the information in the publication; and
  - (iii) the work-seeker is entitled to object to any aspect of the information relating to the work-seeker to be included in the publication by informing the agency of the objection;
- (g) where sub-paragraph (f) applies and the work-seeker informs the agency of an objection, the agency shall not charge a fee or include the information in the publication until the work-seeker's reasonable requirements have been addressed (even if addressing the requirements takes longer than the period referred to in that sub-paragraph); and

(h) where an agency includes, or proposes to include, information about a work-seeker in a publication, the work-seeker is entitled to a full refund of the fees paid if the publication including that information is not produced and made available to potential hirers within 60 days from the date on which payment is made by the work-seeker].

[(5A) Where an agency makes available to the work-seeker a copy of the information referred to in paragraph (5)(f)—

(a) during the period referred to in paragraph (5)(e), where the period referred to in paragraph (5)(f) has elapsed without an objection or where the reasonable requirements of the work-seeker have been addressed, paragraph (5)(e) continues to apply; or

(b) after the period referred to in paragraph (5)(e) has elapsed, paragraph (5)(f) applies until the later of, the date on which the period referred to in paragraph (5)(f) has elapsed or, following an objection, the date on which the reasonable requirements of the work-seeker have been addressed.

(5B) Any reference in paragraph (5) to the inclusion of information about a work-seeker in a publication includes the inclusion of a photographic image or audio or video recording of the work-seeker in a publication.

(5C) Paragraph (5B) shall not be construed, when read with paragraph (5), as preventing an agency producing a photographic image or audio or video recording for the purpose of providing a copy of the image or recording to the work-seeker.]

(6) The restrictions on charging fees to work-seekers contained in section 6(1)(a) of the Act shall not apply to any fee consisting of a charge to a work-seeker in respect of the purchase of or subscription for a publication containing information about employers provided that—

(a) this is the only work-finding service provided by the agency or any person connected with it to the work-seeker; and

(b) the agency has made available to the work-seeker a copy of a current edition of the publication (or, where the publication exists only in electronic form, given him access to a current edition of the publication) in advance of the work-seeker purchasing or subscribing for it.

(7) The restriction on charging fees to work-seekers contained in section 6(1)(a) of the Act shall not apply in respect of a fee charged by an agency for the service provided by it of finding or seeking to find a work-seeker employment where—

(a) the work-seeker in question is a company; and

(b) the employment is in an occupation other than any of those occupations listed in Schedule 3.

NOTES

The word in square brackets at the end of sub-para (c) was substituted, and sub-para (5)(d) was added, by the Conduct of Employment Agencies and Employment Businesses (Amendment) Regulations 2007, SI 2007/3575, regs 2, 7.

The first and second words in square brackets in para (5) were inserted, the number omitted from para (5)(c) was revoked, para (5)(d) was substituted, and paras (5)(e)–(h) and paras (5A)–(5C) were inserted, by the Conduct of Employment Agencies and Employment Businesses (Amendment) Regulations 2010, SI 2010/1782, regs 2, 11, as from 1 October 2010.

PART VII
MISCELLANEOUS

27–29 *(Reg 27 (advertisements), reg 28 (confidentiality), and reg 29 (records) outside the scope of this work.)*

[2.774]

30 Civil liability

(1) Without prejudice to—

(a) any right of action; and

(b) any defence,

which exists or may be available apart from the provisions of the Act and these Regulations, contravention of, or failure to comply with, any of the provisions of the Act or of these Regulations by an agency or employment business shall, so far as it causes damage, be actionable.

(2) In this regulation, "damage" includes the death of, or injury to, any person (including any disease and any impairment of that person's physical or mental condition).

[2.775]

31 Effect of prohibited or unenforceable terms and recoverability of monies

(1) Where any term of a contract is prohibited or made unenforceable by these Regulations, the contract shall continue to bind the parties to it if it is capable of continuing in existence without that term.

(2) Where a hirer pays any money pursuant to a contractual term which is unenforceable by virtue of regulation 10, the hirer is entitled to recover that money.

32, 33 (*Reg 32 (application of the Regulations to work-seekers which are incorporated), and reg 33 (electronic and other communications) outside the scope of this work.*)

SCHEDULES

SCHEDULE 1 AND 2

(*Sch 1 (transitional and saving provisions), and Sch 2 (client accounts) outside the scope of this work.*)

SCHEDULE 3
OCCUPATIONS IN RESPECT OF WHICH EMPLOYMENT AGENCIES MAY CHARGE FEES TO WORK-SEEKERS

Regulation 26

[2.776]
Actor, musician, singer, dancer, [background artist, extra, walk-on] or other performer;

Composer, writer, artist, director, production manager, lighting cameraman, camera operator, make up artist, [clothes, hair or make up stylist,] film editor, action arranger or co-ordinator, stunt arranger, costume or production designer, recording engineer, property master, film continuity person, sound mixer, photographer, stage manager, producer, choreographer, theatre designer;

Photographic or fashion model;

Professional sports person.

NOTES

Words in first pair of square brackets inserted by the Conduct of Employment Agencies and Employment Businesses (Amendment) Regulations 2010, SI 2010/1782, regs 2, 14, as from 1 October 2010; words in second pair of square brackets inserted by the Conduct of Employment Agencies and Employment Businesses (Amendment) Regulations 2007, SI 2007/3575, regs 2, 10.

SCHEDULES 4–6

(*Sch 4 (particulars to be included in an agency's or employment business's records relating to work-seekers), Sch 5 (particulars to be included in an agency's or employment business's records relating to hirers), and Sch 6 (particulars to be included in an agency's or employment business's records relating to other agencies or employment businesses) outside the scope of this work.*)

EMPLOYMENT ACT 2002 (DISPUTE RESOLUTION) REGULATIONS 2004 (NOTE)

(SI 2004/752)

[2.777]

NOTES

These Regulations were made on 12 March 2004 under the powers conferred by the Employment Act 2002, ss 31(6), 32(7), 33, 51(1)(a), (b). They came into force on 1 October 2004 and made provision for the application of the statutory dismissal and disciplinary and grievance procedures set out in Sch 2 to the 2002 Act. Note that ss 31–33 of the 2002 Act were repealed by the Employment Act 2008, s 1, as from 6 April 2009. Section 51 of the 2002 Act (Orders and regulations), although still in force, is a purely administrative provision and contains no specific regulation making powers. Accordingly, these Regulations lapsed on 6 April 2009 (although, as of 6 April 2013, they had not been formally revoked). For transitional provisions and savings in relation to the continued application of the pre-April 2009 dispute resolution procedures, see the Employment Act 2008 (Commencement No 1, Transitional Provisions and Savings) Order 2008, SI 2008/3232, Schedule, Pt 1.

See *Harvey* AII(7).

ACAS ARBITRATION SCHEME (GREAT BRITAIN) ORDER 2004

(SI 2004/753)

NOTES

Made: 9 March 2004.
Authority: Trade Union and Labour Relations (Consolidation) Act 1992, s 212A(1), (3), (6), (7), (8), (9).
Commencement: 6 April 2004.
See *Harvey* PI(3).

ARRANGEMENT OF ARTICLES

[2.778]
1 Citation, commencement, interpretation and extent

(1) This Order may be cited as the ACAS Arbitration Scheme (Great Britain) Order 2004 and shall come into force on 6th April 2004.

(2) In this Order—
"the 1996 Act" means the Employment Rights Act 1996;
"basic amount" means such part of an award of compensation made by an arbitrator as comprises the basic amount, determined in accordance with paragraphs 139 to 146 of the Scheme;
"English/Welsh arbitration" means an arbitration under the Scheme, which the parties have agreed shall be determined under the laws of England and Wales;
"the Scheme" means the arbitration scheme set out in the Schedule with the exception of paragraphs 52EW, 110EW, 183EW, 187EW, 194EW, 200EW, 205EW, 209EW, 212EW, 217EW, 223EW and 224EW thereof;
"Scottish arbitration" means an arbitration under the Scheme, which the parties have agreed shall be determined according to the laws of Scotland.

(3) This Order extends to Great Britain.

(4) Paragraphs in the Schedule marked "EW" apply only to English/Welsh arbitrations.

(5) Paragraphs in the Schedule marked "S" apply only to Scottish arbitrations.

(6) Paragraphs in the Schedule not marked "EW" or "S" apply to both English/Welsh arbitrations and Scottish arbitrations.

[2.779]
2 Commencement of the Scheme

The Scheme shall come into effect on 6th April 2004.

[2.780]
3 Revocation

Subject to article 8, the ACAS Arbitration Scheme (England and Wales) Order 2001 is revoked.

[2.781]
4 Application of Part I of the Arbitration Act 1996

The provisions of Part I of the Arbitration Act 1996 referred to in the Schedule at paragraphs 52EW, 110EW, 183EW, 187EW, 194EW, 200EW, 205EW, 209EW, 212EW, 217EW, 223EW and 224EW and shown in italics shall, as modified in those paragraphs, apply to English/Welsh arbitrations conducted in accordance with the Scheme.

[2.782]
5

(1) section 46(1)(b) of the Arbitration Act 1996 shall apply to English/Welsh arbitrations conducted in accordance with the Scheme, subject to the following modification.

(2) For "such other considerations as are agreed by them or determined by the tribunal" in section 46(1)(b) substitute "the Terms of Reference in paragraph 17 of the arbitration scheme set out in the Schedule to the ACAS Arbitration Scheme (Great Britain) Order 2004".

[2.783]
6 Enforcement of re-employment orders

(1) Employment tribunals shall enforce re-employment orders made in arbitrations conducted in accordance with the Scheme in accordance with section 117 of the 1996 Act (enforcement by award of compensation), modified as follows.

(2) In subsection (1)(a), subsection (3) and subsection (8), for the words "section 113" substitute in each case "paragraph 123(i) of the Scheme".

(3) In subsection (2) for "section 124" substitute "section 124(1) and (5) and subsections (9) and (10)".

(4) In subsection (3)(a) for the words "sections 118 to 127A" substitute the words "sections 118 to 123, section 124(1) and (5), sections 126 and 127A and subsections (9) and (11)".

(5) After subsection (8) insert—

> "(9) section 124(1) shall not apply to compensation awarded, or to a compensatory award made, to a person in a case where the arbitrator finds the reason (or, if more than one, the principal reason) for the dismissal (or, in a redundancy case, for which the employee was selected for dismissal) to be a reason specified in any of the enactments mentioned in section 124(1)A.
>
> (10) In the case of compensation awarded to a person under section 117(1) and (2), the limit imposed by section 124(1) may be exceeded to the extent necessary to enable the award fully to reflect the amount specified as payable under the arbitrator's award in accordance with paragraphs 131(i) or 134(iv) of the Scheme.
>
> (11) Where—
>
> (a) a compensatory award is an award under subsection (3)(a) of section 117, and
>
> (b) an additional award falls to be made under subsection (3)(b) of that section, the limit imposed by section 124(1) on the compensatory award may be exceeded to the extent necessary to enable the aggregate of the compensatory award and additional awards fully to reflect the amount specified as payable under the arbitrator's award in accordance with paragraphs 131(i) or 134(iv) of the Scheme.
>
> (12) In this section "the Scheme" means the arbitration scheme set out in the Schedule to the ACAS Arbitration Scheme (Great Britain) Order 2004.".

[2.784]
7 Awards of compensation

An award of a basic amount shall be treated as a basic award of compensation for unfair dismissal for the purposes of section 184(1)(d) of the 1996 Act (which specifies such an award as a debt which the Secretary of State must satisfy if the employer has become insolvent).

[2.785]
8 Transitional provision

(1) The Scheme has effect in any case where the appropriate date falls on or after 6th April 2004.

(2) In a case where the appropriate date falls before 6th April 2004, the arbitration scheme set out in the Schedule to the ACAS Arbitration Scheme (England and Wales) Order 2001 continues to apply.

(3) In this article, the "appropriate date" means the date of the Arbitration Agreement. Where the parties sign the Arbitration Agreement on different dates, the appropriate date is the date of the first signature.

(4) In this article, "Arbitration Agreement" means an agreement to submit the dispute to arbitration, as defined in paragraph 26 of the Scheme.

SCHEDULE

(The Schedule (omitted for reasons of space) sets out the scheme, submitted to the Secretary of State by ACAS pursuant to the Trade Union and Labour Relations (Consolidation) Act 1992, s 212A, providing for arbitration in the case of disputes involving proceedings, or claims which could be the subject of proceedings, before an employment tribunal arising out of a contravention, or alleged contravention, of the Employment Rights Act 1996, Pt X (unfair dismissal). The Scheme does not extend to other kinds of claim related to, or raised at the same time as, a claim of unfair dismissal, for example, sex discrimination cases, and claims for unpaid wages. The Scheme provides a voluntary alternative to the employment tribunal for the resolution by arbitration of such claims where both parties agree. The full text of the scheme was included in the fifteenth edition of this Handbook.)

COMPROMISE AGREEMENTS (DESCRIPTION OF PERSON) ORDER 2004

(SI 2004/754)

NOTES

Made: 12 March 2004.

Authority: Sex Discrimination Act 1975, s 77(4B)(d); Race Relations Act 1976, s 72(4B)(d); Trade Union and Labour Relations (Consolidation) Act 1992, s 288(4)(d); Disability Discrimination Act 1995, s 9(4)(d); Employment Rights Act 1996, s 203(3A)(d); National Minimum Wage Act 1998, s 49(5)(d). Note that the Sex Discrimination Act 1975, the Race Relations Act 1976 and the Disability Discrimination Act 1995 were repealed by the Equality Act 2010, s 211(2), Sch 27, Pt 1, as from 1 October 2010. For transitional provisions see the Equality Act 2010 (Commencement No 4, Savings, Consequential, Transitional, Transitory and Incidental Provisions and Revocation) Order 2010, SI 2010/2317 art 10(6) (at **[2.1563]**) which provides that despite its lapse by virtue of Sch 27 to the 2010 Act, subordinate legislation specified in Sch 2 to the 2010 Order (which includes this Order and the Compromise Agreements (Description of Person) Order 2004 (Amendment) Order 2004 in so far as made under the 1975 and 1976 Acts) continues to have effect so far as it relates to a shipping matter (within the meaning of art 10(1)(a) or (b)) until regulations under s 30(1) of the 2010 Act come into force. See also art 11(3) of the 2010 Order (at **[2.1564]**) which provides that despite its lapse by virtue of Sch 27 to the 2010 Act, subordinate legislation specified in Sch 4 to the 2010 Order continues to have effect, so far as it relates to work on ships, work on hovercraft and seafarers, until regulations under s 81 of the 2010 Act come into force. Again, Sch 4 includes this Order (and the amending 2004 Order) in so far as made under the 1975 and 1976 Acts. Note also that the Equality Act 2010 (Work on Ships and Hovercraft) Regulations 2011 (SI 2011/1771) which were made under s 81 of the 2010 Act (and ss 207(1), (4)(b), 212(1)) came into force on 15 August 2011. As of 6 April 2013, no Regulations had been made under s 30(1) of the 2010 Act.

With regard to the Disability Discrimination Act 1995, note that s 9 was repealed by the Disability Discrimination Act 1995 (Amendment) Regulations 2003, SI 2003/1673. That provision was replaced by a new Sch 3A, Pt 1 to that Act as added by the 2003 Regulations (now also repealed). However, the new Part did not contain a provision similar to the one formerly in s 9(4)(d), ie, a person is a relevant independent adviser for the purposes of that section if he is a person of a description specified in an Order made by the Secretary of State. It was therefore not clear whether this Order (or the amending SI 2004/2515 which was also partly made under that section) continued to have effect in so far as made under the 1995 Act. The situation was clarified by the Compromise Agreements (Description of Person) Order 2005, SI 2005/2364 (made under s 67 of, and Sch 3A, para 2(3)(d) to, the 1995 Act and as amended by SI 2009/3348) which provided that a Fellow of the Institute of Legal Executives practising in a solicitors' practice (including a body recognised under the Administration of Justice Act 1985, s 9), was specified for the purposes of para 2(3)(d). Accordingly, this Order (and the amending SI 2004/2515) had already lapsed in so far as made under the 1995 Act.

Commencement: 6 April 2004.

[2.786]

1 Citation, commencement and interpretation

(1) This Order may be cited as The Compromise Agreements (Description of Person) Order 2004 and shall come into force on 6th April 2004.

(2) In this Order—

- (a) "the 1975 Act" means the Sex Discrimination Act 1975;
- (b) "the 1976 Act" means the Race Relations Act 1976;
- (c) "the 1992 Act" means the Trade Union and Labour Relations (Consolidation) Act 1992;
- (d) "the 1995 Act" means the Disability Discrimination Act 1995;
- (e) "the 1996 Act" means the Employment Rights Act 1996; and
- (f) "the 1998 Act" means the National Minimum Wage Act 1998.

[2.787]

2 Person specified

For the purposes of section 77(4B)(d) of the 1975 Act, section 72(4B)(d) of the 1976 Act, section 288(4)(d) of the 1992 Act, section 9(4)(d) of the 1995 Act, section 203(3A)(d) of the 1996 Act and section 49(5)(d) of the 1998 Act, a Fellow of the Institute of Legal Executives [practising in a solicitor's practice (including a body recognised under section 9 of the Administration of Justice Act 1985)] is specified.

NOTES

Words in square brackets substituted by the Legal Services Act 2007 (Consequential Amendments) Order 2009, SI 2009/3348, art 22, Sch 1, as from 16 December 2009.

3 (*Revoked by the Compromise Agreements (Description of Person) Order 2004 (Amendment) Order 2004, SI 2004/2515, art 2.*)

CIVIL AVIATION (WORKING TIME) REGULATIONS 2004

(SI 2004/756)

NOTES

Made: 11 March 2004.
Authority: European Communities Act 1972, s 2(2).
Commencement: 13 April 2004.

ARRANGEMENT OF REGULATIONS

SCHEDULES

Part 2 Statutory Instruments

[2.788]
1 Citation and commencement

These Regulations may be cited as the Civil Aviation (Working Time) Regulations 2004 and shall come into force on 13th April 2004.

[2.789]
[2 Scope

These Regulations apply to persons employed to act as crew members on board a civil aircraft flying for the purpose of—

(a) public transport; or
(b) the performance of a commercial air transport flight.]

NOTES

Commencement: 28 June 2010.
Substituted by the Civil Aviation (Working Time) (Amendment) Regulations 2010, SI 2010/1226, reg 2(1), (2), as from 28 June 2010.

[2.790]
3 Interpretation

In these Regulations—

"the 1974 Act" means the Health and Safety at Work Act 1974;

"block flying time" means the time between an aircraft first moving from its parking place for the purpose of taking off until it comes to rest on its designated parking position with all its engines stopped;

"the CAA" means the Civil Aviation Authority;

"cabin crew" means a person on board a civil aircraft, other than flight crew, who is carried for the purpose of performing in the interests of the safety of the passengers, duties that are assigned to him for that purpose by the operator or the commander of that aircraft;

"calendar year" means the period of 12 months beginning with 1st January in any year;

"collective agreement" means a collective agreement within the meaning of section 178 of the Trade Union and Labour Relations (Consolidation) Act 1992 the trade union parties to which are independent trade unions within the meaning of section 5 of that Act;
["commercial air transport flight" has the same meaning as in article 255(1) of the Air Navigation Order 2009;]

. . .

"crew member" means a person employed to act as a member of the cabin crew or flight crew on board a civil aircraft by an undertaking established in the United Kingdom;
"employer" means an undertaking established in the United Kingdom by whom a crew member is (or where the employment has ceased, was) employed;
"employment" in relation to a crew member, means employment under his contract, and "employed" shall be construed accordingly;
"the Executive" means both the Health and Safety Executive [referred to in section 10(1)] of the 1974 Act, and the Health and Safety Executive of Northern Ireland;
"flight crew" means a person employed to act as a pilot, flight navigator, flight engineer or flight radiotelephony operator on board a civil aircraft;
"inspector" means a person appointed by the CAA under paragraph 1 of Schedule 2;
["local mean time" means the time to which a crew member is acclimatised for the purposes of a scheme;]

. . .

"protection and prevention services or facilities" means those services or facilities that are designed to preserve the health and safety of the crew member from any hazards that may threaten his health or safety during the course of his undertaking his work and are capable of being provided by his employer;
["public transport" is to be construed in accordance with the conditions set out in article 260(2) of the Air Navigation Order 2009 in relation to an aircraft that is flying on a public transport flight;]
"relevant agreement", in relation to a crew member, means a workforce agreement which applies to him, any provision of a collective agreement which forms part of a contract between him and his employer, or any other agreement in writing which is legally enforceable as between the crew member and his employer;
"the relevant requirements" means regulations 5(2), 6, 7(2)(a), 8, 9 and 10;
"relevant training" means the training required to enable a person to perform the duties of flight crew or cabin crew carried out or undertaken whilst employed by an employer;
"rest break" and "rest period", in relation to a crew member, means a period which is not working time;
"scheme" means a scheme operated by an employer and approved by the CAA pursuant to [article 145(1)(b) or 149(a) of the Air Navigation Order 2009];
"standby", in relation to a crew member, means a crew member who in accordance with the terms of his employment holds himself ready to act as a crew member if called upon to do so by his employer;
"workforce agreement" means an agreement between an employer and crew members employed by him or his representatives in respect of which the conditions set out in Schedule 1 to these Regulations are satisfied;
"working time", in relation to a crew member means—

(a) any period during which he is working at his employer's disposal and carrying out his activity or duties;
(b) any period during which he is receiving relevant training, . . .
(c) any additional period which is to be treated as working time for the purpose of these Regulations under a relevant agreement, [and
(d) subject to regulation 9A, any period during which he is on standby,]

and "work", "works" and "to work" shall be construed accordingly.

NOTES

Definition "the Commission" (omitted) revoked, and words in square brackets in the definition "the Executive" substituted, by the Legislative Reform (Health and Safety Executive) Order 2008, SI 2008/960, art 22, Sch 3.

All other amendments made by the Civil Aviation (Working Time) (Amendment) Regulations 2010, SI 2010/1226, reg 2(1), (3), as from 28 June 2010.

[2.791]

4 Entitlement to annual leave

(1) A crew member is entitled to paid annual leave of at least four weeks, or a proportion of four weeks in respect of a period of employment of less than one year.

(2) Leave to which a crew member is entitled under this regulation—

(a) may be taken in instalments;
(b) may not be replaced by a payment in lieu, except where the crew member's employment is terminated.

[2.792]

5 Health assessments

(1) An employer shall ensure that each crew member employed by him is entitled to a free health assessment before he commences his employment and thereafter at regular intervals of whatever duration may be appropriate in the case of the crew member.

(2) Subject to paragraph (3), no person shall disclose a health assessment referred to in paragraph (1) made in respect of a crew member to any person other than that crew member without that crew member's consent in writing.

(3) A registered medical practitioner who makes a health assessment referred to in paragraph (1) may advise the employer of the crew member in question that the crew member is suffering from health problems which the practitioner considers to be connected with the fact that the crew member works during night time.

(4) Where—

- (a) a registered medical practitioner has advised an employer pursuant to paragraph (3); and
- (b) it is possible for the employer to transfer the crew member to mobile or non-mobile work—
  - (i) for which the crew member is suited, and
  - (ii) which is to be undertaken during periods such that the crew member will cease to work during night time,

then the employer shall transfer the crew member accordingly.

(5) A health assessment referred to in paragraph (1)—

- (a) may be conducted within the National Health Service, and
- (b) is free if it is undertaken at no cost to the crew member to whom it relates.

(6) For the purposes of this regulation, a crew member works during night time when he works at any time between the hours of 2.00 am and 4.59 am local mean time; . . .

NOTES

Para (6): words omitted revoked by the Civil Aviation (Working Time) (Amendment) Regulations 2010, SI 2010/1226, reg 2(1), (4), as from 28 June 2010.

[2.793]

6 Health and safety protection at work

An employer shall ensure that each crew member employed by him is at all times during the course of that employment provided with adequate health and safety protection and prevention services or facilities appropriate to the nature of his employment.

[2.794]

7 Pattern of work

(1) Where an employer intends to organise work according to a certain pattern he shall take into account the general principle of adapting work to the worker to the extent that is relevant to the objective of protecting workers' health and safety.

(2) Without prejudice to the generality of paragraph (1), in a case where an employer intends to organise work according to a certain pattern he shall—

- (a) ensure that pattern affords the crew member adequate rest breaks, and
- (b) take into account the need to ensure, where practicable, that pattern offers the crew member work, within the scope of his duties, that alleviates monotony or working at a pre-determined rate.

[2.795]

8 Provision of information

(1) When requested to do so by the CAA, an employer shall provide the CAA with such information as it may specify relating to the working patterns of crew members in his employ.

(2) Any information which is generated by an employer relating to the working patterns of crew members shall be retained by the employer for a period of not less than two years.

[2.796]

9 Maximum annual working time

An employer shall ensure that in any month—

- (a) no person employed by him shall act as a crew member during the course of his working time, if during the period of 12 months expiring at the end of the month before the month in question the aggregate block flying time of that person exceeds 900 hours; and
- (b) no crew member employed by him shall have a total annual working time of more than 2,000 hours during the period of 12 months expiring at the end of the month before the month in question.

[2.797]
[9A Standby time

(1) For the purpose of calculating the total annual working time under regulation 9(b), time spent by a crew member on standby is to count in full as working time except where paragraph (2) or (3) applies, when it is to count as half the time spent.

(2) This paragraph applies where the period of notice given by the employer to the crew member before the crew member must report for duty is at least 2 hours 15 minutes.

(3) This paragraph applies where time spent by the crew on standby—

(a) is spent—

(i) at home,

(ii) in accommodation provided by the employer away from the place where the crew member is next required to report for duty, or

(iii) in other accommodation arranged by the crew member to stay in while temporarily deployed away from home; and

(b) is between the hours of 10.00 pm and 8.00 am local mean time, and during that time the crew member—

(i) can take undisturbed rest, and

(ii) is not called upon to report for duty.]

NOTES

Commencement: 28 June 2010.

Inserted by the Civil Aviation (Working Time) (Amendment) Regulations 2010, SI 2010/1226, reg 2(1), (5), as from 28 June 2010.

[2.798]
10 Rest days

(1) Without prejudice to regulation 4, an employer shall ensure that all crew members employed by him are notified in writing as soon as possible of their right to rest days which shall be free of all employment duties including acting as a standby.

(2) For the purposes of this regulation, rest days are—

(a) not less than 7 days in each month during which a crew member works for his employer, which may include any rest periods required under [a scheme referred to in article 145(1) or 149 of the Air Navigation Order 2009]; and

(b) not less than 96 days in each calendar year during which a crew member works for his employer, which may include any rest periods required under [a scheme referred to in article 145(1) or 149 of the Air Navigation Order 2009].

NOTES

Para (2): words in square brackets substituted by the Civil Aviation (Working Time) (Amendment) Regulations 2010, SI 2010/1226, reg 2(1), (6), as from 28 June 2010.

[2.799]
11 Enforcement

The provisions of Schedule 2 to these Regulations shall apply in relation to the enforcement of the relevant requirements.

[2.800]
12 Offences

(1) Any person who fails to comply with any of the relevant requirements shall be guilty of an offence.

(2) The provisions of paragraph (3) shall apply where an inspector is exercising or has exercised any power conferred by Schedule 2.

(3) It is an offence for a person—

(a) to contravene any requirement imposed by an inspector under paragraph 2 of Schedule 2;

(b) to prevent or attempt to prevent any other person from appearing before an inspector or from answering any question to which an inspector may by virtue of paragraph 2(2)(e) of Schedule 2 require an answer;

(c) to contravene any requirement or prohibition imposed by an improvement notice or a prohibition notice referred to in paragraphs 3 and 4 of Schedule 2 (including any such notice as is modified on appeal);

(d) intentionally to obstruct an inspector in the exercise or performance of his powers;

(e) to use or disclose any information in contravention of paragraph 8 of Schedule 2;

(f) to make a statement which he knows to be false or recklessly to make a statement which is false where the statement is made in purported compliance with a requirement to furnish any information imposed by or under these Regulations.

(4) Any person guilty of an offence under paragraph (1) shall be liable—

(a) on summary conviction, to a fine not exceeding the statutory maximum;
(b) on conviction on indictment, to a fine.

(5) A person guilty of an offence under paragraph (3)(b) or (d) shall be liable on summary conviction to a fine not exceeding level 5 on the standard scale.

(6) A person guilty of an offence under paragraph (3)(c) shall be liable—
(a) on summary conviction, to imprisonment for a term not exceeding three months, or a fine not exceeding the statutory maximum;
(b) on conviction on indictment, to imprisonment for a term not exceeding two years, or a fine or both.

(7) A person guilty of an offence under paragraph (3)(a), (e) or (f) shall be liable—
(a) on summary conviction, to a fine not exceeding the statutory maximum;
(b) on conviction on indictment—
(i) if the offence is under paragraph (3)(e), to imprisonment for a term not exceeding two years or a fine or both,
(ii) if the offence is under paragraph (3)(a) or (f), to a fine.

(8) The provisions set out in regulations 13 to 17 shall apply in relation to the offences provided for in paragraphs (1) and (3).

[2.801]
13 Offences due to fault of other person

Where the commission by any person of an offence is due to the act or default of some other person, that other person shall be guilty of the offence, and a person may be charged with and convicted of the offence by virtue of this regulation whether or not proceedings are taken against the first mentioned person.

[2.802]
14 Offences by bodies corporate

(1) Where an offence committed by a body corporate is proved to have been committed with the consent or connivance of, or to have been attributable to any neglect on the part of, any director, manager, secretary or other similar officer of the body corporate or a person who was purporting to act in any such capacity, he as well as the body corporate shall be guilty of that offence and shall be liable to be proceeded against and punished accordingly.

(2) Where the affairs of a body corporate are managed by its members, the preceding paragraph shall apply in relation to the acts and defaults of a member in connection with his functions of management as if he were a director of the body corporate.

[2.803]
15 Restriction on institution of proceedings in England and Wales

Proceedings for an offence shall not be instituted in England or Wales except by an inspector or by, or with the consent of, the Director of Public Prosecutions.

[2.804]
16 Prosecution by inspectors

(1) If authorised in that behalf by the CAA, an inspector may prosecute proceedings for an offence before a magistrates' court even though the inspector is not of counsel or a solicitor.

(2) This regulation shall not apply in Scotland.

[2.805]
17 Power of court to order cause of offence to be remedied or, in certain cases, forfeiture

(1) This regulation applies where a person is convicted of an offence in respect of any matter which appears to the court to be a matter which it is in his power to remedy.

(2) In addition to or instead of imposing any punishment, the court may order the person in question to take such steps as may be specified in the order for remedying the said matters within such time as may be fixed by the order.

(3) The time fixed by an order under paragraph (2) may be extended or further extended by order of the court on an application made before the end of that time as originally fixed or as extended under this paragraph, as the case may be.

(4) Where a person is ordered under paragraph (2) to remedy any matters, that person shall not be liable under these Regulations in respect of that matter in so far as it continues during the time fixed by the order or any further time allowed under paragraph (3).

[2.806]
18 Remedies

(1) A crew member may present a complaint to an employment tribunal that his employer has refused to permit him to exercise any right he has under regulation 4, 5(1), (4), 7(1) or 7(2)(b).

(2) An employment tribunal shall not consider a complaint under this regulation unless it is presented—

(a) before the end of the period of three months beginning with the date on which it is alleged—

(i) that the exercise of the right should have been permitted (or in the case of a rest period or annual leave extending over more than one day, the date on which it should have been permitted to begin), or

(ii) the payment under regulation 4(2)(b) should have been made;

as the case may be; or

(b) within such further period as the tribunal considers reasonable in a case where it is satisfied that it was not reasonably practicable for the complaint to be presented before the end of that period of three months.

(3) Where an employment tribunal finds a complaint under regulation 4, 5(1), (4), 7(1) or 7(2)(b) well-founded, the tribunal—

(a) shall make a declaration to that effect; and

(b) may make an award of compensation to be paid by the employer to the crew member.

(4) The amount of the compensation shall be such as the tribunal considers just and equitable in all the circumstances having regard to—

(a) the employer's default in refusing to permit the crew member to exercise his right; and

(b) any loss sustained by the crew member which is attributable to the matters complained of.

SCHEDULE 1
WORKFORCE AGREEMENTS

Regulation 3

[2.807]

1 An agreement is a workforce agreement for the purposes of these Regulations if the following conditions are satisfied—

(a) the agreement is in writing;

(b) it has effect for a specified period not exceeding five years;

(c) it applies either—

(i) to all of the relevant members of the workforce, or

(ii) to all of the relevant members of the workforce who belong to a particular group;

(d) the agreement is signed—

(i) in the case of an agreement of the kind referred to in sub-paragraph (c)(i), by the representatives of the workforce, and in the case of an agreement of the kind referred to in sub-paragraph (c)(ii), by the representatives of the group to which the agreement applies (excluding, in either case, any representative not a relevant member of the workforce on the date on which the agreement was first made available for signature), or

(ii) if the employer employed 20 or fewer individuals on the date referred to in sub-paragraph (d)(i), either by the appropriate representatives in accordance with that sub-paragraph or by the majority of the individuals employed by him; and

(e) before the agreement was made available for signature, the employer provided all the employees to whom it was intended to apply on the date on which it came into effect with copies of the text of the agreement and such guidance as those employees might reasonably require in order to understand it in full.

2 For the purposes of this Schedule—

"a particular group" is a group of the relevant members of a workforce who undertake a particular function, work at a particular workplace or belong to a particular department or unit within their employer's business;

"relevant members of the workforce" are all of the employees employed by a particular employer, excluding any employee whose terms and conditions of employment are provided for, wholly or in part, in a collective agreement;

"representatives of the group" are employees duly elected to represent the members of a particular group;

"representatives of the workforce" are employees duly elected to represent the relevant members of the workforce;

and representatives are "duly elected" if the election at which they were elected satisfied the requirements of paragraph 3.

3 The requirements concerning elections referred to in paragraph 2 are that—

(a) the number of representatives to be elected is determined by the employer;

(b) the candidates for election as representatives of the workforce are relevant members of the workforce, and candidates for election as representatives of the group are members of the group;

(c) no employee who is eligible to be a candidate is unreasonably excluded from standing for election;

(d) all the relevant members of the workforce are entitled to vote for representatives of the workforce, and all the members of a particular group are entitled to vote for representatives of the group;

(e) the employees entitled to vote may vote for as many candidates as there are representatives to be elected; and

(f) the election is conducted so as to secure that—

(i) so far as is reasonably practicable, those voting do so in secret, and

(ii) the votes given at the election are fairly and accurately counted.

4 In this Schedule "employee" means an individual who has entered into or works under a contract of employment.

SCHEDULE 2
ENFORCEMENT

Regulation 11

[2.808]

1 Appointment of inspectors

(1) The CAA may appoint as inspectors (under whatever title it may from time to time determine) such persons having suitable qualifications as it thinks necessary for carrying into effect these Regulations, and may terminate any appointment made under this paragraph.

(2) Every appointment of a person as an inspector under this paragraph shall be made by an instrument in writing specifying which of the powers conferred on inspectors by these Regulations are to be exercisable by the person appointed; and an inspector shall in right of his appointment under this paragraph—

(a) be entitled to exercise only such of those powers as are so specified; and

(b) be entitled to exercise the powers so specified only within the field of responsibility of the CAA.

(3) So much of an inspector's instrument of appointment as specifies the powers which he is entitled to exercise may be varied by the CAA.

(4) An inspector shall, if so required when exercising or seeking to exercise any power conferred on him by these Regulations, produce his instrument of appointment or a duly authenticated copy thereof.

2 Powers of inspectors

(1) Subject to the provisions of paragraph 1 and this paragraph, an inspector may for the purpose of carrying into effect these Regulations exercise the powers set out in sub-paragraph (2).

(2) The powers of an inspector are the following, namely—

(a) at any reasonable time (or in a situation which in his opinion may be dangerous, at any time) to enter any premises which he has reason to believe it is necessary for him to enter for the purposes mentioned in sub-paragraph (1);

(b) to take with him a constable if he has reasonable cause to apprehend any serious obstruction in the execution of his duty;

(c) without prejudice to paragraph (b), on entering any premises by virtue of paragraph (a) to take with him—

(i) any other person duly authorised by the CAA; and

(ii) any equipment or material required for any purpose for which the power of entry is being exercised;

(d) to make such examination and investigation as may in any circumstances be necessary for the purpose mentioned in sub-paragraph (1);

(e) to require any person whom he has reasonable cause to believe to be able to give any information relevant to any examination or investigation under paragraph (d) to answer (in the absence of persons other than a person nominated by him to be present and any persons whom the inspector may allow to be present) such questions as the inspector thinks fit to ask and to sign a declaration of the truth of his answers;

(f) to require the production of, inspect, and take copies of or of any entry in—

(i) any records which by virtue of these Regulations are required to be kept, and

(ii) any other books, records or documents which it is necessary for him to see for the purposes of any examination or investigation under paragraph (d);

(g) to require any person to afford him such facilities and assistance with respect to any matters or things within that person's control or in relation to which that person has responsibilities as are necessary to enable the inspector to exercise any of the powers conferred on him by this sub-paragraph;

(h) any other power which is necessary for the purpose mentioned in sub-paragraph (1).

(3) No answer given by a person in pursuance of a requirement imposed under sub-paragraph (2)(e) shall be admissible in evidence against that person or the husband or wife of that person in any proceedings.

(4) Nothing in this paragraph shall be taken to compel the production by any person of a document of which he would on grounds of legal professional privilege be entitled to withhold production on an order for discovery in an action in the High Court or, as the case may be, an order for the production of documents in an action in the Court of Session.

3 Improvement notices

If an inspector is of the opinion that a person—

(a) is contravening one or more of these Regulations; or

(b) has contravened one or more of these Regulations in circumstances that make it likely that the contravention will continue or be repeated,

he may serve on him a notice (in this Schedule referred to as "an improvement notice") stating that he is of that opinion, specifying the provision or provisions as to which he is of that opinion, giving particulars of the reasons why he is of that opinion, and requiring that person to remedy the contravention or, as the case may be, the matter occasioning it within such period (ending not earlier than the period within which an appeal against the notice can be brought under paragraph (6) as may be specified in the notice.

4 Prohibition notices

(1) This paragraph applies to any activities which are being or are likely to be carried on by or under the control of any person, being activities to or in relation to which any of these Regulations apply or will, if the activities are so carried on, apply.

(2) If as regards any activities to which this paragraph applies an inspector is of the opinion that, as carried on by or under the control of the person in question, the activities involve or, as the case may be, will involve a risk of serious personal injury, the inspector may serve on that person a notice (in this Schedule referred to as "a prohibition notice").

(3) A prohibition notice shall—

(a) state that the inspector is of the said opinion;

(b) specify the matters which in his opinion give or, as the case may be, will give rise to the said risk;

(c) where in his opinion any of those matters involves or, as the case may be, will involve a contravention of any of these Regulations, state that he is of that opinion, specify the regulation or regulations as to which he is of that opinion, and give particulars of the reasons why he is of that opinion; and

(d) direct that the activities to which the notice relates shall not be carried on by or under the control of the person on whom the notice is served unless the matters specified in the notice in pursuance of paragraph (b) and any associated contraventions of provisions so specified in pursuance of paragraph (c) have been remedied.

(4) A direction contained in a prohibition notice in pursuance of sub-paragraph (3)(d) shall take effect—

(a) at the end of the period specified in the notice; or

(b) if the notice so declares, immediately.

5 Provisions supplementary to paragraphs 3 and 4

(1) In this paragraph "a notice" means an improvement notice or a prohibition notice.

(2) A notice may (but need not) include directions as to the measures to be taken to remedy any contravention or matter to which the notice relates; and any such directions—

(a) may be framed to any extent by reference to any approved code of practice; and

(b) may be framed so as to afford the person on whom the notice is served a choice between different ways of remedying the contravention or matter.

(3) Where an improvement notice or prohibition notice which is not to take immediate effect has been served—

(a) the notice may be withdrawn by an inspector at any time before the end of the period specified therein in pursuance of paragraph 3 or paragraph 4(4) as the case may be; and

(b) the period so specified may be extended or further extended by an inspector at any time when an appeal against the notice is not pending.

6 Appeal against improvement or prohibition notice

(1) In this paragraph "a notice" means an improvement or prohibition notice.

(2) A person on whom a notice is served may within 21 days from the date of its service appeal to an employment tribunal; and on such an appeal the tribunal may either cancel or affirm the notice and, if it affirms it, may do so either in its original form or with such modifications as the tribunal may in the circumstances think fit.

(3) Where an appeal under this paragraph is brought against a notice within the period allowed under the preceding sub-paragraph, then—

(a) in the case of an improvement notice, the bringing of the appeal shall have the effect of suspending the operation of the notice until the appeal is finally disposed of or, if the appeal is withdrawn, until the withdrawal of the appeal;

(b) in the case of a prohibition notice, the bringing of the appeal shall have the like effect if, but only if, on the application of the appellant the tribunal so directs (and then only from the giving of the direction).

(4) One or more assessors may be appointed for the purposes of any proceedings brought before an employment tribunal under this paragraph.

7 Power of the CAA to indemnify inspectors

Where an action has been brought against an inspector in respect of an act done in the execution or purported execution of these Regulations and the circumstances are such that he is not legally entitled to require the CAA to indemnify him, then the CAA may, nevertheless, indemnify him against the whole or any part of any damages or costs or expenses which he may have been ordered to pay or may have incurred, if the CAA is satisfied that the inspector honestly believed that the act complained of was within his powers and that his duty as an inspector required or entitled him to do it.

8 Restrictions on disclosure of information

(1) In this paragraph—

"relevant information" means information obtained by an inspector in pursuance of a requirement imposed under paragraph 2; and

"the recipient", in relation to any relevant information, means the person by whom that information was so obtained or to whom that information was so furnished, as the case may be; and

"relevant statutory provisions" means—

(a) the provisions of the 1974 Act and any regulations made under powers contained in that Act; and

(b) while and to the extent that they remain in force, the provisions of the Acts mentioned in Schedule 1 to the 1974 Act and which are specified in the third column of that Schedule and the regulations, orders or other instruments of a legislative character made or having effect under a provision so specified.

(2) Subject to the following sub-paragraph, no relevant information shall be disclosed without the consent of the person by whom it was furnished.

(3) The preceding sub-paragraph shall not apply to—

(a) disclosure of information to . . . the Executive, a government department, or the CAA;

(b) without prejudice to paragraph (a), disclosure by the recipient of information to any person for the purpose of any function conferred on the recipient by or under any of the relevant statutory provisions or under these Regulations;

(c) without prejudice to paragraph (a), disclosure by the recipient of information to a constable authorised by a chief officer of police to receive it; or

(d) disclosure by the recipient of information in a form calculated to prevent it from being identified as relating to a particular person or case.

[(4) In the preceding paragraph, any reference to the Executive, the CAA or a government department includes respectively a reference to an officer of that body, and also, in the case of a reference to the Executive, includes a reference to—

(a) a person performing any of the functions of the Executive by virtue of section 13(3) of the 1974 Act;

(b) an officer of a body which is so performing any such functions; and

(c) an adviser appointed in pursuance of section 13(7) of the 1974 Act.]

(5) A person to whom information is disclosed in pursuance of sub-paragraph (3) shall not use the information for a purpose other than—

(a) in a case falling within sub-paragraph (3)(a), a purpose of . . . the Executive, a government department, or the CAA in question in connection with these Regulations or with the relevant statutory provisions, as the case may be;

(b) in the case of information given to a constable, the purposes of the police in connection with these Regulations, the relevant statutory provisions or any enactment whatsoever relating to working time.

(6) A person shall not disclose any information obtained by him as a result of the exercise of any power conferred by paragraph 2 (including in particular any information with respect to any trade secret obtained by him in any premises entered by him by virtue of any such power) except—

(a) for the purposes of his functions; or

(b) for the purposes of any legal proceedings; or

(c) with the relevant consent.

In this sub-paragraph "the relevant consent" means, in the case of information furnished in pursuance of a requirement imposed under paragraph 2, the consent of the person who furnished it, and, in any other case, the consent of a person having responsibilities in relation to the premises where the information was obtained.

(7) Notwithstanding anything in the preceding sub-paragraph an inspector shall, in circumstances in which it is necessary to do so for the purpose of assisting in keeping persons (or the representatives of persons) adequately informed about matters affecting their health, safety and welfare or working time, give to such persons or their representatives the following descriptions of information, that is to say—

(a) factual information obtained by him as mentioned in that sub-paragraph which relates to their working environment; and

(b) information with respect to any action which he has taken or proposes to take in or in connection with the performance of his functions in relation to their working environment;

and, where an inspector does as aforesaid, he shall give the like information to the employer of the first-mentioned persons.

(8) Notwithstanding anything in sub-paragraph (6), a person who has obtained such information as is referred to in that sub-paragraph may furnish to a person who appears to him to be likely to be a party to any civil proceedings arising out of any accident, occurrence, situation or other matter, a written statement of the relevant facts observed by him in the course of exercising any of the powers referred to in that sub-paragraph.

NOTES

Para 8: words omitted from sub-paras (3)(a), (5)(a) revoked, and sub-para (4) substituted, by the Legislative Reform (Health and Safety Executive) Order 2008, SI 2008/960, art 22, Sch 3.

EMPLOYMENT TRIBUNALS (CONSTITUTION AND RULES OF PROCEDURE) REGULATIONS 2004

(SI 2004/1861)

NOTES

Made: 19 July 2004.

Authority: Health and Safety at Work etc Act 1974, s 24(2); Employment Tribunals Act 1996, ss 1(1), 4(6), (6A), 7(1), (3), (3ZA), (3A), (5), 7A(1), (2), 9(1), (2), (4), 10(2), (5), (6), (7), 10A(1), 11(1), 12(2), 13, 13A(1), (2), 19, 41(4); Government of Wales Act 1998, Sch 8, para 36 (repealed by the Government of Wales Act 2006, s 163, Sch 12, as from 25 May 2007; by virtue of the Interpretation Act 1978, s 17(2)(b), in so far as these regulations were made under the 1998 Act, they now have effect as if made under the Government of Wales Act 2006, Sch 9, para 32); Scotland Act 1998, Sch 6, para 37.

Commencement: 1 October 2004. These Regulations and the Rules contained in Schs 1–6 apply as from that date in relation to all proceedings, whenever commenced, except to the extent provided for by transitional provisions contained in reg 20 at **[2.854]**. The Regulations and Rules apply equally to England and Wales, and to Scotland with such modifications as indicated).

Employment Judges: a person who is a member of a panel of chairmen of employment tribunals which is appointed in accordance with regulations under the Employment Tribunals Act 1996, s 1(1) may be referred to as an Employment Judge; see s 3A of the 1996 Act at **[1.681]** (as inserted by the Tribunals, Courts and Enforcement Act 2007, s 48(1), Sch 8, paras 35, 36, as from 1 December 2007). See also the amendments made by the Tribunals, Courts and Enforcement Act 2007 (Transitional and Consequential Provisions) Order 2008, SI 2008/2683 as noted below.

Note that these Regulations are reproduced as amended by, inter alia, the Employment Tribunals (Constitution and Rules of Procedure) (Amendment) Regulations 2008, 2008/2771 and the Employment Tribunals (Constitution and Rules of Procedure) (Amendment) Regulations 2008, 2008/3240. Both sets of amending Regulations have identical names, but different series numbers.

See *Harvey* PI(1).

Stop Press: these Regulations are revoked, as from 29 July 2013, by the Employment Tribunals (Constitution and Rules of Procedure) Regulations 2013, SI 2013/1237, reg 2, subject to transitional provisions in reg 15 thereof. The 2013 Regulations were published as this Edition was going to press, and are reproduced in full at **[2.1689]** et seq.

ARRANGEMENT OF REGULATIONS

SCHEDULES

[2.809]
1 Citation, commencement and revocation

[(1) These Regulations may be cited as the Employment Tribunals (Constitution and Rules of Procedure) Regulations 2004 and the Rules of Procedure contained in Schedules 1, 2, 3, 4, 5 and 6 to these Regulations may be referred to, respectively, as:—

(a) the Employment Tribunals Rules of Procedure [2004];
(b) the Employment Tribunals (National Security) Rules of Procedure [2004];
(c) the Employment Tribunals (Levy Appeals) Rules of Procedure [2004];
(d) the Employment Tribunals (Health and Safety – Appeals against Improvement and Prohibition Notices) Rules of Procedure [2004];
(e) the Employment Tribunals (Non-Discrimination Notices Appeals) Rules of Procedure [2004]; and
(f) the Employment Tribunals (Equal Value) Rules of Procedure] [2004].

(2) These Regulations shall come into force on 1 October 2004.

(3) Subject to the savings in regulation 20, the Employment Tribunals (Constitution and Rules of Procedure) Regulations 2001 and the Employment Tribunals (Constitution and Rules of Procedure) (Scotland) Regulations 2001 are revoked.

NOTES

Para (1): substituted by the Employment Tribunals (Constitution and Rules of Procedure) (Amendment) Regulations 2004, SI 2004/2351, reg 2(1), (2); date in square brackets in sub-paras (a)–(f) inserted by the Employment Tribunals (Constitution and Rules of Procedure) (Amendment) (No 2) Regulations 2005, SI 2005/1865, reg 2(1), (2).

[2.810]
2 Interpretation

[(1)] [In these Regulations and in Schedules 1, 2, 3, 4, 5 and 6—]

"ACAS" means the Advisory, Conciliation and Arbitration Service referred to in section 247 of TULR(C)A;

"appointing office holder" means, in England and Wales, the Lord Chancellor, and in Scotland, the Lord President; . . .

. . .

"compromise agreement" means an agreement to refrain from continuing proceedings where the agreement meets the conditions in section 203(3) of the Employment Rights Act;

"constructive dismissal" has the meaning set out in section 95(1)(c) of the Employment Rights Act;

. . .

"electronic communication" has the meaning given to it by section 15(1) of the Electronic Communications Act 2000;

"Employment Act" means the Employment Act 2002;

["Employment Judge" has the meaning given in section 3A of the Employment Tribunals Act;]

"Employment Rights Act" means the Employment Rights Act 1996;

"Employment Tribunals Act" means the Employment Tribunals Act 1996;

"Employment Tribunal Office" means any office which has been established for any area in either England & Wales or Scotland specified by the President and which carries out administrative functions in support of functions being carried out by a tribunal or [Employment Judge], and in relation to particular proceedings it is the office notified to the parties in accordance with rule 61(3) of Schedule 1;

"enactment" includes an enactment comprised in, or in an instrument made under, an Act of the Scottish Parliament;

["Equality Act" means the Equality Act 2010;]

"Equal Pay Act" means the Equal Pay Act 1970;

"excluded person" means, in relation to any proceedings, a person who has been excluded from all or part of the proceedings by virtue of:—

(a) a direction of a Minister of the Crown under rule 54(1)(b) or (c) of Schedule 1, or

(b) an order of the tribunal under rule 54(2)(a) read with 54(1)(b) or (c) of Schedule 1;

"hearing" means a case management discussion, pre-hearing review, review hearing or Hearing (as those terms are defined in Schedule 1) or a sitting of [an Employment Judge] or a tribunal duly constituted for the purpose of receiving evidence, hearing addresses and witnesses or doing anything lawful to enable [the Employment Judge] or tribunal to reach a decision on any question;

"legally represented" has the meaning set out in rule 38(5) of Schedule 1;

"Lord President" means the Lord President of the Court of Session;

"misconceived" includes having no reasonable prospect of success;

"national security proceedings" means proceedings in relation to which a direction is given under rule 54(1) of Schedule 1, or an order is made under rule 54(2) of that Schedule;

"old (England & Wales) regulations" means the Employment Tribunals (Constitution and Rules of Procedure) . . . Regulations 2001;

"old (Scotland) regulations" means the Employment Tribunals (Constitution and Rules of Procedure) [(Scotland)] Regulations 2001;

"panel of [Employment Judges]" means a panel referred to in regulation 8(3)(a);

"President" means, in England and Wales, the person [appointed by the Lord Chancellor or nominated by the Lord Chief Justice] to discharge for the time being the functions of the President of Employment Tribunals (England and Wales), and, in Scotland, the person appointed or nominated by the Lord President to discharge for the time being the functions of the President of Employment Tribunals (Scotland);

. . . ;

"Regional [Employment Judge]" means a member of the panel of [Employment Judges] who has been appointed to the position of Regional [Employment Judge] in accordance with regulation 6 or who has been nominated to discharge the functions of a Regional [Employment Judge] in accordance with regulation 6;

"Register" means the Register of judgments and written reasons kept in accordance with regulation 17;

"Secretary" means a person for the time being appointed to act as the Secretary of employment tribunals either in England and Wales or in Scotland;

. . .

"special advocate" means a person appointed in accordance with rule 8 of Schedule 2;

"tribunal" means an employment tribunal established in accordance with regulation 5, and in relation to any proceedings means the tribunal to which the proceedings have been referred by the President, Vice President or a Regional [Employment Judge];

"TULR(C)A" means the Trade Union and Labour Relations (Consolidation) Act 1992;

"Vice President" means a person who has been appointed to the position of Vice President in accordance with regulation 7 or who has been nominated to discharge the functions of the Vice President in accordance with that regulation;

"writing" includes writing delivered by means of electronic communication.

[(2) The Lord Chief Justice may nominate a judicial office holder (as defined in section 109(4) of the Constitutional Reform Act 2005) to exercise his functions under this regulation.]

NOTES

Para (1) is amended as follows:

Numbered as such by the Lord Chancellor (Transfer of Functions and Supplementary Provisions) Order 2006, SI 2006/680, art 2, Sch 1, paras 73, 74(1), (2).

Words in first pair of square brackets substituted by the Employment Tribunals (Constitution and Rules of Procedure) (Amendment) Regulations 2004, SI 2004/2351, reg 2(1), (3).

Definition "chairman" (omitted) revoked by the Tribunals, Courts and Enforcement Act 2007 (Transitional and Consequential Provisions) Order 2008, SI 2008/2683, art 6(1), Sch 1, paras 240, 241(a), as from 3 November 2008.

Definitions "Disability Discrimination Act", "Race Relations Act", and Sex Discrimination Act" (omitted) revoked, and definition "Equality Act" substituted (for original definition "Equal Pay Act"), by the Equality Act 2010 (Commencement No 4, Savings, Consequential, Transitional, Transitory and Incidental Provisions and Revocation) Order 2010, SI 2010/2317, art 24, Sch 8, para 4, as from 1 October 2010.

Definition "Employment Judge" inserted by SI 2008/2683, art 6(1), Sch 1, paras 240, 241(b), as from 3 November 2008.

All other references in para (1) to "Employment Judge", "an Employment Judge", "the Employment Judge", and "Employment Judges" substituted by SI 2008/2683, art 6(1), Sch 1, paras 240, 241(c)–(e), as from 3 November 2008.

Word omitted from definition "old (England & Wales) regulations" revoked, and word in square brackets in definition "old (Scotland) regulations" inserted, by the Employment Tribunals (Constitution and Rules of Procedure) (Amendment) (No 2) Regulations 2005, SI 2005/1865, reg 2(1), (3)(b).

In definition "President" words in square brackets substituted by SI 2006/680, art 2, Sch 1, paras 73, 74(1), (3).

Para (2): added by SI 2006/680, art 2, Sch 1, paras 73, 74(1), (4)

[2.811]

3 Overriding objective

[(1) The overriding objective of these Regulations and the rules in Schedules 1, 2, 3, 4, 5 and 6 is to enable tribunals and [Employment Judges] to deal with cases justly.]

(2) Dealing with a case justly includes, so far as practicable—

- (a) ensuring that the parties are on an equal footing;
- (b) dealing with the case in ways which are proportionate to the complexity or importance of the issues;
- (c) ensuring that it is dealt with expeditiously and fairly; and
- (d) saving expense.

[(3) A tribunal or [Employment Judge] shall seek to give effect to the overriding objective when it or he:

- (a) exercises any power given to it or him by these Regulations or the rules in Schedules 1, 2, 3, 4, 5 and 6; or
- (b) interprets these Regulations or any rule in Schedules 1, 2, 3, 4, 5 and 6.]

(4) The parties shall assist the tribunal or the [Employment Judge] to further the overriding objective.

NOTES

Paras (1), (3) were substituted by the Employment Tribunals (Constitution and Rules of Procedure) (Amendment) Regulations 2004, SI 2004/2351, reg 2(1), (4), (5).

The words "Employment Judges" in para (1) and "Employment Judge" in paras (3), (4) were substituted by the Tribunals, Courts and Enforcement Act 2007 (Transitional and Consequential Provisions) Order 2008, SI 2008/2683, art 6(1), Sch 1, paras 240, 242, as from 3 November 2008.

[2.812]

4 President of Employment Tribunals

(1) There shall be a President of Employment Tribunals (England and Wales), responsible for the administration of justice by tribunals and [Employment Judges] in England and Wales, who shall be appointed by the Lord Chancellor and shall be a person described in paragraph (3).

(2) There shall be a President of Employment Tribunals (Scotland), responsible for the administration of justice by tribunals and [Employment Judges] in Scotland, who shall be appointed by the Lord President and shall be a person described in paragraph (3).

(3) A President shall be a person:—

- [(a) who satisfies the judicial-appointment eligibility condition within the meaning of section 50 of the Tribunals, Courts and Enforcement Act 2007 on a 5-year basis;]
- (b) being an advocate or solicitor admitted in Scotland of at least [five] years standing; or
- (c) being a member of the Bar of Northern Ireland or [solicitor of the Court of Judicature of Northern Ireland] of at least [five] years standing.

(4) A President may resign his office by notice in writing to the appointing office holder.

[(5) If the appointing office holder is satisfied that the President is incapacitated by infirmity of mind or body from discharging the duties of his office, or—

- (a) the President is adjudged to be bankrupt or makes a composition or arrangement with his creditors, or
- (b) a debt relief order (under Part 7A of the Insolvency Act) has been made in respect of the "bankrupt or" insert "a debt relief order (under Part 7A of the Insolvency Act 1986) has been made in respect of him of the President

the appointing office holder may revoke his appointment.]

[(5A) Where the Lord Chancellor is the appointing office holder, he may revoke an appointment in accordance with paragraph (5) only with the concurrence of the Lord Chief Justice.]

(6) The functions of President under these Regulations may, if he is for any reason unable to act or during any vacancy in his office, be discharged by a person nominated for that purpose by the appointing office holder [where that is the Lord President, or, where the appointing office holder is the Lord Chancellor, by the Lord Chief Justice . . .]. [The Lord President or Lord Chief Justice may only make a nomination after consulting the Senior President of Tribunals.]

[(7) The Lord Chief Justice may nominate a judicial office holder (as defined in section 109(4) of the Constitutional Reform Act 2005) to exercise his functions under this regulation.]

NOTES

Paras (1), (2): words in square brackets substituted by the Tribunals, Courts and Enforcement Act 2007 (Transitional and Consequential Provisions) Order 2008, SI 2008/2683, art 6(1), Sch 1, paras 240, 243, as from 3 November 2008.

Para (3): sub-para (a) substituted, and the word "five" in square brackets in sub-paras (b), (c) substituted, by the Employment Tribunals (Constitution and Rules of Procedure) (Amendment) Regulations 2008, SI 2008/2771, regs 2–4, as from 1 December 2008; words in first pair of square brackets in sub-para (c) substituted by the Constitutional Reform Act 2005, s 59(5), Sch 11, Pt 3, para 5, as from 1 October 2009.

Para (5): substituted by the Tribunals, Courts and Enforcement Act 2007 (Consequential Amendments) Order 2012, SI 2012/2404, arts 3(3), 7, Sch 3, para 36, as from 1 October 2012, in relation to a debt relief order the application for which is made after that date.

Para (5A): inserted by the Constitutional Reform Act 2005, s 15(1), Sch 4, Pt 1, para 360.

Para (6): words in first pair of square brackets inserted by the Lord Chancellor (Transfer of Functions and Supplementary Provisions) Order 2006, SI 2006/680, art 2, Sch 1, paras 73, 75(1), (2); words omitted revoked, and words in second pair of square brackets inserted, by the Employment Tribunals (Constitution and Rules of Procedure) (Amendment) Regulations 2008, SI 2008/3240, regs 2, 3(1), as from 6 April 2009.

Para (7): added by SI 2006/680, art 2, Sch 1, paras 73, 75(1), (3).

[2.813]

5 Establishment of employment tribunals

(1) Each President shall, in relation to that part of Great Britain for which he has responsibility, from time to time determine the number of tribunals to be established for the purposes of determining proceedings.

(2) The President, a Regional [Employment Judge] or the Vice President shall determine, in relation to the area specified in relation to him, at what times and in what places in that area tribunals and [Employment Judges] shall sit.

NOTES

Para (2): words in square brackets substituted by the Tribunals, Courts and Enforcement Act 2007 (Transitional and Consequential Provisions) Order 2008, SI 2008/2683, art 6(1), Sch 1, paras 240, 244, as from 3 November 2008.

[2.814]

6 Regional [Employment Judges]

(1) The Lord Chancellor may from time to time appoint Regional [Employment Judges] from the panel of full-time [Employment Judges] and each Regional [Employment Judge] shall be responsible to the President (England and Wales) for the administration of justice by tribunals and [Employment Judges] in the area specified by the President (England and Wales) in relation to him.

(2) The President (England and Wales) or the Regional [Employment Judge] for an area may from time to time nominate a member of the panel of full time [Employment Judges] to discharge for the time being the functions of the Regional [Employment Judge] for that area.

NOTES

Words in square brackets substituted by the Tribunals, Courts and Enforcement Act 2007 (Transitional and Consequential Provisions) Order 2008, SI 2008/2683, art 6(1), Sch 1, paras 240, 245, as from 3 November 2008.

[2.815]

7 Vice President

(1) The Lord President may from time to time appoint a Vice President from the panel of full time [Employment Judges] and the Vice President shall be responsible to the President (Scotland) for the administration of justice by tribunals and [Employment Judges] in Scotland.

(2) The President (Scotland) or the Vice President may from time to time nominate a member of the panel of full time [Employment Judges] to discharge for the time being the functions of the Vice President.

NOTES

Words in square brackets substituted by the Tribunals, Courts and Enforcement Act 2007 (Transitional and Consequential Provisions) Order 2008, SI 2008/2683, art 6(1), Sch 1, paras 240, 246, as from 3 November 2008.

[2.816]

8 Panels of members of tribunals—general

(1) There shall be three panels of members of Employment Tribunals (England and Wales), as set out in paragraph (3).

(2) There shall be three panels of members of Employment Tribunals (Scotland), as set out in paragraph (3).

(3) The panels referred to in paragraphs (1) and (2) are:—

(a) a panel of full-time and part-time [Employment Judges] appointed by the appointing office holder consisting of persons—

[(i) who satisfy the judicial-appointment eligibility condition within the meaning of section 50 of the Tribunals, Courts and Enforcement Act 2007 on a 5-year basis;]

(ii) being an advocate or solicitor admitted in Scotland of at least [five] years standing; or

(iii) being a member of the Bar of Northern Ireland or [solicitor of the Court of Judicature of Northern Ireland] of at least [five] years standing;

(b) a panel of persons appointed by the [Lord Chancellor] after consultation with such organisations or associations of organisations representative of employees as she sees fit; and

(c) a panel of persons appointed by the [Lord Chancellor] after consultation with such organisations or associations of organisations representative of employers as she sees fit.

(4) Members of the panels constituted under these Regulations shall hold and vacate office under the terms of the instrument under which they are appointed but may resign their office by notice in writing, in the case of a member of the panel of [Employment Judges], to the appointing office holder and, in any other case, to the [Lord Chancellor]; and any such member who ceases to hold office shall be eligible for reappointment.

(5) The President may establish further specialist panels of [Employment Judges] and persons referred to in paragraphs (3)(b) and (c) and may select persons from such specialist panels in order to deal with proceedings in which particular specialist knowledge would be beneficial.

NOTES

Para (3) is amended as follows:

Words "Employment Judges" in square brackets in sub-para (a) substituted by the Tribunals, Courts and Enforcement Act 2007 (Transitional and Consequential Provisions) Order 2008, SI 2008/2683, art 6(1), Sch 1, paras 240, 247, as from 3 November 2008.

Sub-para (a)(i) substituted, and words "five" in square brackets in sub-paras (a)(ii), (iii) substituted, by the Employment Tribunals (Constitution and Rules of Procedure) (Amendment) Regulations 2008, SI 2008/2771, regs 2, 5, 6, as from 1 December 2008.

Words in first pair of square brackets in sub-para (a)(iii) substituted by the Constitutional Reform Act 2005, s 59(5), Sch 11, Pt 3, para 5, as from 1 October 2009.

Words "Lord Chancellor" in square brackets in sub-paras (b), (c) substituted by the Employment Tribunals (Constitution and Rules of Procedure) (Amendment) Regulations 2008, SI 2008/3240, regs 2, 3(2), as from 6 April 2009.

Para (4): words in first pair of square brackets substituted by SI 2008/2683, art 6(1), Sch 1, paras 240, 247, as from 3 November 2008; words in second pair of square brackets substituted by SI 2008/3240, regs 2, 3(2), as from 6 April 2009.

Para (5): words in square brackets substituted by SI 2008/2683, art 6(1), Sch 1, paras 240, 247, as from 3 November 2008.

[2.817]

9 Composition of tribunals—general

(1) For each hearing, the President, Vice President or the Regional [Employment Judge] shall select [an Employment Judge], who shall, subject to regulation 11, be a member of the panel of [Employment Judges], and the President, Vice President or the Regional [Employment Judge] may select himself.

(2) In any proceedings which are to be determined by a tribunal comprising [an Employment Judge] and two other members, the President, Regional [Employment Judge] or Vice President shall, subject to regulation 11, select one of those other members from the panel of persons appointed by the [Lord Chancellor] under regulation 8(3)(b) and the other from the panel of persons appointed under regulation 8(3)(c).

(3) In any proceedings which are to be determined by a tribunal whose composition is described in paragraph (2) or, as the case may be, regulation 11(b), those proceedings may, with the consent of the parties, be heard and determined in the absence of any one member other than the [Employment Judge].

(4) The President, Vice President, or a Regional [Employment Judge] may at any time select from the appropriate panel another person in substitution for the [Employment Judge] or other member of the tribunal previously selected to hear any proceedings before a tribunal or [Employment Judge].

NOTES

Words "Lord Chancellor" in square brackets in para (2) substituted by the Employment Tribunals (Constitution and Rules of Procedure) (Amendment) Regulations 2008, SI 2008/3240, regs 2, 3(2), as from 6 April 2009.

All other words in square brackets substituted by the Tribunals, Courts and Enforcement Act 2007 (Transitional and Consequential Provisions) Order 2008, SI 2008/2683, art 6(1), Sch 1, paras 240, 248, as from 3 November 2008.

[2.818]

10 Panels of members of tribunals—national security proceedings

In relation to national security proceedings, the President shall:—

(a) select a panel of persons from the panel of [Employment Judges] to act as [Employment Judges] in such cases; and

(b) select:—

(i) a panel of persons from the panel referred to in regulation 8(3)(b) as persons suitable to act as members in such cases; and

(ii) a panel of persons from the panel referred to in regulation 8(3)(c) as persons suitable to act as members in such cases.

NOTES

Words in square brackets substituted by the Tribunals, Courts and Enforcement Act 2007 (Transitional and Consequential Provisions) Order 2008, SI 2008/2683, art 6(1), Sch 1, paras 240, 249, as from 3 November 2008.

[2.819]

11 Composition of tribunals—national security proceedings

In relation to national security proceedings:—

(a) the President, the Regional [Employment Judge] or the Vice President shall select [an Employment Judge], who shall be a member of the panel selected in accordance with regulation 10(a), and the President, Regional [Employment Judge] or Vice President may select himself; and

(b) in any such proceedings which are to be determined by a tribunal comprising [an Employment Judge] and two other members, the President, Regional [Employment Judge] or Vice President shall select one of those other members from the panel selected in accordance with regulation 10(b)(i) and the other from the panel selected in accordance with regulation 10(b)(ii).

NOTES

Words in square brackets substituted by the Tribunals, Courts and Enforcement Act 2007 (Transitional and Consequential Provisions) Order 2008, SI 2008/2683, art 6(1), Sch 1, paras 240, 250, as from 3 November 2008.

[2.820]

12 Modification of section 4 of the Employment Tribunals Act (national security proceedings)

(1) For the purposes of national security proceedings section 4 of the Employment Tribunals Act shall be modified as follows.

(2) In section 4(1)(a), for the words "in accordance with regulations made under section 1(1)" substitute the words "in accordance with regulation 11(a) of the Employment Tribunals (Constitution and Rules of Procedure) Regulations 2004".

(3) In section 4(1)(b), for the words "in accordance with regulations so made" substitute the words "in accordance with regulation 11(b) of those Regulations".

(4) In section 4(5), for the words "in accordance with Regulations made under section 1(1)" substitute the words "in accordance with regulation 10(a) of the Employment Tribunals (Constitution and Rules of Procedure) Regulations 2004".

[2.821]

13 Practice directions

(1) The President may make practice directions about the procedure of employment tribunals in the area for which he is responsible, including practice directions about the exercise by tribunals or [Employment Judges] of powers under these Regulations or the Schedules to them.

(2) The power of the President to make practice directions under paragraph (1) includes power:—

(a) to vary or revoke practice directions;

(b) to make different provision for different cases or different areas, including different provision for specific types of proceedings.

(3) The President shall publish a practice direction made under paragraph (1), and any revocation or variation of it, in such manner as he considers appropriate for bringing it to the attention of the persons to whom it is addressed.

NOTES

Para (1): words in square brackets substituted by the Tribunals, Courts and Enforcement Act 2007 (Transitional and Consequential Provisions) Order 2008, SI 2008/2683, art 6(1), Sch 1, paras 240, 251, as from 3 November 2008.

Practice Directions: for Practice Directions made under this regulation see **[5.54]**, **[5.55]**, **[5.56]**.

[2.822]

14 Power to prescribe

(1) The Secretary of State may prescribe—

(a) one or more versions of a form, one of which shall be used by all claimants for the purpose of commencing proceedings in an employment tribunal ("claim form") except any claim or proceedings listed in paragraph (3);

(b) one or more versions of a form, one of which shall be used by all respondents to a claim for the purpose of responding to a claim before an employment tribunal ("response form") except respondents to a claim or proceedings listed in paragraph (3); and

(c) that the provision of certain information and answering of certain questions in a claim form or in a response form is mandatory in all proceedings save those listed in paragraph (3).

(2) The Secretary of State shall publish the forms and matters prescribed pursuant to paragraph (1) in such manner as she considers appropriate in order to bring them to the attention of potential claimants, respondents and their advisers.

(3) The proceedings referred to in paragraph (1) are:—

- (a) those referred to an employment tribunal by a court;
- (b) proceedings to which any of Schedules 3 to 5 apply; or
- (c) proceedings brought under any of the following enactments:—
  - (i) sections 19, 20 or 22 of the National Minimum Wage Act 1998;
  - (ii) section 11 of the Employment Rights Act where the proceedings are brought by the employer.

NOTES

Current versions of the claim and response forms prescribed under this regulation (as of 6 April 2013) are at **[5.57]** and **[5.58]** respectively.

[2.823]

15 Calculation of time limits

[(1) Any period of time for doing any act required or permitted to be done under any of the rules in Schedules 1, 2, 3, 4, 5 and 6, or under any decision, order or judgment of a tribunal or [an Employment Judge], shall be calculated in accordance with paragraphs (2) to (6).]

(2) Where any act must or may be done within a certain number of days of or from an event, the date of that event shall not be included in the calculation. For example, a respondent is sent a copy of a claim on 1st October. He must present a response to the Employment Tribunal Office within 28 days of the date on which he was sent the copy. The last day for presentation of the response is 29th October.

(3) Where any act must or may be done not less than a certain number of days before or after an event, the date of that event shall not be included in the calculation. For example, if a party wishes to submit representations in writing for consideration by a tribunal at a hearing, he must submit them not less than 7 days before the hearing. If the hearing is fixed for 8th October, the representations must be submitted no later than 1st October.

(4) Where the tribunal or [an Employment Judge] gives any decision, order or judgment which imposes a time limit for doing any act, the last date for compliance shall, wherever practicable, be expressed as a calendar date.

(5) In rule 14(4) of Schedule 1 the requirement to send the notice of hearing to the parties not less than 14 days before the date fixed for the hearing shall not be construed as a requirement for service of the notice to have been effected not less than 14 days before the hearing date, but as a requirement for the notice to have been placed in the post not less than 14 days before that date. For example, a hearing is fixed for 15th October. The last day on which the notice may be placed in the post is 1st October.

(6) Where any act must or may have been done within a certain number of days of a document being sent to a person by the Secretary, the date when the document was sent shall, unless the contrary is proved, be regarded as the date on the letter from the Secretary which accompanied the document. For example, a respondent must present his response to a claim to the Employment Tribunal Office [within 28 days of the date on which] he was sent a copy of the claim. If the letter from the Secretary sending him a copy of the claim is dated 1st October, the last day for presentation of the response is 29th October.

NOTES

Para (1): substituted by the Employment Tribunals (Constitution and Rules of Procedure) (Amendment) Regulations 2004, SI 2004/2351, reg 2(1), (6)(a); words in square brackets substituted by the Tribunals, Courts and Enforcement Act 2007 (Transitional and Consequential Provisions) Order 2008, SI 2008/2683, art 6(1), Sch 1, paras 240, 252, as from 3 November 2008.

Para (4): words in square brackets substituted by SI 2008/2683, art 6(1), Sch 1, paras 240, 252, as from 3 November 2008.

Para (6): words in square brackets substituted by SI 2004/2351, reg 2(1), (6)(b).

[2.824]

16 Application of Schedules 1–5 to proceedings

(1) [Subject to paragraphs (2), (3) and (4)], the rules in Schedule 1 shall apply in relation to all proceedings before an employment tribunal except where separate rules of procedure made under the provisions of any enactment are applicable.

(2) In proceedings to which the rules in Schedule 1 apply and in which any power conferred on the Minister, the tribunal or [an Employment Judge] by rule 54 (national security proceedings) of Schedule 1 is exercised, Schedule 1 shall be modified in accordance with Schedule 2.

(3) The rules in Schedules 3, 4 and 5 shall apply to modify the rules in Schedule 1 in relation to proceedings which consist, respectively, in:—

(a) an appeal by a person assessed to levy imposed under a levy order made under section 12 of the Industrial Training Act 1982;

(b) an appeal against an improvement or prohibition notice under section 24 of the Health and Safety at Work etc Act 1974; and

[(c) an appeal against an unlawful act notice under section 21 of the Equality Act 2006].

[(4) In proceedings which involve an equal value claim (as defined in rule 2 of Schedule 6), Schedule 1 shall be modified in accordance with Schedule 6.]

NOTES

Para (1): words in square brackets substituted by the Employment Tribunals (Constitution and Rules of Procedure) (Amendment) Regulations 2004, SI 2004/2351, reg 2(1), (7)(a).

Para (2): words in square brackets substituted by the Tribunals, Courts and Enforcement Act 2007 (Transitional and Consequential Provisions) Order 2008, SI 2008/2683, art 6(1), Sch 1, paras 240, 253, as from 3 November 2008.

Para (3): sub-para (c) substituted by the Equality Act 2006 (Dissolution of Commissions and Consequential and Transitional Provisions) Order 2007, SI 2007/2602, art 4(1), Schedule, para 7(a).

Para (4): added by SI 2004/2351, reg 2(1), (7)(b).

[2.825]

17 Register

(1) The Secretary shall maintain a Register which shall be open to the inspection of any person without charge at all reasonable hours.

(2) The Register shall contain a copy of all judgments and any written reasons issued by any tribunal or [Employment Judge] which are required to be entered in the Register in accordance with the rules in Schedules 1 to 5.

(3) The Register, or any part of it, may be kept by means of a computer.

NOTES

Para (2): words in square brackets substituted by the Tribunals, Courts and Enforcement Act 2007 (Transitional and Consequential Provisions) Order 2008, SI 2008/2683, art 6(1), Sch 1, paras 240, 254, as from 3 November 2008.

[2.826]

18 Proof of decisions of tribunals

The production in any proceedings in any court of a document purporting to be certified by the Secretary to be a true copy of an entry of a judgment in the Register shall, unless the contrary is proved, be sufficient evidence of the document and of the facts stated therein.

[2.827]

19 Jurisdiction of tribunals in Scotland and in England & Wales

(1) An employment tribunal in England or Wales shall only have jurisdiction to deal with proceedings (referred to as "English and Welsh proceedings") where—

(a) the respondent or one of the respondents resides or carries on business in England and Wales;

(b) had the remedy been by way of action in the county court, the cause of action would have arisen wholly or partly in England and Wales;

(c) the proceedings are to determine a question which has been referred to the tribunal by a court in England and Wales; or

(d) in the case of proceedings to which Schedule 3, 4 or 5 applies, the proceedings relate to matters arising in England and Wales.

(2) An employment tribunal in Scotland shall only have jurisdiction to deal with proceedings (referred to as "Scottish proceedings") where—

(a) the respondent or one of the respondents resides or carries on business in Scotland;

(b) the proceedings relate to a contract of employment the place of execution or performance of which is in Scotland;

(c) the proceedings are to determine a question which has been referred to the tribunal by a sheriff in Scotland; or

(d) in the case of proceedings to which Schedule 3, 4 or 5 applies, the proceedings relate to matters arising in Scotland.

[2.828]

20 Transitional provisions

(1) [These Regulations and Schedules 1 to 6] to them shall apply in relation to all proceedings to which they relate where those proceedings were commenced on or after 1 October 2004.

(2) These Regulations and Schedules 1 and 2 to them (with the exception of rules 1 to 3 and 38 to 48 of Schedule 1) shall apply to proceedings:—

(a) which were commenced prior to 1 October 2004; and

(b) to which Schedule 1 to either the old (England & Wales) regulations or the old (Scotland) regulations applied;

provided that a copy of the originating application was not sent to the respondent prior to 1 October 2004.

(3) In relation to the proceedings described in paragraph (2), the following provisions of Schedule 1 to the old (England & Wales) regulations or the old (Scotland) regulations (as the case may be) shall continue to apply:—

(a) rule 1 (originating application);

(b) rule 2 (action upon receipt of originating application) with the exception of paragraphs (2), (4) and (5) of that rule; and

(c) rule 14 (costs).

(4) In relation to proceedings described in paragraph (2) but where a copy of the originating application was sent to the respondent prior to 1 October 2004, Schedules 1 and 2 to these Regulations shall apply with the exception of rules 1 to 9, 21 to 24, 33 and 38 to 48 of Schedule 1 and rules 2, 3 and 4 of Schedule 2.

(5) In relation to proceedings described in paragraph (4), the following provisions of the old (England & Wales) regulations or the old (Scotland) regulations (as the case may be) shall continue to apply:—

(a) in Schedule 1:—

(i) rule 1 (originating application);

(ii) rule 2 (action upon receipt of originating application) with the exception of paragraphs (2), (4) and (5) of that rule;

(iii) rule 3 (appearance by respondent);

(iv) rule 8 (national security);

(v) rule 14 (costs); and

(b) rule 1 of Schedule 2.

(6) In relation to proceedings commenced prior to 1 October 2004 and to which Schedule 4, 5 or 6 to the old (England & Wales) regulations or the old (Scotland) regulations (as the case may be) applied, the provisions of those schedules shall continue to apply to such proceedings.

[(7) In relation to proceedings:—

(i) which were commenced prior to 1 October 2004;

(ii) to which Schedule 3 to either the old (England & Wales) regulations or the old (Scotland) regulations applied; and

(iii) in which the tribunal has not, prior to 1 October 2004, required a member of the panel of independent experts to prepare a report under section 2A(1)(b) of the Equal Pay Act;

these Regulations and rules 1 to 13 of Schedule 6, with the exception of rule 4(3)(a), shall apply.

(8) In relation to proceedings:—

(i) which were commenced prior to 1 October 2004;

(ii) to which Schedule 3 to either the old (England & Wales) regulations or the old (Scotland) regulations applied; and

(iii) in which the tribunal has, prior to 1 October 2004, required a member of the panel of independent experts to prepare a report under section 2A(1)(b) of the Equal Pay Act;

Schedule 3 to either the old (England & Wales) regulations or the old (Scotland) regulations (as the case may be) shall continue to apply.

(9) In relation to proceedings described in paragraph (8), the following rules of Schedule 6 shall also apply and shall take precedence over any conflicting provision in Schedule 3 to either the old (England & Wales) regulations or the old (Scotland) regulations, namely:

— rules 3, 11(2), 11(4), 12, 13(1) and 13(3).

(10) Rule 14 of Schedule 6 shall apply to all proceedings to which, in accordance with this regulation, rule 10 of Schedule 2 applies.]

NOTES

Para (1): words in square brackets substituted by the Employment Tribunals (Constitution and Rules of Procedure) (Amendment) Regulations 2004, SI 2004/2351, reg 2(1), (8)(a).

Paras (7)–(10): added by SI 2004/2351, reg 2(1), (8)(b).

SCHEDULES

SCHEDULE 1
THE EMPLOYMENT TRIBUNALS RULES OF PROCEDURE

Regulation 16

NOTES

All references to "Employment Judge", "an Employment Judge", "Employment Judge's", and "Employment Judges" in this Schedule were substituted by the Tribunals, Courts and Enforcement Act 2007 (Transitional and Consequential Provisions) Order 2008, SI 2008/2683, art 6(1), Sch 1, paras 240, 255(a)–(d), as from 3 November 2008.

Other amendments are noted to the rule concerned.

How to bring a claim

[2.829]

1 Starting a claim

(1) A claim shall be brought before an employment tribunal by the claimant presenting to an Employment Tribunal Office the details of the claim in writing. Those details must include all the relevant required information (subject to . . . rule 53 (Employment Agencies Act 1973)).

(2) The claim may only be presented to an Employment Tribunal Office in England and Wales if it relates to English and Welsh proceedings (defined in regulation 19(1)). The claim may only be presented to an Employment Tribunal Office in Scotland if it relates to Scottish proceedings (defined in regulation 19(2)).

(3) Unless it is a claim in proceedings described in regulation 14(3), a claim which is presented on or after [1st October 2005] must be presented on a claim form which has been prescribed by the Secretary of State in accordance with regulation 14.

(4) Subject to . . . rule 53, the required information in relation to the claim is—

- (a) each claimant's name;
- (b) each claimant's address;
- (c) the name of each person against whom the claim is made ("the respondent");
- (d) each respondent's address;
- (e) details of the claim;
- (f)–(i) . . .

(5), (6) . . .

(7) Two or more claimants may present their claims in the same document if their claims arise out of the same set of facts.

(8) . . .

NOTES

Words omitted from para (1) revoked by the Employment Tribunals (Constitution and Rules of Procedure) (Amendment) Regulations 2008, SI 2008/3240, regs 2, 4(1), (2)(a), as from 6 April 2009, except (by virtue of reg 8 thereof) in relation to proceedings where ss 29 to 33 of, and Schs 2 to 4 to, the Employment Act 2002 apply (those provisions were repealed by the Employment Act 2008, as from 6 April 2009, subject to transitional provisions in the Employment Act 2008 (Commencement No 1, Transitional Provisions and Savings) Order 2008, SI 2008/3232).

Words "1st October 2005" in square brackets in para (3) substituted by the Employment Tribunals (Constitution and Rules of Procedure) (Amendment) Regulations 2005, SI 2005/435, reg 2.

First words omitted from para (4) revoked by SI 2008/3240, regs 2, 4(1), (2)(b), as from 6 April 2009, subject to the same savings in SI 2008/3240 as noted above.

Sub-paras (4)(f)–(i), (5), (6), (8) revoked by SI 2008/3240, regs 2, 4(1), (2)(c), (d), as from 6 April 2009, subject to the same savings in SI 2008/3240, reg 8 as noted above.

Acceptance of claim procedure

[2.830]

2 What the tribunal does after receiving the claim

(1) On receiving the claim the Secretary shall consider whether the claim or part of it should be accepted in accordance with rule 3. If a claim or part of one is not accepted the tribunal shall not proceed to deal with any part which has not been accepted (unless it is accepted at a later date). If no part of a claim is accepted the claim shall not be copied to the respondent.

(2) If the Secretary accepts the claim or part of it, he shall—

- (a) send a copy of the claim to each respondent and record in writing the date on which it was sent;
- (b) inform the parties in writing of the case number of the claim (which must from then on be referred to in all correspondence relating to the claim) and the address to which notices and other communications to the Employment Tribunal Office must be sent;
- (c) inform the respondent in writing about how to present a response to the claim, the time limit for doing so, what may happen if a response is not entered within the time limit and that the respondent has a right to receive a copy of any judgment disposing of the claim;
- (d) when any enactment relevant to the claim provides for conciliation, notify the parties that the services of a conciliation officer [may be] available to them; [and]
- (e) . . .
- (f) if only part of the claim has been accepted, inform the claimant and any respondent which parts of the claim have not been accepted and that the tribunal shall not proceed to deal with those parts unless they are accepted at a later date.

[(3) If the claim or part of it is accepted, the Secretary may, if the Secretary considers it appropriate, send a copy of the claim or part of it, to a regulator where the claimant (C) has—

- (a) consented; and
- (b) alleged in the claim that C has made a protected disclosure.

(4) For the purposes of paragraph (3) a regulator means a person listed in the Annex to this Schedule; and a protected disclosure has the meaning given to that expression by section 43A of the 1996 Act.]

NOTES

Words "may be" in square brackets in sub-para (2)(d) substituted, word "and" in square brackets in that paragraph inserted, and sub-para (2)(e) revoked, by the Employment Tribunals (Constitution and Rules of Procedure) (Amendment) Regulations 2008, SI 2008/3240, regs 2, 4(1), (3), as from 6 April 2009.

Paras (3), (4) added by the Employment Tribunals (Constitution and Rules of Procedure) (Amendment) Regulations 2010, SI 2010/131, reg 2(1), (2), as from 6 April 2010, except where the claim is presented to an Employment Tribunal Office before that date.

[2.831]

3 When the claim will not be accepted by the Secretary

(1) When a claim is required by rule 1(3) to be presented using a prescribed form, but the prescribed form has not been used, the Secretary shall not accept the claim and shall return it to the claimant with an explanation of why the claim has been rejected and provide a prescribed claim form.

(2) The Secretary shall not accept the claim (or a relevant part of one) if it is clear to him that one or more of the following circumstances applies—

(a) the claim does not include all the relevant required information; [or]

(b) the tribunal does not have power to consider the claim (or that relevant part of it) . . .

(c) . . . .

(3) If the Secretary decides not to accept a claim or part of one for any of the reasons in paragraph (2), he shall refer the claim together with a statement of his reasons for not accepting it to [an Employment Judge]. The [Employment Judge] shall decide in accordance with the criteria in paragraph (2) whether the claim or part of it should be accepted and allowed to proceed.

(4) If the [Employment Judge] decides that the claim or part of one should be accepted he shall inform the Secretary in writing and the Secretary shall accept the relevant part of the claim and then proceed to deal with it in accordance with rule 2(2).

(5) If the [Employment Judge] decides that the claim or part of it should not be accepted he shall record his decision together with the reasons for it in writing in a document signed by him. The Secretary shall as soon as is reasonably practicable inform the claimant of that decision and the reasons for it in writing together with information on how that decision may be reviewed or appealed.

(6) . . .

(7) Except for the purposes of paragraph . . . (8) or any appeal to the Employment Appeal Tribunal, where [an Employment Judge] has decided that a claim or part of one should not be accepted such a claim (or the relevant part of it) is to be treated as if it had not been received by the Secretary on that occasion.

(8) Any decision by [an Employment Judge] not to accept a claim or part of one may be reviewed in accordance with rules 34 to 36. If the result of such review is that any parts of the claim should have been accepted, then paragraph (7) shall not apply to the relevant parts of that claim and the Secretary shall then accept such parts and proceed to deal with it as described in rule 2(2).

(9) A decision to accept or not to accept a claim or part of one shall not bind any future tribunal or [Employment Judge] where any of the issues listed in paragraph (2) fall to be determined later in the proceedings.

(10) Except in rule 34 (review of other judgments and decisions), all references to a claim in the remainder of these rules are to be read as references to only the part of the claim which has been accepted.

NOTES

The word "or" in square brackets in sub-para (2)(a) was inserted, and sub-para (2)(c) (and the word "or" immediately preceding it) was revoked, by the Employment Tribunals (Constitution and Rules of Procedure) (Amendment) Regulations 2008, SI 2008/3240, regs 2, 4(1), (4)(a), (b), as from 6 April 2009, subject to the same savings in SI 2008/3240, reg 8 as noted at **[2.829]**.

Para (6), and the words omitted from para (7), were revoked by SI 2008/3240, regs 2, 4(1), (4)(c), (d), as from 6 April 2009, subject to the same savings in SI 2008/3240, reg 8 as noted at **[2.829]**.

Response

[2.832]

4 Responding to the claim

(1) If the respondent wishes to respond to the claim made against him he must present his response to the Employment Tribunal Office within 28 days of the date on which he was sent a copy of the claim. The response must include all the relevant required information. The time limit for the respondent to present his response may be extended in accordance with paragraph (4).

(2) Unless it is a response in proceedings described in regulation 14(3), any response presented on or after [1st October 2005] must be on a response form prescribed by the Secretary of State pursuant to regulation 14.

(3) The required information in relation to the response is—

(a) the respondent's full name;
(b) the respondent's address;
(c) whether or not the respondent wishes to resist the claim in whole or in part; and
(d) if the respondent wishes to so resist, on what grounds.

(4) The respondent may apply . . . for an extension of the time limit within which he is to present his response. The application must be presented to the Employment Tribunal Office within 28 days of the date on which the respondent was sent a copy of the claim (unless the application is made under rule 33(1)) and must explain why the respondent cannot comply with the time limit. Subject to rule 33, the [Employment Judge] shall only extend the time within which a response may be presented if he is satisfied that it is just and equitable to do so.

[(4A) When a respondent is legally represented in relation to the application the respondent or the respondent's representative must, at the same time as the application is sent to the Employment Tribunal Office, provide all other parties with the following information in writing—

(a) details of the application and the reasons why it is made;
(b) notification that any objection to the application must be sent to the Employment Tribunal Office within 7 days of receiving the application or, if a hearing of any type is due to take place before the expiry of that 7 day period, before the date of that hearing; and
(c) that any objection to the application must be copied to both the Employment Tribunal Office and all other parties,

and the respondent or that representative must confirm in writing to the Employment Tribunal Office that this rule has been complied with.

(4B) The time limit described in sub-paragraph (4A)(b) may be amended where the Employment Judge or tribunal considers it in the interests of justice to do so.

(4C) Where a respondent is not legally represented in relation to the application, the Secretary shall send a copy of the application to all other parties and inform them of the matters listed in sub-paragraphs (4A)(b) and (c).

(4D) Where a respondent's application under paragraph (4) is refused the Secretary shall inform the parties in writing of such refusal unless the application is refused at a hearing.

(4E) This rule is subject to section 12 of the State Immunity Act 1978.]

(5) A single document may include the response to more than one claim if the relief claimed arises out of the same set of facts, provided that in respect of each of the claims to which the single response relates—

(a) the respondent intends to resist all the claims and the grounds for doing so are the same in relation to each claim; or
(b) the respondent does not intend to resist any of the claims.

(6) A single document may include the response of more than one respondent to a single claim provided that—

(a) each respondent intends to resist the claim and the grounds for doing so are the same for each respondent; or
(b) none of the respondents intends to resist the claim.

NOTES

Words "1st October 2005" in square brackets in para (2) substituted by the Employment Tribunals (Constitution and Rules of Procedure) (Amendment) Regulations 2005, SI 2005/435, reg 2.

Words omitted from para (4) revoked, and paras (4A)–(4E) inserted, by the Employment Tribunals (Constitution and Rules of Procedure) (Amendment) Regulations 2008, SI 2008/3240, regs 2, 4(1), (5), as from 6 April 2009.

Acceptance of response procedure

[2.833]

5 What the tribunal does after receiving the response

(1) On receiving the response the Secretary shall consider whether the response should be accepted in accordance with rule 6. If the response is not accepted it shall be returned to the respondent and (subject to paragraphs (5) and (6) of rule 6) the claim shall be dealt with as if no response to the claim had been presented.

(2) If the Secretary accepts the response he shall send a copy of it to all other parties and record in writing the date on which he does so.

[2.834]
6 When the response will not be accepted by the Secretary

(1) Where a response is required to be presented using a prescribed form by rule 4(2), but the prescribed form has not been used, the Secretary shall not accept the response and shall return it to the respondent with an explanation of why the response has been rejected and provide a prescribed response form.

(2) The Secretary shall not accept the response if it is clear to him that any of the following circumstances apply—

(a) the response does not include all the required information (defined in rule 4(3));
(b) the response has not been presented within the relevant time limit.

(3) If the Secretary decides not to accept a response for either of the reasons in paragraph (2), he shall refer the response together with a statement of his reasons for not accepting the response to [an Employment Judge]. The [Employment Judge] shall decide in accordance with the criteria in paragraph (2) whether the response should be accepted.

(4) If the [Employment Judge] decides that the response should be accepted he shall inform the Secretary in writing and the Secretary shall accept the response and then deal with it in accordance with rule 5(2).

(5) If the [Employment Judge] decides that the response should not be accepted he shall record his decision together with the reasons for it in writing in a document signed by him. The Secretary shall inform both the claimant and the respondent of that decision and the reasons for it. The Secretary shall also inform the respondent of the consequences for the respondent of that decision and how it may be reviewed or appealed.

(6) Any decision by [an Employment Judge] not to accept a response may be reviewed in accordance with rules 34 to 36. If the result of such a review is that the response [is to be] accepted, then the Secretary shall accept the response and proceed to deal with the response as described in rule 5(2).

NOTES

Words "is to be" in square brackets in para (6) substituted by the Employment Tribunals (Constitution and Rules of Procedure) (Amendment) Regulations 2008, SI 2008/3240, regs 2, 4(1), (6), as from 6 April 2009.

Part 2 Statutory Instruments

[2.835]
7 Counterclaims

(1) When a respondent wishes to present a claim against the claimant ("a counterclaim") in accordance with article 4 of the Employment Tribunals Extension of Jurisdiction (England and Wales) Order 1994, or as the case may be, article 4 of the Employment Tribunals Extension of Jurisdiction (Scotland) Order 1994, he must present the details of his counterclaim to the Employment Tribunal Office in writing. Those details must include—

(a) the respondent's name;
(b) the respondent's address;
(c) the name of each claimant whom the counterclaim is made against;
(d) the claimant's address;
(e) details of the counterclaim.

(2) [An Employment Judge] may in relation to particular proceedings by order made under rule 10(1) establish the procedure which shall be followed by the respondent making the counterclaim and any claimant responding to the counterclaim.

(3) The President may by a practice direction made under regulation 13 make provision for the procedure which is to apply to counterclaims generally.

Consequences of a response not being presented or accepted

[2.836]
8 Default judgments

[(1) Subject to paragraphs (2A) and (6), in any proceedings if the relevant time limit for presenting a response has passed, an Employment Judge shall, in the circumstances listed in paragraph (2), issue a default judgment to determine the claim without a hearing.]

[(1A) If the Employment Judge is not satisfied that he has sufficient information to issue a default judgment, he shall make an order (as described in rule 10(2)(b)) requiring such additional information as he considers appropriate to enable him, subject to paragraphs (2A) and (6), to issue a default judgment.

(1B) Where an order is made as described in paragraph (1A), and the additional information requested has not been received within the specified time limit, a default judgment shall be issued in accordance with paragraph (1).]

[(2) [Subject to paragraphs (2A) and (6), those circumstances] are when either—

(a) no response in those proceedings has been presented to the Employment Tribunal Office within the relevant time limit;

(b) a response has been so presented, but a decision has been made not to accept the response either by the Secretary under rule 6(1) or by [an Employment Judge] under rule 6(3), and the Employment Tribunal Office has not received an application under rule 34 to have that decision reviewed; or

(c) a response has been accepted in those proceedings, but the respondent has stated in the response that he does not intend to resist the claim.]

[(2A) No default judgment need be issued where the Employment Judge—

(a) is not satisfied that the tribunal has jurisdiction to consider the claim, or part of it; or

(b) has sufficient evidence to conclude that the claim form has not been received by the respondent.]

(3) A default judgment may determine liability only or it may determine liability and remedy. If a default judgment determines remedy it shall be such remedy as it appears to the [Employment Judge] that the claimant is entitled to on the basis of the information before him.

(4) Any default judgment issued by [an Employment Judge] under this rule shall be recorded in writing and shall be signed by him. The Secretary shall send a copy of that judgment to the parties, to ACAS, and, if the proceedings were referred to the tribunal by a court, to that court. The Secretary shall also inform the parties of their right to [apply to] have the default judgment reviewed under rule 33. The Secretary shall put a copy of the default judgment on the Register (subject to rule 49 (sexual offences and the Register)).

(5) The claimant or respondent may apply to have the default judgment reviewed in accordance with rule 33.

[(6) A default judgment shall not be issued where the parties have settled the proceedings (either by means of a compromise agreement or through ACAS). If a default judgment is issued in these circumstances it shall have no effect.]

(7) When paragraph (6) applies, either party may apply under rule 33 to have the default judgment revoked.

NOTES

Paras (1), (6) substituted by the Employment Tribunals (Constitution and Rules of Procedure) (Amendment) Regulations 2008, SI 2008/3240, regs 2, 4(1), (7)(a), (f), as from 6 April 2009, except (by virtue of reg 9 thereof) in relation to proceedings where those proceedings were commenced on or before 5 April 2009.

Paras (1A), (1B), (2A) inserted by SI 2008/3240, regs 2, 4(1), (7)(b), (d), as from 6 April 2009, subject to the same savings in SI 2008/3240, reg 9 as noted above.

Para (2) substituted by the Employment Tribunals (Constitution and Rules of Procedure) (Amendment) Regulations 2004, SI 2004/2351, reg 2(1), (9)(a); words "Subject to paragraphs (2A) and (6), those circumstances" in square brackets in para (2) substituted by SI 2008/3240, regs 2, 4(1), (7)(c), as from 6 April 2009, subject to the same savings in SI 2008/3240, reg 9 as noted above.

Para (4) words "apply to" in square brackets inserted by SI 2008/3240, regs 2, 4(1), (7)(e), as from 6 April 2009, subject to the same savings in SI 2008/3240, reg 9 as noted above.

[2.837]

9 Taking no further part in the proceedings

A respondent who has not presented a response to a claim or whose response has not been accepted shall not be entitled to take any part in the proceedings except to—

[(aa) make a request under rule 30 (written reasons);]

(a) make an application under rule 33 (review of default judgments);

(b) make an application under rule 35 (preliminary consideration of application for review) in respect of [rule 34(3)(a), (b) or (e)];

(c) be called as a witness by another person; or

(d) be sent a copy of a document or corrected entry in accordance with rule 8(4), 29(2) or 37;

and in these rules the word "party" or "respondent" includes a respondent only in relation to his entitlement to take such a part in the proceedings, and in relation to any such part which he takes.

NOTES

Sub-para (aa) inserted by the Employment Tribunals (Constitution and Rules of Procedure) (Amendment) Regulations 2008, SI 2008/3240, regs 2, 4(1), (8), as from 6 April 2009; words "rule 34(3)(a), (b) or (e)" in square brackets in para (b) substituted by the Employment Tribunals (Constitution and Rules of Procedure) (Amendment) (No 2) Regulations 2005, SI 2005/1865, reg 2(1), (4)(a).

Case management

[2.838]

10 General power to manage proceedings

(1) Subject to the following rules, the [Employment Judge] may at any time either on the application of a party or on his own initiative make an order in relation to any matter which appears to him to be appropriate. Such orders may be any of those listed in paragraph (2) or such other

orders as he thinks fit. Subject to the following rules, orders may be issued as a result of [an Employment Judge] considering the papers before him in the absence of the parties, or at a hearing (see regulation 2 for the definition of "hearing").

(2) Examples of orders which may be made under paragraph (1) are orders—

(a) as to the manner in which the proceedings are to be conducted, including any time limit to be observed;
(b) that a party provide additional information;
(c) requiring the attendance of any person in Great Britain either to give evidence or to produce documents or information;
(d) requiring any person in Great Britain to disclose documents or information to a party [or] to allow a party to inspect such material as might be ordered by a County Court (or in Scotland, by a sheriff);
(e) extending any time limit, whether or not expired (subject to rules 4(4), 11(2), 25(5), 30(5), 33(1), 35(1), 38(7) and 42(5) of this Schedule, and to rule 3(4) of Schedule 2);
(f) requiring the provision of written answers to questions put by the tribunal or [Employment Judge];
(g) . . .
(h) staying (in Scotland, sisting) the whole or part of any proceedings;
(i) that part of the proceedings be dealt with separately;
(j) that different claims be considered together;
(k) that any person who the [Employment Judge] or tribunal considers may be liable for the remedy claimed should be made a respondent in the proceedings;
(l) dismissing the claim against a respondent who is no longer directly interested in the claim;
(m) postponing or adjourning any hearing;
(n) varying or revoking other orders;
(o) giving notice to the parties of a pre-hearing review or the Hearing;
(p) giving notice under rule 19;
(q) giving leave to amend a claim or response;
(r) that any person who the [Employment Judge] or tribunal considers has an interest in the outcome of the proceedings may be joined as a party to the proceedings;
(s) that a witness statement be prepared or exchanged; or
(t) as to the use of experts or interpreters in the proceedings.

(3) An order may specify the time at or within which and the place at which any act is required to be done. An order may also impose conditions and it shall inform the parties of the potential consequences of non-compliance set out in rule 13.

(4) When a requirement has been imposed under paragraph (1) the person subject to the requirement may make an application under rule 11 (applications in proceedings) for the order to be varied or revoked.

(5) An order described in . . . [sub-]paragraph (2)(d) which requires a person other than a party to grant disclosure or inspection of material may be made only when the disclosure sought is necessary in order to dispose fairly of the claim or to save expense.

(6) Any order containing a requirement described in either sub-paragraph (2)(c) or (d) shall state that under section 7(4) of the Employment Tribunals Act, any person who without reasonable excuse fails to comply with the requirement shall be liable on summary conviction to a fine, and the document shall also state the amount of the maximum fine.

(7) An order as described in [sub-]paragraph (2)(j) may be made only if all relevant parties have been given notice that such an order may be made and they have been given the opportunity to make oral or written representations as to why such an order should or should not be made.

(8) Any order made under this rule shall be recorded in writing and signed by the [Employment Judge] and the Secretary shall [(except where the order is for a witness order described in rule 10(2)(c) only)] inform all parties to the proceedings of any order made as soon as is reasonably practicable.

NOTES

Word "or" in square brackets in sub-para (2)(d) inserted by the Employment Tribunals (Constitution and Rules of Procedure) (Amendment) Regulations 2008, SI 2008/3240, regs 2, 4(1), (9)(a), as from 6 April 2009.

Sub-para (2)(g) revoked by SI 2008/3240, regs 2, 4(1), (9)(b), as from 6 April 2009.

Word omitted from para (5) revoked by the Employment Tribunals (Constitution and Rules of Procedure) (Amendment) (No 2) Regulations 2005, SI 2005/1865, reg 2(1), (4)(b).

Word "sub-" in square brackets in paras (5), (7) inserted by SI 2008/3240, regs 2, 4(1), (9)(c), (d), as from 6 April 2009.

Words "(except where the order is for a witness order described in rule 10(2)(c) only)" in square brackets in para (8) inserted by SI 2008/3240, regs 2, 4(1), (9)(e), as from 6 April 2009.

[2.839]
11 Applications in proceedings

(1) At any stage of the proceedings a party may apply for an order to be issued, varied or revoked or for a case management discussion or pre-hearing review to be held.

(2) An application for an order must be made not less than 10 days before the date of the hearing at which it is to be considered (if any) unless it is not reasonably practicable to do so, or the [Employment Judge] or tribunal considers it in the interests of justice that shorter notice be allowed. The application must (unless [an Employment Judge] orders otherwise) be in writing to the Employment Tribunal Office and include the case number for the proceedings and the reasons for the request. If the application is for a case management discussion or a pre-hearing review to be held, it must identify any orders sought.

(3) An application for an order must include an explanation of how the order would assist the tribunal or [Employment Judge] in dealing with the proceedings efficiently and fairly.

(4) When a party is legally represented in relation to the application (except where the application is for a witness order described in rule 10(2)(c) only), that party or his representative must, at the same time as the application is sent to the Employment Tribunal Office, provide all other parties with the following information in writing—

(a) details of the application and the reasons why it is [made];

[(b) notification that any objection to the application must be sent to the Employment Tribunal Office within 7 days of receiving the application or, if a hearing of any type is due to take place before the expiry of that 7 day period, before the date of that hearing];

(c) that any objection to the application must be copied to both the Employment Tribunal Office and all other parties;

and the party or his representative must confirm in writing to the Employment Tribunal Office that this rule has been complied with.

[(4A) The time limit described in sub-paragraph (4)(b) may be amended where the Employment Judge or tribunal considers it in the interests of justice to do so.]

[(5) Where a party is not legally represented in relation to the application, the Secretary shall (except where the application is for a witness order described in rule 10(2)(c) only) send a copy of the application to all other parties and inform them of the matters listed in sub-paragraphs (4)(b) and (c).]

(6) [An Employment Judge] may refuse a party's application and if he does so the Secretary shall inform the parties in writing of such refusal unless the application is refused at a hearing.

NOTES

Word "made" in square brackets in sub-para (4)(a) substituted, sub-para (4)(b) and para (5) substituted, and para (4A) inserted, by the Employment Tribunals (Constitution and Rules of Procedure) (Amendment) Regulations 2008, SI 2008/3240, regs 2, 4(1), (10), as from 6 April 2009.

[2.840]
12 [Employment Judge] acting on his own initiative

(1) Subject to paragraph (2) and to rules 10(7) and 18(7), [an Employment Judge] may make an order on his own initiative with or without hearing the parties or giving them an opportunity to make written or oral representations. He may also decide to hold a case management discussion or pre-hearing review on his own initiative.

(2) Where [an Employment Judge] makes an order without giving the parties the opportunity to make representations—

(a) the Secretary must send to the party affected by such order a copy of the order and a statement explaining the right to make an application under [sub-]paragraph (2)(b); and

(b) a party affected by the order may apply to have it varied or revoked.

(3) An application under [sub-]paragraph (2)(b) must (subject to rule 10(2)(e)) be made before the time at which, or the expiry of the period within which, the order was to be complied with. Such an application must (unless [an Employment Judge] orders otherwise) be made in writing to an Employment Tribunal Office and it must include the reasons for the application. Paragraphs (4) and (5) of rule 11 apply in relation to informing the other parties of the application.

NOTES

Word "sub-" in square brackets in sub-paras (2)(a), (3) inserted by the Employment Tribunals (Constitution and Rules of Procedure) (Amendment) Regulations 2008, SI 2008/3240, regs 2, 4(1), (11), as from 6 April 2009.

[2.841]
13 Compliance with orders and practice directions

(1) If a party does not comply with an order made under these rules, under rule 8 of Schedule 3, rule 7 of Schedule 4 or a practice direction, [an Employment Judge] or tribunal—

(a) may make an order in respect of costs or preparation time under rules 38 to 46; or

(b) may (subject to paragraph (2) and rule 19) at a pre-hearing review or a Hearing make an order to strike out the whole or part of the claim or, as the case may be, the response and, where appropriate, order that a respondent be debarred from responding to the claim altogether.

(2) An order may also provide that unless the order is complied with, the claim or, as the case may be, the response shall be struck out on the date of non-compliance without further consideration of the proceedings or the need to give notice under rule 19 or hold a pre-hearing review or Hearing.

(3) [Employment Judges] and tribunals shall comply with any practice directions issued under regulation 13.

Different types of hearing

[2.842]

14 Hearings—general

(1) [An Employment Judge] or a tribunal (depending on the relevant rule) may hold the following types of hearing—

(a) a case management discussion under rule 17;
(b) a pre-hearing review under rule 18;
[(bb) a hearing dealing with interim relief as described in rule 18A;]
(c) a Hearing under rule 26; or
(d) a review hearing under rule 33 or 36.

(2) So far as it appears appropriate to do so, the [Employment Judge] or tribunal shall seek to avoid formality in his or its proceedings and shall not be bound by any enactment or rule of law relating to the admissibility of evidence in proceedings before the courts.

(3) The [Employment Judge] or tribunal (as the case may be) shall make such enquiries of persons appearing before him or it and of witnesses as he or it considers appropriate and shall otherwise conduct the hearing in such manner as he or it considers most appropriate for the clarification of the issues and generally for the just handling of the proceedings.

(4) Unless the parties agree to shorter notice, the Secretary shall send notice of any hearing (other than a case management discussion) to every party not less than 14 days before the date fixed for the hearing and shall inform them that they have the opportunity to submit written representations and to advance oral argument. The Secretary shall give the parties reasonable notice before a case management discussion is held.

(5) If a party wishes to submit written representations for consideration at a hearing (other than a case management discussion) he shall present them to the Employment Tribunal Office not less than 7 days before the hearing and shall at the same time send a copy to all other parties.

(6) The tribunal or [Employment Judge] may, if it or he considers it appropriate, consider representations in writing which have been submitted otherwise than in accordance with paragraph (5).

NOTES

Sub-para (1)(bb) inserted by the Employment Tribunals (Constitution and Rules of Procedure) (Amendment) Regulations 2008, SI 2008/3240, regs 2, 4(1), (12), as from 6 April 2009.

[2.843]

[15 Use of electronic communications

(1) A hearing may be conducted (in whole or in part) by use of electronic communications provided that the Employment Judge or tribunal conducting the hearing considers it just and equitable to do so.

(2) Where a hearing is required by these rules to be held in public and electronic communications are to be used in accordance with this rule then, subject to rule 16, it must be held in a place to which the public has access and using equipment so that, when oral evidence is given the public is able to see and hear all parties to the communication.

(3) Where a hearing is to be held in private, and electronic communications are to be used in accordance with this rule, when oral evidence is given the tribunal or Employment Judge must be able to see and hear all parties to the communication.]

NOTES

Substituted by the Employment Tribunals (Constitution and Rules of Procedure) (Amendment) Regulations 2008, SI 2008/3240, regs 2, 4(1), (13), as from 6 April 2009.

[2.844]
16 Hearings which may be held in private

(1) A hearing or part of one may be conducted in private for the purpose of hearing from any person evidence or representations which in the opinion of the tribunal or [Employment Judge] is likely to consist of information—

- (a) which he could not disclose without contravening a prohibition imposed by or by virtue of any enactment;
- (b) which has been communicated to him in confidence, or which he has otherwise obtained in consequence of the confidence placed in him by another person; or
- (c) the disclosure of which would, for reasons other than its effect on negotiations with respect to any of the matters mentioned in section 178(2) of TULR(C)A, cause substantial injury to any undertaking of his or any undertaking in which he works.

(2) Where a tribunal or [Employment Judge] decides to hold a hearing or part of one in private, it or he shall give reasons for doing so . . .

NOTES

Words omitted from para (2) revoked by the Tribunals, Courts and Enforcement Act 2007 (Transitional and Consequential Provisions) Order 2008, SI 2008/2683, art 6(1), Sch 1, paras 240, 255(e), as from 3 November 2008.

Case management discussions

[2.845]
17 Conduct of case management discussions

(1) Case management discussions are interim hearings and may deal with matters of procedure and management of the proceedings and they [shall be held in private]. Case management discussions shall be conducted by [an Employment Judge].

(2) Any determination of a person's civil rights or obligations shall not be dealt with in a case management discussion. The matters listed in rule 10(2) are examples of matters which may be dealt with at case management discussions. Orders and judgments listed in rule 18(7) may not be made at a case management discussion.

NOTES

Words "shall be held in private" in square brackets in para (1) substituted by the Employment Tribunals (Constitution and Rules of Procedure) (Amendment) (No 2) Regulations 2005, SI 2005/1865, reg 2(1), (4)(c).

Pre-hearing reviews

[2.846]
18 Conduct of pre-hearing reviews

(1) Pre-hearing reviews are interim hearings and shall be conducted by [an Employment Judge] unless the circumstances in paragraph (3) are applicable. Subject to rule 16, they shall take place in public.

(2) At a pre-hearing review the [Employment Judge] may carry out a preliminary consideration of the proceedings and he may—

- (a) determine any interim or preliminary matter relating to the proceedings;
- (b) issue any order in accordance with rule 10 or do anything else which may be done at a case management discussion;
- (c) order that a deposit be paid in accordance with rule 20 without hearing evidence;
- (d) consider any oral or written representations or evidence;
- (e) . . .

(3) Pre-hearing reviews shall be conducted by a tribunal composed in accordance with section 4(1) . . . of the Employment Tribunals Act if—

- (a) a party has made a request in writing not less than 10 days before the date on which the pre-hearing review is due to take place that the pre-hearing review be conducted by a tribunal instead of [an Employment Judge]; and
- (b) [an Employment Judge] considers that one or more substantive issues of fact are likely to be determined at the pre-hearing review, that it would be desirable for the pre-hearing review to be conducted by a tribunal and he has issued an order that the pre-hearing review be conducted by a tribunal.

(4) If an order is made under paragraph (3), any reference to [an Employment Judge] in relation to a pre-hearing review shall be read as a reference to a tribunal.

(5) Notwithstanding the preliminary or interim nature of a pre-hearing review, at a pre-hearing review the [Employment Judge] may give judgment on any preliminary issue of substance relating to the proceedings. Judgments or orders made at a pre-hearing review may result in the proceedings being struck out or dismissed or otherwise determined with the result that a Hearing is no longer necessary in those proceedings.

(6) Before a judgment or order listed in paragraph (7) is made, notice must be given in accordance with rule 19. The judgments or [orders] listed in paragraph (7) must be made at a pre-hearing review or a Hearing if one of the parties has so requested. If no such request has been made such judgments or [orders] may be made in the absence of the parties.

(7) Subject to paragraph (6), [an Employment Judge] or tribunal may make a judgment or order:—

(a) as to the entitlement of any party to bring or contest particular proceedings;
(b) striking out or amending all or part of any claim or response on the grounds that it is scandalous, or vexatious or has no reasonable prospect of success;
(c) striking out any claim or response (or part of one) on the grounds that the manner in which the proceedings have been conducted by or on behalf of the claimant or the respondent (as the case may be) has been scandalous, unreasonable or vexatious;
(d) striking out a claim which has not been actively pursued;
(e) striking out a claim or response (or part of one) for non-compliance with an order or practice direction;
(f) striking out a claim where the [Employment Judge] or tribunal considers that it is no longer possible to have a fair Hearing in those proceedings;
(g) making a restricted reporting order (subject to rule 50).

(8) A claim or response or any part of one may be struck out under these rules only on the grounds stated in sub-paragraphs (7)(b) to (f).

(9) If at a pre-hearing review a requirement to pay a deposit under rule 20 has been considered, the [Employment Judge] who conducted that pre-hearing review shall not be a member of the tribunal at the Hearing in relation to those proceedings.

NOTES

Sub-para (2)(e) revoked, and words omitted from para (3) revoked, by the Employment Tribunals (Constitution and Rules of Procedure) (Amendment) Regulations 2008, SI 2008/3240, regs 2, 4(1), (14)(a), (b), as from 6 April 2009; word "orders" in square brackets in both places it occurs in para (6) substituted by the Employment Tribunals (Constitution and Rules of Procedure) (Amendment) (No 2) Regulations 2005, SI 2005/1865, reg 2(1), (4)(d).

[2.847]

[18A Interim relief

(1) Hearings dealing with interim relief are interim hearings.

(2) Subject to the provisions applying to interim relief of TULR(C)A, the Employment Rights Act, and the Employment Tribunals Act, these rules shall apply when dealing with the following applications as they apply to pre-hearing reviews—

(a) an application made under section 161 of TULR(C)A or section 128 of the Employment Rights Act for interim relief;
(b) an application made under section 165 of TULR(C)A or section 131 of the Employment Rights Act to vary or revoke an order.]

NOTES

Inserted by the Employment Tribunals (Constitution and Rules of Procedure) (Amendment) Regulations 2008, SI 2008/3240, regs 2, 4(1), (15), as from 6 April 2009.

[2.848]

19 Notice requirements

(1) Before [an Employment Judge] or a tribunal makes a judgment or order described in rule 18(7), except where the order is one described in rule 13(2) or it is a temporary restricted reporting order made in accordance with rule 50, the Secretary shall send notice to the party against whom it is proposed that the order or judgment should be made. The notice shall inform him of the order or judgment to be considered and give him the opportunity to give reasons why the order or judgment should not be made. This paragraph shall not be taken to require the Secretary to send such notice to that party if that party has been given an opportunity to give reasons orally to the [Employment Judge] or the tribunal as to why the order should not be made.

(2) Where a notice required by paragraph (1) is sent in relation to an order to strike out a claim which has not been actively pursued, unless the contrary is proved, the notice shall be treated as if it were received by the addressee if it has been sent to the address specified in the claim as the address to which notices are to be sent (or to any subsequent replacement for that address which has been notified to the Employment Tribunal Office).

Payment of a deposit

[2.849]

20 Requirement to pay a deposit in order to continue with proceedings

(1) At a pre-hearing review if [an Employment Judge] considers that the contentions put forward by any party in relation to a matter required to be determined by a tribunal have little reasonable prospect of success, the [Employment Judge] may make an order against that party requiring the party to pay a deposit of an amount not exceeding [£1,000] as a condition of being permitted to continue to take part in the proceedings relating to that matter.

(2) No order shall be made under this rule unless the [Employment Judge] has taken reasonable steps to ascertain the ability of the party against whom it is proposed to make the order to comply with such an order, and has taken account of any information so ascertained in determining the amount of the deposit.

(3) An order made under this rule, and the chairman's grounds for making such an order, shall be recorded in a document signed by the [Employment Judge]. A copy of that document shall be sent to each of the parties and shall be accompanied by a note explaining that if the party against whom the order is made persists in making those contentions relating to the matter to which the order relates, he may have an award of costs or preparation time made against him and could lose his deposit.

(4) If a party against whom an order has been made does not pay the amount specified in the order to the Secretary either:—

(a) within the period of 21 days of the day on which the document recording the making of the order is sent to him; or

(b) within such further period, not exceeding 14 days, as the [Employment Judge] may allow in the light of representations made by that party within the period of 21 days;

[an Employment Judge] shall strike out the claim or response of that party or, as the case may be, the part of it to which the order relates.

(5) The deposit paid by a party under an order made under this rule shall be refunded to him in full except where rule 47 applies.

NOTES

Sum in square brackets in para (1) substituted (for the original sum "£500") by the Employment Tribunals (Constitution and Rules of Procedure) (Amendment) Regulations 2012, SI 2012/468, reg 2(1), (2), as from 6 April 2012, except in relation to a claim which is presented to an Employment Tribunal Office on or before 5 April 2012 (see SI 2012/468, reg 3).

Conciliation

[2.850]

21 Documents to be sent to conciliators

In proceedings brought under the provisions of any enactment providing for conciliation, the Secretary shall send copies of all documents, orders, judgments, written reasons and notices to an ACAS conciliation officer except where the Secretary and ACAS have agreed otherwise.

22–24 *(Revoked by the Employment Tribunals (Constitution and Rules of Procedure) (Amendment) Regulations 2008, SI 2008/3240, regs 2, 4(1), (16), as from 6 April 2009.)*

Withdrawal of proceedings

[2.851]

25 Right to withdraw proceedings

(1) A claimant may withdraw all or part of his claim at any time – this may be done either orally at a hearing or in writing in accordance with paragraph (2).

(2) To withdraw a claim or part of one in writing the claimant must inform the Employment Tribunal Office of the claim or the parts of it which are to be withdrawn. Where there is more than one respondent the notification must specify against which respondents the claim is being withdrawn.

(3) The Secretary shall inform all other parties of the withdrawal. Withdrawal takes effect on the date on which the Employment Tribunal Office (in the case of written notifications) or the tribunal (in the case of oral notification) receives notice of it and where the whole claim is withdrawn, subject to paragraph (4), proceedings are brought to an end against the relevant respondent on that date. Withdrawal does not affect proceedings as to costs, preparation time or wasted costs.

(4) Where a claim has been withdrawn, a respondent may make an application to have the proceedings against him dismissed. Such an application must be made by the respondent in writing to the Employment Tribunal Office within 28 days of the notice of the withdrawal being sent to the respondent. If the respondent's application is granted and the proceedings are dismissed[, the claimant may not commence a further claim against the respondent for the same, or substantially the same, cause of action (unless the decision to dismiss is successfully reviewed or appealed)].

(5) The time limit in paragraph (4) may be extended by [an Employment Judge] if he considers it just and equitable to do so.

NOTES

Words ", the claimant may not commence a further claim against the respondent for the same, or substantially the same, cause of action (unless the decision to dismiss is successfully reviewed or appealed)" in square brackets in para (4) substituted by the Employment Tribunals (Constitution and Rules of Procedure) (Amendment) Regulations 2008, SI 2008/3240, regs 2, 4(1), (17)(a), as from 6 April 2009.

[2.852]

[25A Automatic dismissal of proceedings following withdrawal of a claim (or part of a claim) where an ACAS settlement has been reached

(1) Where—

(a) the parties settle the whole or part of the proceedings through ACAS;

(b) the settlement is agreed in writing;

(c) the parties to the settlement have confirmed in the settlement agreement, or otherwise in writing, their understanding that the proceedings covered by the settlement will, following the withdrawal of the claim (or relevant part of the claim) by the claimant, be dismissed; and

(d) the claimant withdraws the whole of, or the part of, the claim that is covered by the settlement by informing the Employment Tribunal Office of the withdrawal in accordance with rule 25(2),

the Employment Judge shall dismiss the proceedings covered by the settlement.

(2) The dismissal shall take place no later than 28 days after the date on which the Employment Tribunal Office receives—

(a) written evidence that the requirement described in sub-paragraph (1)(c) has been satisfied; and

(b) the written notification of withdrawal described in sub-paragraph (1)(d).

(3) If proceedings are dismissed under paragraph (1), the claimant may not commence a further claim against the respondent for the same, or substantially the same, cause of action (unless the decision to dismiss is successfully reviewed or appealed).]

NOTES

Inserted by the Employment Tribunals (Constitution and Rules of Procedure) (Amendment) Regulations 2008, SI 2008/3240, regs 2, 4(1), (17)(b), as from 6 April 2009, except (by virtue of reg 10 thereof) where the parties settle the proceedings through ACAS on or before 5 April 2009.

The hearing

[2.853]

26 Hearings

(1) A Hearing is held for the purpose of determining outstanding procedural or substantive issues or disposing of the proceedings. In any proceedings there may be more than one Hearing and there may be different categories of Hearing, such as a Hearing on liability, remedies, costs (in Scotland, expenses) or preparation time.

(2) Any Hearing of a claim shall be heard by a tribunal composed in accordance with section 4(1) and (2) of the Employment Tribunals Act.

(3) Any Hearing of a claim shall take place in public, subject to rule 16.

[(4) The President, Vice President, or Regional Employment Judge shall fix the date, time and place of the Hearing and the Secretary shall send to each party a notice of the Hearing together with information and guidance as to procedure at the Hearing.]

NOTES

Para (4) added by the Employment Tribunals (Constitution and Rules of Procedure) (Amendment) Regulations 2008, SI 2008/3240, regs 2, 4(1), (18), as from 6 April 2009.

[2.854]

27 What happens at the Hearing

(1) . . .

[(1)] Subject to rule 14(3), at the Hearing a party shall be entitled to give evidence, to call witnesses, to question witnesses and to address the tribunal.

[(2) Where a witness is called to give oral evidence, any witness statement of that person shall stand as that witness's evidence in chief unless the tribunal or Employment Judge orders otherwise.]

(3) The tribunal shall require parties and witnesses who attend the Hearing to give their evidence on oath or affirmation.

(4) The tribunal may exclude from the Hearing any person who is to appear as a witness in the proceedings until such time as they give evidence if it considers it in the interests of justice to do so.

(5) If a party fails to attend or to be represented (for the purpose of conducting the party's case at the Hearing) at the time and place fixed for the Hearing, the tribunal may dismiss or dispose of the proceedings in the absence of that party or may adjourn the Hearing to a later date.

(6) If the tribunal wishes to dismiss or dispose of proceedings in the circumstances described in paragraph (5), it shall first consider any information in its possession which has been made available to it by the parties.

(7) At a Hearing a tribunal may exercise any powers which may be exercised by [an Employment Judge] under these rules.

NOTES

Original para (1) revoked by the Employment Tribunals (Constitution and Rules of Procedure) (Amendment) Regulations 2008, SI 2008/3240, regs 2, 4(1), (19), as from 6 April 2009; original para (2) renumbered as para (1) and new para (2) inserted, by the Employment Tribunals (Constitution and Rules of Procedure) (Amendment) Regulations 2012, SI 2012/468, reg 2(1), (3), as from 6 April 2012, except in relation to a claim which is presented to an Employment Tribunal Office on or before 5 April 2012 (see SI 2012/468, reg 3).

Orders, judgments and reasons

[2.855]

28 Orders and judgments

(1) [Employment Judges] or tribunals may issue the following—

(a) a "judgment", which is a final determination of the proceedings or of a particular issue in those proceedings; it may include an award of compensation, a declaration or recommendation and it may also include orders for costs, preparation time or wasted costs;

(b) an "order", which may be issued in relation to interim matters and it will require a person to do or not to do something.

(2) If the parties agree in writing upon the terms of any order or judgment [an Employment Judge] or tribunal may, if he or it thinks fit, make such order or judgment.

(3) At the end of a hearing the [Employment Judge] (or, as the case may be, the tribunal) shall either issue any order or judgment orally or shall reserve the judgment or order to be given in writing at a later date.

(4) Where a tribunal is composed of three persons any order or judgment may be made or issued by a majority; and if a tribunal is composed of two persons only, the [Employment Judge] has a second or casting vote.

[2.856]

29 Form and content of judgments

(1) When judgment is reserved a written judgment shall be sent to the parties as soon as practicable. All judgments (whether issued orally or in writing) shall be recorded in writing and signed by the [Employment Judge].

(2) The Secretary shall provide a copy of the judgment to each of the parties and, where the proceedings were referred to the tribunal by a court, to that court. The Secretary shall include guidance to the parties on how the judgment may be reviewed or appealed.

(3) Where the judgment includes an award of compensation or a determination that one party is required to pay a sum to another (excluding an order for costs, expenses, allowances, preparation time or wasted costs), the document shall also contain a statement of the amount of compensation awarded, or of the sum required to be paid.

[2.857]

30 Reasons

(1) A tribunal or [Employment Judge] must give reasons (either oral or written) for any—

(a) judgment; or

(b) order, if a request for reasons is made before or at the hearing at which the order is made.

(2) Reasons may be given orally at the time of issuing the judgment or order or they may be reserved to be given in writing at a later date. If reasons are reserved, they shall be signed by the [Employment Judge] and sent to the parties by the Secretary.

(3) [[Where oral reasons have been provided], written reasons shall only be provided]:—

(a) in relation to judgments if requested by one of the parties within the time limit set out in paragraph (5); or

(b) in relation to any judgment or order if requested by the Employment Appeal Tribunal at any time.

(4) When written reasons are provided, the Secretary shall send a copy of the reasons to all parties to the proceedings and record the date on which the reasons were sent. Written reasons shall be signed by the [Employment Judge].

(5) A request for written reasons for a judgment must be made by a party either orally at the hearing (if the judgment is issued at a hearing), or in writing within 14 days of the date on which the judgment was sent to the parties. This time limit may be extended by [an Employment Judge] where he considers it just and equitable to do so.

(6) Written reasons for a judgment shall include the following information—

(a) the issues which the tribunal or [Employment Judge] has identified as being relevant to the claim;

(b) if some identified issues were not determined, what those issues were and why they were not determined;

(c) findings of fact relevant to the issues which have been determined;

(d) a concise statement of the applicable law;

(e) how the relevant findings of fact and applicable law have been applied in order to determine the issues; and

(f) where the judgment includes an award of compensation or a determination that one party make a payment to the other, a table showing how the amount or sum has been calculated or a description of the manner in which it has been calculated.

NOTES

Words in first (outer) pair of square brackets in para (3) substituted by the Employment Tribunals (Constitution and Rules of Procedure) (Amendment) Regulations 2004, SI 2004/2351, reg 2(1), (9)(c); words "Where oral reasons have been provided" in second (inner) pair of square brackets in that paragraph substituted by the Employment Tribunals (Constitution and Rules of Procedure) (Amendment) (No 2) Regulations 2005, SI 2005/1865, reg 2(1), (4)(h).

[2.858]

31 Absence of [Employment Judge]

Where it is not possible for a judgment, order or reasons to be signed by the [Employment Judge] due to death, incapacity or absence—

(a) if the [Employment Judge] has dealt with the proceedings alone the document shall be signed by the Regional [Employment Judge], Vice President or President when it is practicable for him to do so; and

(b) if the proceedings have been dealt with by a tribunal composed of two or three persons, the document shall be signed by the other person or persons;

and any person who signs the document shall certify that the [Employment Judge] is unable to sign.

[2.859]

32 The Register

(1) Subject to rule 49, the Secretary shall enter a copy of the following documents in the Register—

(a) any judgment (including any costs, expenses, preparation time or wasted costs order); and

(b) any written reasons provided in accordance with rule 30 in relation to any judgment.

(2) Written reasons for judgments shall be omitted from the Register in any case in which evidence has been heard in private and the tribunal or [Employment Judge] so orders. In such a case the Secretary shall send the reasons to each of the parties and where there are proceedings before a superior court relating to the judgment in question, he shall send the reasons to that court, together with a copy of the entry in the Register of the judgment to which the reasons relate.

Power to review judgments and decisions

[2.860]

33 Review of default judgments

(1) A party may apply to have a default judgment against or in favour of him reviewed. An application must be made in writing and presented to the Employment Tribunal Office within 14 days of the date on which the default judgment was sent to the parties. The 14 day time limit may be extended by [an Employment Judge] if he considers that it is just and equitable to do so.

(2) The application must state the reasons why the default judgment should be varied or revoked. When it is the respondent applying to have the default judgment reviewed, the application must include with it the respondent's proposed response to the claim [(where that has not been received by the Employment Tribunal Office)], an application for an extension of the time limit for presenting the response and an explanation of why rules 4(1) and (4) were not complied with.

[(2A) An application under paragraph (1) may be given preliminary consideration (without the need to hold a hearing) by an Employment Judge, who may refuse the application if the requirements of paragraph (2) have not been met.]

(3) A review of a default judgment shall be conducted by [an Employment Judge] in public [unless all the parties to the proceedings consent in writing to the review without a hearing]. Notice of the hearing and a copy of the application shall be sent by the Secretary to all other parties.

(4) The [Employment Judge] may—

(a) refuse the application for a review;

(b) vary the default judgment;
(c) revoke all or part of the default judgment;
(d) confirm the default judgment;

and all parties to the proceedings shall be informed by the Secretary in writing of the [Employment Judge's] judgment on the application.

(5) A default judgment must be revoked if the whole of the claim was satisfied before the judgment was issued or if rule 8(6) applies. [An Employment Judge] may revoke or vary all or part of a default judgment if the respondent has a reasonable prospect of successfully responding to the claim or part of it.

(6) In considering the application for a review of a default judgment the [Employment Judge] must have regard to whether there was good reason for the response not having been presented within the applicable time limit.

(7) If the [Employment Judge] decides that the default judgment should be varied or revoked and that the respondent should be allowed to respond to the claim the Secretary shall accept the response and proceed in accordance with rule 5(2).

[(8) An Employment Judge may on his own initiative review a default judgment on the grounds listed at rule 34(3)(a), (b) and (e).]

NOTES

Words "(where that has not been received by the Employment Tribunal Office)" in square brackets in para (2) inserted, para (2A) inserted, and words "unless all the parties to the proceedings consent in writing to the review without a hearing" in square brackets in para (3) inserted, by the Employment Tribunals (Constitution and Rules of Procedure) (Amendment) Regulations 2008, SI 2008/3240, regs 2, 4(1), (20)(a)–(c), as from 6 April 2009.

Para (8) inserted by SI 2008/3240, regs 2, 4(1), (20)(d), as from 6 April 2009, except (by virtue of reg 11 thereof) in relation to proceedings where a default judgment has been issued on or before 5 April 2009.

[2.861]

34 Review of other judgments and decisions

(1) Parties may apply to have certain judgments and decisions made by a tribunal or [an Employment Judge] reviewed under rules 34 to 36. Those judgments and decisions are—

(a) a decision not to accept a claim, response or counterclaim;
(b) a judgment (other than a default judgment but including an order for costs, expenses, preparation time or wasted costs); and
(c) a decision made under rule 6(3) of Schedule 4;

and references to "decision" in rules 34 to 37 are references to the above judgments and decisions only. Other decisions or orders may not be reviewed under these rules.

(2) In relation to a decision not to accept a claim or response, only the party against whom the decision is made may apply to have the decision reviewed.

(3) Subject to paragraph (4), decisions may be reviewed on the following grounds only—

(a) the decision was wrongly made as a result of an administrative error;
(b) a party did not receive notice of the proceedings leading to the decision;
(c) the decision was made in the absence of a party;
(d) new evidence has become available since the conclusion of the hearing to which the decision relates, provided that its existence could not have been reasonably known of or foreseen at that time; or
(e) the interests of justice require such a review.

(4) A decision not to accept a claim or response may only be reviewed on the grounds listed in [sub-]paragraphs (3)(a) and (e).

(5) A tribunal or [Employment Judge] may on its or his own initiative review a decision made by it or him on the grounds listed in paragraphs (3) or (4).

NOTES

Word "sub-" in square brackets in para (4) inserted by the Employment Tribunals (Constitution and Rules of Procedure) (Amendment) Regulations 2008, SI 2008/3240, regs 2, 4(1), (21), as from 6 April 2009.

[2.862]

35 Preliminary consideration of application for review

(1) An application under rule 34 to have a decision reviewed must be made to the Employment Tribunal Office within 14 days of the date on which the decision was sent to the parties. The 14 day time limit may be extended by [an Employment Judge] if he considers that it is just and equitable to do so.

(2) The application must be in writing and must identify the grounds of the application in accordance with rule 34(3), but if the decision to be reviewed was made at a hearing, an application may be made orally at that hearing.

(3) The application to have a decision reviewed shall be considered (without the need to hold a hearing) by the [Employment Judge] of the tribunal which made the decision or, if that is not practicable, by —

(a) a Regional [Employment Judge] or the Vice President;
(b) any chairman nominated by a Regional [Employment Judge] or the Vice President; or
(c) the President;

and that person shall refuse the application if he considers that there are no grounds for the decision to be reviewed under rule 34(3) or there is no reasonable prospect of the decision being varied or revoked.

(4) If an application for a review is refused after such preliminary consideration the Secretary shall inform the party making the application in writing of the [Employment Judge's] decision and his reasons for it. If the application for a review is not refused the decision shall be reviewed under rule 36.

[2.863]
36 The review

(1) When a party has applied for a review and the application has not been refused after the preliminary consideration above, the decision shall be reviewed by the [Employment Judge] or tribunal who made the original decision. If that is not practicable a different [Employment Judge] or tribunal (as the case may be) shall be appointed by a Regional [Employment Judge], the Vice President or the President.

(2) Where no application has been made by a party and the decision is being reviewed on the initiative of the tribunal or [Employment Judge], the review must be carried out by the same tribunal or [Employment Judge] who made the original decision and—

(a) a notice must be sent to each of the parties explaining in summary the grounds upon which it is proposed to review the decision and giving them an opportunity to give reasons why there should be no review; and
(b) such notice must be sent before the expiry of 14 days from the date on which the original decision was sent to the parties.

(3) A tribunal or [Employment Judge] who reviews a decision under paragraph (1) or (2) may confirm, vary or revoke the decision. If the decision is revoked, the tribunal or [Employment Judge] must order the decision to be taken again. When an order is made that the original decision be taken again, if the original decision was taken by [an Employment Judge] without a hearing, the new decision may be taken without hearing the parties and if the original decision was taken at a hearing, a new hearing must be held.

[2.864]
37 Correction of judgments, decisions or reasons

(1) Clerical mistakes in any order, judgment, decision or reasons, or errors arising in those documents from an accidental slip or omission, may at any time be corrected by certificate by the [Employment Judge], Regional [Employment Judge], Vice President or President.

(2) If a document is corrected by certificate under paragraph (1), or if a decision is revoked or varied under rules 33 or 36 or altered in any way by order of a superior court, the Secretary shall alter any entry in the Register which is so affected to conform with the certificate or order and send a copy of any entry so altered to each of the parties and, if the proceedings have been referred to the tribunal by a court, to that court.

(3) Where a document omitted from the Register under rules 32 or 49 is corrected by certificate under this rule, the Secretary shall send a copy of the corrected document to the parties; and where there are proceedings before any superior court relating to the decision or reasons in question, he shall send a copy to that court together with a copy of the entry in the Register of the decision, if it has been altered under this rule.

(4) In Scotland, the references in paragraphs (2) and (3) to superior courts shall be read as referring to appellate courts.

Costs orders and orders for expenses

[2.865]
38 General power to make costs and expenses orders

(1) Subject to paragraph (2) and in the circumstances listed in rules 39, 40 and 47 a tribunal or [Employment Judge] may make an order ("a costs order") that—

(a) a party ("the paying party") make a payment in respect of the costs incurred by another party ("the receiving party");
(b) the paying party pay to the Secretary of State, in whole or in part, any allowances (other than allowances paid to members of tribunals) paid by the Secretary of State under section 5(2) or (3) of the Employment Tribunals Act to any person for the purposes of, or in connection with, that person's attendance at the tribunal;

[(c) the paying party make a payment to a witness in respect of some or all of the expenses that witness incurs for the purposes of, or in connection with, that witness's attendance at the tribunal].

(2) A costs order may be made under rules 39, [40(1) to (4)] and 47 only where the receiving party has been legally represented at the Hearing or, in proceedings which are determined without a Hearing, if the receiving party is legally represented when the proceedings are determined. If the receiving party has not been so legally represented a tribunal [or [Employment Judge]] may make a preparation time order (subject to rules 42 to 45). (See rule 46 on the restriction on making a costs order and a preparation time order in the same proceedings.)

(3) For the purposes of these rules "costs" shall mean fees, charges, disbursements or expenses incurred by or on behalf of a party[, including sums paid pursuant to an order under paragraph (1)(c)], in relation to the proceedings. In Scotland all references to costs (except when used in the expression "wasted costs") or costs orders shall be read as references to expenses or orders for expenses.

(4) A costs order may be made against or in favour of a respondent who has not had a response accepted in the proceedings in relation to the conduct of any part which he has taken in the proceedings.

(5) In these rules legally represented means having the assistance of a person (including where that person is the receiving party's employee) who—

(a) has a general qualification within the meaning of section 71 of the Courts and Legal Services Act 1990;

(b) is an advocate or solicitor in Scotland; or

(c) is a member of the Bar of Northern Ireland or a [solicitor of the Court of Judicature of Northern Ireland].

(6) Any costs order made under rules 39, 40 or 47 shall be payable by the paying party and not his representative.

(7) A party may apply for a costs order to be made at any time during the proceedings. An application may be made at the end of a hearing, or in writing to the Employment Tribunal Office. An application for costs which is received by the Employment Tribunal Office later than 28 days from the issuing of the judgment determining the claim shall not be accepted or considered by a tribunal or [Employment Judge] unless it or he considers that it is in the interests of justice to do so.

(8) In paragraph (7), the date of issuing of the judgment determining the claim shall be either—

(a) the date of the Hearing if the judgment was issued orally; or

(b) if the judgment was reserved, the date on which the written judgment was sent to the parties.

(9) No costs order shall be made unless the Secretary has sent notice to the party against whom the order may be made giving him the opportunity to give reasons why the order should not be made. This paragraph shall not be taken to require the Secretary to send notice to that party if the party has been given an opportunity to give reasons orally to the [Employment Judge] or tribunal as to why the order should not be made.

(10) Where a tribunal or [Employment Judge] makes a costs order it or he shall provide written reasons for doing so if a request for written reasons is made within 14 days of the date of the costs order. The Secretary shall send a copy of the written reasons to all parties to the proceedings.

NOTES

Para (1)(c) inserted by the Employment Tribunals (Constitution and Rules of Procedure) (Amendment) Regulations 2012, SI 2012/468, reg 2(1), (4), as from 6 April 2012, except in relation to a claim which is presented to an Employment Tribunal Office on or before 5 April 2012 (see SI 2012/468, reg 3).

Words "40(1) to (4)" in square brackets in para (2) substituted (for the original figure "40") by SI 2012/468, reg 2(1), (5), as from 6 April 2012 (subject to the same exception in reg 3 as noted above).

Word "or" in second (outer) pair of square brackets in para (2) inserted by the Employment Tribunals (Constitution and Rules of Procedure) (Amendment) (No 2) Regulations 2005, SI 2005/1865, reg 2(1), (4)(i).

Words ", including sums paid pursuant to an order under paragraph (1)(c)" in square brackets in para (3) inserted by SI 2012/468, reg 2(1), (6), as from 6 April 2012 (subject to the same exception in reg 3 as noted above).

Words in square brackets in sub-para (5)(c) substituted by the Constitutional Reform Act 2005, s 59(5), Sch 11, Pt 3, para 5, as from 1 October 2009.

[2.866]

39 When a costs or expenses order must be made

(1) Subject to rule 38(2), a tribunal [or [Employment Judge]] must make a costs order against a respondent where in proceedings for unfair dismissal a Hearing has been postponed or adjourned and—

(a) the claimant has expressed a wish to be reinstated or re-engaged which has been communicated to the respondent not less than 7 days before the Hearing; and

(b) the postponement or adjournment of that Hearing has been caused by the respondent's failure, without a special reason, to adduce reasonable evidence as to the availability of the job from which the claimant was dismissed, or of comparable or suitable employment.

(2) A costs order made under paragraph (1) shall relate to any costs incurred as a result of the postponement or adjournment of the Hearing.

NOTES

Word "or" in first (outer) pair of square brackets in para (1) inserted by the Employment Tribunals (Constitution and Rules of Procedure) (Amendment) (No 2) Regulations 2005, SI 2005/1865, reg 2(1), (4)(i).

[2.867]

40 When a costs or expenses order may be made

(1) A tribunal or [Employment Judge] may make a costs order when on the application of a party it has postponed the day or time fixed for or adjourned a Hearing or pre-hearing review. The costs order may be against or, as the case may require, in favour of that party as respects any costs incurred or any allowances paid as a result of the postponement or adjournment.

(2) A tribunal or [Employment Judge] shall consider making a costs order against a paying party where, in the opinion of the tribunal or [Employment Judge] (as the case may be), any of the circumstances in paragraph (3) apply. Having so considered, the tribunal or [Employment Judge] may make a costs order against the paying party if it or he considers it appropriate to do so.

(3) The circumstances referred to in paragraph (2) are where the paying party has in bringing the proceedings, or he or his representative has in conducting the proceedings, acted vexatiously, abusively, disruptively or otherwise unreasonably, or the bringing or conducting of the proceedings by the paying party has been misconceived.

(4) A tribunal or [Employment Judge] may make a costs order against a party who has not complied with an order or practice direction.

[(5) A tribunal or Employment Judge may make a costs order where a witness attends to give oral evidence at a hearing.]

NOTES

Para (5) inserted by the Employment Tribunals (Constitution and Rules of Procedure) (Amendment) Regulations 2012, SI 2012/468, reg 2(1), (7), as from 6 April 2012, except in relation to a claim which is presented to an Employment Tribunal Office on or before 5 April 2012 (see SI 2012/468, reg 3).

[2.868]

41 The amount of a costs or expenses order

(1) The amount of a costs order against the paying party shall be determined in any of the following ways—

(a) the tribunal may specify the sum which the paying party must pay to the receiving party, provided that sum does not exceed [£20,000];

(b) the parties may agree on a sum to be paid by the paying party to the receiving party and if they do so the costs order shall be for the sum so agreed;

(c) the tribunal may order the paying party to pay the receiving party the whole or a specified part of the costs of the receiving party with the amount to be paid being determined by way of detailed assessment in a County Court in accordance with the Civil Procedure Rules 1998 or, in Scotland, as taxed according to such part of the table of fees prescribed for proceedings in the sheriff court as shall be directed by the order.

(2) The tribunal or [Employment Judge] may have regard to the paying party's ability to pay when considering whether it or he shall make a costs order or how much that order should be.

(3) For the avoidance of doubt, the amount of a costs order made under paragraphs (1)(b) or (c) may exceed [£20,000].

NOTES

Sums in square brackets in paras (1)(a), (3) substituted (for the original sum "£10,000") by the Employment Tribunals (Constitution and Rules of Procedure) (Amendment) Regulations 2012, SI 2012/468, reg 2(1), (8), as from 6 April 2012, except in relation to a claim which is presented to an Employment Tribunal Office on or before 5 April 2012 (see SI 2012/468, reg 3).

Preparation time orders

[2.869]

42 General power to make preparation time orders

(1) Subject to paragraph (2) and in the circumstances described in rules 43, 44 and 47 a tribunal or [Employment Judge] may make an order ("a preparation time order") that a party ("the paying party") make a payment in respect of the preparation time of another party ("the receiving party").

(2) A preparation time order may be made under rules 43, 44 or 47 only where the receiving party has not been legally represented at a Hearing or, in proceedings which are determined without a Hearing, if the receiving party has not been legally represented when the proceedings are determined. (See: rules 38 to 41 on when a costs order may be made; rule 38(5) for the definition of legally represented; and rule 46 on the restriction on making a costs order and a preparation time order in the same proceedings).

(3) For the purposes of these rules preparation time shall mean time spent by—

(a) the receiving party or his employees carrying out preparatory work directly relating to the proceedings; and

(b) the receiving party's legal or other advisers relating to the conduct of the proceedings;

up to but not including time spent at any Hearing.

(4) A preparation time order may be made against a respondent who has not had a response accepted in the proceedings in relation to the conduct of any part which he has taken in the proceedings.

(5) A party may apply to the tribunal for a preparation time order to be made at any time during the proceedings. An application may be made at the end of a hearing or in writing to the Secretary. An application for preparation time which is received by the Employment Tribunal Office later than 28 days from the issuing of the judgment determining the claim shall not be accepted or considered by a tribunal or [Employment Judge] unless they consider that it is in the interests of justice to do so.

(6) In paragraph (5) the date of issuing of the judgment determining the claim shall be either—

(a) the date of the Hearing if the judgment was issued orally; or,

(b) if the judgment was reserved, the date on which the written judgment was sent to the parties.

(7) No preparation time order shall be made unless the Secretary has sent notice to the party against whom the order may be made giving him the opportunity to give reasons why the order should not be made. This paragraph shall not be taken to require the Secretary to send notice to that party if the party has been given an opportunity to give reasons orally to the [Employment Judge] or tribunal as to why the order should not be made.

(8) Where a tribunal or [Employment Judge] makes a preparation time order it or he shall provide written reasons for doing so if a request for written reasons is made within 14 days of the date of the preparation time order. The Secretary shall send a copy of the written reasons to all parties to the proceedings.

[2.870]

43 When a preparation time order must be made

(1) Subject to rule 42(2), a tribunal [or [Employment Judge]] must make a preparation time order against a respondent where in proceedings for unfair dismissal a Hearing has been postponed or adjourned and—

(a) the claimant has expressed a wish to be reinstated or re-engaged which has been communicated to the respondent not less than 7 days before the Hearing; and

(b) the postponement or adjournment of that Hearing has been caused by the respondent's failure, without a special reason, to adduce reasonable evidence as to the availability of the job from which the claimant was dismissed, or of comparable or suitable employment.

(2) A preparation time order made under paragraph (1) shall relate to any preparation time spent as a result of the postponement or adjournment of the Hearing.

NOTES

Word "or" in first (outer) pair of square brackets in para (1) inserted by the Employment Tribunals (Constitution and Rules of Procedure) (Amendment) (No 2) Regulations 2005, SI 2005/1865, reg 2(1), (4)(i).

[2.871]

44 When a preparation time order may be made

(1) A tribunal or [Employment Judge] may make a preparation time order when on the application of a party it has postponed the day or time fixed for or adjourned a Hearing or a pre-hearing review. The preparation time order may be against or, as the case may require, in favour of that party as respects any preparation time spent as a result of the postponement or adjournment.

(2) A tribunal or [Employment Judge] shall consider making a preparation time order against a party (the paying party) where, in the opinion of the tribunal or the [Employment Judge] (as the case may be), any of the circumstances in paragraph (3) apply. Having so considered the tribunal or [Employment Judge] may make a preparation time order against that party if it considers it appropriate to do so.

(3) The circumstances described in paragraph (2) are where the paying party has in bringing the proceedings, or he or his representative has in conducting the proceedings, acted vexatiously, abusively, disruptively or otherwise unreasonably, or the bringing or conducting of the proceedings by the paying party has been misconceived.

(4) A tribunal or [Employment Judge] may make a preparation time order against a party who has not complied with an order or practice direction.

[2.872]

45 Calculation of a preparation time order

(1) In order to calculate the amount of preparation time the tribunal or [Employment Judge] shall make an assessment of the number of hours spent on preparation time on the basis of—

- (a) information on time spent provided by the receiving party; and
- (b) the tribunal or [Employment Judge's] own assessment of what it or he considers to be a reasonable and proportionate amount of time to spend on such preparatory work and with reference to, for example, matters such as the complexity of the proceedings, the number of witnesses and documentation required.

(2) Once the tribunal or [Employment Judge] has assessed the number of hours spent on preparation time in accordance with paragraph (1), it or he shall calculate the amount of the award to be paid to the receiving party by applying an hourly rate of £25.00 to that figure (or such other figure calculated in accordance with paragraph (4)). No preparation time order made under these rules may exceed the sum of £10,000.

(3) The tribunal or [Employment Judge] may have regard to the paying party's ability to pay when considering whether it or he shall make a preparation time order or how much that order should be.

(4) For the year commencing on 6th April 2006, the hourly rate of £25 shall be increased by the sum of £1.00 and for each subsequent year commencing on 6 April, the hourly rate for the previous year shall also be increased by the sum of £1.00.

NOTES

Sum in square brackets in para (2) substituted (for the original sum "£10,000") by the Employment Tribunals (Constitution and Rules of Procedure) (Amendment) Regulations 2012, SI 2012/468, reg 2(1), (8), as from 6 April 2012, except in relation to a claim which is presented to an Employment Tribunal Office on or before 5 April 2012 (see SI 2012/468, reg 3).

[2.873]

46 Restriction on making costs or expenses orders and preparation time orders

(1) A tribunal or [Employment Judge] may not make a preparation time order and a costs order in favour of the same party in the same proceedings. However where a preparation time order is made in favour of a party in proceedings, the tribunal or [Employment Judge] may make a costs order in favour of another party or in favour of the Secretary of State under rule 38(1)(b) in the same proceedings.

(2) If a tribunal or [an Employment Judge] wishes to make either a costs order or a preparation time order in proceedings, before the claim has been determined, it or he may make an order that either costs or preparation time be awarded to the receiving party. In such circumstances a tribunal or [Employment Judge] may decide whether the award should be for costs or preparation time after the proceedings have been determined.

[2.874]

47 Costs, expenses or preparation time orders when a deposit has been taken

(1) When:—

- (a) a party has been ordered under rule 20 to pay a deposit as a condition of being permitted to continue to participate in proceedings relating to a matter;
- (b) in respect of that matter, the tribunal or [Employment Judge] has found against that party in its or his judgment; and
- (c) no award of costs or preparation time has been made against that party arising out of the proceedings on the matter;

the tribunal or [Employment Judge] shall consider whether to make a costs or preparation time order against that party on the ground that he conducted the proceedings relating to the matter unreasonably in persisting in having the matter determined; but the tribunal or [Employment Judge] shall not make a costs or preparation time order on that ground unless it has considered the document recording the order under rule 20 and is of the opinion that the grounds which caused the tribunal or [Employment Judge] to find against the party in its judgment were substantially the same as the grounds recorded in that document for considering that the contentions of the party had little reasonable prospect of success.

(2) When a costs or preparation time order is made against a party who has had an order under rule 20 made against him (whether the award arises out of the proceedings relating to the matter in respect of which the order was made or out of proceedings relating to any other matter considered with that matter), his deposit shall be paid in part or full settlement of the costs or preparation time order—

(a) when an order is made in favour of one party, to that party; and

(b) when orders are made in favour of more than one party, to all of them or any one or more of them as the tribunal or [Employment Judge] thinks fit, and if to all or more than one, in such proportions as the tribunal or [Employment Judge] considers appropriate;

and if the amount of the deposit exceeds the amount of the costs or preparation time order, the balance shall be refunded to the party who paid it.

Wasted costs orders against representatives

[2.875]

48 Personal liability of representatives for costs

(1) A tribunal or [Employment Judge] may make a wasted costs order against a party's representative.

(2) In a wasted costs order the tribunal or [Employment Judge] may:—

(a) disallow, or order the representative of a party to meet the whole or part of any wasted costs of any party, including an order that the representative repay to his client any costs which have already been paid; and

(b) order the representative to pay to the Secretary of State, in whole or in part, any allowances (other than allowances paid to members of tribunals) paid by the Secretary of State under section 5(2) or (3) of the Employment Tribunals Act to any person for the purposes of, or in connection with, that person's attendance at the tribunal by reason of the representative's conduct of the proceedings.

(3) "Wasted costs" means any costs incurred by a party:—

(a) as a result of any improper, unreasonable or negligent act or omission on the part of any representative; or

(b) which, in the light of any such act or omission occurring after they were incurred, the tribunal considers it unreasonable to expect that party to pay.

(4) In this rule "representative" means a party's legal or other representative or any employee of such representative, but it does not include a representative who is not acting in pursuit of profit with regard to those proceedings. A person is considered to be acting in pursuit of profit if he is acting on a conditional fee arrangement.

(5) A wasted costs order may be made in favour of a party whether or not that party is legally represented and such an order may also be made in favour of a representative's own client. A wasted costs order may not be made against a representative where that representative is an employee of a party.

(6) Before making a wasted costs order, the tribunal or [Employment Judge] shall give the representative a reasonable opportunity to make oral or written representations as to reasons why such an order should not be made. [The tribunal or [Employment Judge] may also have regard to the representative's ability to pay] when considering whether it shall make a wasted costs order or how much that order should be.

(7) When a tribunal or [Employment Judge] makes a wasted costs order, it must specify in the order the amount to be disallowed or paid.

(8) The Secretary shall inform the representative's client in writing:—

(a) of any proceedings under this rule; or

(b) of any order made under this rule against the party's representative.

(9) Where a tribunal or [Employment Judge] makes a wasted costs order it or he shall provide written reasons for doing so if a request is made for written reasons within 14 days of the date of the wasted costs order. This 14 day time limit may not be extended under rule 10. The Secretary shall send a copy of the written reasons to all parties to the proceedings.

NOTES

Words in second (outer) pair of square brackets in para (6) substituted by the Employment Tribunals (Constitution and Rules of Procedure) (Amendment) Regulations 2004, SI 2004/2351, reg 2(1), (9)(d).

Powers in relation to specific types of proceedings

[2.876]

49 Sexual offences and the Register

In any proceedings appearing to involve allegations of the commission of a sexual offence the tribunal, the [Employment Judge] or the Secretary shall omit from the Register, or delete from the Register or any judgment, document or record of the proceedings, which is available to the public, any identifying matter which is likely to lead members of the public to identify any person affected by or making such an allegation.

[2.877]

50 Restricted reporting orders

(1) A restricted reporting order may be made in the following types of proceedings—

(a) any case which involves allegations of sexual misconduct;

[(b) proceedings under the Equality Act in which evidence of a personal nature is likely to be heard by the tribunal or an Employment Judge—.

(i) on a complaint relating to a contravention of Part 5 so far as relating to disability;

(ii) on a complaint relating to a contravention of section 112 that relates to Part 5 so far as relating to disability].

(2) A party (or where a complaint is made under the [Equality Act], the complainant) may apply for a restricted reporting order (either temporary or full) in writing to the Employment Tribunal Office, or orally at a hearing, or the tribunal or [Employment Judge] may make the order on its or his own initiative without any application having been made.

(3) [An Employment Judge] or tribunal may make a temporary restricted reporting order without holding a hearing or sending a copy of the application to other parties.

(4) Where a temporary restricted reporting order has been made the Secretary shall inform all parties to the proceedings in writing as soon as possible of—

(a) the fact that the order has been made; and

(b) their right to apply to have the temporary restricted reporting order revoked or converted into a full restricted reporting order within 14 days of the temporary order having been made.

(5) If no application under [sub-]paragraph (4)(b) is made within the 14 days, the temporary restricted reporting order shall lapse and cease to have any effect on the fifteenth day after the order was made. If such an application is made the temporary restricted reporting order shall continue to have effect until the pre-hearing review or Hearing at which the application is considered.

(6) All parties must be given an opportunity to advance oral argument at a pre-hearing review or a Hearing before a tribunal or [Employment Judge] decides whether or not to make a full restricted reporting order (whether or not there was previously a temporary restricted reporting order in the proceedings).

(7) Any person may make an application to the [Employment Judge] or tribunal to have a right to make representations before a full restricted reporting order is made. The [Employment Judge] or tribunal shall allow such representations to be made where he or it considers that the applicant has a legitimate interest in whether or not the order is made.

(8) Where a tribunal or [Employment Judge] makes a restricted reporting order—

(a) it shall specify in the order the persons who may not be identified;

(b) a full order shall remain in force until both liability and remedy have been determined in the proceedings unless it is revoked earlier; and

(c) the Secretary shall ensure that a notice of the fact that a restricted reporting order has been made in relation to those proceedings is displayed on the notice board of the employment tribunal with any list of the proceedings taking place before the employment tribunal, and on the door of the room in which the proceedings affected by the order are taking place.

(9) Where a restricted reporting order has been made under this rule and that complaint is being dealt with together with any other proceedings, the tribunal or [Employment Judge] may order that the restricted reporting order applies also in relation to those other proceedings or a part of them.

(10) A tribunal or [Employment Judge] may revoke a restricted reporting order at any time.

(11) For the purposes of this rule liability and remedy are determined in the proceedings on the date recorded as being the date on which the judgment disposing of the claim was sent to the parties, and references to a restricted reporting order include references to both a temporary and a full restricted reporting order.

NOTES

Sub-para (1)(b) substituted, and the words "Equality Act" in square brackets in para (2) substituted, by the Equality Act 2010 (Commencement No 4, Savings, Consequential, Transitional, Transitory and Incidental Provisions and Revocation) Order 2010, SI 2010/2317, art 24, Sch 8, para 5(1)–(3), as from 1 October 2010; word "sub-" in square brackets in para (5) inserted by the

Employment Tribunals (Constitution and Rules of Procedure) (Amendment) Regulations 2008, SI 2008/3240, regs 2, 4(1), (22), as from 6 April 2009.

[2.878]
51 Proceedings involving the National Insurance Fund

The Secretary of State shall be entitled to appear as if she were a party and be heard at any hearing in relation to proceedings which may involve a payment out of the National Insurance Fund, and in that event she shall be treated for the purposes of these rules as if she were a party.

[2.879]
52 Collective agreements

Where a claim includes a complaint under [section 146(1) of the Equality Act so far as relating to sex, gender reassignment, marriage and civil partnership or pregnancy and maternity] relating to a term of a collective agreement, the following persons, whether or not identified in the claim, shall be regarded as the persons against whom a remedy is claimed and shall be treated as respondents for the purposes of these rules, that is to say—

(a) the claimant's employer (or prospective employer); and
(b) every organisation of employers and organisation of workers, and every association of or representative of such organisations, which, if the terms were to be varied voluntarily, would be likely, in the opinion of [an Employment Judge], to negotiate the variation;

provided that such an organisation or association shall not be treated as a respondent if the [Employment Judge], having made such enquiries of the claimant and such other enquiries as he thinks fit, is of the opinion that it is not reasonably practicable to identify the organisation or association.

NOTES

Words "section 146(1) of the Equality Act so far as relating to sex, gender reassignment, marriage and civil partnership or pregnancy and maternity" in square brackets substituted by the Equality Act 2010 (Commencement No 4, Savings, Consequential, Transitional, Transitory and Incidental Provisions and Revocation) Order 2010, SI 2010/2317, art 24, Sch 8, para 5(1), (4), as from 1 October 2010.

[2.880]
53 Employment Agencies Act 1973

In relation to any claim in respect of an application under section 3C of the Employment Agencies Act 1973 for the variation or revocation of a prohibition order, the Secretary of State shall be treated as the respondent in such proceedings for the purposes of these rules. In relation to such an application the claim does not need to include the name and address of the persons against whom the claim is being made.

[2.881]
54 National security proceedings

(1) A Minister of the Crown (whether or not he is a party to the proceedings) may, if he considers it expedient in the interests of national security, direct a tribunal or [Employment Judge] by notice to the Secretary to:—

(a) conduct proceedings in private for all or part of particular Crown employment proceedings;
(b) exclude the claimant from all or part of particular Crown employment proceedings;
(c) exclude the claimant's representative from all or part of particular Crown employment proceedings;
(d) take steps to conceal the identity of a particular witness in particular Crown employment proceedings.

(2) A tribunal or [Employment Judge] may, if it or he considers it expedient in the interests of national security, by order—

(a) do [in relation to particular proceedings before it] anything which can be required by direction to be done [in relation to particular Crown employment proceedings] under paragraph (1);
(b) order any person to whom any document (including any judgment or record of the proceedings) has been provided for the purposes of the proceedings not to disclose any such document or the content thereof:—
    (i) to any excluded person;
    (ii) in any case in which a direction has been given under [sub-]paragraph (1)(a) or an order has been made under [sub-]paragraph (2)(a) read with [sub-]paragraph (1)(a), to any person excluded from all or part of the proceedings by virtue of such direction or order; or
    (iii) in any case in which a Minister of the Crown has informed the Secretary in accordance with paragraph (3) that he wishes to address the tribunal or [Employment Judge] with a view to an order being made under [sub-]paragraph (2)(a) read with [sub-]paragraph (1)(b) or (c), to any person who may be excluded from all or part of

the proceedings by virtue of such an order, if an order is made, at any time before the tribunal or [Employment Judge] decides whether or not to make such an order;

(c) take steps to keep secret all or part of the reasons for its judgment.

The tribunal or [Employment Judge] (as the case may be) shall keep under review any order it or he has made under this paragraph.

(3) In any proceedings in which a Minister of the Crown considers that it would be appropriate for a tribunal or [Employment Judge] to make an order as referred to in paragraph (2), he shall (whether or not he is a party to the proceedings) be entitled to appear before and to address the tribunal or [Employment Judge] thereon. The Minister shall inform the Secretary by notice that he wishes to address the tribunal or [Employment Judge] and the Secretary shall copy the notice to the parties.

(4) When exercising its or his functions, a tribunal or [Employment Judge] shall ensure that information is not disclosed contrary to the interests of national security.

NOTES

Words "in relation to particular proceedings before it" and "in relation to particular Crown employment proceedings" in square brackets in sub-para (2)(a) inserted by the Employment Tribunals (Constitution and Rules of Procedure) (Amendment) (No 2) Regulations 2005, SI 2005/1865, reg 2(1), (4)(j); word "sub-" in square brackets in each place it occurs in sub-para (2)(b) inserted by the Employment Tribunals (Constitution and Rules of Procedure) (Amendment) Regulations 2008, SI 2008/3240, regs 2, 4(1), (23), as from 6 April 2009.

[2.882]

55 Dismissals in connection with industrial action

(1) In relation to a complaint under section 111 of the Employment Rights Act 1996 (unfair dismissal: complaints to employment tribunal) that a dismissal is unfair by virtue of section 238A of TULR(C)A (participation in official industrial action) a tribunal or [Employment Judge] may adjourn the proceedings where civil proceedings have been brought until such time as interim proceedings arising out of the civil proceedings have been concluded.

(2) In this rule—

(a) "civil proceedings" means legal proceedings brought by any person against another person in which it is to be determined whether an act of that other person, which induced the claimant to commit an act, or each of a series of acts, is by virtue of section 219 of TULR(C)A not actionable in tort or in delict; and

(b) the interim proceedings shall not be regarded as having concluded until all rights of appeal have been exhausted or the time for presenting any appeal in the course of the interim proceedings has expired.

[2.883]

56 Devolution issues

(1) In any proceedings in which a devolution issue within the definition of the term in paragraph 1 of Schedule 6 to the Scotland Act 1998 arises, the Secretary shall as soon as reasonably practicable by notice inform the Advocate General for Scotland and the Lord Advocate thereof (unless they are a party to the proceedings) and shall at the same time—

(a) send a copy of the notice to the parties to the proceedings; and

(b) send the Advocate General for Scotland and the Lord Advocate a copy of the claim and the response.

(2) In any proceedings in which a devolution issue within the definition of the term in paragraph 1 of [Schedule 9 to the Government of Wales Act 2006] arises, the Secretary shall as soon as reasonably practicable by notice inform the Attorney General and the [Counsel General to the Welsh Assembly Government] thereof (unless they are a party to the proceedings) and shall at the same time—

(a) send a copy of the notice to the parties to the proceedings; and

(b) send the Attorney General and the [Counsel General to the Welsh Assembly Government] a copy of the claim and the response.

(3) A person to whom notice is given in pursuance of paragraph (1) or (2) may within 14 days of receiving it, by notice to the Secretary, take part as a party in the proceedings, so far as they relate to the devolution issue. The Secretary shall send a copy of the notice to the other parties to the proceedings.

NOTES

Words in square brackets in para (2) substituted by the National Assembly for Wales (Diversion of Functions) (No 2) Order 2007, SI 2007/2142, art 4(1), (2).

[2.884]
57 Transfer of proceedings between Scotland and England & Wales

(1) The President (England and Wales) or a Regional [Employment Judge] may at any time, with the consent of the President (Scotland), order any proceedings in England and Wales to be transferred to an Employment Tribunal Office in Scotland if it appears to him that the proceedings could be (in accordance with regulation 19), and would more conveniently be, determined in an employment tribunal located in Scotland.

(2) The President (Scotland) or the Vice President may at any time, with the consent of the President (England and Wales), order any proceedings in Scotland to be transferred to an Employment Tribunal Office in England and Wales if it appears to him that the proceedings could be (in accordance with regulation 19), and would more conveniently be, determined in an employment tribunal located in England or Wales.

(3) An order under paragraph (1) or (2) may be made by the President, Vice President or Regional [Employment Judge] without any application having been made by a party. A party may apply for an order under paragraph (1) or (2) in accordance with rule 11.

(4) Where proceedings have been transferred under this rule, they shall be treated as if in all respects they had been presented to the Secretary by the claimant.

[2.885]
58 References to the European Court of Justice

Where a tribunal or [Employment Judge] makes an order referring a question to the European Court of Justice for a preliminary ruling under [Article 267 of the Treaty on the Functioning of the European Union], the Secretary shall send a copy of the order to the Registrar of that Court.

NOTES

Words in second pair of square brackets substituted by the Treaty of Lisbon (Changes in Terminology or Numbering) Order 2012, SI 2012/1809, art 3(1), Schedule, Pt 2, as from 1 August 2012.

[2.886]
59 Transfer of proceedings from a court

Where proceedings are referred to a tribunal by a court, these rules shall apply to them as if the proceedings had been sent to the Secretary by the claimant.

General provisions

[2.887]
60 Powers

(1) Subject to the provisions of these rules and any practice directions, a tribunal or [Employment Judge] may regulate its or his own procedure.

(2) At a Hearing, or a pre-hearing review held in accordance with rule 18(3), a tribunal may make any order which [an Employment Judge] has power to make under these rules, subject to compliance with any relevant notice or other procedural requirements.

(3) Any function of the Secretary may be performed by a person acting with the authority of the Secretary.

[(4) Where the Attorney-General, or Lord Advocate, makes a request to search for, inspect and take a copy of any relevant documents within a case file (including documents held electronically) for the purpose of preparing an application or considering whether to make an application under section 42 of the [Senior Courts Act 1981], (or where the request is made by the Lord Advocate, section 1 of the Vexatious Actions (Scotland) Act 1898) or section 33 of the Employment Tribunals Act 1996 (restriction of vexatious proceedings), the Secretary shall send notice of or a copy of any relevant document which relates to any proceedings before the tribunal, or any decision, order or award of the tribunal.]

NOTES

Para (4) inserted by the Employment Tribunals (Constitution and Rules of Procedure) (Amendment) Regulations 2008, SI 2008/3240, regs 2, 4(1), (24), as from 6 April 2009; words in square brackets substituted by the Constitutional Reform Act 2005, s 59(5), Sch 11, Pt 1, para 1(2), as from 1 October 2009.

[2.888]
61 Notices, etc

(1) Any notice given or document sent under these rules shall (unless [an Employment Judge] or tribunal orders otherwise) be in writing and may be given or sent—

(a) by post;
(b) by . . . means of electronic communication; or
(c) by personal delivery.

(2) Where a notice or document has been given or sent in accordance with paragraph (1), that notice or document shall, unless the contrary is proved, be taken to have been received by the party to whom it is addressed—

(a) in the case of a notice or document given or sent by post, on the day on which the notice or document would be delivered in the ordinary course of post;

(b) in the case of a notice or document transmitted by . . . means of electronic communication, on the day on which the notice or document is transmitted;

(c) in the case of a notice or document delivered in person, on the day on which the notice or document is delivered.

(3) All notices and documents required by these rules to be presented to the Secretary or an Employment Tribunal Office, other than a claim, shall be presented at the Employment Tribunal Office as notified by the Secretary to the parties.

(4) All notices and documents required or authorised by these rules to be sent or given to any person listed below may be sent to or delivered at—

(a) in the case of a notice or document directed to the Secretary of State in proceedings to which she is not a party and which are brought under section 170 of the Employment Rights Act, the offices of the Redundancy Payments Directorate of the Insolvency Service at PO Box 203, 21 Bloomsbury Street, London WC1B 3QW, or such other office as may be notified by the Secretary of State;

(b) in the case of any other notice or document directed to the Secretary of State in proceedings to which she is not a party (or in respect of which she is treated as a party for the purposes of these rules by rule 51), the offices of [the Department for Business, Innovation and Skills] ([Legal Services Directorate]) at 1 Victoria Street, London, SW1H 0ET, or such other office as be notified by the Secretary of State;

(c) in the case of a notice or document directed to the Attorney General under rule 56, the Attorney General's Chambers, [20 Victoria Street, London SW1H 0NF];

(d) in the case of a notice or document directed to the [Counsel General to the Welsh Assembly Government] under rule 56, the [Counsel General to the Welsh Assembly Government], Crown Buildings, Cathays Park, Cardiff, CF10 3NQ;

(e) in the case of a notice or document directed to the Advocate General for Scotland under rule 56, the Office of the Solicitor to the Advocate General for Scotland, Victoria Quay, Edinburgh, EH6 6QQ;

(f) in the case of a notice or document directed to the Lord Advocate under rule 56, the Legal Secretariat to the Lord Advocate, 25 Chambers Street, Edinburgh, EH1 1LA;

(g) in the case of a notice or document directed to a court, the office of the clerk of the court;

(h) in the case of a notice or document directed to a party:—

(i) the address specified in the claim or response to which notices and documents are to be sent, or in a notice under paragraph (5); or

(ii) if no such address has been specified, or if a notice sent to such an address has been returned, to any other known address or place of business in the United Kingdom or, if the party is a corporate body, the body's registered or principal office in the United Kingdom, or, in any case, such address or place outside the United Kingdom as the President, Vice President or a Regional [Employment Judge] may allow;

(i) in the case of a notice or document directed to any person (other than a person specified in the foregoing provisions of this paragraph), his address or place of business in the United Kingdom or, if the person is a corporate body, the body's registered or principal office in the United Kingdom;

and a notice or document sent or given to the authorised representative of a party shall be taken to have been sent or given to that party.

(5) A party may at any time by notice to the Employment Tribunal Office and to the other party or parties (and, where appropriate, to the appropriate conciliation officer) change the address to which notices and documents are to be sent or transmitted.

(6) The President, Vice President or a Regional [Employment Judge] may order that there shall be substituted service in such manner as he may deem fit in any case he considers appropriate.

(7) In proceedings which may involve a payment out of the National Insurance Fund, the Secretary shall, where appropriate, send copies of all documents and notices to the Secretary of State whether or not she is a party.

[(8) In proceedings under the [Equality Act of the kind referred to in paragraph (9)], copies of every document sent to the parties under rules 29, 30 or 32 shall be sent by the Secretary to the Commission for Equality and Human Rights.]

[(9) The proceedings referred to in paragraph (8) are—

(a) proceedings on a complaint relating to a breach of an equality clause or rule within the meaning of the Equality Act;

(b) proceedings on a complaint relating to a contravention of that Act so far as relating to sex, gender reassignment, marriage and civil partnership, pregnancy and maternity, race or disability;

(c) proceedings on a complaint under section 146(1) of that Act so far as relating to sex, gender reassignment, marriage and civil partnership, pregnancy and maternity, race or disability.]

[(10) Paragraph (8) shall not apply in any proceedings where—

(a) a Minister of the Crown has given a direction, or a tribunal or an Employment Judge has made an order, under rule 54 in those proceedings; and

(b) either the Security Service, the Secret Intelligence Service or the Government Communications Headquarters is a party to those proceedings.]

NOTES

Words omitted from sub-paras (1)(b), (2)(b) revoked by the Employment Tribunals (Constitution and Rules of Procedure) (Amendment) Regulations 2008, SI 2008/3240, regs 2, 4(1), (25)(a), (b), as from 6 April 2009.

Words "the Department for Business, Innovation and Skills" in square brackets in sub-para (4)(b) substituted by the Secretary of State for Business, Innovation and Skills Order 2009, SI 2009/2748, art 8, Schedule, Pt 2, para 28, as from 13 November 2009.

Words "Legal Services Directorate" in square brackets in sub-para (4)(b) substituted by SI 2008/3240, regs 2, 4(1), (25)(c), as from 6 April 2009.

Words "20 Victoria Street, London SW1H 0NF" in square brackets in sub-para (4)(c) substituted by SI 2008/3240, regs 2, 4(1), (25)(c), as from 6 April 2009.

Words in square brackets in sub-para (4)(d) substituted by the National Assembly for Wales (Diversion of Functions) (No 2) Order 2007, SI 2007/2142, art 4(1), (3).

Para (8) substituted by the Equality Act 2006 (Dissolution of Commissions and Consequential and Transitional Provisions) Order 2007, SI 2007/2602, art 4(1), Schedule, para 7(b).

Words "Equality Act of the kind referred to in paragraph (9)" in square brackets in para (8) substituted, and para (9) added, by the Equality Act 2010 (Commencement No 4, Savings, Consequential, Transitional, Transitory and Incidental Provisions and Revocation) Order 2010, SI 2010/2317, art 24, Sch 8, para 5(1), (5), (6), as from 1 October 2010.

Para (10) inserted by the Employment Tribunals (Constitution and Rules of Procedure) (Amendment) Regulations 2012, SI 2012/468, reg 2(1), (9), as from 6 April 2012, except in relation to a claim which is presented to an Employment Tribunal Office on or before 5 April 2012 (see SI 2012/468, reg 3).

[Annex

List of Regulators

[2.889]

Accounts Commission for Scotland and auditors appointed by the Commission to audit the accounts of local government bodies.

Audit Commission for England and Wales and auditors appointed by the Commission to audit the accounts of local government, and health service, bodies.

Certification Officer.

Charity Commissioners for England and Wales.

The Scottish Ministers.

Chief Executive of the Criminal Cases Review Commission.

Chief Executive of the Scottish Criminal Cases Review Commission.

Civil Aviation Authority.

Office of Communications.

The competent authority under Part IV of the Financial Services and Markets Act 2000.

Commissioners for Her Majesty's Revenue and Customs.

[Comptroller and Auditor General.]

Auditor General for Wales.

Auditor General for Scotland and persons appointed by that person (or on behalf of that person) under the Public Finance and Accountability (Scotland) Act 2000 to act as auditors or examiners for the purposes of sections 21 to 24 of that Act.

Audit Scotland.

Gas and Electricity Markets Authority.

Water Services Regulation Authority.

. . .

Water Industry Commission for Scotland.

Water Industry Commissioner for Scotland.

Director of the Serious Fraud Office.

Lord Advocate, Scotland.

Environment Agency.

Scottish Environment Protection Agency.

Food Standards Agency.

[Financial Conduct Authority.

Prudential Regulation Authority.

The Bank of England in its capacity as a regulator of recognised clearing houses within the meaning of the Financial Services and Markets Act 2000.]

The Financial Reporting Council Limited and its operating bodies the Professional Oversight Board, the Financial Reporting Review Panel and the Accountancy and Actuarial Discipline Board.

. . .

Care Council for Wales.

Scottish Social Services Council.

Children's Commissioner.

Commissioner for Children and Young People in Scotland.

Children's Commissioner for Wales.

Health and Safety Executive.

Regulator of Social Housing.

Local authorities which are responsible for the enforcement of health and safety legislation.

Independent Police Complaints Commission.

Information Commissioner.

Scottish Information Commissioner.

Care Quality Commission.

[Monitor].

National Assembly for Wales.

[Healthcare Improvement Scotland.

Social Care and Social Work Improvement Scotland.]

Pensions Regulator.

Office of Fair Trading.

Office of Rail Regulation.

Standards Board for England.

Local Commissioner in Wales.

Standards Commission for Scotland and the Chief Investigating Officer.

Treasury.

Secretary of State for Business, Innovation and Skills.

Secretary of State for Transport.

Local authorities which are responsible for the enforcement of consumer protection legislation.

Local authorities which are responsible for the enforcement of food standards.

A person (regulator A) carrying out functions, by virtue of legislation, relating to matters in respect of which another regulator (regulator B), who is listed in this Schedule and was previously responsible for carrying out the same or substantially similar functions and has ceased to be so responsible.]

NOTES

The Annex was added by SI 2010/131, reg 2(1), (3), as from 6 April 2010, except where the claim is presented to an Employment Tribunal Office before that date. It has been subsequently amended as follows—

Entry "Comptroller and Auditor General" substituted (for the original entry "Comptroller and Auditor General of the National Audit Office") by the Budget Responsibility and National Audit Act 2011 (Consequential Amendments) Order 2012, SI 2012/725, art 2(8), as from 1 April 2012.

Entry "Convener of the Water Customer Consultation Panels and any member of those Panels" (omitted) revoked by the Public Services Reform (Scotland) Act 2010 (Consequential Modifications of Enactments) Order 2011, SI 2011/2581, art 2, Sch 3, Pt 2, para 4, as from 28 October 2011.

Entries "Financial Conduct Authority", "Prudential Regulation Authority" and "The Bank of England" substituted for original entry "Financial Services Authority", by the Financial Services Act 2012 (Consequential Amendments and Transitional Provisions) Order 2013, SI 2013/472, art 3, Sch 2, para 94, as from 1 April 2013.

Entry "General Social Care Council" (omitted) revoked by the Health and Social Care Act 2012 (Consequential Provision—Social Workers) Order 2012, SI 2012/1479, art 11, Schedule, Pt 2, para 73, as from 1 August 2012.

Entry "Monitor" substituted, for entry "The Independent Regulator of NHS Foundation Trusts" as originally enacted, by the NHS Commissioning Board Authority (Abolition and Transfer of Staff, Property and Liabilities) and the Health and Social Care Act 2012 (Consequential Amendments) Order 2012, SI 2012/1641, art 10, Sch 4, para 9, as from 1 October 2012.

Entries "Healthcare Improvement Scotland" and "Social Care and Social Work Improvement Scotland" substituted (for original entry "Scottish Commission for the Regulation of Care") by SI 2011/2581, art 2, Sch 2, Pt 2, para 41, as from 28 October 2011.

SCHEDULE 2
THE EMPLOYMENT TRIBUNALS (NATIONAL SECURITY) RULES OF PROCEDURE

Regulation 16(2)

[2.890]

1 Application of Schedule 2

(1) The rules in this Schedule only apply to national security proceedings or proceedings where the right in rule 54(3) of Schedule 1 has been exercised.

(2) The rules in this Schedule modify the rules in Schedule 1 in relation to such proceedings. If there is conflict between the rules contained in this Schedule and those in any other Schedule to these Regulations, the rules in this Schedule shall prevail.

(3) Any reference in this Schedule to rule 54 is a reference to rule 54 in Schedule 1.

2 Notification of national security proceedings

When proceedings before an employment tribunal become national security proceedings the Secretary shall inform the parties of that fact in writing as soon as practicable.

3 Responding to a claim

(1) If before the expiry of the period for entering the response—

(a) a direction of a Minister of the Crown under rule 54(1)(b) (exclusion of claimant) applicable to this stage of the proceedings is given; or

(b) a Minister of the Crown has informed the Secretary in accordance with rule 54(3) that he wishes to address the tribunal or [Employment Judge] with a view to the tribunal or [Employment Judge] making an order under rule 54(2) applicable to this stage of the proceedings to exclude the claimant;

rule 4(3)(d) (grounds for the response) of Schedule 1 shall not apply and paragraphs (2) and (3) of this rule shall apply instead.

(2) In a case falling within [sub-]paragraph (1)(b), if the tribunal or [Employment Judge] decides not to make an order under rule 54(2), the respondent shall within 28 days of the decision present to the Employment Tribunal Office the written grounds on which he resists the claim. On receiving the written grounds the Secretary shall send a copy of them to all other parties and they shall be treated as part of the response.

(3) In a case falling within [sub-]paragraph (1)(b) where the tribunal or [Employment Judge] makes the order, or in a case falling within [sub-]paragraph (1)(a), the respondent shall with 44 days of the direction or order being made, present to the Employment Tribunal Office (and, where applicable, to the special advocate) the written grounds on which he resists the claim and they shall be treated as part of the response.

(4) The time limits in paragraphs (2) and (3) may be extended if it is just and equitable to do so and if an application is presented to the Employment Tribunal Office before the expiry of the relevant time limit. The application must explain why the respondent cannot comply with the time limit.

4 Serving of documents by the Secretary

(1) The Secretary shall not send a copy of the response or grounds for the response to any person excluded from all or part of the proceedings by virtue of a direction or order given or made under rule 54.

(2) Where a Minister of the Crown has informed the Secretary in accordance with rule 54(3) that he wishes to address the tribunal or [Employment Judge] with a view to an order being made under rule 54(2)(a) to exclude the claimant's representative from all or part of the proceedings, the Secretary shall not at any time before the tribunal or [Employment Judge] has considered the Minister's representations, send a copy of the response or the grounds for the response to any person who may be excluded from all or part of the proceedings by such an order if it were made.

5 Default judgment

Rule 8(1) (default judgments) of Schedule 1 shall apply in relation to the time limit for presenting a response, but it shall not apply in relation to the time limits in paragraphs (2) and (3) of rule 3 in this Schedule.

6 Witness orders and disclosure of documents

(1) Where—

(a) a Minister has issued a direction or the tribunal or [an Employment Judge] has made an order under rule 54 to exclude a claimant or his representative from all or part of the proceedings; and

(b) [an Employment Judge] or the tribunal is considering whether to make, or has made, an order described in rule 10(2)(c) or (d) of Schedule 1 (requiring a person to attend and give evidence or to produce documents) or under rule 8 of Schedule 3 or rule 7 of Schedule 4;

a Minister of the Crown (whether or not he is a party to the proceedings) may make an application to the tribunal or [Employment Judge] objecting to the imposition of a requirement described in rule 10(2)(c) or (d) of Schedule 1 or under Schedules 3 or 4. If such an order has been made the Minister may make an application to vary or set aside the order.

(2) The tribunal or [Employment Judge] shall hear and determine the Minister's application in private and the Minister shall be entitled to address the tribunal or [Employment Judge]. The application shall be made by notice to the Secretary and the Secretary shall give notice of the application to all parties.

7 Case management discussions and pre-hearing reviews

(1) Rule 14(4) (hearings – general) of Schedule 1 shall be modified in accordance with paragraph (2).

(2) In proceedings in which a special advocate has been appointed in respect of the claimant, if the claimant has been excluded from a case management discussion or a pre-hearing review, at such a hearing the claimant shall not have the right to advance oral argument, but oral argument may be advanced on the claimant's behalf by the special advocate.

8 Special advocate

(1) In any proceedings in which there is an excluded person the tribunal or [Employment Judge] shall inform the Attorney General (or in Scotland, the Advocate General) of the proceedings before it with a view to the Attorney General (or the Advocate General, in Scotland), if he thinks it fit to do so, appointing a special advocate to represent the interests of the claimant in respect of those parts of the proceedings from which—

(a) any representative of his is excluded;

(b) both he and his representative are excluded; or

(c) he is excluded, where he does not have a representative.

(2) A special advocate shall have a general qualification for the purposes of section 71 of the Courts and Legal Services Act 1990 or shall be an advocate or a solicitor admitted in Scotland.

(3) Where the excluded person is the claimant, he shall be permitted to make a statement to the tribunal or [Employment Judge] before the commencement of the proceedings, or the part of the proceedings, from which he is excluded.

(4) Except in accordance with paragraphs (5) to (7), the special advocate may not communicate directly or indirectly with any person (including an excluded person)—

(a) (except in the case of the tribunal, [Employment Judge] and the respondent) on any matter contained in the grounds for the response referred to in rule 3(3);

(b) (except in the case of a person who was present) on any matter discussed or referred to during any part of the proceedings in which the tribunal or [Employment Judge] sat in private in accordance with a direction or an order given or made under rule 54.

(5) The special advocate may apply for orders from the tribunal or [Employment Judge] authorising him to seek instructions from, or otherwise to communicate with, an excluded person—

(a) on any matter contained in the grounds for the response referred to in rule 3(3); or

(b) on any matter discussed or referred to during any part of the proceedings in which the tribunal or [Employment Judge] sat in private in accordance with a direction or an order given or made under rule 54.

(6) An application under paragraph (5) shall be made in writing to the Employment Tribunal Office and shall include the title of the proceedings and the grounds for the application.

(7) The Secretary shall notify the Minister of an application under paragraph (5) and the Minister shall be entitled to address the tribunal or [Employment Judge] on the application.

(8) In these rules and those in Schedule 1, in any case in which a special advocate has been appointed to represent the interests of the claimant in accordance with paragraph (1), any reference to a party shall (save in those references specified in paragraph (9)) include the special advocate.

(9) The following references to "party" or "parties" shall not include the special advocate—

(a) regulation 9(3);

(b) in Schedule 1, rule 2(2)(b), 9, 10(2)(r), 10(3), the first two references in rule 11(4), 11(5), 18(7), 20, 22, 23, 27(3), 27(5), 29(3), 30(6)(f), 33(1), 34(2), all references in rule 38 save that in 38(10), 39, 40, 41, all references in rule 42 save that in rule 42(8), 44 to 48, 51, 54(1), the first reference in rule 54(3), 56(3), 61(3), 61(4)(a) and (b), and 61(7);

(c) in Schedule 4, rule 5(b), 6(5) and 10; and

(d) in Schedule 5, rule 4(b).

9 Hearings

(1) Any hearing of or in connection with a claim shall, subject to any direction of a Minister of the Crown or order of a tribunal or [Employment Judge] under rule 54 that all or part of the proceedings are to take place in private and subject to rule 16 of Schedule 1, take place in public.

(2) A member of the [Administrative Justice and Tribunals Council] shall not be entitled to attend any hearing taking place in private in his capacity as member where the hearing is taking place in private under a direction of a Minister of the Crown or an order of a tribunal or [Employment Judge] under rule 54.

(3) Subject to any direction of a Minister of the Crown or order of a tribunal or [Employment Judge] under rule 54, a party shall be entitled to give evidence, to call witnesses, to question any witnesses and to address the tribunal at a Hearing.

10 Reasons in national security proceedings

(1) This rule applies to written reasons given under rule 30 of Schedule 1 for a judgment or order made by the tribunal or [Employment Judge] in national security proceedings.

(2) Before the Secretary sends a copy of the written reasons ("the full written reasons") to any party, or enters them in the Register under rule 32 of Schedule 1, he shall send a copy of the full written reasons to the Minister.

(3) If the Minister considers it expedient in the interests of national security and he has given a direction or the tribunal or [an Employment Judge] has made an order under rule 54 in those proceedings, the Minister may—

(a) direct the tribunal or [Employment Judge] that the full written reasons shall not be disclosed to persons specified in the direction, and to prepare a further document ("the edited reasons") setting out the reasons for the judgment or order, but with the omission of such of the information as is specified in the direction;

(b) direct the tribunal or [Employment Judge] that the full written reasons shall not be disclosed to persons specified in the direction, but that no further document setting out the tribunal or [Employment Judge's] reasons should be prepared.

(4) Where the Minister has directed the tribunal or [Employment Judge] in accordance with [sub-]paragraph (3)(a), the edited reasons shall be signed by the [Employment Judge] and initialled in each place where an omission has been made.

(5) Where a direction has been made under [sub-]paragraph (3)(a), the Secretary shall—

(a) send a copy of the edited reasons referred to in [sub-]paragraph (3)(a) to any person specified in the direction and to the persons listed in paragraph (7);

(b) enter the edited reasons in the Register, but omit from the Register the full written reasons; and

(c) send a copy of the full written reasons to the persons listed in paragraph (7).

(6) Where a direction has been made under [sub-]paragraph (3)(b), the Secretary shall send a copy of the full written reasons to the persons listed in paragraph (7), but he shall not enter the full written reasons in the Register.

(7) The persons to whom full written reasons should be sent in accordance with paragraph (5) or (6) are—

(a) the respondent;

(b) the claimant or the claimant's representative if they were not specified in the direction made under paragraph (3);

(c) if applicable, the special advocate;

(d) where the proceedings were referred to the tribunal by a court, to that court; and

(e) where there are proceedings before a superior court (or in Scotland, an appellate court) relating to the decision in question, to that court.

11 Correction of written reasons

Where written reasons (whether "full" or "edited") have been omitted from the Register in accordance with rule 10 and they are corrected by certificate under rule 37 of Schedule 1, the Secretary shall send a copy of the corrected reasons to the same persons who had been sent the reasons in accordance with rule 10.

12 Review of judgments or decisions

In rule 34(3) of Schedule 1 (review of other judgments and decisions), the reference in sub-paragraph (c) to decisions being made in the absence of a party does not include reference to decisions being made in the absence of a party where this is done in accordance with a direction given or an order made under rule 54.

NOTES

All references to "Employment Judge" and "an Employment Judge" substituted by the Tribunals, Courts and Enforcement Act 2007 (Transitional and Consequential Provisions) Order 2008, SI 2008/2683, art 6(1), Sch 1, paras 240, 256(a), (b), as from 3 November 2008.

Other amendments to this Schedule are as follows—

Rules 3, 10: word "sub-" in square brackets in all places in which it occurs inserted by SI 2008/3240, regs 2, 5, as from 6 April 2009.

Rule 9: words "Administrative Justice and Tribunals Council" in square brackets in para (2) substituted by SI 2008/2683, art 6(1), Sch 1, paras 240, 256(c), as from 3 November 2008.

SCHEDULE 3
THE EMPLOYMENT TRIBUNALS (LEVY APPEALS) RULES OF PROCEDURE

Regulation 16(3)(a)

For use only in proceedings on levy appeals

[2.891]

1 Application of Schedule 1

Subject to rules 9 and 10 of this Schedule, Schedule 1 shall apply to levy appeals. The rules in this Schedule modify the rules in Schedule 1 in relation to levy appeals. If there is conflict between the rules contained in this Schedule and those in Schedule 1, the rules in this Schedule shall prevail.

2 Definitions

In this Schedule and in relation to proceedings to which this Schedule applies—

"Board" means in relation to an appeal the respondent industrial training board;

"Industrial Training Act" means the Industrial Training Act 1982;

"levy" means a levy imposed under section 11 of the Industrial Training Act;

"levy appeal" means an appeal against an assessment to a levy;

"respondent" means the Board.

3 Notice of Appeal

A person wishing to appeal an assessment to a levy (the appellant) shall do so by sending to the Board two copies of a notice of appeal which must be substantially in accordance with Form 1 in the Annex to this Schedule, and they must include the grounds of their appeal.

4 Action on receipt of appeal

(1) Subject to rules 5 and 6, the Board shall, within 21 days of receiving the notice of appeal send the following documents to the Employment Tribunal Office—

(a) one copy of the notice of appeal;

(b) a copy of the assessment notice and of any notice by the Board allowing further time for appealing;

(c) a notice giving the Board's address for service under these rules where that address is different from the address specified in the assessment notice as the address for service of a notice of appeal; and

(d) any representations in writing relating to the appeal that the Board wishes to submit to the tribunal.

(2) Failure to comply with any provision of this rule or rule 5 shall not make the appeal invalid.

5 Requests for further information

(1) Subject to rule 6, this rule applies when, on receiving the notice of appeal, the Board considers that it requires further information on the appellant's grounds for the appeal and of any facts relevant to those grounds.

(2) The Board shall send the appellant a notice specifying the further information required by the Board within 21 days of receiving the notice of appeal.

(3) The appellant shall send the Board two copies of the further information within 21 days of receiving the notice requesting the information, or within such further period as the Board may allow.

(4) Subject to paragraph (5), within 21 days of receiving the further information the Board shall send the following documents to the Employment Tribunal Office—

(a) the documents listed in rule 4(1);
(b) a copy of the notice requesting further information;
(c) any further information which has been provided to the Board; and
(d) any representations in writing regarding such information which the Board wishes to submit to the tribunal.

(5) If further information is not received by the Board within the time limit, the documents listed in sub-paragraphs (a) and (b) of paragraph (4) shall be sent by the Board to the Employment Tribunal Office—

(a) within 50 days of the receipt of the notice of appeal by the Board; or
(b) if the Board has allowed a further period of time for delivery of further particulars under paragraph (3), within 7 days of the end of that period.

6 Withdrawal of appeal or assessment

(1) The appellant may withdraw the notice of appeal by notice given to the Board at any time and in that event no further action shall be taken in relation to the appeal.

(2) When an assessment is withdrawn by the Board, it shall notify the Employment Tribunal Office and no further action shall be taken in relation to the appeal.

7 Entry of appeal

(1) The Secretary shall as soon as reasonably practicable after receiving from the Board the relevant documents in accordance with rule 4(1), 5(4) or 5(5)—

(a) give notice to the appellant and to the Board of the case number of the appeal (which must from then on be referred to in all correspondence relating to the appeal) and of the address to which notices and other communications to the Employment Tribunal Office shall be sent;
(b) give notice to the appellant of the Board's address for service; and
(c) send to the appellant a copy of any representations in writing that the Board has submitted to the tribunal under rule 4 or 5.

8 Order for further information

(1) In any case in which the appellant has not sent to the Board further information which has been requested by the Board in accordance with rule 5, [an Employment Judge] or tribunal may, on the application of the Board, by notice order the appellant to supply such further information as may be specified in the notice, and the appellant shall send two copies of such information to the Employment Tribunal Office within such time as [the Employment Judge] or tribunal may direct.

(2) As soon as is reasonably practicable after receiving the further information from the appellant, the Secretary shall send a copy of the information to the Board.

(3) An order made under paragraph (1) shall be treated as an order made under rule 10 of Schedule 1 for the purposes of rule 13 of Schedule 1 (compliance with orders and practice directions).

9 Provisions of Schedule 1 which do not apply to levy appeals

The following rules in Schedule 1 shall not apply in relation to levy appeals: rules 1 to 9, 16(1)(c), 18(2)(c) and (e), 20 to 25, 33, 34(1)(a), 34(2), 34(4), 38(4), 39, 42(4), 43, 47, 49 to 53, 55, and paragraphs (4)(a), (7) and (8) of rule 61. All references in Schedule 1 to the rules listed in this rule shall have no effect in relation to a levy appeal.

10 Modification of Schedule 1

Schedule 1 shall be further modified in relation to levy appeals as follows—

(a) all references in Schedule 1 to a claim or claimant shall be read as references to a levy appeal or to an appellant in a levy appeal respectively and as the context may require; and
(b) in rule 61 (Notices, etc) after paragraph 4(i) insert:—

> "(j) in the case of a notice of an appeal brought under the Industrial Training Act, the Board's address for service specified in the assessment notice;
> (k) in the case of any other document directed to the Board, the Board's address for service;".

ANNEX

FORM 1

INDUSTRIAL TRAINING ACT 1982 NOTICE OF APPEAL AGAINST AN ASSESSMENT

TO

*INDUSTRIAL TRAINING BOARD

. . . . [ ] . . . .

. . . .

. . . .

. . . .

AND TO

The Secretary of Tribunals (England and Wales) + (Scotland)

I/We + ... of

. . . . # . . . .

. . . .

hereby give notice that I/we + appeal to an employment tribunal under the Industrial Training Act 1982, section 12, against the assessment to the levy made by the above-mentioned industry training board on . . . . 20 . . . . . . being the assessment numbered . . . . . .

Grounds of appeal

The grounds of my/our + appeal are as follows—

Address for service

All communications regarding the appeal should be addressed to me/us + at. . . . . #
. . . .

. . . .

to my/our + Solicitor(s)Agent(s)~,

. . . . at . . . . # . . . .

Date . . . . 2 . . . .

Signed . . . .

* Insert name of the Board.

[ ] Insert the address of the Board.

+ Delete as relevant.

Insert address applicable.

~ If the notice is signed on behalf of the appellant, the signatory must state in what capacity or what authority he signs.

NOTES

Rule 8: words in square brackets substituted by the Tribunals, Courts and Enforcement Act 2007 (Transitional and Consequential Provisions) Order 2008, SI 2008/2683, art 6(1), Sch 1, paras 240, 257, as from 3 November 2008.

SCHEDULE 4
THE EMPLOYMENT TRIBUNALS (HEALTH AND SAFETY—APPEALS AGAINST IMPROVEMENT AND PROHIBITION NOTICES) RULES OF PROCEDURE

Regulation 16(3)(b)

For use only in proceedings in an appeal against an improvement or prohibition notice

[2.892]

1 Application of Schedule 1

Subject to rules 11 and 12 of this Schedule, Schedule 1 shall apply to appeals against an improvement notice or a prohibition notice. The rules in this Schedule modify the rules in Schedule 1 in relation to such appeals. If there is conflict between the rules contained in this Schedule and those in Schedule 1, the rules in this Schedule shall prevail.

2 Definitions

In this Schedule and in relation to proceedings to which this Schedule applies—

"Health and Safety Act" means the Health and Safety at Work etc Act 1974;

"improvement notice" means a notice under section 21 of the Health and Safety Act;

"inspector" means a person appointed under section 19(1) of the Health and Safety Act;

"prohibition notice" means a notice under section 22 of the Health and Safety Act; and

"respondent" means the inspector who issued the improvement notice or prohibition notice which is the subject of the appeal.

3 Notice of appeal

A person wishing to appeal an improvement notice or a prohibition notice (the appellant) shall do so by sending to the Employment Tribunal Office . . . a notice of appeal which must include the following—

(a) the name and address of the appellant and, if different, an address to which he requires notices and documents relating to the appeal to be sent;

(b) the date of the improvement notice or prohibition notice appealed against and the address of the premises or the place concerned;

(c) the name and address of the respondent;

(d) details of the requirements or directions which are being appealed; and

(e) the grounds for the appeal.

4 Time limit for bringing appeal

(1) Subject to paragraph (2), the notice of appeal must be sent to the Employment Tribunal Office within 21 days from the date of the service on the appellant of the notice appealed against.

(2) A tribunal may extend the time mentioned above where it is satisfied, on an application made in writing to the Secretary either before or after the expiration of that time, that it is or was not reasonably practicable for an appeal to be brought within that time.

5 Action on receipt of appeal

On receiving the notice of appeal the Secretary shall—

(a) send a copy of the notice of appeal to the respondent; and

(b) inform the parties in writing of the case number of the appeal (which must from then on be referred to in all correspondence relating to the appeal) and of the address to which notices and other communications to the Employment Tribunal Office shall be sent.

6 Application for a direction suspending the operation of a prohibition notice

(1) When an appeal is brought against a prohibition notice, an application may be made by the appellant under section 24(3)(b) of the Health and Safety Act for a direction suspending the operation of the prohibition notice until the appeal is determined or withdrawn. The application must be presented to the Employment Tribunal Office in writing and shall include—

(a) the case number of the appeal, or if there is no case number sufficient details to identify the appeal; and

(b) the grounds on which the application is made.

(2) The Secretary shall send a copy of the application to the respondent as soon as practicable after it has been received and shall inform the respondent that he has the opportunity to submit representations in writing if he so wishes, within a specified time but not less than 7 days.

(3) The [Employment Judge] shall consider the application and any representations submitted by the respondent, and may—

(a) order that the application should not be determined separately from the full hearing of the appeal;

(b) order that the operation of the prohibition notice be suspended until the appeal is determined or withdrawn;

(c) dismiss the appellant's application; or

(d) order that the application be determined at a Hearing (held in accordance with rule 26 of Schedule 1).

(4) The [Employment Judge] must give reasons for any decision made under paragraph (3) or made following a Hearing ordered under [sub-]paragraph (3)(d).

(5) A decision made under paragraph (3) or made following a Hearing ordered under [sub-]paragraph (3)(d) shall be treated as a decision which may be reviewed upon the application of a party under rule 34 of Schedule 1.

7 General power to manage proceedings

(1) The [Employment Judge] may at any time on the application of a party, make an order in relation to any matter which appears to him to be appropriate. Such orders may be those listed in rule 10(2) of Schedule 1 (subject to rule 11 below) or such other orders as he thinks fit. Subject to the case management rules in Schedule 1, orders may be issued as a result of [an Employment Judge] considering the papers before him in the absence of the parties, or at a hearing (see regulation 2 for the definition of "hearing").

(2) If the parties agree in writing upon the terms of any decision to be made by the tribunal or [Employment Judge], the [Employment Judge] may, if he thinks fit, decide accordingly.

8 Appointment of an assessor

The President, Vice President or a Regional [Employment Judge] may, if he thinks fit, appoint in accordance with section 24(4) of the Health and Safety Act a person having special knowledge or experience in relation to the subject matter of the appeal to sit with the tribunal or [Employment Judge] as an assessor.

9 Right to withdraw proceedings

(1) An appellant may withdraw all or part of the appeal at any time. This may be done either orally at a hearing or in writing in accordance with paragraph (2).

(2) To withdraw an appeal or part of one in writing the appellant must inform the Employment Tribunal Office in writing of the appeal or the parts of it which are to be withdrawn.

(3) The Secretary shall inform all other parties of the withdrawal. Withdrawal takes effect on the date on which the Employment Tribunal Office (in the case of written notifications) or the tribunal or [Employment Judge] receives notice of it and where the whole appeal is withdrawn proceedings are brought to an end against the respondent on that date and the tribunal or [Employment Judge] shall dismiss the appeal.

10 Costs and expenses

(1) A tribunal or [Employment Judge] may make an order ("a costs order") that a party ("the paying party") make a payment in respect of the costs incurred by another party ("the receiving party").

(2) For the purposes of paragraph (1) "costs" shall mean fees, charges, disbursements [or expenses] incurred by or on behalf of a party in relation to the proceedings. In Scotland all references in this Schedule to costs or costs orders shall be read as references to expenses or orders for expenses.

(3) The amount of a costs order against the paying party can be determined in the following ways—

(a) the tribunal may specify the sum which the party must pay to the receiving party, provided that sum does not exceed £10,000;

(b) the parties may agree on a sum to be paid by the paying party to the receiving party and if they do so the costs order shall be for the sum so agreed;

(c) the tribunal may order the paying party to pay the receiving party the whole or a specified part of the costs of the second party with the amount to be paid being determined by way of detailed assessment in a County Court in accordance with the Civil Procedure Rules or, in Scotland, as taxed according to such part of the table of fees prescribed for proceedings in the sheriff court as shall be directed by the order.

(4) The tribunal or [Employment Judge] shall have regard to the paying party's ability to pay when considering whether it or he shall make a costs order or how much that order should be.

(5) For the avoidance of doubt, the amount of a costs order made under either [sub-]paragraph (4)(b) or (c) may exceed £10,000.

11 Provisions of Schedule 1 which do not apply to appeals against improvement notices or prohibition notices

The following rules in Schedule 1 shall not apply in relation to appeals against improvement and prohibition notices: rules 1 to 9, 10(1), 10(2)(g), (i), (k), (l) and (r), 12, 13, 16(1)(c), 18(2)(c) and (e), 18(8), 20 to 25, 29(3), 33, 34(1)(a), 34(2), 38 to 47, 49 to 53, 55, and 61(4)(a), (7) and (8). All references in Schedule 1 to the rules listed in this rule shall have no effect in relation to an appeal against an improvement notice or a prohibition notice.

12 Modification of Schedule 1

Schedule 1 shall be further modified so that all references in Schedule 1 to a claim shall be read as references to a notice of appeal or to an appeal against an improvement notice or a prohibition notice, as the context may require, and all references to the claimant shall be read as references to the appellant in such an appeal.

NOTES

All references to "Employment Judge" and "an Employment Judge" substituted by the Tribunals, Courts and Enforcement Act 2007 (Transitional and Consequential Provisions) Order 2008, SI 2008/2683, art 6(1), Sch 1, paras 240, 258, as from 3 November 2008.

Other amendments to this Schedule are as follows—

Rule 3: words omitted revoked by the Employment Tribunals (Constitution and Rules of Procedure) (Amendment) Regulations 2004, SI 2004/2351, reg 2(1), (10).

Rule 6: word "sub-" in square brackets in paras (4), (5) inserted by the Employment Tribunals (Constitution and Rules of Procedure) (Amendment) Regulations 2008, SI 2008/3240, regs 2, 6(1), (2), as from 6 April 2009.

Rule 10: words in square brackets in para (2) substituted by the Employment Tribunals (Constitution and Rules of Procedure) (Amendment) (No 2) Regulations 2005, SI 2005/1865, reg 2(1), (5); word in square brackets in para (5) inserted by SI 2008/3240, regs 2, 6(1), (3), as from 6 April 2009.

SCHEDULE 5
THE EMPLOYMENT TRIBUNALS ([UNLAWFUL ACT NOTICES] APPEALS) RULES OF PROCEDURE

Regulation 16(3)(c)

For use only in proceedings in an appeal against [an unlawful act notice]

[2.893]

1 Application of Schedule 1

Subject to rules 5 and 6 of this Schedule, Schedule 1 shall apply to appeals against [an unlawful act notice]. The rules in this Schedule modify the rules in Schedule 1 in relation to such appeals. If there is conflict between the rules contained in this Schedule and those in Schedule 1, the rules in this Schedule shall prevail.

[2 Definitions

In this Schedule and in relation to proceedings to which this Schedule applies—

"appeal", unless the context requires otherwise, means an appeal referred to in section 21 of the Equality Act 2006;

"unlawful act notice" means a notice under that section; and

"respondent" means the Commission for Equality and Human Rights established under section 1 of the Equality Act 2006.]

3 Notice of Appeal

A person wishing to appeal [an unlawful act notice] (the appellant) shall do so by sending to the Employment Tribunal Office . . . a notice of appeal which must be in writing and must include the following—

(a) the name and address of the appellant and, if different, an address to which he requires notices and documents relating to the appeal to be sent;
(b) the date of [the unlawful act notice] appealed against;
(c) the name and address of the respondent;
(d) details of the requirements which are being appealed; and
(e) the grounds for the appeal.

4 Action on receipt of appeal

On receiving the notice of appeal the Secretary shall—

(a) send a copy of the notice of appeal to the respondent; and
(b) inform the parties in writing of the case number of the appeal (which must from then on be referred to in all correspondence relating to the appeal) and of the address to which notices and other communications to the Employment Tribunal Office shall be sent.

5 Provisions of Schedule 1 which do not apply to appeals against [unlawful act notices]

The following rules in Schedule 1 shall not apply in relation to appeals against [an unlawful act notice]: rules 1 to 9, 16(1)(c), 18(2)(c) and (e), 20 to 24, 33, 34(1)(a), 34(2), 34(4), 38(4), 39, 42(4), 43, 47, 49 to 53, 55, and paragraphs (4)(a), (7) and (8) of rule 61. All references in Schedule 1 to the rules listed in this rule shall have no effect in relation to an appeal against [an unlawful act notice].

6 Modification of Schedule 1

Schedule 1 shall be further modified so that all references in Schedule 1 to a claim shall be read as references to a notice of appeal or to an appeal against [an unlawful act notice], as the context may require, and all references to the claimant shall be read as references to the appellant in such an appeal.

NOTES

Headings and rules 1, 3, 5, 6: words in square brackets substituted by the Equality Act 2006 (Dissolution of Commissions and Consequential and Transitional Provisions) Order 2007, SI 2007/2602, art 4(1), Schedule, para 7(c)(i)–(iii).

Rule 2: substituted by SI 2007/2602, art 4(1), Schedule, para 7(c)(iv).

Rule 3: words omitted revoked by the Employment Tribunals (Constitution and Rules of Procedure) (Amendment) Regulations 2004, SI 2004/2351, reg 2(1), (10).

[SCHEDULE 6
THE EMPLOYMENT TRIBUNALS (EQUAL VALUE) RULES OF PROCEDURE

Regulation 16(4)

[2.894]

1 General

The rules in this Schedule shall only apply in proceedings involving an equal value claim and they modify and supplement the rules in Schedule 1. If there is conflict between Schedule 1 and this Schedule, the provisions of this Schedule shall prevail.

2 Interpretation

(1) In this Schedule and in relation to proceedings to which this Schedule applies:

"comparator" means the person of the opposite sex to the claimant in relation to whom the claimant claims that his work is of equal value . . . ;

" . . .

["equal value claim" means a claim relating to a breach of a sex equality clause or rule within the meaning of the Equality Act in a case involving work within section 65(1)(c) of that Act;]

"the facts relating to the question" has the meaning in rule 7(3);

"independent expert" means a member of the panel of independent experts mentioned in [section 131(8) of the Equality Act];

"indicative timetable" means the indicative timetable set out in the Annex to this Schedule;

"the question" means whether the claimant's work is of equal value to that of the comparator . . . ; and

"report" means a report required by a tribunal to be prepared by an independent expert, in accordance with [section 131(2) of the Equality Act].

(2) A reference in this Schedule to a rule, is a reference to a rule in this Schedule unless otherwise provided.

(3) A reference in this Schedule to "these rules" is a reference to the rules in Schedules 1 and 6 unless otherwise provided.

[(4) A reference in this Schedule to one person's work being of equal value to another's is to be construed in accordance with section 65(6) of the Equality Act.]

3 General power to manage proceedings

(1) In addition to the power to make orders described in rule 10 of Schedule 1, the tribunal or [Employment Judge] shall have power (subject to rules 4(3) and 7(4)) to make the following orders:

(a) the standard orders set out in rules 5 or 8, with such addition to, omission or variation of those orders (including specifically variations as to the periods within which actions are to be taken by the parties) as the [Employment Judge] or tribunal considers is appropriate;

(b) that no new facts shall be admitted in evidence by the tribunal unless they have been disclosed to all other parties in writing before a date specified by the tribunal (unless it was not reasonably practicable for a party to have done so);

(c) that the parties may be required to send copies of documents or provide information to the other parties and to the independent expert;

(d) that the respondent is required to grant the independent expert access to his premises during a period specified by the tribunal or [Employment Judge] in order for the independent expert to conduct interviews with persons identified as relevant by the independent expert;

(e) when more than one expert is to give evidence in the proceedings, that those experts present to the tribunal a joint statement of matters which are agreed between them and those matters on which they disagree;

(f) where proceedings have been joined, that lead claimants be identified.

(2) Any reference in Schedule 1 or 2 to an order made under rule 10 of Schedule 1 shall include reference to an order made in accordance with this Schedule.

4 Conduct of stage 1 equal value hearing

(1) When in an equal value claim there is a dispute as to whether [one person's work is of equal value to another's], the tribunal shall conduct a "stage 1 equal value hearing" in accordance with both this rule and the rules applicable to pre-hearing reviews in Schedule 1.

(2) . . .

(3) At the stage 1 equal value hearing the [Employment Judge or] tribunal shall:

(a) where [section 131(6) of the Equality Act] applies, strike out the claim (or the relevant part of it) if, in accordance with [that section] of that Act, the tribunal must determine that the work of the claimant and the comparator are not of equal value;

(b) decide, in accordance with [section 131(2) of the Equality Act], either that:

(i) the tribunal shall determine the question; or

(ii) it shall require a member of the panel of independent experts to prepare a report with respect to the question;

(c) subject to rule 5 and with regard to the indicative timetable, make the standard orders for the stage 1 equal value hearing as set out in rule 5;

(d) if the tribunal has decided to require an independent expert to prepare a report on the question, require the parties to copy to the independent expert all information which they are required by an order to disclose or agree between each other;

(e) if the tribunal has decided to require an independent expert to prepare a report on the question, fix a date for the stage 2 equal value hearing, having regard to the indicative timetable;

(f) if the tribunal has not decided to require an independent expert to prepare a report on the question, fix a date for the Hearing, having regard to the indicative timetable;

(g) consider whether any further orders are appropriate.

(4) Before a claim or part of one is struck out under [sub-]paragraph (3)(a), the Secretary shall send notice to the claimant giving him the opportunity to make representations to the tribunal as to whether the evaluation contained in the study in question falls within paragraph (a) or (b) of [section 131(6) of the Equality Act]. The Secretary shall not be required to send a notice under this paragraph if the claimant has been given an opportunity to make such representations orally to the tribunal as to why such a judgment should not be issued.

(5) The tribunal may, on the application of a party, hear evidence upon and permit the parties to address it upon the issue contained in [section 69 of the Equality Act (defence of material factor)] before determining whether to require an independent expert to prepare a report under paragraph (3)(b)(ii).

(6) When the Secretary gives notice to the parties of the stage 1 equal value hearing under rule 14(4) of Schedule 1, he shall also give the parties notice of the matters which the tribunal may and shall consider at that hearing which are described in paragraphs (3) and (5) of this rule and he shall give the parties notice of the standard orders in rule 5.

(7) The tribunal's power to strike out the claim or part of it under [sub-]paragraph (3)(a) is in addition to powers to strike out a claim under rule 18(7) of Schedule 1.

5 Standard orders for stage 1 equal value hearing

(1) At a stage 1 equal value hearing a tribunal shall, unless it considers it inappropriate to do so and subject to paragraph (2), order that:—

(a) before the end of the period of 14 days after the date of the stage 1 equal value hearing the claimant shall:

(i) disclose in writing to the respondent the name of any comparator, or, if the claimant is not able to name the comparator he shall instead disclose such information as enables the comparator to be identified by the respondent; and

(ii) identify to the respondent in writing the period in relation to which he considers that the claimant's work and that of the comparator are to be compared;

(b) before the end of the period of 28 days after the date of the stage 1 equal value hearing:

(i) where the claimant has not disclosed the name of the comparator to the respondent under sub-paragraph (a), if the respondent has been provided with sufficient detail to be able to identify the comparator, he shall disclose in writing the name of the comparator to the claimant;

(ii) the parties shall provide each other with written job descriptions for the claimant and any comparator;

(iii) the parties shall identify to each other in writing the facts which they consider to be relevant to the question;

(c) the respondent is required to grant access to the claimant and his representative (if any) to his premises during a period specified by the tribunal or [Employment Judge] in order for him or them to interview any comparator;

(d) the parties shall before the end of the period of 56 days after the date of the stage 1 equal value hearing present to the tribunal a joint agreed statement in writing of the following matters:

- (i) job descriptions for the claimant and any comparator;
- (ii) facts which both parties consider are relevant to the question;
- (iii) facts on which the parties disagree (as to the fact or as to the relevance to the question) and a summary of their reasons for disagreeing;

(e) the parties shall, at least 56 days prior to the Hearing, disclose to each other, to any independent or other expert and to the tribunal written statements of any facts on which they intend to rely in evidence at the Hearing; and

(f) the parties shall, at least 28 days prior to the Hearing, present to the tribunal a statement of facts and issues on which the parties are in agreement, a statement of facts and issues on which the parties disagree and a summary of their reasons for disagreeing.

(2) Any of the standard orders for the stage 1 equal value hearing may be added to, varied or omitted as the tribunal considers appropriate.

6 Involvement of independent expert in fact finding

(1) This rule applies only to proceedings in relation to which the tribunal has decided to require an independent expert to prepare a report on the question.

(2) In proceedings to which this rule applies a tribunal or [Employment Judge] may if it or he considers it appropriate at any stage of the proceedings order an independent expert to assist the tribunal in establishing the facts on which the independent expert may rely in preparing his report.

(3) Examples of the circumstances in which the tribunal or [Employment Judge] may make an order described in paragraph (2) may include:

(a) a party not being legally represented;

(b) the parties are unable to reach agreement as required by an order of the tribunal or [Employment Judge];

(c) the tribunal or [Employment Judge] considers that insufficient information may have been disclosed by a party and this may impair the ability of the independent expert to prepare a report on the question;

(d) the tribunal or [Employment Judge] considers that the involvement of the independent expert may promote fuller compliance with orders made by the tribunal or [an Employment Judge].

(4) A party to proceedings to which this rule applies may make an application under rule 11 of Schedule 1 for an order under paragraph (2).

7 Conduct of stage 2 equal value hearing

(1) This rule applies only to proceedings in relation to which the tribunal has decided to require an independent expert to prepare a report on the question. In such proceedings the tribunal shall conduct a "stage 2 equal value hearing" in accordance with both this rule and the rules applicable to pre-hearing reviews in Schedule 1.

(2) Notwithstanding rule 18(1) and (3) of Schedule 1, a stage 2 equal value hearing shall be [conducted by a tribunal] composed in accordance with section 4(1) of the Employment Tribunals Act.

(3) At the stage 2 equal value hearing the tribunal shall make a determination of facts on which the parties cannot agree which relate to the question and shall require the independent expert to prepare his report on the basis of facts which have (at any stage of the proceedings) either been agreed between the parties or determined by the tribunal (referred to as "the facts relating to the question").

(4) At the stage 2 equal value hearing the tribunal shall:

(a) [subject] to rule 8 and having regard to the indicative timetable, make the standard orders for the stage 2 equal value hearing as set out in rule 8;

(b) make any orders which it considers appropriate;

(c) fix a date for the Hearing, having regard to the indicative timetable.

(5) Subject to paragraph (6), the facts relating to the question shall, in relation to the question, be the only facts on which the tribunal shall rely at the Hearing.

(6) At any stage of the proceedings the independent expert may make an application to the tribunal for . . . some or all of the facts relating to the question to be amended, supplemented or omitted.

(7) When the Secretary gives notice to the parties and to the independent expert of the stage 2 equal value hearing under rule 14(4) of Schedule 1, he shall also give the parties notice of the standard orders in rule 8 and draw the attention of the parties to paragraphs (4) and (5) of this rule.

8 Standard orders for stage 2 equal value hearing

(1) At a stage 2 equal value hearing a tribunal shall, unless it considers it inappropriate to do so and subject to paragraph (2), order that:—

(a) by a date specified by the tribunal (with regard to the indicative timetable) the independent expert shall prepare his report on the question and shall (subject to rule 14) have sent copies of it to the parties and to the tribunal; and
(b) the independent expert shall prepare his report on the question on the basis of the facts relating to the question and no other facts which may or may not relate to the question.

(2) Any of the standard orders for the stage 2 equal value hearing may be added to, varied or omitted as the tribunal considers appropriate.

9 The Hearing

(1) In proceedings in relation to which an independent expert has prepared a report, unless the tribunal determines that the report is not based on the facts relating to the question, the report of the independent expert shall be admitted in evidence in those proceedings.

(2) If the tribunal does not admit the report of an independent expert in accordance with paragraph (1), it may determine the question itself or require another independent expert to prepare a report on the question.

(3) The tribunal may refuse to admit evidence of facts or hear argument as to issues which have not been disclosed to the other party as required by these rules or any order made under them, unless it was not reasonably practicable for the party to have so complied.

10 Duties and powers of the independent expert

(1) When a tribunal requires an independent expert to prepare a report with respect to the question or an order is made under rule 6(2), the Secretary shall inform that independent expert of the duties and powers he has under this rule.

(2) The independent expert shall have a duty to the tribunal to:
(a) assist it in furthering the overriding objective in regulation 3;
(b) comply with the requirements of these rules and any orders made by the tribunal or [an Employment Judge] in relation to the proceedings;
(c) keep the tribunal informed of any delay in complying with any order in the proceedings with the exception of minor or insignificant delays in compliance;
(d) comply with any timetable imposed by the tribunal or [Employment Judge] in so far as this is reasonably practicable;
(e) inform the tribunal or [an Employment Judge] on request by it or him of progress in the preparation of the independent expert's report;
(f) prepare a report on the question based on the facts relating to the question and (subject to rule 14) send it to the tribunal and the parties;
(g) make himself available to attend hearings in the proceedings.

(3) The independent expert may make an application for any order or for a hearing to be held as if he were a party to the proceedings.

(4) At any stage of the proceedings the tribunal may, after giving the independent expert the opportunity to make representations, withdraw the requirement on the independent expert to prepare a report. If it does so, the tribunal may itself determine the question, or it may determine that a different independent expert should be required to prepare the report.

(5) When paragraph (4) applies the independent expert who is no longer required to prepare the report shall provide the tribunal with all documentation and work in progress relating to the proceedings by a date specified by the tribunal. Such documentation and work in progress must be in a form which the tribunal is able to use. Such documentation and work in progress may be used in relation to those proceedings by the tribunal or by another independent expert.

(6) When an independent expert has been required to prepare a report in proceedings the Secretary shall give the independent expert notice of all hearings, orders or judgments in those proceedings as if the independent expert were a party to those proceedings and when these rules require a party to provide information to another party, such information shall also be provided to the independent expert.

11 Use of expert evidence

(1) Expert evidence shall be restricted to that which, in the opinion of the tribunal, is reasonably required to resolve the proceedings.

(2) An expert shall have a duty to assist the tribunal on matters within his expertise. This duty overrides any obligation to the person from whom he has received instructions or by whom he is paid.

(3) No party may call an expert or put in evidence an expert's report without the permission of the tribunal. No expert report shall be put in evidence unless it has been disclosed to all other parties and any independent expert at least 28 days prior to the Hearing.

(4) In proceedings in which an independent expert has been required to prepare a report on the question, the tribunal shall not admit evidence of another expert on the question unless such evidence is based on the facts relating to the question. Unless the tribunal considers it inappropriate to do so, any such expert report shall be disclosed to all parties and to the tribunal on the same date on which the independent expert is required to send his report to the parties and to the tribunal.

(5) If an expert (other than an independent expert) does not comply with these rules or an order made by the tribunal or [an Employment Judge], the tribunal may order that the evidence of that expert shall not be admitted.

(6) Where two or more parties wish to submit expert evidence on a particular issue, the tribunal may order that the evidence on that issue is to be given by one joint expert only. When such an order has been made, if the parties wishing to instruct the joint expert cannot agree who should be the expert, the tribunal may select the expert.

12 Written questions to experts

(1) When any expert (including an independent expert) has prepared a report, a party or any other expert (including an independent expert) involved in the proceedings may put written questions about the report to the expert who has prepared the report.

(2) Unless the tribunal or [Employment Judge] agrees otherwise, written questions under paragraph (1):

(a) may be put once only;
(b) must be put within 28 days of the date on which the parties were sent the report;
(c) must be for the purpose only of clarifying the factual basis of the report;
(d) must be copied to all other parties and experts involved in the proceedings at the same time as they are sent to the expert who prepared the report.

(3) When written questions have been put to an expert in accordance with paragraph (2) he shall answer those questions within 28 days of receiving them.

(4) An expert's answers to questions put in accordance with paragraph (2) shall be treated as part of the expert's report.

(5) Where a party has put a written question in accordance with this rule to an expert instructed by another party and the expert does not answer that question, or does not do so within 28 days, the tribunal may order that the party instructing the expert may not rely on the evidence of that expert.

13 Procedural matters

(1) In proceedings in which an independent expert has been required to prepare a report, the Secretary shall send him notices and inform him of any hearing, application, order or judgment in those proceedings as if he were a party to those proceedings.

(2) For the avoidance of doubt, any requirement in this Schedule to hold a stage 1 or a stage 2 equal value hearing does not preclude holding more than one of each of those types of hearing or other hearings from being held in accordance with Schedule 1.

(3) Any power conferred on [an Employment Judge] in Schedule 1 may (subject to the provisions of this Schedule) be carried out by a tribunal or [an Employment Judge] in relation to proceedings to which this Schedule applies.

14 National security proceedings

(1) In equal value cases which are also national security proceedings, if a tribunal has required an independent expert to prepare a report on the question, the independent expert shall send a copy of the report to the tribunal and shall not send it to the parties. In such proceedings if written questions have been put to the independent expert under rule 12, the independent expert shall send any answers to those questions to the tribunal and not to the parties.

(2) Before the Secretary sends to the parties a copy of a report or answers which have been sent to him by the independent expert under paragraph (1), he shall follow the procedure set out in rule 10 of Schedule 2 as if that rule referred to the independent expert's report or answers (as the case may be) instead of written reasons, except that the independent expert's report or answers shall not be entered on the Register.

(3) If the Minister does not give a direction under rule 10(3) of Schedule 2 within the period of 28 days from the date on which the Minister was sent the report or answers to written questions the Secretary shall send a copy of the independent expert's report or answers to written questions (as the case may be) to the parties.

ANNEX

The indicative timetable	
Claims *not* involving an independent expert	Claims involving an independent expert
Claim	Claim
↓	↓
28 days	28 days
↓	↓
Response	Response
↓	↓
3 weeks	3 weeks
↓	↓
Stage 1 equal value hearing	Stage 1 equal value hearing
↓	↓
↓	10 weeks
↓	↓
↓	Stage 2 equal value hearing
↓	↓
↓	[8 weeks]
↓	↓
↓	Independent expert's report
18 weeks	↓
↓	4 weeks
↓	↓
↓	written questions
↓	↓
↓	8 weeks
↓	↓
Hearing	Hearing
Total 25 weeks	Total 37 weeks.]

NOTES

Added by the Employment Tribunals (Constitution and Rules of Procedure) (Amendment) Regulations 2004, SI 2004/2351, reg 2(1), (11).

All references to "Employment Judge" and "an Employment Judge" substituted by the Tribunals, Courts and Enforcement Act 2007 (Transitional and Consequential Provisions) Order 2008, SI 2008/2683, art 6(1), Sch 1, paras 240, 259, as from 3 November 2008.

Other amendments to this Schedule are as follows—

Rule 4 is amended as follows:

Para (2) revoked by the Employment Tribunals (Constitution and Rules of Procedure) (Amendment) Regulations 2008, SI 2008/3240, regs 2, 7(1), (2), as from 6 April 2009, except (by virtue of reg 12 thereof) in relation to proceedings where all the parties have been notified on or before 5 April 2009 that a stage 1 equal value hearing has been listed.

Words "Employment Judge or" in square brackets in para (3) inserted by SI 2008/3240, regs 2, 7(1), (3), as from 6 April 2009, subject to the same savings in reg 12 of the 2008 Regulations as noted above.

Word "sub-" in square brackets in paras (4), (7) inserted by SI 2008/3240, regs 2, 7(1), (4), as from 6 April 2009.

Rule 7: words "conducted by a tribunal" in square brackets in para (2) inserted, word "subject" in square brackets in para (4)(a) substituted, and words omitted from para (6) revoked, by the Employment Tribunals (Constitution and Rules of Procedure) (Amendment) (No 2) Regulations 2005, SI 2005/1865, reg 2(1), (6)(a)–(c).

All other amendments to this Schedule were made by the Equality Act 2010 (Commencement No 4, Savings, Consequential, Transitional, Transitory and Incidental Provisions and Revocation) Order 2010, SI 2010/2317, art 24, Sch 8, para 6, as from 1 October 2010.

Annex: words in square brackets inserted by SI 2005/1865, reg 2(1), (6)(d).

ACAS (FLEXIBLE WORKING) ARBITRATION SCHEME (GREAT BRITAIN) ORDER 2004 (NOTE)

(SI 2004/2333)

[2.895]

NOTES

Made: 6 September 2004.

Authority: Trade Union and Labour Relations (Consolidation) Act 1992, s 212A(3), (6), (7).

Commencement: 1 October 2004.

This Order sets out a revised scheme, submitted to the Secretary of State by ACAS pursuant to s 212A of the 1992, providing for arbitration in the case of disputes involving proceedings, or claims which could be the subject of proceedings, before an employment tribunal arising out of a contravention or alleged contravention of ss 80G(1) or 80H(1)(b) of the Employment Rights Act 1996 (flexible working). This Order extends to Great Britain. The Scheme provides a voluntary alternative to the employment tribunal for the resolution of claims arising out of an application for flexible working made under s 80F(1) of the 1996 Act by arbitration where both parties agree. The Order also provides for certain provisions of the Arbitration Act 1996, as modified by the Order, to apply to arbitrations conducted in accordance with the Scheme, where the parties have agreed that the arbitration will be determined according to the law of England and Wales. This Order has been omitted from this Edition for reasons of space.

Part 2 Statutory Instruments

INFORMATION AND CONSULTATION OF EMPLOYEES REGULATIONS 2004

(SI 2004/3426)

NOTES

Made: 21 December 2004.

Authority: Employment Relations Act 2004, s 42.

Commencement: 6 April 2005 (subject to transitional provisions in Sch 1 at **[2.938]**).

These Regulations are the domestic implementation of European Parliament and Council Directive 2002/14/EC establishing a general framework for informing and consulting employees in the European Community at **[3.386]**.

Conciliation: employment tribunal proceedings and claims which could be the subject of employment tribunal proceedings under regs 29, 33 are proceedings to which the Employment Tribunals Act 1996, s 18 applies; see s 18(1)(p) of that Act at **[1.706]**.

Employment Appeal Tribunal: an appeal lies to the Employment Appeal Tribunal on any question of law arising from any decision of, or in any proceedings before, an employment tribunal under or by virtue of these Regulations; see the Employment Tribunals Act 1996, s 21(1)(q) at **[1.713]**.

As to the application of these Regulations to undertakings with fewer than 150 employees, see regs 3, 4 at **[2.898]**, **[2.900]** and Sch 1 at **[2.938]**.

See *Harvey* CII(6), DII(9), NIII(2), PI(4).

ARRANGEMENT OF REGULATIONS

PART 1
GENERAL

PART II
EMPLOYEE NUMBERS AND ENTITLEMENT TO DATA

PART III

NEGOTIATED AGREEMENTS

PART 1
GENERAL

[2.896]

1 Citation, commencement and extent

(1) These Regulations may be cited as the Information and Consultation of Employees Regulations 2004 and shall come into force on 6th April 2005.

(2) These Regulations extend to Great Britain.

[2.897]

2 Interpretation

In these Regulations—

"the 1996 Act" means the Employment Rights Act 1996;

["agency worker" has the same meaning as in regulation 3 of the Agency Workers Regulations 2010;]

"Appeal Tribunal" means the Employment Appeal Tribunal;

"CAC" means the Central Arbitration Committee;

"consultation" means the exchange of views and establishment of a dialogue between—

(a) information and consultation representatives and the employer; or

(b) in the case of a negotiated agreement which provides as mentioned in regulation 16(1)(f)(ii), the employees and the employer;

"contract of employment" means a contract of service or apprenticeship, whether express or implied, and (if it is express) whether oral or in writing;

"date of the ballot" means the day or last day on which voting may take place and, where voting in different parts of the ballot is arranged to take place on different days or during periods ending on different days, the last of those days;

"employee" means an individual who has entered into or works under a contract of employment and in Part VIII and regulation 40 includes, where the employment has ceased, an individual who worked under a contract of employment;

"employee request" means a request by employees under regulation 7 for the employer to initiate negotiations to reach an agreement under these Regulations;

"employer notification" means a notification by an employer under regulation 11 that he wishes to initiate negotiations to reach an agreement under these Regulations;

"information" means data transmitted by the employer—

(a) to the information and consultation representatives; or

(b) in the case of a negotiated agreement which provides as mentioned in regulation 16(1)(f)(ii), directly to the employees,

in order to enable those representatives or those employees to examine and to acquaint themselves with the subject matter of the data;

"Information and Consultation Directive" means European Parliament and Council Directive 2002/14/EC of 11 March 2002 establishing a general framework for informing and consulting employees in the European Community;

"information and consultation representative" means—

(a) in the case of a negotiated agreement which provides as mentioned in regulation 16(1)(f)(i), a person appointed or elected in accordance with that agreement; or

(b) a person elected in accordance with regulation 19(1);

"negotiated agreement" means—

(a) an agreement between the employer and the negotiating representatives reached through negotiations as provided for in regulation 14 which satisfies the requirements of regulation 16(1); or

(b) an agreement between the employer and the information and consultation representatives referred to in regulation 18(2);

"negotiating representative" means a person elected or appointed pursuant to regulation 14(1)(a);

"parties" means the employer and the negotiating representatives or the information and consultation representatives, as the case may be;

["Pension Schemes Regulations" means the Occupational and Personal Pension Schemes (Consultation by Employers and Miscellaneous Amendment) Regulations 2006;]

"pre-existing agreement" means an agreement between an employer and his employees or their representatives which—

(a) is made prior to the making of an employee request; and

(b) satisfies the conditions set out in regulation 8(1)(a) to (d),

but does not include an agreement concluded in accordance with regulations 17 or 42 to 45 of the Transnational Information and Consultation of Employees Regulations 1999 or a negotiated agreement;

"standard information and consultation provisions" means the provisions set out in regulation 20;

["suitable information relating to the use of agency workers" means information as to—

(a) the number of agency workers working temporarily for and under the supervision and direction of the employer,

(b) the parts of the employer's undertaking in which those agency workers are working, and

(c) the type of work those agency workers are carrying out.]

"undertaking" means a public or private undertaking carrying out an economic activity, whether or not operating for gain;

"valid employee request" means an employee request made to their employer by the employees of an undertaking to which these Regulations apply (under regulation 3) that satisfies the requirements of regulation 7 and is not prevented from being valid by regulation 12.

NOTES

Definitions "agency worker" and "suitable information relating to the use of agency workers" inserted by the Agency Workers Regulations 2010, SI 2010/93, reg 25, Sch 2, Pt 2, paras 21, 22, as from 1 October 2011; definition "Pension Schemes Regulations" inserted by the Information and Consultation of Employees (Amendment) Regulations 2006, SI 2006/514, regs 2, 3.

[2.898]
3 Application

(1) These Regulations apply to undertakings—

(a) employing in the United Kingdom, in accordance with the calculation in regulation 4, at least the number of employees in column 1 of the table in Schedule 1 to these Regulations on or after the corresponding date in column 2 of that table; and

(b) subject to paragraph (2), whose registered office, head office or principal place of business is situated in Great Britain.

(2) Where the registered office is situated in Great Britain and the head office or principal place of business is situated in Northern Ireland or vice versa, these Regulations shall only apply where the majority of employees are employed to work in Great Britain.

(3) In these Regulations, an undertaking to which these Regulations apply is referred to, in relation to its employees, as "the employer".

[2.899]
[3A Agency Workers

(1) Paragraphs (2) and (3) apply to an agency worker whose contract within regulation 3(1)(b) of the Agency Workers Regulations 2010 (contract with the temporary work agency) is not a contract of employment.

(2) For the purposes of regulations 3, 4 and Schedule 1, any agency worker who has a contract with a temporary work agency shall be treated as being employed by that temporary work agency for the duration of that agency worker's assignment with the employer.

(3) In these Regulations "assignment" has the same meaning as in regulation 2 and "temporary work agency" has the same meaning as in regulation 4, of the Agency Workers Regulations 2010.]

NOTES

Commencement: 1 October 2011.

Inserted by the Agency Workers Regulations 2010, SI 2010/93, reg 25, Sch 2, Pt 2, paras 21, 23, as from 1 October 2011.

PART II
EMPLOYEE NUMBERS AND ENTITLEMENT TO DATA

[2.900]
4 Calculation of number of employees

(1) Subject to paragraph (4), the number of employees for the purposes of regulation 3(1) shall be determined by ascertaining the average number of employees employed in the previous twelve months, calculated in accordance with paragraph (2).

(2) Subject to paragraph (3), the average number of employees is to be ascertained by determining the number of employees employed in each month in the previous twelve months (whether they were employed throughout the month or not), adding together those monthly figures and dividing the number by 12.

(3) For the purposes of the calculation in paragraph (2) if, for the whole of a month within the twelve month period, an employee works under a contract by virtue of which he would have worked for 75 hours or less in that month—

(i) were the month to have contained 21 working days;

(ii) were the employee to have had no absences from work; and

(iii) were the employee to have worked no overtime,

the employee may be counted as representing half of a full-time employee for the month in question, if the employer so decides.

(4) If the undertaking has been in existence for less than twelve months, the references to twelve months in paragraphs (1), (2) and (3), and the divisor of 12 referred to in paragraph (2), shall be replaced by the number of months the undertaking has been in existence.

[2.901]
5 Entitlement to data

(1) An employee or an employees' representative may request data from the employer for the purpose of determining the number of people employed by the employer's undertaking in the United Kingdom.

(2) Any request for data made under paragraph (1) must be in writing and be dated.

(3) The employer must provide the employee or the employees' representative who made the request with data to enable him to—

(a) make the calculation of the numbers of employees referred to in regulation 4, and

(b) determine, for the purpose of regulation 7(2), what number of employees constitutes 10% of the employees in the undertaking.

[2.902]

6 Complaint of failure to provide data

(1) An employee or an employees' representative who has requested data under regulation 5 may present a complaint to the CAC that—

(a) the employer has failed to provide the data referred to in regulation 5(3); or

(b) the data which has been provided by the employer is false or incomplete in a material particular.

(2) Where the CAC finds the complaint to be well-founded it shall make an order requiring the employer to disclose data to the complainant which order shall specify—

(a) the data in respect of which the CAC finds that the complaint is well-founded and which is to be disclosed to the complainant;

(b) the date (or if more than one, the earliest date) on which the employer refused or failed to disclose data, or disclosed false or incomplete information;

(c) a date, not being less than one week from the date of the order, by which the employer must disclose the data specified in the order.

(3) The CAC shall not consider a complaint presented under this regulation unless it is made after the expiry of a period of one month beginning on the date on which the complainant made his request for data under regulation 5.

PART III
NEGOTIATED AGREEMENTS

[2.903]

7 Employee request to negotiate an agreement in respect of information and consultation

(1) On receipt of a valid employee request, the employer shall, subject to paragraphs (8) and (9), initiate negotiations by taking the steps set out in regulation 14(1).

(2) Subject to paragraph (3), an employee request is not a valid employee request unless it consists of—

(a) a single request made by at least 10% of the employees in the undertaking; or

(b) a number of separate requests made on the same or different days by employees which when taken together mean that at least 10% of the employees in that undertaking have made requests, provided that the requests are made within a period of six months.

(3) Where the figure of 10% in paragraph (2) would result in less than 15 or more than 2,500 employees being required in order for a valid employee request to be made, that paragraph shall have effect as if, for the figure of 10%, there were substituted the figure of 15, or as the case may be, 2,500.

(4) An employee request is not a valid employee request unless the single request referred to in paragraph (2)(a) or each separate request referred to in paragraph (2)(b)—

(a) is in writing;

(b) is sent to—

(i) the registered office, head office or principal place of business of the employer; or

(ii) the CAC; and

(c) specifies the names of the employees making it and the date on which it is sent.

(5) Where a request is sent to the CAC under paragraph (4)(b)(ii), the CAC shall—

(a) notify the employer that the request has been made as soon as reasonably practicable;

(b) request from the employer such information as it needs to verify the number and names of the employees who have made the request; and

(c) inform the employer and the employees who have made the request how many employees have made the request on the basis of the information provided by the employees and the employer.

(6) Where the CAC requests information from the employer under paragraph (5)(b), the employer shall provide the information requested as soon as reasonably practicable.

(7) The date on which an employee request is made is—

(a) where the request consists of a single request satisfying paragraph (2)(a) or of separate requests made on the same day satisfying paragraph (2)(b), the date on which the request is or requests are sent to the employer by the employees or the date on which the CAC informs the employer and the employees in accordance with paragraph (5)(c) of how many employees have made the request; and

(b) where the request consists of separate requests made on different days, the date on which—

(i) the request which results in paragraph (2)(b) being satisfied is sent to the employer by the employees; or

(ii) the CAC informs the employer and the employees in accordance with paragraph (5)(c) of how many employees have made the request where that request results in paragraph (2)(b) being satisfied.

(8) If the employer decides to hold a ballot under regulation 8 or 9, the employer shall not be required to initiate negotiations unless and until the outcome of the ballot is that in regulation 8(5)(b).

(9) If an application is made to the CAC under regulation 13, the employer shall not be required to initiate negotiations unless and until if the CAC declares that there was a valid employee request or that the employer's notification was valid.

[2.904]

8 Pre-existing agreements: ballot for endorsement of employee request

(1) Subject to regulation 9, this regulation applies where a valid employee request has been made under regulation 7 by fewer than 40% of employees employed in the undertaking on the date that request was made and where there exists one or more pre-existing agreements which—

(a) are in writing;
(b) cover all the employees of the undertaking;
(c) have been approved by the employees; and
(d) set out how the employer is to give information to the employees or their representatives and seek their views on such information.

(2) Where this regulation applies, the employer may, instead of initiating negotiations in accordance with regulation 7(1), hold a ballot to seek the endorsement of the employees of the undertaking for the employee request in accordance with paragraphs (3) and (4).

(3) The employer must—

(a) inform the employees in writing within one month of the date of the employee request that he intends to hold a ballot under this regulation; and
(b) arrange for the ballot to be held as soon as reasonably practicable thereafter, provided that the ballot does not take place before a period of 21 days has passed since the employer informed the employees under sub-paragraph (a).

(4) A ballot must satisfy the following requirements—

(a) the employer must make such arrangements as are reasonably practicable to ensure that the ballot is fair;
(b) all employees of the undertaking on the day on which the votes may be cast in the ballot, or if the votes may be cast on more than one day, on the first day of those days, must be given an entitlement to vote in the ballot;
(c) the ballot must be conducted so as to secure that—
    (i) so far as is reasonably practicable, those voting do so in secret; and
    (ii) the votes given in the ballot are accurately counted.

(5) Where the employer holds a ballot under this regulation—

(a) he must, as soon as reasonably practicable after the date of the ballot, inform the employees of the result; and
(b) if the employees endorse the employee request, the employer is under the obligation in regulation 7(1) to initiate negotiations; and
(c) if the employees do not endorse the employee request, the employer is no longer under the obligation in regulation 7(1) to initiate negotiations.

(6) For the purposes of paragraph (5), the employees are to be regarded as having endorsed the employee request if—

(a) at least 40% of the employees employed in the undertaking; and
(b) the majority of the employees who vote in the ballot,

have voted in favour of endorsing the request.

(7) An employee or an employees' representative who believes that an employer has not, pursuant to paragraph (3)(a), informed his employees that he intends to hold a ballot within the period specified in that paragraph may apply to the CAC for a declaration that the employer is under the duty in regulation 7(1) to initiate negotiations.

(8) Where an employer, acting pursuant to paragraph (3)(a), has informed the employees that he intends to hold a ballot, any employee or employees' representative who believes that the employer has not complied with paragraph (3)(b) may present a complaint to the CAC

(9) Where the CAC finds a complaint under paragraph (8) well-founded it shall make an order requiring the employer to hold the ballot within such period as the order may specify.

[2.905]

[8A Pre-existing agreements: agency workers

Where information about the employment situation is to be provided under a pre-existing agreement by an employer, such information must include suitable information relating to the use of agency workers (if any) in that undertaking.]

NOTES

Commencement: 1 October 2011.

Inserted by the Agency Workers Regulations 2010, SI 2010/93, reg 25, Sch 2, Pt 2, paras 21, 24, as from 1 October 2011.

[2.906]

9 Pre-existing agreements covering groups of undertakings

(1) This regulation applies where—

(a) the requirements of regulation 8(1) are satisfied in relation to an undertaking;

(b) the pre-existing agreement or one of the pre-existing agreements covers employees in one or more undertakings other than the undertaking mentioned in sub-paragraph (a); and

(c) the other undertaking or each of the other undertakings mentioned in sub-paragraph (b) is one in respect of which there is an agreement that satisfied, or are agreements that taken together satisfied, the requirements in sub-paragraphs (a) to (d) of regulation 8(1) on the date on which the valid employee request was made in respect of the undertaking mentioned in sub-paragraph (a); and

(d) the valid employee request in relation to the undertaking mentioned in sub-paragraph (a) either—

(i) alone, or

(ii) aggregated with any requests made by employees in the undertakings mentioned in sub-paragraph (b) within the period of six months preceding the date of the valid employee request mentioned in regulation 8(1),

is made by fewer than 40% of the employees in the undertakings mentioned in paragraph (1)(a) and (b).

(2) Where this regulation applies the employers may hold a combined ballot for endorsement of the employee request in accordance with this regulation and in that event regulation 8 shall apply to the ballot with the modification that references to employees shall be treated as referring to the employees employed in all of the undertakings referred to in paragraph (1)(a) and (b).

(3) Notwithstanding paragraph (2), the undertaking mentioned in paragraph (1)(a) may choose to hold the ballot for endorsement of the employee request in accordance with regulation 8 rather than under this regulation.

[2.907]

10 Complaint about ballot for endorsement of employee request

(1) Any employee in the undertaking referred to in regulation 8(1) or employee in one of the undertakings referred to in regulation 9(1), or representative of such employees, who believes that a requirement has not been satisfied that has to be satisfied in order to entitle either the employer, in accordance with regulation 8(2), to hold a ballot, or the employers, in accordance with regulation 9(2), to hold a combined ballot may, within 21 days of the employer informing the employees of the relevant undertaking under regulation 8(3)(a), present a complaint to the CAC

(2) Any employee or employees' representative who believes that the arrangements for a ballot held under regulation 8 or 9, as the case may be, did not satisfy one or more of the requirements set out in regulation 8(4) may, within 21 days of the date of the ballot, present a complaint to the CAC

(3) Where the CAC finds a complaint under paragraph (1) or (2) well-founded it shall—

(a) in the case of a finding on a complaint under paragraph (1) that any requirement set out in sub-paragraphs (a) to (d) of regulation 8(1) was not satisfied in relation to the undertaking referred to in regulation 8(1) or 9(1)(a), make an order requiring the employer to whom regulation 8(1) or 9(1)(a) relates to initiate negotiations in accordance with regulation 7(1);

(b) in the case of a finding on a complaint under paragraph (1) that any requirement set out in sub-paragraphs (b) to (d) of regulation 9(1) has not been satisfied, make an order that no combined ballot shall take place and requiring the employer to whom regulation 9(1)(a) relates, according to the preference he has expressed, to initiate negotiations in accordance with regulation 7(1) or, within such period as the order may specify, to conduct a ballot under regulation 8; and

(c) in the case of a complaint under paragraph (2)—

(i) where prior to the order being made, the employer referred to in regulation 8(1) or 9(1)(a) makes representations to the CAC that he would prefer to initiate negotiations under regulation 7, make an order requiring that employer to do so; or

(ii) in the absence of such representations, order the employer or employers to hold the ballot under regulation 8 or 9, as the case may be, again within such period as the order may specify.

[2.908]

11 Employer notification of decision to initiate negotiations

(1) The employer may start the negotiation process set out in regulation 14(1) on his own initiative by issuing a written notification satisfying the requirements of paragraph (2), and where the employer issues such a notification regulations 14 to 17 shall apply.

(2) The notification referred to in paragraph (1) must—

(a) state that the employer intends to start the negotiating process and that the notification is given for the purpose of these Regulations;
(b) state the date on which it is issued; and
(c) be published in such a manner as to bring it to the attention of, so far as reasonably practicable, all the employees of the undertaking.

[2.909]
12 Restrictions on employee request and employer notification

(1) Subject to paragraph (2), no employee request or employer notification is valid if it is made or issued, as the case may be,—
(a) where a negotiated agreement applies, within a period of three years from the date of the agreement or, where the agreement is terminated within that period, before the date on which the termination takes effect;
(b) where the standard information and consultation provisions apply within a period of three years from the date on which they started to apply; and
(c) where the employer has held a ballot under regulation 8, or was one of the employers who held a ballot under regulation 9 and the result was that the employees did not endorse the valid employee request referred to in regulation 8(1), within a period of three years from the date of that request.

(2) Paragraph (1) does not apply where there are material changes in the undertaking during the applicable period having the result—
(a) where a ballot held under regulation 8 or 9 had the result that the employees did not endorse the valid employee request, that there is no longer a pre-existing agreement which satisfies paragraph (1)(b) and (c) of regulation 8 or in the case of a ballot held under regulation 9, that there is no longer an agreement satisfying paragraph (1)(b) of that regulation; or
(b) where a negotiated agreement exists, that the agreement no longer complies with the requirement in regulation 16(1) that it must cover all the employees of the undertaking.

[2.910]
13 Dispute about employee request, employer notification or whether obligation in regulation 7(1) applies

(1) If the employer considers that there was no valid employee request—
(a) because the employee request did not satisfy any requirement of regulation 7(2) to (4) or was prevented from being valid by regulation 12, or
(b) because the undertaking was not one to which these Regulations applied (under Regulation 3) on the date on which the employee request was made,

the employer may apply to the CAC for a declaration as to whether there was a valid employee request.

(2) If an employee or an employees' representative considers that an employer notification was not valid because it did not comply with one or more of the requirements in regulation 11(2) or was prevented from being valid by regulation 12, he may apply to the CAC for a declaration as to whether the notification was valid.

(3) The CAC shall only consider an application for a declaration made under paragraph (1) or (2) if the application is made within a one month period beginning on the date of the employee request or the date on which the employer notification is made.

[2.911]
14 Negotiations to reach an agreement

(1) In order to initiate negotiations to reach an agreement under these Regulations the employer must as soon as reasonably practicable—
(a) make arrangements, satisfying the requirements of paragraph (2), for the employees of the undertaking to elect or appoint negotiating representatives; and thereafter
(b) inform the employees in writing of the identity of the negotiating representatives; and
(c) invite the negotiating representatives to enter into negotiations to reach a negotiated agreement.

(2) The requirements for the election or appointment of negotiating representatives under paragraph (1)(a) are that—
(a) the election or appointment of the representatives must be arranged in such a way that, following their election or appointment, all employees of the undertaking are represented by one or more representatives; and
(b) all employees of the undertaking must be entitled to take part in the election or appointment of the representatives and, where there is an election, all employees of the undertaking on the day on which the votes may be cast in the ballot, or if the votes may be cast on more than one day, on the first day of those days, must be given an entitlement to vote in the ballot.

(3) The negotiations referred to in paragraph (1)(c) shall last for a period not exceeding six months commencing at the end of the period of three months beginning with the date on which the valid employee request was made or the valid employer notification was issued; but the following periods shall not count towards the three month period—

(a) where the employer holds a ballot pursuant to regulation 8 or 9, the period between the employer notifying the employees of his decision to hold such a ballot and whichever of the following dates is applicable—

(i) where there is no complaint to the CAC under regulation 10, the date of the ballot;

(ii) where there is a complaint to the CAC under regulation 10 and the complaint is dismissed by the CAC or on appeal, the date on which it is finally dismissed;

(iii) where there is a complaint to the CAC and the outcome, whether of the complaint or of any appeal from it, is an order to hold the ballot under regulation 8 or 9 again, the date of the ballot that most recently took place;

(iv) where there is a complaint to the CAC under regulation 10 and the outcome, whether of the complaint or of any appeal from it, is an order requiring the employer to initiate negotiations in accordance with regulation 7(1), the date on which the order is made;

(b) where an application for a declaration is made to the CAC pursuant to regulation 13, the period between the date of that application and the final decision of the CAC or any appeal from that decision; and

(c) where a complaint about the election or appointment of negotiating representatives is presented pursuant to regulation 15, the time between the date of the complaint and the determination of the complaint, including any appeal and, where the complaint is upheld, the further period until the negotiating representatives are re-elected or re-appointed.

(4) Where a complaint about the ballot for employee approval of a negotiated agreement is presented pursuant to regulation 17, the time between the date the complaint is presented to the CAC and the determination of the complaint (including any appeal and, where the complaint is upheld, the further period until the re-holding of the ballot) shall not count towards the six month period mentioned in paragraph (3).

(5) If, before the end of the six month period referred to in paragraph (3), the employer and a majority of the negotiating representatives agree that that period should be extended, it may be extended by such period as the parties agree and thereafter may be further extended by such period or periods as the parties agree.

(6) Where one or more employers wish to initiate negotiations to reach an agreement to cover employees in more than one undertaking, any employer whose employees have not made a valid employee request and who has not issued a valid employer notification, shall issue such a notification.

(7) Where paragraph (6) applies, the provisions of paragraphs (1) to (5) of this regulation and regulations 15 and 16 apply with the following modifications—

(a) the references to the employees of the undertaking refer to the employees of all the undertakings to be covered by any agreement negotiated; and

(b) references to employees refer to employees of all the undertakings to be covered by any agreement negotiated.

[2.912]

15 Complaints about election or appointment of negotiating representatives

(1) If an employee or an employees' representative considers that one or both of the requirements for the appointment or election of negotiating representatives set out in regulation 14(2) have not been complied with, he may, within 21 days of the election or appointment, present a complaint to the CAC.

(2) Where the CAC finds the complaint well-founded it shall make an order requiring the employer to arrange for the process of election or appointment of negotiating representatives referred to in regulation 14 to take place again within such period as the order shall specify.

[2.913]

16 Negotiated agreements

(1) A negotiated agreement must cover all employees of the undertaking and may consist either of a single agreement or of different parts (each being approved in accordance with paragraph (4)) which, taken together, cover all the employees of the undertaking. The single agreement or each part must—

(a) set out the circumstances in which the employer must inform and consult the employees to which it relates;

(b) be in writing;

(c) be dated;

(d) be approved in accordance with paragraphs (3) to (5);

(e) be signed by or on behalf of the employer; . . .

(f) either—
   (i) provide for the appointment or election of information and consultation representatives to whom the employer must provide the information and whom the employer must consult in the circumstances referred to in sub-paragraph (a); or
   (ii) provide that the employer must provide information directly to the employees to which it relates and consult those employees directly in the circumstances referred to in sub-paragraph (a); [and
(g) provide that where an employer is to provide information about the employment situation, under that agreement or under any part, such information shall include suitable information relating to the use of agency workers (if any) in that undertaking.]

(2) Where a negotiated agreement consist of different parts they may provide differently in relation to the matters referred to in paragraph (1)(a) and (f).

(3) A negotiated agreement consisting of a single agreement shall be treated as being approved for the purpose of paragraph (1)(d) if—
(a) it has been signed by all the negotiating representatives; or
(b) it has been signed by a majority of negotiating representatives and either—
   (i) approved in writing by at least 50% of employees employed in the undertaking, or
   (ii) approved by a ballot of those employees, the arrangements for which satisfied the requirements set out in paragraph (5), in which at least 50% of the employees voting, voted in favour of approval.

(4) A part shall be treated as being approved for the purpose of paragraph (1)(d) if the part—
(a) has been signed by all the negotiating representatives involved in negotiating the part; or
(b) has been signed by a majority of those negotiating representatives and either—
   (i) approved in writing by at least 50% of employees (employed in the undertaking) to which the part relates, or
   (ii) approved by a ballot of those employees, the arrangements for which satisfied the requirements set out in paragraph (5), in which at least 50% of the employees voting, voted in favour of approving the part.

(5) The ballots referred to in paragraphs (3) and (4) must satisfy the following requirements—
(a) the employer must make such arrangements as are reasonably practicable to ensure that the ballot is fair;
(b) all employees of the undertaking or, as the case may be, to whom the part of the agreement relates, on the day on which the votes may be cast in the ballot, or if the votes may be cast on more than one day, on the first day of those days, must be given an entitlement to vote in the ballot; and
(c) the ballot must be conducted so as to secure that—
   (i) so far as is reasonably practicable, those voting do so in secret; and
   (ii) the votes given in the ballot are accurately counted.

(6) Where the employer holds a ballot under this regulation he must, as soon as reasonably practicable after the date of the ballot, inform the employees entitled to vote of the result.

NOTES

Para (1): word omitted from sub-para (e) revoked and sub-para (g), together with word preceding it, inserted by the Agency Workers Regulations 2010, SI 2010/93, reg 25, Sch 2, Pt 2, paras 21, 25, 26, as from 1 October 2011.

[2.914]

17 Complaints about ballot for employee approval of negotiated agreement

(1) Any negotiating representative who believes that the arrangements for a ballot held under regulation 16 did not satisfy one or more of the requirements set out in paragraph (5) of that regulation, may, within 21 days of the date of the ballot, present a complaint to the CAC.

(2) Where the CAC finds the complaint well-founded it shall make an order requiring the employer to hold the ballot referred to in regulation 16 again within such period as the order may specify.

[2.915]

[17A Negotiated agreements and listed changes to pension schemes

(1) A requirement in any negotiated agreement or any part of such an agreement made before 6th April 2006 to inform and consult employees or their representatives about a listed change shall cease to apply once—
(a) the employer is under a duty under any of regulations 7(3) and 11 to 13 of the Pension Schemes Regulations; and
(b) he has notified the information and consultation representatives or, where he must consult employees directly, the employees in writing that he will be complying with his duty under the provisions of the Pension Schemes Regulations referred to in sub-paragraph (a), instead of his obligations under the negotiated agreement, provided that the notification is given on each occasion on which the employer has become or is about to become subject to the duty.

(2) For the purposes of this regulation "listed change" has the meaning given by regulation 6(2) of the Pension Schemes Regulations.]

NOTES

Inserted by the Information and Consultation of Employees (Amendment) Regulations 2006, SI 2006/514, regs 2, 4.

PART IV
STANDARD INFORMATION AND CONSULTATION PROVISIONS

[2.916]

18 Application of standard information and consultation provisions

(1) Subject to paragraph (2)—

(a) where the employer is under a duty, following the making of a valid employee request or issue of a valid employer notification, to initiate negotiations in accordance with regulation 14 but does not do so, the standard information and consultation provisions shall apply from the date—

(i) which is six months from the date on which the valid employee request was made or the valid employer notification was issued, or

(ii) information and consultation representatives are elected under regulation 19,

whichever is the sooner; and

(b) if the parties do not reach a negotiated agreement within the time limit referred to in regulation 14(3) (or that period as extended by agreement under paragraph (5) of that regulation) the standard information and consultation provisions shall apply from the date—

(i) which is six months from the date on which that time limit expires; or

(ii) information and consultation representatives are elected under regulation 19,

whichever is the sooner.

(2) Where the standard information and consultation provisions apply, the employer and the information and consultation representatives elected pursuant to regulation 19 may, at any time, reach an agreement that provisions other than the standard information and consultation provisions shall apply.

(3) An agreement referred to in paragraph (2) shall only have effect if it covers all the employees of the undertaking, complies with the requirements listed in regulation 16(1)(a) to (c), (e) and (f), and is signed by a majority of the information and consultation representatives.

[2.917]

19 Election of information and consultation representatives

(1) Where the standard information and consultation provisions are to apply, the employer shall, before the standard information and consultation provisions start to apply, arrange for the holding of a ballot of its employees to elect the relevant number of information and consultation representatives.

(2) The provisions in Schedule 2 to these Regulations apply in relation to the arrangements for and conduct of any such ballot.

(3) In this regulation the "relevant number of information and consultation representatives" means one representative per fifty employees or part thereof, provided that that number is at least 2 and does not exceed 25.

(4) An employee or an employee's representative may complain to the CAC that the employer has not arranged for the holding of a ballot in accordance with paragraph (1).

(5) Where the CAC finds the complaint well-founded, it shall make an order requiring the employer to arrange, or re-arrange, and hold the ballot.

(6) Where the CAC finds a complaint under paragraph (4) well-founded, the employee or the employee's representative may make an application to the Appeal Tribunal under regulation 22(6) and paragraphs (7) and (8) of that regulation shall apply to any such application.

[2.918]

20 Standard information and consultation provisions

(1) Where the standard information and consultation provisions apply pursuant to regulation 18, the employer must provide the information and consultation representatives with information on—

(a) the recent and probable development of the undertaking's activities and economic situation;

(b) the situation, structure and probable development of employment within the undertaking [(and such information must include suitable information relating to the use of agency workers (if any) in that undertaking)] and on any anticipatory measures envisaged, in particular, where there is a threat to employment within the undertaking; and

(c) subject to paragraph (5), decisions likely to lead to substantial changes in work organisation or in contractual relations, including those referred to in—

(i) sections 188 to 192 of the Trade Union and Labour Relations (Consolidation) Act 1992; and

[(ii) regulations 13 to 16 of the Transfer of Undertakings (Protection of Employment) Regulations 2006].

(2) The information referred to in paragraph (1) must be given at such time, in such fashion and with such content as are appropriate to enable, in particular, the information and consultation representatives to conduct an adequate study and, where necessary, to prepare for consultation.

(3) The employer must consult the information and consultation representatives on the matters referred to in paragraph (1)(b) and (c).

(4) The employer must ensure that the consultation referred to in paragraph (3) is conducted—

(a) in such a way as to ensure that the timing, method and content of the consultation are appropriate;

(b) on the basis of the information supplied by the employer to the information and consultation representatives and of any opinion which those representatives express to the employer;

(c) in such a way as to enable the information and consultation representatives to meet the employer at the relevant level of management depending on the subject under discussion and to obtain a reasoned response from the employer to any such opinion; and

(d) in relation to matters falling within paragraph (1)(c), with a view to reaching agreement on decisions within the scope of the employer's powers.

(5) The duties in this regulation to inform and consult the information and consultation representatives on decisions falling within paragraph (1)(c) cease to apply once the employer is under a duty under—

(a) section 188 of the Act referred to in paragraph (1)(c)(i) (duty of employer to consult representatives); . . .

(b) [regulation 13] of the Regulations referred to in paragraph (1)(c)(ii) (duty to inform and consult representatives), [or

(c) any of regulations 11 to 13 of the Pension Schemes Regulations,]

and he has notified the information and consultation representatives in writing that he will be complying with his duty under the legislation referred to in [sub-paragraph (a), (b) or (c)], as the case may be, instead of under these Regulations, provided that the notification is given on each occasion on which the employer has become or is about to become subject to the duty.

(6) Where there is an obligation in these Regulations on the employer to inform and consult his employees, a failure on the part of a person who controls the employer (either directly or indirectly) to provide information to the employer shall not constitute a valid reason for the employer failing to inform and consult.

NOTES

Para (1): words in square brackets in sub-para (b) inserted by the Agency Workers Regulations 2010, SI 2010/93, reg 25, Sch 2, Pt 2, paras 21, 27, as from 1 October 2011; sub-para (c)(ii) substituted by the Transfer of Undertakings (Protection of Employment) (Consequential Amendments) Regulations 2006, SI 2006/2405, reg 2.

Para (5): word omitted from sub-para (a) revoked, sub-para (c) and the word immediately preceding it inserted, and final words in square brackets substituted, by the Information and Consultation of Employees (Amendment) Regulations 2006, SI 2006/514, regs 2, 5(a); words in square brackets in sub-para (b) substituted by SI 2006/2405.

PART V
DUTY OF CO-OPERATION

[2.919]

21 Co-operation

The parties are under a duty, when negotiating or implementing a negotiated agreement or when implementing the standard information and consultation provisions, to work in a spirit of co-operation and with due regard for their reciprocal rights and obligations, taking into account the interests of both the undertaking and the employees.

PART VI
COMPLIANCE AND ENFORCEMENT

[2.920]

22 Disputes about operation of a negotiated agreement or the standard information and consultation provisions

(1) Where—

(a) a negotiated agreement has been agreed; or

(b) the standard information and consultation provisions apply,

a complaint may be presented to the CAC by a relevant applicant who considers that the employer has failed to comply with the terms of the negotiated agreement or, as the case may be, one or more of the standard information and consultation provisions.

(2) A complaint brought under paragraph (1) must be brought within a period of three months commencing with the date of the alleged failure.

(3) In this regulation—

"failure" means an act or omission; and

"relevant applicant" means—

(a) in a case where information and consultation representatives have been elected or appointed, an information and consultation representative, or

(b) in a case where no information and consultation representatives have been elected or appointed, an employee or an employees' representative.

(4) Where the CAC finds the complaint well-founded it shall make a declaration to that effect and may make an order requiring the employer to take such steps as are necessary to comply with the terms of the negotiated agreement or, as the case may be, the standard information and consultation provisions.

(5) An order made under paragraph (4) shall specify—

(a) the steps which the employer is required to take; and

(b) the period within which the order must be complied with.

(6) If the CAC makes a declaration under paragraph (4) the relevant applicant may, within the period of three months beginning with the date on which the declaration is made, make an application to the Appeal Tribunal for a penalty notice to be issued.

(7) Where such an application is made, the Appeal Tribunal shall issue a written penalty notice to the employer requiring him to pay a penalty to the Secretary of State in respect of the failure unless satisfied, on hearing representations from the employer, that the failure resulted from a reason beyond the employer's control or that he has some other reasonable excuse for his failure.

(8) Regulation 23 shall apply in respect of a penalty notice issued under this regulation.

(9) No order of the CAC under this regulation shall have the effect of suspending or altering the effect of any act done or of any agreement made by the employer or of preventing or delaying any act or agreement which the employer proposes to do or to make.

[2.921]

23 Penalties

(1) A penalty notice issued under regulation 22 shall specify—

(a) the amount of the penalty which is payable;

(b) the date before which the penalty must be paid; and

(c) the failure and period to which the penalty relates.

(2) No penalty set by the Appeal Tribunal under this regulation may exceed £75,000.

(3) Matters to be taken into account by the Appeal Tribunal when setting the amount of the penalty shall include—

(a) the gravity of the failure;

(b) the period of time over which the failure occurred;

(c) the reason for the failure;

(d) the number of employees affected by the failure; and

(e) the number of employees employed by the undertaking or, where a negotiated agreement covers employees in more than one undertaking, the number of employees employed by both or all of the undertakings.

(4) The date specified under paragraph (1)(b) must not be earlier than the end of the period within which an appeal against a declaration or order made by the CAC under regulation 22 may be made.

(5) If the specified date in a penalty notice has passed and—

(a) the period during which an appeal may be made has expired without an appeal having been made; or

(b) such an appeal has been made and determined,

the Secretary of State may recover from the employer, as a civil debt due to him, any amount payable under the penalty notice which remains outstanding.

(6) The making of an appeal suspends the effect of a penalty notice.

(7) Any sums received by the Secretary of State under regulation 22 or this regulation shall be paid into the Consolidated Fund.

[2.922]

24 Exclusivity of remedy

The remedy for infringement of the rights conferred by Parts I to VI of these Regulations is by way of complaint to the CAC, and not otherwise.

PART VII
CONFIDENTIAL INFORMATION

[2.923]
25 Breach of statutory duty

(1) A person to whom the employer, pursuant to his obligations under these Regulations, entrusts any information or document on terms requiring it to be held in confidence shall not disclose that information or document except, where the terms permit him to do so, in accordance with those terms.

(2) In this regulation a person referred to in paragraph (1) to whom information or a document is entrusted is referred to as a "recipient".

(3) The obligation to comply with paragraph (1) is a duty owed to the employer, and a breach of the duty is actionable accordingly (subject to the defences and other incidents applying to actions for breaches of statutory duty).

(4) Paragraph (3) shall not affect any legal liability which any person may incur by disclosing the information or document, or any right which any person may have in relation to such disclosure otherwise than under this regulation.

(5) No action shall lie under paragraph (3) where the recipient reasonably believed the disclosure to be a "protected disclosure" within the meaning given to that expression by section 43A of the 1996 Act.

(6) A recipient to whom the employer has entrusted any information or document on terms requiring it to be held in confidence may apply to the CAC for a declaration as to whether it was reasonable for the employer to require the recipient to hold the information or document in confidence.

(7) If the CAC considers, on an application under paragraph (6), that the disclosure of the information or document by the recipient would not, or would not be likely to, harm the legitimate interests of the undertaking, it shall make a declaration that it was not reasonable for the employer to require the recipient to hold the information or document in confidence.

(8) If a declaration is made under paragraph (7), the information or document shall not at any time thereafter be regarded as having been entrusted to the recipient who made the application under paragraph (6), or to any other recipient, on terms requiring it to be held in confidence.

[2.924]
26 Withholding of information by the employer

(1) The employer is not required to disclose any information or document to a person for the purposes of these Regulations where the nature of the information or document is such that, according to objective criteria, the disclosure of the information or document would seriously harm the functioning of, or would be prejudicial to, the undertaking.

(2) If there is a dispute between the employer and—
- (a) where information and consultation representatives have been elected or appointed, such a representative; or
- (b) where no information and consultation representatives have been elected or appointed, an employee or an employees' representative,

as to whether the nature of the information or document which the employer has failed to provide is such as is described in paragraph (1), the employer or a person referred to in sub-paragraph (a) or (b) may apply to the CAC for a declaration as to whether the information or document is of such a nature.

(3) If the CAC makes a declaration that the disclosure of the information or document in question would not, according to objective criteria, be seriously harmful or prejudicial as mentioned in paragraph (1), the CAC shall order the employer to disclose the information or document.

(4) An order under paragraph (3) shall specify—
- (a) the information or document to be disclosed;
- (b) the person or persons to whom the information or document is to be disclosed;
- (c) any terms on which the information or document is to be disclosed; and
- (d) the date before which the information or document is to be disclosed.

PART VIII
PROTECTIONS FOR INFORMATION AND CONSULTATION REPRESENTATIVES, ETC

[2.925]
27 Right to time off for information and consultation representatives, etc

(1) An employee who is—
- (a) a negotiating representative; or
- (b) an information and consultation representative,

is entitled to be permitted by his employer to take reasonable time off during the employee's working hours in order to perform his functions as such a representative.

(2) For the purposes of this regulation, the working hours of an employee shall be taken to be any time when, in accordance with his contract of employment, the employee is required to be at work.

[2.926]

28 Right to remuneration for time off under regulation 27

(1) An employee who is permitted to take time off under regulation 27 is entitled to be paid remuneration by his employer for the time taken off at the appropriate hourly rate.

(2) Chapter II of Part XIV of the 1996 Act (a week's pay) shall apply in relation to this regulation as it applies in relation to section 62 of the 1996 Act.

(3) The appropriate hourly rate, in relation to an employee, is the amount of one week's pay divided by the number of normal working hours in a week for that employee when employed under the contract of employment in force on the day when time is taken.

(4) But where the number of normal working hours differs from week to week or over a longer period, the amount of one week's pay shall be divided instead by—

- (a) the average number of normal working hours calculated by dividing by twelve the total number of the employee's normal working hours during the period of twelve weeks ending with the last complete week before the day on which the time is taken off; or
- (b) where the employee has not been employed for a sufficient period to enable the calculations to be made under sub-paragraph (a), a number which fairly represents the number of normal working hours in a week having regard to such of the considerations specified in paragraph (5) as are appropriate in the circumstances.

(5) The considerations referred to in paragraph (4)(b) are—

- (a) the average number of normal working hours in a week which the employee could expect in accordance with the terms of his contract; and
- (b) the average number of normal working hours of other employees engaged in relevant comparable employment with the same employer.

(6) A right to any amount under paragraph (1) does not affect any right of an employee in relation to remuneration under his contract of employment ("contractual remuneration").

(7) Any contractual remuneration paid to an employee in respect of a period of time off under regulation 27 goes towards discharging any liability of the employer to pay remuneration under paragraph (1) in respect of that period, and, conversely, any payment of remuneration under paragraph (1) in respect of a period goes towards discharging any liability of the employer to pay contractual remuneration in respect of that period.

[2.927]

29 Right to time off: complaint to tribunals

(1) An employee may present a complaint to an employment tribunal that his employer—

- (a) has unreasonably refused to permit him to take time off as required by regulation 27; or
- (b) has failed to pay the whole or part of any amount to which the employee is entitled under regulation 28.

(2) A tribunal shall not consider a complaint under this regulation unless it is presented—

- (a) before the end of the period of three months beginning with the day on which the time off was taken or on which it is alleged the time off should have been permitted; or
- (b) within such further period as the tribunal considers reasonable in a case where it is satisfied that it was not reasonably practicable for the complaint to be presented before the end of that period of three months.

(3) Where a tribunal finds a complaint under this regulation well-founded, the tribunal shall make a declaration to that effect.

(4) If the complaint is that the employer has unreasonably refused to permit the employee to take time off, the tribunal shall also order the employer to pay to the employee an amount equal to the remuneration to which he would have been entitled under regulation 28 if the employer had not refused.

(5) If the complaint is that the employer has failed to pay the employee the whole or part of any amount to which he is entitled under regulation 28, the tribunal shall also order the employer to pay to the employee the amount it finds due to him.

NOTES

Conciliation: employment tribunal proceedings and claims which could be the subject of employment tribunal proceedings under this regulation are proceedings to which the Employment Tribunals Act 1996, s 18 applies; see s 18(1)(p) of that Act at **[1.706]**.

[2.928]
30 Unfair dismissal

(1) An employee who is dismissed and to whom paragraph (2) or (5) applies shall be regarded, if the reason (or, if more than one, the principal reason) for the dismissal is a reason specified in, respectively, paragraph (3) or (6), as unfairly dismissed for the purposes of Part 10 of the 1996 Act.

(2) This paragraph applies to an employee who is—
- (a) an employees' representative;
- (b) a negotiating representative;
- (c) an information and consultation representative; or
- (d) a candidate in an election in which any person elected will, on being elected, be such a representative.

(3) The reasons are that—
- (a) the employee performed or proposed to perform any functions or activities as such a representative or candidate;
- (b) the employee exercised or proposed to exercise an entitlement conferred on the employee by regulation 27 or 28; or
- (c) the employee (or a person acting on his behalf) made or proposed to make a request to exercise such an entitlement.

(4) Paragraph (1) does not apply in the circumstances set out in paragraph (3)(a) where the reason (or principal reason) for the dismissal is that in the performance, or purported performance, of the employee's functions or activities he has disclosed any information or document in breach of the duty in regulation 25, unless the employee reasonably believed the disclosure to be a "protected disclosure" within the meaning given to that expression by section 43A of the 1996 Act.

(5) This paragraph applies to any employee whether or not he is an employee to whom paragraph (2) applies.

(6) The reasons are that the employee—
- (a) took, or proposed to take, any proceedings before an employment tribunal to enforce a right or secure an entitlement conferred on him by these Regulations;
- (b) exercised, or proposed to exercise, any entitlement to apply or complain to the CAC or the Appeal Tribunal conferred by these Regulations or to exercise the right to appeal in connection with any rights conferred by these Regulations;
- (c) requested, or proposed to request, data in accordance with regulation 5;
- (d) acted with a view to securing that an agreement was or was not negotiated or that the standard information and consultation provisions did or did not become applicable;
- (e) indicated that he supported or did not support the coming into existence of a negotiated agreement or the application of the standard information and consultation provisions;
- (f) stood as a candidate in an election in which any person elected would, on being elected, be a negotiating representative or an information and consultation representative;
- (g) influenced or sought to influence by lawful means the way in which votes were to be cast by other employees in a ballot arranged under these Regulations;
- (h) voted in such a ballot;
- (i) expressed doubts, whether to a ballot supervisor or otherwise, as to whether such a ballot had been properly conducted; or
- (j) proposed to do, failed to do, or proposed to decline to do, any of the things mentioned in sub-paragraphs (d) to (i).

(7) It is immaterial for the purpose of paragraph (6)(a)—
- (a) whether or not the employee has the right or entitlement; or
- (b) whether or not the right has been infringed;

but for that sub-paragraph to apply, the claim to the right and, if applicable, the claim that it has been infringed must be made in good faith.

31 (*Amends the Employment Rights Act 1996, ss 105, 108 at* **[1.915]**, **[1.918]**, *and amended s 109 (repealed).*)

[2.929]
32 Detriment

(1) An employee to whom paragraph (2) or (5) applies has the right not to be subjected to any detriment by any act, or deliberate failure to act, by his employer, done on a ground specified in, respectively, paragraph (3) or (6).

(2) This paragraph applies to an employee who is—
- (a) an employees' representative;
- (b) a negotiating representative;
- (c) an information and consultation representative; or
- (d) a candidate in an election in which any person elected will, on being elected, be such a representative.

(3) The ground is that—

(a) the employee performed or proposed to perform any functions or activities as such a representative or candidate;

(b) the employee exercised or proposed to exercise an entitlement conferred on the employee by regulation 27 or 28; or

(c) the employee (or a person acting on his behalf) made or proposed to make a request to exercise such an entitlement.

(4) Paragraph (1) does not apply in the circumstances set out in paragraph (3)(a) where the ground (or principal ground) for the subjection to detriment is that in the performance, or purported performance, of the employee's functions or activities he has disclosed any information or document in breach of the duty in regulation 25, unless the employee reasonably believed the disclosure to be a "protected disclosure" within the meaning given to that expression by section 43A of the 1996 Act.

(5) This paragraph applies to any employee whether or not he is an employee to whom paragraph (2) applies.

(6) The grounds are that the employee—

(a) took, or proposed to take, any proceedings before an employment tribunal to enforce a right or secure an entitlement conferred on him by these Regulations;

(b) exercised, or proposed to exercise, any entitlement to apply or complain to the CAC or the Appeal Tribunal conferred by these Regulations or to exercise the right to appeal in connection with any rights conferred by these Regulations;

(c) requested, or proposed to request, data in accordance with regulation 5;

(d) acted with a view to securing that an agreement was or was not negotiated or that the standard information and consultation provisions did or did not become applicable;

(e) indicated that he supported or did not support the coming into existence of a negotiated agreement or the application of the standard information and consultation provisions;

(f) stood as a candidate in an election in which any person elected would, on being elected, be a negotiating representative or an information and consultation representative;

(g) influenced or sought to influence by lawful means the way in which votes were to be cast by other employees in a ballot arranged under these Regulations;

(h) voted in such a ballot;

(i) expressed doubts, whether to a ballot supervisor or otherwise, as to whether such a ballot had been properly conducted; or

(j) proposed to do, failed to do, or proposed to decline to do, any of the things mentioned in sub-paragraphs (d) to (i).

(7) It is immaterial for the purpose of paragraph (6)(a)—

(a) whether or not the employee has the right or entitlement; or

(b) whether or not the right has been infringed,

but for that sub-paragraph to apply, the claim to the right and, if applicable, the claim that it has been infringed must be made in good faith.

(8) This regulation does not apply where the detriment in question amounts to dismissal.

[2.930]

33 Detriment: enforcement and subsidiary provisions

(1) An employee may present a complaint to an employment tribunal that he has been subjected to a detriment in contravention of regulation 32.

(2) The provisions of sections 48(2) to (4) and 49(1) to (5) of the 1996 Act (complaints to employment tribunals and remedies) shall apply in relation to a complaint under this regulation as they apply in relation to a complaint under section 48 of the Act but taking references to the employer as references to the employer within the meaning of regulation 32(1) above.

NOTES

Conciliation: employment tribunal proceedings and claims which could be the subject of employment tribunal proceedings under this regulation are proceedings to which the Employment Tribunals Act 1996, s 18 applies; see s 18(1)(p) of that Act at **[1.706]**.

Tribunal jurisdiction: the Employment Act 2002, s 38 applies to proceedings before the employment tribunal relating to a claim under this regulation; see s 38(1) of, and Sch 5 to, the 2002 Act at **[1.1228]**, **[1.1236]**. See also the Trade Union and Labour Relations (Consolidation) Act 1992, s 207A at **[1.474]** (as inserted by the Employment Act 2008). That section provides that in proceedings before an employment tribunal relating to a claim by an employee under any of the jurisdictions listed in Sch A2 to the 1992 Act at **[1.648]** (which includes this regulation) the tribunal may adjust any award given if the employer or the employee has unreasonably failed to comply with the relevant Code of Practice as defined by s 207A(4). See also the revised Acas Code of Practice 1 – Disciplinary and Grievance Procedures (2009) at **[4.1]**.

34 (*Amends the Employment Tribunals Act 1996, s 18 at* **[1.706]**.)

PART IX
MISCELLANEOUS

[2.931]
35 CAC proceedings

(1) Where under these Regulations a person presents a complaint or makes an application to the CAC the complaint or application must be in writing and in such form as the CAC may require.

(2) In its consideration of a complaint or application under these Regulations, the CAC shall make such enquiries as it sees fit and so far as reasonably practicable give any person whom it considers has a proper interest in the complaint or application an opportunity to be heard.

(3) The CAC may draw an adverse inference from a party's failure to comply with any reasonable request to provide information or documents relevant to a complaint presented to it or an application made to it.

(4) A declaration or order made by the CAC under these Regulations may be relied on—
- (a) in relation to an employer whose registered office, head office or principal place of business is in England or Wales, as if it were a declaration or order made by the High Court, and
- (b) in relation to an employer whose registered office, head office or principal place of business is in Scotland as if it were a declaration or order made by the Court of Session.

(5) A declaration or order made by the CAC under these Regulations must be in writing and state the reasons for the CAC's findings.

(6) An appeal lies to the Appeal Tribunal on any question of law arising from any declaration or order of, or arising in any proceedings before, the CAC under these Regulations.

[2.932]
36 Appeal Tribunal: location of certain proceedings under these Regulations

(1) Any proceedings before the Appeal Tribunal arising under these Regulations, other than appeals under paragraph (n) of section 21(1) of the Employment Tribunals Act 1996 (appeals from employment tribunals on questions of law), shall—
- (a) where the registered office or, where there is no registered office, the head office or principal place of business is situated in England and Wales, be held in England and Wales; and
- (b) where the registered office or, where there is no registered office, the head office or principal place of business is situated in Scotland, be held in Scotland.

(2) . . .

NOTES

Para (2): amends the Employment Tribunals Act 1996, s 20 at **[1.712]**.

37 (*Amends the Employment Tribunals Act 1996, s 21 at* **[1.713]**.)

[2.933]
38 ACAS

(1) If on receipt of an application or complaint under these Regulations the CAC is of the opinion that it is reasonably likely to be settled by conciliation or other assistance provided by the Advisory, Conciliation and Arbitration Service ('ACAS') in accordance with paragraph (2), it shall refer the application or complaint to ACAS and shall notify the applicant or complainant and any persons whom it considers have a proper interest in the application or complaint accordingly.

(2) Where the CAC refers an application or complaint to ACAS under paragraph (1), section 210 of the Trade Union and Labour Relations (Consolidation) Act 1992 (power of ACAS to offer assistance to settle disputes) shall apply, and ACAS may offer the parties to the application or complaint its assistance under that section with a view to bringing about a settlement, as if—
- (a) the dispute or difference between the parties amounted to a trade dispute as defined in section 218 of that Act; and
- (b) the parties to the application or complaint had requested the assistance of ACAS under section 210.

(3) If ACAS does not consider it appropriate to offer its assistance in accordance with paragraph (2) it shall inform the CAC.

(4) If ACAS has offered the parties its assistance in accordance with paragraph (2), the application or complaint referred has not thereafter been settled or withdrawn, and ACAS is of the opinion that no provision or further provision of its assistance is likely to result in a settlement or withdrawal, it shall inform the CAC of its opinion.

(5) If—
- (a) an application or complaint is not referred to ACAS, or
- (b) it is so referred, but ACAS informs the CAC as mentioned in paragraph (3) or (4),

the CAC shall proceed to hear and determine the application or complaint.

[2.934]

39 Restrictions on contracting out: general

(1) Any provision in any agreement (whether an employee's contract or not) is void in so far as it purports—

- (a) to exclude or limit the operation of any provision of these Regulations other than a provision of Part VIII; or
- (b) to preclude a person from bringing any proceedings before the CAC or the Appeal Tribunal under any provision of these Regulations other than a provision of Part VIII.

(2) Paragraph (1) does not apply to any agreement to refrain from continuing any proceedings referred to in sub-paragraph (b) of that paragraph made after the proceedings have been instituted.

[2.935]

40 Restrictions on contracting out: Part VIII

(1) Any provision in any agreement (whether an employee's contract or not) is void in so far as it purports—

- (a) to exclude or limit the operation of any provision of Part VIII; or
- (b) to preclude a person from bringing any proceedings before an employment tribunal under that Part.

(2) Paragraph (1) does not apply to any agreement to refrain from instituting or continuing proceedings before an employment tribunal where a conciliation officer has taken action under section 18 of the Employment Tribunals Act 1996 (conciliation).

(3) Paragraph (1) does not apply to any agreement to refrain from instituting or continuing before an employment tribunal proceedings within section 18(1) of the Employment Tribunals Act 1996 (proceedings under these Regulations where conciliation is available) if the conditions regulating compromise agreements under these Regulations are satisfied in relation to the agreement.

(4) For the purposes of paragraph (3) the conditions regulating compromise agreements are that—

- (a) the agreement must be in writing;
- (b) the agreement must relate to the particular proceedings;
- (c) the employee must have received advice from a relevant independent adviser as to the terms and effect of the proposed agreement and, in particular, its effect on his ability to pursue his rights before an employment tribunal;
- (d) there must be in force, when the adviser gives the advice, a contract of insurance, or an indemnity provided for members of a profession or a professional body, covering the risk of a claim by the employee in respect of loss arising in consequence of the advice;
- (e) the agreement must identify the adviser; and
- (f) the agreement must state that the conditions in sub-paragraphs (a) to (e) are satisfied.

(5) A person is a relevant independent adviser for the purposes of paragraph (4)(c)—

- (a) if he is a qualified lawyer;
- (b) if he is an officer, official, employee or member of an independent trade union who has been certified in writing by the trade union as competent to give advice and as authorised to do so on behalf of the trade union; or
- (c) if he works at an advice centre (whether as an employee or as a volunteer) and has been certified in writing by the centre as competent to give advice and as authorised to do so on behalf of the centre.

(6) But a person is not a relevant independent adviser for the purposes of paragraph (4)(c)—

- (a) if he is, is employed by or is acting in the matter for the employer or an associated employer;
- (b) in the case of a person within paragraph (5)(b) or (c), if the trade union or advice centre is the employer or an associated employer; or
- (c) in the case of a person within (5)(c), if the employee makes a payment for the advice received from him.

(7) In paragraph (5)(a), "qualified lawyer" means—

- (a) as respects England and Wales, [a person who, for the purposes of the Legal Services Act 2007), is an authorised person in relation to an activity which constitutes the exercise of a right of audience or the conduct of litigation (within the meaning of that Act)]; and
- (b) as respects Scotland, an advocate (whether in practice as such or employed to give legal advice) or a solicitor who holds a practising certificate.

(8) A person shall be treated as being a qualified lawyer within the meaning of paragraph (7)(a) if he is a Fellow of the Institute of Legal Executives [practising in a solicitor's practice (including a body recognised under section 9 of the Administration of Justice Act 1985)].

(9) For the purposes of paragraph (6) any two employers shall be treated as associated if—

- (a) one is a company of which the other (directly or indirectly) has control; or
- (b) both are companies of which a third person (directly or indirectly) has control;

and "associated employer" shall be construed accordingly.

NOTES

Para (7): words in square brackets substituted by the Legal Services Act 2007 (Consequential Amendments) Order 2009, SI 2009/3348, art 23, Sch 2, as from 1 January 2010.

Para (8): words in square brackets in sub-para (5) substituted by SI 2009/3348, art 22, Sch 1, as from 16 December 2009.

41 (*Amends the Employment Appeal Tribunal Rules 1993, SI 1993/2854, rr 2–5, 7, 16AA, 26, 31, Schedule at* **[2.143]–[2.147]**, **[2.149]**, **[2.159]**, **[2.173]**, **[2.179]**, **[2.194]** *et seq.*)

[2.936]

42 Crown employment

(1) These Regulations have effect in relation to Crown employment and persons in Crown employment as they have effect in relation to other employment and other employees.

(2) In these Regulations "Crown employment" means employment in an undertaking to which these Regulations apply and which is under or for the purposes of a government department or any officer or body exercising on behalf of the Crown functions conferred by a statutory provision.

(3) For the purposes of the application of these Regulations in relation to Crown employment in accordance with paragraph (1)—

(a) references to an employee shall be construed as references to a person in Crown employment; and

(b) references to a contract of employment shall be construed as references to the terms of employment of a person in Crown employment.

[2.937]

43 Exception for merchant navy

(1) Subject to paragraph (3), no long haul crew member shall be—

(a) a negotiating representative; or

(b) an information and consultation representative.

(2) In paragraph (1), a "long haul crew member" means a person who is a member of a merchant navy crew other than—

(a) a ferry worker; or

(b) a person who normally works on voyages the duration of which is less than 48 hours.

(3) Paragraph (1) does not apply where the employer decides that the long haul crew member in question shall be permitted to be, as the case may be, a negotiating representative or an information and consultation representative.

(4) Where paragraph (1) applies, no long haul crew member shall—

(a) stand as a candidate for election as a negotiating representative or an information and consultation representative; or

(b) be appointed or elected to be a negotiating representative or an information and consultation representative.

SCHEDULES

SCHEDULE 1
APPLICATION OF REGULATIONS

Regulation 3

[2.938]

Number of employees	**Date Regulations apply**
At least 150	6 April 2005
At least 100	6 April 2007
At least 50	6 April 2008

SCHEDULE 2
REQUIREMENTS FOR BALLOTS HELD UNDER REGULATION 19

Regulation 19

Ballot Arrangements

[2.939]

1. Ballots held under regulation 19 must comply with the requirements specified in paragraph 2.

2. The requirements referred to in paragraph 1 are that—

(a) the ballot must comprise a single ballot but may instead, if the employer so decides, comprise separate ballots of employees in such constituencies as the employer may decide where the employer considers that if separate ballots were to be held for those constituencies, the information and consultation representatives to be elected would better reflect the interests of the employees as a whole than if a single ballot were held;

(b) if, at any point, it becomes clear that the number of people standing as candidates in the ballot is equal to or fewer than the relevant number of information and consultation representatives (as defined in regulation 19(3)), the obligation on the employer to hold the ballot in regulation 19 will cease and the candidates referred to above will become the information and consultation representatives;

(c) all employees of the undertaking on the day on which the votes may be cast in the ballot, or if the votes may be cast on more than one day, on the first day of those days, must be given an entitlement to vote in the ballot;

(d) any employee who is an employee of the undertaking at the latest time at which a person may become a candidate in the ballot is entitled to stand in the ballot as a candidate as an information and consultation representative;

(e) the employer must, in accordance with paragraph 6, appoint an independent ballot supervisor to supervise the conduct of the ballot;

(f) after the employer has formulated proposals as to the arrangements for the ballot and before he has published the final arrangements under sub-paragraph (g) he must, so far as reasonably practicable, consult with employees' representatives or, if no such representatives exist, the employees, on the proposed arrangements for the ballot; and

(g) the employer must publish the final arrangements for the ballot in such manner as to bring them to the attention of, so far as reasonably practicable, his employees and, where they exist, the employees' representatives.

3. Any employee or an employees' representative who believes that the arrangements for the ballot are defective may, within a period of 21 days beginning on the date on which the employer published the final arrangements under paragraph 2(g), present a complaint to the CAC.

4. Where the CAC finds the complaint well-founded it shall make a declaration to that effect and may make an order requiring the employer to modify the arrangements he has made for the ballot or to satisfy the requirements in sub-paragraphs (a) to (f) of paragraph 2.

5. An order under paragraph 4 shall specify the modifications to the arrangements which the employer is required to make and the requirements he must satisfy.

6. A person is an independent ballot supervisor for the purposes of paragraph 2(e) if the employer reasonably believes that he will carry out any functions conferred on him in relation to the ballot competently and has no reasonable grounds for believing that his independence might reasonably be called into question.

7. For the purposes of paragraph 3 the arrangements for the ballot are defective if any of the requirements specified in sub-paragraphs (a) to (f) of paragraph 2 is not satisfied.

Conduct of the Ballot

8. The employer must—

(a) ensure that a ballot supervisor appointed under paragraph 2(e) carries out his functions under this Schedule and that there is no interference with his carrying out of those functions; and

(b) comply with all reasonable requests made by a ballot supervisor for the purposes of or in connection with the carrying out of those functions.

9. A ballot supervisor's appointment shall require that he—

(a) supervises the conduct of the ballot he is being appointed to supervise, in accordance with the arrangements for the ballot published by the employer under paragraph 2(g) or, where appropriate, in accordance with the arrangements as required to be modified by an order made under paragraph 4;

(b) does not conduct the ballot before the employer has satisfied the requirement specified in paragraph 2(g) and—

   (i) where no complaint has been presented under paragraph 3, before the expiry of 21 days beginning with the date on which the employer published his arrangements under paragraph 2(g); or

   (ii) where a complaint has been presented under paragraph 3, before the complaint has been determined and, where appropriate, the arrangements have been modified as required by an order made as a result of the complaint;

(c) conducts the ballot so as to secure that—

   (i) so far as reasonably practicable, those entitled to vote are given the opportunity to do so;

   (ii) so far as reasonably practicable, those entitled to stand as candidates are given the opportunity to stand;

(iii) so far as reasonably practicable, those voting are able to do so in secret; and
(iv) the votes given in the ballot are fairly and accurately counted.

10. As soon as reasonably practicable after the date of the ballot, the ballot supervisor must publish the results of the ballot in such manner as to make them available to the employer and, so far as reasonably practicable, the employees entitled to vote in the ballot and the persons who stood as candidates in the ballot.

11. A ballot supervisor shall publish a report ("an ineffective ballot report") where he considers (whether or not on the basis of representations made to him by another person) that—

(a) any of the requirements referred to in paragraph 2 was not satisfied with the result that the outcome of the ballot would have been different; or
(b) there was interference with the carrying out of his functions or a failure by the employer to comply with all reasonable requests made by him with the result that he was unable to form a proper judgement as to whether each of the requirements referred to in paragraph 2 was satisfied in the ballot.

12. Where a ballot supervisor publishes an ineffective ballot report the report must be published within a period of one month commencing on the date on which the ballot supervisor publishes the results of the ballot under paragraph 10.

13. A ballot supervisor must publish an ineffective ballot report in such manner as to make it available to the employer and, so far as reasonably practicable, the employees entitled to vote in the ballot and the persons who stood as candidates in the ballot.

14. Where a ballot supervisor publishes an ineffective ballot report, the outcome of the ballot shall be of no effect and—

(a) if there has been a single ballot or an ineffective ballot report has been published in respect of every separate ballot, the outcome of the ballot or ballots shall be of no effect and the employer shall again be under the obligation in regulation 19;
(b) if there have been separate ballots and sub-paragraph (a) does not apply—
 (i) the employer shall arrange for the separate ballot or ballots in respect of which an ineffective ballot report has been issued to be reheld in accordance with regulation 19, and
 (ii) no such ballot shall have effect until it has been reheld and no ineffective ballot report has been published in respect of it.

15. All costs relating to the holding of the ballot, including payments made to a ballot supervisor for supervising the conduct of the ballot, shall be borne by the employer (whether or not an ineffective ballot report has been made).

ROAD TRANSPORT (WORKING TIME) REGULATIONS 2005

(SI 2005/639)

NOTES

Made: 10 March 2005.
Authority: European Communities Act 1972, s 2(2).
Commencement: 4 April 2005.
These Regulations are the domestic implementation of European Parliament and Council Directive 2002/15/EC on the organisation of working time of persons performing mobile transport activities at **[3.401]**.
Regulatory functions: the regulatory functions conferred by these Regulations are subject to the Legislative and Regulatory Reform Act 2006, ss 21, 22 at **[1.1495]**, **[1.1496]**; see the Legislative and Regulatory Reform (Regulatory Functions) Order 2007, SI 2007/3544 (made under s 24(2) of the 2006 Act) for details.
See *Harvey* CI(1).

ARRANGEMENT OF REGULATIONS

SCHEDULES

[2.940]

1 Citation, commencement and extent

(1) These Regulations may be cited as the Road Transport (Working Time) Regulations 2005 and shall come into force on 4th April 2005.

(2) These Regulations extend to Great Britain only.

[2.941]

2 Interpretation

In these Regulations—

"AETR" means the European agreement concerning the work of crews of vehicles engaged in international road transport of 1st July 1970;

"collective agreement" means a collective agreement within the meaning of section 178 of the Trade Union and Labour Relations (Consolidation) Act 1992, the trade union parties to which are independent trade unions within the meaning of section 5 of that Act;

["the Community Drivers' Hours Regulation" means Regulation (EC) No 561/2006 of the European Parliament and of the Council of 15 March 2006 on the harmonisation of certain social legislation relating to road transport (and amending and repealing certain Council Regulations);]

"employer" in relation to a worker, means the person by whom the worker is (or, where the employment has ceased, was) employed;

"employment" in relation to a worker, means employment under his contract, and "employed" shall be construed accordingly;

"goods" includes goods or burden of any description;

"goods vehicle" means a motor vehicle constructed or adapted for use for the carriage of goods, or a trailer so constructed or adapted;

"inspector" means a person appointed under paragraph 1 of Schedule 2;

"mobile worker" means any worker forming part of the travelling staff, including trainees and apprentices, who is in the service of an undertaking which operates transport services for passengers or goods by road for hire or reward or on its own account;

"night time" means in respect of goods vehicles the period between midnight and 4am and in respect of passenger vehicles the period between 1am and 5am;

"motor vehicle" means a mechanically propelled vehicle intended or adapted for use on roads;

"night work" means any work performed during night time;

"passenger vehicle" means a motor vehicle which is constructed or adapted to carry more than eight seated passengers in addition to the driver;

"period of availability" means a period during which the mobile worker [or self-employed driver] is not required to remain at his workstation, [but—

(a) in the case of a mobile worker, is required to be available, or

(b) in the case of a self-employed driver, makes himself available,]

to answer any calls to start or resume driving or to carry out other work, including periods during which the mobile worker [or self-employed driver] is accompanying a vehicle being transported by a ferry or by a train as well as periods of waiting at frontiers and those due to traffic prohibitions;

"reference period" means the period for calculation of the average maximum weekly working time;

"relevant requirements" means regulations 4(8), [4(9)], 7(5), [7(6)], 8(2), [8(3)], 9(4), [9(5)], 10, 11, [11A] and 12;

"self-employed driver" means anyone whose main occupation is to transport passengers or goods by road for hire or reward within the meaning of [EU] legislation under cover of a Community licence or any other professional authorisation to carry out such transport, who is entitled to work for himself and who is not tied to an employer by an employment contract or by any other type of working hierarchical relationship, who is free to organise the relevant working activities, whose income depends directly on the profits made and

Part 2 Statutory Instruments

who has the freedom, individually or through a co-operation between self-employed drivers, to have commercial relations with several customers;

"vehicle" means a goods vehicle or a passenger vehicle;

"week" means a period of seven days beginning at midnight between Sunday and Monday;

"worker" means an individual [who is not a self-employed driver and] who has entered into or works under (or, where employment has ceased, worked under)—

(a) a contract of employment; or

(b) any other contract, whether express or implied and (if it is express) whether oral or in writing, whereby the individual undertakes to do or perform personally any work or services for another party to the contract;

and any reference to a worker's contract shall be construed accordingly;

"workforce agreement" means an agreement between an employer and mobile workers employed by him or their representatives in respect of which the conditions set out in Schedule 1 to these Regulations are satisfied;

["working time" means the time from the beginning to the end of work during which—

(a) the mobile worker or self-employed driver is at his workstation;

(b) the mobile worker is at the disposal of his employer, or (as applicable) the self employed driver is at the disposal of the client; and

(c) the mobile worker or self-employed driver is exercising his functions or activities, being:

(i) time devoted to all road transport activities, including, in particular—

(aa) driving;

(bb) loading and unloading;

(cc) assisting passengers boarding and disembarking from the vehicle;

(dd) cleaning and technical maintenance;

(ee) all other work intended to ensure the safety of the vehicle, its cargo and passengers or to fulfil the legal or regulatory obligations directly linked to the specific transport operation under way, including monitoring of loading and unloading and dealing with administrative formalities with police, customs, immigration officers and others; or

(ii) time during which the mobile worker or self-employed driver cannot dispose freely of his time and is required (or, in relation to a self-employed driver, chooses) to be at his workstation, ready to take up normal work, with certain tasks associated with being on duty, in particular during periods awaiting loading or unloading where their foreseeable duration is not known in advance, that is to say either before departure or just before the actual start of the period in question, or under collective agreements or workforce agreements;

but, in relation to self-employed drivers, general administrative work that is not directly linked to the specific transport operation under way is excluded from working time;]

"workstation" means

(a) [in relation to a mobile worker] the location of the main place of business of the undertaking for which the person performing mobile transport activities carries out duties, together with its various subsidiary places of business, regardless of whether they are located in the same place as its head office or its main place of business; [or]

(b) [in relation to a mobile worker or self-employed driver] the vehicle which the person performing mobile road transport activities uses when he carries out duties; or

(c) [in relation to a mobile worker or self-employed driver] any other place in which activities connected with transport are carried out.

NOTES

Definition "the Community Drivers' Hours Regulation" substituted by the Road Transport (Working Time) (Amendment) Regulations 2007, SI 2007/853, reg 2(1), (2).

Reference in square brackets in definition "self-employed driver" substituted by the Treaty of Lisbon (Changes in Terminology) Order 2011, SI 2011/1043, art 6(2)(b), as from 22 April 2011.

All other amendments to this regulation were made by the Road Transport (Working Time) (Amendment) Regulations 2012, SI 2012/991, regs 2, 3, as from 11 May 2012.

[2.942]

3 Application

(1) These Regulations apply to mobile workers who are employed by, or who do work for, undertakings established in a Member State of the European Union, and to whom paragraph (2) or paragraph (3) applies.

[(1A) These Regulations also apply to self-employed drivers who are established in, or who do work for undertakings established in, a Member State of the European Union, and to whom paragraph (2) or paragraph (3) applies.]

[(2) This paragraph applies to mobile workers [or self-employed drivers] who, in the course of [their employment or working activities], drive or travel in or on vehicles—

(a) which are vehicles within the meaning of Article 4(b) of the Community Drivers' Hours Regulation,

(b) which are not vehicles described in Article 3 of that Regulation, and

(c) [which are not vehicles exempted from the provisions of that Regulation under regulation 2 of the Community Drivers' Hours and Recording Equipment Regulations 2007].]

(3) This paragraph applies to mobile workers [or self-employed drivers], to whom paragraph (2) does not apply, who in the course of [their employment or working activities] drive, or travel in, vehicles

(a) which fall within the meaning of a "vehicle" in Article 1 of the AETR;

(b) which are not referred to in Article 2(2)(b) of the AETR; and

(c) which are performing international transport.

(4) These Regulations do not apply to—

(a) . . .

(b) any [mobile worker or self-employed driver] who does work which is included in the calculation of working time—

(i) where the reference period is shorter than 26 weeks, on fewer than 11 days in a reference period applicable to that [mobile worker or self-employed driver], or

(ii) in any other case on fewer than 16 days in a reference period applicable to that [mobile worker or self-employed driver].

NOTES

Para (2) was substituted by the Road Transport (Working Time) (Amendment) Regulations 2007, SI 2007/853, reg 2(1), (3).

All other amendments to this regulation were made by the Road Transport (Working Time) (Amendment) Regulations 2012, SI 2012/991, regs 2, 4, as from 11 May 2012.

[2.943]

[3A Duty to Review Regulation 3(1A)

(1) The Secretary of State must from time to time—

(a) carry out a review of regulation 3(1A),

(b) set out the conclusions of the review in a report, and

(c) publish the report.

(2) In carrying out the review the Secretary of State must, so far as is reasonable, have regard to how Directive 2002/15/EC, in so far as it applies to self-employed drivers (which is implemented by means of regulation 3(1A)), is implemented in other Member States.

(3) The report must in particular—

(a) set out the objectives intended to be achieved by the regulatory system established by regulation 3(1A),

(b) assess the extent to which those objectives are achieved, and

(c) assess whether those objectives remain appropriate and, if so, the extent to which they could be achieved with a system that imposes less regulation.

(4) The first report under this regulation must be published before the end of the period of five years beginning with the day on which regulation 3(1A) comes into force.

(5) Reports under this regulation are afterwards to be published at intervals not exceeding five years.]

NOTES

Commencement: 11 May 2012.

Inserted by the Road Transport (Working Time) (Amendment) Regulations 2012, SI 2012/991, regs 2, 5, as from 11 May 2012.

[2.944]

4 Working time

(1) Subject to paragraph (2) below, the working time, including overtime, of a mobile worker [or self-employed driver] shall not exceed 60 hours in a week.

(2) In any reference period which is applicable to his case, [the working time of a mobile worker or self-employed driver] shall not exceed an average of 48 hours for each week.

(3) The reference periods which apply . . . shall be—

[(a) in the case of a mobile worker—

(i) where a collective agreement or a workforce agreement provides for the application of this regulation in relation to successive periods of 17 weeks, each such period, or

(ii) in a case where there is no such provision, and the employer gives written notice to the mobile worker in writing that he intends to apply this subparagraph, any period of 17 weeks in the course of the worker's employment,] [(b) in the case of a self-employed driver who elects to apply this subparagraph in relation to any period of 17 weeks or to successive periods of 17 weeks, each such period,]

(c) in any other case [for a mobile worker or self-employed driver,] the period ending at midnight between Sunday 31st July 2005 and Monday 1st August 2005 and thereafter, in each year, the successive periods beginning at midnight at the beginning of the Monday which falls on, or is the first Monday after, a date in column 1 below and ending at midnight at the beginning of the Monday which falls on, or is the first Monday after, the date on the same line in column 2 below.

Column 1 (beginning)	Column 2 (end)
1st December	1st April
1st April	1st August
1st August	1st December

(4) The reference period may be extended in relation to particular mobile workers or groups of mobile workers for objective or technical reasons or reasons concerning the organisation of work, by a collective agreement or a workforce agreement, by the substitution for 17 weeks of a period not exceeding 26 weeks in the application of paragraphs (2) and (3)(a) above.

[(4A) The reference period may be extended in relation to self-employed drivers for objective or technical reasons or reasons concerning the organisation of work, by the substitution for 17 weeks of a period not exceeding 26 weeks in the application of paragraphs (2) and (3)(b) above.]

(5) [The] average weekly working time during a reference period shall be determined according to the formula—

[(**A** + **B**) ÷ **C** for mobile workers, or

A ÷ **C** for self-employed drivers]

where—

A is the aggregate number of hours comprised in . . . working time during the course of the reference period;

B is the number of excluded hours during the reference period; and

C is the number of weeks in the reference period.

(6) In paragraph (5), "excluded hours" means hours comprised in—

(a) any period of annual leave taken by the mobile worker in exercise of entitlement under regulation 13 of the Working Time Regulations 1998;

(b) any period of sick leave taken by the mobile worker;

(c) any period of maternity, paternity, adoption or parental leave taken by the mobile worker;

(7) For the purposes of paragraph (5), the number of hours in a whole day shall be eight and the number of hours in a whole week shall be forty-eight.

(8) An employer shall take all reasonable steps, in keeping with the need to protect the health and safety of the mobile worker, to ensure that the limits specified above are complied with in the case of each mobile worker employed by him.

[(9) A self-employed driver must take all reasonable steps, in keeping with the need to protect his health and safety, to comply with the limits specified above.]

NOTES

All amendments to this regulation were made by the Road Transport (Working Time) (Amendment) Regulations 2012, SI 2012/991, regs 2, 6, as from 11 May 2012.

[2.945]
5

The times of breaks, rests and periods of availability shall not be included in the calculation of working time.

[2.946]
6 Periods of availability

(1) A period shall not be treated as a period of availability unless the mobile worker [or self-employed driver] knows before the start of the relevant period about that period of availability and its reasonably foreseeable duration.

(2) The time spent by a mobile worker [or self-employed driver], who is working as part of a team, travelling in, but not driving, a moving vehicle as part of that team shall be a period of availability for that mobile worker [or self-employed driver].

(3) Subject to paragraph (4) a period of availability shall not include a period of rest or a break.

(4) A period of availability may include a break taken by a mobile worker [or self-employed driver] during waiting time or time which is not devoted to driving by the mobile worker [or self-employed driver] and is spent in a moving vehicle, a ferry or a train.

NOTES

All amendments to this regulation were made by the Road Transport (Working Time) (Amendment) Regulations 2012, SI 2012/991, regs 2, 7, as from 11 May 2012.

[2.947]

7 Breaks

(1) No mobile worker [or self-employed driver] shall work for more than six hours without a break.

[(2) Where the working time of a mobile worker or self-employed driver exceeds six hours but does not exceed nine hours, the mobile worker or self-employed driver must take a break lasting at least 30 minutes and interrupting that period.]

[(3) Where the working time of a mobile worker or self-employed driver exceeds nine hours, the mobile worker or self-employed driver must take a break lasting at least 45 minutes and interrupting that period.]

(4) Each break may be made up of separate periods of not less than 15 minutes each.

(5) An employer shall take all reasonable steps, in keeping with the need to protect the health and safety of the mobile worker, to ensure that the limits specified above are complied with in the case of each mobile worker employed by him.

[(6) A self-employed driver must take all reasonable steps, in keeping with the need to protect his health and safety, to comply with the limits specified above.]

NOTES

All amendments to this regulation were made by the Road Transport (Working Time) (Amendment) Regulations 2012, SI 2012/991, regs 2, 8, as from 11 May 2012.

[2.948]

8 Rest periods

(1) In the application of these Regulations, the provisions of the Community Drivers' Hours Regulation relating to daily and weekly rest shall apply to all mobile workers [and self-employed drivers] to whom they do not apply under that Regulation as they apply to other mobile workers under that Regulation.

(2) An employer shall take all reasonable steps, in keeping with the need to protect the health and safety of the mobile worker, to ensure that those provisions are complied with in the case of each mobile worker employed by him, to whom they are applied by paragraph (1).

[(3) A self-employed driver must take all reasonable steps, in keeping with the need to protect his health and safety, to ensure that he complies with the provisions applied by paragraph (1).]

NOTES

All amendments to this regulation were made by the Road Transport (Working Time) (Amendment) Regulations 2012, SI 2012/991, regs 2, 9, as from 11 May 2012.

[2.949]

9 Night work

(1) The working time of a mobile worker [or self-employed driver], who performs night work in any period of 24 hours, shall not exceed 10 hours during that period.

(2) The period of 10 hours may be extended in relation to particular mobile workers or groups of mobile workers for objective or technical reasons or reasons concerning the organisation of work, by a collective agreement or a workforce agreement.

[(2A) A self-employed driver may elect to extend the period of 10 hours for objective or technical reasons or reasons concerning the organisation of work.

(3) Compensation for night work shall not be given to a mobile worker [or to a self-employed driver] in any manner which is liable to endanger road safety.

(4) An employer shall take all reasonable steps in keeping with the need to protect the health and safety of mobile workers to ensure that the limit specified in paragraph (1), or extended in accordance with paragraph (2), is complied with in the case of each mobile worker employed by him.

[(5) A self-employed driver must take all reasonable steps, in keeping with the need to protect his health and safety, to ensure that the limit specified in paragraph (1), or extended in accordance with paragraph (2A), is complied with.]

NOTES

All amendments to this regulation were made by the Road Transport (Working Time) (Amendment) Regulations 2012, SI 2012/991, regs 2, 10, as from 11 May 2012.

[2.950]
10 Information and records

An employer of mobile workers shall notify each worker of the provisions of these Regulations and the provisions of any collective or workforce agreement which is capable of application to that worker.

[2.951]
11

An employer of a mobile worker shall
- (a) request from each mobile worker details of any time worked by that worker for another employer;
- (b) include time worked for another employer in the calculation of the mobile worker's working time;
- (c) keep records which are adequate to show whether the requirements of these Regulations are being complied with in the case of each mobile worker employed by him to whom they apply;
- (d) retain such records for at least two years after the end of the period covered by those records;
- (e) provide, at the request of a mobile worker, a copy of the record of hours worked by that worker;
- (f) provide to an enforcement officer copies of such records relating to mobile workers as the officer may require;
- (g) provide to a mobile worker or enforcement officer copies of such documentary evidence in the employer's possession as may be requested by the worker or officer in relation to records provided to him in accordance with paragraph (e) or (f) above.

[2.952]
[11A

A self-employed driver must—
- (a) keep records which are adequate to show whether he is complying with the requirements of these Regulations;
- (b) retain such records for at least two years after the end of the period covered by those records;
- (c) provide to an enforcement officer copies of such records as the officer may require.]

NOTES

Commencement: 11 May 2012.

Inserted by the Road Transport (Working Time) (Amendment) Regulations 2012, SI 2012/991, regs 2, 11, as from 11 May 2012.

[2.953]
12

A mobile worker shall, at the request of his employer under regulation 11(a), notify his employer in writing of time worked by the worker for another employer for inclusion in the calculation of the mobile worker's working time.

[2.954]
13

(1) The Secretary of State shall arrange for the publication, in such form and manner as he considers appropriate, of information and advice concerning the operation of these Regulations.

(2) The information and advice shall be such as appear to him best calculated to enable [employers, workers and self-employed drivers] affected by these Regulations to understand their respective rights and obligations.

NOTES

Words in square brackets in para (2) substituted by the Road Transport (Working Time) (Amendment) Regulations 2012, SI 2012/991, regs 2, 12, as from 11 May 2012.

[2.955]
14 Agency workers not otherwise mobile workers

(1) This regulation applies in any case where an individual ("the agency worker")—
- (a) is supplied by a person ("the agent") to do the work of a mobile worker for another ("the principal") under a contract or other arrangements made between the agent and the principal; but
- (b) is not, as respects that work, a worker, because of the absence of a worker's contract between the individual and the agent or the principal; and

(c) is not a party to a contract under which he undertakes to do the work for another party to the contract whose status is, by virtue of the contract, that of a client or customer or any profession or business undertaking carried on by the individual.

(2) In a case where this regulation applies, the other provisions of these Regulations shall have effect as if there were a contract for the doing of the work by the agency worker made between the agency worker and—

(a) whichever of the agent and the principal is responsible for paying the agency worker in respect of the work; or
(b) if neither the agent nor the principal is so responsible, whichever of them pays the agency worker in respect of the work,
(c) and as if that person were the agency worker's employer.

[2.956]
[15 Individual carrying on trade or business

(1) This regulation applies to an individual who—

(a) for the purpose of a trade or business carried on by him, drives a vehicle described in paragraph (2) or (3) of regulation 3, and
(b) is neither—
    (i) a self-employed driver, nor
    (ii) an agency worker within the meaning of regulation 14.

(2) Where this regulation applies, these Regulations shall have effect as if—

(a) the individual were both a mobile worker and the employer of that mobile worker, and
(b) regulations 10, 11(a) and (e) and 12 were omitted.]

NOTES

Substituted by the Road Transport (Working Time) (Amendment) Regulations 2007, SI 2007/853, reg 2(1), (4).

[2.957]
16 Enforcement

(1) It shall be the duty of the Secretary of State to enforce the requirements of these Regulations.

(2) Schedule 2 shall apply in relation to the enforcement of the relevant requirements.

[2.958]
17

(1) Any person who fails to comply with any of the relevant requirements shall be guilty of an offence.

(2) The provisions of paragraph (3) shall apply where an inspector is exercising or has exercised any power conferred by Schedule 2.

(3) It is an offence for a person—

(a) to contravene any requirement imposed by an inspector under paragraph 2 of Schedule 2;
(b) to prevent or attempt to prevent any other person from appearing before an inspector or from answering any question to which an inspector may by virtue of paragraph 2(2)(e) of Schedule 2 require an answer;
(c) to contravene any requirement or prohibition imposed by an improvement notice or a prohibition notice referred to in paragraphs 3 and 4 of Schedule 2 (including any such notice as is modified on appeal);
(d) intentionally to obstruct an inspector in the exercise or performance of his powers;
(e) to use or disclose any information in contravention of paragraph 7 of Schedule 2;
(f) to make a statement which he knows to be false or recklessly to make a statement which is false where the statement is made in purported compliance with a requirement to furnish any information imposed by or under these Regulations.

(4) Any person guilty of an offence under paragraph (1) shall be liable—

(a) on summary conviction, to a fine not exceeding the statutory maximum;
(b) on conviction on indictment, to a fine.

(5) A person guilty of an offence under paragraph (3)(b) or (d) shall be liable on summary conviction to a fine not exceeding level 5 on the standard scale.

(6) A person guilty of an offence under paragraph (3)(c) shall be liable—

(a) on summary conviction, to imprisonment for a term not exceeding three months, or a fine not exceeding the statutory maximum;
(b) on conviction on indictment, to imprisonment for a term not exceeding two years, or a fine or both.

(7) A person guilty of an offence under paragraph (3)(a), (e) or (f) shall be liable—

(a) on summary conviction, to a fine not exceeding the statutory maximum;
(b) on conviction on indictment—

(i) if the offence is under paragraph (3)(e), to imprisonment for a term not exceeding two years or a fine or both,
(ii) if the offence is under paragraph (3)(a) or (f), to a fine.

(8) The provisions set out in regulations 18 to 22 shall apply in relation to the offences provided for in paragraphs (1) and (3).

[2.959]
18 Offences due to fault of other person

Where the commission by any person of an offence is due to the act or default of some other person, that other person shall be guilty of the offence, and a person may be charged with the conviction of the offence by virtue of this regulation whether or not proceedings are taken against the first-mentioned person.

[2.960]
19 Offences by bodies corporate

(1) Where an offence committed by a body corporate is proved to have been committed with the consent or connivance of, or to have been attributable to any neglect on the part of, any director, manager, secretary or other similar officer of the body corporate or a person who was purporting to act in any such capacity, he as well as the body corporate shall be guilty of that offence and shall be liable to be proceeded against and punished accordingly.

(2) Where the affairs of a body corporate are managed by its members, the preceding paragraph shall apply in relation to the acts and defaults of a member in connection with his functions of management as if he were a director of the body corporate.

[2.961]
20 Restriction on institution of proceedings in England and Wales

Proceedings for an offence shall not be instituted in England or Wales except by an inspector or by, or with the consent of, the Director of Public Prosecutions.

[2.962]
21 Prosecution by inspectors

(1) If authorised in that behalf by the Secretary of State an inspector may prosecute proceedings for an offence before a magistrates court even though the inspector is not of counsel or a solicitor.

(2) This regulation shall not apply in Scotland.

[2.963]
22 Power of court to order cause of offence to be remedied

(1) This regulation applies where a person is convicted of an offence in respect of any matter which appears to the court to be a matter which it is in his power to remedy.

(2) In addition to or instead of imposing any punishment, the court may order the person in question to take such steps as may be specified in the order for remedying the said matters within such time as may be fixed by the order.

(3) The time fixed by an order under paragraph (2) may be extended or further extended by order of the court on an application made before the end of that time as originally fixed or as extended under this paragraph, as the case may be.

(4) Where a person is ordered under paragraph (2) to remedy any matters, that person shall not be liable under these Regulations in respect of that matter in so far as it continues during the time fixed by the order or any further time allowed under paragraph (3).

SCHEDULES

SCHEDULE 1
WORKFORCE AGREEMENTS

Regulation 2

[2.964]
1. An agreement is a workforce agreement for the purposes of these Regulations if the following conditions are satisfied—

(a) the agreement is in writing;
(b) it has effect for a specified period not exceeding five years;
(c) it applies either—
  (i) to all of the relevant members of the workforce, or
  (ii) to all of the relevant members of the workforce who belong to a particular group;
(d) the agreement is signed—
  (i) in the case of an agreement of the kind referred to in sub-paragraph (c)(i), by the representatives of the workforce, and in the case of an agreement of the kind referred

to in sub-paragraph (c)(ii), by the representatives of the group to which the agreement applies (excluding, in either case, any representative not a relevant member of the workforce on the date on which the agreement was first made available for signature), or

(ii) if the employer employed 20 or fewer workers on the date referred to in sub-paragraph (d)(i), either by the appropriate representatives in accordance with that sub-paragraph or by the majority of the workers employed by him; and

(e) before the agreement was made available for signature, the employer provided all the workers to whom it was intended to apply on the date on which it came into effect with copies of the text of the agreement and such guidance as those employees might reasonably require in order to understand it in full.

2. For the purposes of this Schedule—

"a particular group" is a group of the relevant members of a workforce who undertake a particular function, work at a particular workplace or belong to a particular department or unit within their employer's business;

"relevant members of the workforce" are all of the workers employed by a particular employer, excluding any worker whose terms and conditions of employment are provided for, wholly or in part, in a collective agreement;

"representatives of the group" are workers duly elected to represent the members of a particular group;

"representatives of the workforce" are workers duly elected to represent the relevant members of the workforce;

and representatives are "duly elected" if the election at which they were elected satisfied the requirements of paragraph 3.

3. The requirements concerning elections referred to in paragraph 2 are that—

(a) the number of representatives to be elected is determined by the employer;

(b) the candidates for election as representatives of the workforce are relevant members of the workforce, and candidates for election as representatives of the group are members of the group;

(c) no worker who is eligible to be a candidate is unreasonably excluded from standing for election;

(d) all the relevant members of the workforce are entitled to vote for representatives of the workforce, and all the members of a particular group are entitled to vote for representatives of the group;

(e) the workers entitled to vote may vote for as many candidates as there are representatives to be elected; and

(f) the election is conducted so as to secure that—

(i) so far as is reasonably practicable, those voting do so in secret, and

(ii) the votes given at the election are fairly and accurately counted.

SCHEDULE 2
ENFORCEMENT

Regulation 16(2)

[2.965]

1 Appointment of inspectors

(1) The Secretary of State may appoint as inspectors (under whatever title he may from time to time determine) such persons having suitable qualifications as he thinks necessary for carrying into effect these Regulations, and may terminate any appointment made under this paragraph.

(2) Every appointment of a person as an inspector under this paragraph shall be made by an instrument in writing specifying which of the powers conferred on inspectors by these Regulations are to be exercisable by the person appointed; and an inspector shall in right of his appointment under this paragraph be entitled to exercise only such of those powers as are so specified.

(3) So much of an inspector's instrument of appointment as specifies the powers which he is entitled to exercise may be varied by the Secretary of State.

(4) An inspector shall, if so required when exercising or seeking to exercise any power conferred on him by these Regulations, produce his instrument of appointment or a duly authenticated copy thereof.

2 Powers of inspectors

(1) Subject to the provisions of paragraph 1 and this paragraph, an inspector may for the purpose of carrying into effect these Regulations exercise the powers set out in sub-paragraph (2).

(2) The powers of an inspector are the following, namely—

(a) at any reasonable time (or in a situation which in his opinion may be dangerous, at any time) to enter any premises which he has reason to believe it is necessary for him to enter for the purposes mentioned in sub-paragraph (1);

(b) to take with him a constable if he has reasonable cause to apprehend any serious obstruction in the execution of his duty;

(c) without prejudice to paragraph (b), on entering any premises by virtue of paragraph (a) to take with him—

(i) any other person duly authorised by the Secretary of State; and

(ii) any equipment or material required for any purpose for which the power of entry is being exercised;

(d) to make such examination and investigation as may in any circumstances be necessary for the purpose mentioned in sub-paragraph (1);

(e) to require any person whom he has reasonable cause to believe to be able to give any information relevant to any examination or investigation under paragraph (d) to answer (in the absence of persons other than a person nominated by him to be present and any persons whom the inspector may allow to be present) such questions as the inspector thinks fit to ask and to sign a declaration of the truth of his answers;

(f) to require the production of, inspect, and take copies of, or of any entry in—

(i) any records which by virtue of these Regulations are required to be kept, and

(ii) any other books, records or documents which it is necessary for him to see for the purposes of any examination or investigation under paragraph (d);

(g) to require any person to afford him such facilities and assistance with respect to any matters or things within that person's control or in relation to which that person has responsibilities as are necessary to enable the inspector to exercise any of the powers conferred on him by this sub-paragraph;

(h) any other power which is necessary for the purpose mentioned in sub-paragraph (1).

(3) No answer given by a person in pursuance of a requirement imposed under sub-paragraph (2)(e) shall be admissible in evidence against that person or the husband or wife of that person in any proceedings.

(4) Nothing in this paragraph shall be taken to compel the production by any person of a document of which he would on grounds of legal professional privilege be entitled to withhold production on an order for discovery in an action in the High Court or, as the case may be, an order for the production of documents in an action in the Court of Session.

3 Improvement notices

If an inspector is of the opinion that a person—

(a) is contravening one or more of these Regulations; or

(b) has contravened one or more of these Regulations in circumstances that make it likely that the contravention will continue or be repeated,

he may serve on him a notice (in this Schedule referred to as "an improvement notice") stating that he is of that opinion, specifying the provision or provisions as to which he is of that opinion, giving particulars of the reasons why he is of that opinion, and requiring that person to remedy the contravention or, as the case may be, the matter occasioning it within such period (ending not earlier than the period within which an appeal against the notice can be brought under paragraph (6)) as may be specified in the notice.

4 Prohibition notices

(1) This paragraph applies to any activities which are being, or are likely to be, carried on by or under the control of any person, being activities to or in relation to which any of these Regulations apply or will, if the activities are so carried on, apply.

(2) If as regards any activities to which this paragraph applies an inspector is of the opinion that, as carried on by or under the control of the person in question, the activities involve or, as the case may be, will involve a risk of serious personal injury, the inspector may serve on that person a notice (in this Schedule referred to as "a prohibition notice").

(3) A prohibition notice shall—

(a) state that the inspector is of the said opinion;

(b) specify the matters which in his opinion give or, as the case may be, will give rise to the said risk;

(c) where in his opinion any of those matters involves or, as the case may be, will involve a contravention of any of these Regulations, state that he is of that opinion, specify the regulation or regulations as to which he is of that opinion, and give particulars of the reasons why he is of that opinion; and

(d) direct that the activities to which the notice relates shall not be carried on by or under the control of the person on whom the notice is served unless the matters specified in the notice in pursuance of paragraph (b) and any associated contraventions of provisions so specified in pursuance of paragraph (c) have been remedied.

(4) A direction contained in a prohibition notice in pursuance of sub-paragraph (3)(d) shall take effect—

(a) at the end of the period specified in the notice; or

(b) if the notice so declares, immediately.

5 Provisions supplementary to paragraphs 3 and 4

(1) In this paragraph "a notice" means an improvement notice or a prohibition notice.

(2) A notice may (but need not) include directions as to the measures to be taken to remedy any contravention or matter to which the notice relates; and any such directions—

(a) may be framed to any extent by reference to any approved code of practice; and

(b) may be framed so as to afford the person on whom the notice is served a choice between different ways of remedying the contravention or matter.

(3) Where an improvement notice or prohibition notice which is not to take immediate effect has been served—

(a) the notice may be withdrawn by an inspector at any time before the end of the period specified therein in pursuance of paragraph 3 or paragraph 4(4) as the case may be; and

(b) the period so specified may be extended or further extended by an inspector at any time when an appeal against the notice is not pending.

6 Appeal against improvement or prohibition notice

(1) In this paragraph "a notice" means an improvement or prohibition notice.

(2) A person on whom a notice is served may within 21 days from the date of its service appeal to an employment tribunal; and on such an appeal the tribunal may either cancel or affirm the notice and, if it affirms it, may do so either in its original form or with such modifications as the tribunal may in the circumstances think fit.

(3) Where an appeal under this paragraph is brought against a notice within the period allowed under the preceding sub-paragraph, then—

(a) in the case of an improvement notice, the bringing of the appeal shall have the effect of suspending the operation of the notice until the appeal is finally disposed of or, if the appeal is withdrawn, until the withdrawal of the appeal;

(b) in the case of a prohibition notice, the bringing of the appeal shall have the like effect if, but only if, on the application of the appellant the tribunal so directs (and then only from the giving of the direction).

(4) One or more assessors may be appointed for the purposes of any proceedings brought before an employment tribunal under this paragraph.

7 Restrictions on disclosure of information

(1) In this paragraph—

"relevant information" means information obtained by an inspector in pursuance of a requirement imposed under paragraph 2;

"relevant statutory provisions" means the provisions of Part 6 of the Transport Act 1968 and of any orders or regulations made under powers contained in that Part; and

"the recipient", in relation to any relevant information, means the person by whom that information was so obtained or to whom that information was so furnished, as the case may be.

(2) Subject to the following sub-paragraph, no relevant information shall be disclosed without the consent of the person by whom it was furnished.

(3) The preceding sub-paragraph shall not apply to—

(a) disclosure of information to a government department;

(b) without prejudice to paragraph (a), disclosure by the recipient of information to any person for the purpose of any function conferred on the recipient by or under any of the relevant statutory provisions or under these Regulations;

(c) without prejudice to paragraph (a), disclosure by the recipient of information to—

(i) an officer of a local authority who is authorised by that authority to receive it: or

(ii) a constable authorised by a chief officer of police to receive it; or

(d) disclosure by the recipient of information in a form calculated to prevent it from being identified as relating to a particular person or case.

(4) A person to whom information is disclosed in pursuance of sub-paragraph (3) shall not use the information for a purpose other than—

(a) in a case falling within sub-paragraph (3)(a), a purpose of a government department or local authority in connection with these Regulations or with the relevant statutory provisions, or any enactment whatsoever relating to working time;

(b) in the case of information given to a constable, the purposes of the police in connection with these Regulations, the relevant statutory provisions or any enactment relating to working time.

(5) A person shall not disclose any information obtained by him as a result of the exercise of any power conferred by paragraph 2 (including in particular any information with respect to any trade secret obtained by him in any premises entered by him by virtue of any such power) except—

(a) for the purposes of his functions; or
(b) for the purposes of any legal proceedings; or
(c) with the relevant consent.

In this sub-paragraph "the relevant consent" means, in the case of information furnished in pursuance of a requirement imposed under paragraph 2, the consent of the person who furnished it, and, in any other case, the consent of a person having responsibilities in relation to the premises where the information was obtained.

(6) Notwithstanding anything in sub-paragraph (5) an inspector shall, in circumstances in which it is necessary to do so for the purpose of assisting in keeping persons (or the representatives of persons) adequately informed about matters affecting their health, safety and welfare or working time, give to such persons or their representatives the following descriptions of information, that is to say—

(a) factual information obtained by him as mentioned in that sub-paragraph which relates to their working environment; and
(b) information with respect to any action which he has taken or proposes to take in or in connection with the performance of his functions in relation to their working environment;

and, where an inspector does as aforesaid, he shall give the like information to the employer of the first-mentioned persons.

(7) Notwithstanding anything in sub-paragraph (5), a person who has obtained such information as is referred to in that sub-paragraph may furnish to a person who appears to him to be likely to be a party to any civil proceedings arising out of any accident, occurrence, situation or other matter, a written statement of the relevant facts observed by him in the course of exercising any of the powers referred to in that sub-paragraph.

TRANSFER OF EMPLOYMENT (PENSION PROTECTION) REGULATIONS 2005

(SI 2005/649)

NOTES

Made: 10 March 2005.
Authority: Pensions Act 2004, ss 258(2)(c)(ii), (7), 315(2), 318(1).
Commencement: 6 April 2005.
See *Harvey* F(6).

[2.966]

1 Citation, commencement, application and interpretation

(1) These Regulations may be cited as the Transfer of Employment (Pension Protection) Regulations 2005 and shall come into force on 6th April 2005.

(2) These Regulations apply in the case of a person ("the employee") in relation to whom section 257 of the Act (conditions for pension protection) applies, that is to say a person who, in the circumstances described in subsection 9(1) of that section, ceases to be employed by the transferor of an undertaking or part of an undertaking and becomes employed by the transferee.

(3) In these Regulations "the Act" means the Pensions Act 2004.

[2.967]

2 Requirements concerning a transferee's pension scheme

(1) In a case where these Regulations apply, and the transferee is the employer in relation to a pension scheme which is not a money purchase scheme, that scheme complies with section 258(2)(c)(ii) of the Act (alternative standard for a scheme which is not a money purchase scheme) if it provides either—

(a) for members to be entitled to benefits the value of which equals or exceeds 6 per cent of pensionable pay for each year of employment together with the total amount of any contributions made by them, and, where members are required to make contributions to the scheme, for them to contribute at a rate which does not exceed 6 per cent of their pensionable pay; or
(b) for the transferee to make relevant contributions to the scheme on behalf of each employee of his who is an active member of it.

(2) In this regulation—

"pensionable pay" means that part of the remuneration payable to a member of a scheme by reference to which the amount of contributions and benefits are determined under the rules of the scheme.

[2.968]

3 Requirements concerning a transferee's pension contributions

(1) In a case where these Regulations apply, the transferee's pension contributions are relevant contributions for the purposes of section 258(2)(b) of the Act in the case of a money purchase scheme, section 258(3) to (5) of the Act in the case of a stakeholder pension scheme, and regulation 2(1)(b) above in the case of a scheme which is not a money purchase scheme, if—

(a) the contributions are made in respect of each period for which the employee is paid remuneration, provided that the employee also contributes to the scheme in respect of that period, and

(b) the amount contributed in respect of each such period is—

(i) in a case where the employee's contribution in respect of that period is less than 6 per cent of the remuneration paid to him, an amount at least equal to the amount of the employee's contribution;

(ii) in a case where the employee's contribution in respect of that period equals or exceeds 6 per cent of the remuneration paid to him, an amount at least equal to 6 per cent of that remuneration.

(2) In calculating the amount of an employee's remuneration for the purposes of paragraph (1)—

(a) only payments made in respect of basic pay shall be taken into account, and bonus, commission, overtime and similar payments shall be disregarded, and

(b) no account shall be taken of any deductions which are made in respect of tax, national insurance or pension contributions.

(3) In calculating the amount of a transferee's pension contributions for the purposes of paragraph (1) in the case of a scheme which is contracted-out by virtue of section 9 of the Pension Schemes Act 1993, minimum payments within the meaning of that Act shall be disregarded.

DISABILITY DISCRIMINATION (PUBLIC AUTHORITIES) (STATUTORY DUTIES) REGULATIONS 2005 (NOTE)

(SI 2005/2966)

[2.969]

NOTES

These Regulations were made on 21 October 2005 under the powers conferred by the Disability Discrimination Act 1995, ss 49D(1), (2), 67(2), (3). They came into force on 5 December 2005. These Regulations applied to England and Wales and, to the extent that the functions of bodies to which they applied extended to Scotland, also to Scotland. They imposed duties on the public authorities listed in Schedule 1 and 2 to the Regulations. Section 49D of the 1995 Act was repealed by the Equality Act 2010, s 211(2), Sch 27, Pt 1, as from 5 April 2011 (s 67 having already been repealed) and, accordingly, these Regulations lapsed on that date.

DISABILITY DISCRIMINATION (PUBLIC AUTHORITIES) (STATUTORY DUTIES) (SCOTLAND) REGULATIONS 2005 (NOTE)

(SSI 2005/565)

[2.970]

NOTES

These Regulations were made by the Scottish Ministers under the Disability Discrimination Act 1995, s 49D(3), (4) and came into force on 5 December 2005. The Regulations applied to the bodies listed in the Schedule which were within the jurisdiction of the Scottish Parliament. The equivalent Regulations for other bodies were the Disability Discrimination (Public Authorities) (Statutory Duties) Regulations 2005, SI 2005/2966 (noted *ante*). Section 49D of the 1995 Act was repealed by the Equality Act 2010, s 211(2), Sch 27, Pt 1, as from 5 April 2011 and, accordingly, these Regulations lapsed on that date.

REGISTER OF JUDGMENTS, ORDERS AND FINES REGULATIONS 2005

(SI 2005/3595)

NOTES

Made: 29 December 2005.

Authority: Courts Act 2003, ss 98(1)–(3), 108(6).

Commencement: 30 December 2005 (for the purposes of regs 1, 2, 4); 6 April 2006 (otherwise).

These Regulations are now included in this work because they have been amended to apply, inter alia, to judgments of employment tribunals as from 1 April 2009; see regs 8, 9A at **[2.977]**, **[2.978]**. The Regulations apply only to England and Wales (see the Courts Act 2003, s 111).

ARRANGEMENT OF REGULATIONS

[2.971]

1 Citation, commencement and duration

These Regulations may be cited as the Register of Judgments, Orders and Fines Regulations 2005.

[2.972]

2

These Regulations shall come into force—

(a) for the purposes of this regulation and regulations 1 and 4, on the day after the day on which these Regulations are made; and

(b) for all other purposes, on 6th April 2006.

NOTES

Note: despite the heading preceding reg 1 there is no indication in this regulation or in reg 1 that these Regulations have a specified duration. Cf the Register of Fines Regulations 2003, SI 2003/3184 which (by reg 1(2) thereof as amended by reg 4 of these Regulations) expired on 6 April 2006.

[2.973]

3 Interpretation

In these Regulations—

"the 1998 Rules" means the Civil Procedure Rules 1998;

"the Act" means the Courts Act 2003;

"Administrative Court" has the same meaning as in Part 54 of the 1998 Rules;

"amendment notice" means the notice given to the Registrar in accordance with regulation 21;

"applicable charge" means the charge fixed by the Lord Chancellor in accordance with section 98(4) of the Act, or in accordance with section 98(4) as applied by section 98(7)(b) of the Act;

"appropriate officer" means—

(a) in the case of the High Court or a county court, an officer of the court in which the judgment is entered [or with which a tribunal decision is filed];

(b) in the case of a registration under paragraph 38(1)(b) of Schedule 5 to the Act—

(i) where a fines officer exercises the power to register following service of a notice under paragraph 37(6)(b) of that Schedule, that officer; or

(ii) where a court exercises the power to register by virtue of paragraph 39(3) or (4) of that Schedule, an officer of that court;

(c) in respect of a liability order designated for the purposes of section 33(5) of the Child Support Act 1991, the Secretary of State;

"appropriate fee" means the fee prescribed under section 92(1) of the Act;

"certificate of satisfaction" means the certificate applied for under regulation 17;

"data protection principles" means the principles set out in Part 1 of Schedule 1 to the Data Protection Act 1998, as read subject to Part 2 of that Schedule and section 27(1) of that Act;

"debt" means the sum of money owed by virtue of a judgment, [administration order, fine or tribunal decision], and "debtor" means the individual, incorporated or unincorporated body liable to pay that sum;

"family proceedings" has the same meaning as in section 63 (interpretation) of the Family Law Act 1996;

"judgment" means any judgment or order of the court for a sum of money and, in respect of a county court, includes a liability order designated by the Secretary of State for the purposes of section 33(5) of the Child Support Act 1991;

"Local Justice Area" means the area specified in an order made under section 8(2) of the Act;

"Registrar" means—

(a) where the Register is kept by a body corporate in accordance with section 98(6) of the Act, that body corporate; or

(b) otherwise, the Lord Chancellor;

"the Register" means the register kept in accordance with section 98(1) of the Act;

"satisfied", in relation to a debt, means that the debt has been paid in full, and "satisfaction" is to be construed accordingly;

"Technology and Construction Court" has the same meaning as in Part 60 of the 1998 Rules;

["tribunal decision" includes an award].

NOTES

Words in square brackets in definition "appropriate officer" inserted, words in square brackets in definition "debt" substituted, and definition "tribunal decision" inserted, by the Register of Judgments, Orders and Fines (Amendment) Regulations 2009, SI 2009/474, regs 2, 3, as from 1 April 2009.

4 *(Amended the Register of Fines Regulations 2003, SI 2003/3184 (expired on 6 April 2006 in accordance with reg 1(2) thereof as amended by this regulation).)*

[2.974]

5 Performance of steps under these Regulations

Any step to be taken under these Regulations by the appropriate officer or the Registrar shall be taken—

(a) in respect of—

(i) the registration of judgments to which regulation 8(1)(a) applies; . . .

(ii) the registration of administration orders to which regulation 8(1)(b) applies; [and

(iii) the registration of tribunal decisions to which regulation 8(1)(d) applies],

within one working day;

(b) in respect of the registration of sums to which regulation 8(1)(c) applies, as soon as may be reasonably practicable.

NOTES

Word omitted from para (a)(i) revoked, and para (a)(iii) and the word immediately preceding it inserted, by the Register of Judgments, Orders and Fines (Amendment) Regulations 2009, SI 2009/474, regs 2, 4, as from 1 April 2009.

[2.975]

6 Manner, etc, in which the Register is to be kept

(1) Where the Registrar is a body corporate, the Register shall be kept in accordance with the terms of the agreement between the Lord Chancellor and that body.

(2) The terms of the agreement between the Lord Chancellor and the body corporate shall specify—

(a) the manner in which the Register is to be kept;

(b) the form of the Register; and

(c) the place at which the Register is to be kept.

[2.976]
7

Where the Registrar is not a body corporate, the Register shall be kept by the Lord Chancellor in such a manner and at such a place as he shall determine.

[2.977]
8 Registration of judgments, [administration orders, fines and tribunal decisions]

(1) The appropriate officer shall send to the Registrar a return of—
- (a) subject to regulation 9, every judgment entered in—
  - (i) the High Court; and
  - (ii) a county court;
- (b) every administration order made under section 112 of the County Courts Act 1984 (power of county courts to make administration orders);
- (c) every sum to be registered by virtue of paragraph 38(1)(b) of Schedule 5 to the Act (further steps available against defaulters)[;
- (d) subject to regulation 9A, every tribunal decision made by—
  - (i) the First-tier Tribunal;
  - (ii) the Upper Tribunal;
  - (iii) an employment tribunal; or
  - (iv) the Employment Appeal Tribunal,

  in pursuance of which a sum of money is payable].

(2) Following receipt of a return sent in accordance with paragraph (1), the Registrar shall record the details of the return as an entry in the Register.

NOTES

Regulation heading: words in square brackets substituted by the Register of Judgments, Orders and Fines (Amendment) Regulations 2009, SI 2009/474, regs 2, 5, as from 1 April 2009.

Para (1): sub-para (d) inserted by SI 2009/474, regs 2, 6, as from 1 April 2009.

9 *(Reg 9 (Exempt judgments—High Court and county courts) outside the scope of this work.)*

[2.978]
[9A Exempt tribunal decisions

Regulation 8(1)(d) does not apply until, pursuant to rule 70.5(2A)(a) of the 1998 Rules—
- (a) in the case of a tribunal decision made by the First-tier Tribunal or the Upper Tribunal, a copy of the tribunal decision is filed with the High Court or a county court; or
- (b) in the case of a tribunal decision made by an employment tribunal or the Employment Appeal Tribunal, a copy of the tribunal decision is filed with a county court.]

NOTES

Commencement: 1 April 2009.

Inserted by the Register of Judgments, Orders and Fines (Amendment) Regulations 2009, SI 2009/474, regs 2, 7, as from 1 April 2009 (subject to transitional provisions in reg 17 of those Regulations in relation to steps taken before 6 April 2009 to enforce a decision).

[2.979]
10 Information contained in the appropriate officer's return

The return sent by virtue of regulation 8(1) shall contain details of—
- (a) the full name and address of the debtor in respect of whom the entry in the Register is to be made;
- (b) if the entry is to be in respect of an individual, that individual's date of birth (where known);
- (c) the amount of the debt;
- (d) the case number;
- (e) in respect of a return sent by virtue of regulation 8(1)(a) regarding a liability order designated under section 33(5) of the Child Support Act 1991, the date of the judgment;
- (f) in respect of all other returns sent by virtue of regulation 8(1)(a)—
  - (i) the name of the court which made the judgment; and
  - (ii) the date of the judgment;
- (g) in respect of a return sent by virtue of regulation 8(1)(b)—
  - (i) the name of the court which made the administration order; and
  - (ii) the date of the order;
- (h) in respect of a return sent by virtue of regulation 8(1)(c)—
  - (i) the Local Justice Area which imposed the fine; and
  - (ii) the date of conviction;
- [(i) in respect of a return sent by virtue of regulation 8(1)(d)—

(i) the name of the court with which the tribunal decision was filed in accordance with regulation 9A; and
(ii) the date on which the tribunal decision was filed with the court].

NOTES

Para (i) inserted by the Register of Judgments, Orders and Fines (Amendment) Regulations 2009, SI 2009/474, regs 2, 8, as from 1 April 2009.

[2.980]
11 Cancellation or endorsement of entries relating to judgments of the High Court or a county court [or tribunal decisions]

(1) This regulation applies where an entry in the Register is one to which regulation 8(1)(a) applies (judgments entered in the High Court or a county court) [or to which regulation 8(1)(d) applies (tribunal decisions)].

(2) Where it comes to the attention of the appropriate officer that—
(a) the debt to which the entry relates has been satisfied one month or less from the date of the judgment [or the date on which the tribunal decision was filed with the court in accordance with regulation 9A;]
(b) the judgment to which the entry relates has been set aside or reversed[; or
(c) the tribunal decision to which the entry relates has been set aside],

that officer shall send a request to the Registrar to cancel the entry.

(3) Where it comes to the attention of the appropriate officer that the debt has been satisfied more than one month from the date of the judgment [or the date on which the tribunal decision was filed with the court in accordance with regulation 9A], that officer shall send a request to the Registrar to endorse the entry as to the satisfaction of the debt.

NOTES

Regulation heading, paras (1), (3): words in square brackets inserted by the Register of Judgments, Orders and Fines (Amendment) Regulations 2009, SI 2009/474, regs 2, 9, 10(a), (c), as from 1 April 2009.

Para (2): words in first pair of square brackets substituted, and words in second pair of square brackets inserted, by SI 2009/474, regs 2, 10(b), as from 1 April 2009.

12, 13 *(Reg 12 (Endorsement of entries relating to county court administration orders) and reg 13 (Cancellation or endorsement of entries relating to fines) outside the scope of this work.)*

[2.981]
14 Cancellation of entries in the Register—additional provisions

Where an entry in the Register is endorsed in accordance with regulations 11(3) or 13(3) and the appropriate officer is later of the opinion that the debt was satisfied one month or less from—
(a) the date of the judgment or administration order; . . .
(b) the date on which the fine was registered[; or
(c) the date on which the tribunal decision was filed with the court in accordance with regulation 9A],

that officer shall send a request to the Registrar to cancel the relevant entry.

NOTES

Word omitted from para (a) revoked, and para (c) and the word immediately preceding it inserted, by the Register of Judgments, Orders and Fines (Amendment) Regulations 2009, SI 2009/474, regs 2, 11, as from 1 April 2009.

[2.982]
15

Where—
(a) it comes to the attention of the appropriate officer that an administrative error has been made; and
(b) he is of the opinion that the error is such to require the cancellation of an entry in the Register,

that officer shall send a request to the Registrar to cancel the relevant entry.

[2.983]
16 Cancellation and endorsement of entries in the Register by the Registrar

Following receipt of a request under—
(a) regulation 11(2), 13(2), 14 or 15 (debt due satisfied in one month or less, etc), the Registrar shall cancel the relevant entry;
(b) regulation 11(3) or 13(3) (debt due satisfied in more than one month), the Registrar shall endorse the relevant entry as to the satisfaction of the debt;
(c) regulation 12(2) (administration order has been varied, revoked or debt has been satisfied), the Registrar shall endorse the relevant entry accordingly.

[2.984]
17 Application for, and issue of, a certificate of satisfaction

(1) A registered debtor may apply to the appropriate officer for a certificate ("certificate of satisfaction") as to the satisfaction of the debt.

(2) An application under paragraph (1) shall be—
- (a) made in writing; and
- (b) accompanied by the appropriate fee.

[2.985]
18

(1) In the case of an application for a certificate of satisfaction in respect of an entry in the Register to which regulation 8(1)(a) applies (judgments entered in the High Court or a county court) [or to which regulation 8(1)(d) applies (tribunal decisions)], the application under regulation 17(1) shall be accompanied by—
- (a) sufficient evidence that the debt has been satisfied;
- (b) a statement that the registered debtor has taken reasonable steps to obtain such evidence, but has been unable to do so; or
- (c) a statement that the registered debtor believes such evidence is already in the possession of the appropriate officer.

(2) For the purposes of paragraph (1)(a), sufficient evidence that the debt has been satisfied includes a signed statement by the creditor to that effect.

(3) Where paragraph (1)(b) applies, the appropriate officer shall send notice of the registered debtor's application under regulation 17(1) to the creditor together with a request that the creditor confirms within one month of the date of the notice whether the debt has been satisfied.

(4) For the purposes of paragraph (1)(c), evidence which is already in the possession of the appropriate officer includes where—
- (a) the debt has been paid as the result of court enforcement proceedings taken under Part 70 of the 1998 Rules;
- (b) payment of the debt has otherwise been made to the court.

NOTES

Para (1): words in square brackets inserted by the Register of Judgments, Orders and Fines (Amendment) Regulations 2009, SI 2009/474, regs 2, 12, as from 1 April 2009.

[2.986]
19

Where an application has been made under regulation 17(1) and—
- (a) the appropriate officer is of the opinion that the debt has been satisfied; or
- (b) a notice has been sent in accordance with regulation 18(3) and the creditor has not responded within the time limit provided,

the appropriate officer shall issue a certificate of satisfaction to the registered debtor.

[2.987]
20 Amendment of the Register in respect of the amount registered

(1) Where it comes to the attention of the appropriate officer that the amount liable to be paid differs from the amount entered in the Register, due to—
- (a) the issue of a final costs certificate; . . .
- (b) an increase in the amount of the debt[; or
- (c) in the case of an entry to which regulation 8(1)(d) applies, a tribunal decision on appeal],

the appropriate officer shall send a return to the Registrar to amend the Register to reflect the revised amount.

(2) The return sent in accordance with paragraph (1) shall contain the same information as prescribed by regulation 10 in respect of the return sent in accordance with regulation 8(1).

(3) Following receipt of a return sent in accordance with this regulation, the Registrar shall amend the Register accordingly.

NOTES

Para (1): word omitted from sub-para (a) revoked, and sub-para (c) and the word immediately preceding it inserted, by the Register of Judgments, Orders and Fines (Amendment) Regulations 2009, SI 2009/474, regs 2, 13, as from 1 April 2009.

[2.988]
21 Correction of registered details of the judgment, [administration order, fine or tribunal decision]

(1) Where it comes to the attention of a registered debtor that the entry in the Register relating to his debt is inaccurate with respect to the details of the judgment, [administration order, fine or tribunal decision], that debtor may give notice to the Registrar requiring an amendment to be made ("amendment notice").

(2) The amendment notice shall—

(a) identify the entry which is alleged to be inaccurate; and
(b) state the amendment which is required.

NOTES

The words in square brackets in the heading preceding this regulation, and in para (1), were substituted by the Register of Judgments, Orders and Fines (Amendment) Regulations 2009, SI 2009/474, regs 2, 14, 15, as from 1 April 2009.

[2.989]
22

Following receipt of an amendment notice in respect of an entry in the Register, the Registrar shall request that the appropriate officer verify the details of that entry.

[2.990]
23

Following receipt of a request for verification under regulation 22, the appropriate officer shall—

(a) check the information contained in the entry against the official records; and
(b) reply to the request, where applicable stating any necessary amendment.

[2.991]
24

(1) Where the appropriate officer informs the Registrar that the entry is inaccurate and requests an amendment, the Registrar shall amend the Register to rectify the inaccuracy.

(2) Following an amendment to the Register in accordance with paragraph (1), the Registrar shall inform the registered debtor of the action taken and the reasons for having taken that action.

[2.992]
25

Where the appropriate officer informs the Registrar that the entry is accurate, the Registrar shall inform the registered debtor that no action is to be taken and the reasons for not taking any action.

[2.993]
26 Removal of entries in the Register

The Registrar shall remove any entry in the Register registered—

(a) by virtue of regulation 8(1)(a) or (b), six years from the date of the judgment;
(b) by virtue of regulation 8(1)(c), five years from the date of conviction[;
(c) by virtue of regulation 8(1)(d), six years from the date on which the tribunal decision was filed with the court in accordance with regulation 9A].

NOTES

Para (c) inserted by the Register of Judgments, Orders and Fines (Amendment) Regulations 2009, SI 2009/474, regs 2, 16, as from 1 April 2009.

[2.994]
27 Searches of the Register

(1) Subject to regulation 29, searches of a section of the Register may be carried out on payment of the applicable charge relevant to the type and method of search.

(2) The types of search which may be carried out are—

(a) at a stated address, against a named individual or unincorporated body;
(b) against a named incorporated body;
(c) a periodical search—
    (i) relating to a named court;
    (ii) within a named county; or
    (iii) with the agreement of the Registrar, against such other criteria as may be requested.

[2.995]
28 Certified copies

On receipt of—

(a) a written request for a certified copy of an entry in the Register; and
(b) the applicable charge for such a request,

the Registrar shall provide a copy of that entry, certified by him as a true and complete copy of the entry in the Register.

[2.996]

29 Refusal of access to the Register and appeals

(1) The Registrar may—

(a) refuse a person access to the Register, or to a part of the Register; and

(b) refuse to carry out a search of the Register,

if he believes that the purpose for which access has been requested or for which the results of the search will be used contravenes—

(i) any of the data protection principles; or

(ii) the provisions of any other enactment.

(2) Where a refusal is made under paragraph (1), the person who has been denied access to, or has been denied a search of, the Register may appeal to a county court against the decision of the Registrar.

TRANSFER OF UNDERTAKINGS (PROTECTION OF EMPLOYMENT) REGULATIONS 2006

(SI 2006/246)

NOTES

Made: 6 February 2006.

Authority: European Communities Act 1972, s 2(2); Employment Relations Act 1999, s 38.

Commencement: 6 April 2006 (subject to the transitional provisions in reg 21 at **[2.1016]**).

These Regulations represent the current domestic implementation of Council Directive 2001/23/EC at **[3.347]**, re-enacting the original Directive 77/187/EEC together with later amendments. They revoke and replace the Transfer of Undertakings (Protection of Employment) Regulations 1981, SI 1981/1794, subject to transitional provisions and savings in reg 21 *post*.

Employment Appeal Tribunal: an appeal lies to the Employment Appeal Tribunal on a question of law arising from any decision of, or arising in any proceedings before, an employment tribunal under or by virtue of these Regulations; see reg 16(2) of these Regulations at **[2.1012]**.

Conciliation: employment tribunal proceedings and claims which could be the subject of employment tribunal proceedings under regulation 15 are proceedings to which the Employment Tribunals Act 1996, s 18 applies; see reg 16(1) of these Regulations at **[2.1012]**.

The rights conferred by these Regulations are "relevant statutory rights" for the purposes of the Employment Rights Act 1996, s 104 (dismissal on grounds of assertion of statutory right); see s 104(4)(e) of that Act at **[1.907]**.

These Regulations have been applied with modifications in a variety of specific circumstances by the following:

(a) the Industrial Training Act 1982, s 3B (application to the transfer of the activities of an industrial training board);

(b) the Ordnance Factories and Military Services Act 1984, s 4, Sch 2, para 2 (application to personnel transferred as a result of a transfer scheme made under s 1(1) of that Act);

(c) the Dockyard Services Act 1986, s 1(4)–(9) (application to transfers of dockyard undertakings under that Act);

(d) the Dartford-Thurrock Crossing Act 1988, Sch 5 (application to any transfer of an undertaking effected, or treated as effected, by s 14 of that Act);

(e) the Atomic Weapons Establishment Act 1991, s 2 (application to the transfer of certain staff employed in the Atomic Weapons Establishment);

(f) the Export and Investment Guarantees Act 1991, s 9 (application to transfers of property, rights or liabilities under a scheme under s 8 of the 1991 Act);

(g) the Ports Act 1991, Sch 1, para 5 (application to certain transfers of port undertakings made under s 2 of that Act);

(h) the Energy Act 2004, s 38(8), Sch 5, para 10 (application to a transfer of an undertaking or part of an undertaking in accordance with a nuclear transfer scheme or a modification agreement under that Act);

(i) the Criminal Proceedings etc (Reform) (Scotland) Act 2007, s 65(4) (application to a scheme for the transfer of the employment to the Scottish Administration of clerks, assessors and other staff of the district court to which an order under s 64(1) of that Act applies);

(j) the Personal Accounts Delivery Authority Winding Up Order 2010, SI 2010/911 (application to the transfer of property, rights and liabilities from the Personal Accounts Delivery Authority to the National Employment Savings Trust Corporation);

(k) the Office of the Renewable Fuels Agency (Dissolution and Transfer of Functions) Order 2011, SI 2011/493, art 6 (application to the transfer of functions of the Office of the Renewable Fuels Agency);

(l) the Local Government (Wales) Measure 2011, s 166(6) (application to transfers of staff etc as a result of local authority amalgamation orders made under that Measure);

(m) Postal Services Act 2011, ss 8(7), 64(4), 73(2), Schs 1, 11 (application to transfer schemes made under the 2011 Act);

(n) the Local Better Regulation Office (Dissolution and Transfer of Functions, Etc) Order 2012, SI 2012/246, art 6 (application to the dissolution of the LBRO and the transfer of functions etc to the Secretary of State);

(o) the Transfer of Undertakings (Protection of Employment) (RCUK Shared Services Centre Limited) Regulations 2012, SI 2012/2413 (transfer of employees of the Department for Business, Innovation and Skills to RCUK Shared Services Centre Limited);

(p) the Transfer of Undertakings (Protection of Employment) (Transfers of Public Health Staff) Regulations 2013, SI 2013/278 at **[2.1654]** (transfers from bodies listed in the Schedule to the Regulations).

As to the application of these Regulations to certain individual financial institutions, see the Orders made under the Banking (Special Provisions) Act 2008 and the Banking Act 2009.

In addition, the Transfer of Undertakings (Protection of Employment) Regulations 1981, SI 1981/1794 which were revoked and replaced by these Regulations were applied by the following: (i) the Coal Industry Act 1994, s 12(8), Sch 2, para 7 (application to any transfer of any undertaking or part of an undertaking in accordance with a restructuring scheme or a modification agreement under Sch 2, that Act); (ii) the Transfer of Undertakings (Protection of Employment) (Rent Officer Service) Regulations 1999, SI 1999/2511 (application to the transfer of the rent officer service from local authorities to the Secretary of State); (iii) the Transfer of Undertakings (Protection of Employment) (Greater London Authority) Order 2000, SI 2000/686 (application to transfers of staff etc under the Greater London Authority Act 1999, ss 408, 409); (iv) the Transfer of Undertakings (Protection of Employment) (Transfer to OFCOM) Regulations 2003, SI 2003/2715 (application to the transfer of those in employment with the Broadcasting Standards Commission, the Independent Television Commission, the Radio Authority, the Radiocommunications Agency and the Director General of Telecommunications when their functions were transferred to the Office of Communications under the Communications Act 2003).

See *Harvey* F.

ARRANGEMENT OF REGULATIONS

[2.997]

1 Citation, commencement and extent

(1) These Regulations may be cited as the Transfer of Undertakings (Protection of Employment) Regulations 2006.

(2) These Regulations shall come into force on 6 April 2006.

(3) These Regulations shall extend to Northern Ireland, except where otherwise provided.

[2.998]

2 Interpretation

(1) In these Regulations—

"assigned" means assigned other than on a temporary basis;

"collective agreement", "collective bargaining" and "trade union" have the same meanings respectively as in the 1992 Act;

"contract of employment" means any agreement between an employee and his employer determining the terms and conditions of his employment;

references to "contractor" in regulation 3 shall include a sub-contractor;

"employee" means any individual who works for another person whether under a contract of service or apprenticeship or otherwise but does not include anyone who provides services under a contract for services and references to a person's employer shall be construed accordingly;

"insolvency practitioner" has the meaning given to the expression by Part XIII of the Insolvency Act 1986;

references to "organised grouping of employees" shall include a single employee;

"recognised" has the meaning given to the expression by section 178(3) of the 1992 Act;

"relevant transfer" means a transfer or a service provision change to which these Regulations apply in accordance with regulation 3 and "transferor" and "transferee" shall be construed accordingly and in the case of a service provision change falling within regulation 3(1)(b), "the transferor" means the person who carried out the activities prior to the service provision change and "the transferee" means the person who carries out the activities as a result of the service provision change;

"the 1992 Act" means the Trade Union and Labour Relations (Consolidation) Act 1992;

"the 1996 Act" means the Employment Rights Act 1996;

"the 1996 Tribunals Act" means the Employment Tribunals Act 1996;

"the 1981 Regulations" means the Transfer of Undertakings (Protection of Employment) Regulations 1981.

(2) For the purposes of these Regulations the representative of a trade union recognised by an employer is an official or other person authorised to carry on collective bargaining with that employer by that trade union.

(3) In the application of these Regulations to Northern Ireland the Regulations shall have effect as set out in Schedule 1.

[2.999]

3 A relevant transfer

(1) These Regulations apply to—

(a) a transfer of an undertaking, business or part of an undertaking or business situated immediately before the transfer in the United Kingdom to another person where there is a transfer of an economic entity which retains its identity;

(b) a service provision change, that is a situation in which—

(i) activities cease to be carried out by a person ("a client") on his own behalf and are carried out instead by another person on the client's behalf ("a contractor");

(ii) activities cease to be carried out by a contractor on a client's behalf (whether or not those activities had previously been carried out by the client on his own behalf) and are carried out instead by another person ("a subsequent contractor") on the client's behalf; or

(iii) activities cease to be carried out by a contractor or a subsequent contractor on a client's behalf (whether or not those activities had previously been carried out by the client on his own behalf) and are carried out instead by the client on his own behalf,

and in which the conditions set out in paragraph (3) are satisfied.

(2) In this regulation "economic entity" means an organised grouping of resources which has the objective of pursuing an economic activity, whether or not that activity is central or ancillary.

(3) The conditions referred to in paragraph (1)(b) are that—

(a) immediately before the service provision change—

(i) there is an organised grouping of employees situated in Great Britain which has as its principal purpose the carrying out of the activities concerned on behalf of the client;

(ii) the client intends that the activities will, following the service provision change, be carried out by the transferee other than in connection with a single specific event or task of short-term duration; and

(b) the activities concerned do not consist wholly or mainly of the supply of goods for the client's use.

(4) Subject to paragraph (1), these Regulations apply to—

(a) public and private undertakings engaged in economic activities whether or not they are operating for gain;

(b) a transfer or service provision change howsoever effected notwithstanding—

(i) that the transfer of an undertaking, business or part of an undertaking or business is governed or effected by the law of a country or territory outside the United Kingdom or that the service provision change is governed or effected by the law of a country or territory outside Great Britain;

(ii) that the employment of persons employed in the undertaking, business or part transferred or, in the case of a service provision change, persons employed in the organised grouping of employees, is governed by any such law;

(c) a transfer of an undertaking, business or part of an undertaking or business (which may also be a service provision change) where persons employed in the undertaking, business or part transferred ordinarily work outside the United Kingdom.

(5) An administrative reorganisation of public administrative authorities or the transfer of administrative functions between public administrative authorities is not a relevant transfer.

(6) A relevant transfer—

(a) may be effected by a series of two or more transactions; and

(b) may take place whether or not any property is transferred to the transferee by the transferor.

(7) Where, in consequence (whether directly or indirectly) of the transfer of an undertaking, business or part of an undertaking or business which was situated immediately before the transfer in the United Kingdom, a ship within the meaning of the Merchant Shipping Act 1995 registered in

the United Kingdom ceases to be so registered, these Regulations shall not affect the right conferred by section 29 of that Act (right of seamen to be discharged when ship ceases to be registered in the United Kingdom) on a seaman employed in the ship.

[2.1000]

4 Effect of relevant transfer on contracts of employment

(1) Except where objection is made under paragraph (7), a relevant transfer shall not operate so as to terminate the contract of employment of any person employed by the transferor and assigned to the organised grouping of resources or employees that is subject to the relevant transfer, which would otherwise be terminated by the transfer, but any such contract shall have effect after the transfer as if originally made between the person so employed and the transferee.

(2) Without prejudice to paragraph (1), but subject to paragraph (6), and regulations 8 and 15(9), on the completion of a relevant transfer—

(a) all the transferor's rights, powers, duties and liabilities under or in connection with any such contract shall be transferred by virtue of this regulation to the transferee; and

(b) any act or omission before the transfer is completed, of or in relation to the transferor in respect of that contract or a person assigned to that organised grouping of resources or employees, shall be deemed to have been an act or omission of or in relation to the transferee.

(3) Any reference in paragraph (1) to a person employed by the transferor and assigned to the organised grouping of resources or employees that is subject to a relevant transfer, is a reference to a person so employed immediately before the transfer, or who would have been so employed if he had not been dismissed in the circumstances described in regulation 7(1), including, where the transfer is effected by a series of two or more transactions, a person so employed and assigned or who would have been so employed and assigned immediately before any of those transactions.

(4) Subject to regulation 9, in respect of a contract of employment that is, or will be, transferred by paragraph (1), any purported variation of the contract shall be void if the sole or principal reason for the variation is—

(a) the transfer itself; or

(b) a reason connected with the transfer that is not an economic, technical or organisational reason entailing changes in the workforce.

(5) Paragraph (4) shall not prevent the employer and his employee, whose contract of employment is, or will be, transferred by paragraph (1), from agreeing a variation of that contract if the sole or principal reason for the variation is—

(a) a reason connected with the transfer that is an economic, technical or organisational reason entailing changes in the workforce; or

(b) a reason unconnected with the transfer.

(6) Paragraph (2) shall not transfer or otherwise affect the liability of any person to be prosecuted for, convicted of and sentenced for any offence.

(7) Paragraphs (1) and (2) shall not operate to transfer the contract of employment and the rights, powers, duties and liabilities under or in connection with it of an employee who informs the transferor or the transferee that he objects to becoming employed by the transferee.

(8) Subject to paragraphs (9) and (11), where an employee so objects, the relevant transfer shall operate so as to terminate his contract of employment with the transferor but he shall not be treated, for any purpose, as having been dismissed by the transferor.

(9) Subject to regulation 9, where a relevant transfer involves or would involve a substantial change in working conditions to the material detriment of a person whose contract of employment is or would be transferred under paragraph (1), such an employee may treat the contract of employment as having been terminated, and the employee shall be treated for any purpose as having been dismissed by the employer.

(10) No damages shall be payable by an employer as a result of a dismissal falling within paragraph (9) in respect of any failure by the employer to pay wages to an employee in respect of a notice period which the employee has failed to work.

(11) Paragraphs (1), (7), (8) and (9) are without prejudice to any right of an employee arising apart from these Regulations to terminate his contract of employment without notice in acceptance of a repudiatory breach of contract by his employer.

[2.1001]

5 Effect of relevant transfer on collective agreements

Where at the time of a relevant transfer there exists a collective agreement made by or on behalf of the transferor with a trade union recognised by the transferor in respect of any employee whose contract of employment is preserved by regulation 4(1) above, then—

(a) without prejudice to sections 179 and 180 of the 1992 Act (collective agreements presumed to be unenforceable in specified circumstances) that agreement, in its application in relation to the employee, shall, after the transfer, have effect as if made by or on behalf of the transferee with that trade union, and accordingly anything done under or in connection with it, in its application in relation to the employee, by or in relation to the transferor before the transfer, shall, after the transfer, be deemed to have been done by or in relation to the transferee; and

(b) any order made in respect of that agreement, in its application in relation to the employee, shall, after the transfer, have effect as if the transferee were a party to the agreement.

[2.1002]
6 Effect of relevant transfer on trade union recognition

(1) This regulation applies where after a relevant transfer the transferred organised grouping of resources or employees maintains an identity distinct from the remainder of the transferee's undertaking.

(2) Where before such a transfer an independent trade union is recognised to any extent by the transferor in respect of employees of any description who in consequence of the transfer become employees of the transferee, then, after the transfer—

(a) the trade union shall be deemed to have been recognised by the transferee to the same extent in respect of employees of that description so employed; and

(b) any agreement for recognition may be varied or rescinded accordingly.

[2.1003]
7 Dismissal of employee because of relevant transfer

(1) Where either before or after a relevant transfer, any employee of the transferor or transferee is dismissed, that employee shall be treated for the purposes of Part X of the 1996 Act (unfair dismissal) as unfairly dismissed if the sole or principal reason for his dismissal is—

(a) the transfer itself; or

(b) a reason connected with the transfer that is not an economic, technical or organisational reason entailing changes in the workforce.

(2) This paragraph applies where the sole or principal reason for the dismissal is a reason connected with the transfer that is an economic, technical or organisational reason entailing changes in the workforce of either the transferor or the transferee before or after a relevant transfer.

(3) Where paragraph (2) applies—

(a) paragraph (1) shall not apply;

(b) without prejudice to the application of section 98(4) of the 1996 Act (test of fair dismissal), the dismissal shall, for the purposes of sections 98(1) and 135 of that Act (reason for dismissal), be regarded as having been for redundancy where section 98(2)(c) of that Act applies, or otherwise for a substantial reason of a kind such as to justify the dismissal of an employee holding the position which that employee held.

(4) The provisions of this regulation apply irrespective of whether the employee in question is assigned to the organised grouping of resources or employees that is, or will be, transferred.

(5) Paragraph (1) shall not apply in relation to the dismissal of any employee which was required by reason of the application of section 5 of the Aliens Restriction (Amendment) Act 1919 to his employment.

(6) Paragraph (1) shall not apply in relation to a dismissal of an employee if the application of section 94 of the 1996 Act to the dismissal of the employee is excluded by or under any provision of the 1996 Act, the 1996 Tribunals Act or the 1992 Act.

NOTES

Aliens Restriction (Amendment) Act 1919: s 5 was repealed by the Merchant Shipping Act 1970, Sch 5, as from 1 August 1995 (see the Merchant Shipping Act 1970 (Commencement No 12) Order 1995, SI 1995/1426).

[2.1004]
8 Insolvency

(1) If at the time of a relevant transfer the transferor is subject to relevant insolvency proceedings paragraphs (2) to (6) apply.

(2) In this regulation "relevant employee" means an employee of the transferor—

(a) whose contract of employment transfers to the transferee by virtue of the operation of these Regulations; or

(b) whose employment with the transferor is terminated before the time of the relevant transfer in the circumstances described in regulation 7(1).

(3) The relevant statutory scheme specified in paragraph (4)(b) (including that sub-paragraph as applied by paragraph 5 of Schedule 1) shall apply in the case of a relevant employee irrespective of the fact that the qualifying requirement that the employee's employment has been terminated is not met and for those purposes the date of the transfer shall be treated as the date of the termination and the transferor shall be treated as the employer.

(4) In this regulation the "relevant statutory schemes" are—

(a) Chapter VI of Part XI of the 1996 Act;
(b) Part XII of the 1996 Act.

(5) Regulation 4 shall not operate to transfer liability for the sums payable to the relevant employee under the relevant statutory schemes.

(6) In this regulation "relevant insolvency proceedings" means insolvency proceedings which have been opened in relation to the transferor not with a view to the liquidation of the assets of the transferor and which are under the supervision of an insolvency practitioner.

(7) Regulations 4 and 7 do not apply to any relevant transfer where the transferor is the subject of bankruptcy proceedings or any analogous insolvency proceedings which have been instituted with a view to the liquidation of the assets of the transferor and are under the supervision of an insolvency practitioner.

[2.1005]

9 Variations of contract where transferors are subject to relevant insolvency proceedings

(1) If at the time of a relevant transfer the transferor is subject to relevant insolvency proceedings these Regulations shall not prevent the transferor or transferee (or an insolvency practitioner) and appropriate representatives of assigned employees agreeing to permitted variations.

(2) For the purposes of this regulation "appropriate representatives" are—
- (a) if the employees are of a description in respect of which an independent trade union is recognised by their employer, representatives of the trade union; or
- (b) in any other case, whichever of the following employee representatives the employer chooses—
  - (i) employee representatives appointed or elected by the assigned employees (whether they make the appointment or election alone or with others) otherwise than for the purposes of this regulation, who (having regard to the purposes for, and the method by which they were appointed or elected) have authority from those employees to agree permitted variations to contracts of employment on their behalf;
  - (ii) employee representatives elected by assigned employees (whether they make the appointment or election alone or with others) for these particular purposes, in an election satisfying requirements identical to those contained in regulation 14 except those in regulation 14(1)(d).

(3) An individual may be an appropriate representative for the purposes of both this regulation and regulation 13 provided that where the representative is not a trade union representative he is either elected by or has authority from assigned employees (within the meaning of this regulation) and affected employees (as described in regulation 13(1)).

(4) . . .

(5) Where assigned employees are represented by non-trade union representatives—
- (a) the agreement recording a permitted variation must be in writing and signed by each of the representatives who have made it or, where that is not reasonably practicable, by a duly authorised agent of that representative; and
- (b) the employer must, before the agreement is made available for signature, provide all employees to whom it is intended to apply on the date on which it is to come into effect with copies of the text of the agreement and such guidance as those employees might reasonably require in order to understand it fully.

(6) A permitted variation shall take effect as a term or condition of the assigned employee's contract of employment in place, where relevant, of any term or condition which it varies.

(7) In this regulation—

"assigned employees" means those employees assigned to the organised grouping of resources or employees that is the subject of a relevant transfer;

"permitted variation" is a variation to the contract of employment of an assigned employee where—
- (a) the sole or principal reason for it is the transfer itself or a reason connected with the transfer that is not an economic, technical or organisational reason entailing changes in the workforce; and
- (b) it is designed to safeguard employment opportunities by ensuring the survival of the undertaking, business or part of the undertaking or business that is the subject of the relevant transfer;

"relevant insolvency proceedings" has the meaning given to the expression by regulation 8(6).

NOTES

Para (4): amends the Trade Union and Labour Relations (Consolidation) Act 1992, s 168 at **[1.432]**.

[2.1006]
10 Pensions

(1) Regulations 4 and 5 shall not apply—

(a) to so much of a contract of employment or collective agreement as relates to an occupational pension scheme within the meaning of the Pension Schemes Act 1993; or

(b) to any rights, powers, duties or liabilities under or in connection with any such contract or subsisting by virtue of any such agreement and relating to such a scheme or otherwise arising in connection with that person's employment and relating to such a scheme.

(2) For the purposes of paragraphs (1) and (3), any provisions of an occupational pension scheme which do not relate to benefits for old age, invalidity or survivors shall not be treated as being part of the scheme.

(3) An employee whose contract of employment is transferred in the circumstances described in regulation 4(1) shall not be entitled to bring a claim against the transferor for—

(a) breach of contract; or

(b) constructive unfair dismissal under section 95(1)(c) of the 1996 Act,

arising out of a loss or reduction in his rights under an occupational pension scheme in consequence of the transfer, save insofar as the alleged breach of contract or dismissal (as the case may be) occurred prior to the date on which these Regulations took effect.

[2.1007]
11 Notification of Employee Liability Information

(1) The transferor shall notify to the transferee the employee liability information of any person employed by him who is assigned to the organised grouping of resources or employees that is the subject of a relevant transfer—

(a) in writing; or

(b) by making it available to him in a readily accessible form.

(2) In this regulation and in regulation 12 "employee liability information" means—

(a) the identity and age of the employee;

(b) those particulars of employment that an employer is obliged to give to an employee pursuant to section 1 of the 1996 Act;

(c) information of any—

(i) disciplinary procedure taken against an employee;

(ii) grievance procedure taken by an employee,

within the previous two years, in circumstances where [a Code of Practice issued under Part IV of the Trade Union and Labour Relations Act 1992 which relates exclusively or primarily to the resolution of disputes applies];

(d) information of any court or tribunal case, claim or action—

(i) brought by an employee against the transferor, within the previous two years;

(ii) that the transferor has reasonable grounds to believe that an employee may bring against the transferee, arising out of the employee's employment with the transferor; and

(e) information of any collective agreement which will have effect after the transfer, in its application in relation to the employee, pursuant to regulation 5(a).

(3) Employee liability information shall contain information as at a specified date not more than fourteen days before the date on which the information is notified to the transferee.

(4) The duty to provide employee liability information in paragraph (1) shall include a duty to provide employee liability information of any person who would have been employed by the transferor and assigned to the organised grouping of resources or employees that is the subject of a relevant transfer immediately before the transfer if he had not been dismissed in the circumstances described in regulation 7(1), including, where the transfer is effected by a series of two or more transactions, a person so employed and assigned or who would have been so employed and assigned immediately before any of those transactions.

(5) Following notification of the employee liability information in accordance with this regulation, the transferor shall notify the transferee in writing of any change in the employee liability information.

(6) A notification under this regulation shall be given not less than fourteen days before the relevant transfer or, if special circumstances make this not reasonably practicable, as soon as reasonably practicable thereafter.

(7) A notification under this regulation may be given—

(a) in more than one instalment;

(b) indirectly, through a third party.

NOTES

Para (2): words in square brackets in sub-para (c) substituted by the Transfer of Undertakings (Protection of Employment) (Amendment) Regulations 2009, SI 2009/592, reg 2(1), (2), as from 6 April 2009.

[2.1008]

12 Remedy for failure to notify employee liability information

(1) On or after a relevant transfer, the transferee may present a complaint to an employment tribunal that the transferor has failed to comply with any provision of regulation 11.

(2) An employment tribunal shall not consider a complaint under this regulation unless it is presented—

(a) before the end of the period of three months beginning with the date of the relevant transfer;

(b) within such further period as the tribunal considers reasonable in a case where it is satisfied that it was not reasonably practicable for the complaint to be presented before the end of that period of three months.

(3) Where an employment tribunal finds a complaint under paragraph (1) well-founded, the tribunal—

(a) shall make a declaration to that effect; and

(b) may make an award of compensation to be paid by the transferor to the transferee.

(4) The amount of the compensation shall be such as the tribunal considers just and equitable in all the circumstances, subject to paragraph (5), having particular regard to—

(a) any loss sustained by the transferee which is attributable to the matters complained of; and

(b) the terms of any contract between the transferor and the transferee relating to the transfer under which the transferor may be liable to pay any sum to the transferee in respect of a failure to notify the transferee of employee liability information.

(5) Subject to paragraph (6), the amount of compensation awarded under paragraph (3) shall be not less than £500 per employee in respect of whom the transferor has failed to comply with a provision of regulation 11, unless the tribunal considers it just and equitable, in all the circumstances, to award a lesser sum.

(6) In ascertaining the loss referred to in paragraph (4)(a) the tribunal shall apply the same rule concerning the duty of a person to mitigate his loss as applies to any damages recoverable under the common law of England and Wales, Northern Ireland or Scotland, as applicable.

(7) Section 18 of the 1996 Tribunals Act (conciliation) shall apply to the right conferred by this regulation and to proceedings under this regulation as it applies to the rights conferred by that Act and the employment tribunal proceedings mentioned in that Act.

[2.1009]

13 Duty to inform and consult representatives

(1) In this regulation and regulations 14 and 15 references to affected employees, in relation to a relevant transfer, are to any employees of the transferor or the transferee (whether or not assigned to the organised grouping of resources or employees that is the subject of a relevant transfer) who may be affected by the transfer or may be affected by measures taken in connection with it; and references to the employer shall be construed accordingly.

(2) Long enough before a relevant transfer to enable the employer of any affected employees to consult the appropriate representatives of any affected employees, the employer shall inform those representatives of—

(a) the fact that the transfer is to take place, the date or proposed date of the transfer and the reasons for it;

(b) the legal, economic and social implications of the transfer for any affected employees;

(c) the measures which he envisages he will, in connection with the transfer, take in relation to any affected employees or, if he envisages that no measures will be so taken, that fact; and

(d) if the employer is the transferor, the measures, in connection with the transfer, which he envisages the transferee will take in relation to any affected employees who will become employees of the transferee after the transfer by virtue of regulation 4 or, if he envisages that no measures will be so taken, that fact.

[(2A) Where information is to be supplied under paragraph (2) by an employer—

(a) this must include suitable information relating to the use of agency workers (if any) by that employer; and

(b) "suitable information relating to the use of agency workers" means—

(i) the number of agency workers working temporarily for and under the supervision and direction of the employer;

(ii) the parts of the employer's undertaking in which those agency workers are working; and

(iii) the type of work those agency workers are carrying out.]

(3) For the purposes of this regulation the appropriate representatives of any affected employees are—

(a) if the employees are of a description in respect of which an independent trade union is recognised by their employer, representatives of the trade union; or

(b) in any other case, whichever of the following employee representatives the employer chooses—
   (i) employee representatives appointed or elected by the affected employees otherwise than for the purposes of this regulation, who (having regard to the purposes for, and the method by which they were appointed or elected) have authority from those employees to receive information and to be consulted about the transfer on their behalf;
   (ii) employee representatives elected by any affected employees, for the purposes of this regulation, in an election satisfying the requirements of regulation 14(1).

(4) The transferee shall give the transferor such information at such a time as will enable the transferor to perform the duty imposed on him by virtue of paragraph (2)(d).

(5) The information which is to be given to the appropriate representatives shall be given to each of them by being delivered to them, or sent by post to an address notified by them to the employer, or (in the case of representatives of a trade union) sent by post to the trade union at the address of its head or main office.

(6) An employer of an affected employee who envisages that he will take measures in relation to an affected employee, in connection with the relevant transfer, shall consult the appropriate representatives of that employee with a view to seeking their agreement to the intended measures.

(7) In the course of those consultations the employer shall—
(a) consider any representations made by the appropriate representatives; and
(b) reply to those representations and, if he rejects any of those representations, state his reasons.

(8) The employer shall allow the appropriate representatives access to any affected employees and shall afford to those representatives such accommodation and other facilities as may be appropriate.

(9) If in any case there are special circumstances which render it not reasonably practicable for an employer to perform a duty imposed on him by any of paragraphs (2) to (7), he shall take all such steps towards performing that duty as are reasonably practicable in the circumstances.

(10) Where—
(a) the employer has invited any of the affected employee to elect employee representatives; and
(b) the invitation was issued long enough before the time when the employer is required to give information under paragraph (2) to allow them to elect representatives by that time,

the employer shall be treated as complying with the requirements of this regulation in relation to those employees if he complies with those requirements as soon as is reasonably practicable after the election of the representatives.

(11) If, after the employer has invited any affected employees to elect representatives, they fail to do so within a reasonable time, he shall give to any affected employees the information set out in paragraph (2).

(12) The duties imposed on an employer by this regulation shall apply irrespective of whether the decision resulting in the relevant transfer is taken by the employer or a person controlling the employer.

NOTES

Para (2A): inserted by the Agency Workers Regulations 2010, SI 2010/93, reg 25, Sch 2, Pt 2, paras 28, 29, as from 1 October 2011.

[2.1010]

14 Election of employee representatives

(1) The requirements for the election of employee representatives under regulation 13(3) are that—
(a) the employer shall make such arrangements as are reasonably practicable to ensure that the election is fair;
(b) the employer shall determine the number of representatives to be elected so that there are sufficient representatives to represent the interests of all affected employees having regard to the number and classes of those employees;
(c) the employer shall determine whether the affected employees should be represented either by representatives of all the affected employees or by representatives of particular classes of those employees;
(d) before the election the employer shall determine the term of office as employee representatives so that it is of sufficient length to enable information to be given and consultations under regulation 13 to be completed;
(e) the candidates for election as employee representatives are affected employees on the date of the election;
(f) no affected employee is unreasonably excluded from standing for election;

(g) all affected employees on the date of the election are entitled to vote for employee representatives;

(h) the employees entitled to vote may vote for as many candidates as there are representatives to be elected to represent them or, if there are to be representatives for particular classes of employees, may vote for as many candidates as there are representatives to be elected to represent their particular class of employee;

(i) the election is conducted so as to secure that—

   (i) so far as is reasonably practicable, those voting do so in secret; and

   (ii) the votes given at the election are accurately counted.

(2) Where, after an election of employee representatives satisfying the requirements of paragraph (1) has been held, one of those elected ceases to act as an employee representative and as a result any affected employees are no longer represented, those employees shall elect another representative by an election satisfying the requirements of paragraph (1)(a), (e), (f) and (i).

[2.1011]

15 Failure to inform or consult

(1) Where an employer has failed to comply with a requirement of regulation 13 or regulation 14, a complaint may be presented to an employment tribunal on that ground—

(a) in the case of a failure relating to the election of employee representatives, by any of his employees who are affected employees;

(b) in the case of any other failure relating to employee representatives, by any of the employee representatives to whom the failure related;

(c) in the case of failure relating to representatives of a trade union, by the trade union; and

(d) in any other case, by any of his employees who are affected employees.

(2) If on a complaint under paragraph (1) a question arises whether or not it was reasonably practicable for an employer to perform a particular duty or as to what steps he took towards performing it, it shall be for him to show—

(a) that there were special circumstances which rendered it not reasonably practicable for him to perform the duty; and

(b) that he took all such steps towards its performance as were reasonably practicable in those circumstances.

(3) If on a complaint under paragraph (1) a question arises as to whether or not an employee representative was an appropriate representative for the purposes of regulation 13, it shall be for the employer to show that the employee representative had the necessary authority to represent the affected employees.

(4) On a complaint under paragraph (1)(a) it shall be for the employer to show that the requirements in regulation 14 have been satisfied.

(5) On a complaint against a transferor that he had failed to perform the duty imposed upon him by virtue of regulation 13(2)(d) or, so far as relating thereto, regulation 13(9), he may not show that it was not reasonably practicable for him to perform the duty in question for the reason that the transferee had failed to give him the requisite information at the requisite time in accordance with regulation 13(4) unless he gives the transferee notice of his intention to show that fact; and the giving of the notice shall make the transferee a party to the proceedings.

(6) In relation to any complaint under paragraph (1), a failure on the part of a person controlling (directly or indirectly) the employer to provide information to the employer shall not constitute special circumstances rendering it not reasonably practicable for the employer to comply with such a requirement.

(7) Where the tribunal finds a complaint against a transferee under paragraph (1) well-founded it shall make a declaration to that effect and may order the transferee to pay appropriate compensation to such descriptions of affected employees as may be specified in the award.

(8) Where the tribunal finds a complaint against a transferor under paragraph (1) well-founded it shall make a declaration to that effect and may—

(a) order the transferor, subject to paragraph (9), to pay appropriate compensation to such descriptions of affected employees as may be specified in the award; or

(b) if the complaint is that the transferor did not perform the duty mentioned in paragraph (5) and the transferor (after giving due notice) shows the facts so mentioned, order the transferee to pay appropriate compensation to such descriptions of affected employees as may be specified in the award.

(9) The transferee shall be jointly and severally liable with the transferor in respect of compensation payable under sub-paragraph (8)(a) or paragraph (11).

(10) An employee may present a complaint to an employment tribunal on the ground that he is an employee of a description to which an order under paragraph (7) or (8) relates and that—

(a) in respect of an order under paragraph (7), the transferee has failed, wholly or in part, to pay him compensation in pursuance of the order;

(b) in respect of an order under paragraph (8), the transferor or transferee, as applicable, has failed, wholly or in part, to pay him compensation in pursuance of the order.

(11) Where the tribunal finds a complaint under paragraph (10) well-founded it shall order the transferor or transferee as applicable to pay the complainant the amount of compensation which it finds is due to him.

(12) An employment tribunal shall not consider a complaint under paragraph (1) or (10) unless it is presented to the tribunal before the end of the period of three months beginning with—

(a) in respect of a complaint under paragraph (1), the date on which the relevant transfer is completed; or

(b) in respect of a complaint under paragraph (10), the date of the tribunal's order under paragraph (7) or (8),

or within such further period as the tribunal considers reasonable in a case where it is satisfied that it was not reasonably practicable for the complaint to be presented before the end of the period of three months.

NOTES

Conciliation: employment tribunal proceedings and claims which could be the subject of employment tribunal proceedings under this regulation are proceedings to which the Employment Tribunals Act 1996, s 18 applies; see reg 16 of these Regulations at **[2.1012]**.

[2.1012]

16 Failure to inform or consult: supplemental

(1) Section 205(1) of the 1996 Act (complaint to be sole remedy for breach of relevant rights) and section 18 of the 1996 Tribunals Act (conciliation) shall apply to the rights conferred by regulation 15 and to proceedings under this regulation as they apply to the rights conferred by those Acts and the employment tribunal proceedings mentioned in those Acts.

(2) An appeal shall lie and shall lie only to the Employment Appeal Tribunal on a question of law arising from any decision of, or arising in any proceedings before, an employment tribunal under or by virtue of these Regulations; and section 11(1) of the Tribunals and Inquiries Act 1992 (appeals from certain tribunals to the High Court) shall not apply in relation to any such proceedings.

(3) "Appropriate compensation" in regulation 15 means such sum not exceeding thirteen weeks' pay for the employee in question as the tribunal considers just and equitable having regard to the seriousness of the failure of the employer to comply with his duty.

(4) Sections 220 to 228 of the 1996 Act shall apply for calculating the amount of a week's pay for any employee for the purposes of paragraph (3) and, for the purposes of that calculation, the calculation date shall be—

(a) in the case of an employee who is dismissed by reason of redundancy (within the meaning of sections 139 and 155 of the 1996 Act) the date which is the calculation date for the purposes of any entitlement of his to a redundancy payment (within the meaning of those sections) or which would be that calculation date if he were so entitled;

(b) in the case of an employee who is dismissed for any other reason, the effective date of termination (within the meaning of sections 95(1) and (2) and 97 of the 1996 Act) of his contract of employment;

(c) in any other case, the date of the relevant transfer.

NOTES

Conciliation: see the note to reg 15 at **[2.1011]**.

[2.1013]

17 Employers' Liability Compulsory Insurance

(1) Paragraph (2) applies where—

(a) by virtue of section 3(1)(a) or (b) of the Employers' Liability (Compulsory Insurance) Act 1969 ("the 1969 Act"), the transferor is not required by that Act to effect any insurance; or

(b) by virtue of section 3(1)(c) of the 1969 Act, the transferor is exempted from the requirement of that Act to effect insurance.

(2) Where this paragraph applies, on completion of a relevant transfer the transferor and the transferee shall be jointly and severally liable in respect of any liability referred to in section 1(1) of the 1969 Act, in so far as such liability relates to the employee's employment with the transferor.

[2.1014]

18 Restriction on contracting out

Section 203 of the 1996 Act (restrictions on contracting out) shall apply in relation to these Regulations as if they were contained in that Act, save for that section shall not apply in so far as these Regulations provide for an agreement (whether a contract of employment or not) to exclude or limit the operation of these Regulations.

19 (*Amends the Employment Rights Act 1996, s 104 at* **[1.907]**.)

[2.1015]

20 Repeals, revocations and amendments

(1) Subject to regulation 21, the 1981 Regulations are revoked.

(2) Section 33 of, and paragraph 4 of Schedule 9 to, the Trade Union Reform and Employment Rights Act 1993 are repealed.

(3) Schedule 2 (consequential amendments) shall have effect.

[2.1016]

21 Transitional provisions and savings

(1) These Regulations shall apply in relation to—

(a) a relevant transfer that takes place on or after 6 April 2006;

(b) a transfer or service provision change, not falling within sub-paragraph (a), that takes place on or after 6 April 2006 and is regarded by virtue of any enactment as a relevant transfer.

(2) The 1981 Regulations shall continue to apply in relation to—

(a) a relevant transfer (within the meaning of the 1981 Regulations) that took place before 6 April 2006;

(b) a transfer, not falling within sub-paragraph (a), that took place before 6 April 2006 and is regarded by virtue of any enactment as a relevant transfer (within the meaning of the 1981 Regulations).

(3) In respect of a relevant transfer that takes place on or after 6 April 2006, any action taken by a transferor or transferee to discharge a duty that applied to them under regulation 10 or 10A of the 1981 Regulations shall be deemed to satisfy the corresponding obligation imposed by regulations 13 and 14 of these Regulations, insofar as that action would have discharged those obligations had the action taken place on or after 6 April 2006.

(4) The duty on a transferor to provide a transferee with employee liability information shall not apply in the case of a relevant transfer that takes place on or before 19 April 2006.

(5) Regulations 13, 14, 15 and 16 shall not apply in the case of a service provision change that is not also a transfer of an undertaking, business or part of an undertaking or business that takes place on or before 4 May 2006.

(6) The repeal of paragraph 4 of Schedule 9 to the Trade Union Reform and Employment Rights Act 1993 does not affect the continued operation of that paragraph so far as it remains capable of having effect.

SCHEDULES 1 AND 2

(Sch 1 (Application of the Regulations to Northern Ireland) outside the scope of this work; Sch 2 contains consequential amendments only and, in so far as relevant to this work, these have been incorporated at the appropriate place.)

OCCUPATIONAL AND PERSONAL PENSION SCHEMES (CONSULTATION BY EMPLOYERS AND MISCELLANEOUS AMENDMENT) REGULATIONS 2006

(SI 2006/349)

NOTES

Made: 15 February 2006.

Authority: Pensions Act 2004, ss 10(5)(a), 259(1), (2), 260(1), 261(2), (4), 286(1), (3)(g), 315(2), (3), (5), 318(1), (4)(a), (5).

Commencement: 6 February 2006 (reg 22); 6 April 2006 (otherwise).

Conciliation: employment tribunal proceedings and claims which could be the subject of employment tribunal proceedings under paras 4 or 8 of the Schedule to these Regulations are proceedings to which the Employment Tribunals Act 1996, s 18 applies; see s 18(1)(q) of that Act at **[1.706]**

Employment Appeal Tribunal: an appeal lies to the Employment Appeal Tribunal on any question of law arising from any decision of, or in any proceedings before, an employment tribunal under or by virtue of the Schedule to these Regulations; see the Employment Tribunals Act 1996, s 21(1)(r) at **[1.713]**.

See *Harvey* CII(6).

ARRANGEMENT OF REGULATIONS

Introductory

Part 2 Statutory Instruments

Introductory

[2.1017]
1 Citation, commencement and extent

(1) These Regulations may be cited as the Occupational and Personal Pension Schemes (Consultation by Employers and Miscellaneous Amendment) Regulations 2006.

(2) Subject to paragraph (3), these Regulations shall come into force on 6th April 2006.

(3) Regulation 22 shall come into force on the day after the day on which these Regulations are made.

(4) Regulation 22 extends to Northern Ireland.

[2.1018]
2 Interpretation

In these Regulations—

"active member"—

(a) in relation to an occupational pension scheme, has the meaning given by section 124 of the Pensions Act 1995 (interpretation), and
(b) in relation to a personal pension scheme, means any member in respect of whom employer contributions fall to be paid;

"affected members" has the meaning given by regulation 7(4);

"employer contributions", in relation to an occupational or personal pension scheme, means contributions payable by or on behalf of the employer in relation to the scheme on his own account (but in respect of one or more employees);

"member contributions", in relation to an occupational or personal pension scheme, means contributions, other than voluntary contributions, by or on behalf of active members of the scheme which are payable out of deductions from the member's earnings;

"listed change" has the meaning given by regulation 6(2);

"multi-employer scheme" has the meaning given by section 307 of the Pensions Act 2004 (modification of Act in relation to certain categories of schemes);

"personal pension scheme" has the meaning given by regulation 3(3);

"prospective member"—

(a) in relation to an occupational pension scheme, means any person who, under the terms of his contract of service or the rules of the scheme—
   (i) is able, at his own option, to become a member of the scheme,
   (ii) will become so able if he continues in the same employment for a sufficiently long period,
   (iii) will be admitted to the scheme automatically unless he makes an election not to become a member, or
   (iv) may be admitted to it subject to the consent of his employer;
(b) in relation to a personal pension scheme, means any person who, under the terms of his contract of service, is eligible if he becomes a member of the scheme for employer contributions to be paid in respect of him;

"the Regulator" means the Pensions Regulator established under section 1 of the Pensions Act 2004 (the Pensions Regulator); and

"relevant employer" has the meaning given by regulation 3(2).

Application of Regulations

[2.1019]

3 Application

(1) These Regulations apply to—

(a) in the case of an occupational pension scheme which is not a multi-employer scheme—

(i) any relevant employer, and

(ii) if there is a relevant employer, the trustees or managers of the scheme;

(b) in the case of a multi-employer scheme in relation to which there are one or more relevant employers—

(i) each relevant employer,

(ii) the trustees or managers of the scheme, and

(iii) any other person who, under the rules of the scheme, has the power to make a listed change affecting the scheme; and

(c) in the case of a personal pension scheme where direct payment arrangements exist in respect of one or more members of the scheme who are his employees, a relevant employer.

[(2) For the purposes of these Regulations "relevant employer" means—

(a) an employer employing in Great Britain at least the number of employees specified in paragraph (2A); and

(b) in the case of—

(i) an occupational pension scheme, an employer in relation to the scheme other than one who is excluded by regulation 4, and

(ii) a personal pension scheme, an employer in relation to the scheme other than one who is excluded by regulation 5.

(2A) The number of employees referred to in paragraph (2)(a) is—

(a) 150 from 6th April 2006 to 5th April 2007,

(b) 100 from 6th April 2007 to 5th April 2008, and

(c) 50 from 6th April 2008 onwards.

(2B) For the purposes of paragraph (2)(a)—

(a) the number of people employed by an employer is to be determined using the same method of calculation as is set out in regulation 4 of the Information and Consultation of Employees Regulations 2004 (calculation of number of employees), but

(b) references in that regulation to the previous twelve months are to be taken as references to the period of twelve months ending with the date of the proposal to make a listed change to which regulation 6 of these Regulations applies.]

(3) In these Regulations references to a personal pension scheme are to a personal pension scheme falling within paragraph (1)(c).

NOTES

Paras (2), (2A), (2B): substituted (for the original para (2)) by the Occupational and Personal Pension Schemes (Miscellaneous Amendments) Regulations 2006, SI 2006/778, reg 10(1), (2).

[2.1020]

4 Excluded employers: occupational pension schemes

(1) This regulation excludes—

(a) any employer in relation to a public service pension scheme;

(b) any employer in relation to a small occupational pension scheme;

(c) any employer in relation to an occupational pension scheme with fewer than two members;

(d) any employer in relation to an occupational pension scheme which is an employer-financed retirement benefits scheme;

(e) any employer in relation to an unregistered occupational pension scheme which has its main administration outside the [EEA states]; and

(f) . . .

(2), (3) . . .

(4) In this regulation—

"employer-financed retirement benefits scheme" has the meaning given by section 393A of the Income Tax (Earnings and Pensions) Act 2003 (employer-financed retirement benefits scheme);

"public service pension scheme" has the meaning given by section 1(1) of the Pension Schemes Act 1993;

"small occupational pension scheme" means—

Part 2 Statutory Instruments

(a) a scheme with fewer than twelve members where all of the members are trustees of the scheme and either—
   (i) the provisions of the scheme provide that [any decision made by the trustees is made by the unanimous agreement of] the trustees who are members of the scheme, or
   (ii) the scheme has a trustee who is independent in relation to the scheme for the purposes of section 23 of the Pensions Act 1995 (power to appoint independent trustees) and is registered in the register maintained by the Regulator in accordance with regulations made under subsection 9(4) of that section;

(b) a scheme with fewer than twelve members [where a company is the sole trustee] of the scheme, and all the members of the scheme are directors of the company and either—
   (i) the provisions of the scheme provide that any decision made by the company in its capacity as trustee [is made by the unanimous agreement of the directors] who are members of the scheme, or
   (ii) [one of the directors of the company] is independent in relation to the scheme for the purposes of section 23 of the Pensions Act 1995 and is registered in the register maintained by the Regulator in accordance with regulations made under subsection 9(4) of that section; and

"unregistered occupational pension scheme" means an occupational pension scheme which is not registered under section 153 of the Finance Act 2004 (registration of pension schemes).

NOTES

Para (1): words in square brackets in sub-para (e) substituted by the Occupational Pension Schemes (EEA States) Regulations 2007, SI 2007/3014, reg 2(b), Schedule, para 9; sub-para (f) revoked by the Occupational and Personal Pension Schemes (Miscellaneous Amendments) Regulations 2006, SI 2006/778, reg 10(1), (3).

Paras (2), (3): revoked by SI 2006/778, reg 10(3).

Para (4): words in square brackets in definition "small occupational pension scheme" substituted by the Occupational and Personal Pension Schemes (Miscellaneous Amendments) Regulations 2007, SI 2007/814, reg 19.

[2.1021]

[5 Excluded employers: personal pension schemes

This regulation excludes any employer in relation to a personal pension scheme where no employer contributions fall to be paid towards the scheme.]

NOTES

Substituted by the Occupational and Personal Pension Schemes (Miscellaneous Amendments) Regulations 2006, SI 2006/778, reg 10(1), (4).

Restriction on Decision-Making Pending Completion of Consultation

[2.1022]

6 Consultation required before decisions to make listed changes affecting schemes

(1) No person falling within regulation 3(1) may decide to make a listed change that affects an occupational or personal pension scheme unless such consultation as is required by regulation 7(3) has been carried out.

(2) For the purposes of these Regulations, a change affecting an occupational or personal pension scheme is a "listed change" if—
   (a) in relation to an occupational pension scheme, it is listed in regulation 8, or
   (b) in relation to a personal pension scheme, it is listed in regulation 9,

and it is not excluded by virtue of regulation 10.

(3) Paragraph (1) does not require consultation to be carried out in any of the four cases described in paragraphs (4) to (7).

[(4) The first case is where the active or prospective members of the scheme to whom—
   (a) a listed change mentioned in regulation 8(1)(h) relates were notified before 6th April 2012 of the proposal to make that change, or
   (b) any other listed change relates were notified before 6th April 2006 of the proposal to make that change.]

(5) The second case is where, in relation to an occupational pension scheme—
   (a) consultation has already been carried out under these Regulations in respect of a proposal to prevent the future accrual of benefits, as described in regulation 8(1)(c), and
   (b) there is a further proposal as a result of that consultation to make a decision to reduce the rate of such accrual, as described in regulation 8(3)(d).

(6) The third case is where, in relation to an occupational pension scheme—
   (a) consultation has already been carried out under these Regulations in respect of a proposal to remove the liability to make employer contributions, as described in regulation 8(1)(d), and

(b) there is a further proposal as a result of that consultation to make a decision to reduce such contributions, as described in regulation 8(2).

(7) The fourth case is where, in relation to a personal pension scheme—

(a) consultation has already been carried out under these Regulations in respect of a proposal to cease employer contributions, as described in regulation 9(a), and

(b) there is a further proposal as a result of that consultation to make a decision to reduce such contributions, as described in regulation 9(b).

NOTES

Para (4): substituted by the Pensions (Institute and Faculty of Actuaries and Consultation by Employers—Amendment) Regulations 2012, SI 2012/692, reg 2(1), (2), as from 6 April 2012.

[2.1023]

7 Notifications to employers and duty to consult

(1) Any person falling within regulation 3(1) who proposes to make a listed change affecting an occupational or personal pension scheme must give written notice of that change to each employer in relation to the scheme.

(2) Paragraph (1) does not apply—

(a) in any of the four cases described in regulation 6(4) to (7), or

(b) where the person proposing the change is a relevant employer in relation to—

(i) an occupational pension scheme which is not a multi-employer scheme, or

(ii) a personal pension scheme[, or

(c) where the person proposing the change employs all the affected members].

[(3) A relevant employer must consult about the listed change in accordance with regulations 11 to 16 if—

(a) it employs all the affected members, or

(b) its employees appear to it to include affected members and it is a relevant employer who—

(i) has been notified under paragraph (1), or

(ii) falls within paragraph (2)(b).]

(4) For the purposes of these Regulations "affected members", in relation to a proposal to make a listed change affecting an occupational or personal pension scheme, means the active or prospective members of the scheme to whom the listed change relates.

NOTES

Para (2): sub-para (c) and the word immediately preceding it inserted by the Occupational and Personal Pension Schemes (Miscellaneous Amendments) Regulations 2011, SI 2011/672, reg 7(a), as from 6 April 2011.

Para (3): substituted by SI 2011/672, reg 7(b), as from 6 April 2011.

[2.1024]

8 Listed changes: occupational pension schemes

(1) Listed changes that affect occupational pension schemes are—

(a) to increase the normal pension age specified in the scheme rules for members or members of a particular description;

(b) to prevent new members, or new members of a particular description, from being admitted to the scheme;

(c) to prevent the future accrual of benefits under the scheme for or in respect of members or members of a particular description;

(d) to remove the liability to make employer contributions towards the scheme in respect of members or members of a particular description;

(e) to introduce member contributions in any circumstances in which no such contributions were previously payable;

(f) to make any increase in member contributions by or on behalf of members or members of a particular description;

(g) to make any change specified in paragraph (2) or (3);

[(h) to change the rate at which—

(i) pensions in payment under the scheme are increased, or

(ii) pensions or other benefits payable under the scheme are revalued,

but only where that change would be, or would be likely to be, less generous to members or members of a particular description].

(2) A listed change affecting only money purchase benefits is to make any reduction in the amount of employer contributions towards the scheme in respect of members or members of a particular description.

(3) Listed changes affecting only benefits which are not money purchase benefits are—

(a) to change to money purchase benefits some or all of the benefits that may be provided under the scheme to or in respect of members or members of a particular description;

(b) to change, in whole or in part, the basis for determining the rate of future accrual of benefits under the scheme for or in respect of members or members of a particular description;

(c) to modify the scheme under section 229(2) of the Pensions Act 2004 (matters requiring agreement of the employer) so as to reduce the rate of future accrual of benefits under the scheme for or in respect of members or members of a particular description;

(d) to make any other reduction in the rate of future accrual of benefit under the scheme for or in respect of members or members of a particular description.

[(e) to change what elements of pay constitute pensionable earnings, or to change the proportion of or limit the amount of any element of pay that forms part of pensionable earnings, for or in respect of members or members of a particular description].

(4) "Normal pension age" has the meaning given by section 180 of the Pension Schemes Act 1993 (normal pension age).

[(5) "Pensionable earnings" means the earnings by reference to which pension benefits are calculated, and an "element of pay" includes basic salary, a pay rise, an overtime payment, and a bonus payment.]

NOTES

Para (1): sub-para (h) inserted by the Pensions (Institute and Faculty of Actuaries and Consultation by Employers—Amendment) Regulations 2012, SI 2012/692, reg 2(1), (3), as from 6 April 2012.

Para (3): sub-para (e) added by the Occupational and Personal Pension Schemes (Miscellaneous Amendments) Regulations 2010, SI 2010/499, reg 7(1), (2), as from 6 April 2010.

Para (5): added by SI 2010/499, reg 7(1), (3), as from 6 April 2010.

[2.1025]

9 Listed changes: personal pension schemes

Listed changes that affect personal pension schemes are—

(a) to cease employer contributions towards the scheme in respect of members or members of a particular description;

(b) to make any reduction in the amount of employer contributions towards the scheme in respect of members or members of a particular description;

(c) to make any increase in member contributions by or on behalf of members or members of a particular description.

[2.1026]

10 Listed changes: exclusions

(1) For the purposes of regulations 8 and 9, no account is to be taken of any change which—

(a) is made for the purposes of complying with a statutory provision,

(b) is made for the purposes of complying with a determination made by the Regulator, or

(c) has no lasting effect on a person's rights to be admitted to a scheme or on the benefits that may be provided under it.

(2) No change which is—

(a) a regulated modification within the meaning of the subsisting rights provisions, and

(b) subject to the requirements of those provisions,

falls within regulation 8.

(3) "Statutory provision" means a provision comprised in—

(a) an Act of Parliament or subordinate legislation made under such an Act, whenever passed or made,

(b) an Act of the Scottish Parliament or subordinate legislation made under such an Act, whenever passed or made.

(4) "Subsisting rights provisions" has the meaning given by section 67 of the Pensions Act 1995 (the subsisting rights provisions).

Information Provision and Consultation

[2.1027]

11 Requirement to provide information

(1) In relation to a proposal to make a listed change affecting an occupational or personal pension scheme, each relevant employer to whom regulation 7(3) applies must provide information about the proposal to—

(a) such of his employees as appear to him to be affected members of the scheme, and

(b) any representatives of such members who are to be consulted under regulation 12(2)(a) or (3) or 13(2).

(2) The information provided under paragraph (1) must—

(a) be in writing,

(b) be provided before the start of consultation under regulation 12 or 13,

(c) describe the listed change and state what effects it would (or would be likely to) have on the scheme and its members,
(d) be accompanied by any relevant background information,
(e) indicate the timescale on which measures giving effect to the change are proposed to be introduced, and
(f) be given in such fashion and with such content as are appropriate to enable, in particular, representatives of affected members to consider, conduct a study of, and give their views to the employer on, the impact of the listed change on such members.

[2.1028]
12 Consultation under existing arrangements

(1) If arrangements specified in paragraph (2) or (3) exist in relation to his employees, each relevant employer to whom regulation 7(3) applies must consult about a listed change in accordance with such one or more of those arrangements as he may choose.

(2) The specified arrangements are arrangements under which employees appearing to the employer to be affected members—
(a) are represented by—
(i) in the case of employees of a description in respect of which an independent trade union is recognised by the employer, the representatives of the trade union,
(ii) in the case of employees of a description which has elected or appointed information and consultation representatives, those representatives, or
(iii) where there exists one or more pre-existing agreements which apply to any of the employees, any representatives identified in accordance with such agreement or agreements; or
(b) are to be consulted directly in accordance with the terms of a negotiated agreement or a pre-existing agreement.

(3) In any case where—
(a) an election of representatives as described in regulation 13(2) has taken place before any arrangements referred to in paragraph (2) are made, and
(b) the interests of affected members are represented by such representatives,
the specified arrangements also include arrangements for consultation of those representatives.

(4) "Independent trade union" and "recognised", in relation to an independent trade union, have the same meaning as in the Trade Union and Labour Relations (Consolidation) Act 1992.

(5) "Information and consultation representatives" and "negotiated agreement" have the same meaning as in the Information and Consultation of Employees Regulations 2004.

(6) "Pre-existing agreement"—
(a) means an agreement between an employer and his employees or their representatives which satisfies the conditions set out in regulation 8(1)(a) to (d) of the Information and Consultation of Employees Regulations 2004 and which has not been superseded, but
(b) does not include an agreement concluded in accordance with regulations 17 or 42 to 45 of the Transnational Information and Consultation of Employees Regulations 1999 or a negotiated agreement.

[2.1029]
13 Consultation in cases not covered by regulation 12

(1) This regulation applies to a relevant employer to whom regulation 7(3) applies if (and only if) any of the employees who appear to the employer to be affected members are not covered by consultation arrangements referred to in regulation 12.

(2) Where, for the purposes of engaging in consultations under these Regulations, representatives of any affected members have been elected in an election which satisfies the requirements of regulation 14(1), the relevant employer must consult with those representatives about a listed change.

(3) If the interests of any affected members are not represented by representatives who are consulted under paragraph (2), the relevant employer must also consult directly with those members.

(4) If no representatives have been elected as described in paragraph (2), the relevant employer must consult directly with the affected members about a listed change.

(5) Consultation under this regulation—
(a) is required only in relation to the affected members falling within paragraph (1), and
(b) is additional to any consultation in relation to other affected members which is required by regulation 12.

[2.1030]

14 Election of representatives

(1) The requirements of this paragraph are that—

(a) the employer must make such arrangements as are reasonably practical to ensure that the election is fair;

(b) the employer must determine the number of representatives to be elected so that there are sufficient representatives to represent the interests of active members and the interests of prospective members;

(c) the employer must determine whether the active and prospective members should be represented by representatives of all such members or by representatives of particular descriptions of such members;

(d) before the election the employer must determine the term of office as representative of active and prospective members;

(e) the candidates for election must be active or prospective members of the scheme on the date of the election;

(f) no active or prospective member may unreasonably be excluded from standing for election;

(g) all active or prospective members on the date of the election are entitled to vote for member representatives;

(h) the members entitled to vote may vote for as many candidates as there are representatives to be elected to represent them or, if there are to be classes of representative for particular descriptions of member, may vote for as many candidates as there are representatives to be elected to represent their particular description of member;

(i) the election is conducted so as to secure that—

(i) so far as is reasonably practicable, those voting do so in secret, and

(ii) the votes given at the election are accurately counted.

(2) Where, after an election of representatives satisfying the requirements of paragraph (1) has been held—

(a) one of those elected ceases to act as a representative, and

(b) the active or prospective members (or any description of them) are no longer represented,

those members must elect another representative by an election satisfying the requirements of paragraph (1)(a), (e), (f) and (i).

(3) The relevant employer must from time to time review the number of representatives determined under paragraph (1)(b) and the number of representatives elected must be adjusted accordingly (whether by members electing one or more other representatives by an election satisfying the requirements of paragraph (1)(a), (e), (f) and (i), by not holding an election under paragraph (2) or otherwise).

[2.1031]

15 Conduct of consultation

(1) Each relevant employer who carries out a consultation must make such arrangements with respect to the persons to be consulted as appear to him to secure that, so far as is reasonably practicable, the consultation covers all affected members.

(2) In the course of consultation, the relevant employer and any person consulted are under a duty to work in a spirit of co-operation, taking into account the interests of both sides.

(3) At the start of any consultation required by these Regulations, the relevant employer must notify the persons to be consulted of any date set for the end of the consultation or for the submission of written comments.

(4) An appropriate period must be allowed for carrying out the consultation which in any event must not be less than 60 days.

(5) If no responses to the consultation are received before the end of the period allowed for the consultation in accordance with paragraphs (3) and (4), the consultation is to be regarded as complete.

[2.1032]

16 End of consultation

(1) Where the relevant employer who carries out a consultation is not the person who proposed the listed change ("P"), the relevant employer must, as soon as reasonably practicable after the consultation is complete—

(a) report to P on the views (if any) which were expressed to the relevant employer otherwise than in writing,

(b) where the responses include written comments, forward those comments to P, and

(c) in any case where no responses were received, notify P accordingly.

(2) In a case falling within paragraph (1), P must take reasonable steps to satisfy himself that each consultation required by these Regulations in relation to the scheme was carried out in accordance with regulations 11 to 15.

(3) After the end of the period allowed for the consultation, the person who proposed the listed change must consider the responses (if any) received in the course of consultation before making his decision as to whether or not to make a listed change.

Miscellaneous

[2.1033]

17 Employment rights and protections in connection with consultation

The Schedule to these Regulations contains provision as to employment rights and protections which, in connection with consultation under these Regulations, apply to the employees of an employer in relation to an occupational or personal pension scheme.

[2.1034]

[18 Remedies for failure to comply]

[(1) The only remedies for a failure to comply with any obligations under regulations 6 to 16 in respect of any proposal or decision to make a listed change are—

(a) making a complaint to the Regulator,

(b) an improvement notice issued under section 13 of the Pensions Act 2004 (improvement notices), and

(c) a penalty imposed under regulation 18A.]

(2) A complaint [under paragraph (1)(a)] may be made by—

(a) any representative of affected members who falls within regulation 12(2)(a) or (3) or 13(2) (including any such representative who is not consulted), and

(b) any active or prospective member of an occupational or personal pension scheme who considers that he is or may be an affected member.

NOTES

Regulation heading, and para (1), substituted, and words in square brackets in para (2) inserted, by the Occupational, Personal and Stakeholder Pensions (Miscellaneous Amendments) Regulations 2009, SI 2009/615, reg 20(1), (2), as from 6 April 2009.

[2.1035]

[18A Penalties

(1) Where a person fails, without reasonable excuse, to comply with a requirement to consult under regulation 7(3), the Regulator may by notice in writing require that person to pay a penalty.

(2) Any such penalty must be paid within 28 days and must not exceed—

(a) in the case of an individual, £5,000; and

(b) in any other case, £50,000.]

NOTES

Commencement: 6 April 2009.

Inserted by the Occupational, Personal and Stakeholder Pensions (Miscellaneous Amendments) Regulations 2009, SI 2009/615, reg 20(1), (3), as from 6 April 2009.

[2.1036]

19 Powers of the Regulator to waive or relax requirements

(1) The Regulator may by order waive or relax any of the requirements of regulations 6 to 16.

(2) The power under paragraph (1) may be exercised only if the Regulator is satisfied that it is necessary to do so in order to protect the interests of the generality of the members of the scheme.

20 (*Adds the Pensions Act 2004, Sch 2, Pt 5.*)

[2.1037]

21 Waiver or relaxation of requirements: prescribed regulatory function

The Regulator's power to make an order under regulation 19 to waive or relax any of the requirements of regulations 6 to 16 is prescribed for the purposes of section 97(5)(u) of the Pensions Act 2004 (special procedure: applicable cases).

22 (*Amends the Financial Assistance Scheme (Internal Review) Regulations 2005, SI 2005/1994, reg 5.*)

SCHEDULE
EMPLOYMENT RIGHTS AND PROTECTIONS IN CONNECTION WITH CONSULTATION

Regulation 17

[2.1038]

1. In this Schedule—

"the 1996 Act" means the Employment Rights Act 1996;

"consulted representative" has the meaning given by paragraph 2(2);

"contract of employment" means a contract of service or apprenticeship whether express or implied and (if it is express) whether oral or in writing;

"employee" means an individual who has entered into or works under a contract of employment and includes, where the employment has ceased, an individual who worked under a contract of employment;

"employment", in relation to an employee, means employment under a contract of employment (and "employed" has a corresponding meaning);

"employer", in relation to an employee, means the person by whom the employee is (or where employment has ceased, was) employed.

Right to Time Off and Remuneration

2. (1) An employee who—

(a) is a representative falling within regulation 12(2)(a) or (3) or 13(2), and

(b) is consulted under these Regulations about a listed change by a relevant employer,

is entitled to be permitted by his employer to take reasonable time off during the employee's working hours in order to perform his functions as such a representative.

(2) In this Schedule "consulted representative" means an employee who satisfies the conditions specified in sub-paragraph (1)(a) and (b).

(3) For the purposes of this paragraph, the working hours of an employee shall be taken to be any time when, in accordance with his contract of employment, the employee is required to be at work.

3. (1) An employee who is permitted to take time off under paragraph 2 is entitled to be paid remuneration by his employer for the time taken off at the appropriate hourly rate.

(2) Chapter 2 of Part 14 of the 1996 Act (a week's pay) shall apply in relation to this paragraph as it applies in relation to section 62 of the 1996 Act (right to remuneration of certain representatives).

(3) The appropriate hourly rate, in relation to an employee, is the amount of one week's pay divided by the number of normal working hours in a week for that employee when employed under the contract of employment in force on the day when the time is taken off.

(4) But where the number of normal working hours differs from week to week or over a longer period, the amount of one week's pay shall be divided instead by—

(a) the average number of normal working hours calculated by dividing by twelve the total number of the employee's normal working hours during the period of twelve weeks ending with the last complete week before the day when the time is taken off, or

(b) where the employee has not been employed for a sufficient period to enable the calculations to be made under paragraph (a), a number which fairly represents the number of normal working hours in a week having regard to such of the considerations specified in sub-paragraph (5) as are appropriate in the circumstances.

(5) The considerations referred to in sub-paragraph (4)(b) are—

(a) the average number of normal working hours in a week which the employee could expect in accordance with the terms of his contract, and

(b) the average number of normal working hours of other employees engaged in relevant comparable employment with the same employer.

(6) A right to any amount under sub-paragraph (1) does not affect any right of an employee in relation to remuneration under his contract of employment ("contractual remuneration").

(7) Any contractual remuneration paid to an employee in respect of a period of time off under paragraph 2 goes towards discharging any liability of the employer to pay remuneration under sub-paragraph (1) in respect of that period, and, conversely, any payment of remuneration under sub-paragraph (1) in respect of a period goes towards discharging any liability of the employer to pay contractual remuneration in respect of that period.

4. (1) An employee may present a complaint to an employment tribunal that his employer—

(a) has unreasonably refused to permit him to take time off as required by paragraph 2, or

(b) has failed to pay the whole or part of any amount to which the employee is entitled under paragraph 3.

(2) A tribunal shall not consider a complaint under this paragraph unless it is presented—

(a) before the end of the period of three months beginning with the day on which the time off was taken or on which it is alleged the time off should have been permitted, or
(b) within such further period as the tribunal considers reasonable in a case where it is satisfied that it was not reasonably practicable for the complaint to be presented before the end of that period of three months.

(3) Where a tribunal finds a complaint under this paragraph well-founded, the tribunal shall make a declaration to that effect.

(4) If the complaint is that the employer has unreasonably refused to permit the employee to take time off, the tribunal shall also order the employer to pay to the employee an amount equal to the remuneration to which he would have been entitled under paragraph 3 if the employer had not refused.

(5) If the complaint is that the employer has failed to pay the employee the whole or part of any amount to which he is entitled under paragraph 3, the tribunal shall also order the employer to pay to the employee the amount it finds due to him.

Protections against Unfair Dismissal

5. (1) An employee who is dismissed and to whom sub-paragraph (2) or (4) applies shall be regarded, if the reason (or if more than one, the principal reason) for the dismissal is a reason specified in, respectively, sub-paragraph (3) or (5), as unfairly dismissed for the purposes of Part 10 of the 1996 Act (which makes provision as to rights and remedies relating to unfair dismissal).

(2) This sub-paragraph applies to an employee who is—
(a) a consulted representative, or
(b) a candidate in an election in which any person elected will, on being elected, be a representative of such description as is referred to in regulation 13(2).

(3) The reasons are that—
(a) the employee performed or proposed to perform any functions or activities under these Regulations in his capacity as such a representative or candidate,
(b) the employee exercised or proposed to exercise an entitlement conferred on the employee by paragraph 2 or 3, or
(c) the employee (or a person acting on his behalf) made or proposed to make a request to exercise such an entitlement.

(4) This sub-paragraph applies to any employee who is an active or prospective member of an occupational or personal pension scheme, whether or not he is an employee to whom sub-paragraph (2) applies.

(5) The reasons are that the employee—
(a) took, or proposed to take, any proceedings before an employment tribunal to enforce a right or secure an entitlement conferred on him by this Schedule,
(b) complained or proposed to complain to the Regulator that any person falling within regulation 3(1)—
(i) has decided to make a listed change affecting an occupational or personal pension scheme in contravention of regulation 6(1), or
(ii) has failed to comply with the requirements of regulation 16(2) or (3),
(c) complained or proposed to complain to the Regulator that any consultation required by these Regulations was not carried out in accordance with the requirements of these Regulations,
(d) stood as a candidate in an election in which any person elected would, on being elected, be a representative of such description as is referred to in regulation 13(2),
(e) influenced or sought to influence by lawful means the way in which votes were to be cast by other employees in an election arranged under regulation 14,
(f) voted in such an election,
(g) expressed doubts, whether to an election supervisor or otherwise, as to whether such an election had been properly conducted, or
(h) proposed to do, failed to do, or proposed to decline to do any of the things mentioned in paragraphs (d) to (g).

(6) It is immaterial for the purpose of sub-paragraph (5)(a)—
(a) whether or not the employee has the right or entitlement, or
(b) whether or not the right has been infringed,
but for that provision to apply, the claim to the right and, if applicable, the claim that it has been infringed must be made in good faith.

6. . . .

Protections from Suffering other Detriment in Employment

7. (1) An employee to whom sub-paragraph (2) or (4) applies has the right not to be subjected to any detriment by any act, or deliberate failure to act, by his employer done on a ground specified in, respectively, sub-paragraph (3) or (5).

(2) This sub-paragraph applies to an employee who is—

(a) a consulted representative, or

(b) a candidate in an election in which any person elected will, on being elected, be a representative of such description as is referred to in regulation 13(2).

(3) The grounds are that—

(a) the employee performed or proposed to perform any functions or activities under these Regulations in his capacity as such a representative or candidate,

(b) the employee exercised or proposed to exercise an entitlement conferred on the employee by paragraph 2 or 3, or

(c) the employee (or a person acting on his behalf) made or proposed to make a request to exercise such an entitlement.

(4) This sub-paragraph applies to any employee who is an active or prospective member of an occupational or personal pension scheme, whether or not he is an employee to whom sub-paragraph (2) applies.

(5) The grounds are that the employee—

(a) took, or proposed to take, any proceedings before an employment tribunal to enforce a right or secure an entitlement conferred on him by this Schedule,

(b) complained or proposed to complain to the Regulator that any person falling within regulation 3(1)—

(i) has decided to make a listed change affecting an occupational or personal pension scheme in contravention of regulation 6(1), or

(ii) has failed to comply with the requirements of regulation 16(2) or (3),

(c) complained or proposed to complain to the Regulator that any consultation required by these Regulations was not carried out in accordance with the requirements of these Regulations,

(d) stood as a candidate in an election in which any person elected would, on being elected, be a representative of such description as is referred to in regulation 13(2),

(e) influenced or sought to influence by lawful means the way in which votes were to be cast by other employees in an election arranged under regulation 14,

(f) voted in such a election,

(g) expressed doubts, whether to an election supervisor or otherwise, as to whether such an election had been properly conducted, or

(h) proposed to do, failed to do, or proposed to decline to do any of the things mentioned in paragraphs (d) to (g).

(6) It is immaterial for the purpose of sub-paragraph (5)(a)—

(a) whether or not the employee has the right or entitlement, or

(b) whether or not the right has been infringed,

but for that provision to apply, the claim to the right and, if applicable, the claim that it has been infringed must be made in good faith.

(7) This paragraph does not apply where the detriment in question amounts to dismissal.

8. (1) An employee may present a complaint to an employment tribunal that he has been subjected to a detriment in contravention of paragraph 7.

(2) The provisions of sections 48(2) to (4) and 49(1) to (5) of the 1996 Act (complaints to employment tribunals and remedies) shall apply in relation to a complaint under this paragraph as they apply in relation to a complaint under section 48 of that Act.

Conciliation and Appeals

9, 10. . . .

Miscellaneous

11. Any provision in any agreement (whether an employee's contract or not) is void in so far as it purports to exclude or limit the operation of any provision of regulations 6 to 16.

12. (1) Any provision in any agreement (whether an employee's contract or not) is void in so far as it purports—

(a) to exclude or limit the operation of any provision of this Schedule, or

(b) to preclude a person from bringing any proceedings before an employment tribunal under this Schedule.

(2) Sub-paragraph (1) does not apply to any agreement to refrain from instituting or continuing proceedings before an employment tribunal where a conciliation officer has taken action under section 18 of the Employment Tribunals Act 1996 (conciliation).

(3) Sub-paragraph (1) does not apply to any agreement to refrain from instituting or continuing before an employment tribunal proceedings within section 18(1) of the Employment Tribunals Act 1996 (which specifies proceedings under these Regulations as being proceedings where conciliation is available) if the conditions specified in paragraph 13 regulating compromise agreements are satisfied in relation to the agreement.

13. (1) For the purposes of paragraph 12(3) the conditions regulating compromise agreements are that—

(a) the agreement must be in writing,

(b) the agreement must relate to the particular proceedings,

(c) the employee must have received advice from a relevant independent adviser as to the terms and effect of the proposed agreement and, in particular, its effect on his ability to pursue his rights before an employment tribunal,

(d) there must be in force, when the adviser gives the advice, a contract of insurance, or an indemnity provided for members of a profession or a professional body, covering the risk of a claim by the employee in respect of loss arising in consequence of the advice,

(e) the agreement must identify the adviser, and

(f) the agreement must state that the conditions in paragraphs (a) to (e) are satisfied.

(2) A person is a relevant independent adviser for the purposes of sub-paragraph (1)(c)—

(a) if he is a qualified lawyer,

(b) if he is an officer, official, employee or member of an independent trade union who has been certified in writing by the trade union as competent to give advice and as authorised to do so on behalf of the trade union, or

(c) if he works at an advice centre (whether as an employee or as a volunteer) and has been certified in writing by the centre as competent to give advice and as authorised to do so on behalf of the centre.

(3) But a person is not a relevant independent adviser for the purposes of sub-paragraph (1)(c)—

(a) if he is, is employed by or is acting in the matter for the employer or an associated employer,

(b) in the case of a person within sub-paragraph (2)(b) or (c), if the trade union or advice centre is the employer or an associated employer, or

(c) in the case of a person within sub-paragraph (2)(c), if the employee makes a payment for the advice received from him.

(4) In sub-paragraph (2)(a) "qualified lawyer" means—

(a) as respects England and Wales, [a person who, for the purposes of the Legal Services Act 2007), is an authorised person in relation to an activity which constitutes the exercise of a right of audience or the conduct of litigation (within the meaning of that Act)];

(b) as respects Scotland, an advocate (whether in practice as such or employed to give legal advice) or a solicitor who holds a practising certificate.

(5) A person shall be treated as being a qualified lawyer within the meaning of sub-paragraph (4)(a) if he is a Fellow of the Institute of Legal Executives [practising in a solicitor's practice (including a body recognised under section 9 of the Administration of Justice Act 1985)].

(6) In this paragraph—

(a) "independent trade union" has the same meaning as in the Trade Union and Labour Relations (Consolidation) Act 1992; and

(b) for the purposes of sub-paragraph (3) any two employers shall be treated as associated if—

(i) one is a company of which the other (directly or indirectly) has control, or

(ii) both are companies of which a third person (directly or indirectly) has control,

and "associated employer" shall be construed accordingly.

NOTES

Para 6: amends the Employment Rights Act 1996, ss 105, 108 at **[1.915]**, **[1.918]**, and amended s 109 (repealed).

Paras 9, 10: amend the Employment Tribunals Act 1996, ss 18, 21 at **[1.706]**, **[1.713]**.

Para 13: words in square brackets in sub-para (4) substituted by the Legal Services Act 2007 (Consequential Amendments) Order 2009, SI 2009/3348, art 23, Sch 2, as from 1 January 2010; words in square brackets in sub-para (5) substituted by SI 2009/3348, art 22, Sch 1, as from 16 December 2009.

Conciliation: employment tribunal proceedings and claims which could be the subject of employment tribunal proceedings under paras 4 or 8 of this Schedule are proceedings to which the Employment Tribunals Act 1996, s 18 applies; see s 18(1)(q) of that Act at **[1.706]**.

Tribunal jurisdiction: the Employment Act 2002, s 38 applies to proceedings before the employment tribunal relating to a claim under para 8 of this Schedule; see s 38(1) of, and Sch 5 to, the 2002 Act at **[1.1228]**, **[1.1236]**. See also the Trade Union and Labour Relations (Consolidation) Act 1992, s 207A at **[1.474]** (as inserted by the Employment Act 2008). That section provides that in proceedings before an employment tribunal relating to a claim by an employee under any of the jurisdictions listed in Sch A2 to the 1992 Act at **[1.648]** (which includes para 8 of this Schedule) the tribunal may adjust any award given if the employer or the employee has unreasonably failed to comply with the relevant Code of Practice as defined by s 207A(4). See also the revised Acas Code of Practice 1 – Disciplinary and Grievance Procedures (2009) at **[4.1]**.

Employment Appeal Tribunal: see the introductory notes to these Regulations.

EMPLOYMENT EQUALITY (AGE) REGULATIONS 2006 (NOTE)

(SI 2006/1031)

[2.1039]

NOTES

Made: 3 April 2006.

Authority: European Communities Act 1972, s 2(2).

Commencement: 1 October 2006 (certain purposes); 1 December 2006 (otherwise).

These Regulations, except Sch 6 (Duty to consider working beyond retirement) and Sch 8 (Amendments to legislation and related transitional provisions) were revoked by the Equality Act 2010, s 211(2), Sch 27, Pt 2, as from 1 October 2010. The Equality Act 2010 (Commencement No 4, Savings, Consequential, Transitional, Transitory and Incidental Provisions and Revocation) Order 2010, SI 2010/2317 (at **[2.1558]** et seq) provides for various transitional provisions and savings in connection with the commencement of the 2010 Act and the revocation of these Regulations. See, in particular, art 15 (saving where the act complained of occurs wholly before 1 October 2010), and Sch 3 (savings in relation to work on ships, hovercraft and in relation to seafarers).

Schedule 6 to these Regulations (along with certain paragraphs in Sch 8) was revoked by the Employment Equality (Repeal of Retirement Age Provisions) Regulations 2011, SI 2011/1069, reg 4(1), as from 6 April 2011. Regulations 5, 6, and 8 of the 2011 Regulations provide for transitional provisions in connection with the continued operation of Sch 6 (see those provisions at **[2.1603]** et seq). As of 6 April 2013, the only part of these Regulations remaining in force is certain paragraphs in Sch 8; the amendments made by these provisions are incorporated where relevant.

EDUCATION (MODIFICATION OF ENACTMENTS RELATING TO EMPLOYMENT) (WALES) ORDER 2006

(SI 2006/1073)

NOTES

Made: 5 April 2006.

Authority: School Standards and Framework Act 1998, ss 81(1), 138(7).

Commencement: 12 May 2006.

Extent: this Order applies to Wales; the equivalent provisions for England are in SI 2003/1964 at **[2.744]**. There is no equivalent Order applying to Scotland.

ARRANGEMENT OF ARTICLES

[2.1040]
1 Citation, commencement, application and revocation

(1) This Order may be cited as the Education (Modification of Enactments Relating to Employment) (Wales) Order 2006 and shall come into force on 12th May 2006.

(2) This Order applies in relation to Wales.

(3) The Education (Modification of Enactments Relating to Employment) Order 1999 is revoked.

[2.1041]
2 Interpretation

(1) In this Order—

"the 1996 Act" means the Employment Rights Act 1996;

"the 1998 Act" means the School Standards and Framework Act 1998;

"the 2006 Regulations" mean the Staffing of Maintained Schools (Wales) Regulations 2006;

"authority" means the [local authority] by which a maintained school is, or a proposed school is to be, maintained;

"governing body" means the governing body of a school which is maintained by a local education authority;

"governing body" means the governing body of a school which is maintained by a [local authority];

(2) In this Order references to employment powers are references to the powers of appointment, suspension, conduct and discipline, capability and dismissal of staff conferred by the 2006 Regulations.

NOTES

Para (1): words in square brackets in definitions "authority" and "governing body" substituted by the Local Education Authorities and Children's Services Authorities (Integration of Functions) (Subordinate Legislation) (Wales) Order 2010, SI 2010/1142, art 2(3), as from 5 May 2010.

[2.1042]
3 General modifications of employment enactments

(1) In their application to a governing body having a right to a delegated budget, the enactments set out in the Schedule have effect as if—

(a) any reference to an employer (however expressed) included a reference to the governing body acting in the exercise of its employment powers and as if that governing body had at all material times been such an employer;

(b) in relation to the exercise of the governing body's employment powers, employment by the authority at a school were employment by the governing body of the school;

(c) references to employees were references to employees at the school in question;

(d) references to dismissal by an employer included references to dismissal by the authority following notification of a determination by a governing body under regulation 17(1) of the 2006 Regulations; and

(e) references to trade unions recognised by an employer were references to trade unions recognised by the authority or the governing body.

(2) Paragraph (1) does not cause the exemption in respect of an employer with fewer employees than is specified in section 7(1) of the Disability Discrimination Act 1995 to apply (without prejudice to whether it applies irrespective of that paragraph).

[2.1043]
4

Without prejudice to the generality of article 3, where an employee employed at a school having a delegated budget is dismissed by the authority following notification of such a determination as is mentioned in article 3(1)(d)—

(a) section 92 of the 1996 Act has effect as if the governing body had dismissed him and as if references to the employer's reasons for dismissing the employee were references to the reasons for which the governing body made its determination; and

(b) Part X of the 1996 Act has effect in relation to the dismissal as if the governing body had dismissed him, and the reason or principal reason for which the governing body did so had been the reason or principal reason for which it made its determination.

[2.1044]
5 Trade disputes

(1) Subject to paragraph (2), a dispute between staff employed to work at a school having a delegated budget and the school's governing body, which relates wholly or mainly to one of the matters set out in section 244(1) of the Trade Union and Labour Relations (Consolidation) Act 1992 is a trade dispute within the meaning of that Act.

(2) In any case where there is a trade dispute only by virtue of this article, nothing in section 219 of that Act prevents an act from being actionable in tort where the inducement, interference or threat mentioned in that section relates to a contract the performance of which does not affect directly or indirectly the school over which the governing body in question exercises its functions.

[2.1045]
6 Applications to Employment Tribunals

(1) Without prejudice to articles 3 and 4, and despite any provision in the Employment Tribunals Act 1996 and any regulations made under section 1(1) of that Act, this article applies in respect of any application to an employment tribunal, and any proceedings pursuant to such an application, in relation to which by virtue of article 3 or 4 a governing body is to be treated as if it were an employer (however expressed).

(2) The application must be made, and the proceedings must be carried on, against that governing body.

(3) Despite paragraph (2), any decision, declaration, order, recommendation or award made in the course of such proceedings except in so far as it requires reinstatement or re-engagement has effect as if made against the authority.

(4) Where any application is made against a governing body under paragraph (2)—

(a) the governing body must notify the authority within 14 days of receiving notification; and

(b) the authority, on written application to the employment tribunal, is entitled to be made an additional party to the proceedings and to take part in the proceedings accordingly.

SCHEDULE

Article 3

[2.1046]

Sex Discrimination Act 1975
sections 6, 7, 9, 41 and 82(1A)

Race Relations Act 1976
sections 4, 5, 7 and 32

Trade Union and Labour Relations (Consolidation) Act 1992
sections 146, 147, 152–154 and 181–185

Disability Discrimination Act 1995
sections 4–6, 11, 12, 16, 55, 57 and 58

Employment Rights Act 1996
sections 66–68, 70, 71, 92, 93 and Part X

Employment Act 2002
sections 29–32 and Schedules 2–4

NOTES

Note that the Employment Act 2002, ss 29–32, Schs 2–4 were repealed by the Employment Act 2008, as from 6 April 2009 (for transitional provisions and savings in connection with the repeal, see the Employment Act 2008 (Commencement No 1, Transitional Provisions and Savings) Order 2008, SI 2008/3232, Schedule, Pt 1).

Sex Discrimination Act 1975, Race Relations Act 1976, Disability Discrimination Act 1995: repealed by the Equality Act 2010, s 211(2), Sch 27, Pt 1.

RACE RELATIONS ACT 1976 (STATUTORY DUTIES) ORDER 2006 (NOTE)

(SI 2006/2471)

[2.1047]

NOTES

This Order was made on 11 September 2006, under the powers conferred by the Race Relations Act 1976, s 71(2), (3). It came into force on 3 October 2006. The Order imposed certain specific duties on bodies who were subject to the general duty under s 71(1) of the 1976 Act to have due regard, when exercising their functions, to the need to eliminate unlawful racial discrimination and to promote equality of opportunity and good relations between persons of different racial groups. Section 71 of the 1976 Act was repealed on 5 April 2011 by the Equality Act 2010, s 211(2), Sch 27, Pt 1 and, accordingly, this Order lapsed on that date.

LOCAL GOVERNMENT (EARLY TERMINATION OF EMPLOYMENT) (DISCRETIONARY COMPENSATION) (ENGLAND AND WALES) REGULATIONS 2006

(SI 2006/2914)

NOTES

Made: 6 November 2006.
Authority: Superannuation Act 1972, s 24.
Commencement: 29 November 2006 (with effect from 1 October 2006).
These Regulations apply to England and Wales only (see **[2.1048]**).

ARRANGEMENT OF REGULATIONS

SCHEDULES

[2.1048]

1 Citation, commencement and extent

(1) These Regulations may be cited as the Local Government (Early Termination of Employment) (Discretionary Compensation) (England and Wales) Regulations 2006.

(2) They shall come into force on 29th November 2006 but shall have effect from 1st October 2006 and extend to England and Wales.

[2.1049]

2 Interpretation

(1) In these Regulations—

"the 1996 Act" means the Employment Rights Act 1996;

Part 2 Statutory Instruments

"the 2000 Regulations" means the Local Government (Early Termination of Employment) (Discretionary Compensation) (England and Wales) Regulations 2000;

["the Benefits Regulations" means the Local Government Pension Scheme (Benefits, Membership and Contributions) Regulations 2007;

"the Administration Regulations" means the Local Government Pension Scheme (Administration) Regulations 2008;]

"employing authority", in relation to a person, means—

[(a) a body listed in Part 1 of Schedule 2 (Scheme employers) to the Administration Regulations by whom the person is employed immediately before the termination date;

(b) a body listed in Part 2 of that Schedule by whom the person is employed immediately before the termination date and who has been designated by the body as being eligible for membership of the Scheme under regulation 4(3) of those Regulations; or

(c) in the case of a person who is eligible to be a Scheme member under [regulation 8(1) of the Administration Regulations], the [local authority] by whom the person is deemed to be employed under regulation 8(2) of those Regulations].

"employment" includes office but does not include a period as—

(a) the Mayor of London,

(b) a member of the London Assembly, or

(c) a councillor member;

. . .

["Scheme member" means a member of the Local Government Pension Scheme constituted by the Benefits Regulations and the Administration Regulations;]

"termination date" in relation to a person means the final day of his employment.

[(2) Expressions not defined in paragraph (1) but used in these Regulations and in the Benefits Regulations or the Administration Regulations or both have the same meaning as in the Benefits Regulations or the Administration Regulations, as the case may be.]

NOTES

In para (c) of the definition "employing authority" words in first pair of square brackets substituted by the Local Government Pension Scheme (Miscellaneous) Regulations 2012, SI 2012/1989, regs 2, 3, as from 1 October 2012, and words in second pair of square brackets substituted by the Local Education Authorities and Children's Services Authorities (Integration of Functions) (Local and Subordinate Legislation) Order 2010, SI 2010/1172, art 5, Sch 3, para 67, as from 5 May 2010.

All other amendments to this regulation were made by the Local Government Pension Scheme (Miscellaneous) Regulations 2009, SI 2009/3150, regs 2, 3.

[2.1050]

3 Application to the Isles of Scilly

These Regulations apply to the Isles of Scilly as if they were a district in the county of Cornwall and the Council of the Isles of Scilly were a council of that district.

[2.1051]

4 Application of the Regulations

(1) Subject to regulation 11(2), these Regulations apply in relation to a person—

(a) whose employment is terminated—

(i) by reason of redundancy,

(ii) in the interests of the efficient exercise of the employing authority's functions, or

(iii) in the case of a joint appointment, because the other holder of the appointment has left it;

(b) who, on the termination date, is—

(i) employed by an employing authority, and

[(ii) eligible to be a Scheme member (whether or not the person is such a member) or would be so eligible but for the giving of a notification under regulation 14 of the Administration Regulations; and]

(c) whose termination date is on or after 1st October 2006,

and in the following provisions of these Regulations, "person" shall be construed accordingly, unless the context indicates that it has a different meaning.

(2) Where an additional requirement is specified in any provision of regulations 5 and 6 in relation to a person, that provision does not apply in relation to him unless he satisfies that additional requirement.

NOTES

Para (1): sub-para (b)(ii) substituted by the Local Government Pension Scheme (Miscellaneous) Regulations 2009, SI 2009/3150, regs 2, 4.

[2.1052]

5 Power to increase statutory redundancy payments

(1) Compensation may be paid in accordance with this regulation to a person who is entitled to a redundancy payment under the 1996 Act on the termination of his employment.

(2) The amount which may be paid must not be more than the difference between—

(a) the redundancy payment to which he is entitled under Part 11 of the 1996 Act; and

(b) the payment to which he would have been entitled if there had been no limit on the amount of a week's pay used in the calculation of his redundancy payment.

(3) The power to pay compensation is exercisable by the employing authority.

[2.1053]

6 Discretionary compensation

(1) This regulation applies where a person—

(a) ceases to hold his employment with an employing authority, and

[(b) in respect of that cessation is not awarded—

(i) an additional period of membership under regulation 12 (power of employing authority to increase total membership of active members); or

(ii) an additional pension under regulation 13 (power of employing authority to award additional pension)

of the Benefits Regulations].

(2) Where this regulation applies, the employing authority may, not later than six months after the termination date, decide to pay compensation under this regulation and in that event shall, as soon as reasonably practicable after the decision, notify the person in whose favour it has been made, giving details of the amount of the compensation.

(3) The amount of compensation must not exceed 104 weeks' pay.

[(4) Chapter 2 (a week's pay) of Part 14 (Interpretation) of the 1996 Act shall apply for the purpose of calculating a person's week's pay as it applies for the purpose of calculating redundancy payments but without the limit on a week's pay imposed by section 227 of that Act.]

(5) If the person in whose favour a decision under paragraph (2) has been made receives a redundancy payment under Part 11 of the 1996 Act or compensation under regulation 5 of these Regulations, the equivalent amount shall be deducted from the compensation otherwise payable to him under this regulation.

(6) Compensation under this regulation shall be paid by the employing authority as soon as practicable after the decision under paragraph (2).

(7) The compensation shall be payable in the form of a lump sum.

NOTES

Para (1): sub-para (b) substituted by the Local Government Pension Scheme (Miscellaneous) Regulations 2009, SI 2009/3150, regs 2, 5(a).

Para (4): substituted by SI 2009/3150, regs 2, 5(b).

[2.1054]

7 Policy Statements

(1) Each employing authority must formulate, publish and keep under review the policy that they apply in the exercise of their discretionary powers under regulations 5 and 6.

(2) If the authority decide to change their policy, they must publish a statement of the amended policy and may not give effect to any policy change until one month after the date of publication.

(3) In formulating and reviewing their policy the authority must—

(a) have regard to the extent to which the exercise of their discretionary powers (in accordance with the policy), unless properly limited, could lead to a serious loss of confidence in the public service; and

(b) be satisfied that the policy is workable, affordable and reasonable having regard to the foreseeable costs.

[2.1055]

8 Payments and repayments

(1) Any compensation payable under these Regulations is payable to or in trust for the person entitled to receive it.

(2) Where any compensation is paid in error to any person—

(a) the employing authority must, as soon as possible after the discovery of the error—

(i) inform the person concerned, by notice in writing, giving details of the relevant calculation,

(ii) where there has been an underpayment, make a further payment,

(iii) where there has been an overpayment, specify a reasonable period for repayment;

(b) a person who has received a notice under sub-paragraph (a) must repay any overpayment within the specified period; and

(c) the employing authority may take such steps as they consider appropriate to recover from the person to whom it was paid any overpayment which has not been repaid within the specified period.

(3) The employing authority shall take into account the person's circumstances (so far as known or reasonably ascertainable) before taking steps under paragraph (2)(c).

[2.1056]
9 Finance

The cost of any payment to be made under these Regulations must not be met out of any pension fund maintained under [the Local Government Pension Scheme (Management and Investment of Funds) Regulations 1998, the Benefits Regulations and the Administration Regulations].

NOTES

Words in square brackets substituted by the Local Government Pension Scheme (Miscellaneous) Regulations 2009, SI 2009/3150, regs 2, 6.

[2.1057]
10 Consequential amendments

Schedule 1 shall have effect for the purpose of making amendments which are consequential on the making of these Regulations.

[2.1058]
11 Revocation of Regulations, transitional provisions and savings

(1) The following are revoked but subject to the transitional provision in paragraph (2) and the savings in Schedule 2—

(a) the 2000 Regulations,

(b) regulation 598 of the Financial Services and Markets Act 2000 (Consequential Amendments and Repeals) Order 2001,

(c) the Local Government (Early Termination of Employment) (Discretionary Compensation) (England and Wales) (Miscellaneous) Regulations 2002,

(d) regulation 9(2) of the Local Government Pension Scheme and Discretionary Compensation (Local Authority Members in England) Regulations 2003, and

(e) regulation 5 of the Local Government Pension Scheme (Civil Partnership) (Amendment) (England and Wales) Regulations 2005

(2) An employing authority may decide to pay compensation under the 2000 Regulations to a person whose employment with them commenced before 1st October 2006 and whose termination date is after 30th September 2006 and before 1st April 2007.

(3) An employing authority may decide to pay compensation under regulation 6 of these Regulations to a person—

(a) whose employment with them terminated after 30th September 2006 and before the date on which these Regulations come into force, and

(b) in respect of whom a decision to pay lump sum compensation has been made and notified under Part 3 of the 2000 Regulations before the date on which these Regulations come into force ("the 2000 lump sum").

(4) The amount that an employing authority may decide to pay under paragraph (3) may not exceed the difference between—

(a) 104 weeks' pay, and

(b) the 2000 lump sum

but if the person in whose favour a decision under paragraph (3) has been made receives a redundancy payment under Part 11 of the 1996 Act or compensation under regulation 5 of the 2000 Regulations or regulation 5 of these Regulations, the equivalent amount shall be deducted from the compensation otherwise payable to him under paragraph (3) if no such adjustment has already been made.

(5) Nothing in these Regulations shall place any individual who is eligible to participate in the benefits for which the 2000 Regulations provide in a worse position than he would have been in if all the provisions of these Regulations had been framed so as to have effect only from the date of their making.

SCHEDULE 1

(Sch 1 contains various amendments to statutory instruments that are outside the scope of this work.)

SCHEDULE 2
SAVINGS

Regulation 11

[2.1059]
1. The revocation of the 2000 Regulations does not affect—
(a) any person whose termination date is before 1st October 2006 and who is eligible for compensation under the provisions of those Regulations,
(b) any person to whom an employing authority have decided that compensation shall be paid under those Regulations in accordance with regulation 11(2) of these Regulations, or
(c) the rights of any person who is entitled to benefits under those Regulations in consequence of the death of such a person

and in relation to such persons those Regulations shall continue to apply.

2. Where—
(a) any provision continues to have effect in relation to any person by virtue of paragraph 1, and
(b) immediately before 1st October 2006 it has effect in relation to him subject to any saving, transitional provision or modification

nothing in these Regulations affects the operation of that saving, transitional provision or modification.

3. The revocation by these Regulations of any provision which previously revoked any provision subject to savings does not affect the continued operation of those savings, in so far as they remain capable of having effect.

SEX DISCRIMINATION ACT 1975 (PUBLIC AUTHORITIES) (STATUTORY DUTIES) ORDER 2006 (NOTE)

(SI 2006/2930)

[2.1060]

NOTES
This Order was made on 7 November 2006 under the powers conferred by the Sex Discrimination Act 1975, ss 76B(1), 76C(2). It applied to England and Wales only and came into force on 6 April 2007. This Order imposed specific duties on the public authorities listed in the Schedule to the Order. Sections 76B, 76C of the 1975 Act were repealed on 5 April 2011 by the Equality Act 2010, s 211(2), Sch 27, Pt 1 and, accordingly, this Order lapsed on that date.

COMPENSATION (REGULATED CLAIMS MANAGEMENT SERVICES) ORDER 2006

(SI 2006/3319)

NOTES
Made: 12 December 2006.
Authority: Compensation Act 2006, ss 4(2)(e), 15(1).
Commencement: 13 December 2006.

[2.1061]
1 Citation

This Order may be cited as the Compensation (Regulated Claims Management Services) Order 2006.

[2.1062]
2 Commencement

This Order comes into force on the day after the day on which it is made.

[2.1063]
3 Definition—"the Act"

In this Order, "the Act" means the Compensation Act 2006.

[2.1064]

4 Regulated services

(1) For the purposes of Part 2 of the Act, services of a kind specified in paragraph (2) are prescribed if rendered in relation to the making of a claim of a kind described in paragraph (3), or in relation to a cause of action that may give rise to such a claim.

(2) The kinds of service are the following—

(a) advertising for, or otherwise seeking out (for example, by canvassing or direct marketing), persons who may have a cause of action;

(b) advising a claimant or potential claimant in relation to his claim or cause of action;

(c) subject to paragraph (4), referring details of a claim or claimant, or a cause of action or potential claimant, to another person, including a person having the right to conduct litigation;

(d) investigating, or commissioning the investigation of, the circumstances, merits or foundation of a claim, with a view to the use of the results in pursuing the claim;

(e) representation of a claimant (whether in writing or orally, and regardless of the tribunal, body or person to or before which or whom the representation is made).

(3) The kinds of claim are the following—

(a) claims for personal injuries, within the meaning in the Civil Procedure Rules 1998;

(b) claims under the Criminal Injuries Compensation Scheme established under the Criminal Injuries Compensation Act 1995;

(c) claims for a benefit specified or referred to in article 3 of the Compensation (Specification of Benefits) Order 2006;

(d) claims in relation to employment (including claims in relation to wages and salaries and other employment-related payments, and claims in relation to wrongful or unfair dismissal, redundancy, discrimination and harassment);

(e) claims for housing disrepair (that is, claims under section 11 of the Landlord and Tenant Act 1985 or section 4 of the Defective Premises Act 1972, claims in relation to the disrepair of premises under a term of a tenancy agreement or lease or under the common law relating to nuisance or negligence, but not claims for statutory nuisance under section 82 of the Environmental Protection Act 1990);

(f) claims in relation to financial products or services.

(4) In spite of paragraph (2)(c), the service of referring a claim's or a claimant's details to another person is not a regulated claims management service if it is not undertaken for or in expectation of a fee, gain or reward.

COMPENSATION (EXEMPTIONS) ORDER 2007

(SI 2007/209)

NOTES

Made: 30 January 2007.
Authority: Compensation Act 2006, s 6.
Commencement: 31 January 2007.

ARRANGEMENT OF ARTICLES

[2.1065]

1 Citation

This Order may be cited as the Compensation (Exemptions) Order 2007.

[2.1066]
2 Commencement

This Order comes into force on the day after the day on which it is made.

[2.1067]
3 Definition "the Act"

In this Order, "the Act" means the Compensation Act 2006.

[2.1068]
4 Legal practitioners

(1) Section 4(1) of the Act does not prevent the provision of a regulated claims management service in the circumstances that—

- (a) the service is provided—
  - (i) by a legal practitioner;
  - (ii) by a firm, organisation or body corporate that provides the service through a legal practitioner; or
  - (iii) by an individual who provides the service at the direction, and under the supervision, of a legal practitioner who is—
    - (aa) his employer or fellow employee; or
    - (bb) a director of a company, or a member of a limited liability partnership, that provides the service and is his employer; and
- (b) the legal practitioner acts in the normal course of practice in a way permitted by the professional rules to which he is subject.

(2) In paragraph (1), "legal practitioner" means—

- (a) a solicitor, barrister or advocate of any part of the United Kingdom;
- (b) a Fellow of the Institute of Legal Executives;
- (c) a European lawyer, as defined in the European Communities (Services of Lawyers) Order 1978;
- (d) a registered foreign lawyer, as defined in section 89(9) of the Courts and Legal Services Act 1990; or
- (e) any other member of a legal profession, of a jurisdiction other than England and Wales, that is recognised by the Law Society or the General Council of the Bar as a regulated legal profession.

[2.1069]
5 Persons providing services regulated under the Financial Services and Markets Act 2000

(1) Section 4(1) of the Act does not prevent the provision of a regulated claims management service by a person if in providing that service, he is carrying on a regulated activity for the purposes of section 19 of the Financial Services and Markets Act 2000 ("FSMA"), or would be doing so except that—

- (a) he is an exempt person (that is, a person who is exempt from the general prohibition under FSMA), or
- (b) he has the benefit of an exclusion under the Financial Services and Markets Act 2000 (Regulated Activities) Order 2001.

(2) In paragraph (1)(a),"general prohibition" has the meaning given by FSMA.

(3) References in paragraph (1) to a regulated activity carried on by a person must be read with—

- (a) section 22 of FSMA;
- (b) any relevant order under that section; and
- (c) Schedule 2 to FSMA.

[2.1070]
6 Charities and not-for-profit advice agencies

(1) Section 4(1) of the Act does not prevent the provision of a regulated claims management service by a not for profit body, that is, a body that, by or under its constitution—

- (a) is required to apply the whole of its net income, and any expendable capital, after payment of outgoings for charitable or public purposes; and
- (b) subject to paragraph (2), is prohibited from distributing, directly or indirectly, any part of its net income by way of profits, or its assets, among any of its members.

(2) A body is not prevented from being a not-for-profit body for the purposes of paragraph (1) if its constitution permits:

- (a) the payment, out of the body's funds, of reasonable and proper remuneration for goods or services supplied to the body by a member;
- (b) in the case of a not-for-profit body that is a charity, the payment to a member of a benefit to which he is entitled because he is a beneficiary of the charity; or
- (c) the purchase, out of the body's funds, of indemnity insurance for trustees of the body.

[2.1071]
7 Independent Complaints Reviewers

Section 4(1) of the Act does not prevent the provision of a regulated claims management service by a person appointed from time to time by a statutory or other public body as an Independent Complaints Reviewer or Independent Case Examiner in the course of carrying out her duties under the appointment.

[2.1072]
8 Motor Insurers Bureau

Section 4(1) of the Act does not prevent the provision of a regulated claims management service by the Motor Insurers Bureau (being the company limited by guarantee mentioned in section 95(2) of the Road Traffic Act 1988).

[2.1073]
9 Medical Protection Society and medical defence unions

Section 4(1) of the Act does not prevent the provision of a regulated claims management service—

(a) by the Medical Protection Society Limited to its members;
(b) by The Medical Defence Union Ltd to its members; or
(c) by The Medical and Dental Defence Union of Scotland Limited to its members.

[2.1074]
10 Independent trade unions

(1) Section 4(1) of the Act does not prevent the provision of a regulated claims management service by an independent trade union to—

(a) a member (including a retired member or a student member) of the trade union;
(b) a member of the family of a member referred to in sub-paragraph (a); or
(c) a former member of the trade union to whom the trade union may, under its rules, provide claims management services, or a member of the family of such a former member.

(2) In paragraph (1), "independent trade union" has the same meaning as in the Trade Union and Labour Relations (Consolidation) Act 1992.

(3) For the purposes of paragraph (1)—

(a) subject to sub-paragraph (b), whether a person is or has been a member (including a retired member or a student member) of a trade union is to be decided in accordance with the rules of the trade union;
(b) "member" of a trade union does not include a person who, under those rules, is a member only for the purpose of pursuing a claim or claims; and
(c) whether a person is a member of the family of a member of a trade union is to be decided in accordance with the rules of the trade union.

(4) An exemption of a trade union under this article is subject to compliance by the trade union with the condition that the trade union, in providing regulated claims management services, must act in accordance with the code of practice for the provision of regulated claims management services by trade unions issued by the Secretary of State on 28th November 2006.

[2.1075]
11 Students' unions

Section 4(1) of the Act does not prevent the provision of a regulated claims management service by a students' union (as defined in section 20 of the Education Act 1994) to a member of the students' union or (in the case of a students' union referred to in section 20(3) of that Act) a member of a constituent or affiliated association or body.

[2.1076]
12 Certain providers of referrals

(1) In this article, "legal practitioner" has the meaning given by article 4(2).

(2) Section 4(1) of the Act does not prevent the provision of the regulated claims management service of referring details of potential claims or potential claimants to another person if—

(a) the person who refers those details ("the introducer") provides no other regulated claims management service;
(b) the provision of the service is incidental to the introducer's main business;
(c) the details are referred to authorised persons or legal practitioners or firms of legal practitioners;
(d) the introducer refers such details only to persons of those kinds;
(e) of the cases that the introducer refers to such persons, he is paid, in money or money's worth, for no more than 25 cases per calendar quarter; and
(f) subject to paragraph (3), the persons to which the details are referred must be satisfied that the introducer obtains those details in a way consistent with the rules prescribed by the Regulator under paragraph 8 of the Schedule to the Act.

(3) Paragraph (2)(f) does not apply in the case of a referral to a legal practitioner or firm of legal practitioners.

[2.1077]

[13 Exemption for claims in certain circumstances

Section 4(1) of the Act does not prevent the provision of a regulated claims management service in the circumstances that—

(a) a claim has been made by a person ("the claimant") against another person ("the defendant"); and

(b) the service is provided to the defendant in connection with—

(i) the making of a counterclaim against the claimant arising out of the same set of facts as the claim referred to in sub-paragraph (a); or

(ii) the making of a claim against a third party (whether for contribution, as a subrogated claim, or otherwise) which is incidental to, or consequent on, the claim referred to in sub-paragraph (a).]

NOTES

Added by the Compensation (Exemptions) (Amendment) (No 1) Order 2007, SI 2007/1090, art 3.

SEX DISCRIMINATION (PUBLIC AUTHORITIES) (STATUTORY DUTIES) (SCOTLAND) ORDER 2007 (NOTE)

(SSI 2007/32)

[2.1078]

NOTES

This Order was made on 30 January 2007 under the powers conferred by the Sex Discrimination Act 1975, ss 76C(3), 81(4). It came into force on 9 April 2007. This Order imposed specific duties on the Scottish public bodies and authorities listed in the Schedule to the Order. Section 76C of the 1975 Act was repealed on 5 April 2011 by the Equality Act 2010, s 211(2), Sch 27, Pt 1 and, accordingly, this Order lapsed on that date.

COMPANIES (CROSS-BORDER MERGERS) REGULATIONS 2007

(SI 2007/2974)

NOTES

Made: 15 October 2007.

Authority: European Communities Act 1972, s 2(2); Companies Act 2006, ss 1102(2), 1105(2)(d), 1106(2).

Commencement: 15 December 2007.

Only the provisions of these Regulations relevant to employment law are reproduced here. For modifications of these Regulations in relation to their application to LLPs, see the Limited Liability Partnerships (Application of Companies Act 2006) Regulations 2009, SI 2009/1804.

Conciliation: employment tribunal proceedings and claims which could be the subject of employment tribunal proceedings under regs 45, 51 are proceedings to which the Employment Tribunals Act 1996, s 18 applies; see s 18(1)(t) of that Act at **[1.706]**.

Employment Appeal Tribunal: an appeal lies to the Employment Appeal Tribunal on any question of law arising from any decision of, or in any proceedings before, an employment tribunal under or by virtue of these Regulations; see the Employment Tribunals Act 1996, s 21(1)(u) at **[1.713]**.

See *Harvey* CII(6), DII(G), NIII(6).

ARRANGEMENT OF REGULATIONS

PART 1
GENERAL

PART 4
EMPLOYEE PARTICIPATION

CHAPTER 1
APPLICATION OF THIS PART

CHAPTER 2
MERGING COMPANIES AND THE SPECIAL NEGOTIATING BODY

CHAPTER 3
NEGOTIATION OF THE EMPLOYEE PARTICIPATION AGREEMENT

CHAPTER 4
ELECTION OF UNITED KINGDOM MEMBERS OF THE SPECIAL NEGOTIATING BODY

CHAPTER 5
STANDARD RULES OF EMPLOYEE PARTICIPATION IN A UK TRANSFEREE COMPANY

CHAPTER 6
CONFIDENTIAL INFORMATION

CHAPTER 7
PROTECTION FOR EMPLOYEES AND MEMBERS OF SPECIAL NEGOTIATING BODY, ETC

CHAPTER 8
COMPLIANCE AND ENFORCEMENT

CHAPTER 9
MISCELLANEOUS

PART 1
GENERAL

[2.1079]

1 Citation and commencement

These Regulations may be cited as the Companies (Cross-Border Mergers) Regulations 2007 and come into force on 15th December 2007.

[2.1080]

2 Meaning of "cross-border merger"

(1) In these Regulations "cross-border merger" means a merger by absorption, a merger by absorption of a wholly-owned subsidiary, or a merger by formation of a new company.

(2) In these Regulations "merger by absorption" means an operation in which—

- (a) there are one or more transferor companies;
- (b) there is an existing transferee company;
- (c) at least one of those companies is a UK company;
- (d) at least one of those companies is an EEA company;
- (e) every transferor company is dissolved without going into liquidation, and on its dissolution transfers all its assets and liabilities to the transferee company; and
- (f) the consideration for the transfer is—
  - (i) shares or other securities representing the capital of the transferee company, and
  - (ii) if so agreed, a cash payment,

  receivable by members of the transferor company.

(3) In these Regulations "merger by absorption of a wholly-owned subsidiary" means an operation in which—

- (a) there is one transferor company, of which all the shares or other securities representing its capital are held by an existing transferee company;
- (b) either the transferor company or the transferee company is a UK company;
- (c) either the transferor company or the transferee company is an EEA company; and
- (d) the transferor company is dissolved without going into liquidation, and on its dissolution transfers all its assets and liabilities to the transferee company.

(4) In these Regulations "merger by formation of a new company" means an operation in which—

- (a) there are two or more transferor companies, at least two of which are each governed by the law of a different EEA State;
- (b) every transferor company is dissolved without going into liquidation, and on its dissolution transfers all its assets and liabilities to a transferee company formed for the purposes of, or in connection with, the operation;
- (c) the consideration for the transfer is—
  - (i) shares or other securities representing the capital of the transferee company, and
  - (ii) if so agreed, a cash payment,

  receivable by members of the transferor company;
- (d) at least one of the transferor companies or the transferee company is a UK company.

[2.1081]

3 Interpretation

(1) In these Regulations—

"the 1996 Act" means the Employment Rights Act 1996;

["agency worker" has the same meaning as in regulation 3 of the Agency Workers Regulations 2010;]

"the Appeal Tribunal" means the Employment Appeal Tribunal;

["assignment" has the same meaning as in regulation 2 of the Agency Workers Regulations 2010;]

"the CAC" means the Central Arbitration Committee;

"the Companies Acts" has the same meaning as in section 2 of the Companies Act 2006;

"competent authority of another EEA State" means a court or other authority designated in accordance with the law of an EEA State other than the United Kingdom as competent for the purposes of Article 8 (appointment of independent expert), Article 10 (issue of pre-merger certificate) or Article 11 (scrutiny of completion of merger) of the Directive;

"the court" means—

- (a) in England and Wales, the High Court,
- (b) in Scotland, the Court of Session, or
- (c) in Northern Ireland, the High Court;

"the Directive" means Directive 2005/56/EC on cross-border mergers of limited liability companies;

"director" has the same meaning as in the Companies Acts (see section 250 of the Companies Act 2006);

"directors' report" means a report prepared and adopted in accordance with regulation 8 (directors' report), and includes any opinion of the employee representatives which must accompany it in accordance with regulation 8(6);

"dismissed" and "dismissal", in relation to an employee, shall be construed in accordance with Part 10 of the 1996 Act;

"draft terms of merger" means a draft of the proposed terms of a cross-border merger drawn up and adopted in accordance with regulation 7 (draft terms of merger);

"EEA company" means a body corporate governed by the law of an EEA State other than the United Kingdom;

"employee" means an individual who has entered into or works under a contract of employment and includes, where the employment has ceased, an individual who worked under a contract of employment;

"employee participation" means the influence of the employees and/or the employee representatives in the transferee company or a merging company by way of the right to—

(a) elect or appoint some of the members of the transferee company's or the merging company's supervisory or administrative organ; or

(b) recommend and/or oppose the appointment of some or all of the members of the transferee's or the merging company's supervisory or administrative organ;

"employee representatives" means—

(a) if the employees are of a description in respect of which an independent trade union is recognised by their employer for the purpose of collective bargaining, representatives of the trade union who normally take part as negotiators in the collective bargaining process, and

(b) any other employees of their employer who are elected or appointed as employee representatives to positions in which they are expected to receive, on behalf of the employees, information—

(i) which is relevant to the terms and conditions of employment of the employees, or

(ii) about the activities of the undertaking which may significantly affect the interests of the employees,

but excluding representatives who are expected to receive information relevant only to a specific aspect of the terms and conditions or interests of the employees, such as health and safety, collective redundancies, or pension schemes;

"existing transferee company" means a transferee company other than one formed for the purposes of, or in connection with, a cross-border merger;

"First Company Law Directive" means First Council Directive on co-ordination of safeguards which, for the protection of the interests of members and others, are required by Member States of companies within the meaning of the second paragraph of Article 58 of the Treaty, with a view to making such safeguards equivalent throughout the Community (68/151/EEC);

"the Gazette" means—

(a) as respects UK companies registered in England and Wales, the London Gazette,

(b) as respects UK companies registered in Scotland, the Edinburgh Gazette, and

(c) as respects UK companies registered in Northern Ireland, the Belfast Gazette;

["hirer" has the same meaning as in regulation 2 of the Agency Workers Regulations 2010;]

"independent expert's report" means a report prepared in accordance with regulation 9 (independent expert's report);

"liabilities" includes duties;

"member" in relation to a UK company has the same meaning as in the Companies Acts (see section 112 of the Companies Act 2006);

"registrar of companies" has the same meaning as in the Companies Acts (see section 1060 of the Companies Act 2006);

"share exchange ratio" means the number of shares or other securities in any transferee company that the draft terms of merger provide to be allotted to members of any transferor company for a given number of their shares or other securities;

"standard rules of employee participation" means the rules in regulation 38;

["suitable information relating to the use of agency workers" means—

(a) the number of agency workers working temporarily for and under the supervision and direction of a merging company or the transferee company (as the case may be);

(b) the parts of the undertaking in which those agency workers are working; and

(c) the type of work those agency workers are carrying out;]

["temporary work agency" has the same meaning as in regulation 4 of the Agency Workers Regulations 2010;]

"transferee company" means a UK company or an EEA company to which assets and liabilities are to be transferred by way of a cross-border merger;

"transferor company" means a UK company or an EEA company whose assets and liabilities are to be transferred by way of a cross-border merger;

"treasury shares" has the same meaning as in the Companies Acts (see section 724 of the Companies Act 2006);

"UK company" means a company within the meaning of the Companies Acts (see section 1 of the Companies Act 2006) other than—

(a) a company limited by guarantee without a share capital (see section 5 of the Companies Act 2006), or

(b) a company being wound up;

"UK employee" means an employee who has entered into or works under a contract of employment with a UK company;

"UK members of the special negotiating body" means members of the special negotiating body, established pursuant to regulation 25, elected or appointed by UK employees; and

"the UK register" means the register within the meaning of the Companies Acts (see section 1080 of the Companies Act 2006).

(2) References in these Regulations to "the merging companies" are—

(a) in relation to a merger by absorption or a merger by absorption of a wholly-owned subsidiary, to the transferor company or companies and the existing transferee company;

(b) in relation to a merger by formation of a new company, to the transferor companies.

(3) References in these Regulations to—

(a) "a UK merging company" are to a merging company which is a UK company;

(b) "a UK transferee company" are to a transferee company which is a UK company;

(c) "a UK transferor company" are to a transferor company which is a UK company.

NOTES

Para (1): definitions in square brackets inserted by the Agency Workers Regulations 2010, SI 2010/93, reg 25, Sch 2, Pt 2, paras 39, 40, as from 1 October 2011.

[2.1082]

4 The Companies Act 2006

(1) The following provisions of the Companies Act 2006 apply for the purposes of these Regulations as they apply for the purposes of the Companies Acts—

(a) section 1081 (annotation of the register);

(b) sections 1102 to 1104 and 1107 (language requirements for documents delivered to registrar);

(c) section 1112 (offence of false statement to registrar);

(d) section 1113 (enforcement of company's filing obligations);

(e) sections 1121 to 1123 (liability of officer in default);

(f) section 1125 (meaning of "daily default fine");

(g) sections 1127 and 1128 (summary proceedings);

(h) section 1129 (legal professional privilege);

(i) section 1130 (proceedings against unincorporated bodies).

(2) Section 1063 of the Companies Act 2006 (fees payable to registrar) applies to the functions conferred on the registrar of companies by these Regulations as it applies to the functions conferred on the registrar of companies by the Companies Acts.

(3) Section 1105 of the Companies Act 2006 (documents that may be drawn up and delivered in other languages) applies to the documents required to be delivered to the registrar of companies under—

(a) regulation 12(1)(b) (draft terms of merger), and

(b) regulation 19(3) (order of competent authority of another EEA State).

(4) The facility described in section 1106 of the Companies Act 2006 (voluntary filing of translations) is available in relation to—

(a) all official languages of EEA States, and

(b) all documents required to be delivered to the registrar of companies under these Regulations.

(5) . . .

(6) Schedule 1 makes transitional modifications to provisions of these Regulations that refer to provisions of the Companies Act 2006 that are not yet in force.

NOTES

Para (5): amends the Companies Act 2006 (Commencement No 3, Consequential Amendments, Transitional Provisions and Savings) Order 2007, SI 2007/2194, art 4.

[2.1083]

5 Unregistered companies

(1) These Regulations apply to an unregistered company as they apply to a UK company.

(2) In the application of these Regulations to an unregistered company any reference to—

(a) a UK company's registered office shall be read as a reference to the unregistered company's principal office in the United Kingdom;

(b) a part of the United Kingdom in which a UK company is registered shall be read as a reference to the part of the United Kingdom in which the unregistered company's principal office is situated and "Gazette" and "registrar of companies" shall be construed accordingly (see regulation 3(1)).

(3) In the application of these Regulations to an unregistered company, regulation 12(1)(c) applies with the omission of item (iv) (duty to state company's registered number).

(4) In this regulation "unregistered company" means a body to which section 1043 of the Companies Act 2006 (unregistered companies) applies.

6–21 *(Regs 6–15 (Part 2: Pre-merger Requirements) and regs 16–21 (Part 3: Court Approval of Cross-border Merger) outside the scope of this work.)*

PART 4
EMPLOYEE PARTICIPATION

CHAPTER 1
APPLICATION OF THIS PART

[2.1084]
22 Application of this Part

(1) Subject to paragraph (2), this Part shall apply where the transferee company is a UK company and where—

(a) a merging company has, in the six months before the publication of the draft terms of merger, an average number of employees that exceeds 500 and has a system of employee participation, or

(b) a UK merging company has a proportion of employee representatives amongst the directors, or

(c) a merging company has employee representatives amongst members of the administrative or supervisory organ or their committees or of the management group which covers the profit units of the company.

[(1A) For the purposes of paragraph (1)(a), agency workers whose contract within regulation 3(1)(b) of the Agency Workers Regulations 2010 was not a contract of employment with one or more temporary work agencies that were merging companies at the relevant time are to be treated as having been employed by such a temporary work agency or agencies for the duration of their assignment with a hirer.]

(2) Chapters 4 and 6 to 9 shall apply to a UK merging company, its employees or their representatives, regardless of whether the transferee company is a UK company.

(3) This Part applies to Northern Ireland with the modifications contained in Schedule 2.

NOTES

Para (1A): inserted by the Agency Workers Regulations 2010, SI 2010/93, reg 25, Sch 2, Pt 2, paras 39, 42, as from 1 October 2011.

CHAPTER 2
MERGING COMPANIES AND THE SPECIAL NEGOTIATING BODY

[2.1085]
23 Duty on merging company to provide information

(1) As soon as possible after adopting the draft terms of merger (see regulation 7), each merging company shall provide information to the employee representatives of that company or, if no such representatives exist, the employees themselves.

(2) The information referred to in paragraph (1) must include, as a minimum, information—

(a) identifying the merging companies,

(b) of any decision taken pursuant to regulation 36 (merging companies may select standard rules of employee participation), and

(c) giving the number of employees employed by each merging company.

(3) When a special negotiating body has been formed in accordance with regulation 25, each merging company must provide that body with such information as is necessary to keep it informed of the plan and progress of establishing the UK transferee company until the date upon which the consequences of the cross-border merger take effect (see regulation 17).

[(4) Where under the provisions of this regulation a merging company is to provide information, such information must include suitable information relating to the use of agency workers (if any) in that company.]

NOTES

Para (4): added by the Agency Workers Regulations 2010, SI 2010/93, reg 25, Sch 2, Pt 2, paras 39, 43, as from 1 October 2011.

[2.1086]

24 Complaint of failure to provide information

(1) An employee representative or, where no such representative exists, any employee may present a complaint to the CAC that—

(a) a merging company has failed to provide information as required by regulation 23; or

(b) the information is false or incomplete in a material particular.

(2) Where the CAC finds the complaint well-founded it shall make an order requiring the company to disclose information to the complainant specifying—

(a) the information in respect of which the CAC finds that the complaint is well-founded and which is to be disclosed to the complainant; and

(b) a date (not being less than one week from the date of the order) by which the company must disclose the information specified in the order.

[2.1087]

25 The special negotiating body

(1) Subject to regulation 36 (merging companies may select standard rules of employee participation), each merging company shall make arrangements for the establishment of a special negotiating body.

(2) The task of the special negotiating body shall be to reach an employee participation agreement with the merging companies (see Chapter 3).

(3) The special negotiating body shall be constituted in accordance with regulation 26.

[2.1088]

26 Composition of the special negotiating body

(1) Employees of merging companies registered in each EEA State (including the UK) shall be given an entitlement to elect one member of the special negotiating body, in accordance with these Regulations, for each 10% or fraction thereof which employees of merging companies registered in that State represent of the total workforce of the merging companies. These members shall be the "constituent members".

(2) If, following an election under paragraph (1), the members elected to the special negotiating body do not include at least one constituent member in respect of each merging company, the employees of any merging company in respect of which there is no constituent member shall be given an entitlement, subject to paragraph (3), to elect an additional member to the special negotiating body.

(3) The number of additional members which the employees of the merging companies are entitled to elect under paragraph (2) shall not exceed 20% of the number of constituent members elected under paragraph (1) and if the number of additional members under paragraph (2) would exceed that percentage the employees who are entitled to elect the additional members shall be—

(a) if one additional member is to be elected, those employed by the merging company not represented under paragraph (1) having the highest number of employees; and

(b) if more than one additional member is to be elected, those employed by the merging companies registered in each EEA State that are not represented under paragraph (1) having the highest number of employees in descending order, starting with the company with the highest number, followed by those employed by the companies registered in each EEA State that are not so represented having the second highest number of employees in descending order, starting with the company (among those companies) with the highest number.

(4) Each merging company shall, as soon as reasonably practicable and in any event no later than one month after the establishment of the special negotiating body, inform their employees of the outcome of any elections held under this regulation.

(5) If, following the election of members to the special negotiating body under this regulation—

(a) changes to the merging companies result in the number of members which employees would be entitled to elect under this regulation either increasing or decreasing, the original election of members of the special negotiating body shall cease to have effect and the employees of the merging companies shall be entitled to elect the new number of members in accordance with the provisions of these Regulations; and

(b) a member of the special negotiating body is no longer willing or able to continue serving as such a member, the employees whom he represents shall be entitled to elect a new member in his place.

[2.1089]
27 Complaint about establishment of special negotiating body

(1) An application may be presented to the CAC for a declaration that the special negotiating body has not been established at all or has not been established properly in accordance with regulation 25 or 26.

(2) Where it is alleged that the failure is attributable to the conduct of the merging company, an application may be presented under this regulation by—

(a) a person elected under regulation 26 to be a member of the special negotiating body; or

(b) an employee representative or, where no such representative exists in respect of the company, an employee of the company.

(3) Where it is alleged that the failure is attributable to the conduct of the employees or the employee representatives, an application may be presented under this regulation by the merging company.

(4) The CAC shall only consider an application made under this regulation if it is made within a period of one month from the date or, if more than one, the last date on which the merging companies complied or should have complied with the obligation to inform their employees under regulation 26(4).

(5) Where the CAC finds an application made under paragraph (2) well-founded it shall make a declaration that the special negotiating body has not been established at all or has not been established properly and the merging companies continue to be under the obligation in regulation 25.

(6) Where the CAC finds an application made under paragraph (3) well-founded it shall make a declaration that the special negotiating body has not been established at all or has not been established properly and the merging companies no longer continue to be under the obligation in regulation 25.

CHAPTER 3
NEGOTIATION OF THE EMPLOYEE PARTICIPATION AGREEMENT

[2.1090]
28 Negotiations to reach an employee participation agreement

(1) In Chapters 3 and 5 the merging companies and the special negotiating body are referred to as "the parties".

(2) Subject to regulations 31 (decision not to open or to terminate negotiations) and 36 (merging companies may select standard rules of employee participation), the parties are under a duty to negotiate in a spirit of cooperation with a view to reaching an employee participation agreement.

(3) The duty referred to in paragraph (2) commences one month after the date or, if more than one, the last date on which the members of the special negotiating body were elected or appointed and applies—

(a) for the period of six months starting with the day on which the duty commenced or, where an employee participation agreement is successfully negotiated within that period, until the completion of the negotiations;

(b) where the parties agree before the end of that six month period that it is to be extended, for the period of twelve months starting with the day on which the duty commenced or, where an employee participation agreement is successfully negotiated within the twelve month period, until the completion of the negotiations.

[2.1091]
29 The employee participation agreement

(1) The employee participation agreement must be in writing.

(2) Without prejudice to the autonomy of the parties, the employee participation agreement shall specify—

(a) the scope of the agreement;

(b) if, during negotiations, the parties decide to establish arrangements for employee participation, the substance of those arrangements including (if applicable) the number of directors of the UK transferee company which the employees will be entitled to elect, appoint, recommend or oppose, the procedures as to how these directors may be elected, appointed, recommended or opposed by the employees, and their rights; and

(c) the date of entry into force of the agreement, its duration, the circumstances, if any in which the agreement is required to be re-negotiated and the procedure for its re-negotiation.

[(2A) Where under the employee participation agreement the transferee company is to provide information on the employment situation in that company, such information must include suitable information relating to the use of agency workers (if any) in that company.]

(3) The employee participation agreement shall not be subject to the standard rules of employee participation (see regulation 38), unless it contains a provision to the contrary.

NOTES

Para (2A): inserted by the Agency Workers Regulations 2010, SI 2010/93, reg 25, Sch 2, Pt 2, paras 39, 44, as from 1 October 2011.

[2.1092]

30 Decisions of the special negotiating body

(1) Each member of the special negotiating body shall have one vote.

(2) Subject to paragraph (3) and regulation 31 (decision not to open or to terminate negotiations), the special negotiating body shall take decisions by an absolute majority vote.

(3) Where at least 25% of the employees of the merging companies have participation rights, any decision which would result in a reduction of participation rights must be taken by a two thirds majority vote.

(4) In paragraph (3), reduction of participation rights means that the proportion of directors of the UK transferee company who may be elected or appointed (or whose appointment may be recommended or opposed) by virtue of employee participation is lower than the proportion of such directors or members in the merging company which had the highest proportion of such directors or members.

(5) The special negotiating body must publish the details of any decision taken under this regulation or under regulation 31 (decision not to open or to terminate negotiations) in such a manner as to bring the decision, so far as reasonably practicable, to the attention of the employees whom they represent and such publication shall take place as soon as reasonably practicable and, in any event no later than 14 days after the decision has been taken.

(6) For the purpose of negotiations, the special negotiating body may be assisted by experts of its choice.

(7) The merging companies shall pay for any reasonable expenses of the functioning of the special negotiating body and any reasonable expenses relating to the negotiations that are necessary to enable the special negotiating body to carry out its functions in an appropriate manner; but where the special negotiating body is assisted by more than one expert the merging companies are not required to pay such expenses in respect of more than one of them.

[2.1093]

31 Decision not to open or to terminate negotiations

(1) The special negotiating body may decide, by a majority vote of two thirds of its members, representing at least two thirds of the employees of the merging companies, including the votes of members representing employees in at least two different EEA States, not to open negotiations pursuant to regulation 28 (negotiations to reach an employee participation agreement) or to terminate negotiations already opened.

(2) Following any decision made under paragraph (1), the duty of the parties set out in regulation 28 to negotiate with a view to establishing an employee participation agreement shall cease as from the date of the decision.

[2.1094]

32 Complaint about decisions of special negotiating body

(1) A member of the special negotiating body, an employee representative, or where there is no such representative in respect of an employee, that employee may present a complaint to the CAC if he believes that the special negotiating body has taken a decision referred to in regulation 30 or 31 and—

- (a) that the decision was not taken by the majority required by regulation 30 or 31; or
- (b) that the special negotiating body failed to publish the decision in accordance with regulation 30(5).

(2) The complaint must be presented to the CAC—

- (a) in the case of a complaint under paragraph (1)(a) (required majority), within 21 days of publication of the decision of the special negotiating body;
- (b) in the case of a complaint under paragraph (1)(b) (failure to publish decision), within 21 days of the date by which the decision should have been published.

(3) Where the CAC finds the complaint well-founded it shall make a declaration that the decision was not taken properly and that it shall have no effect.

CHAPTER 4
ELECTION OF UNITED KINGDOM MEMBERS OF THE SPECIAL NEGOTIATING BODY

[2.1095]
33 Ballot arrangements

(1) The UK members of the special negotiating body shall be elected by balloting the UK employees.

(2) The UK merging company must arrange for the holding of a ballot of those employees in accordance with the requirements of paragraph (3).

(3) The requirements referred to in paragraph (2) are—

- (a) in relation to the election of constituent members of the special negotiating body under regulation 26(1), that—
  - (i) if the number of members which UK employees are entitled to elect to the special negotiating body is equal to the number of UK merging companies, there shall be separate ballots of the UK employees in each UK merging company;
  - (ii) if the number of members which the UK employees are entitled to elect to the special negotiating body is greater than the number of UK merging companies, there shall be separate ballots of the UK employees in each UK merging company and the directors shall ensure, as far as practicable, that at least one member representing each such merging company is elected to the special negotiating body and that the number of members representing each UK company is proportionate to the number of employees in that company;
  - (iii) if the number of members which the UK employees are entitled to elect to the special negotiating body is smaller than the number of UK merging companies—
    - (aa) the number of ballots held shall be equivalent to the number of members to be elected;
    - (bb) a separate ballot shall be held in respect of each of the merging companies with the higher or highest number of employees; and
    - (cc) it shall be ensured that any employees of a merging company in respect of which a ballot does not have to be held are entitled to vote in a ballot held in respect of one of the other merging companies;
- (b) that in relation to the election of additional members under regulation 26(2) the directors shall hold a separate ballot in respect of each UK merging company entitled to elect an additional member;
- (c) that in a ballot in respect of a particular UK merging company, all UK employees employed by that merging company are entitled to vote;
- (d) that in a ballot in respect of a particular UK merging company, any person who is immediately before the latest time at which a person may become a candidate—
  - (i) a UK employee employed by that company; or
  - (ii) if the directors of that company so permit, a representative of a trade union who is not an employee of that company,

  is entitled to stand as a candidate for election as a member of the special negotiating body in that ballot;
- (e) that the directors must, in accordance with paragraph (7), appoint an independent ballot supervisor to supervise the conduct of the ballot of UK employees but may instead, where there is to be more than one ballot, appoint more than one independent ballot supervisor in accordance with that paragraph, each of whom is to supervise such of the separate ballots as the directors may determine, provided that each separate ballot is supervised by a supervisor;
- (f) that after the directors have formulated proposals as to the arrangements for the ballot of UK employees and before they have published the final arrangements under sub-paragraph (g) they must, so far as reasonably practicable, consult with the employee representatives on the proposed arrangements for the ballot of UK employees; and
- (g) that the directors must publish, as soon as reasonably practicable, the final arrangements for the ballot of UK employees in such manner as to bring them to the attention of, so far as reasonably practicable, all UK employees and the employee representatives.

(4) Any UK employee or employee representative who believes that the arrangements for the ballot of the UK employees do not comply with the requirements of paragraph (3)(a) to (e) or that there has been a failure to satisfy the requirements of sub-paragraph (f) or (g) may, within a period of 21 days beginning on the date on which the directors published, or should have published, the final arrangements under sub-paragraph (g), present a complaint to the CAC.

(5) Where the CAC finds the complaint well-founded it shall make a declaration to that effect and may make an order requiring the directors to modify the arrangements they have made for the ballot of UK employees or to satisfy the requirements in sub-paragraph (f) or (g) of paragraph (3).

(6) An order under paragraph (5) shall specify the modifications to the arrangements which the directors are required to make and the requirements they must satisfy.

(7) A person is an independent ballot supervisor for the purposes of paragraph (3)(e) if the directors reasonably believe that he will carry out any functions conferred on him in relation to the ballot competently and have no reasonable grounds for believing that his independence in relation to the ballot might reasonably be called into question.

[2.1096]

34 Conduct of the ballot

(1) The directors must—

(a) ensure that a ballot supervisor appointed under regulation 33(3)(e) carries out his functions under this regulation and that there is no interference with his carrying out of those functions from the directors; and

(b) comply with all reasonable requests made by a ballot supervisor for the purposes of, or in connection with, the carrying out of those functions.

(2) A ballot supervisor's appointment shall require that he—

(a) supervises the conduct of the ballot, or the separate ballots he is being appointed to supervise, in accordance with the arrangements for the ballot of UK employees published by the directors under regulation 33(3)(g) or, where appropriate, in accordance with the arrangements as required to be modified by an order made as a result of a complaint presented under regulation 33(4);

(b) does not conduct the ballot or any of the separate ballots before the directors have satisfied the requirement specified in regulation 33(3)(g) (publication of final arrangements for ballot) and—

(i) where no complaint has been presented under regulation 33(4), before the expiry of a period of 21 days beginning on the date on which the directors published the arrangements under regulation 33(3)(g); or

(ii) where a complaint has been presented under regulation 33(4), before the complaint has been determined and, where appropriate, the arrangements have been modified as required by an order made as a result of that complaint;

(c) conducts the ballot, or each separate ballot so as to secure that—

(i) so far as reasonably practicable, those entitled to vote are given the opportunity to vote;

(ii) so far as reasonably practicable, those entitled to stand as candidates are given the opportunity to stand;

(iii) so far as reasonably practicable, those voting are able to do so in secret; and

(iv) the votes given in the ballot are fairly and accurately counted.

(3) As soon as reasonably practicable after the holding of the ballot, the ballot supervisor must publish the results of the ballot in such manner as to make them available to the directors and, so far as reasonably practicable, the UK employees entitled to vote in the ballot and the persons who stood as candidates.

(4) A ballot supervisor shall publish a report ("an ineffective ballot report") where he considers (whether on the basis of representations made to him by another person or otherwise) that—

(a) any of the requirements referred to in paragraph (2) was not satisfied with the result that the outcome of the ballot would have been different; or

(b) there was interference with the carrying out of his functions or a failure by the directors to comply with all reasonable requests made by him with the result that he was unable to form a proper judgement as to whether each of the requirements referred to in paragraph (2) was satisfied in the ballot.

(5) Where a ballot supervisor publishes an ineffective ballot report the report must be published within a period of one month commencing on the date on which the ballot supervisor publishes the results of the ballot under paragraph (3).

(6) A ballot supervisor shall publish an ineffective ballot report in such manner as to make it available to the directors and, so far as reasonably practicable, the UK employees entitled to vote in the ballot and the persons who stood as candidates in the ballot.

(7) Where a ballot supervisor publishes an ineffective ballot report then—

(a) if there has been a single ballot or an ineffective ballot report has been published in respect of every separate ballot, the outcome of the ballot or ballots shall have no effect and the directors shall again be under the obligation in regulation 33(2) (directors to hold ballot for election of special negotiating body);

(b) if there have been separate ballots and sub-paragraph (a) does not apply—

(i) the directors shall arrange for the separate ballot or ballots in respect of which an ineffective ballot report was published to be re-held in accordance with regulation 33 and this regulation; and

(ii) no such ballot shall have effect until it has been re-held and no ineffective ballot report has been published in respect of it.

(8) All costs relating to the holding of a ballot of UK employees, including payments made to a ballot supervisor for supervising the conduct of the ballot, shall be borne by the UK merging company (whether or not an ineffective ballot report has been published).

[2.1097]
35 Representation of employees

(1) Subject to paragraph (2), a member elected in accordance with regulation 26(1), shall be treated as representing the employees for the time being of the merging company whose employees were entitled to vote in the ballot in which he was elected.

(2) If an additional member is elected in accordance with regulation 26(2) and (3), he, and not any member elected in accordance with regulation 26(1), shall be treated as representing the employees for the time being of the merging company whose employees were entitled to vote in the ballot in which he was elected.

CHAPTER 5
STANDARD RULES OF EMPLOYEE PARTICIPATION IN A UK TRANSFEREE COMPANY

[2.1098]
36 Merging Companies may select standard rules of employee participation

The merging companies may choose, without negotiating with the special negotiating body, the employee representatives or the employees, that a UK transferee company shall be subject to the standard rules of employee participation in regulation 38 (the standard rules of employee participation) from the date upon which the consequences of the cross-border merger take effect (see regulation 17).

[2.1099]
37 Application of the standard rules

(1) Notwithstanding regulation 36 (merging companies may select standard rules of employee participation), the standard rules of employee participation shall apply to a UK transferee company in circumstances where paragraph (2) applies and where—
(a) the parties agree that they should; or
(b) the period specified in regulation 28(3) (duty to negotiate employee participation agreement) has expired without the parties reaching an employee participation agreement and—
(i) the merging companies agree that they should; and
(ii) the special negotiating body has not taken any decision under regulation 31 either not to open or to terminate the negotiations referred to in that regulation.

(2) This paragraph applies where before registration of the UK transferee company, one or more forms of employee participation existed in at least one of the merging companies and either—
(a) that participation applied to at least one third of the total number of employees of the merging companies, or
(b) that participation applied to less than one third of the total number of employees of the merging companies but the special negotiating body has decided that the standard rules of employee participation should apply.

[(2A) For the purposes of paragraph (2), agency workers whose contract within regulation 3(1)(b) of the Agency Workers Regulations 2010 was not a contract of employment with one or more temporary work agencies that were merging companies at the relevant time, are to be treated as having been employed by such a temporary work agency or agencies for the duration of their assignment with a hirer.]

(3) Where the standard rules of employee participation apply and more than one form of employee participation existed in the merging companies, the special negotiating body shall decide which of the existing forms of participation shall apply in the UK transferee company and shall inform the merging companies accordingly.

(4) In circumstances where—
(a) the standard rules of employee participation apply, more than one form of employee participation existed in the merging companies and the special negotiating body has failed to make a decision in accordance with paragraph (3); or
(b) one or more form of employee participation existed in the merging companies and the merging companies have chosen, without any prior negotiation, to be directly subject to the standard rules of employee participation,
the merging companies shall be responsible for determining the form of employee participation in the UK transferee company.

NOTES

Para (2A): inserted by the Agency Workers Regulations 2010, SI 2010/93, reg 25, Sch 2, Pt 2, paras 39, 45, as from 1 October 2011.

[2.1100]

38 The standard rules of employee participation

(1) The employee representatives of the UK transferee company, or if there are no such representatives, the employees, shall have the right to elect, appoint, recommend or oppose the appointment of a number of directors of the transferee company, such number to be equal to the number in the merging company which had the highest proportion of directors (or their EEA equivalent) so elected or appointed (subject to regulation 39).

(2) Subject to paragraph (3), the employee representatives, or if there are no such representatives, the employees, shall, taking into account the proportion of employees of the transferee company formerly employed in each merging company, decide on the allocation of directorships, or on the means by which the transferee's employees may recommend or oppose the appointment of directors.

(3) In making the decision set out in paragraph (2), if the employees of one or more merging company are not covered by the proportional criterion set out in paragraph (2), the employee representatives, or if there are no such representatives, the employees, shall appoint a member from one of those merging companies including one from the United Kingdom, if appropriate.

(4) Every director of the transferee company who has been elected, appointed or recommended by the employee representatives or the employees, shall be a full director with the same rights and obligations as the directors representing shareholders, including the right to vote.

[(5) Where under the standard rules of employee participation the transferee company is to provide information on the employment situation in that company, such information must include suitable information relating to the use of agency workers (if any) in that company.]

NOTES

Para (5): added by the Agency Workers Regulations 2010, SI 2010/93, reg 25, Sch 2, Pt 2, paras 39, 46, as from 1 October 2011.

[2.1101]

39 Limit on level of employee participation

Where, following prior negotiation, the standard rules of employee participation apply, the UK transferee company may limit the proportion of directors elected, appointed, recommended or opposed through employee participation to a level which is the lesser of—

(a) the highest proportion in force in the merging companies prior to registration, and
(b) one third of the directors.

[2.1102]

40 Subsequent domestic mergers

(1) A transferee company resulting from a cross-border merger that operates under an employee participation system shall ensure that employees' rights to employee participation shall not be affected before the end of the period of three years commencing on the date on which the consequences of the cross-border merger have effect (see regulation 17) by any order made by the court under section 899 of the Companies Act 2006 (court sanction for compromise or arrangement) for the purposes of—

(a) a reconstruction of the company or the amalgamation of the company with another company (see section 900 of that Act (reconstruction or amalgamation of company)), or
(b) a merger involving a public company (see sections 902 and 903 and Chapter 2 of Part 27 of that Act).

(2) For the purposes of this regulation, any subsequent order made by the court under section 900(2) of the Companies Act 2006 has effect as if it were an order made under section 899 of that Act.

CHAPTER 6
CONFIDENTIAL INFORMATION

[2.1103]

41 Duty of confidentiality

(1) Where a transferee company or merging company entrusts a person, pursuant to the provisions of this Part, with any information or document on terms requiring it to be held in confidence, the person shall not disclose that information or document except in accordance with the terms on which it was disclosed to him.

(2) In this regulation a person referred to in paragraph (1) to whom information or a document is entrusted is referred to as a "recipient".

(3) The obligation to comply with paragraph (1) is a duty owed to the company that disclosed the information or document to the recipient and a breach of the duty is actionable accordingly (subject to the defences and other incidents applying to actions for breach of statutory duty).

(4) Paragraph (3) does not affect any legal liability which any person may incur by disclosing the information or document, or any right which any person may have in relation to such disclosure otherwise than under this regulation.

(5) No action shall lie under paragraph (3) where the recipient reasonably believed the disclosure to be a protected disclosure within the meaning given to that expression by section 43A of the 1996 Act.

(6) A recipient may apply to the CAC for a declaration as to whether it was reasonable for the company to require the recipient to hold the information or document in confidence.

(7) If the CAC considers that the disclosure of the information or document by the recipient would not, or would not be likely to, harm the legitimate interests of the undertaking, it shall make a declaration that it was not reasonable for the company to require the recipient to hold the information or document in confidence.

(8) If a declaration is made under paragraph (7), the information or document shall not at any time thereafter be regarded as having been entrusted to any recipient on terms requiring it to be held in confidence.

[2.1104]

42 Withholding of information by the transferee or merging company

(1) Neither a transferee company nor a merging company is required to disclose any information or document to a person for the purposes of this Part where the nature of the information or document is such that, according to objective criteria, the disclosure of the information or document would seriously harm the functioning of, or would be prejudicial to the transferee company or merging company.

(2) Where there is a dispute between the transferee company or merging company and—

- (a) where a special negotiating body has been appointed or elected, a member of that body; or
- (b) where no special negotiating body has been elected or appointed, an employee,

as to whether the nature of any information or document is such as is described in paragraph (1), the transferee company or merging company or a person referred to in sub-paragraph (a) or (b) may apply to the CAC for a declaration as to whether the information or document is of such a nature.

(3) If the CAC makes a declaration that the disclosure of the information or document in question would not, according to objective criteria, be seriously harmful or prejudicial as mentioned in paragraph (1), the CAC shall order the transferee company or merging company to disclose the information or document.

(4) An order under paragraph (3) shall specify—

- (a) the information or document to be disclosed;
- (b) the person or persons to whom the information or document is to be disclosed;
- (c) any terms on which the information or document is to be disclosed; and
- (d) the date before which the information or document is to be disclosed.

CHAPTER 7
PROTECTION FOR EMPLOYEES AND MEMBERS OF SPECIAL NEGOTIATING BODY, ETC

[2.1105]

43 Right to time off for members of special negotiating body, etc

(1) An employee who is—

- (a) a member of a special negotiating body;
- (b) a director of a transferee company; or
- (c) a candidate in an election in which any person elected will, on being elected, be such a director or member,

is entitled to be permitted by his employer to take reasonable time off during the employee's working hours in order to perform his functions as such a member, director or candidate.

(2) For the purpose of this regulation the working hours of an employee shall be taken to be any time when, in accordance with his contract of employment, the employee is required to be at work.

[2.1106]

44 Right to remuneration for time off under regulation 43

(1) An employee who is permitted to take time off under regulation 43 is entitled to be paid remuneration by his employer for the time taken off at the appropriate hourly rate.

(2) Chapter 2 of Part 14 of the 1996 Act (a week's pay) shall apply in relation to this regulation as it applies in relation to section 62 of the 1996 Act.

(3) The appropriate hourly rate, in relation to an employee, is the amount of one week's pay divided by the number of normal working hours in a week for that employee when employed under the contract of employment in force on the day when the time is taken.

(4) But where the number of normal working hours differs from week to week or over a longer period, the amount of one week's pay shall be divided instead by—

(a) the average number of normal working hours calculated by dividing by twelve the total number of the employee's normal working hours during the period of twelve weeks ending with the last complete week before the day on which the time off is taken; or

(b) where the employee has not been employed for a sufficient period to enable the calculation to be made under sub-paragraph (a), a number which fairly represents the number of normal working hours in a week having regard to such of the considerations specified in paragraph (5) as are appropriate in the circumstances.

(5) The considerations referred to in paragraph (4)(b) are—

(a) the average number of normal working hours in a week which the employee could expect in accordance with the terms of his contract; and

(b) the average number of normal working hours of other employees engaged in relevant comparable employment with the same employer.

(6) A right to any amount under paragraph (1) does not affect any right of an employee in relation to remuneration under his contract of employment.

(7) Any contractual remuneration paid to an employee in respect of a period of time off under regulation 43 goes towards discharging any liability of the employer to pay remuneration under paragraph (1) in respect of that period, and conversely, any payment of remuneration under paragraph (1) in respect of a period goes towards discharging any liability of the employer to pay contractual remuneration in respect of that period.

[2.1107]

45 Right to time off: complaints to employment tribunals

(1) An employee may present a complaint to an employment tribunal that his employer—

(a) has unreasonably refused to permit him to take time off as required under regulation 43; or

(b) has failed to pay the whole or any part of any amount to which the employee is entitled under regulation 44.

(2) An employment tribunal shall not consider a complaint under this regulation unless it is presented—

(a) before the end of the period of three months beginning with the day on which the time off was taken or on which it is alleged the time off should have been permitted; or

(b) within such further period as the tribunal considers reasonable in a case where it is satisfied that it was not reasonably practicable for the complaint to be presented before the end of that period of three months.

(3) Where an employment tribunal finds a complaint under this regulation well-founded, the tribunal shall make a declaration to that effect.

(4) If the complaint is that the employer has unreasonably refused to permit the employee to take time off, the tribunal shall also order the employer to pay to the employee an amount equal to the remuneration to which he would have been entitled under regulation 44 if the employer had not refused.

(5) If the complaint is that the employer has failed to pay the employee the whole or part of any amount to which he is entitled under regulation 44, the tribunal shall also order him to pay to the employee the amount which it finds is due to him.

NOTES

Conciliation: employment tribunal proceedings and claims which could be the subject of employment tribunal proceedings under this regulation are proceedings to which the Employment Tribunals Act 1996, s 18 applies; see s 18(1)(t) of that Act at **[1.706]**.

[2.1108]

46 Unfair dismissal of employee

(1) An employee who is dismissed shall be regarded as unfairly dismissed for the purposes of Part 10 of the 1996 Act if the reason (or, if more than one, the principal reason) for the dismissal is one specified in paragraph (2).

(2) The reasons are that the employee—

(a) took, or proposed to take, any proceedings before an employment tribunal to enforce any right conferred on him by these Regulations;

(b) exercised, or proposed to exercise, any entitlement to apply or complain to the CAC or the Appeal Tribunal conferred by these Regulations or exercised or proposed to exercise the right to appeal in connection with any rights conferred by these Regulations;

(c) acted with a view to securing that a special negotiating body did or did not come into existence;

(d) indicated that he did or did not support the coming into existence of a special negotiating body;

(e) stood as a candidate in an election in which any person elected would, on being elected, be a member of a special negotiating body or a director of a UK transferee company;
(f) influenced or sought to influence by lawful means the way in which votes were to be cast by other employees in a ballot arranged under these Regulations;
(g) voted in such a ballot;
(h) expressed doubts, whether to a ballot supervisor or otherwise, as to whether such a ballot had been properly conducted; or
(i) proposed to do, failed to do, or proposed to decline to do, any of the things mentioned in sub-paragraphs (e) to (h).

(3) Paragraph (1) does not apply where the reason (or principal reason) for the dismissal is that in the performance, or purported performance, of the employee's functions or activities he has disclosed any information or document in breach of the duty in regulation 41 (duty of confidentiality), unless the employee reasonably believed the disclosure to be a protected disclosure within the meaning given to that expression by section 43A of the 1996 Act.

(4) For the purposes of paragraph (2)(a) it is immaterial—
(a) whether or not the employee has the right or entitlement; or
(b) whether or not the right has been infringed,
but for that sub-paragraph to apply, the claim to the right and, if applicable, the claim that it has been infringed must be made in good faith.

[2.1109]
47 Unfair dismissal of member of special negotiating body, etc

(1) An employee who is—
(a) a member of a special negotiating body;
(b) a director of a transferee company; or
(c) a candidate in an election in which any person elected will, on being elected, be such a director or member,
who is dismissed shall be regarded as unfairly dismissed for the purposes of Part 10 of the 1996 Act if the reason (or, if more than one, the principal reason) for the dismissal is one specified in paragraph (2).

(2) The reasons are that—
(a) the employee performed or proposed to perform any functions or activities as such a member, director or candidate; or
(b) the employee or a person acting on his behalf made or proposed to make a request to exercise an entitlement conferred on the employee by regulation 43 (right to time off work) or 44 (right to remuneration for time off work).

(3) Paragraph (1) does not apply in the circumstances set out in paragraph (2)(a) where the reason (or principal reason) for the dismissal is that in the performance, or purported performance, of the employee's functions or activities he has disclosed any information or document in breach of the duty in regulation 41 (duty of confidentiality), unless the employee reasonably believed the disclosure to be a protected disclosure within the meaning given to that expression by section 43A of the 1996 Act.

48 (*Amends the Employment Rights Act 1996, ss 105, 108 at* **[1.915]**, **[1.918]**.)

[2.1110]
49 Detriment

(1) An employee has the right not to be subjected to any detriment by any act, or deliberate failure to act, by his employer, done on a ground specified in paragraph (2).

(2) The grounds are that the employee—
(a) took, or proposed to take, any proceedings before an employment tribunal to enforce any right conferred on him by these Regulations;
(b) exercised, or proposed to exercise, any entitlement to apply or complain to the CAC or the Appeal Tribunal conferred by these Regulations or exercised or proposed to exercise the right to appeal in connection with any rights conferred by these Regulations;
(c) acted with a view to securing that a special negotiating body did or did not come into existence;
(d) indicated that he did or did not support the coming into existence of a special negotiating body;
(e) stood as a candidate in an election in which any person elected would, on being elected, be a member of a special negotiating body or a director of a UK transferee company;
(f) influenced or sought to influence by lawful means the way in which votes were to be cast by other employees in a ballot arranged under these Regulations;
(g) voted in such a ballot;
(h) expressed doubts, whether to a ballot supervisor or otherwise, as to whether such a ballot had been properly conducted; or

(i) proposed to do, failed to do, or proposed to decline to do, any of the things mentioned in sub-paragraphs (d) to (h).

(3) It is immaterial for the purposes of paragraph (2)(a)—

(a) whether or not the employee has the right or entitlement; or

(b) whether or not the right has been infringed,

but for that sub-paragraph to apply, the claim to the right and, if applicable, the claim that has been infringed must be made in good faith.

(4) This regulation does not apply where the detriment in question amounts to dismissal.

[2.1111]

50 Detriment for member of special negotiating body, etc

(1) An employee who is—

(a) a member of a special negotiating body;

(b) a director of a transferee company; or

(c) a candidate in an election in which any person elected will, on being elected, be such a director or member,

has the right not to be subjected to any detriment by any act, or deliberate failure to act, by his employer, done on a ground specified in paragraph (2).

(2) The ground is that—

(a) the employee performed or proposed to perform any functions or activities as such a director, member or candidate; or

(b) the employee or person acting on his behalf made or proposed to make a request to exercise an entitlement conferred on the employee by regulation 43 (right to time off work) or 44 (right to remuneration for time off work).

(3) Paragraph (1) does not apply in the circumstances set out in paragraph (2)(a) where the ground for the subjection to detriment is that in the performance, or purported performance, of the employee's functions or activities he has disclosed any information or document in breach of the duty in regulation 41 (duty of confidentiality), unless the employee reasonably believed the disclosure to be a protected disclosure within the meaning given to that expression by section 43A of the 1996 Act.

(4) This regulation does not apply where the detriment in question amounts to a dismissal.

[2.1112]

51 Detriment: enforcement and subsidiary provisions

(1) An employee may present a complaint to an employment tribunal that he has been subjected to a detriment in contravention of regulation 49 or 50.

(2) The provisions of section 49(1) to (5) of the 1996 Act shall apply in relation to a complaint under this regulation.

NOTES

Conciliation: employment tribunal proceedings and claims which could be the subject of employment tribunal proceedings under this regulation are proceedings to which the Employment Tribunals Act 1996, s 18 applies; see s 18(1)(t) of that Act at **[1.706]**.

Tribunal jurisdiction: the Employment Act 2002, s 38 applies to proceedings before the employment tribunal relating to a claim under this regulation; see s 38(1) of, and Sch 5 to, the 2002 Act at **[1.1228]**, **[1.1236]**.

52 (*Amends the Employment Tribunals Act 1996, s 18 at* **[1.706]**.)

CHAPTER 8
COMPLIANCE AND ENFORCEMENT

[2.1113]

53 Disputes about operation of an employee participation agreement or the standard rules of employee participation

(1) Where—

(a) an employee participation agreement has been agreed; or

(b) the standard rules of employee participation apply,

a complaint may be presented to the CAC by a relevant applicant who considers that the transferee company has failed to comply with the terms of the employee participation agreement or, where applicable, the standard rules of employee participation.

(2) A complaint brought under paragraph (1) must be brought within a period of 3 months commencing with the date of the alleged failure, or where the failure takes place over a period, the last day of that period.

(3) In this regulation—

"failure" includes failure by means of an act or omission,

"relevant applicant" means—

(a) a special negotiating body; or
(b) in a case where no special negotiating body has been elected or appointed, or has been dissolved, an employee representative or employee of the transferee company.

(4) Where the CAC finds the complaint well-founded it shall make a declaration to that effect and may make an order requiring the transferee company to take such steps as are necessary to comply with the terms of the employee participation agreement or, where applicable, the standard rules of employee participation.

(5) An order made under paragraph (4) shall specify—
(a) the steps which the transferee company is required to take;
(b) the date of the failure; and
(c) the period within which the order must be complied with.

(6) If the CAC makes a declaration under paragraph (4), the relevant applicant may, within the period of three months beginning with the day on which the decision is made, make an application to the Appeal Tribunal for a penalty notice to be issued.

(7) Where such an application is made, the Appeal Tribunal shall issue a written penalty notice to the transferee company requiring it to pay a penalty to the Secretary of State in respect of the failure unless satisfied, on hearing representations from the transferee company, that the failure resulted from a reason beyond its control or that it has some other reasonable excuse for its failure.

(8) Regulation 55 (penalties) shall apply in respect of a penalty notice issued under this regulation.

(9) No order of the CAC under this regulation shall have the effect of suspending or altering the effect of any act done or of any agreement made by the transferee company or merging company.

[2.1114]
54 Misuse of procedures

(1) If an employee representative, or where there is no such representative in relation to an employee, an employee, believes that a transferee company or merging company is misusing or intending to misuse the transferee company or the powers in these Regulations for the purpose of—
(a) depriving the employees of that merging company or the transferee company of their rights to employee participation; or
(b) withholding such rights from any of the people referred to in sub-paragraph (a), he may make a complaint to the CAC.

(2) A complaint must be made to the CAC under paragraph (1) before the date upon which the consequences of the cross-border merger take effect (see regulation 17) or within a period of 12 months after that date.

(3) The CAC shall uphold the complaint unless the respondent proves that it did not misuse or intend to misuse the transferee company or the powers in these Regulations for either of the purposes set out in sub-paragraph (a) or (b) of paragraph (1).

(4) If the CAC finds the complaint to be well-founded it shall make a declaration to that effect and may make an order requiring the transferee company or merging company to take such action as is specified in the order to ensure that the employees referred to in paragraph (1)(a) are not deprived of their rights to employee participation or that such rights are not withheld from them; and

(5) If the CAC makes a declaration under paragraph (4), the complainant under paragraph (1) may, within the period of three months beginning with the day on which the decision is made, make an application to the Appeal Tribunal for a penalty notice to be issued.

(6) Where such an application is made, the Appeal Tribunal shall issue a written penalty notice to the transferee company or merging company requiring it to pay a penalty to the Secretary of State in respect of the failure unless satisfied, on hearing representations from the transferee company or merging company, that the failure resulted from a reason beyond its control or that it has some other reasonable excuse for its failure.

(7) The provisions in regulations 53(8) to (9) and 55 shall apply to the complaint.

[2.1115]
55 Penalties

(1) A penalty notice issued under regulation 53 (disputes) or 54 (misuse of procedures) shall specify—
(a) the amount of the penalty which is payable;
(b) the date before which the penalty must be paid; and
(c) the failure and period to which the penalty relates.

(2) No penalty set by the Appeal Tribunal under this regulation may exceed £75,000.

(3) When setting the amount of the penalty, the Appeal Tribunal shall take into account—
(a) the gravity of the failure;
(b) the period of time over which the failure occurred;
(c) the reason for the failure;

(d) the number of employees affected by the failure; and
(e) the number of employees employed by the undertaking.

(4) The date specified under paragraph (1)(b) above must not be earlier than the end of the period within which an appeal against a decision or order made by the CAC under regulation 53 or 54 may be made.

(5) If the specified date in a penalty notice has passed and—
(a) the period during which an appeal may be made has expired without an appeal having been made; or
(b) such an appeal has been made and determined,
the Secretary of State may recover from the transferee company or merging company, as a civil debt due to him, any amount payable under the penalty notice which remains outstanding.

(6) The making of an appeal suspends the effect of the penalty notice.

(7) Any sums received by the Secretary of State under regulation 53, 54 or this regulation shall be paid into the Consolidated Fund.

[2.1116]
56 Exclusivity of remedy

Where these Regulations provide for a remedy of infringement of any right by way of application or complaint to the CAC, and provide for no other remedy, no other remedy is available for infringement of that right.

CHAPTER 9
MISCELLANEOUS

[2.1117]
57 CAC proceedings

(1) Where under these Regulations a person presents a complaint or makes an application to the CAC the complaint or application must be in writing and in such form as the CAC may require.

(2) In its consideration of a complaint or application under these Regulations, the CAC shall make such enquiries as it sees fit and give any person whom it considers has a proper interest in the complaint or application an opportunity to be heard.

(3) Where a transferee company or merging company has its registered office in England and Wales—
(a) a declaration made by the CAC under these Regulations may be relied on as if it were a declaration or order made by the High Court in England and Wales; and
(b) an order made by the CAC under these Regulations may be enforced in the same way as an order of the High Court in England and Wales.

(4) Where a transferee company or merging company has its registered office in Scotland—
(a) a declaration or order made by the CAC under these Regulations may be relied on as if it were a declaration or order made by the Court of Session; and
(b) an order made by the CAC under these Regulations may be enforced in the same way as an order of the Court of Session.

(5) A declaration or order made by the CAC under these Regulations must be in writing and state the reasons for the CAC's findings.

(6) An appeal lies to the Appeal Tribunal on any question of law arising from any declaration or order of, or arising in any proceedings before, the CAC under these Regulations.

[2.1118]
58 Appeal Tribunal: location of certain proceedings under these Regulations

(1) Any proceedings before the Appeal Tribunal under these Regulations, other than appeals under paragraph (u) of section 21(1) of the Employment Tribunals Act 1996 (appeals from employment tribunals on questions of law), shall—
(a) where the registered office of the transferee company or merging company is situated in England and Wales, be held in England and Wales; and
(b) where the registered office of the transferee company or merging company is situated in Scotland, be held in Scotland.

(2) . . .

NOTES

Para (2): amends the Employment Tribunals Act 1996, s 20 at **[1.712]**.

59 (*Amends the Employment Tribunals Act 1996, s 21* at **[1.713]**.)

Part 2 Statutory Instruments

[2.1119]
60 ACAS

(1) If on receipt of an application or complaint under these Regulations the CAC is of the opinion that it is reasonably likely to be settled by conciliation, it shall refer the application or complaint to the Advisory, Conciliation and Arbitration Service ("ACAS") and shall notify the applicant or complainant and any persons whom it considers have a proper interest in the application or complaint accordingly, whereupon ACAS shall seek to promote a settlement of the matter.

(2) If an application or complaint so referred is not settled or withdrawn and ACAS is of the opinion that further attempts at conciliation are unlikely to result in a settlement, it shall inform the CAC of its opinion.

(3) If—

(a) the application or complaint is not referred to ACAS; or

(b) ACAS informs the CAC of its opinion that further attempts at conciliation are unlikely to result in a settlement,

the CAC shall proceed to hear and determine the application or complaint.

[2.1120]
61 Restrictions on contracting out: general

(1) Any provision in any agreement (whether an employee's contract or not) is void in so far as it purports—

(a) to exclude or limit the operation of any provision of this Part of these Regulations other than a provision of Chapter 7 (protection for employees and members of special negotiating body) (but see regulation 62); or

(b) to preclude a person from bringing any proceedings before the CAC, under any provision of this Part (other than a provision of that Chapter).

(2) Paragraph (1) does not apply to any agreement to refrain from continuing any proceedings referred to in sub-paragraph (b) of that paragraph made after the proceedings have been instituted.

[2.1121]
62 Restrictions on contracting out: Chapter 7 of this Part

(1) Any provision in any agreement (whether an employee's contract or not) is void in so far as it purports—

(a) to exclude or limit the operation of any provision of Chapter 7 of this Part of these Regulations; or

(b) to preclude a person from bringing any proceedings before an employment tribunal under that Chapter.

(2) Paragraph (1) does not apply to any agreement to refrain from instituting or continuing proceedings before an employment tribunal where a conciliation officer has taken action under section 18 of the Employment Tribunals Act 1996 (conciliation).

(3) Paragraph (1) does not apply to any agreement to refrain from instituting or continuing before an employment tribunal proceedings within section 18(1) of the Employment Tribunals Act 1996 if the conditions regulating compromise agreements under these Regulations are satisfied in relation to the agreement.

(4) For the purposes of paragraph (3) the conditions regulating compromise agreements are that—

(a) the agreement must be in writing;

(b) the agreement must relate to the particular proceedings;

(c) the employee must have received advice from a relevant independent adviser as to the terms and effect of the proposed agreement and, in particular, its effect on his ability to pursue his rights before an employment tribunal;

(d) there must be in force, when the adviser gives the advice, a contract of insurance, or an indemnity provided for members of a profession or professional body, covering the risk of a claim by the employee in respect of loss arising in consequence of the advice;

(e) the agreement must identify the adviser; and

(f) the agreement must state that the conditions in sub-paragraphs (a) to (e) are satisfied.

(5) A person is a relevant independent adviser for the purposes of paragraph (4)(c)—

(a) if he is a qualified lawyer;

(b) if he is an officer, official, employee or member of an independent trade union who has been certified in writing by the trade union as competent to give advice and authorised to do so on behalf of the trade union; or

(c) if he works at an advice centre (whether as an employee or as a volunteer) and has been certified in writing by the centre as competent to give advice and authorised to do so on behalf of the centre.

(6) But a person is not a relevant independent adviser for the purposes of paragraph (4)(c) in relation to the employee—

(a) if he is, is employed by or is acting in the matter for the employer or an associated employer; or

(b) in the case of a person within paragraph (5)(b) or (c), if the trade union or advice centre is the employer or an associated employer.

(7) In paragraph (5)(a), a "qualified lawyer" means—

(a) as respects England and Wales, [a person who, for the purposes of the Legal Services Act 2007), is an authorised person in relation to an activity which constitutes the exercise of a right of audience or the conduct of litigation (within the meaning of that Act)]; and

(b) as respects Scotland, an advocate (whether in practice as such or employed to give legal advice) or a solicitor who holds a practising certificate.

(8) A person shall be treated as being a qualified lawyer within paragraph (7)(a) if he is a Fellow of the Institute of Legal Executives [practising in a solicitor's practice (including a body recognised under section 9 of the Administration of Justice Act 1985)].

(9) For the purposes of paragraph (6) any two employers shall be treated as associated if—

(a) one is a company of which the other (directly or indirectly) has control; or

(b) both are companies of which a third person (directly or indirectly) has control, and "associated employer" shall be construed accordingly.

NOTES

Paras (7), (8): words in square brackets substituted by the Legal Services Act 2007 (Consequential Amendments) Order 2009, SI 2009/3348, arts 22, 23, Schs 1, 2, as from 1 January 2010 (in the case of the para (7) amendment), and as from 16 December 2009 (in the case of the para (8) amendment).

63–66 (*Reg 63 amends the Employment Act 2002, Schs 3–5 (note that Schs 3, 4 were repealed by the Employment Act 2008, as from 6 April 2009); reg 64 contains various amendments to the Employment Appeal Tribunal Rules 1993, SI 2003/2854 at* **[2.142]** *et seq; reg 65 amends the Insolvency Act 1986, Sch B1 at* **[1.152]***; reg 66 amends the Insolvency (Northern Ireland) Order 1989.*)

SCHEDULES 1 AND 2

(*Sch 1 (Transitional Modifications where Provisions of Companies Act 2006 Not in Force) and Sch 2 (Application of the Regulations in Relation to Northern Ireland) outside the scope of this work.*)

IMMIGRATION (RESTRICTIONS ON EMPLOYMENT) ORDER 2007

(SI 2007/3290)

NOTES

Made: 15 November 2007.
Authority: Immigration, Asylum and Nationality Act 2006, ss 15(3), (7), 16(3), (5), 19(2), 23(3), 25(d).
Commencement: 29 February 2008.
See *Harvey* AI(5).

ARRANGEMENT OF ARTICLES

Citation, commencement and interpretation

[2.1122]
1

This order may be cited as the Immigration (Restrictions on Employment) Order 2007 and shall come into force on 29 February 2008.

[2.1123]
2

In this order—

"the 2006 Act" means the Immigration, Asylum and Nationality Act 2006; and
"document" means an original document.

Excuse from paying civil penalty

[2.1124]
3

(1) To the extent provided for by paragraph (2) an employer is excused from paying a penalty under section 15 of the 2006 Act if—

(a) the employee or prospective employee produces to the employer any of the documents or combinations of documents described in list A in the Schedule to this Order; and
(b) the employer complies with the requirements set out in article 6 of this order.

(2) An employer will be excused under this article from paying a penalty under section 15 of the 2006 Act—

(a) for the duration of the employment, if the document or combination of documents is produced prior to the commencement of employment; or
(b) subject to article 5, for the remainder of the employment, if the document or combination of documents is produced after the employment has commenced.

[2.1125]
4

(1) To the extent provided for by paragraph (2) an employer is excused from paying a penalty under section 15 of the 2006 Act if—

(a) the employee or prospective employee produces to the employer any of the documents or combination of documents described in list B in the Schedule to this Order; and
(b) the employer complies with the requirements set out in article 6 of this Order.

(2) Subject to article 5 an employer will be excused under this article from paying a penalty under section 15 of the 2006 Act for a period of twelve months, beginning with the date on which the employee produced the document or combination of documents.

[2.1126]
5

An employer is excused from paying a penalty under section 15 of the 2006 Act by virtue of article 3(2)(b) and article 4(2) only if prior to the commencement of employment the employee produced to the employer any of the documents or combination of documents described in the Schedule to this Order.

[2.1127]
6

The requirements in relation to any documents or combinations of documents produced by an employee pursuant to articles 3 or 4 of this order are that—

(a) the employer takes all reasonable steps to check the validity of the document;
(b) the copy or copies are retained securely by the employer for a period of not less than two years after the employment has come to an end;
(c) if a document contains a photograph, the employer has satisfied himself that the photograph is of the prospective employee or employee;
(d) if a document contains a date of birth, the employer has satisfied himself that the date of birth is consistent with the appearance of the prospective employee or employee;
(e) the employer takes all other reasonable steps to check that the prospective employee or employee is the rightful owner of the document;
(f) if the document is not a passport or other travel document the employer retains a copy of whole of the document in a format which cannot be subsequently altered, . . .
[(g) if the document is a passport or other travel document (which is not in the form of a card), the employer retains a copy of the following pages of that document in a format which cannot be subsequently altered—
 (i) the front cover;
 (ii) any page containing the holder's personal details including nationality;
 (iii) any page containing the holder's photograph;
 (iv) any page containing the holder's signature;
 (v) any page containing the date of expiry; and
 (vi) any page containing information indicating the holder has an entitlement to enter or remain in the UK and undertake the work in question.
(h) if the document is a travel document in the form of a card, the employer retains a copy of the whole of that document in a format which cannot be subsequently altered].

NOTES

Word omitted from para (f) revoked, and paras (g), (h) substituted (for the original para (g)) by the Immigration (Restrictions on Employment) (Amendment) Order 2009, SI 2009/2908, arts 2, 3, as from 24 November 2009.

[2.1128]
7

Nothing in this Order permits employers to retain documents produced by an employee for the purposes of articles 3 or 4 for any period longer than is necessary for the purposes of ensuring compliance with article 6.

Objections

[2.1129]
8

The manner prescribed in which the notice of objection must be given is that it must contain—

(a) the reference number of the notice given under section 15(2) of the 2006 Act;
(b) the name and contact address of the employer;
(c) the name and contact address of the employee in respect of whom the penalty was issued;
(d) the full grounds of objection;
(e) where the employer requests permission to pay by instalments, full details of the employer's ability to pay the penalty;
(f) confirmation and details of any appeal made by the employer to a County Court or Sheriff Court on the basis that the employer is not liable to the penalty, he is excused payment by virtue of section 15(3) of the 2006 Act, or that the amount of the penalty is too high; and
(g) any documents to be relied upon in support of the objection.

[2.1130]
9

The prescribed period within which a notice of objection must be given for the purposes of section 16(3)(d) of the 2006 Act is 28 days, beginning with the date specified in the penalty notice as the date upon which it is given.

[2.1131]
10

The period prescribed for the purposes of section 16(5)(b) of the 2006 Act within which the Secretary of State must inform the objector of his decision is 28 days, beginning with the date on which the notice of objection was given to the Secretary of State.

Codes of Practice

[2.1132]
11

The code of practice entitled "Civil Penalties for Employers", issued by the Secretary of State under section 19(1) of the 2006 Act shall come into force on 29 February 2008.

NOTES

The code of practice is reproduced at **[4.107]**.

[2.1133]
12

The code of practice entitled "Guidance for Employers on the Avoidance of Unlawful Discrimination in Employment Practice While Seeking to Prevent Illegal Working", issued by the Secretary of State under section 23(1) of the 2006 Act shall come into force on 29 February 2008.

NOTES

The code of practice is reproduced at **[4.114]**.

SCHEDULE

Articles 3 and 4

List A

[2.1134]

1. [An ID Card (issued to the holder under the Identity Cards Act 2006) or] a passport showing that the holder, or a person named in the passport as the child of the holder, is a British citizen or a citizen of the United Kingdom and Colonies having the right of abode in the United Kingdom.

[**2.** An ID Card (issued to the holder under the Identity Cards Act 2006), a national identity card or a passport which has the effect of identifying the holder, or a person named in the passport as the child of the holder, as a national of the European Economic Area or Switzerland.]

3. A residence permit, registration certificate or document certifying or indicating permanent residence issued by the Home Office or the Border and Immigration Agency to a national of a European Economic Area country or Switzerland.

4. A permanent residence card issued by the Home Office or the Border and Immigration Agency to the family member of a national of a European Economic Area country or Switzerland.

5. A Biometric Immigration Document issued by the Border and Immigration Agency to the holder which indicates that the person named in it is allowed to stay indefinitely in the United Kingdom, or has no time limit on their stay in the United Kingdom.

6. A passport or other travel document endorsed to show that the holder is exempt from immigration control, is allowed to stay indefinitely in the United Kingdom, has the right of abode in the United Kingdom, or has no time limit on their stay in the United Kingdom.

7. An Immigration Status Document issued by the Home Office or the Border and Immigration Agency to the holder with an endorsement indicating that the person named in it is allowed to stay indefinitely in the United Kingdom or has no time limit on their stay in the United Kingdom, when produced in combination with an official document giving the person's permanent National Insurance Number and their name issued by a Government agency or a previous employer.

8. A full birth certificate issued in the United Kingdom which includes the name(s) of at least one of the holder's parents, when produced in combination with an official document giving the person's permanent National Insurance Number and their name issued by a Government agency or a previous employer.

9. A full adoption certificate issued in the United Kingdom which includes the name(s) of at least one of the holder's adoptive parents when produced in combination with an official document giving the person's permanent National Insurance Number and their name issued by a Government agency or a previous employer.

10. A birth certificate issued in the Channel Islands, the Isle of Man or Ireland, when produced in combination with an official document giving the person's permanent National Insurance Number and their name issued by a Government agency or a previous employer.

11. An adoption certificate issued in the Channel Islands, the Isle of Man or Ireland, when produced in combination with an official document giving the person's permanent National Insurance Number and their name issued by a Government agency or a previous employer.

12. A certificate of registration or naturalisation as a British citizen, when produced in combination with an official document giving the person's permanent National Insurance Number and their name issued by a Government agency or a previous employer.

13. A letter issued by the Home Office or the Border and Immigration Agency to the holder which indicates that the person named in it is allowed to stay indefinitely in the United Kingdom when produced in combination with an official document giving the person's permanent National Insurance Number and their name issued by a Government agency or a previous employer.

List B

1. A passport or travel document endorsed to show that the holder is allowed to stay in the United Kingdom and is allowed to do the type of work in question, provided that it does not require the issue of a work permit.

2. A Biometric Immigration Document issued by the Border and Immigration Agency to the holder which indicates that the person named in it can stay in the United Kingdom and is allowed to do the work in question.

3. A work permit or other approval to take employment issued by the Home Office or the Border and Immigration Agency when produced in combination with either a passport or another travel document endorsed to show the holder is allowed to stay in the United Kingdom and is allowed to do the work in question, or a letter issued by the Home Office or the Border and Immigration Agency to the holder or the employer or prospective employer confirming the same.

4. A certificate of application issued by the Home Office or the Border and Immigration Agency to or for [a person who has applied under regulation 18A(1) of the Immigration (European Economic Area) Regulations 2006, or to or for] a family member of a national of a European Economic Area country or Switzerland stating that the holder is permitted to take employment which is less than 6 months old when produced in combination with evidence of verification by the Border and Immigration Agency Employer Checking Service.

5. A residence card or document issued by the Home Office or the Border and Immigration Agency to a family member of a national of a European Economic Area country or Switzerland.

[5A. A derivative residence card issued by the Home Office or the UK Borders Agency to a person.]

6. An Application Registration Card issued by the Home Office or the Border and Immigration Agency stating that the holder is permitted to take employment, when produced in combination with evidence of verification by the Border and Immigration Agency Employer Checking Service.

7. An Immigration Status Document issued by the Home Office or the Border and Immigration Agency to the holder with an endorsement indicating that the person named in it can stay in the United Kingdom, and is allowed to do the type of work in question, when produced in combination with an official document giving the person's permanent National Insurance Number and their name issued by a Government agency or a previous employer.

8. A letter issued by the Home Office or the Border and Immigration Agency to the holder or the employer or prospective employer, which indicates that the person named in it can stay in the United Kingdom and is allowed to do the work in question when produced in combination with an official document giving the person's permanent National Insurance Number and their name issued by a Government agency or a previous employer.

NOTES

In List A, the words in square brackets in para 1 were inserted, and para 2 was substituted, by the Immigration (Restrictions on Employment) (Amendment) Order 2009, SI 2009/2908, arts 2, 4, as from 24 November 2009.

In LIst B, the words in square brackets in para 4 and the whole of para 5A were inserted by the Immigration (European Economic Area) (Amendment) Regulations 2012, SI 2012/1547, reg 4, Sch 2, para 4, as from 16 July 2012.

IMMIGRATION (EMPLOYMENT OF ADULTS SUBJECT TO IMMIGRATION CONTROL) (MAXIMUM PENALTY) ORDER 2008

(SI 2008/132)

NOTES

Made: 22 January 2008.

Authority: Immigration, Asylum and Nationality Act 2006, s 15(2).

Commencement: 29 February 2008.

[2.1135]

1 Citation and Commencement

This Order may be cited as the Immigration (Employment of Adults Subject to Immigration Control) (Maximum Penalty) Order 2008 and shall come into force on 29th February 2008.

[2.1136]

2 Maximum Penalty

For the purposes of section 15(2) of the Immigration, Asylum and Nationality Act 2006 (employment of adults subject to immigration control: penalty notice) the prescribed maximum is £10,000.

OCCUPATIONAL PENSION SCHEMES (INTERNAL DISPUTE RESOLUTION PROCEDURES CONSEQUENTIAL AND MISCELLANEOUS AMENDMENTS) REGULATIONS 2008

(SI 2008/649)

NOTES

Made: 5 March 2008.

Authority: Pension Schemes Act 1993, ss 113(1)(d), 181(1), 182(2), (3); Pensions Act 1995, ss 50(8)(c), (9)(c), 124(1), 174(2), (3).

Commencement: 6 April 2008.

ARRANGEMENT OF REGULATIONS

[2.1137]

1 Citation, commencement and interpretation

(1) These Regulations may be cited as the Occupational Pension Schemes (Internal Dispute Resolution Procedures Consequential and Miscellaneous Amendments) Regulations 2008 and shall come into force on 6th April 2008.

(2) In these Regulations "the Act" means the Pensions Act 1995.

[2.1138]

2 Information requirements

(1) When the trustees or managers of an occupational pension scheme receive (or, as the case may be, the specified person receives) an application under the relevant procedure, they must as soon as is reasonably practicable—

(a) inform the applicant that TPAS (the Pensions Advisory Service) is available to assist members and beneficiaries of the scheme in connection with any difficulty with the scheme, and

(b) give the applicant the contact details for TPAS.

(2) For the purposes of paragraph (1), the relevant procedure is a procedure for the application for the resolution of a pension dispute under section 50(4) of the Act (procedure for resolution of a pensions dispute).

(3) For the purposes of paragraph (1), "member" has the meaning given to it in section 124(1) and 125(4) of the Act (interpretation of Part 1 and supplementary), and "members" is to be construed accordingly.

(4) When the trustees or managers of an occupational pension scheme notify the applicant of their decision on the matters in dispute in accordance with section 50(5)(b) of the Act (dispute resolution arrangements—duties of trustees or managers), the notification shall include—

(a) a statement that the Pensions Ombudsman appointed under section 145(2) of the Pension Schemes Act 1993 may investigate and determine any complaint or dispute of fact or law, in relation to a scheme, made or referred in accordance with that Act, and

(b) the Pensions Ombudsman's contact details.

[2.1139]

3 Exempted schemes

An occupational pension scheme of a description prescribed for the purposes of section 50(8)(c) of the Act (schemes to which section 50 does not apply) is a scheme in relation to which the sole trustee of the scheme is a company and all members of the scheme are directors of that company.

[2.1140]

4 Exempted disputes

A dispute of a description prescribed for the purposes of section 50(9)(c) of the Act (exempted disputes) is a dispute in respect of which a notice of appeal has been issued by the complainant in accordance with—

(a) regulation H2 of the Police Pensions Regulations 1987 (appeal to board of medical referees);

(b) rule H2 of Schedule 2 to the Firemen's Pension Scheme Order 1992 (appeal against opinion on a medical issue);

(c) rule 2 of Part.6 of Schedule 1 to the Firefighters' Compensation Scheme (Scotland) Order 2006 (appeal to medical referee);

(d) regulation 31 of the Police (Injury Benefit) Regulations 2006 (appeal to board of medical referees);

(e) rule 2 of Part 6 of Schedule 1 to the Firefighters' Compensation Scheme (England) Order 2006 (appeal to medical referee);

(f) regulation 72 of the Police Pensions Regulations 2006 (appeal to board of medical referees);

(g) rule 4 of Part 8 of Schedule 1 to the Firefighters' Pension Scheme (England) Order 2006 (appeals against decisions based on medical advice);

(h) regulation 31 of the Police (Injury Benefit) (Scotland) Regulations 2007 (appeal to board of medical referees);

(i) rule 4 of Part 8 of Schedule 1 to the Firefighters' Pension Scheme (Scotland) Order 2007 (appeals against decisions based on medical advice);

(j) regulation 72 of Part 7 of the Police Pensions (Scotland) Regulations 2007 (appeal to board of medical referees);

(k) rule 4 of Part 8 of Schedule 1 to the Firefighters' Pension Scheme (Wales) Order 2007 (appeals against decisions based on medical advice); or

(l) rule 2 of Part 6 of Schedule 1 to the Firefighters' Compensation Scheme (Wales) Order 2007 (appeal to medical referee).

[2.1141]

5 Transitional provisions

(1) Any disagreement which was ongoing before 6th April 2008 under arrangements made and implemented under section 50(1) of the Act shall continue until the procedure under those arrangements comes to an end, as if the relevant legislative provisions governing those arrangements were still in force.

(2) For the purposes of paragraph (1), the relevant legislative provisions are—

(a) section 50 of the Act as it was in force immediately before 6th April 2008; and

(b) the Occupational Pension Schemes (Internal Dispute Resolution Procedures) Regulations 1996.

(3) In the case of any relevant application, regulation 3 of the Personal and Occupational Pension Schemes (Pensions Ombudsman) Regulations 1996 shall apply as it had effect before 6th April 2008.

(4) For the purposes of paragraph (3), "relevant application" means an application concerning a complaint or dispute made—

(a) to an occupational pension scheme under the arrangements required by section 50 of the Act; and

(b) before 6th April 2008.

6, 7 *(Reg 6 (Consequential and miscellaneous amendments) amends the Personal and Occupational Pension Schemes (Pensions Ombudsman) Regulations 1996 SI 1996/2475, reg 3, and contains other amendments to legislation that are outside the scope of this work; reg 7 revokes the Occupational Pension Schemes (Internal Dispute Resolution Procedures) Regulations 1996, SI 1996/1270.)*

CROSS-BORDER RAILWAY SERVICES (WORKING TIME) REGULATIONS 2008 (NOTE)

(SI 2008/1660)

[2.1142]

NOTES

Made: 25 June 2008.

Authority: European Communities Act 1972, s 2(2).

Commencement: 27 July 2008.

These Regulations were included in previous editions of this Handbook, but have been omitted from this edition as it is felt that they are too specialist in application to justify continued inclusion. A brief summary of the Regulations is given below.

These Regulations implement the provisions of Council Directive 2005/47/EC on the Agreement between the Community of European Railways (CER) and the European Transport Workers' Federation (ETF) on certain aspects of the working conditions of mobile workers engaged in interoperable cross-border services in the railway sector. The Regulations apply to workers whose daily shift includes more than one hour on train services going through the Channel Tunnel that require at least two network safety requirement certifications. These workers are referred to as cross-border workers in the Regulations.

Regulations 1 and 2 (and Sch 1) deal with citation commencement and interpretation.

Regulations 3–7 give cross-border workers entitlements to rests and breaks from work.

Regulation 8 obliges the employer to take reasonable steps to ensure the requirements relating to driving time set out in that regulation are complied with.

Regulation 9 requires the employer to keep records and provide copies of the records.

Regulation 10–16 and Sch 2 contain provisions in relation to enforcement. An employer's obligations under regs 8 and 9 are enforceable by the Office of Rail Regulation and an employer's failure to comply with an obligation under either regulation is an offence.

Regulation 17 makes provision in respect of complaints to an employment tribunal.

Regulation 18 prevents contracting out of the provisions of the Regulations, subject to exceptions set out in that regulation.

Regulation 19 introduces Sch 3 which contains various amendments; including amendments to the Employment Rights Act 1996, the Employment Tribunals Act 1996, the Employment Act 2002, and the Working Time Regulations 1998 (SI 1998/1833).

Conciliation: employment tribunal proceedings and claims which could be the subject of employment tribunal proceedings under reg 17 are proceedings to which the Employment Tribunals Act 1996, s 18 applies; see s 18(1)(u) of that Act at **[1.706]**.

Employment Appeal Tribunal: an appeal lies to the Employment Appeal Tribunal on any question of law arising from any decision of, or in any proceedings before, an employment tribunal under or by virtue of these Regulations; see the Employment Tribunals Act 1996, s 21(1)(v) at **[1.713]**.

The rights conferred by these Regulations are "relevant statutory rights" for the purposes of the Employment Rights Act 1996, s 104 (dismissal on grounds of assertion of statutory right); see s 104(4)(d) of that Act at **[1.907]**.

GANGMASTERS (LICENSING CONDITIONS) RULES 2009

(SI 2009/307)

NOTES

Made: 16 February 2009.
Authority: Gangmasters (Licensing) Act 2004, ss 8, 25(2).
Commencement: 6 April 2009.

ARRANGEMENT OF RULES

[2.1143]

1 Citation and commencement

These Rules may be cited as the Gangmasters (Licensing Conditions) Rules 2009; they come into force on 6th April 2009.

NOTES

Commencement: 6 April 2009.

[2.1144]

2 Interpretation

(1) In these Rules—

"business" includes a sole trader, a company, an unincorporated association and a partnership;

"labour user" means a person to whom workers or services are supplied;

"licence holder" means the business granted a licence;

"principal authority" means the individual responsible for the day-to-day management of a business;

"working day" means a day other than a Saturday or a Sunday, Christmas Day or Good Friday, or a date which is a bank holiday under or by virtue of the Banking and Financial Dealings Act 1971.

NOTES

Commencement: 6 April 2009.

[2.1145]

3 Application for a licence

(1) An application for a licence must be made on the form provided by the Authority and contain such information as the Authority requires for the purposes of determining the application.

(2) The form must be signed by the principal authority of the applicant.

(3) For the purposes of determining the application, the Authority may require the applicant—

(a) to permit an inspection of the applicant's business by the Authority or any person acting on its behalf; and

(b) to supply or make available to the Authority or any person acting on its behalf any document or information.

(4) In paragraph (3)(a), "inspection" includes conducting interviews with such persons as the Authority considers appropriate.

(5) A licence may be renewed before it expires.

NOTES

Commencement: 6 April 2009.

[2.1146]

4 Licence conditions

(1) The Schedule (licence conditions) has effect.

(2) A licence is granted subject to the conditions set out in Part 2 of the Schedule.

(3) The Authority may grant a licence subject to such additional conditions as it thinks fit.

NOTES

Commencement: 6 April 2009.

[2.1147]

5 Expiry of licences on change of information

A licence expires if the licence holder's registered number (if it is a company), Unique Tax Reference or Value Added Tax number change.

NOTES

Commencement: 6 April 2009.

[2.1148]

6 Fees

(1) All fees are payable to the Authority.

(2) An applicant for a licence must, at the time of making the application, pay the application fee specified in the table appropriate to its annual turnover.

(3) If an inspection is required under rule 3(3)(a), the applicant must, on demand, pay the fee specified in the table appropriate to its annual turnover.

(4) A licence holder who wishes to renew its licence must, before the licence expires, pay the fee specified in the table appropriate to its annual turnover.

(5) In this rule, "annual turnover" means the turnover in the work sector regulated by the Gangmasters (Licensing) Act 2004 for the previous financial year or, if there has been no such trading in that sector, on the expected turnover in that sector for the forthcoming financial year, as placed in fee band A, B, C or D in the table.

Table

Annual turnover	*Fee Band*	*Application or renewal fee*	*Inspection fee*
£10 million or more	A	£2,600	£2,900
From £5 million to less than £10 million	B	£2,000	£2,400
From £1 million to less than £5 million	C	£1,200	£2,150
Less than £1 million	D	£400	£1,850

NOTES

Commencement: 6 April 2009.

[2.1149]

7 Civil liability

(1) Any contravention of, or failure to comply with, any provision of these Rules (including the conditions in the Schedule) by a licence holder is, so far as it causes damage, actionable.

(2) Paragraph (1) is without prejudice to any right of action or defence which exists or may be available apart from the provisions of the Gangmasters (Licensing) Act 2004 and these Rules.

(3) In paragraph (1), "damage" includes the death of, or injury to, any person (including any disease and any impairment of that person's physical or mental condition).

NOTES

Commencement: 6 April 2009.

[2.1150]
8 Effect of prohibited or unenforceable terms and recoverability of money

(1) Where any term of a contract is prohibited or made unenforceable under these Rules the contract continues to bind the parties if it is capable of continuing in existence without that term.

(2) Where a labour user pays any money pursuant to a contractual term which is unenforceable by virtue of paragraph 10 of the Schedule, the labour user is entitled to recover that money.

NOTES

Commencement: 6 April 2009.

[2.1151]
9 Requirements relating to information and notices

(1) Any notification, notice or document (including a record) required to be given, sent or made under these Rules must be in writing.

(2) Any notification, notice or document required or authorised by these Rules to be given or sent to any person ("the recipient") may be given to or sent—
- (a) by delivering it to the recipient;
- (b) by leaving it at the recipient's last known address;
- (c) by sending it by post to the recipient at that address; or
- (d) by transmitting it by means of an electronic communication, providing that the conditions in paragraph (2) are met.

(3) The conditions are that—
- (a) the recipient has stated a willingness to receive the document by means of an electronic communication;
- (b) the statement has not been withdrawn; and
- (c) the document was transmitted to an electronic address specified by the recipient.

(4) A statement may be—
- (a) limited to documents of a specified description;
- (b) require a document to be in a specified electronic form;
- (c) modified or withdrawn—
  - (i) in a case where the statement was made by being published, by publishing the modification or withdrawal in the same or in a similar manner;
  - (ii) in any other case, by giving a notice to the person to whom the statement was made.

(5) In this rule—

"electronic address" includes any number or address used for the purposes of receiving electronic communications;

"electronic communication" means an electronic communication within the meaning of the Electronic Communications Act 2000;

"specified" means specified in a statement made for the purposes of paragraph (2)(a)."

NOTES

Commencement: 6 April 2009.

[2.1152]
10 Revocations

The Gangmasters (Licensing Conditions) (No 2) Rules 2006 and the Gangmasters (Licensing Conditions) (No 2) (Amendment) Rules 2008 are revoked.

NOTES

Commencement: 6 April 2009.

SCHEDULE
LICENCE CONDITIONS

Rule 4

PART 1
INTERPRETATION

[2.1153]
1 Meaning of connected person

(1) For the purposes of this Schedule a person ("A") is considered to be connected with—
- (a) the members of A's family;
- (b) any individual who employs A or A's employee;
- (c) any person who is in partnership with A;
- (d) any company of which A is an officer and any company connected with that company;
- (e) in the case of a company—

(i) any person who is an officer of that company;
(ii) any subsidiary or holding company both as defined in section 1159 of the Companies Act 2006, of that company and any person who is an officer or an employee of any such subsidiary or holding company; and
(iii) any company of which the same person or persons have control; and

(f) in the case of a trustee of a trust, a beneficiary of the trust and any person to whom the terms of the trust confer a power that may be exercised for that person's benefit.

(2) In sub-paragraph (1), the members of A's family are—

(a) A's spouse or civil partner;
(b) any other person (whether of a different sex or the same sex) with whom A lives as partner in an enduring family relationship;
(c) any child, step-child, parent, grandchild, grandparent, brother, sister, cousin, uncle or aunt of A;
(d) any child or step-child of a person within paragraph (b) (and who is not a child or step-child of A) who lives with A and has not attained the age of 18.

2 Meaning of employee

In this Schedule, "employee" has the same meaning as in section 230(1) of the Employment Rights Act 1996.

3 Meaning of 'work-finding services'

In this Schedule, "work-finding services" means services (whether by the provision of information or otherwise) provided by a licence holder—

(a) to a person for the purpose of finding that person employment or seeking to find that person employment;
(b) to an employee of the licence holder for the purpose of finding or seeking to find another person, with a view to the employee acting for and under the control of that other person;
(c) to a person ("B") for the purpose of finding or seeking to find another person ("C"), with a view to B becoming employed by the licence holder and acting for and under the control of C.

NOTES

Commencement: 6 April 2009.

Part 2 Statutory Instruments

PART 2
CONDITIONS

[2.1154]

4 Obligation to act in a fit and proper manner

(1) The licence holder, principal authority and any person named or otherwise specified in the licence must at all times act in a fit and proper manner.

(2) If the licence holder or any person named or otherwise specified in the licence is a body corporate, an unincorporated association or partnership—

(a) every director, manager, secretary or other similar officer of the body corporate,
(b) every officer of the association or any member of its governing body, and
(c) every partner,

including any person purporting to act in any such capacity, must at all times act in a fit and proper manner.

5 Obligation to provide information

(1) The licence holder must notify the Authority within 20 working days of commencing an activity authorised by the licence.

(2) The licence holder must notify the Authority within 20 working days if there are significant changes to the details submitted with the holder's application, including any changes to the persons named or the positions otherwise specified in the licence.

(3) The licence holder must notify the Authority as soon as reasonably practicable if the holder knows or suspects the holder's licence has been used by someone not authorised to act on behalf of that holder.

(4) The licence holder must, on request, provide details of the holder's licence to any constable, enforcement officer or compliance officer.

6 Inspection of the business

A licence holder must permit the Authority to inspect the business at any reasonable time.

7 Prohibition on charging fees

A licence holder must not charge a fee to a worker for any work-finding services.

8 Restriction on pre-conditions

(1) A licence holder must not make the provision of work-finding services conditional upon the worker—

(a) using other services or hiring or purchasing goods provided by the licence holder or any person with whom the licence holder is connected; or

(b) giving or not withdrawing consent to the disclosure of information relating to the worker.

(2) Where a worker uses services for which these Rules do not prohibit the charging of a fee, a licence holder providing or making provision for such services must ensure that the worker is able to cancel or withdraw from those services at any time without incurring any detriment or penalty, subject to the worker giving to the provider of those services notice of five working days or, for services relating to the provision of living accommodation, notice of ten working days.

9 Restriction on detrimental action relating to workers working elsewhere

(1) A licence holder must not subject or threaten to subject a worker to any detriment on the ground that the worker has—

(a) terminated or given notice to terminate any contract between the worker and the licence holder; or

(b) taken up or proposes to take up employment with any other person.

(2) A licence holder must not require the worker to notify the licence holder, or any person with whom the holder is connected, of the identity of any future employer.

(3) However, in sub-paragraph (1), "detriment" does not include—

(a) the loss of any benefits to which the worker might have become entitled had the worker not terminated the contract;

(b) the recovery of losses incurred by the licence holder as a result of the failure of the worker to perform agreed work; or

(c) a requirement in a contract with the licence holder for the worker to give a reasonable period of notice to terminate the contract.

10 Restriction on providing workers in industrial disputes

(1) A licence holder must not introduce or supply a worker to a labour user to perform the duties normally performed—

(a) by a worker who is taking part in a strike or other industrial action ("the first worker"), or

(b) by any other worker employed by the labour user and who is assigned by the labour user to perform the duties normally performed by the first worker.

(2) However, sub-paragraph (1) does not apply if—

(a) the licence holder does not know, and had no reasonable grounds for knowing, that the first worker is taking part in a strike or other industrial action, or

(b) in relation to the first worker, the strike or other industrial action is an unofficial strike or other unofficial industrial action for the purposes of section 237 of the Trade Union and Labour Relations (Consolidation) Act 1992.

11 Restriction on paying workers' remuneration

(1) A licence holder must not in respect of a worker whom the holder has introduced or supplied to a labour user who has then employed the worker—

(a) pay or make arrangements to pay to the worker the worker's remuneration arising from the employment with the labour user, or

(b) introduce or refer the labour user to any person with whom the licence holder is connected with a view to that person paying, or making arrangements to pay the remuneration to the worker.

(2) However, sub-paragraph (1) does not apply where the labour user and the licence holder are connected.

12 Restriction on charges to labour users

(1) Any term of a contract between a licence holder and a labour user which is contingent on a worker taking up employment with the labour user or working for the labour user pursuant to being supplied by another licence holder is unenforceable by the licence holder in relation to that worker, unless the contract provides that instead of a transfer fee the labour user may by notice to the licence holder elect for a hire period of such length as is specified in the contract during which the worker will be supplied to the labour user—

(a) in a case where there has been no supply, on the terms specified in the contract; or

(b) in any other case, on terms no less favourable to the labour user than those which applied immediately before the licence holder received the notice.

(2) In sub-paragraph (1), "transfer fee" means any payment in connection with the worker taking up employment with the labour user or in connection with the worker working for the labour user pursuant to being supplied by another licence holder.

(3) Any term as mentioned in sub-paragraph (1) is unenforceable where the licence holder does not supply the worker to the labour user, in accordance with the contract, for the duration of the hire period referred to in sub-paragraph (1) unless the licence holder is in no way at fault.

(4) Any term of a contract between a licence holder and a labour user which is contingent on a worker—

(a) taking up employment with the labour user or any other person to whom the labour user has introduced the worker, or

(b) working for the labour user pursuant to being supplied by another licence holder,

is unenforceable by the licence holder in relation to the event concerned where the worker takes up such employment or begins working pursuant to being supplied by another licence holder (as the case may be) after the end of the relevant period.

(5) In sub-paragraph (4), "the relevant period" means the period of—

(a) eight weeks starting on the day after the day on which the worker last worked for the labour user pursuant to being supplied by the licence holder, or

(b) 14 weeks starting on the first day on which the worker worked for the labour user pursuant to the supply of that worker to that labour user by the licence holder,

whichever period ends later.

(6) In determining the "first day" for the purposes of sub-paragraph (5)(b), no account is taken of any supply that occurred prior to a period of more than 42 days during which that worker did not work for that labour user pursuant to being supplied by that licence holder.

(7) A licence holder must not—

(a) seek to enforce against the labour user, or otherwise seek to give effect to, any term of a contract which is unenforceable by virtue of sub-paragraph (1), (3) or (4); or

(b) otherwise directly or indirectly request a payment to which by virtue of this paragraph the licence holder is not entitled.

13 Prohibition on withholding payment to workers

A licence holder must not withhold or threaten to withhold the whole or any part of any payment due to the worker in respect of any work done on any of the following grounds—

(a) non-receipt of payment from the labour user;

(b) the worker's failure to prove that the worker has worked during a particular period of time (but this does not prevent the licence holder from satisfying itself by other means that the worker worked for the particular period in question);

(c) the worker not having worked during any period other than that to which the payment relates; or

(d) any matter within the control of the licence holder.

14 Notification of charges and terms of offers

(1) Subject to sub-paragraph (2), on the first occasion that a licence holder offers to provide or arrange the provision of a service to a worker, the holder must give notice to the worker stating—

(a) whether that service is a work-finding service for which these Rules prohibit the licence holder from charging a fee; and

(b) whether any other services or goods which may be provided by the licence holder or any other person are services or goods for which the holder or other person providing them will or may charge a fee, together with details of any such fee including—

(i) the amount or method of calculation of the fee;

(ii) the identity of the person to whom the fee is or will be payable;

(iii) a description of the services or goods to which the fee relates and a statement of the worker's right to cancel or withdraw from the service and the notice period required; and

(iv) the circumstances in which refunds or rebates are payable to the worker, the scale of such refunds or rebates, and if no refunds or rebates are payable, a statement to that effect.

(2) Sub-paragraph (1) only applies where one or more services or goods referred to in sub-paragraph (1)(b) for which the worker will or may be charged a fee may be provided to the worker.

(3) A licence holder must give a further notice to a worker stating the matters referred to in sub-paragraph (1)(b) where, subsequent to the first occasion that it offers to provide or arrange the provision of a service to the worker, the licence holder or the person providing to the worker any services or goods referred to in sub-paragraph 1(b), introduces or varies any fees in relation to any services or goods referred to in sub-paragraph 1(b).

(4) Where a licence holder offers any gift or makes an offer of any benefit to a worker, in order to induce the worker to engage the licence holder to provide the worker with services, the holder must notify the worker of the terms on which the gift or benefit is offered before the offer is open for acceptance by the worker.

15 Requirement to agree terms with workers

(1) Before supplying a worker to a labour user, a licence holder must agree the terms which will apply between the licence holder and the worker.

(2) The terms must include—

(a) the type of work the licence holder will find or seek to find for the worker;

(b) whether the worker is or will be supplied by the licence holder under a contract of service or a contract for services, and in either case, the terms and conditions which will apply;

(c) an undertaking that the licence holder will pay the worker in respect of work done by the worker, whether or not the licence holder is paid by the labour user in respect of that work;

(d) the length of notice of termination which the worker is obliged to give the licence holder, and entitled to receive from the holder, in respect any particular assignment;

(e) the rate of remuneration payable, or the minimum rate the licence holder reasonably expects to achieve for the worker;

(f) details of the intervals at which remuneration will be paid; and

(g) details of any entitlement to annual holidays and to payment in respect of such holidays.

(3) A licence holder must record all the terms, where possible in one document, and give the worker the written terms before the holder provides any services to the worker.

(4) Those terms may only be varied by written agreement, a copy of which must be provided to the worker as soon as possible and in any event no later than the end of the fifth working day following the day the variation was agreed.

(5) However, sub-paragraph (3) does not apply if the worker has been given a written statement of particulars of employment in accordance with Part I of the Employment Rights Act 1996.

(6) A licence holder must not make the continued provision of any services by it to a worker conditional on the agreement by the worker to any variation.

16 Requirement to agree terms with labour users

(1) Before first providing services (other than providing information in the form of a publication) to a labour user, a licence holder must agree the terms which will apply between the licence holder and labour user.

(2) The terms must include—

(a) details of any fee which may be payable by the labour user to the licence holder including—

(i) the amount or method of calculation of such fee; and

(ii) the circumstances in which refunds or rebates are payable, and their scale, or, if no refunds or rebates are payable, a statement to that effect; and

(b) details of the procedure to be followed if a worker introduced or supplied to the labour user proves unsatisfactory.

(3) The licence holder must record the terms in a single document and send a copy to the labour user as soon as reasonably practicable.

(4) If any variation to those terms is agreed, the licence holder must provide the labour user with a document containing details and the date of the variation as soon as reasonably practicable.

17 Information to be obtained from a labour user

A licence holder must not supply a worker to a labour user unless the holder has obtained the following information—

(a) the identity of the labour user and, if applicable, the nature of the labour user's business;

(b) the date on which the labour user requires a worker to commence work and the duration, or likely duration, of the work;

(c) the position which the labour user seeks to fill, including the type of work a worker in that position would be required to do, the location at which and the hours during which the worker would be required to work;

(d) any risks to health or safety known to the licence holder or labour user and the steps the licence holder or labour user has taken to prevent or control such risks;

(e) the experience, training, qualifications and any authorisation which the licence holder or labour user considers are necessary, or which are required by law or by any professional body, for a worker to possess in order to work in the position; and

(f) any expenses payable by or to the worker.

18 Confirmation to be obtained about a worker

A licence holder must not supply a worker to a labour user unless the holder has obtained confirmation—

(a) of the identity of the worker;

(b) that the worker has the experience, training, qualifications and any authorisation which the licence holder or labour user considers are necessary, or which are required by law or by any professional body, to work in the position which the labour user seeks to fill; and

(c) that the worker is willing to work in the position which the labour user seeks to fill.

19 Steps to be taken for the protection of the worker and the labour user

(1) Before any work is commenced, a licence holder must have—

(a) taken all reasonably practicable steps to ensure that the worker and the labour user are each aware of any requirements imposed by law, or by any professional body, which must be satisfied; and

(b) made all reasonably practicable enquiries to ensure that it would not be detrimental to the interests of the worker or the labour user for the worker to work in the position which the labour user seeks to fill.

(2) Sub-paragraph (1)(a) is without prejudice to any of the licence holder's duties under any enactment or rule of law in relation to health and safety at work.

(3) Where a licence holder receives or obtains information which—

(a) gives the holder reasonable grounds to believe that a worker is unsuitable for the position with a labour user for which the worker is being supplied, or

(b) does not give such reasonable grounds but otherwise indicates that the worker may be unsuitable for that position,

the holder must without delay inform the labour user and any intermediaries of that information.

(4) If sub-paragraph (3)(a) applies, the licence holder must also end the supply of that worker to the labour user.

(5) If sub-paragraph (3)(b) applies, the licence holder must also make such further enquiries as are reasonably practicable as to the suitability of the worker for the position concerned.

(6) The licence holder must inform the labour user and any intermediaries about those enquiries and any further information obtained.

(7) Where information resulting from those enquiries gives the licence holder reasonable grounds to believe that the worker is unsuitable for the position concerned, the holder must without delay inform the labour user and any intermediaries of that information and end the supply of that worker to the labour user.

(8) In this paragraph "without delay" means on the same day, or where not reasonably practicable, the next working day.

(9) Nothing in this paragraph authorises the making of a disclosure in contravention of the Data Protection Act 1998.

20 Provision of information to workers and labour users

(1) A licence holder must ensure that at the same time as the holder supplies or proposes to supply a particular worker to a labour user, the holder—

(a) gives to the labour user the information about the worker obtained in accordance with paragraph 18; and

(b) informs the worker whether the worker will be supplied under a contract of service or a contract for services;

(2) A licence holder must ensure that at the same time as it offers a worker a position with a labour user—

(a) the holder gives to the worker (orally or otherwise) all information it has been provided with under paragraph 17; and

(b) if a rate of remuneration has not been agreed with the labour user, the holder informs the worker (orally or otherwise) of the rate of remuneration it will pay the worker to work in that position.

(3) Where any of the information referred to in sub-paragraph (1) was given orally, the licence holder must afterwards provide it in writing as soon as possible and in any event within three working days.

(4) Sub-paragraph (1) does not apply where—

(a) the worker has performed the same type of work with the labour user during the previous five working days, and

(b) the information required is the same as the information which the worker and labour user have already received,

unless the worker or labour user request otherwise.

(5) Subject to sub-paragraphs (4) and (6), where a licence holder intends to introduce or supply a worker to a labour user for an assignment of five consecutive working days' duration or less—

(a) sub-paragraph (1)(a) may be satisfied by the holder giving to the labour user (orally or otherwise) the name of the worker to be supplied and a written confirmation by the holder that the holder has complied with paragraph 18; and

(b) sub-paragraph (1)(b) may be satisfied, where the holder has previously provided the worker with the information referred to under that sub-paragraph and that information remains unchanged, by the employment business giving to the worker in writing the information referred to in paragraph 17(a) and (b).

(6) Where, after it has started, an assignment to which sub-paragraph (5) applies is extended beyond a duration of five working days, the information referred to in sub-paragraph (1) which has not already been provided must be provided in writing by the end of the eighth working day of the assignment, or by the end of the assignment if sooner.

21 Situations where workers are provided with travel or required to live away from home

(1) A licence holder must not arrange for a worker to take up a position other than as a labour user's employee if, in order to take up that position, the worker has to occupy accommodation other than the worker's home, unless the conditions in sub-paragraph (2) are satisfied.

(2) The conditions are that the licence holder has taken all reasonably practicable steps to ensure that—

(a) suitable accommodation will be available for the worker and details have been provided to the worker, including the terms on which it is offered and any cost; and

(b) suitable arrangements have been made for the worker to travel to such accommodation.

(3) Where a worker is—

(a) to be supplied to a labour user other than as the labour user's employee, or is under the age of 18; and

(b) the licence holder, labour user or any intermediary has arranged free travel or payment of fares for the worker's journey to the place of work,

the licence holder must, if the work does not start or upon it ending, either arrange free travel for the worker's return journey, pay the worker's return fare or obtain an undertaking from the labour user or any intermediary to arrange free travel or pay the return fare.

(4) The licence holder must give notice to the worker setting out the details of the free travel or payment of fares including any conditions on which the same are offered.

(5) If a labour user or intermediary does not comply with an undertaking given under sub-paragraph (3), the licence holder must either arrange free travel for the return journey of the worker or pay the worker's fare.

(6) A licence holder must not arrange for a worker who is under the age of 18 to take up a position which will require the worker to live away from home unless the parent or guardian of the worker has consented in writing.

(7) If a worker is loaned money by the licence holder, the labour user or any intermediary to meet travel or other expenses in order to take up a position—

(a) the worker must be provided with details in writing of the amount loaned and repayment terms; and

(b) the worker must not be asked to repay a greater sum than the amount loaned.

22 Records relating to workers

Every licence holder must record, as soon as reasonably practicable, the following details in relation to every application received from a worker—

(a) the date terms are agreed between the licence holder and the worker;

(b) the worker's name, address and, if under 22, date of birth;

(c) any terms which apply or will apply between the licence holder and the worker, and any document recording any variation;

(d) any relevant details of the worker's training, experience or qualifications and any authorisation to undertake particular work (and copies of any documentary evidence of the same obtained by the licence holder);

(e) details of any requirements specified by the worker in relation to taking up employment;

(f) the names of labour users or sub-contractors to whom the worker is supplied;

(g) details of any resulting engagement and the date from which it takes effect;

(h) the date the contract was terminated (where applicable); and

(i) details of any enquiries made under paragraphs 18 and 19 about the worker and the position concerned, with copies of all relevant documents and dates they were received or sent.

23 Records relating to labour user

Every licence holder must record, as soon as reasonably practicable, the following details relating to labour users—

(a) the date terms are agreed between the licence holder and the labour user;

(b) the labour user's name and address, and location of the place of work if different;

(c) details of any sub-contractors;

(d) details of the position the labour user seeks to fill;

(e) the duration or likely duration of the work;

(f) any experience, training, ability, qualifications, or authorisation required by the licence holder or labour user by law, or by any professional body; and any other conditions attaching to the position the labour user seeks to fill;

(g) the terms offered in respect of the position the labour user seeks to fill;

(h) a copy of the terms between the licence holder and the labour user, and any document recording any variation;
(i) the names of workers supplied;
(j) details of enquiries under paragraphs 17 and 19 about the labour user and the position the labour user seeks to fill, with copies of all relevant documents and dates of their receipt;
(k) the details of each resulting engagement and date from which it takes effect; and
(l) dates of requests by the licence holder for fees or other payment from the labour user and of receipt of such fees or other payments, and copies of statements or invoices.

24 Records relating to dealings with other licence holders

(1) Every licence holder must record, as soon as reasonably practicable, the names of any other licence holders whose services the licence holder uses, and details of enquiries made to ascertain that the other licence holder is licensed.

(2) A licence holder who has assigned or sub-contracted any of its obligations under any contract or arrangement with a worker or labour user to another licence holder must ensure that the terms upon which those obligations are assigned or sub-contracted are recorded, where possible in a single document.

25 General provisions relating to records

(1) A licence holder must keep all records for at least one year from creation or, where they have been supplied by another person, from last supply.

(2) If the records are kept other than at premises a licence holder uses for or in connection with the carrying on of its business, the licence holder must ensure that they are readily accessible and capable of being delivered to the licence holder's premises in the United Kingdom or to the Authority within two working days.

26 Conditions which apply to gathering shellfish

(1) This paragraph applies to licences granted in relation to shellfish gathering.

(2) The licence holder must ensure that there is a competent supervisor for each individual group of workers.

(3) The supervisor must be named on the licence.

(4) The supervisor must—
(a) accompany the workers at all times to the work area;
(b) be familiar with the use of any equipment or procedures used when gathering shellfish or accessing the work area; and
(c) be able to communicate directly with every one of the group of workers.

(5) The licence holder or the supervisor must notify the Maritime and Coastguard Agency Rescue and Coordination Centre of—
(a) the licence holder's licence number;
(b) contact details for the licence holder or supervisor;
(c) the number of workers in the group;
(d) the location of the work area; and
(e) the times the group is going out and returning from the work area.

(6) In this paragraph, the "work area" means the place where the shellfish are gathered.

(7) If a fisheries permit or licence is required to gather shellfish the licence holder must ensure that workers comply with the provisions of that permit or licence.

NOTES

Commencement: 6 April 2009.

EUROPEAN COMMUNITIES (DEFINITION OF TREATIES) (UNITED NATIONS CONVENTION ON THE RIGHTS OF PERSONS WITH DISABILITIES) ORDER 2009

(SI 2009/1181)

NOTES

Made: 13 May 2009.

Authority: European Communities Act 1972, s 1(3).

Commencement: Article 45 of the United Nations Convention on the Rights of Persons with Disabilities (at **[5.27]**) provides that: (1) this Convention shall enter into force on the thirtieth day after the deposit of the twentieth instrument of ratification or accession; and (2) for each State etc ratifying, formally confirming or acceding to the Convention after the deposit of the twentieth such instrument, the Convention shall enter into force on the thirtieth day after the deposit of its own such instrument. The Convention entered into force on 3 May 2008 in accordance with (1) above. Note that the UK ratified the Treaty on 8 June 2009 and, therefore, it entered into force in the UK on 8 July 2009 in accordance with (2) above.

[2.1155]

1 Citation and commencement

(1) This Order may be cited as The European Communities (Definition of Treaties) (United Nations Convention on the Rights of Persons with Disabilities) Order 2009.

(2) This Order shall come into force on the date on which the treaty specified in article 2 enters into force for the United Kingdom. This date will be notified in the London, Edinburgh and Belfast Gazettes.

NOTES

Commencement: 8 July 2009.

[2.1156]

2 Specification as one of the [EU] Treaties

The United Nations Convention on the Rights of Persons with Disabilities signed in New York by the European Community and by the United Kingdom on 30 March 2007 is to be regarded as one of the [EU] Treaties as defined in section 1(2) of the European Communities Act 1972.

NOTES

Commencement: 8 July 2009.

References in square brackets substituted by the Treaty of Lisbon (Changes in Terminology) Order 2011, SI 2011/1043, art 6(1)(a), as from 22 April 2011.

ECCLESIASTICAL OFFICES (TERMS OF SERVICE) REGULATIONS 2009

(SI 2009/2108)

NOTES

Made: 29 July 2009.

Authority: Ecclesiastical Offices (Terms of Service) Measure 2009, s 2.

Commencement: 1 January 2010.

ARRANGEMENT OF REGULATIONS

PART I
INTRODUCTORY

PART II
PARTICULARS OF OFFICE

Right to statement of particulars of office

PART I
INTRODUCTORY

[2.1157]

1 Citation and coming into force

These Regulations may be cited as the Ecclesiastical Offices (Terms of Service) Regulations 2009 and shall come into force on 1st January 2010.

NOTES

Commencement: 1 January 2010.

[2.1158]

2 Interpretation

(1) In these Regulations—

"capability procedures" means the procedures described in regulation 31 below;

"grievance procedures" means the procedures described in regulation 32 below;

"working day" means any day which is not a rest day or part of a rest period or which is not taken as part of annual or special leave or any such leave as is referred to in regulation 23(1) below and cognate expressions shall be construed accordingly;

"the Measure" means the Ecclesiastical Offices (Terms of Service) Measure 2009.

(2) [Subject to paragraph (3) below,] these Regulations apply to all office holders holding office subject to Common Tenure, whenever appointed to their office, and the following provisions of these Regulations (except regulation 33(3) below) shall apply to an office holder who becomes subject to Common Tenure whilst holding his or her office as if he or she had taken up that office on the day on which he or she became subject to Common Tenure.

[(3) Where an office holder holds an office in pursuance of a contract of employment, these Regulations shall not apply to the office holder in respect of that office, without prejudice to the application of the Regulations in respect of any other office held by that office holder.]

NOTES

Commencement: 1 January 2010.

Words in square brackets in para (2) inserted, and para (3) added, by the Ecclesiastical Offices (Terms of Service) (Amendment) (No 2) Regulations 2010, SI 2010/2848, reg 2, as from 31 January 2011.

PART II
PARTICULARS OF OFFICE

Right to statement of particulars of office

[2.1159]

3 Statement of initial particulars of office

(1) An office holder shall be given a written statement of particulars of office by—

- (a) an officer of the diocese nominated for that purpose by the diocesan bishop, or
- (b) in the case of an office holder who is an archbishop or a diocesan bishop, by an officer of the province nominated by the registrar of the province in which the diocese is situated.

(2) The statement may be given in instalments and (whether or not given in instalments) shall be given not later than the relevant date.

(3) The relevant date for the purposes of paragraph (2) above shall be the expiry of the period of one month from the date on which the office holder took up the office.

(4) The statement shall contain particulars of—

- (a) the name of the office holder and the title or description of the officer nominated by the bishop or registrar under paragraph (1) above and the body which is to be treated, for the purpose of these Regulations, as the respondent in any proceedings brought by the office holder before an employment tribunal,
- (b) the title of the office to which the office holder has been appointed, and
- (c) the date when the appointment took effect.

(5) The statement shall also contain particulars, as at a specified date not more than seven days before the statement (or the instalment containing them) is given, of—

- (a) whether the office holder is entitled to a stipend and, if so, the amount of the stipend or the method of calculating it,
- (b) the person or body responsible for the payment of the stipend,
- (c) the intervals at which any stipend is payable (that is, weekly, monthly or other specified intervals),
- (d) whether the office holder is entitled to receive parochial fees and the relationship, if any, of the receipt of such fees to any stipend,
- (e) any terms and conditions relating to the reimbursement of expenses incurred in connection with the exercise of the office,
- (f) whether the office is full-time or part-time and, in the case of part-time posts, and of posts for which special provision has been made for hours of work, any terms and conditions relating to hours of work (including any terms and conditions relating to normal working hours),
- (g) any terms and conditions relating to any of the following—
    - (i) entitlement to rest periods and holidays, including public holidays,
    - (ii) incapacity for work due to sickness or injury, including any provision for sick pay,
    - (iii) pensions and pensions schemes, including, where the office holder comes within either the Church of England Pensions Scheme or the Church of England Funded Pensions Scheme, or both, a statement to that effect, and
    - (iv) entitlements to maternity, paternity, parental and adoption leave [and time off work to care for dependants] in accordance with regulation 23 below,
- (h) where the office holder is required, for the better performance of his or her duties, to occupy any particular residence, details of the address of the property concerned, the person or body to whom or which it belongs, the terms of occupation and any contents to be provided by the relevant housing provider,
- (i) the length of notice which the office holder is required to give and, if applicable, receive to terminate the appointment, and
- (j) where the appointment is not intended to be permanent, the circumstances in which it may be terminated or, if it is for a fixed term, the date when it is to end.

NOTES

Commencement: 1 January 2010.

Para (5): words in square brackets in sub-para (g)(iv) inserted by the Ecclesiastical Offices (Terms of Service) (Amendment) Regulations 2010, SI 2010/2407, reg 2, as from 1 January 2011.

[2.1160]

4 Statement of initial particulars: supplementary

(1) If, in the case of a statement under regulation 3 above, there are no particulars to be entered under any of the paragraphs of that regulation or any of the heads of any such paragraph, that fact shall be stated.

(2) A statement under regulation 3 above may refer the office holder for particulars of any of the matters mentioned in it to these Regulations, to any Measure or Canon, to other regulations of the General Synod or specified provisions thereof or to the provisions of some other document which is reasonably accessible to the office holder.

(3) A statement shall be given to an office holder even if his or her appointment ends before the end of the period within which the statement is required to be given.

NOTES

Commencement: 1 January 2010.

[2.1161]

5 Note about disciplinary, capability and grievance procedures and pensions

(1) A statement under regulation 3 above shall include a note—

- (a) in the case of office holders to whom the provisions of the Ecclesiastical Jurisdiction Measure 1963 relating to offences or of the Clergy Discipline Measure 2003 relating to misconduct apply specifying those provisions,
- (b) in the case of office holders other than those referred to in paragraph (a) above, specifying any disciplinary rules or procedures applicable to the office held by the office holder, and
- (c) in the case of all office holders, specifying any capability or grievance procedures relating to office holders.

(2) A note included in a statement under paragraph (1) above may comply with that paragraph by referring the office holder to any such laws or documents as are referred to in regulation 4(2) above.

(3) The note shall also state whether there is in force a contracting-out certificate (issued in accordance with Chapter I of Part III of the Pensions Schemes Act 1993) stating that the office held by the office holder is contracted-out employment for the purposes of that Part of that Act.

NOTES

Commencement: 1 January 2010.

[2.1162]

6 Statement of changes

(1) If, after the material date, there is a change in any of the matters particulars of which are required by regulations 3 to 5 above to be included or referred to in a statement under regulation 3, the officer nominated by the bishop or registrar under regulation 3(1) shall give to the office holder a written statement containing particulars of the change.

(2) For the purposes of paragraph (1) above—

- (a) in relation to a matter particulars of which are included or referred to in a statement given under regulation 3 other than in instalments, the material date is the date to which the statement relates,
- (b) in relation to a matter particulars of which are included or referred to in an instalment of a statement given under regulation 3, the material date is the date to which the instalment relates, and
- (c) in relation to any other matter, the material date is the date by which a statement under regulation 3 is required to be given.

(3) A statement under paragraph (1) above shall be given at the earliest opportunity and, in any event, not later than one month after the change in question.

(4) A statement under paragraph (1) may refer the office holder to any such laws or documents as are referred to in regulation 4(2) above.

NOTES

Commencement: 1 January 2010.

[2.1163]

7 Reasonably accessible document

In regulation 4 above the reference to a document which is reasonably accessible to an office holder is a reference to a document which—

(a) the office holder has reasonable opportunities of reading in the course of the exercise of his or her office, or

(b) where details of a website have been provided to the office holder, the office holder can gain access to without incurring unreasonable expense, or

(c) is made reasonably accessible to the office holder in some other way.

NOTES

Commencement: 1 January 2010.

[2.1164]

8 Right to itemised statement of stipend

(1) An office holder to whom a stipend is payable has the right to receive from the person or body who or which is responsible for the payment of the stipend, at or before the time at which any payment of stipend is made to him or her, a written itemised statement of stipend.

(2) The statement shall contain particulars of—

(a) the gross amount of the stipend,

(b) the amounts of any deductions from that gross amount and the purposes for which they are made, and

(c) the net amount of stipend payable.

NOTES

Commencement: 1 January 2010.

Enforcement

[2.1165]

9 References to employment tribunals

(1) Where the officer nominated under regulation 3 above does not give an office holder a statement as required by regulation 3 or 6 or where the office holder is not given a statement as required by regulation 8 (either because the person or body concerned gives no statement or because the statement which is given does not comply with what is required), the office holder may require a reference to be made to an employment tribunal to determine what particulars ought to have been included or referred to in a statement so as to comply with the requirements of the provision concerned.

(2) Where—

(a) a statement purporting to be a statement under regulation 3 or 6 above, or a statement of stipend purporting to comply with regulation 8, has been given to an office holder, and

(b) a question arises as to the particulars which ought to have been included or referred to in the statement so as to comply with the requirements of this Part of these Regulations,

either the person or body concerned or the office holder may require the question to be referred to and determined by an employment tribunal.

(3) For the purposes of this paragraph—

(a) a question as to the particulars which ought to have been included in the note required by regulation 5 above to be included in the statement under regulation 3 does not include any question whether the office is, has been or will be treated as contracted-out employment (for the purposes of Part III of the Pensions Schemes Act 1993), and

(b) a question as to the particulars which ought to have been included in a statement of stipend does not include a question solely as to the accuracy of an amount stated in any such particulars.

(4) An employment tribunal shall not consider a reference under this section in a case where the appointment to which the reference relates has ended unless an application requiring the reference to be made was made—

(a) before the end of the period of three months beginning with the date on which the appointment ended, or

(b) within such period as the tribunal considers reasonable in a case where it is satisfied that it was not reasonably practicable for the application to be made before the end of that period of three months.

NOTES

Commencement: 1 January 2010.

[2.1166]

10 Determination of references

(1) Where, on a reference under regulation 9 above, an employment tribunal determines particulars as being those which ought to have been included or referred to in a statement given under regulation 3 or 6 above, the officer nominated under regulation 3 shall be deemed to have given the office holder a statement in which those particulars were included, or referred to, as specified in the decision of the tribunal.

(2) On determining a reference under regulation 9(2) above relating to a statement purporting to be a statement under regulation 3 or 6, an employment tribunal may—

(a) confirm the particulars as included or referred to in the statement given by the person nominated under regulation 3,

(b) amend those particulars, or

(c) substitute other particulars for them,

as the tribunal may determine to be appropriate; and the statement shall be deemed to have been given by that person to the office holder in accordance with the decision of the tribunal.

(3) Where on a reference under regulation 9 above an employment tribunal finds—

(a) that the person or body responsible has failed to give an office holder a statement of stipend in accordance with regulation 8, or

(b) that a statement of stipend does not, in relation to any deduction, contain the particulars required to be included in that statement by that regulation,

the tribunal shall make a declaration to that effect.

(4) Where on a reference in a case to which paragraph (3) above applies the tribunal further finds that any un-notified deductions have been made from the stipend of the office holder during the period of thirteen weeks immediately preceding the date of the application for the reference (whether or not the deductions were made in breach of the terms and conditions of the appointment), the tribunal may order the person or body who or which is responsible for the payment of the stipend to pay the office holder a sum not exceeding the aggregate of the un-notified deductions so made.

(5) For the purposes of paragraph (4) above a deduction is an un-notified deduction if it is made without the person or body concerned giving the office holder, in any statement of stipend, the particulars of the deduction required by regulation 8.

NOTES

Commencement: 1 January 2010.

PART III
RIGHT TO STIPEND AND PROVISION OF ACCOMMODATION

Entitlement to stipend

[2.1167]

11 Entitlement to stipend of office holders

(1) Subject to paragraph (3), an office holder who is occupying a full-time stipendiary post which is stated to be such in his or her terms of appointment shall be entitled to receive an annual stipend of an amount—

(a) which is not less than the National Minimum Stipend, or

(b) which, together with any income received by the office holder from other sources which is related to or derived from the duties of the office, is not less than the National Minimum Stipend.

(2) In sub-paragraph (1) above "National Minimum Stipend" means the amount specified from time to time by the Archbishops' Council, in exercise of its functions as the Central Stipends Authority, as the National Minimum Stipend, and the circumstances in which income is treated, for the purposes of paragraph (1)(b) above, as to be taken into account for the purpose of calculating an office holder's entitlement, shall be specified from time to time by the Council in the exercise of those functions.

(3) An office holder who is occupying a part-time post shall be entitled to such stipend as may be specified in the statement of particulars of office given under regulation 3 above.

(4) Paragraphs (1) and (3) above do not apply to an office holder who is serving a sentence of imprisonment following a conviction for a criminal offence.

(5) Any directions given by a diocesan bishop under section 5(2) of the Diocesan Stipends Funds Measure 1953 with respect to providing or augmenting the stipends of the office holders mentioned in that section shall be consistent with the provisions of this regulation.

NOTES

Commencement: 1 January 2010.

12–20 *(Regs 12–17 (Provision of accommodation, etc) and regs 18–20 (Part IV: Ministerial development review, education and training) outside the scope of this work.)*

PART V
TIME OFF WORK, TIME SPENT ON OTHER DUTIES AND SICKNESS

Time off and annual leave

[2.1168]

21 Weekly rest period

(1) An office holder shall be entitled to an uninterrupted rest period of not less than 24 hours in any period of seven days, but the statement of particulars of office issued under regulation 3 above may specify that any rest period may not be taken on or include a Sunday or any or all of the principal Feasts of the Church of England or Ash Wednesday or Good Friday.

NOTES

Commencement: 1 January 2010.

[2.1169]

22 Annual leave

(1) An office holder occupying a full-time post shall be entitled to thirty six days annual leave or such greater amount as may be specified in the statement of particulars of office in any calendar year without any deduction of any stipend to which the office holder is entitled, but the statement of particulars may specify particular days on which annual leave shall or may not be taken and may, in particular, specify the maximum number of Sundays on which annual leave may be taken.

(2) During the first calendar year of the appointment, the amount of leave which an office holder may take at any time in exercise of the entitlement under paragraph (1) above is limited to the amount which is deemed to have accrued in his or her case at that time under paragraph (3) below, as modified by paragraph (4) where that paragraph applies, less the amount of leave (if any) that he or she has already taken during that year.

(3) For the purposes of paragraph (2) above leave is deemed to accrue over the course of the first year of the appointment at a rate which is proportionate to the proportion of the calendar year remaining after the date on which the appointment begins.

(4) Where the amount of leave that has accrued in a particular case includes a fraction of a day the fraction shall be treated as a whole day.

(5) For the purposes of paragraph (1) above, the amount of leave allowed by that paragraph shall exclude any period of special leave allowed by the diocesan bishop (or in the case of an office holder who is a diocesan bishop, the archbishop of the province in which the diocese is situated), including any such leave granted for the purposes of removal and re-settlement.

(6) Paragraphs (3) and (4) above shall apply during the final calendar year of the appointment as they apply during the first such year.

(7) An office holder occupying a part-time post shall be entitled to such period of annual leave as may be specified in the statement of particulars of office given to the office holder under regulation 3 above and paragraphs (2) to (5) above shall apply accordingly.

NOTES

Commencement: 1 January 2010.

Maternity, paternity, parental and adoption leave and time spent on public duties

[2.1170]

23 Entitlement to maternity, paternity, parental and adoption leave

(1) An office holder shall be entitled to maternity, paternity, parental and adoption leave and time off work to care for dependants in accordance with directions given by the Archbishops' Council, in the exercise of its functions as the Central Stipends Authority, and any directions given by the Council under this paragraph may—

- (a) provide for the payment of his or her stipend during any such periods of leave,
- (b) impose conditions on any such entitlement, and
- (c) impose requirements as to the procedures for applying for any such entitlement.

(2) In giving any directions under paragraph (1) above the Council shall have regard to the corresponding rights given to employees under Part VIII of the Employment Rights Act 1996.

(3) A draft of any directions proposed to be made by the Archbishops' Council under this regulation shall be laid before the General Synod and, if they are approved by the General Synod, whether with or without amendment, the draft directions as so approved shall be referred to the Archbishops' Council.

(4) Where the draft directions are referred to the Archbishops' Council under paragraph (3) above then—

(a) if they have been approved by the General Synod without any amendment, the Archbishops' Council shall, by applying its seal, make the directions;
(b) if they have been approved by the General Synod with amendment, the Archbishops' Council may either—
    (i) by applying its seal make the directions as so amended, or
    (ii) withdraw the draft directions for further consideration in view of any amendment by the General Synod;

and the directions shall not come into force until they have been sealed by the Archbishops' Council.

(5) Where the Business Committee of the General Synod determines that draft directions do not need to be debated by the General Synod, then, unless—
(a) notice is given by a member of the General Synod in accordance with its Standing Orders that he or she wishes the draft directions to be debated, or
(b) notice is give by any such member that he or she wishes to move an amendment to the draft directions,

the draft directions shall, for the purposes of paragraphs (3) and (4) above, be deemed to have been approved by the General Synod without amendment.

(6) The Statutory Instruments Act 1946 shall apply to any directions sealed by the Archbishops' Council under paragraph (4) above as if they were a statutory instrument and were made when sealed by the Archbishops' Council and as if these regulations were an Act providing that any such directions shall be subject to annulment in pursuance of a resolution of either House of Parliament.

NOTES

Commencement: 1 January 2010.

Directions: the Ecclesiastical offices (Terms of Service) Directions 2010, SI 2010/1923 at **[2.1503]**.

[2.1171]
24 Right to time spent on public duties

(1) An office holder may, subject to paragraph (2) below, spend time on public duties other than the duties of his or her office.

(2) The amount of time which an office holder may spend on public duties under this regulation, the occasions on which and any conditions subject to which the time may be spent, are those that are reasonable in all the circumstances, having regard, in particular, to—
(a) how much time is required for the performance of the particular public duty;
(b) how much time has already been spent on public duties under this regulation;
(c) the nature of the office and its duties and the effect of the absence of the office holder on the performance of the duties of the office; and
(d) any remuneration which the office holder is entitled to receive in connection with the duties of the office.

(3) In the event of any dispute as to any of the matters referred to in sub-paragraph (2) above, the matter shall be determined by the diocesan bishop or, in the case of an office holder who is a diocesan bishop, the archbishop of the province in which the diocese is situated.

(4) In this regulation "public duties" means—
(a) any work done for a public authority, including membership of a court or tribunal, or for a charity within the meaning of the Charities Act 2006 or an incorporated or a registered friendly society, and
(b) any work done in connection with the activities of an independent trade union representing office holders of a description which includes the person in question.

NOTES

Commencement: 1 January 2010.

[2.1172]
25 Right to time off for ante-natal care

(1) An office holder who—
(a) is pregnant, and
(b) has, on the advice of a registered medical practitioner, registered midwife or registered health visitor, made an appointment to attend at any place for the purpose of receiving ante-natal care,

is entitled to take time off during her working hours in order to enable her to keep the appointment.

(2) As soon as is reasonably practicable after the office holder's pregnancy is confirmed, she shall notify the officer of the diocese nominated under regulation 3(1)(a) above.

NOTES

Commencement: 1 January 2010.

[2.1173]

26 Payment of stipend during time off or time spent on public duties

(1) An office holder who takes any time off or spends time on public duties to which he or she is entitled under regulations 24 or 25 above and who is, under the terms of his or her service, entitled to the payment of a stipend, shall not suffer any reduction in his or her stipend during the time off or time spent on public duties, as the case may be, except, in the case of time spent on public duties, such reduction, if any, as may be specified in the statement of particulars of office given under regulation 3 above (including any statement of changes given under regulation 6 above).

NOTES

Commencement: 1 January 2010.

Sickness

[2.1174]

27 Sickness

(1) If an office holder who is in receipt of a stipend is unable to perform the duties of his or her office because of illness for a period of one working day or longer he or she must report the absence to the person nominated for the purposes of [this regulation], who shall inform the Commissioners and, if the report is in writing, send them a copy thereof.

[(1A) The person nominated under paragraph (1) above shall be nominated—

(a) in the case of an office holder other than the diocesan bishop, by the diocesan bishop, and

(b) in the case of an office holder who is a diocesan bishop, by the registrar of the province in which the diocese is situated.]

(2) If an office holder is absent from work because of illness for a continuous period of more than seven days he or she must supply the person nominated as aforesaid with a certificate signed by a qualified medical practitioner and that person shall send a copy of the certificate to the Commissioners.

(3) An office holder who is absent from work because of illness must use all reasonable endeavours to make arrangements for the duties of the office to be performed by another person during the absence which may, where appropriate, consist of notifying a responsible person or authority of the absence.

(4) If an office holder is entitled to receive statutory sick pay under Part XI of the Social Security and Contributions and Benefits Act 1992 for any period of absence from work, the office holder shall be entitled during that period to receive in full any stipend which is payable in respect of the office.

(5) The diocesan bishop or, in the case of an office holder who is a diocesan bishop, the archbishop of the province in which the diocese is situated, may, if he is satisfied that the office holder is, by reason of illness, unable adequately to discharge the duties of his or her office, permit the office holder to be absent from work for such period as he thinks appropriate and may make provision for the discharge of those duties during the period of absence of the office holder.

(6) When giving any directions under section 5(2) of the Diocesan Stipends Funds Measure 1953 in relation to the payment of a stipend to an office holder who is absent from work for illness for any period after the date on which he or she is entitled to receive statutory sick pay under the said Part XI, a diocesan bishop shall have regard to any guidance issued by the Archbishops' Council in the exercise of its functions as the Central Stipends Authority.

NOTES

Commencement: 1 January 2010.

Words in square brackets in para (1) substituted, and para (1A) inserted, by the Ecclesiastical Offices (Terms of Service) (Amendment) Regulations 2010, SI 2010/2407, reg 4, as from 1 January 2011.

[2.1175]

28 Medical examination

(1) The diocesan bishop or, in the case of an office holder who is a diocesan bishop, the archbishop of the province in which the diocese is situated may, if he has reasonable grounds for concern about the physical or mental health of an office holder, direct that the office holder shall undergo a medical examination by a medical practitioner selected by agreement between the bishop (or archbishop) and the office holder or, in default of agreement, by medical practitioners consisting of a practitioner chosen by each party.

[(1A) The archbishop of either province may, if he has reasonable grounds for concern about the physical or mental health of the archbishop of the other province, direct that that archbishop shall undergo a medical examination by a medical practitioner selected by agreement between both archbishops or, in default of agreement, by medical practitioners consisting of a practitioner chosen by each archbishop.]

(2) If an office holder fails to comply with a direction given under paragraph (1) [or (1A)] above or fails to disclose or authorise the disclosure of any relevant medical records, when requested to do so, any person or body responsible for operating any capability procedures in respect of the office holder may draw such inferences as appear to that person or body to be appropriate having regard to all the circumstances.

NOTES

Commencement: 1 January 2010.

Para (1A) and words in square brackets in para (2) inserted, by the Ecclesiastical Offices (Terms of Service) (Amendment) Regulations 2010, SI 2010/2407, reg 5, as from 1 January 2011.

PART VI
DURATION AND TERMINATION OF APPOINTMENTS AND COMPENSATION

Limited appointments and termination of appointments

[2.1176]

29 Fixed and other limited term appointments

(1) A person who holds or is to hold office under Common Tenure may be appointed for a fixed term or under terms which provide for the appointment to be terminated on the occurrence of a specified event if—

- (a) the office holder occupies a post which is designated as a post created in order to cover an office holder's authorised absence from work,
- (b) the office holder has attained the age of seventy years and is occupying a post under a licence granted by the diocesan bishop,
- (c) the office is designated as a training post,
- (d) the office is designated as a post subject to sponsorship funding,
- (e) the office is designated as a probationary office,
- (f) the office is created by a bishop's mission order made under section 47 or 50 of the Dioceses, Pastoral and Mission Measure 2007, . . .
- (g) the office holder holds a post which is designated as a post which is held in connection or conjunction with another office or employment,
- [(h) the office holder does not have the right of abode, or unlimited leave to enter or remain, in the United Kingdom; or
- (i) the office holder occupies a post which is designated as a Locally Supported Ministry Post,]

and section 1(1) of the Ecclesiastical Offices (Age Limit) Measure 1975 shall have effect subject to sub-paragraph (b) above.

(2) Where a person holds office in any circumstances mentioned in paragraph (1) above the statement of particulars of office required to be given to the office holder under regulation 3 above shall, in addition, contain particulars of any relevant term mentioned in that paragraph.

(3) An office may be designated as a training post if the office holder is required by the diocesan bishop to undertake initial ministerial education.

(4) An office may be designated as a post subject to sponsorship funding if—

- (a) the holder of the post is a person referred to in section 1(1)(g) or (h) of the Measure (other than a vicar in a team ministry), and
- (b) any part of the cost of the holder's stipend or other remuneration, pension, housing accommodation or other expenses is defrayed by a person or body other than a diocesan board of finance, parsonages board, parochial church council or the Commissioners.

(5) An office may be designated as a probationary office if, on the date of the appointment of the office holder to the office, the office holder has not held any ecclesiastical office in any place during the period of twelve months immediately preceding that date.

(6) An office may be designated as a probationary office if the office holder has been removed from a previous office by a final adjudication under the capability procedures and the office designated as a probationary office under this paragraph is the first office occupied by the office holder after his or her removal from office.

(7) An office may be designated as a probationary office if—

- (a) the office holder has been the subject of a complaint under the Ecclesiastical Jurisdiction Measure 1963 and has had a censure of prohibition, inhibition or suspension imposed on him or her or he or she has resigned, or
- (b) the office holder has had imposed on him or her a penalty of removal from office, prohibition for a limited term or revocation of his or her licence under the Clergy Discipline Measure 2003 or he or she has resigned in accordance with that Measure,

and appointment to the office is made on the recommendation of the diocesan bishop with a view to facilitating his or her return to the ministry.

[(7A) An office may be designated as a Locally Supported Ministry Post if—

(a) the post is held by an assistant curate who is not in sole or principal charge of the parish in which he or she serves,

(b) the parochial church council of that parish has entered into a legally binding agreement with the diocesan board of finance of the diocese in which the parish is situated to pay the whole cost of the office holder's stipend or other remuneration and expenses, including any pension and housing accommodation and other expenses, and

(c) the designation is in writing, signed by the bishop of the diocese, acting with the consent of the office holder and the parochial church council.]

(8) The term of office of any office holder appointed for a fixed term or until the occurrence of a specified event shall terminate on the expiry of the fixed term (unless that term is extended for a further period or periods) or on the occurrence of the event, as the case may be.

NOTES

Commencement: 1 January 2010.

Word omitted from sub-para (1)(f) revoked, sub-paras (1)(h), (i) inserted, and para (7A) inserted, by the Ecclesiastical Offices (Terms of Service) (Amendment) Regulations 2010, SI 2010/2407, reg 6, as from 1 January 2011.

Compensation for loss of certain offices

[2.1177]

30 Posts subject to potential pastoral reorganisation and priests-in-charge

(1) Where—

(a) an office holder is appointed to hold office as an archdeacon or incumbent or a vicar in a team ministry or a deacon in a team ministry . . .

(b) at the time when the appointment is made, the mission and pastoral committee of the diocese in which the office is situated has invited the views of the interested parties before submitting proposals to the diocesan bishop in accordance with section 3 of that Measure for inclusion in a draft pastoral scheme or order which might affect the office,

the diocesan bishop may designate the office as an office which is subject to potential pastoral reorganisation and the statement of particulars required to be given to the office holder under regulation 3 above shall contain a declaration of that designation.

(2) If an office designated under paragraph (1) above ceases to exist in consequence of a pastoral scheme or order the office holder shall, provided that he is in receipt of a stipend or other emoluments, be entitled to compensation calculated in accordance with Schedule 4 to the Pastoral Measure 1983, except that any periodical payments or lump sum payable under paragraph 7(1) of that Schedule shall be based on the loss of one year's service in his or her post and paragraph 13(1)(b) and (c), all the words following sub-sub-paragraph (c) and sub-paragraphs (2) to (6) of that paragraph shall not apply.

(3) If, following the designation of an office under paragraph (1) above, no pastoral scheme or order is made affecting the office within such period not exceeding five years immediately following the appointment of the office holder as may be specified by the bishop, the bishop shall notify the office holder that the office is no longer designated under that paragraph.

(4) Where notification is given to the office holder under paragraph (3) above, section 26 of and Schedule 4 to the Pastoral Measure 1983 shall apply to the office holder instead of paragraph (2) above.

(5) Paragraph (2) above shall also apply to any other office holder whose office ceases to exist in consequence of a pastoral scheme or order and who is not otherwise entitled to compensation under section 26 of and Schedule 4 to the Pastoral Measure 1983.

(6) Where the licence of a priest-in-charge appointed to a benefice during a vacancy is revoked, in accordance with section 3(4) of the Measure, the priest-in-charge shall be entitled to compensation calculated on the same basis as that on which compensation is calculated under paragraph (2) above.

NOTES

Commencement: 1 January 2010.

Words omitted from sub-para (1)(a) revoked by the Ecclesiastical Offices (Terms of Service) (Amendment) Regulations 2010, SI 2010/2407, reg 7, as from 1 January 2011.

PART VII
CAPABILITY AND GRIEVANCE PROCEDURES

Capability procedures

[2.1178]

31 Capability procedures to be conducted in accordance with Codes of Practice

(1) The diocesan bishop may, if he considers that the performance of an office holder affords grounds for concern, instigate an inquiry into the capability of an office holder to perform the duties of his or her office in accordance with the following provisions of this regulation.

[(1A) Where the office holder is a diocesan bishop or an archbishop an inquiry may be instigated under paragraph (1)above—

(a) in the case of an office holder who is a diocesan bishop, by the archbishop of the province in which the diocese is situated, and

(b) in the case of an office holder who is an archbishop, by the archbishop of the other province.]

(2) An office holder who is the subject of an inquiry under paragraph (1) above shall be entitled, before the inquiry begins, to be informed in writing of—

(a) any matters relating to the office holder's performance which are to be taken into account in assessing his or her performance;

(b) the procedure which is to be followed in assessing his or her performance, which shall include the opportunity of a meeting between the office holder and the person or authority which is to carry out the procedure and the appointment of a panel or other body to adjudicate on issues concerning the officer holder's capability;

(c) the identity of the person or authority who or which is to carry out the procedure;

(d) any action which may be taken following the completion of the procedure; and

(e) the office holder's rights of appeal against the decision to take any action against the office holder.

(3) Any inquiry instituted under paragraph (1) above shall be conducted in accordance with a Code of Practice issued under section 8 of the Measure.

(4) Any Code of Practice issued under paragraph (3) above may provide for different procedures for different circumstances and may make provision for any other matters which the Archbishops' Council considers appropriate.

(5) When issuing any Code of Practice under paragraph (3) above the Archbishops' Council shall endeavour to ensure that an office holder who is the subject of the capability procedures under this regulation is placed in a position which is no less favourable than that in which an employee would be placed under a Code of Practice issued under Chapter III of Part IV of the Trade Union and Labour Relations (Consolidation) Act 1992.

NOTES

Commencement: 1 January 2010.

Para (1A): inserted by the Ecclesiastical Offices (Terms of Service) (Amendment) Regulations 2010, SI 2010/2407, reg 8, as from 1 January 2011.

Grievance procedures

[2.1179]

32 Archbishops' Council to issue Codes of Practice concerning grievance procedures

(1) The Archbishops' Council shall issue a Code of Practice under section 8 of the Measure containing procedures for enabling an office holder to seek redress for grievances.

(2) Any Code of Practice issued under paragraph (1) above shall make provision for—

(a) the office holder to state his or her grievance in writing;

(b) informing the office holder of the person or authority to whom or to which the office holder is to address the grievance;

(c) informing the office holder of the procedures to be followed in discussing the grievance and for taking any action to redress it, including the opportunity for a meeting between the office holder and the person or authority to whom or to which the grievance is to be addressed;

(d) rights of appeal against the decision relating to the grievance and informing the office holder of such rights; and

(e) informing the office holder of any action which may be taken following the completion of the procedure.

(3) Any Code of Practice issued under paragraph (1) above may provide for different procedures for different circumstances and may make provision for any other matters which the Archbishops' Council considers appropriate.

(4) When issuing a Code of Practice under paragraph (1) above the Archbishops' Council shall endeavour to ensure that an office holder who seeks redress under this regulation is placed in a position which is no less favourable than that in which an employee would be placed under a Code of Practice issued under Chapter III of Part IV of the Trade Union and Labour Relations (Consolidation) Act 1992.

NOTES

Commencement: 1 January 2010.

PART VIII
UNFAIR DISMISSAL

Rights on unfair dismissal

[2.1180]
33 Right to apply to employment tribunal

(1) Where the appointment of an office holder has been terminated by notice given under section 3(6) of the Measure following adjudication under procedures carried out under regulation 31 above, the office holder shall have the right not to be unfairly dismissed.

(2) Subject to paragraph (3) and (4) below Part X of the Employment Rights Act 1996 (in this regulation referred to as "the 1996 Act") shall apply in relation to an office holder who is dismissed in the circumstances described in paragraph (1) above as it applies to an employee who is dismissed for a reason relating to the capability of the employee in accordance with section 98(2) of the 1996 Act and as if in that Act—

(a) any reference to an employee were a reference to the office holder;

(b) except in the case of a person holding office in a cathedral, any reference to an employer were a reference to the Diocesan Board of Finance for the diocese in which, on the date on which the office was terminated, the office holder exercised his office;

(c) in the case of a person holding office in a cathedral, any reference to an employer were a reference to the Chapter of the cathedral; and

(d) any reference to employment were a reference to the holding of an office;

and as if the office holder had been dismissed by that Diocesan Board of Finance or that Chapter, as the case may be, and the reason or principal reason stated in the notice referred to in paragraph (1) above were the reason or principal reason for the dismissal.

(3) Section 108 of the 1996 Act shall not apply in relation to an office holder who has the right not to be unfairly dismissed under this regulation and for the purposes of Part X of that Act the office holder shall be treated as if the period of continuous holding of the office were the period beginning with the date on which the office holder was appointed and ending with the date of the notice referred to in paragraph (1) above.

(4) This regulation shall not apply to any office holder who has attained the retirement age specified in relation to the office holder's office in section 1 of the Ecclesiastical Offices (Age Limit) Measure 1975.

NOTES

Commencement: 1 January 2010.

EUROPEAN PUBLIC LIMITED-LIABILITY COMPANY (EMPLOYEE INVOLVEMENT) (GREAT BRITAIN) REGULATIONS 2009

(SI 2009/2401)

NOTES

Made: 9 September 2009.

Authority: European Communities Act 1972, s 2(2).

Commencement: 1 October 2009.

Employment Appeal Tribunal: an appeal lies to the Employment Appeal Tribunal on any question of law arising from any decision of, or in any proceedings before, an employment tribunal under or by virtue of these Regulations; see the Employment Tribunals Act 1996, s 21(1)(w) at **[1.713]**.

Conciliation: employment tribunal proceedings and claims which could be the subject of employment tribunal proceedings under regs 28, 32 are proceedings to which the Employment Tribunals Act 1996, s 18 applies; see s 18(1)(v) of that Act at **[1.706]**.

See *Harvey* NIII(4).

ARRANGEMENT OF REGULATIONS

PART 1
INTRODUCTORY PROVISIONS

PART 2
PARTICIPATING COMPANIES AND THE SPECIAL NEGOTIATING BODY

PART 1
INTRODUCTORY PROVISIONS

[2.1181]
1 Citation, commencement and extent

(1) These Regulations may be cited as the European Public Limited-Liability Company (Employee Involvement) (Great Britain) Regulations 2009.

(2) These Regulations come into force on 1st October 2009.

(3) These Regulations extend to the whole of Great Britain.

NOTES
Commencement: 1 October 2009.

[2.1182]
2 EC Directive and EC Regulation

(1) In these Regulations—

"the EC Directive" means Council Directive 2001/86/EC of 8 October 2001 supplementing the Statute for a European Company with regard to the involvement of employees;

"the EC Regulation" means Council Regulation 2157/2001/EC of 8 October 2001 on the Statute for a European Company.

(2) References in these Regulations to numbered Articles are, unless otherwise specified, references to Articles in the EC Regulation.

NOTES
Commencement: 1 October 2009.

[2.1183]
3 Interpretation

(1) In these Regulations—

"absolute majority vote" means a vote passed by a majority of the total membership of the special negotiating body where the members voting with that majority represent the majority of the employees of the participating companies and their concerned subsidiaries and establishments employed in the EEA states;

["agency worker" has the same meaning as in regulation 3 of the Agency Workers Regulations 2010;]

"Appeal Tribunal" means the Employment Appeal Tribunal;

"CAC" means the Central Arbitration Committee;

"dismissed" and "dismissal", in relation to an employee, have the same meaning as in Part 10 of the Employment Rights Act 1996;

"employee" means an individual who has entered into or works under a contract of employment and includes, where the employment has ceased, an individual who worked under a contract of employment;

"employee involvement agreement" means an agreement reached between the special negotiating body and the competent organs of the participating companies governing the arrangements for the involvement of employees within the SE;

"employees' representatives" means—

(a) if the employees are of a description in respect of which an independent trade union is recognised by their employer for the purpose of collective bargaining, representatives of the trade union who normally take part as negotiators in the collective bargaining process, and

(b) any other employees of their employer who are elected or appointed as employee representatives to positions in which they are expected to receive, on behalf of the employees, information—

(i) which is relevant to the terms and conditions of employment of the employees, or

(ii) about the activities of the undertaking which may significantly affect the interests of the employees,

but excluding representatives who are expected to receive information relevant only to a specific aspect of the terms and conditions or interests of the employees, such as health and safety or collective redundancies;

"information and consultation representative" has the meaning given to it in regulation 15(5);

"participation" means the influence of the representative body and the employees' representatives in the SE or a participating company by way of the right to—

(a) elect or appoint some of the members of the SE's or the participating company's supervisory or administrative organ, or

(b) recommend or oppose the appointment of some or all of the members of the SE's or the participating company's supervisory or administrative organ;

"representative body" means the persons elected or appointed under the employee involvement agreement or under the standard rules on employee involvement;

"SE" means a European Public Limited-Liability Company (or Societas Europaea) within the meaning of the EC Regulation;

"SE established by merger" means an SE established in accordance with Article 2(1);

"SE established by formation of a holding company or subsidiary company" means an SE established in accordance with Article 2(2) or 2(3), as the case may be;

"SE established by transformation" means an SE established in accordance with Article 2(4);

"standard rules on employee involvement" means the rules in the Schedule to these Regulations;

["suitable information relating to the use of agency workers" means—

(a) the number of agency workers working temporarily for and under the supervision and direction of the undertaking;

(b) the parts of the undertaking in which those agency workers are working; and

(c) the type of work those agency workers are carrying out;]

"two thirds majority vote" means a vote passed by a majority of at least two thirds of the total membership of the special negotiating body where the members voting with that majority—

(a) represent at least two thirds of the employees of the participating companies and their concerned subsidiaries and establishments employed in the EEA states, and

(b) include members representing employees employed in at least two EEA states;

"UK employee" means an employee employed to work in the United Kingdom;

"UK members of the special negotiating body" means members of the special negotiating body elected or appointed by UK employees.

(2) In these Regulations the following expressions have the meaning given by Article 2 of the EC Directive—

"participating companies",
"subsidiary",
"special negotiating body",
"involvement of employees",
"information",
"consultation",

and references to a "concerned subsidiary" or a "concerned establishment" are to be construed in accordance with the definition of "concerned subsidiary or establishment" in the EC Directive.

(3) Except as otherwise provided, words and expressions used in the EC Regulation or the EC Directive have the same meaning in these Regulations as they have in that Regulation or Directive.

(4) Except as otherwise provided, references in these Regulations to an SE are to an SE that is to be, or is, registered in Great Britain.

NOTES

Commencement: 1 October 2009.

Para (1): definitions "agency worker" and "suitable information relating to the use of agency workers" inserted by the Agency Workers Regulations 2010, SI 2010/93, reg 25, Sch 2, Pt 2, paras 47, 48, as from 1 October 2011.

[2.1184]

4 Application of these Regulations

(1) These Regulations apply where—

(a) a participating company intends to establish an SE whose registered office is to be in Great Britain, or

(b) an SE has its registered office in Great Britain.

(2) Where there are UK employees, Part 3 also applies (regardless of where the registered office is to be situated) in relation to the election or appointment of UK members of the special negotiating body, unless the majority of those employees is employed to work in Northern Ireland.

(3) Parts 6 to 9 also apply (regardless of where the registered office of the SE is, or is intended to be situated) if any of the following is registered or, as the case may be, situated in Great Britain—

(a) a participating company, its concerned subsidiaries or establishments;

(b) a subsidiary of an SE;

(c) an establishment of an SE;

(d) an employee or an employees' representative.

NOTES

Commencement: 1 October 2009.

PART 2
PARTICIPATING COMPANIES AND THE SPECIAL NEGOTIATING BODY

[2.1185]

5 Duty on participating company to provide information

(1) When the competent organ of a participating company decides to form an SE, that organ must, as soon as possible after—

(a) publishing the draft terms of merger,

(b) creating a holding company, or

(c) agreeing a plan to form a subsidiary or to transform into an SE,

provide information to the employees' representatives of the participating company, its concerned subsidiaries and establishments or, if no such representatives exist, the employees themselves.

(2) The information referred to in paragraph (1) must include, as a minimum, information—

(a) identifying the participating companies, concerned subsidiaries and establishments,

(b) giving the number of employees employed by each participating company and concerned subsidiary and at each concerned establishment, . . .

(c) giving the number of employees employed to work in each EEA State;

[(d) the number of agency workers working temporarily for and under the supervision and direction of the undertaking;

(e) the parts of the undertaking in which those agency workers are working; and

(f) the type of work those agency workers are carrying out].

(3) When a special negotiating body has been formed in accordance with regulation 8, the competent organs of each participating company must provide that body with such information as is necessary to keep it informed of the plan and progress of establishing the SE up to the time the SE has been registered.

NOTES

Commencement: 1 October 2009.

Para (2): the word omitted from sub-para (b) was revoked, and sub-paras (d)–(f) were added, by the Agency Workers Regulations 2010, SI 2010/93, reg 25, Sch 2, Pt 2, paras 47, 49, as from 1 October 2011.

[2.1186]

6 Complaint of failure to provide information

(1) An employees' representative, or an employee for whom there is no such representative, may present a complaint to the CAC that—

(a) the competent organ of a participating company has failed to provide the information referred to in regulation 5, or

(b) the information provided by the competent organ of a participating company for the purpose of complying with regulation 5 is false or incomplete in a material particular.

(2) If the CAC finds the complaint well-founded, it must make an order requiring the competent organ to disclose information to the complainant.

(3) The order must specify—

(a) the information in respect of which the CAC finds that the complaint is well-founded and which is to be disclosed to the complainant, and

(b) a date (not less than one week after the date of the order) by which the competent organ must disclose the information specified in the order.

NOTES

Commencement: 1 October 2009.

[2.1187]

7 Function of the special negotiating body

The special negotiating body and the competent organs of the participating companies have the task of reaching an employee involvement agreement.

NOTES

Commencement: 1 October 2009.

[2.1188]

8 Composition of the special negotiating body

(1) The competent organs of the participating companies must make arrangements for the establishment of a special negotiating body constituted in accordance with the following provisions of this regulation.

(2) In each EEA state in which employees of a participating company or concerned subsidiary are employed to work, those employees must be given an entitlement to elect or appoint one member of the special negotiating body for each 10%, or fraction of 10%, which those employees represent of the total workforce. These members are the "ordinary members".

(3) If, in the case of an SE to be established by merger, following an election or appointment under paragraph (2), the members elected or appointed to the special negotiating body do not include at least one eligible member in respect of each relevant company, the employees of any relevant company in respect of which there is no eligible member must be given an entitlement, subject to paragraph (4), to elect or appoint an additional member to the special negotiating body.

(4) The number of additional members which the employees are entitled to elect or appoint under paragraph (3) must not exceed 20% of the number of ordinary members elected or appointed under paragraph (2). If the number of additional members under paragraph (3) would exceed that percentage, the employees who are entitled to appoint or elect the additional members are—

(a) if one additional member is to be appointed or elected, those employed by the company not represented under paragraph (3) having the highest number of employees;

(b) if more than one additional member is to be appointed or elected, those employed by the companies in each EEA state that are not represented under paragraph (3) having the highest number of employees in descending order, starting with the company with the highest number, followed by those employed by the companies in each EEA state that are not so represented having the second highest number of employees in descending order, starting with the company (among those companies) with the highest number.

(5) The competent organs of the participating companies must, as soon as reasonably practicable and in any event no later than one month after the establishment of the special negotiating body, inform their employees and those of their concerned subsidiaries of the identity of the members of the special negotiating body.

(6) If, following the appointment or election of members to the special negotiating body in accordance with this regulation, changes to the participating companies, concerned subsidiaries or concerned establishments result in the number of ordinary or additional members which employees would be entitled to elect or appoint under this regulation either increasing or decreasing—

(a) the original appointment or election of members of the special negotiating body ceases to have effect, and

(b) those employees are entitled to elect or appoint the new number of members in accordance with the provisions of these Regulations.

(7) If a member of the special negotiating body is no longer willing or able to continue serving as such a member, the employees whom the member represents are entitled to elect or appoint a new member in place of that member.

(8) In this regulation—

"eligible member" means a person who is—

(a) in the case of a relevant company registered in an EEA state whose legislation allows representatives of trade unions who are not employees to be elected to the special negotiating body, an employee of the relevant company or a trade union representative;

(b) in the case of a relevant company not registered in such an EEA state, an employee of the relevant company;

"relevant company" means a participating company which has employees in the EEA state in which it is registered and which it is proposed will cease to exist on or following the registration of the SE;

"the total workforce" means the total number of employees employed by all participating companies and concerned subsidiaries throughout all EEA states.

NOTES

Commencement: 1 October 2009.

[2.1189]

9 Complaint about establishment of special negotiating body

(1) An application may be presented to the CAC for a declaration that the special negotiating body has not been established at all or has not been established properly in accordance with regulation 8.

(2) An application may be presented under this regulation by any of the following—

(a) a person elected or appointed to be a member of the special negotiating body;

(b) an employees' representative;

(c) where there is no employees' representative in respect of a participating company or concerned subsidiary, an employee of that participating company or concerned subsidiary;

(d) the competent organ of a participating company or concerned subsidiary.

(3) The CAC may only consider an application made under paragraph (1) if it is made within a period of one month following the date or, if more than one, the last date on which the participating companies complied or should have complied with the obligation to inform their employees under regulation 8(5).

(4) If the CAC finds the application well-founded—

(a) it must make a declaration that the special negotiating body has not been established at all or has not been established properly, and

(b) the competent organs of the participating companies continue to be under the obligation in regulation 8(1).

NOTES

Commencement: 1 October 2009.

PART 3
ELECTION OR APPOINTMENT OF UK MEMBERS OF THE SPECIAL NEGOTIATING BODY

[2.1190]

10 Ballot arrangements

(1) Subject to regulation 11, the UK members of the special negotiating body must be elected by balloting the UK employees.

(2) The management of the participating companies that employ UK employees ("the management") must arrange for the holding of a ballot or ballots of those employees in accordance with the requirements specified in paragraph (3).

(3) The requirements are—

(a) in relation to the election of ordinary members under regulation 8(2), that—

(i) if the number of members which UK employees are entitled to elect to the special negotiating body is equal to the number of participating companies which have UK employees, there must be separate ballots of the UK employees in each participating company;

(ii) if the number of members which the UK employees are entitled to elect to the special negotiating body is greater than the number of participating companies which have UK employees, there must be separate ballots of the UK employees in each participating company and the management must ensure, as far as practicable, that at least one member representing each such participating company is elected to the special negotiating body and that the number of members representing each company is proportionate to the number of employees in that company;

(iii) if the number of members which the UK employees are entitled to elect to the special negotiating body is smaller than the number of participating companies which have employees in the United Kingdom—

(aa) the number of ballots held must be equivalent to the number of members to be elected,

(bb) a separate ballot must be held in respect of each of the participating companies with the higher or highest number of employees, and

(cc) it must be ensured that any employees of a participating company in respect of which a ballot does not have to be held are entitled to vote in a ballot held in respect of one of the other participating companies;

(iv) if there are any UK employees employed by a concerned subsidiary or establishment of non-UK participating companies, the management must ensure that those employees are entitled to vote in a ballot held pursuant to this regulation;

(b) that in relation to the ballot of additional members under regulation 8(3) the management must hold a separate ballot in respect of each participating company entitled to elect an additional member;

(c) that, in a ballot in respect of a particular participating company, all UK employees employed by that participating company or by its concerned subsidiaries or at its concerned establishments are entitled to vote;

(d) that a person is entitled to stand as a candidate for election as a member of the special negotiating body in a ballot in respect of a particular participating company if, immediately before the latest time at which a person may become a candidate, the person is—

(i) a UK employee employed by that participating company, by any of its concerned subsidiaries or at any of its concerned establishments, or

(ii) if the management of that participating company so permits, a representative of a trade union who is not an employee of that participating company or any of its concerned subsidiaries;

(e) that the management must appoint in accordance with paragraph (7) a person (a "ballot supervisor")—

(i) to supervise the conduct of the ballot of UK employees, or
(ii) where there is to be more than one ballot, to supervise the conduct of each of the separate ballots,

and, in a case falling within paragraph (ii), may appoint different persons to supervise the conduct of such different separate ballots as the management may determine;

(f) that after the management has formulated proposals as to the arrangements for the ballot of UK employees and before it has published the final arrangements under sub-paragraph (g) it must, so far as reasonably practicable, consult the UK employees' representatives on the proposed arrangements for the ballot of UK employees; and

(g) that the management must publish the final arrangements for the ballot of UK employees in such manner as to bring them to the attention of, so far as reasonably practicable, all UK employees and the UK employees' representatives.

(4) Any UK employee or UK employees' representative who believes that the arrangements for the ballot of the UK employees do not comply with the requirements of paragraph (3) may, within a period of 21 days beginning on the date on which the management published the final arrangements under sub-paragraph (g) of that paragraph, present a complaint to the CAC.

(5) If the CAC finds the complaint well-founded, it must make a declaration to that effect and may make an order requiring the management to modify the arrangements it has made for the ballot of UK employees or to satisfy the requirements in sub-paragraph (f) or (g) of paragraph (3).

(6) An order under paragraph (5) must specify—

(a) the modifications to the arrangements which the management is required to make, and
(b) the requirements it must satisfy.

(7) The management may appoint a person to be a ballot supervisor for the purposes of paragraph (3)(e) only if the management—

(a) reasonably believes that the person will carry out competently any functions conferred on the person in relation to the ballot, and
(b) has no reasonable grounds for believing that the person's independence in relation to the ballot might reasonably be called into question.

NOTES

Commencement: 1 October 2009.

[2.1191]

11 Conduct of the ballot

(1) The management must—

(a) ensure that a ballot supervisor appointed under regulation 10(3)(e) carries out the functions conferred or imposed on the ballot supervisor under this regulation;
(b) ensure that there is no interference from the management with the ballot supervisor's carrying out of those functions;
(c) comply with all reasonable requests made by a ballot supervisor for the purposes of, or in connection with, the carrying out of those functions.

(2) A ballot supervisor's appointment must require that the ballot supervisor—

(a) supervises the conduct of the ballot, or the separate ballots, that the ballot supervisor is being appointed to supervise, in accordance with the arrangements for the ballot of UK employees published by the management under regulation 10(3)(g) or, where appropriate, in accordance with the arrangements as required to be modified by an order made as a result of a complaint presented under regulation 10(4);
(b) does not conduct the ballot or any of the separate ballots before the management has satisfied the requirement specified in regulation 10(3)(g) and—
   (i) where no complaint has been presented under regulation 10(4), before the expiry of a period of 21 days beginning on the date on which the management published its arrangements under regulation 10(3)(g), or
   (ii) where a complaint has been presented under regulation 10(4), before the complaint has been determined and, where appropriate, the arrangements have been modified as required by an order made as a result of that complaint;
(c) conducts the ballot, or each separate ballot, so as to secure that—
   (i) so far as reasonably practicable, those entitled to vote are given the opportunity to vote,
   (ii) so far as reasonably practicable, those entitled to stand as candidates are given the opportunity to stand,
   (iii) so far as reasonably practicable, those voting are able to do so in secret, and
   (iv) the votes given in the ballot are fairly and accurately counted.

(3) As soon as reasonably practicable after the holding of the ballot, the ballot supervisor must publish the results of the ballot in such manner as to make them available to the management and, so far as reasonably practicable, to the UK employees entitled to vote in the ballot and the persons who stood as candidates.

(4) If a ballot supervisor considers (whether on the basis of representations made to the ballot supervisor by another person or otherwise)—

(a) that any of the requirements referred to in paragraph (2) was not satisfied, with the result that the outcome of the ballot would have been different, or

(b) that there was interference with the carrying out of the ballot supervisor's functions, or a failure by the management to comply with all reasonable requests made by the ballot supervisor, with the result that the ballot supervisor was unable to form a proper judgement as to whether each of the requirements referred to in paragraph (2) was satisfied in the ballot,

the ballot supervisor must publish a report ("an ineffective ballot report").

(5) Where a ballot supervisor publishes an ineffective ballot report, the report must be published within a period of one month commencing on the date on which the ballot supervisor publishes the results of the ballot under paragraph (3).

(6) A ballot supervisor must publish an ineffective ballot report in such manner as to make it available to the management and, so far as reasonably practicable, to the UK employees entitled to vote in the ballot and the persons who stood as candidates in the ballot.

(7) Where a ballot supervisor publishes an ineffective ballot report, then—

(a) if there has been a single ballot, or if an ineffective ballot report has been published in respect of every separate ballot, the outcome of the ballot or ballots has no effect and the management is again under the obligation in regulation 10(2);

(b) if there have been separate ballots and sub-paragraph (a) does not apply—

(i) the management must arrange for the separate ballot or ballots in respect of which an ineffective ballot report was published to be re-held in accordance with regulation 10 and this regulation, and

(ii) no such ballot has effect until it has been re-held and no ineffective ballot report has been published in respect of it.

(8) All costs relating to the holding of a ballot, including payments made to a ballot supervisor for supervising the conduct of the ballot, must be borne by the management (whether or not an ineffective ballot report has been published).

NOTES

Commencement: 1 October 2009.

[2.1192]

12 Appointment of UK members by a consultative committee

(1) This regulation applies where—

(a) regulation 10(3)(a)(i) or (ii) or (b) would (apart from this regulation) require a ballot to be held, but

(b) there exists in the participating company in respect of which a ballot would be held under regulation 10, a consultative committee.

(2) Where this regulation applies—

(a) the election provided for in regulation 10 must not take place;

(b) the consultative committee is entitled to appoint the UK member or members of the special negotiating body who would otherwise be elected pursuant to regulation 10;

(c) any such appointment by the consultative committee must comply with paragraph (3).

(3) The consultative committee may appoint as a member of the special negotiating body—

(a) one of their number, or

(b) if the management of the participating company in respect of which the consultative committee exists so permits, a trade union representative who is not an employee of that company.

(4) In this regulation a "consultative committee" means a body of persons—

(a) whose normal functions include or comprise the carrying out of an information and consultation function,

(b) which is able to carry out its information and consultation function without interference from the management of the participating company,

(c) which, in carrying out its information and consultation function, represents all the employees of the participating company, and

(d) which consists wholly of persons who are employees of the participating company or its concerned subsidiaries.

(5) In paragraph (4) "information and consultation function" means the function of—

(a) receiving, on behalf of all the employees of the participating company, information which may significantly affect the interests of the employees of that company, but excluding information which is relevant only to a specific aspect of the interests of the employees, such as health and safety or collective redundancies, and

(b) being consulted by the management of the participating company on the information referred to in sub-paragraph (a).

(6) The consultative committee must publish the names of the persons whom it has appointed to be members of the special negotiating body in such a manner as to bring them to the attention of the management of the participating company and, so far as reasonably practicable, the employees and the employees' representatives of that company and its concerned subsidiaries.

(7) Where the management of the participating company, or an employee or an employees' representative, believes that—

(a) the consultative committee does not satisfy the requirements in paragraph (4), or

(b) any of the persons appointed by the consultative committee is not entitled to be appointed,

the management of the participating company or, as the case may be, the employee or the employees' representative may present a complaint to the CAC within a period of 21 days beginning on the date on which the consultative committee published under paragraph (6) the names of the persons appointed.

(8) If the CAC finds the complaint well-founded it must make a declaration to that effect.

(9) Where the CAC has made a declaration under paragraph (8)—

(a) any appointment made by the consultative committee is ineffective, and

(b) the members of the special negotiating body must be elected by a ballot of the employees in accordance with regulation 10.

(10) Where the consultative committee appoints any person to be a member of the special negotiating body, that appointment has effect—

(a) where no complaint has been presented under paragraph (7), after the expiry of a period of 21 days beginning on the date on which the consultative committee published under paragraph (6) the names of the persons appointed;

(b) where a complaint has been presented under paragraph (7), as from the day on which the complaint has been determined without a declaration under paragraph (8) being made.

NOTES

Commencement: 1 October 2009.

[2.1193]

13 Representation of employees

(1) A member elected in a ballot in accordance with regulation 8(2) is treated as representing the employees for the time being of the participating company and of any concerned subsidiary or establishment whose employees were entitled to vote in the ballot in which the member was elected.

(2) If an additional member is elected in accordance with regulation 8(3) and (4), that additional member, and not any member elected in accordance with regulation 8(2), is treated as representing the employees for the time being of the participating company and of any concerned subsidiary or establishment whose employees were entitled to vote in the ballot in which the additional member was elected.

(3) When a member of the special negotiating body is appointed by a consultative committee in accordance with regulation 12, the employees whom the consultative committee represents and the employees of any concerned subsidiary are treated as being represented by the member so appointed.

NOTES

Commencement: 1 October 2009.

PART 4
NEGOTIATION OF THE EMPLOYEE INVOLVEMENT AGREEMENT

[2.1194]

14 Negotiations to reach an employee involvement agreement

(1) In this regulation and in regulation 15 the competent organs of the participating companies and the special negotiating body are referred to as "the parties".

(2) The parties are under a duty to negotiate in a spirit of cooperation with a view to reaching an employee involvement agreement.

(3) The duty referred to in paragraph (2) commences one month after the date or, if more than one, the last date on which the members of the special negotiating body were elected or appointed and applies—

(a) for the period of six months starting with the day on which the duty commenced or, where an employee involvement agreement is successfully negotiated within that period, until the completion of the negotiations;

(b) where the parties agree before the end of that six month period that it is to be extended, for the period of twelve months starting with the day on which the duty commenced or, where an employee involvement agreement is successfully negotiated within the twelve month period, until the completion of the negotiations.

NOTES

Commencement: 1 October 2009.

[2.1195]

15 The employee involvement agreement

(1) The employee involvement agreement must be in writing.

(2) The employee involvement agreement must specify each of the following—

(a) the scope of the agreement;

(b) the composition, number of members and allocation of seats on the representative body;

(c) the functions and the procedure for the information and consultation of the representative body;

(d) the frequency of meetings of the representative body;

(e) the financial and material resources to be allocated to the representative body;

(f) if, during negotiations, the parties decide to establish one or more information and consultation procedures instead of a representative body, the arrangements for implementing those procedures;

(g) if, during negotiations, the parties decide to establish arrangements for participation, the substance of those arrangements including (if applicable) the number of members in the SE's administrative or supervisory body which the employees will be entitled to elect, appoint, recommend or oppose, the procedures as to how these members may be elected, appointed, recommended or opposed by the employees, and their rights;

(h) the date of entry into force of the agreement and its duration, the circumstances, if any, in which the agreement is required to be re-negotiated and the procedure for its re-negotiation.

This paragraph is without prejudice to the autonomy of the parties and is subject to paragraph (4).

(3) The employee involvement agreement is not subject to the standard rules on employee involvement, unless it contains a provision to the contrary.

[(3A) Where under the employee involvement agreement the competent organ of the SE is to provide information on the employment situation in that company, such information must include suitable information relating to the use of agency workers (if any) in that company.]

(4) In relation to an SE to be established by way of transformation, the employee involvement agreement must provide for the elements of employee involvement at all levels to be at least as favourable as those which exist in the company to be transformed into an SE.

(5) If—

(a) the parties decide, in accordance with paragraph (2)(f), to establish one or more information and consultation procedures instead of a representative body, and

(b) those procedures include a provision for representatives to be elected or appointed to act in relation to information and consultation,

those representatives are "information and consultation representatives".

NOTES

Commencement: 1 October 2009.

Para (3A): inserted by the Agency Workers Regulations 2010, SI 2010/93, reg 25, Sch 2, Pt 2, paras 47, 50, as from 1 October 2011.

[2.1196]

16 Decisions of the special negotiating body

(1) Each member of the special negotiating body has one vote.

(2) The special negotiating body must take decisions by an absolute majority vote, except in those cases where paragraph (3) or regulation 17 provides otherwise.

(3) In the following circumstances any decision which would result in a reduction of participation rights must be taken by a two thirds majority vote—

(a) where an SE is to be established by merger and at least 25% of the employees employed to work in the EEA states by the participating companies which are due to merge have participation rights;

(b) where an SE is to be established by formation of a holding company or of a subsidiary company and at least 50% of the total number of employees employed to work in the EEA states by the participating companies have participation rights.

In this paragraph, "reduction of participation rights" means that the body representative of the employees has participation rights in relation to a smaller proportion of members of the supervisory or administrative organs of the SE than the employees' representatives had in the participating company which gave participation rights in relation to the highest proportion of such members in that company.

(4) Where the special negotiating body takes a decision under this regulation or under regulation 17—

- (a) it must publish the details of the decision in such a manner as to bring the decision, so far as reasonably practicable, to the attention of the employees whom it represents, and
- (b) such publication must take place as soon as reasonably practicable and, in any event, no later than 14 days after the decision has been taken.

(5) For the purpose of negotiations, the special negotiating body may be assisted by experts of its choice.

(6) The participating company or companies must pay for—

- (a) any reasonable expenses of the functioning of the special negotiating body, and
- (b) any reasonable expenses relating to the negotiations that are necessary to enable the special negotiating body to carry out its functions in an appropriate manner,

but where the special negotiating body is assisted by more than one expert the participating company is not required to pay such expenses in respect of more than one of them.

NOTES

Commencement: 1 October 2009.

[2.1197]

17 Decision not to open, or to terminate, negotiations

(1) The special negotiating body may decide, by a two thirds majority vote,—

- (a) not to open negotiations with the competent organs of the participating companies, or
- (b) to terminate any such negotiations.

(2) The special negotiating body cannot take the decision referred to in paragraph (1) in relation to an SE to be established by transformation if any employees of the company to be transformed have participation rights.

(3) Any decision made under paragraph (1) has the following effects—

- (a) the duty in regulation 14(2) to negotiate with a view to reaching an employee involvement agreement ceases as from the date of the decision;
- (b) any rules relating to the information and consultation of employees in an EEA state in which employees of the SE are employed apply to the employees of the SE in that EEA state;
- (c) the special negotiating body is to be reconvened only if a request that meets the conditions in paragraph (4) is made by employees or employees' representatives.

(4) The conditions are that the request is made—

- (a) in writing;
- (b) by at least 10% of the employees of—
  - (i) the participating companies and their concerned subsidiaries, or
  - (ii) where the SE has been registered, the SE and its subsidiaries,

  or by employees' representatives representing at least that percentage of those employees;
- (c) no earlier than two years after the decision made under paragraph (1) was or should have been published in accordance with regulation 16(4) unless—
  - (i) the special negotiating body, and
  - (ii) the competent organs of every participating company or, where the SE has been registered, the SE,

  agree to the special negotiating body being reconvened earlier.

NOTES

Commencement: 1 October 2009.

[2.1198]

18 Complaint about decisions of special negotiating body

(1) If a person who is a member of the special negotiating body, or who is an employees' representative or an employee for whom there is no such representative, believes that the special negotiating body has taken a decision referred to in regulation 16 or 17 and—

- (a) that the decision was not taken by the majority required by regulation 16 or 17, as the case may be, or
- (b) that the special negotiating body failed to publish the decision in accordance with regulation 16(4),

the person may present a complaint to the CAC within 21 days after the date on which the special negotiating body published their decision in accordance with regulation 16(4) or, if they have not done so, the date by which they should have so published their decision.

(2) Where the CAC finds the complaint well-founded, it must make a declaration that the decision was not taken properly and that it is of no effect.

NOTES

Commencement: 1 October 2009.

PART 5
STANDARD RULES ON EMPLOYEE INVOLVEMENT

[2.1199]

19 Standard rules on employee involvement

(1) Where this regulation applies, the competent organ of the SE and its subsidiaries and establishments must make arrangements for the involvement of employees of the SE and its subsidiaries and establishments in accordance with the standard rules on employee involvement.

This paragraph is without prejudice to paragraph (3).

(2) This regulation applies in the following circumstances—

(a) where the parties agree that the standard rules on employee involvement are to apply; or

(b) where the period specified in regulation 14(3)(a) or, where applicable, (b) has expired without the parties reaching an employee involvement agreement and—

(i) the competent organs of each of the participating companies agree that the standard rules on employee involvement are to apply and so continue with the registration of the SE, and

(ii) the special negotiating body has not taken any decision under regulation 17(1) either not to open, or to terminate, the negotiations referred to in that regulation.

(3) The standard rules set out in Part 3 of the Schedule to these Regulations (standard rules on participation) apply only in the following circumstances—

(a) in the case of an SE established by merger if, before registration of the SE, one or more forms of participation existed in at least one of the participating companies and either—

(i) that participation applied to at least 25% of the total number of employees of the participating companies employed in the EEA states, or

(ii) that participation applied to less than 25% of the total number of employees of the participating companies employed in the EEA states but the special negotiating body has decided that the standard rules on participation will apply to the employees of the SE; or

(b) in the case of an SE established by formation of a holding company or subsidiary company if, before registration of the SE, one or more forms of employee participation existed in at least one of the participating companies and either—

(i) that participation applied to at least 50% of the total number of employees of the participating companies employed in the EEA states, or

(ii) that participation applied to less than 50% of the total number of employees of the participating companies employed in the EEA states but the special negotiating body has decided that the standard rules on participation will apply to the employees of the SE.

[(3A) This paragraph applies to an agency worker whose contract within regulation 3(1)(b) of the Agency Workers Regulations 2010 (contract with the temporary work agency) is not a contract of employment—

(a) for the purposes of paragraph (3)(a) and (b), any agency worker who has a contract with a temporary work agency, which was at the relevant time a participating company, is to be treated as having been employed by that temporary work agency for the duration of their assignment with a hirer, and

(b) in this paragraph "assignment" and "hirer" have the same meaning as in regulation 2, and "temporary work agency" has the same meaning as in regulation 4, of the Agency Workers Regulations 2010.]

(4) Where—

(a) the standard rules on participation apply, and

(b) more than one form of employee participation exists in the participating companies,

the special negotiating body must decide which of the existing forms of participation is to exist in the SE and must inform the competent organs of the participating companies accordingly.

NOTES

Commencement: 1 October 2009.

Para (3A): inserted by the Agency Workers Regulations 2010, SI 2010/93, reg 25, Sch 2, Pt 2, paras 47, 51, as from 1 October 2011.

PART 6
COMPLIANCE AND ENFORCEMENT

[2.1200]

20 Disputes about the operation of an employee involvement agreement or the standard rules on employee involvement

(1) Where—

(a) an employee involvement agreement has been agreed, or

(b) the standard rules on employee involvement apply,

a complaint may be presented to the CAC by a relevant applicant who considers that the competent organ of a participating company or of the SE has failed to comply with the terms of the employee involvement agreement or, as the case may be, one or more of the standard information and consultation provisions.

(2) A complaint brought under paragraph (1) must be brought within the period of 3 months commencing with—

(a) the date of the alleged failure, or

(b) where the failure takes place over a period, the last day of that period.

(3) In this regulation—

"failure" means an act or omission;

"relevant applicant" means—

(a) in a case where a representative body has been appointed or elected, a member of that body;

(b) in a case where no representative body has been elected or appointed, an information and consultation representative or an employee of the SE.

(4) Where it finds the complaint well-founded, the CAC—

(a) must make a declaration to that effect, and

(b) may make an order requiring the SE to take such steps as are necessary to comply with the terms of the employee involvement agreement or, as the case may be, the standard rules on employee involvement.

(5) An order made under paragraph (4) must specify—

(a) the steps which the SE is required to take;

(b) the date of the failure;

(c) the period within which the order must be complied with.

(6) If the CAC makes a declaration under paragraph (4), the relevant applicant may, within the period of three months beginning with the day on which the decision is made, make an application to the Appeal Tribunal for a penalty notice to be issued.

(7) Where such an application is made, the Appeal Tribunal must issue a written penalty notice to the SE requiring it to pay a penalty to the Secretary of State in respect of the failure, unless the Appeal Tribunal is satisfied, on hearing representations from the SE,—

(a) that the failure resulted from a reason beyond its control, or

(b) that it has some other reasonable excuse for its failure.

(8) Regulation 21 applies in respect of a penalty notice issued under this regulation.

(9) No order of the CAC under this regulation has the effect of suspending or altering the effect of any act done or of any agreement made by the participating company or the SE.

NOTES

Commencement: 1 October 2009.

[2.1201]

21 Penalties

(1) A penalty notice issued under regulation 20 must specify—

(a) the amount of the penalty which is payable;

(b) the date before which the penalty must be paid;

(c) the failure and period to which the penalty relates.

(2) No penalty set by the Appeal Tribunal under this regulation may exceed £75,000.

(3) When setting the amount of the penalty, the Appeal Tribunal must take into account—

(a) the gravity of the failure;

(b) the period of time over which the failure occurred;

(c) the reason for the failure;

(d) the number of employees affected by the failure;

(e) the number of employees employed by the undertaking.

(4) The date specified under paragraph (1)(b) must not be earlier than the end of the period within which an appeal against a decision or order made by the CAC under regulation 20 may be made.

(5) If the specified date in a penalty notice has passed and —

(a) the period during which an appeal may be made has expired without an appeal having been made, or

(b) such an appeal has been made and determined,

the Secretary of State may recover from the SE, as a civil debt due to the Secretary of State, any amount payable under the penalty notice which remains outstanding.

(6) The making of an appeal suspends the effect of the penalty notice.

(7) Any sums received by the Secretary of State under regulation 20 or this regulation must be paid into the Consolidated Fund.

NOTES

Commencement: 1 October 2009.

[2.1202]

22 Misuse of procedures

(1) If an employees' representative, or an employee for whom there is no such representative, believes that a participating company or an SE is misusing or intending to misuse the SE or the powers in these Regulations for the purpose of—

(a) depriving the employees of that participating company or of any of its concerned subsidiaries or, as the case may be, of the SE or of any of its subsidiaries of their rights to employee involvement, or

(b) withholding rights from any of the employees referred to in sub-paragraph (a),

the representative or, as the case may be, the employee may make a complaint to the CAC.

(2) Where a complaint is made to the CAC under paragraph (1)—

(a) before registration of the SE, or

(b) within the period of 12 months following the date of its registration,

the CAC must uphold the complaint unless the respondent proves that it did not misuse or intend to misuse the SE or the powers in these Regulations for a purpose specified in sub-paragraph (a) or (b) of paragraph (1).

(3) If it finds the complaint to be well founded, the CAC—

(a) must make a declaration to that effect, and

(b) may make an order requiring the participating company or the SE, as the case may be, to take such action as is specified in the order to ensure that the employees referred to in paragraph (1)(a) are not deprived of their rights to employee involvement or that such rights are not withheld from them,

and the provisions of regulations 20(6) to (9) and 21 apply where the CAC makes a declaration or order under this paragraph as they apply where it makes a declaration or order under regulation 20(4).

NOTES

Commencement: 1 October 2009.

[2.1203]

23 Exclusivity of remedy

The remedy for infringement of the rights conferred by these Regulations is by way of complaint to the CAC in accordance with these Regulations and not otherwise.

NOTES

Commencement: 1 October 2009.

PART 7
CONFIDENTIAL INFORMATION

[2.1204]

24 Breach of statutory duty

(1) Where a body which is—

(a) an SE,

(b) a subsidiary of an SE,

(c) a participating company, or

(d) a concerned subsidiary,

entrusts a person, pursuant to the provisions of these Regulations, with any information or document on terms requiring it to be held in confidence, the person must not disclose that information or document except in accordance with the terms on which it was disclosed to the person.

(2) In this regulation a person referred to in paragraph (1) to whom information or a document is entrusted is referred to as a "recipient".

(3) Where paragraph (1) applies—

(a) the obligation to comply with that paragraph is a duty owed to the body that disclosed the information or document to the recipient, and

(b) a breach of the duty is actionable accordingly (subject to the defences and other incidents applying to actions for breach of statutory duty).

(4) Paragraph (3) does not affect—

(a) any legal liability which any person may incur otherwise than under this regulation by disclosing the information or document, or

(b) any right which any person may have in relation to such disclosure otherwise than under this regulation.

(5) No action lies under paragraph (3) where the recipient reasonably believed the disclosure to be a "protected disclosure" within the meaning given by section 43A of the Employment Rights Act 1996.

(6) A recipient to whom a body mentioned in paragraph (1) has, pursuant to the provisions of these Regulations, entrusted any information or document on terms requiring it to be held in confidence may apply to the CAC for a declaration as to whether it was reasonable for the body to require the recipient to hold the information or document in confidence.

(7) If the CAC considers that the disclosure of the information or the document by the recipient would not, or would not be likely to, harm the legitimate interests of the undertaking, it must make a declaration that it was not reasonable for the body to require the recipient to hold the information or document in confidence.

(8) If a declaration is made under paragraph (7), the information or document is not at any time after the making of the declaration to be regarded as having been entrusted to the recipient who made the application under paragraph (6), or to any other recipient, on terms requiring it to be held in confidence.

NOTES

Commencement: 1 October 2009.

[2.1205]

25 Withholding of information

(1) Neither an SE nor a participating company is required to disclose any information or document to a person for the purposes of these Regulations where the nature of the information or document is such that, according to objective criteria, the disclosure of the information or document would seriously harm the functioning of, or would be prejudicial to,—

(a) the SE or any subsidiary or establishment of the SE, or

(b) the participating company or any subsidiary or establishment of the participating company.

(2) Where there is a dispute between the SE or a participating company and—

(a) where a representative body has been appointed or elected, a member of that body, or

(b) where a representative body has not been appointed or elected, an information and consultation representative or an employee,

and the dispute is as to whether the nature of the information or document which the SE or the participating company has failed to provide is such as is described in paragraph (1), the SE or participating company, or a person referred to in sub-paragraph (a) or (b), may apply to the CAC for a declaration as to whether the information or document is of such a nature.

(3) If the CAC makes a declaration that the disclosure of the information or document in question would not, according to objective criteria, be seriously harmful or prejudicial as mentioned in paragraph (1), the CAC must order the company to disclose the information or document.

(4) An order under paragraph (3) must specify—

(a) the information or document to be disclosed;

(b) the person or persons to whom the information or document is to be disclosed;

(c) any terms on which the information or document is to be disclosed;

(d) the date before which the information or document is to be disclosed.

NOTES

Commencement: 1 October 2009.

PART 8
PROTECTION FOR MEMBERS OF SPECIAL NEGOTIATING BODY ETC

[2.1206]

26 Right to time off for members of special negotiating body etc

(1) Where an employee is any of the following—

(a) a member of a special negotiating body,

(b) a member of a representative body,

(c) an information and consultation representative,

(d) an employee member on a supervisory or administrative organ,

(e) a candidate in an election in which any person elected will, on being elected, be such a member or a representative,

the employee is entitled to be permitted by the employer to take reasonable time off during working hours in order to perform functions as such a member, representative or candidate.

(2) In this regulation "working hours" means any time when, in accordance with the employee's contract of employment, the employee is required to be at work.

NOTES

Commencement: 1 October 2009.

[2.1207]

27 Right to remuneration for time off under regulation 26

(1) An employee who is permitted to take time off under regulation 26 is entitled to be paid remuneration by the employer for the time taken off at the appropriate hourly rate.

(2) Chapter 2 of Part 14 of the Employment Rights Act 1996 (a week's pay) applies in relation to this regulation as it applies in relation to section 62 of that Act.

(3) The appropriate hourly rate, in relation to an employee, is the amount of one week's pay divided by the number of normal working hours in a week for that employee when employed under the contract of employment in force on the day when the time is taken.

(4) But where the number of normal working hours differs from week to week or over a longer period, the amount of one week's pay is to be divided instead by—

(a) the average number of normal working hours calculated by dividing by twelve the total number of the employee's normal working hours during the period of twelve weeks ending with the last complete week before the day on which the time off is taken, or

(b) where the employee has not been employed for a sufficient period to enable the calculation to be made under sub-paragraph (a), a number which fairly represents the number of normal working hours in a week having regard to such of the considerations specified in paragraph (5) as are appropriate in the circumstances.

(5) The considerations are—

(a) the average number of normal working hours in a week which the employee could expect in accordance with the terms of the contract;

(b) the average number of normal working hours of other employees engaged in relevant comparable employment with the same employer.

(6) A right to any amount under paragraph (1) does not affect any right of an employee in relation to remuneration under the employee's contract of employment.

(7) But—

(a) any contractual remuneration paid to an employee in respect of a period of time off under regulation 26 goes towards discharging any liability of the employer to pay remuneration under paragraph (1) in respect of that period, and

(b) conversely, any payment of remuneration under paragraph (1) in respect of a period goes towards discharging any liability of the employer to pay contractual remuneration in respect of that period.

NOTES

Commencement: 1 October 2009.

[2.1208]

28 Right to time off: complaints to tribunals

(1) An employee may present a complaint to an employment tribunal that the employer—

(a) has unreasonably refused to permit the employee to take time off as required under regulation 26, or

(b) has failed to pay the whole or any part of any amount to which the employee is entitled under regulation 27.

(2) A tribunal must not consider a complaint under this regulation unless it is presented—

(a) before the end of the period of three months beginning with the day on which the time off was taken or on which it is alleged the time off should have been permitted, or

(b) within such further period as the tribunal considers reasonable in a case where it is satisfied that it was not reasonably practicable for the complaint to be presented before the end of that period of three months.

(3) Where a tribunal finds a complaint under this regulation well-founded, the tribunal must make a declaration to that effect.

(4) If the complaint is that the employer has unreasonably refused to permit the employee to take time off, the tribunal must also order the employer to pay to the employee an amount equal to the remuneration to which the employee would have been entitled under regulation 27 if the employer had not refused.

(5) If the complaint is that the employer has failed to pay the employee the whole or part of any amount to which the employee is entitled under regulation 27, the tribunal must also order the employer to pay to the employee the amount which it finds is due to the employee.

NOTES

Commencement: 1 October 2009.

Conciliation: employment tribunal proceedings and claims which could be the subject of employment tribunal proceedings under this regulation are proceedings to which the Employment Tribunals Act 1996, s 18 applies; see s 18(1)(g) of that Act at **[1.706]**.

[2.1209]

29 Unfair dismissal

(1) An employee who is dismissed is to be regarded as unfairly dismissed for the purposes of Part 10 of the Employment Rights Act 1996 if—

(a) paragraph (2) applies to the employee and the reason (or, if more than one, the principal reason) for the dismissal is a reason specified in paragraph (3), or

(b) paragraph (5) applies to the employee and the reason (or, if more than one, the principal reason) for the dismissal is a reason specified in paragraph (6).

(2) This paragraph applies to an employee who is any of the following—

(a) a member of a special negotiating body;

(b) a member of a representative body;

(c) an information and consultation representative;

(d) an employee member in a supervisory or administrative organ;

(e) a candidate in an election in which any person elected will, on being elected, be such a member or a representative.

(3) The reasons are—

(a) that the employee performed, or proposed to perform, any functions or activities as such a member, representative or candidate (but see paragraph (4));

(b) that the employee, or a person acting on behalf of the employee, made or proposed to make a request to exercise an entitlement conferred on the employee by regulation 26 or 27.

(4) Paragraph (3)(a) does not apply if—

(a) the reason (or principal reason) for the dismissal is that, in the performance or purported performance of the employee's functions or activities, the employee has disclosed any information or document in breach of the duty in regulation 24, and

(b) the case is not one where the employee reasonably believed the disclosure to be a "protected disclosure" within the meaning given by section 43A of the Employment Rights Act 1996.

(5) This paragraph applies to any employee (whether or not paragraph (2) also applies).

(6) The reasons are that the employee did any of the following—

(a) took, or proposed to take, any proceedings before an employment tribunal to enforce any right conferred on the employee by these Regulations;

(b) exercised, or proposed to exercise, any entitlement to apply or complain to the CAC or the Appeal Tribunal conferred by these Regulations or exercised, or proposed to exercise, the right to appeal in connection with any rights conferred by these Regulations;

(c) acted with a view to securing that a special negotiating body, a representative body or an information and consultation procedure did or did not come into existence;

(d) indicated that the employee did or did not support the coming into existence of a special negotiating body, a representative body or an information and consultation procedure;

(e) stood as a candidate in an election in which any person elected would, on being elected, be a member of a special negotiating body or a representative body, an employee member on a supervisory or administrative organ, or an information and consultation representative;

(f) influenced, or sought to influence, by lawful means the way in which votes were to be cast by other employees in a ballot arranged under these Regulations;

(g) voted in such a ballot;

(h) expressed doubts, whether to a ballot supervisor or otherwise, as to whether such a ballot had been properly conducted;

(i) proposed to do, failed to do, or proposed to decline to do, any of the things mentioned in sub-paragraphs (d) to (h).

(7) It is immaterial for the purposes of sub-paragraph (a) of paragraph (6)—

(a) whether or not the employee has the right, or

(b) whether or not the right has been infringed,

but for that sub-paragraph to apply, the claim to the right and, if applicable, the claim that it has been infringed must be made in good faith.

NOTES

Commencement: 1 October 2009.

30 (*Amends the Employment Rights Act 1996, ss 105, 108 at* **[1.915]**, **[1.918]**.)

[2.1210]
31 Detriment

(1) An employee to whom paragraph (2) or (5) applies has the right not to be subjected to any detriment by any act, or deliberate failure to act, by the employer, done on a ground specified in, respectively, paragraph (3) or (6).

(2) This paragraph applies to an employee who is any of the following—
- (a) a member of a special negotiating body;
- (b) a member of a representative body;
- (c) an information and consultation representative;
- (d) an employee member on a supervisory or administrative organ;
- (e) a candidate in an election in which any person elected will, on being elected, be such a member or representative.

(3) The grounds are—
- (a) that the employee performed or proposed to perform any functions or activities as such a member, representative or candidate (but see paragraph (4));
- (b) that the employee, or a person acting on behalf of the employee, made or proposed to make a request to exercise an entitlement conferred on the employee by regulation 26 or 27.

(4) Paragraph (3)(a) does not apply if—
- (a) the ground for the subjection to detriment is that in the performance, or purported performance, of the employee's functions or activities the employee has disclosed any information or document in breach of the duty in regulation 24, and
- (b) the case is not one where the employee reasonably believed the disclosure to be a "protected disclosure" within the meaning given by section 43A of the Employment Rights Act 1996.

(5) This paragraph applies to any employee (whether or not paragraph (2) also applies).

(6) The grounds are that the employee did any of the following—
- (a) took, or proposed to take, any proceedings before an employment tribunal to enforce any right conferred on the employee by these Regulations;
- (b) exercised, or proposed to exercise, any entitlement to apply or complain to the CAC or the Appeal Tribunal conferred by these Regulations or exercised, or proposed to exercise, the right to appeal in connection with any rights conferred by these Regulations;
- (c) acted with a view to securing that a special negotiating body, a representative body or an information and consultation procedure did or did not come into existence;
- (d) indicated that the employee did or did not support the coming into existence of a special negotiating body, a representative body or an information and consultation procedure;
- (e) stood as a candidate in an election in which any person elected would, on being elected, be a member of a special negotiating body or a representative body, an employee member on a supervisory or administrative organ, or an information and consultation representative;
- (f) influenced, or sought to influence, by lawful means the way in which votes were to be cast by other employees in a ballot arranged under these Regulations;
- (g) voted in such a ballot;
- (h) expressed doubts, whether to a ballot supervisor or otherwise, as to whether such a ballot had been properly conducted;
- (i) proposed to do, failed to do, or proposed to decline to do, any of the things mentioned in sub-paragraphs (d) to (h).

(7) It is immaterial for the purposes of sub-paragraph (a) of paragraph (6)—
- (a) whether or not the employee has the right, or
- (b) whether or not the right has been infringed,

but for that sub-paragraph to apply, the claim to the right and, if applicable, the claim that it has been infringed must be made in good faith.

(8) This regulation does not apply where the detriment in question amounts to dismissal.

NOTES

Commencement: 1 October 2009.

[2.1211]
32 Detriment: enforcement and subsidiary provisions

(1) An employee may present a complaint to an employment tribunal that the employee has been subjected to a detriment in contravention of regulation 31.

(2) The provisions of section 48(2) to (4) of the Employment Rights Act 1996 (complaints to employment tribunals) apply in relation to a complaint under this regulation as they apply in relation to a complaint under section 48 of that Act but taking references in those provisions to the employer as references to the employer within the meaning of regulation 31(1).

(3) The provisions of section 49(1) to (5) of the Employment Rights Act 1996 (remedies) apply in relation to a complaint under this regulation.

NOTES

Commencement: 1 October 2009.

Conciliation: employment tribunal proceedings and claims which could be the subject of employment tribunal proceedings under this regulation are proceedings to which the Employment Tribunals Act 1996, s 18 applies; see s 18(1)(g) of that Act at **[1.706]**.

33 (*Amends the Employment Tribunals Act 1996, s 18 at* **[1.706]**.)

PART 9
MISCELLANEOUS

[2.1212]

34 CAC proceedings

(1) Where under these Regulations a person presents a complaint or makes an application to the CAC, the complaint or application must be in writing and in such form as the CAC may require.

(2) In its consideration of a complaint or application under these Regulations, the CAC must—

- (a) make such enquiries as it sees fit, and
- (b) give any person whom it considers has a proper interest in the complaint or application an opportunity to be heard.

(3) Where the participating company, concerned subsidiary or establishment or the SE has its registered office in England and Wales—

- (a) a declaration made by the CAC under these Regulations may be relied on as if it were a declaration or order made by the High Court in England and Wales, and
- (b) an order made by the CAC under these Regulations may be enforced in the same way as an order of the High Court in England and Wales.

(4) Where a participating company or concerned subsidiary or an SE has its registered office in Scotland—

- (a) a declaration or order made by the CAC under these Regulations may be relied on as if it were a declaration or order made by the Court of Session, and
- (b) an order made by the CAC under these Regulations may be enforced in the same way as an order of the Court of Session.

(5) A declaration or order made by the CAC under these Regulations must be in writing and state the reasons for the CAC's findings.

(6) An appeal lies to the Appeal Tribunal on any question of law arising from any declaration or order of, or arising in any proceedings before, the CAC under these Regulations.

NOTES

Commencement: 1 October 2009.

[2.1213]

35 Appeal Tribunal: location of certain proceedings under these Regulations

(1) Any proceedings before the Appeal Tribunal under these Regulations, other than appeals under paragraph (w) of section 21(1) of the Employment Tribunals Act 1996 (appeals from employment tribunals on questions of law), must—

- (a) where the registered office of the participating company, concerned subsidiary or the SE is situated in England and Wales, be held in England and Wales, and
- (b) where the registered office of the participating company, concerned subsidiary or the SE is situated in Scotland, be held in Scotland.

(2) (*Amends the Employment Tribunals Act 1996, s 20 at* **[1.712]**.)

NOTES

Commencement: 1 October 2009.

36 (*Amends the Employment Tribunals Act 1996, s 21 at* **[1.713]**.)

[2.1214]

37 ACAS

(1) If, on receipt of an application or complaint under these Regulations, the CAC is of the opinion that it is reasonably likely to be settled by conciliation, it must—

- (a) refer the application or complaint to the Advisory, Conciliation and Arbitration Service ("ACAS"), and
- (b) notify the applicant or complainant and any persons whom it considers have a proper interest in the application or complaint accordingly,

and ACAS must seek to promote a settlement of the matter.

(2) If—

(a) an application or complaint so referred is not settled or withdrawn, and

(b) ACAS is of the opinion that further attempts at conciliation are unlikely to result in a settlement,

ACAS must inform the CAC of that opinion.

(3) If—

(a) the application or complaint is not referred to ACAS, or

(b) it is so referred, but ACAS informs the CAC of its opinion that further attempts at conciliation are unlikely to result in a settlement,

the CAC must proceed to hear and determine the application or complaint.

NOTES

Commencement: 1 October 2009.

[2.1215]

38 Restrictions on contracting out: general

(1) Any provision in any agreement (whether an employee's contract or not) is void in so far as it purports—

(a) to exclude or limit the operation of any provision of these Regulations, other than a provision of Part 8, or

(b) to preclude a person from bringing any proceedings before the CAC under any provision of these Regulations other than a provision of that Part.

(2) Paragraph (1) does not apply to any agreement to refrain from continuing any proceedings referred to in sub-paragraph (b) of that paragraph made after the proceedings have been instituted.

NOTES

Commencement: 1 October 2009.

[2.1216]

39 Restrictions on contracting out: Part 8

(1) Any provision in any agreement (whether an employee's contract or not) is void in so far as it purports—

(a) to exclude or limit the operation of any provision of Part 8 of these Regulations, or

(b) to preclude a person from bringing any proceedings before an employment tribunal under that Part.

(2) Paragraph (1) does not apply to any agreement to refrain from instituting or continuing proceedings before an employment tribunal where a conciliation officer has taken action under section 18 of the Employment Tribunals Act 1996 (conciliation).

(3) Paragraph (1) does not apply to any agreement to refrain from instituting or continuing before an employment tribunal proceedings within section 18(1)(v) of the Employment Tribunals Act 1996 (proceedings under these Regulations where conciliation is available) if the conditions regulating compromise agreements under these Regulations are satisfied in relation to the agreement.

(4) For the purposes of paragraph (3) the conditions regulating compromise agreements are as follows—

(a) the agreement must be in writing;

(b) the agreement must relate to the particular proceedings;

(c) the employee must have received advice from a relevant independent adviser as to the terms and effect of the proposed agreement and, in particular, its effect on the ability of the employee to pursue the employee's rights before an employment tribunal;

(d) there must be in force, when the adviser gives the advice, a contract of insurance, or an indemnity provided for members of a profession or professional body, covering the risk of a claim by the employee in respect of loss arising in consequence of the advice;

(e) the agreement must identify the adviser;

(f) the agreement must state that the conditions in sub-paragraphs (a) to (e) are satisfied.

(5) For the purposes of paragraph (4)(c) a "relevant independent adviser" is a person who is any of the following—

(a) a qualified lawyer;

(b) an officer, official, employee or member of an independent trade union who has been certified in writing by the trade union as competent to give advice and authorised to do so on behalf of the trade union;

(c) a person who works at an advice centre (whether as an employee or as a volunteer) and has been certified in writing by the centre as competent to give advice and authorised to do so on behalf of the centre;

but this is subject to paragraph (6).

(6) A person is not a relevant independent adviser for the purposes of paragraph (4)(c) in relation to the employee in any of the following cases—

(a) if the person is, is employed by, or is acting in the matter for, the employer or an associated employer;

(b) in the case of a person within paragraph (5)(b) or (c), if the trade union or advice centre is the employer or an associated employer;

(c) in the case of a person within paragraph (5)(c), if the employee makes a payment for the advice received.

(7) In paragraph (5)(a) "qualified lawyer" means any of the following—

(a) as respects England and Wales—

(i) a barrister (whether in practice as such or employed to give legal advice);

(ii) a solicitor who holds a practising certificate;

(iii) a person, other than a barrister or solicitor, who is an authorised advocate or authorised litigator (within the meaning of the Courts and Legal Services Act 1990);

(b) as respects Scotland—

(i) an advocate (whether in practice as such or employed to give legal advice); or

(ii) a solicitor who holds a practising certificate.

(8) For the purposes of paragraph (6) any two employers are "associated" if—

(a) one is a company of which the other (directly or indirectly) has control, or

(b) both are companies of which a third person (directly or indirectly) has control,

and "associated employer" is to be construed accordingly.

NOTES

Commencement: 1 October 2009.

40 (*Substitutes the Transnational Information and Consultation of Employees Regulations 1999, SI 1999/3323, reg 46A at* **[2.558]**.)

[2.1217]

41 Existing employee involvement rights

(1) Nothing in these Regulations affects involvement rights of employees of an SE, its subsidiaries or establishments provided for by law or practice in the EEA state in which they were employed immediately prior to the registration of the SE.

(2) Paragraph (1) does not apply to rights to participation.

NOTES

Commencement: 1 October 2009.

SCHEDULE
STANDARD RULES ON EMPLOYEE INVOLVEMENT

Regulation 19(3)

PART 1
COMPOSITION OF THE REPRESENTATIVE BODY

[2.1218]

1. (1) The management of the SE must arrange for the establishment of a representative body in accordance with the following provisions.

(2) The representative body must be composed of employees of the SE and its subsidiaries and establishments.

(3) The representative body must be composed of one member for each 10%, or fraction of 10%, of employees of the SE, its subsidiaries and establishments employed for the time being in each EEA state.

(4) The members of the representative body must be elected or appointed by the members of the special negotiating body.

(5) The election or appointment is to be carried out by whatever method the special negotiating body decides.

2. Where its size so warrants, the representative body must elect a select committee from among its members comprising at most 3 members.

3. The representative body must adopt rules of procedure.

4. The representative body must inform the competent organ of the SE of the composition of the representative body and any changes in its composition.

5. (1) Four years after its establishment, the representative body must decide—

(a) whether to open negotiations with the competent organ of the SE to reach an employee involvement agreement, or

(b) whether the standard rules in Part 2 of this Schedule and, where applicable, Part 3 of this Schedule are to continue to apply.

(2) Where a decision is taken under sub-paragraph (1) to open negotiations, regulations 14 to 16 and 18 apply to the representative body as they apply to the special negotiating body.

NOTES

Commencement: 1 October 2009.

PART 2
STANDARD RULES FOR INFORMATION AND CONSULTATION

[2.1219]

6. (1) The competence of the representative body is limited to—

(a) questions which concern the SE itself and any of its subsidiaries or establishments in another EEA state, and

(b) questions which exceed the powers of the decision-making organ in a single EEA state.

(2) For the purpose of informing and consulting under sub-paragraph (1), the competent organ of the SE must—

(a) prepare and provide to the representative body regular reports on the progress of the business of the SE and the SE's prospects;

(b) provide the representative body with the agenda for meetings of the administrative or, where appropriate, the management or supervisory organs and copies of all documents submitted to the general meeting of its shareholders;

(c) inform the representative body when there are exceptional circumstances affecting the employees' interests to a considerable extent, particularly in the event of relocations, transfers, the closure of establishments or undertakings or collective redundancies.

7. (1) The competent organ must, if the representative body so desires, meet with that body at least once a year to discuss the reports referred to in paragraph 6(2)(a).

This sub-paragraph is without prejudice to paragraph 8.

(2) The meetings must relate in particular to the structure, economic and financial situation, the probable development of business and of production and sales, the situation and probable trend of employment, investments and substantial changes concerning organisation, introduction of new working methods or production processes, transfers of production, mergers, cut-backs or closures of undertakings or establishments, or important parts of undertakings or establishments, and collective redundancies.

8. (1) In the circumstances set out in paragraph 6(2)(c), the representative body may decide, for reasons of urgency, to allow the select committee to meet the competent organ and it has the right to meet a more appropriate level of management within the SE rather than the competent organ itself.

(2) In the event of the competent organ not acting in accordance with the opinion expressed by the representative body, the two bodies must meet again to seek an agreement, if the representative body so wishes.

(3) In the circumstances set out in sub-paragraph (1), if the select committee attends the meeting, any other members of the representative body who represent employees who are directly concerned by the measures being discussed also have the right to participate in the meeting.

(4) Before any meeting referred to in this paragraph, the members of the representative body or the select committee, as the case may be, are entitled to meet without the representatives of the competent organ being present.

[8A. Where under the provisions of this Part, the competent organ of the SE is to provide information on the employment situation in that company, such information must include suitable information relating to the use of agency workers (if any) in that company.]

9. Without prejudice to regulations 24 and 25, the members of the representative body must inform the employees' representatives or, if no such representatives exist, the employees of the SE and its subsidiaries and establishments, of the content and outcome of the information and consultation procedures.

10. The representative body and the select committee may each be assisted by experts of its choice.

11. (1) The costs of the representative body must be borne by the SE which must also provide the members of that body with financial and material resources needed to enable them to perform their duties in an appropriate manner, including (unless agreed otherwise) the cost of organising meetings, providing interpretation facilities and accommodation and travelling expenses.

(2) However, where the representative body or the select committee is assisted by more than one expert, the SE is not required to pay the expenses of more than one of them.

NOTES

Commencement: 1 October 2009.

Para 8A: inserted by the Agency Workers Regulations 2010, SI 2010/93, reg 25, Sch 2, Pt 2, paras 47, 52, as from 1 October 2011.

PART 3
STANDARD RULES FOR PARTICIPATION

[2.1220]

12. (1) In the case of an SE established by transformation, if the rules of a Member State relating to employee participation in the administrative or supervisory body applied before registration, all aspects of employee participation continue to apply to the SE.

(2) Paragraph 13 applies to that end with the necessary modifications.

13. (1) In the case where—

(a) an SE is established otherwise than by transformation, and

(b) the employees or their representatives of at least one of the participating companies had participation rights,

the representative body has the right to elect, appoint, recommend or oppose the appointment of a number of members of the administrative or supervisory body of the SE.

(2) Their number must be equal to the highest proportion in force in the participating companies concerned before the registration of the SE.

14. (1) The representative body must decide on the allocation of seats within the administrative or supervisory body.

(2) In doing so, the representative body must take into account the proportion of employees of the SE employed in each EEA state.

(3) If the employees of one or more EEA states are not covered by that proportional criterion, the representative body, in making its decision under sub-paragraph (1), must appoint a member from one of those EEA states including one from the EEA state in which the SE is registered, if appropriate.

(4) Every member of the administrative body or, where appropriate, the supervisory body of the SE who has been elected, appointed or recommended by the representative body or the employees is to be a full member with the same rights and obligations as the members representing shareholders, including the right to vote.

NOTES

Commencement: 1 October 2009.

SCHOOL STAFFING (ENGLAND) REGULATIONS 2009

(SI 2009/2680)

NOTES

Made: 2 October 2009.

Authority: School Standards and Framework Act 1998, ss 72, 138(7); Education Act 2002, ss 19(3), 26, 34(5), 35(4), (5), 36(4), (5), 210(7).

Commencement: 2 November 2009.

These Regulations apply only to England.

In relation to the application of these Regulations, with modifications, to the staffing of federations, see the School Governance (Federations) (England) Regulations 2012, SI 2012/1035, reg 25, Sch 7.

ARRANGEMENT OF REGULATIONS

PART 1
GENERAL

Part 2 Statutory Instruments

PART 1
GENERAL

[2.1221]

1 Citation, commencement and application

(1) These Regulations may be cited as the School Staffing (England) Regulations 2009 and they come into force on 2nd November 2009.

(2) These Regulations apply only in relation to England.

NOTES

Commencement: 2 November 2009.

[2.1222]

2 Revocations and amendments

The Regulations specified in Schedule 1 are revoked to the extent specified in the third column of that Schedule.

NOTES

Commencement: 2 November 2009.

[2.1223]

3 Interpretation

(1) In these Regulations—

"PA 1997" means the Police Act 1997;

"EA 2002" means the Education Act 2002;

"authority" means the [local authority] by which a maintained school is, or a proposed school is to be, maintained;

"dismissal" is to be interpreted in accordance with sections 95 and 136 of the Employment Rights Act 1996;

"employment business" has the meaning given by section 13(3) of the Employment Agencies Act 1973;

"enhanced criminal record certificate" means an enhanced criminal record certificate within the meaning of section 113B of PA 1997 which includes suitability information relating to children within the meaning of section 113BA(2) of that Act;

"safer recruitment training" means training provided by a person approved by the Secretary of State for the purpose of ensuring that those who undertake it know how to take proper account of the need to safeguard children when recruiting staff;

"support staff" means any member of a school's staff other than a teacher;

"teacher" means—

(a) a person who is a school teacher for the purposes of section 122 of EA 2002 Act; and

(b) a person who would fall within paragraph (a) but for the fact that the other party to the contract is not an authority or a governing body of a school falling within Part 3 of these Regulations.

(2) References to a vacancy in any post include a prospective vacancy in the post.

(3) A person is to be treated as meeting any staff qualification requirements if the person—

(a) fulfils any requirements with respect to qualifications or registration which apply to the person as a result of regulations made under sections 132 to 135 of EA 2002 and regulations made under section 19 of the Teaching and Higher Education Act 1998;

(b) meets any conditions with respect to health and physical capacity which apply to the person as a result of regulations made under section 141 of the 2002 Act; and

(c) is not barred from regulated activity relating to children in accordance with section 3(2) of the Safeguarding Vulnerable Groups Act 2006 or subject to any direction made under section 142 of EA 2002 or any prohibition, restriction or order having effect as such a direction.

(4) References to support staff include support staff employed, or engaged otherwise than under a contract of employment, to provide community facilities and services under section 27 of EA 2002.

(5) For the purposes of these Regulations a person applies for an enhanced criminal record certificate if—

(a) the person countersigns an application for the certificate as a registered person, within the meaning of section 120 of PA 1997, or an application is countersigned on the person's behalf; and

(b) the application is submitted to the Secretary of State in accordance with Part 5 of that Act.

NOTES

Commencement: 2 November 2009.

Para (1): words in square brackets in definition "authority" substituted by the Local Education Authorities and Children's Services Authorities (Integration of Functions) (Local and Subordinate Legislation) Order 2010, SI 2010/1172, art 4(3)(a), as from 5 May 2010.

[2.1224]

4 Delegation of authority

(1) The governing body may delegate—

(a) any of the functions conferred upon it by these Regulations other than those conferred by [regulations 5 to 8 and 9], 15(3) and (5) and 27(3) and (5); and
(b) its power to appoint or dismiss any member of staff at a school to which Part 3 applies.

(2) Subject to paragraph (4), any delegation under paragraph (1) may be to—
(a) the head teacher,
(b) one or more governors; or
(c) one or more governors acting together with the head teacher.

(3) Where the governing body has made any delegation under paragraph (1) to one or more governors and the function being delegated does not directly concern the head teacher—
(a) the head teacher may attend and offer advice at all relevant proceedings; and
(b) the governor or governors to whom the delegation has been made must consider any such advice.

(4) Any delegation under paragraph (1) of—
(a) the determination that the head teacher should cease to work at the school; or
(b) the power to appoint or dismiss the head teacher,
may be to one or more governors, other than a governor who is the head teacher.

NOTES
Commencement: 2 November 2009.
Para (1): words in square brackets in sub-para (a) substituted by the School Staffing (England) (Amendment) Regulations 2012, SI 2012/1740, reg 2(1), (2), as from 1 September 2012.

[2.1225]
5 Head teacher duties and entitlements

(1) The governing body must ensure that the head teacher at the school—
(a) complies with the duties imposed upon the head teacher; and
(b) benefits from any entitlement conferred upon the head teacher,
by any order under section 122 of the EA 2002 (teachers' pay and conditions).

(2) In discharging its duty under paragraph (1)(a), the governing body must have regard to the desirability of the head teacher being able to achieve a satisfactory balance between the time spent discharging the professional duties of a head teacher and the time spent by the head teacher pursuing personal interests outside work.

NOTES
Commencement: 2 November 2009.

[2.1226]
6 Performance of head teacher

(1) Where the authority has any serious concerns about the performance of the head teacher of a school it must—
(a) make a written report of its concerns to the governing body of the school; and
(b) at the same time, send a copy of the report to the head teacher.

(2) The governing body must notify the authority in writing of the action it proposes to take in the light of the authority's report.

NOTES
Commencement: 2 November 2009.

[2.1227]
7 Conduct and discipline of staff

(1) The governing body must establish procedures—
(a) for the regulation of the conduct and discipline of staff at the school; and
(b) by which staff may seek redress for any grievance relating to their work at the school.

(2) Where the implementation of any determination made by the governing body in operation of the procedures requires any action which—
(a) is not within the functions exercisable by the governing body by or under EA 2002; but
(b) is within the power of the authority,
the authority must take that action at the request of the governing body.

NOTES
Commencement: 2 November 2009.

[2.1228]
8 Capability of staff

The governing body must establish procedures for dealing with lack of capability on the part of staff at the school.

NOTES

Commencement: 2 November 2009.

[2.1229]

[8A Provision of information about staff capability

(1) This regulation applies where a member of the teaching staff at a school (School A) applies for a teaching post at another school (School B), where School B is a maintained school or an Academy school.

(2) The governing body of School A must, at the request of the governing body or proprietor (as the case may be) of School B—

(a) advise in writing whether or not that member of staff has, in the preceding two years, been the subject of the procedures established by the governing body in accordance with regulation 8 and, if so,

(b) provide written details of the concerns which gave rise to this, the duration of the proceedings and their outcome.]

NOTES

Commencement: 1 September 2012.

Inserted by the School Staffing (England) (Amendment) Regulations 2012, SI 2012/1740, reg 2(1), (3), as from 1 September 2012.

[2.1230]

9 Safer recruitment training

With effect from 1st January 2010, the governing body must ensure that—

(a) any person who interviews an applicant for any post under these Regulations has completed the safer recruitment training; or

(b) in the case where—

(i) a selection panel is appointed for that purpose under regulation 15 or 26; or

(ii) the governing body delegates the appointment of a member of staff to two or more governors or one or more governors and the head teacher under regulation 4(1),

at least one member of that panel or group has completed the safer recruitment training.

NOTES

Commencement: 2 November 2009.

10 *(Amends the School Governance (Procedures) (England) Regulations 2003, SI 2003/1377 (outside the scope of this work).)*

PART 2
PROVISIONS RELATING TO COMMUNITY, VOLUNTARY CONTROLLED, COMMUNITY SPECIAL AND MAINTAINED NURSERY SCHOOLS

[2.1231]

11 Application of Part 2

This Part applies to community, voluntary controlled, community special and maintained nursery schools.

NOTES

Commencement: 2 November 2009.

[2.1232]

12 Manner of appointment

(1) Where a governing body approves, identifies, selects or recommends a person for appointment under regulation 15(5), 15(7), 16(3) or 17(1), it must determine whether that person is to be appointed—

(a) under a contract of employment with the authority;

(b) by the authority otherwise than under a contract of employment; or

(c) by the governing body otherwise than under a contract of employment.

(2) The governing body must check—

(a) the identity of any such person;

(b) that the person meets all relevant staff qualification requirements; and

(c) that the person has a right to work in the United Kingdom.

(3) The governing body must obtain an enhanced criminal record certificate in respect of any such person before, or as soon as practicable after, the person's appointment.

(4) In the case of any such person for whom, by reason of having lived outside the United Kingdom, obtaining such a certificate is not sufficient to establish that person's suitability to work in a school, the governing body must make such further checks as the authority consider appropriate, having regard to any guidance issued by the Secretary of State.

(5) The governing body must complete the checks referred to in paragraphs (2) and (4) before a person is appointed.

(6) Paragraphs (3) and (4) do not apply to a person who has worked in—

- (a) a school in England in a post—
  - (i) which brought the person regularly into contact with children or young persons; or
  - (ii) to which the person was appointed on or after 12th May 2006 and which did not bring the person regularly into contact with children or young persons; or
- (b) an institution within the further education sector in England[, or in a 16 to 19 Academy,] in a post which involved the provision of education which brought the person regularly into contact with children or young persons,

during a period which ended not more than three months before the person's appointment.

(7) The governing body must keep a register containing the information specified in Schedule 2.

NOTES

Commencement: 2 November 2009.

Para (6): words in square brackets in sub-para (b) inserted by the Alternative Provision Academies and 16 to 19 Academies (Consequential Amendments to Subordinate Legislation) (England) Order 2012, SI 2012/979, art 2, Schedule, para 26, as from 1 May 2012.

[2.1233]

13 Application of regulation 12 to other appointments

Regulation 12(2) to (6) and (7) (insofar as it relates to paragraphs 2 to 4, 7 and 8 of Schedule 2) also applies in relation to—

- (a) any person appointed by an authority for the purpose of working at a school to which this Part applies in the temporary absence of a member of staff of the school; and
- (b) any person appointed by an authority to work at a school as a member of the school meals staff.

NOTES

Commencement: 2 November 2009.

[2.1234]

14 Authority's entitlement to offer advice

(1) A representative of the authority may attend and offer advice at all proceedings relating to the selection or dismissal of any teacher.

(2) The governing body must consider any advice offered by the authority pursuant to paragraph (1).

NOTES

Commencement: 2 November 2009.

[2.1235]

15 Appointment of head teacher and deputy head teacher

(1) The governing body must notify the authority in writing of—

- (a) any vacancy for the head teacher; and
- (b) any post for a deputy head teacher which it has identified as one to be filled.

(2) The governing body must advertise any such vacancy or post in such manner as it considers appropriate unless it has good reason not to.

(3) Where the governing body advertises any such vacancy or post, it must appoint a selection panel, consisting of at least three of its members, other than a governor who is the head teacher or (as the case may be) a deputy head teacher, to—

- (a) select for interview such applicants for the post as it thinks fit and, where the post is that of head teacher, notify the authority in writing of the names of the applicants selected;
- (b) interview those applicants who attend for that purpose; and
- (c) where it considers it appropriate, recommend to the governing body for appointment one of the applicants interviewed.

(4) If, within a period of seven days beginning with the date when it receives notification under paragraph (3)(a), the authority makes written representations to the selection panel that any applicant is not a suitable person for the post, the selection panel must—

- (a) consider those representations; and
- (b) where it decides to recommend for appointment any person about whom representations have been made, notify the governing body and authority in writing of its reasons.

(5) Subject to regulation 12(2) and, where appropriate, regulation 12(4), where the person recommended by the selection panel is approved by the governing body for appointment, the authority must appoint that person, unless the governing body has determined that the person is to be appointed by the governing body otherwise than under a contract of employment pursuant to regulation 12(1)(c).

(6) If—

(a) the selection panel does not recommend a person to the governing body;

(b) the governing body declines to approve the person recommended by the selection panel; or

(c) the authority declines to appoint the person that the governing body approves,

the selection panel may recommend another person for appointment in accordance with this regulation (but this does not prevent it from recommending an existing applicant).

(7) Subject to regulation 12(2) and, where appropriate, regulation 12(4), where the governing body decides for good reason not to advertise and conduct a selection process to fill the vacancy or post in accordance with paragraphs (2) to (4), the authority must appoint the person identified by the governing body to fill the vacancy or post, unless the governing body has determined that the person is to be appointed by the governing body otherwise than under a contract of employment pursuant to regulation 12(1)(c).

NOTES

Commencement: 2 November 2009.

[2.1236]

16 Appointment of other teachers

(1) This regulation applies to any post of teacher, other than a post of head teacher or deputy head teacher.

(2) Where the governing body identifies any such post to be filled for a period of more than four months, it must provide the authority with a specification for the post.

(3) Subject to regulation 12(2) and, where appropriate, regulation 12(4), where a person is selected by the governing body for appointment, the authority must appoint that person, unless the governing body has determined that the person is to be appointed by the governing body otherwise than under a contract of employment pursuant to regulation 12(1)(c).

(4) If the authority declines to appoint a person that the governing body selects, the governing body may select another person for appointment in accordance with this regulation (but this does not prevent it from selecting an existing applicant).

NOTES

Commencement: 2 November 2009.

[2.1237]

17 Appointment of support staff

(1) Subject to regulation 21, where the governing body identifies a support staff post to be filled, it may recommend a person to the authority for appointment.

(2) Where the governing body recommends a person to the authority for appointment under paragraph (1) it must provide the authority with—

(a) the name of any person it recommends pursuant to paragraph (1); and

(b) a job specification for the post, which must include the governing body's recommendations as to—

(i) the duties to be performed,

(ii) the hours of work (where the post is part-time),

(iii) the duration of the appointment,

(iv) the grade; and

(v) the remuneration.

(3) The grade must be on the scale of grades applicable in relation to employment with the authority and such as the governing body considers appropriate.

(4) Where the authority has discretion with respect to remuneration, it must exercise that discretion in accordance with the governing body's recommendation.

(5) The authority may be regarded as having discretion with respect to remuneration if any provisions regulating the rates of remuneration or allowances payable to persons in the authority's employment—

(a) do not apply in relation to that appointment; or

(b) leave to the authority any degree of discretion as to the rate of remuneration.

(6) If, within a period of seven days after receiving the job specification, the authority makes written representations to the governing body relating to the grade or remuneration to be paid, the governing body must—

(a) consider those representations; and

(b) where it decides not to change the grade or remuneration to be paid, notify the authority in writing of its reasons.

(7) Subject to regulation 12(2) and, where appropriate, regulation 12(4), the authority must appoint the person recommended by the governing body to the post, unless the governing body has determined that the person is to be appointed by the governing body otherwise than under a contract of employment pursuant to regulation 12(1)(c).

NOTES

Commencement: 2 November 2009.

[2.1238]

18 Supply staff

(1) The governing body must ensure that no person supplied by an employment business to a school is allowed to begin work as a teacher or member of support staff at the school unless the authority or (as the case may be) the governing body has received—

(a) written notification from the employment business in relation to that person—

(i) that it has made the checks referred to in paragraph 5(a)(i) of Schedule 2;

(ii) that it or another employment business has applied for an enhanced criminal record certificate or has obtained such a certificate in response to an application made by that or another employment business; and

(iii) whether, if the employment business has obtained such a certificate before the person is due to begin work at the school, it disclosed any matter or information, or any information was provided to the employment business in accordance with section 113B(6) of PA 1997; and

(b) where the employment business has obtained an enhanced criminal record certificate before the person is due to begin work at the school which disclosed any matter or information or any information was provided to the employment business in accordance with section 113B(6) of PA 1997, a copy of the certificate.

(2) Subject to paragraph (3), the certificate referred to in paragraph (1)(a)(ii) must have been obtained not more than three months before the person is due to begin work at the school.

(3) Paragraph (2) does not apply in relation to a person who has worked in—

(a) a school in England in a post—

(i) which brought the person regularly into contact with children or young persons; or

(ii) to which the person was appointed on or after 12th May 2006 and which did not bring the person regularly into contact with children or young persons; or

(b) an institution within the further education sector in England[, or in a 16 to 19 Academy,] in a post which involved the provision of education which brought the person regularly into contact with children or young persons,

during a period which ended not more than three months before the person is due to begin work at the school.

(4) Before a person offered for supply by an employment business may begin work at the school the governing body must check the person's identity (whether or not the employment business made such a check before the person was offered for supply).

(5) The authority or (as the case may be) the governing body must, either in the contract or in other arrangements which it makes with any employment business, require it, in respect of any person whom the employment business supplies to the school—

(a) to provide the notification referred to in paragraph (1)(a); and

(b) if any enhanced criminal record certificate which the employment business obtains contains any matter or information, or if any information was provided to the employment business in accordance with section 113B(6) of PA 1997, to provide a copy of the certificate.

NOTES

Commencement: 2 November 2009.

Para (3): words in square brackets in sub-para (b) inserted by the Alternative Provision Academies and 16 to 19 Academies (Consequential Amendments to Subordinate Legislation) (England) Order 2012, SI 2012/979, art 2, Schedule, para 26, as from 1 May 2012.

[2.1239]

19 Suspension of staff

(1) Subject to regulation 21, the governing body or the head teacher may suspend any person employed or engaged otherwise than under a contract of employment to work at the school where, in the opinion of the governing body or (as the case may be) the head teacher, such suspension is required.

(2) The governing body or (as the case may be) the head teacher must immediately inform the authority and the head teacher or (as the case may be) the governing body when a person is suspended under paragraph (1).

(3) Only the governing body may end a suspension under paragraph (1).

(4) On ending such a suspension, the governing body must immediately inform the authority and the head teacher.

(5) In this regulation "suspend" means suspend without loss of emoluments.

NOTES

Commencement: 2 November 2009.

[2.1240]

20 Dismissal of staff

(1) Subject to regulation 21, where the governing body determines that any person employed or engaged by the authority to work at the school should cease to work there, it must notify the authority in writing of its determination and the reasons for it.

(2) If the person concerned is employed or engaged to work solely at the school (and does not resign), the authority must, before the end of the period of fourteen days beginning with the date of the notification under paragraph (1), either—

- (a) terminate the person's contract with the authority, giving such notice as is required under that contract; or
- (b) terminate such contract without notice if the circumstances are such that it is entitled to do so by reason of the person's conduct.

(3) If the person concerned is not employed or engaged by the authority to work solely at the school, the authority must require the person to cease to work at the school.

NOTES

Commencement: 2 November 2009.

[2.1241]

21 School meals staff

(1) Subject to paragraphs (2) to (5), the authority is responsible for the appointment, discipline, suspension and dismissal of school meals staff who work or are to work at a school.

(2) Before exercising any such function the authority must consult the school's governing body to such extent as the authority thinks fit.

(3) Where an order is in force under section 512A(1) of the Education Act 1996 imposing on the governing body of a school a duty corresponding to a duty of the authority mentioned in section 512(3) and (4) of that Act (duty to provide school lunches) or section 512ZB(1) of that Act (duty to provide school lunches free of charge), paragraph (4) or (5) applies as appropriate.

(4) Where the governing body and the authority have agreed that the authority will provide lunches at the school and the governing body determines that any member of the school meals staff should cease to work at the school—

- (a) the governing body must notify the authority in writing of its determination and the reasons for it; and
- (b) the authority must require the person to cease to work at the school.

(5) Where no such agreement has been made, regulations 7, 17, 19 and 20 apply in relation to school meals staff.

NOTES

Commencement: 2 November 2009.

[2.1242]

22 Checks on change of post

Where a member of the school staff who was appointed before 12th May 2006 moves from a post which did not bring the person regularly into contact with children or young persons to a post which does, the governing body must obtain an enhanced criminal record certificate in respect of the person before, or as soon as practicable after the move.

NOTES

Commencement: 2 November 2009.

PART 3
PROVISIONS RELATING TO FOUNDATION, VOLUNTARY AIDED AND FOUNDATION SPECIAL SCHOOLS

[2.1243]

23 Application of Part 3

This Part applies to foundation, voluntary aided and foundation special schools.

NOTES

Commencement: 2 November 2009.

[2.1244]

24 Manner of appointment

(1) Where the governing body has selected a person for appointment it may appoint that person either—

(a) under a contract of employment; or
(b) otherwise than under a contract of employment.

(2) The governing body must check—

(a) the identity of any such person;
(b) that the person meets all relevant staff qualification requirements; and
(c) that the person has a right to work in the United Kingdom.

(3) The governing body must obtain an enhanced criminal record certificate in respect of any such person, before, or as soon as practicable after, the person's appointment.

(4) In the case of any such person for whom, by reason of having lived outside the United Kingdom, obtaining such a certificate is not sufficient to establish the person's suitability to work in a school, the governing body must make such further checks as it considers appropriate, having regard to any guidance issued by the Secretary of State.

(5) The governing body must complete the checks referred to in paragraphs (2) and (4) before a person is appointed.

(6) Paragraphs (3) and (4) do not apply to a person who has worked in—

(a) a school in England in a post—
 (i) which brought the person regularly into contact with children or young persons; or
 (ii) to which the person was appointed on or after 12th May 2006 and which did not bring the person regularly into contact with children or young persons; or
(b) an institution within the further education sector in England[, or in a 16 to 19 Academy,] in a post which involved the provision of education which brought the person regularly into contact with children or young persons,

during a period which ended not more than three months before the person's appointment.

(7) The governing body must keep a separate register which contains the information specified in Schedule 2.

NOTES

Commencement: 2 November 2009.

Para (6): words in square brackets in sub-para (b) inserted by the Alternative Provision Academies and 16 to 19 Academies (Consequential Amendments to Subordinate Legislation) (England) Order 2012, SI 2012/979, art 2, Schedule, para 26, as from 1 May 2012.

[2.1245]

25 Application of regulation 24 to other appointments

Regulation 24(2) to (6) and (7) (insofar as it relates to paragraphs 2 to 4, 7 and 8 of Schedule 2) also applies in relation to any person appointed by an authority for the purpose of working at a school to which this Part applies in the temporary absence of a member of staff of the school.

NOTES

Commencement: 2 November 2009.

[2.1246]

26 Authority's entitlement to offer advice

(1) The authority may offer advice to the governing body in relation to the exercise of the governing body's functions of appointment and dismissal of any teacher, to the extent provided by, and subject to, any relevant agreement.

(2) A "relevant agreement" is an agreement in writing between the authority and the governing body which entitles the authority to offer advice to the governing body in relation to the exercise of any such function to the extent provided, and which has not been terminated by the governing body by notice in writing to the authority.

(3) The governing body must consider any advice offered by the authority pursuant to paragraph (1).

NOTES

Commencement: 2 November 2009.

[2.1247]

27 Appointment of head teacher and deputy head teacher

(1) The governing body must notify the authority in writing of—

(a) any vacancy for the head teacher; and

(b) any post of deputy head teacher which it has identified as one to be filled.

(2) The governing body must advertise any such vacancy or post in such manner as it considers appropriate unless it has good reason not to.

(3) Where the governing body advertises any such vacancy or post, it must appoint a selection panel, consisting of at least three of its members, other than a governor who is the head teacher or (as the case may be) a deputy head teacher, to—

(a) select for interview such applicants for the post as it thinks fit and, where the post is that of head teacher, notify the authority in writing of the names of the applicants so selected;

(b) interview those applicants who attend for that purpose; and

(c) where it considers it appropriate to do so, recommend to the governing body for appointment one of the applicants interviewed.

(4) If, within a period of seven days beginning with the date when it receives notification under paragraph (3)(a), the authority makes written representations to the selection panel that any of the applicants is not a suitable person for the post, the selection panel must—

(a) consider those representations; and

(b) where it decides to recommend for appointment the person about whom the representations have been made, notify the authority in writing of its reasons.

(5) Subject to regulation 24(2) and, where appropriate, regulation 12(4), the governing body may appoint the person recommended by the selection panel to the vacancy or the post to be filled.

(6) If—

(a) the selection panel does not recommend a person to the governing body; or

(b) the governing body declines to appoint the person recommended by the selection panel,

the selection panel may recommend another person for appointment in accordance with this regulation (but this does not prevent it from recommending an existing applicant).

(7) Subject to regulation 24(2) and, where appropriate, regulation 12(4), if the governing body decides, for good reason, not to advertise and conduct a selection process to fill the vacancy or post in accordance with paragraphs (2) to (4), it may appoint the person it has identified to the vacancy or post to be filled.

(8) Paragraphs (2) to (7) are subject to regulation 34.

NOTES

Commencement: 2 November 2009.

[2.1248]

28 Appointment of other teachers

Where the governing body identifies any post of teacher (other than head teacher or deputy head teacher) which is to be filled for a period of more than four months, it must send a specification for the post to the authority.

NOTES

Commencement: 2 November 2009.

[2.1249]

29 Appointment of support staff

The governing body is responsible for the appointment of support staff unless the governing body and the authority agree that the authority will make such appointments.

NOTES

Commencement: 2 November 2009.

[2.1250]

30 Supply staff

(1) The governing body must ensure that no person supplied by an employment business to a school is allowed to begin work as a teacher or member of support staff at the school unless the governing body has received—

(a) written notification from the employment business in relation to that person—

(i) that it has made the checks referred to in paragraph 5(a)(i) of Schedule 2;

(ii) that it or another employment business has applied for an enhanced criminal record certificate or has obtained such a certificate in response to an application made by that or another employment business; and

(iii) whether, if the employment business has obtained such a certificate before the person is due to begin work at the school, it disclosed any matter or information, or any information was provided to the employment business in accordance with section 113B(6) of PA 1997; and

(b) where the employment business has obtained such a certificate before the person is due to begin work at the school which disclosed any matter or information, or any information was provided to the employment business in accordance with section 113B(6) of PA 1997, a copy of the certificate.

(2) Subject to paragraph (3), the certificate referred to in paragraph (1)(a)(ii) must have been obtained not more than three months before the person is due to begin work at the school.

(3) Paragraph (2) does not apply in relation to a person who has worked in—

(a) a school in England in a post—

(i) which brought the person regularly into contact with children or young persons; or

(ii) to which the person was appointed on or after 12th May 2006 and which did not bring the person regularly into contact with children or young persons; or

(b) an institution within the further education sector in England[, or in a 16 to 19 Academy,] in a post which involved the provision of education which brought the person regularly into contact with children or young persons,

during a period which ended not more than three months before the person is due to begin work at the school.

(4) Before a person offered for supply by an employment business may begin work at the school the governing body must check the person's identity (whether or not the employment business made such a check before the person was offered for supply).

(5) The governing body must, either in the contract or in other arrangements which it makes with any employment business, require it, in respect of any person whom the employment business supplies to the school—

(a) to provide the notification referred to in paragraph (1)(a); and

(b) where the employment business obtains an enhanced criminal record certificate which discloses any matter or information, or if any information is provided to the employment business in accordance with section 113B(6) of PA 1997, to provide a copy of the certificate.

NOTES

Commencement: 2 November 2009.

Para (3): words in square brackets in sub-para (b) inserted by the Alternative Provision Academies and 16 to 19 Academies (Consequential Amendments to Subordinate Legislation) (England) Order 2012, SI 2012/979, art 2, Schedule, para 26, as from 1 May 2012.

[2.1251]

31 Suspension of staff

(1) The governing body or the head teacher may suspend any person employed or engaged otherwise than under a contract of employment to work at the school where, in the opinion of the governing body or (as the case may be) the head teacher, the person's suspension from the school is required.

(2) The governing body or (as the case may be) head teacher must immediately inform the head teacher or (as the case may be) the governing body when a person is suspended under paragraph (1).

(3) Only the governing body may end a suspension under paragraph (1).

(4) On ending such a suspension, the governing body must inform the head teacher.

(5) In this regulation "suspend" means suspend without loss of emoluments.

NOTES

Commencement: 2 November 2009.

[2.1252]

32 Suspension and dismissal of authority staff

In the case of staff employed, or engaged otherwise than under a contract of employment, by the authority in accordance with regulation 29, regulation 19 (in place of regulation 31) and regulation 20 apply as they apply to schools referred to in regulation 11.

NOTES

Commencement: 2 November 2009.

[2.1253]

33 Checks on change of post

Where a member of the school staff who was appointed before 12th May 2006 moves from a post which did not bring the person regularly into contact with children or young persons to a post which does, the governing body must obtain an enhanced criminal record certificate in respect of the person before, or as soon as practicable after, the move.

NOTES

Commencement: 2 November 2009.

[2.1254]

34 Appointment of head teachers for schools of Roman Catholic Religious Orders

(1) This regulation applies in relation to a voluntary aided school if the trustees under a trust deed relating to the school are also trustees of a Roman Catholic Religious Order ("the Order").

(2) Subject to paragraph (5), paragraphs (3) and (4) have effect in relation to the filling of a vacancy in the post of head teacher of the school, in place of regulation 27(2) to (7).

(3) The governing body must notify the Major Superior of the vacancy in writing.

(4) The governing body must—

(a) interview such persons who are members of the Order as are proposed as candidates for appointment to the post by the Major Superior; and

(b) appoint to the post one of the persons so interviewed unless, by virtue of regulation 24(2) or otherwise, the governing body has good reason for not making any such appointment.

(5) If the governing body does not make an appointment under paragraph (4)(b), regulation 27(2) to (7), has effect in relation to the filling of the vacancy.

(6) In this regulation—

"the Major Superior" means the Major Superior of the Order;

"Roman Catholic Religious Order" means a Roman Catholic religious institute or society of apostolic life.

NOTES

Commencement: 2 November 2009.

PART 4
COLLABORATION BETWEEN SCHOOLS

[2.1255]

35 General

(1) Where two or more governing bodies agree to collaborate on the discharge of any function relating to individual members of the school staff, these Regulations apply, subject to this Part.

(2) In this Part—

"collaborating governing bodies" means two or more governing bodies which arrange for any of their functions to be discharged jointly;

"relevant school" means the school or schools to which any member of staff is, or is to be, appointed.

NOTES

Commencement: 2 November 2009.

[2.1256]

36 Appointment of head teacher and deputy head teacher

(1) In relation to the appointment of a head teacher or a deputy head teacher under regulation 15 or 27—

(a) the collaborating governing bodies may delegate the notification to the authority and the advertisement of any vacancy or post to—

(i) the head teacher of one or more of the collaborating schools;

(ii) one or more governors from any of the collaborating schools;

(iii) one or more head teachers acting together with one or more governors from any of the collaborating schools;

(b) the selection panel must consist of at least three governors taken from any of the collaborating governing bodies other than a governor who is the head teacher or (as the case may be) a deputy head teacher of the relevant school; and

(c) the selection panel must make its recommendation to the governing body of the relevant school.

(2) If the governing body does not approve the recommendation the selection panel of the collaborating governing bodies must repeat the selection process unless the relevant school's governing body withdraws from the agreement to collaborate.

NOTES

Commencement: 2 November 2009.

[2.1257]

37 Appointment of other teachers and support staff

(1) The collaborating governing bodies may delegate the appointment of any teacher (other than the head teacher and deputy head teacher) and the appointment of any member of the support staff to—

(a) the head teacher of one or more of the collaborating schools;

(b) one or more governors from any of the collaborating schools;

(c) one or more head teachers acting together with one or more governors from any of the collaborating schools.

(2) Where the collaborating governing bodies have delegated the appointment of a member of staff, other than to the head teacher of the relevant school—

(a) the head teacher of the relevant school may attend all relevant proceedings and offer advice; and

(b) the person or persons to whom the delegation has been made must consider any such advice.

NOTES

Commencement: 2 November 2009.

[2.1258]

38 Dismissal of staff

(1) The collaborating governing bodies may delegate—

(a) the determination that a member of staff (other than the head teacher) should cease to work at a relevant school; or

(b) the power to dismiss a member of staff (other than the head teacher) from a relevant school.

(2) Any such delegation may be to—

(a) the head teacher of one or more of the collaborating schools;

(b) one or more governors from any of the collaborating schools;

(c) one or more head teachers acting together with one or more governors from any of the collaborating schools.

(3) The collaborating governing bodies may delegate—

(a) the determination that the head teacher should cease to work at a relevant school; or

(b) the power to dismiss the head teacher from a relevant school,

to one or more governors.

NOTES

Commencement: 2 November 2009.

[2.1259]

39 Authority's entitlement to offer advice

(1) Where the authority is entitled to offer advice to any individual governing body in relation to the exercise of any function under regulation 14 or 26, it is also entitled to offer advice to any other collaborating governing bodies in relation to the exercise of any such function.

(2) The collaborating governing bodies must consider any advice offered by the authority pursuant to paragraph (1).

NOTES

Commencement: 2 November 2009.

PART 5
STAFFING OF NEW SCHOOLS

[2.1260]

40 Interpretation of provisions applied by Part 5

Any provision of these Regulations or Schedule 2 to EA 2002 which applies in relation to a proposed school as a result of this Part has effect for that purpose as if—

(a) any reference to a "governing body" were a reference to a temporary governing body; and

(b) any reference to a "governor" were a reference to a temporary governor.

NOTES

Commencement: 2 November 2009.

[2.1261]

41 Staffing of proposed community, voluntary controlled, community special and maintained nursery schools having delegated budgets

Where a proposed community, voluntary controlled, community special or maintained nursery school has a delegated budget, regulations 4 to 9 and 12 to 22 apply.

NOTES

Commencement: 2 November 2009.

[2.1262]

42 Staffing of proposed foundation, voluntary aided and foundation special schools having delegated budgets

Where a proposed foundation, voluntary aided or foundation special school has a delegated budget, regulations 4 to 9 and 24 to 34 apply.

NOTES

Commencement: 2 November 2009.

[2.1263]

43 Staffing of proposed community, voluntary controlled, community special and maintained nursery schools without delegated budgets

Where a proposed community, voluntary controlled, community special or maintained nursery school does not have a delegated budget, the provisions of Part 1 of Schedule 2 to EA 2002 apply.

NOTES

Commencement: 2 November 2009.

[2.1264]

44 Staffing of proposed foundation, voluntary aided or foundation special schools without delegated budgets

Where a proposed foundation, voluntary aided or foundation special school does not have a delegated budget, the provisions of Part 2 of Schedule 2 to EA 2002 apply.

NOTES

Commencement: 2 November 2009.

SCHEDULES

SCHEDULE 1

(Sch 1 (Revocations) outside the scope of this work.)

SCHEDULE 2
INFORMATION TO BE RECORDED IN THE REGISTER

Regulations 12(7) and 24(7)

[2.1265]

1. The register referred to in regulations 12(7) and 24(7) must contain the following information.

2. In relation to each member of staff appointed on or after 1st January 2007, whether—

(a) a check was made to establish the person's identity;
(b) a check was made to establish that the person is not barred from regulated activity relating to children in accordance with section 3(2) of the Safeguarding Vulnerable Groups Act 2006 or subject to any direction made under section 142 of EA 2002 or any prohibition, restriction or order having effect as such a direction;
(c) checks were made to establish that the person meets the requirements with respect to qualifications or registration mentioned in regulation 3(3)(a);
(d) an enhanced criminal record certificate was obtained in respect of the person;
(e) further checks were made pursuant to regulation 12(4) or 24(4), as the case may be;
(f) a check was made to establish the person's right to work in the United Kingdom and
(g) the date on which each such check was completed or the certificate obtained.

3. Subject to paragraph 4, in relation to each member of staff in post on 1st April 2007 who was appointed at any time before 1st January 2007—

(a) whether each check referred to in paragraph 2 was made;
(b) whether an enhanced criminal record certificate was obtained; and
(c) the date on which each such check was completed or certificate obtained.

4. Paragraph 3 applies, in the case of a member of staff who was appointed at any time before 12th May 2006, only if the work brings the person regularly into contact with children or young persons.

5. In relation to any person supplied by an employment business to work at the school—
(a) whether written notification has been received from the employment business that—
(i) it has made checks corresponding to those which paragraph 2(a) to (c), (e) and (f) requires to be recorded in relation to a member of staff of a school; and
(ii) it or another employment business has applied for an enhanced criminal record certificate or has obtained such a certificate in response to an application made by that or another employment business; and
(b) the date on which such notification was received.

6. Where written notification has been received from the employment business in accordance with a contract or other arrangements made pursuant to regulation 18(5) that it has obtained an enhanced criminal record certificate which disclosed any matter or information, or that information was provided to it in accordance with section 113B(6) of PA 1997, whether the employment business provided a copy of the certificate to the school.

7. It is immaterial for the purposes of paragraphs 2 and 3 whether the check was made or certificate obtained pursuant to a legal obligation.

8. The register may be kept in electronic form, provided that the information so recorded is capable of being reproduced in legible form.

NOTES
Commencement: 2 November 2009.

LAW APPLICABLE TO CONTRACTUAL OBLIGATIONS (ENGLAND AND WALES AND NORTHERN IRELAND) REGULATIONS 2009

(SI 2009/3064)

NOTES
Made: 15 November 2009.
Authority: European Communities Act 1972, s 2(2).
Commencement: 17 December 2009.

[2.1266]
1 Citation, commencement and extent

(1) These Regulations may be cited as the Law Applicable to Contractual Obligations (England and Wales and Northern Ireland) Regulations 2009, and shall come into force on 17 December 2009.

(2) Regulation 3 extends to England and Wales only.

(3) Regulation 4 extends to Northern Ireland only.

(4) Otherwise, these Regulations extend to England and Wales and Northern Ireland.

NOTES
Commencement: 17 December 2009.

2–4 *(Reg 2 inserts the Contracts (Applicable Law) Act 1990, s 4A at* **[1.184]***; reg 3 amends the Foreign Limitation Periods Act 1984, s 8; reg 4 amends the Foreign Limitation Periods (Northern Ireland) Order 1985, art 9.)*

[2.1267]
5 Application of the Regulation (EC) No 593/2008: conflicts falling within Article 22(2)

(1) Notwithstanding Article 22(2) of Regulation (EC) No 593/2008 of the European Parliament and of the Council on the law applicable to contractual obligations, that Regulation shall apply in the case of conflicts between—
(a) the laws of different parts of the United Kingdom, or
(b) the laws of one or more parts of the United Kingdom and Gibraltar,
as it applies in the case of conflicts between the laws of other countries.

(2) Paragraph (1) shall not apply to contracts falling within Article 7 of Regulation (EC) No 593/2008 (insurance contracts).

NOTES

Commencement: 17 December 2009.

LAW APPLICABLE TO CONTRACTUAL OBLIGATIONS (SCOTLAND) REGULATIONS 2009

(SSI 2009/410)

NOTES

Made: 23 November 2009.
Authority: European Communities Act 1972, s 2(2).
Commencement: 17 December 2009.

[2.1268]
1 Citation, commencement and extent

(1) These Regulations may be cited as the Law Applicable to Contractual Obligations (Scotland) Regulations 2009 and come into force on 17th December 2009.
(2) These Regulations extend to Scotland only.

NOTES

Commencement: 17 December 2009.

2, 3 *(Reg 2 inserts the Contracts (Applicable Law) Act 1990, s 4B at* **[1.185]**, *and amends s 8 of that Act; reg 3 amends the Prescription and Limitation (Scotland) Act 1973, s 23A.)*

[2.1269]
4 Conflicts falling within Article 22(2) of Regulation (EC) No 593/2008

Notwithstanding Article 22(2) of Regulation (EC) No 593/2008 of the European Parliament and of the Council on the law applicable to contractual obligations (Rome I), that Regulation shall, with the exception of Article 7 (insurance contracts), apply in the case of conflicts between—

(a) the laws of different parts of the United Kingdom, or
(b) the laws of one or more parts of the United Kingdom and Gibraltar,

as it applies in the case of conflicts between the laws of other countries.

NOTES

Commencement: 17 December 2009.

EMPLOYERS' DUTIES (IMPLEMENTATION) REGULATIONS 2010

(SI 2010/4)

NOTES

Made: 5 January 2010.
Authority: Pensions Act 2008, ss 12, 29(2), (4), 30(8), 99, 144(2), (4).
Commencement: 1 June 2012. Note that, as originally enacted, these Regulations were due to come into force on 1 September 2012. Regulation 1 of these Regulations (Citation, commencement and interpretation) was amended by the Automatic Enrolment (Miscellaneous Amendments) Regulations 2012, SI 2012/215, reg 3(a) with the effect that the commencement date became 1 June 2012. Note also that other amendments made to these Regulations by the 2012 Regulations also came into force on 1 June 2012 (immediately before the commencement of these Regulations by virtue of the amendment made by reg 3(a)). These amendments have, therefore, been incorporated into the text below as they came into force before these Regulations come into force. See further reg 1 (as amended) and reg 4 at **[2.1270]** and **[2.1273]**.

ARRANGEMENT OF REGULATIONS

Part 2 Statutory Instruments

[2.1270]

1 Citation, commencement and interpretation

(1) These Regulations may be cited as the Employers' Duties (Implementation) Regulations 2010 and shall come into force on [1st June 2012, immediately after the time when the amendments to these Regulations made by the Automatic Enrolment (Miscellaneous Amendments) Regulations 2012 come into force].

(2) In these Regulations—

"the Act" means the Pensions Act 2008;

"employer" has the meaning given by—

(a) section 88(7) of the Act; and

(b) regulation 2(2);

"the employers' duties" means sections 2 to 9 of the Act;

"HMRC" means Her Majesty's Revenue and Customs;

"PAYE income" has the same meaning as in section 683 of the Income Tax (Earnings and Pensions) Act 2003;

"PAYE reference number" means a number issued by HMRC to a corresponding PAYE scheme, enabling an employer to pay over amounts deducted to HMRC;

"PAYE scheme" means the HMRC record [applicable] to an employer who—

(a) employs; or

(b) intends to employ,

a worker or workers to whom PAYE income is payable;

"scheme administrator" has the same meaning as in section 270 of the Finance Act 2004; and

["staging date" means the date prescribed in accordance with regulation 2(1) on which the employers' duties apply to employers.]

NOTES

Commencement: 1 June 2012 (see also the introductory notes to these Regulations and reg 4 at **[2.1273]**).

Para (1): words in square brackets substituted by the Automatic Enrolment (Miscellaneous Amendments) Regulations 2012, SI 2012/215, regs 2, 3(a), as from 1 June 2012 (immediately after the other amendments made to these Regulations by the 2012 Regulations (see reg 1(2)(b) thereof)).

Para (2): word in square brackets in definition "PAYE scheme" substituted by SI 2012/215, regs 2, 3(b), as from 1 June 2012; definition "staging date" substituted by the Employers' Duties (Implementation) (Amendment) Regulations 2012, SI 2012/1813, reg 2(1), (2), as from 1 October 2012.

[2.1271]

2 Application of the employers' duties to employers

[(1) Except where an employer satisfies the conditions for early automatic enrolment in regulation 3, the employers' duties do not apply to employers described in the first column of the table in regulation 4 until—

(a) the corresponding staging date prescribed in the final column of that table; or

(b) in a case to which paragraph (1A) applies—

(i) the corresponding staging date prescribed in the final column of that table in regulation 4; or

(ii) where the employer so chooses, the corresponding staging date prescribed in the final column of the table as modified by regulation 4A.]

[(1A) This paragraph applies in a case where, on 1st April 2012, the employer—

(a) had less than 50 workers; and

(b) had, or was part of, one or more PAYE schemes in which there were 50 or more persons.]

(2) For the purposes of these Regulations, an employer is a person within the meaning of section 88(7) of the Act who—

(a) has[, or is part of,] a PAYE scheme of any size, determined by the Regulator in accordance with paragraphs (3) and (4); or

(b) meets any other description contained in the first column of the table in regulation 4 (including having no PAYE scheme).

(3) The size of an employer's PAYE scheme means the number of persons within that scheme.

(4) The number of persons within a PAYE scheme is based on the latest information available to the Regulator, as at 1st April 2012.

(5) Where—

(a) the employers' duties first apply to an employer in accordance with the table in regulation 4; and

(b) for any reason, an employer has another PAYE scheme (or schemes),

the employers' duties apply to that employer in respect of the scheme (or schemes) mentioned in subparagraph (b) from the staging date applicable in relation to subparagraph (a) (and this is so even where the staging date mentioned in the table for any such scheme (or schemes) is later than the staging date referred to in subparagraph (a)).

(6) Any employer who first pays PAYE income in respect of a worker between—

(a) 1st April 2012; and
(b) up to (but not including) [1st October 2017],

is to be treated as a new employer in accordance with the relevant entry in the first column of the table in regulation 4.

(7) Where paragraph (6) applies, the employers' duties do not apply to such an employer until PAYE income is first payable in respect of any worker and then only in accordance with the table in regulation 4.

(8) Where—
(a) an employer pays PAYE income in respect of any worker from [1st October 2017]; and
(b) the employers' duties do not already apply to that employer,

the employers' duties apply to that employer from the day on which PAYE income is payable.

[(9) This paragraph applies in the case of an employer who does not have a PAYE scheme in respect of any worker after 1st April 2017.

(10) Where paragraph (9) applies and the employers' duties do not already apply to that employer, the employers' duties apply to that employer from the date on which qualifying earnings are payable to any worker.]

NOTES

Commencement: 1 June 2012 (see also the introductory notes to these Regulations and reg 4 at **[2.1273]**).

Para (1): substituted by the Employers' Duties (Implementation) (Amendment) Regulations 2012, SI 2012/1813, reg 2(1), (3)(a), as from 1 October 2012.

Para (1A): inserted by SI 2012/1813, reg 2(1), (3)(b), as from 1 October 2012.

Para (2): words in square brackets in sub-para (a) inserted by the Automatic Enrolment (Miscellaneous Amendments) Regulations 2012, SI 2012/215, regs 2, 4, as from 1 June 2012.

Paras (6), (8): words in square brackets substituted by SI 2012/1813, reg 2(1), (3)(c), (d), as from 1 October 2012.

Paras (9), (10): added by SI 2012/1813, reg 2(1), (3)(e), as from 1 October 2012.

[2.1272]
3 Early automatic enrolment

[(1) Where the conditions in paragraphs (3) and (4) are both satisfied, the employers' duties apply to an employer from the early automatic enrolment date referred to in paragraph (5).]

[(1A) This regulation does not apply where the employer has chosen a staging date in accordance with regulation 2(1)(b)(ii).]

(2) Where the condition in paragraph (3) is satisfied but the condition in paragraph (4) is not satisfied, the employers' duties apply to an employer from the staging date corresponding to that employer's description . . . .

(3) The first condition is that an employer must fall within any description in the first column of the table in regulation 4.

(4) The second condition is that an employer has chosen an early automatic enrolment date [referred to in paragraph (5)] for the employers' duties to apply, which is earlier than the date mentioned in the final column of that table corresponding to that employer, and has—
(a) . . .
(b) secured the agreement of the [trustees or managers] (or scheme administrator or provider) of [a pension scheme] that that scheme was to be used by the employer to comply with those duties from that early automatic enrolment date; and
[(c) notified the Regulator accordingly in writing, at any time—
(i) where paragraph (5)(a) applies, before the date specified in the second column of the table in regulation 4 corresponding to that earlier date;
(ii) where paragraph (5)(b) applies, before 1st November 2012; or
(iii) where paragraph (5)(c) applies, no later than the first day of the period of one month before the date specified in that sub-paragraph.]

[(5) The early automatic enrolment date is—
(a) any date in the final column of the table in regulation 4 which is earlier than the staging date corresponding to that employers' description;
(b) 1st December 2012; or
(c) in the case of an employer of 50,000 or more persons by PAYE scheme size or any other description, one of the following dates to be chosen by the employer—
(i) 1st July 2012;
(ii) 1st August 2012; or
(iii) 1st September 2012.]

NOTES

Commencement: 1 June 2012 (see also the introductory notes to these Regulations and reg 4 at **[2.1273]**).

Para (1): substituted by the Automatic Enrolment (Miscellaneous Amendments) Regulations 2012, SI 2012/215, regs 2, 5(a), as from 1 June 2012.

Para (1A): inserted by the Employers' Duties (Implementation) (Amendment) Regulations 2012, SI 2012/1813, reg 2(1), (4)(a), as from 1 October 2012.

Para (2): words omitted revoked by SI 2012/215, regs 2, 5(b), as from 1 June 2012.

Para (4): words in first and second pairs of square brackets substituted, sub-para (a) revoked and sub-para (c) substituted, by SI 2012/215, regs 2, 5(c), as from 1 June 2012; words in third pair of square brackets substituted by SI 2012/1813, reg 2(1), (4)(b), as from 1 October 2012.

Para (5): added by SI 2012/215, regs 2, 5(d), as from 1 June 2012.

[2.1273]

4 Staging of the employers' duties

(1) The table in this regulation sets out the application of the employers' duties.

(2) Where a date prescribed in the second column of the following table falls on a day which is not a working day, that date is to be treated as the next working day (and for the purposes of this paragraph "working day" means a day which is not a Saturday, Sunday, bank holiday or other public holiday).

(3) In this regulation, "bank holiday" means a day specified in paragraphs 1 and 2 of Schedule 1 to the Banking and Financial Dealings Act 1971.

Table

Employer (by PAYE scheme size or other description)	***Date before which notification to automatically enrol early must be sent***	***Staging date***
120,000 or more	1st September 2012	1st October 2012
50,000–119,999	1st October 2012	1st November 2012
30,000–49,999	1st December 2012	1st January 2013
20,000–29,999	1st January 2013	1st February 2013
10,000–19,999	1st February 2013	1st March 2013
6,000–9,999	1st March 2013	1st April 2013
4,100–5,999	1st April 2013	1st May 2013
4,000–4,099	1st May 2013	1st June 2013
3,000–3,999	1st June 2013	1st July 2013
2,000–2,999	1st July 2013	1st August 2013
1,250–1,999	1st August 2013	1st September 2013
800–1,249	1st September 2013	1st October 2013
500–799	1st October 2013	1st November 2013
350–499	1st December 2013	1st January 2014
250–349	1st January 2014	1st February 2014
[160–249	1st March 2014	1st April 2014
90–159	1st April 2014	1st May 2014
62–89	1st June 2014	1st July 2014
61	1st July 2014	1st August 2014
60	1st September 2014	1st October 2014
59	1st October 2014	1st November 2014
58	1st December 2014	1st January 2015
54–57	1st February 2015	1st March 2015
50–53	1st March 2015	1st April 2015
Less than 30 with the last 2 characters in their PAYE reference numbers 92, A1-A9, B1-B9, AA-AZ, BA-BW, M1-M9, MA-MZ, Z1-Z9, ZA-ZZ, 0A-0Z, 1A-1Z or 2A-2Z	1st May 2015	1st June 2015
Less than 30 with the last 2 characters in their PAYE reference numbers BX	1st June 2015	1st July 2015
40–49	1st July 2015	1st August 2015
Less than 30 with the last 2 characters in their PAYE reference numbers BY	1st August 2015	1st September 2015
30–39	1st September 2015	1st October 2015

Employer (by PAYE scheme size or other description)	*Date before which notification to automatically enrol early must be sent*	*Staging date*
Less than 30 with the last 2 characters in their PAYE reference numbers BZ	1st October 2015	1st November 2015
Less than 30 with the last 2 characters in their PAYE reference numbers 02-04, C1-C9, D1-D9, CA-CZ, or DA-DZ	1st December 2015	1st January 2016
Less than 30 with the last 2 characters in their PAYE reference numbers 00, 05-07, E1-E9 or EA-EZ	1st January 2016	1st February 2016
Less than 30 with the last 2 characters in their PAYE reference numbers 01, 08-11, F1-F9, G1-G9, FA-FZ or GA-GZ	1st February 2016	1st March 2016
Less than 30 with the last 2 characters in their PAYE reference numbers 12-16, 3A-3Z, H1-H9 or HA-HZ	1st March 2016	1st April 2016
Less than 30 with the last 2 characters in their PAYE reference numbers I1-I9 or IA-IZ	1st April 2016	1st May 2016
Less than 30 with the last 2 characters in their PAYE reference numbers 17-22, 4A-4Z, J1-J9 or JA-JZ	1st May 2016	1st June 2016
Less than 30 with the last 2 characters in their PAYE reference numbers 23-29, 5A-5Z, K1-K9 or KA-KZ	1st June 2016	1st July 2016
Less than 30 with the last 2 characters in their PAYE reference numbers 30-37, 6A-6Z, L1-L9 or LA-LZ	1st July 2016	1st August 2016
Less than 30 with the last 2 characters in their PAYE reference numbers N1-N9 or NA-NZ	1st August 2016	1st September 2016
Less than 30 with the last 2 characters in their PAYE reference numbers 38-46, 7A-7Z, O1-O9 or OA-OZ	1st September 2016	1st October 2016
Less than 30 with the last 2 characters in their PAYE reference numbers 47-57, 8A-8Z, Q1-Q9, R1-R9, S1-S9, T1-T9, QA-QZ, RA-RZ, SA-SZ or TA-TZ	1st October 2016	1st November 2016
Less than 30 with the last 2 characters in their PAYE reference numbers 58-69, 9A-9Z, U1-U9, V1-V9, W1-W9, UA-UZ, VA-VZ or WA-WZ	1st December 2016	1st January 2017
Less than 30 with the last 2 characters in their PAYE reference numbers 70-83, X1-X9, Y1-Y9, XA-XZ, or YA-YZ	1st January 2017	1st February 2017
Less than 30 with the last 2 characters in their PAYE reference numbers P1-P9 or PA-PZ	1st February 2017	1st March 2017

Employer (by PAYE scheme size or other description)	*Date before which notification to automatically enrol early must be sent*	*Staging date*
Less than 30 with the last 2 characters in their PAYE reference numbers 84-91 or 93-99	1st March 2017	1st April 2017
Less than 30 persons in the PAYE scheme not meeting any other description contained in the first column of this table	1st March 2017	1st April 2017
Employer who does not have a PAYE scheme	1st March 2017	1st April 2017
New employer (PAYE income first payable between 1st April 2012 and 31st March 2013)	1st April 2017	1st May 2017
New employer (PAYE income first payable between 1st April 2013 and 31st March 2014)	1st June 2017	1st July 2017
New employer (PAYE income first payable between 1st April 2014 and 31st March 2015)	1st July 2017	1st August 2017
New employer (PAYE income first payable between 1st April 2015 and 31st December 2015)	1st September 2017	1st October 2017
New employer (PAYE income first payable between 1st January 2016 and 30th September 2016)	1st October 2017	1st November 2017
New employer (PAYE income first payable between 1st October 2016 and 30th June 2017)	1st December 2017	1st January 2018
New employer (PAYE income first payable between 1st July 2017 and 30th September 2017)	1st January 2018	1st February 2018]

NOTES

Commencement: 1 June 2012 (see also the introductory notes to these Regulations and the text of this regulation).

Entries in square brackets in the Table substituted by the Employers' Duties (Implementation) (Amendment) Regulations 2012, SI 2012/1813, reg 2(1), (5), as from 1 October 2012.

[2.1274]
[4A

(1) For the purposes of regulation 2(1)(b)(ii), the date in the final column of the table in regulation 4 is modified in accordance with paragraph (2).

(2) Where the staging date in the final column of the table in regulation 4 is in the period—

(a) beginning with 1st October 2012 and ending on 1st November 2012, the modified date is 1st August 2015;

(b) beginning with 1st January 2013 and ending on 1st February 2013, the modified date is 1st October 2015;

(c) beginning with 1st March 2013 and ending on 1st April 2013, the modified date is 1st January 2016;

(d) beginning with 1st May 2013 and ending on 1st June 2013, the modified date is 1st February 2016;

(e) beginning with 1st July 2013 and ending on 1st August 2013, the modified date is 1st March 2016;

(f) beginning with 1st September 2013 and ending on 1st October 2013, the modified date is 1st April 2016;

(g) beginning with 1st November 2013 and ending on 1st January 2014, the modified date is 1st May 2016;

(h) beginning with 1st February 2014 and ending on 1st April 2014, the modified date is 1st July 2016;

(i) beginning with 1st May 2014 and ending on 1st July 2014, the modified date is 1st September 2016;

(j) beginning with 1st August 2014 and ending on 1st October 2014, the modified date is 1st November 2016;

(k) beginning with 1st November 2014 and ending on 1st January 2015, the modified date is 1st February 2017; or

(l) beginning with 1st March 2015 and ending on 1st April 2015, the modified date is 1st April 2017.]

NOTES

Commencement: 1 October 2012.

Inserted by the Employers' Duties (Implementation) (Amendment) Regulations 2012, SI 2012/1813, reg 2(1), (6), as from 1 October 2012.

[2.1275]

5 Transitional periods for money purchase and personal pension schemes

For the purposes of section 29 of the Act (transitional periods for money purchase and personal pension schemes)—

(a) the first transitional period is [five years and three months], beginning with the coming into force of section 20 (quality requirement: UK money purchase schemes); and

(b) the second transitional period is one year, beginning with the end of the first transitional period.

NOTES

Commencement: 1 June 2012 (see also the introductory notes to these Regulations and reg 4 at **[2.1273]**).

Words in square brackets substituted by the Employers' Duties (Implementation) (Amendment) Regulations 2012, SI 2012/1813, reg 2(1), (7), as from 1 October 2012.

[2.1276]

6 Transitional period for defined benefits and hybrid schemes

For the purposes of section 30 of the Act (transitional period for defined benefits and hybrid schemes), the transitional period for defined benefits and hybrid schemes is [five years and three months], beginning with the day on which section 3 (automatic enrolment) comes into force.

NOTES

Commencement: 1 June 2012 (see also the introductory notes to these Regulations and reg 4 at **[2.1273]**).

Words in square brackets substituted by the Employers' Duties (Implementation) (Amendment) Regulations 2012, SI 2012/1813, reg 2(1), (8), as from 1 October 2012.

AGENCY WORKERS REGULATIONS 2010

(SI 2010/93)

NOTES

Made: 20 January 2010.

Authority: European Communities Act 1972, s 2(2); Health and Safety at Work etc Act 1974, ss 5(1), (2), (5), 82(3), Sch 3, paras 7, 8, 15(1).

Commencement: 1 October 2011.

Employment Appeal Tribunal: an appeal lies to the Employment Appeal Tribunal on any question of law arising from any decision of, or in any proceedings before, an employment tribunal under or by virtue of these Regulations; see the Employment Tribunals Act 1996, s 21(1)(y) at **[1.713]**.

Conciliation: employment tribunal proceedings and claims which could be the subject of employment tribunal proceedings under regs 5, 12, 13 or 17(2) of these Regulations are proceedings to which the Employment Tribunals Act 1996, s 18 applies; see s 18(1)(x) of that Act at **[1.706]**.

See *Harvey* AI(4).

ARRANGEMENT OF REGULATIONS

PART 1
GENERAL AND INTERPRETATION

PART 2
RIGHTS

Part 2 Statutory Instruments

PART 1
GENERAL AND INTERPRETATION

[2.1277]

1 Citation, commencement and extent

(1) These Regulations may be cited as the Agency Workers Regulations 2010 and shall come into force on 1st October 2011.

(2) These Regulations extend to England and Wales and Scotland only, save as provided for in Schedule 1 (provisions extending to England and Wales, Scotland and Northern Ireland).

NOTES

Commencement: 1 October 2011.

[2.1278]

2 Interpretation

In these Regulations—

"the 1996 Act" means the Employment Rights Act 1996;

"assignment" means a period of time during which an agency worker is supplied by one or more temporary work agencies to a hirer to work temporarily for and under the supervision and direction of the hirer;

"contract of employment" means a contract of service or of apprenticeship, whether express or implied, and (if it is express) whether oral or in writing;

"employee" means an individual who has entered into or works under or, where the employment has ceased, worked under a contract of employment;

"employer", in relation to an employee or worker, means the person by whom the employee or worker is (or where the employment has ceased, was) employed;

"employment"—

(a) in relation to an employee, means employment under a contract of employment, and

(b) in relation to a worker, means employment under that worker's contract,

and "employed" shall be construed accordingly;

"hirer" means a person engaged in economic activity, public or private, whether or not operating for profit, to whom individuals are supplied, to work temporarily for and under the supervision and direction of that person; and

"worker" means an individual who is not an agency worker but who has entered into or works under (or where the employment has ceased, worked under)—

(a) a contract of employment, or

(b) any other contract, whether express or implied and (if it is express) whether oral or in writing, whereby the individual undertakes to do or perform personally any work or services for another party to the contract whose status is not by virtue of the contract that of a client or customer of any profession or business undertaking carried on by the individual,

and any reference to a worker's contract shall be construed accordingly.

NOTES

Commencement: 1 October 2011.

[2.1279]

3 The meaning of agency worker

(1) In these Regulations "agency worker" means an individual who—

(a) is supplied by a temporary work agency to work temporarily for and under the supervision and direction of a hirer; and

(b) has a contract with the temporary work agency which is—

(i) a contract of employment with the agency, or

[(ii) any other contract with the agency to perform work or services personally].

(2) But an individual is not an agency worker if—

(a) the contract the individual has with the temporary work agency has the effect that the status of the agency is that of a client or customer of a profession or business undertaking carried on by the individual; or

(b) there is a contract, by virtue of which the individual is available to work for the hirer, having the effect that the status of the hirer is that of a client or customer of a profession or business undertaking carried on by the individual.

(3) For the purposes of paragraph (1)(a) an individual shall be treated as having been supplied by a temporary work agency to work temporarily for and under the supervision and direction of a hirer if—

(a) the temporary work agency initiates or is involved as an intermediary in the making of the arrangements that lead to the individual being supplied to work temporarily for and under the supervision and direction of the hirer, and

(b) the individual is supplied by an intermediary, or one of a number of intermediaries, to work temporarily for and under the supervision and direction of the hirer.

(4) An individual treated by virtue of paragraph (3) as having been supplied by a temporary work agency, shall be treated, for the purposes of paragraph (1)(b), as having a contract with the temporary work agency.

(5) An individual is not prevented from being an agency worker—

(a) because the temporary work agency supplies the individual through one or more intermediaries;

(b) because one or more intermediaries supply that individual;

(c) because the individual is supplied pursuant to any contract or other arrangement between the temporary work agency, one or more intermediaries and the hirer;

(d) because the temporary work agency pays for the services of the individual through one or more intermediaries; or

(e) because the individual is employed by or otherwise has a contract with one or more intermediaries.

(6) Paragraph (5) does not prejudice the generality of paragraphs (1) to (4).

NOTES

Commencement: 1 October 2011.

Para (1): sub-para (b)(ii) substituted by the Agency Workers (Amendment) Regulations 2011, SI 2011/1941, reg 2(1), (2), as from 1 September 2011.

[2.1280]

4 The meaning of temporary work agency

(1) In these Regulations "temporary work agency" means a person engaged in the economic activity, public or private, whether or not operating for profit, and whether or not carrying on such activity in conjunction with others, of—

(a) supplying individuals to work temporarily for and under the supervision and direction of hirers; or

(b) paying for, or receiving or forwarding payment for, the services of individuals who are supplied to work temporarily for and under the supervision and direction of hirers.

(2) Notwithstanding paragraph (1)(b) a person is not a temporary work agency if the person is engaged in the economic activity of paying for, or receiving or forwarding payments for, the services of individuals regardless of whether the individuals are supplied to work for hirers.

NOTES

Commencement: 1 October 2011.

PART 2
RIGHTS

[2.1281]

5 Rights of agency workers in relation to the basic working and employment conditions

(1) Subject to regulation 7, an agency worker (A) shall be entitled to the same basic working and employment conditions as A would be entitled to for doing the same job had A been recruited by the hirer—

(a) other than by using the services of a temporary work agency; and
(b) at the time the qualifying period commenced.

(2) For the purposes of paragraph (1), the basic working and employment conditions are—

(a) where A would have been recruited as an employee, the relevant terms and conditions that are ordinarily included in the contracts of employees of the hirer;
(b) where A would have been recruited as a worker, the relevant terms and conditions that are ordinarily included in the contracts of workers of the hirer,

whether by collective agreement or otherwise, including any variations in those relevant terms and conditions made at any time after the qualifying period commenced.

(3) Paragraph (1) shall be deemed to have been complied with where—

(a) an agency worker is working under the same relevant terms and conditions as an employee who is a comparable employee, and
(b) the relevant terms and conditions of that comparable employee are terms and conditions ordinarily included in the contracts of employees, who are comparable employees of the hirer, whether by collective agreement or otherwise.

(4) For the purposes of paragraph (3) an employee is a comparable employee in relation to an agency worker if at the time when the breach of paragraph (1) is alleged to take place—

(a) both that employee and the agency worker are—
  (i) working for and under the supervision and direction of the hirer, and
  (ii) engaged in the same or broadly similar work having regard, where relevant, to whether they have a similar level of qualification and skills; and
(b) the employee works or is based at the same establishment as the agency worker or, where there is no comparable employee working or based at that establishment who satisfies the requirements of sub-paragraph (a), works or is based at a different establishment and satisfies those requirements.

(5) An employee is not a comparable employee if that employee's employment has ceased.

(6) This regulation is subject to regulation 10.

NOTES

Commencement: 1 October 2011.

Conciliation: employment tribunal proceedings and claims which could be the subject of employment tribunal proceedings under this regulation are proceedings to which the Employment Tribunals Act 1996, s 18 applies; see s 18(1)(x) of that Act at **[1.706]**.

[2.1282]

6 Relevant terms and conditions

(1) In regulation 5(2) and (3) "relevant terms and conditions" means terms and conditions relating to—

(a) pay;
(b) the duration of working time;
(c) night work;
(d) rest periods;
(e) rest breaks; and
(f) annual leave.

(2) For the purposes of paragraph (1)(a), "pay" means any sums payable to a worker of the hirer in connection with the worker's employment, including any fee, bonus, commission, holiday pay or other emolument referable to the employment, whether payable under contract or otherwise, but excluding any payments or rewards within paragraph (3).

(3) Those payments or rewards are—

(a) any payment by way of occupational sick pay;
(b) any payment by way of a pension, allowance or gratuity in connection with the worker's retirement or as compensation for loss of office;
(c) any payment in respect of maternity, paternity or adoption leave;
(d) any payment referable to the worker's redundancy;
(e) any payment or reward made pursuant to a financial participation scheme;

(f) any bonus, incentive payment or reward which is not directly attributable to the amount or quality of the work done by a worker, and which is given to a worker for a reason other than the amount or quality of work done such as to encourage the worker's loyalty or to reward the worker's long-term service;
(g) any payment for time off under Part 6 of the 1996 Act or section 169 of the Trade Union and Labour Relations (Consolidation) Act 1992 (payment for time off for carrying out trade union duties etc);
(h) a guarantee payment under section 28 of the 1996 Act;
(i) any payment by way of an advance under an agreement for a loan or by way of an advance of pay (but without prejudice to the application of section 13 of the 1996 Act to any deduction made from the worker's wages in respect of any such advance);
(j) any payment in respect of expenses incurred by the worker in carrying out the employment; and
(k) any payment to the worker otherwise than in that person's capacity as a worker.

(4) For the purposes of paragraphs (2) and (3) any monetary value attaching to any payment or benefit in kind furnished to a worker by the hirer shall not be treated as pay of the worker except any voucher or stamp which is—
(a) of fixed value expressed in monetary terms, and
(b) capable of being exchanged (whether on its own or together with other vouchers, stamps or documents, and whether immediately or only after a time) for money, goods or services (or for any combination of two or more of those things).

(5) In this regulation—
"financial participation scheme" means any scheme that offers workers of the hirer—
(a) a distribution of shares or options, or
(b) a share of profits in cash or in shares;
"night time", in relation to an individual, means—
(a) a period—
(i) the duration of which is not less than seven hours, and
(ii) which includes the period between midnight and 5 am,
which is determined for the purposes of these Regulations by a working time agreement, or
(b) in default of such a determination, the period between 11 pm and 6 am;
"night work" means work during night time;
"relevant training" means work experience provided pursuant to a training course or programme, training for employment, or both, other than work experience or training—
(a) the immediate provider of which is an educational institution or a person whose main business is the provision of training, and
(b) which is provided on a course run by that institution or person;
"rest period", in relation to an individual, means a period which is not working time, other than a rest break or leave to which that individual is entitled either under the Working Time Regulations 1998 or under the contract between that individual and the employer of that individual;
"working time", in relation to an individual means—
(a) any period during which that individual is working, at the disposal of the employer of that individual and carrying out the activity or duties of that individual,
(b) any period during which that individual is receiving relevant training, and
(c) any additional period which is to be treated as working time for the purposes of the Working Time Regulations 1998 under a working time agreement; and
"working time agreement", in relation to an individual, means a workforce agreement within the meaning of regulation 2(1) of the Working Time Regulations 1998, which applies to the individual any provision of—
(a) a collective agreement which forms part of a contract between that individual and the employer of that individual, or
(b) any other agreement in writing which is legally enforceable as between the individual and the employer of that individual.

NOTES

Commencement: 1 October 2011.

[2.1283]

7 Qualifying period

(1) Regulation 5 does not apply unless an agency worker has completed the qualifying period.

(2) To complete the qualifying period the agency worker must work in the same role with the same hirer for 12 continuous calendar weeks, during one or more assignments.

(3) For the purposes of this regulation and regulations 8 and 9, the agency worker works in "the same role" unless—

(a) the agency worker has started a new role with the same hirer, whether supplied by the same or by a different temporary work agency;
(b) the work or duties that make up the whole or the main part of that new role are substantively different from the work or duties that made up the whole or the main part of the previous role; and
(c) the temporary work agency has informed the agency worker in writing of the type of work the agency worker will be required to do in the new role.

(4) For the purposes of this regulation and regulation 10, any week during the whole or part of which an agency worker works during an assignment is counted as a calendar week.

(5) For the purposes of this regulation and regulations 8 and 9, when calculating whether any weeks completed with a particular hirer are continuous, where—
(a) the agency worker has started working during an assignment, and there is a break, either between assignments or during an assignment, when the agency worker is not working,
(b) paragraph (8) applies to that break, and
(c) the agency worker returns to work in the same role with the same hirer,
any continuous weeks during which the agency worker worked for that hirer before the break shall be carried forward and treated as continuous with any weeks during which the agency worker works for that hirer after the break.

(6) For the purposes of this regulation and regulation 8, when calculating the number of weeks during which the agency worker has worked, where the agency worker has—
(a) started working in a role during an assignment, and
(b) is unable to continue working for a reason described in paragraph (8)(c) or (8)(d)(i), (ii) or (iii),
for the period that is covered by one or more such reasons, that agency worker shall be deemed to be working in that role with the hirer, for the original intended duration, or likely duration of the assignment, whichever is the longer.

(7) Where—
(a) an assignment ends on grounds which are maternity grounds within the meaning of section 68A of the 1996 Act, and
(b) the agency worker is deemed to be working in that role in accordance with paragraph (6),
the fact that an agency worker is actually working in another role, whether for the same or a different hirer during the period mentioned in paragraph (6) or any part of that period, does not affect the operation of that paragraph.

(8) This paragraph applies where there is a break between assignments, or during an assignment, when the agency worker is not working, and the break is—
(a) for any reason and the break is not more than six calendar weeks;
(b) wholly due to the fact that the agency worker is incapable of working in consequence of sickness or injury, and the requirements of paragraph (9) are satisfied;
(c) related to pregnancy, childbirth or maternity and is at a time in a protected period;
(d) wholly for the purpose of taking time off or leave, whether statutory or contractual, to which the agency worker is otherwise entitled which is—
    (i) ordinary, compulsory or additional maternity leave;
    (ii) ordinary or additional adoption leave;
    (iii) paternity leave;
    (iv) time off or other leave not listed in sub-paragraph (d)(i), (ii) or (iii); or
    (v) for more than one of the reasons listed in sub-paragraph (d)(i) to (iv);
(e) wholly due to the fact that the agency worker is required to attend at any place in pursuance of being summoned for service as a juror under the Juries Act 1974, the Coroners Act 1988, the Court of Session Act 1988 or the Criminal Procedure (Scotland) Act 1995, and the break is 28 calendar weeks or less;
(f) wholly due to a temporary cessation in the hirer's requirement for any worker to be present at the establishment and work in a particular role, for a pre-determined period of time according to the established custom and practices of the hirer; or
(g) wholly due to a strike, lock-out or other industrial action at the hirer's establishment; or
(h) wholly due to more than one of the reasons listed in sub-paragraphs (b), (c), (d), (e), (f) or (g).

(9) Paragraph (8)(b) only applies where—
(a) the break is 28 calendar weeks or less;
(b) paragraph (8)(c) does not apply; and
(c) if required to do so by the temporary work agency, the agency worker has provided such written medical evidence as may reasonably be required.

(10) For the purposes of paragraph (8)(c), a protected period begins at the start of the pregnancy, and the protected period associated with any particular pregnancy ends at the end of the 26 weeks beginning with childbirth or, if earlier, when the agency worker returns to work.

(11) For the purposes of paragraph (10) "childbirth" means the birth of a living child or the birth of a child whether living or dead after 24 weeks of pregnancy.

(12) Time spent by an agency worker working during an assignment before 1st October 2011 does not count for the purposes of this regulation.

NOTES

Commencement: 1 October 2011.

[2.1284]

8 Completion of the qualifying period and continuation of the regulation 5 rights

Where an agency worker has completed the qualifying period with a particular hirer, the rights conferred by regulation 5 shall apply and shall continue to apply to that agency worker in relation to that particular hirer unless—

(a) that agency worker is no longer working in the same role, within the meaning of regulation 7(3), with that hirer; or

(b) there is a break between assignments, or during an assignment, when the agency worker is not working, to which regulation 7(8) does not apply.

NOTES

Commencement: 1 October 2011.

[2.1285]

9 Structure of assignments

(1) Notwithstanding paragraphs (1) and (2) of regulation 7, and regulation 8, if paragraphs (3) and (4) apply an agency worker shall be treated as having completed the qualifying period from the time at which the agency worker would have completed the qualifying period but for the structure of the assignment or assignments mentioned in paragraph (3).

(2) Notwithstanding paragraphs (1) and (2) of regulation 7, and regulation 8, if paragraphs (3) and (4) apply an agency worker who has completed the qualifying period and—

(a) is no longer entitled to the rights conferred by regulation 5, but

(b) would be so entitled but for the structure of the assignment or assignments mentioned in paragraph (3),

shall be treated as continuing to be entitled to those rights from the time at which the agency worker completed that period.

(3) This paragraph applies when an agency worker has—

(a) completed two or more assignments with a hirer (H),

(b) completed at least one assignment with H and one or more earlier assignments with hirers connected to H, or

(c) worked in more than two roles during an assignment with H, and on at least two occasions has worked in a role that was not the "same role" as the previous role within the meaning of regulation 7(3).

(4) This paragraph applies where—

(a) the most likely explanation for the structure of the assignment, or assignments, mentioned in paragraph (3) is that H, or the temporary work agency supplying the agency worker to H, or, where applicable, H and one or more hirers connected to H, intended to prevent the agency worker from being entitled to, or from continuing to be entitled to, the rights conferred by regulation 5; and

(b) the agency worker would be entitled to, or would continue to be entitled to, the rights conferred by regulation 5 in relation to H, but for that structure.

(5) The following matters in particular shall be taken into account in determining whether the structure of the assignment or assignments mentioned in paragraph (3) shows that the most likely explanation for it is that mentioned in paragraph (4)(a)—

(a) the length of the assignments;

(b) the number of assignments with H and, where applicable, hirers connected to H;

(c) the number of times the agency worker has worked in a new role with H and, where applicable, hirers connected to H, and that new role is not the "same role" within the meaning of regulation 7(3);

(d) the number of times the agency worker has returned to work in the same role within the meaning of regulation 7(3) with H and, where applicable, hirers connected to H;

(e) the period of any break between assignments with H and, where applicable, hirers connected to H.

(6) For the purposes of this regulation hirers are connected to a hirer if one hirer (directly or indirectly) has control of the other hirer or a third person (directly or indirectly) has control of both hirers.

NOTES

Commencement: 1 October 2011.

[2.1286]
10 Permanent contracts providing for pay between assignments

(1) To the extent to which it relates to pay, regulation 5 does not have effect in relation to an agency worker who has a permanent contract of employment with a temporary work agency if—

(a) the contract of employment was entered into before the beginning of the first assignment under that contract and includes terms and conditions in writing relating to—
   (i) the minimum scale or rate of remuneration or the method of calculating remuneration,
   (ii) the location or locations where the agency worker may be expected to work,
   (iii) the expected hours of work during any assignment,
   (iv) the maximum number of hours of work that the agency worker may be required to work each week during any assignment,
   (v) the minimum hours of work per week that may be offered to the agency worker during any assignment provided that it is a minimum of at least one hour, and
   (vi) the nature of the work that the agency worker may expect to be offered including any relevant requirements relating to qualifications or experience;

(b) the contract of employment contains a statement that the effect of entering into it is that the employee does not, during the currency of the contract, have any entitlement to the rights conferred by regulation 5 insofar as they relate to pay;

(c) during any period under the contract [after the end of the first assignment under that contract] in which the agency worker is not working temporarily for and under the supervision and direction of a hirer but is available to do so—
   (i) the temporary work agency takes reasonable steps to seek suitable work for the agency worker,
   (ii) if suitable work is available, the temporary work agency offers the agency worker to be proposed to a hirer who is offering such work, and
   (iii) the temporary work agency pays the agency worker a minimum amount of remuneration in respect of that period ("the minimum amount"); and

(d) the temporary work agency does not terminate the contract of employment until it has complied with its obligations in sub-paragraph (c) for an aggregate of not less than four calendar weeks during the contract.

(2) For work to be suitable for the purposes of paragraph (1)(c) the nature of the work, and the terms and conditions applicable to the agency worker whilst performing the work, must not differ from the nature of the work and the terms and conditions included in the contract of employment under paragraph (1)(a).

NOTES

Commencement: 1 October 2011.

Para (1): words in square brackets in sub-para (c) inserted by the Agency Workers (Amendment) Regulations 2011, SI 2011/1941, reg 2(1), (3), as from 1 September 2011.

[2.1287]
11 Calculating the minimum amount of pay

(1) Subject to paragraph (3), the minimum amount to be paid to the agency worker during a pay reference period falling within a period to which regulation 10(1)(c) applies shall not be less than 50% of the pay paid to the agency worker in the relevant pay reference period.

(2) For the purposes of paragraph (1), the relevant pay reference period shall be the pay reference period in which the agency worker received the highest level of pay which fell—

(a) within the 12 weeks immediately preceding the end of the previous assignment, where the assignment lasted for longer than 12 weeks, or

(b) during the assignment, where the assignment lasted for 12 or fewer weeks.

[(3) The minimum amount shall be not less than the amount that the agency worker would have been entitled to for the hours worked in the relevant pay reference period if the provisions of the National Minimum Wage Regulations 1999 . . . applied.]

(4) For the purposes of calculating the minimum amount as set out in paragraph (1), only payments in respect of basic pay whether by way of annual salary, payments for actual time worked or by reference to output or otherwise shall be taken into account.

(5) For the purposes of this regulation, "pay reference period" is a month or, in the case of a worker who is paid wages by reference to a period shorter than a month, that period.

NOTES

Commencement: 1 October 2011.

Para (3): substituted by the National Minimum Wage Regulations 1999 (Amendment) Regulations 2010, SI 2010/1901, reg 8, as from 1 October 2010; words omitted revoked by the National Minimum Wage (Amendment) Regulations 2012, SI 2012/2397, reg 3, as from 1 October 2012.

[2.1288]

12 Rights of agency workers in relation to access to collective facilities and amenities

(1) An agency worker has during an assignment the right to be treated no less favourably than a comparable worker in relation to the collective facilities and amenities provided by the hirer.

(2) The rights conferred by paragraph (1) apply only if the less favourable treatment is not justified on objective grounds.

(3) "Collective facilities and amenities" includes, in particular—

- (a) canteen or other similar facilities;
- (b) child care facilities; and
- (c) transport services.

(4) For the purposes of paragraph (1) an individual is a comparable worker in relation to an agency worker if at the time when the breach of paragraph (1) is alleged to take place—

- (a) both that individual and the agency worker are—
  - (i) working for and under the supervision and direction of the hirer, and
  - (ii) engaged in the same or broadly similar work having regard, where relevant, to whether they have a similar level of qualification and skills;
- (b) that individual works or is based at the same establishment as the agency worker or, where there is no comparable worker working or based at that establishment who satisfies the requirements of sub-paragraph (a), works or is based at a different establishment and satisfies those requirements; and
- (c) that individual is an employee of the hirer or, where there is no employee satisfying the requirements of sub-paragraphs (a) and (b), is a worker of the hirer and satisfies those requirements.

Part 2 Statutory Instruments

NOTES

Commencement: 1 October 2011.

Conciliation: employment tribunal proceedings and claims which could be the subject of employment tribunal proceedings under this regulation are proceedings to which the Employment Tribunals Act 1996, s 18 applies; see s 18(1)(x) of that Act at **[1.706]**.

[2.1289]

13 Rights of agency workers in relation to access to employment

(1) An agency worker has during an assignment the right to be informed by the hirer of any relevant vacant posts with the hirer, to give that agency worker the same opportunity as a comparable worker to find permanent employment with the hirer.

(2) For the purposes of paragraph (1) an individual is a comparable worker in relation to an agency worker if at the time when the breach of paragraph (1) is alleged to take place—

- (a) both that individual and the agency worker are—
  - (i) working for and under the supervision and direction of the hirer, and
  - (ii) engaged in the same or broadly similar work having regard, where relevant, to whether they have a similar level of qualification and skills;
- (b) that individual works or is based at the same establishment as the agency worker; and
- (c) that individual is an employee of the hirer or, where there is no employee satisfying the requirements of sub-paragraphs (a) and (b), is a worker of the hirer and satisfies those requirements.

(3) For the purposes of paragraph (1), an individual is not a comparable worker if that individual's employment with the hirer has ceased.

(4) For the purposes of paragraph (1) the hirer may inform the agency worker by a general announcement in a suitable place in the hirer's establishment.

NOTES

Commencement: 1 October 2011.

Conciliation: employment tribunal proceedings and claims which could be the subject of employment tribunal proceedings under this regulation are proceedings to which the Employment Tribunals Act 1996, s 18 applies; see s 18(1)(x) of that Act at **[1.706]**.

PART 3
LIABILITY, PROTECTIONS AND REMEDIES

[2.1290]

14 Liability of temporary work agency and hirer

(1) [Subject to paragraph (3),] a temporary work agency shall be liable for any breach of regulation 5, to the extent that it is responsible for that breach.

(2) . . . The hirer shall be liable for any breach of regulation 5, to the extent that it is responsible for that breach.

(3) A temporary work agency shall not be liable for a breach of regulation 5 where it is established that the temporary work agency—

[(a) obtained, or has taken reasonable steps to obtain, relevant information from the hirer—
  (i) about the basic working and employment conditions in force in the hirer;
  (ii) if needed to assess compliance with regulation 5, about the relevant terms and conditions under which an employee of the hirer is working where—
    (aa) that employee is considered to be a comparable employee in relation to that agency worker for the purposes of regulation 5(4), and
    (bb) those terms and conditions are ordinarily included in the contract of such a comparable employee;

  and
  (iii) which explains the basis on which it is considered that the employee referred to in sub-paragraph (ii)(aa) is a comparable employee;]

(b) where it has received such information, has acted reasonably in determining what the agency worker's basic working and employment conditions should be at the end of the qualifying period and during the period after that until, in accordance with regulation 8, the agency worker ceases to be entitled to the rights conferred by regulation 5; and

(c) ensured that where it has responsibility for applying those basic working and employment conditions to the agency worker, that agency worker has been treated in accordance with the determination described in sub-paragraph (b),

and to the extent that the temporary work agency is not liable under this provision, the hirer shall be liable.

(4) . . .

(5) Where more than one temporary work agency is a party to the proceedings, when deciding whether or not each temporary work agency is responsible in full or in part, the employment tribunal shall have regard to the extent to which each agency was responsible for the determination, or application, of any of the agency worker's basic working and employment conditions.

(6) The hirer shall be liable for any breach of regulation 12 or 13.

(7) In relation to the rights conferred by regulation 17—

(a) a temporary work agency shall be liable for any act, or any deliberate failure to act, of that temporary work agency; and

(b) the hirer shall be liable for any act, or any deliberate failure to act, of the hirer.

NOTES

Commencement: 1 October 2011.

The words in square brackets in para (1) were inserted, the words omitted from para (2) were revoked, para (3)(a) was substituted, and para (4) was revoked, by the Agency Workers (Amendment) Regulations 2011, SI 2011/1941, reg 2(1), (4), as from 1 September 2011.

[2.1291]

15 Restrictions on contracting out

Section 203 of the 1996 Act (restrictions on contracting out) shall apply in relation to these Regulations as if they were contained in that Act.

NOTES

Commencement: 1 October 2011.

[2.1292]

16 Right to receive information

(1) An agency worker who considers that the hirer or a temporary work agency may have treated that agency worker in a manner which infringes a right conferred by regulation 5, may make a written request to the temporary work agency for a written statement containing information relating to the treatment in question.

(2) A temporary work agency that receives such a request from an agency worker shall, within 28 days of receiving it, provide the agency worker with a written statement setting out—

(a) relevant information relating to the basic working and employment conditions of the workers of the hirer,

(b) the factors the temporary work agency considered when determining the basic working and employment conditions which applied to the agency worker at the time when the breach of regulation 5 is alleged to have taken place, and

(c) where the temporary work agency seeks to rely on regulation 5(3), relevant information which—
  (i) explains the basis on which it is considered that an individual is a comparable employee, and
  (ii) describes the relevant terms and conditions, which apply to that employee.

(3) If an agency worker has made a request under paragraph (1) and has not been provided with such a statement within 30 days of making that request, the agency worker may make a written request to the hirer for a written statement containing information relating to the relevant basic working and employment conditions of the workers of the hirer.

(4) A hirer that receives a request made in accordance with paragraph (3) shall, within 28 days of receiving it, provide the agency worker with such a statement.

(5) An agency worker who considers that the hirer may have treated that agency worker in a manner which infringes a right conferred by regulation 12 or 13, may make a written request to the hirer for a written statement containing information relating to the treatment in question.

(6) A hirer that receives such a request from an agency worker shall, within 28 days of receiving it, provide the agency worker with a written statement setting out—

(a) all relevant information relating to the rights of a comparable worker in relation to the rights mentioned in regulation 12 or, as the case may be, regulation 13, and

(b) the particulars of the reasons for the treatment of the agency worker in respect of the right conferred by regulation 12 or, as the case may be, regulation 13.

(7) Paragraphs (1) and (3) apply only to an agency worker who at the time that worker makes such a request is entitled to the right conferred by regulation 5.

(8) Information provided under this regulation, whether in the form of a written statement or otherwise, is admissible as evidence in any proceedings under these Regulations.

(9) If it appears to the tribunal in any proceedings under these Regulations—

(a) that a temporary work agency or the hirer (as the case may be) deliberately, and without reasonable excuse, failed to provide information, whether in the form of a written statement or otherwise, or

(b) that any written statement supplied is evasive or equivocal,

it may draw any inference which it considers it just and equitable to draw, including an inference that that temporary work agency or hirer (as the case may be) has infringed the right in question.

NOTES

Commencement: 1 October 2011.

[2.1293]

17 Unfair dismissal and the right not to be subjected to detriment

(1) An agency worker who is an employee and is dismissed shall be regarded as unfairly dismissed for the purposes of Part 10 of the 1996 Act if the reason (or, if more than one, the principal reason) for the dismissal is a reason specified in paragraph (3).

(2) An agency worker has the right not to be subjected to any detriment by, or as a result of, any act, or any deliberate failure to act, of a temporary work agency or the hirer, done on a ground specified in paragraph (3).

(3) The reasons or, as the case may be, grounds are—

(a) that the agency worker—

(i) brought proceedings under these Regulations;

(ii) gave evidence or information in connection with such proceedings brought by any agency worker;

(iii) made a request under regulation 16 for a written statement;

(iv) otherwise did anything under these Regulations in relation to a temporary work agency, hirer, or any other person;

(v) alleged that a temporary work agency or hirer has breached these Regulations;

(vi) refused (or proposed to refuse) to forgo a right conferred by these Regulations; or

(b) that the hirer or a temporary work agency believes or suspects that the agency worker has done or intends to do any of the things mentioned in sub-paragraph (a).

(4) Where the reason or principal reason for subjection to any act or deliberate failure to act is that mentioned in paragraph (3)(a)(v), or paragraph 3(b) so far as it relates to paragraph (3)(a)(v), neither paragraph (1) nor paragraph (2) applies if the allegation made by the agency worker is false and not made in good faith.

(5) Paragraph (2) does not apply where the detriment in question amounts to a dismissal of an employee within the meaning of Part 10 of the 1996 Act.

NOTES

Commencement: 1 October 2011.

Conciliation: employment tribunal proceedings and claims which could be the subject of employment tribunal proceedings under para (2) are proceedings to which the Employment Tribunals Act 1996, s 18 applies; see s 18(1)(x) of that Act at **[1.706]**.

[2.1294]

18 Complaints to employment tribunals etc

(1) In this regulation "respondent" includes the hirer and any temporary work agency.

(2) Subject to regulation 17(5), an agency worker may present a complaint to an employment tribunal that a temporary work agency or the hirer has infringed a right conferred on the agency worker by regulation 5, 12, 13 or 17 (2).

(3) An agency worker may present a complaint to an employment tribunal that a temporary work agency has—

- (a) breached a term of the contract of employment described in regulation 10(1)(a); or
- (b) breached a duty under regulation 10(1)(b), (c) or (d).

(4) Subject to paragraph (5), an employment tribunal shall not consider a complaint under this regulation unless it is presented before the end of the period of three months beginning—

- (a) in the case of an alleged infringement of a right conferred by regulation 5, 12 or 17(2) or a breach of a term of the contract described in regulation 10(1)(a) or of a duty under regulation 10(1)(b), (c) or (d), with the date of the infringement, detriment or breach to which the complaint relates or, where an act or failure to act is part of a series of similar acts or failures comprising the infringement, detriment or breach, the last of them;
- (b) in the case of an alleged infringement of the right conferred by regulation 13, with the date, or if more than one the last date, on which other individuals, whether or not employed by the hirer, were informed of the vacancy.

(5) A tribunal may consider any such complaint which is out of time if, in all the circumstances of the case, it considers that it is just and equitable to do so.

(6) For the purposes of calculating the date of the infringement, detriment or breach, under paragraph (4)(a)—

- (a) where a term in a contract infringes a right conferred by regulation 5, 12 or 17(2), or breaches regulation 10(1), that infringement or breach shall be treated, subject to sub-paragraph (b), as taking place on each day of the period during which the term infringes that right or breaches that duty;
- (b) a deliberate failure to act that is contrary to regulation 5, 12 or 17(2) or 10(1) shall be treated as done when it was decided on.

(7) In the absence of evidence establishing the contrary, a person (P) shall be taken for the purposes of paragraph (6)(b) to decide not to act—

- (a) when P does an act inconsistent with doing the failed act; or
- (b) if P has done no such inconsistent act, when the period expires within which P might reasonably have been expected to have done the failed act if it was to be done.

(8) Where an employment tribunal finds that a complaint presented to it under this regulation is well founded, it shall take such of the following steps as it considers just and equitable—

- (a) making a declaration as to the rights of the complainant in relation to the matters to which the complaint relates;
- (b) ordering the respondent to pay compensation to the complainant;
- (c) recommending that the respondent take, within a specified period, action appearing to the tribunal to be reasonable, in all the circumstances of the case, for the purpose of obviating or reducing the adverse effect on the complainant of any matter to which the complaint relates.

(9) Where a tribunal orders compensation under paragraph (8)(b), and there is more than one respondent, the amount of compensation payable by each or any respondent shall be such as may be found by the tribunal to be just and equitable having regard to the extent of each respondent's responsibility for the infringement to which the complaint relates.

(10) Subject to paragraphs (12) and (13), where a tribunal orders compensation under paragraph (8)(b), the amount of the compensation awarded shall be such as the tribunal considers just and equitable in all the circumstances having regard to—

- (a) the infringement or breach to which the complaint relates; and
- (b) any loss which is attributable to the infringement.

(11) The loss shall be taken to include—

- (a) any expenses reasonably incurred by the complainant in consequence of the infringement or breach; and
- (b) loss of any benefit which the complainant might reasonably be expected to have had but for the infringement or breach.

(12) Subject to paragraph (13), where a tribunal orders compensation under paragraph (8)(b), any compensation which relates to an infringement or breach of the rights—

- (a) conferred by regulation 5 or 10; or
- (b) conferred by regulation 17(2) to the extent that the infringement or breach relates to regulation 5 or 10,

shall not be less than two weeks' pay, calculated in accordance with regulation 19.

(13) Paragraph (12) does not apply where the tribunal considers that in all the circumstances of the case, taking into account the conduct of the claimant and respondent, two weeks' pay is not a just and equitable amount of compensation, and the amount shall be reduced as the tribunal consider appropriate.

(14) Where a tribunal finds that regulation 9(4) applies and orders compensation under paragraph (8)(b), the tribunal may make an additional award of compensation under paragraph 8(b), which shall not be more than £5,000, and where there is more than one respondent the proportion of any additional compensation awarded that is payable by each of them shall be such as the tribunal considers just and equitable having regard to the extent to which it considers each to have been responsible for the fact that regulation 9(4)(a) applies.

[(14A) In relation to an infringement or breach for which a tribunal orders a respondent to pay compensation under paragraph (8)(b), the tribunal may order the respondent also to pay a penalty under section 12A of the Employment Tribunals Act 1996 only if the tribunal decides not to exercise the power under paragraph (14) to make an additional award of compensation against the respondent.]

(15) Compensation in respect of treating an agency worker in a manner which infringes the right conferred by regulation 5, 12 or 13 or breaches regulation 10(1)(b), (c) or (d), or breaches a term of the contract described in regulation 10(1)(a), shall not include compensation for injury to feelings.

(16) In ascertaining the loss the tribunal shall apply the same rule concerning the duty of a person to mitigate loss as applies to damages recoverable under the common law of England and Wales or (as the case may be) the law of Scotland.

(17) Where the tribunal finds that the act, or failure to act, to which the complaint relates was to any extent caused or contributed to by action of the complainant, it shall reduce the amount of the compensation by such proportion as it considers just and equitable having regard to that finding.

(18) If a temporary work agency or the hirer fails, without reasonable justification, to comply with a recommendation made by an employment tribunal under paragraph (8)(c) the tribunal may, if it thinks it just and equitable to do so—

- (a) increase the amount of compensation required to be paid to the complainant in respect of the complaint, where an order was made under paragraph (8)(b); or
- (b) make an order under paragraph (8)(b).

NOTES

Commencement: 1 October 2011.

Para (14A): inserted by the Enterprise and Regulatory Reform Act 2013, s 16(2), Sch 3, para 6, as from a day to be appointed.

[2.1295]

19 Calculating a week's pay

(1) For the purposes of regulation 18(12)—

- (a) a week's pay shall be the higher of—
  - (i) the average weekly pay received by the agency worker, in relation to the assignment to which the claim relates, in the relevant period; and
  - (ii) the average weekly pay the agency worker should have been receiving by virtue of regulation 5, in relation to the assignment to which the claim relates, in the relevant period; and
- (b) for the purposes of this paragraph, only payments in respect of basic pay whether by way of annual salary, payments for actual time worked or by reference to output or otherwise shall be taken into account.

(2) The relevant period is—

- (a) where the assignment has ended on or before the date the complaint was presented to the tribunal under regulation 18(2), the four week period (or in a case where the assignment was shorter than four weeks, that period) ending with the last day of the assignment to which the claim relates; or
- (b) where the assignment has not so ended the four week period (or in the case where that assignment was shorter than four weeks, that period) ending with the date of the complaint.

NOTES

Commencement: 1 October 2011.

[2.1296]

20 Liability of employers and principals

(1) Anything done by a person in the course of employment shall be treated for the purposes of these Regulations as also done by their employer, whether or not it was done with that employer's knowledge or approval.

(2) Anything done by a person as agent for the employer with the authority of the employer shall be treated for the purposes of these Regulations as also done by the employer.

(3) In proceedings under these Regulations against any person in respect of an act alleged to have been done by an employee of that person, it shall be a defence for that person to prove that he or she took such steps as were reasonably practicable to prevent the employee from—

(a) doing that act; or

(b) doing, in the course of his or her employment, acts of that description.

NOTES

Commencement: 1 October 2011.

PART 4
SPECIAL CLASSES OF PERSON

[2.1297]

21 Crown employment and service as a member of the armed forces

(1) These Regulations have effect in relation to—

(a) Crown employment,

(b) service as a member of the armed forces of the Crown,

(c) persons in Crown employment, and

(d) persons in service as a member of the armed forces of the Crown,

as they have effect in relation to other employment and other employees.

(2) In paragraph (1) "Crown employment" means employment under or for the purposes of a government department or any officer or body exercising on behalf of the Crown functions conferred by a statutory provision but subject to paragraph (4).

(3) For the purposes of the application of the provisions of these Regulations in relation to Crown employment and service as a member of the armed forces of the Crown in accordance with paragraph (1)—

(a) references to an employee shall be construed as references to a person in Crown employment or in service as a member of the armed forces of the Crown to whom the definition of employee is appropriate; and

(b) references to a contract in relation to an employee shall be construed as references to the terms of employment of a person in Crown employment or in service as a member of the armed forces of the Crown to whom the definition of employee is appropriate.

(4) Crown employment—

(a) does not include service as a member of the armed forces of the Crown, but

(b) does include employment by an association established for the purposes of Part 11 of the Reserve Forces Act 1996.

NOTES

Commencement: 1 October 2011.

[2.1298]

22 House of Lords staff

(1) These Regulations have effect in relation to employment as a relevant member of the House of Lords staff as they have effect in relation to other employment.

(2) In this regulation "relevant member of the House of Lords staff" means any person who is employed under a contract with the Corporate Officer of the House of Lords by virtue of which he is a worker.

NOTES

Commencement: 1 October 2011.

[2.1299]

23 House of Commons staff

(1) These Regulations have effect in relation to employment as a relevant member of the House of Commons staff as they have effect in relation to other employment.

(2) In this regulation "relevant member of the House of Commons staff" means any person—

(a) who was appointed by the House of Commons Commission; or

(b) who is a member of the Speaker's personal staff.

NOTES

Commencement: 1 October 2011.

[2.1300]

24 Police service

(1) For the purposes of these Regulations, the holding, otherwise than under a contract of employment, of the office of constable or an appointment as a police cadet shall be treated as employment, under a contract of employment, by the relevant officer.

(2) For the purposes of these Regulations, any constable or other person who has been seconded to SOCA to serve as a member of its staff shall be treated as employed by SOCA, in respect of actions taken by, or on behalf of, SOCA.

(3) For the purposes of regulation 20—

(a) the secondment of any constable or other person to SOCA to serve as a member of its staff shall be treated as employment by SOCA (and not as being employment by any other person); and

(b) anything done by a person so seconded in the performance, or purported performance, of his functions shall be treated as done in the course of that employment.

(4) In this regulation "the relevant officer" means—

(a) in relation to a member of the police force or a special constable or police cadet appointed for a police area, the chief officer of police (or, in Scotland, the chief constable); and

(b) in relation to any other person holding the office of constable or an appointment as a police cadet, the person who has the direction and control of the body of constables or cadets in question.

(5) In this regulation "SOCA" means the Serious Organised Crime Agency.

NOTES

Commencement: 1 October 2011.

25 *(Introduces Sch 2 (Consequential Amendments).)*

SCHEDULES 1 AND 2

(Sch 1 (Provisions Extending to England and Wales, Scotland and Northern Ireland) outside the scope of this work; Sch 2 contains consequential amendments which, in so far as relevant to this Handbook, have been incorporated at the appropriate place. Note that Sch 2, para 16 (which amends the Employment Rights Act 1996, s 108) was amended by the Agency Workers (Amendment) Regulations 2011, SI 2011/1941, reg 2(1), (5), as from 1 September 2011 to correct a drafting error in the original paragraph – see that section ante.)

ADDITIONAL STATUTORY PATERNITY PAY (NATIONAL HEALTH SERVICE EMPLOYEES) REGULATIONS 2010

(SI 2010/152)

NOTES

Made: 28 January 2010.
Authority: Social Security Contributions and Benefits Act 1992, s 171ZJ(9), (10).
Commencement: 6 April 2010.

ARRANGEMENT OF REGULATIONS

[2.1301]

1 Citation, commencement and interpretation

(1) These Regulations may be cited as the Additional Statutory Paternity Pay (National Health Service Employees) Regulations 2010 and come into force on 6th April 2010.

(2) In these Regulations—

"the 2006 Act" means the National Health Service Act 2006;

"the 2006 (Wales) Act" means the National Health Service (Wales) Act 2006;

"the Act" means the Social Security Contributions and Benefits Act 1992;

Part 2 Statutory Instruments

"additional statutory paternity pay" means additional statutory paternity pay payable in accordance with the provisions of Part 12ZA of the Act where the conditions specified in section 171ZEA(2) or 171ZEB(2) are satisfied;

"additional statutory paternity pay period" means the period, determined in accordance with section 171ZEE of the Act and with regulations made under that section, as the period in respect of which additional statutory paternity pay is payable;

"Local Health Board" means a Local Health Board established under section 11 of the 2006 (Wales) Act;

"Primary Care Trust" means a Primary Care Trust continuing in existence or established under section 18 of the 2006 Act;

"Special Health Authority" means, in relation to England, a Special Health Authority established under section 28 of the 2006 Act and, in relation to Wales, a Special Health Authority established under section 22 of the 2006 (Wales) Act; and

"Strategic Health Authority" means a Strategic Health Authority continuing in existence or established under section 13 of the 2006 Act.

(3) References in these Regulations to Part 12ZA of the Act are references to sections 171ZEA to 171ZEE and, in so far as they concern additional statutory paternity pay, to sections 171ZF to 171ZJ of the Act.

NOTES

Commencement: 6 April 2010.

[2.1302]

2 Treatment of more than one contract of employment as one contract

Where—

(a) in consequence of the establishment of one or more National Health Service trusts under section 25 of the 2006 Act or section 18 of the 2006 (Wales) Act, a person's contract of employment is treated by a scheme under paragraph 8 of Schedule 4 to the 2006 Act or paragraph 8 of Schedule 3 to the 2006 (Wales) Act as divided so as to constitute two or more contracts, or

(b) an order under paragraph 26(1) of Schedule 3 to the 2006 Act provides that a person's contract is so divided, that person may elect for all those contracts to be treated as one contract for the purposes of Part 12ZA of the Act.

NOTES

Commencement: 6 April 2010.

[2.1303]

3 Notification of election

A person who makes an election under regulation 2 above shall give written notification of that election to each of their employers under the two or more contracts of employment mentioned in that regulation at least 28 days before the beginning of the additional statutory paternity pay period or, if in the particular circumstances that is not practicable, as soon as is reasonably practicable.

NOTES

Commencement: 6 April 2010.

[2.1304]

4 Provision of information

A person who makes an election under regulation 2 above shall, within 28 days of giving notification of that election or, if in the particular circumstances that is not practicable, as soon as is reasonably practicable thereafter, provide each of their employers under the two or more contracts of employment mentioned in that regulation with the following information—

(a) the name and address of each of those employers;

(b) the date their employment with each of those employers commenced; and

(c) details of their normal weekly earnings during the relevant period from each employer, and for this purpose the expressions "normal weekly earnings" and "relevant period" have the same meanings as they have for the purposes of Part 12ZA of the Act.

NOTES

Commencement: 6 April 2010.

[2.1305]

5 Treatment of two or more employers as one

The employer to be regarded for the purposes of additional statutory paternity pay as the employer under the one contract where two or more contracts of employment are treated as one in accordance with regulation 2 shall be—

(a) in the case of a person whose contract of employment is treated by a scheme under paragraph 8 of Schedule 4 to the 2006 Act or paragraph 8 of Schedule 3 to the 2006 (Wales) Act as divided—
   (i) the Special Health Authority, Primary Care Trust or Local Health Board from which the person was transferred, in a case where any one of the contracts is with such a body; or
   (ii) the first NHS trust to which a contract was transferred in a case where none of the contracts is with such a body; or
(b) in the case of a person whose contract of employment is divided as provided by an order under paragraph 26(1) of Schedule 3 to the 2006 Act—
   (i) the Strategic Health Authority, NHS trust or Primary Care Trust from which the person was transferred, in a case where any one of the contracts is with such a body; or
   (ii) the first Primary Care Trust to which a contract was transferred in a case where none of the contracts is with the body from which the person was transferred.

NOTES

Commencement: 6 April 2010.

[2.1306]

6 Time for which an election is to have effect

An election made under regulation 2 shall lapse at the end of the additional statutory paternity pay period.

NOTES

Commencement: 6 April 2010.

ADDITIONAL STATUTORY PATERNITY PAY (BIRTH, ADOPTION AND ADOPTIONS FROM OVERSEAS) (ADMINISTRATION) REGULATIONS 2010

(SI 2010/154)

NOTES

Made: 28 January 2010.

Authority: Employment Act 2002, ss 7, 8, 10, 51(1); Social Security Contributions (Transfer of Functions, etc) Act 1999, ss 8(1)(f), (ga), 25.

Commencement: 6 April 2010.

See *Harvey* J(8).

ARRANGEMENT OF REGULATIONS

[2.1307]

1 Citation and commencement

These Regulations may be cited as the Additional Statutory Paternity Pay (Birth, Adoption and Adoptions from Overseas) (Administration) Regulations 2010 and shall come into force on 6th April 2010.

NOTES

Commencement: 6 April 2010.

[2.1308]
2 Interpretation

(1) In these Regulations—

"the 1992 Act" means the Social Security Contributions and Benefits Act 1992;

"the 1996 Act" means the Employment Rights Act 1996;

"the 2002 Act" means the Employment Act 2002;

"additional statutory paternity pay period" means the period determined in accordance with section 171ZEE(2) of the 1992 Act, or section 171ZEE(2) of the 1992 Act as it applies to adoptions from overseas, as the period in respect of which additional statutory paternity pay is payable to a person;

"additional statutory paternity pay" means any payment under section 171ZEA or section 171ZEB of the 1992 Act, or under section 171ZEB of the 1992 Act as it applies to adoptions from overseas;

"adoption from overseas" means the adoption of a child who enters Great Britain from outside the United Kingdom in connection with or for the purposes of adoption which does not involve placement of the child for adoption under the law of any part of the United Kingdom;

"the Commissioners" means the Commissioners for Her Majesty's Revenue and Customs;

"contributions payments" has the same meaning as in section 7 of the 2002 Act;

"the Contributions Regulations" means the Social Security (Contributions) Regulations 2001;

"income tax month" means the period beginning on the 6th day of any calendar month and ending on the 5th day of the following calendar month;

"income tax quarter" means the period beginning on the 6th day of April and ending on the 5th day of July, the period beginning on the 6th day of July and ending on the 5th day of October, the period beginning on the 6th day of October and ending on the 5th day of January or the period beginning on the 6th day of January and ending on the 5th day of April;

"tax year" means the 12 months beginning with 6th April in any year;

"writing" includes writing delivered by means of electronic communications approved by directions issued by the Commissioners pursuant to regulations under section 132 of the Finance Act 1999.

(2) Any reference in these Regulations to the employees of an employer includes the employer's former employees.

NOTES

Commencement: 6 April 2010.

[2.1309]
3 Funding of employers' liabilities to make payments of additional statutory paternity pay

(1) An employer who has made any payment of additional statutory paternity pay shall be entitled—

(a) to an amount equal to 92% of such payment; or

(b) if the payment qualifies for small employer's relief by virtue of section 7(3) of the 2002 Act—

  (i) to an amount equal to such payment; and

  (ii) to an additional payment equal to the amount to which the employer would have been entitled under section 167(2)(b) of the 1992 Act had the payment been a payment of statutory maternity pay.

(2) The employer shall be entitled in either case (a) or case (b) to apply for advance funding in respect of such payment in accordance with regulation 4, or to deduct it in accordance with regulation 5 from amounts otherwise payable by the employer.

NOTES

Commencement: 6 April 2010.

[2.1310]
4 Application for funding from the Commissioners

(1) If an employer is entitled to a payment determined in accordance with regulation 3 in respect of additional statutory paternity pay which the employer is required to pay to an employee or employees for an income tax month or income tax quarter, and the payment exceeds the aggregate of—

(a) the total amount of tax which the employer is required to pay to the collector of taxes in respect of the deductions from the emoluments of employees in accordance with the Income Tax (Pay as You Earn) Regulations 2003 for the same income tax month or income tax quarter,

(b) the total amount of the deductions made by the employer from the emoluments of employees for the same income tax month or income tax quarter in accordance with regulations under section 22(5) of the Teaching and Higher Education Act 1998 or section 73B of the Education (Scotland) Act 1980 or in accordance with article 3(5) of the Education (Student Support) (Northern Ireland) Order 1998,

(c) the total amount of contributions payments which the employer is required to pay to the collector of taxes in respect of the emoluments of employees (whether by means of deduction or otherwise) in accordance with the Contributions Regulations for the same income tax month or income tax quarter, and

(d) the total amount of payments which the employer is required to pay to the collector of taxes in respect of the deductions made on account of tax from payments to sub-contractors in accordance with section 61 of the Finance Act 2004 for the same income tax month or income tax quarter,

the employer may apply to the Commissioners in accordance with paragraph (2) for funds to pay the additional statutory paternity pay (or so much of it as remains outstanding) to the employee or employees.

(2) Where—

(a) the condition in paragraph (1) is satisfied, or

(b) the employer considers that the condition in paragraph (1) will be satisfied on the date of any subsequent payment of emoluments to one or more employees who are entitled to payment of additional statutory paternity pay,

the employer may apply to the Commissioners for funding in a form approved for that purpose by the Commissioners.

(3) An application by an employer under paragraph (2) shall be for an amount up to, but not exceeding, the amount of the payment to which the employer is entitled in accordance with regulation 3 in respect of additional statutory paternity pay which the employer is required to pay to an employee or employees for the income tax month or income tax quarter to which the payment of emoluments relates.

NOTES

Commencement: 6 April 2010.

[2.1311]

5 Deductions from payments to the Commissioners

An employer who is entitled to a payment determined in accordance with regulation 3 may recover such payment by making one or more deductions from the aggregate of the amounts specified in sub-paragraphs (a) to (d) of regulation 4(1) except where and in so far as—

(a) those amounts relate to earnings paid before the beginning of the income tax month or income tax quarter in which the payment of additional statutory paternity pay was made;

(b) those amounts are paid by the employer later than six years after the end of the tax year in which the payment of additional statutory paternity pay was made;

(c) the employer has received payment from the Commissioners under regulation 4; or

(d) the employer has made a request in writing under regulation 4 that the payment to which the employer is entitled in accordance with regulation 3 be paid and the employer has not received notification by the Commissioners that the request is refused.

NOTES

Commencement: 6 April 2010.

[2.1312]

6 Payments to employers by the Commissioners

If the total amount which an employer is or would otherwise be entitled to deduct under regulation 5 is less than the payment to which the employer is entitled in accordance with regulation 3 in an income tax month or income tax quarter, and the Commissioners are satisfied that this is so, then provided that the employer has in writing requested them to do so, the Commissioners shall pay the employer such amount as the employer was unable to deduct.

NOTES

Commencement: 6 April 2010.

[2.1313]

7 Date when certain contributions are to be treated as paid

Where an employer has made a deduction from a contributions payment under regulation 5, the date on which it is to be treated as having been paid for the purposes of section 7(5) of the 2002 Act (when amount deducted from contributions payment to be treated as paid and received by the Commissioners) is—

(a) in a case where the deduction did not extinguish the contributions payment, the date on which the remainder of the contributions payment or, as the case may be, the first date on which any part of the remainder of the contributions payment was paid; and

(b) in a case where the deduction extinguished the contributions payment, the 14th day after the end of the income tax month or income tax quarter during which there were paid the earnings in respect of which the contributions payment was payable.

NOTES

Commencement: 6 April 2010.

[2.1314]

8 Overpayments

(1) This regulation applies where funds have been provided to the employer pursuant to regulation 4 in respect of one or more employees and it appears to an officer of Revenue and Customs that the employer has not used the whole or part of those funds to pay additional statutory paternity pay.

(2) An officer of Revenue and Customs shall decide to the best of the officer's judgement the amount of funds provided pursuant to regulation 4 and not used to pay additional statutory paternity pay and shall serve notice in writing of this decision on the employer.

(3) A decision under this regulation may cover funds provided pursuant to regulation 4—

(a) for any one income tax month or income tax quarter, or more than one income tax month or income tax quarter, in a tax year, and

(b) in respect of a class or classes of employees specified in the decision notice (without naming the individual employees), or in respect of one or more employees named in the decision notice.

(4) Subject to the following provisions of this regulation, Part 6 of the Taxes Management Act 1970 (collection and recovery) shall apply with any necessary modifications to a decision under this regulation as if it were an assessment and as if the amount of funds determined were income tax charged on the employer.

(5) Where an amount of funds determined under this regulation relates to more than one employee, proceedings may be brought for the recovery of that amount without distinguishing the amounts making up that sum which the employer is liable to repay in respect of each employee and without specifying the employee in question, and the amount determined under this regulation shall be one cause of action or one matter of complaint for the purposes of proceedings under section 65, 66 or 67 of the Taxes Management Act 1970.

(6) Nothing in paragraph (5) prevents the bringing of separate proceedings for the recovery of any amount which the employer is liable to repay in respect of each employee.

NOTES

Commencement: 6 April 2010.

[2.1315]

9 Records to be maintained by employers

Every employer shall maintain for three years after the end of a tax year in which the employer made payments of additional statutory paternity pay to any employee a record of—

(a) if the employee's additional statutory paternity pay period began in that year—

(i) the date on which that period began, and

(ii) the evidence of entitlement to additional statutory paternity pay provided by the employee pursuant to regulations made under section 171ZEC(3)(c) of the 1992 Act or under section 171ZEC(3)(c) of the 1992 Act as it applies to adoptions from overseas;

(b) the weeks in that tax year in which additional statutory paternity pay was paid to the employee and the amount paid in each week; and

(c) any week in that tax year which was within the employee's additional statutory paternity pay period but for which no payment of additional statutory paternity pay was made to the employee and the reason no payment was made.

NOTES

Commencement: 6 April 2010.

[2.1316]

10 Inspection of employers' records

(1) Every employer, whenever called upon to do so by any authorised officer of Revenue and Customs, shall produce the documents and records specified in paragraph (2) to that officer for inspection, at such time as that officer may reasonably require, at the prescribed place.

(2) The documents and records specified in this paragraph are—

- (a) all wages sheets, deductions working sheets, records kept in accordance with regulation 9 and other documents and records whatsoever relating to the calculation or payment of additional statutory paternity pay to employees in respect of the years specified by such officer; or
- (b) such of those wages sheets, deductions working sheets, or other documents and records as may be specified by the authorised officer.

(3) The "prescribed place" mentioned in paragraph (1) means—

- (a) such place in Great Britain as the employer and the authorised officer may agree upon; or
- (b) in default of such agreement, the place in Great Britain at which the documents and records referred to in paragraph (2)(a) are normally kept; or
- (c) in default of such agreement and if there is no such place as is referred to in sub-paragraph (b), the employer's principal place of business in Great Britain.

(4) The authorised officer may—

- (a) take copies of, or make extracts from, any document or record produced to the authorised officer for inspection in accordance with paragraph (1);
- (b) remove any document or record so produced if it appears to the authorised officer to be necessary to do so, at a reasonable time and for a reasonable period.

(5) Where any document or record is removed in accordance with paragraph (4)(b), the authorised officer shall provide—

- (a) a receipt for the document or record so removed; and
- (b) a copy of the document or record, free of charge, within seven days, to the person by whom it was produced or caused to be produced where the document or record is reasonably required for the proper conduct of a business.

(6) Where a lien is claimed on a document produced in accordance with paragraph (1), the removal of the document under paragraph (4)(b) shall not be regarded as breaking the lien.

(7) Where records are maintained by computer, the person required to make them available for inspection shall provide the authorised officer with all facilities necessary for obtaining information from them.

NOTES

Commencement: 6 April 2010.

[2.1317]

11 Provision of information relating to entitlement to additional statutory paternity pay

(1) Where an employer, who has been given evidence of entitlement to additional statutory paternity pay pursuant to regulations made under section 171ZEC(3)(c) of the 1992 Act or under section 171ZEC(3)(c) of the 1992 Act as it applies to adoptions from overseas by a person who is or has been an employee, decides that they have no liability to make payments of additional statutory paternity pay to the employee, the employer shall furnish the employee with details of the decision and the reasons for it.

(2) Where an employer who has been given such evidence of an entitlement to additional statutory paternity pay has made one or more payments of additional statutory paternity pay to the employee but decides, before the end of the additional statutory paternity pay period, that they have no liability to make further payments to the employee because the employee has been detained in legal custody or sentenced to a term of imprisonment which was not suspended, the employer shall furnish the employee with—

- (a) details of the employer's decision and the reasons for it; and
- (b) details of the last week in respect of which a liability to pay additional statutory paternity pay arose and the total number of weeks within the additional statutory paternity pay period in which such a liability arose.

(3) The employer shall—

- (a) return to the employee any evidence provided by the employee as referred to in paragraph (1) or (2); and
- (b) comply with the requirements imposed by paragraph (1) within 28 days of the day the employee gave notice of intended absence; and
- (c) comply with the requirements imposed by paragraph (2) within seven days of being notified of the employee's detention or sentence.

NOTES

Commencement: 6 April 2010.

[2.1318]

12 Application for the determination of any issue arising as to, or in connection with, entitlement to additional statutory paternity pay

(1) An application for the determination of any issue arising as to, or in connection with, entitlement to additional statutory paternity pay may be submitted to an officer of Revenue and Customs by the employee concerned.

(2) Such an issue shall be decided by an officer of Revenue and Customs only on the basis of such an application or on their own initiative.

NOTES

Commencement: 6 April 2010.

[2.1319]

13 Applications in connection with additional statutory paternity pay

(1) An application for the determination of any issue referred to in regulation 12 shall be made in a form approved for the purpose by the Commissioners.

(2) Where such an application is made by an employee, it shall—

(a) be made to an officer of Revenue and Customs within six months of the earliest day in respect of which entitlement to additional statutory paternity pay is in issue;

(b) state the period in respect of which entitlement to additional statutory paternity pay is in issue; and

(c) state the grounds (if any) on which the applicant's employer had denied liability for additional statutory paternity pay in respect of the period specified in the application.

NOTES

Commencement: 6 April 2010.

[2.1320]

14 Provision of information

(1) Any person specified in paragraph (2) shall, where information or documents are reasonably required from the person to ascertain whether additional statutory paternity pay is or was payable, furnish that information or those documents within 30 days of receiving a notification from an officer of Revenue and Customs requesting such information or documents.

(2) The requirement to provide such information or documents applies to—

(a) any person claiming to be entitled to additional statutory paternity pay;

(b) any person who is, or has been, the spouse, civil partner or partner of such a person as is specified in paragraph (a);

(c) any person who is, or has been, an employer of such a person as is specified in paragraph (a);

(d) any person carrying on an agency or other business for the introduction or supply to persons requiring them of persons available to do work or to perform services; and

(e) any person who is a servant or agent of any such person as is specified in paragraphs (a) to (d).

NOTES

Commencement: 6 April 2010.

EMPLOYEE STUDY AND TRAINING (PROCEDURAL REQUIREMENTS) REGULATIONS 2010

(SI 2010/155)

NOTES

Made: 25 January 2010.

Authority: Employment Rights Act 1996, ss 63F(3), (4), 63H(3).

Commencement: 6 April 2010.

Note that the enabling provisions under which these Regulations are made have (as at 6 April 2013) only been brought into force with regard to employers with at least 250 employees; see the note to s 63D of the 1996 Act at **[1.840]**. Note also that the government has announced that it does not intend to bring these provisions into force for other employers.

See *Harvey* CII(8).

ARRANGEMENT OF REGULATIONS

[2.1321]

1 Citation and commencement

These Regulations may be cited as The Employee Study and Training (Procedural Requirements) Regulations 2010 and come into force on 6th April 2010.

NOTES

Commencement: 6 April 2010 (see further the introductory notes to these Regulations).

[2.1322]

2 Interpretation

(1) In these Regulations—

"the 1996 Act" means the Employment Rights Act 1996;

"companion" means a person who satisfies the requirements in regulation 16(2);

"electronic communication" means an electronic communication within the meaning of section 15(1) of the Electronic Communications Act 2000;

"employee" means an individual who has entered into or works under (or, where the employment has ceased, worked under) a contract of employment;

"employer" means the person by whom an employee is (or, where the employment has ceased, was) employed;

"worker" means an individual who has entered into or works under (or where the employment has ceased, worked under)—

(a) a contract of employment; or

(b) any other contract, whether express or implied and (if it is express) whether oral or in writing, whereby the individual undertakes to do or perform personally any work or services for another party to the contract whose status is not by virtue of the contract that of a client or customer of any profession or business undertaking carried on by the individual:

"writing" includes writing delivered by means of electronic communication.

(2) A section 63D application is taken as having been received—

(a) in relation to an application transmitted by electronic communication, on the day on which it is transmitted; and

(b) in relation to an application sent by post, on the day on which the application would be delivered in the ordinary course of post.

(3) A notice is taken as being given—
  (a) in relation to a notice transmitted by electronic communication, on the day on which it is transmitted; and
  (b) in relation to a notice sent by post, on the day on which the section 63D application would be delivered in the ordinary course of post.

NOTES

Commencement: 6 April 2010 (see further the introductory notes to these Regulations).

[2.1323]

3 Circumstances in which employer must ignore earlier application

(1) For the purposes of section 63F(1) of the 1996 Act, at an employee's request, an employer must ignore an earlier application if paragraphs (2) or (4) apply.

(2) This paragraph applies where the employee failed to start the agreed study or training due to—
  (a) an emergency or unforeseen circumstance beyond the employee's control; or
  (b) cancellation of the study or training by—
    (i) the employer;
    (ii) the institution at which the employee was due to undertake a course;
    (iii) the person whom it was agreed would supervise the training; or
    (iv) any other proposed provider or facilitator of the proposed study or training.

(3) Paragraph (2)(b) does not apply where the cancellation of the study or training is attributable to the employee's own conduct in relation to the study or training.

(4) This paragraph applies where the employee—
  (a) by mistake, submitted a section 63D application ("the earlier application") too soon after a previous section 63D application for the employer to be required to consider it under section 63F of the 1996 Act;
  (b) submits a further section 63D application ("the current application") which the employer would be required to consider but for the earlier application; and
  (c) at the time of making the current application, notifies the employer that—
    (i) the earlier application was submitted too early by mistake; and
    (ii) the employee wishes to withdraw the earlier application.

NOTES

Commencement: 6 April 2010 (see further the introductory notes to these Regulations).

[2.1324]

4 Meeting to discuss application

(1) Subject to paragraph (2) and regulation 15, an employer to whom a section 63D application is submitted shall hold a meeting to discuss the application within 28 days after the date on which the application is received.

(2) Paragraph (1) does not apply where the employer agrees to the section 63D application and notifies the employee accordingly in writing within the period referred to in that paragraph.

NOTES

Commencement: 6 April 2010 (see further the introductory notes to these Regulations).

[2.1325]

5 Notice of employer's decision following meeting

Where a meeting is held to discuss a section 63D application, the employer must give the employee notice of the employer's decision on the application within 14 days after the date of the meeting.

NOTES

Commencement: 6 April 2010 (see further the introductory notes to these Regulations).

[2.1326]

6 Form of decision notice

(1) A notice under regulation 5 must—
  (a) be in writing; and
  (b) be dated.

(2) Where the employer's decision is to agree the section 63D application, a notice under regulation 5 must—
  (a) give the following details of the agreed study or training—
    (i) the subject of the study or training;
    (ii) where and when it will take place;
    (iii) who will provide or supervise it; and
    (iv) what qualification (if any) it will lead to; and

(b) make clear—
   (i) whether any remuneration under the employee's contract of employment will be paid for the time spent undertaking the agreed study or training;
   (ii) any changes to the employee's working hours in order to accommodate the agreed study or training; and
   (iii) how any tuition fees or other direct costs of the agreed study or training will be met.

(3) Where the decision is to refuse the section 63D application, a notice under regulation 5 must—
   (a) state which of the grounds for refusal specified in section 63F(7) of the 1996 Act are considered by the employer to apply;
   (b) contain a sufficient explanation as to why those grounds apply; and
   (c) set out the appeal procedure.

(4) Where the employer's decision is to agree part of a section 63D application and refuse part of a section 63D application, a notice under regulation 5 must—
   (a) make clear which part of the application is agreed to;
   (b) make clear which part of the application is refused;
   (c) give, in respect of the part which is agreed to, the information required under paragraph (2); and
   (d) include, in respect of the part which is refused, the details required under paragraph (3).

NOTES

Commencement: 6 April 2010 (see further the introductory notes to these Regulations).

[2.1327]

7 Variation by agreement

(1) An employer and employee may agree to dispose of a section 63D application, or part of a section 63D application, by the employer granting a varied form of it.

(2) Where agreement is reached by the employer and employee to a varied form of the application, the notice of the employer's decision under regulation 5 must—
   (a) make clear the variation agreed to;
   (b) be supported by written evidence of the employee's agreement to that variation; and
   (c) make clear—
      (i) whether any remuneration under the employee's contract of employment will be paid for the time spent undertaking the agreed study or training;
      (ii) any changes to the employee's working hours in order to accommodate the agreed study or training; and
      (iii) how any tuition fees or other direct costs of the agreed study or training will be met.

NOTES

Commencement: 6 April 2010 (see further the introductory notes to these Regulations).

[2.1328]

8 Appeals

An employee is entitled to appeal against the employer's decision to refuse a section 63D application, or part of a section 63D application, by giving notice in accordance with regulation 9 within 14 days after the date on which notice of the decision is given.

NOTES

Commencement: 6 April 2010 (see further the introductory notes to these Regulations).

[2.1329]

9

A notice of appeal under regulation 8 must—
   (a) be in writing;
   (b) set out the grounds of appeal; and
   (c) be dated.

NOTES

Commencement: 6 April 2010 (see further the introductory notes to these Regulations).

[2.1330]

10

(1) Subject to paragraph (2), the employer must hold a meeting with the employee to discuss the appeal within 14 days after the date on which notice under regulation 8 is given.

(2) Paragraph (1) does not apply where, within 14 days after the date on which notice under regulation 8 is given, the employer—

(a) upholds the appeal; and
(b) notifies the employee in writing of the employer's decision, specifying the information required by regulation 6(2).

NOTES

Commencement: 6 April 2010 (see further the introductory notes to these Regulations).

[2.1331]
11

Where a meeting is held to discuss the appeal, the employer must notify the employee of the employer's decision on the appeal within 14 days after the date of the meeting.

NOTES

Commencement: 6 April 2010 (see further the introductory notes to these Regulations).

[2.1332]
12

(1) Notice under regulation 11 must—
(a) be in writing; and
(b) be dated.

(2) Where the employer upholds the appeal, notice under regulation 11 must specify the information required by regulation 6(2).

(3) Where the employer dismisses the appeal, notice under regulation 11 must—
(a) state the grounds for the decision; and
(b) contain a sufficient explanation as to why those grounds apply.

NOTES

Commencement: 6 April 2010 (see further the introductory notes to these Regulations).

[2.1333]
13 Time and place of meetings

The time and place of a meeting under regulation 4(1) or 10(1) must be convenient to the employer and the employee.

NOTES

Commencement: 6 April 2010 (see further the introductory notes to these Regulations).

[2.1334]
14 Extension of periods

(1) An employer and employee may agree to an extension of any of the time periods referred to in regulations 4, 5, 8, 10, 11 and 15.

(2) An agreement under paragraph (1) must be recorded in writing by the employer.

(3) The employer's record referred to in paragraph (2) must—
(a) specify what period the extension relates to;
(b) specify the date on which the extension is to end;
(c) be dated; and
(d) be given to the employee.

NOTES

Commencement: 6 April 2010 (see further the introductory notes to these Regulations).

[2.1335]
15

Where the individual who would ordinarily consider a section 63D application is absent from work on annual leave or on sick leave on the day on which the application is received, the period referred to in regulation 4(1) commences on the day the individual returns to work or 28 days after the application is received, whichever is the sooner.

NOTES

Commencement: 6 April 2010 (see further the introductory notes to these Regulations).

[2.1336]
16 Right to be accompanied

(1) This regulation applies where—
(a) a meeting is held under regulation 4(1) or 10(1); and
(b) the employee reasonably requests to be accompanied at the meeting.

(2) Where this regulation applies, the employer must permit the employee to be accompanied at the meeting by a single companion who—

(a) is chosen by the employee to attend the relevant meeting; and
(b) is a worker employed by the same employer as the employee.

(3) A companion may—

(a) address the meeting;
(b) confer with the employee during the meeting.

(4) When addressing a meeting, a companion may not answer questions independently of the employee.

(5) If—

(a) an employee has a right under this regulation to be accompanied at a meeting;
(b) his chosen companion will not be available at the time proposed for the meeting by the employer; and
(c) the employee proposes an alternative time which satisfies paragraph (6),

the employer must postpone the meeting to the time proposed by the employee.

(6) An alternative time must—

(a) be convenient for employer, employee and companion; and
(b) fall before the end of the period of seven days beginning with the first day after the day proposed by the employer.

(7) An employer shall permit a worker to take time off during working hours for the purpose of accompanying an employee in accordance with a request under paragraph (1)(b).

(8) Sections 168(3) and (4), 169 and 171 to 173 of the Trade Union and Labour Relations (Consolidation) Act 1992 (time off for carrying out trade union duties) apply in relation to paragraph (7) above as they apply in relation to section 168(1) of that Act.

NOTES

Commencement: 6 April 2010 (see further the introductory notes to these Regulations).

[2.1337]

17 Complaint to employment tribunal

(1) An employee may present a complaint to an employment tribunal that the employer has failed, or threatened to fail, to comply with regulation 16(2), (3), or (5).

(2) A tribunal must not consider a complaint under this regulation in relation to a failure or threat unless the complaint is presented—

(a) before the end of the period of three months beginning with the date of the failure or threat; or
(b) within such further period as the tribunal considers reasonable in a case where it is satisfied that it was not reasonably practicable for the complaint to be presented before the end of that period of three months.

(3) Where a tribunal finds that a complaint under this regulation is well-founded, it must order the employer to pay compensation to the worker of an amount not exceeding two weeks' pay.

(4) In applying Chapter 2 of Part 14 of the 1996 Act (calculation of a week's pay) for the purposes of paragraph (3), the calculation date shall be taken to be the date on which the relevant meeting took place (or was to have taken place).

(5) The limit in section 227(1) of the 1996 Act (maximum amount of a week's pay) shall apply for the purposes of paragraph (3).

NOTES

Commencement: 6 April 2010 (see further the introductory notes to these Regulations).

[2.1338]

18 Detriment and dismissal

(1) A person has the right not to be subjected to any detriment by any act, or any deliberate failure to act, by the person's employer done on the ground that the person—

(a) exercised or sought to exercise the right under regulation 16(2) or (5); or
(b) at the employee's request, accompanied or sought to accompany an employee at a meeting held under regulation 4(1) or 10(1).

(2) Section 48 of the 1996 Act applies in relation to contraventions of paragraph (1) as it applies in relation to contraventions of certain sections of that Act.

(3) A person who is dismissed is to be treated for the purposes of Part 10 of the 1996 Act as unfairly dismissed if the reason (or, if more than one, the principal reason) for the dismissal is that the person—

(a) exercised or sought to exercise his right under regulation 16(2) or (5); or
(b) at the employee's request, accompanied or sought to accompany an employee at a meeting held under regulation 4(1) or 10(1).

(4) Section 108 of the 1996 Act (qualifying period of employment) does not apply in relation to paragraph (3).

(5) Sections 128 to 132 of the 1996 Act (interim relief) apply in relation to dismissal for the reason specified in paragraph (3)(a) or (b) as they apply in relation to dismissal for a reason specified in section 128(1)(b) of that Act.

(6) In the application of Chapter 2 of Part 10 of the 1996 Act in relation to paragraph (3), a reference to an employee is to be treated as a reference to a worker.

NOTES

Commencement: 6 April 2010 (see further the introductory notes to these Regulations).

[2.1339]

19 Withdrawal of application by the employee

(1) An employer must treat a section 63D application as withdrawn where the employee has—

- (a) notified the employer either orally or in writing that the employee is withdrawing the application;
- (b) without reasonable cause, failed to attend a meeting under regulation 4(1) or 10(1) more than once; or
- (c) without reasonable cause, refused to provide the employer with information the employer requires in order to assess whether the application should be agreed to.

(2) An employer must confirm the withdrawal of the section 63D application to the employee in writing unless the employee has provided him with written notice of the withdrawal under paragraph (1)(a).

NOTES

Commencement: 6 April 2010 (see further the introductory notes to these Regulations).

[2.1340]

20 Employee's duties to inform employer

(1) An employee must inform the employee's employer within 14 days of an event listed in s 63H(2) of the 1996 Act occurring.

(2) Notice under paragraph (1) must—

- (a) be in writing; and
- (b) be dated.

NOTES

Commencement: 6 April 2010 (see further the introductory notes to these Regulations).

EMPLOYEE STUDY AND TRAINING (ELIGIBILITY, COMPLAINTS AND REMEDIES) REGULATIONS 2010

(SI 2010/156)

NOTES

Made: 25 January 2010.

Authority: Employment Rights Act 1996, ss 63E(4)(c), (5)(a), 63I(3)(b), 63J(3).

Commencement: 6 April 2010.

Note that the enabling provisions under which these Regulations are made have (as at 6 April 2013) only been brought into force with regard to employers with at least 250 employees; see the note to s 63D of the 1996 Act at **[1.840]**. Note also that the government has announced that it does not intend to bring these provisions into force for other employers.

See *Harvey* CII(8).

ARRANGEMENT OF REGULATIONS

[2.1341]

1 Citation and commencement

These Regulations may be cited as the Employee Study and Training (Eligibility, Complaints and Remedies) Regulations 2010 and come into force on 6th April 2010.

NOTES

Commencement: 6 April 2010 (see further the introductory notes to these Regulations).

[2.1342]

2 Interpretation

(1) In these Regulations—

"the 1996 Act" means the Employment Rights Act 1996;

"the Procedure Regulations" means The Employee Study and Training (Procedural Requirements) Regulations 2010.

NOTES

Commencement: 6 April 2010 (see further the introductory notes to these Regulations).

[2.1343]

3 Further information which the application must contain

(1) An employee must set out in the section 63D application—

(a) the date on which the employee's last section 63D application (if any) was submitted to their employer; and

(b) the method by which that application was submitted.

(2) For the purposes of paragraph (1) an employee submits a section 63D application by sending, delivering or otherwise transmitting it to their employer.

NOTES

Commencement: 6 April 2010 (see further the introductory notes to these Regulations).

[2.1344]

4 Form of the application

A section 63D application must—

(a) be made in writing; and

(b) be dated.

NOTES

Commencement: 6 April 2010 (see further the introductory notes to these Regulations).

[2.1345]

5 Breaches of the Procedure Regulations by the employer entitling an employee to make a complaint to an employment tribunal

The breaches of the Procedure Regulations which entitle an employee to make a complaint to an employment tribunal under section 63I of the 1996 Act notwithstanding the fact that the employee's section 63D application has not been disposed of by agreement or withdrawn are—

(a) failure to hold a meeting in accordance with regulation 4(1) and 10(1) of the Procedure Regulations;

(b) failure to notify a decision in accordance with regulations 5 or 11 of the Procedure Regulations.

NOTES

Commencement: 6 April 2010 (see further the introductory notes to these Regulations).

[2.1346]

6 Compensation

(1) The maximum amount of compensation that an employment tribunal may award under section 63J of the 1996 Act where it finds a complaint by an employee under section 63I of the Act well-founded is 8 weeks' pay.

NOTES

Commencement: 6 April 2010 (see further the introductory notes to these Regulations).

EMPLOYMENT RELATIONS ACT 1999 (BLACKLISTS) REGULATIONS 2010

(SI 2010/493)

NOTES

Made: 1 March 2010.

Authority: Employment Relations Act 1999, s 3.

Commencement: 2 March 2010.

Employment Appeal Tribunal: an appeal lies to the Employment Appeal Tribunal on any question of law arising from any decision of, or in any proceedings before, an employment tribunal under or by virtue of these Regulations; see the Employment Tribunals Act 1996, s 21(1)(x) at **[1.713]**.

Conciliation: employment tribunal proceedings and claims which could be the subject of employment tribunal proceedings under regs 5, 6, or 9 are proceedings to which the Employment Tribunals Act 1996, s 18 applies; see s 18(1)(w) of that Act at **[1.706]**.

See *Harvey* NI(4)(H).

ARRANGEMENT OF REGULATIONS

Introductory provisions

[2.1347]

1 Citation, commencement and extent

These Regulations—

(a) may be cited as the Employment Relations Act 1999 (Blacklists) Regulations 2010,
(b) come into force on the day after the day on which they are made, and
(c) extend to Great Britain.

NOTES

Commencement: 2 March 2010.

[2.1348]

2 Interpretation

(1) In these Regulations—

"'employment agency'" means a person who, for profit or not, provides services for the purposes of finding employment for workers or supplying employers with workers, and does not include a trade union by reason only of the services a trade union provides only for and in relation to its members;

"'office'", in relation to a trade union, means any position—

(a) by virtue of which the holder is an official of the trade union, or

(b) to which Chapter 4 of Part 1 of the Trade Union and Labour Relations (Consolidation) Act 1992 (duty to hold elections) applies,

and "'official'" has the meaning given by section 119 of that Act;

"'prohibited list'" has the meaning given by regulation 3(2);

"'services'", in relation to an employment agency, means services for the purposes of finding employment for workers or supplying employers with workers;

"'use'", in relation to a prohibited list, includes use of information contained in the list.

(2) References in these regulations to information supplied by a person who contravenes regulation 3 include information supplied by a person who would contravene that regulation if that person's actions took place in Great Britain.

NOTES

Commencement: 2 March 2010.

General prohibition

[2.1349]

3 General prohibition

(1) Subject to regulation 4, no person shall compile, use, sell or supply a prohibited list.

(2) A "'prohibited list'" is a list which—

(a) contains details of persons who are or have been members of trade unions or persons who are taking part or have taken part in the activities of trade unions, and

(b) is compiled with a view to being used by employers or employment agencies for the purposes of discrimination in relation to recruitment or in relation to the treatment of workers.

(3) "'Discrimination'" means treating a person less favourably than another on grounds of trade union membership or trade union activities.

(4) In these Regulations references to membership of a trade union include references to—

(a) membership of a particular branch or section of a trade union, and

(b) membership of one of a number of particular branches or sections of a trade union;

and references to taking part in the activities of a trade union have a corresponding meaning.

NOTES

Commencement: 2 March 2010.

[2.1350]

4 Exceptions to general prohibition

(1) A person does not contravene regulation 3 in the following cases.

(2) The first case is where a person supplies a prohibited list, but—

(a) does not know they are supplying a prohibited list, and

(b) could not reasonably be expected to know they are supplying a prohibited list.

(3) The second case is where a person compiles, uses or supplies a prohibited list, but—

(a) in doing so, that person's sole or principal purpose is to make known a contravention of regulation 3 or the possibility of such a contravention,

(b) no information in relation to a person whose details are included in the prohibited list is published without the consent of that person, and

(c) in all the circumstances compiling, using or supplying the prohibited list is justified in the public interest.

(4) The third case is where a person compiles, uses, sells or supplies a prohibited list, but in doing so that person's sole or principal purpose is to apply a requirement either—

(a) that a person may not be considered for appointment to an office or for employment unless that person has experience or knowledge of trade union matters, and in all the circumstances it is reasonable to apply such a requirement, or

(b) that a person may not be considered for appointment or election to an office in a trade union unless he is a member of the union.

(5) The fourth case is where a person compiles, uses, sells or supplies a prohibited list, but the compilation, use, sale or supply of the prohibited list is required or authorised—

(a) under an enactment,

(b) by any rule of law, or

(c) by an order of the court.

(6) The fifth case is where a person uses or supplies a prohibited list—

(a) for the purpose of, or in connection with, legal proceedings (including prospective legal proceedings), or

(b) for the purpose of giving or obtaining legal advice,

where the use or supply is necessary in order to determine whether these regulations have been, are being or will be complied with.

NOTES

Commencement: 2 March 2010.

Refusal of employment or employment agency services

[2.1351]

5 Refusal of employment

(1) A person (P) has a right of complaint to an employment tribunal against another (R) if R refuses to employ P for a reason which relates to a prohibited list, and either—

(a) R contravenes regulation 3 in relation to that list, or

(b) R—

(i) relies on information supplied by a person who contravenes that regulation in relation to that list, and

(ii) knows or ought reasonably to know that the information relied on is supplied in contravention of that regulation.

(2) R shall be taken to refuse to employ P if P seeks employment of any description with R and R—

(a) refuses or deliberately omits to entertain and process P's application or enquiry;

(b) causes P to withdraw or cease to pursue P's application or enquiry;

(c) refuses or deliberately omits to offer P employment of that description;

(d) makes P an offer of such employment the terms of which are such as no reasonable employer who wished to fill the post would offer and which is not accepted; or

(e) makes P an offer of such employment but withdraws it or causes P not to accept it.

(3) If there are facts from which the tribunal could conclude, in the absence of any other explanation, that R contravened regulation 3 or relied on information supplied in contravention of that regulation, the tribunal must find that such a contravention or reliance on information occurred unless R shows that it did not.

NOTES

Commencement: 2 March 2010.

Conciliation: employment tribunal proceedings and claims which could be the subject of employment tribunal proceedings under this regulation are proceedings to which the Employment Tribunals Act 1996, s 18 applies; see s 18(1)(w) of that Act at **[1.706]**.

[2.1352]

6 Refusal of employment agency services

(1) A person (P) has a right of complaint to an employment tribunal against an employment agency (E) if E refuses P any of its services for a reason which relates to a prohibited list, and either—

(a) E contravenes regulation 3 in relation to that list, or

(b) E—

(i) relies on information supplied by a person who contravenes that regulation in relation to that list, and

(ii) knows or ought reasonably to know that information relied on is supplied in contravention of that regulation.

(2) E shall be taken to refuse P a service if P seeks to make use of the service and E—

(a) refuses or deliberately omits to make the service available to P;

(b) causes P not to make use of the service or to cease to make use of it; or

(c) does not provide P the same service, on the same terms, as is provided to others.

(3) If there are facts from which the tribunal could conclude, in the absence of any other explanation, that E contravened regulation 3 or relied on information supplied in contravention of that regulation, the tribunal must find that such a contravention or reliance on information occurred unless E shows that it did not.

NOTES

Commencement: 2 March 2010.

Conciliation: employment tribunal proceedings and claims which could be the subject of employment tribunal proceedings under this regulation are proceedings to which the Employment Tribunals Act 1996, s 18 applies; see s 18(1)(w) of that Act at **[1.706]**.

[2.1353]

7 Time limit for proceedings under regulation 5 or 6

(1) Subject to paragraph (2), an employment tribunal shall not consider a complaint under regulation 5 or 6 unless it is presented to the tribunal before the end of the period of three months beginning with the date of the conduct to which the complaint relates.

(2) An employment tribunal may consider a complaint under regulation 5 or 6 that is otherwise out of time if, in all the circumstances of the case, it considers that it is just and equitable to do so.

(3) The date of the conduct to which a complaint under regulation 5 relates shall be taken to be—

- (a) in the case of an actual refusal, the date of the refusal;
- (b) in the case of a deliberate omission—
  - (i) to entertain and process P's application or enquiry, or
  - (ii) to offer employment,

  the end of the period within which it was reasonable to expect R to act;
- (c) in the case of conduct causing P to withdraw or cease to pursue P's application or enquiry, the date of that conduct;
- (d) in a case where R made but withdrew an offer, the date R withdrew the offer;
- (e) in any other case where R made an offer which was not accepted, the date on which R made the offer.

(4) The date of the conduct to which a complaint under regulation 6 relates shall be taken to be—

- (a) in the case of an actual refusal, the date of the refusal;
- (b) in the case of a deliberate omission to make a service available, the end of the period within which it was reasonable to expect E to act;
- (c) in the case of conduct causing P not make use of a service or to cease to make use of it, the date of that conduct;
- (d) in the case of failure to provide the same service, on the same terms, as is provided to others, the date or last date on which the service in fact was provided.

NOTES

Commencement: 2 March 2010.

[2.1354]

8 Remedies in proceedings under regulation 5 or 6

(1) Where an employment tribunal finds that a complaint under regulation 5 or 6 is well-founded, it shall make a declaration to that effect and may make such of the following as it considers just and equitable—

- (a) an order requiring the respondent to pay compensation;
- (b) a recommendation that the respondent take within a specified period action appearing to the tribunal to be practicable for the purpose of obviating or reducing the adverse effect on the complainant of any conduct to which the complaint relates.

(2) Compensation shall be assessed on the same basis as damages for breach of statutory duty and may include compensation for injury to feelings.

(3) Where an award of compensation is made, the amount of compensation before any increase or reduction is made under paragraph (4), (5) or (6) shall not be less than £5,000.

(4) If the respondent fails without reasonable justification to comply with a recommendation under paragraph (1)(b), the tribunal may increase its award of compensation or, if it has not made such an award, make one.

(5) Where the tribunal considers that any conduct of the complainant before the refusal to which the complaint under regulation 5 or 6 relates was such that it would be just and equitable to reduce the award of compensation, the tribunal shall reduce that amount accordingly.

(6) The amount of compensation shall be reduced or further reduced by the amount of any compensation awarded by the tribunal under section 140 of the Trade Union and Labour Relations (Consolidation) Act 1992 in respect of the same refusal.

(7) The total amount of compensation shall not exceed £65,300.

NOTES

Commencement: 2 March 2010.

Detriment

[2.1355]

9 Detriment

(1) A person (P) has a right of complaint to an employment tribunal against P's employer (D) if D, by any act or any deliberate failure to act, subjects P to a detriment for a reason which relates to a prohibited list, and either—

- (a) D contravenes regulation 3 in relation to that list, or
- (b) D—
  - (i) relies on information supplied by a person who contravenes that regulation in relation to that list, and
  - (ii) knows or ought reasonably to know that information relied on is supplied in contravention of that regulation.

Part 2 Statutory Instruments

(2) If there are facts from which the tribunal could conclude, in the absence of any other explanation, that D contravened regulation 3 or relied on information supplied in contravention of that regulation, the tribunal must find that such a contravention or reliance on information occurred unless D shows that it did not.

(3) This regulation does not apply where the detriment in question amounts to the dismissal of an employee within the meaning in Part 10 of the Employment Rights Act 1996.

NOTES

Commencement: 2 March 2010.

Conciliation: employment tribunal proceedings and claims which could be the subject of employment tribunal proceedings under this regulation are proceedings to which the Employment Tribunals Act 1996, s 18 applies; see s 18(1)(w) of that Act at **[1.706]**.

Tribunal jurisdiction: the Trade Union and Labour Relations (Consolidation) Act 1992, s 207A at **[1.474]** (as inserted by the Employment Act 2008) provides that in proceedings before an employment tribunal relating to a claim by an employee under any of the jurisdictions listed in Sch A2 of the 1992 Act at **[1.648]** (which includes this regulation) the tribunal may adjust any award given if the employer or the employee has unreasonably failed to comply with the relevant Code of Practice issued for the purposes of Chapter III of the 1992 Act. See also the revised Acas Code of Practice 1 – Disciplinary and Grievance Procedures (2009) at **[4.1]**.

[2.1356]

10 Time limit for proceedings under regulation 9

(1) Subject to paragraph (2), an employment tribunal shall not consider a complaint under regulation 9 unless it is presented before the end of the period of three months beginning with the date of the act or failure to which the complaint relates or, where that act or failure is part of a series of similar acts or failures (or both) the last of them.

(2) An employment tribunal may consider a complaint under regulation 9 that is otherwise out of time if, in all the circumstances of the case, it considers that it is just and equitable to do so.

(3) For the purposes of paragraph (1)—

(a) where an act extends over a period, the reference to the date of the act is a reference to the last day of the period;

(b) a failure to act shall be treated as done when it was decided on.

(4) For the purposes of paragraph (3), in the absence of evidence establishing the contrary D shall be taken to decide on a failure to act—

(a) when D does an act which is inconsistent with doing the failed act, or

(b) if D has done no such inconsistent act, when the period expires within which D might reasonably have been expected to do the failed act if it was done.

NOTES

Commencement: 2 March 2010.

[2.1357]

11 Remedies in proceedings under regulation 9

(1) Where the employment tribunal finds that a complaint under regulation 9 is well-founded, it shall make a declaration to that effect and may make an award of compensation to be paid by D to P in respect of the act or failure complained of.

(2) Subject to the following paragraphs, the amount of the compensation awarded shall be such as the tribunal considers just and equitable in all the circumstances having regard to the act or failure complained of and to any loss sustained by P which is attributable to D's act or failure.

(3) The loss shall be taken to include—

(a) any expenses P reasonably incurred in consequence of the act or failure complained of; and

(b) loss of any benefit which P might reasonably be expected to have had but for that act or failure.

(4) In ascertaining the loss, the tribunal shall apply the same rule concerning the duty of a person to mitigate his loss as applies to damages recoverable under the common law of England and Wales or Scotland.

(5) Where an award of compensation is made, the amount of compensation before any increase or reduction is made under paragraphs (6), (7) and (8) of this regulation and section 207A of the Trade Union and Labour Relations (Consolidation) Act 1992 shall not be less than £5,000.

(6) Where the conduct of P before the act or failure complained of was such that it would be just and equitable to reduce the amount of compensation, the tribunal shall reduce that amount accordingly.

(7) Where the tribunal finds that the act or failure complained of was to any extent caused or contributed to by action of P, it shall reduce or further reduce the amount of the compensation by such proportion as it considers just and equitable having regard to that finding.

(8) The amount of compensation shall be reduced or further reduced by the amount of any compensation awarded by the tribunal under section 149 of the Trade Union and Labour Relations (Consolidation) Act 1992 in respect of the same act or failure.

(9) In determining the amount of compensation to be awarded no account shall be taken of any pressure exercised on D by calling, organising, procuring or financing a strike or other industrial action, or by threatening to do so; and that question shall be determined as if no such pressure had been exercised.

(10) Where P is a worker and the detriment to which P is subjected is the termination of P's contract, and that contract is not a contract of employment, the compensation awarded to P under this regulation shall not exceed £65,300.

NOTES

Commencement: 2 March 2010.

12 *(Reg 12 inserts the Employment Rights Act 1996, s 104F at* **[1.913]**, *and amends ss 105, 108, 111, 120, 122, 128 and 129 in Part X of that Act (see Part X (Unfair dismissal) at* **[1.894]** *et seq).)*

Action for breach of statutory duty

[2.1358]

13 Action for breach of statutory duty

(1) A contravention of regulation 3 is actionable as a breach of statutory duty.

(2) If there are facts from which the court could conclude, in the absence of any other explanation, that the defendant has contravened, or is likely to contravene, regulation 3, the court must find that such a contravention occurred, or is likely to occur, unless the defendant shows that it did not, or is not likely to, occur.

(3) In proceedings brought by virtue of this regulation, the court may (without prejudice to any of its other powers)—

- (a) make such order as it considers appropriate for the purpose of restraining or preventing the defendant from contravening regulation 3; and
- (b) award damages, which may include compensation for injured feelings.

(4) A person may complain to an employment tribunal under regulation 5, 6 or 9, or under Part 10 of the Employment Rights Act 1996 (unfair dismissal) as it applies by virtue of these Regulations and bring an action for breach of statutory duty in respect of the same conduct for the purpose of restraining or preventing the defendant from contravening regulation 3.

(5) Except as mentioned in paragraph (4), a person may not bring an action for breach of statutory duty and complain to an employment tribunal under regulation 5, 6 or 9, or under Part 10 of the Employment Rights Act 1996 (unfair dismissal) as it applies by virtue of these Regulations, in respect of the same conduct.

NOTES

Commencement: 2 March 2010.

Supplementary provisions

[2.1359]

14 Complaint against employer and employment agency

(1) Where P has a right of complaint under regulation 5 or 6 against R and E arising out of the same facts, P may present a complaint against either R or E or against R and E jointly.

(2) If P presents a complaint against only one party, that party or P may request the tribunal to join or sist the other as a party to the proceedings.

(3) The request shall be granted if it is made before the hearing of the complaint begins, but may be refused if it is made after that time; and no such request may be made after the tribunal has made its decision as to whether the complaint is well-founded.

(4) Where P brings a complaint against R and E jointly, or where P brings a complaint against one of them and the other is joined or sisted as a party to the proceedings, and the tribunal—

- (a) finds that the complaint is well-founded as against R and E, and
- (b) awards compensation,

the tribunal may order that the compensation shall be paid by R, by E, or partly by R and partly by E, as the tribunal may consider just and equitable in all the circumstances.

NOTES

Commencement: 2 March 2010.

[2.1360]

15 Awards against third parties in tribunal proceedings

(1) If in proceedings on a complaint under regulation 5, 6 or 9, or under Part 10 of the Employment Rights Act 1996 as it applies by virtue of these regulations, either the respondent or complainant claims that another person contravened regulation 3 in respect of the prohibited list to which the complaint relates, the complainant or respondent may request the tribunal to direct that other person be joined or sisted as a party to the proceedings.

(2) The request shall be granted if it is made before the hearing of the complaint begins, but may be refused if it is made after that time; and no such request may be made if it is made after the tribunal has made a decision as to whether the complaint is well-founded.

(3) Where a person has been so joined or sisted as a party to the proceedings and the tribunal—

- (a) finds that the complaint is well-founded,
- (b) awards compensation, and
- (c) finds the claim in paragraph (1) is well-founded,

the tribunal shall make a declaration to that effect and may award such of the remedies mentioned in paragraph (4) as it considers just and equitable.

(4) The remedies the tribunal may award are—

- (a) an order that compensation shall be paid by the person joined (or sisted) instead of by the respondent, or partly by that person and partly by the respondent;
- (b) a recommendation that within a specified period the person joined (or sisted) takes action appearing to the tribunal to be practicable for the purpose of obviating or reducing the adverse effect on the complainant of any conduct to which the complaint relates.

(5) If the person joined (or sisted) fails without reasonable justification to comply with a recommendation to take action, the tribunal may increase its award of compensation or, if it has not made such an award, make one.

(6) Where by virtue of regulation 14 (complaint against employer and employment agency) there is more than one respondent, the above provisions apply to either or both of them.

NOTES

Commencement: 2 March 2010.

[2.1361]

16 Restrictions on contracting out

Section 288 of the Trade Union and Labour Relations (Consolidation) Act 1992 (restrictions on contracting out) applies in relation to regulations 5, 6 and 9 as if they were contained in that Act.

NOTES

Commencement: 2 March 2010.

17 *(Reg 17 amends the Employment Tribunals Act 1996, ss 10, 16, 18, 21 at* **[1.694]**, **[1.704]**, **[1.706]**, **[1.713]**, *and the Trade Union and Labour Relations (Consolidation) Act 1992, Sch A2 at* **[1.648]**.*)*

OCCUPATIONAL AND PERSONAL PENSION SCHEMES (AUTOMATIC ENROLMENT) REGULATIONS 2010

(SI 2010/772)

NOTES

Made: 11 March 2010.

Authority: Pension Schemes Act 1993, ss 111A(15)(b), 181, 182(2), (3); Pensions Act 1995, ss 49(8), 124(1), 174(2), (3); Pensions Act 2008, ss 2(3), 3(2), (5), (6), 4(1), (3), 5(2), (4), (6), (7), (8), 6(1)(b), (2), 7(4), (5), (6), 8(2)(b), (3), (4), (5), (6), 9(3), 10, 15, 16(2), (3)(c), 18(c), 22(4)–(7), 23(1)(b), (3), 24(1)(a), (b), 25, 27, 30(6)(c), 33(2), 37(3), 99, 144(2), (4).

Commencement: 1 July 2012 (see reg 1 at **[2.1362]**).

Only certain regulations of relevance to employment law are reproduced here. For reasons of space, the subject matter of regulations not printed is not annotated.

ARRANGEMENT OF REGULATIONS

PART 1

CITATION, COMMENCEMENT AND INTERPRETATION

PART 1
CITATION, COMMENCEMENT AND INTERPRETATION

[2.1362]

1 Citation, commencement[, expiry] and interpretation

(1) These Regulations may be cited as the Occupational and Personal Pension Schemes (Automatic Enrolment) Regulations 2010 and shall come into force on [1st July 2012, immediately after the time when the amendments made by the Occupational and Personal Pension Schemes (Automatic Enrolment) (Amendment) Regulations 2012 come into force].

[(1A), (1B) . . .]

(2) In these Regulations—

"the Act" means the Pensions Act 2008;

"the 1993 Act" means the Pension Schemes Act 1993;

"the 1995 Act" means the Pensions Act 1995;

"applicable pay reference period" means—

(a) a period of one week; or

(b) in the case of a jobholder who is paid their regular wage or salary by reference to a period longer than a week, that period;

"automatic enrolment date" has the meaning given by section 3(7) (automatic enrolment) of the Act;

"automatic re-enrolment date" means the date determined in accordance with regulation 12;

"enrolment date" means the date determined in accordance with regulation 18(6);

"enrolment information" has the meaning given by regulation 2;

"jobholder information" has the meaning given by regulation 3;

"joining notice" means a notice given under section 9(2) (workers without qualifying earnings) of the Act;

"opt in" means the jobholder's right under section 7(3) of the Act (jobholder's right to opt in) by notice to require the employer to arrange for the jobholder to become an active member of an automatic enrolment scheme;

"opt in notice" means a notice given under section 7(3) (jobholder's right to opt in) of the Act;

"opt out" means the jobholder's right to give notice under section 8 (jobholder's right to opt out) of the Act;

"opt out notice" means a notice in the form set out in [Schedule 1];

"opt out period" means the period determined in accordance with regulation 9(2) or (3);

"staging date" means the date on which sections 2 to 8 of the Act first apply in relation to the employer.

NOTES

Commencement: 1 July 2012.

Regulation heading: word in square brackets inserted by the Occupational and Personal Pension Schemes (Automatic Enrolment) (Amendment) Regulations 2012, SI 2012/1257, regs 2, 3(a), as from 1 July 2012.

Para (1): words in square brackets substituted by SI 2012/1257, regs 2, 3(b), as from 1 July 2012.

Paras (1A), (1B): inserted by SI 2012/1257, regs 2, 3(c), as from 1 July 2012. These paras relate to the expiry of reg 52 of these Regulations, which is outside the scope of this work.

Para (2): words in square brackets in definition "opt out notice" substituted by the Automatic Enrolment (Miscellaneous Amendments) Regulations 2012, SI 2012/215, regs 17, 43(1), as from 1 July 2012.

[2.1363]

[2 Enrolment information

In these Regulations "enrolment information" means the information described in paragraphs 1–15, 24 and 25 of Schedule 2.]

NOTES

Commencement: 1 July 2012.

Substituted by the Automatic Enrolment (Miscellaneous Amendments) Regulations 2012, SI 2012/215, regs 17, 18, as from 1 July 2012.

[2.1364]

3 Jobholder information

(1) In these Regulations "jobholder information" is the jobholder's—

(a) name;
(b) date of birth;
(c) postal residential address;
(d) gender;
(e) automatic enrolment date, automatic re-enrolment date or enrolment date, as the case may be, or for a jobholder to whom regulation 28 or 29 applies, the date mentioned in regulation 7(1) as modified by regulation 28 or 29, as the case may be;
(f) national insurance number;
(g) the gross earnings due to the jobholder in any applicable pay reference period;
(h) the value of any contributions payable to the scheme by the employer and the jobholder in any applicable pay reference period, where this information is available to the employer;
(i) postal work address;
(j) individual work e-mail address, where an individual work e-mail address is allocated to that jobholder; and
(k) personal e-mail address, where the employer holds this information.

(2) For the purposes of paragraph (1)(h), "the value" of contributions may be expressed as a fixed amount or a percentage of any qualifying earnings or pensionable pay due to the jobholder in any applicable pay reference period.

NOTES

Commencement: 1 July 2012.

[2.1365]

4 Pay reference periods for the purposes of [sections 1(1)(c), 3(1)(c) and 5(1)(c)] of the Act

(1) The pay reference period for the purposes of [sections 1(1)(c), 3(1)(c) and 5(1)(c) of the Act (jobholders, automatic enrolment and automatic re-enrolment)] is—

(a) in the case of a person who is paid their regular wage or salary by reference to a period of a week, the period of one week;
(b) in the case of a person who is paid their regular wage or salary by reference to a period longer than a week, that period.

(2)–(7) . . .

NOTES

Commencement: 1 July 2012.

The words in square brackets in the regulation heading and in para (1) were substituted, and paras (2)–(7) were revoked, by the Automatic Enrolment (Miscellaneous Amendments) Regulations 2012, SI 2012/215, regs 17, 19, as from 1 July 2012.

[2.1366]

[5 Pay reference periods for the purposes of section 20(1)(b) and (c) and section 26(4)(b) and (5)(b) of the Act

(1) The pay reference periods for the purposes of section 20(1)(b) and (c) (quality requirement: UK money purchase schemes) and section 26(4)(b) and (5)(b) (quality requirement: UK personal pension schemes) of the Act are as follows.

(2) In relation to any person—

(a) the person's first pay reference period is to begin—
 (i) on the first day, on or after the staging date, that a person is both a jobholder and an active member of a qualifying scheme; or

(ii) where there has been a period beginning after that first day, during which the requirements of section 1(1)(a) or (c) of the Act were not met but the person remained an active member of a qualifying scheme, on the day following the last day of that period; and

(b) the person's subsequent pay reference periods begin on the anniversary of the employer's staging date.

(3) The pay reference period in relation to any person ends on the day on which the person ceases to be a jobholder of the employer or ceases to be an active member of a qualifying scheme.]

NOTES

Commencement: 1 July 2012.

Substituted by the Automatic Enrolment (Miscellaneous Amendments) Regulations 2012, SI 2012/215, regs 17, 20, as from 1 July 2012.

[PART 1A
EXEMPTION

[2.1367]

5A Exemption of European employers

Sections 2(1), 3(2), 5(2), 7(3), 9(2) and 54 of the Act (employer's obligations regarding membership of a qualifying scheme) do not apply in relation to a person's employment of an individual in relation to whom the person is a European employer.]

NOTES

Commencement: 2 July 2012.

Part 1A (reg 5A) inserted by the Occupational and Personal Pension Schemes (Automatic Enrolment) (Amendment) (No 2) Regulations 2012, SI 2012/1477, reg 2, as from 2 July 2012.

PART 2
AUTOMATIC ENROLMENT, OPT OUT AND REFUNDS

[2.1368]

6 Arrangements to achieve active membership

(1) The arrangements the employer must make in accordance with section 3(2) (automatic enrolment) of the Act are to enter into arrangements with—

(a) the trustees or managers of an automatic enrolment scheme which is an occupational pension scheme, so that before the end of a period of one month beginning with the automatic enrolment date the jobholder to whom section 3 of the Act applies becomes an active member of that scheme with effect from the automatic enrolment date; or

(b) the provider of an automatic enrolment scheme which is a personal pension scheme, so that before the end of a period of one month beginning with the automatic enrolment date the jobholder to whom section 3 of the Act applies is given information about the terms and conditions of the agreement to be deemed to exist under paragraph (2).

(2) Where the employer enters into arrangements with a personal pension scheme provider under paragraph (1)(b), the jobholder is deemed to have entered into an agreement to be an active member of that scheme with effect from the automatic enrolment date, on the later of—

(a) the date on which the personal pension scheme provider gives the information required by paragraph (1)(b); or

(b) the date on which the employer gives the jobholder the enrolment information in accordance with regulation 7(1)(a).

(3) The terms and conditions of an agreement deemed to exist under paragraph (2) must, as a minimum—

(a) explain the purpose of the personal pension scheme;

(b) specify the services to be provided by the personal pension scheme provider;

(c) specify the value of any contributions payable by the jobholder, where this information is available to the personal pension scheme provider;

(d) specify the charges which may be payable to the personal pension scheme provider; and

(e) in the absence of a choice made by the jobholder, explain the investment strategy adopted by the personal pension scheme provider in relation to any contributions payable to the scheme by or in respect of the jobholder.

(4) In paragraph (1)(b) the reference to "terms and conditions" is a reference to the terms and conditions mentioned in paragraph (3).

NOTES

Commencement: 1 July 2012.

[2.1369]
7

(1) Subject to paragraph (2), for the purposes of the arrangements under section 3(2) of the Act, at any time before the end of a period of one month beginning with the automatic enrolment date, the employer must give—

(a) the jobholder the enrolment information in writing; and
(b) the trustees or managers of the occupational pension scheme or the personal pension scheme provider the jobholder information in writing.

(2) The requirement in paragraph (1)(b) does not apply in relation to the information specified in regulation 3(1)(g), (h), (i), (j) or (k), where the trustees or managers of the occupational pension scheme notify, or the personal pension scheme provider notifies, the employer that they do not require that piece of information for the purposes of arrangements under section 3(2) of the Act.

(3) Where the information referred to in regulation 3(1)(f) is not available to the employer on the automatic enrolment date, the employer must give the trustees or managers of the occupational pension scheme or the personal pension scheme provider that information within one month from the date on which the employer receives it.

NOTES

Commencement: 1 July 2012.

[2.1370]
8

An employer must, on or after the automatic enrolment date, deduct any contributions payable by the jobholder to the scheme, from any qualifying earnings or pensionable pay due to the jobholder in any applicable pay reference period.

NOTES

Commencement: 1 July 2012.

[2.1371]
9 Opting Out

(1) A jobholder who has become an active member of an occupational pension scheme or a personal pension scheme in accordance with arrangements under section 3(2) of the Act, may opt out by giving their employer a valid opt out notice obtained and given in accordance with this regulation.

(2) Where the jobholder has become an active member of an occupational pension scheme, the jobholder must give their employer a valid opt out notice within a period of one month beginning with the later of—

(a) the date on which the jobholder became an active member of the scheme in accordance with regulation 6(1)(a), or
(b) the date on which the jobholder was given the enrolment information.

(3) Where the jobholder has become an active member of a personal pension scheme, the jobholder must give their employer a valid opt out notice within a period of one month beginning with the date on which the agreement was deemed to exist under regulation 6(2).

(4) Subject to paragraph (5), the jobholder may only obtain an opt out notice from the scheme in which the jobholder is an active member.

(5) Where the jobholder is an active member of a scheme which is an occupational pension scheme and that scheme has, in its trust instrument, expressly delegated its administrative functions to the employer, the jobholder may obtain an opt out notice from that employer.

(6) An opt out notice is valid if—

(a) it is in the form set out in [Schedule 1];
(b) it includes the jobholder's name;
(c) it includes the jobholder's national insurance number or date of birth;
(d) it is signed by the jobholder or, where the notice is in an electronic format, it must include a statement confirming that the jobholder personally submitted the notice; and
(e) it is dated.

(7) Where the employer is given an opt out notice which is not valid—

(a) the employer must inform the jobholder of the reason for the invalidity, and
(b) paragraphs (2) and (3) are modified so that for the reference to "one month" there is substituted "6 weeks".

NOTES

Commencement: 1 July 2012.

Para (6): words in square brackets in sub-para (a) substituted by the Automatic Enrolment (Miscellaneous Amendments) Regulations 2012, SI 2012/215, regs 17, 43(1), as from 1 July 2012.

[2.1372]
10

Where an employer is given a valid opt out notice, the employer must inform the scheme in which the jobholder is an active member that a valid opt out notice has been received.

NOTES

Commencement: 1 July 2012.

[2.1373]
11 Refunds

(1) Where an employer receives a valid opt out notice, that employer must refund to the jobholder before the refund date any contributions paid to the scheme by the jobholder and any contributions made on behalf of the jobholder, except where any of those refunds are required to be paid as tax.

(2) Where a scheme receives the information required by regulation 10, the trustees or managers of the occupational pension scheme or the provider of the personal pension scheme, as the case may be, must refund to the employer before the refund date any contributions made to the scheme by the jobholder and any contributions made to the scheme by the employer on behalf or in respect of the jobholder.

(3) For the purposes of this regulation "the refund date" is—

(a) the date one month from the date on which the employer is given a valid opt out notice; or

(b) where the opt out notice is given to the employer after the employer's payroll arrangements have closed, the last day of the second applicable pay reference period following the date on which a valid opt out notice is given.

NOTES

Commencement: 1 July 2012.

PART 3
AUTOMATIC RE-ENROLMENT

[2.1374]
12 Automatic re-enrolment dates

(1) Subject to paragraphs . . . (3) and (4), the automatic re-enrolment date for the purposes of section 5 (automatic re-enrolment) of the Act—

(a) is the date chosen at the discretion of the employer, within a period [beginning 3 months before, and ending at the end of the period of 3 months beginning with,] the third anniversary of the staging date; and

(b) thereafter, is the date chosen at the discretion of the employer, within a period [beginning 3 months before, and ending at the end of the period of 3 months beginning with,] the third anniversary of the date chosen for the previous automatic re-enrolment date.

(2) . . .

(3) In a case under section 6(4) of the Act, the automatic re-enrolment date for the purposes of section 5 is the day after the day on which [the jobholder ceases to be an active member of the scheme].

(4) In a case under section 6(5) of the Act, the automatic re-enrolment date for the purposes of section 5 is the first day on which all the requirements of section 1(1) (jobholders) of the Act are met (so that the person is a jobholder from that date).

NOTES

Commencement: 1 July 2012.

Words omitted revoked, and words in square brackets substituted, by the Automatic Enrolment (Miscellaneous Amendments) Regulations 2012, SI 2012/215, regs 17, 21, as from 1 July 2012.

[2.1375]
13 Arrangements to achieve active membership

(1) Except where the jobholder becomes an active member of an automatic enrolment scheme under paragraph (2), the arrangements in regulations 6, 7 and 8 are the arrangements prescribed to achieve active membership for the purposes of section 5 of the Act, but with the following modifications—

(a) in regulation 6 for all references to "section 3" substitute "section 5";

(b) in regulations 6, 7 and 8 for all references to "section 3(2)" substitute "section 5(2)"; and

(c) in regulations 6, 7 and 8 for all references to "the automatic enrolment date" substitute "the automatic re-enrolment date".

(2) Subject to paragraph (3), where before the jobholder's automatic re-enrolment date, the jobholder is a member of a personal pension scheme, or in a case under section 6(5) of the Act a member of a personal pension scheme or an occupational pension scheme, the employer may meet the obligation in section 5(2) of the Act by—

(a) before the end of a period of one month beginning with the automatic re-enrolment date, entering into arrangements with the provider or the trustees or managers of the scheme of which the jobholder is a member so that—

(i) the scheme is an automatic enrolment scheme; and

(ii) the jobholder is an active member of that scheme; and

(b) satisfying the requirements of regulation 7, as if for all references in regulation 7 to "section 3(2)" there was substituted "section 5(2)" and for all references to "the automatic enrolment date" there was substituted "the automatic re-enrolment date".

(3) Paragraph (2)(b) does not apply in a case under section 6(5) of the Act.

NOTES

Commencement: 1 July 2012.

[2.1376]

[14 Jobholders excluded from automatic re-enrolment

(1) Section 5(2) of the Act does not apply in the cases to which paragraphs (2) and (3) apply.

(2) This paragraph applies where, in relation to re-enrolment in a case under section 5(1) of the Act, within the period of 12 months before the automatic re-enrolment date referred to in regulation 12(1)—

(a) the jobholder ceased to be an active member of a qualifying scheme because of an action or omission by the jobholder or by the employer at the jobholder's request; or

(b) the jobholder gave notice under section 8 of the Act.

(3) This paragraph applies where, in relation to re-enrolment in a case under section 5(1B) of the Act, the jobholder has ceased to be an active member of the qualifying scheme in question because of any action or omission by the employer and the action or omission was at the jobholder's request.]

NOTES

Commencement: 1 July 2012.

Substituted by the Automatic Enrolment (Miscellaneous Amendments) Regulations 2012, SI 2012/215, regs 17, 22, as from 1 July 2012.

[2.1377]

15 Opting out

The arrangements in regulations 9 and 10 are the arrangements for the purposes of section 8 (jobholder's right to opt out) of the Act in relation to a jobholder who has become an active member of an automatic enrolment scheme under section 5 of the Act, but with the modification that in paragraph (1) of regulation 9 for "section 3(2)" substitute "section 5(2)".

NOTES

Commencement: 1 July 2012.

[2.1378]

16 Refunds

The arrangements in regulation 11 are the arrangements for the purposes of section 8 of the Act in relation to a jobholder who has become an active member of an automatic enrolment scheme under section 5 of the Act.

NOTES

Commencement: 1 July 2012.

17–53 *(The following Parts have been omitted for reasons of space: Part 4 (Jobholders Opting in to Pension Saving); Part 5 (Workers Joining Pension Saving); Part 6 (Postponement of Automatic Enrolment); Part 7 (Automatic Enrolment Following the Transitional Period for Defined Benefit and Hybrid Schemes); Part 7A (Certification that a Quality or Alternative Requirement is Satisfied); Part 8 (Existing Members of Qualifying Schemes); Part 9 (Automatic Enrolment Schemes); Part 10 (Exclusion as a Qualifying Scheme); Part 11 (Test Scheme); Part 12 (Hybrid Schemes); Part 13 (Non-UK Pension Schemes); Part 14 (Due Dates); Part 15 (Special Occupations); Part 16 (Review).)*

SCHEDULES

[SCHEDULE 1]
FORM OF OPT OUT NOTICE

Regulation 9(6)(a)

[2.1379]

Notice to opt out of pension saving

IF YOU WANT TO OPT OUT OF PENSION SAVING FILL IN THIS FORM AND GIVE IT TO YOUR EMPLOYER

Your full name . . . .

Your employer's name . . . .

Your national insurance number or date of birth . . . .

I wish to opt out of pension saving.

I understand that if I opt out I will lose the right to pension contributions from my employer.

I understand that if I opt out I may have a lower income when I retire.

SIGNED . . . .

DATE . . . .

WHAT YOU NEED TO KNOW

Your employer cannot ask you or force you to opt out.

If you are asked or forced to opt out you can tell the Pensions Regulator – see www.thepensionsregulator.gov.uk.

If you change your mind you may be able to opt back in – write to your employer if you want to do this.

If you stay opted out your employer will normally put you back into pension saving in around 3 years.

If you change job your new employer will normally put you back into pension saving straight away.

If you have another job your other employer might also put you into pension saving, now or in the future. This notice only opts you out of pension saving with the employer you name above. A separate notice must be filled out and given to any other employer you work for if you wish to opt out of that pension saving as well.

NOTES

Commencement: 1 July 2012.

This Schedule was numbered as Schedule 1 by the Automatic Enrolment (Miscellaneous Amendments) Regulations 2012, SI 2012/215, regs 17, 43(2), as from 1 July 2012.

[SCHEDULE 2
INFORMATION

Regulation 2, 17, 21, 24, 27 and 33

[2.1380]

1. A statement that the jobholder has been or will be automatically enrolled, automatically re-enrolled or enrolled, as the case may be, into a pension scheme to help save for the jobholder's retirement.

2. The jobholder's automatic enrolment date, automatic re-enrolment date or enrolment date, as the case may be or, for a jobholder to whom regulation 28 or 29 applies, the day or date mentioned in regulation 6 as modified by regulation 28 or 29, as the case may be.

3. The name, address, telephone number and electronic contact details of the scheme in respect of which the jobholder is or will be an active member.

4. (1) The value of any contributions payable to the scheme by the employer and the jobholder in any applicable pay reference period.

(2) The information to be given to the jobholder under sub-paragraph (1) includes information on any change in the value of any contributions payable to the scheme by the employer or jobholder in any applicable pay reference period which will occur as the result of any changes to contributions brought about by the transitional periods for money purchase and personal pension schemes under section 29 of the Act (transitional periods for money purchase and personal pension schemes).

(3) The "value" of contributions may be expressed as a fixed amount or a percentage of any qualifying earnings or pensionable pay due to the jobholder in any applicable pay reference period.

Part 2 Statutory Instruments

5. A statement that any contributions payable to the scheme by the jobholder have been or will be deducted from any qualifying earnings or pensionable pay due to the jobholder.

6. Confirmation as to whether tax relief is or will be given in accordance with section 192 (relief at source) or 193 (relief under net pay arrangements) of the Finance Act 2004.

7. A statement that if the jobholder, on a date, ceases to be an active member of a qualifying scheme (without the jobholder ceasing to be employed by the employer) by reason of something other than an action or omission by the jobholder, the employer must make arrangements by which the jobholder becomes an active member of an automatic enrolment scheme with effect from the day following that date.

8. A statement that the jobholder has the right to opt out of the scheme during the opt out period.

9. A statement indicating the start and end dates of the opt out period applicable to the jobholder if that information is known to the employer but if not, a statement that the opt out period is the period determined in accordance with regulation 9(2) or (3) of the Occupational and Personal Pension Schemes (Automatic Enrolment) Regulations 2010.

10. Where the opt out notice may be obtained.

11. A statement that opting out means that the jobholder will be treated for all purposes as not having become an active member of the scheme on that occasion.

12. A statement that after a valid opt out notice is given to the employer in accordance with regulation 9(2) or (3) any contributions paid by the jobholder will be refunded to the jobholder by the employer.

13. A statement that where the jobholder opts out the jobholder may opt in, in which case the employer will be required to arrange for that jobholder to become an active member of an automatic enrolment scheme once in any 12 month period.

14. A statement that, after the opt out period, the jobholder may cease to make contributions in accordance with scheme rules.

15. A statement that a jobholder who opts out or who ceases active membership of the scheme will normally be automatically re-enrolled into an automatic enrolment scheme by the employer in accordance with regulations made under section 5 of the Act (automatic re-enrolment).

16. A statement that the jobholder may, by giving written notice to the employer, require the employer to make arrangements for the jobholder to become an active member of an automatic enrolment scheme and that the jobholder will be entitled to employer's contributions.

17. A statement that the worker may, where they are working or ordinarily work in Great Britain and are aged at least 16 and under 75 and are not a member of a pension scheme that satisfies the requirements of section 9 of the Act, by giving written notice to the employer, require the employer to make arrangements for the worker to become an active member of such a pension scheme.

18. A statement that, by giving a written notice to the employer, the worker may—

(a) where they earn more than the amount specified in section 13(1)(a) of the Act (and the amount must be given) and are a jobholder and not an active member of a qualifying scheme, opt in to an automatic enrolment scheme and that the jobholder will be entitled to employer's contributions;

(b) where they are not a jobholder, for the sole reason that they earn no more than the amount specified in section 13(1)(a) of the Act (and the amount must be given), and are not a member of a pension scheme that satisfies the requirements of section 9 of the Act, require the employer to make arrangements for the worker to become an active member of such a pension scheme.

19. A statement where the worker is a jobholder and an active member of a qualifying scheme and, on a date, ceases to be such a member (without the jobholder ceasing to be employed by the employer) by reason of something other than an action or omission by the jobholder, the employer must make arrangements by which the jobholder becomes an active member of an automatic enrolment scheme with effect from the day following that date.

20. A statement that the employer has deferred automatic enrolment until the deferral date (and the date must be given).

21. A statement that the employer will automatically enrol the worker into an automatic enrolment scheme if, on the deferral date, the worker is aged 22 or more but less than state pension age, is working or ordinarily works in Great Britain, earnings of more than the amount specified in section 3(1)(c) of the Act (and the amount must be given) are payable to the worker and the worker is not already an active member of a qualifying scheme.

22. A statement that the employer intends to defer automatic enrolment in respect of that jobholder until the end of the transitional period for defined benefit and hybrid schemes.

23. Confirmation that the jobholder is an active member of a qualifying scheme.

24. A statement that a written notice from the worker must be signed by the worker or, if it is given by means of an electronic communication, must include a statement that the worker personally submitted the notice.

25. Where to obtain further information about pensions and saving for retirement.]

NOTES

Commencement: 1 July 2012.

Added by the Automatic Enrolment (Miscellaneous Amendments) Regulations 2012, SI 2012/215, regs 17, 43(3), Schedule, as from 1 July 2012.

EMPLOYEE STUDY AND TRAINING (QUALIFYING PERIOD OF EMPLOYMENT) REGULATIONS 2010

(SI 2010/800)

NOTES

Made: 15 March 2010.

Authority: Employment Rights Act 1996, s 63D(6)(a).

Commencement: 6 April 2010.

Note that the enabling provisions under which these Regulations are made have (as at 6 April 2013) only been brought into force with regard to employers with at least 250 employees; see the note to s 63D of the 1996 Act at **[1.840]**. Note also that the government has announced that it does not intend to bring these provisions into force for other employers.

[2.1381]

1 Citation, commencement and interpretation

(1) These Regulations may be cited as the Employee Study and Training (Qualifying Period of Employment) Regulations 2010 and come into force on 6th April 2010.

(2) In these Regulations, "the 1996 Act" means the Employment Rights Act 1996.

NOTES

Commencement: 6 April 2010 (see further the introductory notes to these Regulations).

[2.1382]

2 Duration of employment

(1) For the purposes of section 63D(6) of the 1996 Act, in order to be a qualifying employee, an employee must have been continuously employed for a period of not less than 26 weeks.

(2) In paragraph (1), a period of continuous employment means a period computed in accordance with Chapter 1 of Part 14 of the 1996 Act, as if that paragraph were a provision of that Act.

NOTES

Commencement: 6 April 2010 (see further the introductory notes to these Regulations).

NATIONAL EMPLOYMENT SAVINGS TRUST ORDER 2010

(SI 2010/917)

NOTES

Made: 22 March 2010.

Authority: Pensions Act 2008, ss 67(1), (8), 68(1)–(3), (5), 69(1)–(3), (5), 70(1), (2), 144(2)–(4), 145(1).

Commencement: 5 July 2010.

ARRANGEMENT OF ARTICLES

PART 1
GENERAL

PART 2
ESTABLISHMENT, CONSTITUTION OF THE SCHEME AND APPOINTMENTS

PART 1
GENERAL

[2.1383]
1 Citation and commencement

(1) This Order may be cited as the National Employment Savings Trust Order 2010.

(2) Article 20 shall come into force on 5th July 2010 and cease to have effect on [1st March 2018].

(3) The remaining provisions of this Order shall come into force on 5th July 2010.

NOTES

Commencement: 5 July 2010.

Para (2): words in square brackets substituted by the National Employment Savings Trust (Amendment) Order 2013, SI 2013/597, art 2(1), (2), as from 1 April 2013.

[2.1384]
2 Interpretation

In this Order—

"the 1999 Act" means the Welfare Reform and Pensions Act 1999;

"the 1999 Order" means the Welfare Reform and Pensions (Northern Ireland) Order 1999;

"the Act" means the Pensions Act 2008;

"the NI Act" means the Pensions (No 2) Act (Northern Ireland) 2008;

"the corporation" means the National Employment Savings Trust Corporation established under section 75 of the Act;

"data" and "personal data" have the same meanings as in section 1 of the Data Protection Act 1998;

"employers' panel" means the panel referred to in article 6(2)(b);

"jobholder" has the meaning given by—

(a) in relation to Great Britain, section 1(1) of the Act; or

(b) in relation to Northern Ireland, section 1(1) of the NI Act;

"member of the Scheme" means a person who has been admitted as a member of the Scheme under article 19 and whose pension account has not yet been fully discharged through the provision of one or more benefits under article 32;

"members' panel" means the panel referred to in article 6(2)(a);

"member's pension account" means an account maintained by the Trustee for a member of the Scheme comprising—

(a) the member's contributions;

(b) contributions made by any participating employer;

(c) any sums transferred into the Scheme in respect of the member;

(d) investment returns; and

(e) any other amounts paid to the Trustee to be applied to the member's pension account,

less any expenses and outgoings properly deducted by the Trustee;

"the panels" means the members' panel and the employers' panel;

["participating employer" means an employer that has been admitted to participation in the Scheme and, except in articles 8 and 19, may include an employer that was formerly participating in the Scheme;]

"pension credit" means a credit—

(a) in relation to Great Britain, under section 29 of the 1999 Act; or

(b) in relation to Northern Ireland, under Article 26 of the 1999 Order;

"qualifying arrangement" has the same meaning—

(a) in relation to Great Britain, as in paragraph 6(1) of Schedule 5 to the 1999 Act; or

(b) in relation to Northern Ireland, as in paragraph 6(1) of Schedule 5 to the 1999 Order;

["qualifying person" and "qualifying self-employed person" have the same meanings as—

(a) in Great Britain, in regulation 2(1) of the Occupational Pension Schemes (Cross-border Activities) Regulations 2005; or

(b) in Northern Ireland, in regulation 2(1) of the Occupational Pension Schemes (Cross-border Activities) Regulations (Northern Ireland) 2005;

"quality requirement" means the quality requirement under—

(a) in relation to Great Britain, Part 1 of the Act; or

(b) in relation to Northern Ireland, Part 1 of the NI Act;]

"rules" means rules made under section 67 of the Act;

"the Scheme" means the pension scheme established by article 3(1); and

"the Trustee" means the person appointed as trustee of the Scheme.

NOTES

Commencement: 5 July 2010.

Definition "participating employer" substituted and definitions "qualifying person", "qualifying self-employed person" and "quality requirement" inserted, by the National Employment Savings Trust (Amendment) Order 2013, SI 2013/597, art 2(1), (3), as from 1 April 2013.

PART 2
ESTABLISHMENT, CONSTITUTION OF THE SCHEME AND APPOINTMENTS

[2.1385]

3 Establishment of the National Employment Savings Trust

(1) There is to be a pension scheme known as the National Employment Savings Trust.

(2) The purpose of the Scheme is the provision of pensions and other benefits in relation to its members.

NOTES

Commencement: 5 July 2010.

[2.1386]

4 Trustee

The corporation is appointed as trustee of the Scheme.

NOTES

Commencement: 5 July 2010.

[2.1387]

5 Appointment of members of the corporation

Where the members' panel has been established, then, in relation to the appointment by the corporation of an individual as a member of the corporation, or a member of the corporation as chair of the corporation—

(a) the corporation must consult the members' panel with respect to any job description or selection criteria that the corporation proposes to use;

(b) the members' panel must nominate one of their members to participate in any meeting or other discussion that is to be held by the corporation with respect to the creation of a shortlist of candidates, and in any interview of a candidate; and

(c) the corporation must supply that member with a copy of any documents that the corporation is to consider when it decides who should be included in the shortlist, or who should be appointed, and must take into account any views expressed by that member before it makes its decision.

NOTES

Commencement: 5 July 2010.

[2.1388]

6 Consultation of members and employers

(1) The Trustee must make and maintain such arrangements as the Trustee considers expedient for consulting members of the Scheme and participating employers about the operation, development or amendment of the Scheme.

(2) Those arrangements must include the establishment and maintenance of—

(a) a panel to represent members of the Scheme (the members' panel); and

(b) a panel to represent participating employers (the employers' panel).

NOTES

Commencement: 5 July 2010.

[2.1389]

7 Establishment of the panels

The Trustee must take all reasonable steps to establish the panels as soon as practicable and, in any event, within 12 months after the first day on which a contribution is made to the Scheme by, or on behalf or in respect of, a member of the Scheme.

NOTES

Commencement: 5 July 2010.

[2.1390]

8 Composition and functions of the panels

(1) The Trustee must make provision in relation to—

(a) the composition of the panels;

(b) the selection, appointment and removal of their members; and

(c) the functions of the panels.

(2) Such provision must—

(a) ensure that, in relation to each panel, the minimum number of members of the panel is 9 and the maximum number is 15;

(b) ensure that the members' panel cannot be comprised entirely of individuals who are not members of the Scheme;

(c) ensure that the employers' panel cannot be comprised entirely of individuals who are not a participating employer or connected with such an employer;

(d) provide for the functions of the employers' panel to include—

(i) without prejudice to the generality of paragraph (ii), providing comments to the Trustee where the employers' panel is consulted by the Trustee on the preparation or revision of a statement of investment principles; and

(ii) giving any assistance or advice that the Trustee may require or that the panel may consider expedient, in connection with the operation, development or amendment of the Scheme.

(e) provide for the functions of the members' panel to include—

(i) in relation to each financial year, making a report on the extent to which the Trustee has taken into account the views of members of the Scheme and the views of the members' panel (with respect to views which the panel is able to express pursuant to its functions), when the Trustee makes decisions about the operation, development or amendment of the Scheme;

(ii) participating in the process for the appointment of an individual as a member or chair of the corporation, as set out in article 5;

(iii) without prejudice to the generality of paragraph (iv), providing comments to the Trustee where the panel is consulted by it on the preparation or revision of a statement of investment principles; and

(iv) giving any assistance or advice which the Trustee may require or which the panel may consider expedient, in connection with the operation, development or amendment of the Scheme.

(3) In relation to the report referred to in paragraph (2)(e)(i)—

(a) the Trustee must make provision for the members' panel to send a copy of it to the Secretary of State and the Trustee;

(b) the Trustee must make it available by—

(i) placing a copy of it on the internet; and

(ii) subject to sub-paragraph (c), sending a copy of it to any person who requests a copy; and

(c) where the Trustee makes a charge in connection with the sending under sub-paragraph (b)(ii) of a copy of the report, the Trustee is not obliged to send the copy until the Trustee has received payment of the charge.

(4) Where the members' panel has been established, the Trustee must, before it prepares or revises a statement of investment principles, consult that panel.

(5) In this article—

(a) "financial year" means the 12 months ending on 31st March in each year; and

(b) "statement of investment principles"—

(i) in Great Britain, has the same meaning as in section 35 of the Pensions Act 1995; and

(ii) in Northern Ireland, has the same meaning as in Article 35 of the Pensions (Northern Ireland) Order 1995.

NOTES

Commencement: 5 July 2010.

[2.1391]

9 Payments to members of the panels

(1) The Trustee may make provision for reasonable payments to be made to members of the panels.

(2) Any payments made under paragraph (1) shall be regarded as part of the general costs of administration and management of the Scheme for the purposes of article 27.

NOTES

Commencement: 5 July 2010.

PART 3
FUNCTIONS OF THE TRUSTEE

[2.1392]

10 Disclosure of requested data to the Secretary of State

(1) This article applies where the Secretary of State (S) requests the disclosure of data held by the Trustee ("requested data") which are—

(a) not personal data; and

(b) in any event, anonymised.

(2) The Trustee must disclose requested data to S if those data are necessary for S or the Trustee—

(a) to comply with any—

(i) legal obligation (in particular the duty of S to establish a pension scheme, contained in section 67 of the Act); or

(ii) requirement to notify or otherwise inform another person,

which, if S did not receive those data, would result in a breach of that obligation or requirement; or

(b) to comply with any request made by a person appointed by S under section 74 of the Act to review any of the matters listed in subsection (1) of that section.

(3) The Trustee must disclose requested data to S for the purpose of the matters listed in paragraph (5) where the Trustee considers that to comply with S's request would not involve disproportionate cost, time or effort.

(4) Where the Trustee—

(a) considers that to comply with S's request would involve disproportionate cost, time or effort; and

(b) gives to S its reasons for considering that this is the case, it need disclose to S only so much of the requested data as is agreed with S.

(5) The matters are—

(a) the assessment by S of the performance, administration or management of the Scheme; or

(b) the use by S for functions relating to private pensions policy or retirement planning.

(6) In this article, "private pensions policy" has the same meaning as in paragraph 4 of Schedule 10 to the Pensions Act 2004 and "retirement planning" has the same meaning as in paragraph 2 of that Schedule.

NOTES

Commencement: 5 July 2010.

[2.1393]

11 Disclosure of relevant personal data to the Secretary of State

(1) This article applies where the Trustee is requested by the Secretary of State (S) to obtain the consent of one or more—

(a) members of the Scheme; or

(b) participating employers,

in order that those members or participating employers may be contacted by S for the purpose of research.

(2) The Trustee may contact any number of members or participating employers to obtain their consent, as the Trustee sees fit to comply with the request of S.

(3) Where—

(a) consent is given, the Trustee may then disclose relevant personal data to S; or

(b) consent is not given, the Trustee must not disclose any relevant personal data to S.

(4) Where paragraph (3)(a) applies—

(a) the Trustee must only disclose relevant personal data to S after satisfying itself that there is a secure means of disclosing them, agreed with S;

(b) S may contact the person from whom the consent was obtained; and

(c) S must state to that person S's specified and lawful purposes related to research.

(5) In this article, "relevant personal data" means personal data which enable S to contact a member of the Scheme or a participating employer of a member of the Scheme, and may include a person's—

(a) email address;

(b) address; or

(c) telephone number.

NOTES

Commencement: 5 July 2010.

[2.1394]

12 Disclosure: references to the Secretary of State

(1) In articles 10 and 11, references to the Secretary of State apply equally to—

(a) a person providing services to, or on behalf of, the Secretary of State or the Northern Ireland Department; or

(b) the Northern Ireland Department.

(2) In this article, "the Northern Ireland Department" means the Department for Social Development in Northern Ireland.

NOTES

Commencement: 5 July 2010.

[2.1395]

13 Protection

(1) Subject to paragraph (3), the Trustee and the members and staff of the corporation shall not be liable for any act or omission in connection with the administration or management of the Scheme except—

(a) an act or omission which amounts to a breach of trust and arises from its or their own wilful act or omission, fraud or dishonesty; or

(b) where the liability is a liability that cannot be excluded or restricted, by virtue of—

(i) in Great Britain, section 33 of the Pensions Act 1995; or

(ii) in Northern Ireland, Article 33 of the Pensions (Northern Ireland) Order 1995.

(2) Without prejudice to the generality of paragraph (1), the reference in paragraph (1) to liability for any act or omission in connection with the administration or management of the Scheme includes a reference to liability for any loss, however caused, occasioned to a member of the Scheme by—

(a) the arrangement by the Trustee of investment funds under article 29(2); or

(b) the member's choice to direct assets of the Scheme attributable to their pension account to any particular investment fund.

(3) In so far as paragraph (1) would exclude liability for the acts or defaults of a fund manager in the exercise of a discretion delegated to such a person under—

(a) in Great Britain, section 34(5)(b) of the Pensions Act 1995; or

(b) in Northern Ireland, Article 34(5)(b) of the Pensions (Northern Ireland) Order 1995,

liability for such acts or defaults is only excluded provided that the steps set out in the provision specified in paragraph (4) have been taken by the Trustee.

(4) The specified provision is—

(a) in Great Britain, section 34(6) of the Pensions Act 1995; and

(b) in Northern Ireland, Article 34(6) of the Pensions (Northern Ireland) Order 1995.

(5) The Trustee may in accordance with [paragraph (7)] indemnify itself or the members or staff of the corporation against any losses, costs and damages it or they may incur in connection with the administration or management of the Scheme except for losses, costs or damages arising from—

(a) an act or omission which amounts to a breach of trust and arises from its or their own wilful act or omission, fraud or dishonesty;

(b) a liability which cannot be excluded or restricted, by virtue of—

(i) in Great Britain, section 33 of the Pensions Act 1995; or

(ii) in Northern Ireland, Article 33 of the Pensions (Northern Ireland) Order 1995; or

(c) a liability to pay a fine or penalty—

(i) in Great Britain, as described in section 256(1) of the Pensions Act 2004; or

(ii) in Northern Ireland, as described in Article 233(1) of the Pensions (Northern Ireland) Order 2005.

(6) The Trustee may insure—

(a) the Scheme against any loss caused by itself, the members or staff of the corporation, or its agents; or

(b) itself, the members or staff of the corporation against any losses, costs or damages arising from a liability in connection with the administration or management of the Scheme except for a liability—

(i) which arises from an act or omission which amounts to a breach of trust and arises from its or their own wilful act or omission, fraud or dishonesty;

(ii) that cannot be excluded or restricted, by virtue of section 33 of the Pensions Act 1995 (in relation to Great Britain) or Article 33 of the Pensions (Northern Ireland) Order 1995 (in relation to Northern Ireland); or

(iii) to pay a fine or penalty as described in section 256(1) of the Pensions Act 2004 (in relation to Great Britain) or Article 233(1) of the Pensions (Northern Ireland) Order 2005 (in relation to Northern Ireland).

(7) Where the Trustee decides to indemnify itself, or the members or staff of the corporation, under paragraph (5), the losses, costs or damages in question shall be regarded for the purposes of article 27 as part of the general costs of administration and management of the Scheme.

(8) Where the Trustee decides to take out insurance under paragraph (6), the costs of taking out the insurance shall be regarded, for the purposes of article 27, as part of the general costs of administration and management of the Scheme.

NOTES

Commencement: 5 July 2010.

Para (5): words in square brackets substituted by the National Employment Savings Trust (Amendment) Order 2013, SI 2013/597, art 2(1), (4), as from 1 April 2013.

[2.1396]

14 Steps for increasing awareness of the Scheme

The Trustee may take such steps as it considers appropriate for increasing awareness and understanding of the Scheme in order that employers and individuals who may be admitted as members of the Scheme may assess whether they wish to use the Scheme.

NOTES

Commencement: 5 July 2010.

[2.1397]

15 Power to make rules

The Trustee may make rules and may revoke, amend or re-enact any rules made by it or the Secretary of State.

NOTES

Commencement: 5 July 2010.

[2.1398]
16 Application of the Trustee Act 2000

The Trustee Act 2000 applies as if this Order and any rules were a trust instrument.

NOTES
Commencement: 5 July 2010.

[2.1399]
17 Information about the Scheme

(1) The Trustee must as soon as possible following the preparation of any of the documents specified in paragraph (2), make the document available by placing a copy of it on the internet.

(2) The specified documents are—
- (a) a document of the kind referred to—
  - (i) in Great Britain, in regulation 6(1) of the Occupational Pension Schemes (Disclosure of Information) Regulations 1996; or
  - (ii) in Northern Ireland, in regulation 6(1) of the Occupational Pension Schemes (Disclosure of Information) Regulations (Northern Ireland) 1997;
- (b) the annual report of the corporation sent to the Secretary of State under paragraph 17 of Schedule 1 to the Act; and
- (c) the annual statement of accounts of the corporation prepared under paragraph 20 of Schedule 1 to the Act.

NOTES
Commencement: 5 July 2010.

PART 4
SCHEME MEMBERSHIP AND EMPLOYER PARTICIPATION

[2.1400]
18 Duty to admit employers

(1) Subject to paragraph (2), the Trustee must admit to participation in the Scheme, on condition that the employer agrees to employer terms and conditions—
- (a) an employer of a jobholder that wishes to comply with its duty in relation to the jobholder under—
  - (i) in relation to Great Britain, section 3(2), 5(2) or 7(3) of the Act; or
  - (ii) in relation to Northern Ireland, section 3(2), 5(2) or 7(3) of the NI Act,

  by arranging for the jobholder to become a member of the Scheme or by making arrangements in relation to the jobholder as referred to in article 19(6);
- (b) an employer of a jobholder that wishes to arrange for the jobholder to become a member of the Scheme or to make arrangements in relation to the jobholder as referred to in article 19(6), for the purposes of—
  - (i) in relation to Great Britain, section 2(3) of the Act (in connection with the duty under section 2(1) of the Act); or
  - (ii) in relation to Northern Ireland, section 2(3) of the NI Act (in connection with the duty under section 2(1) of the NI Act); and
- (c) an employer of a worker that wishes to comply with its duty in relation to the worker under—
  - (i) in relation to Great Britain, section 9(2) of the Act; or
  - (ii) in relation to Northern Ireland, section 9(2) of the NI Act,

  by arranging for the worker to become a member of the Scheme or by making arrangements in relation to the worker as referred to in article 19(6).

(2) Where paragraph (1)(a), (b) or (c) applies and the relevant duty arises by virtue of the employer satisfying the conditions in [regulation 3(3) and (4)] of the Employers' Duties (Implementation) Regulations 2010 (or, in Northern Ireland, the conditions in [regulation 3(3) and (4)] of the Employers' Duties (Implementation) Regulations (Northern Ireland) 2010), then paragraph (1) applies as if—
- (a) for "must admit" there were substituted "may admit"; and
- (b) "on condition that the employer agrees to employer terms and conditions" were omitted.

(3) Where—
- (a) in relation to Great Britain, sections 2 to 9 of the Act; or
- (b) in relation to Northern Ireland, sections 2 to 9 of the NI Act,

do not yet apply in relation to an employer, the Trustee may admit the employer to participation in the Scheme in the circumstances specified in paragraph (4).

(4) The specified circumstances are where—
- (a) the employer is an employer of a worker who—
  - (i) works or ordinarily works in the United Kingdom under the worker's contract; and

(ii) is aged at least 16 and under 75; and

(b) the employer wishes to arrange for the worker to become a member of the Scheme or wishes to make arrangements in relation to the worker as referred to in article 19(6).

(5) Where an employer is admitted to participation in the Scheme under this article, it is admitted with respect to any jobholder or worker of the employer who may at any time be admitted as a member of the Scheme, or with respect to whom arrangements may at any time be made as referred to in article 19(6).

[(5A) A participating employer may, by giving notice to the Trustee, terminate its participation in the Scheme in accordance with rules.]

(6) In this article, "employer terms and conditions" means terms and conditions, provided for by rules, for admittance of employers to participation in the Scheme.

NOTES

Commencement: 5 July 2010.

Para (2): words in square brackets substituted by the National Employment Savings Trust (Amendment) Order 2013, SI 2013/597, art 2(1), (5)(a), as from 1 April 2013.

Para (5A): inserted by SI 2013/597, art 2(1), (5)(b), as from 1 April 2013.

[2.1401]

19 Duty to admit members

(1) Subject to paragraph (6), the Trustee must admit as a member of the Scheme—

(a) a jobholder employed by a participating employer, where the employer wishes to comply with its duty in relation to the jobholder under—

(i) in relation to Great Britain, section 3(2), 5(2) or 7(3) of the Act; or

(ii) in relation to Northern Ireland, section 3(2), 5(2) or 7(3) of the NI Act,

by arranging for the jobholder to become a member of the Scheme;

(b) a jobholder employed by a participating employer, where the employer wishes to make arrangements for the jobholder to become a member of the Scheme for the purposes of—

(i) in relation to Great Britain, section 2(3) of the Act (in connection with the duty in section 2(1) of the Act); or

(ii) in relation to Northern Ireland, section 2(3) of the NI Act (in connection with the duty in section 2(1) of the NI Act); and

(c) a worker employed by a participating employer, where the employer wishes to comply with its duty in relation to the worker under—

(i) in relation to Great Britain, section 9(2) of the Act;

(ii) in relation to Northern Ireland, section 9(2) of the NI Act,

by arranging for the worker to become a member of the Scheme.

(2) Subject to paragraph (6), where—

(a) in relation to Great Britain, sections 2 to 9 of the Act; or

(b) in relation to Northern Ireland, sections 2 to 9 of the NI Act,

do not yet apply in relation to a participating employer, the Trustee may admit as a member of the Scheme a worker employed by the employer in the circumstances specified in paragraph (3).

(3) The specified circumstances are where—

(a) the worker is a worker who—

(i) is working or ordinarily works in the United Kingdom under the worker's contract; and

(ii) is aged at least 16 and under 75; and

(b) the employer and the worker wish the worker to become a member of the Scheme.

[(4) Subject to paragraph (6), the Trustee must admit as a member a person who wishes to join the Scheme and who is—,

(a) a self-employed person aged at least 16 and under 75, who is working or ordinarily works in the United Kingdom and who is not a qualifying self-employed person;

(b) a single person director aged at least 16 and under 75, who is working or ordinarily works in the United Kingdom and who is not a qualifying person; or

(c) a person entitled to a pension credit as referred to in article 31(1)(a)(i).]

(5) In this article—

(a) a person is self-employed if the person is in employment but is not employed [in relation to that employment] by someone else;

(b) in sub-paragraph (a), "employment" includes any trade, business, profession, office or vocation;

(c) a "single person director" means a person who is—

(i) a director of a company; and

(ii) employed by the company under a contract of employment,

where the company does not employ any other persons under a contract of employment;

(d) in sub-paragraph (c), a company includes any body corporate.

(6) Where a person has already been admitted as a member of the Scheme with respect to an employment or a case as described in paragraph (4), then the Trustee must not admit the person afresh but instead must make arrangements whereby contributions may be made by, or on behalf or in respect of, the member as appropriate, in relation to the new employment or new instance in which one of the cases described in paragraph (4) applies.

(7) . . .

NOTES

Commencement: 5 July 2010.

Para (4): substituted by the National Employment Savings Trust (Amendment) Order 2013, SI 2013/597, art 2(1), (6)(a), as from 1 April 2013.

Para (5): words in square brackets inserted by SI 2013/597, art 2(1), (6)(b), as from 1 April 2013.

Para (7): revoked by SI 2013/597, art 2(1), (6)(c), as from 1 April 2013.

[2.1402]

20 Transitory provision

Article 19(4) shall apply as if—

(a) . . .

(b) for "the Trustee must" there were substituted "the Trustee may".

NOTES

Commencement: 5 July 2010.

Words omitted revoked by the National Employment Savings Trust (Amendment) Order 2013, SI 2013/597, art 2(1), (7), as from 1 April 2013.

Note that this article ceases to have effect on 1 March 2018; see art 1 *ante*.

[2.1403]

21 Members' accounts

(1) When a person is admitted as a member of the Scheme, the Trustee must allocate a member's pension account to that person.

(2) Subject to articles 22 to 26 and [paragraphs (2A) and (3)], the Trustee must accept all contributions made by—

(a) a member of the Scheme;

(b) a participating employer of a member of the Scheme, on behalf or in respect of the member, where the member is working or ordinarily works in the United Kingdom; or

[(c) any other person in respect of the member.]

[(2A) The Trustee may refuse to accept contributions which relate to the employment of a member of the Scheme in which the member is—

(a) a qualifying person; or

(b) a qualifying self-employed person.]

(3) The Trustee may determine—

(a) the form in which or the method by which the contributions referred to in paragraph (2) are to be made; or

(b) subject to paragraphs (4) and (5), that, in such cases as are determined by the Trustee, the Trustee may on any occasion refuse to accept a contribution from any of the persons specified in paragraph (2) where the contribution is below such amount as the Trustee determines.

(4) The Trustee must ensure that any determination that it makes under paragraph (3)(b) does not prevent the Scheme from satisfying the quality requirement . . .

(a) . . .

(b) . . .

in relation to a jobholder.

(5) Where the Trustee makes a determination under paragraph (3)(b), it must have regard to the cost of administering contributions.

(6) Contributions as referred to in paragraph (2) must be applied to the relevant member's pension account.

(7) Subject to paragraph (8) and to articles 24 and 26, in the cases specified in paragraph (9) the Trustee may provide a refund of contributions from a member's pension account—

[(a) to the member, where the contributions were made by the member;]

(b) to a participating employer of the member, where the contributions were made by the employer [on behalf of or in respect of the member; or]

[(c) to the person who made the contributions, where the contributions have been made in respect of the member by a person other than the member or a participating employer.]

[(8) In the case specified in paragraph (9)(a), the Trustee must provide a refund of contributions—

(a) where the contributions were made by a participating employer in respect of or on behalf of the member, to the participating employer with respect to which the notice was given;

(b) where the member has made contributions to the Scheme on the member's own behalf, to the member; or

(c) where the contributions have been made by a person other than the member or a participating employer, to the person who made the contributions.]

(9) The specified cases are where—

(a) the member has given notice under—

(i) in Great Britain, section 8 of the Act; or

(ii) in Northern Ireland, section 8 of the NI Act;

(b) the Trustee determines that the contributions have been paid in error; or

(c) the Trustee otherwise determines that a refund is appropriate in all the circumstances.

NOTES

Commencement: 5 July 2010.

Para (2): words in square brackets substituted by the National Employment Savings Trust (Amendment) Order 2013, SI 2013/597, art 2(1), (8)(a), as from 1 April 2013.

Para (2A): inserted by SI 2013/597, art 2(1), (8)(b), as from 1 April 2013.

Para (4): words omitted revoked by SI 2013/597, art 2(1), (8)(c), as from 1 April 2013.

Para (7): sub-para (a) and words in square brackets in sub-para (b) substituted, and sub-para (c) inserted, by SI 2013/597, art 2(1), (8)(d)–(f), as from 1 April 2013.

Para (8): substituted by SI 2013/597, art 2(1), (8)(g), as from 1 April 2013.

PART 5
THE SCHEME FUND

[2.1404]

22 Annual contribution limit

(1) Subject to the following paragraphs, the maximum amount of contributions which may be made by, or on behalf or in respect of, a member of the Scheme in a tax year ("annual contribution limit") is £3,600.

(2) The figure in paragraph (1) is based on the average earnings index for December 2005.

(3) The annual contribution limit must be adjusted by the Trustee in accordance with changes in the average earnings index—

(a) on the first occasion, at any time before the first day on which contributions are paid to the Scheme by, or on behalf or in respect of, members of the Scheme; and

(b) by the start of every subsequent tax year.

(4) The Trustee must—

(a) pursuant to [paragraph (3)], calculate the annual contribution limit, following any relevant provision relating to calculation contained in rules where such provision is made; and

(b) publish that limit in any document considered appropriate by the Trustee.

(5) The Trustee may determine that paragraph (1) does not apply to a member or class of member, in relation to a particular tax year.

(6) In this article, "average earnings index" means the general index of average earnings (for all employees: whole economy: seasonally adjusted) published by the Office for National Statistics or, if that general index is not published for a month for which it is relevant for the purposes of this article, any index or index figures published by that Office in substitution for that general index.

NOTES

Commencement: 5 July 2010.

Para (4): words in square brackets substituted by the National Employment Savings Trust (Amendment) Order 2013, SI 2013/597, art 2(1), (9), as from 1 April 2013.

[2.1405]

23 Annual contribution limit: meaning of contributions

(1) For the purposes of counting towards the annual contribution limit in article 22, "contributions" means any contributions made by, or on behalf or in respect of, a member of the Scheme . . .

(2) But for the same purposes "contributions" do not include—

(a) a cash transfer sum—

(i) in Great Britain, within the meaning of section 101AB(3) of the Pension Schemes Act 1993, used in the way described in section 101AE(2)(a) of that Act; or

(ii) in Northern Ireland, within the meaning of section 97AB(3) of the Pension Schemes (Northern Ireland) Act 1993, used in the way described in section 97AE(2)(a) of that Act;

(b) the discharge by the trustees or managers of a scheme of their liability in respect of a pension credit—

(i) in Great Britain, to which Schedule 5 to the 1999 Act applies; or

(ii) in Northern Ireland, to which Schedule 5 to the 1999 Order applies, by taking the action specified in paragraph (3);

(c) any other transfer of any sum held for the purposes of, or representing accrued rights under, a pension scheme so as to become held for the purposes of, or to represent rights under, the Scheme;

(d) any payment of contributions refunded—
(i) in Great Britain, in accordance with requirements prescribed under section 8(2)(b) of the Act; or
(ii) in Northern Ireland, in accordance with requirements prescribed under section 8(2)(b) of the NI Act;

(e) any payment of contributions made pursuant to a compliance notice issued to a person—
(i) in Great Britain, under section 35 of the Act; or
(ii) in Northern Ireland, under section 35 of the NI Act,
where the appropriate date to which that notice relates is not in the same tax year as that in which the payment of contributions pursuant to the notice takes place;

(f) any payment of contributions made pursuant to an unpaid contributions notice—
(i) in Great Britain, issued to an employer under section 37 of the Act; or
(ii) in Northern Ireland, issued to an employer under section 37 of the NI Act,
where the appropriate date to which that notice relates is not in the same tax year as that in which the payment of contributions pursuant to the notice takes place;

(g) any payment of contributions made pursuant to a third party compliance notice issued under—
(i) in Great Britain, section 36 of the Act; or
(ii) in Northern Ireland, section 36 of the NI Act,
where the payment of contributions under that notice is not in the same tax year in which those contributions were first payable;

(h) any contributions payable by a participating employer under any provision of—
(i) in Great Britain, Chapter 1 of Part 1 of the Act; or
(ii) in Northern Ireland, Chapter 1 of Part 1 of the NI Act,
where the contributions are not paid in the same tax year in which those contributions were first payable;

(i) any contributions not made to the Scheme on or before the due date, where the tax year in which that due date falls has already ended, unless the Trustee determines otherwise;

(j) any payments made in error which are refunded by the Scheme;

(k) any contributions which are refunded under article 24 in respect of the same tax year in which those contributions were made; or

(l) any sum which exceeded the annual contribution limit as a result of the member of the Scheme being in multiple employment within the meaning of article 26, provided that such sum consists of contributions made by a participating employer either on behalf or in respect of that member of the Scheme.

(3) For the purposes of paragraph (2)(b), the specified action is—
(a) conferring appropriate rights under that scheme on a person entitled to the credit; or
(b) paying the amount of the credit to the person responsible for a qualifying arrangement with a view to acquiring rights under that arrangement for the person entitled to the credit.

(4) In this article—
(a) "appropriate date" has the same meaning—
(i) in Great Britain, as in section 38(5) of the Act; or
(ii) in Northern Ireland, as in section 38(5) of the NI Act;
(b) "due date" means the date on or before which payment of a contribution is to be made; and
(c) "relevant pay reference period" has the meaning given in regulations made under—
(i) in Great Britain, section 15(1) of the Act; or
(ii) in Northern Ireland, section 15(1) of the NI Act.

NOTES

Commencement: 5 July 2010.

Para (1): words omitted revoked by the National Employment Savings Trust (Amendment) Order 2013, SI 2013/597, art 2(1), (10), as from 1 April 2013.

[2.1406]

24 Annual contribution limit: refund of excess contributions

(1) This article applies in relation to contributions made in any tax year in excess of the annual contribution limit for that year.

(2) Subject to paragraph (2) of article 26, contributions made to the Scheme in excess of the annual contribution limit by—
(a) a member of the Scheme;
(b) a participating employer on behalf of a member of the Scheme; or
[(c) any other person in respect of a member,]

must not be applied to the member's pension account in respect of that same tax year and may be refunded to the member [or, where the contributions were made in respect of a member by a person other than the member or a participating employer, to the person who made the contributions.]

(3) Contributions made to the Scheme (in excess of the annual contribution limit) by a participating employer in respect of a member of the Scheme may be refunded to the employer but only once contributions by—

- (a) the member;
- (b) a participating employer on behalf of the member; or
- [(c) any other person in respect of the member,]

have already been refunded under paragraph (2).

(4) The Trustee may determine not to refund contributions under this article if the annual contribution limit is exceeded by an amount determined by the Trustee to be disproportionate to the cost of making a refund.

(5) In the event that contributions have already been applied to a member's pension account (whether or not in error), the Trustee may determine that contributions be—

- (a) retained in the member's pension account;
- (b) refunded to the member; . . .
- (c) refunded to the participating employer[; or]
- [(d) refunded to the person who made the contributions in respect of the member.]

NOTES

Commencement: 5 July 2010.

Para (2): sub-para (c) substituted and final words in square brackets added by the National Employment Savings Trust (Amendment) Order 2013, SI 2013/597, art 2(1), (11)(a), (b), as from 1 April 2013.

Para (3): sub-para (c) substituted by SI 2013/597, art 2(1), (11)(c), as from 1 April 2013.

Para (5): word omitted revoked and words in square brackets inserted by SI 2013/597, art 2(1), (11)(d), as from 1 April 2013.

[2.1407]

25 Timing of contributions

All contributions counting towards the annual contribution limit are to be treated as made to the Scheme when they are received by the Trustee.

NOTES

Commencement: 5 July 2010.

[2.1408]

26 Multiple employment

(1) A person is in multiple employment during a tax year if during that year—

- (a) they are a member of the Scheme;
- (b) they are in employment with more than one participating employer; and
- (c) more than one of those participating employers makes contributions to the Scheme on behalf or in respect of that person.

(2) Where a person is in multiple employment, the Trustee may continue to accept contributions (including minimum contributions) made by a participating employer on behalf or in respect of that person, even if such contributions are made in excess of the annual contribution limit.

(3) Where paragraph (2) applies, the Trustee—

- (a) must retain contributions of an amount equal to minimum contributions made by a participating employer on behalf or in respect of the member which exceed the annual contribution limit, and must apply those contributions to the member's pension account; and
- (b) may refund any contributions in excess of the amount referred to in sub-paragraph (a) to either a participating employer or the member.

(4) . . .

[(5) In this article, "minimum contributions" means contributions made to the Scheme by a participating employer on behalf or in respect of a member of the Scheme which enable the Scheme to satisfy the quality requirement.]

NOTES

Commencement: 5 July 2010.

Para (4): revoked by the National Employment Savings Trust (Amendment) Order 2013, SI 2013/597, art 2(1), (12)(a), as from 1 April 2013.

Para (5): substituted by SI 2013/597, art 2(1), (12)(b), as from 1 April 2013.

[2.1409]

27 Deductions from members' accounts

(1) The Trustee must make deductions from members' pension accounts to contribute to the general costs of the setting up, administration and management of the Scheme.

(2) The Secretary of State must determine the method of calculating how to make deductions during an initial period and for how long that initial period applies.

(3) After the initial period, the Trustee may determine subsequent methods of calculating how to make deductions.

(4) The Trustee must determine the level of deductions to be made from members' pension accounts, using the method of calculation determined by the Secretary of State or the Trustee thereafter.

(5) Subject to paragraph (6), the Trustee must set the deductions at a level that—

(a) meets the general costs of the setting up, administration and management of the Scheme; and

(b) allows it to maintain such reserve as it reasonably considers is needed in order to ensure that the Trustee is able to meet its costs where there are unexpected changes in income to, or costs payable by, the Scheme.

(6) In determining the level, the Trustee must have regard to any other sources of income to, and costs payable from, the Scheme.

(7) The Trustee may make further deductions from members' pension accounts to meet the costs of providing a service with respect to members' pension accounts in a particular case or class of case.

(8) In determining a method of calculating how to make deductions, determining the level of deductions under paragraph (4) and making deductions under paragraph (7), the Secretary of State or the Trustee, as the case may be, must ensure that—

(a) deductions will be applied on a consistent basis between members' pension accounts; and

(b) a pension account of a member of the Scheme (A) will not be subject to a different level or amount of deduction to another member's pension account solely on the basis of—

(i) where A is a worker, the number of persons who are or may in the future become members of the Scheme and workers in relation to A's employer;

(ii) the amount of time during which contributions may be made by, or on behalf or in respect of, A;

(iii) where A is a worker, the amount of time during which contributions may be made by, or on behalf or in respect of, other persons who are or may in the future become members of the Scheme and workers in relation to A's employer;

(iv) the income that is, or may in the future be, earned by A; or

(v) where A is a worker, the income that is or may be earned by other persons, as referred to in paragraph (9),

or solely on the basis of more than one of paragraphs (i) to (v) above, in any combination.

(9) The income referred to is income that—

(a) is, or may in the future be, earned by other members of the Scheme who are workers in relation to A's employer; or

(b) may in the future be earned by other persons who may become members of the Scheme and workers in relation to A's employer,

(10) Where the Secretary of State—

(a) has given financial assistance in the form of a loan to the Trustee pursuant to paragraph 18 of Schedule 1 to the Act for the purposes of setting up, administering and managing the Scheme and such assistance is still ongoing; and

(b) is of the opinion that the level of deductions under paragraph (4) is, or the deductions under paragraph (7) are, unreasonably high in the circumstances, having regard in particular to the principle that the cost of participation in the Scheme to members should be minimised,

the Secretary of State may determine an upper limit to the level of deductions under paragraph (4) or deductions under paragraph (7) that may be made from members' pension accounts.

(11) Where the Secretary of State—

(a) has given financial assistance in the form of a loan to the Trustee pursuant to paragraph 18 of Schedule 1 to the Act for the purposes of setting up, administering and managing the scheme and such assistance is still ongoing; and

(b) is of the opinion that the trustee is in breach of any condition of the loan,

the Secretary of State may determine a lower limit to the level of deductions under paragraph (4) or deductions under paragraph (7) that may be made from members' pension accounts.

(12) Where the Secretary of State determines an upper limit, the Trustee may not exceed that limit in the level of deductions it determines or the deductions which it makes.

(13) Where the Secretary of State determines a lower limit, the Trustee must determine a level of deductions, or make deductions, at or above that limit.

(14) Where the Secretary of State determines an upper or lower limit—

(a) the Secretary of State may make a further determination removing that limit; and

(b) on the date any financial assistance given or ongoing for the purposes of paragraphs (10) and (11) is repaid to the Secretary of State, such a further determination shall be deemed to have been made removing that limit.

(15) The Trustee must consult with the members' panel before—

(a) determining subsequent methods of calculating how to make deductions, as referred to in paragraph (3); or

(b) making changes to the level of deductions from members' pension accounts under paragraph (4) or to deductions under paragraph (7).

(16) The Trustee must make available the information specified in paragraph (17) by placing it on the internet.

(17) The specified information is information about—

(a) the method of calculating how to make deductions, determined under paragraph (2), and any subsequent method of calculating how to make deductions, determined under paragraph (3); and

(b) the level of deductions determined under paragraph (4) and any deductions made or to be made under paragraph (7), as they have effect from time to time.

NOTES

Commencement: 5 July 2010.

[2.1410]

28 Power to invest the Scheme's assets

(1) The Trustee has the power to invest all the assets of the Scheme.

(2) Subject to paragraph (3), for the purposes of this power, the assets of the Scheme include—

(a) contributions as referred to in article 21(2);

(b) any other monies received by the Trustee, including under articles 30 and 31; and

(c) returns from any investments of assets referred to in sub-paragraph (a) or (b).

(3) For the purposes of this power, the assets of the Scheme do not include any financial assistance given to the Trustee pursuant to paragraph 18 of Schedule 1 to the Act.

(4) Without prejudice to the generality of the power conferred on the trustees of a trust scheme—

(a) in Great Britain, under section 34 of the Pensions Act 1995; or

(b) in Northern Ireland, under Article 34 of the Pensions (Northern Ireland) Order 1995,

the power in paragraph (1) includes power to take the action specified in paragraph (5).

(5) The specified action is to—

(a) underwrite or sub-underwrite the subscription, offer or issue of any stocks, shares or other securities or investments, as the Trustee may determine;

(b) give any warranty or indemnity the Trustee determines as appropriate in connection with the exercise of that power (or any other power conferred on it by law), to any person;

(c) participate in stock lending arrangements within the meaning of section 263B of the Taxation of Chargeable Gains Act 1992; and

(d) invest in derivative instruments—

(i) in Great Britain, as defined by regulation 4(11) of the Occupational Pension Schemes (Investment) Regulations 2005; or

(ii) in Northern Ireland, as defined by regulation 4(11) of the Occupational Pension Schemes (Investment) Regulations (Northern Ireland) 2005.

NOTES

Commencement: 5 July 2010.

[2.1411]

29 Investment and default investment funds

(1) The Trustee may establish any number of notional funds, by reference to such investment principles and criteria as the Trustee determines ("investment funds").

(2) Subject to the following paragraphs, investment funds may be arranged by the Trustee in such number, combination or type as the Trustee determines.

(3) From time to time, the Trustee may make different arrangements (including closing, withdrawing or terminating the availability of any investment funds).

(4) The Trustee must, subject to the provisions in the following paragraphs, direct assets of the Scheme to at least one investment fund.

(5) Where a member of the Scheme does not express a choice as to where assets of the Scheme attributable to their pension account are to be directed, the investment funds to which those assets of the Scheme are directed shall be known as default investment funds.

(6) Any assets of the Scheme which the Trustee has the power to invest are to be invested by the Trustee in at least one default investment fund, except where—

(a) the member of the Scheme expresses a choice that assets of the Scheme attributable to their pension account be directed to an investment fund other than a default investment fund, in which case paragraph (7) applies;
(b) contributions are made to the member's pension account during the period prescribed in regulations—
(i) in Great Britain, made by virtue of section 8(5)(b) of the Act; or
(ii) in Northern Ireland, made by virtue of section 8(5)(b) of the NI Act;
(c) assets of the Scheme are not attributable to a member's pension account; or
(d) the Trustee decides to invest the assets of the Scheme in cash or on deposit in circumstances where liquid reserves are required for the purposes of the Scheme,

and where sub-paragraph (b), (c) or (d) applies, assets of the Scheme are to be invested as the Trustee determines.

(7) Where a member of the Scheme expresses a choice as to where assets of the Scheme attributable to their pension account are to be directed—
(a) the Trustee may determine—
(i) the form in, and method by, which a member expresses that choice;
(ii) any limits on the number of occasions on which a member may express that choice; and
(iii) the number of investment funds to which assets of the Scheme may be directed, having regard to the value of the assets of the Scheme attributable to a member's pension account; and
(b) subject to the member's choice complying with any determination made by the Trustee for the purposes of sub-paragraph (a), the Trustee must accept that choice unless the Trustee is of the opinion that in doing so it would breach any of its legal obligations, including those imposed—
(i) in Great Britain, by regulation 4 of the Occupational Pension Schemes (Investment) Regulations 2005; or
(ii) in Northern Ireland, by regulation 4 of the Occupational Pension Schemes (Investment) Regulations (Northern Ireland) 2005.

NOTES
Commencement: 5 July 2010.

[2.1412]
30 Acceptance by trustee of cash transfer sums

The Trustee may accept, in relation to a member of the Scheme, a cash transfer sum within the meaning of—
(a) in Great Britain, section 101AB(3) of the Pension Schemes Act 1993, used in the way described in section 101AE(2)(a) of that Act; or
(b) in Northern Ireland, section 97AB(3) of the Pension Schemes (Northern Ireland) Act 1993, used in the way described in section 97AE(2)(a) of that Act.

NOTES
Commencement: 5 July 2010.

[2.1413]
31 Pension sharing

(1) Where a pension credit derives—
(a) from the Scheme, the Trustee may—
(i) confer appropriate rights on the person entitled to the pension credit; or
(ii) pay the amount of the credit to the person responsible for a qualifying arrangement with a view to acquiring rights under that arrangement for the person entitled to the credit, in accordance with paragraph 1(3) of Schedule 5 to the 1999 Act (in Great Britain) or to the 1999 Order (in Northern Ireland); or
(b) from another scheme, the Trustee may accept a payment of the amount of the pension credit by the trustees or managers of the scheme from which the pension credit derives, provided that the person to whom that pension credit relates is already a member of the Scheme.

(2) In this article, "appropriate rights" has the same meaning—
(a) in Great Britain, as in paragraph 5 of Schedule 5 to the 1999 Act; or
(b) in Northern Ireland, as in paragraph 5 of Schedule 5 to the 1999 Order.

NOTES
Commencement: 5 July 2010.

[2.1414]

32 Benefits

(1) Without prejudice to article 31, the Trustee may, in the circumstances set out in rules, use a member's pension account in order to provide the benefits described in paragraph (2) (and only those benefits).

(2) The benefits are—

(a) where a member is alive—

(i) the payment to the member of a lump sum or the purchase of a lifetime annuity policy in the name of the member, or both; or

(ii) the transfer of the cash equivalent of the member's pension account to another pension scheme, where the member meets the conditions specified in paragraph (3);

(b) where a member has died—

(i) the payment of a lump sum to a person nominated by the member or to the personal representatives of that member;

(ii) the payment of a lump sum to any one or more [persons to be determined by the Trustee in accordance with rules];

(iii) the payment of a charity lump sum death benefit; or

(iv) the purchase of a dependants' annuity.

(3) The specified conditions are those—

(a) in Great Britain, in regulation 2(2) or (3) of the Transfer Values (Disapplication) Regulations 2010; or

(b) in Northern Ireland, in regulation 2(2) or (3) of the Transfer Values (Disapplication) Regulations (Northern Ireland) 2010.

(4) In this article—

"dependants' annuity" has the same meaning as in paragraph 17 of Schedule 28 to the Finance Act 2004;

"charity lump sum death benefit" has the same meaning as in paragraph 18 of Schedule 29 to the Finance Act 2004; [and]

"lifetime annuity" has the same meaning as in paragraph 3 of Schedule 28 to the Finance Act 2004; . . .

. . .

NOTES

Commencement: 5 July 2010.

Para (2): words in square brackets substituted by the National Employment Savings Trust (Amendment) Order 2013, SI 2013/597, art 2(1), (13)(a), as from 1 April 2013.

Para (4): word in square brackets inserted and words omitted revoked by SI 2013/597, art 2(1), (13)(b), as from 1 April 2013.

ADDITIONAL PATERNITY LEAVE REGULATIONS 2010

(SI 2010/1055)

NOTES

Made: 24 March 2010.

Authority: Employment Rights Act 1996, ss 47C(2), 80AA, 80BB, 80C, 80D, 80E, 99.

Commencement: 6 April 2010 (see further reg 3 at **[2.1417]**).

See *Harvey* J(8).

ARRANGEMENT OF REGULATIONS

PART 1
GENERAL

PART 2
ADDITIONAL PATERNITY LEAVE (BIRTH)

PART 1
GENERAL

[2.1415]
1 Citation, commencement and extent

These Regulations may be cited as the Additional Paternity Leave Regulations 2010 and shall come into force on 6th April 2010.

NOTES

Commencement: 6 April 2010.

[2.1416]
2 Interpretation

(1) In these Regulations—

"the 1996 Act" means the Employment Rights Act 1996;

"additional paternity leave" means leave under regulation 4 or regulation 14;

"adopter", in relation to a child, means a person who has been matched with the child for adoption and who has elected to take adoption leave in order to care for the child;

"adoption agency" has the meaning given, in relation to England and Wales, by section 2 of the Adoption and Children Act 2002, and in relation to Scotland, by section 119(1) of the Adoption and Children (Scotland) Act 2007;

"adoption leave" means ordinary adoption leave under section 75A of the 1996 Act or additional adoption leave under section 75B of that Act;

"child" means a person who is, or when placed with an adopter for adoption was, under the age of eighteen;

"expected week", in relation to the birth of a child, means the week beginning with midnight between Saturday and Sunday, in which it is expected that the child will be born;

"job", in relation to an employee returning after additional paternity leave, means the nature of the work which the employee is employed to do in accordance with the employee's contract of employment and the capacity and place in which the employee is so employed;

"maternity allowance" has the meaning given in section 35(1) of the Social Security Contributions and Benefits Act 1992;

"maternity leave" means ordinary maternity leave under section 71 of the 1996 Act or additional maternity leave under section 73 of that Act;

"parental leave" means leave under regulation 13(1) of the Maternity and Parental Leave etc Regulations 1999;

"partner" in relation to a child's mother or adopter, means a person (whether of a different sex or the same sex) who lives with the mother or adopter and the child in an enduring family relationship but is not a relative of the mother or adopter of a kind specified in paragraph (2);

"processing", in relation to information, has the meaning given in section 1(1) of the Data Protection Act 1998;

"statutory adoption pay" has the meaning given in section 171ZL of the Social Security Contributions and Benefits Act 1992;

"statutory maternity pay" has the meaning given in section 164(1) of the Social Security Contributions and Benefits Act 1992; and

"statutory leave" means leave provided for in Part 8 of the 1996 Act.

(2) The relatives of a child's mother or adopter referred to in the definition of "partner" in paragraph (1) are the mother's or adopter's parent, grandparent, sister, brother, aunt or uncle.

(3) References to relationships in paragraph (2)—

(a) are to relationships of the full blood or half blood or, in the case of an adopted person, such of those relationships as would exist but for the adoption, and

(b) include the relationship of a child with the child's adoptive, or former adoptive parents, but do not include any other adoptive relationships.

(4) For the purposes of these Regulations—

(a) a person is matched with a child for adoption when an adoption agency decides that that person would be a suitable adoptive parent for the child;

(b) a person is notified of having been matched with a child on the date on which the person receives notification of the agency's decision, under regulation 33(3)(a) of the Adoption Agencies Regulations 2005, regulation 28(3) of the Adoption Agencies (Wales) Regulations 2005 or regulation 8(5) of the Adoption Agencies (Scotland) Regulations 2009.

(5) A reference in any provision of these Regulations to a period of continuous employment is to a period computed in accordance with Chapter 1 of Part 14 of the 1996 Act, as if that provision were a part of that Act.

NOTES

Commencement: 6 April 2010.

[2.1417]

3 Application

(1) The provisions relating to additional paternity leave under regulation 4 have effect only in relation to children whose expected week of birth begins on or after 3rd April 2011.

(2) The provisions relating to additional paternity leave under regulation 14 have effect only in relation to children matched with a person who is notified of having been matched on or after 3rd April 2011.

(3) Regulation 33 (protection from detriment) has effect only in relation to an act or failure to act which takes place on or after 6th April 2010.

(4) For the purposes of paragraph (3)—

(a) where an act extends over a period, the reference to the date of the act is a reference to the last day of that period, and

(b) a failure to act is to be treated as done when it is decided upon.

(5) For the purposes of paragraph (4), in the absence of evidence establishing the contrary an employer shall be taken to decide on a failure to act—

(a) when the employer does an act inconsistent with doing the failed act, or

(b) if the employer has done no such inconsistent act, when the period expires within which the employer might reasonably have been expected to do the failed act if it was to be done.

(6) Regulation 34 (unfair dismissal) has effect only in relation to dismissals where the effective date of termination (within the meaning of section 97 of the 1996 Act) falls on or after 6th April 2010.

NOTES

Commencement: 6 April 2010.

PART 2
ADDITIONAL PATERNITY LEAVE (BIRTH)

[2.1418]
4 Entitlement to additional paternity leave (birth)

(1) An employee ("P") is entitled to be absent from work for the purpose of caring for a child ("C") if—

(a) P satisfies the conditions specified in paragraph (2);
(b) P has complied with the requirements in regulation 6 and, where applicable, regulation 7; and
(c) C's mother ("M") satisfies the conditions specified in paragraph (5) and has signed the mother declaration referred to in regulation 6.

(2) The conditions referred to in paragraph (1)(a) are that P—

(a) has been continuously employed with an employer for a period of not less than 26 weeks ending with the relevant week;
(b) remains in continuous employment with that employer until the week before the first week of P's additional paternity leave;
(c) is either—
  (i) C's father, or
  (ii) married to or the partner or civil partner of M, but not C's father; and
(d) has, or expects to have, the main responsibility (apart from any responsibility of M) for the upbringing of C.

(3) The references in this regulation to the relevant week are to the week immediately preceding the 14th week before C's expected week of birth.

(4) P shall be treated as having satisfied the condition in paragraph (2)(a) on the date of C's birth, notwithstanding the fact that P has not then been continuously employed for the period referred to in that paragraph, where—

(a) the date on which C is born is earlier than the relevant week; and
(b) P would have been continuously employed for such a period if P's employment had continued until the relevant week.

(5) The conditions referred to in paragraph (1)(c) are that M—

(a) is entitled by reference to becoming pregnant with C to one or more of the following—
  (i) maternity leave;
  (ii) statutory maternity pay; or
  (iii) maternity allowance; and
(b) has, or is treated as having, returned to work under regulation 25.

(6) P's entitlement to leave under this regulation shall not be affected by the birth, or expected birth, of more than one child as the result of the same pregnancy.

NOTES

Commencement: 6 April 2010 (see further reg 3 at **[2.1417]**).

[2.1419]
5 Options in respect of leave under regulation 4

(1) P may take leave under regulation 4 at any time within the period which begins 20 weeks after the date on which C is born and ends 12 months after that date.

(2) The minimum period of leave which may be taken is two weeks and the maximum period is 26 weeks.

(3) The leave must be taken in multiples of complete weeks and must be taken as one continuous period.

(4) The leave may not be taken until eight weeks after the date P gave leave notice under regulation 6(1).

(5) This regulation is subject to regulation 24 (disrupted placement or death of a child).

NOTES

Commencement: 6 April 2010 (see further reg 3 at **[2.1417]**).

[2.1420]
6 Notice and evidential requirements for leave under regulation 4

(1) P must, not less than eight weeks before the start date chosen by P for the period of leave, give P's employer ("E")—

(a) a leave notice;
(b) an employee declaration; and
(c) a mother declaration.

(2) In this regulation—

(a) "a leave notice" means a written notice specifying—
   (i) the week which was C's expected week of birth;
   (ii) C's date of birth;
   (iii) the dates P has chosen in accordance with regulation 5 as the start date and end date for the period of leave.

(b) "an employee declaration" means a written declaration signed by P, stating—
   (i) that the purpose of the period of leave will be to care for C, and
   (ii) that P satisfies the conditions in regulation 4(2)(c) and (d).

(c) "mother declaration" means a written declaration by M stating—
   (i) M's name and address;
   (ii) the date M intends to return to work (within the meaning of regulation 25);
   (iii) M's National Insurance number;
   (iv) that P satisfies the conditions in regulation 4(2)(c) and (d);
   (v) that P is to M's knowledge the only person exercising the entitlement to additional paternity leave in respect of C; and
   (vi) that M consents to E processing such of M's information as is contained in the declaration.

(3) Where E makes a request within 28 days of receiving P's leave notice, P must, within 28 days of E's request, give E such of the following as E may request—
(a) a copy of C's birth certificate; and
(b) the name and address of M's employer (or, if M is self-employed, M's business address).

(4) After giving leave notice, P must give E written notice ("withdrawal notice") as soon as reasonably practicable if—
(a) P no longer satisfies the conditions in regulation 4(2)(c) or (d); or
(b) M no longer satisfies the conditions in regulation 4(5).

(5) E may require P to take a period of leave where—
(a) P has given E withdrawal notice less than six weeks before the start date specified in P's leave notice or, where applicable, last varied in accordance with regulation 7, and
(b) it is not reasonably practicable for E to accommodate the change in P's arrangements.

(6) Leave that E may require P to take under paragraph (5)—
(a) shall be treated as additional paternity leave for the purpose of these Regulations;
(b) shall start on the start date specified in P's leave notice, or, where applicable, last varied in accordance with regulation 7; and
(c) shall end no later than—
   (i) six weeks after the date on which withdrawal notice was given to E, or
   (ii) the end date specified in P's leave notice or, where applicable, last varied in accordance with regulation 7,

   whichever is the earlier.

(7) E may require P to remain on leave where—
(a) P has given E withdrawal notice after P's period of additional paternity leave has begun, and
(b) it is not reasonably practicable for E to accommodate the change in P's arrangements.

(8) The period for which E may require P to remain on leave under paragraph (7)—
(a) shall end no later than the earlier of—
   (i) six weeks after the date on which P gave E withdrawal notice, or
   (ii) the end date specified in P's leave notice or, where applicable, last varied in accordance with regulation 7; and
(b) shall be treated as additional paternity leave for the purpose of these Regulations.

NOTES

Commencement: 6 April 2010 (see further reg 3 at **[2.1417]**).

[2.1421]

7 Variation or cancellation of leave under regulation 4 before leave period has begun

(1) Before P's leave period has begun, P may cancel P's leave notice, or vary the dates notified as the start and end date for the period of leave, provided that P gives E written notice ("subsequent notice")—
(a) before the earlier of—
   (i) six weeks before the date cancelled or varied, or
   (ii) six weeks before the new date, or,
(b) if it is not reasonably practicable for P to give notice in accordance with sub-paragraph (a), as soon as is reasonably practicable.

(2) Where P has given subsequent notice, but—
(a) the notice does not comply with paragraph (1)(a), and
(b) it is not reasonably practicable for E to accommodate the change in P's arrangements,

E may require that P take a period of additional paternity leave.

(3) Additional paternity leave which P is required to take under paragraph (2)—

(a) shall start—

(i) on the start date specified by P in the leave notice, or

(ii) where applicable, the start date specified in the most recent subsequent notice given by P in compliance with the requirements of paragraph (1)(a); and

(b) shall end no later than—

(i) six weeks after P gave notice under paragraph (1), or

(ii) the end date specified in the leave notice or, where applicable, the most recent subsequent notice given by P in compliance with the requirements of paragraph (1)(a),

whichever is the earlier.

(4) In this regulation, "leave notice" has the meaning given by regulation 6(2).

NOTES

Commencement: 6 April 2010 (see further reg 3 at **[2.1417]**).

[2.1422]

8 Employer's confirmation of period of leave under regulation 4

(1) Subject to paragraph (2), where P gives leave notice under regulation 6(1) or subsequent notice under regulation 7(1) to E, E shall, within 28 days of receipt of the notice, confirm the relevant dates to P in writing.

(2) Where E requires P to take leave under regulations 6(5) or 7(2), E shall notify P of the dates of that leave as soon as reasonably practicable, and at any event before the start of the leave that P is required to take under regulations 6(5) or 7(2).

NOTES

Commencement: 6 April 2010 (see further reg 3 at **[2.1417]**).

[2.1423]

9 Commencement of leave under regulation 4

Save where regulations 6(5) or 7(2) apply, P's period of additional paternity leave under regulation 4 begins—

(a) on the start date specified in P's leave notice under regulation 6(1), or,

(b) where applicable, the date specified in P's most recent subsequent notice under regulation 7(1).

NOTES

Commencement: 6 April 2010 (see further reg 3 at **[2.1417]**).

[2.1424]

10 Entitlement to additional paternity leave (birth) in the event of the mother's death

(1) In a case where M has died before the end of the period of twelve months beginning with C's birth, the provisions in regulations 4 to 9 shall apply with the following modifications.

(2) In regulation 4 (entitlement to additional paternity leave (birth))—

(a) paragraph (1)(b) shall apply as if the references in that paragraph—

(i) to regulation 6 were references to regulation 12;

(ii) to regulation 7 were references to regulation 13;

(b) paragraph (1)(c) shall be replaced by—

"(c) C's mother ("M") satisfied, before her death, one or more of the conditions specified in paragraph (5)(a) (or would have satisfied such conditions but for the fact that M has died).";

(c) the condition in paragraph (2)(c)(ii) shall be taken to be satisfied if it would have been satisfied but for the fact that M has died; and

(d) paragraph (5)(b) shall be omitted.

(3) Regulation 5 (options in respect of leave) shall be replaced by regulation 11.

(4) Regulation 6 (notice and evidential requirements for leave) shall be replaced by regulation 12.

(5) Regulation 7 (variation or cancellation of leave) shall be replaced by regulation 13.

(6) Regulations 8 (confirmation of leave) and 9 (commencement of leave) apply as if the references in those regulations—

(a) to regulation 6(1) were references to regulation 12(1);

(b) to regulation 6(5) were references to regulation 12(7);

(c) to regulation 7(1) were references to regulation 13(2); and

(d) to regulation 7(2) were references to regulation 13(3).

NOTES

Commencement: 6 April 2010 (see further reg 3 at **[2.1417]**).

[2.1425]

11 Options in respect of leave under regulation 4 in the event of the mother's death

(1) P may take leave under regulation 4, as modified by regulation 10, at any time within the period beginning with the date of M's death and ending 12 months after the date of C's birth.

(2) The minimum period of leave which may be taken is two weeks and the maximum period is 52 weeks.

(3) The leave must be taken as one continuous period and must be taken in multiples of complete weeks.

(4) P shall not be entitled to leave in accordance with regulation 4, as modified by regulation 10, if P has already taken a period of additional paternity leave in respect of C which has ended before the date of M's death.

(5) If P is on leave under regulation 4 on the date of M's death, P shall be entitled to extend the leave to include a further period of leave in accordance with regulation 4, as modified by regulation 10, provided—

(a) P satisfies the conditions for eligibility set out in regulation 4 as so modified;

(b) that further period of leave immediately follows the first, together with which it forms one continuous period of additional paternity leave;

(c) the total period of additional paternity leave taken does not exceed 52 weeks; and

(d) the entire period of additional paternity leave is taken within the period of 12 months after the date of C's birth.

(6) This regulation is subject to regulation 24 (disrupted placement or death of a child).

NOTES

Commencement: 6 April 2010 (see further reg 3 at **[2.1417]**).

[2.1426]

12 Notice and evidential requirements for leave under regulation 4 in the event of the mother's death

(1) As soon as reasonably practicable after the date of M's death, and in any event, on or before the relevant date, P must give P's employer ("E"), in writing—

(a) a leave notice; and

(b) an employee declaration.

(2) In this regulation—

(a) "a leave notice" means a written notice specifying—

(i) the week which was C's expected week of birth;

(ii) C's date of birth;

(iii) the dates P has chosen in accordance with regulation 11 as the start date and end date for the period of leave.

(b) "an employee declaration" means a written declaration signed by P, stating—

(i) that the purpose of the period of leave will be to care for C;

(ii) that P satisfies the conditions in regulation 4(2)(c) and (d), as modified by regulation 10;

(iii) M's name and last address;

(iv) the date of M's death; and

(v) M's National Insurance number.

(c) "the relevant date" is eight weeks after the date of M's death.

(3) Where E makes a request within 28 days of receiving P's leave notice, P must, within 28 days of E's request, give E such of the following as E may request—

(a) a copy of C's birth certificate; and

(b) the name and address of M's employer (or, if M was self-employed, M's business address).

(4) If P takes leave before the relevant date, P shall be taken to have complied with the requirements of paragraph (1), if P, as soon as reasonably practicable, informs E that M has died and, before the relevant date, gives leave notice and the employee declaration.

(5) Notwithstanding paragraph (1), P may give E leave notice and the employee declaration after the relevant date, provided that P gives E written notice at least six weeks before the start date chosen by P for the period of leave.

(6) If P, after giving leave notice, no longer satisfies the conditions in regulation 4(2)(c) or (d) as modified by regulation 10, P must give E written notice (withdrawal notice) as soon as reasonably practicable.

(7) E may require that P take a period of leave where—

(a) P has given E withdrawal notice—
  (i) less than six weeks before the start date specified in P's leave notice, or, where applicable, last varied in accordance with regulation 13, and
  (ii) after the relevant date, and
(b) it is not reasonably practicable for E to accommodate the change in P's arrangements.

(8) Leave that E may require P to take under paragraph (7)—
(a) shall be treated as additional paternity leave for the purpose of these Regulations;
(b) shall start on the start date specified in P's leave notice, or, where applicable, last varied in accordance with regulation 13; and
(c) shall end no later than—
  (i) six weeks after the date on which withdrawal notice was given to E, or
  (ii) the end date specified in P's leave notice, or, where applicable, last varied in accordance with regulation 13,

whichever is the earlier.

(9) E may require P to remain on leave where—
(a) P has given E withdrawal notice—
  (i) after P's period of additional paternity leave has begun, and
  (ii) after the relevant date, and
(b) it is not reasonably practicable for E to accommodate the change in P's arrangements.

(10) The period for which E may require P to remain on leave under regulation (9)—
(a) shall end no later than the earlier of—
  (i) six weeks after the date on which P gave E withdrawal notice, or
  (ii) the end date specified in P's leave notice, or, where applicable, last varied in accordance with regulation 13; and
(b) shall be treated as additional paternity leave for the purpose of these Regulations.

NOTES

Commencement: 6 April 2010 (see further reg 3 at **[2.1417]**).

[2.1427]

13 Variation or cancellation of leave under regulation 4 in the event of the mother's death

(1) Notwithstanding regulation 9 as modified by regulation 10, P may, on or before the relevant date, cancel P's leave notice, or vary the dates notified as the start and end dates for the period of leave, by notifying E in writing on or before any date that is varied or cancelled.

(2) After the relevant date, but before P's leave period has begun, P may cancel P's leave notice, or vary the dates notified as the start and end date for the period of leave, provided that P gives E written notice ("subsequent notice")—
(a) before the earlier of—
  (i) six weeks before the date cancelled or varied, or
  (ii) six weeks before the new date, or,
(b) if it is not reasonably practicable for P to give notice in accordance with sub-paragraph (a), as soon as is reasonably practicable.

(3) Where P has given subsequent notice, but—
(a) the notice does not comply with paragraph (2)(a), and
(b) it is not reasonably practicable for E to accommodate the change in P's arrangements,

E may require that P take a period of additional paternity leave.

(4) Additional paternity leave which P is required to take under paragraph (3)—
(a) shall start—
  (i) on the start date specified by P in the leave notice, or
  (ii) where applicable, the start date specified in the most recent subsequent notice given by P in compliance with the requirements of paragraphs (1) or (2)(a); and
(b) shall end no later than—
  (i) six weeks after P gave notice under paragraph (2), or
  (ii) the end date specified in the leave notice or, where applicable, the most recent subsequent notice given by P in compliance with the requirements of paragraphs (1) or (2)(a),

whichever is the earlier.

(5) In this regulation, the terms "relevant date" and "leave notice" have the meanings given by regulation 12(2).

NOTES

Commencement: 6 April 2010 (see further reg 3 at **[2.1417]**).

PART 3
ADDITIONAL PATERNITY LEAVE (ADOPTION)

[2.1428]

14 Entitlement to additional paternity leave (adoption)

(1) An employee ("P") is entitled to be absent from work for the purpose of caring for a child placed for adoption ("C") if—

- (a) P satisfies the conditions specified in paragraph (2);
- (b) P has complied with the requirements in regulation 16 and, where applicable, regulation 17; and
- (c) C's adopter ("A") satisfies the conditions specified in paragraph (4) and has signed the adopter declaration referred to in regulation 16.

(2) The conditions referred to in paragraph (1)(a) are that P—

- (a) has been continuously employed with an employer for a period of not less than 26 weeks ending with the relevant week;
- (b) remains in continuous employment with that employer from the relevant week until the week before the first week of P's additional paternity leave;
- (c) is married to, or is the partner or civil partner of, A; and
- (d) has been matched with C for adoption.

(3) The references in paragraph (2) above to the relevant week are to the week, beginning with Sunday, in which P is notified of having been matched with C.

(4) The conditions referred to in paragraph (1)(c) are that A—

- (a) is entitled by reference to the adoption of C to one or both of—
  - (i) adoption leave; or
  - (ii) statutory adoption pay; and
- (b) has, or is treated as having, returned to work under regulation 25.

(5) P's entitlement to leave under this regulation shall not be affected by the placement for adoption of more than one child as part of the same arrangement.

NOTES

Commencement: 6 April 2010 (see further reg 3 at **[2.1417]**).

[2.1429]

15 Options in respect of leave under regulation 14

(1) P may choose to take leave under regulation 14 at any time within the period which begins 20 weeks after the date of C's placement for adoption and ends 12 months after that date.

(2) The minimum period of leave which may be taken is two weeks and the maximum period is 26 weeks.

(3) The leave must be taken in multiples of complete weeks and must be taken as one continuous period.

(4) The leave may not be taken until eight weeks after the date of P's leave notice under regulation 16(1).

(5) This regulation is subject to regulation 24 (disrupted placement or death of a child).

NOTES

Commencement: 6 April 2010 (see further reg 3 at **[2.1417]**).

[2.1430]

16 Notice and evidential requirements for leave under regulation 14

(1) P must, not less than eight weeks before the start date chosen by P for the period of leave, give P's employer ("E")—

- (a) a leave notice;
- (b) an employee declaration; and
- (c) an adopter declaration.

(2) In this regulation—

- (a) "a leave notice" means a written notice specifying—
  - (i) the date on which P was notified of having been matched with C;
  - (ii) the date on which C was placed with P;
  - (iii) the dates which P has chosen in accordance with regulation 15 as the start date and end date for the period of leave.
- (b) "an employee declaration" means a written declaration signed by P, stating—
  - (i) that the purpose of the period of leave will be to care for C; and
  - (ii) that P satisfies the conditions in regulation 14(2)(c) and (d).
- (c) "an adopter declaration" means a written declaration by A stating—
  - (i) A's name and address;

(ii) the date A intends to return to work (within the meaning of regulation 25);
(iii) A's National Insurance number;
(iv) that P satisfies the conditions in regulation 14(2)(c); and
(v) that A consents to E processing such of A's information as is contained in the declaration.

(3) Where E makes a request within 28 days of receiving P's leave notice, P must, within 28 days of E's request, give E such of the following as E may request—

(a) evidence, in the form of one or more documents issued by the adoption agency that matched P with C, of—
(i) the name and address of the agency;
(ii) the date on which P was notified that P had been matched with C;
(iii) the date given by the agency as that on which it expected to place C for adoption with A and P; and

(b) the name and address of A's employer (or, if A is self-employed, A's business address).

(4) After giving leave notice, P must give E written notice ("withdrawal notice") as soon as reasonably practicable if—

(a) P no longer satisfies the conditions in regulation 14(2)(c) or (d);
(b) A no longer satisfies the conditions in regulation 14(4).

(5) E may require P to take a period of leave where—

(a) P has given E withdrawal notice less than six weeks before the start date specified in P's leave notice, or, where applicable, last varied in accordance with regulation 17, and
(b) it is not reasonably practicable for E to accommodate the change in P's arrangements.

(6) Leave that E may require P to take under paragraph (5)—

(a) shall be treated as additional paternity leave for the purpose of these Regulations;
(b) shall start on the start date specified in P's leave notice, or last varied in accordance with regulation 17; and
(c) shall end no later than—
(i) six weeks after the date on which withdrawal notice was given to E, or
(ii) the end date specified in P's leave notice, or, where applicable, last varied in accordance with regulation 17,

whichever is the earlier.

(7) E may require P to remain on leave where—

(a) P has given E withdrawal notice after P's period of additional paternity leave has begun, and
(b) it is not reasonably practicable for E to accommodate the change in P's arrangements.

(8) The period for which E may require P to remain on leave under paragraph (7)—

(a) shall end no later than the earlier of—
(i) six weeks after the date on which P gave E withdrawal notice, or
(ii) the end date specified in P's leave notice or, where applicable, last varied in accordance with regulation 17, and
(b) shall be treated as additional paternity leave for the purpose of these Regulations.

NOTES

Commencement: 6 April 2010 (see further reg 3 at **[2.1417]**).

[2.1431]

17 Variation or cancellation of leave under regulation 14 before leave period has begun

(1) Before P's leave period has begun, P may cancel P's leave notice, or vary the dates notified as the start and end date for the period of leave, provided that P gives E written notice ("subsequent notice")—

(a) before the earlier of—
(i) six weeks before the date cancelled or varied, or
(ii) six weeks before the new date, or,
(b) if it is not reasonably practicable for P to give notice in accordance with sub-paragraph (a), as soon as is reasonably practicable.

(2) Where P has given subsequent notice, but—

(a) the notice does not comply with paragraph (1)(a), and
(b) it is not reasonably practicable for E to accommodate the change in P's arrangements,

E may require that P take a period of additional paternity leave.

(3) Additional paternity leave which P is required to take under paragraph (2)—

(a) shall start—
(i) on the start date specified by P in the leave notice, or
(ii) where applicable, the start date specified in the most recent subsequent notice given by P in compliance with the requirements of paragraph (1)(a); and
(b) shall end no later than—

(i) six weeks after P gave notice under paragraph (1), or

(ii) the end date specified in the leave notice or, where applicable, the most recent subsequent notice given by P in compliance with the requirements of paragraph (1)(a),

whichever is the earlier.

(4) In this regulation, "leave notice" has the meaning given by regulation 16(2).

NOTES

Commencement: 6 April 2010 (see further reg 3 at **[2.1417]**).

[2.1432]

18 Employer's confirmation of period of leave under regulation 14

(1) Subject to paragraph (2), where P gives leave notice under regulation 16(1) or subsequent notice under regulation 17(1) to E, E shall, within 28 days of receipt of the notice, confirm the relevant dates to P in writing.

(2) Where E requires P to take leave under regulations 16(5) or 17(2), E shall notify P of the dates of that leave as soon as reasonably practicable, and at any event before the start of the leave that P is required to take under regulations 16(5) or 17(2).

NOTES

Commencement: 6 April 2010 (see further reg 3 at **[2.1417]**).

[2.1433]

19 Commencement of leave under regulation 14

Save where regulations 16(5) and 17(2) apply, P's period of additional paternity leave under regulation 14 begins—

(a) on the start date notified in P's leave notice under regulation 16(1), or,

(b) where applicable, the date specified in P's most recent subsequent notice under regulation 17(1).

NOTES

Commencement: 6 April 2010 (see further reg 3 at **[2.1417]**).

[2.1434]

20 Entitlement to additional paternity leave (adoption) in the event of the death of the adopter

(1) In a case where A has died before the end of the period of 12 months beginning with C's placement for adoption, the provisions in regulations 14 to 19 shall apply with the following modifications.

(2) In regulation 14 (entitlement to additional paternity leave (adoption))—

(a) paragraph (1)(b) shall apply as if the references in that paragraph—

(i) to regulation 16 were references to regulation 22;

(ii) to regulation 17 were references to regulation 23;

(b) paragraph (1)(c) shall read—

"(c) C's adopter ("A") satisfied, before A's death, one or more of the conditions specified in paragraph (4)(a) (or would have satisfied such conditions but for the fact that A has died).";

(c) the condition in paragraph (2)(c) shall be taken to be satisfied if it would have been satisfied but for the fact that A has died; and

(d) the requirement in paragraph (4)(b) shall be omitted.

(3) Regulation 15 (options in respect of leave) shall be replaced by regulation 21.

(4) Regulation 16 (notice and evidential requirements for leave) shall be replaced by regulation 22.

(5) Regulation 17 (variation or cancellation of leave) shall be replaced by regulation 23.

(6) Regulations 18 (employer's confirmation) and 19 (commencement of leave) apply as if the references in those regulations—

(a) to regulation 6(1) were references to regulation 22(1);

(b) to regulation 16(5) were references to regulation 22(7);

(c) to regulation 17(1) were references to regulation 23(2); and

(d) to regulation 17(2) were references to regulation 23(3).

NOTES

Commencement: 6 April 2010 (see further reg 3 at **[2.1417]**).

[2.1435]

21 Options in respect of leave under regulation 14 where the adopter has died

(1) P may take leave under regulation 14, as modified by regulation 20, at any time within the period beginning with the date of A's death and ending 12 months after the date of C's placement for adoption.

(2) The minimum period of leave which may be taken is two weeks and the maximum period is 52 weeks.

(3) The leave must be taken as one continuous period and must be taken in multiples of complete weeks.

(4) P shall not be entitled to leave in accordance with regulation 14, as modified by regulation 20, if P has already taken a period of additional paternity leave in respect of C which has ended before the date of A's death.

(5) If P is on leave under regulation 14 on the date of A's death, P shall be entitled to extend the leave to include a further period of leave in accordance with regulation 14, as modified by regulation 20, provided—

- (a) P satisfies the conditions for eligibility set out in regulation 14 as so modified;
- (b) that further period of leave immediately follows the first, together with which it forms one continuous period of additional paternity leave;
- (c) the total period of additional paternity leave taken does not exceed 52 weeks; and
- (d) the entire period of additional paternity leave is taken within the period of 12 months after the date of C's placement for adoption.

(6) This regulation is subject to regulation 24 (disrupted placement or death of a child).

NOTES

Commencement: 6 April 2010 (see further reg 3 at **[2.1417]**).

[2.1436]

22 Notice and evidential requirements for leave under regulation 14 in the event of the death of the adopter

(1) As soon as reasonably practicable after the date of A's death, and in any event, on or before the relevant date, P must give P's employer ("E"), in writing—

- (a) a leave notice; and
- (b) an employee declaration.

(2) In this regulation—

- (a) "a leave notice" means a written notice specifying—
  - (i) the date on which P was notified of having been matched with C;
  - (ii) the date on which C was placed with P;
  - (iii) the dates P has chosen in accordance with regulation 21 as the start date and end date for the period of leave.
- (b) "an employee declaration" means a written declaration signed by P, stating—
  - (i) that the purpose of the period of leave will be to care for C;
  - (ii) that P satisfies the conditions in regulation 14(2)(c) and (d), as modified by regulation 20;
  - (iii) A's name and last address;
  - (iv) the date of A's death; and
  - (v) A's National Insurance number.
- (c) "the relevant date" is eight weeks after the date of A's death.

(3) Where E makes a request within 28 days of receiving P's leave notice, P must, within 28 days of E's request, give E such of the following as E may request—

- (a) evidence, in the form of one or more documents issued by the adoption agency that matched P with C, of—
  - (i) the name and address of the agency;
  - (ii) the date on which P was notified of having been matched with C;
  - (iii) the date given by the agency as that on which it expected to place C for adoption with A and P; and
- (b) the name and address of A's last employer (or, if A was self-employed, A's business address).

(4) If P takes leave before the relevant date, P shall be taken to have complied with the requirements of paragraph (1), if P, as soon as reasonably practicable, informs E of A's death and, before the relevant date, gives leave notice and the employee declaration.

(5) Notwithstanding paragraph (1), P may give E leave notice and the employee declaration after the relevant date, provided that P gives E written notice at least six weeks before the start date chosen by P for the period of leave.

(6) If P, after giving leave notice, no longer satisfies the conditions in regulation 14(2)(c) or (d) as modified by regulation 20, P must give E written notice ("withdrawal notice") as soon as reasonably practicable.

(7) E may require that P take a period of leave where—
- (a) P has given E withdrawal notice –
  - (i) less than six weeks before the start date specified in P's leave notice, or, where applicable, last varied in accordance with regulation 23, and
  - (ii) after the relevant date, and
- (b) it is not reasonably practicable for E to accommodate the change in P's arrangements.

(8) Leave that E may require P to take under paragraph (7)—
- (a) shall be treated as additional paternity leave for the purpose of these Regulations;
- (b) shall start on the start date specified in P's leave notice, or, where applicable, last varied in accordance with regulation 23; and
- (c) shall end no later than—
  - (i) six weeks after the date on which withdrawal notice was given to E, or
  - (ii) the end date specified in P's leave notice, or, where applicable, last varied in accordance with regulation 23,

  whichever is the earlier.

(9) E may require P to remain on leave where—
- (a) P has given E withdrawal notice—
  - (i) after P's period of additional paternity leave has begun, and
  - (ii) after the relevant date, and
- (b) it is not reasonably practicable for E to accommodate the change in P's arrangements.

(10) The period for which E may require P to remain on leave under regulation (9)—
- (a) shall end no later than the earlier of—
  - (i) six weeks after the date on which P gave E withdrawal notice, or
  - (ii) the end date specified in P's leave notice, or, where applicable, last varied in accordance with regulation 23; and
- (b) shall be treated as additional paternity leave for the purpose of these Regulations.

NOTES

Commencement: 6 April 2010 (see further reg 3 at **[2.1417]**).

[2.1437]

23 Variation or cancellation of leave under regulation 14 in the event of the death of the adopter

(1) Notwithstanding regulation 19 as modified by regulation 20, P may, on or before the relevant date, cancel P's leave notice, or vary the dates notified as the start and end dates for the period of leave, by notifying E in writing on or before any date that is varied or cancelled.

(2) After the relevant date, but before P's leave period has begun, P may cancel P's leave notice, or vary the dates notified as the start and end date for the period of leave, provided that P gives E written notice ("subsequent notice")—
- (a) before the earlier of—
  - (i) six weeks before the date cancelled or varied, or
  - (ii) six weeks before the new date, or,
- (b) if it is not reasonably practicable for P to give notice in accordance with sub-paragraph (a), as soon as is reasonably practicable.

(3) Where P has given subsequent notice, but—
- (a) the notice does not comply with paragraph (2)(a), and
- (b) it is not reasonably practicable for E to accommodate the change in P's arrangements,

E may require that P take a period of additional paternity leave.

(4) Additional paternity leave which P is required to take under paragraph (3)—
- (a) shall start—
  - (i) on the start date specified by P in the leave notice, or
  - (ii) where applicable, the start date specified in the most recent subsequent notice given by P in compliance with the requirements of paragraphs (1) or (2)(a); and
- (b) shall end no later than—
  - (i) six weeks after P gave notice under paragraph (2), or
  - (ii) the end date specified in the leave notice or, where applicable, the most recent subsequent notice given by P in compliance with the requirements of paragraphs (1) or (2)(a),

  whichever is the earlier.

(5) In this regulation, the terms "relevant date" and "leave notice" have the meanings given by regulation 22(2).

NOTES
Commencement: 6 April 2010 (see further reg 3 at **[2.1417]**).

PART 4
PROVISIONS APPLICABLE TO BOTH TYPES OF ADDITIONAL PATERNITY LEAVE

[2.1438]
24 Disrupted placement or death of a child in the course of additional paternity leave

(1) This regulation applies where, during an employee ("P's") leave notice period or additional paternity leave period in respect of a child ("C")—
- (a) C dies, or
- (b) where C has been placed for adoption, C is returned to the adoption agency under sections 32, 33 or 34(3) of the Adoption and Children Act 2002 or section 25(6) of the Adoption and Children (Scotland) Act 2007.

(2) Subject to regulation 29 (dismissal during additional leave period), in a case where this regulation applies—
- (a) where the end date of P's leave occurs less than eight weeks after the relevant week, P's additional paternity leave period ends on the end date,
- (b) where the end date of P's leave occurs eight or more weeks after the relevant week, P's additional paternity leave period ends eight weeks after the end of the relevant week.

(3) For the purposes of paragraph (2)—
- (a) the relevant week means the period of seven days beginning with Sunday, during which—
  - (i) in a case falling within paragraph (1)(a), C dies,
  - (ii) in a case falling within paragraph (1)(b), C is returned to the adoption agency.
- (b) the end date of P's leave is—
  - (i) the end date notified by P in accordance with regulation 6(1), 12(1), 16(1) or 22(1),
  - (ii) where P has varied the end date, that most recently varied in accordance with regulation 7(1), 13(1), 13(2), 17(1), 23(1), or 23(2),
  - (iii) where E required P to take leave, or remain on leave, the end date determined by E in accordance with regulation 6(5), 6(7), 7(2), 12(7), 12(9), 13(3), 16(5), 16(7), 17(2), 22(7), 22(9) and 23(3) and notified to P in accordance with regulation 8(2), 8(2) as modified by regulation 10, 18(2) or 18(2) as modified by regulation 20 as applicable, or
  - (iv) where applicable, the end date determined under regulation 30.

(4) In paragraph (1), P's leave notice period is the period starting on the day P notifies E in accordance with regulation 6(1), 12(1), 16(1) or 22(1) of P's intention to take additional paternity leave and ending on the day before the day that leave begins.

NOTES
Commencement: 6 April 2010 (see further reg 3 at **[2.1417]**).

[2.1439]
25 Return to work

For the purposes of these Regulations, a mother ("M") or adopter ("A") is treated as returning to work if one of the following situations applies—
- (a) in a case where M or A is entitled to maternity leave or to adoption leave in respect of a child ("C"), the leave period has ended;
- (b) in a case where M or A is entitled, in respect of C, to payment of:
  - (i) maternity allowance, that payment is not payable by virtue of regulations made under section 35(3)(a)(i) of the Social Security Contributions and Benefits Act 1992;
  - (ii) statutory maternity pay, that payment is not payable in accordance with section 165(4) or (6) of the Social Security Contributions and Benefits Act 1992; or
  - (iii) statutory adoption pay, that payment is not payable in accordance with section 171ZN(3) or (5) of the Social Security Contributions and Benefits Act 1992;
- (c) in a case where both (a) and (b) apply, the conditions in both (a) and (b) are satisfied.

NOTES
Commencement: 6 April 2010 (see further reg 3 at **[2.1417]**).

[2.1440]
26 Work during an additional paternity leave period

(1) P may carry out up to ten days' work for P's employer ("E") during P's additional paternity leave period without bringing the additional paternity leave period to an end.

(2) For the purposes of this regulation, any work carried out on any day shall constitute a day's work.

(3) Subject to paragraph (4), for the purposes of this regulation, work means any work done under the contract of employment and may include training or any activity undertaken for the purposes of keeping in touch with the workplace.

(4) Reasonable contact from time to time between P and E which either party is entitled to make during an additional paternity leave period (for example to discuss P's return to work) shall not bring that period to an end.

(5) This regulation does not confer any right on E to require that any work be carried out during the additional paternity leave period, nor any right on P to work during the additional paternity leave period.

(6) Any days' work carried out under this regulation shall not have the effect of extending the total duration of the additional paternity leave period.

NOTES

Commencement: 6 April 2010 (see further reg 3 at **[2.1417]**).

[2.1441]

27 Application of terms and conditions during additional paternity leave

(1) During the period of additional paternity leave, P—

- (a) is entitled to the benefit of all of the terms and conditions of employment which would have applied if P had not been absent, and
- (b) is bound by any obligations arising under those terms and conditions, subject only to the exception in section 80C(1)(b) of the 1996 Act.

(2) In paragraph (1)(a), "terms and conditions of employment" has the meaning given by section 80C(5) of the 1996 Act, and accordingly does not include terms and conditions about remuneration.

(3) For the purposes of section 80C of the 1996 Act, only sums payable to P by way of wages or salary are to be treated as remuneration.

(4) In the case of accrual of rights under an employment-related benefit scheme within the meaning given by paragraph 7 of Schedule 5 to the Social Security Act 1989, nothing in paragraph (1)(a) shall be taken to impose a requirement which exceeds the requirements of paragraph 5A of that Schedule.

NOTES

Commencement: 6 April 2010 (see further reg 3 at **[2.1417]**).

[2.1442]

28 Redundancy during additional paternity leave

(1) This regulation applies where, during P's additional paternity leave period, it is not practicable by reason of redundancy for E to continue to employ P under P's existing contract of employment.

(2) Where there is a suitable alternative vacancy, P is entitled to be offered (before the end of P's employment under P's existing contract) alternative employment with E or E's successor, or an associated employer, under a new contract of employment which complies with paragraph (3) and takes effect immediately on the ending of P's employment under the previous contract.

(3) The new contract of employment must be such that—

- (a) the work to be done under it is of a kind which is both suitable in relation to P and appropriate for P to do in the circumstances, and
- (b) its provisions as to the capacity and place in which P is to be employed, and as to the other terms and conditions of P's employment, are not substantially less favourable to P than if P had continued to be employed under the previous contract.

NOTES

Commencement: 6 April 2010 (see further reg 3 at **[2.1417]**).

[2.1443]

29 Dismissal during additional paternity leave

Where P is dismissed after P's additional paternity leave period has begun but before the time when (apart from this regulation) that period would end, the period ends at the time of the dismissal.

NOTES

Commencement: 6 April 2010 (see further reg 3 at **[2.1417]**).

[2.1444]
30 Early return from additional paternity leave period

(1) Subject to regulations 13(1) and 23(1) (variation or cancellation of leave in the event of death of the mother or adopter), where, after P's additional leave period has begun, P intends to return to work earlier than the end of P's additional paternity leave period, P must give E at least six weeks' notice of the date on which P intends to return.

(2) If P attempts to return to work earlier than the end of P's additional paternity leave period without complying with paragraph (1), E is entitled to postpone P's return to a date such as will secure, subject to paragraph (5), that E has six weeks' notice of P's return.

(3) Where P complies with P's obligations in paragraph (1), or where E has postponed P's return in the circumstances described in paragraph (2), if P then decides to return to work—

(a) earlier than the original return date, P must give E not less than six weeks' notice of the date on which P now intends to return;

(b) later than the original return date, P must give E not less than six weeks' notice ending with the original return date.

(4) In paragraph (3) the "original return date" means the date which P notified E as the date of P's return to work under paragraph (1) or the date to which P's return was postponed by E under paragraph (2).

(5) In a case where P's return to work has been postponed under paragraph (2) and P—

(a) has been notified that P is not to return to work before the date to which P's return was postponed, and

(b) returns to work before that date,

E is under no contractual obligation to pay P's remuneration until the date to which P's return was postponed.

(6) This regulation does not apply in a case where E fails to notify P of the date on which P's additional paternity leave period ends, in accordance with regulation 8, regulation 8 as modified by regulation 10, regulation 18 or regulation 18 as modified by regulation 20 (confirmation of period of leave), as applicable.

NOTES

Commencement: 6 April 2010 (see further reg 3 at **[2.1417]**).

[2.1445]
31 Right to return after additional paternity leave

(1) In a case where P returns to work after a period of additional paternity leave, lasting no longer than 26 weeks, which was—

(a) an isolated period of leave, or

(b) the last of two or more consecutive periods of statutory leave, which did not include any period of additional maternity leave or additional adoption leave or a period of parental leave of more than four weeks,

P is entitled to return from leave to the job in which P was employed before P's absence.

(2) In a case where P returns to work after a period of additional paternity leave not falling within the description in paragraph (1)(a) or (b) above, P is entitled to return from leave to the job in which P was employed before P's absence, or, if it is not reasonably practicable for E to permit P to return to that job, to another job which is both suitable for P and appropriate for P to do in the circumstances.

(3) The reference in paragraphs (1) and (2) to the job in which P was employed before P's absence is a reference to the job in which P was employed—

(a) if P's return is from an isolated period of additional paternity leave, immediately before that period began,

(b) if P's return is from consecutive periods of statutory leave, immediately before the first such period.

(4) This regulation does not apply where regulation 28 applies.

NOTES

Commencement: 6 April 2010 (see further reg 3 at **[2.1417]**).

[2.1446]
32 Incidents of the right to return after additional paternity leave

(1) P's right to return under regulation 31 is a right to return—

(a) with P's seniority, pension rights and similar rights as they would have been if P had not been absent, and

(b) on terms and conditions not less favourable than those which would have applied if P had not been absent.

(2) In the case of accrual of rights under an employment-related benefit scheme within the meaning given by paragraph 7 of Schedule 5 to the Social Security Act 1989, nothing in paragraph (1)(a) shall be taken to impose a requirement which exceeds the requirements of paragraphs 5 to 6 of that Schedule.

(3) The provisions in paragraph (1)(a) for P to be treated as if P had not been absent refer to P's absence—

(a) if P's return is from an isolated period of additional paternity leave, since the beginning of that period,

(b) if P's return is from consecutive periods of statutory leave, since the beginning of the first such period.

NOTES

Commencement: 6 April 2010 (see further reg 3 at **[2.1417]**).

[2.1447]

33 Protection from detriment

(1) P is entitled under section 47C of the 1996 Act not to be subjected to any detriment by any act, or any deliberate failure to act, by E because—

(a) P took, sought to take or made use of the benefits of additional paternity leave;

(b) E believed that P was likely to take additional paternity leave;

(c) P failed to return after a period of additional paternity leave in a case where—

(i) E did not notify P, in accordance with regulations 8, 8 as modified by regulation 10, 18, 18 as modified by regulation 20, or otherwise, of the date on which that period ended, and P reasonably believed that the period had not ended, or

(ii) E gave P less than 28 days' notice of the date on which the period would end, and it was not reasonably practicable for P to return on that date;

(d) P undertook, considered undertaking or refused to undertake work in accordance with regulation 26.

(2) For the purposes of paragraph (1)(a), P makes use of the benefits of additional paternity leave if, during P's additional paternity leave period, P benefits from any of the terms and conditions of P's employment preserved by section 80C of the 1996 Act and regulation 27 during that period.

(3) Paragraph (1) does not apply where the detriment in question amounts to dismissal within the meaning of Part 10 of the 1996 Act.

NOTES

Commencement: 6 April 2010 (see further reg 3 at **[2.1417]**).

[2.1448]

34 Unfair dismissal

(1) In a case where P is dismissed, P is entitled under section 99 of the 1996 Act to be regarded for the purpose of Part 10 of that Act as unfairly dismissed if—

(a) the reason or principal reason for the dismissal is of a kind specified in paragraph (3), or

(b) the reason or principal reason for the dismissal is that P is redundant and regulation 28 has not been complied with.

(2) In a case where P is dismissed, P shall also be regarded for the purposes of Part 10 of the 1996 Act as unfairly dismissed if—

(a) the reason (or, if more than one, the principal reason) for the dismissal is that P was redundant,

(b) it is shown that the circumstances constituting the redundancy applied equally to one or more employees in the same undertaking who had positions similar to that held by P and who have not been dismissed by E, and

(c) it is shown that the reason (or if more than one, the principal reason) for which P was selected for dismissal was a reason of a kind specified in paragraph (3).

(3) The kinds of reason referred to in paragraph (1) and (2) are reasons connected with any of the following facts—

(a) that P took, sought to take or made use of the benefits of, additional paternity leave;

(b) that E believed that P was likely to take additional paternity leave;

(c) that P failed to return after a period of additional paternity leave in a case where—

(i) E did not notify P, in accordance with regulations 8, 8 as modified by regulation 10, 18, 18 as modified by regulation 20, or otherwise, of the date on which that period ended, and P reasonably believed that the period had not ended, or

(ii) that E gave P less than 28 days' notice of the date on which the period would end, and it was not reasonably practicable for P to return on that date; or

(d) that P undertook, considered undertaking or refused to undertake work in accordance with regulation 26.

(4) For the purposes of paragraph (3)(a), P makes use of the benefits of additional paternity leave if, during P's additional paternity leave period, P benefits from any of the terms and conditions of P's employment preserved by section 80C of the 1996 Act and regulation 27 during that period.

(5) Paragraph (1) does not apply in relation to P if—

(a) it is not reasonably practicable for a reason other than redundancy for E (who may be E or a successor of E) to permit P to return to a job which is both suitable for P and appropriate for P to do in the circumstances,

(b) an associated employer offers P a job of that kind, and

(c) P accepts or unreasonably refuses that offer.

(6) Where, on a complaint of unfair dismissal, any question arises as to whether the operation of paragraph (1) is excluded by the provisions of paragraph (5), it is for E to show that the provision in question was satisfied in relation to the complainant.

NOTES

Commencement: 6 April 2010 (see further reg 3 at **[2.1417]**).

[2.1449]

35 Contractual rights to additional paternity leave

(1) This regulation applies where P is entitled to additional paternity leave (referred to in paragraph (2) as a "statutory right") and also to a right which corresponds to that right and which arises under P's contract of employment or otherwise.

(2) In a case where this regulation applies—

(a) P may not exercise the statutory right and the corresponding right separately but may, in taking the leave for which the two rights provide, take advantage of whichever right is, in any particular respect, the more favourable, and

(b) the provisions of the 1996 Act and of these Regulations relating to the statutory right apply, subject to any modifications necessary to give effect to any more favourable contractual terms, to the exercise of the composite right described in sub-paragraph (a) as they apply to the exercise of the statutory right.

NOTES

Commencement: 6 April 2010 (see further reg 3 at **[2.1417]**).

[2.1450]

36 Calculation of a week's pay

Where—

(a) under Chapter 2 of Part 14 of the 1996 Act, the amount of a week's pay of an employee falls to be calculated by reference to the average rate of remuneration, or the average amount of remuneration, payable to the employee in respect of a period of 12 weeks ending on a particular date (referred to as "the calculation date"),

(b) during a week in that period, the employee was absent from work on additional paternity leave, and

(c) remuneration is payable to the employee in respect of that week under the employee's contract of employment, but the amount payable is less than the amount that would be payable if the employee were working,

that week shall be disregarded for the purpose of the calculation and account shall be taken of remuneration in earlier weeks so as to bring up to twelve the number of weeks of which account is taken.

NOTES

Commencement: 6 April 2010 (see further reg 3 at **[2.1417]**).

ADDITIONAL STATUTORY PATERNITY PAY (GENERAL) REGULATIONS 2010

(SI 2010/1056)

NOTES

Made: 25 March 2010.

Authority: Social Security Contributions and Benefits Act 1992, ss 171ZEA(1)–(3), 171ZEB(1)–(3), 171ZEC(1), (3), 171ZED(2), (3), 171ZEE(2), (4), (7), 171ZG(3), 171ZJ(3), (4), (7), (8), 175(4); Social Security Administration Act 1992, s 5(1)(g)(i), (p).

Commencement: 6 April 2010 (see further reg 3 at **[2.1453]**).

See *Harvey* J(8).

ARRANGEMENT OF REGULATIONS

PART 1
INTRODUCTION

PART 2
ADDITIONAL STATUTORY PATERNITY PAY (BIRTH)

PART 3
ADDITIONAL STATUTORY PATERNITY PAY (ADOPTION)

PART 4
ADDITIONAL STATUTORY PATERNITY PAY: PROVISIONS APPLICABLE TO BOTH ADDITIONAL STATUTORY PATERNITY PAY (BIRTH) AND ADDITIONAL STATUTORY PATERNITY PAY (ADOPTION)

PART 1
INTRODUCTION

[2.1451]

1 Citation and commencement

These Regulations may be cited as the Additional Statutory Paternity Pay (General) Regulations 2010 and come into force on 6th April 2010.

NOTES

Commencement: 6 April 2010 (see further reg 3 at **[2.1453]**).

[2.1452]

2 Interpretation

(1) In these Regulations—

"the Act" means the Social Security Contributions and Benefits Act 1992;

"actual week of birth", in relation to a child, means the week beginning with midnight between Saturday and Sunday, in which the child is born;

"additional statutory paternity pay" means additional statutory paternity pay (adoption) or additional statutory paternity pay (birth);

"additional statutory paternity pay (adoption)" means additional statutory paternity pay payable in accordance with the provisions of Part 12ZA of the Act where the conditions specified in section 171ZEB(2) of the Act are satisfied;

"additional statutory paternity pay (birth)" means additional statutory paternity pay payable in accordance with the provisions of Part 12ZA of the Act where the conditions specified in section 171ZEA(2) of the Act are satisfied;

"additional statutory paternity pay period" means an additional statutory paternity pay period (adoption) or an additional statutory paternity pay period (birth);

"additional statutory paternity pay period (adoption)" means the period in respect of which additional statutory paternity pay (adoption) is payable;

"additional statutory paternity pay period (birth)" means the period in respect of which additional statutory paternity pay (birth) is payable;

"adopter", in relation to a child, means a person who has been matched with a child for adoption and who has elected to take adoption leave in order to care for the child;

"adoption agency" has the meaning given, in relation to England and Wales, by section 2 of the Adoption and Children Act 2002 and, in relation to Scotland, by section 119(1) of the Adoption and Children (Scotland) Act 2007;

"adoption leave" means ordinary adoption leave under section 75A of the Employment Rights Act 1996 or additional adoption leave under section 75B of that Act;

"adoption pay period" has the meaning given by regulation 21 of the Statutory Paternity Pay and Statutory Adoption Pay (General) Regulations 2002;

"child" means a person who is, or when placed with an adopter for adoption was, under the age of eighteen;

"the Commissioners" means the Commissioners for Her Majesty's Revenue and Customs;

"the Contributions Regulations" means the Social Security (Contributions) Regulations 2001;

"expected week of birth", in relation to a child, means the week, beginning with midnight between Saturday and Sunday, in which, as appropriate, it is expected that the child will be born, or was expected that the child would be born;

"maternity allowance period" means the period for which maternity allowance is payable under section 35 of the Act;

"maternity pay period" has the meaning given by regulation 2 of the Statutory Maternity Pay (General) Regulations 1986;

"ordinary statutory paternity pay" means ordinary statutory paternity pay payable in accordance with the provisions of Part 12ZA of the Act where the conditions specified in section 171ZA(2) or 171ZB(2) are satisfied;

"partner", in relation to a child's mother or adopter, means a person (whether of a different sex or the same sex) who lives with the mother or adopter and the child in an enduring family relationship but is not a relative of the mother or adopter of a kind specified in paragraph (2); and

"processing", in relation to information, has the meaning given by section 1(1) of the Data Protection Act 1998.

(2) The relatives of a child's mother or adopter referred to in the definition of "partner" in paragraph (1) are the mother's or adopter's parent, grandparent, sister, brother, aunt or uncle.

(3) References to relationships in paragraph (2)—

(a) are to relationships of the full blood or half blood or, in the case of an adopted person, such of those relationships as would exist but for the adoption, and

(b) include the relationship of a child with his adoptive, or former adoptive parents, but do not include any other adoptive relationships.

(4) References to Part 12ZA of the Act in these Regulations are references to sections 171ZEA to 171ZEE and, in so far as they concern additional statutory paternity pay, to sections 171ZF to 171ZJ of the Act.

(5) For the purposes of these Regulations—

(a) a person is matched with a child for adoption when an adoption agency decides that that person would be a suitable adoptive parent for the child, and

(b) a person is notified of having been matched with a child on the date on which that person receives notification of the agency's decision, under regulation 33(3)(a) of the Adoption Agencies Regulations 2005, regulation 28(3) of the Adoption Agencies (Wales) Regulations 2005 or regulation 24 of the Adoption Agencies (Scotland) Regulations 2009.

NOTES

Commencement: 6 April 2010 (see further reg 3 at **[2.1453]**).

[2.1453]

3 Application

Subject to the provisions of Part 12ZA of the Act and of these Regulations, there is entitlement to—

(a) additional statutory paternity pay (birth) in respect of children whose expected week of birth begins on or after 3rd April 2011;

(b) additional statutory paternity pay (adoption) in respect of children matched with a person who is notified of having been matched on or after 3rd April 2011.

NOTES

Commencement: 6 April 2010 (see further this regulation).

PART 2
ADDITIONAL STATUTORY PATERNITY PAY (BIRTH)

[2.1454]

4 Entitlement to additional statutory paternity pay (birth)

(1) A person ("P") is entitled to additional statutory paternity pay (birth) if—

(a) P satisfies the conditions—

(i) as to relationship with a child ("C") and with C's mother ("M") specified in paragraph (2); and

(ii) as to continuity of employment and normal weekly earnings specified in paragraph (3);

(b) M satisfies the conditions specified in regulation 6;

(c) P intends to care for C during the additional statutory paternity pay period (birth) in respect of C;

(d) M has signed the declaration referred to in regulation 8(1)(c); and

(e) P has complied with the requirements of regulation 8 including, where applicable, the requirements in regulation 8(3).

(2) The conditions referred to in paragraph (1)(a)(i) are that—

(a) P is either—

(i) C's father; or

(ii) is married to, or is the civil partner or the partner of, M but is not C's father; and

(b) P has, or expects to have, the main responsibility (apart from any responsibility of M) for the upbringing of C.

(3) Subject to regulation 5, the conditions referred to in paragraph (1)(a)(ii) are that—

(a) P has been in employed earner's employment with an employer for a continuous period of at least 26 weeks ending with the relevant week;

(b) P's normal weekly earnings for the period of eight weeks ending with the relevant week are not less than the lower earnings limit in force under section 5(1)(a) of the Act at the end of the relevant week; and

(c) P continues in employed earner's employment with the employer by reference to whom the condition in sub-paragraph (a) is satisfied for a continuous period beginning with the relevant week and ending with the week before the additional statutory paternity pay period (birth) in respect of C begins.

(4) The references in paragraph (3) to the relevant week are to the week immediately preceding the 14th week before C's expected week of birth.

NOTES

Commencement: 6 April 2010 (see further reg 3 at **[2.1453]**).

[2.1455]

5 Modification of entitlement conditions: early birth

(1) Where C's birth occurs earlier than the 14th week before C's expected week of birth, regulation 4(3) shall have effect as if, for the conditions set out there, there were substituted the conditions that—

(a) P would have been in employed earner's employment with an employer for a continuous period of at least 26 weeks ending with the relevant week had C been born after the relevant week;

(b) P's normal weekly earnings for the period of eight weeks ending with the week immediately preceding C's actual week of birth are not less than the lower earnings limit in force under section 5(1)(a) of the Act immediately before the commencement of C's actual week of birth; and

(c) P continues in employed earner's employment with the employer by reference to whom the condition in sub-paragraph (a) is satisfied for a continuous period beginning with the date of C's birth and ending with the week before the additional statutory paternity pay period (birth) in respect of C begins.

(2) The references in paragraph 5(1)(a) to the relevant week are to the week immediately preceding the 14th week before C's expected week of birth.

NOTES

Commencement: 6 April 2010 (see further reg 3 at **[2.1453]**).

[2.1456]

6 Conditions to be satisfied by the child's mother

The conditions referred to in regulation 4(1)(b) are that M—

(a) became entitled, by reference to becoming pregnant with C, to—

(i) a maternity allowance, or

(ii) statutory maternity pay;

(b) has taken action constituting a return to work within the meaning of regulation 19;

(c) has taken the action referred to in paragraph (b) not less than two weeks after the birth of C; and

(d) has at least two weeks of her maternity allowance period or maternity pay period which remain unexpired.

NOTES

Commencement: 6 April 2010 (see further reg 3 at **[2.1453]**).

[2.1457]

7 Additional statutory paternity pay period (birth)

(1) For the purposes of section 171ZEE(2)(a) of the Act, the date on which the additional statutory paternity pay period (birth) in respect of C begins is—

(a) the date specified by P in accordance with regulation 8(2)(d) or last varied in accordance with regulation 8(6), or

(b) if later, the date of M's taking action constituting a return to work within the meaning of regulation 19,

being, in either case, a date which falls no earlier than 20 weeks after the date of C's birth.

(2) For the purposes of section 171ZEE(2)(b)(ii) of the Act, the date on which the additional statutory paternity pay period (birth) in respect of C ends is the date specified by P in accordance with regulation 8(2)(e) or last varied in accordance with regulation 8(6).

(3) For the purposes of section 171ZEE(4)(a) of the Act, the additional statutory paternity pay period (birth) shall not last longer than 26 weeks.

(4) This paragraph applies instead of paragraph (2) where—

(a) M dies after the beginning but before the end of the additional statutory paternity pay period (birth) in respect of C; and

(b) as soon as reasonably practicable after M's death, P gives the person paying P additional statutory paternity pay (birth) notice in writing of M's death.

(5) Where paragraph (4) applies, the date on which the additional statutory paternity pay period (birth) in respect of C ends is the date—

(a) on which the maternity allowance period or maternity pay period in respect of C, which would have applied but for M's death, would have ended; or

(b) if earlier, such date which, for the purposes of section 171ZEE(2)(b)(ii) of the Act, P may specify in the notice given under paragraph (4)(b).

NOTES

Commencement: 6 April 2010 (see further reg 3 at **[2.1453]**).

[2.1458]

8 Application for, and evidence of entitlement to, additional statutory paternity pay (birth)

(1) P shall apply for additional statutory paternity pay (birth) to the person ("E") who will be liable to pay P such pay by providing to E—

(a) the information, in writing, specified in paragraph (2);

(b) a written declaration, signed by P—

(i) that that information is correct;

(ii) that P intends to care for C during the additional statutory paternity pay period (birth) in respect of C; and

(iii) that P meets the conditions in regulation 4(2); and

(c) a written declaration, signed by M—

(i) that she has given notice to her employer that she is returning to work;

(ii) that she satisfies the condition in regulation 6(a);

(iii) specifying her name, address and National Insurance number;

(iv) specifying the start date of her maternity allowance period or maternity pay period in respect of C;

(v) specifying the date on which she intends to return to work;

(vi) confirming that, in relation to C, P is, to M's knowledge, the sole applicant for additional statutory paternity pay; and

(vii) providing M's consent as regards the processing by E of the information provided pursuant to paragraphs (i) to (vi).

(2) The information referred to in paragraph (1)(a) is as follows—

(a) P's name;

(b) C's expected week of birth;

(c) C's date of birth;

(d) the date on which P expects that E's liability to pay additional statutory paternity pay (birth) will begin; and

(e) the date on which P expects that E's liability to pay additional statutory paternity pay (birth) will end.

(3) P shall also provide, if E so requests within 28 days of receiving the information and declarations referred to in paragraph (1)—

(a) a copy of C's birth certificate; and

(b) the name and business address of M's employer (or, if M is self-employed, her business address).

(4) The information and declarations referred to in paragraph (1) must be provided to E at least eight weeks before the date specified by P pursuant to paragraph (2)(d).

(5) P must give E what is requested under paragraph (3) within 28 days of E requesting it.

(6) P may, after applying for additional statutory paternity pay (birth) under paragraph (1), withdraw that application, vary the date on which it is expected that E's liability to pay additional statutory paternity pay (birth) will begin, or (before the additional statutory paternity pay period (birth) in respect of C has begun), vary the date on which it is expected that E's liability to pay additional statutory paternity pay will end, by notice in writing to E given—

(a) if withdrawing an application, at least six weeks before the date specified by P pursuant to paragraph (2)(d), or

(b) if varying the date on which it is expected that E's liability to pay additional statutory paternity pay (birth) will begin, at least six weeks before the earlier of the date varied or the new date, or

(c) if varying the date on which it is expected that E's liability to pay additional statutory paternity pay (birth) will end, at least six weeks before the earlier of the date varied or the new date, or

(d) in a case where it was not reasonably practicable to give notice in accordance with sub-paragraph (a), (b) or (c), as soon as is reasonably practicable.

(7) When P has applied for additional statutory paternity pay (birth) under paragraph (1), P must give E written notice as soon as reasonably practicable if at any time—

(a) P no longer satisfies the conditions in regulation 4(2); or

(b) M no longer intends to take action constituting a return to work within the meaning of regulation 19.

(8) When E has been provided with all of the information and the declarations referred to in paragraph (1) (together with, if applicable, what E has requested under paragraph (3)), E must, within 28 days, confirm the start and end dates of E's liability to pay P additional statutory paternity pay (birth) by notice in writing to P.

NOTES

Commencement: 6 April 2010 (see further reg 3 at **[2.1453]**).

[2.1459]

9 Entitlement to additional statutory paternity pay (birth) in the event of the death of the mother

(1) In a case where M dies before the end of her maternity allowance period or maternity pay period in respect of C (but before the additional statutory paternity pay period (birth) in respect of C has begun)—

(a) the provisions in regulations 4 to 6 shall apply, subject to the following modifications—

(i) regulation 4(1)(d) shall not apply;

(ii) regulation 4(1)(e) shall apply—

(aa) as if the references to regulation 8 were references to regulation 10; and

(bb) in a case where the date of which P informs E pursuant to regulation 10(1)(a) is earlier than the date by which P has complied with the other requirements of regulation 10, as if such other requirements had been complied with on such earlier date provided that they are complied with as soon as reasonably practicable thereafter;

(iii) the condition in regulation 4(2)(a)(ii) shall be taken to be satisfied if it would have been satisfied but for the fact that M had died;

(iv) the condition in regulation 6(a) shall be taken to be satisfied if M would have satisfied it but for the fact that M had died; and

(v) regulation 6(b), (c) and (d) shall not apply;

(b) regulation 7 shall not apply;

(c) for the purposes of section 171ZEE(2)(a) of the Act, the date on which the additional statutory paternity pay period (birth) in respect of C begins is such date, being the date of M's death or a later date, as P informs E of in accordance with regulation 10(1)(a) or as is last varied in accordance with regulation 10(7) or 10(8);

(d) for the purposes of section 171ZEE(2)(b)(ii) of the Act, the date on which the additional statutory paternity pay period (birth) in respect of C ends is, where earlier than the relevant date, the date specified by P in accordance with regulation 10(2)(d) or last varied in accordance with regulation 10(7) or 10(8);

(e) for the purposes of section 171ZEE(4)(a) of the Act, the additional statutory paternity pay period (birth) in respect of C shall not last longer than 39 weeks; and

(f) regulation 8 shall be replaced by regulation 10.

(2) In paragraph (1)(d), "the relevant date" means the date on which the maternity allowance period or maternity pay period in respect of C which would have applied but for M's death, would have ended.

(3) References in this regulation to M's maternity allowance period or maternity pay period in respect of C include, where M's death occurred before her maternity allowance period or maternity pay period in respect of C started, references to such period as would have existed but for the fact that M had died.

NOTES

Commencement: 6 April 2010 (see further reg 3 at **[2.1453]**).

[2.1460]

10 Application for, and evidence of entitlement to, additional statutory paternity pay (birth) in the event of the death of the mother

(1) P shall apply for additional statutory paternity pay (birth) to the person ("E") who will be liable to pay P such pay by—

(a) informing E of the date on which P wishes the additional statutory paternity pay period (birth) in respect of C to begin or the date (if in the past) on which P wishes such period to have begun;

(b) providing E with the information, in writing, specified in paragraph (2); and

(c) providing E with a written declaration, signed by P—

(i) that the information referred to in sub-paragraph (b) is correct;
(ii) that P intends to care for C during the additional statutory paternity pay period (birth) in respect of C; and
(iii) that P meets the conditions in regulation 4(2) (as modified by regulation 9(1)(a)(iii)).

(2) The information referred to in paragraph (1)(b) is as follows—
(a) P's name;
(b) C's expected week of birth;
(c) C's date of birth;
(d) the date on which P expects that E's liability to pay additional statutory paternity pay (birth) will end;
(e) M's name, address, and national insurance number;
(f) the start date of M's maternity pay period or maternity allowance period in respect of C, or, where M's death occurred before her maternity allowance period or maternity pay period in respect of C started, the date that that period would have started but for the fact that M had died; and
(g) the date of M's death.

(3) P shall also provide, if E so requests within 28 days of receiving the information and declaration referred to in paragraph (1)—
(a) a copy of C's birth certificate; and
(b) the name and business address of M's employer (or, if M was self-employed, her business address).

(4) Subject to paragraph (5), the information and declaration referred to in paragraph (1) must be provided to E as soon as reasonably practicable after, and in any event within eight weeks of, the date of M's death.

(5) If provided at least six weeks before the date of which P informs E pursuant to paragraph (1)(a), the information and declaration referred to in paragraph (1)(b) and (c) may be provided more than eight weeks after the date of M's death.

(6) P must give E what is requested under paragraph (3) within 28 days of E requesting it.

(7) Within eight weeks of the date of M's death, P may, after applying for additional statutory paternity pay (birth) under paragraph (1) and by giving E notice in writing, withdraw that application, vary the date (if in the future) on which P wishes the additional statutory paternity pay period (birth) in respect of C to begin, or (either before or after such period has begun) vary the date on which it is expected that E's liability to pay additional statutory paternity pay (birth) will end, with immediate effect.

(8) More than eight weeks after the date of M's death, P may, after applying for additional statutory paternity pay (birth) under paragraph (1), withdraw that application, vary the date (if in the future) on which P wishes the additional statutory paternity pay period (birth) in respect of C to begin, or (before such period has begun), vary the date on which it is expected that E's liability to pay additional statutory paternity pay (birth) will end, by notice in writing to E given—
(a) if withdrawing an application, at least six weeks before the date of which P has informed E pursuant to paragraph (1)(a), or
(b) if varying the date on which P wishes the additional statutory paternity pay period (birth) in respect of C to begin, at least six weeks before the earlier of the date varied or the new date, or
(c) if varying the date on which it is expected that E's liability to pay additional statutory paternity pay (birth) will end, at least six weeks before the earlier of the date varied or the new date, or
(d) in a case where it was not reasonably practicable to give notice in accordance with sub-paragraph (a), (b) or (c), as soon as is reasonably practicable.

(9) When E has been provided with all of the information and the declaration referred to in paragraph (1) (together with, if applicable, what E has requested under paragraph (3)), E must, within 28 days, confirm the date on which the additional statutory paternity pay period (birth) in respect of C begins or began and the date on which E's liability to pay P additional statutory paternity pay (birth) ends, by notice in writing to P.

NOTES

Commencement: 6 April 2010 (see further reg 3 at **[2.1453]**).

[2.1461]

11 Entitlement to additional statutory paternity pay (birth) where there is more than one employer

(1) Additional statutory paternity pay (birth) shall be payable to a person in respect of a statutory pay week during any part of which that person works only for an employer—
(a) who is not liable to pay that person additional statutory paternity pay (birth); and

(b) for whom that person worked in the week immediately preceding the 14th week before the expected week of birth.

(2) In this regulation, "statutory pay week" means a week that that person has chosen as a week in respect of which additional statutory paternity pay (birth) shall be payable.

NOTES

Commencement: 6 April 2010 (see further reg 3 at **[2.1453]**).

PART 3
ADDITIONAL STATUTORY PATERNITY PAY (ADOPTION)

[2.1462]
12 Entitlement to additional statutory paternity pay (adoption)

(1) A person ("P") is entitled to additional statutory paternity pay (adoption) if—

- (a) P satisfies the conditions—
  - (i) as to relationship with a child placed for adoption ("C") and the child's adopter ("A") specified in paragraph (2); and
  - (ii) as to continuity of employment and normal weekly earnings specified in paragraph (3);
- (b) A satisfies the conditions specified in regulation 13;
- (c) P intends to care for C during the additional statutory paternity pay period (adoption) in respect of C;
- (d) A has signed the declaration referred to in regulation 15(1)(c); and
- (e) P has complied with the requirements in regulation 15, including, where applicable, the requirements in regulation 15(3).

(2) The conditions referred to in paragraph (1)(a)(i) are that—

- (a) P is married to, or is the civil partner or the partner of, A; and
- (b) P has been matched with C for adoption.

(3) The conditions referred to in paragraph (1)(a)(ii) are that—

- (a) P has been in employed earner's employment with an employer for a continuous period of at least 26 weeks ending with the relevant week;
- (b) P's normal weekly earnings for the period of eight weeks ending with the relevant week are not less than the lower earnings limit in force under section 5(1)(a) of the Act at the end of the relevant week; and
- (c) P continues in employed earner's employment with the employer by reference to whom the condition in sub-paragraph (a) is satisfied for a continuous period beginning with the relevant week and ending with the week before the additional statutory paternity pay period (adoption) in respect of C begins.

(4) The references in paragraph (3) to the relevant week are to the week in which P was notified of having been matched with C.

NOTES

Commencement: 6 April 2010 (see further reg 3 at **[2.1453]**).

[2.1463]
13 Conditions to be satisfied by the child's adopter

The conditions referred to in regulation 12(1)(b) are that A—

- (a) became entitled, by reference to the adoption of C, to statutory adoption pay;
- (b) has taken action constituting a return to work within the meaning of regulation 19;
- (c) has taken the action referred to in paragraph (b) not less than two weeks after the date C was placed for adoption with A; and
- (d) has at least two weeks of their adoption pay period which remain unexpired.

NOTES

Commencement: 6 April 2010 (see further reg 3 at **[2.1453]**).

[2.1464]
14 Additional statutory paternity pay period (adoption)

(1) For the purposes of section 171ZEE(2)(a) of the Act, the date on which the additional statutory paternity pay period (adoption) in respect of C begins is—

- (a) the date specified by P in accordance with regulation 15(2)(d) or last varied in accordance with regulation 15(6); or
- (b) if later, the date of A's taking action constituting a return to work within the meaning of regulation 19,

being, in either case, a date which falls no earlier than 20 weeks [after] the date on which C was placed for adoption.

(2) For the purposes of section 171ZEE(2)(b)(ii) of the Act, the date on which the additional statutory paternity pay period (adoption) in respect of C ends is the date specified by P in accordance with regulation 15(2)(e) or last varied in accordance with regulation 15(6).

(3) For the purposes of section 171ZEE(4)(a) of the Act, the additional statutory paternity pay period (adoption) in respect of C shall not last longer than 26 weeks.

(4) This paragraph applies instead of paragraph (2) where—

(a) A dies after the beginning but before the end of the additional statutory paternity pay period (adoption) in respect of C; and

(b) as soon as reasonably practicable after A's death, P gives the person paying P additional statutory paternity pay (adoption) notice in writing of A's death.

(5) Where paragraph (4) applies, the date on which the additional statutory paternity pay period (adoption) in respect of C ends is the date—

(a) on which the adoption pay period in respect of C, which would have applied but for A's death, would have ended; or

(b) if earlier, such date which, for the purposes of section 171ZEE(2)(b)(ii) of the Act, P may specify in the notice given under paragraph (4)(b).

NOTES

Commencement: 6 April 2010 (see further reg 3 at **[2.1453]**).

Para (1): word in square brackets substituted by the Additional Statutory Paternity Pay (General) (Amendment) Regulations 2011, SI 2011/678, reg 2, as from 1 April 2011.

[2.1465]

15 Application for, and evidence of entitlement to, additional statutory paternity pay (adoption)

(1) P shall apply for additional statutory paternity pay (adoption) to the person ("E") who will be liable to pay P such pay by providing to E—

(a) the information, in writing, specified in paragraph (2);

(b) a written declaration, signed by P—

(i) that that information is correct;

(ii) that P intends to care for C during the additional statutory paternity pay period (adoption) in respect of C; and

(iii) that P meets the conditions in regulation 12(2);

(c) a written declaration, signed by A—

(i) that they have given notice to their employer that they are returning to work;

(ii) that they satisfy the condition in regulation 13(a);

(iii) specifying their name, address and National Insurance Number;

(iv) specifying the start date of their adoption pay period in respect of C;

(v) specifying the date on which they intend to return to work;

(vi) confirming that, in relation to C, P is, to A's knowledge, the sole applicant for additional statutory paternity pay; and

(vii) providing A's consent as regards the processing by E of the information provided pursuant to paragraphs (i) to (vi).

(2) The information referred to in paragraph (1)(a) is as follows—

(a) P's name;

(b) the date on which P was notified that they had been matched with C;

(c) the date of C's placement for adoption;

(d) the date on which P expects that E's liability to pay additional statutory paternity pay (adoption) will begin; and

(e) the date on which P expects that E's liability to pay additional statutory paternity pay (adoption) will end.

(3) P shall also provide, if E so requests within 28 days of receiving the information and declarations referred to in paragraph (1)—

(a) evidence, in the form of one or more documents issued by the adoption agency that matched P with C, of—

(i) the name and address of the agency;

(ii) the date on which P was notified that they had been matched with C; and

(iii) the date on which the agency was expecting to place C with A and P; and

(b) the name and business address of A's employer (or, if A is self-employed, A's business address).

(4) The information and declarations referred to in paragraph (1) must be provided to E at least eight weeks before the date specified by P pursuant to paragraph (2)(d).

(5) P must give E what is requested under paragraph (3) within 28 days of E requesting it.

(6) P may, after applying for additional statutory paternity pay (adoption) under paragraph (1), withdraw that application, vary the date on which it is expected that E's liability to pay additional statutory paternity pay (adoption) will begin, or (before the additional statutory paternity pay period (adoption) in respect of C has begun) vary the date on which it is expected that E's liability to pay additional statutory paternity pay (adoption) will end, by notice in writing to E given—

(a) if withdrawing an application, at least six weeks before the date specified by P pursuant to paragraph (2)(d), or

(b) if varying the date on which it is expected that E's liability to pay additional statutory paternity pay (adoption) will begin, at least six weeks before the earlier of the date varied or the new date, or

(c) if varying the date on which it is expected that E's liability to pay additional statutory paternity pay (adoption) will end, at least six weeks before the earlier of the date varied or the new date, or

(d) in a case where it was not reasonably practicable to give notice in accordance with sub-paragraph (a), (b) or (c), as soon as is reasonably practicable.

(7) When P has applied for additional statutory paternity pay (adoption) under paragraph (1), P must give E written notice as soon as reasonably practicable if at any time—

(a) P no longer satisfies the conditions in regulation 12(2); or

(b) A no longer intends to take action constituting a return to work within the meaning of regulation 19.

(8) When E has been provided with all of the information and the declarations referred to in paragraph (1) (together with, if applicable, what E has requested under paragraph (3)), E must, within 28 days, confirm the start and end dates of E's liability to pay P additional statutory paternity pay (adoption), by notice in writing to P.

NOTES

Commencement: 6 April 2010 (see further reg 3 at **[2.1453]**).

[2.1466]

16 Entitlement to additional statutory paternity pay (adoption) in the event of the death of the adopter

(1) In a case where A dies before the end of their adoption pay period in respect of C (but before the additional statutory paternity pay period (adoption) in respect of C has begun)—

(a) the provisions in regulations 12 and 13 shall apply, subject to the following modifications—

(i) regulation 12(1)(d) shall not apply;

(ii) regulation 12(1)(e) shall apply—

(aa) as if the references to regulation 15 were references to regulation 17; and

(bb) in a case where the date of which P informs E pursuant to regulation 17(1)(a) is earlier than the date by which P has complied with the other requirements of regulation 17, as if such other requirements had been complied with on such earlier date provided that they are complied with as soon as reasonably practicable thereafter;

(iii) the condition in regulation 12(2)(a) shall be taken to be satisfied if it would have been satisfied but for the fact that A had died;

(iv) the condition in regulation 13(a) shall be taken to be satisfied if A would have satisfied it but for the fact that A had died; and.

(v) regulation 13(b), (c) and (d) shall not apply;

(b) regulation 14 shall not apply;

(c) for the purposes of section 171ZEE(2)(a) of the Act, the date on which the additional statutory paternity pay period (adoption) in respect of C begins is such date, being the date of A's death or a later date, as P informs E of in accordance with regulation 17(1)(a) or as is last varied in accordance with regulation 17(7) or 17(8);

(d) for the purposes of section 171ZEE(2)(b)(ii) of the Act, the date on which the additional statutory paternity pay period (adoption) in respect of C ends is, where earlier than the relevant date, the date specified by P in accordance with regulation 17(2)(d) or last varied in accordance with regulation 17(7) or 17(8);

(e) for the purposes of section 171ZEE(4)(a) of the Act, the additional statutory paternity pay period (adoption) in respect of C shall not last longer than 39 weeks; and

(f) regulation 15 shall be replaced by regulation 17.

(2) In paragraph (1)(d), "the relevant date" means the date on which the adoption pay period in respect of C which would have applied but for A's death, would have ended.

(3) References in this regulation to A's adoption pay period in respect of C include, where A's death occurred before A's adoption pay period in respect of C started, references to such period as would have existed but for the fact that A had died.

NOTES

Commencement: 6 April 2010 (see further reg 3 at **[2.1453]**).

[2.1467]

17 Application for, and evidence of entitlement to, additional statutory paternity pay (adoption) in the event of the death of the adopter

(1) P shall apply for additional statutory paternity pay (adoption) to the person ("E") who will be liable to pay P such pay by—

- (a) informing E of the date on which P wishes the additional statutory paternity pay period (adoption) in respect of C to begin or the date (if in the past) on which P wishes such period to have begun;
- (b) providing E with the information, in writing, specified in paragraph (2); and
- (c) providing E with a written declaration, signed by P—
  - (i) that the information referred to in sub-paragraph (b) is correct;
  - (ii) that P intends to care for C during the additional statutory paternity pay period (adoption) in respect of C; and
  - (iii) that P meets the conditions in regulation 12(2) (as modified by regulation 16(1)(a)(iii)).

(2) The information referred to in paragraph (1)(b) is as follows—

- (a) P's name;
- (b) the date on which P was notified that they had been matched with C;
- (c) the date of C's placement for adoption;
- (d) the date on which P expects that E's liability to pay additional statutory paternity pay (adoption) will end;
- (e) A's name, address, and National Insurance number;
- (f) the start date of A's adoption pay period in respect of C or, where A's death occurred before their adoption pay period in respect of C started, the date that that period would have started but for the fact that A had died; and
- (g) the date of A's death.

(3) P shall also provide, if E so requests within 28 days of receiving the information and declaration referred to in paragraph (1)—

- (a) evidence, in the form of one or more documents issued by the adoption agency that matched P with C, of
  - (i) the name and address of the agency;
  - (ii) the date on which P was notified that they had been matched with C; and
  - (iii) the date on which the agency was expecting to place C with A and P; and
- (b) the name and business address of A's employer (or, if A was self-employed, A's business address).

(4) Subject to paragraph (5), the information and declaration referred to in paragraph (1) must be provided to E as soon as reasonably practicable after, and in any event within eight weeks of, the date of A's death.

(5) If provided at least six weeks before the date of which P informs E pursuant to paragraph (1)(a), the information and evidence referred to in paragraph (1)(b) and (c) may be provided more than eight weeks after the date of A's death.

(6) P must give E what is requested under paragraph (3) within 28 days of E requesting it.

(7) Within eight weeks of the date of A's death, P may, after applying for additional statutory paternity pay (adoption) under paragraph (1) and by giving E notice in writing, withdraw that application, vary the date (if in the future) on which P wishes the additional statutory paternity pay period (adoption) in respect of C to begin, or (either before or after such period has begun) vary the date on which it is expected that E's liability to pay additional statutory paternity pay (adoption) will end, with immediate effect.

(8) More than eight weeks after the date of A's death, P may, after applying for additional statutory paternity pay (adoption) under paragraph (1), withdraw that application, vary the date (if in the future) on which P wishes the additional statutory paternity pay period (adoption) in respect of C to begin, or (before such period has begun), vary the date on which it is expected that E's liability to pay additional statutory paternity pay (adoption) will end, by notice in writing to E given—

- (a) if withdrawing an application, at least six weeks before the date of which P informs E pursuant to paragraph (1)(a), or
- (b) if varying the date on which P wishes the additional statutory paternity pay period (adoption) in respect of C to begin, at least six weeks before the earlier of the date varied or the new date, or

(c) if varying the date on which it is expected that E's liability to pay additional statutory paternity pay (adoption) will end, at least six weeks before the earlier of the date varied or the new date, or

(d) in a case where it was not reasonably practicable to give notice in accordance with sub-paragraph (a), (b) or (c), as soon as is reasonably practicable.

(9) When E has been provided with all of the information and the declaration referred to in paragraph (1) (together with, if applicable, what E has requested under paragraph (3)), E must, within 28 days, confirm the date on which the additional statutory paternity pay period (adoption) in respect of C begins or began and the date on which E's liability to pay P additional statutory paternity pay (adoption) ends, by notice in writing to P.

NOTES

Commencement: 6 April 2010 (see further reg 3 at **[2.1453]**).

[2.1468]

18 Entitlement to additional statutory paternity pay (adoption) where there is more than one employer

(1) Additional statutory paternity pay (adoption) shall be payable to a person in respect of a statutory pay week during any part of which that person works only for an employer—

(a) who is not liable to pay that person additional statutory paternity pay (adoption); and

(b) for whom that person worked in the week immediately preceding the 14th week before the expected week of the placement for adoption.

(2) In this regulation "statutory pay week" means a week that that person has chosen in respect of which additional statutory paternity pay (adoption) shall be payable.

NOTES

Commencement: 6 April 2010 (see further reg 3 at **[2.1453]**).

PART 4
ADDITIONAL STATUTORY PATERNITY PAY: PROVISIONS APPLICABLE TO BOTH ADDITIONAL STATUTORY PATERNITY PAY (BIRTH) AND ADDITIONAL STATUTORY PATERNITY PAY (ADOPTION)

[2.1469]

19 Return to work

For the purposes of these Regulations, a mother or adopter is treated as returning to work if one of the following situations applies—

(a) in a case where a mother is entitled to maternity allowance, that allowance is not payable to her by virtue of regulations made under section 35(3)(a)(i) of the Act;

(b) in a case where an adopter is entitled to statutory adoption pay, that payment is not payable to that person in accordance with section 171ZN(3) or (5) of the Act;

(c) in a case where a mother is entitled to statutory maternity pay, that payment is not payable to her in accordance with section 165(4) or (6) of the Act.

NOTES

Commencement: 6 April 2010 (see further reg 3 at **[2.1453]**).

[2.1470]

20 Work during the additional statutory paternity pay period

(1) In a case where additional statutory paternity pay is being paid to a person who works during the additional statutory paternity pay period for an employer who is not liable to pay that person additional statutory paternity pay and who does not fall within, as appropriate, regulation 11(1)(b) or regulation 18(1)(b), there shall be no liability to pay additional statutory paternity pay in respect of the week in which the person does that work.

(2) In a case falling within paragraph (1), the person shall notify the person liable to pay additional statutory paternity pay within seven days of the first day during which the former works during the additional statutory paternity pay period.

(3) The notification mentioned in paragraph (2) shall be in writing, if the person who has been liable to pay additional statutory paternity pay so requests.

(4) In a case where an employee does any work on any day, under a contract of service with an employer who is liable to pay that employee additional statutory paternity pay, for not more than ten such days during the employee's additional statutory paternity pay period, whether consecutive or not, additional statutory paternity pay shall continue to be payable to the employee by the employer.

NOTES

Commencement: 6 April 2010 (see further reg 3 at **[2.1453]**).

[2.1471]

21 Cases where there is no liability to pay additional statutory paternity pay

(1) There shall be no liability to pay additional statutory paternity pay in respect of any week—

(a) during any part of which the person entitled to it is entitled to statutory sick pay under Part 11 of the Act;

(b) following that in which the person claiming it has died; or

(c) subject to paragraph (2), during any part of which the person entitled to it is detained in legal custody or sentenced to a term of imprisonment (except where the sentence is suspended).

(2) There shall be liability to pay additional statutory paternity pay in respect of any week during any part of which the person entitled to it is detained in legal custody where that person—

(a) is released subsequently without charge;

(b) is subsequently found not guilty of any offence and is released; or

(c) is convicted of an offence but does not receive a custodial sentence.

NOTES

Commencement: 6 April 2010 (see further reg 3 at **[2.1453]**).

[2.1472]

22 Additional statutory paternity pay and contractual remuneration

(1) For the purposes of section 171ZG(1) and (2) of the Act (as such provisions apply to additional statutory paternity pay), the payments which are to be treated as contractual remuneration are sums payable under a contract of service—

(a) by way of remuneration;

(b) for incapacity for work due to sickness or injury; and

(c) by reason of birth or adoption of a child.

NOTES

Commencement: 6 April 2010 (see further reg 3 at **[2.1453]**).

Note: this regulation is reproduced as it appears in the Queen's Printer's copy, ie, there is no para (2).

[2.1473]

23 Avoidance of liability for additional statutory paternity pay

(1) A former employer shall be liable to make payments of additional statutory paternity pay to a former employee in any case where the employee had been employed for a continuous period of at least eight weeks and the employee's contract of service was brought to an end by the former employer solely, or mainly, for the purpose of avoiding liability for additional statutory paternity pay or ordinary statutory paternity pay, or both.

(2) In a case falling within paragraph (1)—

(a) the employee shall be treated as if they had been employed for a continuous period ending with the earliest date that they could have been entitled to additional statutory paternity pay; and

(b) their normal weekly earnings shall be calculated by reference to their normal weekly earnings for the period of eight weeks ending with the last day in respect of which they were paid under their former contract of service.

NOTES

Commencement: 6 April 2010 (see further reg 3 at **[2.1453]**).

[2.1474]

24 Treatment of persons as employees

(1) Subject to paragraph (2), in a case where, and in so far as, a person is treated as an employed earner by virtue of the Social Security (Categorisation of Earners) Regulations 1978 that person shall be treated as an employee for the purposes of Part 12ZA of the Act, and in a case where, and in so far as, such a person is treated otherwise than as an employed earner by virtue of those regulations, that person shall not be treated as an employee for the purposes of Part 12ZA of the Act.

(2) Paragraph (1) shall have effect in relation to a person who—

(a) is under the age of 16; and

(b) would or, as the case may be, would not have been treated as an employed earner by virtue of the Social Security (Categorisation of Earners) Regulations 1978 had they been over that age, as it has effect in relation to a person who is or, as the case may be, is not so treated.

(3) A person who is in employed earner's employment under a contract of apprenticeship shall be treated as an employee for the purposes of Part 12ZA of the Act.

(4) A person who is in employed earner's employment but whose employer—

(a) does not fulfil the conditions prescribed in regulation 145(1) of the Contributions Regulations in so far as that provision relates to residence or presence in Great Britain; or

(b) is a person who, by reason of any international treaty to which the United Kingdom is a party or of any international convention binding the United Kingdom—

(i) is exempt from the provisions of the Act; or

(ii) is a person against whom the provisions of the Act are not enforceable,

shall not be treated as an employee for the purposes of Part 12ZA of the Act.

NOTES

Commencement: 6 April 2010 (see further reg 3 at **[2.1453]**).

[2.1475]

25 Continuous employment

(1) Subject to the following provisions of this regulation, where in any week a person is, for the whole or part of the week—

(a) incapable of work in consequence of sickness or injury;

(b) absent from work on account of a temporary cessation of work;

(c) absent from work in circumstances such that, by arrangement or custom, that person is regarded as continuing in the employment of their employer for all or any purposes,

and returns to work for their employer after the incapacity for or absence from work, that week shall be treated for the purposes of sections 171ZEA and 171ZEB of the Act as part of a continuous period of employment with that employer, notwithstanding that no contract of service exists with that employer in respect of that week.

(2) Incapacity for work which lasts for more than 26 consecutive weeks shall not count for the purposes of paragraph (1)(a).

(3) Where a person—

(a) is an employee in employed earner's employment in which the custom is for the employer—

(i) to offer work for a fixed period of not more than 26 consecutive weeks;

(ii) to offer work for such period on two or more occasions in a year for periods which do not overlap; and

(iii) to offer the work available to those persons who had worked for the employer during the last or a recent such period, but

(b) is absent from work because of incapacity arising from some specific disease or bodily or mental disablement,

then in that case paragraph (1) shall apply as if the words "and returns to work for their employer after the incapacity for or absence from work," were omitted.

NOTES

Commencement: 6 April 2010 (see further reg 3 at **[2.1453]**).

[2.1476]

26 Continuous employment and unfair dismissal

(1) This regulation applies to a person in relation to whose dismissal an action is commenced which consists—

(a) of the presentation by that person of a complaint under section 111(1) of the Employment Rights Act 1996;

(b) of their making a claim in accordance with a dismissal procedures agreement designated by an order under section 110 of that Act; or

(c) of any action taken by a conciliation officer under section 18 of the Employment Tribunals Act 1996.

(2) If, in consequence of an action of the kind specified in paragraph (1), a person is reinstated or re-engaged by their employer or by a successor or associated employer of that employer, the continuity of their employment shall be preserved for the purposes of Part 12ZA of the Act, and any week which falls within the interval beginning with the effective date of termination and ending with the date of reinstatement or re-engagement, as the case may be, shall count in the computation of their period of continuous employment.

(3) In this regulation—

dismissal procedures agreement" and "successor" have the same meanings as in section 235 of the Employment Rights Act 1996; and

"associated employer" shall be construed in accordance with section 231 of the Employment Rights Act 1996.

NOTES

Commencement: 6 April 2010 (see further reg 3 at **[2.1453]**).

[2.1477]

27 Continuous employment and stoppages of work

(1) Where, for any week or part of a week a person does not work because there is a stoppage of work due to a trade dispute within the meaning of section 35(1) of the Jobseekers Act 1995 at their place of employment, that person's continuity of employment shall, subject to paragraph (2), be treated, for the purposes of Part 12ZA of the Act, as continuing throughout the stoppage but, subject to paragraph (3), no such week shall count in the computation of their period of employment.

(2) Subject to paragraph (3), where during the stoppage of work a person is dismissed from their employment, that person's continuity of employment shall not be treated in accordance with paragraph (1) as continuing beyond the commencement of the day they stopped work.

(3) The provisions of paragraph (1), to the extent that they provide that a week in which the stoppage of work occurred shall not count in the computation of a period of employment, and paragraph (2) shall not apply to a person who proves that at no time did they have a direct interest in the trade dispute in question.

NOTES

Commencement: 6 April 2010 (see further reg 3 at **[2.1453]**).

[2.1478]

28 Change of employer

A person's employment shall, notwithstanding a change of employer, be treated, for the purposes of Part 12ZA of the Act, as continuous employment with the second employer where—

(a) the employer's trade or business or an undertaking (whether or not it is an undertaking established by or under an Act of Parliament) is transferred from one person to another;

(b) by or under an Act of Parliament, whether public or local and whenever passed, a contract of employment between any body corporate and the person is modified and some other body corporate is substituted as that person's employer;

(c) on the death of their employer, the person is taken into the employment of the personal representatives or trustees of the deceased;

(d) the person is employed by partners, personal representatives or trustees and there is a change in the partners, or, as the case may be, personal representatives or trustees;

(e) the person is taken into the employment of an employer who is, at the time they entered that employer's employment, an associated employer of their previous employer, and for this purpose "associated employer" shall be construed in accordance with section 231 of the Employment Rights Act 1996; or

(f) on the termination of the person's employment with an employer they are taken into the employment of another employer and those employers are governors of a school maintained by a local education authority.

NOTES

Commencement: 6 April 2010 (see further reg 3 at **[2.1453]**).

[2.1479]

29 Reinstatement after service with the armed forces etc

If a person who is entitled to apply to their employer under the Reserve Forces (Safeguard of Employment) Act 1985 enters the employment of that employer within the six month period mentioned in section 1(4)(b) of that Act, their previous period of employment with that employer (or if there was more than one such period, the last of those periods) and the period of employment beginning in that six-month period shall be treated as continuous.

NOTES

Commencement: 6 April 2010 (see further reg 3 at **[2.1453]**).

[2.1480]

30 Treatment of two or more employers or two or more contracts of service as one

(1) In a case where the earnings paid to a person in respect of two or more employments are aggregated and treated as a single payment of earnings under regulation 15(1) of the Contributions Regulations, the employers of that person in respect of those employments shall be treated as one for the purposes of Part 12ZA of the Act.

(2) Where two or more employers are treated as one under the provisions of paragraph (1), liability for additional statutory paternity pay shall be apportioned between them in such proportions as they may agree, or in default of agreement, in the proportions which the person's earnings from each employment bear to the amount of the aggregated earnings.

(3) Where two or more contracts of service exist concurrently between one employer and one employee, they shall be treated as one for the purposes of Part 12ZA of the Act, except where, by virtue of regulation 14 of the Contributions Regulations, the earnings from those contracts of service are not aggregated for the purposes of earnings-related contributions.

NOTES

Commencement: 6 April 2010 (see further reg 3 at **[2.1453]**).

[2.1481]

31 Meaning of "earnings"

(1) For the purposes of section 171ZJ(6) of the Act (as such provision applies to additional statutory paternity pay) (normal weekly earnings for the purposes of Part 12ZA of the Act), the expression "earnings" shall be construed in accordance with the following provisions of this regulation.

(2) The expression "earnings" refers to gross earnings and includes any remuneration or profit derived from a person's employment except any payment or amount which is—

- (a) excluded from the computation of a person's earnings under regulation 25 of and Schedule 3 to, and regulation 123 of, the Contributions Regulations (payments to be disregarded) and regulation 27 of those Regulations (payments to directors to be disregarded) (or would have been so excluded had they not been under the age of 16);
- (b) a chargeable emolument under section 10A of the Act except where, in consequence of such a chargeable emolument being excluded from earnings, a person would not be entitled to additional statutory paternity pay (or where such a payment or amount would have been so excluded and in consequence the person would not have been entitled to additional statutory paternity pay had they not been under the age of 16).

(3) For the avoidance of doubt, "earnings" includes—

- (a) any amount retrospectively treated as earnings by regulations made by virtue of section 4B(2) of the Act;
- (b) any sum payable in respect of arrears of pay in pursuance of an order for reinstatement or re-engagement under the Employment Rights Act 1996;
- (c) any sum payable by way of pay in pursuance of an order made under the Employment Rights Act 1996 for the continuation of a contract of employment;
- (d) any sum payable by way of remuneration in pursuance of a protective award under section 189 of the Trade Union and Labour Relations (Consolidation) Act 1992;
- (e) any sum payable by way of statutory sick pay, including sums payable in accordance with regulations made under section 151(6) of the Act;
- (f) any sum payable by way of statutory maternity pay;
- (g) any sum payable by way of ordinary statutory paternity pay;
- (h) any sum payable by way of additional statutory paternity pay; and
- (i) any sum payable by way of statutory adoption pay.

NOTES

Commencement: 6 April 2010 (see further reg 3 at **[2.1453]**).

[2.1482]

32 Normal weekly earnings

(1) For the purposes of Part 12ZA of the Act, a person's normal weekly earnings shall be calculated in accordance with the following provisions of this regulation.

(2) In this regulation—

"the appropriate date" means—

- (a) in relation to additional statutory paternity pay (birth), the first day of the 14th week before the expected week of the child's birth or the first day in the week in which the child is born, whichever is the earlier;
- (b) in relation to additional statutory paternity pay (adoption), the first day of the week after the week in which the adopter is notified of being matched with the child for the purposes of adoption;

"day of payment" means a day on which the person was paid; and

"normal pay day" means a day on which the terms of a person's contract of service require that person to be paid, or the practice in that person's employment is for that person to be paid, if any payment is due to them.

(3) Subject to paragraph (4), the relevant period for the purposes of section 171ZJ(6) (as such provision applies to additional statutory paternity pay) is the period between—

(a) the last normal pay day to fall before the appropriate date; and
(b) the last normal pay day to fall at least eight weeks earlier than the normal pay day mentioned in sub-paragraph (a),

including the normal pay day mentioned in sub-paragraph (a) but excluding that first mentioned in sub-paragraph (b).

(4) In a case where a person has no identifiable normal pay day, paragraph (3) shall have effect as if the words "day of payment" were substituted for the words "normal pay day" in each place where they occur.

(5) In a case where a person has normal pay days at intervals of or approximating to one or more calendar months (including intervals of or approximating to a year) that person's normal weekly earnings shall be calculated by dividing their earnings in the relevant period by the number of calendar months in that period (or, if it is not a whole number, the nearest whole number), multiplying the result by 12 and dividing by 52.

(6) In a case to which paragraph (5) does not apply and the relevant period is not an exact number of weeks, the person's normal weekly earnings shall be calculated by dividing their earnings in the relevant period by the number of days in the relevant period and multiplying the result by seven.

(7) In any case where a person receives a back-dated pay increase which includes a sum in respect of a relevant period, normal weekly earnings shall be calculated as if such a sum was paid in that relevant period even though received after that period.

NOTES

Commencement: 6 April 2010 (see further reg 3 at **[2.1453]**).

[2.1483]

33 Payment of additional statutory paternity pay

Payments of additional statutory paternity pay may be made in a like manner to payments of remuneration but shall not include payment in kind or by way of the provision of board or lodgings or of services or other facilities.

NOTES

Commencement: 6 April 2010 (see further reg 3 at **[2.1453]**).

[2.1484]

34 Time when additional statutory paternity pay is to be paid

(1) In this regulation, "pay day" means a day on which it has been agreed, or it is the normal practice between an employer or former employer and a person who is or was an employee of theirs, that payments by way of remuneration are to be made, or, where there is no such agreement or normal practice, the last day of a calendar month.

(2) In any case where—
(a) a decision has been made by an officer of Revenue and Customs under section 8(1) of the Social Security Contributions (Transfer of Functions, etc) Act 1999 as a result of which a person is entitled to an amount of additional statutory paternity pay; and
(b) the time for bringing an appeal against the decision has expired and either—
(i) no such appeal has been brought; or
(ii) such an appeal has been brought and has been finally disposed of,

that amount of additional statutory paternity pay shall be paid within the time specified in paragraph (3).

(3) Subject to paragraphs (4) and (5), the employer or former employer shall pay the amount not later than the first pay day after—
(a) where an appeal has been brought, the day on which the employer or former employer receives notification that it has been finally disposed of;
(b) where leave to appeal has been refused and there remains no further opportunity to apply for leave, the day on which the employer or former employer receives notification of the refusal; and
(c) in any other case, the day on which the time for bringing an appeal expires.

(4) Subject to paragraph (5), where it is impracticable, in view of the employer's or former employer's methods of accounting for and paying remuneration, for the requirement of payment referred to in paragraph (3) to be met by the pay day referred to in that paragraph, it shall be met not later than the next following pay day.

(5) Where the employer or former employer would not have remunerated the employee for their work in the week in question as early as the pay day specified in paragraph (3) or (if it applies) paragraph (4), the requirement of payment shall be met on the first day on which the employee would have been remunerated for his work in that week.

NOTES

Commencement: 6 April 2010 (see further reg 3 at **[2.1453]**).

[2.1485]

35 Liability of the Commissioners to pay additional statutory paternity pay

(1) Where—

(a) an officer of Revenue and Customs has decided that an employer is liable to make payments of additional statutory paternity pay;

(b) the time for appealing against the decision has expired; and

(c) no appeal against the decision has been lodged or leave to appeal against the decision is required and has been refused,

then for any week in respect of which the employer was liable to make payments of additional statutory paternity pay but did not do so, and for any subsequent weeks in the additional statutory paternity pay period, the liability to make those payments shall, notwithstanding section 171ZED of the Act, be that of the Commissioners and not the employer.

(2) Liability to make payments of additional statutory paternity pay shall, notwithstanding section 171ZED of the Act, be a liability of the Commissioners and not the employer as from the week in which the employer first becomes insolvent until the end of the additional statutory paternity pay period.

(3) For the purposes of paragraph (2) an employer shall be taken to be insolvent if, and only if—

(a) in England and Wales—

(i) the employer has been adjudged bankrupt or has made a composition or arrangement with its creditors;

(ii) the employer has died and the employer's estate falls to be administered in accordance with an order made under section 421 of the Insolvency Act 1986; or

(iii) where an employer is a company or a limited liability partnership, a winding-up order is made or a resolution for a voluntary winding-up is passed (or, in the case of a limited liability partnership, a determination for a voluntary winding-up has been made) with respect to it, or it enters administration, or a receiver or a manager of its undertaking is duly appointed, or possession is taken, by or on behalf of the holders of any debentures secured by a floating charge, of any property of the company or limited liability partnership comprised in or subject to the charge, or a voluntary arrangement proposed for the purposes of Part 1 of the Insolvency Act 1986 is approved under that Part of that Act;

(b) in Scotland—

(i) an award of sequestration is made on the employer's estate or the employer executes a trust deed for its creditors or enters into a composition contract;

(ii) the employer has died and a judicial factor appointed under section 11A of the Judicial Factors (Scotland) Act 1889 is required by that section to divide the employer's insolvent estate among the employer's creditors; or

(iii) where the employer is a company or a limited liability partnership, a winding-up order is made or a resolution for voluntary winding-up is passed (or, in the case of a limited liability partnership, a determination for a voluntary winding-up is made) with respect to it, or it enters administration, or a receiver of its undertaking is duly appointed, or a voluntary arrangement proposed for the purposes of Part 1 of the Insolvency Act 1986 is approved under that Part.

NOTES

Commencement: 6 April 2010 (see further reg 3 at **[2.1453]**).

[2.1486]

36 Liability of the Commissioners to pay additional statutory paternity pay in cases of legal custody or imprisonment

(1) Where—

(a) there is liability to pay additional statutory paternity pay in respect of a period which is subsequent to the last week falling within paragraph (1)(c) of regulation 21, or

(b) there is liability to pay additional statutory paternity pay during a period of detention in legal custody by virtue of the provisions of paragraph (2) of that regulation,

that liability, notwithstanding section 171ZED of the Act, shall be that of the Commissioners and not the employer.

NOTES

Commencement: 6 April 2010 (see further reg 3 at **[2.1453]**).

Note: this regulation is reproduced as it appears in the Queen's Printer's copy, ie, there is no para (2).

[2.1487]

37 Payments by the Commissioners

Where the Commissioners become liable in accordance with regulation 35 or 36 to make payments of additional statutory paternity pay to a person, the first payment shall be made as soon as reasonably practicable after they become so liable, and payments thereafter shall be made at weekly intervals, by means of an instrument of payment or by such other means as appears to the Commissioners to be appropriate in the circumstance of any particular case.

NOTES

Commencement: 6 April 2010 (see further reg 3 at **[2.1453]**).

[2.1488]

38 Persons unable to act

(1) Where to any person—

(a) additional statutory paternity pay is payable or it is alleged that additional statutory paternity pay is payable;

(b) that person is unable for the time being to act; and

(c) either—

(i) no deputy has been appointed by the Court of Protection with power to receive additional statutory paternity pay on their behalf, or

(ii) in Scotland, their estate is not being administered by a guardian acting or appointed under the Adults with Incapacity (Scotland) Act 2000,

the Commissioners may, upon written application to the Commissioners by a person who, if a natural person, is over the age of 18, appoint that person to exercise, on behalf of the person unable to act, any right to which the person unable to act may be entitled under Part 12ZA of the Act and to deal on behalf of the person unable to act with any sums payable to the person unable to act.

(2) Where the Commissioners have made an appointment under paragraph (1)—

(a) they may at any time in their absolute discretion revoke it;

(b) the person appointed may resign their office after having given one month's notice in writing to the Commissioners of their intention to do so; and

(c) the appointment shall terminate when the Commissioners are notified that a deputy or other person to whom paragraph (1)(c) applies has been appointed.

(3) Anything required by Part 12ZA of the Act to be done by or to any person who is unable to act may be done by or to the person appointed under this regulation to act on behalf of the person unable to act, and the receipt of the person so appointed shall be a good discharge to the employer or former employer of the person unable to act for any sum paid.

NOTES

Commencement: 6 April 2010 (see further reg 3 at **[2.1453]**).

[2.1489]

39 Service of notices by post

A notice given in accordance with the provisions of these Regulations in writing contained in an envelope which is properly addressed and sent by prepaid post shall be treated as having been given on the day on which it is posted.

NOTES

Commencement: 6 April 2010 (see further reg 3 at **[2.1453]**).

ADDITIONAL STATUTORY PATERNITY PAY (WEEKLY RATES) REGULATIONS 2010

(SI 2010/1060)

NOTES

Made: 24 March 2010.

Authority: Social Security Contributions and Benefits Act 1992, s 171ZEE(1); Social Security Administration Act 1992, s 5(1)(l).

Commencement: 6 April 2010.

See *Harvey* J(8).

[2.1490]

1 Citation and commencement

These Regulations may be cited as the Additional Statutory Paternity Pay (Weekly Rates) Regulations 2010 and come into force on 6th April 2010.

NOTES

Commencement: 6 April 2010.

[2.1491]

2 Weekly rate of payment of additional statutory paternity pay

The weekly rate of payment of additional statutory paternity pay shall be the smaller of the following two amounts—

(a) [£136.78];

(b) 90% of the normal weekly earnings of the person claiming additional statutory paternity pay, determined in accordance with regulations 31 and 32 of the Additional Statutory Paternity Pay (General) Regulations 2010.

NOTES

Commencement: 6 April 2010.

Sum in square brackets in para (a) substituted by the Social Security Benefits Up-rating Order 2013, SI 2013/574, art 10(2), as from 7 April 2013. The previous amounts were: £135.45 (as from 1 April 2012, see SI 2012/780, art 11(2)), £128.73 (as from 3 April 2011, see SI 2011/821, art 11(2)) and £124.88 (applying from the commencement of these Regulations).

[2.1492]

3 Rounding of fractional amounts

Where any payment of additional statutory paternity pay is made on the basis of a calculation at—

(a) the weekly rate specified in regulation 2(b); or

(b) the daily rate of one-seventh of the weekly rate specified in regulation 2(a) or (b),

and that amount includes a fraction of a penny, the payment shall be rounded up to the nearest whole number of pence.

NOTES

Commencement: 6 April 2010.

DAMAGES-BASED AGREEMENTS REGULATIONS 2010

(SI 2010/1206)

NOTES

Made: 7 April 2010.

Authority: Courts and Legal Services Act 1990, ss 58AA(4), 120(3).

Commencement: 8 April 2010.

These Regulations are revoked by the Damages-Based Agreements Regulations 2013, SI 2013/609, reg 2, as from 1 April 2013, but continue to have effect in respect of any damages-based agreement to which they applied and which was signed before 1 April 2013 (see reg 2 of the 2013 Regulations at **[2.1663]**).

ARRANGEMENT OF REGULATIONS

[2.1493]

1 Citation, commencement, interpretation and application

(1) These Regulations may be cited as the Damages-Based Agreements Regulations 2010 and come into force on the day after the day on which they are made.

(2) In these Regulations—

"the Act" means the Courts and Legal Services Act 1990;

"client" means the person who has instructed the representative to provide advocacy services, litigation services (within the meaning of section 119 of the Act) or claims management services (within the meaning of section 4(2)(b) of the Compensation Act 2006) and is liable to make a payment for those services;

"costs" means the total of the representative's time reasonably spent, in respect of the claim or proceedings, multiplied by the reasonable hourly rate of remuneration of the representative;

"damages-based agreement" means a damages-based agreement which relates to an employment matter;

"expenses" means disbursements incurred by the representative, including counsel's fees and the expense of obtaining an expert's report;

"payment" means a part of the sum recovered in respect of the claim or damages awarded that the client agrees to pay the representative and excludes expenses;

"representative" means the person providing the advocacy services, litigation services or claims management services to which the damages-based agreement relates.

(3) These Regulations apply to all damages-based agreements signed on or after the date on which these Regulations come into force.

NOTES

Commencement: 8 April 2010.

Revoked as noted at the beginning of these Regulations.

[2.1494]

2 Requirements of an agreement

The requirements prescribed for the purposes of section 58AA(4)(c) of the Act are that the terms and conditions of a damages-based agreement must specify—

(a) the claim or proceedings or parts of them to which the agreement relates;

(b) the circumstances in which the representative's payment, expenses and costs, or part of them, are payable; and

(c) the reason for setting the amount of the payment at the level agreed, including having regard to, where appropriate, whether the claim or proceedings is one of several similar claims or proceedings.

NOTES

Commencement: 8 April 2010.

Revoked as noted at the beginning of these Regulations.

[2.1495]

3 Information to be given before an agreement is made

(1) The information prescribed for the purposes of section 58AA(4)(d) of the Act is—

(a) information, to be provided to the client in writing, about the matters in paragraph (2); and

(b) such further explanation, advice or other information about any of those matters as the client may request.

(2) Those matters are—

(a) the circumstances in which the client may seek a review of the costs and expenses of the representative and the procedure for doing so;

(b) the dispute resolution service provided by the Advisory, Conciliation and Arbitration Service (ACAS) in regard to actual and potential claims;

(c) whether other methods of pursuing the claim or financing the proceedings, including—

(i) advice under the Community Legal Service,

(ii) legal expenses insurance,

(iii) pro bono representation, or

(iv) trade union representation,

are available, and, if so, how they apply to the client and the claim or proceedings in question;

(d) the point at which expenses become payable; and

(e) a reasonable estimate of the amount that is likely to be spent upon expenses, inclusive of VAT.

NOTES

Commencement: 8 April 2010.

Revoked as noted at the beginning of these Regulations.

[2.1496]
4 Additional causes of action

Any amendment to a damages-based agreement to cover additional causes of action must be in writing and signed by the client and the representative.

NOTES

Commencement: 8 April 2010.
Revoked as noted at the beginning of these Regulations.

[2.1497]
5 The payment

The amount prescribed for the purposes of section 58AA(4)(b) of the Act is the amount which, including VAT, is equal to 35% of the sum ultimately recovered by the client in the claim or proceedings.

NOTES

Commencement: 8 April 2010.
Revoked as noted at the beginning of these Regulations.

[2.1498]
6 Terms and conditions of termination

(1) The additional requirements prescribed for the purposes of section 58AA(4)(c) of the Act are that the terms and conditions of a damages-based agreement must be in accordance with paragraphs (2), (3) and (4).

(2) If the agreement is terminated, the representative may not charge the client more than the representative's costs and expenses for the work undertaken in respect of the client's claim or proceedings.

(3) The client may not terminate the agreement—
(a) after settlement has been agreed; or
(b) within seven days before the start of the tribunal hearing.

(4) The representative may not terminate the agreement and charge costs unless the client has behaved or is behaving unreasonably.

(5) Paragraphs (3) and (4) are without prejudice to any right of either party under the general law of contract to terminate the agreement.

NOTES

Commencement: 8 April 2010.
Revoked as noted at the beginning of these Regulations.

EQUALITY ACT 2010 (OFFSHORE WORK) ORDER 2010

(SI 2010/1835)

NOTES

Made: 21 July 2010.
Authority: Equality Act 2010, ss 82, 207(8).
Commencement: 1 October 2010.

ARRANGEMENT OF ARTICLES

[2.1499]
1 Citation, commencement, interpretation and extent

(1) This Order may be cited as the Equality Act 2010 (Offshore Work) Order 2010 and shall come into force on 1st October 2010.

(2) In this Order—
"the Equality Act" means the Equality Act 2010;

"Renewable Energy Zone" has the meaning given in section 84(4) of the Energy Act 2004.

(3) This Order does not extend to Northern Ireland.

NOTES

Commencement: 1 October 2010.

[2.1500]

2 Application of provisions

(1) Part 5 of the Equality Act applies to offshore work as if the work were taking place in Great Britain unless it—

(a) takes place in the Northern Irish Area as defined by the Civil Jurisdiction (Offshore Activities) Order 1987; or

(b) is in connection with a ship which is in the course of navigation or a ship which is engaged in dredging or fishing.

(2) In paragraph (1)(b), "dredging" does not include the excavation of the sea-bed or its subsoil in the course of pipe laying.

NOTES

Commencement: 1 October 2010.

[2.1501]

3 Jurisdiction over complaints arising in relation to offshore work within section 82(3)(a) and (b) of the Equality Act

In relation to offshore work within section 82(3)(a) and (b) of the Equality Act—

(1) The employment tribunal in England and Wales shall have jurisdiction to determine a complaint arising from an act taking place in the English area as defined in the Civil Jurisdiction (Offshore Activities) Order 1987, as it would have if that act had taken place in England and Wales.

(2) The employment tribunal in Scotland shall have jurisdiction to determine a complaint arising from an act taking place in the Scottish area as defined in the Civil Jurisdiction (Offshore Activities) Order 1987, as it would have if that act had taken place in Scotland.

NOTES

Commencement: 1 October 2010.

[2.1502]

4 Jurisdiction over claims arising in relation to offshore work within section 82(3)(c) of the Equality Act

In relation to offshore work within section 82(3)(c) of the Equality Act—

(1) The High Court shall have jurisdiction to determine a claim arising from an act taking place in the English area as it would have if that act had taken place in England or Wales.

(2) The Court of Session shall have jurisdiction to determine a claim arising from an act taking place in the Scottish area as it would have if that act had taken place in Scotland.

(3) For purposes of this Article—

"offshore area" means—

(a) tidal waters and parts of the sea in or adjacent to Great Britain up to the seaward limits of the territorial sea;

(b) waters in the Renewable Energy Zone as designated by the Renewable Energy Zone (Designation of Area) Order 2004;

"the English area" means such of the offshore area adjacent to England and Wales which lies to the south of the Scottish border;

"the Scottish area" means such of the offshore area adjacent to Scotland which lies to the north of the Scottish border;

"the Scottish border" has the meaning in the Schedule to this Order.

NOTES

Commencement: 1 October 2010.

SCHEDULE

(Definition of the Scottish border by means of points of longitude and latitude: outside the scope of this work.)

ECCLESIASTICAL OFFICES (TERMS OF SERVICE) DIRECTIONS 2010

(SI 2010/1923)

NOTES

Made: 27 July 2010.
Authority: Ecclesiastical Offices (Terms of Service) Regulations 2009, reg 23(1).
Commencement: 1 January 2011.

[2.1503]

1 Citation, coming into force and interpretation

(1) These Directions may be cited as the Ecclesiastical Offices (Terms of Service) Directions 2010 and shall come into force on 1st January 2011.

(2) In these Directions "the 1996 Act" means the Employment Rights Act 1996 and any reference to the 1996 Act or to regulations made under it is a reference to that Act or, as the case may be, to regulations as it has or they have effect on the date of the coming into force of these Directions.

NOTES

Commencement: 1 January 2011.

[2.1504]

2 Entitlement to maternity, paternity, parental and adoption leave

(1) Subject to the provisions of this paragraph, an office holder shall be entitled to maternity, paternity, parental and adoption, leave for the same periods and subject to the same conditions as apply in the case of an employee under the 1996 Act or any regulations made under that Act.

(2) An office holder who exercises any entitlement to leave conferred by sub-paragraph (1) shall, in consultation with a responsible person or authority, use all reasonable endeavours to make arrangements for the duties of the office to be performed by another person or persons during the period of leave.

NOTES

Commencement: 1 January 2011.

[2.1505]

3 Time off work for caring for dependants

(1) An office holder may request the appropriate authority to allow him or her to take time off work or to make adjustments to the duties of the office to care for a dependant.

(2) The request under sub-paragraph (1) shall be in writing and the Archbishops' Council may impose such other conditions as it thinks fit as to the manner in which the request is to be made, including any information which is to be supplied with the request.

(3) The appropriate authority shall be under a duty to consider the request under sub-paragraph (1) and may grant such time off work or adjustments to the duties of the office as appears to the appropriate authority to be reasonable and may impose reasonable conditions on the grant, including any appropriate variations in the stipend which would otherwise be payable to the office holder.

(4) In this paragraph "the appropriate authority" means—

- (a) in the case of an office holder holding any office other than an office in a cathedral, the bishop of the diocese,
- (b) in the case of an office holder holding office in a cathedral (other than the dean), the dean of the cathedral, and
- (c) in the case of the dean of a cathedral, the bishop of the diocese.

(5) In the case of an office other than an office in a cathedral, the bishop shall, before granting a request for time off work under sub-paragraph (3), consult the parochial church council or councils of the parish or parishes belonging to the benefice concerned.

(6) In this paragraph "dependant" has the same meaning as in section 57A of the 1996 Act.

NOTES

Commencement: 1 January 2011.

EQUALITY ACT 2010 (DISABILITY) REGULATIONS 2010

(SI 2010/2128)

NOTES

Made: 25 August 2010.
Authority: Equality Act 2010, ss 22(2)(a), (e), 207(1), (2), (4), 212(1), Sch 1, paras 1, 2(4), 3(2), 4, 7(1), Sch 21, para 6.
Commencement: 1 October 2010.
See *Harvey* L(1), (2)(B).

ARRANGEMENT OF REGULATIONS

Part 2 Statutory Instruments

PART 1
INTRODUCTORY

[2.1506]

1 Citation and Commencement

These Regulations may be cited as the Equality Act 2010 (Disability) Regulations 2010 and shall come into force on 1st October 2010.

NOTES

Commencement: 1 October 2010.

[2.1507]

2 Interpretation

In these Regulations—

"the Act" means the Equality Act 2010;

"addiction" includes a dependency;

"building" means an erection or structure of any kind;

"consultant ophthalmologist" means a consultant or honorary consultant appointed in the medical speciality of ophthalmology, who is employed for the purposes of providing any service as part of the health service continued under section 1(1) and (2) of the National Health Service Act 2006, section 1(1) and (2) of the National Health Service (Wales) Act 2006, section 1(1) of the National Health Service (Scotland) Act 1978 or section 2(1)(a) of the Health and Social Care (Reform) Act (Northern Ireland) 2009;

"a second requirement duty" means a duty to comply with the second requirement contained in any of the following provisions of the Act—

(a) paragraph 2 of Schedule 2;

(b) paragraph 2 of Schedule 8;
(c) paragraph 3 of Schedule 13;
(d) paragraph 2 of Schedule 15.

NOTES

Commencement: 1 October 2010.

PART 2
DETERMINATION OF DISABILITY

[2.1508]
3 Addictions

(1) Subject to paragraph (2) below, addiction to alcohol, nicotine or any other substance is to be treated as not amounting to an impairment for the purposes of the Act.

(2) Paragraph (1) above does not apply to addiction which was originally the result of administration of medically prescribed drugs or other medical treatment.

NOTES

Commencement: 1 October 2010.

[2.1509]
4 Other conditions not to be treated as impairments

(1) For the purposes of the Act the following conditions are to be treated as not amounting to impairments:—
(a) a tendency to set fires,
(b) a tendency to steal,
(c) a tendency to physical or sexual abuse of other persons,
(d) exhibitionism, and
(e) voyeurism.

(2) Subject to paragraph (3) below, for the purposes of the Act the condition known as seasonal allergic rhinitis shall be treated as not amounting to an impairment.

(3) Paragraph (2) above shall not prevent that condition from being taken into account for the purposes of the Act where it aggravates the effect of any other condition.

NOTES

Commencement: 1 October 2010.

[2.1510]
5 Tattoos and piercings

For the purposes of paragraph 3 of Schedule 1 to the Act, a severe disfigurement is not to be treated as having a substantial adverse effect on the ability of the person concerned to carry out normal day-to-day activities if it consists of—
(a) a tattoo (which has not been removed), or
(b) a piercing of the body for decorative or other non-medical purposes, including any object attached through the piercing for such purposes.

NOTES

Commencement: 1 October 2010.

[2.1511]
6 Babies and young children

For the purposes of the Act, where a child under six years of age has an impairment which does not have a substantial and long-term adverse effect on the ability of that child to carry out normal day-to-day activities, the impairment is to be taken to have a substantial and long-term adverse effect on the ability of that child to carry out normal day-to-day activities where it would normally have that effect on the ability of a person aged 6 years or over to carry out normal day-to-day activities.

NOTES

Commencement: 1 October 2010.

[2.1512]
7 Persons deemed to have a disability

A person is deemed to have a disability, and hence to be a disabled person, for the purposes of the Act where that person is certified as blind, severely sight impaired, sight impaired or partially sighted by a consultant ophthalmologist.

NOTES

Commencement: 1 October 2010.

PART 3
AUXILIARY AIDS OR SERVICES

[2.1513]

8 Auxiliary aids or services

(1) The following are to be treated as auxiliary aids or services for the purposes of paragraphs 2 to 4 of Schedule 4 to the Act—

(a) the removal, replacement or (subject to paragraph (2)) provision of any furniture, furnishings, materials, equipment and other chattels;

(b) the replacement or provision of any signs or notices;

(c) the replacement of any taps or door handles;

(d) the replacement, provision or adaptation of any door bell, or any door entry system;

(e) changes to the colour of any surface (such as, for example, a wall or door).

(2) Paragraph (1)(a) does not include the provision of any item which would be a fixture when installed.

(3) It is reasonable to regard a request for a matter falling within paragraph (1) as a request for a controller of premises to take steps in order to provide an auxiliary aid or service.

(4) In paragraph (3), the "controller of premises" means—

(a) in relation to paragraph 2 of Schedule 4 to the Act, the controller of let premises;

(b) in relation to paragraph 3 of Schedule 4 to the Act, the controller of premises that are to let; and,

(c) in relation to paragraph 4 of Schedule 4 to the Act, the commonhold association.

NOTES

Commencement: 1 October 2010.

PART 4
REASONABLE ADJUSTMENTS TO PHYSICAL FEATURES

[2.1514]

9 Reasonableness and design standards

(1) This regulation prescribes particular circumstances, for the purposes of paragraph 2 of Schedule 2 and paragraph 2 of Schedule 15 to the Act, in which it is not reasonable for a provider of services, a public authority carrying out its functions or an association to have to take the steps specified in this regulation.

(2) It is not reasonable for a provider of services, a public authority carrying out its functions or an association to have to remove or alter a physical feature where the feature concerned—

(a) was provided in or in connection with a building for the purpose of assisting people to have access to the building or to use facilities provided in the building; and

(b) satisfies the relevant design standard.

(3) Whether a physical feature satisfies the relevant design standard shall be determined in accordance with the Schedule.

NOTES

Commencement: 1 October 2010.

[2.1515]

10 Landlord withholding consent

(1) This regulation prescribes particular circumstances in which a relevant landlord (L) is to be taken, for the purposes of Schedule 21 to the Act, to have withheld consent for alterations to premises.

(2) Subject to paragraph (3), L is to be taken to have withheld such consent where, within the period of 42 days beginning with the date on which L receives the application for consent, L—

(a) fails to reply consenting to or refusing the alteration; or

(b)

(i) replies consenting to the alteration subject to obtaining the consent of another person required under a superior leave or pursuant to a binding obligation, but

(ii) fails to seek that consent.

(3) L is not to be taken to have withheld consent for the purposes of paragraph (2) where—

(a) the applicant fails to submit with the application such plans and specifications as it is reasonable for L to require before consenting to the alteration, and

(b) within the period of 21 days beginning with the date on which he receives the application, L replies requesting the applicant to submit such plans and specifications.

(4) However, where such plans and specifications are submitted to L in response to a request made in accordance with paragraph (3)(b), L shall be taken to have withheld consent to the alteration where, within the period of 42 days beginning with the date on which he receives those plans and specifications L—

(a) fails to reply consenting or refusing the alteration; or

(b)

(i) replies consenting to the alteration subject to obtaining the consent of another person required under a superior lease or pursuant to a binding obligation, but

(ii) fails to seek that consent.

(5) L, who having sought the consent of the other person referred to in paragraphs (2)(b) or (4)(b), receives that consent, shall be taken to have withheld consent to the alteration where, within the period of 14 days beginning with the day on which he receives the consent, L fails to inform the applicant in writing that it has been received.

(6) L who, but for the requirements as to time, complies with the requirements of paragraphs (2), (4) or (5) shall be taken to have withheld consent until such time as he so complies.

(7) For the purposes of this regulation—

(a) L is to be treated as not having sought another's consent unless he—

(i) has applied in writing to that person indicating that—

(aa) the occupier has applied for consent to the alteration of the premises in order to comply with a second requirement duty; and

(bb) L has given his consent conditionally upon obtaining the other person's consent; and

(ii) submits to that other person any plans and specifications which have been submitted to L;

(b) "to reply" means to reply in writing.

NOTES

Commencement: 1 October 2010.

[2.1516]

11 Landlord withholding consent unreasonably

(1) This regulation prescribes particular circumstances in which a relevant landlord (L) is to be taken, for the purposes of Schedule 21 to the Act, to have acted unreasonably in withholding consent for alterations to the premises.

(2) The circumstances so prescribed are that the lease provides that L shall give his consent to an alteration of the kind in question and L has withheld his consent to that alteration.

NOTES

Commencement: 1 October 2010.

[2.1517]

12 Landlord withholding consent reasonably

(1) This regulation prescribes particular circumstances in which a relevant landlord (L) is to be taken, for the purposes of Schedule 21 to the Act, to have acted reasonably in withholding consent for alterations to premises.

(2) The circumstances so prescribed are where—

(a)

(i) there is a binding obligation requiring the consent of any person to the alteration;

(ii) L has taken steps to obtain that consent; and

(iii) that consent has not been given, or has been given subject to a condition making it reasonable for L to withhold consent; or

(b) L does not know, and could not reasonably be expected to know, that the alteration is one which the occupier proposes to make to comply with a second requirement duty.

NOTES

Commencement: 1 October 2010.

[2.1518]

13 Landlord's consent subject to conditions

(1) This regulation prescribes particular circumstances in which a condition, subject to which a relevant landlord (L) has given consent to alterations to premises, is to be taken, for the purposes of Schedule 21 to the Act, to be reasonable.

(2) The circumstances so prescribed are where the condition is to the effect that—

(a) the occupier must obtain any necessary planning permission and any other consent or permission required by or under any enactment;
(b) the work must be carried out in accordance with any plans or specifications approved by the L;
(c) L must be permitted a reasonable opportunity to inspect the work (whether before or after it is completed);
(d) the consent of another person required under a superior lease or a binding agreement must be obtained;
(e) the occupier must repay to the L the costs reasonably incurred in connection with the giving of the consent.

NOTES

Commencement: 1 October 2010.

[2.1519]

14 Modification of Schedule 21

(1) In relation to any case where the occupier occupies premises under a sub-tenancy, the provisions of Schedule 21 to the Act shall have effect as if they contained the following modifications.

(2) In paragraph 3(3) and (4) and 4(1), for "the landlord" substitute "the immediate landlord" in each place it occurs.

(3) After paragraph 3(3), insert the following sub-paragraph—

"(3A) Except to the extent to which it expressly so provides, any superior lease in respect of the premises shall have effect in relation to the landlord and tenant who are parties to that superior lease as if it provided—
(a) for the tenant to be entitled to give his consent to the alteration with the written consent of the landlord;
(b) for the tenant to have to make a written application to the landlord for consent if he wishes to give his consent to the alteration;
(c) if such an application is made, for the landlord not to withhold his consent unreasonably; and
(d) for the landlord to be entitled to make his consent subject to reasonable conditions.".

(4) After paragraph 4(2), insert the following sub-paragraph—

"(2A) Where the tenant of any superior lease in relation to the premises has applied in writing to his landlord for consent to the alteration and—
(a) That consent has been refused, or
(b) The landlord has made his consent subject to one or more conditions,
the occupier, tenant or a disabled person who has an interest in the alteration being made may refer the matter to a county court or, in Scotland, the sheriff.".

(5) In paragraph 5—
(a) In sub-paragraph (2), for 'the landlord' substitute "any landlord (including any superior landlord)";
(b) In sub-paragraph (3), for paragraph (a), substitute—

"(a) must grant the request if it is made before the hearing of the complaint or claim begins, unless it considers that another landlord should be joined or sisted as a party to the proceedings.".

NOTES

Commencement: 1 October 2010.

[2.1520]

15 Revocation

(1) The Regulations listed in paragraph (2) are revoked.

(2) The Regulations referred to in paragraph (1) are—
(i) the Disability Discrimination (Meaning of Disability) Regulations 1996;
(ii) the Disability Discrimination (Providers of Services) (Adjustment of Premises) Regulations 2001;
(iii) the Disability Discrimination (Blind and Partially Sighted Persons) Regulations 2003;
(iv) the Disability Discrimination (Employment Field) (Leasehold Premises) Regulations 2004;
(v) the Disability Discrimination (Educational Institutions) (Alteration of Leasehold Premises) Regulations 2005;
(vi) the Disability Discrimination (Service Providers and Public Authorities Carrying Out Functions) Regulations 2005;

(vii) the Disability Discrimination (Private Clubs etc) Regulations 2005;
(viii) the Disability Discrimination (Premises) Regulations 2006.

NOTES

Commencement: 1 October 2010.

SCHEDULE
REMOVAL OR ALTERATION OF PHYSICAL FEATURES: DESIGN STANDARDS

Regulation 9(3)

[2.1521]

1. Definition of "relevant design standard"

(1) Subject to sub-paragraph (3), a physical feature, in relation to a building situated in England or Wales, satisfies the relevant design standard for the purpose of regulation 9(2) where it accords with the relevant objectives, design considerations and provisions in Approved Document M.

(2) Subject to sub-paragraph (3), a physical feature, in relation to a building situated in Scotland, satisfies the relevant design standard for the purposes of regulation 9(2) where—

(a) it was provided in or in connection with the building on or after 30th June 1994 and before 1st May 2005 in accordance with the Technical Standards relevant in relation to that feature; or

(b) it was provided in or in connection with the building on or after 1st May 2005 in accordance with the relevant functional standards and guidance in the Technical Handbook.

(3) A physical feature does not satisfy the relevant design standard where more than 10 years have elapsed since—

(a) the day on which construction or installation of the feature was completed; or

(b) in the case of a physical feature provided as part of a larger building project, the day on which the works in relation to that project were completed.

2. Buildings in England and Wales

(1) For the purposes of this paragraph and paragraph 1(1)—

(a) "Approved Document M" means—

(i) the 1992 edition of the document of that title approved by the Secretary of State as practical guidance on meeting the requirements of Part M of Schedule 1 to the Building Regulations 1991, first published for the Department of the Environment by Her Majesty's Stationery Office in 1991 (ISBN 011 752447 6); or

(ii) the 1999 edition of the document of that title approved by the Secretary of State as practical guidance on meeting the requirements of Part M of Schedule 1 to the Building Regulations 1991, first published for the Department of the Environment, Transport and the Regions by The Stationery Office under licence from the Controller of Her Majesty's Stationery Office in 1998 (ISBN 011 753469 2); or

(iii) the 2004 edition of the document of that title approved by the Secretary of State as practical guidance on meeting the requirements of Part M of Schedule 1 to the Building Regulations 2000, first published for the Office of the Deputy Prime Minister by the Stationery Office under licence from the Controller of Her Majesty's Stationery Office 2003 (ISBN 011 753901 5);

(b) "the Building Regulations" means the Building Regulations 1991 or the Building Regulations 2000.

(2) In the case of a physical feature provided as part of building works to which the Building Regulations applied, for the purposes of paragraph 1(1) Approved Document M is whichever edition is the practical guidance which was relevant in relation to meeting the requirements of the Building Regulations which applied to those building works.

(3) In any other case, for the purposes of paragraph 1(1) Approved Document M is whichever edition was the last edition published at the time when the physical feature was provided either in or in connection with the building.

(4) For the purposes of sub-paragraph (3), a physical feature is deemed to be provided in or in connection with the building on—

(a) the day upon which the works to install or construct the feature were commenced; or

(b) in the case of a physical feature provided as part of a larger building project, the day upon which the works in relation to that project were commenced.

(5) Where in relation to the physical feature in question any provision of Approved Document M refers to a standard or specification (in whole or in part), that standard or specification shall be construed as referring to any equivalent standard or specification recognised for use in any EEA state.

3. Buildings in Scotland

(1) For the purposes of this paragraph and paragraph 1(2)—

(a) "Technical standards" means the Technical Standards defined by regulation 2(1) of the Building Standards (Scotland) Regulations 1990 in effect at the time when the physical feature was provided in or in connection with the building;

(b) "Technical Handbook" means the following Technical Handbooks for non-domestic buildings issued by the Scottish Ministers as guidance meeting the requirements of the Building (Scotland) Regulations 2004:

(i) the 2004 edition of the document of that title published by Astron (ISBN 09546292 3 X); or

(ii) the 2007 edition of the document of that title published by The Stationery Office (ISBN 9780114973384); or

(iii) the 2010 edition of the document of that title published by The Stationery Office (ISBN 9780114973568).

(2) For the purposes of paragraph 1(2) and sub-paragraph (1)(a), and subject to sub-paragraph (3), a physical feature is deemed to be provided in or in connection with the building on—

(a) the day upon which the works to install or construct the feature was commenced; or

(b) in the case of a physical feature provided as part of a larger building project, the day upon which the works in relation to that project were commenced.

(3) In a case where the physical feature is provided as part of building works in relation to which an application for a warrant for the construction or conversion of the building has been made and granted, the works are deemed to have been commenced on the day upon which the application for the warrant was granted.

(4) Where in relation to the physical feature in question any provision of the Technical Standards or Technical Handbook refers to a standard or specification (in whole or in part), that standard or specification shall be construed as referring to any equivalent standard or specification recognised for use in any EEA state.

NOTES

Commencement: 1 October 2010.

Part 2 Statutory Instruments

EQUALITY ACT 2010 (SEX EQUALITY RULE) (EXCEPTIONS) REGULATIONS 2010

(SI 2010/2132)

NOTES

Made: 25 August 2010.
Authority: Equality Act 2010, ss 207(1), 212(1), Sch 7, paras 4, 5.
Commencement: 1 October 2010.
See *Harvey* BI(9)(B)(11).

[2.1522]

1 Citation, commencement and interpretation

(1) These Regulations may be cited as the Equality Act 2010 (Sex Equality Rule) (Exceptions) Regulations 2010 and shall come into force on 1st October 2010.

(2) In these Regulations—

"the Act" means the Equality Act 2010;

"the additional pension of a Category A retirement pension" has the same meaning as in Part II of the Contributions and Benefits Act;

"Category A retirement pension" has the same meaning as in Part II of the Contributions and Benefits Act;

"the Contributions and Benefits Act" means the Social Security Contributions and Benefits Act 1992;

"normal pension age" has the meaning given in section 180 of the Pensions Schemes Act 1993;

"pensionable age" shall be construed in accordance with section 122(1) of the Contributions and Benefits Act;

"pensionable service" includes any service in respect of which transfer credits have been allowed by the scheme;

"personal pension scheme" has the meaning given in section 1(1) of the Pension Schemes Act 1993;

"salary-related contracted-out scheme" means an occupational pension scheme which is contracted-out by virtue of satisfying section 9(2) of the Pension Schemes Act 1993 and includes a scheme which was formerly a salary-related contracted-out scheme which is subject to supervision in accordance with section 53 of that Act;

"scheme" means an occupational pension scheme;

"transfer credits" has the meaning given in section 124(1) of the Pensions Act 1995.

NOTES
Commencement: 1 October 2010.

[2.1523]
2 Exceptions to the sex equality rule: bridging pensions
The following circumstances are prescribed for the purposes of paragraph 4 of Part 2 of Schedule 7 to the Act (State retirement pensions)—
- (a) the man is in receipt of a pension from the scheme and has not attained pensionable age but would have attained pensionable age if he were a woman; and
- (b) an additional amount of pension is paid to the man which does not exceed the amount of Category A retirement pension that would be payable to a woman with earnings the same as the man's earnings in respect of his period of pensionable service under the scheme (assuming that the requirements for entitlement to Category A retirement pension were satisfied and a claim made).

NOTES
Commencement: 1 October 2010.

[2.1524]
3 Exceptions to the sex equality rule: effect of indexation
(1) The following circumstances are prescribed for the purposes of paragraph 4 of Part 2 of Schedule 7 to the Act (state retirement pensions)—
- (a) the scheme is a salary-related contracted-out scheme under which the annual rate of a pension payable to or in respect of a member is increased by more than it would have been increased had the recipient been of the other sex; and
- (b) the amount by which the pension increase exceeds any increase that would have applied had the member been of the other sex, does not exceed the relevant amount.

(2) In this regulation, the relevant amount means the amount by which X exceeds Y where—
X is the amount by which the additional pension of a Category A retirement pension attributable to the member's earnings factors during the member's period of pensionable service under the scheme would have been increased following an order made under section 150(9) of the Social Security Administration Act 1992 if the member had been of the other sex; and
Y is the amount (if any) by which the member's entitlement to the additional pension of a Category A retirement pension attributable to the member's earnings factors during the member's period of pensionable service under the scheme is increased following an order made under section 150(9) of that Act.

NOTES
Commencement: 1 October 2010.

[2.1525]
4 Exceptions to the sex equality rule: use of actuarial factors which differ for men and women
(1) The factors prescribed for the purposes of paragraph 5(1) of Part 2 of Schedule 7 to the Act (actuarial factors) are actuarial factors which differ for men and women in respect of the differences in the average life expectancy of men and women and which are determined with a view to providing equal periodical pension benefits for men and women.
(2) The following benefits are prescribed for the purposes of paragraph 5(2) of Part 2 of Schedule 7 to the Act—
- (a) a lump sum payment which consists of a commuted periodical pension or part of such a pension;
- (b) a periodical pension granted in exchange for a lump sum payment;
- (c) money purchase benefits within the meaning of section 181(1) of the Pension Schemes Act 1993;
- (d) transfer credits and any rights allowed to a member by reference to a transfer from a personal pension scheme;
- (e) a transfer payment including a cash equivalent within the meaning of section 94 of the Pension Schemes Act 1993;
- (f) a periodical pension payable in respect of a member who opts to take such benefits before normal pension age or in respect of a member who defers taking such benefits until after normal pension age;
- (g) benefits payable to another person in exchange for part of a member's benefits and the part of the member's benefits given up for that purpose.

NOTES

Commencement: 1 October 2010.

EQUALITY ACT (AGE EXCEPTIONS FOR PENSION SCHEMES) ORDER 2010

(SI 2010/2133)

NOTES

Made: 25 August 2010.
Authority: Equality Act 2010, ss 61(8), 207(1), (2), (4)(a), Sch 9, para 16.
Commencement: 1 October 2010.
See *Harvey* BI(9)(B)(11), L(4)(c).

ARRANGEMENT OF ARTICLES

SCHEDULES

[2.1526]

1 Citation and commencement

This Order may be cited as the Equality Act (Age Exceptions for Pension Schemes) Order 2010 and shall come into force on 1st October 2010.

NOTES

Commencement: 1 October 2010.

[2.1527]

2 Interpretation

(1) In this Order, subject to paragraph (2), "occupational pension scheme" means an occupational pension scheme within the meaning of section 1 of the Pension Schemes Act 1993.

(2) In relation to rules, practices, actions or decisions identified at paragraph 1(a) of Schedule 1, "occupational pension scheme" means an occupational pension scheme within the meaning of section 1 of the Pension Schemes Act 1993 under which only retirement-benefit activities within the meaning of section 255(4) of the Pensions Act 2004 are carried out.

(3) In this Order, "schemes" means an occupational pension scheme, construed in accordance with paragraphs (1) and (2).

(4) In this Order, in relation to a scheme—

["abolition date" means the day appointed for the commencement of section 15(1) of the Pensions Act 2007;]

"active member" has the meaning given by section 124 of the Pensions Act 1995, but in paragraph 8 of Schedule 1 also includes an active member within the meaning of section 151(2) of the Finance Act;

"additional state retirement pension" means the additional pension in the Category A retirement pension within the meaning of sections 44 and 45 of the Social Security Contributions and Benefits Act 1992;

"age related benefit" means benefit provided from a scheme to a member—

- (a) on or following the member's retirement (including early retirement on grounds of ill health or otherwise),
- (b) on the member reaching a particular age, or
- (c) on termination of the member's service in an employment;

"basic statement retirement pension" means the basic pension in the Category A retirement pension within the meaning of section 44 of the Social Security Contributions and Benefits Act 1992;

"block transfer" means a transfer in a single transaction or series of transactions from a scheme of all the sums or assets held for the purposes of, or representing, or derived from—

(a) all accrued rights under a scheme,

(b) contracted-out rights, or

(c) rights which are not contracted-out rights,

relating to a period of continuous pensionable service (or pensionable service which is treated as continuous) or one or more of a number of separate periods of such pensionable service which relate to a member and at least one other member;

["contracted-out rights" are such rights under, or derived from, an occupational pension scheme as fall within the following categories—

(a) entitlement to payment of, or accrued rights to, guaranteed minimum pensions; or

(b) section 9(2B) rights;]

"death benefit" means benefit payable from a scheme in respect of a member, in consequence of that member's death;

"defined benefits arrangement" has the meaning given by section 152(6) of the Finance Act, but the reference in that section to an arrangement shall be read as referring to an arrangement in respect of a member under a scheme as defined in section 1 of the Pension Schemes Act 1993 rather than in respect of a member under a pension scheme as defined in section 150(1) of the Finance Act;

"dependant" means a widow, widower or surviving civil partner, or a dependant as defined in the scheme rules;

"early retirement pivot age" means, in relation to age related benefit provided under a scheme, an age specified in the scheme rules (or otherwise determined) as the earliest age at which entitlement arises—

(a) without consent (whether of an employer, trustee or managers of the scheme or otherwise), and

(b) without an actuarial reduction,

but disregarding any special provision as to early payment on grounds of ill health or otherwise;

"the Finance Act" means the Finance Act 2004;

"guaranteed minimum pension" has the meaning given in section 8(2) of the Pension Schemes Act 1993;

"late retirement pivot age" means an age specified in the scheme rules (or otherwise determined) above which benefit becomes payable with actuarial enhancement;

"lower earnings limit" means the amount specified for the tax year in question in regulations made under section 5(1)(a)(i) of the Social Security Contributions and Benefits Act 1992 (earnings limits and thresholds for Class 1 contributions);

"member" means any active member, deferred member, or pensioner member, but in paragraph 7 includes any active, deferred or pensioner member within the meaning of section 151(2) to (4) of the Finance Act;

"money purchase arrangement" has the meaning given by section 152(2) of the Finance Act, but the reference in that section to an arrangement shall be read as referring to an arrangement in respect of a member under a scheme as defined in section 1 of the Pension Schemes Act 1993 rather than in respect of a member under a pension scheme as defined in section 150(1) of the Finance Act;

"non-discrimination rule" means the rule in section 61 of the Equality Act 2010 as it applies to the protected characteristic of age under that Act;

"normal pension age" has the meaning given by section 180 of the Pension Schemes Act 1993;

"normal retirement age", in relation to a member, means the age at which workers in the undertaking for which the member worked at the time of the member's retirement, and who held the same kind of position as the member held at retirement, were normally required to retire;

"pensionable pay" means that part of a member's pay which counts as pensionable pay under the scheme rules;

"prospective member" means any person who, under the terms of the person's employment, or the scheme rules, or both—

(a) is able, at the person's option, to become a member of the scheme,

(b) shall become so able if the person continues in the same employment for a sufficient period of time,

(c) shall be so admitted to it automatically unless the person makes an election not to become a member, or

(d) may be admitted to it subject to the consent of any person;

"protected rights" has the meaning given in section 10 of the Pension Schemes Act 1993 [as it had effect immediately prior to the abolition date];

"redundancy" means being dismissed by reason of redundancy for the purposes of the Employment Rights Act 1996;

"relevant transfer" has the meaning given in—

(a) regulation 2(1) of the Transfer of Undertakings (Protection of Employment) Regulations 1981 (a relevant transfer), or as the case may be,

(b) regulation 2(1) of the Transfer of Undertakings (Protection of Employment) Regulations 2006 (a relevant transfer);

"section 9(2B) rights" are—

(a) rights to the payment of pensions and accrued rights to pension (other than rights attributable to voluntary contributions) under a scheme contracted-out by virtue of section 9(2B) of the Pension Schemes Act 1993, so far as attributable to an earner's service in contracted-out employment on or after 6th April 1997; and

(b) where a transfer payment has been made to such a scheme, any rights arising under the scheme as a consequence of that payment which are derived directly or indirectly from—

(i) such rights as are referred to in sub-paragraph (a) under another scheme contracted-out by virtue of section 9(2B) of that Act; or

(ii) protected rights under another occupational pension scheme or under a personal pension scheme attributable to payments or contributions in respect of employment on or after 6th April 1997 [where the transfer took place before the abolition date];

"upper earnings limit" means the amount specified for the tax year in question in regulations made under section 5(1)(a)(iii) of the Social Security Contributions and Benefits Act 1992 (earnings limits and thresholds for Class 1 contributions).

(5) In this Order, "registered pension scheme" has the meaning given by section 150(2) of the Finance Act, and references to contributions under a money purchase arrangement shall be construed as including amounts credited to a member's account whether or not they reflect payments actually made under the scheme.

NOTES

Commencement: 1 October 2010.

Para (4): definition "abolition date" inserted, definition "contracted-out rights" substituted, and words in square brackets in definitions "protected rights" and "section 9(2B) rights" inserted, by the Pensions Act 2008 (Abolition of Protected Rights) (Consequential Amendments) Order 2011, SI 2011/1246, art 24, as from 6 April 2012.

[2.1528]

3 Occupational pension schemes: excepted rules, practices, actions and decisions

It is not a breach of the non-discrimination rule for the employer, or the trustees or managers of a scheme, to maintain or use in relation to the scheme,

[(a)] those rules, practices, actions or decisions set out in Schedule 1[; or

(b) rules, practices, actions or decisions as they relate to rights accrued, or benefits payable, in respect of periods of pensionable service prior to 1st December 2006 that would breach the non-discrimination rule but for this paragraph].

NOTES

Commencement: 1 October 2010.

Words in square brackets inserted by the Equality Act (Age Exceptions for Pension Schemes) (Amendment) Order 2010, SI 2010/2285, art 2(1), (2), as from 1 October 2010.

[2.1529]

4 Contributions by employers to personal pension schemes: excepted practices, actions and decisions

It is not an age contravention for the employer, in relation to the payment of contributions to any personal pension scheme in respect of a worker, to maintain or use those practices, actions or decisions set out in Schedule 2.

NOTES

Commencement: 1 October 2010.

[2.1530]

5 Unlawfulness of rules, practices, actions or decisions

(1) The inclusion of a rule, practice, action or decision in Schedule 1 (Occupational Pension Schemes: excepted rules, practices, actions or decisions) shall not be taken to mean that, but for the exemption in Schedule 1, the use or maintenance by an employer or the trustees or managers of a scheme of the rule, practice, action or decision in relation to the scheme, would be unlawful.

(2) The inclusion of a practice, action or decision in Schedule 2 (Contributions by Employers to Personal Pension Schemes: excepted practices, actions or decisions) shall not be taken to mean that, but for the exemption in Schedule 2, the use or maintenance by an employer of the practice, action or decision in relation to the payment of contributions to a personal pension scheme in respect of a worker, would be unlawful.

NOTES

Commencement: 1 October 2010.

[2.1531]

[6 Length of service exceptions

(1) Paragraph (2) is subject to paragraph (3).

(2) In addition to the excepted rules, practices, actions or decisions contained in Schedules 1 and 2, none of the following is a breach of the non-discrimination rule or is an age contravention, as applicable—

(a) any rule, practice, action or decision of the trustees or managers ("A") of an occupational pension scheme regarding—

(i) admission to that scheme ("admission terms"); or

(ii) the accrual of, or eligibility for, any benefit under the scheme ("benefit terms"),

where the admission terms or the benefit terms put a member ("B") of the scheme at a disadvantage when compared with another member ("C") if and to the extent that the disadvantage suffered by B is because B's length of service with an employer ("D") in relation to the scheme is less than that of C;

(b) any rule, practice, action or decision of an employer ("E") in relation to an occupational pension scheme regarding the admission terms or benefit terms where it puts a member ("F") of that scheme at a disadvantage when compared with another member ("G") if and to the extent that the disadvantage suffered by F is because F's length of service with E is less than that of G; or

(c) any practice, action or decision of an employer ("H") regarding payment of contributions in respect of a worker ("I") to a personal pension scheme or to a money purchase arrangement ("contribution terms") where it puts I at a disadvantage when compared with another worker ("J") if and to the extent that the disadvantage suffered by I is because I's length of service with H is less than that of J.

(3) Where B's, or as the case may be, F's or I's, length of service exceeds 5 years and a length of service criterion in the admission terms or, as the case may be, the benefit terms or contribution terms, puts B or F or I at a disadvantage—

(a) where paragraph (2)(a) applies, A—

(i) must ask D to confirm whether the length of service criterion reasonably appears to D to fulfil a business need of D's undertaking (for example by encouraging the loyalty or motivation, or rewarding the experience, of some or all of his workers); and

(ii) may rely on D's confirmation;

(b) for the purposes of sub-paragraph (a)(i), D must—

(i) calculate B's length of service;

(ii) provide A with details of B's length of service; and

(iii) respond to A's request within a reasonable time;

(c) where paragraph (2)(a) or (b) or (c) applies, it must reasonably appear to D or, as the case may be, E or H, that the length of service criterion applies in such a way that it fulfils a business need of his undertaking (for example by encouraging the loyalty or motivation, or rewarding the experience, of some or all of his workers).

(4) When calculating B's or, as the case may be, F's or I's, length of service, D or, as the case may be, E or H, must calculate—

(a) the length of time the member or worker has been working for that employer doing work which that employer reasonably considers to be at or above a particular level (assessed by reference to the demands made on the member or worker, for example, in terms of effort, skills and decision making); or

(b) the length of time the member or worker has been working for that employer in total,

and it is for D or, as the case may be, E or H to decide which of sub-paragraphs (a) or (b) to use.

(5) For the purposes of paragraph (4), D or, as the case may be, E or H, shall calculate the length of time a member or worker has been working for that employer in accordance with sub-paragraphs (4) to (6) of paragraph 10 of Schedule 9 to the Equality Act 2010 (benefits based on length of service) and any reference in those sub-paragraphs to—

(a) "A" shall be read as if it were a reference to "D" or, as the case may be, "E" or "H"; and

(b) "person" (except in the phrase "person other than A") shall, where paragraph (2)(a) or (b) applies, be read as if it were a reference to "member".

(6) For the purposes of this article, a "member" shall include a "prospective member".]

NOTES

Commencement: 1 October 2010.

Inserted by the Equality Act (Age Exceptions for Pension Schemes) (Amendment) Order 2010, SI 2010/2285, art 2(1), (3), as from 1 October 2010.

SCHEDULES

SCHEDULE 1
OCCUPATIONAL PENSION SCHEMES: EXCEPTED RULES, PRACTICES, ACTIONS AND DECISIONS

Article 3

Admission to schemes

[2.1532]

1. In relation to admission to a scheme—

(a) a minimum or maximum age for admission, including different ages for admission for different groups or categories of worker;

(b) a minimum level of pensionable pay for admission where that minimum—

(i) does not exceed one and a half times the lower earnings limit;

(ii) does not exceed an amount calculated by reference to the lower earnings limit where the aim is more or less to reflect the amount of the basic state retirement pension; or

(iii) does not exceed an amount calculated more or less to reflect the amount of the basic state retirement pension plus the additional state retirement pension.

The use of age criteria in actuarial calculations

2. The use of age criteria in actuarial calculations in a scheme, for example in the actuarial calculation of—

(a) any age related benefit commencing before any early retirement pivot age or enhancement of such benefit commencing after any late retirement pivot age;

(b) member or employer contributions by or in respect of a member to a scheme; or

(c) any age related benefit commuted in exchange for the payment of any lump sum.

Contributions

3. Any difference in the rate of member or employer contributions, to a scheme, by or in respect of different members to the extent that this is attributable to any differences in the pensionable pay or, where paragraph 18 applies, different accrual rates of those members.

Contributions under money purchase arrangements

4. Under a money purchase arrangement—

(a) different rates of member or employer contributions according to the age of the members by or in respect of whom contributions are made where the aim in setting the different rates is—

(i) to equalise the amount of age related benefit in respect of comparable aggregate periods of pensionable service to which members of different ages who are otherwise in a comparable situation will become entitled under the arrangement, or

(ii) to make more nearly equal the amount of the age related benefit, in respect of comparable aggregate periods of pensionable service, to which members of different ages who are otherwise in a comparable situation will become entitled under the arrangement;

(b) equal rates of member or employer contributions irrespective of the age of the members by or in respect of whom contributions are made;

(c) any limitation on any employer contributions in respect of a member or member contributions by reference to a maximum level of pensionable pay.

Contributions under defined benefits arrangements

5. Under a defined benefits arrangement, different rates of member or employer contributions according to the age of the members by or in respect of whom contributions are made, to the extent that—

(a) each year of pensionable service entitles members in a comparable situation to accrue a right to defined benefits based on the same fraction of pensionable pay, and

(b) the aim in setting the different rates is to reflect the increasing cost of providing the defined benefits in respect of members as they get older.

6. Any limitation on employer contributions in respect of a member or member contributions to a defined benefit arrangement by reference to a maximum level of pensionable pay.

Rules, practices, actions and decisions relating to benefit

7. (1) Subject to sub-paragraph (4), a minimum age for any member of a scheme to be entitled to a particular age related benefit that is paid in accordance with sub-paragraph (2) and is paid—

(a) either with or without consent (whether of an employer, the trustees or managers of the scheme or otherwise), and

(b) before the early retirement pivot age relevant to that age related benefit.

(2) The age related benefit must—

(a) be actuarially reduced on the basis that the aim is to reflect that it is paid on a date before the applicable early retirement pivot age; and

(b) not be enhanced by crediting the member with any additional periods of pensionable service or additional benefits.

(3) Sub-paragraph (1) shall also apply to different minimum ages for different groups or categories of members.

(4) Sub-paragraph (1) shall not apply to any member who retires on the grounds to which paragraph 8, 9 or 12 apply.

8. (1) A minimum age for any active or prospective members of a scheme for payment of or entitlement to a particular age related benefit before the early retirement pivot age relevant to that age related benefit where—

(a) the entitlement to the age related benefit at a minimum age applies to a member who is an active or prospective member of the scheme on 1st December 2006;

(b) the age related benefit may be paid, at a minimum age, to the active or prospective member either with or without consent (whether of an employer, the trustees or managers of the scheme or otherwise); and

(c) the age related benefit is enhanced in one or more of the ways specified in sub-paragraph (2).

(2) For the purposes of sub-paragraph (1)(c) the specified ways are the enhancement of any age related benefit payable to or in respect of the member calculated in one or more of the following ways—

(a) by reference to some or all of the years of prospective pensionable service a member would have completed if that member had remained in pensionable service until normal pension age;

(b) by reference to a fixed number of years of prospective pensionable service;

(c) by making an actuarial reduction which is smaller than if early retirement had been on grounds to which paragraph 7 applies; or

(d) by not making any actuarial reduction for early retirement.

(3) Sub-paragraph (1) shall also apply to different minimum ages for different groups or categories of active or prospective members.

9. Paragraph 8 shall continue to apply to any member who after 1st December 2006—

(a) joins a scheme as a result of a block transfer or relevant transfer;

(b) joins a scheme as a result of a block transfer or relevant transfer from a scheme to which paragraph (a) applied; or

(c) joins a scheme on the basis that it will provide the same benefits as those provided by the scheme to which paragraph 8 applied.

10. (1) A minimum age for any member of a scheme for payment of or entitlement to a particular age related benefit on the grounds of redundancy where it is enhanced in accordance with sub-paragraph (2) and paid either with or without consent (whether of an employer, the trustees or managers of the scheme or otherwise).

(2) The enhancement of any age related benefit payable to or in respect of a member on the grounds of redundancy where the enhancement is calculated in one or more of the following ways—

(a) by reference to the years of prospective pensionable service a member would have completed if that member had remained in pensionable service until normal pension age;

(b) by reference to a fixed number of years of prospective pensionable service;

(c) by making an actuarial reduction which is smaller than if early retirement had been on grounds to which paragraph 7 applies; or

(d) by not making any actuarial reduction for early retirement.

(3) Sub-paragraph (1) shall also apply to different minimum ages for different groups or categories of members.

11. An early retirement pivot age or a late retirement pivot age including—

(a) different such ages for different groups or categories of member, and

(b) any early retirement pivot age or late retirement pivot age for deferred members which is different than for active members.

12. (1) A minimum age for any member of a scheme for payment of or entitlement to a particular age related benefit on the grounds of ill health where the age related benefit is enhanced in accordance with sub-paragraph (2) and paid either with or without consent (whether of an employer, the trustees or managers of the scheme or otherwise).

(2) The enhancement of any age related benefit payable to or in respect of a member on the grounds of ill health where the enhancement is calculated in one or more of the following ways—

(a) by reference to some or all of the years of prospective pensionable service a member would have completed if he had remained in pensionable service until normal pension age;

(b) by reference to a fixed number of years of prospective pensionable service;

(c) by making an actuarial reduction which is smaller than if early retirement had been on the grounds to which paragraph 7 applies; or

(d) by not making any actuarial reduction for early retirement.

(3) Sub-paragraph (1) shall also apply to different minimum ages for different groups or categories of members.

13. (1) The calculation of any death benefit payable in respect of a member—

(a) by reference to some or all of the years of prospective pensionable service a member would have completed if that member had remained in service until normal pension age; or

(b) by reference to a fixed number of years of prospective pensionable service.

(2) Payment after a member's death of a death benefit calculated by reference to the period remaining in a pension guarantee period.

(3) For the purposes of sub-paragraph (2), a pension guarantee period means a fixed period specified in or permitted by the scheme rules beginning on—

(a) the date on which the payment of pension to or in respect of the member began, or

(b) if specified in the scheme rules, the date of the member's death on or after normal pension age where payment of pension to or in respect of that member had not begun.

(4) Any difference between the death benefits payable in respect of deferred members who die before normal pension age and the death benefits payable in respect of deferred members who die on or after normal pension age.

14. (1) Any rule, practice, action or decision where—

(a) the rate of pension to which a pensioner member is entitled is reduced at any time between age 60 and 65 ("the reduction date"), by either—

(i) an amount not exceeding the relevant state retirement pension rate at the reduction date, or

(ii) the rate of the pension in payment where on the reduction date the relevant state retirement pension rate is greater than the rate of that pension;

(b) from the date a member is entitled to present payment of a pension from a scheme that member is entitled to an additional amount of pension which does not exceed the amount of the basic state retirement pension plus the additional state retirement pension that would be payable at state pension age; or

(c) a member who reaches his state pension age is not entitled to, or no longer entitled to, an additional amount of pension which does not exceed the amount of the basic state retirement pension plus the additional state retirement pension that would be payable at state pension age.

(2) For the purposes of paragraph (1)—

"relevant state retirement pension rate" has the same meaning as in paragraph 2(5) of Schedule 28 to the Finance Act;

"state pension age" means the pensionable age specified in the rules in paragraph 1 of Schedule 4 to the Pensions Act 1995.

15. The actuarial reduction of any pension payable from a scheme in consequence of a member's death to any dependant of the member where that dependant is more than a specified number of years younger than the member.

16. In relation to pensioner members who have retired from a scheme on ill health grounds, discontinuation of any life assurance cover once any such members reach the normal retirement age which applied to them at the time they retired, or in relation to members to whom no such normal retirement age applied, once such members reach the age of 65.

Other rules, practices, actions and decisions relating to benefit

17. Any difference in the amount of any age related benefit or death benefit payable under a scheme to or in respect of members with different lengths of pensionable service to the extent that the difference in amount is attributable to their differing lengths of service, provided that, for each year of pensionable service, members in a comparable situation are entitled to accrue a right to benefit based upon the same fraction of pensionable pay.

18. (1) Any differences in—

(a) the fraction of pensionable pay at which any age related benefit accrues, or

(b) the amount of death benefit,

to or in respect of active or prospective members of a scheme where the differences are attributable to the aim specified in sub-paragraph (2).

(2) The aim referred to in sub-paragraph (1) is that members in a comparable situation will have the right to age related benefit or death benefit equal to the same fraction, proportion or multiple of pensionable pay—

(a) without regard to each member's length of pensionable service under the scheme, and

(b) provided that each member continues in pensionable service under the scheme until normal pension age.

(3) Any differences in age related benefits which accrue, or entitlement to any death benefits which arises, to or in respect of active or prospective members of a scheme who are in a comparable situation where—

(a) those differences are attributable to the aim specified in sub-paragraph (2), and

(b) the member's pensionable service under the arrangement ceases before normal pension age.

(4) Where sub-paragraph (1) applies, any limitation on the amount of any age related benefit or death benefit payable from a scheme where the limitation arises from imposing one or both of the following—

(a) a maximum amount on the age related benefit or death benefit which is equal to a fraction, proportion or multiple of the member's pensionable pay, or

(b) a minimum period of pensionable service.

19. Where paragraph 18 applies, different rates of member or employer contributions according to the age of the members by, or in respect of whom, contributions are made, where for each year of pensionable service members in comparable situations accrue different fractions of pensionable pay.

20. Any difference in the amount of any age related benefit or death benefit payable from a scheme to or in respect of different members to the extent that the difference in amount is attributable to differences over time in the pensionable pay of those members.

21. (1) Any limitation on the amount of any age related benefit or death benefit payable from a scheme where either or both sub-paragraphs (2) and (3) apply.

(2) The limitation results from imposing a maximum number of years of pensionable service by reference to which the age related benefit or death benefit may be calculated.

(3) The limitation arises from imposing a maximum amount on the age related benefit or death benefit which is equal to a fraction, proportion or multiple of a member's pensionable pay.

22. Any rule, practice, action or decision where any age related benefit or death benefit is only payable from a scheme where a member is entitled to short service benefit under section 71 of the Pension Schemes Act 1993 (basic principles as to short service benefit).

23. When determining a member's pensionable pay by reference to which any age related benefit or death benefit payable to or in respect of a member is calculated, to exclude from the member's remuneration an amount which—

(a) does not exceed one and a half times the lower earnings limit;

(b) does not exceed an amount calculated by reference to the lower earnings limit where the aim is more or less to reflect the amount of the basic state retirement pension; or

(c) does not exceed an amount calculated more or less to reflect the amount of the basic state retirement pension plus the additional state retirement pension.

24. Any difference in the amount of age related benefit or death benefit payable under a scheme to or in respect of members where the difference is attributable to accrual of age related benefit at a higher fraction of pensionable pay for pensionable pay over the upper earnings limit (and a lower fraction of pensionable pay for pensionable pay under the upper earnings limit) where the aim is to reflect the additional state retirement pension.

25. Any limitation on the amount of any age related benefit or death benefit payable from a scheme where the limitation—

(a) relates to—

(i) all members who joined or who became eligible to join the scheme on, after or before a particular date; or

(ii) any group or category of members who joined or who became eligible to join the scheme on, after or before a particular date; and

(b) results from imposing a maximum level of pensionable pay by reference to which the age related benefit or death benefit may be calculated.

Closure of schemes

26. The closure of a scheme, from a particular date, to workers who have not already joined it.

Closure of sections of schemes

27. (1) The closure of any section of a scheme, from a particular date, to workers who have not already joined it.

(2) For the purposes of paragraph (1)—

(a) a scheme may be divided into two or more sections, and

(b) a section of a scheme shall mean any of the groups in sub-paragraph (3).

(3) A section of a scheme shall mean any of the following—

(a) any group of members who became eligible to join, or who joined, the scheme on, after or before a particular date on the basis that particular benefits will be provided to or in respect of those members or that a particular level of contributions will be paid in respect of those members; or

(b) any group of members who became eligible to join, or who joined, the scheme as a result of a block transfer or relevant transfer.

Other rules, practices, actions and decisions

28. Increases of pensions in payment which are made to members over 55 but not to members below that age.

29. Any difference in the rate of increase of pensions in payment for members of different ages to the extent that the aim in setting the different rates is to maintain or more nearly maintain the relative value of members' pensions.

30. Any difference in the rate of increase of pensions in payment for members whose pensions have been in payment for different lengths of time to the extent that the aim in setting the different rates is to maintain or more nearly maintain the relative value of members' pensions.

31. The application of an age limit for transfer of the value of a member's accrued rights into or out of a scheme, provided that any such age limit is not more than one year before the member's normal pension age.

Registered pension schemes

32. Any rules, practices, actions or decisions relating to entitlement to or payment of benefits under a scheme which is a registered pension scheme insofar as compliance is necessary to secure any tax relief or exemption available under Part 4 of the Finance Act or to prevent any charge to tax arising under that Part of that Act, whoever is liable in relation to such charge.

33 . . .

NOTES

Commencement: 1 October 2010.

Para 33: revoked by the Equality Act (Age Exceptions for Pension Schemes) (Amendment) Order 2010, SI 2010/2285, art 2(1), (4), as from 1 October 2010.

SCHEDULE 2
CONTRIBUTIONS BY EMPLOYERS TO PERSONAL PENSION SCHEMES: EXCEPTED PRACTICES, ACTIONS OR DECISIONS

Article 4

Contributions by employers

[2.1533]

1. Different rates of contributions by an employer to a personal pension scheme according to the age of the workers in respect of whom the contributions are made where the aim in setting the different rates is—

(a) to equalise the amount of age related benefit, derived from contributions made each year by the employer, to which workers of different ages who are otherwise in a comparable situation will become entitled under their personal pension schemes, or

(b) to make more nearly equal the amount of the age related benefit, derived from contributions made each year by the employer, to which workers of different ages who are otherwise in a comparable situation will become entitled under their personal pension schemes.

2. Any difference in the rate of contributions by an employer to a personal pension scheme in respect of different workers to the extent that this is attributable to any differences in remuneration payable to those workers.

Part 2 Statutory Instruments

3. Any limitation on any contributions by an employer, to a personal pension scheme, by reference to a maximum level of remuneration.

4. A minimum age for commencement of payment of contributions by an employer to a personal pension scheme in respect of a worker.

5. Different minimum ages for commencement of payment of contributions by an employer to a personal pension scheme in respect of different groups or categories of workers.

6. Equal rates of contributions by an employer to a personal pension scheme irrespective of the age of the workers in respect of whom contributions are made.

NOTES

Commencement: 1 October 2010.

EQUALITY ACT 2010 (QUALIFYING COMPROMISE CONTRACT SPECIFIED PERSON) ORDER 2010

(SI 2010/2192)

NOTES

Made: 2 September 2010.
Authority: Equality Act 2010, ss 147(4)(d), 207(1).
Commencement: 1 October 2010.

[2.1534]

1 Citation and commencement

This Order may be cited as the Equality Act 2010 (Qualifying Compromise Contract Specified Person) Order 2010 and comes into force on 1st October 2010.

NOTES

Commencement: 1 October 2010.

[2.1535]

2 Person specified

For the purpose of section 147(4)(d) of the Equality Act 2010, a Fellow of the Institute of Legal Executives practising in a solicitor's practice (including a recognised body under section 9(1) of the Administration of Justice Act 1985) is specified.

NOTES

Commencement: 1 October 2010.

EQUALITY ACT 2010 (OBTAINING INFORMATION) ORDER 2010

(SI 2010/2194)

NOTES

Made: 2 September 2010.
Authority: Authority: Equality Act 2010, ss 138(2), (5)(d), (e), (7), 207(1), (4)(a).
Commencement: 1 October 2010.
See *Harvey* L(5)(c).

ARRANGEMENT OF ARTICLES

SCHEDULES

[2.1536]

1 Citation, commencement and interpretation

(1) This Order may be cited as the Equality Act 2010 (Obtaining Information) Order 2010 and comes into force on 1st October 2010.

(2) In the Order "the Act" means the Equality Act 2010.

NOTES

Commencement: 1 October 2010.

[2.1537]

2 Forms for obtaining information—prohibited conduct

In relation to a contravention of the Act other than a breach of an equality clause or rule—

(a) the form prescribed for the purposes of section 138(2)(a) of the Act is the form set out in Part 1 of Schedule 1 or a form to the like effect with such variations as the circumstances may require, and

(b) the form prescribed for the purposes of section 138(2)(b) of the Act is the form set out in Part 2 of Schedule 1 or a form to the like effect with such variations as the circumstances may require.

NOTES

Commencement: 1 October 2010.

[2.1538]

3 Forms for obtaining information—equality of terms

In relation to a breach of an equality clause or rule—

(a) the form prescribed for the purposes of section 138(2)(a) of the Act is the form set out in Part 1 of Schedule 2 or a form to the like effect with such variations as the circumstances may require, and

(b) the form prescribed for the purposes of section 138(2)(b) of the Act is the form set out in Part 2 of Schedule 2 or a form to the like effect with such variations as the circumstances may require.

NOTES

Commencement: 1 October 2010.

[2.1539]

4 Period for service of questions

In order to be admissible under section 138(3) of the Act a question must be served—

(a) before proceedings under the Act relating to the contravention are commenced, or

(b) where proceedings under the Act relating to the contravention have been commenced, before—

  (i) the end of the period of 28 days beginning on the day on which proceedings were commenced, or

  (ii) such later time as the court or tribunal specifies.

NOTES

Commencement: 1 October 2010.

[2.1540]

5 Manner of service for questions and answers

(1) P may serve a question on R—

(a) by delivering it to R or by sending it by post to R at R's usual or last-known residence or place of business, or

(b) if R has indicated in writing to P that R is willing to accept service of the question by electronic means, by sending it by electronic means to the number, address or other electronic identification given by R for the purpose.

(2) R may serve an answer on P—

(a) by delivering it to P or by sending it by post to P at the address stated on the document containing the question, or, if no address is stated, at P's usual or last-known residence or place of business, or

(b) if P has stated on the document containing the question or has otherwise indicated in writing to R that P is willing to accept service of the answer by electronic means, by sending it by electronic means to the number, address or other electronic identification given by P for the purpose.

(3) Where P or R is acting by a solicitor, a question or answer may be served—

(a) by delivering it at, or by sending it by post to, the solicitor's address for service, or

(b) if the solicitor has indicated in writing to P or R as the case may be that he or she is willing to accept service of the question or answer by electronic means, by sending it by electronic means to the number, address or other electronic identification given by the solicitor for the purpose.

(4) Where P or R is a body corporate, or is a trade union or employers' association within the meaning of the Trade Union and Labour Relations (Consolidation) Act 1992, a question or answer may be served—

(a) by delivering it to the secretary or clerk of the body, union or association at its registered or principal office, or by sending it by post to the secretary or clerk at that office, or

(b) if the secretary or clerk has indicated in writing to P or R as the case may be that he or she is willing to accept service of the question or answer by electronic means, by sending it by electronic means to the number, address or other electronic identification given by the secretary or clerk for the purpose.

(5) For the purposes of service by electronic means—

(a) the following are to be taken as sufficient written indications—

(i) a number, address or other electronic identification set out on the writing paper of the person to be served, or, in the case of P, on the document containing the question, or

(ii) where the person to be served is acting by a solicitor, a number, address or other electronic identification set out on the writing paper of the solicitor, but for service other than by fax, only where it is stated that the number, address or other electronic identification may be used for service.

(b) a question or answer is deemed to be served—

(i) if it is sent on a business day before 4:30pm, on that day, or

(ii) in any other case, on the next business day after the day on which it was sent.

(6) For the purpose of paragraph (5)(b)—

(a) "business day" means any day except Saturday, Sunday, a bank holiday, Good Friday or Christmas Day, and

(b) "bank holiday" means a bank holiday under the Banking and Financial Dealings Act 1971 in the part of the United Kingdom where service is to take place.

NOTES

Commencement: 1 October 2010.

[2.1541]

6 National security

For the purposes of section 138(5)(d) and (e) of the Act the circumstances specified are where R reasonably asserts that the reason for failing to answer or for giving an evasive or equivocal answer is the purpose of safeguarding national security.

NOTES

Commencement: 1 October 2010.

SCHEDULES

SCHEDULE 1

[2.1542]

Article 2

Obtaining information on prohibited conduct

PART 1

Questions Form

(For P)

1. To...*(name of the person to be questioned (R))*
of...*(address)*

2. I... *(name of the person asking questions (P))*
of...*(address)*

think that you may have treated me in a way which is unlawful under the Equality Act 2010.

3. I think that the treatment I received may have been unlawful under the Act because of:

Age ☐ Disability ☐ Gender Reassignment ☐
Marriage and Civil Partnership ☐ Pregnancy and Maternity ☐ Race ☐
Religion or Belief ☐ Sex ☐ Sexual Orientation ☐

4. I think that the treatment I received amounted to:

Direct Discrimination ☐ Indirect Discrimination ☐ Harassment ☐
Victimisation ☐ Failure to make Reasonable Adjustments for Disabled Persons ☐
Gender Reassignment Discrimination ☐ Discrimination arising from Disability ☐
Pregnancy and Maternity Discrimination ☐

5. *(If applicable)* I think that you instructed, caused or induced or that you aided another person to treat me in a way which is unlawful under the Act as set out in paragraphs 3 and 4 of this questions form. ☐

6. *(Give date, approximate time and factual description of the treatment received and of the circumstances leading up to the treatment)*

7. *(If possible, give the reason(s) why you think that the treatment you have received was unlawful under the Act)*

8. My questions to you are:

(1) Do you agree that the statement at paragraph 6 above is an accurate description of what happened?

(2) If not, in what respect do you disagree or what is your version of what happened?

(3) Do you agree that your treatment of me was unlawful under the Act as set out at paragraphs 3 to 5 above? If not:

(a) why not?

(b) what was the reason for your treatment of me?

(c) did considerations of the protected characteristic stated in paragraph 3 affect your treatment of me and if so, how?

(4) *(Any other relevant question(s) to R)*

9. Please send your answers to my home address above ☐

or

Please send your answers to the following address:

....*(address)*

....*(signature of P)*

....*(date)*

(If applicable)

Please send your answers to .... *(name of P's representative)*

of ....*(address)*

.... *(signature of P's representative)*

....*(date)*

By virtue of section 138(3) and (4) of the Act, these questions and any answers are admissible as evidence in proceedings under the Act. A court or tribunal may draw an inference from a failure by R to answer a question by P before the end of the period of 8 weeks beginning with the day on which the question was served or from an evasive or equivocal answer.

2

NOTES

Commencement: 1 October 2010.

[2.1543]

Article 2

Obtaining information on prohibited conduct

PART 2

Answers Form

(For R)

1. To...(*name of the person asking questions (P)*)
of...(*address of the person asking questions*)

2. I..(*name of the person answering questions(R)*)
of ....(*address*)
acknowledge receipt of the questions form signed by you and dated ....(*date*)
which was served on me on ....(*date*)

3. My answers to the questions at paragraphs 8(1) and (2) of the questions form are:

(1) I agree in full / in part* that the statement at paragraph 6 of the questions form is an accurate description of what happened ☐
(If applicable) I agree in full / in part* because ....
....

(2) I do not agree that the statement at paragraph 6 of the questions form is an accurate description of what happened ☐
(If applicable) I do not agree because..
....

4. My answers to the questions at paragraph 8(3) of the questions form are:

(1) I agree in full / in part* that my treatment of you was unlawful under the Act ☐
(If applicable) I agree in full / in part* because...
....

(2) I do not agree that my treatment of you was unlawful under the Act ☐
(If applicable) I do not agree because ....
....

(3) The reasons for your treatment by me and the answers to the other questions at paragraph 8(3) of the questions form are ....
....

5. *(If applicable)* My answer(s) to the question(s) at paragraph 8(4) of the questions form are: ....
....

6. I am unable / unwilling* to answer the question(s) numbered ....
of the questions form because...

*(*delete as appropriate)*

....(*signature of R*)
....(*date*)
(If applicable)
.... (*name of R's representative*)
of ....(*address*)
.... (*signature of R's representative*)
....(*date*)

NOTES
Commencement: 1 October 2010.

SCHEDULE 2

[2.1544]

Article 3

Obtaining information on equality of terms

PART 1

Questions Form

(For P)

1. To...*(name of the person to be questioned (R))*
of...*(address)*

2. I... *(name of the person asking questions (P))*
of...*(address)*
think that I may not have received equality of terms in accordance with the Equality Act 2010 for the following reasons:..
....
(Give a summary of the reasons why you think that you may not have received equality of terms)

3. I am claiming equality of terms with the following comparator(s):.................................
....
(Give the name(s) or, if not known, the job title(s) of the person(s) with whom you are claiming equality of terms)

4. My questions are:

(1) Do you agree that I have not received equality of terms in accordance with the Equality Act 2010?

(2) Do you agree that my work is equal to that of my comparator(s)?

(3) If you do not agree, please explain why you disagree.

(4) Do you agree that I have received less favourable pay or other contractual terms than my comparator(s)?

(5) If you agree that I have received less favourable pay or other contractual terms than my comparator(s), please explain the reason(s) for this difference.

(6) If you do not agree that I have received less favourable pay or other contractual terms than my comparator(s), please explain why you disagree.

5. *(Any other relevant question(s) to R)*

6. Please send your answers to my home address above ☐
or
Please send your answers to the following address:
....*(address)*
....*(signature of P)*
....*(date)*
(If applicable)
Please send your answers to .... *(name of P's representative)*

of ....*(address)*
.... *(signature of P's representative)*
....*(date)*

By virtue of section 138(3) and (4) of the Act, these questions and any answers are admissible as evidence in proceedings under the Act. A court or tribunal may draw an inference from a failure by R to answer a question by P before the end of the period of 8 weeks beginning with the day on which the question was served or from an evasive or equivocal answer.

2

NOTES

Commencement: 1 October 2010.

[2.1545]

Article 3

Obtaining information on equality of terms

PART 2

Answers Form

(For R)

1.To ……………………………………………………*(name of the person asking question(s) (P))*
of …………………………………………………………………………………………*(address)*

2. I…………………………………………………*(name of the person answering question(s) (R))*
of …………………………………………………………………………………………*(address)*

acknowledge receipt of the questions form signed by you and dated …………………………*(date)*
which was served on me on……………………………………………………………………*(date)*

3. My answers to your questions at paragraph 4 of the questions form are:

(1) I agree / do not agree* that you have not received equality of terms in accordance with the Equality Act 2010.

(2) I agree / do not agree* that you are doing equal work to that of your comparator(s).

(3) I do not agree that you are doing equal work to that of your comparator(s) because……..
……………………………………………………………………………………………………

(4) I agree / do not agree* that you have received less favourable pay or other contractual terms than your comparator(s).

(5) *(If applicable)* I agree that you have received less favourable pay or other contractual terms than your comparator(s) and the reason for this difference is……………………………
……………………………………………………………………………………………………

(6) *(If applicable)* I do not agree that you have received less favourable pay or other contractual terms than your comparator(s) because ………………………………………………
……………………………………………………………………………………………………

4. *(Answers to any questions at paragraph 5 of the questions form)*

5. *(If applicable)* I am unable / unwilling* to answer the question(s) numbered…………………
in the questions form because……………………………………………………………………

*(*delete as appropriate)*

……………………………………………………………………………………*(signature of R)*
…………………………………………………………………………………………*(date)*

(If applicable)
…………………………………………………………………… *(name of R's representative)*
of …………………………………………………………………………………………*(address)*

…………………………………………………………………… *(signature of R's representative)*
…………………………………………………………………………………………*(date)*

NOTES

Commencement: 1 October 2010.

EQUALITY ACT 2010 (GENERAL QUALIFICATIONS BODIES REGULATOR AND RELEVANT QUALIFICATIONS) (WALES) REGULATIONS 2010

(SI 2010/2217)

NOTES

Made: 6 September 2010.
Authority: Equality Act 2010, ss 96(10), 97(3).
Commencement: 1 October 2010.

[2.1546]

1 Title, commencement and application

(1) The title of these Regulations is the Equality Act 2010 (General Qualifications Bodies Regulator and Relevant Qualifications) (Wales) Regulations 2010.

(2) These Regulations come into force on 1 October 2010 and apply in relation to Wales.

NOTES

Commencement: 1 October 2010.

[2.1547]

2 The appropriate regulator

The Welsh Ministers are prescribed as the appropriate regulator in relation to a qualifications body that confers qualifications in Wales.

NOTES

Commencement: 1 October 2010.

[2.1548]

3 Relevant Qualifications

The qualifications listed in the Schedule are prescribed as relevant qualifications in relation to conferments of qualifications in Wales.

NOTES

Commencement: 1 October 2010.

SCHEDULE

regulation 3

[2.1549]

1. Advanced Extension Awards

2. Entry level certificate qualifications

3. Free Standing Maths Qualifications

4. Functional Skills

5. General Certificate of Education Advanced level (A and AS levels)

6. General Certificate of Secondary Education

7. The International Baccalaureate

8. Key Skills and Essential Skills Wales

9. Principal Learning and Project Qualifications

10. The Welsh Baccalaureate Qualification Core Certificate

NOTES

Commencement: 1 October 2010.

EQUALITY ACT 2010 (GENERAL QUALIFICATIONS BODIES) (APPROPRIATE REGULATOR AND RELEVANT QUALIFICATIONS) REGULATIONS 2010

(SI 2010/2245)

NOTES

Made: 9 September 2010.
Authority: Equality Act 2010, ss 96(10)(a), 97(3)(a).
Commencement: 1 October 2010.

[2.1550]

1 Citation, commencement and application

(1) These Regulations may be cited as the Equality Act 2010 (General Qualifications Bodies) (Appropriate Regulator and Relevant Qualifications) Regulations 2010 and come into force on 1st October 2010.

(2) Regulations 3 and 4 apply in relation to England only.

NOTES

Commencement: 1 October 2010.

[2.1551]

2 Manner of publishing matters specified under section 96(7) of the Equality Act 2010

An appropriate regulator must publish any matter specified under section 96(7) of the Equality Act 2010 on the regulator's website.

NOTES

Commencement: 1 October 2010.

[2.1552]

3 The appropriate regulator

The appropriate regulator in relation to a qualifications body that confers qualifications in England is the Office of Qualifications and Examinations Regulation.

NOTES

Commencement: 1 October 2010.

[2.1553]

4 Relevant qualifications

Relevant qualifications in relation to conferments in England are those qualifications listed in the Schedule.

NOTES

Commencement: 1 October 2010.

SCHEDULE 1

Regulation 4

[2.1554]

14–19 Diploma Principal Learning

Advanced Extension Awards

Cambridge International Certificate

Cambridge Pre-University qualification

Certificate in Adult Literacy

Certificate in Adult Numeracy

Entry level certificates in GCSE subjects

Extended projects

Foundation Projects

Free Standing Maths Qualifications

Functional Skills

General Certificate of Education Advanced level (Advanced and Advanced Subsidiary levels)

General Certificate of Secondary Education

General National Vocational Qualifications

Higher projects

International Baccalaureate Diploma

Key Skills

Welsh Baccalaureate Qualification Core Certificate

NOTES

Commencement: 1 October 2010.
Note: despite this Schedule being numbered as Schedule 1, these Regulations do not contain a Schedule 2.

EQUALITY ACT 2010 (QUALIFICATIONS BODY REGULATOR AND RELEVANT QUALIFICATIONS) (SCOTLAND) REGULATIONS 2010

(SSI 2010/315)

NOTES

Made: 6 September 2010.
Authority: Equality Act 2010, ss 96(10)(a), 97(3)(a).
Commencement: 1 October 2010.

[2.1555]

1 Citation and commencement

These Regulations may be cited as the Equality Act 2010 (Qualifications Body Regulator and Relevant Qualifications) (Scotland) Regulations 2010 and come into force on 1st October 2010.

NOTES

Commencement: 1 October 2010.

[2.1556]

2 Appropriate Regulator

The Scottish Qualifications Authority is prescribed for the purposes of section 96(10)(c) as appropriate regulator in relation to a qualifications body that confers qualifications in Scotland.

NOTES

Commencement: 1 October 2010.

[2.1557]

3 Relevant Qualification

Those qualifications known as "National Qualifications in Scotland" are prescribed for the purposes of section 97(3)(c) as relevant qualifications in relation to conferments in Scotland.

NOTES

Commencement: 1 October 2010.

EQUALITY ACT 2010 (COMMENCEMENT NO 4, SAVINGS, CONSEQUENTIAL, TRANSITIONAL, TRANSITORY AND INCIDENTAL PROVISIONS AND REVOCATION) ORDER 2010

(SI 2010/2317)

NOTES

Made: 20 September 2010.
Authority: Equality Act 2010, ss 207(4), (6), 216(3).
Commencement: 1 October 2010.
See *Harvey* L(1)(A)(7).

ARRANGEMENT OF ARTICLES

SCHEDULES

[2.1558]

1 Citation, commencement and interpretation

(1) This Order may be cited as the Equality Act 2010 (Commencement No 4, Savings, Consequential, Transitional, Transitory and Incidental Provisions and Revocation) Order 2010.

(2) This Order comes into force on 1st October 2010 immediately after the commencement of the 2010 Order.

(3) In this Order—

"the 1970 Act" means the Equal Pay Act 1970;
"the 1975 Act" means the Sex Discrimination Act 1975;
"the 1976 Act" means the Race Relations Act 1976;
"the 1986 Act" means the Sex Discrimination Act 1986;
"the 1989 Act" means the Employment Act 1989;
"the 1995 Act" means the Disability Discrimination Act 1995;
"the Religion or Belief Regulations" means the Employment Equality (Religion or Belief) Regulations 2003;
"the 2003 Sexual Orientation Regulations" means the Employment Equality (Sexual Orientation) Regulations 2003;
"the 2006 Act" means the Equality Act 2006;
"the Age Regulations" means the Employment Equality (Age) Regulations 2006;
"the 2007 Sexual Orientation Regulations" means the Equality Act (Sexual Orientation) Regulations 2007;
"the 2010 Act" means the Equality Act 2010;
"the 2010 Order" means the Equality Act 2010 (Consequential Amendments, Saving and Supplementary Provisions) Order 2010;
"previous enactment" means—

(a) the 1970 Act;
(b) the 1975 Act;
(c) the 1976 Act;
(d) the 1986 Act;
(e) the 1995 Act;
(f) the 2006 Act;

(g) the Religion or Belief Regulations;
(h) the 2003 Sexual Orientation Regulations;
(i) the Age Regulations;
(j) the 2007 Sexual Orientation Regulations.

NOTES

Commencement: 1 October 2010.

[2.1559]

2 Provisions coming into force on 1st October 2010

(1) Subject to articles 3 to 25, the relevant provisions of the 2010 Act, as set out in the following paragraphs, come into force on 1st October 2010.

(2) In Part 2 (equality: key concepts), the relevant provisions are—
- (a) sections 4 and 5;
- (b) section 6 in so far as it is not already in force;
- (c) sections 7 to 13;
- (d) sections 15 to 21;
- (e) section 22 in so far as it is not already in force;
- (f) sections 23 to 27;
- (g) Schedule 1 in so far as it is not already in force.

(3) In Part 3 (services and public functions), all the provisions are relevant provisions except—
- (a) so far as they apply to the protected characteristic of age;
- (b) paragraph 2 of Schedule 2 so far as it relates to the third requirement in a case where A is—
  - (i) a local authority in England or Wales exercising functions under the Education Acts, or
  - (ii) an education authority exercising functions under an enactment specified in paragraph 10(2) of Schedule 3 to the 2010 Act.

(4) In Part 4 (premises), the relevant provisions are—
- (a) sections 32 to 35;
- (b) section 36(1)(a) to (c), (2) to (4), (7) and (8);
- (c) section 38(1) to (7) and (9);
- (d) section 38(8) in so far as it relates to the provisions set out in paragraph (e);
- (e) in Schedule 4—
  - (i) paragraphs 1 to 4;
  - (ii) paragraph 8 except so far as it relates to paragraph 5(4)(c);
  - (iii) paragraph 9 in so far as it is not already in force;
- (f) Schedule 5.

(5) In Part 5 (work), the relevant provisions are—
- (a) sections 39 to 60;
- (b) section 61 in so far as it is not already in force;
- (c) sections 62 to 77;
- (d) section 79;
- (e) sections 80 to 83 in so far as they are not already in force;
- (f) Schedule 6;
- (g) Schedule 7 in so far as it is not already in force;
- (h) Schedule 8;
- (i) Schedule 9 in so far as it is not already in force.

(6) In Part 6 (education), the relevant provisions are—
- (a) sections 84 to 93;
- (b) section 94 in so far as it is not already in force;
- (c) section 95;
- (d) sections 96 and 97 in so far as they are not already in force;
- (e) section 98 (except as provided in paragraph (i));
- (f) section 99;
- (g) Schedules 10 and 11;
- (h) Schedule 12 in so far as it is not already in force;
- (i) Schedule 13 except—
  - (i) paragraph 2 so far as it relates to the third requirement;
  - (ii) paragraph 5 so far as it relates to the third requirement in a case where A is the governing body of a maintained school (within the meaning of section 92 of the 2010 Act);
- (j) Schedule 14.

(7) In Part 7 (associations), the relevant provisions are—
- (a) sections 100 to 105 except so far as they apply to the protected characteristic of age;
- (b) section 107 except so far as it applies to the protected characteristic of age;
- (c) Schedule 15;

(d) Schedule 16 except so far as it applies to the protected characteristic of age.

(8) In Part 8 (prohibited conduct: ancillary), all the provisions are relevant provisions.

(9) In Part 9 (enforcement), the relevant provisions are—

(a) sections 113 to 115;
(b) section 116(1)(a) and (b) and (2);
(c) section 116(1)(c) so far as it relates to, and for the purpose of, making rules under Part 3 of Schedule 17 to the 2010 Act;
(d) section 116(3) in so far as it relates to the provisions set out in paragraph (k));
(e) section 117 in so far as it is not already in force;
(f) sections 118 to 135;
(g) section 136(1) to (6)(a) to (e);
(h) section 137;
(i) section 138 in so far as it is not already in force;
(j) sections 139 to 141;
(k) in Schedule 17—
 (i) Parts 1 and 2 in so far as they are not already in force;
 (ii) Part 3 so far as it confers or relates to the power to make rules under paragraph 10 of that Schedule;
 (iii) Part 4.

(10) In Part 10 (contracts, etc), the relevant provisions are—

(a) sections 142 to 146;
(b) section 147 in so far as it is not already in force;
(c) section 148.

(11) In Part 11 (advancement of equality), the relevant provisions are—

(a) section 158;
(b) section 159(3) for the purposes of section 158(4)(a) only.

(12) In Part 12 (disabled persons: transport), the relevant provisions are—

(a) section 161 so far as it confers the power to make regulations;
(b) section 165 so far as it relates to, and for the purpose of, the issue of exemption certificates under section 166;
(c) section 166;
(d) section 167(1) to (5), and (7), so far as it relates to, and for the purpose of, the issue of exemption certificates under section 166;
(e) section 167(6);
(f) sections 168 to 185;
(g) sections 187 and 188.

(13) In Part 13 (disability: miscellaneous), the relevant provisions are—

(a) section 189 in so far as it is not already in force;
(b) section 190;
(c) Schedule 21 in so far as it is not already in force.

(14) In Part 14 (general exceptions), the relevant provisions are—

(a) section 191 (except as provided in paragraph (d));
(b) sections 192 to 195;
(c) section 196 (except as provided in paragraph (e));
(d) Schedule 22 except so far as it applies to the protected characteristic of age in Parts 3 and 7 of the 2010 Act;
(e) Schedule 23 except so far as it applies to the protected characteristic of age in Parts 3 and 7 of the 2010 Act.

(15) In Part 16 (general and miscellaneous), the relevant provisions are—

(a) section 206;
(b) section 211(1) in so far as it relates to the provisions set out in paragraph (e));
(c) section 211(2) (except as provided in paragraph (f));
(d) Schedule 25;
(e) in Schedule 26—
 (i) paragraphs 1 to 8;
 (ii) paragraphs 13 to 60;
 (iii) paragraph 61 in so far as it is not already in force;
 (iv) paragraphs 62 to 64;
 (v) paragraph 65(4);
 (vi) paragraphs 66 to 72;
 (vii) paragraph 75;
 (viii) paragraph 76 except so far as it relates to section 34(2)(a) and (b) of the 2006 Act, as substituted by sub-paragraph (3)(b) of that paragraph;
 (ix) paragraphs 77 to 81;
 (x) paragraph 82 except so far as it relates to sections 84 and 85 of the 2006 Act;

(xi) paragraphs 83 to 107;

(f) Schedule 27 except so far as it repeals—

(i) sections 76A to 76C of the 1975 Act (and section 81 of that Act so far as relating to those sections);

(ii) sections 71 to 71B of, and Schedule 1A to, the 1976 Act;

(iii) sections 17(8), 18 and 19(10) of the Local Government Act 1988;

(iv) sections 49A to 49D of the 1995 Act;

(v) section 404 of the Greater London Authority Act 1999;

(vi) sections 84 and 85 of the 2006 Act;

(vii) sections 55 and 56 of the Local Transport Act 2008.

NOTES

Commencement: 1 October 2010.

3–6 *(Arts 3, 4 (Commencement and savings relating to the Additional Support Needs Tribunal for Scotland) and arts 5, 6 (Savings and consequential amendments relating to Wales) are outside the scope of this work.)*

[2.1560]

7 Transitional provisions

Part 9 of the 2010 Act (enforcement) applies where—

(a) an act carried out before 1st October 2010 is unlawful under a previous enactment, and

(b) that act continues on or after 1st October 2010 and is unlawful under the 2010 Act.

NOTES

Commencement: 1 October 2010.

[2.1561]

8

(1) Paragraph (2) applies to the following acts—

(a) bringing proceedings under a previous enactment;

(b) giving evidence or information in connection with proceedings under a previous enactment;

(c) doing any other thing for the purposes of or in connection with a previous enactment;

(d) making an allegation (whether or not express) that another person has contravened a previous enactment.

(2) Section 27 of the 2010 Act (victimisation) applies in relation to an act to which this paragraph applies, and for that purpose the references in that section to "this Act" are to be read as references to the relevant previous enactment.

NOTES

Commencement: 1 October 2010.

[2.1562]

9 Transitory provision relating to the public sector equality duty

Pending the commencement of paragraph 76 of Schedule 26 to the 2010 Act so far as it relates to section 34(2)(b) of the 2006 Act, as substituted by sub-paragraph (3) of that paragraph, section 34 of the 2006 Act, and section 33(1) of that Act so far as it applies to that section, apply in relation to duties under or by virtue of—

(a) sections 76A to 76C of the 1975 Act;

(b) section 71 of the 1976 Act; and

(c) sections 49A to 49D of the 1995 Act.

NOTES

Commencement: 1 October 2010.

[2.1563]

10 Transitory provisions relating to ships and hovercraft

(1) In this article, "shipping matter" means—

(a) transporting people by ship or hovercraft,

(b) a service provided on a ship or hovercraft, or

(c) the exercise of a public function in relation to a ship or hovercraft that is not the provision of a service to the public or a section of the public.

(2) Despite their repeal or revocation by Schedule 27 to the 2010 Act, the provisions set out in Schedule 1 continue to have effect so far as they relate to a shipping matter within paragraph 1(a) or (b) until regulations under section 30(1) of the 2010 Act come into force.

(3) Despite their repeal by Schedule 27 to the 2010 Act, the provisions of the 1995 Act set out in Schedule 1, so far as they relate to discrimination within the meaning of section 21D of that Act, continue to have effect so far as they relate to a shipping matter within paragraph 1(c) until regulations under section 30(2) of the 2010 Act come into force.

(4) The following provisions of Schedule 26 to the 2010 Act do not come into force in relation to a shipping matter within paragraph 1(a) or (b) until regulations under section 30(1) of the 2010 Act come into force—

(a) paragraph 67 (amendment of section 21(2)(b) of the 2006 Act) and paragraph 61 so far as relating to that paragraph; and

(b) paragraphs 69 and 70 (repeal of sections 25 and 26 of the 2006 Act) and paragraph 61 so far as relating to those paragraphs.

(5) Paragraphs 67, 69 and 70 of Schedule 26 to the 2010 Act, and paragraph 61 of that Schedule so far as relating to those paragraphs, so far as they relate to disability discrimination, do not come into force in relation to a shipping matter within paragraph 1(c) until regulations under section 30(2) of the 2010 Act come into force.

(6) Despite its lapse by virtue of Schedule 27 to the 2010 Act, subordinate legislation specified in Schedule 2 continues to have effect so far as it relates to a shipping matter within paragraph 1(a) or (b) until regulations under section 30(1) of the 2010 Act come into force.

(7) Despite its lapse by virtue of Schedule 27 to the 2010 Act, subordinate legislation made under the 1995 Act that is specified in Schedule 2, so far as it relates to discrimination within the meaning of section 21D of that Act, continues to have effect so far as it relates to a shipping matter within paragraph (1)(c) until regulations under section 30(2) of the 2010 Act come into force.

(8) Despite their amendment by the 2010 Order, the following provisions continue to apply in the form immediately before their amendment by that Order, so far as they relate to a shipping matter within paragraph 1(a) or (b), until regulations under section 30(1) of the 2010 Act come into force—

(a) sections 76A to 76C of the 1975 Act;

(b) sections 71 to 71B of, and Schedule 1A to, the 1976 Act;

(c) sections 49A to 49D of the 1995 Act.

(9) Despite their amendment by the 2010 Order, sections 49A to 49D of the 1995 Act, so far as they relate to discrimination within the meaning of section 21D of that Act, continue to apply in the form immediately before their amendment by that Order, so far as they relate to a shipping matter within paragraph (1)(c), until regulations under section 30(2) of the 2010 Act come into force.

NOTES

Commencement: 1 October 2010.

[2.1564]
11

(1) Despite their repeal or revocation by Schedule 27 to the 2010 Act, the provisions set out in Schedule 3 continue to have effect so far as they relate to work on ships, work on hovercraft and seafarers until regulations under section 81 of the 2010 Act come into force.

(2) The following provisions of Schedule 26 to the 2010 Act do not come into force in relation to work on ships, work on hovercraft and seafarers until regulations under section 81 of the 2010 Act come into force—

(a) paragraph 15 (amendment of section 12 of the 1989 Act) and paragraph 13 so far as relating to that paragraph;

(b) paragraph 67 (amendment of section 21(2)(b) of the 2006 Act) and paragraph 61 so far as relating to that paragraph;

(c) paragraphs 69 and 70 (repeal of sections 25 and 26 of the 2006 Act) and paragraph 61 so far as relating to those paragraphs.

(3) Despite its lapse by virtue of Schedule 27 to the 2010 Act, subordinate legislation specified in Schedule 4 continues to have effect, so far as it relates to work on ships, work on hovercraft and seafarers, until regulations under section 81 of the 2010 Act come into force.

(4) Despite their amendment by the 2010 Order, the following provisions continue to apply in the form immediately before their amendment by that Order, so far as they relate to work on ships, work on hovercraft and seafarers, until regulations under section 81 of the 2010 Act come into force—

(a) sections 76A to 76C of the 1975 Act;

(b) sections 71 to 71B of, and Schedule 1A to, the 1976 Act;

(c) sections 49A to 49D of the 1995 Act.

[(5) Despite their amendment by article 24 and Schedule 8, the Employment Tribunals (Constitution and Rules of Procedure) Regulations 2004 continue to apply in the form immediately before their amendment by those provisions, so far as they relate to work on ships, work on hovercraft and seafarers, until regulations under section 81 of the 2010 Act come into force.]

NOTES

Commencement: 1 October 2010.

Para (5): added by the Equality Act 2010 (Commencement No 4, Savings, Consequential, Transitional, Transitory and Incidental Provisions and Revocation) Order 2010 (Amendment) Order 2010, SI 2010/2337, art 2, as from 1 October 2010.

[2.1565]
12 Transitory provision relating to taxis and private hire vehicles

Despite their repeal by Schedule 27 to the 2010 Act, sections 36 and 36A of the 1995 Act, and section 38 of the 1995 Act in so far as it relates to appeals against decisions of licensing authorities under section 36 or 36A of that Act, continue to have effect until section 165 of the 2010 Act comes fully into force.

NOTES

Commencement: 1 October 2010.

[2.1566]
13 Transitory provisions relating to guidance

(1) Until guidance under section 6(5) of the 2010 Act (disability) comes into force, the guidance referred to in paragraph (2) has effect for the purposes of that section.

(2) The guidance is "Guidance on matters to be taken into account in determining questions relating to the definition of disability".

(3) Despite its repeal by Schedule 27 to the 2010 Act, section 3 of the 1995 Act continues to have effect, so far as it confers power to issue that guidance.

NOTES

Commencement: 1 October 2010.

[2.1567]
14

(1) Until guidance issued under paragraph 22(3)(b) of Schedule 3 to the 2010 Act (insurance: sex, gender reassignment, pregnancy and maternity) comes into force, the guidance referred to in paragraph (2) has effect for the purposes of paragraph 22(3)(b).

(2) The guidance is "Guidance on the publication of data associated with the use of gender in the assessment of insurance risks"; and for that purpose—

- (a) a reference to section 29 or 29(1) of the 1975 Act should be read as a reference to section 29 of the 2010 Act,
- (b) a reference to section 45(3) or 45(3)(a) of the 1975 Act should be read as a reference to paragraph 22(3) of Schedule 3 to the 2010 Act,
- (c) paragraph 4.1 should be read as beginning with the words "The Equality Act 2010 and",
- (d) the heading after paragraph 4.4, paragraphs 4.5 to 4.8 and paragraph 4.10 should be ignored,
- (e) in paragraph 4.9, "But" should be ignored,
- (f) in paragraph 4.12, the words "corresponding amendments are made to the relevant provisions of" should be read as "corresponding provisions can be found in",
- (g) in paragraph 4.15, the words "The Regulations amending the Sex Discrimination Act 1975" should be read as "The Equality Act 2010", and
- (h) in paragraph 4.22, the words "the Regulations" should be read as "the applicable legislation and guidance".

(3) Despite its repeal by Schedule 27 to the 2010 Act, section 45(3)(a) of the 1975 Act continues to have effect, so far as it confers power to issue that guidance.

NOTES

Commencement: 1 October 2010.

[2.1568]
15 Savings

The 2010 Act does not apply where the act complained of occurs wholly before 1st October 2010 so that—

- (a) nothing in the 2010 Act affects—
  - (i) the operation of a previous enactment or anything duly done or suffered under a previous enactment;
  - (ii) any right, obligation or liability acquired or incurred under a previous enactment;
  - (iii) any penalty incurred in relation to any unlawful act under a previous enactment;
  - (iv) any investigation, legal proceeding or remedy in respect of any such right, obligation, liability or penalty; and

(b) any such investigation, legal proceeding or remedy may be instituted, continued or enforced, and any such penalty may be imposed, as if the 2010 Act had not been commenced.

NOTES

Commencement: 1 October 2010.

[2.1569]
16

(1) The repeals and revocations made by Schedule 27 to the 2010 Act do not affect the operation of a transitional provision or saving relating to the commencement of a provision for which there is corresponding provision in the 2010 Act, in so far as the transitional provision or saving is not expressly restated in the 2010 Act but remains capable of having effect.

(2) The repeal or revocation by Schedule 27 to the 2010 Act of a provision previously repealed or revoked subject to a saving does not affect the continued operation of that saving.

(3) The repeal or revocation by Schedule 27 to the 2010 Act of a saving on the previous repeal or revocation of a provision does not affect the saving in so far as it is not expressly restated in the 2010 Act but remains capable of having effect.

NOTES

Commencement: 1 October 2010.

[2.1570]
17

Despite the repeal of section 1 of the 1989 Act (overriding of pre-1975 statutory requirements which conflict with the 1975 Act) by Schedule 27 to the 2010 Act, any provision which, immediately before that repeal, is of no effect as a result of that section continues to be of no effect.

NOTES

Commencement: 1 October 2010.

18 *(Applies to insurance policies and is outside the scope of this work.)*

[2.1571]
19

Despite their repeal by Schedule 27 to the 2010 Act, the following provisions of the 1995 Act continue to have effect—

(a) section 30(5) (amendment of section 62 of the Further and Higher Education Act 1992) and section 30(1) so far as relating to it;
(b) section 39 (amendments of section 20 of the Civic Government (Scotland) Act 1982);
(c) section 61 (amendment of section 15 of the Disabled Persons (Employment) Act 1944);
(d) in Schedule 1, paragraph 7(1) to (4), and (7) (persons on register of disabled persons on 12th January 1995 and on date of commencement of paragraph 7 deemed to have disability etc); and
(e) in Schedule 6, paragraph 1(a) (amendment of section 12(1) of the Employment and Training Act 1973) and paragraph 6 (amendment of section 16 of the Enterprise and New Towns (Scotland) Act 1990).

NOTES

Commencement: 1 October 2010.

[2.1572]
20

Despite their revocation by Schedule 27 to the 2010 Act, regulations 2(2) and 44 to 46 of the Age Regulations continue to have effect so far as they relate to Schedule 6 to those Regulations.

NOTES

Commencement: 1 October 2010.

21–23 *(Outside the scope of this work.)*

[2.1573]
24 Revocation and consequential provisions

The amendments in Schedule 8 have effect.

NOTES

Commencement: 1 October 2010.

[2.1574]
25

A reference in any other subordinate legislation to a previous enactment is, so far as the context allows, to be read as a reference to the 2010 Act so far as corresponding to the previous enactment (and the context of the reference is to be read as being subject to such consequential alterations as are required).

NOTES

Commencement: 1 October 2010.

SCHEDULES

SCHEDULE 1
SAVINGS OF PREVIOUS ENACTMENTS IN RELATION TO A SHIPPING MATTER

Article 10(2) and (3)

[2.1575]

Provision of the 1975 Act	*Provision of the 1976 Act*	*Provision of the 1986 Act*
Sections 1 to 3	Part I	Section 6
Sections 3B to 5	Section 20	Section 10
Section 29	Sections 22 and 23	
Sections 34 to 35ZA	Section 27	
Sections 35C to 36	Part IV	
Part IV	Section 34	
Sections 43 and 44	Sections 40 to 42	
Sections 46 to 52	Section 53	
Section 62	Sections 57 and 57ZA	
Sections 66 to 66B	Section 65	
Section 74	Sections 67 to 69	
Section 76	Sections 72 and 72A	
Section 77	Sections 73 to 75	
Sections 80 to 82	Section 78	
Section 85	Section 80	
Section 87		

Provision of the 1995 Act	*Provision of the 2006 Act*	*Provision of the 2007 Sexual Orientation Regulations*
Part I	Sections 44 to 46	Regulations 1 to 4
Sections 19 to 21ZA	Sections 53 to 57	Regulation 6
Sections 21B to 21E	Section 58	Regulation 8
Sections 25 and 26	Section 60	Regulations 9 to 12
Part VII	Sections 63 to 66	Regulation 14
Section 64	Sections 68 to 74	Regulations 18 to 20
Section 67	Sections 76 to 81	Regulations 22 to 26
Section 68		Regulations 29 and 30
Section 70		Regulations 33 and 34
Schedules 1 and 2		Schedule 2
Part II of Schedule 3		
Schedule 3A		
Part II of Schedule 4		

NOTES

Commencement: 1 October 2010.

SCHEDULE 2
SAVINGS OF SUBORDINATE LEGISLATION IN RELATION TO A SHIPPING MATTER

Article 10(6) and (7)

[2.1576]

The 1975 Act	*The 1976 Act*	*The 1995 Act*	*The 2006 Act*
Sex Discrimination (Questions and Replies) Order 1975	Race Relations (Questions and Replies) Order 1977	Disability Discrimination (Providers of Services) (Adjustments of Premises) Regulations 2001	Religion or Belief (Questions and Replies) Order 2007
Compromise Agreements (Description of Person) Order 2004	Civil Courts Order 1983	Disability Discrimination (Questions and Replies) Order 2004	
Compromise Agreements (Description of Person) Order 2004 (Amendment) Order 2004	Civil Courts (Amendment) Order 1988	Disability Discrimination (Questions and Replies) Order 2005	
	Civil Courts (Amendment No 2) Order 1989	Disability Discrimination (Service Providers and Public Authorities Carrying out Public Functions) Regulations 2005	
	Civil Courts (Amendment) Order 1998	Disability Discrimination (Guidance on the Definition of Disability) Appointed Day Order 2006	
	Compromise Agreements (Description of Person) Order 2004	Disability Discrimination (Guidance on the Definition of Disability) Revocation Order 2006	
	Compromise Agreements (Description of Person) Order 2004 (Amendment) Order 2004		
	Civil Courts (Amendment) Order 2006		

NOTES

Commencement: 1 October 2010.

SCHEDULE 3
SAVINGS OF PREVIOUS ENACTMENTS IN RELATION TO WORK ON SHIPS, WORK ON HOVERCRAFT AND SEAFARERS

Article 11(1)

[2.1577]

Provision of the 1970 Act	*Provision of the 1975 Act*	*Provision of the 1976 Act*	*Provision of the 1986 Act*
The whole Act	Sections 1 to 3A	Part I	Section 6
	Sections 4 to 9	Sections 4 to 7	Section 10
	Section 10(1) to (4), and (8)	Section 8(1) to (4)	
	Sections 10A to 16	Section 9(1) to (2), and (4) to (5)	
	Sections 19 to 20A	Sections 10 to 15	
	Part IV	Parts IV to VI	
	Sections 43 and 44	Sections 53 to 54A	
	Sections 46 to 52A	Section 56	
	Sections 62 to 63A	Section 65	
	Section 65	Sections 67 to 69	
	Section 74	Sections 72 and 72A	
	Section 76	Sections 73 to 75	
	Section 77	Sections 76 and 76ZA	
	Sections 80 to 82	Section 78	
	Section 85	Section 80	
	Section 87		

Provision of the 1995 Act	*Provision of the Religion or Belief Regulations*	*Provision of the 2003 Sexual Orientation Regulations*	*Provision of the Age Regulations*
Part I	Parts I to IV	Parts I to IV	Parts 1 to 4
Sections 3A to 4K	Regulations 27 to 30	Regulations 27 to 30	Regulations 35 to 38
Sections 6A to 6C	Regulations 33 to 36	Regulations 33 to 36	Regulations 41 to 44
Sections 7A to 7D	Schedule 1A	Schedules 1A to 4	Schedules 2 to 5
Sections 13 to 14D	Schedules 2 to 4		
Sections 15A to 15C			
Sections 16A to 16C			
Section 17A			
Section 17C			
Sections 18B to 18D			
Part VII			
Section 64			
Section 67			
Section 68			
Section 70			
Schedules 1 and 2			
Part I of Schedule 3			
Schedule 3A			

NOTES

Commencement: 1 October 2010.

SCHEDULE 4
SAVINGS OF SUBORDINATE LEGISLATION IN RELATION TO WORK ON SHIPS, WORK ON HOVERCRAFT AND SEAFARERS

Article 11(3)

[2.1578]

The 1970 Act	*The 1975 Act*	*The 1976 Act*	*The 1995 Act*
Equal Pay (Complaints to Industrial Tribunals) (Armed Forces) Regulations 1977	Sex Discrimination (Questions and Replies) Order 1975	Race Relations (Questions and Replies) Order 1977	Disability Discrimination (Questions and Replies) Order 2004
Equal Pay (Questions and Replies) Order 2003	Sex Discrimination (Complaints to Industrial Tribunals) (Armed Forces) Regulations 1997	Civil Courts Order 1983	Disability Discrimination (Questions and Replies) Order 2005
	Compromise Agreements (Description of Person) Order 2004	Civil Courts (Amendment) Order 1988	Disability Discrimination (Guidance on the Definition of Disability) Appointed Day Order 2006
	Compromise Agreements (Description of Person) Order 2004 (Amendment) Order 2004	Civil Courts (Amendment No 2) Order 1989	Disability Discrimination (Guidance on the Definition of Disability) Revocation Order 2006
		Employment Tribunals (Interest on Awards in Discrimination Cases) Regulations 1996	
		Race Relations (Complaints to Industrial Tribunals (Armed Forces) Regulations 1997	
		Civil Courts (Amendment) Order 1998	
		Compromise Agreements (Description of Person) Order 2004	
		Compromise Agreements (Description of Person) Order 2004 (Amendment) Order 2004	
		Civil Courts (Amendment) Order 2006	

NOTES

Commencement: 1 October 2010.

SCHEDULES 5–8

(Schs 5, 6 (Savings of Previous Enactments and subordinate legislation in relation to existing insurance policies) is outside the scope of this work; Sch 7 (Saving of subordinate legislation) is outside the scope of this work (note, however, that Sch 7 does provide that despite the repeal of the Race Relations Act 1976 and the Disability Discrimination Act 1995, the Employment Tribunals (Interest on Awards in Discrimination Cases) Regulations 1996, SI 1996/2803 shall continue in force and have effect as if made under s 139 of the Equality Act 2010); Sch 8 (Consequential etc Provisions) contains various amendments which, in so far as relevant to this work, have been incorporated at the appropriate place.)

EQUALITY ACT 2010 (STATUTORY DUTIES) (WALES) REGULATIONS 2011

(SI 2011/1064)

NOTES

Made: 3 April 2011.
Authority: Equality Act 2006, ss 153(2), 207(4).
Commencement: 6 April 2011.

ARRANGEMENT OF REGULATIONS

[2.1579]

1 Title, commencement and application

(1) The title of these Regulations is the Equality Act 2010 (Statutory Duties) (Wales) Regulations 2011.

(2) These Regulations come into force on 6 April 2011.

NOTES

Commencement: 6 April 2011.

[2.1580]

2 Interpretation

In these Regulations—

"authority" ("*awdurdod*") means an authority specified in Part 2 of Schedule 19 to the Equality Act 2010 and "authorities" ("*awdurdodau*") is to be construed accordingly;

"employment" ("*cyflogaeth*"), "employees" ("*cyflogeion*") and "persons employed" ("*personau a gyflogir*") are to be construed in accordance with section 83 of the Equality Act 2010;

"gender pay difference" ("*gwahaniaeth cyflog rhwng y rhywiau*") means any difference between the pay of—

(a) a woman and a man; or
(b) women and men,

who are employed by an authority and where either the first or second condition is met.

The first condition is that the difference is for a reason that is related to the protected characteristic of sex.

The second condition is that it appears to the authority to be reasonably likely that the difference is for a reason that is related to the protected characteristic of sex;

"the general duty" ("*y ddyletswydd gyffredinol*") means the duty in section 149(1) of the Equality Act 2010;

"gender pay equality objective" ("*amcan cyflog cyfartal rhwng y rhywiau*") means an equality objective—

(i) that relates to the need to address the causes of any gender pay difference; and
(ii) which the authority has published;

"relevant date" ("*dyddiad perthnasol*") means 31 March;

"relevant information" ("*gwybodaeth berthnasol*") means information that relates to compliance (or otherwise) by the authority with the general duty; and

"reporting period" ("*cyfnod adrodd*") means the period 1 April to 31 March except in relation to the reporting period ending 31 March 2012 in which case "reporting period" means the period 6 April 2011 to 31 March 2012.

NOTES

Commencement: 6 April 2011.

[2.1581]

3 Equality objectives

(1) An authority must publish objectives that are designed to enable it to better perform the general duty.

(2) The authority must also—

(a) publish a statement setting out—

(i) the steps that it has taken or intends to take in order to fulfil each objective; and

(ii) how long the authority expects it will take in order to fulfil each objective;

(b) make such arrangements as it considers appropriate for monitoring the progress that it makes and the effectiveness of the steps that it takes in order to fulfil its equality objectives.

In these Regulations such objectives are referred to as "equality objectives".

(3) If an authority does not publish an equality objective in respect of one or more of the protected characteristics it must publish reasons for its decision not to do so.

(4) Paragraph (3) applies even if an authority publishes an equality objective for the purpose referred to in regulation 11(1) (and for that reason such an objective is to be ignored for the purpose of paragraph (3)).

NOTES

Commencement: 6 April 2011.

[2.1582]

4 Preparation and review etc of equality objectives

(1) When considering what its equality objectives should be and when designing any equality objective (or any revision to such an objective) the authority must—

(a) comply with the engagement provisions (*see* regulation 5); and

(b) have due regard to relevant information that it holds.

(2) An authority must comply with regulation 3(1) by publishing equality objectives—

(a) not later than 2 April 2012; and

(b) subsequently as it considers appropriate.

(3) An authority must review each of its equality objectives—

(a) not later than the end of the period of four years beginning with the date that the objective was first published; and

(b) subsequently at intervals not later than the end of the period of four years beginning with the date of the last review of the objective.

(4) An authority may carry out a review of any of its equality objectives at any other time.

(5) An authority may revise or remake an equality objective at any time.

(6) If an authority revises an objective without remaking it then the authority must, as soon as possible after making the revision, publish the revision or the objective as revised (as it considers appropriate).

(7) If an authority does any of the things referred to in paragraph (5) it must either amend the statement published by it under regulation 3(2) or publish a new statement.

NOTES

Commencement: 6 April 2011.

[2.1583]

5 Engagement provisions

(1) The provisions in paragraph (2) are referred to in these Regulations as "the engagement provisions".

(2) Where any provision of these Regulations requires an authority to comply with the engagement provisions in carrying out any activity (see for example regulation 4(1)(a)), compliance with those provisions means that in carrying out that activity the authority—

(a) must involve such persons as the authority considers—

(i) represent the interests of persons who share one or more of the protected characteristics; and

(ii) have an interest in the way that the authority carries out its functions;

(b) may involve such other persons as the authority considers appropriate;
(c) may consult such persons as the authority considers appropriate.

(3) In reaching a decision under paragraph (2)(b) or (c) the authority must have regard to the need to involve or consult (as the case may be), so far as is reasonably practicable to do so, persons who—

(a) share one or more of the protected characteristics; and
(b) have an interest in the way that the authority carries out its functions.

NOTES

Commencement: 6 April 2011.

[2.1584]

6 Accessibility of published information

(1) This regulation applies to any document or information that an authority is required by these Regulations to publish.

(2) The authority must take all reasonable steps to ensure that the document or information is accessible by persons who share one or more protected characteristics.

NOTES

Commencement: 6 April 2011.

[2.1585]

7 Arrangements for collection etc of information about compliance with the general duty

(1) An authority must make such arrangements as it considers appropriate to ensure that, from time to time, it—

(a) identifies relevant information that it holds;
(b) identifies and collects relevant information that it does not hold; and
(c) publishes relevant information that it holds and which it considers appropriate to publish.

For further provision about what the arrangements must contain see also regulation 11(2).

(2) For the purposes of these Regulations an authority holds relevant information if—

(a) it is held by the authority, otherwise than on behalf of another person;
(b) it is held by another person on behalf of the authority; or
(c) it is held by the authority on behalf of another person and—
  (i) that person has consented to the authority using the information for the purpose of compliance by the authority with the general duty and the duties under these Regulations; or
  (ii) use of the information by the authority for the purpose of compliance by it with those duties meets the conditions in paragraph (3).

(3) The conditions referred to in paragraph (2)(c)(ii) are that the use of the information by the authority—

(a) is not contrary to law; and
(b) is reasonable, having regard to all the circumstances including, in particular, the nature of the information and the circumstances in which it was obtained by the authority.

(4) The identification of relevant information includes identifying such information by means of carrying out an assessment of whether there are—

(a) things done by the authority that contribute to the authority complying (or otherwise) with the general duty; and
(b) things that it could do that would be likely to contribute to compliance by the authority with that duty.

(5) When carrying out an assessment referred to in paragraph (4), the authority must—

(a) comply with the engagement provisions; and
(b) have due regard to relevant information that it holds.

(6) The arrangements referred to in paragraph (1) must ensure that, not later than 2 April 2012, the authority—

(a) carries out an assessment referred to in paragraph (4); and
(b) publishes relevant information that it holds and which it considers appropriate to publish.

NOTES

Commencement: 6 April 2011.

[2.1586]

8 Impact and monitoring of policies and practices

(1) An authority must make such arrangements as it considers appropriate for—

(a) assessing the likely impact of its proposed policies and practices on its ability to comply with the general duty;

(b) assessing the impact of any—
 (i) policy or practice that the authority has decided to review,
 (ii) revision that the authority proposes to make to a policy or practice,
 on its ability to comply with that duty;

(c) monitoring the impact of its policies and practices on its ability to comply with that duty; and

(d) publishing reports in respect of any assessment that—
 (i) is referred to in sub-paragraph (a) or (b); and
 (ii) shows that the impact or likely impact (as the case may be) on the authority's ability to comply with that duty is substantial.

(2) Reports under paragraph (1)(d) must set out, in particular—

(a) the purpose of—
 (i) the proposed policy or practice;
 (ii) the policy or practice; or
 (iii) the proposed revision to a policy or practice,
 that has been assessed;

(b) a summary of the steps that the authority has taken to carry out the assessment;

(c) a summary of the information that the authority has taken into account in the assessment;

(d) the results of the assessment; and

(e) any decisions taken by the authority in relation to those results.

(3) When carrying out an assessment referred to in paragraph (1)(a) or (b) the authority must—

(a) comply with the engagement provisions; and

(b) have due regard to relevant information that it holds.

NOTES

Commencement: 6 April 2011.

[2.1587]

9 Training and collection of employment information

(1) An authority must, in each year, collect the following information—

(a) the number of persons employed by the authority at the relevant date in that year;

(b) the number of persons employed by the authority at that date broken down by—
 (i) job;
 (ii) grade but only where an authority operates a grade system in respect of its employees;
 (iii) pay;
 (iv) contract type (including, but not limited to permanent and fixed-term contracts); and
 (v) working pattern (including, but not limited to full-time, part-time and other flexible working arrangements).

(c) the number, during the reporting period ending with the relevant date in that year, of—
 (i) persons who have applied for employment with the authority (excluding persons already employed by the authority);
 (ii) the authority's employees who have changed position within the authority including the number who applied to change position and the number who were successful (or otherwise) in their application;
 (iii) the authority's employees who have applied for training and the number who were successful (or otherwise) in their application;
 (iv) the authority's employees who completed the training;
 (v) the authority's employees who were or are involved in grievance procedures by reason of either being the person who made an accusation against another or being the person against whom an accusation was made;
 (vi) the authority's employees who were or are the subject of disciplinary proceedings; and
 (vii) the authority's employees who left the employment of the authority.

(2) In paragraph (1) (other than paragraph (1)(b)) any reference to the number of persons or employees includes, in respect of each protected characteristic, the numbers who share the protected characteristic.

(3) In paragraph (1)(b) the reference to the number of persons employed includes, in respect of the protected characteristic of sex, the number who are women and the number who are men.

(4) The authority must publish the information it has collected in accordance with paragraphs (1), (2) and (3).

(5) Nothing in this regulation is to be relied upon by an authority so as to require any person to whom this paragraph applies to provide information to the authority.

(6) Paragraph (5) applies to—

(a) any employee of the authority; and

(b) any person who applies for employment with the authority.

NOTES

Commencement: 6 April 2011.

[2.1588]

10

An authority must make such arrangements as it considers appropriate for—

(a) promoting amongst its employees knowledge and understanding of the general duty and the duties in these Regulations; and

(b) for using its performance assessment procedures (if any) to identify and address the training needs of its employees in relation to those duties.

NOTES

Commencement: 6 April 2011.

[2.1589]

11 Pay and action plans

(1) An authority must, when considering what its equality objectives should be, have due regard to the need to have equality objectives that address the causes of any differences between the pay of any person or persons employed by the authority ("P") who (as the case may be)—

(a) has a protected characteristic;

(b) share a protected characteristic,

and those who do not where either the first or second condition is met.

The first condition is that the difference is for a reason that is related to the fact that P has or share that protected characteristic (as the case may be).

The second condition is that it appears to the authority to be reasonably likely that the difference is for a reason that is related to the fact that P has or share that protected characteristic (as the case may be).

(2) The arrangements referred to in regulation 7(1) must also contain arrangements for identifying and collecting information about—

(a) any differences between the pay of persons referred to in paragraph (1); and

(b) the causes of any such differences.

(3) Where an authority—

(a) has, in accordance with paragraph (1), identified any gender pay difference; and

(b) has not published an equality objective to address the causes of that difference,

the authority must publish reasons for its decision not to publish such an objective.

NOTES

Commencement: 6 April 2011.

[2.1590]

12

(1) An authority must publish an action plan setting out—

(a) any policy of the authority that relates to the need to address the causes of any gender pay difference;

(b) any gender pay equality objective published by it;

(c) any revision to a gender pay equality objective or any revised gender pay equality objective it is required to publish in accordance with regulation 4(6);

(d) information it is required to publish in accordance with regulation 3(2)(a) in respect of any gender pay equality objective;

(e) any reasons it is required to publish in accordance with regulation 11(3).

(2) If, in respect of a gender pay equality objective, an authority does any of the things referred to in regulation 4(5) it must either amend the action plan published by it or publish a new action plan.

NOTES

Commencement: 6 April 2011.

[2.1591]

13 Review etc of arrangements

(1) An authority must keep the arrangements to which this regulation applies under review.

(2) An authority may, at any time, revise or remake the arrangements to which this regulation applies.

(3) This regulation applies to arrangements that the authority has made to comply with—

(i) regulation 3(2)(b);

(ii) regulation 7(1);

(iii) regulation 8(1); and
(iv) regulation 10.

NOTES
Commencement: 6 April 2011.

[2.1592]
14 Strategic Equality Plans

(1) Not later than 2 April 2012, an authority must make a Strategic Equality Plan (SEP).

(2) The SEP must contain a statement setting out—
(a) a description of the authority;
(b) the authority's equality objectives;
(c) in respect of each of those objectives—
(i) the steps that the authority has taken or intends to take in order to fulfil the objective; and
(ii) how long the authority expects it will take in order to fulfil the objective;
(d) the arrangements that it has made or intends to make to comply with—
(i) regulation 3(2)(b);
(ii) regulation 7(1);
(iii) regulation 8(1);
(iv) regulation 10, and
(e) the authority's action plan referred to in regulation 12.

(3) The SEP may contain such other matters that are relevant to compliance with the general duty as the authority considers appropriate.

(4) The authority may revise or remake its SEP at any time.

NOTES
Commencement: 6 April 2011.

[2.1593]
15 Preparation, publication and review of SEPs

(1) In making, remaking or revising a SEP the authority must—
(a) comply with the engagement provisions; and
(b) have due regard to relevant information that it holds.

(2) An authority must publish its SEP as soon as possible after the SEP is made or remade.

(3) If an authority revises its SEP without remaking it then the authority must, as soon as possible after making the revisions, publish the revisions or the SEP as revised (as it considers appropriate).

(4) An authority may comply with the duty to publish its SEP by setting out the SEP as part of another published document or within a number of other published documents.
For the purpose of this paragraph "SEP" includes any revisions to the SEP.

(5) The authority must keep under review—
(a) its SEP; and
(b) any revisions made to the SEP.

(6) In complying with the duty in paragraph (5) the authority must have due regard to—
(i) relevant information that it holds; and
(ii) any other information that the authority considers would be likely to assist it in the review.

NOTES
Commencement: 6 April 2011.

[2.1594]
16 Reports by authorities on compliance with the general duty

(1) An authority must, in respect of each reporting period, publish a report not later than the relevant date in the year following the year in which that reporting period ends.

(2) The report must set out—
(a) the steps that the authority has taken to identify and collect relevant information;
(b) in respect of relevant information that it holds, how the authority has used that information for the purpose of complying with the general duty and the duties in these Regulations;
(c) the authority's reasons for not collecting any relevant information that it has identified but does not hold;
(d) the progress that the authority has made in order to fulfil each of its equality objectives;
(e) a statement by the authority of the effectiveness of—
(i) its arrangements for identifying and collecting relevant information; and
(ii) the steps it has taken in order to fulfil each of its equality objectives; and

(f) the information that the authority is required to publish by regulation 9(4) unless the authority has already published that information.

(3) The authority may, if it considers it appropriate to do so, include in a report any other matter that is relevant to compliance by the authority with the general duty and the duties in these Regulations.

(4) The authority may comply with the duty to publish a report under paragraph (1) by setting out its report (including any matter referred to in paragraph (3)) as part of another published document or within a number of other published documents.

NOTES

Commencement: 6 April 2011.

[2.1595]

17 Reports by Welsh Ministers on compliance with the general duty etc by authorities

(1) The Welsh Ministers must, in accordance with paragraph (2), publish reports that set out an overview of the progress made by authorities towards compliance by those authorities with the general duty.

(2) Reports under paragraph (1) must—

(a) be published—

(i) not later than 31 December 2014; and

(ii) subsequently at intervals not later than the end of each successive period of four years beginning with the date that the last report was published in accordance with this sub-paragraph; and

(b) be published—

(i) not later than 31 December 2016; and

(ii) subsequently at intervals not later than the end of each successive period of four years beginning with the date that the last report was published in accordance with this sub-paragraph.

(3) Reports under paragraph (1), other than the first reports in accordance with paragraph (2)(a)(i) and (b)(i), must cover the period since the date that the last report under paragraph (2)(b) was published.

(4) The Welsh Ministers must publish a report, not later than 31 December 2011, setting out—

(a) an overview of the progress made by authorities towards compliance by them with the general duty so far as it relates to persons who share the protected characteristic of disability; and

(b) information relating to the period 2 December 2008 to 5 April 2011 that the Welsh Ministers would have been required to include in a report under regulation 5 of the Disability Discrimination (Public Authorities) (Statutory Duties) Regulations 2005 by virtue of regulation 5(2)(a) of those regulations if those regulations were in force.

(5) Reports under this regulation must also set out the Welsh Ministers' proposals for the coordination of action by authorities so as to bring about further progress towards compliance by those authorities with the general duty.

NOTES

Commencement: 6 April 2011.

[2.1596]

18 Public procurement

(1) Where an authority that is a contracting authority proposes to enter into a relevant agreement on the basis of an offer which is the most economically advantageous it must have due regard to whether the award criteria should include considerations relevant to its performance of the general duty.

(2) Where an authority that is a contracting authority proposes to stipulate conditions relating to the performance of a relevant agreement it must have due regard to whether the conditions should include considerations relevant to its performance of the general duty.

(3) In this regulation—

"contracting authority" ("*awdurdod contractio*"), "framework agreement" ("*cytundeb fframwaith*") and "public contracts" ("*contractau cyhoeddus*") have the same meaning as in the Public Sector Directive; and

"relevant agreement" ("*cytundeb perthnasol*") means the award of a public contract or the conclusion of a framework agreement that is regulated by the Public Sector Directive.

NOTES

Commencement: 6 April 2011.

[2.1597]
19 Compliance with duties by Welsh Ministers etc

Where the Welsh Ministers, the First Minister for Wales and the Counsel General to the Welsh Assembly Government are required by these Regulations to prepare a SEP, publish a report or do any other thing, they may comply with the duty by acting jointly.

NOTES

Commencement: 6 April 2011.

[2.1598]
20 Disclosure of information

Nothing in these Regulations is to be taken to require an authority to publish information if—

(a) to do so would constitute a breach—
  (i) of confidence actionable by any person; or
  (ii) of the Data Protection Act 1998; or
(b) the authority would be entitled to refuse to produce the information in or for the purposes of proceedings in a court or tribunal in England and Wales.

NOTES

Commencement: 6 April 2011.

EMPLOYMENT EQUALITY (REPEAL OF RETIREMENT AGE PROVISIONS) REGULATIONS 2011

(SI 2011/1069)

NOTES

Made: 5 April 2011.
Authority: European Communities Act 1972, s 2(2).
Commencement: 6 April 2011.
Although amending only, these Regulations are, because of their importance and their transitional provisions, reproduced in full text.
See *Harvey* L(4)(C).

ARRANGEMENT OF REGULATIONS

[2.1599]
1 Citation, commencement and extent

(1) These Regulations may be cited as the Employment Equality (Repeal of Retirement Age Provisions) Regulations 2011 and come into force on 6th April 2011.

(2) These Regulations extend to England and Wales and Scotland.

NOTES

Commencement: 6 April 2011.

[2.1600]
2 Amendments to the Equality Act 2010

(1) Schedule 9 to the Equality Act 2010 (work: exceptions relating to age) is amended as follows.

(2) Omit paragraph 8 (retirement).

(3) Omit paragraph 9 (applicants at or approaching retirement age).

(4) For paragraph 14 (life assurance), substitute—

> **"14 Insurance etc**
>
> (1) It is not an age contravention for an employer to make arrangements for, or afford access to, the provision of insurance or a related financial service to or in respect of an employee for a period ending when the employee attains whichever is the greater of—
>
> (a) the age of 65, and
> (b) the state pensionable age.

(2) It is not an age contravention for an employer to make arrangements for, or afford access to, the provision of insurance or a related financial service to or in respect of only such employees as have not attained whichever is the greater of—

(a) the age of 65, and

(b) the state pensionable age.

(3) Sub-paragraphs (1) and (2) apply only where the insurance or related financial service is, or is to be, provided to the employer's employees or a class of those employees—

(a) in pursuance of an arrangement between the employer and another person, or

(b) where the employer's business includes the provision of insurance or financial services of the description in question, by the employer.

(4) The state pensionable age is the pensionable age determined in accordance with the rules in paragraph 1 of Schedule 4 to the Pensions Act 1995.".

NOTES

Commencement: 6 April 2011.

[2.1601]

3 Amendments to the Employment Rights Act 1996

(1) The Employment Rights Act 1996 is amended as follows.

(2) In section 98 (fairness of dismissals: general)—

(a) omit subsections (2)(ba), (2A) and (3A), and

(b) in subsection (4), for "In any other case where" substitute "Where".

(3) Omit sections 98ZA to 98ZH (retirement dismissals).

(4) In section 105 (redundancy) omit subsection (7IA).

(5) In section 108 (qualifying period of employment) omit subsection (3)(n).

(6) In section 112 (remedies for unfair dismissal: orders for compensation), omit subsections (5) and (6).

(7) In section 120 (basic award in certain cases), omit subsections (1A) and (1B).

NOTES

Commencement: 6 April 2011.

[2.1602]

4 Amendments to the Employment Equality (Age) Regulations 2006

(1) Schedule 6 to the Employment Equality (Age) Regulations 2006 (duty of employer to consider employee's request to work beyond retirement) is revoked.

(2) Omit paragraphs 22 to 24, 26 and 28 of Schedule 8 to those Regulations.

NOTES

Commencement: 6 April 2011.

[2.1603]

5 Transitional provisions

(1) Despite regulations 2 to 4, the provisions mentioned in paragraph (2) continue to have effect in relation to the employment of a person if—

(a) notification in respect of that employment has been given under paragraph 2 or 4 of Schedule 6 to the Employment Equality (Age) Regulations 2006 before the date of the commencement of these Regulations, and

(b) that person has attained the age limit or will attain it before 1st October 2011.

(2) The provisions are—

(a) sections 98(2)(ba), (2A) and (3A), 98ZA to 98ZD, 98ZF to 98ZH, 105(7IA), 108(3)(n), 112(5) and (6) and 120(1A) and (1B) of the Employment Rights Act 1996,

(b) Schedule 6 to the Employment Equality (Age) Regulations 2006, and

(c) paragraph 8 of Schedule 9 to the Equality Act 2010.

(3) The age limit is whichever is the greater of—

(a) the age of 65, and

(b) the normal retirement age in the case of the employment concerned.

(4) Despite this regulation—

(a) an employer may not issue a notification under paragraph 2 or 4 of Schedule 6 to the Employment Equality (Age) Regulations 2006 on or after 6th April 2011 in respect of the employment of a person to which this regulation applies; and

(b) an employee may not make a request under paragraph 5 of Schedule 6 to the Employment Equality (Age) Regulations 2006 on or after 5th January 2012 in respect of the employment to which this regulation applies.

(5) In this regulation, "normal retirement age" has the meaning given in section 98ZH of the Employment Rights Act 1996.

(6) This regulation does not apply to the employment of a person if section 98ZE of the Employment Rights Act 1996 would (but for regulation 3(3)) apply to a dismissal from that employment.

NOTES

Commencement: 6 April 2011.

[2.1604]
6

(1) Despite regulations 3 and 4, the provisions mentioned in paragraph (2) continue to have effect in relation to the employment of a person if—

(a) notification in respect of that employment has been given under paragraph 2 or 4 of Schedule 6 to the Employment Equality (Age) Regulations 2006 before the date of the commencement of these Regulations, and

(b) section 98ZE of the Employment Rights Act 1996 would (but for regulation 3(3)) apply to a dismissal from that employment.

(2) The provisions are—

(a) sections 98(2)(ba), (2A) and (3A), 98ZE to 98ZH, 105(7IA), 108(3)(n), 112(5) and (6) and 120(1A) and (1B) of the Employment Rights Act 1996, and

(b) Schedule 6 to the Employment Equality (Age) Regulations 2006.

NOTES

Commencement: 6 April 2011.

[2.1605]
7

Despite regulation 3(6) and (7), sections 112(5) and (6) and 120(1A) and (1B) of the Employment Rights Act 1996 continue to have effect so far as necessary for the transitional provisions in Part 1 of the Schedule to the Employment Act 2008 (Commencement No 1, Transitional Provisions and Savings) Order 2008.

NOTES

Commencement: 6 April 2011.

[2.1606]
8

Despite regulation 4, paragraphs 9, 12 and 13 of Schedule 6 to the Employment Equality (Age) Regulations 2006 (right of employee to be accompanied at meeting with employer) continue to have effect in a case where paragraph 9 of that Schedule applies immediately before the commencement of these Regulations.

NOTES

Commencement: 6 April 2011.

[2.1607]
9

Regulations 5 to 8 do not affect the general operation of section 16 of the Interpretation Act 1978.

NOTES

Commencement: 6 April 2011.

Note: section 16 of the interpretation Act 1978 provides that (without prejudice to s 15) where an Act repeals an enactment, the repeal does not, unless the contrary intention appears (a) revive anything not in force or existing at the time at which the repeal takes effect; (b) affect the previous operation of the enactment repealed or anything duly done or suffered under that enactment; (c) affect any right, privilege, obligation or liability acquired, accrued or incurred under that enactment; (d) affect any penalty, forfeiture or punishment incurred in respect of any offence committed against that enactment; (e) affect any investigation, legal proceeding or remedy in respect of any such right, privilege, obligation, liability, penalty, forfeiture or punishment; and any such investigation, legal proceeding or remedy may be instituted, continued or enforced, and any such penalty, forfeiture or punishment may be imposed, as if the repealing Act had not been passed.

EQUALITY ACT 2010 (GUIDANCE ON THE DEFINITION OF DISABILITY) APPOINTED DAY ORDER 2011

(SI 2011/1159)

NOTES

Made: 26 April 2011.
Authority: Equality Act 2010, ss 6(5), 207(1), (4), Sch 1, paras 11, 15.
Commencement: 1 May 2011.

[2.1608]

1 Citation and interpretation

(1) This Order may be cited as the Equality Act 2010 (Guidance on the Definition of Disability) Appointed Day Order 2011.

(2) In this Order—

"Guidance" means the guidance on matters to be taken into account in determining questions relating to the definition of disability;

"the 1995 Act" means the Disability Discrimination Act 1995;

"the 2010 Act" means the Equality Act 2010;

"the 2010 Order" means the Equality Act 2010 (Commencement No 4, Savings, Consequential, Transitional, Transitory and Incidental Provisions and Revocation) Order 2010;

"the 1996 Guidance" means the Guidance on matters to be taken into account in determining questions relating to the definition of disability which was issued by the Secretary of State under the 1995 Act on 29th March 2006;

"adjudicating body" has the same meaning as in section 3(3A) of the 1995 Act in relation to any proceedings brought under the 1995 Act, and is defined in paragraph 12(2) of Schedule 1 to the 2010 Act in relation to any proceedings brought under the 2010 Act.

NOTES

Commencement: 1 May 2011.

[2.1609]

2 Appointed Day

(1) 1st May 2011 is the day appointed for the coming into force of the Guidance laid before Parliament in draft on 10th February 2011 and issued under paragraph 14(3) of Schedule 1 to the 2010 Act on 7th April 2011.

(2) Paragraph (1) has effect subject to the provisions of article 3.

NOTES

Commencement: 1 May 2011.
For the Guidance, see **[4.238]**.

[2.1610]

3 Transitional provision

(1) This article applies in relation to any proceedings arising from a complaint presented to an adjudicating body, whenever presented, alleging that a person has, before 1st May 2011, committed an act which is unlawful discrimination or harassment.

(2) A reference to an act in paragraph (1) of this article includes a reference to a continuing act which began before 1st May 2011.

(3) A reference to proceedings in paragraph (1) of this article is a reference to—

(a) Proceedings brought under the 1995 Act by virtue of article 15 of the 2010 Order, or
(b) Proceedings brought under the 2010 Act by virtue of article 7 of the 2010 Order, or
(c) Proceedings brought under the 2010 Act otherwise than by virtue of article 7 of the 2010 Order, and in which the act complained of occurred, or in which the continuing act complained of began, before 1st May 2011.

(4) Where this article applies, the Guidance referred to in article 2(1) of this Order shall not have effect for the purposes of section 3 of the 1995 Act or paragraph 12(1) of Schedule 1 to the 2010 Act.

(5) Where this article applies, the 1996 Guidance is to continue to have effect for the purposes referred to in paragraph (4) of this article.

NOTES

Commencement: 1 May 2011.
The 1996 Guidance was reproduced in the twentieth edition of this Handbook.

EQUALITY ACT 2010 (WORK ON SHIPS AND HOVERCRAFT) REGULATIONS 2011

(SI 2011/1771)

NOTES

Made: 18 July 2011.
Authority: Equality Act 2010, ss 81, 207(1), (4)(b), 212(1).
Commencement: 1 August 2011.

ARRANGEMENT OF REGULATIONS

[2.1611]

1 Citation and commencement

These Regulations may be cited as the Equality Act 2010 (Work on Ships and Hovercraft) Regulations 2011 and come into force fourteen days after the day on which they are made.

NOTES

Commencement: 1 August 2011.

[2.1612]

2 Interpretation

(1) In these Regulations—

"the Act" means the Equality Act 2010;

"British citizen" has the same meaning as in the British Nationality Act 1981;

"designated state" means the countries of the African, Caribbean and Pacific Group of States, the Kingdom of Morocco, Montenegro, the Most Serene Republic of San Marino, the People's Democratic Republic of Algeria, the Principality of Andorra, the Republic of Albania, the Republic of Croatia, the Republic of Macedonia, the Republic of Tunisia, the Republic of Turkey, the Russian Federation or the Swiss Confederation;

"United Kingdom ship" means a ship registered in the United Kingdom under Part II of the Merchant Shipping Act 1995, and

"United Kingdom waters" means the sea or other waters within the seaward limits of the territorial sea of the United Kingdom.

(2) For the purposes of regulations 3(3)(c) and 4(2)(b)—

(a) the legal relationship of the seafarer's employment is located within Great Britain if the contract under which the seafarer is employed—

(i) was entered into in Great Britain; or

(ii) takes effect in Great Britain,

(b) whether the legal relationship of the seafarer's employment retains a sufficiently close link with Great Britain is to be determined by reference to all relevant factors including—

(i) where the seafarer is subject to tax;

(ii) where the employer or principal is incorporated;

(iii) where the employer or principal is established;

(iv) where the ship or hovercraft on which the seafarer works is registered.

NOTES

Commencement: 1 August 2011.

[2.1613]

3 Application of Part 5 of the Act to seafarers working wholly or partly in Great Britain and adjacent waters

(1) Part 5 of the Act applies to a seafarer who works wholly or partly within Great Britain (including United Kingdom waters adjacent to Great Britain) if the seafarer is on—

(a) a United Kingdom ship and the ship's entry in the register maintained under section 8 of the Merchant Shipping Act 1995 specifies a port in Great Britain as the ship's port of choice, or

(b) a hovercraft registered in the United Kingdom and operated by a person whose principal place of business, or ordinary residence, is in Great Britain.

(2) Part 5 of the Act, except in relation to the protected characteristic of marriage and civil partnership, also applies to a seafarer who works wholly or partly within Great Britain (including United Kingdom waters adjacent to Great Britain) and who is on—

(a) a ship registered in or entitled to fly the flag of an EEA State other than the United Kingdom, or

(b) a hovercraft registered in an EEA State other than the United Kingdom,

if paragraph (3) applies.

(3) This paragraph applies if—

(a) the ship or hovercraft is in United Kingdom waters adjacent to Great Britain,

(b) the seafarer is a British citizen, or a national of an EEA State other than the United Kingdom or of a designated state, and

(c) the legal relationship of the seafarer's employment is located within Great Britain or retains a sufficiently close link with Great Britain.

NOTES

Commencement: 1 August 2011.

[2.1614]

4 Application of Part 5 of the Act to seafarers working wholly outside Great Britain and adjacent waters

(1) Part 5 of the Act applies to a seafarer who works wholly outside Great Britain and United Kingdom waters adjacent to Great Britain if the seafarer is on—

(a) a United Kingdom ship and the ship's entry in the register maintained under section 8 of the Merchant Shipping Act 1995 specifies a port in Great Britain as the ship's port of choice, or

(b) a hovercraft registered in the United Kingdom and operated by a person whose principal place of business, or ordinary residence, is in Great Britain,

and paragraph (2) applies.

(2) This paragraph applies if—

(a) the seafarer is a British citizen, or a national of an EEA State other than the United Kingdom or of a designated state, and

(b) the legal relationship of the seafarer's employment is located within Great Britain or retains a sufficiently close link with Great Britain.

NOTES

Commencement: 1 August 2011.

[2.1615]

5 Differentiation in relation to pay

It is not a contravention of section 39(1)(b) or (2)(a) or 41(1)(a) of the Act, as applied by regulations 3 and 4, for an employer or principal to offer to pay or to pay a person (A) at a lower rate than that at which the employer or principal offers to pay or pays another person (B) because A is of a different nationality from B, if—

(a) A—

(i) applied for work as a seafarer, or

(ii) was recruited as a seafarer,

outside Great Britain, and

(b) A is not—

(i) a British Citizen,

(ii) a national of another EEA State, or

(iii) a national of a designated state.

NOTES

Commencement: 1 August 2011.

[2.1616]

6 Review

(1) Before the end of each review period, the Secretary of State must—

(a) carry out a review of regulations 3 to 5,

(b) set out the conclusions of the review in a report, and

(c) publish the report.

(2) In carrying out the review the Secretary of State must, so far as is reasonable, have regard to how—

(a) Council Directive 2000/43/EC of 29 June 2000 implementing the principle of equal treatment between persons irrespective of racial or ethnic origin,
(b) Council Directive 2000/78/EC of 27 November 2000 establishing a general framework of equal treatment in employment and occupation, and
(c) Directive 2006/54/EC of the European Parliament and of the Council of 5 July 2006 on the implementation of the principle of equal opportunities and equal treatment of men and women in matters of employment and occupation (recast),

are implemented in other member States in relation to work on ships and hovercraft and seafarers.

(3) The report must in particular—
(a) set out the objectives intended to be achieved by applying Part 5 of the Act to work on ships and hovercraft and seafarers,
(b) assess the extent to which those objectives are achieved, and
(c) assess whether those objectives remain appropriate and, if so, the extent to which they could be achieved by imposing less regulation.

(4) "Review period" means—
(a) the period of five years beginning with the day on which these Regulations come into force, and
(b) subject to paragraph (5), each successive period of five years.

(5) If a report under this regulation is published before the last day of the review period to which it relates, the following review period is to begin with the day on which that report is published.

NOTES
Commencement: 1 August 2011.

EQUALITY ACT 2010 (SPECIFIC DUTIES) REGULATIONS 2011

(SI 2011/2260)

NOTES
Made: 9 September 2011.
Authority: Equality Act 2010, ss 153(1), 154(2), 207(4).
Commencement: 10 September 2011.

ARRANGEMENT OF REGULATIONS

SCHEDULES

[2.1617]
1 Citation, commencement and interpretation

(1) These Regulations may be cited as the Equality Act 2010 (Specific Duties) Regulations 2011 and come into force on the day after the day they are made.

(2) In these Regulations "the Act" means the Equality Act 2010.

NOTES
Commencement: 10 September 2011.

[2.1618]
2 Publication of information

(1) Each public authority listed in either Schedule to these Regulations must publish information to demonstrate its compliance with the duty imposed by section 149(1) of the Act.

(2) A public authority listed in Schedule 1 to these Regulations must publish the information—
(a) not later than 31st January 2012; and
(b) subsequently at intervals of not greater than one year beginning with the date of last publication.

(3) A public authority listed in Schedule 2 to these Regulations must publish the information—
(a) not later than 6th April 2012; and

(b) subsequently at intervals of not greater than one year beginning with the date of last publication.

(4) The information a public authority publishes in compliance with paragraph (1) must include, in particular, information relating to persons who share a relevant protected characteristic who are

(a) its employees;

(b) other persons affected by its policies and practices.

(5) Paragraph (4)(a) does not apply to a public authority with fewer than 150 employees.

NOTES

Commencement: 10 September 2011.

[2.1619]

3 Equality objectives

(1) Each public authority listed in either Schedule to these Regulations must prepare and publish one or more objectives it thinks it should achieve to do any of the things mentioned in paragraphs (a) to (c) of subsection (1) of section 149 of the Act.

(2) The objectives must be published—

(a) not later than 6th April 2012; and

(b) subsequently at intervals of not greater than four years beginning with the date of last publication.

(3) An objective published by a public authority in compliance with paragraph (1) must be specific and measurable.

NOTES

Commencement: 10 September 2011.

[2.1620]

4 Manner of publication

(1) Each public authority listed in either Schedule to these Regulations must publish the information referred to in regulations 2 and 3 in such a manner that the information is accessible to the public.

(2) A public authority may comply with a duty to publish information imposed by regulation 2 or 3 by publishing the information within another published document.

NOTES

Commencement: 10 September 2011.

SCHEDULES

SCHEDULE 1
PUBLIC AUTHORITIES REQUIRED TO PUBLISH INFORMATION BY 31ST JANUARY 2012

Regulation 2(2)

[2.1621]

Armed forces

Any of the armed forces other than any part of the armed forces which is, in accordance with a requirement of the Secretary of State, assisting the Government Communications Headquarters.

Broadcasting

The British Broadcasting Corporation ("BBC"), except in respect of functions relating to the provision of a content service (within the meaning given by section 32(7) of the Communications Act 2003); and the reference to the BBC includes a reference to a body corporate which—

(a) is a wholly owned subsidiary of the BBC,

(b) is not operated with a view to generating a profit, and

(c) undertakes activities primarily in order to promote the BBC's public purposes.

The Channel Four Television Corporation, except in respect of—

(a) functions relating to the provision of a content service (within the meaning given by section 32(7) of the Communications Act 2003), and

(b) the function of carrying on the activities referred to in section 199 of that Act.

The Welsh Authority (as defined by section 56(1) of the Broadcasting Act 1990), except in respect of functions relating to the provision of a content service (within the meaning given by section 32(7) of the Communications Act 2003).

Civil liberties

The Commission for Equality and Human Rights.

The Information Commissioner.

Court services and legal services

The Children and Family Court Advisory and Support Service.

The Judicial Appointments Commission.

The Legal Services Board.

. . .

Criminal justice

Her Majesty's Chief Inspector of Constabulary.

Her Majesty's Chief Inspector of the Crown Prosecution Service.

Her Majesty's Chief Inspector of Prisons.

Her Majesty's Chief Inspector of Probation for England and Wales.

The Parole Board for England and Wales.

A probation trust established by an order made under section 5(1) of the Offender Management Act 2007.

The Youth Justice Board for England and Wales.

Environment, housing and development

The Environment Agency.

The Homes and Communities Agency.

Natural England.

. . .

The Olympic Delivery Authority.

Health, social care and social security

The Care Quality Commission.

The Child Maintenance and Enforcement Commission.

[Monitor].

NHS Blood and Transplant.

The NHS Business Services Authority.

An NHS foundation trust within the meaning given by section 30 of the National Health Service Act 2006.

An NHS trust established under section 25 of that Act.

[A clinical commissioning group established under section 14D of that Act.

The National Health Service Commissioning Board.

The National Institute for Health and Care Excellence.

The Health and Social Care Information Centre.]

. . .

A Special Health Authority established under section 28 of that Act (other than NHS Blood and Transplant and the NHS Business Services Authority).

. . .

Industry, business, finance etc

The Advisory, Conciliation and Arbitration Service.

The Bank of England, in respect of its public functions.

The Civil Aviation Authority.

[The Financial Conduct Authority.]

The National Audit Office.

The Office for Budget Responsibility.

The Office of Communications.

[The Prudential Regulation Authority.]

Local government

The Audit Commission for Local Authorities and the National Health Service in England.

A body corporate established pursuant to an order under section 67 of the Local Government Act 1985.

The Common Council of the City of London in its capacity as a local authority or port health authority.

The Council of the Isles of Scilly.

A county council or district council in England.

A fire and rescue authority constituted by a scheme under section 2 of the Fire and Rescue Services Act 2004, or a scheme to which section 4 of that Act applies, for an area in England.

The Greater London Authority.

A joint committee constituted in accordance with section 102(1)(b) of the Local Government Act 1972 for an area in England.

A London borough council.

The London Development Agency.

The London Fire and Emergency Planning Authority.

A National Park authority established by an order under section 63 of the Environment Act 1995 for an area in England.

A Passenger Transport Executive for an integrated transport area in England (within the meaning of Part 2 of the Transport Act 1968).

A regional development agency established by the Regional Development Agencies Act 1998 (other than the London Development Agency).

The Standards Board for England.

Transport for London.

Ministers of the Crown and government departments

A government department other than the Security Service, the Secret Intelligence Service or the Government Communications Headquarters.

A Minister of the Crown.

Other educational bodies

The governing body of an institution in England within the further education sector (within the meaning of section 91(3) of the Further and Higher Education Act 1992).

The governing body of an institution in England within the higher education sector (within the meaning of section 91(5) of that Act).

The Higher Education Funding Council for England.

The Student Loans Company Limited.

Parliamentary and devolved bodies

The National Assembly for Wales Commission (Comisiwn Cynulliad Cenedlaethol Cymru).

The Scottish Parliamentary Corporate Body.

Police

The British Transport Police Force.

A chief constable of a police force maintained under section 2 of the Police Act 1996.

The Chief Inspector of the UK Border Agency.

The Civil Nuclear Police Authority.

The Commissioner of Police for the City of London.

The Commissioner of Police of the Metropolis.

The Common Council of the City of London in its capacity as a police authority.

The Independent Police Complaints Commission.

The Metropolitan Police Authority established under section 5B of the Police Act 1996.

A police authority established under section 3 of that Act.

The Serious Organised Crime Agency.

Regulators

The General Council of the Bar, in respect of its public functions.

The Health and Safety Executive.

The Law Society of England and Wales, in respect of its public functions.

NOTES

Commencement: 10 September 2011.

Under the heading "Court services and legal services", the entry "The Legal Services Commission" (omitted) was revoked by the Legal Aid, Sentencing and Punishment of Offenders Act 2012 (Consequential, Transitional and Saving Provisions) Regulations 2013, SI 2013/534, reg 14(1), Schedule, para 10, as from 1 April 2013.

Under the heading "Environment, housing and development", the entry "The Office for Tenants and Social Landlords" (omitted) was revoked by the Localism Act 2011 (Regulation of Social Housing) (Consequential Provisions) Order 2012, SI 2012/641, art 2(7), as from 1 April 2012.

Under the heading "Health, social care and social security", the entry "Monitor" in first pair of square brackets was substituted, for entry "The Independent Regulator of NHS Foundation Trusts" as originally enacted, by the NHS Commissioning Board Authority (Abolition and Transfer of Staff, Property and Liabilities) and the Health and Social Care Act 2012 (Consequential Amendments) Order 2012, SI 2012/1641, art 10, Sch 4, para 20, as from 1 October 2012; entries in second pair of square brackets inserted and entries omitted revoked by the National Treatment Agency (Abolition) and the Health and Social Care Act 2012 (Consequential, Transitional and Saving Provisions) Order 2013, SI 2013/235, art 11, Sch 2, Pt 1, para 166, as from 1 April 2013.

Under the heading "Industry, business, finance etc", the entry "The Financial Conduct Authority" was substituted for original entry "The Financial Services Authority" and the entry "The Prudential Regulation Authority" was inserted by the Financial Services Act 2012 (Consequential Amendments and Transitional Provisions) Order 2013, SI 2013/472, art 3, Sch 2, para 215, as from 1 April 2013.

See further the Budget Responsibility and National Audit Act 2011 (Consequential Amendments) Order 2012, SI 2012/725, art 2 which provides that the reference in this Schedule to the National Audit Office should be read as a reference to the NAO established by the Budget Responsibility and National Audit Act 2011, s 20 (and not the NAO established by the National Audit Act 1983, s 3).

SCHEDULE 2
PUBLIC AUTHORITIES REQUIRED TO PUBLISH INFORMATION BY 6TH APRIL 2012

Regulation 2(3)

[2.1622]

Educational institutions

The governing body of an educational establishment maintained by an English local authority (within the meaning of section 162 of the Education and Inspections Act 2006).

A local authority with respect to the pupil referral units it establishes and maintains by virtue of section 19 of the Education Act 1996.

The proprietor of a City Technology College, City College for Technology or the Arts, or an Academy.

NOTES

Commencement: 10 September 2011.

EQUALITY ACT 2010 (AMENDMENT) ORDER 2012 (NOTE)

(SI 2012/334)

[2.1623]

NOTES

This Order was made on the 8 February 2012 under the powers conferred by the European Communities Act 1972, s 2(2).

Article 1 provides for citation, commencement and extent. The Order comes into force on 6 April 2012 and extends to England and Wales and Scotland.

Article 2 amends the Equality Act 2010, s 147. That section makes provision as to what is a "qualifying compromise contract" ("QCC"), ie, a contract that may be used to settle a complaint within s 120 of the 2010 Act. Section 120 of the 2010 Act grants jurisdiction to an employment tribunal to determine a complaint relating to an unlawful act under Part 5 (Work), namely an act of discrimination, harassment or victimisation. One requirement of s 147 is that the complainant must have received advice from an independent adviser before entering into a QCC (s 147(3)(c)). Section 147(4) and (5) sets out who may act as an independent adviser for these purposes.

The interpretation of s 147 has given rise to uncertainty as to whether a complainant's lawyer is precluded from being an "independent adviser" to the complainant for the purposes of a QCC. This Order seeks to clarify that the "person" referred to in s 147(5)(a) could not include the "complainant" and that, accordingly, a complainant's legal adviser is not precluded from being an "independent adviser" to the complainant.

The wording of art 2 of this Order is as follows—

"(1) Section 147 of the Equality Act 2010 (meaning of "qualifying compromise contract") is amended in accordance with paragraphs (2) and (3).
(2) In subsection (5), after "independent adviser" insert "to the complainant".
(3) In subsection (5)(a), after "person" insert "(other than the complainant)".".

Section 147 of the 2010 Act is at **[1.1733]**.

APPRENTICESHIPS (FORM OF APPRENTICESHIP AGREEMENT) REGULATIONS 2012

(SI 2012/844)

NOTES

Made: 15 March 2012.
Authority: Apprenticeships, Skills, Children and Learning Act 2009, ss 32(2)(b), 36(4), 262(1).
Commencement: 6 April 2012.

[2.1624]

1 Citation, commencement and interpretation

(1) These Regulations may be cited as the Apprenticeships (Form of Apprenticeship Agreement) Regulations 2012 and come into force on 6th April 2012.

(2) In these Regulations—

"the Act" means the Apprenticeships, Skills, Children and Learning Act 2009; and
"the 1996 Act" means the Employment Rights Act 1996.

NOTES

Commencement: 6 April 2012.

[2.1625]

2 Form of the apprenticeship agreement

(1) The prescribed form of an apprenticeship agreement for the purposes of section 32(2)(b) of the Act is—

- (a) a written statement of particulars of employment given to an employee for the purposes of section 1 of the 1996 Act; or
- (b) a document in writing in the form of a contract of employment or letter of engagement where the employer's duty under section 1 of the 1996 Act is treated as met for the purposes of section 7A of the 1996 Act.

(2) An apprenticeship agreement must include a statement of the skill, trade or occupation for which the apprentice is being trained under the apprenticeship framework.

(3) This regulation does not apply where regulation 4 applies.

NOTES

Commencement: 6 April 2012.

[2.1626]

3 Form of the apprenticeship agreement for Crown servants and Parliamentary staff

(1) For the purposes of persons falling within section 36(1)(a) and (c)(ii) of the Act, regulation 2 applies, subject to the following provisions.

(2) In relation to an apprenticeship agreement under which a person undertakes Crown employment, a reference to—

(a) a contract of service shall be construed as a reference to the terms of employment of an apprentice in Crown employment;

(b) an apprentice shall be construed as a reference to an apprentice in Crown employment.

(3) In relation to an apprenticeship agreement under which a person undertakes employment as a relevant member of the House of Commons staff, a reference to—

(a) a contract of service shall be construed as including a reference to the terms of employment of a relevant member of the House of Commons staff;

(b) an apprentice shall be construed as a reference to a relevant member of the House of Commons staff;

(c) an employer will be to—

(i) the House of Commons Commission, for a person appointed by the Commission; or

(ii) the Speaker, for a member of the Speaker's personal staff and any person employed in the refreshment department, where that person was not appointed by the Commission.

NOTES

Commencement: 6 April 2012.

[2.1627]

4 Form of the apprenticeship agreement for persons who are members of the naval, military or air forces of the Crown

For the purposes of persons falling within section 36(1)(b) of the Act, the prescribed form of an apprenticeship agreement for the purposes of section 32(2)(b) is the agreement signed by the member of the naval, military or air forces of the Crown which specifies the name of the apprenticeship framework.

NOTES

Commencement: 6 April 2012.

UNFAIR DISMISSAL AND STATEMENT OF REASONS FOR DISMISSAL (VARIATION OF QUALIFYING PERIOD) ORDER 2012 (NOTE)

(SI 2012/989)

[2.1628]

NOTES

This Order was made on the 30 March 2012 under the powers conferred by the Employment Rights Act 1996, ss 209(1)(c), (5), 236(5). It came into force on 6 April 2012 (Article 1: Citation and commencement).

The effect of this order is to increase from one year to two years the qualifying period of continuous employment needed: (a) for the entitlement, on request, to a written statement of reasons for dismissal, and (b) to acquire the right not to be unfairly dismissed.

Article 2 of this Order (Qualifying period for right to written statement of reasons for dismissal) and article 3 (Qualifying period for right to claim unfair dismissal) amend ss 92(3) (at **[1.892]**) and 108(1), (2) (at **[1.918]**) of the Employment Rights Act 1996 respectively by substituting a reference to "two years" for the previous reference to "one year".

Article 4 (Transitional provision) provides that arts 2, 3 and 5 of this Order do not have effect in any case where the period of continuous employment begins before 6 April 2012.

Article 5 (Revocation) revokes the Unfair Dismissal and Statement of Reasons for Dismissal (Variation of Qualifying Period) Order 1999 (SI 1999/1436).

HEALTH AND SAFETY (FEES) REGULATIONS 2012

(SI 2012/1652)

NOTES

Made: 25 June 2012.
Authority: European Communities Act 1972, s 2(2); Health and Safety at Work etc Act 1974, ss 43(2), (4)–(6), 82(3)(a).
Commencement: 1 October 2012.

[2.1629]

1 Citation, commencement and interpretation

(1) These Regulations may be cited as the Health and Safety (Fees) Regulations 2012 and come into force on 1st October 2012.

(2) They cease to have effect at the end of the period of five years beginning with the day on which these Regulations come into force.

(3) In these Regulations—

"approval" includes the amendment of an approval, and "amendment of an approval" includes the issue of a new approval replacing the original and incorporating one or more amendments;

"employment medical adviser" means an employment medical adviser appointed under section 56(1) of the 1974 Act;

"the mines and quarries provisions" means such of the relevant statutory provisions as relate exclusively to—

(a) mines within the meaning of section 180 of the Mines and Quarries Act 1954;

(b) tips and quarries within the meaning of regulations 2(1) and 3 respectively of the Quarries Regulations 1999; and

(c) tips within the meaning of section 2(1) of the Mines and Quarries (Tips) Act 1969;

and includes regulations, rules and orders relating to a particular mine, whether they are continued in force by regulation 7(3) of the Mines and Quarries Acts 1954 to 1971 (Repeals and Modifications) Regulations 1974 or are health and safety regulations;

"original approval" and "original type approval" do not include an amendment of an approval; and

"working days" does not include weekends or public holidays.

(4) Any reference in these Regulations to the renewal of an approval, explosives certificate, licence or registration (each referred to in this paragraph as an "authorisation") means the granting of the authorisation concerned to follow a previous authorisation of the same kind without any amendment or gap in time.

NOTES

Commencement: 1 October 2012.

2–22 (*Outside the scope of this work.*)

[2.1630]

23 Fees for intervention

(1) Subject to regulation 24, if—

(a) a person is contravening or has contravened one or more of the relevant statutory provisions for which the Executive is the enforcing authority; and

(b) an inspector is of the opinion that that person is doing so or has done so, and notifies that person in writing of that opinion,

a fee is payable by that person to the Executive for its performance of the functions described in paragraphs (2) and (3).

(2) The fee referred to in paragraph (1) is payable for the performance by the Executive of any function conferred on it by the relevant statutory provisions, in consequence of any contravention referred to in the opinion notified to that person pursuant to paragraph (1)(b).

(3) Where, during a site-visit, an inspector forms the opinion that a person is contravening or has contravened one or more of the relevant statutory provisions, the fee referred to in paragraph (1) is payable for the performance by the Executive, during that site-visit, of any function conferred on it by the relevant statutory provisions for which no fee is payable by virtue of paragraph (2).

(4) For the purposes of paragraph (6) and (7) and regulations 24 and 25, "fee for intervention" means the fee described in paragraphs (1) to (3).

(5) An inspector of the opinion that a person is contravening or has contravened one or more of the relevant statutory provisions must have regard, when deciding whether to notify that person in writing of that opinion, to the guidance entitled "HSE 47—Guidance on the application of Fee for Intervention" (1st edition) approved by the Executive on 11th June 2012.

(6) A written notification under paragraph (1) must—

(a) specify the provision or provisions to which that inspector's opinion relates;
(b) give particulars of the reasons for that opinion; and
(c) inform the person to whom it is given that fee for intervention is payable to the Executive in accordance with this regulation and regulation 24.

(7) Fee for intervention is payable by a person in respect of the functions described in paragraph (3) only to the extent that the performance of any such function by the Executive is reasonably attributable to that person.

NOTES

Commencement: 1 October 2012.

[2.1631]
24 Provisions supplementary to regulation 23

(1) Fee for intervention is not to exceed the sum of the costs reasonably incurred by the Executive for its performance of the functions referred to in paragraphs (2) and (3) of regulation 23.

(2) Fee for intervention is payable within 30 days from the date of each invoice that the Executive has sent or given to the person who must pay that fee, and such invoices must include a statement of the work done and the costs incurred, including the period to which the statement relates.

(3) No fee for intervention is payable by a person to the extent that an opinion of an inspector that that person is contravening or has contravened one or more of the relevant statutory provisions relates to any contravention which, having regard to the guidance specified in regulation 23(5), should not have been notified in writing to that person.

(4) No fee for intervention is payable in relation to any contravention of the relevant statutory provisions in consequence of which the Executive performed any function prior to the day on which these Regulations come into force.

(5) No fee for intervention is payable for the performance by any inspector not employed by the Executive of any function conferred on it by the relevant statutory provisions.

(6) No fee for intervention payable for or in connection with any contravention of the relevant statutory provisions is to include any costs connected with—
(a) in England and Wales, any criminal investigation or prosecution, incurred (in either case) from the date on which any information is laid or, as the case may be, any written charge is issued;
(b) in Scotland, any criminal investigation or prosecution, incurred (in either case) after such time as the Executive submits a report to the Procurator Fiscal for a decision as to whether a prosecution should be brought;
(c) any appeal pursuant to section 24 of the 1974 Act (appeal against improvement or prohibition notice) and regulation 16(1) and (3)(b) of, and Schedules 1 and 4 to, the Employment Tribunals (Constitution and Rules of Procedure) Regulations 2004; or
(d) any functions performed from the date on which the Executive formally notifies a person that, but for section 48(1) of the 1974 Act, it would have commenced a criminal prosecution against that person in relation to any such contravention.

(7) No fee for intervention is payable by a person in respect of any contravention of the relevant statutory provisions by that person in his or her capacity as an employee.

(8) No fee for intervention is payable by a self-employed person in respect of any contravention by that self-employed person of the relevant statutory provisions which does not and did not expose any other person to a health or safety risk.

(9) Subject to paragraph (10), no fee for intervention is payable for the performance by the Executive of any function conferred on it by the relevant statutory provisions to the extent that, in respect of any such function—
(a) another fee is payable or has been paid; or
(b) expenses are repayable, or have been repaid, pursuant to section 24A of the Nuclear Installations Act 1965.

(10) No fee for intervention is payable for the performance by the Executive of any function conferred on it by the relevant statutory provisions in respect of which fee for intervention is payable or has been paid in consequence of an opinion previously notified in accordance with paragraphs (1), (5) and (6) of regulation 23.

(11) No fee for intervention is payable in respect of any contravention of the relevant statutory provisions which relates to any activity involving genetic modification.

(12) In paragraph (11), "activity involving genetic modification" has the same meaning as in the Genetically Modified Organisms (Contained Use) Regulations 2000.

(13) No fee for intervention is payable in respect of any contravention of the relevant statutory provisions which relates to any of the activities specified in paragraph 3(3) of Part 1 of Schedule 3 to the Control of Substances Hazardous to Health Regulations 2002.

(14) No fee for intervention is payable by a person who holds a licence to undertake work with asbestos in respect of any contravention of the relevant statutory provisions which relates to licensable work with asbestos.

(15) In paragraph (14), "licensable work with asbestos" has the same meaning as in the Control of Asbestos Regulations 2012, and "work with asbestos" is to be construed in accordance with regulation 2(2) of those Regulations.

(16) No fee for intervention is payable for the performance by the Executive of any function conferred on the Executive by—

(a) the Control of Major Accident Hazards Regulations 1999;
(b) the Genetically Modified Organisms (Contained Use) Regulations 2000;
(c) the Biocidal Products Regulations 2001; and
(d) the Chemicals (Hazard Information and Packaging for Supply) Regulations 2009.

NOTES

Commencement: 1 October 2012.

[2.1632]

25 Repayments and disputes

(1) Subject to paragraph (2), if a person is—

(a) charged with, but not convicted of, a criminal offence; or
(b) served with an enforcement notice that is subsequently cancelled,

the Executive must repay such part of any fee for intervention paid as is wholly and exclusively attributable to the performance by the Executive of functions relating only to that criminal offence or, as the case may be, that enforcement notice.

(2) If—

(a) a person is charged with, but not convicted of, more than one criminal offence; or
(b) two or more enforcement notices served on a person are subsequently cancelled,

the Executive must repay such part of any fee for intervention paid as is wholly and exclusively attributable to the performance by the Executive of functions relating only to the criminal offences of which that person is not convicted or, as the case may be, the enforcement notices that are cancelled.

(3) Where all or part of any fee for intervention paid to the Executive was paid in error, the Executive must repay that fee for intervention or, as the case may be, that part of that fee for intervention.

(4) Where a person has been charged with one or more criminal offences or served with one or more enforcement notices, that person is not obliged to pay fee for intervention to the extent that that fee, when paid, would be repayable in accordance with paragraph (1) or (2) because—

(a) that person has not been convicted of one or more of those criminal offences; or
(b) one or more of those enforcement notices has been cancelled.

(5) The Executive must provide a procedure by which disputes relating to fee for intervention will be considered.

(6) If a dispute relating to fee for intervention is not upheld, the fee for intervention payable is to include the time spent by the Executive (including any inspector or other member of staff) in handling the dispute.

(7) In this regulation, "enforcement notice" means an improvement notice or a prohibition notice.

NOTES

Commencement: 1 October 2012.

[2.1633]

26 Review

(1) Before the end of the review period, the Secretary of State must—

(a) carry out a review of these Regulations;
(b) set out the conclusions in a report; and
(c) publish the report.

(2) The report must in particular—

(a) set out the objectives intended to be achieved by the regulatory system established by these Regulations;
(b) assess the extent to which those objectives are achieved; and
(c) assess whether those objectives remain appropriate and, if so, the extent to which they could be achieved with a system that imposes less regulation.

(3) "Review period" means the period of three years beginning with the day on which these Regulations come into force.

NOTES
Commencement: 1 October 2012.

27 (*Revokes the Health and Safety (Fees) Regulations 2010, SI 2010/579.*)

SCHEDULES 1–17

(*Schs 1–17 outside the scope of this work.*)

EMPLOYMENT RIGHTS (INCREASE OF LIMITS) ORDER 2012

(SI 2012/3007)

NOTES
Made: 29 November 2012.
Authority: Employment Relations Act 1999, s 34.
Commencement: 1 February 2013.

[2.1634]
1 Citation, commencement and interpretation

(1) This Order may be cited as the Employment Rights (Increase of Limits) Order 2012 and shall come into force on 1st February 2013.

(2) In this Order—
- (a) "the 1992 Act" means the Trade Union and Labour Relations (Consolidation) Act 1992; and
- (b) "the 1996 Act" means the Employment Rights Act 1996.

NOTES
Commencement: 1 February 2013.

2 (*Revokes the Employment Rights (Increase of Limits) Order 2011, SI 2011/3006.*)

[2.1635]
3 Increase of limits

In the provisions set out in column 1 of the Schedule to this Order (generally described in column 2), for the sums specified in column 3 substitute the sums specified in column 4.

NOTES
Commencement: 1 February 2013.

[2.1636]
4 Transitional provisions

(1) The revocation in article 2 and the substitutions made by article 3 do not have effect in relation to a case where the appropriate date falls before 1st February 2013.

(2) In this article "the appropriate date" means—
- (a) in the case of an application made under section 67(1) of the 1992 Act (compensation for unjustifiable discipline by a trade union), the date of the determination infringing the applicant's right;
- (b) in the case of a complaint presented under section 70C(1) of the 1992 Act (failure by an employer to consult with a trade union on training matters), the date of the failure;
- (c) in the case of a complaint presented under section 137(2) of the 1992 Act (refusal of employment on grounds related to union membership) or section 138(2) of that Act (refusal of service of employment agency on grounds related to union membership), the date of the conduct to which the complaint relates, as determined under section 139 of that Act;
- (d) in the case of an award under section 145E(2)(b) of the 1992 Act (award to worker in respect of offer made by employer in contravention of section 145A or 145B of that Act), the date of the offer;
- (e) in the case of an application for an award of compensation under section 176(2) of the 1992 Act (compensation for exclusion or expulsion from a trade union), the date of the exclusion or expulsion from the union;
- (f) in the case of an award under paragraph 159(1) of Schedule A1 to the 1992 Act, where a worker has suffered a detriment that is the termination of the worker's contract, the date of the termination;

(g) in the case of a guarantee payment to which an employee is entitled under section 28(1) of the 1996 Act (right to guarantee payment in respect of workless day), the day in respect of which the payment is due;

(h) in the case of an award of compensation under section 49(1)(b) of the 1996 Act by virtue of section 24(2) of the National Minimum Wage Act 1998, where a worker has suffered a detriment that is the termination of the worker's contract, the date of the termination;

(i) in the case of an award of compensation under section 63J(1)(b) of the 1996 Act (employer's failure, refusal or part refusal following request in relation to study or training), the date of the failure, refusal or part refusal (as the case may be);

(j) in the case of an award of compensation under section 80I(1)(b) of the 1996 Act (complaint to an employment tribunal relating to an application for contract variation), the date of the failure in relation to the application or of the decision to reject the application;

(k) in the case of an award under section 112(4) or (5) of the 1996 Act (award in relation to unfair dismissal), the effective date of termination as defined by section 97 of that Act;

(l) in the case of an award under section 117(1) or (3) of the 1996 Act, where an employer has failed to comply fully with the terms of an order for reinstatement or re-engagement or has failed to reinstate or re-engage the complainant in accordance with such an order, the date by which the order for reinstatement (specified under section 114(2)(c) of that Act) or, as the case may be, re-engagement (specified under section 115(2)(f) of that Act), should have been complied with;

(m) in the case of entitlement to a redundancy payment by virtue of section 135(1)(a) of the 1996 Act (dismissal by reason of redundancy), the relevant date as defined by section 145 of that Act;

(n) in the case of entitlement to a redundancy payment by virtue of section 135(1)(b) of the 1996 Act (eligibility for a redundancy payment by reason of being laid off or kept on short-time), the relevant date as defined by section 153 of that Act;

(o) in the case of entitlement to a payment under section 182 of the 1996 Act (payments by the Secretary of State), the appropriate date as defined by section 185 of that Act;

(p) in the case of a complaint presented under section 11(1) of the Employment Relations Act 1999 (failure or threatened failure to allow the worker to be accompanied at the disciplinary or grievance hearing, to allow the companion to address the hearing or confer with the worker, or to postpone the hearing), the date of the failure or threat;

(q) in the case of an award made under section 38(2) of the Employment Act 2002 (failure to give statement of employment particulars etc), the date the proceedings to which that section applies were begun;

(r) in the case of an increase in an award in pursuance of section 38(3) of the Employment Act 2002 (failure to give statement of employment particulars etc), the date the proceedings to which that section applies were begun;

(s) in the case of a complaint presented under regulation 15 of the Flexible Working (Procedural Requirements) Regulations 2002 (failure or threatened failure to allow an employee to be accompanied at a meeting, to allow the companion to address the meeting or confer with the employee, or to postpone the meeting), the date of the failure or threat;

(t) in the case of a complaint presented under paragraph 11(1) of Schedule 6 to the Employment Equality (Age) Regulations 2006 (failure of employer to comply with duty to notify employee of date on which he intends employee to retire or of right to make request not to retire on the intended date), the date of the failure; and

(u) in the case of a complaint presented under paragraph 12(1) of Schedule 6 to the Employment Equality (Age) Regulations 2006 (failure or threatened failure to allow an employee to be accompanied at a meeting, to allow the companion to address the meeting or confer with the employee, or to postpone the meeting), the date of the failure or threat.

NOTES

Commencement: 1 February 2013.

SCHEDULE

Article 3

[2.1637]

Column 1 Relevant statutory provision		*Column 2 Subject of provision*	*Column 3 Old limit*	*Column 4 New limit*
1	Section 145E(3) of the 1992 Act	Amount of award for unlawful inducement relating to trade union membership or activities, or for unlawful inducement relating to collective bargaining.	£3,500	£3,600
2	Section 156(1) of the 1992 Act	Minimum amount of basic award of compensation where dismissal is unfair by virtue of section 152(1) or 153 of the 1992 Act.	£5,300	£5,500
3	Section 176(6A) of the 1992 Act	Minimum amount of compensation where individual excluded or expelled from union in contravention of section 174 of the 1992 Act and not admitted or re-admitted by date of tribunal application.	£8,100	£8,400
4	Section 31(1) of the 1996 Act	Limit on amount of guarantee payment payable to an employee in respect of any day.	£23.50	£24.20
5	Section 120(1) of the 1996 Act	Minimum amount of basic award of compensation where dismissal is unfair by virtue of section 100(1)(a) and (b), 101A(d), 102(1) or 103 of the 1996 Act.	£5,300	£5,500
6	Section 124(1) of the 1996 Act	Limit on amount of compensatory award for unfair dismissal.	£72,300	£74,200
7	Paragraphs (a) and (b) of section 186(1) of the 1996 Act	Limit on amount in respect of any one week payable to an employee in respect of a debt to which Part XII of the 1996 Act applies and which is referable to a period of time.	£430	£450
8	Section 227(1) of the 1996 Act	Maximum amount of "a week's pay" for the purpose of calculating a redundancy payment or for various awards including the basic or additional award of compensation for unfair dismissal.	£430	£450

NOTES

Commencement: 1 February 2013.

EQUALITY ACT 2010 (SPECIFIC DUTIES) (SCOTLAND) REGULATIONS 2012

(SSI 2012/162)

NOTES

Made: 23 May 2012.
Authority: Equality Act 2010, ss 153(3), 155(1)(c), (2), 207(4).
Commencement: 27 May 2012.

ARRANGEMENT OF REGULATIONS

[2.1638]
1 Citation and commencement

These Regulations may be cited as the Equality Act 2010 (Specific Duties) (Scotland) Regulations 2012 and come into force on 27th May 2012.

NOTES

Commencement: 27 May 2012.

[2.1639]
2 Interpretation

In these Regulations—

"the Act" means the Equality Act 2010;

"employee" is to be construed in accordance with section 83 of the Act except that it is also to include a constable (including a chief constable) and a police cadet of a police force maintained under section 1 of the Police (Scotland) Act 1967;

"listed authority" means a public authority listed in the Schedule to these Regulations;

"relevant protected characteristic" is to be construed in accordance with section 149(7) of the Act; and

"the equality duty" means the duty of the listed authority to have, in the exercise of its functions, due regard to the needs mentioned in section 149(1) of the Act.

NOTES

Commencement: 27 May 2012.

[2.1640]
3 Duty to report progress on mainstreaming the equality duty

A listed authority must publish a report on the progress it has made to make the equality duty integral to the exercise of its functions so as to better perform that duty—

(a) not later than 30th April 2013; and

(b) subsequently, at intervals of not more than 2 years, beginning with the date on which it last published a report under this regulation.

NOTES

Commencement: 27 May 2012.

[2.1641]
4 Duty to publish equality outcomes and report progress

(1) A listed authority must publish a set of equality outcomes which it considers will enable it to better perform the equality duty—

(a) not later than 30th April 2013; and

(b) subsequently, at intervals of not more than 4 years, beginning with the date on which it last published a set of equality outcomes under this paragraph.

(2) In preparing a set of equality outcomes under paragraph (1), a listed authority must—

(a) take reasonable steps to involve persons who share a relevant protected characteristic and any person who appears to the authority to represent the interests of those persons; and

(b) consider relevant evidence relating to persons who share a relevant protected characteristic.

(3) If a set of equality outcomes published by a listed authority does not seek to further the needs mentioned in section 149(1) of the Act in relation to every relevant protected characteristic, the authority must publish its reasons for proceeding in this way.

(4) A listed authority must publish a report on the progress made to achieve the equality outcomes published by it under paragraph (1)—

(a) not later than 30th April 2015; and

(b) subsequently, at intervals of not more than 2 years, beginning with the date on which it last published a report under this paragraph.

(5) In this regulation, "equality outcome" means a result that the listed authority aims to achieve in order to further one or more of the needs mentioned in section 149(1) of the Act.

NOTES

Commencement: 27 May 2012.

[2.1642]

5 Duty to assess and review policies and practices

(1) A listed authority must, where and to the extent necessary to fulfil the equality duty, assess the impact of applying a proposed new or revised policy or practice against the needs mentioned in section 149(1) of the Act.

(2) In making the assessment, a listed authority must consider relevant evidence relating to persons who share a relevant protected characteristic (including any received from those persons).

(3) A listed authority must, in developing a policy or practice, take account of the results of any assessment made by it under paragraph (1) in respect of that policy or practice.

(4) A listed authority must publish, within a reasonable period, the results of any assessment made by it under paragraph (1) in respect of a policy or practice that it decides to apply.

(5) A listed authority must make such arrangements as it considers appropriate to review and, where necessary, revise any policy or practice that it applies in the exercise of its functions to ensure that, in exercising those functions, it complies with the equality duty.

(6) For the purposes of this regulation, any consideration by a listed authority as to whether or not it is necessary to assess the impact of applying a proposed new or revised policy or practice under paragraph (1) is not to be treated as an assessment of its impact.

NOTES

Commencement: 27 May 2012.

[2.1643]

6 Duty to gather and use employee information

(1) A listed authority must take steps to gather information on—

(a) the composition of the authority's employees (if any); and

(b) the recruitment, development and retention of persons as employees of the authority,

with respect to, in each year, the number and relevant protected characteristics of such persons.

(2) The authority must use this information to better perform the equality duty.

(3) A report published by the listed authority in accordance with regulation 3 must include—

(a) an annual breakdown of information gathered by it in accordance with paragraph (1) which has not been published previously in such a report; and

(b) details of the progress that the authority has made in gathering and using that information to enable it to better perform the equality duty.

NOTES

Commencement: 27 May 2012.

[2.1644]

7 Duty to publish gender pay gap information

(1) A listed authority must publish information on the percentage difference among its employees between men's average hourly pay (excluding overtime) and women's average hourly pay (excluding overtime).

(2) The information is to be published no later than 30th April in—

(a) 2013; and

(b) each second year after that.

(3) The information published must be based on the most recent data available for a date when the authority had at least 150 employees.

(4) No publication is necessary if, throughout the period since these Regulations came into force or since publication was last due, the authority did not have 150 or more employees at any point.

(5) The Scottish Ministers must review from time to time whether the figure of "150" in paragraphs (3) and (4) should be amended.

NOTES

Commencement: 27 May 2012.

[2.1645]

8 Duty to publish statements on equal pay, etc

(1) A listed authority must publish a statement containing the information specified in paragraph (2) no later than 30th April in—

(a) 2013; and
(b) each fourth year after that.

(2) The statement must specify—
(a) the authority's policy on equal pay among its employees between—
(i) men and women;
(ii) persons who are disabled and persons who are not; and
(iii) persons who fall into a minority racial group and persons who do not; and
(b) occupational segregation among its employees, being the concentration of—
(i) men and women;
(ii) persons who are disabled and persons who are not; and
(iii) persons who fall into a minority racial group and persons who do not,

in particular grades and in particular occupations.

(3) The information published must be based on the most recent data available for a date when the authority had at least 150 employees.

(4) No publication is necessary if, throughout the period since these Regulations came into force or since publication was last due, the authority did not have 150 or more employees at any point.

(5) Paragraphs (2)(a)(ii) and (iii) and (2)(b)(ii) and (iii) apply only in relation to the second and subsequent statements published by a listed authority under paragraph (1).

(6) In paragraph (2), "racial group" is to be construed in accordance with section 9 of the Act.

(7) The Scottish Ministers must review from time to time whether the matters specified in paragraph (2) and the figure of "150" in paragraphs (3) and (4) should be amended.

NOTES

Commencement: 27 May 2012.

[2.1646]

9 Duty to consider award criteria and conditions in relation to public procurement

(1) Where a listed authority is a contracting authority and proposes to enter into a relevant agreement on the basis of an offer which is the most economically advantageous, it must have due regard to whether the award criteria should include considerations to enable it to better perform the equality duty.

(2) Where a listed authority is a contracting authority and proposes to stipulate conditions relating to the performance of a relevant agreement, it must have due regard to whether the conditions should include considerations to enable it to better perform the equality duty.

(3) Nothing in this regulation imposes any requirement on a listed authority where in all the circumstances such a requirement would not be related to and proportionate to the subject matter of the proposed agreement.

(4) In this regulation—

"contracting authority", "framework agreement" and "public contract" have the same meaning as in the Public Contracts (Scotland) Regulations 2012; and

"relevant agreement" means a public contract or a framework agreement that is regulated by the Public Contracts (Scotland) Regulations 2012.

NOTES

Commencement: 27 May 2012.

[2.1647]

10 Duty to publish in a manner that is accessible, etc

(1) A listed authority must comply with its duty to publish under regulations 3, 4, 7 and 8 in a manner that makes the information published accessible to the public.

(2) A listed authority must, so far as practicable, comply with its duty to publish under regulations 3, 4, 7 and 8 by employing an existing means of public performance reporting.

NOTES

Commencement: 27 May 2012.

[2.1648]

11 Duty to consider other matters

In carrying out its duties under these Regulations, a listed authority may be required to consider such matters as may be specified from time to time by the Scottish Ministers.

NOTES

Commencement: 27 May 2012.

[2.1649]

12 Duty of the Scottish Ministers to publish proposals to enable better performance

(1) The Scottish Ministers must publish proposals for activity to enable a listed authority to better perform the equality duty—

(a) not later than 31st December 2013; and

(b) subsequently, at intervals of not more than 4 years, beginning with the date on which it last published proposals under this paragraph.

(2) The Scottish Ministers must publish a report on progress in relation to the activity—

(a) not later than 31st December 2015; and

(b) subsequently, at intervals of not more than 4 years, beginning with the date on which it last published a report under this paragraph.

NOTES

Commencement: 27 May 2012.

SCHEDULE
LIST OF PUBLIC AUTHORITIES

Regulation 2

[2.1650]

Scottish Administration

The Scottish Ministers.

Keeper of the Records of Scotland.

Keeper of the Registers of Scotland.

Registrar General of Births, Deaths and Marriages for Scotland.

Scottish Court Service.

National Health Service

A Health Board constituted under section 2 of the National Health Service (Scotland) Act 1978.

A Special Health Board constituted under that section.

Local government

A council constituted under section 2 of the Local Government etc (Scotland) Act 1994.

A joint board within the meaning of section 235(1) of the Local Government (Scotland) Act 1973.

A joint fire and rescue board constituted by a scheme under section 2(1) of the Fire (Scotland) Act 2005.

A licensing board established under section 5 of the Licensing (Scotland) Act 2005, or continued in being by virtue of that section.

A National Park authority established by a designation order made under section 6 of the National Parks (Scotland) Act 2000.

Scottish Enterprise and Highlands and Islands Enterprise, established under the Enterprise and New Towns (Scotland) Act 1990.

Other educational bodies

An education authority in Scotland (within the meaning of section 135(1) of the Education (Scotland) Act 1980).

The managers of a grant-aided school (within the meaning of that section).

The board of management of a college of further education (within the meaning of section 36(1) of the Further and Higher Education (Scotland) Act 1992) which is a fundable body (within the meaning of section 6(2) of the Further and Higher Education (Scotland) Act 2005).

In the case of such a college of further education not under the management of a board of management, the board of governors of the college or any person responsible for the management of the college, whether or not formally constituted as a governing body or board of governors.

The governing body of an institution within the higher education sector (within the meaning of Part 2 of the Further and Higher Education (Scotland) Act 1992) which is a fundable body (within the meaning of section 6(2) of the Further and Higher Education (Scotland) Act 2005).

Police

A police authority established under section 2 of the Police (Scotland) Act 1967.

Other bodies and offices

Accounts Commission for Scotland.

Audit Scotland.

Board of Trustees for the National Galleries of Scotland.

Board of Trustees of the National Museums of Scotland.

Bòrd na Gáidhlig.

A Chief Constable of a police force maintained under section 1 of the Police (Scotland) Act 1967.

A chief officer of a community justice authority.

A Chief Officer of a relevant authority appointed under section 7 of the Fire (Scotland) Act 2005.

Commissioner for Children and Young People in Scotland.

The Common Services Agency for the Scottish Health Service.

A community justice authority.

Creative Scotland.

Healthcare Improvement Scotland.

The Mental Welfare Commission for Scotland.

A regional Transport Partnership created by an order under section 1(1) of the Transport (Scotland) Act 2005.

Scottish Children's Reporter Administration.

The Scottish Criminal Cases Review Commission.

Scottish Environment Protection Agency.

Scottish Further and Higher Education Funding Council

The Scottish Legal Aid Board.

Scottish Natural Heritage.

Scottish Qualifications Authority.

The Scottish Social Services Council.

The Scottish Sports Council.

Scottish Water.

Skills Development Scotland.

Social Care and Social Work Improvement Scotland.

The Trustees of the National Library of Scotland.

VisitScotland.

NOTES

Commencement: 27 May 2012.

OFFERS TO SETTLE IN CIVIL PROCEEDINGS ORDER 2013

(SI 2013/93)

NOTES

Made: 21 January 2013.
Authority: Legal Aid, Sentencing and Punishment of Offenders Act 2012, s 55.
Commencement: 12 February 2013.

[2.1651]

1 Citation and commencement

This Order may be cited as the Offers to Settle in Civil Proceedings Order 2013 and shall come into force on 12th February 2013.

NOTES

Commencement: 12 February 2013.

[2.1652]

2 Additional amount to be paid where a claim is only for an amount of money

Where rules of court make provision for a court to order a defendant in civil proceedings to pay an additional amount to a claimant in those proceedings and the claim is for (and only for) an amount of money then, for the purposes of section 55(3) of the Legal Aid, Sentencing and Punishment of Offenders Act 2012, the prescribed percentage shall be—

Amount awarded by the court	*Prescribed percentage*
Up to £500,000	10% of the amount awarded.
Above £500,000, up to £1,000,000	10% of the first £500,000 and 5% of the amount awarded above that figure.
Above £1,000,000	7.5% of the first £1,000,000 and 0.001% of the amount awarded above that figure.

NOTES

Commencement: 12 February 2013.

[2.1653]

3 Amount to be paid where a claim is or includes a non-monetary claim

(1) Rules of court may make provision for a court to order a defendant in civil proceedings to pay an amount to a claimant ("the amount to be paid") in those proceedings where—

(a) the claim is or includes a non-monetary claim;
(b) judgment is given in favour of the claimant; and
(c) the judgment in respect of the claim is at least as advantageous as an offer to settle the claim which the claimant made in accordance with rules of court and has not withdrawn in accordance with those rules.

(2) The amount to be paid shall be calculated as prescribed in paragraph (4).

(3) Rules made under paragraph (1) may—

(a) include provision as to the assessment of whether a judgment is at least as advantageous as an offer to settle; and
(b) make provision as to the calculation of the value of a non-monetary benefit awarded to a claimant.

(4) Subject to subparagraph (5), the amount to be paid shall be—

(a) if a claim includes both a claim for an amount of money and a non-monetary claim, the following percentages of the amount awarded to the claimant by the court (excluding any amount awarded in respect of the claimant's costs)—

Amount awarded by the court	*Amount to be paid by the defendant*
Up to £500,000	10% of the amount awarded.
Above £500,000, up to £1,000,000	10% of the first £500,000 and 5% of the amount awarded above that figure; and

(b) in a non-monetary claim only, the following percentages of any costs ordered by the court to be paid to the claimant by the defendant—

Costs ordered to be paid to the claimant	*Amount to be paid by the defendant*
Up to £500,000	10% of the costs ordered to be paid.
Above £500,000, up to £1,000,000	10% of the first £500,000 and 5% of any costs ordered to be paid above that figure.

(5) The amount to be paid shall not exceed £75,000.

NOTES

Commencement: 12 February 2013.

TRANSFER OF UNDERTAKINGS (PROTECTION OF EMPLOYMENT) (TRANSFERS OF PUBLIC HEALTH STAFF) REGULATIONS 2013

(SI 2013/278)

NOTES

Made: 10 February 2013.
Authority: Employment Relations Act 1999, s 38.
Commencement: 1 April 2013.

ARRANGEMENT OF REGULATIONS

[2.1654]

1 Citation, commencement and interpretation

(1) These Regulations may be cited as the Transfer of Undertakings (Protection of Employment) (Transfers of Public Health Staff) Regulations 2013 and come into force on 1st April 2013.

(2) In these Regulations—

"the 1996 Act" means the Employment Rights Act 1996;

"relevant transferor" means, in relation to a person to whom these Regulations apply, the transferor which employs that person immediately before the transfer date;

"specialist dental public health consultant services" means the provision of services by a specialist dental public health practitioner which—

(a) are for the purpose of promoting the oral health of the public, and

(b) involve the assessment of dental health needs and the undertaking of activity to ensure that dental services provided as part of the health service meet those needs;

"transfer date" means 1st April 2013;

"transferor" means a body listed in column (1) of the table in the Schedule;

"the TUPE Regulations" means the Transfer of Undertakings (Protection of Employment) Regulations 2006.

NOTES

Commencement: 1 April 2013.

[2.1655]

2 Application of Regulations

These Regulations apply to any person who—

(a) immediately before the transfer date—

(i) is employed by a transferor, and

(ii) assigned to a unit, or engaged in an activity, specified in the entry in column (2) of the table in the Schedule which relates to the transferor; and

(b) has been notified by that transferor before the transfer date that they are to transfer to the employment of the Secretary of State.

NOTES

Commencement: 1 April 2013.

[2.1656]

3 Transfer of employment

(1) Any person to whom these Regulations apply is on the transfer date transferred to the employment of the Secretary of State.

(2) Subject to paragraph (4), the contract of employment of a person whose employment has transferred to the Secretary of State under paragraph (1)—

(a) is not terminated by that transfer; and

(b) has effect from the transfer date as if originally made between that person and the Secretary of State.

(3) Without prejudice to paragraph (2)—

(a) all the rights, powers, duties and liabilities of the relevant transferor under, or in connection with, the contract of employment of any person whose employment transfers to the Secretary of State on the transfer date under paragraph (1), are transferred to the Secretary of State; and

(b) any act or omission before the transfer date by, or in relation to, the relevant transferor, in respect of that person or that person's contract of employment, is deemed to have been an act or omission of, or in relation to, the Secretary of State.

(4) Paragraphs (1) to (3) do not operate to transfer the contract of employment of a person to whom these Regulations apply, or any rights, powers, duties and liabilities under or in connection with that contract, if, before the transfer date, the person informs the relevant transferor or the Secretary of State that they object to becoming employed by the Secretary of State.

(5) Where a person to whom these Regulations apply has objected as described in paragraph (4), the transfer operates so as to terminate that person's contract of employment with the relevant transferor.

(6) Subject to paragraph (7), a person whose contract of employment is terminated in accordance with paragraph (5) is not to be treated, for any purpose, as having been dismissed by the relevant transferor.

(7) Where the transfer involves or would involve a substantial change in working conditions to the material detriment of a person whose employment is or would have transferred under paragraph (1), that person may treat the contract of employment as having been terminated, and that person is to be treated for any purpose as having been dismissed by that person's employer.

(8) No damages are to be payable by the relevant transferor or the Secretary of State as a result of a dismissal falling within paragraph (7) in respect of any failure by the relevant transferor or the Secretary of State to pay wages to a person in respect of a notice period which the person has failed to work.

(9) Paragraphs (1), (2) and (4) to (7) are without prejudice to any right of a person arising apart from this regulation to terminate that person's contract of employment without notice in acceptance of a repudiatory breach of contract by that person's employer.

NOTES

Commencement: 1 April 2013.

[2.1657]

4 Pensions

A person whose contract of employment is transferred by regulation 3 is to be treated as if regulation 10 of the TUPE Regulations (pensions) applied in relation to that transfer, with the modification that for the reference to regulations 4 and 5 of TUPE Regulations there were substituted a reference to regulation 3 of these Regulations.

NOTES

Commencement: 1 April 2013.

[2.1658]

5 Information and consultation

(1) Any transfer effected by regulation 3 is to be treated as a relevant transfer to which regulations 11 to 16 of the TUPE Regulations apply.

(2) Where before the transfer date, a transferor has notified the Secretary of State of employee liability information (within the meaning of the TUPE Regulations) in the form and manner required by regulation 11 of the TUPE Regulations (notification of employee liability information), the transferor shall be treated as having complied with that regulation.

(3) Information provided or consultation undertaken by the transferor or the Secretary of State before the transfer date, if provided or carried out in the form or manner required by regulation 13 of the TUPE Regulations (duty to inform and consult representatives), is to be treated as effective for the purposes of that regulation.

NOTES

Commencement: 1 April 2013.

SCHEDULE
RELEVANT TRANSFERORS AND PUBLIC HEALTH UNITS & ACTIVITIES

Regulations 1(2) and 2

[2.1659]

Column (1) **Transferor**	*Column (2)* **Unit to which employee assigned, or activity in which employee is engaged**
Barts Health National Health Service Trust	London Cancer Screening Programmes Quality Assurance Reference Centre
Birmingham Women's NHS Foundation Trust	(1) West Midlands Public Health Observatory (2) West Midlands Cancer Screening Quality Assurance Reference Centre (3) West Midlands Cancer Intelligence Unit
Bolton Hospitals NHS Foundation Trust	North West Bowel Cancer Screening Quality Assurance Reference Centre
The Christie NHS Foundation Trust	North West Cancer Intelligence Service
County Durham & Darlington NHS Foundation Trust	Specialist dental public health consultant services
Dartford and Gravesham National Health Service Trust	Specialist dental public health consultant services
Durham University	North East Public Health Observatory
East Sussex Healthcare National Health Service Trust	South East Coast Cancer Screening Quality Assurance Reference Centre
Gloucestershire Hospitals NHS Foundation Trust	(1) UK National Screening Programmes - Diabetic Retinopathy Programme (DRP) (2) UK National Screening Programmes - Abdominal Aortic Aneurysm (AAA) (3) UK National Screening Programmes—Ante Natal and New Born (ANNB)
Great Ormond Street Hospital for Children NHS Foundation Trust	UK Newborn Screening Programme Centre (UKNSPC)
Imperial College Healthcare National Health Service Trust	(1) UK National Screening Committee (2) UK National Screening Programmes - Infectious Diseases in Pregnancy
King's College London	(1) Thames Cancer Registry (2) UK National Screening Programmes - NHS Sickle Cell and Thalassaemia Screening Programme (SCT)
The Leeds Teaching Hospitals National Health Service Trust	Northern & Yorkshire Cancer Registry
Liverpool Women's NHS Foundation Trust	North West Cervical Screening Quality Assurance Reference Centre
Liverpool John Moores University	North West Public Health Observatory
The Newcastle upon Tyne Hospitals NHS Foundation Trust	North East Public Health Observatory
North Bristol National Health Service Trust	South West Cervical Screening Quality Assurance Reference Centre
Nottingham University Hospitals National Health Service Trust	East Midlands Breast Screening Quality Assurance Reference Centre

Column (1) **Transferor**	*Column (2)* **Unit to which employee assigned, or activity in which employee is engaged**
Plymouth University Peninsula Schools of Medicines and Dentistry	Specialist dental public health consultant services
Royal Devon and Exeter NHS Foundation Trust	UK National Screening Programmes - NHS Foetal Anomaly Screening Programme (FASP)
Royal Free London NHS Foundation Trust	(1) UK National Screening Programmes - Newborn Infant Physical Examination (NIPE) (2) UK National Screening Programmes - Newborn Hearing Screening (NHSP)
Sheffield Teaching Hospitals NHS Foundation Trust	(1) Trent Cancer Registry (2) East Midlands Bowel and Cervical Screening Quality Assurance Reference Centre
Tees, Esk and Wear Valleys NHS Foundation Trust	North East Public Health Observatory
University Hospital Southampton NHS Foundation Trust	(1) National End of Life Care Intelligence Network (2) South West Public Health Observatory (3) South West Cervical Screening Quality Assurance Reference Centre (4) South West Cancer Intelligence Service
University of Oxford	National Registry of Childhood Tumours (part of Childhood Cancer Research Group

NOTES

Commencement: 1 April 2013.

PARENTAL LEAVE (EU DIRECTIVE) REGULATIONS 2013 (NOTE)

(SI 2013/283)

[2.1660]

NOTES

These Regulations were made on 13 February 2013 under the powers conferred by the European Communities Act 1972, s 2(2) and the Employment Rights Act 1996, s 76(2). The Regulations came into force on 8 March 2013 (see reg 1) and they implement Council Directive 2010/18/EU on the revised framework agreement on parental leave at **[3.625]** et seq.

Reg 2 amends the Employment Rights Act 1996, s 80F at **[1.882]**.

Reg 3 amends the Maternity and Parental Leave etc Regulations 1999, SI 1999/3312 at **[2.484]** et seq.

NATIONAL EMPLOYMENT SAVINGS TRUST (AMENDMENT) ORDER 2013 (NOTE)

(SI 2013/597)

[2.1661]

NOTES

This Order was made on 11 March 2013 under the powers conferred by the Pensions Act 2008, ss 67(1), (8), 68(3), (5), 144(2)–(4) and comes into force on 1 April 2013. It amends the National Employment Savings Trust Order 2010, SI 2010/917 at **[2.1383]** et seq.

DAMAGES-BASED AGREEMENTS REGULATIONS 2013

(SI 2013/609)

NOTES

Made: 13 March 2013.
Authority: Courts and Legal Services Act 1990, ss 58AA(4), (5), 120(3).
Commencement: 1 April 2013.

ARRANGEMENT OF REGULATIONS

[2.1662]

1 Citation, commencement, interpretation and application

(1) These Regulations may be cited as the Damages-Based Agreements Regulations 2013 and come into force on 1st April 2013.

(2) In these Regulations—

"the Act" means the Courts and Legal Services Act 1990;

"claim for personal injuries" has the same meaning as in Rule 2.3 of the Civil Procedure Rules 1998;

"client" means the person who has instructed the representative to provide advocacy services, litigation services (within section 119 of the Act) or claims management services (within the meaning of section 4(2)(b) of the Compensation Act 2006) and is liable to make a payment for those services;

"costs" means the total of the representative's time reasonably spent, in respect of the claim or proceedings, multiplied by the reasonable hourly rate of remuneration of the representative;

"employment matter" means a matter that is, or could become, the subject of proceedings before an employment tribunal;

"expenses" means disbursements incurred by the representative, including the expense of obtaining an expert's report and, in an employment matter only, counsel's fees;

"payment" means that part of the sum recovered in respect of the claim or damages awarded that the client agrees to pay the representative, and excludes expenses but includes, in respect of any claim or proceedings to which these regulations apply other than an employment matter, any disbursements incurred by the representative in respect of counsel's fees;

"representative" means the person providing the advocacy services, litigation services or claims management services to which the damages-based agreement relates.

(3) Subject to paragraphs (4), (5) and (6), these Regulations shall apply to all damages-based agreements entered into on or after the date on which these Regulations come into force.

(4) Subject to paragraph (6), these Regulations shall not apply to any damages-based agreement to which section 57 of the Solicitors Act 1974 (non-contentious business agreements between solicitor and client) applies.

(5) In these Regulations—

(a) regulation 4 does not apply; and

(b) regulations 5, 6, 7 and 8 only apply,

to any damages-based agreement in respect of an employment matter.

(6) Where these Regulations relate to an employment matter, they apply to all damages-based agreements signed on or after the date on which these Regulations come into force.

NOTES

Commencement: 1 April 2013.

[2.1663]

2 Revocation of 2010 Regulations and transitional provision

(1) Subject to paragraph (2), the Damages-Based Agreements Regulations 2010 ("the 2010 Regulations") are revoked.

(2) The 2010 Regulations shall continue to have effect in respect of any damages-based agreement to which those Regulations applied and which was signed before the date on which these Regulations come into force.

NOTES

Commencement: 1 April 2013.

The Damages-Based Agreements Regulations 2010, SI 2010/1206 are reproduced at **[2.1493]**.

[2.1664]

3 Requirements of an agreement in respect of all damages-based agreements

The requirements prescribed for the purposes of section 58AA(4)(c) of the Act are that the terms and conditions of a damages-based agreement must specify—

(a) the claim or proceedings or parts of them to which the agreement relates;

(b) the circumstances in which the representative's payment, expenses and costs, or part of them, are payable; and

(c) the reason for setting the amount of the payment at the level agreed, which, in an employment matter, shall include having regard to, where appropriate, whether the claim or proceedings is one of several similar claims or proceedings.

NOTES

Commencement: 1 April 2013.

4 *((Payment in respect of claims or proceedings other than an employment matter) Outside the scope of this work.)*

[2.1665]

5 Information required to be given before an agreement is made in an employment matter

(1) In an employment matter, the requirements prescribed for the purposes of section 58AA(4)(d) of the Act are to provide—

(a) information to the client in writing about the matters in paragraph (2); and

(b) such further explanation, advice or other information about any of those matters as the client may request.

(2) Those matters are—

(a) the circumstances in which the client may seek a review of costs and expenses of the representative and the procedure for doing so;

(b) the dispute resolution service provided by the Advisory, Conciliation and Arbitration Service (ACAS) in regard to actual and potential claims;

(c) whether other methods of pursuing the claim or financing the proceedings, including—

(i) advice under the Community Legal Service,

(ii) legal expenses insurance,

(iii) pro bono representation, or

(iv) trade union representation,

are available, and, if so, how they apply to the client and the claim or proceedings in question; and

(d) the point at which expenses become payable; and

(e) a reasonable estimate of the amount that is likely to be spent upon expenses, inclusive of VAT.

NOTES

Commencement: 1 April 2013.

[2.1666]

6 Additional causes of action in an employment matter

In an employment matter, any amendment to a damages-based agreement to cover additional causes of action must be in writing and signed by the client and the representative.

NOTES

Commencement: 1 April 2013.

[2.1667]

7 Payment in an employment matter

In an employment matter, a damages-based agreement must not provide for a payment above an amount which, including VAT, is equal to 35% of the sums ultimately recovered by the client in the claim or proceedings.

NOTES

Commencement: 1 April 2013.

[2.1668]

8 Terms and conditions of termination in an employment matter

(1) In an employment matter, the additional requirements prescribed for the purposes of section 58AA(4)(c) of the Act are that the terms and conditions of a damages-based agreement must be in accordance with paragraphs (2), (3) and (4).

(2) If the agreement is terminated, the representatives may not charge the client more than the representative's costs and expenses for the work undertaken in respect of the client's claim or proceedings.

(3) The client may not terminate the agreement—

(a) after settlement has been agreed; or

(b) within seven days before the start of the tribunal hearing.

(4) The representative may not terminate the agreement and charge costs unless the client has behaved or is behaving unreasonably.

(5) Paragraphs (3) and (4) are without prejudice to any right of either party under general law of contract to terminate the agreement.

NOTES

Commencement: 1 April 2013.

AUTOMATIC ENROLMENT (EARNINGS TRIGGER AND QUALIFYING EARNINGS BAND) ORDER 2013

(SI 2013/667)

NOTES

Made: 18 March 2013.
Authority: Pensions Act 2008, ss 14(2), 15A(1), 144(4).
Commencement: 6 April 2013.

[2.1669]

1 Citation, commencement and interpretation

(1) This Order may be cited as the Automatic Enrolment (Earnings Trigger and Qualifying Earnings Band) Order 2013 and comes into force on 6th April 2013.

(2) In this Order "the Act" means the Pensions Act 2008.

NOTES

Commencement: 6 April 2013.

2 (*Amends the Pensions Act 2008, ss 3, 5, 13 at* **[1.1540]**, **[1.1542]**, **[1.1550]**.)

[2.1670]

3 Rounding of figures

For the purposes of sections 3(6B), 5(7B) and 13(2) of the Act, in the case of a pay reference period of a length described in the first row of the table, the rounded figure in respect of the provision of the Act mentioned in the first column of the table is that which appears below the pay reference period which corresponds to that provision.

Table

	1 week	*2 weeks*	*4 weeks*	*1 month*	*3 months*	*6 months*
Sections 3(6B) and 5(7B)	£182	£364	£727	£787	£2,360	£4,720
Section 13(2) (referring to section 13(1)(a))	£109	£218	£436	£473	£1,417	£2,834
Section 13(2) (referring to section 13(1)(b))	£797	£1,594	£3,188	£3,454	£10,363	£20,725

NOTES

Commencement: 6 April 2013.

4 (*Outside the scope of this work.*)

CONDITIONAL FEE AGREEMENTS ORDER 2013

(SI 2013/689)

NOTES

Made: 19 March 2013.
Authority: Courts and Legal Services Act 1990, ss 58(4)(a), (c), 58(4A)(b), (4B)(c), (d), 120(3).
Commencement: 1 April 2013.

ARRANGEMENT OF ARTICLES

[2.1671]

1 Citation, commencement, interpretation and application

(1) This Order may be cited as the Conditional Fee Agreements Order 2013 and will come into force on 1st April 2013.

(2) In this Order—

"the 1986 Act" means the Insolvency Act 1986;

"the 1990 Act" means the Courts and Legal Services Act 1990;

"claim for personal injuries" has the same meaning as in Rule 2.3 of the Civil Procedure Rules 1998;

"company" means a company within the meaning of section 1 of the Companies Act 2006 or a company which may be wound up under Part V of the 1986 Act;

"diffuse mesothelioma" has the same meaning as in section 48(2) of the Legal Aid, Sentencing and Punishment of Offenders Act 2012;

"news publisher" means a person who publishes a newspaper, magazine or website containing news or information about or comment on current affairs;

"publication and privacy proceedings" means proceedings for—

(a) defamation;
(b) malicious falsehood;
(c) breach of confidence involving publication to the general public;
(d) misuse of private information; or
(e) harassment, where the defendant is a news publisher.

"representative" means the person or persons providing the advocacy services or litigation services to which the conditional fee agreement relates.

NOTES

Commencement: 1 April 2013.

[2.1672]

2 Agreements providing for a success fee

All proceedings which, under section 58 of the Act, can be the subject of an enforceable conditional fee agreement, except proceedings under section 82 of the Environmental Protection Act 1990, are proceedings specified for the purpose of section 58(4)(a) of the Act.

NOTES

Commencement: 1 April 2013.

[2.1673]

3 Amount of success fee

In relation to all proceedings specified in article 2, the percentage specified for the purposes of section 58(4)(c) of the Act is 100%.

NOTES

Commencement: 1 April 2013.

[2.1674]

4 Specified proceedings

A claim for personal injuries shall be proceedings specified for the purpose of section 58(4A)(b) of the Act.

NOTES

Commencement: 1 April 2013.

[2.1675]

5 Amount of success fee in specified proceedings

(1) In relation to the proceedings specified in article 4, the percentage prescribed for the purposes of section 58(4B)(c) of the Act is—

(a) in proceedings at first instance, 25%; and

(b) in all other proceedings, 100%.

(2) The descriptions of damages specified for the purposes of section 58(4B)(d) of the Act are—

(a) general damages for pain, suffering, and loss of amenity; and

(b) damages for pecuniary loss, other than future pecuniary loss,

net of any sums recoverable by the Compensation Recovery Unit of the Department for Work and Pensions.

NOTES

Commencement: 1 April 2013.

[2.1676]

6 Transitional and saving provisions

(1) Articles 4 and 5 do not apply to a conditional fee agreement which is entered into before the date upon which this Order comes into force if—

(a) the agreement was entered into specifically for the purposes of the provision to a person ("P") of advocacy or litigation services in connection with the matter which is the subject of the proceedings; or

(b) advocacy or litigation services were provided to P under the agreement in connection with those proceedings before that date.

(2) Articles 4 and 5 do not apply to any conditional fee agreement entered into in relation to—

(a) proceedings relating to a claim for damages in respect of diffuse mesothelioma;

(b) publication and privacy proceedings;

(c) proceedings in England and Wales brought by a person acting in the capacity of—

(i) a liquidator of a company which is being wound up in England and Wales or Scotland under Parts IV or V of the 1986 Act; or

(ii) a trustee of a bankrupt's estate under Part IX of the 1986 Act;

(d) proceedings brought by a person acting in the capacity of an administrator appointed pursuant to the provisions of Part II of the 1986 Act;

(e) proceedings in England and Wales brought by a company which is being wound up in England and Wales or Scotland under Parts IV or V of the 1986 Act; or

(f) proceedings brought by a company which has entered administration under Part II of the 1986 Act.

NOTES

Commencement: 1 April 2013.

7 (*Revokes the Conditional Fee Agreements Order 2000, SI 2000/823.*)

TRADE UNION AND LABOUR RELATIONS (CONSOLIDATION) ACT 1992 (AMENDMENT) ORDER 2013

(SI 2013/763)

NOTES

Made: 27 March 2013.
Authority: Trade Union and Labour Relations (Consolidation) Act 1992, ss 197(1)(a), 286(2).
Commencement: 6 April 2013.

[2.1677]

1 Citation and commencement

This Order may be cited as the Trade Union and Labour Relations (Consolidation) Act 1992 (Amendment) Order 2013 and comes into force on 6th April 2013.

NOTES

Commencement: 6 April 2013.

[2.1678]
2 Application

(1) The amendments made by paragraphs (2) and (3) of article 3 below apply to proposals to dismiss as redundant 100 or more employees at one establishment within a period of 90 days or less which are made on or after 6th April 2013.

(2) The amendment made by paragraph (4) of article 3 below applies to proposals to dismiss as redundant 20 or more employees at one establishment within a period of 90 days or less which are made on or after 6th April 2013.

NOTES

Commencement: 6 April 2013.

3 *(Amends the Trade Union and Labour Relations (Consolidation) Act 1992, ss 188, 193 at* **[1.453]**, **[1.459]** *and substitutes s 282 thereof at* **[1.563]**.

REHABILITATION OF OFFENDERS ACT 1974 (EXCLUSIONS AND EXCEPTIONS) (SCOTLAND) ORDER 2013

(SSI 2013/50)

NOTES

Made: 13 February 2013.

Authority: Rehabilitation of Offenders Act 1974, ss 4(4), 7(4), 10(1).

Commencement: 14 February 2013.

This Order extends to Scotland only and, in so far as it extends beyond Scotland, it does so only as a matter of Scots law (see art 1 at **[2.1679]**). The equivalent English and Welsh Order is at **[2.15]**.

ARRANGEMENT OF ARTICLES

SCHEDULES

[2.1679]
1 Citation, commencement and extent

(1) This Order may be cited as the Rehabilitation of Offenders Act 1974 (Exclusions and Exceptions) (Scotland) Order 2013, and comes into force the day after the day on which it is made.

(2) This Order extends to Scotland and, in so far as it extends beyond Scotland, it does so only as a matter of Scots law.

NOTES

Commencement: 14 February 2013.

[2.1680]
2 Interpretation

(1) In this Order—

"the 2000 Act" means the Financial Services and Markets Act 2000;

"the 2001 Act" means the Regulation of Care (Scotland) Act 2001;

"the 2007 Act" means the Protection of Vulnerable Groups (Scotland) Act 2007;

"the 2010 Act" means the Public Services Reform (Scotland) Act 2010;

"the Act" means the Rehabilitation of Offenders Act 1974;

"actuary" means a member of the Institute and Faculty of Actuaries;

"accountant" means a member of—

(a) the Association of Chartered Certified Accountants;

(b) the Institute of Chartered Accountants of Scotland;

(c) the Institute of Chartered Accountants in England and Wales;
(d) the Chartered Institute of Public Finance and Accountancy; or
(e) the Chartered Institute of Management Accountants;

"adopt" includes any arrangements to adopt a child, including arrangements for adoption where the proposed adopter is a relative of the child, whether under the Adoption and Children (Scotland) Act 2007 or the Adoptions with a Foreign Element (Scotland) Regulations 2009;

"approved regulator" has the meaning given in Part 2 of the Legal Services (Scotland) Act 2010;

"associate", in relation to a person ("A"), means someone who is a controller, director or a manager of A or, where A is a partnership, any partner of A;

"authorised electronic money institution" has the meaning given by regulation 2(1) of the Electronic Money Regulations 2011;

"authorised payment institution" has the meaning given by regulation 2(1) of the Payment Services Regulations 2009;

"care service" has the meaning given in section 47 of the 2010 Act;

"collective investment scheme" has the meaning given in section 235 of the 2000 Act;

"the competent authority for listing" means the competent authority for the purposes of Part VI of the 2000 Act (official listing);

"contracting authority" means a contracting authority within the meaning of Article 1(9) of Directive 2004/18/EC;

"contracting entity" means a contracting entity within the meaning of Article 2(2) of Directive 2004/17/EC;

"controller" has the meaning given in section 422 of the 2000 Act;

"Council of Lloyd's" means the council constituted by section 3 of the Lloyd's Act 1982;

"Directive 2004/17/EC" means Directive 2004/17/EC of the European Parliament and of the Council of 31st March 2004;

"Directive 2004/18/EC" means Directive 2004/18/EC of the European Parliament and of the Council of 31st March 2004;

"director" has the meaning given in section 417 of the 2000 Act;

"electronic money institution" has the meaning given in regulation 2(1) of the Electronic Money Regulations 2011;

"enactment" includes an Act of the Scottish Parliament and any order, regulation or other instrument having effect by virtue of such an Act;

"firearms dealer" has the meaning given in section 57(4) of the Firearms Act 1968;

"Head of Practice" has the meaning given in Part 2 of the Legal Services Act;

"health services" means services provided under the National Health Service (Scotland) Act 1978 and similar services provided otherwise than under the National Health Service;

"Her Majesty's Inspectors" has the meaning given in section 135 of the Education (Scotland) Act 1980;

"judicial appointment" means an appointment to any office by virtue of which the holder has power (whether alone or with others) under any enactment or rule of law to determine any question affecting the rights, privileges, obligations or liabilities of any person;

"key worker", in relation to any body ("A"), means any individual who is likely, in the course of the duties of that individual's office or employment—

(a) where A is the Financial Services Authority, to play a significant role in the decision making process of the Authority in relation to the exercise of the Authority's public functions (within the meaning of section 349(5) of the 2000 Act) under any provision of the 2000 Act other than Part VI, or to support directly such a person;
(b) where A is the competent authority for listing, to play a significant role in the decision making process of the competent authority for listing in relation to the exercise of its functions under Part VI of the 2000 Act, or to support directly such a person;

"lay representative", for the purposes of sheriff court proceedings, has the meaning given in section 32A(3) of the Sheriff Courts (Scotland) Act 1971 and, for the purposes of Court of Session proceedings, has the meaning given in section 5A(3) of the Court of Session Act 1988;

"the Legal Services Act" means the Legal Services (Scotland) Act 2010;

"licensed legal services provider" has the meaning given in Part 2 of the Legal Services Act;

"manager" has the meaning given in section 423 of the 2000 Act;

"non-solicitor investor" has the meaning given in Part 2 of the Legal Services Act;

"open-ended investment company" has the meaning given in section 236 of the 2000 Act;

"Part IV permission" has the meaning given in section 40(4) of the 2000 Act;

"payment services" has the meaning given in regulation 2(1) of the Payment Services Regulations 2009;

"personal information" means any information (in any form) which relates to a living individual who can be identified from that data, which is of a confidential nature and is not in the public domain;

"Practice Committee" has the meaning given in Part 2 of the Legal Services Act;

"private hire driver" means a driver of a private hire car, as defined by section 23(1) of the Civic Government (Scotland) Act 1982, who is required to be licensed by a licensing authority under the provisions of that Act;

"prosecutor" has the meaning given in section 307 of the Criminal Procedure (Scotland) Act 1995;

"registered chiropractor" has the meaning given in section 43 of the Chiropractors Act 1994;

"registered European lawyer" has the meaning given in section 65 of the Solicitors (Scotland) Act 1980;

"registered foreign lawyer" has the meaning given in section 65 of the Solicitors (Scotland) Act 1980;

"registered osteopath" has the meaning given in section 41 of the Osteopaths Act 1993;

"registered pharmacist" means a person who is registered as a pharmacist in Part 1 or 4 of the register maintained under article 19 of the Pharmacy Order 2010;

"registered pharmacy technician" means a person who is registered in Part 2 or 5 of the register maintained under article 19 of the Pharmacy Order 2010;

"registered teacher" means a teacher registered under the Public Services Reform (General Teaching Council for Scotland) Order 2011;

"regulated work with adults" has the meaning given in section 91(3) of the 2007 Act;

"regulated work with children" has the meaning given in section 91(2) of the 2007 Act;

"relevant collective investment scheme" means a collective investment scheme which is recognised under section 264 (schemes constituted in other EEA States), 270 (schemes authorised in designated countries or territories) or 272 (individually recognised overseas schemes) of the 2000 Act;

"Scottish Social Services Council" has the meaning given in section 43 of the 2001 Act;

"small electronic money institution" has the meaning given in regulation 2(1) of the Electronic Money Regulations 2011;

"small payment institution" has the meaning given in regulation 2(1) of the Payment Services Regulations 2009;

"Social Care and Social Work Improvement Scotland" has the meaning given in section 44 of the 2010 Act;

"social service worker" has the meaning given in section 77 of the 2001 Act;

"social worker" has the meaning given in section 77 of the 2001 Act;

"taxi driver" means a driver of a taxi as defined by section 23(1) of the Civic Government (Scotland) Act 1982, who is required to be licensed by a licensing authority under the provisions of that Act;

"trustee", in relation to a unit trust scheme, has the meaning given in section 237(2) of the 2000 Act;

"UK recognised clearing house" means a clearing house in relation to which a recognition order under section 290 of the 2000 Act, otherwise than by virtue of section 292(2) (overseas clearing houses) of that Act, is in force;

"UK recognised investment exchange" means an investment exchange in relation to which a recognition order under section 290 of the 2000 Act, otherwise than by virtue of section 292(2) (overseas investment exchanges) of that Act, is in force;

"work" includes work of any kind, whether paid or unpaid and whether under a contract of service or apprenticeship, under a contract for services, or otherwise than under a contract.

(2) Any reference in this Order to a numbered article or Schedule is, unless the context otherwise requires, a reference to the article or Schedule so numbered in this Order.

NOTES

Commencement: 14 February 2013.

[2.1681]

3 Exclusion of section 4(1) of the Act

The application of section 4(1) of the Act is excluded in relation to—

- (a) any proceedings specified in Schedule 1; and
- (b) any proceedings with respect to a decision or a proposed decision specified in Part 1 of Schedule 2—
  - (i) to the extent that there falls to be determined in those proceedings any issue relating to a spent conviction or to circumstances ancillary thereto; and
  - (ii) to the extent that section 4(1) renders inadmissible any evidence relating to the conviction or circumstances or removes the requirement to answer any question relating to the conviction or circumstances.

NOTES

Commencement: 14 February 2013.

[2.1682]
4 Exclusion of section 4(2)(a) and (b) of the Act

The application of section 4(2)(a) and (b) of the Act is excluded in relation to questions put in the circumstances to which Schedule 3 applies.

NOTES
Commencement: 14 February 2013.

[2.1683]
5 Exceptions from section 4(3) of the Act

There is excepted from the provisions of section 4(3)(b) of the Act—
- (a) any profession, office, employment or occupation specified in Schedule 4;
- (b) any action taken for the purpose of safeguarding national security; and
- (c) any decision or proposed decision taken by a person specified in Part 1 of Schedule 2 to do or to refuse to do anything specified in that Part.

NOTES
Commencement: 14 February 2013.

6 (*Outside the scope of this work.*)

SCHEDULE 1
PROCEEDINGS

Article 3(a)

[2.1684]
1. Proceedings in respect of a person's admission to, or disciplinary proceedings against a member of, any profession specified in Part 1 of Schedule 4 to this Order.

2. Disciplinary proceedings against a constable.

3–10. . . .

11. Proceedings by way of appeal against, or review of, any decision taken, by virtue of any of the provisions of this Order, on consideration of a spent conviction.

12. Proceedings held for the receipt of evidence affecting the determination of any question arising in any proceedings specified in this Schedule.

13–28. . . .

NOTES
Commencement: 14 February 2013.
Paras 3–10, 13–28: outside the scope of this work.

SCHEDULE 2

(*Sch 2 (Financial Services) outside the scope of this work.*)

SCHEDULE 3
EXCLUSIONS OF SECTION 4(2)(A) AND (B) OF THE ACT

Article 4

[2.1685]
1 Application

Subject to paragraph 2, this Schedule applies, for the purposes of article 4, to the circumstances set out in paragraphs 3 to 15.

2 Requirements to inform

(1) This Schedule applies only where the person questioned is informed at the time the question is asked that, by virtue of this Order, spent convictions are to be disclosed.

(2) In the case of questions put in the circumstances to which paragraph 6 applies, the person questioned is also to be informed at that time that spent convictions are to be disclosed in the interests of national security.

3 Specified professions etc

(1) Any question asked in order to assess the suitability—
- (a) of the person to whom the question relates for a profession specified in Part 1 of Schedule 4;

(b) of the person to whom the question relates for any office or employment specified in Part 2 of Schedule 4;

(c) of the person to whom the question relates or of any other person to pursue any occupation specified in Part 3 of Schedule 4 or to pursue it subject to a particular condition or restriction; and

(d) of the person to whom the question relates or of any other person to be placed on a register or to hold a licence, certificate or permit specified in sub-paragraph (3) or to be placed on it or hold it subject to a particular condition or restriction.

(2) For the avoidance of doubt, references in sub-paragraph (1) to the suitability of a person for any profession or for any office, employment or occupation include the suitability of that person for training for such profession or, as the case may be, for training for such office, employment or occupation.

(3) The register, licences, certificates or permits referred to in sub-paragraph (1)(d) are—

(a) firearm certificates and shot gun certificates issued under the Firearms Act 1968, and permits issued under section 7(1), 9(2) or 13(1)(c) of that Act;

(b) licences issued under section 25 (restrictions on persons under eighteen going abroad for the purpose of performing for profit) of the Children and Young Persons Act 1933;

(c) explosives certificates issued by a chief officer of police pursuant to regulation 4 of the Control of Explosives Regulations 1991 as to the fitness of a person to acquire or acquire and keep explosives;

(d) licences granted under section 8 of the Private Security Industry Act 2001; or

(e) licences issued under, and the register of approved instructors referred to in, Part V (driving instruction) of the Road Traffic Act 1988.

4, 5 . . .

6 National Security

(1) Any question asked by or on behalf of—

(a) the Crown, the United Kingdom Atomic Energy Authority, the Financial Services Authority or a universal service provider within the meaning of section 65 of the Postal Services Act 2011, in order to assess, for the purpose of safeguarding national security, the suitability of the person to whom the question relates or of any other person for any office or employment;

(b) the Civil Aviation Authority;

(c) any other person authorised to provide air traffic services under section 4 or 5 of the Transport Act 2000 (in any case where such person is a company, an "authorised company"); or

(d) subject to sub-paragraph (3)—

(i) any company which is a subsidiary, within the meaning given by section 1159(1) of the Companies Act 2006, of an authorised company; and

(ii) any company of which an authorised company is a subsidiary,

in the circumstances set out in sub-paragraph (2).

(2) The circumstances are that the question is put in order to assess, for the purpose of safeguarding national security, the suitability of the person to whom the question relates or of any other person for any office or employment.

(3) Where the question is put on behalf of a company mentioned in sub-paragraph (1)(d), this paragraph applies only where the question is put in relation to the provision of air traffic services.

7–15 . . .

NOTES

Commencement: 14 February 2013.

Paras 4, 5, 7–15: outside the scope of this work.

SCHEDULE 4
EXCEPTED PROFESSIONS, OFFICES, EMPLOYMENTS AND OCCUPATIONS

Article 5(a)

PART 1
PROFESSIONS

[2.1686]

1. Medical practitioner.

2. Advocate, solicitor.

3. Accountant.

4. Dentist or any profession complementary to dentistry for which a title is specified in regulations under section 36A(2) of the Dentists Act 1984 (professions complementary to dentistry) by virtue of section 36A(3) of that Act.

5. Veterinary surgeon.

6. Nurse or midwife.

7. Ophthalmic optician, dispensing optician.

8. Registered pharmacist.

9. Registered pharmacy technician.

10. Registered teacher.

11. Any profession to which the Health Professions Order 2001 applies and which is undertaken following registration under that Order.

12. Registered osteopath.

13. Registered chiropractor.

14. Actuary.

15. Registered European lawyer, registered foreign lawyer.

16. Social worker.

17. Social service worker.

NOTES

Commencement: 14 February 2013.

PART 2
OFFICES AND EMPLOYMENTS

[2.1687]

1. Judicial appointments.

2. Prosecutors, officers assisting prosecutors, and officers assisting in the work of the Crown Office.

3. Justices of the Peace and members of local authorities with signing functions under section 76 of the Criminal Proceedings etc (Reform) (Scotland) Act 2007.

4. Clerks (including depute and assistant clerks) and officers of the High Court of Justiciary, the Court of Session and the justice of the peace court, sheriff clerks (including sheriff clerks depute) and their clerks and assistants and other support officers assisting in the work of the Scottish Court Service.

5. Precognition agents.

6. Constables, police custody and security officers, persons appointed as police cadets to undergo training with a view to becoming constables, persons employed for the purposes of a police force established under any enactment, persons appointed to assist in the carrying out of police functions and naval, military and air force police.

7. Any office, employment or work which is concerned with the administration of, or is otherwise normally carried out wholly or partly within the precincts of a prison, remand centre, young offenders institution, detention centre or removal centre, and members of visiting committees for prisons appointed under rules made under section 39 of the Prisons (Scotland) Act 1989 and members of visiting committees for remand centres and young offenders institutions appointed under section 19(3) of that Act.

8. Traffic wardens appointed under or in accordance with section 95 of the Road Traffic Regulation Act 1984.

9. Any employment or work which is concerned with the provision of a care service.

10. Any employment or work which is concerned with the provision of health services and which is of such a kind as to enable the holder to have access to persons in receipt of such services in the course of that person's normal duties.

11. Any regulated work with children.

12. Any employment or work in the Scottish Society for the Prevention of Cruelty to Animals where the person employed or working, as part of his or her duties, may carry out the killing of animals.

13. Any office, employment or work in the Serious Fraud Office.

14. Any office, employment or work in the Serious Organised Crime Agency.

15. Any office, employment or work in Her Majesty's Revenue and Customs.

16. Any employment which is concerned with the monitoring, for the purposes of child protection, of communications by means of the internet.

17. Any office or employment in the Scottish Social Services Council.

18. Her Majesty's Inspectors, or any person appointed by the Scottish Ministers for the purposes of section 66 of the Education (Scotland) Act 1980 or section 9 of the Standards in Scotland's Schools etc Act 2000, or members of any Management Board established to assist either Her Majesty's Inspectors or any such person, or any individual undertaking employment or work for Her Majesty's Inspectors or any such person in relation to the carrying out of inspections under section 66 of the Education (Scotland) Act 1980, section 9 of the Standards in Scotland's Schools etc Act 2000 or section 115 of the 2010 Act, or otherwise in regard to matters associated with such inspections.

19. The Principal Reporter or officers appointed under section 128(5) of the Local Government etc (Scotland) Act 1994 to assist that officer.

20. Members of a panel established by virtue of section 101(1) of the Children (Scotland) Act 1995 (panels for curators *ad litem*, reporting officers and safeguarders).

21. Any office or employment in the Risk Management Authority.

22. Any office or employment in the Scottish Criminal Cases Review Commission.

23. Any office or employment in a relevant authority as defined in section 6 of the Fire (Scotland) Act 2005.

24. Any employment or work in a body concerned primarily with the provision of counselling or other support to individuals who are or appear to be victims of, or witnesses to, offences, and which involves having access to personal information about such individuals.

25. Any regulated work with adults.

26. Members mentioned in section 35(4)(c) of the Judiciary and Courts (Scotland) Act 2008 of a tribunal constituted under section 35(1) of that Act to consider the fitness for judicial office of a person holding a judicial office mentioned in section 35(2) of that Act.

27. Members mentioned in section 12A(4)(d) of the Sheriff Courts (Scotland) Act 1971 of a tribunal constituted under section 12A(1) of that Act to consider the fitness for shrieval office of a person holding a shrieval office mentioned in section 12A(2) of that Act.

28. Lay members of the Judicial Appointments Board for Scotland appointed by the Scottish Ministers under paragraph 2 of schedule 1 to the Judiciary and Courts (Scotland) Act 2008.

29. Non-judicial members of the Scottish Court Service mentioned in paragraph 2(3)(d) of schedule 3 to the Judiciary and Courts (Scotland) Act 2008.

30. Any office or employment in Social Care and Social Work Improvement Scotland.

31. Any office or employment in the General Teaching Council for Scotland.

32. A Head of Practice or a member of a Practice Committee of a licensed legal services provider.

NOTES

Commencement: 14 February 2013.

PART 3
OCCUPATIONS

[2.1688]

1. Firearms dealer.

2. Any occupation in respect of which an application to the Gambling Commission for a licence, certificate or registration is required by or under any enactment.

3. Any occupation which is concerned with the management of a place in respect of which the approval of the Scottish Ministers is required by section 1 of the Abortion Act 1967.

4. Any occupation in respect of which the holder is required pursuant to regulation 4 of the Control of Explosives Regulations 1991 to obtain from the chief officer of police an explosives certificate certifying that person to be a fit person to acquire or acquire and keep explosives.

5. Taxi driver or private hire driver.

6. Any occupation in respect of which an application to the Security Industry Authority for a licence is required by the Private Security Industry Act 2001.

7. Any occupation which is concerned with visiting persons detained in police stations, for the purposes of examining and reporting on the conditions under which they are held.

8. Any occupation in respect of which a licence or registration is required by or under Part V (driving instruction) of the Road Traffic Act 1988.

NOTES

Commencement: 14 February 2013.

SCHEDULE 5

(Sch 5 (Revocations) outside the scope of this work.)

EMPLOYMENT TRIBUNALS (CONSTITUTION AND RULES OF PROCEDURE) REGULATIONS 2013

(SI 2013/1237)

NOTES

Made: 28 May 2013.

Authority: Health and Safety at Work etc Act 1974, s 24(2); Employment Tribunals Act 1996, ss 1(1), 4(6), (6A), 7(1), (3), (3ZA), (3A), (3AA), (3AB), (3B), (3C), (5), 7A(1), (2), 7B(1), (2), 9(1), (2), 10(2), (5)–(7), 10A(1), 11(1), 12(2), 13, 13A, 19, 41(4); Scotland Act 1998, Sch 6, para 37; Government of Wales Act 2006, Sch 9, para 32.

Commencement: 1 July 2013 (regs 1, 3 11) and 29 July 2013 (remainder); see reg 1(2) below.

Note: these Regulations were published as this Edition was going to press. They are reproduced in full below but it has not been possible to include entries for the Regulations in the Index. For transitional provisions see reg 15 at **[2.1703]**.

[2.1689]

1 Citation and commencement

(1) These Regulations may be cited as the Employment Tribunals (Constitution and Rules of Procedure) Regulations 2013 and the Rules of Procedure contained in Schedules 1, 2 and 3 may be referred to, respectively, as—

(a) the Employment Tribunals Rules of Procedure 2013;
(b) the Employment Tribunals (National Security) Rules of Procedure 2013; and
(c) the Employment Tribunals (Equal Value) Rules of Procedure 2013.

(2) This regulation and regulations 3 and 11 come into force on 1st July 2013 and the remainder of these Regulations (including the Schedules) come into force on 29th July 2013.

NOTES

Commencement: 1 July 2013.

[2.1690]
2 Revocation

Subject to the savings in regulation 15 the Employment Tribunals (Constitution and Rules of Procedure) Regulations 2004 are revoked.

NOTES

Commencement: 29 July 2013.

[2.1691]
3 Interpretation

Except in the Schedules which are subject to the definitions contained in the Schedules, in these Regulations—

"2004 Regulations" means the Employment Tribunals (Constitution and Rules of Procedure) Regulations 2004;

"appointing office holder" means, in England and Wales, the Lord Chancellor, and in Scotland, the Lord President;

"Employment Tribunals Act" means the Employment Tribunals Act 1996;

"Lord President" means the Lord President of the Court of Session;

"national security proceedings" means proceedings in relation to which a direction is given, or an order is made, under rule 94 of Schedule 1;

"President" means either of the two presidents appointed from time to time in accordance with regulation 5(1);

"Regional Employment Judge" means a person appointed or nominated in accordance with regulation 6(1) or (2);

"Senior President of Tribunals" means the person appointed in accordance with section 2 of the Tribunals, Courts and Enforcement Act 2007;

"Tribunal" means an employment tribunal established in accordance with regulation 4 and, in relation to any proceedings, means the Tribunal responsible for the proceedings in question, whether performing administrative or judicial functions;

"Vice President" means a person appointed or nominated in accordance with regulation 6(3) or (4).

NOTES

Commencement: 1 July 2013.

[2.1692]
4 Establishment of employment tribunals

There are to be tribunals known as employment tribunals.

NOTES

Commencement: 29 July 2013.

[2.1693]
5 President of Employment Tribunals

(1) There shall be a President of Employment Tribunals, responsible for Tribunals in England and Wales, and a President of Employment Tribunals, responsible for Tribunals in Scotland, appointed by the appointing office holder.

(2) A President shall be—

(a) a person who satisfies the judicial-appointment eligibility condition within the meaning of section 50 of the Tribunals, Courts and Enforcement Act 2007 on a 5-year basis;

(b) an advocate or solicitor admitted in Scotland of at least five years standing; or

(c) a member of the Bar of Northern Ireland or solicitor of the Supreme Court of Northern Ireland of at least five years standing.

(3) A President may at any time resign from office by giving the appointing officer holder notice in writing to that effect.

(4) The appointing officer holder may remove a President from office on the ground of inability or misbehaviour, or if the President is adjudged to be bankrupt or makes a composition or arrangement with his creditors.

(5) Where a President is unable to carry out the functions set out in these Regulations, those functions may be discharged by a person nominated by the appointing office holder (save that any nomination in relation to England and Wales shall be made by the Lord Chief Justice following consultation with the Senior President of Tribunals, rather than by the Lord Chancellor).

(6) The Lord Chief Justice may nominate a judicial office holder (as defined in section 109(4) of the Constitutional Reform Act 2005) to exercise his functions under this regulation.

NOTES

Commencement: 29 July 2013.

[2.1694]

6 Regional Employment Judges and the Vice President

(1) The Lord Chancellor may appoint Regional Employment Judges.

(2) The President (England and Wales) or the Regional Employment Judge for an area may nominate an Employment Judge to discharge the functions of the Regional Employment Judge for that area.

(3) The Lord President may appoint a Vice President.

(4) The President (Scotland) or the Vice President may nominate an Employment Judge to discharge the functions of the Vice President.

(5) Appointments and nominations under this regulation shall be from the full-time Employment Judges on the panel referred to in regulation 8(2)(a).

NOTES

Commencement: 29 July 2013.

[2.1695]

7 Responsibilities of the Presidents, Regional Employment Judges and Vice President

(1) The President shall, in relation to the area for which the President is responsible, use the resources available to—

(a) secure, so far as practicable, the speedy and efficient disposal of proceedings;
(b) determine the allocation of proceedings between Tribunals; and
(c) determine where and when Tribunals shall sit.

(2) The President (England and Wales) may direct Regional Employment Judges, and the President (Scotland) may direct the Vice President, to take action in relation to the fulfilment of the responsibilities in paragraph (1) and the Regional Employment Judges and Vice President shall follow such directions.

NOTES

Commencement: 29 July 2013.

[2.1696]

8 Panels of members for tribunals

(1) There shall be three panels of members for the Employment Tribunals (England and Wales) and three panels of members for the Employment Tribunals (Scotland).

(2) The panels of members shall be—

(a) a panel of chairmen who satisfy the criteria set out in regulation 5(2) and are appointed by the appointing office holder (in these Regulations (including the Schedules) referred to as "Employment Judges");
(b) a panel of persons appointed by the Lord Chancellor after consultation with organisations or associations representative of employees; and
(c) a panel of persons appointed by the Lord Chancellor after consultation with organisations or associations representative of employers.

(3) Members of the panels shall hold and vacate office in accordance with the terms of their appointment, but may resign from office by written notice to the person who appointed them under paragraph (2), and any member who ceases to hold office shall be eligible for reappointment.

(4) The President may establish further specialist panels of members referred to in paragraph (2) and may select persons from those panels to deal with proceedings in which particular specialist knowledge would be beneficial.

NOTES

Commencement: 29 July 2013.

[2.1697]

9 Composition of tribunals

(1) Where proceedings are to be determined by a Tribunal comprising an Employment Judge and two other members, the President, Vice President or a Regional Employment Judge shall select—

(a) an Employment Judge; and
(b) one member from each of the panels referred to in regulation 8(2)(b) and (c),

and for all other proceedings shall select an Employment Judge.

(2) The President, Vice President or a Regional Employment Judge may select him or herself as the Employment Judge required under paragraph (1).

(3) The President, Vice President or a Regional Employment Judge may select from the appropriate panel a substitute for a member previously selected to hear any proceedings.

(4) This regulation does not apply in relation to national security proceedings (see regulation 10(2)).

NOTES

Commencement: 29 July 2013.

[2.1698]

10 National security proceedings—panel of members and composition of tribunals

(1) The President shall select—

(a) a panel of persons from the panel referred to in regulation 8(2)(a);
(b) a panel of persons from the panel referred to in regulation 8(2)(b); and
(c) a panel of persons from the panel referred to in regulation 8(2)(c),

who may act in national security proceedings.

(2) Where proceedings become national security proceedings, the President, Vice President or a Regional Employment Judge shall—

(a) select an Employment Judge from the panel referred to in paragraph (1)(a) and may select him or herself; and
(b) where the proceedings are to be determined by a Tribunal comprising an Employment Judge and two other members, select in addition one member from each of the panels referred to in sub-paragraphs (b) and (c) of paragraph (1).

NOTES

Commencement: 29 July 2013.

[2.1699]

11 Practice directions

(1) The President may make, vary or revoke practice directions about the procedure of the Tribunals in the area for which the President is responsible, including—

(a) practice directions about the exercise by Tribunals of powers under these Regulations (including the Schedules); and
(b) practice directions about the provision by Employment Judges of mediation, in relation to disputed matters in a case that is the subject of proceedings, and may permit an Employment Judge to act as mediator in a case even though they have been selected to decide matters in that case.

(2) Practice directions may make different provision for different cases, different areas, or different types of proceedings.

(3) Any practice direction made, varied or revoked shall be published by the President in an appropriate manner to bring it to the attention of the persons to whom it is addressed.

NOTES

Commencement: 1 July 2013.

[2.1700]

12 Power to prescribe

(1) The Secretary of State may prescribe—

(a) one or more versions of a form which shall be used by claimants to start proceedings in a Tribunal;
(b) one or more versions of a form which shall be used by respondents to respond to a claim before a Tribunal; and
(c) that the provision of certain information on the prescribed forms is mandatory.

(2) It is not necessary to use a form prescribed under paragraph (1) if the proceedings are—

(a) referred to a Tribunal by a court;
(b) proceedings in which a Tribunal will be exercising its appellate jurisdiction; or
(c) proceedings brought by an employer under section 11 of the Employment Rights Act 1996.

(3) The Secretary of State shall publish the prescribed forms in an appropriate manner to bring them to the attention of prospective claimants, respondents and their advisers.

NOTES

Commencement: 29 July 2013.

[2.1701]

13 Application of Schedules 1 to 3

(1) Subject to paragraph (2), Schedule 1 applies to all proceedings before a Tribunal except where separate rules of procedure made under the provisions of any enactment are applicable.

(2) Schedules 2 and 3 apply to modify the rules in Schedule 1 in relation, respectively, to proceedings which are—

(a) national security proceedings; or

(b) proceedings which involve an equal value claim (as defined in rule 1 of Schedule 3).

NOTES

Commencement: 29 July 2013.

[2.1702]

14 Register and proof of judgments

(1) The Lord Chancellor shall maintain a register containing a copy of all judgments and written reasons issued by a Tribunal which are required to be entered in the register under Schedules 1 to 3.

(2) The Lord Chancellor shall delete any entry in the register six years from the date of judgment.

(3) A document purporting to be certified by a member of staff of a Tribunal to be a true copy of an entry of a judgment in the register shall, unless the contrary is proved, be sufficient evidence of the document and its contents.

NOTES

Commencement: 29 July 2013.

[2.1703]

15 Transitional provisions

(1) Subject to paragraphs (2) and (3), these Regulations and the Rules of Procedure contained in Schedules 1 to 3 apply in relation to all proceedings to which they relate.

(2) Where a respondent receives from a Tribunal a copy of the claim form before 29th July 2013, rules 23 to 25 of Schedule 1 do not apply to the proceedings and rule 7 of Schedule 1 to the 2004 Regulations continues to apply.

(3) Where in accordance with Schedules 3 to 5 of the 2004 Regulations, a notice of appeal was presented to a Tribunal before 29th July 2013, Schedule 1 does not apply to the proceedings and Schedule 3, 4 or 5, as appropriate, of the 2004 Regulations continues to apply.

NOTES

Commencement: 29 July 2013.

SCHEDULE 1
THE EMPLOYMENT TRIBUNALS RULES OF PROCEDURE

Regulation 13(1)

INTRODUCTORY AND GENERAL

[2.1704]

Interpretation

1 (1) In these Rules—

"ACAS" means the Advisory, Conciliation and Arbitration Service referred to in section 247 of the Trade Union and Labour Relations (Consolidation) Act 1992;

"claim" means any proceedings before an Employment Tribunal making a complaint;

"claimant" means the person bringing the claim;

"Commission for Equality and Human Rights" means the body established under section 1 of the Equality Act 2006;

"complaint" means anything that is referred to as a claim, complaint, reference, application or appeal in any enactment which confers jurisdiction on the Tribunal;

"Employment Appeal Tribunal" means the Employment Appeal Tribunal established under section 87 of the Employment Protection Act 1975 and continued in existence under section 135 of the Employment Protection (Consolidation) Act 1978 and section 20(1) of the Employment Tribunals Act;

"electronic communication" has the meaning given to it by section 15(1) of the Electronic Communications Act 2000;

"employee's contract claim" means a claim brought by an employee in accordance with articles 3 and 7 of the Employment Tribunals Extension of Jurisdiction (England and Wales) Order 1994 or articles 3 and 7 of the Employment Tribunals Extension of Jurisdiction (Scotland) Order 1994;

"employer's contract claim" means a claim brought by an employer in accordance with articles 4 and 8 of the Employment Tribunals Extension of Jurisdiction (England and Wales) Order 1994 or articles 4 and 8 of the Employment Tribunals Extension of Jurisdiction (Scotland) Order 1994;

"Employment Tribunal" or "Tribunal" means an employment tribunal established in accordance with regulation 4, and in relation to any proceedings means the Tribunal responsible for the proceedings in question, whether performing administrative or judicial functions;
"Employment Tribunals Act" means the Employment Tribunals Act 1996;
"Equality Act" means the Equality Act 2010;
"full tribunal" means a Tribunal constituted in accordance with section 4(1) of the Employment Tribunals Act;
"Health and Safety Act" means the Health and Safety at Work etc Act 1974;
"improvement notice" means a notice under section 21 of the Health and Safety Act;
"levy appeal" means an appeal against an assessment to a levy imposed under section 11 of the Industrial Training Act 1982;
"Minister" means Minister of the Crown;
"prescribed form" means any appropriate form prescribed by the Secretary of State in accordance with regulation 12;
"present" means deliver (by any means permitted under rule 85) to a tribunal office;
"President" means either of the two presidents appointed from time to time in accordance with regulation 5(1);
"prohibition notice" means a notice under section 22 of the Health and Safety Act;
"Regional Employment Judge" means a person appointed or nominated in accordance with regulation 6(1) or (2);
"Register" means the register of judgments and written reasons kept in accordance with regulation 14;
"remission application" means any application which may be made under any enactment for remission or part remission of a Tribunal fee;
"respondent" means the person or persons against whom the claim is made;
"Tribunal fee" means any fee which is payable by a party under any enactment in respect of a claim, employer's contract claim, application or judicial mediation in an Employment Tribunal;
"tribunal office" means any office which has been established for any area in either England and Wales or Scotland and which carries out administrative functions in support of the Tribunal, and in relation to particular proceedings it is the office notified to the parties as dealing with the proceedings;
"unlawful act notice" means a notice under section 21 of the Equality Act 2006;
"Vice President" means a person appointed or nominated in accordance with regulation 6(3) or (4);
"writing" includes writing delivered by means of electronic communication.

(2) Any reference in the Rules to a Tribunal applies to both a full tribunal and to an Employment Judge acting alone (in accordance with section 4(2) or (6) of the Employment Tribunals Act).

(3) An order or other decision of the Tribunal is either—

(a) a "case management order", being an order or decision of any kind in relation to the conduct of proceedings, not including the determination of any issue which would be the subject of a judgment; or

(b) a "judgment", being a decision, made at any stage of the proceedings (but not including a decision under rule 13 or 19), which finally determines—

(i) a claim, or part of a claim, as regards liability, remedy or costs (including preparation time and wasted costs); or

(ii) any issue which is capable of finally disposing of any claim, or part of a claim, even if it does not necessarily do so (for example, an issue whether a claim should be struck out or a jurisdictional issue).

Overriding objective

2 The overriding objective of these Rules is to enable Employment Tribunals to deal with cases fairly and justly. Dealing with a case fairly and justly includes, so far as practicable—

(a) ensuring that the parties are on an equal footing;
(b) dealing with cases in ways which are proportionate to the complexity and importance of the issues;
(c) avoiding unnecessary formality and seeking flexibility in the proceedings;
(d) avoiding delay, so far as compatible with proper consideration of the issues; and
(e) saving expense.

A Tribunal shall seek to give effect to the overriding objective in interpreting, or exercising any power given to it by, these Rules. The parties and their representatives shall assist the Tribunal to further the overriding objective and in particular shall co-operate generally with each other and with the Tribunal.

Alternative dispute resolution

3 A Tribunal shall wherever practicable and appropriate encourage the use by the parties of the services of ACAS, judicial or other mediation, or other means of resolving their disputes by agreement.

Time

4 (1) Unless otherwise specified by the Tribunal, an act required by these Rules, a practice direction or an order of a Tribunal to be done on or by a particular day may be done at any time before midnight on that day. If there is an issue as to whether the act has been done by that time, the party claiming to have done it shall prove compliance.

(2) If the time specified by these Rules, a practice direction or an order for doing any act ends on a day other than a working day, the act is done in time if it is done on the next working day. "Working day" means any day except a Saturday or Sunday, Christmas Day, Good Friday or a bank holiday under section 1 of the Banking and Financial Dealings Act 1971.

(3) Where any act is required to be, or may be, done within a certain number of days of or from an event, the date of that event shall not be included in the calculation. (For example, a response shall be presented within 28 days of the date on which the respondent was sent a copy of the claim: if the claim was sent on 1st October the last day for presentation of the response is 29th October.)

(4) Where any act is required to be, or may be, done not less than a certain number of days before or after an event, the date of that event shall not be included in the calculation. (For example, if a party wishes to present representations in writing for consideration by a Tribunal at a hearing, they shall be presented not less than 7 days before the hearing: if the hearing is fixed for 8th October, the representations shall be presented no later than 1st October.)

(5) Where the Tribunal imposes a time limit for doing any act, the last date for compliance shall, wherever practicable, be expressed as a calendar date.

(6) Where time is specified by reference to the date when a document is sent to a person by the Tribunal, the date when the document was sent shall, unless the contrary is proved, be regarded as the date endorsed on the document as the date of sending or, if there is no such endorsement, the date shown on the letter accompanying the document.

Extending or shortening time

5 The Tribunal may, on its own initiative or on the application of a party, extend or shorten any time limit specified in these Rules or in any decision, whether or not (in the case of an extension) it has expired.

Irregularities and non-compliance

6 A failure to comply with any provision of these Rules (except rule 8(1), 16(1), 23 or 25) or any order of the Tribunal (except for an order under rules 38 or 39) does not of itself render void the proceedings or any step taken in the proceedings. In the case of such non-compliance, the Tribunal may take such action as it considers just, which may include all or any of the following—

- (a) waiving or varying the requirement;
- (b) striking out the claim or the response, in whole or in part, in accordance with rule 37;
- (c) barring or restricting a party's participation in the proceedings;
- (d) awarding costs in accordance with rules 74 to 84.

Presidential Guidance

7 The Presidents may publish guidance for England and Wales and for Scotland, respectively, as to matters of practice and as to how the powers conferred by these Rules may be exercised. Any such guidance shall be published by the Presidents in an appropriate manner to bring it to the attention of claimants, respondents and their advisers. Tribunals must have regard to any such guidance, but they shall not be bound by it.

STARTING A CLAIM

Presenting the claim

8 (1) A claim shall be started by presenting a completed claim form (using a prescribed form) in accordance with any practice direction made under regulation 11 which supplements this rule.

(2) A claim may be presented in England and Wales if—

- (a) the respondent, or one of the respondents, resides or carries on business in England and Wales;
- (b) one or more of the acts or omissions complained of took place in England and Wales;
- (c) the claim relates to a contract under which the work is or has been performed partly in England and Wales; or
- (d) the Tribunal has jurisdiction to determine the claim by virtue of a connection with Great Britain and the connection in question is at least partly a connection with England and Wales.

(3) A claim may be presented in Scotland if—

(a) the respondent, or one of the respondents, resides or carries on business in Scotland;
(b) one or more of the acts or omissions complained of took place in Scotland;
(c) the claim relates to a contract under which the work is or has been performed partly in Scotland; or
(d) the Tribunal has jurisdiction to determine the claim by virtue of a connection with Great Britain and the connection in question is at least partly a connection with Scotland.

Multiple claimants

9 Two or more claimants may make their claims on the same claim form if their claims are based on the same set of facts. Where two or more claimants wrongly include claims on the same claim form, this shall be treated as an irregularity falling under rule 6.

Rejection: form not used or failure to supply minimum information

10 (1) The Tribunal shall reject a claim if—
(a) it is not made on a prescribed form; or
(b) it does not contain all of the following information—
(i) each claimant's name;
(ii) each claimant's address;
(iii) each respondent's name;
(iv) each respondent's address.

(2) The form shall be returned to the claimant with a notice of rejection explaining why it has been rejected. The notice shall contain information about how to apply for a reconsideration of the rejection.

Rejection: absence of Tribunal fee or remission application

11 (1) The Tribunal shall reject a claim if it is not accompanied by a Tribunal fee or a remission application.

(2) Where a claim is accompanied by a Tribunal fee but the amount paid is lower than the amount payable for the presentation of that claim, the Tribunal shall send the claimant a notice specifying a date for payment of the additional amount due and the claim, or part of it in respect of which the relevant Tribunal fee has not been paid, shall be rejected by the Tribunal if the amount due is not paid by the date specified.

(3) If a remission application is refused in part or in full, the Tribunal shall send the claimant a notice specifying a date for payment of the Tribunal fee and the claim shall be rejected by the Tribunal if the Tribunal fee is not paid by the date specified.

(4) If a claim, or part of it, is rejected, the form shall be returned to the claimant with a notice of rejection explaining why it has been rejected.

Rejection: substantive defects

12 (1) The staff of the tribunal office shall refer a claim form to an Employment Judge if they consider that the claim, or part of it, may be—
(a) one which the Tribunal has no jurisdiction to consider; or
(b) in a form which cannot sensibly be responded to or is otherwise an abuse of the process.

(2) The claim, or part of it, shall be rejected if the Judge considers that the claim, or part of it, is of a kind described in sub-paragraphs (a) or (b) of paragraph (1).

(3) If the claim is rejected, the form shall be returned to the claimant together with a notice of rejection giving the Judge's reasons for rejecting the claim, or part of it. The notice shall contain information about how to apply for a reconsideration of the rejection.

Reconsideration of rejection

13 (1) A claimant whose claim has been rejected (in whole or in part) under rule 10 or 12 may apply for a reconsideration on the basis that either—
(a) the decision to reject was wrong; or
(b) the notified defect can be rectified.

(2) The application shall be in writing and presented to the Tribunal within 14 days of the date that the notice of rejection was sent. It shall explain why the decision is said to have been wrong or rectify the defect and if the claimant wishes to request a hearing this shall be requested in the application.

(3) If the claimant does not request a hearing, or an Employment Judge decides, on considering the application, that the claim shall be accepted in full, the Judge shall determine the application without a hearing. Otherwise the application shall be considered at a hearing attended only by the claimant.

(4) If the Judge decides that the original rejection was correct but that the defect has been rectified, the claim shall be treated as presented on the date that the defect was rectified.

Protected disclosure claims: notification to a regulator

14 If a claim alleges that the claimant has made a protected disclosure, the Tribunal may, with the consent of the claimant, send a copy of any accepted claim to a regulator listed in Schedule 1 to the Public Interest Disclosure (Prescribed Persons) Order 1999. "Protected disclosure" has the meaning given to it by section 43A of the Employment Rights Act 1996.

THE RESPONSE TO THE CLAIM

Sending claim form to respondents

15 Unless the claim is rejected, the Tribunal shall send a copy of the claim form, together with a prescribed response form, to each respondent with a notice which includes information on—

(a) whether any part of the claim has been rejected; and

(b) how to submit a response to the claim, the time limit for doing so and what will happen if a response is not received by the Tribunal within that time limit.

Response

16 (1) The response shall be on a prescribed form and presented to the tribunal office within 28 days of the date that the copy of the claim form was sent by the Tribunal.

(2) A response form may include the response of more than one respondent if they are responding to a single claim and either they all resist the claim on the same grounds or they do not resist the claim.

(3) A response form may include the response to more than one claim if the claims are based on the same set of facts and either the respondent resists all of the claims on the same grounds or the respondent does not resist the claims.

Rejection: form not used or failure to supply minimum information

17 (1) The Tribunal shall reject a response if—

(a) it is not made on a prescribed form; or

(b) it does not contain all of the following information—

(i) the respondent's full name;

(ii) the respondent's address;

(iii) whether the respondent wishes to resist any part of the claim.

(2) The form shall be returned to the respondent with a notice of rejection explaining why it has been rejected. The notice shall explain what steps may be taken by the respondent, including the need (if appropriate) to apply for an extension of time, and how to apply for a reconsideration of the rejection.

Rejection: form presented late

18 (1) A response shall be rejected by the Tribunal if it is received outside the time limit in rule 16 (or any extension of that limit granted within the original limit) unless an application for extension has already been made under rule 20 or the response includes or is accompanied by such an application (in which case the response shall not be rejected pending the outcome of the application).

(2) The response shall be returned to the respondent together with a notice of rejection explaining that the response has been presented late. The notice shall explain how the respondent can apply for an extension of time and how to apply for a reconsideration.

Reconsideration of rejection

19 (1) A respondent whose response has been rejected under rule 17 or 18 may apply for a reconsideration on the basis that the decision to reject was wrong or, in the case of a rejection under rule 17, on the basis that the notified defect can be rectified.

(2) The application shall be in writing and presented to the Tribunal within 14 days of the date that the notice of rejection was sent. It shall explain why the decision is said to have been wrong or rectify the defect and it shall state whether the respondent requests a hearing.

(3) If the respondent does not request a hearing, or the Employment Judge decides, on considering the application, that the response shall be accepted in full, the Judge shall determine the application without a hearing. Otherwise the application shall be considered at a hearing attended only by the respondent.

(4) If the Judge decides that the original rejection was correct but that the defect has been rectified, the response shall be treated as presented on the date that the defect was rectified (but the Judge may extend time under rule 5).

Applications for extension of time for presenting response

20 (1) An application for an extension of time for presenting a response shall be presented in writing and copied to the claimant. It shall set out the reason why the extension is sought and shall, except where the time limit has not yet expired, be accompanied by a draft of the response which the respondent wishes to present or an explanation of why that is not possible and if the respondent wishes to request a hearing this shall be requested in the application.

(2) The claimant may within 7 days of receipt of the application give reasons in writing explaining why the application is opposed.

(3) An Employment Judge may determine the application without a hearing.

(4) If the decision is to refuse an extension, any prior rejection of the response shall stand. If the decision is to allow an extension, any judgment issued under rule 21 shall be set aside.

Effect of non-presentation or rejection of response, or case not contested

21 (1) Where on the expiry of the time limit in rule 16 no response has been presented, or any response received has been rejected and no application for a reconsideration is outstanding, or where the respondent has stated that no part of the claim is contested, paragraphs (2) and (3) shall apply.

(2) An Employment Judge shall decide whether on the available material (which may include further information which the parties are required by a Judge to provide), a determination can properly be made of the claim, or part of it. To the extent that a determination can be made, the Judge shall issue a judgment accordingly. Otherwise, a hearing shall be fixed before a Judge alone.

(3) The respondent shall be entitled to notice of any hearings and decisions of the Tribunal but, unless and until an extension of time is granted, shall only be entitled to participate in any hearing to the extent permitted by the Judge.

Notification of acceptance

22 Where the Tribunal accepts the response it shall send a copy of it to all other parties.

EMPLOYER'S CONTRACT CLAIM

Making an employer's contract claim

23 Any employer's contract claim shall be made as part of the response, presented in accordance with rule 16, to a claim which includes an employee's contract claim. An employer's contract claim may be rejected on the same basis as a claimant's claim may be rejected under rule 12, in which case rule 13 shall apply.

Notification of employer's contract claim

24 When the Tribunal sends the response to the other parties in accordance with rule 22 it shall notify the claimant that the response includes an employer's contract claim and include information on how to submit a response to the claim, the time limit for doing so, and what will happen if a response is not received by the Tribunal within that time limit.

Responding to an employer's contract claim

25 A claimant's response to an employer's contract claim shall be presented to the tribunal office within 28 days of the date that the response was sent to the claimant. If no response is presented within that time limit, rules 20 and 21 shall apply.

INITIAL CONSIDERATION OF CLAIM FORM AND RESPONSE

Initial consideration

26 (1) As soon as possible after the acceptance of the response, the Employment Judge shall consider all of the documents held by the Tribunal in relation to the claim, to confirm whether there are arguable complaints and defences within the jurisdiction of the Tribunal (and for that purpose the Judge may order a party to provide further information).

(2) Except in a case where notice is given under rule 27 or 28, the Judge conducting the initial consideration shall make a case management order (unless made already), which may deal with the listing of a preliminary or final hearing, and may propose judicial mediation or other forms of dispute resolution.

Dismissal of claim (or part)

27 (1) If the Employment Judge considers either that the Tribunal has no jurisdiction to consider the claim, or part of it, or that the claim, or part of it, has no reasonable prospect of success, the Tribunal shall send a notice to the parties—

(a) setting out the Judge's view and the reasons for it; and

(b) ordering that the claim, or the part in question, shall be dismissed on such date as is specified in the notice unless before that date the claimant has presented written representations to the Tribunal explaining why the claim (or part) should not be dismissed.

(2) If no such representations are received, the claim shall be dismissed from the date specified without further order (although the Tribunal shall write to the parties to confirm what has occurred).

(3) If representations are received within the specified time they shall be considered by an Employment Judge, who shall either permit the claim (or part) to proceed or fix a hearing for the purpose of deciding whether it should be permitted to do so. The respondent may, but need not, attend and participate in the hearing.

(4) If any part of the claim is permitted to proceed the Judge shall make a case management order.

Dismissal of response (or part)

28 (1) If the Employment Judge considers that the response to the claim, or part of it, has no reasonable prospect of success the Tribunal shall send a notice to the parties—

- (a) setting out the Judge's view and the reasons for it;
- (b) ordering that the response, or the part in question, shall be dismissed on such date as is specified in the notice unless before that date the respondent has presented written representations to the Tribunal explaining why the response (or part) should not be dismissed; and
- (c) specifying the consequences of the dismissal of the response, in accordance with paragraph (5) below.

(2) If no such representations are received, the response shall be dismissed from the date specified without further order (although the Tribunal shall write to the parties to confirm what has occurred).

(3) If representations are received within the specified time they shall be considered by an Employment Judge, who shall either permit the response (or part) to stand or fix a hearing for the purpose of deciding whether it should be permitted to do so. The claimant may, but need not, attend and participate in the hearing.

(4) If any part of the response is permitted to stand the Judge shall make a case management order.

(5) Where a response is dismissed, the effect shall be as if no response had been presented, as set out in rule 21 above.

CASE MANAGEMENT ORDERS AND OTHER POWERS

Case management orders

29 The Tribunal may at any stage of the proceedings, on its own initiative or on application, make a case management order. The particular powers identified in the following rules do not restrict that general power. A case management order may vary, suspend or set aside an earlier case management order where that is necessary in the interests of justice, and in particular where a party affected by the earlier order did not have a reasonable opportunity to make representations before it was made.

Applications for case management orders

30 (1) An application by a party for a particular case management order may be made either at a hearing or presented in writing to the Tribunal.

(2) Where a party applies in writing, they shall notify the other parties that any objections to the application should be sent to the Tribunal as soon as possible.

(3) The Tribunal may deal with such an application in writing or order that it be dealt with at a preliminary or final hearing.

Disclosure of documents and information

31 The Tribunal may order any person in Great Britain to disclose documents or information to a party (by providing copies or otherwise) or to allow a party to inspect such material as might be ordered by a county court or, in Scotland, by a sheriff.

Requirement to attend to give evidence

32 The Tribunal may order any person in Great Britain to attend a hearing to give evidence, produce documents, or produce information.

Evidence from other EU Member States

33 The Tribunal may use the procedures for obtaining evidence prescribed in Council Regulation (EC) No 1026/2001 of 28 May 2001 on cooperation between the courts of the Member States in the taking of evidence in civil or commercial matters.

Addition, substitution and removal of parties

34 The Tribunal may on its own initiative, or on the application of a party or any other person wishing to become a party, add any person as a party, by way of substitution or otherwise, if it appears that there are issues between that person and any of the existing parties falling within the jurisdiction of the Tribunal which it is in the interests of justice to have determined in the proceedings; and may remove any party apparently wrongly included.

Other persons

35 The Tribunal may permit any person to participate in proceedings, on such terms as may be specified, in respect of any matter in which that person has a legitimate interest.

Lead cases

36 (1) Where a Tribunal considers that two or more claims give rise to common or related issues of fact or law, the Tribunal or the President may make an order specifying one or more of those claims as a lead case and staying, or in Scotland sisting, the other claims ("the related cases").

(2) When the Tribunal makes a decision in respect of the common or related issues it shall send a copy of that decision to each party in each of the related cases and, subject to paragraph (3), that decision shall be binding on each of those parties.

(3) Within 28 days after the date on which the Tribunal sent a copy of the decision to a party under paragraph (2), that party may apply in writing for an order that the decision does not apply to, and is not binding on the parties to, a particular related case.

(4) If a lead case is withdrawn before the Tribunal makes a decision in respect of the common or related issues, it shall make an order as to—

(a) whether another claim is to be specified as a lead case; and

(b) whether any order affecting the related cases should be set aside or varied.

Striking out

37 (1) At any stage of the proceedings, either on its own initiative or on the application of a party, a Tribunal may strike out all or part of a claim or response on any of the following grounds—

(a) that it is scandalous or vexatious or has no reasonable prospect of success;

(b) that the manner in which the proceedings have been conducted by or on behalf of the claimant or the respondent (as the case may be) has been scandalous, unreasonable or vexatious;

(c) for non-compliance with any of these Rules or with an order of the Tribunal;

(d) that it has not been actively pursued;

(e) that the Tribunal considers that it is no longer possible to have a fair hearing in respect of the claim or response (or the part to be struck out).

(2) A claim or response may not be struck out unless the party in question has been given a reasonable opportunity to make representations, either in writing or, if requested by the party, at a hearing.

(3) Where a response is struck out, the effect shall be as if no response had been presented, as set out in rule 21 above.

Unless orders

38 (1) An order may specify that if it is not complied with by the date specified the claim or response, or part of it, shall be dismissed without further order. If a claim or response, or part of it, is dismissed on this basis the Tribunal shall give written notice to the parties confirming what has occurred.

(2) A party whose claim or response has been dismissed, in whole or in part, as a result of such an order may apply to the Tribunal in writing, within 14 days of the date that the notice was sent, to have the order set aside on the basis that it is in the interests of justice to do so. Unless the application includes a request for a hearing, the Tribunal may determine it on the basis of written representations.

(3) Where a response is dismissed under this rule, the effect shall be as if no response had been presented, as set out in rule 21.

Deposit orders

39 (1) Where at a preliminary hearing (under rule 53) the Tribunal considers that any specific allegation or argument in a claim or response has little reasonable prospect of success, it may make an order requiring a party ("the paying party") to pay a deposit not exceeding £1,000 as a condition of continuing to advance that allegation or argument.

(2) The Tribunal shall make reasonable enquiries into the paying party's ability to pay the deposit and have regard to any such information when deciding the amount of the deposit.

(3) The Tribunal's reasons for making the deposit order shall be provided with the order and the paying party must be notified about the potential consequences of the order.

(4) If the paying party fails to pay the deposit by the date specified the specific allegation or argument to which the deposit order relates shall be struck out. Where a response is struck out, the consequences shall be as if no response had been presented, as set out in rule 21.

(5) If the Tribunal at any stage following the making of a deposit order decides the specific allegation or argument against the paying party for substantially the reasons given in the deposit order—

(a) the paying party shall be treated as having acted unreasonably in pursuing that specific allegation or argument for the purpose of rule 76, unless the contrary is shown; and

(b) the deposit shall be paid to the other party (or, if there is more than one, to such other party or parties as the Tribunal orders),

otherwise the deposit shall be refunded.

(6) If a deposit has been paid to a party under paragraph (5)(b) and a costs or preparation time order has been made against the paying party in favour of the party who received the deposit, the amount of the deposit shall count towards the settlement of that order.

Non-payment of fees

40 (1) Subject to rule 11, where a party has not paid a relevant Tribunal fee or presented a remission application in respect of that fee the Tribunal will send the party a notice specifying a date for payment of the Tribunal fee or presentation of a remission application.

(2) If at the date specified in a notice sent under paragraph (1) the party has not paid the Tribunal fee and no remission application in respect of that fee has been presented—

(a) where the Tribunal fee is payable in relation to a claim, the claim shall be dismissed without further order;

(b) where the Tribunal fee is payable in relation to an employer's contract claim, the employer's contract claim shall be dismissed without further order;

(c) where the Tribunal fee is payable in relation to an application, the application shall be dismissed without further order;

(d) where the Tribunal fee is payable in relation to judicial mediation, the judicial mediation shall not take place.

(3) Where a remission application is refused in part or in full, the Tribunal shall send the claimant a notice specifying a date for payment of the Tribunal fee.

(4) If at the date specified in a notice sent under paragraph (3) the party has not paid the Tribunal fee, the consequences shall be those referred to in sub-paragraphs (a) to (d) of paragraph (2).

(5) In the event of a dismissal under paragraph (2) or (4) a party may apply for the claim or response, or part of it, which was dismissed to be reinstated and the Tribunal may order a reinstatement. A reinstatement shall be effective only if the Tribunal fee is paid, or a remission application is presented and accepted, by the date specified in the order.

RULES COMMON TO ALL KINDS OF HEARING

General

41 The Tribunal may regulate its own procedure and shall conduct the hearing in the manner it considers fair, having regard to the principles contained in the overriding objective. The following rules do not restrict that general power. The Tribunal shall seek to avoid undue formality and may itself question the parties or any witnesses so far as appropriate in order to clarify the issues or elicit the evidence. The Tribunal is not bound by any rule of law relating to the admissibility of evidence in proceedings before the courts.

Written representations

42 The Tribunal shall consider any written representations from a party, including a party who does not propose to attend the hearing, if they are delivered to the Tribunal and to all other parties not less than 7 days before the hearing.

Witnesses

43 Where a witness is called to give oral evidence, any witness statement of that person ordered by the Tribunal shall stand as that witness's evidence in chief unless the Tribunal orders otherwise. Witnesses shall be required to give their oral evidence on oath or affirmation. The Tribunal may exclude from the hearing any person who is to appear as a witness in the proceedings until such time as that person gives evidence if it considers it in the interests of justice to do so.

Inspection of witness statements

44 Subject to rules 50 and 94, any witness statement which stands as evidence in chief shall be available for inspection during the course of the hearing by members of the public attending the hearing unless the Tribunal decides that all or any part of the statement is not to be admitted as evidence, in which case the statement or that part shall not be available for inspection.

Timetabling

45 A Tribunal may impose limits on the time that a party may take in presenting evidence, questioning witnesses or making submissions, and may prevent the party from proceeding beyond any time so allotted.

Hearings by electronic communication

46 A hearing may be conducted, in whole or in part, by use of electronic communication (including by telephone) provided that the Tribunal considers that it would be just and equitable to do so and provided that the parties and members of the public attending the hearing are able to hear what the Tribunal hears and see any witness as seen by the Tribunal.

Non-attendance

47 If a party fails to attend or to be represented at the hearing, the Tribunal may dismiss the claim or proceed with the hearing in the absence of that party. Before doing so, it shall consider any information which is available to it, after any enquiries that may be practicable, about the reasons for the party's absence.

Conversion from preliminary hearing to final hearing and vice versa

48 A Tribunal conducting a preliminary hearing may order that it be treated as a final hearing, or vice versa, if the Tribunal is properly constituted for the purpose and if it is satisfied that neither party shall be materially prejudiced by the change.

Majority decisions

49 Where a Tribunal is composed of three persons any decision may be made by a majority and if it is composed of two persons the Employment Judge has a second or casting vote.

Privacy and restrictions on disclosure

50 (1) A Tribunal may at any stage of the proceedings, on its own initiative or on application, make an order with a view to preventing or restricting the public disclosure of any aspect of those proceedings so far as it considers necessary in the interests of justice or in order to protect the Convention rights of any person or in the circumstances identified in section 10A of the Employment Tribunals Act.

(2) In considering whether to make an order under this rule, the Tribunal shall give full weight to the principle of open justice and to the Convention right to freedom of expression.

(3) Such orders may include—

(a) an order that a hearing that would otherwise be in public be conducted, in whole or in part, in private;

(b) an order that the identities of specified parties, witnesses or other persons referred to in the proceedings should not be disclosed to the public, by the use of anonymisation or otherwise, whether in the course of any hearing or in its listing or in any documents entered on the Register or otherwise forming part of the public record;

(c) an order for measures preventing witnesses at a public hearing being identifiable by members of the public;

(d) a restricted reporting order within the terms of section 11 or 12 of the Employment Tribunals Act.

(4) Any party, or other person with a legitimate interest, who has not had a reasonable opportunity to make representations before an order under this rule is made may apply to the Tribunal in writing for the order to be revoked or discharged, either on the basis of written representations or, if requested, at a hearing.

(5) Where an order is made under paragraph (3)(d) above—

(a) it shall specify the person whose identity is protected; and may specify particular matters of which publication is prohibited as likely to lead to that person's identification;

(b) it shall specify the duration of the order;

(c) the Tribunal shall ensure that a notice of the fact that such an order has been made in relation to those proceedings is displayed on the notice board of the Tribunal with any list of the proceedings taking place before the Tribunal, and on the door of the room in which the proceedings affected by the order are taking place; and

(d) the Tribunal may order that it applies also to any other proceedings being heard as part of the same hearing.

(6) "Convention rights" has the meaning given to it in section 1 of the Human Rights Act 1998.

WITHDRAWAL

End of claim

51 Where a claimant informs the Tribunal, either in writing or in the course of a hearing, that a claim, or part of it, is withdrawn, the claim, or part, comes to an end, subject to any application that the respondent may make for a costs, preparation time or wasted costs order.

Dismissal following withdrawal

52 Where a claim, or part of it, has been withdrawn under rule 51, the Tribunal shall issue a judgment dismissing it (which means that the claimant may not commence a further claim against the respondent raising the same, or substantially the same, complaint) unless—

(a) the claimant has expressed at the time of withdrawal a wish to reserve the right to bring such a further claim and the Tribunal is satisfied that there would be legitimate reason for doing so; or

(b) the Tribunal believes that to issue such a judgment would not be in the interests of justice.

PRELIMINARY HEARINGS

Scope of preliminary hearings

53 (1) A preliminary hearing is a hearing at which the Tribunal may do one or more of the following—

(a) conduct a preliminary consideration of the claim with the parties and make a case management order (including an order relating to the conduct of the final hearing);

(b) determine any preliminary issue;

(c) consider whether a claim or response, or any part, should be struck out under rule 37;

(d) make a deposit order under rule 39;

(e) explore the possibility of settlement or alternative dispute resolution (including judicial mediation).

(2) There may be more than one preliminary hearing in any case.

(3) "Preliminary issue" means, as regards any complaint, any substantive issue which may determine liability (for example, an issue as to jurisdiction or as to whether an employee was dismissed).

Fixing of preliminary hearings

54 A preliminary hearing may be directed by the Tribunal on its own initiative following its initial consideration (under rule 26) or at any time thereafter or as the result of an application by a party. The Tribunal shall give the parties reasonable notice of the date of the hearing and in the case of a hearing involving any preliminary issues at least 14 days notice shall be given and the notice shall specify the preliminary issues that are to be, or may be, decided at the hearing.

Constitution of tribunal for preliminary hearings

55 Preliminary hearings shall be conducted by an Employment Judge alone, except that where notice has been given that any preliminary issues are to be, or may be, decided at the hearing a party may request in writing that the hearing be conducted by a full tribunal in which case an Employment Judge shall decide whether that would be desirable.

When preliminary hearings shall be in public

56 Preliminary hearings shall be conducted in private, except that where the hearing involves a determination under rule 53(1)(b) or (c), any part of the hearing relating to such a determination shall be in public (subject to rules 50 and 94) and the Tribunal may direct that the entirety of the hearing be in public.

FINAL HEARING

Scope of final hearing

57 A final hearing is a hearing at which the Tribunal determines the claim or such parts as remain outstanding following the initial consideration (under rule 26) or any preliminary hearing. There may be different final hearings for different issues (for example, liability, remedy or costs).

Notice of final hearing

58 The Tribunal shall give the parties not less than 14 days' notice of the date of a final hearing.

When final hearing shall be in public

59 Any final hearing shall be in public, subject to rules 50 and 94.

DECISIONS AND REASONS

Decisions made without a hearing

60 Decisions made without a hearing shall be communicated in writing to the parties, identifying the Employment Judge who has made the decision.

Decisions made at or following a hearing

61 (1) Where there is a hearing the Tribunal may either announce its decision in relation to any issue at the hearing or reserve it to be sent to the parties as soon as practicable in writing.

(2) If the decision is announced at the hearing, a written record (in the form of a judgment if appropriate) shall be provided to the parties (and, where the proceedings were referred to the Tribunal by a court, to that court) as soon as practicable. (Decisions concerned only with the conduct of a hearing need not be identified in the record of that hearing unless a party requests that a specific decision is so recorded.)

(3) The written record shall be signed by the Employment Judge.

Reasons

62 (1) The Tribunal shall give reasons for its decision on any disputed issue, whether substantive or procedural (including any decision on an application for reconsideration or for orders for costs, preparation time or wasted costs).

(2) In the case of a decision given in writing the reasons shall also be given in writing. In the case of a decision announced at a hearing the reasons may be given orally at the hearing or reserved to be given in writing later (which may, but need not, be as part of the written record of the decision). Written reasons shall be signed by the Employment Judge.

(3) Where reasons have been given orally, the Employment Judge shall announce that written reasons will not be provided unless they are asked for by any party at the hearing itself or by a written request presented by any party within 14 days of the sending of the written record of the decision. The written record of the decision shall repeat that information. If no such request is received, the Tribunal shall provide written reasons only if requested to do so by the Employment Appeal Tribunal or a court.

(4) The reasons given for any decision shall be proportionate to the significance of the issue and for decisions other than judgments may be very short.

(5) In the case of a judgment the reasons shall: identify the issues which the Tribunal has determined, state the findings of fact made in relation to those issues, concisely identify the relevant law, and state how that law has been applied to those findings in order to decide the issues. Where the judgment includes a financial award the reasons shall identify, by means of a table or otherwise, how the amount to be paid has been calculated.

Absence of Employment Judge

63 If it is impossible or not practicable for the written record or reasons to be signed by the Employment Judge as a result of death, incapacity or absence, it shall be signed by the other member or members (in the case of a full tribunal) or by the President, Vice President or a Regional Employment Judge (in the case of a Judge sitting alone).

Consent orders and judgments

64 If the parties agree in writing or orally at a hearing upon the terms of any order or judgment a Tribunal may, if it thinks fit, make such order or judgment, in which case it shall be identified as having been made by consent.

When a judgment or order takes effect

65 A judgment or order takes effect from the day when it is given or made, or on such later date as specified by the Tribunal.

Time for compliance

66 A party shall comply with a judgment or order for the payment of an amount of money within 14 days of the date of the judgment or order, unless—

(a) the judgment, order, or any of these Rules, specifies a different date for compliance; or
(b) the Tribunal has stayed (or in Scotland sisted) the proceedings or judgment.

The Register

67 Subject to rules 50 and 94, a copy shall be entered in the Register of any judgment and of any written reasons for a judgment.

Copies of judgment for referring court

68 Where the proceedings were referred to the Tribunal by a court a copy of any judgment and of any written reasons shall be provided to that court.

Correction of clerical mistakes and accidental slips

69 An Employment Judge may at any time correct any clerical mistake or other accidental slip or omission in any order, judgment or other document produced by a Tribunal. If such a correction is made, any published version of the document shall also be corrected. If any document is corrected under this rule, a copy of the corrected version, signed by the Judge, shall be sent to all the parties.

RECONSIDERATION OF JUDGMENTS

Principles

70 A Tribunal may, either on its own initiative (which may reflect a request from the Employment Appeal Tribunal) or on the application of a party, reconsider any judgment where it is necessary in the interests of justice to do so. On reconsideration, the decision ("the original decision") may be confirmed, varied or revoked. If it is revoked it may be taken again.

Application

71 Except where it is made in the course of a hearing, an application for reconsideration shall be presented in writing (and copied to all the other parties) within 14 days of the date on which the written record, or other written communication, of the original decision was sent to the parties or within 14 days of the date that the written reasons were sent (if later) and shall set out why reconsideration of the original decision is necessary.

Process

72 (1) An Employment Judge shall consider any application made under rule 71. If the Judge considers that there is no reasonable prospect of the original decision being varied or revoked (including, unless there are special reasons, where substantially the same application has already been made and refused), the application shall be refused and the Tribunal shall inform the parties of the refusal. Otherwise the Tribunal shall send a notice to the parties setting a time limit for any response to the application by the other parties and seeking the views of the parties on whether the application can be determined without a hearing. The notice may set out the Judge's provisional views on the application.

(2) If the application has not been refused under paragraph (1), the original decision shall be reconsidered at a hearing unless the Employment Judge considers, having regard to any response to the notice provided under paragraph (1), that a hearing is not necessary in the interests of justice. If the reconsideration proceeds without a hearing the parties shall be given a reasonable opportunity to make further written representations.

(3) Where practicable, the consideration under paragraph (1) shall be by the Employment Judge who made the original decision or, as the case may be, chaired the full tribunal which made it; and any reconsideration under paragraph (2) shall be made by the Judge or, as the case may be, the full tribunal which made the original decision. Where that is not practicable, the President, Vice President or a Regional Employment Judge shall appoint another Employment Judge to deal with the application or, in the case of a decision of a full tribunal, shall either direct that the reconsideration be by such members of the original Tribunal as remain available or reconstitute the Tribunal in whole or in part.

Reconsideration by the Tribunal on its own initiative

73 Where the Tribunal proposes to reconsider a decision on its own initiative, it shall inform the parties of the reasons why the decision is being reconsidered and the decision shall be reconsidered in accordance with rule 72(2) (as if an application had been made and not refused).

COSTS ORDERS, PREPARATION TIME ORDERS AND WASTED COSTS ORDERS

Definitions

74 (1) "Costs" means fees, charges, disbursements or expenses incurred by or on behalf of the receiving party (including expenses that witnesses incur for the purpose of, or in connection with, attendance at a Tribunal hearing). In Scotland all references to costs (except when used in the expression "wasted costs") shall be read as references to expenses.

(2) "Legally represented" means having the assistance of a person (including where that person is the receiving party's employee) who—

(a) has a right of audience in relation to any class of proceedings in any part of the Senior Courts of England and Wales, or all proceedings in county courts or magistrates' courts;

(b) is an advocate or solicitor in Scotland; or

(c) is a member of the Bar of Northern Ireland or a solicitor of the Court of Judicature of Northern Ireland.

(3) "Represented by a lay representative" means having the assistance of a person who does not satisfy any of the criteria in paragraph (2) and who charges for representation in the proceedings.

Costs orders and preparation time orders

75 (1) A costs order is an order that a party ("the paying party") make a payment to—

(a) another party ("the receiving party") in respect of the costs that the receiving party has incurred while legally represented or while represented by a lay representative;

(b) the receiving party in respect of a Tribunal fee paid by the receiving party; or

(c) another party or a witness in respect of expenses incurred, or to be incurred, for the purpose of, or in connection with, an individual's attendance as a witness at the Tribunal.

Part 2 Statutory Instruments

(2) A preparation time order is an order that a party ("the paying party") make a payment to another party ("the receiving party") in respect of the receiving party's preparation time while not legally represented. "Preparation time" means time spent by the receiving party (including by any employees or advisers) in working on the case, except for time spent at any final hearing.

(3) A costs order under paragraph (1)(a) and a preparation time order may not both be made in favour of the same party in the same proceedings. A Tribunal may, if it wishes, decide in the course of the proceedings that a party is entitled to one order or the other but defer until a later stage in the proceedings deciding which kind of order to make.

When a costs order or a preparation time order may or shall be made

76 (1) A Tribunal may make a costs order or a preparation time order, and shall consider whether to do so, where it considers that—

- (a) a party (or that party's representative) has acted vexatiously, abusively, disruptively or otherwise unreasonably in either the bringing of the proceedings (or part) or the way that the proceedings (or part) have been conducted; or
- (b) any claim or response had no reasonable prospect of success.

(2) A Tribunal may also make such an order where a party has been in breach of any order or practice direction or where a hearing has been postponed or adjourned on the application of a party.

(3) Where in proceedings for unfair dismissal a final hearing is postponed or adjourned, the Tribunal shall order the respondent to pay the costs incurred as a result of the postponement or adjournment if—

- (a) the claimant has expressed a wish to be reinstated or re-engaged which has been communicated to the respondent not less than 7 days before the hearing; and
- (b) the postponement or adjournment of that hearing has been caused by the respondent's failure, without a special reason, to adduce reasonable evidence as to the availability of the job from which the claimant was dismissed or of comparable or suitable employment.

(4) A Tribunal may make a costs order of the kind described in rule 75(1)(b) where a party has paid a Tribunal fee in respect of a claim, employer's contract claim or application and that claim, counterclaim or application is decided in whole, or in part, in favour of that party.

(5) A Tribunal may make a costs order of the kind described in rule 75(1)(c) on the application of a party or the witness in question, or on its own initiative, where a witness has attended or has been ordered to attend to give oral evidence at a hearing.

Procedure

77 A party may apply for a costs order or a preparation time order at any stage up to 28 days after the date on which the judgment finally determining the proceedings in respect of that party was sent to the parties. No such order may be made unless the paying party has had a reasonable opportunity to make representations (in writing or at a hearing, as the Tribunal may order) in response to the application.

The amount of a costs order

78 (1) A costs order may—

- (a) order the paying party to pay the receiving party a specified amount, not exceeding £20,000, in respect of the costs of the receiving party;
- (b) order the paying party to pay the receiving party the whole or a specified part of the costs of the receiving party, with the amount to be paid being determined, in England and Wales, by way of detailed assessment carried out either by a county court in accordance with the Civil Procedure Rules 1998, or by an Employment Judge applying the same principles; or, in Scotland, by way of taxation carried out either by the auditor of court in accordance with the Act of Sederunt (Fees of Solicitors in the Sheriff Court)(Amendment and Further Provisions) 1993, or by an Employment Judge applying the same principles;
- (c) order the paying party to pay the receiving party a specified amount as reimbursement of all or part of a Tribunal fee paid by the receiving party;
- (d) order the paying party to pay another party or a witness, as appropriate, a specified amount in respect of necessary and reasonably incurred expenses (of the kind described in rule 75(1)(c)); or
- (e) if the paying party and the receiving party agree as to the amount payable, be made in that amount.

(2) Where the costs order includes an amount in respect of fees charged by a lay representative, for the purposes of the calculation of the order, the hourly rate applicable for the fees of the lay representative shall be no higher than the rate under rule 79(2).

(3) For the avoidance of doubt, the amount of a costs order under sub-paragraphs (b) to (e) of paragraph (1) may exceed £20,000.

The amount of a preparation time order

79 (1) The Tribunal shall decide the number of hours in respect of which a preparation time order should be made, on the basis of—

- (a) information provided by the receiving party on time spent falling within rule 75(2) above; and
- (b) the Tribunal's own assessment of what it considers to be a reasonable and proportionate amount of time to spend on such preparatory work, with reference to such matters as the complexity of the proceedings, the number of witnesses and documentation required.

(2) The hourly rate is £33 and increases on 6 April each year by £1.

(3) The amount of a preparation time order shall be the product of the number of hours assessed under paragraph (1) and the rate under paragraph (2).

When a wasted costs order may be made

80 (1) A Tribunal may make a wasted costs order against a representative in favour of any party ("the receiving party") where that party has incurred costs—

- (a) as a result of any improper, unreasonable or negligent act or omission on the part of the representative; or
- (b) which, in the light of any such act or omission occurring after they were incurred, the Tribunal considers it unreasonable to expect the receiving party to pay.

Costs so incurred are described as "wasted costs".

(2) "Representative" means a party's legal or other representative or any employee of such representative, but it does not include a representative who is not acting in pursuit of profit with regard to the proceedings. A person acting on a contingency or conditional fee arrangement is considered to be acting in pursuit of profit.

(3) A wasted costs order may be made in favour of a party whether or not that party is legally represented and may also be made in favour of a representative's own client. A wasted costs order may not be made against a representative where that representative is representing a party in his or her capacity as an employee of that party.

Effect of a wasted costs order

81 A wasted costs order may order the representative to pay the whole or part of any wasted costs of the receiving party, or disallow any wasted costs otherwise payable to the representative, including an order that the representative repay to its client any costs which have already been paid. The amount to be paid, disallowed or repaid must in each case be specified in the order.

Procedure

82 A wasted costs order may be made by the Tribunal on its own initiative or on the application of any party. A party may apply for a wasted costs order at any stage up to 28 days after the date on which the judgment finally determining the proceedings as against that party was sent to the parties. No such order shall be made unless the representative has had a reasonable opportunity to make representations (in writing or at a hearing, as the Tribunal may order) in response to the application or proposal. The Tribunal shall inform the representative's client in writing of any proceedings under this rule and of any order made against the representative.

Allowances

83 Where the Tribunal makes a costs, preparation time, or wasted costs order, it may also make an order that the paying party (or, where a wasted costs order is made, the representative) pay to the Secretary of State, in whole or in part, any allowances (other than allowances paid to members of the Tribunal) paid by the Secretary of State under section 5(2) or (3) of the Employment Tribunals Act to any person for the purposes of, or in connection with, that person's attendance at the Tribunal.

Ability to pay

84 In deciding whether to make a costs, preparation time, or wasted costs order, and if so in what amount, the Tribunal may have regard to the paying party's (or, where a wasted costs order is made, the representative's) ability to pay.

DELIVERY OF DOCUMENTS

Delivery to the Tribunal

85 (1) Subject to paragraph (2), documents may be delivered to the Tribunal—

- (a) by post;
- (b) by direct delivery to the appropriate tribunal office (including delivery by a courier or messenger service); or
- (c) by electronic communication.

(2) A claim form may only be delivered in accordance with the practice direction made under regulation 11 which supplements rule 8.

(3) The Tribunal shall notify the parties following the presentation of the claim of the address of the tribunal office dealing with the case (including any fax or email or other electronic address) and all documents shall be delivered to either the postal or the electronic address so notified. The Tribunal may from time to time notify the parties of any change of address, or that a particular form of communication should or should not be used, and any documents shall be delivered in accordance with that notification.

Delivery to parties

86 (1) Documents may be delivered to a party (whether by the Tribunal or by another party)—

(a) by post;

(b) by direct delivery to that party's address (including delivery by a courier or messenger service);

(c) by electronic communication; or

(d) by being handed personally to that party, if an individual and if no representative has been named in the claim form or response; or to any individual representative named in the claim form or response; or, on the occasion of a hearing, to any person identified by the party as representing that party at that hearing.

(2) For the purposes of sub-paragraphs (a) to (c) of paragraph (1), the document shall be delivered to the address given in the claim form or response (which shall be the address of the party's representative, if one is named) or to a different address as notified in writing by the party in question.

(3) If a party has given both a postal address and one or more electronic addresses, any of them may be used unless the party has indicated in writing that a particular address should or should not be used.

Delivery to non-parties

87 Subject to the special cases which are the subject of rule 88, documents shall be sent to non-parties at any address for service which they may have notified and otherwise at any known address or place of business in the United Kingdom or, if the party is a corporate body, at its registered or principal office in the United Kingdom or, if permitted by the President, at an address outside the United Kingdom.

Special cases

88 Addresses for serving the Secretary of State, the Law Officers, and the Counsel General to the Welsh Assembly Government, in cases where they are not parties, shall be issued by practice direction.

Substituted service

89 Where no address for service in accordance with the above rules is known or it appears that service at any such address is unlikely to come to the attention of the addressee, the President, Vice President or a Regional Employment Judge may order that there shall be substituted service in such manner as appears appropriate.

Date of delivery

90 Where a document has been delivered in accordance with rule 85 or 86, it shall, unless the contrary is proved, be taken to have been received by the addressee—

(a) if sent by post, on the day on which it would be delivered in the ordinary course of post;

(b) if sent by means of electronic communication, on the day of transmission;

(c) if delivered directly or personally, on the day of delivery.

Irregular service

91 A Tribunal may treat any document as delivered to a person, notwithstanding any non-compliance with rules 86 to 88, if satisfied that the document in question, or its substance, has in fact come to the attention of that person.

Correspondence with the Tribunal: copying to other parties

92 Where a party sends a communication to the Tribunal (except an application under rule 32) it shall send a copy to all other parties, and state that it has done so (by use of "cc" or otherwise). The Tribunal may order a departure from this rule where it considers it in the interests of justice to do so.

MISCELLANEOUS

ACAS

93 (1) Where proceedings concern an enactment which provides for conciliation, the Tribunal shall—

(a) send a copy of the claim form and the response to an ACAS conciliation officer; and

(b) inform the parties that the services of an ACAS conciliation officer are available to them.

(2) Subject to rules 50 and 94, a representative of ACAS may attend any preliminary hearing.

National security proceedings

94 (1) Where in relation to particular Crown employment proceedings a Minister considers that it would be expedient in the interests of national security, the Minister may direct a Tribunal to—
  (a) conduct all or part of the proceedings in private;
  (b) exclude a person from all or part of the proceedings;
  (c) take steps to conceal the identity of a witness in the proceedings.

(2) Where the Tribunal considers it expedient in the interests of national security, it may order—
  (a) in relation to particular proceedings (including Crown employment proceedings), anything which can be required to be done under paragraph (1);
  (b) a person not to disclose any document (or the contents of any document), where provided for the purposes of the proceedings, to any other person (save for any specified person).

Any order made must be kept under review by the Tribunal.

(3) Where the Tribunal considers that it may be necessary to make an order under paragraph (2) in relation to particular proceedings (including Crown employment proceedings), the Tribunal may consider any material provided by a party (or where a Minister is not a party, by a Minister) without providing that material to any other person. Such material shall be used by the Tribunal solely for the purposes of deciding whether to make that order (unless that material is subsequently used as evidence in the proceedings by a party).

(4) Where a Minister considers that it would be appropriate for the Tribunal to make an order under paragraph (2), the Minister may make an application for such an order.

(5) Where a Minister has made an application under paragraph (4), the Tribunal may order—
  (a) in relation to the part of the proceedings preceding the outcome of the application, anything which can be required to be done under paragraph (1);
  (b) a person not to disclose any document (or the contents of any document) to any other person (save for any specified person), where provided for the purposes of the proceedings preceding the outcome of the application.

(6) Where a Minister has made an application under paragraph (4) for an order to exclude any person from all or part of the proceedings, the Tribunal shall not send a copy of the response to that person, pending the decision on the application.

(7) If before the expiry of the time limit in rule 16 a Minister makes a direction under paragraph (1) or makes an application under paragraph (4), the Minister may apply for an extension of the time limit in rule 16.

(8) A direction under paragraph (1) or an application under paragraph (4) may be made irrespective of whether or not the Minister is a party.

(9) Where the Tribunal decides not to make an order under paragraph (2), rule 6 of Schedule 2 shall apply to the reasons given by the Tribunal under rule 62 for that decision, save that the reasons will not be entered on the Register.

(10) The Tribunal must ensure that in exercising its functions, information is not disclosed contrary to the interests of national security.

Interim relief proceedings

95 When a Tribunal hears an application for interim relief (or for its variation or revocation) under section 161 or section 165 of the Trade Union and Labour Relations (Consolidation) Act 1992 or under section 128 or section 131 of the Employment Rights Act 1996, rules 53 to 56 apply to the hearing and the Tribunal shall not hear oral evidence unless it directs otherwise.

Proceedings involving the National Insurance Fund

96 The Secretary of State shall be entitled to appear and be heard at any hearing in relation to proceedings which may involve a payment out of the National Insurance Fund and shall be treated as a party for the purposes of these Rules.

Collective agreements

97 Where a claim includes a complaint under section 146(1) of the Equality Act relating to a term of a collective agreement, the following persons, whether or not identified in the claim, shall be regarded as the persons against whom a remedy is claimed and shall be treated as respondents for the purposes of these Rules—
  (a) the claimant's employer (or prospective employer); and
  (b) every organisation of employers and organisation of workers, and every association of or representative of such organisations, which, if the terms were to be varied voluntarily, would be likely, in the opinion of an Employment Judge, to negotiate the variation.

An organisation or association shall not be treated as a respondent if the Judge, having made such enquiries of the claimant and such other enquiries as the Judge thinks fit, is of the opinion that it is not reasonably practicable to identify the organisation or association.

Devolution issues

98 (1) Where a devolution issue arises, the Tribunal shall as soon as practicable send notice of that fact and a copy of the claim form and response to the Advocate General for Scotland and the Lord Advocate, where it is a Scottish devolution issue, or to the Attorney General and the Counsel General to the Welsh Assembly Government, where it is a Welsh devolution issue, unless they are a party to the proceedings.

(2) A person to whom notice is sent may be treated as a party to the proceedings, so far as the proceedings relate to the devolution issue, if that person sends notice to the Tribunal within 14 days of receiving a notice under paragraph (1).

(3) Any notices sent under paragraph (1) or (2) must at the same time be sent to the parties.

(4) "Devolution issue" has the meaning given to it in paragraph 1 of Schedule 6 to the Scotland Act 1998 (for the purposes of a Scottish devolution issue), and in paragraph 1 of Schedule 9 to the Government of Wales Act 2006 (for the purposes of a Welsh devolution issue).

Transfer of proceedings between Scotland and England & Wales

99 (1) The President (England and Wales) or a Regional Employment Judge may at any time, on their own initiative or on the application of a party, with the consent of the President (Scotland), transfer to a tribunal office in Scotland any proceedings started in England and Wales which could (in accordance with rule 8(3)) have been started in Scotland and which in that person's opinion would more conveniently be determined there.

(2) The President (Scotland) or the Vice President may at any time, on their own initiative or on the application of a party, with the consent of the President (England and Wales), transfer to a tribunal office in England and Wales any proceedings started in Scotland which could (in accordance with rule 8(2)) have been started in England and Wales and in that person's opinion would more conveniently be determined there.

References to the Court of Justice of the European Union

100 Where a Tribunal decides to refer a question to the Court of Justice of the European Union for a preliminary ruling under Article 267 of the Treaty on the Functioning of the European Union, a copy of that decision shall be sent to the registrar of that court.

Transfer of proceedings from a court

101 Where proceedings are referred to a Tribunal by a court, these Rules apply as if the proceedings had been presented by the claimant.

Vexatious litigants

102 The Tribunal may provide any information or documents requested by the Attorney General, the Solicitor General or the Lord Advocate for the purpose of preparing an application or considering whether to make an application under section 42 of the Senior Courts Act 1981, section 1 of the Vexatious Actions (Scotland) Act 1898 or section 33 of the Employment Tribunals Act.

Information to the Commission for Equality and Human Rights

103 The Tribunal shall send to the Commission for Equality and Human Rights copies of all judgments and written reasons relating to complaints under section 120, 127 or 146 of the Equality Act. That obligation shall not apply in any proceedings where a Minister of the Crown has given a direction, or a Tribunal has made an order, under rule 94; and either the Security Service, the Secret Intelligence Service or the Government Communications Headquarters is a party to the proceedings.

Application of this Schedule to levy appeals

104 For the purposes of a levy appeal, references in this Schedule to a claim or claimant shall be read as references to a levy appeal or to an appellant in a levy appeal respectively.

Application of this Schedule to appeals against improvement and prohibition notices

105 (1) A person ("the appellant") may appeal an improvement notice or a prohibition notice by presenting a claim to a tribunal office—

(a) before the end of the period of 21 days beginning with the date of the service on the appellant of the notice which is the subject of the appeal; or

(b) within such further period as the Tribunal considers reasonable where it is satisfied that it was not reasonably practicable for an appeal to be presented within that time.

(2) For the purposes of an appeal against an improvement notice or a prohibition notice, this Schedule shall be treated as modified in the following ways—

(a) references to a claim or claimant shall be read as references to an appeal or to an appellant in an appeal respectively;

(b) references to a respondent shall be read as references to the inspector appointed under section 19(1) of the Health and Safety Act who issued the notice which is the subject of the appeal.

Application of this Schedule to appeals against unlawful act notices

106 For the purposes of an appeal against an unlawful act notice, this Schedule shall be treated as modified in the following ways—

(a) references in this Schedule to a claim or claimant shall be read as references to a notice of appeal or to an appellant in an appeal against an unlawful act notice respectively;

(b) references to a respondent shall be read as references to the Commission for Equality and Human Rights.

NOTES

Commencement: 29 July 2013.

For transitional provisions (affecting in particular rules 23–25 above and proceedings to which Schs 3, 4 or 5 to the previous (2004) Rules of Procedure at **[2.840]**, **[2.841]** and **[2.842]** respectively apply) see reg 15 at **[2.1703]**.

SCHEDULE 2
THE EMPLOYMENT TRIBUNALS (NATIONAL SECURITY) RULES OF PROCEDURE

Regulation 13(2)

[2.1705]

Application of Schedule 2

1 (1) This Schedule applies to proceedings in relation to which a direction is given, or order is made, under rule 94 and modifies the rules in Schedule 1 in relation to such proceedings.

(2) References in this Schedule to rule numbers are to those in Schedule 1.

(3) The definitions in rule 1 apply to terms in this Schedule and in this Schedule—

"excluded person" means, in relation to any proceedings, a person who has been excluded from all or part of the proceedings by virtue of a direction under rule 94(1)(b) or an order under rule 94(2)(a) (read with rule 94(1)(b)).

Serving of documents

2 The Tribunal shall not send a copy of the response to any excluded person.

Witness orders and disclosure of documents

3 (1) Where a person or their representative has been excluded under rule 94 from all or part of the proceedings and a Tribunal is considering whether to make an order under rule 31 or 32, a Minister (whether or not he is a party to the proceedings) may make an application to the Tribunal objecting to that order. If such an order has been made, the Minister may make an application to vary or set aside the order.

(2) The Tribunal shall hear and determine the Minister's application in private and the Minister shall be entitled to address the Tribunal.

Special advocate

4 (1) The Tribunal shall inform the relevant Law Officer if a party becomes an excluded person. For the purposes of this rule, "relevant Law Officer" means, in relation to England and Wales, the Attorney General, and, in relation to Scotland, the Advocate General.

(2) The relevant Law Officer may appoint a special advocate to represent the interests of a person in respect of those parts of the proceedings from which—

(a) a person's representative is excluded;

(b) a person and their representative are excluded;

(c) a person is excluded and is unrepresented.

(3) A special advocate shall be a person who has a right of audience in relation to any class of proceedings in any part of the Senior Courts or all proceedings in county courts or magistrates' courts, or shall be an advocate or a solicitor admitted in Scotland.

(4) An excluded person (where that person is a party) may make a statement to the Tribunal before the commencement of the proceedings or the relevant part of the proceedings.

(5) The special advocate may communicate, directly or indirectly, with an excluded person at any time before receiving material from a Minister in relation to which the Minister states an objection to disclosure to the excluded person ("closed material").

(6) After receiving closed material, the special advocate must not communicate with any person about any matter connected with the proceedings, except in accordance with paragraph (7) or (9) or an order of the Tribunal.

(7) The special advocate may communicate about the proceedings with—

(a) the Tribunal;

(b) the Minister, or their representative;

(c) the relevant Law Officer, or their representative;

(d) any other person, except for an excluded person or his representative, with whom it is necessary for administrative purposes to communicate about matters not connected with the substance of the proceedings.

(8) The special advocate may apply for an order from the Tribunal to authorise communication with an excluded person or with any other person and if such an application is made—

(a) the Tribunal must notify the Minister of the request; and

(b) the Minister may, within a period specified by the Tribunal, present to the Tribunal and serve on the special advocate notice of any objection to the proposed communication.

(9) After the special advocate has received closed material, an excluded person may only communicate with the special advocate in writing and the special advocate must not reply to the communication, except that the special advocate may send a written acknowledgment of receipt to the legal representative.

(10) References in these Regulations and Schedules 1 and 2 to a party shall include any special advocate appointed in particular proceedings, save that the references to "party" or "parties" in rules 3, 6(c), 22, 26, 34, 36(2), 36(3), the first reference in rule 37, 38, 39, 40, 41, 45, 47, 64, 74 to 84, 86, 96 and 98(3) shall not include the special advocate.

Hearings

5 (1) Subject to any order under rule 50 or any direction or order under rule 94, any hearing shall take place in public, and any party may attend and participate in the hearing.

(2) A member of the Administrative Justice and Tribunals Council shall not be entitled to attend any hearing conducted in private.

Reasons in national security proceedings

6 (1) The Tribunal shall send a copy of the written reasons given under rule 62 to the Minister and allow 42 days for the Minister to make a direction under paragraph (3) below before sending them to any party or entering them onto the Register.

(2) If the Tribunal considers it expedient in the interests of national security, it may by order take steps to keep secret all or part of the written reasons.

(3) If the Minister considers it expedient in the interests of national security, the Minister may direct that the written reasons—

(a) shall not be disclosed to specified persons and require the Tribunal to prepare a further document which sets out the reasons for the decision, but omits specified information ("the edited reasons");

(b) shall not be disclosed to specified persons and that no further document setting out the reasons for the decision should be prepared.

(4) Where the Minister has directed the Tribunal to prepare edited reasons, the Employment Judge shall initial each omission.

(5) Where a direction has been made under paragraph (3)(a), the Tribunal shall—

(a) send the edited reasons to the specified persons;

(b) send the edited reasons and the written reasons to the relevant persons listed in paragraph (7); and

(c) where the written reasons relate to a judgment, enter the edited reasons on the Register but not enter the written reasons on the Register.

(6) Where a direction has been made under paragraph (3)(b), the Tribunal shall send the written reasons to the relevant persons listed in paragraph (7), but not enter the written reasons on the Register.

(7) The relevant persons are—

(a) the respondent or the respondent's representative, provided that they were not specified in the direction made under paragraph (3);

(b) the claimant or the claimant's representative, provided that they were not specified in the direction made under paragraph (3);

(c) any special advocate appointed in the proceedings; and

(d) where the proceedings were referred to the Tribunal by a court, to that court.

(8) Where written reasons or edited reasons are corrected under rule 69, the Tribunal shall send a copy of the corrected reasons to the same persons who had been sent the reasons.

NOTES

Commencement: 29 July 2013.

[2.1706]

SCHEDULE 3
THE EMPLOYMENT TRIBUNALS (EQUAL VALUE) RULES OF PROCEDURE

Regulation 13(2)

Application of Schedule 3

1 (1) This Schedule applies to proceedings involving an equal value claim and modifies the rules in Schedule 1 in relation to such proceedings.

(2) The definitions in rule 1 of Schedule 1 apply to terms in this Schedule and in this Schedule—

"comparator" means the person of the opposite sex to the claimant in relation to whom the claimant alleges that his or her work is of equal value;

"equal value claim" means a claim relating to a breach of a sex equality clause or rule within the meaning of the Equality Act in a case involving work within section 65(1)(c) of that Act;

"the facts relating to the question" has the meaning in rule 6(1)(a);

"independent expert" means a member of the panel of independent experts mentioned in section 131(8) of the Equality Act;

"the question" means whether the claimant's work is of equal value to that of the comparator; and

"report" means a report required by a Tribunal to be prepared in accordance with section 131(2) of the Equality Act.

(3) A reference in this Schedule to a rule, is a reference to a rule in this Schedule unless otherwise provided.

(4) A reference in this Schedule to "these rules" is a reference to the rules in Schedules 1 and 3 unless otherwise provided.

General power to manage proceedings

2 (1) The Tribunal may (subject to rules 3(1) and 6(1)) order—

(a) that no new facts shall be admitted in evidence by the Tribunal unless they have been disclosed to all other parties in writing before a date specified by the Tribunal (unless it was not reasonably practicable for a party to have done so);

(b) the parties to send copies of documents or provide information to the independent expert;

(c) the respondent to grant the independent expert access to the respondent's premises during a period specified in the order to allow the independent expert to conduct interviews with persons identified as relevant by the independent expert;

(d) when more than one expert is to give evidence in the proceedings, that those experts present to the Tribunal a joint statement of matters which are agreed between them and matters on which they disagree.

(2) In managing the proceedings, the Tribunal shall have regard to the indicative timetable in the Annex to this Schedule.

Conduct of stage 1 equal value hearing

3 (1) Where there is a dispute as to whether one person's work is of equal value to another's (equal value being construed in accordance with section 65(6) of the Equality Act), the Tribunal shall conduct a hearing, which shall be referred to as a "stage 1 equal value hearing", and at that hearing shall—

(a) strike out the claim (or the relevant part of it) if in accordance with section 131(6) of the Equality Act the Tribunal must determine that the work of the claimant and the comparator are not of equal value;

(b) determine the question or require an independent expert to prepare a report on the question;

(c) if the Tribunal has decided to require an independent expert to prepare a report on the question, fix a date for a further hearing, which shall be referred to as a "stage 2 equal value hearing"; and

(d) if the Tribunal has not decided to require an independent expert to prepare a report on the question, fix a date for the final hearing.

(2) Before a claim or part is struck out under sub-paragraph (1)(a), the Tribunal shall send notice to the claimant and allow the claimant to make representations to the Tribunal as to whether the evaluation contained in the study in question falls within paragraph (a) or (b) of section 131(6) of the Equality Act. The Tribunal shall not be required to send a notice under this paragraph if the claimant has been given an opportunity to make such representations orally to the Tribunal.

(3) The Tribunal may, on the application of a party, hear evidence and submissions on the issue contained in section 69 of the Equality Act before determining whether to require an independent expert to prepare a report under paragraph (1)(b).

(4) The Tribunal shall give the parties reasonable notice of the date of the stage 1 equal value hearing and the notice shall specify the matters that are to be, or may be, considered at the hearing and give notice of the standard orders in rule 4.

Standard orders for stage 1 equal value hearing

4 (1) At a stage 1 equal value hearing a Tribunal shall, unless it considers it inappropriate to do so, order that—

(a) before the end of the period of 14 days the claimant shall—
   (i) disclose in writing to the respondent the name of any comparator, or, if the claimant is not able to name the comparator, disclose information which enables the respondent to identify the comparator; and
   (ii) identify to the respondent in writing the period in relation to which the claimant considers that the claimant's work and that of the comparator are to be compared;

(b) before the end of the period of 28 days—
   (i) where the claimant has not disclosed the name of the comparator to the respondent under sub-paragraph (a) and the respondent has been provided with sufficient detail to be able to identify the comparator, the respondent shall disclose in writing the name of the comparator to the claimant;
   (ii) the parties shall provide each other with written job descriptions for the claimant and any comparator;
   (iii) the parties shall identify to each other in writing the facts which they consider to be relevant to the question;

(c) the respondent shall grant access to the respondent's premises during a period specified in the order to allow the claimant and his or her representative to interview any comparator;

(d) the parties shall before the end of the period of 56 days present to the Tribunal an agreed written statement specifying—
   (i) job descriptions for the claimant and any comparator;
   (ii) the facts which both parties consider are relevant to the question;
   (iii) the facts on which the parties disagree (as to the fact or as to the relevance to the question) and a summary of their reasons for disagreeing;

(e) the parties shall, at least 56 days before the final hearing, disclose to each other, to any independent or other expert and to the Tribunal written statements of any facts on which they intend to rely in evidence at the final hearing; and

(f) the parties shall, at least 28 days before the final hearing, present to the Tribunal a statement of facts and issues on which the parties are in agreement, a statement of facts and issues on which the parties disagree and a summary of their reasons for disagreeing.

(2) The Tribunal may add to, vary or omit any of the standard orders in paragraph (1).

Involvement of independent expert in fact finding

5 Where the Tribunal has decided to require an independent expert to prepare a report on the question, it may at any stage of the proceedings, on its own initiative or on the application of a party, order the independent expert to assist the Tribunal in establishing the facts on which the independent expert may rely in preparing the report.

Conduct of stage 2 equal value hearing

6 (1) Any stage 2 equal value hearing shall be conducted by a full tribunal and at the hearing the Tribunal shall—

(a) make a determination of facts on which the parties cannot agree which relate to the question and shall require the independent expert to prepare the report on the basis of facts which have (at any stage of the proceedings) either been agreed between the parties or determined by the Tribunal (referred to as "the facts relating to the question"); and

(b) fix a date for the final hearing.

(2) Subject to paragraph (3), the facts relating to the question shall, in relation to the question, be the only facts on which the Tribunal shall rely at the final hearing.

(3) At any stage of the proceedings the independent expert may make an application to the Tribunal for some or all of the facts relating to the question to be amended, supplemented or omitted.

(4) The Tribunal shall give the parties reasonable notice of the date of the stage 2 equal value hearing and the notice shall draw the attention of the parties to this rule and give notice of the standard orders in rule 7.

Standard orders for stage 2 equal value hearing

7 (1) At a stage 2 equal value hearing a Tribunal shall, unless it considers it inappropriate to do so, order that—

(a) by a specified date the independent expert shall prepare his report on the question and shall (subject to rule 13) send copies of it to the parties and to the Tribunal; and

(b) the independent expert shall prepare his report on the question on the basis only of the facts relating to the question.

(2) The Tribunal may add to, vary or omit any of the standard orders in paragraph (1).

Final hearing

8 (1) Where an independent expert has prepared a report, unless the Tribunal determines that the report is not based on the facts relating to the question, the report of the independent expert shall be admitted in evidence.

(2) If the Tribunal does not admit the report of an independent expert in accordance with paragraph (1), it may determine the question itself or require another independent expert to prepare a report on the question.

(3) The Tribunal may refuse to admit evidence of facts or hear submissions on issues which have not been disclosed to the other party as required by these rules or any order (unless it was not reasonably practicable for a party to have done so).

Duties and powers of the independent expert

9 (1) When a Tribunal makes an order under rule 3(1)(b) or 5, it shall inform that independent expert of the duties and powers under this rule.

(2) The independent expert shall have a duty to the Tribunal to—
- (a) assist it in furthering the overriding objective set out in rule 2 of Schedule 1;
- (b) comply with the requirements of these rules and any orders made by the Tribunal;
- (c) keep the Tribunal informed of any delay in complying with any order (with the exception of minor or insignificant delays in compliance);
- (d) comply with any timetable imposed by the Tribunal in so far as this is reasonably practicable;
- (e) when requested, inform the Tribunal of progress in the preparation of the report;
- (f) prepare a report on the question based on the facts relating to the question and (subject to rule 13) send it to the Tribunal and the parties; and
- (g) attend hearings.

(3) The independent expert may make an application for any order or for a hearing to be held as if he were a party to the proceedings.

(4) At any stage of the proceedings the Tribunal may, after giving the independent expert the opportunity to make representations, withdraw the requirement on the independent expert to prepare a report. If it does so, the Tribunal may itself determine the question, or it may require a different independent expert to prepare the report.

(5) When paragraph (4) applies the independent expert who is no longer required to prepare the report shall provide the Tribunal with all documentation and work in progress relating to the proceedings by a specified date. Such documentation and work in progress must be in a form which the Tribunal is able to use and may be used in relation to those proceedings by the Tribunal or by another independent expert.

Use of expert evidence

10 (1) The Tribunal shall restrict expert evidence to that which it considers is reasonably required to resolve the proceedings.

(2) An expert shall have a duty to assist the Tribunal on matters within the expert's expertise. This duty overrides any obligation to the person from whom the expert has received instructions or by whom the expert is paid.

(3) No party may call an expert or put in evidence an expert's report without the permission of the Tribunal. No expert report shall be put in evidence unless it has been disclosed to all other parties and any independent expert at least 28 days before the final hearing.

(4) In proceedings in which an independent expert has been required to prepare a report on the question, the Tribunal shall not admit evidence of another expert on the question unless such evidence is based on the facts relating to the question. Unless the Tribunal considers it inappropriate to do so, any such expert report shall be disclosed to all parties and to the Tribunal on the same date on which the independent expert is required to send his report to the parties and to the tribunal.

(5) If an expert (other than an independent expert) does not comply with these rules or an order made by the Tribunal, the Tribunal may order that the evidence of that expert shall not be admitted.

(6) Where two or more parties wish to submit expert evidence on a particular issue, the Tribunal may order that the evidence on that issue is to be given by one joint expert only and if the parties wishing to instruct the joint expert cannot agree an expert, the Tribunal may select an expert.

Written questions to experts (including independent experts)

11 (1) When an expert has prepared a report, a party or any other expert involved in the proceedings may put written questions about the report to the expert who has prepared the report.

(2) Unless the Tribunal agrees otherwise, written questions under paragraph (1)—
- (a) may be put once only;
- (b) must be put within 28 days of the date on which the parties were sent the report;
- (c) must be for the purpose only of clarifying the factual basis of the report; and
- (d) must be copied to all other parties and experts involved in the proceedings at the same time as they are sent to the expert who prepared the report.

(3) An expert shall answer written questions within 28 days of receipt and the answers shall be treated as part of the expert's report.

(4) Where a party has put a written question to an expert instructed by another party and the expert does not answer that question within 28 days, the Tribunal may order that the party instructing that expert may not rely on the evidence of that expert.

Procedural matters

12 (1) Where an independent expert has been required to prepare a report, the Tribunal shall send that expert notice of any hearing, application, order or judgment in the proceedings as if the independent expert were a party to those proceedings and when these rules or an order requires a party to provide information to another party, such information shall also be provided to the independent expert.

(2) There may be more than one stage 1 or stage 2 equal value hearing in any case.

(3) Any power conferred on an Employment Judge by Schedule 1 may (subject to the provisions of this Schedule) in an equal value claim be carried out by a full tribunal or an Employment Judge.

National security proceedings

13 Where in an equal value claim a direction is given, or order is made, under rule 94 of Schedule 1—

(a) any independent expert appointed shall send a copy of any report and any responses to written questions to the Tribunal only; and

(b) before the Tribunal sends the parties a copy of a report or answers which have been received from an independent expert, it shall follow the procedure set out in rule 6 of Schedule 2 as if that rule referred to the independent expert's report or answers (as the case may be) instead of written reasons, except that the independent expert's report or answers shall not be entered on the Register.

NOTES

Commencement: 29 July 2013.

ANNEX
THE INDICATIVE TIMETABLE

Claims not involving an independent expert

Claim → 28 days → Response → 3 weeks → Stage 1 equal value hearing → 18 weeks → Hearing → Total 25 weeks

Claims involving an independent expert

Claim → 28 days → Response → 3 weeks → Stage 1 equal value hearing → 10 weeks → Stage 2 equal value hearing → 8 weeks → Independent expert's report → 4 weeks → written questions → 8 weeks →Hearing → →Total 37 weeks

EMPLOYMENT TRIBUNALS AND THE EMPLOYMENT APPEAL TRIBUNAL FEES ORDER 2013

(DRAFT)

[2.1707]

NOTES

Authority: Tribunals, Courts and Enforcement Act 2007, ss 42(1)(d), (2), 49(3).

The Government has announced that the date for implementation of this draft Order will be 29 July 2013 (subject to Parliamentary approval).

PART 1
GENERAL

1 Citation and commencement

This Order may be cited as the Employment Tribunals and the Employment Appeal Tribunal Fees Order 2013 and shall come into force on the day after the date on which it is made.

2 Interpretation

In this Order—

"the 2007 Act" means the Tribunals, Courts and Enforcement Act 2007;

"appellant" means a person who appeals to the Employment Appeal Tribunal against a decision of an employment tribunal;

"claim" means any proceedings brought before an employment tribunal and includes an appeal, application, complaint, reference or question, and "claimant" shall be construed accordingly;

"claim form" means the form by means of which a person presents a claim;

"employer's contract claim" means a claim brought by an employer in accordance with articles 4 and 8 of the Employment Tribunals Extension of Jurisdiction (England and Wales) Order 1994 or articles 4 and 8 of the Employment Tribunals Extension of Jurisdiction (Scotland) Order 1994;

"fee group" means—

(a) in relation to the payment of the issue fee, the group of persons named as claimants in the claim form at the time the claim was presented;

(b) subject to article 12(2), in relation to the payment of a hearing fee, the group of persons each of whom—

(i) were named as claimants in the claim form at the time the claim was presented; and

(ii) are named as claimants in the notification of the listing of the final hearing.

"final hearing" means the first hearing at which an employment tribunal will determine liability, remedy or costs;

"notice of appeal" means the notice referred to in rule 3(1)(a) of the Employment Appeal Tribunal Rules 1993; and

"single claimant" means a claimant who is the only claimant named in the claim form.

3 Matters in relation to which fees are payable

Fees are payable in respect of any claim presented to an employment tribunal, or an appeal to the Employment Appeal Tribunal, as provided for in this Order.

PART 2
FEES IN EMPLOYMENT TRIBUNALS

4 Fee charging occasions

(1) A fee is payable by a single claimant or a fee group—

(a) when a claim form is presented to an employment tribunal ("the issue fee"); and

(b) on a date specified in a notice accompanying the notification of the listing of a final hearing of the claim ("the hearing fee").

(2) A fee is payable by the party making an application listed in column 1 of Schedule 1 on a date specified by the Lord Chancellor in a notice following the making of the application.

(3) A fee of £600 is payable by the respondent on a date specified in a notice accompanying a notification of listing for judicial mediation.

5 Fees payable

Table 1 in Schedule 2 has effect for the purpose of defining expressions used in Table 2 in that Schedule.

6

The issue fee and hearing fee payable by a single claimant in respect of a claim listed in Table 2 in Schedule 2 ("a type A claim") is the amount specified in column 2 of Table 3 in Schedule 2.

7

The issue fee and hearing fee payable by a single claimant in respect of any claim other than one listed in Table 2 in Schedule 2 ("a type B claim") is the amount specified in column 3 of Table 3 in Schedule 2.

8

Subject to articles 9 and 10, the issue fee and hearing fee payable by a fee group is the amount calculated by reference to Table 4 in Schedule 2.

9

Subject to article 10, where, on the date on which a fee is payable in accordance with article 4, the claim form contains—

(a) one or more type A claim and one or more type B claim, the total amount of the fees payable in respect of all the claims is the fee specified in respect of a type B claim; or

(b) more than one claim of the same type, then the total amount of the fees payable in respect of all the claims is the amount specified in Table 3 or, in the case of a fee group, Table 4 in Schedule 2 for that type of claim.

10

Any fee payable by a fee group under article 8 or 9—

(a) must not exceed an amount equal to the sum of the fees which the members of the fee group would have been liable to pay as single claimants; and

(b) where one or more members of the group is entitled to remission in accordance with Schedule 3, must not exceed an amount equal to the sum of the fees which the members of the fee group would be liable to pay as single claimants, taking into account any remission which would have been granted to individual members of the group if they were single claimants.

11

(1) The fee payable in relation to an application listed in column 1 of Schedule 1, irrespective of the number of claims or of claimants named in the application is the amount specified in the relevant part of column 2 of Schedule 1.

(2) Where an application referred to in paragraph (1) is made in respect of one or more type A claims and one or more type B claims, the amount of the fee payable in respect of the application is the amount specified in column 2 of Schedule 1 in respect of a type B claim.

12 Fee group – failure to pay fee

(1) Where a fee payable by a fee group remains unpaid after the date specified in accordance with article 4, a member of that fee group may, before the date on which the claim to which the fee relates is liable to be struck out for non payment, notify the Lord Chancellor of that member's decision no longer to be part of the group.

(2) Where a notice is received by the Lord Chancellor before the date on which the claim is liable to be struck out, the member of the fee group who has given the notification shall be treated as a single claimant for the purposes of the claim to which the notice referred to in paragraph (1) relates.

PART 3
FEES IN THE EMPLOYMENT APPEAL TRIBUNAL

13 Fees payable

A fee of £400 is payable by an appellant on the date specified in a notice issued by the Lord Chancellor, following the receipt by the Employment Appeal Tribunal of a notice of appeal.

14

A fee of £1200 is payable by an appellant on the date specified in a notice issued by the Lord Chancellor, following a direction by the Employment Appeal Tribunal that a matter proceed to an oral hearing at which the appeal is to be finally disposed of.

PART 4
TRANSITIONAL ARRANGEMENTS, REMISSION ETC

15 Transitional arrangements

No fee is payable in respect of a claim where the claim form was presented before the date this Order comes into force.

16

No fee is payable in respect of proceedings in the Employment Appeal Tribunal where a notice of appeal was received by that Tribunal before the date on which this Order comes into force.

17 Remission provisions

(1) Schedule 3 applies for the purposes of determining whether a person is entitled to a remission or part remission of any fee otherwise payable under this Order.

(2) Where an application for remission is made by a member of a fee group, Schedule 3 is to have effect for the purposes of determining whether or not the member of the group would be entitled to remission (whether wholly or in part) if that person was a single claimant.

18

The Lord Chancellor may disregard an application for remission by a member of a fee group if the amount of the fee payable by the fee group would not be altered in consequence of the application being granted.

19 International obligations

Where by any Convention, treaty or other instrument entered into by Her Majesty with any foreign power it is provided that no fee is required to be paid in respect of any proceedings, the fees specified in this Order are not payable in respect of those proceedings.

SCHEDULE 1
EMPLOYMENT TRIBUNALS – OTHER FEES

Articles 4 and 11

Fee(s) payable by applicant

Column 1	*Column 2*	
Type of application	*Type A claim*	*Type B claim*
Reconsideration of a default judgment	£100	£100
Reconsideration of a judgment following a final hearing	£100	£350
Dismissal following withdrawal	£60	£60
An employer's contract claim made by way of application as part of the response to the employee's contract claim	£160	—

SCHEDULE 2
EMPLOYMENT TRIBUNALS – ISSUE AND HEARING FEE

Articles 4 to 9

TABLE 1 – ABBREVIATIONS USED IN TABLE 2 IN THIS SCHEDULE

CAR	Civil Aviation (Working Time) Regulations 2004
CCBR	Companies (Cross-Border Mergers) Regulations 2007
CEC	Colleges of Education (Compensation) Regulations 1975
COMAH	Control of Major Accident Hazards Regulations 1999
EA 2006	Equality Act 2006
EA 2010	Equality Act 2010
EAA	Employment Agencies Act 1973
ECSR	European Cooperative Society (Involvement of Employees) Regulations 2006
EJOs	Employment Tribunals Extension of Jurisdiction (England and Wales) Order 1994; and Employment Tribunals Extension of Jurisdiction (Scotland) Order 1994
EOR	Ecclesiastical Offices (Terms of Service) Regulations 2009
ELLR	European Public Limited-Liability Company (Employee Involvement) (Great Britain) Regulations 2009
ERA	Employment Rights Act 1996
ETA	Employment Tribunals Act 1996
FVR	Fishing Vessels (Working Time: Sea-fishermen) Regulations 2004
HSCE	Health and Safety (Consultation with Employees) Regulations 1996
HSWA	Health and Safety at Work etc Act 1974
ICR	Information and Consultation of Employees Regulations 2004
ITA	Industrial Training Act 1982
MSR	Merchant Shipping (Working Time: Inland Waterways) Regulations 2003

NMWA	National Minimum Wage Act 1998
OPR	Occupational and Personal Pension Schemes (Consultation by Employers and Miscellaneous Amendment) Regulations 2006
OPS(CO)R	Occupational Pension Schemes (Contracting-Out) Regulations 1996
OPS(DI)R	Occupational Pensions Schemes (Disclosure of Information) Regulations 1996
PSA	Pension Schemes Act 1993
REACHER	REACH Enforcement Regulations 2008(
RTR	Road Transport (Working Time) Regulations 2005
SRSC	Safety Representatives and Safety Committees Regulations 1977
TULR(C)A	Trade Union and Labour Relations (Consolidation) Act 1992
TUPE	Transfer of Undertakings (Protection of Employment) Regulations 2006
WTR	Working Time Regulations 1998

TABLE 2 TYPE A CLAIMS

Column 1 *Description of claim*	*Column 2* *Provision identifying the rights of the claimant*	*Column 3* *Provision conferring jurisdiction on tribunal*
Application by the Secretary of State to prohibit a person from running an Employment Agency	Sections 3A EAA	Sections 3A EAA
Application by a person subject to a prohibition order to vary or set it aside	Section 3C EAA	Section 3C EAA
Appeal against improvement or prohibition notice	Section 24 HSWA	Section 24 HSWA
Appeal against assessment of training levy	Section 12 ITA	Section 12 ITA
Complaint of deduction of unauthorised subscriptions	Section 68 TULR(C)A	Section 68A TULR(C)A
Complaint relating to failure to deduct or refuse to deduct an amount to a political fund	Section 86 TULR(C)A	Section 87 TULR(C)A
Complaint that an employer has failed to permit time off for carrying out trade union duties	Section 168 TULR(C)A	Section 168 TULR(C)A
Complaint that an employer has failed to permit time off for union learning representatives	Section 168A TULR(C)A	Section 168A TULR(C)A
Complaint that an employer has failed to pay for time off for union learning representatives	Section 169 TULR(C)A	Section 169 TULR(C)A
Complaint that an employer has failed to permit time off for trade union activities	Section 170 TULR(C)A	Section 170 TULR(C)A
Complaint that employer has failed, wholly or in part, to pay remuneration under a protective award	Section 190 TULR(C)A	Section 192 TULR(C)A

Column 1 *Description of claim*	*Column 2* *Provision identifying the rights of the claimant*	*Column 3* *Provision conferring jurisdiction on tribunal*
Complaint that the Secretary of State has not paid, or has paid less than, the amount of relevant contributions which should have been paid into a pension scheme	Section 124 PSA	Section 126 PSA
Breach of contract, except where the employer's contract claim is made made by way of application as part of the employer's response to the employee's contract claim (as to which, see instead article 4 and Schedule 1 to this Order)		Section 3 ETA; Articles 3 and 4 of each of the EJOs
Reference to determine what particulars ought to be included in a statement of employment particulars or changes to particulars	Sections 1 and 4 ERA	Section 11 ERA
Reference to determine what particulars ought to be included in an itemised pay statement	Section 8 ERA	Section 11 ERA
Complaint of unauthorised deductions from wages	Section 13 ERA	Section 23 ERA
Complaint that employer has received unauthorised payments	Section 15 ERA	Section 23 ERA
Complaint that employer has failed to pay guaranteed payment	Section 28 ERA	Section 34 ERA
Complaint that employer has failed to permit time off for public duties	Section 50 ERA	Section 51 ERA
Complaint that employer has refused to permit, or has failed to pay for, time off to look for work or arrange training	Sections 52 and 53 ERA	Section 54 ERA
Complaint that employer has refused to allow, or has failed to pay for, time off for antenatal care	Sections 55, 56, 57ZA and 57ZB ERA	Sections 57 and 57ZC ERA
Complaint that employer has refused to allow time off for dependants	Section 57A ERA	Section 57B ERA
Complaint that employer has failed to allow, or to pay for, time off for trustee of pension scheme	Sections 58 and 59 ERA	Section 60 ERA
Complaint that employer has failed to allow, or to pay for, time off for employee representative	Sections 61 and 62 ERA	Section 63 ERA
Complaint that employer has failed to allow, or to pay for, time off for young people in Wales and Scotland	Section 63A and 63B ERA	Section 63C ERA

Column 1 ***Description of claim***	***Column 2*** ***Provision identifying the rights of the claimant***	***Column 3*** ***Provision conferring jurisdiction on tribunal***
Complaint that employer has failed to pay for time off on medical or maternity grounds	Sections 64, 68 and 68C ERA	Sections 70 and 70A ERA
Complaint that employer has failed to allow time of for studies or training or the refusal is based on incorrect facts	Section 63D to 63H ERA	Section 63I ERA
Complaint that employer has unreasonably failed to provide a written statement of reasons for dismissal or the particulars are inadequate or untrue	Section 92 ERA	Section 93 ERA
Reference in respect of a right to redundancy payment	Section 135 ERA	Sections 163 and 177 ERA
Reference related to payment out of National Insurance Fund	Section 166 ERA	Section 170 ERA
References related to payments equivalent to redundancy payments	Sections 167, 168 and 177 ERA	Section 177 ERA
Complaint that the Secretary of State has failed to make any, or insufficient, payment of out the National Insurance Fund	Section 182 ERA	Section 188 ERA
Appeal against a notice of underpayment	Section 19C NMWA	Section 19C NMWA
Appeal against a notice issued by the Commission for Equality and Human Rights where the notice relates to an unlawful act	Section 21 EA 2006	Section 21 EA 2006
Complaint that prospective employer made enquiries about disability or health	Section 60 EA 2010	Section 120 EA 2010
Application in relation to the effect of a non-discrimination rule in an occupational pension scheme	Section 61 EA 2010	Section 120 EA 2010
Complaint in relation to a breach of a sex equality clause	Section 66 EA 2010	Section 127 EA 2010
Complaint in relation to a breach of, or application in relation to the effect of, a sex equality rule in an occupational pension scheme	Section 67 EA 2010	Section 127 EA 2010
Complaint in relation to a breach of a maternity equality clause	Section 73 EA 2010	Section 127 EA 2010
Complaint in relation to a breach of, or application in relation to the effect of, a maternity equality rule in an occupational pension scheme	Section 75 EA 2010	Section 127 EA 2010

Column 1 ***Description of claim***	***Column 2*** ***Provision identifying the rights of the claimant***	***Column 3*** ***Provision conferring jurisdiction on tribunal***
Complaint in relation to terms prohibiting discussions about pay	Section 77 EA 2010	Section 120 EA 2010
Complaint that a term in a collective agreement is void or unenforceable	Section 145 EA 2010	Section 146 EA 2010
Appeal of decision of compensating authority	Regulation 42 CEC	Regulation 42 CEC
Complaint that employer has failed to pay for remunerated time off for safety representative	Regulation 4(2) of, and Schedule 2 to, the SRSC	Regulation 11 SRSC
Reference that there has been a failure to consult with employee representatives about contracting out of pension scheme	Regulation 4 OPS(CO)R and regulation 9 of OPS(DI)R	Regulation 4 OPS(CO)R and regulation 9 of OPS(DI)R
Complaint that employer has failed to pay for time off to carry out Safety Representative duties or undertake training	Regulation 7 of, and Schedule 1 to, the HSCE	Schedule 2 to the HSCE
Complaint that employer has refused to allow annual leave, compensation, payment, compensatory rest	Regulations 13, 13A,14, 16, 24, 24A, 27 and 27A WTR	Regulation 30 WTR
Appeal against improvement or prohibition notice	Paragraph 6 of Schedule 3 to WTR	Paragraph 6 of Schedule 3 to WTR
Appeal against improvement or prohibition notice	Regulation 18 COMAH	Regulation 18 COMAH
Complaint in relation to refusal of annual leave or to make payment	Regulation 11 MSR	Regulation 18 MSR
Complaint in relation to refusal to provide paid annual leave	Regulation 4 CAR	Regulation 18 CAR
Complaint in relation to failure to provide free health assessments	Regulation 5 CAR	Regulation 18 CAR
Complaint in relation to refusal of annual leave or to make payment	Regulation 11 FVR	Regulation 19 FVR
Complaint that employer has refused to allow or failed to pay for time off for information and consultation or negotiating representatives	Regulations 27 and 28 ICR	Regulation 29 ICR
Appeal against improvement notice	Paragraph 6(2) of Schedule 2 to the RTR	Paragraph 6(2) of Schedule 2 to the RTR
Complaint in relation to failure of employer to inform or consult	Regulation 13 TUPE	Regulation 15 TUPE
Complaint that employer has failed to allow, or pay for, time off for functions as employee representative	Paragraphs 2 and 3 of the Schedule to OPR	Paragraph 4 of the Schedule to OPR

Column 1 *Description of claim*	*Column 2* *Provision identifying the rights of the claimant*	*Column 3* *Provision conferring jurisdiction on tribunal*
Complaint that employer has failed to allow, or pay for, time off for members of special negotiating body	Regulations 28 and 29 ECSR	Regulation 30 ECSR
Complaint that employer has failed to allow, or pay for, time off for members of special negotiating body	Regulations 43 and 44 CCBR	Regulation 45 CCBR
Appeal against notice from Health and Safety Executive or a local authority	Regulation 21 and Part 2 of Schedule 8 to REACHER	Regulation 21 and Part 2 of Schedule 8 to REACHER
Reference to determine what particulars ought to be included in an itemised statement of stipend	Regulation 6 EOR	Regulation 9 EOR
Reference to determine what particulars ought to be included in a statement of particulars or changes to particulars	Regulations 3 and 6 EOR	Regulation 9 EOR
Complaint that employer has failed to allow, or pay for, time off for members of special negotiating body	Regulations 26 and 27 ELLR	Regulation 28 ELLR

TABLE 3 AMOUNT OF FEE – CLAIM MADE BY A SINGLE CLAIMANT

Column 1 *Fee type*	*Column 2* *Type A claim*	*Column 3* *Type B claim*
1. Issue fee	£160	£250
2. Hearing fee	£230	£950

TABLE 4 AMOUNT OF FEE – FEE GROUP
PART A – TYPE A CLAIM

Column 1 *Type of fee*	*Column 2* *Number of claimants/amount of fee*		
	2-10	11-200	Over 200
Issue fee	£320	£640	£960
Hearing fee	£460	£920	£1380

PART B – TYPE B CLAIM

Column 1 *Type of fee*	*Column 2* *Number of claimants/amount of fee*		
	2-10	11-200	Over 200
Issue fee	£500	£1,000	£1,500
Hearing fee	£1900	£3,800	£5,700

SCHEDULE 3
REMISSIONS AND PART REMISSIONS

Article 17

1. Interpretation

(1) In this Schedule—

"child" means a child or young person in respect of whom a party is entitled to receive child benefit in accordance with section 141, and regulations made under section 142, of the Social Security Contributions and Benefits Act 1992;

"child care costs" has the meaning given in Part 3 of the Criminal Legal Aid (Financial Resources) Regulations 2013;

"couple" has the meaning given in section 3(5A) of the Tax Credits Act 2002;

"disposable monthly income" has the meaning given in paragraph 5;

"excluded benefits" means—

- (a) any of the following benefits payable under the Social Security Contributions and Benefits Act 1992—
  - (i) attendance allowance paid under section 64;
  - (ii) severe disablement allowance;
  - (iii) carer's allowance;
  - (iv) disability living allowance;
  - (v) constant attendance allowance paid under section 104 as an increase to a disablement pension;
  - (vi) council tax benefit;
  - (vii) any payment made out of the social fund;
  - (viii) housing benefit;
- (b) any direct payment made under the Community Care, Services for Carers and Children's Services (Direct Payments) (England) Regulations 2009, the Community Care, Services for Carers and Children's Services (Direct Payments) (Wales) Regulations 2011, or section 12B(1) of the Social Work (Scotland) Act 1968;
- (c) a back to work bonus payable under section 26 of the Jobseekers Act 1995;
- (d) any exceptionally severe disablement allowance paid under the Personal Injuries (Civilians) Scheme 1983;
- (e) any pension paid under the Naval, Military and Air Forces etc. (Disablement and Death) Service Pension Order 2006;
- (f) any payment made from the Independent Living Funds; and
- (g) any financial support paid under an agreement for the care of a foster child;

"gross annual income" means total annual income, for the 12 months preceding the application for remission or part remission, from all sources other than receipt of any of the excluded benefits;

"gross monthly income" means total monthly income, for the month in which the application for remission or part remission is made, from all sources other than receipt of any of the excluded benefits;

"the Independent Living Funds" means any payment made from the funds listed at regulation 20(2)(b) of the Criminal Legal Aid (Financial Resources) Regulations 2013;

"partner" means a person with whom the party lives as a couple and includes a person with whom the party is not currently living but from whom the party is not living separate and apart;

"party" means the individual who would, but for this Schedule, be liable to pay the fee required under this Order.

(2) Paragraphs 2, 3 and 4 do not apply to a party for whom civil legal services, for which a certificate has been issued under the Civil Legal Aid (Procedure) Regulations 2012, have been made available under arrangements made for the purposes of Part 1 of the Legal Aid, Sentencing and Punishment of Offenders Act 2012 for the purposes of the proceedings.

2. Full remission of fees—qualifying benefits

(1) No fee is payable under this Order if, at the time when a fee would otherwise be payable, the party is in receipt of a qualifying benefit.

(2) The following are qualifying benefits for the purposes of sub-paragraph (1)—

- (a) income support under the Social Security Contributions and Benefits Act 1992;
- (b) working tax credit, provided that no child tax credit is being paid to the party;
- (c) income-based jobseeker's allowance under the Jobseekers Act 1995;
- (d) guarantee credit under the State Pension Credit Act 2002; and
- (e) income-related employment and support allowance under the Welfare Reform Act 2007.

3. Full remission of fees—gross annual income

(1) No fee is payable under this Order if, at the time when the fee would otherwise be payable, the party has the number of children specified in column 1 of the following table and—

- (a) if the party is single, the gross annual income of the party does not exceed the amount set out in the appropriate row of column 2; or
- (b) if the party is one of a couple, the gross annual income of the couple does not exceed the amount set out in the appropriate row of column 3.

Column 1 *Number of children of party*	*Column 2* *Single*	*Column 3* *Couple*
no children	£13,000	£18,000
1 child	£15,930	£20,930
2 children	£18,860	£23,860
3 children	£21,790	£26,790
4 children	£24,720	£29,720

(2) If the party has more than 4 children then the relevant amount of gross annual income is the amount specified in the table for 4 children plus the sum of £2,930 for each additional child.

4. Full and part remission of fees—disposable monthly income

(1) No fee is payable under this Order if, at the time when the fee would otherwise be payable, the disposable monthly income of the party is £50 or less.

(2) The maximum amount of fee payable is—

(a) if the disposable monthly income of the party is more than £50 but does not exceed £210, an amount equal to one-quarter of every £10 of the party's disposable monthly income up to a maximum of £50; and

(b) if the disposable monthly income is more than £210, an amount equal to £50 plus one-half of every £10 over £200 of the party's disposable monthly income.

(3) Where the fee that would otherwise be payable under this Order is greater than the maximum fee which a party is required to pay as calculated in sub-paragraph (2), the fee will be remitted to the amount payable under that sub-paragraph.

5. Disposable monthly income

(1) A party's disposable monthly income is the gross monthly income of the party for the month in which the fee becomes payable ("the period") less the deductions referred to in subparagraphs (2) and (3).

(2) There are to be deducted from the gross monthly income—

(a) income tax paid or payable in respect of the period;

(b) any contributions estimated to have been paid under Part 1 of the Social Security Contributions and Benefits Act 1992 in respect of the period;

(c) either—

(i) monthly rent or monthly payment in respect of a mortgage debt or hereditable security, payable in respect of the only or main dwelling of the party, less any housing benefit paid under the Social Security Contributions and Benefits Act 1992; or

(ii) the monthly cost of the living accommodation of the party;

(d) any child care costs paid or payable in respect of the period;

(e) if the party is making bona fide payments for the maintenance of a child who is not a member of the household of the party, the amount of such payments paid or payable in respect of the period; and

(f) any amount paid or payable by the party, in respect of the period, in pursuance of a court order.

(3) There will be deducted from the gross monthly income an amount representing the cost of living expenses in respect of the period being—

(a) £315; plus

(b) £244 for each child of the party; plus

(c) £159, if the party has a partner.

6. Resources of partners

(1) For the purpose of determining whether a party is entitled to the remission or part remission of a fee in accordance with this Schedule, the income of a partner, if any, is to be included as income of the party.

(2) The receipt by a partner of a qualifying benefit does not entitle a party to remission of a fee.

7. Application for remission or part remission of fees

(1) A party is only relieved by paragraphs 2 to 4 of liability to pay a fee if that party makes an application for remission in accordance with this paragraph.

(2) An application for remission or part remission of a fee must be made to the Lord Chancellor at the time when the fee would otherwise be payable.

(3) Where a claim for full remission of fees is made, the party must provide documentary evidence of, as the case may be—

(a) entitlement to a qualifying benefit; or

(b) gross annual income and, if applicable, the children included for the purposes of paragraph 3.

(4) Where a claim for full or part remission of fees under paragraph 4 is made, the party must provide documentary evidence of—

(a) such of the party's gross monthly income as is derived from—
   (i) employment;
   (ii) rental or other income received from persons living with the party by reason of their residence in the party's home;
   (iii) a pension; or
   (iv) a state benefit, not being an excluded benefit; and

(b) any expenditure being deducted from the gross monthly income in accordance with paragraph 5(2).

8. Remission in exceptional circumstances

A fee specified in this Order may be reduced or remitted where the Lord Chancellor is satisfied there are exceptional circumstances which justify doing so.

9. Time for payment following remission application

(1) Where a person applies for remission on or before the date on which a fee is payable, the date for payment of the fee specified in article 4 is disapplied.

(2) Where the Lord Chancellor refuses remission or grants part remission of a fee, the amount of the fee which remains unremitted must be paid within such period as may be notified in writing by the Lord Chancellor to the party or the fee group (as the case may be).

10. Refunds

(1) Subject to sub-paragraph (3), where a party has not provided the documentary evidence required by paragraph 7 and a fee has been paid at a time when, under paragraph 2, 3 or 4, it was not payable, the fee must be refunded if documentary evidence relating to the time when the fee became payable is provided at a later date.

(2) Subject to sub-paragraph (3), where a fee has been paid at a time where the Lord Chancellor, if all the circumstances had been known, would have reduced or remitted the fee under paragraph 8, the fee or the amount by which the fee would have been reduced, as the case may be, must be refunded.

(3) No refund shall be made under this paragraph unless the party who paid the fee applies within 6 months of paying the fee.

(4) The Lord Chancellor may extend the period of 6 months mentioned in sub-paragraph (3) if the Lord Chancellor considers that there is a good reason for an application being made after the end of the period of 6 months.

ADDED TRIBUNALS (EMPLOYMENT TRIBUNALS AND EMPLOYMENT APPEAL TRIBUNAL) ORDER 2013

(DRAFT)

[2.1708]

NOTES

Authority: Tribunals, Courts and Enforcement Act 2007, s 42(3).

The Government has announced that the date for implementation of this draft Order will be 29 July 2013 (subject to Parliamentary approval).

1 Citation and commencement

This Order may be cited as the Added Tribunals (Employment Tribunals and Employment Appeal Tribunal) Order 2013.

2 Employment tribunals and the Employment Appeal Tribunal to be "added tribunals"

Employment tribunals and the Employment Appeal Tribunal are "added tribunals" for the purpose of section 42 of the 2007 Act.

PART 3
EU MATERIALS

A. CONSTITUTIONAL MATERIALS

CONSOLIDATED VERSION OF THE TREATY ON EUROPEAN UNION

NOTES

Date of publication in OJ: OJ C326, 26.10.2012, p 13.

Commencement: 1 December 2009.

This is the Treaty on European Union as consolidated following the amendments made by the Treaty of Lisbon, which came into force on 1 December 2009. Only those Articles of particular relevance to employment law are printed here.

Cross-references to the equivalent article in the pre-Lisbon Treaty version of the Treaty are given at the beginning of each of the Articles reproduced which have such equivalents; these cross-references are part of the official text. For further information on the derivation of Articles reproduced here see the Table of Equivalences at **[3.12]**.

TITLE I
COMMON PROVISIONS

[3.1]
Article 1
(ex Article 1 TEU)

By this Treaty, the HIGH CONTRACTING PARTIES establish among themselves a EUROPEAN UNION, hereinafter called "the Union", on which the Member States confer competences to attain objectives they have in common.

This Treaty marks a new stage in the process of creating an ever closer union among the peoples of Europe, in which decisions are taken as openly as possible and as closely as possible to the citizen.

The Union shall be founded on the present Treaty and on the Treaty on the Functioning of the European Union (hereinafter referred to as "the Treaties"). Those two Treaties shall have the same legal value. The Union shall replace and succeed the European Community.

[3.2]
Article 2

The Union is founded on the values of respect for human dignity, freedom, democracy, equality, the rule of law and respect for human rights, including the rights of persons belonging to minorities. These values are common to the Member States in a society in which pluralism, non-discrimination, tolerance, justice, solidarity and equality between women and men prevail.

[3.3]
Article 3
(ex Article 2 TEU)

1. The Union's aim is to promote peace, its values and the well-being of its peoples.
2. The Union shall offer its citizens an area of freedom, security and justice without internal frontiers, in which the free movement of persons is ensured in conjunction with appropriate measures with respect to external border controls, asylum, immigration and the prevention and combating of crime.
3. The Union shall establish an internal market. It shall work for the sustainable development of Europe based on balanced economic growth and price stability, a highly competitive social market economy, aiming at full employment and social progress, and a high level of protection and improvement of the quality of the environment. It shall promote scientific and technological advance.

It shall combat social exclusion and discrimination, and shall promote social justice and protection, equality between women and men, solidarity between generations and protection of the rights of the child.

It shall promote economic, social and territorial cohesion, and solidarity among Member States.

It shall respect its rich cultural and linguistic diversity, and shall ensure that Europe's cultural heritage is safeguarded and enhanced.

4. The Union shall establish an economic and monetary union whose currency is the euro.
5. In its relations with the wider world, the Union shall uphold and promote its values and interests and contribute to the protection of its citizens. It shall contribute to peace, security, the sustainable development of the Earth, solidarity and mutual respect among peoples, free and fair trade, eradication of poverty and the protection of human rights, in particular the rights of the child, as well as to the strict observance and the development of international law, including respect for the principles of the United Nations Charter.

6. The Union shall pursue its objectives by appropriate means commensurate with the competences which are conferred upon it in the Treaties.

[3.4]
Article 4
1. In accordance with Article 5, competences not conferred upon the Union in the Treaties remain with the Member States.
2. The Union shall respect the equality of Member States before the Treaties as well as their national identities, inherent in their fundamental structures, political and constitutional, inclusive of regional and local self-government. It shall respect their essential State functions, including ensuring the territorial integrity of the State, maintaining law and order and safeguarding national security. In particular, national security remains the sole responsibility of each Member State.
3. Pursuant to the principle of sincere cooperation, the Union and the Member States shall, in full mutual respect, assist each other in carrying out tasks which flow from the Treaties.

The Member States shall take any appropriate measure, general or particular, to ensure fulfilment of the obligations arising out of the Treaties or resulting from the acts of the institutions of the Union.

The Member States shall facilitate the achievement of the Union's tasks and refrain from any measure which could jeopardise the attainment of the Union's objectives.

[3.5]
Article 5
(ex Article 5 TEC)
1. The limits of Union competences are governed by the principle of conferral. The use of Union competences is governed by the principles of subsidiarity and proportionality.
2. Under the principle of conferral, the Union shall act only within the limits of the competences conferred upon it by the Member States in the Treaties to attain the objectives set out therein. Competences not conferred upon the Union in the Treaties remain with the Member States.
3. Under the principle of subsidiarity, in areas which do not fall within its exclusive competence, the Union shall act only if and in so far as the objectives of the proposed action cannot be sufficiently achieved by the Member States, either at central level or at regional and local level, but can rather, by reason of the scale or effects of the proposed action, be better achieved at Union level.

The institutions of the Union shall apply the principle of subsidiarity as laid down in the Protocol on the application of the principles of subsidiarity and proportionality. National Parliaments ensure compliance with the principle of subsidiarity in accordance with the procedure set out in that Protocol.
4. Under the principle of proportionality, the content and form of Union action shall not exceed what is necessary to achieve the objectives of the Treaties.

The institutions of the Union shall apply the principle of proportionality as laid down in the Protocol on the application of the principles of subsidiarity and proportionality.

[3.6]
Article 6
(ex Article 6 TEU)
1. The Union recognises the rights, freedoms and principles set out in the Charter of Fundamental Rights of the European Union of 7 December 2000, as adapted at Strasbourg, on 12 December 2007, which shall have the same legal value as the Treaties.

The provisions of the Charter shall not extend in any way the competences of the Union as defined in the Treaties.

The rights, freedoms and principles in the Charter shall be interpreted in accordance with the general provisions in Title VII of the Charter governing its interpretation and application and with due regard to the explanations referred to in the Charter, that set out the sources of those provisions.
2. The Union shall accede to the European Convention for the Protection of Human Rights and Fundamental Freedoms. Such accession shall not affect the Union's competences as defined in the Treaties.
3. Fundamental rights, as guaranteed by the European Convention for the Protection of Human Rights and Fundamental Freedoms and as they result from the constitutional traditions common to the Member States, shall constitute general principles of the Union's law.

TITLE III
PROVISIONS ON THE INSTITUTIONS

[3.7]
Article 13
1. The Union shall have an institutional framework which shall aim to promote its values, advance its objectives, serve its interests, those of its citizens and those of the Member States, and ensure the consistency, effectiveness and continuity of its policies and actions.

The Union's institutions shall be:
— the European Parliament,
— the European Council,
— the Council,
— the European Commission (hereinafter referred to as "the Commission"),
— the Court of Justice of the European Union,
— the European Central Bank,
— the Court of Auditors.

2. Each institution shall act within the limits of the powers conferred on it in the Treaties, and in conformity with the procedures, conditions and objectives set out in them. The institutions shall practice mutual sincere cooperation.

3. The provisions relating to the European Central Bank and the Court of Auditors and detailed provisions on the other institutions are set out in the Treaty on the Functioning of the European Union.

4. The European Parliament, the Council and the Commission shall be assisted by an Economic and Social Committee and a Committee of the Regions acting in an advisory capacity.

[3.8]
Article 14

1. The European Parliament shall, jointly with the Council, exercise legislative and budgetary functions. It shall exercise functions of political control and consultation as laid down in the Treaties. It shall elect the President of the Commission.

2. The European Parliament shall be composed of representatives of the Union's citizens. They shall not exceed seven hundred and fifty in number, plus the President. Representation of citizens shall be degressively proportional, with a minimum threshold of six members per Member State. No Member State shall be allocated more than ninety-six seats.

The European Council shall adopt by unanimity, on the initiative of the European Parliament and with its consent, a decision establishing the composition of the European Parliament, respecting the principles referred to in the first subparagraph.

3. The members of the European Parliament shall be elected for a term of five years by direct universal suffrage in a free and secret ballot.

4. The European Parliament shall elect its President and its officers from among its members.

[3.9]
Article 15

1. The European Council shall provide the Union with the necessary impetus for its development and shall define the general political directions and priorities thereof. It shall not exercise legislative functions.

2. The European Council shall consist of the Heads of State or Government of the Member States, together with its President and the President of the Commission. The High Representative of the Union for Foreign Affairs and Security Policy shall take part in its work.

3. The European Council shall meet twice every six months, convened by its President. When the agenda so requires, the members of the European Council may decide each to be assisted by a minister and, in the case of the President of the Commission, by a member of the Commission. When the situation so requires, the President shall convene a special meeting of the European Council.

4. Except where the Treaties provide otherwise, decisions of the European Council shall be taken by consensus.

5. The European Council shall elect its President, by a qualified majority, for a term of two and a half years, renewable once. In the event of an impediment or serious misconduct, the European Council can end the President's term of office in accordance with the same procedure.

6. The President of the European Council:
(a) shall chair it and drive forward its work;
(b) shall ensure the preparation and continuity of the work of the European Council in cooperation with the President of the Commission, and on the basis of the work of the General Affairs Council;
(c) shall endeavour to facilitate cohesion and consensus within the European Council;
(d) shall present a report to the European Parliament after each of the meetings of the European Council.

The President of the European Council shall, at his level and in that capacity, ensure the external representation of the Union on issues concerning its common foreign and security policy, without prejudice to the powers of the High Representative of the Union for Foreign Affairs and Security Policy.

The President of the European Council shall not hold a national office.

[3.10]
Article 16

1. The Council shall, jointly with the European Parliament, exercise legislative and budgetary functions. It shall carry out policy-making and coordinating functions as laid down in the Treaties.
2. The Council shall consist of a representative of each Member State at ministerial level, who may commit the government of the Member State in question and cast its vote.
3. The Council shall act by a qualified majority except where the Treaties provide otherwise.
4. As from 1 November 2014, a qualified majority shall be defined as at least 55% of the members of the Council, comprising at least fifteen of them and representing Member States comprising at least 65% of the population of the Union.

A blocking minority must include at least four Council members, failing which the qualified majority shall be deemed attained.

The other arrangements governing the qualified majority are laid down in Article 238(2) of the Treaty on the Functioning of the European Union.

5. The transitional provisions relating to the definition of the qualified majority which shall be applicable until 31 October 2014 and those which shall be applicable from 1 November 2014 to 31 March 2017 are laid down in the Protocol on transitional provisions.

6–9. . . .

NOTES

Paras 6–9: outside the scope of this work.

[3.11]
Article 19

1. The Court of Justice of the European Union shall include the Court of Justice, the General Court and specialised courts. It shall ensure that in the interpretation and application of the Treaties the law is observed.

Member States shall provide remedies sufficient to ensure effective legal protection in the fields covered by Union law.

2. The Court of Justice shall consist of one judge from each Member State. It shall be assisted by Advocates-General.

The General Court shall include at least one judge per Member State.

The Judges and the Advocates-General of the Court of Justice and the Judges of the General Court shall be chosen from persons whose independence is beyond doubt and who satisfy the conditions set out in Articles 253 and 254 of the Treaty on the Functioning of the European Union. They shall be appointed by common accord of the governments of the Member States for six years. Retiring Judges and Advocates-General may be reappointed.

3. The Court of Justice of the European Union shall, in accordance with the Treaties:
   (a) rule on actions brought by a Member State, an institution or a natural or legal person;
   (b) give preliminary rulings, at the request of courts or tribunals of the Member States, on the interpretation of Union law or the validity of acts adopted by the institutions;
   (c) rule in other cases provided for in the Treaties.

TREATY ON EUROPEAN UNION TABLE OF EQUIVALENCES

[3.12]

NOTES

Date of publication in OJ: OJ C326, 26.10.2012, p 363.

This table shows in column (1) provisions of the Treaty on European Union prior to consolidation, and in column (2) the new numbering of relevant provisions of the Treaty as reproduced in this work.

The abbreviations used in this Table and the related notes are as follows:

— "TEC" means the Treaty establishing the European Community;
— "TEU" means the Treaty on European Union;
— "TFEU" means the Treaty on the Functioning of the European Union.

(1) **Old numbering of the Treaty on European Union**	(2) **New numbering of the Treaty on European Union**
Title I Common Provisions	Title I Common Provisions
Article 1	Article 1
—	Article 2
Article 2	Article 3
Article 3 (repealed)[1]	—
—	Article 4
—	Article 5[2]
Article 4 (repealed)[3]	—
Article 5 (repealed)[4]	—
Article 6	Article 6
Title III Provisions amending the Treaty establishing the European Coal and Steel Community	Title III Provisions on the Institutions
Article 9 (repealed)[5]	Article 13
—	Article 14[6]
—	Article 15[7]
—	Article 16[8]
—	Article 19[9]

1 Replaced, in substance, by Article 7 TFEU and by Articles 13(1) and 21, para 3, second subparagraph of TEU.

2 Replaces Article 5 TEC.

3 Replaced, in substance, by Article 15.

4 Replaced, in substance, by Article 13, paragraph 2.

5 The current Article 9 TEU amended the Treaty establishing the European Coal and Steel Community. This latter expired on 23 July 2002. Article 9 is repealed and the number thereof is used to insert another provision.

6 Paras 1 and 2 replace, in substance, Article 189 TEC; paras 1 to 3 replace, in substance, paras 1 to 3 of Article 190 TEC; para 1 replaces, in substance, the first sub-para of Article 192 TEC; para 4 replaces, in substance, the first sub-para of Article 197 TEC.

7 Replaces, in substance, Article 4.

8 Para 1 replaces, in substance, the first and second indents of Article 202 TEC; paras 2 and 9 replace, in substance, Article 203 TEC; paras 4 and 5 replace, in substance, paras 2 and 4 of Article 205 TEC.

9 Replaces, in substance, Article 220 TEC. The first sub-para of para 2 replaces, in substance, the first sub-para of Article 221 TEC.

CONSOLIDATED VERSION OF THE TREATY ON THE FUNCTIONING OF THE EUROPEAN UNION

NOTES

Date of publication in OJ: OJ C326, 26.10.2012, p 47.

Commencement: 1 December 2009.

Formerly titled the "Treaty Establishing the European Community" (Treaty of Rome).

This is the Treaty currently in force which is the successor to the Treaty of Rome, as consolidated following the amendments to and the renaming of the Treaty by the Treaty of Lisbon, which came into force on 1 December 2009.

Only those Articles of particular relevance to employment law are printed here. These include those relating to the free movement of persons and the right of establishment; social policy; the legislative powers of the European Union; and the powers of the Court of Justice of the European Union.

Cross-references to the equivalent article in the pre-Lisbon Treaty version of the Treaty are given at the beginning of each of the Articles reproduced which have such equivalents; these cross-references are part of the official text. A Table of Equivalences showing derivation of the provisions included in this work is at **[3.58]**.

PART ONE
PRINCIPLES

TITLE II
PROVISIONS HAVING GENERAL APPLICATION

[3.13]
Article 7
The Union shall ensure consistency between its policies and activities, taking all of its objectives into account and in accordance with the principle of conferral of powers.

[3.14]
Article 8
(ex Article 3(2) TEC)
In all its activities, the Union shall aim to eliminate inequalities, and to promote equality, between men and women.

[3.15]
Article 9
In defining and implementing its policies and activities, the Union shall take into account requirements linked to the promotion of a high level of employment, the guarantee of adequate social protection, the fight against social exclusion, and a high level of education, training and protection of human health.

[3.16]
Article 10
In defining and implementing its policies and activities, the Union shall aim to combat discrimination based on sex, racial or ethnic origin, religion or belief, disability, age or sexual orientation.

PART TWO
NON-DISCRIMINATION AND CITIZENSHIP OF THE UNION

[3.17]
Article 18
(ex Article 12 TEC)
Within the scope of application of the Treaties, and without prejudice to any special provisions contained therein, any discrimination on grounds of nationality shall be prohibited.

The European Parliament and the Council, acting in accordance with the ordinary legislative procedure, may adopt rules designed to prohibit such discrimination.

[3.18]
Article 19
(ex Article 13 TEC)
1. Without prejudice to the other provisions of the Treaties and within the limits of the powers conferred by them upon the Union, the Council, acting unanimously in accordance with a special legislative procedure and after obtaining the consent of the European Parliament, may take appropriate action to combat discrimination based on sex, racial or ethnic origin, religion or belief, disability, age or sexual orientation.

2. By way of derogation from paragraph 1, the European Parliament and the Council, acting in accordance with the ordinary legislative procedure, may adopt the basic principles of Union incentive measures, excluding any harmonisation of the laws and regulations of the Member States, to support action taken by the Member States in order to contribute to the achievement of the objectives referred to in paragraph 1.

PART THREE
UNION POLICIES AND INTERNAL ACTIONS

TITLE I
THE INTERNAL MARKET

[3.19]
Article 26
(ex Article 14 TEC)

1. The Union shall adopt measures with the aim of establishing or ensuring the functioning of the internal market, in accordance with the relevant provisions of the Treaties.
2. The internal market shall comprise an area without internal frontiers in which the free movement of goods, persons, services and capital is ensured in accordance with the provisions of the Treaties.
3. The Council, on a proposal from the Commission, shall determine the guidelines and conditions necessary to ensure balanced progress in all the sectors concerned.

TITLE IV
FREE MOVEMENT OF PERSONS, SERVICES AND CAPITAL

CHAPTER 1
WORKERS

[3.20]
Article 45
(ex Article 39 TEC)

1. Freedom of movement for workers shall be secured within the Union.
2. Such freedom of movement shall entail the abolition of any discrimination based on nationality between workers of the Member States as regards employment, remuneration and other conditions of work and employment.
3. It shall entail the right, subject to limitations justified on grounds of public policy, public security or public health:
   (a) to accept offers of employment actually made;
   (b) to move freely within the territory of Member States for this purpose;
   (c) to stay in a Member State for the purpose of employment in accordance with the provisions governing the employment of nationals of that State laid down by law, regulation or administrative action;
   (d) to remain in the territory of a Member State after having been employed in that State, subject to conditions which shall be embodied in regulations to be drawn up by the Commission.
4. The provisions of this Article shall not apply to employment in the public service.

CHAPTER 2
RIGHT OF ESTABLISHMENT

[3.21]
Article 49
(ex Article 43 TEC)

Within the framework of the provisions set out below, restrictions on the freedom of establishment of nationals of a Member State in the territory of another Member State shall be prohibited. Such prohibition shall also apply to restrictions on the setting-up of agencies, branches or subsidiaries by nationals of any Member State established in the territory of any Member State.

Freedom of establishment shall include the right to take up and pursue activities as self-employed persons and to set up and manage undertakings, in particular companies or firms within the meaning of the second paragraph of Article 54, under the conditions laid down for its own nationals by the law of the country where such establishment is effected, subject to the provisions of the Chapter relating to capital.

CHAPTER 3
SERVICES

[3.22]
Article 56
(ex Article 49 TEC)

Within the framework of the provisions set out below, restrictions on freedom to provide services within the Union shall be prohibited in respect of nationals of Member States who are established in a Member State other than that of the person for whom the services are intended.

The European Parliament and the Council, acting in accordance with the ordinary legislative procedure, may extend the provisions of the Chapter to nationals of a third country who provide services and who are established within the Union.

[3.23]
Article 57
(ex Article 50 TEC)

Services shall be considered to be 'services' within the meaning of the Treaties where they are normally provided for remuneration, in so far as they are not governed by the provisions relating to freedom of movement for goods, capital and persons.

'Services' shall in particular include:

(a) activities of an industrial character;
(b) activities of a commercial character;
(c) activities of craftsmen;
(d) activities of the professions.

Without prejudice to the provisions of the Chapter relating to the right of establishment, the person providing a service may, in order to do so, temporarily pursue his activity in the Member State where the service is provided, under the same conditions as are imposed by that State on its own nationals.

TITLE V
AREA OF FREEDOM, SECURITY AND JUSTICE

CHAPTER 3
JUDICIAL COOPERATION IN CIVIL MATTERS

[3.24]
Article 81
(ex Article 65 TEC)

1. The Union shall develop judicial cooperation in civil matters having cross-border implications, based on the principle of mutual recognition of judgments and of decisions in extrajudicial cases. Such cooperation may include the adoption of measures for the approximation of the laws and regulations of the Member States.

2. For the purposes of paragraph 1, the European Parliament and the Council, acting in accordance with the ordinary legislative procedure, shall adopt measures, particularly when necessary for the proper functioning of the internal market, aimed at ensuring:

(a) the mutual recognition and enforcement between Member States of judgments and of decisions in extrajudicial cases;
(b) the cross-border service of judicial and extrajudicial documents;
(c) the compatibility of the rules applicable in the Member States concerning conflict of laws and of jurisdiction;
(d) cooperation in the taking of evidence;
(e) effective access to justice;
(f) the elimination of obstacles to the proper functioning of civil proceedings, if necessary by promoting the compatibility of the rules on civil procedure applicable in the Member States;
(g) the development of alternative methods of dispute settlement;
(h) support for the training of the judiciary and judicial staff.

3. . . .

NOTES

Para 3: outside the scope of this work.

TITLE VII

COMMON RULES ON COMPETITION, TAXATION AND APPROXIMATION OF LAWS

CHAPTER 3

APPROXIMATION OF LAWS

[3.25]

Article 114

(ex Article 95 TEC)

1. Save where otherwise provided in the Treaties, the following provisions shall apply for the achievement of the objectives set out in Article 26. The European Parliament and the Council shall, acting in accordance with the ordinary legislative procedure and after consulting the Economic and Social Committee, adopt the measures for the approximation of the provisions laid down by law, regulation or administrative action in Member States which have as their object the establishment and functioning of the internal market.

2. Paragraph 1 shall not apply to fiscal provisions, to those relating to the free movement of persons nor to those relating to the rights and interests of employed persons.

3. The Commission, in its proposals envisaged in paragraph 1 concerning health, safety, environmental protection and consumer protection, will take as a base a high level of protection, taking account in particular of any new development based on scientific facts. Within their respective powers, the European Parliament and the Council will also seek to achieve this objective.

4. If, after the adoption of a harmonisation measure by the European Parliament and the Council, by the Council or by the Commission, a Member State deems it necessary to maintain national provisions on grounds of major needs referred to in Article 36, or relating to the protection of the environment or the working environment, it shall notify the Commission of these provisions as well as the grounds for maintaining them.

5. Moreover, without prejudice to paragraph 4, if, after the adoption of a harmonisation measure by the European Parliament and the Council, by the Council or by the Commission, a Member State deems it necessary to introduce national provisions based on new scientific evidence relating to the protection of the environment or the working environment on grounds of a problem specific to that Member State arising after the adoption of the harmonisation measure, it shall notify the Commission of the envisaged provisions as well as the grounds for introducing them.

6. The Commission shall, within six months of the notifications as referred to in paragraphs 4 and 5, approve or reject the national provisions involved after having verified whether or not they are a means of arbitrary discrimination or a disguised restriction on trade between Member States and whether or not they shall constitute an obstacle to the functioning of the internal market.

In the absence of a decision by the Commission within this period the national provisions referred to in paragraphs 4 and 5 shall be deemed to have been approved.

When justified by the complexity of the matter and in the absence of danger for human health, the Commission may notify the Member State concerned that the period referred to in this paragraph may be extended for a further period of up to six months.

7. When, pursuant to paragraph 6, a Member State is authorised to maintain or introduce national provisions derogating from a harmonisation measure, the Commission shall immediately examine whether to propose an adaptation to that measure.

8. When a Member State raises a specific problem on public health in a field which has been the subject of prior harmonisation measures, it shall bring it to the attention of the Commission which shall immediately examine whether to propose appropriate measures to the Council.

9. By way of derogation from the procedure laid down in Articles 258 and 259, the Commission and any Member State may bring the matter directly before the Court of Justice of the European Union if it considers that another Member State is making improper use of the powers provided for in this Article.

10. The harmonisation measures referred to above shall, in appropriate cases, include a safeguard clause authorising the Member States to take, for one or more of the non-economic reasons referred to in Article 36, provisional measures subject to a Union control procedure.

[3.26]

Article 115

(ex Article 94 TEC)

Without prejudice to Article 114, the Council shall, acting unanimously in accordance with a special legislative procedure and after consulting the European Parliament and the Economic and Social Committee, issue directives for the approximation of such laws, regulations or administrative provisions of the Member States as directly affect the establishment or functioning of the internal market.

TITLE X
SOCIAL POLICY

[3.27]
Article 151
(ex Article 136 TEC)
The Union and the Member States, having in mind fundamental social rights such as those set out in the European Social Charter signed at Turin on 18 October 1961 and in the 1989 Community Charter of the Fundamental Social Rights of Workers, shall have as their objectives the promotion of employment, improved living and working conditions, so as to make possible their harmonisation while the improvement is being maintained, proper social protection, dialogue between management and labour, the development of human resources with a view to lasting high employment and the combating of exclusion.

To this end the Union and the Member States shall implement measures which take account of the diverse forms of national practices, in particular in the field of contractual relations, and the need to maintain the competitiveness of the Union's economy.

They believe that such a development will ensue not only from the functioning of the internal market, which will favour the harmonisation of social systems, but also from the procedures provided for in the Treaties and from the approximation of provisions laid down by law, regulation or administrative action.

[3.28]
Article 152
The Union recognises and promotes the role of the social partners at its level, taking into account the diversity of national systems. It shall facilitate dialogue between the social partners, respecting their autonomy.

The Tripartite Social Summit for Growth and Employment shall contribute to social dialogue.

[3.29]
Article 153
(ex Article 137 TEC)
1. With a view to achieving the objectives of Article 151, the Union shall support and complement the activities of the Member States in the following fields:
   (a) improvement in particular of the working environment to protect workers' health and safety;
   (b) working conditions;
   (c) social security and social protection of workers;
   (d) protection of workers where their employment contract is terminated;
   (e) the information and consultation of workers;
   (f) representation and collective defence of the interests of workers and employers, including co-determination, subject to paragraph 5;
   (g) conditions of employment for third-country nationals legally residing in Union territory;
   (h) the integration of persons excluded from the labour market, without prejudice to Article 166;
   (i) equality between men and women with regard to labour market opportunities and treatment at work;
   (j) the combating of social exclusion;
   (k) the modernisation of social protection systems without prejudice to point (c).
2. To this end, the European Parliament and the Council:
   (a) may adopt measures designed to encourage cooperation between Member States through initiatives aimed at improving knowledge, developing exchanges of information and best practices, promoting innovative approaches and evaluating experiences, excluding any harmonisation of the laws and regulations of the Member States;
   (b) may adopt, in the fields referred to in paragraph 1(a) to (i), by means of directives, minimum requirements for gradual implementation, having regard to the conditions and technical rules obtaining in each of the Member States. Such directives shall avoid imposing administrative, financial and legal constraints in a way which would hold back the creation and development of small and medium-sized undertakings.

The European Parliament and the Council shall act in accordance with the ordinary legislative procedure after consulting the Economic and Social Committee and the Committee of the Regions.

In the fields referred to in paragraph 1(c), (d), (f) and (g), the Council shall act unanimously, in accordance with a special legislative procedure, after consulting the European Parliament and the said Committees.

The Council, acting unanimously on a proposal from the Commission, after consulting the European Parliament, may decide to render the ordinary legislative procedure applicable to paragraph 1(d), (f) and (g).

3. A Member State may entrust management and labour, at their joint request, with the implementation of directives adopted pursuant to paragraph 2, or, where appropriate, with the implementation of a Council decision adopted in accordance with Article 155.

In this case, it shall ensure that, no later than the date on which a directive or a decision must be transposed or implemented, management and labour have introduced the necessary measures by agreement, the Member State concerned being required to take any necessary measure enabling it at any time to be in a position to guarantee the results imposed by that directive or that decision.

4. The provisions adopted pursuant to this Article:

— shall not affect the right of Member States to define the fundamental principles of their social security systems and must not significantly affect the financial equilibrium thereof,

— shall not prevent any Member State from maintaining or introducing more stringent protective measures compatible with the Treaties.

5. The provisions of this Article shall not apply to pay, the right of association, the right to strike or the right to impose lock-outs.

[3.30]
Article 154
(ex Article 138 TEC)

1. The Commission shall have the task of promoting the consultation of management and labour at Union level and shall take any relevant measure to facilitate their dialogue by ensuring balanced support for the parties.

2. To this end, before submitting proposals in the social policy field, the Commission shall consult management and labour on the possible direction of Union action.

3. If, after such consultation, the Commission considers Union action advisable, it shall consult management and labour on the content of the envisaged proposal. Management and labour shall forward to the Commission an opinion or, where appropriate, a recommendation.

4. On the occasion of the consultation referred to in paragraphs 2 and 3, management and labour may inform the Commission of their wish to initiate the process provided for in Article 155. The duration of this process shall not exceed nine months, unless the management and labour concerned and the Commission decide jointly to extend it.

[3.31]
Article 155
(ex Article 139 TEC)

1. Should management and labour so desire, the dialogue between them at Union level may lead to contractual relations, including agreements.

2. Agreements concluded at Union level shall be implemented either in accordance with the procedures and practices specific to management and labour and the Member States or, in matters covered by Article 153, at the joint request of the signatory parties, by a Council decision on a proposal from the Commission. The European Parliament shall be informed.

The Council shall act unanimously where the agreement in question contains one or more provisions relating to one of the areas for which unanimity is required pursuant to Article 153(2).

[3.32]
Article 156
(ex Article 140 TEC)

With a view to achieving the objectives of Article 151 and without prejudice to the other provisions of the Treaties, the Commission shall encourage cooperation between the Member States and facilitate the coordination of their action in all social policy fields under this Chapter, particularly in matters relating to:

— employment,
— labour law and working conditions,
— basic and advanced vocational training,
— social security,
— prevention of occupational accidents and diseases,
— occupational hygiene,
— the right of association and collective bargaining between employers and workers.

To this end, the Commission shall act in close contact with Member States by making studies, delivering opinions and arranging consultations both on problems arising at national level and on those of concern to international organisations, in particular initiatives aiming at the establishment of guidelines and indicators, the organisation of exchange of best practice, and the preparation of the necessary elements for periodic monitoring and evaluation. The European Parliament shall be kept fully informed.

Before delivering the opinions provided for in this Article, the Commission shall consult the Economic and Social Committee.

[3.33]
Article 157
(ex Article 141 TEC)

1. Each Member State shall ensure that the principle of equal pay for male and female workers for equal work or work of equal value is applied.

2. For the purpose of this Article, 'pay' means the ordinary basic or minimum wage or salary and any other consideration, whether in cash or in kind, which the worker receives directly or indirectly, in respect of his employment, from his employer.

Equal pay without discrimination based on sex means:

(a) that pay for the same work at piece rates shall be calculated on the basis of the same unit of measurement;

(b) that pay for work at time rates shall be the same for the same job.

3. The European Parliament and the Council, acting in accordance with the ordinary legislative procedure, and after consulting the Economic and Social Committee, shall adopt measures to ensure the application of the principle of equal opportunities and equal treatment of men and women in matters of employment and occupation, including the principle of equal pay for equal work or work of equal value.

4. With a view to ensuring full equality in practice between men and women in working life, the principle of equal treatment shall not prevent any Member State from maintaining or adopting measures providing for specific advantages in order to make it easier for the under-represented sex to pursue a vocational activity or to prevent or compensate for disadvantages in professional careers.

[3.34]
Article 158
(ex Article 142 TEC)

Member States shall endeavour to maintain the existing equivalence between paid holiday schemes.

PART SIX
INSTITUTIONAL AND FINANCIAL PROVISIONS

TITLE I
INSTITUTIONAL PROVISIONS

CHAPTER 1
THE INSTITUTIONS

Section 5
The Court Of Justice Of The European Union

[3.35]
Article 251
(ex Article 221 TEC)

The Court of Justice shall sit in chambers or in a Grand Chamber, in accordance with the rules laid down for that purpose in the Statute of the Court of Justice of the European Union.

When provided for in the Statute, the Court of Justice may also sit as a full Court.

[3.36]
Article 252
(ex Article 222 TEC)

The Court of Justice shall be assisted by eight Advocates-General. Should the Court of Justice so request, the Council, acting unanimously, may increase the number of Advocates-General.

It shall be the duty of the Advocate-General, acting with complete impartiality and independence, to make, in open court, reasoned submissions on cases which, in accordance with the Statute of the Court of Justice of the European Union, require his involvement.

[3.37]
Article 253
(ex Article 223 TEC)

The Judges and Advocates-General of the Court of Justice shall be chosen from persons whose independence is beyond doubt and who possess the qualifications required for appointment to the highest judicial offices in their respective countries or who are jurisconsults of recognised competence; they shall be appointed by common accord of the governments of the Member States for a term of six years, after consultation of the panel provided for in Article 255.

Every three years there shall be a partial replacement of the Judges and Advocates-General, in accordance with the conditions laid down in the Statute of the Court of Justice of the European Union.

The Judges shall elect the President of the Court of Justice from among their number for a term of three years. He may be re-elected.

Retiring Judges and Advocates-General may be reappointed.

The Court of Justice shall appoint its Registrar and lay down the rules governing his service.

The Court of Justice shall establish its Rules of Procedure. Those Rules shall require the approval of the Council.

[3.38]
Article 254
(ex Article 224 TEC)

The number of Judges of the General Court shall be determined by the Statute of the Court of Justice of the European Union. The Statute may provide for the General Court to be assisted by Advocates-General.

The members of the General Court shall be chosen from persons whose independence is beyond doubt and who possess the ability required for appointment to high judicial office. They shall be appointed by common accord of the governments of the Member States for a term of six years, after consultation of the panel provided for in Article 255. The membership shall be partially renewed every three years. Retiring members shall be eligible for reappointment.

The Judges shall elect the President of the General Court from among their number for a term of three years. He may be re-elected.

The General Court shall appoint its Registrar and lay down the rules governing his service.

The General Court shall establish its Rules of Procedure in agreement with the Court of Justice. Those Rules shall require the approval of the Council.

Unless the Statute of the Court of Justice of the European Union provides otherwise, the provisions of the Treaties relating to the Court of Justice shall apply to the General Court.

[3.39]
Article 258
(ex Article 226 TEC)

If the Commission considers that a Member State has failed to fulfil an obligation under the Treaties, it shall deliver a reasoned opinion on the matter after giving the State concerned the opportunity to submit its observations.

If the State concerned does not comply with the opinion within the period laid down by the Commission, the latter may bring the matter before the Court of Justice of the European Union.

[3.40]
Article 259
(ex Article 227 TEC)

A Member State which considers that another Member State has failed to fulfil an obligation under the Treaties may bring the matter before the Court of Justice of the European Union.

Before a Member State brings an action against another Member State for an alleged infringement of an obligation under the Treaties, it shall bring the matter before the Commission.

The Commission shall deliver a reasoned opinion after each of the States concerned has been given the opportunity to submit its own case and its observations on the other party's case both orally and in writing.

If the Commission has not delivered an opinion within three months of the date on which the matter was brought before it, the absence of such opinion shall not prevent the matter from being brought before the Court.

[3.41]
Article 260
(ex Article 228 TEC)

1. If the Court of Justice of the European Union finds that a Member State has failed to fulfil an obligation under the Treaties, the State shall be required to take the necessary measures to comply with the judgment of the Court.

2. If the Commission considers that the Member State concerned has not taken the necessary measures to comply with the judgment of the Court, it may bring the case before the Court after giving that State the opportunity to submit its observations. It shall specify the amount of the lump sum or penalty payment to be paid by the Member State concerned which it considers appropriate in the circumstances.

If the Court finds that the Member State concerned has not complied with its judgment it may impose a lump sum or penalty payment on it.

This procedure shall be without prejudice to Article 259.

3. When the Commission brings a case before the Court pursuant to Article 258 on the grounds that the Member State concerned has failed to fulfil its obligation to notify measures transposing a directive adopted under a legislative procedure, it may, when it deems appropriate, specify the amount of the lump sum or penalty payment to be paid by the Member State concerned which it considers appropriate in the circumstances.

If the Court finds that there is an infringement it may impose a lump sum or penalty payment on the Member State concerned not exceeding the amount specified by the Commission. The payment obligation shall take effect on the date set by the Court in its judgment.

[3.42]
Article 263
(ex Article 230 TEC)
The Court of Justice of the European Union shall review the legality of legislative acts, of acts of the Council, of the Commission and of the European Central Bank, other than recommendations and opinions, and of acts of the European Parliament and of the European Council intended to produce legal effects vis-à-vis third parties. It shall also review the legality of acts of bodies, offices or agencies of the Union intended to produce legal effects vis-à-vis third parties.

It shall for this purpose have jurisdiction in actions brought by a Member State, the European Parliament, the Council or the Commission on grounds of lack of competence, infringement of an essential procedural requirement, infringement of the Treaties or of any rule of law relating to their application, or misuse of powers.

The Court shall have jurisdiction under the same conditions in actions brought by the Court of Auditors, by the European Central Bank and by the Committee of the Regions for the purpose of protecting their prerogatives.

Any natural or legal person may, under the conditions laid down in the first and second paragraphs, institute proceedings against an act addressed to that person or which is of direct and individual concern to them, and against a regulatory act which is of direct concern to them and does not entail implementing measures.

Acts setting up bodies, offices and agencies of the Union may lay down specific conditions and arrangements concerning actions brought by natural or legal persons against acts of these bodies, offices or agencies intended to produce legal effects in relation to them.

The proceedings provided for in this Article shall be instituted within two months of the publication of the measure, or of its notification to the plaintiff, or, in the absence thereof, of the day on which it came to the knowledge of the latter, as the case may be.

[3.43]
Article 264
(ex Article 231 TEC)
If the action is well founded, the Court of Justice of the European Union shall declare the act concerned to be void.

However, the Court shall, if it considers this necessary, state which of the effects of the act which it has declared void shall be considered as definitive.

[3.44]
Article 267
(ex Article 234 TEC)
The Court of Justice of the European Union shall have jurisdiction to give preliminary rulings concerning:

(a) the interpretation of the Treaties;
(b) the validity and interpretation of acts of the institutions, bodies, offices or agencies of the Union;

Where such a question is raised before any court or tribunal of a Member State, that court or tribunal may, if it considers that a decision on the question is necessary to enable it to give judgment, request the Court to give a ruling thereon.

Where any such question is raised in a case pending before a court or tribunal of a Member State against whose decisions there is no judicial remedy under national law, that court or tribunal shall bring the matter before the Court.

If such a question is raised in a case pending before a court or tribunal of a Member State with regard to a person in custody, the Court of Justice of the European Union shall act with the minimum of delay.

[3.45]
Article 270
(ex Article 236 TEC)
The Court of Justice of the European Union shall have jurisdiction in any dispute between the Union and its servants within the limits and under the conditions laid down in the Staff Regulations of Officials and the Conditions of Employment of other servants of the Union.

[3.46]
Article 278
(ex Article 242 TEC)
Actions brought before the Court of Justice of the European Union shall not have suspensory effect. The Court may, however, if it considers that circumstances so require, order that application of the contested act be suspended.

[3.47]
Article 279
(ex Article 243 TEC)
The Court of Justice of the European Union may in any cases before it prescribe any necessary interim measures.

CHAPTER 2
LEGAL ACTS OF THE UNION, ADOPTION PROCEDURES AND OTHER PROVISIONS

Section 1
The Legal Acts Of The Union

[3.48]
Article 288
(ex Article 249 TEC)
To exercise the Union's competences, the institutions shall adopt regulations, directives, decisions, recommendations and opinions.

A regulation shall have general application. It shall be binding in its entirety and directly applicable in all Member States.

A directive shall be binding, as to the result to be achieved, upon each Member State to which it is addressed, but shall leave to the national authorities the choice of form and methods.

A decision shall be binding in its entirety. A decision which specifies those to whom it is addressed shall be binding only on them.

Recommendations and opinions shall have no binding force.

[3.49]
Article 289
1. The ordinary legislative procedure shall consist in the joint adoption by the European Parliament and the Council of a regulation, directive or decision on a proposal from the Commission. This procedure is defined in Article 294.
2. In the specific cases provided for by the Treaties, the adoption of a regulation, directive or decision by the European Parliament with the participation of the Council, or by the latter with the participation of the European Parliament, shall constitute a special legislative procedure.
3. Legal acts adopted by legislative procedure shall constitute legislative acts.
4. In the specific cases provided for by the Treaties, legislative acts may be adopted on the initiative of a group of Member States or of the European Parliament, on a recommendation from the European Central Bank or at the request of the Court of Justice or the European Investment Bank.

Section 2
Procedures For The Adoption Of Acts And Other Provisions

[3.50]
Article 293
(ex Article 250 TEC)
1. Where, pursuant to the Treaties, the Council acts on a proposal from the Commission, it may amend that proposal only by acting unanimously, except in the cases referred to in paragraphs 10 and 13 of Article 294, in Articles 310, 312 and 314 and in the second paragraph of Article 315.
2. As long as the Council has not acted, the Commission may alter its proposal at any time during the procedures leading to the adoption of a Union act.

[3.51]
Article 294
(ex Article 251 TEC)
1. Where reference is made in the Treaties to the ordinary legislative procedure for the adoption of an act, the following procedure shall apply.
2. The Commission shall submit a proposal to the European Parliament and the Council.
First reading
3. The European Parliament shall adopt its position at first reading and communicate it to the Council.

4. If the Council approves the European Parliament's position, the act concerned shall be adopted in the wording which corresponds to the position of the European Parliament.
5. If the Council does not approve the European Parliament's position, it shall adopt its position at first reading and communicate it to the European Parliament.
6. The Council shall inform the European Parliament fully of the reasons which led it to adopt its position at first reading. The Commission shall inform the European Parliament fully of its position.

Second reading

7. If, within three months of such communication, the European Parliament:
   (a) approves the Council's position at first reading or has not taken a decision, the act concerned shall be deemed to have been adopted in the wording which corresponds to the position of the Council;
   (b) rejects, by a majority of its component members, the Council's position at first reading, the proposed act shall be deemed not to have been adopted;
   (c) proposes, by a majority of its component members, amendments to the Council's position at first reading, the text thus amended shall be forwarded to the Council and to the Commission, which shall deliver an opinion on those amendments.
8. If, within three months of receiving the European Parliament's amendments, the Council, acting by a qualified majority:
   (a) approves all those amendments, the act in question shall be deemed to have been adopted;
   (b) does not approve all the amendments, the President of the Council, in agreement with the President of the European Parliament, shall within six weeks convene a meeting of the Conciliation Committee.
9. The Council shall act unanimously on the amendments on which the Commission has delivered a negative opinion.

Conciliation

10. The Conciliation Committee, which shall be composed of the members of the Council or their representatives and an equal number of members representing the European Parliament, shall have the task of reaching agreement on a joint text, by a qualified majority of the members of the Council or their representatives and by a majority of the members representing the European Parliament within six weeks of its being convened, on the basis of the positions of the European Parliament and the Council at second reading.
11. The Commission shall take part in the Conciliation Committee's proceedings and shall take all necessary initiatives with a view to reconciling the positions of the European Parliament and the Council.
12. If, within six weeks of its being convened, the Conciliation Committee does not approve the joint text, the proposed act shall be deemed not to have been adopted.

Third reading

13. If, within that period, the Conciliation Committee approves a joint text, the European Parliament, acting by a majority of the votes cast, and the Council, acting by a qualified majority, shall each have a period of six weeks from that approval in which to adopt the act in question in accordance with the joint text. If they fail to do so, the proposed act shall be deemed not to have been adopted.
14. The periods of three months and six weeks referred to in this Article shall be extended by a maximum of one month and two weeks respectively at the initiative of the European Parliament or the Council.

Special provisions

15. Where, in the cases provided for in the Treaties, a legislative act is submitted to the ordinary legislative procedure on the initiative of a group of Member States, on a recommendation by the European Central Bank, or at the request of the Court of Justice, paragraph 2, the second sentence of paragraph 6, and paragraph 9 shall not apply.

In such cases, the European Parliament and the Council shall communicate the proposed act to the Commission with their positions at first and second readings. The European Parliament or the Council may request the opinion of the Commission throughout the procedure, which the Commission may also deliver on its own initiative. It may also, if it deems it necessary, take part in the Conciliation Committee in accordance with paragraph 11.

[3.52]
Article 295

The European Parliament, the Council and the Commission shall consult each other and by common agreement make arrangements for their cooperation. To that end, they may, in compliance with the Treaties, conclude interinstitutional agreements which may be of a binding nature.

[3.53]
Article 296
(ex Article 253 TEC)

Where the Treaties do not specify the type of act to be adopted, the institutions shall select it on a case-by-case basis, in compliance with the applicable procedures and with the principle of proportionality.

Legal acts shall state the reasons on which they are based and shall refer to any proposals, initiatives, recommendations, requests or opinions required by the Treaties.

When considering draft legislative acts, the European Parliament and the Council shall refrain from adopting acts not provided for by the relevant legislative procedure in the area in question.

[3.54]
Article 297
(ex Article 254 TEC)

1. Legislative acts adopted under the ordinary legislative procedure shall be signed by the President of the European Parliament and by the President of the Council.

Legislative acts adopted under a special legislative procedure shall be signed by the President of the institution which adopted them.

Legislative acts shall be published in the Official Journal of the European Union. They shall enter into force on the date specified in them or, in the absence thereof, on the twentieth day following that of their publication.

2. Non-legislative acts adopted in the form of regulations, directives or decisions, when the latter do not specify to whom they are addressed, shall be signed by the President of the institution which adopted them.

Regulations and directives which are addressed to all Member States, as well as decisions which do not specify to whom they are addressed, shall be published in the Official Journal of the European Union. They shall enter into force on the date specified in them or, in the absence thereof, on the twentieth day following that of their publication.

Other directives, and decisions which specify to whom they are addressed, shall be notified to those to whom they are addressed and shall take effect upon such notification.

PART SEVEN
GENERAL AND FINAL PROVISIONS

[3.55]
Article 352
(ex Article 308 TEC)

1. If action by the Union should prove necessary, within the framework of the policies defined in the Treaties, to attain one of the objectives set out in the Treaties, and the Treaties have not provided the necessary powers, the Council, acting unanimously on a proposal from the Commission and after obtaining the consent of the European Parliament, shall adopt the appropriate measures. Where the measures in question are adopted by the Council in accordance with a special legislative procedure, it shall also act unanimously on a proposal from the Commission and after obtaining the consent of the European Parliament.

2. Using the procedure for monitoring the subsidiarity principle referred to in Article 5(3) of the Treaty on European Union, the Commission shall draw national Parliaments' attention to proposals based on this Article.

3. Measures based on this Article shall not entail harmonisation of Member States' laws or regulations in cases where the Treaties exclude such harmonisation.

4. This Article cannot serve as a basis for attaining objectives pertaining to the common foreign and security policy and any acts adopted pursuant to this Article shall respect the limits set out in Article 40, second paragraph, of the Treaty on European Union.

PROTOCOL (NO 30) ON THE APPLICATION OF THE CHARTER OF FUNDAMENTAL RIGHTS OF THE EUROPEAN UNION TO POLAND AND TO THE UNITED KINGDOM

[3.56]

THE HIGH CONTRACTING PARTIES,

WHEREAS in Article 6 of the Treaty on European Union, the Union recognises the rights, freedoms and principles set out in the Charter of Fundamental Rights of the European Union,

WHEREAS the Charter is to be applied in strict accordance with the provisions of the aforementioned Article 6 and Title VII of the Charter itself,

WHEREAS the aforementioned Article 6 requires the Charter to be applied and interpreted by the courts of Poland and of the United Kingdom strictly in accordance with the explanations referred to in that Article,

WHEREAS the Charter contains both rights and principles,

WHEREAS the Charter contains both provisions which are civil and political in character and those which are economic and social in character,

WHEREAS the Charter reaffirms the rights, freedoms and principles recognised in the Union and makes those rights more visible, but does not create new rights or principles,

RECALLING the obligations devolving upon Poland and the United Kingdom under the Treaty on European Union, the Treaty on the Functioning of the European Union, and Union law generally,

NOTING the wish of Poland and the United Kingdom to clarify certain aspects of the application of the Charter,

DESIROUS therefore of clarifying the application of the Charter in relation to the laws and administrative action of Poland and of the United Kingdom and of its justiciability within Poland and within the United Kingdom,

REAFFIRMING that references in this Protocol to the operation of specific provisions of the Charter are strictly without prejudice to the operation of other provisions of the Charter,

REAFFIRMING that this Protocol is without prejudice to the application of the Charter to other Member States,

REAFFIRMING that this Protocol is without prejudice to other obligations devolving upon Poland and the United Kingdom under the Treaty on European Union, the Treaty on the Functioning of the European Union, and Union law generally,

HAVE AGREED UPON the following provisions, which shall be annexed to the Treaty on European Union and to the Treaty on the Functioning of the European Union:

Article 1

1. The Charter does not extend the ability of the Court of Justice of the European Union, or any court or tribunal of Poland or of the United Kingdom, to find that the laws, regulations or administrative provisions, practices or action of Poland or of the United Kingdom are inconsistent with the fundamental rights, freedoms and principles that it reaffirms.
2. In particular, and for the avoidance of doubt, nothing in Title IV of the Charter creates justiciable rights applicable to Poland or the United Kingdom except in so far as Poland or the United Kingdom has provided for such rights in its national law.

Article 2

To the extent that a provision of the Charter refers to national laws and practices, it shall only apply to Poland or the United Kingdom to the extent that the rights or principles that it contains are recognised in the law or practices of Poland or of the United Kingdom.

PROTOCOL (NO 36) ON TRANSITIONAL PROVISIONS

[3.57]

THE HIGH CONTRACTING PARTIES,

WHEREAS, in order to organise the transition from the institutional provisions of the Treaties applicable prior to the entry into force of the Treaty of Lisbon to the provisions contained in that Treaty, it is necessary to lay down transitional provisions,

HAVE AGREED UPON the following provisions, which shall be annexed to the Treaty on European Union, to the Treaty on the Functioning of the European Union and to the Treaty establishing the European Atomic Energy Community:

Article 1

In this Protocol, the words "the Treaties" shall mean the Treaty on European Union, the Treaty on the Functioning of the European Union and the Treaty establishing the European Atomic Energy Community.

Article 2
(*Outside the scope of this work.*)

Article 3
1. In accordance with Article 16(4) of the Treaty on European Union, the provisions of that paragraph and of Article 238(2) of the Treaty on the Functioning of the European Union relating to the definition of the qualified majority in the European Council and the Council shall take effect on 1 November 2014.
2. Between 1 November 2014 and 31 March 2017, when an act is to be adopted by qualified majority, a member of the Council may request that it be adopted in accordance with the qualified majority as defined in paragraph 3. In that case, paragraphs 3 and 4 shall apply.
3. Until 31 October 2014, the following provisions shall remain in force, without prejudice to the second subparagraph of Article 235(1) of the Treaty on the Functioning of the European Union.

For acts of the European Council and of the Council requiring a qualified majority, members' votes shall be weighted as follows:

Belgium	12
Bulgaria	10
Czech Republic	12
Denmark	7
Germany	29
Estonia	4
Ireland	7
Greece	12
Spain	27
France	29
Italy	29
Cyprus	4
Latvia	4
Lithuania	7
Luxembourg	4
Hungary	12
Malta	3
Netherlands	13
Austria	10
Poland	27
Portugal	12
Romania	14
Slovenia	4
Slovakia	7
Finland	7
Sweden	10
United Kingdom	29

Acts shall be adopted if there are at least 255 votes in favour representing a majority of the members where, under the Treaties, they must be adopted on a proposal from the Commission. In other cases decisions shall be adopted if there are at least 255 votes in favour representing at least two thirds of the members.

A member of the European Council or the Council may request that, where an act is adopted by the European Council or the Council by a qualified majority, a check is made to ensure that the Member States comprising the qualified majority represent at least 62% of the total population of the Union. If that proves not to be the case, the act shall not be adopted.
4. Until 31 October 2014, the qualified majority shall, in cases where, under the Treaties, not all the members of the Council participate in voting, namely in the cases where reference is made to the qualified majority as defined in Article 238(3) of the Treaty on the Functioning of the European

Union, be defined as the same proportion of the weighted votes and the same proportion of the number of the Council members and, if appropriate, the same percentage of the population of the Member States concerned as laid down in paragraph 3 of this Article.

Articles 4–10
(*Outside the scope of this work.*)

TREATY ON THE FUNCTIONING OF THE EUROPEAN UNION TABLE OF EQUIVALENCES

[3.58]

NOTES

Date of publication in OJ: OJ C326, 26.10.2012, p 368.

This table shows in column (1) the provisions of the Treaty establishing the European Community which were reproduced in previous editions of this Handbook, and in column (2) the new numbering of provisions of that Treaty as consolidated and renamed the "Treaty on the Functioning of the European Union".

The abbreviations used in this Table and the related notes are as follows:

(i) "TEU" means the Treaty on European Union;

(ii) "TFEU" means the Treaty on the Functioning of the European Union.

(1) **Old numbering of the Treaty establishing the European Community**	(2) **New numbering of the Treaty on the Functioning of the European Union**
PART ONE	PART ONE
PRINCIPLES	PRINCIPLES
Article 1 (repealed)	—
—	Article 1
Article 2 (repealed)[1]	—
—	Title I
	Categories and areas of union competence
—	Article 2
—	Article 3
—	Article 4
—	Article 5
—	Article 6
—	Title II
	Provisions having general application
—	Article 7
Article 3, paragraph 1 (repealed)[2]	—
Article 3, paragraph 2	Article 8
—	Article 9
—	Article 10
PART TWO	PART TWO
CITIZENSHIP OF THE UNION	NON-DISCRIMINATION AND CITIZENSHIP OF THE UNION
Article 12 (moved)	Article 18
Article 13 (moved)	Article 19
PART THREE	PART THREE
COMMUNITY POLICIES	POLICIES AND INTERNAL ACTIONS OF THE UNION
—	Title I
	The internal market
Article 14 (moved)	Article 26
Title III	Title IV
Free movement of persons, services and capital	Free movement of persons, services and capital
Chapter 1	Chapter 1
Workers	Workers
Article 39	Article 45
Article 40	Article 46
Article 41	Article 47
Article 42	Article 48
Chapter 2	Chapter 2
Right of establishment	Right of establishment
Article 43	Article 49
Chapter 3	Chapter 3
Services	Services
Article 49	Article 56

(1) **Old numbering of the Treaty establishing the European Community**	(2) **New numbering of the Treaty on the Functioning of the European Union**
Article 50	Article 57
Article 54	Article 61
Title IV	Title V
Visas, asylum, immigration and other policies related to free movement of persons	Area of freedom, security and justice
—	Chapter 3
	Judicial cooperation in civil matters
Article 65	Article 81
Title VI	Title VII
Common rules on competition, taxation and approximation of laws	Common rules on competition, taxation and approximation of laws
Chapter 3	Chapter 3
Approximation of laws	Approximation of laws
Article 95 (moved)	Article 114
Article 94 (moved)	Article 115
Title VIII	Title IX
Employment	Employment
Article 125	Article 145
Article 126	Article 146
Article 127	Article 147
Article 128	Article 148
Article 129	Article 149
Article 130	Article 150
Title XI	Title X
Social policy, education, vocational training and youth	Social policy
Chapter 1	
social provisions (repealed)	—
Article 136	Article 151
—	Article 152
Article 137	Article 153
Article 138	Article 154
Article 139	Article 155
Article 140	Article 156
Article 141	Article 157
Article 142	Article 158
Article 143	Article 159
Article 144	Article 160
Article 145	Article 161
PART FIVE	PART SIX
INSTITUTIONS OF THE COMMUNITY	INSTITUTIONAL AND FINANCIAL PROVISIONS
Title I	Title I
Institutional provisions	Institutional provisions
Chapter 1	Chapter 1
The institutions	The institutions
Section 4	Section 5
The Court of Justice	The Court of Justice of the European Union
Article 220 (repealed)[3]	—
Article 221, first paragraph (repealed)[4]	—
Article 221, second and third paragraphs	Article 251
Article 222	Article 252
Article 223	Article 253
Article 224[5]	Article 254

(1) **Old numbering of the Treaty establishing the European Community**	(2) **New numbering of the Treaty on the Functioning of the European Union**
Article 226	Article 258
Article 227	Article 259
Article 228	Article 260
Article 229	Article 261
Article 229a	Article 262
Article 230	Article 263
Article 231	Article 264
Article 234	Article 267
Article 236	Article 270
Article 242	Article 278
Article 243	Article 279
Chapter 2	Chapter 2
Provisions common to several institutions	Legal acts of the Union, adoption procedures and other provisions
—	Section 1
	The legal acts of the Union
Article 249	Article 288
—	Article 289
—	Section 2
	Procedures for the adoption of acts and other provisions
Article 250	Article 293
Article 251	Article 294
Article 252 (repealed)	—
—	Article 295
Article 253	Article 296
Article 254	Article 297
PART SIX	PART SEVEN
GENERAL AND FINAL PROVISIONS	GENERAL AND FINAL PROVISIONS
Article 308	Article 352

1 Replaced, in substance, by Article 3 TEU.

2 Replaced, in substance, by Articles 3 to 6 TFEU.

3 Replaced, in substance, by Article 19 TEU.

4 Replaced, in substance, by Article 19, paragraph 2, first subparagraph, of the TEU.

5 The first sentence of the first subparagraph is replaced, in substance, by Article 19, paragraph 2, second subparagraph of the TEU.

COMMUNITY CHARTER OF THE FUNDAMENTAL SOCIAL RIGHTS OF WORKERS

[10 December 1989]

NOTES

This "Social Charter" was adopted in December 1989 by the Heads of Government of all member states of the Community except the United Kingdom. It was subsequently adopted by the United Kingdom in 1998. There is no express legal provision for such a charter in the Treaty and it does not have any direct legal status except as instructions to the Commission to prepare a programme of measures to implement its objectives. It is included for its general interest and because of the importance of the Community instruments it may generate and has generated, including the Protocol to the Maastricht Treaty on Social Policy 1992, and because of its relevance to issues arising on the legality or interpretation of EU measures before the Court.

[3.59]

THE HEADS OF STATE AND GOVERNMENT OF THE MEMBER STATES OF THE EUROPEAN COMMUNITY MEETING AT STRASBOURG ON 10 DECEMBER 1989

Whereas, under the terms of Article 117 of the EEC Treaty, the Member States have agreed on the need to promote improved living and working conditions for workers so as to make possible their harmonisation while the improvement is being maintained;

Whereas following on from the conclusions of the European Councils of Hanover and Rhodes the European Council of Madrid considered that, in the context of the establishment of the single European market, the same importance must be attached to the social aspects as to the economic aspects and whereas, therefore, they must be developed in a balanced manner;

Having regard to the Resolutions of the European Parliament of 15 March 1989 and 14 September 1989 and to the Opinion of the Economic and Social Committee of 22 February 1989;

Whereas the completion of the internal market is the most effective means of creating employment and ensuring maximum well-being in the Community; whereas employment development and creation must be given first priority in the completion of the internal market; whereas it is for the Community to take up the challenges of the future with regard to economic competitiveness, taking into account, in particular, regional imbalances;

Whereas the social consensus contributes to the strengthening of the competitiveness of undertakings and of the economy as a whole and to the creation of employment; whereas in this respect it is an essential condition for ensuring sustained economic development;

Whereas the completion of the internal market must favour the approximation of improvements in living and working conditions, as well as economic and social cohesion within the European Community, while avoiding distortions of competition;

Whereas the completion of the internal market must offer improvements in the social field for workers of the European Community, especially in terms of freedom of movement, living and working conditions, health and safety at work, social protection, education and training;

Whereas, in order to ensure equal treatment, it is important to combat every form of discrimination, including discrimination on grounds of sex, colour, race, opinion and beliefs, and whereas, in a spirit of solidarity, it is important to combat social exclusion;

Whereas it is for Member States to guarantee that workers from non-member countries and members of their families who are legally resident in a Member State of the European Community are able to enjoy, as regards their living and working conditions, treatment comparable to that enjoyed by workers who are nationals of the Member State concerned;

Whereas inspiration should be drawn from the Conventions of the International Labour Organisation and from the European Social Charter of the Council of Europe;

Whereas the Treaty, as amended by the Single European Act, contains provisions laying down the powers of the Community relating, inter alia, to the freedom of movement of workers (Articles 7, 48–51), to the right of establishment (Articles 52–58), to the social field under the conditions laid down in Articles 117–122—in particular as regards the improvement of health and safety in the working environment (Article 118a), the development of the dialogue between management and labour at European level (Article 118b), equal pay for men and women for equal work (Article 119)—to the general principles for implementing a common vocational training policy (Article 128), to economic and social cohesion (Article 130a to 130e) and, more generally, to the approximation of legislation (Articles 100, 100a and 235); whereas the implementation of the Charter must not entail an extension of the Community's powers as defined by the Treaties;

Whereas the aim of the present Charter is on the one hand to consolidate the progress made in the social field, through action by the Member States, the two sides of industry and the Community;

Whereas its aim is on the other hand to declare solemnly that the implementation of the Single European Act must take full account of the social dimension of the Community and that it is necessary in this context to ensure at appropriate levels the development of the social rights of workers of the European Community, especially employed workers and self-employed persons;

Whereas, in accordance with the conclusions of the Madrid European Council, the respective roles of Community rules, national legislation and collective agreements must be clearly established;

Whereas, by virtue of the principle of subsidiarity, responsibility for the initiatives to be taken with regard to the implementation of these social rights lies with the Member States or their constituent parts and, within the limits of its powers, with the European Community; whereas such implementation may take the form of laws, collective agreements or existing practices at the various appropriate levels and whereas it requires in many spheres the active involvement of the two sides of industry;

Whereas the solemn proclamation of fundamental social rights at European Community level may not, when implemented, provide grounds for any retrogression compared with the situation currently existing in each Member State.

HAVE ADOPTED THE FOLLOWING DECLARATION CONSTITUTING THE "COMMUNITY CHARTER OF THE FUNDAMENTAL SOCIAL RIGHTS OF WORKERS"—

TITLE I
FUNDAMENTAL SOCIAL RIGHTS OF WORKERS

FREEDOM OF MOVEMENT

[3.60]
1. Every worker of the European Community shall have the right to freedom of movement throughout the territory of the Community, subject to restrictions justified on grounds of public order, public safety or public health.

2. The right to freedom of movement shall enable any worker to engage in any occupation or profession in the Community in accordance with the principles of equal treatment as regards access to employment, working conditions and social protection in the host country.

3. The right of freedom of movement shall also imply—
- harmonisation of conditions of residence in all Member States, particularly those concerning qualifications;
- elimination of obstacles arising from the non-recognition of diplomas or equivalent occupational qualifications;
- improvement of the living and working conditions of frontier workers.

EMPLOYMENT AND REMUNERATION

[3.61]
4. Every individual shall be free to choose and engage in an occupation according to the regulations governing each occupation.

5. All employment shall be fairly remunerated.

To this effect, in accordance with arrangements applying in each country—
- workers shall be assured of an equitable wage, ie a wage sufficient to enable them to have a decent standard of living;
- workers subject to terms of employment other than an open-ended full time contract shall receive an equitable reference wage;
- wages may be withheld, seized or transferred only in accordance with the provisions of national law; such provisions should entail measures enabling the worker concerned to continue to enjoy the necessary means of subsistence for himself and his family.

6. Every individual must be able to have access to public placement services free of charge.

IMPROVEMENT OF LIVING AND WORKING CONDITIONS

[3.62]
7. The completion of the internal market must lead to an improvement in the living and working conditions of workers in the European Community. This process must result from an approximation of these conditions while the improvement is being maintained, as regards in particular the duration and organisation of working time and forms of employment other than open-ended contracts, such as fixed-term contracts, part-time working, temporary work and seasonal work.

The improvement must cover, where necessary, the development of certain aspects of employment regulations such as procedures for collective redundancies and those regarding bankruptcies.

8. Every worker of the European Community shall have a right to a weekly rest period and to annual paid leave, the duration of which must be harmonised in accordance with national practices while the improvement is being maintained.

9. The conditions of employment of every worker of the European Community shall be stipulated in laws, in a collective agreement or in a contract of employment, according to arrangements applying in each country.

SOCIAL PROTECTION

[3.63]
According to the arrangements applying in each country—

10. Every worker of the European Community shall have a right to adequate social protection and shall, whatever his status and whatever the size of the undertaking in which he is employed, enjoy an adequate level of social security benefits.

Persons who have been unable either to enter or re-enter the labour market and have no means of subsistence must be able to receive sufficient resources and social assistance in keeping with their particular situation.

FREEDOM OF ASSOCIATION AND COLLECTIVE BARGAINING

[3.64]
11. Employers and workers of the European Community shall have the right of association in order to constitute professional organisations or trade unions of their choice for the defence of their economic and social interests.

Every employer and every worker shall have the freedom to join or not to join such organisations without any personal or occupational damage being thereby suffered by him.

12. Employers or employers' organisations, on the one hand, and workers' organisations, on the other, shall have the right to negotiate and conclude collective agreements under the conditions laid down by national legislation and practice.

The dialogue between the two sides of industry at European level which must be developed, may, if the parties deem it desirable, result in contractual relations, in particular at inter-occupational and sectoral level.

13. The right to resort to collective action in the event of a conflict of interests shall include the right to strike, subject to the obligations arising under national regulations and collective agreements.

In order to facilitate the settlement of industrial disputes the establishment and utilisation at the appropriate levels of conciliation, mediation and arbitration procedures should be encouraged in accordance with national practice.

14. The internal legal order of the Member States shall determine under which conditions and to what extent the rights provided for in Articles 11 to 13 apply to the armed forces, the police and the civil service.

VOCATIONAL TRAINING

[3.65]
15. Every worker of the European Community must be able to have access to vocational training and to receive such training throughout his working life. In the conditions governing access to such training there may be no discrimination on grounds of nationality.

The competent public authorities, undertakings or the two sides of industry each within their own sphere of competence, should set up continuing and permanent training systems enabling every person to undergo retraining more especially through leave for training purposes, to improve his skills or to acquire new skills, particularly in the light of technical developments.

EQUAL TREATMENT FOR MEN AND WOMEN

[3.66]
16. Equal treatment for men and women must be assured. Equal opportunities for men and women must be developed.

To this end, action should be intensified wherever necessary to ensure the implementation of the principle of equality between men and women as regards in particular access to employment, remuneration, working conditions, social protection, education, vocational training and career development.

Measures should also be developed enabling men and women to reconcile their occupational and family obligations.

INFORMATION, CONSULTATION AND PARTICIPATION FOR WORKERS

[3.67]
17. Information, consultation and participation for workers must be developed along appropriate lines, taking account of the practice in force in the various Member States.

This shall apply especially in companies or groups of companies having establishments or companies in several Member States of the European Community.

18. Such information, consultation and participation must be implemented in due time, particularly in the following cases—

- when technological changes which, from the point of view of working conditions and work organisation, have major implications for the work force are introduced into undertakings;
- in connection with restructuring operations in undertakings or in cases of mergers having an impact on the employment of workers;
- in cases of collective redundancy procedures;
- when transfrontier workers in particular are affected by employment policies pursued by the undertaking where they are employed.

HEALTH PROTECTION AND SAFETY AT THE WORKPLACE

[3.68]

19. Every worker must enjoy satisfactory health and safety conditions in his working environment. Appropriate measures must be taken in order to achieve further harmonisation of conditions in this area while maintaining the improvements made.

These measures shall take account, in particular, of the need for the training, information, consultation and balanced participation of workers as regards the risks incurred and the steps taken to eliminate or reduce them.

The provisions regarding implementation of the internal market shall help to ensure such protection.

PROTECTION OF CHILDREN AND ADOLESCENTS

[3.69]

20. Without prejudice to such rules as may be more favourable to young people, in particular those ensuring their preparation for work through vocational training, and subject to derogations limited to certain light work, the minimum employment age must not be lower than the minimum school-leaving age and, in any case, not lower than 15 years.

21. Young people who are in gainful employment must receive equitable remuneration in accordance with national practice.

22. Appropriate measures must be taken to adjust labour regulations applicable to young workers so that their specific needs regarding development, vocational training and access to employment are met.

The duration of work must, in particular, be limited—without it being possible to circumvent this limitation through recourse to overtime—and night work prohibited in the case of workers of under eighteen years of age, save in the case of certain jobs laid down in national legislation or regulations.

23. Following the end of compulsory education, young people must be entitled to receive initial vocational training of a sufficient duration to enable them to adapt to the requirements of their future working life; for young workers, such training should take place during working hours.

ELDERLY PERSONS

[3.70]

According to the arrangements applying in each country—

24. Every worker of the European Community must, at the time of retirement, be able to enjoy resources affording him or her a decent standard of living.

25. Every person who has reached retirement age but who is not entitled to a pension or who does not have other means of subsistence, must be entitled to sufficient resources and to medical and social assistance specifically suited to his needs.

DISABLED PERSONS

[3.71]

26. All disabled persons, whatever the origin and nature of their disablement, must be entitled to additional concrete measures aimed at improving their social and professional integration.

These measures must concern, in particular, according to the capacities of the beneficiaries, vocational training, ergonomics, accessibility, mobility, means of transport and housing.

TITLE II
IMPLEMENTATION OF THE CHARTER

[3.72]

27. It is more particularly the responsibility of the Member States, in accordance with the national practices, notably through legislative measures or collective agreements, to guarantee the fundamental social rights in this Charter and to implement the social measures indispensable to the smooth operation of the internal market as part of a strategy of economic and social cohesion.

28. The European Council invites the Commission to submit as soon as possible initiatives which fall within its powers, as provided for in the Treaties, with a view to the adoption of legal instruments for the effective implementation, as and when the internal market is completed, of those rights which come within the Community's area of competence.

29. The Commission shall establish each year, during the last three months, a report on the application of the Charter by the Member States and by the European Community.

30. The report of the Commission shall be forwarded to the European Council, the European Parliament and the Economic and Social Committee.

CHARTER OF FUNDAMENTAL RIGHTS OF THE EUROPEAN UNION (2010)

NOTES

Date of publication in OJ: OJ C326, 26.10.2012, p 391.

Commencement: 1 December 2009.

This Charter, originally adopted in 2001, is printed as amended by the Treaty of Lisbon, to which it is annexed. As to the legal status of the Charter, see Protocol No 30 to the Treaty on the Functioning of the European Union, at **[3.56]**.

Only those Articles potentially relevant to matters within the scope of this work are included. Articles omitted are not annotated.

[3.73]

THE EUROPEAN PARLIAMENT, THE COUNCIL AND THE COMMISSION SOLEMNLY PROCLAIM THE FOLLOWING TEXT AS THE CHARTER OF FUNDAMENTAL RIGHTS OF THE EUROPEAN UNION.

PREAMBLE

The peoples of Europe, in creating an ever closer union among them, are resolved to share a peaceful future based on common values.

Conscious of its spiritual and moral heritage, the Union is founded on the indivisible, universal values of human dignity, freedom, equality and solidarity; it is based on the principles of democracy and the rule of law. It places the individual at the heart of its activities, by establishing the citizenship of the Union and by creating an area of freedom, security and justice.

The Union contributes to the preservation and to the development of these common values while respecting the diversity of the cultures and traditions of the peoples of Europe as well as the national identities of the Member States and the organisation of their public authorities at national, regional and local levels; it seeks to promote balanced and sustainable development and ensures free movement of persons, services, goods and capital, and the freedom of establishment.

To this end, it is necessary to strengthen the protection of fundamental rights in the light of changes in society, social progress and scientific and technological developments by making those rights more visible in a Charter.

This Charter reaffirms, with due regard for the powers and tasks of the Union and for the principle of subsidiarity, the rights as they result, in particular, from the constitutional traditions and international obligations common to the Member States, the European Convention for the Protection of Human Rights and Fundamental Freedoms, the Social Charters adopted by the Union and by the Council of Europe and the case-law of the Court of Justice of the European Union and of the European Court of Human Rights. In this context the Charter will be interpreted by the courts of the Union and the Member States with due regard to the explanations prepared under the authority of the Praesidium of the Convention which drafted the Charter and updated under the responsibility of the Praesidium of the European Convention.

Enjoyment of these rights entails responsibilities and duties with regard to other persons, to the human community and to future generations.

The Union therefore recognises the rights, freedoms and principles set out hereafter.

TITLE I
DIGNITY

[3.74]
Article 1
Human dignity
Human dignity is inviolable. It must be respected and protected.

[3.75]
Article 5
Prohibition of slavery and forced labour
1. No one shall be held in slavery or servitude.
2. No one shall be required to perform forced or compulsory labour.
3. Trafficking in human beings is prohibited.

TITLE II
FREEDOMS

[3.76]
Article 6
Right to liberty and security
Everyone has the right to liberty and security of person.

[3.77]
Article 7
Respect for private and family life
Everyone has the right to respect for his or her private and family life, home and communications.

[3.78]
Article 8
Protection of personal data
1. Everyone has the right to the protection of personal data concerning him or her.
2. Such data must be processed fairly for specified purposes and on the basis of the consent of the person concerned or some other legitimate basis laid down by law. Everyone has the right of access to data which has been collected concerning him or her, and the right to have it rectified.
3. Compliance with these rules shall be subject to control by an independent authority.

[3.79]
Article 9
Right to marry and right to found a family
The right to marry and the right to found a family shall be guaranteed in accordance with the national laws governing the exercise of these rights.

[3.80]
Article 10
Freedom of thought, conscience and religion
1. Everyone has the right to freedom of thought, conscience and religion. This right includes freedom to change religion or belief and freedom, either alone or in community with others and in public or in private, to manifest religion or belief, in worship, teaching, practice and observance.
2. The right to conscientious objection is recognised, in accordance with the national laws governing the exercise of this right.

[3.81]
Article 11
Freedom of expression and information
1. Everyone has the right to freedom of expression. This right shall include freedom to hold opinions and to receive and impart information and ideas without interference by public authority and regardless of frontiers.
2. The freedom and pluralism of the media shall be respected.

[3.82]
Article 12
Freedom of assembly and of association
1. Everyone has the right to freedom of peaceful assembly and to freedom of association at all levels, in particular in political, trade union and civic matters, which implies the right of everyone to form and to join trade unions for the protection of his or her interests.
2. Political parties at Union level contribute to expressing the political will of the citizens of the Union.

[3.83]
Article 13
Freedom of the arts and sciences
The arts and scientific research shall be free of constraint. Academic freedom shall be respected.

[3.84]
Article 14
Right to education
1. Everyone has the right to education and to have access to vocational and continuing training.
2. This right includes the possibility to receive free compulsory education.
3. The freedom to found educational establishments with due respect for democratic principles and the right of parents to ensure the education and teaching of their children in conformity with their religious, philosophical and pedagogical convictions shall be respected, in accordance with the national laws governing the exercise of such freedom and right.

[3.85]
Article 15
Freedom to choose an occupation and right to engage in work
1. Everyone has the right to engage in work and to pursue a freely chosen or accepted occupation.
2. Every citizen of the Union has the freedom to seek employment, to work, to exercise the right of establishment and to provide services in any Member State.
3. Nationals of third countries who are authorised to work in the territories of the Member States are entitled to working conditions equivalent to those of citizens of the Union.

[3.86]
Article 16
Freedom to conduct a business
The freedom to conduct a business in accordance with Union law and national laws and practices is recognised.

TITLE III
EQUALITY

[3.87]
Article 20
Equality before the law
Everyone is equal before the law.

[3.88]
Article 21
Non-discrimination
1. Any discrimination based on any ground such as sex, race, colour, ethnic or social origin, genetic features, language, religion or belief, political or any other opinion, membership of a national minority, property, birth, disability, age or sexual orientation shall be prohibited.
2. Within the scope of application of the Treaties and without prejudice to any of their specific provisions, any discrimination on grounds of nationality shall be prohibited.

[3.89]
Article 22
Cultural, religious and linguistic diversity
The Union shall respect cultural, religious and linguistic diversity.

[3.90]
Article 23
Equality between women and men
Equality between women and men must be ensured in all areas, including employment, work and pay.

The principle of equality shall not prevent the maintenance or adoption of measures providing for specific advantages in favour of the under-represented sex.

[3.91]
Article 26
Integration of persons with disabilities
The Union recognises and respects the right of persons with disabilities to benefit from measures designed to ensure their independence, social and occupational integration and participation in the life of the community.

TITLE IV
SOLIDARITY

[3.92]
Article 27
Workers' right to information and consultation within the undertaking
Workers or their representatives must, at the appropriate levels, be guaranteed information and consultation in good time in the cases and under the conditions provided for by Union law and national laws and practices.

[3.93]
Article 28
Right of collective bargaining and action
Workers and employers, or their respective organisations, have, in accordance with Union law and national laws and practices, the right to negotiate and conclude collective agreements at the appropriate levels and, in cases of conflicts of interest, to take collective action to defend their interests, including strike action.

[3.94]
Article 29
Right of access to placement services
Everyone has the right of access to a free placement service.

[3.95]
Article 30
Protection in the event of unjustified dismissal
Every worker has the right to protection against unjustified dismissal, in accordance with Union law and national laws and practices.

[3.96]
Article 31
Fair and just working conditions
1. Every worker has the right to working conditions which respect his or her health, safety and dignity.
2. Every worker has the right to limitation of maximum working hours, to daily and weekly rest periods and to an annual period of paid leave.

[3.97]
Article 32
Prohibition of child labour and protection of young people at work
The employment of children is prohibited. The minimum age of admission to employment may not be lower than the minimum school-leaving age, without prejudice to such rules as may be more favourable to young people and except for limited derogations.

Young people admitted to work must have working conditions appropriate to their age and be protected against economic exploitation and any work likely to harm their safety, health or physical, mental, moral or social development or to interfere with their education.

[3.98]
Article 33
Family and professional life
1. The family shall enjoy legal, economic and social protection.
2. To reconcile family and professional life, everyone shall have the right to protection from dismissal for a reason connected with maternity and the right to paid maternity leave and to parental leave following the birth or adoption of a child.

TITLE VI
JUSTICE

[3.99]
Article 47
Right to an effective remedy and to a fair trial
Everyone whose rights and freedoms guaranteed by the law of the Union are violated has the right to an effective remedy before a tribunal in compliance with the conditions laid down in this Article.

Everyone is entitled to a fair and public hearing within a reasonable time by an independent and impartial tribunal previously established by law. Everyone shall have the possibility of being advised, defended and represented.

Legal aid shall be made available to those who lack sufficient resources in so far as such aid is necessary to ensure effective access to justice.

TITLE VII
GENERAL PROVISIONS GOVERNING THE INTERPRETATION AND APPLICATION OF THE CHARTER

[3.100]
Article 51
Field of application
1. The provisions of this Charter are addressed to the institutions, bodies, offices and agencies of the Union with due regard for the principle of subsidiarity and to the Member States only when they are implementing Union law. They shall therefore respect the rights, observe the principles and promote the application thereof in accordance with their respective powers and respecting the limits of the powers of the Union as conferred on it in the Treaties.
2. The Charter does not extend the field of application of Union law beyond the powers of the Union or establish any new power or task for the Union, or modify powers and tasks as defined in the Treaties.

[3.101]
Article 52
Scope and interpretation of rights and principles
1. Any limitation on the exercise of the rights and freedoms recognised by this Charter must be provided for by law and respect the essence of those rights and freedoms. Subject to the principle of proportionality, limitations may be made only if they are necessary and genuinely meet objectives of general interest recognised by the Union or the need to protect the rights and freedoms of others.
2. Rights recognised by this Charter for which provision is made in the Treaties shall be exercised under the conditions and within the limits defined by those Treaties.
3. In so far as this Charter contains rights which correspond to rights guaranteed by the Convention for the Protection of Human Rights and Fundamental Freedoms, the meaning and scope of those rights shall be the same as those laid down by the said Convention. This provision shall not prevent Union law providing more extensive protection.
4. In so far as this Charter recognises fundamental rights as they result from the constitutional traditions common to the Member States, those rights shall be interpreted in harmony with those traditions.
5. The provisions of this Charter which contain principles may be implemented by legislative and executive acts taken by institutions, bodies, offices and agencies of the Union, and by acts of Member States when they are implementing Union law, in the exercise of their respective powers. They shall be judicially cognisable only in the interpretation of such acts and in the ruling on their legality.
6. Full account shall be taken of national laws and practices as specified in this Charter.
7. The explanations drawn up as a way of providing guidance in the interpretation of this Charter shall be given due regard by the courts of the Union and of the Member States.

[3.102]
Article 53
Level of protection
Nothing in this Charter shall be interpreted as restricting or adversely affecting human rights and fundamental freedoms as recognised, in their respective fields of application, by Union law and international law and by international agreements to which the Union or all the Member States are party, including the European Convention for the Protection of Human Rights and Fundamental Freedoms, and by the Member States' constitutions.

[3.103]
Article 54
Prohibition of abuse of rights
Nothing in this Charter shall be interpreted as implying any right to engage in any activity or to perform any act aimed at the destruction of any of the rights and freedoms recognised in this Charter or at their limitation to a greater extent than is provided for herein.

B. REGULATIONS, DIRECTIVES AND RECOMMENDATIONS

COUNCIL DIRECTIVE

(79/7/EEC)

of 19 December 1978

on the progressive implementation of the principle of equal treatment for men and women in matters of social security

NOTES

Date of publication in OJ: OJ L6, 10.1.1979, p 24.

[3.104]

THE COUNCIL OF THE EUROPEAN COMMUNITIES,

Having regard to the Treaty establishing the European Economic Community, and in particular Article 235 thereof;

Having regard to the proposal from the Commission;[1]

Having regard to the opinion of the European Parliament;[2]

Having regard to the opinion of the Economic and Social Committee;[3]

Whereas Article 1(2) of Council Directive 76/207/EEC of 9 February 1976 on the implementation of the principle of equal treatment for men and women as regards access to employment, vocational training and promotion, and working conditions[4] provides that, with a view to ensuring the progressive implementation of the principle of equal treatment in matters of social security, the Council, acting on a proposal from the Commission, will adopt provisions defining its substance, its scope and the arrangements for its application; whereas the Treaty does not confer the specific powers required for this purpose;

Whereas the principle of equal treatment in matters of social security should be implemented in the first place in the statutory schemes which provide protection against the risks of sickness, invalidity, old age, accidents at work, occupational diseases and unemployment, and in social assistance in so far as it is intended to supplement or replace the abovementioned schemes;

Whereas the implementation of the principle of equal treatment in matters of social security does not prejudice the provisions relating to the protection of women on the ground of maternity; whereas, in this respect, Member States may adopt specific provisions for women to remove existing instances of unequal treatment,

NOTES

1 OJ C34, 11.2.77, p 3.

2 OJ C299, 12.12.77, p 13.

3 OJ C180, 28.7.77, p 36.

4 OJ L39, 14.2.76, p 40.

HAS ADOPTED THIS DIRECTIVE—

[3.105]

Article 1

The purpose of this Directive is the progressive implementation, in the field of social security and other elements of social protection provided for in Article 3, of the principle of equal treatment for men and women in matters of social security, hereinafter referred to as 'the principle of equal treatment'.

[3.106]

Article 2

This Directive shall apply to the working population—including self-employed persons, workers and self-employed persons whose activity is interrupted by illness, accident or involuntary unemployment and persons seeking employment—and to retired or invalided workers and self-employed persons.

[3.107]

Article 3

1. This Directive shall apply to—
   (a) statutory schemes which provide protection against the following risks—
      — sickness,
      — invalidity,

Part 3 EU Materials

— old age,
— accidents at work and occupational diseases,
— unemployment;

(b) social assistance, in so far as it is intended to supplement or replace the schemes referred to in (a).

2. This Directive shall not apply to the provisions concerning survivors' benefits nor to those concerning family benefits, except in the case of family benefits granted by way of increases of benefits due in respect of the risks referred to in paragraph 1(a).

3. With a view to ensuring implementation of the principle of equal treatment in occupational schemes, the Council, acting on a proposal from the Commission, will adopt provisions defining its substance, its scope and the arrangements for its application.

[3.108]
Article 4

1. The principle of equal treatment means that there shall be no discrimination whatsoever on ground of sex either directly, or indirectly by reference in particular to marital or family status, in particular as concerns—

— the scope of the schemes and the conditions of access thereto,
— the obligation to contribute and the calculation of contributions,
— the calculation of benefits including increases due in respect of a spouse and for dependants and the conditions governing the duration and retention of entitlement to benefits.

2. The principle of equal treatment shall be without prejudice to the provisions relating to the protection of women on the grounds of maternity.

[3.109]
Article 5

Member States shall take the measures necessary to ensure that any laws, regulations and administrative provisions contrary to the principle of equal treatment are abolished.

[3.110]
Article 6

Member States shall introduce into their national legal systems such measures as are necessary to enable all persons who consider themselves wronged by failure to apply the principle of equal treatment to pursue their claims by judicial process, possibly after recourse to other competent authorities.

[3.111]
Article 7

1. This Directive shall be without prejudice to the right of Member States to exclude from its scope—

(a) the determination of pensionable age for the purposes of granting old-age and retirement pensions and the possible consequences thereof for other benefits;

(b) advantages in respect of old-age pension schemes granted to persons who have brought up children; the acquisition of benefit entitlements following periods of interruption of employment due to the bringing up of children;

(c) the granting of old-age or invalidity benefit entitlements by virtue of the derived entitlements of a wife;

(d) the granting of increases of long-term invalidity, old-age, accidents at work and occupational disease benefits for a dependent wife;

(e) the consequences of the exercise, before the adoption of this Directive, of a right of option not to acquire rights to incur obligations under a statutory scheme.

2. Member States shall periodically examine matters excluded under paragraph 1 in order to ascertain, in the light of social developments in the matter concerned, whether there is justification for maintaining the exclusions concerned.

[3.112]
Article 8

1. Member States shall bring into force the laws, regulations and administrative provisions necessary to comply with this Directive within six years of its notification. They shall immediately inform the Commission thereof.

2. Member States shall communicate to the Commission the text of laws, regulations and administrative provisions which they adopt in the field covered by this Directive, including measures adopted pursuant to Article 7(2).

They shall inform the Commission of their reasons for maintaining any existing provisions on the matters referred to in Article 7(1) and of the possibilities for reviewing them at a later date.

[3.113]
Article 9
Within seven years of notification of this Directive, Member States shall forward all information necessary to the Commission to enable it to draw up a report on the application of this Directive for submission to the Council and to propose such further measures as may be required for the implementation of the principle of equal treatment.

[3.114]
Article 10
This Directive is addressed to the Member States.

COUNCIL DIRECTIVE

(89/391/EEC)
of 12 June 1989

on the introduction of measures to encourage improvements in the safety and health of workers at work

NOTES
Date of publication in OJ: OJ L183, 29.6.1989, p 1. The text of this Directive incorporates the corrigendum published in OJ L275, 5.10.1990, p 42.
For the domestic implementation of this Directive see in particular the Management of Health and Safety at Work Regulations 1999, SI 1999/3242 at **[2.454]**, the Employment Rights Act 1996, ss 44, 100 at **[1.801]**, **[1.900]**, and the Health and Safety (Consultation with Employees) Regulations 1996, SI 1996/1513 at **[2.233]**.

[3.115]
THE COUNCIL OF THE EUROPEAN COMMUNITIES,

Having regard to the Treaty establishing the European Economic Community, and in particular Article 118a thereof,

Having regard to the proposal from the Commission,[1] drawn up after consultation with the Advisory Committee on Safety, Hygiene and Health Protection at Work,

In cooperation with the European Parliament,[2]

Having regard to the opinion of the Economic and Social Committee,[3]

Whereas Article 118a of the Treaty provides that the Council shall adopt, by means of Directives, minimum requirements for encouraging improvements, especially in the working environment, to guarantee a better level of protection of the safety and health of workers;

Whereas this Directive does not justify any reduction in levels of protection already achieved in individual Member States, the Member State being committed, under the Treaty, to encouraging improvements in conditions in this area and to harmonising conditions while maintaining the improvements made;

Whereas it is known that workers can be exposed to the effects of dangerous environmental factors at the work place during the course of their working life;

Whereas, pursuant to Article 118a of the Treaty, such Directives must avoid imposing administrative, financial and legal constraints which would hold back the creation and development of small and medium-sized undertakings;

Whereas the communication from the Commission on its programme concerning safety, hygiene and health at work[4] provides for the adoption of Directives designed to guarantee the safety and health of workers;

Whereas the Council, in its resolution of 21 December 1987 on safety, hygiene and health at work,[5] took note of the Commission's intention to submit to the Council in the near future a Directive on the organisation of the safety and health of workers at the work place;

Whereas in February 1988 the European Parliament adopted four resolutions following the debate on the internal market and worker protection; whereas these resolutions specifically invited the Commission to draw up a framework Directive to serve as a basis for more specific Directives covering all the risks connected with safety and health at the work place;

Whereas Member States have a responsibility to encourage improvements in the safety and health of workers on their territory; whereas taking measures to protect the health and safety of workers at work also helps, in certain cases, to preserve the health and possibly the safety of persons residing with them;

Whereas Member States' legislative systems covering safety and health at the work place differ widely and need to be improved; whereas national provisions on the subject, which often include technical specifications and/or self-regulatory standards, may result in different levels of safety and health protection and allow competition at the expense of safety and health;

Whereas the incidence of accidents at work and occupational diseases is still too high; whereas preventive measures must be introduced or improved without delay in order to safeguard the safety and health of workers and ensure a higher degree of protection;

Whereas, in order to ensure an improved degree of protection, workers and/or their representatives must be informed of the risks to their safety and health and of the measures required to reduce or eliminate these risks; whereas they must also be in a position to contribute, by means of balanced participation in accordance with national laws and/or practices, to seeing that the necessary protective measures are taken;

Whereas information, dialogue and balanced participation on safety and health at work must be developed between employers and workers and/or their representatives by means of appropriate procedures and instruments, in accordance with national laws and/or practices;

Whereas the improvement of workers' safety, hygiene and health at work is an objective which should not be subordinated to purely economic considerations;

Whereas employers shall be obliged to keep themselves informed of the latest advances in technology and scientific findings concerning work-place design, account being taken of the inherent dangers in their undertaking, and to inform accordingly the workers' representatives exercising participation rights under this Directive, so as to be able to guarantee a better level of protection of workers' health and safety;

Whereas the provisions of this Directive apply, without prejudice to more stringent present or future Community provisions, to all risks, and in particular to those arising from the use at work of chemical, physical and biological agents covered by Directive 80/1107/EEC,[6] as last amended by Directive 88/642/EEC;[7]

Whereas, pursuant to Decision 74/325/EEC,[8] the Advisory Committee on Safety, Hygiene and Health Protection at Work is consulted by the Commission on the drafting of proposals in this field;

Whereas a Committee composed of members nominated by the Member States needs to be set up to assist the Commission in making the technical adaptations to the individual Directives provided for in this Directive.

NOTES

1 OJ C141, 30.5.88, p 1.

2 OJ C326, 19.12.88, p 102 and OJ C158, 26.6.89.

3 OJ C175, 4.7.88, p 22.

4 OJ C28, 3.2.88, p 3.

5 OJ C28, 3.2.88, p 1.

6 OJ L327, 3.12.80, p 8.

7 OJ L356, 24.12.88, p 74.

8 OJ L185, 9.7.74, p 15.

HAS ADOPTED THIS DIRECTIVE—

SECTION I
GENERAL PROVISIONS

[3.116]
Article 1
Object

1. The object of this Directive is to introduce measures to encourage improvements in the safety and health of workers at work.

2. To that end it contains general principles concerning the prevention of occupational risks, the protection of safety and health, the elimination of risk and accident factors, the informing, consultation, balanced participation in accordance with national laws and/or practices and training of workers and their representatives, as well as general guidelines for the implementation of the said principles.

3. This Directive shall be without prejudice to existing or future national and Community provisions which are more favourable to protection of the safety and health of workers at work.

[3.117]
Article 2
Scope

1. This Directive shall apply to all sectors of activity, both public and private (industrial, agricultural, commercial, administrative, service, educational, cultural, leisure, etc).

2. This Directive shall not be applicable where characteristics peculiar to certain specific service activities, such as the armed forces or the police, or to certain specific activities in the civil protection services inevitably conflict with it.

In that event, the safety and health of workers must be ensured as far as possible in the light of the objectives of this Directive.

[3.118]
Article 3
Definitions

For the purposes of this Directive, the following terms shall have the following meanings—

(a) worker: any person employed by an employer, including trainees and apprentices but excluding domestic servants;
(b) employer: any natural or legal person who has an employment relationship with the worker and has responsibility for the undertaking and/or establishment;
(c) workers' representative with specific responsibility for the safety and health of workers: any person elected, chosen or designated in accordance with national laws and/or practices to represent workers where problems arise relating to the safety and health protection of workers at work;
(d) prevention: all the steps or measures taken or planned at all stages of work in the undertaking to prevent or reduce occupational risks.

[3.119]
Article 4

1. Member States shall take the necessary steps to ensure that employers, workers and workers' representatives are subject to the legal provisions necessary for the implementation of this Directive.
2. In particular, Member States shall ensure adequate controls and supervision.

SECTION II
EMPLOYERS' OBLIGATIONS

[3.120]
Article 5
General provision

1. The employer shall have a duty to ensure the safety and health of workers in every aspect related to the work.
2. Where, pursuant to Article 7(3), an employer enlists competent external services or persons, this shall not discharge him from his responsibilities in this area.
3. The workers' obligations in the field of safety and health at work shall not affect the principle of the responsibility of the employer.
4. This Directive shall not restrict the option of Member States to provide for the exclusion or the limitation of employers' responsibility where occurrences are due to unusual and unforeseeable circumstances, beyond the employers' control, or to exceptional events, the consequences of which could not have been avoided despite the exercise of all due care.

Member States need not exercise the option referred to in the first sub-paragraph.

[3.121]
Article 6
General obligations on employers

1. Within the context of his responsibilities, the employer shall take the measures necessary for the safety and health protection of workers, including prevention of occupational risks and provision of information and training, as well as provision of the necessary organisation and means.

The employer shall be alert to the need to adjust these measures to take account of changing circumstances and aim to improve existing situations.

2. The employer shall implement the measures referred to in the first subparagraph of paragraph 1 on the basis of the following general principles of prevention—

(a) avoiding risks;
(b) evaluating the risks which cannot be avoided;
(c) combating the risk at source;
(d) adapting the work to the individual, especially as regards the design of work places, the choice of work equipment and the choice of working and production methods, with a view, in particular, to alleviating monotonous work and work at a predetermined work-rate and to reducing their effect on health;
(e) adapting to technical progress;
(f) replacing the dangerous by the non-dangerous or the less dangerous;
(g) developing a coherent overall prevention policy which covers technology, organisation of work, working conditions, social relationships and the influence of factors related to the working environment;
(h) giving collective protective measures priority over individual protective measures;
(i) giving appropriate instructions to the workers.

3. Without prejudice to the other provisions of this Directive, the employers shall, taking into account the nature of the activities of the enterprise and/or establishment—

(a) evaluate the risks to the safety and health of workers, *inter alia* in the choice of work equipment, the chemical substances or preparations used, and the fitting-out of work places.

Subsequent to this evaluation and as necessary, the preventive measures and the working and production methods implemented by the employer must—

— assure an improvement in the level of protection afforded to workers with regard to safety and health,

— be integrated into all the activities of the undertaking and/or establishment and at all hierarchical levels;

(b) where he entrusts tasks to a worker, take into consideration the worker's capabilities as regards health and safety;

(c) ensure that the planning and introduction of new technologies are the subject of consultation with the workers and/or their representatives, as regards the consequences of the choice of equipment, the working conditions and the working environment for the safety and health of workers;

(d) take appropriate steps to ensure that only workers who have received adequate instructions may have access to areas where there is serious and specific danger.

4. Without prejudice to the other provisions of this Directive, where several undertakings share a work place, the employers shall co-operate in implementing the safety, health and occupational hygiene provisions and, taking into account the nature of the activities, shall coordinate their actions in matters of the protection and prevention of occupational risks, and shall inform one another and their respective workers and/or workers' representatives of these risks.

5. Measures related to safety, hygiene and health at work may in no circumstances involve the workers in financial cost.

[3.122]
Article 7
Protective and preventive services

1. Without prejudice to the obligations referred to in Articles 5 and 6, the employer shall designate one or more workers to carry out activities related to the protection and prevention of occupational risks for the undertaking and/or establishment.

2. Designated workers may not be placed at any disadvantage because of their activities related to the protection and prevention of occupational risks.

Designated workers shall be allowed adequate time to enable them to fulfil their obligations arising from this Directive.

3. If such protective and preventive measures cannot be organised for lack of competent personnel in the undertaking and/or establishment, the employer shall enlist competent external services or persons.

4. Where the employer enlists such services or persons, he shall inform them of the factors known to affect, or suspected of affecting, the safety and health of the workers and they must have access to the information referred to in Article 10(2).

5. In all cases—

— the workers designated must have the necessary capabilities and the necessary means,

— the external services or persons consulted must have the necessary aptitudes and the necessary personal and professional means, and

— the workers designated and the external services or persons consulted must be sufficient in number

to deal with the organisation of protective and preventive measures, taking into account the size of the undertaking and/or establishment and/or the hazards to which the workers are exposed and their distribution throughout the entire undertaking and/or establishment.

6. The protection from, and prevention of, the health and safety risks which form the subject of this Article shall be the responsibility of one or more workers, of one service or of separate services whether from inside or outside the undertaking and/or establishment.

The worker(s) and/or agency(ies) must work together whenever necessary.

7. Member States may define, in the light of the nature of the activities and size of the undertakings, the categories or undertakings in which the employer, provided he is competent, may himself take responsibility for the measures referred to in paragraph 1.

8. Member States shall define the necessary capabilities and aptitudes referred to in paragraph 5.

They may determine the sufficient number referred to in paragraph 5.

[3.123]
Article 8
First aid, fire-fighting and evacuation of workers, serious and imminent danger

1. The employer shall—

— take the necessary measures for first aid, fire-fighting and evacuation of workers, adapted to the nature of the activities and the size of the undertaking and/or establishment and taking into account other persons present;

— arrange any necessary contacts with external services, particularly as regards first aid, emergency medical care, rescue work and fire-fighting.

2. Pursuant to paragraph 1, the employer shall, *inter alia*, for first aid, fire-fighting and the evacuation of workers, designate the workers required to implement such measures.

The number of such workers, their training and the equipment available to them shall be adequate, taking account of the size and/or specific hazards of the undertaking and/or establishment.

3. The employer shall—

(a) as soon as possible, inform all workers who are, or may be, exposed to serious and imminent danger of the risk involved and of the steps taken or to be taken as regards protection;

(b) take action and give instructions to enable workers in the event of serious, imminent and unavoidable danger to stop work and/or immediately to leave the work place and proceed to a place of safety;

(c) save in exceptional cases for reasons duly substantiated, refrain from asking workers to resume work in a working situation where there is still a serious and imminent danger.

4. Workers who, in the event of serious, imminent and unavoidable danger, leave their workstation and/or a dangerous area may not be placed at any disadvantage because of their action and must be protected against any harmful and unjustified consequences, in accordance with national laws and/or practices.

5. The employer shall ensure that all workers are able, in the event of serious and imminent danger to their own safety and/or that of other persons, and where the immediate superior responsible cannot be contacted, to take the appropriate steps in the light of their knowledge and the technical means at their disposal, to avoid the consequences of such danger.

Their actions shall not place them at any disadvantage, unless they acted carelessly or there was negligence on their part.

[3.124]

Article 9

Various obligations on employers

1. The employer shall—

(a) be in possession of an assessment of the risks to safety and health at work, in including those facing groups of workers exposed to particular risks;

(b) decide on the protective measures to be taken and, if necessary, the protective equipment to be used;

(c) keep a list of occupational accidents resulting in a worker being unfit for work for more than three working days;

(d) draw up, for the responsible authorities and in accordance with national laws and/or practices, reports on occupational accidents suffered by his workers.

2. Member States shall define, in the light of the nature of the activities and size of the undertaking, the obligations to be met by the different categories of undertakings in respect of the drawing-up of the documents provided for in paragraph 1(a) and (b) and when preparing the documents provided for in paragraph 1(c) and (d).

[3.125]

Article 10

Worker information

1. The employer shall take appropriate measures so that workers and/or their representatives in the undertaking and/or establishment receive in accordance with national laws and/or practices which may take account, *inter alia*, of the size of the undertaking and/or establishment, all the necessary information concerning—

(a) the safety and health risks and protective and preventive measures and activities in respect of both the undertaking and/or establishment in general and each type of workstati and/or job;

(b) the measures taken pursuant to Article 8(2).

2. The employer shall take appropriate measures so that employers of workers from a undertakings and/or establishments engaged in work in his undertaking and/or e receive, in accordance with national laws and/or practices, adequate information points referred to in paragraph 1(a) and (b) which is to be provided to the work

3. The employer shall take appropriate measures so that workers with protecting the safety and health of workers, or workers' representatives wit for the safety and health of workers shall have access, to carry out their fu with national laws and/or practices, to—

(a) the risk assessment and protective measures referred to in

(b) the list and reports referred to in Article 9(1)(c) and (d);

(c) the information yielded by protective and preventive bodies responsible for safety and health.

[3.126]
Article 11
Consultation and participation of workers

1. Employers shall consult workers and/or their representatives and allow them to take part in discussions on all questions relating to safety and health at work.

This presupposes—

— the consultation of workers,
— the right of workers and/or their representatives to make proposals,
— balanced participation in accordance with national laws and/or practices.

2. Workers or workers' representatives with specific responsibility for the safety and health of workers shall take part in a balanced way, in accordance with national laws and/or practices, or shall be consulted in advance and in good time by the employer with regard to—

(a) any measure which may substantially affect safety and health;
(b) the designation of workers referred to in Articles 7(1) and 8(2) and the activities referred to in Article 7(1);
(c) the information referred to in Articles 9(1) and 10;
(d) the enlistment, where appropriate, of the competent services or persons outside the undertaking and/or establishment, as referred to in Article 7(3);
(e) the planning and organisation of the training referred to in Article 12.

3. Workers' representatives with specific responsibility for the safety and health of workers shall have the right to ask the employer to take appropriate measures and to submit proposals to him to that end to mitigate hazards for workers and/or to remove sources of danger.

4. The workers referred to in paragraph 2 and the workers' representatives referred to in paragraphs 2 and 3 may not be placed at a disadvantage because of their respective activities referred to in paragraphs 2 and 3.

5. Employers must allow workers' representatives with specific responsibility for the safety and health of workers adequate time off work, without loss of pay, and provide them with the necessary means to enable such representatives to exercise their rights and functions deriving from this Directive.

6. Workers and/or their representatives are entitled to appeal, in accordance with national law and/or practice, to the authority responsible for safety and health protection at work if they consider that the measures taken and the means employed by the employer are inadequate for the purposes of ensuring safety and health at work.

Workers' representatives must be given the opportunity to submit their observations during inspection visits by the competent authority.

[3.127]
Article 12
Training of workers

1. The employer shall ensure that each worker receives adequate safety and health training, in particular in the form of information and instructions specific to his workstation or job—

— on recruitment,
— in the event of a transfer or a change of job,
— in the event of the introduction of new work equipment or a change in equipment,
— in the event of the introduction of any new technology.

The training shall be—

— adapted to take account of new or changed risks, and
— repeated periodically if necessary.

from outside undertakings and/or establishments establishment have in fact received appropriate during their activities in his undertaking and/or

in protecting the safety and health of workers shall

3 may not be at the workers' expense or at that of

take place during working hours.
take place during working hours or in accordance he undertaking and/or the establishment.

ION III
OBLIGATIONS

o take care as far as possible of his own safety and acts or omissions at work in accordance with his yer.

2. To this end, workers must in particular, in accordance with their training and the instructions given by their employer—
   (a) make correct use of machinery, apparatus, tools, dangerous substances, transport equipment and other means of production;
   (b) make correct use of the personal protective equipment supplied to them and, after use, return it to its proper place;
   (c) refrain from disconnecting, changing or removing arbitrarily safety devices fitted, eg to machinery, apparatus, tools, plant and buildings, and use such safety devices correctly;
   (d) immediately inform the employer and/or the workers with specific responsibility for the safety and health of workers of any work situation they have reasonable grounds for considering represents a serious and immediate danger to safety and health and of any shortcomings in the protection arrangements;
   (e) co-operate, in accordance with national practice, with the employer and/or workers with specific responsibility for the safety and health of workers, for as long as may be necessary to enable any tasks or requirements imposed by the competent authority to protect the safety and health of workers at work to be carried out;
   (f) co-operate, in accordance with national practice, with the employer and/or workers with specific responsibility for the safety and health of workers, for as long as may be necessary to enable the employer to ensure that the working environment and working conditions are safe and pose no risk to safety and health within their field of activity.

SECTION IV
MISCELLANEOUS PROVISIONS

[3.129]
Article 14
Health surveillance
1. To ensure that workers receive health surveillance appropriate to the health and safety risks they incur at work, measures shall be introduced in accordance with national law and/or practices.
2. The measures referred to in paragraph 1 shall be such that each worker, if he so wishes, may receive health surveillance at regular intervals.
3. Health surveillance may be provided as part of a national health system.

[3.130]
Article 15
Risk groups
Particularly sensitive risk groups must be protected against the dangers which specifically affect them.

[3.131]
Article 16
Individual Directives—Amendments—General scope of this Directive
1. The Council, acting on a proposal from the Commission based on Article 118a of the Treaty, shall adopt individual Directives, *inter alia*, in the areas listed in the Annex.
2. This Directive and, without prejudice to the procedure referred to in Article 17 concerning technical adjustments, the individual Directives may be amended in accordance with the procedure provided for in Article 118a of the Treaty.
3. The provisions of this Directive shall apply in full to all the areas covered by the individual Directives, without prejudice to more stringent and/or specific provisions contained in these individual Directives.

NOTES
Article 118a: see now Art 154 at **[3.30]**.

[3.132]
[Article 17
Committee procedure
1. The Commission shall be assisted by a committee to make purely technical adjustments to the individual directives provided for in Article 16(1) in order to take account of:
   (a) the adoption of directives in the field of technical harmonisation and standardisation;
   (b) technical progress, changes in international regulations or specifications and new findings.

Those measures, designed to amend non-essential elements of the individual directives, shall be adopted in accordance with the regulatory procedure with scrutiny referred to in paragraph 2. On imperative grounds of urgency, the Commission may have recourse to the urgency procedure referred to in paragraph 3.
2. Where reference is made to this paragraph, Article 5a(1) to (4) and Article 7 of Decision 1999/468/EC shall apply, having regard to the provisions of Article 8 thereof.

3. Where reference is made to this paragraph, Article 5a(1), (2), (4) and (6) and Article 7 of Decision 1999/468/EC shall apply, having regard to the provisions of Article 8 thereof.]

NOTES

Substituted by European Parliament and Council Regulation 1137/2008/EC, Art 1, Annex, para 2, as from 11 December 2008.

[3.133]
[Article 17a
Implementation reports

1. Every five years, the Member States shall submit a single report to the Commission on the practical implementation of this Directive and individual Directives within the meaning of Article 16(1), indicating the points of view of the social partners. The report shall assess the various points related to the practical implementation of the different Directives and, where appropriate and available, provide data disaggregated by gender.
2. The structure of the report, together with a questionnaire specifying its content, shall be defined by the Commission, in cooperation with the Advisory Committee on Safety and Health at Work.

The report shall include a general part on the provisions of this Directive relating to the common principles and points applicable to all of the Directives referred to in paragraph 1.

To complement the general part, specific chapters shall deal with implementation of the particular aspects of each Directive, including specific indicators, where available.
3. The Commission shall submit the structure of the report, together with the above-mentioned questionnaire specifying its content, to the Member States at least six months before the end of the period covered by the report. The report shall be transmitted to the Commission within 12 months of the end of the five-year period that it covers.
4. Using these reports as a basis, the Commission shall evaluate the implementation of the Directives concerned in terms of their relevance, of research and of new scientific knowledge in the various fields in question. It shall, within 36 months of the end of the five-year period, inform the European Parliament, the Council, the European Economic and Social Committee and the Advisory Committee on Safety and Health at Work of the results of this evaluation and, if necessary, of any initiatives to improve the operation of the regulatory framework.
5. The first report shall cover the period 2007 to 2012.]

NOTES

Inserted by European Parliament and Council Directive 2007/30/EC, Art 1.

[3.134]
Article 18
Final provisions

1. Member States shall bring into force the laws, regulations and administrative provisions necessary to comply with this Directive by 31 December 1992.

They shall forthwith inform the Commission thereof.
2. Member States shall communicate to the Commission the texts of the provisions of rational law which they have already adopted or adopt in the field covered by this Directive.
3, 4. . . .

NOTES

Paras 3, 4: repealed by European Parliament and Council Directive 2007/30/EC, Art 3(1).

[3.135]
Article 19

This Directive is addressed to the Member States.

ANNEX
LIST OF AREAS REFERRED TO IN ARTICLE 16(1)

[3.136]

— Work places

— Work equipment

— Personal protective equipment

— Work with visual display units

— Handling of heavy loads involving risk of back injury

— Temporary or mobile work sites

— Fisheries and agriculture.

COUNCIL DIRECTIVE

(91/533/EEC)

of 14 October 1991

on an employer's obligation to inform employees of the conditions applicable to the contract or employment relationship

NOTES

Date of publication in OJ: OJ L288, 18.10.1991, p 32.

There is no specific domestic legislation introduced to implement this Directive as its provisions were already reflected in what is now Part I of the Employment Rights Act 1996 (qv, at **[1.743]**–**[1.756]**).

See also *Harvey* AII(3).

[3.137]

THE COUNCIL OF THE EUROPEAN COMMUNITIES,

Having regard to the Treaty establishing the European Economic Community, and in particular Article 100 thereof,

Having regard to the proposal from the Commission,[1]

Having regard to the opinion of the European Parliament,[2]

Having regard to the opinion of the Economic and Social Committee,[3]

Whereas the development, in the Member States, of new forms of work has led to an increase in the number of types of employment relationship;

Whereas, faced with this development, certain Member States have considered it necessary to subject employment relationships to formal requirements; whereas these provisions are designed to provide employees with improved protection against possible infringements of their rights and to create greater transparency on the labour market;

Whereas the relevant legislation of the Member States differs considerably on such fundamental points as the requirement to inform employees in writing of the main terms of the contract or employment relationship;

Whereas differences in the legislation of Member States may have a direct effect on the operation of the common market;

Whereas Article 117 of the Treaty provides for the Member States to agree upon the need to promote improved working conditions and an improved standard of living for workers, so as to make possible their harmonisation while the improvement is being maintained;

Whereas point 9 of the Community Charter of Fundamental Social Rights for Workers, adopted at the Strasbourg European Council on 9 December 1989 by the Heads of State and Government of 11 Member States, states—

'The conditions of employment of every worker of the European Community shall be stipulated in laws, a collective agreement or a contract of employment, according to arrangements applying in each country.';

Whereas it is necessary to establish at Community level the general requirement that every employee must be provided with a document containing information on the essential elements of his contract or employment relationship;

Whereas, in view of the need to maintain a certain degree of flexibility in employment relationships, Member States should be able to exclude certain limited cases of employment relationship from this Directive's scope of application;

Whereas the obligation to provide information may be met by means of a written contract, a letter of appointment or one or more other documents or, if they are lacking, a written statement signed by the employer;

Whereas, in the case of expatriation of the employee, the latter must, in addition to the main terms of this contract or employment relationship, be supplied with relevant information connected with his secondment;

Whereas, in order to protect the interests of employees with regard to obtaining a document, any change in the main terms of the contract or employment relationship must be communicated to them in writing;

Whereas it is necessary for Member States to guarantee that employees can claim the rights conferred on them by this Directive;

Whereas Member States are to adopt the laws, regulations and legislative provisions necessary to comply with this Directive or are to ensure that both sides of industry set up the necessary provisions by agreement, with Member States being obliged to take the necessary steps enabling them at all times to guarantee the results imposed by this Directive,

NOTES

1 OJ C24, 31.1.1991, p 3.

2 OJ C240, 16.9.1991, p 21.

Part 3 EU Materials

[3] OJ C159, 17.6.1991, p 32.

HAS ADOPTED THIS DIRECTIVE—

[3.138]
Article 1
Scope
1. This Directive shall apply to every paid employee having a contract or employment relationship defined by the law in force in a Member State and/or governed by the law in force in a Member State.
2. Member States may provide that this Directive shall not apply to employees having a contract or employment relationship—
- (a) with a total duration not exceeding one month, and/or with a working week not exceeding eight hours; or
- (b) of a casual and/or specific nature provided, in these cases, that its non-application is justified by objective considerations.

[3.139]
Article 2
Obligation to provide information
1. An employer shall be obliged to notify an employee to whom this Directive applies, hereinafter referred to as 'the employee', of the essential aspects of the contract or employment relationship.
2. The information referred to in paragraph 1 shall cover at least the following—
- (a) the identities of the parties;
- (b) the place of work; where there is no fixed or main place of work, the principle that the employee is employed at various places and the registered place of business or, where appropriate, the domicile of the employer;
- (c)
  - (i) the title, grade, nature or category of the work for which the employee is employed; or
  - (ii) a brief specification or description of the work;
- (d) the date of commencement of the contract or employment relationship;
- (e) in the case of a temporary contract or employment relationship, the expected duration thereof;
- (f) the amount of paid leave to which the employee is entitled or, where this cannot be indicated when the information is given, the procedures for allocating and determining such leave;
- (g) the length of the periods of notice to be observed by the employer and the employee should their contract or employment relationship be terminated or, where this cannot be indicated when the information is given, the method for determining such periods of notice;
- (h) the initial basic amount, the other component elements and the frequency of payment of the remuneration to which the employee is entitled;
- (i) the length of the employee's normal working day or week;
- (j) where appropriate—
  - (i) the collective agreements governing the employee's conditions of work; or
  - (ii) in the case of collective agreements concluded outside the business by special joint bodies or institutions, the name of the competent body or joint institution within which the agreements were concluded.

3. The information referred to in paragraph 2(f), (g), (h) and (i) may, where appropriate, be given in the form of a reference to the laws, regulations and administrative or statutory provisions or collective agreements governing those particular points.

[3.140]
Article 3
Means of information
1. The information referred to in Article 2(2) may be given to the employee, not later than two months after the commencement of employment, in the form of—
- (a) a written contract of employment; and/or
- (b) a letter of engagement; and/or
- (c) one or more other written documents, where one of these documents contains at least all the information referred to in Article 2(2)(a), (b), (c), (d), (h) and (i).

2. Where none of the documents referred to in paragraph 1 is handed over to the employee within the prescribed period, the employer shall be obliged to give the employee, not later than two months after the commencement of employment, a written declaration signed by the employer and containing at least the information referred to in Article 2(2).

Where the document(s) referred to in paragraph 1 contain only part of the information required, the written declaration provided for in the first subparagraph of this paragraph shall cover the remaining information.

3. Where the contract or employment relationship comes to an end before expiry of a period of two months as from the date of the start of work, the information provided for in Article 2 and in this Article must be made available to the employee by the end of this period at the latest.

[3.141]
Article 4
Expatriate employees

1. Where an employee is required to work in a country or countries other than the Member State whose law and/or practice governs the contract or employment relationship, the document(s) referred to in Article 3 must be in his/her possession before his/her departure and must include at least the following additional information—

(a) the duration of the employment abroad;
(b) the currency to be used for the payment of remuneration;
(c) where appropriate, the benefits in cash or kind attendant on the employment abroad;
(d) where appropriate, the conditions governing the employee's repatriation.

2. The information referred to in paragraph 1(b) and (c) may, where appropriate, be given in the form of a reference to the laws, regulations and administrative or statutory provisions or collective agreements governing those particular points.
3. Paragraphs 1 and 2 shall not apply if the duration of the employment outside the country whose law and/or practice governs the contract or employment relationship is one month or less.

[3.142]
Article 5
Modification of aspects of the contract or employment relationship

1. Any change in the details referred to in Articles 2(2) and 4(1) must be the subject of a written document to be given by the employer to the employee at the earliest opportunity and not later than one month after the date of entry into effect of the change in question.
2. The written document referred to in paragraph 1 shall not be compulsory in the event of a change in the laws, regulations and administrative or statutory provisions or collective agreements cited in the documents referred to in Article 3, supplemented, where appropriate, pursuant to Article 4(1).

[3.143]
Article 6
Form and proof of the existence of a contract or employment relationship and procedural rules

This Directive shall be without prejudice to national law and practice concerning—

— the form of the contract or employment relationship,
— proof as regards the existence and content of a contract or employment relationship,
— the relevant procedural rules.

[3.144]
Article 7
More favourable provisions

This Directive shall not affect Member States' prerogative to apply or to introduce laws, regulations or administrative provisions which are more favourable to employees or to encourage or permit the application of agreements which are more favourable to employees.

[3.145]
Article 8
Defence of rights

1. Member States shall introduce into their national legal systems such measures as are necessary to enable all employees who consider themselves wronged by failure to comply with the obligations arising from this Directive to pursue their claims by judicial process after possible recourse to other competent authorities.
2. Member States may provide that access to the means of redress referred to in paragraph 1 are subject to the notification of the employer by the employee and the failure by the employer to reply within 15 days of notification.

However, the formality of prior notification may in no case be required in the cases referred to in Article 4, neither for workers with a temporary contract or employment relationship, nor for employees not covered by a collective agreement or by collective agreements relating to the employment relationship.

[3.146]
Article 9
Final provisions

1. Member States shall adopt the laws, regulations and administrative provisions necessary to comply with this Directive no later than 30 June 1993 or shall ensure by that date that the employers' and workers' representatives introduce the required provisions by way of agreement, the Member States being obliged to take the necessary steps enabling them at all times to guarantee the results imposed by this Directive.

They shall forthwith inform the Commission thereof.

2. Member States shall take the necessary measures to ensure that, in the case of employment relationships in existence upon entry into force of the provisions that they adopt, the employer gives the employee, on request, within two months of receiving that request; any of the documents referred to in Article 3, supplemented, where appropriate, pursuant to Article 4(1).

3. When Member States adopt the measures referred to in paragraph 1, such measures shall contain a reference to this Directive or shall be accompanied by such reference on the occasion of their official publication. The methods of making such a reference shall be laid down by the Member States.

4. Member States shall forthwith inform the Commission of the measures they take to implement this Directive.

[3.147]
Article 10

This Directive is addressed to the Member States.

COMMISSION RECOMMENDATION

(92/131/EEC)

of 27 November 1991

on the protection of the dignity of women and men at work

NOTES

Date of publication in OJ: OJ L49, 24.2.1992, p 1.

[3.148]

THE COMMISSION OF THE EUROPEAN COMMUNITIES

Having regard to the Treaty establishing the European Economic Community and the second indent of Article 155 thereof;

Whereas unwanted conduct of a sexual nature, or other conduct based on sex affecting the dignity of women and men at work, including the conduct of superiors and colleagues, is unacceptable and may, in certain circumstances, be contrary to the principle of equal treatment within the meaning of Articles 3, 4 and 5 of Council Directive 76/207/EEC of 9 February 1976 on the implementation of the principle of equal treatment for men and women as regards access to employment, vocational training and promotion and working conditions,[1] a view supported by case law in some Member States;

Whereas, in accordance with the Council Recommendation of 13 December 1984 on the promotion of positive action for women,[2] many Member States have carried out a variety of positive action measures and actions having a bearing, inter alia, on respect for the dignity of women at the workplace;

Whereas the European Parliament, in its resolution of 11 June 1986 on violence against women,[3] has called upon national governments, equal opportunities committees and trade unions to carry out concerted information campaigns to create a proper awareness of the individual rights of all members of the labour force;

Whereas the Advisory Committee on Equal Opportunities for Women and Men, in its opinion of 20 June 1988, has unanimously recommended that there should be a Recommendation and code of conduct on sexual harassment in the workplace covering harassment of both sexes;

Whereas the Commission in its action programme relating to the implementation of the Community Charter of Basic Social Rights for workers undertook to examine the protection of workers and their dignity at work, having regard to the reports and recommendations prepared on various aspect of implementation of Community law;[4]

Whereas the Council, in its resolution of 29 May 1990 on the protection of the dignity of women and men at work, affirms that conduct based on sex affecting the dignity of women and men at work,[5] including conduct of superiors and colleagues, constitutes an intolerable violation of the dignity of workers or trainees, and calls on the Member States and the institutions and organs of the European Communities to develop positive measures designed to create a climate at work in which women and men respect one another's human integrity;

Whereas the Commission, in its third action programme on equal opportunities for women and men, 1991–1995 and pursuant to paragraph 3.2 of the said Council Resolution of 29 May 1990, resolved to draw up a code of conduct on the protection of the dignity of women and men at work,[6] based on experience and best practice in the Member States, to provide guidance on initiating and pursuing positive measures designed to create a climate at work in which women and men respect one another's human integrity;

Whereas the European Parliament, on 22 October 1991, adopted a Resolution on the protection of the dignity of women and men at work;[7]

Whereas the Economic and Social Committee, on 30 October 1991, adopted an Opinion on the protection of the dignity of women and men at work,[8]

NOTES

1 OJ L39, 14.2.76, p 40.

2 OJ L331, 19.12.84, p 34.

3 OJ C176, 14.7.86, p 79.

4 COM(89) final, 29.11.1989. For example, "The dignity of women at work: A report on the problem of sexual harassment in the Member States of the European Communities", October 1987, by Michael Rubenstein (ISBN 92-825-8764-9).

5 OJ C157, 27.6.90, p 3.

6 COM(90) 449 final, 6.11.90.

7 OJ C305, 25.11.91.

8 OJ C14, 20.1.92.

RECOMMENDS AS FOLLOWS—

[3.149]
Article 1

It is recommended that the Member State take action to promote awareness that conduct of a sexual nature, or other conduct based on sex affecting the dignity of women and men at work, including conduct of superiors and colleagues, is unacceptable if—

(a) such conduct is unwanted, unreasonable and offensive to the recipient;

(b) a person's rejection of or submission to such conduct on the part of employers or workers (including superiors or colleagues) is used explicitly or implicitly as a basis for a decision which affects that person's access to vocational training, access to employment, continued employment, promotion, salary or other employment decisions; and/or

(c) such conduct creates an intimidating, hostile or humiliating work environment for the recipient;

and that such conduct may, in certain circumstances, be contrary to the principle of equal treatment within the meaning of Articles 3, 4 and 5 of Directive 76/207/EEC.

[3.150]
Article 2

It is recommended that Member States should take action, in the public sector, to implement the Commission's Code of Practice on the protection of the dignity of women and men at work, annexed hereto. The action of the Member States, in thus initiating and pursuing positive measures designed to create a climate at work in which women and men respect one another's human integrity, should serve as an example to the private sector.

[3.151]
Article 3

It is recommended that Member States encourage employers and employee representatives to develop measures to implement the Commission's Code of Practice on the protection of the dignity of women and men at work.

[3.152]
Article 4

The Member States shall inform the Commission within three years of the date of this Recommendation of the measures taken to give effect to it, in order to allow the Commission to draw up a report on all such measures. The Commission shall, within this period, ensure the widest possible circulation of the Code of Practice. The report should examine the degree of awareness of the Code, its perceived effectiveness, its degree of application and the extent of its use in collective bargaining between the social partners.

[3.153]
Article 5

This Recommendation is addressed to the Member States.

ANNEX
COMMISSION CODE OF PRACTICE ON PROTECTING THE DIGNITY OF WOMEN AND MEN AT WORK

A CODE OF PRACTICE ON MEASURES TO COMBAT SEXUAL HARASSMENT

1. Introduction

[3.154]

This code of practice is issued in accordance with the resolution of the Council of Ministers on the protection of the dignity of women and men at work,[1] and to accompany the Commission's Recommendations on this issue.

Its purpose is to give practical guidance to employers, trade unions, and employees on the protection of the dignity of women and men at work. The Code is intended to be applicable in both the public and the private sector and employers are encouraged to follow the recommendations contained in the Code in a way which is appropriate to the size and structure of their organisation. It may be particularly relevant for small and medium-sized enterprises to adapt some of the practical steps to their specific needs.

The aim is to ensure that sexual harassment does not occur and, if it does occur, to ensure that adequate procedures are readily available to deal with the problem and prevent its recurrence. The Code thus seeks to encourage the development and implementation of policies and practices which establish working environments free of sexual harassment and in which women and men respect one another's human integrity.

The expert report carried out on behalf of the Commission found that sexual harassment is a serious problem for many working women in the European Community[2] and research in Member States has proven beyond doubt that sexual harassment at work is not an isolated phenomenon. On the contrary, it is clear that for millions of women in the European Community, sexual harassment is an unpleasant and unavoidable part of their working lives. Men too may suffer sexual harassment and should, of course, have the same rights as women to the protection of their dignity.

Some specific groups are particularly vulnerable to sexual harassment. Research in several Member States, which documents the link between the risk of sexual harassment and the recipient's perceived vulnerability, suggests that divorced and separated women, young women and new entrants to the labour market and those with irregular or precarious employment contracts, women in non-traditional jobs, women with disabilities, lesbians and women from racial minorities are disproportionately at risk. Gay men and young men are also vulnerable to harassment. It is undeniable that harassment on grounds of sexual orientation undermines the dignity at work of those affected and it is impossible to regard such harassment as appropriate workplace behaviour.

Sexual harassment pollutes the working environment and can have a devastating effect upon the health, confidence, morale and performance of those affected by it. The anxiety and stress produced by sexual harassment commonly leads to those subjected to it taking time off work due to sickness, being less efficient at work, or leaving their job to seek work elsewhere. Employees often suffer the adverse consequences of the harassment itself and short- and long-term damage to their employment prospects if they are forced to change jobs. Sexual harassment may also have a damaging impact on employees not themselves the object of unwanted behaviour but who are witness to it or have a knowledge of the unwanted behaviour.

There are also adverse consequences arising from sexual harassment for employers. It has a direct impact on the profitability of the enterprise where staff take sick leave or resign their posts because of sexual harassment, and on the economic efficiency of the enterprise where employees' productivity is reduced by having to work in a climate in which individuals' integrity is not respected.

In general terms, sexual harassment is an obstacle to the proper integration of women into the labour market and the Commission is committed to encouraging the development of comprehensive measures to improve such integration.[3]

NOTES

1 OJ C157, 27.6.90, p 3.

2 "The dignity of women at work: A report on the problem of sexual harassment in the Member States of the European Communities", October 1987, by Michael Rubenstein (ISBN 92-825-8764-9).

3 Third action programme on equal opportunities for women and men, 1991 to 1995, COM(90) 449, 6.11.1990.

2. Definition

[3.155]

Sexual harassment means "unwanted conduct of a sexual nature, or other conduct based on sex affecting the dignity of women and men at work".[1] This can include unwelcome physical, verbal or non-verbal conduct.

Thus, a range of behaviour may be considered to constitute sexual harassment. It is unacceptable if such conduct is unwanted, unreasonable and offensive to the recipient; a person's rejection of or submission to such conduct on the part of employers or workers (including superiors or colleagues) is used explicitly or implicitly as a basis for a decision which affects that person's access to vocational training or to employment, continued employment, promotion, salary or any other employment decisions; and/or such conduct creates an intimidating, hostile or humiliating working environment for the recipient.

The essential characteristic of sexual harassment is that it is unwanted by the recipient, that it is for each individual to determine what behaviour is acceptable to them and what they regard as offensive. Sexual attention becomes sexual harassment if it is persisted in once it has been made clear that it is regarded by the recipient as offensive, although one incident of harassment may constitute sexual harassment if sufficiently serious. It is the unwanted nature of the conduct which distinguishes sexual harassment from friendly behaviour, which is welcome and mutual.

NOTES

1 Council resolution on the protection of the dignity of men and women at work (OJ C157, 27.6.90, point 1.)

3. The law and employers' responsibilities

[3.156]
Conduct of a sexual nature or other conduct based on sex affecting the dignity of women and men at work may be contrary to the principle of equal treatment within the meaning of Articles 3, 4 and 5 of Council Directive 76/207/EEC of 9 February 1976 on the implementation of the principle of equal treatment for men and women as regards access to employment, vocational training and promotion and working conditions.[1] This principle means that there shall be no discrimination whatsoever on grounds of sex either directly or indirectly by reference in particular to marital or family status.

In certain circumstances, and depending upon national law, sexual harassment may also be a criminal offence or may contravene other obligations imposed by the law, such as health and safety duties, or a duty, contractual or otherwise, to be a good employer. Since sexual harassment is a form of employee misconduct, employers have a responsibility to deal with it as they do with any other form of employee misconduct as well as to refrain from harassing employees themselves. Since sexual harassment is a risk to health and safety, employers have a responsibility to take steps to minimise the risk as they do with other hazards. Since sexual harassment often entails an abuse of power, employers may have a responsibility for the misuse of the authority they delegate.

This Code, however, focuses on sexual harassment as a problem of sex discrimination. Sexual harassment is sex discrimination because the gender of the recipient is the determining factor in who is harassed. Conduct of a sexual nature or other conduct based on sex affecting the dignity of women and men at work in some Member States already has been found to contravene national equal treatment laws and employers have a responsibility to seek to ensure that the work environment is free from such conduct.[2]

As sexual harassment is often a function of women's status in the employment hierarchy, policies to deal with sexual harassment are likely to be most effective where they are linked to a broader policy to promote equal opportunities and to improve the position of women. Advice on steps which can be taken generally to implement an equal opportunities policy is set out in the Commission's guide to positive action.[3]

Similarly, a procedure to deal with complaints of sexual harassment should be regarded as only one component of a strategy to deal with the problem. The prime objective should be to change behaviour and attitudes, to seek to ensure the prevention of sexual harassment.

NOTES

1 OJ L39, 14.2.76, p 40.

2 Third action programme on equal opportunities for women and men, 1991 to 1995, COM(90) 449, 6.11.1990.

3 Positive action: Equal opportunities for women in employment—a guide, Office for Official Publications of the European Communities, 1988.

4. Collective bargaining

[3.157]
The majority of the recommendations contained in this Code are for action by employers, since employers have clear responsibilities to ensure the protection of the dignity of women and men at work.

Trade unions also have responsibilities to their members and they can and should play an important role in the prevention of sexual harassment in the workplace. It is recommended that the question of including appropriate clauses in agreements is examined in the context of the collective bargaining process, with the aim of achieving a work environment free from unwanted conduct of a sexual nature or other conduct based on sex affecting the dignity of women and men at work and free from victimisation of a complainant or of a person wishing to give, or giving, evidence in the event of a complaint.

5. Recommendations to employers

[3.158]
The policies and procedures recommended below should be adopted, where appropriate, after consultation or negotiation with trade unions or employee representatives. Experience suggests that strategies to create and maintain a working environment in which the dignity of employees is respected are most likely to be effective where they are jointly agreed.

It should be emphasised that a distinguishing characteristic of sexual harassment is that employees subjected to it often will be reluctant to complain. An absence of complaints about sexual harassment in a particular organisation, therefore, does not necessarily mean an absence of sexual harassment. It may mean that the recipients of sexual harassment think that there is no point in complaining because nothing will be done about it, or because it will be trivialised or the complainant subjected to ridicule, or because they fear reprisals. Implementing the preventative and procedural recommendations outlined below should facilitate the creation of a climate at work in which such concerns have no place.

A Prevention

[3.159]
(i) Policy statements

As a first step in showing senior management's concern and their commitment to dealing with the problem of sexual harassment, employers should issue a policy statement which expressly states that all employees have a right to be treated with dignity, that sexual harassment at work will not be permitted or condoned and that employees have a right to complain about it should it occur.

It is recommended that the policy statement makes clear what is considered inappropriate behaviour at work, and explain that such behaviour, in certain circumstances, may be unlawful. It is advisable for the statement to set out a positive duty on managers and supervisors to implement the policy and to take corrective action to ensure compliance with it. It should also place a positive duty on all employees to comply with the policy and to ensure that their colleagues are treated with respect and dignity.

In addition, it is recommended that the statement explains the procedure which should be followed by employees subjected to sexual harassment at work in order to obtain assistance and to whom they should complain; that it contain an undertaking that allegations of sexual harassment will be dealt with seriously, expeditiously and confidentially; and that employees will be protected against victimisation or retaliation for bringing a complaint of sexual harassment.

It should also specify that appropriate disciplinary measures will be taken against employees found guilty of sexual harassment.

(ii) Communicating the policy

Once the policy has been developed, it is important to ensure that it is communicated effectively to all employees, so that they are aware that they have a right to complain and to whom they should complain; that their complaint will be dealt with promptly and fairly; and so that employees are made aware of the likely consequences of engaging in sexual harassment. Such communication will highlight management's commitment to eliminating sexual harassment, thus enhancing a climate in which it will not occur.

(iii) Responsibility

All employees have a responsibility to help ensure a working environment in which the dignity of employees is respected and managers (including supervisors) have a particular duty to ensure that sexual harassment does not occur in work areas for which they are responsible. It is recommended that managers should explain the organisation's policy to their staff and take steps to positively promote the policy. Managers should also be responsive and supportive to any member of staff who complains about sexual harassment; provide full and clear advice on the procedure to be adopted; maintain confidentiality in any cases of sexual harassment; and ensure that there is no further problem of sexual harassment or any victimisation after a complaint has been resolved.

(iv) Training

An important means of ensuring that sexual harassment does not occur and that, if it does occur, the problem is resolved efficiently is through the provision of training for managers and supervisors. Such training should aim to identify the factors which contribute to a working environment free of sexual harassment and to familiarise participants with their responsibilities under the employer's policy and any problems they are likely to encounter.

In addition, those playing an official role in any formal complaints procedure in respect of sexual harassment should receive specialist training, such as that outlined above.

It is also good practice to include information as to the organisation's policy on sexual harassment and procedures for dealing with it as part of appropriate induction and training programmes.

B Procedures

[3.160]
The development of clear and precise procedures to deal with sexual harassment once it has occurred is of great importance. The procedures should ensure the resolution of problems in an efficient and effective manner. Practical guidance for employees on how to deal with sexual harassment when it occurs and with its aftermath will make it more likely that it will be dealt with at an early stage. Such guidance should of course draw attention to an employee's legal rights and to any time limits within which they must be exercised.

(i) Resolving problems informally

Most recipients of harassment simply want the harassment to stop. Both informal and formal methods of resolving problems should be available.

Employees should be advised that, if possible, they should attempt to resolve the problem informally in the first instance. In some cases, it may be possible and sufficient for the employee to explain clearly to the person engaging in the unwanted conduct that the behaviour in question is not welcome, that it offends them or makes them uncomfortable, and that it interferes with their work.

In circumstances where it is too difficult or embarrassing for an individual to do this on their own behalf, an alternative approach would be to seek support from, or for an initial approach to be made by, a sympathetic friend or confidential counsellor.

If the conduct continues or if it is not appropriate to resolve the problem informally, it should be raised through the formal complaints procedure.

(ii) Advice and assistance

It is recommended that employers should designate someone to provide advice and assistance to employees subjected to sexual harassment, where possible, with responsibilities to assist in the resolution of any problems, whether through informal or formal means. It may be helpful if the officer is designated with the agreement of the trade unions or employees, as this is likely to enhance their acceptability. Such officers could be selected from personnel departments or equal opportunities departments for example. In some organisations they are designated as 'confidential counsellors' or 'sympathetic friends'. Often such a role may be played by someone from the employee's trade union or by women's support groups.

Whatever the location of this responsibility in the organisation, it is recommended that the designated officer receives appropriate training in the best means of resolving problems and in the detail of the organisation's policy and procedures, so that they can perform their role effectively. It is also important that they are given adequate resources to carry out their function, and protection against victimisation for assisting any recipient of sexual harassment.

(iii) Complaints procedure

It is recommended that, where the complainant regards attempts at informal resolution as inappropriate, where informal attempts at resolution have been refused, or where the outcome has been unsatisfactory, a formal procedure for resolving the complaint should be provided. The procedure should give employees confidence that the organisation will take allegations of sexual harassment seriously.

By its nature sexual harassment may make the normal channels of complaint difficult to use because of embarrassment, fears of not being taken seriously, fears of damage to reputation, fears of reprisal or the prospect of damaging the working environment. Therefore, a formal procedure should specify to whom the employee should bring a complaint, and it should also provide an alternative if in the particular circumstances the normal grievance procedure may not be suitable, for example because the alleged harasser is the employee's line manager. It is also advisable to make provision for employees to bring a complaint in the first instance to someone of their own sex, should they so choose.

It is good practice for employers to monitor and review complaints of sexual harassment and how they have been resolved, in order to ensure that their procedures are working effectively.

(iv) Investigations

It is important to ensure that internal investigations of any complaints are handled with sensitivity and with due respect for the rights of both the complainant and the alleged harasser. The investigation should be seen to be independent and objective. Those carrying out the investigation should not be connected with the allegation in any way, and every effort should be made to resolve complaints speedily—grievances should be handled promptly and the procedure should set a time limit within which complaints will be processed, with due regard for any time limits set by national legislation for initiating a complaint through the legal system.

It is recommended as good practice that both the complainant and the alleged harasser have the right to be accompanied and/or represented, perhaps by a representative of their trade union or a friend or colleague; that the alleged harasser be given full details of the nature of the complaint and the opportunity to respond; and that strict confidentiality be maintained throughout any investigation into an allegation. Where it is necessary to interview witnesses, the importance of confidentiality should be emphasised.

It must be recognised that recounting the experience of sexual harassment is difficult and can damage the employee's dignity. Therefore, a complainant should not be required to repeatedly recount the events complained of where this is unnecessary.

The investigation should focus on the facts of the complaint and it is advisable for the employer to keep a complete record of all meetings and investigations.

(v) Disciplinary offence

It is recommended that violations of the organisation's policy protecting the dignity of employees at work should be treated as a disciplinary offence; and the disciplinary rules should make clear what is regarded as inappropriate behaviour at work. It is also good practice to ensure that the range of penalties to which offenders will be liable for violating the rule is clearly stated and also to make it clear that it will be considered a disciplinary offence to victimise or retaliate against an employee for bringing a complaint of sexual harassment in good faith.

Where a complaint is upheld and it is determined that it is necessary to relocate or transfer one party, consideration should be given, wherever practicable, to allowing the complainant to choose whether he or she wishes to remain in their post or be transferred to another location. No element of penalty should be seen to attach to a complainant whose complaint is upheld and in addition, where a complaint is upheld, the employer should monitor the situation to ensure that the harassment has stopped.

Even where a complaint is not upheld, for example because the evidence is regarded as inconclusive, consideration should be given to transferring or rescheduling the work of one of the employees concerned rather than requiring them to continue to work together against the wishes of either party.

6. Recommendations to trade unions

[3.161]

Sexual harassment is a trade union issue as well as an issue for employers. It is recommended as good practice that trade unions should formulate and issue clear policy statements on sexual harassment and take steps to raise awareness of the problem of sexual harassment in the workplace, in order to help create a climate in which it is neither condoned nor ignored. For example, trade unions could aim to give all officers and representatives training on equality issues, including dealing with sexual harassment and include such information in union-sponsored or approved training courses, as well as information on the union's policy. Trade unions should consider declaring that sexual harassment is inappropriate behaviour and educating members and officials about its consequences is recommended as good practice.

Trade unions should also raise the issue of sexual harassment with employers and encourage the adoption of adequate policies and procedures to protect the dignity of women and men at work in the organisation. It is advisable for trade unions to inform members of their right not to be sexually harassed at work and provide members with clear guidance as to what to do if they are sexually harassed, including guidance on any relevant legal rights.

Where complaints arise, it is important for trade unions to treat them seriously and sympathetically and ensure that the complainant has the opportunity of representation if a complaint is to be pursued. It is important to create an environment in which members feel able to raise such complaints knowing they will receive a sympathetic and supportive response from local union representatives. Trade unions could consider designating specially-trained officials to advise and counsel members with complaints of sexual harassment and act on their behalf if required. This will provide a focal point for support. It is also a good idea to ensure that there are sufficient female representatives to support women subjected to sexual harassment.

It is recommended too, where the trade union is representing both the complainant and the alleged harasser for the purpose of the complaints procedure, that it be made clear that the union is not condoning offensive behaviour by providing representation. In any event, the same official should not represent both parties.

It is good practice to advise members that keeping a record of incidents by the harassed worker will assist in bringing any formal or informal action to a more effective conclusion; and that the union wishes to be informed of any incident of sexual harassment and that such information will be kept confidential. It is also good practice for the union to monitor and review the union's record in responding to complaints and in representing alleged harassers and the harassed, in order to ensure its responses are effective.

7. Employees' responsibilities

[3.162]

Employees have a clear role to play in helping to create a climate at work in which sexual harassment is unacceptable. They can contribute to preventing sexual harassment through an awareness and sensitivity towards the issue and by ensuring that standards of conduct for themselves and for colleagues do not cause offence.

Employees can do much to discourage sexual harassment by making it clear that they find such behaviour unacceptable and by supporting colleagues who suffer such treatment and are considering making a complaint.

Employees who are themselves recipients of harassment should, where practicable, tell the harasser that the behaviour is unwanted and unacceptable. Once the offender understands clearly that the behaviour is unwelcome, this may be enough to put an end to it. If the behaviour is persisted in, employees should inform management and/or their employee representative through the appropriate channels and request assistance in stopping the harassment, whether through informal or formal means.

COUNCIL DIRECTIVE

(92/85/EEC)

of 19 October 1992

on the introduction of measures to encourage improvements in the safety and health of pregnant workers and workers who have recently given birth or are breastfeeding (tenth individual Directive within the meaning of Article 16(1) of Directive 89/391)

NOTES

Date of publication in OJ: OJ L348, 28.11.1992, p 1.

For the domestic implementation of this Directive see now the Employment Rights Act 1996, ss 66–75 at **[1.850]** et seq; the Management of Health and Safety at Work Regulations 1999, SI 1999/3242, regs 16–18 at **[2.469]**–**[2.473]**; and the Social Security Contributions and Benefits Act 1992, Pt XII, at **[1.201]**, and Regulations made thereunder.

See also *Harvey* J(2), (3), (4), (5), (6).

[3.163]

THE COUNCIL OF THE EUROPEAN COMMUNITIES,

Having regard to the Treaty establishing the European Economic Community, and in particular Article 118a thereof,

Having regard to the proposal from the Commission, drawn up after consultation with the Advisory Committee on Safety, Hygiene and Health Protection at work,[1]

In cooperation with the European Parliament,[2]

Having regard to the opinion of the Economic and Social Committee,[3]

Whereas Article 118a of the Treaty provides that the Council shall adopt, by means of directives, minimum requirements for encouraging improvements, especially in the working environment, to protect the safety and health of workers;

Whereas this Directive does not justify any reduction in levels of protection already achieved in individual Member States, the Member States being committed, under the Treaty, to encouraging improvements in conditions in this area and to harmonizing conditions while maintaining the improvements made;

Whereas, under the terms of Article 118a of the Treaty, the said directives are to avoid imposing administrative, financial and legal constraints in a way which would hold back the creation and development of small and medium-sized undertakings;

Whereas, pursuant to Decision 74/325/EEC,[4] as last amended by the 1985 Act of Accession, the Advisory Committee on Safety, Hygiene and Health Protection at Work is consulted by the Commission on the drafting of proposals in this field;

Whereas the Community Charter of the fundamental social rights of workers, adopted at the Strasbourg European Council on 9 December 1989 by the Heads of State or Government of 11 Member States, lays down, in paragraph 19 in particular, that—

'Every worker must enjoy satisfactory health and safety conditions in his working environment. Appropriate measures must be taken in order to achieve further harmonization of conditions in this area while maintaining the improvements made';

Whereas the Commission, in its action programme for the implementation of the Community Charter of the fundamental social rights of workers, has included among its aims the adoption by the Council of a Directive on the protection of pregnant women at work;

Whereas Article 15 of Council Directive 89/391/EEC of 12 June 1989 on the introduction of measures to encourage improvements in the safety and health of workers at work[5] provides that particularly sensitive risk groups must be protected against the dangers which specifically affect them;

Whereas pregnant workers, workers who have been recently given birth or who are breastfeeding must be considered a specific risk group in many respects, and measures must be taken with regard to their safety and health;

Whereas the protection of the safety and health of pregnant workers, workers who have recently given birth or workers who are breastfeeding should not treat women on the labour market unfavourably nor work to the detriment of directives concerning equal treatment for men and women;

Whereas some types of activities may pose a specific risk, for pregnant workers, workers who have recently given birth or workers who are breastfeeding, of exposure to dangerous agents, processes or working conditions; whereas such risks must therefore be assessed and the result of such assessment communicated to female workers and/or their representatives;

Whereas, further, should the result of this assessment reveal the existence of a risk to the safety or health of the female worker, provision must be made for such worker to be protected;

Whereas pregnant workers and workers who are breastfeeding must not engage in activities which have been assessed as revealing a risk of exposure, jeopardising safety and health, to certain particularly dangerous agents or working conditions;

Whereas provision should be made for pregnant workers, workers who have recently given birth or workers who are breastfeeding not to be required to work at night where such provision is necessary from the point of view of their safety and health;

Whereas the vulnerability of pregnant workers, workers who have recently given birth or who are breastfeeding makes it necessary for them to be granted the right to maternity leave of at least 14 continuous weeks, allocated before and/or after confinement, and renders necessary the compulsory nature of maternity leave of at least two weeks, allocated before and/or after confinement;

Whereas the risk of dismissal for reasons associated with their condition may have harmful effects on the physical and mental state of pregnant workers, workers who have recently given birth or who are breastfeeding; whereas provision should be made for such dismissal to be prohibited;

Whereas measures for the organization of work concerning the protection of the health of pregnant workers, workers who have recently given birth or workers who are breastfeeding would serve no purpose unless accompanied by the maintenance of rights linked to the employment contract, including maintenance of payment and/or entitlement to an adequate allowance;

Whereas, moreover, provision concerning maternity leave would also serve no purpose unless accompanied by the maintenance of rights linked to the employment contract and/or entitlement to an adequate allowance;

Whereas the concept of an adequate allowance in the case of maternity leave must be regarded as a technical point of reference with a view to fixing the minimum level of protection and should in no circumstances be interpreted as suggesting an analogy between pregnancy and illness,

NOTES

1 OJ C281, 9.11.90, p 3; and OJ C25, 1.2.91, p 9.

2 OJ C19, 28.1.91, p 177; and OJ C150, 15.6.92, p 99.

3 OJ C41, 18.2.91, p 29.

4 OJ L185, 9.7.74, p 15.

5 OJ L183, 29.6.89, p 1.

HAS ADOPTED THIS DIRECTIVE—

SECTION I
PURPOSE AND DEFINITIONS

[3.164]
Article 1
Purpose

1. The purpose of this Directive, which is the tenth individual Directive within the meaning of Article 16(1) of Directive 89/391/EEC, is to implement measures to encourage improvements in the safety and health at work of pregnant workers and workers who have recently given birth or who are breastfeeding.

2. The provisions of Directive 89/391/EEC, except for Article 2(2) thereof, shall apply in full to the whole area covered by paragraph 1, without prejudice to any more stringent and/or specific provisions contained in this Directive.

3. This Directive may not have the effect of reducing the level of protection afforded to pregnant workers, workers who have recently given birth or who are breastfeeding as compared with the situation which exists in each Member State on the date on which this Directive is adopted.

[3.165]
Article 2
Definitions

For the purposes of this Directive—

(a) *pregnant worker* shall mean a pregnant worker who informs her employer of her condition, in accordance with national legislation and/or national practice;

(b) *worker who has recently given birth* shall mean a worker who has recently given birth within the meaning of national legislation and/or national practice and who informs her employer of her condition, in accordance with that legislation and/or practice;
(c) *worker who is breastfeeding* shall mean a worker who is breastfeeding within the meaning of national legislation and/or national practice and who informs her employer of her condition, in accordance with that legislation and/or practice.

SECTION II
GENERAL PROVISIONS

[3.166]
Article 3
Guidelines

1. In consultation with the Member States and assisted by the Advisory Committee on Safety, Hygiene and Health Protection at Work, the Commission shall draw up guidelines on the assessment of the chemical, physical and biological agents and industrial process considered hazardous for the safety or health of workers within the meaning of Article 2.

The guidelines referred to in the first subparagraph shall also cover movements and postures, mental and physical fatigue and other types of physical and mental stress connected with the work done by workers within the meaning of Article 2.

2. The purpose of the guidelines referred to in paragraph 1 is to serve as a basis for the assessment referred to in Article 4(1).

To this end, Member States shall bring these guidelines to the attention of all employers and all female workers and/or their representatives in the respective Member State.

[3.167]
Article 4
Assessment and information

1. For all activities liable to involve a specific risk of exposure to the agents, processes or working conditions of which a non-exhaustive list is given in Annex 1, the employer shall assess the nature, degree and duration of exposure, in the undertaking and/or establishment concerned, or workers within the meaning of Article 2, either directly or by way of the protective and preventative services referred to in Article 7 of Directive 89/391/EEC, in order to—

— assess any risks to the safety or health and any possible effect on the pregnancies or breastfeeding of workers within the meaning of Article 2,
— decide what measures should be taken.

2. Without prejudice to Article 10 of Directive 89/391/EEC, workers within the meaning of Article 2 and workers likely to be in one of the situations referred to in Article 2 in the undertaking and/or establishment concerned and/or their representatives shall be informed of the results of the assessment referred to in paragraph 1 and of all measures to be taken concerning health and safety at work.

[3.168]
Article 5
Action further to the results of the assessment

1. Without prejudice to Article 6 of Directive 89/391/EEC, if the results of the assessment referred to in Article 4(1) reveal a risk to the safety or health or an effect on the pregnancy or breastfeeding of a worker within the meaning of Article 2, the employer shall take the necessary measures to ensure that, by temporarily adjusting the working conditions and/or the working hours of the worker concerned, the exposure of that worker to such risks is avoided.

2. If the adjustment of her working conditions and/or working hours is not technically and/or objectively feasible, or cannot reasonably be required on duly substantiated grounds, the employer shall take the necessary measures to move the worker concerned to another job.

3. If moving her to another job is not technically and/or objectively feasible or cannot reasonably be required on duly substantiated grounds, the worker concerned shall be granted leave in accordance with national legislation and/or national practice for the whole of the period necessary to protect her safety or health.

4. The provisions of this Article shall apply *mutatis mutandis* to the case where a worker pursuing an activity which is forbidden pursuant to Article 6 becomes pregnant or starts breastfeeding and informs her employer thereof.

[3.169]
Article 6
Cases in which exposure is prohibited

In addition to the general provisions concerning the protection of workers, in particular those relating to the limit values for occupational exposure—

1. pregnant workers within the meaning of Article 2(a) may under no circumstances be obliged to perform duties for which the assessment has revealed a risk of exposure, which would jeopardize safety or health, to the agents and working conditions listed in Annex II, Section A;
2. workers who are breastfeeding, within the meaning of Article 2(c), may under no circumstances be obliged to perform duties for which the assessment has revealed a risk of exposure, which would jeopardize safety or health, to the agents and working conditions listed in Annex II, Section B.

[3.170]
Article 7
Night work

1. Member States shall take the necessary measures to ensure that workers referred to in Article 2 are not obliged to perform night work during their pregnancy and for a period following childbirth which shall be determined by the national authority competent for safety and health, subject to submission, in accordance with the procedures laid down by the Member States, of a medical certificate stating that this is necessary for the safety or health of the worker concerned.
2. The measures referred to in paragraph 1 must entail the possibility, in accordance with national legislation and/or national practice, of—
   (a) transfer to daytime work; or
   (b) leave from work or extension of maternity leave where such a transfer is not technically and/or objectively feasible or cannot reasonably be required on duly substantiated grounds.

[3.171]
Article 8
Maternity leave

1. Member States shall take the necessary measures to ensure that workers within the meaning of Article 2 are entitled to a continuous period of maternity leave of at least 14 weeks allocated before and/or after confinement in accordance with national legislation and/or practice.
2. The maternity leave stipulated in paragraph 1 must include compulsory maternity leave of at least two weeks allocated before and/or after confinement in accordance with national legislation and/or practice.

[3.172]
Article 9
Time off for ante-natal examinations

Member States shall take the necessary measures to ensure that pregnant workers within the meaning of Article 2(a) are entitled to, in accordance with national legislation and/or practice, time off, without loss of pay, in order to attend ante-natal examinations, if such examinations have to take place during working hours.

[3.173]
Article 10
Prohibition of dismissal

In order to guarantee workers, within the meaning of Article 2, the exercise of their health and safety protection rights as recognized under this Article, it shall be provided that—

1. Member States shall take the necessary measures to prohibit the dismissal of workers, within the meaning of Article 2, during the period from the beginning of their pregnancy to the end of the maternity leave referred to in Article 8(1) save in exceptional cases not connected with their condition which are permitted under national legislation and/or practice and, where applicable, provided that the competent authority has given its consent;
2. if a worker, within the meaning of Article 2, is dismissed during the period referred to in point 1, the employer must cite duly substantiated grounds for her dismissal in writing;
3. Member States shall take the necessary measures to protect workers, within the meaning of Article 2, from consequences of dismissal which is unlawful by virtue of point 1.

[3.174]
Article 11
Employment rights

In order to guarantee workers within the meaning of Article 2 the exercise of their health and safety protection rights as recognized in this Article, it shall be provided that—

1. in the cases referred to in Articles 5, 6 and 7, the employment rights relating to the employment contract, including the maintenance of a payment to, and/or entitlement to an adequate allowance for, workers within the meaning of Article 2, must be ensured in accordance with national legislation and/or national practice;
2. in the case referred to in Article 8, the following must be ensured—
   (a) the rights connected with the employment contract of workers within the meaning of Article 2, other than those referred to in point (b) below;

(b) maintenance of a payment to, and/or entitlement to an adequate allowance for, workers within the meaning of Article 2;

3. the allowance referred to in point 2(b) shall be deemed adequate if it guarantees income at least equivalent to that which the worker concerned would receive in the event of a break in her activities on grounds connected with her state of health, subject to any ceiling laid down under national legislation;

4. Member States may make entitlement to pay or the allowance referred to in points 1 and 2(b) conditional upon the worker concerned fulfilling the conditions of eligibility for such benefits laid down under national legislation.

These conditions may under no circumstances provide for periods of previous employment in excess of 12 months immediately prior to the presumed date of confinement.

NOTES

The Council and Commission issued the following formal statement at the 1608th meeting of the Council on 19 October 1992 (OJ L348/92, p 8)—

THE COUNCIL AND THE COMMISSION stated that—

"In determining the level of the allowances referred to in Article 11(2)(b) and (3), reference shall be made, for purely technical reasons, to the allowance which a worker would receive in the event of a break in her activities on grounds connected with her state of health. Such a reference is not intended in any way to imply that pregnancy and childbirth be equated with sickness. The national social security legislation of all Member States provides for an allowance to be paid during an absence from work due to sickness. The link with such allowance in the chosen formulation is simply intended to serve as a concrete, fixed reference amount in all Member States for the determination of the minimum amount of maternity allowance payable. In so far as allowances are paid in individual Member States which exceed those provided for in the Directive, such allowances are, of course, retained. This is clear from Article 1(3) of the Directive.".

[3.175]
Article 12
Defence of rights

Member States shall introduce into their national legal systems such measures as are necessary to enable all workers who should themselves wronged by failure to comply with the obligations arising from this Directive to pursue their claims by judicial process (and/or, in accordance with national laws and/or practices) by recourse to other competent authorities.

NOTE

This Article is printed as in the *Official Journal*: presumably the word "consider" ought to have been inserted after the word "should".

[3.176]
Article 13
Amendments to the Annexes

1. Strictly technical adjustments to Annex I as a result of technical progress, changes in international regulations or specifications and new findings in the area covered by this Directive shall be adopted in accordance with the procedure laid down in Article 17 of Directive 89/391/EEC.

2. Annex II may be amended only in accordance with the procedure laid down in Article 118a of the Treaty.

NOTES

Article 118a: see now Art 154 at **[3.30]**.

[3.177]
Article 14
Final provisions

1. Member States shall bring into force the laws, regulations and administrative provisions necessary to comply with this Directive not later than two years after the adoption thereof or ensure, at the latest two years after the adoption of this Directive, that the two sides of industry introduce the requisite provisions by means of collective agreements, with Member States being required to make all the necessary provisions to enable them at all times to guarantee the results laid down by this Directive. They shall forthwith inform the Commission thereof.

2. When Member States adopt the measure referred to in paragraph 1, they shall contain a reference of this Directive or shall be accompanied by such reference on the occasion of their official publication. The methods of making such a reference shall be laid down by the Member States.

3. Member States shall communicate to the Commission the texts of the essential provisions of national law which they have already adopted or adopt in the field governed by this Directive.

4–6. . . .

NOTES

Paras 4–6: repealed by European Parliament and Council Directive 2007/30/EC, Art 3(11).

[3.178]

Article 15

The Directive is addressed to the Member States.

ANNEX I
NON-EXHAUSTIVE LIST OF AGENTS, PROCESSES AND WORKING CONDITIONS

(referred to in Article 4(1))

[3.179]

A. Agents

1. Physical agents where these are regarded as agents causing foetal lesions and/or likely to disrupt placental attachment, and in particular—

(a) shocks, vibration or movement;
(b) handling of loads entailing risks, particularly of a dorsolumbar nature;
(c) noise;
(d) ionising radiation;[1]
(e) non-ionising radiation;
(f) extremes of cold or heat;
(g) movements and postures, travelling—either inside or outside the establishment— mental and physical fatigue and other physical burdens connected with the activity of the worker within the meaning of Article 2 of the Directive.

2. Biological agents

Biological agents of risk groups 2, 3 and 3 [*] within the meaning of Article 2(d) numbers 2, 3 and 4 of Directive 90/679/EEC,[2] in so far as it is known that these agents or the therapeutic measures necessitated by such agents endanger the health of pregnant women and the unborn child and in so far as they do not yet appear in Annex II.

3. Chemical agents

The following chemical agents in so far as it is known that they endanger the health of pregnant women and the unborn child and in so far as they do not yet appear in Annex II—

(a) substances labelled R 40, R 45, R 46, and R 47 under Directive 67/548/EEC[3] in so far as they do not yet appear in Annex II;
(b) chemical agents in Annex I to Directive 90/394/EEC;[4]
(c) mercury and mercury derivatives;
(d) antimitotic drugs;
(e) carbon monoxide;
(f) chemical agents of known and dangerous percutaneous absorption.

B. Processes

Industrial processes listed in Annex I to Directive 90/394/EEC.

C. Working Conditions

Underground mining work.

NOTES

1 See Directive 80/836/Euratom (OJ L246, 17.9.80, p 1).

2 OJ L374, 31.12.90, p 1.

3 OJ L196, 16.8.67, p 1. Directive as last amended by Directive 90/517/EEC (OJ L287, 19.10.90, p 37).

4 OJ L196, 26.7.90, p 1.

* Text printed as in the Official Journal.

ANNEX II
NON-EXHAUSTIVE LIST OF AGENTS AND WORKING CONDITIONS

(referred to in Article 6)

[3.180]

A. Pregnant workers within the meaning of Article 2(A)

1. Agents

(a) Physical agents
Work in hyperbaric atmosphere, eg pressurized enclosures and underwater diving.

(b) Biological agents
The following biological agents—
— toxoplasma,
— rubella virus,
unless the pregnant workers are proved to be adequately protected against such agents by immunization.

(c) Chemical agents
Lead and lead derivatives in so far as these agents are capable of being absorbed by the human organism.

2. *Working conditions*
Underground mining work.

B. Workers who are breastfeeding within the meaning of Article 2(C)

1. *Agents*
   (a) Chemical agents
   Lead and lead derivatives in so far as these agents are capable of being absorbed by the human organism.

2. *Working conditions*
Underground mining work.

COUNCIL DIRECTIVE

(94/33/EC)

of 22 June 1994

on the protection of young people at work

NOTES

Date of publication in OJ: OJ L 216, 20.8.1994, p 12.

For the domestic implementation of those parts of this Directive within the scope of this work, see in particular the Working Time Regulations 1998, SI 1998/1833, at **[2.269]** et seq.

See *Harvey* AI(6), CI(1).

[3.181]

THE COUNCIL OF THE EUROPEAN UNION,

Having regard to the Treaty establishing the European Community, and in particular Article 118a thereof,

Having regard to the proposal from the Commission,[1]

Having regard to the opinion, of the Economic and Social Committee,[2]

Acting in accordance with the procedure referred to in Article 189c of the Treaty,[3]

Whereas Article 118a of the Treaty provides that the Council shall adopt, by means of directives, minimum requirements to encourage improvements, especially in the working environment, as regards the health and safety of workers;

Whereas, under that Article, such directives must avoid imposing administrative, financial and legal constraints in a way which would hold back the creation and development of small and medium-sized undertakings;

Whereas points 20 and 22 of the Community Charter of the Fundamental Social Rights of Workers, adopted by the European Council in Strasbourg on 9 December 1989, state that—

'20. Without prejudice to such rules as may be more favourable to young people, in particular those ensuring their preparation for work through vocational training, and subject to derogations limited to certain light work, the minimum employment age must not be lower than the minimum school-leaving age and, in any case, not lower than 15 years;

22. Appropriate measures must be taken to adjust labour regulations applicable to young workers so that their specific development and vocational training and access to employment needs are met.

The duration of work must, in particular, be limited—without it being possible to circumvent this limitation through recourse to overtime—and night work prohibited in the case of workers of under eighteen years of age, save in the case of certain jobs laid down in national legislation or regulations.';

Whereas account should be taken of the principles of the International Labour Organisation regarding the protection of young people at work, including those relating to the minimum age for access to employment or work;

Whereas, in its Resolution on child labour,[4] the European Parliament summarised the various aspects of work by young people and stressed its effects on their health, safety and physical and intellectual development, and pointed to the need to adopt a Directive harmonising national legislation in the field;

Whereas Article 15 of Council Directive 89/391/EEC of 12 June 1989 on the introduction of measures to encourage improvements in the safety and health of workers at work[5] provides that particularly sensitive risk groups must be protected against the dangers which specifically affect them;

Whereas children and adolescents must be considered specific risk groups, and measures must be taken with regard to their safety and health;

Whereas the vulnerability of children calls for Member States to prohibit their employment and ensure that the minimum working or employment age is not lower than the minimum age at which compulsory schooling as imposed by national law ends or 15 years in any event; whereas derogations from the prohibition on child labour may be admitted only in special cases and under the conditions stipulated in this Directive; whereas, under no circumstances, may such derogations be detrimental to regular school attendance or prevent children benefiting fully from their education;

Whereas, in view of the nature of the transition from childhood to adult life, work by adolescents should be strictly regulated and protected;

Whereas every employer should guarantee young people working conditions appropriate to their age;

Whereas employers should implement the measures necessary to protect the safety and health of young people on the basis on an assessment of work-related hazards to the young;

Whereas Member States should protect young people against any specific risks arising from their lack of experience, absence of awareness of existing or potential risks, or from their immaturity;

Whereas Member States should therefore prohibit the employment of young people for the work specified by this Directive;

Whereas the adoption of specific minimal requirements in respect of the organisation of working time is likely to improve working conditions for young people;

Whereas the maximum working time of young people should be strictly limited and night work by young people should be prohibited, with the exception of certain jobs specified by national legislation or rules;

Whereas Member States should take the appropriate measures to ensure that the working time of adolescents receiving school education does not adversely affect their ability to benefit from that education;

Whereas time spent on training by young persons working under a theoretical and/or practical combined work/training scheme or an in-plant work-experience should be counted as working time;

Whereas, in order to ensure the safety and health of young people, the latter should be granted minimum daily, weekly and annual periods of rest and adequate breaks;

Whereas, with respect to the weekly rest period, due account should be taken of the diversity of cultural, ethnic, religious and other factors prevailing in the Member States; whereas in particular, it is ultimately for each Member State to decide whether Sunday should be included in the weekly rest period, and if so to what extent;

Whereas appropriate work experience may contribute to the aim of preparing young people for adult working and social life, provided it is ensured that any harm to their safety, health and development is avoided;

Whereas, although derogations from the bans and limitations imposed by this Directive would appear indispensable for certain activities or particular situations, applications thereof must not prejudice the principles underlying the established protection system;

Whereas this Directive constitutes a tangible step towards developing the social dimension of the internal market;

Whereas the application in practice of the system of protection laid down by this Directive will require that Member States implement a system of effective and proportionate measures;

Whereas the implementation of some provisions of this Directive poses particular problems for one Member State with regard to its system of protection for young people at work; whereas that Member State should therefore be allowed to refrain from implementing the relevant provisions for a suitable period,

NOTES

1 OJ C84, 4.4.92, p 7.

2 OJ C313, 30.11.92, p 70.

3 Opinion of the European Parliament of 17 December 1992 (OJ C21, 25.1.93, p 167). Council Common Position of 23 November 1993 (not yet published in the Official Journal) and Decision of the European Parliament of 9 March 1994 (OJ C 91, 28.3.94, p 89).

4 OJ C190, 20.7.87, p 44.

5 OJ L183, 29.6.89, p 1.

HAS ADOPTED THIS DIRECTIVE—

SECTION I

[3.182]
Article 1
Purpose

1. Member States shall take the necessary measures to prohibit work by children.

They shall ensure, under the conditions laid down by this Directive, that the minimum working or employment age is not lower than the minimum age at which compulsory full-time schooling as imposed by national law ends or 15 years in any event.

2. Member States ensure that work by adolescents is strictly regulated and protected under the conditions laid down in this Directive.

3. Member States shall ensure in general that employers guarantee that young people have working conditions which suit their age.

They shall ensure that young people are protected against economic exploitation and against any work likely to harm their safety, health or physical, mental, moral or social development or to jeopardise their education.

[3.183]
Article 2
Scope

1. This Directive shall apply to any person under 18 years of age having an employment contract or an employment relationship defined by the law in force in a Member State and/or governed by the law in force in a Member State.
2. Member States may make legislative or regulatory provision for this Directive not to apply, within the limits and under the conditions which they set by legislative or regulatory provision, to occasional work or short-term work involving—
   (a) domestic service in a private household, or
   (b) work regarded as not being harmful, damaging or dangerous to young people in a family undertaking.

[3.184]
Article 3
Definitions

For the purposes of this Directive—
   (a) 'young person' shall mean any person under 18 years of age referred to in Article 2(1);
   (b) 'child' shall mean any young person of less than 15 years of age or who is still subject to compulsory full-time schooling under national law;
   (c) 'adolescent' shall mean any young person of at least 15 years of age but less than 18 years of age who is no longer subject to compulsory full-time schooling under national law;
   (d) 'light work' shall mean all work which, on account of the inherent nature of the tasks which it involves and the particular conditions under which they are performed—
      (i) is not likely to be harmful to the safety, health or development of children, and
      (ii) is not such as to be harmful to their attendance at school, their participation in vocational guidance or training programmes approved by the competent authority or their capacity to benefit from the instruction received;
   (e) 'working time' shall mean any period during which the young person is at work, at the employer's disposal and carrying out his activity or duties in accordance with national legislation and/or practice;
   (f) 'rest period' shall mean any period which is not working time.

[3.185]
Article 4
Prohibition of work by children

1. Member States shall adopt the measures necessary to prohibit work by children.
2. Taking into account the objectives set out in Article 1, Member States may make legislative or regulatory provision for the prohibition of work by children not to apply to—
   (a) children pursuing the activities set out in Article 5;
   (b) children of at least 14 years of age working under a combined work/ training scheme or an in-plant work-experience scheme, provided that such work is done in accordance with the conditions laid down by the competent authority;
   (c) children of at least 14 years of age performing light work other than that covered by Article 5; light work other than that covered by Article 5 may, however, be performed by children of 13 years of age for a limited number of hours per week in the case of categories of work determined by national legislation.
3. Member States that make use of the opinion referred to in paragraph 2(c) shall determine, subject to the provisions of this Directive, the working conditions relating to the light work in question.

[3.186]
Article 5
Cultural or similar activities

1. The employment of children for the purposes of performance in cultural, artistic, sports or advertising activities shall be subject to prior authorisation to be given by the competent authority in individual cases.
2. Member States shall by legislative or regulatory provision lay down the working conditions for children in the cases referred to in paragraph 1 and the details of the prior authorisation procedure, on condition that the activities—
   (i) are not likely to be harmful to the safety, health or development of children, and

(ii) are not such as to be harmful to their attendance at school, their participation in vocational guidance or training programmes approved by the competent authority or their capacity to benefit from the instruction received.

3. By way of derogation from the procedure laid down in paragraph 1, in the case of children of at least 13 years of age, Member States may authorise, by legislative or regulatory provision, in accordance with conditions which they shall determine, the employment of children for the purposes of performance in cultural, artistic, sports or advertising activities.

4. The Member States which have a specific authorisation system for modelling agencies with regard to the activities of children may retain that system.

SECTION II

[3.187]

Article 6

General obligations on employers

1. Without prejudice to Article 4 (1), the employer shall adopt the measures necessary to protect the safety and health of young people, taking particular account of the specific risks referred to in Article 7(1).

2. The employer shall implement the measures provided for in paragraph 1 on the basis of an assessment of the hazards to young people in connection with their work.

The assessment must be made before young people begin work and when there is any major change in working conditions and must pay particular attention to the following points—

(a) the fitting-out and layout of the workplace and the workstation;
(b) the nature, degree and duration of exposure to physical, biological and chemical agents;
(c) the form, range and use of work equipment, in particular agents, machines, apparatus and devices, and the way in which they are handled;
(d) the arrangement of work processes and operations and the way in which these are combined (organisation of work);
(e) the level of training and instruction given to young people.

Where this assessment shows that there is a risk to the safety, the physical or mental health or development of young people, an appropriate free assessment and monitoring of their health shall be provided at regular intervals without prejudice to Directive 89/391/EEC.

The free health assessment and monitoring may form part of a national health system.

3. The employer shall inform young people of possible risks and of all measures adopted concerning their safety and health.

Furthermore, he shall inform the legal representatives of children of possible risks and of all measures adopted concerning children's safety and health.

4. The employer shall involve the protective and preventive services referred to in Article 7 of Directive 89/391/EEC in the planning, implementation and monitoring of the safety and health conditions applicable to young people.

[3.188]

Article 7

Vulnerability of young people—Prohibition of work

1. Member States shall ensure that young people are protected from any specific risks to their safety, health and development which are a consequence of their lack of experience, of absence of awareness of existing or potential risks or of the fact that young people have not yet fully matured.

2. Without prejudice to Article 4(1), Member States shall to this end prohibit the employment of young people for—

(a) work which is objectively beyond their physical or psychological capacity;
(b) work involving harmful exposure to agents which are toxic, carcinogenic, cause heritable genetic damage, or harm to the unborn child or which in any other way chronically affect human health;
(c) work involving harmful exposure to radiation;
(d) work involving the risk of accidents which it may be assumed cannot be recognised or avoided by young persons owing to their insufficient attention to safety or lack of experience or training; or
(e) work in which there is a risk to health from extreme cold or heat, or from noise or vibration.

Work which is likely to entail specific risks for young people within the meaning of paragraph I includes—

— work involving harmful exposure to the physical, biological and chemical agents referred to in point I of the Annex, and
— processes and work referred to in point II of the Annex.

3. Member States may, by legislative or regulatory provision, authorise derogations from paragraph 2 in the case of adolescents where such derogations are indispensable for their vocational training, provided that protection of their safety and health is ensured by the fact that the work is performed under the supervision of a competent person within the meaning of Article 7 of Directive 89/391/EEC and provided that the protection afforded by that Directive is guaranteed.

SECTION III

[3.189]
Article 8
Working time

1. Member States which make use of the option in Article 4(2)(b) or (c) shall adopt the measures necessary to limit the working time of children to—
   (a) eight hours a day and 40 hours a week for work performed under a combined work/training scheme or an in-plant work-experience scheme;
   (b) two hours on a school day and 12 hours a week for work performed in term-time outside the hours fixed for school attendance, provided that this is not prohibited by national legislation and/or practice;

in no circumstances may the daily working time exceed seven hours; this limit may be raised to eight hours in the case of children who have reached the age of 15;
   (c) seven hours a day and 35 hours a week for work performed during a period of at least a week when school is not operating; these limits may be raised to eight hours a day and 40 hours a week in the case of children who have reached the age of 15;
   (d) seven hours a day and 35 hours a week for light work performed by children no longer subject to compulsory full-time schooling under national law.

2. Member States shall adopt the measures necessary to limit the working time of adolescents to eight hours a day and 40 hours a week.

3. The time spent on training by a young person working under a theoretical and/or practical combined work/training scheme or an in-plant work-experience scheme shall be counted as working time.

4. Where a young person is employed by more than one employer, working days and working time shall be cumulative.

5. Member States may, by legislative or regulatory provision, authorise derogations from paragraph 1(a) and paragraph 2 either by way of exception or where there are objective grounds for so doing.

Member States shall, by legislative or regulatory provision, determine the conditions, limits and procedure for implementing such derogations.

[3.190]
Article 9
Night work

1.
   (a) Member States which make use of the option in Article 4(2)(b) or (c) shall adopt the measures necessary to prohibit work by children between 8 pm and 6 am.
   (b) Member States shall adopt the measures necessary to prohibit work by adolescents either between 10 pm and 6 am or between 11 pm and 7 am.

2.
   (a) Member States may, by legislative or regulatory provision, authorise work by adolescents in specific areas of activity during the period in which night work is prohibited as referred to in paragraph 1(b).

   In that event, Member States shall take appropriate measures to ensure that the adolescent is supervised by an adult where such supervision is necessary for the adolescent's protection.
   (b) If point (a) is applied, work shall continue to be prohibited between midnight and 4 am.

   However, Member States may, by legislative or regulatory provision, authorise work by adolescents during the period in which night work is prohibited in the following cases, where there are objective grounds for so doing and provided that adolescents are allowed suitable compensatory rest time and that the objectives set out in Article 1 are not called into question—
   — work performed in the shipping or fisheries sectors;
   — work performed in the context of the armed forces or the police;
   — work performed in hospitals or similar establishments;
   — cultural, artistic, sports or advertising activities.

3. Prior to any assignment to night work and at regular intervals thereafter, adolescents shall be entitled to a free assessment of their health and capacities, unless the work they do during the period during which work is prohibited is of an exceptional nature.

[3.191]
Article 10
Rest period
1.
(a) Member States which make use of the option in Article 4(2), (b) or (c) shall adopt the measures necessary to ensure that, for each 24 hour period, children are entitled to a minimum rest period of 14 consecutive hours.
(b) Member States shall adopt the measures necessary to ensure that, for each 24-hour period, adolescents are entitled to a minimum rest period of 12 consecutive hours.
2. Member States shall adopt the measures necessary to ensure that, for each seven-day period—
— children in respect of whom they have made use of the option in Article 4(2)(b) or (c), and
— adolescents
are entitled to a minimum rest period of two days, which shall be consecutive if possible.

Where justified by technical or organisation reasons, the minimum rest period may be reduced, but may in no circumstances be less than 36 consecutive hours.

The minimum rest period referred to in the first and second subparagraphs shall in principle include Sunday.

3. Member States may, by legislative or regulatory provision, provide for the minimum rest periods referred to in paragraphs 1 and 2 to be interrupted in the case of activities involving periods of work that are split up over the day or are of short duration.

4. Member States may make legislative or regulatory provision for derogations from paragraph 1(b) and paragraph 2 in respect of adolescents in the following cases, where there are objective grounds for so doing and provided that they are granted appropriate compensatory rest time and that the objectives set out in Article 1 are not called into question—
(a) work performed in the shipping or fisheries sectors;
(b) work performed in the context of the armed forces or the police;
(c) work performed in hospitals or similar establishments;
(d) work performed in agriculture;
(e) work performed in the tourism industry or in the hotel, restaurant and café sector;
(f) activities involving periods of work split up over the day.

[3.192]
Article 11
Annual rest
Member States which make use of the option referred to in Article 4(2)(b) or (c) shall see to it that a period free of any work is included, as far as possible, in the school holidays of children subject to compulsory full-time schooling under national law.

[3.193]
Article 12
Breaks
Member States shall adopt the measures necessary to ensure that, where daily working time is more than four and a half hours, young people are entitled to a break of at least 30 minutes, which shall be consecutive if possible.

[3.194]
Article 13
Work by adolescents in the event of *force majeure*
Member States may, by legislative or regulatory provision, authorise derogations from Article 8(2), Article 9(l)(b), Article 10(1)(b) and, in the case of adolescents, Article 12, for work in the circumstances referred to in Article 5(4) of Directive 89/391/EEC, provided that such work is of a temporary nature and must be performed immediately, that adult workers are not available and that the adolescents are allowed equivalent compensatory rest time within the following three weeks.

SECTION IV

[3.195]
Article 14
Measures
Each Member State shall lay down any necessary measures to be applied in the event of failure to comply with the provisions adopted in order to implement this Directive; such measures must be effective and proportionate.

[3.196]
Article 15
Adaptation of the Annex
Adaptations of a strictly technical nature to the Annex in the light of technical progress, changes in international rules or specifications and advances in knowledge in the field covered by this

Directive shall be adopted in accordance with the procedure provided for in Article 17 of Directive 89/391/EEC.

[3.197]
Article 16
Non-reducing clause
Without prejudice to the right of Member States to develop, in the light of changing circumstances, different provisions on the protection of young people, as long as the minimum requirements provided for by this Directive are complied with, the implementation of this Directive shall not constitute valid grounds for reducing the general level of protection afforded to young people.

[3.198]
Article 17
Final provisions
1.
- (a) Member States shall bring into force the laws, regulations and administrative provisions necessary to comply with this Directive not later than 22 June 1996 or ensure, by that date at the latest, that the two sides of industry introduce the requisite provisions by means of collective agreements, with Member States being required to make all the necessary provisions to enable them at all times to guarantee the results laid down by this Directive.
- (b) The United Kingdom may refrain from implementing the first subparagraph of Article 8(1)(b) with regard to the provision relating to the maximum weekly working time, and also Article 8(2) and Article 9(1)(b) and (2) for a period of four years from the date specified in subparagraph (a).

  The Commission shall submit a report on the effects of this provision.

  The Council, acting in accordance with the conditions laid down by the Treaty, shall decide whether this period should be extended.
- (c) Member States shall forthwith inform the Commission thereof.

2. When Member States adopt the measures referred to in paragraph 1, such measures shall contain a reference to this Directive or shall be accompanied by such reference on the occasion of their official publication. The methods of making such reference shall be laid down by Member States.
3. Member States shall communicate to the Commission the texts of the main provisions of national law which they have already adopted or adopt in the field governed by this Directive.
4, 5. . . .

NOTES
Paras 4, 5: repealed by European Parliament and Council Directive 2007/30/EC, Art 3(15).

[3.199]
[Article 17a
Implementation report
Every five years, the Member States shall submit to the Commission a report on the practical implementation of this Directive in the form of a specific chapter of the single report referred to in Article 17a(1), (2) and (3) of Directive 89/391/EEC, which serves as a basis for the Commission's evaluation, in accordance with Article 17a(4) of that Directive.]

NOTES
Inserted by European Parliament and Council Directive 2007/30/EC, Art 2(4).

[3.200]
Article 18
This Directive is addressed to the Member States.

ANNEX
NON-EXHAUSTIVE LIST OF AGENTS, PROCESSES AND WORK (ARTICLE 7(2), SECOND SUBPARAGRAPH)

[3.201]
I. Agents
1. *Physical agents*
   - (a) Ionising radiation;
   - (b) Work in a high-pressure atmosphere, eg in pressurised containers, diving.
2. *Biological agents*
   - (a) Biological agents belonging to groups 3 and 4 within the meaning of Article 2(d) of Council Directive 90/679/EEC of 26 November 1990 on the protection of workers from risks related to exposure to biological agents at work (Seventh individual Directive within the meaning of Article 16(1) of Directive 89/391/EEC).[1]

3. *Chemical agents*

(a) Substances and preparations classified according to Council Directive 67/548/EEC of 27 June 1967 on the approximation of laws, regulations and administrative provisions relating to the classification, packaging and labelling of dangerous substances[2] with amendments and Council Directive 88/379/EEC of 7 June 1988 on the approximation of the laws, regulations and administrative provisions of the Member States relating to the classification, packaging and labelling of dangerous preparations[3] as toxic (T), very toxic (Tx), corrosive (C) or explosive (E);

(b) Substances and preparations classified according to Directives 67/548/EEC and 88/379/EEC as harmful (Xn) and with one or more of the following risk phrases—
- danger of very serious irreversible effects (R39),
- possible risk of irreversible effects (R40),
- may cause sensitisation by inhalation (R42),
- may cause sensitisation by skin contact (R43),
- may cause cancer (R45),
- may cause heritable genetic damage (R46),
- danger of serious damage to health by prolonged exposure (R48),
- may impair fertility (R60),
- may cause harm to the unborn child (R61);

(c) Substances and preparations classified according to Directives 67/548/EEC and 88/379/EEC as irritant (Xi) and with one or more of the following risk phrases—
- highly flammable (R12);
- may cause sensitisation by inhalation (R42),
- may cause sensitisation by skin contact (R43);

(d) Substances and preparations referred to Article 2(c) of Council Directive 90/394/EEC of 28 June 1990 on the protection of workers from the risks related to exposure to carcinogens at work (Sixth individual Directive within the meaning of Article 16(1) of Directive 89/391/EEC);[4]

(e) Lead and compounds thereof, inasmuch as the agents in question are absorbable by the human organism;

(f) Asbestos.

II. Processes and work

1. Processes at work referred to in Annex I to Directive 90/394/EEC.
2. Manufacture and handling of devices, fireworks or other objects containing explosives.
3. Work with fierce or poisonous animals.
4. Animal slaughtering on an industrial scale.
5. Work involving the handling of equipment for the production, storage or application of compressed, liquefied or dissolved gases.
6. Work with vats, tanks, reservoirs or carboys containing chemical agents referred to in 1.3.
7. Work involving a risk of structural collapse.
8. Work involving high-voltage electrical hazards.
9. Work the pace of which is determined by machinery and involving payment by results.

NOTES

1 OJ L374, 31.12.90, p 1.

2 OJ L196, 16.8.67, p 1. Directive as last amended by Directive 93/679/EEC (OJ L268, 29.10.93, p 71).

3 OJ L187, 16.7.88, p 14. Directive as last amended by Directive 93/18/EEC (OJ L104, 29.4.93, p 46).

4 OJ L196, 26.7.90, p 1.

COUNCIL DIRECTIVE

(94/45/EC)

of 22 September 1994

on the establishment of a European Works Council or a procedure in Community-scale undertakings and Community-scale groups of undertakings for the purposes of informing and consulting employees (Note)

[3.202]

NOTES

Date of publication in OJ: OJ L254, 30.9.1994, p 64.

This Directive was repealed and replaced by European Parliament and Council Directive 2009/38/EC at **[3.601]**, with effect from 6 June 2011 (see Art 17 thereof at **[3.618]**). See also Annex III (Correlation Table) at **[3.624]**.

See *Harvey* NI(3).

DIRECTIVE OF THE EUROPEAN PARLIAMENT AND OF THE COUNCIL

(95/46/EC)

of 24 October 1995

on the protection of individuals with regard to the processing of personal data and on the free movement of such data

NOTES

Date of publication in OJ: OJ L281, 23.11.1995, p 31.

For the domestic implementation of this Directive, see the Data Protection Act 1998 at **[1.1078]**.

[3.203]

THE EUROPEAN PARLIAMENT AND THE COUNCIL OF THE EUROPEAN UNION,

Having regard to the Treaty establishing the European Community, and in particular Article 100a thereof,

Having regard to the proposal from the Commission,[1]

Having regard to the opinion of the Economic and Social Committee,[2]

Acting in accordance with the procedure referred to in Article 189b of the Treaty,

(1) Whereas the objectives of the Community, as laid down in the Treaty, as amended by the Treaty on European Union, include creating an ever closer union among the peoples of Europe, fostering closer relations between the States belonging to the Community, ensuring economic and social progress by common action to eliminate the barriers which divide Europe, encouraging the constant improvement of the living conditions of its peoples, preserving and strengthening peace and liberty and promoting democracy on the basis of the fundamental rights recognised in the constitution and laws of the Member States and in the European Convention for the Protection of Human Rights and Fundamental Freedoms;

(2) Whereas data-processing systems are designed to serve man; whereas they must, whatever the nationality or residence of natural persons, respect their fundamental rights and freedoms, notably the right to privacy, and contribute to economic and social progress, trade expansion and the well-being of individuals;

(3) Whereas the establishment and functioning of an internal market in which, in accordance with Article 7a of the Treaty, the free movement of goods, persons, services and capital is ensured require not only that personal data should be able to flow freely from one Member State to another, but also that the fundamental rights of individuals should be safeguarded;

(4) Whereas increasingly frequent recourse is being had in the Community to the processing of personal data in the various spheres of economic and social activity; whereas the progress made in information technology is making the processing and exchange of such data considerably easier;

(5) Whereas the economic and social integration resulting from the establishment and functioning of the internal market within the meaning of Article 7a of the Treaty will necessarily lead to a substantial increase in cross-border flows of personal data between all those involved in a private or public capacity in economic and social activity in the Member States; whereas the exchange of personal data between undertakings in different Member States is set to increase; whereas the national authorities in the various Member States are being called upon by virtue of Community law to collaborate and exchange personal data so as to be able to perform their duties or carry out tasks on behalf of an authority in another Member State within the context of the area without internal frontiers as constituted by the internal market;

(6) Whereas, furthermore, the increase in scientific and technical cooperation and the coordinated introduction of new telecommunications networks in the Community necessitate and facilitate cross-border flows of personal data;

(7) Whereas the difference in levels of protection of the rights and freedoms of individuals, notably the right to privacy, with regard to the processing of personal data afforded in the Member States may prevent the transmission of such data from the territory of one Member State to that of another Member State; whereas this difference may therefore constitute an obstacle to the pursuit of a number of economic activities at Community level, distort competition and impede authorities in the discharge of their responsibilities under Community law; whereas this difference in levels of protection is due to the existence of a wide variety of national laws, regulations and administrative provisions;

(8) Whereas, in order to remove the obstacles to flows of personal data, the level of protection of the rights and freedoms of individuals with regard to the processing of such data must be equivalent in all Member States; whereas this objective is vital to the internal market but cannot be achieved by the Member States alone, especially in view of the scale of the divergences which currently exist between the relevant laws in the Member States and the need to coordinate the laws

of the Member States so as to ensure that the cross-border flow of personal data is regulated in a consistent manner that is in keeping with the objective of the internal market as provided for in Article 7a of the Treaty; whereas Community action to approximate those laws is therefore needed;

(9) Whereas, given the equivalent protection resulting from the approximation of national laws, the Member States will no longer be able to inhibit the free movement between them of personal data on grounds relating to protection of the rights and freedoms of individuals, and in particular the right to privacy; whereas Member States will be left a margin for manoeuvre, which may, in the context of implementation of the Directive, also be exercised by the business and social partners; whereas Member States will therefore be able to specify in their national law the general conditions governing the lawfulness of data processing; whereas in doing so the Member States shall strive to improve the protection currently provided by their legislation; whereas, within the limits of this margin for manoeuvre and in accordance with Community law, disparities could arise in the implementation of the Directive, and this could have an effect on the movement of data within a Member State as well as within the Community;

(10) Whereas the object of the national laws on the processing of personal data is to protect fundamental rights and freedoms, notably the right to privacy, which is recognised both in Article 8 of the European Convention for the Protection of Human Rights and Fundamental Freedoms and in the general principles of Community law; whereas, for that reason, the approximation of those laws must not result in any lessening of the protection they afford but must, on the contrary, seek to ensure a high level of protection in the Community;

(11) Whereas the principles of the protection of the rights and freedoms of individuals, notably the right to privacy, which are contained in this Directive, give substance to and amplify those contained in the Council of Europe Convention of 28 January 1981 for the Protection of Individuals with regard to Automatic Processing of Personal Data;

(12) Whereas the protection principles must apply to all processing of personal data by any person whose activities are governed by Community law; whereas there should be excluded the processing of data carried out by a natural person in the exercise of activities which are exclusively personal or domestic, such as correspondence and the holding of records of addresses;

(13) Whereas the activities referred to in Titles V and VI of the Treaty on European Union regarding public safety, defence, State security or the activities of the State in the area of criminal laws fall outside the scope of Community law, without prejudice to the obligations incumbent upon Member States under Article 56(2), Article 57 or Article 100a of the Treaty establishing the European Community; whereas the processing of personal data that is necessary to safeguard the economic well-being of the State does not fall within the scope of this Directive where such processing relates to State security matters;

(14) Whereas, given the importance of the developments under way, in the framework of the information society, of the techniques used to capture, transmit, manipulate, record, store or communicate sound and image data relating to natural persons, this Directive should be applicable to processing involving such data;

(15) Whereas the processing of such data is covered by this Directive only if it is automated or if the data processed are contained or are intended to be contained in a filing system structured according to specific criteria relating to individuals, so as to permit easy access to the personal data in question;

(16) Whereas the processing of sound and image data, such as in cases of video surveillance, does not come within the scope of this Directive if it is carried out for the purposes of public security, defence, national security or in the course of State activities relating to the area of criminal law or of other activities which do not come within the scope of Community law;

(17) Whereas, as far as the processing of sound and image data carried out for purposes of journalism or the purposes of literary or artistic expression is concerned, in particular in the audiovisual field, the principles of the Directive are to apply in a restricted manner according to the provisions laid down in Article 9;

(18) Whereas, in order to ensure that individuals are not deprived of the protection to which they are entitled under this Directive, any processing of personal data in the Community must be carried out in accordance with the law of one of the Member States; whereas, in this connection, processing carried out under the responsibility of a controller who is established in a Member State should be governed by the law of that State;

(19) Whereas establishment on the territory of a Member State implies the effective and real exercise of activity through stable arrangements; whereas the legal form of such an establishment, whether simply branch or a subsidiary with a legal personality, is not the determining factor in this respect; whereas, when a single controller is established on the territory of several Member States, particularly by means of subsidiaries, he must ensure, in order to avoid any circumvention of national rules, that each of the establishments fulfils the obligations imposed by the national law applicable to its activities;

(20) Whereas the fact that the processing of data is carried out by a person established in a third country must not stand in the way of the protection of individuals provided for in this Directive; whereas in these cases, the processing should be governed by the law of the Member State in which the means used are located, and there should be guarantees to ensure that the rights and obligations provided for in this Directive are respected in practice;

(21) Whereas this Directive is without prejudice to the rules of territoriality applicable in criminal matters;

(22) Whereas Member States shall more precisely define in the laws they enact or when bringing into force the measures taken under this Directive the general circumstances in which processing is lawful; whereas in particular Article 5, in conjunction with Articles 7 and 8, allows Member States, independently of general rules, to provide for special processing conditions for specific sectors and for the various categories of data covered by Article 8;

(23) Whereas Member States are empowered to ensure the implementation of the protection of individuals both by means of a general law on the protection of individuals as regards the processing of personal data and by sectorial laws such as those relating, for example, to statistical institutes;

(24) Whereas the legislation concerning the protection of legal persons with regard to the processing data which concerns them is not affected by this Directive;

(25) Whereas the principles of protection must be reflected, on the one hand, in the obligations imposed on persons, public authorities, enterprises, agencies or other bodies responsible for processing, in particular regarding data quality, technical security, notification to the supervisory authority, and the circumstances under which processing can be carried out, and, on the other hand, in the right conferred on individuals, the data on whom are the subject of processing, to be informed that processing is taking place, to consult the data, to request corrections and even to object to processing in certain circumstances;

(26) Whereas the principles of protection must apply to any information concerning an identified or identifiable person; whereas, to determine whether a person is identifiable, account should be taken of all the means likely reasonably to be used either by the controller or by any other person to identify the said person; whereas the principles of protection shall not apply to data rendered anonymous in such a way that the data subject is no longer identifiable; whereas codes of conduct within the meaning of Article 27 may be a useful instrument for providing guidance as to the ways in which data may be rendered anonymous and retained in a form in which identification of the data subject is no longer possible;

(27) Whereas the protection of individuals must apply as much to automatic processing of data as to manual processing; whereas the scope of this protection must not in effect depend on the techniques used, otherwise this would create a serious risk of circumvention; whereas, nonetheless, as regards manual processing, this Directive covers only filing systems, not unstructured files; whereas, in particular, the content of a filing system must be structured according to specific criteria relating to individuals allowing easy access to the personal data; whereas, in line with the definition in Article 2(c), the different criteria for determining the constituents of a structured set of personal data, and the different criteria governing access to such a set, may be laid down by each Member State; whereas files or sets of files as well as their cover pages, which are not structured according to specific criteria, shall under no circumstances fall within the scope of this Directive;

(28) Whereas any processing of personal data must be lawful and fair to the individuals concerned; whereas, in particular, the data must be adequate, relevant and not excessive in relation to the purposes for which they are processed; whereas such purposes must be explicit and legitimate and must be determined at the time of collection of the data; whereas the purposes of processing further to collection shall not be incompatible with the purposes as they were originally specified;

(29) Whereas the further processing of personal data for historical, statistical or scientific purposes is not generally to be considered incompatible with the purposes for which the data have previously been collected provided that Member States furnish suitable safeguards; whereas these safeguards must in particular rule out the use of the data in support of measures or decisions regarding any particular individual;

(30) Whereas, in order to be lawful, the processing of personal data must in addition be carried out with the consent of the data subject or be necessary for the conclusion or performance of a contract binding on the data subject, or as a legal requirement, or for the performance of a task carried out in the public interest or in the exercise of official authority, or in the legitimate interests of a natural or legal person, provided that the interests or the rights and freedoms of the data subject are not overriding; whereas, in particular, in order to maintain a balance between the interests involved while guaranteeing effective competition, Member States may determine the circumstances in which personal data may be used or disclosed to a third party in the context of the legitimate ordinary business activities of companies and other bodies; whereas Member States may similarly specify the conditions under which personal data may be disclosed to a third party for the purposes of marketing whether carried out commercially or by a charitable organisation or by any other association or foundation, of a political nature for example, subject to the provisions allowing a data

subject to object to the processing of data regarding him, at no cost and without having to state his reasons;

(31) Whereas the processing of personal data must equally be regarded as lawful where it is carried out in order to protect an interest which is essential for the data subject's life;

(32) Whereas it is for national legislation to determine whether the controller performing a task carried out in the public interest or in the exercise of official authority should be a public administration or another natural or legal person governed by public law, or by private law such as a professional association;

(33) Whereas data which are capable by their nature of infringing fundamental freedoms or privacy should not be processed unless the data subject gives his explicit consent; whereas, however, derogations from this prohibition must be explicitly provided for in respect of specific needs, in particular where the processing of these data is carried out for certain health-related purposes by persons subject to a legal obligation of professional secrecy or in the course of legitimate activities by certain associations or foundations the purpose of which is to permit the exercise of fundamental freedoms;

(34) Whereas Member States must also be authorised, when justified by grounds of important public interest, to derogate from the prohibition on processing sensitive categories of data where important reasons of public interest so justify in areas such as public health and social protection—especially in order to ensure the quality and cost-effectiveness of the procedures used for settling claims for benefits and services in the health insurance system—scientific research and government statistics; whereas it is incumbent on them, however, to provide specific and suitable safeguards so as to protect the fundamental rights and the privacy of individuals;

(35) Whereas, moreover, the processing of personal data by official authorities for achieving aims, laid down in constitutional law or international public law, of officially recognised religious associations is carried out on important grounds of public interest;

(36) Whereas where, in the course of electoral activities, the operation of the democratic system requires in certain Member States that political parties compile data on people's political opinion, the processing of such data may be permitted for reasons of important public interest, provided that appropriate safeguards are established;

(37) Whereas the processing of personal data for purposes of journalism or for purposes of literary of artistic expression, in particular in the audiovisual field, should qualify for exemption from the requirements of certain provisions of this Directive in so far as this is necessary to reconcile the fundamental rights of individuals with freedom of information and notably the right to receive and impart information, as guaranteed in particular in Article 10 of the European Convention for the Protection of Human Rights and Fundamental Freedoms; whereas Member States should therefore lay down exemptions and derogations necessary for the purpose of balance between fundamental rights as regards general measures on the legitimacy of data processing, measures on the transfer of data to third countries and the power of the supervisory authority; whereas this should not, however, lead Member States to lay down exemptions from the measures to ensure security of processing; whereas at least the supervisory authority responsible for this sector should also be provided with certain ex-post powers, eg to publish a regular report or to refer matters to the judicial authorities;

(38) Whereas, if the processing of data is to be fair, the data subject must be in a position to learn of the existence of a processing operation and, where data are collected from him, must be given accurate and full information, bearing in mind the circumstances of the collection;

(39) Whereas certain processing operations involve data which the controller has not collected directly from the data subject; whereas, furthermore, data can be legitimately disclosed to a third party, even if the disclosure was not anticipated at the time the data were collected from the data subject; whereas, in all these cases, the data subject should be informed when the data are recorded or at the latest when the data are first disclosed to a third party;

(40) Whereas, however, it is not necessary to impose this obligation of the data subject already has the information; whereas, moreover, there will be no such obligation if the recording or disclosure are expressly provided for by law or if the provision of information to the data subject proves impossible or would involve disproportionate efforts, which could be the case where processing is for historical, statistical or scientific purposes; whereas, in this regard, the number of data subjects, the age of the data, and any compensatory measures adopted may be taken into consideration;

(41) Whereas any person must be able to exercise the right of access to data relating to him which are being processed, in order to verify in particular the accuracy of the data and the lawfulness of the processing; whereas, for the same reasons, every data subject must also have the right to know the logic involved in the automatic processing of data concerning him, at least in the case of the automated decisions referred to in Article 15(1); whereas this right must not adversely affect trade secrets or intellectual property and in particular the copyright protecting the software; whereas these considerations must not, however, result in the data subject being refused all information;

(42) Whereas Member States may, in the interest of the data subject or so as to protect the rights and freedoms of others, restrict rights of access and information; whereas they may, for example, specify that access to medical data may be obtained only through a health professional;

(43) Whereas restrictions on the rights of access and information and on certain obligations of the controller may similarly be imposed by Member States in so far as they are necessary to safeguard, for example, national security, defence, public safety, or important economic or financial interests of a Member State or the Union, as well as criminal investigations and prosecutions and action in respect of breaches of ethics in the regulated professions; whereas the list of exceptions and limitations should include the tasks of monitoring, inspection or regulation necessary in the three last-mentioned areas concerning public security, economic or financial interests and crime prevention; whereas the listing of tasks in these three areas does not affect the legitimacy of exceptions or restrictions for reasons of State security or defence;

(44) Whereas Member States may also be led, by virtue of the provisions of Community law, to derogate from the provisions of this Directive concerning the right of access, the obligation to inform individuals, and the quality of data, in order to secure certain of the purposes referred to above;

(45) Whereas, in cases where data might lawfully be processed on grounds of public interest, official authority or the legitimate interests of a natural or legal person, any data subject should nevertheless be entitled, on legitimate and compelling grounds relating to his particular situation, to object to the processing of any data relating to himself; whereas Member States may nevertheless lay down national provisions to the contrary;

(46) Whereas the protection of the rights and freedoms of data subjects with regard to the processing of personal data requires that appropriate technical and organisational measures be taken, both at the time of the design of the processing system and at the time of the processing itself, particularly in order to maintain security and thereby to prevent any unauthorised processing; whereas it is incumbent on the Member States to ensure that controllers comply with these measures; whereas these measures must ensure an appropriate level of security, taking into account the state of the art and the costs of their implementation in relation to the risks inherent in the processing and the nature of the data to be protected;

(47) Whereas where a message containing personal data is transmitted by means of a telecommunications or electronic mail service, the sole purpose of which is the transmission of such messages, the controller in respect of the personal data contained in the message will normally be considered to be the person from whom the message originates, rather than the person offering the transmission services; whereas, nevertheless, those offering such services will normally be considered controllers in respect of the processing of the additional personal data necessary for the operation of the service;

(48) Whereas the procedures for notifying the supervisory authority are designed to ensure disclosure of the purposes and main features of any processing operation for the purpose of verification that the operation is in accordance with the national measures taken under this Directive;

(49) Whereas, in order to avoid unsuitable administrative formalities, exemptions from the obligation to notify and simplification of the notification required may be provided for by Member States in cases where processing is unlikely adversely to affect the rights and freedoms of data subjects, provided that it is in accordance with a measure taken by a Member State specifying its limits; whereas exemption or simplification may similarly be provided for by Member States where a person appointed by the controller ensures that the processing carried out is not likely adversely to affect the rights and freedoms of data subjects; whereas such a data protection official, whether or not an employee of the controller, must be in a position to exercise his functions in complete independence;

(50) Whereas exemption or simplification could be provided for in cases of processing operations whose sole purpose is the keeping of a register intended, according to national law, to provide information to the public and open to consultation by the public or by any person demonstrating a legitimate interest;

(51) Whereas, nevertheless, simplification or exemption from the obligation to notify shall not release the controller from any of the other obligations resulting from this Directive;

(52) Whereas, in this context, *ex post facto* verification by the competent authorities must in general be considered a sufficient measure;

(53) Whereas, however, certain processing operation are likely to pose specific risks to the rights and freedoms of data subjects by virtue of their nature, their scope or their purposes, such as that of excluding individuals from a right, benefit or a contract, or by virtue of the specific use of new technologies; whereas it is for Member States, if they so wish, to specify such risks in their legislation;

(54) Whereas with regard to all the processing undertaken in society, the amount posing such specific risks should be very limited; whereas Member States must provide that the supervisory authority, or the data protection official in cooperation with the authority, check such processing

prior to it being carried out; whereas following this prior check, the supervisory authority may, according to its national law, give an opinion or an authorisation regarding the processing; whereas such checking may equally take place in the course of the preparation either of a measure of the national parliament or of a measure based on such a legislative measure, which defines the nature of the processing and lays down appropriate safeguards;

(55) Whereas, if the controller fails to respect the rights of data subjects, national legislation must provide for a judicial remedy; whereas any damage which a person may suffer as a result of unlawful processing must be compensated for by the controller, who may be exempted from liability if he proves that he is not responsible for the damage, in particular in cases where he establishes fault on the part of the data subject or in case of *force majeure*; whereas sanctions must be imposed on any person, whether governed by private of public law, who fails to comply with the national measures taken under this Directive;

(56) Whereas cross-border flows of personal data are necessary to the expansion of international trade; whereas the protection of individuals guaranteed in the Community by this Directive does not stand in the way of transfers of personal data to third countries which ensure an adequate level of protection; whereas the adequacy of the level of protection afforded by a third country must be assessed in the light of all the circumstances surrounding the transfer operation or set of transfer operations;

(57) Whereas, on the other hand, the transfer of personal data to a third country which does not ensure an adequate level of protection must be prohibited;

(58) Whereas provisions should be made for exemptions from this prohibition in certain circumstances where the data subject has given his consent, where the transfer is necessary in relation to a contract or a legal claim, where protection of an important public interest so requires, for example in cases of international transfers of data between tax or customs administrations or between services competent for social security matters, or where the transfer is made from a register established by law and intended for consultation by the public or persons having a legitimate interest; whereas in this case such a transfer should not involve the entirety of the data or entire categories of the data contained in the register and, when the register is intended for consultation by persons having a legitimate interest, the transfer should be made only at the request of those persons or if they are to be the recipients;

(59) Whereas particular measures may be taken to compensate for the lack of protection in a third country in cases where the controller offers appropriate safeguards; whereas, moreover, provision must be made for procedures for negotiations between the Community and such third countries;

(60) Whereas, in any event, transfers to third countries may be effected only in full compliance with the provisions adopted by the Member States pursuant to this Directive, and in particular Article 8 thereof;

(61) Whereas Member States and the Commission, in their respective spheres of competence, must encourage the trade associations and other representative organisations concerned to draw up codes of conduct so as to facilitate the application of this Directive, taking account of the specific characteristics of the processing carried out in certain sectors, and respecting the national provisions adopted for its implementation;

(62) Whereas the establishment in Member States of supervisory authorities, exercising their functions with complete independence, is an essential component of the protection of individuals with regard to the processing of personal data;

(63) Whereas such authorities must have the necessary means to perform their duties, including powers of investigation and intervention, particularly in cases of complaints from individuals, and powers to engage in legal proceedings; whereas such authorities must help to ensure transparency of processing in the Member States within whose jurisdiction they fall;

(64) Whereas the authorities in the different Member States will need to assist one another in performing their duties so as to ensure that the rules of protection are properly respected throughout the European Union;

(65) Whereas, at Community level, a Working Party on the Protection of Individuals with regard to the Processing of Personal Data must be set up and be completely independent in the performance of its functions; whereas, having regard to its specific nature, it must advise the Commission and, in particular, contribute to the uniform application of the national rules adopted pursuant to this Directive;

(66) Whereas, with regard to the transfer of data to third countries, the application of this Directive calls for the conferment of powers of implementation on the Commission and the establishment of a procedure as laid down in Council Decision 87/373/EEC;[3]

(67) Whereas an agreement on a *modus vivendi* between the European Parliament, the Council and the Commission concerning the implementing measures for acts adopted in accordance with the procedure laid down in Article 189b of the EC Treaty was reached on 20 December 1994;

(68) Whereas the principles set out in this Directive regarding the protection of the rights and freedoms of individuals, notably their right to privacy, with regard to the processing of personal data may be supplemented or clarified, in particular as far as certain sectors are concerned, by specific rules based on those principles;

(69) Whereas Member States should be allowed a period of not more than three years from the entry into force of the national measures transposing this Directive in which to apply such new national rules progressively to all processing operations already under way; whereas, in order to facilitate their cost-effective implementation, a further period expiring 12 years after the date on which this Directive is adopted will be allowed to Member States to ensure the conformity of existing manual filing systems with certain of the Directive's provisions; whereas, where data contained in such filing systems are manually processed during this extended transition period, those systems must be brought into conformity with these provisions at the time of such processing;

(70) Whereas it is not necessary for the data subject to give his consent again so as to allow the controller to continue to process, after the national provisions taken pursuant to this Directive enter into force, any sensitive data necessary for the performance of a contract concluded on the basis of free and informed consent before the entry into force of these provisions;

(71) Whereas this Directive does not stand in the way of a Member State's regulating marketing activities aimed at consumers residing in territory in so far as such regulation does not concern the protection of individuals with regard to the processing of personal data;

(72) Whereas this Directive allows the principle of public access to official documents to be taken into account when implementing the principles set out in this Directive,

NOTES

[1] OJ C277, 5.11.90, p 3 and OJ C311, 27.11.92, p 30.

[2] OJ C159, 17.6.91, p 38.

[3] OJ L197, 18.7.87, p 33.

HAVE ADOPTED THIS DIRECTIVE—

CHAPTER I
GENERAL PROVISIONS

[3.204]
Article 1
Object of the Directive

1. In accordance with this Directive, Member States shall protect the fundamental rights and freedoms of natural persons, and in particular their right to privacy with respect to the processing of personal data.
2. Member States shall neither restrict nor prohibit the free flow of personal data between Member States for reasons connected with the protection afforded under paragraph 1.

[3.205]
Article 2
Definitions

For the purposes of this Directive—

(a) "personal data" shall mean any information relating to an identified or identifiable natural person ("data subject"); an identifiable person is one who can be identified, directly or indirectly, in particular by reference to an identification number or to one or more factors specific to his physical, physiological, mental, economic, cultural or social identity;

(b) "processing of personal data" ("processing") shall mean any operation or set of operations which is performed upon personal data, whether or not by automatic means, such as collection, recording, organisation, storage, adaptation or alteration, retrieval, consultation, use, disclosure by transmission, dissemination or otherwise making available, alignment or combination, blocking, erasure or destruction;

(c) "personal data filing system" ("filing system") shall mean any structured set of personal data which are accessible according to specific criteria, whether centralised, decentralised or dispersed on a functional or geographical basis;

(d) "controller" shall mean the natural or legal person, public authority, agency or any other body which alone or jointly with others determines the purposes and means of the processing of personal data; where the purposes and means of processing are determined by national or Community laws or regulations, the controller or the specific criteria for his nomination may be designated by national or Community law;

(e) "processor" shall mean a natural or legal person, public authority, agency or any other body which processes personal data on behalf of the controller;

(f) "third party" shall mean any natural or legal person, public authority, agency or any other body other than the data subject, the controller, the processor and the persons who, under the direct authority of the controller or the processor, are authorised to process the data;
(g) "recipient" shall mean a natural or legal person, public authority, agency or any other body to whom data are disclosed, whether a third party or not; however, authorities which may receive data in the framework of a particular inquiry shall not be regarded as recipients;
(h) "the data subject's consent" shall mean any freely given specific and informed indication of his wishes by which the data subject signifies his agreement to personal data relating to him being processed.

[3.206]
Article 3
Scope
1. This Directive shall apply to the processing of personal data wholly or partly by automatic means, and to the processing otherwise than by automatic means of personal data which form part of a filing system or are intended to form part of a filing system.
2. This Directive shall not apply to the processing of personal data—
— in the course of an activity which falls outside the scope of Community law, such as those provided for by Titles V and VI of the Treaty on European Union and in any case to processing operations concerning public security, defence, State security (including the economic well-being of the State when the processing operation relates to State security matters) and the activities of the State in areas of criminal law,
— by a natural person in the course of a purely personal or household activity.

[3.207]
Article 4
National law applicable
1. Each Member State shall apply the national provisions it adopts pursuant to this Directive to the processing of personal data where—
(a) the processing is carried out in the context of the activities of an establishment of the controller on the territory of the Member State; when the same controller is established on the territory of several Member States, he must take the necessary measures to ensure that each of these establishments complies with the obligations laid down by the national law applicable;
(b) the controller is not established on the Member State's territory, but in a place where its national law applies by virtue of international public law;
(c) the controller is not established on Community territory and, for purposes of processing personal data makes use of equipment, automated or otherwise, situated on the territory of the said Member State, unless such equipment is used only for purposes of transit through the territory of the Community.
2. In the circumstances referred to in paragraph 1(c), the controller must designate a representative established in the territory of that Member State, without prejudice to legal actions which could be initiated against the controller himself.

CHAPTER II
GENERAL RULES ON THE LAWFULNESS OF THE PROCESSING OF PERSONAL DATA

[3.208]
Article 5
Member States shall, within the limits of the provisions of this Chapter, determine more precisely the conditions under which the processing of personal data is lawful.

SECTION I
PRINCIPLES RELATING TO DATA QUALITY

[3.209]
Article 6
1. Member States shall provide that personal data must be—
(a) processed fairly and lawfully;
(b) collected for specified, explicit and legitimate purposes and not further processed in a way incompatible with those purposes. Further processing of data for historical, statistical or scientific purposes shall not be considered as incompatible provided that Member States provide appropriate safeguards;
(c) adequate, relevant and not excessive in relation to the purposes for which they are collected and/or further processed;

(d) accurate and, where necessary, kept up to date; every reasonable step must be taken to ensure that data which are inaccurate or incomplete, having regard to the purposes for which they were collected or for which they are further processed, are erased or rectified;

(e) kept in a form which permits identification of data subjects for no longer than is necessary for the purposes for which the data were collected or for which they are further processed. Member States shall lay down appropriate safeguards for personal data stored for longer periods for historical, statistical or scientific use.

2. It shall be for the controller to ensure that paragraph 1 is complied with.

SECTION II
CRITERIA FOR MAKING DATA PROCESSING LEGITIMATE

[3.210]
Article 7

Member States shall provide that personal data may be processed only if—

(a) the data subject has unambiguously given his consent; or

(b) processing is necessary for the performance of a contract to which the data subject is party or in order to take steps at the request of the data subject prior to entering into a contract; or

(c) processing is necessary for compliance with a legal obligation to which the controller is subject; or

(d) processing is necessary in order to protect the vital interests of the data subject; or

(e) processing is necessary for the performance of a task carried out in the public interest or in the exercise of official authority vested in the controller or in a third party to whom the data are disclosed; or

(f) processing is necessary for the purposes of the legitimate interests pursued by the controller or by the third party or parties to whom the data are disclosed, except where such interests are overridden by the interests for fundamental rights and freedoms of the data subject which require protection under Article 1(1).

SECTION III
SPECIAL CATEGORIES OF PROCESSING

[3.211]
Article 8
The processing of special categories of data

1. Member States shall prohibit the processing of personal data revealing racial or ethnic origin, political opinions, religious or philosophical beliefs, trade-union membership, and the processing of data concerning health or sex life.

2. Paragraph 1 shall not apply where—

(a) the data subject has given his explicit consent to the processing of those data, except where the laws of the Member State provide that the prohibition referred to in paragraph 1 may not be lifted by the data subject's giving his consent; or

(b) processing is necessary for the purposes of carrying out the obligations and specific rights of the controller in the field of employment law in so far as it is authorised by national law providing for adequate safeguards; or

(c) processing is necessary to protect the vital interests of the data subject or of another person where the data subject is physically or legally incapable of giving his consent; or

(d) processing is carried out in the course of its legitimate activities with appropriate guarantees by a foundation, association or any other non-profit-seeking body with a political, philosophical, religious or trade-union aim and on condition that the processing relates solely to the members of the body or to persons who have regular contact with it in connection with its purposes and that the data are not disclosed to a third party without the consent of the data subjects; or

(e) the processing relates to data which are manifestly made public by the data subject or is necessary for the establishment, exercise or defence of legal claims.

3. Paragraph 1 shall not apply where processing of the data is required for the purposes of preventive medicine, medical diagnosis, the provision of care or treatment or the management of health-care services, and where those data are processed by a health professional subject under national law or rules established by national competent bodies to the obligation of professional secrecy or by another person also subject to an equivalent obligation of secrecy.

4. Subject to the provision of suitable safeguards, Member States may, for reasons of substantial public interest, lay down exemptions in addition to those laid down in paragraph 2 either by national law or by decision of the supervisory authority.

5. Processing of data relating to offences, criminal convictions or security measures may be carried out only under the control of official authority, or if suitable specific safeguards are provided under national law, subject to derogations which may be granted by the Member State under national provisions providing suitable specific safeguards. However, a complete register of criminal convictions may be kept only under the control of official authority.

Member States may provide that data relating to administrative sanctions or judgements in civil cases shall also be processed under the control of official authority.

6. Derogations from paragraph 1 provided for in paragraphs 4 and 5 shall be notified to the Commission.

7. Member States shall determine the conditions under which a national identification number or any other identifier of general application may be processed.

[3.212]
Article 9
Processing of personal data and freedom of expression

Member States shall provide for exemptions or derogations from the provisions of this Chapter, Chapter IV and Chapter VI for the processing of personal data carried out solely for journalistic purposes or the purpose of artistic or literary expression only if they are necessary to reconcile the right to privacy with the rules governing freedom of expression.

SECTION IV
INFORMATION TO BE GIVEN TO THE DATA SUBJECT

[3.213]
Article 10
Information in cases of collection of data from the data subject

Member States shall provide that the controller or his representative must provide a data subject from whom data relating to himself are collected with at least the following information, except where he already has it—

(a) the identity of the controller and of his representative, if any;
(b) the purposes of the processing for which the data are intended;
(c) any further information such as
- the recipients or categories of recipients of the data,
- whether replies to the questions are obligatory or voluntary, as well as the possible consequences of failure to reply,
- the existence of the right of access to and the right to rectify the data concerning him

in so far as such further information is necessary, having regard to the specific circumstances in which the data are collected, to guarantee fair processing in respect of the data subject.

[3.214]
Article 11
Information where the data have not been obtained from the data subject

1. Where the data have not been obtained from the data subject, Member States shall provide that the controller or his representative must at the time of undertaking the recording of personal data or if a disclosure to a third party is envisaged, no later than the time when the data are first disclosed provide the data subject with at least the following information, except where he already has it—

(a) the identity of the controller and of his representative, if any;
(b) the purposes of the processing;
(c) any further information such as
- the categories of data concerned,
- the recipients or categories of recipients,
- the existence of the right of access to and the right to rectify the data concerning him

in so far as such further information is necessary, having regard to the specific circumstances in which the data are processed, to guarantee fair processing in respect of the data subject.

2. Paragraph 1 shall not apply where, in particular for processing for statistical purposes or for the purposes of historical or scientific research, the provision of such information proves impossible or would involve a disproportionate effort or if recording or disclosure is expressly laid down by law. In these cases Member States shall provide appropriate safeguards.

SECTION V
THE DATA SUBJECT'S RIGHT OF ACCESS TO DATA

[3.215]
Article 12
Right of access

Member States shall guarantee every data subject the right to obtain from the controller—

(a) without constraint at reasonable intervals and without excessive delay or expense—

— confirmation as to whether or not data relating to him are being processed and information at least as to the purposes of the processing, the categories of data concerned, and the recipients or categories of recipients to whom the data are disclosed,
— communication to him in an intelligible form of the data undergoing processing and of any available information as to their source,
— knowledge of the logic involved in any automatic processing of data concerning him at least in the case of the automated decisions referred to in Article 15(1);

(b) as appropriate the rectification, erasure or blocking of data the processing of which does not comply with the provisions of this Directive, in particular because of the incomplete or inaccurate nature of the data;
(c) notification to third parties to whom the data have been disclosed of any rectification, erasure or blocking carried out in compliance with (b), unless this proves impossible or involves a disproportionate effort.

SECTION VI
EXEMPTIONS AND RESTRICTIONS

[3.216]
Article 13
Exemptions and restrictions
1. Member States may adopt legislative measures to restrict the scope of the obligations and rights provided for in Articles 6(1), 10, 11(1), 12 and 21 when such a restriction constitutes a necessary measures to safeguard—
(a) national security;
(b) defence;
(c) public security;
(d) the prevention, investigation, detection and prosecution of criminal offences, or of breaches of ethics for regulated professions;
(e) an important economic or financial interest of a Member State or of the European Union, including monetary, budgetary and taxation matters;
(f) a monitoring, inspection or regulatory function connected, even occasionally, with the exercise of official authority in cases referred to in (c), (d) and (e);
(g) the protection of the data subject or of the rights and freedoms of others.

2. Subject to adequate legal safeguards, in particular that the data are not used for taking measures or decisions regarding any particular individual, Member States may, where there is clearly no risk of breaching the privacy of the data subject, restrict by a legislative measure the rights provided for in Article 12 when data are processed solely for purposes of scientific research or are kept in personal form for a period which does not exceed the period necessary for the sole purpose of creating statistics.

SECTION VII
THE DATA SUBJECT'S RIGHT TO OBJECT

[3.217]
Article 14
The data subject's right to object
Member States shall grant the data subject the right—
(a) at least in the cases referred to in Article 7(e) and (f), to object at any time on compelling legitimate grounds relating to his particular situation to the processing of data relating to him, save where otherwise provided by national legislation. Where there is a justified objection, the processing instigated by the controller may no longer involve those data;
(b) to object, on request and free of charge, to the processing of personal data relating to him which the controller anticipates being processed for the purposes of direct marketing, or to be informed before personal data are disclosed for the first time to third parties or used on their behalf for the purposes of direct marketing, and to be expressly offered the right to object free of charge to such disclosures or uses.

Member States shall take the necessary measures to ensure that data subjects are aware of the existence of the right referred to in the first subparagraph of (b).

[3.218]
Article 15
Automated individual decisions
1. Member States shall grant the right to every person not to be subject to a decision which produces legal effects concerning him or significantly affects him and which is based solely on automated processing of data intended to evaluate certain personal aspects relating to him, such as his performance at work, creditworthiness, reliability, conduct, etc.

2. Subject to the other Articles of this Directive, Member States shall provide that a person may be subjected to a decision of the kind referred to in paragraph 1 if that decision—
  (a) is taken in the course of the entering into or performance of a contract, provided the request for the entering into or the performance of the contract, lodged by the data subject, has been satisfied or that there are suitable measures to safeguard his legitimate interests, such as arrangements allowing him to put his point of view; or
  (b) is authorised by a law which also lays down measures to safeguard the data subject's legitimate interests.

SECTION VIII
CONFIDENTIALITY AND SECURITY OF PROCESSING

[3.219]
Article 16
Confidentiality of processing
Any person acting under the authority of the controller or of the processor, including the processor himself, who has access to personal data must not process them except on instructions from the controller, unless he is required to do so by law.

[3.220]
Article 17
Security of processing
1. Member States shall provide that the controller must implement appropriate technical and organisational measures to protect personal data against accidental or unlawful destruction or accidental loss, alteration, unauthorised disclosure or access, in particular where the processing involves the transmission of data over a network, and against all other unlawful forms of processing.

Having regard to the state of the art and the cost of their implementation, such measures shall ensure a level of security appropriate to the risks represented by the processing and the nature of the data to be protected.

2. The Member States shall provide that the controller must, where processing is carried out on his behalf, choose a processor providing sufficient guarantees in respect of the technical security measures and organisational measures governing the processing to be carried out, and must ensure compliance with those measures.

3. The carrying out of processing by way of a processor must be governed by a contract or legal act binding the processor to the controller and stipulating in particular that—
- the processor shall act only on instructions from the controller,
- the obligations set out in paragraph 1, as defined by the law of the Member State in which the processor is established, shall also be incumbent on the processor.

4. For the purposes of keeping proof, the parts of the contract or the legal act relating to data protection and the requirements relating to the measures referred to in paragraph 1 shall be in writing or in another equivalent form.

SECTION IX
NOTIFICATION

[3.221]
Article 18
Obligation to notify the supervisory authority
1. Member States shall provide that the controller or his representative, if any, must notify the supervisory authority referred to in Article 28 before carrying out any wholly or partly automatic processing operation or set of such operations intended to serve a single purpose or several related purposes.

2. Member States may provide for the simplification of or exemption from notification only in the following cases and under the following conditions—
- where, for categories of processing operations which are unlikely, taking account of the data to be processed, to affect adversely the rights and freedoms of data subjects, they specify the purposes of the processing, the data or categories of data undergoing processing, the category or categories of data subject, the recipients or categories of recipient to whom the data are to be disclosed and the length of time the data are to be stored, and/or
- where the controller, in compliance with the national law which governs him, appoints a personal data protection official, responsible in particular—
  - for ensuring in an independent manner the internal application of the national provisions taken pursuant to this Directive
  - for keeping the register of processing operations carried out by the controller, containing the items of information referred to in Article 21(2),

  thereby ensuring that the rights and freedoms of the data subjects are unlikely to be adversely affected by the processing operations.

3. Member States may provide that paragraph 1 does not apply to processing whose sole purpose is the keeping of a register which according to laws or regulations is intended to provide information to the public and which is open to consultation either by the public in general or by any person demonstrating a legitimate interest.

4. Member States may provide for an exemption from the obligation to notify or a simplification of the notification in the case of processing operations referred to in Article 8(2)(d).

5. Member States may stipulate that certain or all non-automatic processing operations involving personal data shall be notified, or provide for these processing operations to be subject to simplified notification.

[3.222]
Article 19
Contents of notification

1. Member States shall specify the information to be given in the notification. It shall include at least—

(a) the name and address of the controller and of his representative, if any;
(b) the purpose or purposes of the processing;
(c) a description of the category or categories of data subject and of the data or categories of data relating to them;
(d) the recipients or categories of recipient to whom the data might be disclosed;
(e) proposed transfers of data to third countries;
(f) a general description allowing a preliminary assessment to be made of the appropriateness of the measures taken pursuant to Article 17 to ensure security of processing.

2. Member States shall specify the procedures under which any change affecting the information referred to in paragraph 1 must be notified to the supervisory authority.

[3.223]
Article 20
Prior checking

1. Member States shall determine the processing operations likely to present specific risks to the rights and freedoms of data subjects and shall check that these processing operations are examined prior to the start thereof.

2. Such prior checks shall be carried out by the supervisory authority following receipt of a notification from the controller or by the data protection official, who, in cases of doubt, must consult the supervisory authority.

3. Member States may also carry out such checks in the context of preparation either of a measure of the national parliament or of a measure based on such a legislative measure, which define the nature of the processing and lay down appropriate safeguards.

[3.224]
Article 21
Publicising of processing operations

1. Member States shall take measures to ensure that processing operations are publicised.

2. Member States shall provide that a register of processing operations notified in accordance with Article 18 shall be kept by the supervisory authority.

The register shall contain at least the information listed in Article 19(1)(a) to (e).

The register may be inspected by any person.

3. Member States shall provide, in relation to processing operations not subject to notification, that controllers or another body appointed by the Member States make available at least the information referred to in Article 19(1)(a) to (e) in an appropriate form to any person on request.

Member States may provide that this provision does not apply to processing whose sole purpose is the keeping of a register which according to laws or regulations is intended to provide information to the public and which is open to consultation either by the public in general or by any person who can provide proof of a legitimate interest.

CHAPTER III
JUDICIAL REMEDIES, LIABILITY AND SANCTIONS

[3.225]
Article 22
Remedies

Without prejudice to any administrative remedy for which provision may be made, *inter alia* before the supervisory authority referred to in Article 28, prior to referral to the judicial authority, Member States shall provide for the right of every person to a judicial remedy for any breach of the rights guaranteed him by the national law applicable to the processing in question.

[3.226]
Article 23
Liability

1. Member States shall provide that any person who has suffered damage as a result of an unlawful processing operation or of any act incompatible with the national provisions adopted pursuant to this Directive is entitled to receive compensation from the controller for the damage suffered.
2. The controller may be exempted from this liability, in whole or in part, if he proves that he is not responsible for the event giving rise to the damage.

[3.227]
Article 24
Sanctions

The Member States shall adopt suitable measures to ensure the full implementation of the provisions of this Directive and shall in particular lay down the sanctions to be imposed in case of infringement of the provisions adopted pursuant to this Directive.

CHAPTER IV
TRANSFER OF PERSONAL DATA TO THIRD COUNTRIES

[3.228]
Article 25
Principles

1. The Member States shall provide that the transfer to a third country of personal data which are undergoing processing or are intended for processing after transfer may take place only if, without prejudice to compliance with the national provisions adopted pursuant to the other provisions of this Directive, the third country in question ensures an adequate level of protection.
2. The adequacy of the level of protection afforded by a third country shall be assessed in the light of all the circumstances surrounding a data transfer operation or set of data transfer operations; particular consideration shall be given to the nature of the data, the purpose and duration of the proposed processing operation or operations, the country of origin and country of final destination, the rules of law, both general and sectoral, in force in the third country in question and the professional rules and security measures which are complied with in that country.
3. The Member States and the Commission shall inform each other of cases where they consider that a third country does not ensure an adequate level of protection within the meaning of paragraph 2.
4. Where the Commission finds, under the procedure provided for in Article 31(2), that a third country does not ensure an adequate level of protection within the meaning of paragraph 2 of this Article, Member States shall take the measures necessary to prevent any transfer of data of the same type to the third country in question.
5. At the appropriate time, the Commission shall enter into negotiations with a view to remedying the situation resulting from the finding made pursuant to paragraph 4.
6. The Commission may find, in accordance with the procedure referred to in Article 31(2), that a third country ensures an adequate level of protection within the meaning of paragraph 2 of this Article, by reason of its domestic law or of the international commitments it has entered into, particularly upon conclusion of the negotiations referred to in paragraph 5, for the protection of the private lives and basic freedoms and rights of individuals.

Member States shall take the measures necessary to comply with the Commission's decision.

[3.229]
Article 26
Derogations

1. By way of derogation from Article 25 and save where otherwise provided by domestic law governing particular cases, Member States shall provide that a transfer or a set of transfers of personal data to a third country which does not ensure an adequate level of protection within the meaning of Article 25(2) may take place on condition that—
   (a) the data subject has given his consent unambiguously to the proposed transfer; or
   (b) the transfer is necessary for the performance of a contract between the data subject and the controller or the implementation of precontractual measures taken in response to the data subject's request; or
   (c) the transfer is necessary for the conclusion or performance of a contract concluded in the interest of the data subject between the controller and a third party; or
   (d) the transfer is necessary or legally required on important public interest grounds, or for the establishment, exercise or defence of legal claims; or
   (e) the transfer is necessary in order to protect the vital interests of the data subject; or

(f) the transfer is made from a register which according to laws or regulations is intended to provide information to the public and which is open to consultation either by the public in general or by any person who can demonstrate legitimate interest, to the extent that the conditions laid down in law for consultation are fulfilled in the particular case.

2. Without prejudice to paragraph 1, a Member State may authorise a transfer or a set of transfers of personal data to a third country which does not ensure an adequate level of protection within the meaning of Article 25(2), where the controller adduces adequate safeguards with respect to the protection of the privacy and fundamental rights and freedoms of individuals and as regards the exercise of the corresponding rights; such safeguards may in particular result from appropriate contractual clauses.

3. The Member State shall inform the Commission and the other Member States of the authorisations it grants pursuant to paragraph 2.

If a Member State or the Commission objects on justified grounds involving the protection of the privacy and fundamental rights and freedoms of individuals, the Commission shall take appropriate measures in accordance with the procedure laid down in Article 31(2).

Member States shall take the necessary measures to comply with the Commission's decision.

4. Where the Commission decides, in accordance with the procedure referred to in Article 31(2), that certain standard contractual clauses offer sufficient safeguards as required by paragraph 2, Member States shall take the necessary measures to comply with the Commission's decision.

CHAPTER V
CODES OF CONDUCT

[3.230]
Article 27

1. The Member States and the Commission shall encourage the drawing up of codes of conduct intended to contribute to the proper implementation of the national provisions adopted by the Member States pursuant to this Directive, taking account of the specific features of the various sectors.

2. Member States shall make provision for trade associations and other bodies representing other categories of controllers which have drawn up draft national codes or which have the intention of amending or extending existing national codes to be able to submit them to the opinion of the national authority.

Member States shall make provision for this authority to ascertain, among other things, whether the drafts submitted to it are in accordance with the national provisions adopted pursuant to this Directive. If it sees fit, the authority shall seek the views of data subjects or their representatives.

3. Draft Community codes, and amendments or extensions to existing Community codes, may be submitted to the Working Party referred to in Article 29. This Working Party shall determine, among other things, whether the drafts submitted to it are in accordance with the national provisions adopted pursuant to this Directive. If it sees fit, the authority shall seek the views of data subjects or their representatives. The Commission may ensure appropriate publicity for the codes which have been approved by the Working Party.

CHAPTER VI
SUPERVISORY AUTHORITY AND WORKING PARTY ON THE PROTECTION OF INDIVIDUALS WITH REGARD TO THE PROCESSING OF PERSONAL DATA

[3.231]
Article 28
Supervisory authority

1. Each Member State shall provide that one or more public authorities are responsible for monitoring the application within its territory of the provisions adopted by the Member States pursuant to this Directive.

These authorities shall act with complete independence in exercising the functions entrusted to them.

2. Each Member State shall provide that the supervisory authorities are consulted when drawing up administrative measures or regulations relating to the protection of individuals' rights and freedoms with regard to the processing of personal data.

3. Each authority shall in particular be endowed with—

— investigative powers, such as powers of access to data forming the subject-matter of processing operations and powers to collect all the information necessary for the performance of its supervisory duties,

— effective powers of intervention, such as, for example, that of delivering opinions before processing operations are carried out, in accordance with Article 20, and ensuring appropriate publication of such opinions, of ordering the blocking, erasure or destruction of data, of imposing a temporary or definitive ban on processing, of warning or admonishing the controller, or that of referring the matter to national parliaments or other political institutions,

— the power to engage in legal proceedings where the national provisions adopted pursuant to this Directive have been violated or to bring these violations to the attention of the judicial authorities.

Decisions by the supervisory authority which give rise to complaints may be appealed against through the courts.

4. Each supervisory authority shall hear claims lodged by any person, or by an association representing that person, concerning the protection of his rights and freedoms in regard to the processing of personal data. The person concerned shall be informed of the outcome of the claim.

Each supervisory authority shall, in particular, hear claims for checks on the lawfulness of data processing lodged by any person when the national provisions adopted pursuant to Article 13 of this Directive apply. The person shall at any rate be informed that a check has taken place.

5. Each supervisory authority shall draw up a report on its activities at regular intervals. The report shall be made public.

6. Each supervisory authority is competent, whatever the national law applicable to the processing in question, to exercise, on the territory of its own Member State, the powers conferred on it in accordance with paragraph 3. Each authority may be requested to exercise its powers by an authority of another Member State.

The supervisory authorities shall cooperate with one another to the extent necessary for the performance of their duties, in particular by exchanging all useful information.

7. Member States shall provide that the members and staff of the supervisory authority, even after their employment has ended, are to be subject to a duty of professional secrecy with regard to confidential information to which they have access.

[3.232]
Article 29
Working Party on the Protection of Individuals with regard to the Processing of Personal Data

1. A Working Party on the Protection of Individuals with regard to the Processing of Personal Data, hereinafter referred to as "the Working Party", is hereby set up.

It shall have advisory status and act independently.

2. The Working Party shall be composed of a representative of the supervisory authority or authorities designated by each Member State and of a representative of the authority or authorities established for the Community institutions and bodies, and of a representative of the Commission.

Each member of the Working Party shall be designated by the institution, authority or authorities which he represents. Where a Member State has designated more than one supervisory authority, they shall nominate a joint representative. The same shall apply to the authorities established for Community institutions and bodies.

3. The Working Party shall take decisions by a simple majority of the representatives of the supervisory authorities.

4. The Working Party shall elect its chairman. The chairman's term of office shall be two years. His appointment shall be renewable.

5. The Working Party's secretariat shall be provided by the Commission.

6. The Working Party shall adopt its own rules of procedure.

7. The Working Party shall consider items placed on its agenda by its chairman, either on his own initiative or at the request of a representative of the supervisory authorities or at the Commission's request.

[3.233]
Article 30

1. The Working Party shall—
   (a) examine any question covering the application of the national measures adopted under this Directive in order to contribute to the uniform application of such measures;
   (b) give the Commission an opinion on the level of protection in the Community and in third countries;
   (c) advise the Commission on any proposed amendment of this Directive, on any additional or specific measures to safeguard the rights and freedoms of natural persons with regard to the processing of personal data and on any other proposed Community measures affecting such rights and freedoms;
   (d) give an opinion on codes of conduct drawn up at Community level.

2. If the Working Party finds that divergences likely to affect the equivalence of protection for persons with regard to the processing of personal data in the Community are arising between the laws or practices of Member States, it shall inform the Commission accordingly.

3. The Working Party may, on its own initiative, make recommendations on all matters relating to the protection of persons with regard to the processing of personal data in the Community.

4. The Working Party's opinions and recommendations shall be forwarded to the Commission and to the committee referred to in Article 31.

5. The Commission shall inform the Working Party of the action it has taken in response to its opinions and recommendations. It shall do so in a report which shall also be forwarded to the European Parliament and the Council. The report shall be made public.
6. The Working Party shall draw up an annual report on the situation regarding the protection of natural persons with regard to the processing of personal data in the Community and in third countries, which it shall transmit to the Commission, the European Parliament and the Council. The report shall be made public.

CHAPTER VII
COMMUNITY IMPLEMENTING MEASURES

[3.234]
[Article 31
The Committee
1. The Commission shall be assisted by a committee.
2. Where reference is made to this Article, Articles 4 and 7 of Decision 1999/468/EC(36) shall apply, having regard to the provisions of Article 8 thereof.
The period laid down in Article 4(3) of Decision 1999/468/EC shall be set at three months.
3. The Committee shall adopt its rules of procedure.]

NOTES
Substituted by European Parliament and Council Regulation 1882/2003/EC, Art 2, Annex II, para 18.

FINAL PROVISIONS

[3.235]
Article 32
1. Member States shall bring into force the laws, regulations and administrative provisions necessary to comply with this Directive at the latest at the end of a period of three years from the date of its adoption.
When Member States adopt these measures, they shall contain a reference to this Directive or be accompanied by such reference on the occasion of their official publication. The methods of making such reference shall be laid down by the Member States.
2. Member States shall ensure that processing already under way on the date the national provisions adopted pursuant to this Directive enter into force, is brought into conformity with these provisions within three years of this date.
By way of derogation from the preceding subparagraph, Member States may provide that the processing of data already held in manual filing systems on the date of entry into force of the national provisions adopted in implementation of this Directive shall be brought into conformity with Articles 6, 7 and 8 of this Directive within 12 years of the date on which it is adopted. Member States shall, however, grant the data subject the right to obtain, at his request and in particular at the time of exercising his right of access, the rectification, erasure or blocking of data which are incomplete, inaccurate or stored in a way incompatible with the legitimate purposes pursued by the controller.
3. By way of derogation from paragraph 2, Member States may provide, subject to suitable safeguards, that data kept for the sole purpose of historical research need not be brought into conformity with Articles 6, 7 and 8 of this Directive.
4. Member States shall communicate to the Commission the text of the provisions of domestic law which they adopt in the field covered by this Directive.

[3.236]
Article 33
The Commission shall report to the Council and the European Parliament at regular intervals, starting not later than three years after the date referred to in Article 32(1), on the implementation of this Directive, attaching to its report, if necessary, suitable proposals for amendments. The report shall be made public.
The Commission shall examine, in particular, the application of this Directive to the data processing of sound and image data relating to natural persons and shall submit any appropriate proposals which prove to be necessary, taking account of developments in information technology and in the light of the state of progress in the information society.

[3.237]
Article 34
This Directive is addressed to the Member States.

COUNCIL DIRECTIVE

(96/34/EC)

of 3 June 1996

on the framework agreement on parental leave concluded by UNICE, CEEP and the ETUC (Note)

[3.238]

NOTES

Date of publication in OJ: OJ L145, 19.6.1996, p 4.

This Directive was repealed and replaced by Council Directive 2010/18/EU at **[3.625]**, with effect from 8 March 2012 (see Art 4 thereof at **[3.629]**).

DIRECTIVE OF THE EUROPEAN PARLIAMENT AND OF THE COUNCIL

(96/71/EC)

of 16 December 1996

concerning the posting of workers in the framework of the provision of services

NOTES

Date of publication in OJ: OJ L18, 21.1.1997, p 1.

[3.239]

THE EUROPEAN PARLIAMENT AND THE COUNCIL OF THE EUROPEAN UNION,

Having regard to the Treaty establishing the European Community, and in particular Articles 57(2) and 66 thereof,

Having regard to the proposal from the Commission,[1]

Having regard to the opinion of the Economic and Social Committee,[2]

Acting in accordance with the procedure laid down in Article 189b of the Treaty,[3]

(1) Whereas, pursuant to Article 3(c) of the Treaty, the abolition, as between Member States, of obstacles to the free movement of persons and services constitutes one of the objectives of the Community;

(2) Whereas, for the provision of services, any restrictions based on nationality or residence requirements are prohibited under the Treaty with effect from the end of the transitional period;

(3) Whereas the completion of the internal market offers a dynamic environment for the transnational provision of services, prompting a growing number of undertakings to post employees abroad temporarily to perform work in the territory of a Member State other than the State in which they are habitually employed;

(4) Whereas the provision of services may take the form either of performance of work by an undertaking on its account and under its direction, under a contract concluded between that undertaking and the party for whom the services are intended, or of the hiring-out of workers for use by an undertaking in the framework of a public or a private contract;

(5) Whereas any such promotion of the transnational provision of services requires a climate of fair competition and measures guaranteeing respect for the rights of workers;

(6) Whereas the transnationalization of the employment relationship raises problems with regard to the legislation applicable to the employment relationship; whereas it is in the interests of the parties to lay down the terms and conditions governing the employment relationship envisaged;

(7) Whereas the Rome Convention of 19 June 1980 on the law applicable to contractual obligations,[4] signed by 12 Member States, entered into force on 1 April 1991 in the majority of Member States;

(8) Whereas Article 3 of that Convention provides, as a general rule, for the free choice of law made by the parties; whereas, in the absence of choice, the contract is to be governed, according to Article 6(2), by the law of the country, in which the employee habitually carries out his work in performance of the contract, even if he is temporarily employed in another country, or, if the employee does not habitually carry out his work in any one country, by the law of the country in which the place of business through which he was engaged is situated, unless it appears from the circumstances as a whole that the contract is more closely connected with another country, in which case the contract is to be governed by the law of that country;

(9) Whereas, according to Article 6(1) of the said Convention, the choice of law made by the

parties is not to have the result of depriving the employee of the protection afforded to him by the mandatory rules of the law which would be applicable under paragraph 2 of that Article in the absence of choice;

(10) Whereas Article 7 of the said Convention lays down, subject to certain conditions, that effect may be given, concurrently with the law declared applicable, to the mandatory rules of the law of another country, in particular the law of the Member State within whose territory the worker is temporarily posted;

(11) Whereas, according to the principle of precedence of Community law laid down in its Article 20, the said Convention does not affect the application of provisions which, in relation to a particular matter, lay down choice-of-law rules relating to contractual obligations and which are or will be contained in acts of the institutions of the European Communities or in national laws harmonized in implementation of such acts;

(12) Whereas Community law does not preclude Member States from applying their legislation, or collective agreements entered into by employers and labour, to any person who is employed, even temporarily, within their territory, although his employer is established in another Member State; whereas Community law does not forbid Member Stares to guarantee the observance of those rules by the appropriate means;

(13) Whereas the laws of the Member States must be coordinated in order to lay down a nucleus of mandatory rules for minimum protection to be observed in the host country by employers who post workers to perform temporary work in the territory of a Member State where the services are provided; whereas such coordination can be achieved only by means of Community law;

(14) Whereas a 'hard core' of clearly defined protective rules should be observed by the provider of the services notwithstanding the duration of the worker's posting;

(15) Whereas it should be laid down that, in certain clearly defined cases of assembly and/or installation of goods, the provisions on minimum rates of pay and minimum paid annual holidays do nor apply;

(16) Whereas there should also be some flexibility in application of the provisions concerning minimum rates of pay and the minimum length of paid annual holidays; whereas, when the length of the posting is not more than one month, Member States may, under certain conditions, derogate from the provisions concerning minimum rates of pay or provide for the possibility of derogation by means of collective agreements; whereas, where the amount of work to be done is not significant, Member States may derogate from the provisions concerning minimum rates of pay and the minimum length of paid annual holidays;

(17) Whereas the mandatory rules for minimum protection in force in the host country must not prevent the application of terms and conditions of employment which are more favourable to workers;

(18) Whereas the principle that undertakings established outside the Community must not receive more favourable treatment than undertakings established in the territory of a Member State should be upheld;

(19) Whereas, without prejudice to other provisions of Community law, this Directive does not entail the obligation to give legal recognition to the existence of temporary employment undertakings, nor does it prejudice the application by Member States of their laws concerning the hiring-out of workers and temporary employment undertakings to undertakings not established in their territory but operating therein in the framework of the provision of services;

(20) Whereas this Directive does not affect either the agreements concluded by the Community with third countries or the laws of Member States concerning the access to their territory of third-country providers of services; whereas this Directive is also without prejudice to national laws relating to the entry, residence and access to employment of third-country workers;

(21) Whereas Council Regulation (EEC) No 1408/71 of 14 June 1971 on the application of social security schemes to employed persons and their families moving within the Community[5] lays down the provisions applicable with regard to social security benefits and contributions;

(22) Whereas this Directive is without prejudice to the law of the Member States concerning collective action to defend the interests of trades and professions;

(23) Whereas competent bodies in different Member States must cooperate with each other in the application of this Directive; whereas Member States must provide for appropriate remedies in the event of failure to comply with this Directive;

(24) Whereas it is necessary to guarantee proper application of this Directive and to that end to make provision for close collaboration between the Commission and the Member States;

(25) Whereas five years after adoption of this Directive at the latest the Commission must review the detailed rules for implementing this Directive with a view to proposing, where appropriate, the necessary amendments,

NOTES

1 OJ C225, 30.8.91, p 6 and OJ C187, 9.7.93, p 5.

2 OJ C49, 24.2.92, p 41.

3 Opinion of the European Parliament of 10 February 1993 (OJ C72, 15.3.93, p 78), Council common position of 3 June 1996 (OJ C220, 29.7.96, p 1) and Decision of the European Parliament of 18 September 1996 (not yet published in the Official Journal). Council Decision of 24 September 1996.

4 OJ L266, 9.10.80, p 1.

5 OJ L149, 5.7.71, p 2; Special Edition 1971 (II), p 416. Regulation as last amended by Regulation 3096/95/EC (OJ L335, 30.12.95, p 10).

HAVE ADOPTED THIS DIRECTIVE—

[3.240]
Article 1
Scope

1. This Directive shall apply to undertakings established in a Member State which, in the framework of the transnational provision of services, post workers, in accordance with paragraph 3, to the territory of a Member State.
2. This Directive shall not apply to merchant navy undertakings as regards seagoing personnel.
3. This Directive shall apply to the extent that the undertakings referred to in paragraph 1 take one of the following transnational measures—
   (a) post workers to the territory of a Member State on their account and under their direction, under a contract concluded between the undertaking making the posting and the party for whom the services are intended, operating in that Member State, provided there is an employment relationship between the undertaking making the posting and the worker during the period of posting; or
   (b) post workers to an establishment or to an undertaking owned by the group in the territory of a Member State, provided there is an employment relationship between the undertaking making the posting and the worker during the period of posting; or
   (c) being a temporary employment undertaking or placement agency, hire out a worker to a user undertaking established or operating in the territory of a Member State, provided there is an employment relationship between the temporary employment undertaking or placement agency and the worker during the period of posting.
4. Undertakings established in a non-member State must not be given more favourable treatment than undertakings established in a Member State.

[3.241]
Article 2
Definition

1. For the purposes of this Directive, 'posted worker' means a worker who, for a limited period, carries out his work in the territory of a Member State other than the State in which he normally works.
2. For the purposes of this Directive, the definition of a worker is that which applies in the law of the Member State to whose territory the worker is posted.

[3.242]
Article 3
Terms and conditions of employment

1. Member States shall ensure that, whatever the law applicable to the employment relationship, the undertakings referred to in Article 1(1) guarantee workers posted to their territory the terms and conditions of employment covering the following matters which, in the Member State where the work is carried out, are laid down—
   — by law, regulation or administrative provision, and/or
   — by collective agreements or arbitration awards which have been declared universally applicable within the meaning of paragraph 8, insofar as they concern the activities referred to in the Annex—
      (a) maximum work periods and minimum rest periods;
      (b) minimum paid annual holidays;
      (c) the minimum rates of pay, including overtime rates; this point does not apply to supplementary occupational retirement pension schemes;
      (d) the conditions of hiring-out of workers, in particular the supply of workers by temporary employment undertakings;
      (e) health, safety and hygiene at work;
      (f) protective measures with regard to the terms and conditions of employment of pregnant women or women who have recently given birth, of children and of young people;

(g) equality of treatment between men and women and other provisions on non-discrimination.

For the purposes of this Directive, the concept of minimum rates of pay referred to in paragraph 1(c) is defined by the national law and/or practice of the Member State to whose territory the worker is posted.

2. In the case of initial assembly and/or first installation of goods where this is an integral part of a contract for the supply of goods and necessary for taking the goods supplied into use and carried out by the skilled and/or specialist workers of the supplying undertaking, the first subparagraph of paragraph 1(b) and (c) shall not apply, if the period of posting does not exceed eight days.

This provision shall not apply to activities in the field of building work listed in the Annex.

3. Member States may, after consulting employers and labour, in accordance with the traditions and practices of each Member State, decide not to apply the first subparagraph of paragraph 1(c) in the cases referred to in Article 1(3)(a) and (b) when the length of the posting does not exceed one month.

4. Member States may, in accordance with national laws and/or practices, provide that exemptions may be made from the first subparagraph of paragraph 1(c) in the cases referred to in Article 1(3)(a) and (b) and from a decision by a Member State within the meaning of paragraph 3 of this Article, by means of collective agreements within the meaning of paragraph 8 of this Article, concerning one or more sectors of activity, where the length of the posting does not exceed one month.

5. Member States may provide for exemptions to be granted from the first subparagraph of paragraph 1(b) and (c) in the cases referred to in Article 1(3)(a) and (b) on the grounds that the amount of work to be done is not significant.

Member States availing themselves of the option referred to in the first subparagraph shall lay down the criteria which the work to be performed must meet in order to be considered as 'non-significant'.

6. The length of the posting shall be calculated on the basis of a reference period of one year from the beginning of the posting.

For the purpose of such calculations, account shall be taken of any previous periods for which the post has been filled by a posted worker.

7. Paragraphs 1 to 6 shall not prevent application of terms and conditions of employment which are more favourable to workers.

Allowances specific to the posting shall be considered to be part of the minimum wage, unless they are paid in reimbursement of expenditure actually incurred on account of the posting, such as expenditure on travel, board and lodging.

8. 'Collective agreements or arbitration awards which have been declared universally applicable' means collective agreements or arbitration awards which must be observed by all undertakings in the geographical area and in the profession or industry concerned.

In the absence of a system for declaring collective agreements or arbitration awards to be of universal application within the meaning of the first subparagraph, Member States may, if they so decide, base themselves on—

— collective agreements or arbitration awards which are generally applicable to all similar undertakings in the geographical area and in the profession or industry concerned, and/or
— collective agreements which have been concluded by the most representative employers' and labour organizations at national level and which are applied throughout national territory,

provided that their application to the undertakings referred to in Article 1(1) ensures equality of treatment on matters listed in the first subparagraph of paragraph 1 of this Article between those undertakings and the other undertakings referred to in this subparagraph which are in a similar position.

Equality of treatment, within the meaning of this Article, shall be deemed to exist where national undertakings in a similar position—

— are subject, in the place in question or in the sector concerned, to the same obligations as posting undertakings as regards the matters listed in the first subparagraph of paragraph 1, and
— are required to fulfil such obligations with the same effects.

9. Member States may provide that the undertakings referred to in Article 1(1) must guarantee workers referred to in Article 1(3)(c) the terms and conditions which apply to temporary workers in the Member State where the work is carried out.

10. This Directive shall not preclude the application by Member States, in compliance with the Treaty, to national undertakings and to the undertakings of other States, on a basis of equality of treatment, of—

— terms and conditions of employment on matters other than those referred to in the first subparagraph of paragraph 1 in the case of public policy provisions,
— terms and conditions of employment laid down in the collective agreements or arbitration awards within the meaning of paragraph 8 and concerning activities other than those referred to in the Annex.

[3.243]
Article 4
Cooperation on information

1. For the purposes of implementing this Directive, Member States shall, in accordance with national legislation and/or practice, designate one or more liaison offices or one or more competent national bodies.

2. Member States shall make provision for cooperation between the public authorities which, in accordance with national legislation, are responsible for monitoring the terms and conditions of employment referred to in Article 3. Such cooperation shall in particular consist in replying to reasoned requests from those authorities for information on the transnational hiring-out of workers, including manifest abuses or possible cases of unlawful transnational activities.

The Commission and the public authorities referred to in the first subparagraph shall cooperate closely in order to examine any difficulties which might arise in the application of Article 3(10).

Mutual administrative assistance shall be provided free of charge.

3. Each Member State shall take the appropriate measures to make the information on the terms and conditions of employment referred to in Article 3 generally available.

4. Each Member State shall notify the other Member States and the Commission of the liaison offices and/or competent bodies referred to in paragraph 1.

[3.244]
Article 5
Measures

Member States shall take appropriate measures in the event of failure to comply with this Directive.

They shall in particular ensure that adequate procedures are available to workers and/or their representatives for the enforcement of obligations under this Directive.

[3.245]
Article 6
Jurisdiction

In order to enforce the right to the terms and conditions of employment guaranteed in Article 3, judicial proceedings may be instituted in the Member State in whose territory the worker is or was posted, without prejudice, where applicable, to the right, under existing international conventions on jurisdiction, to institute proceedings in another State.

[3.246]
Article 7
Implementation

Member States shall adopt the laws, regulations and administrative provisions necessary to comply with this Directive by 16 December 1999 at the latest. They shall forthwith inform the Commission thereof.

When Member States adopt these provisions, they shall contain a reference to this Directive or shall be accompanied by such reference on the occasion of their official publication. The methods of making such reference shall be laid down by Member States.

[3.247]
Article 8
Commission review

By 16 December 2001 at the latest, the Commission shall review the operation of this Directive with a view to proposing the necessary amendments to the Council where appropriate.

[3.248]
Article 9

This Directive is addressed to the Member States.

ANNEX

[3.249]

The activities mentioned in Article 3(1), second indent, include all building work relating to the construction, repair, upkeep, alteration or demolition of buildings, and in particular the following work—

1. excavation

2. earthmoving

3. actual building work

4. assembly and dismantling of prefabricated elements

5. fitting out or installation

6. alterations
7. renovation
8. repairs
9. dismantling
10. demolition
11. maintenance
12. upkeep, painting and cleaning work
13. improvements.

COUNCIL DIRECTIVE

(97/81/EC)

of 15 December 1997

concerning the Framework Agreement on part-time work concluded by UNICE, CEEP and the ETUC

NOTES

Date of publication in OJ: OJ L14, 20.1.1998, p 9.

This Directive implements a Framework Agreement made by the Social Partners (the Union of Industrial and Employers' Confederations of Europe (UNICE), since renamed Business Europe), the European Centre of Enterprises with Public Participation (CEEP), and the European Trade Union Confederation (ETUC) in accordance with Art 4 of the Agreement on Social Policy annexed to Protocol 14 to the Treaty of Union 1992 and, therefore, did not bind the United Kingdom. It was subsequently extended to the UK by Directive 98/23/EC with a required date of transposition of 7 April 2000 (see Art 2(1A) of this Directive at **[3.252]**). For the domestic implementation of this Directive as extended to the UK by Directive 98/23/EC, see the Employment Relations Act 1999, ss 19–21 at **[1.1197]–[1.1199]** and the Part-time Workers (Prevention of Less Favourable Treatment) Regulations 2000, SI 2000/1551 at **[2.575]**.

[3.250]

THE COUNCIL OF THE EUROPEAN UNION,

Having regard to the Agreement on social policy annexed to the Protocol (No 14) on social policy, annexed to the Treaty establishing the European Community, and in particular Article 4(2) thereof,

Having regard to the proposal from the Commission,

(1) Whereas on the basis of the Protocol on social policy annexed to the Treaty establishing the European Community, the Member States, with the exception of the United Kingdom of Great Britain and Northern Ireland (hereinafter referred to as 'the Member States'), wishing to continue along the path laid down in the 1989 Social Charter, have concluded an agreement on social policy;

(2) Whereas management and labour (the social partners) may, in accordance with Article 4(2) of the Agreement on social policy, request jointly that agreements at Community level be implemented by a Council decision on a proposal from the Commission;

(3) Whereas point 7 of the Community Charter of the Fundamental Social Rights of Workers provides, *inter alia*, that 'the completion of the internal market must lead to an improvement in the living and working conditions of workers in the European Community. This process must result from an approximation of these conditions while the improvement is being maintained, as regards in particular (. . .) forms of employment other than open-ended contracts, such as fixed-term contracts, part-time working, temporary work and seasonal work';

(4) Whereas the Council has not reached a decision on the proposal for a Directive on certain employment relationships with regard to distortions of competition,[1] as amended,[2] nor on the proposal for a Directive on certain employment relationships with regard to working conditions;[3]

(5) Whereas the conclusions of the Essen European Council stressed the need to take measures to promote employment and equal opportunities for women and men, and called for measures with a view to increasing the employment-intensiveness of growth, in particular by a more flexible organization of work in a way which fulfils both the wishes of employees and the requirements of competition;

(6) Whereas the Commission, in accordance with Article 3(2) of the Agreement on social policy, has consulted management and labour on the possible direction of Community action with regard to flexible working time and job security;

(7) Whereas the Commission, considering after such consultation that Community action was desirable, once again consulted management and labour at Community level on the substance of the

envisaged proposal in accordance with Article 3(3) of the said Agreement;

(8) Whereas the general cross-industry organizations, the Union of Industrial and Employer's Confederations of Europe (UNICE), the European Centre of Enterprises with Public Participation (CEEP) and the European Trade Union Confederation (ETUC) informed the Commission in their joint letter of 19 June 1996 of their desire to initiate the procedure provided for in Article 4 of the Agreement on social policy; whereas they asked the Commission, in a joint letter dated 12 March 1997, for a further three months; whereas the Commission complied with this request;

(9) Whereas the said cross-industry organizations concluded, on 6 June 1997, a Framework Agreement on part-time work; whereas they forwarded to the Commission their joint request to implement this Framework Agreement by a Council decision on a proposal from the Commission, in accordance with Article 4(2) of the said Agreement;

(10) Whereas the Council, in its Resolution of 6 December 1994 on prospects for a European Union social policy: contribution to economic and social convergence in the Union,[4] asked management and labour to make use of the opportunities for concluding agreements, since they are as a rule closer to social reality and to social problems;

(11) Whereas the signatory parties wished to conclude a framework agreement on part-time work setting out the general principles and minimum requirements for part-time working; whereas they have demonstrated their desire to establish a general framework for eliminating discrimination against part-time workers and to contribute to developing the potential for part-time work on a basis which is acceptable for employers and workers alike;

(12) Whereas the social partners wished to give particular attention to part-time work, while at the same time indicating that it was their intention to consider the need for similar agreements for other flexible forms of work;

(13) Whereas, in the conclusions of the Amsterdam European Council, the Heads of State and Government of the European Union strongly welcomed the agreement concluded by the social partners on part-time work;

(14) Whereas the proper instrument for implementing the Framework Agreement is a Directive within the meaning of Article 189 of the Treaty; whereas it therefore binds the Member States as to the result to be achieved, whilst leaving national authorities the choice of form and methods;

(15) Whereas, in accordance with the principles of subsidiarity and proportionality as set out in Article 3(b) of the Treaty, the objectives of this Directive cannot be sufficiently achieved by the Member States and can therefore be better achieved by the Community; whereas this Directive does not go beyond what is necessary for the attainment of those objectives;

(16) Whereas, with regard to terms used in the Framework Agreement which are not specifically defined therein, this Directive leaves Member States free to define those terms in accordance with national law and practice, as is the case for other social policy Directives using similar terms, providing that the said definitions respect the content of the Frame-work Agreement;

(17) Whereas the Commission has drafted its proposal for a Directive, in accordance with its Communication of 14 December 1993 concerning the application of the Protocol (No 14) on social policy and its Communication of 18 September 1996 concerning the development of the social dialogue at Community level, taking into account the representative status of the signatory parties and the legality of each clause of the Framework Agreement;

(18) Whereas the Commission has drafted its proposal for a Directive in compliance with Article 2(2) of the Agreement on social policy which provides that Directives in the social policy domain 'shall avoid imposing administrative, financial and legal constraints in a way which would hold back the creation and development of small and medium-sized undertakings';

(19) Whereas the Commission, in accordance with its Communication of 14 December 1993 concerning the application of the Protocol (No 14) on social policy, informed the European Parliament by sending it the text of its proposal for a Directive containing the Framework Agreement;

(20) Whereas the Commission also informed the Economic and Social Committee;

(21) Whereas Clause 6.1 of the Framework Agreement provides that Member States and/or the social partners may maintain or introduce more favourable provisions;

(22) Whereas Clause 6.2 of the Framework Agreement provides that implementation of this Directive may not serve to justify any regression in relation to the situation which already exists in each Member State;

(23) Whereas the Community Charter of the Fundamental Social Rights of Workers recognizes the importance of the fight against all forms of discrimination, especially based on sex, colour, race, opinion and creed;

(24) Whereas Article F(2) of the Treaty on European Union states that the Union shall respect fundamental rights, as guaranteed by the European Convention for the Protection of Human Rights

and Fundamental Freedoms and as they result from the constitutional traditions common to the Member States, as general principles of Community law;

(25) Whereas the Member States may entrust the social partners, at their joint request, with the implementation of this Directive, provided that the Member States take all the necessary steps to ensure that they can at all times guarantee the results imposed by this Directive;

(26) Whereas the implementation of the Framework Agreement contributes to achieving the objectives under Article 1 of the Agreement on social policy,

NOTES

1 OJ C224, 8.9.90, p 6.

2 OJ C305, 5.12.90, p 8.

3 OJ C224, 8.9.90, p 4.

4 OJ C368, 23.12.94, p 6.

HAS ADOPTED THIS DIRECTIVE—

[3.251]
Article 1
The purpose of this Directive is to implement the Framework Agreement on part-time work concluded on 6 June 1997 between the general cross-industry organizations (UNICE, CEEP and the ETUC) annexed hereto.

[3.252]
Article 2
1. Member States shall bring into force the laws, regulations and administrative provisions necessary to comply with this Directive not later than 20 January 2000, or shall ensure that, by that date at the latest, the social partners have introduced the necessary measures by agreement, the Member States being required to take any necessary measures to enable them at any time to be in a position to guarantee the results imposed by this Directive. They shall forthwith inform the Commission thereof.

Member States may have a maximum of one more year, if necessary, to take account of special difficulties or implementation by a collective agreement.

They shall inform the Commission forthwith in such circumstances.

When Member States adopt the measures referred to in the first subparagraph, they shall contain a reference to this Directive or shall be accompanied by such reference on the occasion of their official publication. The methods of making such a reference shall be laid down by the Member States.

[1A. As regards the United Kingdom of Great Britain and Northern Ireland, the date of 20 January 2000 in paragraph 1 shall be replaced by the date of 7 April 2000.]

2. Member States shall communicate to the Commission the text of the main provisions of domestic law which they have adopted or which they adopt in the field governed by this Directive.

NOTES

Para 1A: inserted by Council Directive 98/23/EC, Art 2.

[3.253]
Article 3
This Directive shall enter into force on the day of its publication in the *Official Journal of the European Communities*.

[3.254]
Article 4
This Directive is addressed to the Member States.

ANNEX
UNION OF INDUSTRIAL AND EMPLOYERS' CONFEDERATIONS OF EUROPE
EUROPEAN TRADE UNION CONFEDERATION
EUROPEAN CENTRE OF ENTERPRISES WITH PUBLIC PARTICIPATION

FRAMEWORK AGREEMENT ON PART-TIME WORK

[3.255]
Preamble
This Framework Agreement is a contribution to the overall European strategy on employment. Part-time work has had an important impact on employment in recent years. For this reason, the parties to this agreement have given priority attention to this form of work. It is the intention of the parties to consider the need for similar agreements relating to other forms of flexible work.

Recognizing the diversity of situations in Member States and acknowledging that part-time work is a feature of employment in certain sectors and activities, this Agreement sets out the general principles and minimum requirements relating to part-time work. It illustrates the willingness of the social partners to establish a general framework for the elimination of discrimination against part-time workers and to assist the development of opportunities for part-time working on a basis acceptable to employers and workers.

This Agreement relates to employment conditions of part-time workers recognizing that matters concerning statutory social security are for decision by the Member States. In the context of the principle of non-discrimination, the parties to this Agreement have noted the Employment Declaration of the Dublin European Council of December 1996, wherein the Council inter alia emphasized the need to make social security systems more employment-friendly by 'developing social protection systems capable of adapting to new patterns of work and of providing appropriate protection to people engaged in such work'. The parties to this Agreement consider that effect should be given to this Declaration.

ETUC, UNICE and CEEP request the Commission to submit this Framework Agreement to the Council for a decision making these requirements binding in the Member States which are party to the Agreement on social policy annexed to the Protocol (No 14) on social policy annexed to the Treaty establishing the European Community.

The parties to this Agreement ask the Commission, in its proposal to implement this Agreement, to request that Member States adopt the laws, regulations and administrative provisions necessary to comply with the Council decision within a period of two years from its adoption or ensure[1] that the social partners establish the necessary measures by way of agreement by the end of this period. Member States may, if necessary to take account of particular difficulties or implementation by collective agreement, have up to a maximum of one additional year to comply with this provision.

Without prejudice to the role of national courts and the Court of Justice, the parties to this agreement request that any matter relating to the interpretation of this agreement at European level should, in the first instance, be referred by the Commission to them for an opinion.

NOTES

1 Within the meaning of Article 2(4) of the agreement on social policy of the Treaty establishing the European Community.

[3.256]

General considerations

1. Having regard to the Agreement on social policy annexed to the Protocol (No 14) on social policy annexed to the Treaty establishing the European Community, and in particular Articles 3(4) and 4(2) thereof;

2. Whereas Article 4(2) of the Agreement on social policy provides that agreements concluded at Community level may be implemented, at the joint request of the signatory parties, by a Council decision on a proposal from the Commission.

3. Whereas, in its second consultation document on flexibility of working time and security for workers, the Commission announced its intention to propose a legally binding Community measure;

4. Whereas the conclusions of the European Council meeting in Essen emphasized the need for measures to promote both employment and equal opportunities for women and men, and called for measures aimed at 'increasing the employment intensiveness of growth, in particular by more flexible organization of work in a way which fulfils both the wishes of employees and the requirements of competition';

5. Whereas the parties to this agreement attach importance to measures which would facilitate access to part-time work for men and women in order to prepare for retirement, reconcile professional and family life, and take up education and training opportunities to improve their skills and career opportunities for the mutual benefit of employers and workers and in a manner which would assist the development of enterprises;

6. Whereas this Agreement refers back to Member States and social partners for the arrangements for the application of these general principles, minimum requirements and provisions, in order to take account of the situation in each Member State;

7. Whereas this Agreement takes into consideration the need to improve social policy requirements, to enhance the competitiveness of the Community economy and to avoid imposing administrative, financial and legal constraints in a way which would hold back the creation and development of small and medium-sized undertakings;

8. Whereas the social partners are best placed to find solutions that correspond to the needs of both employers and workers and must therefore be given a special role in the implementation and application of this Agreement.

THE SIGNATORY PARTIES HAVE AGREED THE FOLLOWING:

[3.257]

Clause 1: Purpose

The purpose of this Framework Agreement is—

(a) to provide for the removal of discrimination against part-time workers and to improve the quality of part-time work;

(b) to facilitate the development of part-time work on a voluntary basis and to contribute to the flexible organization of working time in a manner which takes into account the needs of employers and workers.

Clause 2: Scope

1. This Agreement applies to part-time workers who have an employment contract or employment relationship as defined by the law, collective agreement or practice in force in each Member State.

2. Member States, after consultation with the social partners in accordance with national law, collective agreements or practice, and/or the social partners at the appropriate level in conformity with national industrial relations practice may, for objective reasons, exclude wholly or partly from the terms of this Agreement part-time workers who work on a casual basis. Such exclusions should be reviewed periodically to establish if the objective reasons for making them remain valid.

Clause 3: Definitions

For the purpose of this agreement—

1. The term 'part-time worker' refers to an employee whose normal hours of work, calculated on a weekly basis or on average over a period of employment of up to one year, are less than the normal hours of work of a comparable full-time worker.
2. The term 'comparable full-time worker' means a full-time worker in the same establishment having the same type of employment contract or relationship, who is engaged in the same or a similar work/occupation, due regard being given to other considerations which may include seniority and qualification/skills.

Where there is no comparable full-time worker in the same establishment, the comparison shall be made by reference to the applicable collective agreement or, where there is no applicable collective agreement, in accordance with national law, collective agreements or practice.

Clause 4: Principle of non-discrimination

1. In respect of employment conditions, part-time workers shall not be treated in a less favourable manner than comparable full-time workers solely because they work part time unless different treatment is justified on objective grounds.

2. Where appropriate, the principle of *pro rata temporis* shall apply.

3. The arrangements for the application of this clause shall be defined by the Member States and/or social partners, having regard to European legislation, national law, collective agreements and practice.

4. Where justified by objective reasons, Member States after consultation of the social partners in accordance with national law, collective agreements or practice and/or social partners may, where appropriate, make access to particular conditions of employment subject to a period of service, time worked or earnings qualification. Qualifications relating to access by part-time workers to particular conditions of employment should be reviewed periodically having regard to the principle of non-discrimination as expressed in Clause 4.1.

Clause 5: Opportunities for part-time work

1. In the context of Clause 1 of this Agreement and of the principle of non-discrimination between part-time and full-time workers—

(a) Member States, following consultations with the social partners in accordance with national law or practice, should identify and review obstacles of a legal or administrative nature which may limit the opportunities for part-time work and, where appropriate, eliminate them;

(b) the social partners, acting within their sphere of competence and through the procedures set out in collective agreements, should identify and review obstacles which may limit opportunities for part-time work and, where appropriate, eliminate them.

2. A worker's refusal to transfer from full-time to part-time work or vice-versa should not in itself constitute a valid reason for termination of employment, without prejudice to termination in accordance with national law, collective agreements and practice, for other reasons such as may arise from the operational requirements of the establishment concerned.

3. As far as possible, employers should give consideration to—

(a) requests by workers to transfer from full-time to part-time work that becomes available in the establishment;

(b) requests by workers to transfer from part-time to full-time work or to increase their working time should the opportunity arise;

(c) the provision of timely information on the availability of part-time and full-time positions in the establishment in order to facilitate transfers from full-time to part-time or vice versa;

(d) measures to facilitate access to part-time work at all levels of the enterprise, including skilled and managerial positions, and where appropriate, to facilitate access by part-time workers to vocational training to enhance career opportunities and occupational mobility;

(e) the provision of appropriate information to existing bodies representing workers about part-time working in the enterprise.

Clause 6: Provisions on implementation

1. Member States and/or social partners may maintain or introduce more favourable provisions than set out in this agreement.
2. Implementation of the provisions of this Agreement shall not constitute valid grounds for reducing the general level of protection afforded to workers in the field of this agreement. This does not prejudice the right of Member States and/or social partners to develop different legislative, regulatory or contractual provisions, in the light of changing circumstances, and does not prejudice the application of Clause 5.1 as long as the principle of non-discrimination as expressed in Clause 4.1 is complied with.
3. This Agreement does not prejudice the right of the social partners to conclude, at the appropriate level, including European level, agreements adapting and/or complementing the provisions of this Agreement in a manner which will take account of the specific needs of the social partners concerned.
4. This Agreement shall be without prejudice to any more specific Community provisions, and in particular Community provisions concerning equal treatment or opportunities for men and women.
5. The prevention and settlement of disputes and grievances arising from the application of this Agreement shall be dealt with in accordance with national law, collective agreements and practice.
6. The signatory parties shall review this Agreement, five years after the date of the Council decision, if requested by one of the parties to this Agreement.

COUNCIL DIRECTIVE

(98/59/EC)

of 20 July 1998

on the approximation of the laws of the Member States relating to collective redundancies

NOTES

Date of publication in OJ: OJ L225, 12.8.1998, p 16. The text of this Directive incorporates the corrigendum published in OJ L59, 27.2.2007, p 84. Note that the Recitals are reproduced as they appear in the official OJ version of this Directive.

This Directive is essentially a consolidation of Directive 75/129/EEC as amended by Directive 92/56/EEC. For the domestic implementation of those Directives, see the Trade Union and Labour Relations (Consolidation) Act 1992, ss 188–198 at **[1.453]**–**[1.464]**.

See *Harvey* E(17).

[3.258]

THE COUNCIL OF THE EUROPEAN UNION,

Having regard to the Treaty establishing the European Community, and in particular Article 100 thereof,

Having regard to the proposal from the Commission,

Having regard to the opinion of the European Parliament,[1]

Having regard to the opinion of the Economic and Social Committee,[2]

(1) Whereas for reasons of clarity and rationality Council Directive 75/129/EEC of 17 February 1975 on the approximation of the laws of the Member States relating to collective redundancies[3] should be consolidated;

(2) Whereas it is important that greater protection should be afforded to workers in the event of collective redundancies while taking into account the need for balanced economic and social development within the Community;

(3) Whereas, despite increasing convergence, differences still remain between the provisions in force in the Member States concerning the practical arrangements and procedures for such redundancies and the measures designed to alleviate the consequences of redundancy for workers;

(4) Whereas these differences can have a direct effect on the functioning of the internal market;

(5) Whereas the Council resolution of 21 January 1974 concerning a social action programme[4] made provision for a directive on the approximation of Member States' legislation on collective redundancies;

(6) Whereas the Community Charter of the fundamental social rights of workers, adopted at the European Council meeting held in Strasbourg on 9 December 1989 by the Heads of State or Government of 11 Member States, states, *inter alia*, in point 7, first paragraph, first sentence, and second paragraph; in point 17, first paragraph; and in point 18, third indent—

"7. The completion of the internal market must lead to an improvement in the living and working conditions of workers in the European Community (. . .).

The improvement must cover, where necessary, the development of certain aspects of employment regulations such as procedures for collective redundancies and those regarding bankruptcies.

(. . .)

17. Information, consultation and participation for workers must be developed along appropriate lines, taking account of the practices in force in the various Member States.

(. . .)

18. Such information, consultation and participation must be implemented in due time, particularly in the following cases—

(. . .)

(. . .)

— in cases of collective redundancy procedures;

(. . .)";

(7) Whereas this approximation must therefore be promoted while the improvement is being maintained within the meaning of Article 117 of the Treaty;

(8) Whereas, in order to calculate the number of redundancies provided for in the definition of collective redundancies within the meaning of this Directive, other forms of termination of employment contracts on the initiative of the employer should be equated to redundancies, provided that there are at least five redundancies;

(9) Whereas it should be stipulated that this Directive applies in principle also to collective redundancies resulting where the establishment's activities are terminated as a result of a judicial decision;

(10) Whereas the Member States should be given the option of stipulating that workers' representatives may call on experts on grounds of the technical complexity of the matters which are likely to be the subject of the informing and consulting;

(11) Whereas it is necessary to ensure that employers' obligations as regards information, consultation and notification apply independently of whether the decision on collective redundancies emanates from the employer or from an undertaking which controls that employer;

(12) Whereas Member States should ensure that workers' representatives and/or workers have at their disposal administrative and/or judicial procedures in order to ensure that the obligations laid down in this Directive are fulfilled;

(13) Whereas this Directive must not affect the obligations of the Member States concerning the deadlines for transposition of the Directives set out in Annex I, Part B,

NOTES

[1] OJ C210, 6.7.98.

[2] OJ C158, 26.5.97, p 11.

[3] OJ L48, 22.2.75, p 29. Directive as amended by Directive 92/56/EEC (OJ L245, 26.8.92, p 3).

[4] OJ C13, 12.2.74, p 1.

HAS ADOPTED THIS DIRECTIVE—

SECTION I
DEFINITIONS AND SCOPE

[3.259]

Article 1

1. For the purposes of this Directive—
   (a) 'collective redundancies' means dismissals effected by an employer for one or more reasons not related to the individual workers concerned where, according to the choice of the Member States, the number of redundancies is—
      (i) either, over a period of 30 days—
         — at least 10 in establishments normally employing more than 20 and less than 100 workers,
         — at least 10% of the number of workers in establishments normally employing at least 100 but less than 300 workers,
         — at least 30 in establishments normally employing 300 workers or more,
      (ii) or, over a period of 90 days, at least 20, whatever the number of workers normally employed in the establishments in question;
   (b) 'workers' representatives' means the workers' representatives provided for by the laws or practices of the Member States.

For the purpose of calculating the number of redundancies provided for in the first subparagraph of point (a), terminations of an employment contract which occur on the employer's initiative for one or more reasons not related to the individual workers concerned shall be assimilated to redundancies, provided that there are at least five redundancies.

2. This Directive shall not apply to—

(a) collective redundancies effected under contracts of employment concluded for limited periods of time or for specific tasks except where such redundancies take place prior to the date of expiry or the completion of such contracts;
(b) workers employed by public administrative bodies or by establishments governed by public law (or, in Member States where this concept is unknown, by equivalent bodies);
(c) the crews of seagoing vessels.

SECTION II
INFORMATION AND CONSULTATION

[3.260]
Article 2
1. Where an employer is contemplating collective redundancies, he shall begin consultations with the workers' representatives in good time with a view to reaching an agreement.
2. These consultations shall, at least, cover ways and means of avoiding collective redundancies or reducing the number of workers affected, and of mitigating the consequences by recourse to accompanying social measures aimed, *inter alia*, at aid for redeploying or retraining workers made redundant.

Member States may provide that the workers' representatives may call on the services of experts in accordance with national legislation and/or practice.
3. To enable workers' representatives to make constructive proposals, the employers shall in good time during the course of the consultations—
(a) supply them with all relevant information and
(b) in any event notify them in writing of—
   (i) the reasons for the projected redundancies;
   (ii) the number and categories of workers to be made redundant;
   (iii) the number and categories of workers normally employed;
   (iv) the period over which the projected redundancies are to be effected;
   (v) the criteria proposed for the selection of the workers to be made redundant in so far as national legislation and/or practice confers the power therefore upon the employer;
   (vi) the method for calculating any redundancy payments other than those arising out of national legislation and/or practice.

The employer shall forward to the competent public authority a copy of, at least, the elements of the written communication which are provided for in the first subparagraph, point (b), sub-points (i) to (v).
4. The obligations laid down in paragraphs 1, 2 and 3 shall apply irrespective of whether the decision regarding collective redundancies is being taken by the employer or by an undertaking controlling the employer.

In considering alleged breaches of the information, consultation and notification requirements laid down by this Directive, account shall not be taken of any defence on the part of the employer on the ground that the necessary information has not been provided to the employer by the undertaking which took the decision leading to collective redundancies.

SECTION III
PROCEDURE FOR COLLECTIVE REDUNDANCIES

[3.261]
Article 3
1. Employers shall notify the competent public authority in writing of any projected collective redundancies.

However, Member States may provide that in the case of planned collective redundancies arising from termination of the establishment's activities as a result of a judicial decision, the employer shall be obliged to notify the competent public authority in writing only if the latter so requests.

This notification shall contain all relevant information concerning the projected collective redundancies and the consultations with workers' representatives provided for in Article 2, and particularly the reasons for the redundancies, the number of workers to be made redundant, the number of workers normally employed and the period over which the redundancies are to be effected.
2. Employers shall forward to the workers' representatives a copy of the notification provided for in paragraph 1.

The workers' representatives may send any comments they may have to the competent public authority.

[3.262]
Article 4
1. Projected collective redundancies notified to the competent public authority shall take effect not earlier than 30 days after the notification referred to in Article 3(1) without prejudice to any provisions governing individual rights with regard to notice of dismissal.

Member States may grant the competent public authority the power to reduce the period provided for in the preceding subparagraph.

2. The period provided for in paragraph 1 shall be used by the competent public authority to seek solutions to the problems raised by the projected collective redundancies.

3. Where the initial period provided for in paragraph 1 is shorter than 60 days, Member States may grant the competent public authority the power to extend the initial period to 60 days following notification where the problems raised by the projected collective redundancies are not likely to be solved within the initial period.

Member States may grant the competent public authority wider powers of extension.

The employer must be informed of the extension and the grounds for it before expiry of the initial period provided for in paragraph 1.

4. Member States need not apply this Article to collective redundancies arising from termination of the establishment's activities where this is the result of a judicial decision.

SECTION IV
FINAL PROVISIONS

[3.263]
Article 5
This Directive shall not affect the right of Member States to apply or to introduce laws, regulations or administrative provisions which are more favourable to workers or to promote or to allow the application of collective agreements more favourable to workers.

[3.264]
Article 6
Member States shall ensure that judicial and/or administrative procedures for the enforcement of obligations under this Directive are available to the workers' representatives and/or workers.

[3.265]
Article 7
Member States shall forward to the Commission the text of any fundamental provisions of national law already adopted or being adopted in the area governed by this Directive.

[3.266]
Article 8
1. The Directives listed in Annex I, Part A, are hereby repealed without prejudice to the obligations of the Member States concerning the deadlines for transposition of the said Directive set out in Annex I, Part B.

2. References to the repealed Directives shall be construed as references to this Directive and shall be read in accordance with the correlation table in Annex II.

[3.267]
Article 9
This Directive shall enter into force on the 20th day following its publication in the *Official Journal of the European Communities*.

[3.268]
Article 10
This Directive is addressed to the Member States.

ANNEX I

PART A

REPEALED DIRECTIVES
(REFERRED TO BY ARTICLE 8)

[3.269]
Council Directive 75/129/EEC and its following amendment:

Council Directive 92/56/EEC.

PART B

DEADLINES FOR TRANSPOSITION INTO NATIONAL LAW
(REFERRED TO BY ARTICLE 8)

[3.270]

Directive	*Deadline for transposition*
75/129/EEC (OJ L48, 22.2.1975, p 29)	19 February 1977
92/56/EEC (OJ L245, 26.8.1992, p 3)	24 June 1994

ANNEX II

CORRELATION TABLE

[3.271]

Directive 75/129/EEC	*This Directive*
Article 1(1), first subparagraph, point (a), first indent, point 1	Article 1(1), first subparagraph, point (a)(i), first indent
Article 1(1), first subparagraph, point (a), first indent, point 2	Article 1(1), first subparagraph, point (a)(i), second indent
Article 1(1), first subparagraph, point (a), first indent, point 3	Article 1(1), first subparagraph, point (a)(i), third indent
Article 1(1), first subparagraph, point (a), second indent	Article 1(1), first subparagraph, point (a)(ii)
Article 1(1), first subparagraph, point (b)	Article 1(1), first subparagraph, point (b)
Article 1(1), second subparagraph	Article 1(1), second subparagraph
Article 1(2)	Article 1(2)
Article 2	Article 2
Article 3	Article 3
Article 4	Article 4
Article 5	Article 5
Article 5a	Article 6
Article 6(1)	—
Article 6(2)	Article 7
Article 7	—
—	Article 8
—	Article 9
—	Article 10
—	Annex I
—	Annex II

COUNCIL DIRECTIVE

(99/70/EC)

of 28 June 1999

concerning the framework agreement on fixed-term work concluded by ETUC, UNICE and CEEP

NOTES

Date of publication in OJ: OJ L175, 10.7.1999, p 43. The text of this Directive incorporates the corrigendum published in OJ L244, 16.9.1999, p 64 (see further Article 2 below).

For the domestic implementation of this Directive, see the Fixed-term Employees (Prevention of Less Favourable Treatment) Regulations 2002, SI 2002/2034 at **[2.597]**.

[3.272]

THE COUNCIL OF THE EUROPEAN UNION,

Having regard to the Treaty establishing the European Community, and in particular Article 139(2) thereof,

Having regard to the proposal from the Commission,

Whereas:

(1) Following the entry into force of the Treaty of Amsterdam the provisions of the Agreement on social policy annexed to the Protocol on social policy, annexed to the Treaty establishing the European Community have been incorporated into Articles 136 to 139 of the Treaty establishing the European Community;

(2) Management and labour (the social partners) may, in accordance with Article 139(2) of the Treaty, request jointly that agreements at Community level be implemented by a Council decision on a proposal from the Commission;

(3) Point 7 of the Community Charter of the Fundamental Social Rights of Workers provides, *inter alia*, that 'the completion of the internal market must lead to an improvement in the living and working conditions of workers in the European Community. This process must result from an approximation of these conditions while the improvement is being maintained, as regards in particular forms of employment other than open-ended contracts, such as fixed-term contracts, part-time working, temporary work and seasonal work';

(4) The Council has been unable to reach a decision on the proposal for a Directive on certain employment relationships with regard to distortions of competition,[1] nor on the proposal for a Directive on certain employment relationships with regard to working conditions;[2]

(5) The conclusions of the Essen European Council stressed the need to take measures with a view to 'increasing the employment-intensiveness of growth, in particular by a more flexible organisation of work in a way which fulfils both the wishes of employees and the requirements of competition';

(6) The Council Resolution of 9 February 1999 on the 1999 Employment Guidelines invites the social partners at all appropriate levels to negotiate agreements to modernise the organisation of work, including flexible working arrangements, with the aim of making undertakings productive and competitive and achieving the required balance between flexibility and security;

(7) The Commission, in accordance with Article 3(2) of the Agreement on social policy, has consulted management and labour on the possible direction of Community action with regard to flexible working time and job security;

(8) The Commission, considering after such consultation that Community action was desirable, once again consulted management and labour on the substance of the envisaged proposal in accordance with Article 3(3) of the said Agreement;

(9) The general cross-industry organisations, namely the Union of Industrial and Employers' Confederations of Europe (UNICE), the European Centre of Enterprises with Public Participation (CEEP) and the European Trade Union Confederation (ETUC), informed the Commission in a joint letter dated 23 March 1998 of their desire to initiate the procedure provided for in Article 4 of the said Agreement; they asked the Commission, in a joint letter, for a further period of three months; the Commission complied with this request extending the negotiation period to 30 March 1999;

(10) The said cross-industry organisations on 18 March 1999 concluded a framework agreement on fixed-term work; they forwarded to the Commission their joint request to implement the framework agreement by a Council Decision on a proposal from the Commission, in accordance with Article 4(2) of the Agreement on social policy;

(11) The Council, in its Resolution of 6 December 1994 on 'certain aspects for a European Union social policy: a contribution to economic and social convergence in the Union',[3] asked management and labour to make use of the opportunities for concluding agreements, since they are as a rule closer to social reality and to social problems;

(12) The signatory parties, in the preamble to the framework agreement on part-time work concluded on 6 June 1997, announced their intention to consider the need for similar agreements relating to other forms of flexible work;

(13) Management and labour wished to give particular attention to fixed-term work, while at the same time indicating that it was their intention to consider the need for a similar agreement relating to temporary agency work;

(14) The signatory parties wished to conclude a framework agreement on fixed-term work setting out the general principles and minimum requirements for fixed-term employment contracts and employment relationships; they have demonstrated their desire to improve the quality of fixed-term work by ensuring the application of the principle of non-discrimination, and to establish a framework to prevent abuse arising from the use of successive fixed-term employment contracts or relationships;

(15) The proper instrument for implementing the framework agreement is a directive within the meaning of Article 249 of the Treaty; it therefore binds the Member States as to the result to be achieved, whilst leaving them the choice of form and methods;

(16) In accordance with the principles of subsidiarity and proportionality as set out in Article 5

of the Treaty, the objectives of this Directive cannot be sufficiently achieved by the Member States and can therefore be better achieved by the Community; this Directive limits itself to the minimum required for the attainment of those objectives and does not go beyond what is necessary for that purpose;

(17) As regards terms used in the framework agreement but not specifically defined therein, this Directive allows Member States to define such terms in conformity with national law or practice as is the case for other Directives on social matters using similar terms, provided that the definitions in question respect the content of the framework agreement;

(18) The Commission has drafted its proposal for a Directive, in accordance with its Communication of 14 December 1993 concerning the application of the agreement on social policy and its Communication of 20 May 1998 on adapting and promoting the social dialogue at Community level, taking into account the representative status of the contracting parties, their mandate and the legality of each clause of the framework agreement; the contracting parties together have a sufficiently representative status;

(19) The Commission informed the European Parliament and the Economic and Social Committee by sending them the text of the agreement, accompanied by its proposal for a Directive and the explanatory memorandum, in accordance with its communication concerning the implementation of the Protocol on social policy;

(20) On 6 May 1999 the European Parliament adopted a Resolution on the framework agreement between the social partners;

(21) The implementation of the framework agreement contributes to achieving the objectives in Article 136 of Treaty,

NOTES

[1] OJ C224, 8.9.90, p 6 and OJ C305, 5.12.90, p 8.

[2] OJ C224, 8.9.90, p 4.

[3] OJ C368, 23.12.94, p 6.

HAS ADOPTED THIS DIRECTIVE—

[3.273]
Article 1
The purpose of the Directive is to put into effect the framework agreement on fixed-term contracts concluded on 18 March 1999 between the general cross-industry organisations (ETUC, UNICE and CEEP) annexed hereto.

[3.274]
Article 2
Member States shall bring into force the laws, regulations and administrative provisions necessary to comply with this Directive by 10 July 2001, or shall ensure that, by that date at the latest, management and labour have introduced the necessary measures by agreement, the Member States being required to take any necessary measures to enable them at any time to be in a position to guarantee the results imposed by this Directive. They shall forthwith inform the Commission thereof.

Member States may have a maximum of one more year, if necessary, and following consultation with management and labour, to take account of special difficulties or implementation by a collective agreement. They shall inform the Commission forthwith in such circumstances.

When Member States adopt the provisions referred to in the first paragraph, these shall contain a reference to this Directive or shall be accompanied by such reference at the time of their official publication. The procedure for such reference shall be adopted by the Member States.

NOTES

The date of 10 July 2001 in the first paragraph is by virtue of the Corrigendum to Council Directive 1999/70/EC of 28 June 1999 concerning the framework agreement on fixed-term work concluded by ETUC, UNICE and CEEP. The original date (as published in the Official Journal) was 10 July 1999.

[3.275]
Article 3
This Directive shall enter into force on the day of its publication in the *Official Journal of the European Communities*.

[3.276]
Article 4
This Directive is addressed to the Member States.

ANNEX
ETUC-UNICE-CEEP

FRAMEWORK AGREEMENT ON FIXED-TERM WORK

[3.277]
Preamble
This framework agreement illustrates the role that the social partners can play in the European employment strategy agreed at the 1997 Luxembourg extra-ordinary summit and, following the framework agreement on part-time work, represents a further contribution towards achieving a better balance between "flexibility in working time and security for workers".

The parties to this agreement recognise that contracts of an indefinite duration are, and will continue to be, the general form of employment relationship between employers and workers. They also recognise that fixed-term employment contracts respond, in certain circumstances, to the needs of both employers and workers.

This agreement sets out the general principles and minimum requirements relating to fixed-term work, recognising that their detailed application needs to take account of the realities of specific national, sectoral and seasonal situations. It illustrates the willingness of the Social Partners to establish a general framework for ensuring equal treatment for fixed-term workers by protecting them against discrimination and for using fixed-term employment contracts on a basis acceptable to employers and workers.

This agreement applies to fixed-term workers with the exception of those placed by a temporary work agency at the disposition of a user enterprise. It is the intention of the parties to consider the need for a similar agreement relating to temporary agency work.

This agreement relates to the employment conditions of fixed-term workers, recognising that matters relating to statutory social security are for decision by the Member States. In this respect the Social Partners note the Employment Declaration of the Dublin European Council in 1996 which emphasised *inter alia*, the need to develop more employment-friendly social security systems by "developing social protection systems capable of adapting to new patterns of work and providing appropriate protection to those engaged in such work". The parties to this agreement reiterate the view expressed in the 1997 part-time agreement that Member States should give effect to this Declaration without delay.

In addition, it is also recognised that innovations in occupational social protection systems are necessary in order to adapt them to current conditions, and in particular to provide for the transferability of rights.

The ETUC, UNICE and CEEP request the Commission to submit this framework agreement to the Council for a decision making these requirements binding in the Member States which are party to the Agreement on social policy annexed to the Protocol (No 14) on social policy annexed to the Treaty establishing the European Community.

The parties to this agreement ask the Commission, in its proposal to implement the agreement, to request Member States to adopt the laws, regulations and administrative provisions necessary to comply with the Council decision within two years from its adoption or ensure[1] that the social partners establish the necessary measures by way of agreement by the end of this period. Member States may, if necessary and following consultation with the social partners, and in order to take account of particular difficulties or implementation by collective agreement have up to a maximum of one additional year to comply with this provision.

The parties to this agreement request that the social partners are consulted prior to any legislative, regulatory or administrative initiative taken by a Member State to conform to the present agreement.

Without prejudice to the role of national courts and the Court of Justice, the parties to this agreement request that any matter relating to the interpretation of this agreement at European level, should in the first instance, be referred by the Commission to them for an opinion.

NOTES

[1] Within the meaning of Article 2.4 of the Agreement on social policy annexed to the Protocol (No 14) on social policy annexed to the Treaty establishing the European Community.

[3.278]
General considerations
1. Having regard to the Agreement on social policy annexed to the Protocol (No 14) on social policy annexed to the Treaty establishing the European Community, and in particular Article 3.4 and 4.2 thereof;
2. Whereas Article 4.2 of the Agreement on social policy provides that agreements concluded at Community level may be implemented, at the joint request of the signatory parties, by a Council decision on a proposal from the Commission;
3. Whereas, in its second consultation document on flexibility in working time and security for workers, the Commission announced its intention to propose a legally-binding Community measure;

4. Whereas in its opinion on the proposal for a directive on part-time work, the European Parliament invited the Commission to submit immediately proposals for directives on other forms of flexible work, such as fixed-term work and temporary agency work;
5. Whereas in the conclusions of the extraordinary summit on employment adopted in Luxembourg, the European Council invited the social partners to negotiate agreements to "modernise the organisation of work, including flexible working arrangements, with the aim of making undertakings productive and competitive and achieving the required balance between flexibility and security";
6. Whereas employment contracts of an indefinite duration are the general form of employment relationships and contribute to quality of life of the workers concerned and improve performance;
7. Whereas the use of fixed-term employment contracts based on objective reasons is a way to prevent abuse;
8. Whereas fixed-term employment contracts are a feature of employment in certain sectors, occupations and activities which can suit both employers and workers;
9. Whereas more than half of fixed-term workers in the European Union are women and this agreement can therefore contribute to improving equality of opportunities between women and men;
10. Whereas this agreement refers back to Member States and social partners for the arrangements for the application of its general principles, minimum requirements and provisions, in order to take account of the situation in each Member State and the circumstances of particular sectors and occupations, including the activities of a seasonal nature;
11. Whereas this agreement takes into consideration the need to improve social policy requirements, to enhance the competitiveness of the Community economy and to avoid imposing administrative, financial and legal constraints in a way which would hold back the creation and development of small and medium-sized undertakings;
12. Whereas the social partners are best placed to find solutions that correspond to the needs of both employers and workers and shall therefore be given a special role in the implementation and application of this agreement.

The signatory parties have agreed the following

[3.279]
Purpose (clause 1)
The purpose of this framework agreement is to—

(1) improve the quality of fixed-term work by ensuring the application of the principle of non-discrimination;
(2) establish a framework to prevent abuse arising from the use of successive fixed-term employment contracts or relationships.

Scope (clause 2)
1. This agreement applies to fixed-term workers who have an employment contract or employment relationship as defined in law, collective agreements or practice in each Member State.
2. Member States after consultation with the social partners and/or the social partners may provide that this agreement does not apply to—

(a) initial vocational training relationships and apprenticeship schemes;
(b) employment contracts and relationships which have been concluded within the framework of a specific public or publicly-supported training, integration and vocational retraining programme.

Definitions (clause 3)
1. For the purpose of this agreement the term "fixed-term worker" means a person having an employment contract or relationship entered into directly between an employer and a worker where the end of the employment contract or relationship is determined by objective conditions such as reaching a specific date, completing a specific task, or the occurrence of a specific event.
2. For the purpose of this agreement, the term "comparable permanent worker" means a worker with an employment contract or relationship of an indefinite duration, in the same establishment, engaged in the same or similar work/occupation, due regard being given to qualifications/skills.

Where there is no comparable permanent worker in the same establishment, the comparison shall be made by reference to the applicable collective agreement, or where there is no applicable collective agreement, in accordance with national law, collective agreements or practice.

Principle of non-discrimination (clause 4)
1. In respect of employment conditions, fixed-term workers shall not be treated in a less favourable manner than comparable permanent workers solely because they have a fixed-term contract or relation unless justified on objective grounds.
2. Where appropriate, the principle of *pro rata temporis* shall apply.
3. The arrangements for the application of this clause shall be defined by the Member States after consultation with the social partners and/or the social partners, having regard to Community law, national law, collective agreements and practice.

4. Period of service qualifications relating to particular conditions of employment shall be the same for fixed-term workers as for permanent workers except where different length of service qualifications are justified on objective grounds.

Measures to prevent abuse (clause 5)

1. To prevent abuse arising from the use of successive fixed-term employment contracts or relationships, Member States, after consultation with social partners in accordance with national law, collective agreements or practice, and/or the social partners, shall, where there are no equivalent legal measures to prevent abuse, introduce in a manner which takes account of the needs of specific sectors and/or categories of workers, one or more of the following measures—

(a) objective reasons justifying the renewal of such contracts or relationships;

(b) the maximum total duration of successive fixed-term employment contracts or relationships;

(c) the number of renewals of such contracts or relationships.

2. Member States after consultation with the social partners and/or the social partners, shall, where appropriate, determine under what conditions fixed-term employment contracts or relationships—

(a) shall be regarded as "successive";

(b) shall be deemed to be contracts or relationships of indefinite duration.

Information and employment opportunities (clause 6)

1. Employers shall inform fixed-term workers about vacancies which become available in the undertaking or establishment to ensure that they have the same opportunity to secure permanent positions as other workers. Such information may be provided by way of a general announcement at a suitable place in the undertaking or establishment.

2. As far as possible, employers should facilitate access by fixed-term workers to appropriate training opportunities to enhance their skills, career development and occupational mobility.

Information and consultation (clause 7)

1. Fixed-term workers shall be taken into consideration in calculating the threshold above which workers' representative bodies provided for in national and Community law may be constituted in the undertaking as required by national provisions.

2. The arrangements for the application of clause 7.1 shall be defined by Member States after consultation with the social partners and/or the social partners in accordance with national law, collective agreements or practice and having regard to clause 4.1.

3. As far as possible, employers should give consideration to the provision of appropriate information to existing workers' representative bodies about fixed-term work in the undertaking.

Provisions on implementation (clause 8)

1. Member States and/or the social partners can maintain or introduce more favourable provisions for workers than set out in this agreement.

2. This agreement shall be without prejudice to any more specific Community provisions, and in particular Community provisions concerning equal treatment or opportunities for men and women.

3. Implementation of this agreement shall not constitute valid grounds for reducing the general level of protection afforded to workers in the field of the agreement.

4. The present agreement does not prejudice the right of the social partners to conclude at the appropriate level, including European level, agreements adapting and/or complementing the provisions of this agreement in a manner which will take account of the specific needs of the social partners concerned.

5. The prevention and settlement of disputes and grievances arising from the application of this agreement shall be dealt with in accordance with national law, collective agreements and practice.

6. The signatory parties shall review the application of this agreement five years after the date of the Council decision if requested by one of the parties to this agreement.

18 March 1999

COUNCIL DIRECTIVE

(2000/43/EC)

of 29 June 2000

implementing the principle of equal treatment between persons irrespective of racial or ethnic origin

NOTES

Date of publication in OJ: OJ L180, 19.7.2000, p 22.

For the domestic implementation of this Directive, see now the Equality Act 2010, s 9, Part 2, Chapter 2, and Part 5 (the 2010 Act is at **[1.1618]**).

See *Harvey* L(2)(e), (3), (4), (5).

[3.280]

THE COUNCIL OF THE EUROPEAN UNION,

Having regard to the Treaty establishing the European Community and in particular Article 13 thereof,

Having regard to the proposal from the Commission,[1]

Having regard to the opinion of the European Parliament,[2]

Having regard to the opinion of the Economic and Social Committee,[3]

Having regard to the opinion of the Committee of the Regions,[4]

Whereas:

(1) The Treaty on European Union marks a new stage in the process of creating an ever closer union among the peoples of Europe.

(2) In accordance with Article 6 of the Treaty on European Union, the European Union is founded on the principles of liberty, democracy, respect for human rights and fundamental freedoms, and the rule of law, principles which are common to the Member States, and should respect fundamental rights as guaranteed by the European Convention for the protection of Human Rights and Fundamental Freedoms and as they result from the constitutional traditions common to the Member States, as general principles of Community Law.

(3) The right to equality before the law and protection against discrimination for all persons constitutes a universal right recognised by the Universal Declaration of Human Rights, the United Nations Convention on the Elimination of all forms of Discrimination Against Women, the International Convention on the Elimination of all forms of Racial Discrimination and the United Nations Covenants on Civil and Political Rights and on Economic, Social and Cultural Rights and by the European Convention for the Protection of Human Rights and Fundamental Freedoms, to which all Member States are signatories.

(4) It is important to respect such fundamental rights and freedoms, including the right to freedom of association. It is also important, in the context of the access to and provision of goods and services, to respect the protection of private and family life and transactions carried out in this context.

(5) The European Parliament has adopted a number of Resolutions on the fight against racism in the European Union.

(6) The European Union rejects theories which attempt to determine the existence of separate human races. The use of the term "racial origin" in this Directive does not imply an acceptance of such theories.

(7) The European Council in Tampere, on 15 and 16 October 1999, invited the Commission to come forward as soon as possible with proposals implementing Article 13 of the EC Treaty as regards the fight against racism and xenophobia.

(8) The Employment Guidelines 2000 agreed by the European Council in Helsinki, on 10 and 11 December 1999, stress the need to foster conditions for a socially inclusive labour market by formulating a coherent set of policies aimed at combating discrimination against groups such as ethnic minorities.

(9) Discrimination based on racial or ethnic origin may undermine the achievement of the objectives of the EC Treaty, in particular the attainment of a high level of employment and of social protection, the raising of the standard of living and quality of life, economic and social cohesion and solidarity. It may also undermine the objective of developing the European Union as an area of freedom, security and justice.

(10) The Commission presented a communication on racism, xenophobia and anti-Semitism in December 1995.

(11) The Council adopted on 15 July 1996 Joint Action (96/443/JHA) concerning action to combat racism and xenophobia[5] under which the Member States undertake to ensure effective

judicial cooperation in respect of offences based on racist or xenophobic behaviour.

(12) To ensure the development of democratic and tolerant societies which allow the participation of all persons irrespective of racial or ethnic origin, specific action in the field of discrimination based on racial or ethnic origin should go beyond access to employed and self-employed activities and cover areas such as education, social protection including social security and healthcare, social advantages and access to and supply of goods and services.

(13) To this end, any direct or indirect discrimination based on racial or ethnic origin as regards the areas covered by this Directive should be prohibited throughout the Community. This prohibition of discrimination should also apply to nationals of third countries, but does not cover differences of treatment based on nationality and is without prejudice to provisions governing the entry and residence of third-country nationals and their access to employment and to occupation.

(14) In implementing the principle of equal treatment irrespective of racial or ethnic origin, the Community should, in accordance with Article 3(2) of the EC Treaty, aim to eliminate inequalities, and to promote equality between men and women, especially since women are often the victims of multiple discrimination.

(15) The appreciation of the facts from which it may be inferred that there has been direct or indirect discrimination is a matter for national judicial or other competent bodies, in accordance with rules of national law or practice. Such rules may provide in particular for indirect discrimination to be established by any means including on the basis of statistical evidence.

(16) It is important to protect all natural persons against discrimination on grounds of racial or ethnic origin. Member States should also provide, where appropriate and in accordance with their national traditions and practice, protection for legal persons where they suffer discrimination on grounds of the racial or ethnic origin of their members.

(17) The prohibition of discrimination should be without prejudice to the maintenance or adoption of measures intended to prevent or compensate for disadvantages suffered by a group of persons of a particular racial or ethnic origin, and such measures may permit organisations of persons of a particular racial or ethnic origin where their main object is the promotion of the special needs of those persons.

(18) In very limited circumstances, a difference of treatment may be justified where a characteristic related to racial or ethnic origin constitutes a genuine and determining occupational requirement, when the objective is legitimate and the requirement is proportionate. Such circumstances should be included in the information provided by the Member States to the Commission.

(19) Persons who have been subject to discrimination based on racial and ethnic origin should have adequate means of legal protection. To provide a more effective level of protection, associations or legal entities should also be empowered to engage, as the Member States so determine, either on behalf or in support of any victim, in proceedings, without prejudice to national rules of procedure concerning representation and defence before the courts.

(20) The effective implementation of the principle of equality requires adequate judicial protection against victimisation.

(21) The rules on the burden of proof must be adapted when there is a prima facie case of discrimination and, for the principle of equal treatment to be applied effectively, the burden of proof must shift back to the respondent when evidence of such discrimination is brought.

(22) Member States need not apply the rules on the burden of proof to proceedings in which it is for the court or other competent body to investigate the facts of the case. The procedures thus referred to are those in which the plaintiff is not required to prove the facts, which it is for the court or competent body to investigate.

(23) Member States should promote dialogue between the social partners and with non-governmental organisations to address different forms of discrimination and to combat them.

(24) Protection against discrimination based on racial or ethnic origin would itself be strengthened by the existence of a body or bodies in each Member State, with competence to analyse the problems involved, to study possible solutions and to provide concrete assistance for the victims.

(25) This Directive lays down minimum requirements, thus giving the Member States the option of introducing or maintaining more favourable provisions. The implementation of this Directive should not serve to justify any regression in relation to the situation which already prevails in each Member State.

(26) Member States should provide for effective, proportionate and dissuasive sanctions in case of breaches of the obligations under this Directive.

(27) The Member States may entrust management and labour, at their joint request, with the implementation of this Directive as regards provisions falling within the scope of collective agreements, provided that the Member States take all the necessary steps to ensure that they can at all times guarantee the results imposed by this Directive.

(28) In accordance with the principles of subsidiarity and proportionality as set out in Article 5 of the EC Treaty, the objective of this Directive, namely ensuring a common high level of protection against discrimination in all the Member States, cannot be sufficiently achieved by the Member States and can therefore, by reason of the scale and impact of the proposed action, be better achieved by the Community. This Directive does not go beyond what is necessary in order to achieve those objectives,

NOTES

[1] Not yet published in the Official Journal.

[2] Opinion delivered on 18.5.2000 (not yet published in the Official Journal).

[3] Opinion delivered on 12.4.2000 (not yet published in the Official Journal).

[4] Opinion delivered on 31.5.2000 (not yet published in the Official Journal).

[5] OJ L185, 24.7.96, p 5.

HAS ADOPTED THIS DIRECTIVE—

CHAPTER I
GENERAL PROVISIONS

[3.281]
Article 1
Purpose

The purpose of this Directive is to lay down a framework for combating discrimination on the grounds of racial or ethnic origin, with a view to putting into effect in the Member States the principle of equal treatment.

[3.282]
Article 2
Concept of discrimination

1. For the purposes of this Directive, the principle of equal treatment shall mean that there shall be no direct or indirect discrimination based on racial or ethnic origin.
2. For the purposes of paragraph 1—
   (a) direct discrimination shall be taken to occur where one person is treated less favourably than another is, has been or would be treated in a comparable situation on grounds of racial or ethnic origin;
   (b) indirect discrimination shall be taken to occur where an apparently neutral provision, criterion or practice would put persons of a racial or ethnic origin at a particular disadvantage compared with other persons, unless that provision, criterion or practice is objectively justified by a legitimate aim and the means of achieving that aim are appropriate and necessary.
3. Harassment shall be deemed to be discrimination within the meaning of paragraph 1, when an unwanted conduct related to racial or ethnic origin takes place with the purpose or effect of violating the dignity of a person and of creating an intimidating, hostile, degrading, humiliating or offensive environment. In this context, the concept of harassment may be defined in accordance with the national laws and practice of the Member States.
4. An instruction to discriminate against persons on grounds of racial or ethnic origin shall be deemed to be discrimination within the meaning of paragraph 1.

[3.283]
Article 3
Scope

1. Within the limits of the powers conferred upon the Community, this Directive shall apply to all persons, as regards both the public and private sectors, including public bodies, in relation to—
   (a) conditions for access to employment, to self-employment and to occupation, including selection criteria and recruitment conditions, whatever the branch of activity and at all levels of the professional hierarchy, including promotion;
   (b) access to all types and to all levels of vocational guidance, vocational training, advanced vocational training and retraining, including practical work experience;
   (c) employment and working conditions, including dismissals and pay;
   (d) membership of and involvement in an organisation of workers or employers, or any organisation whose members carry on a particular profession, including the benefits provided for by such organisations;
   (e) social protection, including social security and healthcare;
   (f) social advantages;
   (g) education;
   (h) access to and supply of goods and services which are available to the public, including housing.

2. This Directive does not cover difference of treatment based on nationality and is without prejudice to provisions and conditions relating to the entry into and residence of third-country nationals and stateless persons on the territory of Member States, and to any treatment which arises from the legal status of the third-country nationals and stateless persons concerned.

[3.284]
Article 4
Genuine and determining occupational requirements
Notwithstanding Article 2(1) and (2), Member States may provide that a difference of treatment which is based on a characteristic related to racial or ethnic origin shall not constitute discrimination where, by reason of the nature of the particular occupational activities concerned or of the context in which they are carried out, such a characteristic constitutes a genuine and determining occupational requirement, provided that the objective is legitimate and the requirement is proportionate.

[3.285]
Article 5
Positive action
With a view to ensuring full equality in practice, the principle of equal treatment shall not prevent any Member State from maintaining or adopting specific measures to prevent or compensate for disadvantages linked to racial or ethnic origin.

[3.286]
Article 6
Minimum requirements
1. Member States may introduce or maintain provisions which are more favourable to the protection of the principle of equal treatment than those laid down in this Directive.
2. The implementation of this Directive shall under no circumstances constitute grounds for a reduction in the level of protection against discrimination already afforded by Member States in the fields covered by this Directive.

CHAPTER II
REMEDIES AND ENFORCEMENT

[3.287]
Article 7
Defence of rights
1. Member States shall ensure that judicial and/or administrative procedures, including where they deem it appropriate conciliation procedures, for the enforcement of obligations under this Directive are available to all persons who consider themselves wronged by failure to apply the principle of equal treatment to them, even after the relationship in which the discrimination is alleged to have occurred has ended.
2. Member States shall ensure that associations, organisations or other legal entities, which have, in accordance with the criteria laid down by their national law, a legitimate interest in ensuring that the provisions of this Directive are complied with, may engage, either on behalf or in support of the complainant, with his or her approval, in any judicial and/or administrative procedure provided for the enforcement of obligations under this Directive.
3. Paragraphs 1 and 2 are without prejudice to national rules relating to time limits for bringing actions as regards the principle of equality of treatment.

[3.288]
Article 8
Burden of proof
1. Member States shall take such measures as are necessary, in accordance with their national judicial systems, to ensure that, when persons who consider themselves wronged because the principle of equal treatment has not been applied to them establish, before a court or other competent authority, facts from which it may be presumed that there has been direct or indirect discrimination, it shall be for the respondent to prove that there has been no breach of the principle of equal treatment.
2. Paragraph 1 shall not prevent Member States from introducing rules of evidence which are more favourable to plaintiffs.
3. Paragraph 1 shall not apply to criminal procedures.
4. Paragraphs 1, 2 and 3 shall also apply to any proceedings brought in accordance with Article 7(2).
5. Member States need not apply paragraph 1 to proceedings in which it is for the court or competent body to investigate the facts of the case.

[3.289]
Article 9
Victimisation

Member States shall introduce into their national legal systems such measures as are necessary to protect individuals from any adverse treatment or adverse consequence as a reaction to a complaint or to proceedings aimed at enforcing compliance with the principle of equal treatment.

[3.290]
Article 10
Dissemination of information

Member States shall take care that the provisions adopted pursuant to this Directive, together with the relevant provisions already in force, are brought to the attention of the persons concerned by all appropriate means throughout their territory.

[3.291]
Article 11
Social dialogue

1. Member States shall, in accordance with national traditions and practice, take adequate measures to promote the social dialogue between the two sides of industry with a view to fostering equal treatment, including through the monitoring of workplace practices, collective agreements, codes of conduct, research or exchange of experiences and good practices.
2. Where consistent with national traditions and practice, Member States shall encourage the two sides of the industry without prejudice to their autonomy to conclude, at the appropriate level, agreements laying down anti-discrimination rules in the fields referred to in Article 3 which fall within the scope of collective bargaining. These agreements shall respect the minimum requirements laid down by this Directive and the relevant national implementing measures.

[3.292]
Article 12
Dialogue with non-governmental organisations

Member States shall encourage dialogue with appropriate non-governmental organisations which have, in accordance with their national law and practice, a legitimate interest in contributing to the fight against discrimination on grounds of racial and ethnic origin with a view to promoting the principle of equal treatment.

CHAPTER III
BODIES FOR THE PROMOTION OF EQUAL TREATMENT

[3.293]
Article 13

1. Member States shall designate a body or bodies for the promotion of equal treatment of all persons without discrimination on the grounds of racial or ethnic origin. These bodies may form part of agencies charged at national level with the defence of human rights or the safeguard of individuals' rights.
2. Member States shall ensure that the competences of these bodies include—
   — without prejudice to the right of victims and of associations, organisations or other legal entities referred to in Article 7(2), providing independent assistance to victims of discrimination in pursuing their complaints about discrimination,
   — conducting independent surveys concerning discrimination,
   — publishing independent reports and making recommendations on any issue relating to such discrimination.

CHAPTER IV
FINAL PROVISIONS

[3.294]
Article 14
Compliance

Member States shall take the necessary measures to ensure that—
   (a) any laws, regulations and administrative provisions contrary to the principle of equal treatment are abolished;
   (b) any provisions contrary to the principle of equal treatment which are included in individual or collective contracts or agreements, internal rules of undertakings, rules governing profit-making or non-profit-making associations, and rules governing the independent professions and workers' and employers' organisations, are or may be declared, null and void or are amended.

[3.295]
Article 15
Sanctions

Member States shall lay down the rules on sanctions applicable to infringements of the national provisions adopted pursuant to this Directive and shall take all measures necessary to ensure that they are applied. The sanctions, which may comprise the payment of compensation to the victim, must be effective, proportionate and dissuasive. The Member States shall notify those provisions to the Commission by 19 July 2003 at the latest and shall notify it without delay of any subsequent amendment affecting them.

[3.296]
Article 16
Implementation

Member States shall adopt the laws, regulations and administrative provisions necessary to comply with this Directive by 19 July 2003 or may entrust management and labour, at their joint request, with the implementation of this Directive as regards provisions falling within the scope of collective agreements. In such cases, Member States shall ensure that by 19 July 2003, management and labour introduce the necessary measures by agreement, Member States being required to take any necessary measures to enable them at any time to be in a position to guarantee the results imposed by this Directive. They shall forthwith inform the Commission thereof.

When Member States adopt these measures, they shall contain a reference to this Directive or be accompanied by such a reference on the occasion of their official publication. The methods of making such a reference shall be laid down by the Member States.

[3.297]
Article 17
Report

1. Member States shall communicate to the Commission by 19 July 2005, and every five years thereafter, all the information necessary for the Commission to draw up a report to the European Parliament and the Council on the application of this Directive.

2. The Commission's report shall take into account, as appropriate, the views of the European Monitoring Centre on Racism and Xenophobia, as well as the viewpoints of the social partners and relevant non-governmental organisations. In accordance with the principle of gender mainstreaming, this report shall, inter alia, provide an assessment of the impact of the measures taken on women and men. In the light of the information received, this report shall include, if necessary, proposals to revise and update this Directive.

[3.298]
Article 18
Entry into force

This Directive shall enter into force on the day of its publication in the *Official Journal of the European Communities*.

[3.299]
Article 19
Addressees

This Directive is addressed to the Member States.

COUNCIL DIRECTIVE

(2000/78/EC)

of 27 November 2000

establishing a general framework for equal treatment in employment and occupation

NOTES

Date of publication in OJ: OJ L303, 2.12.2000, p 16.

For the domestic implementation of this Directive, see now the Equality Act 2010, Parts 2, 5 and 9 (the 2010 Act is at **[1.1618]**).

See *Harvey* L.

[3.300]
THE COUNCIL OF THE EUROPEAN UNION,

Having regard to the Treaty establishing the European Community, and in particular Article 13 thereof,

Having regard to the proposal from the Commission,[1]

Having regard to the Opinion of the European Parliament,[2]

Having regard to the Opinion of the Economic and Social Committee,[3]
Having regard to the Opinion of the Committee of the Regions,[4]
Whereas—

(1) In accordance with Article 6 of the Treaty on European Union, the European Union is founded on the principles of liberty, democracy, respect for human rights and fundamental freedoms, and the rule of law, principles which are common to all Member States and it respects fundamental rights, as guaranteed by the European Convention for the Protection of Human Rights and Fundamental Freedoms and as they result from the constitutional traditions common to the Member States, as general principles of Community law.

(2) The principle of equal treatment between women and men is well established by an important body of Community law, in particular in Council Directive 76/207/EEC of 9 February 1976 on the implementation of the principle of equal treatment for men and women as regards access to employment, vocational training and promotion, and working conditions.[5]

(3) In implementing the principle of equal treatment, the Community should, in accordance with Article 3(2) of the EC Treaty, aim to eliminate inequalities, and to promote equality between men and women, especially since women are often the victims of multiple discrimination.

(4) The right of all persons to equality before the law and protection against discrimination constitutes a universal right recognised by the Universal Declaration of Human Rights, the United Nations Convention on the Elimination of All Forms of Discrimination against Women, United Nations Covenants on Civil and Political Rights and on Economic, Social and Cultural Rights and by the European Convention for the Protection of Human Rights and Fundamental Freedoms, to which all Member States are signatories. Convention No 111 of the International Labour Organisation (ILO) prohibits discrimination in the field of employment and occupation.

(5) It is important to respect such fundamental rights and freedoms. This Directive does not prejudice freedom of association, including the right to establish unions with others and to join unions to defend one's interests.

(6) The Community Charter of the Fundamental Social Rights of Workers recognises the importance of combating every form of discrimination, including the need to take appropriate action for the social and economic integration of elderly and disabled people.

(7) The EC Treaty includes among its objectives the promotion of coordination between employment policies of the Member States. To this end, a new employment chapter was incorporated in the EC Treaty as a means of developing a coordinated European strategy for employment to promote a skilled, trained and adaptable workforce.

(8) The Employment Guidelines for 2000 agreed by the European Council at Helsinki on 10 and 11 December 1999 stress the need to foster a labour market favourable to social integration by formulating a coherent set of policies aimed at combating discrimination against groups such as persons with disability. They also emphasise the need to pay particular attention to supporting older workers, in order to increase their participation in the labour force.

(9) Employment and occupation are key elements in guaranteeing equal opportunities for all and contribute strongly to the full participation of citizens in economic, cultural and social life and to realising their potential.

(10) On 29 June 2000 the Council adopted Directive 2000/43/EC[6] implementing the principle of equal treatment between persons irrespective of racial or ethnic origin. That Directive already provides protection against such discrimination in the field of employment and occupation.

(11) Discrimination based on religion or belief, disability, age or sexual orientation may undermine the achievement of the objectives of the EC Treaty, in particular the attainment of a high level of employment and social protection, raising the standard of living and the quality of life, economic and social cohesion and solidarity, and the free movement of persons.

(12) To this end, any direct or indirect discrimination based on religion or belief, disability, age or sexual orientation as regards the areas covered by this Directive should be prohibited throughout the Community. This prohibition of discrimination should also apply to nationals of third countries but does not cover differences of treatment based on nationality and is without prejudice to provisions governing the entry and residence of third-country nationals and their access to employment and occupation.

(13) This Directive does not apply to social security and social protection schemes whose benefits are not treated as income within the meaning given to that term for the purpose of applying Article 141 of the EC Treaty, nor to any kind of payment by the State aimed at providing access to employment or maintaining employment.

(14) This Directive shall be without prejudice to national provisions laying down retirement ages.

(15) The appreciation of the facts from which it may be inferred that there has been direct or indirect discrimination is a matter for national judicial or other competent bodies, in accordance with

rules of national law or practice. Such rules may provide, in particular, for indirect discrimination to be established by any means including on the basis of statistical evidence.

(16) The provision of measures to accommodate the needs of disabled people at the workplace plays an important role in combating discrimination on grounds of disability.

(17) This Directive does not require the recruitment, promotion, maintenance in employment or training of an individual who is not competent, capable and available to perform the essential functions of the post concerned or to undergo the relevant training, without prejudice to the obligation to provide reasonable accommodation for people with disabilities.

(18) This Directive does not require, in particular, the armed forces and the police, prison or emergency services to recruit or maintain in employment persons who do not have the required capacity to carry out the range of functions that they may be called upon to perform with regard to the legitimate objective of preserving the operational capacity of those services.

(19) Moreover, in order that the Member States may continue to safeguard the combat effectiveness of their armed forces, they may choose not to apply the provisions of this Directive concerning disability and age to all or part of their armed forces. The Member States which make that choice must define the scope of that derogation.

(20) Appropriate measures should be provided, ie effective and practical measures to adapt the workplace to the disability, for example adapting premises and equipment, patterns of working time, the distribution of tasks or the provision of training or integration resources.

(21) To determine whether the measures in question give rise to a disproportionate burden, account should be taken in particular of the financial and other costs entailed, the scale and financial resources of the organisation or undertaking and the possibility of obtaining public funding or any other assistance.

(22) This Directive is without prejudice to national laws on marital status and the benefits dependent thereon.

(23) In very limited circumstances, a difference of treatment may be justified where a characteristic related to religion or belief, disability, age or sexual orientation constitutes a genuine and determining occupational requirement, when the objective is legitimate and the requirement is proportionate. Such circumstances should be included in the information provided by the Member States to the Commission.

(24) The European Union in its Declaration No 11 on the status of churches and non-confessional organisations, annexed to the Final Act of the Amsterdam Treaty, has explicitly recognised that it respects and does not prejudice the status under national law of churches and religious associations or communities in the Member States and that it equally respects the status of philosophical and non-confessional organisations. With this in view, Member States may maintain or lay down specific provisions on genuine, legitimate and justified occupational requirements which might be required for carrying out an occupational activity.

(25) The prohibition of age discrimination is an essential part of meeting the aims set out in the Employment Guidelines and encouraging diversity in the workforce. However, differences in treatment in connection with age may be justified under certain circumstances and therefore require specific provisions which may vary in accordance with the situation in Member States. It is therefore essential to distinguish between differences in treatment which are justified, in particular by legitimate employment policy, labour market and vocational training objectives, and discrimination which must be prohibited.

(26) The prohibition of discrimination should be without prejudice to the maintenance or adoption of measures intended to prevent or compensate for disadvantages suffered by a group of persons of a particular religion or belief, disability, age or sexual orientation, and such measures may permit organisations of persons of a particular religion or belief, disability, age or sexual orientation where their main object is the promotion of the special needs of those persons.

(27) In its Recommendation 86/379/EEC of 24 July 1986 on the employment of disabled people in the Community,[7] the Council established a guideline framework setting out examples of positive action to promote the employment and training of disabled people, and in its Resolution of 17 June 1999 on equal employment opportunities for people with disabilities,[8] affirmed the importance of giving specific attention inter alia to recruitment, retention, training and lifelong learning with regard to disabled persons.

(28) This Directive lays down minimum requirements, thus giving the Member States the option of introducing or maintaining more favourable provisions. The implementation of this Directive should not serve to justify any regression in relation to the situation which already prevails in each Member State.

(29) Persons who have been subject to discrimination based on religion or belief, disability, age or sexual orientation should have adequate means of legal protection. To provide a more effective level of protection, associations or legal entities should also be empowered to engage in proceedings,

as the Member States so determine, either on behalf or in support of any victim, without prejudice to national rules of procedure concerning representation and defence before the courts.

(30) The effective implementation of the principle of equality requires adequate judicial protection against victimisation.

(31) The rules on the burden of proof must be adapted when there is a prima facie case of discrimination and, for the principle of equal treatment to be applied effectively, the burden of proof must shift back to the respondent when evidence of such discrimination is brought. However, it is not for the respondent to prove that the plaintiff adheres to a particular religion or belief, has a particular disability, is of a particular age or has a particular sexual orientation.

(32) Member States need not apply the rules on the burden of proof to proceedings in which it is for the court or other competent body to investigate the facts of the case. The procedures thus referred to are those in which the plaintiff is not required to prove the facts, which it is for the court or competent body to investigate.

(33) Member States should promote dialogue between the social partners and, within the framework of national practice, with non-governmental organisations to address different forms of discrimination at the workplace and to combat them.

(34) The need to promote peace and reconciliation between the major communities in Northern Ireland necessitates the incorporation of particular provisions into this Directive.

(35) Member States should provide for effective, proportionate and dissuasive sanctions in case of breaches of the obligations under this Directive.

(36) Member States may entrust the social partners, at their joint request, with the implementation of this Directive, as regards the provisions concerning collective agreements, provided they take any necessary steps to ensure that they are at all times able to guarantee the results required by this Directive.

(37) In accordance with the principle of subsidiarity set out in Article 5 of the EC Treaty, the objective of this Directive, namely the creation within the Community of a level playing-field as regards equality in employment and occupation, cannot be sufficiently achieved by the Member States and can therefore, by reason of the scale and impact of the action, be better achieved at Community level. In accordance with the principle of proportionality, as set out in that Article, this Directive does not go beyond what is necessary in order to achieve that objective.

NOTES

1 OJ C177 E, 27.6.2000, p 42.

2 Opinion delivered on 12 October 2000 (not yet published in the Official Journal).

3 OJ C204, 18.7.2000, p 82.

4 OJ C226, 8.8.2000, p 1.

5 OJ L9, 14.2.1976, p 40.

6 OJ L180, 19.7.2000, p 22.

7 OJ L225, 12.8.1986, p 43.

8 OJ C186, 2.7.1999, p 3.

HAS ADOPTED THIS DIRECTIVE—

CHAPTER I
GENERAL PROVISIONS

[3.301]
Article 1
Purpose

The purpose of this Directive is to lay down a general framework for combating discrimination on the grounds of religion or belief, disability, age or sexual orientation as regards employment and occupation, with a view to putting into effect in the Member States the principle of equal treatment.

[3.302]
Article 2
Concept of discrimination

1. For the purposes of this Directive, the "principle of equal treatment" shall mean that there shall be no direct or indirect discrimination whatsoever on any of the grounds referred to in Article 1.

2. For the purposes of paragraph 1—

(a) direct discrimination shall be taken to occur where one person is treated less favourably than another is, has been or would be treated in a comparable situation, on any of the grounds referred to in Article 1;

(b) indirect discrimination shall be taken to occur where an apparently neutral provision, criterion or practice would put persons having a particular religion or belief, a particular disability, a particular age, or a particular sexual orientation at a particular disadvantage compared with other persons unless—
   (i) that provision, criterion or practice is objectively justified by a legitimate aim and the means of achieving that aim are appropriate and necessary, or
   (ii) as regards persons with a particular disability, the employer or any person or organisation to whom this Directive applies, is obliged, under national legislation, to take appropriate measures in line with the principles contained in Article 5 in order to eliminate disadvantages entailed by such provision, criterion or practice.

3. Harassment shall be deemed to be a form of discrimination within the meaning of paragraph 1, when unwanted conduct related to any of the grounds referred to in Article 1 takes place with the purpose or effect of violating the dignity of a person and of creating an intimidating, hostile, degrading, humiliating or offensive environment. In this context, the concept of harassment may be defined in accordance with the national laws and practice of the Member States.
4. An instruction to discriminate against persons on any of the grounds referred to in Article 1 shall be deemed to be discrimination within the meaning of paragraph 1.
5. This Directive shall be without prejudice to measures laid down by national law which, in a democratic society, are necessary for public security, for the maintenance of public order and the prevention of criminal offences, for the protection of health and for the protection of the rights and freedoms of others.

[3.303]
Article 3
Scope

1. Within the limits of the areas of competence conferred on the Community, this Directive shall apply to all persons, as regards both the public and private sectors, including public bodies, in relation to—
   (a) conditions for access to employment, to self-employment or to occupation, including selection criteria and recruitment conditions, whatever the branch of activity and at all levels of the professional hierarchy, including promotion;
   (b) access to all types and to all levels of vocational guidance, vocational training, advanced vocational training and retraining, including practical work experience;
   (c) employment and working conditions, including dismissals and pay;
   (d) membership of, and involvement in, an organisation of workers or employers, or any organisation whose members carry on a particular profession, including the benefits provided for by such organisations.

2. This Directive does not cover differences of treatment based on nationality and is without prejudice to provisions and conditions relating to the entry into and residence of third-country nationals and stateless persons in the territory of Member States, and to any treatment which arises from the legal status of the third-country nationals and stateless persons concerned.
3. This Directive does not apply to payments of any kind made by state schemes or similar, including state social security or social protection schemes.
4. Member States may provide that this Directive, in so far as it relates to discrimination on the grounds of disability and age, shall not apply to the armed forces.

[3.304]
Article 4
Occupational requirements

1. Notwithstanding Article 2(1) and (2), Member States may provide that a difference of treatment which is based on a characteristic related to any of the grounds referred to in Article 1 shall not constitute discrimination where, by reason of the nature of the particular occupational activities concerned or of the context in which they are carried out, such a characteristic constitutes a genuine and determining occupational requirement, provided that the objective is legitimate and the requirement is proportionate.
2. Member States may maintain national legislation in force at the date of adoption of this Directive or provide for future legislation incorporating national practices existing at the date of adoption of this Directive pursuant to which, in the case of occupational activities within churches and other public or private organisations the ethos of which is based on religion or belief, a difference of treatment based on a person's religion or belief shall not constitute discrimination where, by reason of the nature of these activities or of the context in which they are carried out, a person's religion or belief constitute a genuine, legitimate and justified occupational requirement, having regard to the organisation's ethos. This difference of treatment shall be implemented taking account of Member States' constitutional provisions and principles, as well as the general principles of Community law, and should not justify discrimination on another ground.

Provided that its provisions are otherwise complied with, this Directive shall thus not prejudice the right of churches and other public or private organisations, the ethos of which is based on religion or belief, acting in conformity with national constitutions and laws, to require individuals working for them to act in good faith and with loyalty to the organisation's ethos.

[3.305]
Article 5
Reasonable accommodation for disabled persons
In order to guarantee compliance with the principle of equal treatment in relation to persons with disabilities, reasonable accommodation shall be provided. This means that employers shall take appropriate measures, where needed in a particular case, to enable a person with a disability to have access to, participate in, or advance in employment, or to undergo training, unless such measures would impose a disproportionate burden on the employer. This burden shall not be disproportionate when it is sufficiently remedied by measures existing within the framework of the disability policy of the Member State concerned.

[3.306]
Article 6
Justification of differences of treatment on grounds of age
1. Notwithstanding Article 2(2), Member States may provide that differences of treatment on grounds of age shall not constitute discrimination, if, within the context of national law, they are objectively and reasonably justified by a legitimate aim, including legitimate employment policy, labour market and vocational training objectives, and if the means of achieving that aim are appropriate and necessary.

Such differences of treatment may include, among others—

(a) the setting of special conditions on access to employment and vocational training, employment and occupation, including dismissal and remuneration conditions, for young people, older workers and persons with caring responsibilities in order to promote their vocational integration or ensure their protection;

(b) the fixing of minimum conditions of age, professional experience or seniority in service for access to employment or to certain advantages linked to employment;

(c) the fixing of a maximum age for recruitment which is based on the training requirements of the post in question or the need for a reasonable period of employment before retirement.

2. Notwithstanding Article 2(2), Member States may provide that the fixing for occupational social security schemes of ages for admission or entitlement to retirement or invalidity benefits, including the fixing under those schemes of different ages for employees or groups or categories of employees, and the use, in the context of such schemes, of age criteria in actuarial calculations, does not constitute discrimination on the grounds of age, provided this does not result in discrimination on the grounds of sex.

[3.307]
Article 7
Positive action
1. With a view to ensuring full equality in practice, the principle of equal treatment shall not prevent any Member State from maintaining or adopting specific measures to prevent or compensate for disadvantages linked to any of the grounds referred to in Article 1.
2. With regard to disabled persons, the principle of equal treatment shall be without prejudice to the right of Member States to maintain or adopt provisions on the protection of health and safety at work or to measures aimed at creating or maintaining provisions or facilities for safeguarding or promoting their integration into the working environment.

[3.308]
Article 8
Minimum requirements
1. Member States may introduce or maintain provisions which are more favourable to the protection of the principle of equal treatment than those laid down in this Directive.
2. The implementation of this Directive shall under no circumstances constitute grounds for a reduction in the level of protection against discrimination already afforded by Member States in the fields covered by this Directive.

CHAPTER II
REMEDIES AND ENFORCEMENT

[3.309]
Article 9
Defence of rights

1. Member States shall ensure that judicial and/or administrative procedures, including where they deem it appropriate conciliation procedures, for the enforcement of obligations under this Directive are available to all persons who consider themselves wronged by failure to apply the principle of equal treatment to them, even after the relationship in which the discrimination is alleged to have occurred has ended.
2. Member States shall ensure that associations, organisations or other legal entities which have, in accordance with the criteria laid down by their national law, a legitimate interest in ensuring that the provisions of this Directive are complied with, may engage, either on behalf or in support of the complainant, with his or her approval, in any judicial and/or administrative procedure provided for the enforcement of obligations under this Directive.
3. Paragraphs 1 and 2 are without prejudice to national rules relating to time limits for bringing actions as regards the principle of equality of treatment.

[3.310]
Article 10
Burden of proof

1. Member States shall take such measures as are necessary, in accordance with their national judicial systems, to ensure that, when persons who consider themselves wronged because the principle of equal treatment has not been applied to them establish, before a court or other competent authority, facts from which it may be presumed that there has been direct or indirect discrimination, it shall be for the respondent to prove that there has been no breach of the principle of equal treatment.
2. Paragraph 1 shall not prevent Member States from introducing rules of evidence which are more favourable to plaintiffs.
3. Paragraph 1 shall not apply to criminal procedures.
4. Paragraphs 1, 2 and 3 shall also apply to any legal proceedings commenced in accordance with Article 9(2).
5. Member States need not apply paragraph 1 to proceedings in which it is for the court or competent body to investigate the facts of the case.

[3.311]
Article 11
Victimisation

Member States shall introduce into their national legal systems such measures as are necessary to protect employees against dismissal or other adverse treatment by the employer as a reaction to a complaint within the undertaking or to any legal proceedings aimed at enforcing compliance with the principle of equal treatment.

[3.312]
Article 12
Dissemination of information

Member States shall take care that the provisions adopted pursuant to this Directive, together with the relevant provisions already in force in this field, are brought to the attention of the persons concerned by all appropriate means, for example at the workplace, throughout their territory.

[3.313]
Article 13
Social dialogue

1. Member States shall, in accordance with their national traditions and practice, take adequate measures to promote dialogue between the social partners with a view to fostering equal treatment, including through the monitoring of workplace practices, collective agreements, codes of conduct and through research or exchange of experiences and good practices.
2. Where consistent with their national traditions and practice, Member States shall encourage the social partners, without prejudice to their autonomy, to conclude at the appropriate level agreements laying down anti-discrimination rules in the fields referred to in Article 3 which fall within the scope of collective bargaining. These agreements shall respect the minimum requirements laid down by this Directive and by the relevant national implementing measures.

[3.314]
Article 14
Dialogue with non-governmental organisations

Member States shall encourage dialogue with appropriate non-governmental organisations which have, in accordance with their national law and practice, a legitimate interest in contributing to the fight against discrimination on any of the grounds referred to in Article 1 with a view to promoting the principle of equal treatment.

CHAPTER III
PARTICULAR PROVISIONS

[3.315]
Article 15
Northern Ireland

1. In order to tackle the under-representation of one of the major religious communities in the police service of Northern Ireland, differences in treatment regarding recruitment into that service, including its support staff, shall not constitute discrimination insofar as those differences in treatment are expressly authorised by national legislation.

2. In order to maintain a balance of opportunity in employment for teachers in Northern Ireland while furthering the reconciliation of historical divisions between the major religious communities there, the provisions on religion or belief in this Directive shall not apply to the recruitment of teachers in schools in Northern Ireland in so far as this is expressly authorised by national legislation.

CHAPTER IV
FINAL PROVISIONS

[3.316]
Article 16
Compliance

Member States shall take the necessary measures to ensure that—

(a) any laws, regulations and administrative provisions contrary to the principle of equal treatment are abolished;

(b) any provisions contrary to the principle of equal treatment which are included in contracts or collective agreements, internal rules of undertakings or rules governing the independent occupations and professions and workers' and employers' organisations are, or may be, declared null and void or are amended.

[3.317]
Article 17
Sanctions

Member States shall lay down the rules on sanctions applicable to infringements of the national provisions adopted pursuant to this Directive and shall take all measures necessary to ensure that they are applied. The sanctions, which may comprise the payment of compensation to the victim, must be effective, proportionate and dissuasive. Member States shall notify those provisions to the Commission by 2 December 2003 at the latest and shall notify it without delay of any subsequent amendment affecting them.

[3.318]
Article 18
Implementation

Member States shall adopt the laws, regulations and administrative provisions necessary to comply with this Directive by 2 December 2003 at the latest or may entrust the social partners, at their joint request, with the implementation of this Directive as regards provisions concerning collective agreements. In such cases, Member States shall ensure that, no later than 2 December 2003, the social partners introduce the necessary measures by agreement, the Member States concerned being required to take any necessary measures to enable them at any time to be in a position to guarantee the results imposed by this Directive. They shall forthwith inform the Commission thereof.

In order to take account of particular conditions, Member States may, if necessary, have an additional period of 3 years from 2 December 2003, that is to say a total of 6 years, to implement the provisions of this Directive on age and disability discrimination. In that event they shall inform the Commission forthwith. Any Member State which chooses to use this additional period shall report annually to the Commission on the steps it is taking to tackle age and disability discrimination and on the progress it is making towards implementation. The Commission shall report annually to the Council.

When Member States adopt these measures, they shall contain a reference to this Directive or be accompanied by such reference on the occasion of their official publication. The methods of making such reference shall be laid down by Member States.

[3.319]
Article 19
Report

1. Member States shall communicate to the Commission, by 2 December 2005 at the latest and every five years thereafter, all the information necessary for the Commission to draw up a report to the European Parliament and the Council on the application of this Directive.

2. The Commission's report shall take into account, as appropriate, the viewpoints of the social partners and relevant non-governmental organisations. In accordance with the principle of gender mainstreaming, this report shall, inter alia, provide an assessment of the impact of the measures taken on women and men. In the light of the information received, this report shall include, if necessary, proposals to revise and update this Directive.

[3.320]
Article 20
Entry into force

This Directive shall enter into force on the day of its publication in the *Official Journal of the European Communities*.

[3.321]
Article 21
Addressees

This Directive is addressed to the Member States.

COUNCIL REGULATION

(44/2001/EC)

of 22 December 2000

on jurisdiction and the recognition and enforcement of judgments in civil and commercial matters

NOTES

Date of publication in OJ: OJ L12, 16.01.2001, p 1.

This Regulation is repealed by European Parliament and Council Regulation 1215/2012/EU, Art 80 at **[3.684]**, with effect from 10 January 2015 and subject to transitional provisions: see Arts 66, 81 at **[3.682]**, **[3.685]**.

Only those parts of this Regulation of most relevance to this work are included.

See *Harvey* H(3).

[3.322]

THE COUNCIL OF THE EUROPEAN UNION,

Having regard to the Treaty establishing the European Community, and in particular Article 61(c) and Article 67(1) thereof,

Having regard to the proposal from the Commission,[1]

Having regard to the opinion of the European Parliament,[2]

Having regard to the opinion of the Economic and Social Committee,[3]

Whereas:

(1) The Community has set itself the objective of maintaining and developing an area of freedom, security and justice, in which the free movement of persons is ensured. In order to establish progressively such an area, the Community should adopt, amongst other things, the measures relating to judicial cooperation in civil matters which are necessary for the sound operation of the internal market.

(2) Certain differences between national rules governing jurisdiction and recognition of judgments hamper the sound operation of the internal market. Provisions to unify the rules of conflict of jurisdiction in civil and commercial matters and to simplify the formalities with a view to rapid and simple recognition and enforcement of judgments from Member States bound by this Regulation are essential.

(3) This area is within the field of judicial cooperation in civil matters within the meaning of Article 65 of the Treaty.

(4) In accordance with the principles of subsidiarity and proportionality as set out in Article 5 of the Treaty, the objectives of this Regulation cannot be sufficiently achieved by the Member States and can therefore be better achieved by the Community. This Regulation confines itself to the minimum required in order to achieve those objectives and does not go beyond what is necessary for that purpose.

(5) On 27 September 1968 the Member States, acting under Article 293, fourth indent, of the Treaty, concluded the Brussels Convention on Jurisdiction and the Enforcement of Judgments in

Civil and Commercial Matters, as amended by Conventions on the Accession of the New Member States to that Convention (hereinafter referred to as the "Brussels Convention").[4] *On 16 September 1988 Member States and EFTA States concluded the Lugano Convention on Jurisdiction and the Enforcement of Judgments in Civil and Commercial Matters, which is a parallel Convention to the 1968 Brussels Convention. Work has been undertaken for the revision of those Conventions, and the Council has approved the content of the revised texts. Continuity in the results achieved in that revision should be ensured.*

(6) In order to attain the objective of free movement of judgments in civil and commercial matters, it is necessary and appropriate that the rules governing jurisdiction and the recognition and enforcement of judgments be governed by a Community legal instrument which is binding and directly applicable.

(7) The scope of this Regulation must cover all the main civil and commercial matters apart from certain well-defined matters.

(8) There must be a link between proceedings to which this Regulation applies and the territory of the Member States bound by this Regulation. Accordingly common rules on jurisdiction should, in principle, apply when the defendant is domiciled in one of those Member States.

(9) A defendant not domiciled in a Member State is in general subject to national rules of jurisdiction applicable in the territory of the Member State of the court seised, and a defendant domiciled in a Member State not bound by this Regulation must remain subject to the Brussels Convention.

(10) For the purposes of the free movement of judgments, judgments given in a Member State bound by this Regulation should be recognised and enforced in another Member State bound by this Regulation, even if the judgment debtor is domiciled in a third State.

(11) The rules of jurisdiction must be highly predictable and founded on the principle that jurisdiction is generally based on the defendant's domicile and jurisdiction must always be available on this ground save in a few well-defined situations in which the subject-matter of the litigation or the autonomy of the parties warrants a different linking factor. The domicile of a legal person must be defined autonomously so as to make the common rules more transparent and avoid conflicts of jurisdiction.

(12) In addition to the defendant's domicile, there should be alternative grounds of jurisdiction based on a close link between the court and the action or in order to facilitate the sound administration of justice.

(13) In relation to insurance, consumer contracts and employment, the weaker party should be protected by rules of jurisdiction more favourable to his interests than the general rules provide for.

(14) The autonomy of the parties to a contract, other than an insurance, consumer or employment contract, where only limited autonomy to determine the courts having jurisdiction is allowed, must be respected subject to the exclusive grounds of jurisdiction laid down in this Regulation.

(15) In the interests of the harmonious administration of justice it is necessary to minimise the possibility of concurrent proceedings and to ensure that irreconcilable judgments will not be given in two Member States. There must be a clear and effective mechanism for resolving cases of lis pendens and related actions and for obviating problems flowing from national differences as to the determination of the time when a case is regarded as pending. For the purposes of this Regulation that time should be defined autonomously.

(16) Mutual trust in the administration of justice in the Community justifies judgments given in a Member State being recognised automatically without the need for any procedure except in cases of dispute.

(17) By virtue of the same principle of mutual trust, the procedure for making enforceable in one Member State a judgment given in another must be efficient and rapid. To that end, the declaration that a judgment is enforceable should be issued virtually automatically after purely formal checks of the documents supplied, without there being any possibility for the court to raise of its own motion any of the grounds for non-enforcement provided for by this Regulation.

(18) However, respect for the rights of the defence means that the defendant should be able to appeal in an adversarial procedure, against the declaration of enforceability, if he considers one of the grounds for non-enforcement to be present. Redress procedures should also be available to the claimant where his application for a declaration of enforceability has been rejected.

(19) Continuity between the Brussels Convention and this Regulation should be ensured, and transitional provisions should be laid down to that end. The same need for continuity applies as regards the interpretation of the Brussels Convention by the Court of Justice of the European Communities and the 1971 Protocol[5] *should remain applicable also to cases already pending when this Regulation enters into force.*

(20) The United Kingdom and Ireland, in accordance with Article 3 of the Protocol on the

position of the United Kingdom and Ireland annexed to the Treaty on European Union and to the Treaty establishing the European Community, have given notice of their wish to take part in the adoption and application of this Regulation.

(21)–(29) (*Outside the scope of this work.*)

NOTES

Repealed as noted at the beginning of this Regulation.

[1] OJ C376, 28.12.1999, p 1.

[2] Opinion delivered on 21 September 2000 (not yet published in the Official Journal).

[3] OJ C117, 26.4.2000, p 6.

[4] OJ L299, 31.12.1972, p 32; OJ L304, 30.10.1978, p 1; OJ L388, 31.12.1982, p 1; OJ L285, 3.10.1989, p 1; OJ C15, 15.1.1997, p 1; for a consolidated text, see OJ C27, 26.1.1998, p 1.

[5] OJ L204, 2.8.1975, p 28; OJ L304, 30.10.1978, p 1; OJ L388, 31.12.1982, p 1; OJ L285, 3.10.1989, p 1; OJ C15, 15.1.1997, p 1; for a consolidated text see OJ C27, 26.1.1998, p 28.

HAS ADOPTED THIS REGULATION:

CHAPTER I
SCOPE

[3.323]
Article 1

1. This Regulation shall apply in civil and commercial matters whatever the nature of the court or tribunal. It shall not extend, in particular, to revenue, customs or administrative matters.

2. The Regulation shall not apply to:

- *(a) the status or legal capacity of natural persons, rights in property arising out of a matrimonial relationship, wills and succession;*
- *(b) bankruptcy, proceedings relating to the winding-up of insolvent companies or other legal persons, judicial arrangements, compositions and analogous proceedings;*
- *(c) social security;*
- *(d) arbitration.*

3. In this Regulation, the term "Member State" shall mean Member States with the exception of Denmark.

NOTES

Repealed as noted at the beginning of this Regulation.

CHAPTER II
JURISDICTION

SECTION 1
GENERAL PROVISIONS

[3.324]
Article 2

1. Subject to this Regulation, persons domiciled in a Member State shall, whatever their nationality, be sued in the courts of that Member State.

2. Persons who are not nationals of the Member State in which they are domiciled shall be governed by the rules of jurisdiction applicable to nationals of that State.

NOTES

Repealed as noted at the beginning of this Regulation.

[3.325]
Article 3

1. Persons domiciled in a Member State may be sued in the courts of another Member State only by virtue of the rules set out in Sections 2 to 7 of this Chapter.

2. In particular the rules of national jurisdiction set out in Annex I shall not be applicable as against them.

NOTES

Repealed as noted at the beginning of this Regulation.

[3.326]
Article 4

1. If the defendant is not domiciled in a Member State, the jurisdiction of the courts of each Member State shall, subject to Articles 22 and 23, be determined by the law of that Member State.

2. As against such a defendant, any person domiciled in a Member State may, whatever his nationality, avail himself in that State of the rules of jurisdiction there in force, and in particular those specified in Annex I, in the same way as the nationals of that State.

NOTES

Repealed as noted at the beginning of this Regulation.

SECTION 2
SPECIAL JURISDICTION

[3.327]
Article 5

A person domiciled in a Member State may, in another Member State, be sued:

1.

(a) in matters relating to a contract, in the courts for the place of performance of the obligation in question;

(b) for the purpose of this provision and unless otherwise agreed, the place of performance of the obligation in question shall be:

— *in the case of the sale of goods, the place in a Member State where, under the contract, the goods were delivered or should have been delivered,*

— *in the case of the provision of services, the place in a Member State where, under the contract, the services were provided or should have been provided,*

(c) if subparagraph (b) does not apply then subparagraph (a) applies;

2. in matters relating to maintenance, in the courts for the place where the maintenance creditor is domiciled or habitually resident or, if the matter is ancillary to proceedings concerning the status of a person, in the court which, according to its own law, has jurisdiction to entertain those proceedings, unless that jurisdiction is based solely on the nationality of one of the parties;

3. in matters relating to tort, delict or quasi-delict, in the courts for the place where the harmful event occurred or may occur;

4. as regards a civil claim for damages or restitution which is based on an act giving rise to criminal proceedings, in the court seised of those proceedings, to the extent that that court has jurisdiction under its own law to entertain civil proceedings;

5. as regards a dispute arising out of the operations of a branch, agency or other establishment, in the courts for the place in which the branch, agency or other establishment is situated;

6. as settlor, trustee or beneficiary of a trust created by the operation of a statute, or by a written instrument, or created orally and evidenced in writing, in the courts of the Member State in which the trust is domiciled;

7. as regards a dispute concerning the payment of remuneration claimed in respect of the salvage of a cargo or freight, in the court under the authority of which the cargo or freight in question:

(a) has been arrested to secure such payment, or

(b) could have been so arrested, but bail or other security has been given;

provided that this provision shall apply only if it is claimed that the defendant has an interest in the cargo or freight or had such an interest at the time of salvage.

NOTES

Repealed as noted at the beginning of this Regulation.

[3.328]
Article 6

A person domiciled in a Member State may also be sued:

1. where he is one of a number of defendants, in the courts for the place where any one of them is domiciled, provided the claims are so closely connected that it is expedient to hear and determine them together to avoid the risk of irreconcilable judgments resulting from separate proceedings;

2. as a third party in an action on a warranty or guarantee or in any other third party proceedings, in the court seised of the original proceedings, unless these were instituted solely with the object of removing him from the jurisdiction of the court which would be competent in his case;

3. on a counter-claim arising from the same contract or facts on which the original claim was based, in the court in which the original claim is pending;

4. in matters relating to a contract, if the action may be combined with an action against the same defendant in matters relating to rights in rem in immovable property, in the court of the Member State in which the property is situated.

NOTES

Repealed as noted at the beginning of this Regulation.

[3.329]

Article 7

Where by virtue of this Regulation a court of a Member State has jurisdiction in actions relating to liability from the use or operation of a ship, that court, or any other court substituted for this purpose by the internal law of that Member State, shall also have jurisdiction over claims for limitation of such liability.

NOTES

Repealed as noted at the beginning of this Regulation.

Articles 8–17 *(Outside the scope of this work.)*

SECTION 5
JURISDICTION OVER INDIVIDUAL CONTRACTS OF EMPLOYMENT

[3.330]

Article 18

1. In matters relating to individual contracts of employment, jurisdiction shall be determined by this Section, without prejudice to Article 4 and point 5 of Article 5.

2. Where an employee enters into an individual contract of employment with an employer who is not domiciled in a Member State but has a branch, agency or other establishment in one of the Member States, the employer shall, in disputes arising out of the operations of the branch, agency or establishment, be deemed to be domiciled in that Member State.

NOTES

Repealed as noted at the beginning of this Regulation.

[3.331]

Article 19

An employer domiciled in a Member State may be sued:

1. in the courts of the Member State where he is domiciled; or

2. in another Member State:

(a) in the courts for the place where the employee habitually carries out his work or in the courts for the last place where he did so, or

(b) if the employee does not or did not habitually carry out his work in any one country, in the courts for the place where the business which engaged the employee is or was situated.

NOTES

Repealed as noted at the beginning of this Regulation.

[3.332]

Article 20

1. An employer may bring proceedings only in the courts of the Member State in which the employee is domiciled.

2. The provisions of this Section shall not affect the right to bring a counter-claim in the court in which, in accordance with this Section, the original claim is pending.

NOTES

Repealed as noted at the beginning of this Regulation.

[3.333]

Article 21

The provisions of this Section may be departed from only by an agreement on jurisdiction:

1. which is entered into after the dispute has arisen; or

2. which allows the employee to bring proceedings in courts other than those indicated in this Section.

NOTES

Repealed as noted at the beginning of this Regulation.

Article 22 *(Outside the scope of this work.)*

SECTION 7
PROROGATION OF JURISDICTION

[3.334]
Article 23

1. If the parties, one or more of whom is domiciled in a Member State, have agreed that a court or the courts of a Member State are to have jurisdiction to settle any disputes which have arisen or which may arise in connection with a particular legal relationship, that court or those courts shall have jurisdiction. Such jurisdiction shall be exclusive unless the parties have agreed otherwise. Such an agreement conferring jurisdiction shall be either:

(a) in writing or evidenced in writing; or

(b) in a form which accords with practices which the parties have established between themselves; or

(c) in international trade or commerce, in a form which accords with a usage of which the parties are or ought to have been aware and which in such trade or commerce is widely known to, and regularly observed by, parties to contracts of the type involved in the particular trade or commerce concerned.

2. Any communication by electronic means which provides a durable record of the agreement shall be equivalent to "writing".

3. Where such an agreement is concluded by parties, none of whom is domiciled in a Member State, the courts of other Member States shall have no jurisdiction over their disputes unless the court or courts chosen have declined jurisdiction.

4. The court or courts of a Member State on which a trust instrument has conferred jurisdiction shall have exclusive jurisdiction in any proceedings brought against a settlor, trustee or beneficiary, if relations between these persons or their rights or obligations under the trust are involved.

5. Agreements or provisions of a trust instrument conferring jurisdiction shall have no legal force if they are contrary to Articles 13, 17 or 21, or if the courts whose jurisdiction they purport to exclude have exclusive jurisdiction by virtue of Article 22.

NOTES

Repealed as noted at the beginning of this Regulation.

[3.335]
Article 24

Apart from jurisdiction derived from other provisions of this Regulation, a court of a Member State before which a defendant enters an appearance shall have jurisdiction. This rule shall not apply where appearance was entered to contest the jurisdiction, or where another court has exclusive jurisdiction by virtue of Article 22.

NOTES

Repealed as noted at the beginning of this Regulation.

SECTION 8
EXAMINATION AS TO JURISDICTION AND ADMISSIBILITY

[3.336]
Article 25

Where a court of a Member State is seised of a claim which is principally concerned with a matter over which the courts of another Member State have exclusive jurisdiction by virtue of Article 22, it shall declare of its own motion that it has no jurisdiction.

NOTES

Repealed as noted at the beginning of this Regulation.

[3.337]
Article 26

1. Where a defendant domiciled in one Member State is sued in a court of another Member State and does not enter an appearance, the court shall declare of its own motion that it has no jurisdiction unless its jurisdiction is derived from the provisions of this Regulation.

2. The court shall stay the proceedings so long as it is not shown that the defendant has been able to receive the document instituting the proceedings or an equivalent document in sufficient time to enable him to arrange for his defence, or that all necessary steps have been taken to this end.

3. Article 19 of Council Regulation (EC) No 1348/2000 of 29 May 2000 on the service in the Member States of judicial and extrajudicial documents in civil or commercial matters[1] shall apply instead of the provisions of paragraph 2 if the document instituting the proceedings or an equivalent document had to be transmitted from one Member State to another pursuant to this Regulation.

4. Where the provisions of Regulation (EC) No 1348/2000 are not applicable, Article 15 of the Hague Convention of 15 November 1965 on the Service Abroad of Judicial and Extrajudicial Documents in Civil or Commercial Matters shall apply if the document instituting the proceedings or an equivalent document had to be transmitted pursuant to that Convention.

NOTES

Repealed as noted at the beginning of this Regulation.

[1] OJ L160, 30.6.2000, p 37.

SECTION 9
LIS PENDENS — RELATED ACTIONS

[3.338]
Article 27

1. Where proceedings involving the same cause of action and between the same parties are brought in the courts of different Member States, any court other than the court first seised shall of its own motion stay its proceedings until such time as the jurisdiction of the court first seised is established.

2. Where the jurisdiction of the court first seised is established, any court other than the court first seised shall decline jurisdiction in favour of that court.

NOTES

Repealed as noted at the beginning of this Regulation.

[3.339]
Article 28

1. Where related actions are pending in the courts of different Member States, any court other than the court first seised may stay its proceedings.

2. Where these actions are pending at first instance, any court other than the court first seised may also, on the application of one of the parties, decline jurisdiction if the court first seised has jurisdiction over the actions in question and its law permits the consolidation thereof.

3. For the purposes of this Article, actions are deemed to be related where they are so closely connected that it is expedient to hear and determine them together to avoid the risk of irreconcilable judgments resulting from separate proceedings.

NOTES

Repealed as noted at the beginning of this Regulation.

[3.340]
Article 29

Where actions come within the exclusive jurisdiction of several courts, any court other than the court first seised shall decline jurisdiction in favour of that court.

NOTES

Repealed as noted at the beginning of this Regulation.

[3.341]
Article 30

For the purposes of this Section, a court shall be deemed to be seised:

1. at the time when the document instituting the proceedings or an equivalent document is lodged with the court, provided that the plaintiff has not subsequently failed to take the steps he was required to take to have service effected on the defendant, or

2. if the document has to be served before being lodged with the court, at the time when it is received by the authority responsible for service, provided that the plaintiff has not subsequently failed to take the steps he was required to take to have the document lodged with the court.

NOTES

Repealed as noted at the beginning of this Regulation.

SECTION 10
PROVISIONAL, INCLUDING PROTECTIVE, MEASURES

[3.342]
Article 31

Application may be made to the courts of a Member State for such provisional, including protective, measures as may be available under the law of that State, even if, under this Regulation, the courts of another Member State have jurisdiction as to the substance of the matter.

NOTES
Repealed as noted at the beginning of this Regulation.

Articles 32–58 (*Outside the scope of this work.*)

CHAPTER V
GENERAL PROVISIONS

[3.343]
Article 59
1. In order to determine whether a party is domiciled in the Member State whose courts are seised of a matter, the court shall apply its internal law.
2. If a party is not domiciled in the Member State whose courts are seised of the matter, then, in order to determine whether the party is domiciled in another Member State, the court shall apply the law of that Member State.

NOTES
Repealed as noted at the beginning of this Regulation.

[3.344]
Article 60
1. For the purposes of this Regulation, a company or other legal person or association of natural or legal persons is domiciled at the place where it has its:
(a) statutory seat, or
(b) central administration, or
(c) principal place of business.
2. For the purposes of the United Kingdom and Ireland "statutory seat" means the registered office or, where there is no such office anywhere, the place of incorporation or, where there is no such place anywhere, the place under the law of which the formation took place.
3. In order to determine whether a trust is domiciled in the Member State whose courts are seised of the matter, the court shall apply its rules of private international law.

NOTES
Repealed as noted at the beginning of this Regulation.

Articles 61–75 (*Outside the scope of this work.*)

CHAPTER VIII
FINAL PROVISIONS

[3.345]
Article 76
This Regulation shall enter into force on 1 March 2002.
This Regulation is binding in its entirety and directly applicable in the Member States in accordance with the Treaty establishing the European Community.

NOTES
Repealed as noted at the beginning of this Regulation.

[ANNEX I
RULES OF JURISDICTION REFERRED TO IN ARTICLES 3(2) AND 4(2)

[3.346]
— *in Belgium: Articles 5 through 14 of the Law of 16 July 2004 on private international law,*

— *in Bulgaria: Article 4, paragraph 1, point 2 of the Private International Law Code,*

— *in the Czech Republic: Article 86 of Act No 99/1963 Coll, the Code of Civil Procedure ('občanský soudní řád'), as amended,*

— *in Denmark: Article 246(2) and (3) of the Administration of Justice Act (lov om rettens pleje'),*

— *in Germany: Article 23 of the code of civil procedure ('Zivilprozeßordnung'),*

— *in Estonia: Article 86 of the Code of Civil Procedure ('tsiviilkohtumenetluse seadustik'),*

— *in Ireland: the rules which enable jurisdiction to be founded on the document instituting the proceedings having been served on the defendant during his temporary presence in Ireland,*

— *in Greece: Article 40 of the code of civil procedure ('Κώδικας Πολιτικής Δικονομίας');*

— *in France: Articles 14 and 15 of the civil code ('Code civil'),*

— *in Italy: Articles 3 and 4 law 218 of 31 May 1995,*

— *in Cyprus: section 21(2) of the Courts of Justice Law No 14 of 1960, as amended,*

— *in Latvia: section 27 and paragraphs 3, 5, 6 and 9 of section 28 of the Civil Procedure Law ('Civilprocesa likums'),*

— *in Lithuania: Article 31 of the Code of Civil Procedure ('Civilinio proceso kodeksas'),*

— *in Luxembourg: Articles 14 and 15 of the civil code ('Code civil'),*

— *in Hungary: Article 57 of Law Decree No 13 of 1979 on International Private Law ('a nemzetközi magánjogról szóló 1979. évi 13. törvényerejű rendelet'),]*

— *in Malta: Articles 742, 743 and 744 of the Code of Organisation and Civil Procedure – Chapter 12 ('Kodiċi ta' Organizzazzjoni u Proċedura Ċivili–Kap. 12') and Article 549 of the Commercial Code – Chapter 13 ('Kodiċi tal-kummerċ–Kap. 13'),*

— *in Austria: Article 99 of the Law on Court Jurisdiction ('Jurisdiktionsnorm'),*

— *in Poland: Article 1103, paragraph 4 of the Code of Civil Procedure ('Kodeksu postępowania cywilnego'),*

— *in Portugal: Article 65(1)(b) of the Code of Civil Procedure ('Código de Processo Civil') in so far as it may encompass exorbitant grounds of jurisdiction, such as the courts for the place in which the branch, agency or other establishment is situated (if situated in Portugal) when the central administration (if situated in a foreign State) is the party sued and Article 10 of the Code of Labour Procedure ('Código de Processo do Trabalho') in so far as it may encompass exorbitant grounds of jurisdiction, such as the courts for the place where the plaintiff is domiciled in proceedings relating to individual contracts of employment brought by the employee against the employer,*

— *in Romania: Articles 148–157 of Law No 105/1992 on Private International Law Relations,*

— *in Slovenia: Article 48(2) of the Private International Law and Procedure Act ('Zakon o medarodnem zasebnem pravu in postopku') in relation to Article 47(2) of the Civil Procedure Act ('Zakon o pravdnem postopku') and Article 58 of the Private International Law and Procedure Act ('Zakon o medarodnem zasebnem pravu in postopku') in relation to Article 59 of the Civil Procedure Act ('Zakon o pravdnem postopku'),*

— *in Slovakia: Articles 37 to 37e of Act No 97/1963 on Private International Law and the Rules of Procedure relating thereto,*

— *in Finland: paragraphs 1 and 2 of Section 18(1) of Chapter 10 of the Code of Judicial Procedure ('oikeudenkäymiskaari/rättegångsbalken'),*

— *in Sweden: the first sentence of the first paragraph of Section 3 of Chapter 10 of the Code of Judicial Procedure ('rättegångsbalken'),*

— *in the United Kingdom: the rules which enable jurisdiction to be founded on:*
- *(a) the document instituting the proceedings having been served on the defendant during his temporary presence in the United Kingdom; or*
- *(b) the presence within the United Kingdom of property belonging to the defendant; or*
- *(c) the seizure by the plaintiff of property situated in the United Kingdom.]*

NOTES

Repealed as noted at the beginning of this Regulation.

Substituted by Commission Regulation 156/2012/EU, Art 1, Annex I, as from 14 March 2012.

ANNEXES II–VI

(Annexes II–VI outside the scope of this work.)

COUNCIL DIRECTIVE

(2001/23/EC)

of 12 March 2001

on the approximation of the laws of the Member States relating to the safeguarding of employees' rights in the event of transfers of undertakings, businesses or parts of undertakings or businesses

NOTES

Date of publication in OJ: OJ L82, 22.03.2001, p 16.

This Directive consolidates Directive 77/187/EC ('the Acquired Rights Directive') as amended by Directive 98/50/EC. Annex II at **[3.364]** is a table correlating the provisions in the former and current Directives. For the domestic implementation of this Directive, see the Transfer of Undertakings (Protection of Employment) Regulations 2006, SI 2006/246 at **[2.997]**.

See *Harvey* F.

[3.347]

THE COUNCIL OF THE EUROPEAN UNION,

Having regard to the Treaty establishing the European Community, and in particular Article 94 thereof,

Having regard to the proposal from the Commission,

Having regard to the opinion of the European Parliament,[1]

Having regard to the opinion of the Economic and Social Committee,[2]

Whereas:

(1) Council Directive 77/187/EEC of 14 February 1977 on the approximation of the laws of the Member States relating to the safeguarding of employees' rights in the event of transfers of undertakings, businesses or parts of undertakings or businesses[3] has been substantially amended.[4] In the interests of clarity and rationality, it should therefore be codified.

(2) Economic trends are bringing in their wake, at both national and Community level, changes in the structure of undertakings, through transfers of undertakings, businesses or parts of undertakings or businesses to other employers as a result of legal transfers or mergers.

(3) It is necessary to provide for the protection of employees in the event of a change of employer, in particular, to ensure that their rights are safeguarded.

(4) Differences still remain in the Member States as regards the extent of the protection of employees in this respect and these differences should be reduced.

(5) The Community Charter of the Fundamental Social Rights of Workers adopted on 9 December 1989 ("Social Charter") states, in points 7, 17 and 18 in particular that: "The completion of the internal market must lead to an improvement in the living and working conditions of workers in the European Community. The improvement must cover, where necessary, the development of certain aspects of employment regulations such as procedures for collective redundancies and those regarding bankruptcies. Information, consultation and participation for workers must be developed along appropriate lines, taking account of the practice in force in the various Member States. Such information, consultation and participation must be implemented in due time, particularly in connection with restructuring operations in undertakings or in cases of mergers having an impact on the employment of workers".

(6) In 1977 the Council adopted Directive 77/187/EEC to promote the harmonisation of the relevant national laws ensuring the safeguarding of the rights of employees and requiring transferors and transferees to inform and consult employees' representatives in good time.

(7) That Directive was subsequently amended in the light of the impact of the internal market, the legislative tendencies of the Member States with regard to the rescue of undertakings in economic difficulties, the case-law of the Court of Justice of the European Communities, Council Directive 75/129/EEC of 17 February 1975 on the approximation of the laws of the Member States relating to collective redundancies[5] and the legislation already in force in most Member States.

(8) Considerations of legal security and transparency required that the legal concept of transfer be clarified in the light of the case-law of the Court of Justice. Such clarification has not altered the scope of Directive 77/187/EEC as interpreted by the Court of Justice.

(9) The Social Charter recognises the importance of the fight against all forms of discrimination, especially based on sex, colour, race, opinion and creed.

(10) This Directive should be without prejudice to the time limits set out in Annex I Part B within which the Member States are to comply with Directive 77/187/EEC, and the act amending it,

NOTES

1 Opinion delivered on 25 October 2000 (not yet published in the Official Journal).

2 OJ C367, 20.12.2000, p 21.

3 OJ L61, 5.3.1977, p 26.

4 See Annex I, Part A.

5 OJ L48, 22.2.1975, p 29. Directive replaced by Directive 98/59/EC (OJ L225, 12.8.1998, p 16).

HAS ADOPTED THIS DIRECTIVE—

CHAPTER I
SCOPE AND DEFINITIONS

[3.348]
Article 1

1.
- (a) This Directive shall apply to any transfer of an undertaking, business, or part of an undertaking or business to another employer as a result of a legal transfer or merger.
- (b) Subject to subparagraph (a) and the following provisions of this Article, there is a transfer within the meaning of this Directive where there is a transfer of an economic entity which retains its identity, meaning an organised grouping of resources which has the objective of pursuing an economic activity, whether or not that activity is central or ancillary.
- (c) This Directive shall apply to public and private undertakings engaged in economic activities whether or not they are operating for gain. An administrative reorganisation of public administrative authorities, or the transfer of administrative functions between public administrative authorities, is not a transfer within the meaning of this Directive.

2. This Directive shall apply where and in so far as the undertaking, business or part of the undertaking or business to be transferred is situated within the territorial scope of the Treaty.

3. This Directive shall not apply to seagoing vessels.

[3.349]
Article 2

1. For the purposes of this Directive—
- (a) "transferor" shall mean any natural or legal person who, by reason of a transfer within the meaning of Article 1(1), ceases to be the employer in respect of the undertaking, business or part of the undertaking or business;
- (b) "transferee" shall mean any natural or legal person who, by reason of a transfer within the meaning of Article 1(1), becomes the employer in respect of the undertaking, business or part of the undertaking or business;
- (c) "representatives of employees" and related expressions shall mean the representatives of the employees provided for by the laws or practices of the Member States;
- (d) "employee" shall mean any person who, in the Member State concerned, is protected as an employee under national employment law.

2. This Directive shall be without prejudice to national law as regards the definition of contract of employment or employment relationship.

However, Member States shall not exclude from the scope of this Directive contracts of employment or employment relationships solely because—
- (a) of the number of working hours performed or to be performed,
- (b) they are employment relationships governed by a fixed-duration contract of employment within the meaning of Article 1(1) of Council Directive 91/383/EEC of 25 June 1991 supplementing the measures to encourage improvements in the safety and health at work of workers with a fixed-duration employment relationship or a temporary employment relationship, or

they are temporary employment relationships within the meaning of Article 1(2) of Directive 91/383/EEC, and the undertaking, business or part of the undertaking or business transferred is, or is part of, the temporary employment business which is the employer.

CHAPTER II
SAFEGUARDING OF EMPLOYEES' RIGHTS

[3.350]
Article 3

1. The transferor's rights and obligations arising from a contract of employment or from an employment relationship existing on the date of a transfer shall, by reason of such transfer, be transferred to the transferee.

Member States may provide that, after the date of transfer, the transferor and the transferee shall be jointly and severally liable in respect of obligations which arose before the date of transfer from a contract of employment or an employment relationship existing on the date of the transfer.

2. Member States may adopt appropriate measures to ensure that the transferor notifies the transferee of all the rights and obligations which will be transferred to the transferee under this Article, so far as those rights and obligations are or ought to have been known to the transferor at the time of the transfer. A failure by the transferor to notify the transferee of any such right or obligation shall not affect the transfer of that right or obligation and the rights of any employees against the transferee and/or transferor in respect of that right or obligation.

3. Following the transfer, the transferee shall continue to observe the terms and conditions agreed in any collective agreement on the same terms applicable to the transferor under that agreement, until the date of termination or expiry of the collective agreement or the entry into force or application of another collective agreement.

Member States may limit the period for observing such terms and conditions with the proviso that it shall not be less than one year.

4.

(a) Unless Member States provide otherwise, paragraphs 1 and 3 shall not apply in relation to employees' rights to old-age, invalidity or survivors' benefits under supplementary company or intercompany pension schemes outside the statutory social security schemes in Member States.

(b) Even where they do not provide in accordance with subparagraph (a) that paragraphs 1 and 3 apply in relation to such rights, Member States shall adopt the measures necessary to protect the interests of employees and of persons no longer employed in the transferor's business at the time of the transfer in respect of rights conferring on them immediate or prospective entitlement to old age benefits, including survivors' benefits, under supplementary schemes referred to in subparagraph (a).

[3.351]
Article 4

1. The transfer of the undertaking, business or part of the undertaking or business shall not in itself constitute grounds for dismissal by the transferor or the transferee. This provision shall not stand in the way of dismissals that may take place for economic, technical or organisational reasons entailing changes in the workforce.

Member States may provide that the first subparagraph shall not apply to certain specific categories of employees who are not covered by the laws or practice of the Member States in respect of protection against dismissal.

2. If the contract of employment or the employment relationship is terminated because the transfer involves a substantial change in working conditions to the detriment of the employee, the employer shall be regarded as having been responsible for termination of the contract of employment or of the employment relationship.

[3.352]
Article 5

1. Unless Member States provide otherwise, Articles 3 and 4 shall not apply to any transfer of an undertaking, business or part of an undertaking or business where the transferor is the subject of bankruptcy proceedings or any analogous insolvency proceedings which have been instituted with a view to the liquidation of the assets of the transferor and are under the supervision of a competent public authority (which may be an insolvency practitioner authorised by a competent public authority).

2. Where Articles 3 and 4 apply to a transfer during insolvency proceedings which have been opened in relation to a transferor (whether or not those proceedings have been instituted with a view to the liquidation of the assets of the transferor) and provided that such proceedings are under the supervision of a competent public authority (which may be an insolvency practitioner determined by national law) a Member State may provide that—

(a) notwithstanding Article 3(1), the transferor's debts arising from any contracts of employment or employment relationships and payable before the transfer or before the opening of the insolvency proceedings shall not be transferred to the transferee, provided that such proceedings give rise, under the law of that Member State, to protection at least equivalent to that provided for in situations covered by Council Directive 80/987/EEC of 20 October 1980 on the approximation of the laws of the Member States relating to the protection of employees in the event of the insolvency of their employer, and, or alternatively, that,

(b) the transferee, transferor or person or persons exercising the transferor's functions, on the one hand, and the representatives of the employees on the other hand may agree alterations, in so far as current law or practice permits, to the employees' terms and conditions of employment designed to safeguard employment opportunities by ensuring the survival of the undertaking, business or part of the undertaking or business.

3. A Member State may apply paragraph 20(b) to any transfers where the transferor is in a situation of serious economic crisis, as defined by national law, provided that the situation is declared by a competent public authority and open to judicial supervision, on condition that such provisions already existed in national law on 17 July 1998.

The Commission shall present a report on the effects of this provision before 17 July 2003 and shall submit any appropriate proposals to the Council.

4. Member States shall take appropriate measures with a view to preventing misuse of insolvency proceedings in such a way as to deprive employees of the rights provided for in this Directive.

[3.353]

Article 6

1. If the undertaking, business or part of an undertaking or business preserves its autonomy, the status and function of the representatives or of the representation of the employees affected by the transfer shall be preserved on the same terms and subject to the same conditions as existed before the date of the transfer by virtue of law, regulation, administrative provision or agreement, provided that the conditions necessary for the constitution of the employee's representation are fulfilled.

The first subparagraph shall not supply if, under the laws, regulations, administrative provisions or practice in the Member States, or by agreement with the representatives of the employees, the conditions necessary for the reappointment of the representatives of the employees or for the reconstitution of the representation of the employees are fulfilled.

Where the transferor is the subject of bankruptcy proceedings or any analogous insolvency proceedings which have been instituted with a view to the liquidation of the assets of the transferor and are under the supervision of a competent public authority (which may be an insolvency practitioner authorised by a competent public authority), Member States may take the necessary measures to ensure that the transferred employees are properly represented until the new election or designation of representatives of the employees.

If the undertaking, business or part of an undertaking or business does not preserve its autonomy, the Member States shall take the necessary measures to ensure that the employees transferred who were represented before the transfer continue to be properly represented during the period necessary for the reconstitution or reappointment of the representation of employees in accordance with national law or practice.

2. If the term of office of the representatives of the employees affected by the transfer expires as a result of the transfer, the representatives shall continue to enjoy the protection provided by the laws, regulations, administrative provisions or practice of the Member States.

CHAPTER III
INFORMATION AND CONSULTATION

[3.354]

Article 7

1. The transferor and transferee shall be required to inform the representatives of their respective employees affected by the transfer of the following—

— the date or proposed date of the transfer,
— the reasons for the transfer,
— the legal, economic and social implications of the transfer for the employees,
— any measures envisaged in relation to the employees.

The transferor must give such information to the representatives of his employees in good time, before the transfer is carried out.

The transferee must give such information to the representatives of his employees in good time, and in any event before his employees are directly affected by the transfer as regards their conditions of work and employment.

2. Where the transferor or the transferee envisages measures in relation to his employees, he shall consult the representatives of this employees in good time on such measures with a view to reaching an agreement.

3. Member States whose laws, regulations or administrative provisions provide that representatives of the employees may have recourse to an arbitration board to obtain a decision on the measures to be taken in relation to employees may limit the obligations laid down in paragraphs 1 and 2 to cases where the transfer carried out gives rise to a change in the business likely to entail serious disadvantages for a considerable number of the employees.

The information and consultations shall cover at least the measures envisaged in relation to the employees.

The information must be provided and consultations take place in good time before the change in the business as referred to in the first subparagraph is effected.

4. The obligations laid down in this Article shall apply irrespective of whether the decision resulting in the transfer is taken by the employer or an undertaking controlling the employer.

In considering alleged breaches of the information and consultation requirements laid down by this Directive, the argument that such a breach occurred because the information was not provided by an undertaking controlling the employer shall not be accepted as an excuse.

5. Member States may limit the obligations laid down in paragraphs 1, 2 and 3 to undertakings or businesses which, in terms of the number of employees, meet the conditions for the election or nomination of a collegiate body representing the employees.
6. Member States shall provide that, where there are no representatives of the employees in an undertaking or business through no fault of their own, the employees concerned must be informed in advance of—
- the date or proposed date of the transfer,
- the reason for the transfer,
- the legal, economic and social implications of the transfer for the employees,
- any measures envisaged in relation to the employees.

CHAPTER IV
FINAL PROVISIONS

[3.355]
Article 8
This Directive shall not affect the right of Member States to apply or introduce laws, regulations or administrative provisions which are more favourable to employees or to promote or permit collective agreements or agreements between social partners more favourable to employees.

[3.356]
Article 9
Member States shall introduce into their national legal systems such measures as are necessary to enable all employees and representatives of employees who consider themselves wronged by failure to comply with the obligations arising from this Directive to pursue their claims by judicial process after possible recourse to other competent authorities.

[3.357]
Article 10
The Commission shall submit to the Council an analysis of the effect of the provisions of this Directive before 17 July 2006. It shall propose any amendment which may seem necessary.

[3.358]
Article 11
Member States shall communicate to the Commission the texts of the laws, regulations and administrative provisions which they adopt in the field covered by this Directive.

[3.359]
Article 12
Directive 77/187/EEC, as amended by the Directive referred to in Annex I, Part A, is repealed, without prejudice to the obligations of the Member States concerning the time limits for implementation set out in Annex I, Part B.

References to the repealed Directive shall be construed as references to this Directive and shall be read in accordance with the correlation table in Annex II.

[3.360]
Article 13
This Directive shall enter into force on the 20th day following its publication in the *Official Journal of the European Communities*.

[3.361]
Article 14
This Directive is addressed to the Member States.

ANNEX I

PART A
REPEALED DIRECTIVE AND ITS AMENDING DIRECTIVE

(referred to in Article 12)

[3.362]
Council Directive 77/187/EEC (OJ L 61, 5.3.1977, p. 26)

Council Directive 98/50/EC (OJ L 201, 17.7.1998, p. 88)

PART B
DEADLINES FOR TRANSPOSITION INTO NATIONAL LAW

(referred to in Article 12)

[3.363]

Directive	*Deadline for transposition*
77/187/EEC	16 February 1979
98/50/EC	17 July 2001

ANNEX II
CORRELATION TABLE

[3.364]

Directive 77/187/EEC	*This Directive*
Article 1	Article 1
Article 2	Article 2
Article 3	Article 3
Article 4	Article 4
Article 4a	Article 5
Article 5	Article 6
Article 6	Article 7
Article 7	Article 8
Article 7a	Article 9
Article 7b	Article 10
Article 8	Article 11
—	Article 12
—	Article 13
—	Article 14
—	Annex I
—	Annex II

COUNCIL DIRECTIVE

(2001/86/EC)

of 8 October 2001

supplementing the Statute for a European company with regard to the involvement of employees

NOTES

Date of publication in OJ: OJ L294, 10.11.2001, p 22.

For the domestic implementation of this Directive see the European Public Limited-Liability Company (Employee Involvement) (Great Britain) Regulations 2009, SI 2009/2401 at **[2.1181]**.

See *Harvey* NIII(4).

[3.365]

THE COUNCIL OF THE EUROPEAN UNION,

Having regard to the Treaty establishing the European Community, and in particular Article 308 thereof,

Having regard to the amended proposal from the Commission,[1]

Having regard to the opinion of the European Parliament,[2]

Having regard to the opinion of the Economic and Social Committee,[3]

Whereas:

(1) In order to attain the objectives of the Treaty, Council Regulation (EC) No 2157/2001[4] establishes a Statute for a European company (SE).

(2) That Regulation aims at creating a uniform legal framework within which companies from different Member States should be able to plan and carry out the reorganisation of their business on a Community scale.

(3) In order to promote the social objectives of the Community, special provisions have to be set,

notably in the field of employee involvement, aimed at ensuring that the establishment of an SE does not entail the disappearance or reduction of practices of employee involvement existing within the companies participating in the establishment of an SE. This objective should be pursued through the establishment of a set of rules in this field, supplementing the provisions of the Regulation.

(4) Since the objectives of the proposed action, as outlined above, cannot be sufficiently achieved by the Member States, in that the object is to establish a set of rules on employee involvement applicable to the SE, and can therefore, by reason of the scale and impact of the proposed action, be better achieved at Community level, the Community may adopt measures, in accordance with the principle of subsidiarity as set out in Article 5 of the Treaty. In accordance with the principle of proportionality, as set out in that Article, this Directive does not go beyond what is necessary to achieve these objectives.

(5) The great diversity of rules and practices existing in the Member States as regards the manner in which employees' representatives are involved in decision-making within companies makes it inadvisable to set up a single European model of employee involvement applicable to the SE.

(6) Information and consultation procedures at transnational level should nevertheless be ensured in all cases of creation of an SE.

(7) If and when participation rights exist within one or more companies establishing an SE, they should be preserved through their transfer to the SE, once established, unless the parties decide otherwise.

(8) The concrete procedures of employee transnational information and consultation, as well as, if applicable, participation, to apply to each SE should be defined primarily by means of an agreement between the parties concerned or, in the absence thereof, through the application of a set of subsidiary rules.

(9) Member States should still have the option of not applying the standard rules relating to participation in the case of a merger, given the diversity of national systems for employee involvement. Existing systems and practices of participation where appropriate at the level of participating companies must in that case be maintained by adapting registration rules.

(10) The voting rules within the special body representing the employees for negotiation purposes, in particular when concluding agreements providing for a level of participation lower than the one existing within one or more of the participating companies, should be proportionate to the risk of disappearance or reduction of existing systems and practices of participation. That risk is greater in the case of an SE established by way of transformation or merger than by way of creating a holding company or a common subsidiary.

(11) In the absence of an agreement subsequent to the negotiation between employees' representatives and the competent organs of the participating companies, provision should be made for certain standard requirements to apply to the SE, once it is established. These standard requirements should ensure effective practices of transnational information and consultation of employees, as well as their participation in the relevant organs of the SE if and when such participation existed before its establishment within the participating companies.

(12) Provision should be made for the employees' representatives acting within the framework of the Directive to enjoy, when exercising their functions, protection and guarantees which are similar to those provided to employees' representatives by the legislation and/or practice of the country of employment. They should not be subject to any discrimination as a result of the lawful exercise of their activities and should enjoy adequate protection as regards dismissal and other sanctions.

(13) The confidentiality of sensitive information should be preserved even after the expiry of the employees' representatives terms of office and provision should be made to allow the competent organ of the SE to withhold information which would seriously harm, if subject to public disclosure, the functioning of the SE.

(14) Where an SE and its subsidiaries and establishments are subject to Council Directive 94/45/EC of 22 September 1994 on the establishment of a European Works Council or a procedure in Community-scale undertakings and Community-scale groups of undertakings for the purposes of informing and consulting employees,[5] the provisions of that Directive and the provision transposing it into national legislation should not apply to it nor to its subsidiaries and establishments, unless the special negotiating body decides not to open negotiations or to terminate negotiations already opened.

(15) This Directive should not affect other existing rights regarding involvement and need not affect other existing representation structures, provided for by Community and national laws and practices.

(16) Member States should take appropriate measures in the event of failure to comply with the obligations laid down in this Directive.

(17) The Treaty has not provided the necessary powers for the Community to adopt the proposed Directive, other than those provided for in Article 308.

(18) It is a fundamental principle and stated aim of this Directive to secure employees' acquired rights as regards involvement in company decisions. Employee rights in force before the establishment of SEs should provide the basis for employee rights of involvement in the SE (the "before and after" principle). Consequently, that approach should apply not only to the initial establishment of an SE but also to structural changes in an existing SE and to the companies affected by structural change processes.

(19) Member States should be able to provide that representatives of trade unions may be members of a special negotiating body regardless of whether they are employees of a company participating in the establishment of an SE. Member States should in this context in particular be able to introduce this right in cases where trade union representatives have the right to be members of, and to vote in, supervisory or administrative company organs in accordance with national legislation.

(20) In several Member States, employee involvement and other areas of industrial relations are based on both national legislation and practice which in this context is understood also to cover collective agreements at various national, sectoral and/or company levels,

NOTES

1 OJ C138, 29.5.1991, p 8.

2 OJ C342, 20.12.1993, p 15.

3 OJ C124, 21.5.1990, p 34.

4 See page 1 of this Official Journal.

5 OJ L254, 30.9.1994, p 64. Directive as last amended by Directive 97/74/EC (OJ L10, 16.1.1998, p 22).

HAS ADOPTED THIS DIRECTIVE:

SECTION I
GENERAL

[3.366]
Article 1
Objective

1. This Directive governs the involvement of employees in the affairs of European public limited-liability companies (Societas Europaea, hereinafter referred to as "SE"), as referred to in Regulation (EC) No 2157/2001.
2. To this end, arrangements for the involvement of employees shall be established in every SE in accordance with the negotiating procedure referred to in Articles 3 to 6 or, under the circumstances specified in Article 7, in accordance with the Annex.

[3.367]
Article 2
Definitions

For the purposes of this Directive—

(a) "SE" means any company established in accordance with Regulation (EC) No 2157/2001;
(b) "participating companies" means the companies directly participating in the establishing of an SE;
(c) "subsidiary" of a company means an undertaking over which that company exercises a dominant influence defined in accordance with Article 3(2) to (7) of Directive 94/45/EC;
(d) "concerned subsidiary or establishment" means a subsidiary or establishment of a participating company which is proposed to become a subsidiary or establishment of the SE upon its formation;
(e) "employees' representatives" means the employees' representatives provided for by national law and/or practice;
(f) "representative body" means the body representative of the employees set up by the agreements referred to in Article 4 or in accordance with the provisions of the Annex, with the purpose of informing and consulting the employees of an SE and its subsidiaries and establishments situated in the Community and, where applicable, of exercising participation rights in relation to the SE;
(g) "special negotiating body" means the body established in accordance with Article 3 to negotiate with the competent body of the participating companies regarding the establishment of arrangements for the involvement of employees within the SE;
(h) "involvement of employees" means any mechanism, including information, consultation and participation, through which employees' representatives may exercise an influence on decisions to be taken within the company;

(i) "information" means the informing of the body representative of the employees and/or employees' representatives by the competent organ of the SE on questions which concern the SE itself and any of its subsidiaries or establishments situated in another Member State or which exceed the powers of the decision-making organs in a single Member State at a time, in a manner and with a content which allows the employees' representatives to undertake an in-depth assessment of the possible impact and, where appropriate, prepare consultations with the competent organ of the SE;

(j) "consultation" means the establishment of dialogue and exchange of views between the body representative of the employees and/or the employees' representatives and the competent organ of the SE, at a time, in a manner, and with a content which allows the employees' representatives, on the basis of information provided, to express an opinion on measures envisaged by the competent organ which may be taken into account in the decision-making process within the SE;

(k) "participation" means the influence of the body representative of the employees and/or the employees' representatives in the affairs of a company by way of—
- — the right to elect or appoint some of the members of the company's supervisory or administrative organ, or
- — the right to recommend and/or oppose the appointment of some or all of the members of the company's supervisory or administrative organ.

SECTION II
NEGOTIATING PROCEDURE

[3.368]
Article 3
Creation of a special negotiating body

1. Where the management or administrative organs of the participating companies draw up a plan for the establishment of an SE, they shall as soon as possible after publishing the draft terms of merger or creating a holding company or after agreeing a plan to form a subsidiary or to transform into an SE, take the necessary steps, including providing information about the identity of the participating companies, concerned subsidiaries or establishments, and the number of their employees, to start negotiations with the representatives of the companies' employees on arrangements for the involvement of employees in the SE.

2. For this purpose, a special negotiating body representative of the employees of the participating companies and concerned subsidiaries or establishments shall be created in accordance with the following provisions—

(a) in electing or appointing members of the special negotiating body, it must be ensured—

(i) that these members are elected or appointed in proportion to the number of employees employed in each Member State by the participating companies and concerned subsidiaries or establishments, by allocating in respect of a Member State one seat per portion of employees employed in that Member State which equals 10%, or a fraction thereof, of the number of employees employed by the participating companies and concerned subsidiaries or establishments in all the Member States taken together;

(ii) that in the case of an SE formed by way of merger, there are such further additional members from each Member State as may be necessary in order to ensure that the special negotiating body includes at least one member representing each participating company which is registered and has employees in that Member State and which it is proposed will cease to exist as a separate legal entity following the registration of the SE, in so far as—
- — the number of such additional members does not exceed 20% of the number of members designated by virtue of point (i), and
- — the composition of the special negotiating body does not entail a double representation of the employees concerned.

If the number of such companies is higher than the number of additional seats available pursuant to the first subparagraph, these additional seats shall be allocated to companies in different Member States by decreasing order of the number of employees they employ;

(b) Member States shall determine the method to be used for the election or appointment of the members of the special negotiating body who are to be elected or appointed in their territories. They shall take the necessary measures to ensure that, as far as possible, such members shall include at least one member representing each participating company which has employees in the Member State concerned. Such measures must not increase the overall number of members.

Member States may provide that such members may include representatives of trade unions whether or not they are employees of a participating company or concerned subsidiary or establishment.

Without prejudice to national legislation and/or practice laying down thresholds for the establishing of a representative body, Member States shall provide that employees in undertakings or establishments in which there are no employees' representatives through no fault of their own have the right to elect or appoint members of the special negotiating body.

3. The special negotiating body and the competent organs of the participating companies shall determine, by written agreement, arrangements for the involvement of employees within the SE.

To this end, the competent organs of the participating companies shall inform the special negotiating body of the plan and the actual process of establishing the SE, up to its registration.

4. Subject to paragraph 6, the special negotiating body shall take decisions by an absolute majority of its members, provided that such a majority also represents an absolute majority of the employees. Each member shall have one vote. However, should the result of the negotiations lead to a reduction of participation rights, the majority required for a decision to approve such an agreement shall be the votes of two thirds of the members of the special negotiating body representing at least two thirds of the employees, including the votes of members representing employees employed in at least two Member States—

- in the case of an SE to be established by way of merger, if participation covers at least 25% of the overall number of employees of the participating companies, or
- in the case of an SE to be established by way of creating a holding company or forming a subsidiary, if participation covers at least 50% of the overall number of employees of the participating companies.

Reduction of participation rights means a proportion of members of the organs of the SE within the meaning of Article 2(k), which is lower than the highest proportion existing within the participating companies.

5. For the purpose of the negotiations, the special negotiating body may request experts of its choice, for example representatives of appropriate Community level trade union organisations, to assist it with its work. Such experts may be present at negotiation meetings in an advisory capacity at the request of the special negotiating body, where appropriate to promote coherence and consistency at Community level. The special negotiating body may decide to inform the representatives of appropriate external organisations, including trade unions, of the start of the negotiations.

6. The special negotiating body may decide by the majority set out below not to open negotiations or to terminate negotiations already opened, and to rely on the rules on information and consultation of employees in force in the Member States where the SE has employees. Such a decision shall stop the procedure to conclude the agreement referred to in Article 4. Where such a decision has been taken, none of the provisions of the Annex shall apply.

The majority required to decide not to open or to terminate negotiations shall be the votes of two thirds of the members representing at least two thirds of the employees, including the votes of members representing employees employed in at least two Member States.

In the case of an SE established by way of transformation, this paragraph shall not apply if there is participation in the company to be transformed.

The special negotiating body shall be reconvened on the written request of at least 10% of the employees of the SE, its subsidiaries and establishments, or their representatives, at the earliest two years after the abovementioned decision, unless the parties agree to negotiations being reopened sooner. If the special negotiating body decides to reopen negotiations with the management but no agreement is reached as a result of those negotiations, none of the provisions of the Annex shall apply.

7. Any expenses relating to the functioning of the special negotiating body and, in general, to negotiations shall be borne by the participating companies so as to enable the special negotiating body to carry out its task in an appropriate manner.

In compliance with this principle, Member States may lay down budgetary rules regarding the operation of the special negotiating body. They may in particular limit the funding to cover one expert only.

[3.369]

Article 4

Content of the agreement

1. The competent organs of the participating companies and the special negotiating body shall negotiate in a spirit of cooperation with a view to reaching an agreement on arrangements for the involvement of the employees within the SE.

2. Without prejudice to the autonomy of the parties, and subject to paragraph 4, the agreement referred to in paragraph 1 between the competent organs of the participating companies and the special negotiating body shall specify—

(a) the scope of the agreement;

(b) the composition, number of members and allocation of seats on the representative body which will be the discussion partner of the competent organ of the SE in connection with arrangements for the information and consultation of the employees of the SE and its subsidiaries and establishments;

(c) the functions and the procedure for the information and consultation of the representative body;
(d) the frequency of meetings of the representative body;
(e) the financial and material resources to be allocated to the representative body;
(f) if, during negotiations, the parties decide to establish one or more information and consultation procedures instead of a representative body, the arrangements for implementing those procedures;
(g) if, during negotiations, the parties decide to establish arrangements for participation, the substance of those arrangements including (if applicable) the number of members in the SE's administrative or supervisory body which the employees will be entitled to elect, appoint, recommend or oppose, the procedures as to how these members may be elected, appointed, recommended or opposed by the employees, and their rights;
(h) the date of entry into force of the agreement and its duration, cases where the agreement should be renegotiated and the procedure for its renegotiation.

3. The agreement shall not, unless provision is made otherwise therein, be subject to the standard rules referred to in the Annex.

4. Without prejudice to Article 13(3)(a), in the case of an SE established by means of transformation, the agreement shall provide for at least the same level of all elements of employee involvement as the ones existing within the company to be transformed into an SE.

[3.370]
Article 5
Duration of negotiations

1. Negotiations shall commence as soon as the special negotiating body is established and may continue for six months thereafter.

2. The parties may decide, by joint agreement, to extend negotiations beyond the period referred to in paragraph 1, up the total of one year from the establishment of the special negotiating body.

[3.371]
Article 6
Legislation applicable to the negotiation procedure

Except where otherwise provided in this Directive, the legislation applicable to the negotiation procedure provided for in Articles 3 to 5 shall be the legislation of the Member State in which the registered office of the SE is to be situated.

[3.372]
Article 7
Standard rules

1. In order to achieve the objective described in Article 1, Member States shall, without prejudice to paragraph 3 below, lay down standard rules on employee involvement which must satisfy the provisions set out in the Annex.

The standard rules as laid down by the legislation of the Member State in which the registered office of the SE is to be situated shall apply from the date of the registration of the SE where either—

(a) the parties so agree; or
(b) by the deadline laid down in Article 5, no agreement has been concluded, and—
  — the competent organ of each of the participating companies decides to accept the application of the standard rules in relation to the SE and so to continue with its registration of the SE, and
  — the special negotiating body has not taken the decision provided in Article 3(6).

2. Moreover, the standard rules fixed by the national legislation of the Member State of registration in accordance with part 3 of the Annex shall apply only—

(a) in the case of an SE established by transformation, if the rules of a Member State relating to employee participation in the administrative or supervisory body applied to a company transformed into an SE;
(b) in the case of an SE established by merger—
  — if, before registration of the SE, one or more forms of participation applied in one or more of the participating companies covering at least 25% of the total number of employees in all the participating companies, or
  — if, before registration of the SE, one or more forms of participation applied in one or more of the participating companies covering less than 25% of the total number of employees in all the participating companies and if the special negotiating body so decides,
(c) in the case of an SE established by setting up a holding company or establishing a subsidiary—
  — if, before registration of the SE, one or more forms of participation applied in one or more of the participating companies covering at least 50% of the total number of employees in all the participating companies; or

— if, before registration of the SE, one or more forms of participation applied in one or more of the participating companies covering less than 50% of the total number of employees in all the participating companies and if the special negotiating body so decides.

If there was more than one form of participation within the various participating companies, the special negotiating body shall decide which of those forms must be established in the SE. Member States may fix the rules which are applicable in the absence of any decision on the matter for an SE registered in their territory. The special negotiating body shall inform the competent organs of the participating companies of any decisions taken pursuant to this paragraph.

3. Member States may provide that the reference provisions in part 3 of the Annex shall not apply in the case provided for in point (b) of paragraph 2.

SECTION III
MISCELLANEOUS PROVISIONS

[3.373]

Article 8

Reservation and confidentiality

1. Member States shall provide that members of the special negotiating body or the representative body, and experts who assist them, are not authorised to reveal any information which has been given to them in confidence.

The same shall apply to employees' representatives in the context of an information and consultation procedure.

This obligation shall continue to apply, wherever the persons referred to may be, even after the expiry of their terms of office.

2. Each Member State shall provide, in specific cases and under the conditions and limits laid down by national legislation, that the supervisory or administrative organ of an SE or of a participating company established in its territory is not obliged to transmit information where its nature is such that, according to objective criteria, to do so would seriously harm the functioning of the SE (or, as the case may be, the participating company) or its subsidiaries and establishments or would be prejudicial to them.

A Member State may make such dispensation subject to prior administrative or judicial authorisation.

3. Each Member State may lay down particular provisions for SEs in its territory which pursue directly and essentially the aim of ideological guidance with respect to information and the expression of opinions, on condition that, on the date of adoption of this Directive, such provisions already exist in the national legislation.

4. In applying paragraphs 1, 2 and 3, Member States shall make provision for administrative or judicial appeal procedures which the employees' representatives may initiate when the supervisory or administrative organ of an SE or participating company demands confidentiality or does not give information.

Such procedures may include arrangements designed to protect the confidentiality of the information in question.

[3.374]

Article 9

Operation of the representative body and procedure for the information and consultation of employees

The competent organ of the SE and the representative body shall work together in a spirit of cooperation with due regard for their reciprocal rights and obligations.

The same shall apply to cooperation between the supervisory or administrative organ of the SE and the employees' representatives in conjunction with a procedure for the information and consultation of employees.

[3.375]

Article 10

Protection of employees' representatives

The members of the special negotiating body, the members of the representative body, any employees' representatives exercising functions under the information and consultation procedure and any employees' representatives in the supervisory or administrative organ of an SE who are employees of the SE, its subsidiaries or establishments or of a participating company shall, in the exercise of their functions, enjoy the same protection and guarantees provided for employees' representatives by the national legislation and/or practice in force in their country of employment.

This shall apply in particular to attendance at meetings of the special negotiating body or representative body, any other meeting under the agreement referred to in Article 4(2)(f) or any meeting of the administrative or supervisory organ, and to the payment of wages for members employed by a participating company or the SE or its subsidiaries or establishments during a period of absence necessary for the performance of their duties.

[3.376]
Article 11
Misuse of procedures

Member States shall take appropriate measures in conformity with Community law with a view to preventing the misuse of an SE for the purpose of depriving employees of rights to employee involvement or withholding such rights.

[3.377]
Article 12
Compliance with this Directive

1. Each Member State shall ensure that the management of establishments of an SE and the supervisory or administrative organs of subsidiaries and of participating companies which are situated within its territory and the employees' representatives or, as the case may be, the employees themselves abide by the obligations laid down by this Directive, regardless of whether or not the SE has its registered office within its territory.

2. Member States shall provide for appropriate measures in the event of failure to comply with this Directive; in particular they shall ensure that administrative or legal procedures are available to enable the obligations deriving from this Directive to be enforced.

[3.378]
Article 13
Link between this Directive and other provisions

1. Where an SE is a Community-scale undertaking or a controlling undertaking of a Community-scale group of undertakings within the meaning of Directive 94/45/EC or of Directive 97/74/EC[1] extending the said Directive to the United Kingdom, the provisions of these Directives and the provisions transposing them into national legislation shall not apply to them or to their subsidiaries.

However, where the special negotiating body decides in accordance with Article 3(6) not to open negotiations or to terminate negotiations already opened, Directive 94/45/EC or Directive 97/74/EC and the provisions transposing them into national legislation shall apply.

2. Provisions on the participation of employees in company bodies provided for by national legislation and/or practice, other than those implementing this Directive, shall not apply to companies established in accordance with Regulation (EC) No 2157/2001 and covered by this Directive.

3. This Directive shall not prejudice—
   (a) the existing rights to involvement of employees provided for by national legislation and/or practice in the Member States as enjoyed by employees of the SE and its subsidiaries and establishments, other than participation in the bodies of the SE;
   (b) the provisions on participation in the bodies laid down by national legislation and/or practice applicable to the subsidiaries of the SE.

4. In order to preserve the rights referred to in paragraph 3, Member States may take the necessary measures to guarantee that the structures of employee representation in participating companies which will cease to exist as separate legal entities are maintained after the registration of the SE.

NOTES

[1] OJ L10, 16.1.1998, p 22.

[3.379]
Article 14
Final provisions

1. Member States shall adopt the laws, regulations and administrative provisions necessary to comply with this Directive no later than 8 October 2004, or shall ensure by that date at the latest that management and labour introduce the required provisions by way of agreement, the Member States being obliged to take all necessary steps enabling them at all times to guarantee the results imposed by this Directive. They shall forthwith inform the Commission thereof.

2. When Member States adopt these measures, they shall contain a reference to this Directive or shall be accompanied by such reference on the occasion of their official publication. The methods of making such reference shall be laid down by the Member States.

[3.380]
Article 15
Review by the Commission

No later than 8 October 2007, the Commission shall, in consultation with the Member States and with management and labour at Community level, review the procedures for applying this Directive, with a view to proposing suitable amendments to the Council where necessary.

[3.381]
Article 16
Entry into force
This Directive shall enter into force on the day of its publication in the *Official Journal of the European Communities*.

[3.382]
Article 17
Addressees
This Directive is addressed to the Member States.

ANNEX
STANDARD RULES

(referred to in Article 7)

[3.383]
Part 1: Composition of the body representative of the employees
In order to achieve the objective described in Article 1, and in the cases referred to in Article 7, a representative body shall be set up in accordance with the following rules.

(a) The representative body shall be composed of employees of the SE and its subsidiaries and establishments elected or appointed from their number by the employees' representatives or, in the absence thereof, by the entire body of employees.
(b) The election or appointment of members of the representative body shall be carried out in accordance with national legislation and/or practice.

Member States shall lay down rules to ensure that the number of members of, and allocation of seats on, the representative body shall be adapted to take account of changes occurring within the SE and its subsidiaries and establishments.

(c) Where its size so warrants, the representative body shall elect a select committee from among its members, comprising at most three members.
(d) The representative body shall adopt its rules of procedure.
(e) The members of the representative body are elected or appointed in proportion to the number of employees employed in each Member State by the participating companies and concerned subsidiaries or establishments, by allocating in respect of a Member State one seat per portion of employees employed in that Member State which equals 10%, or a fraction thereof, of the number of employees employed by the participating companies and concerned subsidiaries or establishments in all the Member States taken together.
(f) The competent organ of the SE shall be informed of the composition of the representative body.
(g) Four years after the representative body is established, it shall examine whether to open negotiations for the conclusion of the agreement referred to in Articles 4 and 7 or to continue to apply the standard rules adopted in accordance with this Annex.

Articles 3(4) to (7) and 4 to 6 shall apply, mutatis mutandis, if a decision has been taken to negotiate an agreement according to Article 4, in which case the term "special negotiating body" shall be replaced by "representative body". Where, by the deadline by which the negotiations come to an end, no agreement has been concluded, the arrangements initially adopted in accordance with the standard rules shall continue to apply.

[3.384]
Part 2: Standard rules for information and consultation
The competence and powers of the representative body set up in an SE shall be governed by the following rules.

(a) The competence of the representative body shall be limited to questions which concern the SE itself and any of its subsidiaries or establishments situated in another Member State or which exceed the powers of the decision-making organs in a single Member State.
(b) Without prejudice to meetings held pursuant to point (c), the representative body shall have the right to be informed and consulted and, for that purpose, to meet with the competent organ of the SE at least once a year, on the basis of regular reports drawn up by the competent organ, on the progress of the business of the SE and its prospects. The local managements shall be informed accordingly.

The competent organ of the SE shall provide the representative body with the agenda for meetings of the administrative, or, where appropriate, the management and supervisory organ, and with copies of all documents submitted to the general meeting of its shareholders.

The meeting shall relate in particular to the structure, economic and financial situation, the probable development of the business and of production and sales, the situation and probable trend of employment, investments, and substantial changes concerning organisation, introduction of new working methods or production processes, transfers of production, mergers, cut-backs or closures of undertakings, establishments or important parts thereof, and collective redundancies.

(c) Where there are exceptional circumstances affecting the employees' interests to a considerable extent, particularly in the event of relocations, transfers, the closure of establishments or undertakings or collective redundancies, the representative body shall have the right to be informed. The representative body or, where it so decides, in particular for reasons of urgency, the select committee, shall have the right to meet at its request the competent organ of the SE or any more appropriate level of management within the SE having its own powers of decision, so as to be informed and consulted on measures significantly affecting employees' interests.

Where the competent organ decides not to act in accordance with the opinion expressed by the representative body, this body shall have the right to a further meeting with the competent organ of the SE with a view to seeking agreement.

In the case of a meeting organised with the select committee, those members of the representative body who represent employees who are directly concerned by the measures in question shall also have the right to participate.

The meetings referred to above shall not affect the prerogatives of the competent organ.

(d) Member States may lay down rules on the chairing of information and consultation meetings.

Before any meeting with the competent organ of the SE, the representative body or the select committee, where necessary enlarged in accordance with the third subparagraph of paragraph (c), shall be entitled to meet without the representatives of the competent organ being present.

(e) Without prejudice to Article 8, the members of the representative body shall inform the representatives of the employees of the SE and of its subsidiaries and establishments of the content and outcome of the information and consultation procedures.

(f) The representative body or the select committee may be assisted by experts of its choice.

(g) In so far as this is necessary for the fulfilment of their tasks, the members of the representative body shall be entitled to time off for training without loss of wages.

(h) The costs of the representative body shall be borne by the SE, which shall provide the body's members with the financial and material resources needed to enable them to perform their duties in an appropriate manner.

In particular, the SE shall, unless otherwise agreed, bear the cost of organising meetings and providing interpretation facilities and the accommodation and travelling expenses of members of the representative body and the select committee.

In compliance with these principles, the Member States may lay down budgetary rules regarding the operation of the representative body. They may in particular limit funding to cover one expert only.

[3.385]

Part 3: Standard rules for participation

Employee participation in an SE shall be governed by the following provisions.

(a) In the case of an SE established by transformation, if the rules of a Member State relating to employee participation in the administrative or supervisory body applied before registration, all aspects of employee participation shall continue to apply to the SE. Point (b) shall apply mutatis mutandis to that end.

(b) In other cases of the establishing of an SE, the employees of the SE, its subsidiaries and establishments and/or their representative body shall have the right to elect, appoint, recommend or oppose the appointment of a number of members of the administrative or supervisory body of the SE equal to the highest proportion in force in the participating companies concerned before registration of the SE.

If none of the participating companies was governed by participation rules before registration of the SE, the latter shall not be required to establish provisions for employee participation.

The representative body shall decide on the allocation of seats within the administrative or supervisory body among the members representing the employees from the various Member States or on the way in which the SE's employees may recommend or oppose the appointment of the members of these bodies according to the proportion of the SE's employees in each Member State. If the employees of one or more Member States are not covered by this proportional criterion, the representative body shall appoint a member from one of those Member States, in particular the Member State of the SE's registered office where that is appropriate. Each Member State may determine the allocation of the seats it is given within the administrative or supervisory body.

Every member of the administrative body or, where appropriate, the supervisory body of the SE who has been elected, appointed or recommended by the representative body or, depending on the circumstances, by the employees shall be a full member with the same rights and obligations as the members representing the shareholders, including the right to vote.

DIRECTIVE OF THE EUROPEAN PARLIAMENT AND OF THE COUNCIL

(2002/14/EC)

of 11 March 2002

establishing a general framework for informing and consulting employees in the European Community

NOTES

Date of publication in OJ: OJ L80, 23.3.2002, p 29.

For the domestic implementation of this Directive, see the Information and Consultation of Employees Regulations 2004, SI 2004/3426 at **[2.896]**.

See *Harvey* CII(7), N(III)(2).

[3.386]

THE EUROPEAN PARLIAMENT AND THE COUNCIL OF THE EUROPEAN UNION,

Having regard to the Treaty establishing the European Community, and in particular Article 137(2) thereof,

Having regard to the proposal from the Commission,[1]

Having regard to the opinion of the Economic and Social Committee,[2]

Having regard to the opinion of the Committee of the Regions,[3]

Acting in accordance with the procedure referred to in Article 251,[4] and in the light of the joint text approved by the Conciliation Committee on 23 January 2002,

Whereas—

(1) Pursuant to Article 136 of the Treaty, a particular objective of the Community and the Member States is to promote social dialogue between management and labour.

(2) Point 17 of the Community Charter of Fundamental Social Rights of Workers provides, inter alia, that information, consultation and participation for workers must be developed along appropriate lines, taking account of the practices in force in different Member States.

(3) The Commission consulted management and labour at Community level on the possible direction of Community action on the information and consultation of employees in undertakings within the Community.

(4) Following this consultation, the Commission considered that Community action was advisable and again consulted management and labour on the contents of the planned proposal; management and labour have presented their opinions to the Commission.

(5) Having completed this second stage of consultation, management and labour have not informed the Commission of their wish to initiate the process potentially leading to the conclusion of an agreement.

(6) The existence of legal frameworks at national and Community level intended to ensure that employees are involved in the affairs of the undertaking employing them and in decisions which affect them has not always prevented serious decisions affecting employees from being taken and made public without adequate procedures having been implemented beforehand to inform and consult them.

(7) There is a need to strengthen dialogue and promote mutual trust within undertakings in order to improve risk anticipation, make work organisation more flexible and facilitate employee access to training within the undertaking while maintaining security, make employees aware of adaptation needs, increase employees' availability to undertake measures and activities to increase their employability, promote employee involvement in the operation and future of the undertaking and increase its competitiveness.

(8) There is a need, in particular, to promote and enhance information and consultation on the situation and likely development of employment within the undertaking and, where the employer's evaluation suggests that employment within the undertaking may be under threat, the possible anticipatory measures envisaged, in particular in terms of employee training and skill development, with a view to offsetting the negative developments or their consequences and increasing the employability and adaptability of the employees likely to be affected.

(9) Timely information and consultation is a prerequisite for the success of the restructuring and adaptation of undertakings to the new conditions created by globalisation of the economy, particularly through the development of new forms of organisation of work.

(10) The Community has drawn up and implemented an employment strategy based on the

concepts of "anticipation", "prevention" and "employability", which are to be incorporated as key elements into all public policies likely to benefit employment, including the policies of individual undertakings, by strengthening the social dialogue with a view to promoting change compatible with preserving the priority objective of employment.

(11) Further development of the internal market must be properly balanced, maintaining the essential values on which our societies are based and ensuring that all citizens benefit from economic development.

(12) Entry into the third stage of economic and monetary union has extended and accelerated the competitive pressures at European level. This means that more supportive measures are needed at national level.

(13) The existing legal frameworks for employee information and consultation at Community and national level tend to adopt an excessively a posteriori approach to the process of change, neglect the economic aspects of decisions taken and do not contribute either to genuine anticipation of employment developments within the undertaking or to risk prevention.

(14) All of these political, economic, social and legal developments call for changes to the existing legal framework providing for the legal and practical instruments enabling the right to be informed and consulted to be exercised.

(15) This Directive is without prejudice to national systems regarding the exercise of this right in practice where those entitled to exercise it are required to indicate their wishes collectively.

(16) This Directive is without prejudice to those systems which provide for the direct involvement of employees, as long as they are always free to exercise the right to be informed and consulted through their representatives.

(17) Since the objectives of the proposed action, as outlined above, cannot be adequately achieved by the Member States, in that the object is to establish a framework for employee information and consultation appropriate for the new European context described above, and can therefore, in view of the scale and impact of the proposed action, be better achieved at Community level, the Community may adopt measures in accordance with the principle of subsidiarity as set out in Article 5 of the Treaty. In accordance with the principle of proportionality, as set out in that Article, this Directive does not go beyond what is necessary in order to achieve these objectives.

(18) The purpose of this general framework is to establish minimum requirements applicable throughout the Community while not preventing Member States from laying down provisions more favourable to employees.

(19) The purpose of this general framework is also to avoid any administrative, financial or legal constraints which would hinder the creation and development of small and medium-sized undertakings. To this end, the scope of this Directive should be restricted, according to the choice made by Member States, to undertakings with at least 50 employees or establishments employing at least 20 employees.

(20) This takes into account and is without prejudice to other national measures and practices aimed at fostering social dialogue within companies not covered by this Directive and within public administrations.

(21) However, on a transitional basis, Member States in which there is no established statutory system of information and consultation of employees or employee representation should have the possibility of further restricting the scope of the Directive as regards the numbers of employees.

(22) A Community framework for informing and consulting employees should keep to a minimum the burden on undertakings or establishments while ensuring the effective exercise of the rights granted.

(23) The objective of this Directive is to be achieved through the establishment of a general framework comprising the principles, definitions and arrangements for information and consultation, which it will be for the Member States to comply with and adapt to their own national situation, ensuring, where appropriate, that management and labour have a leading role by allowing them to define freely, by agreement, the arrangements for informing and consulting employees which they consider to be best suited to their needs and wishes.

(24) Care should be taken to avoid affecting some specific rules in the field of employee information and consultation existing in some national laws, addressed to undertakings or establishments which pursue political, professional, organisational, religious, charitable, educational, scientific or artistic aims, as well as aims involving information and the expression of opinions.

(25) Undertakings and establishments should be protected against disclosure of certain particularly sensitive information.

(26) The employer should be allowed not to inform and consult where this would seriously damage the undertaking or the establishment or where he has to comply immediately with an order issued to him by a regulatory or supervisory body.

(27) Information and consultation imply both rights and obligations for management and labour at undertaking or establishment level.

(28) Administrative or judicial procedures, as well as sanctions that are effective, dissuasive and proportionate in relation to the seriousness of the offence, should be applicable in cases of infringement of the obligations based on this Directive.

(29) This Directive should not affect the provisions, where these are more specific, of Council Directive 98/59/EC of 20 July 1998 on the approximation of the laws of the Member States relating to collective redundancies[5] and of Council Directive 2001/23/EC of 12 March 2001 on the approximation of the laws of the Member States relating to the safeguarding of employees' rights in the event of transfers of undertakings, businesses or parts of undertakings or businesses.[6]

(30) Other rights of information and consultation, including those arising from Council Directive 94/45/EEC of 22 September 1994 on the establishment of a European Works Council or a procedure in Community-scale undertakings and Community-scale groups of undertakings for the purposes of informing and consulting employees,[7] should not be affected by this Directive.

(31) Implementation of this Directive should not be sufficient grounds for a reduction in the general level of protection of workers in the areas to which it applies,

NOTES

1 OJ C2, 5.1.1999, p 3.

2 OJ C258, 10.9.1999, p 24.

3 OJ C144, 16.5.2001, p 58.

4 Opinion of the European Parliament of 14 April 1999 (OJ C219, 30.7.1999, p 223), confirmed on 16 September 1999 (OJ C54, 25.2.2000, p 55), Council Common Position of 27 July 2001 (OJ C307, 31.10.2001, p 16) and Decision of the European Parliament of 23 October 2001 (not yet published in the Official Journal). Decision of the European Parliament of 5 February 2002 and Decision of the Council of 18 February 2002.

5 OJ L225, 12.8.1998, p 16.

6 OJ L82, 22.3.2001, p 16.

7 OJ L254, 30.9.1994, p 64. Directive as amended by Directive 97/74/EC (OJ L10, 16.1.1998, p 22.

HAVE ADOPTED THIS DIRECTIVE:

[3.387]
Article 1
Object and principles

1. The purpose of this Directive is to establish a general framework setting out minimum requirements for the right to information and consultation of employees in undertakings or establishments within the Community.
2. The practical arrangements for information and consultation shall be defined and implemented in accordance with national law and industrial relations practices in individual Member States in such a way as to ensure their effectiveness.
3. When defining or implementing practical arrangements for information and consultation, the employer and the employees' representatives shall work in a spirit of cooperation and with due regard for their reciprocal rights and obligations, taking into account the interests both of the undertaking or establishment and of the employees.

[3.388]
Article 2
Definitions

For the purposes of this Directive—

(a) "undertaking" means a public or private undertaking carrying out an economic activity, whether or not operating for gain, which is located within the territory of the Member States;
(b) "establishment" means a unit of business defined in accordance with national law and practice, and located within the territory of a Member State, where an economic activity is carried out on an ongoing basis with human and material resources;
(c) "employer" means the natural or legal person party to employment contracts or employment relationships with employees, in accordance with national law and practice;
(d) "employee" means any person who, in the Member State concerned, is protected as an employee under national employment law and in accordance with national practice;
(e) "employees' representatives" means the employees' representatives provided for by national laws and/or practices;
(f) "information" means transmission by the employer to the employees' representatives of data in order to enable them to acquaint themselves with the subject matter and to examine it;
(g) "consultation" means the exchange of views and establishment of dialogue between the employees' representatives and the employer.

[3.389]
Article 3
Scope

1. This Directive shall apply, according to the choice made by Member States, to—
   (a) undertakings employing at least 50 employees in any one Member State, or
   (b) establishments employing at least 20 employees in any one Member State.

   Member States shall determine the method for calculating the thresholds of employees employed.

2. In conformity with the principles and objectives of this Directive, Member States may lay down particular provisions applicable to undertakings or establishments which pursue directly and essentially political, professional organisational, religious, charitable, educational, scientific or artistic aims, as well as aims involving information and the expression of opinions, on condition that, at the date of entry into force of this Directive, provisions of that nature already exist in national legislation.

3. Member States may derogate from this Directive through particular provisions applicable to the crews of vessels plying the high seas.

[3.390]
Article 4
Practical arrangements for information and consultation

1. In accordance with the principles set out in Article 1 and without prejudice to any provisions and/or practices in force more favourable to employees, the Member States shall determine the practical arrangements for exercising the right to information and consultation at the appropriate level in accordance with this Article.

2. Information and consultation shall cover—
   (a) information on the recent and probable development of the undertaking's or the establishment's activities and economic situation;
   (b) information and consultation on the situation, structure and probable development of employment within the undertaking or establishment and on any anticipatory measures envisaged, in particular where there is a threat to employment;
   (c) information and consultation on decisions likely to lead to substantial changes in work organisation or in contractual relations, including those covered by the Community provisions referred to in Article 9(1).

3. Information shall be given at such time, in such fashion and with such content as are appropriate to enable, in particular, employees' representatives to conduct an adequate study and, where necessary, prepare for consultation.

4. Consultation shall take place—
   (a) while ensuring that the timing, method and content thereof are appropriate;
   (b) at the relevant level of management and representation, depending on the subject under discussion;
   (c) on the basis of information supplied by the employer in accordance with Article 2(f) and of the opinion which the employees' representatives are entitled to formulate;
   (d) in such a way as to enable employees' representatives to meet the employer and obtain a response, and the reasons for that response, to any opinion they might formulate;
   (e) with a view to reaching an agreement on decisions within the scope of the employer's powers referred to in paragraph 2(c).

[3.391]
Article 5
Information and consultation deriving from an agreement

Member States may entrust management and labour at the appropriate level, including at undertaking or establishment level, with defining freely and at any time through negotiated agreement the practical arrangements for informing and consulting employees. These agreements, and agreements existing on the date laid down in Article 11, as well as any subsequent renewals of such agreements, may establish, while respecting the principles set out in Article 1 and subject to conditions and limitations laid down by the Member States, provisions which are different from those referred to in Article 4.

[3.392]
Article 6
Confidential information

1. Member States shall provide that, within the conditions and limits laid down by national legislation, the employees' representatives, and any experts who assist them, are not authorised to reveal to employees or to third parties, any information which, in the legitimate interest of the undertaking or establishment, has expressly been provided to them in confidence. This obligation shall continue to apply, wherever the said representatives or experts are, even after expiry of their terms of office. However, a Member State may authorise the employees' representatives and anyone assisting them to pass on confidential information to employees and to third parties bound by an obligation of confidentiality.

2. Member States shall provide, in specific cases and within the conditions and limits laid down by national legislation, that the employer is not obliged to communicate information or undertake consultation when the nature of that information or consultation is such that, according to objective criteria, it would seriously harm the functioning of the undertaking or establishment or would be prejudicial to it.
3. Without prejudice to existing national procedures, Member States shall provide for administrative or judicial review procedures for the case where the employer requires confidentiality or does not provide the information in accordance with paragraphs 1 and 2. They may also provide for procedures intended to safeguard the confidentiality of the information in question.

[3.393]
Article 7
Protection of employees' representatives
Member States shall ensure that employees' representatives, when carrying out their functions, enjoy adequate protection and guarantees to enable them to perform properly the duties which have been assigned to them.

[3.394]
Article 8
Protection of rights
1. Member States shall provide for appropriate measures in the event of non-compliance with this Directive by the employer or the employees' representatives. In particular, they shall ensure that adequate administrative or judicial procedures are available to enable the obligations deriving from this Directive to be enforced.
2. Member States shall provide for adequate sanctions to be applicable in the event of infringement of this Directive by the employer or the employees' representatives. These sanctions must be effective, proportionate and dissuasive.

[3.395]
Article 9
Link between this Directive and other Community and national provisions
1. This Directive shall be without prejudice to the specific information and consultation procedures set out in Article 2 of Directive 98/59/EC and Article 7 of Directive 2001/23/EC.
2. This Directive shall be without prejudice to provisions adopted in accordance with Directives 94/45/EC and 97/74/EC.
3. This Directive shall be without prejudice to other rights to information, consultation and participation under national law.
4. Implementation of this Directive shall not be sufficient grounds for any regression in relation to the situation which already prevails in each Member State and in relation to the general level of protection of workers in the areas to which it applies.

[3.396]
Article 10
Transitional provisions
Notwithstanding Article 3, a Member State in which there is, at the date of entry into force of this Directive, no general, permanent and statutory system of information and consultation of employees, nor a general, permanent and statutory system of employee representation at the workplace allowing employees to be represented for that purpose, may limit the application of the national provisions implementing this Directive to—

(a) undertakings employing at least 150 employees or establishments employing at least 100 employees until 23 March 2007, and
(b) undertakings employing at least 100 employees or establishments employing at least 50 employees during the year following the date in point (a).

[3.397]
Article 11
Transposition
1. Member States shall adopt the laws, regulations and administrative provisions necessary to comply with this Directive not later than 23 March 2005 or shall ensure that management and labour introduce by that date the required provisions by way of agreement, the Member States being obliged to take all necessary steps enabling them to guarantee the results imposed by this Directive at all times. They shall forthwith inform the Commission thereof.
2. Where Member States adopt these measures, they shall contain a reference to this Directive or shall be accompanied by such reference on the occasion of their official publication. The methods of making such reference shall be laid down by the Member States.

[3.398]
Article 12
Review by the Commission
Not later than 23 March 2007, the Commission shall, in consultation with the Member States and the social partners at Community level, review the application of this Directive with a view to proposing any necessary amendments.

[3.399]
Article 13
Entry into force
This Directive shall enter into force on the day of its publication in the *Official Journal of the European Communities*.

[3.400]
Article 14
Addressees
This Directive is addressed to the Member States.

DIRECTIVE OF THE EUROPEAN PARLIAMENT AND OF THE COUNCIL

(2002/15/EC)

of 11 March 2002

on the organisation of the working time of persons performing mobile road transport activities

NOTES
Date of publication in OJ: OJ L80, 23.3.2002, p 35.
For the domestic implementation of this Directive, see the Road Transport (Working Time) Regulations 2005, SI 2005/639 at **[2.940]**.
See *Harvey* CI(1).

[3.401]
THE EUROPEAN PARLIAMENT AND THE COUNCIL OF THE EUROPEAN UNION,
Having regard to the Treaty establishing the European Community, and in particular Article 71 and Article 137(2) thereof,
Having regard to the proposal from the Commission,[1]
Having regard to the opinion of the Economic and Social Committee,[2]
Following consultation of the Committee of the Regions,
Acting in accordance with the procedure laid down in Article 251 of the Treaty,[3] and in the light of the joint text approved by the Conciliation Committee on 16 January 2002,
Whereas:

(1) Council Regulation (EEC) No 3820/85 of 20 December 1985 on the harmonisation of certain social legislation relating to road transport[4] laid down common rules on driving times and rest periods for drivers; that Regulation does not cover other aspects of working time for road transport.

(2) Council Directive 93/104/EC of 23 November 1993 concerning certain aspects of the organisation of working time[5] makes it possible to adopt more specific requirements for the organisation of working time. Bearing in mind the sectoral nature of this Directive, the provisions thereof take precedence over Directive 93/104/EC by virtue of Article 14 thereof.

(3) Despite intensive negotiations between the social partners, it has not been possible to reach agreement on the subject of mobile workers in road transport.

(4) It is therefore necessary to lay down a series of more specific provisions concerning the hours of work in road transport intended to ensure the safety of transport and the health and safety of the persons involved.

(5) Since the objectives of the proposed action cannot be sufficiently achieved by the Member States and can therefore, by reason of the scale and effects of the proposed action, be better achieved at Community level, the Community may adopt measures, in accordance with the principle of subsidiarity as set out in Article 5 of the Treaty. In accordance with the principle of proportionality, as set out in that Article, this Directive does not go beyond what is necessary in order to achieve those objectives.

(6) The scope of this Directive covers only mobile workers employed by transport undertakings established in a Member State participating in mobile road transport activities covered by Regulation (EEC) No 3820/85 or, failing that, by the European agreement concerning the work of crews of

vehicles engaged in international road transport (AETR).

(7) It should be made clear that mobile workers excluded from the scope of this Directive, other than self-employed drivers, benefit from the basic protection provided for in Directive 93/104/EC. That basic protection includes the existing rules on adequate rest, the maximum average working week, annual leave and certain basic provisions for night workers including health assessment.

(8) As self-employed drivers are included within the scope of Regulation (EEC) No 3820/85 but excluded from that of Directive 93/104/EC, they should be excluded temporarily from the scope of this Directive in accordance with the provisions of Article 2(1).

(9) The definitions used in this Directive are not to constitute a precedent for other Community regulations on working time.

(10) In order to improve road safety, prevent the distortion of competition and guarantee the safety and health of the mobile workers covered by this Directive, the latter should know exactly which periods devoted to road transport activities constitute working time and which do not and are thus deemed to be break times, rest times or periods of availability. These workers should be granted minimum daily and weekly periods of rest, and adequate breaks. It is also necessary to place a maximum limit on the number of weekly working hours.

(11) Research has shown that the human body is more sensitive at night to environmental disturbances and also to certain burdensome forms of organisation and that long periods of night work can be detrimental to the health of workers and can endanger their safety and also road safety in general.

(12) As a consequence, there is a need to limit the duration of periods of night work and to provide that professional drivers who work at night should receive appropriate compensation for their activity and should not be disadvantaged as regards training opportunities.

(13) Employers should keep records of instances when the maximum average working week applicable to mobile workers is exceeded.

(14) The provisions of Regulation (EEC) No 3820/85 on driving time in international and national passenger transport, other than regular services, should continue to apply.

(15) The Commission should monitor the implementation of this Directive and developments in this field in the Member States and submit to the European Parliament, the Council, the Economic and Social Committee and the Committee of the Regions a report on the application of the rules and the consequences of the provisions on night work.

(16) It is necessary to provide that certain provisions may be subject to derogations adopted, according to the circumstances, by the Member States or the two sides of industry. As a general rule, in the event of a derogation, the workers concerned must be given compensatory rest periods,

NOTES

1 OJ C43, 17.2.1999, p 4.

2 OJ C138, 18.5.1999, p 33.

3 Opinion of the European Parliament of 14 April 1999 (OJ C219, 30.7.1999, p 235), as confirmed on 6 May 1999 (OJ C279, 1.10.1999, p 270), Council Common Position of 23 March 2001 (OJ C142, 15.5.2001, p 24) and Decision of the European Parliament of 14 June 2001 (not yet published in the Official Journal). Decision of the European Parliament of 5 February 2002 and Council Decision of 18 February 2002.

4 OJ L370, 31.12.1985, p 1.

5 OJ L307, 13.12.1993, p 18. Directive as last amended by Directive 2000/34/EC of the European Parliament and of the Council (OJ L195, 1.8.2000, p 41).

HAVE ADOPTED THIS DIRECTIVE:

[3.402]
Article 1
Purpose

The purpose of this Directive shall be to establish minimum requirements in relation to the organisation of working time in order to improve the health and safety protection of persons performing mobile road transport activities and to improve road safety and align conditions of competition.

[3.403]
Article 2
Scope

1. This Directive shall apply to mobile workers employed by undertakings established in a Member State, participating in road transport activities covered by Regulation (EEC) No 3820/85 or, failing that, by the AETR Agreement.

Without prejudice to the provisions of following subparagraph, this Directive shall apply to self-employed drivers from 23 March 2009.

At the latest two years before this date, the Commission shall present a report to the European Parliament and the Council. This report shall analyse the consequences of the exclusion of self-employed drivers from the scope of the Directive in respect of road safety, conditions of competition, the structure of the profession as well as social aspects. The circumstances in each Member State relating to the structure of the transport industry and to the working environment of the road transport profession shall be taken into account. On the basis of this report, the Commission shall submit a proposal, the aim of which may be either, as appropriate

— to set out the modalities for the inclusion of the self-employed drivers within the scope of the Directive in respect of certain self-employed drivers who are not participating in road transport activities in other Member States and who are subject to local constraints for objective reasons, such as peripheral location, long internal distances and a particular competitive environment, or
— not to include self-employed drivers within the scope of the Directive.

2. The provisions of Directive 93/104/EC shall apply to mobile workers excluded from the scope of this Directive.
3. In so far as this Directive contains more specific provisions as regards mobile workers performing road transport activities it shall, pursuant to Article 14 of Directive 93/104/EC, take precedence over the relevant provisions of that Directive.
4. This Directive shall supplement the provisions of Regulation (EEC) No 3820/85 and, where necessary, of the AETR Agreement, which take precedence over the provisions of this Directive.

[3.404]
Article 3
Definitions

For the purposes of this Directive:

(a) "working time" shall mean:

1. in the case of mobile workers: the time from the beginning to the end of work, during which the mobile worker is at his workstation, at the disposal of the employer and exercising his functions or activities, that is to say:
   — the time devoted to all road transport activities. These activities are, in particular, the following:
     (i) driving;
     (ii) loading and unloading;
     (iii) assisting passengers boarding and disembarking from the vehicle;
     (iv) cleaning and technical maintenance;
     (v) all other work intended to ensure the safety of the vehicle, its cargo and passengers or to fulfil the legal or regulatory obligations directly linked to the specific transport operation under way, including monitoring of loading and unloading, administrative formalities with police, customs, immigration officers etc,
   — the times during which he cannot dispose freely of his time and is required to be at his workstation, ready to take up normal work, with certain tasks associated with being on duty, in particular during periods awaiting loading or unloading where their foreseeable duration is not known in advance, that is to say either before departure or just before the actual start of the period in question, or under the general conditions negotiated between the social partners and/or under the terms of the legislation of the Member States;
2. in the case of self-employed drivers, the same definition shall apply to the time from the beginning to the end of work, during which the self employed driver is at his workstation, at the disposal of the client and exercising his functions or activities other than general administrative work that is not directly linked to the specific transport operation under way.

   The break times referred to in Article 5, the rest times referred to in Article 6 and, without prejudice to the legislation of Member States or agreements between the social partners providing that such periods should be compensated or limited, the periods of availability referred to in (b) of this Article, shall be excluded from working time;

(b) "periods of availability" shall mean:

— periods other than those relating to break times and rest times during which the mobile worker is not required to remain at his workstation, but must be available to answer any calls to start or resume driving or to carry out other work. In particular such periods of availability shall include periods during which the mobile worker is accompanying a vehicle being transported by ferryboat or by train as well as periods of waiting at frontiers and those due to traffic prohibitions.

  These periods and their foreseeable duration shall be known in advance by the mobile worker, that is to say either before departure or just before the actual start of the period in question, or under the general conditions negotiated between the social partners and/or under the terms of the legislation of the Member States,

— for mobile workers driving in a team, the time spent sitting next to the driver or on the couchette while the vehicle is in motion;

(c) "workstation" shall mean:

— the location of the main place of business of the undertaking for which the person performing mobile road transport activities carries out duties, together with its various subsidiary places of business, regardless of whether they are located in the same place as its head office or main place of business,

— the vehicle which the person performing mobile road transport activities uses when he carries out duties, and

— any other place in which activities connected with transportation are carried out;

(d) "mobile worker" shall mean any worker forming part of the travelling staff, including trainees and apprentices, who is in the service of an undertaking which operates transport services for passengers or goods by road for hire or reward or on its own account;

(e) "self-employed driver" shall mean anyone whose main occupation is to transport passengers or goods by road for hire or reward within the meaning of Community legislation under cover of a Community licence or any other professional authorisation to carry out the aforementioned transport, who is entitled to work for himself and who is not tied to an employer by an employment contract or by any other type of working hierarchical relationship, who is free to organise the relevant working activities, whose income depends directly on the profits made and who has the freedom to, individually or through a cooperation between self-employed drivers, have commercial relations with several customers.

For the purposes of this Directive, those drivers who do not satisfy these criteria shall be subject to the same obligations and benefit from the same rights as those provided for mobile workers by this Directive;

(f) "person performing mobile road transport activities" shall mean any mobile worker or self-employed driver who performs such activities;

(g) "week" shall mean the period between 00.00 hours on Monday and 24.00 hours on Sunday;

(h) "night time" shall mean a period of at least four hours, as defined by national law, between 00.00 hours and 07.00 hours;

(i) "night work" shall mean any work performed during night time.

[3.405]
Article 4
Maximum weekly working time

Member States shall take the measures necessary to ensure that:

(a) the average weekly working time may not exceed 48 hours. The maximum weekly working time may be extended to 60 hours only if, over four months, an average of 48 hours a week is not exceeded. The fourth and fifth subparagraphs of Article 6(1) of Regulation (EEC) No 3820/85 or, where necessary, the fourth subparagraph of Article 6(1) of the AETR Agreement shall take precedence over this Directive, in so far as the drivers concerned do not exceed an average working time of 48 hours a week over four months;

(b) working time for different employers is the sum of the working hours. The employer shall ask the mobile worker concerned in writing for an account of time worked for another employer. The mobile worker shall provide such information in writing.

[3.406]
Article 5
Breaks

1. Member States shall take the measures necessary to ensure that, without prejudice to the level of protection provided by Regulation (EEC) No 3820/85 or, failing that, by the AETR Agreement, persons performing mobile road transport activities, without prejudice to Article 2(1), in no circumstances work for more than six consecutive hours without a break. Working time shall be interrupted by a break of at least 30 minutes, if working hours total between six and nine hours, and of at least 45 minutes, if working hours total more than nine hours.

2. Breaks may be subdivided into periods of at least 15 minutes each.

[3.407]
Article 6
Rest periods

For the purposes of this Directive, apprentices and trainees shall be covered by the same provisions on rest time as other mobile workers in pursuance of Regulation (EEC) No 3820/85 or, failing that, of the AETR Agreement.

[3.408]
Article 7
Night work

1. Member States shall take the measures necessary to ensure that:

— if night work is performed, the daily working time does not exceed ten hours in each 24 period,
— compensation for night work is given in accordance with national legislative measures, collective agreements, agreements between the two sides of industry and/or national practice, on condition that such compensation is not liable to endanger road safety.

2. By 23 March 2007, the Commission shall, within the framework of the report which it draws up in accordance with Article 13(2), assess the consequences of the provisions laid down in paragraph 1 above. The Commission shall, if necessary, submit appropriate proposals along with that report.
3. The Commission shall present a proposal for a Directive containing provisions relating to the training of professional drivers, including those who perform night work, and laying down the general principles of such training.

[3.409]
Article 8
Derogations

1. Derogations from Articles 4 and 7 may, for objective or technical reasons or reasons concerning the organisation of work, be adopted by means of collective agreements, agreements between the social partners, or if this is not possible, by laws, regulations or administrative provisions provided there is consultation of the representatives of the employers and workers concerned and efforts are made to encourage all relevant forms of social dialogue.
2. The option to derogate from Article 4 may not result in the establishment of a reference period exceeding six months, for calculation of the average maximum weekly working time of forty-eight hours.

[3.410]
Article 9
Information and records

Member States shall ensure that:
(a) mobile workers are informed of the relevant national requirements, the internal rules of the undertaking and agreements between the two sides of industry, in particular collective agreements and any company agreements, reached on the basis of this Directive, without prejudice to Council Directive 91/533/EEC of 14 October 1991 on an employer's obligation to inform employees of the conditions applicable to the contract or employment relationship;[1]
(b) without prejudice to Article 2(1), the working time of persons performing mobile road transport activities is recorded. Records shall be kept for at least two years after the end of the period covered. Employers shall be responsible for recording the working time of mobile workers. Employers shall upon request provide mobile workers with copies of the records of hours worked.

NOTES
[1] OJ L288, 18.10.1991, p 32.

[3.411]
Article 10
More favourable provisions

This Directive shall not affect Member States' right to apply or introduce laws, regulations or administrative provisions more favourable to the protection of the health and safety of persons performing mobile road transport activities, or their right to facilitate or permit the application of collective agreements or other agreements concluded between the two sides of industry which are more favourable to the protection of the health and safety of mobile workers. Implementation of this Directive shall not constitute valid grounds for reducing the general level of protection afforded to workers referred to in Article 2(1).

[3.412]
Article 11
Penalties

Member States shall lay down a system of penalties for breaches of the national provisions adopted pursuant to this Directive and shall take all the measures necessary to ensure that these penalties are applied. The penalties thus provided for shall be effective, proportional and dissuasive.

[3.413]
Article 12
Negotiations with third countries

Once this Directive has entered into force, the Community shall begin negotiations with the relevant third countries with a view to the application of rules equivalent to those laid down in this Directive to mobile workers employed by undertakings established in a third country.

[3.414]
Article 13
Reports
1. Member States shall report to the Commission every two years on the implementation of this Directive, indicating the views of the two sides of industry. The report must reach the Commission no later than 30 September following the date on which the two-year period covered by the report expires. The two-year period shall be the same as that referred to in Article 16(2) of Regulation (EEC) No 3820/85.
2. The Commission shall produce a report every two years on the implementation of this Directive by Member States and developments in the field in question. The Commission shall forward this report to the European Parliament, the Council, the Economic and Social Committee and the Committee of the Regions.

[3.415]
Article 14
Final provisions
1. Member States shall adopt the laws, regulations and administrative provisions necessary to comply with this Directive by 23 March 2005 or shall ensure by that date that the two sides of industry have established the necessary measures by agreement, the Member States being obliged to take any steps to allow them to be able at any time to guarantee the results required by this Directive. When Member States adopt the measures referred to in the first subparagraph, they shall contain a reference to this Directive or shall be accompanied by such reference on the occasion of their official publication. The methods of making such reference shall be laid down by Member States.
2. Member States shall communicate to the Commission the provisions of national law which they have already adopted or which they adopt in the field covered by this Directive.
3. Member States shall take care that consignors, freight forwarders, prime contractors, subcontractors and enterprises which employ mobile workers comply with the relevant provisions of this Directive.

[3.416]
Article 15
Entry into force
This Directive shall enter into force on the day of its publication in the *Official Journal of the European Communities*.

[3.417]
Article 16
Addressees
This Directive is addressed to the Member States.

DIRECTIVE OF THE EUROPEAN PARLIAMENT AND OF THE COUNCIL

(2003/88/EC)

of 4 November 2003

concerning certain aspects of the organisation of working time

NOTES
Date of publication in OJ: OJ L229, 18.11.2003, p 9.
This Directive is a consolidation of Directive 93/104/EEC, as amended by Council Directive 2000/34/EC ('the Working Time Directive' and 'the 'Horizontal Amending Directive'). A correlation table is in Annex II at **[3.451]**. For the domestic implementation of this Directive and its predecessor in the United Kingdom, see the Working Time Regulations 1998, SI 1998/1833 at **[2.269]**.
See *Harvey* CI(1).

[3.418]
THE EUROPEAN PARLIAMENT AND THE COUNCIL OF THE EUROPEAN UNION,
Having regard to the Treaty establishing the European Community, and in particular Article 137(2) thereof,
Having regard to the proposal from the Commission,
Having regard to the opinion of the European Economic and Social Committee,[1]
Having consulted the Committee of the Regions,
Acting in accordance with the procedure referred to in Article 251 of the Treaty,[2]
Whereas:

(1) Council Directive 93/104/EC of 23 November 1993, concerning certain aspects of the organisation of working time,[3] which lays down minimum safety and health requirements for the organisation of working time, in respect of periods of daily rest, breaks, weekly rest, maximum weekly working time, annual leave and aspects of night work, shift work and patterns of work, has been significantly amended. In order to clarify matters, a codification of the provisions in question should be drawn up.

(2) Article 137 of the Treaty provides that the Community is to support and complement the activities of the Member States with a view to improving the working environment to protect workers' health and safety. Directives adopted on the basis of that Article are to avoid imposing administrative, financial and legal constraints in a way which would hold back the creation and development of small and medium-sized undertakings.

(3) The provisions of Council Directive 89/391/EEC of 12 June 1989 on the introduction of measures to encourage improvements in the safety and health of workers at work[4] remain fully applicable to the areas covered by this Directive without prejudice to more stringent and/or specific provisions contained herein.

(4) The improvement of workers' safety, hygiene and health at work is an objective which should not be subordinated to purely economic considerations.

(5) All workers should have adequate rest periods. The concept of "rest" must be expressed in units of time, ie in days, hours and/or fractions thereof. Community workers must be granted minimum daily, weekly and annual periods of rest and adequate breaks. It is also necessary in this context to place a maximum limit on weekly working hours.

(6) Account should be taken of the principles of the International Labour Organisation with regard to the organisation of working time, including those relating to night work.

(7) Research has shown that the human body is more sensitive at night to environmental disturbances and also to certain burdensome forms of work organisation and that long periods of night work can be detrimental to the health of workers and can endanger safety at the workplace.

(8) There is a need to limit the duration of periods of night work, including overtime, and to provide for employers who regularly use night workers to bring this information to the attention of the competent authorities if they so request.

(9) It is important that night workers should be entitled to a free health assessment prior to their assignment and thereafter at regular intervals and that whenever possible they should be transferred to day work for which they are suited if they suffer from health problems.

(10) The situation of night and shift workers requires that the level of safety and health protection should be adapted to the nature of their work and that the organisation and functioning of protection and prevention services and resources should be efficient.

(11) Specific working conditions may have detrimental effects on the safety and health of workers. The organisation of work according to a certain pattern must take account of the general principle of adapting work to the worker.

(12) A European Agreement in respect of the working time of seafarers has been put into effect by means of Council Directive 1999/63/EC of 21 June 1999 concerning the Agreement on the organisation of working time of seafarers concluded by the European Community Shipowners' Association (ECSA) and the Federation of Transport Workers' Unions in the European Union (FST)[5] based on Article 139(2) of the Treaty. Accordingly, the provisions of this Directive should not apply to seafarers.

(13) In the case of those "share-fishermen" who are employees, it is for the Member States to determine, pursuant to this Directive, the conditions for entitlement to, and granting of, annual leave, including the arrangements for payments.

(14) Specific standards laid down in other Community instruments relating, for example, to rest periods, working time, annual leave and night work for certain categories of workers should take precedence over the provisions of this Directive.

(15) In view of the question likely to be raised by the organisation of working time within an undertaking, it appears desirable to provide for flexibility in the application of certain provisions of this Directive, whilst ensuring compliance with the principles of protecting the safety and health of workers.

(16) It is necessary to provide that certain provisions may be subject to derogations implemented, according to the case, by the Member States or the two sides of industry. As a general rule, in the event of a derogation, the workers concerned must be given equivalent compensatory rest periods.

(17) This Directive should not affect the obligations of the Member States concerning the deadlines for transposition of the Directives set out in Annex I, part B,

NOTES

1 OJ C61, 14.3.2003, p 123.

2 Opinion of the European Parliament of 17 December 2002 (not yet published in the Official Journal) and Council Decision of 22 September 2003.

3 OJ L307, 13.12.1993, p 18. Directive as amended by Directive 2000/34/EC of the European Parliament and of the Council (OJ L195, 1.8.2000, p 41).

4 OJ L183, 29.6.1989, p 1.

5 OJ L167, 2.7.1999, p 33.

HAVE ADOPTED THIS DIRECTIVE:

CHAPTER 1
SCOPE AND DEFINITIONS

[3.419]

Article 1
Purpose and scope

1. This Directive lays down minimum safety and health requirements for the organisation of working time.

2. This Directive applies to:
   (a) minimum periods of daily rest, weekly rest and annual leave, to breaks and maximum weekly working time; and
   (b) certain aspects of night work, shift work and patterns of work.

3. This Directive shall apply to all sectors of activity, both public and private, within the meaning of Article 2 of Directive 89/391/EEC, without prejudice to Articles 14, 17, 18 and 19 of this Directive.

This Directive shall not apply to seafarers, as defined in Directive 1999/63/EC without prejudice to Article 2(8) of this Directive.

4. The provisions of Directive 89/391/EEC are fully applicable to the matters referred to in paragraph 2, without prejudice to more stringent and/or specific provisions contained in this Directive.

[3.420]

Article 2
Definitions

For the purposes of this Directive, the following definitions shall apply:

1. "working time" means any period during which the worker is working, at the employer's disposal and carrying out his activity or duties, in accordance with national laws and/or practice;
2. "rest period" means any period which is not working time;
3. "night time" means any period of not less than seven hours, as defined by national law, and which must include, in any case, the period between midnight and 5.00;
4. "night worker" means:
   (a) on the one hand, any worker, who, during night time, works at least three hours of his daily working time as a normal course; and
   (b) on the other hand, any worker who is likely during night time to work a certain proportion of his annual working time, as defined at the choice of the Member State concerned:
      (i) by national legislation, following consultation with the two sides of industry; or
      (ii) by collective agreements or agreements concluded between the two sides of industry at national or regional level;
5. "shift work" means any method of organising work in shifts whereby workers succeed each other at the same work stations according to a certain pattern, including a rotating pattern, and which may be continuous or discontinuous, entailing the need for workers to work at different times over a given period of days or weeks;
6. "shift worker" means any worker whose work schedule is part of shift work;
7. "mobile worker" means any worker employed as a member of travelling or flying personnel by an undertaking which operates transport services for passengers or goods by road, air or inland waterway;
8. "offshore work" means work performed mainly on or from offshore installations (including drilling rigs), directly or indirectly in connection with the exploration, extraction or exploitation of mineral resources, including hydrocarbons, and diving in connection with such activities, whether performed from an offshore installation or a vessel;

9. "adequate rest" means that workers have regular rest periods, the duration of which is expressed in units of time and which are sufficiently long and continuous to ensure that, as a result of fatigue or other irregular working patterns, they do not cause injury to themselves, to fellow workers or to others and that they do not damage their health, either in the short term or in the longer term.

CHAPTER 2
MINIMUM REST PERIODS—OTHER ASPECTS OF THE ORGANISATION OF WORKING TIME

[3.421]
Article 3
Daily rest
Member States shall take the measures necessary to ensure that every worker is entitled to a minimum daily rest period of 11 consecutive hours per 24-hour period.

[3.422]
Article 4
Breaks
Member States shall take the measures necessary to ensure that, where the working day is longer than six hours, every worker is entitled to a rest break, the details of which, including duration and the terms on which it is granted, shall be laid down in collective agreements or agreements between the two sides of industry or, failing that, by national legislation.

[3.423]
Article 5
Weekly rest period
Member States shall take the measures necessary to ensure that, per each seven-day period, every worker is entitled to a minimum uninterrupted rest period of 24 hours plus the 11 hours' daily rest referred to in Article 3.

If objective, technical or work organisation conditions so justify, a minimum rest period of 24 hours may be applied.

[3.424]
Article 6
Maximum weekly working time
Member States shall take the measures necessary to ensure that, in keeping with the need to protect the safety and health of workers:

(a) the period of weekly working time is limited by means of laws, regulations or administrative provisions or by collective agreements or agreements between the two sides of industry;

(b) the average working time for each seven-day period, including overtime, does not exceed 48 hours.

[3.425]
Article 7
Annual leave
1. Member States shall take the measures necessary to ensure that every worker is entitled to paid annual leave of at least four weeks in accordance with the conditions for entitlement to, and granting of, such leave laid down by national legislation and/or practice.
2. The minimum period of paid annual leave may not be replaced by an allowance in lieu, except where the employment relationship is terminated.

CHAPTER 3
NIGHT WORK—SHIFT WORK—PATTERNS OF WORK

[3.426]
Article 8
Length of night work
Member States shall take the measures necessary to ensure that:

(a) normal hours of work for night workers do not exceed an average of eight hours in any 24-hour period;

(b) night workers whose work involves special hazards or heavy physical or mental strain do not work more than eight hours in any period of 24 hours during which they perform night work.

For the purposes of point (b), work involving special hazards or heavy physical or mental strain shall be defined by national legislation and/or practice or by collective agreements or agreements concluded between the two sides of industry, taking account of the specific effects and hazards of night work.

[3.427]
Article 9
Health assessment and transfer of night workers to day work

1. Member States shall take the measures necessary to ensure that:
   (a) night workers are entitled to a free health assessment before their assignment and thereafter at regular intervals;
   (b) night workers suffering from health problems recognised as being connected with the fact that they perform night work are transferred whenever possible to day work to which they are suited.

2. The free health assessment referred to in paragraph 1(a) must comply with medical confidentiality.

3. The free health assessment referred to in paragraph 1(a) may be conducted within the national health system.

[3.428]
Article 10
Guarantees for night-time working

Member States may make the work of certain categories of night workers subject to certain guarantees, under conditions laid down by national legislation and/or practice, in the case of workers who incur risks to their safety or health linked to night-time working.

[3.429]
Article 11
Notification of regular use of night workers

Member States shall take the measures necessary to ensure that an employer who regularly uses night workers brings this information to the attention of the competent authorities if they so request.

[3.430]
Article 12
Safety and health protection

Member States shall take the measures necessary to ensure that:
   (a) night workers and shift workers have safety and health protection appropriate to the nature of their work;
   (b) appropriate protection and prevention services or facilities with regard to the safety and health of night workers and shift workers are equivalent to those applicable to other workers and are available at all times.

[3.431]
Article 13
Pattern of work

Member States shall take the measures necessary to ensure that an employer who intends to organise work according to a certain pattern takes account of the general principle of adapting work to the worker, with a view, in particular, to alleviating monotonous work and work at a predetermined work-rate, depending on the type of activity, and of safety and health requirements, especially as regards breaks during working time.

CHAPTER 4
MISCELLANEOUS PROVISIONS

[3.432]
Article 14
More specific Community provisions

This Directive shall not apply where other Community instruments contain more specific requirements relating to the organisation of working time for certain occupations or occupational activities.

[3.433]
Article 15
More favourable provisions

This Directive shall not affect Member States' right to apply or introduce laws, regulations or administrative provisions more favourable to the protection of the safety and health of workers or to facilitate or permit the application of collective agreements or agreements concluded between the two sides of industry which are more favourable to the protection of the safety and health of workers.

[3.434]
Article 16
Reference periods

Member States may lay down:

(a) for the application of Article 5 (weekly rest period), a reference period not exceeding 14 days;

(b) for the application of Article 6 (maximum weekly working time), a reference period not exceeding four months.

The periods of paid annual leave, granted in accordance with Article 7, and the periods of sick leave shall not be included or shall be neutral in the calculation of the average;

(c) for the application of Article 8 (length of night work), a reference period defined after consultation of the two sides of industry or by collective agreements or agreements concluded between the two sides of industry at national or regional level.

If the minimum weekly rest period of 24 hours required by Article 5 falls within that reference period, it shall not be included in the calculation of the average.

CHAPTER 5
DEROGATIONS AND EXCEPTIONS

[3.435]
Article 17
Derogations

1. With due regard for the general principles of the protection of the safety and health of workers, Member States may derogate from Articles 3 to 6, 8 and 16 when, on account of the specific characteristics of the activity concerned, the duration of the working time is not measured and/or predetermined or can be determined by the workers themselves, and particularly in the case of:

(a) managing executives or other persons with autonomous decision-taking powers;

(b) family workers; or

(c) workers officiating at religious ceremonies in churches and religious communities.

2. Derogations provided for in paragraphs 3, 4 and 5 may be adopted by means of laws, regulations or administrative provisions or by means of collective agreements or agreements between the two sides of industry provided that the workers concerned are afforded equivalent periods of compensatory rest or that, in exceptional cases in which it is not possible, for objective reasons, to grant such equivalent periods of compensatory rest, the workers concerned are afforded appropriate protection.

3. In accordance with paragraph 2 of this Article derogations may be made from Articles 3, 4, 5, 8 and 16:

(a) in the case of activities where the worker's place of work and his place of residence are distant from one another, including offshore work, or where the worker's different places of work are distant from one another;

(b) in the case of security and surveillance activities requiring a permanent presence in order to protect property and persons, particularly security guards and caretakers or security firms;

(c) in the case of activities involving the need for continuity of service or production, particularly:

(i) services relating to the reception, treatment and/or care provided by hospitals or similar establishments, including the activities of doctors in training, residential institutions and prisons;

(ii) dock or airport workers;

(iii) press, radio, television, cinematographic production, postal and telecommunications services, ambulance, fire and civil protection services;

(iv) gas, water and electricity production, transmission and distribution, household refuse collection and incineration plants;

(v) industries in which work cannot be interrupted on technical grounds;

(vi) research and development activities;

(vii) agriculture;

(viii) workers concerned with the carriage of passengers on regular urban transport services;

(d) where there is a foreseeable surge of activity, particularly in:

(i) agriculture;

(ii) tourism;

(iii) postal services;

(e) in the case of persons working in railway transport:

(i) whose activities are intermittent;

(ii) who spend their working time on board trains; or

(iii) whose activities are linked to transport timetables and to ensuring the continuity and regularity of traffic;

(f) in the circumstances described in Article 5(4) of Directive 89/391/EEC;

(g) in cases of accident or imminent risk of accident.

4. In accordance with paragraph 2 of this Article derogations may be made from Articles 3 and 5:

(a) in the case of shift work activities, each time the worker changes shift and cannot take daily and/or weekly rest periods between the end of one shift and the start of the next one;

(b) in the case of activities involving periods of work split up over the day, particularly those of cleaning staff.

5. In accordance with paragraph 2 of this Article, derogations may be made from Article 6 and Article 16(b), in the case of doctors in training, in accordance with the provisions set out in the second to the seventh subparagraphs of this paragraph.

With respect to Article 6 derogations referred to in the first subparagraph shall be permitted for a transitional period of five years from 1 August 2004.

Member States may have up to two more years, if necessary, to take account of difficulties in meeting the working time provisions with respect to their responsibilities for the organisation and delivery of health services and medical care. At least six months before the end of the transitional period, the Member State concerned shall inform the Commission giving its reasons, so that the Commission can give an opinion, after appropriate consultations, within the three months following receipt of such information. If the Member State does not follow the opinion of the Commission, it will justify its decision. The notification and justification of the Member State and the opinion of the Commission shall be published in the *Official Journal of the European Union* and forwarded to the European Parliament.

Member States may have an additional period of up to one year, if necessary, to take account of special difficulties in meeting the responsibilities referred to in the third subparagraph. They shall follow the procedure set out in that subparagraph.

Member States shall ensure that in no case will the number of weekly working hours exceed an average of 58 during the first three years of the transitional period, an average of 56 for the following two years and an average of 52 for any remaining period.

The employer shall consult the representatives of the employees in good time with a view to reaching an agreement, wherever possible, on the arrangements applying to the transitional period. Within the limits set out in the fifth subparagraph, such an agreement may cover:

(a) the average number of weekly hours of work during the transitional period; and
(b) the measures to be adopted to reduce weekly working hours to an average of 48 by the end of the transitional period.

With respect to Article 16(b) derogations referred to in the first subparagraph shall be permitted provided that the reference period does not exceed 12 months, during the first part of the transitional period specified in the fifth subparagraph, and six months thereafter.

[3.436]
Article 18
Derogations by collective agreements

Derogations may be made from Articles 3, 4, 5, 8 and 16 by means of collective agreements or agreements concluded between the two sides of industry at national or regional level or, in conformity with the rules laid down by them, by means of collective agreements or agreements concluded between the two sides of industry at a lower level.

Member States in which there is no statutory system ensuring the conclusion of collective agreements or agreements concluded between the two sides of industry at national or regional level, on the matters covered by this Directive, or those Member States in which there is a specific legislative framework for this purpose and within the limits thereof, may, in accordance with national legislation and/or practice, allow derogations from Articles 3, 4, 5, 8 and 16 by way of collective agreements or agreements concluded between the two sides of industry at the appropriate collective level.

The derogations provided for in the first and second subparagraphs shall be allowed on condition that equivalent compensating rest periods are granted to the workers concerned or, in exceptional cases where it is not possible for objective reasons to grant such periods, the workers concerned are afforded appropriate protection.

Member States may lay down rules:

(a) for the application of this Article by the two sides of industry; and
(b) for the extension of the provisions of collective agreements or agreements concluded in conformity with this Article to other workers in accordance with national legislation and/or practice.

[3.437]
Article 19
Limitations to derogations from reference periods

The option to derogate from Article 16(b), provided for in Article 17(3) and in Article 18, may not result in the establishment of a reference period exceeding six months.

However, Member States shall have the option, subject to compliance with the general principles relating to the protection of the safety and health of workers, of allowing, for objective or technical reasons or reasons concerning the organisation of work, collective agreements or agreements concluded between the two sides of industry to set reference periods in no event exceeding 12 months.

Before 23 November 2003, the Council shall, on the basis of a Commission proposal accompanied by an appraisal report, re-examine the provisions of this Article and decide what action to take.

[3.438]
Article 20
Mobile workers and offshore work

1. Articles 3, 4, 5 and 8 shall not apply to mobile workers.

Member States shall, however, take the necessary measures to ensure that such mobile workers are entitled to adequate rest, except in the circumstances laid down in Article 17(3)(f) and (g).

2. Subject to compliance with the general principles relating to the protection of the safety and health of workers, and provided that there is consultation of representatives of the employer and employees concerned and efforts to encourage all relevant forms of social dialogue, including negotiation if the parties so wish, Member States may, for objective or technical reasons or reasons concerning the organisation of work, extend the reference period referred to in Article 16(b) to 12 months in respect of workers who mainly perform offshore work.

3. Not later than 1 August 2005 the Commission shall, after consulting the Member States and management and labour at European level, review the operation of the provisions with regard to offshore workers from a health and safety perspective with a view to presenting, if need be, the appropriate modifications.

[3.439]
Article 21
Workers on board seagoing fishing vessels

1. Articles 3 to 6 and 8 shall not apply to any worker on board a seagoing fishing vessel flying the flag of a Member State.

Member States shall, however, take the necessary measures to ensure that any worker on board a seagoing fishing vessel flying the flag of a Member State is entitled to adequate rest and to limit the number of hours of work to 48 hours a week on average calculated over a reference period not exceeding 12 months.

2. Within the limits set out in paragraph 1, second subparagraph, and paragraphs 3 and 4 Member States shall take the necessary measures to ensure that, in keeping with the need to protect the safety and health of such workers:

(a) the working hours are limited to a maximum number of hours which shall not be exceeded in a given period of time; or

(b) a minimum number of hours of rest are provided within a given period of time.

The maximum number of hours of work or minimum number of hours of rest shall be specified by law, regulations, administrative provisions or by collective agreements or agreements between the two sides of the industry.

3. The limits on hours of work or rest shall be either:

(a) maximum hours of work which shall not exceed:
  (i) 14 hours in any 24-hour period; and
  (ii) 72 hours in any seven-day period; or

(b) minimum hours of rest which shall not be less than:
  (i) 10 hours in any 24-hour period; and
  (ii) 77 hours in any seven-day period.

4. Hours of rest may be divided into no more than two periods, one of which shall be at least six hours in length, and the interval between consecutive periods of rest shall not exceed 14 hours.

5. In accordance with the general principles of the protection of the health and safety of workers, and for objective or technical reasons or reasons concerning the organisation of work, Member States may allow exceptions, including the establishment of reference periods, to the limits laid down in paragraph 1, second subparagraph, and paragraphs 3 and 4. Such exceptions shall, as far as possible, comply with the standards laid down but may take account of more frequent or longer leave periods or the granting of compensatory leave for the workers. These exceptions may be laid down by means of:

(a) laws, regulations or administrative provisions provided there is consultation, where possible, of the representatives of the employers and workers concerned and efforts are made to encourage all relevant forms of social dialogue; or

(b) collective agreements or agreements between the two sides of industry.

6. The master of a seagoing fishing vessel shall have the right to require workers on board to perform any hours of work necessary for the immediate safety of the vessel, persons on board or cargo, or for the purpose of giving assistance to other vessels or persons in distress at sea.

7. Members States may provide that workers on board seagoing fishing vessels for which national legislation or practice determines that these vessels are not allowed to operate in a specific period of the calendar year exceeding one month, shall take annual leave in accordance with Article 7 within that period.

[3.440]
Article 22
Miscellaneous provisions

1. A Member State shall have the option not to apply Article 6, while respecting the general principles of the protection of the safety and health of workers, and provided it takes the necessary measures to ensure that:

(a) no employer requires a worker to work more than 48 hours over a seven-day period, calculated as an average for the reference period referred to in Article 16(b), unless he has first obtained the worker's agreement to perform such work;
(b) no worker is subjected to any detriment by his employer because he is not willing to give his agreement to perform such work;
(c) the employer keeps up-to-date records of all workers who carry out such work;
(d) the records are placed at the disposal of the competent authorities, which may, for reasons connected with the safety and/or health of workers, prohibit or restrict the possibility of exceeding the maximum weekly working hours;
(e) the employer provides the competent authorities at their request with information on cases in which agreement has been given by workers to perform work exceeding 48 hours over a period of seven days, calculated as an average for the reference period referred to in Article 16(b).

Before 23 November 2003, the Council shall, on the basis of a Commission proposal accompanied by an appraisal report, re-examine the provisions of this paragraph and decide on what action to take.

2. Member States shall have the option, as regards the application of Article 7, of making use of a transitional period of not more than three years from 23 November 1996, provided that during that transitional period:

(a) every worker receives three weeks' paid annual leave in accordance with the conditions for the entitlement to, and granting of, such leave laid down by national legislation and/or practice; and
(b) the three-week period of paid annual leave may not be replaced by an allowance in lieu, except where the employment relationship is terminated.

3. If Member States avail themselves of the options provided for in this Article, they shall forthwith inform the Commission thereof.

CHAPTER 6
FINAL PROVISIONS

[3.441]
Article 23
Level of Protection

Without prejudice to the right of Member States to develop, in the light of changing circumstances, different legislative, regulatory or contractual provisions in the field of working time, as long as the minimum requirements provided for in this Directive are complied with, implementation of this Directive shall not constitute valid grounds for reducing the general level of protection afforded to workers.

[3.442]
Article 24
Reports

1. Member States shall communicate to the Commission the texts of the provisions of national law already adopted or being adopted in the field governed by this Directive.

2. Member States shall report to the Commission every five years on the practical implementation of the provisions of this Directive, indicating the viewpoints of the two sides of industry.

The Commission shall inform the European Parliament, the Council, the European Economic and Social Committee and the Advisory Committee on Safety, Hygiene and Health Protection at Work thereof.

3. Every five years from 23 November 1996 the Commission shall submit to the European Parliament, the Council and the European Economic and Social Committee a report on the application of this Directive taking into account Articles 22 and 23 and paragraphs 1 and 2 of this Article.

[3.443]
Article 25
Review of the operation of the provisions with regard to workers on board seagoing fishing vessels

Not later than 1 August 2009 the Commission shall, after consulting the Member States and management and labour at European level, review the operation of the provisions with regard to workers on board seagoing fishing vessels, and, in particular examine whether these provisions remain appropriate, in particular, as far as health and safety are concerned with a view to proposing suitable amendments, if necessary.

[3.444]
Article 26
Review of the operation of the provisions with regard to workers concerned with the carriage of passengers
Not later than 1 August 2005 the Commission shall, after consulting the Member States and management and labour at European level, review the operation of the provisions with regard to workers concerned with the carriage of passengers on regular urban transport services, with a view to presenting, if need be, the appropriate modifications to ensure a coherent and suitable approach in the sector.

[3.445]
Article 27
Repeal
1. Directive 93/104/EC, as amended by the Directive referred to in Annex I, part A, shall be repealed, without prejudice to the obligations of the Member States in respect of the deadlines for transposition laid down in Annex I, part B.
2. The references made to the said repealed Directive shall be construed as references to this Directive and shall be read in accordance with the correlation table set out in Annex II.

[3.446]
Article 28
Entry into force
This Directive shall enter into force on 2 August 2004.

[3.447]
Article 29
Addressees
This Directive is addressed to the Member States.

ANNEX I

PART A
REPEALED DIRECTIVE AND ITS AMENDMENT

(Article 27)

[3.448]

Council Directive 93/104/EC	(OJ L307, 13.12.1993, p 18)
Directive 2000/34/EC of the European Parliament and of the Council	(OJ L195, 1.8.2000, p 41)

PART B
DEADLINES FOR TRANSPOSITION INTO NATIONAL LAW

(Article 27)

[3.449]

Directive	*Deadline for transposition*
93/104/EC	23 November 1996
2000/34/EC	1 August 2003[1]

NOTES

[1] 1 August 2004 in the case of doctors in training. See Article 2 of Directive 2000/34/EC.

ANNEX II
CORRELATION TABLE

[3.450]

Directive 93/104/EC	*This Directive*
Articles 1 to 5	Articles 1 to 5
Article 6, introductory words	Article 6, introductory words
Article 6(1)	Article 6(a)
Article 6(2)	Article 6(b)
Article 7	Article 7

Directive 93/104/EC	***This Directive***
Article 8, introductory words	Article 8, introductory words
Article 8(1)	Article 8(a)
Article 8(2)	Article 8(b)
Articles 9, 10 and 11	Articles 9, 10 and 11
Article 12, introductory words	Article 12, introductory words
Article 12(1)	Article 12(a)
Article 12(2)	Article 12(b)
Articles 13, 14 and 15	Articles 13, 14 and 15
Article 16, introductory words	Article 16, introductory words
Article 16(1)	Article 16(a)
Article 16(2)	Article 16(b)
Article 16(3)	Article 16(c)
Article 17(1)	Article 17(1)
Article 17(2), introductory words	Article 17(2)
Article 17(2)(1)	Article 17(3)(a) to (e)
Article 17(2)(2)	Article 17(3)(f) to (g)
Article 17(2)(3)	Article 17(4)
Article 17(2)(4)	Article 17(5)
Article 17(3)	Article 18
Article 17(4)	Article 19
Article 17a(1)	Article 20(1), first subparagraph
Article 17a(2)	Article 20(1), second subparagraph
Article 17a(3)	Article 20(2)
Article 17a(4)	Article 20(3)
Article 17b(1)	Article 21(1), first subparagraph
Article 17b(2)	Article 21(1), second subparagraph
Article 17b(3)	Article 21(2)
Article 17b(4)	Article 21(3)
Article 17b(5)	Article 21(4)
Article 17b(6)	Article 21(5)
Article 17b(7)	Article 21(6)
Article 17b(8)	Article 21(7)
Article 18(1)(a)	—
Article 18(1)(b)(i)	Article 22(1)
Article 18(1)(b)(ii)	Article 22(2)
Article 18(1)(c)	Article 22(3)
Article 18(2)	—
Article 18(3)	Article 23
Article 18(4)	Article 24(1)
Article 18(5)	Article 24(2)
Article 18(6)	Article 24(3)
—	Article 25[1]
—	Article 26[2]
—	Article 27
—	Article 28
Article 19	Article 29
—	Annex I
—	Annex II

NOTES

[1] Directive 2000/34/EC, Article 3.

[2] Directive 2000/34/EC, Article 4.

COUNCIL DIRECTIVE

(2004/113/EC)

of 13 December 2004

implementing the principle of equal treatment between men and women in the access to and supply of goods and services

NOTES

Date of publication in OJ: OJ L373, 21.12.2004, p 37.

For the domestic implementation of this Directive, see now the Equality Act 2010, Parts 3, 9 and 10 (the 2010 Act is at **[1.1618]**).

[3.451]

THE COUNCIL OF THE EUROPEAN UNION,

Having regard to the Treaty establishing the European Community and in particular Article 13(1) thereof,

Having regard to the proposal from the Commission,

Having regard to the Opinion of the European Parliament,[1]

Having regard to the Opinion of the European Economic and Social Committee,[2]

Having regard to the opinion of the Committee of the Regions,[3]

Whereas:

(1) In accordance with Article 6 of the Treaty on European Union, the Union is founded on the principles of liberty, democracy, respect for human rights and fundamental freedoms and the rule of law, principles which are common to the Member States, and respects fundamental rights as guaranteed by the European Convention for the Protection of Human Rights and Fundamental Freedoms and as they result from the constitutional traditions common to the Member States as general principles of Community law.

(2) The right to equality before the law and protection against discrimination for all persons constitutes a universal right recognised by the Universal Declaration of Human Rights, the United Nations Convention on the Elimination of all forms of Discrimination Against Women, the International Convention on the Elimination of all forms of Racial Discrimination and the United Nations Covenants on Civil and Political Rights and on Economic, Social and Cultural Rights and by the European Convention for the Protection of Human Rights and Fundamental Freedoms, to which all Member States are signatories.

(3) While prohibiting discrimination, it is important to respect other fundamental rights and freedoms, including the protection of private and family life and transactions carried out in that context and the freedom of religion.

(4) Equality between men and women is a fundamental principle of the European Union. Articles 21 and 23 of the Charter of Fundamental Rights of the European Union prohibit any discrimination on grounds of sex and require equality between men and women to be ensured in all areas.

(5) Article 2 of the Treaty establishing the European Community provides that promoting such equality is one of the Community's essential tasks. Similarly, Article 3(2) of the Treaty requires the Community to aim to eliminate inequalities and to promote equality between men and women in all its activities.

(6) The Commission announced its intention of proposing a directive on sex discrimination outside of the labour market in its Communication on the Social Policy Agenda. Such a proposal is fully consistent with Council Decision 2001/51/EC of 20 December 2000 establishing a Programme relating to the Community framework strategy on gender equality (2001–2005)[4] covering all Community policies and aimed at promoting equality for men and women by adjusting these policies and implementing practical measures to improve the situation of men and women in society.

(7) At its meeting in Nice of 7 and 9 December 2000, the European Council called on the Commission to reinforce equality-related rights by adopting a proposal for a directive on promoting gender equality in areas other than employment and professional life.

(8) The Community has adopted a range of legal instruments to prevent and combat sex

discrimination in the labour market. These instruments have demonstrated the value of legislation in the fight against discrimination.

(9) Discrimination based on sex, including harassment and sexual harassment, also takes place in areas outside of the labour market. Such discrimination can be equally damaging, acting as a barrier to the full and successful integration of men and women into economic and social life.

(10) Problems are particularly apparent in the area of the access to and supply of goods and services. Discrimination based on sex, should therefore be prevented and eliminated in this area. As in the case of Council Directive 2000/43/EC of 29 June 2000 implementing the principle of equal treatment between persons irrespective of racial and ethnic origin,[5] this objective can be better achieved by means of Community legislation.

(11) Such legislation should prohibit discrimination based on sex in the access to and supply of goods and services. Goods should be taken to be those within the meaning of the provisions of the Treaty establishing the European Community relating to the free movement of goods. Services should be taken to be those within the meaning of Article 50 of that Treaty.

(12) To prevent discrimination based on sex, this Directive should apply to both direct discrimination and indirect discrimination. Direct discrimination occurs only when one person is treated less favourably, on grounds of sex, than another person in a comparable situation. Accordingly, for example, differences between men and women in the provision of healthcare services, which result from the physical differences between men and women, do not relate to comparable situations and therefore, do not constitute discrimination.

(13) The prohibition of discrimination should apply to persons providing goods and services, which are available to the public and which are offered outside the area of private and family life and the transactions carried out in this context. It should not apply to the content of media or advertising nor to public or private education.

(14) All individuals enjoy the freedom to contract, including the freedom to choose a contractual partner for a transaction. An individual who provides goods or services may have a number of subjective reasons for his or her choice of contractual partner. As long as the choice of partner is not based on that person's sex, this Directive should not prejudice the individual's freedom to choose a contractual partner.

(15) There are already a number of existing legal instruments for the implementation of the principle of equal treatment between men and women in matters of employment and occupation. Therefore, this Directive should not apply in this field. The same reasoning applies to matters of self-employment insofar as they are covered by existing legal instruments. The Directive should apply only to insurance and pensions which are private, voluntary and separate from the employment relationship.

(16) Differences in treatment may be accepted only if they are justified by a legitimate aim. A legitimate aim may, for example, be the protection of victims of sex-related violence (in cases such as the establishment of single-sex shelters), reasons of privacy and decency (in cases such as the provision of accommodation by a person in a part of that person's home), the promotion of gender equality or of the interests of men or women (for example single-sex voluntary bodies), the freedom of association (in cases of membership of single-sex private clubs), and the organisation of sporting activities (for example single-sex sports events). Any limitation should nevertheless be appropriate and necessary in accordance with the criteria derived from case law of the Court of Justice of the European Communities.

(17) The principle of equal treatment in the access to goods and services does not require that facilities should always be provided to men and women on a shared basis, as long as they are not provided more favourably to members of one sex.

(18) The use of actuarial factors related to sex is widespread in the provision of insurance and other related financial services. In order to ensure equal treatment between men and women, the use of sex as an actuarial factor should not result in differences in individuals' premiums and benefits. To avoid a sudden readjustment of the market, the implementation of this rule should apply only to new contracts concluded after the date of transposition of this Directive.

(19) Certain categories of risks may vary between the sexes. In some cases, sex is one but not necessarily the only determining factor in the assessment of risks insured. For contracts insuring those types of risks, Member States may decide to permit exemptions from the rule of unisex premiums and benefits, as long as they can ensure that underlying actuarial and statistical data on which the calculations are based, are reliable, regularly up-dated and available to the public. Exemptions are allowed only where national legislation has not already applied the unisex rule. Five years after transposition of this Directive, Member States should re-examine the justification for these exemptions, taking into account the most recent actuarial and statistical data and a report by the Commission three years after the date of transposition of this Directive.

(20) Less favourable treatment of women for reasons of pregnancy and maternity should be considered a form of direct discrimination based on sex and therefore prohibited in insurance and

related financial services. Costs related to risks of pregnancy and maternity should therefore not be attributed to the members of one sex only.

(21) Persons who have been subject to discrimination based on sex should have adequate means of legal protection. To provide a more effective level of protection, associations, organisations and other legal entities should also be empowered to engage in proceedings, as the Member States so determine, either on behalf or in support of any victim, without prejudice to national rules of procedure concerning representation and defence before the courts.

(22) The rules on the burden of proof should be adapted when there is a prima facie case of discrimination and for the principle of equal treatment to be applied effectively, the burden of proof should shift back to the defendant when evidence of such discrimination is brought.

(23) The effective implementation of the principle of equal treatment requires adequate judicial protection against victimisation.

(24) With a view to promoting the principle of equal treatment, Member States should encourage dialogue with relevant stakeholders, which have, in accordance with national law and practice, a legitimate interest in contributing to the fight against discrimination on grounds of sex in the area of access to and supply of goods and services.

(25) Protection against discrimination based on sex should itself be strengthened by the existence of a body or bodies in each Member State, with competence to analyse the problems involved, to study possible solutions and to provide concrete assistance for the victims. The body or bodies may be the same as those with responsibility at national level for the defence of human rights or the safeguarding of individuals' rights, or the implementation of the principle of equal treatment.

(26) This Directive lays down minimum requirements, thus giving the Member States the option of introducing or maintaining more favourable provisions. The implementation of this Directive should not serve to justify any regression in relation to the situation, which already prevails in each Member State.

(27) Member States should provide for effective, proportionate and dissuasive penalties in cases of breaches of the obligations under this Directive.

(28) Since the objectives of this Directive, namely to ensure a common high level of protection against discrimination in all the Member States, cannot be sufficiently achieved by the Member States and can, therefore, by reason of the scale and effects of the action, be better achieved at Community level, the Community may adopt measures, in accordance with the principle of subsidiarity as set out in Article 5 of the Treaty. In accordance with the principle of proportionality, as set out in that Article, this Directive does not go beyond what is necessary in order to achieve those objectives.

(29) In accordance with paragraph 34 of the interinstitutional agreement on better law-making,[6] Member States are encouraged to draw up, for themselves and in the interest of the Community, their own tables, which will, as far as possible, illustrate the correlation between the Directive and the transposition measures and to make them public,

NOTES

1 Opinion delivered on 30 March 2004 (not yet published in the Official Journal).

2 OJ C241, 28.9.2004, p 44.

3 OJ C121, 30.4.2004, p 27.

4 OJ L17, 19.1.2001, p 22.

5 OJ L180, 19.7.2000, p 22.

6 OJ C321, 31.12.2003, p 1.

HAS ADOPTED THIS DIRECTIVE:

CHAPTER I
GENERAL PROVISIONS

[3.452]
Article 1
Purpose

The purpose of this Directive is to lay down a framework for combating discrimination based on sex in access to and supply of goods and services, with a view to putting into effect in the Member States the principle of equal treatment between men and women.

[3.453]
Article 2
Definitions

For the purposes of this Directive, the following definitions shall apply:

(a) direct discrimination: where one person is treated less favourably, on grounds of sex, than another is, has been or would be treated in a comparable situation;
(b) indirect discrimination: where an apparently neutral provision, criterion or practice would put persons of one sex at a particular disadvantage compared with persons of the other sex, unless that provision, criterion or practice is objectively justified by a legitimate aim and the means of achieving that aim are appropriate and necessary;
(c) harassment: where an unwanted conduct related to the sex of a person occurs with the purpose or effect of violating the dignity of a person and of creating an intimidating, hostile, degrading, humiliating or offensive environment;
(d) sexual harassment: where any form of unwanted physical, verbal, non-verbal or physical conduct of a sexual nature occurs, with the purpose or effect of violating the dignity of a person, in particular when creating an intimidating, hostile, degrading, humiliating or offensive environment.

[3.454]
Article 3
Scope
1. Within the limits of the powers conferred upon the Community, this Directive shall apply to all persons who provide goods and services, which are available to the public irrespective of the person concerned as regards both the public and private sectors, including public bodies, and which are offered outside the area of private and family life and the transactions carried out in this context.
2. This Directive does not prejudice the individual's freedom to choose a contractual partner as long as an individual's choice of contractual partner is not based on that person's sex.
3. This Directive shall not apply to the content of media and advertising nor to education.
4. This Directive shall not apply to matters of employment and occupation. This Directive shall not apply to matters of self-employment, insofar as these matters are covered by other Community legislative acts.

[3.455]
Article 4
Principle of equal treatment
1. For the purposes of this Directive, the principle of equal treatment between men and women shall mean that
(a) there shall be no direct discrimination based on sex, including less favourable treatment of women for reasons of pregnancy and maternity;
(b) there shall be no indirect discrimination based on sex.
2. This Directive shall be without prejudice to more favourable provisions concerning the protection of women as regards pregnancy and maternity.
3. Harassment and sexual harassment within the meaning of this Directive shall be deemed to be discrimination on the grounds of sex and therefore prohibited. A person's rejection of, or submission to, such conduct may not be used as a basis for a decision affecting that person.
4. Instruction to direct or indirect discrimination on the grounds of sex shall be deemed to be discrimination within the meaning of this Directive.
5. This Directive shall not preclude differences in treatment, if the provision of the goods and services exclusively or primarily to members of one sex is justified by a legitimate aim and the means of achieving that aim are appropriate and necessary.

[3.456]
Article 5
Actuarial factors
1. Member States shall ensure that in all new contracts concluded after 21 December 2007 at the latest, the use of sex as a factor in the calculation of premiums and benefits for the purposes of insurance and related financial services shall not result in differences in individuals' premiums and benefits.
2. Notwithstanding paragraph 1, Member States may decide before 21 December 2007 to permit proportionate differences in individuals' premiums and benefits where the use of sex is a determining factor in the assessment of risk based on relevant and accurate actuarial and statistical data. The Member States concerned shall inform the Commission and ensure that accurate data relevant to the use of sex as a determining actuarial factor are compiled, published and regularly updated. These Member States shall review their decision five years after 21 December 2007, taking into account the Commission report referred to in Article 16, and shall forward the results of this review to the Commission.
3. In any event, costs related to pregnancy and maternity shall not result in differences in individuals' premiums and benefits.

Member States may defer implementation of the measures necessary to comply with this paragraph until two years after 21 December 2007 at the latest. In that case the Member States concerned shall immediately inform the Commission.

[3.457]
Article 6
Positive action

With a view to ensuring full equality in practice between men and women, the principle of equal treatment shall not prevent any Member State from maintaining or adopting specific measures to prevent or compensate for disadvantages linked to sex.

[3.458]
Article 7
Minimum requirements

1. Member States may introduce or maintain provisions which are more favourable to the protection of the principle of equal treatment between men and women than those laid down in this Directive.
2. The implementation of this Directive shall in no circumstances constitute grounds for a reduction in the level of protection against discrimination already afforded by Member States in the fields covered by this Directive.

CHAPTER II
REMEDIES AND ENFORCEMENT

[3.459]
Article 8
Defence of rights

1. Member States shall ensure that judicial and/or administrative procedures, including where they deem it appropriate conciliation procedures, for the enforcement of the obligations under this Directive are available to all persons who consider themselves wronged by failure to apply the principle of equal treatment to them, even after the relationship in which the discrimination is alleged to have occurred has ended.
2. Member States shall introduce into their national legal systems such measures as are necessary to ensure real and effective compensation or reparation, as the Member States so determine, for the loss and damage sustained by a person injured as a result of discrimination within the meaning of this Directive, in a way which is dissuasive and proportionate to the damage suffered. The fixing of a prior upper limit shall not restrict such compensation or reparation.
3. Member States shall ensure that associations, organisations or other legal entities, which have, in accordance with the criteria laid down by their national law, a legitimate interest in ensuring that the provisions of this Directive are complied with, may engage, on behalf or in support of the complainant, with his or her approval, in any judicial and/or administrative procedure provided for the enforcement of obligations under this Directive.
4. Paragraphs 1 and 3 shall be without prejudice to national rules on time limits for bringing actions relating to the principle of equal treatment.

[3.460]
Article 9
Burden of proof

1. Member States shall take such measures as are necessary, in accordance with their national judicial systems, to ensure that, when persons who consider themselves wronged because the principle of equal treatment has not been applied to them establish, before a court or other competent authority, facts from which it may be presumed that there has been direct or indirect discrimination, it shall be for the respondent to prove that there has been no breach of the principle of equal treatment.
2. Paragraph 1 shall not prevent Member States from introducing rules of evidence, which are more favourable to plaintiffs.
3. Paragraph 1 shall not apply to criminal procedures.
4. Paragraphs 1, 2 and 3 shall also apply to any proceedings brought in accordance with Article 8(3).
5. Member States need not apply paragraph 1 to proceedings in which it is for the court or other competent authority to investigate the facts of the case.

[3.461]
Article 10
Victimisation

Member States shall introduce into their national legal systems such measures as are necessary to protect persons from any adverse treatment or adverse consequence as a reaction to a complaint or to legal proceedings aimed at enforcing compliance with the principle of equal treatment.

[3.462]
Article 11
Dialogue with relevant stakeholders
With a view to promoting the principle of equal treatment, Member States shall encourage dialogue with relevant stakeholders which have, in accordance with national law and practice, a legitimate interest in contributing to the fight against discrimination on grounds of sex in the area of access to and supply of goods and services.

CHAPTER III
BODIES FOR THE PROMOTION OF EQUAL TREATMENT

[3.463]
Article 12
1. Member States shall designate and make the necessary arrangements for a body or bodies for the promotion, analysis, monitoring and support of equal treatment of all persons without discrimination on the grounds of sex. These bodies may form part of agencies charged at national level with the defence of human rights or the safeguard of individuals' rights, or the implementation of the principle of equal treatment.
2. Member States shall ensure that the competencies of the bodies referred to in paragraph 1 include:
- (a) without prejudice to the rights of victims and of associations, organisations or other legal entities referred to in Article 8(3), providing independent assistance to victims of discrimination in pursuing their complaints about discrimination;
- (b) conducting independent surveys concerning discrimination;
- (c) publishing independent reports and making recommendations on any issue relating to such discrimination.

CHAPTER IV
FINAL PROVISIONS

[3.464]
Article 13
Compliance
Member States shall take the necessary measures to ensure that the principle of equal treatment is respected in relation to the access to and supply of goods and services within the scope of this Directive, and in particular that:
- (a) any laws, regulations and administrative provisions contrary to the principle of equal treatment are abolished;
- (b) any contractual provisions, internal rules of undertakings, and rules governing profit-making or non-profit-making associations contrary to the principle of equal treatment are, or may be, declared null and void or are amended.

[3.465]
Article 14
Penalties
Member States shall lay down the rules on penalties applicable to infringements of the national provisions adopted pursuant to this Directive and shall take all measures necessary to ensure that they are applied. The penalties, which may comprise the payment of compensation to the victim, shall be effective, proportionate and dissuasive. Member States shall notify those provisions to the Commission by 21 December 2007 at the latest and shall notify it without delay of any subsequent amendment affecting them.

[3.466]
Article 15
Dissemination of information
Member States shall take care that the provisions adopted pursuant to this Directive, together with the relevant provisions already in force, are brought to the attention of the persons concerned by all appropriate means throughout their territory.

[3.467]
Article 16
Reports
1. Member States shall communicate all available information concerning the application of this Directive to the Commission, by 21 December 2009. and every five years thereafter.

The Commission shall draw up a summary report, which shall include a review of the current practices of Member States in relation to Article 5 with regard to the use of sex as a factor in the

calculation of premiums and benefits. It shall submit this report to the European Parliament and to the Council no later 21 December 2010. Where appropriate, the Commission shall accompany its report with proposals to modify the Directive.
2. The Commission's report shall take into account the viewpoints of relevant stakeholders.

[3.468]
Article 17
Transposition
1. Member States shall bring into force the laws, regulations and administrative provisions necessary to comply with this Directive by 21 December 2007 at the latest. They shall forthwith communicate to the Commission the text of those provisions.

When Member States adopt these measures, they shall contain a reference to this Directive or be accompanied by such a reference on the occasion of their official publication. The methods of making such publication of reference shall be laid down by the Member States.
2. Member States shall communicate to the Commission the text of the main provisions of national law which they adopt in the field covered by this Directive.

[3.469]
Article 18
Entry into force
This Directive shall enter into force on the day of its publication in the *Official Journal of the European Union*.

[3.470]
Article 19
Addressees
This Directive is addressed to the Member States.

DIRECTIVE OF THE EUROPEAN PARLIAMENT AND OF THE COUNCIL

(2006/54/EC)

of 5 July 2006

on the implementation of the principle of equal opportunities and equal treatment of men and women in matters of employment and occupation (recast)

NOTES

Date of publication in OJ: OJ L204, 26.7.2006, p 23.

This Directive consolidates and updates the four major directives on gender equality, the Equal Pay Directive (75/117/EEC), the Equal Treatment Directive (76/207/EEC), the Directive on Equal Treatment in Occupational Social Security Schemes (86/378/EEC) and the Burden of Proof Directive (97/80/EC), in each case as subsequently amended. These Directives are repealed by Art 34 of, and Annex I, Pt A to, this Directive, with effect from 15 August 2009 (see **[3.505]** and **[3.508]**). From that date, references in other EU legislation are to be read as references to the corresponding provisions in this Directive. Note that, apparently by oversight, Art 34 of this Directive does not list the amending Directives 96/97/EC, 98/52/EC or 2002/73/EC. However, it appears from Annex I, Pt A of this Directive that the amending Directives are also intended to be repealed.

This Directive came into force on 15 August 2006 (20 days after its publication in the Official Journal on 26 July 2006). The deadline for transposition was 15 August 2008. Article 33 (at **[3.504]**) makes it clear that the obligations for transposition of provisions that are contained in the original Directives on the dates provided for in those Directives are not affected by this. The original dates for transposition are set out in a table in Annex I, Pt B (at **[3.510]**). The new obligation to transpose only applies to 'those provisions which represent a substantive change compared with the earlier Directives'. These are not specifically identified within the Directive. No additional or amending legislation was introduced by the UK government in relation to this Directive, presumably because none was considered necessary.

For the domestic implementation of this Directive, see now the Equality Act 2010, Parts 2, 5, 9, 10 and 11 (the 2010 Act is at **[1.1618]**).

See *Harvey* K, L.

[3.471]
THE EUROPEAN PARLIAMENT AND THE COUNCIL OF THE EUROPEAN UNION,

Having regard to the Treaty establishing the European Community, and in particular Article 141(3) thereof,

Having regard to the proposal from the Commission,

Having regard to the opinion of the European Economic and Social Committee,[1]

Acting in accordance with the procedure laid down in Article 251 of the Treaty,[2]

Whereas:

(1) Council Directive 76/207/EEC of 9 February 1976 on the implementation of the principle of equal treatment for men and women as regards access to employment, vocational training and promotion, and working conditions[3] and Council Directive 86/378/EEC of 24 July 1986 on the

implementation of the principle of equal treatment for men and women in occupational social security schemes[4] have been significantly amended.[5] Council Directive 75/117/EEC of 10 February 1975 on the approximation of the laws of the Member States relating to the application of the principle of equal pay for men and women[6] and Council Directive 97/80/EC of 15 December 1997 on the burden of proof in cases of discrimination based on sex[7] also contain provisions which have as their purpose the implementation of the principle of equal treatment between men and women. Now that new amendments are being made to the said Directives, it is desirable, for reasons of clarity, that the provisions in question should be recast by bringing together in a single text the main provisions existing in this field as well as certain developments arising out of the case-law of the Court of Justice of the European Communities (hereinafter referred to as the Court of Justice).

(2) Equality between men and women is a fundamental principle of Community law under Article 2 and Article 3(2) of the Treaty and the case-law of the Court of Justice. Those Treaty provisions proclaim equality between men and women as a "task" and an "aim" of the Community and impose a positive obligation to promote it in all its activities.

(3) The Court of Justice has held that the scope of the principle of equal treatment for men and women cannot be confined to the prohibition of discrimination based on the fact that a person is of one or other sex. In view of its purpose and the nature of the rights which it seeks to safeguard, it also applies to discrimination arising from the gender reassignment of a person.

(4) Article 141(3) of the Treaty now provides a specific legal basis for the adoption of Community measures to ensure the application of the principle of equal opportunities and equal treatment in matters of employment and occupation, including the principle of equal pay for equal work or work of equal value.

(5) Articles 21 and 23 of the Charter of Fundamental Rights of the European Union also prohibit any discrimination on grounds of sex and enshrine the right to equal treatment between men and women in all areas, including employment, work and pay.

(6) Harassment and sexual harassment are contrary to the principle of equal treatment between men and women and constitute discrimination on grounds of sex for the purposes of this Directive. These forms of discrimination occur not only in the workplace, but also in the context of access to employment, vocational training and promotion. They should therefore be prohibited and should be subject to effective, proportionate and dissuasive penalties.

(7) In this context, employers and those responsible for vocational training should be encouraged to take measures to combat all forms of discrimination on grounds of sex and, in particular, to take preventive measures against harassment and sexual harassment in the workplace and in access to employment, vocational training and promotion, in accordance with national law and practice.

(8) The principle of equal pay for equal work or work of equal value as laid down by Article 141 of the Treaty and consistently upheld in the case-law of the Court of Justice constitutes an important aspect of the principle of equal treatment between men and women and an essential and indispensable part of the *acquis communautaire*, including the case-law of the Court concerning sex discrimination. It is therefore appropriate to make further provision for its implementation.

(9) In accordance with settled case-law of the Court of Justice, in order to assess whether workers are performing the same work or work of equal value, it should be determined whether, having regard to a range of factors including the nature of the work and training and working conditions, those workers may be considered to be in a comparable situation.

(10) The Court of Justice has established that, in certain circumstances, the principle of equal pay is not limited to situations in which men and women work for the same employer.

(11) The Member States, in collaboration with the social partners, should continue to address the problem of the continuing gender-based wage differentials and marked gender segregation on the labour market by means such as flexible working time arrangements which enable both men and women to combine family and work commitments more successfully. This could also include appropriate parental leave arrangements which could be taken up by either parent as well as the provision of accessible and affordable child-care facilities and care for dependent persons.

(12) Specific measures should be adopted to ensure the implementation of the principle of equal treatment in occupational social security schemes and to define its scope more clearly.

(13) In its judgment of 17 May 1990 in Case C-262/88,[8] the Court of Justice determined that all forms of occupational pension constitute an element of pay within the meaning of Article 141 of the Treaty.

(14) Although the concept of pay within the meaning of Article 141 of the Treaty does not encompass social security benefits, it is now clearly established that a pension scheme for public servants falls within the scope of the principle of equal pay if the benefits payable under the scheme are paid to the worker by reason of his/her employment relationship with the public employer, notwithstanding the fact that such scheme forms part of a general statutory scheme. According to the judgments of the Court of Justice in Cases C-7/93[9] and C-351/00,[10] that condition will be satisfied if the pension scheme concerns a particular category of workers and its benefits are directly related

to the period of service and calculated by reference to the public servant's final salary. For reasons of clarity, it is therefore appropriate to make specific provision to that effect.

(15) The Court of Justice has confirmed that whilst the contributions of male and female workers to a defined-benefit pension scheme are covered by Article 141 of the Treaty, any inequality in employers' contributions paid under funded defined-benefit schemes which is due to the use of actuarial factors differing according to sex is not to be assessed in the light of that same provision.

(16) By way of example, in the case of funded defined-benefit schemes, certain elements, such as conversion into a capital sum of part of a periodic pension, transfer of pension rights, a reversionary pension payable to a dependant in return for the surrender of part of a pension or a reduced pension where the worker opts to take earlier retirement, may be unequal where the inequality of the amounts results from the effects of the use of actuarial factors differing according to sex at the time when the scheme's funding is implemented.

(17) It is well established that benefits payable under occupational social security schemes are not to be considered as remuneration insofar as they are attributable to periods of employment prior to 17 May 1990, except in the case of workers or those claiming under them who initiated legal proceedings or brought an equivalent claim under the applicable national law before that date. It is therefore necessary to limit the implementation of the principle of equal treatment accordingly.

(18) The Court of Justice has consistently held that the Barber Protocol[11] does not affect the right to join an occupational pension scheme and that the limitation of the effects in time of the judgment in Case C-262/88 does not apply to the right to join an occupational pension scheme. The Court of Justice also ruled that the national rules relating to time limits for bringing actions under national law may be relied on against workers who assert their right to join an occupational pension scheme, provided that they are not less favourable for that type of action than for similar actions of a domestic nature and that they do not render the exercise of rights conferred by Community law impossible in practice. The Court of Justice has also pointed out that the fact that a worker can claim retroactively to join an occupational pension scheme does not allow the worker to avoid paying the contributions relating to the period of membership concerned.

(19) Ensuring equal access to employment and the vocational training leading thereto is fundamental to the application of the principle of equal treatment of men and women in matters of employment and occupation. Any exception to this principle should therefore be limited to those occupational activities which necessitate the employment of a person of a particular sex by reason of their nature or the context in which they are carried out, provided that the objective sought is legitimate and complies with the principle of proportionality.

(20) This Directive does not prejudice freedom of association, including the right to establish unions with others and to join unions to defend one's interests. Measures within the meaning of Article 141(4) of the Treaty may include membership or the continuation of the activity of organisations or unions whose main objective is the promotion, in practice, of the principle of equal treatment between men and women.

(21) The prohibition of discrimination should be without prejudice to the maintenance or adoption of measures intended to prevent or compensate for disadvantages suffered by a group of persons of one sex. Such measures permit organisations of persons of one sex where their main object is the promotion of the special needs of those persons and the promotion of equality between men and women.

(22) In accordance with Article 141(4) of the Treaty, with a view to ensuring full equality in practice between men and women in working life, the principle of equal treatment does not prevent Member States from maintaining or adopting measures providing for specific advantages in order to make it easier for the under-represented sex to pursue a vocational activity or to prevent or compensate for disadvantages in professional careers. Given the current situation and bearing in mind Declaration No 28 to the Amsterdam Treaty, Member States should, in the first instance, aim at improving the situation of women in working life.

(23) It is clear from the case-law of the Court of Justice that unfavourable treatment of a woman related to pregnancy or maternity constitutes direct discrimination on grounds of sex. Such treatment should therefore be expressly covered by this Directive.

(24) The Court of Justice has consistently recognised the legitimacy, as regards the principle of equal treatment, of protecting a woman's biological condition during pregnancy and maternity and of introducing maternity protection measures as a means to achieve substantive equality. This Directive should therefore be without prejudice to Council Directive 92/85/EEC of 19 October 1992 on the introduction of measures to encourage improvements in the safety and health at work of pregnant workers and workers who have recently given birth or are breastfeeding.[12] This Directive should further be without prejudice to Council Directive 96/34/EC of 3 June 1996 on the framework agreement on parental leave concluded by UNICE, CEEP and the ETUC.[13]

(25) For reasons of clarity, it is also appropriate to make express provision for the protection of the employment rights of women on maternity leave and in particular their right to return to the same

or an equivalent post, to suffer no detriment in their terms and conditions as a result of taking such leave and to benefit from any improvement in working conditions to which they would have been entitled during their absence.

(26) In the Resolution of the Council and of the Ministers for Employment and Social Policy, meeting within the Council, of 29 June 2000 on the balanced participation of women and men in family and working life,[14] Member States were encouraged to consider examining the scope for their respective legal systems to grant working men an individual and non-transferable right to paternity leave, while maintaining their rights relating to employment.

(27) Similar considerations apply to the granting by Member States to men and women of an individual and non-transferable right to leave subsequent to the adoption of a child. It is for the Member States to determine whether or not to grant such a right to paternity and/or adoption leave and also to determine any conditions, other than dismissal and return to work, which are outside the scope of this Directive.

(28) The effective implementation of the principle of equal treatment requires appropriate procedures to be put in place by the Member States.

(29) The provision of adequate judicial or administrative procedures for the enforcement of the obligations imposed by this Directive is essential to the effective implementation of the principle of equal treatment.

(30) The adoption of rules on the burden of proof plays a significant role in ensuring that the principle of equal treatment can be effectively enforced. As the Court of Justice has held, provision should therefore be made to ensure that the burden of proof shifts to the respondent when there is a prima facie case of discrimination, except in relation to proceedings in which it is for the court or other competent national body to investigate the facts. It is however necessary to clarify that the appreciation of the facts from which it may be presumed that there has been direct or indirect discrimination remains a matter for the relevant national body in accordance with national law or practice. Further, it is for the Member States to introduce, at any appropriate stage of the proceedings, rules of evidence which are more favourable to plaintiffs.

(31) With a view to further improving the level of protection offered by this Directive, associations, organisations and other legal entities should also be empowered to engage in proceedings, as the Member States so determine, either on behalf or in support of a complainant, without prejudice to national rules of procedure concerning representation and defence.

(32) Having regard to the fundamental nature of the right to effective legal protection, it is appropriate to ensure that workers continue to enjoy such protection even after the relationship giving rise to an alleged breach of the principle of equal treatment has ended. An employee defending or giving evidence on behalf of a person protected under this Directive should be entitled to the same protection.

(33) It has been clearly established by the Court of Justice that in order to be effective, the principle of equal treatment implies that the compensation awarded for any breach must be adequate in relation to the damage sustained. It is therefore appropriate to exclude the fixing of any prior upper limit for such compensation, except where the employer can prove that the only damage suffered by an applicant as a result of discrimination within the meaning of this Directive was the refusal to take his/her job application into consideration.

(34) In order to enhance the effective implementation of the principle of equal treatment, Member States should promote dialogue between the social partners and, within the framework of national practice, with non-governmental organisations.

(35) Member States should provide for effective, proportionate and dissuasive penalties for breaches of the obligations under this Directive.

(36) Since the objectives of this Directive cannot be sufficiently achieved by the Member States and can therefore be better achieved at Community level, the Community may adopt measures in accordance with the principle of subsidiarity as set out in Article 5 of the Treaty. In accordance with the principle of proportionality, as set out in that Article, this Directive does not go beyond what is necessary in order to achieve those objectives.

(37) For the sake of a better understanding of the different treatment of men and women in matters of employment and occupation, comparable statistics disaggregated by sex should continue to be developed, analysed and made available at the appropriate levels.

(38) Equal treatment of men and women in matters of employment and occupation cannot be restricted to legislative measures. Instead, the European Union and the Member States should continue to promote the raising of public awareness of wage discrimination and the changing of public attitudes, involving all parties concerned at public and private level to the greatest possible extent. The dialogue between the social partners could play an important role in this process.

(39) The obligation to transpose this Directive into national law should be confined to those provisions which represent a substantive change as compared with the earlier Directives. The

obligation to transpose the provisions which are substantially unchanged arises under the earlier Directives.

(40) This Directive should be without prejudice to the obligations of the Member States relating to the time limits for transposition into national law and application of the Directives set out in Annex I, Part B.

(41) In accordance with paragraph 34 of the Inter-institutional agreement on better law-making,[15] Member States are encouraged to draw up, for themselves and in the interest of the Community, their own tables, which will, as far as possible, illustrate the correlation between this Directive and the transposition measures and to make them public,

NOTES

1 OJ C157, 28.6.2005, p 83.

2 Opinion of the European Parliament of 6 July 2005 (not yet published in the Official Journal), Council Common Position of 10 March 2006 (OJ C126E, 30.5.2006, p 33) and Position of the European Parliament of 1 June 2006 (not yet published in the Official Journal).

3 OJ L39, 14.2.1976, p 40. Directive as amended by Directive 2002/73/EC of the European Parliament and of the Council (OJ L269, 5.10.2002, p 15).

4 OJ L225, 12.8.1986, p 40. Directive as amended by Directive 96/97/EC (OJ L46, 17.2.1997, p 20).

5 See Annex I Part A.

6 OJ L45, 19.2.1975, p 19.

7 OJ L14, 20.1.1998, p 6. Directive as amended by Directive 98/52/EC (OJ L205, 22.7.1998, p 66).

8 C-262/88: *Barber v Guardian Royal Exchange Assurance Group* (1990 ECR I-1889).

9 C-7/93: *Bestuur van het Algemeen Burgerlijk Pensioenfonds v G. A. Beune* (1994 ECR I-4471).

10 C-351/00: *Pirkko Niemi* (2002 ECR I-7007).

11 Protocol 17 concerning Article 141 of the Treaty establishing the European Community (1992).

12 OJ L348, 28.11.1992, p 1.

13 OJ L145, 19.6.1996, p 4. Directive as amended by Directive 97/75/EC (OJ L10, 16.1.1998, p 24).

14 OJ C218, 31.7.2000, p 5.

15 OJ C321, 31.12.2003, p 1.

HAVE ADOPTED THIS DIRECTIVE:

TITLE I
GENERAL PROVISIONS

[3.472]
Article 1
Purpose

The purpose of this Directive is to ensure the implementation of the principle of equal opportunities and equal treatment of men and women in matters of employment and occupation.

To that end, it contains provisions to implement the principle of equal treatment in relation to:

(a) access to employment, including promotion, and to vocational training;
(b) working conditions, including pay;
(c) occupational social security schemes.

It also contains provisions to ensure that such implementation is made more effective by the establishment of appropriate procedures.

[3.473]
Article 2
Definitions

1. For the purposes of this Directive, the following definitions shall apply:

(a) 'direct discrimination': where one person is treated less favourably on grounds of sex than another is, has been or would be treated in a comparable situation;
(b) 'indirect discrimination': where an apparently neutral provision, criterion or practice would put persons of one sex at a particular disadvantage compared with persons of the other sex, unless that provision, criterion or practice is objectively justified by a legitimate aim, and the means of achieving that aim are appropriate and necessary;
(c) 'harassment': where unwanted conduct related to the sex of a person occurs with the purpose or effect of violating the dignity of a person, and of creating an intimidating, hostile, degrading, humiliating or offensive environment;
(d) 'sexual harassment': where any form of unwanted verbal, non-verbal or physical conduct of a sexual nature occurs, with the purpose or effect of violating the dignity of a person, in particular when creating an intimidating, hostile, degrading, humiliating or offensive environment;

(e) 'pay': the ordinary basic or minimum wage or salary and any other consideration, whether in cash or in kind, which the worker receives directly or indirectly, in respect of his/her employment from his/her employer;

(f) 'occupational social security schemes': schemes not governed by Council Directive 79/7/EEC of 19 December 1978 on the progressive implementation of the principle of equal treatment for men and women in matters of social security[1] whose purpose is to provide workers, whether employees or self-employed, in an undertaking or group of undertakings, area of economic activity, occupational sector or group of sectors with benefits intended to supplement the benefits provided by statutory social security schemes or to replace them, whether membership of such schemes is compulsory or optional.

2. For the purposes of this Directive, discrimination includes:

(a) harassment and sexual harassment, as well as any less favourable treatment based on a person's rejection of or submission to such conduct;

(b) instruction to discriminate against persons on grounds of sex;

(c) any less favourable treatment of a woman related to pregnancy or maternity leave within the meaning of Directive 92/85/EEC.

NOTES

1 OJ L6, 10.1.1979, p 24.

[3.474]
Article 3
Positive action

Member States may maintain or adopt measures within the meaning of Article 141(4) of the Treaty with a view to ensuring full equality in practice between men and women in working life.

TITLE II
SPECIFIC PROVISIONS

CHAPTER 1
EQUAL PAY

[3.475]
Article 4
Prohibition of discrimination

For the same work or for work to which equal value is attributed, direct and indirect discrimination on grounds of sex with regard to all aspects and conditions of remuneration shall be eliminated.

In particular, where a job classification system is used for determining pay, it shall be based on the same criteria for both men and women and so drawn up as to exclude any discrimination on grounds of sex.

CHAPTER 2
EQUAL TREATMENT IN OCCUPATIONAL SOCIAL SECURITY SCHEMES

[3.476]
Article 5
Prohibition of discrimination

Without prejudice to Article 4, there shall be no direct or indirect discrimination on grounds of sex in occupational social security schemes, in particular as regards:

(a) the scope of such schemes and the conditions of access to them;

(b) the obligation to contribute and the calculation of contributions;

(c) the calculation of benefits, including supplementary benefits due in respect of a spouse or dependants, and the conditions governing the duration and retention of entitlement to benefits.

[3.477]
Article 6
Personal scope

This Chapter shall apply to members of the working population, including self-employed persons, persons whose activity is interrupted by illness, maternity, accident or involuntary unemployment and persons seeking employment and to retired and disabled workers, and to those claiming under them, in accordance with national law and/or practice.

[3.478]
Article 7
Material scope

1. This Chapter applies to:

(a) occupational social security schemes which provide protection against the following risks:

- (i) sickness,
- (ii) invalidity,
- (iii) old age, including early retirement,
- (iv) industrial accidents and occupational diseases,
- (v) unemployment;

(b) occupational social security schemes which provide for other social benefits, in cash or in kind, and in particular survivors' benefits and family allowances, if such benefits constitute a consideration paid by the employer to the worker by reason of the latter's employment.

2. This Chapter also applies to pension schemes for a particular category of worker such as that of public servants if the benefits payable under the scheme are paid by reason of the employment relationship with the public employer. The fact that such a scheme forms part of a general statutory scheme shall be without prejudice in that respect.

[3.479]
Article 8
Exclusions from the material scope

1. This Chapter does not apply to:

(a) individual contracts for self-employed persons;
(b) single-member schemes for self-employed persons;
(c) insurance contracts to which the employer is not a party, in the case of workers;
(d) optional provisions of occupational social security schemes offered to participants individually to guarantee them:
- (i) either additional benefits,
- (ii) or a choice of date on which the normal benefits for self-employed persons will start, or a choice between several benefits;

(e) occupational social security schemes in so far as benefits are financed by contributions paid by workers on a voluntary basis.

2. This Chapter does not preclude an employer granting to persons who have already reached the retirement age for the purposes of granting a pension by virtue of an occupational social security scheme, but who have not yet reached the retirement age for the purposes of granting a statutory retirement pension, a pension supplement, the aim of which is to make equal or more nearly equal the overall amount of benefit paid to these persons in relation to the amount paid to persons of the other sex in the same situation who have already reached the statutory retirement age, until the persons benefiting from the supplement reach the statutory retirement age.

[3.480]
Article 9
Examples of discrimination

1. Provisions contrary to the principle of equal treatment shall include those based on sex, either directly or indirectly, for:

(a) determining the persons who may participate in an occupational social security scheme;
(b) fixing the compulsory or optional nature of participation in an occupational social security scheme;
(c) laying down different rules as regards the age of entry into the scheme or the minimum period of employment or membership of the scheme required to obtain the benefits thereof;
(d) laying down different rules, except as provided for in points (h) and (j), for the reimbursement of contributions when a worker leaves a scheme without having fulfilled the conditions guaranteeing a deferred right to long-term benefits;
(e) setting different conditions for the granting of benefits or restricting such benefits to workers of one or other of the sexes;
(f) fixing different retirement ages;
(g) suspending the retention or acquisition of rights during periods of maternity leave or leave for family reasons which are granted by law or agreement and are paid by the employer;
(h) setting different levels of benefit, except in so far as may be necessary to take account of actuarial calculation factors which differ according to sex in the case of defined-contribution schemes; in the case of funded defined-benefit schemes, certain elements may be unequal where the inequality of the amounts results from the effects of the use of actuarial factors differing according to sex at the time when the scheme's funding is implemented;
(i) setting different levels for workers' contributions;
(j) setting different levels for employers' contributions, except:
- (i) in the case of defined-contribution schemes if the aim is to equalise the amount of the final benefits or to make them more nearly equal for both sexes,
- (ii) in the case of funded defined-benefit schemes where the employer's contributions are intended to ensure the adequacy of the funds necessary to cover the cost of the benefits defined;

(k) laying down different standards or standards applicable only to workers of a specified sex, except as provided for in points (h) and (j), as regards the guarantee or retention of entitlement to deferred benefits when a worker leaves a scheme.

2. Where the granting of benefits within the scope of this Chapter is left to the discretion of the scheme's management bodies, the latter shall comply with the principle of equal treatment.

[3.481]
Article 10
Implementation as regards self-employed persons

1. Member States shall take the necessary steps to ensure that the provisions of occupational social security schemes for self-employed persons contrary to the principle of equal treatment are revised with effect from 1 January 1993 at the latest or for Member States whose accession took place after that date, at the date that Directive 86/378/EEC became applicable in their territory.

2. This Chapter shall not preclude rights and obligations relating to a period of membership of an occupational social security scheme for self-employed persons prior to revision of that scheme from remaining subject to the provisions of the scheme in force during that period.

[3.482]
Article 11
Possibility of deferral as regards self-employed persons

As regards occupational social security schemes for self-employed persons, Member States may defer compulsory application of the principle of equal treatment with regard to:

(a) determination of pensionable age for the granting of old-age or retirement pensions, and the possible implications for other benefits:
  (i) either until the date on which such equality is achieved in statutory schemes,
  (ii) or, at the latest, until such equality is prescribed by a directive;

(b) survivors' pensions until Community law establishes the principle of equal treatment in statutory social security schemes in that regard;

(c) the application of Article 9(1)(i) in relation to the use of actuarial calculation factors, until 1 January 1999 or for Member States whose accession took place after that date until the date that Directive 86/378/EEC became applicable in their territory.

[3.483]
Article 12
Retroactive effect

1. Any measure implementing this Chapter, as regards workers, shall cover all benefits under occupational social security schemes derived from periods of employment subsequent to 17 May 1990 and shall apply retroactively to that date, without prejudice to workers or those claiming under them who have, before that date, initiated legal proceedings or raised an equivalent claim under national law. In that event, the implementation measures shall apply retroactively to 8 April 1976 and shall cover all the benefits derived from periods of employment after that date. For Member States which acceded to the Community after 8 April 1976, and before 17 May 1990, that date shall be replaced by the date on which Article 141 of the Treaty became applicable in their territory.

2. The second sentence of paragraph 1 shall not prevent national rules relating to time limits for bringing actions under national law from being relied on against workers or those claiming under them who initiated legal proceedings or raised an equivalent claim under national law before 17 May 1990, provided that they are not less favourable for that type of action than for similar actions of a domestic nature and that they do not render the exercise of rights conferred by Community law impossible in practice.

3. For Member States whose accession took place after 17 May 1990 and which were on 1 January 1994 Contracting Parties to the Agreement on the European Economic Area, the date of 17 May 1990 in the first sentence of paragraph 1 shall be replaced by 1 January 1994.

4. For other Member States whose accession took place after 17 May 1990, the date of 17 May 1990 in paragraphs 1 and 2 shall be replaced by the date on which Article 141 of the Treaty became applicable in their territory.

[3.484]
Article 13
Flexible pensionable age

Where men and women may claim a flexible pensionable age under the same conditions, this shall not be deemed to be incompatible with this Chapter.

CHAPTER 3
EQUAL TREATMENT AS REGARDS ACCESS TO EMPLOYMENT, VOCATIONAL TRAINING AND PROMOTION AND WORKING CONDITIONS

[3.485]
Article 14
Prohibition of discrimination

1. There shall be no direct or indirect discrimination on grounds of sex in the public or private sectors, including public bodies, in relation to:
   (a) conditions for access to employment, to self-employment or to occupation, including selection criteria and recruitment conditions, whatever the branch of activity and at all levels of the professional hierarchy, including promotion;
   (b) access to all types and to all levels of vocational guidance, vocational training, advanced vocational training and retraining, including practical work experience;
   (c) employment and working conditions, including dismissals, as well as pay as provided for in Article 141 of the Treaty;
   (d) membership of, and involvement in, an organisation of workers or employers, or any organisation whose members carry on a particular profession, including the benefits provided for by such organisations.
2. Member States may provide, as regards access to employment including the training leading thereto, that a difference of treatment which is based on a characteristic related to sex shall not constitute discrimination where, by reason of the nature of the particular occupational activities concerned or of the context in which they are carried out, such a characteristic constitutes a genuine and determining occupational requirement, provided that its objective is legitimate and the requirement is proportionate.

[3.486]
Article 15
Return from maternity leave

A woman on maternity leave shall be entitled, after the end of her period of maternity leave, to return to her job or to an equivalent post on terms and conditions which are no less favourable to her and to benefit from any improvement in working conditions to which she would have been entitled during her absence.

[3.487]
Article 16
Paternity and adoption leave

This Directive is without prejudice to the right of Member States to recognise distinct rights to paternity and/or adoption leave. Those Member States which recognise such rights shall take the necessary measures to protect working men and women against dismissal due to exercising those rights and ensure that, at the end of such leave, they are entitled to return to their jobs or to equivalent posts on terms and conditions which are no less favourable to them, and to benefit from any improvement in working conditions to which they would have been entitled during their absence.

TITLE III
HORIZONTAL PROVISIONS

CHAPTER 1
REMEDIES AND ENFORCEMENT

SECTION 1
REMEDIES

[3.488]
Article 17
Defence of rights

1. Member States shall ensure that, after possible recourse to other competent authorities including where they deem it appropriate conciliation procedures, judicial procedures for the enforcement of obligations under this Directive are available to all persons who consider themselves wronged by failure to apply the principle of equal treatment to them, even after the relationship in which the discrimination is alleged to have occurred has ended.
2. Member States shall ensure that associations, organisations or other legal entities which have, in accordance with the criteria laid down by their national law, a legitimate interest in ensuring that the provisions of this Directive are complied with, may engage, either on behalf or in support of the complainant, with his/her approval, in any judicial and/or administrative procedure provided for the enforcement of obligations under this Directive.

3. Paragraphs 1 and 2 are without prejudice to national rules relating to time limits for bringing actions as regards the principle of equal treatment.

[3.489]
Article 18
Compensation or reparation

Member States shall introduce into their national legal systems such measures as are necessary to ensure real and effective compensation or reparation as the Member States so determine for the loss and damage sustained by a person injured as a result of discrimination on grounds of sex, in a way which is dissuasive and proportionate to the damage suffered. Such compensation or reparation may not be restricted by the fixing of a prior upper limit, except in cases where the employer can prove that the only damage suffered by an applicant as a result of discrimination within the meaning of this Directive is the refusal to take his/her job application into consideration.

SECTION 2
BURDEN OF PROOF

[3.490]
Article 19
Burden of proof

1. Member States shall take such measures as are necessary, in accordance with their national judicial systems, to ensure that, when persons who consider themselves wronged because the principle of equal treatment has not been applied to them establish, before a court or other competent authority, facts from which it may be presumed that there has been direct or indirect discrimination, it shall be for the respondent to prove that there has been no breach of the principle of equal treatment.
2. Paragraph 1 shall not prevent Member States from introducing rules of evidence which are more favourable to plaintiffs.
3. Member States need not apply paragraph 1 to proceedings in which it is for the court or competent body to investigate the facts of the case.
4. Paragraphs 1, 2 and 3 shall also apply to:
   (a) the situations covered by Article 141 of the Treaty and, insofar as discrimination based on sex is concerned, by Directives 92/85/EEC and 96/34/EC;
   (b) any civil or administrative procedure concerning the public or private sector which provides for means of redress under national law pursuant to the measures referred to in (a) with the exception of out-of-court procedures of a voluntary nature or provided for in national law.
5. This Article shall not apply to criminal procedures, unless otherwise provided by the Member States.

CHAPTER 2
PROMOTION OF EQUAL TREATMENT—DIALOGUE

[3.491]
Article 20
Equality bodies

1. Member States shall designate and make the necessary arrangements for a body or bodies for the promotion, analysis, monitoring and support of equal treatment of all persons without discrimination on grounds of sex. These bodies may form part of agencies with responsibility at national level for the defence of human rights or the safeguard of individuals' rights.
2. Member States shall ensure that the competences of these bodies include:
   (a) without prejudice to the right of victims and of associations, organisations or other legal entities referred to in Article 17(2), providing independent assistance to victims of discrimination in pursuing their complaints about discrimination;
   (b) conducting independent surveys concerning discrimination;
   (c) publishing independent reports and making recommendations on any issue relating to such discrimination;
   (d) at the appropriate level exchanging available information with corresponding European bodies such as any future European Institute for Gender Equality.

[3.492]
Article 21
Social dialogue

1. Member States shall, in accordance with national traditions and practice, take adequate measures to promote social dialogue between the social partners with a view to fostering equal treatment, including, for example, through the monitoring of practices in the workplace, in access to employment, vocational training and promotion, as well as through the monitoring of collective agreements, codes of conduct, research or exchange of experience and good practice.

2. Where consistent with national traditions and practice, Member States shall encourage the social partners, without prejudice to their autonomy, to promote equality between men and women, and flexible working arrangements, with the aim of facilitating the reconciliation of work and private life, and to conclude, at the appropriate level, agreements laying down anti-discrimination rules in the fields referred to in Article 1 which fall within the scope of collective bargaining. These agreements shall respect the provisions of this Directive and the relevant national implementing measures.
3. Member States shall, in accordance with national law, collective agreements or practice, encourage employers to promote equal treatment for men and women in a planned and systematic way in the workplace, in access to employment, vocational training and promotion.
4. To this end, employers shall be encouraged to provide at appropriate regular intervals employees and/or their representatives with appropriate information on equal treatment for men and women in the undertaking.

Such information may include an overview of the proportions of men and women at different levels of the organisation; their pay and pay differentials; and possible measures to improve the situation in cooperation with employees' representatives.

[3.493]
Article 22
Dialogue with non-governmental organisations
Member States shall encourage dialogue with appropriate non-governmental organisations which have, in accordance with their national law and practice, a legitimate interest in contributing to the fight against discrimination on grounds of sex with a view to promoting the principle of equal treatment.

CHAPTER 3
GENERAL HORIZONTAL PROVISIONS

[3.494]
Article 23
Compliance
Member States shall take all necessary measures to ensure that:

(a) any laws, regulations and administrative provisions contrary to the principle of equal treatment are abolished;
(b) provisions contrary to the principle of equal treatment in individual or collective contracts or agreements, internal rules of undertakings or rules governing the independent occupations and professions and workers' and employers' organisations or any other arrangements shall be, or may be, declared null and void or are amended;
(c) occupational social security schemes containing such provisions may not be approved or extended by administrative measures.

[3.495]
Article 24
Victimisation
Member States shall introduce into their national legal systems such measures as are necessary to protect employees, including those who are employees' representatives provided for by national laws and/or practices, against dismissal or other adverse treatment by the employer as a reaction to a complaint within the undertaking or to any legal proceedings aimed at enforcing compliance with the principle of equal treatment.

[3.496]
Article 25
Penalties
Member States shall lay down the rules on penalties applicable to infringements of the national provisions adopted pursuant to this Directive, and shall take all measures necessary to ensure that they are applied. The penalties, which may comprise the payment of compensation to the victim, must be effective, proportionate and dissuasive. The Member States shall notify those provisions to the Commission by 5 October 2005 at the latest and shall notify it without delay of any subsequent amendment affecting them.

[3.497]
Article 26
Prevention of discrimination
Member States shall encourage, in accordance with national law, collective agreements or practice, employers and those responsible for access to vocational training to take effective measures to prevent all forms of discrimination on grounds of sex, in particular harassment and sexual harassment in the workplace, in access to employment, vocational training and promotion.

[3.498]
Article 27
Minimum requirements

1. Member States may introduce or maintain provisions which are more favourable to the protection of the principle of equal treatment than those laid down in this Directive.
2. Implementation of this Directive shall under no circumstances be sufficient grounds for a reduction in the level of protection of workers in the areas to which it applies, without prejudice to the Member States' right to respond to changes in the situation by introducing laws, regulations and administrative provisions which differ from those in force on the notification of this Directive, provided that the provisions of this Directive are complied with.

[3.499]
Article 28
Relationship to Community and national provisions

1. This Directive shall be without prejudice to provisions concerning the protection of women, particularly as regards pregnancy and maternity.
2. This Directive shall be without prejudice to the provisions of Directive 96/34/EC and Directive 92/85/EEC.

[3.500]
Article 29
Gender mainstreaming

Member States shall actively take into account the objective of equality between men and women when formulating and implementing laws, regulations, administrative provisions, policies and activities in the areas referred to in this Directive.

[3.501]
Article 30
Dissemination of information

Member States shall ensure that measures taken pursuant to this Directive, together with the provisions already in force, are brought to the attention of all the persons concerned by all suitable means and, where appropriate, at the workplace.

TITLE IV
FINAL PROVISIONS

[3.502]
Article 31
Reports

1. By 15 February 2011, the Member States shall communicate to the Commission all the information necessary for the Commission to draw up a report to the European Parliament and the Council on the application of this Directive.
2. Without prejudice to paragraph 1, Member States shall communicate to the Commission, every four years, the texts of any measures adopted pursuant to Article 141(4) of the Treaty, as well as reports on these measures and their implementation. On the basis of that information, the Commission will adopt and publish every four years a report establishing a comparative assessment of any measures in the light of Declaration No 28 annexed to the Final Act of the Treaty of Amsterdam.
3. Member States shall assess the occupational activities referred to in Article 14(2), in order to decide, in the light of social developments, whether there is justification for maintaining the exclusions concerned. They shall notify the Commission of the results of this assessment periodically, but at least every 8 years.

[3.503]
Article 32
Review

By 15 February 2011 at the latest, the Commission shall review the operation of this Directive and if appropriate, propose any amendments it deems necessary.

[3.504]
Article 33
Implementation

Member States shall bring into force the laws, regulations and administrative provisions necessary to comply with this Directive by 15 August 2008 at the latest or shall ensure, by that date, that management and labour introduce the requisite provisions by way of agreement. Member States may, if necessary to take account of particular difficulties, have up to one additional year to comply with this Directive. Member States shall take all necessary steps to be able to guarantee the results imposed by this Directive. They shall forthwith communicate to the Commission the texts of those measures.

When Member States adopt these measures, they shall contain a reference to this Directive or be accompanied by such reference on the occasion of their official publication. They shall also include a statement that references in existing laws, regulations and administrative provisions to the Directives repealed by this Directive shall be construed as references to this Directive. Member States shall determine how such reference is to be made and how that statement is to be formulated.

The obligation to transpose this Directive into national law shall be confined to those provisions which represent a substantive change as compared with the earlier Directives. The obligation to transpose the provisions which are substantially unchanged arises under the earlier Directives.

Member States shall communicate to the Commission the text of the main provisions of national law which they adopt in the field covered by this Directive.

[3.505]
Article 34
Repeal

1. With effect from 15 August 2009 Directives 75/117/EEC, 76/207/EEC, 86/378/EEC and 97/80/EC shall be repealed without prejudice to the obligations of the Member States relating to the time-limits for transposition into national law and application of the Directives set out in Annex I, Part B.
2. References made to the repealed Directives shall be construed as being made to this Directive and should be read in accordance with the correlation table in Annex II.

[3.506]
Article 35
Entry into force

This Directive shall enter into force on the 20th day following its publication in the *Official Journal of the European Union.*

[3.507]
Article 36
Addressees

This Directive is addressed to the Member States.

ANNEX I

PART A
REPEALED DIRECTIVES WITH THEIR SUCCESSIVE AMENDMENTS

[3.508]

Council Directive 75/117/EEC	OJ L45, 19.2.1975, p 19
Council Directive 76/207/EEC	OJ L39, 14.2.1976, p 40
Directive 2002/73/EC of the European Parliament and of the Council	OJ L269, 5.10.2002, p 15
Council Directive 86/378/EEC	OJ L225, 12.8.1986, p 40
Council Directive 96/97/EC	OJ L46, 17.2.1997, p 20
Council Directive 97/80/EC	OJ L14, 20.1.1998, p 6
Council Directive 98/52/EC	OJ L205, 22.7.1998, p 66

PART B
LIST OF TIME LIMITS FOR TRANSPOSITION INTO NATIONAL LAW AND APPLICATION DATES

(referred to in Article 34(1))

[3.509]

Directive	Time-limit for transposition	Date of application
Directive 75/117/EEC	19.2.1976	
Directive 76/207/EEC	14.8.1978	
Directive 86/378/EEC	1.1.1993	
Directive 96/97/EC	1.7.1997	17.5.1990 in relation to workers, except for those workers or those claiming under them who had before that date initiated legal proceedings or raised an equivalent claim under national law.

Directive	**Time-limit for transposition**	**Date of application**
		Article 8 of Directive 86/378/EEC – 1.1.1993 at the latest. Article 6(1)(i), first indent of Directive 86/378/EEC – 1.1.1999 at the latest.
Directive 97/80/EC	1.1.2001	As regards the United Kingdom of Great Britain and Northern Ireland 22.7.2001
Directive 98/52/EC	22.7.2001	
Directive 2002/73/EC	5.10.2005	

ANNEX II
CORRELATION TABLE

[3.510]

Directive 75/117/EEC	**Directive 76/207/EEC**	**Directive 86/378/EEC**	**Directive 97/80/EC**	**This Directive**
—	Article 1(1)	Article 1	Article 1	Article 1
—	Article 1(2)	—	—	—
—	Article 2(2), first indent	—	—	Article 2(1)(a)
—	Article 2(2), second indent	—	Article 2(2)	Article 2(1)(b)
—	Article 2(2), third and fourth indents	—	—	Article 2(1)(c) and (d)
—	—	—	—	Article 2(1)(e)
—	—	Article 2(1)	—	Article 2(1)(f)
—	Article 2(3) and (4) and Article 2(7) third subparagraph	—	—	Article 2(2)
—	Article 2(8)	—	—	Article 3
Article 1	—	—	—	Article 4
—	—	Article 5(1)	—	Article 5
—	—	Article 3	—	Article 6
—	—	Article 4	—	Article 7(1)
—	—	—	—	Article 7(2)
		Article 2(2)		Article 8(1)
—	—	Article 2(3)	—	Article 8(2)
—	—	Article 6	—	Article 9
—	—	Article 8	—	Article 10
—	—	Article 9	—	Article 11
—	—	(Article 2 of Directive 96/97/EC)	—	Article 12
—	—	Article 9a	—	Article 13
—	Articles 2(1) and 3(1)	—	Article 2(1)	Article 14(1)
—	Article 2(6)	—	—	Article 14(2)
—	Article 2(7), second subparagraph	—	—	Article 15
—	Article 2(7), fourth subparagraph, second and third sentence	—	—	Article 16
Article 2	Article 6(1)	Article 10	—	Article 17(1)
—	Article 6(3)	—	—	Article 17(2)

Directive 75/117/EEC	Directive 76/207/EEC	Directive 86/378/EEC	Directive 97/80/EC	This Directive
—	Article 6(4)	—	—	Article 17(3)
—	Article 6(2)	—	—	Article 18
—	—	—	Articles 3 and 4	Article 19
—	Article 8a	—	—	Article 20
—	Article 8b	—	—	Article 21
—	Article 8c	—	—	Article 22
Articles 3 and 6	Article 3(2)(a)	—	—	Article 23(a)
Article 4	Article 3(2)(b)	Article 7(a)	—	Article 23(b)
—	—	Article 7(b)	—	Article 23(c)
Article 5	Article 7	Article 11	—	Article 24
Article 6	—	—	—	—
—	Article 8d	—	—	Article 25
	Article 2(5)			Article 26
—	Article 8e(1)	—	Article 4(2)	Article 27(1)
—	Article 8e(2)	—	Article 6	Article 27(2)
—	Article 2(7) first subparagraph	Article 5(2)	—	Article 28(1)
—	Article 2(7) fourth subparagraph first sentence			Article 28(2)
—	Article 1(1a)			Article 29
Article 7	Article 8	—	Article 5	Article 30
Article 9	Article 10	Article 12(2)	Article 7, fourth subparagraph	Article 31(1) and (2)
—	Article 9(2)	—	—	Article 31(3)
—	—	—	—	Article 32
Article 8	Article 9(1), first subparagraph and 9(2) and (3)	Article 2(1)	Article 7, first, second and third subparagraphs	Article 33
—	Article 9(1), second subparagraph	—	—	—
—	—	—	—	Article 34
—	—	—	—	Article 35
—	—	—	—	Article 36
—	—	Annex	—	—

REGULATION OF THE EUROPEAN PARLIAMENT AND OF THE COUNCIL

(864/2007/EC)

of 11 July 2007

on the law applicable to non-contractual obligations (Rome II)

NOTES

Date of publication in OJ: OJ L199, 31.07.2007, p 40.

The provisions of the Regulation reproduced here came into force on 11 January 2009 (see Art 32 at **[3.537]**) but apply only in relation to events giving rise to damage which occur after the entry into force of the Regulation (see Art 31 at **[3.536]**).

This Regulation is included for the provisions it makes for determining the applicable law in disputes relating to employment issues, including in particular industrial action. Only those parts of the Regulation within the scope of this work are reproduced here.

See *Harvey* H(3).

[3.511]

THE EUROPEAN PARLIAMENT AND THE COUNCIL OF THE EUROPEAN UNION,

Having regard to the Treaty establishing the European Community, and in particular Articles 61(c) and 67 thereof,

Having regard to the proposal from the Commission,

Having regard to the opinion of the European Economic and Social Committee,[1]

Acting in accordance with the procedure laid down in Article 251 of the Treaty in the light of the joint text approved by the Conciliation Committee on 25 June 2007,[2]

Whereas:

(1) The Community has set itself the objective of maintaining and developing an area of freedom, security and justice. For the progressive establishment of such an area, the Community is to adopt measures relating to judicial cooperation in civil matters with a cross-border impact to the extent necessary for the proper functioning of the internal market.

(2) According to Article 65(b) of the Treaty, these measures are to include those promoting the compatibility of the rules applicable in the Member States concerning the conflict of laws and of jurisdiction.

(3) The European Council meeting in Tampere on 15 and 16 October 1999 endorsed the principle of mutual recognition of judgments and other decisions of judicial authorities as the cornerstone of judicial cooperation in civil matters and invited the Council and the Commission to adopt a programme of measures to implement the principle of mutual recognition.

(4) On 30 November 2000, the Council adopted a joint Commission and Council programme of measures for implementation of the principle of mutual recognition of decisions in civil and commercial matters.[3] The programme identifies measures relating to the harmonisation of conflict-of-law rules as those facilitating the mutual recognition of judgments.

(5) The Hague Programme,[4] adopted by the European Council on 5 November 2004, called for work to be pursued actively on the rules of conflict of laws regarding non-contractual obligations (Rome II).

(6) The proper functioning of the internal market creates a need, in order to improve the predictability of the outcome of litigation, certainty as to the law applicable and the free movement of judgments, for the conflict-of-law rules in the Member States to designate the same national law irrespective of the country of the court in which an action is brought.

(7) The substantive scope and the provisions of this Regulation should be consistent with Council Regulation (EC) No 44/2001 of 22 December 2000 on jurisdiction and the recognition and enforcement of judgments in civil and commercial matters[5] (Brussels I) and the instruments dealing with the law applicable to contractual obligations.

(8) This Regulation should apply irrespective of the nature of the court or tribunal seised.

(9) Claims arising out of *acta iure imperii* should include claims against officials who act on behalf of the State and liability for acts of public authorities, including liability of publicly appointed office-holders. Therefore, these matters should be excluded from the scope of this Regulation.

(10) Family relationships should cover parentage, marriage, affinity and collateral relatives. The reference in Article 1(2) to relationships having comparable effects to marriage and other family relationships should be interpreted in accordance with the law of the Member State in which the court is seised.

(11) The concept of a non-contractual obligation varies from one Member State to another. Therefore for the purposes of this Regulation non-contractual obligation should be understood as an autonomous concept. The conflict-of-law rules set out in this Regulation should also cover non-contractual obligations arising out of strict liability.

(12) The law applicable should also govern the question of the capacity to incur liability in tort/delict.

(13) Uniform rules applied irrespective of the law they designate may avert the risk of distortions of competition between Community litigants.

(14) The requirement of legal certainty and the need to do justice in individual cases are essential elements of an area of justice. This Regulation provides for the connecting factors which are the most appropriate to achieve these objectives. Therefore, this Regulation provides for a general rule but also for specific rules and, in certain provisions, for an "escape clause" which allows a departure from these rules where it is clear from all the circumstances of the case that the tort/delict is manifestly more closely connected with another country. This set of rules thus creates a flexible framework of conflict-of-law rules. Equally, it enables the court seised to treat individual cases in an appropriate manner.

(15) The principle of the *lex loci delicti commissi* is the basic solution for non-contractual obligations in virtually all the Member States, but the practical application of the principle where the

component factors of the case are spread over several countries varies. This situation engenders uncertainty as to the law applicable.

(16) Uniform rules should enhance the foreseeability of court decisions and ensure a reasonable balance between the interests of the person claimed to be liable and the person who has sustained damage. A connection with the country where the direct damage occurred (lex loci damni) strikes a fair balance between the interests of the person claimed to be liable and the person sustaining the damage, and also reflects the modern approach to civil liability and the development of systems of strict liability.

(17) The law applicable should be determined on the basis of where the damage occurs, regardless of the country or countries in which the indirect consequences could occur. Accordingly, in cases of personal injury or damage to property, the country in which the damage occurs should be the country where the injury was sustained or the property was damaged respectively.

(18) The general rule in this Regulation should be the *lex loci damni* provided for in Article 4(1). Article 4(2) should be seen as an exception to this general principle, creating a special connection where the parties have their habitual residence in the same country. Article 4(3) should be understood as an 'escape clause' from Article 4(1) and (2), where it is clear from all the circumstances of the case that the tort/delict is manifestly more closely connected with another country.

(19) Specific rules should be laid down for special torts/delicts where the general rule does not allow a reasonable balance to be struck between the interests at stake.

(20)–(25) (*Outside the scope of this work.*)

(26) Regarding infringements of intellectual property rights, the universally acknowledged principle of the *lex loci protectionis* should be preserved. For the purposes of this Regulation, the term 'intellectual property rights' should be interpreted as meaning, for instance, copyright, related rights, the *sui generis* right for the protection of databases and industrial property rights.

(27) The exact concept of industrial action, such as strike action or lock-out, varies from one Member State to another and is governed by each Member State's internal rules. Therefore, this Regulation assumes as a general principle that the law of the country where the industrial action was taken should apply, with the aim of protecting the rights and obligations of workers and employers.

(28) The special rule on industrial action in Article 9 is without prejudice to the conditions relating to the exercise of such action in accordance with national law and without prejudice to the legal status of trade unions or of the representative organisations of workers as provided for in the law of the Member States.

(29) Provision should be made for special rules where damage is caused by an act other than a tort/delict, such as unjust enrichment, *negotiorum gestio* and *culpa in contrahendo.*

(30) *Culpa in contrahendo* for the purposes of this Regulation is an autonomous concept and should not necessarily be interpreted within the meaning of national law. It should include the violation of the duty of disclosure and the breakdown of contractual negotiations. Article 12 covers only non-contractual obligations presenting a direct link with the dealings prior to the conclusion of a contract. This means that if, while a contract is being negotiated, a person suffers personal injury, Article 4 or other relevant provisions of this Regulation should apply.

(31) To respect the principle of party autonomy and to enhance legal certainty, the parties should be allowed to make a choice as to the law applicable to a non-contractual obligation. This choice should be expressed or demonstrated with reasonable certainty by the circumstances of the case. Where establishing the existence of the agreement, the court has to respect the intentions of the parties. Protection should be given to weaker parties by imposing certain conditions on the choice.

(32) Considerations of public interest justify giving the courts of the Member States the possibility, in exceptional circumstances, of applying exceptions based on public policy and overriding mandatory provisions. In particular, the application of a provision of the law designated by this Regulation which would have the effect of causing non-compensatory exemplary or punitive damages of an excessive nature to be awarded may, depending on the circumstances of the case and the legal order of the Member State of the court seised, be regarded as being contrary to the public policy (*ordre public*) of the forum.

(33)–(35) (*Outside the scope of this work.*)

(36) Respect for international commitments entered into by the Member States means that this Regulation should not affect international conventions to which one or more Member States are parties at the time this Regulation is adopted. To make the rules more accessible, the Commission should publish the list of the relevant conventions in the *Official Journal of the European Union* on the basis of information supplied by the Member States.

(37) The Commission will make a proposal to the European Parliament and the Council concerning the procedures and conditions according to which Member States would be entitled to negotiate and conclude on their own behalf agreements with third countries in individual and

exceptional cases, concerning sectoral matters, containing provisions on the law applicable to non-contractual obligations.

(38) Since the objective of this Regulation cannot be sufficiently achieved by the Member States, and can therefore, by reason of the scale and effects of this Regulation, be better achieved at Community level, the Community may adopt measures, in accordance with the principle of subsidiarity set out in Article 5 of the Treaty. In accordance with the principle of proportionality set out in that Article, this Regulation does not go beyond what is necessary to attain that objective.

(39) In accordance with Article 3 of the Protocol on the position of the United Kingdom and Ireland annexed to the Treaty on European Union and to the Treaty establishing the European Community, the United Kingdom and Ireland are taking part in the adoption and application of this Regulation.

(40) In accordance with Articles 1 and 2 of the Protocol on the position of Denmark, annexed to the Treaty on European Union and to the Treaty establishing the European Community, Denmark does not take part in the adoption of this Regulation, and is not bound by it or subject to its application,

NOTES

1 OJ C241, 28.9.2004, p 1.

2 Opinion of the European Parliament of 6 July 2005 (OJ C157 E, 6.7.2006, p 371), Council Common Position of 25 September 2006 (OJ C289 E, 28.11.2006, p 68) and Position of the European Parliament of 18 January 2007 (not yet published in the Official Journal). European Parliament Legislative Resolution of 10 July 2007 and Council Decision of 28 June 2007.

3 OJ C12, 15.1.2001, p 1.

4 OJ C53, 3.3.2005, p 1.

5 OJ L12, 16.1.2001, p 1. Regulation as last amended by Regulation (EC) No 1791/2006 (OJ L363, 20.12.2006, p 1).

HAVE ADOPTED THIS REGULATION:

CHAPTER I
SCOPE

[3.512]
Article 1
Scope

1. This Regulation shall apply, in situations involving a conflict of laws, to non-contractual obligations in civil and commercial matters. It shall not apply, in particular, to revenue, customs or administrative matters or to the liability of the State for acts and omissions in the exercise of State authority (*acta iure imperii*).

2. The following shall be excluded from the scope of this Regulation:
   (a) non-contractual obligations arising out of family relationships and relationships deemed by the law applicable to such relationships to have comparable effects including maintenance obligations;
   (b) non-contractual obligations arising out of matrimonial property regimes, property regimes of relationships deemed by the law applicable to such relationships to have comparable effects to marriage, and wills and succession;
   (c) non-contractual obligations arising under bills of exchange, cheques and promissory notes and other negotiable instruments to the extent that the obligations under such other negotiable instruments arise out of their negotiable character;
   (d) non-contractual obligations arising out of the law of companies and other bodies corporate or unincorporated regarding matters such as the creation, by registration or otherwise, legal capacity, internal organisation or winding-up of companies and other bodies corporate or unincorporated, the personal liability of officers and members as such for the obligations of the company or body and the personal liability of auditors to a company or to its members in the statutory audits of accounting documents;
   (e) non-contractual obligations arising out of the relations between the settlors, trustees and beneficiaries of a trust created voluntarily;
   (f) non-contractual obligations arising out of nuclear damage;
   (g) non-contractual obligations arising out of violations of privacy and rights relating to personality, including defamation.

3. This Regulation shall not apply to evidence and procedure, without prejudice to Articles 21 and 22.

4. For the purposes of this Regulation, "Member State" shall mean any Member State other than Denmark.

[3.513]
Article 2
Non-contractual obligations

1. For the purposes of this Regulation, damage shall cover any consequence arising out of tort/delict, unjust enrichment, *negotiorum gestio* or *culpa in contrahendo*.
2. This Regulation shall apply also to non-contractual obligations that are likely to arise.
3. Any reference in this Regulation to:
   (a) an event giving rise to damage shall include events giving rise to damage that are likely to occur; and
   (b) damage shall include damage that is likely to occur.

[3.514]
Article 3
Universal application

Any law specified by this Regulation shall be applied whether or not it is the law of a Member State.

CHAPTER II
TORTS/DELICTS

[3.515]
Article 4
General rule

1. Unless otherwise provided for in this Regulation, the law applicable to a non-contractual obligation arising out of a tort/delict shall be the law of the country in which the damage occurs irrespective of the country in which the event giving rise to the damage occurred and irrespective of the country or countries in which the indirect consequences of that event occur.
2. However, where the person claimed to be liable and the person sustaining damage both have their habitual residence in the same country at the time when the damage occurs, the law of that country shall apply.
3. Where it is clear from all the circumstances of the case that the tort/delict is manifestly more closely connected with a country other than that indicated in paragraphs 1 or 2, the law of that other country shall apply. A manifestly closer connection with another country might be based in particular on a pre-existing relationship between the parties, such as a contract, that is closely connected with the tort/delict in question.

Articles 5–7 (*Outside the scope of this work.*)

[3.516]
Article 8
Infringement of intellectual property rights

1. The law applicable to a non-contractual obligation arising from an infringement of an intellectual property right shall be the law of the country for which protection is claimed.
2. In the case of a non-contractual obligation arising from an infringement of a unitary Community intellectual property right, the law applicable shall, for any question that is not governed by the relevant Community instrument, be the law of the country in which the act of infringement was committed.
3. The law applicable under this Article may not be derogated from by an agreement pursuant to Article 14.

[3.517]
Article 9
Industrial action

Without prejudice to Article 4(2), the law applicable to a non-contractual obligation in respect of the liability of a person in the capacity of a worker or an employer or the organisations representing their professional interests for damages caused by an industrial action, pending or carried out, shall be the law of the country where the action is to be, or has been, taken.

CHAPTER III
UNJUST ENRICHMENT, *NEGOTIORUM GESTIO* AND *CULPA IN CONTRAHENDO*

[3.518]
Article 10
Unjust enrichment

1. If a non-contractual obligation arising out of unjust enrichment, including payment of amounts wrongly received, concerns a relationship existing between the parties, such as one arising out of a contract or a tort/delict, that is closely connected with that unjust enrichment, it shall be governed by the law that governs that relationship.

2. Where the law applicable cannot be determined on the basis of paragraph 1 and the parties have their habitual residence in the same country when the event giving rise to unjust enrichment occurs, the law of that country shall apply.
3. Where the law applicable cannot be determined on the basis of paragraphs 1 or 2, it shall be the law of the country in which the unjust enrichment took place.
4. Where it is clear from all the circumstances of the case that the non-contractual obligation arising out of unjust enrichment is manifestly more closely connected with a country other than that indicated in paragraphs 1, 2 and 3, the law of that other country shall apply.

[3.519]
Article 11
Negotiorum gestio
1. If a non-contractual obligation arising out of an act performed without due authority in connection with the affairs of another person concerns a relationship existing between the parties, such as one arising out of a contract or a tort/delict, that is closely connected with that non-contractual obligation, it shall be governed by the law that governs that relationship.
2. Where the law applicable cannot be determined on the basis of paragraph 1, and the parties have their habitual residence in the same country when the event giving rise to the damage occurs, the law of that country shall apply.
3. Where the law applicable cannot be determined on the basis of paragraphs 1 or 2, it shall be the law of the country in which the act was performed.
4. Where it is clear from all the circumstances of the case that the non-contractual obligation arising out of an act performed without due authority in connection with the affairs of another person is manifestly more closely connected with a country other than that indicated in paragraphs 1, 2 and 3, the law of that other country shall apply.

[3.520]
Article 12
Culpa in contrahendo
1. The law applicable to a non-contractual obligation arising out of dealings prior to the conclusion of a contract, regardless of whether the contract was actually concluded or not, shall be the law that applies to the contract or that would have been applicable to it had it been entered into.
2. Where the law applicable cannot be determined on the basis of paragraph 1, it shall be:
   (a) the law of the country in which the damage occurs, irrespective of the country in which the event giving rise to the damage occurred and irrespective of the country or countries in which the indirect consequences of that event occurred; or
   (b) where the parties have their habitual residence in the same country at the time when the event giving rise to the damage occurs, the law of that country; or
   (c) where it is clear from all the circumstances of the case that the non-contractual obligation arising out of dealings prior to the conclusion of a contract is manifestly more closely connected with a country other than that indicated in points (a) and (b), the law of that other country.

[3.521]
Article 13
Applicability of Article 8
For the purposes of this Chapter, Article 8 shall apply to non-contractual obligations arising from an infringement of an intellectual property right.

CHAPTER IV
FREEDOM OF CHOICE

[3.522]
Article 14
Freedom of choice
1. The parties may agree to submit non-contractual obligations to the law of their choice:
   (a) by an agreement entered into after the event giving rise to the damage occurred;
   or
   (b) where all the parties are pursuing a commercial activity, also by an agreement freely negotiated before the event giving rise to the damage occurred.

The choice shall be expressed or demonstrated with reasonable certainty by the circumstances of the case and shall not prejudice the rights of third parties.
2. Where all the elements relevant to the situation at the time when the event giving rise to the damage occurs are located in a country other than the country whose law has been chosen, the choice of the parties shall not prejudice the application of provisions of the law of that other country which cannot be derogated from by agreement.

3. Where all the elements relevant to the situation at the time when the event giving rise to the damage occurs are located in one or more of the Member States, the parties' choice of the law applicable other than that of a Member State shall not prejudice the application of provisions of Community law, where appropriate as implemented in the Member State of the forum, which cannot be derogated from by agreement.

CHAPTER V
COMMON RULES

[3.523]
Article 15
Scope of the law applicable

The law applicable to non-contractual obligations under this Regulation shall govern in particular:

(a) the basis and extent of liability, including the determination of persons who may be held liable for acts performed by them;
(b) the grounds for exemption from liability, any limitation of liability and any division of liability;
(c) the existence, the nature and the assessment of damage or the remedy claimed;
(d) within the limits of powers conferred on the court by its procedural law, the measures which a court may take to prevent or terminate injury or damage or to ensure the provision of compensation;
(e) the question whether a right to claim damages or a remedy may be transferred, including by inheritance;
(f) persons entitled to compensation for damage sustained personally;
(g) liability for the acts of another person;
(h) the manner in which an obligation may be extinguished and rules of prescription and limitation, including rules relating to the commencement, interruption and suspension of a period of prescription or limitation.

[3.524]
Article 16
Overriding mandatory provisions

Nothing in this Regulation shall restrict the application of the provisions of the law of the forum in a situation where they are mandatory irrespective of the law otherwise applicable to the non-contractual obligation.

[3.525]
Article 17
Rules of safety and conduct

In assessing the conduct of the person claimed to be liable, account shall be taken, as a matter of fact and in so far as is appropriate, of the rules of safety and conduct which were in force at the place and time of the event giving rise to the liability.

[3.526]
Article 18
Direct action against the insurer of the person liable

The person having suffered damage may bring his or her claim directly against the insurer of the person liable to provide compensation if the law applicable to the non-contractual obligation or the law applicable to the insurance contract so provides.

[3.527]
Article 19
Subrogation

Where a person (the creditor) has a non-contractual claim upon another (the debtor), and a third person has a duty to satisfy the creditor, or has in fact satisfied the creditor in discharge of that duty, the law which governs the third person's duty to satisfy the creditor shall determine whether, and the extent to which, the third person is entitled to exercise against the debtor the rights which the creditor had against the debtor under the law governing their relationship.

[3.528]
Article 20
Multiple liability

If a creditor has a claim against several debtors who are liable for the same claim, and one of the debtors has already satisfied the claim in whole or in part, the question of that debtor's right to demand compensation from the other debtors shall be governed by the law applicable to that debtor's non-contractual obligation towards the creditor.

[3.529]
Article 21
Formal validity
A unilateral act intended to have legal effect and relating to a non-contractual obligation shall be formally valid if it satisfies the formal requirements of the law governing the non-contractual obligation in question or the law of the country in which the act is performed.

[3.530]
Article 22
Burden of proof
1. The law governing a non-contractual obligation under this Regulation shall apply to the extent that, in matters of non-contractual obligations, it contains rules which raise presumptions of law or determine the burden of proof.
2. Acts intended to have legal effect may be proved by any mode of proof recognised by the law of the forum or by any of the laws referred to in Article 21 under which that act is formally valid, provided that such mode of proof can be administered by the forum.

CHAPTER VI
OTHER PROVISIONS

[3.531]
Article 23
Habitual residence
1. For the purposes of this Regulation, the habitual residence of companies and other bodies, corporate or unincorporated, shall be the place of central administration.

Where the event giving rise to the damage occurs, or the damage arises, in the course of operation of a branch, agency or any other establishment, the place where the branch, agency or any other establishment is located shall be treated as the place of habitual residence.
2. For the purposes of this Regulation, the habitual residence of a natural person acting in the course of his or her business activity shall be his or her principal place of business.

[3.532]
Article 24
Exclusion of renvoi
The application of the law of any country specified by this Regulation means the application of the rules of law in force in that country other than its rules of private international law.

[3.533]
Article 25
States with more than one legal system
1. Where a State comprises several territorial units, each of which has its own rules of law in respect of non-contractual obligations, each territorial unit shall be considered as a country for the purposes of identifying the law applicable under this Regulation.
2. A Member State within which different territorial units have their own rules of law in respect of non-contractual obligations shall not be required to apply this Regulation to conflicts solely between the laws of such units.

[3.534]
Article 26
Public policy of the forum
The application of a provision of the law of any country specified by this Regulation may be refused only if such application is manifestly incompatible with the public policy (*ordre public*) of the forum.

[3.535]
Article 27
Relationship with other provisions of Community law
This Regulation shall not prejudice the application of provisions of Community law which, in relation to particular matters, lay down conflict-of-law rules relating to non-contractual obligations.

Article 28 (*Outside the scope of this work.*)

CHAPTER VII
FINAL PROVISIONS

Articles 29, 30 (*Outside the scope of this work.*)

[3.536]
Article 31
Application in time

This Regulation shall apply to events giving rise to damage which occur after its entry into force.

[3.537]
Article 32
Date of application

This Regulation shall apply from 11 January 2009, except for Article 29, which shall apply from 11 July 2008.

This Regulation shall be binding in its entirety and directly applicable in the Member States in accordance with the Treaty establishing the European Community.

(*Commission Statement on the review clause; Commission Statement on road accidents; Commission Statement on the treatment of foreign law; outside the scope of this work.*)

REGULATION OF THE EUROPEAN PARLIAMENT AND OF THE COUNCIL

(593/2008/EC)

of 17 June 2008

on the law applicable to contractual obligations (Rome I)

NOTES

Date of publication in OJ: OJ L177, 4.7.2008, p 6. The text of this Directive incorporates the corrigendum published in OJ L309, 24.11.2009, p 87.

Only those provisions within the scope of this work are reproduced.

Application to the United Kingdom: Commission Decision 2009/26/EC of 22 December 2008 (OJ L10, 15.1.2009, p 22) provides that:

> "**Article 1**
> Regulation (EC) No 593/2008 shall apply to the United Kingdom in accordance with Article 2.
> **Article 2** Regulation (EC) No 593/2008 shall enter into force in the United Kingdom from the date of notification of this Decision. It shall apply from 17 December 2009, except for Article 26 which shall apply from 17 June 2009.".

The Regulation applies to contracts concluded as from 17 December 2009: see Art 28 at **[3.563]**.

For the domestic implementation of this Directive, see the Contracts (Applicable Law) Act 1990, ss 4A, 4B at **[1.184]** and **[1.185]**.

See *Harvey* H(3).

[3.538]

THE EUROPEAN PARLIAMENT AND THE COUNCIL OF THE EUROPEAN UNION,

Having regard to the Treaty establishing the European Community, and in particular Article 61(c) and the second indent of Article 67(5) thereof,

Having regard to the proposal from the Commission,

Having regard to the opinion of the European Economic and Social Committee,[1]

Acting in accordance with the procedure laid down in Article 251 of the Treaty,[2]

Whereas:

(1) The Community has set itself the objective of maintaining and developing an area of freedom, security and justice. For the progressive establishment of such an area, the Community is to adopt measures relating to judicial cooperation in civil matters with a cross-border impact to the extent necessary for the proper functioning of the internal market.

(2) According to Article 65, point (b) of the Treaty, these measures are to include those promoting the compatibility of the rules applicable in the Member States concerning the conflict of laws and of jurisdiction.

(3) The European Council meeting in Tampere on 15 and 16 October 1999 endorsed the principle of mutual recognition of judgments and other decisions of judicial authorities as the cornerstone of judicial cooperation in civil matters and invited the Council and the Commission to adopt a programme of measures to implement that principle.

(4) On 30 November 2000 the Council adopted a joint Commission and Council programme of measures for implementation of the principle of mutual recognition of decisions in civil and commercial matters.[3] The programme identifies measures relating to the harmonisation of conflict-of-law rules as those facilitating the mutual recognition of judgments.

(5) The Hague Programme,[4] adopted by the European Council on 5 November 2004, called for work to be pursued actively on the conflict-of-law rules regarding contractual obligations (Rome I).

(6) The proper functioning of the internal market creates a need, in order to improve the predictability of the outcome of litigation, certainty as to the law applicable and the free movement of judgments, for the conflict-of-law rules in the Member States to designate the same national law irrespective of the country of the court in which an action is brought.

(7) The substantive scope and the provisions of this Regulation should be consistent with Council Regulation (EC) No 44/2001 of 22 December 2000 on jurisdiction and the recognition and enforcement of judgments in civil and commercial matters[5] (Brussels I) and Regulation (EC) No 864/2007 of the European Parliament and of the Council of 11 July 2007 on the law applicable to non-contractual obligations (Rome II).[6]

(8) Family relationships should cover parentage, marriage, affinity and collateral relatives. The reference in Article 1(2) to relationships having comparable effects to marriage and other family relationships should be interpreted in accordance with the law of the Member State in which the court is seised.

(9) Obligations under bills of exchange, cheques and promissory notes and other negotiable instruments should also cover bills of lading to the extent that the obligations under the bill of lading arise out of its negotiable character.

(10) Obligations arising out of dealings prior to the conclusion of the contract are covered by Article 12 of Regulation (EC) No 864/2007. Such obligations should therefore be excluded from the scope of this Regulation.

(11) The parties' freedom to choose the applicable law should be one of the cornerstones of the system of conflict-of-law rules in matters of contractual obligations.

(12) An agreement between the parties to confer on one or more courts or tribunals of a Member State exclusive jurisdiction to determine disputes under the contract should be one of the factors to be taken into account in determining whether a choice of law has been clearly demonstrated.

(13) This Regulation does not preclude parties from incorporating by reference into their contract a non-State body of law or an international convention.

(14) Should the Community adopt, in an appropriate legal instrument, rules of substantive contract law, including standard terms and conditions, such instrument may provide that the parties may choose to apply those rules.

(15) Where a choice of law is made and all other elements relevant to the situation are located in a country other than the country whose law has been chosen, the choice of law should not prejudice the application of provisions of the law of that country which cannot be derogated from by agreement. This rule should apply whether or not the choice of law was accompanied by a choice of court or tribunal. Whereas no substantial change is intended as compared with Article 3(3) of the 1980 Convention on the Law Applicable to Contractual Obligations[7] (the Rome Convention), the wording of this Regulation is aligned as far as possible with Article 14 of Regulation (EC) No 864/2007.

(16) To contribute to the general objective of this Regulation, legal certainty in the European judicial area, the conflict-of-law rules should be highly foreseeable. The courts should, however, retain a degree of discretion to determine the law that is most closely connected to the situation.

(17) As far as the applicable law in the absence of choice is concerned, the concept of 'provision of services' and 'sale of goods' should be interpreted in the same way as when applying Article 5 of Regulation (EC) No 44/2001 in so far as sale of goods and provision of services are covered by that Regulation. Although franchise and distribution contracts are contracts for services, they are the subject of specific rules.

(18) As far as the applicable law in the absence of choice is concerned, multilateral systems should be those in which trading is conducted, such as regulated markets and multilateral trading facilities as referred to in Article 4 of Directive 2004/39/EC of the European Parliament and of the Council of 21 April 2004 on markets in financial instruments,[8] regardless of whether or not they rely on a central counterparty.

(19) Where there has been no choice of law, the applicable law should be determined in accordance with the rule specified for the particular type of contract. Where the contract cannot be categorised as being one of the specified types or where its elements fall within more than one of the specified types, it should be governed by the law of the country where the party required to effect the characteristic performance of the contract has his habitual residence. In the case of a contract consisting of a bundle of rights and obligations capable of being categorised as falling within more than one of the specified types of contract, the characteristic performance of the contract should be determined having regard to its centre of gravity.

(20) Where the contract is manifestly more closely connected with a country other than that indicated in Article 4(1) or (2), an escape clause should provide that the law of that other country is to apply. In order to determine that country, account should be taken, inter alia, of whether the

contract in question has a very close relationship with another contract or contracts.

(21) In the absence of choice, where the applicable law cannot be determined either on the basis of the fact that the contract can be categorised as one of the specified types or as being the law of the country of habitual residence of the party required to effect the characteristic performance of the contract, the contract should be governed by the law of the country with which it is most closely connected. In order to determine that country, account should be taken, inter alia, of whether the contract in question has a very close relationship with another contract or contracts.

(22) (*Outside the scope of this work.*)

(23) As regards contracts concluded with parties regarded as being weaker, those parties should be protected by conflict-of-law rules that are more favourable to their interests than the general rules.

(24)–(33) (*Outside the scope of this work.*)

(34) The rule on individual employment contracts should not prejudice the application of the overriding mandatory provisions of the country to which a worker is posted in accordance with Directive 96/71/EC of the European Parliament and of the Council of 16 December 1996 concerning the posting of workers in the framework of the provision of services.[9]

(35) Employees should not be deprived of the protection afforded to them by provisions which cannot be derogated from by agreement or which can only be derogated from to their benefit.

(36) As regards individual employment contracts, work carried out in another country should be regarded as temporary if the employee is expected to resume working in the country of origin after carrying out his tasks abroad. The conclusion of a new contract of employment with the original employer or an employer belonging to the same group of companies as the original employer should not preclude the employee from being regarded as carrying out his work in another country temporarily.

(37) Considerations of public interest justify giving the courts of the Member States the possibility, in exceptional circumstances, of applying exceptions based on public policy and overriding mandatory provisions. The concept of 'overriding mandatory provisions' should be distinguished from the expression 'provisions which cannot be derogated from by agreement' and should be construed more restrictively.

(38) In the context of voluntary assignment, the term 'relationship' should make it clear that Article 14(1) also applies to the property aspects of an assignment, as between assignor and assignee, in legal orders where such aspects are treated separately from the aspects under the law of obligations. However, the term 'relationship' should not be understood as relating to any relationship that may exist between assignor and assignee. In particular, it should not cover preliminary questions as regards a voluntary assignment or a contractual subrogation. The term should be strictly limited to the aspects which are directly relevant to the voluntary assignment or contractual subrogation in question.

(39) For the sake of legal certainty there should be a clear definition of habitual residence, in particular for companies and other bodies, corporate or unincorporated. Unlike Article 60(1) of Regulation (EC) No 44/2001, which establishes three criteria, the conflict-of-law rule should proceed on the basis of a single criterion; otherwise, the parties would be unable to foresee the law applicable to their situation.

(40) A situation where conflict-of-law rules are dispersed among several instruments and where there are differences between those rules should be avoided. This Regulation, however, should not exclude the possibility of inclusion of conflict-of-law rules relating to contractual obligations in provisions of Community law with regard to particular matters.

This Regulation should not prejudice the application of other instruments laying down provisions designed to contribute to the proper functioning of the internal market in so far as they cannot be applied in conjunction with the law designated by the rules of this Regulation. The application of provisions of the applicable law designated by the rules of this Regulation should not restrict the free movement of goods and services as regulated by Community instruments, such as Directive 2000/31/EC of the European Parliament and of the Council of 8 June 2000 on certain legal aspects of information society services, in particular electronic commerce, in the Internal Market (Directive on electronic commerce).[10]

(41) Respect for international commitments entered into by the Member States means that this Regulation should not affect international conventions to which one or more Member States are parties at the time when this Regulation is adopted. To make the rules more accessible, the Commission should publish the list of the relevant conventions in the *Official Journal of the European Union* on the basis of information supplied by the Member States.

(42) The Commission will make a proposal to the European Parliament and to the Council concerning the procedures and conditions according to which Member States would be entitled to negotiate and conclude, on their own behalf, agreements with third countries in individual and exceptional cases, concerning sectoral matters and containing provisions on the law applicable to contractual obligations.

(43) Since the objective of this Regulation cannot be sufficiently achieved by the Member States and can therefore, by reason of the scale and effects of this Regulation, be better achieved at Community level, the Community may adopt measures, in accordance with the principle of subsidiarity as set out in Article 5 of the Treaty. In accordance with the principle of proportionality, as set out in that Article, this Regulation does not go beyond what is necessary to attain its objective.

(44) In accordance with Article 3 of the Protocol on the position of the United Kingdom and Ireland, annexed to the Treaty on European Union and to the Treaty establishing the European Community, Ireland has notified its wish to take part in the adoption and application of the present Regulation.

(45) In accordance with Articles 1 and 2 of the Protocol on the position of the United Kingdom and Ireland, annexed to the Treaty on European Union and to the Treaty establishing the European Community, and without prejudice to Article 4 of the said Protocol, the United Kingdom is not taking part in the adoption of this Regulation and is not bound by it or subject to its application.

(46) In accordance with Articles 1 and 2 of the Protocol on the position of Denmark, annexed to the Treaty on European Union and to the Treaty establishing the European Community, Denmark is not taking part in the adoption of this Regulation and is not bound by it or subject to its application,

NOTES

1 OJ C318, 23.12.2006, p 56.

2 Opinion of the European Parliament of 29 November 2007 (not yet published in the Official Journal) and Council Decision of 5 June 2008.

3 OJ C12, 15.1.2001, p 1.

4 OJ C53, 3.3.2005, p 1.

5 OJ L12, 16.1.2001, p 1. Regulation as last amended by Regulation (EC) No 1791/2006 (OJ L363, 20.12.2006, p 1).

6 OJ L199, 31.7.2007, p 40.

7 OJ C334, 30.12.2005, p 1.

8 OJ L145, 30.4.2004, p 1. Directive as last amended by Directive 2008/10/EC (OJ L76, 19.3.2008, p 33).

9 OJ L18, 21.1.1997, p 1.

10 OJ L178, 17.7.2000, p 1.

HAVE ADOPTED THIS REGULATION:

CHAPTER I
SCOPE

[3.539]

Article 1 Material scope

1. This Regulation shall apply, in situations involving a conflict of laws, to contractual obligations in civil and commercial matters.

It shall not apply, in particular, to revenue, customs or administrative matters.

2. The following shall be excluded from the scope of this Regulation:

(a) questions involving the status or legal capacity of natural persons, without prejudice to Article 13;

(b) obligations arising out of family relationships and relationships deemed by the law applicable to such relationships to have comparable effects, including maintenance obligations;

(c) obligations arising out of matrimonial property regimes, property regimes of relationships deemed by the law applicable to such relationships to have comparable effects to marriage, and wills and succession;

(d) obligations arising under bills of exchange, cheques and promissory notes and other negotiable instruments to the extent that the obligations under such other negotiable instruments arise out of their negotiable character;

(e) arbitration agreements and agreements on the choice of court;

(f) questions governed by the law of companies and other bodies, corporate or unincorporated, such as the creation, by registration or otherwise, legal capacity, internal organisation or winding-up of companies and other bodies, corporate or unincorporated, and the personal liability of officers and members as such for the obligations of the company or body;

(g) the question whether an agent is able to bind a principal, or an organ to bind a company or other body corporate or unincorporated, in relation to a third party;

(h) the constitution of trusts and the relationship between settlors, trustees and beneficiaries;

(i) obligations arising out of dealings prior to the conclusion of a contract;

(j) insurance contracts arising out of operations carried out by organisations other than undertakings referred to in Article 2 of Directive 2002/83/EC of the European Parliament and of the Council of 5 November 2002 concerning life assurance[1] the object of which is to provide benefits for employed or self-employed persons belonging to an undertaking or group of undertakings, or to a trade or group of trades, in the event of death or survival or of discontinuance or curtailment of activity, or of sickness related to work or accidents at work.

3. This Regulation shall not apply to evidence and procedure, without prejudice to Article 18.

4. In this Regulation, the term 'Member State' shall mean Member States to which this Regulation applies. However, in Article 3(4) and Article 7 the term shall mean all the Member States.

NOTES

[1] OJ L345, 19.12.2002, p 1. Directive as last amended by Directive 2008/19/EC (OJ L76, 19.3.2008, p 44).

[3.540]
Article 2
Universal application

Any law specified by this Regulation shall be applied whether or not it is the law of a Member State.

CHAPTER II
UNIFORM RULES

[3.541]
Article 3
Freedom of choice

1. A contract shall be governed by the law chosen by the parties. The choice shall be made expressly or clearly demonstrated by the terms of the contract or the circumstances of the case. By their choice the parties can select the law applicable to the whole or to part only of the contract.

2. The parties may at any time agree to subject the contract to a law other than that which previously governed it, whether as a result of an earlier choice made under this Article or of other provisions of this Regulation. Any change in the law to be applied that is made after the conclusion of the contract shall not prejudice its formal validity under Article 11 or adversely affect the rights of third parties.

3. Where all other elements relevant to the situation at the time of the choice are located in a country other than the country whose law has been chosen, the choice of the parties shall not prejudice the application of provisions of the law of that other country which cannot be derogated from by agreement.

4. Where all other elements relevant to the situation at the time of the choice are located in one or more Member States, the parties' choice of applicable law other than that of a Member State shall not prejudice the application of provisions of Community law, where appropriate as implemented in the Member State of the forum, which cannot be derogated from by agreement.

5. The existence and validity of the consent of the parties as to the choice of the applicable law shall be determined in accordance with the provisions of Articles 10, 11 and 13.

[3.542]
Article 4
Applicable law in the absence of choice

1. To the extent that the law applicable to the contract has not been chosen in accordance with Article 3 and without prejudice to Articles 5 to 8, the law governing the contract shall be determined as follows:

(a) a contract for the sale of goods shall be governed by the law of the country where the seller has his habitual residence;

(b) a contract for the provision of services shall be governed by the law of the country where the service provider has his habitual residence;

(c) a contract relating to a right in rem in immovable property or to a tenancy of immovable property shall be governed by the law of the country where the property is situated;

(d) notwithstanding point (c), a tenancy of immovable property concluded for temporary private use for a period of no more than six consecutive months shall be governed by the law of the country where the landlord has his habitual residence, provided that the tenant is a natural person and has his habitual residence in the same country;

(e) a franchise contract shall be governed by the law of the country where the franchisee has his habitual residence;

(f) a distribution contract shall be governed by the law of the country where the distributor has his habitual residence;

(g) a contract for the sale of goods by auction shall be governed by the law of the country where the auction takes place, if such a place can be determined;

(h) a contract concluded within a multilateral system which brings together or facilitates the bringing together of multiple third-party buying and selling interests in financial instruments, as defined by Article 4(1), point (17) of Directive 2004/39/EC, in accordance with non-discretionary rules and governed by a single law, shall be governed by that law.

2. Where the contract is not covered by paragraph 1 or where the elements of the contract would be covered by more than one of points (a) to (h) of paragraph 1, the contract shall be governed by the law of the country where the party required to effect the characteristic performance of the contract has his habitual residence.

3. Where it is clear from all the circumstances of the case that the contract is manifestly more closely connected with a country other than that indicated in paragraphs 1 or 2, the law of that other country shall apply.

4. Where the law applicable cannot be determined pursuant to paragraphs 1 or 2, the contract shall be governed by the law of the country with which it is most closely connected.

Articles 5–7 (*Outside the scope of this work.*)

[3.543]

Article 8

Individual employment contracts

1. An individual employment contract shall be governed by the law chosen by the parties in accordance with Article 3. Such a choice of law may not, however, have the result of depriving the employee of the protection afforded to him by provisions that cannot be derogated from by agreement under the law that, in the absence of choice, would have been applicable pursuant to paragraphs 2, 3 and 4 of this Article.

2. To the extent that the law applicable to the individual employment contract has not been chosen by the parties, the contract shall be governed by the law of the country in which or, failing that, from which the employee habitually carries out his work in performance of the contract. The country where the work is habitually carried out shall not be deemed to have changed if he is temporarily employed in another country.

3. Where the law applicable cannot be determined pursuant to paragraph 2, the contract shall be governed by the law of the country where the place of business through which the employee was engaged is situated.

4. Where it appears from the circumstances as a whole that the contract is more closely connected with a country other than that indicated in paragraphs 2 or 3, the law of that other country shall apply.

[3.544]

Article 9

Overriding mandatory provisions

1. Overriding mandatory provisions are provisions the respect for which is regarded as crucial by a country for safeguarding its public interests, such as its political, social or economic organisation, to such an extent that they are applicable to any situation falling within their scope, irrespective of the law otherwise applicable to the contract under this Regulation.

2. Nothing in this Regulation shall restrict the application of the overriding mandatory provisions of the law of the forum.

3. Effect may be given to the overriding mandatory provisions of the law of the country where the obligations arising out of the contract have to be or have been performed, in so far as those overriding mandatory provisions render the performance of the contract unlawful. In considering whether to give effect to those provisions, regard shall be had to their nature and purpose and to the consequences of their application or non-application.

[3.545]

Article 10

Consent and material validity

1. The existence and validity of a contract, or of any term of a contract, shall be determined by the law which would govern it under this Regulation if the contract or term were valid.

2. Nevertheless, a party, in order to establish that he did not consent, may rely upon the law of the country in which he has his habitual residence if it appears from the circumstances that it would not be reasonable to determine the effect of his conduct in accordance with the law specified in paragraph 1.

[3.546]

Article 11

Formal validity

1. A contract concluded between persons who, or whose agents, are in the same country at the time of its conclusion is formally valid if it satisfies the formal requirements of the law which governs it in substance under this Regulation or of the law of the country where it is concluded.

2. A contract concluded between persons who, or whose agents, are in different countries at the time of its conclusion is formally valid if it satisfies the formal requirements of the law which governs it in substance under this Regulation, or of the law of either of the countries where either of the parties or their agent is present at the time of conclusion, or of the law of the country where either of the parties had his habitual residence at that time.
3. A unilateral act intended to have legal effect relating to an existing or contemplated contract is formally valid if it satisfies the formal requirements of the law which governs or would govern the contract in substance under this Regulation, or of the law of the country where the act was done, or of the law of the country where the person by whom it was done had his habitual residence at that time.
4. Paragraphs 1, 2 and 3 of this Article shall not apply to contracts that fall within the scope of Article 6. The form of such contracts shall be governed by the law of the country where the consumer has his habitual residence.
5. Notwithstanding paragraphs 1 to 4, a contract the subject matter of which is a right in rem in immovable property or a tenancy of immovable property shall be subject to the requirements of form of the law of the country where the property is situated if by that law:
- (a) those requirements are imposed irrespective of the country where the contract is concluded and irrespective of the law governing the contract; and
- (b) those requirements cannot be derogated from by agreement.

[3.547]
Article 12
Scope of the law applicable
1. The law applicable to a contract by virtue of this Regulation shall govern in particular:
- (a) interpretation;
- (b) performance;
- (c) within the limits of the powers conferred on the court by its procedural law, the consequences of a total or partial breach of obligations, including the assessment of damages in so far as it is governed by rules of law;
- (d) the various ways of extinguishing obligations, and prescription and limitation of actions;
- (e) the consequences of nullity of the contract.

2. In relation to the manner of performance and the steps to be taken in the event of defective performance, regard shall be had to the law of the country in which performance takes place.

[3.548]
Article 13
Incapacity
In a contract concluded between persons who are in the same country, a natural person who would have capacity under the law of that country may invoke his incapacity resulting from the law of another country, only if the other party to the contract was aware of that incapacity at the time of the conclusion of the contract or was not aware thereof as a result of negligence.

[3.549]
Article 14
Voluntary assignment and contractual subrogation
1. The relationship between assignor and assignee under a voluntary assignment or contractual subrogation of a claim against another person (the debtor) shall be governed by the law that applies to the contract between the assignor and assignee under this Regulation.
2. The law governing the assigned or subrogated claim shall determine its assignability, the relationship between the assignee and the debtor, the conditions under which the assignment or subrogation can be invoked against the debtor and whether the debtor's obligations have been discharged.
3. The concept of assignment in this Article includes outright transfers of claims, transfers of claims by way of security and pledges or other security rights over claims.

[3.550]
Article 15
Legal subrogation
Where a person (the creditor) has a contractual claim against another (the debtor) and a third person has a duty to satisfy the creditor, or has in fact satisfied the creditor in discharge of that duty, the law which governs the third person's duty to satisfy the creditor shall determine whether and to what extent the third person is entitled to exercise against the debtor the rights which the creditor had against the debtor under the law governing their relationship.

[3.551]
Article 16
Multiple liability

If a creditor has a claim against several debtors who are liable for the same claim, and one of the debtors has already satisfied the claim in whole or in part, the law governing the debtor's obligation towards the creditor also governs the debtor's right to claim recourse from the other debtors. The other debtors may rely on the defences they had against the creditor to the extent allowed by the law governing their obligations towards the creditor.

[3.552]
Article 17
Set-off

Where the right to set-off is not agreed by the parties, set-off shall be governed by the law applicable to the claim against which the right to set-off is asserted.

[3.553]
Article 18
Burden of proof

1. The law governing a contractual obligation under this Regulation shall apply to the extent that, in matters of contractual obligations, it contains rules which raise presumptions of law or determine the burden of proof.
2. A contract or an act intended to have legal effect may be proved by any mode of proof recognised by the law of the forum or by any of the laws referred to in Article 11 under which that contract or act is formally valid, provided that such mode of proof can be administered by the forum.

CHAPTER III
OTHER PROVISIONS

[3.554]
Article 19
Habitual residence

1. For the purposes of this Regulation, the habitual residence of companies and other bodies, corporate or unincorporated, shall be the place of central administration.

The habitual residence of a natural person acting in the course of his business activity shall be his principal place of business.
2. Where the contract is concluded in the course of the operations of a branch, agency or any other establishment, or if, under the contract, performance is the responsibility of such a branch, agency or establishment, the place where the branch, agency or any other establishment is located shall be treated as the place of habitual residence.
3. For the purposes of determining the habitual residence, the relevant point in time shall be the time of the conclusion of the contract.

[3.555]
Article 20
Exclusion of renvoi

The application of the law of any country specified by this Regulation means the application of the rules of law in force in that country other than its rules of private international law, unless provided otherwise in this Regulation.

[3.556]
Article 21
Public policy of the forum

The application of a provision of the law of any country specified by this Regulation may be refused only if such application is manifestly incompatible with the public policy (*ordre public*) of the forum.

[3.557]
Article 22
States with more than one legal system

1. Where a State comprises several territorial units, each of which has its own rules of law in respect of contractual obligations, each territorial unit shall be considered as a country for the purposes of identifying the law applicable under this Regulation.
2. A Member State where different territorial units have their own rules of law in respect of contractual obligations shall not be required to apply this Regulation to conflicts solely between the laws of such units.

[3.558]
Article 23
Relationship with other provisions of Community law
With the exception of Article 7, this Regulation shall not prejudice the application of provisions of Community law which, in relation to particular matters, lay down conflict-of-law rules relating to contractual obligations.

[3.559]
Article 24
Relationship with the Rome Convention
1. This Regulation shall replace the Rome Convention in the Member States, except as regards the territories of the Member States which fall within the territorial scope of that Convention and to which this Regulation does not apply pursuant to Article 299 of the Treaty.
2. In so far as this Regulation replaces the provisions of the Rome Convention, any reference to that Convention shall be understood as a reference to this Regulation.

[3.560]
Article 25
Relationship with existing international conventions
1. This Regulation shall not prejudice the application of international conventions to which one or more Member States are parties at the time when this Regulation is adopted and which lay down conflict-of-law rules relating to contractual obligations.
2. However, this Regulation shall, as between Member States, take precedence over conventions concluded exclusively between two or more of them in so far as such conventions concern matters governed by this Regulation.

[3.561]
Article 26
List of Conventions
1. By 17 June 2009, Member States shall notify the Commission of the conventions referred to in Article 25(1). After that date, Member States shall notify the Commission of all denunciations of such conventions.
2. Within six months of receipt of the notifications referred to in paragraph 1, the Commission shall publish in the *Official Journal of the European Union*:
- (a) a list of the conventions referred to in paragraph 1;
- (b) the denunciations referred to in paragraph 1.

[3.562]
Article 27
Review clause
1. By 17 June 2013, the Commission shall submit to the European Parliament, the Council and the European Economic and Social Committee a report on the application of this Regulation. If appropriate, the report shall be accompanied by proposals to amend this Regulation. The report shall include:
- (a) a study on the law applicable to insurance contracts and an assessment of the impact of the provisions to be introduced, if any; and
- (b) an evaluation on the application of Article 6, in particular as regards the coherence of Community law in the field of consumer protection.

2. By 17 June 2010, the Commission shall submit to the European Parliament, the Council and the European Economic and Social Committee a report on the question of the effectiveness of an assignment or subrogation of a claim against third parties and the priority of the assigned or subrogated claim over a right of another person. The report shall be accompanied, if appropriate, by a proposal to amend this Regulation and an assessment of the impact of the provisions to be introduced.

[3.563]
Article 28
Application in time
This Regulation shall apply to contracts concluded as from 17 December 2009.

CHAPTER IV
FINAL PROVISIONS

[3.564]
Article 29
Entry into force and application
This Regulation shall enter into force on the 20th day following its publication in the *Official Journal of the European Union*.

It shall apply from 17 December 2009 except for Article 26 which shall apply from 17 June 2009.

This Regulation shall be binding in its entirety and directly applicable in the Member States in accordance with the Treaty establishing the European Community.

DIRECTIVE OF THE EUROPEAN PARLIAMENT AND OF THE COUNCIL

(2008/94/EC)

of 22 October 2008

on the protection of employees in the event of the insolvency of their employer

(Codified version) Text with EEA relevance

NOTES

Date of publication in OJ: OJ L283, 28.10.2008, p 36.

This Directive consolidates and replaces Directive 80/987/EC as amended. A correlation table for the provisions of Directive 80/987/EC is at Annex II (at **[3.585]**). For the domestic implementation of the provisions consolidated see the Employment Rights Act 1996, ss 166–170 at **[1.973]**–**[1.977]** and Part XII at **[1.989]**. The Directive came into force on 17 November 2008 (20 days after publication in the *Official Journal*): see Art 17 at **[3.582]**.

See *Harvey* E(16), G.

[3.565]

THE EUROPEAN PARLIAMENT AND THE COUNCIL OF THE EUROPEAN UNION,

Having regard to the Treaty establishing the European Community, and in particular Article 137(2) thereof,

Having regard to the proposal from the Commission,

Having regard to the opinion of the European Economic and Social Committee,[1]

After consultation of the Committee of the Regions,

Acting in accordance with the procedure laid down in Article 251 of the Treaty,[2]

Whereas:

(1) Council Directive 80/987/EEC of 20 October 1980 on the protection of employees in the event of the insolvency of their employer[3] has been substantially amended several times.[4] In the interests of clarity and rationality the said Directive should be codified.

(2) The Community Charter of Fundamental Social Rights for Workers adopted on 9 December 1989 states, in point 7, that the completion of the internal market must lead to an improvement in the living and working conditions of workers in the Community and that this improvement must cover, where necessary, the development of certain aspects of employment regulations such as procedures for collective redundancies and those regarding bankruptcies.

(3) It is necessary to provide for the protection of employees in the event of the insolvency of their employer and to ensure a minimum degree of protection, in particular in order to guarantee payment of their outstanding claims, while taking account of the need for balanced economic and social development in the Community. To this end, the Member States should establish a body which guarantees payment of the outstanding claims of the employees concerned.

(4) In order to ensure equitable protection for the employees concerned, the state of insolvency should be defined in the light of the legislative trends in the Member States and that concept should also include insolvency proceedings other than liquidation. In this context, Member States should, in order to determine the liability of the guarantee institution, be able to lay down that where an insolvency situation results in several insolvency proceedings, the situation is to be treated as a single insolvency procedure.

(5) It should be ensured that the employees referred to in Council Directive 97/81/EC of 15 December 1997 concerning the Framework Agreement on part-time work concluded by UNICE, CEEP and the ETUC,[5] Council Directive 1999/70/EC of 28 June 1999 concerning the framework agreement on fixed-term work concluded by the ETUC, UNICE and CEEP[6] and Council Directive 91/383/EEC of 25 June 1991 supplementing the measures to encourage improvements in the safety and health at work of workers with a fixed-duration employment relationship or a temporary employment relationship[7] are not excluded from the scope of this Directive.

(6) In order to ensure legal certainty for employees in the event of insolvency of undertakings pursuing their activities in a number of Member States, and to strengthen employees' rights in line with the established case-law of the Court of Justice of the European Communities, provisions should be laid down which expressly state which institution is responsible for meeting pay claims in these cases and establish as the aim of cooperation between the competent administrative authorities of the Member States the early settlement of employees' outstanding claims. Furthermore

it is necessary to ensure that the relevant arrangements are properly implemented by making provision for collaboration between the competent administrative authorities in the Member States.

(7) Member States may set limitations on the responsibility of the guarantee institutions. Those limitations must be compatible with the social objective of the Directive and may take into account the different levels of claims.

(8) In order to make it easier to identify insolvency proceedings, in particular in situations with a cross-border dimension, provision should be made for the Member States to notify the Commission and the other Member States about the types of insolvency proceedings which give rise to intervention by the guarantee institution.

(9) Since the objective of the action to be taken cannot be sufficiently achieved by the Member States and can therefore be better achieved at Community level, the Community may adopt measures, in accordance with the principle of subsidiarity as set out in Article 5 of the Treaty. In accordance with the principle of proportionality, as set out in that Article, this Directive does not go beyond what is necessary in order to achieve that objective.

(10) The Commission should submit to the European Parliament and the Council a report on the implementation and application of this Directive in particular as regards the new forms of employment emerging in the Member States.

(11) This Directive should be without prejudice to the obligations of the Member States relating to the time-limits for transposition into national law and application of the Directives set out in Annex I, Part C,

NOTES

1 OJ C161, 13.7.2007, p 75.

2 Opinion of the European Parliament of 19 June 2007 (OJ C146 E, 12.6.2008, p 71) and Council Decision of 25 September 2008.

3 OJ L283, 28.10.1980, p 23.

4 See Annex I, Parts A and B.

5 OJ L14, 20.1.1998, p 9.

6 OJ L175, 10.7.1999, p 43.

7 OJ L206, 29.7.1991, p 19.

HAVE ADOPTED THIS DIRECTIVE:

CHAPTER I
SCOPE AND DEFINITIONS

[3.566]
Article 1

1. This Directive shall apply to employees' claims arising from contracts of employment or employment relationships and existing against employers who are in a state of insolvency within the meaning of Article 2(1).

2. Member States may, by way of exception, exclude claims by certain categories of employee from the scope of this Directive, by virtue of the existence of other forms of guarantee if it is established that these offer the persons concerned a degree of protection equivalent to that resulting from this Directive.

3. Where such provision already applies in their national legislation, Member States may continue to exclude from the scope of this Directive:

(a) domestic servants employed by a natural person;

(b) share-fishermen.

[3.567]
Article 2

1. For the purposes of this Directive, an employer shall be deemed to be in a state of insolvency where a request has been made for the opening of collective proceedings based on insolvency of the employer, as provided for under the laws, regulations and administrative provisions of a Member State, and involving the partial or total divestment of the employer's assets and the appointment of a liquidator or a person performing a similar task, and the authority which is competent pursuant to the said provisions has:

(a) either decided to open the proceedings; or

(b) established that the employer's undertaking or business has been definitively closed down and that the available assets are insufficient to warrant the opening of the proceedings.

2. This Directive is without prejudice to national law as regards the definition of the terms "employee", "employer", "pay", "right conferring immediate entitlement" and "right conferring prospective entitlement".

However, the Member States may not exclude from the scope of this Directive:

(a) part-time employees within the meaning of Directive 97/81/EC;
(b) employees with a fixed-term contract within the meaning of Directive 1999/70/EC;
(c) employees with a temporary employment relationship within the meaning of Article 1(2) of Directive 91/383/EEC.

3. Member States may not set a minimum duration for the contract of employment or the employment relationship in order for employees to qualify for claims under this Directive.

4. This Directive does not prevent Member States from extending employee protection to other situations of insolvency, for example where payments have been de facto stopped on a permanent basis, established by proceedings different from those mentioned in paragraph 1 as provided for under national law.

Such procedures shall not however create a guarantee obligation for the institutions of the other Member States in the cases referred to in Chapter IV.

CHAPTER II
PROVISIONS CONCERNING GUARANTEE INSTITUTIONS

[3.568]
Article 3
Member States shall take the measures necessary to ensure that guarantee institutions guarantee, subject to Article 4, payment of employees' outstanding claims resulting from contracts of employment or employment relationships, including, where provided for by national law, severance pay on termination of employment relationships.

The claims taken over by the guarantee institution shall be the outstanding pay claims relating to a period prior to and/or, as applicable, after a given date determined by the Member States.

[3.569]
Article 4
1. Member States shall have the option to limit the liability of the guarantee institutions referred to in Article 3.

2. If Member States exercise the option referred to in paragraph 1, they shall specify the length of the period for which outstanding claims are to be met by the guarantee institution. However, this may not be shorter than a period covering the remuneration of the last three months of the employment relationship prior to and/or after the date referred to in the second paragraph of Article 3.

Member States may include this minimum period of three months in a reference period with a duration of not less than six months.

Member States having a reference period of not less than 18 months may limit the period for which outstanding claims are met by the guarantee institution to eight weeks. In this case, those periods which are most favourable to the employee shall be used for the calculation of the minimum period.

3. Member States may set ceilings on the payments made by the guarantee institution. These ceilings must not fall below a level which is socially compatible with the social objective of this Directive.

If Member States exercise this option, they shall inform the Commission of the methods used to set the ceiling.

[3.570]
Article 5
Member States shall lay down detailed rules for the organisation, financing and operation of the guarantee institutions, complying with the following principles in particular:

(a) the assets of the institutions must be independent of the employers' operating capital and be inaccessible to proceedings for insolvency;
(b) employers must contribute to financing, unless it is fully covered by the public authorities;
(c) the institutions' liabilities must not depend on whether or not obligations to contribute to financing have been fulfilled.

CHAPTER III
PROVISIONS CONCERNING SOCIAL SECURITY

[3.571]
Article 6
Member States may stipulate that Articles 3, 4 and 5 shall not apply to contributions due under national statutory social security schemes or under supplementary occupational or inter-occupational pension schemes outside the national statutory social security schemes.

[3.572]
Article 7
Member States shall take the measures necessary to ensure that non-payment of compulsory contributions due from the employer, before the onset of his insolvency, to their insurance

institutions under national statutory social security schemes does not adversely affect employees' benefit entitlement in respect of these insurance institutions in so far as the employees' contributions have been deducted at source from the remuneration paid.

[3.573]
Article 8
Member States shall ensure that the necessary measures are taken to protect the interests of employees and of persons having already left the employer's undertaking or business at the date of the onset of the employer's insolvency in respect of rights conferring on them immediate or prospective entitlement to old-age benefits, including survivors' benefits, under supplementary occupational or inter-occupational pension schemes outside the national statutory social security schemes.

CHAPTER IV
PROVISIONS CONCERNING TRANSNATIONAL SITUATIONS

[3.574]
Article 9
1. If an undertaking with activities in the territories of at least two Member States is in a state of insolvency within the meaning of Article 2(l), the institution responsible for meeting employees' outstanding claims shall be that in the Member State in whose territory they work or habitually work.
2. The extent of employees' rights shall be determined by the law governing the competent guarantee institution.
3. Member States shall take the measures necessary to ensure that, in the cases referred to in paragraph 1 of this Article, decisions taken in the context of insolvency proceedings referred to in Article 2(1), which have been requested in another Member State, are taken into account when determining the employer's state of insolvency within the meaning of this Directive.

[3.575]
Article 10
1. For the purposes of implementing Article 9, Member States shall make provision for the sharing of relevant information between their competent administrative authorities and/or the guarantee institutions mentioned in the first paragraph of Article 3, making it possible in particular to inform the guarantee institution responsible for meeting the employees' outstanding claims.
2. Member States shall notify the Commission and the other Member States of the contact details of their competent administrative authorities and/or guarantee institutions. The Commission shall make that information publicly accessible.

CHAPTER V
GENERAL AND FINAL PROVISIONS

[3.576]
Article 11
This Directive shall not affect the option of Member States to apply or introduce laws, regulations or administrative provisions which are more favourable to employees.

Implementation of this Directive shall not under any circumstances be sufficient grounds for a regression in relation to the current situation in the Member States and in relation to the general level of protection of employees in the area covered by it.

[3.577]
Article 12
This Directive shall not affect the option of Member States:
(a) to take the measures necessary to avoid abuses;
(b) to refuse or reduce the liability referred to in the first paragraph of Article 3 or the guarantee obligation referred to in Article 7 if it appears that fulfilment of the obligation is unjustifiable because of the existence of special links between the employee and the employer and of common interests resulting in collusion between them;
(c) to refuse or reduce the liability referred to in the first paragraph of Article 3 or the guarantee obligation referred to in Article 7 in cases where the employee, on his or her own or together with his or her close relatives, was the owner of an essential part of the employer's undertaking or business and had a considerable influence on its activities.

[3.578]
Article 13
Member States shall notify the Commission and the other Member States of the types of national insolvency proceedings falling within the scope of this Directive, and of any amendments relating thereto.

The Commission shall publish these communications in the *Official Journal of the European Union*.

[3.579]
Article 14
Member States shall communicate to the Commission the text of the laws, regulations and administrative provisions which they adopt in the field covered by this Directive.

[3.580]
Article 15
By 8 October 2010 at the latest, the Commission shall submit to the European Parliament and to the Council a report on the implementation and application in the Member States of Articles 1 to 4, 9 and 10, Article 11, second paragraph, Article 12, point (c), and Articles 13 and 14.

[3.581]
Article 16
Directive 80/987/EEC, as amended by the acts listed in Annex I, is repealed, without prejudice to the obligations of the Member States relating to the time-limits for transposition into national law and application of the Directives set out in Annex I, Part C.

References to the repealed Directive shall be construed as references to this Directive and shall be read in accordance with the correlation table in Annex II.

[3.582]
Article 17
This Directive shall enter into force on the 20th day following its publication in the *Official Journal of the European Union*.

[3.583]
Article 18
This Directive is addressed to the Member States.

ANNEX I

PART A
REPEALED DIRECTIVE WITH ITS SUCCESSIVE AMENDMENTS

(referred to in Article 16)
[3.584]

Council Directive 80/987/EEC	(OJ L283, 28.10.1980, p 23).
Council Directive 87/164/EEC	(OJ L66, 11.3.1987, p 11).
Directive 2002/74/EC of the European Parliament and of the Council	(OJ L270, 8.10.2002, p 10).

PART B
NON-REPEALED AMENDING ACT

(referred to in Article 16)

1994 Act of Accession

PART C
TIME-LIMITS FOR TRANSPOSITION INTO NATIONAL LAW AND APPLICATION

(referred to in Article 16)

Directive	*Time-limit for transposition*	*Date of application*
80/987/EEC	23 October 1983	
87/164/EEC		1 January 1986
2002/74/EC	7 October 2005	

ANNEX II
CORRELATION TABLE

[3.585]

Directive 80/987/EEC	*This Directive*
Article 1	Article 1
Article 2	Article 2
Article 3	Article 3
Article 4	Article 4
Article 5	Article 5
Article 6	Article 6
Article 7	Article 7
Article 8	Article 8
Article 8a	Article 9
Article 8b	Article 10
Article 9	Article 11
Article 10	Article 12
Article 10a	Article 13
Article 11(1)	—
Article 11(2)	Article 14
Article 12	—
—	Article 15
—	Article 16
—	Article 17
Article 13	Article 18
—	Annex I
—	Annex II

DIRECTIVE OF THE EUROPEAN PARLIAMENT AND OF THE COUNCIL

(2008/104/EC)

of 19 November 2008

on temporary agency work

NOTES

Date of publication in OJ: OJ L327, 5.12.2008, p 9.

For the domestic implementation of this Directive see the Agency Workers Regulations 2010, SI 2010/93 at **[2.1277]**.

See *Harvey* AI(4).

[3.586]

THE EUROPEAN PARLIAMENT AND THE COUNCIL OF THE EUROPEAN UNION,

Having regard to the Treaty establishing the European Community, and in particular Article 137(2) thereof,

Having regard to the proposal from the Commission,

Having regard to the opinion of the European Economic and Social Committee,[1]

After consulting the Committee of the Regions,

Acting in accordance with the procedure laid down in Article 251 of the Treaty,[2]

Whereas:

(1) This Directive respects the fundamental rights and complies with the principles recognised by the Charter of Fundamental Rights of the European Union.[3] In particular, it is designed to ensure full compliance with Article 31 of the Charter, which provides that every worker has the right to working conditions which respect his or her health, safety and dignity, and to limitation of maximum working hours, to daily and weekly rest periods and to an annual period of paid leave.

(2) The Community Charter of the Fundamental Social Rights of Workers provides, in point 7 thereof, inter alia, that the completion of the internal market must lead to an improvement in the living and working conditions of workers in the European Community; this process will be achieved

by harmonising progress on these conditions, mainly in respect of forms of work such as fixed-term contract work, part-time work, temporary agency work and seasonal work.

(3) On 27 September 1995, the Commission consulted management and labour at Community level in accordance with Article 138(2) of the Treaty on the course of action to be adopted at Community level with regard to flexibility of working hours and job security of workers.

(4) After that consultation, the Commission considered that Community action was advisable and on 9 April 1996, further consulted management and labour in accordance with Article 138(3) of the Treaty on the content of the envisaged proposal.

(5) In the introduction to the framework agreement on fixed-term work concluded on 18 March 1999, the signatories indicated their intention to consider the need for a similar agreement on temporary agency work and decided not to include temporary agency workers in the Directive on fixed-term work.

(6) The general cross-sector organisations, namely the Union of Industrial and Employers' Confederations of Europe (UNICE),[4] the European Centre of Enterprises with Public Participation and of Enterprises of General Economic Interest (CEEP) and the European Trade Union Confederation (ETUC), informed the Commission in a joint letter of 29 May 2000 of their wish to initiate the process provided for in Article 139 of the Treaty. By a further joint letter of 28 February 2001, they asked the Commission to extend the deadline referred to in Article 138(4) by one month. The Commission granted this request and extended the negotiation deadline until 15 March 2001.

(7) On 21 May 2001, the social partners acknowledged that their negotiations on temporary agency work had not produced any agreement.

(8) In March 2005, the European Council considered it vital to relaunch the Lisbon Strategy and to refocus its priorities on growth and employment. The Council approved the Integrated Guidelines for Growth and Jobs 2005–2008, which seek, inter alia, to promote flexibility combined with employment security and to reduce labour market segmentation, having due regard to the role of the social partners.

(9) In accordance with the Communication from the Commission on the Social Agenda covering the period up to 2010, which was welcomed by the March 2005 European Council as a contribution towards achieving the Lisbon Strategy objectives by reinforcing the European social model, the European Council considered that new forms of work organisation and a greater diversity of contractual arrangements for workers and businesses, better combining flexibility with security, would contribute to adaptability. Furthermore, the December 2007 European Council endorsed the agreed common principles of flexicurity, which strike a balance between flexibility and security in the labour market and help both workers and employers to seize the opportunities offered by globalisation.

(10) There are considerable differences in the use of temporary agency work and in the legal situation, status and working conditions of temporary agency workers within the European Union.

(11) Temporary agency work meets not only undertakings' needs for flexibility but also the need of employees to reconcile their working and private lives. It thus contributes to job creation and to participation and integration in the labour market.

(12) This Directive establishes a protective framework for temporary agency workers which is non-discriminatory, transparent and proportionate, while respecting the diversity of labour markets and industrial relations.

(13) Council Directive 91/383/EEC of 25 June 1991 supplementing the measures to encourage improvements in the safety and health at work of workers with a fixed-duration employment relationship or a temporary employment relationship[5] establishes the safety and health provisions applicable to temporary agency workers.

(14) The basic working and employment conditions applicable to temporary agency workers should be at least those which would apply to such workers if they were recruited by the user undertaking to occupy the same job.

(15) Employment contracts of an indefinite duration are the general form of employment relationship. In the case of workers who have a permanent contract with their temporary-work agency, and in view of the special protection such a contract offers, provision should be made to permit exemptions from the rules applicable in the user undertaking.

(16) In order to cope in a flexible way with the diversity of labour markets and industrial relations, Member States may allow the social partners to define working and employment conditions, provided that the overall level of protection for temporary agency workers is respected.

(17) Furthermore, in certain limited circumstances, Member States should, on the basis of an agreement concluded by the social partners at national level, be able to derogate within limits from the principle of equal treatment, so long as an adequate level of protection is provided.

(18) The improvement in the minimum protection for temporary agency workers should be

accompanied by a review of any restrictions or prohibitions which may have been imposed on temporary agency work. These may be justified only on grounds of the general interest regarding, in particular the protection of workers, the requirements of safety and health at work and the need to ensure that the labour market functions properly and that abuses are prevented.

(19) This Directive does not affect the autonomy of the social partners nor should it affect relations between the social partners, including the right to negotiate and conclude collective agreements in accordance with national law and practices while respecting prevailing Community law.

(20) The provisions of this Directive on restrictions or prohibitions on temporary agency work are without prejudice to national legislation or practices that prohibit workers on strike being replaced by temporary agency workers.

(21) Member States should provide for administrative or judicial procedures to safeguard temporary agency workers' rights and should provide for effective, dissuasive and proportionate penalties for breaches of the obligations laid down in this Directive.

(22) This Directive should be implemented in compliance with the provisions of the Treaty regarding the freedom to provide services and the freedom of establishment and without prejudice to Directive 96/71/EC of the European Parliament and of the Council of 16 December 1996 concerning the posting of workers in the framework of the provision of services.[6]

(23) Since the objective of this Directive, namely to establish a harmonised Community-level framework for protection for temporary agency workers, cannot be sufficiently achieved by the Member States and can therefore, by reason of the scale or effects of the action, be better achieved at Community level by introducing minimum requirements applicable throughout the Community, the Community may adopt measures in accordance with the principle of subsidiarity as set out in Article 5 of the Treaty. In accordance with the principle of proportionality, as set out in that Article, this Directive does not go beyond what is necessary in order to achieve that objective,

NOTES

1 OJ 61, 14.3.2003, p 124.

2 Opinion of the European Parliament of 21 November 2002 (OJ C25E, 29.1.2004, p 368), Council Common Position of 15 September 2008 and Position of the European Parliament of 22 October 2008 (not yet published in the Official Journal).

3 OJ C303, 14.12.2007, p 1.

4 UNICE changed its name to BUSINESSEUROPE in January 2007.

5 OJ L206, 29.7.1991, p 19.

6 OJ L18, 21.1.1997, p 1.

HAVE ADOPTED THIS DIRECTIVE:

CHAPTER I
GENERAL PROVISIONS

[3.587]
Article 1
Scope

1. This Directive applies to workers with a contract of employment or employment relationship with a temporary-work agency who are assigned to user undertakings to work temporarily under their supervision and direction.
2. This Directive applies to public and private undertakings which are temporary-work agencies or user undertakings engaged in economic activities whether or not they are operating for gain.
3. Member States may, after consulting the social partners, provide that this Directive does not apply to employment contracts or relationships concluded under a specific public or publicly supported vocational training, integration or retraining programme.

[3.588]
Article 2
Aim

The purpose of this Directive is to ensure the protection of temporary agency workers and to improve the quality of temporary agency work by ensuring that the principle of equal treatment, as set out in Article 5, is applied to temporary agency workers, and by recognising temporary-work agencies as employers, while taking into account the need to establish a suitable framework for the use of temporary agency work with a view to contributing effectively to the creation of jobs and to the development of flexible forms of working.

[3.589]
Article 3
Definitions

1. For the purposes of this Directive:
   (a) "worker" means any person who, in the Member State concerned, is protected as a worker under national employment law;
   (b) "temporary-work agency" means any natural or legal person who, in compliance with national law, concludes contracts of employment or employment relationships with temporary agency workers in order to assign them to user undertakings to work there temporarily under their supervision and direction;
   (c) "temporary agency worker" means a worker with a contract of employment or an employment relationship with a temporary-work agency with a view to being assigned to a user undertaking to work temporarily under its supervision and direction;
   (d) "user undertaking" means any natural or legal person for whom and under the supervision and direction of whom a temporary agency worker works temporarily;
   (e) "assignment" means the period during which the temporary agency worker is placed at the user undertaking to work temporarily under its supervision and direction;
   (f) "basic working and employment conditions" means working and employment conditions laid down by legislation, regulations, administrative provisions, collective agreements and/or other binding general provisions in force in the user undertaking relating to:
      (i) the duration of working time, overtime, breaks, rest periods, night work, holidays and public holidays;
      (ii) pay.

2. This Directive shall be without prejudice to national law as regards the definition of pay, contract of employment, employment relationship or worker.

Member States shall not exclude from the scope of this Directive workers, contracts of employment or employment relationships solely because they relate to part-time workers, fixed-term contract workers or persons with a contract of employment or employment relationship with a temporary-work agency.

[3.590]
Article 4
Review of restrictions or prohibitions

1. Prohibitions or restrictions on the use of temporary agency work shall be justified only on grounds of general interest relating in particular to the protection of temporary agency workers, the requirements of health and safety at work or the need to ensure that the labour market functions properly and abuses are prevented.
2. By 5 December 2011, Member States shall, after consulting the social partners in accordance with national legislation, collective agreements and practices, review any restrictions or prohibitions on the use of temporary agency work in order to verify whether they are justified on the grounds mentioned in paragraph 1.
3. If such restrictions or prohibitions are laid down by collective agreements, the review referred to in paragraph 2 may be carried out by the social partners who have negotiated the relevant agreement.
4. Paragraphs 1, 2 and 3 shall be without prejudice to national requirements with regard to registration, licensing, certification, financial guarantees or monitoring of temporary-work agencies.
5. The Member States shall inform the Commission of the results of the review referred to in paragraphs 2 and 3 by 5 December 2011.

CHAPTER II
EMPLOYMENT AND WORKING CONDITIONS

[3.591]
Article 5
The principle of equal treatment

1. The basic working and employment conditions of temporary agency workers shall be, for the duration of their assignment at a user undertaking, at least those that would apply if they had been recruited directly by that undertaking to occupy the same job.

For the purposes of the application of the first subparagraph, the rules in force in the user undertaking on:
   (a) protection of pregnant women and nursing mothers and protection of children and young people; and
   (b) equal treatment for men and women and any action to combat any discrimination based on sex, race or ethnic origin, religion, beliefs, disabilities, age or sexual orientation;

must be complied with as established by legislation, regulations, administrative provisions, collective agreements and/or any other general provisions.

2. As regards pay, Member States may, after consulting the social partners, provide that an exemption be made to the principle established in paragraph 1 where temporary agency workers who have a permanent contract of employment with a temporary-work agency continue to be paid in the time between assignments.
3. Member States may, after consulting the social partners, give them, at the appropriate level and subject to the conditions laid down by the Member States, the option of upholding or concluding collective agreements which, while respecting the overall protection of temporary agency workers, may establish arrangements concerning the working and employment conditions of temporary agency workers which may differ from those referred to in paragraph 1.
4. Provided that an adequate level of protection is provided for temporary agency workers, Member States in which there is either no system in law for declaring collective agreements universally applicable or no such system in law or practice for extending their provisions to all similar undertakings in a certain sector or geographical area, may, after consulting the social partners at national level and on the basis of an agreement concluded by them, establish arrangements concerning the basic working and employment conditions which derogate from the principle established in paragraph 1. Such arrangements may include a qualifying period for equal treatment.

The arrangements referred to in this paragraph shall be in conformity with Community legislation and shall be sufficiently precise and accessible to allow the sectors and firms concerned to identify and comply with their obligations. In particular, Member States shall specify, in application of Article 3(2), whether occupational social security schemes, including pension, sick pay or financial participation schemes are included in the basic working and employment conditions referred to in paragraph 1. Such arrangements shall also be without prejudice to agreements at national, regional, local or sectoral level that are no less favourable to workers.
5. Member States shall take appropriate measures, in accordance with national law and/or practice, with a view to preventing misuse in the application of this Article and, in particular, to preventing successive assignments designed to circumvent the provisions of this Directive. They shall inform the Commission about such measures.

[3.592]
Article 6
Access to employment, collective facilities and vocational training

1. Temporary agency workers shall be informed of any vacant posts in the user undertaking to give them the same opportunity as other workers in that undertaking to find permanent employment. Such information may be provided by a general announcement in a suitable place in the undertaking for which, and under whose supervision, temporary agency workers are engaged.
2. Member States shall take any action required to ensure that any clauses prohibiting or having the effect of preventing the conclusion of a contract of employment or an employment relationship between the user undertaking and the temporary agency worker after his assignment are null and void or may be declared null and void.

This paragraph is without prejudice to provisions under which temporary agencies receive a reasonable level of recompense for services rendered to user undertakings for the assignment, recruitment and training of temporary agency workers.
3. Temporary-work agencies shall not charge workers any fees in exchange for arranging for them to be recruited by a user undertaking, or for concluding a contract of employment or an employment relationship with a user undertaking after carrying out an assignment in that undertaking.
4. Without prejudice to Article 5(1), temporary agency workers shall be given access to the amenities or collective facilities in the user undertaking, in particular any canteen, child-care facilities and transport services, under the same conditions as workers employed directly by the undertaking, unless the difference in treatment is justified by objective reasons.
5. Member States shall take suitable measures or shall promote dialogue between the social partners, in accordance with their national traditions and practices, in order to:

(a) improve temporary agency workers' access to training and to child-care facilities in the temporary-work agencies, even in the periods between their assignments, in order to enhance their career development and employability;
(b) improve temporary agency workers' access to training for user undertakings' workers.

[3.593]
Article 7
Representation of temporary agency workers

1. Temporary agency workers shall count, under conditions established by the Member States, for the purposes of calculating the threshold above which bodies representing workers provided for under Community and national law and collective agreements are to be formed at the temporary-work agency.

2. Member States may provide that, under conditions that they define, temporary agency workers count for the purposes of calculating the threshold above which bodies representing workers provided for by Community and national law and collective agreements are to be formed in the user undertaking, in the same way as if they were workers employed directly for the same period of time by the user undertaking.
3. Those Member States which avail themselves of the option provided for in paragraph 2 shall not be obliged to implement the provisions of paragraph 1.

[3.594]
Article 8
Information of workers' representatives
Without prejudice to national and Community provisions on information and consultation which are more stringent and/or more specific and, in particular, Directive 2002/14/EC of the European Parliament and of the Council of 11 March 2002 establishing a general framework for informing and consulting employees in the European Community,[1] the user undertaking must provide suitable information on the use of temporary agency workers when providing information on the employment situation in that undertaking to bodies representing workers set up in accordance with national and Community legislation.

NOTES
[1] OJ L80, 23.3.2002, p. 29.

CHAPTER III
FINAL PROVISIONS

[3.595]
Article 9
Minimum requirements
1. This Directive is without prejudice to the Member States' right to apply or introduce legislative, regulatory or administrative provisions which are more favourable to workers or to promote or permit collective agreements concluded between the social partners which are more favourable to workers.
2. The implementation of this Directive shall under no circumstances constitute sufficient grounds for justifying a reduction in the general level of protection of workers in the fields covered by this Directive. This is without prejudice to the rights of Member States and/or management and labour to lay down, in the light of changing circumstances, different legislative, regulatory or contractual arrangements to those prevailing at the time of the adoption of this Directive, provided always that the minimum requirements laid down in this Directive are respected.

[3.596]
Article 10
Penalties
1. Member States shall provide for appropriate measures in the event of non-compliance with this Directive by temporary-work agencies or user undertakings. In particular, they shall ensure that adequate administrative or judicial procedures are available to enable the obligations deriving from this Directive to be enforced.
2. Member States shall lay down rules on penalties applicable in the event of infringements of national provisions implementing this Directive and shall take all necessary measures to ensure that they are applied. The penalties provided for must be effective, proportionate and dissuasive. Member States shall notify these provisions to the Commission by 5 December 2011. Member States shall notify to the Commission any subsequent amendments to those provisions in good time. They shall, in particular, ensure that workers and/or their representatives have adequate means of enforcing the obligations under this Directive.

[3.597]
Article 11
Implementation
1. Member States shall adopt and publish the laws, regulations and administrative provisions necessary to comply with this Directive by 5 December 2011, or shall ensure that the social partners introduce the necessary provisions by way of an agreement, whereby the Member States must make all the necessary arrangements to enable them to guarantee at any time that the objectives of this Directive are being attained. They shall forthwith inform the Commission thereof.
2. When Member States adopt these measures, they shall contain a reference to this Directive or shall be accompanied by such reference on the occasion of their official publication. The methods of making such reference shall be laid down by Member States.

[3.598]
Article 12
Review by the Commission
By 5 December 2013, the Commission shall, in consultation with the Member States and social partners at Community level, review the application of this Directive with a view to proposing, where appropriate, the necessary amendments.

[3.599]
Article 13
Entry into force
This Directive shall enter into force on the day of its publication in the *Official Journal of the European Union.*

[3.600]
Article 14
Addressees
This Directive is addressed to the Member States.

DIRECTIVE OF THE EUROPEAN PARLIAMENT AND OF THE COUNCIL

(2009/38/EC)

of 6 May 2009

on the establishment of a European Works Council or a procedure in Community-scale undertakings and Community-scale groups of undertakings for the purposes of informing and consulting employees

(Recast) (Text with EEA relevance)

NOTES
Date of publication in OJ: OJ L122, 16.05.2009, p 28.
This Directive is a recast replacement of Directive 94/45/EC which was repealed and replaced on 6 June 2011 following the coming into force of this Directive on 5 June 2011: see Art 16(1) at **[3.617]** and Art 17 at **[3.618]**. A Table of Correlations for the previous Directive is at Annex III (at **[3.624]**).
For the domestic implementation of this Directive see the Transnational Information and Consultation of Employees Regulations 1999, SI 1999/3323 (as amended to implement this Directive) at **[2.509]**.
See *Harvey* NIII(3).

[3.601]
THE EUROPEAN PARLIAMENT AND THE COUNCIL OF THE EUROPEAN UNION,
Having regard to the Treaty establishing the European Community, and in particular Article 137 thereof,
Having regard to the proposal from the Commission,
Having regard to the opinion of the European Economic and Social Committee,[1]
Having consulted the Committee of the Regions,
Acting in accordance with the procedure referred to in Article 251 of the Treaty,[2]
Whereas:

(1) A number of substantive changes are to be made to Council Directive 94/45/EC of 22 September 1994 on the establishment of a European Works Council or a procedure in Community-scale undertakings and Community-scale groups of undertakings for the purposes of informing and consulting employees.[3] In the interests of clarity, that Directive should be recast.

(2) Pursuant to Article 15 of Directive 94/45/EC, the Commission has, in consultation with the Member States and with management and labour at European level, reviewed the operation of that Directive and, in particular, examined whether the workforce size thresholds are appropriate, with a view to proposing suitable amendments where necessary.

(3) Having consulted the Member States and management and labour at European level, the Commission submitted, on 4 April 2000, a report on the application of Directive 94/45/EC to the European Parliament and to the Council.

(4) Pursuant to Article 138(2) of the Treaty, the Commission consulted management and labour at Community level on the possible direction of Community action in this area.

(5) Following this consultation, the Commission considered that Community action was advisable and again consulted management and labour at Community level on the content of the planned proposal, pursuant to Article 138(3) of the Treaty.

(6) Following this second phase of consultation, management and labour have not informed

the Commission of their shared wish to initiate the process which might lead to the conclusion of an agreement, as provided for in Article 138(4) of the Treaty.

(7) It is necessary to modernise Community legislation on transnational information and consultation of employees with a view to ensuring the effectiveness of employees' transnational information and consultation rights, increasing the proportion of European Works Councils established while enabling the continuous functioning of existing agreements, resolving the problems encountered in the practical application of Directive 94/45/EC and remedying the lack of legal certainty resulting from some of its provisions or the absence of certain provisions, and ensuring that Community legislative instruments on information and consultation of employees are better linked.

(8) Pursuant to Article 136 of the Treaty, one particular objective of the Community and the Member States is to promote dialogue between management and labour.

(9) This Directive is part of the Community framework intended to support and complement the action taken by Member States in the field of information and consultation of employees. This framework should keep to a minimum the burden on undertakings or establishments while ensuring the effective exercise of the rights granted.

(10) The functioning of the internal market involves a process of concentrations of undertakings, cross-border mergers, take-overs, joint ventures and, consequently, a transnationalisation of undertakings and groups of undertakings. If economic activities are to develop in a harmonious fashion, undertakings and groups of undertakings operating in two or more Member States must inform and consult the representatives of those of their employees who are affected by their decisions.

(11) Procedures for informing and consulting employees as embodied in legislation or practice in the Member States are often not geared to the transnational structure of the entity which takes the decisions affecting those employees. This may lead to the unequal treatment of employees affected by decisions within one and the same undertaking or group of undertakings.

(12) Appropriate provisions must be adopted to ensure that the employees of Community-scale undertakings or Community-scale groups of undertakings are properly informed and consulted when decisions which affect them are taken in a Member State other than that in which they are employed.

(13) In order to guarantee that the employees of undertakings or groups of undertakings operating in two or more Member States are properly informed and consulted, it is necessary to set up European Works Councils or to create other suitable procedures for the transnational information and consultation of employees.

(14) The arrangements for informing and consulting employees need to be defined and implemented in such a way as to ensure their effectiveness with regard to the provisions of this Directive. To that end, informing and consulting the European Works Council should make it possible for it to give an opinion to the undertaking in a timely fashion, without calling into question the ability of undertakings to adapt. Only dialogue at the level where directions are prepared and effective involvement of employees' representatives make it possible to anticipate and manage change.

(15) Workers and their representatives must be guaranteed information and consultation at the relevant level of management and representation, according to the subject under discussion. To achieve this, the competence and scope of action of a European Works Council must be distinct from that of national representative bodies and must be limited to transnational matters.

(16) The transnational character of a matter should be determined by taking account of both the scope of its potential effects, and the level of management and representation that it involves. For this purpose, matters which concern the entire undertaking or group or at least two Member States are considered to be transnational. These include matters which, regardless of the number of Member States involved, are of importance for the European workforce in terms of the scope of their potential effects or which involve transfers of activities between Member States.

(17) It is necessary to have a definition of "controlling undertaking" relating solely to this Directive, without prejudice to the definitions of "group" or "control" in other acts.

(18) The mechanisms for informing and consulting employees in undertakings or groups of undertakings operating in two or more Member States must encompass all of the establishments or, as the case may be, the group's undertakings located within the Member States, regardless of whether the undertaking or the group's controlling undertaking has its central management inside or outside the territory of the Member States.

(19) In accordance with the principle of autonomy of the parties, it is for the representatives of employees and the management of the undertaking or the group's controlling undertaking to determine by agreement the nature, composition, the function, mode of operation, procedures and financial resources of European Works Councils or other information and consultation procedures so as to suit their own particular circumstances.

(20) In accordance with the principle of subsidiarity, it is for the Member States to determine who the employees' representatives are and in particular to provide, if they consider appropriate, for a balanced representation of different categories of employees.

(21) It is necessary to clarify the concepts of information and consultation of employees, in accordance with the definitions in the most recent Directives on this subject and those which apply within a national framework, with the objectives of reinforcing the effectiveness of dialogue at transnational level, permitting suitable linkage between the national and transnational levels of dialogue and ensuring the legal certainty required for the application of this Directive.

(22) The definition of "information" needs to take account of the goal of allowing employees representatives to carry out an appropriate examination, which implies that the information be provided at such time, in such fashion and with such content as are appropriate without slowing down the decision-making process in undertakings.

(23) The definition of "consultation" needs to take account of the goal of allowing for the expression of an opinion which will be useful to the decision-making process, which implies that the consultation must take place at such time, in such fashion and with such content as are appropriate.

(24) The information and consultation provisions laid down in this Directive must be implemented in the case of an undertaking or a group's controlling undertaking which has its central management outside the territory of the Member States by its representative agent, to be designated if necessary, in one of the Member States or, in the absence of such an agent, by the establishment or controlled undertaking employing the greatest number of employees in the Member States.

(25) The responsibility of undertakings or groups of undertakings in the transmission of the information required to commence negotiations must be specified in a way that enables employees to determine whether the undertaking or group of undertakings where they work is a Community-scale undertaking or group of undertakings and to make the necessary contacts to draw up a request to commence negotiations.

(26) The special negotiating body must represent employees from the various Member States in a balanced fashion. Employees' representatives must be able to cooperate to define their positions in relation to negotiations with the central management.

(27) Recognition must be given to the role that recognised trade union organisations can play in negotiating and renegotiating the constituent agreements of European Works Councils, providing support to employees' representatives who express a need for such support. In order to enable them to monitor the establishment of new European Works Councils and promote best practice, competent trade union and employers' organisations recognised as European social partners shall be informed of the commencement of negotiations. Recognised competent European trade union and employers' organisations are those social partner organisations that are consulted by the Commission under Article 138 of the Treaty. The list of those organisations is updated and published by the Commission.

(28) The agreements governing the establishment and operation of European Works Councils must include the methods for modifying, terminating, or renegotiating them when necessary, particularly where the make-up or structure of the undertaking or group of undertakings is modified.

(29) Such agreements must lay down the arrangements for linking the national and transnational levels of information and consultation of employees appropriate for the particular conditions of the undertaking or group of undertakings. The arrangements must be defined in such a way that they respect the competences and areas of action of the employee representation bodies, in particular with regard to anticipating and managing change.

(30) Those agreements must provide, where necessary, for the establishment and operation of a select committee in order to permit coordination and greater effectiveness of the regular activities of the European Works Council, together with information and consultation at the earliest opportunity where exceptional circumstances arise.

(31) Employees' representatives may decide not to seek the setting-up of a European Works Council or the parties concerned may decide on other procedures for the transnational information and consultation of employees.

(32) Provision should be made for certain subsidiary requirements to apply should the parties so decide or in the event of the central management refusing to initiate negotiations or in the absence of agreement subsequent to such negotiations.

(33) In order to perform their representative role fully and to ensure that the European Works Council is useful, employees' representatives must report to the employees whom they represent and must be able to receive the training they require.

(34) Provision should be made for the employees' representatives acting within the framework of this Directive to enjoy, when exercising their functions, the same protection and guarantees as those provided to employees' representatives by the legislation and/or practice of the country of employment. They must not be subject to any discrimination as a result of the lawful exercise of their

activities and must enjoy adequate protection as regards dismissal and other sanctions.

(35) The Member States must take appropriate measures in the event of failure to comply with the obligations laid down in this Directive.

(36) In accordance with the general principles of Community law, administrative or judicial procedures, as well as sanctions that are effective, dissuasive and proportionate in relation to the seriousness of the offence, should be applicable in cases of infringement of the obligations arising from this Directive.

(37) For reasons of effectiveness, consistency and legal certainty, there is a need for linkage between the Directives and the levels of informing and consulting employees established by Community and national law and/or practice. Priority must be given to negotiations on these procedures for linking information within each undertaking or group of undertakings. If there are no agreements on this subject and where decisions likely to lead to substantial changes in work organisation or contractual relations are envisaged, the process must be conducted at both national and European level in such a way that it respects the competences and areas of action of the employee representation bodies. Opinions expressed by the European Works Council should be without prejudice to the competence of the central management to carry out the necessary consultations in accordance with the schedules provided for in national legislation and/or practice. National legislation and/or practice may have to be adapted to ensure that the European Works Council can, where applicable, receive information earlier or at the same time as the national employee representation bodies, but must not reduce the general level of protection of employees.

(38) This Directive should be without prejudice to the information and consultation procedures referred to in Directive 2002/14/EC of the European Parliament and of the Council of 11 March 2002 establishing a general framework for informing and consulting employees in the European Community[4] and to the specific procedures referred to in Article 2 of Council Directive 98/59/EC of 20 July 1998 on the approximation of the laws of the Member States relating to collective redundancies[5] and Article 7 of Council Directive 2001/23/EC of 12 March 2001 on the approximation of the laws of the Member States relating to the safeguarding of employees' rights in the event of transfers of undertakings, businesses or parts of undertakings or businesses.[6]

(39) Special treatment should be accorded to Community-scale undertakings and groups of undertakings in which there existed, on 22 September 1996, an agreement, covering the entire workforce, providing for the transnational information and consultation of employees.

(40) Where the structure of the undertaking or group of undertakings changes significantly, for example, due to a merger, acquisition or division, the existing European Works Council(s) must be adapted. This adaptation must be carried out as a priority pursuant to the clauses of the applicable agreement, if such clauses permit the required adaptation to be carried out. If this is not the case and a request establishing the need is made, negotiations, in which the members of the existing European Works Council(s) must be involved, will commence on a new agreement. In order to permit the information and consultation of employees during the often decisive period when the structure is changed, the existing European Works Council(s) must be able to continue to operate, possibly with adaptations, until a new agreement is concluded. Once a new agreement is signed, the previously established councils must be dissolved, and the agreements instituting them must be terminated, regardless of their provisions on validity or termination.

(41) Unless this adaptation clause is applied, the agreements in force should be allowed to continue in order to avoid their obligatory renegotiation when this would be unnecessary. Provision should be made so that, as long as agreements concluded prior to 22 September 1996 under Article 13(1) of Directive 94/45/EC or under Article 3(1) of Directive 97/74/EC[7] remain in force, the obligations arising from this Directive should not apply to them. Furthermore, this Directive does not establish a general obligation to renegotiate agreements concluded pursuant to Article 6 of Directive 94/45/EC between 22 September 1996 and 5 June 2011.

(42) Without prejudice to the possibility of the parties to decide otherwise, a European Works Council set up in the absence of agreement between the parties must, in order to fulfil the objective of this Directive, be kept informed and consulted on the activities of the undertaking or group of undertakings so that it may assess the possible impact on employees' interests in at least two different Member States. To that end, the undertaking or controlling undertaking must be required to communicate to the employees' appointed representatives general information concerning the interests of employees and information relating more specifically to those aspects of the activities of the undertaking or group of undertakings which affect employees' interests. The European Works Council must be able to deliver an opinion at the end of the meeting.

(43) Certain decisions having a significant effect on the interests of employees must be the subject of information and consultation of the employees' appointed representatives as soon as possible.

(44) The content of the subsidiary requirements which apply in the absence of an agreement and serve as a reference in the negotiations must be clarified and adapted to developments in the needs and practices relating to transnational information and consultation. A distinction should be made

between fields where information must be provided and fields where the European Works Council must also be consulted, which involves the possibility of obtaining a reasoned response to any opinions expressed. To enable the select committee to play the necessary coordinating role and to deal effectively with exceptional circumstances, that committee must be able to have up to five members and be able to consult regularly.

(45) Since the objective of this Directive, namely the improvement of the right to information and to consultation of employees in Community-scale undertakings and Community-scale groups of undertakings, cannot be sufficiently achieved by the Member States and can therefore be better achieved at Community level, the Community may adopt measures, in accordance with the principle of subsidiarity as set out in Article 5 of the Treaty. In accordance with the principle of proportionality as set out in that Article, this Directive does not go beyond what is necessary in order to achieve that objective.

(46) This Directive respects fundamental rights and observes in particular the principles recognised by the Charter of Fundamental Rights of the European Union. In particular, this Directive seeks to ensure full respect for the right of workers or their representatives to be guaranteed information and consultation in good time at the appropriate levels in the cases and under the conditions provided for by Community law and national laws and practices (Article 27 of the Charter of Fundamental Rights of the European Union).

(47) The obligation to transpose this Directive into national law should be confined to those provisions which represent a substantive change as compared with the earlier Directives. The obligation to transpose the provisions which are unchanged arises under the earlier Directives.

(48) In accordance with point 34 of the Interinstitutional Agreement on better law-making,[8] Member States are encouraged to draw up, for themselves and in the interests of the Community, tables illustrating, as far as possible, the correlation between this Directive and the transposition measures, and to make them public.

(49) This Directive should be without prejudice to the obligations of the Member States relating to the time limits set out in Annex II, Part B for transposition into national law and application of the Directives,

NOTES

1 Opinion of 4 December 2008 (not yet published in the Official Journal).

2 Opinion of the European Parliament of 16 December 2008 (not yet published in the Official Journal) and Council Decision of 17 December 2008.

3 OJ L254, 30.9.1994, p 64.

4 OJ L80, 23.3.2002, p 29.

5 OJ L225, 12.8.1998, p 16.

6 OJ L82, 22.3.2001, p 16.

7 Council Directive 97/74/EC of 15 December 1997 extending, to the United Kingdom of Great Britain and Northern Ireland, Directive 94/45/EC on the establishment of a European Works Council or a procedure in Community-scale undertakings and Community-scale groups of undertakings for the purposes of informing and consulting employees (OJ L10, 16.1.1998, p 22).

8 OJ C321, 31.12.2003, p 1.

HAVE ADOPTED THIS DIRECTIVE:

SECTION I
GENERAL

[3.602]
Article 1
Objective

1. The purpose of this Directive is to improve the right to information and to consultation of employees in Community-scale undertakings and Community-scale groups of undertakings.

2. To that end, a European Works Council or a procedure for informing and consulting employees shall be established in every Community-scale undertaking and every Community-scale group of undertakings, where requested in the manner laid down in Article 5(1), with the purpose of informing and consulting employees. The arrangements for informing and consulting employees shall be defined and implemented in such a way as to ensure their effectiveness and to enable the undertaking or group of undertakings to take decisions effectively.

3. Information and consultation of employees must occur at the relevant level of management and representation, according to the subject under discussion. To achieve that, the competence of the European Works Council and the scope of the information and consultation procedure for employees governed by this Directive shall be limited to transnational issues.

4. Matters shall be considered to be transnational where they concern the Community-scale undertaking or Community-scale group of undertakings as a whole, or at least two undertakings or establishments of the undertaking or group situated in two different Member States.
5. Notwithstanding paragraph 2, where a Community-scale group of undertakings within the meaning of Article 2(1)(c) comprises one or more undertakings or groups of undertakings which are Community-scale undertakings or Community-scale groups of undertakings within the meaning of Article 2(1)(a) or (c), a European Works Council shall be established at the level of the group unless the agreements referred to in Article 6 provide otherwise.
6. Unless a wider scope is provided for in the agreements referred to in Article 6, the powers and competence of European Works Councils and the scope of information and consultation procedures established to achieve the purpose specified in paragraph 1 shall, in the case of a Community-scale undertaking, cover all the establishments located within the Member States and, in the case of a Community-scale group of undertakings, all group undertakings located within the Member States.
7. Member States may provide that this Directive shall not apply to merchant navy crews.

[3.603]
Article 2
Definitions
1. For the purposes of this Directive:
- (a) "Community-scale undertaking" means any undertaking with at least 1000 employees within the Member States and at least 150 employees in each of at least two Member States;
- (b) "group of undertakings" means a controlling undertaking and its controlled undertakings;
- (c) "Community-scale group of undertakings" means a group of undertakings with the following characteristics:
  - — at least 1000 employees within the Member States,
  - — at least two group undertakings in different Member States, and
  - — at least one group undertaking with at least 150 employees in one Member State and at least one other group undertaking with at least 150 employees in another Member State;
- (d) "employees' representatives" means the employees' representatives provided for by national law and/or practice;
- (e) "central management" means the central management of the Community-scale undertaking or, in the case of a Community-scale group of undertakings, of the controlling undertaking;
- (f) "information" means transmission of data by the employer to the employees' representatives in order to enable them to acquaint themselves with the subject matter and to examine it; information shall be given at such time, in such fashion and with such content as are appropriate to enable employees' representatives to undertake an in-depth assessment of the possible impact and, where appropriate, prepare for consultations with the competent organ of the Community-scale undertaking or Community-scale group of undertakings;
- (g) "consultation" means the establishment of dialogue and exchange of views between employees' representatives and central management or any more appropriate level of management, at such time, in such fashion and with such content as enables employees' representatives to express an opinion on the basis of the information provided about the proposed measures to which the consultation is related, without prejudice to the responsibilities of the management, and within a reasonable time, which may be taken into account within the Community-scale undertaking or Community-scale group of undertakings;
- (h) "European Works Council" means a council established in accordance with Article 1(2) or the provisions of Annex I, with the purpose of informing and consulting employees;
- (i) "special negotiating body" means the body established in accordance with Article 5(2) to negotiate with the central management regarding the establishment of a European Works Council or a procedure for informing and consulting employees in accordance with Article 1(2).

2. For the purposes of this Directive, the prescribed thresholds for the size of the workforce shall be based on the average number of employees, including part-time employees, employed during the previous two years calculated according to national legislation and/or practice.

[3.604]
Article 3
Definition of "controlling undertaking"
1. For the purposes of this Directive, "controlling undertaking" means an undertaking which can exercise a dominant influence over another undertaking (the controlled undertaking) by virtue, for example, of ownership, financial participation or the rules which govern it.
2. The ability to exercise a dominant influence shall be presumed, without prejudice to proof to the contrary, when an undertaking, in relation to another undertaking directly or indirectly:

(a) holds a majority of that undertaking's subscribed capital;
(b) controls a majority of the votes attached to that undertaking's issued share capital; or
(c) can appoint more than half of the members of that undertaking's administrative, management or supervisory body.

3. For the purposes of paragraph 2, a controlling undertaking's rights as regards voting and appointment shall include the rights of any other controlled undertaking and those of any person or body acting in his or its own name but on behalf of the controlling undertaking or of any other controlled undertaking.

4. Notwithstanding paragraphs 1 and 2, an undertaking shall not be deemed to be a "controlling undertaking" with respect to another undertaking in which it has holdings where the former undertaking is a company referred to in Article 3(5)(a) or (c) of Council Regulation (EC) No 139/2004 of 20 January 2004 on the control of concentrations between undertakings.[1]

5. A dominant influence shall not be presumed to be exercised solely by virtue of the fact that an office holder is exercising his functions, according to the law of a Member State relating to liquidation, winding up, insolvency, cessation of payments, compositions or analogous proceedings.

6. The law applicable in order to determine whether an undertaking is a controlling undertaking shall be the law of the Member State which governs that undertaking.

Where the law governing that undertaking is not that of a Member State, the law applicable shall be the law of the Member State within whose territory the representative of the undertaking or, in the absence of such a representative, the central management of the group undertaking which employs the greatest number of employees is situated.

7. Where, in the case of a conflict of laws in the application of paragraph 2, two or more undertakings from a group satisfy one or more of the criteria laid down in that paragraph, the undertaking which satisfies the criterion laid down in point (c) thereof shall be regarded as the controlling undertaking, without prejudice to proof that another undertaking is able to exercise a dominant influence.

NOTES

[1] OJ L24, 29.1.2004, p 1.

SECTION II
ESTABLISHMENT OF A EUROPEAN WORKS COUNCIL OR AN EMPLOYEE INFORMATION AND CONSULTATION PROCEDURE

[3.605]
Article 4
Responsibility for the establishment of a European Works Council or an employee information and consultation procedure

1. The central management shall be responsible for creating the conditions and means necessary for the setting-up of a European Works Council or an information and consultation procedure, as provided for in Article 1(2), in a Community-scale undertaking and a Community-scale group of undertakings.

2. Where the central management is not situated in a Member State, the central management's representative agent in a Member State, to be designated if necessary, shall take on the responsibility referred to in paragraph 1.

In the absence of such a representative, the management of the establishment or group undertaking employing the greatest number of employees in any one Member State shall take on the responsibility referred to in paragraph 1.

3. For the purposes of this Directive, the representative or representatives or, in the absence of any such representatives, the management referred to in the second subparagraph of paragraph 2, shall be regarded as the central management.

4. The management of every undertaking belonging to the Community-scale group of undertakings and the central management or the deemed central management within the meaning of the second subparagraph of paragraph 2 of the Community-scale undertaking or group of undertakings shall be responsible for obtaining and transmitting to the parties concerned by the application of this Directive the information required for commencing the negotiations referred to in Article 5, and in particular the information concerning the structure of the undertaking or the group and its workforce. This obligation shall relate in particular to the information on the number of employees referred to in Article 2(1)(a) and (c).

[3.606]
Article 5
Special negotiating body

1. In order to achieve the objective set out in Article 1(1), the central management shall initiate negotiations for the establishment of a European Works Council or an information and consultation procedure on its own initiative or at the written request of at least 100 employees or their representatives in at least two undertakings or establishments in at least two different Member States.

2. For this purpose, a special negotiating body shall be established in accordance with the following guidelines:

(a) The Member States shall determine the method to be used for the election or appointment of the members of the special negotiating body who are to be elected or appointed in their territories.

Member States shall provide that employees in undertakings and/or establishments in which there are no employees' representatives through no fault of their own, have the right to elect or appoint members of the special negotiating body.

The second subparagraph shall be without prejudice to national legislation and/or practice laying down thresholds for the establishment of employee representation bodies.

(b) The members of the special negotiating body shall be elected or appointed in proportion to the number of employees employed in each Member State by the Community-scale undertaking or Community-scale group of undertakings, by allocating in respect of each Member State one seat per portion of employees employed in that Member State amounting to 10%, or a fraction thereof, of the number of employees employed in all the Member States taken together;

(c) The central management and local management and the competent European workers' and employers' organisations shall be informed of the composition of the special negotiating body and of the start of the negotiations.

3. The special negotiating body shall have the task of determining, with the central management, by written agreement, the scope, composition, functions, and term of office of the European Works Council(s) or the arrangements for implementing a procedure for the information and consultation of employees.

4. With a view to the conclusion of an agreement in accordance with Article 6, the central management shall convene a meeting with the special negotiating body. It shall inform the local managements accordingly.

Before and after any meeting with the central management, the special negotiating body shall be entitled to meet without representatives of the central management being present, using any necessary means for communication.

For the purpose of the negotiations, the special negotiating body may request assistance from experts of its choice which can include representatives of competent recognised Community-level trade union organisations. Such experts and such trade union representatives may be present at negotiation meetings in an advisory capacity at the request of the special negotiating body.

5. The special negotiating body may decide, by at least two-thirds of the votes, not to open negotiations in accordance with paragraph 4, or to terminate the negotiations already opened.

Such a decision shall stop the procedure to conclude the agreement referred to in Article 6. Where such a decision has been taken, the provisions in Annex I shall not apply.

A new request to convene the special negotiating body may be made at the earliest two years after the abovementioned decision unless the parties concerned lay down a shorter period.

6. Any expenses relating to the negotiations referred to in paragraphs 3 and 4 shall be borne by the central management so as to enable the special negotiating body to carry out its task in an appropriate manner.

In compliance with this principle, Member States may lay down budgetary rules regarding the operation of the special negotiating body. They may in particular limit the funding to cover one expert only.

[3.607]
Article 6
Content of the agreement

1. The central management and the special negotiating body must negotiate in a spirit of cooperation with a view to reaching an agreement on the detailed arrangements for implementing the information and consultation of employees provided for in Article 1(1).

2. Without prejudice to the autonomy of the parties, the agreement referred to in paragraph 1 and effected in writing between the central management and the special negotiating body shall determine:

(a) the undertakings of the Community-scale group of undertakings or the establishments of the Community-scale undertaking which are covered by the agreement;

(b) the composition of the European Works Council, the number of members, the allocation of seats, taking into account where possible the need for balanced representation of employees with regard to their activities, category and gender, and the term of office;
(c) the functions and the procedure for information and consultation of the European Works Council and the arrangements for linking information and consultation of the European Works Council and national employee representation bodies, in accordance with the principles set out in Article 1(3);
(d) the venue, frequency and duration of meetings of the European Works Council;
(e) where necessary, the composition, the appointment procedure, the functions and the procedural rules of the select committee set up within the European Works Council;
(f) the financial and material resources to be allocated to the European Works Council;
(g) the date of entry into force of the agreement and its duration, the arrangements for amending or terminating the agreement and the cases in which the agreement shall be renegotiated and the procedure for its renegotiation, including, where necessary, where the structure of the Community-scale undertaking or Community-scale group of undertakings changes.

3. The central management and the special negotiating body may decide, in writing, to establish one or more information and consultation procedures instead of a European Works Council.

The agreement must stipulate by what method the employees' representatives shall have the right to meet to discuss the information conveyed to them.

This information shall relate in particular to transnational questions which significantly affect workers' interests.

4. The agreements referred to in paragraphs 2 and 3 shall not, unless provision is made otherwise therein, be subject to the subsidiary requirements of Annex I.

5. For the purposes of concluding the agreements referred to in paragraphs 2 and 3, the special negotiating body shall act by a majority of its members.

[3.608]
Article 7
Subsidiary requirements

1. In order to achieve the objective set out in Article 1(1), the subsidiary requirements laid down by the legislation of the Member State in which the central management is situated shall apply:
— where the central management and the special negotiating body so decide,
— where the central management refuses to commence negotiations within six months of the request referred to in Article 5(1), or
— where, after three years from the date of this request, they are unable to conclude an agreement as laid down in Article 6 and the special negotiating body has not taken the decision provided for in Article 5(5).

2. The subsidiary requirements referred to in paragraph 1 as adopted in the legislation of the Member States must satisfy the provisions set out in Annex I.

SECTION III
MISCELLANEOUS PROVISIONS

[3.609]
Article 8
Confidential information

1. Member States shall provide that members of special negotiating bodies or of European Works Councils and any experts who assist them are not authorised to reveal any information which has expressly been provided to them in confidence.

The same shall apply to employees' representatives in the framework of an information and consultation procedure.

That obligation shall continue to apply, wherever the persons referred to in the first and second subparagraphs are, even after the expiry of their terms of office.

2. Each Member State shall provide, in specific cases and under the conditions and limits laid down by national legislation, that the central management situated in its territory is not obliged to transmit information when its nature is such that, according to objective criteria, it would seriously harm the functioning of the undertakings concerned or would be prejudicial to them.

A Member State may make such dispensation subject to prior administrative or judicial authorisation.

3. Each Member State may lay down particular provisions for the central management of undertakings in its territory which pursue directly and essentially the aim of ideological guidance with respect to information and the expression of opinions, on condition that, at the date of adoption of this Directive such particular provisions already exist in the national legislation.

[3.610]
Article 9
Operation of the European Works Council and the information and consultation procedure for workers

The central management and the European Works Council shall work in a spirit of cooperation with due regard to their reciprocal rights and obligations.

The same shall apply to cooperation between the central management and employees' representatives in the framework of an information and consultation procedure for workers.

[3.611]
Article 10
Role and protection of employees' representatives

1. Without prejudice to the competence of other bodies or organisations in this respect, the members of the European Works Council shall have the means required to apply the rights arising from this Directive, to represent collectively the interests of the employees of the Community-scale undertaking or Community-scale group of undertakings.

2. Without prejudice to Article 8, the members of the European Works Council shall inform the representatives of the employees of the establishments or of the undertakings of a Community-scale group of undertakings or, in the absence of representatives, the workforce as a whole, of the content and outcome of the information and consultation procedure carried out in accordance with this Directive.

3. Members of special negotiating bodies, members of European Works Councils and employees' representatives exercising their functions under the procedure referred to in Article 6(3) shall, in the exercise of their functions, enjoy protection and guarantees similar to those provided for employees' representatives by the national legislation and/or practice in force in their country of employment.

This shall apply in particular to attendance at meetings of special negotiating bodies or European Works Councils or any other meetings within the framework of the agreement referred to in Article 6(3), and the payment of wages for members who are on the staff of the Community-scale undertaking or the Community-scale group of undertakings for the period of absence necessary for the performance of their duties.

4. In so far as this is necessary for the exercise of their representative duties in an international environment, the members of the special negotiating body and of the European Works Council shall be provided with training without loss of wages.

[3.612]
Article 11
Compliance with this Directive

1. Each Member State shall ensure that the management of establishments of a Community-scale undertaking and the management of undertakings which form part of a Community-scale group of undertakings which are situated within its territory and their employees' representatives or, as the case may be, employees abide by the obligations laid down by this Directive, regardless of whether or not the central management is situated within its territory.

2. Member States shall provide for appropriate measures in the event of failure to comply with this Directive; in particular, they shall ensure that adequate administrative or judicial procedures are available to enable the obligations deriving from this Directive to be enforced.

3. Where Member States apply Article 8, they shall make provision for administrative or judicial appeal procedures which the employees' representatives may initiate when the central management requires confidentiality or does not give information in accordance with that Article.

Such procedures may include procedures designed to protect the confidentiality of the information in question.

[3.613]
Article 12
Relationship with other Community and national provisions

1. Information and consultation of the European Works Council shall be linked to those of the national employee representation bodies, with due regard to the competences and areas of action of each and to the principles set out in Article 1(3).

2. The arrangements for the links between the information and consultation of the European Works Council and national employee representation bodies shall be established by the agreement referred to in Article 6. That agreement shall be without prejudice to the provisions of national law and/or practice on the information and consultation of employees.

3. Where no such arrangements have been defined by agreement, the Member States shall ensure that the processes of informing and consulting are conducted in the European Works Council as well as in the national employee representation bodies in cases where decisions likely to lead to substantial changes in work organisation or contractual relations are envisaged.

4. This Directive shall be without prejudice to the information and consultation procedures referred to in Directive 2002/14/EC and to the specific procedures referred to in Article 2 of Directive 98/59/EC and Article 7 of Directive 2001/23/EC.
5. Implementation of this Directive shall not be sufficient grounds for any regression in relation to the situation which already prevails in each Member State and in relation to the general level of protection of workers in the areas to which it applies.

[3.614]
Article 13
Adaptation

Where the structure of the Community-scale undertaking or Community-scale group of undertakings changes significantly, and either in the absence of provisions established by the agreements in force or in the event of conflicts between the relevant provisions of two or more applicable agreements, the central management shall initiate the negotiations referred to in Article 5 on its own initiative or at the written request of at least 100 employees or their representatives in at least two undertakings or establishments in at least two different Member States.

At least three members of the existing European Works Council or of each of the existing European Works Councils shall be members of the special negotiating body, in addition to the members elected or appointed pursuant to Article 5(2).

During the negotiations, the existing European Works Council(s) shall continue to operate in accordance with any arrangements adapted by agreement between the members of the European Works Council(s) and the central management.

[3.615]
Article 14
Agreements in force

1. Without prejudice to Article 13, the obligations arising from this Directive shall not apply to Community-scale undertakings or Community-scale groups of undertakings in which, either
   (a) an agreement or agreements covering the entire workforce, providing for the transnational information and consultation of employees have been concluded pursuant to Article 13(1) of Directive 94/45/EC or Article 3(1) of Directive 97/74/EC, or where such agreements are adjusted because of changes in the structure of the undertakings or groups of undertakings; or
   (b) an agreement concluded pursuant to Article 6 of Directive 94/45/EC is signed or revised between 5 June 2009 and 5 June 2011.

The national law applicable when the agreement is signed or revised shall continue to apply to the undertakings or groups of undertakings referred to in point (b) of the first subparagraph.

2. Upon expiry of the agreements referred to in paragraph 1, the parties to those agreements may decide jointly to renew or revise them. Where this is not the case, the provisions of this Directive shall apply.

[3.616]
Article 15
Report

No later than 5 June 2016, the Commission shall report to the European Parliament, the Council and the European Economic and Social Committee on the implementation of this Directive, making appropriate proposals where necessary.

[3.617]
Article 16
Transposition

1. Member States shall bring into force the laws, regulations and administrative provisions necessary to comply with Article 1(2), (3) and (4), Article 2(1), points (f) and (g), Articles 3(4), Article 4(4), Article 5(2), points (b) and (c), Article 5(4), Article 6(2), points (b), (c), (e) and (g), and Articles 10, 12, 13 and 14, as well as Annex I, point 1(a), (c) and (d) and points 2 and 3, no later than 5 June 2011 or shall ensure that management and labour introduce on that date the required provisions by way of agreement, the Member States being obliged to take all necessary steps enabling them at all times to guarantee the results imposed by this Directive.

When Member States adopt those provisions, they shall contain a reference to this Directive or be accompanied by such a reference on the occasion of their official publication. They shall also include a statement that references in existing laws, regulations and administrative provisions to the directive repealed by this Directive shall be construed as references to this Directive. Member States shall determine how such reference is to be made and how that statement is to be formulated.

2. Member States shall communicate to the Commission the text of the main provisions of national law which they adopt in the field covered by this Directive.

[3.618]
Article 17
Repeal
Directive 94/45/EC, as amended by the Directives listed in Annex II, Part A, is repealed with effect from 6 June 2011 without prejudice to the obligations of the Member States relating to the time limit for transposition into national law of the Directives set out in Annex II, Part B.

References to the repealed Directive shall be construed as references to this Directive and shall be read in accordance with the correlation table in Annex III.

[3.619]
Article 18
Entry into force
This Directive shall enter into force on the 20th day following its publication in the *Official Journal of the European Union.*

Article 1(1), (5), (6) and (7), Article 2(1), points (a) to (e), (h) and (i), Article 2(2), Articles 3(1), (2), (3), (5), (6) and (7), Article 4(1), (2) and (3), Article 5(1), (3), (5) and (6), Article 5(2), point (a), Article 6(1), Article 6(2), points (a), (d) and (f), and Article 6(3), (4) and (5), and Articles 7, 8, 9 and 11, as well as Annex I, point 1(b), (e) and (f), and points 4, 5 and 6, shall apply from 6 June 2011.

[3.620]
Article 19
Addressees
This Directive is addressed to the Member States.

ANNEX I
SUBSIDIARY REQUIREMENTS (REFERRED TO IN ARTICLE 7)

[3.621]
1. In order to achieve the objective set out in Article 1(1) and in the cases provided for in Article 7(1), the establishment, composition and competence of a European Works Council shall be governed by the following rules:

(a) The competence of the European Works Council shall be determined in accordance with Article 1(3).
The information of the European Works Council shall relate in particular to the structure, economic and financial situation, probable development and production and sales of the Community-scale undertaking or group of undertakings. The information and consultation of the European Works Council shall relate in particular to the situation and probable trend of employment, investments, and substantial changes concerning organisation, introduction of new working methods or production processes, transfers of production, mergers, cut-backs or closures of undertakings, establishments or important parts thereof, and collective redundancies.
The consultation shall be conducted in such a way that the employees' representatives can meet with the central management and obtain a response, and the reasons for that response, to any opinion they might express;

(b) The European Works Council shall be composed of employees of the Community-scale undertaking or Community-scale group of undertakings elected or appointed from their number by the employees' representatives or, in the absence thereof, by the entire body of employees.
The election or appointment of members of the European Works Council shall be carried out in accordance with national legislation and/or practice;

(c) The members of the European Works Council shall be elected or appointed in proportion to the number of employees employed in each Member State by the Community-scale undertaking or Community-scale group of undertakings, by allocating in respect of each Member State one seat per portion of employees employed in that Member State amounting to 10%, or a fraction thereof, of the number of employees employed in all the Member States taken together;

(d) To ensure that it can coordinate its activities, the European Works Council shall elect a select committee from among its members, comprising at most five members, which must benefit from conditions enabling it to exercise its activities on a regular basis.
It shall adopt its own rules of procedure;

(e) The central management and any other more appropriate level of management shall be informed of the composition of the European Works Council;

(f) Four years after the European Works Council is established it shall examine whether to open negotiations for the conclusion of the agreement referred to in Article 6 or to continue to apply the subsidiary requirements adopted in accordance with this Annex.
Articles 6 and 7 shall apply, mutatis mutandis, if a decision has been taken to negotiate an

agreement according to Article 6, in which case "special negotiating body" shall be replaced by "European Works Council".

2. The European Works Council shall have the right to meet with the central management once a year, to be informed and consulted, on the basis of a report drawn up by the central management, on the progress of the business of the Community-scale undertaking or Community-scale group of undertakings and its prospects. The local managements shall be informed accordingly.

3. Where there are exceptional circumstances or decisions affecting the employees' interests to a considerable extent, particularly in the event of relocations, the closure of establishments or undertakings or collective redundancies, the select committee or, where no such committee exists, the European Works Council shall have the right to be informed. It shall have the right to meet, at its request, the central management, or any other more appropriate level of management within the Community-scale undertaking or group of undertakings having its own powers of decision, so as to be informed and consulted.

Those members of the European Works Council who have been elected or appointed by the establishments and/or undertakings which are directly concerned by the circumstances or decisions in question shall also have the right to participate where a meeting is organised with the select committee.

This information and consultation meeting shall take place as soon as possible on the basis of a report drawn up by the central management or any other appropriate level of management of the Community-scale undertaking or group of undertakings, on which an opinion may be delivered at the end of the meeting or within a reasonable time.

This meeting shall not affect the prerogatives of the central management.

The information and consultation procedures provided for in the above circumstances shall be carried out without prejudice to Article 1(2) and Article 8.

4. The Member States may lay down rules on the chairing of information and consultation meetings.

Before any meeting with the central management, the European Works Council or the select committee, where necessary enlarged in accordance with the second paragraph of point 3, shall be entitled to meet without the management concerned being present.

5. The European Works Council or the select committee may be assisted by experts of its choice, in so far as this is necessary for it to carry out its tasks.

6. The operating expenses of the European Works Council shall be borne by the central management.

The central management concerned shall provide the members of the European Works Council with such financial and material resources as enable them to perform their duties in an appropriate manner.

In particular, the cost of organising meetings and arranging for interpretation facilities and the accommodation and travelling expenses of members of the European Works Council and its select committee shall be met by the central management unless otherwise agreed.

In compliance with these principles, the Member States may lay down budgetary rules regarding the operation of the European Works Council. They may in particular limit funding to cover one expert only.

ANNEX II

PART A
REPEALED DIRECTIVE WITH ITS SUCCESSIVE AMENDMENTS (REFERRED TO IN ARTICLE 17)

[3.622]

Council Directive 94/45/EC	(OJ L254, 30.9.1994, p 64)
Council Directive 97/74/EC	(OJ L10, 16.1.1998, p 22)
Council Directive 2006/109/EC	(OJ L363, 20.12.2006, p 416)

PART B
TIME LIMITS FOR TRANSPOSITION INTO NATIONAL LAW (REFERRED TO IN ARTICLE 17)

[3.623]

Directive	Time limit for transposition
94/45/EC	22.9.1996
97/74/EC	15.12.1999

Directive	Time limit for transposition
2006/109/EC	1.1.2007

ANNEX III
CORRELATION TABLE

[3.624]

Directive 94/45/EC	This Directive
Article 1(1)	Article 1(1)
Article 1(2)	Article 1(2), first sentence
—	Article 1(2), second sentence
—	Article 1(3) and (4)
Article 1(3)	Article 1(5)
Article 1(4)	Article 1(6)
Article 1(5)	Article 1(7)
Article 2(1)(a) to (e)	Article 2(1)(a) to (e)
—	Article 2(1)(f)
Article 2(1)(f)	Article 2(1)(g)
Article 2(1)(g) and (h)	Article 2(1)(h) and (i)
Article 2(2)	Article 2(2)
Article 3	Article 3
Article 4(1), (2) and (3)	Article 4(1), (2) and (3)
Article 11(2)	Article 4(4)
Article 5(1) and (2)(a)	Article 5(1) and (2)(a)
Article 5(2)(b) and (c)	Article 5(2)(b)
Article 5(2)(d)	Article 5(2)(c)
Article 5(3)	Article 5(3)
Article 5(4), first subparagraph	Article 5(4), first subparagraph
—	Article 5(4), second subparagraph
Article 5(4), second subparagraph	Article 5(4), third subparagraph
Article 5(5) and (6)	Article 5(5) and (6)
Article 6(1) and (2)(a)	Article 6(1) and (2)(a)
Article 6(2)(b)	Article 6(2)(b)
Article 6(2)(c)	Article 6(2)(c)
Article 6(2)(d)	Article 6(2)(d)
—	Article 6(2)(e)
Article 6(2)(e)	Article 6(2)(f)
Article 6(2)(f)	Article 6(2)(g)
Article 6(3), (4) and (5)	Article 6(3), (4) and (5)
Article 7	Article 7
Article 8	Article 8
Article 9	Article 9
—	Article 10(1) and (2)
Article 10	Article 10(3)
—	Article 10(4)
Article 11(1)	Article 11(1)
Article 11(2)	Article 4(4)
Article 11(3)	Article 11(2)
Article 11(4)	Article 11(3)
Article 12(1) and (2)	—
—	Article 12(1) to (5)
—	Article 13

Directive 94/45/EC	This Directive
Article 13(1)	Article 14(1)
Article 13(2)	Article 14(2)
—	Article 15
Article 14	Article 16
—	Article 17
—	Article 18
Article 16	Article 19
Annex	Annex I
Point 1, introductory wording	Point 1, introductory wording
Point 1(a) (partly) and point 2, second paragraph (partly)	Point 1(a) (partly)
Point 1(b)	Point 1(b)
Point 1(c) (partly) and point 1(d)	Point 1(c)
Point 1(c) (partly)	Point 1(d)
Point 1(e)	Point 1(e)
Point 1(f)	Point 1(f)
Point 2, first paragraph	Point 2
Point 3	Point 3
Point 4	Point 4
Point 5	—
Point 6	Point 5
Point 7	Point 6
—	Annexes II and III

COUNCIL DIRECTIVE

(2010/18/EU)

of 8 March 2010

implementing the revised Framework Agreement on parental leave concluded by BUSINESSEUROPE, UEAPME, CEEP and ETUC and repealing Directive 96/34/EC

(Text with EEA relevance)

NOTES

Date of publication in OJ: OJ L68, 18.03.2010, p 13.

This Directive replaced Council Directive 96/34/EC with effect from 8 March 2012. For the domestic implementation of the provisions in the Directive replaced by this Directive see the Employment Rights Act 1996, ss 57A, 57B, 76–80 at **[1.829]**, **[1.830]**, **[1.870]**–**[1.874]**. See also the Parental Leave (EU Directive) Regulations 2013, SI 2013/283 at **[2.1660]**.

See *Harvey* J(1), (7).

[3.625]

THE COUNCIL OF THE EUROPEAN UNION,

Having regard to the Treaty on the Functioning of the European Union, and in particular Article 155(2) thereof,

Having regard to the proposal from the European Commission,

Whereas:

(1) Article 153 of the Treaty on the Functioning of the European Union (the "TFEU") enables the Union to support and complement the activities of the Member States, inter alia in the field of equality between men and women with regard to labour market opportunities and treatment at work.

(2) Social dialogue at Union level may, in accordance with Article 155(1) of the TFEU, lead to contractual relations, including agreements, should management and labour (the "social partners") so desire. The social partners may, in accordance with Article 155(2) of the TFEU, request jointly that agreements concluded by them at Union level in matters covered by Article 153 of the TFEU be implemented by a Council decision on a proposal from the Commission.

(3) A Framework Agreement on parental leave was concluded by the European cross-industry

social partner organisations (ETUC, UNICE and CEEP) on 14 December 1995 and was given legal effect by Council Directive 96/34/EC of 3 June 1996 on the framework agreement on parental leave concluded by UNICE, CEEP and the ETUC.[1] That Directive was amended and extended to the United Kingdom of Great Britain and Northern Ireland by Council Directive 97/75/EC.[2] Directive 96/34/EC contributed greatly to improving the opportunities available to working parents in the Member States to better reconcile their work and family responsibilities through leave arrangements.

(4) In accordance with Article 138(2) and (3) of the Treaty establishing the European Community (the "EC Treaty"),[3] the Commission consulted the European social partners in 2006 and 2007 on ways of further improving the reconciliation of work, private and family life and, in particular, the existing Community legislation on maternity protection and parental leave, and on the possibility of introducing new types of family-related leave, such as paternity leave, adoption leave and leave to care for family members.

(5) The three European general cross-industry social partner organisations (ETUC, CEEP and BUSINESSEUROPE, formerly named UNICE) and the European cross-industry social partner organisation representing a certain category of undertakings (UEAPME) informed the Commission on 11 September 2008 of their wish to enter into negotiations, in accordance with Article 138(4) and Article 139 of the EC Treaty,[4] with a view to revising the Framework Agreement on parental leave concluded in 1995.

(6) On 18 June 2009, those organisations signed the revised Framework Agreement on parental leave (the "revised Framework Agreement") and addressed a joint request to the Commission to submit a proposal for a Council decision implementing that revised Framework Agreement.

(7) In the course of their negotiations, the European social partners completely revised the 1995 Framework Agreement on parental leave. Therefore Directive 96/34/EC should be repealed and replaced by a new directive rather than being simply amended.

(8) Since the objectives of the Directive, namely to improve the reconciliation of work, private and family life for working parents and equality between men and women with regard to labour market opportunities and treatment at work across the Union, cannot be sufficiently achieved by the Member States and can therefore be better achieved at Union level, the Union may adopt measures, in accordance with the principle of subsidiarity as set out in Article 5 of the Treaty on European Union. In accordance with the principle of proportionality, as set out in that Article, this Directive does not go beyond what is necessary in order to achieve those objectives.

(9) When drafting its proposal for a Directive, the Commission took account of the representative status of the signatory parties to the revised Framework Agreement, their mandate and the legality of the clauses in that revised Framework Agreement and its compliance with the relevant provisions concerning small and medium-sized undertakings.

(10) The Commission informed the European Parliament and the European Economic and Social Committee of its proposal.

(11) Clause 1(1) of the revised Framework Agreement, in line with the general principles of Union law in the social policy area, states that the Agreement lays down minimum requirements.

(12) Clause 8(1) of the revised Framework Agreement states that the Member States may apply or introduce more favourable provisions than those set out in the Agreement.

(13) Clause 8(2) of the revised Framework Agreement states that the implementation of the provisions of the Agreement shall not constitute valid grounds for reducing the general level of protection afforded to workers in the field covered by the Agreement.

(14) Member States should provide for effective, proportionate and dissuasive penalties in the event of any breach of the obligations under this Directive.

(15) Member States may entrust the social partners, at their joint request, with the implementation of this Directive, as long as such Member States take all the steps necessary to ensure that they can at all times guarantee the results imposed by this Directive.

(16) In accordance with point 34 of the Interinstitutional agreement on better law-making,[5] Member States are encouraged to draw up, for themselves and in the interests of the Union, their own tables which will, as far as possible, illustrate the correlation between this Directive and the transposition measures, and to make them public,

NOTES

1 OJ L145, 19.6.1996, p 4.

2 OJ L10, 16.1.1998, p 24.

3 Renumbered: Article 154(2) and (3) of the TFEU.

4 Renumbered: Articles 154(4) and 155 of the TFEU.

5 OJ C321, 31.12.2003, p 1.

HAS ADOPTED THIS DIRECTIVE:

[3.626]
Article 1
This Directive puts into effect the revised Framework Agreement on parental leave concluded on 18 June 2009 by the European cross-industry social partner organisations (BUSINESSEUROPE, UEAPME, CEEP and ETUC), as set out in the Annex.

[3.627]
Article 2
Member States shall determine what penalties are applicable when national provisions enacted pursuant to this Directive are infringed. The penalties shall be effective, proportionate and dissuasive.

[3.628]
Article 3
1. Member States shall bring into force the laws, regulations and administrative provisions necessary to comply with this Directive or shall ensure that the social partners have introduced the necessary measures by agreement by 8 March 2012 at the latest. They shall forthwith inform the Commission thereof.

When those provisions are adopted by Member States, they shall contain a reference to this Directive or shall be accompanied by such reference on the occasion of their official publication. The methods of making such reference shall be laid down by Member States.

2. Member States may have a maximum additional period of one year to comply with this Directive, if this is necessary to take account of particular difficulties or implementation by collective agreement. They shall inform the Commission thereof by 8 March 2012 at the latest, stating the reasons for which an additional period is required.

3. Member States shall communicate to the Commission the text of the main provisions of national law which they adopt in the field covered by this Directive.

[3.629]
Article 4
Directive 96/34/EC shall be repealed with effect from 8 March 2012. References to Directive 96/34/EC shall be construed as references to this Directive.

[3.630]
Article 5
This Directive shall enter into force on the 20th day following its publication in the *Official Journal of the European Union.*

[3.631]
Article 6
This Directive is addressed to the Member States.

ANNEX
FRAMEWORK AGREEMENT ON PARENTAL LEAVE (REVISED) 18 JUNE 2009

[3.632]
Preamble
This framework agreement between the European social partners, BUSINESSEUROPE, UEAPME, CEEP and ETUC (and the liaison committee Eurocadres/CEC) revises the framework agreement on parental leave, concluded on 14 December 1995, setting out the minimum requirements on parental leave, as an important means of reconciling professional and family responsibilities and promoting equal opportunities and treatment between men and women.

The European social partners request the Commission to submit this framework agreement to the Council for a Council decision making these requirements binding in the Member States of the European Union.

I. General considerations

1. Having regard to the EC Treaty and in particular Articles 138 and 139 thereof;[1]

2. Having regard to Articles 137(1)(c) and 141 of the EC Treaty[2] and the principle of equal treatment (Articles 2, 3 and 13 of the EC Treaty)[3] and the secondary legislation based on this, in particular Council Directive 75/117/EEC on the approximation of the laws of the Member States relating to the application of the principle of equal pay for men and women;[4] Council Directive 92/85/EEC on the introduction of measures to encourage improvements in the safety and health at work of pregnant workers and workers who have recently given birth or are breastfeeding;[5] Council Directive 96/97/EC amending Directive 86/378/EEC on the implementation of the principle of equal treatment for men and women in occupational social security schemes;[6] and Directive 2006/54/EC on the implementation of the principle of equal opportunities and equal treatment of men and women in matters of employment and occupation (recast);[7]

3. Having regard to the Charter of Fundamental Rights of the European Union of 7 December 2000 and Articles 23 and 33 thereof relating to equality between men and women and reconciliation of professional, private and family life;
4. Having regard to the 2003 Report from the Commission on the Implementation of Council Directive 96/34/EC of 3 June 1996 on the framework agreement on parental leave concluded by UNICE, CEEP and the ETUC;
5. Having regard to the objective of the Lisbon strategy on growth and jobs of increasing overall employment rates to 70%, women's employment rates to 60% and the employment rates of older workers to 50%; to the Barcelona targets on the provision of childcare facilities; and to the contribution of policies to improve reconciliation of professional, private and family life in achieving these targets;
6. Having regard to the European social partners' Framework of Actions on Gender Equality of 22 March 2005 in which supporting work-life balance is addressed as a priority area for action, while recognising that, in order to continue to make progress on the issue of reconciliation, a balanced, integrated and coherent policy mix must be put in place, comprising of leave arrangements, working arrangements and care infrastructures;
7. Whereas measures to improve reconciliation are part of a broader policy agenda to address the needs of employers and workers and improve adaptability and employability, as part of a flexicurity approach;
8. Whereas family policies should contribute to the achievement of gender equality and be looked at in the context of demographic changes, the effects of an ageing population, closing the generation gap, promoting women's participation in the labour force and the sharing of care responsibilities between women and men;
9. Whereas the Commission has consulted the European social partners in 2006 and 2007 in a first and second stage consultation on reconciliation of professional, private and family life, and, among other things, has addressed the issue of updating the regulatory framework at Community level, and has encouraged the European social partners to assess the provisions of their framework agreement on parental leave with a view to its review;
10. Whereas the Framework agreement of the European social partners of 1995 on parental leave has been a catalyst for positive change, ensured common ground on work life balance in the Member States and played a significant role in helping working parents in Europe to achieve better reconciliation; however, on the basis of a joint evaluation, the European social partners consider that certain elements of the agreement need to be adapted or revised in order to better achieve its aims;
11. Whereas certain aspects need to be adapted, taking into account the growing diversity of the labour force and societal developments including the increasing diversity of family structures, while respecting national law, collective agreements and/or practice;
12. Whereas in many Member States encouraging men to assume an equal share of family responsibilities has not led to sufficient results; therefore, more effective measures should be taken to encourage a more equal sharing of family responsibilities between men and women;
13. Whereas many Member States already have a wide variety of policy measures and practices relating to leave facilities, childcare and flexible working arrangements, tailored to the needs of workers and employers and aiming to support parents in reconciling their professional, private and family life; these should be taken into account when implementing this agreement;
14. Whereas this framework agreement provides one element of European social partners' actions in the field of reconciliation;
15. Whereas this agreement is a framework agreement setting out minimum requirements and provisions for parental leave, distinct from maternity leave, and for time off from work on grounds of force majeure, and refers back to Member States and social partners for the establishment of conditions for access and modalities of application in order to take account of the situation in each Member State;
16. Whereas the right of parental leave in this agreement is an individual right and in principle non-transferable, and Member States are allowed to make it transferable. Experience shows that making the leave non-transferable can act as a positive incentive for the take up by fathers, the European social partners therefore agree to make a part of the leave non-transferable;
17. Whereas it is important to take into account the special needs of parents with children with disabilities or long term illness;
18. Whereas Member States should provide for the maintenance of entitlements to benefits in kind under sickness insurance during the minimum period of parental leave;
19. Whereas Member States should also, where appropriate under national conditions and taking into account the budgetary situation, consider the maintenance of entitlements to relevant social security benefits as they stand during the minimum period of parental leave as well as the role of income among other factors in the take-up of parental leave when implementing this agreement;
20. Whereas experiences in Member States have shown that the level of income during parental leave is one factor that influences the take up by parents, especially fathers;

21. Whereas the access to flexible working arrangements makes it easier for parents to combine work and parental responsibilities and facilitates the reintegration into work, especially after returning from parental leave;
22. Whereas parental leave arrangements are meant to support working parents during a specific period of time, aimed at maintaining and promoting their continued labour market participation; therefore, greater attention should be paid to keeping in contact with the employer during the leave or by making arrangements for return to work;
23. Whereas this agreement takes into consideration the need to improve social policy requirements, to enhance the competitiveness of the European Union economy and to avoid imposing administrative, financial and legal constraints in a way which would hold back the creation and development of small and medium sized undertakings;
24. Whereas the social partners are best placed to find solutions that correspond to the needs of both employers and workers and shall therefore play a special role in the implementation, application, monitoring and evaluation of this agreement, in the broader context of other measures to improve the reconciliation of professional and family responsibilities and to promote equal opportunities and treatment between men and women.

The signatory parties have agreed the following:

II. Content

Clause 1: Purpose and scope

1. This agreement lays down minimum requirements designed to facilitate the reconciliation of parental and professional responsibilities for working parents, taking into account the increasing diversity of family structures while respecting national law, collective agreements and/or practice.
2. This agreement applies to all workers, men and women, who have an employment contract or employment relationship as defined by the law, collective agreements and/or practice in force in each Member State.
3. Member States and/or social partners shall not exclude from the scope and application of this agreement workers, contracts of employment or employment relationships solely because they relate to part-time workers, fixed-term contract workers or persons with a contract of employment or employment relationship with a temporary agency.

Clause 2: Parental leave

1. This agreement entitles men and women workers to an individual right to parental leave on the grounds of the birth or adoption of a child to take care of that child until a given age up to eight years to be defined by Member States and/or social partners.
2. The leave shall be granted for at least a period of four months and, to promote equal opportunities and equal treatment between men and women, should, in principle, be provided on a non-transferable basis. To encourage a more equal take-up of leave by both parents, at least one of the four months shall be provided on a non-transferable basis. The modalities of application of the non-transferable period shall be set down at national level through legislation and/or collective agreements taking into account existing leave arrangements in the Member States.

Clause 3: Modalities of application

1. The conditions of access and detailed rules for applying parental leave shall be defined by law and/or collective agreements in the Member States, as long as the minimum requirements of this agreement are respected. Member States and/or social partners may, in particular:
   (a) decide whether parental leave is granted on a full-time or part-time basis, in a piecemeal way or in the form of a time-credit system, taking into account the needs of both employers and workers;
   (b) make entitlement to parental leave subject to a period of work qualification and/or a length of service qualification which shall not exceed one year; Member States and/or social partners shall ensure, when making use of this provision, that in case of successive fixed term contracts, as defined in Council Directive 1999/70/EC on fixed-term work, with the same employer the sum of these contracts shall be taken into account for the purpose of calculating the qualifying period;
   (c) define the circumstances in which an employer, following consultation in accordance with national law, collective agreements and/or practice, is allowed to postpone the granting of parental leave for justifiable reasons related to the operation of the organisation. Any problem arising from the application of this provision should be dealt with in accordance with national law, collective agreements and/or practice;
   (d) in addition to (c), authorise special arrangements to meet the operational and organisational requirements of small undertakings.
2. Member States and/or social partners shall establish notice periods to be given by the worker to the employer when exercising the right to parental leave, specifying the beginning and the end of the period of leave. Member States and/or social partners shall have regard to the interests of workers and of employers in specifying the length of such notice periods.
3. Member States and/or social partners should assess the need to adjust the conditions for access and modalities of application of parental leave to the needs of parents of children with a disability or a long-term illness.

Clause 4: Adoption

1. Member States and/or social partners shall assess the need for additional measures to address the specific needs of adoptive parents.

Clause 5: Employment rights and non-discrimination

1. At the end of parental leave, workers shall have the right to return to the same job or, if that is not possible, to an equivalent or similar job consistent with their employment contract or employment relationship.
2. Rights acquired or in the process of being acquired by the worker on the date on which parental leave starts shall be maintained as they stand until the end of parental leave. At the end of parental leave, these rights, including any changes arising from national law, collective agreements and/or practice, shall apply.
3. Member States and/or social partners shall define the status of the employment contract or employment relationship for the period of parental leave.
4. In order to ensure that workers can exercise their right to parental leave, Member States and/or social partners shall take the necessary measures to protect workers against less favourable treatment or dismissal on the grounds of an application for, or the taking of, parental leave in accordance with national law, collective agreements and/or practice.
5. All matters regarding social security in relation to this agreement are for consideration and determination by Member States and/or social partners according to national law and/or collective agreements, taking into account the importance of the continuity of the entitlements to social security cover under the different schemes, in particular health care.

All matters regarding income in relation to this agreement are for consideration and determination by Member States and/or social partners according to national law, collective agreements and/or practice, taking into account the role of income – among other factors – in the take-up of parental leave.

Clause 6: Return to work

1. In order to promote better reconciliation, Member States and/or social partners shall take the necessary measures to ensure that workers, when returning from parental leave, may request changes to their working hours and/or patterns for a set period of time. Employers shall consider and respond to such requests, taking into account both employers' and workers' needs.

The modalities of this paragraph shall be determined in accordance with national law, collective agreements and/or practice.

2. In order to facilitate the return to work following parental leave, workers and employers are encouraged to maintain contact during the period of leave and may make arrangements for any appropriate reintegration measures, to be decided between the parties concerned, taking into account national law, collective agreements and/or practice.

Clause 7: Time off from work on grounds of force majeure

1. Member States and/or social partners shall take the necessary measures to entitle workers to time off from work, in accordance with national legislation, collective agreements and/or practice, on grounds of force majeure for urgent family reasons in cases of sickness or accident making the immediate presence of the worker indispensable.
2. Member States and/or social partners may specify the conditions of access and detailed rules for applying clause 7.1 and limit this entitlement to a certain amount of time per year and/or per case.

Clause 8: Final provisions

1. Member States may apply or introduce more favourable provisions than those set out in this agreement.
2. Implementation of the provisions of this agreement shall not constitute valid grounds for reducing the general level of protection afforded to workers in the field covered by this agreement. This shall not prejudice the right of Member States and/or social partners to develop different legislative, regulatory or contractual provisions, in the light of changing circumstances (including the introduction of non-transferability), as long as the minimum requirements provided for in the present agreement are complied with.
3. This agreement shall not prejudice the right of social partners to conclude, at the appropriate level including European level, agreements adapting and/or complementing the provisions of this agreement in order to take into account particular circumstances.
4. Member States shall adopt the laws, regulations and administrative provisions necessary to comply with the Council decision within a period of two years from its adoption or shall ensure that social partners introduce the necessary measures by way of agreement by the end of this period. Member States may, if necessary to take account of particular difficulties or implementation by collective agreements, have up to a maximum of one additional year to comply with this decision.
5. The prevention and settlement of disputes and grievances arising from the application of this agreement shall be dealt with in accordance with national law, collective agreements and/or practice.

6. Without prejudice to the respective role of the Commission, national courts and the European Court of Justice, any matter relating to the interpretation of this agreement at European level should, in the first instance, be referred by the Commission to the signatory parties who will give an opinion.
7. The signatory parties shall review the application of this agreement five years after the date of the Council decision if requested by one of the parties to this agreement.

NOTES

1 Renumbered: Articles 154 and 155 of the TFEU.

2 Renumbered: Articles 153(1)c and 157 of the TFEU.

3 Article 2 of the EC Treaty is repealed and replaced, in substance, by Article 3 of the Treaty on the European Union. Article 3(1) of the EC Treaty is repealed and replaced, in substance, by Articles 3 to 6 of the TFEU. Article 3(2) of the EC Treaty is renumbered as Article 8 of the TFEU. Article 13 of the EC Treaty is renumbered as Article 19 of the TFEU.

4 OJ L45, 19.2.1975, p 19–20.

5 OJ L348, 28.11.1992, p 1–8.

6 OJ L46, 17.2.1997, p 20–24.

7 OJ L204, 26.7.2006, p 23–36.

DIRECTIVE OF THE EUROPEAN PARLIAMENT AND OF THE COUNCIL

(2010/41/EU)

of 7 July 2010

on the application of the principle of equal treatment between men and women engaged in an activity in a self-employed capacity and repealing Council Directive 86/613/EEC

NOTES

Date of publication in OJ: OJ L180, 15.7.2010, p 1.

The deadline for domestic implementation of this Directive was 5 August 2012 (see Article 16 at **[3.649]**). No specific domestic implementing measures have been introduced, presumably because it was considered that the Directive was sufficiently implemented by existing law.

[3.633]

THE EUROPEAN PARLIAMENT AND THE COUNCIL OF THE EUROPEAN UNION,

Having regard to the Treaty on the Functioning of the European Union, and in particular Article 157(3) thereof,

Having regard to the proposal from the European Commission,

Having regard to the opinion of the European Economic and Social Committee,[1]

Acting in accordance with the ordinary legislative procedure,[2]

Whereas:

(1) Council Directive 86/613/EEC of 11 December 1986 on the application of the principle of equal treatment between men and women engaged in an activity, including agriculture, in a self-employed capacity, and on the protection of self-employed women during pregnancy and motherhood[3] ensures application in Member States of the principle of equal treatment as between men and women engaged in an activity in a self-employed capacity, or contributing to the pursuit of such activity. As far as self-employed workers and spouses of self-employed workers are concerned, Directive 86/613/EEC has not been very effective and its scope should be reconsidered, as discrimination based on sex and harassment also occur in areas outside salaried work. In the interest of clarity, Directive 86/613/EEC should be replaced by this Directive.

(2) In its Communication of 1 March 2006 entitled 'Roadmap for equality between women and men', the Commission announced that in order to improve governance of gender equality, it would review the existing Union gender equality legislation not included in the 2005 recast exercise with a view to updating, modernising and recasting where necessary. Directive 86/613/EEC was not included in the recasting exercise.

(3) In its conclusions of 5 and 6 December 2007 on 'Balanced roles of women and men for jobs, growth and social cohesion', the Council called on the Commission to consider the need to revise, if necessary, Directive 86/613/EEC in order to safeguard the rights related to motherhood and fatherhood of self-employed workers and their helping spouses.

(4) The European Parliament has consistently called on the Commission to review Directive 86/613/EEC, in particular so as to boost maternity protection for self- employed women and to improve the situation of spouses of self-employed workers.

(5) The European Parliament has already stated its position on these matters in its resolution of

21 February 1997 on the situation of the assisting spouses of the self- employed.[4]

(6) In its Communication of 2 July 2008 entitled 'Renewed Social Agenda: Opportunities, access and solidarity in 21st century Europe', the Commission has affirmed the need to take action on the gender gap in entrepreneurship as well as to improve the reconciliation of private and professional life.

(7) There are already a number of existing legal instruments for the implementation of the principle of equal treatment which cover self-employment activities, in particular Council Directive 79/7/EEC of 19 December 1978 on the progressive implementation of the principle of equal treatment for men and women in matters of social security[5] and Directive 2006/54/EC of the European Parliament and of the Council of 5 July 2006 on the implementation of the principle of equal opportunities and equal treatment of men and women in matters of employment and occupation.[6] This Directive should therefore not apply to the areas already covered by other directives.

(8) This Directive is without prejudice to the powers of the Member States to organise their social protection systems. The exclusive competence of the Member States with regard to the organisation of their social protection systems includes, inter alia decisions on the setting up, financing and management of such systems and related institutions as well as on the substance and delivery of benefits, the level of contributions and the conditions for access.

(9) This Directive should apply to self-employed workers and to their spouses or, when and in so far as recognised by national law, their life partners, where they, under the conditions laid down by national law, habitually participate in the activities of the business. In order to improve the situation for these spouses and, when and in so far as recognised by national law, the life partners of self-employed workers, their work should be recognised.

(10) This Directive should not apply to matters covered by other Directives implementing the principle of equal treatment between men and women, notably Council Directive 2004/113/EC of 13 December 2004 implementing the principle of equal treatment between men and women in the access to and supply of goods and services,[7] inter alia, Article 5 of Directive 2004/113/EC on insurance and related financial services remains applicable.

(11) To prevent discrimination based on sex, this Directive should apply to both direct and indirect discrimination. Harassment and sexual harassment should be considered discrimination and therefore prohibited.

(12) This Directive should be without prejudice to the rights and obligations deriving from marital or family status as defined in national law.

(13) The principle of equal treatment should cover the relationships between the self-employed worker and third parties within the remit of this Directive, but not relationships between the self-employed worker and his or her spouse or life partner.

(14) In the area of self-employment, the application of the principle of equal treatment means that there must be no discrimination on grounds of sex, for instance in relation to the establishment, equipment or extension of a business or the launching or extension of any other form of self-employed activity.

(15) Member States may, under Article 157(4) of the Treaty on the Functioning of the European Union, maintain or adopt measures providing for specific advantages in order to make it easier for the under-represented sex to engage in self-employed activities or to prevent or compensate for disadvantages in their professional careers. In principle, measures such as positive action aimed at achieving gender equality in practice should not be seen as being in breach of the legal principle of equal treatment between men and women.

(16) It is necessary to ensure that the conditions for setting up a company between spouses or, when and in so far as recognised by national law, life partners, are not more restrictive than the conditions for setting up a company between other persons.

(17) In view of their participation in the activities of the family business, the spouses or, when and in so far as recognised by national law, the life partners of self- employed workers who have access to a system for social protection, should also be entitled to benefit from social protection. Member States should be required to take the necessary measures to organise this social protection in accordance with national law. In particular, it is up to Member States to decide whether this social protection should be implemented on a mandatory or voluntary basis. Member States may provide that this social protection may be proportional to the participation in the activities of the self-employed worker and/or the level of contribution.

(18) The economic and physical vulnerability of pregnant self- employed workers and pregnant spouses and, when and in so far as recognised by national law, pregnant life partners of self-employed workers, makes it necessary for them to be granted the right to maternity benefits. The Member States remain competent to organise such benefits, including establishing the level of contributions and all the arrangements concerning benefits and payments, provided the minimum requirements of this Directive are complied with. In particular, they may determine in which period

before and/or after confinement the right to maternity benefits is granted.

(19) The length of the period during which female self- employed workers and female spouses or, when and in so far as recognised by national law, female life partners of self-employed workers, are granted maternity benefits is similar to the duration of maternity leave for employees currently in place at Union level. In case the duration of maternity leave provided for employees is modified at Union level, the Commission should report to the European Parliament and the Council assessing whether the duration of maternity benefits for female self-employed workers and female spouses and life partners referred to in Article 2 should also be modified.

(20) In order to take the specificities of self-employed activities into account, female self-employed workers and female spouses or, when and in so far as recognised by national law, female life partners of self-employed workers should be given access to any existing services supplying temporary replacement enabling interruptions in their occupational activity owing to pregnancy or motherhood, or to any existing national social services. Access to those services can be an alternative to or a part of the maternity allowance.

(21) Persons who have been subject to discrimination based on sex should have suitable means of legal protection. To provide more effective protection, associations, organisations and other legal entities should be empowered to engage in proceedings, as Member States so determine, either on behalf or in support of any victim, without prejudice to national rules of procedure concerning representation and defence before the courts.

(22) Protection of self-employed workers and spouses of self- employed workers and, when and in so far as recognised by national law, the life partners of self-employed workers, from discrimination based on sex should be strengthened by the existence of a body or bodies in each Member State with competence to analyse the problems involved, to study possible solutions and to provide practical assistance to the victims. The body or bodies may be the same as those with responsibility at national level for the implementation of the principle of equal treatment.

(23) This Directive lays down minimum requirements, thus giving the Member States the option of introducing or maintaining more favourable provisions.

(24) Since the objective of the action to be taken, namely to ensure a common high level of protection from discrimination in all the Member States, cannot be sufficiently achieved by the Member States and can be better achieved at Union level, the Union may adopt measures, in accordance with the principle of subsidiarity as set out in Article 5 of the Treaty on European Union. In accordance with the principle of proportionality, as set out in that Article, this Directive does not go beyond what is necessary in order to achieve that objective,

NOTES

[1] OJ C228, 22.9.2009, p 107.

[2] Position of the European Parliament of 6 May 2009 (not yet published in the Official Journal), Position of the Council at first reading of 8 March 2010 (OJ C123 E, 12.5.2010, p 5), Position of the European Parliament of 18 May 2010.

[3] OJ L359, 19.12.1986, p 56.

[4] OJ C85, 17.3.1997, p 186.

[5] OJ L6, 10.1.1979, p 24.

[6] OJ L204, 26.7.2006, p 23.

[7] OJ L373, 21.12.2004, p 37.

HAVE ADOPTED THIS DIRECTIVE:

[3.634]
Article 1
Subject matter

1. This Directive lays down a framework for putting into effect in the Member States the principle of equal treatment between men and women engaged in an activity in a self-employed capacity, or contributing to the pursuit of such an activity, as regards those aspects not covered by Directives 2006/54/EC and 79/7/EEC.
2. The implementation of the principle of equal treatment between men and women in the access to and supply of goods and services remains covered by Directive 2004/113/EC.

[3.635]
Article 2
Scope

This Directive covers:

(a) self-employed workers, namely all persons pursuing a gainful activity for their own account, under the conditions laid down by national law;

(b) the spouses of self-employed workers or, when and in so far as recognised by national law, the life partners of self- employed workers, not being employees or business partners, where they habitually, under the conditions laid down by national law, participate in the activities of the self-employed worker and perform the same tasks or ancillary tasks.

[3.636]
Article 3
Definitions

For the purposes of this Directive, the following definitions shall apply:

(a) 'direct discrimination': where one person is treated less favourably on grounds of sex than another is, has been or would be, treated in a comparable situation;
(b) 'indirect discrimination': where an apparently neutral provision, criterion or practice would put persons of one sex at a particular disadvantage compared with persons of the other sex, unless that provision, criterion or practice is objectively justified by a legitimate aim, and the means of achieving that aim are appropriate and necessary;
(c) 'harassment': where unwanted conduct related to the sex of a person occurs with the purpose, or effect, of violating the dignity of that person, and of creating an intimidating, hostile, degrading, humiliating or offensive environment;
(d) 'sexual harassment': where any form of unwanted verbal, non-verbal, or physical, conduct of a sexual nature occurs, with the purpose or effect of violating the dignity of a person, in particular when creating an intimidating, hostile, degrading, humiliating or offensive environment.

[3.637]
Article 4
Principle of equal treatment

1. The principle of equal treatment means that there shall be no discrimination whatsoever on grounds of sex in the public or private sectors, either directly or indirectly, for instance in relation to the establishment, equipment or extension of a business or the launching or extension of any other form of self-employed activity.
2. In the areas covered by paragraph 1, harassment and sexual harassment shall be deemed to be discrimination on grounds of sex and therefore prohibited. A person's rejection of, or submission to, such conduct may not be used as a basis for a decision affecting that person.
3. In the areas covered by paragraph 1, an instruction to discriminate against persons on grounds of sex shall be deemed to be discrimination.

[3.638]
Article 5
Positive action

Member States may maintain or adopt measures within the meaning of Article 157(4) of the Treaty on the Functioning of the European Union with a view to ensuring full equality in practice between men and women in working life, for instance aimed at promoting entrepreneurship initiatives among women.

[3.639]
Article 6
Establishment of a company

Without prejudice to the specific conditions for access to certain activities which apply equally to both sexes, the Member States shall take the measures necessary to ensure that the conditions for the establishment of a company between spouses, or between life partners when and in so far as recognised by national law, are not more restrictive than the conditions for the establishment of a company between other persons.

[3.640]
Article 7
Social protection

1. Where a system for social protection for self-employed workers exists in a Member State, that Member State shall take the necessary measures to ensure that spouses and life partners referred to in Article 2(b) can benefit from a social protection in accordance with national law.
2. The Member States may decide whether the social protection referred to in paragraph 1 is implemented on a mandatory or voluntary basis.

[3.641]
Article 8
Maternity benefits

1. The Member States shall take the necessary measures to ensure that female self-employed workers and female spouses and life partners referred to in Article 2 may, in accordance with national law, be granted a sufficient maternity allowance enabling interruptions in their occupational activity owing to pregnancy or motherhood for at least 14 weeks.

2. The Member States may decide whether the maternity allowance referred to in paragraph 1 is granted on a mandatory or voluntary basis.
3. The allowance referred to in paragraph 1 shall be deemed sufficient if it guarantees an income at least equivalent to:
   (a) the allowance which the person concerned would receive in the event of a break in her activities on grounds connected with her state of health and/or;
   (b) the average loss of income or profit in relation to a comparable preceding period subject to any ceiling laid down under national law and/or;
   (c) any other family related allowance established by national law, subject to any ceiling laid down under national law.
4. The Member States shall take the necessary measures to ensure that female self-employed workers and female spouses and life partners referred to in Article 2 have access to any existing services supplying temporary replacements or to any existing national social services. The Member States may provide that access to those services is an alternative to or a part of the allowance referred to in paragraph 1 of this Article.

[3.642]
Article 9
Defence of rights
1. The Member States shall ensure that judicial or administrative proceedings, including, where Member States consider it appropriate, conciliation procedures, for the enforcement of the obligations under this Directive are available to all persons who consider they have sustained loss or damage as a result of a failure to apply the principle of equal treatment to them, even after the relationship in which the discrimination is alleged to have occurred has ended.
2. The Member States shall ensure that associations, organisations and other legal entities which have, in accordance with the criteria laid down by their national law, a legitimate interest in ensuring that this Directive is complied with may engage, either on behalf or in support of the complainant, with his or her approval, in any judicial or administrative proceedings provided for the enforcement of obligations under this Directive.
3. Paragraphs 1 and 2 shall be without prejudice to national rules on time limits for bringing actions relating to the principle of equal treatment.

[3.643]
Article 10
Compensation or reparation
The Member States shall introduce such measures into their national legal systems as are necessary to ensure real and effective compensation or reparation, as Member States so determine, for the loss or damage sustained by a person as a result of discrimination on grounds of sex, such compensation or reparation being dissuasive and proportionate to the loss or damage suffered. Such compensation or reparation shall not be limited by the fixing of a prior upper limit.

[3.644]
Article 11
Equality bodies
1. The Member States shall take the necessary measures to ensure that the body or bodies designated in accordance with Article 20 of Directive 2006/54/EC are also competent for the promotion, analysis, monitoring and support of equal treatment of all persons covered by this Directive without discrimination on grounds of sex.
2. The Member States shall ensure that the tasks of the bodies referred to in paragraph 1 include:
   (a) providing independent assistance to victims of discrimination in pursuing their complaints of discrimination, without prejudice to the rights of victims and of associations, organisations and other legal entities referred to in Article 9(2);
   (b) conducting independent surveys on discrimination;
   (c) publishing independent reports and making recommendations on any issue relating to such discrimination;
   (d) exchanging, at the appropriate level, the information available with the corresponding European bodies, such as the European Institute for Gender Equality.

[3.645]
Article 12
Gender mainstreaming
The Member States shall actively take into account the objective of equality between men and women when formulating and implementing laws, regulations, administrative provisions, policies and activities in the areas referred to in this Directive.

[3.646]
Article 13
Dissemination of information

The Member States shall ensure that the provisions adopted pursuant to this Directive, together with the relevant provisions already in force, are brought by all appropriate means to the attention of the persons concerned throughout their territory.

[3.647]
Article 14
Level of protection

The Member States may introduce or maintain provisions which are more favourable to the protection of the principle of equal treatment between men and women than those laid down in this Directive.

The implementation of this Directive shall under no circumstances constitute grounds for a reduction in the level of protection against discrimination already afforded by Member States in the fields covered by this Directive.

[3.648]
Article 15
Reports

1. Member States shall communicate all available information concerning the application of this Directive to the Commission by 5 August 2015.

The Commission shall draw up a summary report for submission to the European Parliament and to the Council no later than 5 August 2016. That report should take into account any legal change concerning the duration of maternity leave for employees. Where appropriate, that report shall be accompanied by proposals for amending this Directive.

2. The Commission's report shall take the viewpoints of the stakeholders into account.

[3.649]
Article 16
Implementation

1. The Member States shall bring into force the laws, regulations and administrative provisions necessary to comply with this Directive by 5 August 2012 at the latest. They shall forthwith communicate to the Commission the text of those provisions.

When the Member States adopt those provisions, they shall contain a reference to this Directive or be accompanied by such a reference on the occasion of their official publication. Member States shall determine how such reference is to be made.

2. Where justified by particular difficulties, the Member States may, if necessary, have an additional period of two years until 5 August 2014 in order to comply with Article 7, and in order to comply with Article 8 as regards female spouses and life partners referred to in Article 2(b).

3. The Member States shall communicate to the Commission the text of the main provisions of national law which they adopt in the field covered by this Directive.

[3.650]
Article 17
Repeal

Directive 86/613/EEC shall be repealed, with effect from 5 August 2012.

References to the repealed Directive shall be construed as references to this Directive.

[3.651]
Article 18
Entry into force

This Directive shall enter into force on the 20th day following its publication in the *Official Journal of the European Union.*

[3.652]
Article 19
Addressees

This Directive is addressed to the Member States.

DIRECTIVE OF THE EUROPEAN PARLIAMENT AND OF THE COUNCIL

(2010/76/EU)

of 24 November 2010

amending Directives 2006/48/EC and 2006/49/EC as regards capital requirements for the trading book and for re-securitisations, and the supervisory review of remuneration policies

(Text with EEA relevance)

NOTES

Date of publication in OJ: OJ L329, 14.12.2010, p 3.

Only those parts of the Directive within the scope of this work are reproduced. Provisions not included are not annotated.

For the domestic implementation of those provisions of this Directive that are within the scope of this work, see the Remuneration Code SYSC 19A at **[4.163]**.

[3.653]

THE EUROPEAN PARLIAMENT AND THE COUNCIL OF THE EUROPEAN UNION,

Having regard to the Treaty on the Functioning of the European Union, and in particular Article 53(1) thereof,

Having regard to the proposal from the European Commission,

Having regard to the opinion of the European Central Bank,[1]

Having regard to the opinion of the European Economic and Social Committee,[2]

Acting in accordance with the ordinary legislative procedure,[3]

Whereas:

(1) Excessive and imprudent risk-taking in the banking sector has led to the failure of individual financial institutions and systemic problems in Member States and globally. While the causes of such risk-taking are many and complex, there is agreement by supervisors and regulatory bodies, including the G-20 and the Committee of European Banking Supervisors (CEBS), that the inappropriate remuneration structures of some financial institutions have been a contributory factor. Remuneration policies which give incentives to take risks that exceed the general level of risk tolerated by the institution can undermine sound and effective risk management and exacerbate excessive risk-taking behaviour. The internationally agreed and endorsed Financial Stability Board (FSB) Principles for Sound Compensation Practices (the FSB principles) are therefore of particular importance.

(2) Directive 2006/48/EC of the European Parliament and of the Council of 14 June 2006 relating to the taking up and pursuit of the business of credit institutions[4] requires credit institutions to have arrangements, strategies, processes and mechanisms to manage the risks to which they are exposed. By virtue of Directive 2006/49/EC of the European Parliament and of the Council of 14 June 2006 on the capital adequacy of investment firms and credit institutions,[5] that requirement applies to investment firms within the meaning of Directive 2004/39/EC of the European Parliament and of the Council of 21 April 2004 on markets in financial instruments.[6] Directive 2006/48/EC requires competent authorities to review those arrangements, strategies, processes and mechanisms, and to determine whether the own funds held by the credit institution or investment firm concerned ensure a sound management and coverage of the risks to which the institution or firm is or might be exposed. That supervision is carried out on a consolidated basis in relation to banking groups, and includes financial holding companies and affiliated financial institutions in all jurisdictions.

(3) In order to address the potentially detrimental effect of poorly designed remuneration structures on the sound management of risk and control of risk-taking behaviour by individuals, the requirements of Directive 2006/48/EC should be supplemented by an express obligation for credit institutions and investment firms to establish and maintain, for categories of staff whose professional activities have a material impact on their risk profile, remuneration policies and practices that are consistent with effective risk management. Those categories of staff should include at least senior management, risk takers, staff engaged in control functions and any employee whose total remuneration, including discretionary pension benefit provisions, takes them into the same remuneration bracket as senior management and risk takers.

(4) Because excessive and imprudent risk-taking may undermine the financial soundness of credit institutions or investment firms and destabilise the banking system, it is important that the new obligation concerning remuneration policies and practices should be implemented in a consistent manner and should cover all aspects of remuneration including salaries, discretionary pension benefits and any similar benefits. In that context, discretionary pension benefits should mean discretionary payments granted by a credit institution or investment firm to an employee on an individual basis payable by reference to or expectation of retirement and which can be assimilated

to variable remuneration. It is therefore appropriate to specify clear principles on sound remuneration to ensure that the structure of remuneration does not encourage excessive risk-taking by individuals or moral hazard and is aligned with the risk appetite, values and long-term interests of the credit institution or investment firm. Remuneration should be aligned with the role of the financial sector as the mechanism through which financial resources are efficiently allocated in the economy. In particular, the principles should provide that the design of variable remuneration policies ensures that incentives are aligned with the long-term interests of the credit institution or investment firm and that payment methods strengthen its capital base. Performance-based components of remuneration should also help enhance fairness within the remuneration structures of the credit institution or investment firm. The principles should recognise that credit institutions and investment firms may apply the provisions in different ways according to their size, internal organisation and the nature, scope and complexity of their activities and, in particular, that it may not be proportionate for investment firms referred to in Article 20(2) and (3) of Directive 2006/49/EC to comply with all of the principles. In order to ensure that the design of remuneration policies is integrated in the risk management of the credit institution or investment firm, the management body, in its supervisory function, of each credit institution or investment firm should adopt and periodically review the principles to be applied. In that context, it should be possible, where applicable and in accordance with national company law, for the management body in its supervisory function to be understood as the supervisory board.

(5) Credit institutions and investment firms that are significant in terms of their size, internal organisation and the nature, the scope and the complexity of their activities should be required to establish a remuneration committee as an integral part of their governance structure and organisation.

(6) By 1 April 2013, the Commission should review the principles on remuneration policy with particular regard to their efficiency, implementation and enforcement, taking into account international developments including any further proposals from the FSB and the implementation of the FSB principles in other jurisdictions including the link between the design of variable remuneration and excessive risk-taking behaviour.

(7) Remuneration policy should aim at aligning the personal objectives of staff members with the long-term interests of the credit institution or investment firm concerned. The assessment of the performance-based components of remuneration should be based on longer-term performance and take into account the outstanding risks associated with the performance. The assessment of performance should be set in a multi-year framework of at least three to 5 years, in order to ensure that the assessment process is based on longer term performance and that the actual payment of performance-based components of remuneration is spread over the business cycle of the credit institution or investment firm. To align incentives further, a substantial portion of variable remuneration of all staff members covered by those requirements should consist of shares, share-linked instruments of the credit institution or investment firm, subject to the legal structure of the credit institution or investment firm concerned or, in the case of a non-listed credit institution or investment firm, other equivalent non-cash instruments and, where appropriate, other long-dated financial instruments that adequately reflect the credit quality of the credit institution or investment firm. It should be possible for such instruments to include a capital instrument which, where the institution is subject to severe financial problems, is converted into equity or otherwise written down. In cases where the credit institution concerned does not issue long-dated financial instruments, it should be permitted to issue the substantial portion of variable remuneration in shares and share-linked instruments and other equivalent non-cash instruments. The Member States or their competent authorities should be able to place restrictions on the types and designs of those instruments or prohibit certain instruments, as appropriate.

(8) To minimise incentives for excessive risk-taking, variable remuneration should constitute a balanced proportion of total remuneration. It is essential that an employee's fixed salary represents a sufficiently high proportion of his total remuneration to allow the operation of a fully flexible variable remuneration policy, including the possibility to pay no variable remuneration. In order to ensure coherent remuneration practices throughout the sector, it is appropriate to specify certain clear requirements. Guaranteed variable remuneration is not consistent with sound risk management or the pay-for-performance principle and should, as a general rule, be prohibited.

(9) A substantial portion of the variable remuneration component, such as 40 to 60%, should be deferred over an appropriate period of time. That portion should increase significantly with the level of seniority or responsibility of the person remunerated. Moreover, a substantial portion of the variable remuneration component should consist of shares, share-linked instruments of the credit institution or investment firm, subject to the legal structure of the credit institution or investment firm concerned or, in the case of a non-listed credit institution or investment firm, other equivalent non-cash instruments and, where appropriate, other long-dated financial instruments that adequately reflect the credit quality of the credit institution or investment firm. In that context, the principle of proportionality is of great importance since it may not always be appropriate to apply those requirements in the context of small credit institutions and investment firms. Taking into account the

restrictions that limit the amount of variable remuneration payable in cash and payable upfront, the amount of variable remuneration which can be paid in cash or cash equivalent not subject to deferral should be limited in order to further align the personal objectives of staff with the long-term interest of the credit institution or investment firm.

(10) Credit institutions and investment firms should ensure that the total variable remuneration does not limit their ability to strengthen their capital base. The extent to which capital needs to be built up should be a function of the current capital position of the credit institution or investment firm. In that context, Member States' competent authorities should have the power to limit variable remuneration, inter alia, as a percentage of total net revenue when it is inconsistent with the maintenance of a sound capital base.

(11) Credit institutions and investment firms should require their staff to undertake not to use personal hedging strategies or insurance to undermine the risk alignment effects embedded in their remuneration arrangements.

(12) Regarding entities that benefit from exceptional government intervention, priority should be given to building up their capital base and providing for recovery of taxpayer assistance. Any variable remuneration payments should reflect those priorities.

(13) The principles regarding sound remuneration policies set out in the Commission Recommendation of 30 April 2009 on remuneration policies in the financial services sector[7] are consistent with and complement the principles set out in this Directive.

(14) The provisions on remuneration should be without prejudice to the full exercise of fundamental rights guaranteed by the Treaties, in particular Article 153(5) of the Treaty on the Functioning of the European Union (TFEU), general principles of national contract and labour law, legislation regarding shareholders' rights and involvement and the general responsibilities of the administrative and supervisory bodies of the institution concerned, as well as the rights, where applicable, of the social partners to conclude and enforce collective agreements, in accordance with national law and customs.

(15) In order to ensure fast and effective enforcement, the competent authorities should also have the power to impose or apply financial or non-financial penalties or other measures for breach of a requirement under Directive 2006/48/EC, including the requirement to have remuneration policies that are consistent with sound and effective risk management. Those measures and penalties should be effective, proportionate and dissuasive. In order to ensure consistency and a level playing field, the Commission should review the adoption and application by the Member States of such measures and penalties on an aggregate basis with regard to their consistency across the Union.

(21) Good governance structures, transparency and disclosure are essential for sound remuneration policies. In order to ensure adequate transparency to the market of their remuneration structures and the associated risk, credit institutions and investments firms should disclose detailed information on their remuneration policies, practices and, for reasons of confidentiality, aggregated amounts for those members of staff whose professional activities have a material impact on the risk profile of the credit institution or investment firm. That information should be made available to all stakeholders (shareholders, employees and the general public). However, that obligation should be without prejudice to Directive 95/46/EC of the European Parliament and of the Council of 24 October 1995 on the protection of individuals with the regard to the processing of personal data and on the free movement of such data.[8]

(22) In order to guarantee their full effectiveness and in order to avoid any discriminatory effect in their application, the provisions on remuneration laid down in this Directive should be applied to remuneration due on the basis of contracts concluded before the date of their effective implementation in each Member State and awarded or paid after that date. Moreover, in order to safeguard the objectives pursued by this Directive, especially effective risk management, in respect of periods still characterised by a high degree of financial instability, and in order to avoid any risk of circumvention of the provisions on remuneration laid down in this Directive during the period prior to their implementation, it is necessary to apply those provisions to remuneration awarded, but not yet paid, before the date of their effective implementation in each Member State, for services provided in 2010.

(23) The review of risks to which the credit institution might be exposed should result in effective supervisory measures. It is therefore necessary that further convergence be reached with a view to supporting joint decisions by supervisors and ensuring equal conditions of competition within the Union.

NOTES

1 OJ C291, 1.12.2009, p 1.

2 Opinion of 20 January 2010 (not yet published in the Official Journal).

3 Position of the European Parliament of 7 July 2010 (not yet published in the Official Journal) and decision of the Council of 11 October 2010.

4 OJ L177, 30.6.2006, p 1.

[5] OJ L177, 30.6.2006, p 201.

[6] OJ L145, 30.4.2004, p 1.

[7] OJ L120, 15.5.2009, p 22.

[8] OJ L281, 23.11.1995, p 31.
Note that the original footnote 9 occurs within paragraph (38) of these recitals and has therefore been omitted as outside the scope of this work.

HAVE ADOPTED THIS DIRECTIVE:

[3.654]
Article 1
Amendments to Directive 2006/48/EC
Directive 2006/48/EC is hereby amended as follows:
20. The Annexes are amended as set out in Annex I to this Directive.

[3.655]
Article 3
Transposition
1. Member States shall bring into force the laws, regulations and administrative provisions necessary to comply with:
   (a) points 3, 4, 16 and 17 of Article 1 and points 1, 2(c), 3 and 5(b)(iii) of Annex I, by 1 January 2011; and
   (b) the provisions of this Directive other than those specified in point (a), by 31 December 2011.

When Member States adopt the measures referred to in this paragraph, they shall contain a reference to this Directive or shall be accompanied by such reference on the occasion of their official publication. The methods of making such reference shall be laid down by Member States.
2. The laws, regulations and administrative provisions necessary to comply with point 1 of Annex I shall require credit institutions to apply the principles laid down therein to:
   (i) remuneration due on basis of contracts concluded before the effective date of implementation in each Member State and awarded or paid after that date; and
   (ii) for services provided in 2010, remuneration awarded, but not yet paid, before the date of effective implementation in each Member State.
3. Member States shall communicate to the Commission the text of the main provisions of national law which they adopt in the field covered by this Directive.

[3.656]
Article 4
Report
With regard to the international nature of the Basel framework and the risks associated with a non-simultaneous implementation of the changes to that framework in major jurisdictions, the Commission shall report to the European Parliament and the Council by 31 December 2010 on progress made towards the international implementation of the changes to the capital adequacy framework, together with any appropriate proposals.

[3.657]
Article 5
Entry into force
This Directive shall enter into force on the day following its publication in the *Official Journal of the European Union*.

[3.658]
Article 6
Addressees
This Directive is addressed to the Member States.

ANNEX I

[3.659]
Annexes V, VI, VII, IX and XII to Directive 2006/48/EC are amended as follows:

1. In Annex V, the following Section is added:

"11. Remuneration policies

23. When establishing and applying the total remuneration policies, inclusive of salaries and discretionary pension benefits, for categories of staff including senior management, risk takers, staff engaged in control functions and any employee receiving total remuneration that takes them into the same remuneration bracket as senior management and risk takers, whose

professional activities have a material impact on their risk profile, credit institutions shall comply with the following principles in a way and to the extent that is appropriate to their size, internal organisation and the nature, the scope and the complexity of their activities:

(a) the remuneration policy is consistent with and promotes sound and effective risk management and does not encourage risk-taking that exceeds the level of tolerated risk of the credit institution;

(b) the remuneration policy is in line with the business strategy, objectives, values and long-term interests of the credit institution, and incorporates measures to avoid conflicts of interest;

(c) the management body, in its supervisory function, of the credit institution adopts and periodically reviews the general principles of the remuneration policy and is responsible for its implementation;

(d) the implementation of the remuneration policy is, at least annually, subject to central and independent internal review for compliance with policies and procedures for remuneration adopted by the management body in its supervisory function;

(e) staff engaged in control functions are independent from the business units they oversee, have appropriate authority, and are remunerated in accordance with the achievement of the objectives linked to their functions, independent of the performance of the business areas they control;

(f) the remuneration of the senior officers in the risk management and compliance functions is directly overseen by the remuneration committee referred to in point (24) or, if such a committee has not been established, by the management body in its supervisory function;

(g) where remuneration is performance related, the total amount of remuneration is based on a combination of the assessment of the performance of the individual and of the business unit concerned and of the overall results of the credit institution and when assessing individual performance, financial and non-financial criteria are taken into account;

(h) the assessment of the performance is set in a multi-year framework in order to ensure that the assessment process is based on longer-term performance and that the actual payment of performance-based components of remuneration is spread over a period which takes account of the underlying business cycle of the credit institution and its business risks;

(i) the total variable remuneration does not limit the ability of the credit institution to strengthen its capital base;

(j) guaranteed variable remuneration is exceptional and occurs only when hiring new staff and is limited to the first year of employment;

(k) in the case of credit institutions that benefit from exceptional government intervention:

  (i) variable remuneration is strictly limited as a percentage of net revenue where it is inconsistent with the maintenance of a sound capital base and timely exit from government support;

  (ii) the relevant competent authorities require credit institutions to restructure remuneration in a manner aligned with sound risk management and long-term growth, including, where appropriate, establishing limits to the remuneration of the persons who effectively direct the business of the credit institution within the meaning of Article 11(1);

  (iii) no variable remuneration is paid to the persons who effectively direct the business of the credit institution within the meaning of Article 11(1) unless justified;

(l) fixed and variable components of total remuneration are appropriately balanced and the fixed component represents a sufficiently high proportion of the total remuneration to allow the operation of a fully flexible policy, on variable remuneration components, including the possibility to pay no variable remuneration component.

Credit institutions shall set the appropriate ratios between the fixed and the variable component of the total remuneration;

(m) payments related to the early termination of a contract reflect performance achieved over time and are designed in a way that does not reward failure;

(n) the measurement of performance used to calculate variable remuneration components or pools of variable remuneration components includes an adjustment for all types of current and future risks and takes into account the cost of the capital and the liquidity required.

The allocation of the variable remuneration components within the credit institution shall also take into account all types of current and future risks;

(o) a substantial portion, and in any event at least 50%, of any variable remuneration shall consist of an appropriate balance of:
   (i) shares or equivalent ownership interests, subject to the legal structure of the credit institution concerned or share-linked instruments or equivalent non-cash instruments, in case of a non- listed credit institution, and
   (ii) where appropriate, other instruments within the meaning of Article 66(1a)(a), that adequately reflect the credit quality of the credit institution as a going concern.

   The instruments referred to in this point shall be subject to an appropriate retention policy designed to align incentives with the longer-term interests of the credit institution. Member States or their competent authorities may place restrictions on the types and designs of those instruments or prohibit certain instruments as appropriate. This point shall be applied to both the portion of the variable remuneration component deferred in accordance with point (p) and the portion of the variable remuneration component not deferred;

(p) a substantial portion, and in any event at least 40%, of the variable remuneration component is deferred over a period which is not less than three to 5 years and is correctly aligned with the nature of the business, its risks and the activities of the member of staff in question.

   Remuneration payable under deferral arrangements shall vest no faster than on a pro-rata basis. In the case of a variable remuneration component of a particularly high amount, at least 60% of the amount shall be deferred. The length of the deferral period shall be established in accordance with the business cycle, the nature of the business, its risks and the activities of the member of staff in question;

(q) the variable remuneration, including the deferred portion, is paid or vests only if it is sustainable according to the financial situation of the credit institution as a whole, and justified according to the performance of the credit institution, the business unit and the individual concerned.

   Without prejudice to the general principles of national contract and labour law, the total variable remuneration shall generally be considerably contracted where subdued or negative financial performance of the credit institution occurs, taking into account both current remuneration and reductions in payouts of amounts previously earned, including through malus or clawback arrangements;

(r) the pension policy is in line with the business strategy, objectives, values and long-term interests of the credit institution.

   If the employee leaves the credit institution before retirement, discretionary pension benefits shall be held by the credit institution for a period of 5 years in the form of instruments referred to in point (o). In case of an employee reaching retirement, discretionary pension benefits shall be paid to the employee in the form of instruments referred to in point (o) subject to a five-year retention period;

(s) staff members are required to undertake not to use personal hedging strategies or remuneration-and liability-related insurance to undermine the risk alignment effects embedded in their remuneration arrangements;

(t) variable remuneration is not paid through vehicles or methods that facilitate the avoidance of the requirements of this Directive.

   The principles set out in this point shall be applied by credit institutions at group, parent company and subsidiary levels, including those established in offshore financial centres.

24. Credit institutions that are significant in terms of their size, internal organisation and the nature, the scope and the complexity of their activities shall establish a remuneration committee. The remuneration committee shall be constituted in such a way as to enable it to exercise competent and independent judgment on remuneration policies and practices and the incentives created for managing risk, capital and liquidity.

The remuneration committee shall be responsible for the preparation of decisions regarding remuneration, including those which have implications for the risk and risk management of the credit institution concerned and which are to be taken by the management body in its supervisory function. The Chair and the members of the remuneration committee shall be members of the management body who do not perform any executive functions in the credit institution concerned. When preparing such decisions, the remuneration committee shall take into account the long-term interests of shareholders, investors and other stakeholders in the credit institution.".

5. Annex XII is amended as follows:

(a) the title is replaced by the following:

"Technical Criteria on Transparency and Disclosure";

(b) Part 2 is amended as follows:

(iii) the following point is added:

"15. The following information, including regular, at least annual, updates, shall be disclosed to the public regarding the remuneration policy and practices of the credit institution for those categories of staff whose professional activities have a material impact on its risk profile:

(a) information concerning the decision-making process used for determining the remuneration policy, including if applicable, information about the composition and the mandate of a remuneration committee, the external consultant whose services have been used for the determination of the remuneration policy and the role of the relevant stakeholders;

(b) information on link between pay and performance;

(c) the most important design characteristics of the remuneration system, including information on the criteria used for performance measurement and risk adjustment, deferral policy and vesting criteria;

(d) information on the performance criteria on which the entitlement to shares, options or variable components of remuneration is based;

(e) the main parameters and rationale for any variable component scheme and any other non-cash benefits;

(f) aggregate quantitative information on remuneration, broken down by business area;

(g) aggregate quantitative information on remuneration, broken down by senior management and members of staff whose actions have a material impact on the risk profile of the credit institution, indicating the following:

(i) the amounts of remuneration for the financial year, split into fixed and variable remuneration, and the number of beneficiaries;

(ii) the amounts and forms of variable remuneration, split into cash, shares, share-linked instruments and other types;

(iii) the amounts of outstanding deferred remuneration, split into vested and unvested portions;

(iv) the amounts of deferred remuneration awarded during the financial year, paid out and reduced through performance adjustments;

(v) new sign-on and severance payments made during the financial year, and the number of beneficiaries of such payments; and

(vi) the amounts of severance payments awarded during the financial year, number of beneficiaries and highest such award to a single person.

For credit institutions that are significant in terms of their size, internal organisation and the nature, scope and the complexity of their activities, the quantitative information referred to in this point shall also be made available to the public at the level of persons who effectively direct the business of the credit institution within the meaning of Article 11(1).

Credit institutions shall comply with the requirements set out in this point in a manner that is appropriate to their size, internal organisation and the nature, scope and complexity of their activities and without prejudice to Directive 95/46/EC.".

EUROPEAN PARLIAMENT AND COUNCIL REGULATION

(1215/2012/EU)

of 12 December 2012

on jurisdiction and the recognition and enforcement of judgments in civil and commercial matters

(recast)

NOTES

Date of publication in OJ: OJ L351, 20.12.2012, p 1.

Only those parts of this Regulation of most relevance to this work are included.

This Regulation is a recast replacement of Council Regulation 44/2001/EC at **[3.322]**, which is repealed with effect from 10 January 2015, subject to transitional provisions: see Arts 66, 80, 81 of this Regulation at **[3.682]**, **[3.684]**, **[3.685]**. A Table of Correlations for the relevant parts of the 2001 Regulation is in Annex III (at **[3.686]**). Note that the provisions of this Regulation reproduced here will only come into effect from 10 January 2015 (see Art 81 at **[3.685]**).

[3.660]

THE EUROPEAN PARLIAMENT AND THE COUNCIL OF THE EUROPEAN UNION,

Having regard to the Treaty on the Functioning of the European Union, and in particular Article 67(4) and points (a), (c) and (e) of Article 81(2) thereof,

Having regard to the proposal from the European Commission,

After transmission of the draft legislative act to the national parliaments,

Having regard to the opinion of the European Economic and Social Committee,[1]

Acting in accordance with the ordinary legislative procedure,[2]

Whereas:

(1) On 21 April 2009, the Commission adopted a report on the application of Council Regulation (EC) No 44/2001 of 22 December 2000 on jurisdiction and the recognition and enforcement of judgments in civil and commercial matters.[3] The report concluded that, in general, the operation of that Regulation is satisfactory, but that it is desirable to improve the application of certain of its provisions, to further facilitate the free circulation of judgments and to further enhance access to justice. Since a number of amendments are to be made to that Regulation it should, in the interests of clarity, be recast.

(2) At its meeting in Brussels on 10 and 11 December 2009, the European Council adopted a new multiannual programme entitled "The Stockholm Programme – an open and secure Europe serving and protecting citizens".[4] In the Stockholm Programme the European Council considered that the process of abolishing all intermediate measures (the exequatur) should be continued during the period covered by that Programme. At the same time the abolition of the exequatur should also be accompanied by a series of safeguards.

(3) The Union has set itself the objective of maintaining and developing an area of freedom, security and justice, inter alia, by facilitating access to justice, in particular through the principle of mutual recognition of judicial and extra-judicial decisions in civil matters. For the gradual establishment of such an area, the Union is to adopt measures relating to judicial cooperation in civil matters having cross-border implications, particularly when necessary for the proper functioning of the internal market.

(4) Certain differences between national rules governing jurisdiction and recognition of judgments hamper the sound operation of the internal market. Provisions to unify the rules of conflict of jurisdiction in civil and commercial matters, and to ensure rapid and simple recognition and enforcement of judgments given in a Member State, are essential.

(5) Such provisions fall within the area of judicial cooperation in civil matters within the meaning of Article 81 of the Treaty on the Functioning of the European Union (TFEU).

(6) In order to attain the objective of free circulation of judgments in civil and commercial matters, it is necessary and appropriate that the rules governing jurisdiction and the recognition and enforcement of judgments be governed by a legal instrument of the Union which is binding and directly applicable.

(7) On 27 September 1968, the then Member States of the European Communities, acting under Article 220, fourth indent, of the Treaty establishing the European Economic Community, concluded the Brussels Convention on Jurisdiction and the Enforcement of Judgments in Civil and Commercial Matters, subsequently amended by conventions on the accession to that Convention of new Member States[5] ("the 1968 Brussels Convention"). On 16 September 1988, the then Member States of the European Communities and certain EFTA States concluded the Lugano Convention on Jurisdiction and the Enforcement of Judgments in Civil and Commercial Matters[6] ("the 1988 Lugano Convention"), which is a parallel convention to the 1968 Brussels Convention. The 1988 Lugano Convention became applicable to Poland on 1 February 2000.

Part 3 EU Materials

(8) On 22 December 2000, the Council adopted Regulation (EC) No 44/2001, which replaces the 1968 Brussels Convention with regard to the territories of the Member States covered by the TFEU, as between the Member States except Denmark. By Council Decision 2006/325/EC,[7] the Community concluded an agreement with Denmark ensuring the application of the provisions of Regulation (EC) No 44/2001 in Denmark. The 1988 Lugano Convention was revised by the Convention on Jurisdiction and the Recognition and Enforcement of Judgments in Civil and Commercial Matters,[8] signed at Lugano on 30 October 2007 by the Community, Denmark, Iceland, Norway and Switzerland ("the 2007 Lugano Convention").

(9) The 1968 Brussels Convention continues to apply to the territories of the Member States which fall within the territorial scope of that Convention and which are excluded from this Regulation pursuant to Article 355 of the TFEU.

(10) The scope of this Regulation should cover all the main civil and commercial matters apart from certain well-defined matters, in particular maintenance obligations, which should be excluded from the scope of this Regulation following the adoption of Council Regulation (EC) No 4/2009 of 18 December 2008 on jurisdiction, applicable law, recognition and enforcement of decisions and cooperation in matters relating to maintenance obligations.[9]

(11) For the purposes of this Regulation, courts or tribunals of the Member States should include courts or tribunals common to several Member States, such as the Benelux Court of Justice when it exercises jurisdiction on matters falling within the scope of this Regulation. Therefore, judgments given by such courts should be recognised and enforced in accordance with this Regulation.

(12) This Regulation should not apply to arbitration. Nothing in this Regulation should prevent the courts of a Member State, when seised of an action in a matter in respect of which the parties have entered into an arbitration agreement, from referring the parties to arbitration, from staying or dismissing the proceedings, or from examining whether the arbitration agreement is null and void, inoperative or incapable of being performed, in accordance with their national law.

A ruling given by a court of a Member State as to whether or not an arbitration agreement is null and void, inoperative or incapable of being performed should not be subject to the rules of recognition and enforcement laid down in this Regulation, regardless of whether the court decided on this as a principal issue or as an incidental question.

On the other hand, where a court of a Member State, exercising jurisdiction under this Regulation or under national law, has determined that an arbitration agreement is null and void, inoperative or incapable of being performed, this should not preclude that court's judgment on the substance of the matter from being recognised or, as the case may be, enforced in accordance with this Regulation. This should be without prejudice to the competence of the courts of the Member States to decide on the recognition and enforcement of arbitral awards in accordance with the Convention on the Recognition and Enforcement of Foreign Arbitral Awards, done at New York on 10 June 1958 ("the 1958 New York Convention"), which takes precedence over this Regulation.

This Regulation should not apply to any action or ancillary proceedings relating to, in particular, the establishment of an arbitral tribunal, the powers of arbitrators, the conduct of an arbitration procedure or any other aspects of such a procedure, nor to any action or judgment concerning the annulment, review, appeal, recognition or enforcement of an arbitral award.

(13) There must be a connection between proceedings to which this Regulation applies and the territory of the Member States. Accordingly, common rules of jurisdiction should, in principle, apply when the defendant is domiciled in a Member State.

(14) A defendant not domiciled in a Member State should in general be subject to the national rules of jurisdiction applicable in the territory of the Member State of the court seised.

However, in order to ensure the protection of consumers and employees, to safeguard the jurisdiction of the courts of the Member States in situations where they have exclusive jurisdiction and to respect the autonomy of the parties, certain rules of jurisdiction in this Regulation should apply regardless of the defendant's domicile.

(15) The rules of jurisdiction should be highly predictable and founded on the principle that jurisdiction is generally based on the defendant's domicile. Jurisdiction should always be available on this ground save in a few well-defined situations in which the subject-matter of the dispute or the autonomy of the parties warrants a different connecting factor. The domicile of a legal person must be defined autonomously so as to make the common rules more transparent and avoid conflicts of jurisdiction.

(16) In addition to the defendant's domicile, there should be alternative grounds of jurisdiction based on a close connection between the court and the action or in order to facilitate the sound administration of justice. The existence of a close connection should ensure legal certainty and avoid the possibility of the defendant being sued in a court of a Member State which he could not reasonably have foreseen. This is important, particularly in disputes concerning non-contractual obligations arising out of violations of privacy and rights relating to personality, including defamation.

(17) The owner of a cultural object as defined in Article 1(1) of Council Directive 93/7/EEC of

15 March 1993 on the return of cultural objects unlawfully removed from the territory of a Member State[10] should be able under this Regulation to initiate proceedings as regards a civil claim for the recovery, based on ownership, of such a cultural object in the courts for the place where the cultural object is situated at the time the court is seised. Such proceedings should be without prejudice to proceedings initiated under Directive 93/7/EEC.

(18) In relation to insurance, consumer and employment contracts, the weaker party should be protected by rules of jurisdiction more favourable to his interests than the general rules.

(19) The autonomy of the parties to a contract, other than an insurance, consumer or employment contract, where only limited autonomy to determine the courts having jurisdiction is allowed, should be respected subject to the exclusive grounds of jurisdiction laid down in this Regulation.

(20) Where a question arises as to whether a choice-of-court agreement in favour of a court or the courts of a Member State is null and void as to its substantive validity, that question should be decided in accordance with the law of the Member State of the court or courts designated in the agreement, including the conflict-of-laws rules of that Member State.

(21) In the interests of the harmonious administration of justice it is necessary to minimise the possibility of concurrent proceedings and to ensure that irreconcilable judgments will not be given in different Member States. There should be a clear and effective mechanism for resolving cases of lis pendens and related actions, and for obviating problems flowing from national differences as to the determination of the time when a case is regarded as pending. For the purposes of this Regulation, that time should be defined autonomously.

(22) However, in order to enhance the effectiveness of exclusive choice-of-court agreements and to avoid abusive litigation tactics, it is necessary to provide for an exception to the general lis pendens rule in order to deal satisfactorily with a particular situation in which concurrent proceedings may arise. This is the situation where a court not designated in an exclusive choice-of-court agreement has been seised of proceedings and the designated court is seised subsequently of proceedings involving the same cause of action and between the same parties. In such a case, the court first seised should be required to stay its proceedings as soon as the designated court has been seised and until such time as the latter court declares that it has no jurisdiction under the exclusive choice-of-court agreement. This is to ensure that, in such a situation, the designated court has priority to decide on the validity of the agreement and on the extent to which the agreement applies to the dispute pending before it. The designated court should be able to proceed irrespective of whether the non-designated court has already decided on the stay of proceedings.

This exception should not cover situations where the parties have entered into conflicting exclusive choice-of-court agreements or where a court designated in an exclusive choice-of-court agreement has been seised first. In such cases, the general lis pendens rule of this Regulation should apply.

(23) This Regulation should provide for a flexible mechanism allowing the courts of the Member States to take into account proceedings pending before the courts of third States, considering in particular whether a judgment of a third State will be capable of recognition and enforcement in the Member State concerned under the law of that Member State and the proper administration of justice.

(24) When taking into account the proper administration of justice, the court of the Member State concerned should assess all the circumstances of the case before it. Such circumstances may include connections between the facts of the case and the parties and the third State concerned, the stage to which the proceedings in the third State have progressed by the time proceedings are initiated in the court of the Member State and whether or not the court of the third State can be expected to give a judgment within a reasonable time.

That assessment may also include consideration of the question whether the court of the third State has exclusive jurisdiction in the particular case in circumstances where a court of a Member State would have exclusive jurisdiction.

(25)–(33) (*Outside the scope of this work.*)

(34) Continuity between the 1968 Brussels Convention, Regulation (EC) No 44/2001 and this Regulation should be ensured, and transitional provisions should be laid down to that end. The same need for continuity applies as regards the interpretation by the Court of Justice of the European Union of the 1968 Brussels Convention and of the Regulations replacing it.

(35) Respect for international commitments entered into by the Member States means that this Regulation should not affect conventions relating to specific matters to which the Member States are parties.

(36) Without prejudice to the obligations of the Member States under the Treaties, this Regulation should not affect the application of bilateral conventions and agreements between a third State and a Member State concluded before the date of entry into force of Regulation (EC) No 44/2001 which concern matters governed by this Regulation.

(37) In order to ensure that the certificates to be used in connection with the recognition or enforcement of judgments, authentic instruments and court settlements under this Regulation are kept up-to-date, the power to adopt acts in accordance with Article 290 of the TFEU should be delegated to the Commission in respect of amendments to Annexes I and II to this Regulation. It is of particular importance that the Commission carry out appropriate consultations during its preparatory work, including at expert level. The Commission, when preparing and drawing up delegated acts, should ensure a simultaneous, timely and appropriate transmission of relevant documents to the European Parliament and to the Council.

(38) This Regulation respects fundamental rights and observes the principles recognised in the Charter of Fundamental Rights of the European Union, in particular the right to an effective remedy and to a fair trial guaranteed in Article 47 of the Charter.

(39) Since the objective of this Regulation cannot be sufficiently achieved by the Member States and can be better achieved at Union level, the Union may adopt measures in accordance with the principle of subsidiarity as set out in Article 5 of the Treaty on European Union (TEU). In accordance with the principle of proportionality, as set out in that Article, this Regulation does not go beyond what is necessary in order to achieve that objective.

(40) The United Kingdom and Ireland, in accordance with Article 3 of the Protocol on the position of the United Kingdom and Ireland, annexed to the TEU and to the then Treaty establishing the European Community, took part in the adoption and application of Regulation (EC) No 44/2001. In accordance with Article 3 of Protocol No 21 on the position of the United Kingdom and Ireland in respect of the area of freedom, security and justice, annexed to the TEU and to the TFEU, the United Kingdom and Ireland have notified their wish to take part in the adoption and application of this Regulation.

(41) In accordance with Articles 1 and 2 of Protocol No 22 on the position of Denmark annexed to the TEU and to the TFEU, Denmark is not taking part in the adoption of this Regulation and is not bound by it or subject to its application, without prejudice to the possibility for Denmark of applying the amendments to Regulation (EC) No 44/2001 pursuant to Article 3 of the Agreement of 19 October 2005 between the European Community and the Kingdom of Denmark on jurisdiction and the recognition and enforcement of judgments in civil and commercial matters,[11]

NOTES

1 OJ C218, 23.7.2011, p 78.

2 Position of the European Parliament of 20 November 2012 (not yet published in the Official Journal) and decision of the Council of 6 December 2012.

3 OJ L12, 16.1.2001, p 1.

4 OJ C115, 4.5.2010, p 1.

5 OJ L299, 31.12.1972, p 32, OJ L304, 30.10.1978, p 1, OJ L388, 31.12.1982, p 1, OJ L285, 3.10.1989, p 1, OJ C15, 15.1.1997, p 1. For a consolidated text, see OJ C27, 26.1.1998, p 1.

6 OJ L319, 25.11.1988, p 9.

7 OJ L120, 5.5.2006, p 22.

8 OJ L147, 10.6.2009, p 5.

9 OJ L7, 10.1.2009, p 1.

10 OJ L74, 27.3.1993, p 74.

11 OJ L299, 16.11.2005, p 62.

HAVE ADOPTED THIS REGULATION:

CHAPTER I
SCOPE AND DEFINITIONS

[3.661]
Article 1

1. This Regulation shall apply in civil and commercial matters whatever the nature of the court or tribunal. It shall not extend, in particular, to revenue, customs or administrative matters or to the liability of the State for acts and omissions in the exercise of State authority (*acta iure imperii*).
2. The Regulation shall not apply to:
   (a) the status or legal capacity of natural persons, rights in property arising out of a matrimonial relationship or out of a relationship deemed by the law applicable to such relationship to have comparable effects to marriage;
   (b) bankruptcy, proceedings relating to the winding-up of insolvent companies or other legal persons, judicial arrangements, compositions and analogous proceedings;
   (c) social security;
   (d) arbitration;
   (e) maintenance obligations arising from a family relationship, parentage, marriage or affinity;

(f) wills and succession, including maintenance obligations arising by reason of death.

[3.662]
Article 2
For the purposes of this Regulation:

(a) "judgment" means any judgment given by a court or tribunal of a Member State, whatever the judgment may be called, including a decree, order, decision or writ of execution, as well as a decision on the determination of costs or expenses by an officer of the court.

For the purposes of Chapter III, "judgment" includes provisional, including protective, measures ordered by a court or tribunal which by virtue of this Regulation has jurisdiction as to the substance of the matter. It does not include a provisional, including protective, measure which is ordered by such a court or tribunal without the defendant being summoned to appear, unless the judgment containing the measure is served on the defendant prior to enforcement;

(b) "court settlement" means a settlement which has been approved by a court of a Member State or concluded before a court of a Member State in the course of proceedings;

(c) "authentic instrument" means a document which has been formally drawn up or registered as an authentic instrument in the Member State of origin and the authenticity of which:
   (i) relates to the signature and the content of the instrument; and
   (ii) has been established by a public authority or other authority empowered for that purpose;

(d) "Member State of origin" means the Member State in which, as the case may be, the judgment has been given, the court settlement has been approved or concluded, or the authentic instrument has been formally drawn up or registered;

(e) "Member State addressed" means the Member State in which the recognition of the judgment is invoked or in which the enforcement of the judgment, the court settlement or the authentic instrument is sought;

(f) "court of origin" means the court which has given the judgment the recognition of which is invoked or the enforcement of which is sought.

[3.663]
Article 3
For the purposes of this Regulation, "court" includes the following authorities to the extent that they have jurisdiction in matters falling within the scope of this Regulation:

(a) in Hungary, in summary proceedings concerning orders to pay (fizetési meghagyásos eljárás), the notary (közjegyző);

(b) in Sweden, in summary proceedings concerning orders to pay (betalningsföreläggande) and assistance (handräckning), the Enforcement Authority (Kronofogdemyndigheten).

CHAPTER II
JURISDICTION

SECTION 1
GENERAL PROVISIONS

[3.664]
Article 4
1. Subject to this Regulation, persons domiciled in a Member State shall, whatever their nationality, be sued in the courts of that Member State.
2. Persons who are not nationals of the Member State in which they are domiciled shall be governed by the rules of jurisdiction applicable to nationals of that Member State.

[3.665]
Article 5
1. Persons domiciled in a Member State may be sued in the courts of another Member State only by virtue of the rules set out in Sections 2 to 7 of this Chapter.
2. In particular, the rules of national jurisdiction of which the Member States are to notify the Commission pursuant to point (a) of Article 76(1) shall not be applicable as against the persons referred to in paragraph 1.

[3.666]
Article 6
1. If the defendant is not domiciled in a Member State, the jurisdiction of the courts of each Member State shall, subject to Article 18(1), Article 21(2) and Articles 24 and 25, be determined by the law of that Member State.

2. As against such a defendant, any person domiciled in a Member State may, whatever his nationality, avail himself in that Member State of the rules of jurisdiction there in force, and in particular those of which the Member States are to notify the Commission pursuant to point (a) of Article 76(1), in the same way as nationals of that Member State.

SECTION 2
SPECIAL JURISDICTION

[3.667]
Article 7
A person domiciled in a Member State may be sued in another Member State:

(1)
- (a) in matters relating to a contract, in the courts for the place of performance of the obligation in question;
- (b) for the purpose of this provision and unless otherwise agreed, the place of performance of the obligation in question shall be:
  - — in the case of the sale of goods, the place in a Member State where, under the contract, the goods were delivered or should have been delivered,
  - — in the case of the provision of services, the place in a Member State where, under the contract, the services were provided or should have been provided;
- (c) if point (b) does not apply then point (a) applies;

(2) in matters relating to tort, delict or quasi-delict, in the courts for the place where the harmful event occurred or may occur;

(3) as regards a civil claim for damages or restitution which is based on an act giving rise to criminal proceedings, in the court seised of those proceedings, to the extent that that court has jurisdiction under its own law to entertain civil proceedings;

(4) as regards a civil claim for the recovery, based on ownership, of a cultural object as defined in point 1 of Article 1 of Directive 93/7/EEC initiated by the person claiming the right to recover such an object, in the courts for the place where the cultural object is situated at the time when the court is seised;

(5) as regards a dispute arising out of the operations of a branch, agency or other establishment, in the courts for the place where the branch, agency or other establishment is situated;

(6) as regards a dispute brought against a settlor, trustee or beneficiary of a trust created by the operation of a statute, or by a written instrument, or created orally and evidenced in writing, in the courts of the Member State in which the trust is domiciled;

(7) as regards a dispute concerning the payment of remuneration claimed in respect of the salvage of a cargo or freight, in the court under the authority of which the cargo or freight in question:
- (a) has been arrested to secure such payment; or
- (b) could have been so arrested, but bail or other security has been given;

provided that this provision shall apply only if it is claimed that the defendant has an interest in the cargo or freight or had such an interest at the time of salvage.

[3.668]
Article 8
A person domiciled in a Member State may also be sued:

(1) where he is one of a number of defendants, in the courts for the place where any one of them is domiciled, provided the claims are so closely connected that it is expedient to hear and determine them together to avoid the risk of irreconcilable judgments resulting from separate proceedings;

(2) as a third party in an action on a warranty or guarantee or in any other third-party proceedings, in the court seised of the original proceedings, unless these were instituted solely with the object of removing him from the jurisdiction of the court which would be competent in his case;

(3) on a counter-claim arising from the same contract or facts on which the original claim was based, in the court in which the original claim is pending;

(4) in matters relating to a contract, if the action may be combined with an action against the same defendant in matters relating to rights in rem in immovable property, in the court of the Member State in which the property is situated.

[3.669]
Article 9
Where by virtue of this Regulation a court of a Member State has jurisdiction in actions relating to liability from the use or operation of a ship, that court, or any other court substituted for this purpose by the internal law of that Member State, shall also have jurisdiction over claims for limitation of such liability.

Articles 10–19 (*Outside the scope of this work.*)

SECTION 5
JURISDICTION OVER INDIVIDUAL CONTRACTS OF EMPLOYMENT

[3.670]
Article 20
1. In matters relating to individual contracts of employment, jurisdiction shall be determined by this Section, without prejudice to Article 6, point 5 of Article 7 and, in the case of proceedings brought against an employer, point 1 of Article 8.
2. Where an employee enters into an individual contract of employment with an employer who is not domiciled in a Member State but has a branch, agency or other establishment in one of the Member States, the employer shall, in disputes arising out of the operations of the branch, agency or establishment, be deemed to be domiciled in that Member State.

[3.671]
Article 21
1. An employer domiciled in a Member State may be sued:
  (a) in the courts of the Member State in which he is domiciled; or
  (b) in another Member State:
    (i) in the courts for the place where or from where the employee habitually carries out his work or in the courts for the last place where he did so; or
    (ii) if the employee does not or did not habitually carry out his work in any one country, in the courts for the place where the business which engaged the employee is or was situated.
2. An employer not domiciled in a Member State may be sued in a court of a Member State in accordance with point (b) of paragraph 1.

[3.672]
Article 22
1. An employer may bring proceedings only in the courts of the Member State in which the employee is domiciled.
2. The provisions of this Section shall not affect the right to bring a counter-claim in the court in which, in accordance with this Section, the original claim is pending.

[3.673]
Article 23
The provisions of this Section may be departed from only by an agreement:
  (1) which is entered into after the dispute has arisen; or
  (2) which allows the employee to bring proceedings in courts other than those indicated in this Section.

Article 24 (*Outside the scope of this work.*)

SECTION 7
PROROGATION OF JURISDICTION

[3.674]
Article 25
1. If the parties, regardless of their domicile, have agreed that a court or the courts of a Member State are to have jurisdiction to settle any disputes which have arisen or which may arise in connection with a particular legal relationship, that court or those courts shall have jurisdiction, unless the agreement is null and void as to its substantive validity under the law of that Member State. Such jurisdiction shall be exclusive unless the parties have agreed otherwise. The agreement conferring jurisdiction shall be either:
  (a) in writing or evidenced in writing;
  (b) in a form which accords with practices which the parties have established between themselves; or
  (c) in international trade or commerce, in a form which accords with a usage of which the parties are or ought to have been aware and which in such trade or commerce is widely known to, and regularly observed by, parties to contracts of the type involved in the particular trade or commerce concerned.
2. Any communication by electronic means which provides a durable record of the agreement shall be equivalent to 'writing'.
3. The court or courts of a Member State on which a trust instrument has conferred jurisdiction shall have exclusive jurisdiction in any proceedings brought against a settlor, trustee or beneficiary, if relations between those persons or their rights or obligations under the trust are involved.

4. Agreements or provisions of a trust instrument conferring jurisdiction shall have no legal force if they are contrary to Articles 15, 19 or 23, or if the courts whose jurisdiction they purport to exclude have exclusive jurisdiction by virtue of Article 24.
5. An agreement conferring jurisdiction which forms part of a contract shall be treated as an agreement independent of the other terms of the contract.

The validity of the agreement conferring jurisdiction cannot be contested solely on the ground that the contract is not valid.

[3.675]
Article 26
1. Apart from jurisdiction derived from other provisions of this Regulation, a court of a Member State before which a defendant enters an appearance shall have jurisdiction. This rule shall not apply where appearance was entered to contest the jurisdiction, or where another court has exclusive jurisdiction by virtue of Article 24.
2. In matters referred to in Sections 3, 4 or 5 where the policyholder, the insured, a beneficiary of the insurance contract, the injured party, the consumer or the employee is the defendant, the court shall, before assuming jurisdiction under paragraph 1, ensure that the defendant is informed of his right to contest the jurisdiction of the court and of the consequences of entering or not entering an appearance.

Articles 27, 28 (*Outside the scope of this work.*)

SECTION 9
LIS PENDENS — RELATED ACTIONS

[3.676]
Article 29
1. Without prejudice to Article 31(2), where proceedings involving the same cause of action and between the same parties are brought in the courts of different Member States, any court other than the court first seised shall of its own motion stay its proceedings until such time as the jurisdiction of the court first seised is established.
2. In cases referred to in paragraph 1, upon request by a court seised of the dispute, any other court seised shall without delay inform the former court of the date when it was seised in accordance with Article 32.
3. Where the jurisdiction of the court first seised is established, any court other than the court first seised shall decline jurisdiction in favour of that court.

[3.677]
Article 30
1. Where related actions are pending in the courts of different Member States, any court other than the court first seised may stay its proceedings.
2. Where the action in the court first seised is pending at first instance, any other court may also, on the application of one of the parties, decline jurisdiction if the court first seised has jurisdiction over the actions in question and its law permits the consolidation thereof.
3. For the purposes of this Article, actions are deemed to be related where they are so closely connected that it is expedient to hear and determine them together to avoid the risk of irreconcilable judgments resulting from separate proceedings.

[3.678]
Article 31
1. Where actions come within the exclusive jurisdiction of several courts, any court other than the court first seised shall decline jurisdiction in favour of that court.
2. Without prejudice to Article 26, where a court of a Member State on which an agreement as referred to in Article 25 confers exclusive jurisdiction is seised, any court of another Member State shall stay the proceedings until such time as the court seised on the basis of the agreement declares that it has no jurisdiction under the agreement.
3. Where the court designated in the agreement has established jurisdiction in accordance with the agreement, any court of another Member State shall decline jurisdiction in favour of that court.
4. Paragraphs 2 and 3 shall not apply to matters referred to in Sections 3, 4 or 5 where the policyholder, the insured, a beneficiary of the insurance contract, the injured party, the consumer or the employee is the claimant and the agreement is not valid under a provision contained within those Sections.

[3.679]
Article 32
1. For the purposes of this Section, a court shall be deemed to be seised:
  (a) at the time when the document instituting the proceedings or an equivalent document is lodged with the court, provided that the claimant has not subsequently failed to take the steps he was required to take to have service effected on the defendant; or

(b) if the document has to be served before being lodged with the court, at the time when it is received by the authority responsible for service, provided that the claimant has not subsequently failed to take the steps he was required to take to have the document lodged with the court.

The authority responsible for service referred to in point (b) shall be the first authority receiving the documents to be served.

2. The court, or the authority responsible for service, referred to in paragraph 1, shall note, respectively, the date of the lodging of the document instituting the proceedings or the equivalent document, or the date of receipt of the documents to be served.

[3.680]
Article 33

1. Where jurisdiction is based on Article 4 or on Articles 7, 8 or 9 and proceedings are pending before a court of a third State at the time when a court in a Member State is seised of an action involving the same cause of action and between the same parties as the proceedings in the court of the third State, the court of the Member State may stay the proceedings if:

(a) it is expected that the court of the third State will give a judgment capable of recognition and, where applicable, of enforcement in that Member State; and

(b) the court of the Member State is satisfied that a stay is necessary for the proper administration of justice.

2. The court of the Member State may continue the proceedings at any time if:

(a) the proceedings in the court of the third State are themselves stayed or discontinued;

(b) it appears to the court of the Member State that the proceedings in the court of the third State are unlikely to be concluded within a reasonable time; or

(c) the continuation of the proceedings is required for the proper administration of justice.

3. The court of the Member State shall dismiss the proceedings if the proceedings in the court of the third State are concluded and have resulted in a judgment capable of recognition and, where applicable, of enforcement in that Member State.

4. The court of the Member State shall apply this Article on the application of one of the parties or, where possible under national law, of its own motion.

[3.681]
Article 34

1. Where jurisdiction is based on Article 4 or on Articles 7, 8 or 9 and an action is pending before a court of a third State at the time when a court in a Member State is seised of an action which is related to the action in the court of the third State, the court of the Member State may stay the proceedings if:

(a) it is expedient to hear and determine the related actions together to avoid the risk of irreconcilable judgments resulting from separate proceedings;

(b) it is expected that the court of the third State will give a judgment capable of recognition and, where applicable, of enforcement in that Member State; and

(c) the court of the Member State is satisfied that a stay is necessary for the proper administration of justice.

2. The court of the Member State may continue the proceedings at any time if

(a) it appears to the court of the Member State that there is no longer a risk of irreconcilable judgments;

(b) the proceedings in the court of the third State are themselves stayed or discontinued;

(c) it appears to the court of the Member State that the proceedings in the court of the third State are unlikely to be concluded within a reasonable time; or

(d) the continuation of the proceedings is required for the proper administration of justice.

3. The court of the Member State may dismiss the proceedings if the proceedings in the court of the third State are concluded and have resulted in a judgment capable of recognition and, where applicable, of enforcement in that Member State.

4. The court of the Member State shall apply this Article on the application of one of the parties or, where possible under national law, of its own motion.

Articles 35–65 (*Outside the scope of this work.*)

CHAPTER VI
TRANSITIONAL PROVISIONS

[3.682]
Article 66

1. This Regulation shall apply only to legal proceedings instituted, to authentic instruments formally drawn up or registered and to court settlements approved or concluded on or after 10 January 2015.

2. Notwithstanding Article 80, Regulation (EC) No 44/2001 shall continue to apply to judgments given in legal proceedings instituted, to authentic instruments formally drawn up or registered and to court settlements approved or concluded before 10 January 2015 which fall within the scope of that Regulation.

CHAPTER VII
RELATIONSHIP WITH OTHER INSTRUMENTS

Article 67 (*Outside the scope of this work.*)

[3.683]
Article 68
1. This Regulation shall, as between the Member States, supersede the 1968 Brussels Convention, except as regards the territories of the Member States which fall within the territorial scope of that Convention and which are excluded from this Regulation pursuant to Article 355 of the TFEU.
2. In so far as this Regulation replaces the provisions of the 1968 Brussels Convention between the Member States, any reference to that Convention shall be understood as a reference to this Regulation.

Articles 69–73 (*Outside the scope of this work.*)

CHAPTER VIII
FINAL PROVISIONS

Articles 74–79 (*Outside the scope of this work.*)

[3.684]
Article 80
This Regulation shall repeal Regulation (EC) No 44/2001. References to the repealed Regulation shall be construed as references to this Regulation and shall be read in accordance with the correlation table set out in Annex III.

[3.685]
Article 81
This Regulation shall enter into force on the twentieth day following that of its publication in the *Official Journal of the European Union*.

It shall apply from 10 January 2015, with the exception of Articles 75 and 76, which shall apply from 10 January 2014.

This Regulation shall be binding in its entirety and directly applicable in the Member States in accordance with the Treaties.

ANNEXES I, II

(*Annexes I, II outside the scope of this work.*)

ANNEX III

CORRELATION TABLE

[3.686]

NOTES

Only those entries which relate to the provisions of Regulation 44/2001/EC and Regulation 1215/2012/EU reproduced in this work are listed below.

Regulation 44/2001/EC	*This Regulation*
Article 1(1)	Article 1(1)
Article 1(2), introductory words	Article 1(2), introductory words
Article 1(2) point (a)	Article 1(2), points (a) and (f)
Article 1(2), points (b) to (d)	Article 1(2), points (b) to (d)
—	Article 1(2), point (e)
Article 1(3)	—
—	Article 2
Article 2	Article 4
Article 3	Article 5
Article 4	Article 6
Article 5, introductory words	Article 7, introductory words

Regulation 44/2001/EC	*This Regulation*
Article 5, point (1)	Article 7, point (1)
Article 5, point (2)	—
Article 5, points (3) and (4)	Article 7, points (2) and (3)
—	Article 7, point (4)
Article 5, points (5) to (7)	Article 7, points (5) to (7)
Article 6	Article 8
Article 7	Article 9
. . .	. . .
Article 18	Article 20
Article 19, points (1) and (2)	Article 21(1)
—	Article 21(2)
Article 20	Article 22
Article 21	Article 23
. . .	. . .
Article 23(1) and (2)	Article 25(1) and (2)
Article 23(3)	—
Article 23(4) and (5)	Article 25(3) and (4)
—	Article 25(5)
Article 24	Article 26(1)
—	Article 26(2)
Article 25	Article 27
Article 26	Article 28
Article 27(1)	Article 29(1)
—	Article 29(2)
Article 27(2)	Article 29(3)
Article 28	Article 30
Article 29	Article 31(1)
—	Article 31(2)
—	Article 31(3)
—	Article 31(4)
Article 30	Article 32(1), points (a) and (b)
—	Article 32(1), second subparagraph
—	Article 32(2)
—	Article 33
—	Article 34
Article 31	Article 35
Article 32	Article 2, point (a)
. . .	. . .
Article 59	Article 62
Article 60	Article 63
. . .	. . .
Article 76	Article 81
Annex I	Article 76(1), point (a)
. . .	. . .
—	Annex III

PART 4
STATUTORY CODES OF PRACTICE

PART 4
STATUTORY CODES OF PRACTICE

A. ACAS

ACAS CODE OF PRACTICE 1
DISCIPLINARY AND GRIEVANCE PROCEDURES (2009)

[4.1]

NOTES

This is the fifth version of the Code originally produced by ACAS in 1977, and reissued in 1998, 2000 and 2004.

This version was produced under the authority given to ACAS by TULR(C)A 1992, s 199 at **[1.465]** and approved by the Secretary of State and by Parliament in accordance with s 200(2) and (4) at **[1.466]** (see the Employment Code of Practice (Disciplinary and Grievance Procedures) Order 2009, SI 2009/771). It came into effect on 6 April 2009, but does not have effect in circumstances where ss 29–33 of, and Schs 2–4 to, the Employment Act 2002 apply (all repealed). See for the circumstances in which those provisions apply after 5 April 2009 the Employment Act 2008 (Commencement, Transitional Provisions and Savings) Order 2008, SI 2008/3232. For the legal status of the Code see s 207 of the 1992 Act at **[1.473]**. Note also that by s 207A of that Act at **[1.474]**, as inserted by s 2 of the Employment Act 2008, an employment tribunal may in the circumstances there provided increase or decrease any compensation awarded by up to 25% where there has been unreasonable failure to comply with any relevant provision of the Code.

The Code is reproduced here in full, but it should be noted that the Foreword does not form part of the Code for the purpose of the legal effects of the Code under ss 207 and 207A of the 1992 Act. The Guide issued by ACAS to amplify the Code is at **[4.6]** below.

FOREWORD

[4.2]

The Acas statutory Code of Practice on discipline and grievance is set out at paras 1 to 45 on the following pages. It provides basic practical guidance to employers, employees and their representatives and sets out principles for handling disciplinary and grievance situations in the workplace. The Code does not apply to dismissals due to redundancy or the non-renewal of fixed term contracts on their expiry. Guidance on handling redundancies is contained in Acas' advisory booklet on Redundancy handling.

The Code is issued under section 199 of the Trade Union and Labour Relations (Consolidation) Act 1992 and was laid before both Houses of Parliament on 9 December 2008. It comes into effect by order of the Secretary of State on 6 April 2009 and replaces the Code issued in 2004.

A failure to follow the Code does not, in itself, make a person or organisation liable to proceedings. However, employment tribunals will take the Code into account when considering relevant cases. Tribunals will also be able to adjust any awards made in relevant cases by up to 25 per cent for unreasonable failure to comply with any provision of the Code. This means that if the tribunal feels that an employer has unreasonably failed to follow the guidance set out in the Code they can increase any award they have made by up to 25 per cent. Conversely, if they feel an employee has unreasonably failed to follow the guidance set out in the code they can reduce any award they have made by up to 25 per cent.

Employers and employees should always seek to resolve disciplinary and grievance issues in the workplace. Where this is not possible employers and employees should consider using an independent third party to help resolve the problem. The third party need not come from outside the organisation but could be an internal mediator, so long as they are not involved in the disciplinary or grievance issue. In some cases, an external mediator might be appropriate.

Many potential disciplinary or grievance issues can be resolved informally. A quiet word is often all that is required to resolve an issue. However, where an issue cannot be resolved informally then it may be pursued formally. This Code sets out the basic requirements of fairness that will be applicable in most cases; it is intended to provide the standard of reasonable behaviour in most instances.

Employers would be well advised to keep a written record of any disciplinary or grievances cases they deal with.

Organisations may wish to consider dealing with issues involving bullying, harassment or whistleblowing under a separate procedure.

More comprehensive advice and guidance on dealing with disciplinary and grievance situations is contained in the Acas booklet, 'Discipline and grievances at work: the Acas guide'. The booklet also contains sample disciplinary and grievance procedures. Copies of the guidance can be obtained from Acas.

Unlike the Code employment tribunals are not required to have regard to the Acas guidance booklet. However, it provides more detailed advice and guidance that employers and employees will often find helpful both in general terms and in individual cases.

THE CODE OF PRACTICE

INTRODUCTION

[4.3]

1. This Code is designed to help employers, employees and their representatives deal with disciplinary and grievance situations in the workplace.

- Disciplinary situations include misconduct and/or poor performance. If employers have a separate capability procedure they may prefer to address performance issues under this procedure. If so, however, the basic principles of fairness set out in this Code should still be followed, albeit that they may need to be adapted.
- Grievances are concerns, problems or complaints that employees raise with their employers.

The Code does not apply to redundancy dismissals or the non renewal of fixed term contracts on their expiry.

2. Fairness and transparency are promoted by developing and using rules and procedures for handling disciplinary and grievance situations. These should be set down in writing, be specific and clear. Employees and, where appropriate, their representatives should be involved in the development of rules and procedures. It is also important to help employees and managers understand what the rules and procedures are, where they can be found and how they are to be used.

3. Where some form of formal action is needed, what action is reasonable or justified will depend on all the circumstances of the particular case. Employment tribunals will take the size and resources of an employer into account when deciding on relevant cases and it may sometimes not be practicable for all employers to take all of the steps set out in this Code.

4. That said, whenever a disciplinary or grievance process is being followed it is important to deal with issues fairly. There are a number of elements to this:

- Employers and employees should raise and deal with issues **promptly** and should not unreasonably delay meetings, decisions or confirmation of those decisions.
- Employers and employees should act **consistently**.
- Employers should carry out any necessary **investigations**, to establish the facts of the case.
- Employers should **inform** employees of the basis of the problem and give them an opportunity to **put their case** in response before any decisions are made.
- Employers should allow employees to be **accompanied** at any formal disciplinary or grievance meeting.
- Employers should allow an employee to **appeal** against any formal decision made.

DISCIPLINE

KEYS TO HANDLING DISCIPLINARY ISSUES IN THE WORKPLACE

Establish the facts of each case

[4.4]

5. It is important to carry out necessary investigations of potential disciplinary matters without unreasonable delay to establish the facts of the case. In some cases this will require the holding of an investigatory meeting with the employee before proceeding to any disciplinary hearing. In others, the investigatory stage will be the collation of evidence by the employer for use at any disciplinary hearing.

6. In misconduct cases, where practicable, different people should carry out the investigation and disciplinary hearing.

7. If there is an investigatory meeting this should not by itself result in any disciplinary action. Although there is no statutory right for an employee to be accompanied at a formal investigatory meeting, such a right may be allowed under an employer's own procedure.

8. In cases where a period of suspension with pay is considered necessary, this period should be as brief as possible, should be kept under review and it should be made clear that this suspension is not considered a disciplinary action.

Inform the employee of the problem

9. If it is decided that there is a disciplinary case to answer, the employee should be notified of this in writing. This notification should contain sufficient information about the alleged misconduct or poor performance and its possible consequences to enable the employee to prepare to answer the case at a disciplinary meeting. It would normally be appropriate to provide copies of any written evidence, which may include any witness statements, with the notification.

10. The notification should also give details of the time and venue for the disciplinary meeting and advise the employee of their right to be accompanied at the meeting.

Hold a meeting with the employee to discuss the problem

11. The meeting should be held without unreasonable delay whilst allowing the employee reasonable time to prepare their case.

12. Employers and employees (and their companions) should make every effort to attend the meeting. At the meeting the employer should explain the complaint against the employee and go through the evidence that has been gathered. The employee should be allowed to set out their case and answer any allegations that have been made. The employee should also be given a reasonable opportunity to ask questions, present evidence and call relevant witnesses. They should also be given an opportunity to raise points about any information provided by witnesses. Where an employer or employee intends to call relevant witnesses they should give advance notice that they intend to do this.

Allow the employee to be accompanied at the meeting

13. Workers have a statutory right to be accompanied by a companion where the disciplinary meeting could result in:

- a formal warning being issued; or
- the taking of some other disciplinary action; or
- the confirmation of a warning or some other disciplinary action (appeal hearings).

14. The chosen companion may be a fellow worker, a trade union representative, or an official employed by a trade union. A trade union representative who is not an employed official must have been certified by their union as being competent to accompany a worker.

15. To exercise the statutory right to be accompanied workers must make a reasonable request. What is reasonable will depend on the circumstances of each individual case. However, it would not normally be reasonable for workers to insist on being accompanied by a companion whose presence would prejudice the hearing nor would it be reasonable for a worker to ask to be accompanied by a companion from a remote geographical location if someone suitable and willing was available on site.

16. The companion should be allowed to address the hearing to put and sum up the worker's case, respond on behalf of the worker to any views expressed at the meeting and confer with the worker during the hearing. The companion does not, however, have the right to answer questions on the worker's behalf, address the hearing if the worker does not wish it or prevent the employer from explaining their case.

Decide on appropriate action

17. After the meeting decide whether or not disciplinary or any other action is justified and inform the employee accordingly in writing.

18. Where misconduct is confirmed or the employee is found to be performing unsatisfactorily it is usual to give the employee a written warning. A further act of misconduct or failure to improve performance within a set period would normally result in a final written warning.

19. If an employee's first misconduct or unsatisfactory performance is sufficiently serious, it may be appropriate to move directly to a final written warning. This might occur where the employee's actions have had, or are liable to have, a serious or harmful impact on the organisation.

20. A first or final written warning should set out the nature of the misconduct or poor performance and the change in behaviour or improvement in performance required (with timescale). The employee should be told how long the warning will remain current. The employee should be informed of the consequences of further misconduct, or failure to improve performance, within the set period following a final warning. For instance that it may result in dismissal or some other contractual penalty such as demotion or loss of seniority.

21. A decision to dismiss should only be taken by a manager who has the authority to do so. The employee should be informed as soon as possible of the reasons for the dismissal, the date on which the employment contract will end, the appropriate period of notice and their right of appeal.

22. Some acts, termed gross misconduct, are so serious in themselves or have such serious consequences that they may call for dismissal without notice for a first offence. But a fair disciplinary process should always be followed, before dismissing for gross misconduct.

23. Disciplinary rules should give examples of acts which the employer regards as acts of gross misconduct. These may vary according to the nature of the organisation and what it does, but might include things such as theft or fraud, physical violence, gross negligence or serious insubordination.

24. Where an employee is persistently unable or unwilling to attend a disciplinary meeting without good cause the employer should make a decision on the evidence available.

Provide employees with an opportunity to appeal

25. Where an employee feels that disciplinary action taken against them is wrong or unjust they should appeal against the decision. Appeals should be heard without unreasonable delay and ideally at an agreed time and place. Employees should let employers know the grounds for their appeal in writing.

26. The appeal should be dealt with impartially and wherever possible, by a manager who has not previously been involved in the case.

27. Workers have a statutory right to be accompanied at appeal hearings.

28. Employees should be informed in writing of the results of the appeal hearing as soon as possible.

Special cases

29. Where disciplinary action is being considered against an employee who is a trade union representative the normal disciplinary procedure should be followed. Depending on the circumstances, however, it is advisable to discuss the matter at an early stage with an official employed by the union, after obtaining the employee's agreement.

30. If an employee is charged with, or convicted of a criminal offence this is not normally in itself reason for disciplinary action. Consideration needs to be given to what effect the charge or conviction has on the employee's suitability to do the job and their relationship with their employer, work colleagues and customers.

GRIEVANCE

KEYS TO HANDLING GRIEVANCES IN THE WORKPLACE

Let the employer know the nature of the grievance

[4.5]

31. If it is not possible to resolve a grievance informally employees should raise the matter formally and without unreasonable delay with a manager who is not the subject of the grievance. This should be done in writing and should set out the nature of the grievance.

Hold a meeting with the employee to discuss the grievance

32. Employers should arrange for a formal meeting to be held without unreasonable delay after a grievance is received.

33. Employers, employees and their companions should make every effort to attend the meeting. Employees should be allowed to explain their grievance and how they think it should be resolved. Consideration should be given to adjourning the meeting for any investigation that may be necessary.

Allow the employee to be accompanied at the meeting

34. Workers have a statutory right to be accompanied by a companion at a grievance meeting which deals with a complaint about a duty owed by the employer to the worker. So this would apply where the complaint is, for example, that the employer is not honouring the worker's contract, or is in breach of legislation.

35. The chosen companion may be a fellow worker, a trade union representative or an official employed by a trade union. A trade union representative who is not an employed official must have been certified by their union as being competent to accompany a worker.

36. To exercise the right to be accompanied a worker must first make a reasonable request. What is reasonable will depend on the circumstances of each individual case. However it would not normally be reasonable for workers to insist on being accompanied by a companion whose presence would prejudice the hearing nor would it be reasonable for a worker to ask to be accompanied by a companion from a remote geographical location if someone suitable and willing was available on site.

37. The companion should be allowed to address the hearing to put and sum up the worker's case, respond on behalf of the worker to any views expressed at the meeting and confer with the worker during the hearing. The companion does not however, have the right to answer questions on the worker's behalf, address the hearing if the worker does not wish it or prevent the employer from explaining their case.

Decide on appropriate action

38. Following the meeting decide on what action, if any, to take. Decisions should be communicated to the employee, in writing, without unreasonable delay and, where appropriate, should set out what action the employer intends to take to resolve the grievance. The employee should be informed that they can appeal if they are not content with the action taken.

Allow the employee to take the grievance further if not resolved

39. Where an employee feels that their grievance has not been satisfactorily resolved they should appeal. They should let their employer know the grounds for their appeal without unreasonable delay and in writing.

40. Appeals should be heard without unreasonable delay and at a time and place which should be notified to the employee in advance.

41. The appeal should be dealt with impartially and wherever possible by a manager who has not previously been involved in the case.

42. Workers have a statutory right to be accompanied at any such appeal hearing.

43. The outcome of the appeal should be communicated to the employee in writing without unreasonable delay.

Overlapping grievance and disciplinary cases

44. Where an employee raises a grievance during a disciplinary process the disciplinary process may be temporarily suspended in order to deal with the grievance. Where the grievance and disciplinary cases are related it may be appropriate to deal with both issues concurrently.

Collective grievances

45. The provisions of this code do not apply to grievances raised on behalf of two or more employees by a representative of a recognised trade union or other appropriate workplace representative. These grievances should be handled in accordance with the organisation's collective grievance process.

ACAS GUIDE: DISCIPLINE AND GRIEVANCES AT WORK (2011)

[4.6]

NOTES

This Guide was issued by ACAS to supplement the statutory guidance provided by the Code of Practice at **[4.1]** above. It has no statutory force but provides detailed guidance as to the application of the Code of Practice; see further the notes to that Code, *ante*. Throughout this Guide there are cross-references to other pages of the Guide. Those cross-references are to the Guide as published on the ACAS website; the equivalent paragraph in this work is also given. Footnotes are as in the original.

CONTENTS

INTRODUCTION

[4.7]

This guide provides good practice advice for dealing with discipline and grievances in the workplace. It complements the *Acas Code of Practice on disciplinary and grievance procedures.* Extracts from the Code of Practice are reproduced in shaded boxes accompanied by further practical advice and guidance.

Extract: Acas Code of Practice on disciplinary and grievance procedures
This Code is designed to help employers, employees and their representatives deal with disciplinary and grievance situations in the workplace.

The Acas Code of Practice sets out principles for handling disciplinary and grievance situations in the workplace. This guide provides more detailed advice and guidance that employers and employees will often find helpful both in general terms and in individual cases.

Employment tribunals are legally required to take the Acas Code of Practice into account when considering relevant cases. Tribunals will also be able to adjust any compensatory awards made in these cases by up to 25 per cent for unreasonable failure to comply with any provision of the Code. This means that if the tribunal feels that an employer has unreasonably failed to follow the guidance set out in the Code they can increase any award they have made by up to 25 per cent. Conversely, if they feel an employee has unreasonably failed to follow the guidance set out in the code they can reduce any award they have made by up to 25 per cent.

Employment tribunals are not required to have regard to guidance in this booklet that does not form part of the Code.

The law on unfair dismissal requires employers to act reasonably when dealing with disciplinary issues. What is classed as reasonable behaviour will depend on the circumstances of each case, and is ultimately a matter for employment tribunals to decide. However, the core principles are set out in the Acas Code of Practice.

The foreword to the Code and this guide emphasise that employers and employees should always seek to resolve disciplinary and grievance issues in the workplace. If discipline and grievance issues are settled at an early stage they are normally less time-consuming and less likely to damage working relationships.

Good employment relations practices – including for recruitment, induction training, communications and consultation – can prevent many discipline and grievance problems arising. Organisations are also more likely to have positive employment relationships if they make efforts to gain their employees' commitment through:

- showing them clear leadership and letting them know how they can contribute
- engaging them in their work and giving them the power to make some decisions themselves rather than trying to control and restrict them
- showing them respect and appreciation
- giving them ways to voice their views and concerns.

Acas provides comprehensive guidance on employment issues in its publications or on its website and information about suitable training. For further details see the Acas website www.acas.org.uk or call the Acas Helpline **08457 47 47 47**.

Handling discipline – an overview

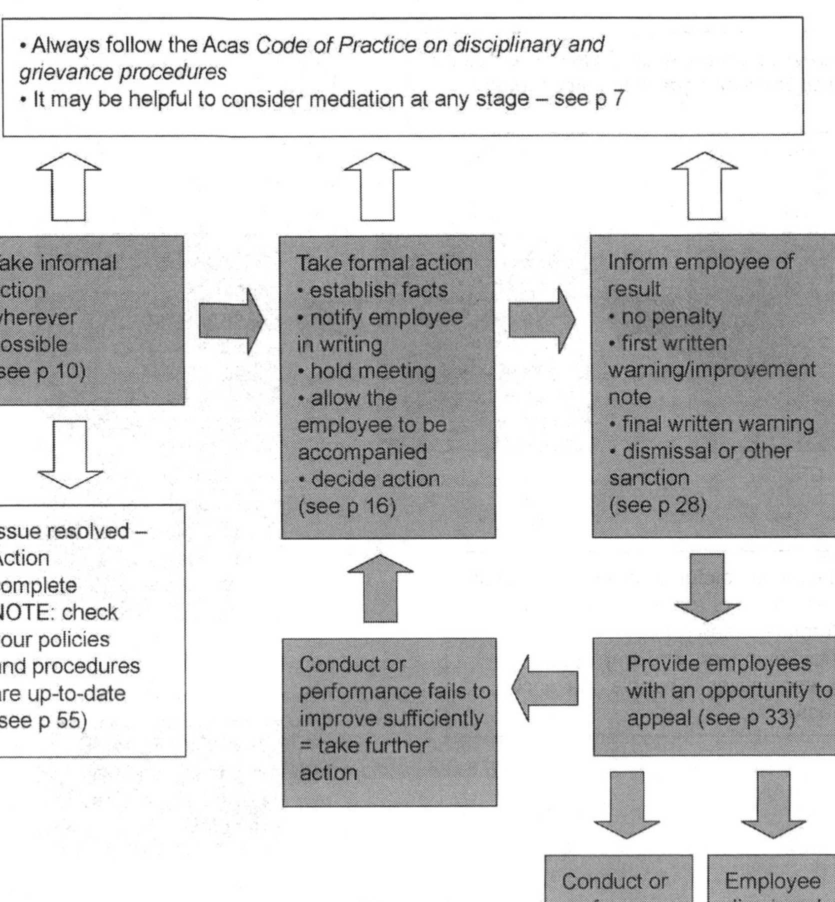
• Always follow the Acas *Code of Practice on disciplinary and grievance procedures*
• It may be helpful to consider mediation at any stage – see p 7
Take informal action wherever possible (see p 10)
Take formal action
• establish facts
• notify employee in writing
• hold meeting
• allow the employee to be accompanied
• decide action
(see p 16)
Inform employee of result
• no penalty
• first written warning/improvement note
• final written warning
• dismissal or other sanction
(see p 28)
Issue resolved – Action complete NOTE: check your policies and procedures are up-to-date (see p 55)
Conduct or performance fails to improve sufficiently = take further action
Provide employees with an opportunity to appeal (see p 33)
Conduct or performance improve = action complete
Employee dismissed

Handling grievances – an overview

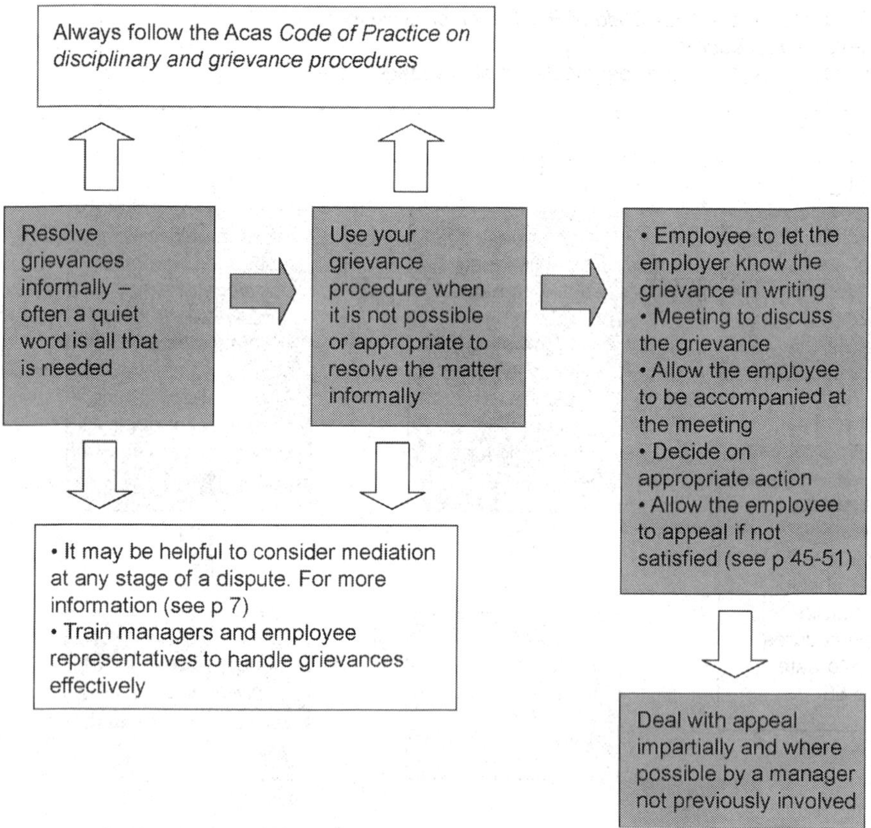

Always follow the Acas *Code of Practice on disciplinary and grievance procedures*
Resolve grievances informally – often a quiet word is all that is needed
Use your grievance procedure when it is not possible or appropriate to resolve the matter informally
• Employee to let the employer know the grievance in writing
• Meeting to discuss the grievance
• Allow the employee to be accompanied at the meeting
• Decide on appropriate action
• Allow the employee to appeal if not satisfied (see p 45-51)
• It may be helpful to consider mediation at any stage of a dispute. For more information (see p 7)
• Train managers and employee representatives to handle grievances effectively
Deal with appeal impartially and where possible by a manager not previously involved

USING MEDIATION

An independent third party or mediator can sometimes help resolve disciplinary or grievance issues. Mediation is a voluntary process where the mediator helps two or more people in dispute to attempt to reach an agreement. Any agreement comes from those in dispute, not from the mediator. The mediator is not there to judge, to say one person is right and the other wrong, or to tell those involved in the mediation what they should do. The mediator is in charge of the process of seeking to resolve the problem but not the outcome.

Mediators may be employees trained and accredited by an external mediation service who act as internal mediators in addition to their day jobs. Or they may be from an external mediation provider. They can work individually or in pairs as co-mediators.

There are no hard-and-fast rules for when mediation is appropriate but it can be used:

- for conflict involving colleagues of a similar job or grade, or between a line manager and their staff
- at any stage in the conflict as long as any ongoing formal procedures are put in abeyance, or where mediation is included as a stage in the procedures themselves
- to rebuild relationships after a formal dispute has been resolved
- to address a range of issues, including relationship breakdown, personality clashes, communication problems, bullying and harassment.

In some organisations mediation is written into formal discipline and grievance procedures as an optional stage. Where this is not the case, it is useful to be clear about whether the discipline and grievance procedure can be suspended if mediation is deemed to be an appropriate method of resolving the dispute.

Grievances most obviously lend themselves to the possibility of mediation. Managers may not always see it as appropriate to surrender their discretion in relation to disciplinary issues where they believe a point of principle is at stake, such as misconduct or poor performance. However, disciplinary and grievance issues can become blurred, and the employer may prefer to tackle the underlying relationship issues by means of mediation.

Cases unsuitable for mediation

Mediation may not be suitable if:

- used as a first resort – because people should be encouraged to speak to each other and talk to their manager before they seek a solution via mediation
- it is used by a manager to avoid their managerial responsibilities
- a decision about right or wrong is needed, for example where there is possible criminal activity
- the individual bringing a discrimination or harassment case wants it investigated
- the parties do not have the power to settle the issue
- one side is completely intransigent and using mediation will only raise unrealistic expectations of a positive outcome.

For more information about mediation see the Acas website at www.acas.org.uk and the Acas/CIPD guide *Mediation: An employer's guide* which can be downloaded from the website.

DISCIPLINE
KEYS TO HANDLING DISCIPLINARY PROBLEMS IN THE WORKPLACE

RESOLVE DISCIPLINE ISSUES INFORMALLY

[4.8]
Cases of minor misconduct or unsatisfactory performance are usually best dealt with informally. A quiet word is often all that is required to improve an employee's conduct or performance. In some cases additional training, coaching and advice may be what is needed. An informal approach may be particularly helpful in small firms, where problems can be resolved quickly and confidentially. There will be situations where matters are more serious or where an informal approach has been tried but is not working.

If informal action does not bring about an improvement, or the misconduct or unsatisfactory performance is considered too serious to be classed as minor, employers should provide employees with a clear signal of their dissatisfaction by taking formal action.

Discipline in practice 1

A valued and generally reliable employee is late for work on a number of occasions causing difficulty for other staff who have to provide cover.

You talk to the employee on his own and he reveals that he has recently split up with his wife and he now has to take the children to school on the way to work. You agree a temporary adjustment to his start and finish times and he undertakes to make arrangements for 'school run' cover which solves the problem. You decide that formal disciplinary action is not appropriate.

How should it be done?

Talk to the employee in private. This should be a two-way discussion, aimed at discussing possible shortcomings in conduct or performance and encouraging improvement. Criticism should be constructive, with the emphasis being on finding ways for the employee to improve and for the improvement to be sustained.

Listen to whatever the employee has to say about the issue. It may become evident there is no problem – if so make this clear to the employee.

Where improvement is required make sure the employee understands what needs to be done, how their performance or conduct will be reviewed, and over what period. It may be useful to confirm in writing what has been decided.

Be careful that any informal action does not turn into formal disciplinary action, as this may unintentionally deny the employee certain rights, such as the right to be accompanied (see p 23 (**[4.28]**)). If, during the discussion, it becomes obvious that the matter may be more serious, the meeting should be adjourned. The employee should be told that the matter will be continued under the formal disciplinary procedure.

Keep brief notes of any agreed informal action for reference purposes. There should be reviews of progress over specified periods.

Consider at any stage whether the use of an independent mediator may be helpful (see p 7 (**[4.6]**)).

DEVELOP RULES AND PROCEDURES

[4.9]

Extract: Acas Code of Practice on disciplinary and grievance procedures

Fairness and transparency are promoted by developing and using rules and procedures for handling disciplinary and grievance situations. These should be set down in writing, be specific and clear. Employees and, where appropriate, their representatives should be involved in the development of rules and procedures. It is also important to help employees and managers understand what the rules and procedures are, where they can be found and how they are to be used.

Rules and performance standards

Clear rules benefit employees and set standards of conduct. They also help employers to act fairly and consistently.

Employers should also set standards of performance so that employees know what is expected of them. This is usually done as part of an organisation's performance management which will involve agreeing objectives and reviewing performance on a regular basis.

What should rules cover?

Different organisations will have different requirements but rules often cover such matters as:

- timekeeping
- absence[1]
- health and safety
- use of organisation facilities
- discrimination, bullying and harassment
- personal appearance
- the types of conduct that might be considered as 'gross misconduct' (see p 31 (**[4.42]**)).

How should rules be drawn up and communicated?

Rules are likely to be more effective if they are accepted as reasonable by those covered by them and those who operate them. It is good practice to develop rules in consultation with employees (and their representatives where appropriate) and those who will have responsibility for applying them.

Unless there are reasons why different sets of rules apply to different groups they should apply to all employees at all levels in the organisation.

The rules should not discriminate on the grounds of sex, transgender, marital or civil partnership status, racial group, sexual orientation, religion or belief, disability[2] or age.[3]

Writing down the rules helps both managers and employees to know what is expected of them. The rules should be made clear to employees. Ideally employees should be given their own printed copy of the rules or written information about how to access them – eg on the organisation's Intranet or in their handbook. Employees are entitled to a written statement of employment particulars which must include a note about disciplinary rules and procedures.[4]

In a small organisation, it may be sufficient for rules to be displayed in a prominent place. See Appendix 1 for a checklist 'Disciplinary rules for small organisations'.

Special attention should be paid to ensure that rules are understood by any employees without recent experience of working life (for instance young people or those returning to work after a lengthy break), and by employees whose English or reading ability is limited or who have a disability such as visual impairment.

Why have a disciplinary procedure?

A disciplinary procedure is the means by which rules are observed and standards are maintained. The procedure should be used primarily to help and encourage employees to improve rather than just as a way of imposing punishment. It provides a method of dealing with any apparent shortcomings in conduct or performance and can help an employee to become effective again. The procedure should be fair, effective, and consistently applied.

Extract: Acas Code of Practice on disciplinary and grievance procedures

Disciplinary situations include misconduct and/or poor performance. If employers have a separate capability procedure they may prefer to address performance issues under this procedure. If so, however, the basic principles of fairness set out in this Code should still be followed, albeit that they may need to be adapted.

NOTES

1 For detailed advice on absence see the Acas Advisory Booklet *Managing attendance and employee turnover.*

2 Further advice and Codes of Practice may be obtained from the Equality and Human Rights Commission at www.equalityhumanrights.com. Acas' Equality Direct Helpline can also give help and advice to employers. Tel 08456 00 33 44.

3 See the Acas Guidance on *Age and the workplace: putting the Equality Act 2010 and the removal of the default retirement age (DRA) 2011 into practice.*

4 Guidance on what the written statement must include is provided on the Department for Business, Enterprise and Regulatory Reform (BERR) website at www.berr.gov.uk.

What should disciplinary procedures contain?

[4.10]
When drawing up and applying procedures, employers should always bear in mind principles of fairness. For example, employees should be informed of the allegations against them, together with the supporting evidence, in advance of the meeting. Employees should be given the opportunity to challenge the allegations before decisions are reached and should be provided with a right to appeal. Good disciplinary procedures should:

- be in writing
- be non-discriminatory
- provide for matters to be dealt with speedily
- allow for information to be kept confidential
- tell employees what disciplinary action might be taken
- say what levels of management have the authority to take the various forms of disciplinary action
- require employees to be informed of the complaints against them and supporting evidence, before a disciplinary meeting
- give employees a chance to have their say before management reaches a decision
- provide employees with the right to be accompanied
- provide that no employee is dismissed for a first breach of discipline, except in cases of gross misconduct
- require management to investigate fully before any disciplinary action is taken
- ensure that employees are given an explanation for any sanction and allow employees to appeal against a decision
- apply to all employees, irrespective of their length of service, status or say if there are different rules for different groups and ensure that:
  - any investigatory period of suspension is with pay, and specify how pay is to be calculated during this period. If, exceptionally, suspension is to be without pay, this must be provided for in the contract of employment
  - any suspension is brief, and is never used as a sanction against the employee prior to a disciplinary meeting and decision. Keep the employee informed of progress
  - the employee will be heard in good faith and that there is no pre-judgement of the issue
  - where the facts are in dispute, no disciplinary penalty is imposed until the case has been carefully investigated, and there is a reasonably held belief that the employee committed the act in question.

Samples of disciplinary procedures are at Appendix 2 – Sample disciplinary and grievance procedures, and may be adapted according to the requirements of the organisation.

Reviewing rules and procedures

[4.11]
Keep rules and procedures under review to make sure they are always relevant and effective. Address any shortcomings as they arise. Employees and their representatives should be consulted before new or additional rules are introduced.

Training

[4.12]
Good training helps managers achieve positive outcomes, reducing the need for any further disciplinary action. Those responsible for using and operating the disciplinary rules and procedures, including managers at all levels, should be trained for the task. Ignoring or circumventing the procedures when dismissing an employee is likely to have a bearing on the outcome of any subsequent employment tribunal claim. If the organisation recognises trade unions, or there is any other form of employee representation, it can be useful to undertake training on a joint basis –

everyone then has the same understanding and has an opportunity to work through the procedure, clarifying any issues that might arise. For information about suitable training see the Acas website www.acas.org.uk.

KEEPING WRITTEN RECORDS

What records should be kept?

[4.13]
The foreword to the Code of Practice advises employers to keep a written record of any disciplinary or grievances cases they deal with.

Records should include:

- the complaint against the employee
- the employee's defence
- findings made and actions taken
- the reason for actions taken
- whether an appeal was lodged
- the outcome of the appeal
- any grievances raised during the disciplinary procedure
- subsequent developments
- notes of any formal meetings.

Records should be treated as confidential and be kept no longer than necessary in accordance with the Data Protection Act 1998. This Act gives individuals the right to request and have access to certain personal data. The Information Commissioner has produced Codes of Practice covering recruitment and selection, employment records, monitoring at work and information about an employee's health.[5] The data protection principles are outlined at Appendix 5.

Copies of meeting records should be given to the employee including copies of any formal minutes that may have been taken. In certain circumstances (for example to protect a witness) the employer might withhold some information.

NOTES

5 The recommendations for good practice can be obtained from the Information Commissioner's Office, Wycliffe House, Water Lane, Wilmslow, Cheshire SK9 5AF Tel 01625 545700 www.ico.gov.uk.

DEALING FAIRLY WITH FORMAL DISCIPLINARY ACTION

[4.14]

Extract: Acas Code of Practice on disciplinary and grievance procedures
Where some form of formal action is needed, what action is reasonable or justified will depend on all the circumstances of the particular case. Employment tribunals will take the size and resources of an employer into account when deciding on relevant cases and it may sometimes not be practicable for all employers to take all of the steps set out in this Code. That said, whenever a disciplinary or grievance process is being followed it is important to deal with issues fairly. There are a number of elements to this: • Employers and employees should raise and deal with issues **promptly** and should not unreasonably delay meetings, decisions or confirmation of those decisions. • Employers and employees should act **consistently**. • Employers should carry out any necessary **investigations**, to establish the facts of the case. • Employers should **inform** employees of the basis of the problem and give them an opportunity to **put their case** in response before any decisions are made. • Employers should allow employees to be **accompanied** at any formal disciplinary or grievance meeting. • Employers should allow an employee to appeal against any formal decision made.

The following pages give detailed guidance on handling formal disciplinary issues. Always bear in mind the need for fairness when following procedures taking account of the elements from the Acas Code of Practice reproduced above. Dealing with absence is only one of any number of issues where disciplinary action may be considered. It can, however, raise particular problems and is dealt with separately at Appendix 4 – Dealing with absence.

ESTABLISHING THE FACTS

[4.15]

Extract: Acas Code of Practice on disciplinary and grievance procedures
It is important to carry out necessary investigations of potential disciplinary matters without unreasonable delay to establish the facts of the case. In some cases this will require the holding of an investigatory meeting with the employee before proceeding to any disciplinary hearing. In others, the investigatory stage will be the collation of evidence by the employer for use at any disciplinary hearing.
In misconduct cases, where practicable, different people should carry out the investigation and disciplinary hearing.
If there is an investigatory meeting this should not by itself result in any disciplinary action. Although there is no statutory right for an employee to be accompanied at a formal investigatory meeting, such a right may be allowed under an employer's own procedure.
In cases where a period of suspension with pay is considered necessary, this period should be as brief as possible, should be kept under review and it should be made clear that this suspension is not considered a disciplinary action.

Investigating cases

[4.16]

When investigating a disciplinary matter take care to deal with the employee in a fair and reasonable manner. The nature and extent of the investigations will depend on the seriousness of the matter and the more serious it is then the more thorough the investigation should be. It is important to keep an open mind and look for evidence which supports the employee's case as well as evidence against.

It is not always necessary to hold an investigatory meeting (often called a fact finding meeting). If a meeting is held, give the employee advance warning and time to prepare.

Any investigatory meeting should be conducted by a management representative and should be confined to establishing the facts of the case. It is important that disciplinary action is not considered at an investigatory meeting. If it becomes apparent that formal disciplinary action may be needed then this should be dealt with at a formal meeting at which the employee will have the statutory right to be accompanied. See also 'Use of external consultants' on p 37 (**[4.53]**).

Suspension

[4.17]

There may be instances where suspension with pay is necessary while investigations are carried out. For example where relationships have broken down, in gross misconduct cases or where there are risks to an employee's or the company's property or responsibilities to other parties. Exceptionally you may wish to consider suspension with pay where you have reasonable grounds for concern that evidence has been tampered with, destroyed or witnesses pressurised before the meeting.

Suspension with pay should only be imposed after careful consideration and should be reviewed to ensure it is not unnecessarily protracted. It should be made clear that suspension is not an assumption of guilt and is not considered a disciplinary sanction.

INFORMING THE EMPLOYEE

[4.18]

Extract: Acas Code of Practice on disciplinary and grievance procedures
If it is decided that there is a disciplinary case to answer, the employee should be notified of this in writing. This notification should contain sufficient information about the alleged misconduct or poor performance and its possible consequences to enable the employee to prepare to answer the case at a disciplinary meeting. It would normally be appropriate to provide copies of any written evidence, which may include any witness statements, with the notification.
The notification should also give details of the time and venue for the disciplinary meeting and advise the employee of their right to be accompanied at the meeting.

As well notifying the nature of the complaint and the right to be accompanied (see p 23 (**[4.28]**)) the employee should also be told about the procedure to be followed.

A sample letter inviting an employee to a meeting is at Appendix 3.

HOLDING A DISCIPLINARY MEETING

[4.19]

Extract: Acas Code of Practice on disciplinary and grievance procedures

The meeting should be held without unreasonable delay whilst allowing the employee reasonable time to prepare their case.

Employers and employees (and their companions) should make every effort to attend the meeting. At the meeting the employer should explain the complaint against the employee and go through the evidence that has been gathered. The employee should be allowed to set out their case and answer any allegations that have been made. The employee should also be given a reasonable opportunity to ask questions, present evidence and call relevant witnesses. They should also be given an opportunity to raise points about any information provided by witnesses. Where an employer or employee intends to call relevant witnesses they should give advance notice that they intend to do this.

Preparing for the meeting

[4.20]

You should:

- ensure that all the relevant facts are available, such as disciplinary records and any other relevant documents (for instance absence or sickness records) and, where appropriate, written statements from witnesses
- where possible arrange for someone who is not involved in the case to take a note of the meeting and to act as a witness to what was said
- check if there are any special circumstances to be taken into account. For example, are there personal or other outside issues affecting performance or conduct?
- be careful when dealing with evidence from a person who wishes to remain anonymous. Take written statements, seek corroborative evidence and check that the person's motives are genuine[6]
- consider what explanations may be offered by the employee, and if possible check them out beforehand
- allow the employee time to prepare his or her case. Copies of any relevant papers and witness statements should be made available to the employee in advance
- if the employee concerned is a trade union representative discuss the case with a trade union full-time official after obtaining the employee's agreement. This is because the action may be seen as an attack on the union
- arrange a time for the meeting, which should be held as privately as possible, in a suitable room, and where there will be no interruptions. The employee may offer a reasonable alternative time within five days of the original date if their chosen companion cannot attend. You may also arrange another meeting if an employee fails to attend through circumstances outside their control, such as illness
- try and get a written statement from any witness from outside the organisation who is not prepared to or is unable to attend the meeting
- allow the employee to call witnesses or submit witness statements
- consider the provision of an interpreter or facilitator if there are understanding or language difficulties (perhaps a friend of the employee, or a co-employee). This person may need to attend in addition to the companion though ideally one person should carry out both roles
- make provision for any reasonable adjustments to accommodate the needs of a person with disabilities
- think about the structure of the meeting and make a list of points you will wish to cover.

NOTES

[6] Guidance given by the Employment Appeal Tribunal in *Linfood Cash and Carry v Thomson* [1989] IRLR 235, sets out the approach that should be taken with anonymous informants. In particular statements should be in writing, available to the accused employee and give details of time/place/dates as appropriate. The employer should enquire as to the character of the informant and assess the credibility and weight to be attached to the evidence.

What if an employee repeatedly fails to attend a meeting?

[4.21]

There may be occasions when an employee is repeatedly unable or unwilling to attend a meeting. This may be for various reasons, including genuine illness or a refusal to face up to the issue. Employers will need to consider all the facts and come to a reasonable decision on how to proceed. Considerations may include:

- any rules the organisation has for dealing with failure to attend disciplinary meetings
- the seriousness of the disciplinary issue under consideration
- the employee's disciplinary record (including current warnings), general work record, work experience, position and length of service

- medical opinion on whether the employee is fit to attend the meeting
- how similar cases in the past have been dealt with.

Where an employee continues to be unavailable to attend a meeting the employer may conclude that a decision will be made on the evidence available. The employee should bc informed where this is to be the case. See also Appendix 4 'Dealing with absence'.

How should the disciplinary meeting be conducted?

Remember that the point of the meeting is to establish the facts, not catch people out. The meetings may not proceed in neat, orderly stages but it is good practice to:

- introduce those present to the employee and explain why they are there
- introduce and explain the role of the accompanying person if present
- explain that the purpose of the meeting is to consider whether disciplinary action should be taken in accordance with the organisation's disciplinary procedure
- explain how the meeting will be conducted.

Statement of the complaint

[4.22]
State precisely what the complaint is and outline the case briefly by going through the evidence that has been gathered. Ensure that the employee and his or her representative or accompanying person are allowed to see any statements made by witnesses and question them.

Employee's reply

[4.23]
Give the employee the opportunity to state their case and answer any allegations that have been made. They should be able to ask questions, present evidence and call witnesses. The accompanying person may also ask questions and should be able to confer privately with the employee. Listen carefully and be prepared to wait in silence for an answer as this can be a constructive way of encouraging the employee to be more forthcoming.

Establish whether the employee is prepared to accept that they may have done something wrong or are not performing to the required standard. Then agree the steps which should be taken to remedy the situation.

If it is not practical for witnesses to attend, consider proceeding if it is clear that their verbal evidence will not affect the substance of the complaint. Alternatively, consider an adjournment to allow questions to be put to a witness who cannot attend in person but who has submitted a witness statement.

General questioning and discussion

[4.24]
You should:

- use this stage to establish all the facts
- ask the employee if they have any explanation for the alleged misconduct or unsatisfactory performance, or if there are any special circumstances to be taken into account
- if it becomes clear during this stage that the employee has provided an adequate explanation or there is no real evidence to support the allegation, bring the proceedings to a close
- keep the approach formal and polite and encourage the employee to speak freely with a view to establishing the facts. A properly conducted disciplinary meeting should be a two-way process. Use questions to clarify the issues and to check that what has been said is understood. Ask open-ended questions, for example, 'what happened then?' to get the broad picture. Ask precise, closed questions requiring a yes/no answer only when specific information is needed
- do not get involved in arguments and do not make personal or humiliating remarks. Avoid physical contact or gestures which could be misinterpreted or misconstrued as judgemental.

If new facts emerge, it may be necessary to adjourn the meeting to investigate them and reconvene the meeting when this has been done.

Summing up

[4.25]
Summarise the main points of the discussion after questioning is completed. This allows all parties to be reminded of the nature of the offence, the arguments and evidence put forward and to ensure nothing is missed. Ask the employee if they have anything further to say. This should help to demonstrate to the employee that they have been treated reasonably.

Adjournment before decision

[4.26]
Adjourn before a decision is taken about whether a disciplinary penalty is appropriate. This allows

time for reflection and proper consideration. It also allows for any further checking of any matters raised, particularly if there is any dispute over facts.

What problems may arise and how should they be handled?

[4.27]

Extract: Acas Code of Practice on disciplinary and grievance procedures
Where an employee raises a grievance during a disciplinary process the disciplinary process may be temporarily suspended in order to deal with the grievance. Where the grievance and disciplinary cases are related, it may be appropriate to deal with both issues concurrently.

When an employee raises a grievance during the meeting it may sometimes be appropriate to consider stopping the meeting and suspending the disciplinary procedure – for example when:

- the grievance relates to a conflict of interest that the manager holding the disciplinary meeting is alleged to have
- bias is alleged in the conduct of the disciplinary meeting
- management have been selective in the evidence they have supplied to the manager holding the meeting
- there is possible discrimination.

It would not be appropriate to suspend the meeting where the employee makes an invalid point. For example if they mistakenly claim that they have the right to be legally represented or that a collectively agreed and applicable procedure does not apply to them because they are not a union member.

It is possible that the disciplinary meeting may not proceed smoothly – people may be upset or angry. If the employee becomes upset or distressed allow time for them to regain composure before continuing. If the distress is too great to continue then adjourn and reconvene at a later date – however, the issues should not be avoided. Clearly during the meeting there may be some 'letting off steam', and this can be helpful in finding out what has actually happened. However, abusive language or conduct should not be tolerated.

ALLOWING THE EMPLOYEE TO BE ACCOMPANIED

[4.28]

Extract: Acas Code of Practice on disciplinary and grievance procedures
Workers have a statutory right to be accompanied by a companion where the disciplinary meeting could result in: • a formal warning being issued; or • the taking of some other disciplinary action; or • the confirmation of a warning or some other disciplinary action (appeal hearings). The chosen companion may be a fellow worker, a trade union representative, or an official employed by a trade union. A trade union representative who is not an employed official must have been certified by their union as being competent to accompany a worker. To exercise the statutory right to be accompanied workers must make a reasonable request. What is reasonable will depend on the circumstances of each individual case. However, it would not normally be reasonable for workers to insist on being accompanied by a companion whose presence would prejudice the hearing nor would it be reasonable for a worker to ask to be accompanied by a companion from a remote geographical location if someone suitable and willing was available on site. The companion should be allowed to address the hearing to put and sum up the workers case, respond on behalf of the worker to any views expressed at the meeting and confer with the worker during the hearing. The companion does not, however, have the right to answer questions on the worker's behalf, address the hearing if the worker does not wish it or prevent the employer from explaining their case.

What is the right to be accompanied?

[4.29]

Workers have a statutory right to be accompanied where they are required or invited by their employer to attend certain disciplinary or grievance meetings. The chosen companion may be a fellow worker, a trade union representative, or an official employed by a trade union. A trade union representative who is not an employed official must have been certified by their union as being competent to accompany a worker. Workers must make a reasonable request to their employer to be accompanied.

When does the right apply?

[4.30]
Employees have the right to be accompanied at meetings that could result in:

- a formal warning being issued to a worker (ie a warning that will be placed on the worker's record);
- the taking of some other disciplinary action (such as suspension without pay, demotion or dismissal) or other action; or
- the confirmation of a warning or some other disciplinary action (such as an appeal hearing).

Informal discussions, counselling sessions or investigatory meetings do not attract the right to be accompanied. Meetings to investigate an issue are not disciplinary meetings. If it becomes apparent that formal disciplinary action may be needed then this should be dealt with at a formal meeting at which the employee will have the statutory right to be accompanied.

What is a reasonable request?

[4.31]
Whether a request for a companion is reasonable will depend on the circumstances of the individual case and, ultimately, it is a matter for the courts and tribunals to decide. However, when workers are choosing a companion, they should bear in mind that it would not be reasonable to insist on being accompanied by a colleague whose presence would prejudice the hearing or who might have a conflict of interest. Nor would it be reasonable for a worker to ask to be accompanied by a colleague from a geographically remote location when someone suitably qualified was available on site. The request to be accompanied does not have to be in writing.

The companion

[4.32]
The companion may be:

- a fellow worker (ie another of the employer's workers)
- an official employed by a trade union
- a workplace trade union representative, as long as they have been reasonably certified in writing by their union as having experience of, or having received training in, acting as a worker's companion at disciplinary or grievance hearings. Certification may take the form of a card or letter.

Some workers may, however, have additional contractual rights to be accompanied by persons other than those listed above (for instance a partner, spouse or legal representative).

Reasonable adjustment may be needed for a worker with a disability (and possibly for their companion if they are disabled). For example the provision of a support worker or advocate with knowledge of the disability and its effects.

Workers may ask an official from any trade union to accompany them at a disciplinary or grievance hearing, regardless of whether or not they are a member or the union is recognised.

Fellow workers or trade union officials do not have to accept a request to accompany a worker, and they should not be pressurised to do so.

Trade unions should ensure that their officials are trained in the role of acting as a worker's companion. Even when a trade union official has experience of acting in the role, there may still be a need for periodic refresher training. Employers should consider allowing time off for this training.

A worker who has agreed to accompany a colleague employed by the same employer is entitled to take a reasonable amount of paid time off to fulfil that responsibility. This should cover the hearing and it is also good practice to allow time for the companion to familiarise themselves with the case and confer with the worker before and after the hearing.

A lay trade union official is permitted to take a reasonable amount of paid time off to accompany a worker at a hearing, as long as the worker is employed by the same employer. In cases where a lay official agrees to accompany a worker employed by another organisation, time off is a matter for agreement by the parties concerned.

Applying the right

[4.33]
The employer should allow a companion to have a say about the date and time of a hearing. If the companion cannot attend on a proposed date, the worker can suggest an alternative time and date so long as it is reasonable and it is not more than five working days after the original date.

Before the hearing takes place, the worker should tell the employer who they have chosen as a companion. In certain circumstances (for instance when the companion is an official of a non-recognised trade union) it can be helpful for the companion and employer to make contact before the hearing.

The companion should be allowed to address the hearing in order to:

- put the worker's case
- sum up the worker's case
- respond on the worker's behalf to any view expressed at the hearing.

The companion can also confer with the worker during the hearing. It is good practice to allow the companion to participate as fully as possible in the hearing, including asking witnesses questions. The employer is, however, not legally required to permit the companion to answer questions on the worker's behalf, or to address the hearing if the worker does not wish it, or to prevent the employer from explaining their case.

Workers whose employers fail to comply with a reasonable request to be accompanied may present a complaint to an employment tribunal. Workers may also complain to a tribunal if employers fail to re-arrange a hearing to a reasonable date proposed by the worker when a companion cannot attend on the date originally proposed. The tribunal may order compensation of up to two weeks' pay.

It is unlawful to disadvantage workers for using their right to be accompanied or for being companions. This could lead to a claim to an employment tribunal.

TAKING ACTION AFTER THE DISCIPLINARY MEETING

[4.34]

Extract: Acas Code of Practice on disciplinary and grievance procedures
After the meeting decide whether or not disciplinary or any other action is justified and inform the employee accordingly in writing.
Where misconduct is confirmed or the employee is found to be performing unsatisfactorily it is usual to give the employee a written warning. A further act of misconduct or failure to improve performance within a set period would normally result in a final written warning.
If an employee's first misconduct or unsatisfactory performance is sufficiently serious, it may be appropriate to move directly to a final written warning. This might occur where the employee's actions have had, or are liable to have, a serious or harmful impact on the organisation.
A first or final written warning should set out the nature of the misconduct or poor performance and the change in behaviour or improvement in performance required (with timescale). The employee should be told how long the warning will remain current. The employee should be informed of the consequences of further misconduct, or failure to improve performance, within the set period following a final warning. For instance that it may result in dismissal or some other contractual penalty such as demotion or loss of seniority.
A decision to dismiss should only be taken by a manager who has the authority to do so. The employee should be informed as soon as possible of the reasons for the dismissal, the date on which the employment contract will end, the appropriate period of notice and their right of appeal.
Some acts, termed gross misconduct, are so serious in themselves or have such serious consequences that they may call for dismissal without notice for a first offence. But a fair disciplinary process, should always be followed, before dismissing for gross misconduct.
Disciplinary rules should give examples of acts which the employer regards as acts of gross misconduct. These may vary according to the nature of the organisation and what it does, but might include things such as theft or fraud, physical violence, gross negligence or serious insubordination.
Where an employee is persistently unable or unwilling to attend a disciplinary meeting without good cause the employer should make a decision on the evidence available.

What should be considered before deciding any disciplinary penalty?

[4.35]
When deciding whether a disciplinary penalty is appropriate and what form it should take, consideration should be given to:

- whether the rules of the organisation indicate what the likely penalty will be as a result of the particular misconduct
- the penalty imposed in similar cases in the past
- whether standards of other employees are acceptable, and that this employee is not being unfairly singled out
- the employee's disciplinary record (including current warnings), general work record, work experience, position and length of service
- any special circumstances which might make it appropriate to adjust the severity of the penalty
- whether the proposed penalty is reasonable in view of all the circumstances

- whether any training, additional support or adjustments to the work are necessary.

It should be clear what the normal organisational practice is for dealing with the kind of misconduct or unsatisfactory performance under consideration. This does not mean that similar offences will always call for the same disciplinary action: each case must be looked at on its own merits and any relevant circumstances taken into account. Such relevant circumstances may include health or domestic problems, provocation, justifiable ignorance of the rule or standard involved or inconsistent treatment in the past.

If guidance is needed on formal disciplinary action, seek advice, where possible, from someone who will not be involved in hearing any potential appeal. Call the Acas helpline on **08457 47 47 47** to talk to one of our advisers.

IMPOSING THE DISCIPLINARY PENALTY

First formal action – unsatisfactory performance

[4.36]
In cases of unsatisfactory performance an employee should be given an 'improvement note', setting out:

- the performance problem
- the improvement that is required
- the timescale for achieving this improvement
- a review date and
- any support, including any training, that the employer will provide to assist the employee.

The employee should be informed that the note represents the first stage of a formal procedure and is equivalent to a first written warning and that failure to improve could lead to a final written warning and, ultimately, dismissal. A copy of the note should be kept and used as the basis for monitoring and reviewing performance over a specified period (eg, six months).

If an employee's unsatisfactory performance – or its continuance – is sufficiently serious, for example because it is having, or is likely to have, a serious harmful effect on the organisation, it may be justifiable to move directly to a final written warning.

Discipline in practice 2

A member of staff in accounts makes a number of mistakes on invoices to customers. You bring the mistakes to his attention, make sure he has had the right training and impress on him the need for accuracy but the mistakes continue. You invite the employee to a disciplinary meeting and inform him of his right to be accompanied by a colleague or employee representative. At the meeting the employee does not give a satisfactory explanation for the mistakes so you decide to issue an improvement note setting out: the problem, the improvement required, the timescale for improvement, the support available and a review date. You inform the employee that a failure to improve may lead to a final written warning.

First formal action – misconduct

[4.37]
In cases of misconduct, employees should be given a written warning setting out the nature of the misconduct and the change in behaviour required.

The warning should also inform the employee that a final written warning may be considered if there is further misconduct. A record of the warning should be kept, but it should be disregarded for disciplinary purposes after a specified period (eg, six months).

Discipline in practice 3

An employee in a small firm makes a series of mistakes in letters to one of your key customers promising impossible delivery dates. The customer is upset at your firm's failure to meet delivery dates and threatens to take his business elsewhere.

You are the owner of the business and carry out an investigation and invite the employee to a disciplinary meeting. You inform her of her right to be accompanied by a colleague or employee representative.

Example outcome of meeting

At the meeting the employee does not give a satisfactory explanation for the mistakes and admits that her training covered the importance of agreeing realistic delivery dates with her manager.

During your investigation, her team leader and section manager told you they had stressed to the employee the importance of agreeing delivery dates with them before informing the customer. In view of the seriousness of the mistakes and the possible impact on the business, you issue the employee with a final written warning. You inform the employee that failure to improve will lead to dismissal and of her right to appeal.

Example outcome of meeting in different circumstances

At the meeting, the employee reveals that her team leader would not let her attend training as the section was too busy. Subsequently the team leader was absent sick and the employee asked the section manager for help with setting delivery dates. The manager said he was too busy and told the employee to 'use her initiative'. Your other investigations support the employee's explanation. You inform the employee that you will not be taking disciplinary action and will make arrangements for her to be properly trained. You decide to carry out a review of general management standards on supervision and training.

Final written warning

[4.38]

If the employee has a current warning about conduct or performance then further misconduct or unsatisfactory performance (whichever is relevant) may warrant a final written warning. This may also be the case where 'first offence' misconduct is sufficiently serious, but would not justify dismissal. Such a warning should normally remain current for a specified period, for example, 12 months, and contain a statement that further misconduct or unsatisfactory performance may lead to dismissal.

Discipline in practice 4

A member of your telephone sales team has been to lunch to celebrate success in an exam. He returns from lunch in a very merry mood, is slurring his speech and is evidently not fit to carry out his duties. You decide to send him home and invite him in writing to a disciplinary meeting setting out his alleged behaviour of gross misconduct for which he could be dismissed. Your letter includes information about his right to be accompanied by a colleague or employee representative.

At the meeting he admits he had too much to drink, is very apologetic and promises that such a thing will not happen again. He is one of your most valued members of staff and has an exemplary record over his 10 years service with you. You know that being unfit for work because of excessive alcohol is listed in your company rules as gross misconduct. In view of the circumstances and the employee's record, however, you decide not to dismiss him but give him a final written warning. You inform the employee of his right to appeal.

Dismissal or other sanction

[4.39]

If the employee has received a final written warning further misconduct or unsatisfactory performance may warrant dismissal. Alternatively the contract may allow for a different disciplinary penalty instead. Such a penalty may include disciplinary transfer, disciplinary suspension without pay,[7] demotion, loss of seniority or loss of increment. These sanctions may only be applied if allowed for in the employee's contract or with the employee's agreement.

Any penalty should be confirmed in writing, and the procedure and time limits for appeal set out clearly.

There may be occasions when, depending on the seriousness of the misconduct involved, it will be appropriate to consider dismissal without notice (see over).

NOTES

7 Special consideration should be given before imposing disciplinary suspension without pay. It must be allowed for in the worker's contract of employment, and no suspension should exceed the maximum period set out in the contract. It must not be unreasonably prolonged, since it would then be open to the worker to take action for breach of contract or resign and claim constructive dismissal.

Dismissal with notice

[4.40]

Employees should only be dismissed if, despite warnings, conduct or performance does not improve to the required level within the specified time period. Dismissal must be reasonable in all the circumstances of the case.

Unless the employee is being dismissed for reasons of gross misconduct, he or she should receive the appropriate period of notice or payment in lieu of notice.

Dismissal without notice

[4.41]
Employers should give all employees a clear indication of the type of misconduct which, in the light of the requirements of the employer's business, will warrant dismissal without the normal period of notice or pay in lieu of notice. So far as possible the types of offences which fall into this category of 'gross misconduct' should be clearly specified in the rules, although such a list cannot normally be exhaustive.

What is gross misconduct?

[4.42]
Gross misconduct is generally seen as misconduct serious enough to overturn the contract between the employer and the employee thus justifying summary dismissal. Acts which constitute gross misconduct must be very serious and are best determined by organisations in the light of their own particular circumstances. However, examples of gross misconduct might include:

- theft or fraud
- physical violence or bullying
- deliberate and serious damage to property
- serious misuse of an organisation's property or name
- deliberately accessing internet sites containing pornographic, offensive or obscene material
- serious insubordination
- unlawful discrimination or harassment
- bringing the organisation into serious disrepute
- serious incapability at work brought on by alcohol or illegal drugs
- causing loss, damage or injury through serious negligence
- a serious breach of health and safety rules
- a serious breach of confidence.

If an employer considers an employee guilty of gross misconduct and thus liable for summary dismissal, it is still important to follow a fair procedure as for any other disciplinary offence. This will include establishing the facts of the case before taking any action, holding a meeting with the employee and allowing the employee the right of appeal. It should be made clear to the employee that dismissal is a possibility. A short period of suspension with full pay to help establish the facts or to allow tempers to cool may be helpful. However, such a period of suspension should only be imposed after careful consideration and should be kept under review. It should be made clear to the employee that the suspension is not a disciplinary action and does not involve any prejudgement.

How should the employee be informed of the disciplinary decision?

[4.43]
Details of any disciplinary action should be given in writing to the employee as soon as the decision is made. See example letters at Appendix 3. A copy of the notification should be retained by the employer. The written notification should specify:

- the nature of the misconduct
- any period of time given for improvement and the improvement expected
- the disciplinary penalty and, where appropriate, how long it will last
- the likely consequences of further misconduct
- the timescale for lodging an appeal and how it should be made.

The organisation may wish to require the employee to acknowledge receipt of the written notification.

Written reasons for dismissal

[4.44]
Employees with one year's service or more have the right to request a 'written statement of reasons for dismissal'. Employers are required by law to comply within 14 days of the request being made, unless it is not reasonably practicable. It is good practice to give written reasons for all dismissals.

A woman who is dismissed during pregnancy or maternity or adoption leave is automatically entitled to the written statement without having to request it and irrespective of length of service.[8]

The written statement can be used in evidence in any subsequent proceedings, for example, in relation to a complaint of unfair dismissal.

NOTES

8 Section 92 of the Employment Rights Act 1996 refers. More details of employees' Rights to notice and reasons for dismissal is provided on the Department for Business, Enterprise and Regulatory Reform (BERR) website at

www.berr.gov.uk.

Time limits for warnings

[4.45]
Except in agreed special circumstances, any disciplinary action taken should be disregarded for disciplinary purposes after a specified period of satisfactory conduct or performance. This period should be established clearly when the disciplinary procedure is being drawn up. A decision to dismiss should not be based on an expired warning but the fact that there is an expired warning may explain why the employer does not substitute a lesser sanction.

Normal practice is for different types of warnings to remain in force for different periods. For example, a first written warning might be valid for up to six months while a final written warning may remain in force for 12 months (or more in exceptional circumstances). Warnings should cease to be 'live' following the specified period of satisfactory conduct.

There may be occasions where an employee's conduct is satisfactory throughout the period the warning is in force, only to lapse very soon thereafter. Where a pattern emerges and/or there is evidence of abuse, the employee's disciplinary record should be borne in mind in deciding how long any warning should last.

PROVIDE EMPLOYEES WITH AN OPPORTUNITY TO APPEAL

[4.46]

Extract: Acas Code of Practice on disciplinary and grievance procedures
Where an employee feels that disciplinary action taken against them is wrong or unjust they should appeal against the decision. Appeals should be heard without unreasonable delay and ideally at an agreed time and place. Employees should let employers know the grounds for their appeal in writing. The appeal should be dealt with impartially and wherever possible, by a manager who has not previously been involved in the case. Workers have a statutory right to be accompanied at appeal hearings. Employees should be informed in writing of the results of the appeal hearing as soon as possible.

The opportunity to appeal against a disciplinary decision is essential to natural justice, and appeals may be raised by employees on any number of grounds, for instance new evidence, undue severity or inconsistency of the penalty. The appeal may either be a review of the disciplinary sanction or a re-hearing depending on the grounds of the appeal.

An appeal must never be used as an opportunity to punish the employee for appealing the original decision, and it should not result in any increase in penalty as this may deter individuals from appealing.

What should an appeals procedure contain?

[4.47]
It should:

- specify a time-limit within which the appeal should be lodged (five working days is commonly felt appropriate although this may be extended in particular circumstances)
- provide for appeals to be dealt with speedily, particularly those involving suspension or dismissal
- wherever possible provide for the appeal to be heard by someone senior in authority to the person who took the disciplinary decision and, if possible, someone who was not involved in the original meeting or decision
- spell out what action may be taken by those hearing the appeal
- set out the right to be accompanied at any appeal meeting
- provide that the employee, or a companion if the employee so wishes, has an opportunity to comment on any new evidence arising during the appeal before any decision is taken.

Small organisations

[4.48]
In small organisations, even if there is no more senior manager available, another manager should, if possible, hear the appeal. If this is not possible consider whether the owner or, in the case of a charity, the board of trustees, should hear the appeal. Whoever hears the appeal should consider it as impartially as possible.

How should an appeal hearing be conducted?

[4.49]

Before the appeal ensure that the individual knows when and where it is to be held, and of their statutory right to be accompanied (see p 23 (**[4.28]**)). Hold the meeting in a place which will be free from interruptions. Make sure the relevant records and notes of the original meeting are available for all concerned. See sample letters at Appendix 3.

At the meeting

You should:

- introduce those present to each other, explaining their presence if necessary
- explain the purpose of the meeting, how it will be conducted, and the powers the person/people hearing the appeal have
- ask the employee why he or she is appealing
- pay particular attention to any new evidence that has been introduced, and ensure the employee has the opportunity to comment on it
- once the relevant issues have been thoroughly explored, summarise the facts and call an adjournment to consider the decision
- change a previous decision if it becomes apparent that it was not soundly based – such action does not undermine authority but rather makes clear the independent nature of the appeal. If the decision is overturned consider whether training for managers needs to be improved, if rules need clarification, or are if there other implications to be considered?
- inform the employee of the results of the appeal and the reasons for the decision and confirm it in writing. Make it clear, if this is the case, that this decision is final. See sample letters at Appendix 3.

DEALING WITH SPECIAL CASES

[4.50]

Extract: Acas Code of Practice on disciplinary and grievance procedures
Where disciplinary action is being considered against an employee who is a trade union representative the normal disciplinary procedure should be followed. Depending on the circumstances, however, it is advisable to discuss the matter at an early stage with an official employed by the union, after obtaining the employee's agreement. If an employee is charged with, or convicted of a criminal offence this is not normally in itself reason for disciplinary action. Consideration needs to be given to what effect the charge or conviction has on the employee's suitability to do the job and their relationship with their employer, work colleagues and customers.

Trade union officials

[4.51]

Although normal disciplinary standards apply to their conduct as employees, disciplinary action against a trade union representative can be construed as an attack on the union if not handled carefully (see also p 19 (**[4.20]**)).

Criminal charges or convictions

[4.52]

An employee should not be dismissed or otherwise disciplined solely because he or she has been charged with or convicted of a criminal offence. The question to be asked in such cases is whether the employee's conduct or conviction merits action because of its employment implications.

Where it is thought the conduct warrants disciplinary action the following guidance should be borne in mind:

- the employer should investigate the facts as far as possible, come to a view about them and consider whether the conduct is sufficiently serious to warrant instituting the disciplinary procedure
- where the conduct requires prompt attention the employer need not await the outcome of the prosecution before taking fair and reasonable action
- where the police are called in they should not be asked to conduct any investigation on behalf of the employer, nor should they be present at any meeting or disciplinary meeting.

In some cases the nature of the alleged offence may not justify disciplinary action – for example, off-duty conduct which has no bearing on employment – but the employee may not be available for work because he or she is in custody or on remand. In these cases employers should decide whether, in the light of the needs of the organisation, the employee's job can be held open. Where a criminal conviction leads, for example, to the loss of a licence so that continued employment in a particular job would be illegal, employers should consider whether alternative work is appropriate and available.

Where an employee, charged with or convicted of a criminal offence, refuses or is unable to cooperate with the employer's disciplinary investigations and proceedings, this should not deter an employer from taking action. The employee should be advised in writing that unless further information is provided, a disciplinary decision will be taken on the basis of the information available and could result in dismissal.

Where there is little likelihood of an employee returning to employment, it may be argued that the contract of employment has been terminated through 'frustration'.[9] However, the doctrine is normally accepted by the courts only where the frustrating event renders all performance of the employment contract clearly impossible. It is normally better for the employer to take disciplinary action.

An employee who has been charged with, or convicted of, a criminal offence may become unacceptable to colleagues, resulting in workforce pressure to dismiss and threats of industrial action. Employers should bear in mind that they may have to justify the reasonableness of any decision to dismiss and that an employment tribunal will ignore threats of, and actual industrial action when determining the fairness of a decision (Section 107, Employment Rights Act 1996). They should consider all relevant factors, not just disruption to production, before reaching a reasonable decision.

NOTES

9 In law, frustration occurs when, without the fault of either party, some event, which was not reasonably foreseeable at the time of the contract, renders future performance either impossible or something radically different from what was contemplated originally. Legal advice should be sought if it is thought frustration of the employment contract has occurred.

Use of external consultants

[4.53]

In some instances employers may wish to bring in external consultants to carry out an investigation. Employers will still be responsible for any inappropriate or discriminatory behaviour if the investigation is carried out by consultants. Make arrangements for the investigation to be overseen by a representative of management. Make sure that the consultants follow the organisation's disciplinary policies and procedures and deal with the case fairly in accordance with the Acas Code of Practice.

Employees to whom the full procedure is not immediately available

[4.54]

It may be sensible to arrange time off with pay so that employees who are in isolated locations or on shifts can attend a disciplinary meeting on the main site in normal working hours. Alternatively, if a number of witnesses need to attend it may be better to hold the disciplinary meeting on the nightshift or at the particular location.

GRIEVANCES
KEYS TO HANDLING GRIEVANCES IN THE WORKPLACE

RESOLVE GRIEVANCES INFORMALLY

[4.55]

In organisations where managers have an open policy for communication and consultation problems and concerns are often raised and settled as a matter of course.

Employees should aim to settle most grievances informally with their line manager. Many problems can be raised and settled during the course of everyday working relationships. This also allows for problems to be settled quickly.

In some cases outside help such as an independent mediator can help resolve problems especially those involving working relationships. See p 7 ([**4.6**]) for more information.

DEVELOP RULES AND PROCEDURES

[4.56]

Extract: Acas Code of Practice on disciplinary and grievance procedures
Fairness and transparency are promoted by developing and using rules and procedures for handling disciplinary and grievance situations. These should be set down in writing, be specific and clear. Employees and, where appropriate, their representatives should be involved in the development of rules and procedures. It is also important to help employees and managers understand what the rules and procedures are, where they can be found and how they are to be used.

WHAT IS A GRIEVANCE AND WHY HAVE A PROCEDURE?

[4.57]

Extract: Acas Code of Practice on disciplinary and grievance procedures
Grievances are concerns, problems or complaints that employees raise with their employers.

Anybody working in an organisation may, at some time, have problems or concerns about their work, working conditions or relationships with colleagues that they wish to talk about with management. They want the grievance to be addressed, and if possible, resolved. It is also clearly in management's interests to resolve problems before they can develop into major difficulties for all concerned.

Issues that may cause grievances include:

- terms and conditions of employment
- health and safety
- work relations
- bullying and harassment
- new working practices
- working environment
- organisational change
- discrimination.

Grievances may occur at all levels and the Acas Code of Practice, and this guidance, applies equally to management and employees.

A written procedure can help clarify the process and help to ensure that employees are aware of their rights such as to be accompanied at grievance meetings (see p 47 (**[4.68]**) on the right to be accompanied). Some organisations use, or may wish to use, external mediators to help resolve grievances (see p 7 (**[4.6]**)). Where this is the case the procedure should explain how and when mediators may be used.

Employees might raise issues about matters not entirely within the control of the organisation, such as client or customer relationships (for instance where an employee is working on another employer's site). These should be treated in the same way as grievances within the organisation, with the employer/manager investigating as far as possible and taking action if required. The organisation should make it very clear to any third party that grievances are taken seriously and action will be taken to protect their employees.

Extract: Acas Code of Practice on disciplinary and grievance procedures
The provisions of this Code do not apply to grievances raised on behalf of two or more employees by a representative of a recognised trade union or other appropriate workplace representative. These grievances should be handled in accordance with the organisation's collective grievance process.

Occasionally a collective grievance may arise where a number of people have the same grievance at the same time. If there is a grievance which applies to more than one person this should be resolved in accordance with the organisation's collective grievance process – where one exists.

Training for dealing with grievances

[4.58]
Management and employee representatives who may be involved in grievance matters should be trained for the task. They should be familiar with the provisions of the grievance procedure, and know how to conduct or represent at grievance hearings. Consideration might be given to training managers and employee representatives jointly. For information about suitable training see the Acas website at www.acas.org.uk.

KEEPING WRITTEN RECORDS

What records should be kept?

[4.59]
The foreword to the Code of Practice advises employers to keep a written record of any disciplinary or grievances cases they deal with.

Records should include:

- the nature of the grievance
- what was decided and actions taken
- the reason for the actions
- whether an appeal was lodged

- the outcome of the appeal
- any subsequent developments.

Records should be treated as confidential and be kept no longer than necessary in accordance with the Data Protection Act 1998. This Act gives individuals the right to request and have access to certain personal data. The Information Commissioner has produced Codes of Practice covering recruitment and selection, employment records, monitoring at work and information about an employee's health.[10]

Copies of meeting records should be given to the employee including copies of any formal minutes that may have been taken. In certain circumstances (for example to protect a witness) the employer might withhold some information.

NOTES

[10] The recommendations for good practice can be obtained from the Information Commissioner's Office, Wycliffe House, Water Lane, Wilmslow, Cheshire SK9 5AF. Tel 01625 545700 www.ico.gov.uk.

DEALING WITH FORMAL GRIEVANCES

[4.60]

Extract: Acas Code of Practice on disciplinary and grievance procedures

Where some form of formal action is needed, what action is reasonable or justified will depend on all the circumstances of the particular case. Employment tribunals will take the size and resources of an employer into account when deciding on relevant cases and it may sometimes not be practicable for all employers to take all of the steps set out in this Code.

That said, whenever a disciplinary or grievance process is being followed it is important to deal with issues fairly. There are a number of elements to this:

- Employers and employees should raise and deal with issues **promptly** and should not unreasonably delay meetings, decisions or confirmation of those decisions.
- Employers and employees should act **consistently**.
- Employers should carry out any necessary **investigations**, to establish the facts of the case.
- Employers should inform employees of the basis of the problem and give them an opportunity to **put their case** in response before any decisions are made.
- Employers should allow employees to be **accompanied** at any formal disciplinary or grievance meeting.
- Employers should allow an employee to appeal against any formal decision made.

The following pages give detailed guidance on handling formal grievances. Always bear in mind the need for fairness when following procedures, taking account of the elements from the Acas Code of Practice reproduced above.

LET THE EMPLOYER KNOW THE NATURE OF THE GRIEVANCE

[4.61]

Extract: Acas Code of Practice on disciplinary and grievance procedures

If it is not possible to resolve a grievance informally employees should raise the matter formally and without unreasonable delay with a manager who is not the subject of the grievance. This should be done in writing and should set out the nature of the grievance.

Where a grievance is serious or an employee has attempted to raise a problem informally without success, the employee should raise it formally with management in writing.

Where employees have difficulty expressing themselves because of language or other difficulties they may like to seek help from trade union or other employee representatives or from colleagues.

When stating their grievance, employees should stick to the facts and avoid language which may be considered insulting or abusive.

Where the grievance is against the line manager the employee may approach another manager or raise the issue with their HR department if there is one. It is helpful if the grievance procedure sets out who the individual should approach in these circumstances.

In small firms run by an owner/manager there will be no alternative manager to raise a grievance with. It is in the interests of such employers to make it clear that they will treat all grievances fairly and objectively even if the grievance is about something they have said or done.

HOLDING A GRIEVANCE MEETING

[4.62]

Extract: Acas Code of Practice on disciplinary and grievance procedures
Employers should arrange for a formal meeting to be held without unreasonable delay after a grievance is received. Employers, employees and their companions should make every effort to attend the meeting. Employees should be allowed to explain their grievance and how they think it should be resolved. Consideration should be given to adjourning the meeting for any investigation that may be necessary.

What is a grievance meeting?

[4.63]
In general terms a grievance meeting deals with any grievance raised by an employee. For the purposes of the legal right to be accompanied, a grievance meeting is defined as a meeting where an employer deals with a complaint about a 'duty owed by them to a worker' (see p 47 ([**4.68**])).

Preparing for the meeting

[4.64]
Managers should:

- arrange a meeting, ideally within five working days, in private where there will not be interruptions
- consider arranging for someone who is not involved in the case to take a note of the meeting and to act as a witness to what was said
- whether similar grievances have been raised before, how they have been resolved, and any follow-up action that has been necessary. This allows consistency of treatment
- consider arranging for an interpreter where the employee has difficulty speaking English
- consider whether any reasonable adjustments are necessary for a person who is disabled and/or their companion
- consider whether to offer independent mediation – see p 7 ([**4.6**]).

Conduct of the meeting

[4.65]
Managers should:

- remember that a grievance hearing is not the same as a disciplinary hearing, and is an occasion when discussion and dialogue may lead to an amicable solution
- make introductions as necessary
- invite the employee to re-state their grievance and how they would like to see it resolved
- put care and thought into resolving grievances. They are not normally issues calling for snap decisions, and the employee may have been holding the grievance for a long time. Make allowances for any reasonable 'letting off steam' if the employee is under stress
- consider adjourning the meeting if it is necessary to investigate any new facts which arise
- sum up the main points
- tell the employee when they might reasonably expect a response if one cannot be made at the time, bearing in mind the time limits set out in the organisation's procedure.

Be calm, fair and follow the procedure

[4.66]
In smaller organisations, grievances can sometimes be taken as personal criticism – employers should be careful to hear any grievance in a calm and objective manner, being as fair to the employee as possible in the resolution of the problem. Following the grievance procedure can make this easier.

Grievances in practice 1

You are the owner of a small firm. An employee has been complaining that she is being given too much work and can't complete it in time. You have told the employee that her predecessor had no problem completing the same amount of work and that things will get easier with experience. The employee is not happy and puts her grievance to you in writing.

You invite the employee to a meeting to discuss the grievance and inform her of her right to be accompanied. At the meeting you discover that the employee is working on a different computer from her predecessor. The computer is slower and uses an old version of the software required to carry out the work. You agree to upgrade the software, provide training and to review progress in a month. You confirm what was agreed in writing and inform the employee of her right to an appeal meeting if she feels her grievance has not been satisfactorily resolved.

Grievances about fellow employees

[4.67]
These can be made easier by following the grievance procedure. An employee may be the cause of grievances among his or her co-employees – perhaps on grounds of personal hygiene, attitude, or capability for the job. Employers must deal with these cases carefully and should generally start by talking privately to the individual about the concerns of fellow employees. This may resolve the grievance. Alternatively, if those involved are willing, an independent mediator may be able to help (see p 7 (**[4.6]**)). Care needs to be taken that any discussion with someone being complained about does not turn into a meeting at which they would be entitled to be accompanied (see p 47 (**[4.68]**)).

ALLOW THE EMPLOYEE TO BE ACCOMPANIED AT THE GRIEVANCE MEETING
[4.68]

Extract: Acas Code of Practice on disciplinary and grievance procedures

Workers have a statutory right to be accompanied by a companion at a grievance meeting which deals with a complaint about a duty owed by the employer to the worker. So this would apply where the complaint is, for example, that the employer is not honouring the worker's contract, or is in breach of legislation.

The chosen companion may be a fellow worker a trade union representative or an official employed by a trade union. A trade union representative who is not an employed official must have been certified by their union as being competent to accompany a worker.

To exercise the right to be accompanied a worker must first make a reasonable request. What is reasonable will depend on the circumstances of each individual case. However it would not normally be reasonable for workers to insist on being accompanied by a companion whose presence would prejudice the hearing nor would it be reasonable for a worker to ask to be accompanied by a companion from a remote geographical location if someone suitable and willing was available on site.

The companion should be allowed to address the hearing to put and sum up the worker's case, respond on behalf of the worker to any views expressed at the meeting and confer with the worker during the hearing. The companion does not however have the right to answer questions on the workers behalf, address the hearing if the worker does not wish it or prevent the employer from explaining their case.

When do workers have the right to be accompanied?

[4.69]
For the purposes of this right, a grievance hearing is a meeting at which an employer deals with a complaint about a duty owed by them to a worker, whether the duty arises from statute or common law (for example contractual commitments).

For instance, an individual's request for a pay rise is unlikely to fall within the definition, unless a right to an increase is specifically provided for in the contract or the request raises an issue about equal pay. Equally, most employers will be under no legal duty to provide their workers with car parking facilities, and a grievance about such facilities would carry no right to be accompanied at a hearing by a companion. However, if a worker were disabled and needed a car to get to and from work, they probably would be entitled to a companion at a grievance hearing, as an issue might arise as to whether the employer was meeting their obligations under the Equality Act 2010.

It is generally good practice to allow workers to be accompanied at a formal grievance meeting even when the statutory right does not apply.

What is a reasonable request?

[4.70]
Whether a request for a companion is reasonable will depend on the circumstances of the individual case and, ultimately, it is a matter for the courts and tribunals to decide. However, when workers are choosing a companion, they should bear in mind that it would not be reasonable to insist on being accompanied by a colleague whose presence would prejudice the hearing or who might have a conflict of interest. Nor would it usually be reasonable for a worker to ask to be accompanied by a colleague from a geographically remote location when someone suitably qualified was available on site. The request to be accompanied does not have to be in writing.

The companion

[4.71]

The companion may be:

- a fellow worker (ie another of the employer's workers)
- an official employed by a trade union
- a workplace trade union representative, as long as they have been reasonably certified in writing by their union as having experience of, or having received training in, acting as a worker's companion at disciplinary or grievance hearings. Certification may take the form of a card or letter.

Some workers may, however, have additional contractual rights to be accompanied by persons other than those listed above (for instance a partner, spouse or legal representative).

Reasonable adjustment may be needed for a worker with a disability (and possibly for their companion if they are disabled). For example the provision of a support worker or advocate with knowledge of the disability and its effects.

Workers may ask an official from any trade union to accompany them at a disciplinary or grievance hearing, regardless of whether or not they are a member or the union is recognised.

Fellow workers or trade union officials do not have to accept a request to accompany a worker, and they should not be pressurised to do so.

Trade unions should ensure that their officials are trained in the role of acting as a worker's companion. Even when a trade union official has experience of acting in the role, there may still be a need for periodic refresher training. Employers should consider allowing time off for this training.

A worker who has agreed to accompany a colleague employed by the same employer is entitled to take a reasonable amount of paid time off to fulfil that responsibility. This should cover the hearing and it is also good practice to allow time for the companion to familiarise themselves with the case and confer with the worker before and after the hearing. A lay trade union official is permitted to take a reasonable amount of paid time off to accompany a worker at a hearing, as long as the worker is employed by the same employer. In cases where a lay official agrees to accompany a worker employed by another organisation, time off is a matter for agreement by the parties concerned.

Applying the right

[4.72]

Where possible, the employer should allow a companion to have a say in the date and time of a hearing. If the companion cannot attend on a proposed date, the worker can suggest an alternative time and date so long as it is reasonable and it is not more than five working days after the original date.

Before the hearing takes place, the worker should tell the employer who they have chosen as a companion. In certain circumstances (for instance when the companion is an official of a non-recognised trade union) it can be helpful for the companion and employer to make contact before the hearing.

The companion should be allowed to address the meeting in order to:

- put the worker's case
- sum up the worker's case
- respond on the worker's behalf to any view expressed at the hearing
- confer with the worker during the meeting.

The companion can also confer with the worker during the hearing. It is good practice to allow the companion to participate as fully as possible in the hearing, including asking witnesses questions. The employer is, however, not legally required to permit the companion to answer questions on the worker's behalf, or to address the hearing if the worker does not wish it, or to prevent the employer from explaining their case.

Workers whose employers fail to comply with a reasonable request to be accompanied may present a complaint to an employment tribunal. Workers may also complain to a tribunal if employers fail to re-arrange a hearing to a reasonable date proposed by the worker when a companion cannot attend on the date originally proposed. The tribunal may order compensation of up to two weeks' pay.

Employers should be careful not to disadvantage workers for using their right to be accompanied or for being companions, as this is against the law and could lead to a claim to an employment tribunal.

DECIDE ON APPROPRIATE ACTION

[4.73]

Extract: Acas Code of Practice on disciplinary and grievance procedures
Following the meeting decide on what action, if any, to take. Decisions should be communicated to the employee, in writing, without unreasonable delay and, where appropriate, should set out what action the employer intends to take to resolve the grievance. The employee should be informed that they can appeal if they are not content with the action taken.

It is generally good practice to adjourn a meeting before a decision is taken about how to deal with an employee's grievance. This allows time for reflection and proper consideration. It also allows for any further checking of any matters raised.

Set out clearly in writing any action that is to be taken and the employee's right of appeal. Where an employee's grievance is not upheld make sure the reasons are carefully explained.

Bear in mind that actions taken to resolve a grievance may have an impact on other individuals, who may also feel aggrieved.

If the grievance highlights any issues concerning policies, procedures or conduct (even if not sufficiently serious to merit separate disciplinary procedures) they should be addressed as soon as possible.

Ensure any action taken is monitored and reviewed, as appropriate, so that it deals effectively with the issues.

ALLOW THE EMPLOYEE TO TAKE THE GRIEVANCE FURTHER IF NOT RESOLVED

[4.74]

Extract: Acas Code of Practice on disciplinary and grievance procedures
Where an employee feels that their grievance has not been satisfactorily resolved they should appeal. They should let their employer know the grounds for their appeal without unreasonable delay and in writing. Appeals should be heard without unreasonable delay and at a time and place which should be notified to the employee in advance. The appeal should be dealt with impartially and wherever possible by a manager who has not previously been involved in the case. Workers have a statutory right to be accompanied at any such appeal hearing. The outcome of the appeal should be communicated to the employee in writing without unreasonable delay.

Arranging an appeal

[4.75]

If an employee informs the employer that they are unhappy with the decision after a grievance meeting, the employer should arrange an appeal. As far as reasonably practicable the appeal should be with a more senior manager than the one who dealt with the original grievance.

In small organisations, even if there is no more senior manager available, another manager should, if possible, hear the appeal. If this is not possible consider whether the owner or, in the case of a charity, the board of trustees, should hear the appeal. Whoever hears the appeal should consider it as impartially as possible.

At the same time as inviting the employee to attend the appeal, the employer should remind them of their right to be accompanied at the appeal meeting.

As with the first meeting, the employer should write to the employee with a decision on their grievance as soon as possible. They should also tell the employee if the appeal meeting is the final stage of the grievance procedure.

Large organisations may wish to allow a further appeal to a higher level of management, such as a director. However, in smaller firms the first appeal will usually mark the end of the grievance procedure. Sample grievance procedure (small organisation) is at Appendix 2.

Dealing with special cases

[4.76]

The foreword to the Code of Practice points out that organisations may wish to consider dealing with issues involving bullying, harassment[11] or whistleblowing under a separate procedure. For further advice about how to deal with bullying and harassment see the Acas advice leaflet *Bullying and harassment at work: a guide for managers and employers* available to order or download from the Acas website www.acas.org.uk.

Clearly confidentiality is of prime importance when handling any such grievance, although the outcome may need to be made known if, for instance, someone is found to have bullied or harassed an individual and the result is disciplinary action. Mediation may be particularly useful in these types of cases see p 7 ([4.6]).

NOTES

[11] See advice leaflet – *Bullying and harassment at work: a guide for managers and employers.*

APPENDIX 1
DISCIPLINARY RULES FOR SMALL ORGANISATIONS

CHECKLIST

[4.77]
As a minimum, rules should:

- be simple, clear and in writing
- be displayed prominently in the workplace
- be known and understood by all employees
- cover issues such as absences, timekeeping, health and safety and use of organisational facilities and equipment (add any other items relevant to your organisation)
- indicate examples of the type of conduct which will normally lead to disciplinary action other than dismissal – for instance lateness or unauthorised absence
- indicate examples of the type of conduct which will normally lead to dismissal without notice – examples may include working dangerously, stealing or fighting – although much will depend on the circumstances of each offence.

APPENDIX 2
SAMPLE DISCIPLINARY AND GRIEVANCE PROCEDURES

SAMPLE DISCIPLINARY PROCEDURE (ANY ORGANISATION)

1. Purpose and scope

[4.78]
This procedure is designed to help and encourage all employees to achieve and maintain standards of conduct, attendance and job performance. The company rules (a copy of which is displayed in the office) and this procedure apply to all employees. The aim is to ensure consistent and fair treatment for all in the organisation.

2. Principles

[4.79]
Informal action will be considered, where appropriate, to resolve problems.

No disciplinary action will be taken against an employee until the case has been fully investigated.

For formal action the employee will be advised of the nature of the complaint against him or her and will be given the opportunity to state his or her case before any decision is made at a disciplinary meeting.

Employees will be provided, where appropriate, with written copies of evidence and relevant witness statements in advance of a disciplinary meeting.

At all stages of the procedure the employee will have the right to be accompanied by a trade union representative, or work colleague.

No employee will be dismissed for a first breach of discipline except in the case of gross misconduct, when the penalty will be dismissal without notice or payment in lieu of notice.

An employee will have the right to appeal against any disciplinary action.

The procedure may be implemented at any stage if the employee's alleged misconduct warrants this.

3. The Procedure

First stage of formal procedure

[4.80]
This will normally be either:

- *an improvement note for unsatisfactory performance* if performance does not meet acceptable standards. This will set out the performance problem, the improvement that is required, the timescale, any help that may be given and the right of appeal. The individual will be advised that it constitutes the first stage of the formal procedure. A record of the improvement note will be kept for . . . months, but will then be considered spent – subject to achieving and sustaining satisfactory performance, or

- *a first warning for misconduct* if conduct does not meet acceptable standards. This will be in writing and set out the nature of the misconduct and the change in behaviour required and the right of appeal. The warning will also inform the employee that a final written warning may be considered if there is no sustained satisfactory improvement or change. A record of the warning will be kept, but it will be disregarded for disciplinary purposes after a specified period (eg, six months).

Final written warning

If the offence is sufficiently serious, or if there is further misconduct or a failure to improve performance during the currency of a prior warning, a final written warning may be given to the employee. This will give details of the complaint, the improvement required and the timescale. It will also warn that failure to improve may lead to dismissal (or some other action short of dismissal) and will refer to the right of appeal. A copy of this written warning will be kept by the supervisor but will be disregarded for disciplinary purposes after . . . months subject to achieving and sustaining satisfactory conduct or performance.

Dismissal or other sanction

If there is still further misconduct or failure to improve performance the final step in the procedure may be dismissal or some other action short of dismissal such as demotion or disciplinary suspension or transfer (as allowed in the contract of employment). Dismissal decisions can only be taken by the appropriate senior manager, and the employee will be provided in writing with reasons for dismissal, the date on which the employment will terminate, and the right of appeal.

If some sanction short of dismissal is imposed, the employee will receive details of the complaint, will be warned that dismissal could result if there is no satisfactory improvement, and will be advised of the right of appeal. A copy of the written warning will be kept by the supervisor but will be disregarded for disciplinary purposes after . . . months subject to achievement and sustainment of satisfactory conduct or performance.

Gross misconduct

The following list provides some examples of offences which are normally regarded as gross misconduct:

- theft or fraud
- physical violence or bullying
- deliberate and serious damage to property
- serious misuse of an organisation's property or name
- deliberately accessing internet sites containing pornographic, offensive or obscene material
- serious insubordination
- unlawful discrimination or harassment
- bringing the organisation into serious disrepute
- serious incapability at work brought on by alcohol or illegal drugs
- causing loss, damage or injury through serious negligence
- a serious breach of health and safety rules
- a serious breach of confidence.

If you are accused of an act of gross misconduct, you may be suspended from work on full pay, normally for no more than five working days, while the alleged offence is investigated. If, on completion of the investigation and the full disciplinary procedure, the organisation is satisfied that gross misconduct has occurred, the result will normally be summary dismissal without notice or payment in lieu of notice.

Appeals

An employee who wishes to appeal against a disciplinary decision must do so within five working days. The senior manager will hear all appeals and his/her decision is final. At the appeal any disciplinary penalty imposed will be reviewed.

SAMPLE DISCIPLINARY PROCEDURE (SMALL ORGANISATION)

1. Purpose and scope

[4.81]
The organisation's aim is to encourage improvement in individual conduct or performance. This procedure sets out the action which will be taken when disciplinary rules are breached.

2. Principles

(a) The procedure is designed to establish the facts quickly and to deal consistently with disciplinary issues. No disciplinary action will be taken until the matter has been fully investigated.

(b) At every stage employees will be informed in writing of what is alleged and have the opportunity to state their case at a disciplinary meeting and be represented or accompanied, if they wish, by a trade union representative or a work colleague.

(c) An employee has the right to appeal against any disciplinary penalty.

3. The Procedure

Stage 1 – first warning

If conduct or performance is unsatisfactory, the employee will be given a written warning or performance note. Such warnings will be recorded, but disregarded after . . . months of satisfactory service. The employee will also be informed that a final written warning may be considered if there is no sustained satisfactory improvement or change. (Where the first offence is sufficiently serious, for example because it is having, or is likely to have, a serious harmful effect on the organisation, it may be justifiable to move directly to a final written warning.)

Stage 2 – final written warning

If the offence is serious, or there is no improvement in standards, or if a further offence of a similar kind occurs, a final written warning will be given which will include the reason for the warning and a note that if no improvement results within . . . months, action at Stage 3 will be taken.

Stage 3 – dismissal or action short of dismissal

If the conduct or performance has failed to improve, the employee may suffer demotion, disciplinary transfer, loss of seniority (as allowed in the contract) or dismissal.

Gross misconduct

If, after investigation, it is confirmed that an employee has committed an offence of the following nature (the list is not exhaustive), the normal consequence will be dismissal without notice or payment in lieu of notice:

— theft, damage to property, fraud, incapacity for work due to being under the influence of alcohol or illegal drugs, physical violence, bullying and gross insubordination.

While the alleged gross misconduct is being investigated, the employee may be suspended, during which time he or she will be paid their normal pay rate. Any decision to dismiss will be taken by the employer only after full investigation.

Appeals

An employee who wishes to appeal against any disciplinary decision must do so to the named person in the organisation within five working days. The employer will hear the appeal and decide the case as impartially as possible.

SAMPLE GRIEVANCE PROCEDURE (SMALL ORGANISATION)

Dealing with grievances informally

If you have a grievance or complaint to do with your work or the people you work with you should, wherever possible, start by talking it over with your manager. You may be able to agree a solution informally between you.

Formal grievance

If the matter is serious and/or you wish to raise the matter formally you should set out the grievance in writing to your manager. You should stick to the facts and avoid language that is insulting or abusive.

Where your grievance is against your manager and you feel unable to approach him or her you should talk to another manager or the owner.

Grievance hearing

Your manager will call you to a meeting, normally within five days, to discuss your grievance. You have the right to be accompanied by a colleague or trade union representative at this meeting if you make a reasonable request.

After the meeting the manager will give you a decision in writing, normally within 24 hours.

Appeal

If you are unhappy with your manager's decision and you wish to appeal you should let your manager know.

You will be invited to an appeal meeting, normally within five days, and your appeal will be heard by a more senior manager (or the company owner). You have the right to be accompanied by a colleague or trade union representative at this meeting if you make a reasonable request.

After the meeting the manager (or owner) will give you a decision, normally within 24 hours. The manager's (or owner's) decision is final.

APPENDIX 3
SAMPLE LETTERS

(1) NOTICE OF DISCIPLINARY MEETING

[4.82]
Date . . . .

Dear . . . .

I am writing to tell you that you are required to attend a disciplinary meeting on . . . . at . . . . am/pm which is to be held in . . . . At this meeting the question of disciplinary action against you, in accordance with the Company Disciplinary Procedure, will be considered with regard to:. . . . .

. . . .

I enclose the following documents*:. . . . .

. . . .

The possible consequences arising from this meeting might be: . . . .

. . . .

You are entitled, if you wish, to be accompanied by another work colleague or a trade union representative.

Yours sincerely

Signed Manager . . . .

Note:

** Delete if not applicable*

(2) NOTICE OF WRITTEN WARNING OR FINAL WRITTEN WARNING

Date . . . .

Dear . . . .

You attended a disciplinary hearing on . . . . I am writing to inform you of your written warning/final written warning*.

This warning will be placed in your personal file but will be disregarded for disciplinary purposes after a period of . . . . months, provided your conduct improves/performance reaches a satisfactory level**.

(a) The nature of the unsatisfactory conduct or performance was:
. . . .

(b) The conduct or performance improvement expected is:
. . . .

(c) The timescale within which the improvement is required is:
. . . .

(d) The likely consequence of further misconduct or insufficient improvement is:
. . . .

Final written warning/dismissal

You have the right to appeal against this decision (in writing**) to . . . . within . . . . days of receiving this disciplinary decision.

Yours sincerely

Signed Manager . . . .

Note:

** The wording should be amended as appropriate*

*** Delete as appropriate*

(3) NOTICE OF APPEAL MEETING AGAINST WARNING

Date . . . .

Dear . . . .

You have appealed against the written warning/ final written warning* confirmed to you in writing on . . . .

Your appeal will be heard by . . . . in . . . . on . . . . at . . . .

You are entitled to be accompanied by a work colleague or trade union representative.

The decision of this appeal hearing is final and there is no further right of review.

Yours sincerely

Signed Manager . . . .

Note:

** The wording should be amended as appropriate*

(4) NOTICE OF RESULT OF APPEAL AGAINST WARNING

Date . . . .

Dear . . . .

You appealed against the decision of the disciplinary hearing that you be given a . . . . warning/in accordance with the Company Disciplinary Procedure. The appeal hearing was held on . . . .

I am now writing to inform you of the decision taken by the Manager who conducted the appeal hearing, namely that the decision to . . . . stands*/the decision to. . . . . be revoked* [specify if no disciplinary action is being taken or what the new disciplinary action is].

You have now exercised your right of appeal under the Company Disciplinary Procedure and this decision is final.

Yours sincerely

Signed Manager . . . .

Note:

** The wording should be amended as appropriate*

(5) LETTER TO BE SENT BY THE EMPLOYER TO ARRANGE A MEETING WHERE DISMISSAL OR ACTION SHORT OF DISMISSAL* IS BEING CONSIDERED

Date . . . .

Dear . . . .

I am writing to tell you that . . . . [insert organisation name] is considering dismissing OR taking disciplinary action [insert proposed action] against you.

This action is being considered with regard to the following circumstances: . . . .

. . . .

You are invited to attend a disciplinary meeting on . . . . at . . . . am/pm which is to be held in . . . . where this will be discussed.

You are entitled, if you wish, to be accompanied by another work colleague or your trade union representative.

Yours sincerely

Signed Manager . . . .

Note:

** Action other than a warning such as transfer or demotion (see p 30)*

(6) LETTER TO BE SENT BY THE EMPLOYER AFTER THE DISCIPLINARY MEETING ARRANGED IN LETTER 5

Date . . . .

Dear . . . .

On . . . . you were informed that . . . . [insert organisation name] was considering dismissing OR taking disciplinary action [insert proposed action] against you.

This was discussed in a meeting on . . . . At this meeting, it was decided that: [delete as applicable]

Your conduct/performance/etc was still unsatisfactory and that you be dismissed.

Your conduct/performance/etc was still unsatisfactory and that the following disciplinary action would be taken against you . . . .

No further action would be taken against you.

I am therefore writing to you to confirm the decision that you be dismissed and that your last day of service with the Company will be . . . .

The reasons for your dismissal are: . . . .

I am therefore writing to you to confirm the decision that disciplinary action will be taken against you. The action will be . . . . The reasons for this disciplinary action are: . . . .

You have the right of appeal against this decision. Please [write] to . . . . within . . . . days of receiving this disciplinary decision

Yours sincerely

Signed Manager . . . .

(7) NOTICE OF APPEAL MEETING AGAINST DISMISSAL/DISCIPLINARY ACTION*

Date . . . .

Dear . . . .

You have appealed against your dismissal/disciplinary action [delete as appropriate] on . . . . confirmed to you in writing on . . . . Your appeal will be heard by . . . . in . . . . on . . . . at . . . .

You are entitled, if you wish, to be accompanied by another work colleague or a trade union representative.

The decision of this appeal meeting is final and there is no further right of review.

Yours sincerely

Signed Manager . . . .

Note:

* *Action other than a warning such as transfer or demotion (see p 30)*

(8) NOTICE OF RESULT OF APPEAL AGAINST DISMISSAL/DISCIPLINARY ACTION*

Date . . . .

Dear . . . .

You appealed against the decision of the disciplinary hearing that you be dismissed/subject to disciplinary action [delete as appropriate].

The appeal meeting was held on . . . .

I am now writing to inform you of the decision taken by . . . . [insert name of the manager] who conducted the appeal meeting, namely that the decision to . . . . stands/ the decision to . . . . be revoked [specify if no disciplinary action is being taken or what the new disciplinary action is].

You have now exercised your right of appeal under the Company Disciplinary Procedure and this decision is final.

Yours sincerely

Signed Manager . . . .

Note:

* *Action other than a warning such as transfer or demotion (see p 30)*

(9) LETTER OF ENQUIRY REGARDING LIKELY CAUSE OF ABSENCE ADDRESSED TO A WORKER'S GENERAL PRACTITIONER

Date . . . .

Doctor's name . . . .

Address . . . .

PLEASE ACKNOWLEDGE RECEIPT OF THIS LETTER IF THERE IS LIKELY TO BE ANY DELAY IN REPLYING

Re . . . .

Name . . . .

Address . . . .

To administer Statutory Sick Pay, and the Company's sick pay scheme, and to plan the work in the department, it would be helpful to have a report on your patient, who works for our organisation.

His/her work as a . . . . has the following major features:

Management responsibility for

Seated/standing/mobile

Light/medium/heavy effort required

Day/shift/night work

Clerical/secretarial duties

Group I (private)/Group II (professional) driver

Other

The absence record for the past year is summarised as:

Total days lost

This month

Previous months

Attached is your patient's permission to enquire. He/she wishes/does not wish to have access to the report under the Access to Medical Reports Act 1988:

What is the likely date of return to work?

Will there be any disability at that time?

How long is it likely to last?

Are there any reasonable adjustments we could make to accommodate the disability?

Is there any underlying medical reason for this attendance record?

Is he/she likely to be able to render regular and efficient service in the future?

Is there any specific recommendation you wish to make about him/her which would help in finding him/her an alternative job, if that is necessary, and if there is an opportunity for redeployment (for instance no climbing ladders, no driving).

I would be grateful for an early reply and enclose a stamped addressed envelope. Please attach your account to the report (following the BMA guidance on fees).

Yours sincerely

Signed Name (BLOCK LETTERS) . . . .

Role in the company . . . .

Note:

Please amend/delete where necessary

APPENDIX 4
DEALING WITH ABSENCE

[4.83]
This appendix considers how to handle problems of absence and gives guidance about unauthorised short-term and long-term absences, and the failure to return from extended leave. More extensive advice on attendance management is available in the Acas advisory booklet *Managing attendance and employee turnover* available to purchase or download on the Acas website www.acas.org.uk. A distinction should be made between absence on grounds of illness or injury and absence for no good reason which may call for disciplinary action. Where disciplinary action is called for, the normal disciplinary procedure should be used. Where the employee is absent because of illness or injury, the guidance in this section of the booklet should be followed. The organisation should be aware of the requirements of the Equality Act 2010 when making any decisions that affect someone who may be disabled as defined by the Act.[12]

Records showing lateness and the duration of and reasons for all spells of absence should be kept to help monitor absence levels. These enable management to check levels of absence or lateness so that problems can be spotted and addressed at an early stage (the Information Commissioner[13] has produced a Code of Practice on employment records).

NOTES

[12] For further information see the Equality and Human Rights Commission website at www.equalityhumanrights.com.

[13] See the Information Commissioner's website at www.ico.gov.uk.

HOW SHOULD FREQUENT AND PERSISTENT SHORT-TERM ABSENCE BE HANDLED?

- unexpected absences should be investigated promptly and the employee asked for an explanation at a return-to-work interview
- if there are no acceptable reasons then the employer may wish to treat the matter as a conduct issue and deal with it under the disciplinary procedure
- where there is no medical certificate to support frequent short-term, self-certified, absences then the employee should be asked to see a doctor to establish whether treatment is necessary and whether the underlying reason for the absence is work-related. If no medical support is forthcoming the employer should consider whether to take action under the disciplinary procedure
- if the absence could be disability related the employer should consider what reasonable adjustments could be made in the workplace to help the employee (this might be something as simple as an adequate, ergonomic chair, or a power-assisted piece of equipment.[14] Reasonable adjustment also means redeployment to a different type of work if necessary
- if the absence is because of temporary problems relating to dependants, the employee may be entitled to have time off under the provisions of the Employment Rights Act 1996 relating to time off for dependants
- if the absence is because the employee has difficulty managing both work and home responsibilities then the employer should give serious consideration to more flexible ways of working. Employees who are parents of children aged 16 and under (disabled children under 18) and carers of adults have the right to request flexible working arrangements – including job-sharing, part-time working, flexi-time, working from home/teleworking and school time contracts – and employers must have a good business reason for rejecting any application
- in all cases the employee should be told what improvement in attendance is expected and warned of the likely consequences if this does not happen
- if there is no improvement, the employee's length of service, performance, the likelihood of a change in attendance, the availability of suitable alternative work where appropriate, and the effect of past and future absences on the organisation should all be taken into account in deciding appropriate action.

In order to show both the employee concerned, and other employees, that absence is regarded as a serious matter and may result in dismissal, it is very important that persistent absence is dealt with promptly, firmly and consistently.

An examination of records will identify those employees who are frequently absent and may show an absence pattern.

NOTES

[14] For further information see the Equality and Human Rights Commission website at www.equalityhumanrights.com.

HOW SHOULD LONGER-TERM ABSENCE THROUGH ILL HEALTH BE HANDLED?

[4.84]
Where absence is due to medically certificated illness, the issue becomes one of capability rather than conduct. Employers need to take a more sympathetic and considerate approach, particularly if the employee is disabled and where reasonable adjustments at the workplace might enable them to return to work.

There are certain steps an employer should take when considering the problem of long-term absence:

- employee and employer should keep in regular contact with each other
- the employee must be kept fully informed if there is any risk to employment
- if the employer wishes to contact the employee's doctor, he or she must notify the employee in writing that they intend to make such an application and they must secure the employee's consent in writing.[15] The employer must inform the individual that he or she has:
    - — the right to withhold consent to the application being made
    - — the right to state that he or she wishes to have access to the report. (The Access to Medical Reports Act 1988 also gives the individual the right to have access to the medical practitioner's report for up to six months after it was supplied)
    - — rights concerning access to the report before (and/or after) it is supplied

  - the right to withhold consent to the report being supplied to the employer
  - the right to request amendments to the report
- where the employee states that he or she wishes to have access to the report, the employer must let the GP know this when making the application and at the same time let the employee know that the report has been requested
- the letter of enquiry reproduced in Appendix 3 – Sample letters, and approved by the British Medical Association, may be used, and the employee's permission to the enquiry should be attached to the letter[16]
- the employee must contact the GP within 21 days of the date of application to make arrangement to see the report. Otherwise the rights under the 1988 Act will be lost
- if the employee considers the report to be incorrect or misleading, the employee may make a written request to the GP to make appropriate amendments
- if the GP refuses, the employee has the right to ask the GP to attach a statement to the report reflecting the employee's view on any matters of disagreement
- the employee may withhold consent to the report being supplied to the employer
- on the basis of the GP's report the employer should consider whether alternative work is available
- the employer is not expected to create a special job for the employee concerned, nor to be a medical expert, but to take action on the basis of the medical evidence
- where there is a reasonable doubt about the nature of the illness or injury, the employee should be asked if he or she would agree to be examined by a doctor to be appointed by the organisation
- where an employee refuses to cooperate in providing medical evidence, or to undergo an independent medical examination, the employee should be told in writing that a decision will be taken on the basis of the information available and that it could result in dismissal
- where the employee is allergic to a product used in the workplace the employer should consider remedial action or a transfer to alternative work
- where the employee's job can no longer be held open, and no suitable alternative work is available, the employee should be informed of the likelihood of dismissal
- where dismissal action is taken the employee should be given the period of notice to which he or she is entitled by statute or contract and informed of any right of appeal.

Where an employee has been on long-term sick absence and there is little likelihood of he or she becoming fit enough to return, it may be argued that the contract of employment has been terminated through 'frustration'. However, the doctrine of frustration should not be relied on since the courts are generally reluctant to apply it where a procedure exists for termination of the contract. It is therefore better for the employer to take dismissal action after following proper procedures.

NOTES

15 Access to Medical Reports Act 1988

16 The GP should return the report via the company doctor. If there is not one the employer should make it clear to the employee, when seeking permission to approach the GP, that the report will be sent direct to the employer. Employers who wish to seek advice on securing the services of a company doctor should contact the Faculty of Occupational Medicine at 6 St Andrews Place, Regents Park, London NW1 4LB. Tel 020 7317 5890 www.facoccmed.ac.uk.

SPECIFIC HEALTH PROBLEMS

[4.85]

Consideration should be given to introducing measures to help employees, regardless of status or seniority, who are suffering from alcohol or drug abuse, or from stress. The aim should be to identify employees affected and encourage them to seek help and treatment. See the Acas advisory booklet *Health, work and wellbeing* available to purchase or download on the Acas website www.acas.org.uk Employers should consider whether it is appropriate to treat the problem as a medical rather than a disciplinary matter.

There is sometimes workforce pressure to dismiss an employee because of a medical condition, or even threats of industrial action. If such an employee is dismissed, then he or she may be able to claim unfair dismissal before an employment tribunal, or breach of contract. Also, the Equality Act 2010 makes it unlawful for an employer of any size to treat a disabled person less favourably for a reason relating to their disability, without a justifiable reason. Employers are required to make a reasonable adjustment to working conditions or the workplace where that would help to accommodate a particular disabled person.[17]

NOTES

17 For further information see the Equality and human rights commission website at www.equalityhumanrights.com.

FAILURE TO RETURN FROM EXTENDED LEAVE ON THE AGREED DATE

[4.86]
Employers may have policies which allow employees extended leave of absence without pay, for example to visit relatives in their countries of origin, or relatives who have emigrated to other countries, or to nurse a sick relative. There is no general statutory right to such leave without pay, except to deal with an initial emergency relating to a dependant under the Employment Rights Act 1996.

Where a policy of extended leave is in operation, the following points should be borne in mind:

- the policy should apply to all employees, irrespective of their age, sex, marital or civil partnership status, racial group, disability, sexual orientation or religion or belief
- any conditions attaching to the granting of extended leave should be carefully explained to the employee, using interpreters if necessary, and the employee's signature should be obtained as an acknowledgement that he or she understands and accepts them. Employers should be aware that agreed extended leave can preserve continuity of employment, even when such leave is unpaid and other terms and conditions of employment are suspended for the duration of the leave
- if an employee fails to return on the agreed date, this should be approached in the same way as any other failure to abide by the rules and the circumstances should be investigated in the normal way, with disciplinary procedures being followed if appropriate
- care should be taken to ensure that foreign medical certificates are not treated in a discriminatory way: employees can fall ill while abroad just as they can fall ill in this country
- before deciding to dismiss an employee who overstays leave, the employee's experience, length of service, reliability record and any explanation given should all be taken into account
- failure to return from ordinary maternity leave does not of itself terminate the contract of employment. Employers should try and find out the reason for the failure and take action if necessary as in any other case of failing to return from leave (whether extended/additional maternity/holiday/parental/time off for dependants).

An agreement that an employee should return to work on a particular date will not prevent a complaint of unfair dismissal to an employment tribunal if the employee is dismissed for failing to return as agreed. In all such cases, all the factors mentioned above and the need to act reasonably should be borne in mind before any dismissal action is taken.

APPENDIX 5
BASIC PRINCIPLES OF THE DATA PROTECTION ACT 1998 AND THE EQUALITY ACT 2010

DATA PROTECTION ACT 1998

[4.87]
The Data Protection Act gives individuals the right to know what information is held about them. It provides a framework to ensure that personal information is handled properly.

The Act works in two ways. Firstly, it states that anyone who processes personal information must comply with eight principles, which make sure that personal information is:

- fairly and lawfully processed
- processed for limited purposes
- adequate, relevant and not excessive
- accurate and up to date
- not kept for longer than is necessary
- processed in line with your rights
- secure
- not transferred to other countries without adequate protection.

The second area covered by the Act provides individuals with important rights, including the right to find out what personal information is held on computer and most paper records.

Should an individual or organisation feel they're being denied access to personal information they're entitled to, or feel their information has not been handled according to the eight principles, they can contact the Information Commissioner's Office for help. Complaints are usually dealt with informally, but if this isn't possible, enforcement action can be taken.

Full details are available from the Information Commissioner's Office, Wycliffe House, Water Lane, Wilmslow, Cheshire SK9 5AF, Information line 01625 545700. The website, www.ico.gov.uk provides comprehensive advice including details of the Code of Practice on the Use of Personal Data in Employer/Employee Relationships and other Codes of Practice on recruitment and selection, employment records, monitoring at work and medical information.

THE EQUALITY ACT 2010

[4.88]
The Equality Act gives disabled people rights in employment. A disabled person is defined in the Act as 'anyone with a physical or mental impairment which has a substantial and long-term adverse effect upon his or her ability to carry out normal day-to-day activities'.

However, disability does not necessarily affect someone's health, so insisting on a medical report purely on the basis of the disability may be unlawful discrimination. If your organisation believes that preemployment health screening is necessary, you must make sure it is carried out in a non-discriminatory way. It is unlawful to ask health related questions before making a job offer (whether condition or unconditional), except in order to:

- determine if a candidate can carry out a function which is essential to the job
- ask whether candidates need special arrangements for any part of the application process
- anonymously monitor whether candidates are disabled
- take positive action to assist disabled people
- check that a candidate has a disability where this is a genuine requirement of the job.

If a report from any individual's doctor is sought, then permission must be given by the individual, and they have the right to see the report (Access to Medical Reports Act 1988).

Discrimination means treating someone less favourably without any justification, and the Act requires that employers make reasonable adjustments if that will then remove the reason for the unfavourable treatment. An example of a reasonable adjustment could be the provision of a suitable computer keyboard to an operator who had difficulty through disability in using a conventional keyboard.

In relation to discipline and grievance procedures, employers must clearly ensure they do not discriminate in any area of practice which could lead to dismissal or any other detriment (for example warnings).

The Act also covers people who become disabled during the course of their employment, and this is particularly relevant to the absence handling section of this handbook. It is vital that the employer should discuss with the worker what their needs really are and what effect, if any, the disability may have on future work with the organisation. Any dismissal of a disabled employee for a reason relating to the disability would have to be justified, and the reason for it would have to be one which could not be removed or made less than substantial by any reasonable adjustment.

The Equality and Human Rights Commission provides information and advice about all aspects of the Equality Act 2010, as well as signposting specialist organisations where necessary. In addition, it can offer good practice advice on the employment of disabled people.

Tel: England 0845 604 6610, Scotland 0845 604 5510 and for Wales 0845 604 8810.

GLOSSARY

[4.89]
capability: an employee's ability or qualification to do their job. Most often referred to in discipline cases where there is a lack of capability

conduct: an employee's behaviour in the workplace

disciplinary action: formal action against an employee: for example issuing a first written warning for misconduct or dismissing someone for gross misconduct

disciplinary procedure: is a procedure for organisations to follow to deal with cases of misconduct or unsatisfactory performance. It helps employers deal with discipline cases fairly and consistently

employees: are people who work for an employer under a contract of employment. The term is used throughout Sections 1 & 2 of the handbook and the Code of Practice

grievance: is a problem or concern that an employee has about their work, working conditions or relationships with colleagues

grievance procedure: is a procedure for organisations to use to consider employees' grievances. It helps employers deal with grievances fairly and consistently

gross misconduct: are acts which are so serious as to justify possible dismissal see example list on p 31 (**[4.42]**)

improvement note: in cases of unsatisfactory performance an employee should be given an improvement note setting out the performance problem, the improvement that is required, the timescale for achieving this improvement, a review date and any support the employer will provide to assist the employee

natural justice: refers to the basic fundamental principles of fair treatment. These principles include the duty to give someone a fair hearing; the duty to ensure that the matter is decided by someone who is impartial; and the duty to allow an appeal against a decision

reasonable adjustments: a way of preventing discrimination against disabled employees by making changes to ensure that they are not at a disadvantage. For example, a specialist keyboard would count as a reasonable adjustment for a disabled employee unable to use a conventional keyboard

sanction: is a punishment imposed on an employee as a result of unsatisfactory performance or misconduct. Sanctions may include dismissal or actions short of dismissal such as loss of pay or demotion

summary dismissal: is dismissal without notice – usually only justifiable for gross misconduct. Summary is not necessarily the same as instant and incidents of gross misconduct should be investigated as part of a formal procedure

workers: is a term that includes employees and also other groups such as agency workers or anyone carrying out work who is not genuinely self-employed. Workers might include those involved in seasonal work – such as farm labourers or shop assistants.

ACAS CODE OF PRACTICE 2
DISCLOSURE OF INFORMATION TO TRADE UNIONS FOR COLLECTIVE BARGAINING PURPOSES (1998)

[4.90]

NOTES

This revised Code was issued on 28 October 1997, and was brought into force on 5 February 1998 by the Employment Protection Code of Practice (Disclosure of Information) Order 1998, SI 1998/45. It replaces the similarly named Code of 1977. Despite a statement on the version of this Code on the ACAS website that it was brought into effect in April 2003, that is not the case. That statement appears to refer to ACAS Code of Practice 3 (see SI 2003/1191 (spent)), now replaced by the 2010 reissue of the Code printed at **[4.98]**.

Authority: Trade Union and Labour Relations (Consolidation) Act 1992, s 201. For the legal status of this Code, see s 207 of the 1992 Act at **[1.473]**.

Text in bold type summarises statutory provisions on the disclosure of information, while practical guidance is set out in ordinary type. Notes are as in the Code.

CONTENTS

INTRODUCTION

[4.91]

1. Under the Trade Union and Labour Relations (Consolidation) Act 1992 the Advisory, Conciliation and Arbitration Service (ACAS) may issue Codes of Practice containing such practical guidance as the Service thinks fit for the purpose of promoting the improvement of industrial relations. In particular, the Service has a duty to provide practical guidance on the information to be disclosed by employers to trade union representatives in accordance with sections 181 and 182 of that Act, for the purposes of collective bargaining.

2. The Act and the Code apply to employers operating in both the public and private sectors of industry. They do not apply to collective bargaining between employers' associations and trade unions, although the parties concerned may wish to follow the guidelines contained in the Code.

3. The information which employers may have a duty to disclose under section 181 is information which it would be in accordance with good industrial relations practice to disclose. In determining what would be in accordance with good industrial relations practice, regard is to be had to any relevant provisions of the Code. However, the Code imposes no legal obligations on an employer to disclose any specific item of information. Failure to observe the Code does not by itself render anyone liable to proceedings, but the Act requires any relevant provisions to be taken into account in proceedings before the Central Arbitration Committee.[1]

NOTES

[1] Trade Union and Labour Relations (Consolidation) Act 1992, sections 181(2)(b), 181(4) and 207(1) and (2).

This Code replaces the Code of Practice on Disclosure of Information to Trade Unions for Collective Bargaining Purposes, issued by the Service in 1977.

PROVISIONS OF THE ACT

[4.92]

4. The Act places a general duty on an employer who recognises an independent trade union to disclose, for the purposes of all stages of collective bargaining about matters, and in relation to descriptions of workers, in respect of which the union is recognised by him, information requested by representatives of the union. The representative of the union is an official or other person authorised by the union to carry on such collective bargaining.

5. The information requested has to be in the employer's possession, or in the possession of any associated employer, and must relate to the employer's undertaking. The information to be disclosed is that without which a trade union representative would be impeded to a material extent in bargaining and which it would be in accordance with good industrial relations practice to disclose for the purpose of collective bargaining. In determining what is in accordance with good industrial relations practice, any relevant provisions of this Code are to be taken into account.

6. No employer is required to disclose any information which: would be against the interests of national security; would contravene a prohibition imposed by or under an enactment; was given to an employer in confidence, or was obtained by the employer in consequence of the confidence reposed in him by another person; relates to an individual unless he has consented to its disclosure; would cause substantial injury to the undertaking (or national interest in respect of Crown employment) for reasons other than its effect on collective bargaining; or was obtained for the purpose of any legal proceedings.

7. In providing information the employer is not required to produce original documents for inspection or copying. Nor is he required to compile or assemble information which would entail work or expenditure out of reasonable proportion to the value of the information in the conduct of collective bargaining. The union representative can request that the information be given in writing by the employer or be confirmed in writing. Similarly, an employer can ask the trade union representative to make the request for information in writing or confirm it in writing.

8. If the trade union considers that an employer has failed to disclose to its representatives information which he was required to disclose by section 181 of the Act, or to confirm such information in writing in accordance with that section, it may make a complaint to the Central Arbitration Committee. The Committee may ask the Advisory, Conciliation and Arbitration Service to conciliate. If conciliation does not lead to a settlement of the complaint, the Service shall inform the Committee accordingly who shall proceed to hear and determine the complaint. If the complaint is upheld by the Committee, it is required to specify the information that should have been disclosed or confirmed in writing, the date the employer failed to disclose, or confirm in writing, any of the information and a period of time within which the employer ought to disclose the information, or confirm it in writing. If the employer does not disclose the information, or confirm it in writing, within the specified time, the union (except in relation to Crown employment and Parliamentary staff) may present a further complaint to the Committee and may also present a claim for improved terms and conditions. If the further complaint is upheld by the Committee, an award, which would have effect as part of the contract of employment, may be made against the employer on the terms and conditions specified in the claim, or other terms and conditions which the Committee considers appropriate.

PROVIDING INFORMATION

[4.93]

9. The absence of relevant information about an employer's undertaking may to a material extent impede trade unions in collective bargaining, particularly if the information would influence the formulation, presentation or pursuance of a claim, or the conclusion of an agreement. The provision of relevant information in such circumstances would be in accordance with good industrial relations practice.

10. To determine what information will be relevant, negotiators should take account of the subject-matter of the negotiations and the issues raised during them; the level at which negotiations take place (department, plant, division, or company level); the size of the company; and the type of business the company is engaged in.

11. Collective bargaining within an undertaking can range from negotiations on specific matters arising daily at the workplace affecting particular sections of the workforce, to extensive periodic negotiations on terms and conditions of employment affecting the whole workforce in multi-plant companies. The relevant information and the depth, detail and form in which it could be presented to negotiators will vary accordingly. Consequently, it is not possible to compile a list of items that should be disclosed in all circumstances. Some examples of information relating to the undertaking which could be relevant in certain collective bargaining situations are given below:

(i) *Pay and benefits*: principles and structure of payment systems; job evaluation systems and grading criteria; earnings and hours analysed according to work-group, grade, plant, sex, out-workers and homeworkers, department or division, giving, where appropriate, distributions and make-up of pay showing any additions to basic rate or salary; total pay bill; details of fringe benefits and non-wage labour costs.

(ii) *Conditions of service*: policies on recruitment, redeployment, redundancy, training, equal opportunity, and promotion; appraisal systems; health, welfare and safety matters.

(iii) *Manpower*: numbers employed analysed according to grade, department, location, age and sex; labour turnover; absenteeism; overtime and short-time; manning standards; planned changes in work methods, materials, equipment or organisation; available manpower plans; investment plans.

(iv) *Performance*: productivity and efficiency data; savings from increased productivity and output, return on capital invested; sales and state of order book.

(v) *Financial*: cost structures; gross and net profits; sources of earnings; assets; liabilities; allocation of profits; details of government financial assistance; transfer prices; loans to parent or subsidiary companies and interest charged.

12. These examples are not intended to represent a check list of information that should be provided for all negotiations. Nor are they meant to be an exhaustive list of types of information as other items may be relevant in particular negotiations.

RESTRICTIONS ON THE DUTY TO DISCLOSE

[4.94]

13. Trade unions and employers should be aware of the restrictions on the general duty to disclose information for collective bargaining.[2]

14. Some examples of information which if disclosed in particular circumstances might cause substantial injury are: cost information on individual products; detailed analysis of proposed investment, marketing or pricing policies; and price quotas or the make-up of tender prices. Information which has to be made available publicly, for example under the Companies Acts, would not fall into this category.

15. Substantial injury may occur if, for example, certain customers would be lost to competitors, or suppliers would refuse to supply necessary materials, or the ability to raise funds to finance the company would be seriously impaired as a result of disclosing certain information. The burden of establishing a claim that disclosure of certain information would cause substantial injury lies with the employer.

NOTES

[2] Trade Union and Labour Relations (Consolidation) Act 1992, section 182. See paragraphs 6 and 7 of this Code.

TRADE UNIONS' RESPONSIBILITIES

[4.95]

16. Trade unions should identify and request the information they require for collective bargaining in advance of negotiations whenever practicable. Misunderstandings can be avoided, costs reduced, and time saved, if requests state as precisely as possible all the information required, and the reasons why the information is considered relevant. Requests should conform to an agreed procedure. A reasonable period of time should be allowed for employers to consider a request and to reply.

17. Trade unions should keep employers informed of the names of the representatives authorised to carry on collective bargaining on their behalf.

18. Where two or more trade unions are recognised by an employer for collective bargaining purposes they should co-ordinate their requests for information whenever possible.

19. Trade unions should review existing training programmes or establish new ones to ensure negotiators are equipped to understand and use information effectively.

EMPLOYERS' RESPONSIBILITIES[3]

[4.96]

20. Employers should aim to be as open and helpful as possible in meeting trade union requests for information. Where a request is refused, the reasons for the refusal should be explained as far as possible to the trade union representatives concerned and be capable of being substantiated should the matter be taken to the Central Arbitration Committee.

21. Information agreed as relevant to collective bargaining should be made available as soon as possible once a request for the information has been made by an authorised trade union representative. Employers should present information in a form and style which recipients can reasonably be expected to understand.

NOTES

[3] The Stock Exchange has drawn attention to the need for employers to consider any obligations which they may have under their Listing Agreement.

JOINT ARRANGEMENTS FOR DISCLOSURE OF INFORMATION

[4.97]

22. Employers and trade unions should endeavour to arrive at a joint understanding on how the provisions on the disclosure of information can be implemented most effectively. They should consider what information is likely to be required, what is available, and what could reasonably be made available. Consideration should also be given to the form in which the information will be presented, when it should be presented and to whom. In particular, the parties should endeavour to reach an understanding on what information could most appropriately be provided on a regular basis.

23. Procedures for resolving possible disputes concerning any issues associated with the disclosure of information should be agreed. Where possible such procedures should normally be related to any existing arrangements within the undertaking or industry and the complaint, conciliation and arbitration procedure described in the Act.[4]

NOTES

[4] Trade Union and Labour Relations (Consolidation) Act 1992, sections 183 to 185. See paragraph 8 of this Code.

ACAS CODE OF PRACTICE 3 TIME OFF FOR TRADE UNION DUTIES AND ACTIVITIES (INCLUDING GUIDANCE ON TIME OFF FOR UNION LEARNING REPRESENTATIVES) (2010)

[4.98]

NOTES

This Code was originally issued by ACAS under the Employment Protection Act 1975, s 6 (repealed) and was brought into effect on 1 April 1978 (by SI 1977/2076). The present Code is the fourth reissue. The statutory authority for the making of the Code and its revision is TULR(C)A 1992, s 199 at **[1.465]**, and its legal status is, as for the other ACAS Codes, as set out in s 207 at **[1.473]**. This Code came into effect on 1 January 2010 (see the Employment Protection Code of Practice (Time Off for Trade Union Duties and Activities) Order 2009, SI 2009/3223).

CONTENTS

INTRODUCTION

[4.99]

1. Under section 199 of the Trade Union and Labour Relations (Consolidation) Act 1992 the Advisory, Conciliation and Arbitration Service (Acas) has a duty to provide practical guidance on the time off to be permitted by an employer:

(a) to a trade union official in accordance with section 168 of the Trade Union and Labour Relations (Consolidation) Act 1992; and

(b) to a trade union member in accordance with section 170 of the Trade Union and Labour Relations (Consolidation) Act 1992.

Section 199 of the Act, as amended by the Employment Act 2002, also provides for Acas to issue practical guidance on time off and training for Union Learning Representatives.

This Code, which replaces the Code of Practice issued by Acas in 2003, is intended to provide such guidance. Advice on the role and responsibilities of employee representatives is provided in two Acas Guides: *Trade union representation in the workplace: a guide to managing time off, training* and facilities and *Non-union representation in the workplace: a guide to managing time off, training and facilities.*

TERMINOLOGY

2. In this Code the term 'Trade union official', is replaced by 'union representative'. In practice there is often confusion between an 'official' and an 'officer' of a union and the term 'representative' is commonly used in practice. Section 119 of the Trade Union and Labour Relations (Consolidation) Act 1992 defines an official as '(a) an officer of the union or of a branch or section of the union, or (b) a person elected or appointed in accordance with the rules of the union to be a representative of its members or of some of them, and includes a person so elected or appointed who is an employee of the same employer as the members or one or more of the members whom he is to represent'. Section 181(1) of the same Act defines a 'representative', for the purposes of sections 181–185 of the Act, as 'an official or other person authorised by the union to carry on such collective bargaining'.

In this Code a union representative means an employee who has been elected or appointed in accordance with the rules of the independent union to be a representative of all or some of the union's members in the particular company or workplace, or agreed group of workplaces where the union is recognised for collective bargaining purposes. This is intended to equate with the legal term 'trade union official' for the purposes of this Code.

The term 'union full-time officer' in this Code means a trade union official who is employed by an independent trade union to represent members in workplaces, or groups of workplaces, where the union is recognised for collective bargaining purposes.

A Union Learning Representative is an employee who is a member of an independent trade union recognised by the employer who has been elected or appointed in accordance with the rules of the union to be a learning representative of the union at the workplace.

THE BACKGROUND

3. Union representatives have had a statutory right to reasonable paid time off from employment to carry out trade union duties and to undertake trade union training since the Employment Protection Act 1975. Union representatives and members were also given a statutory right to reasonable unpaid time off when taking part in trade union activities. Union duties must relate to matters covered by collective bargaining agreements between employers and trade unions and relate to the union representative's own employer, unless agreed otherwise in circumstances of multi-employer bargaining, and not, for example, to any associated employer. All the time off provisions were brought together in sections 168–170 of the Trade Union and Labour Relations (Consolidation) Act 1992. Section 43 of the Employment Act 2002 added a new right for Union Learning Representatives to take paid time off during working hours to undertake their duties and to undertake relevant training. The rights to time off for the purpose of carrying out trade union duties, and to take time off for training, were extended to union representatives engaged in duties related to redundancies under Section 188 of the amended 1992 Act and to duties relating to the Transfer of Undertakings (Protection of Employment) Regulations 2006.

GENERAL PURPOSE OF THE CODE

4. The general purpose of the statutory provisions and this Code of Practice is to aid and improve the effectiveness of relationships between employers and trade unions. Employers and unions have a joint responsibility to ensure that agreed arrangements work to mutual advantage by specifying how reasonable time off for union duties and activities and for training will work.

STRUCTURE OF THE CODE

5. Section 1 of this Code provides guidance on time off for trade union duties. Section 2 deals with time off for training of trade union representatives and offers guidance on sufficient training for Union Learning Representatives. Section 3 considers time off for trade union activities. In each case the amount and frequency of time off, and the purposes for which and any conditions subject to which time off may be taken, are to be those that are reasonable in all the circumstances. Section 4 describes the responsibilities which employers and trade unions share in considering reasonable time off. Section 5 notes the advantages of reaching formal agreements on time off. Section 6 deals with industrial action and Section 7 with methods of appeal.

6. The annex to this Code reproduces the relevant statutory provisions on time off. To help differentiate between these and practical guidance, the summary of statutory provisions relating to time off which appears in the main text of the Code is in **bold type**. Practical guidance is in ordinary type. While every effort has been made to ensure that the summary of the statutory provisions included in this Code is accurate, only the courts can interpret the law authoritatively.

STATUS OF THE CODE

7. The provisions of this Code are admissible in evidence in proceedings before an Employment Tribunal relating to time off for trade union duties and activities. Any provisions of the Code which appear to the Tribunal to be relevant shall be taken into account. However, failure to observe any provision of the Code does not of itself render a person liable to any proceedings.

SECTION 1
TIME OFF FOR TRADE UNION DUTIES

[4.100]
Union representatives undertake a variety of roles in collective bargaining and in working with management, communicating with union members, liaising with their trade union and in handling individual disciplinary and grievance matters on behalf of employees. There are positive benefits for employers, employees and for union members in encouraging the efficient performance of union representatives' work, for example in aiding the resolution of problems and conflicts at work. The role can be both demanding and complex. In order to perform effectively union representatives need to have reasonable paid time off from their normal job in appropriate circumstances.

ENTITLEMENT

8. Employees who are union representatives of an independent trade union recognised by their employer are to be permitted reasonable time off during working hours to carry out certain trade union duties.

9. Union representatives are entitled to time off where the duties are concerned with:
- **negotiations with the employer about matters which fall within section 178(2) of the Trade Union and Labour Relations (Consolidation) Act 1992 (TULR(C)A) and for which the union is recognised for the purposes of collective bargaining by the employer;**
- **any other functions on behalf of employees of the employer which are related to matters falling within section 178(2) TULR(C)A and which the employer has agreed the union may perform;**
- **the receipt of information from the employer and consultation by the employer under section 188 TULR(C)A, related to redundancy or under the Transfer of Undertakings (Protection of Employment) Regulations 2006 that applies to employees of the employer;**
- **negotiations with a view to entering into an agreement under regulation 9 of the Transfer of Undertakings (Protection of Employment) Regulations 2006 that applies to employees of the employer; or**
- **the performance on behalf of employees of the employer of functions related to or connected with the making of an agreement under regulation 9 of the Transfer of Undertakings (Protection or Employment) Regulations 2006.**

Matters falling within section 178(2) TULR(C)A are listed in the sub headings of paragraph 13 below.

10. The Safety Representatives and Safety Committees Regulations 1977 regulation 4(2)(a) requires that employers allow union health and safety representatives paid time, as is necessary, during working hours, to perform their functions.

Further advice on time off provisions for health and safety representatives is provided by the Health and Safety Executive in their approved Code and Guidance 'Consulting workers on health and safety'. This is not covered in this Acas Code.

11. An independent trade union is recognised by an employer when it is recognised to any extent for the purposes of collective bargaining. Where a trade union is not so recognised by an employer, employees have no statutory right to time off to undertake any duties except that of accompanying a worker at a disciplinary or grievance hearing (see para 20).

EXAMPLES OF TRADE UNION DUTIES

12. Subject to the recognition or other agreement, trade union representatives should be allowed to take reasonable time off for duties concerned with negotiations or, where their employer has agreed, for duties concerned with other functions related to or connected with the subjects of collective bargaining.

13. The subjects connected with collective bargaining may include one or more of the following:

(a) **terms and conditions of employment, or the physical conditions in which workers are required to work.** Examples could include:
- pay
- hours of work
- holidays and holiday pay
- sick pay arrangements
- pensions
- learning and training
- equality and diversity
- notice periods
- the working environment
- operation of digital equipment and other machinery;

(b) **engagement or non engagement, or termination or suspension of employment or the duties of employment, of one or more workers.** Examples could include:
- recruitment and selection policies
- human resource planning
- redundancy and dismissal arrangements;

(c) **allocation of work or the duties of employment as between workers or groups of workers.** Examples could include:
- job grading
- job evaluation
- job descriptions
- flexible working practices
- work-life balance;

(d) **matters of discipline.** Examples could include:
- disciplinary procedures
- arrangements for representing or accompanying employees at internal interviews
- arrangements for appearing on behalf of trade union members, or as witnesses, before agreed outside appeal bodies or employment tribunals;

(e) **trade union membership or non membership.** Examples could include:
- representational arrangements
- any union involvement in the induction of new workers;

(f) **facilities for trade union representatives.** Examples could include any agreed arrangements for the provision of:
- accommodation
- equipment
- names of new workers to the union;

(g) **machinery for negotiation or consultation and other procedures.** Examples could include arrangements for:
- collective bargaining at the employer and/or multi-employer level
- grievance procedures
- joint consultation
- communicating with members
- communicating with other union representatives and union full-time officers concerned with collective bargaining with the employer.

14. The duties of a representative of a recognised trade union must be connected with or related to negotiations or the performance of functions both in time and subject matter. Reasonable time off may be sought, for example, to:
- prepare for negotiations, including attending relevant meetings
- inform members of progress and outcomes
- prepare for meetings with the employer about matters for which the trade union has only representational rights.

15. Trade union duties will also be related to the receipt of information and consultation related to the handling of collective redundancies where an employer is proposing to dismiss as redundant 20 or more employees at one establishment within a period of 90 days, and where the Transfer of Undertakings (Protection of Employees) Regulations apply but also including the negotiations with a view to entering an agreement under regulation 9 of the Regulations (variation of contract in insolvency).

UNION LEARNING REPRESENTATIVES

16. Employees who are members of an independent trade union recognised by the employer can take reasonable time off to undertake the duties of a Union Learning Representative, provided that the union has given the employer notice in writing that the employee is a learning representative of the trade union and the training condition is met (see paras 28–33 for further information on the training condition). **The functions for which time off as a Union Learning Representative is allowed are:**
- **analysing learning or training needs**
- **providing information and advice about learning or training matters**
- **arranging learning or training**
- **promoting the value of learning or training**
- **consulting the employer about carrying on any such activities**
- **preparation to carry out any of the above activities**
- **undergoing relevant training.**

In practice, the roles and responsibilities of Union Learning Representatives will often vary by union and by workplace but must include one or more of these functions. In some cases it may be helpful if Union Learning Representatives attend meetings concerned with agreeing and promoting learning agreements. Employers may also see it in their interests to grant paid time off for these representatives to attend meetings with external partners concerned with the development and provision of workforce training.

Recognition needs to be given to the varying roles of Union Learning Representatives where the post holder also undertakes additional duties as a union representative.

17. Many employers have in place well established training and development programmes for their employees. Union Learning Representatives should liaise with their employers to ensure that their respective training activities complement one another and that the scope for duplication is minimised.

PAYMENT FOR TIME OFF FOR TRADE UNION DUTIES

18. An employer who permits union representatives time off for trade union duties must pay them for the time off taken. The employer must pay either the amount that the union representative would have earned had they worked during the time off taken or, where earnings vary with the work done, an amount calculated by reference to the average hourly earnings for the work they are employed to do.

The calculation of pay for the time taken for trade union duties should be undertaken with due regard to the type of payment system applying to the union representative including, as appropriate, shift premia, performance related pay, bonuses and commission earnings. Where pay is linked to the achievement of performance targets it may be necessary to adjust such targets to take account of the reduced time the representative has to achieve the desired performance.

19. There is no statutory requirement to pay for time off where the duty is carried out at a time when the union representative would not otherwise have been at work unless the union representative works flexible hours, such as night shift, but needs to perform representative duties during normal hours. Staff who work part time will be entitled to be paid if staff who work full time would be entitled to be paid. In all cases the amount of time off must be reasonable.

TIME OFF TO ACCOMPANY WORKERS AT DISCIPLINARY OR GRIEVANCE HEARINGS

20. Trade union representatives are statutorily entitled to take a reasonable amount of paid time off to accompany a worker at a disciplinary or grievance hearing so long as they have been certified by their union as being capable of acting as a worker's companion. The right to time off in these situations applies regardless of whether the certified person belongs to a recognised union or not although the worker being accompanied must be employed by the same employer. Time off for a union representative or a certified person to accompany a worker of another employer is a matter for voluntary agreement between the parties concerned.

SECTION 2
TRAINING OF UNION REPRESENTATIVES IN ASPECTS OF EMPLOYMENT RELATIONS AND EMPLOYEE DEVELOPMENT

[4.101]
Training is important for union representatives to enable them to carry out their duties effectively. Training should be available both to newly appointed and to more established union representatives. It is desirable, from time to time where resources permit it, for joint training and development activities between union representatives and managers to occur.

ENTITLEMENT

21. Employees who are union representatives of an independent trade union recognised by their employer are to be permitted reasonable time off during working hours to undergo training in aspects of industrial relations relevant to the carrying out of their trade union duties. These duties must be concerned with:

— **negotiations with the employer about matters which fall within section 178(2) TULR(C)A and for which the union is recognised to any extent for the purposes of collective bargaining by the employer; or**
— **any other functions on behalf of employees of the employer which are related to matters falling within section 178(2) TULR(C)A and which the employer has agreed the union may perform;**
— **matters associated with information and consultation concerning collective redundancy and the Transfer of Undertakings, and the negotiation of an agreement under Regulation 9 of the Transfer of Undertakings (Protection of Employees) Regulations.**

Matters falling within section 178(2) TULR(C)A are set out in paragraph 13 above.

22. The Safety Representatives and Safety Committees Regulations 1977 regulation 4(2)(b) requires that employers allow union health and safety representatives to undergo training in aspects of their functions that is 'reasonable in all the circumstances'.

Further advice on the training of health and safety representatives is provided by the Health and Safety Executive in their approved Code and Guidance 'Consulting workers on health and safety'. This is not covered in this Acas Code.

23. Employees who are Trade Union Learning Representatives are also permitted reasonable time off during working hours to undergo training relevant to their functions as a Union Learning Representative.

WHAT IS RELEVANT EMPLOYMENT RELATIONS TRAINING?

24. Training should be in aspects of employment relations relevant to the duties of a union representative. There is no one recommended syllabus for training as a union representative's duties will vary according to:

— the collective bargaining arrangements at the place of work, particularly the scope of the recognition or other agreement
— the structure of the union
— the role of the union representative
— the handling of proposed collective redundancies or the transfer of undertakings.

25. The training must also be approved by the Trades Union Congress or by the independent trade union of which the employee is a union representative.

26. Union representatives are more likely to carry out their duties effectively if they possess skills and knowledge relevant to their duties. In particular, employers should be prepared to consider releasing union representatives for initial training in basic representational skills as soon as possible after their election or appointment, bearing in mind that suitable courses may be infrequent. Reasonable time off could also be considered, for example:

— for training courses to develop the union representative's skills in representation, accompaniment, negotiation and consultation
— for further training particularly where the union representative has special responsibilities, for example in collective redundancy and transfer of undertakings circumstances
— for training courses to familiarise or update union representatives on issues reflecting the developing needs of the workforce they represent
— for training where there are proposals to change the structure and topics of negotiation about matters for which the union is recognised; or where significant changes in the organisation of work are being contemplated
— for training where legal change may affect the conduct of employment relations at the place of work and may require the reconsideration of existing agreements
— for training where a union representative undertakes the role of accompanying employees in grievance and disciplinary hearings.

27. E-learning tools, related to the role of union representatives, should be used where available and appropriate. However, their best use is as an additional learning aid rather than as a replacement to attendance at approved trade union and Trades Union Congress training courses. Time needs to be given during normal working hours for union representatives to take advantage of e-learning where it is available.

TRAINING FOR UNION LEARNING REPRESENTATIVES

28. Employees who are members of an independent trade union recognised by the employer are entitled to reasonable paid time off to undertake the functions of a Union Learning Representative. To qualify for paid time off the member must be sufficiently trained to carry out duties as a learning representative:

— either at the time when their trade union gives notice to their employer in writing that they are a learning representative of the trade union
— or within six months of that date.

29. In the latter case, the trade union is required to give the employer notice in writing that the employee will be undergoing such training and when the employee has done so to give the employer notice of that fact. During the six month period in which he or she is undergoing this training, the Union Learning Representative must be allowed time off to perform their duties. It should be confirmed by the union in a letter that the training undertaken is sufficient to allow the Learning Representative to undertake their role and it is good practice for the union to give details of the training which has been completed and any previous training that has been taken into account. In the interests of good practice, the six month qualifying period may be extended, with agreement, to take into account any significant unforeseen circumstances such as prolonged absence from work due to ill health, pregnancy, bereavement or unavoidable delays in arranging an appropriate training course.

30. To satisfy this training requirement an employee will need to be able to demonstrate to their trade union that they have received sufficient training to enable them to operate competently in one or more of the following areas of activity relevant to their duties as a Union Learning Representative:

analysing learning or training needs;

— this could for example include understanding the different methods for identifying learning interests or needs, being able to effectively identify and record individual learning needs or being able to draw up a plan to meet identified learning requirements.

providing information and advice about learning or training matters;

— including, for example, the development of communication and interviewing skills

— knowledge of available opportunities, in order to be able to provide accurate information to members about learning opportunities within and outside the workplace

— the ability to signpost members to other sources of advice and guidance where additional support is needed, for example, basic skills tutors or fuller in depth professional career guidance.

arranging and supporting learning and training;

— for example, obtaining and providing information on learning opportunities including e-learning where available, supporting and encouraging members to access learning opportunities and helping to develop and improve local learning opportunities;

— promoting the value of learning and training;

— some examples of this activity could be, understanding current initiatives for the development of learning and skills in the workplace, promoting the value of learning to members and within trade union networks and structures, working with employers to meet the learning and skill needs of both individuals and the organisation, and appreciating the value of learning agreements and how they may be developed.

31. An employee could demonstrate to their trade union that they have received sufficient training to enable them to operate competently in one or more of these areas of activity by:

— completing a training course approved by the Trades Union Congress or by the independent trade union of which the employee is a Union Learning Representative, or by

— showing that they have previously gained the relevant expertise and experience to operate effectively as a learning representative.

In the latter case, previous experience and expertise gained in areas such as teaching, training, counselling, providing careers advice and guidance or human resource development, may well be relevant, as may periods of extensive on-the-job training and experience gained in shadowing an experienced Union Learning Representative.

32. Reasonable time off should also be considered for further training to help Union Learning Representatives develop their skills and competencies.

33. Although not required by law it is recognised that there would be clear advantages both to the individual and the organisation if training undertaken leads to a recognised qualification standard.

PAYMENT FOR TIME OFF FOR TRAINING

34. An employer who permits union representatives or Union Learning Representatives time off to attend relevant training, must pay them for the time off taken. The employer must pay either the amount that the union representative or the Union Learning Representative would have earned had they worked during the time off taken or, where earnings vary with the work done, an amount calculated by reference to the average hourly earnings for the work they are employed to do.

The calculation of pay for the time taken for training should be undertaken with due regard to the type of payment system applying to the union representative and Union Learning Representative including, as appropriate, shift premia, performance related pay, bonuses and commission earnings. Where pay is linked to the achievement of performance targets it may be necessary to adjust such targets to take account of the reduced time the representative has to achieve the desired performance.

35. There is no statutory requirement to pay for time off where training is undertaken at a time when the union representative or Union Learning Representative would not otherwise have been at work unless the union representative or Union Learning Representative works flexible hours, such as night shift, but needs to undertake training during normal hours. Staff who work part time will be entitled to be paid if staff who work full time would be entitled to be paid. In all cases, the amount of time off must be reasonable.

SECTION 3
TIME OFF FOR TRADE UNION ACTIVITIES

[4.102]

To operate effectively and democratically, trade unions need the active participation of members. It can also be very much in employers' interests that such participation is assured and help is given to promote effective communication between union representatives and members in the workplace.

ENTITLEMENT

36. An employee who is a member of an independent trade union recognised by the employer in respect of that description of employee is to be permitted reasonable time off during working hours to take part in any trade union activity. An employee who is a member of an independent and recognised trade union is also permitted to take reasonable time off during working hours

for the purposes of accessing the services of a Union Learning Representative (provided those services are services for which the Union Learning Representative is entitled to time off).

WHAT ARE EXAMPLES OF TRADE UNION ACTIVITIES?

37. The activities of a trade union member can be, for example:
— attending workplace meetings to discuss and vote on the outcome of negotiations with the employer. Where relevant, and with the employer's agreement, this can include attending such workplace meetings at the employer's neighbouring locations.
— meeting full time officers to discuss issues relevant to the workplace
— voting in union elections
— having access to services provided by a Union Learning representative.

38. Where the member is acting as a representative of a recognised union, activities can be, for example, taking part in:
— branch, area or regional meetings of the union where the business of the union is under discussion
— meetings of official policy making bodies such as the executive committee or annual conference
— meetings with full time officers to discuss issues relevant to the workplace.

39. There is no right to time off for trade union activities which themselves consist of industrial action.

PAYMENT FOR TIME OFF FOR TRADE UNION ACTIVITIES

40. Paragraphs 18 and 19 set out the statutory entitlement to payment for time off to undertake trade union duties.

41. There is no statutory requirement that union members or representatives be paid for time off taken on trade union activities. Nevertheless employers may want to consider payment in certain circumstances, for example to ensure that workplace meetings are fully representative or to ensure that employees have access to services provided by Union Learning Representatives.

SECTION 4
THE RESPONSIBILITIES OF EMPLOYERS AND TRADE UNIONS

[4.103]
Employers, trade unions, union representatives and line managers should work together to ensure that time off provisions, including training, operate effectively and for mutual benefit. Union representatives need to be able to communicate with management, each other, their trade union and employees. To do so they need to be able to use appropriate communication media and other facilities.

GENERAL CONSIDERATIONS

42. The amount and frequency of time off should be reasonable in all the circumstances. Although the statutory provisions apply to all employers without exception as to size and type of business or service, trade unions should be aware of the wide variety of difficulties and operational requirements to be taken into account when seeking or agreeing arrangements for time off, for example:
— the size of the organisation and the number of workers
— the production process
— the need to maintain a service to the public
— the need for safety and security at all times.

43. Employers in turn should have in mind the difficulties for trade union representatives and members in ensuring effective representation and communications with, for example:
— shift workers
— part-time workers
— home workers
— teleworkers or workers not working in a fixed location
— those employed at dispersed locations
— workers with particular domestic commitments including those on leave for reasons of maternity, paternity or care responsibilities
— workers with special needs such as disabilities or language requirements.

44. For time off arrangements to work satisfactorily trade unions should:
— ensure that union representatives are aware of their role, responsibilities and functions
— inform management, in writing, as soon as possible of appointments or resignations of union representatives
— ensure that union representatives receive any appropriate written credentials promptly
— ensure that employers receive details of the functions of union representatives where they carry out special duties or functions.

45. Employers should ensure that, where necessary, work cover and/or work load reductions are provided when time off is required. This can include the allocation of duties to other employees, rearranging work to a different time or a reduction in workloads.

46. While there is no statutory right for facilities for union representatives, except for representatives engaged in duties related to collective redundancies and the Transfer of Undertakings, employers should, where practical, make available to union representatives the facilities necessary for them to perform their duties efficiently and communicate effectively with their members, colleague union representatives and full-time officers. Where resources permit the facilities should include:

— accommodation for meetings which could include provision for Union Learning Representatives and a union member(s) to meet to discuss relevant training matters
— access to a telephone and other communication media used or permitted in the workplace such as email, intranet and internet
— the use of noticeboards
— where the volume of the union representative's work justifies it, the use of dedicated office space
— confidential space where an employee involved in a grievance or disciplinary matter can meet their representative or to discuss other confidential matters
— access to members who work at a different location
— access to e-learning tools where computer facilities are available.

47. When using facilities provided by the employer for the purposes of communication with their members or their trade union, union representatives must comply with agreed procedures both in respect of the use of such facilities and also in respect of access to and use of company information. The agreed procedures will be either those agreed between the union and the employer as part of an agreement on time off (see section 6) or comply with general rules applied to all employees in the organisation. In particular, union representatives must respect and maintain the confidentiality of information they are given access to where, the disclosure would seriously harm the functioning of, or would be prejudicial to, the employer's business interests. The disclosure of information for collective bargaining purposes is covered by the Acas Code of Practice on that topic. Union representatives should understand that unauthorised publication risks damaging the employer's business, straining relations with the representative body concerned, possible breaches of individual contracts of employment and, in extreme cases such as unauthorised publication of price sensitive information, the commission of criminal offences.

48. Union representatives will have legitimate expectations that they and their members are entitled to communicate without intrusion in the form of monitoring by their employer. Rules concerning the confidentiality of communications involving union representatives should be agreed between the employer and the union. Guidance on this is set out in paragraphs 49 and 57 below.

49. Employers must respect the confidential and sensitive nature of communications between union representatives and their members and trade union. They should not normally carry out regular or random monitoring of union emails. Only in exceptional circumstances may employers require access to communications but such access should be subject to the general rules set out in statute and the Employment Practices Code issued by the Information Commissioner's Office. In the context of the Data Protection Act 1998 whether a person is a member of a trade union or not is defined as sensitive personal data. This also applies to data concerning individuals, for example communications concerned with possible or actual grievance and disciplinary issues. There are therefore very strict provisions on how such data can be used and monitored in compliance with the law.

REQUESTING TIME OFF

50. Trade union representatives and members requesting time off to pursue their duties or activities or to access the services of a Union Learning Representative should provide management, especially their line manager, with as much notice as practically possible concerning:

— the purpose of such time off, while preserving personal confidential information relating to individuals in grievance or disciplinary matters
— the intended location
— the timing and duration of time off required.

51. Union representatives should minimise business disruption by being prepared to be as flexible as possible in seeking time off in circumstances where the immediate or unexpected needs of the business make it difficult for colleagues or managers to provide cover for them in their absence. Equally employers should recognise the mutual obligation to allow union representatives to undertake their duties.

52. In addition, union representatives who request paid time off to undergo relevant training should:

— give at least a few weeks' notice to management of nominations for training courses
— provide details of the contents of the training course.

53. When deciding whether requests for paid time off should be granted, consideration would need to be given as to their reasonableness, for example to ensure adequate cover for safety or to safeguard the production process or the provision of service. Consideration should also be given to allowing Union Learning Representatives access to a room in which they can discuss training in a confidential manner with an employee. Similarly, managers and unions should seek to agree a mutually convenient time which minimises the effect on production or services. Where workplace meetings are requested, consideration should be given to holding them, for example:

— towards the end of a shift or the working week
— before or after a meal break.

54. For their part line managers should be familiar with the rights and duties of union representatives regarding time off. They should be encouraged to take reasonable steps as necessary in the planning and management of representatives' time off and the provision of cover or work load reduction, taking into account the legitimate needs of such union representatives to discharge their functions and receive training efficiently and effectively.

55. Employers need to consider each application for time off on its merits; they should also consider the reasonableness of the request in relation to agreed time off already taken or in prospect.

SECTION 5
AGREEMENTS ON TIME OFF

[4.104]

To take account of the wide variety of circumstances and problems which can arise, there can be positive advantages for employers and trade unions in establishing agreements on time off in ways that reflect their own situations. It should be borne in mind, however, that the absence of a formal agreement on time off does not in itself deny an individual any statutory entitlement. Nor does any agreement supersede statutory entitlement to time off.

56. A formal agreement can help to:

— provide clear guidelines against which applications for time off can be determined
— establish realistic expectations on the part of union representatives and managers
— avoid misunderstanding
— facilitate better planning
— ensure fair and reasonable treatment.

57. Agreements should specify:

— the amount of time off permitted recognising that this will vary according the fluctuations in demand on the union representatives' role
— the occasions on which time off can be taken including meetings with management, meetings with other union representatives, time needed to prepare for meetings, communicating with members and their trade union, time to undertake e-learning if appropriate and to attend approved training events
— in what circumstances time off will be paid
— arrangements for taking time off at short notice
— how pay is to be calculated
— to whom time off will be paid
— the facilities and equipment to be provided and limits to their use, if any
— arrangements for ensuring confidentiality of communications involving union representatives. These should include agreed rules on the use of data and the exceptional cases where monitoring may be necessary, for example in cases of suspected illegal use, specifying the circumstances where such monitoring may be undertaken and the means by which it is to be done, for example by company IT or security personnel
— the role of line managers in granting permission to legitimate requests for time off and, where appropriate and practical, ensuring that adequate cover or work load reductions are provided
— the procedure for requesting time off
— the procedure for resolving grievances about time off.

58. In addition, it would be sensible for agreements to make clear:

— arrangements for the appropriate payment to be made when time off relates in part to union duties and in part to union activities
— how and in what circumstances payment might be made to shift and part time employees undertaking trade union duties outside their normal working hours.

59. Agreements for time off and other facilities for union representation should be consistent with wider agreements which deal with such matters as constituencies, number of representatives and the election of officials.

60. The operation of time off agreements or arrangements should be jointly reviewed by the parties from time to time.

61. In smaller organisations, it might be thought more appropriate for employers and unions to reach understandings about how requests for time off are to be made; and more broadly to agree flexible arrangements which can accommodate their particular circumstances.

SECTION 6
INDUSTRIAL ACTION

[4.105]

62. Employers and unions have a responsibility to use agreed procedures to settle problems and avoid industrial action. Time off may therefore be permitted for this purpose particularly where there is a dispute. **There is no right to time off for trade union activities which themselves consist of industrial action.** However, where a union representative is not taking part in industrial action but represents members involved, normal arrangements for time off with pay for the union representatives should apply.

SECTION 7
RESOLVING DISPUTES

[4.106]

There is advantage in agreeing ways in which disputes concerning time off arrangements, including training and access to facilities, can be settled and any appropriate procedures to resolve disputes should be followed.

63. Every effort should be made to resolve any dispute or grievance in relation to time off work for union duties or activities. **Where the grievance remains unresolved, union representatives, Union Learning Representatives or members have a right to complain to an employment tribunal that their employer has failed to allow reasonable time off or, in the case of a Union Learning Representative or union representative, has failed to pay for all or part of the time off taken. Such complaints may be resolved by conciliation by Acas or through a compromise agreement and, if this is successful, no tribunal hearing will be necessary.** Acas assistance may also be sought without the need for a formal complaint to a tribunal.

ANNEX

(The Annex sets out the law on time off for trade union duties and activities, ie, TULR(C)A 1992, ss 168, 168A, 169, 170, 178(1)–(3) and 173(1) and the definition of 'official' in s 119. The 1992 Act is set out at **[1.241]** *et seq.)*

B. BORDER & IMMIGRATION AGENCY

BORDER & IMMIGRATION AGENCY CODE OF PRACTICE: CIVIL PENALTIES FOR EMPLOYERS (FEBRUARY 2008)

PREVENTION OF ILLEGAL WORKING

IMMIGRATION, ASYLUM AND NATIONALITY ACT 2006

[4.107]

NOTES

This Code of Practice, and the Code immediately following at **[4.114]**, were issued by the Border and Immigration Agency (now the UK Border Agency, and part of the Home Office). This Code is made under the authority of s 19 of the Immigration, Asylum and Nationality Act 2006; the Parliamentary authority for the Codes is SI 2007/3290, regs 11 and 12 respectively at **[2.1132]** and **[2.1133]**. The Codes came into force on 29 February 2008. The Codes have no specific statutory status. They replace the previous Code issued by the Home Office under the Asylum and Immigration Act 1996. The new Codes do not apply in respect of those employees continuously employed since a date prior to 29 February 2008. Notes are as in the original Code.

CONTENTS

1. INTRODUCTION

[4.108]

1.1 The Government is introducing civil penalties for employers of illegal migrant workers as part of a fundamental reform of our immigration system, in which the rights and responsibilities of employers are clearly set out and penalties are proportionate to the level of non-compliance or illegal behaviour.

1.2 As an employer, you have a responsibility to prevent illegal working in the United Kingdom. The illegal working provisions of the Immigration, Asylum and Nationality Act 2006 ('the 2006 Act') came into effect on 29 February 2008 and replaced the previous offence under section 8 of the Asylum and Immigration Act 1996,[1] ('the 1996 Act'), **which has now been repealed**. Section 15 of the 2006 Act allows the Secretary of State to serve an employer with a notice requiring the payment of a penalty of a specified amount where they have employed a person aged 16 or over, who is subject to immigration control unless:

- that person has been given valid and subsisting leave to be in the United Kingdom by the Government, and that leave does not restrict them from taking the job in question; **or**
- the person comes into a category where employment is also allowed.

1.3 For the purposes of the 2006 Act, an 'employer' is defined as a person who employs an individual under a contract of employment. This can be a contract of service or apprenticeship, whether express or implied. If the contract is expressed, this can be either orally or in writing. In most cases, it should be clear when you are entering into such a contract of service with an employee.

1.4 This Code of practice has been issued under section 19 of the 2006 Act. The Code has been prepared to set out the factors that may be considered when determining the level of penalty to be imposed in each case. This Code has been produced alongside other guidance documents and sources of information. You may wish to refer to this Code alongside that guidance and information.

1.5 This is a statutory Code. This means that it has been approved by the Secretary of State and laid before Parliament. The Code does not impose any legal obligations on employers, nor is it an authoritative statement of the law; only the courts can provide that. However, the Code can be used as evidence in legal proceedings and courts must take account of any part of the Code that might be relevant.

NOTES

[1] As amended by section 22 of the Immigration and Asylum Act 1999, section 147 of the Nationality, Immigration and Asylum Act 2002 and section 6 of the Asylum and Immigration (Treatment of Claimants, etc) Act 2004).

2. HOW THE LEVEL OF PENALTY MAY BE DETERMINED

[4.109]

2.1 If we find you to be employing illegal migrant workers, we may look at certain factors when deciding the level of your civil penalty.

2.2 Table 1 is a framework designed to assist the Border and Immigration Agency with the assessment of whether to issue a penalty notice to an employer, and if so, at what level. It provides a sliding scale with minimum and maximum penalties, but the actual amount will be decided by the Border and Immigration Agency on a case by case basis. The framework is provided for guidance purposes (explanatory flow charts are also attached at Appendix 2). The level of penalty to be imposed per worker may be increased or reduced according to different criteria. For example, the penalty can be increased according to the number of times you are found with illegal migrant workers in your workforce and have failed to establish a statutory excuse.

Table 1- framework for assessment of level of civil penalty

OCCASION ON WHICH WARNING/PENALTY ISSUED		NATURE OF CHECKS COMPLETED				
		FULL	PARTIAL		NO	
	3RD+	No penalty	Maximum penalty of **£10,000** per worker		Maximum penalty of **£10,000** per worker	
			Reduced by up to **£1,250** per worker reported	Reduced by up to **£1,250** per worker, with co-operation		
			Minimum penalty of **£7,500** per worker			
	2ND	No penalty	Maximum penalty of **£7,500** per worker		Maximum penalty of **£10,000** per worker	
			Reduced by up to **£1,250** per worker reported	Reduced by up to **£1,250** per worker, with co-operation	Reduced by up to **£1,250** per worker reported	Reduced by up to **£1,250** per worker, with co-operation
			Minimum penalty of **£5,000** per worker		Minimum penalty of **£7,500** per worker	
	1ST	No penalty	Maximum penalty of **£5,000** per worker		Maximum penalty of **£7,500** per worker	
			Reduced by up to **£2,500** per worker reported	Reduced by up to **£2,500** per worker, with co-operation	Reduced by up to **£2,500** per worker reported	Reduced by up to **£2,500** per worker, with co-operation
			No penalty warning letter issued		Minimum penalty of **£2,500** per worker	

2.3 Where an objection is made against the imposition of a civil penalty, reference will be made to this framework, in addition to factors listed at Appendix 4. The factors we will take into account are:

(A) the nature of checks that you have conducted; **and**
(B) reporting suspected illegal workers to the Border and Immigration Agency; **and**
(C) your co-operation with the Border and Immigration Agency; **and**
(D) the number of offences you have committed in the past.

A. THE NATURE OF CHECKS CONDUCTED

2.4 The system of civil penalties is designed to encourage employers to comply with their legal obligations, without criminalising those who are less than diligent in operating their recruitment and employment practices. Under the 2006 Act, an employer may establish a statutory excuse by checking original documents presented by a potential or existing employee. Details of what documents are acceptable and how to do this are provided in Appendix 1.

2.5 In all cases, you must undertake these steps **before** a person begins employment to establish the statutory excuse and, where a document or documents from List B are provided, you must also carry out a follow-up check at least once every **12 months** after the initial check to retain the statutory excuse.

2.6 The Government is soon to begin introducing identity cards for foreign nationals on a compulsory basis. However, before full roll-out of the cards, if you are presented with a false travel document or visa, you will only be subject to legal action if the falsity is reasonably apparent. The falsity would be considered to be 'reasonably apparent' if an individual who is untrained in the identification of false documents, examining it carefully, but briefly and without the use of technological aids, could reasonably be expected to realise that the document in question is not genuine.

2.7 Equally, where a potential employee presents a document and it is reasonably apparent that the person presenting the document is not the rightful holder of that document, then you may also be subject to enforcement action, even if the document itself is genuine. Therefore, you should examine the photograph and personal details in the document and compare these with the holder in order to detect any impersonation.

Full and partial checks

2.8 A **full check** shall be considered to have been conducted where you can provide copies of certain documents, as described in Appendix 1, for all relevant employees and the official is satisfied that the specified steps were taken when checking these documents. If a full check has been conducted, then the employer will be entitled to a statutory excuse and no penalty may be payable, even if illegal migrant workers are found to be working.

2.9 However, the provision of such records **does not** provide a statutory excuse if you **knew** that the employee was not permitted to take the work in question. You may receive a penalty or be prosecuted for a criminal offence, including the offence of knowingly employing an illegal migrant worker, or facilitating a breach of UK immigration law. Action will be taken against any employer where there is sufficient evidence available and where prosecution would be in the public interest.

2.10 Where only a partial check has been carried out for migrant workers who are found to be working illegally, the employer may be subject to a civil penalty. A **partial check** shall be considered to have been conducted where, for example, you have only checked and copied one of a specified combination of two original documents that are required to establish the statutory excuse, or failed to conduct a follow-up check on a worker with temporary immigration status, after having conducted a full document check at the point of recruitment.

2.11 If you cannot provide a record of having conducted the prescribed document checks prior to recruitment, or you have accepted a document which clearly does not belong to the holder, or it is reasonably apparent that the document is false, or shows that the person does not have a current entitlement to work in this country, you shall be considered to have conducted no check for the purpose of imposing a penalty. Where **no check** has been conducted, the employer may be subject to the maximum level of penalty.

2.12 In each case, it is for you to show that you have complied with the requirements to establish a statutory excuse.

B. REPORTING SUSPECTED ILLEGAL WORKERS TO THE BORDER AND IMMIGRATION AGENCY

2.13 As shown in Table 1, the civil penalty may be reduced at the discretion of the Border and Immigration Agency, having regard to the suggested minimum and maximum penalties. If more than one employee is found working illegally, you may be penalised for each worker found, but any reduction made may be applied proportionately for each illegal migrant worker detected.

2.14 If you report any suspicions about your employees' entitlement to work in the UK, or to undertake the work in question to the Border and Immigration Agency, a sum may be deducted from the amount of penalty due for each worker. This information must have been reported to the Employers' Helpline on **0845 010 6677**[2] **before** any immigration visit is made to the employer. When reporting, you will be given a call reference and this must be referred to when applying a reduction in penalty.

C. CO-OPERATION WITH THE BORDER AND IMMIGRATION AGENCY IN CONDUCTING AN OPERATION

2.15 The penalty due for each worker can also be reduced where you have co-operated with the Border and Immigration Agency in any investigation, or in any consequent operation to detect and detain illegal migrant workers within your workforce.

2.16 The level of any reduction made will depend on whether you have been found to be employing illegal migrant workers within the previous three years. The sliding scale also allows for a warning letter to be issued instead of a civil penalty in cases where:

- It is the first occasion on which you are found with illegal migrant workers in your workforce; **and**

- You have conducted partial checks on the workers; **and**
- You have reported suspected illegal workers; **and**
- There is no evidence of deliberate wrong doing by you; **and**
- You have co-operated with the Border and Immigration Agency.

2.17 Where it can be established that you have conducted full checks and did not knowingly employ an illegal worker, you will receive no penalty or warning.

D. PREVIOUS OFFENCES

2.18 When considering whether a higher level of penalty should apply to an employer who has been visited before, previous penalties or warnings will not be considered if they were issued more than three years before the date of the new visit. Where an employer is revisited, and has received a penalty or warning within three years of the current visit, those penalties and warnings will be counted.

Multiple premises

2.19 A company with multiple premises where recruitment is devolved to each site, will not be liable to a cumulative penalty if illegal workers are detected at different sites, unless this can be attributed to a general failure in the company's centrally set recruitment practices.

Transfer Of Undertakings

2.20 Employers who acquire staff as a result of a Transfer of Undertakings (Protection of Employment) transfer are provided with a period of 28 days grace to undertake the appropriate document checks.

NOTES

[2] For current information, please visit www.bia.homeoffice.gov.uk

APPENDIX 1: DOCUMENTS REQUIRED FOR THE PURPOSE OF ESTABLISHING THE STATUTORY EXCUSE

[4.110]

Any one of the documents, or combination of documents described in **List A** or **List B** will provide you with a statutory excuse if you take reasonable steps to check the validity of the original document and that the person presenting the document is the rightful holder, then make a copy of the relevant page, or pages before employing an individual.

For identity cards, passports and travel documents, a copy should be taken of:

- the document's front cover; **and**
- any page containing the holder's personal details including nationality, his or her photograph, date of birth and/or signature; **and**
- any biometric details; **and**
- the date of expiry; **and**
- any relevant UK immigration endorsements.

Other documents should be copied in their entirety.

All copies of documents should be kept securely. If your potential employee gives you two documents which have different names, ask them for a further document to explain the reason for this. The further document could be a marriage certificate, a divorce decree, or a deed poll document.

By doing this, the Border and Immigration Agency will be able to examine your right to the statutory excuse if they detect any illegal migrants working for you.

If reasonable steps are taken to check the validity of a document or documents from **List A**, the statutory excuse will have been established for the duration of the employment **and no further checks will be required**.

Each time that a document or combination of documents from **List B** is provided, you must note the date on which you carried out the original document check. In order to retain your excuse against a penalty for employing that individual, you must carry out a follow-up check at least once every **12 months** after the initial check. Again, this will involve asking the employee to produce a valid original document, or documents either from **List A**, or from **List B** and copying it for your records. If a document, or documents, from **List A** are subsequently presented and reasonable steps are taken to check the validity of the document or documents, the statutory excuse will have been established for the remainder of the employment and **no further checks will be required**.

Please note the references to the provision of a National Insurance number in Lists A and B. **The provision of a National Insurance number in isolation is never sufficient for the purpose of establishing a statutory excuse**. The National Insurance number can only be used for this purpose when presented in combination with one of the documents, as appropriate, specified in Lists A and B.

All references to the documents issued by the Home Office in Lists A and B, also include documents issued by the former Immigration and Nationality Directorate (IND) and Work Permits (UK).

LIST A DOCUMENTS

1. A passport showing that the holder, or a person named in the passport as the child of the holder, is a British citizen or a citizen of the United Kingdom and Colonies having the right of abode in the United Kingdom; **or**

2. A passport or national identity card showing that the holder, or a person named in the passport as the child of the holder, is a national of a European Economic Area country or Switzerland; **or**

3. A residence permit, registration certificate or document certifying or indicating permanent residence issued by the Home Office or the Border and Immigration Agency to a national of a European Economic Area country or Switzerland; **or**

4. A permanent residence card issued by the Home Office or the Border and Immigration Agency to the family member of a national of a European Economic Area country or Switzerland; **or**

5. A Biometric Immigration Document issued by the Border and Immigration Agency to the holder which indicates that the person named in it is allowed to stay indefinitely in the United Kingdom, or has no time limit on their stay in the United Kingdom; **or**

6. A passport or other travel document endorsed to show that the holder is exempt from immigration control, is allowed to stay indefinitely in the United Kingdom, has the right of abode in the United Kingdom, or has no time limit on their stay in the United Kingdom; **or**

7. An Immigration Status Document issued by the Home Office or the Border and Immigration Agency to the holder with an endorsement indicating that the person named in it is allowed to stay indefinitely in the United Kingdom, or has no time limit on their stay in the United Kingdom, **when produced in combination with** an official document giving the person's permanent National Insurance Number and their name issued by a Government agency or a previous employer (eg P45, P60, National Insurance Card); **or**

8. A full birth certificate issued in the United Kingdom which includes the name(s) of at least one of the holder's parents, **when produced in combination with** an official document giving the person's permanent National Insurance Number and their name issued by a Government agency or a previous employer (eg P45, P60, National Insurance Card); **or**

9. A full adoption certificate issued in the United Kingdom which includes the name(s) of at least one of the holder's adoptive parents, **when produced in combination with** an official document giving the person's permanent National Insurance Number and their name issued by a Government agency or a previous employer (eg P45, P60, National Insurance Card); **or**

10. A birth certificate issued in the Channel Islands, the Isle of Man, or Ireland, **when produced in combination with** an official document giving the person's permanent National Insurance Number and their name issued by a Government agency or a previous employer (eg P45, P60, National Insurance Card); **or**

11. An adoption certificate issued in the Channel Islands, the Isle of Man, or Ireland, **when produced in combination with** an official document giving the person's permanent National Insurance Number and their name issued by a Government agency or a previous employer (eg P45, P60, National Insurance Card); **or**

12. A certificate of registration or naturalisation as a British citizen, **when produced in combination with** an official document giving the person's permanent National Insurance Number and their name issued by a Government agency or a previous employer (eg P45, P60, National Insurance Card); **or**

13. A letter issued by the Home Office or the Border and Immigration Agency to the holder which indicates that the person named in it is allowed to stay indefinitely in the United Kingdom, or has no time limit on their stay, **when produced in combination with** an official document giving the person's permanent National Insurance Number and their name issued by a Government agency or a previous employer (eg P45, P60, National Insurance Card).

LIST B DOCUMENTS

1. A passport or other travel document endorsed to show that the holder is allowed to stay in the United Kingdom and is allowed to do the work in question, provided that it does not require the issue of a work permit; **or**

2. A Biometric Immigration Document, issued by the Border and Immigration Agency to the holder which indicates that the person named in it can stay in the United Kingdom and is allowed to do the work in question; **or**

3. A work permit or other approval to take employment issued by the Home Office or the Border and Immigration Agency, **when produced in combination with** either a passport or another travel document endorsed to show that the holder is allowed to stay in the United Kingdom and is allowed to do the work in question, or a letter issued by the Home Office or the Border and Immigration Agency to the holder, or the employer or prospective employer confirming the same; **or**

4. A certificate of application issued by the Home Office or the Border and Immigration Agency to or for a family member of a national of a European Economic Area country or Switzerland, stating that the holder is permitted to take employment, which is less than 6 months old, when produced in combination with evidence of verification by the Border and Immigration Agency Employer Checking Service; **or**

5. A residence card or document issued by the Home Office or the Border and Immigration Agency to a family member of a national of a European Economic Area country or Switzerland; **or**

6. An Application Registration Card (ARC) issued by the Home Office or the Border and Immigration Agency stating that the holder is permitted to take employment, **when produced in combination with** evidence of verification by the Border and Immigration Agency Employer Checking Service; **or**

7. An Immigration Status Document issued by the Home Office or the Border and Immigration Agency to the holder with an endorsement indicating that the person named in it can stay in the United Kingdom, and is allowed to do the work in question, **when produced in combination with** an official document giving the person's permanent National Insurance Number and their name issued by a Government agency or previous employer (eg P45, P60, National Insurance Card); **or**

8. A letter issued by the Home Office or the Border and Immigration Agency to the holder or the employer or prospective employer, which indicates that the person named in it can stay in the United Kingdom and is allowed to do the work in question, **when produced in combination with** an official document giving the person's permanent National Insurance Number and their name issued by a Government agency or previous employer (eg P45, P60, National Insurance Card).

APPENDIX 2: FLOWCHARTS FOR DETERMINATION OF THE CIVIL PENALTY

[4.111]

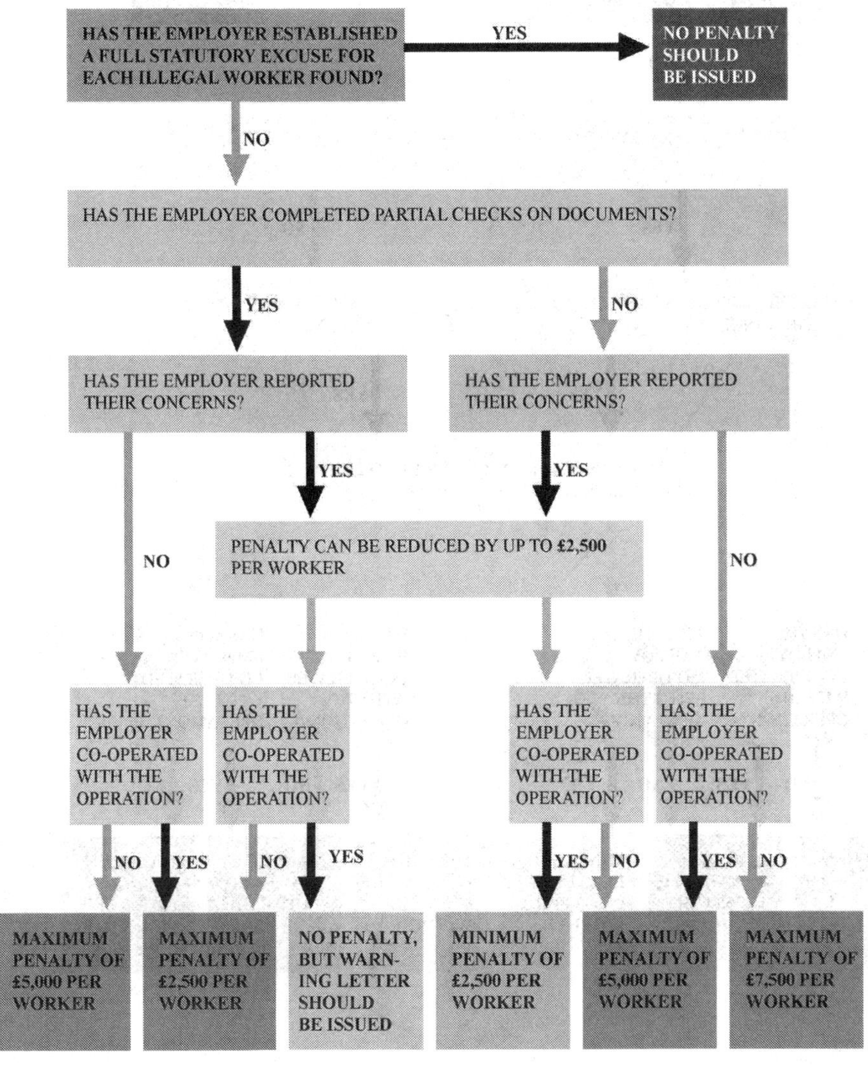

FIRST VISIT TO EMPLOYER
HAS THE EMPLOYER ESTABLISHED A FULL STATUTORY EXCUSE FOR EACH ILLEGAL WORKER FOUND?
YES
NO PENALTY SHOULD BE ISSUED
NO
HAS THE EMPLOYER COMPLETED PARTIAL CHECKS ON DOCUMENTS?
YES
NO
HAS THE EMPLOYER REPORTED THEIR CONCERNS?
HAS THE EMPLOYER REPORTED THEIR CONCERNS?
YES
YES
NO
PENALTY CAN BE REDUCED BY UP TO £2,500 PER WORKER
NO
HAS THE EMPLOYER CO-OPERATED WITH THE OPERATION?
HAS THE EMPLOYER CO-OPERATED WITH THE OPERATION?
HAS THE EMPLOYER CO-OPERATED WITH THE OPERATION?
HAS THE EMPLOYER CO-OPERATED WITH THE OPERATION?
NO
YES
NO
YES
YES
NO
YES
NO
MAXIMUM PENALTY OF £5,000 PER WORKER
MAXIMUM PENALTY OF £2,500 PER WORKER
NO PENALTY, BUT WARN-ING LETTER SHOULD BE ISSUED
MINIMUM PENALTY OF £2,500 PER WORKER
MAXIMUM PENALTY OF £5,000 PER WORKER
MAXIMUM PENALTY OF £7,500 PER WORKER

SECOND VISIT TO EMPLOYER (WITHIN THREE YEARS OF FIRST VISIT)

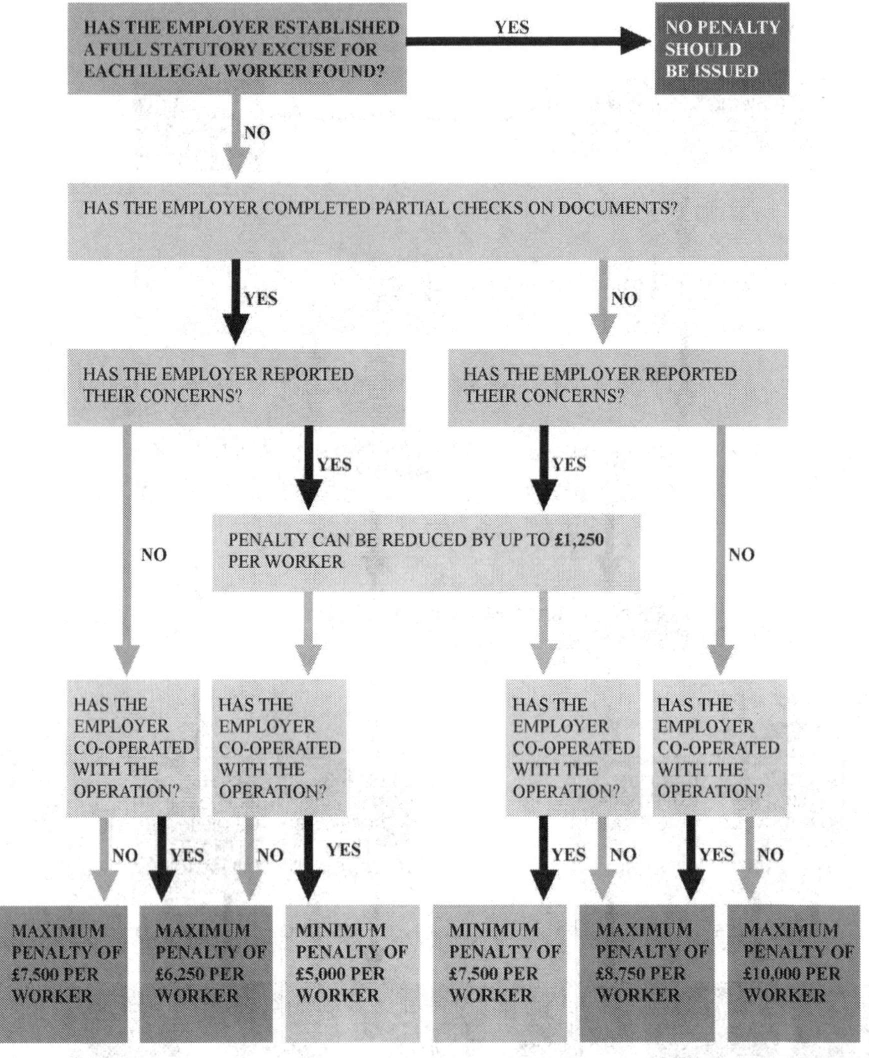
HAS THE EMPLOYER ESTABLISHED A FULL STATUTORY EXCUSE FOR EACH ILLEGAL WORKER FOUND?
YES
NO PENALTY SHOULD BE ISSUED
NO
HAS THE EMPLOYER COMPLETED PARTIAL CHECKS ON DOCUMENTS?
YES
NO
HAS THE EMPLOYER REPORTED THEIR CONCERNS?
HAS THE EMPLOYER REPORTED THEIR CONCERNS?
YES
YES
NO
PENALTY CAN BE REDUCED BY UP TO £1,250 PER WORKER
NO
HAS THE EMPLOYER CO-OPERATED WITH THE OPERATION?
HAS THE EMPLOYER CO-OPERATED WITH THE OPERATION?
HAS THE EMPLOYER CO-OPERATED WITH THE OPERATION?
HAS THE EMPLOYER CO-OPERATED WITH THE OPERATION?
NO
YES
NO
YES
YES
NO
YES
NO
MAXIMUM PENALTY OF £7,500 PER WORKER
MAXIMUM PENALTY OF £6,250 PER WORKER
MINIMUM PENALTY OF £5,000 PER WORKER
MINIMUM PENALTY OF £7,500 PER WORKER
MAXIMUM PENALTY OF £8,750 PER WORKER
MAXIMUM PENALTY OF £10,000 PER WORKER

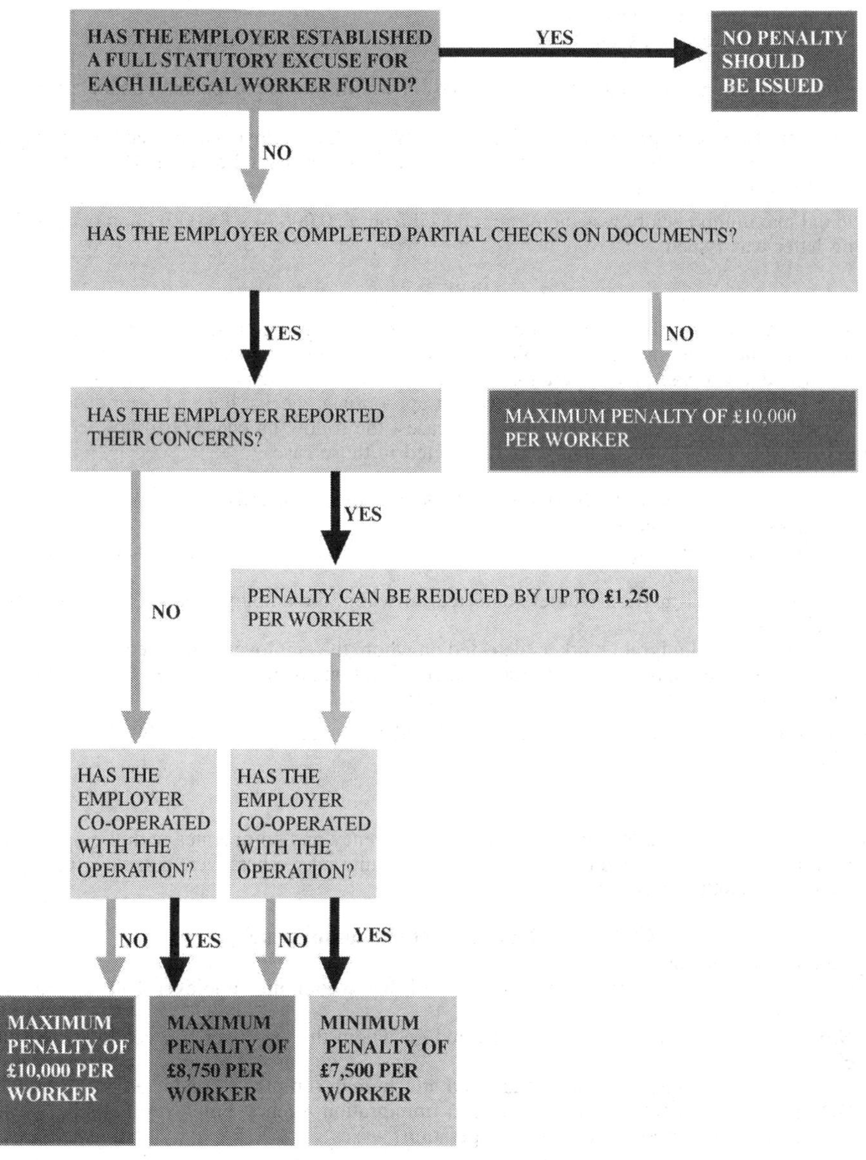
THIRD AND EVERY SUBSEQUENT VISIT TO EMPLOYER
(WITHIN THREE YEARS OF FIRST VISIT)
HAS THE EMPLOYER ESTABLISHED A FULL STATUTORY EXCUSE FOR EACH ILLEGAL WORKER FOUND?
YES
NO PENALTY SHOULD BE ISSUED
NO
HAS THE EMPLOYER COMPLETED PARTIAL CHECKS ON DOCUMENTS?
YES
NO
HAS THE EMPLOYER REPORTED THEIR CONCERNS?
MAXIMUM PENALTY OF £10,000 PER WORKER
YES
NO
PENALTY CAN BE REDUCED BY UP TO £1,250 PER WORKER
HAS THE EMPLOYER CO-OPERATED WITH THE OPERATION?
HAS THE EMPLOYER CO-OPERATED WITH THE OPERATION?
NO
YES
NO
YES
MAXIMUM PENALTY OF £10,000 PER WORKER
MAXIMUM PENALTY OF £8,750 PER WORKER
MINIMUM PENALTY OF £7,500 PER WORKER

APPENDIX 3: CASE SCENARIOS

[4.112]

In any scenario where the full checks have been completed and the employer did not knowingly employ an illegal migrant worker, the employer will not be liable to a civil penalty. The following scenarios provide examples of potential maximum penalty amounts, however, the penalties set out in these scenarios are only intended as guidelines and each case will be considered on its merits.

CASE A

A company contacts the Border and Immigration Agency Employers' Helpline with concerns that a number of its employees may be working illegally. In co-operation with the employer, the Border and Immigration Agency find that four workers on the staff lists are illegal migrant workers and mount an operation to collect these individuals for removal. The company had not been visited previously by the Border and Immigration Agency. All these employees were taken on or after

29 February 2008 and the company had accepted letters issued by the Home Office from these employees as evidence of their entitlement to work in each case, rather than as part of a specified combination.

CASE A RESULT: No penalty, warning letter issued, advice provided.

- Number of previous visits – 0
- Number of illegal migrant workers detected for whom the employer had a statutory excuse – 0
- Number of illegal migrant workers detected on whom the employer had conducted partial checks – 4
- Number of illegal migrant workers detected on whom the employer conducted no checks – 0
- Did the company approach the Border and Immigration Agency Employer Helpline? – Yes
- Did the company co-operate with the operation? – Yes

The potential maximum penalty was therefore reduced from £20,000 (4 x £5,000) to no penalty, but a warning letter was issued.

CASE B

A company is visited by the Border and Immigration Agency, but had not approached them beforehand and they had no prior warnings or penalties. The company co-operates with the investigation and the consequent operation to pick up illegal workers. Ten illegal workers are detected; in six cases, the company had carried out appropriate checks, but had been deceived by high quality forgeries. However, in the other four cases, the follow-up checks had not been made, indicating that only partial checks had been completed in those cases.

CASE B RESULT: £10,000 maximum penalty

- Number of previous visits – 0
- Number of illegal migrant workers detected for whom the employer had a statutory excuse – 6
- Number of illegal migrant workers detected on whom the employer had conducted partial checks – 4
- Number of illegal migrant workers detected on whom the employer conducted no checks – 0
- Did the company approach the Border and Immigration Agency Employer Helpline? – No
- Did the company co-operate with the operation? – Yes

The potential maximum penalty was therefore reduced from £20,000 (4 x £5,000) to a £10,000 (4 x £2,500)

CASE C

An employer is visited by the Border and Immigration Agency and co-operates with the operation. The employer had not been visited previously. Six illegal migrant workers were detected, for whom the employer had conducted no checks.

CASE C RESULT: £30,000 maximum penalty

- Number of previous visits – 0
- Number of illegal migrant workers detected for whom the employer had a statutory excuse – 0
- Number of illegal migrant workers detected on whom the employer had conducted partial checks – 0
- Number of illegal migrant workers detected on whom the employer conducted no checks – 6
- Did the company approach the Border and Immigration Agency Employer Helpline? – No
- Did the company co-operate with the operation? – Yes

The potential maximum penalty was therefore reduced from £45,000 (6 x £7,500) to a £30,000 penalty (6 x £5,000).

CASE D

The same employer as case C contacts the Border and Immigration Agency six months later to report suspicions about some members of staff. The employer co-operates with the subsequent operation, which results in the detection of three illegal migrant workers. The employer provides evidence of checks for these workers, having improved their processes, but the checks had only been partial.

CASE D RESULT: £15,000 maximum penalty

- Number of previous visits – 1
- Number of illegal migrant workers detected for whom the employer had a statutory excuse – 0
- Number of illegal migrant workers detected on whom the employer had conducted partial checks – 3

- Number of illegal migrant workers detected on whom the employer conducted no checks – 0
- Did the company approach the Border and Immigration Agency Employer Helpline? – Yes
- Did the company co-operate with the operation? – Yes

The potential maximum penalty was therefore reduced from £22,500 (3 x £7,500) to a £15,000 penalty (3 x £5,000).

CASE E

The same employer as in cases C and D is visited again six months later. The employer did not approach the Border and Immigration Agency this time, but co-operates with the enforcement operation. Two illegal workers are detected and the checks made were only partial.

CASE E RESULT: £17,500 maximum penalty

- Number of previous visits – 2
- Number of illegal migrant workers detected for whom the employer had a statutory excuse – 0
- Number of illegal migrant workers detected on whom the employer had conducted partial checks – 2
- Number of illegal migrant workers detected on whom the employer conducted no checks – 0
- Did the company approach the Border and Immigration Agency Employer Helpline? – No
- Did the company co-operate with the operation? – Yes

The potential maximum penalty was therefore reduced from £20,000 (2 x £10,000) to a £17,500 penalty (2 x £8,750).

CASE F

An employer is visited by the Border and Immigration Agency and co-operates. Two illegal migrant workers are detected whose leave expired over a year ago and began their employment after the Immigration (Restrictions on Employment) Order 2007 came into force. The employer can provide evidence of full checks at the point of recruitment, but has carried out no follow-up checks within the past 12 months. The employer has not been visited previously.

CASE F RESULT: £5,000 maximum penalty

- Number of previous visits – 0
- Number of illegal migrant workers detected for whom the employer had a statutory excuse – 0
- Number of illegal migrant workers detected on whom the employer had conducted partial checks – 2
- Number of illegal migrant workers detected on whom the employer conducted no checks – 0
- Did the company approach the Border and Immigration Agency Employer Helpline? – No
- Did the company co-operate with the operation? – Yes

The potential maximum penalty was therefore reduced from £10,000 (2 x £5,000) to a £5,000 penalty (2 x £2,500).

APPENDIX 4: ADDITIONAL FACTORS TO BE CONSIDERED WHEN DETERMINING THE LEVEL OF A CIVIL PENALTY

[4.113]
Each case will be examined in context, and consideration must be given to the fairness of the financial penalty to be imposed on the employer. Therefore, the following factors may be considered by an official when determining the level of penalty appropriate for each illegal migrant worker detected:

- whether full or partial document checks have been completed by the employer;
- whether any previous penalties or warnings have been issued to the employer within the previous three years, and if there has been any subsequent improvement in their procedures;
- whether the Civil Penalty Code of practice has been adhered to;
- if the employer reported any suspected illegal workers;
- if the employer has not obstructed the Border and Immigration Agency in conducting any operation to apprehend the illegal workers in question;
- whether the migrant worker is living and working in the UK illegally;
- whether the migrant worker is legally resident in the UK, but has been found to be working in breach of their employment restrictions;
- the proportionality of the level of penalty given;
- whether previous civil penalties have been paid in full;
- the ability of the employer to pay; and
- the thoroughness and/or consistency of the employers' existing employment processes.

BORDER & IMMIGRATION AGENCY CODE OF PRACTICE: GUIDANCE FOR EMPLOYERS ON THE AVOIDANCE OF UNLAWFUL DISCRIMINATION IN EMPLOYMENT PRACTICE WHILE SEEKING TO PREVENT ILLEGAL WORKING (FEBRUARY 2008)

PREVENTION OF ILLEGAL WORKING

IMMIGRATION, ASYLUM AND NATIONALITY ACT 2006

[4.114]

NOTES

This Code of Practice was issued under section 23 of the Immigration, Asylum and Nationality Act 2006. For further details see the notes to the preceding Code of Practice at **[4.107]**.

CONTENTS

1. INTRODUCTION

[4.115]

1.1 This Code has been issued by the Border and Immigration Agency and aims to provide employers with guidance on how to avoid a civil penalty for employing an illegal migrant worker, in a way that **does not result in unlawful race discrimination.**[1]

1.2 Failing to carry out identity checks on potential employees is not a criminal offence, but those employers who only carry out checks on workers who they believe are not British citizens, for example, on the basis of race or ethnicity, could find that this is used against them as evidence in any proceedings brought under the Race Relations Act 1976. This is why we recommend that employers obtain a statutory excuse for all potential employees; this not only protects the employer from liability for a civil penalty, but also demonstrates consistent, transparent and non-discriminatory recruitment practices.

1.3 Legal migrant workers make a substantial contribution to this country's economy. However, those who use illegal migrant workers are often guilty of breaking other laws relating to health and safety, exploitation and tax evasion. The United Kingdom, like many other countries around the world, has laws to deal with illegal migrant working.

1.4 It is important to remember that the population of the UK is ethnically diverse. Many people from ethnic minorities in this country are British citizens and many non-British citizens from black and minority ethnic communities are entitled to work here. Therefore, it must not be assumed that someone from an ethnic minority is an immigrant, or that someone born abroad is not entitled to work in the UK.

NOTES

1 This Code draws on the previous Code, entitled 'Immigration and Asylum Act 1999 – Section 22 Code of Practice: For all employers on the avoidance of race discrimination in recruitment practice while seeking to prevent illegal working'. This document was issued by the Home Office in June 2001. This Code also draws on the 'Statutory Code of Practice on Racial Equality in Employment', which was published by the CRE in April 2006. Further information and details are contained in Appendix 2.

2. PURPOSE AND STATUS OF THIS CODE

[4.116]

2.1 The purpose of this Code is to give you practical guidance on how to avoid unlawful racial discrimination whilst also complying with the law to prevent illegal migrant working.

2.2 This is a statutory Code. This means that it has been approved by the Secretary of State and laid before Parliament. The Code does not impose any legal obligations on employers, nor is it an authoritative statement of the law; only the courts and Employment Tribunals can provide that. However, the Code can be used as evidence in legal proceedings. Courts and Employment Tribunals must take account of any part of the Code that might be relevant on matters of racial discrimination in employment practices.

2.3 This Code, which is issued under section 23 of the Immigration, Asylum and Nationality Act 2006 ('the 2006 Act'), is intended to strengthen the safeguards against unlawful discrimination by re-emphasising your statutory duty to avoid discrimination in your employment practices.

2.4 The Equality and Human Rights Commission (EHRC), also known as the Commission for Equality and Human Rights,[2] the Equality Commission for Northern Ireland and the members of the Illegal Working Group (IWG),[3] which is comprised of representatives from a range of business sectors, government departments and voluntary organisations, have been consulted on the contents of this Code, as required by section 23 of the 2006 Act. Their comments and recommendations have been incorporated, where appropriate.

2.5 This Code applies to all employers in England, Scotland, Wales and Northern Ireland. It also applies to certain organisations, such as employment businesses, employment and recruitment agencies (including on-line agencies). An employment agency or business practising unlawful discrimination will be liable, even if it is acting on the instructions of an employer.

2.6 Whilst some smaller organisations may wish to adapt the guidance to suit their particular circumstances, it should be noted that no allowances can be made for smaller companies when considering their liability under the law. We recommend that smaller organisations ensure that their employment practices do not discriminate on grounds of race and that they follow the advice given in this Code.

2.7 Public authorities are also subject to the requirements of this Code. They also have a general statutory duty to promote equality of opportunity and good race relations, which includes a requirement to monitor specified employment procedures and practices.

2.8 This Code outlines your legal obligations under the Race Relations Act 1976 ("the 1976 Act"),[4] Race Relations (Northern Ireland) Order 1997, the 2006 Act and the Immigration (Restrictions on Employment) Order 2007. However, it is not intended to be a comprehensive statement of the law.

2.9 This Code has been produced alongside other guidance documents and sources of information, details of which are provided in Appendix 2. You may wish to refer to this Code alongside that guidance and information.

NOTES

2 Formerly known as the Commission for Racial Equality (CRE).

3 Formerly known as the Illegal Working Steering Group and the Illegal Working Stakeholder Group.

4 Any reference in this Code to the Race Relations Act includes all subsequent amending legislation.

3. YOUR RESPONSIBILITY AS AN EMPLOYER UNDER THE LAW: THE RACE RELATIONS ACT 1976 AND RACE RELATIONS (NORTHERN IRELAND) ORDER 1997

[4.117]

3.1 Under section 4 of the 1976 Act, and section 6 of the 1997 Order, **it is unlawful** to discriminate in employment practices on racial grounds. That means that an employer cannot discriminate against a potential or existing employee on the following grounds:

- race;
- colour;
- nationality (including citizenship);
- ethnic origin;
- national origin.

Race discrimination may be either **direct** or **indirect**.

3.2 **Direct discrimination** means treating a person less favourably on racial grounds, for example by rejecting all job applicants who do not have British nationality, or by refusing to consider any non-European job applicants. Treatment based on racial or national stereotypes can also constitute direct discrimination. Examples include:

- where the assumption is made that people from certain nationalities or ethnic groups cannot work as a team;
- where individuals are only recruited from one nationality or ethnic group;
- where all refugees are automatically rejected;
- where an employee with limited leave to remain in the UK is given a more degrading form of work to do in comparison with workers with unlimited leave;
- where it is assumed that overseas qualifications and experience are inferior to those gained in the UK.[5]

3.3 Indirect discrimination means imposing a condition or requirement which applies equally to everyone, but is harder for people from particular racial groups to satisfy and which cannot be justified. For example, it would be discriminatory to ask for a very high standard of English when the job does not require this, or to reject an applicant who has an unfamiliar accent.

3.4 It is unlawful to victimise or harass a person because he or she has made or supported a complaint of racial discrimination. **It is also unlawful** to instruct or induce another person to discriminate, or to publish an advertisement or notice that indicates an intention to discriminate.

3.5 Employers must not discriminate on racial grounds or subject a person to harassment in:
(a) the arrangements they make to decide who should be offered employment; or
(b) the terms on which they offer to employ a person; or
(c) by refusing or deliberately failing to offer employment.

3.6 It is also unlawful for employers to discriminate on racial grounds against a worker, or to subject him or her to harassment:
(a) in the terms of employment provided; or
(b) in the way they make opportunities for training, promotion, transfer, facilities, services or other benefits available; or
(c) by refusing access to such opportunities, benefits, facilities or services; or
(d) by dismissing the worker, or subjecting him to some other detriment.

3.7 Under the 1976 Act and the 1997 Order, discrimination committed by an **employee** in the course of his or her employment, is treated as having been committed by the **employer** as well as by the individual employee, **whether or not the employer knew or approved the acts of discrimination**. You can avoid this liability if you can prove that you took sufficient and reasonable steps to prevent such discrimination, for example, by applying consistent checks to all potential employees. A complaint to an Employment Tribunal may be made against both the employer and the individual employee who is alleged to have discriminated.

3.8 Separate legislation similarly outlaws discrimination on grounds of religious affiliation, gender, sexual orientation, disability and age[6] in employment practices. Although this Code only addresses racial discrimination, you should be mindful of other forms of discrimination, particularly religious discrimination, when applying the provisions of the 2006 Act. If people affected by religious discrimination are from a particular racial group, the discrimination might also amount to indirect racial discrimination.

NOTES

5 If you are unsure about the UK equivalent of an overseas qualification, you could consult the National Recognition Information Centre (NARIC) website at: www.naric.org.uk, which provides useful information.

6 Regulations on age discrimination came into force on 1 October 2006. See the Equality Act 2006 for further details.

4. RIGHT OF COMPLAINT

[4.118]
4.1 Anyone who believes that he or she has been discriminated against, either directly or indirectly, by an employer, a prospective employer, or an employment agency, may bring a complaint before an Employment Tribunal, or an Industrial Tribunal in Northern Ireland. If the complaint is upheld, the Tribunal will normally order the employer to pay compensation, for which there is no upper limit.

4.2 The EHRC and the Northern Ireland Equality Commission can also bring proceedings against an employer who publishes a discriminatory advertisement, or who instructs or induces another person to discriminate.

4.3 Where an employer has been found to have committed an act of unlawful racial discrimination, the Public Procurement Regulations 2006 provide that public authorities may disqualify the organisation from entering into public procurement contracts.

5. YOUR RESPONSIBILITY AS AN EMPLOYER UNDER THE LAW: SECTION 15 AND SECTION 21 OF THE IMMIGRATION, ASYLUM AND NATIONALITY ACT 2006 EXPLAINED

[4.119]
5.1 The 2006 Act has strengthened the law on the prevention of illegal migrant working by replacing the previous controls under section 8 of the Asylum and Immigration Act 1996 ('the 1996 Act'). There is now a system of civil penalties for employers who employ an illegal migrant worker (section 15) without having obtained a statutory excuse, and a separate criminal offence of knowingly employing an illegal migrant worker (section 21).

The 2006 Act sets out the changes to the law on the prevention of illegal migrant working. You will be committing an offence if you are found to be employing a person aged 16 or over who is subject to immigration control[7] unless:

- that person has current and valid permission to be in the United Kingdom, **and**
- the person has valid permission to do the type of work offered.

Under section 15, you may be liable for a civil penalty in respect of each illegal migrant worker employed.[8]

5.2 Section 15 can also provide you with a statutory excuse against liability for a civil penalty. This can be done by checking and copying one of the original documents, or a specified combination of original documents from **List A** or **Lists B** (provided in Appendix 1), **before** employing that person. Those people who have restrictions on their time in the UK may be subject to repeat checks. If you can show that you complied with the requirements, you may be excused from liability for the penalty, even if it turns out that the person being employed is subject to immigration control and is working without the necessary permission.

5.3 However, the excuse is not available if you knew, at any time during the period of employment, that the employment was not allowed. **If you know that you are employing a person without the required permission to work, you could be served with a civil penalty or prosecuted under section 21 for the offence of knowingly employing an illegal migrant worker, for which there is a maximum prison sentence of two years and an unlimited fine.**

5.4 Section 21 deals with cases involving the intentional use of illegal workers, which are often linked to exploitation, or other forms of illegal activity. The offence is committed by a person where he or she employed an individual knowing that they did not have current leave to enter or remain, or that their conditions of stay prevented them from undertaking the employment offered.

5.5 There is a difference between the entitlement of asylum seekers and refugees to work in the United Kingdom. The term asylum seeker is used to describe those who have made a claim for asylum under the Refugee Convention or under Article 3 of the European Convention on Human Rights.

5.6 For the purposes of sections 15 and 21, a person who has been granted temporary admission to the United Kingdom, or temporary release from immigration detention, such as an asylum seeker, may only be employed if the Home Office or the Border and Immigration Agency has lifted restrictions on their taking employment.[9]

5.7 In the case of the minority of asylum seekers who enjoy permission to work, this will be clearly indicated on their Application Registration Card (ARC). As part of the checks required to obtain or retain a statutory excuse under section 15, you should contact the Employer Checking Service to verify whether the employee continues to be entitled to work in the United Kingdom.[10] You must inform your employee that you are undertaking this check before doing so.

5.8 Since 1 May 2004, neither the Standard Acknowledgement Letter (SAL), nor the form entitled IS96(W) have been acceptable as evidence that an asylum seeker has permission to work in the UK. If a potential, or current employee, presents one of these documents to you, please refer them to the Border and Immigration Agency on **0151 237 6375** for further advice on how they can obtain an appropriate ARC.

5.9 Those who have been granted refugee status, or have been allowed to remain exceptionally on humanitarian grounds, will have no restriction on the type of work that they can do, whilst their leave remains valid.

NOTES

7 A person subject to immigration control is a person who, under the Immigration Act 1971, requires leave to enter or remain in the UK.

8 Further information on the civil penalty scheme is available in the *'Prevention of illegal working. Immigration, Asylum and Nationality Act 2006: Civil Penalties for Employers Code of Practice* – Border and Immigration Agency, 2008.' See Appendix 2.

9 An asylum applicant may apply to the Secretary of State for permission to take up employment (which shall not include permission to become self-employed, or to engage in a business or professional activity) only in exceptional circumstances, for example, if a decision has not been taken on the applicant's asylum application within one year of the date on which it was recorded. The Secretary of State shall only consider such an application if, in his opinion, any delay in reaching a decision at first instance cannot be attributed to the applicant.

10 The Border and Immigration Agency will issue separate guidance to employers detailing the procedure to be followed.

6. MAKING THE DOCUMENT CHECKS

[4.120]

6.1 In order to establish the statutory excuse against liability for a civil penalty, you must check the original document(s) presented from **List A**, or **Lists B** (see Appendix 1) before the person starts their employment and make a paper copy, or electronic record of the document(s) and store it securely. In certain circumstances, you may retain the document(s).[11] Further details are provided in the Immigration (Restrictions on Employment) Order 2007.

6.2 You should undertake basic visual checks to ensure that the document or documents, relate to the applicant by comparing any photographs in the document or documents, and dates of birth against the appearance and apparent age of the applicant. You should check for any obvious discrepancy in age. You should also check that any United Kingdom Government endorsements (stamps, vignettes etc.) entitle the potential employee to do the type of work offered and that any expiry date has not passed.

6.3 Where a job applicant has produced an original document or documents from **List A**, you have checked and copied the relevant parts of the document or documents, and you are satisfied that the person is entitled to take the job offered, you will have established an excuse in relation to your employment of that person and will not need to carry out any subsequent document checks. This is because the documents from **List A** show that there are no time restrictions on the individual's ability to take up employment in the UK.

6.4 Where an employee produces an original document or documents from **Lists B**, you must note the date on which you carry out the original document check. In order to retain your excuse against a penalty for employing that individual, you must carry out a follow-up check at least once every **12 months** after the initial check. Again, this will involve asking the employee to produce an original document or documents either from **List A**, or **Lists B**. This is because the documents from **Lists B** show that there are restrictions on the length of time the individual can stay in the UK and you will need to ensure that your employee has retained their entitlement to work.

6.5 The same visual checks should be carried out to ensure that each document is not false and that it relates to the holder. You should take another copy of the document, recording the date on which the check was made. These follow-up checks must be repeated:

- no later than **12 months** after the previous check, **or**
- until the employee produces a document on **List A**, **or**
- until the employee leaves your employment.

6.6 There may be occasions when an employee is unable to produce a document from **List A** or **Lists B** when requested to as part of a follow-up check, and claims that this is due to having an outstanding application for leave to remain with the Border and Immigration Agency. If this happens you can use the Employer Checking Service to verify whether the employee continues to enjoy the right to work in the United Kingdom. It is the employers' responsibility to inform the employee, or potential employee, that they may be making the checks.

6.7 The checks you need to make to claim the statutory excuse are in most cases straightforward and can be built into your normal employment procedures. **These document checks are not compulsory, but they are advisable as part of good employment practice. If you do not make these checks at the point of recruitment, you will not have the benefit of the statutory excuse if you are later found to be employing illegal migrant workers.**

When you make pre-recruitment checks, you should ensure that they are made in a non-discriminatory manner by applying them to all applicants and at the same point of the recruitment process.

6.8 We don't expect employers to act as Immigration Officers. Responsibility for immigration control lies firmly with the Border and Immigration Agency. If you are worried that a document you have been shown does not relate to the holder, you do not have to employ that person. The Employer Checking Service is available to employers who may wish to clarify an individual's right to work.

6.9 Further details on obtaining a statutory excuse are available in guidance produced by the Home Office and the Border and Immigration Agency. Details are contained in Appendix 2.

NOTES

[11] It is not appropriate to retain a person's original documents indefinitely. The only exception to this is when an individual provides a P45 as part of a combination of documents. In these circumstances, the employer may retain part 2 of the P45 for their records, otherwise, an employer may only obtain a person's documents for the purpose of copying them. The employer must also have facilities for keeping the documents and copies of documents safe. A job applicant's original documents must not be kept for longer than a day. If an employer deliberately appropriates a person's passport or other original documents belonging to them, or retains these without their consent, then they may be guilty of an offence under the Theft Act 1968, or under section 25(5) of the Identity Cards Act 2006.

7. HOW TO AVOID RACIAL DISCRIMINATION

[4.121]

7.1 As a matter of good employment practice, you should have clear written procedures for the recruitment and selection of all staff, based on equal and fair treatment for all applicants. Copies of these procedures should be made available to all relevant staff.

7.2 All job selections should be on the basis of suitability for the post. You should ensure that no prospective job applicants are discouraged or excluded, either directly or indirectly, because of their personal appearance or accent. You should not make assumptions about a person's right to work or immigration status on the basis of their colour, race, nationality, or ethnic or national origins, or the length of time they have been resident in the UK.

7.3 The best way to ensure that you do not discriminate is to treat all applicants in the same way at each stage of the recruitment process. For example, if you provide information to prospective applicants, or if you supply an application form, you could also include a reminder that the successful applicant, or short-listed applicants, will be required to produce an original document or documents included in **List A** or **Lists B**.

7.4 You may ask applicants to provide the specified document(s) to obtain a statutory excuse at any stage **before** they start work. Depending on your recruitment processes, you may find it most convenient to request documents from all those called to a first interview, or just from those called to a second interview, or only from persons short-listed to fill the vacancy. Original documents should be checked before employment commences. If you ask for documents from one applicant, you should make sure you ask for documents from all applicants being considered at that stage.

7.5 Job applicants should not be treated less favourably if they produce a document or documents from **Lists B** rather than **List A**. A person producing document(s) from **Lists B** will have a time limit on their legal ability to stay and work in the UK, but it is possible for certain categories of entrant to obtain an extension to their entitlement to remain and work in this country.

7.6 Once a person who has limited leave to remain has established their initial and ongoing entitlement to work, they should not be treated less favourably during their employment, including the terms of employment provided, opportunities for training, promotion or transfer, benefits, facilities or services, or by dismissing the worker or subjecting them to some other detriment, other than the repeat checks.

7.7 You should only ask questions about an applicant's or employee's immigration status, where necessary, to determine whether their status imposes limitations on the number of hours they are entitled to work each week, or on the length of time they are permitted to work within their overall period or type of leave given. For example, those granted leave as students undertaking full-time undergraduate study in the UK should not work for more than 20 hours per week during term time, except where the placement is a necessary part of their studies and is undertaken with the educational institution's express agreement.

7.8 If a person is not able to produce the appropriate listed document(s), you should not assume that he or she is living or working in the UK illegally. You should instead refer the person to the Border and Immigration Agency through the Immigration Enquiry Bureau on **0870 606 7766**, or a Citizens Advice Bureau for advice. You should try to keep the job open for as long as possible, but you are not obliged to do so if you need to recruit someone urgently. **It is ultimately the decision of the employer whether or not to employ an individual**.

8. MONITORING APPLICATIONS

[4.122]
8.1 As a matter of good practice, you should monitor the ethnicity of applications during the recruitment and selection process of job applicants. This will help you to know whether you are reaching a wide range of potential job applicants. This can then be used in reviewing recruitment procedures. It is also good practice to take measures to encourage an integrated and diverse workforce and provide English language teaching for those who need it.

(Appendix 1 (Documents required for the purpose of establishing the statutory excuse) is identical to the Appendix 1 in the Code of Practice on Civil Penalties for Employers (see that Appendix at **[4.110]***). Appendix 2 (Other sources of information) omitted for reasons of space.)*

C. EQUALITY & HUMAN RIGHTS COMMISSION

DISABILITY DISCRIMINATION ACT 1995 REVISED CODE OF PRACTICE: TRADE ORGANISATIONS, QUALIFICATIONS BODIES AND GENERAL QUALIFICATIONS BODIES (2008)

Equality and Human Rights Commission

[4.123]

NOTES

This Code was issued by the Equality and Human Rights Commission on 16 May 2008. The Code was approved by the Secretary of State and by Parliament in accordance with the Equality Act 2006, s 14 and came into effect on 23 June 2008 (see the Disability Discrimination Code of Practice (Trade Organisations, Qualifications Bodies and General Qualifications Bodies) (Commencement) Order 2008, SI 2008/1335). For the legal status of the Code see s 15(4) of the 2006 Act at **[1.1364]**.

It replaces the Disability Rights Commission Code of Practice: Trade Organisations and Qualifications Bodies 2004 which was revoked, as from 23 June 2008, by the Disability Discrimination Code of Practice (Trade Organisations and Qualifications Bodies) (Revocation) Order 2008, SI 2008/1336, subject to transitional provisions in relation to proceedings under Part 2 of the Disability Discrimination Act 1995 to the extent they relate to events taking place before 23 June 2008 and had not been determined by that date.

Note that the Disability Discrimination Act 1995 was repealed by the Equality Act 2010, s 211(2), Sch 27, Pt 1, as from 1 October 2010. Note, however, that this Code has not been replaced or updated since the repeal of the 1995 Act.

See *Harvey* L.

CONTENTS

1. INTRODUCTION

PURPOSE OF PART 2 AND CHAPTER 2A OF PART 4 OF THE ACT

[4.124]

1.1 The Disability Discrimination Act 1995 (the Act) brought in measures to prevent discrimination against disabled people. Part 2 of the Act is based on the principle that disabled people should not be discriminated against in employment or when seeking employment. Part 4 of the Act (as amended by the Special Education Needs and Disability Act 2002 and the Disability Discrimination Act 2005 and regulations made under both Acts) is based on similar principles that disabled people should not be discriminated against in accessing education opportunities or discriminated against during the course of their education in schools, colleges and universities. A person's prospects of gaining employment, or of progressing in or retaining employment, may be affected by his ability to become a member of a trade organisation or to take advantage of its membership services. A person's employment prospects may also be affected by his ability to obtain a general, professional or trade qualification.

1.2 It is for this reason that, in addition to imposing duties on employers which are intended to prevent discrimination against disabled people, Part 2 sets out a number of duties with which trade organisations and bodies which confer professional or trade qualifications must comply for the same purpose, and new provisions under Chapter 2A of Part 4 of the Act set out similar duties in respect of general qualifications bodies. The extension of Part 2 to cover qualifications bodies as from October 2004, and the extension of Part 4 to cover general qualification bodies as from September 2007, represents a change in the law.

PURPOSE OF THE CODE

1.3 This Code of Practice (the Code) gives practical guidance on how to prevent discrimination against disabled people by trade organisations, qualifications bodies and general qualifications bodies. It describes the duties on such organisations and bodies in this regard. The Code helps disabled people to understand the law and what they can do if they feel that they have been discriminated against. By encouraging good practice, the Code assists trade organisations, qualifications bodies and general qualifications bodies to avoid complaints being made against them and to work towards the elimination of discrimination against disabled people.

1.4 The Code also gives guidance on the law which is intended to help lawyers when advising their clients, and to assist courts and tribunals when interpreting new legal concepts. The Code explains the operation and effect of technical statutory provisions – some of which only came into force on October 2004 (for qualifications bodies) and September 2007 (for general qualifications bodies), and many of which have a complex legal effect. Because of this, the Code is necessarily comprehensive and detailed.

1.5 [s 14 Equality Act 2006] The Commission for Equality and Human Rights has prepared and issued this revised Code under the Equality Act 2006 on the basis of a request by the Lord Privy Seal. It applies to England, Wales and Scotland. A similar but separate Code applies to Northern Ireland.

1.6 As employers themselves, trade organisations, qualifications bodies and general qualifications bodies have duties under Part 2 in respect of disabled people whom they employ, or who apply to them for employment. However, these matters are not considered in the Code – which is concerned only with the duties of trade organisations, qualifications bodies and general qualifications bodies acting in their capacity as such. Guidance on the application of the Act to employers is given in a separate code of practice issued by the Disability Rights Commission (DRC) (see Appendix B for details). It is possible that a number of individuals, organisations and bodies may be involved at different stages in matters concerning the legal duties described within this Code, particularly in respect of general qualifications bodies, and the Code attempts to explain each party's responsibilities under these duties.

STATUS OF THE CODE

1.7 [s 15(4) Equality Act 2006] The Code does not impose legal obligations. Nor is it an authoritative statement of the law – that is a matter for the courts and tribunals. However, the Code can be used in evidence in legal proceedings under the Act. Courts and employment tribunals must take into account any part of the Code that appears to them relevant to any question arising in those proceedings. If trade organisations, qualifications bodies and general qualifications bodies follow the guidance in the Code, it may help to avoid an adverse decision by a court or tribunal in such proceedings.

HOW TO USE THE CODE

1.8 This chapter gives an introduction to the Code. Chapter 2 sets out some general guidance on how to avoid discrimination. Chapter 3 contains an overview of the relevant provisions of the Act, and those provisions are examined in more detail in subsequent chapters.

1.9 Chapter 4 details what is meant by discrimination and harassment, and Chapter 5 explains the duty to make reasonable adjustments for disabled people. Chapter 6 examines the relevance of justification under Part 2 and Chapter 2A of Part 4. Chapters 7, 8 and 9 focus on particular issues relating to discrimination by trade organisations, qualifications bodies and general qualifications bodies respectively. Chapters 8 and 9 provide further information about competence standards.

1.10 Chapter 10 looks at issues concerning adjustments to premises, and Chapter 11 deals with various other points and explains what happens if discrimination is alleged.

1.11 Appendix A gives more information on what is meant by 'disability' and by 'disabled person'. Separate statutory guidance relating to the definition of disability has been issued under the Act (see paragraph 3.6). Appendix B lists other sources of relevant information about matters referred to in the Code.

1.12 Each chapter of the Code should be viewed as part of an overall explanation of the relevant provisions of the Act and the regulations made under them. In order to understand the law properly it is necessary to read the Code as a whole. The Code should not be read too narrowly or literally. It is intended to explain the principles of the law, to illustrate how the Act might operate in certain situations and to provide general guidance on good practice. There are some questions which the Code cannot resolve and which must await the authoritative interpretation of the courts and tribunals. The Code is not intended to be a substitute for taking appropriate advice on the legal consequences of particular situations.

EXAMPLES IN THE CODE

1.13 Examples of good practice and how the Act is likely to work are given in boxes. They are intended simply to illustrate the principles and concepts used in the legislation and should be read in that light. The examples should not be treated as complete or authoritative statements of the law.

1.14 While the examples refer to particular situations, they should be understood more widely as demonstrating how the law is likely to be applied generally. They can often be used to test how the law might apply in similar circumstances involving different disabilities or situations. The examples attempt to use as many different varieties of disabilities and situations as possible to demonstrate the breadth and scope of the Act. Examples relating to men or women are given for realism and could, of course, apply to people of either gender.

REFERENCES IN THE CODE

1.15 References to the Act are shown in the margins. For example, s 1(1) means section 1(1) of the Act and Sch means Schedule to the Act. References to Part 2, 3 or 4 refer to the relevant Part of the Act. Where reference is made to regulations, the appropriate Statutory Instrument (SI) number is shown in the margin.

CHANGES TO THE LEGISLATION

1.16 The Code refers to the Disability Discrimination Act as of 1 October 2004 and as amended to September 2007. There may be changes to the Act or to other legislation, for example to the range of people who are considered to be disabled under the Act, which may have an effect on the duties explained in the Code. You will need to ensure that you keep up to date with any developments that affect the Act's provisions.

FURTHER INFORMATION

1.17 Copies of the Act and regulations made under it can be purchased from The Stationery Office (see Appendix B for contact details). Separate codes covering other aspects of the Act, and guidance relating to the definition of disability are also available from The Stationery Office.

2. HOW CAN DISCRIMINATION BE AVOIDED?

INTRODUCTION

[4.125]

2.1 There are various actions which trade organisations, qualifications bodies and general qualifications bodies can take in order to avoid discriminating against disabled people. By doing so, organisations and bodies are not only likely to minimise the incidence of expensive and time-consuming litigation, but will also improve their general performance and the quality of the services they provide.

2.2 In addition, these actions will assist organisations and bodies who are public authorities (including any organisation certain of whose functions are functions of a public nature) to comply with the disability equality duty. The duty requires all such public authorities when carrying out their functions to have due regard to the need to:

- promote equality of opportunity between disabled persons and other persons;
- eliminate discrimination that is unlawful under the Act;
- eliminate harassment of disabled persons that is related to their disabilities;
- promote positive attitudes towards disabled persons;
- encourage participation by disabled persons in public life; and
- take steps to take account of disabled persons' disabilities, even where that involves treating disabled persons more favourably than other persons.

2.3 To assist certain public authorities (including statutory regulators responsible for professional, trade and general qualifications in complying with the above duty – known as the general duty), regulations lay down certain steps which these authorities must take. These are known as the 'specific duties'. They include the obligation to produce a Disability Equality Scheme which, amongst other things, requires public authorities to set out the steps which they will take (the action plan) to comply with the general duty. The general and specific duties do not create any individual rights for disabled people, but the Equality and Human Rights Commission can enforce both the general and the specific duties, and a failure to comply with the general duties may result in actions in the High Court (in England and Wales) or the Court of Session (in Scotland) by way of judicial review proceedings.

2.4 This chapter sets out some guidance on ways to help ensure that disabled people are not discriminated against. It also addresses only some of the aspects of the disability equality duty. Organisations and bodies should refer to the **Statutory Codes of Practice: The Duty to Promote Disability Equality** (England and Wales) and (Scotland) for full details of the obligations which they must comply with in relation to the duty.

UNDERSTANDING THE SOCIAL DIMENSION OF DISABILITY

2.5 The concept of discrimination in the Act reflects an understanding that functional limitations arising from disabled people's impairments do not inevitably restrict their ability to participate fully in society. Rather than the limitations of an impairment it is often environmental factors (such as the structure of a building, or an organisation's practices) which unnecessarily lead to these social restrictions. This principle underpins the duty to make reasonable adjustments described in

Chapter 5. Understanding this will assist trade organisations, qualifications bodies and general qualifications bodies to avoid discrimination. It is as important to consider which aspects of an organisation or body's activities create difficulties for a disabled person as it is to understand the particular nature of an individual's disability.

RECOGNISING THE DIVERSE NATURE OF DISABILITY

2.6 There are more than eight million disabled adults in our society. The nature and extent of their disabilities vary widely, as do their requirements for overcoming any difficulties they may face. If trade organisations, qualifications bodies and general qualifications bodies are to avoid discriminating, they need to understand this, and to be aware of the effects their decisions and actions – and those of their agents and employees – may have on disabled people. The evidence shows that many of the steps that can be taken to avoid discrimination cost little or nothing and are easy to implement.

AVOIDING MAKING ASSUMPTIONS

2.7 It is advisable to avoid making assumptions about disabled people. Impairments will often affect different people in different ways and their needs may be different as well. The following suggestions may help to avoid discrimination:

- Do not assume that because a person does not look disabled, he is not disabled.
- Do not assume that most disabled people use wheelchairs.
- Do not assume that all blind people read Braille or have guide dogs.
- Do not assume that all deaf people use sign language.
- Do not assume that disabled people have lesser abilities and career aspirations than non-disabled people.
- Do not assume that people with certain types of disability (such as mental health problems or epilepsy) present a health and safety risk.
- Do not assume that because you are unaware of any disabled members of an organisation there are none.
- Do not assume that because you are unaware of any disabled people who are engaged in a particular profession or trade there are none.

FINDING OUT ABOUT DISABLED PEOPLE'S NEEDS

2.8 As explained later in the Code (see paragraphs 5.14 and 8.22 for example), the Act requires trade organisations, qualifications bodies and general qualification bodies to think about ways of complying with their legal duties. Listening carefully to disabled people and finding out what they want will help organisations and bodies to meet their obligations by identifying the best way of meeting disabled people's needs. There is a better chance of reaching the best outcome if discussions are held with disabled people at an early stage.

2.9 Often, discussing with disabled people what is required to meet their needs will reassure a trade organisation, qualifications body or general qualifications body that suitable adjustments can be carried out cheaply and with very little inconvenience.

2.10 There are various ways in which the views of disabled people can be obtained. Many trade unions and professional bodies and general qualifications bodies may have established formal structures for seeking and representing the views of disabled people. These may take the form of an advisory committee, perhaps a sub-committee of the equal opportunities committee or national governing body. Some organisations have a standing national forum for disabled members as well as arranging periodic conferences. In addition, the specific duties regulations require prescribed public authorities to involve disabled people in the development of the Disability Equality Scheme.

SEEKING EXPERT ADVICE

2.11 It may be possible to avoid discrimination by using personal or in-house knowledge and expertise – particularly if information or views are obtained from the disabled person concerned. However, although the Act does not specifically require anyone to obtain expert advice about meeting the needs of disabled people, in practice it may sometimes be necessary to do so in order to comply with the principal duties set out in the Act. Expert advice might be especially useful if a person is newly disabled or if the effects of a person's disability become more marked. Local and national disability organisations in particular may be able to give useful advice about the needs of disabled people and steps that can be taken to meet those needs.

PLANNING AHEAD

2.12 The duties which the Act places on trade organisations, qualifications bodies and general qualifications bodies are owed to the individual disabled people with whom those organisations and bodies have dealings. There is no duty owed to disabled people in general. Nevertheless, it is likely to be cost effective for trade organisations and qualifications bodies to plan ahead. Considering the needs of a range of disabled people when planning for change (such as when planning a building refurbishment, a new IT system, or the design of a website) is likely to make it easier to implement adjustments for individuals when the need arises. In addition, the disability equality duty requires organisations and bodies that are public authorities to have due regard to the need to promote equality of opportunity – including the need to eliminate discrimination. This requirement may require public authorities to adopt a proactive approach, anticipating the needs of disabled people.

2.13 It is good practice for trade organisations, qualifications bodies and general qualifications bodies to check whether access audits have been carried out to identify any improvements which can be made to a building to make it more accessible. Access audits should be carried out by suitably qualified people, such as those listed in the National Register of Access Consultants (see Appendix B for details). Websites and intranet sites can also be reviewed to see how accessible they are to disabled people using access software.

A trade organisation is re-fitting its premises including its facilities for members. The architects are asked to comply with British Standard 8300 to ensure that facilities such as the entrance, reception, meeting rooms, lecture theatre and toilets are accessible to a wide range of disabled visitors. BS8300 is a code of practice on the design of buildings and their approaches to meet the needs of disabled people (see Appendix B for details).

A qualifications body is re-designing its website. In doing so it ensures that the new website is easy to read for people with a variety of access software; has the website checked for accessibility; and invites disabled readers of the website to let the qualifications body know if they find any part of it inaccessible.

As part of the approval process for centres to deliver examinations and assessments for general qualifications, a general qualifications body asks a prospective centre to give details of the accessibility of its premises. Where there are concerns with the accessibility of the premises, the prospective centre is advised of the need to identify and make any improvements. The general qualifications body provides a leaflet with further information for centres on where to get advice and assistance in relation to access audits.

IMPLEMENTING ANTI-DISCRIMINATORY POLICIES AND PRACTICES

2.14 Trade organisations, qualifications bodies and general qualifications bodies are more likely to comply with their duties under the Act, and to avoid the risk of legal action being taken against them, if they implement anti-discriminatory policies and practices. These are often referred to as equality policies or diversity policies. Additionally, in the event that legal action is taken, trade organisations, qualifications bodies and general qualifications bodies may be asked to demonstrate to an employment tribunal or county/sheriff court that they have effective policies and procedures in place to minimise the risk of discrimination.

As part of the approval process for centres to deliver general qualifications, a general qualifications body advises centres that learners with disabilities should be accommodated in examination rooms that are appropriate to their needs. For example, a candidate with learning difficulties, who relies on the use of a prompter, is best accommodated in a room with few distractions, away from other candidates.

An inspector working on behalf of the general qualifications bodies visits a centre to ensure that the examinations are being carried out in accordance with relevant requirements. His checklist includes a check that any candidate with a disability has access to suitable accommodation. He reports to the general qualifications bodies any circumstances where unsuitable accommodation has been provided and they take up this issue with the centre.

RECOMMENDED STEPS FOR ALL TRADE ORGANISATIONS, QUALIFICATIONS BODIES AND GENERAL QUALIFICATIONS BODIES

2.15 Anti-discriminatory policies and practices will vary depending on the nature of the organisation (for example, on whether it is a trade organisation, qualifications body or general qualifications body and on the size and nature of its membership). However, it is advisable for all trade organisations, qualifications bodies and general qualifications bodies to take the following steps:

- Establish a policy which aims to prevent discrimination against disabled people and which is communicated to all employees and agents of the organisation or body.
- Provide disability awareness and equality training to all employees. In addition, train employees and agents so that they understand the organisation or body's policy on disability, their obligations under the Act and the practice of reasonable adjustments.
- Ensure that members and potential members of the organisation (or, in the case of a qualifications body and general qualifications body, people who wish to have a qualification conferred on them and people who already hold a qualification) are informed about the organisation or body's disability policy.
- Ensure that people within the organisation or body who have responsibility for liaising with members or applicants have more in-depth training about the organisation's duties under the Act.
- Inform all employees and agents that conduct which breaches the anti-discrimination policy will not be tolerated, and respond quickly and effectively to any such breaches.
- Monitor the implementation and effectiveness of such a policy.
- Address acts of disability discrimination by employees as part of disciplinary rules and procedures.
- Have complaints and grievance procedures which are easy for disabled people to use and which are designed to resolve issues effectively.
- Regularly review the effectiveness of reasonable adjustments made for disabled people in accordance with the Act, and act on the findings of those reviews.
- Keep clear records of decisions taken in respect of each of these matters.

ADDITIONAL RECOMMENDED STEPS FOR TRADE UNIONS

2.16 Trade unions are a particular kind of trade organisation. In addition to taking the general steps outlined in paragraph 2.15, it is advisable for trade unions to:

- Have (and inform local branches about) a central budget or 'access fund' to pay for adjustments for disabled members in circumstances where it would be too expensive for the adjustments to be funded by local branches.
- Ensure that union representatives understand the Act's provisions on employment and occupation so that they are able to support union members who encounter disability discrimination at work.
- Ensure that health and safety representatives have a proper understanding of the principles of risk assessment and reasonable adjustments, so that health and safety issues are not used to discriminate against disabled people in the workplace or when participating in union activities.

The above considerations apply just as much to unpaid union representatives in the workplace as to salaried employees of a union.

2.17 Trade unions should not enter into collective agreements containing terms which discriminate against disabled people (see paragraphs 11.14 to 11.16). In addition, European law encourages trade unions to enter into collective agreements at national and local level in respect of anti-discriminatory policies and practices. It is advisable for trade unions to monitor the effectiveness of any such agreements.

ADDITIONAL RECOMMENDED STEPS FOR QUALIFICATIONS BODIES

2.18 The general steps outlined in paragraph 2.15 are recommended for trade organisations and qualifications bodies alike. However, there are additional steps which it is advisable for qualifications bodies to take. These are to:

- Ensure that there are effective systems in place for disabled people to request reasonable adjustments for examinations or practical tests, so that qualifications bodies are in a position to respond quickly and effectively to individual requests for specific adjustments. This may involve establishing procedures with educational institutions to ensure that institutions request relevant information from their students and then pass this on to the qualifications bodies (see paragraph 8.23).
- Regularly review any competence standards which relate to particular professional or trade qualifications to ensure that they are framed in a way which does not unnecessarily exclude disabled people from being able to meet them. This will involve carefully scrutinising each competence standard to check that it is not discriminatory. Consideration should be given to whether each standard can be objectively justified. Disabled people who work in the relevant profession or trade could be consulted to learn from their experiences, and factors such as changes in technology, which can enable people to do jobs in different ways, should be taken into account.

Further advice about how to avoid discrimination in relation to competence standards is given at paragraph 8.41.

ADDITIONAL RECOMMENDED STEPS FOR GENERAL QUALIFICATIONS BODIES

2.19 The context within which general qualifications bodies operate is summarised in paragraph 3.30 and set out in more detail in Chapter 9. The general steps outlined in paragraph 2.15 are also recommended for general qualifications bodies. However, there are also additional steps specifically recommended for general qualifications bodies to take. These are to:

- Regularly review with their regulators the requirements for relevant general qualifications to ensure that they are framed in a way which does not unnecessarily exclude disabled people from being able to meet them. This will involve carefully scrutinising each requirement to check that it is not discriminatory. Consideration should be given to whether each requirement is objectively reasonable or, in the case of competence standards, legitimate and proportionate.
- Ensure that there are effective systems in place for disabled people to request reasonable adjustments for examinations or practical tests, so that general qualifications bodies are in a position to respond quickly and effectively to individual requests for specific adjustments. This may well involve establishing procedures for direct contact between disabled people, general qualifications bodies and educational institutions to ensure that all relevant information reaches the general qualifications bodies. In practice, most requests for adjustments may be received through educational institutions.
- Ensure that disabled people have effective recourse to the general qualifications bodies appeal procedures in respect of examinations and assessment results.

Further advice about how to avoid discrimination in relation to competence standards is given at paragraphs 9.57 to 9.82.

AUDITING POLICIES AND PROCEDURES

2.20 Although there is no duty under Part 2 (and Part 4 in respect of general qualifications bodies) to anticipate the needs of disabled people in general, it is a good idea for trade organisations and qualifications bodies to keep all their policies under review, and to consider the needs of such disabled people as part of this process. It is advisable for organisations and bodies to do this in addition to having a specific policy to prevent discrimination. In addition, the disability equality duty requires organisations and bodies that are public authorities to have due regard to the need to promote equality of opportunity – including the need to eliminate discrimination. This requirement may require public authorities to adopt a proactive approach, anticipating the needs of disabled people. Trade organisations and qualifications bodies are likely to have policies about matters such as:

- emergency evacuation procedures
- procurement of equipment, IT systems and websites
- information provision
- service standards for members.

> A trade organisation has a policy to ensure that all members are kept informed about the organisation's activities through a website. The policy states that the website should be accessible to disabled people, including those who use access software (such as speech synthesis).
>
> The website editor is given additional training in accessible website design.

> A trade organisation has a policy outlining the level of service that all members and potential members should receive. It includes standards of service for disabled members and potential members, such as provision of application forms in accessible formats.

A new procurement policy requires a number of factors to be taken into account in procuring equipment and IT systems. These factors include cost and energy efficiency. It is good practice for such factors to include accessibility for disabled people as well.

A trade union reviews its procedures for organising conferences to ensure that access for disabled members is taken into account at all stages.

2.21 Much of what is stated about auditing policies and procedures in paragraph 2.20 also applies to general qualifications bodies, apart from the fact that the relevant provisions of Chapter 2A of Part 4, and not Part 2, apply to general qualifications bodies. General qualifications bodies are particularly likely to have policies about matters such as:

- testing, assessment and examination arrangements
- adjustments to the testing, assessment and examination process
- standards for qualifications
- their relationship with those who are responsible for conducting examinations, testing and assessments (eg schools and colleges).

A general qualifications body is updating its exam timetable. It ensures that the guidance to centres on timetabling refers to the flexibility available to candidates who may require adjustments to the timetable for a reason related to their impairment.

MONITORING

2.22 Monitoring of members or, in the case of qualifications bodies and general qualifications bodies, people applying for a qualification or people who hold qualifications, is an important way of determining whether anti-discrimination measures taken by an organisation or body are effective, and ensuring that disability equality is a reality. Information must be gathered sensitively, with appropriately worded questions, and confidentiality must be ensured. Knowing the proportion of disabled people and their status in respect of an organisation or body can help it determine where practices and policies need to be improved.

2.23 In addition, where applicable, the disability equality specific duties require public authorities to set out the following in their Disability Equality Schemes:

- arrangements for gathering information on the extent to which the services it provides and those other functions it performs take account of the needs of disabled persons.

2.24 It is important to understand that information gathering is not an end in itself but that the information obtained must be analysed and used as the basis for preparing disability action plans, and reviewing the effectiveness of those actions taken. The information gathered is in fact evidence of an authority's progress in relation to disability equality. For this reason the Disability Equality Scheme is also required to include a statement of the public authority's arrangements for making use of the information gathered in these ways and in particular its arrangements for reviewing on a regular basis the effectiveness of the action plan and preparing subsequent Disability Equality Schemes.

2.25 Information must be gathered sensitively, with appropriately worded questions, and confidentiality must be ensured.

2.26 Monitoring will be more effective if disabled people feel comfortable about disclosing information about their disabilities. This is more likely to be the case if the trade organisation, qualifications body or general qualifications body explains the purpose of the monitoring and if members and applicants believe that it genuinely supports equality for disabled people and is using the information gathered to create positive change.

By monitoring of its membership, a professional association becomes aware that disabled people are under-represented at fellowship level. The association uses this information to review its criteria for awarding fellowships, and carries out research into the barriers facing disabled people at senior levels of the profession.

A trade union becomes aware, through monitoring, that disabled people are under-represented as conference delegates. It uses this information to find out from disabled members how arrangements for conferences can be improved to enable fuller participation.

A general qualifications body monitors the numbers of disabled people who take their qualifications. The general qualifications body finds that disabled people are less likely to choose certain courses. It uses the information to involve disabled people to consider and review the accessibility of the syllabuses/specifications and the nature of the assessment of the qualifications in question.

2.27 Some organisations choose to monitor by broad type of disability to understand the barriers faced by people with different types of impairment.

A general qualifications body decides to monitor the numbers of issues raised by disabled people and groups representing disabled people. It finds that most of these issues relate to a particular examination paper which included materials that created an unnecessary barrier to assessment and one which was not required. It reviews the results of the candidates affected and then requires the subject team to check questions as they are written so that the problem can be avoided in future.

Through monitoring of people applying for and achieving registration, a qualifications body becomes aware that people with certain disabilities are significantly under-represented as applicants for, and holders of, a particular qualification. The qualifications body uses this information to review its competence standards to ensure that they do not present unnecessary barriers to disabled people.

2.28 Public authorities are required to put into effect arrangements for gathering information and making use of it. In their annual reporting on the disability equality duty, they must set out the results of the information gathering which they have carried out, detailing the evidence which has been obtained and the use to which it has been put – such as the actions which will be taken to address the issues raised by the evidence.

2.29 Gathering information on students is a different process to gathering information from individual disabled students about their reasonable adjustments requirements. The processes should be separate and it should be clear to students and applicants why the information is being collected.

PROMOTING EQUALITY

2.30 Organisations or bodies not subject to the disability equality duty may nevertheless have an important part to play in promoting equality of opportunity (and they may also find that they are required to do so in relation to contractual arrangements with public authorities). In order to enhance disabled people's opportunities for gaining, retaining and progressing in employment, trade organisations, qualifications bodies and general qualifications bodies need to consider equality of opportunity for disabled people from two perspectives. First, such organisations and bodies should ensure that disabled people have equal access to membership, and to the benefits of membership, or (as the case may be) to opportunities for gaining and retaining a general, professional or trade qualification. Secondly, it is good practice for a trade organisation, qualifications body or general qualifications body to seek to promote equality for disabled people within the trade, profession or employment/ education sector in which it operates.

A general qualifications body advises schools and colleges which can enter candidates for its qualifications about the variety of ways in which it delivers the course and its assessment in ways which meet the particular needs of disabled people with a variety of impairments.

A trade organisation in the tourism sector holds a conference in association with employers in that sector and disability organisations to promote opportunities for disabled people within the tourism industry.

A trade union representing people in the broadcasting trades ensures that its promotional literature and its website show positive images of disabled people carrying out a variety of jobs within this industry.

A qualifications body in the health sector promotes a scheme through which disabled people are encouraged to apply to train as health professionals.

2.31 Organisations and bodies should be ensuring that any marketing activity, such as advertising a course, which features students or prospective students positively represents disabled students within that. As well as contributing to the overall goal of equality of opportunity, promoting such attitudes will ensure that organisations and bodies demonstrate that they are aware of the needs of disabled people. This will, in turn, generate broader representation of disabled people in terms of the activities of organisations and bodies, and will also encourage participation of disabled people in their monitoring activities in particular. For organisations and bodies that are public authorities, one of the aspects of the disability equality duty, as outlined above, is the need to promote positive attitudes towards disabled people.

RESOLVING DISPUTES

2.32 Although the Act does not require trade organisations, qualifications bodies or general qualifications bodies to resolve disputes within the organisation or body, it is in the interests of such an organisation or body wherever possible to resolve problems as they arise. This should be done in a non-discriminatory way to comply with the requirements of the Act.

2.33 Grievance procedures can provide an open and fair way for concerns to be made known. Such procedures may be particularly appropriate for use by members of trade organisations, and can enable grievances to be resolved quickly before they become major problems. Use of the procedures may highlight areas in which the duty to make reasonable adjustments has not been observed, and can prevent misunderstandings leading to complaints to tribunals and courts.

2.34 Chapter 11 contains further information about grievance procedures and about resolving disputes under the Act.

3. DISCRIMINATION BY TRADE ORGANISATIONS, QUALIFICATIONS BODIES AND GENERAL QUALIFICATIONS BODIES – AN OVERVIEW

INTRODUCTION

[4.126]

3.1 This chapter gives an overview of those provisions of the Act which are relevant to trade organisations, qualifications bodies and general qualifications bodies. It explains who has rights and duties under those provisions and outlines what is made unlawful by them. Later chapters explain the provisions in greater detail.

WHO HAS RIGHTS UNDER THE ACT?

Disabled people

3.2 [ss 1 and 2 and Sch 1 and 2] The Act gives protection from discrimination to a 'disabled' person within the meaning of the Act. A disabled person is someone who has a physical or mental impairment which has an effect on his or her ability to carry out normal day-to-day activities. That effect must be:

- substantial (that is, more than minor or trivial), and
- adverse, and long term (that is, it has lasted or is likely to last for at least a year or for the rest of the life of the person affected).

3.3 Physical or mental impairment includes sensory impairment. Hidden impairments are also covered (for example, mental illness or mental health problems, learning disabilities, dyslexia, diabetes and epilepsy).

3.4 The definition of disability used in the Act is not the same as other definitions of disabled persons in other legislation that applies to education in schools and colleges – for example in relation to the special educational needs framework in England and Wales, or the Additional Support for Learning in Scotland. It is possible that some people may be covered by more than one definition, and others may be covered by only one of these definitions. In considering its duties under the Act, a trade organisation, qualifications body and general qualifications body should not use any definition of 'disabled person' which is narrower than that in the Act. If such an organisation or body is asked to make a disability-related adjustment, it may ask the person requesting it for evidence that the impairment is one which meets the definition of disability in the Act. It may be appropriate to do so where the disability is not obvious. However, it is not appropriate to ask for more information about the impairment than is necessary for this purpose. Nor should evidence of disability be asked for where it ought to be obvious that the Act will apply.

People who have had a disability in the past

3.5 People who have had a disability within the meaning of the Act (as set out in Appendix A) in the past are protected from discrimination even if they no longer have the disability.

More information about the meaning of disability

3.6 For a fuller understanding of the concept of disability under the Act, reference should be made to Appendix A. A government publication, *Guidance on matters to be taken into account in determining questions relating to the definition of disability*, provides additional help in understanding the concept of disability and in identifying who is a disabled person. Where relevant, the Guidance must be taken into account in any legal proceedings.

People who have been victimised

3.7 The Act also gives rights to people who have been victimised, whether or not they have a disability or have had one in the past (see paragraphs 4.31 to 4.34).

WHO HAS OBLIGATIONS UNDER THE ACT?

Trade organisations

3.8 **[s 13(4)]** The Act defines a trade organisation as an organisation of workers or of employers, or any other organisation whose members carry on a particular profession or trade for the purposes of which the organisation exists. Bodies like trade unions, employers' associations and chartered professional institutions are all trade organisations because they exist for the purposes of the profession or trade which their members carry on. Examples of trade organisations include the Law Society, the Royal College of Nursing, the Swimming Teachers' Association, the Society of Floristry, the British Computer Society, and the Institute of Carpenters. The Act applies to all trade organisations, no matter how many (or how few) members they may have.

Qualifications bodies

3.9 **[s 14A(5)]** The Act defines a qualifications body as an authority or body which can confer, renew or extend a professional or trade qualification. For this purpose a professional or trade qualification is an authorisation, qualification, recognition, registration, enrolment, approval or certification which is needed for, or which facilitates engagement in, a particular profession or trade. What this means in practice is considered in paragraphs 8.5 to 8.7. Qualifications bodies include examination boards, the General Medical Council, the Nursing and Midwifery Council, and the Driving Standards Agency. Other examples are City and Guilds, the Institute of the Motor Industry, the Hospitality Awarding Body and the Guild of Cleaners and Launderers.

3.10 **[s 14A(5)]** Nevertheless, certain bodies are not regarded as qualifications bodies for the purposes of Part 2, even though they may perform some of the functions mentioned in paragraph 3.9. These are listed in the Act. Broadly speaking, they comprise local education authorities in England and Wales, education authorities in Scotland, and other bodies having responsibility for schools and colleges. This is because discrimination by such bodies is the concern of Part 4 of the Act, which relates to discrimination in the provision of education. The DRC has issued two separate codes of practice giving guidance on the operation of Part 4 (see Appendix B for details).

3.11 Clearly, certain trade organisations (such as the Law Society) also confer professional or trade qualifications. Consequently, the same organisation or body can be both a trade organisation and a qualifications body. Where this is the case, the application of the Act's provisions depends upon the capacity in which the organisation or body is acting at the time in question. For example, if an alleged act of discrimination relates to conferring, renewing or extending a professional or trade qualification, the relevant provisions are those relating to discrimination by qualifications bodies – the fact that the body is also a trade organisation is irrelevant in this context.

General qualifications bodies

3.12 [s 31AA(4) and (6) and Reg 2 and Sch of SI 2007/1764] The Act defines a general qualifications body as an authority or body which can confer, renew or extend a relevant qualification, or authenticate a relevant qualification awarded by another person. For this purpose a relevant qualification is an authorisation, qualification, approval or certification which is listed in the regulations, and is one of the following qualifications:

- GCEs (General Certificate of Education)
- Advanced level (A and AS levels)
- VCEs (Vocational Certificate of Education)
- AEAs (Advanced Extension Awards)
- GCSEs (General Certificate of Secondary Education)
- Free standing Maths Qualifications
- Entry level qualifications
- Key Skills
- Certificates in Adult Literacy and Numeracy Entry Levels, Level 1, 2 and 3
- GNVQs (General National Vocational Qualifications)
- The National Qualifications framework in Scotland
- The Welsh Baccalaureate Qualification
- The International Baccalaureate.

[s 31AA(6)(i)–(iv)] In line with paragraph 3.10, under the Act certain bodies are deemed not to be general qualifications bodies. These include responsible bodies within the meaning of Chapters 1 and 2 of Part 4 of the Act (responsible bodies of schools and further and higher education institutions), local education authorities in England and Wales and education authorities in Scotland. **[s 31AA(5)]** A relevant general qualification cannot be a professional and trade qualification within the meaning given by s 14A(5) of the Act.

Employers and others to whom Part 2 applies

3.13 The primary focus of Part 2 is, of course, on the duties of employers to disabled people. As mentioned at paragraph 1.6, however, that is not the subject of this Code. Guidance on the application of the Act to employers (as well as its application to people and bodies concerned with certain occupations and to persons such as the trustees or managers of occupational pension schemes and the providers of group insurance services) is given in a separate code of practice issued by the DRC (see Appendix B for details). It has already been noted that, as employers themselves, trade organisations, qualifications bodies and general qualifications bodies have duties under Part 2 in respect of disabled people whom they employ, or who apply to them for employment. Those duties are governed by the employment provisions of the Act.

Education institutions to whom Chapter 2A of Part 4 applies

3.14 Part 4 of the Act is largely concerned with the duties of education providers ('responsible bodies'). However, this is also not the subject of this Code. Guidance on the application of the Act to education providers is given in two separate codes of practice issued by the DRC (see Appendix B for details).

WHAT DOES THE ACT SAY ABOUT DISCRIMINATION BY TRADE ORGANISATIONS, QUALIFICATIONS BODIES AND GENERAL QUALIFICATIONS BODIES?

Effect of the Act

3.15 The Act makes it unlawful for a trade organisation to **discriminate** against a disabled person in relation to membership of the organisation or access to membership benefits. The Act also makes it unlawful for a qualifications body and a general qualifications body to **discriminate** against a disabled person in relation to conferring professional or trade qualifications and relevant general qualifications respectively.

3.16 However, the Act does not prevent organisations or bodies from treating disabled people more favourably than those who are not disabled.

Forms of discrimination

3.17 The four forms of discrimination which are unlawful under Part 2 (and unlawful under Part 4 in relation to general qualifications bodies) are:

- direct discrimination (the meaning of which is explained at paragraphs 4.4 to 4.21)
- failure to comply with a duty to make reasonable adjustments (explained in Chapter 5)
- 'disability-related discrimination' (see paragraphs 4.25 to 4.30), and
- victimisation of a person (whether or not he is disabled) – what the Act says about victimisation is explained at paragraphs 4.31 to 4.34.

Discrimination by trade organisations

3.18 **[s 13(1)]** The Act says that it is unlawful for a trade organisation to discriminate against a disabled person:

- in the arrangements it makes for the purpose of determining who should be offered membership of the organisation, or
- in the terms on which it is prepared to admit him to membership, or
- by refusing to accept, or deliberately not accepting, his application for membership.

3.19 **[s 13(2)]** The Act also says that it is unlawful for a trade organisation to discriminate against a disabled member:

- in the way it affords the member access to any benefits or by refusing or deliberately omitting to afford access to them, or
- by depriving the member of membership, or varying the terms of his membership, or
- by subjecting the member to any other detriment.

What this means in practice is explained in Chapter 7.

3.20 It should be noted that the Act does not protect corporate members of trade organisations, even if a disabled person is a representative of a corporate member.

> A trade organisation in the building industry has both individual and corporate members. A disabled employee of a company which is a member of this trade organisation would not have protection from discrimination by the trade organisation under Part 2, whereas an individual member of the organisation would have such protection.

Discrimination by qualifications bodies

3.21 **[s 14A(1)]** In relation to conferring, renewing, or extending professional or trade qualifications (abbreviated to 'conferring'), the Act says that it is unlawful for a qualifications body to discriminate against a disabled person:

- in the arrangements it makes for the purpose of determining upon whom to confer a professional or trade qualification, or
- in the terms on which it is prepared to confer such a qualification, or
- by refusing or deliberately omitting to grant any application by him for a professional or trade qualification, or
- by withdrawing such a qualification from him or varying the terms on which he holds it.

What this means in practice is explained in Chapter 8.

Discrimination by general qualifications bodies

3.22 **[s 31AA(1)]** In relation to conferring, renewing, or extending a general qualification (collectively referred to in this code as 'conferring'), the Act says that it is unlawful for a general qualifications body to discriminate against a disabled person:

- in the arrangements it makes for the purpose of determining upon whom to confer a relevant general qualification, or
- in the terms on which it is prepared to confer such a qualification, or
- by refusing or deliberately omitting to grant any application by him for a relevant general qualification, or
- by withdrawing such a qualification from him or varying the terms on which he holds it.

What this means in practice is explained in Chapter 9.

WHAT ELSE IS UNLAWFUL UNDER THE RELEVANT PROVISIONS OF THE ACT?

Harassment

3.23 **[s 13(3) and s 14A(2) and s 31AA(2)]** In addition to what it says about discrimination, Part 2 (and Part 4) makes it unlawful for a trade organisation, qualifications body or general qualifications body to subject a disabled person to **harassment** for a reason which relates to his disability. What the Act says about harassment is explained in more detail at paragraphs 4.36 and 4.37. The Act treats disability-related harassment as a separate concept, and this is not one of the forms of discrimination.

Instructions and pressure to discriminate

3.24 **[s 16C and s 17B(1)]** It is also unlawful for a person who has authority or influence over another to instruct him, or put pressure on him, to act unlawfully under the provisions of Part 2 – this provision **does not** apply to general qualifications bodies. Where these duties apply they cover pressure to discriminate, whether applied directly to the person concerned, or indirectly but in a way in which he is likely to hear of it. However, the Act does not give individual disabled people the right to take legal action in respect of unlawful instructions or pressure to discriminate. Such action may only be taken by the Equality and Human Rights Commission (see paragraphs 11.26 to 11.28).

> A trade union is holding a conference. The conference organiser, who is a paid employee of the union working in the events department, instructs the branch representatives not to send any wheelchair users to the conference as the venue is not wheelchair accessible. This is likely to be unlawful as it is an instruction to discriminate.

Discriminatory advertisements

3.25 **[s 16B]** The Act does not prevent advertisements for membership of trade organisations, or for general, professional or trade qualifications from saying that applications from disabled people are welcome. However, in respect of trade organisations and qualifications bodies (but **not** in respect of general qualifications bodies) it does say that it is unlawful for those seeking members for an organisation (or seeking candidates for professional and trade qualifications) to publish an advertisement (or cause it to be published) which indicates, or might reasonably be understood to indicate:

- that the success of a person's application may depend to any extent on his not having any disability, or any particular disability, or
- that the person determining the application is reluctant to make reasonable adjustments.

3.26 This applies to every form of advertisement or notice, whether to the public or not. However, an advertisement may still be lawful even if it does indicate that having a particular disability will adversely affect an applicant's prospects of success. This will be the case where, for example, the particular circumstances are such that the trade organisation or qualifications body is entitled to take the effects of the disability into account when assessing the suitability of applicants.

> A qualifications body in the tourism industry advertises in a trade publication, inviting readers to apply to take a course leading to a qualification accredited by that body. The advertisement says that candidates 'must have excellent written and spoken English'. This would exclude people who used British Sign Language as their first language, or people who had dyslexia, and may be unlawful.

> However a qualifications body advertising a course in tree surgery, would not be discriminating by stipulating that candidates 'must not be afraid of heights', even if this would exclude people who had vertigo as a result of their disability.

3.27 It is good practice to consider carefully what information should be included in advertisements and where they should be placed.

3.28 **[s 17B(1)]** The Act does not give individual applicants for membership of trade organisations or applicants for professional or trade qualifications the right to take legal action in respect of discriminatory advertisements. Such action may only be taken by the Equality and Human Rights Commission (see paragraphs 11.26 to 11.28).

WHO IS LIABLE FOR UNLAWFUL ACTS?

Responsibility for the acts of others

3.29 **[s 58]** Trade organisations, qualifications bodies and general qualifications bodies who act through agents are liable for the actions of their agents done with the express or implied authority of the organisation or body in question – this can include the actions of unpaid union representatives in the workplace or education institutions (and/or their employees) in respect of exams and testing.

3.30 General qualifications bodies may directly provide, or contract with third parties to organise and to provide, examination and assessment facilities, and to undertake examinations and assessments that may result in conferring relevant general qualifications. In addition, statutory regulators may set criteria which general qualifications bodies use to determine examination and assessment objectives. Chapter 9 provides further information about the context in which general qualifications bodies operate and the duties that they have under the DDA.

A person employed by an examination centre to invigilate an examination for a GCSE qualification refuses to allow a candidate with a severe disfigurement into the examination hall as he believes this candidate's disability would be off-putting for other candidates. This is likely to constitute unlawful direct disability discrimination. The invigilator in question is acting on behalf of the examination centre in relation to delivery of the examination and, therefore, he is likely to be acting as an agent of the general qualifications body who ultimately confer the GCSE qualification. The general qualifications body would be liable under the Act for the unlawful actions of the invigilator, who, together with the examination centre, would also be individually liable.

3.31 The Act also says that trade organisations, qualifications bodies and general qualifications bodies are responsible for the actions of their employees in the course of their employment. For example, a trade union is responsible for the actions of its salaried officials in the course of their employment.

3.32 However, in legal proceedings against a trade organisation, qualifications body or general qualifications body, based on the actions of an employee, it is a defence that the organisation or body took 'such steps as were reasonably practicable' to prevent such actions. It is not a defence simply to show that the action took place without the knowledge or approval of the organisation or body.

A trade union has a disability policy which states that it will pay for sign language interpreters to interpret at branch meetings, should the need arise, from a central union fund. This policy, and the arrangements available for paying for sign language interpreters (and for other adjustments), is explained to all branch representatives and new members. In addition all branch representatives are required to undergo basic training in the policy. A deaf union member requests a sign language interpreter for a branch meeting, but the branch representative who has undergone this training says that this is not possible as there are insufficient funds in the branch to pay for this adjustment. In this case the union could demonstrate that it had taken 'such steps as were reasonably practicable' to prevent such actions and it is likely that it has not acted unlawfully. The branch representative, however, is likely to be acting unlawfully (see paragraphs 3.29 and 3.30).

An Examiner working for a Scottish general qualifications body refuses to allow a pupil with a severe speech impediment to have extra time to answer in a French Speaking Test. The Examiner is employed by the general qualifications body so the body will be liable for the potentially discriminatory actions of the Examiner (in failing to make a reasonable adjustment), unless it could demonstrate that it had taken such steps as were reasonably practicable to prevent such actions (see paragraphs 3.29 and 3.30).

Aiding an unlawful act

3.33 **[s 57]** A person who knowingly helps another to do something made unlawful by the Act will be treated as having done the same kind of unlawful act. This means that, where a trade organisation, qualifications body or general qualifications body is liable for an unlawful act of its employee or agent, that employee or agent will be liable for aiding the unlawful act of the organisation or body.

3.34 Where an employee of a trade organisation, qualifications body or general qualifications body discriminates against or harasses a disabled person, it is the employing organisation or body which will be liable for that unlawful act – unless it can show that it took such steps as were reasonable to prevent the unlawful act in question. But the employee who committed the discrimination or harassment will be liable for aiding the unlawful act – and this will be the case even if the trade organisation, qualifications body or general qualifications body is able to show that it took reasonable steps to prevent the act.

In the last-but-one example, where the union has taken steps to ensure that disabled members can participate in branch meetings, it is likely that the branch representative would be acting unlawfully in aiding an unlawful act by the union, even though the union itself has avoided liability by taking reasonably practicable steps.

ENFORCING RIGHTS UNDER PART 2 OF THE ACT

3.35 **[s 17A]** Enforcement of rights under Part 2 takes place in the employment tribunals. More information about enforcement is given in Chapter 11.

ENFORCING RIGHTS UNDER PART 4 OF THE ACT (IN RESPECT OF GENERAL QUALIFICATIONS BODIES)

3.36 **[s 31ADA(4) and (5) and Reg 3 of SI 2007/2405]** Enforcement of rights under Part 4 in respect of general qualifications bodies takes place in the County Courts in England and Wales (or in the Sheriff Courts in Scotland). More information about enforcement is given in Chapter 11.

4. WHAT IS DISCRIMINATION AND HARASSMENT?

INTRODUCTION

[4.127]

4.1 The forms of discrimination by trade organisations, qualifications bodies and general qualifications bodies which the Act makes unlawful are:

- direct discrimination
- failure to comply with a duty to make reasonable adjustments
- disability-related discrimination, and victimisation.

4.2 This chapter describes these four forms of discrimination in more detail, and explains the differences between them. It explores, in particular, the distinction between direct discrimination and disability-related discrimination (see paragraphs 4.25 to 4.30, and 4.35). These two forms of discrimination both depend on the way in which the disabled person concerned is treated – both require the disabled person to have been treated less favourably than other people are (or would be) treated. However, whether such treatment amounts to one of these forms of discrimination or the other (and, indeed, whether the treatment is unlawful in the first place) depends on the circumstances in which it arose.

4.3 The chapter examines the four forms of discrimination in the order in which they are listed in paragraph 4.1. This is because less favourable treatment which does not amount to direct discrimination can sometimes be justified. (In contrast, neither direct discrimination nor a failure to comply with a duty to make a reasonable adjustment is justifiable. Victimisation cannot be justified either.) In deciding whether the treatment is justified, and therefore whether there has been disability-related discrimination, the Act requires the question of reasonable adjustments to be taken into account (see paragraphs 6.5 and 6.6 where this is explained in more detail). Consequently, although the chapter describes direct discrimination first, it touches on the subject of reasonable adjustments before moving on to disability-related discrimination. This chapter also explains what the Act means by 'harassment'.

WHAT DOES THE ACT MEAN BY 'DIRECT DISCRIMINATION'?

What does the Act say?

4.4 **[s 3A(5) and 31AB(8)]** The Act says that treatment of a disabled person by a trade organisation, qualifications body or general qualifications body amounts to direct discrimination if:

- it is on the ground of his disability
- the treatment is less favourable than the way in which a person not having that particular disability is (or would be) treated, and
- the relevant circumstances, including the abilities, of the person with whom the comparison is made are the same as, or not materially different from, those of the disabled person.

4.5 It follows that direct discrimination depends on treatment of a disabled person by a trade organisation, qualifications body or general qualifications body being on the ground of his disability. It also depends on a comparison of that treatment with the way in which the organisation or body treats (or would treat) an appropriate comparator. If, on the ground of his disability, the disabled person is treated less favourably than the comparator is (or would be) treated, the treatment amounts to direct discrimination.

When is direct discrimination likely to occur?

4.6 Treatment of a disabled person is 'on the ground of' his disability if it is caused by the fact that he is disabled or has the disability in question. In general, this means that treatment is on the ground of disability if a disabled person would not have received it but for his disability. However, disability does not have to be the only (or even the main) cause of the treatment complained of – provided that it is an effective cause, determined objectively from all the circumstances.

4.7 Consequently, if the less favourable treatment occurs because of generalised, or stereotypical, assumptions about the disability or its effects, it is likely to be direct discrimination. This is because a trade organisation, qualifications body or general qualifications body would not normally make such assumptions about a non-disabled person, but would instead consider his individual abilities.

> A trade union member who has a mental health condition – which her branch secretary is aware of – is refused admission to a meeting because the branch secretary wrongly assumes that she would seriously disrupt the meeting with loud interjections. The branch secretary has treated her less favourably than other members by refusing her entry to the meeting. The treatment was on the ground of the woman's disability (because assumptions would not have been made about a non-disabled person).

> A general qualifications body has a blanket policy not to allow candidates with epilepsy to take practical chemistry examinations. A candidate with epilepsy is refused the opportunity to take practical chemistry examinations. This is based on an assumption that all people with epilepsy present an unacceptable health and safety risk in this context. This amounts to direct discrimination.

> A general qualifications body has a practice of not allowing wheelchair users to undertake a GCSE qualification in Dance, because it has assumed all wheelchair users are not capable of undertaking this qualification, and it has operated this policy without considering the individual circumstances of each person. This amounts to direct discrimination.

4.8 In addition, less favourable treatment which is disability-specific, or which arises out of prejudice about disability (or about a particular type of disability), is also likely to amount to direct discrimination.

> An applicant for a professional hairdressing qualification is told that he would not be suitable for the qualification because he has a disability and thus the qualifications body refuses to confer the qualification upon him. This refusal is unrelated to any competence standard which is applied by the body when conferring the qualification, but arises instead from prejudice about the applicant's disability. This amounts to direct discrimination.

> A person with a severe visible disfigurement is not allowed to undertake a GNVQ in leisure and tourism because the body conferring this qualification believes this disability will prevent the person from gaining employment in this sector. This amounts to direct discrimination.

> A general qualifications body tells an applicant for a GCSE in biology that she should not take the course because she has HIV. This refusal arises from prejudice about the applicant's disability. This amounts to direct discrimination.

4.9 In some cases, an apparently neutral reason for less favourable treatment of a disabled person may, on investigation, turn out to be a pretext for direct discrimination.

> A disabled member of a professional body wishes to represent the body publicly by giving a television interview but is told that only people who have been members for at least three years are permitted to do this. However, she discovers that another member, who is not disabled, has given a public presentation on behalf of the professional body even though he had only been a member for two years at the time. Although the reason given to the disabled member (that she had not been a member of the body for long enough to represent it publicly) appeared to be a neutral

one, it would seem that the reason was actually a pretext for direct discrimination, and is therefore unlawful.

4.10 Direct discrimination will often occur where the trade organisation, qualifications body or general qualifications body is aware that the disabled person has a disability, and this is the reason for its treatment of him. Direct discrimination need not be conscious – people may hold prejudices that they do not admit, even to themselves. Thus, a person may behave in a discriminatory way while believing that he would never do so. Moreover, direct discrimination may sometimes occur even though the trade organisation, qualifications body or general qualifications body is unaware of a person's disability.

4.11 In situations such as those described in the above examples, it will often be readily apparent that the disabled person concerned has been treated less favourably on the ground of his disability. In other cases, however, this may be less obvious. Whether or not the basis for the treatment in question appears to be clear, a useful way of telling whether or not it is discriminatory (and of establishing what kind of discrimination it is), is to focus on the person with whom the disabled person should be compared. That person may be real or hypothetical (see paragraph 4.17).

Identifying comparators in respect of direct discrimination

4.12 In determining whether a disabled person has been treated less favourably in the context of direct discrimination, his treatment must be compared with that of an appropriate comparator. This must be someone who does not have the same disability. It could be a non-disabled person or a person with other disabilities.

4.13 It follows that, in the great majority of cases, some difference will exist between the circumstances (including the abilities) of the comparator and those of the disabled person – there is no need to find a comparator whose circumstances are the same as those of the disabled person in every respect. What matters is that the comparator's **relevant** circumstances (including his abilities) must be the same as, or not materially different from, those of the disabled person.

4.14 Once an appropriate comparator is identified, it is clear that the situations described in the examples at paragraph 4.7 amounts to direct discrimination:

In the example about the trade union member who is refused admission to a meeting because she has a mental health problem, there is direct discrimination because the woman was treated less favourably on the ground of her disability than an appropriate comparator (that is, a person who does not have a mental health problem but whose relevant circumstances (including abilities) are otherwise the same): such a person would not have been refused admission to the meeting in the same circumstances.

In the example about the general qualifications body with a blanket policy not allowing candidates with epilepsy to take practical chemistry examinations, there is direct discrimination because the candidate was treated less favourably on the ground of her disability than an appropriate comparator (that is, a person who does not have epilepsy but whose relevant circumstances (including abilities) are otherwise the same): such a person would not have been prevented from taking the assessment.

In the example about the general qualifications body with a blanket policy that does not allow wheelchair users to undertake a GCSE qualification in Dance, there is direct discrimination because a candidate who does not use a wheelchair with the same abilities as the candidate using a wheelchair would have been treated more favourably: such a person would have been allowed on to the course.

4.15 The examples of direct discrimination in paragraph 4.8 also become clearer when the appropriate comparator is identified:

In the example about the applicant for a professional hairdressing qualification who is told that he would not be suitable for the qualification because he has a disability, there is direct discrimination because the man was treated less favourably on the ground of his disability than an appropriate comparator (that is, a person who does not have the same disability, but whose relevant abilities in respect of the qualification are the same): such a person would not have been treated in this way.

In the example about the person with a severe visible disfigurement not being allowed to undertake a GNVQ in leisure and tourism, there is direct discrimination because the applicant with the severe disfigurement is treated less favourably than someone with the same abilities who does not have a severe disfigurement: such a person would have been allowed to undertake this course.

In the example about the applicant for a GCSE in biology who is told she should not take the course because she has HIV, there is direct discrimination because the applicant was treated less favourably on the ground of her disability. An appropriate comparator would be a person who does not have the same disability, but whose relevant abilities in respect of the qualification are the same, and who was not treated in the same way.

4.16 The comparator used in relation to direct discrimination under the Act is the same as it is for other types of direct discrimination – such as direct sex discrimination. It is, however, made explicit in the Act that the comparator must have the same relevant abilities as the disabled person.

4.17 It may not be possible to identify an actual comparator whose relevant circumstances are the same as (or not materially different from) those of the disabled person in question. In such cases a hypothetical comparator may be used. Evidence which helps to establish how a hypothetical comparator would have been treated is likely to include details of how other people (not satisfying the statutory comparison test) were treated in circumstances which were broadly similar.

In the example at paragraph 4.9, there is nobody who has represented the professional body in television interviews with whom the disabled person can be compared. Nevertheless, the treatment of the member who had only two years' membership but was able to give a public presentation on behalf of the body might be evidence of discrimination: it might be used as evidence that a hypothetical non-disabled member who wanted to participate in a television interview would not have been treated in the same way as the disabled member was treated.

4.18 It should be noted that the type of comparator described in the preceding paragraphs is only relevant to disability discrimination when assessing whether there has been **direct** discrimination. A different comparison falls to be made when assessing whether there has been a failure to comply with a duty to make reasonable adjustments (see paragraphs 5.2 and 5.3) or when considering disability-related discrimination (see paragraph 4.29).

Focusing on relevant circumstances

4.19 As stated in paragraph 4.13, direct discrimination only occurs where the **relevant** circumstances of the comparator, including his abilities, are the same as, or not materially different from, those of the disabled person himself. It is therefore important to focus on those circumstances which are, in fact, relevant to the matter to which the less favourable treatment relates. Although, in some cases, the effects of the disability may be relevant, the fact of the disability itself is not a relevant circumstance for these purposes. This is because the comparison must be with a person **not** having that particular disability.

A woman who has a severe facial disfigurement applies for membership of a professional association in the tourism industry. Despite meeting the formal requirements for membership, she is told that her disability would not create a good impression and her application is rejected. The correct comparator in a claim for direct discrimination would be a person who does not have a facial disfigurement but who meets the formal requirements for membership of the professional association

A pupil who has arthrogryposis (a muscular-skeletal condition) is credited with very high marks for a practical demonstration of swimming abilities. The general qualifications body queries the mark believing that there must have been an error. The correct comparator in a claim for direct discrimination would be a person who does not have this impairment, but whose abilities in respect of the swimming assessment are the same, or not materially different, from the person with arthrogryposis.

Relevance of reasonable adjustments to comparison

4.20 In making the comparison in respect of a claim of direct discrimination, the disabled person's abilities must be considered **as they in fact are**. In some cases, there will be particular reasonable adjustments which a trade organisation, qualifications body or general qualifications body was required by the Act to make, but in fact failed to make. It may be that those adjustments would have had an effect on the disabled person's relevant abilities. But in making the comparison, the disabled person's abilities should be considered as they **in fact** were, and not as they would or might have been had those adjustments been made. On the other hand, if adjustments have **in fact** been made which have had the effect of enhancing the disabled person's abilities, then it is those enhanced abilities which should be considered. The disabled person's abilities are being considered as they in fact are (and not as they might have been if the adjustments had not been made).

A disabled person has to sit an examination in order to obtain a relevant general qualification. Because of her disability she has difficulty writing, and asks to be allowed to type her answers or given extra time to complete the examination. The general qualifications body does not permit this (even though it would have been reasonable for it to do so) and, as a result, the woman is unable to complete the examination in time. This is not direct discrimination, as the comparator for the purposes of this claim is a non-disabled person who also fails to complete the examination in time. (But the woman would be likely to have good claims in respect of two other forms of discrimination – failure to make reasonable adjustments and disability-related discrimination – see paragraph 4.35.)

Can direct discrimination be justified?

4.21 [s 3A(4) and s 31AB(7)] Treatment of a disabled person which amounts to direct discrimination under the Act is unlawful. It can never be justified.

FAILURE TO MAKE REASONABLE ADJUSTMENTS – RELATIONSHIP TO DISCRIMINATION

4.22 For the reason given in paragraph 4.3, it may be necessary to consider whether a trade organisation, qualifications body or general qualifications body has failed to comply with a duty to make a reasonable adjustment in order to determine whether disability related discrimination has occurred.

4.23 [s 3A(2) and s 31AB(2)] Irrespective of its relevance to disability-related discrimination, however, a failure to comply with a duty to make a reasonable adjustment in respect of a disabled person amounts to discrimination in its own right. Such a failure is therefore unlawful. Chapter 5 explains the circumstances in which a trade organisation, qualifications body or general qualifications body has such a duty, and gives guidance as to what they need to do when the duty arises. Chapters 7, 8 and 9 also give further guidance on when an adjustment might be considered reasonable in relation to trade organisations, qualifications and general qualifications bodies respectively.

4.24 As with direct discrimination, the Act does not permit an organisation or body to justify a failure to comply with a duty to make a reasonable adjustment (see paragraphs 5.26 and 5.27).

WHAT IS DISABILITY-RELATED DISCRIMINATION?

What does the Act say?

4.25 [s 3A(1) and s 31AB(1)] The Act says that treatment of a disabled person by a trade organisation, qualifications body or general qualifications body amounts to discrimination if:

- it is for a reason related to his disability
- the treatment is less favourable than the way in which the trade organisation, qualifications body or general qualifications body treats (or would treat) others to whom that reason does not (or would not) apply, and
- the organisation or body cannot show that the treatment is justified.

4.26 Although the Act itself does not use the term 'disability-related discrimination', this expression is used in the Code when referring to treatment of a disabled person which:

- is unlawful because each of the conditions listed in paragraph 4.25 is satisfied, but

- does **not** amount to direct discrimination under the Act.

4.27 In general, direct discrimination occurs when the reason for the less favourable treatment in question is the disability, while disability-related discrimination occurs when the reason relates to the disability but is not the disability itself. The expression 'disability-related discrimination' therefore distinguishes less favourable treatment which amounts to direct discrimination from a wider class of less favourable treatment which, although not amounting to direct discrimination, is nevertheless unlawful.

When does disability-related discrimination occur?

4.28 In determining whether disability related discrimination has occurred, the treatment of the disabled person must be compared with that of a person **to whom the disability-related reason does not apply**. This contrasts with direct discrimination, which requires a comparison to be made with a person without the disability in question but whose relevant circumstances are the same. The comparator may be non-disabled or disabled – but the key point is that the disability-related reason for the less favourable treatment must not apply to him.

A trade union refuses to allow a disabled person, who has a severe back condition and has been unable to carry out branch activities for the past couple of months due to her disability, to go on a training course. The union says that anyone who had not been carrying out their branch activities for this amount of time would have been refused training. The disability related reason for the less favourable treatment is the fact that the woman has not been carrying out branch activities, and the correct comparator is a person to whom that reason does not apply – that is, someone who had been carrying out branch activities. Consequently, unless the trade union can show that the treatment is justified, it will amount to disability-related discrimination because the comparator would not have been refused the opportunity to go on the training course. However, the reason for the treatment is not the disability itself (it is only a matter related thereto, namely not carrying out branch activities). So there is no direct discrimination.

A general qualifications body has set a start time of 9am for pupils/students undertaking an examination and refuses to allow anyone to take this examination other than at this time. A disabled pupil who requires regular medical treatment (dialysis) at this time in the morning cannot attend the examination. Refusing to allow him to attend at a different time would constitute less favourable treatment for disability related reasons and would amount to disability-related discrimination unless the general qualifications body could justify the treatment. The reason for the treatment is not the disability itself, so there is no direct discrimination.

4.29 The relationship between a disabled person's disability and the treatment of him by the organisation or body in question must be judged objectively. The reason for any less favourable treatment may well relate to the disability even if the organisation or body does not have knowledge of the disability as such, or of whether its salient features are such that it meets the definition of disability in the Act. Less favourable treatment which is not itself direct discrimination will still be unlawful (subject to justification) if, in fact, the reason for it relates to the person's disability.

In the first example at paragraph 4.28, the trade union did not know that the reason why the woman had not been carrying out branch activities was disability-related. Nevertheless, its refusal to allow her to attend the training course is less favourable treatment for a disability-related reason, and would be unlawful unless it can be justified.

In the second example at paragraph 4.28, the general qualifications body did not know why (and didn't make any appropriate enquiries) as to why the pupil could not attend the examination at 9am and that the reason was disability related. Nevertheless, the refusal to allow the pupil to take the examination at another time is disability-related less favourable treatment and would be unlawful unless it can be justified.

4.30 The circumstances in which justification may be possible are explained in Chapter 6. However, it is worth noting that the possibility of justifying potential discrimination only arises at all when the form of discrimination being considered is disability-related discrimination, rather than direct discrimination or failure to make reasonable adjustments.

WHAT DOES THE ACT SAY ABOUT VICTIMISATION?

4.31 **[s 55(1) and (2)]** Victimisation is a special form of discrimination which is made unlawful by the Act. It is unlawful for one person to treat another ('the victim') less favourably than he treats or would treat other people in the same circumstances because the victim has:

- brought, or given evidence or information in connection with, proceedings under the Act (whether or not proceedings are later withdrawn)
- done anything else under the Act, or
- alleged someone has contravened the Act (whether or not the allegation is later dropped),

or because the person believes or suspects that the victim has done or intends to do any of these things.

> A member of a trade organisation brings a claim of discrimination against the organisation. He is accompanied to the hearing of the claim by a friend who is also a member of the organisation. This person is subsequently refused a place on a course run by the organisation because he accompanied the claimant to the hearing. This amounts to victimisation.

> A non-disabled pupil at a school supports his disabled colleague in respect of a complaint of disability discrimination made against a general qualifications body. Thereafter, because the general qualifications body in question has taken exception to this, they refuse to re-mark an examination paper that the non-disabled pupil has completed. This amounts to victimisation.

4.32 **[s 55(4)]** It is not victimisation to treat a person less favourably because that person has made an allegation which was false and not made in good faith.

4.33 However, the fact that a person has given evidence on behalf of an applicant in a claim which was unsuccessful does not, of itself, prove that his evidence was false or that it was not given in good faith.

4.34 **[s 55(5)]** Unlike the other forms of discrimination which are made unlawful by the Act, victimisation may be claimed by people who are not disabled as well as by those who are.

HOW DO THE DIFFERENT FORMS OF DISCRIMINATION COMPARE IN PRACTICE?

4.35 The way in which the different forms of discrimination which are unlawful under the Act may operate in practice can be demonstrated by the following series of examples.

> A disabled person who has multiple sclerosis applies to go to a union conference which lasts for one week. She mentions her disability on the booking form, but says that it would not affect her ability to attend. Nevertheless, the conference organiser wrongly assumes that the woman's disability will prevent her from participating at the conference and she is refused a place. This is direct discrimination.
>
> In the situation described above, the woman states on the booking form that she will have to miss one day of the conference in order to have hospital treatment in relation to her disability. Because full attendance is required of all conference participants, she is refused a place. This is not direct discrimination, as the reason for the refusal of a place was not the woman's disability, but the fact that she would not be able to attend the conference in full.
>
> However, the trade union has a duty to make reasonable adjustments. In order to prevent the disabled woman being substantially disadvantaged by the union's policy of only allowing people to attend the conference if they can attend it in full, it may be a reasonable adjustment for the union to waive this requirement. If so, the union will be unlawfully discriminating against the woman by refusing to do this.
>
> Although there is no direct discrimination, the union has still treated the woman less favourably for a reason relating to her disability (namely, the fact that she cannot attend the conference in full). This will be disability-related discrimination unless the union can show that it is justified – and the union will be unable to show this if it would have been reasonable for it to have waived the requirement for full attendance.
>
> Because of the way in which she has been treated, the woman makes a claim against the trade union under Part 2 of the Act. Some time later, however, she asks for union representation in relation to a grievance at work. Her request is rejected because she has previously made a claim

against the union. This is victimisation.

A disabled sixth form student is studying for an A level. Before the disabled student began studying, staff at the college met with him to discuss the reasonable adjustments that he would require in order to study there. However, the general qualifications body wrongly assumes that the student's disability will prevent his full participation in the A level course and it does not accept his entry onto the examination. This is likely to be direct discrimination.

In the situation above the student mentions to the college that he will need a more flexible course programme, because his health condition means that he has to make regular hospital visits and he will not, therefore, be able to attend all lessons and hand all course work in on time. The college makes a request for varying the deadline (for the disabled student to hand in his coursework) to the general qualifications body conferring this qualification. The general qualifications body decides not to allow the student to have this flexibility because they require all coursework deadlines to be strictly adhered to and they subsequently refuse to confer the qualification because this student's coursework has been submitted after the deadline.

The duty on the general qualifications body to make reasonable adjustments means that in order to prevent the disabled student from being substantially disadvantaged by this policy it may be reasonable to waive the requirement that all coursework deadlines must be strictly adhered to. If the general qualifications body refuses to make the possible reasonable adjustments that could be made, it will be unlawfully discriminating.

Although there is no direct discrimination because the requirement to meet coursework deadlines applies equally to everyone, the general qualifications body has still treated him less favourably for a reason relating to his disability. This is because the refusal to confer the qualification is due to the fact that the disabled student could not hand his coursework in on time due to regular hospital appointments and this, in turn, is for reasons related to his disability. This will constitute unlawful disability-related discrimination, unless the general qualifications body can show that the treatment is justified. If it would be reasonable to allow flexibility in the deadlines for the submission of coursework, it would not be able to show that this requirement was justified.

Because of the way in which he has been treated, the student makes a claim of disability discrimination against the general qualifications body. A few years later, an application is made on his behalf to enter for a GCSE qualification that is administered by the same general qualifications body. His entry is denied because he has previously made a disability discrimination claim in good faith against the general qualifications body. This is victimisation.

WHAT DOES THE ACT SAY ABOUT HARASSMENT?

4.36 **[s 3B(1) and s 31AC(1)]** The Act says that harassment occurs where, for a reason which relates to a person's disability, another person engages in unwanted conduct which has the purpose or effect of:

- violating the disabled person's dignity, or
- creating an intimidating, hostile, degrading, humiliating or offensive environment for him.

4.37 **[s 3B(2) and s 31AC(2)]** If the conduct in question was engaged in with the intention that it should have either of these effects, then it amounts to harassment irrespective of its actual effect on the disabled person. In the absence of such intention, however, the conduct will only amount to harassment if it should reasonably be considered as having either of these effects. Regard must be had to all the circumstances in order to determine whether this is the case. Those circumstances include, in particular, the perception of the disabled person.

An assessor from a motor mechanics qualifications body is judging a number of practical tasks performed in the workplace by a trainee motor mechanic who has a speech impairment. The assessor imitates the mechanic's manner of speech and makes offensive remarks about him to the trainee's line manager. This is harassment, whether or not the disabled man was present when the comments were made, because they were made with the intention of humiliating him.

At an awards ceremony of a trade organisation, a member of the organisation makes a speech including derogatory remarks about people with schizophrenia. A woman with schizophrenia who is a member of the trade organisation and who is present in the audience complains about the speech but is told that the comments were made as a joke and that the speaker did not have any intention of causing offence. Nevertheless the experience of the woman is likely to amount to harassment because the comments made by the speaker could reasonably be considered as having either of the effects mentioned above.

A trade union member with HIV uses another member's mug at a union meeting. The other member then makes a point of being seen washing the mug with bleach, which is not something she would do if anyone else used her mug. She also makes offensive comments about having her mug used by someone with HIV. This is likely to amount to harassment.

A trade union branch representative circulates a joke about people with autism by email to branch members. A member with autism receives the email and finds the joke offensive. This is likely to amount to harassment.

During the course of an examination a teacher invigilating the examination – who is acting as an agent of the general qualifications body – makes a disabled candidate who is incontinent explain, in front of his colleagues and peers, why he needs to use the toilet. This is likely to amount to harassment.

A general qualifications body offers resources and guidance for exam officers on exam administration. The materials suggest that candidates with dyslexia may be more likely to cheat and abuse the reasonable adjustments that they are offered. This is harassment, whether or not the disabled person was present when the written comments were made, because they were made with the intention of humiliating people with dyslexia.

WHAT DOES THE ACT SAY ABOUT STATUTORY OBLIGATIONS?

4.38 **[s 59]** Nothing is made unlawful by the Act if it is required by an express statutory obligation. However, it is only in cases where a statutory obligation is specific in its requirements, leaving a trade organisation, qualifications body or general qualifications body with no choice other than to act in a particular way that the provisions of the Act may be overridden. The provision in section 59 of the Act is thus of narrow application, and it is likely to permit disability discrimination only in rare circumstances.

WHAT EVIDENCE IS NEEDED TO PROVE THAT DISCRIMINATION OR HARASSMENT HAS OCCURRED?

4.39 A person who brings a claim for unlawful discrimination or harassment must show that discrimination or harassment has occurred. He must prove this on the balance of probabilities in order to succeed with a claim.

4.40 **[s 17A(1C), s 31ADA(2) and Reg 3 of SI 2007/2405]** However, in relation to trade organisations, qualifications bodies and general qualifications bodies, the Act says that, when such a claim is heard by a tribunal or court, the tribunal or court must uphold the claim if:

- the claimant/pursuer proves facts from which the tribunal or court could conclude in the absence of an adequate explanation that the person against whom the claim is made (the respondent or defendant/defender) has acted unlawfully, and
- the respondent/defendant/defender fails to prove that he did not act in that way.

A disabled man with autism is the only trade union branch member in the workplace not to be sent an email inviting him to stand for election as a branch representative. Unless the union demonstrates a non-discriminatory reason for this omission, unlawful discrimination will be inferred in these circumstances.

4.41 Consequently, where a disabled person is able to prove on the balance of probabilities facts from which an inference of unlawful discrimination or harassment could be drawn, the burden of proof shifts to the respondent/defendant/defender, who must then show that it is more likely than not that its conduct was not unlawful. This principle applies to allegations in respect of all forms of discrimination, including victimisation, and to harassment. Its practical effect in relation to the three principal forms of disability discrimination can be summarised as follows:

- To prove an allegation of **direct discrimination**, a claimant/pursuer must prove facts from which it could be inferred in the absence of an adequate explanation that he has been treated less favourably on the ground of his disability than an appropriate comparator has been, or would be, treated. If the claimant/pursuer does this, the claim will succeed unless the respondent/defendant/defender can show that disability was not any part of the reason for the treatment in question.
- To prove an allegation that there has been a **failure to comply with a duty to make reasonable adjustments**, a claimant/pursuer must prove facts from which it could be inferred in the absence of an adequate explanation that such a duty has arisen, and that it has been breached. If the claimant/pursuer does this, the claim will succeed unless the respondent/defendant/defender can show that it did not fail to comply with its duty in this regard.
- To prove an allegation of **disability-related discrimination**, a claimant/ pursuer must prove facts from which it could be inferred in the absence of an adequate explanation that, for a reason relating to his disability, he has been treated less favourably than a person to whom that reason does not apply has been, or would be, treated. If the claimant/pursuer does this, the burden of proof shifts, and it is for the respondent/defendant/defender to show that the claimant has not received less favourable treatment for a disability related reason. Even if the respondent/defendant/defender cannot show this, however, the claim will not succeed if the respondent/defendant/defender shows that the treatment was justified.

4.42 [s 56] The Act provides a means by which a disabled person can seek evidence about whether he has been discriminated against, or subjected to harassment, under Part 2. However, no equivalent procedure exists in relation to Part 4 in respect of general qualifications bodies. Where such an opportunity to seek evidence arises under the Act, a person may do this by using a questionnaire to obtain further information from a person he thinks has acted unlawfully in relation to him (see paragraph 11.5). If there has been a failure to provide a satisfactory response to questions asked by the disabled person in this way, inferences may be drawn from that failure.

4.43 In addition, the fact that there has been a failure to comply with a relevant provision of the Code must be taken into account by a court or tribunal, where it considers it relevant, in determining whether there has been discrimination or harassment (see paragraph 1.7).

5. WHAT IS THE DUTY TO MAKE REASONABLE ADJUSTMENTS?

INTRODUCTION

[4.128]
5.1 One of the ways in which discrimination occurs under Part 2 or Part 4 of the Act is when a trade organisation, qualifications body or a general qualifications body fails to comply with a duty imposed on it to make 'reasonable adjustments' in relation to the disabled person. This chapter examines the circumstances in which a duty to make reasonable adjustments arises and outlines what a trade organisation, qualifications body or general qualifications body needs to do in order to discharge such a duty.

WHEN DOES THE DUTY TO MAKE REASONABLE ADJUSTMENTS ARISE?

5.2 [s 14(1), s 14B(1), s 31AD(1) and (3)] Subject to what is said in paragraph 5.7 about competence standards, the duty to make reasonable adjustments arises where a provision, criterion or practice applied by or on behalf of a trade organisation, qualifications body or general qualifications body, or any physical feature of premises which it occupies, places a disabled person at a substantial disadvantage compared with people who are not disabled. The trade organisation, qualifications body or general qualifications body has to take such steps as it is reasonable for it to have to take in all the circumstances to prevent that disadvantage – in other words it has to make a 'reasonable adjustment'. Where the duty arises, an organisation or body cannot justify a failure to make a reasonable adjustment.

> A trade organisation for hairdressers arranges a one-day training course in colouring techniques for its members. A disabled member wishes to attend this course, but the programme for the day does not allow him sufficient rest breaks. He would therefore be at a substantial disadvantage because of his disability. The trade organisation rearranges the programme for the day to include

more breaks. This is likely to be a reasonable adjustment for it to make.

A trade organisation for carpenters has an application form with several paragraphs in small print. A partially sighted carpenter cannot read the whole form and is therefore at a substantial disadvantage because he cannot fill it in correctly. The trade organisation provides him with an application form in large print. This is likely to be a reasonable adjustment for it to make.

A qualifications body holds an awards ceremony at its headquarters. A newly qualified woman who uses a wheelchair wants to attend the ceremony but is at a substantial disadvantage because the stage where the awards are presented is only accessible by stairs. The qualifications body provides a ramp up to the stage. This is likely to be a reasonable adjustment for the qualifications body to make.

A disabled woman who is unable to use public transport wishes to attend a trade fair in central London, organised by a trade organisation of which she is a member. There is very little parking in the area and the information brochure suggests that 'visitors to the trade fair are advised to come by public transport'. The woman asks the trade organisation if it can arrange a parking space and it does so. This is likely to be a reasonable adjustment for the trade organisation to make.

A candidate for a general qualification with a visual impairment requests a range of reasonable adjustments to take a written test. In preparation for a test, the exams officer at the centre discusses with the candidate his requirements for the test in advance and then discusses these requirements with the general qualifications body. When he sits the paper, he is provided with a large print paper, additional time, a desk lamp and a rest break. These are likely to be reasonable adjustments.

A general qualifications body allows a person with Chronic Fatigue Syndrome who, due to effects of her impairment, is unable to travel to an examination venue to take the examination (which is properly invigilated by a teacher from her college) at her home. She is also granted extra time to undertake the examination. These are likely to be reasonable adjustments for the general qualifications body to make.

5.3 It does not matter if a disabled person cannot point to an actual nondisabled person compared with whom he is at a substantial disadvantage. The fact that a non-disabled person, or even another disabled person, would not be substantially disadvantaged by the provision, criterion or practice or by the physical feature in question is irrelevant. The duty is owed specifically to the individual disabled person.

WHICH DISABLED PEOPLE DOES THE DUTY PROTECT?

5.4 In order to avoid discrimination, it is prudent not to attempt to make a fine judgement as to whether a particular individual falls within the statutory definition of disability, but to focus instead on meeting the needs of each individual with whom a trade organisation, qualifications body or general qualifications body has dealings. However, the Act says that the duties are owed to the following people:

- **[s 14(2)]** disabled people who are members of trade organisations, or who are applicants, or potential applicants, for membership of such organisations, and
- **[s 14B(2)]** disabled people who are holders of professional or trade qualifications, or who are applicants, or potential applicants, for such qualifications.
- **[s 31AD(2) and (3)]** disabled people who are holders of general qualifications, or who are applicants, or potential applicants, for such qualifications.

5.5 The extent of the duty to make reasonable adjustments depends on the circumstances of the disabled person in question. For example, more extensive duties are owed to members of trade organisations and holders of professional or trade qualifications than to people who are merely thinking about applying. However, for general qualifications bodies more extensive duties are owed to people seeking to enter for relevant general qualifications and candidates taking examinations and assessments potentially leading to such qualifications, than to people who already hold such qualifications. More extensive duties are also owed to current members and qualification holders than to past members or to people who no longer hold a qualification. The extent to which trade organisations, qualifications bodies and general qualifications bodies have knowledge of relevant circumstances is also a factor. These issues are explained in more detail in Chapters 7, 8 and 9.

WHAT ARE 'PROVISIONS, CRITERIA AND PRACTICES'?

5.6 [s 18D(2) and s 31AD(5)] Provisions, criteria and practices include arrangements, for example for determining who to accept as a member of a trade organisation, or upon whom to confer a general, professional or trade qualification, as well as the rules of membership of an organisation. The duty to make reasonable adjustments applies, for example, to selection and interview procedures for trade organisations and to examination and assessment procedures used by qualifications bodies and general qualifications bodies. In addition, the duty applies to premises used for such procedures.

A trade union requires its members to be either employed or seeking employment in a specific sector. A woman with a spinal injury as a result of an accident is not in work or looking for work, because she is adjusting to her newly acquired disability, but nevertheless would like to remain a member of the union, as it would help her to maintain contact with the sector in which she worked prior to her accident. The union agrees that she can retain her membership. This is likely to be a reasonable adjustment for the trade union to make to a criterion (in this case a membership criterion).

A general qualifications body receives an application from a centre wishing to enter disabled candidates for an examination which, if successfully undertaken, will lead to a relevant general qualification. A candidate with a physical impairment affecting her ability to write cannot complete the written examination papers. The general qualifications body allows the centre to provide a scribe for this individual. This is likely to be a reasonable adjustment for the general qualifications body to make.

A general qualifications body regularly publishes a list of the approved access arrangements. In the light of comments from candidates, centres and organisations representing disabled people, it regularly reviews these arrangements to ensure that the criteria set out are fit for purpose. It also ensures that there are arrangements in place for requests for reasonable adjustments that are not covered in the guidance on access arrangements.

5.7 [s 14B(1) and s 31AD(1) and (2) and s 31AB(9)] It should be noted that, in relation to both qualifications bodies and general qualifications bodies, there is no duty to make any adjustment to a provision, criterion or practice of a kind which the Act defines as a 'competence standard'. What the Act says about competence standards is considered in more detail in respect of qualifications bodies in paragraphs 8.27 to 8.41 and in respect of general qualifications bodies in paragraphs 9.57 to 9.82.

WHAT IS A 'PHYSICAL FEATURE'?

5.8 [s 18D(2) and Reg 4 of SI 2007/1764] The Act says that the following are to be treated as a physical feature:

- any feature arising from the design or construction of a building on the premises occupied by the trade organisation, qualifications body
- or general qualifications body any feature on the premises of any approach to, exit from, or access to such a building
- any fixtures, fittings, furnishings, furniture, equipment or materials in or on the premises, and
- any other physical element or quality of any land comprised in the premises occupied by the trade organisation, qualifications body or general qualifications body.

All these features are covered, whether temporary or permanent. Considerations which need to be taken into account when making adjustments to premises are explained in Chapter 10.

> The design of a professional association's training facility makes it difficult for a person with a visual impairment to find his way around, as there are glass doors, glass panels and reflecting surfaces. That is a substantial disadvantage caused by the physical features of the professional association's premises.

5.9 Physical features will include steps, stairways, kerbs, exterior surfaces and paving, parking areas, building entrances and exits (including emergency escape routes), internal and external doors, gates, toilet and washing facilities, lighting and ventilation, lifts and escalators, floor coverings, signs, furniture, and temporary or movable items. This is not an exhaustive list.

WHAT DISADVANTAGES GIVE RISE TO THE DUTY?

5.10 The Act says that only substantial disadvantages give rise to the duty. Substantial disadvantages are those which are not minor or trivial. Whether or not such a disadvantage exists in a particular case is a question of fact. What matters is not that a provision, criterion or practice or a physical feature is capable of causing a substantial disadvantage to the disabled person in question, but that it actually has (or would have) this effect on him.

IS KNOWLEDGE OF THE DISABILITY A FACTOR?

5.11 **[s 14(3) and s 14B(3) and s 31AD(4)]** Although (as explained in paragraphs 4.10 and 4.29) less favourable treatment can occur even if a trade organisation, qualifications body or general qualifications body does not know that the person is disabled, the organisation or body only has a duty to make an adjustment if it knows, or could reasonably be expected to know, that the person has a disability and is likely to be placed at a substantial disadvantage. A trade organisation, qualifications body or general qualifications body must, however, do all it can reasonably be expected to do to find out whether this is the case. More information is given in Chapters 7, 8 and 9 about the relationship between the knowledge of a trade organisation, qualifications body or general qualifications body and its duties under the Act.

WHAT ADJUSTMENTS MIGHT HAVE TO BE MADE?

5.12 **[s 18B(2)]** Part 2 of the Act gives a number of examples of adjustments, or 'steps', which trade organisations and qualifications bodies may have to take, if it is reasonable for them to have to do so (see paragraphs 5.14 to 5.25). Many of these examples may also be relevant to general qualifications bodies and indicative of the type of adjustments that they may have to think about, even though no equivalent examples are listed in Chapter 2A of Part 4 of the Act. Any necessary adjustments should be implemented in a timely fashion, and it may also be necessary to make more than one adjustment. It is advisable for the appropriate body to agree any proposed adjustments with the disabled person in question before they are made. The Act does not give an exhaustive list of the steps which may have to be taken to discharge the duty. Not all of the steps listed in the Act are likely to be relevant to trade organisations and qualifications bodies. By the same token, steps other than those listed, or a combination of steps, will sometimes have to be taken. However, the steps in the Act which it is likely to be reasonable for trade organisations or qualifications bodies to have to take are:

- making adjustments to premises which they occupy

> A trade organisation or qualifications body might have to make structural or other physical changes such as: widening a doorway, providing a ramp or moving furniture for a wheelchair user; relocating light switches, door handles or shelves for someone who has difficulty in reaching; providing appropriate contrast in décor to help the safe mobility of a visually impaired person.

- giving, or arranging for, training or mentoring (whether for the disabled person or any other person)

> This could be training in the use of particular pieces of equipment which the disabled person uses while participating in activities as a benefit of their membership of the trade organisation, or training which any member can take part in but which needs altering for the disabled person because of their disability. For example, all members might have the opportunity to be trained to use the trade organisation's library computer system but the trade organisation might have to

provide longer or different training for a disabled person.

A trade union provides training for a branch in conducting meetings in a way that enables a deaf branch member to participate.

A disabled member of a professional association wishes to become a fellow of the organisation but has concerns about the requirement to pass an assessment – an oral presentation to fellows of the association with questions and answers – as she has a speech impairment. The professional association arranges for her to see a mentor (in this case a disabled fellow of the same organisation) to support her in achieving fellowship status.

- acquiring or modifying equipment

A trade organisation or qualifications body might have to arrange to provide, or consent to the provision of special equipment for a disabled person to enable him to take part in activities or benefit from services provided by the organisation or body. There is no requirement to provide or modify equipment for personal purposes unconnected with the person's dealings with the trade organisation or qualifications body, for example to provide a wheelchair if a person needs one in any event but does not have one.

- modifying instructions or reference manuals

The way instructions are normally given might need to be revised when telling a disabled person how to do a task. The format of instructions or reference manuals may need to be modified (eg produced in Braille or on audio tape) and instructions for people with learning disabilities may need to be conveyed orally with individual demonstration.

- modifying procedures for testing or assessment

This could involve ensuring that particular testing methods do not adversely affect particular disabled people. For example, a person with restricted manual dexterity might be disadvantaged by a hand written test and would need to have an alternative arrangement such as an oral test or to be permitted to use a computer with voice recognition software. More information about how the Act affects testing and examinations is set out in Chapters 8 and 9.

- providing a reader or interpreter

This could involve the provision of a sign language interpreter for meetings, talks or training; or could involve provision of a reader for a visually impaired person.

- providing supervision or other support

This could involve the provision of a support worker to enable a disabled person to participate in a conference, meeting, training session, interview, examination, assessment or social event; or extra support for a disabled trade union representative to enable that person to fulfil their role on an on going basis.

5.13 As mentioned above, it may be reasonable for a trade organisation, qualifications body or general qualifications body to take steps which are not given as examples in the Act. Such steps might include:

- arranging or consenting to a proper assessment of what reasonable adjustments may be required
- modifying the arrangements for meetings, and
- making adjustments to the way in which information is provided.

Further examples of the way in which reasonable adjustments work in practice are given in Chapters 7, 8 and 9.

WHEN IS IT 'REASONABLE' FOR A TRADE ORGANISATION, QUALIFICATIONS BODY OR GENERAL QUALIFICATIONS BODY TO HAVE TO MAKE ADJUSTMENTS?

5.14 Whether it is reasonable for a trade organisation, qualifications body or general qualifications body to make any particular adjustment will depend on a number of things, such as its cost and effectiveness. However, if an adjustment is one which it is reasonable to make, then the organisation or body must do so. Where a disabled person is placed at a substantial disadvantage by a provision, criterion or practice of the organisation or body, or by a physical feature of the premises it occupies, the organisation or body must consider whether any reasonable adjustments can be made to overcome that disadvantage. There is no onus on the disabled person to suggest what adjustments should be made but, where the disabled person does so, the organisation or body must consider whether such adjustments would help overcome the disadvantage, and whether they are reasonable.

5.15 Nevertheless, an organisation or body may not know enough about the disabled person to determine what adjustments are appropriate. It is therefore good practice to ask a disabled person whether he requires any adjustments to be made. It is also a good idea for a disabled person to make suggestions about adjustments which would be helpful. Schools and colleges may request information about the needs of disabled candidates and should seek their permission to pass this information on to the general qualifications body.

5.16 Effective and practicable adjustments for disabled people often involve little or no cost or disruption and are therefore very likely to be reasonable for a trade organisation, qualifications body or general qualifications body to have to make. Many adjustments do not involve making physical changes to premises. However, where such changes do need to be made, trade organisations, qualifications bodies and general qualifications bodies may need to take account of the considerations explained in Chapter 10, which deals with issues about making alterations to premises.

> A qualifications body allows a student to have extra time to take a written test because the student has dyslexia. This adjustment only involves the cost of paying an invigilator for the extra time in question, and is likely to be a reasonable one to make.

> A trade union member with a hearing impairment requests a seat at the front of the conference hall, so that she can lip read. This is likely to be a reasonable adjustment for the trade union to make and would involve no additional cost and no disruption to the union.

> A member of a professional association attending a meeting at that association asks for a mug half full of tea, rather than a china tea cup and saucer, because she has a hand tremor due to a neurological condition. This would involve very little cost or disruption to the professional association and is likely to be a reasonable adjustment to make.

5.17 **[SI 1999/3242]** If making a particular adjustment would increase the risks to the health and safety of any person (including the disabled person in question) then this is a relevant factor in deciding whether it is reasonable to make that adjustment. Suitable and sufficient risk assessments, such as those carried out for the purposes of the Management of Health and Safety at Work Regulations 999, should be used to help determine whether such risks are likely to arise.

5.18 **[s 18B(1)]** Part 2 of the Act lists a number of factors which may, in particular, have a bearing on whether it will be reasonable to have to make a particular adjustment. These factors make a useful checklist, particularly when considering more substantial adjustments. Many of these factors may also be relevant to general qualifications bodies when they consider reasonableness of adjustments, even though no equivalent factors are listed in Chapter 2A of Part 4 of the Act. The effectiveness and practicability of a particular adjustment might be considered first. If it is practicable and effective, the financial aspects might be looked at as a whole – the cost of the adjustment and resources available to fund it. Other factors might also have a bearing. The factors in the Act include the following:

The effectiveness of the step in preventing the disadvantage

5.19 It is unlikely to be reasonable to have to make an adjustment involving little benefit to the disabled person. However, such an adjustment may be one of several adjustments which, when looked at together, would be effective and, in that case, it is likely to be reasonable to have to make it.

> A candidate for a general qualification, who has a condition that causes fatigue (ME), makes enquiries with the exams centre as to what adjustments are available for her during examinations. One of the adjustments she needs is ensuring that non-fluorescent lighting is used in the exams hall. However, there is little benefit in having this or additional time on its own, but if these adjustments are provided together with a reader, the measures taken as a whole could be suitable to overcome the particular disadvantages that she experiences during examinations.

The practicability of the step

5.20 It is more likely to be reasonable to have to take a step which is easy to take than one which is difficult. In some circumstances it may be reasonable to have to take a step, even though it is difficult.

> A trade organisation is asked by a woman with a severe allergy to many commonly found substances (such as latex) to ensure that a venue for a lecture is free of all these substances. This is likely to be an impractical step to take. However, it may instead be reasonable for the trade organisation to provide the woman with a video of the lecture.

> A candidate for a GCSE qualification with a practical element requires treatment at a hospital during the exam period and asks to take the examination at the hospital. It would be impracticable to do this though, and it would also be impracticable to rearrange the timetabling of the exams, so the general qualifications body arranges for the candidate to sit the exams at a different centre nearer to the hospital.

The financial and other costs of the adjustment and the extent of any disruption caused

5.21 If an adjustment costs little or nothing and is not disruptive, it would be reasonable unless some other factor (such as practicability or effectiveness) made it unreasonable. It may, of course, be reasonable to have to make more expensive adjustments in some circumstances. The costs to be taken into account include those for staff and other resources. The significance of the cost of a step may depend in part on what the trade organisation, qualifications body or general qualifications body might otherwise spend in the circumstances. In assessing the likely costs of making an adjustment, the availability of external funding should be taken into account.

The extent of the financial or other resources available to the trade organisation, qualifications body or general qualifications body

5.22 It is more likely to be reasonable for a trade organisation, qualifications body or general qualifications body with substantial financial resources to have to make an adjustment with a significant cost, than for one with fewer resources. The resources in practice available to the organisation or body as a whole should be taken into account as well as other calls on those resources. It is good practice for organisations and bodies to have a specific budget for reasonable adjustments – but limitations on the size of any such budget will not affect the existence of the duties owed to disabled people. The reasonableness of an adjustment will depend not only on the resources in practice available for the adjustment but also on all other relevant factors (such as effectiveness and practicability).

> A large professional association with 300,000 members and considerable funds would be expected to make more substantial changes to its premises, in order to make them accessible for a member, than would a small trade organisation with only fifty members and very limited funds.

> A union branch is sending a disabled representative to a regional three-day conference. The disabled person, who has cerebral palsy, requires a support worker to accompany her to the

conference. Although the cost of providing this support would be relatively high compared to the resources available to the branch, the cost is unlikely to be seen as unreasonably high when assessed against the overall funds of the union.

The availability of financial or other assistance to help make an adjustment

5.23 The availability of outside help may well be a relevant factor. This help may be financial or practical. Disability organisations may be able to provide further information or assistance.

5.24 A disabled person is not required to contribute to the cost of a reasonable adjustment. However, if a disabled person has a particular piece of special or adapted equipment which he is prepared to use, this might make it reasonable for a trade organisation, qualifications body or general qualifications body to have to take some other step (as well as allowing the use of the equipment).

A blind person wishes to go to an event organised by a trade organisation of which she is a member. She wishes to take notes at this event using a laptop computer. The trade organisation provides her with a table to put the computer on while she takes notes. This is likely to be a reasonable adjustment for the organisation to make.

The nature of the activities of the organisation or body, and the size of its undertaking

5.25 The size of an organisation or body's undertaking and the nature of its activities may be relevant in determining the reasonableness of a particular step.

CAN FAILURE TO MAKE A REASONABLE ADJUSTMENT EVER BE JUSTIFIED?

5.26 **[s 3A(2) and s 31AB(5)]** The Act does not permit a trade organisation, qualifications body or general qualifications body to justify a failure to comply with a duty to make a reasonable adjustment. For trade organisations this is a change in the law.

5.27 Clearly, however, an organisation or body will only breach such a duty if the adjustment in question is one which it is reasonable for it to have to make. So, where the duty applies, it is the question of 'reasonableness' which alone determines whether the adjustment has to be made.

A woman with severe back pain wishes to attend a trade union conference. The only adjustment she needs is for a space to be made available for her to set up a portable couch on which she can lie down during the conference proceedings. This is likely to be a reasonable adjustment for the trade union to make. It involves no cost and little disruption for the union. Nevertheless, the union does not allow this as it says 'nobody has ever needed this adjustment before and there may be health and safety implications'. The trade union will be acting unlawfully.

6. JUSTIFICATION

INTRODUCTION

[4.129]
6.1 Most conduct which is potentially unlawful under Part 2 of the Act and Part 4 of the Act (in respect of most post-16 education and general qualifications bodies) cannot be justified. Conduct which amounts to:

- direct discrimination
- failure to comply with a duty to make a reasonable adjustment
- victimisation
- harassment
- instructions or pressure to discriminate, or
- aiding an unlawful act

is unlawful irrespective of the reason or motive for it.

WHEN DOES THE ACT PERMIT JUSTIFICATION?

6.2 Paragraph 4.25 explains that one of the forms of discrimination which is unlawful under Part 2 and Chapter 2A of Part 4 is disability-related discrimination. However, the conduct of a trade organisation, qualifications body or a general qualifications body towards a disabled person does not amount to disability-related discrimination if it can be justified. This chapter explains the limited circumstances in which this may happen.

6.3 **[s 3A(3) and (4), s 31AB(3) and (7)]** Where less favourable treatment of a disabled person is capable of being justified (that is, where it is not direct discrimination), the Act says that it will, in fact, be justified if, but only if, the reason for the treatment is both material to the circumstances of the particular case and substantial. This is an objective test. 'Material' means that there must be a reasonably strong connection between the reason given for the treatment and the circumstances of the particular case. 'Substantial' means, in the context of justification, that the reason must carry real weight and be of substance.

Competence standards

6.4 [s 14A(3) and s 31AB(4) and s 31AB(9)] This general principle is subject to one exception – which relates to the application of a 'competence standard' to a disabled person by a qualifications body and general qualifications body. The Act says that less favourable treatment of a disabled person in this regard will be justified only if the qualifications body or general qualifications body can show that the standard is (or would be) applied equally to people who do not have the disabled person's disability, and that its application is a proportionate means of achieving a legitimate aim. What the Act says about competence standards is considered in more detail in paragraphs 8.27 to 8.4 and paragraphs 9.57 to 9.82.

Justification and reasonable adjustments

6.5 In certain circumstances, the existence of a material and substantial reason for less favourable treatment is not enough to justify that treatment. This is the case where a trade organisation, qualifications body or general qualifications body is also under a duty to make reasonable adjustments in relation to the disabled person but fails to comply with that duty.

6.6 [s 3A(6) and s 31AB(5)] In those circumstances, it is necessary to consider not only whether there is a material and substantial reason for the less favourable treatment, but also whether the treatment would still have been justified even if the organisation or body had complied with its duty to make reasonable adjustments. In effect, it is necessary to ask the question 'would a reasonable adjustment have made any difference?' If a reasonable adjustment would have made a difference to the reason that is being used to justify the treatment, then the less favourable treatment cannot be justified.

6.7 In relation to disability-related discrimination, the fact that a trade organisation, qualifications body or general qualifications body has failed to comply with a duty to make a reasonable adjustment means that the sequence of events for justifying disability-related less favourable treatment is as follows:

- The disabled person proves facts from which it could be inferred in the absence of an adequate explanation that:
  - (a) for a reason related to his disability, he has been treated less favourably than a person to whom that reason does not apply has been, or would be, treated, and
  - (b) a duty to make a reasonable adjustment has arisen in respect of him and the organisation or body has failed to comply with it.
- The trade organisation, qualifications body or general qualifications body will be found to have discriminated unless it proves that:
  - (a) the reason for the treatment is both material to the circumstances of the particular case and substantial, and
  - (b) the reason would still have applied if the reasonable adjustment had been made.

CAN HEALTH AND SAFETY CONCERNS JUSTIFY LESS FAVOURABLE TREATMENT?

6.8 Stereotypical assumptions about the health and safety implications of disability should be avoided, both in general terms and in relation to particular types of disability. Indeed, less favourable treatment which is based on such assumptions may itself amount to direct discrimination – which is incapable of justification (see paragraph 4.4). The fact that a person has a disability does not necessarily mean that he represents an additional risk to health and safety.

> A person with bi-polar affective disorder applies for registration as a health professional with a professional association. The association refuses to register her, simply on the basis that she has mentioned her disability on a health questionnaire. The association makes an assumption that her disability would present a health and safety risk, without making any attempt to find out whether or how it would present such a risk, or indeed whether she had made a recovery. This is likely to be direct discrimination and therefore likely to be unlawful.

> A young person with cerebral palsy is undertaking a Scottish Higher general qualification in chemistry. The general qualifications body refuses his application for entry for the general qualification because they assume that his cerebral palsy would present a health and safety risk,

without making any attempt to find out whether there are, in fact, any health and safety risks. This is likely to be direct discrimination and, therefore, likely to be unlawful.

6.9 Genuine concerns about the health and safety of anybody (including a disabled person) may be relevant when seeking to establish that disability related less favourable treatment of a disabled person is justified. However, it is important to remember that health and safety legislation does not require the removal of all conceivable risk but that risk is properly appreciated, understood and managed. Further information can be obtained from the Health and Safety Executive (see Appendix B for details).

6.10 Paragraphs 6.11 to 6.15 examine the circumstances in which concerns about health and safety may justify less favourable treatment of a disabled person, and this is followed by a consideration of the relevance of medical information in this context. As noted in paragraph 6.4, however, the basis upon which a qualifications body may justify less favourable treatment of a disabled person in the application of a competence standard differs from that which usually applies under the Act. The following principles do not have the same relevance to justification in those circumstances, but regard should instead be had to paragraphs 8.35 to 8.40 (in respect of qualifications bodies) and paragraphs 9.67 to 9.73 (in respect of general qualifications bodies).

6.11 It is the trade organisation, qualifications body or general qualifications body which must decide what action to take, or to decide what advice to give an examination centre, in response to concerns about health and safety in relation to the examination. However, leaving aside the question of competence standards, it is prudent for a trade organisation, qualifications body or general qualifications body to have, or arrange for, a risk assessment to be carried out by a suitably qualified person in circumstances where it has reason to think that the effects of a person's disability may give rise to an issue about health and safety. This is because:

- If a trade organisation, qualifications body or general qualifications body treats a disabled person less favourably merely on the basis of generalised assumptions about the health and safety implications of having a disability, such treatment may itself amount to direct discrimination – which is incapable of justification.

A qualifications body refuses to issue a certificate to operate heavy machinery to a man with epilepsy. No attempt is made to find out the actual circumstances of the individual through a risk assessment. The qualifications body merely makes an assumption that it would be a health and safety risk to let someone with epilepsy operate heavy machinery. This is likely to be direct discrimination and therefore to be unlawful.

- Even where there is no direct discrimination, an organisation or body which treats a disabled person less favourably without having a suitable and sufficient risk assessment carried out is unlikely to be able to show that its concerns about health and safety justify the less favourable treatment.

6.12 Nevertheless, a trade organisation, qualifications body or general qualifications body should not subject a disabled person to a risk assessment if this is not merited by the particular circumstances of the case.

A man who has diabetes applies to go on a residential training course in accounting provided by a professional association of which he is a member. The man's condition is stable and he has successfully managed it for many years. Nevertheless, the association says that it has health and safety concerns; that it wants to undertake a risk assessment; and that it needs further medical evidence from the man's doctor. This is likely to be unlawful, as the circumstances of the case do not indicate that there would be any health and safety risk.

6.13 A risk assessment must be suitable and sufficient. It should identify the risks associated with a particular activity, taking account of any reasonable adjustments put in place for the disabled person, and should be specific for the individual carrying out a particular task. It is therefore unlikely that a trade organisation, qualifications body or general qualifications body which has a **general** policy of treating people with certain disabilities (such as epilepsy, diabetes or mental health problems) less favourably than other people will be able to justify doing so – even if that policy is in accordance with the advice of an occupational health adviser.

6.14 A 'blanket' policy of this nature will usually be unlawful. This is because it is likely to amount to direct discrimination (which cannot ever be justified) or to disability-related less favourable treatment which is not justifiable in the circumstances – ie disability-related discrimination.

> A qualifications body for social care professionals has a policy of asking applicants for registration to fill out a health questionnaire. Any applicant who states that they have had treatment for a mental health problem is refused registration without any investigation into their individual circumstances. The qualifications body is applying a blanket policy, which is likely to amount to direct discrimination

> A general qualifications body issues guidance that states that the qualification in ICT which they offer will be unsuitable to any candidate with a visual impairment and that people with visual impairments should not apply for the course. The general qualifications body is applying a blanket policy, which is likely to amount to direct discrimination.

6.15 Reasonable adjustments made by a trade organisation, qualifications body or general qualifications body may remove or reduce health and safety risks related to a person's disability. A suitable and sufficient assessment of such risks therefore needs to take account of the impact which making any reasonable adjustments would have. If a risk assessment is not conducted on this basis, then an organisation or body is unlikely to be able to show that its concerns about health and safety justify less favourable treatment of the disabled person.

CAN MEDICAL INFORMATION JUSTIFY LESS FAVOURABLE TREATMENT?

6.16 Consideration of medical information (such as a doctor's report or the answers to a medical questionnaire) is likely to form part of an assessment of health and safety risks. In most cases, however, having a disability does not adversely affect a person's general health. In other cases, its effect on a person's health may fluctuate. Although medical information about a disability may justify an adverse decision, it will not do so if there is no effect on the person's relevant skills and abilities (or if any effect is less than substantial), no matter how great the effects of the disability are in other ways. Indeed, less favourable treatment of a disabled person in a case where his disability has no effect on his relevant skills and abilities may well amount to direct discrimination – which is incapable of being justified.

6.17 In addition, where medical information is available, trade organisations, qualifications bodies and general qualifications bodies must weigh it up in the context of the relevant circumstances, and the capabilities of the individual. An organisation or body should also consider whether reasonable adjustments could be made in order to overcome any problems which may have been identified as a result of the medical information. It should not be taken for granted that the person who provides the medical information will be aware that trade organisations, qualifications bodies and general qualifications bodies have a duty to make reasonable adjustments, or what these adjustments might be. It is good practice, therefore, to ensure that medical advisers are made aware of these matters. Information provided by a medical adviser should only be relied on if the adviser has the appropriate knowledge and expertise.

6.18 In any event, although medical evidence may generally be considered as an 'expert contribution', it should not ordinarily be the sole factor influencing a decision by a trade organisation, qualifications body or general qualifications body. The views of the disabled person (about his/her own capabilities and possible adjustments) should also be sought. It may also be possible to seek help from disability organisations. Ultimately, it is for the trade organisation, qualifications body or general qualifications body – and not the medical adviser – to take decisions.

7. DISCRIMINATION BY TRADE ORGANISATIONS

INTRODUCTION

[4.130]

7.1 Chapter 3 explains what the Act means by 'trade organisation', and that the Act makes it unlawful for a trade organisation to discriminate against a disabled person who is a member of the organisation or an applicant for membership. Chapter 3 also explains that the Act says it is unlawful for a trade organisation to subject such a person to harassment, or to victimise any person – whether disabled or not.

7.2 This chapter looks at discrimination by trade organisations in more detail. In order to do so (and after considering an important point about the relationship of trade organisations to qualifications bodies), it is necessary to look at the different aspects of a trade organisation's functions, from those which relate to becoming a member of the organisation to those which concern the benefits of membership once achieved. It is also necessary to consider issues relating to the variation and withdrawal of membership.

TRADE ORGANISATIONS AS QUALIFICATIONS BODIES

7.3 It has already been noted (at paragraph 3.11) that some trade organisations confer professional or trade qualifications and that, as a consequence, such organisations can be subject to the Act's provisions about trade organisations or, depending upon the context, to those about qualifications bodies.

7.4 However, it should also be noted that membership of certain trade organisations (for example, the Institute of Linguists or the Chartered Institute of Personnel and Development) itself amounts to a professional or trade qualification for the reasons explained at paragraph 8.6. Where this is the case, decisions about granting, varying or withdrawing membership of the trade organisation will also be subject to the rules about conferring professional or trade qualifications. This fact is likely to be of particular significance where such decisions result from the application of a 'competence standard' (see paragraphs 8.27 to 8.41).

BECOMING A MEMBER

What does the Act say?

7.5 **[s 13(1)]** The Act says that it is unlawful for a trade organisation to discriminate against a disabled person:

- in the arrangements it makes for the purpose of determining who should be offered membership of the organisation

> A trade organisation asks a woman with a learning disability to take an additional test before allowing her membership, even though she already meets the entry criteria for that organisation. This is likely to be unlawful.

- in the terms on which it is prepared to admit him to membership

> A trade organisation for journalists asks a partially sighted woman to pay an extra fee for membership because of the cost of putting information onto audio tape. This is likely to be unlawful.

- by refusing to accept, or deliberately not accepting, his application for membership.

> A nursing organisation refuses to admit a woman with a history of mental health problems – without further enquiry. This is likely to be unlawful.

7.6 **[s 16B]** As explained at paragraphs 3.22 to 3.25, the Act also makes it unlawful in certain circumstances to publish a discriminatory advertisement for membership of a trade organisation.

What amounts to direct discrimination?

7.7 **[s 3A(5)]** A trade organisation may wish to differentiate between individuals when dealing with applications for membership of the organisation. However, in doing so, it should avoid discriminating against disabled applicants or potential applicants. As explained in Chapter 4, treating a disabled person in a different way from the way in which other people are (or would be) treated amounts to discrimination in certain circumstances. In particular, such treatment is unlawful if it amounts to direct discrimination under Part 2. As explained at paragraph 4.4, treatment of a disabled person amounts to direct discrimination if:

- it is on the ground of his disability
- the treatment is less favourable than the way in which a person not having that particular disability is (or would be) treated, and
- the relevant circumstances, including the abilities, of the person with whom the comparison is made are the same as, or not materially different from, those of the disabled person.

> A trade organisation refuses to let a woman who has schizophrenia become a member, even though the woman has shown that she has sufficient qualifications and experience to gain membership. This is likely to amount to direct discrimination, because she is being treated less favourably on the ground of her disability. The treatment is less favourable than the way in which someone who does not have schizophrenia would be treated; the relevant circumstances of the

woman (in this case her qualifications and experience) are the same as those of other candidates who do not have schizophrenia.

What amounts to disability-related discrimination?

7.8 [s 3A(1)] Less favourable treatment of a disabled person may be unlawful under the Act even if it does not amount to direct discrimination. This will be the case if it amounts to disability-related discrimination instead. As explained at paragraph 4.25, this is less favourable treatment which is for a reason related to the person's disability. However, unlike treatment which amounts to direct discrimination (and which is therefore incapable of justification), a trade organisation's treatment of a disabled person does not amount to disability-related discrimination if the organisation can show that it is justified. The circumstances in which this may be possible are explained in Chapter 6.

7.9 In summary, less favourable treatment of a disabled person will be unlawful if it amounts either to direct discrimination or to disability related discrimination, and involves:

- a trade organisation's arrangements for selecting new members
- the terms on which membership is offered, or
- the rejection or non-acceptance of an application for membership.

When does the duty to make reasonable adjustments apply to applicants and potential applicants for membership?

7.10 [s 14] The duty of a trade organisation to make reasonable adjustments obviously applies in respect of its disabled members. However, the duty also applies in respect of any disabled person who is, or has notified the organisation that he may be, an applicant for membership.

A disabled man, who is unable to write because of his disability, requests an electronic application form from a trade organisation so that he can fill it in on his computer. The organisation may have a duty to make this reasonable adjustment because it knows that this man is a potential applicant for membership.

7.11 [s 14(3)] The duty only applies in respect of a disabled person if the trade organisation knows that the person is, or may be, an applicant for membership. 'Knowledge', in this context, means that the organisation knows, or could reasonably be expected to know, about this. Likewise, the duty applies only if the organisation knows that the person has a disability which is likely to place him at a substantial disadvantage in comparison with people who are not disabled.

7.12 Where a trade organisation has knowledge that a person may be an applicant for membership, the duty to make reasonable adjustments applies to provisions, criteria or practices for determining to whom membership should be offered. However, reasonable adjustments to premises are only required in respect of existing members and actual applicants for membership of whom the organisation has knowledge.

7.13 Where it applies, the duty to make reasonable adjustments is likely to affect arrangements in relation to, for example, advertisements, application forms and interviews for membership of the organisation. This is not a complete list of everything which could be covered by the duty (and which would be relevant in connection with becoming a member of a trade organisation), but it is intended as an indication of the likely relevant areas.

A man with a speech impairment applies for membership of a professional association. The association normally conducts a short interview for its potential members. Because the man has difficulty with verbal communication he asks if he can have the interview in the form of written questions and answers. This is likely to be a reasonable adjustment to the organisation's membership arrangements.

7.14 As explained in paragraphs 5.26 and 5.27, a trade organisation is never able to justify a failure to comply with a duty to make a reasonable adjustment under the Act.

MEMBERSHIP BENEFITS

What does the Act say?

7.15 [s 13(2)] The Act says that it is unlawful for a trade organisation to discriminate against a disabled person who is a member of the organisation:

- in the way it affords him access to any benefits or by refusing or deliberately omitting to afford him access to them, or

- by subjecting him to any other detriment.

An employee of a trade organisation deliberately fails to invite a member with schizophrenia to an annual dinner, because she thinks that other members may be offended by this person's behaviour, even though she has never met the member and knows nothing about his behaviour. This is likely to be unlawful.

7.16 The Act does not define what a benefit is (although it does say that benefits include facilities and services). Whether something is a benefit will depend on all the relevant circumstances, including an organisation's rules and practices. However, the following are likely to amount to benefits: training facilities, welfare or insurance services, participation at meetings and other events and invitations to attend those events, information about the organisation's activities, and assistance to members in employers' disciplinary or dismissal procedures.

When does less favourable treatment in relation to membership benefits amount to discrimination?

7.17 **[s 3A]** A trade organisation needs to take care if it differentiates between members in relation to the provision of membership benefits. For example, if the organisation's treatment of a disabled member in this regard amounts to direct discrimination under the Act (see paragraph 7.7) it will be unlawful.

7.18 Even where it is not directly discriminatory, treatment of a disabled person will be unlawful if it amounts to disability-related discrimination (see paragraph 4.25).

When does the duty to make reasonable adjustments apply in respect of membership benefits?

7.19 **[s 14]** A trade organisation has a duty to make reasonable adjustments in respect of the way it makes benefits available to its members. It owes this duty to a disabled member of the organisation if it has knowledge of the fact that he has a disability and is likely to be placed at a substantial disadvantage in comparison with people who are not disabled. The duty is likely to apply, for example, in respect of the provision of the benefits mentioned in paragraph 7.16. Where the duty does apply, the trade organisation must take such steps as are reasonable to prevent the provision, criterion or practice, or the physical feature (as the case may be) from placing the disabled member at a substantial disadvantage.

A trade union has a website through which it informs members about its services. A member with a learning disability requests that a summary of the information on the website is provided in a format that is easy for her to understand (Easy Read). This is likely to be a reasonable adjustment for the union to make.

A trade organisation organises a trade fair. A blind member requests assistance at the trade fair to find his way around. This is likely to be a reasonable adjustment for the trade organisation to make.

A deaf woman, who is a union member, has a problem at work which she wants to discuss in depth with a trade union representative. The trade union pays for and arranges a sign language interpreter for the meeting. This is likely to be a reasonable adjustment for the union to make.

7.20 For many members, the manner in which a trade organisation makes information available to them is likely to be an important issue. If this information is not provided in forms accessible to disabled people they are likely to be placed at a substantial disadvantage. However, recent technological developments have meant that it is increasingly practicable to produce material in alternative formats quickly and cheaply. Disability organisations and bodies like the Equality and Human Rights Commission are able to advise trade organisations about practicable methods of providing information in an accessible way. What is reasonable will depend on the individual circumstances of the case.

> A trade organisation provides a magazine for its members. A blind member of the organisation asks for the magazine to be sent to him electronically as an email attachment so that he can read it using access software on his home computer. This is likely to be a reasonable adjustment for the trade organisation to make.

7.21 In some cases a reasonable adjustment will not work without the co-operation of other members of the organisation. Members may therefore have an important role in helping to ensure that a reasonable adjustment is carried out in practice. Subject to considerations about confidentiality (explained at paragraphs 7.34 to 7.36), trade organisations must ensure that this happens. It is unlikely to be a valid defence to a claim under the Act that members were obstructive or unhelpful when the trade organisation tried to make reasonable adjustments. A trade organisation would at least need to be able to show that it took such behaviour seriously and dealt with it appropriately. Trade organisations will be more likely to be able to do this if they establish and implement the type of policies and practices described at paragraph 2.15 (and, in the case of trade unions, 2.16).

> A professional association organises a question and answer session with a panel of experts, to which it invites members. The event is organised at a venue with an induction loop to enable a deaf member who uses a hearing aid to participate. The Chair of the event reminds all contributors to speak in turn, and only when they are holding the microphone to enable everyone present to follow the proceedings. When a member persistently speaks out of turn, without the microphone, she is reminded that the organisation has a disability policy and that contributions will not be taken from her if she continues to ignore the rules laid down for the session which were designed to enable disabled people to participate.

VARIATION AND WITHDRAWAL OF MEMBERSHIP

What does the Act say?

7.22 **[s 13(2)]** The Act says that it is unlawful for a trade organisation to discriminate against a disabled person who is a member of the organisation:

- by depriving him of membership, or varying the terms on which he is a member, or
- by subjecting him to any other detriment.

> A man who is a member of a trade organisation becomes disabled after a spinal injury. His membership is withdrawn without any consideration or consultation with him about whether or how he can still meet the membership requirements. This is likely to be direct discrimination and therefore to be unlawful.

7.23 **[s 16A]** The Act also says that, where a disabled person's membership of a trade organisation has come to an end, it is still unlawful for the trade organisation:

- to discriminate against him by subjecting him to a detriment, or
- to subject him to harassment

if the discrimination or harassment arises out of his former membership of the organisation and is closely connected to it.

7.24 **[s 55]** It is also unlawful to victimise a person (whether or not he is disabled) after he has ceased to be a member of a trade organisation (see paragraphs 4.31 to 4.34).

When does less favourable treatment in relation to variation or withdrawal of membership amount to discrimination?

7.25 **[s 3A]** If a trade organisation varies the terms on which a disabled person is a member of the organisation, or withdraws his membership, it may be treating him less favourably than it treats other members. Depending upon the circumstances, the organisation may be discriminating against the disabled person by treating him in this way. For example, if the organisation's treatment of a disabled member amounts to direct discrimination under the Act (see paragraph 7.7) it will be unlawful.

7.26 Even where it does not amount to direct discrimination, treatment of a disabled person will be unlawful if it amounts to disability-related discrimination (see paragraph 4.25).

> A member of a trade union complains about another member who has Asperger's syndrome (a form of autism) after a conference, saying that the fellow member behaved in an inappropriate

way whilst at the conference hotel. The man's behaviour was related to his disability but she was not aware of this at the time. The trade union disciplines the disabled man and his membership is withdrawn, even though the union knows about his disability. This is likely to be less favourable treatment for a disability-related reason and is therefore likely to be unlawful, unless the trade union can show that the treatment was justified.

When does the duty to make reasonable adjustments apply in respect of the variation or withdrawal of membership?

7.27 **[s 14]** The duty of a trade organisation to make reasonable adjustments for a member who it knows to have a disability extends to the way in which it operates grievance and disciplinary procedures, or procedures for the variation or withdrawal of membership. Where a provision, criterion or practice, or a physical feature, places a disabled member at a substantial disadvantage in this regard, the trade organisation must take such steps as are reasonable to prevent this.

A disabled doctor has a meeting to discuss his continued membership of a professional association. The venue is changed to one that is accessible to the doctor, who has a mobility impairment. This is likely to be a reasonable adjustment for the association to make.

A disabled woman has a grievance hearing at the offices of a trade union. She is provided with a car parking space at the venue because her disability makes it impossible for her to use public transport. This is likely to be a reasonable adjustment for the union to make, whether or not the grievance was related to her disability.

7.28 **[s 16A(4)–(6)]** A trade organisation's duty to make reasonable adjustments may also apply in respect of a former member who is a disabled person. This will be the case where:

- the disabled person is placed at a substantial disadvantage in comparison with other former members:
  - (a) by a provision, practice or criterion applied by the trade organisation to the disabled person in relation to any matter arising out of his former membership, or
  - (b) by a physical feature of premises occupied by the organisation, and the organisation either knows, or could reasonably be expected to know, that the former member in question has a disability and is likely to be affected in this way.

A newly disabled person wishes to attend a conference of a trade organisation of which he is a former member. This conference is open to former members. He explains to the conference organisers that he is now partially sighted. They arrange for a guide to accompany him at the conference and produce conference papers in large print. These are likely to be reasonable adjustments for the trade organisation to make.

7.29 The former members with whom the position of the disabled person should be compared must be people who are not disabled, but who are former members of the same organisation. If it is not possible to identify an actual comparator for this purpose, then a hypothetical comparator may be used (see paragraph 4.17).

KNOWLEDGE OF DISABILITY

7.30 **[s 14(3)]** The point has been made a number of times in this chapter that a trade organisation only has a duty to make a reasonable adjustment if it knows, or could reasonably be expected to know, that a person is, or may be, an applicant for membership or has a disability and is likely to be placed at a substantial disadvantage in comparison with people who are not disabled. However, a trade organisation will be deemed to have that knowledge in certain circumstances.

Obtaining information

7.31 It is good practice for a trade organisation to invite its members to tell it about their disability-related needs. In any event, where information which should alert a trade organisation to the circumstances mentioned in paragraph 7.30 is available to it, or would be if it were reasonably alert, the organisation cannot simply ignore it. It is therefore in the interests of a trade organisation to be aware of the possibility that people it is dealing with may have a disability and to make reasonable enquiries if circumstances suggest this may be the case. It also means that it is a good idea for disabled people, if they wish to take full advantage of the provisions of the Act, to let trade organisations know of their disability and of substantial disadvantages at which they are likely to be placed. The earlier a trade organisation is told about a disability and its effects, the more likely it is to be able to make effective adjustments.

> A trade union has questions on its membership application form asking if the applicant is disabled or needs information in an accessible format (such as large print, Braille, tape or email). It also asks if the applicant has any additional disability-related needs.

> A professional association sends its members invitations to a conference. The invitation contains general details about access for disabled people, and the booking form asks about access requirements – such as whether delegate information is required in an accessible format, and whether delegates have any specific dietary requirements.

7.32 If a trade organisation's agent or employee (such as a trade union representative) knows, in that capacity, of a member's disability, the organisation will not usually be able to claim that it does not know of the disability. The same applies in respect of actual or potential applicants for membership of the organisation. Trade organisations therefore need to ensure that where information about disabled people may come through different channels, there is a means – suitably confidential – for bringing the information together, to make it easier for the organisation to fulfil its duties under the Act.

> A trade union member tells her branch secretary that she is unable to climb stairs due to her mobility impairment. The branch secretary arranges for the member to go on a training course organised by the union's education department. When the member arrives at the training session, she is unable to gain access to the building because of a flight of stairs. The union would be unable to claim that it did not know about the member's disability.

7.33 Information will not be imputed to a trade organisation if it is gained by a person providing services to members independently of the organisation. This is the case even if the organisation has arranged for those services to be provided.

> A trade organisation member uses a counselling Helpline which is independent of the organisation but which is provided as a benefit of membership. During his conversation with the counsellor the member discusses his worries about his worsening sight problem. The trade organisation itself should not be assumed to know about his need for the organisation's magazine to be in an accessible format, on the basis of this conversation.

Confidential information

7.34 The extent to which a trade organisation is entitled to let other members know about a fellow member's disability will depend partly on the terms of membership. An organisation could be discriminating against the member by revealing such information if it would not reveal similar information about another person for an equally legitimate purpose; or if the organisation revealed such information without consulting the individual, instead of adopting the usual practice of talking to a member before revealing personal information about him. Trade organisations also need to be aware that they have obligations under the Data Protection Act in respect of personal data.

> A member of a trade union wishes to go on a residential weekend conference, travelling there on a coach arranged by the union. The union member has to take dialysis equipment with her because she has had kidney failure. Another member needs to be informed, in order to help her load and unload the equipment. The disabled member gives her permission for another union member to be told that she is taking medical equipment with her, so that she can be helped with the equipment.

7.35 However, as noted at paragraph 7.21, sometimes a reasonable adjustment will not work without the co-operation of other members. In order to secure such co-operation, it may be necessary for a trade organisation to tell one or more of a disabled person's fellow members (in confidence) about a disability which is not obvious. Who it might be appropriate to tell will depend on the nature of the disability and the reason they need to know about it. In any event, a trade organisation must not disclose confidential details about a member without his consent. A disabled person's refusal to give such consent may impact upon the effectiveness of the adjustments which the trade organisation is able to make or its ability to make adjustments at all.

7.36 The Act does not prevent a disabled person keeping a disability confidential from a trade organisation. But this is likely to mean that unless the organisation could reasonably be expected to know about the person's disability anyway, it will not be under a duty to make a reasonable adjustment. If a disabled person expects a trade organisation to make a reasonable adjustment, he will need to provide the organisation – or someone acting on its behalf – with sufficient information to carry out that adjustment.

THE ROLE OF TRADE UNIONS

7.37 Trade unions are obvious examples of what the Act means by trade organisations. Representing the interests of their members in the workplace is one of the most important functions of trade unions, and so union representatives need to be familiar with the Act's provisions on employment and occupation. They need to be able to recognise potential claims under the Act and to know how to respond appropriately. Union representatives should also understand the need to make reasonable adjustments at branch meetings, for example, and that the reasonableness of the cost of making an adjustment should be assessed having regard to the union's overall resources, and to any access funds which may be available (see paragraphs 2.15 and 2.16).

7.38 It is important for trade unions to ensure that union representatives receive proper training on the Act and that they are aware of the DRC's code of practice on the Act's provisions on employment and occupation (see Appendix B). It is also advisable for trade unions to have arrangements in place so that appropriate cases are referred to the union's solicitors.

8. DISCRIMINATION BY QUALIFICATIONS BODIES

INTRODUCTION

[4.131]
8.1 Chapter 3 describes the meaning of 'qualifications body', and explains that it is unlawful for such a body to discriminate against a disabled person in relation to conferring professional or trade qualifications, or to subject him to harassment, or to victimise any person – whether disabled or not. This chapter does not concern the duties in respect of those bodies conferring of relevant general qualifications – these duties are considered further in Chapter 9.

8.2 This chapter looks at the provisions about qualifications bodies in more detail. It explains what the definition of 'professional or trade qualification' covers in practice. It considers when less favourable treatment of a disabled person by a qualifications body is unlawful, and when the duty to make reasonable adjustments arises. Finally, it examines the meaning and significance of 'competence standards'.

8.3 **[s 17A(1A)]** It should be noted that a disabled person is not permitted to bring a claim in an employment tribunal about alleged discrimination or harassment by a qualifications body if a statutory appeal is available in respect of the matter in question. For example, the Medical Act 1983 sets out specific mechanisms for appealing decisions of the General Medical Council or its committees regarding the registration of medical practitioners. A complaint to which these appeal mechanisms applied could not, therefore, be brought instead in an employment tribunal.

8.4 It should also be noted that the provisions of the Act which relate specifically to qualifications bodies' focus only on the functions of conferring professional or trade qualifications. The performance of other functions by such bodies may be subject to other provisions of the Act. For example, where a qualifications body is also a trade organisation, regard must also be had to what the Act says about trade organisations – and to Chapter 7 of the Code in particular.

WHAT IS A PROFESSIONAL OR TRADE QUALIFICATION?

8.5 **[s 14A(5)]** As noted at paragraph 3.9, the key feature of a qualifications body is that it confers professional or trade qualifications. The Act says that such a qualification is an authorisation, qualification, recognition, registration, enrolment, approval or certification which is needed for, or which facilitates engagement in, a particular profession or trade. Clearly, therefore, the expression includes those qualifications etc, which are conferred solely in anticipation of furthering a particular career. However, it is also capable of including more general qualifications if attaining them facilitates engagement in a particular profession or trade and if these general qualifications are not relevant general qualifications (see chapter 9 for further details). In order to decide whether a particular qualification is a professional or trade qualification for the purposes of the Act, it is necessary to address the following three questions:

- What is the profession or trade?

- What is the qualification?
- Does possession of that particular qualification make it easier to work in that particular profession or trade (rather than merely assisting general advancement in that or any other career)?

8.6 The word 'qualification' should not be interpreted narrowly – attaining a professional or trade qualification need not involve passing formal examinations or tests. In some cases, simply being a member of an organisation or body may amount to such a qualification if membership itself facilitates engagement in a particular profession or trade.

8.7 The following list (which is not intended to be exhaustive) gives examples of qualifications which would or could count as professional or trade qualifications under the Act provided that the criteria set out in paragraph 8.5 are met:

- Registration with the Nursing and Midwifery Council
- A certificate to practise as a solicitor issued by the Law Society
- Registration with the Council for Registered Gas Installers (CORGI)
- NVQs
- BTECs
- City and Guilds
- Scottish Vocational Qualifications
- HGV driving licences
- Membership, registration or fellowship of trade or professional bodies (eg Fellow of the Institute of Linguists).

8.8 In relation to certain professions or trades, educational institutions or other bodies may devise, run and examine their own courses, although approval for entry into the profession or trade is controlled by an external body. Because of the wide definition of 'professional or trade qualification', such external bodies are likely to be qualifications bodies if they perform any of the following functions:

- maintaining a register of people who are qualified to practice in the profession or trade
- conducting additional tests for people who have qualified, or who wish to qualify, into the profession or trade, such as basic skills tests or medical checks, or
- giving approval for a person's qualification to his course provider.

WHAT AMOUNTS TO DIRECT DISCRIMINATION?

8.9 **[s 14A(1)]** It is obvious that a qualifications body will differentiate between individuals when conferring, renewing or extending professional or trade qualifications. However, in doing so, it should avoid discriminating against disabled people – it is unlawful for a qualifications body to discriminate against a disabled person in respect of a number of matters which are specified in the Act (and listed in paragraph 3.19).

8.10 **[s 3A(5)]** As explained in Chapter 4, treating a disabled person in a different way from the way in which other people are (or would be) treated amounts to discrimination in certain circumstances. In particular, such treatment is unlawful if it amounts to direct discrimination under Part 2. As explained at paragraph 4.4, treatment of a disabled person amounts to direct discrimination if:

- it is on the ground of his disability
- the treatment is less favourable than the way in which a person not having that particular disability is (or would be) treated, and
- the relevant circumstances, including the abilities, of the person with whom the comparison is made are the same as, or not materially different from, those of the disabled person.

> A qualifications body recommends to a college of higher education that a man with a mobility impairment should not be allowed on to a social work course, as they wrongly assume that he may have difficulty visiting the homes of clients. This is likely to amount to direct discrimination.

WHAT AMOUNTS TO DISABILITY-RELATED DISCRIMINATION?

8.11 **[s 3A(1)]** Less favourable treatment of a disabled person may be unlawful under the Act even if it does not amount to direct discrimination. This will be the case if it amounts to disability-related discrimination instead. As explained at paragraph 4.25, this is less favourable treatment which is for a reason related to the person's disability. However, unlike treatment which amounts to direct discrimination (and which is therefore incapable of justification), a qualifications body's treatment of a disabled person does not amount to disability-related discrimination if the body can show that it is justified. The general circumstances in which this may be possible are explained in Chapter 6. However, special rules apply in respect of justification of less favourable treatment in the application of a competence standard (see paragraphs 8.35 to 8.40).

8.12 In summary, less favourable treatment of a disabled person will be unlawful if it amounts to either direct discrimination or disability related discrimination, and involves:

- the arrangements for determining upon whom to confer a professional or trade qualification
- the terms upon which a qualifications body confers, renews or extends such a qualification
- a refusal or deliberate omission by such a body to grant his application for a qualification, or
- the withdrawal of a qualification from him or a variation of the terms on which he holds it.

> A professional association which maintains a register of approved acupuncturists withdraws registration from a woman who, because of treatment for cancer, has not been able to work for a year. The association has a policy of withdrawing registration from anyone who has not practised for this length of time. The treatment of the woman is for a disability-related reason (her lack of recent practice is due to her disability). The treatment is less favourable than the way in which someone who had practised recently would have been treated. It would therefore amount to disability-related discrimination unless the association (acting as a qualifications body) can justify it.

8.13 **[s 16A]** The Act also says that, where a disabled person ceases to hold a professional or trade qualification, it is still unlawful for the qualifications body which conferred it:

- to discriminate against him by subjecting him to a detriment, or
- to subject him to harassment

if the discrimination or harassment arises out of his having formerly held the qualification and is closely connected to it.

8.14 It is also unlawful to victimise a person (whether or not he is disabled) after he has ceased to hold such a qualification (see paragraphs 4.31 to 4.34).

HOW DOES THE DUTY TO MAKE REASONABLE ADJUSTMENTS APPLY TO QUALIFICATIONS BODIES?

In respect of which disabled people is the duty owed?

8.15 **[s 14B(1)]** A qualifications body has a duty to make reasonable adjustments to the way it confers, renews or extends professional or trade qualifications (except in respect of competence standards). It owes this duty to a disabled person who holds a qualification conferred by it and to a disabled applicant or potential applicant for such a qualification.

8.16 **[s 14B(2)]** The duty extends to holders of a qualification conferred by the body and to applicants for such a qualification. However, in the case of a provision, criterion or practice for determining on whom a qualification is to be conferred, the duty only applies to a disabled person who has either applied for the qualification or has notified the body that he may apply.

8.17 **[s 14B(3)]** The duty only applies if the qualifications body knows, or could reasonably be expected to know, that the disabled person concerned is, or may be, an applicant for a professional or trade qualification. Likewise, the duty only applies if the body knows or should know that the person has a disability and is likely to be placed at a substantial disadvantage compared with people who are not disabled.

8.18 **[s 16A(4)–(6)]** The duty of a qualifications body to make reasonable adjustments may also extend to a disabled person who formerly held a professional or trade qualification. This is the case where a provision, practice or criterion, or a physical feature of premises occupied by the qualifications body, places the disabled person at a substantial disadvantage compared with others in the same position. The duty only applies, however, if the qualifications body knows, or could reasonably be expected to know, that the person concerned has a disability and is likely to be affected in this way.

8.19 The people with whom the position of the disabled person should be compared must be people who are not disabled, but who also formerly held the same professional or trade qualification conferred by the qualifications body in question. If it is not possible to identify an actual comparator for this purpose, then a hypothetical comparator may be used (see paragraph 4.17).

What is the effect of the duty?

8.20 Where it applies, the duty to make reasonable adjustments is likely to affect arrangements in relation to, for example, taking tests and examinations, and renewing qualifications where it is necessary to do so. However, there is no duty to make adjustments to competence standards applied to a disabled person by a qualifications body. Where the duty does apply, however, the qualifications body must take such steps as are reasonable to prevent the provision, criterion or practice, or the physical feature (as the case may be) from placing the disabled person in question at a substantial disadvantage.

> A woman with a mental health problem is informed that an oral examination for a diploma in interpreting and translation has been arranged for 8:30 am. The timing of the examination would substantially disadvantage the woman, because a side effect of her medication is extreme drowsiness for several hours after taking her morning dose – which prevents her from concentrating well. The qualifications body agrees to her request to take the examination later in the day.

> A man who lip-reads because of his hearing impairment is due to have a practical test as part of his beauty therapy course. The qualifications body instructs an assessor working on its behalf to face the man when she issues instructions during the assessment and to talk clearly.

> An advanced craft test for carpentry consists of a seven hour practical examination. A woman with arthritis who is only able to work part-time as a result of her disability wishes to take this test as two sessions of three and a half hours on two consecutive days. The qualifications body awarding the qualification allows the test to be taken in this way.

> A candidate for a written examination as part of a jewellery-making course has dyslexia. The qualifications body allows her extra time to sit the examination, and also permits the use of a reader and an amanuensis (someone to write on her behalf) as the candidate is not able to read and write well because of her dyslexia.

> A woman with a learning disability is allowed extra time by a qualifications body to take a written examination. This is likely to be a reasonable adjustment for the qualifications body to make, because the trade which the woman wants to enter would not require written work to be done in a short amount of time, so the ability to write quickly is not a competence standard.

> A disabled man asks for twice as much time for a test in shorthand because his disability makes it impossible for him to write quickly. This is unlikely to be a reasonable adjustment for the qualifications body to make, because speed is an essential element of the shorthand qualification – in other words, it is likely to be a competence standard, and thus the duty to make reasonable adjustments does not apply.

What are the practical implications of the duty?

8.21 Although there is no duty on a qualifications body to make a reasonable adjustment if it does not have the requisite knowledge (see paragraph 8.17), it will be deemed to have that knowledge in certain circumstances.

8.22 Where information is available which should alert a qualifications body to the circumstances mentioned in paragraph 8.17, or would be if it were reasonably alert, the body cannot simply ignore it. It is thus a good idea for disabled people, if they wish to take full advantage of the provisions of the Act, to let educational institutions and qualifications bodies know of their disability and of substantial disadvantages that are likely to arise. The earlier a qualifications body is told about a disability and its effects, the more likely it is to be able to make effective adjustments.

8.23 As mentioned at paragraph 2.15, it is also advisable for qualifications bodies to set up systems for working with educational institutions and other bodies with whom they work to ensure that qualifications bodies obtain the information they need to make adjustments for disabled students who are taking examinations or other assessments in order to obtain a professional or trade qualification. For example, such a system could comprise the following steps:

- Well in advance of the examination or assessment in question, the qualifications body asks educational institutions to seek information from candidates about whether they have disabilities which make reasonable adjustments necessary.
- Each educational institution requests this information from its students, together with their individual consent to inform the qualifications body. The information is then passed on to the qualifications body.
- Students may be given a contact at the qualifications body with whom they can discuss their requirements further.
- The qualifications body uses the information it obtains to decide what adjustments should be made. It then notifies educational institutions of its decision, and discusses with them how such adjustments will be implemented.

A body which confers qualifications in accountancy asks a college for information about students who may require reasonable adjustments. The college seeks this information from its students. A student with cerebral palsy has difficulty writing, and therefore asks to be allowed to take the examinations using a computer. The colleges relays this request to the qualifications body, which gives its consent and liaises with the college to ensure that the college can provide him with appropriate facilities to take the examinations.

8.24 Educational institutions or other bodies often provide education, training or other services (such as facilities for taking examinations or assessments) which lead to the attainment of a professional or trade qualification, even though they do not themselves confer the qualification. Such institutions or bodies are likely to have separate duties under Part 3 or Part 4 in respect of the education, training or other services they provide. To ensure full compliance with the Act, it is advisable for such institutions or bodies to inform qualifications bodies at an early stage about an applicant's disability and its relevant implications – subject, of course, to obtaining the applicant's consent first.

8.25 In practice, the needs of a disabled person who is taking an examination, test or assessment can only be met fully if the educational institution or body and the qualifications body concerned work together to achieve an appropriate outcome.

A partially sighted man requests a test paper in large print and a desk light. The qualifications body provides a large print test paper and liaises with the college where the man is sitting the test to ensure that it provides a desk light.

A partially sighted man on another course has always had course information provided to him in large print by the college as a reasonable adjustment (under Chapter or 2 of Part 4 of the Act), and has used a desk light when taking internal tests as part of his course. With the man's consent, the college informs the qualifications body that the man needs an examination paper in large print for examinations set by the qualifications body. The college provides him with a desk light for such examinations.

8.26 The Act does not prevent a disabled person keeping a disability confidential from a qualifications body (although other legislation may require its disclosure – in relation to an application for a driving licence, for example). But this is likely to mean that unless the qualifications body could reasonably be expected to know about the person's disability anyway, it will not be under a duty to make a reasonable adjustment. If a disabled person expects a qualifications body to make a reasonable adjustment, he will need to provide it with sufficient information to carry out that adjustment.

WHAT DOES THE ACT SAY ABOUT COMPETENCE STANDARDS?

What is a competence standard?

8.27 **[s 14A(5)]** The Act says that a competence standard is an academic, medical, or other standard applied by or on behalf of a qualifications body for the purpose of determining whether or not a person has a particular level of competence or ability. So, for example, having a certain standard of eyesight is a competence standard required for a pilot's qualification. Having a certain level of knowledge of the UK taxation system is a competence standard for an accountancy qualification.

8.28 Qualifications bodies are likely to impose various requirements and conditions upon the conferment of a professional or trade qualification. However, any such requirement or condition only amounts to a competence standard if its purpose is to demonstrate a particular level of competence or ability. A requirement that a person has a particular level of knowledge of a subject, for example, or has the strength or ability to carry out a particular task or activity within a set period of time, would probably be a competence standard.

8.29 On the other hand, a condition that a person has, for example, a certain length of experience of doing something will not be a competence standard if it does not determine a particular level of competence or ability. The following are examples of requirements which are therefore unlikely to amount to competence standards:

- a requirement that a candidate must have at least ten years continuous experience (a person who has two periods of experience which total ten years may have equivalent ability and experience)
- a requirement that a candidate must complete twelve qualifying sessions (for qualification as a barrister)
- a requirement that a candidate must be currently professionally employed in a particular field.

8.30 Generally, there is a difference between a competence standard and the process by which attainment of the standard is determined. For example, the conferment of many qualifications is dependent upon passing an academic examination. Having the requisite level of knowledge to pass the examination is a competence standard. However, the examination itself (as opposed to performance in it) may not involve a competence standard – because the mechanical process of sitting the examination is unlikely to be relevant to the determination of a relevant competence or ability.

8.31 Sometimes, of course, the process of assessing whether a competence standard has been achieved is inextricably linked to the standard itself. The conferment of some qualifications is conditional upon having a practical skill or ability which must be demonstrated by completing a practical test. The ability to take the test may itself amount to a competence standard.

> An oral examination for a person training to be a Russian interpreter cannot be done in an alternative way, eg as a written examination, because the examination is to ascertain whether someone can speak Russian.

> A driving test for a heavy goods vehicle licence cannot be done solely as a written test because the purpose of the test is to ascertain whether someone can actually drive a heavy goods vehicle.

> A practical test in tree surgery cannot be taken on the ground because the test is to ascertain whether someone can actually cut the branches of trees, including the high branches.

What is the significance of this distinction?

8.32 Special rules apply in relation to the application of a competence standard to a disabled person by or on behalf of a qualifications body. The effect of the Act is that:

- there is no duty to make reasonable adjustments in respect of the application of a competence standard, and
- in the limited circumstances in which less favourable treatment of a disabled person in the application of such a standard may be justified, justification is assessed by reference to a special statutory test (see paragraph 8.36).

8.33 It follows that it is very important to ascertain whether a particular provision, criterion or practice of a qualifications body is a competence standard and, if so, whether the matter at issue concerns the application of that standard to the disabled person concerned. Although there is no duty to make reasonable adjustments in respect of the application of a competence standard, such a duty is likely to apply in respect of the process by which competence is assessed.

> A woman taking a written test for a qualification in office administration asks the relevant qualifications body for extra time for the test because she has dyslexia. This is likely to be a reasonable adjustment for the qualifications body to make. She also asks if she can leave out the questions asking her to write a business letter and to précis a document, because she feels these questions would substantially disadvantage her because of her dyslexia. The qualifications body

would not have to make this adjustment because these questions are there to determine her competence at writing and précising, so are part of the competence standard being tested.

8.34 As noted in paragraphs 8.23 and 8.24, it is advisable for qualifications bodies and, where relevant, educational institutions to ensure that they have adequate information to assess their responsibilities to disabled people. Even though a qualifications body has no duty to alter a competence standard, it needs to obtain enough information about a person's disability to decide whether a reasonable adjustment should be made to some other aspect of the process by which it confers the qualification in question. A qualifications body must ascertain whether a person's disability impacts upon a competence standard in the first place. However, as noted at paragraph 8.31, there may be an overlap between a competence standard and any process by which an individual is assessed against that standard.

When can less favourable treatment be justified in relation to competence standards?

8.35 **[s 3A(4) applied by s 14A(4)]** Less favourable treatment of a disabled person can never be justified if it amounts to direct discrimination under Part 2 (see paragraph 8.10) – as where the treatment is based on generalised, or stereotypical, assumptions about the disability or its effects. This principle applies to the way that a disabled person is treated in the application of a competence standard in the same way that it applies to treatment of him in other respects.

8.36 **[s 14A(3)]** To the extent that it does not amount to direct discrimination, the Act says that, where the application of a competence standard to a disabled person amounts to less favourable treatment of him for a reason which relates to his disability, that treatment is justified if, but only if, the qualifications body can show that:

- the standard is (or would be) applied equally to people who do not have his particular disability, and
- its application is a proportionate means of achieving a legitimate aim.

A qualifications body refuses to grant a qualification to a man who fails a fitness test. This does not amount to direct discrimination because anyone, disabled or non-disabled, failing the fitness test would be treated in the same way. But it is less favourable treatment for a reason related to the man's disability. The treatment could be justified if the fitness test was applied equally to all candidates and the fitness test was a proportionate way of showing that the person was fit enough to carry out the essential requirements of the job to which the qualification relates.

In the above situation the qualifications body had not reviewed the fitness standards to see if they were proportionate to the requirements of the job. If it had done so, it would have found that the fitness standard demanded was much higher than many people actually working in that job could now achieve (even though these people achieved that standard at the time of qualification). The qualifications body would therefore be unlikely to be able to justify this competence standard.

8.37 The effect of these provisions is that, in the limited circumstances in which justification may be possible, less favourable treatment which is disability-related and which arises from the application of a competence standard is capable of justification on an objective basis. Justification does not depend on an individual assessment of the disabled person's circumstances, but depends instead on an assessment of the purpose and effect of the competence standard itself.

8.38 These special rules about justification are only relevant to the actual application of a competence standard. If a qualifications body applies a competence standard incorrectly, then it is not, in fact, applying the standard and these rules do not operate. Instead, the more usual test of justification operates (assuming, of course, that the incorrect application of the standard is not directly discriminatory, but that it is disability related less favourable treatment).

8.39 The application of a competence standard concerning a medical requirement may, depending on the circumstances, result in less favourable treatment of a disabled person. Medical requirements which are based on stereotypical assumptions about the health and safety implications of disability generally, or about particular types of disability, are likely to be directly discriminatory – less favourable treatment of a disabled person resulting from the application of such a requirement will therefore be unlawful.

A man studying to become a social care professional has epilepsy. His condition is controlled by medication and he has not had a seizure for two years. Nevertheless the relevant qualifications body prevents him from carrying on with his training for the qualification on health and safety grounds. It does this without first undertaking a risk assessment. This is likely to be unlawful.

8.40 Nevertheless, genuine concerns about health and safety may be relevant to the justification of a competence standard concerning a medical requirement. Assuming that it does not amount to direct discrimination, the application of such a requirement to a disabled person will be justified only if the body can show that the requirement applies (or would apply) equally to people who do not have that disability. It would also be necessary to show that the requirement serves a valid purpose and is a legitimate means of achieving that purpose. The qualifications body would have to provide cogent evidence that the standard is genuinely fundamental to the needs of the profession or trade in order to ensure the competence of practitioners.

How can qualifications bodies avoid discrimination in relation to competence standards?

8.41 If unlawful discrimination is to be avoided when the application of a competence standard results in less favourable treatment of a disabled person, the qualifications body concerned will have to show two things. First, it will have to show that the application of the standard does not amount to direct discrimination. Second, it will be necessary to show that the standard can be objectively justified. This is more likely to be possible where a qualifications body has considered the nature and effects of its competence standards in advance of an issue arising in practice. It would be advisable for qualifications bodies to review and evaluate competence standards. This process might involve:

- identifying the specific purpose of each competence standard which is applied, and examining the manner in which the standard achieves that purpose
- considering the impact which each competence standard may have on disabled people and, in the case of a standard which may have an adverse impact, asking whether the application of the standard is absolutely necessary
- reviewing the purpose and effect of each competence standard in the light of changing circumstances – such as developments in technology examining whether the purpose for which any competence standard is applied could be achieved in a way which does not have an adverse impact on disabled people, and
- documenting the manner in which these issues have been addressed, the conclusions which have been arrived at, and the reasons for those conclusions.

(Section 9 Discrimination by general qualifications bodies: outside the scope of this work.)

10. MAKING REASONABLE ADJUSTMENTS TO PREMISES – LEGAL CONSIDERATIONS

INTRODUCTION

[4.132]

10.1 In Chapter 5 it was explained that one of the situations in which there is a duty to make reasonable adjustments arises where a physical feature of premises occupied by a trade organisation, qualifications body or general qualifications body places a disabled person at a substantial disadvantage compared with people who are not disabled. In such circumstances the organisation or body must consider whether any reasonable steps can be taken to overcome that disadvantage. Making adjustments to premises may be a reasonable step to have to take. This chapter addresses the issues of how leases, building regulations and other statutory requirements affect the duty to make reasonable adjustments to premises.

10.2 The issues dealt with in this chapter largely concern the need to obtain consent to the making of reasonable adjustments where a trade organisation, qualifications body or general qualifications body occupies premises under a lease or other binding obligation. However, such organisations and bodies should remember that even where consent is not given for altering a physical feature, they still have a duty to consider taking other steps to overcome the disadvantage which the feature causes in respect of the disabled person.

WHAT ABOUT THE NEED TO OBTAIN STATUTORY CONSENT FOR SOME BUILDING CHANGES?

10.3 **[s 59]** A trade organisation, qualifications body or general qualifications body might have to obtain statutory consent before making adjustments involving changes to premises. Such consents include planning permission, building regulations approval or a building warrant in Scotland, listed building consent, scheduled monument consent and fire regulations approval. The Act does not override the need to obtain such consents.

10.4 Organisations and bodies should plan for and anticipate the need to obtain consent to make a particular adjustment. It might take time to obtain such consent, but it could be reasonable to make an interim or other adjustment – one that does not require consent – in the meantime.

> A trade organisation occupies premises with steps up to the main entrance. These premises have facilities for members, such as a conference room and a library. The trade organisation is not aware of any members who have a mobility impairment and does not do anything to make its premises more accessible. When a new member notifies the organisation that she walks with

crutches and wishes to use the premises, the organisation tries to obtain statutory consent to install a ramp with a handrail. It takes several months to obtain such permission. Because it cannot make this adjustment in time, it decides to make a temporary adjustment – making an existing side entrance, without steps, available for the disabled member to use. If the trade organisation had anticipated that this need was very likely to arise (through carrying out an access audit, for example), it would have been able to make this adjustment sooner.

10.5 Where consent has been refused, there is likely to be a means of appeal. Whether or not the duty to take such steps as it is reasonable to take includes pursuing an appeal will depend on the circumstances of the case.

BUILDING REGULATIONS AND BUILDING DESIGN

10.6 **[SI 2000/2531]** The design and construction of a new building, or the material alteration of an existing one, must comply with Building Regulations. For buildings in England or Wales, Part M of the Building Regulations (access to and use of buildings) is intended to ensure that reasonable provision is made for people to gain access to and use buildings. A similar provision applies in Scotland under the Technical Standards for compliance with the Building Standards (Scotland) Regulations 990 and, from May 2005, under the Building (Scotland) Regulations 2004 and relevant functional standards and guidance in the associated Technical Handbooks.

10.7 Nevertheless, the fact that the design and construction of a building (or a physical feature of a building) which a trade organisation, qualifications body or general qualifications body occupies meets the requirements of the Building Regulations does not diminish its duty to make reasonable adjustments in respect of the building's physical features. In particular, it should be noted that the partial exemption from the duty to remove or alter physical features which applies to service providers under Part 3 of the Act does not apply to trade organisations, qualifications bodies under Part 2 of the Act or general qualifications bodies under Part 4 of the Act.

10.8 The Building Regulations building standards provide only a baseline standard of accessibility, which is not intended to address the specific needs of individual disabled people. It is therefore good practice for trade organisations, qualifications bodies and general qualifications bodies to carry out an assessment of the access needs of each disabled person with whom it has dealings, and to consider what alterations can be made to the features of its buildings in order to meet those needs. It is also good practice to anticipate the needs of disabled people when planning building or refurbishment works.

10.9 When assessing the access requirements of disabled people, it is likely to be helpful to refer to British Standard 8300:2001, **Design of buildings and their approaches to meet the needs of disabled people – Code of Practice**. Indeed, it is unlikely to be reasonable for a trade organisation, qualifications body or general qualifications body to have to make an adjustment to a physical feature of a building which it occupies if the design and construction of the physical features of the building is in accordance with BS8300. Further information about BS8300 can be found in Appendix B.

10.10 In addition, although less comprehensive than BS8300, guidance accompanying the Building Regulations (known as 'Approved Document M') sets out a number of 'provisions' as suggested ways in which the requirements of the Regulations might be met. It is unlikely to be reasonable for a trade organisation, qualifications body or general qualifications body to have to make an adjustment to a physical feature of a building which it occupies if that feature accords with the relevant provisions of the most up to date version of Approved Document M.

WHAT IF A BINDING OBLIGATION OTHER THAN A LEASE PREVENTS A BUILDING BEING ALTERED?

10.11 **[s 18B(3) and Sch 4, Part 4, para 12]** A trade organisation or qualifications body may be bound by the terms of an agreement or other legally binding obligation (for example, a mortgage, charge or restrictive covenant or, in Scotland, a real burden) under which it cannot alter the premises without someone else's consent. In these circumstances, the Part 2 of the Act provides that it is always reasonable for the organisation or body to have to request that consent, but that it is never reasonable for it to have to make an alteration before having obtained that consent. Under Chapter 2A of Part 4 of the Act, it may also be necessary for general qualifications bodies to obtain consent pursuant to a binding obligation and the Act does not override the need to obtain such consent.

WHAT HAPPENS IF A LEASE SAYS THAT CERTAIN CHANGES TO PREMISES CANNOT BE MADE?

10.12 **[s 18A(2) and s 31ADB(2)]** Special provisions apply where a trade organisation, qualifications body or general qualifications body occupies premises under a lease, the terms of which prevent it from making an alteration to the premises. In such circumstances, if the alteration is one which the organisation or body proposes to make in order to comply with a duty of reasonable adjustment, the Act overrides the terms of the lease so as to entitle it to make the alteration with the consent of its landlord ('the lessor'). In such a case the organisation or body must first write to the lessor asking for consent to make the alteration. The lessor cannot unreasonably withhold consent but may attach reasonable conditions to the consent.

10.13 [Sch 4, Part I, para 1 and Sch 4, Part 4, para 15] If a trade organisation, qualifications body or general qualifications body fails to make a written application to the lessor for consent to the alteration, it will not be able to rely upon the fact that the lease has a term preventing it from making alterations to the premises to defend its failure to make an alteration. In these circumstances, anything in the lease which prevents that alteration being made must be ignored in deciding whether it was reasonable for the organisation or body to have made the alteration.

WHAT HAPPENS IF THE LESSOR HAS A 'SUPERIOR' LESSOR?

10.14 The lessor may itself hold a lease the terms of which prevent it from consenting to the alteration without the consent of its landlord ('the superior lessor'). In such circumstances the effect of the superior lease is modified so as to require the lessee of that lease to apply in writing to its lessor (the 'superior lessor' in this context) if it wishes to consent to the alteration. As with the lessor of the trade organisation, qualifications body or general qualifications body, the superior lessor must not withhold such consent unreasonably but may attach reasonable conditions to the consent.

10.15 Where a superior lessor receives an application from its lessee, the provisions described in paragraphs 10.16 to 10.30 apply as if its lessee were the trade organisation, qualifications body or general qualifications body.

HOW DO ARRANGEMENTS FOR GAINING CONSENT WORK?

10.16 [SI 2004/153 and SI 2007/2405] Regulations made under the Act concerning trade organisations, qualifications bodies and general qualifications bodies govern the procedure for obtaining consent. These Regulations (the Disability Discrimination (Employment Field) (Leasehold Premises) Regulations 2004) and Disability Discrimination Act 1995 (Amendment etc) (General Qualifications Bodies) (Alternation of Premises and Enforcement) Regulations 2007 are commonly referred to in this chapter as the 'Leasehold Premises Regulations'. For the sake of clarity, references below to particular provisions in these regulations refer to the 2004 regulations and then the 2007 regulations.

10.17 [Reg 4 and Reg 9] In relation to trade organisations and qualifications bodies, the Leasehold Premises Regulations say that, once the application has been made, the lessor has 21 days, beginning with the day on which it receives the application, to reply in writing to the trade organisation, qualifications body (or the person who made the application on its behalf). If it fails to do so it is taken to have unreasonably withheld its consent to the alteration. However, where it is reasonable to do so, the lessor is permitted to take more than 21 days to reply to the request. Under the different duties applicable to general qualifications bodies, a lessor has 42 days to reply to an application for the lessor's consent made by a general qualifications body, beginning with the day on which it receives the application. However, the lessor has 21 days to make a written request for any plans and specifications that it is reasonable for him to require and which were not included within the general qualifications body's application.

10.18 If the lessor replies to a trade organisation or qualifications body's request by consenting to the application subject to obtaining the consent of another person (required under a superior lease or because of a binding obligation), but fails to seek the consent of the other person within 21 days of receiving the application (or such longer period as may be reasonable), it will also be taken to have withheld its consent. For general qualifications bodies, the relevant period for the lessor to seek the consent of another person is 42 days, and not 21 days, and the distinct duties applying to general qualifications bodies make no allowance for extending the period either for such longer period as may be reasonable, or at all.

10.19 The Leasehold Premises Regulations provide that a lessor will be treated as not having sought the consent of another person unless the lessor has applied in writing to the other person indicating that the occupier has asked for consent for an alteration in order to comply with a duty to make reasonable adjustments, and that the lessor has given its consent conditionally upon obtaining the other person's consent.

10.20 [Reg 6 and Reg 11] If the lessor replies refusing consent to the alteration, the trade organisation, qualifications body or general qualifications body must inform the disabled person of this, but has no further obligation to make the alteration (but see paragraph 10.2).

WHEN IS IT UNREASONABLE FOR A LESSOR TO WITHHOLD CONSENT?

10.21 Whether withholding consent will be reasonable or not will depend on the specific circumstances. For example, if a particular adjustment is likely to result in a substantial permanent reduction in the value of the lessor's interest in the premises, the lessor is likely to be acting reasonably in withholding consent. The lessor is also likely to be acting reasonably if it withholds consent because an adjustment would cause significant disruption or inconvenience to other tenants (for example, where the premises consist of multiple adjoining units).

> A particular adjustment helps make a public building more accessible generally and is therefore likely to benefit the landlord. It is likely to be unreasonable for consent to be withheld in these circumstances.

> A particular adjustment is likely to result in a substantial permanent reduction in the value of the landlord's interest in the premises. The landlord is likely to be acting reasonably in withholding consent.

> A particular adjustment would cause significant disruption or major inconvenience to other tenants (for example, where the premises consist of multiple adjoining units). The landlord is likely to be acting reasonably in withholding consent.

10.22 A trivial or arbitrary reason would almost certainly be unreasonable. Many reasonable adjustments to premises will not harm the lessor's interests and so it would generally be unreasonable to withhold consent for them.

10.23 **[Reg 5 and Reg 10]** The Leasehold Premises Regulations say that, provided the consent has been sought in the way required by the lease, it is unreasonable for a lessor to withhold consent in circumstances where the lease says that consent will be given to alterations of the kind for which consent has been sought.

10.24 **[Reg 6]** The Leasehold Premises Regulations concerning trade organisations and qualifications bodies only specifically provide that withholding consent will be reasonable where:

- there is a binding obligation requiring the consent of any person to the alteration
- the lessor has taken steps to seek consent, and
- consent has not been given or has been given subject to a condition making it reasonable for the lessor to withhold its consent.

It will also be reasonable for a lessor to withhold consent where it is bound by an agreement under which it would have to make a payment in order to give the consent, but which prevents it from recovering the cost from the trade organisation, qualifications body. **[Reg 11]** This particular requirement does not apply to an application for the lessor's consent made by a general qualifications body. In this specific context, a lessor may reasonably withhold consent where it does not know, and could not reasonably know, that the alteration is one that the general qualifications body proposes to make in order to comply with the duty to make reasonable adjustments.

WHAT CONDITIONS WOULD IT BE REASONABLE FOR A LESSOR TO MAKE WHEN GIVING CONSENT?

10.25 The Leasehold Premises Regulations set out some conditions which it is reasonable for a lessor to make. Depending on the circumstances of the case there may be other conditions which it would also be reasonable for a lessor to require a trade organisation, qualifications body or general qualifications body to make. Where a lessor imposes other conditions, their reasonableness may be challenged in the course of subsequent employment tribunal proceedings (where trade organisations and qualifications bodies are concerned) or county/sheriff court proceedings (where general qualifications bodies are concerned) – see paragraph 10.27.

10.26 **[Reg 7 and Reg 12]** The conditions set out in the Leasehold Premises Regulations as ones which a lessor may reasonably require a trade organisation, qualifications body or general qualifications body to meet are that it:

- obtains any necessary planning permission and other statutory consents
- submits plans and specifications for the lessor's approval (provided that such approval will not be unreasonably withheld) and thereafter carries out the work in accordance with them
- allows the lessor a reasonable opportunity to inspect the work after it is completed, or
- reimburses the lessor's reasonable costs incurred in connection with the giving of consent.

In the case of general qualifications bodies only, there is a further condition that the consent of another person required under a superior lease or binding obligation must be obtained. In addition, in a case where it would be reasonable for the lessor to withhold consent, the lessor may give such consent subject to a condition that the premises are reinstated to their original condition at the end of the lease. This condition does not apply to general qualifications bodies.

WHAT HAPPENS IF THE LESSOR REFUSES CONSENT OR ATTACHES CONDITIONS TO CONSENT?

10.27 [Sch 4, Part I, para 2 and Sch 4, Part 4, para 17] Where a disabled person brings legal proceedings against a trade organisation, qualifications body or general qualifications body under Part 2 or Part 4 – and those proceedings involve a failure to make an alteration to premises – he may ask the employment tribunal or County/Sheriff Court hearing the case to bring in the lessor as an additional party to the proceedings. The organisation or body may also make such a request. The tribunal or court will grant that request if it is made before the hearing of the case begins – save where the court can refuse the request if the court considers that another lessor should be brought into the proceedings. It may refuse the request if it is made after the hearing of the claim begins. The request will not be granted if it is made after the tribunal or court has determined the claim.

Reference to court

10.28 [Sch 4, Part 4, para 16] If a general qualifications body has written to the lessor for consent to make an alteration and the lessor has refused consent or has attached conditions to his consent, the general qualifications body or a disabled person who has an interest in the proposed alteration may refer the matter to a County Court or, in Scotland, the Sheriff Court. The court will decide whether the lessor's refusal or any of the conditions are unreasonable. If it decides that they are, it may make an appropriate declaration or authorise the general qualifications body to make the alteration under a court order (which may impose conditions on the general qualifications body). Where the general qualifications body occupies premises under a sub-lease or sub-tenancy, these provisions are modified to apply also to the general qualifications body's landlord.

10.29 Where the lessor has been made a party to the proceedings, the employment tribunal or County/Sheriff Court may determine whether the lessor has unreasonably refused consent to the alteration or has consented subject to unreasonable conditions. In either case, the tribunal or court can:

- make an appropriate declaration
- make an order authorising the organisation or body to make a specified alteration
- order the lessor to pay compensation to the disabled person.

10.30 The tribunal or court may require the organisation or body to comply with any conditions specified in the order. If the tribunal or court orders the lessor to pay compensation, it cannot also order the organisation or body to do so.

COMPARISON WITH THE PROCEDURE FOR OBTAINING CONSENT UNDER PART 3

10.31 There are similar provisions which govern the procedure by which a service provider may obtain consent to an alteration which it proposes to make in order to comply with a duty of reasonable adjustment under Part 3 of the Act. These procedures are broadly similar to procedures under Part 4 of the Act that apply to general qualifications bodies. However, it should be noted that the procedures for obtaining consent under Parts 2 and 3 respectively differ in certain ways. In particular:

- the periods within which the lessor must respond to an application for consent are not the same – under Part 3 (and in relation to Part 4 duties concerning general qualifications bodies) the relevant period is 42 days beginning with the day on which the application is received
- Under Part 3 (and in relation to Part 4 duties concerning general qualifications bodies) the lessor may require plans and specifications to be submitted **before** it decides whether to give consent
- Under Part 3 (and in relation to Part 4 duties concerning general qualifications bodies) it is possible to make a freestanding reference to the court if the lessor has either refused consent or attached conditions to it. Under Part 2, the question of consent to alterations can only be considered by an employment tribunal in the course of a complaint of discrimination.

11. OTHER RELEVANT PROVISIONS

[4.133]

11.1 Additional provisions of the Act (and provisions of other legislation) are relevant to understanding the protection from discrimination afforded to disabled people in relation to trade organisations, qualifications bodies and general qualifications bodies. This chapter describes those provisions, and focuses in particular on the way in which disputes under the Act should be resolved. It should be noted at the outset that the duties imposed on trade organisations and qualifications bodies are contained in Part 2 of the Act (and are enforceable through employment tribunals), whereas the duties imposed on general qualifications bodies are contained in Chapter 2A of Part 4 of the Act (and are enforceable through the county courts in England and Wales and the sheriff courts in Scotland).

RESOLVING DISPUTES UNDER PART 2 OF THE ACT

11.2 Chapter 2 explained that, broadly speaking, the Act does not require the internal resolution of disputes by trade organisations and qualifications bodies, but that it is desirable for grievance procedures to be used where possible. Where grievance or disciplinary procedures exist, they must not discriminate against disabled people. Trade organisations and qualifications bodies may have to make reasonable adjustments to enable disabled people to use such procedures effectively, or to ensure that they do not place disabled people at a substantial disadvantage compared with others.

11.3 **[s 17A(1) and s 55 and Sch 3, para 3]** The Act says that a person who believes that someone has unlawfully discriminated against him (which includes victimising him or failing to make a reasonable adjustment) or has subjected him to harassment, may make an application to an employment tribunal. Such an application must normally be made within three months of the date when the incident complained about occurred.

11.4 **[s 17A(1A)]** This is subject to one proviso. In cases of alleged discrimination or harassment by a qualifications body, the Act says that no application may be made to an employment tribunal if a statutory appeal is available in respect of the matter in question.

11.5 Before making an application to an employment tribunal (or within 28 days of lodging it), a disabled person can request information relevant to his claim from the person against whom the claim is made. This is known as the 'questionnaire procedure'. There is a standard form of questionnaire (DL56) and accompanying booklet which explains how the procedure works (see Appendix B for details).

11.6 When an application to an employment tribunal has been made, a conciliation officer from the Advisory, Conciliation and Arbitration Service (ACAS) will try to promote settlement of the dispute without a tribunal hearing. However, if a hearing becomes necessary – and if the application is upheld – the tribunal may:

- **[s 7A(2)]** declare the rights of the disabled person (the applicant), and the other person (the respondent) in relation to the application
- order the respondent to pay the applicant compensation, and
- recommend that, within a specified time, the respondent takes reasonable action to prevent or reduce the adverse effect in question.

11.7 **[s 17A(4)]** The Act allows compensation for injury to feelings to be awarded whether or not other compensation is awarded.

11.8 **[s 17A(5)]** The Act also says that if a respondent fails, without reasonable justification, to comply with an employment tribunal's recommendation, the tribunal may:

- increase the amount of compensation to be paid, or
- order the respondent to pay compensation if it did not make such an order earlier.

11.9 Sources of information about how to make an application to an employment tribunal are listed in Appendix B.

OTHER PROVISIONS FOR PART 2 OF THE ACT

Anti-avoidance provisions

11.10 **[Sch 3A, Part 1]** Generally speaking, a disabled person cannot waive his rights (or the duties of a trade organisation or qualifications body) under the Act. The Act says that any term of a contract is 'void' (ie not valid) where:

- making the contract is unlawful under Part 2 because of the inclusion of the term
- the term is included in furtherance of an act which is
- itself unlawful under Part 2, or
- the term provides for the doing of an act which is unlawful under Part 2.

11.11 Trade organisations and qualifications bodies should not include in an agreement any provision intended to avoid obligations under the Act, or to prevent someone from fulfilling obligations. An agreement should not, therefore, be used to try to justify less favourable treatment or deem an adjustment unreasonable. Even parts of agreements which unintentionally have such an effect are unenforceable if they would restrict the working of Part 2. However, as explained in Chapter 10, special arrangements cover leases and other agreements which might restrict the making of adjustments to premises.

Compromise agreements

11.12 **[Sch 3A, Part 1]** The effect of the Act's provisions is also to make a contract term unenforceable if it would prevent anyone from making an application to an employment tribunal under Part 2, or a claim to a county/sheriff Court under Chapter 2A of Part 4, or would force them to discontinue such an application or claim (see paragraphs 11.3 and 11.24). There is a limited exception to this principle relating to settlement agreements concerning Part 2 claims which have either been brokered by an ACAS conciliation officer, or which are made in circumstances where the following conditions are satisfied:

- the disabled person has received advice from a relevant independent adviser about the terms and effects of the agreement, particularly its effect on his ability to apply to a tribunal
- the adviser has a contract of insurance or an indemnity provided for members of a profession or professional body, and

- the agreement is in writing, relates to the application, identifies the adviser and says that these conditions are satisfied.

[Sch 3A, Part 1] In this regard the Act defines the circumstances in which a person is a 'relevant independent adviser' for this purpose.

Variation of contracts

11.13 **[Sch 3A, para 3]** A disabled person interested in a contract which contains a term of the kind mentioned in paragraph 11.10 may apply to a county court or, in Scotland, a sheriff court, for an order removing or modifying that term.

Collective agreements and rules of undertakings

11.14 **[Sch 3A, Part 2]** There are also anti-avoidance provisions in the Act relating to the terms of collective agreements, and to rules made by trade organisations or qualifications bodies which apply to all or any of an organisation's members or prospective members, or (as the case may be), to all or any of the people on whom a body has conferred qualifications, or who are seeking qualifications from it.

11.15 The Act says that any such term or rule is void where:

- making the collective agreement is unlawful under Part 2 because of the inclusion of the term
- the term or rule is included in furtherance of an act which is itself unlawful under Part 2, or
- the term or rule provides for the doing of an act which is unlawful under Part 2.

11.16 It does not matter whether the collective agreement was entered into, or the rule was made, before or after these provisions became law – the term or rule in question can still be challenged under the Act. In addition, where these provisions apply, certain disabled people may ask an employment tribunal to make a declaration that a discriminatory term or rule is void if they believe that it may affect them in the future. The Act specifies which disabled people may make such an application.

RESOLVING DISPUTES UNDER CHAPTER 2A OF PART 4 OF THE ACT

Introduction

11.17 This part of the chapter explains what happens if someone makes a complaint against a general qualifications body, and what routes of redress exist. It also explains what action may be taken to put right any discrimination that is found to have taken place.

Resolving disputes

11.18 It is good practice (and a legal requirement under the Civil Procedure Rules in England and Wales) to attempt to resolve disputes without resorting to legal proceedings. Complainants may, therefore, want to raise complaints directly with general qualifications bodies before resorting to legal proceedings. Many general qualifications bodies will have complaints procedures which aid the speedy resolution of disputes.

11.19 General qualifications bodies must make reasonable adjustments to any internal complaints procedures to prevent a disabled person from being placed at a substantial disadvantage in comparison with people who are not disabled. Failure to do so will itself amount to a breach of the Act.

11.20 So, for example, it is likely to be a reasonable adjustment for a general qualifications body to allow a disabled person who has communication difficulties some assistance to make a written statement of a complaint he wishes to make (such as by providing him with assistance via a neutral party). Depending on the circumstances, it may be reasonable to allow a disabled person with learning disabilities to be accompanied to a meeting by a family member or friend, or to send written communications to a blind or visually impaired person in a format which is accessible to him.

11.21 Although, as stated above, it is good practice to try to resolve disputes internally wherever possible, there may be exceptional occasions where this will not be practical or appropriate.

CONCILIATION

Equality Act 2006

11.22 The Equality and Human Rights Commission is empowered by the Act to set up an independent conciliation service for disputes arising under Part 4 of the Act to promote the settlement of disputes without recourse to the courts, and has done so. Conciliation is made available locally around the country, and disputes may be referred to conciliation by the Equality and Human Rights Commission if both the complainant and the general qualifications body agree to this. The Equality and Human Rights Commission has no power to impose a settlement on either party.

11.23 Agreeing to participate in the conciliation process does not prevent a complainant from pursuing a case through the courts. The time limit for bringing an action in court is extended by three months if the conciliation process has been started within six months of a discriminatory act. No information disclosed to a conciliator during the conciliation process may be used in any subsequent court case without the permission of the person who disclosed it.

MAKING A CLAIM UNDER CHAPTER 2A OF PART 4 OF THE ACT

11.24 **[s 31ADA and SI 2007/2405]** The Act says that a person who believes that a general qualifications body has discriminated against him or has subjected him to harassment, may bring civil proceedings. Those proceedings take place in a County Court (in England and Wales) or the Sheriff Court (in Scotland). Similar proceedings may also be brought against a person who has aided someone else to commit an unlawful act. A claim must be lodged within six months of the alleged discrimination. Where there has been a continuing process of discrimination which takes place over a period of time, the six months begins at the date of the last discriminatory act. A court has the discretion to allow claims made outside of the six-month time limitation period to proceed, where they decide that it is just and equitable to do so.

11.25 If a complaint cannot be resolved and it is heard and determined by a court, the court may:

- declare the rights of the disabled person (the claimant in England and Wales and the pursuer in Scotland) and the other person (the defendant in England and Wales or the defender in Scotland) in relation to the claim (ie make a declaration of discrimination)
- order the defendant/defender to pay the claimant/pursuer compensation, including compensation for injury to feelings; and
- impose an injunction (in England and Wales) or specific implement or interdict (in Scotland) requiring a general qualifications body to take positive action or to prevent the general qualifications body from repeating any discriminatory act in the future.

Sources of information about how to make a claim to the courts are listed in Appendix B.

ENFORCEMENT OF CERTAIN PROVISIONS UNDER PART 2 OF THE ACT

11.26 In addition, the Equality and Human Rights Commission has a direct involvement in the enforcement of the provisions of Part 2 relating to:

- instructing or pressurising other people to act unlawfully (see paragraph 3.24), and
- discriminatory advertisements (see paragraphs 3.25 and 3.28).

11.27 **[s 25(2) Equality Act 2006]** Only the Equality and Human Rights Commission may bring proceedings in respect of these matters. Where it does so, the Equality and Human Rights Commission may seek:

- a declaration from an employment tribunal as to whether a contravention has occurred, and
- an injunction from a County Court (or, in Scotland, an order from a Sheriff Court) restraining further contraventions.

11.28 The Equality and Human Rights Commission may only apply for an injunction or order if it has first obtained a declaration from an employment tribunal that an unlawful act has occurred, and then only if it appears to the Equality and Human Rights Commission that a further unlawful act is likely to occur unless the person concerned is restrained.

(Appendix A (The meaning of disability) outside the scope of this work. Appendix B (Further information) omitted; see Useful addresses at **[5.61]**.*)*

EQUALITY AND HUMAN RIGHTS COMMISSION: CODE OF PRACTICE ON EQUAL PAY (2011)

[4.134]

NOTES

This Code of Practice was prepared by the Equality and Human Rights Commission to accompany the Equality Act 2010. It replaces the Equal Opportunities Commission's *Code of Practice on Equal Pay*, issued in 2003.

The new Code was brought into effect on 6 April 2011 by the Equality Act 2010 Codes of Practice (Services, Public Functions and Associations, Employment and Equal Pay) Order 2011, SI 2011/857 and applies in relation to all matters occurring on or after that date. The former Equal Pay Code was revoked with effect immediately before the coming into force of the new Code, by the Former Equality Commissions' Codes of Practice (Employment, Equal Pay and Rights of Access for Disabled Persons) (Revocation) Order 2011, SI 2011/776. The old Code, which is no longer reproduced for reasons of space, continues to have effect in relation to matters occurring before the date of revocation (see SI 2011/776, art 3).

Note that the original Code contains references to sections and Schedules of the Equality Act 2010 (and other legislation) in the margin of the page, next to the paragraph to which they relate. These have been reproduced at the beginning of the paragraph in question in this Handbook (in bold and within square brackets). Note also that where there are more than two section (etc) references separated by a semi-colon, the second reference relates to a second (or subsequent) sentence within the paragraph in question.

Note also that the Code is reproduced here as per the original; ie, Part 1 begins at paragraph 23 even though the introduction ends with paragraph 24.

See *Harvey* K.

INTRODUCTION

[4.135]

1. The Equality Act 2010 (the Act) gives women (and men) a right to equal pay for equal work. It replaces previous legislation, including the Equal Pay Act 1970 and the Sex Discrimination Act 1975, and the equality provisions in the Pensions Act 1995.

2. [Part 5 Chapter 3 Equality Act 2006] The provisions explained in this code are those set out in the Act under the heading 'Equality of terms'. They apply to pay and all the other terms of a person's contract of employment, but this code uses the language of 'equal pay' in the interests of both continuity and brevity.

POWERS OF THE COMMISSION

3. [ss 8, 9 & 10 Equality Act 2006] The Equality and Human Rights Commission (the Commission) was set up under the Equality Act 2006 to work towards the elimination of unlawful discrimination and promote equality and human rights.

[ss 16 & 20 Equality Act 2006] The Commission has powers to carry out inquiries, for example into the extent and causes of pay gaps in particular sectors or areas, and to conduct investigations of an employer it suspects of having unlawfully discriminatory pay practices.

The Commission uses its powers of investigation and inquiry strategically to promote equality and human rights, and to tackle entrenched discrimination and pay inequality.

4. [Schedule 2 Equality Act 2006] As part of an investigation or inquiry the Commission can require the employer to provide information about its policies or practices. This could include information about the pay of its employees. The employer cannot refuse to provide such information unless the Commission's request is unnecessary given the purpose of the inquiry or investigation or otherwise unreasonable.

It has previously used these powers to require companies in the financial services sector to provide data on pay gaps between men and women.[1]

5. [ss 31, 32 Equality Act 2006] The Commission has powers to assess and enforce compliance with the gender equality duty, including the duty to have due regard to the need to eliminate unlawful discrimination. It may also issue guidance.

6. [ss 28, 30 Equality Act 2006] The Commission may provide assistance to individuals taking legal action to enforce their right to equal pay, and may institute or intervene in legal proceedings to support an individual or help interpret and clarify the law.

NOTES

1 Financial Services Inquiry, Sex Discrimination and Gender Pay Gap Report of the Equality and Human Rights Commission, September 2009.

PURPOSE OF THE EQUAL PAY PROVISIONS OF THE ACT

7. The full-time gender pay gap has narrowed since 1975 when equal pay legislation first came into force but there remains a gap of over 16 per cent between women's and men's pay.[2]

8. Historically, women have often been paid less than men for doing the same or equivalent work and this inequality has persisted in some areas.

9. The Act's provisions on equal pay and sex discrimination are intended to ensure that pay and other employment terms are determined without sex discrimination or bias.

10. There are sound business as well as legal reasons for implementing equal pay. Pay systems that are transparent and value the entire workforce send positive messages about an organisation's values and ways of working. Fair and non-discriminatory systems represent good management practice and contribute to the efficient achievement of business objectives by encouraging maximum productivity from all employees.

11. Although this code relates to equal pay between women and men, pay systems may be open to challenge on grounds of race, age or other protected characteristics under the Equality Act 2010.

NOTES

2 There are several ways of measuring the pay gap. The figure quoted is the mean gender pay gap between full-time employees' earnings in the UK, based on the Office for National Statistics (ONS) Annual Survey of Hours and Earnings 2009. The hourly pay gap is bigger if women working part time are included.

PURPOSE OF THE CODE

12. The purpose of Part 1 of this code is to help employers, advisers, trade union representatives, human resources departments and others who need to understand and apply the law on equal pay, and to assist courts and tribunals when interpreting the law. Employees may also find it useful.

13. It is in everyone's interests to avoid litigation and Part 2 of the code – good equal pay practice – provides guidance on how to prevent or eliminate discriminatory pay practices and ensure that there are no unjustifiable pay inequalities.

14. The Equality and Human Rights Commission recommends that all employers regularly review and monitor their pay practices, although this is not a formal legal requirement. Involving trade unions or other employee representatives can help make pay systems more transparent. This code (Part 2) suggests that equal pay audits may be the most effective means of ensuring that a pay system delivers equal pay.

15. The Commission has extensive practical guidance available on its website to help employers to implement equal pay for women and men in their organisations.

STATUS OF THE CODE

16. This is a statutory code issued by the Commission under s 14 Equality Act 2006. It was approved by the Secretary of State and laid before Parliament on 27 July 2010. The code does not itself impose legal obligations. However it helps explain the legal obligations under the Equality Act 2010. Tribunals and courts considering an equal pay claim are obliged to take into account any part of the code that appears relevant to the proceedings. If employers and others who have obligations under the Act's equal pay provisions follow the guidance in the code, it may help to avoid an adverse decision by a tribunal or court in such proceedings.

17. This code applies to England, Scotland and Wales.

LARGE AND SMALL EMPLOYERS

18. The equal pay for equal work provisions of the Act apply to all employers regardless of size,[3] but the way employers discharge their obligation to avoid sex discrimination in pay may in practice vary according to the size of the organisation. Small employers are less likely to have a human resources team, and may have fewer written policies and more informal practices than large employers. They may also have less complex pay systems and may (though not necessarily) have narrower gender pay gaps.

NOTES

3 Except the reserve power in s 78 to require employers to report on their gender pay gap applies only to employers with 250 or more employees.

PUBLIC SECTOR EMPLOYERS

19. Employers in the public sector, and organisations in the private and voluntary sectors that exercise public functions, are subject to the gender equality duty in respect of those functions. They must have due regard to the need to eliminate discrimination and promote equality, and certain listed authorities have a particular duty in relation to reducing gender pay inequality.[4] This is explained in the Commission's Gender Equality Duty Code of Practice 2006.[5]

NOTES

4 Sex Discrimination Act (SDA) 1975 Public Authorities (Statutory Duties) Order 2006. Reg 2(5): 'A listed authority shall when formulating its objectives for the purposes of paragraph (4) consider the need to have objectives that address the

causes of any differences between the pay of men and women that are related to their sex.'

5 The Equality Act 2010 contains a single public sector equality duty which will apply to all characteristics except marriage and civil partnership. However, at the time of issue of this code, this duty has not been commenced. The Gender Equality Duty Code of Practice 2006 has effect until replaced by any new public sector equality duty code.

MEN AND WOMEN

20. The equal pay provisions in the Equality Act 2010 apply to both men and women but to avoid repetition and for clarity, this code is written as though the claimant is a woman comparing her work and pay with those of a man, referred to as the male comparator.

USE OF THE WORDS 'EMPLOYER' AND 'EMPLOYEE'

21. The equal pay provisions of the Act apply to some people who are 'workers' but not employees in the legal sense – such as office-holders, police officers and those serving in the armed forces. In this code, these people are also referred to as 'employees' for convenience. Similarly, people who recruit or 'employ' these people are referred to as 'employers'.

REFERENCES IN THE CODE

22. In this Code, 'the Act' means the Equality Act 2010. References to particular sections (marked as 's.') and schedules of the Act are shown in the margins. Other legislation or regulations are also referenced in the margins.

FURTHER INFORMATION

23. Copies of the Act and regulations made under it can be purchased from The Stationery Office. Separate codes covering other aspects of the Act are also available from The Stationery Office. The text of all the Equality and Human Rights Commission's codes (including this Code) and guidance relating to the codes can also be downloaded free of charge from the Commission's website where Word and PDF versions are also available: www.equalityhumanrights.com

24. Free information about the Equality Act can be obtained by contacting the Equality and Human Right Commission's Helpline, details of which are below.

England

Equality and Human Rights Commission Helpline

FREEPOST RRLL-GHUX-CTRX

Arndale House, Arndale Centre, Manchester M4 3AQ

Main number 0845 604 6610

Textphone 0845 604 6620

Fax 0845 604 6630

Scotland

Equality and Human Rights Commission Helpline

FREEPOST RSAB-YJEJ-EXUJ

The Optima Building, 58 Robertson Street, Glasgow G2 8DU

Main number 0845 604 5510

Textphone 0845 604 5520

Fax 0845 604 5530

Wales

Equality and Human Rights Commission Helpline

FREEPOST RRLR-UEYB-UYZL

3rd Floor, 3 Callaghan Square, Cardiff CF10 5BT

Main number 0845 604 8810

Textphone 0845 604 8820

Fax 0845 604 8830

PART 1: EQUAL PAY LAW

OVERVIEW OF EQUAL PAY LAW

[4.136]

23. The principle that women and men are entitled to equal pay for doing equal work is embedded in British law and European Union law. Eliminating discrimination in pay is crucial to achieving gender equality and dignity for women.

24. Courts and tribunals will interpret equal pay law purposively because the legislation is grounded in European Union law, and in particular treaty provisions that have a broad social purpose.

British domestic law must conform to European Union law, which imposes specific obligations in respect of equal pay which can have direct effect. So, in considering equal pay claims under the Equality Act 2010, the British courts must take into account the relevant provisions of the Treaty,[6] relevant Directives and decisions of the Court of Justice of the European Union (formerly the European Court of Justice). If domestic law does not give full effect to these rulings then a woman may be able to rely on European Union law in British Courts.[7]

25. Pay is defined broadly under European Union law and includes pensions. Article 4 of the recast Equal Treatment Directive[8] requires that:

'For the same work or for work to which equal value is attributed, direct and indirect discrimination on grounds of sex with regard to all aspects and conditions of remuneration shall be eliminated.'

26. The equal pay provisions in the Act apply to all contractual terms not just those directly related to remuneration, such as holiday entitlement. This is why the Act calls them 'equality of terms'.

27. Although the law on equal pay may seem complicated its purpose is simple – to ensure that where women and men are doing equal work they should receive the same rewards for it.

NOTES

[6] Article 157 of the Treaty of the Functioning of European Union; formerly Article 141 of the EC Treaty.

[7] See for example *Levez v TH Jennings (Harlow Pools) Ltd (No 2)* [1999] IRLR 764 EAT.

[8] The recast Equal Treatment Directive (No 2006/54/EC) on the implementation of the principle of equal opportunities and equal treatment of men and women in matters of employment and occupation consolidates a number of Directives on gender equality.

SEX EQUALITY CLAUSE

28. A woman doing equal work with a man in the same employment is entitled to equality in pay and other contractual terms, unless the employer can show that there is a material reason for the difference which does not discriminate on the basis of her sex.

29. [s 66] Where there is equal work, the Act implies a sex equality clause automatically into the woman's contract of employment, modifying it where necessary to ensure her pay and all other contractual terms are no less favourable than the man's.

30. Where a woman doing equal work shows that she is receiving less pay or other less favourable terms in her contract, or identifies a contract term from which her comparator benefits and she does not (for example he is entitled to a company car and she is not), the employer will have to show why this is. If the employer is unable to show that the difference is due to a material factor which has nothing to do with her sex, then the equality clause takes effect.

31. These equal pay provisions apply to all contractual terms including wages and salaries, non-discretionary bonuses, holiday pay, sick pay, overtime, shift payments, and occupational pension benefits, and to non-monetary terms such as leave entitlements or access to sports and social benefits.

32. [s 70] Other sex discrimination provisions apply to non-contractual pay and benefits such as purely discretionary bonuses, promotions, transfers and training and offers of employment or appointments to office.

Example: A female sales manager is entitled under her contract of employment to an annual bonus calculated by reference to a specified number of sales. She discovers that a male sales manager working for the same employer and in the same office receives a higher bonus under his contract for the same number of sales. She would bring her claim under the equality of terms (equal pay) provisions.

However, if the female sales manager is not paid a discretionary Christmas bonus that the male manager is paid, she could bring a claim under the sex discrimination at work provisions rather than an equal pay claim because it is not about a contractual term.

33. [s 71] Where an equality clause cannot operate, because for example the woman cannot identify an actual male comparator for an equal pay claim, but she has evidence of direct sex discrimination, she can bring a discrimination claim (see paragraph 61).

WHAT IS EQUAL WORK?

34. [s 65(1)] A woman can claim equal pay and other contract terms with a male comparator doing work that is:

- The same or broadly similar, provided that where there are any differences in the work these are not of practical importance (known as **'like work'**)

- Different, but which is rated under the same job evaluation scheme as being work of equal value (known as '**work rated as equivalent**')
- Different, but of equal value in terms of factors such as effort, skill and decision-making (known as '**work of equal value**').

The comparator must be in the 'same employment' as the claimant, the meaning of which is explained at paragraph 51.

LIKE WORK

35. [s 65(2), (3)] There are two questions to ask when determining 'like work'.

The first question is whether the woman and her male comparator are employed on work that is the same or of a broadly similar nature. This involves a general consideration of the work and the knowledge and skills needed to do it.

If the woman shows that the work is broadly similar, the second question is whether any differences between her work and that done by her comparator are of practical importance having regard to:

- the frequency with which any differences occur in practice, and
- the nature and extent of those differences.

36. It is for the employer to show that there are differences of practical importance in the work actually performed. Differences such as additional duties, level of responsibility, skills, the time at which work is done, qualifications, training and physical effort could be of practical importance.

A difference in workload does not itself preclude a like work comparison, unless the increased workload represents a difference in responsibility or other difference of practical importance.

EXAMPLES OF 'LIKE WORK'

Like work comparisons that have succeeded, in the particular circumstances of the case, include:

- Male and female drivers where the men were more likely to work at weekends.[9]
- A woman cook preparing lunches for directors and a male chef cooking breakfast, lunch and tea for employees.[10]
- Male and female supermarket employees who perform similar tasks, requiring similar skill levels, although the men may lift heavier objects from time to time.
- Male and female laboratory assistants where the man spent some time on the shop floor.[11]

The differences were not found to be of practical importance in relation to their pay.

37. A detailed examination of the nature and extent of the differences and how often they arise in practice is required. A contractual obligation on a man to do additional duties is not sufficient, it is what happens in practice that counts.

Example: A woman working as a primary school administrator claimed equal pay with a male secondary school administrator. The courts found they were not doing like work. Although the work was broadly similar, the latter role carried greater financial and managerial responsibilities and was in a much larger school. The primary school administrator had more routine, term-time tasks while the secondary school administrator's work was year round and more strategic. These differences were considered to be of practical importance so the equal pay for like work claim failed.[12]

However where men but not women were obliged under their contracts to transfer to different duties and work compulsory overtime, this did not amount to a difference of practical importance because the flexibility was not used in practice.[13]

NOTES

9 *Hatch v Wadham Stringer Commercials (Ashford) Ltd ET* Case No 40171/77.

10 *Capper Pass Ltd v Allan* [1980] ICR 194 EAT.

11 *Crook v Dexter Paints Ltd COET* 2089/166.

12 *Morgan v Middlesborough Borough Council* 2005 EWCA Civ 1432.

13 *Electrolux Ltd v Hutchinson and others* [1976] IRLR 410 EAT.

WORK RATED AS EQUIVALENT

38. [s 65(4)] woman's work is rated as equivalent to a man's if the employer's job evaluation study gives an equal value to their work in terms of the demands made on the workers, by reference to factors such as effort, skill and decision-making.

39. [s 80(5)] Job evaluation is a way of systematically assessing the relative value of different jobs. Work is rated as equivalent if the jobs have been assessed as scoring the same number of points and/or as falling within the same job evaluation grade. A small difference may or may not reflect a material difference in the value of the jobs, depending on the nature of the job evaluation exercise.

40. A job evaluation study will rate the demands made by jobs under headings such as skill, effort and decision-making. Because the focus is on the demands of the job rather than the nature of the job overall, jobs which may seem to be of a very different type may be rated as equivalent.

Example: The work of an occupational health nurse might be rated as equivalent to that of a production supervisor when components of the job such as skill, responsibility and effort are assessed by a valid job evaluation scheme.

41. To be valid, a job evaluation study must:

- encompass both the woman's job and her comparator's
- be thorough in its analysis and capable of impartial application[14]
- take into account factors connected only with the requirements of the job rather than the person doing the job (so for example how well someone is doing the job is not relevant), and
- be analytical in assessing the component parts of particular jobs, rather than their overall content on a 'whole job' basis.[15]

42. [s 131(5) & (6)] If a job evaluation study has assessed the woman's job as being of lower value than her male comparator's job, then an equal value claim will fail unless the Employment Tribunal has reasonable grounds for suspecting that the evaluation was tainted by discrimination or was in some other way unreliable.

43. [s 65(5)] Job evaluation studies must be non-discriminatory and not influenced by gender stereotyping or assumptions about women's and men's work. There has historically been a tendency to undervalue or overlook qualities inherent in work traditionally undertaken by women (for example, caring). A scheme which results in different points being allocated to jobs because it values certain demands of work traditionally undertaken by women differently from demands of work traditionally undertaken by men would be discriminatory. Such a scheme will not prevent a woman claiming that her work would be rated as equivalent to that of a male comparator if the sex-specific values were removed.

Example: A job evaluation study rated the jobs of female classroom teaching assistants and their better paid male physical education instructors as not equivalent. This was because the study had given more points to the physical effort involved in the men's jobs than it had to the intellectual and caring work involved in the jobs predominantly done by women. Because it uses a sex-biased points system, this job evaluation would not prevent the women succeeding in an equal pay claim.

44. [s 65(4)(b)] A woman's work can be treated as rated as equivalent if she can show that the work would have been assessed as being of equal value, had the evaluation not been itself discriminatory in setting different values for the demands being made of men and women.

45. A woman may also bring a claim of equal pay where her job is rated higher than that of a comparator under a job evaluation scheme but she is paid less. However, this will not entitle her, if an equality clause applies, to better terms than those her comparator has.[16]

Detailed guidance on designing, implementing and monitoring non-discriminatory job-evaluation schemes is available from the Commission's website. The Advisory, Conciliation and Arbitration Service (ACAS) and trade unions can also advise on job evaluation.

NOTES

14 *Eaton Ltd v Nuttall* 1977 ICR 272 EAT.

15 *Bromley v Quick* [1988] IRLR 249 CA.

16 *Evesham v North Hertfordshire Health Authority and another* [2000] ICR 612 CA.

WORK OF EQUAL VALUE

46. [s 65(6)(a)] A woman can claim equal pay with a man if she can show that her work is of equal value with his in terms of the demands made on her.

47. [s 65(6)(b)] This means that the jobs done by a woman and her comparator are different but can be regarded as being of equal worth, having regard to the nature of the work performed, the training or skills necessary to do the job, the conditions of work and the decision-making that is part of the role.

48. In some cases the jobs being compared may appear fairly equivalent (such as a female head of personnel and a male head of finance). More commonly, entirely different types of job (such as manual and administrative) can turn out to be of equal value when analysed in terms of the demands made on the employee.

Guidance on how to tell if jobs are of equal value is available from the Commission.

The Employment Tribunal Equal Value Rules of Procedure[17] apply to equal pay claims where a woman is claiming work of equal value.

49. A woman can claim equal pay using any or all of these methods of comparison. For example, a woman working as an office manager in a garage could claim 'like work' with a male office manager working alongside her and 'equal value' with a male garage mechanic.

NOTES

17 Employment Tribunals (Constitution and Rules of Procedure) Regulations 2004, Schedule 6.

WHO IS THE COMPARATOR?

50. [s 79] A woman can claim equal pay for equal work with a man or men in the same employment. It is for her to select the man or men with whom she wishes to be compared.

European Union law also allows a woman to compare herself to a man who is not in the same employment but where the difference in pay is attributable to 'a single source' which has the power to rectify the difference (see paragraph 57).

IN THE SAME EMPLOYMENT

51. [s 79] A woman can compare herself with a man employed:

- by the same or an associated employer at the same establishment or workplace, or
- by the same or an associated employer at a different establishment or workplace, provided that common terms and conditions apply either generally between employees or as between the woman and her comparator.

52. [s 79(9)] An associated employer means a company over which another company has control, or companies over which a third party has control (for example, the employer's parent company).

53. The definition of establishment is not restricted to a single physical location. For example, a woman may claim equal pay with a man doing equal work employed by the same council but working in a different geographic location.[18]

54. Where the woman and her comparator work at different establishments, she has to show that common terms and conditions apply. An example of common terms and conditions is where they are governed by the same collective agreement, but the concept is not limited to this type of arrangement.[19]

55. A woman can also compare herself with a comparator working at a different establishment if she can show that, had he been employed at the same establishment as her, he would have been working under the same common terms and conditions as those he and others in the comparator group are currently working under. The woman does not have to be working to the same common terms as him, and does not have to show that the comparator ever would, in reality, be employed at the same establishment as her.[20]

56. The Equality Act does not specify the geographical scope of the equal pay provisions but in most cases the woman and her male comparator will be based in Great Britain.

NOTES

18 *City of Edinburgh Council v Wilkinson and others*, EAT, 20/5/2010.

19 Per Lord Bridge in *Leverton*, relied on in *Barclays Bank plc v James* [1990] IRLR 90 EAT; *British Coal Corporation v Smith and others* [1996] ICR 515 HL; *South Tyneside Metropolitan Borough Council v Anderson* [2007] IRLR 715 CA.

20 *British Coal Corporation v Smith and others* [1996] ICR 515 HL.

COMPARING ACROSS EMPLOYERS: SINGLE SOURCE

57. Under European Union law differences in pay must be attributable to a single source which is capable of remedying an unlawful inequality. If this is different from the 'same employment' test in British domestic law, European Union law may be applied to produce a remedy. In practice, a woman and her comparator whose pay can be equalised by a single source are likely to be in the same employment.[21]

Example: A woman teacher can compare herself to a man employed by a different education authority where the difference in their pay is due to terms and conditions set by a national scheme and can be remedied by a national negotiating body.

NOTES

21 *Lawrence and others v Regent Office Care Ltd and others* [2003] ICR 1092 ECJ.

CHOICE OF COMPARATOR

58. A woman must select the man or men with whom she wishes to make a comparison, although she does not have to identify them by name at the outset.

The selected comparator could be representative of a group of workers or he could be the only person doing the particular type of work.

59. A woman can select more than one comparator and from her point of view this may be prudent. Multiple comparators may be necessary for a term-by-term comparison of a woman's contract. However, an Employment Tribunal can strike out a claim with a particular comparator, or could in exceptional cases require a claimant who unreasonably cites too many comparators to pay some costs.

60. **[s 64(2)]** The chosen comparator does not have to be working at the same time as the woman, so he may for example be her predecessor in the job.

61. **[s 71]** Where a woman has evidence of direct sex discrimination in relation to her contractual pay but there is no actual comparator doing equal work, so that a sex equality clause cannot operate, she can claim sex discrimination based on a hypothetical comparator.

Example: A woman's employer tells her that she would be paid more if she were a man. There are no men employed on equal work so she cannot claim equal pay using a comparator. However, she could claim direct sex discrimination as the less favourable treatment she has received is clearly based on her sex.

PART-TIME WORK AND EQUAL PAY

62. A pay practice that treats part-time workers less favourably than comparable full-time workers is likely to be indirectly discriminatory against women, as more women than men work part time. Unless an employer can objectively justify the pay differential or practice, it will be unlawful.

It is unlikely that an employer could justify a different basic hourly rate for full-time and part-time workers.

In most cases where a part-time worker is paid less (pro-rata) than a full-time worker, the Part-time Workers (Prevention of Less Favourable Treatment) Regulations would also apply.[22] These prohibit less favourable treatment of part-time workers (male or female) unless it can be objectively justified.

NOTES

[22] SI 2000/1551. Implementing the Part-time work Directive (97/81/EC).

EQUAL PAY AND OCCUPATIONAL PENSION SCHEMES

General

63. **[Pensions Act 1995]** Occupational pension schemes are also subject to the equal pay for equal work principle. Most occupational pension schemes are trust-based schemes where the scheme is legally separate from the employer and is administered by trustees, who are bound to implement equal treatment between women and men. The benefits will be in the form of pensions and lump sums.

Sex equality rule

64. **[s 67(1), (2)]** The sex equality rule operates to ensure that comparable women and men are treated equally in both access to and benefits of an occupational pension scheme. If an occupational pension scheme, or a term of it, is less favourable to a woman than it is to a male comparator, then the term is modified so that it is not less favourable.

65. The exclusion of part-time workers from an occupational pension scheme has been held to be indirectly discriminatory and unlawful.[23]

66. **[s 67(3), (4)]** Also, a discretion that is capable of being exercised in a way that would be less favourable to the woman than to her male comparator is modified so as to prevent the exercise of the discretion in that way.

67. **[s 69(4)]** However, if the trustees or managers of the scheme can show that the difference in treatment is because of a material factor which is not the difference in sex, then the sex equality rule will not apply to that difference.

68. The effect is that men and women are treated equally to comparable members of the opposite sex in relation both to the terms on which they are permitted to join the scheme and to the terms on which they are treated once they have become scheme members.

So a rule that provides for men and women to draw their benefits from the scheme at different ages, or on satisfying different conditions, is not consistent with the sex equality rule. The rule would be overridden to require benefits to be provided at the more favourable age or on the person satisfying the conditions applicable to either men or women.

69. **[s 67(5) & (6)]** The terms on which benefits are provided to dependants of members, and associated discretions, are also covered by the sex equality rule.

70. **[s 67(7) & (8)]** Where people of the same sex are treated differently according to their family, marital or civil partnership status, a woman must select a male comparator who has the same status. So if a scheme provides a particular benefit only to members who are married or in civil partnerships, a woman who is not married or in a civil partnership cannot choose as a comparator a man who is married or in a civil partnership for a claim in relation to that benefit.

71. **[s 67(9)]** A successful claim for access to an occupational pension scheme can result in the granting of retrospective access in respect of any period going back to 8 April 1976.

72. **[s 67(10)]** Equality in pension benefits can only be claimed for service from 17 May 1990.

73. **[Schedule 7 Part 2]** There is an exception to the sex equality rule that allows a difference in occupational pension contributions for women and men because of prescribed actuarial factors. For example, an employer may have to pay higher contributions for female than male employees because of their longer life expectancy.[24]

NOTES

[23] *Preston and others v Wolverhampton Healthcare NHS Trust and others (No 3)* [2004] ICR 993; *Bilka-Kaufhaus GmbH v Weber von Hartz* [1986] IRLR 317 ECJ.

[24] *Neath v Hugh Steeper Ltd* [1995] IRLR 91 ECJ.

DEFENCES TO AN EQUAL PAY CLAIM

74. The possible defences that an employer may raise in response to an equal pay claim are:

- the woman and her comparator are not doing equal work;
- the chosen comparator is not one allowed by law (for example he is not in the same employment);
- the difference in pay is genuinely due to a material factor, which is not related to the sex of the jobholders.

MATERIAL FACTOR DEFENCE

75. **[s 69]** Once a woman has shown that she is doing equal work with her male comparator, the equality clause will take effect unless her employer can prove that the difference in pay or other contractual terms is due to a material factor which does not itself discriminate against her either directly or indirectly because of her sex.

76. The employer must identify the factor(s) and prove[25]:

- it is the real reason for the difference in pay and not a sham or pretence
- it is causative of the difference in pay between the woman and her comparator
- it is material: that is, significant and relevant, and
- it does not involve direct or indirect sex discrimination.

Example: If an employer argues that it was necessary to pay the comparator more because of a skill shortage, they will have to provide evidence of actual difficulties in recruiting and retaining people to do the job being done by the higher-paid man. The employer will also need to monitor the discrepancy to ensure it is still justified.

77. Personal differences between the workers concerned such as experience and qualifications may be material factors.

Other examples of possible material factors are:

- geographical differences, for example London weighting
- unsocial hours, rotating shifts and night working.

78. Whether the defence is made out will depend on the specific circumstances in each case.

79. If the material factor accounts for only part of the variation in pay, the woman is entitled to a pay increase to the extent that that the defence is not made out.[26]

80. To be a valid defence, the material factor must not be directly discriminatory and if it is indirectly discriminatory, the difference in terms must be justified.

81. For example, if an employer argues that the difference in pay is due to market forces, but gender segregation in the workforce means that women are still concentrated in lower paid jobs, this defence may be discriminatory. An employer cannot pay women less than men for equal work just because a competitor does so.[27]

82. **[s 69(1)(a)]** A material factor will be directly discriminatory where it is based on treating women and men differently because of their sex.

A directly discriminatory material factor cannot provide a defence to an equal pay claim, and it is not open to an employer to provide objective justification.

Example: Male maintenance workers in a bank were paid more than female administrators because the bank had always regarded and rewarded men as family breadwinners. This is directly discriminatory and cannot be justified.

83. Even if the employer can show that a material factor is not directly discriminatory, a woman claiming equal pay may be able to show that it is indirectly discriminatory.

84. **[s 69(2)]** Indirect discrimination arises where a pay system, policy or arrangement has a disproportionate adverse impact on women compared to their male comparators. If the employer cannot objectively justify it, the defence will not be made out.

85. Statistical analysis which demonstrates a difference in the terms offered to men and women doing equal work but where one job is predominantly carried out by one sex, is one way of showing disproportionate adverse impact but it is not the only way.

86. Where the disadvantaged group is predominately women, and the group of advantaged comparators is predominantly men, it will be difficult for the employer to prove an absence of sex discrimination.[28]

Example: Women employed as carers by a local authority, whose work was rated as equivalent to men employed as street cleaners and gardeners, were paid at a lower rate. The difference was due to a productivity bonus scheme which did not apply to carers, who were predominantly women. As the scheme had a disproportionately adverse effect on the women, the employer would have to provide objective justification for it. That is, they would need to prove that it is a proportionate means to achieve a legitimate end.[29]

87. [s 69(1)(b)] An employer can justify an indirectly discriminatory factor by showing that it is a proportionate means of achieving a legitimate aim.

Example: If an employer can show that the only way to ensure adequate staffing of unsocial hours shifts is to pay a shift premium, then even if there is evidence that more men than women work those shifts and receive the extra payments, the material factor defence may succeed.[30]

Example: A firm of accountants structures employees' pay on the basis of success in building client relationships. It uses as one of the key indicators of that success the number of functions attended out of hours. Due to childcare responsibilities, fewer women than men can participate in these functions and women's pay is much lower. The firm cannot show that attendance at these functions produces better client relationships or other business outcomes that warrant the pay premium, taking into account the disadvantage to women. It is unlikely in these circumstances to be able to justify the payment.

88. [s 69(3)] There is no list of aims that are accepted to be legitimate, and whether or not an employer's pay practice pursues a legitimate aim will depend on the facts and circumstances in a particular case. However, the Act does specify that, for the purpose of justifying reliance upon a material factor, the long-term objective of reducing inequality between men's and women's terms of work is always to be regarded as a legitimate aim.

The employer must be able to show that the measure was in fact adopted to reduce inequality.

89. Even where the aim is legitimate, the employer must be able to show that the means it adopts to achieve the aim is proportionate in the circumstances.

Example: A process to phase out historical disparity in pay and benefits between men and women, which involves a period of pay protection for men to cushion the impact on them of the new arrangements, has the long-term objective of reducing inequality between the sexes. This is a legitimate aim. However, the employer will have to prove on the facts of the case that the approach to achieving that aim is proportionate. It may be difficult to prove that protecting the men's higher pay for any length of time is a proportionate means of achieving the aim where the reason for the original pay disparity is sex discrimination.[31]

90. Where a material factor applies at a particular point in time but subsequently ceases to apply, it will no longer provide a defence to differences in contractual terms.[32]

Example: An employer recruits a new employee at a lower than normal rate of salary due to severe financial constraints at the time of recruitment. Later, the employer's financial position improves. Once the reason for the difference in pay ceases to exist the employer cannot continue to rely upon that factor to explain differences in pay or other contractual terms.

NOTES

25 *Glasgow City Council v Marshall* [2000] IRLR 272, HL.

26 *Enderby and Others v Frenchay Health Authority and Another* [1993] IRLR 591ECJ.

27 *Ratcliffe and others v North Yorkshire County Council* [1995] IRLR 439 HL. For information about gender segregation in the workforce and the undervaluing of women's work see, for example, the Women and Work Commission report Shaping a Fairer Future, 2006.

28 Lord Justice Pill in *Gibson and others v Sheffield City Council* [2010] IRLR 311 CA; *Enderby and Others v Frenchay Health Authority and Another* [1993] IRLR 591ECJ.

29 *Gibson and others v Sheffield City Council* [2010] IRLR 311 CA.

30 *Blackburn v Chief Constable of West Midlands Police* [2008] ICR 505 CA.

31 *Redcar and Cleveland Borough Council v Bainbridge & Others* [2008] EWCA Civ 885.

32 *Benveniste v University of Southampton* [1989] IRLR 123 CA.

PREGNANCY, MATERNITY LEAVE AND EQUAL PAY

91. [s 73] A woman should not receive lower pay or inferior contractual terms for a reason relating to her pregnancy and a maternity equality clause is implied into her contract to ensure this. There is no need to show equal work with a comparator in this situation.

92. [ss 74, 74(10) & 18] The maternity equality clause applies to:

- the calculation of contractual maternity-related pay
- bonus payments during maternity leave, and
- pay increases following maternity leave.

Maternity leave includes compulsory, ordinary and additional maternity leave.[33]

93. During maternity leave a woman's entitlement to receive her usual contractual remuneration (that is, salary or other benefits with a transferable cash value such as a car allowance or luncheon vouchers) stops unless her contract provides for maternity-related pay.[34]

94. [s 74(6), (7)] However she is entitled to any pay rise or contractual bonus payment awarded during her maternity leave period, or that would have been awarded had she not been on maternity leave.

95. [s 74(9)] Maternity-related pay means pay other than statutory maternity pay to which a woman is entitled as a result of being pregnant or being on maternity leave.[35]

96. [s 74(3)] Any pay increase a woman receives or would have received had she not been on maternity leave must be taken into account in the calculation of her maternity-related pay.

Example: Early in her maternity leave a woman receiving maternity-related pay becomes entitled to an increase in pay. If her terms of employment do not already provide for the increase to be reflected in her maternity-related pay, the employer must recalculate her maternity pay to take account of the pay increase.

97. [s 74] Similarly any pay or bonus related to time before the maternity leave starts, during compulsory maternity leave or after maternity leave ends must be paid without delay. So if a woman becomes entitled to a contractual bonus for work she undertook before she went on maternity leave, she should receive it when it would have been paid had she not been on maternity leave.

Example: A woman goes on maternity leave on 1 June. The contractual bonus for the year ending 30 April is payable on 1 July. Her employer says he will pay the bonus to her when she is back in a few months. The law requires the employer to pay the bonus on 1 July as it would if the woman was not on maternity leave. If this does not happen, she can claim equal pay relying on the maternity equality clause provisions.

98. [s 74(8)] On her return to work a woman should receive any pay increases which would have been paid to her had she not been on maternity leave.

99. [s 76] Unfavourable treatment because of pregnancy or maternity in relation to non-contractual pay and benefits is covered by the employment discrimination provisions in the Act.

Example: [s 18] A woman who has been approved for a promotion tells her employer that she is pregnant. The employer responds that he will not now promote her because she will be absent on maternity leave during a very busy period. This would be pregnancy discrimination at work and any claim would be brought by the woman under those provisions of the Equality Act.

However, if the same woman is promoted and her increased salary takes effect after the commencement of her maternity leave, her maternity-related pay will need to be recalculated to take account of the salary increase, and the salary increase will be payable to the woman on her return to work from maternity leave. If this does not happen, she can claim equal pay relying on the maternity equality clause provisions.

NOTES

[33] The statutory maternity leave scheme is set out in Part VIII of the Employment Rights Act 1996 (ERA) and in the Maternity and Parental Leave etc Regulations 1991 SI 1999/3312.

[34] *Gillespie and others v Northern Health and Social Services Board and others* 1996, ECJ. Note that the law on women's entitlement to full pay during their maternity leave may continue to evolve.

[35] Earnings-related Statutory Maternity Pay must also be recalculated to reflect a pay rise awarded to a woman after the end of the calculation period but before the end of her maternity leave. *Alabaster v Barclays Bank* [2005] ICR 1246. This is explained in the HMRC Employer Helpbook for Statutory Maternity Pay.

MATERNITY EQUALITY IN PENSION SCHEMES

100. [s 75(1)–(6)] An occupational pension scheme is treated as including a maternity equality rule if it does not have such a rule already. The effect of this is to ensure that a woman on paid maternity leave is treated as if she were at work for pension purposes.

101. [s 75(9)] The only time a woman on maternity leave may be treated differently is when she is on a period of unpaid additional maternity leave, when she is not entitled to accrue occupational pension benefits as of right.[36]

NOTES

[36] However, this is a developing area of domestic and EU law, so advice should be sought on whether pension accrual should be maintained throughout the entire maternity leave period.

PAY TRANSPARENCY

102. The Court of Justice of the European Union has held that pay systems that are not transparent are particularly at risk of being found to be discriminatory. Transparency means that pay and benefit systems should be capable of being understood by everyone (employers, workers and their trade unions). It should be clear to individuals how each element of their pay contributes to their total earnings in a pay period.

Where the pay structure is not transparent and a woman is able to show some indication of sex discrimination in her pay, the employer carries the burden of proving that the pay system does not discriminate.[37]

NOTES

[37] *Handels og Kontorfunktionaerernes Forbund i Danmark v Dansk Arbejdsgiverforening (acting for Danfoss)* [1989] IRLR 532, [1991] ICR 74.

DISCUSSING EQUAL PAY ISSUES WITH COLLEAGUES OR TRADE UNION REPRESENTATIVES

103. The Act introduces limits to the enforceability of what are often called 'gagging clauses' or 'secrecy clauses' that some employers use to restrict discussions about pay packages and differentials. Restricting use of these clauses is intended to promote openness and dialogue about pay and bring an end to opaque pay structures.

104. [s 77] Any term of a contract which prohibits or restricts a person from making a 'relevant pay disclosure' to anyone, including a trade union representative, or from seeking such a disclosure from a colleague, including a former colleague, is unenforceable.

105. Colleague is not defined in the Act but is likely to have similar scope to the definition of a comparator, as the intention is to protect the seeking of pay information for the purpose of identifying pay discrimination.

106. [s 77(3)] A relevant pay disclosure is one which is:

- about pay, and
- made for the purpose of finding out whether or to what extent there is a connection between pay and having (or not having) a protected characteristic.

107. The pay discussions that are protected in this way are those aimed at establishing whether or not there is pay discrimination. This provision is not confined to the protected characteristic of sex.

Example: A discussion between a woman and a man for the purpose of establishing whether the man is being paid more than the woman could involve a relevant pay disclosure. However, two male colleagues simply comparing their respective salaries are unlikely to be making a relevant pay disclosure, unless they are investigating pay disparities which may be linked to race or another protected characteristic.

108. Involvement in a relevant pay disclosure can include but is not limited to:

- asking a colleague to provide information about his/her pay and/or benefits
- providing information to a trade union representative about pay and/or benefits, and
- receiving information from a colleague about pay and/or benefits.

109. If an employer takes action against an employee for making or seeking to make such a disclosure, or for receiving information as a result of such a disclosure, the employee may claim victimisation.

Example: A female airline pilot believes she is underpaid compared with a male colleague. She asks him what he is paid, and he tells her. The airline takes disciplinary action against the man as a result. The man can bring a claim for victimisation against the employer for disciplining him.

Example: A female estate agent believes she may have received a smaller bonus than she should have. She asks her male colleagues what bonus payments they received. She then approaches her employer and complains about the discrepancy. She is reprimanded for discussing her pay and told she will not receive a bonus at all next year. She can claim victimisation, as well as making a discrimination or equal pay claim in respect of the bonus if she now has or can obtain sufficient evidence to do so.

Example: A male construction engineer employed by a road haulage company discloses information about his pay to a competitor company in breach of a confidentiality obligation. He would not be protected from disciplinary action, as the disclosure was unlikely to have been made for the purpose of finding out whether or to what extent there was pay discrimination in his workplace.

110. Guidance on protected pay discussions and disclosures is available on the Commission's website.

EQUAL PAY – OBTAINING INFORMATION

111. [s 138] A woman who believes she is not receiving equal pay can write to her employer asking for information that will help to establish whether this is the case and if so, the reasons for the pay difference.

112. A trade union equality representative or other trade union representative can assist in this process.

113. There is a procedure set out in the Act and there are forms prescribed by the accompanying Order that can be used by people to seek information. However, there is no restriction on the form or manner in which questions can be posed or answers given. A question or reply is admissible as evidence in Tribunal proceedings whether or not they are contained in the statutory question or reply form. So if similar questions are asked in a letter rather than using the form, that letter and any response that the employer provides can still be put before the Employment Tribunal for them to consider provided it is sent within the relevant time limits.

114. **[s 138(4) & (5)]** If the employer fails to answer the questions within eight weeks or answers in an evasive or equivocal way, an Employment Tribunal can draw an inference, including an inference that the employer is in breach of the equal pay provisions. Standard forms and guidance on their use are available on the Government Equalities Office website.

115. A woman can use the statutory question and reply process to request key information and in many cases an employer will be able to answer detailed questions in general terms, while still preserving the anonymity and confidentiality of other employees.

116. The statutory question and reply process cannot be used to require an employer to disclose an employee's personal details, unless an Employment Tribunal orders the employer to do so, or the employee concerned consents to such information being disclosed.

117. Guidance on using the Data Protection Act 1998 and Freedom of Information Act 2000 in employment discrimination cases, including equal pay, is available on the Commission's website.

118. The Information Commissioner also has helpful guidance ('When should salaries be disclosed?') on its website.

USING THE GRIEVANCE PROCEDURE

119. Before making a complaint to the Employment Tribunal about equal pay, a woman should consider trying to resolve the issue with her employer.

If informal resolution is not possible, a woman should lodge a formal written grievance.

120. It is not necessary for the woman to name her male comparator at the grievance stage.

121. The ACAS Code of Practice on disciplinary and grievance procedures includes guidance for employees and employers on raising and dealing with complaints about pay or contractual terms.

122. Employees may seek advice and help from employee or trade union representatives.

123. Employers and employees can also seek advice from an ACAS conciliator. ACAS advisors can provide guidance on implementing equal pay too. ACAS can be contacted at www.acas.org.uk.

124. **[s 207A Trade Union Labour Relations (Consolidation) Act 1992]** If Employment Tribunal proceedings are commenced and there has been an unreasonable failure by either party to adhere to the ACAS Code this could affect any compensation awarded.

125. The time limit for making a complaint to the Employment Tribunal is not extended to take account of the time taken to complete a grievance procedure.

126. It can be unclear whether a particular term or benefit is contractual or not and in this case a woman would be well advised to make a claim for both equal pay and sex discrimination.

127. When responding either to a grievance or to a statutory question form, employers need to:

- decide whether or not they agree that the woman and her comparator are doing equal work, and, if not, explain in what way the work is not equal
- consider the reasons for any difference in pay/benefits or other contractual terms and whether (if necessary) these can be objectively justified, and
- explain the reasons for the difference.

BURDEN OF PROOF

128. A woman claiming equal pay must prove facts from which an Employment Tribunal could decide that her employer has paid her less than a male comparator in the same employment doing equal work. It is then for her employer, if the claim is denied, to prove that the difference in pay and/or other terms is for a material reason other than sex. If the employer proves that there is a non-discriminatory material factor which has resulted in the difference in pay the woman's claim will fail.

129. If the woman asserts that the material factor is indirectly discriminatory it is for her to provide evidence of this, statistical or otherwise. The employer will then need to objectively justify the difference in terms (that is, prove that it is a proportionate means of achieving a legitimate aim).

EMPLOYMENT TRIBUNALS

130. **[s 131(5), (6) & (7)]** If an equal pay claim is made, the Employment Tribunal will assess the evidence about:

- the work done by the woman and her comparator
- the application and validity of the job evaluation study if the claim is for work rated as equivalent
- the value placed on the work (sometimes with the advice of an independent expert), in terms of the demands of the jobs if the claim is for work of equal value
- the pay and/or other contract terms of the woman and her comparator and how they are determined, and
- the reasons for the difference in pay and/or contract terms if the employer raises a material factor defence.

131. There are special Tribunal procedures for work of equal value claims.[38] These can be obtained from www.employmenttribunals.gov.uk

132. **[s 131]** Once a woman has lodged an equal pay claim, she can seek relevant information about pay and other contractual terms from her employer in a number of ways. These include:

- disclosure
- requests for additional information, and
- requests for written answers.

NOTES

38 The Employment Tribunals (Equal Value) Rules of Procedure, Schedule 6 of the Employment Tribunals (Constitution and Rules of Procedure) Regulations 2004 (SI 2004/1861).

PROCEDURE

133. **[ss 127(1), (9) & 128]** A claim relating to a breach of an equality clause or rule is usually made to an Employment Tribunal. Where a claim is made to the civil court, the court may refer it to the tribunal which has more expertise in employment matters.

134. **[s 127(6)]** Members of the armed forces must make a service complaint before an Employment Tribunal can consider an equal pay or pensions claim from them, and cannot withdraw the service complaint if they wish the Employment Tribunal to hear their claim.

TIME LIMITS FOR EQUAL PAY CLAIMS

135. **[ss 129 & 123]** A complaint to an Employment Tribunal about equal pay must be made within six months of the end of what is known as the 'qualifying period'. In a 'standard case', this is six months from the last day of employment. This is different from sex discrimination claims for which the time limit is ordinarily three months from the last act of discrimination.

136. **[s 129(3)]** The date from which the six-month time limit starts to run is affected by the circumstances set out below.

137. **[s 130(3) & (10)]** In a stable work case (that is, where there have been breaks in what would otherwise have been continuous employment with the same employer), the six months would start to run from the date on which the stable employment relationship ended, not on the date a particular contract ended.

Whether it is a stable work case will depend on the facts.

For example, where a woman is on a series of contracts in what is essentially the same job (for example a teaching assistant on a series of annual contracts) or a progression within the same job (for example an administrative assistant who progresses to administrative officer), time will not start to run with the issue of a new contract.

Where a woman reduces her hours following a period of maternity leave and is issued with a new contract, this will not trigger the time limit as it is a stable employment relationship.

Example: Ms Smith had been continuously employed since 1980 by the local council as a cook in a residential home. In 2007, she wanted to reduce her hours of work. It was agreed to vary her contractual hours from 37 to 30 hours per week and reduce her days from five to four per week. She was issued with a letter headed 'Contract of employment' which stated that this superseded any previous contract. While this signed document did amount to a new contract, an uninterrupted succession of contracts is a stable employment relationship. She had done the same work for the same council over many years without any break in the work. The only variation made in the new contract was the reduction of working hours. Because Ms Smith had a stable employment relationship with the council the time limit would not be triggered until the end of this stable employment.

Example: Ms Auster was employed by her local council as a relief home carer from November 2000. In April 2009, she was appointed as a permanent home carer. With this change of status she became entitled to sick pay. Otherwise her terms of employment were unchanged. She signed a new contract stating that previous contracts were superseded. There was no gap or break in the continuity of her work for the council but because her status changed and some of her employment terms, a stable working relationship cannot necessarily be said to exist.[39]

138. A variation in terms and conditions will not start the six-month time limit running, providing the variation is not so significant as to amount to a termination of the previous contract.[40]

139. Where a woman is transferred to a new employer under the Transfer of Undertakings (Protection of Employment) Regulations 2006, and the equal pay claim relates to her employment with the transferor, if the liability for that claim passes under the Regulations, the equal pay claim must be lodged against the transferee within six months of the date of the transfer.

If the new employer, the transferee, fails to honour her pre-existing contractual right under the equality clause, she will have a separate claim against the transferee in respect of this breach. The six-month time limit for bringing that claim will not start to run until the end of her employment with the transferee.[41]

140. Example: Ms Jones worked for an NHS Trust as a domestic cleaner in a hospital. In January 2001, under a contracting-out arrangement, Ms Jones was transferred to the employment of a private cleaning company. She continued to work as before at the same hospital. In September 2006, she brought an equal pay claim against the cleaning company, relying on male comparators who had not transferred over to the company and were still employed by the NHS Trust. Ms Jones was paid £2 an hour less than men doing equal work for the Trust. Her claim relating to her employment with the Trust before the transfer is time-barred, as the six-month time limit ran from January 2001, the date of the transfer. The cleaning company, as transferee, is obliged to honour the equality clause, where it passes to them, and, if they fail to do so, she could bring a claim against them up to six months after the end of her employment with them.

141. [s 130(4)] Where the fact of the pay inequality was deliberately concealed and the woman could not reasonably have been expected to discover it, the time starts to run from the date she actually discovered or could reasonably have discovered the inequality. This is referred to as a concealment case.

142. [s 130(7)] Where the woman has an incapacity the time starts to run from the end of the incapacity.

[s 141(6)] 'Has an incapacity' in England and Wales means the woman has not attained the age of 18 or lacks capacity within the meaning of the Mental Capacity Act 2005.

[s 141(7)] In Scotland it means she has not attained the age of 16 or is incapable within the meaning of the Adults with Incapacity (Scotland) Act 2000.

143. [s 129(4)] Members of the armed forces have nine months from their last day of service to make their application to the Employment Tribunal provided that they raise a service complaint as mentioned at paragraph 134.

144. Civilians working with the armed forces are not governed by these rules and must make an application to an Employment Tribunal on the same basis as other people.

145. It is the claimant's responsibility to ensure their claim is made in time. Individuals and their representatives should be alert to the importance of observing these time limits, and err on the side of caution if there is any ambiguity or uncertainty about when time starts to run.

It should be noted that using an employer's grievance procedure does not extend the time limit for lodging a claim, nor does serving a statutory question and reply form.

NOTES

[39] *Cumbria County Council v Dow (No 2)* [2009] IRLR 463, CA.

[40] *Potter and others (appellants) v North Cumbria Acute Hospitals NHS Trust and others (respondents) (No 2)* [2009] IRLR 900, EAT.

[41] *Sodexo Ltd v Gutridge* [2008] IRLR 752, CA.

EQUAL PAY AWARDS AND REMEDIES

146. [s 132] If an equal pay claim is heard by an Employment Tribunal and upheld, the Tribunal may:

- make a declaration as to the rights of the woman and/or her employer in relation to the claim brought. For example, a pay rise to the level of the comparator's pay (including any occupational pension rights) or the inclusion of any beneficial term not in the woman's contract, and
- order the employer to pay arrears of pay or damages to the person who has brought the claim.

147. A declaration may be made even if the Employment Tribunal decides not to award any compensation.

148. An Employment Tribunal cannot make an award for injury to feelings for breach of an equality clause.

149. [s 132(4)] In England and Wales, the Tribunal can award arrears of pay or damages going back not longer than six years before the date that proceedings were started in the Employment Tribunal.

This is extended to the day on which the breach first occurred where incapacity or concealment applies (see paragraphs 141 and 142).

[s 132(5)] In Scotland, the Employment Tribunal can award arrears of pay or damages going back not longer than five years from the date that proceedings were brought in the Employment Tribunal. This is extended to 20 years where the employee had a relevant incapacity or there was a fraud or error.

150. [Employment Tribunals (Interest on Awards in Discrimination Cases) Regulations 1996] As in other discrimination cases, equal pay awards can be made subject to interest. An award of arrears of pay will generally only attract interest for about half the arrears period. Interest will be calculated as simple interest accruing day to day in accordance with prescribed statutory rates.

151. [s 133] In cases involving occupational pension entitlements, an Employment Tribunal may make a declaration as to the rights of the parties concerned. The rules as to what compensation can be ordered or may be agreed are complicated so it is important to seek advice.

152. [s 133(8)] Where an Employment Tribunal makes a declaration about the terms on which a member of an occupational scheme must be treated, the employer must provide such resources to the scheme as are necessary to secure that person's rights without further contribution by her or any other members.

PROTECTION AGAINST VICTIMISATION

153. [s 27] It is unlawful for an employer to victimise a worker for bringing an equal pay or discrimination claim or for giving evidence about such a complaint.

Victimisation arises if a person is subjected to a detriment, because that person has done a protected act, or is believed to have done a protected act.

A protected act includes the following:

- bringing proceedings under the Act
- giving evidence or information in connection with such proceedings
- doing any other thing for the purposes of or in connection with the Act, and
- making an allegation that someone is in breach of the Act.

This means that protection from victimisation does not start only when a claim is filed with the Employment Tribunal. Protected acts can include any discussion or correspondence about the matter between the woman and her employer.

154. [s 77(4)] Workers who seek or make a relevant pay disclosure, or who receive information that is a relevant pay disclosure, are protected from victimisation. For explanation of what is a 'relevant pay disclosure' see paragraph 106.

155. There is no requirement for a comparator in a victimisation complaint.

156. In considering whether an act has caused detriment, the focus is on the effect on the alleged victim, rather than any intent or purpose on the part of the employer.

Example: A group of women employed by a local authority brought equal pay claims. Some of the women settled, the others proceeded with their claim. Shortly before the Tribunal hearing, the employer wrote to the latter group warning of the potential consequences of the case for the council's finances. The women experienced this as pressure to drop the case and were distressed by the letter. The House of Lords found that this did amount to victimisation.[42]

157. The protection against victimisation includes not only the woman bringing the claim, but also any person who assists her, for example, a comparator.

NOTES

[42] *Derbyshire and others v St Helens Metropolitan Borough Council* [2007] UKHL 16.

PART 2: GOOD EQUAL PAY PRACTICE

INTRODUCTION

[4.137]

158. Despite the implementation of equal pay and sex discrimination legislation in the 1970s, there is still a significant gender pay gap. It could take an estimated 20 years to close the gap without further corrective action. This section of the code of practice therefore provides information and guidance on steps that employers can take which go beyond compliance with legal requirements. These steps, taken in consultation with the workforce and trade union or other employee representatives, should help accelerate the achievement of substantive gender equality at work.

159. The financial loss to women arising out of unequal pay is well documented, but organisations also lose out by failing to properly value and reward the range of skills and experience that women bring to the workforce.

The most commonly recognised risk of failing to ensure that pay is determined without sex discrimination is the risk of time-consuming and costly litigation equal pay litigation. The direct costs to an organisation of a claim can include not only any eventual equal pay award to the woman or women bringing the claim but also the costs of time spent responding to the claim, and the costs of legal representation.

The indirect costs are harder to quantify, but could include lower productivity on the part of those employees who consider that they are not getting equal pay and on the part of managers whose time is taken up in dealing with staff dissatisfaction and other repercussions.

160. Tackling unequal pay can also increase efficiency and productivity by attracting the best employees, reducing staff turnover, increasing commitment, and reducing absenteeism. Pay is one of the key factors affecting motivation and relationships at work. It is therefore important to develop pay arrangements that are right for the organisation and that reward employees fairly. Providing equal pay for equal work is central to the concept of rewarding people fairly for what they do.

161. Employers should not discriminate on any protected ground in their pay arrangements. The information on good practice set out here focuses on eliminating gender pay inequalities, which are the subject of this code of practice. However, the methods used to identify and remedy unlawful gender pay discrimination can also be used to remedy unlawful pay discrimination on other grounds.

REVIEWING OR AUDITING PAY

162. Employers are responsible for providing equal pay for equal work and for ensuring that pay systems are transparent. Where a pay system lacks transparency the employer must be able to prove there is no sex discrimination behind a pay differential.[43]

Pay arrangements are often complicated and the features that can give rise to discrimination in pay are not always obvious. A structured pay system, based on sound, bias-free job evaluation, is more transparent and more likely to provide equal pay than a system that relies primarily on managerial discretion.

ACAS can advise on how to structure a pay system.

163. Most employers believe that they provide equal pay for equal work, irrespective of the sex of the job holders or whether they work full or part time. An equal pay audit is the most effective way of establishing whether an organisation is in fact providing equal pay.

Organisations subject to the gender equality duty must pay due regard to the need to eliminate sex discrimination in pay. Although conducting an equal pay audit is not mandatory, it demonstrates appropriate action to identify and eliminate gender pay discrimination.[44] It provides a risk assessment tool for pay structures.

The Commission recommends all employers carry out regular equal pay audits. A model for carrying out an equal pay audit is described below.

164. A number of common pay practices, listed below, pose risks in terms of potential non-compliance with an employer's legal obligations:

- Lack of transparency and unnecessary secrecy over grading and pay.
- Discretionary pay systems (for example, merit pay and performance-related pay) unless they are clearly structured and based on objective criteria.
- Different non-basic pay, terms and conditions for different groups of employees (for example, attendance allowances, overtime or unsocial hours payments).
- More than one grading and pay system within the organisation
- Long pay scales or ranges.
- Overlapping pay scales or ranges, where the maximum of the lower pay scale is higher than the minimum of the next higher scale, including 'broad-banded' structures where there are significant overlaps.
- Managerial discretion over starting salaries.
- Market-based pay systems or supplements not underpinned by job evaluation.
- Job evaluation systems which have been incorrectly implemented or not kept up to date.
- Pay protection policies.

There is detailed guidance on the Commission's website about the law and risk management in relation to these issues. In many cases, this will involve carrying out a few straightforward checks or reviewing a relevant policy.

165. Risks of equal pay challenges generally arise not out of any intention to discriminate, but through pay systems not being kept under review and up to date. ACAS provides basic advice on the various different types of pay systems and on job evaluation.

NOTES

[43] See Part 1 of the code, paragraph 102. The key legal authority for this is known as Danfoss, the full case name is *Handels og Kontorfunktionaerernes Forbund i Danmark v Dansk Arbejdsgiverforening (acting for Danfoss)* [1989] IRLR 532, [1991] ICR 74. See also *Barton v Investec Henderson Crosthwaite Securities Ltd* 2003 ICR 1205, EAT.

[44] See Gender Equality Code of Practice England and Wales, EOC 2006, paragraphs 3.40–3.52, which has effect until replaced by any new public sector equality duty code.

THE BENEFITS OF CONDUCTING AN EQUAL PAY AUDIT

166. The benefits to an organisation of carrying out an equal pay audit include:
- identifying, explaining and, where unjustifiable, eliminating pay inequalities
- having rational, fair and transparent pay arrangements
- demonstrating to employees and to potential employees a commitment to equality, and
- demonstrating the organisation's values to those it does business with.

167. An equal pay audit may be the most effective method of ensuring that a pay system is free from unlawful bias. An audit should include:
- comparing the pay of men and women doing equal work – ensuring that this considers work that is the same or broadly similar (like work), work rated as equivalent and work that can be shown to be of equal value or worth
- identifying and explaining any pay differences, and
- eliminating those pay inequalities that cannot be explained on non-discriminatory grounds.

168. A process that does not include these features cannot claim to be an equal pay audit. The Commission's extensive guidance for employers on conducting equal pay audits is available on its website.

169. An equal pay audit is not simply a data collection exercise. It entails a commitment to put right any unjustified pay inequalities. This means that the audit must have the involvement and support of managers who have the authority to deliver the necessary changes.

170. The validity of the audit and the success of subsequent action taken will be enhanced if the pay system is understood and accepted by the managers who operate the system, by the employees and by their unions. Employers should therefore aim to secure the involvement of employees and, where possible, trade union and other employee representatives, when carrying out an equal pay audit.

A MODEL FOR CARRYING OUT AN EQUAL PAY AUDIT

171. The Commission recommends a five-step equal pay audit model.

Step 1: Decide the scope of the audit and identify the information required.

Step 2: Determine where men and women are doing equal work.

Step 3: Collect and compare pay data to identify any significant pay inequalities between roles of equal value.

Step 4: Establish the causes of any significant pay inequalities and assess the reasons for them.

Step 5: Develop an equal pay action plan to remedy any direct or indirect pay discrimination.

The Commission's Equal Pay Resources and Audit Toolkit provides detailed guidance on how to conduct an audit.

STEP 1: DECIDE THE SCOPE OF THE AUDIT AND IDENTIFY THE INFORMATION REQUIRED

172. This is a particularly important aspect of the audit, especially if it is the first audit that an organisation has undertaken. It is worth investing time and thought at this stage. In scoping the audit, employers need to decide:
- Which employees are going to be included? It is advisable to include all employees who are deemed to be in the same employment or whose pay can be attributed to a single source (see paragraphs 51-57 of Part 1 of the code). If a comprehensive audit is not possible, or is deemed unnecessary, then a sample of roles may be audited but the basis for selecting the sample must be clear.
- What information will be needed and what tools are available? Employers will need to collect and compare two broad types of information about their employees: the jobs they do, and what they are paid (ensure that this information is collected about part-time as well as full-time workers):
  - All the various elements of their pay, including pensions and other benefits.
  - The sex of each employee; their job, grade or pay band.
- In addition, where there is gender pay inequality, it will be helpful to collect data on: qualifications related to the job; hours of work; length of service; any performance ratings and so on.

173. The Commission has produced guidance that explains an employer's legal obligations regarding data protection when carrying out an equal pay audit, which is available on its website.

174. The key tool for conducting pay audits is the Commission's equal pay audit kit and its five-step process. Guidelines on conducting equal pay audits have also been published by various bodies including Local Government Employers, and the Joint Negotiating Committee for Higher Education Staff, the TUC and individual trade unions. These contain useful additional sector specific advice.

175. The employer needs to consider carefully what resources are needed.

- Who should be involved in carrying out the audit? An equal pay audit requires different types of input from people with different perspectives, including those with knowledge and understanding of:
    - the organisation's pay and grading arrangements
    - any job evaluation system(s) in use
    - payroll and human resource information systems, and
    - key equality issues, such as occupational segregation and the systemic tendency to undervalue work done by women.
- When should the workforce be involved? Employers need to consider when to involve the trade unions or other employee representatives.
- Is expert advice needed? Employers may also wish to consider whether to bring in outside expertise. ACAS, the employment relations experts, offer practical, independent and impartial help to help bring pay systems up to date.

STEP 2: DETERMINE WHERE WOMEN AND MEN ARE DOING EQUAL WORK

176. In Step 2 an employer needs to check whether women and men are doing:

- like work – that is work that is the same or broadly similar, or
- work rated as equivalent under a valid job evaluation scheme, or
- work of broadly equal value or worth, considering factors such as effort, skill and decision-making.

These checks determine where women and men are doing equal work. They are the foundation of an equal pay audit.

Employers who do not have analytical job evaluation schemes designed with equal value in mind will need to find an alternative means of assessing whether men and women are doing equal work. The Commission's Equal Pay audit toolkit includes suggestions as to how this can be done.

Employers who do use analytical job evaluation schemes need to check that their scheme has been designed and implemented in such a way as not to discriminate on grounds of sex. The Commission's toolkit provides helpful guidance on this.

STEP 3: COLLECT AND COMPARE PAY DATA TO IDENTIFY ANY SIGNIFICANT PAY INEQUALITIES BETWEEN ROLES OF EQUAL VALUE

177. Once employers have determined which male and female employees are doing equal work, they need to collate and compare pay information to identify any significant inequalities by:

- calculating average basic pay and total earnings, and
- comparing access to and amounts received of each element of the pay package.

178. To ensure comparisons are consistent, when calculating average basic pay and average total earnings for men and women separately, employers should do this either on an hourly basis or on a full-time equivalent salary basis (grossing up or down for those who work fewer, or more, hours per week – excluding overtime - than the norm).

179. Employers then need to review the pay comparisons to identify any gender pay inequalities and decide if any are significant enough to warrant further investigation. It is advisable to record all the significant or patterned pay inequalities that have been identified. The Commission's toolkit gives detailed advice and guidance on collecting and comparing pay information and when pay gaps may be regarded as significant.

180. Modern software allows for speedy and in-depth investigation of pay inequalities on any protected ground and also provides an essential tool for equality impact assessments.

STEP 4: ESTABLISH THE CAUSES OF ANY SIGNIFICANT PAY INEQUALITIES AND ASSESS THE REASONS FOR THEM

181. In Step 4 employers need to:

- find out if there is a real, material reason for the difference in pay that has nothing to do with the sex of the jobholders, and
- examine their pay systems to find out which pay policies and practices may have caused or may be contributing to any gender pay inequalities.

182. Pay systems vary considerably. Pay systems that group jobs into pay grades or bands have traditionally treated jobs in the same grade or band as being of broadly equal value, either because they have been evaluated with similar scores under a job evaluation scheme, or because they are simply regarded as equivalent. However, recent years have seen a trend towards structures with fewer, broader grades or bands and greater use of performance pay and market factors.

A single broad band or grade may contain jobs or roles of significantly different value because it encompasses a wide range of job evaluation scores. This, combined with a wider use of other determinants of pay and more complex methods of pay progression, means employers should check all aspects of the pay system from a variety of standpoints: design, implementation, and differential impact on men and women.

183. The Commission has produced a series of checklists and guidance notes to help employers deal with the more common causes of unequal pay in the workplace (see paragraph 164).

STEP 5: DEVELOP AN EQUAL PAY ACTION PLAN TO REMEDY ANY DIRECT OR INDIRECT PAY DISCRIMINATION

184. Where the reason for the pay difference is connected with the employee's sex (or another protected ground), employers will need to remedy this and provide equal pay for current and future employees doing equal work.

If the pay differential arises from a factor that has an adverse impact on women, then it has to be objectively justified. For example, if an employee is entitled to a premium for working unsocial hours and fewer women than men can do this because of their caring responsibilities, it will be indirectly discriminatory and the employer will have to be able to prove it is justified. Further explanation of what this means is in Part 1 of the code (paragraph 83–89) and in other Commission guidance.

185. Employers who find no inequalities between men's and women's pay, or on other protected grounds, or who find pay differences for which there are genuinely non-discriminatory reasons, should nevertheless keep their pay systems under review by introducing regular monitoring undertaken jointly with trade unions. This will ensure that the pay system remains free of bias.

(List of contacts omitted; see Part 5, Section F at **[5.61]**.*)*

EQUALITY AND HUMAN RIGHTS COMMISSION: CODE OF PRACTICE ON EMPLOYMENT (2011)

This code applies to the provisions in the Equality Act 2010 that were commenced on 1st October 2010.

[4.138]

NOTES

This Code of Practice was prepared by the Equality and Human Rights Commission to accompany the Equality Act 2010. It replaces Codes issued by the Equal Opportunities Commission in 1985 (*Code of Practice for the elimination of discrimination on the grounds of sex and marriage and the promotion of equality of opportunity in employment*), the Commission for Racial Equality in 2005 (*Code of Practice on racial equality in employment*), and the Disability Rights Commission in 2004 (*Employment and Occupation*), but not that on Equal Pay, which is the subject of a separate new Code (see **[4.134]**). The Employment Code covers all of the strands of employment discrimination covered by the Equality Act other than equal pay.

The new Code was brought into effect on 6 April 2011 by the Equality Act 2010 Codes of Practice (Services, Public Functions and Associations, Employment, and Equal Pay) Order 2011, SI 2011/857 and applies in relation to all matters occurring on or after that date. The former Codes, referred to above, were revoked with effect immediately before the coming into force of the new Code, by the Former Equality Commissions' Codes of Practice (Employment, Equal Pay and Rights of Access for Disabled Persons) (Revocation) Order 2011, SI 2011/776. The old Codes, which are no longer reproduced for reasons of space, continue to have effect in relation to matters occurring before the date of revocation (see SI 2011/776, art 3).

Note that the original Code contains references to sections and Schedules of the Equality Act 2010 (and other legislation) in the margin of the page, next to the paragraph to which they relate. These have been reproduced at the beginning of the paragraph in question in this Handbook (in bold and within square brackets). Note also that where there are more than two section (etc) references separated by a semi-colon, the second reference relates to a second (or subsequent) sentence within the paragraph in question.

See *Harvey* L.

CONTENTS

CHAPTER 1 INTRODUCTION

PURPOSE OF THE EQUALITY ACT 2010

[4.139]

1.1 The Equality Act 2010 (the Act) consolidates and replaces most of the previous discrimination legislation for England, Scotland and Wales. The Act covers discrimination because of age, disability, gender reassignment, marriage and civil partnership, pregnancy and maternity, race, religion or belief, sex and sexual orientation. These categories are known in the Act as 'protected characteristics'.

1.2 An important purpose of the Act is to unify the legislation outlawing discrimination against people with different protected characteristics, where this is appropriate. There are, however, some significant differences and exceptions, which this Code explains.

1.3 As well as consolidating existing law, the Act makes discrimination unlawful in circumstances not covered previously. Discrimination in most areas of activity is now unlawful, subject to certain exceptions. These areas of activity include, for example: employment and other areas of work; education; housing; the provision of services, the exercise of public functions and membership of associations.

1.4 Different areas of activity are covered under different parts of the Act. Part 3 of the Act deals with discrimination in the provision of services and public functions. Part 4 deals with discrimination in the sale, letting, management and occupation of premises, including housing. Part 5 covers employment and other work-related situations. Part 6 covers education including schools, further education, higher education, and general qualifications bodies. Part 7 deals with discrimination by membership associations. An organisation may have duties under more than one area of the Act because, for example, it employs people and provides services to customers.

SCOPE OF THE CODE

1.5 This Code covers discrimination in employment and work-related activities under Part 5 of the Act. Part 5 is based on the principle that people with the protected characteristics set out in the Act should not be discriminated against in employment, when seeking employment, or when engaged in occupations or activities related to work.

1.6 In Part 5 of the Act, there are some provisions relating to equal pay between men and women. These provisions create an implied sex equality clause in employment contracts, in order to ensure equality in pay and other contractual terms for women and men doing equal work. Equal pay between men and women is covered in the Equal Pay Code published by the Equality and Human Rights Commission ('the Commission').

1.7 Part 5 also contains sections which make discrimination by trade organisations (including trade unions) and vocational qualifications bodies unlawful. Because the duties of qualifications bodies and trade organisations are different to the duties of employers, these will be covered by a separate Code.

1.8 This Code applies to England, Scotland and Wales.

PURPOSE OF THE CODE

1.9 The main purpose of this Code is to provide a detailed explanation of the Act. This will assist courts and tribunals when interpreting the law and help lawyers, advisers, trade union representatives, human resources departments and others who need to apply the law and understand its technical detail.

1.10 The Commission has also produced practical guidance for workers and employers which assumes no knowledge of the law and which may be more helpful and accessible for people who need an introduction to the Act. It can be obtained from the Commission, or downloaded from the Commission's website.

1.11 The Code, together with the practical guidance produced by the Commission will:

- help employers and others understand their responsibilities and avoid disputes in the workplace;
- help individuals to understand the law and what they can do if they believe they have been discriminated against;
- help lawyers and other advisers to advise their clients;
- give Employment Tribunals and courts clear guidance on good equal opportunities practice in employment; and
- ensure that anyone who is considering bringing legal proceedings under the Act, or attempting to negotiate equality in the workplace, understands the legislation and is aware of good practice in employment.

STATUS OF THE CODE

1.12 The Commission has prepared and issued this Code on the basis of its powers under the Equality Act 2006. It is a statutory Code. This means it has been approved by the Secretary of State and laid before Parliament.

1.13 The Code does not impose legal obligations. Nor is it an authoritative statement of the law; only the tribunals and the courts can provide such authority. However, the Code can be used in evidence in legal proceedings brought under the Act. Tribunals and courts must take into account any part of the Code that appears to them relevant to any questions arising in proceedings.

1.14 If employers and others who have duties under the Act follow the guidance in the Code, it may help them avoid an adverse decision by a tribunal or court.

ROLE OF THE EQUALITY AND HUMAN RIGHTS COMMISSION

1.15 The Commission was set up under the Equality Act 2006 to work towards the elimination of unlawful discrimination and promote equality and human rights.

1.16 In relation to equality, the Commission has duties to promote awareness and understanding and encourage good practice, as well as a power to provide advice and guidance on the law. It also has powers to enforce discrimination law in some circumstances.

HUMAN RIGHTS

1.17 Public authorities have a duty under the Human Rights Act 1998 (HRA) not to act incompatibly with rights under the European Convention for the Protection of Human Rights and Fundamental Freedoms (the Convention).

1.18 Courts and tribunals have a duty to interpret primary legislation (including the Equality Act 2010) and secondary legislation in a way that is compatible with the Convention rights, unless it is impossible to do so. This duty applies to courts and tribunals whether a public authority is involved in the case or not. So in any employment discrimination claim made under the Act, the court or tribunal must ensure that it interprets the Act compatibly with the Convention rights, where it can.

1.19 In practice, human rights issues in the workplace are likely to arise in relation to forced labour, privacy and data protection, freedom of expression and thought, trade union activity and harassment.

LARGE AND SMALL EMPLOYERS

1.20 While all employers have the same legal duties under the Act, the way that these duties are put into practice may be different. Small employers may have more informal practices, have fewer written policies, and may be more constrained by financial resources. This Code should be read with awareness that large and small employers may carry out their duties in different ways, but that no employer is exempt from these duties because of size.

HOW TO USE THE CODE

1.21 **Section 1** of the Code, comprising **Chapters 2 to 15**, gives a detailed explanation of the Act.

Chapter 2 explains the protected characteristics of age, disability, gender reassignment, marriage and civil partnership, pregnancy and maternity, race, religion or belief, sex and sexual orientation.

Chapters 3 to 9 cover different types of conduct that are prohibited under the Act. **Chapter 3** explains direct discrimination. **Chapter 4** deals with indirect discrimination as well as explaining the objective justification test. **Chapter 5** covers discrimination arising from disability and **Chapter 6** sets out the duty to make adjustments for disabled people. **Chapter 7** explains the provisions on harassment. **Chapter 8** deals with pregnancy and maternity discrimination. **Chapter 9** covers the remaining types of unlawful conduct: victimisation; instructing, causing or inducing discrimination; aiding contraventions of the Act; and gender reassignment discrimination (absence from work).

Chapter 10 explains the obligations and liabilities of the employer and the corresponding rights of workers. **Chapter 11** deals with the wider work relationships covered by Part 5 of the Act. **Chapter 12** sets out the legal provisions relating to positive action and how employers adopting positive action measures can ensure that such measures are lawful under the Act.

Chapter 13 explains occupational requirements and other exceptions related to work. **Chapter 14** covers pay and benefits including several specific exceptions to the work provisions of the Act. **Chapter 15** explains how the Act can be enforced by individuals or the Commission and gives an overview of alternatives to litigation.

Section 2, comprising **Chapters 16 to 19**, sets out recommended practice for employers, to help them comply with the Act and to achieve equality of opportunity and outcomes over the whole employment cycle. Public sector employers have specific obligations under the public sector equality duties and will find that this section helps them to meet these obligations.

Chapter 16 discusses how employers can avoid discrimination during the recruitment process. **Chapter 17** explains how discrimination can be avoided during employment and deals with issues such as working hours, accommodating workers' needs, training and development and disciplinary and grievance matters. **Chapter 18** discusses equality policies and implementation of such policies in the workplace. **Chapter 19** explains how discrimination can be avoided during termination of employment.

Additional information is appended at the end of the Code. **Appendix 1** gives further information on the definition of disability under the Act; **Appendix 2** provides information about diversity monitoring; and **Appendix 3** explains how leases and other legal obligations affect the duty to make reasonable adjustments to premises.

EXAMPLES IN THE CODE

1.22 Examples of good practice and how the Act is likely to work are included in the Code. They are intended simply to illustrate the principles and concepts used in the legislation and should be read in that light. The examples use different protected characteristics and work-related situations to demonstrate the breadth and scope of the Act.

USE OF THE WORDS 'EMPLOYER' AND 'WORKER'

1.23 The Act imposes obligations on people who are not necessarily employers in the legal sense – such as partners in firms, people recruiting their first worker, or people using contract workers. In this Code, these people are also referred to as 'employers' for convenience. The term 'employment' is also used to refer to these wider work-related relationships, except where it is specified that the provision in question does not apply to these wider relationships.

1.24 Similarly, the Code uses the term 'worker' to refer to people who are working for an 'employer', whether or not this is under a contract of employment with that 'employer'. These people include, for example, contract workers, police officers and office holders. The word 'workers' may also include job applicants, except where it is clear that the provision in question specifically excludes them. Where there is a reference to 'employees' in the Code, this indicates that only employees (within the strict meaning of the word) are affected by the particular provision.

REFERENCES IN THE CODE

1.25 In this Code, 'the Act' means the Equality Act 2010. References to particular Sections and Schedules of the Act are shown in the margins, abbreviated as 's' and 'Sch' respectively. Occasionally other legislation is also referenced in the margins.

CHANGES TO THE LAW

1.26 This Code refers to the provisions of the Equality Act 2010 that came into force on 1 October 2010. There may be subsequent changes to the Act or to other legislation which may have an effect on the duties explained in the Code.

1.27 The Act contains provisions on dual discrimination (also known as combined discrimination) and the new public sector equality duty. These provisions are not expected to come into force before April 2011. The government is considering how these provisions can be implemented in the best way for business and the public sector respectively.

1.28 Readers of this Code will therefore need to keep up to date with any developments that affect the Act's provisions and should be aware of the other Codes issued by the Commission. Further information can be obtained from the Commission (see below for contact details).

FURTHER INFORMATION

1.29 Copies of the Act and regulations made under it can be purchased from The Stationery Office. Separate codes covering other aspects of the Act are also available from The Stationery Office. The text of all the Equality and Human Rights Commission's codes (including this Code) and guidance relating to the codes can also be downloaded free of charge from the Commission's website where Word and PDF versions are also available: www.equalityhumanrights.com

1.30 (*Addresses and telephone numbers of the Equality and Human Right Commission have been omitted; see 'Useful Addresses' in Part 5 at* **[5.61]**.)

PART 1: CODE OF PRACTICE ON EMPLOYMENT

CHAPTER 2
PROTECTED CHARACTERISTICS

INTRODUCTION

[4.140]
2.1 This chapter outlines the characteristics which are protected under the Act and which are relevant to the areas covered by this Code.

2.2 The 'protected characteristics' are: age; disability; gender reassignment; marriage and civil partnership; pregnancy and maternity; race; religion or belief; sex; and sexual orientation.

AGE

What the Act says

2.3 **[s 5(1)]** Age is defined in the Act by reference to a person's age group. In relation to age, when the Act refers to people who share a protected characteristic, it means that they are in the same age group.

2.4 [s 5(2)] An age group can mean people of the same age or people of a range of ages. Age groups can be wide (for example, 'people under 50'; 'under 18s'). They can also be quite narrow (for example, 'people in their mid-40s'; 'people born in 1952'). Age groups may also be relative (for example, 'older than me' or 'older than us').

2.5 The meaning of certain age-related terms may differ according to the context. For example, whether someone is seen as 'youthful' can depend on their role: compare a youthful bartender with a youthful CEO. Age groups can also be linked to actual or assumed physical appearance, which may have little relationship with chronological age – for example, 'the grey workforce'.

2.6 There is some flexibility in the definition of a person's age group. For example, a 40 year old could be described as belonging to various age groups, including '40 year olds'; 'under 50s'; '35 to 45 year olds'; 'over 25s'; or 'middle-aged'. Similarly, a 16 year old could be seen as belonging to groups that include: 'children'; 'teenagers'; 'under 50s'; 'under 25s'; 'over 14s' or '16 year olds'.

Example: A female worker aged 25 could be viewed as sharing the protected characteristic of age with a number of different age groups. These might include '25 year olds'; 'the under 30s'; 'the over 20s'; and 'younger workers'.

Example: A man of 86 could be said to share the protected characteristic of age with the following age groups: '86 year olds'; 'over 80s'; 'over 65s'; 'pensioners'; 'senior citizens'; 'older people'; and 'the elderly'.

2.7 Where it is necessary to compare the situation of a person belonging to a particular age group with others, the Act does not specify the age group with which comparison should be made. It could be everyone outside the person's age group, but in many cases the choice of comparator age group will be more specific; this will often be led by the context and circumstances. (More detail on how to identify a comparator in direct discrimination cases is set out in paragraphs 3.22 to 3.31.)

Example: In the first example above, the 25 year old woman might compare herself to the 'over 25s', or 'over 35s', or 'older workers'. She could also compare herself to 'under 25s' or '18 year olds'.

DISABILITY

What the Act says

2.8 [s 6, s 6(3)(b)] Only a person who meets the Act's definition of disability has the protected characteristic of disability. When the Act refers to people who share a protected characteristic in relation to disability, it means they share the same disability.

2.9 [s 6(4)] In most circumstances, a person will have the protected characteristic of disability if they have had a disability in the past, even if they no longer have the disability.

2.10 People who currently have a disability are protected because of this characteristic against harassment and discrimination – including discrimination arising from disability (see Chapter 5) and a failure to comply with the duty to make reasonable adjustments (see Chapter 6). People who have had a disability in the past are also protected against harassment and discrimination (see paragraph 21.3).

2.11 Non-disabled people are protected against direct disability discrimination only where they are perceived to have a disability or are associated with a disabled person (see paragraphs 3.11 to 3.21). In some circumstances, a non-disabled person may be protected where they experience harassment (see Chapter 7) or some other unlawful act such as victimisation (see Chapter 9).

2.12 [s 6(1)] The Act says that a person has a disability if they have a physical or mental impairment which has a long-term and substantial adverse effect on their ability to carry out normal day-to-day activities. Physical or mental impairment includes sensory impairments such as those affecting sight or hearing.

2.13 [Sch 1, para 3] An impairment which consists of a severe disfigurement is treated as having a substantial adverse effect on the ability of the person concerned to carry out normal day-to-day activities.

2.14 [Sch 1, para 2(1)] Long-term means that the impairment has lasted or is likely to last for at least 12 months or for the rest of the affected person's life.

2.15 [s 212(1)] Substantial means more than minor or trivial.

2.16 [Sch 1, para 5] Where a person is taking measures to treat or correct an impairment (other than by using spectacles or contact lenses) and, but for those measures, the impairment would be likely to have a substantial adverse effect on the ability to carry out normal day to day activities, it is still to be treated as though it does have such an effect.

2.17 This means that 'hidden' impairments (for example, mental illness or mental health conditions, diabetes and epilepsy) may count as disabilities where they meet the definition in the Act.

2.18 [Sch 1, para 6] Cancer, HIV infection, and multiple sclerosis are deemed disabilities under the Act from the point of diagnosis. In some circumstances, people who have a sight impairment are automatically treated under the Act as being disabled.

2.19 [Sch 1, paras 2(2) & 8] Progressive conditions and those with fluctuating or recurring effects will amount to disabilities in certain circumstances.

2.20 For more on the concept of disability, see Appendix 1 to this Code. Guidance on matters to be taken into account in determining questions relating to the definition of disability is also available from the Office for Disability Issues:
www.officefordisability.gov.uk/docs/wor/new/ea-guide.pdf

GENDER REASSIGNMENT

What the Act says

2.21 [s 7(1)] The Act defines gender reassignment as a protected characteristic. People who are proposing to undergo, are undergoing, or have undergone a process (or part of a process) to reassign their sex by changing physiological or other attributes of sex have the protected characteristic of gender reassignment.

2.22 [s 7(2)] A reference to a transsexual person is a reference to a person who has the protected characteristic of gender reassignment.

2.23 Under the Act 'gender reassignment' is a personal process, that is, moving away from one's birth sex to the preferred gender, rather than a medical process.

2.24 The reassignment of a person's sex may be proposed but never gone through; the person may be in the process of reassigning their sex; or the process may have happened previously. It may include undergoing the medical gender reassignment treatments, but it does not require someone to undergo medical treatment in order to be protected.

Example: A person who was born physically female decides to spend the rest of his life as a man. He starts and continues to live as a man. He decides not to seek medical advice as he successfully passes as a man without the need for any medical intervention. He would be protected as someone who has the protected characteristic of gender reassignment.

2.25 The Act requires that a person should have at least proposed to undergo gender reassignment. It does not require such a proposal to be irrevocable. People who start the gender reassignment process but then decide to stop still have the protected characteristic of gender reassignment.

Example: A person born physically male lets her friends know that she intends to reassign her sex. She attends counselling sessions to start the process. However, she decides to go no further. She is protected under the law because she has undergone part of the process of reassigning her sex.

2.26 Protection is provided where, as part of the process of reassigning their sex, someone is driven by their gender identity to cross-dress, but not where someone chooses to cross-dress for some other reason.

2.27 In order to be protected under the Act, there is no requirement for a transsexual person to inform their employer of their gender reassignment status. However, if a worker is proposing to undergo gender reassignment or is still in the process of transitioning, they may want to discuss their needs with their employer so the employer can support them during the process.

Example: Before a formal dinner organised by his employer, a worker tells his colleagues that he intends to come to the event dressed as a woman 'for a laugh'. His manager tells him not to do this, as it would create a bad image of the company. Because the worker has no intention of undergoing gender reassignment, he would not have a claim for discrimination.

On the other hand, if the employer had said the same thing to a worker driven by their gender identity to cross-dress as a woman as part of the process of reassigning their sex, this could amount to direct discrimination because of gender reassignment.

2.28 Where an individual has been diagnosed as having 'Gender Dysphoria' or 'Gender Identity Disorder' and the condition has a substantial and long-term adverse impact on their ability to carry out normal day-to-day activities, they may also be protected under the disability discrimination provisions of the Act.

Gender recognition certificates

2.29 The Gender Recognition Act 2004 (GRA) provides that where a person holds a gender recognition certificate they must be treated according to their acquired gender (see the GRA for details on those who are covered by that Act; see also the Data Protection Act 1998 which deals with processing sensitive personal information).

2.30 Transsexual people should not be routinely asked to produce their gender recognition certificate as evidence of their legal gender. Such a request would compromise a transsexual person's right to privacy. If an employer requires proof of a person's legal gender, then their (new) birth certificate should be sufficient confirmation.

MARRIAGE AND CIVIL PARTNERSHIP

What the Act says

2.31 **[s 8(1)]** A person who is married or in a civil partnership has the protected characteristic of marriage and civil partnership.

2.32 Marriage will cover any formal union of a man and woman which is legally recognised in the UK as a marriage. A civil partnership refers to a registered civil partnership under the Civil Partnership Act 2004, including those registered outside the UK.

2.33 **[s 13(4)]** Only people who are married or in a civil partnership are protected against discrimination on this ground. The status of being unmarried or single is not protected. People who only intend to marry or form a civil partnership, or who have divorced or had their civil partnership dissolved, are not protected on this ground.

2.34 **[s 8(2)(b)]** People who are married or in a civil partnership share the same protected characteristic. For example, a married man and a woman in a civil partnership share the protected characteristic of marriage and civil partnership.

PREGNANCY AND MATERNITY

What the Act says

2.35 **[s 4; s 18(6)]** The Act lists pregnancy and maternity as a protected characteristic. It is unlawful for an employer to subject a woman to unfavourable treatment during the 'protected period' as defined by the Act. Pregnancy and maternity discrimination in the workplace is considered in detail in Chapter 8.

RACE

What the Act says

2.36 **[s 9(1)(a)–(c)]** The Act defines 'race' as including colour, nationality and ethnic or national origins.

2.37 **[s 9(2)]** A person has the protected characteristic of race if they fall within a particular racial group. A racial group can also be made up of two or more distinct racial groups. See paragraph 2.46 for the meaning of 'racial group'.

Nationality

2.38 Nationality (or citizenship) is the specific legal relationship between a person and a state through birth or naturalisation. It is distinct from national origins (see paragraph 2.43 below).

Ethnic origins

2.39 Everyone has an ethnic origin but the provisions of the Act only apply where a person belongs to an 'ethnic group' as defined by the courts. This means that the person must belong to an ethnic group which regards itself and is regarded by others as a distinct and separate community because of certain characteristics. These characteristics usually distinguish the group from the surrounding community.

2.40 There are two essential characteristics which an ethnic group must have: a long shared history and a cultural tradition of its own. In addition, an ethnic group may have one or more of the following characteristics: a common language; a common literature; a common religion; a common geographical origin; or being a minority; or an oppressed group.

2.41 An ethnic group or national group could include members new to the group, for example, a person who marries into the group. It is also possible for a person to leave an ethnic group.

2.42 The courts have confirmed that the following are protected ethnic groups: Sikhs, Jews, Romany Gypsies, Irish Travellers, Scottish Gypsies, and Scottish Travellers.

National origins

2.43 National origins must have identifiable elements, both historic and geographic, which at least at some point in time indicate the existence or previous existence of a nation. For example, as England and Scotland were once separate nations, the English and the Scots have separate national origins. National origins may include origins in a nation that no longer exists (for example, Czechoslovakia) or in a 'nation' that was never a nation state in the modern sense.

2.44 National origin is distinct from nationality. For example, people of Chinese national origin may be citizens of China but many are citizens of other countries.

2.45 A person's own national origin is not something that can be changed, though national origin can change through the generations.

Meaning of 'racial group'

2.46 **[s 9(3)]** A racial group is a group of people who have or share a colour, nationality or ethnic or national origins. For example, a racial group could be 'British' people. All racial groups are protected from unlawful discrimination under the Act.

2.47 A person may fall into more than one racial group. For example, a 'Nigerian' may be defined by colour, nationality or ethnic or national origin.

2.48 **[s 9(4)]** A racial group can be made up of two or more distinct racial groups. For example, a racial group could be 'black Britons' which would encompass those people who are both black and who are British citizens. Another racial group could be 'South Asian' which may include Indians, Pakistanis, Bangladeshis and Sri Lankans.

2.49 Racial groups can also be defined by exclusion, for example, those of 'non-British' nationality could form a single racial group.

RELIGION OR BELIEF

What the Act says

2.50 **[s 10(1) & (2)]** The protected characteristic of religion or belief includes any religion and any religious or philosophical belief. It also includes a lack of any such religion or belief.

2.51 For example, Christians are protected against discrimination because of their Christianity and non-Christians are protected against discrimination because they are not Christians, irrespective of any other religion or belief they may have or any lack of one.

2.52 The meaning of religion and belief in the Act is broad and is consistent with Article 9 of the European Convention on Human Rights (which guarantees freedom of thought, conscience and religion).

Meaning of religion

2.53 **[s 10(1)]** 'Religion' means any religion and includes a lack of religion. The term 'religion' includes the more commonly recognised religions in the UK such as the Baha'i faith, Buddhism, Christianity, Hinduism, Islam, Jainism, Judaism, Rastafarianism, Sikhism and Zoroastrianism. It is for the courts to determine what constitutes a religion.

2.54 A religion need not be mainstream or well known to gain protection as a religion. However, it must have a clear structure and belief system. Denominations or sects within religions, such as Methodists within Christianity or Sunnis within Islam, may be considered a religion for the purposes of the Act.

Meaning of belief

2.55 **[s 10(2)]** Belief means any religious or philosophical belief and includes a lack of belief.

2.56 'Religious belief' goes beyond beliefs about and adherence to a religion or its central articles of faith and may vary from person to person within the same religion.

2.57 A belief which is not a religious belief may be a philosophical belief. Examples of philosophical beliefs include Humanism and Atheism.

2.58 A belief need not include faith or worship of a God or Gods, but must affect how a person lives their life or perceives the world.

2.59 For a philosophical belief to be protected under the Act:

- it must be genuinely held;
- it must be a belief and not an opinion or viewpoint based on the present state of information available;
- it must be a belief as to a weighty and substantial aspect of human life and behaviour;
- it must attain a certain level of cogency, seriousness, cohesion and importance;
- it must be worthy of respect in a democratic society, not incompatible with human dignity and not conflict with the fundamental rights of others.

Example: A woman believes in a philosophy of racial superiority for a particular racial group. It is a belief around which she centres the important decisions in her life. This is not compatible with human dignity and conflicts with the fundamental rights of others. It would therefore not constitute a 'belief' for the purposes of the Act.

Manifestation of religion or belief

2.60 While people have an absolute right to hold a particular religion or belief under Article 9 of the European Convention on Human Rights, manifestation of that religion or belief is a qualified right which may in certain circumstances be limited. For example, it may need to be balanced against other Convention rights such as the right to respect for private and family life (Article 8) or the right to freedom of expression (Article 10).

2.61 Manifestations of a religion or belief could include treating certain days as days for worship or rest; following a certain dress code; following a particular diet; or carrying out or avoiding certain practices. There is not always a clear line between holding a religion or belief and the manifestation of that religion or belief. Placing limitations on a person's right to manifest their religion or belief may amount to unlawful discrimination; this would usually amount to indirect discrimination.

Example: An employer has a 'no headwear' policy for its staff. Unless this policy can be objectively justified, this will be indirect discrimination against Sikh men who wear the turban, Muslim women who wear a headscarf and observant Jewish men who wear a skullcap as manifestations of their religion.

SEX

What the Act says

2.62 **[ss 11(a) & (b), 212(1)]** Sex is a protected characteristic and refers to a male or female of any age. In relation to a group of people it refers to either men and/or boys, or women and/or girls.

2.63 A comparator for the purposes of showing sex discrimination will be a person of the opposite sex. Sex does not include gender reassignment (see paragraph 2.21) or sexual orientation (see paragraph 2.64).

SEXUAL ORIENTATION

What the Act says

2.64 **[s 12(1)]** Sexual orientation is a protected characteristic. It means a person's sexual orientation towards:

- persons of the same sex (that is, the person is a gay man or a lesbian);
- persons of the opposite sex (that is, the person is heterosexual); or
- persons of either sex (that is, the person is bisexual).

2.65 Sexual orientation relates to how people feel as well as their actions.

2.66 Sexual orientation discrimination includes discrimination because someone is of a particular sexual orientation, and it also covers discrimination connected with manifestations of that sexual orientation. These may include someone's appearance, the places they visit or the people they associate with.

2.67 **[s 12(2)]** When the Act refers to the protected characteristic of sexual orientation, it means the following:

- a reference to a person who has a particular protected characteristic is a reference to a person who is of a particular sexual orientation; and
- a reference to people who share a protected characteristic is a reference to people who are of the same sexual orientation.

2.68 Gender reassignment is a separate protected characteristic and unrelated to sexual orientation – despite a common misunderstanding that the two characteristics are related (see paragraph 2.21).

RESTRICTIONS ON PROTECTION UNDER THE ACT

2.69 For some protected characteristics, the Act does not provide protection in relation to all types of prohibited conduct.

- In relation to marriage and civil partnership, there is no protection from discrimination if a person is unmarried or single (see paragraph 2.33).
- For marriage and civil partnership, there is no protection from direct discrimination by association or perception (see paragraphs 3.18 and 3.21) or harassment (see paragraph 7.5). However, harassment related to civil partnership would amount to harassment related to sexual orientation.
- For pregnancy and maternity, there is no express protection from direct discrimination by association or perception (see paragraphs 3.18 and 3.21); indirect discrimination (see paragraph 4.1); or harassment (see paragraph 7.5). However, in these three situations, a worker may be protected under the sex discrimination provisions.
- Apart from discrimination by association or perception, protection from direct discrimination because of disability only applies to disabled people (see paragraph 3.35).
- Indirect disability discrimination and discrimination arising from disability only apply to disabled people (see Chapters 4 and 5).
- An employer is only under a duty to make reasonable adjustments for a disabled worker or an actual or potential disabled job applicant (see Chapter 6).

CHAPTER 3
DIRECT DISCRIMINATION

INTRODUCTION

[4.141]

3.1 This chapter explains what the Act says about direct discrimination in employment for all of the protected characteristics. It discusses how the requirement for a comparator may be met.

WHAT THE ACT SAYS

3.2 **[s 13(1)]** Direct discrimination occurs when a person treats another less favourably than they treat or would treat others because of a protected characteristic.

3.3 Direct discrimination is generally unlawful. However, it may be lawful in the following circumstances:

- **[s 13(2)]** where the protected characteristic is age, and the less favourable treatment can be justified as a proportionate means of achieving a legitimate aim (see paragraphs 3.36 to 3.41);
- **[s 13(3)]** in relation to the protected characteristic of disability, where a disabled person is treated more favourably than a non-disabled person (see paragraph 3.35);
- where the Act provides an express exception which permits directly discriminatory treatment that would otherwise be unlawful (see Chapters 12 to 14).

WHAT IS 'LESS FAVOURABLE' TREATMENT?

3.4 To decide whether an employer has treated a worker 'less favourably', a comparison must be made with how they have treated other workers or would have treated them in similar circumstances. If the employer's treatment of the worker puts the worker at a clear disadvantage compared with other workers, then it is more likely that the treatment will be less favourable: for example, where a job applicant is refused a job. Less favourable treatment could also involve being deprived of a choice or excluded from an opportunity.

Example: At a job interview, an applicant mentions she has a same sex partner. Although she is the most qualified candidate, the employer decides not to offer her the job. This decision treats her less favourably than the successful candidate, who is a heterosexual woman. If the less favourable treatment of the unsuccessful applicant is because of her sexual orientation, this would amount to direct discrimination.

3.5 The worker does not have to experience actual disadvantage (economic or otherwise) for the treatment to be less favourable. It is enough that the worker can reasonably say that they would have preferred not to be treated differently from the way the employer treated – or would have treated – another person.

Example: A female worker's appraisal duties are withdrawn while her male colleagues at the same grade continue to carry out appraisals. Although she was not demoted and did not suffer any financial disadvantage, she feels demeaned in the eyes of those she managed and in the eyes of her colleagues. The removal of her appraisal duties may be treating her less favourably than her male colleagues. If the less favourable treatment is because of her sex, this would amount to direct discrimination.

3.6 Under the Act, it is not possible for the employer to balance or eliminate less favourable treatment by offsetting it against more favourable treatment – for example, extra pay to make up for loss of job status.

Example: A saleswoman informs her employer that she intends to spend the rest of her life living as a man. As a result of this, she is demoted to a role without client contact. The employer increases her salary to make up for the loss of job status. Despite the increase in pay, the demotion will constitute less favourable treatment because of gender reassignment.

3.7 **[s 18]** For direct discrimination because of pregnancy and maternity, the test is whether the treatment is **unfavourable** rather than less favourable. There is no need for the woman to compare her treatment with that experienced by other workers (see Chapter 8).

Segregation

3.8 **[s 13(5)]** When the protected characteristic is race, deliberately segregating a worker or group of workers from others of a different race automatically amounts to less favourable treatment. There is no need to identify a comparator, because racial segregation is always discriminatory. But it must be a deliberate act or policy rather than a situation that has occurred inadvertently.

Example: A British marketing company which employs predominantly British staff recruits Polish nationals and seats them in a separate room nicknamed 'Little Poland'. The company argues that they have an unofficial policy of seating the Polish staff separately from British staff so that they can speak amongst themselves in their native language without disturbing the staff who speak English. This is segregation, as the company has a deliberate policy of separating staff because of race.

3.9 Segregation linked to other protected characteristics **may** be direct discrimination. However, it is necessary to show that it amounts to less favourable treatment.

SHARED PROTECTED CHARACTERISTICS

3.10 **[s 24(1)]** Direct discrimination can take place even though the employer and worker share the same protected characteristic giving rise to the less favourable treatment.

Example: A Muslim businessman decides not to recruit a Muslim woman as his personal assistant, even though she is the best qualified candidate. Instead he recruits a woman who has no particular religious or non-religious belief. He believes that this will create a better impression with clients and colleagues, who are mostly Christian or have no particular religious or non-religious belief. This could amount to direct discrimination because of religion or belief, even though the businessman shares the religion of the woman he has rejected.

'BECAUSE OF' A PROTECTED CHARACTERISTIC

3.11 'Because of' a protected characteristic has the same meaning as the phrase 'on grounds of' (a protected characteristic) in previous equality legislation. The new wording does not change the legal meaning of what amounts to direct discrimination. The characteristic needs to be a cause of the less favourable treatment, but does not need to be the only or even the main cause.

3.12 In some instances, the discriminatory basis of the treatment will be obvious from the treatment itself.

Example: If an employer were to state in a job advert 'Gypsies and Travellers need not apply', this could amount to direct discrimination because of race against a Gypsy or Traveller who might have been eligible to apply for the job but was deterred from doing so because of the statement in the advert. In this case, the discriminatory basis of the treatment is obvious from the treatment itself.

3.13 In other cases, the link between the protected characteristic and the treatment will be less clear and it will be necessary to look at why the employer treated the worker less favourably to determine whether this was because of a protected characteristic.

Example: During an interview, a job applicant informs the employer that he has multiple sclerosis. The applicant is unsuccessful and the employer offers the job to someone who does not have a disability. In this case, it will be necessary to look at why the employer did not offer the job to the unsuccessful applicant with multiple sclerosis to determine whether the less favourable treatment was because of his disability.

3.14 Direct discrimination is unlawful, no matter what the employer's motive or intention, and regardless of whether the less favourable treatment of the worker is conscious or unconscious. Employers may have prejudices that they do not even admit to themselves or may act out of good intentions – or simply be unaware that they are treating the worker differently because of a protected characteristic.

Example: An angling magazine produced by an all-male team does not recruit a female journalist. They are genuinely concerned that she would feel unhappy and uncomfortable in an all-male environment. Although they appear to be well-intentioned in their decision not to recruit her, this is likely to amount to direct sex discrimination.

3.15 Direct discrimination also includes less favourable treatment of a person based on a stereotype relating to a protected characteristic, whether or not the stereotype is accurate.

Example: An employer believes that someone's memory deteriorates with age. He assumes – wrongly – that a 60-year-old manager in his team can no longer be relied on to undertake her role competently. An opportunity for promotion arises, which he does not mention to the manager. The employer's conduct is influenced by a stereotyped view of the competence of 60 year olds. This is likely to amount to less favourable treatment because of age.

3.16 An employer cannot base their treatment on another criterion that is discriminatory – for example, where the treatment in question is based on a decision to follow a discriminatory external rule.

Example: A chemical company operates a voluntary redundancy scheme which provides enhanced terms to women aged 55 or older and men aged 60 or older. A woman of 56 is able to take advantage of the scheme and leave on enhanced terms but a man of 56 cannot do this. The company argues that their scheme is based on the original state pension age of 60 for women and 65 for men. The scheme discriminates because of sex against the male workers. The company cannot rely on an external policy which is itself discriminatory to excuse this discrimination, even though that external policy in this case may be lawful.

3.17 A worker experiencing less favourable treatment 'because of' a protected characteristic does not have to possess the characteristic themselves. For example, the person might be associated with someone who has the characteristic ('discrimination by association'); or the person might be wrongly perceived as having the characteristic ('discrimination by perception').

Discrimination by association

3.18 It is direct discrimination if an employer treats a worker less favourably because of the worker's association with another person who has a protected characteristic; however, this does not apply to marriage and civil partnership or pregnancy and maternity. In the case of pregnancy and maternity, a worker treated less favourably because of association with a pregnant woman, or a woman who has recently given birth, may have a claim for sex discrimination.

3.19 Discrimination by association can occur in various ways – for example, where the worker has a relationship of parent, son or daughter, partner, carer or friend of someone with a protected characteristic. The association with the other person need not be a permanent one.

Example: A lone father caring for a disabled son has to take time off work whenever his son is sick or has medical appointments. The employer appears to resent the fact that the worker needs to care for his son and eventually dismisses him. The dismissal may amount to direct disability discrimination against the worker by association with his son.

Example: A manager treats a worker (who is heterosexual) less favourably because she has been seen out with a person who is gay. This could be direct sexual orientation discrimination against the worker because of her association with this person.

3.20 Direct discrimination because of a protected characteristic could also occur if a worker is treated less favourably because they campaigned to help someone with a particular protected characteristic or refused to act in a way that would disadvantage a person or people who have (or whom the employer believes to have) the characteristic. The provisions of the Act on instructing, causing or inducing discrimination may also be relevant here (see paragraphs 9.16 to 9.24).

Example: An employer does not short-list an internal applicant for a job because the applicant – who is not disabled himself – has helped to set up an informal staff network for disabled workers. This could amount to less favourable treatment because of disability.

Discrimination by perception

3.21 It is also direct discrimination if an employer treats a worker less favourably because the employer mistakenly thinks that the worker has a protected characteristic. However, this does not apply to pregnancy and maternity or marriage and civil partnership.

Example: An employer rejects a job application form from a white woman whom he wrongly thinks is black, because the applicant has an African-sounding name. This would constitute direct race discrimination based on the employer's mistaken perception.

Example: A masculine-looking woman applies for a job as a sales representative. The sales manager thinks that she is transsexual because of her appearance and does not offer her the job, even though she performed the best at interview. The woman would have a claim for direct discrimination because of perceived gender reassignment, even though she is not in fact transsexual.

COMPARATORS

3.22 [s 13(1)] In most circumstances direct discrimination requires that the employer's treatment of the worker is less favourable than the way the employer treats, has treated or would treat another worker to whom the protected characteristic does not apply. This other person is referred to as a 'comparator'. However, no comparator is needed in cases of racial segregation (see paragraph 3.8) or pregnancy and maternity discrimination (see paragraph 3.7 and Chapter 8).

Who will be an appropriate comparator?

3.23 [s 23(1)] The Act says that, in comparing people for the purpose of direct discrimination, there must be no material difference between the circumstances relating to each case. However, it is not necessary for the circumstances of the two people (that is, the worker and the comparator) to be identical in every way; what matters is that the circumstances which are relevant to the treatment of the worker are the same or nearly the same for the worker and the comparator.

Example: When an employer has a vacancy for an IT supervisor, both the senior IT workers apply for promotion to the post. One of them is Scottish and the other is English. Both are of a similar age, have no disability, are male, heterosexual, and are non-practising Christians. However, the English worker has more experience than his Scottish counterpart. When the Scottish man is promoted, the English worker alleges direct race discrimination because of his national origin. In this case, the comparator's circumstances are sufficiently similar to enable a valid comparison to be made.

Example: The head office of a Japanese company seconds a limited number of staff from Japan to work for its UK subsidiary, alongside locally recruited UK staff. One of these local workers complains that his salary and benefits are lower than those of a secondee from Japan employed at the same grade. Although the two workers are working for the same company at the same grade, the circumstances of the Japanese secondee are materially different. He has been recruited in Japan, reports at least in part to the Japanese parent company, has a different career path and his salary and benefits reflect the fact that he is working abroad. For these reasons, he would not be a suitable comparator.

Hypothetical comparators

3.24 In practice it is not always possible to identify an actual person whose relevant circumstances are the same or not materially different, so the comparison will need to be made with a hypothetical comparator.

3.25 In some cases a person identified as an actual comparator turns out to have circumstances that are not materially the same. Nevertheless their treatment may help to construct a hypothetical comparator.

Example: A person who has undergone gender reassignment works in a restaurant. She makes a mistake on the till, resulting in a small financial loss to her employer, because of which she is dismissed. The situation has not arisen before, so there is no actual comparator. But six months earlier, the employer gave a written warning to another worker for taking home items of food without permission. That person's treatment might be used as evidence that the employer would not have dismissed a hypothetical worker who is not transsexual for making a till error.

3.26 Constructing a hypothetical comparator may involve considering elements of the treatment of several people whose circumstances are similar to those of the claimant, but not the same. Looking at these elements together, an Employment Tribunal may conclude that the claimant was less favourably treated than a hypothetical comparator would have been treated.

Example: An employer dismissed a worker at the end of her probation period because she had lied on one occasion. While accepting she had lied, the worker explained that this was because the employer had undermined her confidence and put her under pressure. In the absence of an actual comparator, the worker compared her treatment to two male comparators; one had behaved dishonestly but had not been dismissed, and the other had passed his probation in spite of his performance being undermined by unfair pressure from the employer. Elements of the treatment of these two comparators could allow a tribunal to construct a hypothetical comparator showing the worker had been treated less favourably because of sex.

3.27 Who could be a hypothetical comparator may also depend on the reason why the employer treated the claimant as they did. In many cases it may be more straightforward for the Employment Tribunal to establish the reason for the claimant's treatment first. This could include considering the employer's treatment of a person whose circumstances are not the same as the claimant's to shed light on the reason why that person was treated in the way they were. If the reason for the treatment is found to be because of a protected characteristic, a comparison with the treatment of hypothetical comparator(s) can then be made.

Example: After a dispute over an unreasonably harsh performance review carried out by his line manager, a worker of Somali origin was subjected to disciplinary proceedings by a second manager which he believes were inappropriate and unfair. He makes a claim for direct race discrimination. An Employment Tribunal might first of all look at the reason for the atypical conduct of the two managers, to establish whether it was because of race. If this is found to be the case, they would move on to consider whether the worker was treated less favourably than hypothetical comparator(s) would have been treated.

3.28 Another way of looking at this is to ask, 'But for the relevant protected characteristic, would the claimant have been treated in that way?'

Comparators in disability cases

3.29 **[s 23(2)(a)]** The comparator for direct disability discrimination is the same as for other types of direct discrimination. However, for disability, the relevant circumstances of the comparator and the disabled person, including their abilities, must not be materially different. An appropriate comparator will be a person who does not have the disabled person's impairment but who has the same abilities or skills as the disabled person (regardless of whether those abilities or skills arise from the disability itself).

3.30 It is important to focus on those circumstances which are, in fact, relevant to the less favourable treatment. Although in some cases, certain abilities may be the result of the disability itself, these may not be relevant circumstances for comparison purposes.

Example: A disabled man with arthritis who can type at 30 words per minute applies for an administrative job which includes typing, but is rejected on the grounds that his typing is too slow. The correct comparator in a claim for direct discrimination would be a person without arthritis who has the same typing speed with the same accuracy rate. In this case, the disabled man is unable to lift heavy weights, but this is not a requirement of the job he applied for. As it is not relevant to the circumstances, there is no need for him to identify a comparator who cannot lift heavy weights.

Comparators in sexual orientation cases

3.31 **[s 23(3)]** For sexual orientation, the Act says that the fact that one person is a civil partner while another is married is not a material difference between the circumstances relating to each case.

Example: A worker who is gay and in a civil partnership complains that he was refused promotion because of his sexual orientation. His married colleague is promoted instead. The fact that the worker is in a civil partnership and the colleague is married will not be a material difference in their circumstances, so he would be able to refer to his married colleague as a comparator in this case.

ADVERTISING AN INTENTION TO DISCRIMINATE

3.32 If an employer makes a statement in an advertisement that in offering employment they will treat applicants less favourably because of a protected characteristic, this would amount to direct discrimination. Only people who are eligible to apply for the job in question can make a claim for discrimination under the Act.

Example: A marketing company places an advert on its web site offering jobs to 'young graduates'. This could be construed as advertising an intention to discriminate because of age. An older graduate who is put off applying for the post, even though they are eligible to do so, could claim direct discrimination.

3.33 The question of whether an advertisement is discriminatory depends on whether a reasonable person would consider it to be so. An advertisement can include a notice or circular, whether to the public or not, in any publication, on radio, television or in cinemas, via the internet or at an exhibition.

Example: A dress manufacturing company places an advertisement in a local newspaper for a Turkish machinist. A reasonable person would probably view this as advertising an intention to discriminate because of race.

MARRIAGE AND CIVIL PARTNERSHIP

3.34 **[s 13(4); s 8(2)]** In relation to employment, if the protected characteristic is marriage and civil partnership, direct discrimination only covers less favourable treatment of a worker because the worker themselves is married or a civil partner. Single people and people in relationships outside of marriage or civil partnership (whether or not they are cohabiting), are not protected from direct discrimination because of their status.

Example: An employer offers 'death in service' benefits to the spouses and civil partners of their staff members. A worker who lives with her partner, but is not married to him, wants to nominate him for death in service benefits. She is told she cannot do this as she is not married. Because being a cohabitee is not a protected characteristic, she would be unable to make a claim for discrimination.

WHEN IS IT LAWFUL TO TREAT A PERSON MORE FAVOURABLY?

More favourable treatment of disabled people

3.35 **[s 13(3)]** In relation to disability discrimination, the Act only protects disabled people, so it is not discrimination to treat a disabled person more favourably than a non-disabled person.

Example: An employer with 60 staff has no disabled workers. When they advertise for a new office administrator, they guarantee all disabled applicants an interview for the post. This would not amount to direct discrimination because of disability.

Justifiable direct discrimination because of age

3.36 **[s 13(2)]** A different approach applies to the protected characteristic of age, because some age-based rules and practices are seen as justifiable. Less favourable treatment of a person because of their age is not direct discrimination if the employer can show the treatment is a proportionate means of achieving a legitimate aim. This is often called the 'objective justification test'.

3.37 In considering direct discrimination because of age, it is important to distinguish a rule or practice affecting workers in a particular age group from a neutral provision, criterion or practice applied equally to everyone that may give rise to indirect discrimination (see paragraph 4.6).

3.38 The objective justification test, which also applies to other areas of discrimination law, is explained in more detail in paragraphs 4.25 to 4.32.

3.39 The question of whether an age-based rule or practice is 'objectively justified' – that is, a proportionate means of achieving a legitimate aim – should be approached in two stages:

- First, is the aim of the rule or practice legal and non-discriminatory, and one that represents a real, objective consideration?
- Second, if the aim is legitimate, is the means of achieving it proportionate – that is, appropriate and necessary in all the circumstances?

3.40 The following is an illustration of an age-based rule that might well satisfy the objective justification test.

Example: A building company has a policy of not employing under-18s on its more hazardous building sites. The aim behind this policy is to protect young people from health and safety risks associated with their lack of experience and less developed physical strength. This aim is supported by accident statistics for younger workers on building sites and is likely to be a legitimate one. Imposing an age threshold of 18 would probably be a proportionate means of achieving the aim if this is supported by the evidence. Had the threshold been set at 25, the proportionality test would not necessarily have been met.

3.41 The following examples illustrate age-based rules that would probably fail the objective justification test.

Example: A haulage company introduces a blanket policy forcing its drivers to stop driving articulated lorries at 55, because statistical evidence suggests an increased risk of heart attacks over this age. The aim of public safety would be a legitimate one which is supported by evidence of risk. However, the company would have to show that its blanket ban was a proportionate means of achieving this objective. This might be difficult, as medical checks for individual drivers could offer a less discriminatory means of achieving the same aim.

Example: A fashion retailer rejects a middle-aged woman as a sales assistant on the grounds that she is 'too old' for the job. They tell her that they need to attract the young customer base at which their clothing is targeted. If this corresponds to a real business need on the part of the retailer, it could qualify as a legitimate aim. However, rejecting this middle-aged woman is unlikely to be a proportionate means of achieving this aim; a requirement for all sales assistants to have knowledge of the products and fashion awareness would be a less discriminatory means of making sure the aim is achieved.

Occupational requirements

3.42 **[Sch 9, para 1]** The Act creates a general exception to the prohibition on direct discrimination in employment for occupational requirements that are genuinely needed for the job. See Chapter 13 for details.

CHAPTER 4
INDIRECT DISCRIMINATION

INTRODUCTION

[4.142]
4.1 This chapter explains indirect discrimination and 'objective justification'. The latter concept applies to indirect discrimination, direct discrimination because of age, discrimination arising from disability and to some of the exceptions permitted by the Act.

4.2 Indirect discrimination applies to all the protected characteristics apart from pregnancy and maternity (although, in pregnancy and maternity situations, indirect sex discrimination may apply).

WHAT THE ACT SAYS

4.3 **[s 19(1) & (2)]** Indirect discrimination may occur when an employer applies an apparently neutral provision, criterion or practice which puts workers sharing a protected characteristic at a particular disadvantage.

4.4 **[s 19(2)]** For indirect discrimination to take place, four requirements must be met:

- the employer applies (or would apply) the provision, criterion or practice equally to everyone within the relevant group including a particular worker;
- the provision, criterion or practice puts, or would put, people who share the worker's protected characteristic at a particular disadvantage when compared with people who do not have that characteristic;
- the provision, criterion or practice puts, or would put, the worker at that disadvantage; and
- the employer cannot show that the provision, criterion or practice is a proportionate means of achieving a legitimate aim.

WHAT CONSTITUTES A PROVISION, CRITERION OR PRACTICE?

4.5 The first stage in establishing indirect discrimination is to identify the relevant provision, criterion or practice. The phrase 'provision, criterion or practice' is not defined by the Act but it should be construed widely so as to include, for example, any formal or informal policies, rules, practices, arrangements, criteria, conditions, prerequisites, qualifications or provisions. A provision, criterion or practice may also include decisions to do something in the future – such as a policy or criterion that has not yet been applied – as well as a 'one-off' or discretionary decision.

Example: A factory owner announces that from next month staff cannot wear their hair in dreadlocks, even if the locks are tied back. This is an example of a policy that has not yet been implemented but which still amounts to a provision, criterion or practice. The decision to introduce the policy could be indirectly discriminatory because of religion or belief, as it puts the employer's Rastafarian workers at a particular disadvantage. The employer must show that the provision, criterion or practice can be objectively justified.

Is the provision, criterion or practice a neutral one?

4.6 The provision, criterion or practice must be applied to everyone in the relevant group, whether or not they have the protected characteristic in question. On the face of it, the provision, criterion or practice must be neutral. If it is not neutral in this way, but expressly applies to people with a specific protected characteristic, it is likely to amount to direct discrimination.

Example: A bus company adopts a policy that all female drivers must re-sit their theory and practical tests every five years to retain their category D licence. Such a policy would amount to direct discrimination because of sex. In contrast, another bus company adopts a policy that drivers on two particular routes must re-sit the theory test. Although this provision is apparently neutral, it turns out that the drivers on these two routes are nearly all women. This could amount to indirect sex discrimination unless the policy can be objectively justified.

WHAT DOES 'WOULD PUT' MEAN?

4.7 **[s 19(2)(b)]** It is a requirement of the Act that the provision, criterion or practice puts **or would put** people who share the worker's protected characteristic at a particular disadvantage when compared with people who do not have that characteristic. The Act also requires that it puts **or would put** the particular worker at that disadvantage. This allows challenges to provisions, criteria or practices which have not yet been applied but which would have a discriminatory effect if they were.

4.8 **[s 19(2)(c)]** However, for a claim of indirect discrimination to succeed, the worker must show that they would experience a disadvantage if the provision, criterion or practice were applied to them.

Example: The contracts for senior buyers at a department store have a mobility clause requiring them to travel at short notice to any part of the world. A female senior buyer with young children considers that the mobility clause puts women at a disadvantage as they are more likely to be the carers of children and so less likely to be able to travel abroad at short notice. She may challenge the mobility clause even though she has not yet been asked to travel abroad at short notice.

By contrast, a female manager in customer services at the same store might agree that the mobility clause discriminates against women – but, as she is not a senior buyer, she cannot challenge the clause.

WHAT IS A DISADVANTAGE?

4.9 'Disadvantage' is not defined by the Act. It could include denial of an opportunity or choice, deterrence, rejection or exclusion. The courts have found that 'detriment', a similar concept, is something that a reasonable person would complain about – so an unjustified sense of grievance would not qualify. A disadvantage does not have to be quantifiable and the worker does not have to experience actual loss (economic or otherwise). It is enough that the worker can reasonably say that they would have preferred to be treated differently.

4.10 Sometimes, a provision, criterion or practice is intrinsically liable to disadvantage a group with a particular protected characteristic.

Example: At the end of the year, an employer decides to invite seasonal workers employed during the previous summer to claim a bonus within a 30 day time limit. By writing to these workers at their last known address, the employer is liable to disadvantage migrant workers. This is because these workers normally return to their home country during the winter months, and so they are unlikely to apply for the bonus within the specified period. This could amount to indirect race discrimination, unless the practice can be objectively justified.

4.11 In some situations, the link between the protected characteristic and the disadvantage might be obvious; for example, dress codes create a disadvantage for some workers with particular religious beliefs. In other situations it will be less obvious how people sharing a protected characteristic are put (or would be put) at a disadvantage, in which case statistics or personal testimony may help to demonstrate that a disadvantage exists.

Example: A hairdresser refuses to employ stylists who cover their hair, believing it is important for them to exhibit their flamboyant haircuts. It is clear that this criterion puts at a particular disadvantage both Muslim women and Sikh men who cover their hair. This may amount to indirect discrimination unless the criterion can be objectively justified.

Example: A consultancy firm reviews the use of psychometric tests in their recruitment procedures and discovers that men tend to score lower than women. If a man complains that the test is indirectly discriminatory, he would not need to explain the reason for the lower scores or how the lower scores are connected to his sex to show that men have been put at a disadvantage; it is sufficient for him to rely on the statistical information.

4.12 Statistics can provide an insight into the link between the provision, criterion or practice and the disadvantage that it causes. Statistics relating to the workplace in question can be obtained through the questions procedure (see paragraphs 15.5 to 15.10). It may also be possible to use national or regional statistics to throw light on the nature and extent of the particular disadvantage.

4.13 However, a statistical analysis may not always be appropriate or practicable, especially when there is inadequate or unreliable information, or the numbers of people are too small to allow for a statistically significant comparison. In this situation, the Employment Tribunal may find it helpful for an expert to provide evidence as to whether there is any disadvantage and, if so, the nature of it.

4.14 There are other cases where it may be useful to have evidence (including, if appropriate, from an expert) to help the Employment Tribunal to understand the nature of the protected characteristic or the behaviour of the group sharing the characteristic – for example, evidence about the principles of a particular religious belief.

Example: A Muslim man who works for a small manufacturing company wishes to undertake the Hajj. However, his employer only allows their staff to take annual leave during designated shutdown periods in August and December. The worker considers that he has been subjected to indirect religious discrimination. In assessing the case, the Employment Tribunal may benefit from expert evidence from a Muslim cleric or an expert in Islam on the timing of the Hajj and whether it is of significance.

THE COMPARATIVE APPROACH

4.15 **[s 19(2)(b); s 23(1)]** Once it is clear that there is a provision, criterion or practice which puts (or would put) people sharing a protected characteristic at a particular disadvantage, then the next stage is to consider a comparison between workers with the protected characteristic and those without it. The circumstances of the two groups must be sufficiently similar for a comparison to be made and there must be no material differences in circumstances.

4.16 It is important to be clear which protected characteristic is relevant. In relation to disability, this would not be disabled people as a whole but people with a particular disability – for example, with an equivalent level of visual impairment. For race, it could be all Africans or only Somalis, for example. For age, it is important to identify the age group that is disadvantaged by the provision, criterion or practice.

Example: If an employer were to advertise a position requiring at least five GCSEs at grades A to C without permitting any equivalent qualifications, this criterion would put at a particular disadvantage everyone born before 1971, as they are more likely to have taken O level examinations rather than GCSEs. This might be indirect age discrimination if the criterion could not be objectively justified.

The 'pool for comparison'

4.17 The people used in the comparative exercise are usually referred to as the 'pool for comparison'.

4.18 In general, the pool should consist of the group which the provision, criterion or practice affects (or would affect) either positively or negatively, while excluding workers who are not affected by it, either positively or negatively. In most situations, there is likely to be only one appropriate pool, but there may be circumstances where there is more than one. If this is the case, the Employment Tribunal will decide which of the pools to consider.

Example: A marketing company employs 45 women, 10 of whom are part-timers, and 55 men who all work full-time. One female receptionist works Mondays, Wednesdays and Thursdays. The annual leave policy requires that all workers take time off on public holidays, at least half of which fall on a Monday every year. The receptionist argues that the policy is indirectly discriminatory against women and that it puts her at a personal disadvantage because she has proportionately less control over when she can take her annual leave. The appropriate pool for comparison is all the workers affected by the annual leave policy. The pool is not all receptionists or all part-time workers, because the policy does not only affect these groups.

Making the comparison

4.19 Looking at the pool, a comparison must be made between the impact of the provision, criterion or practice on people **without** the relevant protected characteristic, and its impact on people **with** the protected characteristic.

4.20 The way that the comparison is carried out will depend on the circumstances, including the protected characteristic concerned. It may in some circumstances be necessary to carry out a formal comparative exercise using statistical evidence.

Carrying out a formal comparative exercise

4.21 If the Employment Tribunal is asked to undertake a formal comparative exercise to decide an indirect discrimination claim, it can do this in a number of ways. One established approach involves the Employment Tribunal asking these questions:

- What proportion of the pool has the particular protected characteristic?
- Within the pool, does the provision, criterion or practice affect workers without the protected characteristic?
- How many of these workers are (or would be) disadvantaged by it? How is this expressed as a proportion ('x')?
- Within the pool, how does the provision, criterion or practice affect people who share the protected characteristic?
- How many of these workers are (or would be) put at a disadvantage by it? How is this expressed as a proportion ('y')?

4.22 Using this approach, the Employment Tribunal will then compare (x) with (y). It can then decide whether the group with the protected characteristic experiences a 'particular disadvantage' in comparison with others. Whether a difference is significant will depend on the context, such as the size of the pool and the numbers behind the proportions. It is not necessary to show that that the majority of those within the pool who share the protected characteristic are placed at a disadvantage.

Example: A single mother of two young children is forced to resign from her job as a train driver when she cannot comply with her employer's new shift system.

The shift system is a provision, criterion or practice which causes particular disadvantage to this single mother. In an indirect discrimination claim, an Employment Tribunal must carry out a comparative exercise to decide whether the shift system puts (or would put) workers who share her protected characteristic of sex at a particular disadvantage when compared with men.

The Employment Tribunal decides to use as a pool for comparison all the train drivers working for the same employer. There are 20 female train drivers, while 2,000 are men.

It is accepted as common knowledge that men are far less likely than women to be single parents with childcare responsibilities.

- Of the 2,000 male drivers, two are unable to comply with the new shift system. This is expressed as a proportion of 0.001
- Of the 20 female train drivers, five are unable to comply with the new shift system. This is expressed as a proportion of 0.25

It is clear that a higher proportion of female drivers (0.25) than male drivers (0.001) are unable to comply with the shift system.

Taking all this into account, the Employment Tribunal decides that female train drivers – in comparison to their male counterparts – are put at a particular disadvantage by the shift system.

IS THE WORKER CONCERNED PUT AT THAT DISADVANTAGE?

4.23 It is not enough that the provision, criterion or practice puts (or would put) at a particular disadvantage a group of people who share a protected characteristic. It must also have that effect (or be capable of having it) on the individual worker concerned. So it is not enough for a worker merely to establish that they are a member of the relevant group. They must also show they have personally suffered (or could suffer) the particular disadvantage as an individual.

Example: An airline operates a dress code which forbids workers in customer-facing roles from displaying any item of jewellery. A Sikh cabin steward complains that this policy indirectly discriminates against Sikhs by preventing them from wearing the Kara bracelet. However, because he no longer observes the Sikh articles of faith, the steward is not put at a particular disadvantage by this policy and could not bring a claim for indirect discrimination.

THE INTENTION BEHIND THE PROVISION, CRITERION OR PRACTICE IS IRRELEVANT

4.24 Indirect discrimination is unlawful, even where the discriminatory effect of the provision, criterion or practice is not intentional, unless it can be objectively justified. If an employer applies the provision, criterion or practice without the intention of discriminating against the worker, the Employment Tribunal may decide not to order a payment of compensation (see paragraph 15.44).

Example: An employer starts an induction session for new staff with an ice-breaker designed to introduce everyone in the room to the others. Each worker is required to provide a picture of themselves as a toddler. One worker is a transsexual woman who does not wish her colleagues to know that she was brought up as a boy. When she does not bring in her photo, the employer criticises her in front of the group for not joining in. It would be no defence that it did not occur to the employer that this worker may feel disadvantaged by the requirement to disclose such information.

WHEN CAN A PROVISION, CRITERION OR PRACTICE BE OBJECTIVELY JUSTIFIED?

4.25 **[s 19(2)(d)]** If the person applying a provision, criterion or practice can show that it is 'a proportionate means of achieving a legitimate aim', then it will not amount to indirect discrimination. This is often known as the 'objective justification' test. The test applies to other areas of discrimination law; for example, direct discrimination because of age (see paragraphs 3.36 to 3.41) and discrimination arising from disability (see Chapter 5).

4.26 If challenged in the Employment Tribunal, it is for the employer to justify the provision, criterion or practice. So it is up to the employer to produce evidence to support their assertion that it is justified. Generalisations will not be sufficient to provide justification. It is not necessary for that justification to have been fully set out at the time the provision, criterion or practice was applied. If challenged, the employer can set out the justification to the Employment Tribunal.

4.27 The question of whether the provision, criterion or practice is a proportionate means of achieving a legitimate aim should be approached in two stages:

- Is the aim of the provision, criterion or practice legal and non-discriminatory, and one that represents a real, objective consideration?
- If the aim is legitimate, is the means of achieving it proportionate – that is, appropriate and necessary in all the circumstances?

What is a legitimate aim?

4.28 The concept of 'legitimate aim' is taken from European Union (EU) law and relevant decisions of the Court of Justice of the European Union (CJEU) – formerly the European Court of Justice (ECJ). However, it is not defined by the Act. The aim of the provision, criterion or practice should be legal, should not be discriminatory in itself, and must represent a real, objective consideration. The health, welfare and safety of individuals may qualify as legitimate aims provided that risks are clearly specified and supported by evidence.

4.29 Although reasonable business needs and economic efficiency may be legitimate aims, an employer solely aiming to reduce costs cannot expect to satisfy the test. For example, the employer cannot simply argue that to discriminate is cheaper than avoiding discrimination.

Example: Solely as a cost-saving measure, an employer requires all staff to work a full day on Fridays, so that customer orders can all be processed on the same day of the week. The policy puts observant Jewish workers at a particular disadvantage in the winter months by preventing them from going home early to observe the Sabbath, and could amount to indirect discrimination unless it can be objectively justified. The single aim of reducing costs is not a legitimate one; the employer cannot just argue that to discriminate is cheaper than avoiding discrimination.

What is proportionate?

4.30 Even if the aim is a legitimate one, the means of achieving it must be proportionate. Deciding whether the means used to achieve the legitimate aim are proportionate involves a balancing exercise. An Employment Tribunal may wish to conduct a proper evaluation of the discriminatory effect of the provision, criterion or practice as against the employer's reasons for applying it, taking into account all the relevant facts.

4.31 Although not defined by the Act, the term 'proportionate' is taken from EU Directives and its meaning has been clarified by decisions of the CJEU (formerly the ECJ). EU law views treatment as proportionate if it is an 'appropriate and necessary' means of achieving a legitimate aim. But 'necessary' does not mean that the provision, criterion or practice is the only possible way of achieving the legitimate aim; it is sufficient that the same aim could not be achieved by less discriminatory means.

4.32 The greater financial cost of using a less discriminatory approach cannot, by itself, provide a justification for applying a particular provision, criterion or practice. Cost can only be taken into account as part of the employer's justification for the provision, criterion or practice if there are other good reasons for adopting it.

Example: A food manufacturer has a rule that beards are forbidden for people working on the factory floor. Unless it can be objectively justified, this rule may amount to indirect religion or belief discrimination against the Sikh and Muslim workers in the factory. If the aim of the rule is to meet food hygiene or health and safety requirements, this would be legitimate. However, the employer would need to show that the ban on beards is a proportionate means of achieving this aim. When considering whether the policy is justified, the Employment Tribunal is likely to examine closely the reasons given by the employer as to why they cannot fulfil the same food hygiene or health and safety obligations by less discriminatory means, for example by providing a beard mask or snood.

CHAPTER 5
DISCRIMINATION ARISING FROM DISABILITY

INTRODUCTION

[4.143]
5.1 This chapter explains the duty of employers not to treat disabled people unfavourably because

of something connected with their disability. Protection from this type of discrimination, which is known as 'discrimination arising from disability', only applies to disabled people.

WHAT THE ACT SAYS

5.2 **[s 15]** The Act says that treatment of a disabled person amounts to discrimination where:

- an employer treats the disabled person unfavourably;
- this treatment is because of something arising in consequence of the disabled person's disability; and
- the employer cannot show that this treatment is a proportionate means of achieving a legitimate aim,

[s 15(2)] unless the employer does not know, and could not reasonably be expected to know, that the person has the disability.

How does it differ from direct discrimination?

5.3 Direct discrimination occurs when the employer treats someone less favourably because of disability itself (see Chapter 3). By contrast, in discrimination arising from disability, the question is whether the disabled person has been treated unfavourably because of something arising in consequence of their disability.

Example: An employer dismisses a worker because she has had three months' sick leave. The employer is aware that the worker has multiple sclerosis and most of her sick leave is disability-related. The employer's decision to dismiss is not because of the worker's disability itself. However, the worker has been treated unfavourably because of something arising in consequence of her disability (namely, the need to take a period of disability-related sick leave).

How does it differ from indirect discrimination?

5.4 Indirect discrimination occurs when a disabled person is (or would be) disadvantaged by an unjustifiable provision, criterion or practice applied to everyone, which puts (or would put) people sharing the disabled person's disability at a particular disadvantage compared to others, and puts (or would put) the disabled person at that disadvantage (see Chapter 4).

5.5 In contrast, discrimination arising from disability only requires the disabled person to show they have experienced unfavourable treatment because of something connected with their disability. If the employer can show that they did not know and could not reasonably have been expected to know that the disabled person had the disability, it will not be discrimination arising from disability (see paragraphs 5.13 to 5.19). However, as with indirect discrimination, the employer may avoid discrimination arising from disability if the treatment can be objectively justified as a proportionate means of achieving a legitimate aim (see paragraph 5.11)

Is a comparator required?

5.6 Both direct and indirect discrimination require a comparative exercise. But in considering discrimination arising from disability, there is no need to compare a disabled person's treatment with that of another person. It is only necessary to demonstrate that the unfavourable treatment is because of something arising in consequence of the disability.

Example: In considering whether the example of the disabled worker dismissed for disability-related sickness absence (see paragraph 5.3) amounts to discrimination arising from disability, it is irrelevant whether or not other workers would have been dismissed for having the same or similar length of absence. It is not necessary to compare the treatment of the disabled worker with that of her colleagues or any hypothetical comparator.

The decision to dismiss her will be discrimination arising from disability if the employer cannot objectively justify it.

WHAT IS 'UNFAVOURABLE TREATMENT'?

5.7 **[s 15(1)(a)]** For discrimination arising from disability to occur, a disabled person must have been treated 'unfavourably'. This means that he or she must have been put at a disadvantage. Often, the disadvantage will be obvious and it will be clear that the treatment has been unfavourable; for example, a person may have been refused a job, denied a work opportunity or dismissed from their employment. But sometimes unfavourable treatment may be less obvious. Even if an employer thinks that they are acting in the best interests of a disabled person, they may still treat that person unfavourably.

WHAT DOES 'SOMETHING ARISING IN CONSEQUENCE OF DISABILITY' MEAN?

5.8 **[s 15(1)(a)]** The unfavourable treatment must be because of something that arises in consequence of the disability. This means that there must be a connection between whatever led to the unfavourable treatment and the disability.

5.9 The consequences of a disability include anything which is the result, effect or outcome of a disabled person's disability. The consequences will be varied, and will depend on the individual effect upon a disabled person of their disability. Some consequences may be obvious, such as an inability to walk unaided or inability to use certain work equipment. Others may not be obvious, for example, having to follow a restricted diet.

Example: A woman is disciplined for losing her temper at work. However, this behaviour was out of character and is a result of severe pain caused by cancer, of which her employer is aware. The disciplinary action is unfavourable treatment. This treatment is because of something which arises in consequence of the worker's disability, namely her loss of temper. There is a connection between the 'something' (that is, the loss of temper) that led to the treatment and her disability. It will be discrimination arising from disability if the employer cannot objectively justify the decision to discipline the worker.

5.10 So long as the unfavourable treatment is because of something arising in consequence of the disability, it will be unlawful unless it can be objectively justified, or unless the employer did not know or could not reasonably have been expected to know that the person was disabled (see paragraph 5.13).

WHEN CAN DISCRIMINATION ARISING FROM DISABILITY BE JUSTIFIED?

5.11 **[s 15(1)(b)]** Unfavourable treatment will not amount to discrimination arising from disability if the employer can show that the treatment is a 'proportionate means of achieving a legitimate aim'. This 'objective justification' test is explained in detail in paragraphs 4.25 to 4.32.

5.12 It is for the employer to justify the treatment. They must produce evidence to support their assertion that it is justified and not rely on mere generalisations.

WHAT IF THE EMPLOYER DOES NOT KNOW THAT THE PERSON IS DISABLED?

5.13 **[s 15(2)]** If the employer can show that they:

- did not know that the disabled person had the disability in question; and
- could not reasonably have been expected to know that the disabled person had the disability,

then the unfavourable treatment does not amount to discrimination arising from disability.

5.14 It is not enough for the employer to show that they did not know that the disabled person had the disability. They must also show that they could not reasonably have been expected to know about it. Employers should consider whether a worker has a disability even where one has not been formally disclosed, as, for example, not all workers who meet the definition of disability may think of themselves as a 'disabled person'.

5.15 An employer must do all they can reasonably be expected to do to find out if a worker has a disability. What is reasonable will depend on the circumstances. This is an objective assessment. When making enquiries about disability, employers should consider issues of dignity and privacy and ensure that personal information is dealt with confidentially.

Example: A disabled man who has depression has been at a particular workplace for two years. He has a good attendance and performance record. In recent weeks, however, he has become emotional and upset at work for no apparent reason. He has also been repeatedly late for work and has made some mistakes in his work. The worker is disciplined without being given any opportunity to explain that his difficulties at work arise from a disability and that recently the effects of his depression have worsened.

The sudden deterioration in the worker's time-keeping and performance and the change in his behaviour at work should have alerted the employer to the possibility that that these were connected to a disability. It is likely to be reasonable to expect the employer to explore with the worker the reason for these changes and whether the difficulties are because of something arising in consequence of a disability.

5.16 **[s 60]** However, employers should note that the Act imposes restrictions on the types of health or disability-related enquiries that can be made prior to making someone a job offer or including someone in a pool of successful candidates to be offered a job when one becomes available (see paragraphs 10.25 to 10.43).

When can an employer be assumed to know about disability?

5.17 If an employer's agent or employee (such as an occupational health adviser or a HR officer) knows, in that capacity, of a worker's or applicant's or potential applicant's disability, the employer will not usually be able to claim that they do not know of the disability, and that they cannot therefore have subjected a disabled person to discrimination arising from disability.

5.18 Therefore, where information about disabled people may come through different channels, employers need to ensure that there is a means – suitably confidential and subject to the disabled person's consent – for bringing that information together to make it easier for the employer to fulfil their duties under the Act.

Example: An occupational health (OH) adviser is engaged by a large employer to provide them with information about their workers' health. The OH adviser becomes aware of a worker's disability that is relevant to his work, and the worker consents to this information being disclosed to the employer. However, the OH adviser does not pass that information on to Human Resources or to the worker's line manager. As the OH adviser is acting as the employer's agent, it is not a defence for the employer to claim that they did not know about the worker's disability. This is because the information gained by the adviser on the employer's behalf is attributed to the employer.

5.19 Information will not be attributed ('imputed') to the employer if it is gained by a person providing services to workers independently of the employer. This is the case even if the employer has arranged for those services to be provided.

Example: An employer contracts with an agency to provide an independent counselling service to workers. The contract states that the counsellors are not acting on the employer's behalf while in the counselling role. Any information obtained by a counsellor during such counselling would not be attributed to the employer.

RELEVANCE OF REASONABLE ADJUSTMENTS

5.20 Employers can often prevent unfavourable treatment which would amount to discrimination arising from disability by taking prompt action to identify and implement reasonable adjustments (see Chapter 6).

5.21 If an employer has failed to make a reasonable adjustment which would have prevented or minimised the unfavourable treatment, it will be very difficult for them to show that the treatment was objectively justified.

5.22 Even where an employer has complied with a duty to make reasonable adjustments in relation to the disabled person, they may still subject a disabled person to unlawful discrimination arising from disability. This is likely to apply where, for example, the adjustment is unrelated to the particular treatment complained of.

Example: The employer in the example at paragraph 5.3 made a reasonable adjustment for the worker who has multiple sclerosis. They adjusted her working hours so that she started work at 9.30am instead of 9am.

However, this adjustment is not relevant to the unfavourable treatment – namely, her dismissal for disability-related sickness absence – which her claim concerns. And so, despite the fact that reasonable adjustments were made, there will still be discrimination arising from disability unless the treatment is justified.

CHAPTER 6
DUTY TO MAKE REASONABLE ADJUSTMENTS

INTRODUCTION

[4.144]

6.1 This chapter describes the principles and application of the duty to make reasonable adjustments for disabled people in employment.

6.2 The duty to make reasonable adjustments is a cornerstone of the Act and requires employers to take positive steps to ensure that disabled people can access and progress in employment. This goes beyond simply avoiding treating disabled workers, job applicants and potential job applicants unfavourably and means taking additional steps to which non-disabled workers and applicants are not entitled.

6.3 The duty to make reasonable adjustments applies to employers of all sizes, but the question of what is reasonable may vary according to the circumstances of the employer. Part 2 of the Code has more information about good practice in making reasonable adjustments in different work situations, such as in recruitment or during employment.

WHAT THE ACT SAYS

6.4 **[s 21(2)]** Discrimination against a disabled person occurs where an employer fails to comply with a duty to make reasonable adjustments imposed on them in relation to that disabled person.

WHAT IS THE DUTY TO MAKE REASONABLE ADJUSTMENTS?

6.5 The duty to make reasonable adjustments comprises three requirements. Employers are required to take reasonable steps to:

- **[s 20(3)]** Avoid the substantial disadvantage where a provision, criterion or practice applied by or on behalf of the employer puts a disabled person at a substantial disadvantage compared to those who are not disabled.
- **[s 20(4)]** Remove or alter a physical feature or provide a reasonable means of avoiding such a feature where it puts a disabled person at a substantial disadvantage compared to those who are not disabled.

- **[s 20(5)]** Provide an auxiliary aid (which includes an auxiliary service - see paragraph 6.13) where a disabled person would, but for the provision of that auxiliary aid, be put at a substantial disadvantage compared to those who are not disabled.

Accessible information

6.6 [s 20(6)] The Act states that where the provision, criterion or practice or the need for an auxiliary aid relates to the provision of information, the steps which it is reasonable for the employer to take include steps to ensure that the information is provided in an accessible format; for example, providing letters, training materials or recruitment forms in Braille or on audio-tape.

Avoiding substantial disadvantages caused by physical features

6.7 [s 20(9)] The Act says that avoiding a substantial disadvantage caused by a physical feature includes:

- removing the physical feature in question;
- altering it; or
- providing a reasonable means of avoiding it.

WHICH DISABLED PEOPLE DOES THE DUTY PROTECT?

6.8 [Sch 8, paras 4 & 5] The duty to make reasonable adjustments applies in recruitment and during all stages of employment, including dismissal. It may also apply after employment has ended. The duty relates to all disabled workers of an employer and to any disabled applicant for employment. The duty also applies in respect of any disabled person who has notified the employer that they may be an applicant for work.

6.9 In order to avoid discrimination, it would be sensible for employers not to attempt to make a fine judgment as to whether a particular individual falls within the statutory definition of disability, but to focus instead on meeting the needs of each worker and job applicant.

WHAT IS A PROVISION, CRITERION OR PRACTICE?

6.10 The phrase 'provision, criterion or practice' is not defined by the Act but should be construed widely so as to include, for example, any formal or informal policies, rules, practices, arrangements or qualifications including one-off decisions and actions (see also paragraph 4.5).

Example: An employer has a policy that designated car parking spaces are only offered to senior managers. A worker who is not a manager, but has a mobility impairment and needs to park very close to the office, is given a designated car parking space. This is likely to be a reasonable adjustment to the employer's car parking policy.

WHAT IS A 'PHYSICAL FEATURE'?

6.11 [s 20(10), s 20(12)] The Act says that the following are to be treated as a physical feature of the premises occupied by the employer:

- any feature of the design or construction of a building;
- any feature of an approach to, exit from or entrance to a building;
- a fixture or fitting, or furniture, furnishings, materials, equipment or other chattels (moveable property in Scotland) in or on the premises;
- any other physical element or quality of the premises.

All these features are covered, whether temporary or permanent.

6.12 Physical features will include steps, stairways, kerbs, exterior surfaces and paving, parking areas, building entrances and exits (including emergency escape routes), internal and external doors, gates, toilet and washing facilities, lighting and ventilation, lifts and escalators, floor coverings, signs, furniture and temporary or moveable items. This is not an exhaustive list.

Example: Clear glass doors at the end of a corridor in a particular workplace present a hazard for a visually impaired worker. This is a substantial disadvantage caused by the physical features of the workplace.

WHAT IS AN 'AUXILIARY AID'?

6.13 [s 20(11)] An auxiliary aid is something which provides support or assistance to a disabled person. It can include provision of a specialist piece of equipment such as an adapted keyboard or text to speech software. Auxiliary aids include auxiliary services; for example, provision of a sign language interpreter or a support worker for a disabled worker.

WHAT DISADVANTAGE GIVES RISE TO THE DUTY?

6.14 [s 20(3), s 20(4), s 20(5)] The duty to make adjustments arises where a provision, criterion, or practice, any physical feature of work premises or the absence of an auxiliary aid puts a disabled person at a substantial disadvantage compared with people who are not disabled.

6.15 **[s 212(1)]** The Act says that a substantial disadvantage is one which is more than minor or trivial. Whether such a disadvantage exists in a particular case is a question of fact, and is assessed on an objective basis.

6.16 **[s 23(1)]** The purpose of the comparison with people who are not disabled is to establish whether it is because of disability that a particular provision, criterion, practice or physical feature or the absence of an auxiliary aid disadvantages the disabled person in question. Accordingly – and unlike direct or indirect discrimination – under the duty to make adjustments there is no requirement to identify a comparator or comparator group whose circumstances are the same or nearly the same as the disabled person's.

WHAT IF THE EMPLOYER DOES NOT KNOW THAT A DISABLED PERSON IS AN ACTUAL OR POTENTIAL JOB APPLICANT?

6.17 **[Sch 8, para 20(1)(a)]** An employer only has a duty to make an adjustment if they know, or could reasonably be expected to know, that a disabled person is, or may be, an applicant for work.

6.18 There are restrictions on when health or disability-related enquiries can be made prior to making a job offer or including someone in a pool of people to be offered a job. However, questions are permitted to determine whether reasonable adjustments need to be made in relation to an assessment, such as an interview or other process designed to give an indication of a person's suitability for the work concerned. These provisions are explained in detail in paragraphs 10.25 to 10.43.

WHAT IF THE EMPLOYER DOES NOT KNOW THE WORKER IS DISABLED?

6.19 **[Sch 8, para 20(1)(b)]** For disabled workers already in employment, an employer only has a duty to make an adjustment if they know, or could reasonably be expected to know, that a worker has a disability and is, or is likely to be, placed at a substantial disadvantage. The employer must, however, do all they can reasonably be expected to do to find out whether this is the case. What is reasonable will depend on the circumstances. This is an objective assessment. When making enquiries about disability, employers should consider issues of dignity and privacy and ensure that personal information is dealt with confidentially.

Example: A worker who deals with customers by phone at a call centre has depression which sometimes causes her to cry at work. She has difficulty dealing with customer enquiries when the symptoms of her depression are severe. It is likely to be reasonable for the employer to discuss with the worker whether her crying is connected to a disability and whether a reasonable adjustment could be made to her working arrangements.

6.20 The Act does not prevent a disabled person keeping a disability confidential from an employer. But keeping a disability confidential is likely to mean that unless the employer could reasonably be expected to know about it anyway, the employer will not be under a duty to make a reasonable adjustment. If a disabled person expects an employer to make a reasonable adjustment, they will need to provide the employer – or someone acting on their behalf – with sufficient information to carry out that adjustment.

When can an employer be assumed to know about disability?

6.21 If an employer's agent or employee (such as an occupational health adviser, a HR officer or a recruitment agent) knows, in that capacity, of a worker's or applicant's or potential applicant's disability, the employer will not usually be able to claim that they do not know of the disability and that they therefore have no obligation to make a reasonable adjustment. Employers therefore need to ensure that where information about disabled people may come through different channels, there is a means – suitably confidential and subject to the disabled person's consent – for bringing that information together to make it easier for the employer to fulfil their duties under the Act.

Example: In the example in paragraph 5.18, if the employer's working arrangements put the worker at a substantial disadvantage because of the effects of his disability and he claims that a reasonable adjustment should have been made, it will not be a defence for the employer to claim that they were unaware of the worker's disability. Because the information gained by the OH adviser on the employer's behalf is assumed to be shared with the employer, the OH adviser's knowledge means that the employer's duty under the Act applies.

6.22 Information will not be 'imputed' or attributed to the employer if it is gained by a person providing services to employees independently of the employer. This is the case even if the employer has arranged for those services to be provided.

WHAT IS MEANT BY 'REASONABLE STEPS'?

6.23 The duty to make adjustments requires employers to take such steps as it is reasonable to have to take, in all the circumstances of the case, in order to make adjustments. The Act does not specify any particular factors that should be taken into account. What is a reasonable step for an employer to take will depend on all the circumstances of each individual case.

6.24 There is no onus on the disabled worker to suggest what adjustments should be made (although it is good practice for employers to ask). However, where the disabled person does so, the employer should consider whether such adjustments would help overcome the substantial disadvantage, and whether they are reasonable.

6.25 Effective and practicable adjustments for disabled workers often involve little or no cost or disruption and are therefore very likely to be reasonable for an employer to have to make. Even if an adjustment has a significant cost associated with it, it may still be cost-effective in overall terms – for example, compared with the costs of recruiting and training a new member of staff – and so may still be a reasonable adjustment to have to make.

6.26 **[Sch 21]** Many adjustments do not involve making physical changes to premises. However, where such changes need to be made and an employer occupies premises under a lease or other binding obligation, the employer may have to obtain consent to the making of reasonable adjustments. These provisions are explained in Appendix 3.

6.27 If making a particular adjustment would increase the risk to health and safety of any person (including the disabled worker in question) then this is a relevant factor in deciding whether it is reasonable to make that adjustment. Suitable and sufficient risk assessments should be used to help determine whether such risk is likely to arise.

6.28 The following are some of the factors which might be taken into account when deciding what is a reasonable step for an employer to have to take:

- whether taking any particular steps would be effective in preventing the substantial disadvantage;
- the practicability of the step;
- the financial and other costs of making the adjustment and the extent of any disruption caused;
- the extent of the employer's financial or other resources;
- the availability to the employer of financial or other assistance to help make an adjustment (such as advice through Access to Work); and
- the type and size of the employer.

6.29 Ultimately the test of the 'reasonableness' of any step an employer may have to take is an objective one and will depend on the circumstances of the case.

CAN FAILURE TO MAKE A REASONABLE ADJUSTMENT EVER BE JUSTIFIED?

6.30 The Act does not permit an employer to justify a failure to comply with a duty to make a reasonable adjustment. However, an employer will only breach such a duty if the adjustment in question is one which it is reasonable for the employer to have to make. So, where the duty applies, it is the question of 'reasonableness' which alone determines whether the adjustment has to be made.

WHAT HAPPENS IF THE DUTY IS NOT COMPLIED WITH?

6.31 **[s 21]** If an employer does not comply with the duty to make reasonable adjustments they will be committing an act of unlawful discrimination. A disabled worker will have the right to take a claim to the Employment Tribunal based on this.

REASONABLE ADJUSTMENTS IN PRACTICE

6.32 It is a good starting point for an employer to conduct a proper assessment, in consultation with the disabled person concerned, of what reasonable adjustments may be required. Any necessary adjustments should be implemented in a timely fashion, and it may also be necessary for an employer to make more than one adjustment. It is advisable to agree any proposed adjustments with the disabled worker in question before they are made.

6.33 Examples of steps it might be reasonable for employers to have to take include:

Making adjustments to premises

Example: An employer makes structural or other physical changes such as widening a doorway, providing a ramp or moving furniture for a wheelchair user.

Providing information in accessible formats

Example: The format of instructions and manuals might need to be modified for some disabled workers (for example, produced in Braille or on audio tape) and instructions for people with learning disabilities might need to be conveyed orally with individual demonstration or in Easy Read. Employers may also need to arrange for recruitment materials to be provided in alternative formats.

Allocating some of the disabled person's duties to another worker

Example: An employer reallocates minor or subsidiary duties to another worker as a disabled worker has difficulty doing them because of his disability. For example, the job involves occasionally going onto the open roof of a building but the employer transfers this work away from a worker whose disability involves severe vertigo.

Transferring the disabled worker to fill an existing vacancy

Example: An employer should consider whether a suitable alternative post is available for a worker who becomes disabled (or whose disability worsens), where no reasonable adjustment would enable the worker to continue doing the current job. Such a post might also involve retraining or other reasonable adjustments such as equipment for the new post or transfer to a position on a higher grade.

Altering the disabled worker's hours of work or training

Example: An employer allows a disabled person to work flexible hours to enable him to have additional breaks to overcome fatigue arising from his disability. It could also include permitting part-time working or different working hours to avoid the need to travel in the rush hour if this creates a problem related to an impairment. A phased return to work with a gradual build-up of hours might also be appropriate in some circumstances.

Assigning the disabled worker to a different place of work or training or arranging home working

Example: An employer relocates the workstation of a newly disabled worker (who now uses a wheelchair) from an inaccessible third floor office to an accessible one on the ground floor. It may be reasonable to move his place of work to other premises of the same employer if the first building is inaccessible. Allowing the worker to work from home might also be a reasonable adjustment for the employer to make.

Allowing the disabled worker to be absent during working or training hours for rehabilitation, assessment or treatment

Example: An employer allows a person who has become disabled more time off work than would be allowed to non-disabled workers to enable him to have rehabilitation training. A similar adjustment may be appropriate if a disability worsens or if a disabled person needs occasional treatment anyway.

Giving, or arranging for, training or mentoring (whether for the disabled person or any other worker)

This could be training in particular pieces of equipment which the disabled person uses, or an alteration to the standard workplace training to reflect the worker's particular disability.

Example: All workers are trained in the use of a particular machine but an employer provides slightly different or longer training for a worker with restricted hand or arm movements. An employer might also provide training in additional software for a visually impaired worker so that he can use a computer with speech output.

Acquiring or modifying equipment

Example: An employer might have to provide special equipment such as an adapted keyboard for someone with arthritis, a large screen for a visually impaired worker, or an adapted telephone for someone with a hearing impairment, or other modified equipment for disabled workers (such as longer handles on a machine).

There is no requirement to provide or modify equipment for personal purposes unconnected with a worker's job, such as providing a wheelchair if a person needs one in any event but does not have one. The disadvantages in such a case do not flow from the employer's arrangements or premises.

Modifying procedures for testing or assessment

Example: A worker with restricted manual dexterity would be disadvantaged by a written test, so the employer gives that person an oral test instead.

Providing a reader or interpreter

Example: An employer arranges for a colleague to read mail to a worker with a visual impairment at particular times during the working day. Alternatively, the employer might hire a reader.

Providing supervision or other support

Example: An employer provides a support worker or arranges help from a colleague, in appropriate circumstances, for someone whose disability leads to uncertainty or lack of confidence in unfamiliar situations, such as on a training course.

Allowing a disabled worker to take a period of disability leave

Example: A worker who has cancer needs to undergo treatment and rehabilitation. His employer allows a period of disability leave and permits him to return to his job at the end of this period.

Participating in supported employment schemes, such as Workstep

Example: A man applies for a job as an office assistant after several years of not working because of depression. He has been participating in a supported employment scheme where he saw the post advertised. He asks the employer to let him make private phone calls during the working day to a support worker at the scheme and the employer allows him to do so as a reasonable adjustment.

Employing a support worker to assist a disabled worker

Example: An adviser with a visual impairment is sometimes required to make home visits to clients. The employer employs a support worker to assist her on these visits.

Modifying disciplinary or grievance procedures for a disabled worker

Example: A worker with a learning disability is allowed to take a friend (who does not work with her) to act as an advocate at a meeting with her employer about a grievance. The employer also ensures that the meeting is conducted in a way that does not disadvantage or patronise the disabled worker.

Adjusting redundancy selection criteria for a disabled worker

Example: Because of his condition, a man with an autoimmune disease has taken several short periods of absence during the year. When his employer is taking the absences into account as a criterion for selecting people for redundancy, they discount these periods of disability-related absence.

Modifying performance-related pay arrangements for a disabled worker

Example: A disabled worker who is paid purely on her output needs frequent short additional breaks during her working day – something her employer agrees to as a reasonable adjustment. It may be a reasonable adjustment for her employer to pay her at an agreed rate (for example, her average hourly rate) for these breaks.

6.34 It may sometimes be necessary for an employer to take a combination of steps.

Example: A worker who is blind is given a new job with her employer in an unfamiliar part of the building. The employer:

- arranges facilities for her assistance dog in the new area;
- arranges for her new instructions to be in Braille; and
- provides disability equality training to all staff.

6.35 In some cases, a reasonable adjustment will not succeed without the co-operation of other workers. Colleagues as well as managers may therefore have an important role in helping ensure that a reasonable adjustment is carried out in practice. Subject to considerations about confidentiality, employers must ensure that this happens. It is unlikely to be a valid defence to a claim under the Act to argue that an adjustment was unreasonable because staff were obstructive or unhelpful when the employer tried to implement it. An employer would at least need to be able to show that they took such behaviour seriously and dealt with it appropriately. Employers will be more likely to be able to do this if they establish and implement the type of policies and practices described in Chapter 18.

Example: An employer ensures that a worker with autism has a structured working day as a reasonable adjustment. As part of this adjustment, it is the responsibility of the employer to ensure that other workers co-operate with this arrangement.

THE ACCESS TO WORK SCHEME

6.36 The Access to Work scheme may assist an employer to decide what steps to take. If financial assistance is available from the scheme, it may also make it reasonable for an employer to take certain steps which would otherwise be unreasonably expensive.

6.37 However, Access to Work does not diminish any of an employer's duties under the Act. In particular:

- The legal responsibility for making a reasonable adjustment remains with the employer – even where Access to Work is involved in the provision of advice or funding in relation to the adjustment.
- It is likely to be a reasonable step for the employer to help a disabled person in making an application for assistance from Access to Work and to provide on-going administrative support (by completing claim forms, for example).

6.38 It may be unreasonable for an employer to decide not to make an adjustment based on its cost before finding out whether financial assistance for the adjustment is available from Access to Work or another source.

6.39 More information about the Access to Work scheme is available from:
www.direct.gov.uk/en/DisabledPeople/Employmentsupport/WorkSchemesAndProgrammes/DG_4000347

CHAPTER 7
HARASSMENT

INTRODUCTION

[4.145]
7.1 This chapter explains the Act's general test for harassment. It also explains the provisions on

harassment related to a relevant protected characteristic, the provisions on sexual harassment, and less favourable treatment for rejecting or submitting to harassment.

7.2 Unlike direct discrimination, harassment does not require a comparative approach; it is not necessary for the worker to show that another person was, or would have been, treated more favourably. For an explanation of direct discrimination, please see Chapter 4.

WHAT THE ACT SAYS

7.3 The Act prohibits three types of harassment. These are:

- **[s 26(1)]** harassment related to a 'relevant protected characteristic';
- **[s 26(2)]** sexual harassment; and
- **[s 26(3)]** less favourable treatment of a worker because they submit to, or reject, sexual harassment or harassment related to sex or gender reassignment.

7.4 **[s 26(5)]** 'Relevant protected characteristics' are:

- Age
- Disability
- Gender Reassignment
- Race
- Religion or Belief
- Sex
- Sexual Orientation

7.5 Pregnancy and maternity and marriage and civil partnership are not protected directly under the harassment provisions. However, pregnancy and maternity harassment would amount to harassment related to sex, and harassment related to civil partnership would amount to harassment related to sexual orientation.

HARASSMENT RELATED TO A PROTECTED CHARACTERISTIC

7.6 **[s 26(1)]** This type of harassment of a worker occurs when a person engages in unwanted conduct which is related to a relevant protected characteristic and which has the purpose or the effect of:

- violating the worker's dignity; or
- creating an intimidating, hostile, degrading, humiliating or offensive environment for that worker.

7.7 Unwanted conduct covers a wide range of behaviour, including spoken or written words or abuse, imagery, graffiti, physical gestures, facial expressions, mimicry, jokes, pranks, acts affecting a person's surroundings or other physical behaviour.

7.8 The word 'unwanted' means essentially the same as 'unwelcome' or 'uninvited'. 'Unwanted' does not mean that express objection must be made to the conduct before it is deemed to be unwanted. A serious one-off incident can also amount to harassment.

Example: In front of her male colleagues, a female electrician is told by her supervisor that her work is below standard and that, as a woman, she will never be competent to carry it out. The supervisor goes on to suggest that she should instead stay at home to cook and clean for her husband. This could amount to harassment related to sex as such a statement would be self-evidently unwanted and the electrician would not have to object to it before it was deemed to be unlawful harassment.

'RELATED TO'

7.9 Unwanted conduct 'related to' a protected characteristic has a broad meaning in that the conduct does not have to be because of the protected characteristic. It includes the following situations:

a) Where conduct is related to the worker's own protected characteristic.

Example: If a worker with a hearing impairment is verbally abused because he wears a hearing aid, this could amount to harassment related to disability.

7.10 Protection from harassment also applies where a person is generally abusive to other workers but, in relation to a particular worker, the form of the unwanted conduct is determined by that worker's protected characteristic.

Example: During a training session attended by both male and female workers, a male trainer directs a number of remarks of a sexual nature to the group as a whole. A female worker finds the comments offensive and humiliating to her as a woman. She would be able to make a claim for harassment, even though the remarks were not specifically directed at her.

b) Where there is any connection with a protected characteristic.

Protection is provided because the conduct is dictated by a relevant protected characteristic, whether or not the worker has that characteristic themselves. This means that protection against unwanted conduct is provided where the worker does not have the relevant protected characteristic, including where the employer knows that the worker does not have the relevant characteristic. Connection with a protected characteristic may arise in several situations:

- The worker may be associated with someone who has a protected characteristic.

Example: A worker has a son with a severe disfigurement. His work colleagues make offensive remarks to him about his son's disability. The worker could have a claim for harassment related to disability.

- The worker may be wrongly perceived as having a particular protected characteristic.

Example: A Sikh worker wears a turban to work. His manager wrongly assumes he is Muslim and subjects him to Islamaphobic abuse. The worker could have a claim for harassment related to religion or belief because of his manager's perception of his religion.

- The worker is known not to have the protected characteristic but nevertheless is subjected to harassment related to that characteristic.

Example: A worker is subjected to homophobic banter and name calling, even though his colleagues know he is not gay. Because the form of the abuse relates to sexual orientation, this could amount to harassment related to sexual orientation.

- The unwanted conduct related to a protected characteristic is not directed at the particular worker but at another person or no one in particular.

Example: A manager racially abuses a black worker. As a result of the racial abuse, the black worker's white colleague is offended and could bring a claim of racial harassment.

- The unwanted conduct is related to the protected characteristic, but does not take place because of the protected characteristic.

Example: A female worker has a relationship with her male manager. On seeing her with another male colleague, the manager suspects she is having an affair. As a result, the manager makes her working life difficult by continually criticising her work in an offensive manner. The behaviour is not because of the sex of the female worker, but because of the suspected affair which is related to her sex. This could amount to harassment related to sex.

7.11 In all of the circumstances listed above, there is a connection with the protected characteristic and so the worker could bring a claim of harassment where the unwanted conduct creates for them any of the circumstances defined in paragraph 7.6

SEXUAL HARASSMENT

7.12 **[s 26(2)]** Sexual harassment occurs when a person engages in unwanted conduct as defined in paragraph 7.6 and which is of a sexual nature.

7.13 Conduct 'of a sexual nature' can cover verbal, non-verbal or physical conduct including unwelcome sexual advances, touching, forms of sexual assault, sexual jokes, displaying pornographic photographs or drawings or sending emails with material of a sexual nature.

LESS FAVOURABLE TREATMENT FOR REJECTING OR SUBMITTING TO UNWANTED CONDUCT

7.14 **[s 26(3)]** The third type of harassment occurs when a worker is treated less favourably by their employer because that worker submitted to, or rejected unwanted conduct of a sexual nature, or unwanted conduct which is related to sex or to gender reassignment, and the unwanted conduct creates for them any of the circumstances defined in paragraph 7.6.

Example: A shopkeeper propositions one of his shop assistants. She rejects his advances and then is turned down for a promotion which she believes she would have got if she had accepted her boss's advances. The shop assistant would have a claim for harassment.

7.15 **[s 26(3)(a)]** Under this type of harassment, the initial unwanted conduct may be committed by the person who treats the worker less favourably or by another person.

Example: A female worker is asked out by her team leader and she refuses. The team leader feels resentful and informs the Head of Division about the rejection. The Head of Division subsequently fails to give the female worker the promotion she applies for, even though she is the best candidate. She knows that the team leader and the Head of Division are good friends and believes that her refusal to go out with the team leader influenced the Head of Division's decision. She could have a claim of harassment over the Head of Division's actions.

'PURPOSE OR EFFECT'

7.16 For all three types of harassment, if the **purpose** of subjecting the worker to the conduct is to create any of the circumstances defined in paragraph 7.6, this will be sufficient to establish unlawful harassment. It will not be necessary to inquire into the effect of that conduct on that worker.

7.17 Regardless of the intended purpose, unwanted conduct will also amount to harassment if it has the **effect** of creating any of the circumstances defined in paragraph 7.6.

Example: Male members of staff download pornographic images on to their computers in an office where a woman works. She may make a claim for harassment if she is aware that the images are being downloaded and the effect of this is to create a hostile and humiliating environment for her. In this situation, it is irrelevant that the male members of staff did not have the purpose of upsetting the woman, and that they merely considered the downloading of images as 'having a laugh'.

7.18 In deciding whether conduct had that effect, each of the following must be taken into account:

(a) **[s 26(4)(a)]** The perception of the worker; that is, did they regard it as violating their dignity or creating an intimidating (etc) environment for them. This part of the test is a subjective question and depends on how the worker regards the treatment.

(b) **[s 26(4)(b)]** The other circumstances of the case; circumstances that may be relevant and therefore need to be taken into account can include the personal circumstances of the worker experiencing the conduct; for example, the worker's health, including mental health; mental capacity; cultural norms; or previous experience of harassment; and also the environment in which the conduct takes place.

(c) **[s 26(4)(c)]** Whether it is reasonable for the conduct to have that effect; this is an objective test. A tribunal is unlikely to find unwanted conduct has the effect, for example, of offending a worker if the tribunal considers the worker to be hypersensitive and that another person subjected to the same conduct would not have been offended.

7.19 Where the employer is a public authority, it may also be relevant in cases of alleged harassment whether the alleged perpetrator was exercising any of her/his Convention rights protected under the Human Rights Act 1998. For example, the right to freedom of thought, conscience and religion or freedom of speech of the alleged harasser will need to be taken into account when considering all relevant circumstances of the case.

LIABILITY OF EMPLOYERS FOR HARASSMENT BY THIRD PARTIES

7.20 Employers may be liable for harassment of their employees or job applicants by third parties – such as customers – who are not directly under their control. This is explained in paragraphs 10.19 to 10.24.

CHAPTER 8
PREGNANCY AND MATERNITY

INTRODUCTION

[4.146]

8.1 Specific provisions in the Act protect women from discrimination at work because of pregnancy or maternity leave. These apply during the protected period explained at paragraphs 8.9 to 8.13.

8.2 There is also a statutory regime setting out pregnant employees' rights to health and safety protection, time off for antenatal care, maternity leave and unfair dismissal protection.

8.3 European law, including the Pregnant Workers Directive (92/85/EEC) and the recast Equal Treatment Directive (2006/54/EC), gives women who are pregnant or on maternity leave protected status in employment. For example, Article 10 of the Pregnant Workers Directive prohibits the dismissal of pregnant workers and workers on maternity leave other than in exceptional circumstances not connected with their pregnancy or maternity leave.

WHAT THE ACT SAYS

8.4 **[s 18(1)–(4)]** It is unlawful discrimination to treat a woman unfavourably because of her pregnancy or a related illness, or because she is exercising, has exercised or is seeking or has sought to exercise her right to maternity leave.

8.5 In considering whether there has been pregnancy and maternity discrimination, the employer's motive or intention is not relevant, and neither are the consequences of pregnancy or maternity leave. Such discrimination cannot be justified.

8.6 The meaning of 'because of' is discussed in paragraph 3.11. However, unlike in cases of direct sex discrimination, there is no need to compare the way a pregnant worker is treated with the treatment of any other workers. If she is treated unfavourably by her employer because of her pregnancy or maternity leave, this is automatically discrimination.

8.7 **[s 18(7)]** Unfavourable treatment of a woman because of her pregnancy or maternity leave during 'the protected period' is unlawful pregnancy and maternity discrimination. This cannot be treated as direct sex discrimination (for which a comparator, actual or hypothetical, is required).

8.8 **[s 13(6)(b)]** In some cases, employers have to treat workers who are pregnant or have recently given birth more favourably than other workers. This is explained at paragraph 8.43. Men cannot make a claim for sex discrimination in relation to any special treatment given to a woman in connection with pregnancy or childbirth, such as maternity leave or additional sick leave.

THE PROTECTED PERIOD

8.9 [s 18(6)] The protected period starts when a woman becomes pregnant and continues until the end of her maternity leave, or until she returns to work if that is earlier (but see paragraphs 8.14 and 8.15 below).

8.10 The maternity leave scheme is set out in Part VIII of the Employment Rights Act 1996 (ERA) and the Maternity and Parental Leave (etc) Regulations 1999 (MPLR).

8.11 [s 213] The Act refers to the three kinds of maternity leave regulated by the ERA:

- Compulsory maternity leave – the minimum two-week period (four weeks for factory workers) immediately following childbirth when a woman must not work for her employer. All employees entitled to Ordinary Maternity Leave must take compulsory maternity leave.
- Ordinary maternity leave – all pregnant employees are entitled to 26 weeks ordinary maternity leave (which includes the compulsory leave period), provided they give proper notice.
- Additional maternity leave – all pregnant employees are entitled to a further 26 weeks maternity leave, provided they give proper notice.

8.12 There is no minimum period of qualifying service for ordinary and additional maternity leave but only employees are eligible to take it.

8.13 [s 18(6)] The protected period in relation to a woman's pregnancy ends either:

- if she is entitled to ordinary and additional maternity leave, at the end of the additional maternity leave period; or
- when she returns to work after giving birth, if that is earlier; or
- if she is not entitled to maternity leave, for example because she is not an employee, two weeks after the baby is born.

Unfavourable treatment outside the protected period

8.14 [s 18(7)] Outside the protected period, unfavourable treatment of a woman in employment because of her pregnancy would be considered as sex discrimination rather than pregnancy and maternity discrimination.

8.15 [s 18(5)] However, if a woman is treated unfavourably because of her pregnancy (or a related illness) after the end of the protected period, but due to a decision made during it, this is regarded as occurring during the protected period.

'PREGNANCY OF HERS'

8.16 [s 18(2)] For pregnancy and maternity discrimination, the unfavourable treatment must be because of the woman's own pregnancy. However, a worker treated less favourably because of association with a pregnant woman, or a woman who has recently given birth, may have a claim for sex discrimination.

KNOWLEDGE OF PREGNANCY

8.17 [Reg 4 Maternity and Parental Leave etc Regulations 1999 (MPLR)] There is no obligation on a job applicant or employee to inform the employer of her pregnancy until 15 weeks before the baby is due. However, telling the employer triggers the legal protection, including the employer's health and safety obligations.

8.18 Unfavourable treatment will only be unlawful if the employer is aware the woman is pregnant. The employer must know, believe or suspect that she is pregnant – whether this is by formal notification or through the grapevine.

NO NEED FOR COMPARISON

8.19 It is not necessary to show that the treatment was unfavourable compared with the treatment of a man, with that of a woman who is not pregnant or with any other worker. However, evidence of how others have been treated may be useful to help determine if the unfavourable treatment is in fact related to pregnancy or maternity leave.

Example: A company producing office furniture decides to exhibit at a trade fair. A pregnant member of the company's sales team, who had expected to be asked to attend the trade fair to staff the company's stall and talk to potential customers, is not invited. In demonstrating that, but for her pregnancy, she would have been invited, it would help her to show that other members of the company's sales team, either male or female but not pregnant, were invited to the trade fair.

NOT THE ONLY REASON

8.20 A woman's pregnancy or maternity leave does not have to be the only reason for her treatment, but it does have to be an important factor or effective cause.

Example: An employer dismisses an employee on maternity leave shortly before she is due to return to work because the locum covering her absence is regarded as a better performer. Had the employee not been absent on maternity leave she would not have been sacked. Her dismissal is therefore unlawful, even if performance was a factor in the employer's decision-making.

UNFAVOURABLE TREATMENT

8.21 An employer must not demote or dismiss a woman, or deny her training or promotion opportunities, because she is pregnant or on maternity leave. Nor must an employer take into account any period of pregnancy-related sickness absence when making a decision about her employment.

8.22 As examples only, it will amount to pregnancy and maternity discrimination to treat a woman unfavourably during the protected period for the following reasons:

- the fact that, because of her pregnancy, the woman will be temporarily unable to do the job for which she is specifically employed whether permanently or on a fixed-term contract;
- the pregnant woman is temporarily unable to work because to do so would be a breach of health and safety regulations;
- the costs to the business of covering her work;
- any absence due to pregnancy related illness;
- her inability to attend a disciplinary hearing due to morning sickness or other pregnancy-related conditions;
- performance issues due to morning sickness or other pregnancy-related conditions.

This is not an exhaustive list but indicates, by drawing on case law, the kinds of treatment that have been found to be unlawful.

8.23 The following are further examples of unlawful discrimination:

- failure to consult a woman on maternity leave about changes to her work or about possible redundancy;
- disciplining a woman for refusing to carry out tasks due to pregnancy related risks;
- assuming that a woman's work will become less important to her after childbirth and giving her less responsible or less interesting work as a result;
- depriving a woman of her right to an annual assessment of her performance because she was on maternity leave;
- excluding a pregnant woman from business trips.

OTHER EMPLOYMENT RIGHTS FOR PREGNANT WOMEN

8.24 [s 99 & 47(c) ERA] There are separate legal provisions in the ERA protecting employees from dismissal and other disadvantage (except relating to pay) where the reason or principal reason is related to pregnancy or maternity leave. These ERA rights can overlap with the discrimination provisions and if they are breached this may also constitute pregnancy and maternity discrimination.

Example: If an employer fails to consult a woman about threatened redundancy because she is absent on maternity leave, this will be unlawful discrimination.

8.25 [MPLR, regs 10 & 20(1)(b)] An employee who is made redundant while on statutory maternity leave is entitled to be offered any suitable alternative vacancy, in preference to other employees. If she is not offered it, she can claim automatically unfair dismissal.

8.26 [MPLR, regs 18 & 18A] A woman has a statutory right to return to the same job after ordinary maternity leave. After additional maternity leave, she has a right to return to the same job unless that is not reasonably practicable. If that is the case, she is entitled to be offered a suitable alternative job, on terms and conditions which are not less favourable than her original job. If a woman seeks to return on different terms where she does not have a specific contractual right to do so, a refusal could constitute direct discrimination because of sex, depending on the circumstances.

8.27 In addition, depending on the circumstances, refusing to allow a woman to return to work part-time could be indirect sex discrimination.

8.28 [ERA 1996, Part 8A] Parents of dependent children have a right to request flexible working set out in the ERA. This right entitles a woman returning from maternity leave to make a request to change her hours and if she does so, her employer must consider her request (see paragraphs 17.8 to 17.12).

8.29 [MPLR, reg 12A] An employee on statutory maternity or adoption leave may by agreement work for her employer for up to ten 'keeping in touch' (KIT) days without bringing the leave to an end. This can include training or attending staff meetings, for example.

HEALTH AND SAFETY AT WORK

8.30 [Sch 22, para 2] The Act permits differential treatment of women at work where it is necessary to comply with laws protecting the health and safety of women who are pregnant, who have recently given birth or are breastfeeding.

8.31 Steps taken to protect pregnant workers' health and safety should not result in them being treated unfavourably.

8.32 [Pregnant Workers Directive, incl Annex II MHSW Regs; The Workplace (Health, Safety and Welfare) Regs 1992, reg 25(4)] Employers have specific obligations to protect the health and safety of pregnant women and women who have recently given birth. Where a workplace includes women of childbearing age, and the work or workplace conditions are of a kind that could involve risk to a pregnant woman, a woman who has given birth within the previous six months or who is breastfeeding, or create a risk to her baby, the employer's general risk assessment must include an assessment of such risks. There is a non-exhaustive list of the working conditions, processes, and physical, chemical or biological agents that may pose a risk in Annexes I and II to the Pregnant Workers Directive.

8.33 [MHSW Regs, reg 18] In addition, where an employee has given notice in writing that she is pregnant, has given birth within the last six months, or is breastfeeding, the employer must consider the risks in relation to that individual and take action to avoid them. This may involve altering her working conditions or hours of work. For example, as a result of a risk assessment an employer may ensure that the worker takes extra breaks, refrains from lifting, or spends more time sitting rather than standing.

8.34 If it is not reasonable to do this, or it would not avoid the risk, the employer must suspend the woman from work for as long as is necessary to avoid the risk.

8.35 [s 67 ERA 1996] Before being suspended on maternity grounds, a woman is entitled to be offered suitable alternative work if it is available. If she unreasonably refuses an offer of alternative work, she will lose the statutory right to be paid during any period of maternity suspension.

8.36 The Health and Safety Executive produces guidance on New and Expectant Mothers at Work. This is available from:
www.hse.gov.uk/mothers/mothers/htm

PAY AND CONDITIONS DURING MATERNITY LEAVE

8.37 Employers are obliged to maintain a woman's benefits except contractual remuneration during both ordinary and additional maternity leave. Unless otherwise provided in her contract of employment, a woman does not have a legal right to continue receiving her full pay during maternity leave.

8.38 [SMP (General) Regs (Amendment) 2005] If a woman receives a pay rise between the start of the calculation period for Statutory Maternity Pay (SMP) and the end of her maternity leave, she is entitled to have her SMP recalculated and receive any extra SMP due. She may also, as a result of recalculation following such a pay rise, become eligible for SMP where previously she was not. Employers are reimbursed all or some of the cost of SMP.

Non-contractual payments during maternity leave

8.39 [Sch 9, para 17(5)] The Act has a specific exception relating to non-contractual payments to women on maternity leave. There is no obligation on an employer to extend to a woman on maternity leave any non-contractual benefit relating to pay, such as a discretionary bonus. For the purposes of this exception, 'pay' means a payment of money by way of wages or salary.

8.40 [Sch 9, para 17(2)(a), (6)] However, this exception does not apply to any maternity-related pay (whether statutory or contractual), to which a woman is entitled as a result of being pregnant or on maternity leave. Nor does it apply to any maternity-related pay arising from an increase that the woman would have received had she not been on maternity leave.

Example: A woman on maternity leave is receiving contractual maternity pay, which is worked out as a percentage of her salary. The date of her employer's annual review of staff pay falls while she is on maternity leave. All other staff are awarded a 2% pay rise with immediate effect. If the woman on maternity leave does not receive the increase, this would be unlawful discrimination. Her contractual maternity pay should be recalculated so that it is based on her salary plus the 2% increase given to all her colleagues. Any other benefits linked to salary should also be adjusted to take into account the pay rise. When she returns to work her normal pay must reflect the pay rise.

8.41 [Sch 9, para 17(2)(b) & (c)] Any non-contractual bonus relating to the period of compulsory maternity leave is not covered by the exception, so the employer would have to pay this. Neither does the exception apply to pay relating to times when a woman is not on maternity leave.

8.42 [ss 72–76] Further information on equal treatment and what may be unlawful discrimination in terms and conditions for pregnant women and women on maternity leave is set out in the Equal Pay Code.

SPECIAL TREATMENT IN CONNECTION WITH PREGNANCY AND CHILDBIRTH IS LAWFUL

8.43 [s 13(6)(b)] An employer does not discriminate against a man where it affords a woman 'special treatment' in connection with childbirth and pregnancy.

Example: A man who is given a warning for being repeatedly late to work in the mornings alleges that he has been treated less favourably than a pregnant woman who has also been repeatedly late for work, but who was not given a warning. The man cannot compare himself to the pregnant woman, because her lateness is related to her morning sickness. The correct comparator in his case would be a non-pregnant woman who was also late for work.

8.44 Treating a woman unfavourably because she is undergoing in vitro fertilisation (IVF) or other fertility treatment would not count as pregnancy and maternity discrimination. This is because a woman is not deemed pregnant until the fertilised ova have been implanted in her uterus. However, such unfavourable treatment could amount to sex discrimination (see paragraph 17.28).

Breastfeeding

8.45 There is no statutory right for workers to take time off to breastfeed. However, employers should try to accommodate women who wish to do so, bearing in mind the following:

- As explained above in paragraph 8.30, where risks to the health and safety of an employee who is breastfeeding have been identified in the employer's risk assessment, and where she has given written notice that she is breastfeeding, it may be reasonable for the employer to alter her working conditions or hours of work. If this is not reasonable or would not avoid the risks identified, the employer should suspend the employee from work for so long as is necessary to avoid the risks; as above, this is subject to the right to be offered alternative work if it is available.
- Employers have a duty to provide suitable workplace rest facilities for women at work who are breastfeeding mothers to use.
- A refusal to allow a woman to express milk or to adjust her working conditions to enable her to continue to breastfeed may amount to unlawful sex discrimination.

Example: An employer refused a request from a woman to return from maternity leave part-time to enable her to continue breastfeeding her child who suffered from eczema. The woman told her employer that her GP had advised that continued breastfeeding would benefit the child's medical condition. The employer refused the request without explanation. Unless the employer's refusal can be objectively justified, this is likely to be indirect sex discrimination.

CHAPTER 9
VICTIMISATION AND OTHER UNLAWFUL ACTS

INTRODUCTION

[4.147]
9.1 This chapter explains what the Act says about the unlawful acts of victimisation, instructing, causing or inducing discrimination, and aiding contraventions. It also sets out the provisions on gender reassignment discrimination (absence from work).

VICTIMISATION

What the Act says

9.2 **[s 27(1)]** The Act prohibits victimisation. It is victimisation for an employer to subject a worker to a detriment because the worker has done a 'protected act' or because the employer believes that the worker has done or may do a protected act in the future.

9.3 **[s 27(2)(c) & (d)]** A worker need not have a particular protected characteristic in order to be protected against victimisation under the Act; to be unlawful, victimisation must be linked to a 'protected act' (see paragraph 9.5). Making an allegation or doing something related to the Act does not have to involve an explicit reference to the legislation.

Example: A non-disabled worker gives evidence on behalf of a disabled colleague at an Employment Tribunal hearing where disability discrimination is claimed. If the non-disabled worker is subsequently refused a promotion because of that action, they would have suffered victimisation in contravention of the Act.

9.4 Former workers are also protected from victimisation.

Example: A grocery shop worker resigns after making a sexual harassment complaint against the owner. Several weeks later, she tries to make a purchase at the shop but is refused service by the owner because of her complaint. This could amount to victimisation.

What is a 'protected act'?

9.5 A protected act is any of the following:

- **[s 27(2)(a)]** bringing proceedings under the Act;
- **[s 27(2)(b)]** giving evidence or information in connection with proceedings brought under the Act;
- **[s 27(2)(c)]** doing anything which is related to the provisions of the Act;
- **[s 27(2)(d)]** making an allegation (whether or not express) that another person has done something in breach of the Act; or

- **[s 77(3)]** making or seeking a 'relevant pay disclosure' to or from a colleague (including a former colleague).

9.6 A 'relevant pay disclosure' is explained in paragraph 14.11 and in the Equal Pay Code.

9.7 Protected acts can occur in any field covered by the Act and in relation to any part of the Act. An employer must therefore not victimise a person who has done a protected act in relation to services, for example.

What is a 'detriment'?

9.8 'Detriment' in the context of victimisation is not defined by the Act and could take many forms. Generally, a detriment is anything which the individual concerned might reasonably consider changed their position for the worse or put them at a disadvantage. This could include being rejected for promotion, denied an opportunity to represent the organisation at external events, excluded from opportunities to train, or overlooked in the allocation of discretionary bonuses or performance-related awards.

Example: A senior manager hears a worker's grievance about harassment. He finds that the worker has been harassed and offers a formal apology and directs that the perpetrators of the harassment be disciplined and required to undertake diversity training. As a result, the senior manager is not put forward by his director to attend an important conference on behalf of the company. This is likely to amount to detriment.

9.9 A detriment might also include a threat made to the complainant which they take seriously and it is reasonable for them to take it seriously. There is no need to demonstrate physical or economic consequences. However, an unjustified sense of grievance alone would not be enough to establish detriment.

Example: An employer threatens to dismiss a staff member because he thinks she intends to support a colleague's sexual harassment claim. This threat could amount to victimisation, even though the employer has not actually taken any action to dismiss the staff member and may not really intend to do so.

9.10 Detrimental treatment amounts to victimisation if a 'protected act' is one of the reasons for the treatment, but it need not be the only reason.

What other factors are involved in proving that victimisation has occurred?

9.11 Victimisation does not require a comparator. The worker need only show that they have experienced a detriment because they have done a protected act or because the employer believes (rightly or wrongly) that they have done or intend to do a protected act.

9.12 There is no time limit within which victimisation must occur after a person has done a protected act. However, a complainant will need to show a link between the detriment and the protected act.

Example: In 2006, a trade union staff representative acted on behalf of a colleague in a claim of age discrimination. In 2009, he applies for a promotion but is rejected. He asks for his interview notes which make a reference to his loyalty to the company and in brackets were written the words 'tribunal case'. This could amount to victimisation despite the three-year gap between the protected act and the detriment.

9.13 **[s 27(3)]** A worker cannot claim victimisation where they have acted in bad faith, such as maliciously giving false evidence or information or making a false allegation of discrimination. Any such action would not be a protected act.

9.14 However, if a worker gives evidence, provides information or makes an allegation in good faith but it turns out that it is factually wrong, or provides information in relation to proceedings which are unsuccessful, they will still be protected from victimisation.

9.15 A worker is protected from victimisation by an employer or prospective employer where they do a protected act which is not in relation to employment. For example, a protected act may be linked to accessing goods, facilities and services provided by the employer.

INSTRUCTING, CAUSING OR INDUCING DISCRIMINATION

What the Act says

9.16 **[s 111(1)]** It is unlawful to instruct someone to discriminate against, harass or victimise another person because of a protected characteristic or to instruct a person to help another person to do an unlawful act. Such an instruction would be unlawful even if it is not acted on.

Example: A GP instructs his receptionist not to register anyone with an Asian name. The receptionist would have a claim against the GP if she experienced a detriment as a result of not following the instruction. A potential patient would also have a claim against the GP under the services provisions of the Act if she discovered the instruction had been given and was put off from applying to register.

9.17 **[s 111(2), (3) & (8)]** The Act also makes it unlawful to cause or induce, or to attempt to cause or induce, someone to discriminate against or harass a third person because of a protected characteristic or to victimise a third person because they have done a protected act.

9.18 **[s 111(4)]** An inducement may amount to no more than persuasion and need not involve a benefit or loss. Nor does the inducement have to be applied directly: it may be indirect. It is enough if it is applied in such a way that the other person is likely to come to know about the inducement.

Example: The managing partner of an accountancy firm is aware that the head of the administrative team is planning to engage a senior receptionist with a physical disability. The managing partner does not issue any direct instruction but suggests to the head of administration that to do this would reflect poorly on his judgement and so affect his future with the firm. This is likely to amount to causing or attempting to cause the head of administration to act unlawfully.

9.19 It is also unlawful for a person to instruct, cause or induce a person to commit an act of discrimination or harassment in the context of relationships which have come to an end (see paragraphs 10.57 to 10.62).

9.20 **[s 111(1)–(3)]** The Act also prohibits a person from causing or inducing someone to help another person to do an unlawful act (see paragraph 9.26 below).

9.21 **[s 111(6)]** It does not matter whether the person who is instructed, caused or induced to commit an unlawful act carries it out. This is because instructing, causing or inducing an unlawful act is in itself unlawful. However, if the person does commit the unlawful act, they may be liable. The person who instructed, caused or induced them to carry it out will also be liable for it.

When does the Act apply?

9.22 **[s 111(7)]** For the Act to apply, the relationship between the person giving the instruction, or causing or inducing the unlawful act, and the recipient must be one in which discrimination, harassment or victimisation is prohibited. This will include employment relationships, the provision of services and public functions, and other relationships governed by the Act.

Who is protected?

9.23 **[s 111(5)]** The Act provides a remedy for:

(a) the person to whom the causing, instruction or inducement is addressed; and

(b) the person who is subjected to the discrimination or harassment or victimisation if it is carried out,

provided that they suffer a detriment as a result.

Example: In the example in paragraph 9.18, if the head of administration were to experience a detriment as a result of the managing partner's actions, he would be entitled to a remedy against the managing partner. The disabled candidate is also entitled to a remedy if she suffers a detriment as a result of the managing partner's actions.

9.24 **[s 111(5)(c)]** In addition, the Equality and Human Rights Commission has the power to bring proceedings regardless of whether an individual has actually experienced a detriment.

AIDING CONTRAVENTIONS

What the Act says

9.25 **[s 112(1)]** The Act makes it unlawful knowingly to help someone discriminate against, harass or victimise another person. A person who helps another in this way will be treated as having done the act of discrimination, harassment or victimisation themselves. It is also unlawful to help a person to discriminate against or harass another person after a relationship covered by the Act has ended, where the discrimination or harassment arises from and is closely connected to the relationship.

9.26 **[s 112(1)]** The Act also makes it unlawful to help with an instruction to discriminate or with causing or inducing discrimination.

What does it mean to help someone commit an unlawful act?

9.27 'Help' should be given its ordinary meaning. It does not have the same meaning as to procure, induce or cause an unlawful act. The help given to someone to discriminate, harass or victimise a person will be unlawful even if it is not substantial or productive, so long as it is not negligible.

Example: A company manager wants to ensure that a job goes to a female candidate because he likes to be surrounded by women in the office. However the company's Human Resources (HR) department, in accordance with their equal opportunities policy, has ensured that the application forms contain no evidence of candidates' sex. The manager asks a clerical worker to look in the HR files and let him know the sex of each candidate, explaining that he wants to filter out the male candidates. It may be unlawful for the clerical worker to give the manager this help, even if the manager is unsuccessful in excluding the male candidates.

What does the helper need to know to be liable?

9.28 For the help to be unlawful, the person giving the help must know at the time they give the help that discrimination, harassment or victimisation is a probable outcome. But the helper does not have to intend that this outcome should result from the help.

Example: In the example above, the help will be unlawful unless the clerical worker fails to realise that an act of discrimination is a likely outcome of her actions. But she only needs to understand that discrimination is a likely outcome; she does not have to intend that discrimination should occur as a result of her help.

Reasonable reliance on another's statement

9.29 **[s 112(2), (3)]** If the helper is told that they are assisting with a lawful act and it is reasonable for them to rely on this statement, then the help they give will not be unlawful even if it transpires that it assisted with a contravention of the Act. It is a criminal offence to knowingly or recklessly make a false or misleading statement as to the lawfulness of an act.

Example: In the example above, the manager might tell the clerical worker that he has a responsibility as manager to balance the sexes in the workforce and the HR department is mistaken in its approach. If it is reasonable for the worker to believe this, she will escape liability for the discrimination. Whether it is reasonable to believe this depends on all the relevant circumstances, including the nature of the action and the relationship of the helper to the person seeking help to carry out an unlawful act.

If the manager tells the clerical worker that it is all right for her to get the information, either knowing that that is not true or simply not caring whether it is true or not, the manager will not only have civil liability under the Act for discrimination but will also commit a criminal offence.

9.30 'Reasonable' means having regard to all the circumstances, including the nature of the act and how obviously discriminatory it is, the authority of the person making the statement and the knowledge that the helper has or ought to have.

GENDER REASSIGNMENT DISCRIMINATION - ABSENCE FROM WORK

What the Act says

9.31 **[s 16(2)(a)]** If a transsexual worker is absent from work because of gender reassignment, it is unlawful to treat them less favourably than they would be treated if they were absent due to an illness or injury.

Example: A transsexual worker takes time off to attend a Gender Identity Clinic as part of the gender reassignment process. His employer cannot treat him less favourably than she would treat him for absence due to illness or injury, for example by paying him less than he would have received if he were off sick.

9.32 **[s 16(2)(b)]** It is also discrimination for an employer to treat a transsexual person less favourably for being absent because of gender reassignment, compared to how they would treat the same worker for being absent for a reason other than sickness or injury and it is unreasonable to treat them less favourably.

Example: A transsexual worker tells her boss that she intends to undergo gender reassignment and asks him if she can take an afternoon off as annual leave to attend counselling. The request is brusquely refused although there are sufficient staff members on duty that day to cover for her absence. This could amount to gender reassignment discrimination.

9.33 The Act does not define a minimum or maximum time which must be allowed for absence because of gender reassignment. It would be good practice for employers to discuss with transsexual staff how much time they will need to take off in relation to the gender reassignment process and accommodate those needs in accordance with their normal practice and procedures.

CHAPTER 10
OBLIGATIONS AND LIABILITIES UNDER THE ACT

INTRODUCTION

[4.148]

10.1 Part 5 of the Act sets out the prohibited conduct as it applies in the employment context. It introduces new forms of obligations on employers to protect job applicants and employees from harassment by third parties during the course of employment, and not to enquire about the disability or health of applicants during the recruitment process. Part 8 sets out the circumstances in which liability for breaches of the Act might be incurred and the defences available against allegations of breaches of the Act.

10.2 This chapter explains the obligations of employers to job applicants and employees; liability of employers, principals, employees and agents for breaches of the Act; and the statutory defences available. In addition, this chapter explains employers' obligations when entering into contracts and the territorial scope of the Act.

DEFINITION OF EMPLOYMENT

10.3 **[s 83]** The Act defines employment broadly and covers a wide category of relationships that constitute work. Employment is defined in the Act as:
(a) employment under a contract of employment, a contract of apprenticeship or a contract personally to do work;
(b) Crown employment;
(c) employment as a relevant member of the House of Commons staff; or
(d) employment as a relevant member of the House of Lords staff.

10.4 The definition of employment in the Act is wider than under many other employment law provisions. So, for example, it covers a wider group of workers than are covered by the unfair dismissal provisions in the Employment Rights Act 1996.

10.5 The fact that a contract of employment is illegal or performed in an illegal manner will not exclude an Employment Tribunal having jurisdiction to hear an employment-related discrimination claim. This will be so provided that the discrimination is not inextricably linked to illegal conduct (so as to make an award of compensation appear to condone that conduct).

Example: An employee is aware that her employer is not deducting income tax or National Insurance contributions from her wages which, in this particular situation, is illegal. She queries this but her employer tells her: 'It's the way we do business.' Subsequently, she is dismissed after her employer becomes aware that she is pregnant. She alleges that the reason for her dismissal was her pregnancy and claims discrimination because of her pregnancy. While she knew that her employer was not paying tax on her wages, she did not actively participate in her employer's illegal conduct. The illegal performance of the contract was in no way linked to her discrimination claim. In the circumstances, she may be able to pursue her claim, despite her knowledge of her employer's illegal conduct.

OBLIGATIONS OF EMPLOYERS TO JOB APPLICANTS AND EMPLOYEES

10.6 **[ss 39 & 40; s 83(4)]** An employer has obligations not to discriminate against, victimise or harass job applicants and employees. These obligations also apply to a person who is seeking to recruit employees even if they are not yet an employer.

Example: A man sets up a new gardening business and advertises for men to work as gardeners. A woman gardener applies for a job but is rejected because of her sex. She would be able to make a claim for direct discrimination even though the businessman is not yet an employer as he does not yet have any employees.

WHAT THE ACT SAYS ABOUT EMPLOYERS' OBLIGATIONS TO JOB APPLICANTS

10.7 **[s 39(1) & (3)]** Employers must not discriminate against or victimise job applicants in:
(a) the arrangements they make for deciding who should be offered employment;
(b) in the terms on which they offer employment; or
(c) by not offering employment to the applicant.

What are arrangements?

10.8 Arrangements refer to the policies, criteria and practices used in the recruitment process including the decision making process. 'Arrangements' for the purposes of the Act are not confined to those which an employer makes in deciding who should be offered a specific job. They also include arrangements for deciding who should be offered employment more generally. Arrangements include such things as advertisements for jobs, the application process and the interview stage.

What are terms on which employment is offered?

10.9 **[s 39(6)]** The terms on which an employer might offer employment include such things as pay, bonuses and other benefits. In respect of discrimination because of sex or pregnancy and maternity, a term of an offer of employment that relates to pay is treated as discriminatory where, if accepted by the employee, it would give rise to an equality clause or rule; or where the term does not give rise to an equality clause or rule but it nevertheless amounts to direct discrimination. For more information on sex equality and maternity clauses, please see the Equal Pay Code.

10.10 **[s 60]** Employers' obligations to job applicants extend to them not making enquiries about disability or health before the offer of a job is made. This is discussed at paragraph 10.25 below.

What the Act says about employers' obligations to employees

10.11 **[s 39(2) & (4)]** Employers must not discriminate against or victimise an employee:
(a) as to the terms of employment;
(b) in the way they make access to opportunities for promotion, transfer or training or for receiving any other benefit, facility or service;
(c) by dismissing the employee; or

(d) subjecting them to any other detriment.

Terms of employment

10.12 The terms of employment include such things as pay, working hours, bonuses, occupational pensions, sickness or maternity and paternity leave and pay. The Act has specific provisions on equality of contractual terms between women and men, which are explained in the Code of Practice on Equal Pay.

Dismissals

10.13 **[s 39(7) & (8)]** A dismissal for the purposes of the Act includes:

(a) direct termination of employment by the employer (with or without notice);

(b) **[s 39(7)(a) & (8)]** termination of employment through the expiry of a fixed term contract (including a period defined by reference to an event or circumstance) unless the contract is immediately renewed; and

(c) **[s 39(7)(b)]** constructive dismissal – that is, where because of the employer's conduct the employee treats the employment as having come to an immediate end by resigning (whether or not the employee gives notice).

10.14 An employee who is dismissed in breach of the Act does not have to complete a qualifying period of service to bring a claim in the Employment Tribunal.

Example: An employer decides not to confirm a transsexual employee's employment at the end of a six months probationary period because of his poor performance. The employee is consequently dismissed. Yet, at the same time, the employer extends by three months the probationary period of a non-transsexual employee who has also not been performing to standard. This could amount to direct discrimination because of gender reassignment, entitling the dismissed employee to bring a claim to the Employment Tribunal.

Discrimination and unfair dismissal

10.15 Unfair dismissal claims can generally only be brought by employees who have one year or more continuous employment – but many categories of 'automatically unfair' dismissal have no minimum service requirement. For example, where the principal reason for dismissal is related to a request for time off work for family reasons such as maternity or parental leave, there is no minimum qualifying service.

10.16 Provided that the employee had one year or more continuous employment at the date of termination, a dismissal that amounts to a breach of the Act will almost inevitably be an unfair dismissal as well. In such cases, a person can make a claim for unfair dismissal at the same time as a discrimination claim.

Example: An employee who has worked with his employer for five years provides a witness statement in support of a colleague who has raised a grievance about homophobic bullying at work. The employer rejects the grievance and a subsequent appeal. A few months later the employer needs to make redundancies. The employer selects the employee for redundancy because he is viewed as 'difficult' and not a 'team player' because of the support he gave to his colleague in the grievance. It is likely that the redundancy would amount to unlawful victimisation and also be an unfair dismissal.

Detriment

10.17 A detriment is anything which might cause an employee to change their position for the worse or put them at a disadvantage; for example, being excluded from opportunities to progress within their career. The concept of detriment is explained in paragraph 9.8.

Example: An employer does not allow a black male employee an opportunity to act up in a management post, even though he has demonstrated enthusiasm by attending relevant training courses and taking on additional work. He has also expressed an interest in progressing within the business. Instead the employer offers the acting up opportunity to an Asian woman because he perceives Asian people as more hard-working than black people. If the black worker were able to demonstrate that he was better qualified for the acting up position compared to his Asian colleague, he could claim discrimination because of race on the basis that he was subjected to a detriment.

EMPLOYERS' DUTY TO MAKE REASONABLE ADJUSTMENTS

10.18 **[s 39(5)]** Employers have a duty to make reasonable adjustments in the recruitment and selection process and during employment. Making reasonable adjustments in recruitment might mean providing and accepting information in accessible formats. During recruitment, making reasonable adjustments could entail amending employment policies and procedures to ensure disabled employees are not put at a substantial disadvantage compared to non-disabled employees. (See Chapter 6 for a detailed explanation of the duty to make reasonable adjustments, and Chapters 16 and 17 for information on what employers can do to comply with the law.)

Example: An employer's disciplinary policy provides that they will make reasonable adjustments for disabled employees in the disciplinary procedure. When the employer decides to take disciplinary action against an employee with a hearing impairment, they pay for a palantypist to enable the employee to discuss her case with her union representative and to attend all meetings and hearings pertaining to the disciplinary hearing.

HARASSMENT OF JOB APPLICANTS AND EMPLOYEES

10.19 **[s 40]** Employers have a duty not to harass job applicants or their employees. This duty extends to harassment by third parties of job applicants and employees in the course of employment. (Chapter 7 provides a detailed explanation of the provisions on harassment; see paragraph 10.20 below on harassment by third parties.)

Harassment by third parties

10.20 **[s 40(2) & (4)]** Employers may be liable for harassment of job applicants and employees by third parties. A third party is anyone who is not the employer or another employee. It refers to those over whom the employer does not have direct control, such as customers or clients. The duty on employers to prevent third party harassment arises where the employee or job applicant has been harassed by a third party on at least two previous occasions, and the employer is aware of the harassment but fails to take 'reasonably practical steps' to prevent harassment by a third party happening again.

Example: A Ghanaian shop assistant is upset because a customer has come into the shop on Monday and Tuesday and on each occasion has made racist comments to him. On each occasion the shop assistant complained to his manager about the remarks. If his manager does nothing to stop it happening again, the employer would be liable for any further racial harassment perpetrated against that shop assistant by any customer.

10.21 **[s 40(3)]** The employer will be liable for harassment by a third party whether or not it is committed by the same third party or another third party.

Example: An employer is aware that a female employee working in her bar has been sexually harassed on two separate occasions by different customers. The employer fails to take any action and the employee experiences further harassment by yet another customer. The employer is likely to be liable for the further act of harassment.

10.22 It may be difficult to determine whether an employee or job applicant has been subjected to third party harassment. Employers should not wait for harassment by a third party to have occurred on at least two occasions before taking action.

10.23 **[s 40(2)(b)]** Employers will be able to avoid liability for third party harassment of their employees if they can show they took reasonably practical steps to prevent it happening.

10.24 Depending on the size and resources of an employer, reasonably practical steps might include:

- having a policy on harassment;
- notifying third parties that harassment of employees is unlawful and will not be tolerated, for example by the display of a public notice;
- inclusion of a term in all contracts with third parties notifying them of the employer's policy on harassment and requiring them to adhere to it;
- encouraging employees to report any acts of harassment by third parties to enable the employer to support the employee and take appropriate action;
- taking action on every complaint of harassment by a third party.

PRE-EMPLOYMENT ENQUIRIES ABOUT DISABILITY AND HEALTH

10.25 **[s 60]** Except in the specific circumstances set out below, it is unlawful for an employer to ask **any** job applicant about their disability or health until the applicant has been offered a job (on a conditional or unconditional basis) or has been included in a pool of successful candidates to be offered a job when a position becomes available. This includes asking such a question as part of the application process or during an interview. Questions relating to previous sickness absence are questions that relate to disability or health.

10.26 It is also unlawful for an agent or employee of an employer to ask questions about disability or health. This means that an employer cannot refer an applicant to an occupational health practitioner or ask an applicant to fill in a questionnaire provided by an occupational health practitioner before the offer of a job is made (or before acceptance into a pool of successful applicants) except in the circumstances set out below.

10.27 This provision of the Act is designed to ensure that disabled applicants are assessed objectively for their ability to do the job in question, and that they are not rejected because of their disability. There are some limited exceptions to this general rule, which mean that there are specified situations where such questions would be lawful.

EXCEPTIONS TO THE GENERAL RULE PROHIBITING DISABILITY OR HEALTH-RELATED QUESTIONS

10.28 [s 60(6) & (14)] There are six situations when it will be lawful for an employer to ask questions related to disability or health.

Reasonable adjustment needed for the recruitment process

10.29 [s 60(6)(a)] It is lawful for an employer to ask questions relating to reasonable adjustments that would be needed for an assessment such as an interview or other process designed to assess a person's suitability for a job. This means in practice that any information on disability or health obtained by an employer for the purpose of making adjustments to recruitment arrangements should, as far as possible, be held separately. Also it should not form any part of the decision-making process about an offer of employment, whether or not conditional.

10.30 Questions about reasonable adjustments needed for the job itself should not be asked until after the offer of a job has been made (unless these questions relate to a function that is intrinsic to the job – see below at paragraph 10.36). When questions are asked about reasonable adjustments, it is good practice to make clear the purpose of asking the question.

Example: An application form states: 'Please contact us if you are disabled and need any adjustments for the interview'. This would be lawful under the Act.

10.31 [s 60(6)(a)] It is lawful to ask questions about disability or health that are needed to establish whether a person (whether disabled or not) can undertake an assessment as part of the recruitment process, including questions about reasonable adjustments for this purpose.

Example: An employer is recruiting play workers for an outdoor activity centre and wants to hold a practical test for applicants as part of the recruitment process. He asks a question about health in order to ensure that applicants who are not able to undertake the test (for example, because they have a particular mobility impairment or have an injury) are not required to take the test. This would be lawful under the Act.

Monitoring purposes

10.32 [s 60(6)(c)] Questions about disability and health can be asked for the purposes of monitoring the diversity of applicants. (For information on good practice on monitoring, see Chapter 18 and Appendix 2.)

Implementing positive action measures

10.33 [s 60(6)(d)] It is also lawful for an employer to ask if a person is disabled so they can benefit from any measures aimed at improving disabled people's employment rates. This could include the guaranteed interview scheme whereby any disabled person who meets the essential requirements of the job is offered an interview. When asking questions about, for example, eligibility for a guaranteed interview scheme, an employer should make clear that this is the purpose of the question (see Chapter 12).

Occupational requirements

10.34 [s 60(6)(e)] There would be a need to demonstrate an occupational requirement if a person with a particular impairment is required for a job. In such a situation, where an employer can demonstrate that a job has an occupational requirement for a person with a specific impairment, then the employer may ask about a person's health or disability to establish that the applicant has that impairment.

Example: An employer wants to recruit a Deafblind project worker who has personal experience of Deafblindness. This is an occupational requirement of the job and the job advert states that this is the case. It would be lawful under the Act for the employer to ask on the application form or at interview about the applicant's disability.

National security

10.35 [s 60(14)] Questions about disability or health can be asked where there is a requirement to vet applicants for the purposes of national security.

Function intrinsic to the job

10.36 [s 60(6)(b)] Apart from the situations explained above, an employer may only ask about disability or health (before the offer of a job is made or before the person is in a pool of candidates to be offered vacancies when they arise) where the question relates to a person's ability to carry out a function that is intrinsic to that job. As explained in paragraphs 16.5 to 16.9, only functions that can be justified as necessary to a job should be included in a job description. Where a disability or health-related question would determine whether a person can carry out this function with reasonable adjustments in place, then such a question is permitted.

Example: A construction company is recruiting scaffolders. It would be lawful under the Act to ask about disability or health on the application form or at interview if the questions related specifically to an applicant's ability to climb ladders and scaffolding to a significant height. The ability to climb ladders and scaffolding is intrinsic to the job.

10.37 Where a disabled applicant voluntarily discloses information about their disability or health, the employer must ensure that in responding to this disclosure they only ask further questions that are permitted, as explained above. So, for example, the employer may respond by asking further questions about reasonable adjustments that would be required to enable the person to carry out an intrinsic function of the job. The employer must not respond by asking questions about the applicant's disability or health that are irrelevant to the ability to carry out the intrinsic function.

Example: At a job interview for a research post, a disabled applicant volunteers the information that as a reasonable adjustment he will need to use voice activated computer software. The employer responds by asking: 'Why can't you use a keyboard? What's wrong with you?' This would be an unlawful disability-related question, because it does not relate to a requirement that is intrinsic to the job – that is, the ability to produce research reports and briefings, not the requirement to use a keyboard.

If the employer wishes to ask any questions arising from the person's disclosure of a disability they would need to confine them to the permitted circumstances, and this can be explained to the candidate. In this instance, this might include asking about the type of adjustment that might be required to enable him to prepare reports and briefings.

10.38 This exception to the general rule about pre-employment disability or health enquiries should be applied narrowly because, in practice, there will be very few situations where a question about a person's disability or health needs to be asked – as opposed to a question about a person's ability to do the job in question with reasonable adjustments in place.

DISABILITY AND HEALTH ENQUIRIES AFTER A JOB OFFER

10.39 Although job offers can be made conditional on satisfactory responses to pre-employment disability or health enquiries or satisfactory health checks, employers must ensure they do not discriminate against a disabled job applicant on the basis of any such response. For example, it will amount to direct discrimination to reject an applicant purely on the grounds that a health check reveals that they have a disability. Employers should also consider at the same time whether there are reasonable adjustments that should be made in relation to any disability disclosed by the enquiries or checks.

10.40 If an employer is not in a position to offer a job, but has accepted applicants into a pool of people to be offered a job when one becomes available, it is lawful for the employer to ask disability or health-related questions at that stage.

10.41 Where pre-employment health enquiries are made after an applicant has been conditionally offered a job subject to such enquiries, employers must not use the outcome of the enquiries to discriminate against the person to whom a job offer has been made.

Example: A woman is offered a job subject to a satisfactory completion of a health questionnaire. When completing this questionnaire the woman reveals that she has HIV infection. The employer then decides to withdraw the offer of the job because of this. This would amount to direct discrimination because of disability.

10.42 An employer can avoid discriminating against applicants to whom they have offered jobs subject to satisfactory health checks by ensuring that any health enquiries are relevant to the job in question and that reasonable adjustments are made for disabled applicants (see Chapter 6). It is particularly important that occupational health practitioners who are employees or agents of the employer understand the duty to make reasonable adjustments. If a disabled person is refused a job because of a negative assessment from an occupational health practitioner during which reasonable adjustments were not adequately considered, this could amount to unlawful discrimination if the refusal was because of disability.

Example: An employer requires all successful job applicants to complete a health questionnaire. The questionnaire asks irrelevant questions about mental health and in answering the questions an applicant declares a history of a mental health condition. If the employer then refused to confirm the offer of the job, the unsuccessful disabled applicant would be able to make a claim of direct discrimination because of disability.

10.43 It is good practice for employers and occupational health practitioners to focus on any reasonable adjustments needed even if there is doubt about whether the person falls within the Act's definition of disabled person. (See paragraphs 2.8 to 2.20 and Appendix 1 for further information about the definition of disability).

ARMED FORCES

10.44 **[Sch 9, para 4]** An employer's obligations do not apply to service in the armed forces in relation to the protected characteristics of age or disability (see paragraphs 13.21 to 13.23).

LIABILITY OF EMPLOYERS AND PRINCIPALS UNDER THE ACT

Employers

10.45 [s **109(1)** & (3)] Employers will be liable for unlawful acts committed by their employees in the course of employment, whether or not they know about the acts of their employees.

10.46 The phrase 'in the course of employment' has a wide meaning: it includes acts in the workplace and may also extend to circumstances outside such as work-related social functions or business trips abroad. For example, an employer could be liable for an act of discrimination which took place during a social event organised by the employer, such as an after-work drinks party.

Example: A shopkeeper goes abroad for three months and leaves an employee in charge of the shop. This employee harasses a colleague with a learning disability, by constantly criticising how she does her work. The colleague leaves the job as a result of this unwanted conduct. This could amount to harassment related to disability and the shopkeeper could be responsible for the actions of his employee.

10.47 [s **109(4)**] However, an employer will not be liable for unlawful acts committed by an employee if they can show that they took 'all reasonable steps' to prevent the employee acting unlawfully. It could be a reasonable step for an employer to have an equality policy in place and to ensure it is put into practice. It might also be a reasonable step for an employer to provide training on the Act to employees. (Part 2 of the Code provides detailed explanations of the types of action employers can take to comply with the Act.)

Principals

10.48 [s **109(2)** & (3)] Principals are liable for unlawful acts committed by their agents while acting under the principal's authority. It does not matter whether the principal knows about or approves of the acts of their agents. An agent would be considered to be acting with the principal's authority if the principal consents (whether this consent is expressed or implied) to the agent acting on their behalf. Examples of agents include occupational health advisers engaged but not employed by the employer, or recruitment agencies.

Example: A firm of accountants engages a recruitment agency to find them a temporary receptionist. The agency only puts forward white candidates, even though there are suitably qualified black and minority ethnic candidates on their books. The firm could be liable for the actions of the agency even though they do not know about or approve of the agency's action.

10.49 [s **109(5)**] The liability of employers and principals does not extend to criminal offences. The only exception to this is offences relating to disabled persons and transport under Part 12 of the Act.

How employers and principals can avoid liability

10.50 [s **109(4]**)An employer will not be liable for unlawful acts committed by their employees where the employer has taken 'all reasonable steps' to prevent such acts.

Example: An employer ensures that all their workers are aware of their policy on harassment, and that harassment of workers related to any of the protected characteristics is unacceptable and will lead to disciplinary action. They also ensure that managers receive training in applying this policy. Following implementation of the policy, an employee makes anti-Semitic comments to a Jewish colleague, who is humiliated and offended by the comments. The employer then takes disciplinary action against the employee. In these circumstances the employer may avoid liability because their actions are likely to show that they took all reasonable steps to prevent the unlawful act.

10.51 An employer would be considered to have taken all reasonable steps if there were no further steps that they could have been expected to take. In deciding whether a step is reasonable, an employer should consider its likely effect and whether an alternative step could be more effective. However, a step does not have to be effective to be reasonable.

10.52 Reasonable steps might include:

- implementing an equality policy;
- ensuring workers are aware of the policy;
- providing equal opportunities training;
- reviewing the equality policy as appropriate; and
- dealing effectively with employee complaints.

More information on equality policies is set out in Chapter 18.

10.53 A principal will not be liable for unlawful discrimination carried out by its agents where the agent has acted without the authority of the principal, for example, by acting contrary to the principal's instructions not to discriminate.

Example: An hotel (the principal) uses an agency (the agent) to supply catering staff. The hotel management ensures that the agency is aware of the hotel's equality and diversity policy. Despite this, and without the hotel management's knowledge, the agency decides never to send for interview anyone whom they believe to be gay or lesbian. In this case, the agency has acted without the hotel's authority and the hotel would not, therefore, be liable for the unlawful discrimination by the agency.

Employers' and principals' liability for other unlawful acts

10.54 Employers and principals will be also liable for aiding, causing, instructing or inducing their employees or agents to commit an unlawful act. Employers and principals will also be liable for discrimination or harassment of former workers if the discrimination or harassment arises out of and is closely connected to a relationship covered by the Act which has ended (see paragraph 10.57 to 10.62 below).

LIABILITY OF EMPLOYEES AND AGENTS UNDER THE ACT

10.55 **[s 110(1) & (2)]** Employees and agents may be personally liable for breaches of the Act where the employer or principal is also liable. Employees may be liable for their actions where the employer is able to rely successfully on the 'reasonable steps' defence. An agent may be personally liable for unlawful acts committed under their principal's authority. The principal may avoid liability if they can show that the agent was not acting with their authority.

Example: A line manager fails to make reasonable adjustments for a machine operator with multiple sclerosis, even though the machine operator has made the line manager aware that he needs various adjustments. The line manager is not aware that she has acted unlawfully because she failed to attend equality and diversity training, provided by her employer. The line manager could be liable personally for her actions as her employer's action, in providing training, could be enough to meet the statutory defence.

10.56 **[s 110(3)]** However, if the employee or agent reasonably relies on a statement by the employer or principal that an act is not unlawful, then the employee or agent will not be liable.

Example: In the example above, the line manager has asked the company director if she needs to make these adjustments and the director has wrongly said, 'I don't think he's covered by the Equality Act because he isn't in a wheelchair, so don't bother.' In this situation, the line manager would not be liable, but the employer would be liable.

RELATIONSHIPS THAT HAVE ENDED

What the Act says

10.57 **[s 108]** The Act makes it unlawful for employers to discriminate against or harass employees after a relationship covered by the Act has ended. An employer will be liable for acts of discrimination or harassment arising out of the work relationship and which are 'closely connected to' it.

10.58 The expression 'closely connected to' is not defined in the Act but will be a matter of degree to be judged on a case-by-case basis.

Example: A worker who receives an inaccurate and negative job reference from her former employer because she is a lesbian could have a claim against her former employer for direct discrimination because of sexual orientation.

10.59 **[s 108(3)]** This protection will apply even if the relationship in question came to an end before this section came into force.

10.60 **[s 108(4)]** This protection includes a duty to make reasonable adjustments for disabled ex-employees who are placed at a substantial disadvantage when dealing with their former employer.

Example: A former worker has lifetime membership of a works social club but cannot access it due to a physical impairment. Once the former employer is made aware of the situation, they will need to consider making reasonable adjustments.

10.61 **[s 108(3)]** An employee will be able to enforce protection against discrimination or harassment as if they were still in the relationship which has ended.

10.62 If the conduct or treatment which an individual receives after a relationship has ended amounts to victimisation, this will be covered by the victimisation provisions (see paragraphs 9.2 to 9.15).

CONTRACTS

10.63 **[s 142]** The Act prevents employers from avoiding their responsibilities under the Act by seeking to enter into agreements which permit them to discriminate or commit other unlawful acts.

Unenforceable terms in contracts and other agreements

10.64 **[s 142(1)]** A term of a contract that promotes or provides for treatment that is prohibited by the Act is unenforceable. However, this will not prevent a person who is or would be disadvantaged by an unenforceable term from relying on it to get any benefit to which they are entitled.

10.65 **[s 142(2) & (3)]** In relation to disability only, these provisions on unenforceable terms apply to terms of non-contractual agreements pertaining to the provision of employment services, or group insurance arrangements for employees.

10.66 **[s 142(1) & (4)]** The Act also says that a term of a contract that attempts to exclude or limit the anti-discrimination provisions of the Act is unenforceable by a person in whose favour it would operate. However, this does not prevent the parties to a claim in the Employment Tribunal from entering into an agreement to settle the claim, provided the agreement is made with the assistance of Acas or is a 'qualifying compromise contract' (see also paragraph 15.13).

Removal or modification of unenforceable terms

10.67 **[s 143]** A person who has an interest in or is affected by an unenforceable term in a contract can apply to the county court (or sheriff court in Scotland) to have it modified or removed.

VOID OR UNENFORCEABLE TERMS IN COLLECTIVE AGREEMENTS AND RULES OF UNDERTAKINGS

10.68 **[s 145]** Any term of a collective agreement will be void insofar as it leads to conduct prohibited by the Act. A rule of an undertaking is unenforceable insofar as it also has that effect. A rule of an undertaking is a rule made by a trade organisation, qualifications body or employer which is applied respectively to members or prospective members, holders of relevant qualifications or those seeking them, and employees or prospective employees.

10.69 **[s 146]** Employees and prospective employees can apply to an Employment Tribunal for a declaration that a term is void or that a rule is unenforceable.

TERRITORIAL SCOPE

10.70 The employment provisions in the Act form part of the law of England, Scotland and Wales (Great Britain). The Act leaves it to Employment Tribunals to determine whether these provisions apply to the circumstances being considered, in line with domestic and European case law. This requires that protection be afforded when there is a sufficiently close link between the employment relationship and Great Britain.

10.71 Where an employee works physically wholly within Great Britain, this will be straightforward. Where an employee works partly or wholly outside Great Britain, in considering whether a sufficiently close link exists a tribunal may consider such matters as: where the employee lives and works, where the employer is established, what laws govern the employment relationship in other respects, where tax is paid, and other matters it considers appropriate.

10.72 The protection to be afforded to seafarers and employees who work on an offshore installation, for example an oil rig, a gas rig or a renewable energy installation, ship or hovercraft, will be set out in secondary legislation made under the Act.

CHAPTER 11
DISCRIMINATION IN WORK RELATIONSHIPS OTHER THAN EMPLOYMENT

INTRODUCTION

[4.149]

11.1 As explained in paragraph 1.22, the Act covers a variety of work relationships beyond employment. This Chapter explains the relevant provisions of Part 5 of the Act which focus specifically on these wider work-related provisions. In other respects, however, the employment provisions of the Act apply in the usual way.

DISCRIMINATION AGAINST CONTRACT WORKERS

What the Act says

11.2 **[s 41]** Contract workers are protected to a similar extent to employees against discrimination, harassment and victimisation. They are also entitled to have reasonable adjustments made to avoid being put to a substantial disadvantage compared with non-disabled people.

11.3 **[s 41(1) & (3)]** The Act says that it is unlawful for a 'principal' to discriminate against or victimise a contract worker:

- in the terms on which the principal allows the contract worker to work;
- by not allowing the contract worker to do or continue to do the work;
- in the way the principal affords the contract worker access to benefits in relation to contract work, or by failing to afford the contract worker access to such benefits; or
- by subjecting the contract worker to any other detriment.

11.4 **[s 41(2) & (4)]** The Act also says that it is unlawful for a principal to harass a contract worker and that the duty to make reasonable adjustments applies to a principal.

Example: A meat packing company uses agency workers who are engaged and supplied by an employment business to supplement its own workforce during times of peak demand. The employment business supplies the company with three agency workers, one of whom is gay. The owner of the company discovers this and asks the agency to replace him with someone who is not gay. By not allowing the gay man to continue to work at the meat packing plant, the company will be liable for discrimination as a 'principal'.

Who is a 'principal'?

11.5 [s 41(5)] A 'principal', also known as an 'end-user', is a person who makes work available for an individual who is employed by another person and supplied by that other person under a contract to which the principal is a party (whether or not that other person is a party to it). The contract does not have to be in writing.

Example: A nurse is employed by a private health care company which sometimes uses an employment business to deploy staff to work in the NHS. The employment business arranges for the nurse to work at an NHS Trust. In this case the 'principal' is the NHS Trust.

Who is a contract worker?

11.6 [s 41(7)] A contract worker is a person who is supplied to the principal and is employed by another person who is not the principal. The worker must work wholly or partly for the principal, even if they also work for their employer, but they do not need to be under the managerial power or control of the principal. Contract workers can include employees who are seconded to work for another company or organisation and employees of companies who have a contract for services with an employment business.

11.7 Agency workers engaged by an employment business may also be contract workers as long as they are employed by the employment business. An agency worker supplied to a principal to do work and paid by an employment business under a contract will also be protected. Self-employed workers who are not supplied through employment businesses are not contract workers but may still be covered by the Act (see paragraph 10.3).

Example: An individual owns X company of which he is the sole employee. He has a contract for services with an employment business whereby he has to personally do the work. The employment business supplies him to Y company. Although there is no contract between X and Y companies, the employee of X company would be a contract worker and would be protected under the Act.

Example: A self-employed person is supplied by an employment business to a company. The worker is racially and sexually harassed by an employee of the company. Because the worker is not employed, it is unlikely that she will be protected by the Act unless she is able to convince a tribunal that it is necessary for a contract to be implied between her and the end-user.

11.8 [s 41(5)(b)] There is usually a contract directly between the end-user and supplier, but this is not always the case. Provided there is an unbroken chain of contracts between the individual and the end-user of their services, that end-user is a principal for the purposes of the Act and the individual is therefore a contract worker.

Example: A worker is employed by a perfume concession based in a department store, where the store profited from any sales he made and imposed rules on the way he should behave. In these circumstances, the worker could be a contract worker. The concession would be his employer and the store would be the principal. However, this would not apply if the store simply offered floor space to the concession, the concession paid a fixed fee to the store for the right to sell its own goods in its own way and for its own profit, and concession staff in no way worked for the store.

HOW DOES THE DUTY TO MAKE REASONABLE ADJUSTMENTS APPLY TO DISABLED CONTRACT WORKERS?

11.9 [s 41(4)] The duty to make reasonable adjustments applies to a principal as well as an employer. Therefore, in the case of a disabled contract worker, their employer and the principal to whom they are supplied may each be under a separate duty to make reasonable adjustments.

Example: A travel agency hires a clerical worker from an employment business to fulfil a three month contract to file travel invoices during the busy summer holiday period. The contract worker is a wheelchair user, and is quite capable of doing the job if a few minor, temporary changes are made to the arrangement of furniture in the office. It is likely to be reasonable for the travel agency to make these.

Employer's duty to make reasonable adjustments

11.10 [Sch 8, para 5(1)] A disabled contract worker's employer will have to make reasonable adjustments if the contract worker is substantially disadvantaged by their own provisions, criteria and practices, by a physical feature of the premises they occupy, or by the non-provision of an auxiliary aid (see Chapter 6).

11.11 [Sch 8, para 5(2)–(5)] The employer of a disabled contract worker is also under a duty to make reasonable adjustments where the contract worker is likely to be substantially disadvantaged by:

- a provision, criterion or practice applied by or on behalf of all or most of the principals to whom the contract worker is or might be supplied, and where the disadvantage is the same or similar in the case of each principal;
- a physical feature of the premises occupied by each of the principals to whom the contract worker is or might be supplied, and where the disadvantage is the same or similar in the case of each principal; or
- the non-provision of an auxiliary aid which would cause substantial disadvantage, and that disadvantage would be the same or similar in the case of all or most of the principals to whom the contract worker might be supplied.

Example: A blind secretary is employed by a temping agency which supplies her to other organisations for secretarial work. Her ability to access standard computer equipment places her at a substantial disadvantage at the offices of all or most of the principals to whom she might be supplied. The agency provides her with an adapted portable computer and Braille keyboard, by way of reasonable adjustments.

Principal's duty to make reasonable adjustments

11.12 [Sch 8, para 6] A principal has similar duties to make reasonable adjustments to those of a disabled contract worker's employer, but does not have to make any adjustment which the employer should make. So, in effect, the principal is responsible for any additional reasonable adjustments which are necessary solely because of its own provision, criterion or practice, the physical feature of the premises it occupies or to avoid the non-provision of or failure to provide an auxiliary aid.

Example: In the preceding example, a bank which hired the blind secretary may have to make reasonable adjustments which are necessary to ensure that the computer provided by the employment business is compatible with the system which the bank is already using.

11.13 In deciding whether any, and if so, what, adjustments would be reasonable for a principal to make, the period for which the disabled contract worker will work for the principal is important. It might not be reasonable for a principal to have to make certain adjustments if the worker will be with the principal for only a short time.

Example: An employment business enters into a contract with a firm of accountants to provide an assistant for two weeks to cover an unexpected absence. The employment business proposes a name. The person concerned finds it difficult, because of his disability, to travel during the rush hour and would like his working hours to be modified accordingly. It might not be reasonable for the firm to have to agree, given the short time in which to negotiate and implement the new hours.

11.14 It would be reasonable for a principal and the employer of a contract worker to co-operate with each other with regard to any steps taken by the other to assist the contract worker. It is good practice for the principal and the employer to discuss what adjustments should be made, and who should make them.

Example: The bank and the employment business in the example in paragraphs 11.12 above would need to co-operate with each other so that, for example, the employment business allows the bank to make any necessary adaptations to the equipment which the employment business provided to ensure its compatibility with the bank's existing systems.

DISCRIMINATION AGAINST POLICE OFFICERS

What the Act says

11.15 [s 42(1) & (2); s 109] The Act says that police officers and cadets are to be treated as employees of the chief officer (chief constable in Scotland) under whose direction and control they are serving, or of the 'responsible' authority. Police officers include special constables and those in private constabularies such as the British Transport Police. Police officers and police cadets have the same rights as employees under the Act and therefore have the same protection against discrimination, harassment and victimisation (see Chapter 10) under Part 5. The chief officer (chief constable in Scotland) or the responsible authority is liable for their unlawful acts against police officers, cadets and applicants for appointment. They are also vicariously liable for unlawful acts committed by one officer against another.

11.16 [s 42(4) & (5)]A constable serving with the Serious Organised Crime Agency (SOCA) or Scottish Police Services Authority (SPSA) is treated as employed by those agencies or authorities and is protected by the employment provisions of the Act.

11.17 [s 42(6)] A constable at the Scottish Crime and Drugs Enforcement Agency (SCDEA) is treated as employed by the Director General of SCDEA.

DISCRIMINATION AGAINST PARTNERS IN A FIRM AND MEMBERS OF LIMITED LIABILITY PARTNERSHIPS

11.18 The Act provides protection to partners and members of a limited liability partnership (LLP) and a person seeking to become a partner or member of a LLP, similar to that provided to workers and job applicants against an employer.

What the Act says

11.19 **[ss 44(1), (5), 45(1), (5)]** It is unlawful for a firm, proposed firm, LLP or proposed LLP to discriminate against or victimise a partner or member:

- in the arrangements they make to determine who should be offered the position of partner or member;
- in the terms on which they offer the person a position as partner or member; or
- by not offering the person a position as partner or member.

Example: An African Caribbean candidate with better qualifications than other applicants is not shortlisted for partnership with an accountancy firm. The firm is unable to provide an explanation for the failure to shortlist. This could amount to direct discrimination because of race.

11.20 **[ss 44(2), (6), 45(2), (6)]** Where the person is already a partner or a member of a LLP, it is unlawful to discriminate against or victimise that person:

- in the terms of partnership or membership;
- in the way it affords (or by not affording) the person who is a partner or member access to opportunities for promotion, transfer or training or for receiving any other benefits, facility or service;
- by expelling the person who is a partner or member; or
- by subjecting the person who is a partner or member to any other detriment.

Example: An LLP refuses a Muslim member access to its childcare scheme because all the other children who attend the scheme have Christian parents. This could amount to direct discrimination because of religion or belief.

11.21 **[s 44(4) & 45(4)]** It is also unlawful for a firm, proposed firm, LLP or proposed LLP to subject a partner or member or a person seeking to become a partner or member to harassment.

Example: A lesbian candidate who applies to become a partner is subjected to homophobic banter during her partnership interview. The banter is offensive and degrading of her sexual orientation and creates an offensive and degrading environment for her at interview. This would amount to harassment related to sexual orientation.

HOW DOES THE DUTY TO MAKE REASONABLE ADJUSTMENTS APPLY TO PARTNERS, AND MEMBERS OF AN LLP?

11.22 **[s 44(7) & 45(7)]** The duty to make reasonable adjustments for disabled partners and members applies to a firm, proposed firm, LLP and proposed LLP in the same way as it applies to an employer (see Chapters 6 and 10).

11.23 **[Sch 8, paras 7 & 8]** Where a firm or LLP is required to make adjustments for a disabled partner, disabled prospective partner, disabled member or disabled prospective member, the cost of making the adjustments must be borne by that firm or LLP. Provided that the disabled person is, or becomes, a partner or member, they may be required (because partners or members share the costs of the firm or LLP) to make a reasonable contribution towards this expense. In assessing the reasonableness of any such contribution (or level of such contribution), particular regard should be had to the proportion in which the disabled partner or member is entitled to share in the firm's or LLP's profits, the cost of the reasonable contribution and the size and administrative resources of the firm or LLP.

Example: A disabled person who uses a wheelchair as a result of a mobility impairment joins a firm of architects as a partner, receiving 20% of the firm's profits. He is asked to pay 20% towards the cost of a lift which must be installed so that he can work on the premises. This is likely to be reasonable.

DISCRIMINATION AGAINST BARRISTERS AND ADVOCATES

11.24 In England and Wales, barristers who are tenants and pupil barristers (including persons who apply for pupillage) have rights which are broadly similar to the rights of employees under the Act. Tenants include barristers who are permitted to work in chambers, door tenants and squatters (barristers who can practice from a set of chambers but who are not tenants).

What the Act says

11.25 **[s 47(1) & (4)]** It is unlawful for a barrister or a barrister's clerk to discriminate against or victimise a person applying for a tenancy or pupillage:

- in the arrangements made to determine to whom a tenancy or pupillage should be offered;
- in respect of any terms on which a tenancy or pupillage is offered; or
- by not offering a tenancy or pupillage to them.

Example: A barristers' chambers reject all CVs for pupillages from applicants who completed their law examinations over three years ago. This criterion tends to exclude older applicants and could amount to indirect age discrimination, unless it can be objectively justified.

11.26 [s 47(3)] A barrister or barrister's clerk must not in relation to a tenancy or pupillage harass a tenant or pupil or an applicant for a tenancy or pupillage.

Example: A male barrister pesters a female applicant for pupillage with repeated invitations to dinner and suggests that her application for pupillage would be viewed more favourably by the barristers' chambers if she accepted his invitation to dinner. This could amount to sexual harassment.

11.27 [s 47(2) & (5)] The Act also makes it unlawful for a barrister or barrister's clerk to discriminate against or victimise a tenant or pupil:

(a) in respect of the terms of their tenancy or pupillage;
(b) in the opportunities for training, or gaining experience, which are afforded or denied to them;
(c) in the benefits, facilities or services which are afforded or denied to them;
(d) by terminating their pupillage;
(e) by subjecting them to pressure to leave their chambers; or
(f) by subjecting them to any other detriment.

Example: On receiving a solicitor's instructions on behalf of a Christian client, a clerk puts forward a Christian barrister in his chambers in preference to a Hindu barrister. He does this because he thinks the Hindu barrister's religion would prevent him representing the Christian client properly. This could amount to direct discrimination because of religion or belief as the clerk's action could be a detriment to the Hindu barrister.

11.28 [s 47(6)] The Act also says it is unlawful for a person (for example, an instructing solicitor, firm of solicitors or client) in relation to instructing a barrister to discriminate against that barrister by subjecting them to a detriment, or harass or victimise that barrister. This includes the giving, withholding or termination of instructions.

Example: When a clerk puts forward a male barrister for a pregnancy discrimination case, the firm of solicitors representing the employer asks for a female barrister instead, because they consider the case would be represented better by a woman. This could amount to direct discrimination because of sex on the part of the firm of solicitors.

11.29 [s 48] The provisions applying to barristers and barristers' clerks, set out above, also apply to advocates, advocates' clerks, devils, members of stables and persons seeking to become devils or members of a stable in Scotland.

HOW DOES THE DUTY TO MAKE REASONABLE ADJUSTMENTS APPLY TO BARRISTERS AND CLERKS?

11.30 [ss 47(7), 48(7)] The duty to make reasonable adjustments applies to barristers and barristers' clerks (advocates' clerks in Scotland) in the same way as it applies to an employer (see Chapters 6 and 10).

Example: Barristers' clerks at a set of chambers routinely leave messages for barristers on scraps of paper. This practice is likely to disadvantage visually impaired members of chambers and may need to be altered for individual disabled tenants and pupils.

DISCRIMINATION AGAINST PERSONAL AND PUBLIC OFFICE HOLDERS

11.31 [ss 49–52, Sch 6 paras (1) & (2)] It is unlawful to discriminate against, victimise or harass office holders where they are not protected by other provisions (within Part 5) of the Act. Thus an office holder who is an employee will be protected by the provisions dealing with employment. Whilst an office holder may also be an employee, it is important to note that office holders do not hold their position as employees. An office holder's functions, rights and duties may be defined by the office they hold, instead of or in addition to a contract of employment.

11.32 The Act affords protection to those seeking to be appointed or those appointed to personal offices and public offices. Office holders include offices and posts such as directors, non-executive directors, company secretaries, positions on the board of non-departmental public bodies, some judicial positions and positions held by some ministers of religion.

What is a personal office?

11.33 [s 49(1), (2) & (11)] A personal office is an office or post to which a person is appointed to discharge a function personally under the direction of another person (who may be different from the person who makes the appointment) and is entitled to remuneration other than expenses or compensation for loss of income or benefits.

11.34 **[s 52(4)]** Where a personal office is also a public office it is to be treated as a public office only.

What is a public office?

11.35 **[s 50(1) & (2)]** A public office holder is a person who is appointed by a member of the executive or whose appointment is made on the recommendation of, or with the approval of, a member of the executive or either Houses of Parliament, the National Assembly for Wales, or the Scottish Parliament.

What the Act says

11.36 **[ss 49(3), (5) & 50(3), (5)]** It is unlawful for a person who has the power to make an appointment to a personal or public office to discriminate against or victimise a person:

- in the arrangements which are made for deciding to whom to offer the appointment;
- as to the terms on which the appointment is offered;
- by refusing to offer the person the appointment.

Example: A deaf woman who communicates using British Sign Language applies for appointment as a Chair of a public body. Without interviewing her, the public body making the appointments writes to her saying that she would not be suitable as good communication skills are a requirement. This could amount to discrimination because of disability.

11.37 **[ss 49(4) & 50(4)]** It is unlawful for a person who has the power to make an appointment to a personal or public office to harass a person who is seeking or being considered for appointment in relation to the office.

11.38 **[ss 49(6), (8) & 50(6), (9), (10)]** It is also unlawful for a 'relevant person' in relation to a personal office or public office to discriminate against or victimise an office holder:

- as to the terms of the appointment;
- in the opportunities which are afforded (or refused) for promotion, transfer, training or receiving any other benefit, facility or service;
- by terminating their appointment; or
- by subjecting the person to any other detriment.

11.39 **[ss 49(7) & 50(8)]** The Act also makes it unlawful for a relevant person to harass an appointed office holder in relation to that office.

11.40 **[s 52(6)]** A 'relevant person' is the person who has the power to act on the matter in respect of which unlawful conduct is alleged. Depending on the circumstances, this may be the person who can set the terms of appointment, afford access to an opportunity; terminate the appointment; subject an appointee to a detriment; or harass an appointee.

11.41 **[ss 49(9) & 50(11)]** The duty to make reasonable adjustments applies to those who can make an appointment to personal office and to public office and a 'relevant person' in relation to the needs of disabled office holders.

11.42 **[ss 49(12) & 50(12)]** In respect of sex or pregnancy and maternity discrimination, if an offer of appointment to an office has a term relating to pay that would give rise to an equality clause if it were accepted, this would be treated as discriminatory. If that is not the case, a term relating to pay will be discriminatory where the offer of the term constitutes direct discrimination.

Who can make appointments to a public office?

11.43 **[s 50(2)]** A member of the executive, for example a government Minister, or someone who makes an appointment on the recommendation of or subject to the approval of a member of the executive can make appointments to a public office.

11.44 **[s 50(7), (10); s 52(6)]** Where, in relation to a public office, an appointment is made on the recommendation or is subject to the approval of the House of Commons, the House of Lords, the National Assembly for Wales or the Scottish Parliament, it is unlawful for a relevant person to discriminate against or victimise an office holder in all respects as set out in paragraph 11.38, except by terminating the appointment. However, a relevant person does not include the House of Commons or the House of Lords, the National Assembly for Wales or the Scottish Parliament.

Example: A Secretary of State terminates the appointment of a Commissioner in a non-departmental public body because of the Commissioner's religious beliefs. This could amount to discrimination because of religion or belief.

Recommendations and approvals for the appointment to public offices

11.45 **[s 51(1) & (3)]** The Act says it is unlawful for a member of the executive or a 'relevant body' who has the power to make recommendations or give approval for an appointment, or a member of the executive, to discriminate or victimise a person:

- in the arrangements made for deciding who to recommend for appointment or to whose appointment to give approval;

- by not recommending that person for appointment or by not giving approval to the appointment;
- by making a negative recommendation for appointment.

11.46 [s 51(2)] It is unlawful for a member of the executive or 'relevant body' to harass a person seeking or being considered for a public office in relation to that office.

11.47 [s 51(4)] A 'relevant body' has a duty to make reasonable adjustments to avoid a disabled person being put at a substantial disadvantage compared to non-disabled people.

Example: A selection process is carried out to appoint a chair for a public health body. The best candidate for the appointment is a disabled person with a progressive condition who is not able to work full-time because of her disability. The person who approves the appointment should consider whether it would be a reasonable adjustment to approve the appointment of the disabled person on a job-share or part-time basis.

What is a 'relevant body'?

11.48 [s 51(5)] A relevant body is a body established by or in pursuance of an enactment or by a member of the executive, for example a non-departmental public body.

Example: A statutory commission which makes recommendations to the Minister for the appointment of its CEO would be a relevant body for the purpose of the Act.

Example: It could be direct discrimination for the government Minister responsible for approving the appointment of members of the BBC Trust to refuse to approve the appointment of a person because they are undergoing gender reassignment.

Personal and public offices that are excluded from the Act

11.49 [Sch 6, para 2] Political offices or posts are excluded from the definition of personal or public offices. Political offices and posts include offices of the House of Commons or House of Lords; the office of the leader of the opposition; the Chief or Assistant Opposition Whip; county council offices; an office of the Greater London Authority held by the Mayor of London; or assembly members of the Greater London Authority and offices of registered political parties.

11.50 Life peerages and any dignity or honour awarded by the Crown are also excluded from the definition of personal and public offices.

What the Act says about the termination of an office holder's post

11.51 [s 52(7) & (8)] The provisions on the termination of an office holder's office or post are the same as for termination of employment; that is, it applies to fixed term appointments which are not renewed on the expiration of the term of the appointment, and to termination of the appointment by an office holder because of the conduct of a relevant person.

QUALIFICATIONS BODIES AND TRADE ORGANISATIONS

11.52 [ss 53 & 57] Qualification bodies and trade organisations have the same obligations as employers in their capacity as employers. They also have separate obligations under the Act to members and prospective members and to those on whom they confer qualifications. The nature and effect of the obligations on qualification bodies and trade organisations will be set out in a separate Code of Practice.

EMPLOYMENT SERVICES

11.53 [s 55] The Act places obligations on employment service providers that are similar to those placed on employers. The definition of an employment service is set out in paragraph 11.59 below.

What the Act says

11.54 [s 55(1) & (4)] An employment service provider must not discriminate against or victimise a person in relation to the provision of an employment service:

- in the arrangements that it makes for selecting people to whom it provides, or offers to provide, the service;
- in the terms on which it offers to provide the service to that person;
- by not offering to provide the service to that person.

Example: An employment agency only offers its services to people with European Economic Area (EEA) passports or identity cards. This could be indirect race discrimination as it would put to a particular disadvantage non-European nationals who do not hold a European passport but have the right to live and work in the UK without immigration restrictions. It is unlikely that the policy could be objectively justified.

11.55 [s 55(2) & (5)] In addition, an employment service provider must not in relation to the provision of an employment service, discriminate against or victimise a person:

- as to the terms upon which it provides the service to that person;
- by not providing the service to that person;
- by terminating the provision of the service to that person; or
- by subjecting that person to a detriment.

Example: A headhunting company fails to put forward women for chief executive positions. It believes that women are less likely to succeed in these positions because they will leave to get married and start a family. This could amount to discrimination because of sex.

11.56 **[s 55(3)]** It is also unlawful for an employment service provider to harass, in relation to the provision of an employment service, those who seek to use or who use its services.

Example: An advisor for a careers guidance service is overheard by a transsexual client making offensive and humiliating comments to a colleague about her looks and how she is dressed. This could amount to harassment related to gender reassignment.

11.57 **[s 55(6)]** Under the Act, an employment service provider has a duty to make reasonable adjustments, except when providing a vocational service. The duty to make reasonable adjustments is an anticipatory duty.

Example: A woman who has dyslexia finds it difficult to fill in an employment agency's registration form. An employee of the agency helps her to fill it in. This could be a reasonable adjustment for the employer to make.

11.58 **[s 55(7)]** However, the anticipatory duty to make reasonable adjustments does not apply to vocational training (that is, training for work or work experience), where the duty is the same as in employment.

What are employment services?

11.59 'Employment service' includes:

- **[s 56(2)]** the provision of or making arrangements for the provision of vocational training, that is, training for employment and work experience;
- the provision of or making arrangements for the provision of vocational guidance, such as careers guidance;
- services for finding people employment, such as employment agencies and headhunters. It also includes the services provided by, for example, Jobcentre Plus, the Sector Skills Council and intermediary agencies that provide basic training and work experience opportunities such as the Adult Advancement and Careers Service and other schemes that assist people to find employment;
- services for supplying employers with people to do work, such as those provided by employment businesses.

11.60 **[s 56(8)]** The reference to training applies to facilities for training. Examples of the types of activities covered by these provisions include providing classes on CV writing and interviewing techniques, training in IT/keyboard skills, providing work placements and literacy and numeracy classes to help adults into work.

Which employment services are excluded?

11.61 **[s 56(4) & (5)]** The provision of employment services does not include training or guidance in schools or to students at universities or further and higher education institutions.

11.62 Those concerned with the provision of vocational services are subject to different obligations which are explained further in the code on Services, Public Functions and Associations under Part 3 of the Act (see Code on Services, Public Functions and Associations).

DISCRIMINATION AGAINST LOCAL AUTHORITY MEMBERS

11.63 **[s 58]** Local authority members carrying out their official duties are protected against unlawful discrimination, harassment and victimisation.

What the Act says

11.64 **[s 58(1) & (3)]** A local authority must not discriminate against or victimise a local authority member while they undertake official business:

(a) in the opportunities which are afforded (or refused) for training or receiving any other benefit; or

(b) by subjecting the local authority member to any other detriment.

Example: A councillor of Chinese origin sits on a local council's policy scrutiny committee. Officers of the council often send him papers for meetings late or not at all which means he is often unprepared for meetings and unable to make useful contributions. His colleagues, none of whom are Chinese, do not experience this problem. This could amount to direct discrimination against the councillor by the authority.

11.65 **[s 58(2)]** It is also unlawful for a local authority to harass a local authority member while they undertake official business.

Example: A councillor who is a Humanist regularly gets ridiculed about her beliefs by other councillors and council officers when attending council meetings. This could amount to harassment related to religion or belief.

11.66 **[s 58(4)]** It will not be a detriment if a local authority fails to elect, appoint or nominate a local authority member to an office, committee, sub-committee or body of the local authority.

Example: A local authority councillor who is a Christian fails to get appointed to a planning committee when another councillor who is an Atheist did get appointed. The Christian councillor would not have a claim under the Act.

11.67 **[s 58(6)]** Local authorities are also under a duty to make reasonable adjustments for disabled members of the local authority, who carry out official business, to avoid their being at a substantial disadvantage compared to non-disabled people.

Example: A local authority fails to provide documents for meetings in Braille for a councillor who is blind. As a result the councillor is unable to participate fully in Council business. By not making the documents available in Braille, the local authority would have failed to comply with its duty to make reasonable adjustments.

What is a local authority?

11.68 **[s 59(2)]** 'Local authority' refers to any of the twelve types of body listed in the Act. The government can by order change the list to add, amend or remove bodies which exercise functions that have been conferred on those covered by (a) to (l) of the list.

Who is a local authority member?

11.69 **[s 59(5)]** A local authority 'member' will usually mean an elected member of a local authority such as a councillor. In relation to the Greater London Authority, 'member' means the Mayor of London or a member of the London Assembly.

What is official business?

11.70 **[s 59(4)]** Official business is anything undertaken by a local authority member in their capacity as a member of:
(a) the local authority;
(b) a body to which the local authority member is appointed by their authority or by a group of local authorities, for example a planning committee; or
(c) any other public body.

CHAPTER 12
POSITIVE ACTION

INTRODUCTION

[4.150]
12.1 **[s 158]** The Act permits employers to take positive action measures to improve equality for people who share a protected characteristic. These optional measures can be used by employers, principals, partnerships, LLPs, barristers and advocates, those who make appointments to personal and public offices and employment service providers (the term 'employer' is used to refer to all those covered by the provisions).

12.2 As well as explaining the general positive action provisions in the Act, this chapter outlines the benefits of using these measures, describes the circumstances when positive action could be appropriate and illustrates the law with examples of approaches that employers might consider taking.

12.3 **[s 159]** The specific provisions on positive action in recruitment and promotion will not be in force when the Code is laid before Parliament and therefore are not covered in this Code.

DISTINGUISHING POSITIVE ACTION AND 'POSITIVE DISCRIMINATION'

12.4 Positive action is not the same as positive discrimination, which is unlawful. It may be helpful to consider the Act's positive action provisions within the continuum of actions to improve work opportunities for people who share a protected characteristic.

12.5 First, action taken to benefit those from one particular protected group that does not involve less favourable treatment of those from another protected group, or to eradicate discriminatory policies or practices, will normally be lawful. Examples might include placing a job advertisement in a magazine with a largely lesbian and gay readership as well as placing it in a national newspaper; or reviewing recruitment processes to ensure that they do not contain criteria that discriminate because of any protected characteristic. Such actions would not be classed as 'positive action'.

12.6 Second, there are actions that fall within the framework of the Act's positive action provisions, such as reserving places on a training course for a group sharing a protected characteristic. These actions are only lawful if they meet the statutory conditions for positive action measures and do not exceed the limitations set out in the Act.

Example: A large public sector employer monitors the composition of their workforce and identifies that there are large numbers of visible ethnic minority staff in junior grades and low numbers in management grades. In line with their equality policy, the employer considers the following action to address the low numbers of ethnic minority staff in senior grades:

- Reviewing their policies and practices to establish whether there might be discriminatory criteria which inhibit the progression of visible ethnic minorities;
- Discussing with representatives of the trade union and the black staff support group how the employer can improve opportunities for progression for the under-represented group;
- Devising a positive action programme for addressing under-representation of the target group, which is shared with all staff;
- Including within the programme shadowing and mentoring sessions with members of management for interested members of the target group. The programme also encourages the target group to take advantage of training opportunities such as training in management, which would improve their chances for promotion.

12.7 Third, there are actions – often referred to as 'positive discrimination' – which involve preferential treatment to benefit members of a disadvantaged or under-represented group who share a protected characteristic, in order to address inequality. However, these actions do not meet the statutory requirements for positive action, and will be unlawful unless a statutory exception applies (see Chapters 13 and 14).

Example: An LLP seeks to address the low participation of women partners by interviewing all women regardless of whether they meet the criteria for partnership. This would be positive discrimination and is unlawful.

12.8 It is important to note that it is not unlawful for an employer to treat a disabled person more favourably compared to a non-disabled person (see paragraph 3.35).

Voluntary nature of positive action

12.9 Positive action is optional, not a requirement. However, as a matter of good business practice, public and private sector employers may wish to take positive action measures to help alleviate disadvantage experienced in the labour market by groups sharing a protected characteristic; take action to increase their participation in the workforce where this is disproportionately low; or meet their particular needs relating to employment.

12.10 In addition, employers who use positive action measures may find this brings benefits to their own organisation or business. Benefits could include:

- a wider pool of talented, skilled and experienced people from which to recruit;
- a dynamic and challenging workforce able to respond to changes;
- a better understanding of foreign/global markets;
- a better understanding of the needs of a more diverse range of customers – both nationally and internationally.

WHAT THE ACT SAYS

12.11 Where an employer reasonably thinks that people who share a protected characteristic:

(a) **[s 158(1)(a)]** experience a disadvantage connected to that characteristic; or

(b) **[s 158(1)(b)]** have needs that are different from the needs of persons who do not share that characteristic; or

(c) **[s 158(1)(c)]** have disproportionately low participation in an activity compared to others who do not share that protected characteristic

the employer may take any action which is proportionate to meet the aims stated in the Act (the 'stated aims').

12.12 The 'stated aims' are:

(a) **[s 158(2)(a)]** enabling or encouraging persons who share the protected characteristic to overcome or minimise that disadvantage (referred to in this chapter as 'action to remedy disadvantage');

(b) **[s 158(2)(b)]** meeting those needs ('action to meet needs'); or

(c) **[s 158(2)(c)]** enabling or encouraging persons who share the protected characteristic to participate in that activity ('action to encourage participation in activities').

12.13 Action may be taken when any one or all of these conditions exist. Sometimes the conditions will overlap – for example, people sharing a protected characteristic may be at a disadvantage which may also give rise to a different need or may be reflected in their low level of participation in particular activities.

Example: National research shows that Bangladeshis have low rates of participation in the teaching profession. A local school governing body seeks to tackle this low participation by offering open days in schools to members of the Bangladeshi community who might be interested in teaching as a profession. This would be a form of positive action to encourage participation.

What does 'reasonably think' mean?

12.14 In order to take positive action, an employer must reasonably think that one of the above conditions applies; that is, disadvantage, different needs or disproportionately low participation. This means that some indication or evidence will be required to show that one of these statutory conditions applies. It does not, however, need to be sophisticated statistical data or research. It may simply involve an employer looking at the profiles of their workforce and/or making enquiries of other comparable employers in the area or sector. Additionally, it could involve looking at national data such as labour force surveys for a national or local picture of the work situation for particular groups who share a protected characteristic. A decision could be based on qualitative evidence, such as consultation with workers and trade unions.

12.15 More than one group with a particular protected characteristic may be targeted by an employer, provided that for each group the employer has an indication or evidence of disadvantage, different needs or disproportionately low participation.

ACTION TO REMEDY DISADVANTAGE

What is a disadvantage for these purposes?

12.16 'Disadvantage' is not defined in the Act. It may for example, include exclusion, rejection, lack of opportunity, lack of choice and barriers to accessing employment opportunities. Disadvantage may be obvious in relation to some issues such as legal, social or economic barriers or obstacles which make it difficult for people of a particular protected group to enter into or make progress in an occupation, a trade, a sector or workplace (see also paragraphs 4.9 to 4.14).

What action might be taken to overcome or minimise disadvantage?

12.17 **[s 158(2)(a)]** The Act enables action to be taken to overcome or minimise disadvantage experienced by people who share a protected characteristic. The Act does not limit the action that could be taken, provided it satisfies the statutory conditions and is a proportionate way of achieving the aim of overcoming a genuine disadvantage. Such action could include identifying through monitoring, consultation or a review of policies and practices any possible causes of the disadvantage and then:

- targeting advertising at specific disadvantaged groups, for example advertising jobs in media outlets which are likely to be accessed by the target group;
- making a statement in recruitment advertisements that the employer welcomes applications from the target group, for example 'older people are welcome to apply';
- providing opportunities exclusively to the target group to learn more about particular types of work opportunities with the employer, for example internships or open days;
- providing training opportunities in work areas or sectors for the target group, for example work placements.

Example: Research shows that women in Britain experience significant disadvantage in pursuing careers in engineering, as reflected in their low participation in the profession and their low status within it. Some of the key contributing factors are gender stereotyping in careers guidance and a lack of visible role models. A leading equalities organisation, in partnership with employers in the engineering sector, offers opportunities exclusively to girls and women to learn more about the career choices through a careers fair attended by women working in the profession.

ACTION TO MEET NEEDS

What are 'different' or 'particular' needs?

12.18 A group of people who share a particular protected characteristic have 'different needs' if, due to past or present discrimination or disadvantage or due to factors that especially apply to people who share that characteristic, they have needs that are different to those of other groups. This does not mean that the needs of a group have to be entirely unique from the needs of other groups to be considered 'different'. Needs may also be different because, disproportionately, compared to the needs of other groups, they are not being met or the need is of particular importance to that group.

Example: An employer's monitoring data on training shows that their workers over the age of 60 are more likely to request training in advanced IT skills compared to workers outside this age group. The employer could provide training sessions primarily targeted at this group of workers.

What action might be taken to meet those needs?

12.19 **[s 158(2)(b)]** The Act does not limit the action that employers can take to meet different needs, provided the action satisfies the statutory conditions and is a proportionate means of achieving the aim of meeting genuinely different needs. Such action could include:

- providing exclusive training to the target group specifically aimed at meeting particular needs, for example, English language classes for staff for whom English is a second language;
- the provision of support and mentoring, for example, to a member of staff who has undergone gender reassignment;
- the creation of a work-based support group for members of staff who share a protected characteristic who may have workplace experiences or needs that are different from those of staff who do not share that characteristic. (The Act's provisions on members associations might be relevant here: see the Code on services and public functions).

ACTION TO ENCOURAGE PARTICIPATION IN ACTIVITIES

What activities does this apply to?

12.20 This provision applies to participation in any activity where the participation of those who share a protected characteristic is disproportionately low; this can include employment and training. Action to increase participation might include making available training opportunities, open days or mentoring and shadowing schemes.

What does 'disproportionately low' mean?

12.21 **[s 158(1)(c)]** The Act says that action can only be taken where the employer reasonably thinks that participation in an activity by people sharing a particular protected characteristic is 'disproportionately low.' This means that the employer will need to have some reliable indication or evidence that participation is low compared with that of other groups or compared with the level of participation that could reasonably be expected for people from that protected group.

Example: An employer has two factories, one in Cornwall and one in London. Each factory employs 150 workers. The Cornish factory employs two workers from an ethnic minority background and the London factory employs 20 workers also from an ethnic minority background.

The ethnic minority population is 1% in Cornwall and 25% in London. In the Cornish factory the employer would not be able to meet the test of 'disproportionately low', since the number of its ethnic minority workers is not low in comparison to the size of the ethnic minority population in Cornwall. However, the London factory, despite employing significantly more ethnic minority workers, could show that that the number of ethnic minority workers employed there was still disproportionately low in comparison with their proportion in the population of London overall.

12.22 Participation may be low compared with:

- the proportion of people with that protected characteristic nationally;

Example: A national labour force survey shows women are under-represented at board level in the financial services sector. An employer could take positive action to increase their representation in the sector.

- the proportion of people with that protected characteristic locally;

Example: An employer with a factory in Oldham employs 150 people but only one Asian worker. The employer may be able to show disproportionately low participation of Asian workers by looking at their workforce profile in comparison to the size of the Asian population in Oldham.

- the proportion of people with that protected characteristic in the workforce.

Example: A construction company's workforce monitoring data reveals low participation of women in their workforce. They collaborate with the sector skills council for the electro-technical, heating, ventilation, air conditioning, refrigeration and plumbing industries to provide information targeting women on apprenticeships in construction.

12.23 Employers will need to have some indication or evidence to show low participation. This might be by means of statistics or, where these are not available, by evidence based on monitoring, consultation or national surveys. For more information on evidence, see paragraph 12.14.

What action could be taken?

12.24 **[s 158(2)(c)]** The Act permits action to be taken to enable or encourage people who share the protected characteristic to participate in that activity. Provided that the action is a proportionate means of achieving the aim of enabling or encouraging participation, the Act does not limit what action could be taken. It could include:

- setting targets for increasing participation of the targeted group;
- providing bursaries to obtain qualifications in a profession such as journalism for members of the group whose participation in that profession might be disproportionately low;

- outreach work such as raising awareness of public appointments within the community;
- reserving places on training courses for people with the protected characteristic, for example, in management;
- targeted networking opportunities, for example, in banking;
- working with local schools and FE colleges, inviting students from groups whose participation in the workplace is disproportionately low to spend a day at the company;
- providing mentoring.

WHAT DOES 'PROPORTIONATE' MEAN?

12.25 **[s 158(2)]** To be lawful, any action which is taken under the positive action provisions must be a proportionate means of achieving one of the 'stated aims' described in paragraph 12.12 above.

12.26 'Proportionate' refers to the balancing of competing relevant factors. These factors will vary depending on the basis for the positive action – whether it is to overcome a disadvantage, meet different needs or address under-representation of a particular group. Other relevant factors will include the objective of the action taken, or to be taken, including the cost of the action.

12.27 The seriousness of the relevant disadvantage, the degree to which the need is different and the extent of the low participation in the particular activity will need to be balanced against the impact of the action on other protected groups, and the relative disadvantage, need or participation of these groups.

12.28 Organisations need to consider:

- Is the action an appropriate way to achieve the stated aim?
- If so, is the proposed action reasonably necessary to achieve the aim; that is, in all of the circumstances, would it be possible to achieve the aim as effectively by other actions that are less likely to result in less favourable treatment of others?

12.29 Paragraphs 4.30 to 4.32 provide a more detailed explanation of proportionality.

TIME-LIMITED POSITIVE ACTION

12.30 If positive action continues indefinitely, without any review, it may no longer be proportionate, as the action taken may have already remedied the situation which had been a precondition for positive action. This could make it unlawful to continue to take the action.

12.31 Therefore, when undertaking measures under the positive action provisions, it would be advisable for employers to indicate that they intend to take the action only so long as the relevant conditions apply, rather than indefinitely. During that period they should monitor the impact of their action and review progress towards their aim.

POSITIVE ACTION AND DISABILITY

12.32 **[s 13(3)]** As indicated above at paragraph 3.35, it is not unlawful direct disability discrimination to treat a disabled person more favourably than a non-disabled person. This means that an employer, if they wish, can for example restrict recruitment, training and promotion to disabled people and this will be lawful.

Example: An employer which has a policy of interviewing all disabled candidates who meet the minimum selection criteria for a job would not be acting unlawfully.

12.33 However, the positive action provisions may still be appropriate to achieve equality of opportunity between disabled people with different impairments. This means that an employer can implement positive action measures to overcome disadvantage, meet different needs or increase participation of people with one impairment but not those with other impairments.

POSITIVE ACTION AND THE PUBLIC SECTOR EQUALITY DUTIES

12.34 Public authorities which are subject to the public sector equality duties may wish to consider using positive action to help them comply with those duties.

IMPLEMENTING POSITIVE ACTION LAWFULLY

12.35 An employer does not have to take positive action but if they do, they will need to ensure they comply with the requirements of the Act to avoid unlawful discrimination. To establish whether there is any basis to implement a positive action programme, employers should collate evidence, for example through their monitoring data, and analyse that evidence to decide on the most appropriate course of action to take.

12.36 In considering positive action measures, employers might consider drawing up an action plan which:

- sets out evidence of the disadvantage, particular need and/or disproportionately low levels of participation, as appropriate, and an analysis of the causes;
- sets out specific outcomes which the employer is aiming to achieve;
- identifies possible action to achieve those outcomes;

- shows an assessment of the proportionality of proposed action;
- sets out the steps the employer decides to take to achieve these aims;
- sets out the measurable indicators of progress towards those aims, set against a timetable;
- explains how they will consult with relevant groups such as all staff, including staff support groups and members of the protected group for whom the programme is being established;
- specifies the time period for the programme;
- sets out periods for review of progress of the measures towards the aim to ensure it remains proportionate.

CHAPTER 13
OCCUPATIONAL REQUIREMENTS AND OTHER EXCEPTIONS RELATED TO WORK

INTRODUCTION

[4.151]
13.1 The Act contains a number of exceptions that permit discrimination that would otherwise be prohibited. Any exception to the prohibition on discrimination should generally be interpreted restrictively. Where an exception permits discrimination in relation to one protected characteristic, for example nationality, employers must ensure that they do not discriminate in relation to other protected characteristics.

13.2 This chapter explains occupational requirements and other exceptions related to work. There are other exceptions that apply to a particular characteristic, for example pregnancy and maternity, and these are dealt with in the relevant chapters throughout the code. Exceptions relating to pay and benefits are covered in Chapter 14.

OCCUPATIONAL REQUIREMENTS

13.3 [Sch 9, para 1] In certain circumstances, it is lawful for an employer to require a job applicant or worker to have a particular protected characteristic, provided certain statutory conditions are met.

13.4 The exception may also be used by a principal, a limited liability partnership (LLP), a firm or a person who has the power to appoint or remove office holders and a person who has the power to recommend an appointment to a public office.

What the Act says

13.5 [Sch 9, para 1] An employer may apply, in relation to work, a requirement to have a particular protected characteristic if the employer can show that having regard to the nature or context of the work:
- the requirement is an occupational requirement;
- the application of the requirement is a proportionate means of achieving a legitimate aim (see paragraphs 4.25 to 4.32); and
- the applicant or worker does not meet the requirement; or,
- except in the case of sex, the employer has reasonable grounds for not being satisfied that the applicant or worker meets the requirement.

13.6 [Sch 9, para 1(3)] In the case of gender reassignment and marriage and civil partnership, the requirement is not to be a transsexual person, married or a civil partner.

13.7 The requirement must not be a sham or pretext and there must be a link between the requirement and the job.

13.8 Examples of how the occupational requirement exception may be used include some jobs which require someone of a particular sex for reasons of privacy and decency or where personal services are being provided. For example, a unisex gym could rely on an occupational requirement to employ a changing room attendant of the same sex as the users of that room. Similarly, a women's refuge which lawfully provides services to women only can apply a requirement for all members of its staff to be women.

In what circumstances can an employer apply the occupational requirement exception?

13.9 [Sch 9, para 1(2)] In the case of an employer, firm, LLP or person with the power to appoint or remove an office holder, an occupational requirement may be applied in relation to:
- the arrangements made for deciding whom to offer employment or a position as a partner; or appoint as an office holder;
- an offer of employment, the position of partner or member or appointment of an office holder;
- the provision of access to opportunities for promotion, transfer, training; or
- except in relation to sex, dismissals, expulsions and terminations.

Example: A local council decides to set up a health project which would encourage older people from the Somali community to make more use of health services. The council wants to recruit a person of Somali origin for the post because it involves visiting elderly people in their homes and it is necessary for the post-holder to have a good knowledge of the culture and language of the potential clients. The council does not have a Somali worker already in post who could take on the new duties. They could rely on the occupational requirement exception to recruit a health worker of Somali origin.

13.10 It would be lawful for a principal (end-user) not to allow a contract worker to do work or, except in the case of sex, to continue to do work where the principal relies on the occupational requirement exception.

13.11 In the case of a person who has the power to recommend or approve the appointment of a public office holder, an occupational requirement may only be used in relation to:

- the arrangements that person makes for deciding whom to recommend or approve for appointment;
- not recommending or approving a person for appointment; or
- making a negative recommendation of a person for appointment.

OCCUPATIONAL REQUIREMENTS FOR THE PURPOSES OF AN ORGANISED RELIGION

What the Act says

13.12 [Sch 9, para 2(1)] The Act permits an employer (or a person who makes, recommends or approves appointments of office holders) to apply a requirement for a person to be of a particular sex or not to be a transsexual person, or a requirement relating to marriage, civil partnership or sexual orientation, if the employer can show that:

- the employment is for the purposes of an organised religion;
- the requirement is applied to comply with the doctrines of the religion (the 'compliance principle'); or
- because of the nature or context of the employment, the requirement is applied to avoid conflicting with the strongly held religious convictions of a significant number of the religion's followers (the 'non-conflict principle'); and
- the applicant or worker does not meet the requirement in question; or, except in the case of sex, the employer is not reasonably satisfied that the person meets it.

Example: An orthodox synagogue could apply a requirement for its rabbi to be a man.

Example: An evangelical church could require its ministers to be married or heterosexual if this enables the church to avoid a conflict with the strongly held religious convictions of its congregation.

13.13 The requirement must be a proportionate way of meeting the 'compliance' or 'non-conflict' principle. The occupational requirement exception should only be used for a limited number of posts, such as ministers of religion and a small number of posts outside the clergy including those which exist to promote or represent the religion.

When may the occupational requirement exception be applied for the purpose of an organised religion?

13.14 [Sch 9, para 2(2)] In relation to employment and personal or public offices, the occupational requirement exception may be used in:

- the arrangements made for deciding whom to offer employment or an appointment as an office holder;
- an offer of employment or an appointment to a personal or public office;
- the provision of access to opportunities for promotion, transfer or training; or
- except in the case of sex, the dismissal or termination of an appointment.

13.15 In the case of public offices for which a recommendation is needed for an appointment, the occupational requirement may be used in relation to:

- the arrangements made for deciding whom to recommend or approve for an appointment;
- not recommending or giving approval to an appointment; or
- making a negative recommendation for appointment.

Example: The trustees of a Mosque want to employ two youth workers, one who will provide guidance on the teachings of the Koran and the other purely to organise sporting activities not involving promoting or representing the religion. The trustees apply an occupational requirement for both workers to be heterosexual. It might be lawful to apply the occupational requirement exception to the first post but not the second post because the second post does not engage the 'compliance' or the 'non-conflict' principle.

OCCUPATIONAL REQUIREMENTS RELATING TO RELIGION OR BELIEF

What the Act says

13.16 [Sch 9, para 3] The Act says that where an employer has an ethos based on religion or belief, they are permitted to rely on the occupational requirement exception if they can show that, having regard to that ethos and the nature or context of the work:

- the requirement of having a particular religion or belief is an occupational requirement;
- the application of the requirement is a proportionate means of achieving a legitimate aim; and
- a person does not meet the requirement or the employer has reasonable grounds for not being satisfied that the person meets the requirement.

13.17 To rely on the exception, the employer must be able to show that their ethos is based on a religion or belief, for example, by referring to their founding constitution. An 'ethos' is the important character or spirit of the religion or belief. It may also be the underlying sentiment, conviction or outlook that informs the behaviours, customs, practices or attitudes of followers of the religion or belief.

13.18 The circumstances in which an employer with a religious or belief ethos may apply the exception are the same as those set out at paragraph 13.14.

Example: It could be a lawful use of the exception for a Humanist organisation which promotes Humanist philosophy and principles to apply an occupational requirement for their chief executive to be a Humanist.

WHAT CAN AN EMPLOYER DO TO ENSURE THEY APPLY THE OCCUPATIONAL REQUIREMENT EXCEPTION LAWFULLY?

13.19 A failure to comply with the statutory conditions described above could result in unlawful direct discrimination. Some of the issues that an employer may wish to consider when addressing the question of whether the application of an occupational requirement is proportionate to a legitimate aim are:

- Do any or all of the duties of the job need to be performed by a person with a particular characteristic?
- Could the employer use the skills of an existing worker with the required protected characteristic to do that aspect of the job?

13.20 Employers should not have a blanket policy of applying an occupational requirement exception, such as a policy that all staff of a certain grade should have a particular belief. They should also re-assess the job whenever it becomes vacant to ensure that the statutory conditions for applying the occupational requirement exception still apply.

OTHER WORK-RELATED EXCEPTIONS

ARMED FORCES

13.21 [Sch 9, para 4] The Act permits the armed forces to refuse a woman or a transsexual person employment or access to opportunities for promotion, transfer or training if this is a proportionate way of ensuring the combat effectiveness of the armed forces. This exception does not extend to dismissal or any other detriment.

13.22 The Act disapplies the provisions relating to age and disability to service in the armed forces and the provisions relating to disability to opportunities for work experience in the armed forces.

13.23 Non-service personnel are covered by the Act's provisions on employees (see Chapter 10).

EMPLOYMENT SERVICES

13.24 [Sch 9, para 5] The Act permits employment service providers, which include those providing vocational training, to restrict access to training or services to people with a protected characteristic if the training or services relate to work to which the occupational requirement exception has been applied.

13.25 The employment service provider can rely on this exception by showing that it reasonably relied on a statement from a person who could offer the work or training in question that having the particular protected characteristic was an occupational requirement. It is a criminal offence for such a person to make a statement of that kind which they know to be false or misleading.

DEFAULT RETIREMENT AGE

What the Act says

13.26 [Sch 9, para 8] Forcing someone to retire at a particular age is, on the face of it, age discrimination. However, the Act provides an exception for retirement; an employer is allowed to retire an employee at or over the age of 65, provided the dismissal satisfies all the legal tests for retirement, and provided the correct procedures are followed. This is known as the Default Retirement Age (DRA).

13.27 The DRA applies to 'relevant workers' only; that is:

- employees;
- those in Crown employment; and
- certain parliamentary staff.

13.28 The DRA retirement exception does not apply to any other type of worker, for example a partner, office holder, contract worker or police officer. Forced retirement of these workers is unlawful discrimination unless it can be objectively justified. The circumstances where retirement may be objectively justified are explained further in paragraphs 13.42 to 13.45.

The DRA and normal retirement age

13.29 The DRA means that employers, if they wish, can lawfully operate a 'normal retirement age' of 65 or above – that is, one which is the same as, or higher than, the DRA.

13.30 The 'normal retirement age' is the age at which employees in the same kind of position within an organisation are usually required to retire. It is not necessarily the same as the contractual retirement age, if in practice employees in that position retire at a different age.

Example: An employer has a contractual retirement age of 67, but regularly grants requests from employees to work beyond 67. However there is no consistency as to the age when employees then retire. In these circumstances, the employer's contractual retirement age of 67 would be treated as the normal retirement age.

Example: An employer has a contractual retirement age of 67 but normally grants requests to their senior managers to work until 70. In these circumstances, it is likely that 70 would be treated as the normal retirement age for senior managers.

13.31 Some employers do not operate any 'normal retirement age' for their employees. If this is the case, they can rely on the DRA of 65.

Example: An employer's employment contracts do not mention retirement and there is no fixed age at which employees retire. The employer can rely on the default retirement age of 65 if they wish to enforce a retirement.

13.32 Employers do not have to retire employees when they reach normal retirement age (or, if none applies, the DRA of 65). Indeed, there may be many good business reasons why an employer might benefit from retaining older employees in employment.

Statutory retirement procedure

13.33 Where an employer wants to retire an employee who has reached the DRA of 65 (or a normal retirement age of 65 or above), the employer must follow the retirement procedures that are set out in legislation. A dismissal that does not comply with these requirements may be unjustifiable age discrimination. In addition, the dismissal may not qualify as a 'retirement' and could be unfair.

13.34 **[Employment Equality (Age) Regulations 2006 Sch 6]** In summary, the statutory retirement procedure is as follows:

- The employer must give the employee six to 12 months' written notice of impending retirement and advise them of the 'right to request' that they continue working.
- Within three to six months of the intended retirement date, the employee may request in writing to be allowed to continue working indefinitely or for a stated period, quoting Schedule 6, paragraph 5 of the Employment Equality (Age) Regulations 2006.
- The employer has a duty to consider the written request within a reasonable period of receiving it by holding a meeting with the employee and giving written notice of their decision.
- If the request is refused or employment extended for a shorter period than requested, the employee has a right to appeal by giving written notice.
- The employer must consider any appeal by holding an appeal meeting as soon as is reasonably practicable and giving written notice of the appeal decision.

13.35 The dismissal will not amount to age discrimination provided that:

- the employee will be aged 65 or over at the intended date of retirement (or has reached the normal retirement age if this is higher);
- the employer has complied with the notice requirements and advised the employee of the right to request to continue working;
- the employee's contract is terminated on the intended date of retirement, as previously notified.

Example: An employer normally allows employees to continue working until age 70, but forces one employee to retire at age 65. That employee's dismissal will not qualify as retirement as the employee has been dismissed below the normal retirement age. It is likely to be both age discrimination and an unfair dismissal.

13.36 An employer who gives less than six months' notice of the date of retirement or the employee's right to request to continue working will be liable to pay compensation of up to eight weeks' pay.

13.37 However, even if full notice is not given, the employer might still be able to rely on the exception for retirement to escape liability for age discrimination. They would be expected to give the employee as much written notice as possible (and a minimum of 14 days) of the intended retirement date and of the right to request to continue to work. The employer would then have to comply with all other aspects of the statutory retirement procedure and show that the reason for dismissal is genuinely retirement.

Example: Because of inaccurate records, an employer only becomes aware that an employee is approaching her 65th birthday three months beforehand. The employer immediately issues her with written notice of intended retirement on her 65th birthday and informs her of the right to request to continue working. She does not pursue the request. Because the employer has given three months' notice and followed the correct procedure, this may qualify as a retirement dismissal. But as less than six months' notice was given, they would be liable for compensation of up to eight week's pay. The employer's safest course of action would be to give six months' notice from the date the error was discovered.

13.38 In certain cases, a dismissal may possibly qualify as a retirement but nonetheless be an unfair dismissal:

- where the employer has given the employee much less than six months' notice of the intended date of retirement; or
- where the employer has not followed the 'duty to consider' procedure under the statutory retirement rules.

Example: An employer gives an employee only a week's verbal notice that they intend to retire her on her 70th birthday, and fail to tell her of her right to request to continue working. In this case, because this is a serious breach of the legal requirements, retirement is unlikely to qualify as the reason for dismissal. The dismissal is likely to be unfair, as well as an act of unlawful age discrimination. Having breached the notice requirements, the employer would also be liable for compensation of up to eight weeks' pay.

Example: An employer without a normal retirement age forces an employee to retire at 67 on a month's notice. The employee's request to continue working is ignored. To decide whether the dismissal is a retirement, a tribunal would look at all the circumstances. It would probably find that the retirement was not the reason for the dismissal because the employer failed to consider the request to continue working. Even if the facts do not support a claim of age discrimination, the dismissal would be unfair because of the failure to follow the duty to consider procedure.

RETIREMENT FALLING OUTSIDE THE DRA EXCEPTION

13.39 The following types of retirement do not fall within the DRA exception and would therefore be unlawful age discrimination unless they can be objectively justified:

- the retirement, at any age, of someone who is not a 'relevant worker' (see paragraph 13.27);
- the retirement of a 'relevant worker' at a normal retirement age below 65.

Example: Partners in a law firm are required to retire from the partnership at 70. Partners are not 'relevant workers' for the purposes of the Act and so the retirement age of 70 would have to be objectively justified for it to be lawful.

Example: An airline company has a normal retirement age of 55 for their cabin attendants. As employees of the airline, the cabin attendants are 'relevant workers'. The airline would have to objectively justify the retirement age of 55 for it to be lawful.

13.40 Where there is no normal retirement age and an employee is forced to 'retire' before the age of 65, the reason for their dismissal cannot be retirement. It will be difficult for the employer to objectively justify the employee's dismissal; the dismissal is very likely to be unfair as well as being an act of unlawful age discrimination.

13.41 There are other circumstances where, due to a failure on the employer's part, dismissal of an employee over 65 will not qualify as retirement and is likely to be unfair dismissal and/or unjustifiable age discrimination (see paragraphs 3.36 to 3.41 above).

Objective justification

13.42 To avoid age discrimination, the Act requires employers to objectively justify any retirement that falls outside the DRA exception. This will apply to any normal retirement age below 65, and the forced retirement at any age of those who are not 'relevant workers'.

13.43 **[s 13(2)]** To objectively justify retirement in these circumstances, the employer must show that the retirement decision or policy is a proportionate means of achieving a legitimate aim. This concept is explained in more detail in paragraphs 4.25 to 4.32.

13.44 The first question is whether the aim behind the retirement decision is legitimate. Depending on the situation, the following are examples of aims that might be considered legitimate:

- to facilitate workforce planning, by providing a realistic long-term expectation as to when vacancies will arise;
- to provide sufficient opportunities for promotion, thereby ensuring staff retention at more junior levels.

However, the legitimacy of such aims would depend on all the circumstances of the case.

13.45 Even if the aim is a legitimate one, the second question is whether retiring someone at a particular age is a proportionate means of achieving that aim. In determining this, a balance must be struck between the discriminatory effect of the retirement and the employer's need to achieve the aim – taking into account all the relevant facts. If challenged in the Employment Tribunal, an employer would need to produce evidence supporting their decision.

Example: Partners in a small law firm are required to retire from the partnership at 65. The firm prides itself on its collegiate culture and has structured its partnership agreement to promote this. The fixed retirement age avoids the need to expel partners for performance management reasons, which the firm thinks would undermine the collegiate environment. While it is possible that fostering a collegiate environment may be a legitimate aim, the firm would need to show that compulsory retirement at 65 is a proportionate means of achieving it. For example, evidence would be needed to support the assumption that the performance of partners reduces when they reach the age of 65.

PROVISION OF SERVICES TO THE PUBLIC

13.46 **[Sch 9, para 19]** The Act says that an employer who provides services to the public is not liable for claims of discrimination or victimisation by an employee under Part 5 of the Act (the employment provisions) in relation to those services. Where a worker is discriminated against or victimised in relation to those services, their claim would be in the county court (or sheriff court in Scotland) under Part 3 of the Act relating to services and public functions.

Example: If an employee of a women's clothing retailer is denied the services of the retailer because she is a transsexual woman, her claim would be made under the services provisions of the Act. This means she should bring her claim in the county court.

13.47 However, where the service provided under the terms and conditions of employment differs from that provided to other employees, or is related to training, the worker can bring a claim in the Employment Tribunal under the employment provisions (Part 5).

Example: In the example above, the situation would be different if the same transsexual woman's employment contract provided her with a 20% discount on all clothes purchased from her employer, a discount not available to members of the public. If she tried to use the discount and was refused, then she would bring her claim in the Employment Tribunal under the employment provisions of the Act.

SUPPORTED EMPLOYMENT FOR DISABLED PEOPLE

13.48 **[s 193(3)]** The Act allows some charities to provide employment only to people who have the same disability or a disability of a prescribed description where this is to help disabled people gain employment.

STATUTORY AUTHORITY

13.49 **[Sch 22, para 1]** In relation to age, disability and religion or belief, it is not a contravention of the employment provisions in the Act to do anything that is required under another law. The exception also applies to a requirement or condition imposed pursuant to another law by a Minister of the Crown, a member of the Scottish Executive, the National Assembly for Wales or the Welsh Ministers, the First Minister for Wales or the Counsel General to the Welsh Assembly Government.

EDUCATIONAL APPOINTMENTS FOR RELIGIOUS INSTITUTIONS

13.50 **[Sch 22, para 3]** The Act allows schools and further and higher education institutions (FHEs) to reserve the posts of head teachers and principals for people of a particular religion and certain academic posts for women where the governing instrument provides for this. The exception for academic posts which are reserved for women only applies where the governing instrument was made before 16 January 1990.

13.51 **[Sch 22, para 3]** The Act also allows ordained priests to hold certain professorships where legislation or a university's governing instrument provides for this.

13.52 **[Sch 22, para 4]** Under the Act, faith schools are permitted to take into account religious considerations in employment matters relating to head-teachers and teachers, in accordance with the School Standards and Framework Act 1998. These considerations are different according to the category of school. Voluntary aided and independent faith schools have greater freedom than voluntary controlled and foundation schools. These exceptions only relate specifically to religion or belief – there is no scope in the Act for discrimination because of any other characteristic.

CROWN EMPLOYMENT

13.53 [Sch 22, para 53] The Act permits the Crown or a prescribed public body to restrict employment or the holding of a public office to people of a particular birth, nationality, descent or residence.

NATIONALITY DISCRIMINATION

13.54 [Sch 23, para 1] The Act permits direct nationality discrimination and indirect race discrimination on the basis of residency requirements where other laws, Ministerial arrangements or Ministerial conditions make provision for such discrimination. It does not matter whether the laws, instruments, arrangements or conditions were made before or after the Act was passed.

TRAINING FOR NON-EEA NATIONALS

13.55 [Sch 23, para 4] The Act permits an employer to employ or to contract non-EEA nationals who are not ordinarily resident in an EEA state, where the employment or contract is for the sole or main purpose of training them in skills, for example medical skills. The employer can only rely on the exception if they think that the person does not intend to exercise the skills gained as a result of the training in Great Britain. Where the training provider is the armed forces or the Secretary of State for Defence, the rules differ slightly.

NATIONAL SECURITY

13.56 [s 192] An employer does not contravene the Act only by doing something for the purpose of safeguarding national security and the action is proportionate for that purpose.

COMMUNAL ACCOMMODATION

13.57 [Sch 23, para 3] An employer does not breach the prohibition of sex discrimination or gender reassignment discrimination by doing anything in relation to admitting persons to communal accommodation or to providing any benefit, facility or service linked to the accommodation, if the criteria set out below are satisfied.

13.58 Communal accommodation is residential accommodation which includes dormitories or other shared sleeping accommodation which, for reasons of privacy, should be used only by persons of the same sex. It can also include shared sleeping accommodation for men and for women, ordinary sleeping accommodation and residential accommodation, all or part of which should be used only by persons of the same sex because of the nature of the sanitary facilities serving the accommodation.

13.59 A benefit, facility or service is linked to communal accommodation if it cannot properly and effectively be provided except for those using the accommodation. It can be refused only if the person can lawfully be refused use of the accommodation.

13.60 Where accommodation or a benefit, facility or service is refused to a worker, alternative arrangements must be made in each case where reasonable so as to compensate the person concerned.

Example: At a worksite, the only sleeping accommodation provided is communal accommodation occupied by men. A female worker wishes to attend a training course at the worksite but is refused permission because of the men-only accommodation. Her employer must make alternative arrangements to compensate her where reasonable; for example, by arranging alternative accommodation near the worksite or an alternative course.

13.61 Sex or gender reassignment discrimination in admitting people to communal accommodation is not permitted unless the accommodation is managed in a way which is as fair as possible to both women and men.

13.62 In excluding a person because of sex or gender reassignment, the employer must take account of:

- whether and how far it is reasonable to expect that the accommodation should be altered or extended or that further accommodation should be provided; and
- the relative frequency of demand or need for the accommodation by persons of each sex.

13.63 The Act permits a provider of communal accommodation to exclude people who are proposing to undergo, undergoing or who have undergone gender reassignment from this accommodation. However, to do so will only be lawful where the exclusion is a proportionate means of achieving a legitimate aim. This must be considered on a case-by-case basis; in each case, the provider of communal accommodation must assess whether it is appropriate and necessary to exclude the transsexual person.

CHAPTER 14
PAY AND BENEFITS

INTRODUCTION

[4.152]

14.1 This chapter looks at the implications of the Act for pay and employment benefits, including pensions. Employers must not discriminate directly or indirectly in setting rates of pay or offering benefits to workers. Likewise, they must avoid discrimination arising from disability and, in certain circumstances, may need to consider the duty to make reasonable adjustments to pay or to certain benefits that they provide. The Act also contains a number of specific provisions relating to pay and benefits, including certain exceptions to the general prohibition on discrimination in employment.

PAY

14.2 An employer must not discriminate in setting terms of employment relating to pay, or in awarding pay increases. Pay includes basic pay; non-discretionary bonuses; overtime rates and allowances; performance related benefits; severance and redundancy pay; access to pension schemes; benefits under pension schemes; hours of work; company cars; sick pay; and fringe benefits such as travel allowances.

14.3 Where workers work less than full time hours, employers should ensure that pay and benefits are in direct proportion to the hours worked. This will avoid the risk of the employer putting part-time workers who share a protected characteristic at a disadvantage that could amount to unjustifiable indirect discrimination or that could be unlawful under the Part Time Workers (Prevention of Less Favourable Treatment) Regulations 2000.

Exception for the national minimum wage

14.4 **[Sch 9, para 11]** However, there is an exception in the Act which allows employers to base their pay structures for young workers on the pay bands set out in the National Minimum Wage Regulations 1999.

14.5 These Regulations set minimum hourly wage rates, which are lower for younger workers aged 18 to 20, and lower again for those aged 16 and 17. Employers can use the rates of pay set out in the Regulations or may set pay rates that are higher, provided they are linked to the same age bands. However, the higher rates of pay need not be in proportion to the corresponding rates of the national minimum wage.

Example: A supermarket wants to pay a more attractive rate than the national minimum wage. Their pay scales must be based on the pay bands set out in the National Minimum Wage Regulations 1999. The supermarket opts for the following rates, which would be permissible under the Act:

- 16-17 years of age — 20p per hour more than the national minimum wage for workers in that age band;
- 18-20 years of age — 45p per hour more than the national minimum wage for workers in that age band; and
- 21 years of age or over — 70p per hour more than the national minimum wage for workers aged 21 or over.

14.6 Employed apprentices who are under the age of 19 or in the first year of their apprenticeship are entitled to the apprentice minimum wage which is lower than the ordinary national minimum wage. The apprentice minimum wage applies to all hours of work and training, including training off the job.

Performance related pay and bonuses

14.7 Where an employer operates a pay policy and/or bonus scheme with elements related to individual performance, they must ensure that the policy and/or scheme does not unlawfully discriminate against a worker because of a protected characteristic.

Example: A trade union equality representative obtains statistics which show that the best scores for appraisals are disproportionately awarded to white male workers. As a result, this group is more likely to receive an increase in pay and annual bonuses. The statistics suggest that the policy could be indirectly discriminatory, either through the criteria that have been selected, or the way that these criteria are applied.

14.8 If a worker has a disability which adversely affects their rate of output, the effect may be that they receive less under a performance related pay scheme than other workers. The employer must consider whether there are reasonable adjustments which would overcome this substantial disadvantage.

Example: A disabled man with arthritis works in telephone sales and is paid commission on the value of his sales. His impairment gets worse and he is advised to change his computer equipment. He takes some time to get used to the new equipment and, as a consequence, his sales fall. It is likely to be a reasonable adjustment for his employer to pay him a certain amount of additional commission for the period he needs to get used to the new equipment.

Equal pay

14.9 **[s 64–66]** The Act gives women and men the right to equal pay for equal work.

14.10 The provisions on equal pay operate by implying a sex equality clause into each contract of employment. This clause has the effect of modifying any term that is less favourable than for a comparator of the opposite sex. It also incorporates an equivalent term where the comparator benefits from a term not included in the worker's contract. These provisions are covered in more detail in the Equal Pay Code.

Pay secrecy clauses

14.11 **[s 77]** 'Pay secrecy clauses' or 'gagging clauses' are terms of employment which seek to prevent or restrict workers from discussing or disclosing their pay. Such terms are unenforceable in relation to a person making or seeking a 'relevant pay disclosure'. This is defined by the Act as a disclosure sought or made for the purpose of finding out whether – or to what extent – any pay differences are related to a protected characteristic.

14.12 The disclosure can be made to anyone (including a trade union representative), or requested from a colleague or former colleague. Any action taken by an employer against a worker who makes such a disclosure, or who receives information as a result, may amount to victimisation (see paragraphs 9.2 to 9.15).

Example: An African worker thinks he is underpaid compared to a white colleague and suspects that the difference is connected to race. The colleague reveals his salary, even though the contract of employment forbids this. If the employer takes disciplinary action against the white colleague as the result of this disclosure, this could amount to victimisation. But if he had disclosed pay information to the employer's competitor in breach of a confidentiality obligation, he would not be protected by the Act.

14.13 This provision is designed to improve pay transparency and relates to all protected characteristics. Further guidance in relation to the characteristic of sex can be found in the Equal Pay Code.

BENEFITS

14.14 Employment-related benefits might include canteens, meal vouchers, social clubs and other recreational activities, dedicated car parking spaces, discounts on products, bonuses, share options, hairdressing, clothes allowances, financial services, healthcare, medical assistance/insurance, transport to work, company car, education assistance, workplace nurseries, and rights to special leave. This is not an exhaustive list. Such benefits may be contractual or discretionary.

14.15 **[ss 13(1), 39(2)(b)]** Employers must ensure that they do not deny workers access to benefits because of a protected characteristic. Where denying access to a benefit or offering it on less favourable terms either:

- directly discriminates because of the protected characteristic of age, for example, by imposing an age restriction; or
- indirectly discriminates by putting a group of workers sharing a protected characteristic at a disadvantage when compared with other workers,

[ss 13(2), 19(2)(d)] the employer must be able to objectively justify the rule or practice as a proportionate means of achieving a legitimate aim.

14.16 But cost alone is not sufficient to objectively justify the discriminatory rule or practice. Financial cost may be taken into account only if there are other good reasons for denying or restricting access to the benefit. For more information about the application of the objective justification test, see paragraphs 4.25 to 4.32.

Example: An employer provides a company car to most of their sales staff, but not to those under 25 because of higher insurance costs. This amounts to direct discrimination because of age. The employer may not be able to objectively justify this policy by relying upon cost considerations alone.

14.17 In addition, where a disabled worker is put at a substantial disadvantage in the way that a particular benefit is provided, an employer must take reasonable steps to adjust the way the benefit is provided in order to avoid that disadvantage.

Example: An employer provides dedicated car parking spaces close to the workplace which are generally used by senior managers. A disabled worker finds it very difficult to get to and from the public car park further away. It is likely to be a reasonable adjustment for the employer to allocate one of the dedicated spaces to that worker.

14.18 Some benefits may continue after employment has ended. An employer's duties under the Act extend to its former workers in respect of such benefits.

Example: An employer provides a workplace nursery. Parents who leave their jobs with the employer are always offered the chance of keeping their nursery place until their child's fifth birthday – but this opportunity is not offered to a lesbian mother of a three year old. If this less favourable treatment is because of sexual orientation, it would amount to direct discrimination.

14.19 The Act also provides some specific exceptions to the general prohibition of discrimination in employment benefits, which are explained below. Exceptions relating to pregnancy and maternity are covered in Chapter 8 and in the Equal Pay Code.

Exception for service-related benefits

14.20 **[Sch 9, para 10(1)]** In many cases, employers require a certain length of service before increasing or awarding a benefit, such as pay increments, holiday entitlement, access to company cars or financial advice. On the face of it, such rules could amount to indirect age discrimination because older workers are more likely to have completed the length of service than younger workers. However, the Act provides a specific exception for benefits based on five years' service or less.

14.21 **[Sch 9, para 10(3)]** Length of service can be calculated by the employer in one of two ways:
(a) by the length of time that the person has been working for the employer at or above a particular level; or
(b) by the total length of time that person has been working for the employer.

14.22 Length of service may include employment by a predecessor employer under the Transfer of Undertakings (Protection of Employment) Regulations 2006.

Example: For junior office staff, an employer operates a five-point pay scale to reflect growing experience over the first five years of service. This would be permitted by the Act.

14.23 **[Sch 9, para 10(2)]** However, it may still be lawful for the employer to use length of service above five years to award or increase a benefit, provided they reasonably believe that this 'fulfils a business need'. Examples of a business need could include rewarding higher levels of experience, or encouraging loyalty, or increasing or maintaining the motivation of long-serving staff.

14.24 This test of 'fulfilling a business need' is less onerous than the general test for objective justification for indirect discrimination (see paragraph 14.15 above and paragraphs 4.25 to 4.32). However, an employer would still need evidence to support a reasonable belief that the length of service rule did fulfil a business need. This could include information the employer might have gathered through monitoring, staff attitude surveys or focus groups. An employer would be expected to take into account the interests of their workers and not be motivated simply by financial self-interest.

Example: An employer offers one additional day's holiday for every year of service up to a maximum of four years, to reward loyalty and experience. Although this may mean younger staff having fewer holidays than older workers, this approach is permitted by the Act. The same employer also provides free health insurance to all employees with over five years' service and will have to justify this by showing that it actually fulfils a business need – for example, by rewarding experience, encouraging loyalty or increasing staff motivation.

14.25 **[Sch 9, para 10(7)]** This exception does not apply to service-related termination payments or any other benefits which are provided only by virtue of the worker ceasing employment.

Exception for enhanced redundancy benefits

14.26 **[Sch 9, para 13(1)–(6)]** The Act also provides a specific exception for employers who want to make redundancy payments that are more generous than the statutory scheme. The exception allows an employer to use the formula of the statutory scheme to enhance redundancy payments. One of the following methods must be used:

- removing the statutory scheme's maximum ceiling on a week's pay so that an employee's actual weekly pay is used in the calculation;
- raising the statutory ceiling on a week's pay so that a higher amount of pay is used on the calculation; and/or
- multiplying the appropriate amount for each year of employment set out in the statutory formula by a figure of more than one.

Having done this, the employer may again multiply the total by a figure of one or more.

Example: An employer operates a redundancy scheme which provides enhanced redundancy payments based on employees' actual weekly pay, instead of the (lower) maximum set out in the statutory redundancy scheme. This is lawful under the Act.

Example: Using the statutory redundancy scheme formula and the scheme's maximum weekly wage, another employer calculates every employee's redundancy entitlement, then applies a multiple of two to the total. This is also lawful under the Act.

14.27 **[Sch 9, para 13(3)(b)–(d)]** The exception also allows an employer to make a redundancy payment to an employee who has taken voluntary redundancy or to an employee with less than two years continuous service, where no statutory redundancy payment is required. In such cases, an employer may make a payment equivalent to the statutory minimum, or an enhanced payment based on any of the above methods.

14.28 A redundancy payment will fall outside this exception if an employer's calculation is not based on the statutory scheme, or the method of enhancement differs from those set out in paragraph 14.26 above. As using length of service could amount to indirect age discrimination, the employer needs to show that calculating the redundancy payment in this way is justified as a proportionate means of achieving a legitimate aim. In this context, a legitimate aim might be to reward loyalty or to give larger financial payments to protect older employees because they may be more vulnerable in the job market.

14.29 For the means of achieving the aim to be proportionate, the employer would need to show that they had balanced the reasonable needs of the business against the discriminatory effects on the employees who do not stand to benefit. One factor would be the degree of difference between payments made to different groups of employees and whether that differential was reasonably necessary to achieve the stated aim.

Example: A company's redundancy scheme provides for one and a half weeks' actual pay for each year of employment for employees of all ages. Thus the scheme does not use the formula in the statutory scheme, which has different multipliers for employees under 22 and over 40. Although the company's scheme is less discriminatory because of age and more generous than the statutory scheme, it does not fit in with the calculations permitted by the exception. The company would have to show that their scheme was justified as a proportionate means of achieving a legitimate aim.

Exception relating to life assurance

14.30 [Sch 9, para 14] Some employers provide life assurance cover for their workers. If a worker retires early due to ill health, the employer may continue to provide life assurance cover. The Act provides an exception allowing an employer to stop providing cover when the worker reaches the age at which they would have retired had they not fallen ill. If there is no normal retirement age applicable to the worker's job, the employer can stop providing life assurance cover when the worker reaches 65.

Example: An employer operates a normal retirement age of 67. They provide life assurance cover to all workers up to this age. When one of their managers takes early retirement at 60 because of ill health, the employer continues her life assurance cover until she reaches 67. This is lawful.

Exception relating to child care benefits

14.31 [Sch 9, paras 15(1)–(2)] The Act creates an exception for benefits relating to the provision of childcare facilities that are restricted to children of a particular age group. It applies not only to natural parents, but also to others with parental responsibility for a child.

14.32 [Sch 9, para 15(3)] This exception also applies to actions taken to facilitate the provision of child care, including: the payment for some or all of the cost of the child care; helping a parent to find a suitable person to provide child care; and enabling a parent to spend more time providing care for the child or otherwise assisting the parent with respect to childcare they provide.

14.33 [Sch 9, para 15(4)] The exception covers benefits relating to the provision of care for children aged under 17.

Example: A sales assistant lives with his wife and seven year old stepdaughter, who attends an after school club run by the local authority. He receives childcare vouchers from his employer, but these are restricted to workers with children under 10. This restriction would be lawful. In this case, the sales assistant uses the vouchers to help pay for his stepdaughter's after school club.

Exception for benefits based on marital status

14.34 [Sch 9, para 18(2)] Benefits which are restricted on the basis of a worker's marital status are lawful under the Act, provided workers in a civil partnership have access to the same benefit. Workers who are not married or in a civil partnership can be excluded from such benefits.

Example: An employer gives an additional week's honeymoon leave to a woman who is getting married. Last year, her lesbian colleague who was celebrating a civil partnership was given only one extra day's leave to go on honeymoon. The difference in the treatment would not fall within the marital status exception.

14.35 [Sch 9, para 18(1)] There is also a limited exception for married workers only. This allows employers to provide a benefit exclusively for married workers, provided the benefit in question accrued before 5 December 2005 (the day on which section 1 of the Civil Partnership Act 2004 came into force) or where payment is in respect of periods of service before that date.

Exception for group insurance schemes

14.36 [Sch 9, para 20] Some employers offer their workers insurance-based benefits such as life assurance or accident cover under a group insurance policy. The Act allows employers to provide for differential payment of premiums or award of benefits based on sex, marital/civil partnership status, pregnancy and maternity or gender reassignment. However, the difference in treatment must be reasonable, and be done by reference to actuarial or other data from a source on which it is reasonable to rely.

14.37 [Sch 3, para 20] The Act also clarifies that it is the employer, not the insurer, who is responsible for making sure that provision of benefits under such group insurance schemes complies with the above exception.

Example: An employer arranges for an insurer to provide a group health insurance scheme to workers in their company. The insurer refuses to provide cover on the same terms to one of the workers because she is a transsexual person. The employer, who is responsible for any discrimination in the scheme, would only be acting lawfully if the difference in treatment is reasonable in all the circumstances, and done by reference to reliable actuarial or other data.

PENSIONS

Occupational pension schemes

14.38 Employers may provide benefits to current and former workers and their dependants through occupational pension schemes. The schemes are legally separate from the employers and are administered by trustees and managers. The benefits will be in the form of pensions and lump sums. Special provisions apply to such schemes because of their separate legal status and the nature of the benefits they provide.

14.39 **[s 61(1) & (2)]** An occupational pension scheme is treated as including a 'non-discrimination rule' by which a 'responsible person' must not discriminate against another person in carrying out any functions in relation to the scheme or harass or victimise another person in relation to the scheme.

14.40 **[s 61(4)]** A responsible person includes a trustee or manager of a scheme, the employer of members or potential members and a person who can make appointments to offices.

14.41 **[s 61(3)]** The provisions of an occupational pension scheme have effect subject to the non-discrimination rule. So, for example, if the rules of a scheme provide for a benefit which is less favourable for one member than another because of a protected characteristic, they must be read as though the less favourable provision did not apply.

14.42 There are a number of exceptions and limitations to the non-discrimination rule. The rule does not apply:

- **[s 61(5)]** to persons entitled to benefits awarded under a divorce settlement or on the ending of a civil partnership (although it does apply to the provision of information and the operation of the scheme's dispute resolution procedure in relation to such persons);
- **[s 61(10)]** in so far as an equality rule applies – or would apply if it were not for the exceptions described in part 2 of Schedule 7 (for more information on equality rules, please see the Equal Pay Code);
- **[s 61(8)]** to practices, actions or decisions of trustees or managers or employers relating to age specified by order of a Minister of the Crown, introduced under enabling powers in the Act.

14.43 It is expected that the exceptions relating to age will be based on those that previously applied under Schedule 2 to the Employment Equality (Age) Regulations 2006.

14.44 **[s 61(11)]** In addition to the requirement to comply with the non-discrimination rule, a responsible person is under a duty to make reasonable adjustments to any provision, criterion or practice relating to an occupational pension scheme which puts a disabled person at a substantial disadvantage in comparison with persons who are not disabled.

Example: The rules of an employer's final salary scheme provide that the maximum pension is based on the member's salary in the last year of work. Having worked full-time for 20 years, a worker becomes disabled and has to reduce her working hours two years before her pension age. The scheme's rules put her at a disadvantage as a result of her disability, because her pension will only be calculated on her part-time salary. The trustees decide to convert her part-time salary to its full-time equivalent and make a corresponding reduction in the period of her part-time employment which counts as pensionable. In this way, her full-time earnings will be taken into account. This is likely to be a reasonable adjustment to make.

14.45 **[s 62(1) & (2)]** The Act provides a mechanism for the trustees or managers of occupational pension schemes to make alterations to their schemes to ensure they reflect the non-discrimination rule. As most schemes already give trustees a power of alteration, the mechanism in the Act would only be required if a scheme does not have this. The mechanism would also be needed if the procedure for exercising the power is unduly complex or protracted or involves obtaining consents which cannot be obtained (or which can be obtained only with undue delay or difficulty).

14.46 **[s 62(3) & (4)]** Under this mechanism, the trustees or managers can make the necessary alterations by resolution. The alteration can have effect in relation to a period before the date of the resolution.

14.47 The rules on occupational pensions for women on maternity leave are covered in the Equal Pay Code.

Contributions to personal pension schemes

14.48 **[s 61(8)]** The enabling powers under the Act also allow exceptions to be introduced to the non-discrimination rule in respect of contributions to personal pension schemes or stakeholder pension schemes where the protected characteristic is age. As with exceptions for occupational pension schemes, it is expected that these exceptions will be based on those that previously applied under Schedule 2 to the Employment Equality (Age) Regulations 2006.

CHAPTER 15
ENFORCEMENT

INTRODUCTION

[4.153]
15.1 A worker who considers they have been affected by a breach of the Act has a right to seek redress through the Employment Tribunal (or, in the case of an occupational pension scheme, the county court or sheriff court in Scotland). Employment Tribunals can deal with the unlawful acts that are set out in Chapters 3 to 9. However, because litigation can be a costly and time-consuming exercise, employers should deal with complaints relating to a breach of the Act seriously and rigorously, with support from any recognised trade union, to avoid having recourse to the Employment Tribunal.

15.2 As explained in paragraph 1.22, the term 'employer' refers to all those who have duties in the areas covered by the Code. In this chapter, the term 'claimant' is used to refer to a worker who brings a claim under the Act and the term 'respondent' is used to refer to an employer against whom the claim is made.

15.3 This chapter gives an overview of enforcement by the Employment Tribunals of Part 5 of the Act. It is not intended to be a procedural guide to presenting a claim to an Employment Tribunal. The relevant procedures are set out in Schedule 1 to the Employment Tribunals (Constitution and Rules of Procedure) Regulations 2004.

15.4 This chapter covers the following:

- Obtaining information under the Act
- Settling complaints without recourse to a tribunal
- Jurisdiction for hearing complaints of discrimination related to work
- Time limits
- Burden of proof
- Remedies
- The Commission's enforcement powers
- National security.

THE PROCEDURE FOR OBTAINING INFORMATION

15.5 A worker who has a complaint under the Act should, as far as possible, seek to raise the complaint with the employer in the first instance. To avoid a claim proceeding to the Employment Tribunal, the employer should investigate thoroughly any allegations of a breach of the Act. This would enable the employer to determine whether there is any substance to the complaint and, if so, whether it can be resolved to the satisfaction of the parties.

15.6 **[s 138]** A worker who has a complaint under the Act may request information from their employer about the reason for the treatment which is the subject of the complaint. This is known as the procedure for obtaining information and it is additional to other means of obtaining information under the Employment Tribunal rules.

15.7 There are standard forms for asking and answering questions, as well as guidance which explains how the procedure works. However, standard forms do not have to be used to present questions or answers.

15.8 For the questions and any answers to be admissible in evidence, the questions should be sent to the employer before a claim is made to the Employment Tribunal, at the same time as the claim is made, or within 28 days of it being made; or if later, within the time specified by the tribunal.

15.9 **[s 138(3)]** The questions procedure is a way for workers to obtain information when they believe they have been subjected to conduct which is unlawful under the Act but do not have sufficient information to be sure. It could also assist the worker in their decision about how to proceed with the complaint. The questions and any answers are admissible in evidence in tribunal proceedings.

Example: A lesbian employee who suspects that she has been denied a promotion because of her sexual orientation could use the procedure to ask her employer about their decision not to promote her. This information could support her suspicion or resolve her concerns.

15.10 **[s 138(4); s 138(5)]** A respondent is not obliged to answer the questions. However, if they fail to answer within eight weeks (starting on the day the questions are received), or give equivocal or evasive replies, a tribunal may draw an inference from that, which could be an inference of discrimination. A tribunal must not draw an inference from a failure to answer questions if the answers might prejudice or reveal the reasons for bringing or not bringing criminal proceedings or in other circumstances specified in legislation.

SETTLING COMPLAINTS WITHOUT RECOURSE TO AN EMPLOYMENT TRIBUNAL

15.11 Nothing in the Act prevents the parties settling a claim or potential claim before it is decided by the Employment Tribunal (or the civil courts in the case of a claim relating to an occupational pension scheme). An agreement of this nature can include any terms the parties agree to and can cover compensation, future actions by the respondent, costs and other lawful matters.

Example: A worker raises a grievance with her employers alleging discrimination. The employer investigates this and accepts that there is substance to the complaint. The employer agrees to compensate the worker and undertakes to provide mandatory training for all staff to prevent such a complaint arising again.

15.12 Acas offers a conciliation service for parties in dispute, whether or not a claim has been made to an Employment Tribunal.

15.13 **[s 147]** A claim or potential claim to the Employment Tribunal can also be settled by way of a 'qualifying compromise contract'. Although contracts that seek to exclude or limit the application of the Act are normally unenforceable, this provision does not apply to a compromise contract, provided it fulfils certain conditions:

- the contract is in writing;
- the conditions in the contract are tailored to the circumstances of the claim;
- the claimant has received independent legal advice from a named person who is insured against the risk of a claim arising from that advice; and
- the named legal adviser is a qualified lawyer, a nominated trade union representative, an advice centre worker or another person specified by order under the Act.

JURISDICTION FOR HEARING COMPLAINTS OF DISCRIMINATION IN WORK CASES

15.14 **[s 120(1)]** An Employment Tribunal has jurisdiction to determine complaints related to work about a breach of the Act (that is, discrimination, harassment, victimisation, failure to make reasonable adjustments, breach of an equality clause or rule, instructing, causing or inducing and aiding unlawful acts).

15.15 **[s 120(2); s 120(3)]** An Employment Tribunal also has jurisdiction to determine an application relating to a non-discrimination rule of an occupational pension scheme (see paragraph 14.39). A responsible person (that is, the trustees or managers of an occupational pension scheme, the employer or a person who can make appointments to offices) can make an application to an Employment Tribunal for a declaration as to the rights of that person and a worker or member with whom they are in a dispute about the effect of a non-discrimination rule. An Employment Tribunal can also determine a question that relates to a non-discrimination rule which has been referred to it by a court.

15.16 **[s 120(5)]** Where proceedings relate to a breach of a non-discrimination rule of an occupational pension scheme, the employer is treated as a party to the proceedings and has the right to appear and be heard.

15.17 **[s 120(6)]** The Employment Tribunal's jurisdiction to determine proceedings that relate to a breach of a non-discrimination rule in an occupational pension scheme does not affect the jurisdiction of the High Court or county court, or (in Scotland) the Court of Session or the sheriff court, to also determine such proceedings.

15.18 **[s 121]** An Employment Tribunal will not have jurisdiction to hear a case from a member of the armed forces until a 'service complaint' has been made and not withdrawn (see paragraph 15.21).

15.19 **[s 60(2)]** The Employment Tribunal jurisdiction does not extend to complaints relating to disability or health enquiries under section 60(1) of the Act (see paragraphs 10.25 to 10.43). Only the Equality and Human Rights Commission can enforce a breach of the provisions relating to health or disability enquiries. Cases are brought in the county court in England and Wales or the sheriff court in Scotland. However, the Employment Tribunal will have jurisdiction to hear a complaint of discrimination where the worker is, for example, rejected for a job as a result of responding to a disability or health enquiry that is not permitted.

TIME LIMITS

15.20 **[s 123]** For work-related cases, an Employment Tribunal claim must be started within three months (less one day) of the alleged unlawful act. Where the unlawful act relates to an equality clause or rule different time limits apply; these are dealt with in the Equal Pay Code of Practice.

15.21 **[s 123(2)]** In the case of members of the armed forces, Employment Tribunal proceedings must be started within six months of the date of the alleged unlawful act. The time limit applies whether or not any service complaint has been determined. Civilians working for the armed forces are not governed by these rules and should make their application to an Employment Tribunal within the usual three months time limit.

15.22 **[s 123(1)(b)]** If proceedings are not brought within the prescribed period, the Employment Tribunal still has discretion to hear the proceedings, if it thinks it is just and equitable to do so (see paragraph 15.29 to 15.31 below).

When does the period for bringing the claim start?

15.23 **[s 123(1)(a)]** The Act says that the period for bringing a claim starts with the date of the unlawful act. Generally, this will be the date on which the alleged unlawful act occurred, or the date on which the worker becomes aware that an unlawful act occurred.

Example: A male worker applied for a promotion and was advised on 12 March 2011 that he was not successful. The successful candidate was a woman. He believes that he was better qualified for the promotion than his colleague and that he has been discriminated against because of his sex. He sent a questions form to his employer within two weeks of finding out about the promotion and the answers to the questions support his view. The worker must start proceedings by 11 June 2011.

15.24 **[s 123(3) & (4); s 123(4)(a)]** Sometimes, however, the unlawful act is an employer's failure to do something. The Act says that a failure to do a thing occurs when the person decides not to do it. In the absence of evidence to the contrary, an employer is treated as deciding not to do a thing when they do an act inconsistent with doing the thing.

15.25 **[s 123(4)(b)]** If the employer does not carry out an inconsistent act, they are treated as deciding not to do a thing on the expiry of the period in which they might reasonably have been expected to do the thing.

Example: A wheelchair-user asks her employer to install a ramp to enable her more easily to get over the kerb between the car park and the office entrance. The employer indicates that they will do so but no work at all is carried out. After a period in which it would have been reasonable for the employer to commission the work, even though the employer has not made a positive decision not to install a ramp, they may be treated as having made that decision.

15.26 **[s 123(3)(a)]** In addition, the Act recognises that where conduct extends over a period, it should be treated as being done at the end of that period for the purposes of calculating when the unlawful act occurred.

15.27 If an employer has a policy, rule, or practice (whether formal or informal) in accordance with which decisions are taken from time to time, this might amount to an 'act extended over a period'. So if an employer maintains an unlawful policy which results in a person being discriminated against on a continuing basis or on many occasions, the period for bringing a claim starts when the last act of discrimination occurred, or when the policy, rule or practice is removed.

Example: An employer operates a mortgage scheme for married couples only. A civil partner would be able to bring a claim to an Employment Tribunal at any time while the scheme continued to operate in favour of married couples. However, once the scheme ceased to operate in favour of married couples, the time limit for bringing proceedings would be within three months of that date.

15.28 For these purposes, a continuing state of affairs may constitute an act extended over a period. This means that even if the individual acts relied upon are done by different workers and are done at different places, they may be treated as a single act extending over a period. However, a single unlawful act which has continuing consequences will not extend the time period.

Example: A black worker is graded on lower pay than her Asian counterpart. The time period for starting proceedings is three months from the date the decision was taken to grade the workers or the date the worker discovered that she was being paid at a lower grade.

What happens if the claim is presented outside the correct time limit?

15.29 **[s 123(1)(b) & (2)(b)]** Where a claim is brought outside the time limits referred to above, an Employment Tribunal has discretion to hear the case if it considers it just and equitable to do so.

15.30 In exercising its discretion, a tribunal will consider the prejudice which each party would suffer as a result of the decision to extend the time limit. This means a tribunal will consider what impact hearing the case out of time would have on the respondent and the claimant.

15.31 When a tribunal considers whether to exercise its 'just and equitable' discretion, it will have regard to all the circumstances of the case including in particular:

- the length of and reasons for the delay;
- the extent to which the cogency of the evidence is likely to be affected;
- the extent to which the employer had cooperated with requests for information;
- the promptness with which the claimant bringing the claim acted once they knew of the facts giving rise to the claim;
- the steps taken by the claimant to obtain appropriate legal advice once they knew of the possibility of taking action.

BURDEN OF PROOF

15.32 **[s 136]** A claimant alleging that they have experienced an unlawful act must prove facts from which an Employment Tribunal could decide or draw an inference that such an act has occurred.

Example: A worker of Jain faith applies for promotion but is unsuccessful. Her colleague who is a Mormon successfully gets the promotion. The unsuccessful candidate obtains information using the questions procedure in the Act which shows that she was better qualified for the promotion than her Mormon colleague. The employer will have to explain to the tribunal why the Jain worker was not promoted and that religion or belief did not form any part of the decision.

15.33 An Employment Tribunal will hear all of the evidence from the claimant and the respondent before deciding whether the burden of proof has shifted to the respondent.

15.34 **[s 136(2) & (3)]** If a claimant has proved facts from which a tribunal could conclude that there has been an unlawful act, then the burden of proof shifts to the respondent. To successfully defend a claim, the respondent will have to prove, on the balance of probabilities, that they did not act unlawfully. If the respondent's explanation is inadequate or unsatisfactory, the tribunal must find that the act was unlawful.

15.35 Where the basic facts are not in dispute, an Employment Tribunal may simply consider whether the employer is able to prove, on the balance of probabilities, that they did not commit the unlawful act.

Example: A Jewish trainee solicitor complains that he has not been allowed to take annual leave to celebrate Jewish religious holidays and is able to compare himself to a Hindu trainee solicitor who has been allowed to take annual leave to celebrate Hindu religious holidays. If these facts are not in dispute, a tribunal may proceed directly to consideration of whether the law firm has shown that the treatment was not, in fact, an act of religious discrimination.

15.36 **[s 136(5)]** The above rules on burden of proof do not apply to proceedings following a breach of the Act which gives rise to a criminal offence.

REMEDIES FOR UNLAWFUL ACTS RELATING TO WORK

15.37 An Employment Tribunal may:

- **[s 124(2)(a)]** make a declaration as to the rights of the parties to the claim;
- **[s 124(2)(b)]** award compensation to the claimant for any loss suffered;
- **[s 124(2)(c)]** make an 'appropriate' recommendation, that is a recommendation that a respondent takes specified steps to obviate or reduce the adverse effect of any matter relating to the proceedings on the claimant and/or others who may be affected;
- **[s 139]** award interest on compensation;
- award costs (expenses in Scotland) if appropriate.

15.38 Information on remedies in equal pay claims is contained in the Equal Pay Code.

Declarations of unlawful acts

15.39 **[s 124(2)(a)]** An Employment Tribunal may make a declaration instead of or as well as making an award of compensation or a recommendation.

What compensation can an Employment Tribunal award?

15.40 **[ss 124(6) & 119]** An Employment Tribunal can award a claimant compensation for injury to feelings. An award for compensation may also include:

- past loss of earnings or other financial loss;
- future loss of earnings which may include stigma or 'career damage' losses for bringing a claim;
- personal injury (physical or psychological) caused by the discrimination or harassment;
- aggravated damages (England and Wales only) which are awarded when the respondent has behaved in a high-handed, malicious, insulting or oppressive manner; and
- punitive or exemplary damages (England and Wales only) which are awarded for oppressive, arbitrary or unconstitutional action by servants of the government or where the respondent's conduct has been calculated to make a profit greater than the compensation payable to the claimant.

15.41 Compensation for loss of earnings must be based on the actual loss to the claimant. The aim is, so far as possible by an award of money, to put the claimant in the position they would have been in if they had not suffered the unlawful act.

15.42 Generally, compensation must be directly attributable to the unlawful act. This may be straightforward where the loss is, for example, related to an unlawfully discriminatory dismissal. However, subsequent losses, including personal injury, may be difficult to assess.

15.43 A worker who is dismissed for a discriminatory reason is expected to take reasonable steps to mitigate their loss, for example by looking for new work or applying for state benefits. Failure to take reasonable steps to mitigate loss may reduce compensation awarded by a tribunal. However, it is for the respondent to show that the claimant did not mitigate their loss.

COMPENSATION FOR COMPLAINTS OF INDIRECT DISCRIMINATION

15.44 **[s 124(4) & (5)]** Where an Employment Tribunal makes a finding of indirect discrimination but is satisfied that the provision, criterion or practice was not applied with the intention of discriminating against the claimant, it must not make an award for compensation unless it first considers whether it would be more appropriate to dispose of the case by providing another remedy, such as a declaration or a recommendation. If the tribunal considers that another remedy is not appropriate in the circumstances, it may make an award of damages.

15.45 Indirect discrimination will be intentional where the respondent knew that certain consequences would follow from their actions and they wanted those consequences to follow. A motive, for example, of promoting business efficiency, does not mean that the act of indirect discrimination is unintentional.

EMPLOYMENT TRIBUNAL RECOMMENDATIONS

15.46 **[s 124(3)]** An Employment Tribunal can make an appropriate recommendation requiring the respondent within a specified period to take specific steps to reduce the negative impact of the unlawful act on the claimant or the wider workforce. The power to make a recommendation does not apply to equal pay claims.

15.47 A recommendation might, for example, require a respondent to take steps to implement a harassment policy more effectively; provide equal opportunities training for staff involved in promotion procedures; or introduce more transparent selection criteria in recruitment, transfer or promotion processes.

Example: An Employment Tribunal makes a finding that a respondent employer's probation policy has an indirect discriminatory impact on transsexual people generally and an individual transsexual worker specifically. The Employment Tribunal in addition to making a declaration to this effect makes a recommendation to the employer to review the policy and to take steps to remove the discriminatory provision.

15.48 Employment Tribunal recommendations often focus on processes (such as adoption of an equality policy or discontinuance of a practice or rule).

15.49 Whether a recommendation is made is a matter for the Employment Tribunal's discretion: the claimant does not have a right to have a tribunal recommend a course of action or process even if the tribunal makes a declaration of unlawful discrimination.

Making recommendations affecting the wider workforce

15.50 **[s 124(3)(b)]** As mentioned above, an Employment Tribunal can make recommendations which affect the wider workforce. A tribunal may consider making a wider recommendation if:

- the evidence in the case suggested that wider or structural issues were the cause of the discrimination and that they are likely to lead to further discrimination unless addressed; and
- it is commensurate (or 'proportionate') to the respondent's capacity to implement it.

15.51 A wider recommendation forms part of the Employment Tribunal decision in any particular case.

15.52 A recommendation is not contractually binding between the claimant and respondent (unless the parties make a separate agreement for the decision to have this effect).

What happens if a respondent fails to comply with a tribunal recommendation?

15.53 **[s 124(7)]** If a respondent fails to comply with an Employment Tribunal recommendation which related to the claimant, the tribunal may:

- increase the amount of any compensation awarded to that claimant; or
- order the respondent to pay compensation to the claimant if it did not make such an order earlier.

15.54 A failure to comply with a recommendation could also be adduced in evidence in any later cases against the same organisation.

REMEDIES IN RELATION TO OCCUPATIONAL PENSION SCHEMES

15.56 **[s 126]** If an Employment Tribunal finds that there has been discrimination in relation to:

(a) the terms on which persons become members of an occupational pension scheme; or

(b) the terms on which members are treated;

[s 126(2)] it may, in addition to the remedies it can make generally, declare that the person bringing the claim has a right to be admitted to the scheme or a right to membership without discrimination.

15.57 **[s 126(4)]** The Employment Tribunal's order may also set out the terms of admission or membership for that person. The order may apply to a period before it is made.

15.58 **[s 126(3)]** However, an Employment Tribunal may not make an order for compensation unless it is for injured feelings or for a failure by the recipient of an appropriate recommendation to comply with the recommendation. The tribunal cannot make an order for arrears of benefit.

THE COMMISSION'S POWERS TO ENFORCE BREACHES OF THE ACT

15.59 **[Equality Act (EA) 2006, s 24]** In addition to the rights given to the individual under the Act, the Commission has a power to apply to the court if it thinks that a person is likely to commit an unlawful act for an injunction (interdict in Scotland) to prohibit them from committing that act.

15.60 [EA 2006, s 24A] The Commission also has a power to enforce a breach of the prohibition on pre-employment health and disability enquiries (see paragraphs 10.25 to 10.43).

15.61 [EA 2006, s 24A] The Commission has power to take action even if no identifiable individual has been (or may be) affected by the unlawful act. It can take action in respect of arrangements which would, if they were applied to an individual, amount to an unlawful act; for example, to deal with the publication of an advertisement which suggests that an employer would discriminate (see Chapter 18 on recruitment). This power could also be used to challenge a provision, criterion or practice that indirectly discriminates, even if it has not yet put any particular person at a disadvantage.

15.62 [EA 2006, s 20] If the Commission suspects that an employer has committed an unlawful act, it can conduct an investigation. If it finds that the employer has done so, it can serve a notice requiring them to prepare an action plan to avoid repetition or continuation of that act or recommend that they take action for that purpose.

15.63 [EA 2006, s 23] The Commission may also, if it suspects that an employer is committing an unlawful act, enter into a binding agreement with the employer to avoid such contraventions.

15.64 [EA 2006, s 28] The Commission also has a power to assist a worker who is taking enforcement action against their employer.

NATIONAL SECURITY

15.65 [s 192; Employment Tribunals Rules 2004 (rule 54)] The Act includes an exception for acts for the purpose of safeguarding national security. Special rules apply in cases involving an assertion that national security is involved. The Employment Tribunal rules may allow the tribunal to exclude the claimant and/or their representative from all or part of the proceedings.

15.66 The claimant, and/or their representative who has been excluded, may make a statement to the tribunal before the exclusive part of the proceedings start. The Employment Tribunal may take steps to keep secret all or part of the reasons for its decision.

15.67 The Attorney General for England and Wales or the Advocate General for Scotland may appoint a special advocate to represent the interests of a claimant in the proceedings. However, that representative is not responsible to the claimant whose interest they are appointed to represent.

PART 2: CODE OF PRACTICE ON EMPLOYMENT

CHAPTER 16
AVOIDING DISCRIMINATION IN RECRUITMENT

INTRODUCTION

[4.154]
16.1 Ensuring fair recruitment processes can help employers avoid discrimination. While nothing in the Act prevents an employer from hiring the best person for the job, it is unlawful for an employer to discriminate in any of the arrangements made to fill a vacancy, in the terms of employment that are offered or in any decision to refuse someone a job (see Chapter 10). With certain limited exceptions, employers must not make recruitment decisions that are directly or indirectly discriminatory. As with other stages of employment, employers must also make reasonable adjustments for disabled candidates, where appropriate.

16.2 It is recognised that employers will have different recruitment processes in place depending on their size, resources, and the sector in which they operate. Whichever processes are used, applicants must be treated fairly and in accordance with the Act. This chapter examines the main issues arising in the recruitment of both external and internal applicants and explains the steps that should be taken to avoid unlawful conduct within each of the recruitment stages that are commonly used. It also makes some recommendations for good practice.

16.3 The Act's prohibition on pre-employment health and disability enquiries is covered more fully in Chapter 10.

DEFINING THE JOB

General principles

16.4 The inclusion of requirements in a job description or person specification which are unnecessary or seldom used is likely to lead to indirect discrimination. Employers who use job descriptions and person specifications should therefore review them each time they decide to fill a post. Reliance on an existing person specification or job description, may lead to discrimination if they contain discriminatory criteria.

Example: An employer uses a person specification for an accountant's post that states 'employees must be confident in dealing with external clients' when in fact the job in question does not involve liaising directly with external clients. This requirement is unnecessary and could lead to discrimination against disabled people who have difficulty interacting with others, such as some people with autism.

Job Descriptions

16.5 Job descriptions should accurately describe the job in question. Inclusion of tasks or duties that workers will not, in practice, need to perform has two pitfalls. It may discourage appropriately qualified people from applying because they cannot perform the particular task or fulfil the particular duty specified. It may also lead to discrimination claims if such people believe they have been unfairly denied an opportunity of applying.

16.6 Job titles should not show a predetermined bias for the recruitment of those with a particular characteristic. For example, 'shop girl' suggests a bias towards recruiting a younger woman, and 'office boy' suggests a bias towards recruiting a younger man.

16.7 Tasks and duties set out in the job description should be objectively justifiable as being necessary to that post. This is especially important for tasks and duties which some people may not be able to fulfil, or would be less likely to be able to fulfil, because of a protected characteristic. Similarly, the job description should not overstate a duty which is only an occasional or marginal one.

Example: A job description includes the duty: 'regular Sunday working'. In reality, there is only an occasional need to work on a Sunday. This overstated duty written into the job description puts off Christians who do not wish to work on a Sunday, and so could amount to indirect discrimination unless the requirement can be objectively justified.

16.8 Where there are different ways of performing a task, job descriptions should not specify how the task should be done. Instead, the job description should state what outcome needs to be achieved.

Example: A job description includes the task: 'Using MagicReport software to produce reports about customer complaints'. This particular software is not accessible to some disabled people who use voice-activated software. Discrimination could be avoided by describing the task as 'Producing reports about customer complaints'.

16.9 Job descriptions should not specify working hours or working patterns that are not necessary to the job in question. If a job could be done either part-time, full-time, or through job share arrangements, this should be stated in the job description. As well as avoiding discrimination, this approach can also widen the group of people who may choose to make an application.

Example: A job description for a manager states that the job is full-time. The employer has stated this because all managers are currently full-time and he has not considered whether this is an actual requirement for the role. The requirement to work full-time could put women at a disadvantage compared with men because more women than men work part-time or job share in order to accommodate childcare responsibilities. This requirement could amount to indirect discrimination unless it can be objectively justified.

Person specifications

16.10 Person specifications describe various criteria – including skills, knowledge, abilities, qualifications, experience and qualities – that are considered necessary or desirable for someone fulfilling the role set out in the job description. These criteria must not be discriminatory. Discrimination can be avoided by ensuring that any necessary or desirable criteria can be justified for that particular job.

16.11 Criteria that exclude people because of a protected characteristic may be directly discriminatory unless they are related to occupational requirements (see Chapter 13).

Example: Stating in a job description for a secretary that the person must be under 40 would amount to direct age discrimination against people over 40. In some circumstances, age criteria can be objectively justified, but in this case it is very unlikely.

16.12 Criteria that are less likely to be met by people with certain protected characteristics may amount to indirect discrimination if these criteria cannot be objectively justified.

Example: Asking for 'so many years' experience could amount to indirect discrimination because of age unless this provision can be objectively justified.

Example: A requirement for continuous experience could indirectly discriminate against women who have taken time out from work for reasons relating to maternity or childcare, unless the requirement can be objectively justified.

16.13 The person specification should not include criteria that are wholly irrelevant.

Example: A requirement that the applicant must be 'active and energetic' when the job is a sedentary one is an irrelevant criterion. This requirement could be discriminatory against some disabled people who may be less mobile.

16.14 Employers should ensure that criteria relating to skills or knowledge are not unnecessarily restrictive in specifying particular qualifications that are necessary or desirable. It is advisable to make reference to 'equivalent qualifications' or to 'equivalent levels of skill or knowledge' in order to avoid indirect discrimination against applicants sharing a particular protected characteristic if this group is less likely to have obtained the qualification. The level of qualification needed should not be overstated. Employers should avoid specifying qualifications that were not available a generation ago, such as GCSEs, without stating that equivalent qualifications are also acceptable.

Example: Requiring a UK-based qualification, when equivalent qualifications obtained abroad would also meet the requirement for that particular level of knowledge or skill, may lead to indirect discrimination because of race, if the requirement cannot be objectively justified.

16.15 As far as possible, all the criteria should be capable of being tested objectively. For example, attributes such as 'leadership' should be defined in terms of measurable skills or experience.

Health requirements in person specifications

16.16 The inclusion of health requirements can amount to direct discrimination against disabled people, where such requirements lead to a blanket exclusion of people with particular impairments and do not allow individual circumstances to be considered. Employers should also be aware that, except in specified circumstances, it is unlawful to ask questions about health or disability before the offer of a job is made or a person is placed in a pool of people to be offered a job (see paragraphs 10.25 to 10.43).

Example: A person specification states that applicants must have 'good health'. This criterion is too broad to relate to any specific requirement of the job and is therefore likely to amount to direct discrimination because of disability.

16.17 The inclusion of criteria that relate to health, physical fitness or disability, such as asking applicants to demonstrate a good sickness record, may amount to indirect discrimination against disabled people in particular, unless these criteria can be objectively justified by the requirements of the actual job in question.

16.18 Person specifications that include requirements relating to health, fitness or other physical attributes may discriminate not only against some disabled applicants, but also against applicants with other protected characteristics – unless the requirements can be objectively justified.

Example: A person specification includes a height requirement. This may indirectly discriminate as it would put at a disadvantaged women, some disabled people, and people from certain racial groups if it cannot be objectively justified for the job in question.

ADVERTISING A JOB

16.19 An employer must not discriminate in its arrangements for advertising jobs or by not advertising a job. Neither should they discriminate through the actual content of the job advertisement (see paragraphs 3.32 and 10.6).

Arrangements for advertising

16.20 The practice of recruitment on the basis of recommendations made by existing staff, rather than through advertising, can lead to discrimination. For example, where the workforce is drawn largely from one racial group, this practice can lead to continued exclusion of other racial groups. It is therefore important to advertise the role widely so that the employer can select staff from a wider and more diverse pool.

16.21 Before deciding only to advertise a vacancy internally, an employer should consider whether there is any good reason for doing so. If the workforce is made up of people with a particular protected characteristic, advertising internally will not help diversify the workforce. If there is internal advertising alone, this should be done openly so that everyone in the organisation is given the opportunity to apply.

16.22 Employers should also ensure that people absent from work (including women on maternity leave, those on long-term sick leave, and those working part-time or remotely) are informed of any jobs that become available so they can consider whether to apply. Failure to do so may amount to discrimination.

Content of job advertisements

16.23 Job advertisements should accurately reflect the requirements of the job, including the job description and person specification if the employer uses these. This will ensure that nobody will be unnecessarily deterred from applying or making an unsuccessful application even though they could in fact do the job.

16.24 Advertisements must not include any wording that suggests the employer may directly discriminate by asking for people with a certain protected characteristic, for example by advertising for a 'salesman' or a 'waitress' or saying that the applicant must be 'youthful'.

Example: An employer advertises for a 'waitress'. This suggests that the employer is discriminating against men. By using a gender neutral term such as 'waiting staff' or by using the term 'waiter or waitress', the employer could avoid a claim of discrimination based on this advert.

16.25 Advertisements must not include any wording that suggests the employer might indirectly discriminate. Wording should not, for example, suggest criteria that would disadvantage people of a particular sex, age, or any other protected characteristic unless the requirement can be objectively justified or an exception under the Act applies.

16.26 A job advertisement should not include wording that suggests that reasonable adjustments will not be made for disabled people, or that disabled people will be discriminated against, or that they should not bother to apply.

Example: An employer advertises for an office worker, stating, 'This job is not suitable for wheelchair users because the office is on the first floor'. The employer should state instead, 'Although our offices are on the first floor, we welcome applications from disabled people and are willing to make reasonable adjustments'.

When is it lawful to advertise for someone with a particular protected characteristic?

16.27 Where there is an occupational requirement for a person with a particular protected characteristic that meets the legal test under the Act, then it would be lawful to advertise for such a person; for example, if there is an occupational requirement for a woman (see paragraphs 13.2 to 13.15). Where the job has an occupational requirement, the advertisement should state this so that it is clear that there is no unlawful discrimination.

Example: An employer advertises for a female care worker. It is an occupational requirement for the worker to be female, because the job involves intimate care tasks, such as bathing and toileting women. The advert states: 'Permitted under Schedule 9, part 1 of the Equality Act 2010'.

16.28 An employer can lawfully advertise a job as only open to disabled applicants because of the asymmetrical nature of disability discrimination (see paragraph 3.35).

Example: A private nursery advertises for a disabled childcare assistant. This is lawful under the Act.

16.29 An employer may include statements in a job advertisement encouraging applications from under-represented groups, as a voluntary 'positive action' measure (see Chapter 12). An employer may also include statements about their equality policy or statements that all applications will be considered solely on merit.

Example: The vast majority of workers employed by a national retailer are under the age of 40. Consequently, people over the age of 40 are under-represented in the organisation. The retailer is looking to open new stores and needs to recruit more staff. It would be lawful under the Act for that retailer to place a job advert encouraging applications from all groups, especially applicants over the age of 40.

Recruitment through employment services, careers services or other agencies

16.30 When recruiting through recruitment agencies, job centres, career offices, schools or online agencies, an employer must not instruct them to discriminate, for example by suggesting that certain groups would – or would not be – preferred; or cause or induce them to discriminate (see paragraphs 9.16 to 9.24).

16.31 Any agencies involved in an employer's recruitment should be made aware of the employer's equality policy, as well as other relevant policies. They should also be given copies of the job descriptions and person specifications for posts they are helping the employer to fill.

APPLICATION PROCESS

General principles

16.32 An employer must not discriminate through the application process. A standardised process, whether this is through an application form or using CVs, will enable an employer to make an objective assessment of an applicant's ability to do the job and will assist an employer in demonstrating that they have has assessed applicants objectively. It will also enable applicants to compete on equal terms with each other. A standardised application process does not preclude reasonable adjustments for disabled people (see below).

Example: An application form asks applicants to provide 400 words stating how they meet the job description and person specification. Applicants are marked for each criterion they satisfy and short-listed on the basis of their marks. This is a standardised application process that enables the employer to show that they have assessed all applicants without discriminating.

Reasonable adjustments during the application process

16.33 An employer must make reasonable adjustments for disabled applicants during the application process and must provide and accept information in accessible formats, where this would be a reasonable adjustment.

16.34 Where written information is provided about a job, it is likely to be a reasonable adjustment for that employer to provide, on request, information in a format that is accessible to a disabled applicant (see paragraphs 6.6 and 6.33). Accessible formats could include email, Braille, Easy Read, large print, audio format, and data formats. A disabled applicant's requirements will depend upon their impairment and on other factors too. For example, many blind people do not read Braille and would prefer to receive information by email or in audio format.

16.35 Where an employer invites applications by completing and returning an application form, it is likely to be a reasonable adjustment for them to provide forms and accept applications in accessible formats. However, a disabled applicant might not have a right to submit an application in their preferred format (such as Braille) if they would not be substantially disadvantaged by submitting it in some other format (such as email) which the employer would find easier to access.

16.36 In employment, the duty to make reasonable adjustments is not anticipatory (see Chapter 6). For this reason, employers do not need to keep stocks of job information or application forms in accessible formats, unless they are aware that these formats will be in demand. However, employers are advised to prepare themselves in advance so they can create accessible format documents quickly, allowing a candidate using that format to have their application considered at the same time as other applicants. Otherwise, employers may need to make a further adjustment of allowing extra time for return of the form, if the applicant has been put at a substantial disadvantage by having less time to complete it.

16.37 Where applications are invited by completing and returning a form online, it is likely to be a reasonable adjustment for the form to be made accessible to disabled people. If on-line forms are not accessible to disabled people, the form should be provided in an alternative way.

16.38 Where an application is submitted in an accessible format, an employer must not discriminate against disabled applicants in the way that it deals with these applications.

Personal information requested as part of the application process

16.39 An employer can reduce the possibility of discrimination by ensuring that the section of the application form requesting personal information is detachable from the rest of the form or requested separately. It is good practice for this information to be withheld from the people who are short-listing or interviewing because it could allow them to find out about a person's protected characteristics (such as age or sex). However, where an applicant's protected characteristics are suggested by information in an application form or CV (for example, qualifications or work history) those who are short-listing or interviewing must not use it to discriminate against the applicant.

16.40 Where information for monitoring purposes is requested as part of an online application process, employers should find a way to separate the monitoring process from the application process. For example, a monitoring form could be sent out by email on receipt of a completed application form.

16.41 Any other questions on the main application form about protected characteristics should include a clear explanation as to why this information is needed, and an assurance that the information will be treated in strictest confidence. These questions should only be asked where they reflect occupational requirements for the post. Questions related to an occupational requirement should only seek as much information as is required to establish whether the candidate meets the requirement (see Chapter 13)

16.42 Applicants should not be asked to provide photographs, unless it is essential for selection purposes, for example for an acting job; or for security purposes, such as to confirm that a person who attends for an assessment or interview is the applicant.

SELECTION, ASSESSMENT AND INTERVIEW PROCESS

General principles

16.43 Arrangements for deciding to whom to offer employment include short-listing, selection tests, use of assessment centres and interviews. An employer must not discriminate in any of these arrangements and must make reasonable adjustments so that disabled people are not placed at a substantial disadvantage compared to non-disabled people (see Chapter 10). Basing selection decisions on stereotypical assumptions or prejudice is likely to amount to direct discrimination.

16.44 An employer should ensure that these processes are fair and objective and that decisions are consistent. Employers should also keep records that will allow them to justify each decision and the process by which it was reached and to respond to any complaints of discrimination. If the employer does not keep records of their decisions, in some circumstances, it could result in an Employment Tribunal drawing an adverse inference of discrimination.

16.45 In deciding exactly how long to keep records after a recruitment exercise, employers must balance their need to keep such records to justify selection decisions with their obligations under the Data Protection Act 1998 to keep personal data for no longer than is necessary.

16.46 The records that employers should keep include:

- any job advertisement, job description or person specification used in the recruitment process;
- the application forms or CVs, and any supporting documentation from every candidate applying for the job;
- records of discussions and decisions by an interviewer or members of the selection panel; for example, on marking standards or interview questions;
- notes taken by the interviewer or by each member of the panel during the interviews;
- each interview panel member's marks at each stage of the process; for example, on the application form, any selection tests and each interview question (where a formal marking system is used);
- all correspondence with the candidates.

16.47 An employer is more likely to make consistent and objective decisions if the same staff members are responsible for selection at all stages of the recruitment process for each vacancy. Staff involved in the selection process should receive training on the employer's equality policy (if there is one).

16.48 An employer should ensure that they do not put any applicant at a particular disadvantage in the arrangements they make for holding tests or interviews, or using assessment centres. For example, dates that coincide with religious festivals or tests that favour certain groups of applicants may lead to indirect discrimination, if they cannot be objectively justified.

Example: An all-day assessment that involves a social dinner may amount to indirect discrimination if the employer has not taken account of dietary needs relating to an applicant's religion – unless the arrangements can be objectively justified.

16.49 An employer is not required to make changes in anticipation of applications from disabled people in general – although it would be good practice to do so. It is only if the employer knows or could be reasonably expected to know that a particular disabled person is (or may be) applying, and that the person is likely to be substantially disadvantaged by the employer's premises or arrangements, that the employer must make reasonable adjustments. If an employer fails to ask about reasonable adjustments needed for the recruitment process, but could reasonably have been expected to know that a particular disabled applicant or possible applicant is likely to be disadvantaged compared to non-disabled people, they will still be under a duty to make a reasonable adjustment at the interview.

Short-listing

16.50 It is recommended that employers build the following guidelines for good practice into their selection procedures. By doing so, they will reduce the possibility of unlawful discrimination and avoid an adverse inference being made, should a tribunal claim be made by a rejected applicant.

- Wherever possible, more than one person should be involved in short-listing applicants, to reduce the chance of one individual's bias prejudicing an applicant's chances of being selected.
- The marking system, including the cut-off score for selection, should be agreed before the applications are assessed, and applied consistently to all applications.
- Where more than one person is involved in the selection, applications should be marked separately before a final mark is agreed between the people involved.
- Selection should be based only on information provided in the application form, CV or, in the case of internal applicants, any formal performance assessment reports.
- The weight given to each criterion in the person specification should not be changed during short-listing; for example, in order to include someone who would otherwise not be short-listed.

Guaranteed interviews for disabled applicants

16.51 Some employers operate a guaranteed interview scheme, under which a disabled candidate who wishes to use the scheme will be short-listed for interview automatically if they demonstrate that they meet the minimum criteria for getting the job. As explained above (paragraph 10.33), the Act permits questions to be asked at the application stage to identify disabled applicants who want to use this scheme.

Selection tests and assessment centres

16.52 Ability tests, personality questionnaires and other similar methods should only be used if they are well designed, properly administered and professionally validated and are a reliable method of predicting an applicant's performance in a particular job. If such a test leads to indirect discrimination or discrimination arising from disability, even if such discrimination is not intended and the reason for the discrimination is not understood, the test should not be used unless it can be objectively justified.

16.53 Where tests and assessment centres are used as part of the selection process, it is recommended that employers take account of the following guidelines:

- Tests should correspond to the job in question, and measure as closely as possible the appropriate levels of the skills and abilities included in the person specification.
- The Welsh Language Act 1993 puts Welsh and English on an equal basis in the delivery of public services in Wales and bilingual tests may need to be used for recruitment to some public sector jobs, where the ability to speak Welsh is essential or desirable.
- Where the purpose of a test is not to ascertain a person's level of proficiency in English (or Welsh in Wales), special care should be taken to make sure candidates whose first language is not English (or Welsh in Wales) understand the instructions. Tests that are fair for speakers of English (or Welsh) as a first language may present problems for people who are less proficient in the language.
- Deaf people whose first language is British Sign Language may be at a substantial disadvantage if a test is in English (or Welsh). An employer will need to consider what they should do to comply with the duty to make reasonable adjustments for such applicants.
- All candidates should take the same test unless there is a health and safety reason why the candidate cannot do so, for example because of pregnancy, or unless a reasonable adjustment is required (see below).
- Test papers, assessment notes and records of decisions should be kept on file (see paragraph 17.4).

16.54 Employers should make adjustments where a test or assessment would put a disabled applicant at a substantial disadvantage, if such adjustments would be reasonable (see Chapter 6). Examples of adjustments which may be reasonable include:
- providing written instructions in an accessible format;
- allowing a disabled person extra time to complete the test;
- permitting a disabled person the assistance of a reader or scribe during the test;
- allowing a disabled applicant to take an oral test in writing or a written test orally.

16.55 The extent to which such adjustments would be reasonable may depend on the nature of the disabled person's impairment, how closely the test is related to the job in question and what adjustments the employer would be reasonably required to make if the applicant were given the job.

16.56 However, employers would be well advised to seek professional advice in the light of individual circumstances before making adjustments to psychological or aptitude tests.

Interviews

16.57 An employer must not discriminate at the interview stage. In reality, this is the stage at which it is easiest to make judgements about an applicant based on instant, subjective and sometimes wholly irrelevant impressions. If decisions are based on prejudice and stereotypes and not based on factors relating to the job description or person specification, this could lead to unlawful discrimination. By conducting interviews strictly on the basis of the application form, the job description, the person specification, the agreed weight given to each criterion and the results of any selection tests, an employer will ensure that all applicants are assessed objectively, and solely on their ability to do the job satisfactorily.

16.58 Employers should try to be flexible about the arrangements made for interviews. For example, a woman with childcare responsibilities may have difficulties attending an early morning interview or a person practising a particular religion or belief may have difficulty attending on certain days or at certain times.

16.59 By the interview stage, an employer should already have asked whether reasonable adjustments are needed for the interview itself. This should have been covered on the application form or in the letter inviting a candidate for interview. However, it is still good practice for the interviewer to ask on the day if any adjustments are needed for the interview.

16.60 The practical effects of an employer's duties may be different if a person whom the employer previously did not know to be disabled (and it would not be reasonable to expect them to have known this) arrives for interview and is substantially disadvantaged because of the arrangements. The employer will be under a duty to make a reasonable adjustment from the time that they first learn of the disability and the disadvantage. However, the extent of the duty is less than might have been the case if they had known (or ought to have known) in advance about the disability and its effects.

16.61 An employer can reduce the possibility of unlawful discrimination by ensuring that staff involved in selection panels have had equality training and training about interviews, to help them:
- recognise when they are making stereotypical assumptions about people;
- apply a scoring method objectively;
- prepare questions based on the person specification and job description and the information in the application form; and
- avoid questions that are not relevant to the requirements of the job.

16.62 It is particularly important to avoid irrelevant interview questions that relate to protected characteristics, as this could lead to discrimination under the Act. These could include, for example, questions about childcare arrangements, living arrangements or plans to get married or to have children. Where such information is volunteered, selectors should take particular care not to allow themselves to be influenced by that information. A woman is under no obligation to declare her pregnancy in a recruitment process. If she volunteers that information, it should not be taken into account in deciding her suitability for the job.

16.63 Questions should not be asked, nor should assumptions be made, about whether someone would fit in with the existing workforce.

Example: At a job interview a woman is asked: 'You would be the only woman doing this job, and the men might make sexist jokes. How would you feel about this?' This question could amount to direct sex discrimination.

16.64 Except in particular circumstances, questions about disability or health must not be asked at the interview stage or at any other stage before the offer of a job (whether conditional or not) has been made, or where the person has been accepted into a pool of applicants to be offered a position when one becomes available. This is explained in paragraphs 10.25 to 10.43.

References

16.65 References should only be obtained, and circulated to members of the selection panel, after a selection decision has been reached. This can help ensure that the selection decision is based on objective criteria and is not influenced by other factors, such as potentially subjective judgments about a candidate by referees. Employers should send referees copies of the job description and person specification, requesting evidence of the candidate's ability to meet the specific requirements of the job. This is more likely to ensure that the reference focuses on information that is relevant to the job. Where a reference is subjective and negative, it is good practice to give the successful applicant an opportunity to comment on it.

Eligibility to work in the UK

16.66 Under the Immigration, Asylum and Nationality Act 2006, all employers (including small employers) are required to obtain information about a person's eligibility to work in the UK before employment begins. Many people from ethnic minorities in this country are British citizens or are otherwise entitled to work here. Employers should not make assumptions about a person's right to work in the UK based on race, colour or national origin, because all applicants should be treated equally under the Act.

16.67 Eligibility to work in the UK should be verified in the final stages of the selection process rather than at the application stage, to make sure the appointment is based on merit alone, and is not influenced by other factors. Depending on the employer's recruitment process, and the type of job being filled, candidates might be asked for the relevant documents when they are invited to an interview, or when an offer of employment is made. Employers can, in some circumstances, apply for work permits and should not exclude potentially suitable candidates from the selection process.

16.68 The UK Border Agency has published a code of practice for employers on how to avoid unlawful racial discrimination when complying with this requirement. Please see:
www.ukba.homeoffice.gov.uk/sitecontent/documents/employersandsponsors/preventingillegalworking/

JOB OFFERS

16.69 As stated at the beginning of this chapter, an employer must not discriminate against a person in the terms on which the person is offered employment.

Example: An employer offers a job but extends their usual probation period from three months to six months because the preferred candidate is a woman returning from maternity leave or a person with a disability. This would be discrimination in the terms on which the person is offered employment.

16.70 A refusal to recruit a woman because she is pregnant is unlawful even if she is unable to carry out the job for which she is to be employed. This will be the case even if the initial vacancy was to cover another woman on maternity leave. It is irrelevant that the woman failed to disclose that she was pregnant when she was recruited. A woman is not legally obliged to tell an employer during the recruitment process that she is pregnant because it is not a factor which can lawfully influence the employer's decision (see Chapter 8).

16.71 **[Sch 9, para 9]** Employers do not discriminate because of age by refusing to recruit someone who is older than 64 years and six months old or within six months of the normal retirement age where such normal retirement age is more than 65. This does not alter an existing employee's right to request to work beyond retirement age (see paragraphs 13.26 to 13.38).

Feedback to short-listed unsuccessful candidates

16.72 Having secured a preferred candidate, it is good practice for an employer to offer feedback to unsuccessful short-listed candidates if this is requested. By demonstrating objective reasons for the applicant's lack of success, based on the requirements of the job, an employer can minimise the risk of any claims for unlawful discrimination under the Act.

CHAPTER 17
AVOIDING DISCRIMINATION DURING EMPLOYMENT

INTRODUCTION

[4.155]

17.1 As explained in Chapter 10, the Act prohibits discrimination, victimisation and harassment at all stages and in all aspects of the employment relationship, including in workers' training and development. It also places employers under a duty to make reasonable adjustments for disabled workers. This chapter takes a closer look at the implications of the Act for a range of issues that are central to the relationship between employers and workers: working hours; sickness and absence; arranging leave from work; accommodating workers' needs; induction, training and development; disciplinary and grievance matters. Where appropriate, it also makes recommendations for good practice.

17.2 Many aspects of the employment relationship are governed by the contract of employment between the employer and the worker, which may be verbal or written. Practical day-to-day arrangements or custom and practice in the workplace are also important; in some cases, these features are communicated via written policies and procedures.

17.3 In many workplaces, a trade union is recognised by the employer for collective bargaining purposes. Where changes to policies and procedures are being considered, an employer should consult with a recognised trade union in the first instance. It is also good practice for employers to consult with trade union equality representatives as a first step towards understanding the diverse needs of workers. The role of trade unions in meeting the training and development needs of their members should also be recognised.

17.4 Where resources permit, employers are strongly advised to maintain proper written records of decisions taken in relation to individual workers, and the reasons for these decisions. Keeping written records will help employers reflect on the decisions they are taking and thus help avoid discrimination. In addition, written records will be invaluable if an employer has to defend a claim in the Employment Tribunal.

17.5 It is also useful for employers to monitor overall workplace figures on matters such as requests for flexible working, promotion, training and disciplinary procedures to see if there are significant disparities between groups of people sharing different protected characteristics. If disparities are found, employers should investigate the possible causes in each case and take steps to remove any barriers.

WORKING HOURS

17.6 Working hours are determined by agreement between the employer and the worker, subject to collective agreements negotiated by trade unions on behalf of workers. The Working Time Regulations 1998 set out certain legal requirements; for example, maximum average working hours per week, minimum rest breaks, daily and weekly rest periods and entitlement to annual leave. There are also special provisions for night workers.

17.7 Established working time agreements can be varied either simply by agreement between the employer and worker or following a statutory request for flexible working.

Flexible working

17.8 [ERA 1996 ss 80F–80I] There are statutory rules which give employees with caring responsibilities for children or specified adults the right to have a request for flexible working considered. The right is designed to give employees the opportunity to adopt working arrangements that help them to balance their commitments at work with their need to care for a child or an adult.

17.9 The statutory rules are set out in the Employment Rights Act 1996, and expanded in the Flexible Working (Procedural Requirements) Regulations 2002 and the Flexible Working (Eligibility, Complaints and Remedies) Regulations 2002. Under these rules, employees with caring responsibilities who have at least 26 weeks' continuous service are entitled to make a written request for flexible working; that is, to request changes to hours of work, times of work and the location of work. In practice this might mean:

- part-time working, term-time working or home working;
- adjusting start and finish times;
- adopting a particular shift pattern or extended hours on some days with time off on others.

17.10 Employers have a duty to consider a request for flexible working arrangements within specified timescales, and can refuse only on one of the business-related grounds set out in the statutory rules. The refusal must be in writing and include a sufficient explanation of the decision, based on correct facts. Employers who do not comply with these statutory procedures risk being taken to an Employment Tribunal and possibly having to pay compensation to the employee. For further details of the flexible working procedures, see: www.direct.gov.uk/en/employment/employees/workinghoursandtimeoff/dg_10029491

17.11 It is also important to bear in mind that rigid working patterns may result in indirect discrimination unless they can be objectively justified. Although a flexible working request may legitimately be refused under the statutory rules, such a refusal may still be indirectly discriminatory if the employer is unable to show that the requirement to work certain hours is justified as a proportionate means of achieving a legitimate aim. For example:

- A requirement to work full-time hours may indirectly discriminate against women because they are more likely to have childcare responsibilities.
- A requirement to work full-time hours could indirectly discriminate against disabled people with certain conditions (such as ME). It could also amount to a failure to make reasonable adjustments.
- A requirement to work on certain days may indirectly discriminate against those with particular religious beliefs.

Example: An employee's contractual hours are 9am–3pm. Under the flexible working procedures, she has formally requested to work from 10am–4pm because of childcare needs. Her employer refuses, saying that to provide staff cover in the mornings would involve extra costs. This refusal would be compatible with the flexible working procedures, which do not require a refusal to be objectively justified. However, in some circumstances, this could amount to indirect sex discrimination. Where a refusal to permit certain working patterns would detrimentally affect a larger proportion of women than men, the employer must show that it is based on a legitimate aim, such as providing sufficient staff cover before 10am, and that refusing the request is a proportionate means of achieving that aim.

17.12 Employers should also be particularly mindful of their duty to make reasonable adjustments to working hours for disabled workers.

Example: A worker with a learning disability has a contract to work normal office hours (9am to 5.30pm in this particular office). He wishes to change these hours because the friend whom he needs to accompany him to work is no longer available before 9am. Allowing him to start later is likely to be a reasonable adjustment for that employer to make.

Rest breaks

17.13 Minimum rest break periods are set out in the Working Time Regulations 1998. Some employers operate a policy on rest breaks and lunch breaks that is more generous than the provisions of those Regulations.

17.14 In considering requests for additional or different breaks, employers should ensure that they do not discriminate because of any protected characteristic. In some circumstances, an employer's refusal to allow additional breaks or flexibility as to when they are taken might amount to indirect discrimination unless it can be objectively justified. When dealing with requests for additional breaks, an employer should consider whether it is possible to grant the request by allowing the person to work more flexible hours.

Example: An observant Muslim requests two additional 10-minute breaks every day to allow him to pray at work. The employer allows other workers to take additional smoking breaks of similar length. Refusing this request could amount to direct discrimination because of religion or belief. On the other hand, if the employer took a consistently strict approach to rest breaks, they could allow the prayer breaks on the understanding that the Muslim worker arrives at work 20 minutes earlier or makes up the time at the end of the day.

17.15 Allowing disabled workers to take additional rest breaks is one way that an employer can fulfil their duty to make reasonable adjustments.

Example: A worker has recently been diagnosed with diabetes. As a consequence of her medication and her new dietary requirements, she finds that she gets extremely tired at certain times during the working day. It is likely to be a reasonable adjustment to allow her to take additional rest breaks to control the effects of her impairment.

SICKNESS AND ABSENCE FROM WORK

17.16 Sickness and absence from work may be governed by contractual terms and conditions and/or may be the subject of non-contractual practices and procedures. Regardless of the nature of these policies, it is important to ensure that they are non-discriminatory in design, and applied to workers who are sick or absent for whatever reason without discrimination of any kind. This is particularly important when a policy has discretionary elements such as decisions about stopping sick pay or commencing attendance management procedures.

17.17 To avoid discrimination, sickness and absence procedures should include clear requirements about informing the employer of sickness and providing medical certificates. They should also specify the rate and the maximum period of payment for sick pay.

17.18 In order to defend any claims of discrimination, it is advisable for employers to maintain records of workers' absences. In relation to sick leave, this is a legal requirement under the Statutory Sick Pay (General) Regulations 1982. Particular care is needed to ensure that sensitive medical information about workers is kept confidential and handled in accordance with the Data Protection Act 1998.

17.19 When taking attendance management action against a worker, employers should ensure that they do not discriminate because of a protected characteristic. In particular, it will often be appropriate to manage disability, pregnancy and gender reassignment-related absences differently from other types of absence. Recording the reasons for absences should assist that process.

Disability-related absences

17.20 Employers are not automatically obliged to disregard all disability-related sickness absences, but they must disregard some or all of the absences by way of an adjustment if this is reasonable. If an employer takes action against a disabled worker for disability-related sickness absence, this may amount to discrimination arising from disability (see Chapter 5).

Example: During a six-month period, a man who has recently developed a long-term health condition has a number of short periods of absence from work as he learns to manage this condition. Ignoring these periods of disability-related absence is likely to be a reasonable adjustment for the employer to make. Disciplining this man because of these periods of absence will amount to discrimination arising from disability, if the employer cannot show that this is objectively justified.

17.21 Workers who are absent because of disability-related sickness must be paid no less than the contractual sick pay which is due for the period in question. Although there is no automatic obligation for an employer to extend contractual sick pay beyond the usual entitlement when a worker is absent due to disability-related sickness, an employer should consider whether it would be reasonable for them to do so.

17.22 However, if the reason for absence is due to an employer's delay in implementing a reasonable adjustment that would enable the worker to return to the workplace, maintaining full pay would be a further reasonable adjustment for the employer to make.

Example: A woman who has a visual impairment needs work documents to be enlarged. Her employer fails to make arrangements for a reasonable adjustment to provide her with these. As a result, she has a number of absences from work because of eyestrain. After she has received full sick pay for four months, the employer is considering a reduction to half-pay in line with its sickness policy. It is likely to be a reasonable adjustment to maintain full pay as her absence is caused by the employer's delay in making the original adjustment.

17.23 Disabled workers may sometimes require time out during the working day to attend medical appointments or receive treatment related to their disability. On occasions, it may be necessary for them to attend to access needs such as wheelchair maintenance or care of working dogs. If, for example, a worker needs to take a short period of time off each week over a period of several months it is likely to be reasonable to accommodate the time off.

17.24 However, if a worker needs to take off several days per week over a period of months it may not be reasonable for the employer to accommodate this. Whether or not it is reasonable will depend on the circumstances of both the employer and the worker.

Example: An employer allows a worker who has become disabled after a stroke to have time off for rehabilitation training. Although this is more time off than would be allowed to non-disabled workers, it is likely to be a reasonable adjustment. A similar adjustment may be reasonable if a disability gets worse or if a disabled worker needs occasional but regular long-term treatment.

Pregnancy-related absences

17.25 All pregnancy-related absences must be disregarded for the purposes of attendance management action. Workers who are absent for a pregnancy-related reason have no automatic right to full pay but should receive no less than the contractual sick pay that might be due for the period in question. However, employers have no obligation to extend contractual sick pay beyond what would usually be payable. Sickness absence associated with a miscarriage should be treated as pregnancy-related sickness. Pregnancy-related absence is covered in more detail in Chapter 8.

Example: A worker has been off work because of pregnancy complications since early in her pregnancy. Her employer has now dismissed her in accordance with the sickness policy which allows no more than 20 weeks' continuous absence. This policy is applied regardless of sex. The dismissal is unfavourable treatment because of her pregnancy and would be unlawful even if a man would be dismissed for a similar period of sickness absence, because the employer took into account the worker's pregnancy-related sickness absence in deciding to dismiss.

17.26 Pregnant employees are entitled to paid time off for antenatal care. Antenatal care can include medical examinations, relaxation and parenting classes.

Example: A pregnant employee has booked time off to attend a medical appointment related to her pregnancy. Her employer insists this time must be made up through flexi-time arrangements or her pay will be reduced to reflect the time off. This is unlawful: a pregnant employee is under no obligation to make up time taken off for antenatal appointments and an employer cannot refuse paid time off to attend such classes.

Absences related to gender reassignment

17.27 If a transsexual person is absent from work because they propose to undergo, are undergoing or have undergone gender reassignment, it is unlawful to treat them less favourably than they would be treated if they were absent due to illness or injury, or – if reasonable – than they would be treated for absence for other reasons (see paragraphs 9.31 to 9.33).

Example: A worker undergoing gender reassignment has to take some time off for medical appointments and also for surgery. The employer records all these absences for the purposes of their attendance management policy. However, when another worker breaks his leg skiing the employer disregards his absences because 'it wasn't really sickness and won't happen again'. This indicates that the treatment of the transsexual worker may amount to discrimination because the employer would have treated him more favourably if he had broken his leg than they treated him because of gender reassignment absences.

Absences related to in vitro fertilisation

17.28 There is no statutory entitlement to time off for in vitro fertilisation (IVF) or other fertility treatment. However, in responding to requests for time off from a woman undergoing IVF, an employer must not treat her less favourably than they treat, or would treat, a man in a similar situation as this could amount to sex discrimination. After a fertilised embryo has been implanted, a woman is legally pregnant and from that point is protected from unfavourable treatment because of her pregnancy, including pregnancy-related sickness. She would also be entitled to time off for antenatal care.

17.29 It is good practice for employers to treat sympathetically any request for time off for IVF or other fertility treatment, and consider adopting a procedure to cover this situation. This could include allowing women to take annual leave or unpaid leave when receiving treatment and designating a member of staff whom they can inform on a confidential basis that that they are undergoing treatment.

Example: A female worker who is undergoing IVF treatment has to take time off sick because of its side effects. Her employer treats this as ordinary sickness absence and pays her contractual sick pay that is due to her. Had contractual sick pay been refused, this could amount to sex discrimination.

Example: Recently an employer agreed, as a one-off request, a week's annual leave for a male worker who wanted to undergo cosmetic dental surgery. Two months later, one of his female colleagues asks if she can take a week's annual leave to undergo IVF treatment. The employer refuses this request, even though the worker still has two weeks leave due to her. She may be able show that the employer's refusal to grant her request for annual leave for IVF treatment amounts to sex discrimination, by comparing her treatment to that of her male colleague.

Maternity, paternity, adoption and parental leave

17.30 When dealing with workers who request or take maternity, paternity, adoption or parental leave, employers should ensure that they do not discriminate against the worker because of a protected characteristic.

Example: A lesbian worker has asked her employer for parental leave. She and her partner adopted a child two years ago and she wants to be able to look after her child for part of the summer holidays. The worker made sure the time she has requested would not conflict with parental leave being taken by other workers. In exercising his discretion whether to grant parental leave, the woman's line manager refuses her request because he does not agree with same sex couples being allowed to adopt children. This is likely to be direct discrimination because of sexual orientation.

17.31 Detailed provisions dealing with maternity, paternity, adoption and parental leave and workers' rights during such leave are set out in other statutes and regulations; for example, the Employment Rights Act 1996, Maternity and Parental Leave etc Regulations 1999 (as amended), Paternity and Adoption Leave Regulations 2002 (as amended) and the Management of Health and Safety at Work Regulations 1999. For more information, please see Chapter 8.

Emergency leave

17.32 [ERA 1996 s 57A] Employees have a statutory right to take reasonable unpaid time off which is necessary to deal with immediate emergencies concerning dependants. Dependants include a spouse or civil partner or partner, a child or a parent, or a person living in the employee's household. In dealing with cases where emergency leave is required, employers should ensure that they do not discriminate.

Example: A worker receives a telephone call informing him that his civil partner has been involved in an accident. The worker has been recorded as next of kin on his civil partner's medical notes and is required at the hospital. The employer has a policy that only allows emergency leave to be taken where a spouse, child or parent is affected and refuses the worker's request for leave. This would amount to discrimination because of sexual orientation. It would also be a breach of the worker's statutory rights.

Annual leave

17.33 Annual leave policies and procedures must be applied without discrimination of any kind. It is particularly important for employers to avoid discrimination when dealing with competing requests for annual leave, or requests that relate to a worker's protected characteristic such as religion or belief.

17.34 The Working Time Regulations 1998 provide a minimum annual holiday entitlement of 5.6 weeks, which can include public and bank holidays; however, employers may offer workers more holiday than their minimum legal entitlement. The procedure in the Regulations for requesting annual leave and dealing with such requests may be replaced by agreement between the employer and worker. All policies and procedures for handling annual leave requests should be non-discriminatory in design and the employer must not refuse a request for annual leave because of a protected characteristic.

17.35 A policy leading to a refusal is also an application of a provision, criterion or practice. The policy could be indirectly discriminatory if it places the worker and people sharing the worker's characteristic at a particular disadvantage, unless the provision, criterion or practice is a proportionate means of achieving a legitimate aim.

17.36 A worker may request annual leave for a religious occasion or to visit family overseas. To avoid discrimination, employers should seek to accommodate the request – provided the worker has sufficient holiday due to them and it is reasonable for them to be absent from work during the period requested.

Example: An Australian worker requests three weeks' leave to visit his family in Australia. He works for a large employer, whose annual leave policy normally limits periods of annual leave to a maximum of two weeks at any one time. The two-week limit could be indirectly discriminatory because of nationality, unless it can be objectively justified. In this case, the employer has sufficient staff to cover the additional week's leave. They operate the annual leave policy flexibly, and agree to allow the worker to take three weeks' leave to visit his family.

17.37 Many religions or beliefs have special periods of religious observance, festivals or holidays. Employers should be aware that some of these occasions are aligned with lunar phases. As a result, dates can change from year to year and may not become clear until quite close to the actual day.

Example: Last year, a Sikh worker took annual leave on 1 and 2 March to celebrate Hola Mohalla. This year, he requests annual leave on 6th and 7th March to celebrate the same holiday. No other staff members in his department have requested leave on these dates. The employer refuses the request but says that the worker can take off the same days as he did last year. Festivals in Sikhism are based on the lunar calendar, so the dates on which they fall differ every year. It could be indirect discrimination for the employer to expect the worker to take annual leave on the same days every year, unless this can be objectively justified.

17.38 Employers who require everyone to take leave during an annual closedown should consider whether this creates a particular disadvantage for workers sharing a protected characteristic who need annual leave at other times, for example, during specific school holidays or religious festivals. This practice could amount to indirect discrimination, unless it can be objectively justified. Although the operational needs of the business may be a legitimate aim, employers must consider the needs of workers in assessing whether the closure is a proportionate means of achieving the aim (see paragraphs 4.25 to 4.32).

AVOIDING DISCRIMINATION – ACCOMMODATING WORKERS' NEEDS

Dress and business attire

17.39 Many employers enforce a dress code or uniform with the aim of ensuring that workers dress in a manner that is appropriate to the business or workplace or to meet health and safety requirements. However, dress codes – including rules about jewellery – may indirectly discriminate against workers sharing a protected characteristic. To avoid indirect discrimination, employers should make sure that any dress rules can be justified as a proportionate means of achieving a legitimate aim such as health and safety considerations.

17.40 It is good practice for employers to consult with workers as to how a dress code may impact on different religious or belief groups, and whether any exceptions should be allowed – for example, for religious jewellery.

Example: An employer introduces a 'no jewellery' policy in the workplace. This is not for health and safety reasons but because the employer does not like body piercings. A Sikh worker who wears a Kara bracelet as an integral part of her religion has complained about the rule. To avoid a claim of indirect discrimination, the employer should consider allowing an exception to this rule. A blanket ban on jewellery would probably not be considered a proportionate means of achieving a legitimate aim in these circumstances.

17.41 In some situations, a dress code could amount to direct discrimination because of a protected characteristic. It is not necessarily sex discrimination for a dress code to set out different requirements for men and women (for example, that men have to wear a collar and tie). However, it may be direct discrimination if a dress code requires a different overall standard of dress for men and for women; for example, requiring men to dress in a professional and business-like way but allowing women to wear more casual clothes. It could also be direct discrimination if the dress code is similar for both sexes but applied more strictly to men than women – or the other way round.

17.42 Where men are required to wear suits, it may be less favourable treatment to require women to wear skirts, if an equivalent level of smartness can be achieved by women wearing, for example, a trouser suit. If a male to female transsexual person is prevented from wearing a skirt where other women are permitted to do so, this could amount to direct discrimination because of gender reassignment.

Example: An employer's dress code requires men to wear shirts and ties and women to 'dress smartly'. The dress code is not enforced as strictly against women as against men. A male worker has been suspended for continually failing to wear a tie, while no action is taken against female colleagues for wearing T-shirts. This could amount to direct discrimination because of sex.

17.43 Employers should also be aware of the duty to make reasonable adjustments to a dress code in order to avoid placing disabled workers at a substantial disadvantage. For example, in some cases uniforms made of certain fabrics may cause a reaction in workers with particular skin conditions.

Language in the workplace

17.44 A language requirement for a job may be indirectly discriminatory unless it is necessary for the satisfactory performance of the job. For example, a requirement that a worker have excellent English skills may be indirectly discriminatory because of race; if a worker really only needs a good grasp of English, the requirement for excellent English may not be objectively justified. A requirement for good spoken English may be indirectly discriminatory against certain disabled people, for example, deaf people whose first language is British Sign Language. (See Chapter 4 for more information on indirect discrimination.)

Example: A superstore insists that all its workers have excellent spoken English. This might be a justifiable requirement for those in customer-facing roles. However, for workers based in the stock room, the requirement could be indirectly discriminatory in relation to race or disability as it is less likely to be objectively justified.

17.45 Under the Welsh Language Act 1993, public bodies providing services to the public in Wales must make their services available in Welsh as well as English. This operates as a statutory exception to the Equality Act, and allows a wide range of posts in public bodies in Wales (and some outside Wales) to require workers who can speak, write and read Welsh sufficiently well for the post in question. In some cases, Welsh language skills may be an essential requirement for appointment; in others, the worker may need to agree to learn the language to the required level within a reasonable period of time after appointment. On this issue, employers are recommended to seek advice from the Welsh Language Board.

Example: A local council in Wales requires all its newly recruited receptionists to speak Welsh or be willing to learn the language within a year of being employed. This requirement would be lawful under the Act.

17.46 In fulfilling the duty to make reasonable adjustments, employers may have to take steps to ensure that information is provided in accessible formats. This requirement is covered in more detail in paragraphs 6.6 and 6.33.

17.47 An employer might also wish to impose a requirement on workers to communicate in a common language – generally English. There is a clear business interest in having a common language in the workplace, to avoid misunderstandings, whether legal, financial or in relation to health and safety. It is also conducive to good working relations to avoid excluding workers from conversations that might concern them.

17.48 However, employers should make sure that any requirement involving the use of a particular language during or outside working hours, for example during work breaks, does not amount to unlawful discrimination. Blanket rules involving the use of a particular language may not be objectively justifiable as a proportionate means of achieving a legitimate aim. An employer who prohibits workers from talking casually to each other in a language they do not share with all colleagues, or uses occasions when this happens to trigger disciplinary or capability procedures or to impede workers' career progress, may be considered to be acting disproportionately.

17.49 English is generally the language of business in Britain and is likely to be the preferred means of communication in most workplaces, unless other languages are required for specific business reasons. There may be some circumstances where using a different language might be more practical for a line manager dealing with a particular group of workers with limited English language skills.

Example: A construction company employs a high number of Polish workers on one of its sites. The project manager of the site is also Polish and finds it more practical to speak Polish when giving instructions to those workers. However, the company should not advertise vacancies as being only open to Polish-speaking workers as the requirement is unlikely to be justified and could amount to indirect race discrimination.

17.50 Where the workforce includes people sharing a protected characteristic who experience disadvantage within the workplace because of limited English, employers could consider taking proportionate positive action measures to improve their communication skills. These measures might include providing:

- interpreting and translation facilities; for example, multilingual safety signs and notices, to make sure the workers in question understand health and safety requirements;
- English language classes to improve communication skills.

The provisions on positive action are explained in Chapter 12.

17.51 Inappropriate or derogatory language in the workplace could amount to harassment if it is related to a protected characteristic and is sufficiently serious. Workplace policies – if the employer has these in place – should emphasise that workers should not make inappropriate comments, jokes or use derogatory terms related to a protected characteristic (see Chapter 7 on harassment).

Example: A male worker has made a number of offensive remarks about a worker who is pregnant, such as 'women are only good for making babies'. The employer's equality policy makes it clear that inappropriate and offensive language, comments and jokes related to a protected characteristic can amount to harassment and may be treated as a disciplinary offence. The employer may bring disciplinary proceedings against the male worker for making offensive comments that relate to the pregnant worker's sex.

Understanding a worker's needs

17.52 The employer's duty to make reasonable adjustments continues throughout the disabled worker's employment (see Chapter 6). It is good practice for an employer to encourage disabled workers to discuss their disability so that any reasonable adjustments can be put in place. Disabled workers may be reluctant to disclose their impairment and the Act does not impose any obligation on them to do so. An employer can help overcome any concerns a disabled worker may have in this regard by explaining the reasons why information is being requested (that is, to consider reasonable adjustments). The employer should also reassure the worker that that information about disability is held confidentially.

Example: An office worker has symptomatic HIV and does not wish to tell his employer. His symptoms get worse and he finds it increasingly difficult to work the required number of hours in a week. At his annual appraisal, he raises this problem with his line manager and discloses his medical condition. As a result, a reasonable adjustment is made and his working hours are reduced to overcome the difficulty.

17.53 Sometimes a reasonable adjustment will not succeed without the co-operation of other workers. To secure such co-operation it may be necessary for the employer, with the disabled worker's consent, to tell their colleague(s) in confidence about a disability which is not obvious. This disclosure may be limited to the disabled person's line manager or it may be appropriate to involve other colleagues, depending on the circumstances.

17.54 However, an employer should obtain a worker's consent before revealing any information about their disability. Employers need to be aware that they have obligations under the Data Protection Act 1998 in respect of personal data.

Example: A factory worker with cancer tells her employer that she does not want colleagues to know of her condition. As an adjustment she needs extra time away from work to receive treatment and to rest. Neither her colleagues nor her line manager need to be told the precise reasons for the extra leave but the line manager will need to know that the adjustment is required in order to implement it effectively.

17.55 If a worker is undergoing gender reassignment, it is good practice for the employer to consult with them sensitively about their needs in the workplace and whether there are any reasonable and practical steps the employer can take to help the worker as they undergo their gender reassignment process. For further information on gender reassignment, please refer to paragraphs 2.21 to 2.30 and 9.31 to 9.33.

Example: A worker will soon be undergoing gender reassignment treatment and the employer has accepted that they want to continue working throughout the transition process. To avoid unresolved questions about which toilet facilities the worker should use, their uniform and communications with other members of staff, the employer should arrange to discuss the situation sympathetically with the worker. The discussion could cover setting a date for using different facilities and uniform; the timescale of the treatment; any impact this may have on the worker's job and adjustments that could be made; and how the worker would like to address the issue of their transition with colleagues.

17.56 Consultation will also help an employer understand the requirements of a worker's religion or belief, such as religious observances. This will help avoid embarrassment or difficulties for those who need to practice their religion or belief at the workplace.

Example: A large employer in an urban area is aware that their workers come from varied backgrounds. As part of their induction meeting, new workers are given the option of disclosing their religion or belief and of discussing whether there is anything the company can do to help them – such as allowing flexible breaks to accommodate prayer times. Workers do not have to disclose anything about their religion or belief if they do not want to. All information provided is kept confidential, unless the worker consents to its disclosure.

Quiet rooms

17.57 Some religions or beliefs require their followers to pray at specific times during the day. Workers may therefore request access to an appropriate quiet place (or prayer room) to undertake their religious observance.

17.58 The Act does not require employers to provide a quiet room. However, if a quiet place is available and allowing its use for prayer and contemplation does not cause problems for the business or for other workers, an employer with sufficient resources may be discriminating because of religion or belief by refusing such a request – especially if comparable facilities are provided for other reasons.

17.59 On the other hand, employers should be careful to avoid creating a disadvantage for workers who do not need a quiet room (for example, by converting the only rest room), as this might amount to indirect religion or belief discrimination. It would be good practice to consult with all workers before designating a room for prayer and contemplation and to discuss policies for using it, such as the wearing of shoes. If possible, employers may also wish to consider providing separate storage facilities for ceremonial objects.

Example: A large employer has one meeting room which is generally unused. There is also a separate rest room, and the employer has made provision for smokers by permitting them to use an open porch by the back entrance. A group of Muslim workers has asked the employer to convert the small meeting room into a quiet room. Refusing this request may amount to direct discrimination if the Muslim workers have been treated less favourably because of religion or belief, compared to non-Muslim workers.

Food and fasting

17.60 Some religions or beliefs have specific dietary requirements. If workers with such needs bring food into the workplace, they may need to store and heat it separately from other food. It is good practice for employers to consult their workforce on such issues and find a mutually acceptable way of accommodating such requirements.

Example: An orthodox Jewish worker in a small firm has a religious requirement that her food cannot come into direct contact with pork or indirect contact through items such as cloths or sponges. After discussion with staff, the employer allocates one shelf of a fridge for this worker's food, and separate cupboard space for the plates and cutlery that she uses. They also introduce a policy that any food brought into the workplace should be stored in sealed containers.

17.61 Some religions require extended periods of fasting. Although there is no requirement under the Act, employers may wish to consider how they can support workers through a fasting period. However, employers should take care to ensure that, in doing so, they do not place unreasonable extra burdens on other workers. As well as potentially causing conflict in the workplace, this could amount to less favourable treatment because of religion or belief and give rise to claims of discrimination.

Example: A Muslim teacher is fasting for Ramadan which is an integral part of her religion. The head teacher of the school, in consultation with the other teachers, has agreed to change the dinnertime rota so she does not have to supervise the dining hall during her fasting period. This adjustment to her duties does not amount to unfavourable treatment of non-Muslim staff members, so would not amount to direct discrimination.

Washing and changing facilities

17.62 An employer may require workers to change their clothing and/or shower for reasons of health and safety. Some religions or beliefs do not allow their adherents to undress or shower in the company of others. Insisting upon communal showers and changing facilities, even if segregated by sex, could constitute indirect discrimination as it may put at a particular disadvantage workers sharing a certain religion or belief whose requirement for modesty prevents them from changing their clothing in the presence of others, even others of the same sex. An employer would have to show that this provision, criterion or practice was objectively justified.

17.63 Some needs relating to religion or belief require no change to workplaces. For example, certain religions require people to wash before prayer, which can be done using normal washing facilities. It is good practice for employers to ensure that all workers understand the religion or belief-related observances of their colleagues, to avoid misunderstandings.

Breastfeeding

17.64 Although there is no legal right to take time off to breastfeed, wherever possible employers should try to accommodate workers who wish to do this. Breastfeeding at work is covered in more detail in Chapter 8.

LIABILITY FOR DISCRIMINATION OUTSIDE THE WORKPLACE

17.65 Employers are liable for prohibited conduct that takes place 'in the course of employment'. This may extend to discrimination and harassment occurring away from work premises or outside normal working hours where there is sufficient connection with work – for example, at team building days, social events to which all workers are invited, business trips or client events (see paragraph 10.46).

17.66 To avoid liability for discrimination and harassment outside the workplace, employers should consider taking steps such as: drafting disciplinary and equality policies that refer to acceptable behaviour outside the office; checking dietary requirements to ensure that all workers have appropriate food during work-related events; and making it clear to workers what is required of them to comply with acceptable standards of behaviour. Employers should also consider whether they need to make any reasonable adjustments to accommodate the needs of disabled workers.

Example: A worker aged 17 has a job in a telephone sales company. On Friday nights her team colleagues go to a local club to socialise. During this time they talk mainly about work-related issues. The team manager also buys drinks for the team member who has achieved the most sales that week. The worker cannot attend these events as the club has a strict 'over-18s only' policy; she feels excluded and undervalued. This treatment could amount to unjustifiable age discrimination. The manager should consider organising team social events somewhere that accepts under-18s.

INDUCTION, TRAINING AND DEVELOPMENT

Induction

17.67 It is important to make sure that induction procedures do not discriminate. Employers should ask themselves whether any changes are needed to remove the indirectly discriminatory effect of a provision, criterion or practice. They must also consider whether any reasonable adjustments are required to enable disabled workers to participate fully in any induction arrangements. In addition, employers may want to consider whether there are any proportionate positive action measures that would help remedy disadvantage experienced by workers sharing a protected characteristic (see also Chapter 12 on positive action).

Example: A worker with a hearing impairment is selected for a post as an engineer. He attends the induction course which consists of a video followed by a discussion. The video is not subtitled and thus the worker cannot participate fully in the induction. To avoid discrimination, the employer should have discussed with the worker what type of reasonable adjustment to the format of the induction training would enable him to participate.

Example: A worker with a learning disability finds it hard to assimilate the material in the employer's induction procedure at the same speed as a colleague who started on the same day. In relation to this worker's induction, it is likely to be a reasonable adjustment for the employer to provide more time, personal support and assistance, such as making available induction materials in Easy Read.

17.68 The induction process is also a good opportunity to make sure all new staff members are trained in the employer's equality policy and procedures. For more information on equality policies, see Chapter 18.

Training and development

17.69 Training and development opportunities, including training provided by a trade union to its members, should be made known to all relevant workers including those absent from the office for whatever reason (see paragraph 16.22 above).

Example: An employee who is on maternity leave asked to be kept updated about training opportunities, so her knowledge would be up to date when she returns to work. During her maternity leave, all other workers have been sent emails updating them on the latest training opportunities but she has not. Excluding this employee is unfavourable treatment and would amount to unlawful discrimination because of pregnancy and maternity.

17.70 However, it will not be appropriate for an employer to contact a worker who is absent for a disability-related reason if the employer has agreed to have limited contact.

17.71 To avoid discrimination, employers should ensure that managers and supervisors who select workers for training understand their legal responsibilities under the Act. It is advisable to monitor training applications and take-up by reference to protected characteristics, taking steps to deal with any significant disparities. Selection for training must be made without discrimination because of a protected characteristic.

Example: An employer has opened a new office overseas and is offering managers the chance of a six-month secondment at the new office to assist in the initial set up. They do not select any of the female managers with children who apply for the secondment, as they assume these women would miss their families and would not perform as well as other managers. This is likely to amount to direct discrimination because of sex.

17.72 Employers should be mindful of their duty to make reasonable adjustments in relation to training and development. For example, if a worker with a mobility impairment is expected to be attending a course, it is likely to be a reasonable adjustment for the employer to select a training venue with adequate disabled access. An employer may need to make training manuals, slides or other visual media accessible to a visually impaired worker (perhaps by providing Braille versions or having materials read out), or ensure that an induction loop is available for someone with a hearing impairment.

17.73 Employers should also consider whether opportunities for training are limited by any other potentially discriminatory factors. If food is provided at training events, employers should try to make sure that special dietary requirements are accommodated. If resources permit, training and development opportunities should be offered on a flexible basis, to accommodate those who work part-time, who have atypical working patterns or who cannot attend training on a particular day, for example, because of conflict with a religious festival or a medical appointment.

17.74 Any criteria used to select workers for training should also be regularly reviewed to make sure they do not discriminate.

Example: An employer offers team leading training for staff who wish to develop management skills. Staff must have been with the company for over seven years to apply for a place on this course. This could be indirectly discriminatory because of age, as older staff are likely to have longer service than younger staff. The employer would have to show that the age criterion is objectively justifiable.

17.75 As explained in Chapter 12, employers may want to consider taking positive action to remedy disadvantage, meet different needs or increase the participation of people who share a protected characteristic. Providing training opportunities for a group which is under-represented in the workforce might be one way of doing this. It is also lawful for employers to provide training for disabled workers, regardless of whether the criteria for positive action are met.

Example: A national education provider wishes to recruit science teachers for its chain of private colleges. It has evidence that almost all of its teachers are recently qualified and under 40. The provider decides to take positive action measures to increase the participation of older teachers. It undertakes a targeted recruitment drive to attract older teachers and recruits several teachers who are returning to teaching after working in industry for many years. In order to update their skills, the provider then offers them additional training on current curriculum and teaching practices.

17.76 Workers who have been absent (for example, on maternity or adoption leave, or for childcare or disability-related reasons) may need additional training on their return to work. It is good practice for employers to liaise with the worker either before or shortly after their return to work to consider whether any additional training is needed.

17.77 An employee on statutory maternity or adoption leave may by agreement work for her employer for up to 10 'keeping in touch' days (KIT days) without bringing the leave to an end; see paragraph 8.29.

Appraisals

17.78 An appraisal is an opportunity for a worker and their line manager to discuss the worker's performance and development. Appraisals usually review past behaviour and so provide an opportunity to reflect on recent performance. They also form an important part of a worker's continuing training and development programme.

17.79 The Act does not require employers to conduct appraisals, although it is good practice to do so if resources permit. Where a formal appraisal process is used, the starting point should be that employers take a consistent approach. In particular, they should ensure that in awarding marks for performance they do not discriminate against any worker because of a protected characteristic. This is especially important because low appraisal scores can have a negative impact on pay, bonuses, promotion and development opportunities.

Example: A woman with young children, who works part-time, is given the same performance targets as her full-time colleagues. She fails to meet the targets. When conducting her annual appraisal, her manager gives her a worse score than full-timers. Other part-time workers, who are mainly women, experience similar problems. This practice could amount to indirect sex discrimination; using identical targets regardless of working hours is unlikely to be objectively justified. This could also be considered as less favourable treatment of a part-time worker under the Part-Time Workers (Prevention of Less Favourable Treatment) Regulations 2000.

17.80 Employers should also be aware of the duty to make reasonable adjustments when discussing past performance. For example, they should consider whether performance would have been more effective had a reasonable adjustment been put in place, or introduced earlier. Appraisals may also provide an opportunity for workers to disclose a disability to their employer, and to discuss any adjustments that would be reasonable for the employer to make in future.

Example: An employer installed voice-activated software as a reasonable adjustment to accommodate the needs of a new manager with a visual impairment. The manager takes several weeks to familiarise herself with the software. After six months in post, the manager undergoes an appraisal. In assessing the manager's performance, it would be a reasonable adjustment for the employer to take account of the time the manager needed to become fully familiar with the software.

17.81 To avoid discrimination when conducting appraisals, employers are recommended to:

- make sure that performance is measured by transparent, objective and justifiable criteria using procedures that are consistently applied;
- check that, for all workers, performance is assessed against standards that are relevant to their role;
- ensure that line managers carrying out appraisals receive training and guidance on objective performance assessment and positive management styles; and
- monitor performance assessment results to ensure that any significant disparities in scores apparently linked to a protected characteristic are investigated, and steps taken to deal with possible causes.

PROMOTION AND TRANSFER

17.82 Issues and considerations that arise on recruitment (see Chapter 16) can arise again in respect of promoting or transferring existing workers to new roles. It is unlawful for employers to discriminate against, victimise or harass workers in the way they make opportunities for promotion or transfer available or by refusing or deliberately failing to make them available. An employer may need to make reasonable adjustments to the promotion or transfer process to ensure that disabled workers are not substantially disadvantaged by the process for promotion or transfer or by the way the process is applied.

17.83 Failure to inform workers of opportunities for promotion or transfer may be direct or indirect discrimination. To avoid discrimination, employers are advised to advertise all promotion and transfer opportunities widely throughout the organisation. This includes development or deputising opportunities or secondments that could lead to permanent promotion.

17.84 If an employer has an equal opportunities policy and/or recruitment policy and procedures, it would be good practice to ensure that these policies are followed when internal promotions or transfers are taking place. This can help ensure that that selection is based strictly on demonstrable merit. Unless a temporary promotion is absolutely necessary, employers should avoid bypassing the procedures they have adopted for recruiting other staff.

Example: An employer promotes a male worker to the position of section manager without advertising the vacancy internally. There are several women in the organisation who are qualified for the post and who could have applied if they had known about it. The decision not to advertise internally counts as a provision, criterion or practice and could amount to indirect discrimination: if challenged, the employer would need to be able to objectively justify their decision. Recruiting the man could also amount to direct discrimination, as one or more of the women could argue they have been treated less favourably because of their sex.

17.85 Employers should consider whether it is really necessary to restrict applications for promotion and other development opportunities to staff at a particular grade or level. This restriction would operate as a provision, criterion or practice and, unless it can be objectively justified, could indirectly discriminate by putting workers sharing a protected characteristic at a particular disadvantage.

17.86 Employers must also ensure that women on maternity leave are informed of any jobs that become available and must enable them to apply if they wish to do so. Failure to do so may be unfavourable treatment, and thus could amount to discrimination because of pregnancy and maternity (see also Chapter 8).

17.87 Arrangements for promoting workers or arranging transfers must not discriminate because of disability – either in the practical arrangements relating to selection for promotion or transfer, or in the arrangements for the job itself. It is also important for employers to consider whether there are any reasonable adjustments that should be made in relation to promotion or transfer.

Example: A woman with a disability resulting from a back injury is seeking a transfer to another department. A minor aspect of the role she is seeking is to assist with unloading the weekly delivery van. She is unable to do this because of her disability. In assessing her suitability for transfer, the employer should consider whether reallocating this duty to someone else would be a reasonable adjustment to make.

17.88 Opportunities for promotion and transfer should be made available to all workers regardless of age. Different treatment because of age is only lawful if it can be objectively justified as a proportionate means of achieving a legitimate aim (see paragraphs 3.36 to 3.41).

Example: An employer decides to impose a maximum age of 60 for promotion to the position of technical manager, for which additional training is required. In deciding whether this age restriction is objectively justifiable, the time and costs of training for the post would be relevant, taking into account that an internal candidate would probably need less training than a new recruit. Average staff turnover across all groups should also be considered. The need for a reasonable period of employment before retirement might also be relevant – although employees' right to request to continue working beyond 65 should be factored in.

17.89 It would be good practice for employers to build the following guidelines into any policies and procedures they may have relating to promotion and career development:

- If posts are advertised internally and externally, the same selection procedures and criteria should apply to all candidates.
- If appropriate – especially with larger employers – selection decisions based on performance assessments should be endorsed by the organisation's human resources department.

17.90 Employers should not make assumptions about the suitability of existing workers for promotion or transfer.

Example: An employer makes an assumption that a particular woman is unsuitable for promotion because she appears to be of childbearing age and he assumes she might want to have children in the near future. This would amount to direct discrimination because of sex.

DISCIPLINARY AND GRIEVANCE MATTERS

17.91 It is good practice for employers (irrespective of their size) to have procedures for dealing with grievances and disciplinary hearings together with appeals against decisions under these procedures. Where procedures have been put in place, they should not discriminate against workers either in the way they are designed or how the employer implements them in practice. More information about disciplinary and grievance procedures, including a worker's right to be accompanied by a trade union representative or fellow worker, can be found on the Acas website: www.acas.org.uk/index.aspx?articleid=2174

17.92 An employer may in addition wish to introduce a separate policy designed specifically to deal with harassment. Such policies commonly aim to highlight and eradicate harassment whilst at the same time establishing a procedure for complaints, similar to a grievance procedure, with safeguards to deal with the sensitivities that allegations of harassment often bring.

Example: An employer has a procedure that allows a grievance relating to harassment to be raised with a designated experienced manager. This avoids the possibility of an allegation of harassment having to be raised with a line manager who may be the perpetrator of the harassment.

17.93 Employers should ensure that when conducting disciplinary and grievance procedures they do not discriminate against a worker because of a protected characteristic. For example, employers may need to make reasonable adjustments to procedures to ensure that they do not put disabled workers at a substantial disadvantage. Procedures might also need to be adapted to accommodate a worker at home on maternity leave.

Dealing with grievances

17.94 Employers must not discriminate in the way they respond to grievances. Where a grievance involves allegations of discrimination or harassment, it must be taken seriously and investigated promptly and not dismissed as 'over-sensitivity' on the part of the worker.

17.95 Wherever possible, it is good practice – as well as being in the interests of employers – to resolve grievances as they arise and before they become major problems. Grievance procedures can provide an open and fair way for complainants to make their concerns known, and for their grievances to be resolved quickly, without having to bring legal proceedings.

17.96 It is strongly recommended that employers properly investigate any complaints of discrimination. If a complaint is upheld against an individual co-worker or manager, the employer should consider taking disciplinary action against the perpetrator.

17.97 Whether or not the complaint of discrimination is upheld, raising it in good faith is a 'protected act' and if the worker is subject to any detriment because of having done so, this could amount to victimisation (see paragraphs 9.2 to 9.15).

Disciplinary procedures

17.98 Employers must not discriminate in the way they invoke or pursue a disciplinary process. A disciplinary process is a formal measure and should be followed fairly and consistently, regardless of the protected characteristics of any workers involved. Where a disciplinary process involves allegations of discrimination or harassment, the matter should be thoroughly investigated and the alleged perpetrator should be given a fair hearing.

17.99 If a complaint about discrimination leads to a disciplinary process where the complaint proves to be unfounded, employers must be careful not to subject the complainant (or any witness or informant) to any detriment for having raised the matter in good faith. Such actions qualify as 'protected acts' and detrimental treatment amounts to victimisation if a protected act is an effective cause of the treatment.

Avoiding disputes and conflicts

17.100 To help avoid disputes and conflicts with and between workers with different protected characteristics, employers should treat their workers with dignity and respect and ensure workers treat each other in the same way. If the principle of dignity and respect is embedded into the workplace culture, it can help prevent misunderstandings and behaviour that may lead to prohibited conduct. It is good practice to have a clear policy on 'dignity and respect in the workplace', setting out workers' rights and responsibilities to each other.

17.101 It is also good practice, and in the interests of both employers and their workers, to try to resolve workplace disputes so as to avoid litigation. Employers should have different mechanisms in place for managing disputes, such as mediation or conciliation. Where it is not possible to resolve a dispute using internal procedures, it may be better to seek outside help.

17.102 Employers will sometimes have to deal with complaints about prohibited conduct that arise between members of staff. They can avoid potential conflicts by noticing problems at an early stage and attempting to deal with them by, for example, talking to the people involved in a non-confrontational way. It is important to encourage good communication between workers and managers in order to understand the underlying reasons for potential conflicts. Employers should have effective procedures in place for dealing with grievances if informal methods of resolving the issue fail.

17.103 There may be situations where an employer should intervene to prevent a worker discriminating against another worker or against another person to whom that employer has a duty under the Act (such as a customer). In these circumstances, it may be necessary to take disciplinary action against the worker who discriminates.

CHAPTER 18
EQUALITY POLICIES AND PRACTICE IN THE WORKPLACE

INTRODUCTION

[4.156]
18.1 There is no formal statutory requirement in the Act for an employer to put in place an equality policy. However, a systematic approach to developing and maintaining good practice is the best way of showing that an organisation is taking its legal responsibilities seriously. To help employers and others meet their legal obligations, and avoid the risk of legal action being taken against them, it is recommended, as a matter of good practice, that they draw up an equality policy (also known as an equal opportunities policy or equality and diversity policy) and put this policy into practice.

18.2 This chapter describes why an employer should have an equality policy and how to plan, implement, monitor and review that policy.

WHY HAVE AN EQUALITY POLICY?

18.3 There are a number of reasons why employers should have an equality policy. For example:

- it can give job applicants and workers confidence that they will be treated with dignity and respect;
- it can set the minimum standards of behaviour expected of all workers and outline what workers and job applicants can expect from the employer;
- it is key to helping employers and others comply with their legal obligations;
- it can minimise the risk of legal action being taken against employers and workers; and/or
- if legal action is taken, employers may use the equality policy to demonstrate to an Employment Tribunal that they take discrimination seriously and have taken all reasonable steps to prevent discrimination.

18.4 Equality policies and practices are often drivers of good recruitment and retention practice. Information on these policies, as well as on equality worker network groups, on the organisation's website and/or in induction packs, send a very positive and inclusive signal encouraging people to apply to work for the organisation. This can indicate that the organisation seeks to encourage a diverse workforce and that, for example, applicants with any religion or belief and/or sexual orientation would be welcome in the organisation.

Example: For one organisation which is part of a multi-national corporation, being sensitive to local contexts is an important part of their operation. All their branches aim to reflect the local communities in which they operate in terms of their customers and their staff. In ethnically mixed areas, they aim to reflect this in the products they sell and in the mix of staff. This makes strong business sense since having a greater ethnic diversity of staff will attract more customers from that group.

PLANNING AN EQUALITY POLICY

18.5 It is essential that a written equality policy is backed by a clear programme of action for implementation and continual review. It is a process which consists of four key stages: planning, implementing, monitoring and reviewing the equality policy.

18.6 The content and details of equality policies and practices will vary according to the size, resources and needs of the employer. Some employers will require less formal structures but all employers should identify a time scale against which they aim to review progress and the achievement of their objectives.

18.7 A written equality policy should set out the employer's general approach to equality and diversity issues in the workplace. The policy should make clear that the employer intends to develop and apply procedures which do not discriminate because of any of the protected characteristics, and which provide equality of opportunity for all job applicants and workers.

Planning the content of equality policies

18.8 Most policies will include the following:

- a statement of the employer's commitment to equal opportunity for all job applicants and workers;
- what is and is not acceptable behaviour at work (also referring to conduct near the workplace and at work-related social functions where relevant);
- the rights and responsibilities of everyone to whom the policy applies, and procedures for dealing with any concerns and complaints;
- how the policy may apply to the employer's other policies and procedures;
- how the employer will deal with any breaches of policy;
- who is responsible for the policy; and
- how the policy will be implemented and details of monitoring and review procedures.

Example: An organisation informs new recruits that abuse and harassment are unacceptable and staff who make offensive, racist or homophobic comments are automatically subject to disciplinary proceedings.

18.9 It will help an employer avoid discrimination if the equality policy covers all aspects of employment including recruitment, terms and conditions of work, training and development, promotion, performance, grievance, discipline and treatment of workers when their contract ends. Areas of the employment relationship are covered in more detail in this Code and cross-references to the relevant chapters/sections are provided below:

- monitoring (see paragraph 18.23 and Appendix 2)
- recruitment (see Chapter 16)
- terms and conditions of work (see Chapter 17)
- pay and benefits (see Chapter 14)
- leave and flexible working arrangements (see Chapter 17)
- the availability of facilities, such as quiet/prayer rooms and meal options in staff canteens (see Chapter 17)
- pensions (see Chapter 14)
- dress codes (see Chapter 17)
- training and development (see Chapter 17)
- promotion and transfer (see Chapter 17)
- grievance and disciplinary issues (see Chapter 17)
- treatment of employees when their contract ends (see Chapter 9)
- health and safety (see Chapter 8 in relation to pregnancy and maternity)

Planning an equality policy – protected characteristics

18.10 It is recommended that adopting one equality policy covering all protected characteristics is the most practical approach. Where separate policies are developed, such as a separate race equality or sex equality policy, they should be consistent with each other and with an overall commitment to promoting equality of opportunity in employment.

IMPLEMENTING AN EQUALITY POLICY

18.11 An equality policy should be more than a statement of good intentions; there should also be plans for its implementation. The policy should be in writing and drawn up in consultation with workers and any recognised trade unions or other workplace representatives, including any equality representatives within the workforce.

18.12 Employers will be of different sizes and have different structures but it is advisable for all employers to take the following steps to implement an equality policy:

- audit existing policies and procedures;
- ensure the policy is promoted and communicated to all job applicants and workers and agents of the employer; and
- monitor and review the policy.

Promotion and communication of an equality policy

18.13 Employers should promote and publicise their equality policy as widely as possible and there are a number of ways in which this can be done. Promoting the policy is part of the process of effective implementation and will help an employer demonstrate that they have taken all reasonable steps to prevent discrimination.

18.14 Employers may use a number of methods of communication to promote their policy, including:

- email bulletins
- intranet and/or website
- induction packs
- team meetings
- office notice boards
- circulars, newsletters
- cascade systems
- training
- handbooks
- annual reports.

18.15 These methods of communication may not be appropriate in all cases. Some workers, for example those in customer-facing or shop floor roles, may not have regular access to computers. Alternative methods of communication, such as notice boards and regular staff meetings, should also be considered. Employers must also consider whether reasonable adjustments need to be made for disabled people so that they are able to access the information.

18.16 Promoting and communicating an equality policy should not be a one-off event. It is recommended that employers provide periodic reminders and updates to workers and others such as contractors and suppliers. Employers should also periodically review their advertising, recruitment and application materials and processes.

Responsibility for implementing an equality policy

18.17 The policy should have the explicit backing of people in senior positions such as the chair, owner, chief executive, or board of directors. Senior management should ensure that the policy is implemented, resourced, monitored and reviewed, and that there is regular reporting on its effectiveness.

Example: When a large company introduces a new equality policy, they might ask an external training company to run training sessions for all staff, or they might ask their human resources manager to deliver training to staff on this policy.

Example: A small employer introducing an equality policy asks the managing director to devote a team meeting to explaining the policy to her staff and discussing why it is important and how it will operate.

Implementing an equality policy – training

18.18 Employers should ensure that all workers and agents understand the equality policy, how it affects them and the plans for putting it into practice. The best way to achieve this is by providing regular training.

18.19 Some workers may need more specific training, depending on what they do within the organisation. For example, line managers and senior management should receive detailed training on how to manage equality and diversity issues in the workplace.

18.20 The training should be designed in consultation with workers, their workplace representatives and managers and by incorporating feedback from any previous training into future courses.

18.21 Employers should make sure in-house trainers are themselves trained before running courses for other workers. External trainers also need to be fully informed about the employer's policies, including their equality policy.

18.22 Training on the equality policy may include the following:

- an outline of the law covering all the protected characteristics and prohibited conduct;
- why the policy has been introduced and how it will be put into practice;
- what is and is not acceptable conduct in the workplace;
- the risk of condoning or seeming to approve inappropriate behaviour and personal liability;
- how prejudice can affect the way an employer functions and the impact that generalisations, stereotypes, bias or inappropriate language in day-to-day operations can have on people's chances of obtaining work, promotion, recognition and respect;
- the equality monitoring process (see paragraph 18.23 and Appendix 2).

Example: A large employer trains all their workers in the organisation's equality policy and the Equality Act. They also train all occupational health advisers with whom they work to ensure that the advisers have the necessary expertise about the Act and the organisation's equality policy.

MONITORING AND REVIEWING AN EQUALITY POLICY

18.23 Equality monitoring enables an employer to find out whether their equality policy is working. For example, monitoring may reveal that:

- applicants with a particular religion or belief are not selected for promotion;
- women are concentrated in certain jobs or departments;
- people from a particular ethnic group do not apply for employment or fewer apply than expected;
- older workers are not selected for training and development opportunities.

18.24 Equality monitoring is the process that employers use to collect, store and analyse data about the protected characteristics of job applicants and workers. Employers can use monitoring to:

- establish whether an equality policy is effective in practice;
- analyse the effect of other policies and practices on different groups;
- highlight possible inequalities and investigate their underlying causes;
- set targets and timetables for reducing disparities; and
- send a clear message to job applicants and workers that equality and diversity issues are taken seriously within the organisation.

Example: A large employer notices through monitoring that the organisation has been successful at retaining most groups of disabled people, but not people with mental health conditions. They act on this information by contacting a specialist organisation for advice about good practice in retaining people with mental health conditions.

Monitoring an equality policy – law and good practice

18.25 Public sector employers may find that monitoring assists them in carrying out their obligations under the public sector equality duty. For employers in the private sector, equality monitoring is not mandatory. However, it is recommended that all employers carry out equality monitoring. The methods used will depend on the size of the organisation and can be simple and informal. Smaller organisations may only need a simple method of collecting information about job applicants and workers. Larger organisations are likely to need more sophisticated procedures and computerised systems to capture the full picture across the whole of their organisation.

18.26 Monitoring will be more effective if workers (or job applicants) feel comfortable about disclosing personal information. This is more likely to be the case if the employer explains the purpose of the monitoring and if the workers or job applicants believe that the employer is using the information because they value the diversity of their workforce and want to use the information in a positive way.

18.27 Employers must take full account of the Data Protection Act 1998 (DPA) when they collect, store, analyse and publish data.

Monitoring an equality policy – key areas

18.28 Employers should monitor the key areas of the employment relationship including:

- recruitment and promotion
- pay and remuneration
- training
- appraisals
- grievances
- disciplinary action
- dismissals and other reasons for leaving

18.29 Employers who are carrying out equality monitoring will find it useful to compare progress over a period of time and against progress made by other employers in the same sector or industry.

Monitoring an equality policy – reporting back

18.30 It is important for employers to communicate on a regular basis to managers, workers and trade union representatives on the progress and achievement of objectives of the equality policy. Employers should also consider how the results of any monitoring activity can be communicated to the workforce. However, care should be taken to ensure that individuals are not identifiable from any reports.

Monitoring an equality policy – taking action

18.31 Taking action based on any findings revealed by the monitoring exercise is vital to ensure that an employer's equality policy is practically implemented. There are a number of steps employers can take, including:

- examine decision-making processes, for example recruitment and promotion;
- consider whether training or further guidelines are required on how to avoid discrimination;
- consider whether any positive action measures may be appropriate (see Chapter 12);
- work with network groups and trade union equality representatives to share information and advice;
- set targets on the basis of benchmarking data and develop an action plan.

REVIEWING AN EQUALITY POLICY AND OTHER EMPLOYMENT POLICIES

18.32 It is good practice for employers to keep both their equality policy and all other policies and procedures (such as those listed below) under regular review at least annually and to consider workers' needs as part of the process.

18.33 Policies which should be reviewed in light of an employer's equality policy might include:

- recruitment policies
- leave and flexible working arrangements
- retirement policies
- health and safety, for example, emergency evacuation procedures
- procurement of equipment, IT systems, software and websites
- pay and remuneration
- grievance policies, including harassment and bullying
- disciplinary procedure
- appraisal and performance-related pay systems
- sickness absence policies
- redundancy and redeployment policies
- training and development policies
- employee assistance schemes offering financial or emotional support

18.34 Part of the review process may entail employers taking positive action measures to alleviate disadvantage experienced by workers who share a protected characteristic, meet their particular needs, or increase their participation in relation to particular activities (see Chapter 12). Employers must also ensure they make reasonable adjustments where these are required by individual disabled workers. The review process can help employers to consider and anticipate the needs of disabled workers (see Chapter 6).

CHAPTER 19
TERMINATION OF EMPLOYMENT

INTRODUCTION

[4.157]

19.1 The employment relationship can come to an end in a variety of ways and in a range of situations. A worker may resign under normal circumstances, or resign in response to the employer's conduct and treat the resignation as a constructive dismissal. On the other hand, an employer may dismiss a worker, for example, for reasons of capability, conduct or redundancy. The Act makes it unlawful for an employer to discriminate against or victimise a worker by dismissing them (see paragraphs 10.11 and 10.13 to 10.16).

19.2 This chapter focuses on termination of employment by the employer, including in redundancy situations. It explains how to avoid discrimination in decisions to dismiss and in procedures for dismissal. The question of retirement is dealt with separately in paragraphs 13.26 to 13.45.

TERMINATING EMPLOYMENT

19.3 Those responsible for deciding whether or not a worker should be dismissed should understand their legal obligations under the Act. They should also be made aware of how the Act might apply to situations where dismissal is a possibility. Employers can help avoid discrimination if they have procedures in place for dealing with dismissals and apply these procedures consistently and fairly. In particular, employers should take steps to ensure the criteria they use for dismissal – especially in a redundancy situation – are not indirectly discriminatory (see paragraph 19.11 below).

19.4 It is also important that employers ensure they do not dismiss a worker with a protected characteristic for performance or behaviour which would be overlooked or condoned in others who do not share the characteristic.

Example: A Sikh worker is dismissed for failing to meet her set objectives, which form a part of her annual performance appraisal, in two consecutive years. However, no action is taken against a worker of the Baha'i faith, who has also failed to meet her objectives over the same period of time. This difference in treatment could amount to direct discrimination because of religion or belief.

19.5 Where an employer is considering dismissing a worker who is disabled, they should consider what reasonable adjustments need to be made to the dismissal process (see Chapter 6). In addition, the employer should consider whether the reason for dismissal is connected to or in consequence of the worker's disability. If it is, dismissing the worker will amount to discrimination arising from disability unless it can be objectively justified. In these circumstances, an employer should consider whether dismissal is an appropriate sanction to impose.

Example: A disabled worker periodically requires a limited amount of time off work to attend medical appointments related to the disability. The employer has an attendance management policy which results in potential warnings and ultimately dismissal if the worker's absence exceeds 20 days in any 12-month period. A combination of the worker's time off for disability-related medical appointments and general time off for sickness results in the worker consistently exceeding the 20 day limit by a few days. The worker receives a series of warnings and is eventually dismissed. This is likely to amount to disability discrimination.

19.6 Based on the facts in the example above, it is very likely to have been a reasonable adjustment for the employer to ignore the absences arising out of the worker's disability or increase the trigger points that would invoke the attendance policy. By making one or both of these adjustments, the employer could have avoided the possibility of claims for both a failure to make adjustments and discrimination arising from disability.

19.7 Employers must not discriminate against a transsexual worker when considering whether to dismiss the worker for absences or other conduct because of gender reassignment (see paragraphs 9.31 to 9.33). To avoid discrimination because of gender reassignment when considering the dismissal of a transsexual worker, employers should make provision within their disciplinary policy for dealing with such dismissals.

Example: A transsexual worker who experiences gender dysphoria and is considering gender reassignment takes time off from work because of his condition. The employer's attendance management policy provides that absence exceeding eight days or more in a 12-month rolling period will trigger the capability procedure. As the worker has had over eight days off, the employer invokes the procedure and consequently decides to dismiss him. However, over a previous 12-month rolling period, the worker was absent from work for more than eight days with various minor illnesses. The employer took no action against the worker because they viewed these absences as genuine. The dismissal could amount to an unlawful dismissal because of gender reassignment.

DISMISSAL FOR REASONS OF CAPABILITY AND CONDUCT

19.8 As noted in Chapter 17, employers must not discriminate against or victimise their workers in how they manage capability or conduct issues. To avoid discrimination in any disciplinary decision that leads to a dismissal (or could lead to a dismissal after a subsequent disciplinary matter), employers should have procedures in place for managing capability and conduct issues. They should apply these procedures fairly and in a non-discriminatory way.

Example: A white worker and a black worker are subjected to disciplinary action for fighting. The fight occurred because the black worker had made derogatory remarks about the white worker. The employer has no disciplinary policy and consequently does not investigate the matter. Instead, the employer decides to dismiss the white worker without notice and give the black worker a final written warning. This could amount to a discriminatory dismissal because of race. Had the employer had a disciplinary procedure in place and applied it fairly, they could have avoided a discriminatory outcome.

19.9 Where an employer is considering the dismissal of a disabled worker for a reason relating to that worker's capability or their conduct, they must consider whether any reasonable adjustments need to be made to the performance management or dismissal process which would help improve the performance of the worker or whether they could transfer the worker to a suitable alternative role.

How can discrimination be avoided in capability and conduct dismissals?

19.10 To avoid discrimination when terminating employment, an employer should, in particular:

- apply their procedures for managing capability or conduct fairly and consistently (or use Acas's Guide on Disciplinary and Grievance at Work, if the employer does not have their own procedure);

- ensure that any decision to dismiss is made by more than one individual, and on the advice of the human resources department (if the employer has one);
- keep written records of decisions and reasons to dismiss;
- monitor all dismissals by reference to protected characteristics (see paragraph 18.28 and Appendix 2); and
- encourage leavers to give feedback about their employment; this information could contribute to the monitoring process.

REDUNDANCY

19.11 A redundancy amounts to a dismissal and it is therefore unlawful for an employer to discriminate against or victimise a worker in a redundancy situation. Where an employer is planning dismissals because of redundancy, they should consult affected workers about ways of avoiding dismissals. They should also consult any recognised trade unions (and are required to consult with the unions if planning 20 or more redundancies in a 90-day period).

19.12 To avoid discrimination, an employer should, in consultation with any recognised trade union, adopt a selection matrix containing a number of separate selection criteria rather than just one selection criterion, to reduce the risk of any possible discriminatory impact.

19.13 Employers should ensure that the selection criteria are objective and do not discriminate directly or indirectly. Many of the selection criteria used in redundancy situations carry a risk of discrimination.

19.14 For example, 'last in, first out' may amount to indirect age discrimination against younger employees; indirect sex discrimination against women who may have shorter service due to time out for raising children; or indirect race discrimination where an employer might have only recently adopted policies that have had the effect of increasing the proportion of employees from ethnic minority backgrounds.

19.15 However, used as one criterion among many within a fair selection procedure, 'last in, first out' could be a proportionate means of achieving the legitimate aim of rewarding loyalty and creating a stable workforce. If it is the only or determinant selection criterion, or given disproportionate weight within the selection matrix, it could lead to discrimination.

Example: An employer wishing to make redundancies adopts a selection matrix which includes the following criteria: expertise/knowledge required for posts to be retained; disciplinary records; performance appraisals; attendance and length of service. Each person in the pool of employees who are potentially redundant is scored against each criterion from 1 to 4 points on a range of poor to excellent. There is provision in the matrix for deducting points for episodes of unauthorised absence in the prescribed period. Points are also added for length of service. Although length of service does have the potential to discriminate, in this redundancy selection process it is not obviously dominant or necessarily determinative of who will be selected for redundancy. In this context, length of service is likely to be an objectively justifiable criterion.

19.16 'Flexibility' – for example, willingness to relocate or to work unsocial hours, or ability to carry out a wide variety of tasks – may amount to discrimination because of (or arising from) disability or because of sex.

19.17 When setting criteria for redundancy selection, employers should consider whether any proposed criterion would adversely impact upon a disabled employee. If so, the employer will need to consider what reasonable adjustments will be necessary to avoid such discriminatory impact.

Example: A call centre re-tenders for a large contract and has to reduce its price to secure the work in the face of low-cost competition from overseas. The employer therefore decides that attendance records are a particularly important selection criterion for redundancy. This has the potential to disadvantage disabled employees who require additional time off for medical treatment. It is likely to be a reasonable adjustment to discount some disability-related sickness absence when assessing attendance as part of the redundancy selection exercise.

When should employers offer suitable alternative employment?

19.18 During a redundancy exercise, if alternative vacancies exist within the employer's organisation or with an associated employer, these should be offered to potentially redundant employees using criteria which do not unlawfully discriminate.

19.19 However, where there is a potentially redundant female employee on ordinary or additional maternity leave, she is entitled to be offered any suitable available vacancy with the employer, their successor or any associated employer. The offer must be of a new contract taking effect immediately on the ending of the worker's previous contract and must be such that:

- the work is suitable and appropriate for her to do; and
- the capacity, place of employment and other terms and conditions are not substantially less favourable than under the previous contract.

Example: A company decides to combine their head office and regional teams and create a 'centre of excellence' in Manchester. A new organisation structure is drawn up which involves a reduction in headcount. The company intends that all employees should have the opportunity to apply for posts in the new structure. Those unsuccessful at interview will be made redundant. At the time this is implemented, one of the existing members of the team is on ordinary maternity leave. As such, she has a priority right to be offered a suitable available vacancy in the new organisation without having to go through the competitive interview process.

APPENDICES

APPENDIX 1
THE MEANING OF DISABILITY

[4.158]
1. This Appendix is included to aid understanding about who is covered by the Act. Government guidance on determining questions relating to the definition of disability is also available from the Office of Disability Issues:
www.officefordisability.gov.uk/docs/wor/new/ea-guide.pdf

When is a person disabled?

2. A person has a disability if they have a physical or mental impairment, which has a substantial and long-term adverse effect on their ability to carry out normal day-to-day activities.

3. However, special rules apply to people with some conditions such as progressive conditions (see paragraph 19 of this Appendix) and some people are automatically deemed disabled for the purposes of the Act (see paragraph 18).

What about people who have recovered from a disability?

4. People who have had a disability within the definition are protected from discrimination even if they have since recovered, although those with past disabilities are not covered in relation to Part 12 (transport) and section 190 (improvements to let dwelling houses).

What does 'impairment' cover?

5. It covers physical or mental impairments. This includes sensory impairments, such as those affecting sight or hearing.

Are all mental impairments covered?

6. The term 'mental impairment' is intended to cover a wide range of impairments relating to mental functioning, including what are often known as learning disabilities.

What if a person has no medical diagnosis?

7. There is no need for a person to establish a medically diagnosed cause for their impairment. What it is important to consider is the effect of the impairment, not the cause.

What is a 'substantial' adverse effect?

8. **[s 212]** A substantial adverse effect is something which is more than a minor or trivial effect. The requirement that an effect must be substantial reflects the general understanding of disability as a limitation going beyond the normal differences in ability which might exist among people.

9. Account should also be taken of where a person avoids doing things which, for example, cause pain, fatigue or substantial social embarrassment; or because of a loss of energy and motivation.

10. An impairment may not directly prevent someone from carrying out one or more normal day-to-day activities, but it may still have a substantial adverse long-term effect on how they carry out those activities. For example, where an impairment causes pain or fatigue in performing normal day-to-day activities, the person may have the capacity to do something but suffer pain in doing so; or the impairment might make the activity more than usually fatiguing so that the person might not be able to repeat the task over a sustained period of time.

What is a 'long-term' effect?

11. A long-term effect of an impairment is one:
- which has lasted at least 12 months; or
- where the total period for which it lasts is likely to be at least 12 months; or
- which is likely to last for the rest of the life of the person affected.

12. Effects which are not long-term would therefore include loss of mobility due to a broken limb which is likely to heal within 12 months, and the effects of temporary infections, from which a person would be likely to recover within 12 months.

What if the effects come and go over a period of time?

13. If an impairment has had a substantial adverse effect on normal day-to-day activities but that effect ceases, the substantial effect is treated as continuing if it is likely to recur; that is, if it might well recur.

What are 'normal day-to-day activities'?

14. They are activities which are carried out by most men or women on a fairly regular and frequent basis. The term is not intended to include activities which are normal only for a particular person or group of people, such as playing a musical instrument, or participating in a sport to a professional standard, or performing a skilled or specialised task at work. However, someone who is affected in such a specialised way but is also affected in normal day-to-day activities would be covered by this part of the definition.

15. Day-to-day activities thus include – but are not limited to –activities such as walking, driving, using public transport, cooking, eating, lifting and carrying everyday objects, typing, writing (and taking exams), going to the toilet, talking, listening to conversations or music, reading, taking part in normal social interaction or forming social relationships, nourishing and caring for one's self. Normal day-to-day activities also encompass the activities which are relevant to working life.

What about treatment?

16. Someone with an impairment may be receiving medical or other treatment which alleviates or removes the effects (though not the impairment). In such cases, the treatment is ignored and the impairment is taken to have the effect it would have had without such treatment. This does not apply if substantial adverse effects are not likely to recur even if the treatment stops (that is, the impairment has been cured).

Does this include people who wear spectacles?

17. No. The sole exception to the rule about ignoring the effects of treatment is the wearing of spectacles or contact lenses. In this case, the effect while the person is wearing spectacles or contact lenses should be considered.

Are people who have disfigurements covered?

18. People with severe disfigurements are covered by the Act. They do not need to demonstrate that the impairment has a substantial adverse effect on their ability to carry out normal day-to-day activities. However, they do need to meet the long-term requirement.

Are there any other people who are automatically treated as disabled under the Act?

19. Anyone who has HIV, cancer or multiple sclerosis is automatically treated as disabled under the Act. In some circumstances, people who have a sight impairment are automatically treated as disabled under Regulations made under the Act.

What about people who know their condition is going to get worse over time?

20. Progressive conditions are conditions which are likely to change and develop over time. Where a person has a progressive condition they will be covered by the Act from the moment the condition leads to an impairment which has some effect on ability to carry out normal day-to-day activities, even though not a substantial effect, if that impairment might well have a substantial adverse effect on such ability in the future. This applies provided that the effect meets the long-term requirement of the definition.

APPENDIX 2
MONITORING – ADDITIONAL INFORMATION

WHAT TO MONITOR?

[4.159]
1. It is recommended that employers consider monitoring the list of areas below. This list is not exhaustive and an employer, depending on its size and resources, may wish to consider monitoring additional areas.

Recruitment

- Sources of applications for employment
- Applicants for employment
- Those who are successful or unsuccessful in the short-listing process
- Those who are successful or unsuccessful at test/assessment stage

- Those who are successful or unsuccessful at interview

During employment

- Workers in post
- Workers in post by type of job, location and grade
- Applicants for training
- Workers who receive training
- Applicants for promotion and transfer and success rates for each
- Time spent at a particular grade/level
- Workers who benefit or suffer detriment as a result of performance assessment procedures
- Workers involved in grievance procedures
- Workers who are the subject of disciplinary procedures

Termination of employment

- Workers who cease employment
- Dismissals for gross misconduct
- Dismissals for persistent misconduct
- Dismissals for poor performance
- Dismissals for sickness
- Redundancies
- Retirement
- Resignation
- Termination for other reasons

CONSIDERING CATEGORIES

2. It is recommended that employers ask job applicants and workers to select the group(s) they want to be associated with from a list of categories. The 2001/2011 census provides comprehensive data about the population in England, Scotland and Wales. This is supplemented by the Labour Force Survey and other survey statistics produced by the Office for National Statistics. Employers can therefore use categories which are compatible with the categories contained in these sources, for consistency.

3. Set out below are some of the issues to consider when monitoring particular protected characteristics. Please see the Commission's Non Statutory Guidance for further information.

Age

4. Monitoring age may not initially appear as controversial as some of the other protected characteristics.

The following age bands might provide a useful starting point for employers monitoring the age of job applicants and workers:

- 16–17
- 18–21
- 22–30
- 31–40
- 41–50
- 51–60
- 61–65
- 66–70
- 71+

Disability

5. Disclosing information about disability can be a particularly sensitive issue. Monitoring will be more effective if job applicants and workers feel comfortable about disclosing information about their disabilities. This is more likely to be the case if employers explain the purpose of monitoring and job applicants and workers believe that the employer genuinely values disabled people and is using the information gathered to create positive change. Asking questions about health or disability before the offer of a job is made or a person is placed in a pool of people to be offered a vacancy is not unlawful under the Act where the purpose of asking such questions is to monitor the diversity of applicants (see paragraphs 10.25 to 10.43).

Example: Through monitoring of candidates at the recruitment stage a company becomes aware that, although several disabled people applied for a post, none were short-listed for interview. On the basis of this information, they review the essential requirements for the post.

6. Some employers choose to monitor by broad type of disability to understand the barriers faced by people with different types of impairment.

Example: A large employer notices through monitoring that the organisation has been successful at retaining most groups of disabled people, but not people with mental health conditions. They act on this information by contacting a specialist organisation for advice about good practice in retaining people with mental health conditions.

Race

7. When employers gather data in relation to race, a decision should be made as to which ethnic categories to use. It is recommended that employers use the ethnic categories that were used in the 2001 census (or categories that match them very closely). If different categories are used, it may make it difficult to use the census data or other national surveys, such as the annual Labour Force Survey, as a benchmark (see also Chapter 18).

8. Subgroups are intended to provide greater choice to encourage people to respond. Sticking to broad headings may otherwise hide important differences between subgroups and the level of detail will provide employers with greater flexibility when analysing the data. Employers may wish to add extra categories to the recommended subcategories of ethnic categories. However, this should be considered carefully.

9. Employers should be aware that the way people classify themselves can change over time. It may therefore become necessary to change categories.

Religion and belief

10. Monitoring religion and belief may help employers understand workers' needs (for example, if they request leave for festivals) and ensure that staff turnover does not reflect a disproportionate number of people from specific religion or beliefs.

Sex

11. As well as the male and female categories, employers should consider whether to monitor for part-time working and for staff with caring responsibilities, including child-care, elder-care or care for a spouse or another family member. Both groups are predominantly women at a national level and are likely to be so for many employers as well.

Sexual orientation

12. Sexual orientation (and sexuality) may be considered to be a private issue. However, it is relevant in the workplace, particularly where discrimination and the application of equality policies, and other policies, are concerned. The way in which the question is asked is very important, particularly if employers are to ensure that the monitoring process does not create a further barrier.

13. The recommended way to ask job applicants and workers about their sexual orientation is outlined below:

What is your sexual orientation?

- Bisexual
- Gay man
- Gay woman/lesbian
- Heterosexual/straight
- Other
- Prefer not to say

14. Some employers, as an alternative, provide one option ('gay/lesbian') rather than the two options above, and then cross-reference the results of their data on gender in order to examine differences in experiences between gay men and gay woman.

15. It also acknowledges that some women identify themselves as gay rather than as lesbians. The option of 'other' provides an opportunity for staff to identify their sexual orientation in another way if the categories are not suitable.

16. Employers should note that transsexual or transgender status should not fall within the section on sexual orientation. It should instead have a section on its own (see paragraph 21 below).

17. In some monitoring exercises, for example, staff satisfaction surveys, it may be appropriate to ask a further question about how open an employee is about their sexual orientation:

If you are lesbian, gay or bisexual, are you open about your sexual orientation (Yes, Partially, No)

- At home
- With colleagues
- With your manager
- At work generally

The results from the above question may indicate wider organisational issues which need to be addressed.

Transgender status

18. Monitoring numbers of transsexual staff is a very sensitive area and opinion continues to be divided on this issue. While there is a need to protect an individual's right to privacy, without gathering some form of evidence, it may be difficult to monitor the impact of policies and procedures on transsexual people or employment patterns such as recruitment, training, promotion or leaving rates.

19. Because many transsexual people have had negative experiences in the workplace, many may be reluctant to disclose or may not trust their employers fully. (In order to obtain more reliable results, some employers have chosen to conduct monitoring through a neutral organisation under a guarantee of anonymity.)

20. If employers choose to monitor transsexual staff using their own systems, then privacy, confidentiality and anonymity should be paramount. For example, diversity statistics should not be linked to IT-based personnel records that indicate grade or job title, as the small number of transsexual workers in an organisation may be identified by these or other variables, compromising confidentiality.

21. Employers should note that it is important to recognise that transsexual people will usually identify as men or women, as well as transsexual people. In light of this, it is not appropriate to offer a choice between identifying as male, female or transsexual.

APPENDIX 3
MAKING REASONABLE ADJUSTMENTS TO WORK PREMISES – LEGAL CONSIDERATIONS

Introduction

[4.160]

1. In Chapter 6 it was explained that one of the situations in which a duty to make reasonable adjustments may arise is where a physical feature of premises occupied by an employer places a disabled worker at a substantial disadvantage compared with people who are not disabled. In such circumstances the employer must consider whether any reasonable steps can be taken to overcome that disadvantage. Making physical alterations to premises may be a reasonable step for an employer to have to take. This appendix addresses the issues of how leases and other legal obligations affect the duty to make reasonable adjustments to premises.

What happens if a binding obligation other than a lease prevents a building being altered?

2. An employer may be bound by the terms of an agreement or other legally binding obligation (for example, a mortgage, charge or restrictive covenant or, in Scotland, a feu disposition) under which they cannot alter the premises without someone else's consent.

3. **[Sch 21, para 2]** In these circumstances, the Act provides that it is always reasonable for the employer to have to request that consent, but that it is never reasonable for the employer to have to make an alteration before having obtained that consent.

What happens if a lease says that certain changes to premises cannot be made?

4. **[Sch 21, para 3]** Special provisions apply where an employer occupies premises under a lease, the terms of which prevent them from making an alteration to the premises.

5. In such circumstances, if the alteration is one which the employer proposes to make in order to comply with a duty of reasonable adjustment, the Act enables the lease to be read as if it provided:

- for the employer to make a written application to the landlord for that consent;
- for the landlord not to withhold the consent unreasonably;
- for the landlord to be able to give consent subject to reasonable conditions; and
- for the employer to make the alteration with the written consent of the landlord.

6. If the employer fails to make a written application to the landlord for consent to the alteration, the employer will not be able to rely upon the fact that the lease has a term preventing them from making alterations to the premises to defend their failure to make an alteration. In these circumstances, anything in the lease which prevents that alteration being made must be ignored in deciding whether it was reasonable for the employer to have made the alteration.

7. Whether withholding consent will be reasonable or not will depend on the specific circumstances.

8. For example, if a particular adjustment is likely to result in a substantial permanent reduction in the value of the landlord's interest in the premises, the landlord is likely to be acting reasonably in withholding consent. The landlord is also likely to be acting reasonably if it withholds consent because an adjustment would cause significant disruption or inconvenience to other tenants (for example, where the premises consist of multiple adjoining units).

9. A trivial or arbitrary reason would almost certainly be unreasonable. Many reasonable adjustments to premises will not harm the landlord's interests and so it would generally be unreasonable to withhold consent for them.

10. [Sch 21, para 5] In any legal proceedings on a claim involving a failure to make a reasonable adjustment, the disabled person concerned or the employer may ask the Employment Tribunal to direct that the landlord be made a party to the proceedings. The tribunal will grant that request if it is made before the hearing of the claim begins. It may refuse the request if it is made after the hearing of the claim begins. The request will not be granted if it is made after the tribunal has determined the claim.

11. Where the landlord has been made a party to the proceedings, the tribunal may determine whether the landlord has refused to consent to the alteration, or has consented subject to a condition, and in each case whether the refusal or condition was unreasonable.

12. If the tribunal finds that the refusal or condition is unreasonable it can:

- make an appropriate declaration;
- make an order authorising the employer to make a specified alteration (subject to any conditions); or
- order the landlord to pay compensation to the disabled person.

13. If the tribunal orders the landlord to pay compensation, it cannot also order the employer to do so.

What about the need to obtain statutory consent for some building changes?

14. An employer might have to obtain statutory consent before making adjustments involving changes to premises. Such consents include planning permission, Building Regulations approval (or a building warrant in Scotland), listed building consent, scheduled monument consent and fire regulations approval. The Act does not override the need to obtain such consents.

15. Employers should plan for and anticipate the need to obtain consent to make a particular adjustment. It might take time to obtain such consent, but it could be reasonable to make an interim or other adjustment – one that does not require consent – in the meantime.

16. Employers should remember that even where consent is not given for removing or altering a physical feature, they still have a duty to make all the adjustments that are reasonable to have to make to remove any substantial disadvantage faced by the disabled worker.

(Index and list of contacts omitted; see Part 5, Section F at **[5.61]**.*)*

[illegible] generally be [illegible] consent [illegible].

[illegible] ... the time it would take to make a particular adjustment ... consent ... [illegible] ... in the meantime.

[illegible] see Part [illegible] Section [illegible] of [illegible]

D. FINANCIAL CONDUCT AUTHORITY AND PRUDENTIAL REGULATION AUTHORITY

FINANCIAL CONDUCT AUTHORITY AND PRUDENTIAL REGULATION AUTHORITY HANDBOOKS

[4.161]

NOTES

The Financial Services Authority Handbook which appeared in previous editions of this work, has been split between the Financial Conduct Authority (FCA) and the Prudential Regulation Authority (PRA) to form two new Handbooks. The labels at the beginning of each provision "[FCA]" and/or "[PRA]" indicate whether the provision applies to FCA-regulated firms and/or PRA-regulated firms.

The material in this section is the revised Remuneration Code, introduced, with effect from 1 January 2011, in compliance with the requirements of Annex 1 to the EU Third Capital Requirements Directive (2010/76/EU). The Remuneration Code forms part of the Handbooks, within the section titled Senior Management Arrangements, Systems and Controls (abbreviated as SYSC).

The Code is reproduced including amendments made to it by the Senior Management Arrangements, Systems and Controls (Remuneration Code) (No 4) Instrument 2011 (FSA 2011/62) which came into effect on 1 January 2012. FSA 2011/62 amended SYSC 19A.3.54, SYSC 19A.3.55 and SYSC Annex 1, and inserts a new SYSC 19A.3.53A. It also added the definition "Third country 730k BIPRU firm" to the Glossary.

The style of the FCA and PRA Handbooks is that there is a Glossary of defined words and phrases, and words so defined are printed in italics within the Handbooks. For reasons of space the Glossary is not reproduced in full here, but a selection of the more important of the terms used in the sections of the Handbooks included in this work are reproduced.

The Handbook as a whole, including the Glossary can be accessed at www.fsahandbook.info. The status of the provisions of the Handbook reproduced here is that the requirements are mandatory for those employers to whom the remuneration policy is stated to apply; the letters 'R' and 'G' beside each section indicate whether the text is a Rule or Guidance. As to the coming into effect of the amended policy, see SYSC 19A.1.3-19A.1.5 and SYSC 19A Annex 1.

GLOSSARY (EXTRACTS)

[4.162]

NOTES

The definitions printed below apply to FCA-regulated firms and PRA-regulated firms.

Banking Consolidation Directive

the Directive of the European Parliament and the Council of 14 June 2006 relating to the taking up and pursuit of the business of credit institutions (No 2006/48/EC).

BIPRU

the Prudential sourcebook for Banks, Building Societies and Investment Firms.

BIPRU firm

has the meaning set out BIPRU 1.1.6 R (The definition of a BIPRU firm), which is in summary a *firm* that is:

(a) a *building society*; or
(b) a *bank*; or
(c) a *full scope BIPRU investment firm*; or
(d) a *BIPRU limited licence firm*; or
(e) a *BIPRU limited activity firm*;

but excluding *firms* of the type listed in BIPRU 1.1.7 R (Exclusion of certain types of *firm* from the definition of *BIPRU firm*).

employee

(1) (for all purposes except those in (2)) an individual:
 (a) who is employed or appointed by a *person* in connection with that *person's* business, whether under a contract of service or for services or otherwise; or
 (b) whose services, under an arrangement between that *person* and a third party, are placed at the disposal and under the control of that *person*;

 but excluding an *appointed representative* or a *tied agent* of that *person*.
(2) (for the purposes of:
 (a) COBS 11.7 (Personal account dealing);
 (aa) GEN 4 (Statutory status disclosure);
 (ab) GEN 6.1 (Payment of financial penalties);

(b) SUP 12 (Appointed representatives); and
(c) TC)

an individual:

(i) within (1); or
(ii) who is:
  (A) an *appointed representative* or, where applicable, a *tied agent* of the *person* referred to in (1); or
  (B) employed or appointed by an *appointed representative* or, where applicable, a *tied agent* of that *person*, whether under a contract of service or for services or otherwise, in connection with the business of the *appointed representative* or *tied agent* for which that *person* has accepted responsibility.

governing body

the board of *directors*, committee of management or other governing body of a *firm* or *recognised body*, including, in relation to a *sole trader*, the *sole trader*.

prudential context

(1) For the *FCA*, in relation to activities carried on by a *firm*, the context in which the activities have, or might reasonably be regarded as likely to have, a negative effect on:
(a) the integrity of the *UK financial system*; or
(b) the ability of the *firm* to meet either:
  (i) the 'fit and proper' test in *threshold condition* 5 (Suitability); or
  (ii) the applicable requirements and standards under the *regulatory system* relating to the *firm*'s financial resources.

(2) For the *PRA*, in relation to activities carried on by a *firm*, the context in which the activities have, or might reasonably be regarded as likely to have, a negative effect on:
(a) the safety and soundness of *PRA-authorised persons*; or
(b) the ability of the *firm* to meet either:
  (i) the 'fit and proper' test in *threshold condition* 5 (Suitability); or
  (ii) the applicable requirements and standards under the *regulatory system* relating to the *firm*'s financial resources.

Regulated Activities Order

the Financial Services and Markets Act 2000 (Regulated Activities) Order 2001 (SI 2001/544).

regulated activity

(A) in the PRA Handbook:

(in accordance with section 22 of the *Act* (Regulated Activities) any of the following activities specified in Part II of the *Regulated Activities Order* (Specified Activities):

(a) accepting deposits (article 5);
(aa) issuing electronic money (article 9B);
(b) effecting contracts of insurance (article 10(1));
(c) carrying out contracts of insurance (article 10(2));
(d) dealing in investments as principal (article 14);
(e) dealing in investments as agent (article 21);
(ea) bidding in emissions auctions (article 24A);
(f) arranging (bringing about) deals in investments (article 25(1));
(g) making arrangements with a view to transactions in investments (article 25(2));
(ga) arranging (bringing about) regulated mortgage contracts (article 25A(1));
(gb) making arrangements with a view to regulated mortgage contracts (article 25A(2));
(gc) arranging (bringing about) a home reversion plan (article 25B(1));
(gd) making arrangements with a view to a home reversion plan (article 25B(2));
(ge) arranging (bringing about) a home purchase plan (article 25C(1));
(gf) making arrangements with a view to a home purchase plan (article 25C(2));
(gg) operating a multilateral trading facility (article 25D);
(gh) arranging (bringing about) a regulated sale and rent back agreement (article 25E(1));
(gi) making arrangements with a view to a regulated sale and rent back agreement (article 25E(2));
(h) managing investments (article 37);
(ha) assisting in the administration and performance of a contract of insurance (article 39A);
(i) *safeguarding and administering investments* (article 40); for the purposes of the *permission* regime, this is sub-divided into:
  (i) *safeguarding and administration of assets (without arranging)*;
  (ii) arranging safeguarding and administration of assets;
(j) sending dematerialised instructions (article 45(1));
(k) causing dematerialised instructions to be sent (article 45(2));

(l) *establishing, operating or winding up a collective investment scheme* (article 51(1)(a)); for the purposes of the permission regime, this is sub-divided into:
  (i) *establishing, operating or winding up a regulated collective investment scheme*;
  (ii) *establishing, operating or winding up an unregulated collective investment scheme*;

(m) acting as trustee of an authorised unit trust scheme (article 51(1)(b));
(n) acting as the depositary or sole director of an open-ended investment company (article 51(1)(c));
(o) establishing, operating or winding up a stakeholder pension scheme (article 52(a));
(oa) providing *basic advice* on *stakeholder products* (article 52B);
(ob) establishing, operating or winding up a personal pension scheme (article 52(b));
(p) *advising on investments* (article 53); for the purposes of the *permission* regime, this is sub-divided into:
  (i) *advising on investments* (except pension transfers and pension opt-outs);
  (ii) *advising on pension transfers and pension opt-outs*;
(pa) advising on regulated mortgage contracts (article 53A);
(pb) advising on a home reversion plan (article 53B);
(pc) advising on a home purchase plan (article 53C);
(pd) advising on a regulated sale and rent back agreement (article 53D);
(q) *advising on syndicate participation at Lloyd's* (article 56);
(r) managing the underwriting capacity of a Lloyd's syndicate as a managing agent at Lloyd's (article 57);
(s) arranging deals in contracts of insurance written at Lloyd's (article 58);
(sa) entering into a regulated mortgage contract (article 61(1));
(sb) administering a regulated mortgage contract (article 61(2));
(sc) entering into a home reversion plan (article 63B(1));
(sd) administering a home reversion plan (article 63B(2));
(se) entering into a home purchase plan (article 63F(1));
(sf) administering a home purchase plan (article 63F(2));
(sg) entering into a regulated sale and rent back agreement (article 63J(1));
(sh) administering a regulated sale and rent back agreement (article 63J(2));
(si) *meeting of repayment claims* (article 63N(1)(a));
(sj) managing dormant account funds (including the investment of such funds) (article 63N(1)(b));
(t) entering as provider into a funeral plan contract (article 59);

(B) in the FCA Handbook:

as in (A) with the addition of

(ta) providing information in relation to a specified benchmark;
(tb) administering a specified benchmark;
which is carried on by way of business and, except for (ta) and (tb), relates to a specified investment applicable to that activity or, in the case of (l), (m), (n) and (o), is carried on in relation to property of any kind.
(u) agreeing to carry on a regulated activity (article 64);
which is carried on by way of business and relates to a specified investment applicable to that activity or, in the case of (l), (m), (n) and (o), is carried on in relation to property of any kind.

remuneration

any form of remuneration, including salaries, *discretionary pension benefits* and benefits of any kind. [**Note:** paragraph 23 of Annex V to the *Banking Consolidation Directive*]

Remuneration Code

SYSC 19A (Remuneration Code).

Remuneration Code staff

(for a *BIPRU firm* and a *third country BIPRU firm*) has the meaning given in SYSC 19A.3.4 R.

Remuneration principles proportionality rule

(in SYSC 19A) has the meaning given in SYSC 19A.3.3 R.

Third country BIPRU firm

an *overseas firm* that:

(a) is not an *EEA firm*;
(b) has its head office outside the *EEA*; and
(c) would be a *BIPRU firm* if it had been a *UK domestic firm*, it had carried on all its business in the *United Kingdom* and had obtained whatever authorisations for doing so are required under the *Act*.

Third country 730k BIPRU firm

an *overseas firm* that:

(a) is not an *EEA firm*;
(b) has its head office outside the *EEA*; and
(c) would be a *BIPRU 730k firm* if it had been a *UK domestic firm*, had carried on all its business in the *United Kingdom* and had obtained whatever authorisations for doing so as are required under the *Act*.

SYSC 19A.1 GENERAL APPLICATION AND PURPOSE

WHO? WHAT? WHERE?

[4.163]

SYSC 19A.1.1 R [FCA] [PRA]

(1) The *Remuneration Code* applies to a *BIPRU firm* and a *third country BIPRU firm*.
(2) In relation to a *third country BIPRU firm*, the *Remuneration Code* applies only in relation to activities carried on from an establishment in the United Kingdom.
(3) Otherwise, the *Remuneration Code* applies to a firm within (1) in the same way as SYSC 4.1.1 R (General Requirements).

SYSC 19A.1.2 G [FCA] [PRA]

Part 2 of SYSC 1 Annex 1 provides for the application of SYSC 4.1.1 R (General Requirements). In particular, and subject to the provisions on group risk systems and controls requirements in SYSC 12, this means that:

(1) in relation to what the *Remuneration Code* applies to, it:
    (a) applies in relation to *regulated activities*, activities that constitute *dealing in investments as principal* (disregarding the exclusion in article 15 of the *Regulated Activities Order* (Absence of holding out etc)), *ancillary activities* and (in relation to *MiFID business*) *ancillary services*;
    (b) applies with respect to the carrying on of *unregulated activities* in a *prudential context*; and
    (c) takes into account activities of other *group* members; and
(2) in relation to where the *Remuneration Code* applies, it applies in relation to:
    (a) a *firm's UK* activities;
    (b) a *firm's passported activities* carried on from a *branch* in another *EEA State*; and
    (c) a *UK domestic firm's* activities wherever they are carried on, in a *prudential context*.

WHEN?

SYSC 19A.1.3 R [FCA] [PRA]

A *firm* must apply the *remuneration* requirements in SYSC 19A.3 in relation to:

(1) *remuneration* awarded, whether pursuant to a contract or otherwise, on or after 1 January 2011;
(2) *remuneration* due on the basis of contracts concluded before 1 January 2011 which is awarded or paid on or after 1 January 2011; and
(3) *remuneration* awarded, but not yet paid, before 1 January 2011, for services provided in 2010.

[**Note:** article 3(2) of the Third Capital Requirements Directive (Directive 2010/76/EU)]

SYSC 19A.1.4 G [FCA] [PRA]

Subject to the requirements of SYSC 19A.1.5 R, in the *appropriate regulator's* view SYSC 19A.1.3 R does not require a *firm* to breach requirements of applicable contract or employment law.
[**Note:** recital 14 of the Third Capital Requirements Directive (Directive 2010/76/EU)]

SYSC 19A.1.5 R [FCA] [PRA]

(1) This *rule* applies to a *firm* that is unable to comply with the *Remuneration Code* because of an obligation it owes to a *Remuneration Code staff member* under a provision of an agreement made on or before 29 July 2010 (the "provision").
(2) A *firm* must take reasonable steps to amend or terminate the provision referred to in (1) in a way that enables it to comply with the *Remuneration Code* at the earliest opportunity.
(3) Until the provision referred to in (1) ceases to prevent the *firm* from complying with the *Remuneration Code*, the *firm* must adopt specific and effective arrangements, processes and mechanisms to manage the risks raised by the provision.

PURPOSE

SYSC 19A.1.6 G [FCA] [PRA]

(1) The aim of the *Remuneration Code* is to ensure that *firms* have risk-focused *remuneration* policies, which are consistent with and promote effective risk management and do not expose them to excessive risk. It expands upon the general organisational requirements in SYSC 4.

(2) The *Remuneration Code* implements the main provisions of the Third Capital Requirements Directive (Directive 2010/76/EU) which relate to *remuneration*. The Committee of European Banking Supervisors published Guidelines on Remuneration Policies and Practices on 10 December 2010. Provisions of the Third Capital Requirements Directive relating to Pillar 3 disclosures of information relating to *remuneration* have been implemented through amendments to BIPRU 11 (specifically the *rules* and *guidance* in BIPRU 11.5.18 R to BIPRU 11.5.21 G). Provisions of the Capital Requirements (Amendment) Regulations 2012 (SI 2012/917) together with the European Banking Authority's Guidelines to article 22(3) and (5) of the *Banking Consolidation Directive* relating to the collection of *remuneration* benchmarking information and *high earners* information have been implemented through SUP 16 Annex 33AR and SUP 16 Annex 34AR.

(3) [deleted]

NOTIFICATIONS TO THE APPROPRIATE REGULATOR

SYSC 19A.1.7 G [FCA] [PRA]

(1) The *Remuneration Code* does not contain specific notification requirements. However, general circumstances in which the *appropriate regulator* expects to be notified by *firms* of matters relating to their compliance with requirements under the *regulatory system* are set out in SUP 15.3 (General notification requirements).

(2) In particular, in relation to *remuneration* matters such circumstances should take into account *unregulated activities* as well as *regulated activities* and the activities of other members of a *group* and would include each of the following:
   (a) significant breaches of the *Remuneration Code*, including any breach of a *rule* to which the detailed provisions on voiding and recovery in SYSC 19A Annex 1 apply;
   (b) any proposed *remuneration* policies, procedures or practices which could:
      (i) have a significant adverse impact on the *firm's* reputation; or
      (ii) affect the *firm's* ability to continue to provide adequate services to its *customers* and which could result in serious detriment to a *customer* of the *firm*; or
      (iii) result in serious financial consequences to the *financial system* or to other *firms*;
   (c) any proposed changes to *remuneration* policies, practices or procedures which could have a significant impact on the *firm's* risk profile or resources;
   (d) fraud, errors and other irregularities described in SUP 15.3.17 R which may suggest weaknesses in, or be motivated by, the *firm's remuneration* policies, procedures or practices.

(3) Such notifications should be made immediately the *firm* becomes aware, or has information which reasonably suggests such circumstances have occurred, may have occurred or may occur in the foreseeable future.

INDIVIDUAL GUIDANCE

SYSC 19A.1.8 G [FCA]

The *FCA's* policy on individual *guidance* is set out in SUP 9. *Firms* should in particular note the policy on what the *FCA* considers to be a reasonable request for *guidance* (see SUP 9.2.5 G). For example, where a *firm* is seeking *guidance* on a proposed *remuneration* structure the *FCA* will expect the *firm* to provide a detailed analysis of how the structure complies with the *Remuneration Code*, including the general requirement for *remuneration* policies, procedures and practices to be consistent with and promote sound and effective risk management.

SYSC 19A.2 GENERAL REQUIREMENT

REMUNERATION POLICIES MUST PROMOTE EFFECTIVE RISK MANAGEMENT

[4.164]
SYSC 19A.2.1 R [FCA] [PRA]

A *firm* must establish, implement and maintain *remuneration* policies, procedures and practices that are consistent with and promote sound and effective risk management.
[**Note:** Article 22(1) of the *Banking Consolidation Directive*]

SYSC 19A.2.2 G [FCA] [PRA]

(1) If a *firm's remuneration* policy is not aligned with effective risk management it is likely that *employees* will have incentives to act in ways that might undermine effective risk management.

(2) The *Remuneration Code* covers all aspects of *remuneration* that could have a bearing on effective risk management including salaries, bonuses, long-term incentive plans, options, hiring bonuses, severance packages and pension arrangements. In applying the *Remuneration Code*, a *firm* should have regard to applicable good practice on *remuneration* and corporate governance, such as guidelines on executive contracts and severance produced by the Association of British Insurers (ABI) and the National Association of Pension Funds (NAPF). In considering the risks arising from its *remuneration* policies, a *firm* will also need to take into account its statutory duties in relation to equal pay and non-discrimination.

(3) As with other aspects of a *firm's* systems and controls, in accordance with SYSC 4.1.2 R *remuneration* policies, procedures and practices must be comprehensive and proportionate to the nature, scale and complexity of the *common platform firm's* activities. What a *firm* must do in order to comply with the *Remuneration Code* will therefore vary. For example, while the *Remuneration Code* refers to a *firm's remuneration* committee and risk management function, it may be appropriate for the *governing body* of a smaller *firm* to act as the *remuneration* committee, and for the *firm* not to have a separate risk management function.

(4) The principles in the *Remuneration Code* are used by the *appropriate regulator* to assess the quality of a *firm's remuneration* policies and whether they encourage excessive risk-taking by a *firm's employees*.

(5) The *appropriate regulator* may also ask *remuneration* committees to provide the *appropriate regulator* with evidence of how well the *firm's remuneration* policies meet the *Remuneration Code's* principles, together with plans for improvement where there is a shortfall. The *appropriate regulator* also expects relevant *firms* to use the principles in assessing their exposure to risks arising from their *remuneration* policies as part of the *internal capital adequacy assessment process (ICAAP)*.

(6) The *Remuneration Code* is principally concerned with the risks created by the way *remuneration* arrangements are structured, not with the absolute amount of *remuneration*, which is generally a matter for *firms' remuneration* committees.

SYSC 19A.2.3 G [FCA] [PRA]

(1) The specific *remuneration* requirements in this chapter may apply only in relation to certain categories of *employee*. But the *appropriate regulator* would expect *firms*, in complying with the *Remuneration Code general requirement*, to apply certain principles on a *firm*-wide basis.

(2) In particular, the *appropriate regulator* considers that *firms* should apply the principle relating to guaranteed variable *remuneration* on a *firm*-wide basis (Remuneration Principle 12(c); SYSC 19A.3.40 R to SYSC 19A.3.43 G).

(3) The *appropriate regulator* would also expect *firms* to apply at least the principles relating to risk management and risk tolerance (Remuneration Principle 1); supporting business strategy, objectives, values and long-term interests of the firm (Remuneration Principle 2); conflicts of interest (Remuneration Principle 3); governance (Remuneration Principle 4); risk adjustment (Remuneration Principle 8); pension policy (Remuneration Principle 9); personal investment strategies (Remuneration Principle 10); payments related to early termination (Remuneration Principle 12(e)) and deferral (Remuneration Principle 12(g)) on a *firm*-wide basis.

RECORD-KEEPING

SYSC 19A.2.4 G [FCA] [PRA]

In line with the record-keeping requirements in SYSC 9, a *firm* should ensure that its *remuneration* policies, practices and procedures are clear and documented. Such policies, practices and procedures would include performance appraisal processes and decisions.

INTERPRETATION OF REFERENCES TO REMUNERATION

SYSC 19A.2.5 R [FCA] [PRA]

(1) In this chapter references to *remuneration* include *remuneration* paid, provided or awarded by any *person* to the extent that it is paid, provided or awarded in connection with *employment* by a *firm*.

(2) Paragraph (1) is without prejudice to the meaning of *remuneration* elsewhere in the *Handbook*.

SYSC 19A.2.6 G [FCA] [PRA]

Remuneration includes, for example, payments made by a seconding organisation which is not subject to the *Remuneration Code* to a secondee in respect of their *employment* by a *firm* which is subject to the *Remuneration Code*.

SYSC 19A.3 REMUNERATION PRINCIPLES FOR BANKS, BUILDING SOCIETIES AND INVESTMENT FIRMS

APPLICATION: GROUPS

[4.165]
SYSC 19A.3.1 R [FCA] [PRA]

(1) A *firm* must apply the requirements of this section at *group*, *parent undertaking* and *subsidiary undertaking* levels, including those *subsidiaries* established in a country or territory which is not an *EEA State*.

(2) Paragraph (1) does not limit SYSC 12.1.13 R (2)(dA) (which relates to the application of the *Remuneration Code* within *UK* consolidation groups and *non-EEA sub-groups*).

[**Note:** Paragraph 23 (final, unnumbered point) of Annex V to the *Banking Consolidation Directive*]

SYSC 19A.3.2 G [FCA] [PRA]

SYSC 12.1.13 R (2)(dA) requires the *firm* to ensure that the risk management processes and internal control mechanisms at the level of any *UK consolidation group* or *non-EEA sub-group* of which a *firm* is a member comply with the obligations set out in this section on a consolidated (or sub-consolidated) basis. In the *appropriate regulator's* view, the requirement to apply this section at *group*, *parent undertaking* and *subsidiary undertaking* levels (as provided for in SYSC 19A.3.1 R (1)) is in line with the requirements in article 73(3) of the *Banking Consolidation Directive* concerning the application of systems and controls requirements to *groups* (as implemented in SYSC 12.1.13 R).

APPLICATION: CATEGORIES OF STAFF AND PROPORTIONALITY

SYSC 19A.3.3 R [FCA] [PRA]

(1) This section applies in relation to *Remuneration Code staff*, except as set out in (3).

(2) When establishing and applying the total *remuneration* policies for *Remuneration Code staff*, a *firm* must comply with this section in a way and to the extent that is appropriate to its size, internal organisation and the nature, the scope and the complexity of its activities (the *remuneration principles proportionality rule*).

(3) Paragraphs (1) and (2) do not apply to the requirement for significant *firms* to have a *remuneration* committee (SYSC 19A.3.12 R).

[**Note:** Paragraph 23 of Annex V to the *Banking Consolidation Directive*]
[**Note:** In addition, the *PRA* has set out information on the division of *firms* into categories for the purpose of providing a framework for the operation of the *remuneration principles proportionality rule*.]
[**Note:** In addition to the *guidance* in this section which relates to the *remuneration principles proportionality rule*, the *FSA* gave *guidance* on the division of *firms* into categories for the purpose of providing a framework for the operation of the *remuneration principles proportionality rule*. This *guidance* was published in Policy Statement 10/20 Revising the Remuneration Code and is available at www.fca.org.uk/your-fca.]

SYSC 19A.3.4 R [FCA] [PRA]

Remuneration Code staff comprises categories of staff including senior management, risk takers, staff engaged in control functions and any *employee* receiving total remuneration that takes them into the same *remuneration* bracket as senior management and risk takers, whose professional activities have a material impact on the *firm's* risk profile.
[**Note:** Paragraph 23 of Annex V to the *Banking Consolidation Directive*]

SYSC 19A.3.5 R [FCA] [PRA]

A *firm* must:

(1) maintain a record of its *Remuneration Code staff* in accordance with the general record-keeping requirements (SYSC 9); and

(2) take reasonable steps to ensure that its *Remuneration Code staff* understand the implications of their status as such, including the potential for *remuneration* which does not comply with certain requirements of the *Remuneration Code* to be rendered void and recoverable by the *firm*.

SYSC 19A.3.6 G [FCA] [PRA]

(1) In the *appropriate regulator's* view:

(a) a *firm's* staff includes its *employees*;

(b) a *person* who performs a *significant influence function* for, or is a *senior manager* of, a *firm* would normally be expected to be part of the *firm's Remuneration Code staff*;

(c) the table in (2) provides a non-exhaustive list of examples of key positions that should, subject to (d), be within a *firm's* definition of staff who are risk takers

(d) *firms* should consider how the examples in the table in (2) apply in relation to their own organisational structure (as the description of suggested business lines in the first row may be most appropriate to a *firm* which *deals on its own account* to a significant extent);

(e) *firms* may find it useful to set their own metrics to identify their risk takers based, for example, on trading limits; and

(f) a *firm* should treat a *person* as being *Remuneration Code staff* in relation to *remuneration* in respect of a given performance year if they were *Remuneration Code staff* for any part of that year.

[**Note:** The *FSA* gave *guidance* on the application of particular rules on *remuneration* structures in relation to individuals who are *Remuneration Code staff* for only part of a given performance year. This *guidance* was published in Policy Statement 10/20 Revising the Remuneration Code and is available at www.fca.org.uk/your-fca.]

(2)

High-level category	Suggested business lines
Heads of significant business lines (including regional heads) and any individuals or groups within their control who have a material impact on the *firm's* risk profile	Fixed income
	Foreign exchange
	Commodities
	Securitisation
	Sales areas
	Investment banking (including mergers and acquisitions advisory)
	Commercial banking
	Equities
	Structured finance
	Lending quality
	Trading areas
	Research
Heads of support and control functions and other individuals within their control who have a material impact on the *firm's* risk profile	Credit/market/ operational risk
	Legal
	Treasury controls
	Human resources
	Compliance
	Internal audit

REMUNERATION PRINCIPLE 1: RISK MANAGEMENT AND RISK TOLERANCE

SYSC 19A.3.7 R [FCA] [PRA]

A *firm* must ensure that its *remuneration* policy is consistent with and promotes sound and effective risk management and does not encourage risk-taking that exceeds the level of tolerated risk of the

firm.
[**Note:** Paragraph 23(a) of Annex V to the *Banking Consolidation Directive*]

REMUNERATION PRINCIPLE 2: SUPPORTING BUSINESS STRATEGY, OBJECTIVES, VALUES AND LONG-TERM INTERESTS OF THE FIRM

SYSC 19A.3.8 R [FCA] [PRA]

A *firm* must ensure that its *remuneration* policy is in line with the business strategy, objectives, values and long-term interests of the *firm.*
[**Note:** Paragraph 23(b) of Annex V to the *Banking Consolidation Directive*]

REMUNERATION PRINCIPLE 3: AVOIDING CONFLICTS OF INTEREST

SYSC 19A.3.9 R [FCA] [PRA]

A *firm* must ensure that its *remuneration* policy includes measures to avoid conflicts of interest.
[**Note:** Paragraph 23(b) of Annex V to the *Banking Consolidation Directive*]

REMUNERATION PRINCIPLE 4: GOVERNANCE

SYSC 19A.3.10 R [FCA] [PRA]

A *firm* must ensure that its *governing body* in its *supervisory function* adopts and periodically reviews the general principles of the *remuneration* policy and is responsible for its implementation.
[**Note:** Paragraph 23(c) of Annex V to the *Banking Consolidation Directive* and Standard 1 of the *FSB Compensation Standards*]

SYSC 19A.3.11 R [FCA] [PRA]

A *firm* must ensure that the implementation of the *remuneration* policy is, at least annually, subject to central and independent internal review for compliance with policies and procedures for *remuneration* adopted by the *governing body* in its *supervisory function.*
[**Note:** Paragraph 23(d) of Annex V to the *Banking Consolidation Directive* and Standard 1 of the *FSB Compensation Standards*]

SYSC 19A.3.12 R [FCA] [PRA]

(1) A *firm* that is significant in terms of its size, internal organisation and the nature, the scope and the complexity of its activities must establish a *remuneration* committee.
(2) The *remuneration* committee must be constituted in a way that enables it to exercise competent and independent judgment on *remuneration* policies and practices and the incentives created for managing risk, capital and liquidity.
(3) The chairman and the members of the *remuneration* committee must be members of the *governing body* who do not perform any executive function in the *firm.*
(4) The *remuneration* committee must be responsible for the preparation of decisions regarding *remuneration*, including those which have implications for the risk and risk management of the *firm* and which are to be taken by the *governing body* in its *supervisory function.*
(5) When preparing such decisions, the *remuneration* committee must take into account the long-term interests of shareholders, investors and other stakeholders in the *firm.*

[**Note:** Paragraph 24 of Annex V of the *Banking Consolidation Directive* and Standard 1 of the *FSB Compensation Standards*]
[**Note:** The *guidance* referred to in the Note to SYSC 19A.3.3 R also gives *guidance* on proportionality in relation to *remuneration* committees.]

SYSC 19A.3.13 G [FCA] [PRA]

(1) A *firm* should be able to demonstrate that its decisions are consistent with an assessment of its financial condition and future prospects. In particular, practices by which *remuneration* is paid for potential future revenues whose timing and likelihood remain uncertain should be evaluated carefully and the *governing body* or *remuneration* committee (or both) should work closely with the *firm's* risk function in evaluating the incentives created by its *remuneration* system.
(2) The *governing body* and any *remuneration* committee are responsible for ensuring that the *firm's remuneration* policy complies with the *Remuneration Code* and where relevant should take into account relevant guidance, such as that issued by the Basel Committee on Banking Supervision, the International Association of Insurance Supervisors (IAIS) and the International Organization of Securities Commissions (IOSCO).
(3) The periodic review of the implementation of the *remuneration* policy should assess compliance with the *Remuneration Code.*
(4) Guidance on what the *supervisory function* might involve is set out in SYSC 4.3.3 G.

REMUNERATION PRINCIPLE 5: CONTROL FUNCTIONS

SYSC 19A.3.14 R [FCA] [PRA]

A *firm* must ensure that *employees* engaged in control functions:

(1) are independent from the business units they oversee;
(2) have appropriate authority; and
(3) are *remunerated*:
  (a) adequately to attract qualified and experienced staff; and
  (b) in accordance with the achievement of the objectives linked to their functions, independent of the performance of the business areas they control.

[**Note:** Paragraph 23(e) of Annex V to the *Banking Consolidation Directive* and Standard 2 of the *FSB Compensation Standards*]

SYSC 19A.3.15 E [FCA] [PRA]

(1) A *firm's* risk management and compliance functions should have appropriate input into setting the *remuneration* policy for other business areas. The procedures for setting *remuneration* should allow risk and compliance functions to have significant input into the setting of individual *remuneration* awards where those functions have concerns about the behaviour of the individuals concerned or the riskiness of the business undertaken.
(2) Contravention of (1) may be relied on as tending to establish contravention of the *rule* on *employees* engaged in control functions having appropriate authority (SYSC 19A.3.14 R (2)).

SYSC 19A.3.16 R [FCA] [PRA]

A *firm* must ensure that the *remuneration* of the senior officers in risk management and compliance functions is directly overseen by the *remuneration* committee referred to in SYSC 19A.3.12 R, or, if such a committee has not been established, by the governing body in its *supervisory function*.

[**Note:** Paragraph 23(f) of Annex V to the *Banking Consolidation Directive*]

SYSC 19A.3.17 G [FCA] [PRA]

(1) This Remuneration Principle is designed to manage the conflicts of interest which might arise if other business areas had undue influence over the *remuneration* of *employees* within control functions. Conflicts of interest can easily arise when *employees* are involved in the determination of *remuneration* for their own business area. Where these could arise they need to be managed by having in place independent roles for control functions (including, notably, risk management and compliance) and human resources. It is good practice to seek input from a *firm's* human resources function when setting *remuneration* for other business areas.
(2) The need to avoid undue influence is particularly important where *employees* from the control functions are embedded in other business areas. This Remuneration Principle does not prevent the views of other business areas being sought as an appropriate part of the assessment process.
(3) The *appropriate regulator* would generally expect the ratio of the potential variable component of *remuneration* to the fixed component of *remuneration* to be significantly lower for *employees* in risk management and compliance functions than for *employees* in other business areas whose potential bonus is a significant proportion of their *remuneration*. *Firms* should nevertheless ensure that the total *remuneration* package offered to those *employees* is sufficient to attract and retain staff with the skills, knowledge and expertise to discharge those functions. The requirement that the method of determining the *remuneration* of *relevant persons* involved in the compliance function must not compromise their objectivity or be likely to do so also applies (see SYSC 6.1.4 R (4)).

REMUNERATION PRINCIPLE 6: REMUNERATION AND CAPITAL

SYSC 19A.3.18 R [FCA] [PRA]

A *firm* must ensure that total variable *remuneration* does not limit the *firm's* ability to strengthen its capital base.

[**Note:** Paragraph 23(i) of Annex V to the *Banking Consolidation Directive* and Standard 3 of the *FSB Compensation Standards*]

SYSC 19A.3.19 G [FCA] [PRA]

This Remuneration Principle underlines the link between a *firm's* variable *remuneration* costs and the need to manage its capital base, including forward-looking capital planning measures. Where a *firm* needs to strengthen its capital base, its variable *remuneration* arrangements should be sufficiently flexible to allow it to direct the necessary resources towards capital building.

REMUNERATION PRINCIPLE 7: EXCEPTIONAL GOVERNMENT INTERVENTION

SYSC 19A.3.20 R [FCA] [PRA]

A *firm* that benefits from exceptional government intervention must ensure that:

(1) variable *remuneration* is strictly limited as a percentage of net revenues when it is inconsistent with the maintenance of a sound capital base and timely exit from government support;

(2) it restructures *remuneration* in a manner aligned with sound risk management and long-term growth, including when appropriate establishing limits to the *remuneration* of *senior personnel*; and

(3) no variable *remuneration* is paid to its *senior personnel* unless this is justified.

[**Note:** Paragraph 23(k) of Annex V to the *Banking Consolidation Directive* and Standard 10 of the *FSB Compensation Standards*]

SYSC 19A.3.21 G [FCA] [PRA]

The *appropriate regulator* would normally expect it to be appropriate for the ban on paying variable *remuneration* to *senior personnel* of a *firm* that benefits from exceptional government intervention to apply only in relation to *senior personnel* who were in office at the time that the intervention was required.

REMUNERATION PRINCIPLE 8: PROFIT-BASED MEASUREMENT AND RISK ADJUSTMENT

SYSC 19A.3.22 R [FCA] [PRA]

(1) A *firm* must ensure that any measurement of performance used to calculate variable *remuneration* components or pools of variable *remuneration* components:

  (a) includes adjustments for all types of current and future risks and takes into account the cost and quantity of the capital and the liquidity required; and

  (b) takes into account the need for consistency with the timing and likelihood of the firm receiving potential future revenues incorporated into current earnings.

(2) A *firm* must ensure that the allocation of variable *remuneration* components within the *firm* also takes into account all types of current and future risks.

[**Note:** Paragraph 23(n) of Annex V to the *Banking Consolidation Directive* and Standard 4 of the *FSB Compensation Standards*]

SYSC 19A.3.23 G [FCA] [PRA]

(1) This Remuneration Principle stresses the importance of risk adjustment in measuring performance, and the importance within that process of applying judgment and common sense. A *firm* should ask the risk management function to validate and assess risk-adjustment techniques, and to attend a meeting of the *governing body* or *remuneration* committee for this purpose.

(2) A number of risk-adjustment techniques and measures are available, and a *firm* should choose those most appropriate to its circumstances. Common measures include those based on economic profit or economic capital. Whichever technique is chosen, the full range of future risks should be covered. The *appropriate regulator* expects a *firm* to be able to provide it with details of all adjustments that the *firm* has made under a formulaic approach.

(3) The *appropriate regulator* expects that a *firm* will apply qualitative judgments and common sense in the final decision about the performance-related components of variable *remuneration* pools.

(4) A *firm's governing body* (or *remuneration* committee where appropriate) should take the lead in determining the measures to be used. It should offer the appropriate checks and balances to prevent inappropriate manipulation of the measures used. It should consult closely and frequently with the *firm's* risk management functions, in particular those relating to operational, market, credit and liquidity risk.

SYSC 19A.3.24 G [FCA] [PRA]

(1) Long-term incentive plans should be treated as pools of variable *remuneration*. Many common measures of performance for long-term incentive plans, such as earnings per *share* (EPS), are not adjusted for longer-term risk factors. Total shareholder return (TSR), another common measure, includes in its measurement dividend distributions, which can also be based on unadjusted earnings data. If incentive plans mature within a two to four year period and are based on EPS or TSR, strategies can be devised to boost EPS or TSR during the life of the plan, to the detriment of the true longer-term health of a *firm*. For example, increasing leverage is a technique which can be used to boost EPS and TSR. *Firms* should take account of these factors when developing risk-adjustment methods.

(2) *Firms* that have long-term incentive plans should structure them with vesting subject to appropriate performance conditions, and at least half of the award vesting after not less than five years and the remainder after not less than three years.

(3) Long-term incentive plan awards may be included in the calculation of the deferred portion of variable *remuneration* only if upside incentives are adequately balanced by downside adjustments. The valuation of the award should be based on its value when the award is granted, and determined using an appropriate technique.

SYSC 19A.3.25 R [FCA] [PRA]

Assessments of financial performance used to calculate variable *remuneration* components or pools of variable *remuneration* components must be based principally on profits.

SYSC 19A.3.26 G [FCA] [PRA]

(1) Performance measures based primarily on revenues or turnover are unlikely to pay sufficient regard to the quality of business undertaken or services provided. Profits are a better measure provided they are adjusted for risk, including future risks not adequately captured by accounting profits.

(2) Management accounts should provide profit data at such levels within the *firm's* structure as to enable a *firm* to see as accurate a picture of contributions of relevant staff to a *firm's* performance as is reasonably practicable. If revenue or turnover is used as a component in performance assessment, processes should be in place to ensure that the quality of business undertaken or services provided and their appropriateness for *clients* are taken into account.

SYSC 19A.3.27 R [FCA] [PRA]

A *firm* must ensure that its total variable *remuneration* is generally considerably contracted where subdued or negative financial performance of the *firm* occurs, taking into account both current *remuneration* and reductions in payouts of amounts previously earned.

[**Note:** Paragraph 23(q) of Annex V to the *Banking Consolidation Directive* and Standard 5 of the *FSB Compensation Standards*]

SYSC 19A.3.28 G [FCA] [PRA]

Where a *firm* makes a loss the *appropriate regulator* would generally expect no variable *remuneration* to be awarded. Variable *remuneration* may nevertheless be justified, for example, to incentivise *employees* involved in new business ventures which could be loss-making in their early stages.

REMUNERATION PRINCIPLE 9: PENSION POLICY

SYSC 19A.3.29 R [FCA] [PRA]

A *firm* must ensure that:

(1) its pension policy is in line with its business strategy, objectives, values and long-term interests;

(2) when an *employee* leaves the *firm* before retirement, any *discretionary pension benefits* are held by the *firm* for a period of five years in the form of instruments referred to in SYSC 19A.3.47 R (1); and

(3) in the case of an *employee* reaching retirement, *discretionary pension benefits* are paid to the *employee* in the form of instruments referred to in SYSC 19A.3.47 R (1) and subject to a five-year retention period.

[**Note:** Paragraph 23(r) of Annex V to the *Banking Consolidation Directive*]

REMUNERATION PRINCIPLE 10: PERSONAL INVESTMENT STRATEGIES

SYSC 19A.3.30 R [FCA] [PRA]

(1) A *firm* must ensure that its *employees* undertake not to use personal hedging strategies or *remuneration*- or liability-related *contracts of insurance* to undermine the risk alignment effects embedded in their *remuneration* arrangements.

(2) A *firm* must maintain effective arrangements designed to ensure that *employees* comply with their undertaking.

[**Note:** Paragraph 23(s) of Annex V to the *Banking Consolidation Directive* and Standard 14 of the *FSB Compensation Standards*]

SYSC 19A.3.31 G [FCA] [PRA]

In the *appropriate regulator's* view, circumstances in which a *person* will be using a personal hedging strategy include entering into an arrangement with a third party under which the third party will make payments, directly or indirectly, to that *person* that are linked to or commensurate with the amounts by which the *person's remuneration* is subject to reductions.

REMUNERATION PRINCIPLE 11: AVOIDANCE OF THE REMUNERATION CODE

SYSC 19A.3.32 R [FCA] [PRA]

A *firm* must ensure that variable *remuneration* is not paid through vehicles or methods that facilitate the avoidance of the *Remuneration Code*.

[**Note:** Paragraph 23(t) of Annex V to the *Banking Consolidation Directive*]

REMUNERATION PRINCIPLE 12: REMUNERATION STRUCTURES — INTRODUCTION

SYSC 19A.3.33 G [FCA] [PRA]

Remuneration Principle 12 consists of a series of *rules*, *evidential provisions* and *guidance* relating to *remuneration* structures.

SYSC 19A.3.34 G [FCA] [PRA]

(1) Taking account of the *remuneration principles proportionality rule*, the *appropriate regulator* does not generally consider it necessary for a firm to apply the rules referred to in (2) where, in relation to an individual ('X'), both the following conditions are satisfied:
  (a) Condition 1 is that X's variable *remuneration* is no more than 33% of total *remuneration*; and
  (b) Condition 2 is that X's total *remuneration* is no more than £500,000.

(2) The *rules* referred to in (1) are those relating to:
  (a) guaranteed variable *remuneration* (SYSC 19A.3.40 R);
  (b) retained *shares* or other instruments (SYSC 19A.3.47 R);
  (c) deferral (SYSC 19A.3.49 R); and
  (d) performance adjustment (SYSC 19A.3.51 R).

[**Note:**The *FSA* also gave *guidance* on the application of certain *rules* on *remuneration* structures in relation to individuals who are *Remuneration Code staff* for only part of a given performance year. This guidance was published in Policy Statement 10/20 Revising the Remuneration Code and is available at www.fca.org.uk/your-fca.]

REMUNERATION PRINCIPLE 12(A): REMUNERATION STRUCTURES — GENERAL REQUIREMENT

SYSC 19A.3.35 R [FCA] [PRA]

A *firm* must ensure that the structure of an *employee's remuneration* is consistent with and promotes effective risk management.

REMUNERATION PRINCIPLE 12(B): REMUNERATION STRUCTURES — ASSESSMENT OF PERFORMANCE

SYSC 19A.3.36 R [FCA] [PRA]

A *firm* must ensure that where *remuneration* is performance-related:

(1) the total amount of *remuneration* is based on a combination of the assessment of the performance of:
  (a) the individual;
  (b) the business unit concerned; and
  (c) the overall results of the *firm*; and

(2) when assessing individual performance, financial as well as non-financial criteria are taken into account.

[**Note:** Paragraph 23(g) of Annex V to the *Banking Consolidation Directive* and Standard 6 of the *FSB Compensation Standards*]

SYSC 19A.3.37 G [FCA] [PRA]

Non-financial performance metrics should form a significant part of the performance assessment process and should include adherence to effective risk management and compliance with the *regulatory system* and with relevant overseas regulatory requirements. Poor performance as assessed by non-financial metrics such as poor risk management or other behaviours contrary to *firm* values can pose significant risks for a *firm* and should, as appropriate, override metrics of financial performance. The performance assessment process and the importance of non-financial assessment factors in the process should be clearly explained to relevant *employees* and implemented. A balanced scorecard can be a good technique.

SYSC 19A.3.38 R [FCA] [PRA]

A *firm* must ensure that the assessment of performance is set in a multi-year framework in order to ensure that the assessment process is based on longer-term performance and that the actual payment of performance-based components of *remuneration* is spread over a period which takes account of the underlying business cycle of the *firm* and its business risks.

[**Note:** Paragraph 23(h) of Annex V to the *Banking Consolidation Directive*]

SYSC 19A.3.39 G [FCA] [PRA]

The requirement for assessment of performance to be in a multi-year framework reflects the fact that profits from a *firm's* activities can be volatile and subject to cycles. The financial performance of *firms* and individual *employees* can be exaggerated as a result. Performance assessment on a moving average of results can be a good way of meeting this requirement. However, other techniques such as good quality risk adjustment and deferral of a sufficiently large proportion of *remuneration* may also be useful.

REMUNERATION PRINCIPLE 12(C): REMUNERATION STRUCTURES — GUARANTEED VARIABLE REMUNERATION

SYSC 19A.3.40 R [FCA] [PRA]

A *firm* must not award, pay or provide guaranteed variable *remuneration* unless it:

(1) is exceptional;
(2) occurs in the context of hiring new *Remuneration Code staff*; and
(3) is limited to the first year of service.

[**Note:** Paragraph 23(j) of Annex V to the *Banking Consolidation Directive* and Standard 11 of the *FSB Compensation Standards*]

SYSC 19A.3.41 E [FCA] [PRA]

(1) A *firm* should not award, pay or provide guaranteed variable *remuneration* in the context of hiring new *Remuneration Code staff* (X) unless:
   (a) it has taken reasonable steps to ensure that the *remuneration* is not more generous in either its amount or terms (including any deferral or retention periods) than the variable *remuneration* awarded or offered by X's previous employer; and
   (b) it is subject to appropriate performance adjustment requirements.

(2) Contravention of (1) may be relied on as tending to establish contravention of the *rule* on guaranteed variable *remuneration* (SYSC 19A.3.40 R).

SYSC 19A.3.42 G [FCA] [PRA]

Guaranteed variable *remuneration* should be subject to the same deferral criteria as other forms of variable *remuneration* awarded by the *firm*.

SYSC 19A.3.43 G [FCA] [PRA]

In the *appropriate regulator's* view, variable *remuneration* can be awarded to *Remuneration Code staff* in the form of retention awards where it is compatible with the *Remuneration Code general requirement* to do so. The *appropriate regulator* considers this is likely to be the case only where a *firm* is undergoing a major restructuring and a good case can be made for retention of particular key staff members on prudential grounds. Proposals to give retention awards should form part of any notice of the restructuring proposals required in accordance with Principle 11 and the general notification requirements in SUP 15.3.

REMUNERATION PRINCIPLE 12(D): REMUNERATION STRUCTURES — RATIOS BETWEEN FIXED AND VARIABLE COMPONENTS OF TOTAL REMUNERATION

SYSC 19A.3.44 R [FCA] [PRA]

A *firm* must set appropriate ratios between the fixed and variable components of total *remuneration* and ensure that:

(1) fixed and variable components of total *remuneration* are appropriately balanced; and
(2) the fixed component represents a sufficiently high proportion of the total *remuneration* to allow the operation of a fully flexible policy on variable *remuneration* components, including the possibility to pay no variable *remuneration* component.

[**Note:** Paragraph 23(l) of Annex V to the *Banking Consolidation Directive*]

REMUNERATION PRINCIPLE 12(E): REMUNERATION STRUCTURES — PAYMENTS RELATED TO EARLY TERMINATION

SYSC 19A.3.45 R [FCA] [PRA]

A *firm* must ensure that payments related to the early termination of a contract reflect performance achieved over time and are designed in a way that does not reward failure.

[**Note:** Paragraph 23(m) of Annex V to the *Banking Consolidation Directive* and Standard 12 of the *FSB Compensation Standards*]

SYSC 19A.3.46 G [FCA] [PRA]

Firms should review existing contractual payments related to termination of employment with a view to ensuring that these are payable only where there is a clear basis for concluding that they are consistent with the *Remuneration Code general requirement.*

[**Note:** Standard 12 of the *FSB Compensation Standards*]

REMUNERATION PRINCIPLE 12(F): REMUNERATION STRUCTURES — RETAINED SHARES OR OTHER INSTRUMENTS

SYSC 19A.3.47 R [FCA] [PRA]

(1) A *firm* must ensure that a substantial portion, which is at least 50%, of any variable *remuneration* consists of an appropriate balance of:
  (a) *shares* or equivalent ownership interests, subject to the legal structure of the *firm* concerned, or *share*-linked instruments or equivalent non-cash instruments in the case of a non-listed *firm*; and
  (b) where appropriate, *capital instruments* which are eligible for inclusion at stage B1 of the calculation in the *capital resources table*, where applicable that adequately reflects the credit quality of the *firm* as a going concern.

(2) The instruments in (1) must be subject to an appropriate retention policy designed to align incentives with the longer-term interests of the *firm.*

(3) This *rule* applies to both the portion of the variable *remuneration* component deferred in accordance with SYSC 19A.3.49 R and the portion not deferred.

[**Note:** Paragraph 23(o) of Annex V to the *Banking Consolidation Directive* and Standard 8 of the *FSB Compensation Standards*]

SYSC 19A.3.48 G [FCA] [PRA]

(1) The Committee of European Banking Supervisors has given guidance on the interpretation of the Directive provision transposed by SYSC 19A.3.47 R (3). Its Guidelines provide that this requirement means that the 50% minimum threshold for instruments must be applied equally to the non-deferred and the deferred components; in other words, *firms* must apply the same chosen ratio between instruments and cash for their total variable *remuneration* to both the upfront and deferred components. (Guidelines on Remuneration Policies and Practices, 10 December 2010, paragraph 133.)

(2) This simplified example illustrates the operation of (1). The variable remuneration of a material risk taker (X) is 100, and by SYSC 19A.3.49 R (3) X is required to defer 60%. X's upfront component is 40 and X's deferred component is 60. At least 20 of X's upfront component, and at least 30 of X's deferred component, must be in instruments referred to in SYSC 19A.3.47 R (1).

REMUNERATION PRINCIPLE 12(G): REMUNERATION STRUCTURES — DEFERRAL

SYSC 19A.3.49 R [FCA] [PRA]

(1) A *firm* must not award, pay or provide a variable *remuneration* component unless a substantial portion of it, which is at least 40%, is deferred over a period which is not less than three to five years.

(2) *Remuneration* under (1) must vest no faster than on a pro-rata basis.

(3) In the case of a variable *remuneration* component:
  (a) of a particularly high amount, or
  (b) payable to a *director* of a *firm* that is significant in terms of its size, internal organisation and the nature, scope and complexity of its activities;

  at least 60% of the amount must be deferred.

(4) Paragraph (3)(b) does not apply to a *non-executive director.*

(5) The length of the deferral period must be established in accordance with the business cycle, the nature of the business, its risks and the activities of the *employee* in question.

[**Note:** Paragraph 23(p) of Annex V to the *Banking Consolidation Directive* and Standards 6 and 7 of the *FSB Compensation Standards*]

(6) £500,000 is a particularly high amount for the purpose of (3)(a).

(7) Paragraph (6) is without prejudice to the possibility of lower sums being considered a particularly high amount.

SYSC 19A.3.50 G [FCA] [PRA]

(1) Deferred *remuneration* paid in *shares* or *share*-linked instruments should be made under a scheme which meets appropriate criteria, including risk adjustment of the performance measure used to determine the initial allocation of shares. Deferred *remuneration* paid in cash should also be subject to performance criteria.

(2) The *appropriate regulator* would generally expect a *firm* to have a *firm*-wide policy (and *group*-wide policy, where appropriate) on deferral. The proportion deferred should

generally rise with the ratio of variable *remuneration* to fixed *remuneration* and with the amount of variable *remuneration*. While any variable *remuneration* component of £500,000 or more paid to *Remuneration Code staff* must be subject to 60% deferral, *firms* should also consider whether lesser amounts should be considered to be 'particularly high' taking account, for example, of whether there are significant differences within *Remuneration Code staff* in the levels of variable *remuneration* paid.

REMUNERATION PRINCIPLE 12(H): REMUNERATION STRUCTURES — PERFORMANCE ADJUSTMENT, ETC

SYSC 19A.3.51 R [FCA] [PRA]

A *firm* must ensure that any variable *remuneration*, including a deferred portion, is paid or vests only if it is sustainable according to the financial situation of the *firm* as a whole, and justified according to the performance of the *firm*, the business unit and the individual concerned.

[**Note:** Paragraph 23(q) of Annex V to the *Banking Consolidation Directive* and Standards 6 and 9 of the *FSB Compensation Standards*]

SYSC 19A.3.52 E [FCA] [PRA]

(1) A *firm* should reduce unvested deferred variable *remuneration* when, as a minimum:
  (a) there is reasonable evidence of *employee* misbehaviour or material error; or
  (b) the *firm* or the relevant business unit suffers a material downturn in its financial performance; or
  (c) the *firm* or the relevant business unit suffers a material failure of risk management.

(2) For performance adjustment purposes, awards of deferred variable *remuneration* made in *shares* or other non-cash instruments should provide the ability for the *firm* to reduce the number of *shares* or other non-cash instruments.

(3) Contravention of (1) or (2) may be relied on as tending to establish contravention of the *rule* on performance adjustment (SYSC 19A.3.51 R).

SYSC 19A.3.53 G [FCA] [PRA]

(1) Variable *remuneration* may be justified, for example, to incentivise *employees* involved in new business ventures which could be loss-making in their early stages.

(2) The *governing body* (or, where appropriate, the *remuneration* committee) should approve performance adjustment policies, including the triggers under which adjustment would take place. The *appropriate regulator* may ask *firms* to provide a copy of their policies and expects *firms* to make adequate records of material decisions to operate the adjustments.

EFFECT OF BREACHES OF REMUNERATION PRINCIPLES

SYSC 19A.3.53A R [FCA] [PRA]

SYSC 19A Annex 1 makes provision about voiding and recovery.

SYSC 19A.3.54 R [FCA] [PRA]

(1) Subject to (1A) to (3), the *rules* in SYSC 19A Annex 1.1R to 1.4R apply in relation to the prohibitions on *Remuneration Code staff* being *remunerated* in the ways specified in:
  (a) SYSC 19A.3.40 R (guaranteed variable *remuneration*);
  (b) SYSC 19A.3.49 R (non-deferred variable *remuneration*); and
  (c) SYSC 19A Annex 1.7R (replacing payments recovered or property transferred).

(1A) Paragraph (1) applies only to those prohibitions as they apply in relation to a *firm* that satisfies at least one of the conditions set out in (1B) and (1D).

(1B) Condition 1 is that the *firm* is a *UK bank*, a *building society* or a relevant *BIPRU 730k firm* that has relevant total assets exceeding £50 billion.

(1C) [deleted]

(1D) Condition 2 is that the *firm*:
  (a) is a *full credit institution*, a relevant *BIPRU 730k firm* or a relevant *third country BIPRU 730k firm*; and
  (b) is part of a *group* containing a *firm* that has relevant total assets exceeding £50 billion and that is a *UK bank*, a *building society* or a relevant *BIPRU 730k firm*

(1E) In this rule:
  (a) a "relevant *BIPRU 730k firm*" is any *BIPRU 730k firm* that is not a *limited activity firm* or a *limited licence firm*;
  (b) a "relevant *third country BIPRU 730k firm*" is any *third country BIPRU 730k firm* that is not a *limited activity firm* or a *limited licence firm*; and
  (c) "relevant total assets" means the arithmetic mean of the *firm's* total assets as set out in its balance sheet on its last three *accounting reference dates*.

(2) This *rule* does not apply in relation to the prohibition on *Remuneration Code staff* being *remunerated* in the way specified in SYSC 19A.3.40 R (guaranteed variable *remuneration*) if both the conditions in paragraphs (2) and (3) of that *rule* are met

(3) This *rule* does not apply in relation to *Remuneration Code staff* (X) in respect of whom both the following conditions are satisfied:
   (a) Condition 1 is that X's variable *remuneration* is no more than 33% of total *remuneration*; and
   (b) Condition 2 is that X's total *remuneration* is no more than £500,000.

(4) In relation to (3):
   (a) references to *remuneration* are to *remuneration* awarded or paid in respect of the relevant performance year;
   (b) the amount of any *remuneration* is:
      (i) if it is money, its amount when awarded;
      (ii) otherwise, whichever of the following is greatest: its value to the recipient when awarded; its market value when awarded; and the cost of providing it;
   (c) where *remuneration* is, when awarded, subject to any condition, restriction or other similar provision which causes the amount of the *remuneration* to be less than it otherwise would be, that condition, restriction or provision is to be ignored in arriving at its value; and
   (d) it is to be assumed that the member of *Remuneration Code staff* will remain so for the duration of the relevant performance year.

SYSC 19A.3.55 G [FCA] [PRA]

(1) Sections 137H and 137I of the *Act* enables the *appropriate regulator* to make *rules* that render void any provision of an agreement that contravenes specified prohibitions in the *Remuneration Code*, and that provide for the recovery of any payment made, or other property transferred, in pursuance of such a provision. SYSC 19A.3.53A R and SYSC 19A.3.54 R (together with SYSC 19A Annex 1) are such *rules* and render void provisions of an agreement that contravene the specified prohibitions on guaranteed variable *remuneration*, non-deferred variable *remuneration* and replacing payments recovered or property transferred. This is an exception to the general position set out in section 138E(2) of the *Act* that a contravention of a *rule* does not make any transaction void or unenforceable.

(2) [deleted]

SYSC 19A ANNEX 1 [FCA] [PRA]
DETAILED PROVISIONS ON VOIDING AND RECOVERY (SYSC 19A.3.53AR AND SYSC 19A.3.54R)

[4.166]

Rendering contravening provisions of agreements void			
1	R	Any provision of an agreement that contravenes a prohibition on *persons* being *remunerated* in a way specified in a *rule* to which this *rule* applies (a 'contravening provision') is void.	
1A	R	A contravening provision does not cease to be void because:	
		(1)	the *firm* concerned ceases to satisfy any of the conditions set out in SYSC 19A.3.54R(1B) to (1D); or
		(2)	the member of *Remuneration Code staff* concerned starts to satisfy both of the conditions set out in SYSC 19A.3.54R(3)(a) and (b).
2	R	A contravening provision that, at the time a *rule* to which this *rule* applies was made, is contained in an agreement made before that time is not rendered void by 1R unless it is subsequently amended so as to contravene such a *rule*.	
3	G	The effect of 2R, in accordance with sections 137H and 137I of the *Act*, is to prevent contravening provisions being rendered void retrospectively. Contravening provisions may however be rendered void if they are contained in an agreement made after the *rule* containing the prohibition is made by the *appropriate regulator* but before the *rule* comes into effect. For further relevant transitional provisions, see SYSC TP3.6A.	
3A	R	(1)	A pre-existing provision is not rendered void by 1R.
		(2)	In this Annex a pre-existing provision is any provision of an agreement that would (but for this *rule*) be rendered void by 1R that was agreed at a time when either:
		(a)	the *firm* concerned did not satisfy any of the conditions set out in SYSC 19A.3.54R(1B) to (1D); or
		(b)	the member of *Remuneration Code staff* concerned satisfied both of the conditions set out in SYSC 19A.3.54R(3)(a) and (b).

		(3)	But an amendment to, or in relation to, a pre-existing provision is not to be treated as a pre-existing provision where the amendment is agreed at a time when both:
		(a)	the *firm* concerned satisfies at least one of the conditions set out in SYSC 19A.3.54R(1B) to (1D); and
		(b)	the member of *Remuneration Code staff* concerned does not satisfy both of the conditions set out in SYSC 19A.3.54R(3)(a) and (b).
4	R	For the purposes of this chapter it is immaterial whether the law which (apart from this annex) governs a contravening provision is the law of the *United Kingdom*, or of a part of the *United Kingdom*.	
Recovery of payments made or property transferred pursuant to a void contravening provision			
5	R	In relation to any payment made or other property transferred in pursuance of a contravening provision other than a pre-existing provision, a *firm* must take reasonable steps to:	
		(1)	recover any such payment made or other property transferred by the *firm*; and
		(2)	ensure that any other *person* ("P") recovers any such payment made or other property transferred by that *person*.
5A	R	Paragraph 5R continues to apply in one or both of the following cases:	
		(1)	the *firm* concerned ceases to satisfy any of the conditions set out in SYSC 19A.3.54R(1B) to (1D);
		(2)	the member of *Remuneration Code staff* concerned starts to satisfy both of the conditions set out in SYSC 19A.3.54R(3)(a) and (b).
6	G	The *rule* in 5R(2) would, for example, apply in the context of a secondment. Where a *group* member seconds an individual to a *firm* and continues to be responsible for the individual's *remuneration* in respect of services provided to the *firm*, the *firm* would need to take reasonable steps to ensure that the *group* member recovers from the secondee any *remuneration* paid in pursuance of a contravening provision.	
Replacing payments recovered or property transferred			
7	R	(1)	A *firm* must not award, pay or provide variable *remuneration* to a *person* who has received *remuneration* in pursuance of a contravening provision other than a pre-existing provision (the "contravening *remuneration*") unless the *firm* has obtained a legal opinion stating that the award, payment or provision of the *remuneration* complies with the *Remuneration Code*.
		(2)	This *rule* applies only to variable *remuneration* relating to a performance year to which the contravening *remuneration* related.
		(3)	The legal opinion in (1) must be properly reasoned and be provided by an appropriately qualified independent individual.
		(4)	Paragraph (1) continues to apply in one or both of the following cases:
		(a)	the *firm* concerned ceases to satisfy any of the conditions set out in SYSC 19A.3.54R(1B) to (1D);
		(b)	the member of *Remuneration Code staff* concerned starts to satisfy both of the conditions set out in SYSC 19A.3.54R(3)(a) and (b).
Notification to the appropriate regulator			
8	G	The *appropriate regulator* considers any breach of a *rule* to which this annex applies to be a significant breach which should be notified to the *appropriate regulator* in accordance with SUP 15.3.11 R (Breaches of rules and other requirements in or under the Act). Such a notification should include information on the steps which a *firm* or other *person* has taken or intends to take to recover payments or property in accordance with 5R.	

E. HEALTH AND SAFETY EXECUTIVE

HEALTH AND SAFETY COMMISSION CODE OF PRACTICE: SAFETY REPRESENTATIVES AND SAFETY COMMITTEES (1978)

[4.167]

NOTES

This Code of Practice was issued under the Health and Safety at Work etc Act 1974, s 16 at **[1.43]**, and came into force on 1 October 1978. It has the legal effect indicated in that section. For the Safety Representatives and Safety Committees Regulations 1977, SI 1977/500, see **[2.27]**.

The Health and Safety Commission was abolished and replaced by a new Health and Safety Executive, by the Legislative Reform (Health and Safety Executive) Order 2008, SI 2008/960, art 2. Para 8 of Sch 2 to the 2008 Order provides that codes of practice issued by the Commission under the Health and Safety at Work etc Act 1974, s 16, before 1 April 2008, have effect on or after that date as though they had been issued by the new Executive.

[4.168]

1. The Safety Representatives and Safety Committees Regulations 1977 concern safety representatives appointed in accordance with Section 2(4) of the Act and cover:

(a) prescribed cases in which recognised trade unions may appoint safety representatives from amongst the employees;

(b) prescribed functions of safety representatives.

Section 2(6) of the Act requires an employer to consult with safety representatives with a view to the making and maintenance of arrangements which will enable him and his employees to cooperate effectively in promoting and developing measures to ensure the health and safety at work of the employees, and in checking the effectiveness of such measures. Under section 2(4) safety representatives are required to represent the employees in those consultations.

2. This Code of Practice has been approved by the Health and Safety Commission with the consent of the Secretary of State. It relates to the requirements placed on safety representatives by section 2(4) of the Act and on employers by the Regulations and takes effect on the date the Regulations come into operation.

3. The employer, the recognised trade unions concerned and safety representatives should make full and proper use of the existing agreed industrial relations machinery to reach the degree of agreement necessary to achieve the purpose of the Regulations and in order to resolve any differences.

INTERPRETATION

4.

(a) In this Code, "the 1974 Act" means the Health and Safety at Work etc Act 1974 and "the Regulations" mean the Safety Representatives and Safety Committees Regulations 1977;

(b) words and expressions which are defined in the Act or in the Regulations have the same meaning in this Code unless the context requires otherwise.

FUNCTIONS OF SAFETY REPRESENTATIVES

5. In order to fulfil their functions under section 2(4) of the Act safety representatives should:

(a) take all reasonably practical steps to keep themselves informed of:

   (i) the legal requirements relating to the health and safety of persons at work, particularly the group or groups of persons they directly represent,

   (ii) the particular hazards of the workplace and the measures deemed necessary to eliminate or minimise the risk deriving from these hazards, and

   (iii) the health and safety policy of their employer and the organisation and arrangements for fulfilling that policy;

(b) encourage cooperation between their employer and his employees in promoting and developing essential measures to ensure the health and safety of employees and in checking the effectiveness of these measures;

(c) bring to the employer's notice normally in writing any unsafe or unhealthy conditions or working practices or unsatisfactory arrangements for welfare at work which come to their attention whether on an inspection or day to day observation. The report does not imply that all other conditions and working practices are safe and healthy or that the welfare arrangements are satisfactory in all other respects.

Making a written report does not preclude the bringing of such matters to the attention of the employer or his representative by a direct oral approach in the first instance, particularly in situations where speedy remedial action is necessary. It will also be appropriate for minor matters to be the subject of direct oral discussion without the need for a formal written approach.

INFORMATION TO BE PROVIDED BY EMPLOYERS

6. The Regulations require employers to make information within their knowledge available to safety representatives necessary to enable them to fulfil their functions. Such information should include:

(a) information about the plans and performance of their undertaking and any changes proposed insofar as they affect the health and safety at work of their employees;

(b) information of a technical nature about hazards to health and safety and precautions deemed necessary to eliminate or minimise them, in respect of machinery, plant, equipment, processes, systems of work and substances in use at work, including any relevant information provided by consultants or designers or by the manufacturer, importer or supplier of any article or substance used, or proposed to be used, at work by their employees;

(c) information which the employer keeps relating to the occurrence of any accident, dangerous occurrence or notifiable industrial disease and any statistical records relating to such accidents, dangerous occurrences or cases of notifiable industrial disease;

(d) any other information specifically related to matters affecting the health and safety at work of his employees, including the results of any measurements taken by the employer or persons acting on his behalf in the course of checking the effectiveness of his health and safety arrangements;

(e) information on articles or substances which an employer issues to home-workers.

HEALTH AND SAFETY COMMISSION CODE OF PRACTICE: TIME OFF FOR THE TRAINING OF SAFETY REPRESENTATIVES (1978)

[4.169]

NOTES

This Code of Practice was issued under the Health and Safety at Work etc Act 1974, s 16, at **[1.43]**, and came into force on 1 October 1978. It has the legal effect indicated in that section. For the Safety Representatives and Safety Committees Regulations 1977, SI 1977/500, see **[2.27]**.

The Health and Safety Commission was abolished and replaced by a new Health and Safety Executive by the Legislative Reform (Health and Safety Executive) Order 2008, SI 2008/960, art 2. Para 8 of Sch 2 to the 2008 Order provides that codes of practice issued by the Commission under the Health and Safety at Work etc Act 1974, s 16, before 1 April 2008, have effect on or after that date as though they had been issued by the new Executive.

PREFACE

[4.170]

This document sets out a Code of Practice, which has been approved by the Health and Safety Commission, relating to the time off with pay which a safety representative is to be permitted to take during his working hours for the purpose of undergoing training approved by the TUC or by independent unions. It should be read in conjunction with the Safety Representatives and Safety Committees Regulations 1977, with particular reference to Regulation 4, which sets out the functions of a safety representative and the time off for training necessary to perform these functions.

The Advisory, Conciliation and Arbitration Service has also prepared a Code of Practice on Time Off for trade union duties and activities generally under Section 57 of the Employment Protection Act. However, this Code, approved by the Health and Safety Commission, is concerned with time off for training of safety representatives appointed under the Regulations.

Issues which may arise are covered by paragraph 3 of the Code of Practice on Safety Representatives approved by the Health and Safety Commission. The Schedule to the Regulations deals with the computation of pay for the time off allowed. Regulation 11 contains provisions as to reference of complaints to industrial tribunals about time off and the payment to be made.

To complement training approved by the TUC or by independent unions for safety representatives, an employer should make such arrangements as are necessary to provide training in the technical hazards of the workplace and relevant precautions on safe methods of work, and on his organisation and arrangements for health and safety.

CODE OF PRACTICE

1. The function of safety representatives appointed by recognised trade unions as set out in Section 2(4) of the Health and Safety at Work etc Act 1974 is to represent employees in consultations with employers about health and safety matters. Regulations 4(1) of the Safety Representatives and Safety Committees Regulations (SI 1977/500) prescribes other functions of safety representatives appointed under those Regulations.

2. Under Regulations 4(2)(b) of those Regulations the employer has a duty to permit those safety representatives such time off with pay during the employee's working hours as shall be necessary for the purpose of "undergoing such training in aspects of those functions as may be reasonable in all the circumstances".

3. As soon as possible after their appointment safety representatives should be permitted time off with pay to attend basic training facilities approved by the TUC or by the independent union or unions which appointed the safety representatives. Further training, similarly approved, should be undertaken where the safety representative has special responsibilities or where such training is necessary to meet changes in circumstances or relevant legislation.

4. With regard to the length of training required, this cannot be rigidly prescribed, but basic training should take into account the function of safety representatives placed on them by the Regulations. In particular, basic training should provide an understanding of the role of safety representatives, of safety committees, and of trade union policies and practices in relation to:

(a) the legal requirements relating to the health and safety of persons at work, particularly the group or class of persons they directly represent;

(b) the nature and extent of workplace hazards, and the measures necessary to eliminate or minimise them;

(c) the health and safety policy of employers, and organisation and arrangements for fulfilling those policies.

Additionally, safety representatives will need to acquire new skills in order to carry out their functions, including safety inspections, and in using basic sources of legal and official information and information provided by or through the employer on health and safety matters.

5. Trade unions are responsible for appointing safety representatives and when the trade union wishes a safety representative to receive training relevant to his functions it should inform management of the course it has approved and supply a copy of the syllabus, indicating its contents, if the employer asks for it. It should normally give at least a few weeks' notice of the safety representatives it has nominated for attendance. The number of safety representatives attending training courses at any one time should be that which is reasonable in the circumstances, bearing in mind such factors as the availability of relevant courses and the operational requirements of the employer. Unions and management should endeavour to reach agreement on the appropriate numbers and arrangements and refer any problems which may arise to the relevant agreed procedures.

F. INFORMATION COMMISSIONER

DATA PROTECTION: EMPLOYMENT PRACTICES CODE (2011)

[4.171]

NOTES

A consolidated Code of Practice was issued by the Information Commissioner in June 2005 to replace the four separate Parts originally issued between 2002 and 2004. In November 2011, a new version of the Code was published. The 2011 version is substantively the same as the 2005 version; the only differences being in formatting and updated website addresses etc. The Code is issued under the authority conferred by the Data Protection Act 1998, s 51(3)(b) (at **[1.1104]**). That Act does not confer any specific legal status on the Code, and does not require either ministerial or Parliamentary approval. The Code came into effect on its issue by the Commissioner. The Supplementary Guidance referred to in the Code is not reproduced for reasons of space; it is available on the Commissioner's website (www.ico.org.uk).

Note that where the text of this Code originally cross-referred to a page number within the hardcopy version of the Code, the appropriate paragraph number has been substituted in its place.

CONTENTS

PART 4: INFORMATION ABOUT WORKERS' HEALTH

GOOD PRACTICE RECOMMENDATIONS – PART 4

ABOUT THE CODE

OUR AIM:

[4.172]

This Code is intended to help employers comply with the Data Protection Act and to encourage them to adopt good practice. The Code aims to strike a balance between the legitimate expectations of workers that personal information about them will be handled properly and the legitimate interests of employers in deciding how best, within the law, to run their own businesses. It does not impose new legal obligations.

WHO IS THE CODE FOR?

The Employment Practices Data Protection Code deals with the impact of data protection laws on the employment relationship. It covers such issues as the obtaining of information about workers, the retention of records, access to records and disclosure of them. Not every aspect of the Code will be relevant to every organisation – this will vary according to size and the nature of its business. Some of the issues addressed may arise only rarely – particularly for small businesses. Here the Code is intended to serve as a reference document to be called on when necessary.

THE BENEFITS OF THE CODE

The Data Protection Act 1998 places responsibilities on any organisation to process personal information that it holds in a fair and proper way. Failure to do so can ultimately lead to a criminal offence being committed.

The effect of the Act on how an organisation processes information on its workers is generally straightforward. But in some areas it can be complex and difficult to understand, especially if your organisation has only limited experience of dealing with data protection issues. The Code therefore covers the points you need to check, and what action, if any, you may need to take. Following the Code should produce other benefits in terms of relationships with your workers, compliance with other legislation and efficiencies in storing and managing information.

Following the Code will:

- increase trust in the workplace – there will be transparency about information held on individuals, thus helping to create an open atmosphere where workers have trust and confidence in employment practices.
- encourage good housekeeping – following the Code encourages organisations to dispose of out-of-date information, freeing up both physical and computerised filing systems and making valuable information easier to find.
- protect organisations from legal action – adhering to the Code will help employers to protect themselves from challenges against their data protection practices.
- encourage workers to treat customers' personal data with respect – following the Code will create a general level of awareness of personal data issues, helping to ensure that information about customers is treated properly.
- help organisations to meet other legal requirements – the Code is intended to be consistent with other legislation such as the Human Rights Act 1998 and the Regulation of Investigatory Powers Act 2000 (RIPA).
- assist global businesses to adopt policies and practices which are consistent with similar legislation in other countries – the Code is produced in the light of EC Directive 95/46/EC and ought to be in line with data protection law in other European Union member states.
- help to prevent the illicit use of information by workers – informing them of the principles of data protection, and the consequences of not complying with the Act, should discourage them from misusing information held by the organisation.

WHAT IS THE LEGAL STATUS OF THE CODE?

The Code has been issued by the Information Commissioner under section 51 of the Data Protection Act. This requires him to promote the following of good practice, including compliance with the Act's requirements, by data controllers and empowers him, after consultation, to prepare Codes of Practice giving guidance on good practice.

The basic legal requirement on each employer is to comply with the Act itself. The Code is designed to help. It sets out the Information Commissioner's recommendations as to how the legal requirements of the Act can be met. Employers may have alternative ways of meeting these requirements but if they do nothing they risk breaking the law.

Any enforcement action would be based on a failure to meet the requirements of the Act itself. However, relevant parts of the Code are likely to be cited by the Commissioner in connection with any enforcement action that arises in relation to the processing of personal information in the employment context.

WHO DOES DATA PROTECTION COVER IN THE WORKPLACE?

The Code is concerned with information that employers might collect and keep on any individual who might wish to work, work, or have worked for them. In the Code the term 'worker' includes:

- applicants (successful and unsuccessful)
- former applicants (successful and unsuccessful)
- employees (current and former)
- agency staff (current and former)
- casual staff (current and former)
- contract staff (current and former)

Some of this Code will also apply to others in the workplace, such as volunteers and those on work experience placements.

WHAT INFORMATION IS COVERED BY THE CODE?

Information about individuals, that is kept by an organisation on computer in the employment context, will fall within the scope of the Data Protection Act and therefore, within the scope of this Code. However, information that is kept in simple manual files will often fall outside the Act. Where information falls outside the Act, this Code can do no more than offer advice on good information handling practice.

Personal information

The Code is concerned with 'personal information'. That is, information which:

- is about a living person and affects that person's privacy (whether in his/her personal or family life, business or professional capacity) in the sense that the information has the person as its focus or is otherwise biographical in nature, and
- identifies a person, whether by itself, or together with other information in the organisation's possession or that is likely to come into its possession.

This means that automated and computerised personal information kept about workers by employers is covered by the Act. It also covers personal information put on paper or microfiche and held in any 'relevant filing system'. In addition, information recorded with the intention that it will be put in a relevant filing system or held on computer is covered.

Only a well structured manual system will qualify as a relevant filing system. This means that the system must amount to more than a bundle of documents about each worker filed in date order. There must be some sort of system to guide a searcher to where specific information about a named worker can be found readily. This might take the form of topic dividers within individually named personnel files or name dividers within a file on a particular topic, such as 'Training Applications'.

Processing

The Act applies to personal information that is subject to 'processing'. For the purposes of the Act, the term 'processing' applies to a comprehensive range of activities. It includes the initial obtaining of personal information, the retention and use of it, access and disclosure and final disposal.

Examples of personal information **likely** to be covered by the Act include:

- details of a worker's salary and bank account held on an organisation's computer system
- an e-mail about an incident involving a named worker
- a supervisor's notebook containing information on a worker where there is an intention to put that information in that worker's computerised personnel file
- an individual worker's personnel file where the documents are filed in date order but there is an index to the documents at the front of the file
- an individual worker's personnel file where at least some of the documents are filed behind sub dividers with headings such as application details, leave record and performance reviews
- a set of leave cards where each worker has an individual card and the cards are kept in alphabetical order
- a set of completed application forms, filed in alphabetical order within a file of application forms for a particular vacancy.

Examples of information **unlikely** to be covered by the Act include:

- information on the entire workforce's salary structure, given by grade, where individuals are not named and are not identifiable
- a report on the comparative success of different recruitment campaigns where no details regarding individuals are held
- a report on the results of "exit interviews" where all responses are anonymised and where the results are impossible to trace back to individuals
- a personnel file that contains information about a named worker but where the information is simply filed in date order with nothing to guide a searcher to where specific information, such as the worker's leave entitlement, can be found.

SENSITIVE PERSONAL INFORMATION

What are sensitive data?

Sensitive data are information concerning an individual's:

- racial or ethnic origin
- political opinions
- religious beliefs or other beliefs of a similar nature
- trade union membership (within the meaning of the Trade Union and Labour Relations (Consolidation) Act 1992)
- physical or mental health or condition
- sexual life
- commission or alleged commission of any offence, or
- proceedings for any offence committed or alleged to have been committed, the disposal of such proceedings or the sentence of any court in such proceedings

Sensitive data processed by an employer might typically be about a worker's:

- physical or mental health
  - — as a part of sickness records revealed through monitoring e-mails sent by a worker to his or her manager or to an occupational health advisor
  - — obtained as part of a pre-employment medical questionnaire or examination.
  - — drug or alcohol test results
- criminal convictions
  - — to assess suitability for certain types of employment
- disabilities
  - — to facilitate adaptations in the workplace
  - — to ensure special needs are catered for at interview or selection testing
  - — in monitoring equality of opportunity
- racial origin
  - — to ensure that recruitment processes do not discriminate against particular racial groups
  - — to ensure equality of opportunity
- trade union membership
  - — to enable deduction of subscriptions from payroll
  - — revealed by internet access logs which show that a worker routinely accesses a particular trade union website.

The Act sets out a series of conditions, at least one of which has to apply before an employer can collect, store, use, disclose or otherwise process sensitive data.

See Supplementary Guidance page 72 which explains more about the conditions for processing sensitive data.

WHAT RESPONSIBILITIES DO WORKERS HAVE UNDER THE ACT?

Workers – as well as employers – have responsibilities for data protection under the Act. Line managers have responsibility for the type of personal information they collect and how they use it. No-one at any level should disclose personal information outside the organisation's procedures, or use personal information held on others for their own purposes. Anyone disclosing personal information without the authority of the organisation may commit a criminal offence, unless there is some other legal justification, for example under 'whistle-blowing' legislation.

Of course, applicants for jobs ought to provide accurate information and may breach other laws if they do not. However, the Act does not create any new legal obligation for them to do so.

Managing Data Protection (post) explains more about allocating responsibility.

PARTS OF THE CODE

The 'Employment Practices Code' starts with a section on managing data protection in employment practices. It is then split into four parts;

- **recruitment and selection** – is about job applications and pre-employment vetting

- **employment records** – is about collecting, storing, disclosing and deleting records
- **monitoring at work** – is about monitoring workers' use of telephones, the internet, e-mail systems and vehicles
- **workers' health** – is about occupational health, medical testing, drug and genetic screening.

Each part of the Code has been designed to stand alone. Which parts of the Code you choose to use will depend on the relevance to your organisation of each area covered.

THE GOOD PRACTICE RECOMMENDATIONS

Each part of the Code consists of a series of good practice recommendations. These good practice recommendations may be relevant to either large or small employers, but some of them address activities that are of a more specialist nature than others or may occur only rarely, particularly in a small business, These recommendations are most likely to be relevant to larger organisations. However, how far they are applicable and what is needed to achieve them will, of course, depend very much not just on size but also on the nature of each organisation.

SUPPLEMENTARY GUIDANCE

Supporting guidance, aimed mainly at those in larger organisations who are responsible for ensuring that employment policies and practices comply with data protection law, includes more detailed notes and examples. These notes and examples, do not form part of this Code.

MANAGING DATA PROTECTION

GOOD PRACTICE RECOMMENDATIONS – MANAGING DATA PROTECTION

[4.173]
Data protection compliance should be seen as an integral part of employment practice. It is important to develop a culture in which respect for private life, data protection, security and confidentiality of personal information is seen as the norm.

0.1 Identify the person within the organisation responsible for ensuring that employment policies and procedures comply with the Act and for ensuring that they continue to do so. Put in place a mechanism for checking that procedures are followed in practice.

Key points and possible actions

- The nature and size of the organisation will influence where responsibility should rest.
- Ensure the person responsible reads all relevant parts of the Code.
- Check employment policies and procedures, including unwritten practices, against the relevant parts of the Code.
- Eliminate areas of non-compliance.
- Inform those who need to know why certain procedures have changed.
- Introduce a mechanism for checking that procedures are followed in practice, for example, occasional audits and spot checks and/or a requirement for managers to sign a compliance statement.

0.2 Ensure that business areas and individual line managers who process information about workers understand their own responsibility for data protection compliance and if necessary amend their working practices in the light of this.

Key points and possible actions

- Prepare a briefing to departmental heads and line managers about their responsibilities.

0.3 Assess what personal information about workers is in existence and who is responsible for it.

Key points and possible actions

- Use the various parts of this Code as the framework to assess what personal information your organisation keeps and where responsibility for it lies.
- Remember that personal information may be held in different departments as well as within the personnel/human resource function.

0.4 Eliminate the collection of personal information that is irrelevant or excessive to the employment relationship. If sensitive data are collected ensure that a sensitive data condition is satisfied.

Key points and possible actions

- Consider each type of personal information that is held and decide whether any information could be deleted or not collected in the first place.
- Check that the collection and use of any sensitive personal data satisfies at least one of the sensitive data conditions.

See Supplementary Guidance page 72 which explains more about the conditions for processing sensitive data.

0.5 Ensure that all workers are aware how they can be criminally liable if they knowingly or recklessly disclose personal information outside their employer's policies and procedures. Make serious breaches of data protection rules a disciplinary matter.

Key points and possible actions

- Prepare a guide explaining to workers the consequences of their actions in this area.
- Make sure that the serious infringement of data protection rules is clearly indicated as a disciplinary matter.
- Ensure that the guide is brought to the attention of new workers.
- Ensure that workers can ask questions about the guide.

0.6 Ensure that your organisation has a valid notification in the register of data controllers that relates to the processing of personal information about workers, unless it is exempt from notification.

Key points and possible actions

- Consult the Data Protection Register website – www.ico.gov.uk – to check the notification status of your organisation.
- Check whether your organisation is exempt from notification using the website.
- Check whether all your processing of information about workers is correctly described there – unless your organisation is exempt.
- Allocate responsibility for checking and updating this information on a regular basis, for example every 6 months.

0.7 Consult workers, and/or trade unions or other representatives, about the development and implementation of employment practices and procedures that involve the processing of personal information about workers.

Key points and possible actions

- Consultation is only mandatory under employment law, in limited circumstances and for larger employers but it should nevertheless help to ensure that processing of personal information is fair.
- When formulating new employment practices and procedures, assess the impact on collection and use of personal information.

PART 1: RECRUITMENT AND SELECTION

ABOUT PART 1 OF THE CODE

Data protection in recruitment and selection

[4.174]
The recruitment and selection process necessarily involves an employer in collecting and using information about workers. Much of this information is personal in nature and can affect a worker's privacy. The Act does not prevent an employer from carrying out an effective recruitment exercise but helps to strike a balance between the employer's needs and the applicant's right to respect for his or her private life.

What does this part of the Code cover?

This part of the Code covers all aspects of the recruitment and selection process from the advertising of vacancies through to the deletion of information on unsuccessful applicants. It does not though deal in detail with the collection and use of health information on job applicants. This is covered in Part 4. Nor does it deal in detail with the right of applicants to access to the information that an employer keeps about them. This is essentially no different from the right of access that a worker has once employed or engaged. This is covered in Part 2.

Some recommendations in the Code are only likely to be of relevance to those using sophisticated selection methods such as psychometric testing or to those employing workers with responsibilities that mean that special checks are justified, for example, criminal record checks on those working with children. For this reason some sub sections are likely to be of relevance mainly to larger or specialist organisations.

Verification and vetting

The terms "verification" and "vetting" are both used in this part of the Code. Verification covers the process of checking that details supplied by applicants (eg qualifications) are accurate and complete. Verification, therefore, is limited to checking of information that is sought in the application or supplied later in the recruitment process. As used here the term also includes the taking up of references provided by the applicant. Where an employer is justified in asking an applicant about any criminal convictions the Criminal Records Bureau provides a verification service covering certain, high risk areas of employment.

Vetting covers the employer actively making its own enquiries from third parties about an applicant's background and circumstances. It goes beyond the verification of details addressed above. As such it is particularly intrusive and should be confined to areas of special risk. It is for example used for some government workers who have regular access to highly classified information.

In some sectors vetting may be a necessary and accepted practice. Limited vetting may be a legal requirement for some jobs, for example, child care jobs under the Protection of Children Act 1999. The Department of Health has developed a Protection of Vulnerable Adults list which employers intending to recruit certain types of care workers are required to consult. Such vetting usually takes place through the Criminal Records Bureau.

See Supplementary Guidance, page 17 for background information on the Criminal Records Bureau.

GOOD PRACTICE RECOMMENDATIONS – PART 1

The parts of the Code in this section are:

1.1 Advertising

1.2 Applications

1.3 Verification

1.4 Short-listing

1.5 Interviews

1.6 Pre-employment vetting

1.7 Retention of recruitment records

1.1 Advertising

[4.175]
This sub-section covers any method used to notify potential applicants of job vacancies, using such media as notices, newspapers, radio, television and the internet.

1.1.1 Inform individuals responding to job advertisements of the name of the organisation to which they will be providing their information and how it will be used unless this is self-evident.

Key points and possible actions

- Ensure that the name of your organisation appears in all recruitment advertisements.
- Ensure that your organisation is named on the answerphone message which invites potential applicants to leave details.
- Ensure that your organisation is named on your website before personal information is collected on an online application form.
- To the extent that it is not self evident describe in the advertisement the purposes for which you may use personal information, for example, to market your organisations products and service.

1.1.2 Recruitment agencies, used on behalf of an employer, should identify themselves and explain how personal information they receive will be used and disclosed unless this is self-evident.

Key points and possible actions

- If you use a recruitment agency check that it identifies itself in any advertisement, and that it informs applicants if the information requested is to be used for any purpose of which the applicant is unlikely to be aware.

1.1.3 On receiving identifiable particulars of applicants from an agency ensure, as soon as you can, that the applicants are aware of the name of the organisation holding their information.

Key points and possible actions

- Inform the applicant as soon as you can of the employer's identity and of any uses that the employer might make of the information received that are not self-evident.

OR

- If the employer does not wish to be identified at an early stage in the recruitment process, ensure the agency only sends anonymised information about applicants. Ensure the employer is identified to individuals whose applications are to be pursued further.

1.2 Applications

[4.176]
This sub-section covers CVs sent 'on spec' as well as more formal responses to job advertisements.

1.2.1 State, on any application form, to whom the information is being provided and how it will be used if this is not self-evident.

Key points and possible actions

- Ensure the name of your organisation is stated on the application form.
- If information from the application form will be used for any other purpose than to recruit for a specific job or passed to anyone else, make sure that this purpose is stated on the application form.

1.2.2 Only seek personal information that is relevant to the recruitment decision to be made.

Key points and possible actions

- Determine whether all questions are relevant for all applicants.
- Consider customising application forms where posts justify the collection of more intrusive personal information.
- Remove or amend any questions which require the applicant to provide information extraneous to the recruitment decision.
- Remove questions that are only relevant to people your organisation goes on to employ (eg banking details) but are not relevant to unsuccessful applicants.

1.2.3 Only request information about an applicant's criminal convictions if and to the extent that the information can be justified in terms of the role offered. If this information is justified, make it clear that spent convictions do not have to be declared, unless the job being filled is covered by the Exceptions Order to the Rehabilitation of Offenders Act 1974.

Key points and possible actions

- Consider whether the collection of information about criminal convictions can be justified for each job for which it is sought.
- Check that it is stated that spent convictions do not have to be declared (unless the job is one covered by the Exceptions Order).
- In any case limit the collection of information to offences that have a direct bearing on suitability for the job in question.

See Supplementary Guidance, page 19 for more information on the Exceptions Order.

1.2.4 Explain the nature of and sources from which information might be obtained about the applicant in addition to the information supplied directly by the applicant.

Key points and possible actions

- Ensure there is a clear statement on the application form or surrounding documents, explaining what information will be sought and from whom.

1.2.5 If sensitive data are collected ensure a sensitive data condition is satisfied.

Key points and possible actions

- Assess whether the collection of sensitive data is relevant to the recruitment process.
- Remove any questions about sensitive data that do not have to be asked at the initial application stage.
- Ensure that the purpose of collecting any relevant sensitive data is explained on the application form or surrounding documentation.
- Ensure the purpose of collection satisfies one of the sensitive data conditions.
- If health information is to be collected, refer to Part 4 of the Code: Information About Workers' Health.

See Supplementary Guidance, page 72 which explains more about the conditions for processing sensitive data.

1.2.6 Provide a secure method for sending applications.

Key points and possible actions

- Ensure that a secure method of transmission is used for sending applications online. (Eg encryption-based software).
- Ensure that once electronic applications are received, they are saved in a directory or drive which has access limited to those involved in the recruitment process.
- Ensure that postal applications are given directly to the person or people processing the applications and that these are stored in a locked drawer.

- Ensure that faxed applications are given directly to the person or people processing the applications and that these are stored in a locked drawer.
- If applications are processed by line managers, make sure line managers are aware of how to gather and store applications.

1.3 Verification

[4.177]

1.3.1 Explain to applicants as early as is reasonably practicable in the recruitment process the nature of the verification process and the methods used to carry it out.

Key points and possible actions

- Ensure that information provided to applicants for example on an application form or associated documents explains what information will be verified and how, including in particular any external sources that will be used.
- Do not force applicants to use their subject access rights to obtain records from another organisation (ie by making such a requirement a condition of getting a job).

1.3.2 Where the need to protect the employer's business, customers, clients or others warrants the collection and verification of details of an applicant's criminal convictions use only a disclosure from the Criminal Records Bureau (CRB) or Disclosure Scotland for this verification.

Key points and possible actions

- Do not attempt to obtain information about criminal convictions by forcing an applicant to use his/her subject access right or from sources other than the CRB, Disclosure Scotland or the applicant.
- Confine the obtaining of a disclosure, as far as practicable, to an applicant it is intended to appoint. Avoid requiring all short-listed applicants to obtain a disclosure.
- Do not share with other employers the information obtained through a "disclosure".
- Abide by the CRB or Disclosure Scotland's Code of Practice in obtaining and handling disclosure information.

1.3.3 If it is necessary to secure the release of documents or information from another organisation or person, obtain a signed consent form from the applicant unless consent to their release has been indicated in some other way.

Key points and possible actions

- Ensure applicants provide signed consent if this is required to secure the release of documents to you from another organisation or person.
- Remember that if you mislead another person or organisation into giving you personal information about an applicant you may be committing a criminal offence.

1.3.4 Give the applicant an opportunity to make representations should any of the checks produce discrepancies.

Key points and possible actions

- Ensure that those staff who are involved in verification in your organisation are aware what to do should inconsistencies emerge between what the applicant said in the application and what your checks have discovered.
- Make sure that in this situation, staff inform the applicant and allow them the opportunity to provide an explanation of the inconsistencies.
- Ensure this feedback to the applicant is incorporated into any recruitment procedures.

1.4 Short-listing

[4.178]

1.4.1 Be consistent in the way personal information is used in the process of short-listing candidates for a particular position.

Key points and possible actions

- Check shortlist methods with sources of good practice such as the Equality and Human Rights Commission.

See Supplementary Guidance page 83 for contact details.

1.4.2 Inform applicants if an automated short-listing system will be used as the sole basis of making a decision. Make provisions to consider representations from applicants about this and to take these into account before making the final decision.

Key points and possible actions

- Ensure all the applicants are informed that an automated system is used as the sole basis of short-listing and of how to make representations against any adverse decision.
- Test and keep the results produced by the system under review to ensure they properly and fairly apply your short-listing criteria to all applicants.

1.4.3 Ensure that tests based on the interpretation of scientific evidence, such as psychological tests, are only used and interpreted by those who have received appropriate training.

Key points and possible actions

- Determine which such tests are used within your organisation.
- Ensure all tests are assessed by properly qualified persons.

1.5 Interviews

[4.179]
1.5.1 Ensure that personal information that is recorded and retained following interview can be justified as relevant to, and necessary for, the recruitment process itself, or for defending the process against challenge.

Key points and possible actions

- Ensure that all interviewers are aware that interviewees may have a right to request access to their interview notes.
- Ensure that all interviewers are given instructions on how to store interview notes.
- Make provisions for interview notes to be destroyed after a reasonable time, allowing the organisation to protect itself from any potential claims such as those for race or sex discrimination.
- Explain to interviewers or those in contact with applicants, how to deal with a request for access to interview notes.

1.6 Pre-employment vetting

[4.180]
1.6.1 Only use vetting where there are particular and significant risks involved to the employer, clients, customers or others, and where there is no less intrusive and reasonably practicable alternative.

Key points and possible actions

- Find out for which jobs, if any, pre-employment vetting takes place.
- Consider whether pre-employment vetting is justified for each of these jobs and whether the information could be obtained in a less intrusive way.
- Wherever practicable obtain relevant information directly from the applicant and, if necessary, verify it rather than undertake pre-employment vetting.
- Do not vet workers just because a customer for your products or services imposes a condition requiring you to do so, unless you can satisfy yourself that the condition is justified.

1.6.2 Only carry out pre-employment vetting on an applicant as at late a stage as is practicable in the recruitment process.

Key points and possible actions

- Ascertain at which point pre-employment vetting takes place and who is subject to it. Eliminate any comprehensive pre-employment vetting that takes place for all shortlisted applicants (only the people selected for the job should be submitted to comprehensive pre-employment vetting).

1.6.3 Make it clear early in the recruitment process that vetting will take place and how it will be conducted.

Key points and possible actions

- Provide information about any vetting that might take place on application forms or other recruitment material. This should explain the nature, extent and range of sources to be used to carry out the vetting.
- Make clear the extent to which you will release information about the applicant to the sources you use.

1.6.4 Only use vetting as a means of obtaining specific information, not as a means of general intelligence gathering. Ensure that the extent and nature of information sought is justified.

Key points and possible actions

- Ensure that there are clearly stated objectives in any vetting process.

- Consider the extent and nature of information that is sought against these objectives.
- Eliminate any vetting that consists of general intelligence-gathering. Ensure that it is clearly focused information that will have a significant bearing on the employment decision.

1.6.5 Only seek information from sources where it is likely that relevant information will be revealed. Only approach the applicant's family or close associates in exceptional cases.

Key points and possible actions

- Ensure that those who will seek the information are briefed about which sources to use, ensuring that those sources are likely to produce relevant information.
- Ensure that if family members or close associates are approached it can be justified by the special nature of the job.

1.6.6 Do not place reliance on information collected from possibly unreliable sources. Allow the applicant to make representations regarding information that will affect the decision to finally appoint.

Key points and possible actions

- Ensure that information that has been collected from a vetting process is evaluated in the light of the reliability of the sources.
- Ensure that no recruitment decision is made solely on the basis of information obtained from a source that may be unreliable.
- Ensure that if information received will lead to the applicant not being appointed, then this will be made known to the applicant.
- Put in place a mechanism for providing this feedback, allowing the applicant to respond and obliging those involved in the recruitment decision to take this response into account.

1.6.7 Where information is collected about a person other than the applicant that affects the other person's privacy, ensure so far as practicable that the other person is made aware of this.

Key points and possible actions

- Ensure that those conducting a vetting process are briefed to avoid discovering information about other people unnecessarily.
- Where substantial personal information has been collected about another person and is to be retained, ensure there is a process in place to inform the other person of this and of how the information will be used.

1.6.8 If it is necessary to secure the release of documents or information from a third party, obtain a signed consent from the applicant.

Key points and possible actions

- If you are asking a third party, such as a previous employer, to disclose confidential personal information to you the third party will need the applicant's permission before doing so.
- It may be easier for you to obtain this permission from the applicant and pass it on to the third party than for the third party to obtain permission directly.

1.7 Retention of recruitment records

[4.181]
1.7.1 Establish and adhere to retention periods for recruitment records that are based on a clear business need.

Key points and possible actions

- Assess who in your organisation retains recruitment records (eg are they held centrally, at departmental level or in the line).
- Ensure that no recruitment record is held beyond the statutory period in which a claim arising from the recruitment process may be brought unless there is a clear business reason for exceeding this period.
- Consider anonymising any recruitment information that is to be held longer than the period necessary for responding to claims.

1.7.2 Destroy information obtained by a vetting exercise as soon as possible, or in any case within 6 months. A record of the result of vetting or verification can be retained.

Key points and possible actions

- Check who in your organisation retains information from vetting. Ensure that vetting records are destroyed after 6 months. Manual records should be shredded and electronic files permanently deleted from the system.
- Inform those responsible for the destruction of this information that they may keep a record that vetting was carried out, the result and the recruitment decision taken.

1.7.3 Consider carefully which information contained on an application form is to be transferred to the worker's employment record. Do not retain information that has no bearing on the on-going employment relationship.

Key points and possible actions

- Check how information is transferred from recruitment records to employment records.
- Ensure those responsible for such transfers only move information relevant to on-going employment to employment files.

1.7.4 Delete information about criminal convictions collected in the course of the recruitment process once it has been verified through a Criminal Records Bureau disclosure unless, in exceptional circumstances, the information is clearly relevant to the on-going employment relationship.

Key points and possible actions

- Make sure it is only recorded whether a check has yielded a satisfactory or an unsatisfactory result. Delete other information.

1.7.5 If it is your practice to do so advise unsuccessful applicants that there is an intention to keep their names on file for future vacancies (if appropriate) and give them the opportunity to have their details removed from the file.

Key points and possible actions

- Ensure that application forms or surrounding documentation tell applicants that, should they be unsuccessful, their details will be kept on file unless they specifically request that this should not be the case.

1.7.6 Ensure that personal information received during the recruitment process are securely stored or are destroyed.

Key points and possible actions

- Assess who in your organisation presently processes recruitment information.
- Inform them that manual records should be kept securely, for example in a locked filing cabinet.
- Make sure that electronic files are kept securely, for example by using passwords and other technical security measures.

PART 2: EMPLOYMENT RECORDS

ABOUT PART 2 OF THE CODE

Data protection in employment records

[4.182]
Running a business necessarily involves keeping records about workers. Such records will contain information that is personal in nature and can affect a worker's privacy. The Act does not prevent an employer from collecting, maintaining and using records about workers but helps to strike a balance between the employer's need to keep records and the worker's right to respect for his or her private life. This part of the Code will assist employers not only to comply with the law but also to follow good records management practice.

What does this part of the code cover?

This part of the Code covers all aspects of the collection, holding and use of employment records from the initial obtaining of information once a worker has been employed or engaged through to the ultimate deletion of the former worker's record. It also deals with the rights of job applicants as well as workers to access to information the employer keeps about them. It does not though deal in detail with the collection and use of health information. This is covered in Part 4.

Some recommendations in the Code are only likely to be of relevance to those involved in particular activities such as marketing to their workers or to those who find themselves in particular situations such as a business merger or acquisition. For this reason some sub sections are likely to be of relevance mainly to larger organisations.

Sickness and injury records

For the purposes of this Code it is necessary to distinguish between records that include "sensitive data" and those that do not. The term 'sickness record' is therefore used to describe a record which contains details of the illness or condition responsible for a worker's absence. Similarly, an injury record is a record which contains details of the injury suffered. The term 'absence record' is used to describe a record that may give the reason for absence as 'sickness' or 'accident' but does not include any reference to specific medical conditions.

Many employers keep accident records. Such a record will only be an "injury record" if it includes details of the injury suffered by an identifiable worker.

Sickness and injury records include information about workers' physical or mental health. The holding of sickness or injury records will therefore involve the processing of sensitive personal data. This means one of the conditions for processing sensitive personal data must be satisfied.

Employers are advised as far as practicable to restrict their record keeping to absence records rather than sickness or injury records.

See Supplementary Guidance page 72 which explains more about the conditions for processing sensitive data.

Workers' access to information about themselves

Workers, like any other individuals, have a right to gain access to information that is kept about them. This right is known as subject access. The right applies, for example, to sickness records, disciplinary or training records, appraisal or performance review notes, e-mails, word-processed documents, e-mail logs, audit trails, information held in general personnel files and interview notes, whether held as computerised files, or as structured paper records. A fee of up to £10 can be charged by the employer for giving access.

Responding to a subject access request involves:

- telling the worker if the organisation keeps any personal information about him or her;
- giving the worker a description of the type of information the organisation keeps, the purposes it is used for and the types of organisations which it may be passed on to, if any;
- showing the worker all the information the organisation keeps about him or her, explaining any codes or other unintelligible terms used;
- providing this information in a hard copy or in readily readable, permanent electronic form unless providing it in that way would involve disproportionate effort or the worker agrees to receive it in some other way;
- providing the worker with any additional information the organisation has as to the source of the information kept about him or her.

There are a number of exemptions from the right of subject access which can be relevant in an employment context.

See Supplementary Guidance – Exemptions from the subject access right page 42 for details.

References

The provision of a reference about a worker from one party, such as a present employer, to another, such as a prospective employer, will generally involve the disclosure of personal data. In considering how the Act applies to such disclosure it is important to establish who the reference is being given by or on behalf of.

The Code therefore distinguishes between a reference given in a personal capacity and one given in a corporate capacity. A corporate reference is one given on behalf of the employer by one of its staff. Many employers have rules about who can give such a reference and what it can include. The employer remains legally responsible for compliance with the Data Protection Act.

A personal reference is one given by a member of staff in an individual capacity. It may refer to work done but it is not given on behalf of the employer. References that are given in a personal capacity do not, at least in data protection terms, incur a liability for the employer.

Under a specific exemption in the Act, a worker does not have the right to gain access to a confidential job reference from the organisation which has given it. However, once the reference is with the organisation to which it was sent then no such specific exemption from the right of access exists. That organisation is though entitled to take steps to protect the identity of third parties such as the author of the reference.

Disclosure requests

Employers regularly receive requests for information about individual workers that come from outside the employer's organisation. An employer has a responsibility to its workers to be cautious in responding to such requests. It risks a breach of the Act if it does not take sufficient care to ensure the interests of its workers are safeguarded. In some cases though the employer has no choice but to respond positively to a request for disclosure. This is where there is a legal obligation to disclose. It is not the Data Protection Act but other laws that create such obligations. Where they do so the Act does not stand in the way of disclosure.

In some other cases the employer will have a choice whether or not to disclose but provided sensitive data are not involved it is clear that the Act will not stand in the way of disclosure. This is where the circumstances of the disclosure are covered by one of the exemptions from the 'non-disclosure provisions' of the Act.

See Supplementary Guidance: Exemptions from non-disclosure page 43 for details.

GOOD PRACTICE RECOMMENDATIONS – PART 2

The parts of the Code referred to in this section are:

2.1 Collecting and keeping general records

2.2 Security

2.3 Sickness and injury records

2.4 Pension and insurance schemes

2.5 Equal opportunities monitoring

2.6 Marketing

2.7 Fraud detection

2.8 Workers' access to information about themselves

2.9 References

2.10 Disclosure requests

2.11 Publication and other disclosures

2.12Merger, acquisition, and business re-organisation

2.13 Discipline, grievance and dismissal

2.14 Outsourcing data processing

2.15 Retention of records

2.1 Collecting and keeping general records

[4.183]

2.1.1 Ensure that newly appointed workers are aware of the nature and source of any information stored about them, how it will be used and who it will be disclosed to.

Key points and possible actions

- It is not generally necessary to seek a worker's consent to keep employment records. It will usually be sufficient to ensure that the worker is aware that records are being kept and is given an explanation of the purposes they are kept for and the nature of any intended disclosures.
- It is only if sensitive data are collected that consent may be necessary.
- Decide on how best to inform new workers about how information about them will be held, used and disclosed.
- If your organisation has not done so previously, distribute this information to existing workers.
- In large organisations, randomly check with a sample of workers, that they did in fact receive this information. Rectify any communication gaps.

2.1.2 Inform new workers and remind existing workers about their rights under the Act, including their right of access to the information kept upon them.

Key points and possible actions

- Ensure that information given to new workers includes information about their rights under the Act.
- Set up a system to remind existing workers of their rights.

2.1.3 Ensure that there is a clear and foreseeable need for any information collected from workers and that the information collected actually meets that need.

Key points and possible actions

- Review all forms where information is requested from workers.
- Remove or amend any questions which require the worker to provide information extraneous to your needs.

2.1.4 Provide each worker with a copy of information that may be subject to change, eg personal details such as home address, annually or allow workers to view this on-line. Ask workers to check their records for accuracy and ensure any necessary amendments are made to bring records up-to-date.

Key points and possible actions

- Determine the different types of personal data kept about workers and whether they are likely to be subject to change.
- Decide whether data that change could easily be viewed electronically and make any changes to systems necessary to enable this.
- Ensure that the system restricts access to individuals' records so that each worker can only get access to his or her own record.
- If it is only possible for workers to view data manually, consider how this can best be done.
- Make provision to amend any details that are incorrect on individual workers' files.

2.1.5 Incorporate accuracy, consistency and validity checks into systems.

Key points and possible actions

- Review computerised systems to see if accuracy checks can be easily built in.
- Put in place arrangements to ensure that when systems are updated or new systems purchased they facilitate data protection compliance.
- Remember that legal responsibility for data protection compliance rests with users rather than suppliers of systems.

2.2 Security

[4.184]
2.2.1 Apply security standards that take account of the risks of unauthorised access to, accidental loss of, destruction of, or damage to employment records.

Key points and possible actions

- BS 7799: 1995 (Code of Practice for Information Security Management) provides guidance which, if followed, should address the main security risks.
- Obtain a copy of BS7799 if you do not have one already and compare its recommendations to your own existing procedures.
- Put in place measures to rectify any shortfalls, bearing in mind that not all controls will be relevant to all organisations.

2.2.2 Institute a system of secure cabinets, access controls and passwords to ensure that staff can only gain access to employment records where they have a legitimate business need to do so.

Key points and possible actions

- Review who in your organisation has access to employment records and determine whether it is necessary for everyone who currently has access to retain it.
- Remove access rights from those who have unnecessary or over-extensive access to personal information about others.
- Make sure manual files that hold personal information are securely held with locks and only those who should have access retain the key.
- In the case of computerised records, ensure that passwords or similar controls are set up to limit unauthorised access.

2.2.3 Use the audit trail capabilities of automated systems to track who accesses and amends personal information.

Key points and possible actions

- Check whether computerised systems that retain personal information currently have audit trail capabilities. If they do, check that the audit trail is enabled.
- If they do not, see if it would be possible to create audit trails of who accesses and amends personal information.
- If you have a system with audit trails, ensure that regular checks occur to detect unauthorised or suspicious use. Set up a procedure to investigate patterns of unusual or unauthorised access of personal information.

2.2.4 Take steps to ensure the reliability of staff that have access to workers' records.

Key points and possible actions

- Carry out background checks on staff that will have access to workers' records, for example by taking up references.
- Review the contracts of workers who deal with personal information to ensure they include confidentiality clauses concerning the unauthorised disclosure and use of personal information.
- Set up induction training for these staff that contains explanation about their responsibilities. Organise refresher training as and when necessary.

2.2.5 Ensure that if employment records are taken off-site, eg on laptop computers, this is controlled. Make sure only the necessary information is taken and there are security rules for staff to follow.

Key points and possible actions

- Formulate a procedure for taking laptop computers off-site (or review the existing procedure). Include points regarding the information that may be taken off-site, security of passwords and keeping the laptop in view or secured at all times.
- Inform all workers, including senior staff, of the procedure.

2.2.6 Take account of the risks of transmitting confidential worker information by fax or e-mail. Only transmit information between locations if a secure network or comparable arrangements are in place.

Key points and possible actions

- Check that your security policy properly addresses the risk of sending and receiving worker information by e-mail or fax and review the relevant procedures.
- Ensure that all managers use a secure system if workers' records are to be transmitted by fax.
- In the case of e-mail deploy some technical means of ensuring security, such as effective password protection and encryption.
- Advise all managers about permanently deleting e-mails that contain personal information about workers from their work-stations.
- Check whether deleted e-mails will still be kept on a server. Wherever possible ensure these too can be permanently deleted. In any case, restrict access to them.

2.3 Sickness and injury records

[4.185]
2.3.1 Where possible keep sickness and injury records separate from absence and accident records. Do not use sickness records for a particular purpose when records of absence could be used instead.

Key points and possible actions

- Review how sickness and accident records are currently kept.
- If necessary, change the way information on sickness and accidents is kept so that information on workers' health is not accessed when only information on absence or the circumstances of an accident at work is needed.
- Inform those accessing both sickness/injury and absence records of when it is and is not necessary to access the full sickness or injury records.

2.3.2 Ensure that the holding and use of sickness and injury records satisfies a sensitive data condition.

Key points and possible actions

- Check current practices on the use of sickness and injury records against the sensitive data conditions in the Code.
- Take any remedial action necessary including restricting the purposes for which records can be used and/or deleting records if no condition can be satisfied.
- Inform those handling sickness and injury records of any changes in procedures or practices.

See Supplementary Guidance page 72 which explains more about the sensitive data conditions.

2.3.3 Only disclose information from sickness or injury records about an identifiable worker's illness, medical condition or injury where there is a legal obligation to do so, where it is necessary for legal proceedings or where the worker has given explicit consent to the disclosure.

Key points and possible actions

- Ensure that all those who deal with workers' sickness or injury records are aware in which circumstances there may be a legal obligation to disclose.
- Ensure when appropriate, written consent is obtained from the worker.

2.3.4 Do not make the sickness, injury or absence records of individual workers available to other workers unless it is necessary for them to do their jobs.

Key points and possible actions

- Managers can be provided with information about those who work for them in so far as this is necessary for them to carry out their managerial roles.
- No 'league tables' of individual records should be published.
- Ensure that managers are aware of the sensitive nature of sickness and injury records.

2.4 Pension and insurance schemes

[4.186]
Pension or insurance-based schemes such as those offering private medical care are usually controlled by a third party but can be administered in-house. Some employers also insure their business against sickness by key workers. These recommendations are directed at employers who are party to such schemes rather than at insurance companies or pensions providers.

2.4.1 Do not access personal information required by a third party to administer a scheme, in order to use it for general employment purposes.

Key points and possible actions

- Identify and review schemes currently in operation in your business.
- Identify where information could possibly 'leak' from a scheme to be used for other employment purposes.
- Identify ways of stopping this occurring, for example by passing information in sealed envelopes.

2.4.2 Limit your exchange of information with a scheme provider to the minimum necessary for operation of the scheme bearing in mind the scheme's funding obligations.

Key points and possible actions

- Remember that if information on a worker's sickness, injury or other sensitive data is exchanged a sensitive data condition must be satisfied.
- Bear in mind that your funding of a scheme does not give you a right to receive information about individual scheme members beyond that necessary for the operation of the scheme.
- Review the exchange of information with any scheme providers.
- Identify and eliminate any personal information passed to you by the scheme provider that is not essential to the operation of the scheme.

2.4.3 Do not use information gained from the internal trustees or administrators of pension schemes for general employment purposes.

Key points and possible actions

- Inform trustees and administrators of their general data protection responsibilities. In particular make sure they know they must not use personal information acquired in their capacity as trustee or administrator in their capacity as employer.

2.4.4 If your business takes on the role of broker or your staff act as group secretary for a private medical insurance scheme, ensure that personal information gathered is kept to minimum, limit access to the information and do not use it for general employment purposes.

Key points and possible actions

- Consider carefully what information is actually needed to administer the scheme.
- Limit access to personal data arising from the administration of the scheme and ensure that information gathered in this context is not used for any other purposes.

2.4.5 Ensure that when a worker joins a health or insurance scheme it is made clear what, if any, information is passed between the scheme controller and the employer and how it will be used.

Key points and possible actions

- Assess the information given to workers when they join a health or insurance scheme.
- If no specific mention is made about the transfer of information, amend the documentation about the scheme accordingly.

2.5 Equal opportunities monitoring

[4.187]
2.5.1 Information about a worker's ethnic origin, disability, religion or sexual orientation is sensitive personal data. Ensure that equal opportunities monitoring of these characteristics satisfies a sensitive data condition.

Key points and possible actions

- Check your organisation's current equal opportunities monitoring against the sensitive data conditions in the Code.
- Make any necessary changes to the monitoring procedure to ensure that a sensitive data condition can always be satisfied.

See Supplementary Guidance page 72 for conditions to be satisfied.

2.5.2 Only use information that identifies individual workers where this is necessary to carry out meaningful equal opportunities monitoring. Where practicable, keep the information collected in an anonymised form.

Key points and possible actions

- Review current practices. Check whether any monitoring form gives the impression that information is anonymous, when in fact, it can be traced back to individuals.
- If identifiable information is held but it can be anonymised, do this.
- When there is no reasonable alternative but to be able to identify individuals, check whether the monitoring form states this and explains how the information is to be used.
- Ensure that identifiable information collected for equal opportunities monitoring is not used for any other purposes.
- Make any necessary changes to procedures and ensure that staff involved in monitoring understand why these changes have been made.

2.5.3 Ensure questions are designed so that the personal information collected through them is accurate and not excessive.

Key points and possible actions

- Check that questions allow people to identify themselves accurately. For example, in ethnic origin monitoring, do not limit the range of choices given so that workers are forced to make a choice that does not properly describe them.
- If you assign workers to categories ensure the record is clear that it is your assumption and not a matter of fact.

2.6 Marketing

[4.188]

2.6.1 Inform new workers if your organisation intends to use their personal information to deliver advertising or marketing messages to them. Give workers a clear opportunity to object (an 'opt-out') and respect any objections whenever received.

Key points and possible actions

- Review whether your business markets its, or anyone else's, products or services to current or former workers.
- Ensure that any new worker who will receive marketing information from your company has been informed that this will happen.
- Ensure that a clear procedure for 'opting-out' is made known to all workers.

2.6.2 Do not disclose workers' details to other organisations for their marketing unless individual workers have positively and freely indicated their agreement (an 'opt-in').

Key points and possible actions

- Review whether your business discloses workers' details. If so, put in place a procedure to ensure that a worker's details are not passed on until you have received a positive indication of agreement from him or her.

2.6.3 If you intend to use details of existing workers for marketing for the first time either in ways that were not explained when they first joined or that they would not expect, do not proceed until individual workers have positively and freely indicated their agreement (an 'opt-in').

Key points and possible actions

- When considering this type of campaign, construct an approval form to send to workers. Only direct material to those workers who have given a positive indication of agreement.
- Enclosing details of particular offers within a communication that workers will receive anyway, for example in a pay-slip, is acceptable as long as the offer includes an explanation of how to object.

2.7 Fraud detection

[4.189]

Public sector employers, in particular, use workers' records in the prevention and detection of fraud, for example, in order to check that they are not paying state benefits to those who by virtue of their employment are not entitled to receive them. Such exercises involve the electronic comparison of data sets held for different purposes in order to identify inconsistencies or discrepancies which may indicate fraud. This is known as data matching.

2.7.1 Consult workers, and/or trade unions or other representatives before starting a data matching exercise.

Key points and possible actions

- Inform trade unions and other workers' representatives of any proposed data matching exercise.
- Discuss how the plan will work in detail and take account of legitimate concerns raised before starting the exercise.

2.7.2 Inform new workers of the use of payroll or other information in fraud prevention exercises and remind them of this periodically.

Key points and possible actions

- Explain how fraud prevention exercises operate to new workers as part of information given about data protection.
- Set up regular reminders to workers on how the data matching exercise works – eg prior to the start of each new exercise.

2.7.3 Do not disclose worker information to other organisations for the prevention or detection of fraud unless:—

- you are required by law to make the disclosure, or
- you believe that failure to disclose, in a particular instance, is likely to prejudice the prevention or detection of crime, or
- the disclosure is provided for in workers' contracts of employment.

Key points and possible actions

- Ensure staff who would be approached by outside agencies for this type of information, understand the rules of disclosure.

2.8 Workers' access to information about themselves

[4.190]

Workers, like any other individuals, have a right to gain access to information that is kept about them. This right is known as subject access.

2.8.1 Establish a system that enables your organisation to recognise a subject access request and to locate all the information about a worker in order to be able to respond promptly and in any case within 40 calendar days of receiving a request.

Key points and possible actions

- Assess what personal information about workers is in existence and who is responsible for it (**See recommendation 0.3** ***ante***.)
- Ensure that the information is accessible.
- Establish who in the organisation is responsible for responding to subject access requests.
- Ensure that all workers who are likely to receive subject access requests can recognise them and know who to pass them to.
- Have a checklist in place listing all places where personal information might be held that should be checked.
- Use the checklist to gather all personal information in time to enable a response within 40 days.

2.8.2 Check the identity of anyone making a subject access request to ensure information is only given to the person entitled to it.

Key points and possible actions

- In smaller organisations where workers make access requests in person, identity checks may not be necessary, but in large organisations it should not simply be assumed all requests are genuine.
- Brief anyone responsible for responding to a subject access request on how to check the identity of the person making it.

2.8.3 Provide the worker with a hard copy of the information kept, making clear any codes used and the sources of the information.

Key points and possible actions

- In the checklist used to gather all personal information include a check to ensure that the information supplied is intelligible, that it includes sources and that if at all possible it is in hard copy form.
- Although a hard copy of the subject access information does not have to be provided if this would involve "disproportionate effort" some form of access to the information still has to be given.

2.8.4 Make a judgement as to what information it is reasonable to withhold concerning the identities of third parties.

Key points and possible actions

- Information released to a worker could include information that enables a third party such as another worker to be identified. The employer has to balance the worker's right to know against an expectation of privacy that the third party might have.
- You can use the guidance on Access when Information about Third Parties is involved on page 40 of the Supplementary Guidance to help you make the necessary judgement.
- Brief those handling subject access requests on how to make decisions concerning third party information.

2.8.5 Inform managers and other relevant people in the organisation of the nature of information that will be released to individuals who make subject access requests.

Key points and possible actions

- Managers should be made aware of the extent to which information relating to them might be released to workers.
- If managers and others are aware of the extent and nature of the information that an individual could gain access to it should encourage them to record only what is truly relevant and useful.

2.8.6 Ensure that on request, promptly and in any event within 40 calendar days, workers are provided with a statement of how any automated decision-making process, to which they are subject, is used, and how it works.

Key points and possible actions

- Determine whether your organisation has any automated systems which are used as the sole basis for decision-making, for example during short-listing.
- If so, document how the system works and the basis of its decisions.
- Make this information available to those who are responsible for responding to requests about the process and make sure that they are aware of the requirement to respond within 40 calendar days.

2.8.7 When purchasing a computerised system ensure that the system enables you to retrieve all the information relating to an individual worker without difficulty.

Key points and possible actions

- Ensure that the supplier of a system that you will use to take automated decisions about workers provides the information needed to enable you to respond fully to requests for information about how the system works.
- Put in place arrangements to ensure that when systems are updated or new systems purchased they facilitate responses to subject access requests.

2.9 References

[4.191]

The provision of a reference about a worker from one party, such as a present employer, to another, such as a prospective employer, will generally involve the disclosure of personal data. This sub section of the Code applies not only to references given to prospective employers, but also references given in other circumstances, for example character references given in connection with legal proceedings or financial references given in connection with a worker's application for a mortgage.

References Given:

2.9.1 Set out a clear company policy stating who can give corporate references, in what circumstances, and the policy that applies to the granting of access to them. Make anyone who is likely to become a referee aware of this policy.

Key points and possible actions

- Determine who is allowed to give corporate references, this may, for example, be done by grade. Check whether your organisation distinguishes between corporate and personal references. If not, consider doing so.
- Draw up a policy explaining how reference requests should be handled, outlining the types of information that can be provided and the extent to which workers are given access. Ensure the policy is brought to the attention of anyone who is likely to receive a reference request.

2.9.2 Do not provide confidential references about a worker unless you are sure that this is the worker's wish.

Key points and possible actions

- As part of the policy, include a requirement that all those giving corporate references must be satisfied that the worker wishes the reference to be provided.

- As part of an Exit Policy, include on file a record of whether the worker wishes references to be provided after he/she has left.

References received:

2.9.3 When responding to a request from a worker to see his or her own reference and the reference enables a third party to be identified, make a judgement as to what information it is reasonable to withhold.

Key points and possible actions

- You can use the guidance on Access when Information about Third Parties is Involved on page 40 of the Supplementary Guidance to help you make this judgement.
- Brief those responsible for responding to requests for access to references received on how to make decisions concerning third party information.

2.10 Disclosure requests

[4.192]
This is concerned with requests for information about individual workers that come from outside the employer's organisation.

2.10.1 Establish a disclosure policy to tell staff who are likely to receive requests for information about workers how to respond, and to where they should refer requests that fall outside the policy rules.

Key points and possible actions

- Distribute information, based on this Code, on how to handle disclosure requests and ensure that all those likely to handle such requests receive the information.
- Give examples of situations where a member of staff might need to refer a request to a higher authority within the organisation.
- Provide contact details of whom staff should contact, should they be unsure of how to deal with a disclosure request.

2.10.2 Ensure that disclosure decisions that are not covered by clear policy rules are only taken by staff who are familiar with the Act and this Code, and who are able to give the decision proper consideration.

Key points and possible actions

- Determine who will be responsible for dealing with disclosure requests not covered by the policy.
- Organise any necessary training for those who will take on this role.

2.10.3 Unless you are under a legal obligation to do so, only disclose information about a worker where you conclude that in all the circumstances it is right to do so.

Key points and possible actions

- In some cases you will be under a legal obligation to disclose. Where this is the case you have no choice but to disclose. The Act does not stand in your way provided that you disclose no more than you are obliged to.
- In some cases you will not be under an obligation to disclose but you will be able to rely on an exemption in the Act if you choose to do so. This is most likely to arise in the case of criminal or tax investigations or where legal action is involved.
- Where you can relay on an exemption in the Act you still need to take care with the disclosure of confidential or sensitive information.
- In other cases you could breach the Act if you disclose. Only disclose, if in all the circumstances you are satisfied that it is fair to do so. Bear in mind that the duty of fairness is owed primarily to the worker. Where possible seek and take account of the workers' views.
- Only disclose confidential information if the worker has clearly agreed or you are satisfied that despite the duty of confidence the worker's interest or the wider public interest justifies disclosure.
- Ensure that if you intend to disclose sensitive personal data a sensitive data condition is satisfied.

2.10.4 Where a disclosure is requested in an emergency, make a careful decision as to whether to disclose, considering the nature of the information being requested and the likely impact on the individual of not providing it.

Key points and possible actions

- Make sure staff who are likely to receive such requests know whether they can handle them themselves or if not, who to refer them to. If they handle them themselves make them aware of their responsibility to assess the nature of the emergency and determine whether the request could be submitted in writing.

2.10.5 Make staff aware that those seeking information sometimes use deception to gain access to it. Ensure that they check the legitimacy of any request and the identity and authority of the person making it.

Key points and possible actions

- As part of the disclosure policy, make it a requirement that staff check the identity of any person making a request, the authority of the individual concerned and the basis for the request.
- Ensure that when a request is made on the basis of a stated legal obligation, that it is received in writing, spelling out the legal obligation on which it is based. If the stated legal obligation is in doubt check it against the law.

2.10.6 Where the disclosure involves a transfer of information about a worker to a country outside the European Economic Area (EEA), ensure that there is a proper legal basis for making the transfer.

Key points and possible actions

- The Act restricts the transfer of personal information outside the EEA.
- Review the Information Commissioner's guidance at www.ico.gov.uk, if you intend to pass workers' information outside the EEA.
- Keep a record of the legal basis on which you make the transfer.

2.10.7 Inform the worker before or as soon as is practicable after a request has been received that a non-regular disclosure is to be made, unless prevented by law from doing so, or unless this would constitute a "tip off" prejudicing a criminal or tax investigation.

Key points and possible actions

- For each non-regular disclosure, make a judgment as to whether the worker can be informed and whether a copy of the information can be provided to him or her. (A reminder of this could be placed in any system for handling non-regular disclosures.)
- In cases where the information can be provided to the worker do so as soon as possible.

2.10.8 Keep a record of non-regular disclosures. Regularly check and review this record to ensure that the requirements of the Act are being satisfied.

Key points and possible actions

- Set up a system for non-regular disclosures recording the details of the person who made the disclosure, the person who authorised it, the person requesting the disclosure, the reasons for the disclosure, the information disclosed and the date and time.
- Also set up a system to regularly check and review this record.

2.11 Publication and other disclosures

[4.193]

2.11.1 If publishing information about workers ensure that:

- there is a legal obligation to do so, or
- the information is clearly not intrusive, or
- the worker has consented to disclosure, or
- the information is in a form that does not identify individual workers.

Key points and possible actions

- An employer must balance the benefits of publishing information about workers with the reasonable expectations of its workers that their employer will respect the privacy of their personal information.
- Assess the current information published about named workers (eg in annual reports or on the website or in other publications) and the basis on which this takes place.
- Determine whether it is necessary to obtain consent from workers who are named and if so, set up an arrangement for obtaining consent from workers who are named in publications in the future.

2.11.2 Where information about workers is published on the basis of consent, ensure that when the worker gives consent he or she is made aware of the extent of information that will be published, how it will be published and the implications of this.

Key points and possible actions

- In any arrangement for obtaining consent for the publication of information on named workers, ensure that the worker is made aware of the full extent of any information to be published and where it is to be published. This is particularly important if information is to be published on the internet.

2.11.3 Personal information about workers should only be supplied to a trade union for its recruitment purposes if:

- the trade union is recognised by the employer,
- the information is limited to that necessary to enable a recruitment approach, and
- each worker has been previously told that this will happen and has been given a clear opportunity to object.

Key points and possible actions

- If your organisation has a recognised trade union that is requesting personal information about workers for a recruitment drive, inform all workers and give them an opportunity to object if they so wish.

2.11.4 Where staffing information is supplied to trade unions in the course of collective bargaining, ensure the information is such that individual workers cannot be identified.

Key points and possible actions

- Review your arrangements for the supply of information in connection with collective bargaining to ensure that in future all information on workers is supplied in an anonymised form.

2.12 Merger, acquisition, and business re-organisation

[4.194]

Business mergers and acquisitions will generally involve the disclosure of information about workers. This may take place during evaluation of assets and liabilities prior to the final merger or acquisition decision. Once a decision has been made disclosure is also likely to take place either in the run-up to or at the time of the actual merger or acquisition. A similar situation arises in business re-organisations that involve the transfer of workers' employment from one legal entity to another. This sub-section of the Code will be relevant to such situations.

2.12.1 Ensure, wherever practicable, that information handed over to another organisation in connection with a prospective acquisition, merger or business re-organisation is anonymised.

Key points and possible actions

- Ensure that in any merger or acquisition situation, those responsible for negotiation are aware of the Code, including its provisions on sensitive data.
- Assess any request for personal information from the other organisation. If at all possible, limit the information given to anonymised details.

2.12.2 Only hand over personal information prior to a final merger or acquisition decision after securing assurances that it will be used solely for the evaluation of assets and liabilities, it will be treated in confidence and will not be disclosed to other parties, and it will be destroyed or returned after use.

Key points and possible actions

- Remind those negotiating that they must receive strict assurances about how personal information will be used and what will happen to it should discussions end.
- Consider setting up a "data room" with accompanying rules of access.

2.12.3 Unless it is impractical to do so, tell workers if their employment records are to be disclosed to another organisation before an acquisition, merger or re-organisation takes place. If the acquisition, merger or re-organisation proceeds make sure workers are aware of the extent to which their records are to be transferred to the new employer.

Key points and possible actions

- In some circumstances "insider trading" or similar restrictions will apply. An example is where providing an explanation to workers would alert them to the possibility of a takeover of which they would otherwise be unaware and could thereby affect the price of a company's shares. The obligation to provide an explanation to workers is lifted in such circumstances.

2.12.4 Where a merger, acquisition or re-organisation involves a transfer of information about a worker to a country outside the European Economic Area (EEA) ensure that there is a proper basis for making the transfer.

Key points and possible actions

- Review the Information Commissioner's guidance at www.ico.gov.uk: if you intend to pass workers' information outside the EEA.
- Check that there is a legal basis for the transfer that you intend to make.

2.12.5 New employers should ensure that the records they hold as a result of a merger, acquisition or re-organisation do not include excessive information, and are accurate and relevant.

Key points and possible actions

- Remember that a new employer's use of workers' information acquired as the result of a merger, acquisition or re-organisation is constrained by the expectations the workers will have from their former employer's use of information.
- When taking over an organisation assess what personal information you now hold as outlined in 0.3 and 0.4 (*ante*).

2.13 Discipline, grievance and dismissal

[4.195]
2.13.1 Remember that the Data Protection Act applies to personal information processed in relation to discipline, grievance and dismissal proceedings.

Key points and possible actions

- Assess your organisation's disciplinary procedures and grievance procedures. Consider whether they need to be amended in the light of the Code.
- Ensure that managers are aware that subject access rights apply even if responding to a request might impact on a disciplinary or grievance investigation or on forthcoming proceedings, unless responding would be likely to prejudice a criminal investigation.
- Ensure that those involved in investigating disciplinary matters or grievances are aware that they must not gather information by deception.
- Ensure that records used in the course of proceedings are of good enough quality to support any conclusion drawn from them.
- Ensure that all records are kept securely.
- Check that unsubstantiated allegations have been removed unless there are exceptional reasons for retaining some record.

2.13.2 Do not access or use information you keep about workers merely because it might have some relevance to a disciplinary or grievance investigation if access or use would be either:

- incompatible with the purpose(s) you obtained the information for, or
- disproportionate to the seriousness of the matter under investigation.

Key points and possible actions

- Make those in the organisation who are likely to carry out investigations aware that they do not have an unrestricted right of access to all information held about workers under investigation.
- Put in place a system to ensure that decisions on whether access is justified take into account the provisions of this Code and the Act.

2.13.3 Ensure that there are clear procedures on how "spent" disciplinary warnings are handled.

Key points and possible actions

- Determine what is meant by a "spent" warning in your organisation. Assess the disciplinary procedure and decide whether it needs to be amended to clarify what happens once a warning period has expired.
- Set up a diary system, either manual or computerised, to remove spent warnings from individual's records, if this is a requirement of your procedure.

2.13.4 Ensure that when employment is terminated the reason for this is accurately recorded, and that the record reflects properly what the worker has been told about the termination.

Key points and possible actions

- Ensure that if a worker has resigned, even if asked to do so, that this is recorded on his or her record, as "resigned" rather than "dismissed".

2.14 Outsourcing data processing

[4.196]
Frequently, organisations do not process all the information they hold on workers themselves but outsource this to other organisations. Such organisations are termed 'data processors' in the Data Protection Act.

2.14.1 Satisfy yourself that any data processor you choose adopts appropriate security measures both in terms of the technology it uses and how it is managed.

Key points and possible actions

- Check whether the data processor has in place appropriate security measures. Is it, for example, certified to BS7799?
- Check that the processor actually puts their security measures into practice.

2.14.2 Have in place a written contract with any data processor you choose that requires it to process personal information only on your instructions, and to maintain appropriate security.

Key points and possible actions

- If there is no contract, put one in place.
- Check that any contract you have with a data processor includes clauses ensuring proper data security measures.

2.14.3 Where the use of a data processor would involve a transfer of information about a worker to a country outside the European Economic Area (EEA), ensure that there is a proper basis for making the transfer.

Key points and possible actions

- Review the Information Commissioner guidelines at www.ico.gov.uk: if you intend to pass workers' information outside the EEA.
- Check that there is a legal basis for the transfer that you intend to make.

2.15 Retention of records

[4.197]

See Part 1: Recruitment and Selection for specific recommendations on retention of recruitment records.

2.15.1 Establish and adhere to standard retention times for the various categories of information to be held on the records of workers and former workers. Base the retention times on business need taking into account relevant professional guidelines.

Key points and possible actions

- Remember that the Act does not override any statutory requirement to retain records, for example, in relation to income tax or certain aspects of health and safety.
- Only retain information on records that is still needed; eliminate personal information that is no longer of any relevance, once the employment relationship has ended.
- As far as possible set standard retention times for categories of information held in employment records. Consider basing these on a risk analysis approach.
- Assess who in your organisation retains employment records (**see 0.3** *ante*). Make sure no one retains information beyond the standard retention times unless there is a sound business reason for doing so.
- If possible, set up a computerised system which flags information retained for more than a certain time as due for review or deletion.

2.15.2 Anonymise any information about workers and former workers where practicable.

Key points and possible actions

- Where statistical information only is required, anonymised records should be sufficient.

2.15.3 If the holding of any information on criminal convictions of workers is justified, ensure that the information is deleted once the conviction is 'spent' under the Rehabilitation of Offenders Act.

Key points and possible actions

- Use a computerised or manual system to ensure spent convictions are deleted from the system.
- Identify if your organisation may be justified in making exceptions to this, for example, certain convictions held in connection with workers who work with children.

2.15.4 Ensure that records which are to be disposed of are securely and effectively destroyed.

Key points and possible actions

- Review arrangements for dealing with old records to ensure they are securely disposed of and advise anyone holding employment records of these arrangements for disposal.
- Do not assume that pressing the "delete" key on a computer based system necessarily removes a record completely from the system. Check that computer records that are to be deleted are in practice removed completely.

- Make sure that computer equipment that has held employment records is never sold on unless you are sure the records have been fully removed.

PART 3: MONITORING AT WORK

ABOUT PART 3 OF THE CODE

Data protection and monitoring at work

[4.198]
A number of the requirements of the Data Protection Act will come into play whenever an employer wishes to monitor workers. The Act does not prevent an employer from monitoring workers, but such monitoring must be done in a way which is consistent with the Act. Employers – especially in the public sector – must also bear in mind Article 8 of the European Convention on Human Rights which creates a right to respect for private and family life and for correspondence.

How does the Data Protection Act regulate monitoring?

Monitoring is a recognised component of the employment relationship. Most employers will make some checks on the quantity and quality of work produced by their workers. Workers will generally expect this. Many employers carry out monitoring to safeguard workers, as well as to protect their own interests or those of their customers. For example, monitoring may take place to ensure that those in hazardous environments are not being put at risk through the adoption of unsafe working practices. Monitoring arrangements may equally be part of the security mechanisms used to protect personal information. In other cases, for example in the context of some financial services, the employer may be under legal or regulatory obligations which it can only realistically fulfil if it undertakes some monitoring. However where monitoring goes beyond one individual simply watching another and involves the manual recording or any automated processing of personal information, it must be done in a way that is both lawful and fair to workers.

Monitoring may, to varying degrees, have an adverse impact on workers. It may intrude into their private lives, undermine respect for their correspondence or interfere with the relationship of mutual trust and confidence that should exist between them and their employer. The extent to which it does this may not always be immediately obvious. It is not always easy to draw a distinction between work-place and private information. For example monitoring e-mail messages from a worker to an occupational health advisor, or messages between workers and their trade union representatives, can give rise to concern.

In broad terms, what the Act requires is that any adverse impact on workers is justified by the benefits to the employer and others. This Code is designed to help employers determine when this might be the case.

What does this part of the Code cover?

This part of the Code applies where activities that are commonly referred to as "monitoring" are taking place or are planned. This means activities that set out to collect information about workers by keeping them under some form of observation, normally with a view to checking their performance or conduct. This could be done either directly, indirectly, perhaps by examining their work output, or by electronic means.

This part of Code is primarily directed at employers – especially larger organisations – using or planning some form of **systematic monitoring**. This is where the employer monitors all workers or particular groups of workers as a matter of routine, perhaps by using an electronic system to scan all e-mail messages or by installing monitoring devices in all company vehicles.

The Act still applies to **occasional monitoring**. This is where the employer introduces monitoring as a short term measure in response to a particular problem or need, for example by keeping a watch on the e-mails sent by a worker suspected of racial harassment or by installing a hidden camera when workers are suspected of drug dealing on the employer's premises.

This part of the Code deals with both types of monitoring, but it is likely to be of most relevance to employers involved in systematic monitoring, which will generally be larger organisations.

Examples of monitoring

There is no hard-and-fast definition of 'Monitoring' to which this part of the Code applies. Examples of activities addressed in this part of the Code include:

- gathering information through point of sale terminals, to check the efficiency of individual supermarket check-out operators
- recording the activities of workers by means of CCTV cameras, either so that the recordings can be viewed routinely to ensure that health and safety rules are being complied with, or so that they are available to check on workers in the event of a health and safety breach coming to light

- randomly opening up individual workers' e-mails or listening to their voice-mails to look for evidence of malpractice
- using automated checking software to collect information about workers, for example to find out whether particular workers are sending or receiving inappropriate e-mails
- examining logs of websites visited to check that individual workers are not downloading pornography
- keeping recordings of telephone calls made to or from a call centre, either to listen to as part of workers training, or simply to have a record to refer to in the event of a customer complaint about a worker
- systematically checking logs of telephone numbers called to detect use of premium-rate lines
- videoing workers outside the workplace, to collect evidence that they are not in fact sick
- obtaining information through credit reference agencies to check that workers are not in financial difficulties.

Outside this part of the Code

There are other activities that this part of the Code does not specifically address. Most employers will keep some business records that contain information about workers but are not collected primarily to keep a watch on their performance or conduct. An example could be records of customer transactions – including paper records, computer records or recordings of telephone calls. This part of the Code is **not** concerned with occasional access to records of this type in the course of an investigation into a specific problem, such as a complaint from a customer.

See Part 2: Employment Records, para 2.13, for guidance relating to grievance and disciplinary investigations.

Examples of activities not directly addressed in this part of the Code include;

- looking back through customer records in the event of a complaint, to check that the customer was given the correct advice
- checking a collection of e-mails sent by a particular worker which is stored as a record of transactions, in order to ensure the security of the system or to investigate an allegation of malpractice
- looking back through a log of telephone calls made that is kept for billing purposes, to establish whether a worker suspected of disclosing trade secrets has been contacting a competitor.

Impact assessments

The Data Protection Act does not prevent monitoring. Indeed in some cases monitoring might be necessary to satisfy its requirements. However, any adverse impact of monitoring on individuals must be justified by the benefits to the employer and others. We use the term "impact assessment" to describe the process of deciding whether this is the case.

In all but the most straightforward cases, employers are likely to find it helpful to carry out a formal or informal 'impact assessment' to decide if and how to carry out monitoring. This is the means by which employers can judge whether a monitoring arrangement is a proportionate response to the problem it seeks to address. This Code does not prejudge the outcome of the impact assessment. Each will necessarily depend on the particular circumstances of the employer. Nor does the Code attempt to set out for employers the benefits they might gain from monitoring. What it does do is assist employers in identifying and giving appropriate weight to the other factors they should take into account.

An impact assessment involves;

- identifying clearly the **purpose(s)** behind the monitoring arrangement and the benefits it is likely to deliver
- identifying any likely **adverse impact** of the monitoring arrangement
- considering **alternatives** to monitoring or different ways in which it might be carried out
- taking into account the **obligations** that arise from monitoring
- judging whether monitoring is **justified**.

Adverse impact

Identifying any likely adverse impact means taking into account the consequences of monitoring, not only for workers, but also for others who might be affected by it, such as customers. Consider:

- what intrusion, if any, will there be into the private lives of workers and others, or interference with their private e-mails, telephone calls or other correspondence? Bear in mind that the private lives of workers can, and usually will, extend into the workplace.
- to what extent will workers and others know when either they, or information about them, are being monitored and then be in a position to act to limit any intrusion or other adverse impact on themselves?

- whether information that is confidential, private or otherwise sensitive will be seen by those who do not have a business need to know, eg IT workers involved in monitoring e-mail content
- what impact, if any, will there be on the relationship of mutual trust and confidence that should exist between workers and their employer?
- what impact, if any, will there be on other legitimate relationships, eg between trades union members and their representatives?
- what impact, if any, will there be on individuals with professional obligations of confidentiality or secrecy, eg solicitors or doctors?
- whether the monitoring will be oppressive or demeaning.

Alternatives

Considering alternatives, or different methods of monitoring, means asking questions such as:

- can established or new methods of supervision, effective training and/or clear communication from managers, rather than electronic or other systemic monitoring, deliver acceptable results?
- can the investigation of specific incidents or problems be relied on, for example accessing stored e-mails to follow up an allegation of malpractice, rather than undertaking continuous monitoring?
- can monitoring be limited to workers about whom complaints have been received, or about whom there are other grounds to suspect of wrong-doing?
- can monitoring be targeted at areas of highest risk, eg can it be directed at a few individuals whose jobs mean they pose a particular risk to the business rather than at everyone?
- can monitoring be automated? If so, will it be less intrusive, eg does it mean that private information will be 'seen' only by a machine rather than by other workers?
- can spot-checks or audit be undertaken instead of using continuous monitoring? Remember though that continuous automated monitoring could be less intrusive than spot-check or audit that involves human intervention.

Obligations

Taking into account the obligations that arise from monitoring means considering such matters as:

- whether and how workers will be notified about the monitoring arrangements
- how information about workers collected through monitoring will be kept securely and handled in accordance with the Act.

See Part 2 – Employment Records, para 2.2, for more information on security requirements.

- the implications of the rights that individuals have to obtain a copy of information about them that has been collected through monitoring.

See Part 2 – Employment Records, para 2.8, which explains more about rights to access.

Is monitoring justified?

Making a conscious decision as to whether the current or proposed method of monitoring is justified involves;

- establishing the benefits of the method of monitoring
- considering any alternative method of monitoring
- weighing these benefits against any adverse impact
- placing particular emphasis on the need to be fair to individual workers
- ensuring, particularly where monitoring electronic communications is involved, that any intrusion is no more than absolutely necessary
- bearing in mind that significant intrusion into the private lives of individuals will not normally be justified unless the employer's business is at real risk of serious damage
- taking into account the results of consultation with trade unions or other representatives, if any, or with workers themselves.

See Supplementary Guidance page 57 for a chart to help assess the degree of intrusiveness involved in monitoring the content of various types of communication

Making an impact assessment need not be a complicated or onerous process. It will often be enough for an employer to make a simple mental evaluation of the risks faced by his or her business and to assess whether the carrying out of monitoring would reduce or eradicate those risks. In other cases the impact assessment will be more complicated, for example where an employer faces a number of different risks of varying degrees of seriousness. In such cases appropriate documentation would be advisable.

Is a worker's consent needed?

There are limitations as to how far consent can be relied on in the employment context to justify the processing of personal information. To be valid, for the purposes of the Data Protection Act, consent must be "freely given", which may not be the case in the employment environment. Once given, consent can be withdrawn. In any case, employers who can justify monitoring on the basis of an impact assessment will not generally need the consent of individual workers.

Are there special rules for electronic communications?

Electronic communications are broadly telephone calls, fax messages, e-mails and internet access. Monitoring can involve the 'interception' of such communications. The Regulation of Investigatory Powers Act, and the Lawful Business Practice Regulations made under it, set out when interception can take place despite the general rule that interception without consent is against the law. It should be remembered that – whilst the Regulations deal only with interception – the Data Protection Act is concerned more generally with the processing of personal information. Therefore when monitoring involves an interception which results in the recording of personal information an employer will need to satisfy both the Regulations and the requirements of the Data Protection Act.

See Supplementary Guidance page 58, for more details on The Lawful Business Practice Regulations.

GOOD PRACTICE RECOMMENDATIONS – PART 3

The parts of the Code in this section are:

3.1 The general approach to monitoring

3.2 Monitoring electronic communications

3.3 Video and audio monitoring

3.4 Covert monitoring

3.5 In-vehicle monitoring

3.6 Monitoring through information from third parties

3.1 The general approach to monitoring

[4.199]

Core Principles

- It will usually be intrusive to monitor your workers.
- Workers have legitimate expectations that they can keep their personal lives private and that they are also entitled to a degree of privacy in the work environment.
- If employers wish to monitor their workers, they should be clear about the purpose and satisfied that the particular monitoring arrangement is justified by real benefits that will be delivered.
- Workers should be aware of the nature, extent and reasons for any monitoring, unless (exceptionally) covert monitoring is justified.
- In any event, workers' awareness will influence their expectations.

3.1.1 Identify who within the organisation can authorise the monitoring of workers and ensure they are aware of the employer's responsibilities under the Act.

Key points and possible actions

- There are non-compliance risks if line mangers introduce monitoring arrangements without due authority.
- Those who monitor workers, or who can authorise such monitoring, should be briefed on the Act and this Code.

3.1.2 Before monitoring, identify clearly the purpose(s) behind the monitoring and the specific benefits it is likely to bring. Determine – preferably using an impact assessment – whether the likely benefits justify any adverse impact.

Key points and possible actions

- Identify the monitoring that currently takes place in your organisation.
- Identify any monitoring that you plan to implement.
- Consider conducting an impact assessment on either current or planned monitoring based on the guidance ante.

3.1.3 If monitoring is to be used to enforce the organisation's rules and standards make sure that the rules and standards are clearly set out in a policy which also refers to the nature and extent of any associated monitoring. Ensure workers are aware of the policy.

Key points and possible actions

- Identify which of your organisation's rules and standards are enforced partly or wholly through the use of monitoring.

- Ensure that these rules and standards are set out in policies that are clearly communicated to workers.

3.1.4 Tell workers what monitoring is taking place and why, and keep them aware of this, unless covert monitoring is justified.

Key points and possible actions

- Ensure that workers are aware of the nature and extent of any monitoring.
- Set up a system (for example by using the workers handbook or via an intranet) to ensure workers remain aware that monitoring is being conducted.
- Tell workers when significant changes are introduced.

3.1.5 If sensitive information is collected in the course of monitoring, ensure that a sensitive data condition is satisfied.

Key points and possible actions

- If monitoring workers' performance or conduct results in the collection of information on such matters as health, racial origin, trade union activities or sex life, check that at least one of the sensitive data conditions is met. See Supplementary Guidance page 72 which explains more about the conditions for processing sensitive data.

3.1.6 Keep to a minimum those who have access to personal information obtained through monitoring. Subject them to confidentiality and security requirements and ensure that they are properly trained where the nature of the information requires this.

Key points and possible actions

- Assess whether the organisation could reduce the number of staff involved in monitoring workers.
- Consider whether monitoring is more appropriately carried out by security or personnel functions rather than by line managers.
- Ensure that the training for workers who may come across personal information whilst monitoring makes them aware of data protection obligations.

3.1.7 Do not use personal information collected through monitoring for purposes other than those for which the monitoring was introduced unless:

(a) it is clearly in the individual's interest to do so; or

(b) it reveals activity that no employer could reasonably be expected to ignore.

Key points and possible actions

- Ensure that only senior management can authorise the use of personal information obtained through monitoring for new or different purposes.
- Ensure that they are familiar with the Act and the relevant parts of this Code.

3.1.8 If information gathered from monitoring might have an adverse impact on workers, present them with the information and allow them to make representations before taking action.

Key points and possible actions

- Equipment or systems malfunction can cause information collected through monitoring to be misleading or inaccurate. Information can also be misinterpreted or even deliberately falsified.
- Ensure that, within or alongside disciplinary or grievance procedures, workers can see, and if necessary explain or challenge, the results of any monitoring.

3.1.9 Ensure that the right of access of workers to information about them which is kept for, or obtained through, monitoring is not compromised. Monitoring systems must be capable of meeting this and other data protection requirements.

Key points and possible actions

- Assess whether monitoring systems collect information in a way that enables you to respond readily to access requests.
- If they do not, ensure that a mechanism that will allow you to do so is built into the system.
- Check that any electronic monitoring system, bought 'off-the-shelf', has the capability to enable you to meet access requests.

3.1.10 Do not monitor workers just because a customer for your products or services imposes a condition requiring you to do so, unless you can satisfy yourself that the condition is justified.

Key points and possible actions

- Monitoring is not justified simply because it is a condition of business. Such a condition cannot over-ride the employer's obligations to comply with the Act.

- Consider carrying out an impact assessment to assess whether meeting any external stipulation means that your organisation is in breach of the Act. If so, cease monitoring on this basis.

3.2 Monitoring electronic communications

[4.200]
This sub-section deals with the monitoring of telephone, fax, e-mail, voice-mail, internet access and other forms of electronic communication.

3.2.1 If you wish to monitor electronic communications, establish a policy on their use and communicate it to workers – see 'Policy for the use of electronic communications' below.

Key points and possible actions

- If your organisation does not have a policy on the use of electronic communications, decide whether you should establish one.
- Review any existing policy to ensure that it reflects data protection principles.
- Review any existing policies and actual practices to ensure that they are not out of line, eg whether private calls are banned in the policy but generally accepted in practice.
- Check that workers are aware of the policy and if not bring it to their attention.

Policy for the use of electronic communications

Employers should consider integrating the following data protection features into a policy for the use of electronic communications:

- Set out clearly to workers the circumstances in which they may or may not use the employer's telephone systems (including mobile phones), the e mail system and internet access for private communications.
- Make clear the extent and type of private use that is allowed, for example restrictions on overseas phone calls or limits on the size and/or type of e-mail attachments that they can send or receive.
- In the case of internet access, specify clearly any restrictions on material that can be viewed or copied. A simple ban on 'offensive material' is unlikely to be sufficiently clear for people to know what is and is not allowed. Employers may wish to consider giving examples of the sort of material that is considered offensive, for example material containing racist terminology or nudity.
- Advise workers about the general need to exercise care, about any relevant rules, and about what personal information they are allowed to include in particular types of communication.
- Make clear what alternatives can be used, eg the confidentiality of communications with the company doctor can only be ensured if they are sent by internal post, rather than by e-mail, and are suitably marked.
- Lay down clear rules for private use of the employer's communication equipment when used from home or away from the workplace, eg the use of facilities that enable external dialling into company networks
- Explain the purposes for which any monitoring is conducted, the extent of the monitoring and the means used.
- Outline how the policy is enforced and penalties which exist for a breach of policy.

There may, of course, be other matters that an employer also wants to address in its policy.

3.2.2 Ensure that where monitoring involves the interception of a communication it is not outlawed by the Regulation of Investigatory Powers Act 2000.

Key points and possible actions

- Interception occurs when, in the course of its transmission, the contents of a communication are made available to someone other than the sender or intended recipient. It does not include access to stored e-mails that have been opened.
- The intended recipient may be the business, but it could be a specified individual.
- Check whether any interception is allowed under the Lawful Business Practice Regulations.
- Take any necessary action to bring such monitoring in line with RIPA and these Regulations.

See Supplementary Guidance page 58 for more information about the Lawful Business Practice Regulations.

3.2.3 Consider – preferably using an impact assessment – whether any monitoring of electronic communications can be limited to that necessary to ensure the security of the system and whether it can be automated.

Key points and possible actions

- Automated systems can be used to provide protection from intrusion, malicious code such as viruses and Trojans, and to prevent password misuse. Such systems may be less intrusive than monitoring of communications to or from workers.

3.2.4 If telephone calls or voice-mails are, or are likely to be, monitored, consider – preferably using an impact assessment – whether the benefits justify the adverse impact. If so, inform workers about the nature and extent of such monitoring.

Key points and possible actions

- If telephone calls or voice-mails are monitored, or will be monitored in the future, consider carrying out an impact assessment.
- If voice-mails need to be checked for business calls when workers are away, make sure they know this may happen and that it may be unavoidable that some personal messages are heard.
- In other cases, assess whether it is essential to monitor the content of calls and consider the use of itemised call records instead.
- Ensure that workers are aware of the nature and extent of telephone monitoring.

3.2.5 Ensure that those making calls to, or receiving calls from, workers are aware of any monitoring and the purpose behind it, unless this is obvious.

Key points and possible actions

- Consider the use of recorded messages, informing external callers that calls may be monitored.
- If this is not feasible, encourage workers to tell callers that their conversations may be monitored.

3.2.6 Ensure that workers are aware of the extent to which you receive information about the use of telephone lines in their homes, or mobile phones provided for their personal use, for which your business pays partly or fully. Do not make use of information about private calls for monitoring, unless they reveal activity that no employer could reasonably be expected to ignore.

Key points and possible actions

- Remember that expectations of privacy are likely to be significantly greater at home than in the workplace.
- If any workers using mobiles or home telephone lines, for which you pay, are currently subjected to monitoring ensure that they are aware of the nature and the reasons for monitoring.

3.2.7 If e-mails and/or internet access are, or are likely to be, monitored, consider, preferably using an impact assessment, whether the benefits justify the adverse impact. If so, inform workers about the nature and extent of all e-mail and internet access monitoring.

Key points and possible actions

- If e-mails and/or internet access are presently monitored, or will be monitored in the future, consider carrying out an impact assessment.
- Check that workers are aware of the nature and extent of e-mail and internet access monitoring.

3.2.8 Wherever possible avoid opening e-mails, especially ones that clearly show they are private or personal.

Key points and possible actions

- Ensure that e-mail monitoring is confined to address/heading unless it is essential for a valid and defined reason to examine content.
- Encourage workers to mark any personal e-mails as such and encourage them to tell those who write to them to do the same.
- If workers are allowed to access personal e-mail accounts from the workplace, such e-mails should only be monitored in exceptional circumstances.

3.2.9 Where practicable, and unless this is obvious, ensure that those sending e-mails to workers, as well as workers themselves, are aware of any monitoring and the purpose behind it.

Key points and possible actions

- It may be practicable – for example when soliciting e-mail job applications – to provide information about the nature and extent of monitoring.
- In some cases, those sending e-mails to a work-place address will be aware that monitoring takes place without the need for specific information.

3.2.10 If it is necessary to check the e-mail accounts of workers in their absence, make sure that they are aware that this will happen.

Key points and possible actions

- If e-mail accounts need to be checked in the absence of workers, make sure they know this will happen.
- Encourage the use of a marking system to help protect private or personal communications.
- Avoid, where possible, opening e-mails that clearly show they are private or personal communications.

3.2.11 Inform workers of the extent to which information about their internet access and e-mails is retained in the system and for how long.

Key points and possible actions

- Check whether workers are currently aware of the retention period of e-mail and internet usage.
- If it is not already in place, set up a system (eg displaying information online or in a communication pack) that informs workers of retention periods.

3.3. Video and audio monitoring

[4.201]
Some – though not all – of the data protection issues that arise when carrying out video monitoring in public places will arise in the workplace. Employers carrying out video monitoring of workers will therefore find the guidance in the Information Commissioner's CCTV Code useful. Audio monitoring means the recording of face-to-face conversations, not recording telephone calls.

See www.ico.gov.uk and search for the CCTV Code of Practice.

3.3.1 If video or audio monitoring is (or is likely) to be used, consider – preferably using an impact assessment – whether the benefits justify the adverse impact.

Key points and possible actions

- Where possible, any video or audio monitoring should be targeted at areas of particular risk and confined to areas where expectations of privacy are low.
- Continuous video or audio monitoring of particular individuals is only likely to be justified in rare circumstances.

3.3.2 Give workers a clear notification that video or audio monitoring is being carried out and where and why it is being carried out.

Key points and possible actions

- Unless covert monitoring is justified, ensure that workers are informed of the extent and nature of any monitoring that is taking place and the reasons for it.

3.3.3 Ensure that people other than workers, such as visitors or customers, who may inadvertently be caught by monitoring, are made aware of its operation and why it is being carried out.

Key points and possible actions

- Ensure that there are adequate notices, or other means, to inform such people about the monitoring and its purpose(s).

3.4 Covert monitoring

[4.202]
Covert monitoring means monitoring carried out in a manner calculated to ensure those subject to it are unaware that it is taking place. This sub-section is largely directed at covert video or audio monitoring, but will also be relevant where electronic communications are monitored when workers would not expect it.

3.4.1 Senior management should normally authorise any covert monitoring. They should satisfy themselves that there are grounds for suspecting criminal activity or equivalent malpractice and that notifying individuals about the monitoring would prejudice its prevention or detection.

Key points and possible actions

- Covert monitoring should not normally be considered. It will be rare for covert monitoring of workers to be justified. It should therefore only be used in exceptional circumstances.

3.4.2 Ensure that any covert monitoring is strictly targeted at obtaining evidence within a set timeframe and that the covert monitoring does not continue after the investigation is complete.

Key points and possible actions

- Deploy covert monitoring only as part of a specific investigation and cease once the investigation has been completed.

3.4.3 Do not use covert audio or video monitoring in areas which workers would genuinely and reasonably expect to be private.

Key points and possible actions

- If embarking on covert monitoring with audio or video equipment, ensure that this is not used in places such as toilets or private offices.
- There may be exceptions to this in cases of suspicion of serious crime but there should be an intention to involve the police.

3.4.4 If a private investigator is employed to collect information on workers covertly make sure there is a contract in place that requires the private investigator to only collect information in a way that satisfies the employer's obligations under the Act.

Key points and possible actions

- Check any arrangements for employing private investigators to ensure your contracts with them impose requirements on the investigator to only collect and use information on workers in accordance with your instructions and to keep the information secure.

3.4.5 Ensure that information obtained through covert monitoring is used only for the prevention or detection of criminal activity or equivalent malpractice. Disregard and, where feasible, delete other information collected in the course of monitoring unless it reveals information that no employer could reasonably be expected to ignore.

Key points and possible actions

- In a covert monitoring exercise, limit the number of people involved in the investigation.
- Prior to the investigation, set up clear rules limiting the disclosure and access to information obtained.
- If information is revealed in the course of covert monitoring that is tangential to the original investigation, delete it from the records unless it concerns other criminal activity or equivalent malpractice.

3.5 In-vehicle monitoring

[4.203]

Devices can record or transmit information such as the location of a vehicle, the distance it has covered and information about the user's driving habits. Monitoring of vehicle movements, where the vehicle is allocated to a specific driver, and information about the performance of the vehicle can therefore be linked to a specific individual, will fall within the scope of the Data Protection Act.

3.5.1 If in-vehicle monitoring is or will be used, consider – preferably using an impact assessment – whether the benefits justify the adverse impact.

Key points and possible actions

- Where private use of a vehicle is allowed, monitoring its movements when used privately, without the freely given consent of the user, will rarely be justified.
- If the vehicle is for both private and business use, it ought to be possible to provide a 'privacy button' or similar arrangement to enable the monitoring to be disabled.
- Where an employer is under a legal obligation to monitor the use of vehicles, even if used privately, for example by fitting a tachograph to a lorry, then the legal obligation will take precedence.

3.5.2 Set out a policy that states what private use can be made of vehicles provided by, or on behalf of, the employer, and any conditions attached to use.

Key points and possible actions

- Make sure, either in the policy or separately, that details of the nature and extent of monitoring are set out.
- Check that workers using vehicles are aware of the policy.

3.6 Monitoring through information from third parties

[4.204]

Employers need to take special care when wishing to make use of information held by third parties, such as credit reference or electoral roll information. This section also applies to information held by employers in a non-employment capacity, such as when a bank monitors its workers' bank accounts. Where an employer wishes to obtain information about a worker's criminal convictions, a disclosure must be obtained via the Criminal Records Bureau.

See Part 1 – Recruitment and Selection, para 1.3.2, for more information about the Criminal Records Bureau.

3.6.1 Before undertaking any monitoring which uses information from third parties, ensure – preferably using an impact assessment – that the benefits justify the adverse impact.

Key points and possible actions

- A worker's financial circumstances should not be monitored unless there are firm grounds to conclude that financial difficulties would pose a significant risk to the employer.

3.6.2 Tell workers what information sources are to be used to carry out checks on them and why the checks are to be carried out.

Key points and possible actions

- Set up a system to tell workers the nature and extent of any monitoring which uses information from third parties. (This could be via a workers handbook, notice board or on-line.)
- Where a specific check is to be carried out, the workers should be directly informed, unless to do so would be likely to prejudice the prevention or detection of crime.

3.6.3 Ensure that, if workers are monitored through the use of information held by a credit reference agency, the agency is aware of the use to which the information is put. Do not use a facility provided to conduct credit checks on customers to monitor or vet workers.

Key points and possible actions

- If your organisation uses a credit reference agency to check customers, make sure this facility is not being used to monitor or vet workers. If such practices are in place, stop them immediately.

3.6.4 Take particular care with information about workers which you have as a result of a non-employment relationship with them.

Key points and possible actions

- Check whether your organisation routinely uses information about workers that has been obtained from them because they are also (or have been) your customers, clients or suppliers. If such practices are in place, stop them unless they are justified by a risk you face.

3.6.5 Ensure that workers carrying out monitoring which involves information from third parties are properly trained. Put in place rules preventing the disclosure or inappropriate use of information obtained through such monitoring.

Key points and possible actions

- Identify who may carry out monitoring using information from third parties.
- Assess whether the organisation could reduce the number of workers involved in this activity without compromising necessary monitoring.
- Set up instructions or training for workers involved in this monitoring, making them aware of the data protection principles involved.
- Consider placing confidentiality clauses in the contracts of relevant staff.

3.6.6 Do not retain all the information obtained through such monitoring. Simply record that a check has taken place and the result of this.

Key points and possible actions

- Review procedures on retaining information. Unless there is a legal or regulatory obligation, check that information is not normally retained for more than 6 months.

PART 4: INFORMATION ABOUT WORKERS' HEALTH

ABOUT PART 4 OF THE CODE

Data protection and information about workers' health

[4.205]

The Data Protection Act's sensitive data rules come into play whenever an employer wishes to process information about workers' health. These rules do not prevent the processing of such information but limit the circumstances in which it can take place. The processing must also be consistent with the other requirements of the Act. Employers, especially in the public sector, need to bear in mind Article 8 of the European Convention on Human Rights which creates a right to respect for private and family life.

What does this part of the Code cover?

This part of the Code addresses the collection and subsequent use of information about a worker's physical or mental health or condition. Collection will often be done by some form of medical examination or test, but may involve other means such as health questionnaires.

The issues addressed in this part of the Code will arise typically from the carrying out of medical examination and testing or from the operation of an occupational health scheme. This part of the Code is therefore most likely to be of relevance to larger organisations and those with specific health and safety obligations.

Examples of information about workers' health

This part of the Code applies to information such as:

- a questionnaire completed by workers to detect problems with their health
- information about a worker's disabilities or special needs
- the results of an eye-test taken by a worker using display screens
- records of blood tests carried out to ensure a worker has not been exposed to hazardous substances
- the results of a test carried out to check a worker's exposure to alcohol or drugs
- the results of genetic tests carried out on workers
- an assessment of fitness for work to determine entitlement to benefits or suitability for continued employment
- records of vaccination and immunisation status and history.

Outside the Code

The Data Protection Act only comes into play when personal information is or will be held electronically or recorded in a structured filing system. This will often be the case but sometimes it may not, for example where a line-manager enquires about a worker's health but does not keep, or intend to keep, any record of the conversation, or only keeps a note in a general notebook.

Where samples are taken, as might be the case with drug or alcohol testing, the Code only applies from the point at which samples yield personal information about a worker. This Code does not address consent for any physical intervention involved in taking a sample from a worker in the course of medical testing.

Sensitive data rules

Where information about workers' health is to be processed, one of the Act's sensitive data conditions must be satisfied. There are various conditions. Below we have listed the ones likely to be of most relevance to employers. Employers holding information about workers' health ought to be able to answer 'yes' to one or more of these questions:

- Is the processing necessary to enable the employer to meet its legal obligations, for example to ensure health and safety at work, or to comply with the requirement not to discriminate against workers on the grounds of sex, age, race or disability?
- Is the processing for medical purposes, eg the provision of care or treatment, and undertaken by a health professional or someone working under an equivalent duty of confidentiality, eg an occupational health doctor?
- Is the processing in connection with actual or prospective legal proceedings?
- Has the worker given consent explicitly to the processing of his or her medical information?

This is not an exhaustive list of all the conditions.

See Supplementary Guidance, page 72 for more information on these and other sensitive data conditions.

Relying on the worker's consent

There are limitations as to how far consent can be relied on as a basis for the processing of information about workers' health. To be valid, consent must be:

- **explicit.** This means the worker must have been told clearly what personal data are involved and have been properly informed about the use that will be made of them. The worker must have given a positive indication of agreement, eg a signature.
- **freely given.** This means the worker must have a real choice whether or not to consent and there must be no penalty imposed for refusing to give consent.

See Supplementary Guidance page 75 for further explanation of what this means in practice.

Impact assessments

Once a sensitive data condition is satisfied, an employer then needs to be clear that either:

- it is under a legal duty to process information about workers' health, eg the duty to monitor workers' possible exposure to hazardous materials under the Control of Substances Hazardous to Health Regulations 2002, or

- the benefits gained from processing information about workers' health justify the privacy intrusion or any other adverse impact on them. In other words, the collection and use of information about workers' health must be a proportionate response to a particular problem.

An 'impact assessment' is a useful tool for employers to use to help them to judge whether the second of the above options applies.

Particularly where medical testing is involved, employers are likely to find it helpful to carry out a formal or informal 'impact assessment' to decide how or whether to collect information about workers' health. This Code does not prejudge the outcome of the impact assessment. Each will necessarily depend on the particular circumstances of the employer. Nor does the Code attempt to set out for employers the benefits they might gain from holding information about workers' health. What it does do is assist employers in identifying and giving appropriate weight to the other factors they should take into account.

An impact assessment involves:

- identifying clearly the **purpose(s)** for which health information is to be collected and held and the benefits this is likely to deliver
- identifying any likely **adverse impact** of collecting and holding the information
- considering **alternatives** to collecting and holding such information
- taking into account the **obligations** that arise from collecting and holding health information
- judging whether collecting and holding health information is **justified**.

Purpose(s)

It is important that a realistic assessment is made of the extent to which the collection of health information will actually address the risks it is directed at. Decisions based on, for example, the effect of particular medical conditions on a worker's future employability or the effect of particular drugs on safety should be based on relevant and reputable scientific evidence.

Adverse impact

Identifying any likely adverse impact means taking into account the consequences of collecting and holding health information, not only for workers, but also for others who might be affected by it, such as a worker's family. Consider:

- how extensive will the intrusion into the private lives of workers and others be as a result of collecting information about their health?
- whether health information will be seen by those who do not have a business need to know, eg IT workers involved in maintaining electronic files about workers
- what impact, if any, will the collection of health information have on the relationship of mutual trust and confidence that should exist between workers and their employer?
- whether the collection of health information will be oppressive or demeaning.

Alternatives

Considering whether it is necessary to collect information about workers' health, and if so how to do this in the least intrusive manner, means asking questions such as:

- can health questionnaires rather than tests be used to obtain the information the employer requires?
- can changes in the workplace, for example eliminating exposure to a hazardous substance, remove the need to obtain information through testing?
- can medical testing be targeted at individuals who have exhibited behavioural problems that may be drink or drug related, rather than at all workers?
- can the collection of health information be confined to areas of highest risk, eg can it be directed at a few individuals the nature of whose jobs mean they pose a particular risk rather than at everyone?
- can medical testing be designed to reveal only a narrow range of information that is directly relevant to the purpose for which it is undertaken?
- can access to health information be limited so that it will only be seen by medically qualified staff or those working under specific confidentiality agreements?

Obligations

Taking into account the obligations that arise from collecting information about workers' health means considering such matters as:

- whether and how workers will be notified about the collection of their health information
- how information about workers' health will be kept securely and handled in accordance with the Act.

See Part 2 – Employment Records, para 2.2, for more information on security requirements.

- the implications of the rights that individuals have to obtain a copy of information that has been collected about their health.

See Part 2 – Employment Records, para 2.8, which explains more about rights to access.

Is health information justified?

Making a conscious decision as to whether the current or proposed collection and use of health information is justified involves:

- establishing the benefits the collection and use of health information will bring
- considering any alternative method of obtaining these benefits and/or the information needed
- weighing these benefits against the adverse impact
- placing particular emphasis on the need to be fair to individual workers
- ensuring that the intrusion is no more than absolutely necessary
- bearing in mind that health information can be particularly sensitive, that its obtaining can be particularly intrusive and that significant intrusion will not normally be justified unless the employer's business is at real risk of serious damage
- taking into account the results of consultation with trade unions or other representatives, if any, or with workers themselves.

Making an impact assessment need not be a complicated or onerous process. Even in the context of health information it may sometimes be enough for an employer to make a simple mental evaluation of the risks faced by his or her business and to assess whether the collection and use of information about workers' health would reduce or eradicate those risks or would bring particular benefits. In other cases the impact assessment will be more complicated, for example where an employer faces a number of different risks of varying degrees of seriousness. In such cases appropriate documentation would be advisable.

GOOD PRACTICE RECOMMENDATIONS – PART 4

The parts of the Code in this section are:

4.1 Information about workers' health: general considerations

4.2 Occupational health schemes

4.3 Information from medical examination and testing

4.4 Information from drug & alcohol testing

4.5 Information from genetic testing

Sickness and Injury records are dealt with in Part 2 of the Code. See para 2.3.

4.1 Information about workers' health: general considerations

Core Principles

[4.206]

- It will be intrusive and may be highly intrusive to obtain information about your workers' health.
- Workers have legitimate expectations that they can keep their personal health information private and that employers will respect their privacy.
- If employers wish to collect and hold information on their workers' health, they should be clear about the purpose and satisfied that this is justified by real benefits that will be delivered.
- One of the sensitive data conditions must be satisfied.
- Workers should be aware of the extent to which information about their health is held and the reasons for which it is held.
- Decisions on a worker's suitability for particular work are properly management decisions but the interpretation of medical information should be left to a suitably qualified health professional.

4.1.1 Identify who within the organisation can authorise or carry out the collection of information about workers' health on behalf of the organisation and ensure they are aware of their employer's responsibilities under the Act.

Key points and possible actions

- Those who handle information about workers' health, or who can authorise the collection of such information, should be briefed on the Act and this Code.
- There are non-compliance risks if those lacking proper authority and any necessary training introduce the collection of health information and in particular medical testing.
- Leave the interpretation of medical information to those who are qualified to do this.

4.1.2 If health information is to be collected ensure a sensitive data condition can be satisfied.

Key points and possible actions

- The collection and use of information about workers' health is against the law unless a sensitive data condition is satisfied.

- In general employers should only collect health information where this is necessary for the protection of health and safety, to prevent discrimination on the grounds of disability, to satisfy other legal obligations or if each worker affected has given his or her explicit consent.
- If consent is to be relied on, it must be freely given. That means a worker must be able to say 'no' without penalty and must be able to withdraw consent once given. Blanket consent obtained at the outset of employment cannot always be relied on.
- Consent should not be confined to the testing itself, it should also cover the subsequent recording, use and disclosure of the test results.

See Supplementary Guidance, page 72 which explains more about the conditions for processing sensitive data.

4.1.3 Identify clearly the purposes behind the collection of information about workers' health and the specific business benefits which it is likely to bring.

Key points and possible actions

- Identify the collection and use of information about workers' health that currently takes place in your organisation.
- Identify any collection or use of information about workers' health that you plan to implement.
- Consider conducting an impact assessment on current or planned collection and use of health information.

See above for information on how to carry out an impact assessment.

4.1.4 Protect information about workers' health with appropriate security measures. Ensure that wherever practicable only suitably qualified health professionals have access to medical details.

Key points and possible actions

- Managers should not have access to more information about a worker's health than is necessary for them to carry out their management responsibilities. As far as possible the information should be confined to that necessary to establish fitness to work, rather than consist of more general medical details.
- Safety representatives should be provided with anonymised information unless any workers concerned have consented to the provision of information in an identifiable form.
- Unless the general standard of information security in your organisation is sufficiently high, medical information about workers should be separated from other personnel information, for example by keeping it in a sealed envelope, or subject to additional access controls on an electronic system.
- Information about workers' health collected to run a pension or insurance scheme should not be available to the employer unless this is necessary for the employer's role in administering the scheme.

4.1.5 Do not collect more information about workers' health than is necessary for the purpose(s) behind its collection.

Key points and possible actions

- Review any health questionnaires to ensure that only information that is really needed is collected.
- If commissioning a medical report on a sick employee, seek information on the worker's fitness for continued employment rather than medical details.
- Do not ask workers to consent to the disclosure of their entire general practitioner record as a matter of expediency. Only seek the disclosure of the whole record, or substantial parts of it, where this is genuinely necessary.
- If seeking a report from a worker's general practitioner or other medical practitioner who has been responsible for the care of the worker, ensure that you meet the requirements of the Access to Medical Reports Act 1988. This includes obtaining the worker's consent to your application for a report.

4.2 Occupational health schemes

[4.207]
This sub-section gives good practice recommendations for employers with occupational health schemes. It does not provide detailed professional guidance to doctors, nurses and others involved in such schemes.

4.2.1 Ensure workers are aware of how information about their health will be used and who will have access to it.

Key points and possible actions

- Unless told otherwise workers are entitled to assume that information they give to a doctor, nurse or other health professional will be treated in confidence and not passed to others.
- Set out clearly to workers, preferably in writing, how information they supply in the context of an occupational health scheme will be used, who it might be made available to and why.

4.2.2 Do not compromise any confidentiality of communications between workers and health professionals in an occupational health service.

Key points and possible actions

- If workers are allowed to use telephone or e-mail for confidential communication with their occupational health service, do not compromise this confidentiality by monitoring the contents of these communications.

4.2.3 Act in a way that is consistent with the Guidance on Ethics for Occupational Physicians published by the Faculty of Occupational Medicine.

Key points and possible actions

- Although this is guidance for occupational physicians rather than employers, it should give you a clear understanding of the legal and ethical constraints that apply to the exchange of information when working with occupational health professionals.

4.3 Information from medical examination and testing

[4.208]

This sub-section gives good practice recommendations specific to the collection and handling of information derived from medical examination and testing. The general recommendations in section 4.1 should also be taken into account.

Employers should bear in mind that obtaining a worker's consent or satisfying another sensitive data condition is not, on its own, sufficient to ensure data protection compliance. There is still an obligation to ensure that information obtained through medical examination is relevant, is accurate, is up to date and is kept secure.

See Supplementary Guidance page 72 for more Information on the Sensitive Data Conditions.

4.3.1 Where information obtained from medical testing is used to enforce the organisation's rules and standards make sure that the rules and standards are clearly set out in a policy which workers are aware of.

Key points and possible actions

- Ensure workers understand these rules and standards.
- Set out the circumstances in which medical testing may take place, the nature of the testing, how information obtained through testing will be used, and the safeguards that are in place for the workers that are subject to it.

4.3.2 Only obtain information through medical examination or testing of applicants or other potential workers at an appropriate point in the recruitment process, ie where there is a likelihood of appointing them. You must also be satisfied that the testing is a necessary and justified measure to:

- Determine whether the potential worker is fit or likely to remain fit to carry out the job in question, or
- Meet any legal requirements for testing, or
- Determine the terms on which a potential worker is eligible to join a pension or insurance scheme.

Key points and possible actions

- Record the business purpose for which examination or testing is to be introduced and the sensitive data condition that can be satisfied.
- Consider less intrusive ways of meeting the objectives, for example using a health questionnaire as an alternative to a medical examination or as a means to select those required to undergo a full examination.
- Only carry out a pre-employment medical examination or medical testing where there is a real likelihood that the individual will be appointed.
- Make it clear early on in the recruitment process that individuals may be subjected to medical examination or testing once there is a likelihood that they will be appointed.

4.3.3 Only obtain information through a medical examination or medical testing of current workers if the testing is part of a occupational health and safety programme that workers have a free choice to participate in, or you are satisfied that it is a necessary and justified measure to:

- Prevent a significant risk to the health and safety of the worker, or others, or
- Determine a particular worker's fitness for carrying out his or her job, or
- Determine whether a worker is fit to return to work after a period of sickness absence, or when this might be the case, or
- Determine the worker's entitlement to health related benefits eg sick pay, or
- Prevent discrimination against workers on the grounds of disability or assess the need to make reasonable adjustments to the working environment, or
- Comply with other legal obligations.

Key points and possible actions

- Record the business purpose for which the programme of examination or testing of workers is to be introduced and the sensitive data condition that can be satisfied.
- Establish and document who will be tested, what precisely are they being tested for, the frequency of testing, and the consequences of a positive or negative test.
- Consider less intrusive ways of meeting the employer's objectives, for example collecting information via a health questionnaire either as a first stage or as an alternative to a medical examination.

4.3.4 Do not obtain a sample covertly or use an existing sample, test result or other information obtained through a medical examination for a purpose other than that for which it was originally obtained.

Key points and possible actions

- Be clear about the purpose(s) for which any testing is being carried out and communicate this to workers.
- The covert obtaining of bodily samples for testing is most unlikely ever to be justified.
- If there is a wish to carry out a different test on an existing sample, this can only be done if the worker has been told about it and has freely consented.

4.3.5 Permanently delete information obtained in the course of medical examination or testing that is not relevant for the purpose(s) for which the examination or testing is undertaken.

Key points and possible actions

- Health information that is excessive, irrelevant or out of date should not be retained by an employer.
- If the retention of medical information is necessary only for the operation of an occupational health service, it should be kept in a confidential occupational health file.

4.4 Information from drug and alcohol testing

[4.209]

This part of the Code gives good practice recommendations specific to the collection and handling of information derived from drug and alcohol testing. The recommendations in sub-sections 4.1 and 4.3 should also be taken into account.

4.4.1 Before obtaining information through drug or alcohol testing ensure that the benefits justify any adverse impact, unless the testing is required by law.

Key points and possible actions

- The collection of information through drug and alcohol testing is unlikely to be justified unless it is for health and safety reasons.
- Post-incident testing where there is a reasonable suspicion that drug or alcohol use is a factor is more likely to be justified than random testing.
- Given the intrusive nature of testing employers would be well advised to undertake and document an impact assessment.

See Part 4 above, at [4.205], for information about how to carry out an impact assessment.

4.4.2 Minimise the amount of personal information obtained through drug and alcohol testing.

Key points and possible actions

- Only use drug or alcohol testing where it provides significantly better evidence of impairment than other less intrusive means.
- Use the least intrusive forms of testing practicable to deliver the benefits to the business that the testing is intended to bring.
- Tell workers what drugs they are being tested for.
- Base any testing on reliable scientific evidence of the effect of particular substances on workers.
- Limit testing to those substances and the extent of exposure that will have a significant bearing on the purpose(s) for which the testing is conducted.

4.4.3 Ensure the criteria used for selecting workers for testing are justified, properly documented, adhered to and are communicated to workers.

Key points and possible actions

- It is unfair and deceptive to lead workers to believe that testing is being carried out randomly if, in fact, other criteria are being used.
- If random testing is to be used, ensure that it is carried out in a genuinely random way.
- If other criteria are used to trigger testing, for example suspicion that a worker's performance is impaired as a result of drug or alcohol use, the employer should ensure workers are aware of the true criteria that are used.

4.4.4 Confine the obtaining of information through random testing to those workers who are employed to work in safety critical activities.

Key points and possible actions

- Collecting personal information by testing all workers in a business will not be justified if in fact it is only workers engaged in particular activities that pose a risk.
- Even in safety-critical businesses such as public transport or heavy industry, workers in different jobs will pose different safety risks. Therefore collecting information through the random testing of all workers will rarely be justified.

4.4.5 Gather information through testing designed to ensure safety at work rather than to reveal the illegal use of substances in a worker's private life.

Key points and possible actions

- Very few employers will be justified in testing to detect illegal use rather than on safety grounds. Testing to detect illegal use may, exceptionally, be justified where illegal use would:
  - breach the worker's contract of employment, conditions of employment or disciplinary rules, and
  - cause serious damage to the employer's business, eg by substantially undermining public confidence in the integrity of a law enforcement agency.

4.4.6 Ensure that workers are fully aware that drug or alcohol testing is taking place, and of the possible consequences of being tested.

Key points and possible actions

- Explain your drug or alcohol policy in a staff handbook.
- Explain the consequences for workers of breaching the policy.
- Ensure workers are aware of the blood-alcohol level at which they may be disciplined when being tested for alcohol.
- Do not conduct testing on samples collected without the worker's knowledge.

4.4.7 Ensure that information is only obtained through drug and alcohol testing that is;

- of sufficient technical quality to support any decisions or opinions that are derived from it and,
- subject to rigorous integrity and quality control procedures and,
- conducted under the direction of, and positive test results interpreted by, a person who is suitably qualified and competent in the field of drug testing.

Key points and possible actions

- Use a professional service with qualified staff and that meets appropriate standards.
- Ensure workers have access to a duplicate of any sample taken to enable them to have it independently analysed as a check on the accuracy of the employer's results.
- Do not assume that the tests are infallible and be prepared to deal properly with disputes arising from their use.

4.5 Information from genetic testing

[4.210]

Genetic testing has the potential to provide employers with information predictive of the likely future general health of workers or with information about their genetic susceptibility to occupational diseases. Genetic testing is, though, still under development and in most cases has an uncertain predictive value. It is rarely, if ever, used in the employment context. The Human Genetics Commission advises that employers should not demand that an individual take a genetic test as a condition of employment. It should therefore only be introduced after very careful consideration, if at all. This sub-section supplements sub-sections 4.1 and 4.3.

4.5.1 Do not use genetic testing in an effort to obtain information that is predictive of a worker's future general health.

Key points and possible actions

- Obtaining information through genetic testing is too intrusive and the information's predictive value is insufficiently certain to be relied on to provide information about a worker's future health.

4.5.2 Do not insist that a worker discloses the results of a previous genetic test.

Key points and possible actions

- It is important that workers are not put off taking genetic tests that may be beneficial for their health care by the fear that they may have to disclose the results to a current or future employer.
- You can ask for information that is relevant to your health and safety or other legal duties but the provision of the information should be voluntary.

4.5.3 Only use genetic testing to obtain information where it is clear that a worker with a particular, detectable genetic condition is likely to pose a serious safety risk to others or where it is known that a specific working environment or practice might pose specific risks to workers with particular genetic variations.

Key points and possible actions

- Only seek information through genetic testing as a last resort, where:
  - it is not practicable to make changes to the working environment or practices so as to reduce risks to all workers and
  - it is the only reasonable method to obtain the required information.
- Inform the Human Genetics Commission of any proposals to use genetic testing for employment purposes.

4.5.4 If a genetic test is used to obtain information for employment purposes ensure that it is valid and is subject to assured levels of accuracy and reliability.

Key points and possible actions

- There should be scientific evidence that any genetic test is valid for the purpose for which it is used.
- Ensure the results of any test undertaken are always communicated to the person tested and professional advice is available.
- Ensure test results are carefully interpreted, taking account of how they might be affected by environmental conditions.

(Contact details—omitted; see Useful addresses at **[5.61]**.)

G. SECRETARY OF STATE

CODE OF PRACTICE: PICKETING (1992)

[4.211]

NOTES

This Code was originally made under the Employment Act 1980, s 3 (as amended by the Employment Act 1988, s 18). See now the Trade Union and Labour Relations (Consolidation) Act 1992, ss 201, 202 at **[1.467]**, **[1.468]**.

This Code was made by the Secretary of State for Employment, and came into force on 1 May 1992 (see the Employment Code of Practice (Picketing) Order 1992, SI 1992/476). It replaces the previous Code issued in 1980. For the legal status of the Code, see now the Trade Union and Labour Relations (Consolidation) Act 1992, s 207 at **[1.473]**.

Text and notes printed in green bold in the original Code are reproduced in italics in this work (see the preamble below). Notes are as in the Code.

See *Harvey* NII(11).

CONTENTS

PREAMBLE

[4.212]

The legal framework within which the Code will operate is explained in its text. While every effort has been made to ensure that explanations included in the Code are accurate, only the courts can give authoritative interpretations of the law.

The Code's provisions apply equally to men and to women, but for simplicity the masculine pronoun is used throughout. Wherever it appears in the Code, the word "court" is used to mean the High Court in England and Wales and the Court of Session in Scotland, but without prejudice to the Code's relevance to any proceedings before any other court.

Passages in this Code which are printed [*in italics*] outline or re-state provisions in primary legislation.

On the day on which this Code of Practice comes into operation in pursuance of an order under section 3(5) of the Employment Act 1980, the Code of Practice "Picketing" which came into effect on 17 December 1980 ceases to have effect subject to any transitional provisions or savings made by the order.

SECTION A. INTRODUCTION

[4.213]

1. The purpose of this Code is to provide practical guidance on picketing in trade disputes for those:

— contemplating, organising or taking part in a picket or activities associated with picketing, such as assemblies of demonstrations; and/or

— employers, workers or members of the general public who may be affected by a picket or any associated activities.

2. There is no legal "right to picket" as such, but attendance for the purpose of peaceful picketing has long been recognised to be a lawful activity. However, the law imposes certain limits on how, where and for what purpose such picketing can be undertaken. These limits help ensure proper protection for those who may be affected by picketing—including those who wish to cross a picket line and go to work.

3. It is a **civil** wrong, actionable in the civil courts, to persuade someone to break his contract of employment, or to secure the breaking of a commercial contract. But the law exempts from this liability those acting in contemplation or furtherance of a trade dispute, including—in certain circumstances—pickets themselves.

4. This exemption is provided by means of special "statutory immunities" to prevent liability arising to such **civil law** proceedings. These immunities—which are explained in more detail in Section B of this Code—have the effect that trade unions and individuals can, in certain circumstances, organise or conduct a picket without fear of being successfully sued in the courts. However, this protection applies only to acts of inducing breach, or interference with the performance, of contracts, or threatening to do either of these things.

5. These "statutory immunities" afford no protection for a picket, anyone involved in activities associated with picketing, or anyone organising a picket who commits some other kind of civil wrong—such as trespass or nuisance.[1] Nor do they protect anyone—whether a picket, an employee who decides to take industrial action or to break his contract of employment because he is persuaded to do so by a picket, or anyone else—from the consequences which may follow if they choose to take industrial action or break their contracts of employment. These could include, for example, loss of wages, or other disciplinary action or dismissal from employment.

NOTES

[1] See the further explanation in paragraph 27 in Section B of the Code.

6. The **criminal** law applies to pickets just as it applies to everyone else. No picket, person involved in activities associated with picketing or person organising a picket, has any exemption from the provisions of the criminal law as this applies, for example, to prevent obstruction, preserve public order, or regulate assemblies or demonstrations.

7. This Code outlines aspects of the law on picketing—although it is, of course, for the courts and industrial tribunals to interpret and apply the law in particular cases. Sections B and C, respectively, outline provisions of the civil and criminal law and, where relevant, give guidance on good practice. Section D describes the role of the police in enforcing the law. Sections E, F and G also give guidance on good practice in relation to the conduct of particular aspects of picketing and of certain activities associated with picketing.

8. *The Code itself imposes no legal obligations and failure to observe it does not by itself render anyone liable to proceedings. But statute law provides that any provisions of the Code are to be admissible in evidence and taken into account in proceedings before any court, industrial tribunal or the Central Arbitration Committee where they consider them relevant.*

SECTION B. PICKETING AND THE CIVIL LAW

[4.214]

9. *The law sets out the basic rules which must be observed if picketing is to be carried out, or organised, lawfully. To keep to these rules, attendance for the purpose of picketing may only:*

(i) *be taken in contemplation or furtherance of a trade dispute;*

(ii) *be carried out by a person attending at or near his own place of work; a trade union official, in addition to attending at or near his own place of work, may also attend at or near the place of work of a member of his trade union whom he is accompanying on the picket line and whom he represents.*

Furthermore, the only purpose involved must be peacefully to obtain or communicate information, or peacefully to persuade a person to work or not to work.

10. Picketing commonly involves persuading workers to break, or interfere with the performance of, their contracts of employment by not going into work. Picketing can also disrupt the business of the employer who is being picketed by interfering with the performance of a commercial contract which the employer has with a customer or supplier. If pickets follow the rules outlined in paragraph 9, however, they may have the protection against civil proceedings afforded by the "statutory immunities". These rules, and immunities, are explained more fully in paragraphs 11 to 30 below.

IN CONTEMPLATION OR FURTHERANCE OF A TRADE DISPUTE

11. *Picketing is lawful only if it is carried out in contemplation or furtherance of a "trade dispute". A "trade dispute" is defined in law so as to cover the matters which normally occasion disputes between employers and workers—such as terms and conditions of employment, the allocation of work, matters of discipline, trade union recognition.*

"SECONDARY" ACTION

12. *The "statutory immunities" do not apply to protect a threat of, or call for or other inducement of "secondary" industrial action. The law defines "secondary" action—which is sometimes referred to as "sympathy" or "solidarity" action—as that by workers whose employer is not a party to the trade dispute to which the action relates.*

13. However, a worker employed by a party to a trade dispute, picketing at his own place of work may try to persuade another worker, not employed by that employer, to break, or interfere with the performance of, the second worker's contract of employment, and/or to interfere with the performance of a commercial contract. This could happen, for example, if a picket persuaded a lorry driver employed by another employer not to cross the picket line and deliver goods to be supplied, under a commercial contract, to the employer in dispute. Such an act by a picket would be an unlawful inducement to take secondary action unless provision was made to the contrary.

14. *Accordingly, the law contains provisions which make it lawful for a peaceful picket, at the picket's own place of work, to seek to persuade workers other than those employed by the picket's own employer not to work, or not to work normally. To have such protection, the peaceful picketing must be done:*

(a) *by a worker employed by the employer who is party to the dispute;*[2] *or*

(b) *by a trade union official whose attendance is lawful (see paragraphs 22–23 below).*

NOTES

[2] *However, the peaceful picketing may be done by a worker who is not in employment but was last employed by the employer in dispute in certain circumstances—see paragraph 20.*

15. Where an entrance or exit is used jointly by the workers of more than one employer, the workers who are not involved in the dispute to which a picket relates should not be interfered with by picketing activities. Particular care should be taken to ensure that picketing does not involve calls for a breach, or interference with the performance, of contracts by employees of other employer(s) who are not involved in the dispute. Observing this principle will help avoid consequences which might otherwise be damaging and disruptive to good industrial relations.

ATTENDANCE AT OR NEAR A PICKET'S OWN PLACE OF WORK

16. *It is lawful for a person to induce breach, or interference with the performance, of a contract in the course of attendance for the purpose of picketing only if he pickets at or near his own place of work.*

17. The expression "at or near his own place of work" is not further defined in statute law. The provisions means that, except for those covered by paragraphs 22 and 23 below, lawful picketing must be limited to attendance at, or near, an entrance to or exit from the factory, site or office at which the picket works. Picketing should be confined to a location, or locations, as near as practicable to the place of work.

18. The law does not enable a picket to attend lawfully at an entrance to, or exit from, *any* place of work other than his own. This applies even, for example, if those working at the other place of work are employed by the same employer, or are covered by the same collective bargaining arrangements as the picket.

19. *The law identifies two specific groups in respect of which particular arrangements apply. These groups are:*

— *those (eg mobile workers) who work at more than one place; and*

— *those for whom it is impracticable to picket at their own place of work because of its location.*

The law provides that it is lawful for such workers to picket those premises of their employer from which they work, or those from which their work is administered. In the case of lorry drivers, for example, this will usually mean, in practice, the premises of their employer from which their vehicles operate.

20. Special provisions also apply to people who are not in work, and who have lost their jobs for reasons connected with the dispute which has occasioned the picketing. This might arise, for example, where the dismissal of a group of employees has led directly to the organisation of a picket, or where an employer has dismissed employees because they refuse to work normally, and some or all of those dismissed then wish to set up a picket. *In such cases the law provides that it is lawful for a worker to picket at his former place of work. This special arrangement ceases to apply, however, to any worker who subsequently takes a job at another place of work.*

21. The law does not protect anyone who pickets without permission on or inside any part of premises which are private property. The law will not, therefore, protect pickets who trespass, or those who organise such trespass, from being sued in the civil courts.

TRADE UNION OFFICIALS

22. For the reasons described in Section F of this Code, it may be helpful to the orderly organisation and conduct of picketing for a trade union official[3] to be present on a picket line where his members are picketing. *The law provides that it is lawful for a trade union official to picket at any place of work provided that:*

(i) *he is accompanying members of his trade union who are picketing lawfully at or near their own place of work; and*

(ii) *he personally represents those members.*

NOTES

[3] *The law defines an "official of the union" as a person who is an officer of the union (or of a branch or section of the union), or who, not being such an officer, is a person elected or appointed in accordance with the rules of the union to be a representative of its members (or some of them), including any person so elected or appointed who is an employee*

of the same employer as the members, or one or more of the members, whom he is elected to represent. This could include, for example, a shop steward.

23. If these conditions are satisfied, then a trade union official has the same legal protection as other pickets who picket lawfully at or near their own place of work. *However, the law provides that an official—whether a lay official or an employee of the union—is regarded for this purpose as representing only those members of his union whom he has been specifically* appointed or elected to represent. An official cannot, therefore, claim that he represents a group of members simply because they belong to his trade union. He must represent and be responsible for them in the normal course of his trade union duties. For example, it is lawful for an official—such as a shop steward—who represents members at a particular place of work to be present on a picket line where those members are picketing lawfully; for a branch official to be present only where members of his branch are lawfully picketing; for a national official who represents a particular trade group or section within the union, to be present wherever members of that trade group or section are lawfully picketing; for a regional official to be present only where members of his region are lawfully picketing; and for a national official such as a general secretary or president who represents the whole union to be present wherever any members of his union are picketing lawfully.

LAWFUL PURPOSES OF PICKETING

24. In no circumstances does a picket have power, under the law, to require other people to stop, or to compel them to listen or to do what he asks them to do. A person who decides to cross a picket line must be allowed to do so. *In addition, the law provides a remedy for any union member who is disciplined by his union because he has crossed a picket line.*[4]

NOTES

[4] *A member disciplined for crossing a picket line is "unjustifiably disciplined"; the remedy for unjustifiable discipline is by complaint to an industrial tribunal.* (See also paragraphs 60–61 in Section F of this Code.)

25. The **only** purposes of picketing declared lawful in statute are:
— *peacefully obtaining and communicating information: and*
— *peacefully persuading a person to work or not to work.*

26. The law allows pickets to seek to explain their case to those entering or leaving the picketed premises, and/or to ask them not to enter or leave the premises where the dispute is taking place. This may be done by speaking to people, or it may involve the distribution of leaflets or the carrying of banners or placards putting the pickets' case. **In all cases, however, any such activity must by carried out *peacefully*.**

27. The law protects peaceful communication and persuasion. It does not give pickets, anyone organising or participating in any activity associated with picketing, or anyone organising a picket, protection against civil proceedings being brought against them for any conduct occurring during the picketing, or associated activity, which amounts to a separate civil wrong such as:
— unlawful threat or assault;
— harassment (ie threatening or unreasonable behaviour causing fear or apprehension to those in the vicinity);
— obstruction of a path, road, entrance or exit to premises;
— interference (eg because of noise or crowds) in the rights of those in neighbouring properties (ie "private nuisance");
— trespassing on private property.

28. Both individual pickets, and anyone—including a union—organising a picket or associated activity, should be careful not to commit such civil wrongs. It is possible, for example, that material on placards carried by pickets—or, for that matter, by those involved in activities associated with picketing—could be defamatory or amount to a threat or harassment. Pickets will also have no legal protection if they do or say things, or make offensive gestures at people, which amount to unlawful threat or harassment. Section C of this Code explains that such actions may also give rise to prosecution under the criminal law.

29. Similarly, if the noise or other disturbance caused to residents of an area by pickets, or by those associated with picketing activity, amounts to a civil wrong, those involved or responsible are not protected by the law from proceedings being brought against them.

30. Similar principles apply in respect of any breach of the criminal law by pickets, or their organiser. As explained in Section C of this Code, a picket, or anyone involved in an associated activity, who threatens or intimidates someone, or obstructs an entrance to a workplace, or causes a breach of the peace, commits a criminal offence. Where pickets commit a criminal offence, then in many circumstances they will not be acting peacefully; consequently, any immunity under the civil law will be lost.

SEEKING REDRESS

31. An employer, a worker, or anyone else who is party to a contract which is, or may be, broken or interfered with by unlawful picketing has a civil law remedy. He may apply to the court for an order[5] preventing, or stopping the unlawful picketing, or its organisation. Such a person may also claim damages from those responsible where the activities of the unlawful picket have caused him loss. An order can be sought against the person—which could include a particular trade union or unions—on whose instructions or advice the unlawful picketing is taking place, or will take place.

NOTES

5 An injunction in England and Wales; an interdict in Scotland.

32. In making an order, the court has authority to require a trade union which has acted unlawfully to take such steps as are considered necessary to ensure that there is no further call for, or other organisation of, unlawful picketing. An order may be granted by the court on an interim basis, pending a full hearing of the case.

33. If a court order is made, it can apply not only to the person or union named in the order, but to anyone else acting on his behalf or on his instructions. Thus an organiser of unlawful picketing cannot avoid liability, for example, merely by changing the people on the unlawful picket line from time to time.

34. Similarly, anyone who is wronged in any other way by a picket can seek an order from the court to get the unlawful act stopped or prevented, and/or for damages. Thus, for example, if picketing, or associated activities, give rise to unlawful disturbance to residents in the vicinity, one or more of the residents so affected can apply to the court for such an order and/or for damages. Such proceedings might be taken against individual pickets, or the person—including a union where applicable—responsible for the unlawful act.

35. If a court is not obeyed, or is ignored, those who sought it can go back to court and ask to have those concerned declared in contempt of court. Anyone who is found to be in contempt of court may face heavy fines, or other penalties, which the court may consider appropriate. For example, a union may be deprived of its assets through sequestration, where the union's funds are placed in the control of a person appointed by the court who may, in particular, pay any fines or legal costs arising from the court proceedings. Similarly, if a person knows that such an order had been made against someone, or some union, and yet aids and abets that person to disobey or ignore the order, he may also be found to be acting in contempt of court and liable to be punished by the court.

DETERMINING WHETHER A UNION IS RESPONSIBLE

36. Pickets will usually attend at a place of work for the purpose of persuading others not to work, or not to work normally, and may thereby be inducing them to breach, or interfere with the performance of, contracts. The law lays down rules which determine whether a union will be held liable for any such acts of inducement which are unlawful.

37. *The law provides that a union will be held responsible for such an unlawful act if it is done, authorised or endorsed by:*

(a) *the union's principal executive committee, president, or general secretary;*

(b) *any person given power under the union's own rules to do, authorise or endorse acts of the kind in question; or*

(c) *any other committee of the union, or any official of the union*[6]*—including those who are employed by the union, and those, like shop stewards, who are not.*[7]

A union will be held responsible for such an act by such a body or person regardless of any provisions to the contrary in its own rules, or anything in any other contract or rule of law.

NOTES

6 See footnote at paragraph 22 for the relevant definition of "official". *In this case, however, an act will also be taken to have been done by an "official of the union" if it was done (or authorised or endorsed) by a group of persons, or any member of a group, to which such an official belonged at the relevant time if the group's purposes included organising or co-ordinating industrial action.*

7 *However, if an act which is done (or authorised or endorsed) by a union committee or official is "effectively repudiated" by the union's principal executive committee, president or general secretary, the union will not be held responsible in law. In order to avoid liability in this way, the act concerned must be repudiated by any of these as soon as reasonably practicable after it has come to their knowledge. In addition, the union must, without delay:*

(a) *give written notice of the repudiation to the committee or official in question; and*

(b) *do its best to give individual written notice of the fact and date of the repudiation to: (i) every member of the union who it has reason to believe is taking part – or might otherwise take part – in industrial action as a result of the act; and (ii) the employer of every such member.*

38. Pickets may, of course, commit civil wrongs other than inducing breach, or interference with the performance, of contracts. The question of whether a union will be held responsible for those wrongs will be determined according to common law principles of liability, rather than by reference to the rules described in paragraph 37 above.

THE NEED FOR A BALLOT

39. If what is done in the course of picketing amounts to a call for industrial action, and is an act for which the union is responsible in law, the union can only have the protection of statutory immunity if it has first held a properly-conducted secret ballot.

40. *The law requires that entitlement to vote in such a ballot must be given to all the union members who it is reasonable at the time of the ballot for the union to believe will be called upon to take part in, or continue with, the industrial action, and to no other member. The ballot must produce a majority of those voting which is in favour of taking, or continuing with, industrial action.* These, and other requirements of the law in respect of such ballots, are restated in the statutory Code of Practice "Trade Union Ballots on Industrial Action (1st Revision)" [Note: This has now been replaced by the Code of Practice on "Industrial Action Ballots and Notice to Employers"].

SECTION C. PICKETING AND THE CRIMINAL LAW

[4.215]
41. If a picket commits a criminal offence he is just as liable to be prosecuted as any other member of the public who breaks the law. The immunity provided under the civil law does not protect him in any way.

42. The criminal law protects the rights of every person to go about his lawful daily business free from interference by others. No one is under any obligation to stop when a picket asks him to do so, or, if he does stop, to comply with a request, for example, not to go into work. Everyone has the right, if he wishes to do so, to cross a picket line in order to go into his place of work or to deliver or collect goods. A picket may exercise peaceful persuasion, but if he goes beyond that and tries by means other than peaceful persuasion to deter another person from exercising those rights he may commit a criminal offence.

43. *Among other matters, it is a criminal offence for pickets (as for others):*

— *to use threatening, abusive or insulting words or behaviour, or disorderly behaviour within the sight or hearing of any person—whether a worker seeking to cross a picket line, an employer, an ordinary member of the public, or the police—likely to be caused harassment, alarm or distress by such conduct;*

— *to use threatening, abusive or insulting words or behaviour towards any person with intent to cause fear of violence or to provoke violence;*

— *to use or threaten unlawful violence;*

— *to obstruct the highway or the entrance to premises or to seek physically to bar the passage of vehicles or persons by lying down in the road, linking arms across or circling in the road, or jostling or physically restraining those entering or leaving the premises;*

— *to be in possession of an offensive weapon;*

— *intentionally or recklessly to damage property;*

— *to engage in violent, disorderly or unruly behaviour or to take any action which is likely to lead to a breach of the peace;*

— *to obstruct a police officer in the execution of his duty.*

44. A picket has no right under the law to require a vehicle to stop or to be stopped. The law allows him only to ask a driver to stop by words or signals. A picket may not physically obstruct a vehicle if the driver decides to drive on or, indeed, in any other circumstances. A driver must—as on all other occasions—exercise due care and attention when approaching or driving past a picket line, and may not drive in such a manner as to give rise to a reasonable foreseeable risk of injury.

SECTION D. ROLE OF THE POLICE

[4.216]
45. It is not the function of the police to take a view of the merits of a particular trade dispute. They have a general duty to uphold the law and keep the peace, whether on the picket line or elsewhere. The law gives the police discretion to take whatever measures may reasonable be considered necessary to ensure that picketing remains peaceful and orderly.

46. The police have no responsibility for enforcing the civil law. An employer cannot require the police to help in identifying the pickets against whom he wishes to seek an order from the civil court. Nor is it the job of the police to enforce the terms of an order. Enforcement of an order on the application of a plaintiff is a matter for the court and its officer. The police may, however, decide to assist the officers of the court if they think there may be a breach of the peace.

47. As regards the **criminal law** the police have considerable discretionary powers to limit the numbers of pickets at any one place where they have reasonable cause to fear disorder.[8] The law does not impose a specific limit on the number of people who may picket at any one place; nor does this Code affect in any way the discretion of the police to limit the number of people on a particular picket line. It is for the police to decide, taking into account all the circumstances, whether the number of pickets at any particular place provides reasonable grounds for the belief that a breach of the peace is likely to occur. If a picket does not leave the picket line when asked to do so by the police, he is liable to be arrested for obstruction either of the highway or of a police officer in the execution of his duty if the obstruction is such as to cause, or be likely to cause, a breach of the peace.

NOTES

[8] In *Piddington v Bates (1960)* the High Court upheld the decision of a police constable in the circumstances of that case to limit the number of pickets to two.

SECTION E. LIMITING NUMBERS OF PICKETS

[4.217]

48. Violence and disorder on the picket line is more likely to occur if there are excessive numbers of pickets. Wherever large numbers of people with strong feelings are involved there is danger that the situation will get out of control, and that those concerned will run the risk of committing an offence, with consequent arrest and prosecution, or of committing a civil wrong which exposes them, or anyone organising them, to civil proceedings.

49. This is particularly so wherever people seek by sheer weight of numbers to stop others going into work or delivering or collecting goods. In such cases, what is intended is not peaceful persuasion, but obstruction or harassment—if not intimidation. Such a situation is often described as "mass picketing". In fact, it is not picketing in its lawful sense of an attempt at peaceful persuasion, and may well result in a breach of the peace or other criminal offences.

50. Moreover, anyone seeking to demonstrate support for those in dispute should keep well away from any picket line so as not to create a risk of a breach of the peace or other criminal offence being committed on that picket line. Just as with a picket itself, the numbers involved is any such demonstration should not be excessive, and the demonstration should be conducted lawfully. *Section 14 of the Public Order Act 1986 provides the police with the power to impose conditions (for example, as to numbers, location and duration) on public assemblies of 20 or more people where the assembly is likely to result in serious public disorder; or serious damage to property; or serious disruption to the life of the community; or if its purpose is to coerce.*

51. Large numbers on a picket line are also likely to give rise to fear and resentment amongst those seeking to cross that picket line, even where no criminal offence is committed. They exacerbate disputes and sour relations not only between management and employees but between the pickets and their fellow employees. Accordingly pickets and their organisers should ensure that in general the number of pickets does not exceed six at any entrance to, or exit from, a workplace; frequently a smaller number will be appropriate.

SECTION F. ORGANISATION OF PICKETING

[4.218]

52. Sections B and C of this Code outline aspects of the civil law and the criminal law, as they may apply to pickets, and to anyone, including a trade union, who organises a picket. While it is possible that a picket may be entirely "spontaneous", it is much more likely that it will be organised by an identifiable individual or group.

53. Paragraphs 36–38 in Section B of this Code describe how to identify whether a trade union is, in fact, responsible in terms of civil law liability, for certain acts. As explained in these paragraphs, the law means, for example, that if such an act takes place in the course of picketing, and if a trade union official has done, authorised or endorsed the act, then the official's union will be responsible in law unless the act is "effectively repudiated" by the union's national leadership.

FUNCTIONS OF THE PICKET ORGANISER

54. Wherever picketing is "official" (ie organised by a trade union), an experienced person, preferably a trade union official who represents those picketing, should always be in charge of the picket line. He should have a letter of authority from his union which he can show to the police officers or to people who want to cross the picket line. Even when he is not on the picket line himself he should be available to give the pickets advice if a problem arises.

55. A picket should not be designated as an "official" picket unless it is actually organised by a trade union. Nor should pickets claim the authority and support of a union unless the union is prepared to accept the consequent responsibility. In particular, union authority and support should not be claimed by the pickets if the union has, in fact, repudiated calls to take industrial action made, or being made, in the course of the picketing.

56. Whether a picket is "official" or "unofficial", an organiser of pickets should maintain close contact with the police. Advance consultation with the police is always in the best interests of all concerned. In particular the organiser and the pickets should seek directions from the police on the number of people who should be present on the picket line at any one time and on where they should stand in order to avoid obstructing the highway.

57. The other main functions of the picket organiser should include ensuring that:

— the pickets understand the law and are aware of the provisions of this Code, and that the picketing is conducted peacefully and lawfully;
— badges or armbands, which authorised pickets should wear so that they are clearly identified, are distributed to such pickets and are worn while they are picketing;
— workers from other places of work do not join the picket line, and that any offers of support on the picket line from outsiders are refused;
— the number of pickets at any entrance to, or exit from, a place of work is not so great as to give rise to fear and resentment amongst those seeking to cross that picket line (see paragraph 51 in Section E of this Code);
— close contact with his own union office (if any), and with the officers of other unions if they are involved in the picketing, is established and maintained;
— such special arrangements as may be necessary for essential supplies, services or operations (see paragraphs 62–64 in Section G of this Code) are understood and observed by the pickets.

CONSULTATIONS WITH OTHER TRADE UNIONS

58. Where several unions are involved in a dispute, they should consult each other about the organisation of any picketing. It is important that they should agree how the picketing is to be carried out, how many pickets there should be from each union, and who should have overall responsibility for organising them.

RIGHT TO CROSS PICKET LINES

59. Everyone has the right to decide for himself whether he will cross a picket line. Disciplinary action should not be taken or threatened by a union against a member on the grounds that he has crossed a picket line.

60. *If a union disciplines any member for crossing a picket line, the member will have been "unjustifiably disciplined". In such a case, the individual can make a complaint to an industrial tribunal. If the tribunal finds the complaint well-founded, it will make a declaration to that effect.*

61. *If the union has not lifted the penalty imposed on the member, or if it has not taken all necessary steps to reverse anything done in giving effect to the penalty, an application for compensation should be made to the Employment Appeal Tribunal (EAT). In any other case, the individual can apply to an industrial tribunal for compensation. The EAT or tribunal will award whatever compensation it considers just and equitable in all the circumstances, subject to a specified maximum amount. Where the application is made to the EAT, there will normally be a specified minimum award.*

SECTION G. ESSENTIAL SUPPLIES, SERVICES AND OPERATIONS

[4.219]

62. Pickets, and anyone organising a picket should take very great care to ensure that their activities do not cause distress, hardship or inconvenience to members of the public who are not involved in the dispute. Particular care should be taken to ensure that the movement of essential goods and supplies, the carrying out of essential maintenance of plant and equipment, and the provision of services essential to the life of the community are not impeded, still less prevented.

63. The following list of essential supplies and services is provided as an illustration of the kind of activity which requires special protection to comply with the recommendations in paragraph 62 above. However, **the list is not intended to be comprehensive**. The supplies and services which may need to be protected in accordance with these recommendations could cover different activities in different circumstances. Subject to this *caveat*, "essential supplies, services and operations" include:

— the production, packaging, marketing and/or distribution of medical and pharmaceutical products;
— the provision of supplies and services essential to health and welfare institutions, eg hospitals, old people's homes;
— the provision of heating fuel for schools, residential institutions, medical institutions and private residential accommodation;
— the production and provision of other supplies for which there is a crucial need during a crisis in the interests of public health and safety (eg chlorine, lime and other agents for water purification; industrial and medical gases; sand and salt for road gritting purposes);
— activities necessary to the maintenance of plant and machinery;
— the proper care of livestock;
— necessary safety procedures (including such procedures as are necessary to maintain plant and machinery);
— the production, packaging, marketing and/or distribution of food and animal feeding stuffs;
— the operation of essential services, such as police, fire, ambulance, medical and nursing services, air safety, coastguard and air sea rescue services, and services provided by voluntary bodies (eg Red Cross and St John's ambulances, meals on wheels, hospital car service), and mortuaries, burial and cremation services.

64. Arrangements to ensure these safeguards for essential supplies, services and operations should be agreed in advance between the pickets, or anyone organising the picket, and the employer, or employers, concerned.

CODE OF PRACTICE: ACCESS AND UNFAIR PRACTICES DURING RECOGNITION AND DERECOGNITION BALLOTS (2005)

[4.220]

NOTES

This Code is issued under the power given to the Secretary of State by the Trade Union and Labour Relations (Consolidation) Act 1992, s 203 (at **[1.469]**), with the authority of Parliament. It came into effect on 1 October 2005 (see the Employment Code of Practice (Access and Unfair Practices during Recognition and Derecognition Ballots) Order 2005, SI 2005/2421). The statutory status of the Code is as stated in s 207 of the 1992 Act (at **[1.473]**).

This Code replaces the Code of Practice on Access to Workers during Recognition and Derecognition Ballots (2000). Notes are as in the original.

See *Harvey* NI(7).

CONTENTS

PREAMBLE

[4.221]

This document revises the Code of Practice on Access to Workers during Recognition and Derecognition Ballots, which came into effect on 6 June 2000. It also contains practical guidance on unfair practices during recognition and derecognition ballots, for which the law provides a separate power for the Secretary of State to issue a Code of Practice. These two Codes on access and unfair practices are therefore combined within this single document. For simplicity and ease of reference, the text refers to there being just one Code of Practice dealing with both topics.

This Code supersedes the Code of Practice on Access to Workers during Recognition and Derecognition Ballots, which came into effect on 6 June 2000. Pursuant to section 208(2) of the Trade Union and Labour Relations (Consolidation) Act 1992, that Code shall cease to have effect on the date on which this Code of Practice comes in force.

The legal framework within which this Code will operate is explained in its text. While every effort has made to ensure that explanations included in the Code are accurate, only the courts can give authoritative interpretations of the law.

The Code's provisions apply equally to men and to women, but for simplicity the masculine pronoun is used throughout.

Unless the text specifies otherwise, (i) the term "union" should be read to mean "unions" in cases where two or more unions are seeking to be jointly recognised; (ii) the term "workplace" should be read to mean "workplaces" in cases where a recognition application covers more than one workplace; and (iii) the term "working day" should be read to mean any day other than a Saturday or a Sunday, Christmas Day or Good Friday, or a day which is a bank holiday.

Passages in this Code which appear in italics are extracts from, or re-statements of, provisions in primary legislation.

SECTION A
INTRODUCTION

BACKGROUND

[4.222]

1. Schedule A1 of the Trade Union and Labour Relations (Consolidation) Act 1992, inserted by the Employment Relations Act 1999 and subsequently amended by the Employment Relations Act 2004, sets out the statutory procedure for the recognition and derecognition of trade unions for the purpose of collective bargaining.

RECOGNITION

2. Where an employer and a trade union fail to reach agreement on recognition voluntarily, the statute provides for the union to apply to the Central Arbitration Committee (CAC) to decide whether it should be recognised for collective bargaining purposes. In certain cases, the CAC may award recognition, or dismiss the application, without a ballot. In other cases, the CAC will be obliged to hold a secret ballot of members of the bargaining unit to determine the issue. If a ballot takes place, the CAC will decide whether it should be held at the workplace, by post, or, if special factors make it appropriate, by a combination of the two methods. The ballot must be conducted by a qualified independent person appointed by the CAC.

3. Schedule A1 places various duties and obligations on parties during the period of a recognition ballot including the following:

(a) Paragraph 26(2) of Schedule A1 places a duty on the employer *to co-operate generally, in connection with the ballot, with the union and the independent person appointed to conduct the ballot;*

(b) Paragraph 26(3) of Schedule A1 places a duty on the employer to give a union applying for recognition *such access to the workers constituting the bargaining unit as is reasonable to enable the union to inform the workers of the object of the ballot and to seek their support and their opinions on the issues involved;*

(c) Paragraph 26(4A) of Schedule A1 places a duty on the employer *to refrain from making any offer to any or all of the workers constituting the bargaining unit which (i) has or is likely to have the effect of inducing any or all of them not to attend a relevant meeting between the union and the workers constituting the bargaining unit and (ii) is not reasonable in the circumstances.* A "relevant meeting" is defined as a meeting arranged in accordance with the duty to provide reasonable access to which the employer has agreed, or is required, to permit the worker to attend;

(d) Paragraph 26(4B) of Schedule A1 places a duty on the employer *to refrain from taking or threatening to take any action against a worker solely or mainly on the grounds that he attended or took part in any relevant meeting between the union and the workers in the bargaining unit, or on the grounds that he indicated his intention to attend or take part in such a meeting.* The definition of a "relevant meeting" is the same as at (c);

(e) *Paragraph 27A(1) of Schedule A1 places an obligation on both the employer and the union to refrain from using an unfair practice with a view to influencing the result of a recognition ballot. The unfair practices are defined by paragraph 27A(2) of Schedule A1.*

4. Section 203(1)(a) of the Trade Union and Labour Relations (Consolidation) Act 1992 gives a general power to the Secretary of State to issue Codes of Practice containing practical guidance for the purpose of promoting the improvement of industrial relations. Paragraphs 26(8) and 26(9) of Schedule A1 specify that this general power includes the particular power to issue a Code of Practice giving practical guidance about reasonable access during recognition ballots and about the employer's duty to refrain from making offers to workers not to attend access meetings. In addition, paragraph 27A(5) of Schedule A1 specifies that the general power includes the particular power to issue a Code of Practice about unfair practices for the purposes of paragraph 27A.

DERECOGNITION

5. The CAC can also call a derecognition ballot in cases where an employer, or his workers, are seeking to end recognition arrangements with a union. In general, the duties and obligations on the parties are the same in both recognition and derecognition ballots. Paragraph 118(3) of Schedule A1 contains identical wording to paragraph 26(3) of Schedule A1, placing a duty on the employer to give the recognised union reasonable access to the workers comprising the bargaining unit where the CAC is holding a ballot on derecognition. Similarly, paragraph 118(4A) places a duty on the employer to refrain from making offers to workers not to attend access meetings. And paragraph 119A(1) requires both the employer, the union and, in cases where workers are applying to derecognise the union, those workers to refrain from using an unfair practice during the period of a derecognition ballot. Paragraphs 118(8) and 119(9) and paragraph 119A(5) contain similar provisions to paragraphs 26(8) and 26(9) and 27A(5) enabling the Secretary of State to issue a Code of Practice giving practical guidance about reasonable access and unfair practices during derecognition ballots.

6. For simplicity, most examples and explanations in this Code relate to the case where the union is seeking recognition. However, the guidance contained in this Code applies equally to cases where the ballot is about recognition or derecognition.

GENERAL PURPOSE OF THE CODE

7. This Code covers two related issues: the union's access to workers during the period of recognition or derecognition ballots and the avoidance of unfair practices when campaigning during that period. As regards the first topic of **access**, this Code gives practical guidance about the issues which arise when an employer receives a request by a union to be granted access to his workers at their workplace and/or during their working time. Of course, the union does not need the employer's consent or assistance to arrange access outside the workplace and outside working hours – say, when hiring a public hall to hold a meeting or when using local newspapers and media to put across its case. The Code does not therefore deal with the issues that arise when arranging such access, though those parts of the Code which concern the conduct of parties when campaigning are relevant. This Code deals with the specific circumstances of access during the period of recognition or derecognition ballots. It does not provide guidance on access at other times.

8. Access can take many and varied forms depending largely on the type of workplace involved and the characteristics of the balloted workforce. The overall aim is to ensure that the union can reach the workers involved, but local circumstances will need to be taken into account when deciding what form the access should take. Each case should be looked at on the facts. This Code therefore aims to help the employer and the union arrive at agreed arrangements for access, which can take full account of the circumstances of each individual case.

9. The second purpose of this Code is to help parties avoid committing **unfair practices**. Recognition and derecognition ballots usually occur because the employer and the union cannot agree the way ahead. In some cases a party will wish to communicate its views to the workers concerned through active campaigning once the CAC has informed it that a ballot will be held. This Code aims to encourage reasonable and responsible behaviour by both the employer and the union when undertaking campaigning activity in this period. A failure to follow the Code's guidance on responsible behaviour may not necessarily mean that an unfair practice has occurred. However, responsible campaigning should help ensure that acrimony between the parties is avoided and it greatly reduces the risk that individual workers are exposed to intimidation, threat or other unfair practices when deciding which way to cast their vote. As regards the treatment of individuals, both parties should note that the law provides protections against dismissal or detriment for workers who campaign either for or against recognition. The Code does not cover campaigning activity which occurs before the CAC decides that a ballot should be held. However, parties are still advised to act responsibly when undertaking early campaigning and they may benefit by drawing on the guidance provided by this Code.

10. In order for a ballot to take place, the union must have satisfied the CAC that at least 10% of the proposed bargaining unit are already members of the union, and that a majority of the workers in the proposed bargaining unit would be likely to favour recognition. There is therefore a good chance that recognition will be granted to the union, and that a working relationship between the parties will have to be sustained after the ballot. This longer term perspective should encourage both the employer and the union to behave responsibly and in a co-operative spirit during the balloting period.

STRUCTURE OF THE CODE

11. This Code deals mainly with issues concerning access and unfair practices. These are distinct, though related, matters and all sections of the Code should therefore be read in conjunction. Sections B–D contain guidance on access, whilst Section E provides guidance on conduct to avoid committing an unfair practice. Finally, Section F provides guidance on the resolution of any disputes which might arise about the arrangement of access to the union or to the conduct of either the employer or the union when campaigning during the balloting period.

LEGAL STATUS OF THE CODE

12. *Under paragraphs 27 and 119 of Schedule A1, the CAC may order employers who are breaching their duty to allow reasonable access to take specified, reasonable steps to do so, and can award recognition without a ballot, or can refuse to award derecognition where applied for by the employer, if an employer fails to abide by its orders to remedy a breach. Paragraphs 27C–27F of Schedule A1 provide a number of actions which the CAC may take when it concludes that a party has committed an unfair practice during a recognition or derecognition ballot. For example, the CAC may order a further ballot and it may order a party to take specified actions to help remedy the effects of the unfair practice. In addition, the CAC may award recognition or derecognition (or dismiss an application for recognition or derecognition) where an unfair practice has involved the use of violence or the dismissal of a union official, or where the CAC has found that a party has committed a second unfair practice or failed to comply with a remedial order.*

13. *This Code itself imposes no legal obligations and failure to observe it does not in itself render anyone liable to proceedings. But section 207 of the Trade Union and Labour Relations (Consolidation) Act 1992 provides that any provisions of this Code are to be admissible in evidence and are to be taken into account in proceedings before any court, tribunal or the CAC where they consider them relevant.*

SECTION B
PREPARING FOR ACCESS

WHEN SHOULD PREPARATIONS FOR ACCESS BEGIN?

[4.223]

14. Preparations for access should begin as soon as possible. The CAC is required to give notice to the employer and the union that it intends to arrange for the holding of a ballot. There then follows a period of ten working days before the CAC proceeds with arrangements for the ballot. The parties should make full use of this notification period to prepare for access. The union should request an early meeting with the employer in this period to discuss access arrangements. The employer should agree to arrange the meeting on an early date and at a mutually convenient time. The employer and the union should ensure that the individual or individuals representing them at the meeting are expressly authorised by them to take all relevant decisions regarding access, or are authorised to make recommendations directly to those who take such decisions.

JOINT APPLICATIONS BY TWO OR MORE UNIONS

15. Where there is a joint application for recognition by two or more unions acting together, the unions should act jointly in preparing and implementing the access arrangements. Therefore, unless the employer and the unions agree otherwise, the unions should have common access arrangements. The amount of time needed for access would normally be the same for single or joint applications.

ESTABLISHING AN ACCESS AGREEMENT

16. It would be reasonable for the employer to want to give his prior permission before allowing a full time union official to enter his workplace and talk to his workers. In particular, the employer may have security and health and safety issues to consider. The parties should discuss practical arrangements for the union's activities at the workplace, in advance of the period of access actually beginning.

17. Consideration should be given to establishing an agreement, preferably in written form, on access arrangements. Such an agreement could include:

- the union's programme for where, when and how it will access the workers on site and/or during their working time; and
- a mechanism for resolving disagreements, if any arise, about implementing the agreed programme of access.

When discussions about access arrangements are taking place, parties should also seek to reach understandings about the standards of conduct expected of those individuals who campaign on their behalf (see paragraph 52 below for more guidance on this point).

18. In seeking to reach an agreement, the union should put its proposals for accessing the workers to the employer. The employer should not dismiss the proposals unless he considers the union's requirements to be unreasonable in the circumstances. If the employer rejects the proposals, he should offer alternative arrangements to the union at the earliest opportunity, preferably within three working days of receiving the union's initial proposals. In the course of this dialogue the union will need to reveal its plans for on-site access.

19. It is reasonable for the union to request information from the employer to help it formulate and refine its access proposals. In particular, the employer should disclose to the union information about his typical methods of communicating with his workforce and provide such other practical information as may be needed about, say, workplace premises or patterns of work. Where relevant to the union in framing its plans, the employer should also disclose information about his own plans to put across his views, directly or indirectly, to the workers about the recognition (or derecognition) of the union. The employer should not, however, disclose to the union the names or addresses (postal or e-mail) of the workers who will be balloted, unless the workers concerned have authorised the disclosure.

AMENDING THE ACCESS AGREEMENT

20. Every effort should be made to ensure access agreements are faithfully implemented. To avoid misunderstanding on the ground, the employer should seek to draw the attention of relevant managers to the agreement and the commitments to release workers to attend access meetings. Likewise, the union should take steps to ensure that the relevant union officials and representatives are made aware of the agreed arrangements. However, in some cases, the agreement may need to be changed if circumstances alter. For example, a union official selected to enter the workplace may be unexpectedly called away by his union on other urgent business. Likewise, the employer might wish to re-arrange an event if the selected meeting-room is unexpectedly and unavoidably needed for other important business purposes. If such circumstances arise, the union, or the employer if his situation changes, should notify the other party at the earliest opportunity that a change will need to be made to the agreed access arrangements, and offer alternative suggestions. The other party should generally accept the alternative arrangements, if they are of an equivalent nature to those already agreed.

RESOLVING DIFFERENCES ABOUT AGREEING ACCESS ARRANGEMENTS

21. Where the employer and the union fail to agree access arrangements voluntarily, either party, acting separately or together, may ask the Advisory, Conciliation and Arbitration Service (Acas) to conciliate. Given the limited time available, Acas will respond to the conciliation request as soon as possible, and preferably within one working day of receiving the request. Both parties should give all reasonable assistance to Acas to enable it to help the parties overcome their difficulties through conciliation.

22. Every effort should be made to resolve any procedural difficulties remaining, but, ultimately, where it remains deadlocked, the CAC may be asked to assist. The CAC could, in appropriate circumstances, consider delaying the arrangement of the ballot for a limited period to give extra time for the parties to settle their differences. However, where no agreement is forthcoming, the CAC may be asked to adjudicate and to make an order.

SECTION C
ACCESS IN OPERATION

WHAT IS THE ACCESS PERIOD?

[4.224]
23. *Following the notification period, and providing it does not receive a contrary request from the trade union, the CAC will be required to arrange the holding of the ballot. As soon as is reasonably practicable, the CAC must inform the parties of the fact that it is arranging the ballot, the name of the qualified independent person appointed to conduct the ballot, and the period within which the ballot must be conducted. The ballot must be held within 20 working days from the day after the appointment of the independent person, or longer if the CAC should so decide.*

24. The period of access will begin as soon as the parties have been informed of the arrangements for the ballot as in paragraph 23 above. The CAC will endeavour to inform both parties as soon as the independent person has been appointed. This may be achieved by a telephone call to both parties, followed by a letter of confirmation.

25. If the ballot is to be conducted by post, the period of access will come to an end on the closing date of the balloting period. If the ballot is to be conducted at the workplace, access will continue until the ballot has closed. However, where the ballot is to be conducted at the workplace, and where the union has already had adequate access opportunities, both the employer and the union should largely confine their activities during the actual hours of balloting to the encouragement of workers to vote. They should reduce or cease other campaigning activity at this time. For example, both the employer and the union should avoid scheduling large meetings at such times. This should ensure that the ballot is conducted in a calm and orderly fashion, with minimum disruption to the normal functioning of the workplace.

WHO MAY BE GRANTED ACCESS?

26. The access agreement should specify who should be given access to the workers who will be balloted. Employers should be prepared to give access to:

(a) individual union members employed by the employer, who are nominated by the union as the lead representative of their members at workplaces where the bargaining unit is situated;

(b) individual union members employed by the employer, who are nominated by the union as the lead representative of their members at other workplaces in the employer's business, provided that it is practicable for them to attend events at workplaces where the bargaining unit is situated. The costs of travelling from other workplaces should be met by the individuals or the union; and

(c) "full-time" union officials. (That is, individuals employed by the union, who are officials of the union within the meaning of the Sections 1 and 119 of the Trade Union and Labour Relations (Consolidation) Act 1992).

The number of union representatives entitled to gain access should be proportionate to the scale and nature of the activities or events organised within the agreed access programme.

WHERE WILL THE ACCESS TAKE PLACE?

27. Where practicable in the circumstances, a union should be granted access to the workers at their actual workplace. However, each case will depend largely on the type of workplace concerned, and the union will need to take account of the wide variety of circumstances and operational requirements that are likely to be involved. In particular, consideration will need to be given to the employer's responsibility for health and safety and security issues. In other words, access arrangements should reflect local circumstances and each case should be examined on the facts.

28. Where they are suitable for the purpose, the employer's typical methods of communicating with his workforce should be used as a benchmark for determining how the union should communicate with members of the same workforce during the access period. If the employer follows the custom and practice of holding large workforce meetings in, for example, a meeting room or a canteen, then the employer should make the same facilities available to the union. However, in cases where the workplace is more confined, and it is therefore the employer's custom and practice to hold only small meetings at the workplace, then the union will also be limited to holding similar small meetings at that workplace. In exceptional circumstances, due to the nature of the business or severe space limitations, access may need to be restricted to meetings away from the workplace premises, and the union will need to consider finding facilities off-site at its own expense unless it agrees otherwise with the employer. In these circumstances, the employer should give all reasonable assistance to the union in notifying the workers in advance of where and when such off-site events are to take place. Where such exceptional circumstances exist, it would normally be expected that the employer would not hold similar events at the workplace.

WHEN WILL THE ACCESS TAKE PLACE?

29. The union should ensure that disruption to the business is minimised, especially for small businesses which might find it more difficult to organise cover for absent workers. The union's access to the workers should usually take place during normal working hours but at times which minimise any possible disruption to the activities of the employer. This will ensure that the union is able to communicate with as large a number of the workers as possible. Again, the arrangements should reflect the circumstances of each individual case. Consideration should be given to holding events, particularly those involving a large proportion of the workers in the bargaining unit, during rest periods or towards the end of a shift. In deciding the timing of meetings and other events, the union and the employer should be guided by the employer's custom and practice when communicating with his workforce. If, due to exceptional circumstances, access must be arranged away from the workplace, it might be practicable to arrange events in work time if they are held nearby, within easy walking distance. Otherwise, off-site events should normally occur outside work time.

THE FREQUENCY AND DURATION OF UNION ACTIVITIES

30. The parties will need to establish agreed limits on the duration and frequency of the union's activities during the access period. Subject to the circumstances discussed in paragraphs 27–29 above, the employer should allow the union to hold one meeting of at least 30 minutes in duration for every 10 days of the access period, or part thereof, which all workers or a substantial proportion of them are given the opportunity to attend. In circumstances where the employer or others organise similar large-scale meetings in work time against the recognition application (or in favour of derecognition), then it would be reasonable for the union to hold additional meetings, if necessary, to ensure that in total it has the same number of large-scale meetings as the employer and his supporters.

31. Where they would be appropriate having regard to all the circumstances, union "surgeries" could be organised at the workplace during working hours at which each worker would have the opportunity, if they wish, to meet a union representative for fifteen minutes on an individual basis or in small groups of two or three. The circumstances would include whether there was a demand from the workforce for surgeries, whether the surgeries could be arranged off-site as effectively, whether the holding of surgeries would lead to an unacceptable increase in tension at the workplace and whether the employer, line managers or others use similar one-to-one or small meetings to put across the employer's case. The union should organise surgeries in a systematic way, ensuring that workers attend meetings at pre-determined times, thereby avoiding delays before workers are seen and ensuring that they promptly return to their work stations afterwards. Wherever practicable, the union should seek to arrange surgeries during periods of down-time such as rest or meal breaks. Where surgeries do not take place, the minimum time allowed for each larger scale meeting should be 45 minutes.

32. An employer should ensure that workers who attend a meeting or a "surgery" organised by the union with his agreement during work time, should be paid, in full, for the duration of their absence from work. The employer will not be expected to pay the worker if the meeting or surgery takes place when the worker would not otherwise have been at work, and would not have been receiving payment from the employer.

33. Where the union wishes one of the employer's workers within the meaning of paragraphs 26(a) and 26(b) above to conduct a surgery, the employer should normally give time off with pay to the worker concerned. The worker should ensure that he provides the employer with as much notice as possible, giving details about the timing and location of the surgery. Exceptionally, it may be reasonable for the employer to refuse time off. This will apply if unavoidable situations arise where there is no adequate cover for the worker's absence from the workplace and the production process, or the provision of a service cannot otherwise be maintained. Before refusing permission, the employer should discuss the matter with the union and the worker to explore alternative arrangements.

WHAT ABOUT WRITTEN COMMUNICATION?

34. The union may want to display written material at the place of work. Employers, where practicable, should provide a notice board for the union's use. This notice board should be in a prominent location in the workplace and the union should be able to display material, including references to off-site meetings, without interference from the employer. Often, an existing notice-board could be used for this purpose. The union should also be able to place additional material near to the noticeboard including, for example, copies of explanatory leaflets, which the workers may read or take away with them. If there are no union representatives within the meaning of paragraphs 26(a) and 26(b) above present at the workplace, the employer should allow access to a full time official of the union to display the material.

35. The union may also wish to make use of its web-site pages on the internet for campaigning purposes. An employer should allow his workers access to the union's material in the same way that he explicitly, or tacitly, allows his workers to down-load information in connection with activities not directly related to the performance of their job. If an employer generally disallows all such internet use, he should consider giving permission to one of his workers nominated by the union to down-load the material, and it would be this person's responsibility to disseminate it more widely among other workers.

36. A nominated union representative employed by the employer may also want to make use of internal electronic communication, such as electronic mail or intranets, for campaigning purposes. For example, he may want to remind workers of forthcoming union meetings or surgeries. The employer should allow the representative to make reasonable use of these systems if the employer explicitly, or tacitly, allows his workers to use them for matters which are not directly related to the performance of their job. In cases where such use is disallowed, it would still be reasonable for the representative to use them, if the employer uses such forms of communication to send to the workers information against the union's case. When sending messages in this capacity, the representative should make it clear that the advice comes from the union and not the employer.

WHAT ABOUT SMALL BUSINESSES?

37. Access arrangements for small businesses need not necessarily create difficulties. For example, it may be easier to arrange for a smaller number of workers to meet together. On the other hand, there may be difficulties providing cover for workers in smaller organisations, or in finding accommodation for meetings. In such cases, the employer and the union should try to reach an understanding about how access arrangements can be organised to ensure minimum disruption. Agreements may need to be flexible to accommodate any particular needs of the employer.

ARRANGEMENTS FOR NON-TYPICAL WORKERS

38. Many, or sometimes most, workers in a bargaining unit may not work full time in a standard Monday-Friday working week. Others might rarely visit the employer's premises. The employer should bear in mind the difficulties faced by unions in communicating with:
- shift workers
- part-time workers
- homeworkers
- a dispersed or peripatetic workforce
- those on maternity or parental leave
- those on sick leave.

39. The employer should be receptive to a union's suggestions for securing reasonable access to such "non-typical workers", and allow them, where practicable, to achieve a broadly equivalent level of access to those workers as to typical workers. It would be reasonable for the union to organise its meetings or surgery arrangements on a more flexible basis to cover shift workers or part-time workers. An employer should agree to the maximum flexibility of arrangements, where reasonable in the circumstances. This would not extend to an employer being obliged to meet the travel costs of his workers attending meetings arranged by the union.

40. In addition, the union will be able to make use of the independent person to distribute information to home addresses via the postal service. This will ensure that literature will be received by any workers who are not likely to attend the workplace during the access period, for example those on maternity or sick leave. The CAC will supply the name, address and telephone number of the independent person to both the union and the employer.

WHAT ABOUT JOINT EMPLOYER/UNION ACTIVITIES?

41. There may be scope for the union and the employer to undertake joint activities where they both put across their respective views about recognition or derecognition in a non-confrontational way. Such joint activities can be an efficient method of providing information, minimising business disruption and costs. For example, the parties may wish to consider:
- the arrangement of joint meetings with each party allocated a period of thirty minutes to address the workers; and
- the use of a joint notice-board where an equal amount of space is devoted to the employer and the union.

SECTION D
OTHER ACCESS ISSUES

OBSERVING AN ACCESS AGREEMENT

[4.225]
42. Both parties should ensure they keep to agreements about access arrangements. For example, if the parties agree to hold a meeting lasting 30 minutes in duration, every effort should be made to

ensure that the meeting does not over-run its allocated time. Likewise, neither party should remove, or tamper, with material placed on a notice board by the other party, unless they are obliged to do so for legal reasons.

PRIVACY OF MEETINGS

43. Employers should respect the privacy of access meetings. *Paragraph 26(4D) of Schedule A1 of the Trade Union and Labour Relations (Consolidation) Act 1992 therefore provides that the employer or any representative of his must not attend an access meeting unless invited to do so. Likewise, the employer must not use the union's unwillingness to allow him or his representative to attend as a reason to refuse an access meeting unless it is reasonable to do so. The employer must not record or otherwise be informed of the proceedings of a meeting unless it is reasonable for him to do so.*

44. Supervisors or managers may attend an access meeting, even though they may be seen as representatives of the employer, provided they have been invited to attend by the union. In general, it should be expected that such workers would be invited by the union to attend access meetings where they fall within the bargaining unit and are therefore entitled to vote. However, there may be circumstances – for example, where the attendance of supervisors would deter other workers from expressing their opinions, or where managers are campaigning on behalf of the employer – where it is reasonable for the union not to invite them. In such circumstances, consideration should be given to arranging separate access meetings for the supervisors and managers concerned. In situations where they are not invited to attend meetings with other workers, supervisors or other managers should not insist on attending simply because they are part of the bargaining unit. To avoid uncertainty and the disruption of meetings, the union should consider in advance whether it wishes to exclude such individuals from meetings, taking steps where possible to inform the individuals concerned before the meeting occurs. The union should avoid issuing generalised or loosely drafted invitations to attend access meetings, if its intention is to prevent certain individuals from attending.

45. In small workplaces or in workplaces with no dedicated meeting rooms, it may be difficult to find suitable accommodation on site which can be set aside for the exclusive use of the union to hold a meeting. Achieving privacy in such circumstances may be difficult, but solutions might be found by holding meetings during lunch breaks or at other times when business would not be significantly affected if managers or other work colleagues were required to vacate the premises or meeting area in question. In extreme cases, for example where continuous working is necessary, privacy may be achieved only by holding meetings away from the workplace.

46. Many employers have security cameras or other recording equipment permanently positioned on site to monitor or record workplace activity. Most are installed for reasons of security, health and safety or quality control. Where such equipment is used, and could record meetings, the employer should inform the union accordingly unless key security considerations prevent such disclosure. The employer and the union should then discuss ways to ensure the privacy of meetings. It may be possible, for example, to turn off the equipment in question for the short period of meetings. Alternatively, the employer may wish to ensure that any transmissions from the surveillance equipment during the period of the meeting are not viewed live or recorded. The scope for such measures may be limited in rare cases where security or health and safety may be significantly and unavoidably jeopardised as a result.

47. The employer should not eavesdrop on access meetings or pressurise any of those attending to disclose what occurred at them. Generally, the employer should not seek to question attendees about the proceedings of meetings but, in exceptional cases of, say, alleged harassment or damage to property, there may be a need for the employer to investigate the conduct of meetings. However, it must be recognised that information often circulates quite widely within workplaces and the employer may therefore learn what took place even though he took no specific steps to discover what had occurred. In some cases, individual workers may disclose without prompting what took place at meetings in their ordinary exchanges with line managers or other work colleagues.

BEHAVING RESPONSIBLY

48. Both parties should endeavour to ensure that, wherever possible, potentially acrimonious situations are avoided. For access arrangements to work satisfactorily, the employer and the union should behave responsibly, and give due consideration to the requirements of the other party throughout the access period. For example, neither the union nor the employer should seek to disrupt or interfere with meetings being held by the other party. So, if the union is holding a meeting, the employer should avoid the scheduling of other conflicting meetings or events which would draw workers away from the union's meeting. Unless special factors apply, the employer should not offer inducements to workers not to attend access meetings. For example, where an access meeting is held towards the end of the working day, the employer should not tell workers that they could go home early if they do not attend the union's meeting. However, unforeseen events may arise – an urgent order, for example – where the employer may need to require workers not to attend an access meeting, paying them overtime, or some other additional payment or fringe benefit, for any extra work involved. The offer of additional pay for extra work in such circumstances is reasonable.

Where such exceptional events occur, the employer should explain the position to the union as soon as practicable, and offer alternative but comparable access arrangements for the workers involved.

49. Where it is practicable to hold meetings or surgeries at the workplace, the employer should provide appropriate accommodation, fit for the purpose, which should include adequate heating and lighting, and arrangements to ensure that the meeting is held in private. In turn, the union should ensure that business costs and business disruption are minimised. Unions should be aware of the needs of the employer to maintain the production process, to maintain a level of service, and to ensure safety and security at all times.

SECTION E
RESPONSIBLE CAMPAIGNING AND UNFAIR PRACTICES

[4.226]

50. This Section of the Code provides guidance on those standards of behaviour which are likely to prevent undue influence or other unfair practices from occurring. In places, it also refers to behaviour which, if pursued, may constitute an unfair practice. However, given the range of possible behaviours involved, it is unrealistic for the Code to identify every circumstance which might give rise to undue influence or other unfair practice. In any event, as Section F discusses, it is the task of the Central Arbitration Committee to judge whether an unfair practice has been committed, basing its judgment on the particular facts of a case.

RESPONSIBLE CAMPAIGNING

51. Recognition and derecognition ballots concern important, and sometimes complex, issues. It may help those workers entitled to vote in these ballots to receive information from the employer and the union setting out their views on the implications of recognition and non-recognition. Parties are not required to undertake any campaigning activity during this period. Indeed, a party might choose to desist from campaigning altogether because it wishes to avoid unnecessary acrimony or because it sees an advantage in employment relations terms in leaving the issue to the workers to decide. This Code should not therefore be read as discouraging such behaviour. That said, there will be other cases where parties will wish to campaign and such activity can benefit the balloting process in helping the workers make informed decisions. But active campaigning needs to be responsible or it can lead to the use of unfair practices which distort the balloting process, increase workplace friction and can sour employment relations.

52. Campaigning can expose sharp divisions of opinion, and ill-judged activity can damage trust and long-term employment relations. Parties should therefore discuss with each other at an early stage how they would wish campaigning to be undertaken. This discussion could take place at the same time the parties seek to reach access agreements. There are advantages in parties exchanging information about their approach to campaigning, indicating for example those persons or organisations which are likely to undertake the activity on their behalf. Prior discussion should focus in particular on the standards of conduct expected of campaigners to minimise the risk of intimidation occurring. One way to structure such joint discussions might be for the parties to discuss how they think the guidance in this section of the Code could best be applied to their particular situation. Where they agree standards of conduct, parties should take steps to ensure that those who campaign on their behalf are fully aware of them.

WHAT ARE UNFAIR PRACTICES?

53. *Parties must refrain from using an unfair practice during recognition or derecognition ballots. A party uses an unfair practice if, with a view to influencing the result of the ballot, the party:*

(a) *offers to pay money or give money's worth to a worker entitled to vote in a ballot in return for the worker's agreement to vote in a particular way or to abstain from voting;*

(b) *makes an "outcome-specific" offer to a worker entitled to vote in a ballot. (An "outcome-specific" offer is an offer to pay money or give money's worth which is conditional on the issuing by the CAC of a declaration that the union is entitled to be recognised or is not entitled to be recognised, and such an offer is not conditional on anything which is done or occurs as a result of the declaration in question).* Thus, an offer by either a union (or an employer) to pay each worker £100, provided the ballot does (or does not) result in recognition would be categorised as an unfair practice. In contrast, an undertaking by a union to secure an increase of £1,000 in the annual pay of workers through the collective bargaining process following a vote for recognition would not be captured because the offer clearly depends on other circumstances – in this case, the negotiation of a collective agreement – which is contingent on recognition being awarded;

(c) *coerces or attempts to coerce a worker entitled to vote in a ballot to disclose whether he intends to vote or abstain from voting in the ballot, or how he intends to vote, or how he has voted, in the ballot;*

(d) *dismisses or threatens to dismiss a worker;*

(e) *takes or threatens to take disciplinary action against a worker;*

(f) *subjects or threatens to subject a worker to any other detriment by, for example, threatening to give a worker a lower performance mark or a worse promotional assessment if he supports recognition or non-recognition; or*

(g) *uses or attempts to use undue influence on a worker entitled to vote in a ballot.*[1]

54. The statute refers to the term "money's worth" when defining an unfair offer to a worker. The term covers the making of non-cash offers to workers. Such non-cash offers usually involve the provision of goods and services, for which workers would otherwise need to pay if they procured the goods or services for themselves. Most fringe benefits – say, a better company car, subsidised health insurance or free legal services – would normally fall into this category. In addition, offers to provide additional paid holiday or other paid leave are likely to constitute "money's worth". Of course, providing such "money's worth" for permissible reasons – for example, as a normal inducement to join a union or as a typical bonus for meeting a work target – would not be categorised as an unfair practice.

55. Unfair practices can involve the taking of disciplinary action against workers, where such disciplinary action has the purpose of influencing the result of the ballot. The period of ballots is relatively short and this lessens the scope for disciplinary matters to arise. However, it is worth noting that this unfair practice is not limited just to disciplinary action taken against workers entitled to vote in a ballot. It is possible that an unfair practice could be committed if, say, disciplinary action were taken against a union activist involved in the union's campaign who was not entitled to vote in the ballot. Equally, the employer is not prevented from taking any disciplinary action just because a ballot is occurring. There may be sound grounds for the employer to discipline a worker, which are totally unconnected with the ballot. Likewise, it is possible that a worker's campaigning activity – say, the use of threatening behaviour against other workers or the unauthorised use of work time for campaigning – may itself give rise to disciplinary action which would not constitute an unfair practice. When contemplating disciplinary action, the employer should in addition take note of the guidance provided in the *Acas Code of Practice on Disciplinary and Grievance Procedures*, especially its advice on the disciplining of union officials.

56. The statutory list of unfair practices highlights actions to bribe, pressurise or exert other undue influence on workers to vote in particular ways or not to vote at all. Such conduct, especially the exertion of undue influence, can take many forms. At one extreme, undue influence may take the obvious form of actual or threatened physical violence against workers. It may also take other, and more subtle, forms of behaviour to influence the outcome of the ballot. For example, the introduction of higher pay or better conditions in the ballot period may constitute undue influence if the ballot period is not the normal time for reviewing pay or if there is not some other pressing reason unconnected with the ballot for raising pay.

WHO SHOULD CAMPAIGN?

57. Transparency is an important feature of normal campaigning activity and reduces the risk that a worker might be unduly influenced through subterfuge or misrepresentation. So, those authorised by the employer or a union to campaign on their behalf should take steps to inform the workers involved that they are so authorised and are therefore acting under instruction or at the behest of the party involved. Where there is reason to believe that workers do not understand their role, supervisors and line managers who undertake such work on behalf of the employer should state that they are acting in that capacity when communicating campaign messages to the workforce. In similar circumstances, union members who act as officials of the union or who are otherwise authorised to represent the union in its campaigning work should also explain their role when speaking to other workers in their capacity as campaigners.

58. Sometimes, a party might employ or hire a paid consultant to assist its campaigning work. Such consultants are therefore acting as agents of the party involved. If their behaviour constitutes an unfair practice, then the party who hired their services is also committing an unfair practice where the party expressly or by implication authorised the behaviour. A failure by a party to repudiate and correct misconduct by a consultant can be taken as implying that such conduct is authorised. Parties should therefore monitor the activities of the consultants they hire. Where outside consultants are used by either party, and undertake active campaigning by speaking to the workforce, then they should inform the workers that they have been hired by that party. They should also take steps to inform the workers accurately about the general purpose of their engagement. Whilst there is no need to divulge commercial confidences or to detail the precise contractual remit, if a consultant has been hired to advance the case of the union or the employer in the campaign then that essential fact should be divulged to the workforce when the consultant is communicating with them. It follows that consultants should not present themselves as independent or impartial third parties when undertaking their campaigning work.

59. The employer and the union are usually responsible for the actions of those whom they authorise or hire to campaign on their behalf. They should therefore take steps to brief their representatives or agents accordingly in advance of undertaking such activity. The briefing should not be limited to just the messages or information which the union or employer wish to convey. It should also provide clear advice to representatives or agents on the behavioural standards expected of them and the need to avoid actions which could constitute an unfair practice.

60. The employer and the union should also dissociate themselves from material containing personal attacks or allegations which is circulated on an anonymous basis. The party whose case appears to be favoured by the anonymous material should usually repudiate it, informing all workers in the bargaining unit accordingly.

WHAT ARE THE MAIN FORMS OF CAMPAIGNING?

61. All campaigning involves communication with workers in the bargaining unit. Sometimes, that communication can take the form of face-to-face discussion with a worker or workers. Such encounters can perform useful functions as many workers may feel nervous about asking questions at mass meetings and small scale gatherings may encourage more open debate. Section C therefore refers to the option for unions to access the workforce by holding "surgeries" which individual workers or small groups of workers can attend if they wish. That said, the employer or the union must take particular care when handling one-to-one meetings or encounters with small groups, because a worker may feel more vulnerable in those situations and undue influence may arise if a worker feels threatened as a result. Workers should not normally be required to attend small meetings organised by either the employer or the union for campaigning purposes, and they should not be threatened with sanctions if they fail to attend. Workers who voluntarily attend should be informed that they are under no obligation to answer any direct questions which are put to them. In particular, they should not be required to disclose the way they have voted or their voting intentions.

62. Most small or one-to-one meetings occur at the place of work. But a party might also try to arrange similar encounters outside the workplace to canvass opinion by visiting a worker's home or by ringing a home telephone. When undertaking such activity, unions should note that neither the CAC nor the qualified independent person it employs to run the ballot will disclose to the union the names, addresses or telephone numbers of the workers involved. Whereas canvassing at a worker's home may be an acceptable practice, reflecting perhaps restricted access at work, considerable care needs to be taken by the party involved to avoid possible intimidation, however unintended, which could give rise to undue influence. Where practicable, a party should seek and obtain a worker's permission in advance before visiting him at home. In particular, the number of people visiting a worker's home to campaign or canvass, even where prior permission is obtained, should be limited to one or, perhaps, two people. If a worker does not wish to open or continue a discussion with the campaigners, then that wish must be completely respected. A failure to leave a worker's premises on request would almost certainly be seen as an intimidatory practice. Also, if a worker indicates he does not wish to be revisited at home, or rung again by telephone, then that wish should be respected.

63. The holding of one or two face-to-face meetings, either on site or off it, may not in itself be perceived as placing unwelcome pressure on the worker involved. Indeed, a worker might request further meetings himself to cover the issues fully or to follow up a discussion. However, the frequency of meetings, or frequent requests to attend meetings, can be perceived as potentially threatening by some workers. There may come a point where persistent approaches to workers will be construed as harassment. Parties must therefore be aware that the intensity of their campaigning activity can give rise to problems.

64. Campaigning can also be undertaken by circulating information by e-mails, videos or other mediums. There is nothing intrinsically wrong with communication of that nature. Indeed, because such communication does not require the physical presence of the campaigner, they may well be seen as having less potential to threaten the worker. That said, the content of such communications can still intimidate or threaten the voter, and care should therefore be taken to avoid such effects when drafting written communication or producing videos.

HOW SHOULD CAMPAIGNERS PUT ACROSS THEIR MESSAGE?

65. Campaigning is inherently a partisan activity. Each party is therefore unlikely to put across a completely balanced message to the workforce, and some overstatement or exaggeration may well occur. In general, workers will expect such behaviour and can deal with it. Also, by listening to both sides, they will be able to question and evaluate the material presented to them.

66. Campaigning should focus on the issues at stake. These will mostly concern the workplace, the performance of the union or the running of the employer's business. Sometimes, it will be legitimate to focus on the work behaviours and previous work histories of key individuals. For example, it may be pertinent to refer to the way a proprietor or a senior manager has responded to workplace grievances in the past or to the way a key union official has handled negotiations elsewhere. But campaigning about the personal lives of senior managers or union leaders usually adds nothing beneficial to the discussion of the issues and should be avoided. Personalised attacks and the denigration of individuals may also harm the long-term health of employment relations.

67. Parties, especially the employer, should take particular care if they discuss job losses or the relocation of business activity. Such statements can be seen as directly threatening the livelihoods of the workers involved, and can give rise to undue influence by implicitly threatening to harm the workers concerned. It is a fine line, therefore, to distinguish between fair comment about job prospects and intimidatory behaviour designed primarily to scare the workers to vote against recognition. In general, references to job prospects are more likely to constitute fair comment if they can be clearly linked to the future economic performance of the employer with or without union recognition, and are expressed in measured terms. Unsubstantiated assertions on this particularly sensitive issue should therefore be avoided. So, it might be fair comment to argue that the employer's business may run less successfully if recognition is awarded, and employment may be less secure as a result, because pay levels would rise or work would be organised less flexibly. On the other hand, statements that the employer will make redundancies or relocate simply because a union is recognised should be avoided.

68. Part of a party's normal campaigning is to engage with the arguments put forward by others. That can be helpful and can assist workers in understanding the issues at stake. Each party will therefore try to obtain the campaigning literature of the other party to enable them to discuss the points raised. This should not normally present a problem as literature tends to be widely available either on websites, notice boards or elsewhere. Indeed, parties may often find it mutually advantageous to exchange these materials.

69. Campaigning meetings should be treated as far as possible as private affairs, and there are legislative requirements covering the privacy of access meetings at work (see paragraphs 43–47 in Section D). Meetings or other campaigning activities which occur off-site are generally not covered by the access provisions, but the privacy of those gatherings should be respected. A party should not infiltrate meetings or use other covert methods to monitor another party's campaign. It is also likely to constitute an intimidatory practice for parties to photograph, record or otherwise place workers under surveillance without permission whilst they are undertaking campaigning or attending campaigning events off-site, unless such activity takes place at a location (for example, the entrance to a workplace) where surveillance equipment normally operates for other legitimate reasons. Parties should also not penalise workers, or threaten to penalise them, if they attend or take part in those off-site activities.

NOTES

1 See paragraphs 27A(2) and 119A(2) of Schedule A1 of the Trade Union and Labour Relations (Consolidation) Act 1992.

SECTION F
RESOLVING DISPUTES

INTERVENTION BY THE CAC

Access

[4.227]

70. Disputes may arise between the parties during the access period about the failure to allow reasonable access or to implement access agreements. If these disputes cannot be resolved, the union may ask the CAC to decide whether the employer has failed to perform his statutory duties in relation to the ballot.

71. *If the CAC is satisfied that the employer has failed to perform one or more of his five duties:*

(a) *to co-operate generally with the union and the independent person on the ballot;*
(b) to give the union such access to the workers constituting the bargaining unit as is reasonable to inform them of the object of the ballot and to seek their support and opinions;
(c) *to provide the CAC with the names and home addresses of those workers;*
(d) to refrain from making any offer to any or all of the workers constituting the bargaining unit which (i) has or is likely to have the effect of inducing any or all of them not to attend any relevant meeting between the union and the workers constituting the bargaining unit and (ii) is not reasonable in the circumstances; and
(e) to refrain from taking or threatening to take any action against a worker solely or mainly on the grounds that he (i) attended or took part in any relevant meeting between the union and the workers constituting the bargaining unit, or (ii) indicated his intention to attend or take part in such a meeting.

and the ballot has not been held, the CAC may order the employer to take such steps to remedy the failure as the CAC considers reasonable, and within a time that the CAC considers reasonable. Where the CAC is asked to make an order very shortly before the end of the access period, it may be impracticable for the CAC to consider the request and for the employer and the union to remedy any failure in the short time before the ballot is held. In such circumstances, the CAC may extend the access period by ordering the ballot to be rescheduled for a later date to ensure that access is achieved.

72. *If the employer fails to comply with the CAC's order within the time specified, and the ballot has still not been held, the CAC may issue a declaration that the union is recognised, or that the union is not derecognised.*

73. It is the employer's duty to provide reasonable access, and complaints about a failure to provide such access can be made by unions only. However, in deciding whether the employer has complied with his duty to give the union access, the CAC may take into account all relevant circumstances. This may include the behaviour of the union. The CAC may therefore decide that the employer has complied with the duty in circumstances where, because the union has acted unreasonably, he denies the union access or refuses to implement agreed access arrangements.

UNFAIR PRACTICES

74. Complaints may also surface that a party has committed an unfair practice during the balloting period. Such complaints may be referred by the employer or the union to the CAC to adjudicate though any complaints must be made either before the ballot closes or on the first working day after that. Where time permits, it is a good practice for the parties to try to resolve them locally in the first instance.

75. The CAC must decide that a complaint is well-founded if the party complained against used an unfair practice and the CAC is satisfied that the practice changed or was likely to change, in the case of a worker entitled to vote in a ballot either (i) his intention to vote or to abstain from voting or (ii) his intention to vote in a particular way or (iii) how he voted.

76. *Where it considers a complaint is well-founded, the CAC must issue a declaration to that effect, and it may*

- *issue a remedial order to the party concerned to take such action as it specifies and within a timetable it specifies to mitigate the effect of the unfair practice, and /or*
- *give notice to the parties that it intends to hold a fresh secret ballot* (and thereby replace any which may have been contaminated by the unfair practice).

77. *Where a party either (i) fails to comply with a remedial order or (ii) has committed a second unfair practice in relation to the ballot (or a re-run ballot) or (iii) has committed an unfair practice involving the use of violence or the dismissal of a union official, the CAC may take other sanctions against that party. Where that party is the union, the CAC may declare that the union is not entitled to be recognised. Where that party is the employer, the CAC may declare that the union is entitled to be recognised.*[2]

MINOR DISPUTES

78. Some disputes about access may be minor by nature. For example, the employer may be aggrieved that an access meeting has over-run somewhat. Or a union might have cause to complain if it regards the meeting room provided by the employer as being too small to accommodate everyone in comfort. In such cases, both parties should avoid taking hasty action which might prejudice the implementation of other access arrangements. The union should generally avoid taking minor complaints about access to the CAC as a first course of action.

79. Instead, the parties should make every effort to resolve the dispute between themselves. They should make full use of any mechanism to resolve such disputes which they may have established in the access agreement, and consider the use of Acas's conciliation services. It would generally be a good practice if both the employer and the union nominated a person to act as their lead contact if disagreements or questions arose about the implementation of access arrangements.

80. The period of access will be limited in duration, given that the balloting period will normally be a maximum of 20 working days, and the parties should therefore ensure that disputes are swiftly resolved. The parties should endeavour to inform each other immediately if a dispute arises, and should seek to resolve any disputes as a matter of priority, preferably within one working day of their occurrence.

81. It is also a good practice to follow similar procedures in cases where there are complaints about a person's conduct whilst campaigning. For example, some complaints will be based on a misunderstanding which can be resolved quickly between the parties. And in cases where minor offence has been caused as a result of a careless or unintended remark, then the matter may be simply remedied by the issuing of an apology. Regular and early communication between the parties about the poor behaviour by individual campaigners may also ensure that senior figures on the union and employer sides can prevent repetitions of such behaviour and thereby ensure that unnecessary disputes are avoided.

82. It should be noted that a complaint to the CAC about an unfair practice is unlikely to succeed if it relates to minor aberrations in conduct because such matters are very unlikely to have influenced voting behaviours or intentions. So, for example, a campaigner's use of strong language or swearing (which, perhaps regrettably, is commonplace inside many workplaces and outside them as well) may not in itself constitute the basis for a well-founded complaint.

THE INDEPENDENT PERSON

83. The prime duties of the independent person are to ensure that:

- the names and addresses of the workers comprising the balloting constituency are accurate;
- the ballot is conducted properly and in secret; and
- the CAC is promptly informed of the ballot result.

It is not the function of the independent person to adjudicate disputes about access or unfair practices. That is the CAC's role. However, the independent person may have wide experience and knowledge of balloting arrangements in different settings. The parties might consider informing the independent person about their problems and draw on his experience to identify possible options to resolve their difficulties.

NOTES

[2] There are other sanctions which apply in the special case where a worker has applied to the CAC to derecognise a union.

CODE OF PRACTICE: INDUSTRIAL ACTION BALLOTS AND NOTICE TO EMPLOYERS (2005)

[4.228]

NOTES

This Code is issued under the power given to the Secretary of State by the Trade Union and Labour Relations (Consolidation) Act 1992, s 203 (at **[1.469]**), with the authority of Parliament. It came into effect on 1 October 2005 (see the Employment Code of Practice (Industrial Action Ballots and Notice to Employers) Order 2005, SI 2005/2420). This Code replaces the similarly named Code issued in 2000. The statutory status of the Code is as stated in s 207 of the 1992 Act (at **[1.473]**). Notes are as in the original.

See *Harvey* NII(9).

CONTENTS

PREAMBLE

[4.229]
This document revises and supersedes the Code of Practice on Industrial Action Ballots and Notice to Employers [PL962 (Rev1)], which came into effect on 18 September 2000. Pursuant to section 208(2) of the Trade Union and Labour Relations (Consolidation) Act 1992, that Code shall cease to have effect on the date on which this Code of Practice comes in force.

The legal framework for the operation of this Code is explained in Annex 1 and in its main text. While every effort has been made to ensure that explanations included in the Code are accurate, only the courts can give authoritative interpretations of the law.

The Code's provisions apply equally to men and to women, but for simplicity the masculine pronoun is used throughout. Wherever it appears in the Code the word "court" is used to mean the High Court in England and Wales and the Court of Session in Scotland, but without prejudice to the Code's relevance to any proceedings before any other court.

Passages in this Code which are printed in italic are re-statements of provisions in primary legislation.

SECTION A
INTRODUCTION

[4.230]
1. This Code provides practical guidance to trade unions and employers to promote the improvement of industrial relations and good practice in the conduct of trade union industrial action ballots.

2. A union is legally responsible for organising industrial action only if it "authorises or endorses" the action. Authorisation would take place before the industrial action starts, and endorsement after it has previously started as unofficial action.[1]

3. Apart from certain small accidental failures that are unlikely to affect the result, a failure to satisfy the statutory requirements[2] relating to the ballot or giving employers notice of industrial action will give grounds for proceedings against a union by an employer, a customer or supplier of an employer, or an individual member of the public claiming that an effect or likely effect of the industrial action would be to prevent or delay the supply of goods or services to him or to reduce the quality of goods or services so supplied. With the exception of failures to comply with the requirements to give notice to employers, these will also give grounds for action by the union's members.

4. The Code does not deal with other matters which may affect a union's liability in respect of industrial action. For example, the law will give no protection against proceedings to a union which organises secondary action, intimidatory or violent picketing, industrial action which is not "in contemplation or furtherance of a trade dispute",[3] industrial action to establish or maintain any closed shop practice or in support of a worker dismissed while taking part in unofficial industrial action. Nor does it apply to union election ballots, ballots on union political funds or ballots on union recognition or derecognition arranged for by the Central Arbitration Committee under section 70A of and Schedule A1 to the Trade Union and Labour Relations (Consolidation) Act 1992 ("the 1992 Act").[4] These are subject to separate statutory requirements.

LEGAL STATUS

5. *The Code itself imposes no legal obligations and failure to observe it does not by itself render anyone liable to proceedings. But section 207 of the 1992 Act provides that any provisions of the Code are to be admissible in evidence and are to be taken into account in proceedings before any court where it considers them relevant.*

NOTES

1 A note on trade union legal liability for the organisation of industrial action is set out in Annex 1 to this Code.

2 Set out in sections 226–232A and section 234A of the Trade Union and Labour Relations (Consolidation) Act 1992 as amended by the Trade Union Reform and Employment Rights Act 1993, the Employment Relations Act 1999 and the Employment Relations Act 2004.

3 *The term "trade dispute" is defined in section 244 of the 1992 Act.*

4 Inserted by the Employment Relations Act 1999.

SECTION B
WHETHER A BALLOT IS APPROPRIATE

OBSERVING PROCEDURAL AGREEMENTS

[4.231]

6. An industrial action ballot should not take place until any agreed procedures, whether formal or otherwise, which might lead to the resolution of a dispute without the need for industrial action have been completed and consideration has been given to resolving the dispute by other means, including seeking assistance from the Advisory, Conciliation and Arbitration Service (Acas).[5] A union should hold a ballot on industrial action only if it is contemplating the organisation of industrial action.

BALLOTING BY MORE THAN ONE UNION

7. Where more than one union decides that it wishes to ballot members working for the same employer in connection with the same dispute, the arrangements for the different ballots should be co-ordinated so that, as far as practicable, they are held at the same time and the results are announced simultaneously.

NOTES

5 Acas can provide assistance after the ballot stage as well. Parties should therefore consider using its services at other times during the course of a dispute to avoid industrial action altogether or to bring that action to an end through a negotiated resolution of the issues at dispute.

SECTION C
PREPARING FOR AN INDUSTRIAL ACTION BALLOT

ARRANGING FOR INDEPENDENT SCRUTINY OF THE BALLOT

[4.232]

8. *For a ballot where more than 50 members are given entitlement to vote (see paragraph 21 below), the union must appoint a qualified person as the scrutineer of the ballot.*[6] *For a person to be qualified for appointment as scrutineer of an industrial action ballot, he must be among those specified in an order made by the Secretary of State*[7] *and the union must not have grounds for believing that he will carry out the functions which the law requires other than competently or that his independence in relation to the union might reasonably be called into question.*

9. *The scrutineer's terms of appointment must require him to take such steps as appear appropriate to him for the purpose of enabling him to make a report to the union as soon as reasonably practicable after the date of the ballot (ie the last day on which votes may be cast, if they may be cast on more than one day), and in any event not later than four weeks after that date.*

10. *The union must ensure that the scrutineer carries out the functions required to be part of his terms of appointment, and that there is no interference with this from the union, or any of its members, officials or employees; and comply with all reasonable requests made by the scrutineer for the purpose of carrying out those functions.*

11. It may be desirable to appoint the scrutineer before steps are taken to satisfy any of the other requirements of the law to make it easier for the scrutineer to satisfy himself whether what is done conforms to the legal requirements.

12. In some circumstances, it may help ensure adequate standards for the conduct of the ballot or simplify the balloting process if a union gives the scrutineer additional tasks to carry out on the union's behalf, such as:—

- supervising the production and distribution of voting papers;
- being the person to whom the voting papers are returned by those voting in the ballot; and
- retaining custody of all returned voting papers for a set period after the ballot.

13. Although the scrutiny requirement does not apply to ballots where 50 or fewer members are entitled to vote, a union may want to consider whether the appointment of a scrutineer would still be of benefit in enabling it to demonstrate compliance with the statutory requirements more easily.

PROVIDING BALLOT NOTICE TO EMPLOYERS

14. *The union must take such steps as are reasonably necessary to ensure that any employer who it is reasonable for the union to believe will be the employer of any of its members who will be given entitlement to vote receives written notice of the ballot not later than the seventh day before the intended opening day of the ballot (ie the first day on which a voting paper is sent to any person entitled to vote). That notice must:—*

- *state that the union intends to hold the ballot;*
- *specify the date which the union reasonably believes will be the opening day of the ballot; and*
- *contain either:*
  - (a) *a list of the categories of employee to which the employees concerned belong, a list of the workplaces at which they work and figures (together with an explanation of how they were arrived at) showing the total number of employees concerned, the number of them in each of the categories listed and the number of them that work at each of the workplaces listed; or*
  - (b) *where some or all of the employees concerned are employees from whose wages the employer makes deductions representing payments to the union,* a practice commonly known as "check off" or "DOCAS", other alternatives apply. In such circumstances, the notice must contain either:
    - (i) *those same lists, figures and explanations as set out in (a); or*
    - (ii) *such information as will enable the employer to readily deduce the total number of employees concerned, the categories of employee to which they belong, the number of employees concerned in each of those categories, the workplaces at which the employees concerned work and the number of them at each of these workplaces.*

  Where only some of the employees concerned pay their union contributions by the "check off", the union's notice may include both types of information. That is, the lists, figures and explanations should be provided for those who do not pay their subscriptions through the check off whilst information relating to check off payments may suffice for those who do.

  The "employees concerned" are those whom the union reasonably believes will be entitled to vote in the ballot.

  The lists and figures or information supplied should be as accurate as is reasonably practicable in the light of the information in the union's possession at the time when it complied with subsection 226A(1)(a). Information is "in the union's possession" provided it is held for union purposes in a document (either in electronic or other form) and provided it is in the possession or under the control of an officer or employee of the union. Dependent on the precise status of the individuals concerned, information held by shop stewards or other lay representatives would probably not qualify for these purposes as being "in the union's possession".

  But a notice will not fail to satisfy the requirements simply because it does not name any employees.

15. There are many ways to categorise a group of employees. When deciding which categories it should list in the notice, the union should consider choosing a categorisation which relates to the nature of the employees' work. For example, the appropriate categorisation might be based on the occupation, grade or pay band of the employees involved. The decision might also be informed by the categorisations of the employees typically used by the employer in his dealings with the union. The availability of data to the union is also a legitimate factor in determining the union's choice.

16. When providing an explanation of how the figures in the written notice were arrived at, unions should consider describing the sources of the data used (for example, membership lists held centrally or information held at regional offices, or data collected from surveys or other sources). It is not reasonable to expect union records to be perfectly accurate and to contain detailed information on all members. Where the union's data are known to be incomplete or to contain other inaccuracies, it is a desirable practice for unions to describe in the notices the main deficiencies. In some cases, the figures will be estimates based on assumptions and the notice should therefore describe the main assumptions used when making estimates.

17. To reduce the risk of legal action, the union should allow sufficient time for delivery, use a suitable means of transmission (such as first class post, courier, fax, email or hand delivery) and consider obtaining confirmation that the employer has received the notice, by using recorded delivery or otherwise.

18. It may also reduce the risk of litigation for a union to check that an employer accepts that the information provided complies with the requirements of section 226A(2)(c) of the 1992 Act. Similarly, it would be in the interests of good industrial relations for an employer who believes the notice he has received does not contain sufficient information to comply with the statutory requirements to raise that with the union promptly before pursuing the matter in the court.

PROVIDING SAMPLE VOTING PAPER(S) TO EMPLOYERS

19. *The union must take such steps as are reasonably necessary to ensure that any employer who it is reasonable for the union to believe will be the employer of any of its members who will be given entitlement to vote receives a sample voting paper (and a sample of any variant of that voting paper) not later than the third day before the opening day of the ballot. Where more than one employer's workers are being balloted, it is sufficient to send each employer only the voting paper or papers which will be sent to his employees.*

20. If the sample voting paper is available in time, the union may wish to include it with the notice of intention to ballot. As with the ballot notice, the risk of non-compliance can be reduced by allowing enough time, using appropriate means of transmission and, possibly, by obtaining confirmation of receipt.

ESTABLISHING ENTITLEMENT TO VOTE (THE "BALLOTING CONSTITUENCY")

21. *Entitlement to vote in the ballot must be given to all the union's members who it is reasonable at the time of the ballot for the union to believe will be induced by the union (whether that inducement will be successful or not) to take part in or continue with the industrial action, and to no other members.*[8]

22. *The validity of the ballot will not however be affected if the union subsequently induces members to take part in or continue with industrial action who at the time of the ballot:—*

- *were not members; or*
- *were members but who it was not reasonable to expect would be induced to take action* (for example because they changed jobs after the ballot).

23. *It should also be noted that accidental failures to comply with the requirements on:*

- *in particular, who is given entitlement to vote,*
- *the dispatch of voting papers,*
- *giving members the opportunity to vote conveniently by post, and*
- *balloting merchant seamen employed in a ship at sea or outside Great Britain at some time during the voting period*

will be disregarded if, taken together, they are on a scale unlikely to affect the ballot's result.

BALLOTING MEMBERS AT MORE THAN ONE WORKPLACE

24. *Where the members of a union with different workplaces are to be balloted, a separate ballot will be necessary for each workplace unless one of the conditions set out below is met. Where separate ballots are held, it will be unlawful for the union to organise industrial action at any such workplace where a majority of those voting in the ballot for that workplace have not voted "Yes" in response to the relevant required question (or questions) (see paragraph 30 below). (If an employee works at or from a single set of premises, his workplace is those premises. If not, it is the premises with which his employment has the closest connection.)*

25. *In summary, the conditions for holding a single ballot for more than one workplace are:—*

- *at each of the workplaces covered by the single ballot there is at least one member of the union affected*[9] *by the dispute; or*
- *entitlement to vote in the single ballot is given, and limited, to all of a union's members who, according to the union's reasonable belief, are employed in a particular occupation or occupations by one employer or any of a number of employers with whom the union is in dispute; or*
- *entitlement to vote in the single ballot is given, and limited, to all of a union's members who are employed by a particular employer or any of a number of employers with whom the union is in dispute.*

Where a single ballot across a number of workplaces is held and the majority is in favour of industrial action, it is lawful for the union to organise industrial action at any such workplace.

It is possible for a union to hold more than one ballot on a dispute at a single workplace. If the conditions above are met, some or all of those ballots may also cover members in other workplaces.

THE BALLOTING METHOD

26. *Votes must be recorded by the individual voter marking a voting paper. Voting papers must be sent out by post and members must be enabled conveniently to return them by post at no direct expense to themselves.*[10] In practice, this means that those properly entitled to vote should be supplied with pre-paid reply envelopes in which to return the voting paper.

27. The period between sending out voting papers (ie the opening day of the ballot) and the date by which completed voting papers should be returned should be long enough for the voting papers to be distributed and returned and for the members concerned to consider their vote. The appropriate period may vary according to such factors as the geographical dispersion of the workforce, their familiarity or otherwise with the issues in the dispute, the class of post used and whether the ballot is being held at a time of year when members are more than usually likely to be away from home or the workplace, for example during the summer holidays. Generally, seven days should be the minimum period where voting papers are sent out and returned by first class post and fourteen days where second class post is used, although – very exceptionally – shorter periods may be possible for ballots with very small, concentrated constituencies who can be expected to be familiar with the terms of the dispute.

28. In order to reduce the likelihood of dispute over whether or not sufficient time has been allowed, the union may wish to consider obtaining one or more certificates of posting to confirm the date when voting papers were actually put into the post, and the number sent out.

VOTING PAPERS

29. *The voting paper must:—*

- *where applicable, state the name of the independent scrutineer;*
- *clearly specify the address to which, and the date by which, it is to be returned;*
- *be marked with a number, which is one of series of consecutive numbers used to give a different number to each voting paper;*
- *make clear whether voters are being asked if they are prepared to take part in, or to continue to take part in, industrial action which consists of a strike, or in industrial action short of a strike, which for this purpose includes overtime bans and call-out bans; and*
- *specify the person or persons (and/or class or classes of person/s) who the union intends to have authority to make the first call for industrial action to which the ballot relates, in the event of a vote in favour of industrial action.*[11]

30. *While the question (or questions) may be framed in different ways, the voter must be asked to say by answering "Yes" or "No" whether he is willing to take part in or continue with the industrial action. If the union has not decided whether the industrial action would consist of a strike or action short of a strike (including overtime bans or call-out bans), separate questions in respect of each type of action must appear on the voting paper.*

31. The relevant required question (or questions) should be simply expressed. Neither they, nor anything else which appears on the voting paper, should be presented in such a way as to encourage a voter to answer one way rather than another as a result of that presentation. It is not in general good practice for the union to include additional questions on the voting paper (for example, asking if voters agree with the union's opinion on the merits of the dispute or are prepared to "support" industrial action), but if it chooses to do so they should be clearly separate from the required question(s).

32. *The following words must appear on every voting paper:—*

> *"If you take part in a strike or other industrial action, you may be in breach of your contract of employment. However, if you are dismissed for taking part in strike or other industrial action which is called officially and is otherwise lawful, the dismissal will be unfair if it takes place fewer than twelve weeks after you started taking part in the action, and depending on the circumstances may be unfair if it takes place later."*

This statement must not be qualified or commented upon by anything else on the voting paper.

33. An example voting paper containing the information required by law and other useful information is set out in Annex 2 to this Code. Factual information as indicated would appear in the square brackets and either or both questions could be used as appropriate.

PRINTING AND DISTRIBUTION OF THE VOTING PAPERS

34. The union will wish to ensure that arrangements for producing and distributing voting papers will prevent mistakes which might invalidate the ballot. If in doubt, the independent scrutineer may be able to provide useful advice.

35. If there is no independent scrutineer, or if a union decides that it cannot follow the advice offered by the scrutineer, it should consider:—

- printing the voting papers on a security background to prevent duplication;
- whether the arrangements proposed for printing (or otherwise producing) the voting papers, and for their distribution to those entitled to vote in the ballot, offer all concerned sufficient assurance of security.

COMMUNICATION WITH MEMBERS

36. A union should give relevant information to its members entitled to vote in the ballot, including (so far as practicable):—

- the background to the ballot and the issues to which the dispute relates;
- the nature and timing of the industrial action the union proposes to organise if a majority vote "Yes";
- any considerations in respect of turnout or size of the majority vote in the ballot that will be taken into account in deciding whether to call for industrial action; and
- the possible consequences for workers if they take industrial action.

In doing so, the union should ensure that any information it gives to members in connection with the ballot is accurate and not misleading.

NOTES

6 *Where separate workplace ballots are required, the scrutiny procedures must be followed in respect of each separate ballot if the number of members given entitlement to vote aggregated across all of the ballots is more than 50.*

7 *In broad terms, the current order (SI 1993/1909) covers practising solicitors, qualified accountants and four named bodies (Election.com Limited; Electoral Reform (Ballot Services) Limited; The Involvement and Participation Association; and Popularis Limited)).*

8 *The union may choose whether or not to give a vote to any "overseas member", ie any member (other than a merchant seaman or offshore worker) who is outside Great Britain for the whole of the voting period. However, members who may be called upon to take part in or continue with the industrial action, and will be in Northern Ireland for the whole of the voting period, must be given entitlement to vote in a ballot where: (i) the ballot is a workplace ballot at their workplace in Great Britain; or (ii) they work in Northern Ireland but it is intended that they should be called upon to take part in the industrial action alongside their counterparts in Britain, and the ballot is a general ballot covering places of work in both Northern Ireland and Great Britain.*

9 Section 228A(5) of the 1992 Act defines for this purpose which members are affected by a dispute.

10 *There is a limited exception for the balloting of union members who are merchant seamen, where the union reasonably believes that they will be employed in a ship at sea (or outside Great Britain) at some time in the period during which votes may be cast and that it will be convenient for them to vote while on the ship or where the ship is. So far as reasonably practicable, the union must ensure that, in these circumstances, those members get a voting paper while on board ship (or at the place where the ship is located), and an opportunity to vote on board ship (or at that place). The recommendations in this Code should be applied to such ballots, however, save to the extent that they are irrelevant because the dispatch of voting papers is not by post.*

11 Where a person who has not been not specified on the voting paper calls industrial action before it is first called by a specified person, then – in order to be certain that the ballot will give protection against legal proceedings – the union should if possible ensure that the call by the unspecified person is effectively repudiated.

SECTION D
HOLDING AN INDUSTRIAL ACTION BALLOT

[4.233]

37. *In an industrial action ballot:—*

- *every person entitled to vote must be allowed to do so without interference from, or constraint imposed by, the union or any of its members, officials or employees;*
- *as far as reasonably practicable, every person entitled to vote must be:—*
  - *sent a voting paper by post to his home address, or another address which he has asked the union (in writing) to treat as his postal address;*
  - *given a convenient opportunity to vote by post; and*
  - *allowed to do so without incurring any direct cost to himself (see also paragraph 26); and*
- *as far as reasonably practicable, the ballot must be conducted in such a way as to ensure that those voting do so in secret.*

CHECKS ON NUMBER OF VOTING PAPERS FOR RETURN

38. In order to reduce the risk of failures to satisfy the statutory requirements and invalidating the ballot, the union should establish an appropriate checking system so that:—

- no-one properly entitled to vote is accidentally disenfranchised, for example through the use of an out of date or otherwise inaccurate membership list; and
- votes from anyone not properly entitled to vote are excluded.

The independent scrutineer may provide advice on this.

ENSURING SECRECY OF VOTING

39. Any list of those entitled to vote should be compiled, and the voting papers themselves handled, so as to preserve the anonymity of the voter so far as this is consistent with the proper conduct of the ballot.

40. Steps should be taken to ensure that a voter's anonymity is preserved when a voting paper is returned. This means, for example, that:—

- envelopes in which voting papers are to be posted should have no distinguishing marks from which the identity of the voter could be established; and
- the procedures for counting voting papers should not prejudice the statutory requirement for secret voting.

SECTION E
FOLLOWING AN INDUSTRIAL ACTION BALLOT

[4.234]

41. *The union must:—*

- *ensure that the votes given in an industrial action ballot are fairly and accurately counted;*
- *observe its obligations in connection with the notification of details of the result of an industrial action ballot to all those entitled to vote in the ballot and their employers; and*
- *provide a copy of the scrutineer's report on the ballot to anyone entitled to receive it.*

An inaccuracy in the counting of the votes is to be disregarded if it is both accidental and on a scale which could not affect the result of the ballot. Whether an accidental inaccuracy meets this test in practice will depend on the closeness of the ballot result.

COUNTING VOTES ACCURATELY AND FAIRLY

42. Where the union itself is conducting the ballot, it may wish to apply some or all of the following procedures to secure that the statutory requirements have been complied with:—

- ensuring all unused or unissued voting papers are retained only for so long as is necessary after the time allowed for voting has passed to allow the necessary information for checking the number of voting papers issued and used to be prepared, and that a record is kept of such voting papers when they are destroyed;
- rejection of completed voting papers received after the official close of voting or the time set for receipt of voting papers;
- settlement well in advance of the actual ballot of the organisational arrangements for conducting the count of votes cast, and making available equipment or facilities needed in the conduct of the count to those concerned;
- storage of all voting papers received at the counting location under secure conditions from when they arrive until they are counted;
- setting clear criteria to enable those counting the votes to decide which voting papers are to be rejected as "spoiled", and designating someone who is neither directly affected by the dispute to which the ballot relates nor a union official who regularly represents any of those entitled to vote in the ballot to adjudicate on any borderline cases;
- locking and securing the counting room during the period during which votes are to be counted whenever counting staff are not actually at work; and
- storage of voting papers, once counted, under secure conditions (ie so that they cannot be tampered with in any way and are available for checking if necessary) for at least 6 months after the ballot.

The union may wish to consider putting the counting exercise as a whole into the hands of the independent scrutineer.

ANNOUNCING DETAILS OF THE RESULT OF A BALLOT

43. *A union must, as soon as reasonably practicable after holding an industrial action ballot, take steps to inform all those entitled to vote,*[12] *and their employer(s), of the number of:—*

- *votes cast in the ballot;*
- *individuals answering "Yes" to the required question (or questions);*
- *individuals answering "No" to the required question (or questions); and*
- *spoiled voting papers.*

Where separate workplace ballots are required (see paragraphs 24 and 25 above), these details must be notified separately for each such workplace to those entitled to vote there.

44. To help ensure that its result can be notified as required, the union may wish to consider, for example:—

- designating a "Returning Officer" for the centralised count of votes cast in the ballot (or separate "Returning Officers" for counts conducted at different locations) to whom the results will be notified in the form required prior to their announcement;

- organising the counting of votes in such a way that the information required to satisfy the relevant statutory requirements can be easily obtained after the counting process is over;
- using its own journals, local communications news-sheets, company or union branch notice boards to publicise the details of the ballot result to its members; and
- checking with relevant employers that the ballot result details notified to them have arrived.

45. *Before giving the seven-day notice to employers of intended industrial action, the union must have taken the required steps to notify the relevant employer(s) of the ballot result details. Where the employees of more than one employer have been balloted, a failure to provide the required ballot result details to a particular employer or employers will mean that if the union organises industrial action by the workers of that employer or those employers it will not have the support of a ballot. In cases where it is lawful to hold a single ballot across the workplaces of several or many employers (see paragraph 25 above), the "ballot result" refers to the result aggregated across all the employers and workplaces involved.*

46. *If the inducement of industrial action to which the ballot relates is to be capable of being protected by the law, some part of the action must be induced and start to take place within four weeks from the date of the ballot (ie the last day on which votes may be cast in the ballot) or such longer period not exceeding eight weeks as the union and employer may agree.*[13] (To reduce the risk of misunderstanding, both parties may find it helpful for such agreements to be in writing.) *If a ballot results in a "Yes" vote for both a strike and action short of a strike and action short of a strike is induced and starts to take place within the relevant period, the ballot would also continue to protect strike action subsequently, and vice versa.*

OBTAINING, AND PROVIDING COPIES OF, THE SCRUTINEER'S REPORT

47. *Where more than 50 members are given entitlement to vote, a union must appoint an independent scrutineer, whose terms of appointment must include the production of a report on the conduct of the ballot. This report must be produced as soon as reasonably practicable after the date of the ballot, and in any event not later than four weeks after that date.*

48. *The union must provide a copy of the scrutineer's report to any union member who was entitled to vote in the ballot, or any employer of such a member, who requests one within six months of the date of the ballot. The copy must be supplied as soon as reasonably practicable, and free of charge (or on payment of a reasonable fee specified by the union).*

49. In order to reduce the risk of challenge to a ballot's compliance with the statutory requirements, a union may wish to delay any call for industrial action, following a ballot, until it has obtained the scrutineer's report on the ballot.

IF THE UNION DECIDES TO AUTHORISE OR ENDORSE INDUSTRIAL ACTION

50. *If the union decides to authorise or endorse industrial action following a ballot, it must take such steps as are reasonably necessary to ensure that any employer who it is reasonable for the union to believe employs workers who will be, or have been, called upon to take part in the action receives no less than seven days before the day specified in the notice as the date on which workers are intended to begin to take part in continuous action or as the first date on which they are intended to take part in discontinuous action a written notice from the union which:—*

- *is given by any officer, official or committee of the union for whose act of inducing industrial action the union is responsible in law* (an indication of whom this might cover is given in *Annex 1* to this Code);
- *specifies: (i) whether the union intends the action to be "continuous" or "discontinuous";*[14] and *(ii) the date on which any of the affected employees are intended to begin to take part in the action (where it is continuous action), or all the dates on which any of them are intended to take part (where it is discontinuous action);*
- *states that it is a notice given for the purposes of section 234A of the 1992 Act; and*
- *contains either:—*
    - (a) *a list of the categories of employee to which the affected employees belong, a list of the workplaces at which they work and figures (together with an explanation of how they were arrived at) showing the total number of affected employees, the number of them in each of the categories listed and the number of them that work at each of the workplaces listed; or*
    - (b) *where some or all of the employees are employees from whose wages the employer makes deductions representing payments to the union,* a practice commonly known as "check off" or "DOCAS", *other alternatives apply. In such circumstances the notice must contain either:—*
        - (i) *those same lists, figures and explanations as set out in (a); or*
        - (ii) *such information as will enable the employer to readily deduce the total number of affected employees, the categories of employee to which they belong, the number of employees concerned in each of those categories, the workplaces at which the affected employees work and the number of them at each of these workplaces.*

Where only some of the affected employees pay their union contributions by the "check off", the union's notice may include both types of information. That is, the lists, figures and explanations should be provided for those who do not pay their subscriptions through the check off whilst information relating to check off payments may suffice for those who do.

The "affected employees " are those whom the union reasonably believes will be induced by the union or have been so induced to take part in or continue to take part in the industrial action.

The lists and figures or information supplied should be as accurate as is reasonably practicable in the light of the information in the union's possession at the time when it complied with subsection 234A(1). Information is "in the union's possession" if it is held for union purposes in a document (either in electronic or other form) and it is in the possession or under the control of an officer or employee of the union. Dependent on the precise status of the individuals concerned, information held by shop stewards or other lay representatives would probably not qualify for these purposes as being "in the union's possession".

But a notice will not fail to satisfy the requirements simply because it does not name any employees.

Changes in the union's intentions, for example as to the dates on which action is to be taken, require further notices to be given accordingly.

51. With the exception of the requirements relating to continuous and discontinuous action and to the need to give further notices in the event of changes in the union's intentions, the statutory requirements applying to notice of industrial action are for the most part the same as those applying to notice of industrial action ballots and the guidance in paragraphs 15–18 will be of relevance, taking account of the different circumstances.

52. *Where continuous industrial action is suspended,* for example for further negotiations between the employer and union, *the union must normally give the employer a further notice as in paragraphs 50 and 51 above before resuming the action. There is an exception to this requirement to give further notice, however, where the union agrees with the employer that the industrial action will cease to be authorised or endorsed with effect from a date specified in the agreement but may be authorised or endorsed again on or after another date specified in the agreement and the union:—*

- *ceases to authorise or endorse the action with effect from the specified date; and*
- *subsequently re-authorises or re-endorses the action from a date on or after the originally specified date or such later date as may be agreed with the employer.*

For this exception to apply, the resumed industrial action must be of the same kind as covered in the original notice. That will not be so if, for example, the later action is taken by different or additional descriptions of workers. In order to avoid misunderstanding, both parties may find it helpful for such agreements to be in writing.

SEEKING UNION MEMBERS' VIEWS AFTER A UNION HAS AUTHORISED OR ENDORSED INDUSTRIAL ACTION

53. There is no statutory obligation on a union to ballot, or otherwise consult, its members before it decides to call off industrial action. However, if a union decides to seek its members' views about continuing with industrial action, it may wish to apply the same standards to the process of seeking their views as are set out in this Code.

NOTES

[12] *If overseas members of a trade union have been given entitlement to vote in an industrial action ballot the detailed information about its result need not be sent to them, but the information supplied to non-overseas members in accordance with the statutory requirements must distinguish between votes cast, individuals voting, and spoiled ballot papers to show which details relate to overseas, and which to non-overseas, members. (For these purposes members in Northern Ireland given entitlement to vote do not count as "overseas" members.)*

[13] *A union may be allowed to make its first call for industrial action more than four weeks after the date of the ballot if either (a) the employer and union agree on an extension, for example to enable talks which are making progress to continue, of up to eight weeks after the date of the ballot or (b) an injunction granted by a court or an undertaking given by the union to the court prohibits the union from calling for industrial action during some part, or the whole, of the four weeks following the date of the ballot, and the injunction subsequently lapses or is set aside or the union is released from its undertaking. In the latter case, a union may forthwith apply to the court for an order which, if granted, would provide that the period during which the prohibition had effect would not count towards the four week period for which ballots are normally effective. However, if the court believes that the result of a ballot no longer represents the views of union members, or that something has happened or is likely to happen which would result in union members voting against taking, or continuing with, action if there were a fresh ballot, it may not make such an order. In any case, a ballot can never be effective if a union's first call for industrial action is made more than twelve weeks after the date of the ballot.*

[14] *For these purposes, industrial action is "discontinuous" if it is to involve action other than on all the days when action might be taken by those concerned.* An indefinite strike would, therefore, be "continuous"; an overtime ban might be "continuous" or "discontinuous", depending on whether the ban applied to overtime working on all the days on which overtime would otherwise be worked or to overtime working on only some of those days.

ANNEX 1
TRADE UNION LIABILITY

[4.235]

1. *Section 20 of the Trade Union and Labour Relations (Consolidation) Act 1992 lays down when a union is to be held responsible for the act of inducing, or threatening, a breach or interference with a contract in circumstances where there is no immunity. The union will be held liable for any such act which is done, authorised or endorsed by:—*

- *its Executive Committee, General Secretary, President;*
- *any person given power under the union's rules to do, authorise or endorse acts of the kind in question; or*
- *any committee or official of the union (whether employed by it or not).*

A union will be held responsible for such an act by such a body or person regardless of any term or condition to the contrary in its own rules, or in any other contractual provision or rule of law.

2. *For these purposes:—*

- *a "committee of the union" is any group of persons constituted in accordance with the rules of the union;*
- *an "official of the union" is any person who is an officer of the union or of a branch or section of the union or any person who is elected or appointed in accordance with the union's own rules to be a representative of its members, including any person so elected or appointed who is an employee of the same employer as the members, or one or more of the members, he is elected to represent* (eg a shop steward)*; and*
- *an act will be treated to have been done (or authorised or endorsed) by an official if it was so done (or authorised or endorsed) by a group of persons, or any member of a group, to which an official belonged at the relevant time if the group's purposes included organising or co-ordinating industrial action.*

3. *A union will not be held liable for such an act of any of its committees or officials, however, if its Executive Committee, President or General Secretary repudiates the act as soon as reasonably practicable after it has come to the attention of any of them, and the union takes the steps which the law requires to make that repudiation effective. But the union will not be considered to have "effectively repudiated" an act if the Executive Committee, President or General Secretary subsequently behave in a manner which is inconsistent with the repudiation.*

4. The fact that a union is responsible for organising industrial action to which immunity does not apply does not prevent legal action also being taken against the individual organisers of that action.

"IMMUNITY"

5. A trade union which organises (ie authorises or endorses) industrial action without satisfying the requirements of section 226 (for balloting on industrial action), or 234A (for notice to employers of official industrial action), of the 1992 Act will have no "immunity". Without immunity the trade union will be at risk of legal action by (i) an employer (and/or a customer or supplier of such an employer) who suffers (or may suffer) damage as a consequence of the trade union's unlawful inducement to his workers to break or interfere with the performance of contracts; and/or (ii) any individual who is (or is likely to be) deprived of goods or services because of the industrial action. Such legal proceedings might result in a court order requiring the trade union not to proceed with, and/or desist from, the unlawful inducement of its members to take part or continue with the action, and that no member does anything after the order is made as a result of unlawful inducement prior to the making of the order.

6. Under section 62 of the 1992 Act, a member of a trade union who claims that members of the union, including himself, are likely to be or have been induced by the union to take industrial action which does not have the support of a ballot may apply to the court for an order, which may require the trade union to take steps to ensure that there is no, or no further, unlawful inducement to members to take part or continue to take part in the action, and that no member does anything after the order is made as a result of unlawful inducement prior to the making of the order.

CONTEMPT AND OTHER PROCEEDINGS

7. If a court order issued following legal proceedings as described in paragraphs 5 and 6 above is not obeyed, anyone who sought it can go back to court and ask that those concerned be declared in contempt of court. A union found in contempt of court may face heavy fines, or other penalties which the court may consider appropriate.

8. In addition, any member of the union may have grounds for legal action against the union's trustees if they have caused or permitted the unlawful application of union funds or property.

ANNEX 2
EXAMPLE OF VOTING PAPER FOR BALLOT ON TAKING INDUSTRIAL ACTION

[4.236]

[VOTING PAPER NUMBER]

[NAME OF THE TRADE UNION]

ARE YOU PREPARED TO TAKE PART IN INDUSTRIAL ACTION CONSISTING OF A STRIKE?[15]

YES . . . . NO . . . .

ARE YOU PREPARED TO TAKE PART IN INDUSTRIAL ACTION SHORT OF A STRIKE (which for this purpose is defined to include overtime and call-out bans)?[15]

YES . . . . NO . . . .

Your union intends the following to have authority to make the call for industrial action to which this ballot relates: *[DETAILS OF RELEVANT PERSON, PERSONS, AND/OR CLASS OR CLASSES OF PERSONS]*

If your vote is to count, this voting paper must be returned to *[FULL ADDRESS OF LOCATION TO WHICH THE VOTING PAPER IS TO BE RETURNED]* by *[FULL DATE AND TIME AS APPROPRIATE]*. Please use the enclosed pre-paid envelope provided for this purpose.

The independent scrutineer for this ballot is *[DETAILS OF RELEVANT PERSON]*.

The law requires your union to ensure that your vote is accurately and fairly counted and that you are able to vote without interference from the union or any of its members, officials or employees and, so far as is reasonably practicable, in secret.

If you take part in a strike or other industrial action, you may be in breach of your contract of employment. However, if you are dismissed for taking part in a strike or other industrial action which is called officially and is otherwise lawful, the dismissal will be unfair if it takes place fewer than twelve weeks after you started taking part in the action, and depending on the circumstances may be unfair if it takes place later.

NOTES

15 Either question or both should be included as appropriate.

ANNEX 3
INFORMATION TO BE GIVEN TO EMPLOYERS

[4.237]

The following paragraphs of the Code deal with requirements to provide information to employers:—

	Paragraphs
Ballot notice	14–18
Sample voting papers	19–20
Results of the ballot	43–45
Scrutineer's report on the conduct of the ballot	48
Notice of intention to authorise or endorse industrial action or resume suspended industrial action	50–51

GUIDANCE ON MATTERS TO BE TAKEN INTO ACCOUNT IN DETERMINING QUESTIONS RELATING TO THE DEFINITION OF DISABILITY (2011)

[4.238]

NOTES

This Guidance was issued by the Secretary of State under the Equality Act 2010, s 6(5) and was laid before Parliament on 10 February 2011. It was brought into effect on 1 May 2011 by the Equality Act 2010 (Guidance on the Definition of Disability) Appointed Day Order 2011, SI 2011/1159, art 2 at **[2.1609]**. Art 3 of the 2011 Order (transitional provisions) provides that the 2006 Guidance which it replaces (omitted from this edition) continues to have effect in relation to any proceedings arising from a complaint presented to an adjudicating body, whenever presented, alleging that a person has, before 1 May 2011, committed an act which is unlawful discrimination or harassment.

Notes are as in the original.

See *Harvey* L.

CONTENTS

STATUS AND PURPOSE OF THE GUIDANCE

[4.239]

This guidance is issued by the Secretary of State under section 6(5) of the Equality Act 2010. In this document, any reference to 'the Act' means the Equality Act 2010.

This guidance concerns the definition of disability in the Act. Section 6(5) of the Act enables a Minister of the Crown to issue guidance about matters to be taken into account in determining whether a person is a disabled person. The guidance gives illustrative examples.

This guidance does not impose any legal obligations in itself, nor is it an authoritative statement of the law. However, Schedule 1, Paragraph 12 to the Act requires that an adjudicating body[1] which is determining for any purpose of the Act whether a person is a disabled person, must take into account any aspect of this guidance which appears to it to be relevant.

This guidance applies to England, Wales and Scotland. Similar, but separate, guidance applies to Northern Ireland.

PART 1: INTRODUCTION

THE EQUALITY ACT 2010

[4.240]

1. The Equality Act 2010 prohibits discrimination against people with the protected characteristics that are specified in section 4 of the Act. Disability is one of the specified protected characteristics. Protection from discrimination for disabled people applies to disabled people in a range of circumstances, covering the provision of goods, facilities and services, the exercise of public functions, premises, work, education, and associations. Only those disabled people who are defined as disabled in accordance with section 6 of the Act, and the associated Schedules and regulations made under that section, will be entitled to the protection that the Act provides to disabled people. However, the Act also provides protection for non-disabled people who are subjected to direct discrimination or harassment because of their association with a disabled person or because they are wrongly perceived to be disabled.

USING THE GUIDANCE

2. This guidance is primarily designed for adjudicating bodies which determine cases brought under the Act. The definition of disability for the purposes of the Act is a legal definition and it is only adjudicating bodies which can determine whether a person meets that definition. However, the guidance is also likely to be of value to a range of people and organisations as an explanation of how the definition operates.

3. In the vast majority of cases there is unlikely to be any doubt whether or not a person has or has had a disability, but this guidance should prove helpful in cases where the matter is not entirely clear.

4. The Act generally defines a disabled person as a person with a disability. A person has a disability for the purposes of the Act if he or she has a physical or mental impairment and the impairment has a substantial and long-term adverse effect on his or her ability to carry out normal day-to-day activities. Therefore, the general definition of disability has a number of elements. The Guidance covers each of these elements in turn. Each section contains an explanation of the relevant provisions of the Act which supplement the basic definition. Guidance and illustrative examples are provided where relevant. **Those using this Guidance for the first time should read it all, as each part of the Guidance builds upon the part(s) preceding it.** It is important not to consider any individual element in isolation.

5. Throughout the guidance, descriptions of statutory provisions in the legislation are immediately preceded by bold text and followed by a reference to the relevant provision of the Act or to regulations made under the Act. References to sections of the Act are marked **'S'**; references to schedules are marked **'Sch'**; and references to paragraphs in schedules are marked **'Para'**.

OTHER REFERENCES TO 'DISABILITY'

6. The definition of disability set out in the Act and described in this guidance is the only definition relevant to determining whether someone is a disabled person for the purposes of the Act. References to 'disability' or to mental or physical impairments in the context of other legislation are not necessarily relevant but may assist adjudicating bodies when determining whether someone is a disabled person in accordance with the definition in this Act.

7. There is a range of services, concessions, schemes and financial benefits for which disabled people may qualify. These include, for example: local authority services for disabled people; the Blue Badge parking scheme; tax concessions for people who are blind; and disability-related social security benefits. However, each of these has its own individual eligibility criteria and qualification for any one of them does not automatically confer entitlement to protection under the Act, nor does entitlement to the protection of the Act confer eligibility for benefits, or concessions. Similarly, a child who has been identified as having special educational needs is not necessarily disabled for the purposes of the Act. However, having eligibility for such benefits may assist a person to demonstrate that they meet the definition in the Act.

8. In order to be protected by the Act, a person must have an impairment that meets the Act's definition of disability, or be able to establish that any less favourable treatment or harassment is because of another person's disability or because of a perceived disability.

PART 2: GUIDANCE ON MATTERS TO BE TAKEN INTO ACCOUNT IN DETERMINING QUESTIONS RELATING TO THE DEFINITION OF DISABILITY

SECTION A: THE DEFINITION

Main elements of the definition of disability

[4.241]
A1. The Act defines a disabled person as a person with a disability. A person has a disability for the purposes of the Act if he or she has a physical or mental impairment and the impairment has a substantial and long-term adverse effect on his or her ability to carry out normal day-to-day activities (**S 6(1)**).

A2. This means that, in general:

- the person must have an impairment that is either physical or mental (**see paragraphs A3 to A8**);
- the impairment must have adverse effects which are substantial (**see Section B**);
- the substantial adverse effects must be long-term (**see Section C**); and
- the long-term substantial adverse effects must be effects on normal day-to-day activities (**see Section D**).

This definition is subject to the provisions in **Schedule 1 (Sch 1)**.

All of the factors above must be considered when determining whether a person is disabled.

Meaning of 'impairment'

A3. The definition requires that the effects which a person may experience must arise from a physical or mental impairment. The term mental or physical impairment should be given its ordinary meaning. It is not necessary for the cause of the impairment to be established, nor does the impairment have to be the result of an illness. In many cases, there will be no dispute whether a person has an impairment. Any disagreement is more likely to be about whether the effects of the impairment are sufficient to fall within the definition and in particular whether they are long-term. Even so, it may sometimes be necessary to decide whether a person has an impairment so as to be able to deal with the issues about its effects.

A4. Whether a person is disabled for the purposes of the Act is generally determined by reference to the **effect** that an impairment has on that person's ability to carry out normal day-to-day activities. An exception to this is a person with severe disfigurement (**see paragraph B24**). It is not possible to provide an exhaustive list of conditions that qualify as impairments for the purposes of the Act. Any attempt to do so would inevitably become out of date as medical knowledge advanced.

A5. A disability can arise from a wide range of impairments which can be:

- sensory impairments, such as those affecting sight or hearing;
- impairments with fluctuating or recurring effects such as rheumatoid arthritis, myalgic encephalitis (ME), chronic fatigue syndrome (CFS), fibromyalgia, depression and epilepsy;
- progressive, such as motor neurone disease, muscular dystrophy, and forms of dementia;
- auto-immune conditions such as systemic lupus erythematosis (SLE);
- organ specific, including respiratory conditions, such as asthma, and cardiovascular diseases, including thrombosis, stroke and heart disease;
- developmental, such as autistic spectrum disorders (ASD), dyslexia and dyspraxia;
- learning disabilities;
- mental health conditions with symptoms such as anxiety, low mood, panic attacks, phobias, or unshared perceptions; eating disorders; bipolar affective disorders; obsessive compulsive disorders; personality disorders; post traumatic stress disorder, and some self-harming behaviour;
- mental illnesses, such as depression and schizophrenia;
- produced by injury to the body, including to the brain.

A6. It may not always be possible, nor is it necessary, to categorise a condition as either a physical or a mental impairment. The underlying cause of the impairment may be hard to establish. There may be adverse effects which are both physical and mental in nature. Furthermore, effects of a mainly physical nature may stem from an underlying mental impairment, and vice versa.

A7. It is not necessary to consider how an impairment is caused, even if the cause is a consequence of a condition which is excluded. For example, liver disease as a result of alcohol dependency would count as an impairment, although an addiction to alcohol itself is expressly excluded from the scope of the definition of disability in the Act. What it is important to consider is the effect of an impairment, not its cause — provided that it is not an excluded condition. (**See also paragraph A12 (exclusions from the definition).**)

A woman is obese. Her obesity in itself is not an impairment, but it causes breathing and mobility difficulties which substantially adversely affect her ability to walk.

A man has a borderline moderate learning disability which has an adverse impact on his short-term memory and his levels of literacy and numeracy. For example, he cannot write any original material, as opposed to slowly copying existing text, and he cannot write his address from memory.

It is the effects of these impairments that need to be considered, rather than the underlying conditions themselves.

A8. It is important to remember that not all impairments are readily identifiable. While some impairments, particularly visible ones, are easy to identify, there are many which are not so immediately obvious, for example some mental health conditions and learning disabilities.

Persons with HIV infection, cancer and multiple sclerosis

A9. The Act states that a person who has cancer, HIV infection or multiple sclerosis (MS) is a disabled person. This means that the person is protected by the Act effectively from the point of diagnosis. (**Sch 1, Para 6**). (**See also paragraphs B18 to 23 (progressive conditions).**)

Persons deemed to be disabled

A10. The Act provides for certain people to be deemed to meet the definition of disability without having to show that they have an impairment that has (or is likely to have) a substantial and long-term adverse effect on the ability to carry out normal day-to-day activities. Regulations provide for a person who is certified as blind, severely sight impaired, sight impaired or partially sighted by a consultant ophthalmologist to be deemed to have a disability[2]. (**Sch 1, Para 7**)

A11. Anyone who has an impairment which is not covered by paragraphs A9 and A10 will need to meet the requirements of the definition as set out in paragraph A1 in order to demonstrate that he or she has a disability under the Act. (**But see paragraphs A16 to A17 for details of some people who are treated as having had a past disability.**)

Exclusions from the definition

A12. Certain conditions are not to be regarded as impairments for the purposes of the Act[3]. These are:

- addiction to, or dependency on, alcohol, nicotine, or any other substance (other than in consequence of the substance being medically prescribed);
- the condition known as seasonal allergic rhinitis (e.g. hayfever), except where it aggravates the effect of another condition;
- tendency to set fires;
- tendency to steal;
- tendency to physical or sexual abuse of other persons;
- exhibitionism;
- voyeurism.

A13. The exclusions apply where the tendency to set fires, tendency to steal, tendency to physical or sexual abuse of other persons, exhibitionism, or voyeurism constitute an impairment in themselves. The exclusions also apply where these tendencies arise as a consequence of, or a manifestation of, an impairment that constitutes a disability for the purposes of the Act. It is important to determine the basis for the alleged discrimination. If the alleged discrimination was a result of an excluded condition, the exclusion will apply. However, if the alleged discrimination was specifically related to the actual disability which gave rise to the excluded condition, the exclusion **will not** apply. Whether the exclusion applies will depend on all the facts of the individual case.

A young man has Attention Deficit Hyperactivity Disorder (ADHD) which manifests itself in a number of ways, including exhibitionism and an inability to concentrate. The disorder, as an impairment which has a substantial and long-term adverse effect on the young person's ability to carry out normal day-to-day activities, would be a disability for the purposes of the Act.

The young man is not entitled to the protection of the Act in relation to any discrimination he experiences as a consequence of his exhibitionism, because that is an excluded condition under the Act.

However, he would be protected in relation to any discrimination that he experiences in relation to the non-excluded effects of his condition, such as inability to concentrate. For example, he would be entitled to any reasonable adjustments that are required as a consequence of those effects.

A14. A person with an excluded condition may nevertheless be protected as a disabled person if he or she has an accompanying impairment which meets the requirements of the definition. For example, a person who is addicted to a substance such as alcohol may also have depression, or a physical impairment such as liver damage, arising from the alcohol addiction. While this person would not meet the definition simply on the basis of having an addiction, he or she may still meet the definition as a result of the effects of the depression or the liver damage.

A15. Disfigurements which consist of a tattoo (which has not been removed), non-medical body piercing, or something attached through such piercing, are to be treated as not having a substantial adverse effect on the person's ability to carry out normal day-to-day activities[4]. **(See also paragraphs B24 to B26.)**

People who have had a disability in the past

A16. The Act says that, except for the provisions in Part 12 (Transport[5]) and section 190 (improvements to let dwelling houses), the provisions of the Act also apply in relation to a person who previously has had a disability as defined in paragraphs **A1 and A2 (S 6(4) and Sch 1, Para 9).** This means that someone who is no longer disabled, but who met the requirements of the definition in the past, will still be covered by the Act. Also protected would be someone who continues to experience debilitating effects as a result of treatment for a past disability.

Four years ago, a woman experienced a mental illness that had a substantial and long-term adverse effect on her ability to carry out normal day-to-day activities, so it met the Act's definition of disability. She has experienced no recurrence of the condition, but if she is discriminated against because of her past mental illness she is still entitled to the protection afforded by the Act, as a person with a past disability.

A17. A particular instance of someone who is treated under the Act as having had a disability in the past is someone whose name was on the register of disabled persons under provisions in the Disabled Persons (Employment) Act 1944[6] on both 12 January 1995 and 2 December 1996. The Disability Discrimination Act 1995 provided for such people to be treated as having had a disability in the past, and those provisions have been saved so that they still apply for the purposes of the Equality Act 2010.

SECTION B: SUBSTANTIAL

This section should not be read in isolation but must be considered together with sections A, C and D. Whether a person satisfies the definition of a disabled person for the purposes of the Act will depend upon the full circumstances of the case. That is, whether the adverse effect of the person's impairment on the carrying out of normal day-to-day activities is substantial and long term.

Meaning of 'substantial adverse effect'

[4.242]
B1. The requirement that an adverse effect on normal day-to-day activities should be a substantial one reflects the general understanding of disability as a limitation going beyond the normal differences in ability which may exist among people. A substantial effect is one that is more than a minor or trivial effect. This is stated in the **Act at S 212(1)**. This section looks in more detail at what 'substantial' means. **It should be read in conjunction with Section D which considers what is meant by 'normal day-to-day activities'.**

The time taken to carry out an activity

B2. The time taken by a person with an impairment to carry out a normal day-to-day activity should be considered when assessing whether the effect of that impairment is substantial. It should be compared with the time it might take a person who did not have the impairment to complete an activity.

A ten-year-old child has cerebral palsy. The effects include muscle stiffness, poor balance and unco-ordinated movements. The child is still able to do most things for himself, but he gets tired very easily and it is harder for him to accomplish tasks like eating and drinking, washing, and getting dressed. He has the ability to carry out everyday activities such as these, but everything takes much longer compared to a child of a similar age who does not have cerebral palsy. This amounts to a substantial adverse effect.

The way in which an activity is carried out

B3. Another factor to be considered when assessing whether the effect of an impairment is substantial is the way in which a person with that impairment carries out a normal day-to-day activity. The comparison should be with the way that the person might be expected to carry out the activity compared with someone who does not have the impairment.

A person who has obsessive compulsive disorder (OCD) constantly checks and rechecks that electrical appliances are switched off and that the doors are locked when leaving home. A person without the disorder would not normally carry out these frequent checks. The need to constantly check and recheck has a substantial adverse effect.

Cumulative effects of an impairment

B4. An impairment might not have a substantial adverse effect on a person's ability to undertake a particular day-to-day activity in isolation. However, it is important to consider whether its effects on more than one activity, when taken together, could result in an overall substantial adverse effect.

B5. For example, a person whose impairment causes breathing difficulties may, as a result, experience minor effects on the ability to carry out a number of activities such as getting washed and dressed, going for a walk or travelling on public transport. But taken together, the cumulative result would amount to a substantial adverse effect on his or her ability to carry out these normal day-to-day activities.

A man with depression experiences a range of symptoms that include a loss of energy and motivation that makes even the simplest of tasks or decisions seem quite difficult. He finds it difficult to get up in the morning, get washed and dressed, and prepare breakfast. He is forgetful and cannot plan ahead. As a result he has often run out of food before he thinks of going shopping again. Household tasks are frequently left undone, or take much longer to complete than normal. Together, the effects amount to the impairment having a substantial adverse effect on carrying out normal day-to-day activities.

B6. A person may have more than one impairment, any one of which alone would not have a substantial effect. In such a case, account should be taken of whether the impairments together have a substantial effect overall on the person's ability to carry out normal day-to-day activities. For example, a minor impairment which affects physical co-ordination and an irreversible but minor injury to a leg which affects mobility, when taken together, might have a substantial effect on the person's ability to carry out certain normal day-to-day activities. The cumulative effect of more than one impairment should also be taken into account when determining whether the effect is long-term, **see Section C**.

A person has mild learning disability. This means that his assimilation of information is slightly slower than that of somebody without the impairment. He also has a mild speech impairment that slightly affects his ability to form certain words. Neither impairment on its own has a substantial adverse effect, but the effects of the impairments taken together have a substantial adverse effect on his ability to converse.

Effects of behaviour

B7. Account should be taken of how far a person can **reasonably** be expected to modify his or her behaviour, for example by use of a coping or avoidance strategy, to prevent or reduce the effects of an impairment on normal day-to-day activities. In some instances, a coping or avoidance strategy might alter the effects of the impairment to the extent that they are no longer substantial and the person would no longer meet the definition of disability. In other instances, even with the coping or avoidance strategy, there is still an adverse effect on the carrying out of normal day-to-day activities.

For example, a person who needs to avoid certain substances because of allergies may find the day-to-day activity of eating substantially affected. Account should be taken of the degree to which a person can reasonably be expected to behave in such a way that the impairment ceases to have a substantial adverse effect on his or her ability to carry out normal day-to-day activities. (**See also paragraph B12.**)

When considering modification of behaviour, it would be reasonable to expect a person who has chronic back pain to avoid extreme activities such as skiing. It would not be reasonable to expect the person to give up, or modify, more normal activities that might exacerbate the symptoms; such as shopping, or using public transport.

B8. Similarly, it would be reasonable to expect a person with a phobia to avoid extreme activities or situations that would aggravate their condition. It would not be reasonable to expect him or her to give up, or modify, normal activities that might exacerbate the symptoms.

A person with acrophobia (extreme fear of heights which can induce panic attacks) might reasonably be expected to avoid the top of extremely high buildings, such as the Eiffel Tower, but not to avoid all multi-storey buildings.

B9. Account should also be taken of where a person avoids doing things which, for example, cause pain, fatigue or substantial social embarrassment, or avoids doing things because of a loss of energy and motivation. It would **not** be reasonable to conclude that a person who employed an avoidance strategy was not a disabled person. In determining a question as to whether a person meets the definition of disability **it is important to consider the things that a person cannot do, or can only do with difficulty**.

In order to manage her mental health condition, a woman who experiences panic attacks finds that she can manage daily tasks, such as going to work, if she can avoid the stress of travelling in the rush hour.

In determining whether she meets the definition of disability, consideration should be given to the extent to which it is reasonable to expect her to place such restrictions on her working and personal life.

B10. In some cases, people have coping or avoidance strategies which cease to work in certain circumstances (for example, where someone who has dyslexia is placed under stress). If it is possible that a person's ability to manage the effects of an impairment will break down so that effects will sometimes still occur, this possibility must be taken into account when assessing the effects of the impairment.

(See also paragraphs B12 to B17 (effects of treatment), paragraphs C9 to C11 (likelihood of recurrence) and paragraph D22 (indirect effects).)

Effects of environment

B11. Environmental conditions may exacerbate or lessen the effect of an impairment. Factors such as temperature, humidity, lighting, the time of day or night, how tired the person is, or how much stress he or she is under, may have an impact on the effects. When assessing whether adverse effects of an impairment are substantial, the extent to which such environmental factors, individually or cumulatively, are likely to have an impact on the effects should, therefore, also be considered. The fact that an impairment may have a less substantial effect in certain environments does not necessarily prevent it having an overall substantial adverse effect on day-to-day activities. (**See also paragraphs C5 to C8, meaning of 'long-term' (recurring or fluctuating effects).**)

A woman has had rheumatoid arthritis for the last three years. The effect on her ability to carry out normal day-to-day activities fluctuates according to the weather conditions. The effects are particularly bad during autumn and winter months when the weather is cold and damp. Symptoms are mild during the summer months. It is necessary to consider the overall impact of the arthritis, and the extent to which it has a substantial adverse effect on her ability to carry out day-to-day activities such as walking, undertaking household tasks, and getting washed and dressed.

Effects of treatment

B12. The Act provides that, where an impairment is subject to treatment or correction, the impairment is to be treated as having a substantial adverse effect if, but for the treatment or correction, the impairment is likely to have that effect. In this context, 'likely' should be interpreted as meaning 'could well happen'. The practical effect of this provision is that the impairment should be treated as having the effect that it would have without the measures in question (**Sch 1, Para 5(1)**). **The Act states** that the treatment or correction measures which are to be disregarded for these purposes include, in particular, medical treatment and the use of a prosthesis or other aid (**Sch 1, Para 5(2)**). In this context, medical treatments would include treatments such as counselling, the need to follow a particular diet, and therapies, in addition to treatments with drugs. (**See also paragraphs B7 and B16.**)

B13. This provision applies even if the measures result in the effects being completely under control or not at all apparent. Where treatment is continuing it may be having the effect of masking or ameliorating a disability so that it does not have a substantial adverse effect. If the final outcome of such treatment cannot be determined, or if it is known that removal of the medical treatment would result in either a relapse or a worsened condition, it would be reasonable to disregard the medical treatment in accordance with paragraph 5 of Schedule 1.

B14. For example, if a person with a hearing impairment wears a hearing aid the question as to whether his or her impairment has a substantial adverse effect is to be decided by reference to what the hearing level would be without the hearing aid. Similarly, in the case of someone with diabetes which is being controlled by medication or diet should be decided by reference to what the effects of the condition would be if he or she were not taking that medication or following the required diet.

A person with long-term depression is being treated by counselling. The effect of the treatment is to enable the person to undertake normal day-to-day activities, like shopping and going to work. If the effect of the treatment is disregarded, the person's impairment would have a substantial adverse effect on his ability to carry out normal day-to-day activities.

B15. The Act states that this provision does not apply to sight impairments to the extent that they are capable of correction by spectacles or contact lenses. (**Sch 1, Para 5(3)**). In other words, the only effects on the ability to carry out normal day-to-day activities which are to be considered are those which remain when spectacles or contact lenses are used (or would remain if they were used). This does not include the use of devices to correct sight which are not spectacles or contact lenses.

B16. Account should be taken of where the effect of the continuing medical treatment is to create a permanent improvement rather than a temporary improvement. It is necessary to consider whether, as a consequence of the treatment, the impairment would cease to have a substantial adverse effect. For example, a person who develops pneumonia may be admitted to hospital for treatment including a course of antibiotics. This cures the impairment and no substantial effects remain. (**See also paragraph C11, regarding medical or other treatment that permanently reduces or removes the effects of an impairment.**)

B17. However, if a person receives treatment which cures a condition that would otherwise meet the definition of a disability, the person would be protected by the Act as a person who had a disability in the past. (**See paragraph A16.**)

Progressive conditions

B18. Progressive conditions, which are conditions that have effects which increase in severity over time, are subject to the special provisions set out in **Sch 1, Para 8.** These provisions provide that a person with a progressive condition is to be regarded as having an impairment which has a substantial adverse effect on his or her ability to carry out normal day-to-day activities **before** it actually has that effect.

B19. A person who has a progressive condition, will be treated as having an impairment which has a **substantial** adverse effect from the moment any impairment resulting from that condition first has some adverse effect on his or her ability to carry out normal day-to-day activities, provided that in the future the adverse effect is **likely** to become substantial. Medical prognosis of the likely impact of the condition will be the normal route to establishing protection under this provision. The effect need not be continuous and need not be substantial. (**See also paragraphs C5 to C8 on recurring or fluctuating effects**). The person will still need to show that the impairment meets the long-term condition of the definition. (**Sch 1, Para 2**)

B20. Examples of progressive conditions to which the special provisions apply include systemic lupus erythematosis (SLE), various types of dementia, and motor neurone disease. This list, however, is not exhaustive.

A young boy aged 8 has been experiencing muscle cramps and some weakness. The effects are quite minor at present, but he has been diagnosed as having muscular dystrophy. Eventually it is expected that the resulting muscle weakness will cause substantial adverse effects on his ability to walk, run and climb stairs. Although there is no substantial adverse effect at present, muscular dystrophy is a progressive condition, and this child will still be entitled to the protection of the Act under the special provisions in Sch 1, Para 8 of the Act if it can be shown that the effects are likely to become substantial.

A woman has been diagnosed with systemic lupus erythematosis (SLE) following complaints to her GP that she is experiencing mild aches and pains in her joints. She has also been feeling generally unwell, with some flu-like symptoms. The initial symptoms do not have a substantial adverse effect on her ability to carry out normal day-to-day activities. However, SLE is a progressive condition, with fluctuating effects. She has been advised that the condition may come and go over many years, and in the future the effects may become substantial, including severe joint pain, inflammation, stiffness, and skin rashes. Providing it can be shown that the effects are likely to become substantial, she will be covered by the special provisions relating to progressive conditions. She will also need to meet the 'long-term' condition of the definition in order to be protected by the Act.

B21. The Act provides for a person with one of the progressive conditions of cancer, HIV and multiple sclerosis to be a disabled person from the point at which they have that condition, so effectively from diagnosis. (**See paragraph A9.**)

B22. As set out in paragraph B19, in order for the special provisions covering progressive conditions to apply, there only needs to be **some** adverse effect on the person's ability to carry out normal day to day activities. It does not have to be a substantial adverse effect. If a person with a progressive condition is successfully treated (for example by surgery) so that there are no longer any adverse effects, the special provisions will not apply. However, if the treatment does not remove all adverse effects the provisions will still apply. In addition, where the treatment manages to treat the original condition but leads to other adverse effects the provisions may still apply.

A man has an operation to remove the colon because of progressing and uncontrollable ulcerative colitis. The operation results in his no longer experiencing adverse effects from the colitis. He requires a colostomy, however, which means that his bowel actions can only be controlled by a sanitary appliance.

This requirement for an appliance substantially affects his ability to undertake a normal day-to-day activity and should be taken into account as an adverse effect arising from the original impairment.

B23. Whether the effects of any treatment can qualify for the purposes of **Sch 1, Para 8**, which provides that a person with a progressive condition is to be regarded as having an impairment that has a substantial adverse effect on his or her ability to carry out normal day-to-day activities, will depend on the circumstances of the individual case.

Severe disfigurements

B24. The Act provides that where an impairment consists of a severe disfigurement, it is to be treated as having a substantial adverse effect on the person's ability to carry out normal day-to-day activities. **There is no need to demonstrate such an effect (Sch 1, Para 3).**

> **A lady has significant scarring to her face as a result of a bonfire accident. The woman uses skin camouflage to cover the scars as she is very self conscious about her appearance. She avoids large crowds and bright lights including public transport and supermarkets and she does not socialise with people outside her family in case they notice the mark and ask her questions about it.**
>
> **This amounts to a substantial adverse effect. However, the Act does not require her to show that her disfigurement has this effect because it provides for a severe disfigurement to be treated as having a substantial adverse effect on the person's ability to carry out normal day-to-day activities.**

B25. Examples of disfigurements include scars, birthmarks, limb or postural deformation (including restricted bodily development), or diseases of the skin. Assessing severity will be mainly a matter of the degree of the disfigurement which may involve taking into account factors such as the nature, size, and prominence of the disfigurement. However, it may be necessary to take account of where the disfigurement in question is (e.g. on the back as opposed to the face).

B26. Regulations provide that a disfigurement which consists of a tattoo (which has not been removed) is not to be considered as a severe disfigurement. Also excluded is a piercing of the body for decorative purposes including anything attached through the piercing[7].

SECTION C: LONG-TERM

This section should not be read in isolation but must be considered together with sections A, C and D. Whether a person satisfies the definition of a disabled person for the purposes of the Act will depend upon the full circumstances of the case. That is, whether the adverse effect of the person's impairment on the carrying out of normal day-to-day activities is substantial and long term.

Meaning of 'long-term effects'

[4.243]

C1. The Act states that, for the purpose of deciding whether a person is disabled, a long-term effect of an impairment is one:

- which has lasted at least 12 months; or
- where the total period for which it lasts, from the time of the first onset, is likely to be at least 12 months; or
- which is likely to last for the rest of the life of the person affected (**Sch 1, Para 2**)

Special provisions apply when determining whether the effects of an impairment that has fluctuating or recurring effects are long-term. (**See paragraphs C5 to C11**). Also a person who is deemed to be a disabled person does not need to satisfy the long-term requirement. (**See paragraphs A9 to A10.**)

C2. The cumulative effect of related impairments should be taken into account when determining whether the person has experienced a long-term effect for the purposes of meeting the definition of a disabled person. The substantial adverse effect of an impairment which has developed from, or is likely to develop from, another impairment should be taken into account when determining whether the effect has lasted, or is likely to last at least twelve months, or for the rest of the life of the person affected.

A man experienced an anxiety disorder. This had a substantial adverse effect on his ability to make social contacts and to visit particular places. The disorder lasted for eight months and then developed into depression, which had the effect that he was no longer able to leave his home or go to work. The depression continued for five months. As the total period over which the adverse effects lasted was in excess of 12 months, the long-term element of the definition of disability was met.

A person experiences, over a long period, adverse effects arising from two separate and unrelated conditions, for example a lung infection and a leg injury. These effects should not be aggregated.

Meaning of 'likely'

C3. The meaning of 'likely' is relevant when determining:

- whether an impairment has a long-term effect **(Sch 1, Para 2(1), see also paragraph C1)**;
- whether an impairment has a recurring effect **(Sch 1, Para 2(2), see also paragraphs C5 to C11)**;
- whether adverse effects of a progressive condition will become substantial **(Sch 1, Para 8, see also paragraphs B18 to B23)**; or
- how an impairment should be treated for the purposes of the Act when the effects of that impairment are controlled or corrected by treatment or behaviour **(Sch 1, Para 5(1), see also paragraphs B7 to B17)**.

In these contexts, 'likely', should be interpreted as meaning that it could well happen.

C4. In assessing the likelihood of an effect lasting for 12 months, account should be taken of the circumstances at the time the alleged discrimination took place. Anything which occurs after that time will not be relevant in assessing this likelihood. Account should also be taken of both the typical length of such an effect on an individual, and any relevant factors specific to this individual (for example, general state of health or age).

Recurring or fluctuating effects

C5. The Act states that, if an impairment has had a substantial adverse effect on a person's ability to carry out normal day-to-day activities but that effect ceases, the substantial effect is treated as continuing if it is likely to recur. (In deciding whether a person has had a disability in the past, the question is whether a substantial adverse effect has in fact recurred.) Conditions with effects which recur only sporadically or for short periods can still qualify as impairments for the purposes of the Act, in respect of the meaning of 'long-term' **(Sch 1, Para 2(2), see also paragraphs C3 to C4 (meaning of likely).)**

C6. For example, a person with rheumatoid arthritis may experience substantial adverse effects for a few weeks after the first occurrence and then have a period of remission. **See also example at paragraph B11.** If the substantial adverse effects are likely to recur, they are to be treated as if they were continuing. If the effects are likely to recur beyond 12 months after the first occurrence, they are to be treated as long-term. Other impairments with effects which can recur beyond 12 months, or where effects can be sporadic, include Menieres Disease and epilepsy as well as mental health conditions such as schizophrenia, bipolar affective disorder, and certain types of depression, though this is not an exhaustive list. Some impairments with recurring or fluctuating effects may be less obvious in their impact on the individual concerned than is the case with other impairments where the effects are more constant.

A young man has bipolar affective disorder, a recurring form of depression. The first episode occurred in months one and two of a 13-month period. The second episode took place in month 13. This man will satisfy the requirements of the definition in respect of the meaning of long-term, because the adverse effects have recurred beyond 12 months after the first occurrence and are therefore treated as having continued for the whole period (in this case, a period of 13 months).

In contrast, a woman has two discrete episodes of depression within a ten-month period. In month one she loses her job and has a period of depression lasting six weeks. In month nine

she experiences a bereavement and has a further episode of depression lasting eight weeks. Even though she has experienced two episodes of depression she will not be covered by the Act. This is because, as at this stage, the effects of her impairment have not yet lasted more than 12 months after the first occurrence, and there is no evidence that these episodes are part of an underlying condition of depression which is likely to recur beyond the 12-month period.

However, if there was evidence to show that the two episodes did arise from an underlying condition of depression, the effects of which are likely to recur beyond the 12-month period, she would satisfy the long term requirement.

C7. It is not necessary for the effect to be the same throughout the period which is being considered in relation to determining whether the 'long-term' element of the definition is met. A person may still satisfy the long-term element of the definition even if the effect is not the same throughout the period. It may change: for example activities which are initially very difficult may become possible to a much greater extent. The effect might even disappear temporarily. Or other effects on the ability to carry out normal day-to-day activities may develop and the initial effect may disappear altogether.

A person has Menières Disease. This results in his experiencing mild tinnitus at times, which does not adversely affect his ability to carry out normal day-to-day activities. However, it also causes temporary periods of significant hearing loss every few months. The hearing loss substantially and adversely affects his ability to conduct conversations or listen to the radio or television. Although his condition does not continually have this adverse effect, it satisfies the long-term requirement because it has substantial adverse effects that are likely to recur beyond 12 months after he developed the impairment.

C8. Regulations specifically exclude seasonal allergic rhinitis (e.g. hayfever) except where it aggravates the effects of an existing condition[8]. For example, this may occur in some cases of asthma. (**See also paragraphs A12 to A15 (exclusions).**)

Likelihood of recurrence

C9. Likelihood of recurrence should be considered taking all the circumstances of the case into account. This should include what the person could reasonably be expected to do to prevent the recurrence. For example, the person might reasonably be expected to take action which prevents the impairment from having such effects (e.g. avoiding substances to which he or she is allergic). This may be unreasonably difficult with some substances.

C10. In addition, it is possible that the way in which a person can control or cope with the effects of an impairment may not always be successful. For example, this may be because an avoidance routine is difficult to adhere to, or itself adversely affects the ability to carry out day-to-day activities, or because the person is in an unfamiliar environment. If there is an increased likelihood that the control will break down, it will be more likely that there will be a recurrence. That possibility should be taken into account when assessing the likelihood of a recurrence. (**See also paragraphs B7 to B10 (effects of behaviour), paragraph B11 (environmental effects); paragraphs B12 to B17 (effect of treatment); and paragraphs C3 to C4 (meaning of likely).**)

C11. If medical or other treatment is likely to permanently cure a condition and therefore remove the impairment, so that recurrence of its effects would then be unlikely even if there were no further treatment, this should be taken into consideration when looking at the likelihood of recurrence of those effects. However, if the treatment simply delays or prevents a recurrence, and a recurrence would be likely if the treatment stopped, as is the case with most medication, then the treatment is to be ignored and the effect is to be regarded as likely to recur.

Assessing whether a past disability was long-term

C12. The Act provides that a person who has had a disability within the definition is protected from some forms of discrimination even if he or she has since recovered or the effects have become less than substantial. In deciding whether a past condition was a disability, its effects count as long-term if they lasted 12 months or more after the first occurrence, or if a recurrence happened or continued until more than 12 months after the first occurrence (**S 6(4) and Sch 1, Para 2**). **For the forms of discrimination covered by this provision see paragraph A16.**

A person was diagnosed with a digestive condition that significantly restricted her ability to eat. She received medical treatment for the condition for over a year, but eventually required surgery which cured the condition. As the effects of the condition had lasted for

over 12 months, and they had a substantial adverse effect on her ability to carry out a normal day-to-day activity, the condition met the Act's definition of a disability.

The woman is entitled to the protection of the Act as a person who has had a past disability.

SECTION D: NORMAL DAY-TO-DAY ACTIVITIES

This section should not be read in isolation but must be considered together with sections A, B and C. Whether a person satisfies the definition of a disabled person for the purposes of the Act will depend upon the full circumstances of the case. That is, whether the adverse effect of the person's impairment on the carrying out of normal day-to-day activities is substantial and long term.

[4.244]
D1. The Act looks at a person's impairment and whether it substantially and adversely affects the person's ability to carry out normal day-to-day activities.

Meaning of 'normal day-to-day activities'

D2. The Act does not define what is to be regarded as a 'normal day-to-day activity'. It is not possible to provide an exhaustive list of day-to-day activities, although guidance on this matter is given here and illustrative examples of when it would, and would not, be reasonable to regard an impairment as having a substantial adverse effect on the ability to carry out normal day-to-day activities are shown in the Appendix.

D3. In general, day-to-day activities are things people do on a regular or daily basis, and examples include shopping, reading and writing, having a conversation or using the telephone, watching television, getting washed and dressed, preparing and eating food, carrying out household tasks, walking and travelling by various forms of transport, and taking part in social activities. Normal day-to-day activities can include general work-related activities, and study and education-related activities, such as interacting with colleagues, following instructions, using a computer, driving, carrying out interviews, preparing written documents, and keeping to a timetable or a shift pattern.

A person works in a small retail store. His duties include maintaining stock in a stock room, dealing with customers and suppliers in person and by telephone, and closing the store at the end of the day. Each of these elements of the job would be regarded as a normal day-to-day activity, which could be adversely affected by an impairment.

D4. The term 'normal day-to-day activities' is not intended to include activities which are normal only for a particular person, or a small group of people. In deciding whether an activity is a normal day-to-day activity, account should be taken of how far it is carried out by people on a daily or frequent basis. In this context, 'normal' should be given its ordinary, everyday meaning.

D5. A normal day-to-day activity is not necessarily one that is carried out by a majority of people. For example, it is possible that some activities might be carried out only, or more predominantly, by people of a particular gender, such as breast-feeding or applying make-up, and cannot therefore be said to be normal for most people. They would nevertheless be considered to be normal day-to-day activities.

D6. Also, whether an activity is a normal day-to-day activity should not be determined by whether it is more normal for it to be carried out at a particular time of day. For example, getting out of bed and getting dressed are activities that are normally associated with the morning. They may be carried out much later in the day by workers who work night shifts, but they would still be considered to be normal day-to-day activities.

D7. In considering the ability of a child aged six or over to carry out a normal day-to-day activity, it is necessary to take account of the level of achievement which would be normal for a person of a similar age. (**See also Section E (Disabled children).**)

Specialised activities

D8. Where activities are themselves highly specialised or involve highly specialised levels of attainment, they would not be regarded as normal day-to-day activities for most people. In some instances work-related activities are so highly specialised that they would not be regarded as normal day-to-day activities.

A watch repairer carries out delicate work with highly specialised tools. He develops tenosynovitis. This restricts his ability to carry out delicate work though he is able to carry out activities such as general household repairs using more substantial tools.

Although the delicate work is a normal working activity for a person in his profession, it would not be regarded as a normal day-to-day activity for most people.

D9. The same is true of other specialised activities such as playing a musical instrument to a high standard of achievement; taking part in activities where very specific skills or level of ability are required; or playing a particular sport to a high level of ability, such as would be required for a professional footballer or athlete. Where activities involve highly specialised skills or levels of attainment, they would not be regarded as normal day-to-day activities for most people.

A woman plays the piano to a high standard, and often takes part in public performances. She has developed carpal tunnel syndrome in her wrists. This does not prevent her from playing the piano, but she cannot achieve such a high standard.

This restriction would not be an adverse effect on a normal day-to-day activity, because playing the piano to such a specialised level would not be normal for most people.

D10. However, many types of specialised work-related or other activities may still involve normal day-to-day activities which can be adversely affected by an impairment. For example they may involve normal activities such as: sitting down, standing up, walking, running, verbal interaction, writing, driving; using everyday objects such as a computer keyboard or a mobile phone, and lifting, or carrying everyday objects, such as a vacuum cleaner.

The work of the watch repairer referred to above also includes preparing invoices and counting and recording daily takings. These are normal day-to-day activities. The effects of his tenosynovitis increase in severity over time resulting in greater restriction of movement in his hands. As a consequence he experiences substantial difficulties carrying out these normal day-to-day activities.

Adverse effects on the ability to carry out normal day-to-day activities

D11. This section provides guidance on what should be taken into account in deciding whether a person's ability to carry out normal day-to-day activities might be restricted by the effects of that person's impairment. The examples given are purely illustrative and **should not in any way be considered as a prescriptive or exhaustive list**.

D12. In the Appendix, examples are given of circumstances where it **would be reasonable** to regard the adverse effect on the ability to carry out a normal day-to-day activity as substantial. In addition, examples are given of circumstances where it would **not be reasonable** to regard the effect as substantial. In these examples, the effect described should be thought of as if it were the **only** effect of the impairment.

D13. The examples of what it would, and what it would not, be reasonable to regard as substantial adverse effects on normal day-to-day activities **are indicators and not tests**. They do not mean that if a person can do an activity listed then he or she does not experience any substantial adverse effects: the person may be affected in relation to other activities, and this instead may indicate a substantial effect. Alternatively, the person may be affected in a minor way in a number of different activities, and the cumulative effect could amount to a substantial adverse effect. (**See also paragraphs B4 to B6 (cumulative effects).**)

D14. The examples in this section describe the effect which would occur when the various factors described in Sections A, B and C have been allowed for, including for example disregarding the impact of medical or other treatment.

D15. Some of the examples in this section show how an adverse effect may arise from either a physical or a mental impairment. Where illustrations of both types of impairment have not been given, this does not mean that only one type of impairment could result in that particular effect. **Physical impairments can result in mental effects and mental impairments can have physical manifestations.**

- A person with a physical impairment may, because of pain or fatigue, experience difficulties in carrying out normal activities that involve mental processes.

A journalist has recurrent severe migraines which cause her significant pain. Owing to the pain, she has difficulty maintaining concentration on writing articles and meeting deadlines.

- A person with a mental impairment or learning disability may experience difficulty in carrying out normal day-to-day activities that involve physical activity.

A young man with severe anxiety and symptoms of agoraphobia is unable to go out more than a few times a month. This is because he fears being outside in open spaces and gets panic attacks which mean that he cannot remain in places like theatres and restaurants once they become crowded.

This has a substantial adverse effect on his ability to carry out normal day-to-day activities such as social activities.

A woman has Downs Syndrome and is only able to understand her familiar local bus route. This means that she is unable to travel unaccompanied on other routes, because she gets lost and cannot find her way home without assistance.

This has a substantial adverse effect on her ability to carry out the normal day-to-day activity of using public transport.

D16. Normal day-to-day activities also include activities that are required to maintain personal well-being or to ensure personal safety, or the safety of other people. Account should be taken of whether the effects of an impairment have an impact on whether the person is inclined to carry out or neglect basic functions such as eating, drinking, sleeping, keeping warm or personal hygiene; or to exhibit behaviour which puts the person or other people at risk.

A woman has had anorexia, an eating disorder, for two years and the effects of her impairment restrict her ability to carry out the normal day-to-day activity of eating.

A man has had paranoid schizophrenia for five years. One of the effects of this impairment is an inability to make proper judgements about activities that may result in a risk to his personal safety. For example, he will walk into roads without checking if cars are coming.

This has a substantial adverse effect on his ability to carry out the normal day-to-day activity of crossing the road safely.

D17. Some impairments may have an adverse impact on the ability of a person to carry out normal day-to-day communication activities. For example, they may adversely affect whether a person is able to speak clearly at a normal pace and rhythm and to understand someone else speaking normally in the person's native language. Some impairments can have an adverse effect on a person's ability to understand human non-factual information and non-verbal communication such as body language and facial expressions. Account should be taken of how such factors can have an adverse effect on normal day-to-day activities.

A six-year-old boy has verbal dyspraxia which adversely affects his ability to speak and make himself clear to other people, including his friends and teachers at school.

A woman has bipolar disorder. Her speech sometimes becomes over-excited and irrational, making it difficult for others to understand what she is saying.

A man has had a stammer since childhood. He does not stammer all the time, but his stammer, particularly in telephone calls, goes beyond the occasional lapses in fluency found in the speech of people who do not have the impairment. However, this effect can often be

hidden by his avoidance strategies. He tries to avoid making or taking telephone calls where he believes he will stammer, or he does not speak as much during the calls. He sometimes tries to avoid stammering by substituting words, or by inserting extra words or phrases.

In these cases there are substantial adverse effects on the person's ability to carry out normal day-to-day communication activities.

A man has Asperger's syndrome, a form of autism. He finds it hard to understand non-verbal communications such as facial expressions, and non-factual communication such as jokes. He takes everything that is said very literally. He is given verbal instructions during office banter with his manager, but his ability to understand the instruction is impaired because he is unable to isolate the instruction from the social conversation.

This has a substantial adverse effect on his ability to carry out normal day-to-day communication.

D18. A person's impairment may have an adverse effect on day-to- day activities that require an ability to co-ordinate their movements, to carry everyday objects such as a kettle of water, a bag of shopping, a briefcase, or an overnight bag, or to use standard items of equipment.

A young man who has dyspraxia experiences a range of effects which include difficulty co-ordinating physical movements. He is frequently knocking over cups and bottles of drink and cannot combine two activities at the same time, such as walking while holding a plate of food upright, without spilling the food.

This has a substantial adverse effect on his ability to carry out normal day-to-day activities such as making a drink and eating.

A man with achondroplasia has unusually short stature, and arms which are disproportionate in size to the rest of his body. He has difficulty lifting everyday items like a vacuum cleaner, and he cannot reach a standard height sink or washbasin without a step to stand on.

This has a substantial adverse effect on his ability to carry out normal day-to-day activities, such as cleaning, washing up and washing his hands.

D19. A person's impairment may adversely affect the ability to carry out normal day-to-day activities that involve aspects such as remembering to do things, organising their thoughts, planning a course of action and carrying it out, taking in new knowledge, and understanding spoken or written information. This includes considering whether the person has cognitive difficulties or learns to do things significantly more slowly than a person who does not have an impairment.

A woman with bipolar affective disorder is easily distracted. This results in her frequently not being able to concentrate on performing an activity like making a sandwich or filling in a form without being constantly distracted from the task. Consequently, it takes her significantly longer than a person without the disorder to complete these types of task.

Therefore there is a substantial adverse effect on normal day-to-day activities.

Environmental effects

D20. Environmental conditions may have an impact on how an impairment affects a person's ability to carry out normal day-to-day activities. Consideration should be given to the level and nature of any environmental effect. Account should be taken of whether it is within such a range and of such a type that most people would be able to carry out an activity without an adverse effect. For example, whether background noise or lighting is of a type or level that would enable most people to hear or see adequately. (**See also paragraph B11.**)

A woman has tinnitus which makes it difficult for her to hear or understand normal conversations. She cannot hear and respond to what a supermarket checkout assistant is saying if the two people behind her in the queue are holding a conversation at the same time.

This has a substantial adverse effect on her ability to carry out the normal day-to-day activity of taking part in a conversation.

A man has retinitis pigmentosa (RP), a hereditary eye disorder which affects the retina. The man has difficulty seeing in poor light and experiences a marked reduction in his field of vision (referred to as tunnel vision). As a result he often bumps into furniture and doors when he is in an unfamiliar environment, and can only read when he is in a very well-lit area.

This has a substantial adverse effect on his ability to carry out normal day-to-day activities such as socialising in a cinema or lowly-lit restaurant.

D21. Consideration should be given to whether there may also be an adverse effect on the ability to carry out a normal day-to-day activity outside of that particular environment.

A man works in a factory where chemical fumes cause him to have breathing difficulties. He is diagnosed with occupational asthma. This has a substantial adverse effect while he is at work, because he is no longer able to work where he would be exposed to the fumes.

Even in a non-work situation he finds any general exertion difficult. This has some adverse effect on his ability to carry out a normal day-to-day activity like changing a bed.

Although the substantial effect is only apparent while he is at work, where he is exposed to fumes, the man is able to demonstrate that his impairment has an adverse effect on his ability to carry out normal day-to-day activities.

Indirect effects

D22. An impairment may not directly **prevent** someone from carrying out one or more normal day-to-day activities, but it may still have a substantial adverse effect on how the person carries out those activities. For example:

- pain or fatigue: where an impairment causes pain or fatigue, the person may have the ability to carry out a normal day-to-day activity, but may be restricted in the way that it is carried out because of experiencing pain in doing so. Or the impairment might make the activity more than usually fatiguing so that the person might not be able to repeat the task over a sustained period of time. (**See also paragraphs B7 to B10 (effects of behaviour)**);

A man with osteoarthritis experiences significant pain in his hands undertaking tasks such as using a keyboard at home or work, peeling vegetables, opening jars and writing.

The impairment substantially adversely affects the man's ability to carry out normal day-to-day activities.

A man has had chronic fatigue syndrome for several years. Although he has the physical capability to walk and to stand, he finds these very difficult to sustain for any length of time because he experiences overwhelming fatigue. As a consequence, he is restricted in his ability to take part in normal day-to-day activities such as travelling, so he avoids going out socially, and works from home several days a week.

Therefore there is a substantial adverse effect on normal day-to-day activities.

- medical advice: where a person has been advised by a medical practitioner or other health professional, as part of a treatment plan, to change, limit or refrain from a normal day-to-day activity on account of an impairment or only do it in a certain way or under certain conditions. **(See also paragraphs B12 to B17 (effects of treatment).)**

> **A woman who works as a teacher develops sciatic pain which is attributed to a prolapsed inter-vertebral disc. Despite physiotherapy and traction her pain became worse. As part of her treatment plan her doctor prescribes daily pain relief medication and advises her to avoid carrying moderately heavy items or standing for more than a few minutes at a time.**
>
> **This has a substantial adverse effect on her carrying out a range of normal day-to-day activities such as shopping or standing to address her pupils for a whole lesson.**

- frequency: some impairments may require the person to undertake certain activities, or functions at such frequent intervals that they adversely affect the ability to carry out normal day-to-day activities.

> **A young woman is a sales representative. She has developed colitis, an inflammatory bowel disease. The condition is a chronic one which is subject to periods of remission and flare-ups. During a flare-up she experiences severe abdominal pain and bouts of diarrhoea. This makes it very difficult for her to drive, including for the purposes of her job, as she must ensure she is always close to a lavatory.**
>
> **This has a substantial adverse effect on her ability to carry out normal day-to-day activities.**

Effect of treatment or correction measures

D23. Except as explained below, where a person is receiving treatment or correction measures for an impairment, the effect of the impairment on day-to-day activities is to be taken as that which the person would experience without the treatment or measures. **(See also paragraphs B12 to B17.)**

> **A man has a hearing impairment which has the effect that he cannot hold a conversation with another person even in a quiet environment. He has a hearing aid which overcomes that effect. However, it is the effect of the impairment without the hearing aid that needs to be considered.**
>
> **In this case, the impairment has a substantial adverse effect on the day-to-day activity of holding a conversation.**

D24. If a person's sight is corrected by spectacles or contact lenses, or could be corrected by them, what needs to be considered is any adverse effect that the visual impairment has on the ability to carry out normal day-to-day activities which remains while the person is wearing spectacles or lenses.

SECTION E: DISABLED CHILDREN

[4.245]

E1. The effects of impairments may not be apparent in babies and young children because they are too young to have developed the ability to carry out activities that are normal for older children and adults. Regulations provide that an impairment to a child under six years old is to be treated as having a substantial and long-term adverse effect on the ability of that child to carry out normal day-to-day activities where it would normally have a substantial and long-term adverse effect on the ability of a person aged six years or over to carry out normal day-to-day activities[9].

> **A six month old girl has an impairment that results in her having no movement in her legs. She is not yet at the stage of crawling or walking. So far the impairment does not have an apparent effect on her ability to move around. However, the impairment is to be treated as having a substantial and long-term adverse effect on her ability to carry out a normal day-to-day activity like going for a walk. This is because it would normally have such an adverse effect on the ability of a person aged six years or over to carry out normal day-to-day activities.**

E2. Children aged six and older are subject to the normal requirements of the definition. That is, that they must have an impairment which has a substantial and long-term adverse effect on their ability to carry out normal day-to-day activities. However, in considering the ability of a child aged six or over to carry out a normal day-to-day activity, it is necessary to take account of the level of achievement which would be normal for a person of a similar age.

A six-year-old child has been diagnosed as having autism. He has difficulty communicating through speech and in recognising when someone is happy or sad. When going somewhere new or taking a different route he can become very anxious. Each of these factors amounts to a substantial adverse effect on his ability to carry out normal day-to-day activities, such as holding a conversation or enjoying a day trip, even for such a young child.

E3. Part 6 of the Act provides protection for disabled pupils and students by preventing discrimination against them at school or in post-16 education because of, or for a reason related to, their disability. A pupil or student must satisfy the definition of disability as described in this guidance in order to be protected by Part 6 of the Act. The duties for schools in the Act, including the duty for schools to make reasonable adjustments for disabled children, are designed to dovetail with duties under the Special Educational Needs (SEN) framework which are based on a separate definition of special educational needs. Further information on these duties can be found in the SEN Code of Practice and the Equality and Human Rights Commission's Codes of Practice for Education.

Examples of children in an educational setting where their impairment has a substantial and long-term adverse effect on the ability to carry out normal day-to-day activities:

A 10-year-old girl has a learning disability. She has a short attention span and has difficulty remembering facts from one day to the next. She can read only a few familiar words. Each of these factors has a substantial adverse effect on her ability to participate in learning activities.

A 14-year-old boy has been diagnosed as having attention deficit hyperactivity disorder (ADHD). He often finds it difficult to concentrate and skips from task to task forgetting instructions. Either of these factors has a substantial adverse effect on his ability to participate in class and join in team games in the playground.

A 12-year-old boy has cerebral palsy and has limited movement in his legs. This has a substantial adverse effect on his ability to move around the school and take part in physical sports activities.

SECTION F: DISABILITY AS A PARTICULAR PROTECTED CHARACTERISTIC OR AS A SHARED PROTECTED CHARACTERISTIC

[4.246]

F1. The Act provides protection from discrimination based on a range of protected characteristics and disability, as defined in the Act and related, is a protected characteristic.

F2. Certain provisions in the Act apply where a person has a "particular" protected characteristic. In the case of disability, **the Act states** that a reference to a person with a particular protected characteristic is a reference to a person who has a particular disability (**S 6(3)**).

A disabled man has a mobility impairment. This has a substantial and long-term adverse effect on his ability to carry out normal day-to-day activities like shopping and gardening. Therefore he is protected by the Act in general because he has the protected characteristic of disability.

However, for the purposes of the provisions of the Act that apply specifically to people with a particular protected characteristic, he would have the particular characteristic of being mobility impaired.

F3. Some provisions in the Act apply where persons share a protected characteristic. In the case of disability, **the Act states** that a reference to persons who share a particular characteristic is a reference to persons who have the same disability (**S 6(3)**).

For the purposes of the provisions that apply specifically to people who share a protected characteristic, the disabled man would share the protected characteristic with other people who have mobility impairments.

F4. This may be illustrated by reference to the following provisions in the Act.

- Schedule 9 paragraph 1 of the Act provides that it is not discrimination, under a range of work provisions, for it to be an occupational requirement that the job holder has a particular protected characteristic.

A charitable organisation that provides services to people with HIV and Aids has vacancies for counsellors for which being HIV positive is an occupational requirement.

It is not discriminatory for the organisation to only appoint people who have a particular protected characteristic which, in this instance, is having the particular disability of being HIV positive.

- Schedule 16 paragraph 1 relating to associations or clubs for people who have a single protected characteristic, apply where persons share a protected characteristic.

A group of people with hearing impairments form a private club that provides advice, support and recreational activities specifically for people who have that particular impairment.

For the purposes of the Act, a reference to people who share a protected characteristic would, in this instance, be to people who have hearing impairments.

APPENDIX

AN ILLUSTRATIVE AND NON-EXHAUSTIVE LIST OF FACTORS WHICH, IF THEY ARE EXPERIENCED BY A PERSON, **IT WOULD BE REASONABLE** TO REGARD AS HAVING A SUBSTANTIAL ADVERSE EFFECT ON NORMAL DAY-TO-DAY ACTIVITIES.

[4.247]

Whether a person satisfies the definition of a disabled person for the purposes of the Act will depend upon the full circumstances of the case. That is, whether the substantial adverse effect of the impairment on normal day-to-day activities is long term.

In the following examples, the effect described should be thought of as if it were the **only** effect of the impairment.

- Difficulty in getting dressed, for example, because of physical restrictions, a lack of understanding of the concept, or low motivation;
- Difficulty carrying out activities associated with toileting, or caused by frequent minor incontinence;
- Difficulty preparing a meal, for example, because of restricted ability to do things like open cans or packages, or because of an inability to understand and follow a simple recipe;
- Difficulty eating; for example, because of an inability to co-ordinate the use of a knife and fork, a need for assistance, or the effect of an eating disorder;
- Difficulty going out of doors unaccompanied, for example, because the person has a phobia, a physical restriction, or a learning disability;
- Difficulty waiting or queuing, for example, because of a lack of understanding of the concept, or because of pain or fatigue when standing for prolonged periods;
- Difficulty using transport; for example, because of physical restrictions, pain or fatigue, a frequent need for a lavatory or as a result of a mental impairment or learning disability;
- Difficulty in going up or down steps, stairs or gradients; for example, because movements are painful, fatiguing or restricted in some way;
- A total inability to walk, or an ability to walk only a short distance without difficulty; for example because of physical restrictions, pain or fatigue;
- Difficulty entering or staying in environments that the person perceives as strange or frightening;
- Behaviour which challenges people around the person, making it difficult for the person to be accepted in public places;

- Persistent difficulty crossing a road safely, for example, because of physical restrictions or a failure to understand and manage the risk;
- Persistent general low motivation or loss of interest in everyday activities;
- Difficulty accessing and moving around buildings; for example because of inability to open doors, grip handrails on steps or gradients, or an inability to follow directions;
- Difficulty operating a computer, for example, because of physical restrictions in using a keyboard, a visual impairment or a learning disability;
- Difficulty picking up and carrying objects of moderate weight, such as a bag of shopping or a small piece of luggage, with one hand;
- Inability to converse, or give instructions orally, in the person's native spoken language;
- Difficulty understanding or following simple verbal instructions;
- Difficulty hearing and understanding another person speaking clearly over the voice telephone (where the telephone is not affected by bad reception);
- Persistent and significant difficulty in reading or understanding written material where this is in the person's native written language, for example because of a mental impairment, or learning disability, or a visual impairment (except where that is corrected by glasses or contact lenses);
- Intermittent loss of consciousness;
- Frequent confused behaviour, intrusive thoughts, feelings of being controlled, or delusions;
- Persistently wanting to avoid people or significant difficulty taking part in normal social interaction or forming social relationships, for example because of a mental health condition or disorder;
- Persistent difficulty in recognising, or remembering the names of, familiar people such as family or friends;
- Persistent distractibility or difficulty concentrating;
- Compulsive activities or behaviour, or difficulty in adapting after a reasonable period to minor changes in a routine.

AN ILLUSTRATIVE AND NON-EXHAUSTIVE LIST OF FACTORS WHICH, IF THEY ARE EXPERIENCED BY A PERSON, **IT WOULD NOT BE REASONABLE** TO REGARD AS HAVING A SUBSTANTIAL ADVERSE EFFECT ON NORMAL DAY-TO-DAY ACTIVITIES.

Whether a person satisfies the definition of a disabled person for the purposes of the Act will depend upon the full circumstances of the case. That is, whether the substantial adverse effect of the impairment on normal day-to-day activities is long term.

- Inability to move heavy objects without assistance or a mechanical aid, such as moving a large suitcase or heavy piece of furniture without a trolley;
- Experiencing some discomfort as a result of travelling, for example by car or plane, for a journey lasting more than two hours;
- Experiencing some tiredness or minor discomfort as a result of walking unaided for a distance of about 1.5 kilometres or one mile;
- Minor problems with writing or spelling;
- Inability to reach typing speeds standardised for secretarial work;
- Inability to read very small or indistinct print without the aid of a magnifying glass;
- Inability to fill in a long, detailed, technical document, which is in the person's native language, without assistance;
- Inability to speak in front of an audience simply as a result of nervousness;
- Some shyness and timidity;
- Inability to articulate certain sounds due to a lisp;
- Inability to be understood because of having a strong accent;
- Inability to converse orally in a language which is not the speaker's native spoken language;
- Inability to hold a conversation in a very noisy place, such as a factory floor, a pop concert, sporting event or alongside a busy main road;
- Inability to sing in tune;
- Inability to distinguish a known person across a substantial distance (e.g. across the width of a football pitch);
- Occasionally forgetting the name of a familiar person, such as a colleague;
- Inability to concentrate on a task requiring application over several hours;
- Occasional apprehension about significant heights;
- A person consciously taking a higher than normal risk on their own initiative, such as persistently crossing a road when the signals are adverse, or driving fast on highways for own pleasure;
- Simple inability to distinguish between red and green, which is not accompanied by any other effect such as blurring of vision;
- Infrequent minor incontinence;
- Inability to undertake activities requiring delicate hand movements, such as threading a small needle or picking up a pin.

NOTES

1 Schedule 1, Para 12 defines an 'adjudicating body' as a court, tribunal, or a person (other than a court or tribunal) who may decide a claim relating to a contravention of Part 6 (education).

2 Regulation 7 of The Equality Act 2010 (Disability) Regulations 2010 (SI 2010/2128).

3 The Equality Act 2010 (Disability) Regulations 2010 (SI 2010/2128).

4 Provisions in The Equality Act 2010 (Disability) Regulations 2010 (SI 2010/2128).

5 Covering: taxis etc; public service vehicles and rail transport.

6 The Disability Discrimination Act 1995 (DDA) provided that any individual who was registered as a disabled person under the Disabled Persons (Employment) Act 1944 and whose name appeared on the register both on 12 January 1995 and 2 December 1996 was treated as having a disability for during the period of three years starting on 2 December 1996 (when the DDA employment provisions came into force). This applied regardless of whether the person met the DDA definition of a disabled person during that period. Following the end of the three-year transitional period, those persons who were treated by this provision as being disabled are now treated as having a disability in the past. **This provision is preserved for the purposes of the Equality Act 2010.**

7 See Note 3.

8 See Note 3.

9 See Note 3.

H. CODES MADE BY THE BODIES REPLACED BY THE EHRC

EQUAL OPPORTUNITIES COMMISSION: CODE OF PRACTICE ON SEX DISCRIMINATION EQUAL OPPORTUNITY POLICIES, PROCEDURES AND PRACTICES IN EMPLOYMENT (1985) (NOTE)

[4.248]

NOTES

This Code of Practice was issued by the Equal Opportunities Commission under the Sex Discrimination Act 1975, s 56A (repealed as noted below), and was brought into effect on 30 April 1985 by the Sex Discrimination Code of Practice Order 1985, SI 1985/387.

The statutory provision under which this Code was made was repealed by the Equality Act 2006, ss 40, 91, Sch 3, paras 6, 11, Sch 4; however the Code was continued in force by s 42(3) of the 2006 Act (see **[1.1388]**).

The Code was finally revoked (with effect from 6 April 2011) by the Former Equality Commissions' Codes of Practice (Employment, Equal Pay, and Rights of Access for Disabled Persons) (Revocation) Order 2011, SI 2011/776, art 2.

Article 3 of the 2011 Order makes transitional provision for proceedings arising from alleged contraventions of previous discrimination legislation saved in respect of insurance business in relation to existing insurance policies, or occurring wholly before 1 October 2010, or so far as the previous legislation relates to work on ships, work on hovercraft and seafarers (until Regulations under s 81 of the Equality Act 2010 come into force). The 1985 Code continues to have effect in relation to such proceedings for the purposes of s 15(4)(b) of the Equality Act 2006, which requires a court or tribunal to take a code into account in any case in which it appears to the court or tribunal to be relevant.

With regard to work on ships, work on hovercraft and seafarers, note that the Equality Act 2010 (Work on Ships and Hovercraft) Regulations 2011, SI 2011/1771 (made under s 81 of the 2010 Act) came into force on 15 August 2011.

See now the EHRC's Code of Practice on Employment at **[4.138]**.

The 1985 Code is omitted for reasons of space.

COMMISSION FOR RACIAL EQUALITY: CODE OF PRACTICE ON THE DUTY TO PROMOTE RACE EQUALITY (2002)

[4.249]

NOTES

This Code was issued by the Commission for Racial Equality under the Race Relations Act 1976, s 71C (as inserted by the Race Relations (Amendment) Act 2000 and repealed as noted below). Following Parliamentary approval, the Code was brought into effect by the Race Relations Act 1976 (General Statutory Duty: Code of Practice) Order 2002 (SI 2002/1435) with effect from 30 May 2002.

The statutory provision under which this Code was made was repealed by the Equality Act 2006, ss 40, 91, Sch 3, paras 21, 30, Sch 4; however the Code is continued in force by s 42(3) of the 2006 Act (see **[1.1388]**).

Much of the Code relates to the application of the general statutory duty to the provision of public services and, in particular, education; Section 4 (in Part II) and much of Section 6 (in Part III) have been omitted as outside the scope of this work. The bodies subject to the general statutory duty are listed in Appendix 1 (omitted for reasons of space). Similarly, Appendix 2 (Bodies required to publish a race equality scheme) which reproduces Sch 1 to the Race Relations Act 1976 (Statutory Duties) Order 2001, SI 2001/3458, is omitted for reasons of space. Appendix 3 is included; it lists the bodies subject to the duty to undertake ethnic monitoring of employees, comprising the bodies listed in Sch 1 to the Race Relations Act 1976 (now repealed) *other than* those listed in Sch 3 to the 2001 Order. Appendices 4 and 6 are omitted as outside the scope of this work; Appendix 5, which lists those bodies within Sch 1A to the Act which are Scottish public authorities, is also omitted.

The equivalent Code for Scotland 'The Duty to Promote Race Equality in Scotland' (2003) (applicable to those bodies subject to the authority of the Scottish Parliament) is omitted for reasons of space.

The statutory duties imposed by the Race Relations Act 1976 have been replaced by a general statutory duty in relation to equal treatment under the Equality Act 2010, s 149, and it was originally intended that this Code (and its equivalent for the gender equality duty) would be replaced by a new Code under s 149 of the 2010 Act. However, the Equality and Human Rights Commission has subsequently announced that the Secretary of State is unlikely to approve a new statutory code, and that the new Guidance would be issued on a non-statutory basis. The new Guidance on the equality duty for England, Wales and Scotland is on the EHRC website at:
www.equalityhumanrights.com/advice-and-guidance/public-sector-equality-duty/guidance-on-the-equality-duty/.

Permission to reproduce this Code was kindly granted by the Commission for Racial Equality.

CONTENTS

GLOSSARY

[4.250]

In this Code, the words below have the meanings shown beneath them.

action plan

a practical and realistic plan, with an agreed timetable, showing how an authority is planning to meet its duties.

assessing impact

a systematic way of finding out whether a policy (or proposed policy) affects different racial groups differently. This may include obtaining and analysing data, and consulting people, including staff, on the policy.

complementary

this refers to the fact that the three parts of the general duty support each other and may, in practice, overlap. However, they are different, and public authorities should consider each one individually.

consultation

asking for views on policies or services from staff, colleagues, service-users, or the general public. Different circumstances call for different types of consultation. For example, consultation includes meetings, focus groups, reference groups, citizens' juries, surveys, and questionnaires.

direct discrimination

treating one person less favourably than another on racial grounds (see [below]). Direct discrimination is unlawful under the Race Relations Act.

disciplinary procedures

the arrangements and procedures used to discipline staff. These may include informal and formal disciplinary measures.

duty to promote race equality

the general duty, unless the context suggests otherwise.

ethnic monitoring

the process you use to collect, store and analyse data about people's ethnic backgrounds.

focus groups, reference groups and citizens' juries

various forms of face-to-face consultation with members of the public, service-users, or others.

formal investigation

an investigation by the CRE under sections 49–52 of the Race Relations Act. The investigation can be either a "named person" investigation or a general investigation.

- A "named person" investigation can be carried out if the CRE suspects that an organisation is discriminating on racial grounds. The CRE can ask the organisation for documents and information. If the CRE is satisfied that unlawful discrimination has taken place, or is taking place, the CRE can issue a "non-discrimination notice".
- A general investigation can be carried out, without suspicion of discrimination, to examine practice within an area of activity. At the end of the investigation, the CRE can make recommendations.

functions

the full range of a public authority's duties and powers.

further and higher education institution

the governing body of an institution in the further and higher education sectors (as defined in sections 91(3) and 91(5) of the Further and Higher Education Act).

general duty

the duty as given in section 71(1) of the Race Relations Act (see chapter 3, paragraph 3.1).

grievance procedures

arrangements or procedures for dealing with grievances, such as complaints about bullying, harassment or discrimination; or appeals against decisions on promotion or appraisal marks.

indirect racial discrimination

occurs when a rule or condition which is applied equally to everyone—

- can be met by a considerably smaller proportion of people from a particular racial group;
- is to the disadvantage of that group; and

- cannot be justified on non-racial grounds.

All three conditions must apply.

judicial review

a claim to the High Court or the Scottish Court of Sessions asking the court to review the way a public authority or certain other bodies made a decision. The court will not decide the merits of the decision, only whether it is legal. The court can ask the authority to reconsider the matter.

monitoring

the process of collecting, analysing and evaluating information, to measure performance, progress or change.

non-devolved authorities

public authorities in Scotland whose functions and powers remain the responsibility of the Westminster Parliament rather than the Scottish Parliament.

obligatory

this refers to the fact that public authorities are legally bound to meet the general duty, and must make race equality a central part of their functions.

orders

ministerial directions to apply the law, or to change the way it applies.

performance assessment procedures

formal and informal staff appraisals that are likely to affect career development, pay and benefits.

policies

the formal and informal decisions about how a public authority carries out its duties and uses its powers.

positive action

action permitted by the Race Relations Act that allows a person to—

- provide facilities to meet the special needs of people from particular racial groups in relation to their training, education or welfare (section 35); and
- target job training at people from racial groups that are under-represented in a particular area of work, or encourage them to apply for such work (sections 37 and 38).

promoting race equality

public authorities should have "due regard to the need", in carrying out their functions, to—

- tackle unlawful racial discrimination;
- promote equality of opportunity; and
- promote good relations between people from different racial groups.

proportionate

this refers to the fact that the weight given to race equality should be proportionate to its relevance to a particular function. This approach may mean giving greater consideration and resources to functions or policies that have most effect on the public, or on the authority's employees.

public appointments

appointments to the boards of public bodies. These are bodies that have a role in the processes of national government, but operate at arm's length from government.

public authority

a body named, defined or described in schedule 1A to the Race Relations Act or, depending on the context, a body named, defined or described in one of the schedules to the Race Relations Act 1976 (Statutory Duties) Order 2001.

public functions

functions that affect, or are likely to affect, the public or a section of the public. While only the courts can decide this, public functions would normally not include internal management or contractual matters such as employing staff; purchasing goods, works or services; or buying or selling premises. This term is used to refer to those authorities that are bound by the duties only in relation to their public functions (for example professional representative organisations, such as the Royal College of Surgeons, or broadcasting authorities).

public procurement

the contractual or other arrangements that a public authority makes to obtain goods, works or services from an outside organisation.

publish

making publicly available; for example by producing a written document for distribution.

race equality policy

a written statement of an educational establishment's policy on race equality, which is put into practice and monitored.

race equality scheme

a timetabled and realistic plan, setting out an authority's arrangements for meeting the general and specific duties.

Race Relations Act

the Race Relations Act 1976, as amended by the Race Relations (Amendment) Act 2000.

racial group

a group of people defined by their race, colour, nationality (including citizenship), ethnic or national origins.

racial grounds

reasons of race, colour, nationality (including citizenship), ethnic or national origins.

relevance

this refers to the fact that race equality will be more relevant to some public functions than others. Relevance is about how far a function or policy affects people, as members of the public, and as employees of the authority.

schedule

an appendix to legislation, such as schedule 1A to the Race Relations Act. This schedule lists the public authorities to which the general duty applies.

school

the governing body of an educational establishment maintained by local education authorities in England and Wales, or of a city technology college, a city college for technology of the arts, or a city academy.

Scottish public authority

a public authority whose functions can only be carried out in, or in relation to, Scotland.

specific duty

a duty imposed by the Race Relations Act 1976 (Statutory Duties) Order 2001.

statutory code of practice

a document such as this one, which offers practical guidance on the law, has been approved by Parliament, and is admissible in evidence in a court of law.

statutory duties

duties, either general or specific, which an authority is legally bound to meet.

training

a wide range of career development opportunities, which could include informal in-house training as well as more formal courses.

victimisation

punishing or treating someone unfairly because they have made a complaint of racial discrimination, or are thought to have done so; or because they have supported someone else who has made a complaint of racial discrimination. Victimisation is defined as unlawful discrimination under the Race Relations Act.

PART I
PROMOTING RACE EQUALITY IN ALL LISTED PUBLIC AUTHORITIES

1—INTRODUCTION

[4.251]
1.1 The Race Relations Act (see the glossary) places a general duty on a wide range of public authorities to promote race equality. This duty means that authorities (listed in appendix 1 of this code) must have due regard to the need to—
(a) eliminate unlawful racial discrimination;
(b) promote equality of opportunity; and
(c) promote good relations between people of different racial groups.

1.2. Most public authorities are bound by this duty. Many of them provide major public services, such as education or health. Some of them (for example professional representative organisations, such as the Royal College of Surgeons, or broadcasting authorities) are bound by this duty only so far as their public functions (see the glossary) are concerned.

1.3. The duty aims to make the promotion of race equality central to the way public authorities work. Promoting race equality will improve the way public services are delivered for everyone. In most cases, these authorities should be able to use their existing arrangements – such as those for policy making – to meet the duty's requirements. This should help to avoid any unnecessary or duplicated work.

Benefits of the duty

1.4. The duty will help public authorities to make steady progress in achieving race equality. In relation to policy development and service delivery, the duty will—
(a) encourage policy makers to be more aware of possible problems;
(b) contribute to more informed decision making;
(c) make sure that policies are properly targeted;
(d) improve the authority's ability to deliver suitable and accessible services that meet varied needs;
(e) encourage greater openness about policy making;
(f) increase confidence in public services, especially among ethnic minority communities;
(g) help to develop good practice; and
(h) help to avoid claims of unlawful racial discrimination.

1.5. The duty of public authorities to promote race equality in *employment* will—
(a) help to make the authority's workforce more representative of the communities it serves;
(b) attract able staff;
(c) avoid losing or undervaluing able staff;
(d) improve staff morale and productivity;
(e) improve the way staff are managed;
(f) help to develop good practice; and
(g) help to avoid claims of unlawful racial discrimination.

Purpose of the Code

1.6. Public authorities can decide how they will meet their duty to promote race equality. The Race Relations Act gives the CRE the power to issue codes of practice, with the approval of Parliament.

1.7. This code offers practical guidance to public authorities on how to meet their duty to promote race equality. It includes guidance on both the general duty (see 1.1) and specific duties imposed by the Home Secretary. The code's aim is to help public authorities to adopt good practice and to eliminate racial discrimination. The code should also help the public understand what public authorities have to do, and the role that the public can play.

1.8. The specific duties imposed by order of the Home Secretary came into effect on **3 December 2001**. Public authorities bound by these duties (see appendices 2, 3 and 4) were required to have properly timetabled and realistic plans for meeting these duties in place by **31 May 2002**.

1.9. This code applies to public authorities in England and Wales (see appendix 1) and to "non-devolved" public authorities in Scotland (see the glossary and appendix 1). Chapter 6 of this code applies only to the governing bodies of educational institutions in England and Wales. The Code of Practice for Scotland will apply to devolved public authorities in Scotland (see the glossary).

Nature of the Code

1.10. This code of practice is a "statutory" code. This means that it has been approved by Parliament. It also means that the code is admissible in evidence in any legal action, and a court or tribunal should take the code's recommendations into account. On its own, the code does not place any legal obligations on public authorities. It is not a complete statement of the law, as only the courts can give this. If a public authority does not follow the code's guidance, it may need to be able to show how it has otherwise met its legal obligations under the general duty and any specific duties.

How to use this Code

1.11. The code is divided into five parts, seven chapters and six appendices.

(a) Part I (chapters 2 and 3) applies to all listed public authorities, including schools, and further and higher education institutions.

(b) Part II (chapters 4 and 5) deals with promoting race equality in certain public authorities other than educational institutions.

(c) Part III (chapter 6) deals with promoting race equality in educational institutions.

(d) Part IV (chapter 7) deals with the CRE's role, including enforcing this code.

(e) Part V (appendices 1 to 6) lists the public authorities that are bound by the general duty (appendix 1), the public authorities that are required to publish a race equality scheme (appendix 2), the public authorities bound by the employment duty (appendix 3), the public authorities bound by the duties for educational institutions (appendix 4), Scottish public authorities (appendix 5), and other guidance published by the CRE (appendix 6).

2—THE LEGAL FRAMEWORK

[4.252]

2.1. The Race Relations Act (see the glossary) defines direct and indirect discrimination, and victimisation (see the glossary for each of these terms). It outlaws racial discrimination in employment, training, education, housing, public appointments, and the provision of goods, facilities and services. The Race Relations (Amendment) Act 2000 came into force on 2 April 2001 and since then the Race Relations Act (the Act) has covered all the functions of public authorities (with just a few exceptions).

2.2. Section 71(1) of the Act places a general duty on listed public authorities (see appendix 1). The Act also gives the Home Secretary power to make orders placing specific duties on all or some of these authorities (section 71(2)). Scottish ministers have a similar power over Scottish public authorities (section 71B(1); see the glossary). Under the Race Relations Act 1976 (Statutory Duties) Order 2001, the specific duties discussed in this code came into force on **3 December 2001**.

2.3. The Act gives the CRE enforcement powers over the specific duties imposed by the Home Secretary and Scottish ministers. The Act also gives the CRE power to issue codes of practice containing practical guidance on how public authorities can meet the general duty (see chapter 3) and specific duties (see chapters 4, 5 and 6). This is a statutory code, issued for this purpose.

The general duty to promote race equality

2.4. This general duty applies to all public authorities listed in schedule 1A to the Act (see appendix 1). The duty's aim is to make the promotion of race equality central to the work of the listed public authorities.

Specific duties to promote race equality

2.5. Specific duties have been placed on some public authorities responsible for delivering important public services. The duties involve making arrangements that will help these authorities to meet the general duty to promote race equality.

(a) The public authorities listed in appendix 2 must prepare and publish a race equality scheme. This scheme should set out the "functions" or "policies" (see the glossary for both terms) that are relevant to meeting the general duty, and the arrangements that will help to meet the duty in the areas of policy and service delivery (see chapter 4).

(b) The public authorities listed in appendix 3 must monitor their employment procedures and practice (see chapter 5). Some of these authorities have to produce a race equality scheme. They may find it useful to include the arrangements they make to meet their employment duties in their race equality schemes.

(c) The educational institutions listed in appendix 4 have to prepare a race equality policy and put in place arrangements for meeting their specific duties on policy and employment (see chapter 6).

2.6. Public authorities that introduce effective arrangements, as required under the specific duties, should be able to show that they are meeting the general duty to promote race equality. Taking action to promote race equality should give authorities the evidence they need to show that they are meeting the general duty.

2.7. Chapters 4, 5, and 6 give guidance on the specific duties.

Liability under the Race Relations Act

2.8. Public authorities are responsible for meeting their general and specific duties. Within each public authority, this responsibility will rest with the groups or individuals who are liable (legally responsible) for the authority's acts or failure to act.

Private or voluntary organisations carrying out a public authority's functions

2.9. When a public authority has a contract or other agreement with a private company or voluntary organisation to carry out any of its functions (see the glossary), and the duty to promote race equality applies to those functions, the public authority remains responsible for meeting the general duty and any specific duties that apply to those functions. The authority should therefore consider the arrangements it will need. If the authority's race equality duties are relevant to the functions it is contracting out, it may be appropriate to incorporate those duties among the performance requirements for delivery of the service. For example, a contractor could be required to monitor service users by their racial group, to make sure the authority is meeting its duties. This would not involve requirements concerning the contractor's internal practices. Whatever action the authority takes, it must be consistent with the policy and legal framework for public procurement.

2.10. In addition to specifications for the general duty and any specific duties, public authorities may promote race equality by encouraging contractors to draw up policies that will help them (contractors) to avoid unlawful discrimination, and promote equality of opportunity. Such encouragement should only be within a voluntary framework, once contracts have been awarded, rather than by making specific criteria or conditions part of the selection process. Public authorities should bear in mind that the general duty does not override other laws or regulations on public procurement. In particular, as above, whatever action the authority takes must be consistent with the policy and legal framework for public procurement.

Partnership

2.11. Public authorities should take account of their general duty to promote race equality – and any specific duties – when they work with other public, private or voluntary organisations. There is no similar obligation on private or voluntary-sector partners.

2.12. Public authorities that are involved in partnership work with other public authorities, or with private or voluntary-sector organisations, are still responsible for meeting their general duty to promote race equality, and any specific duties.

2.13. In practice, this will mean that a public authority working within a partnership will need to seek agreement from its partners to arrangements for planning, funding and managing joint work that will allow it to meet its statutory race equality duties. Public authorities should reflect their partnership work in their race equality schemes.

Inspecting and auditing public authorities

2.14. Agencies that audit or inspect public authorities are bound by the duty to promote race equality. These agencies need to consider how the duty fits with their inspection or audit obligations. In most cases, inspection and audit bodies should be able to use their existing inspection arrangements to promote race equality.

3—THE GENERAL DUTY

[4.253]
3.1 This chapter explains what public authorities can do to meet the general duty to promote race equality. The duty is set out in section 71(1) of the Race Relations Act (the Act) and it applies to every public authority listed in schedule 1A to the Act (see appendix 1 of this code). Section 71(1) says—

(1) Every body or other person specified in Schedule 1A or of a description falling within that Schedule shall, in carrying out its functions, have due regard to the need
  (a) to eliminate unlawful racial discrimination; and
  (b) to promote equality of opportunity and good relations between persons of different racial groups.*

* For immigration and nationality functions, the general duty does not include the words "equality of opportunity and" (section 71A(1)).

Guiding principles

3.2. Four principles should govern public authorities' efforts to meet their duty to promote race equality.

(a) Promoting race equality is obligatory for all public authorities listed in schedule 1A to the Act (see appendix 1).
(b) Public authorities must meet the duty to promote race equality in all relevant functions.
(c) The weight given to race equality should be proportionate to its relevance.
(d) The elements of the duty are complementary (which means they are all necessary to meet the whole duty).

"Obligatory"

3.3. Public authorities listed in schedule 1A to the Act must make race equality a central part of their functions (such as planning, policy making, service delivery, regulation, inspection, enforcement, and employment). The general duty does not tell public authorities how to do their work, but it expects them to assess whether race equality is relevant to their functions. If it is, the authority should do everything it can to meet the general duty. The duty should underpin all policy and practice, and it should encourage improvement. It is not necessarily a new responsibility for the authority, just a more effective way of doing what it already does.

"Relevant"

3.4. Race equality will be more relevant to some functions than others. Relevance is about how much a function affects people, as members of the public or as employees of the authority. For example, a local authority may decide that race equality is more relevant to raising educational standards than to its work on highway maintenance. Public authorities should therefore assess whether, and how, race equality is relevant to each of their functions. A public authority may decide that the general duty does not apply to some of its functions; for example those that are purely technical, such as traffic control or weather forecasting.

"Proportionate"

3.5. Under section 71(1) of the Act, public authorities are expected to have "due regard" to the three parts of the duty to promote race equality (see 1.1). This means that the weight given to race equality should be proportionate to its relevance to a particular function. In practice, this approach may mean giving greater consideration and resources to functions or policies that have most effect on the public, or on the authority's employees. The authority's concern should be to ask whether particular policies could affect different racial groups in different ways, and whether the policies will promote good race relations.

3.6. "Due regard" does not mean that race equality is less important when the ethnic minority population is small. It is also not acceptable for a public authority to claim that it does not have enough resources to meet the duty. This is because meeting the general duty is a statutory requirement. In practice, this means that public authorities should draw on work they already do to promote race equality, and build on it, using their existing administrative systems and processes and adjusting their plans and priorities, where necessary.

3.7. The general duty is a continuing duty. What a public authority has to do to meet it may change over time as its functions or policies change, or as the communities it serves change.

"Complementary"

3.8. The general duty has three parts—

(a) eliminating unlawful racial discrimination;
(b) promoting equality of opportunity; and
(c) promoting good relations between people of different racial groups.

3.9. These three parts support each other. And, in practice, they may overlap (for example, promoting equality of opportunity may also eliminate or prevent unlawful racial discrimination, *and* promote good race relations). However, it is important to remember that the three parts are different, and that achieving one of them may not lead to achieving all three. For example, a new equal opportunities policy that is not clearly explained when it is introduced may improve equality of opportunity, but it may also damage race relations and create resentment if staff do not understand how it benefits everyone.

3.10. Public authorities should consider and deal with all three parts of the general duty.

How to meet the general duty

3.11. Public authorities should consider the following four steps to meet the general duty.

(a) Identify which of their functions and policies are relevant to the duty, or, in other words, affect most people.

(b) Put the functions and policies in order of priority, based on how relevant they are to race equality.
(c) Assess whether the way these 'relevant' functions and policies are being carried out meets the three parts of the duty.
(d) Consider whether any changes need to be made to meet the duty, and make the changes.

Identifying relevant functions

3.12. To identify relevant functions, a public authority will find it useful, first, to make a list of all its functions, including employment. It should then assess how relevant each function is to each part of the general duty. As shown in paragraph 3.4, some functions may, by their nature, have little or no relevance.

3.13. A public authority should consider setting priorities, and giving priority to those functions that are most relevant to race equality.

Assessing impact and considering change

3.14. To assess the impact its functions and policies have on race equality, the authority may find it useful to draw up a clear statement of the aims of each function or policy. It should then consider whether it has information about how different racial groups are affected by the function or policy, as employees or users (or possible users) of services. The authority should also consider whether its functions and policies are promoting good race relations. The authority could get this information from various sources; for example previous research, records of complaints, surveys, or local meetings. These methods should help public authorities to assess which of their services are used by which racial groups, or what people think of their services, and whether they are being provided fairly to people from different racial groups. This kind of evidence should help public authorities to decide what they might need to do to meet all three parts of the general duty.

3.15. Public authorities may also need to consider adapting their existing information systems, so that they can provide information about different racial groups and show what progress the authority is making on race equality.

3.16. To assess the effects of a policy, or the way a function is being carried out, public authorities could ask themselves the following questions.
(a) Could the policy or the way the function is carried out have an adverse impact on equality of opportunity for some racial groups? In other words, does it put some racial groups at a disadvantage?
(b) Could the policy or the way the function is carried out have an adverse impact on relations between different racial groups?
(c) Is the adverse impact, if any, unavoidable? Could it be considered to be unlawful racial discrimination? Can it be justified by the aims and importance of the policy or function? Are there other ways in which the authority's aims can be achieved without causing an adverse impact on some racial groups?
(d) Could the adverse impact be reduced by taking particular measures?
(e) Is further research or consultation necessary? Would this research be proportionate to the importance of the policy or function? Is it likely to lead to a different outcome?

3.17. If the assessment suggests that the policy, or the way the function is carried out, should be modified, the authority should do this to meet the general duty.

PART II
PROMOTING RACE EQUALITY IN LISTED PUBLIC AUTHORITIES OTHER THAN EDUCATIONAL INSTITUTIONS

4—SPECIFIC DUTIES: POLICY AND SERVICE DELIVERY

(*Outside the scope of this work.*)

5—SPECIFIC DUTIES: EMPLOYMENT

[4.254]
5.1. The specific duty on employment applies to most of the public authorities bound by the general duty (see appendix 3). Schools and further and higher education institutions are not bound by the employment duty, as they have separate employment responsibilities (see chapter 6). A few, mainly advisory, agencies are also not bound by the employment duty.

5.2. Articles 5(1), 5(2), and 5(3) of the Race Relations Act 1976 (Statutory Duties) Order 2001 say the following—

5

(1) A person to which this article applies shall,
(a) before 31st May 2002, have in place arrangements for fulfilling, as soon as is reasonably practicable, its duties under paragraph (2); and

(b) fulfil those duties in accordance with such arrangements.

(2) It shall be the duty of such a person to monitor, by reference to the racial groups to which they belong,

(a) the numbers of—

(i) staff in post, and

(ii) applicants for employment, training and promotion, from each such group, and

(b) where that person has 150 or more full-time staff, the numbers of staff from each such group who—

(i) receive training;

(ii) benefit or suffer detriment as a result of its performance assessment procedures;

(iii) are involved in grievance procedures;

(iv) are the subject of disciplinary procedures; or

(v) cease employment with that person.

(3) Such a person shall publish annually the results of its monitoring under paragraph (2).

5.3. Public authorities that have to produce race equality schemes may find it useful to include their arrangements for meeting their employment duty in their race equality schemes.

5.4. The specific duties on employment are designed to provide a framework for measuring progress in equality of opportunity in public-sector employment. The specific duties are also aimed at providing monitoring information to guide initiatives that could lead to a more representative public-sector workforce. For example, these initiatives could include setting recruitment targets for under-represented racial groups, or targeting management development courses at racial groups that are under-represented at certain levels. The specific duties on employment set minimum standards. Other issues may also be relevant for good employment practice. This will depend on local circumstances.

5.5. Ethnic monitoring (see the glossary) is central to providing a clear picture of what is happening during the authority's employment cycle – from applying for a job and joining the authority to leaving it. Monitoring helps to measure overall progress and to show whether the authority's equal opportunities policies are effective. Monitoring is the essential tool to assess progress – or lack of it – in removing barriers to equality of opportunity in the public services.

5.6. It is important that the authority explains to applicants and existing staff why they are monitoring employment. People will normally only have to give information about their racial group voluntarily, and the authority should explain the conditions of the Data Protection Act 1998 (about processing this information) to them.

5.7. Wherever possible, the authority should build monitoring information into the information systems it already uses. The authority may be able to publish its monitoring results each year through its existing reporting systems. In its published results, the authority should explain how it is dealing with trends or problems highlighted by its monitoring. The authority may also find it useful to combine and analyse ethnic monitoring data with other data; for example on sex and disability.

5.8. To help meet the specific duty on employment, public authorities should—

(a) collect ethnic monitoring data; and

(b) publish the results of the monitoring each year.

5.9. To check that they are meeting the general duty, public authorities may want to—

(a) analyse the data to find any patterns of inequality; and

(b) take whatever steps are needed to remove barriers and promote equality of opportunity.

5.10. If the monitoring shows that current employment policies, procedures and practice are leading to unlawful racial discrimination, the authority should take steps to end the discrimination. As a first step, the authority should examine each of its procedures closely to find out where and how discrimination might be happening, and then consider what changes to introduce.

5.11. On the other hand, the monitoring may show that current policies, procedures and practice have an adverse impact on equality of opportunity or good race relations (even though they are not causing unlawful discrimination). If this is the case, the authority should consider changing its policies or procedures so that they still meet the same aims, but do not harm equality of opportunity or race relations.

Positive action

5.12. If monitoring reveals that some racial groups are under-represented in the workforce, the authority could consider using "positive action" (see the glossary). This allows employers and others to target their job training and recruitment efforts at those groups that are under-represented in a particular area of work. However, positive action does not allow discrimination when deciding who will be offered a job.

Ethnic categories and the 2001 census

5.13. Public authorities are encouraged to use the same ethnic classification system as the one used in the 2001 census. Some authorities already have systems in place. If an authority chooses to collect more detailed information, it should make sure that the categories are the same as, or similar to, those used in the 2001 census. Any extra ethnic categories it adds to reflect its particular circumstances should fit in with the 2001 census categories.

5.14. Public authorities should make realistic and timetabled plans to adapt their ethnic monitoring systems to meet the specific duties.

5.15. The 2001 census used different ethnic classifications for England and Wales, and Scotland.

PART III
PROMOTING RACE EQUALITY IN EDUCATIONAL INSTITUTIONS

6—SPECIFIC DUTIES: EDUCATIONAL INSTITUTIONS

Introduction

[4.255]

6.1. This part of the code is written mainly for education providers. They are as follows.

(a) The governing bodies of maintained schools (see the glossary) and other educational institutions maintained by a local education authority (LEA) – in other words, all community, foundation and voluntary schools, and special schools maintained by the LEA.

(b) The governing bodies of City Technology Colleges, City Colleges for Technology or the Arts, and City Academies.

(c) The governing bodies of further education institutions (see the glossary).

(d) The governing bodies of higher education institutions (see the glossary).

6.2. Schools and further and higher education institutions must all meet the general duty. Chapter 3 explains what they need to do to meet the duty. The Home Secretary has also placed specific duties on schools (see 6.7–6.22), and on further and higher education institutions (see 6.23–6.44), to help them to meet the general duty.

6.3. The specific duties on employment, described in chapter 5, do not apply directly to schools. The main responsibility for monitoring employment rests with LEAs. All schools are expected to give their LEA ethnic monitoring data on their staff from their regular returns, so that the LEA can meet the duty.

6.4. Further and higher education institutions have other employment duties, which are described in paragraphs 6.39 to 6.41. As well as these duties, further and higher education institutions will have to give bodies such as the higher education funding councils (see 6.45–6.48 for details of the specific duties placed on these bodies), monitoring information about their teaching staff.

6.5. The aim of the general duty is to make race equality central to the way public authorities carry out their functions (see the glossary). Promoting race equality should be a central part of all policy development, service delivery and employment practice.

6.6–6.22. (*Outside the scope of this work.*)

Further and higher education institutions

6.23–6.34. (*Outside the scope of this work.*)

Monitoring admission, recruitment and progress

6.35. Under the duty, further and higher education institutions must monitor, by racial group, student admission and progress, and staff recruitment and career progress (see 6.23).

6.36. Monitoring involves collecting information to measure an institution's performance and effectiveness. The results may suggest how the institution can improve.

6.37. The institution should monitor all stages of the student admissions process, from applications to outcomes. To help interpret the information, the institution might also consider monitoring other areas that could have an adverse impact on students from some racial groups, such as—

(a) choice of subject;

(b) home or international status; and

(c) selection methods.

6.38. The institution should monitor all students' achievements and progress. To help interpret the information, the institution might also consider monitoring other areas that could have an adverse impact on students from some racial groups, such as—

(a) student numbers, transfers and drop-outs;

(b) different methods of assessing students;

(c) work placements;

(d) the results of programmes targeted at people from specific racial groups; and

(e) bullying and racial harassment.

6.39. The institution should monitor all activities that relate to staff recruitment and selection, and to career development and opportunities for promotion. It might consider monitoring for each department as well as the whole institution. This is likely to include—

(a) selecting and training panel members;
(b) applications and appointments;
(c) success rates for the different selection methods;
(d) permanent, temporary or fixed-term appointments; and
(e) home or international status (for institutions that recruit internationally).

6.40. The institution should identify areas where career progress could be affected and monitor those. They might include—
(a) staff, by their grade and type of post;
(b) staff, by their length of service;
(c) staff training and development, including applications and selection, if appropriate;
(d) the results of training and career-development programmes or strategies that target staff from particular racial groups;
(e) staff appraisals; and
(f) staff promotion, including recruitment methods and criteria for choosing candidates.

6.41. The institution will find it useful to assess its monitoring information regularly. This will allow it to evaluate the progress it is making in meeting its race equality targets and aims. These assessments will help the institution to—
(a) highlight any differences between staff and students from different racial groups;
(b) ask why these differences exist;
(c) review how effective its current targets and aims are;
(d) decide what more it can do to improve the performance of students from different racial groups (including positive action as allowed in section 35 of the Race Relations Act; see the glossary) and to improve the recruitment and progression of staff from different racial groups (again including positive action as allowed in sections 37 and 38 of the Race Relations Act; see the glossary); and
(e) decide what further action it may need to take to meet the three parts of the general duty.

6.42–6.44. (*Outside the scope of this work.*)

Employment duties of bodies with specific responsibilities for education

6.45. Local education authorities (LEAs) have a duty to monitor by racial group, for all the maintained schools in their area, the following—
(a) staff in post; and
(b) applicants for employment, training and promotion;
(c) for schools with 150 or more full-time staff, or equivalent, the number of staff—
(i) receiving training;
(ii) benefiting, or suffering a detriment, as a result of performance assessment procedures;
(iii) involved in grievance procedures;
(iv) subject to disciplinary procedures; and
(v) ending employment with these schools.

6.46. LEAs have a duty to take reasonably practicable steps to publish, each year, the results of this monitoring.

6.47. The Department for Education and Skills has a duty to—
(a) monitor, by racial group, the number of teaching staff from each racial group at all maintained schools;
(b) take reasonably practicable steps to use information provided by LEAs for that purpose; and
(c) take reasonably practicable steps to publish, each year, the results of this monitoring.

6.48. The Learning and Skills Council for England, the Higher Education Funding Councils for England and Wales, and the National Council for Education and Training for Wales have a duty to—
(a) monitor, by racial group, the number of teaching staff at all the establishments for which they are responsible; and
(b) take reasonably practicable steps to publish, each year, the results of this monitoring.

PART IV
ROLE OF THE COMMISSION FOR RACIAL EQUALITY

7—ROLE OF THE COMMISSION FOR RACIAL EQUALITY

[4.256]
7.1. The Commission for Racial Equality (CRE) was set up under the Race Relations Act as an independent statutory agency. The CRE reports every year to the Home Secretary, but it is not formally part of the Home Office. The duties of the CRE, as set out in the Act, are to—
(a) work towards eliminating discrimination;
(b) promote equality of opportunity and good relations between persons of different racial groups; and
(c) review the workings of the Act.

7.2. The CRE has both promotional and enforcement powers, and both apply to its work on the duty to promote race equality. This chapter explains how the CRE will use both these powers to help promote race equality.

Partnership

Helping public authorities to meet their duty

7.3. The CRE will—
(a) give practical advice;
(b) work with main parts of the public sector, including the inspectorates, to develop good practice; and
(c) monitor and spread good practice.

Providing practical guidance

7.4. The CRE has issued non-statutory supplementary guides to this code, for public authorities, schools and further and higher education institutions (see appendix 6).

7.5. The CRE will continue to work with public authorities to help them to meet their general and specific duties.

Developing and monitoring good practice

7.6. The CRE works with public authorities to develop and share good practice in a number of ways, for example by—
(a) sharing and demonstrating good practice;
(b) supporting training;
(c) giving information and advice;
(d) updating guidance and publishing other material;
(e) promoting good practice; and
(f) identifying poor practice.

Enforcement

7.7. The CRE is committed to using the full range of its enforcement powers appropriately. The CRE has a new power under the Act to enforce the specific duties to promote race equality.

The general duty

7.8. If a public authority does not meet the general duty, its actions (or failure to act) can be challenged by a claim to the High Court for judicial review (see the glossary). A claim for judicial review can be made by a person or group of people with an interest in the matter, or by the CRE.

Specific duties

7.9. If a public authority does not meet any of its specific duties, it could face enforcement action by the CRE under section 71D of the Race Relations Act.

7.10. If the CRE is satisfied that a public authority has failed (or is failing) to meet any of its specific duties, the CRE can serve a "compliance notice" on that authority. This notice will state that the authority must meet its duty and tell the CRE, within 28 days, what it has done, or is doing, to meet its duty.

7.11. In the compliance notice, the CRE can also ask the authority to give it written information showing that it has met its duty. The notice will state the time by which the CRE should receive the information. The CRE cannot ask for more information than a public authority would have to provide during High Court proceedings in England, or in the Scottish Court of Session.

7.12. If, three months after a compliance notice has been served, the CRE considers that the authority has still not met one or more of its specific duties referred to in the notice, the CRE can apply to the county court (in England) or sheriff court (in Scotland) for an order to obey the notice.

7.13. If the compliance notice says that the authority must provide information, and it has not done so within the given time – or the CRE believes that the authority will not provide the information – the CRE can apply to the county court (in England) or sheriff court (in Scotland) for an order saying that the authority must provide the relevant information.

7.14. The county court or sheriff court may grant the order in the terms that the CRE applied for, or in more limited terms. If the court makes an order and the authority does not keep to it, the authority may be found in contempt of court.

Unlawful discrimination

7.15. The Act gives individuals the right to take legal action against unlawful racial discrimination. The Act also gives the CRE the power to take legal action against certain acts of unlawful discrimination. This power includes the power to carry out formal investigations (see the glossary).

CRE codes of practice

7.16. This and other statutory codes of practice that the CRE issues under the Act are admissible in evidence in court. A court will be expected to take the code of practice into account if it seems relevant to any matter the court is ruling on. Public authorities do not have to follow the guidance in this code of practice. However, they are expected to meet the general duty and any specific duties by which they are bound.

(Appendix 1 (Public authorities bound by the general duty), Appendix 2 (Public authorities required to publish a race equality scheme) omitted: see the introductory notes to this Code.)

APPENDIX 3
PUBLIC AUTHORITIES BOUND BY THE EMPLOYMENT DUTY

MINISTERS OF THE CROWN AND GOVERNMENT DEPARTMENTS

[4.257]
(1) A Minister of the Crown or government department

(2) Sub-paragraph (1) does not include the Security Service, the Intelligence Service or the Government Communications Headquarters

SCOTTISH ADMINISTRATION

(1) An office-holder in the Scottish Administration (within the meaning given by section 126(7)(a) of the Scotland Act 1998)

(2) Members of the staff of the Scottish Administration (within the meaning given by section 126(7)(b) of that Act)

NATIONAL ASSEMBLY FOR WALES

(1) The National Assembly for Wales

(2) An Assembly subsidiary as defined by section 99(4) of the Government of Wales Act 1998

ARMED FORCES

Any of the naval, military or air forces of the Crown

NATIONAL HEALTH SERVICE: ENGLAND AND WALES

A health authority established under section 8 of the National Health Service Act 1977

A National Health Service trust established under section 5 of the National Health Service and Community Care Act 1990

A primary care trust established under section 16A of that Act

A special health authority established under section 11 of that Act

LOCAL GOVERNMENT

A body corporate established pursuant to an order under section 67 of the Local Government Act 1985 (transfer of functions to successors of residuary bodies, etc)

A body corporate established pursuant to an order under section 22 of the Local Government Act 1992 (residuary bodies)

The Broads Authority established by section 1 of the Norfolk and Suffolk Broads Act 1988

Any charter trustees constituted under section 246 of that Act

The Common Council of the City of London in its capacity as a local authority or port health authority

The Council of the Isles of Scilly

A fire authority constituted by a combination scheme under section 5 or 6 of the Fire Services Act 1947

The Greater London Authority

An internal drainage board which is continued in being by virtue of section 1 of the Land Drainage Act 1991

A joint authority established under Part IV of the Local Government Act 1985 (fire services, civil defence and transport)

A joint authority established under section 21 of the Local Government Act 1992

A joint board which is continued in being by virtue of section 263(1) of that Act

A joint committee constituted in accordance with section 102(1)(b) of the Local Government Act 1972

A joint planning board constituted for an area in Wales outside a National Park by an order under section 2(1B) of the Town and Country Planning Act 1990

A local authority (within the meaning of the Local Government Act 1972), namely
(a) in England, a county council, a London borough council, a district council;
(b) in Wales, a county council, a county borough council

A local probation board established under section 4 of the Criminal Justice and Court Services Act 2000

The London Development Agency

The London Fire and Emergency Planning Authority

A magistrates' courts committee established under section 27 of the Justices of the Peace Act 1997

A national park authority established by an order under section 63 of the Environment Act 1995

A passenger transport executive for a passenger transport area (within the meaning of Part II of the Transport Act 1968)

A port health authority constituted by an order under section 2 of the Public Health (Control of Disease) Act 1984

A regional development agency established under the Regional Development Agencies Act 1998 (other than the London Development Agency)

The Sub-Treasurer of the Inner Temple or the Under-Treasurer of the Middle Temple, in his capacity as a local authority

Transport for London

A waste disposal authority established by virtue of an order under section 10(1) of the Local Government Act 1985

EDUCATION

The Adult Learning Inspectorate

The British Educational Communication and Technology Agency

The Construction Industry Training Board

The Engineering Construction Industry Training Board

The General Teaching Council for Scotland

The General Teaching Council for Wales

The Higher Education Funding Council for England

The Higher Education Funding Council for Wales

The Learning and Skills Council for England

The managers of a grant-aided school (within the meaning of section 135 of the Education (Scotland) Act 1980)

The National Council for Education and Training for Wales

The Qualifications and Curriculum Authority

The Qualifications, Curriculum and Assessment Authority for Wales

The Student Loans Company

The Teacher Training Agency

HOUSING BODIES

A housing action trust established under Part III of the Housing Act 1988

The Housing Corporation

POLICE

The British Transport Police

A chief constable of a police force maintained under section 2 of the Police Act 1996

The Chief Constable for the Ministry of Defence Police appointed by the Secretary of State under section 1(3) of the Ministry of Defence Police Act 1987

The Commissioner of Police for the City of London

The Commissioner of Police of the Metropolis

The Common Council of the City of London in its capacity as a police authority

The Metropolitan Police Authority established under section 5B of the Police Act 1996

A police authority established under section 3 of the Police Act 1996

The Police Complaints Authority

The Police Information Technology Organisation

A selection panel for independent members of police authorities

The Service Authority for the National Crime Squad

The Service Authority for the National Criminal Intelligence Service

HEALTH

The Commission for Health Improvement

The Council for Professions Supplementary to Medicine, in respect of its public functions

The Dental Practice Board

The English National Board for Nursing, Midwifery and Health Visiting

The Human Fertilisation and Embryology Authority

The Joint Committee on Postgraduate Training for General Practice

The National Biological Standards Board

The Public Health Laboratory Service Board

The Royal College of Anaesthetists, in respect of its public functions

The Royal College of General Practitioners, in respect of its public functions

The Royal College of Midwives, in respect of its public functions

The Royal College of Nursing, in respect of its public functions

The Royal College of Obstetricians and Gynaecologists, in respect of its public functions

The Royal College of Ophthalmologists, in respect of its public functions

The Royal College of Paediatrics and Child Health, in respect of its public functions

The Royal College of Pathologists, in respect of its public functions

The Royal College of Physicians, in respect of its public functions

The Royal College of Psychiatrists, in respect of its public functions

The Royal College of Radiologists, in respect of its public functions

The Royal College of Speech and Language Therapists, in respect of its public functions

The Royal College of Surgeons of England, in respect of its public functions

The Specialist Training Authority of the Medical Royal Colleges

The Welsh National Board for Nursing, Midwifery and Health Visiting

LIBRARIES, MUSEUMS AND ARTS

The Arts Council of England

The Arts Council of Wales

The British Library

The British Museum

The British Tourist Authority

The Commission for Architecture and the Built Environment

The Countryside Council for Wales The Design Council

English Nature

The English Tourist Board

The Film Council

The Geffrye Museum

The Historic Buildings and Monuments Commission for England

The Historic Royal Palaces Trust

The Horniman Museum

The Imperial War Museum

The Library and Information Services Council (Wales)

The Millennium Commission

The Museum of London

The Museum of Science and Industry in Manchester

The National Endowment for Science, Technology and the Arts

The National Gallery

The National Heritage Memorial Fund

The National Library of Wales

The National Lottery Charities Board

The National Maritime Museum

National Museums and Galleries on Merseyside

National Museums and Galleries of Wales

The National Portrait Gallery

The Natural History Museum

The Registrar of Public Lending Right Resource: The Council for Museums, Archives and Libraries

The Royal Armouries

The Royal Botanic Gardens, Kew

The Royal Commission on Ancient and Historical Monuments of Wales

The Royal Commission on Historical Manuscripts

The Science Museum

Sir John Soane's Museum

Sport England

The Sports Council for Wales

The Tate Gallery

The UK Sports Council

The Victoria and Albert Museum

The Wales Tourist Board

The Wallace Collection

PUBLIC CORPORATIONS AND NATIONALISED INDUSTRIES

The Bank of England, in respect of its public functions

The British Broadcasting Corporation, in respect of its public functions

The Broadcasting Standards Commission, in respect of its public functions

The Channel Four Television Corporation, in respect of its public functions

The Civil Aviation Authority

The Coal Authority

The Covent Garden Market Authority

A Customer Service Committee maintained under section 28 of the Water Industry Act 1991

The Independent Television Commission, in respect of its public functions

The Radio Authority, in respect of its public functions

Sianel Pedwar Cymru (Welsh Fourth Channel Authority), in respect of its public functions

The United Kingdom Atomic Energy Authority, in respect of its public functions

REGULATORY, AUDIT AND INSPECTION

The Advisory, Conciliation and Arbitration Service (ACAS)

The Association of Authorised Public Accountants

The Association of Certified Chartered Accountants

The Association of Child Psychotherapy

The Audit Commission for Local Authorities and the National Health Service in England and Wales

The British Hallmarking Council

The British Standards Institute

The Chartered Institute of Patent Agents, in respect of its public functions

The Council for Licensed Conveyancers, in respect of its public functions

The Engineering Council

The Financial Services Authority

The General Chiropractic Council

The General Council of the Bar of England and Wales, in respect of its public functions

The General Dental Council

The General Medical Council

The General Optical Council

The General Osteopathic Council

The General Social Care Council

The Insolvency Practitioners Association

The Institute of Chartered Accountants in England and Wales

The Institute of Legal Executives, in respect of its public functions

The Institute of Trade Mark Attorneys

The Law Society of England and Wales, in respect of its public functions

Her Majesty's Magistrates' Courts Service Inspectorate

The Master of the Court of the Faculties of the Archbishop of Canterbury, in respect of its public functions

The National Audit Office

The Royal Pharmaceutical Society of Great Britain, in respect of its statutory functions and the regulation of the pharmacy profession

The United Kingdom Central Council for Nursing, Midwifery and Health Visiting, in respect of its public functions

RESEARCH

The Alcohol Education and Research Council

The Apple and Pear Research Council

The Biotechnology and Biological Sciences Research Council

The Council for the Central Laboratory of the Research Councils

The Economic and Social Research Council

The Engineering and Physical Sciences Research Council

The Fire Service Research and Training Trust

The Horticultural Development Council

The Medical Research Council

The Natural Environment Research Council

The Particle Physics and Astronomy Research Council

OTHER BODIES, ETC

A board of visitors established under section 6(2) of the Prison Act 1952

The Britain-Russia Centre

The British Association for Central and Eastern Europe

The British Council

The British Potato Council

The British Waterways Board

The British Wool Marketing Board

The Children and Family Court Advisory and Support Service

The Commission for Racial Equality

The Community Development Foundation

The Criminal Injuries Compensation Authority

The Disability Rights Commission

The Electoral Commission

English Partnerships

The Environment Agency

The Equal Opportunities Commission

Food From Britain

The Gaming Board for Great Britain

The Gas and Electricity Consumer Council

The Great Britain-China Centre

The Health and Safety Commission

The Health and Safety Executive

The Home-Grown Cereals Authority

The Horserace Betting Levy Board

The Horserace Totalisator Board

The Information Commissioner

Investors in People UK

The Joint Nature Conservation Committee

The Legal Services Commission

The Local Government Commission for England

The Marshall Aid Commemoration Commission

The Meat and Livestock Commission

The Milk Development Council

The National Consumer Council

The National Forest Company

The National Radiological Protection Board

The New Opportunities Fund

The Northern Lighthouse Board

The Oil and Pipelines Agency

The Sea Fish Industry Authority

The Strategic Rail Authority

The Trinity House Lighthouse Service

A visiting committee appointed under section 152 of the Immigration and Asylum Act 1999 for an immigration detention centre

The Welsh Development Agency

The Welsh Language Board

The Westminster Foundation for Democracy

The Wine Standards Board of the Vintners' Company

The Youth Justice Board for England and Wales.

(Appendix 4 (Public authorities bound by the duties for educational institutions), Appendix 5 (Scottish public authorities), Appendix 6 (Other guidance published by the CRE) omitted: see the introductory notes to this Code.)

EQUAL OPPORTUNITIES COMMISSION CODE OF PRACTICE ON EQUAL PAY (2003) (NOTE)

[4.258]

NOTES

This Code was a re-issue, significantly expanded and rewritten, of the Equal Opportunities Commission's 1997 Code of Practice on Equal Pay. It came into effect on 1 December 2003 (see the Code of Practice on Equal Pay Order 2003, SI 2003/2865) and was issued under the Sex Discrimination Act 1975, s 56A (repealed as noted below).

The statutory provision under which this Code was made was repealed by the Equality Act 2006, ss 40, 91, Sch 3, paras 6, 11, Sch 4; however the Code was continued in force by s 42(3) of the 2006 Act (see **[1.1388]**).

The Code was finally revoked (with effect from 6 April 2011) by the Former Equality Commissions' Codes of Practice (Employment, Equal Pay, and Rights of Access for Disabled Persons) (Revocation) Order 2011, SI 2011/776, art 2. Article 3 of the 2011 Order makes transitional provision for proceedings arising from alleged contraventions of previous discrimination legislation saved in respect of insurance business in relation to existing insurance policies, or occurring wholly before 1 October 2010, or so far as the previous legislation relates to work on ships, work on hovercraft and seafarers (until Regulations under s 81 of the Equality Act 2010 come into force). The 2003 Code continues to have effect in relation to such proceedings for the purposes of s 15(4)(b) of the Equality Act 2006, which requires a court or tribunal to take a code into account in any case in which it appears to the court or tribunal to be relevant. With regard to work on ships, work on hovercraft and seafarers, note that the Equality Act 2010 (Work on Ships and Hovercraft) Regulations 2011, SI 2011/1771 (made under s 81 of the 2010 Act) came into force on 15 August 2011.

The 2003 Code is omitted for reasons of space. See now the EHRC's Code of Practice on Equal Pay at **[4.134]**.

DISABILITY RIGHTS COMMISSION CODE OF PRACTICE: EMPLOYMENT AND OCCUPATION (2004) (NOTE)

[4.259]

NOTES

This Code of Practice was prepared by the Disability Rights Commission in 2004, under the powers conferred on it by the Disability Discrimination Act 1995, s 53A (inserted by the Disability Rights Commission Act 1999 and repealed as noted below). It replaced the former (1996) Code produced by the then Department for Education and Employment, which was revoked by SI 2004/2300. The Code was approved by the Secretary of State and by Parliament in accordance with s 53A (see the Disability Discrimination Codes of Practice (Employment and Occupation, and Trade Organisations and Qualifications Bodies) Appointed Day Order 2004, SI 2004/2302) and came into effect on 1 October 2004.

The statutory provision under which this Code was made was repealed by the Equality Act 2006, ss 40, 91, Sch 3, paras 41, 52, Sch 4; however the Code was continued in force by s 42(3) of the 2006 Act (see **[1.1388]**).

The Code was finally revoked (with effect from 6 April 2011) by the Former Equality Commissions' Codes of Practice (Employment, Equal Pay, and Rights of Access for Disabled Persons) (Revocation) Order 2011, SI 2011/776, art 2. Article 3 of the 2011 Order makes transitional provision for proceedings arising from alleged contraventions of previous discrimination legislation saved in respect of insurance business in relation to existing insurance policies, or occurring wholly before 1 October 2010, or so far as the previous legislation relates to work on ships, work on hovercraft and seafarers (until Regulations under s 81 of the Equality Act 2010 come into force). The 2004 Code continues to have effect in relation to such proceedings for the purposes of s 15(4)(b) of the Equality Act 2006, which requires a court or tribunal to take a code into account in any case in which it appears to the court or tribunal to be relevant. With regard to work on ships, work on hovercraft and seafarers, note that the Equality Act 2010 (Work on Ships and Hovercraft) Regulations 2011, SI 2011/1771 (made under s 81 of the 2010 Act) came into force on 15 August 2011.

The 2004 Code is omitted for reasons of space. See now the EHRC's Code of Practice on Employment at **[4.138]**.

COMMISSION FOR RACIAL EQUALITY: CODE OF PRACTICE ON RACIAL EQUALITY IN EMPLOYMENT (2005) (NOTE)

[4.260]

NOTES

This Code of Practice was issued by the Commission for Racial Equality under the Race Relations Act 1976, s 47 (repealed as noted below) in November 2005 and came into effect on 6 April 2006 (see the Race Relations Code of Practice relating to Employment (Appointed Day) Order 2006, SI 2006/630).

The statutory provision under which this Code was made was repealed by the Equality Act 2006, ss 40, 91, Sch 3, paras 21, 26, Sch 4, however the Code was continued in force by s 42(3) of the 2006 Act (see **[1.1388]**); its legal effect was provided for by s 15(4) of the 2006 Act at **[1.1364]**.

The Code was finally revoked (with effect from 6 April 2011) by the Former Equality Commissions' Codes of Practice (Employment, Equal Pay, and Rights of Access for Disabled Persons) (Revocation) Order 2011, SI 2011/776, art 2. Article 3 of the 2011 Order makes transitional provision for proceedings arising from alleged contraventions of previous discrimination legislation saved in respect of insurance business in relation to existing insurance policies, or occurring wholly before 1 October 2010, or so far as the previous legislation relates to work on ships, work on hovercraft and seafarers (until Regulations under s 81 of the Equality Act 2010 come into force). The 2005 Code continues to have effect in relation to such proceedings for the purposes of s 15(4)(b) of the Equality Act 2006, which requires a court or tribunal to take a code into account in any case in which it appears to the court or tribunal to be relevant. With regard to work on ships, work on hovercraft and seafarers, note that the Equality Act 2010 (Work on Ships and Hovercraft) Regulations 2011, SI 2011/1771 (made under s 81 of the 2010 Act) came into force on 15 August 2011.

The 2005 Code is omitted for reasons of space. See now the EHRC's Code of Practice on Employment at **[4.138]**.

EQUAL OPPORTUNITIES COMMISSION: GENDER EQUALITY DUTY CODE OF PRACTICE ENGLAND AND WALES (2007)

[4.261]

NOTES

This Code of Practice was issued by the Equal Opportunities Commission under the Sex Discrimination Act 1975, s 76E(1) (repealed as noted below), and was brought into effect, on 6 April 2007, by the Sex Discrimination Code of Practice (Public Authorities) (Duty to Promote Equality) (Appointed Day) Order 2007, SI 2007/741.

The statutory provision under which this Code was made was repealed by the Equality Act 2006, ss 40, 91, Sch 3, paras 6, 16, Sch 4, however the Code is continued in force by s 42(3) of the 2006 Act (see **[1.1388]**); its legal effect is provided for by s 15(4) of the 2006 Act at **[1.1364]**.

The statutory duties imposed by the Sex Discrimination Act 1975 have been replaced by a general statutory duty in relation to equal treatment under the Equality Act 2010, s 149, and it was originally intended that this Code would be replaced by a new Code under s 149 of the 2010 Act. However, the Equality and Human Rights Commission has subsequently announced that the Secretary of State is unlikely to approve a new statutory code, and that the new Guidance would be issued on a non-statutory basis. The new Guidance on the equality duty for England, Wales and Scotland is on the EHRC website at: www.equalityhumanrights.com/advice-and-guidance/public-sector-equality-duty/guidance-on-the-equality-duty/.

Only those parts of the Code of particular relevance to employment law are reproduced. The following are omitted: Foreword; paras 2.53–2.61; paras 3.57–3.74; Chapters 4–6; Appendices C–G.

The equivalent Code for Scotland ('Gender Equality Duty Code of Practice for Scotland') is omitted for reasons of space. It applies to those bodies subject to the authority of the Scottish Parliament.

CONTENTS

CHAPTER 1: OVERVIEW OF THE GENDER EQUALITY DUTY

WHAT THIS CODE IS AND HOW TO USE IT

[4.262]

1.1. This Code of Practice (the Code) gives practical guidance to public authorities on how to meet the legal requirements of the gender equality duty. The Equal Opportunities Commission (EOC) has prepared and issued this Code under the Sex Discrimination Act 1975, as amended by the Equality Act 2006. The Code is expected to come into effect on April 6 2007.

1.2. Those parts of the Code which deal with the general gender equality duty in section 76A of the Sex Discrimination Act 1975 apply (subject to the exceptions set out in Appendix B) to all public authorities in England and Wales and to reserved functions of public authorities in Scotland. A similar but separate code applies to Scotland. Those parts of the Code (primarily Chapter 3) which deal with the specific duties imposed by the Sex Discrimination Act 1975 (Public Authorities) (Statutory Duties) Order 2006 (the Order) apply only to the public authorities listed in the Schedule to that Order. This does not include authorities all of whose functions are public functions in relation to Wales.

1.3. This Code of Practice is a 'statutory' code and has been laid before Parliament before taking effect. This means that the Code is admissible in evidence in any legal action under the Sex Discrimination Act 1975 or the Equal Pay Act 1970, in criminal or civil proceedings before any court or tribunal.

1.4. A court or tribunal must take into account any part of the Code that appears to them to be relevant to any question arising in the proceedings. This includes the question of whether public authorities have breached the law. A tribunal or court may draw an adverse inference that a breach of the law has occurred if a public authority has failed to follow relevant provisions in the Code. If a public authority does not follow the Code's provisions, it will need to show how it has otherwise met its legal obligations under the general duty and any specific duties.

1.5. On its own, the Code does not impose any legal obligations on public authorities. The Code is not a complete statement of the law – only the courts can give this.

1.6. References to the Sex Discrimination Act 1975 (SDA), the Equal Pay Act 1970 (EqPA) and the Equality Act 2006 are shown in the margins.

1.7. Where examples are used, they are intended to illustrate the ways in which different types of public authorities can comply with the duty. They should be read in that light, and not as authoritative statements of the law. Where examples are taken from the voluntary sector, they are intended to illustrate gender equality issues and possible means of addressing them, not to imply that those bodies are covered by the gender duty.

1.8. The EOC will be issuing non-statutory guidance to supplement this Code, to cover particular parts of the public sector, aspects of the duty such as gender impact assessment and how the duty applies to procurement.

WHAT IS THE GENDER EQUALITY DUTY?

1.9. The Equality Act 2006 amends the SDA to place a statutory duty on all public authorities, when carrying out their functions, to have due regard to the need:

- to eliminate unlawful discrimination and harassment
- to promote equality of opportunity between men and women.

1.10. This is known as the 'general duty' and will come into effect on 6 April 2007.

1.11. The duty applies to all public authorities in respect of all of their functions (with limited exceptions described in Appendix B). This means it applies to policy-making, service provision, employment matters, and in relation to enforcement or any statutory discretion and decision-making. It also applies to a public authority in relation to services and functions which are contracted out. In addition, it applies to private and voluntary bodies which are carrying out public functions, but only in respect of those functions. For examples of the kind of public authorities which are covered, see Appendix A.

1.12. Public authorities are expected to have 'due regard' to the need to eliminate unlawful discrimination and harassment and promote equality of opportunity between men and women in all of their functions. Due regard comprises two linked elements: proportionality and relevance. The weight which public authorities give to gender equality should therefore be proportionate to its relevance to a particular function. The greater the relevance of a function to gender equality, the greater regard which should be paid to it. For more detail on due regard and the component parts of the duty, see Chapter 2, paragraphs 2.1–2.16 and 2.21–2.32.

1.13. As part of the duty, public authorities are required to have due regard to the need to eliminate unlawful discrimination and harassment in employment and vocational training (including further and higher education), for people who intend to undergo, are undergoing or have undergone gender reassignment. For the purposes of this Code, the expression 'transsexual people' is used to refer to the people who are covered by those provisions. For more detail, see Chapter 2, paragraphs 2.17–2.20.

1.14. To support progress in delivering the general duty, there is also a series of 'specific duties' which apply to listed public authorities as laid out in the Order in Appendix C. The Order sets out steps those authorities must take to help them meet the general duty.

1.15. Those specific duties, in brief, are:

- **To prepare and publish a gender equality scheme**, showing how it will meet its general and specific duties and setting out its gender equality objectives.
- In formulating its overall objectives, **to consider the need to include objectives to address the causes of any gender pay gap.**
- **To gather and use information** on how the public authority's policies and practices affect gender equality in the workforce and in the delivery of services.
- **To consult stakeholders (ie employees, service users and others, including trade unions) and take account of relevant information** in order to determine its gender equality objectives.
- **To assess the impact of its current and proposed policies and practices** on gender equality.
- **To implement the actions set out in its scheme** within three years, unless it is unreasonable or impracticable to do so.
- **To report** against the scheme every year and **review** the scheme at least every three years.

1.16. The first scheme must be published by 30 April 2007. For more detail on these specific duties and how to meet them, see Chapter 3.

1.17. This document contains guidance on how to meet both the general and the specific duties in Chapters 2 and 3. Even if a public authority is not subject to the specific duties (such as public authorities operating solely in Wales), it will still be expected to provide clear evidence of meeting the general duty. The specific duties laid out in Chapter 3 can act as a framework to assist authorities in complying with the general duty.

WHY HAS THE GENDER EQUALITY DUTY BEEN INTRODUCED?

1.18. The gender equality duty aims to make gender equality central to the way that public authorities work, in order to create:

- better-informed decision-making and policy development
- a clearer understanding of the needs of service users
- better-quality services which meet varied needs
- more effective targeting of policy and resources
- better results and greater confidence in public services
- a more effective use of talent in the workforce.

1.19. The duty is intended to address the fact that, despite 30 years of individual legal rights to sex equality, there is still widespread discrimination – sometimes intentional, sometimes unintentional – and persistent gender inequality. Policies and practices that seem neutral can have a significantly different effect on women and on men, often contributing to greater gender inequality and poor policy outcomes. Individual legal rights have not been enough by themselves to change this.

1.20. The duty is intended to improve this situation, both for men and for women, for boys and for girls. Gender roles and relationships structure men's and women's lives. Women are frequently disadvantaged by policies and practices that do not recognise their greater caring responsibilities, the different pattern of their working lives, their more limited access to resources and their greater vulnerability to domestic violence and sexual assault. Men are also disadvantaged by workplace cultures that do not support their family or childcare responsibilities, by family services that assume they have little or no role in parenting, or by health services which do not recognise their different needs. Both sexes suffer from stereotyping of their roles and needs. The duty should help the public sector, and those working with it, to identify and respond to stereotyping, sex discrimination and sexism, resulting in improvements for all.

1.21. The duty requires public authorities to identify and tackle discrimination, to prevent harassment, and to ensure that their work promotes equality of opportunity between men and women. It is a form of legally enforceable 'gender mainstreaming' – building gender equality into the core business thinking and processes of an organisation. It is different from previous sex equality legislation in two crucial respects:

- public authorities have to be proactive in eliminating discrimination and harassment, rather than waiting for individuals to take cases against them.
- public authorities have to be proactive in promoting equality of opportunity, and not just avoiding discrimination.

OUTCOMES – THE CHANGES TO WHICH THE GENDER EQUALITY DUTY SHOULD LEAD

1.22. The aim of the duty is not to establish processes but to make visible and faster progress towards gender equality. Indicators of progress might include:

- Service-users notice that services are more accessible and better tailored to their needs, and service outcomes by gender begin to improve.
- Women and men are making greater use of services that their sex had previously under-used.
- Service-users with caring responsibilities are receiving appropriate support, such as better pushchair access on public transport and crèche facilities for trainees.
- Fathers receive greater support for their childcare responsibilities from public services and employers.
- Girls have higher aspirations for their future careers.
- Women and men from all groups feel effectively engaged in decision and policy-making around issues that have a direct effect on them.
- Women and men are represented at all levels of the workforce and in all areas of work.
- Harassment and sexual harassment of staff, service users and others is dealt with promptly and systematically, according to agreed procedures, and tolerance of harassment drops within the organisation as a whole.
- The reported level of discrimination experienced by pregnant staff and staff returning from maternity leave reduces significantly and is eventually eliminated.
- The gap between women and men's pay narrows and is eventually eliminated.
- Employees with caring responsibilities are receiving greater support from the public authority, including flexible and part-time working opportunities at all levels of work.
- Transsexual people feel supported and valued as staff and potential staff.
- Barriers to the recruitment and retention of transsexual staff have been identified and removed.
- Employees are aware of the gender equality duty, understand how it will affect their work, and have the skills to implement the duty in their work.

- Gender equality issues, and their budgetary implications, are considered at the beginning of policy-making.
- It is easy to find a wide variety of data and information to assess effectively how certain actions will affect women and men.

HOW THE GENDER EQUALITY DUTY FITS INTO THE BROADER EQUALITY PICTURE

1.23. Women and men, including transsexual women and men, will experience different forms of disadvantage depending on their age, ethnicity, religion or belief, sexual orientation, marital or civil partnership status, and whether or not they have a disability. In order to understand and address questions of gender equality under the duty, public authorities may need to consider that complexity and whether particular groups of women or men are experiencing particular disadvantages.

> Only 47% of disabled women are in employment, compared with 53% of disabled men. Of the disabled women in employment, only 52% work full-time. This compares with an employment rate of 75% for non-disabled women and 86% for non-disabled men. (EOC Facts about women and men in Great Britain 2005)

1.24. The gender equality duty is similar to the existing duties on race and disability equality and all three have the same spirit and intention behind them, requiring public authorities to take action to tackle discrimination, to prevent harassment, and to ensure that their work promotes equality of opportunity across all their functions. The gender equality duty has fewer requirements to set up processes than the race duty, however, in order to ensure that public authorities focus on the achievement of outcomes.

1.25. The gender equality scheme, which is a requirement for listed public authorities under the specific duties, can be published as part of an overall equality scheme, covering the requirements of all three duties. There are, however, slight differences in the requirements of the three duties. Public authorities which choose to take the overall equality scheme approach must ensure that they clearly meet the requirements of the gender equality duty, including specific objectives on gender equality. The scheme should show clearly and specifically which elements of the overall equality scheme refer to gender equality.

WHICH ORGANISATIONS HAVE TO TAKE ACTION ON THE GENERAL DUTY?

S76A Sex Discrimination Act (margin note)

1.26. The general duty applies to all functions of every public authority (bar the exceptions listed in Appendix B). The definition of a public authority is 'any person who has functions of a public nature'. Despite a slight difference in the wording, this is the same approach as the definition of public authorities covered by the Disability Discrimination Act 2005 and the Human Rights Act 1998.

1.27. Because the duty is based on this definition, public authorities covered by the general gender duty are not individually listed. The duty would apply to all of the authorities listed in Schedule 1A to the amended Race Relations Act 1976. Further details on the definition of a public authority are contained in Appendix A.

1.28. The gender duty can also apply directly to certain private or voluntary sector bodies when they are carrying out public functions (the private functions of such bodies being excluded). Further details of who is affected by this are contained in Appendix A.

WHICH PUBLIC AUTHORITIES HAVE TO TAKE ACTION ON THE SPECIFIC DUTIES?

1.29. To find out whether a public authority is covered, check the list at Appendix D. The list will be subject to periodic updating by Government, the relevant order being available on the Stationery Office website.

HOW WILL THE GENDER EQUALITY DUTY BE ENFORCED?

1.30. The general duty is enforceable by judicial review. Any person or body affected by a failure to comply with the general duty by a public authority may take action through judicial review proceedings.

S32 Equality Act (margin note)

1.31. From late 2007, the Commission for Equality and Human Rights (CEHR) will have the power to conduct formal assessments and to issue compliance notices in connection with a breach of the general duty which will be enforceable in the courts.

S76D SDA (margin note)

1.32. The CEHR and EOC will have the power to issue compliance notices in respect of the specific duties. For more detail see Chapter 4.

1.33. In addition it is likely that relevant inspection bodies will require evidence of compliance with the general and specific duties.

FUTURE CHANGES IN THE LEGISLATION

1.34. There may be changes in the future to the sex equality legislation which will affect the definition of unlawful discrimination and harassment under the duty. Public authorities will need to ensure that they keep up-to-date with any developments which affect the duties explained in this Code. Relevant information will be publicised by the EOC on the gender duty section of their website, and will be available from the CEHR in the future. This Code will remain in force after the dissolution of the EOC, however, until the CEHR updates it.

WHERE TO OBTAIN FURTHER INFORMATION NOW AND IN THE FUTURE

1.35. Copies of the Sex Discrimination Act, the Equal Pay Act, the Equality Act and the orders or regulations made under them can be obtained from the Stationery Office. The text of this Code and of the Equal Pay Code of Practice can be downloaded free of charge from the EOC's website on www.eoc.org.uk. There is also supporting guidance available on the EOC website.

1.36. Free information on the duty is available through the EOC Helpline on 0845 601 5901 or by email on info@eoc.org.uk.

1.37. The Equality Act also provides for the dissolution of the EOC and the passing of its functions to the CEHR. This is currently expected to happen in late 2007. Once this transition has occurred, promotion and enforcement of the gender equality duty will pass to the CEHR.

CHAPTER 2: HOW TO MEET THE GENERAL DUTY

INTRODUCTION

[4.263]
2.1. All public authorities and private and voluntary bodies carrying out public functions on behalf of a public authority are subject to the general duty, and this Chapter explains how to meet it.

2.2. All public authorities are legally required, when exercising their functions, to have due regard to the need:

- to eliminate discrimination and harassment that is unlawful under the Sex Discrimination Act 1975 (SDA) and discrimination that is unlawful under the Equal Pay Act 1970 (EqPA)
- to promote equality of opportunity between men and women.

2.3. This means that the duty is not a negative or passive one, but requires public authorities to adopt a proactive approach to meeting the duty. When the EOC (and subsequently the CEHR) and public sector inspectorates are monitoring and evaluating compliance with this duty, they will be looking for evidence of action and positive change. Without such evidence, it will be difficult to establish that the authority is meeting the gender equality duty.

2.4. Smaller public authorities will have fewer resources and this will affect the steps which they take to ensure compliance with the general duty.

HOW THE DIFFERENT PARTS OF THE DUTY WORK TOGETHER

2.5. As stated above the general duty has three parts:

- eliminating unlawful discrimination
- eliminating harassment
- promoting equality of opportunity between men and women

2.6. These three parts support each other, and in practice may overlap. For example, promoting equality of opportunity may also eliminate or prevent unlawful discrimination and harassment. It is important to remember, however, that the three parts are different, and that achieving on one may not lead to achieving all three. Public authorities should consider and deal with all three parts of the gender duty.

UNLAWFUL DISCRIMINATION

2.7. Unlawful discrimination includes discrimination as defined by the SDA, and discrimination that is unlawful under the EqPA. Public authorities are legally required to have due regard to the need to eliminate both forms of discrimination.

2.8. In the SDA, unlawful discrimination is defined as:

- direct and indirect discrimination on grounds of sex
- discrimination on the grounds of pregnancy and maternity leave
- discrimination on the grounds of gender reassignment
- direct and indirect discrimination against married persons and civil partners
- victimisation
- harassment and sexual harassment.

Further details of the above definitions and where they apply can be found in Appendix E.

In the employment field, the SDA prohibits discrimination in non-contractual pay and benefits, such as discretionary bonuses. Sex discrimination related to contractual pay and benefits is dealt with under the EqPA.

2.9. The EqPA (read in the light of article 141 of the Treaty of Rome) gives an individual a right to the same contractual pay and benefits as a person of the opposite sex in the same employment, or where the source of the pay is the same, where the man and the woman are doing:

- the same or broadly similar work
- work which has been rated as equivalent under an analytical job evaluation study
- work that is of equal value (work of equal value is where the work done is different but considered to be of equal value or worth in terms of demands such as effort, skill and decision-making).

A public authority can pay a man more than a woman (or vice versa) in such circumstances if there is a genuine and material factor for doing so which is not attributable to direct or indirect sex discrimination.

HARASSMENT AND SEXUAL HARASSMENT

2.10. Harassment and sexual harassment are unlawful under the SDA and the duty requires public authorities to have due regard to the need to eliminate them. The duty to have due regard to the need to promote equality of opportunity between men and women is also relevant to ensuring that harassment is prevented before it occurs.

2.11. Different legal definitions apply, depending on whether the harassment occurs in:

- employment and related fields, vocational training (including further and higher education) and in the exercise of public functions; or
- schools, the provision of goods, facilities or services, or in the disposal or management of premises.

Appendix E explains the definitions of harassment. Paragraphs 2.69–2.77 provide information on how to meet the duty to have due regard to the need to eliminate harassment.

THE PROMOTION OF EQUALITY OF OPPORTUNITY BETWEEN MEN AND WOMEN

2.12. The term 'sex' is used to describe biological differences between women and men. The term 'gender' refers to the wider social roles and relationships which structure men's and women's lives. Gender inequality exists in all aspects of society and refers to lasting and embedded patterns of advantage and disadvantage.

2.13. The duty on public authorities to have due regard to the need to promote equality of opportunity between men and women is a new aspect of the SDA. In order to achieve actual equality of opportunity, it is necessary to recognise that in certain circumstances women and men, because of their sex or gender roles, are not in the same position. In some circumstances it may therefore be appropriate for public authorities to treat women and men differently, if that action is aimed at overcoming previous disadvantage.

2.14. For example, where one sex is under-represented in particular work, a public authority could promote equality of opportunity by taking positive action to encourage members of the under-represented sex to apply for such work, or to provide training to equip the under-represented sex for such work. It would not, however, be lawful to discriminate in favour of one sex in the actual appointments procedure. See Chapter 6 for more detail.

2.15. As another example, women make up the substantial majority of victims of domestic violence and rape. It would not be appropriate, therefore, for a local council to seek to fund refuge services on a numerically equal basis for men and for women. The promotion of equal opportunities between men and women requires public authorities to recognise that the two groups are not starting from an equal footing and identical treatment would not be appropriate.

2.16. In some instances, promoting equality of opportunity may require separate provision to be offered, as an alternative approach to improve take-up of services by the under-represented sex, where this is permitted under the SDA. An example of this might be to encourage men to increase their low take-up of primary health care services. For more detail, see Chapter 6 on single-sex activities.

THE GENDER EQUALITY DUTY AND GENDER REASSIGNMENT

2.17. The gender equality duty requires public authorities to have due regard to the need to eliminate unlawful discrimination and harassment against transsexual people in the fields of employment and vocational training (including further and higher education). This section gives further details on issues relating to the gender duty and gender reassignment.

S2A SDA (margin note)

2.18. The SDA provides that people who intend to undergo, are undergoing or have undergone gender reassignment are protected against discrimination and harassment in the fields of employment and related areas and in vocational training (including further and higher education). This means that public authorities must have due regard to the need to eliminate unlawful discrimination and harassment in those fields against transsexual people when discharging their gender duty.

2.19. The scope of legal protection against discrimination on grounds of gender reassignment will be extended in the SDA, by 21 December 2007, by the implementation of the Goods and Services Directive 2004/113. As a matter of domestic law, as a consequence, by that date (or the date of implementation if earlier), public authorities will be under a duty to have due regard to the need to eliminate unlawful discrimination and harassment on grounds of gender reassignment in the provision of goods and services.

2.20. Public authorities may wish to take the need to have due regard to the need to eliminate gender reassignment discrimination and harassment into account when discharging their gender equality duty in relation to the provision of goods and services, before they are required to do so following the implementation of the Goods and Services Directive.

WHAT DOES THE GENERAL DUTY MEAN? DUE REGARD, PROPORTIONALITY AND RELEVANCE

S76A SDA (margin note)

2.21. Public authorities will be expected to have due regard to the need to eliminate unlawful discrimination and harassment and promote equality of opportunity between women and men in relation to all their functions and to provide evidence that they have done so. This includes their core functions of policy development, service design and delivery, decision-making and employment, the exercise of statutory discretion, enforcement and any services and functions which have been contracted out. For details on contracted-out services see Chapter 5 on procurement.

2.22. Having due regard means that the weight given to the need to promote gender equality is **proportionate** to its **relevance** to a particular function. In practice, this principle will mean public authorities should prioritise action to address the most significant gender inequalities within their remit, and take actions which are likely to deliver the best gender equality outcomes. This is likely to mean focusing on functions or policies that have most effect on the public, or on the authority's employees, or on a section of the public or on a section of the authority's employees. The authority should ask whether particular functions could affect women and men in different ways, and whether functions can be carried out in a way which promotes equality of opportunity between men and women.

2.23. The general duty applies to public authorities whatever their size, but the way in which it is implemented should be appropriate to the size of the authority and its functions. For example, a primary school may wish to train its staff in gender equality in order to meet the duty, but does not have sufficient budget to meet this training need alongside other competing needs. It decides to meet the duty by arranging gender equality training for the head teacher, who then runs a feedback session for staff and governors at the next in-service training day. This could be a proportionate means of meeting the duty.

2.24. Gender equality will be more relevant to some functions than others. Relevance is about how much a function affects people's gender equality, as members of the public or as employees of the authority. For example, a school may decide that gender equality is more relevant to the way that it designs its teaching methods than to its building maintenance work. Public authorities should therefore assess whether, and how, gender equality is relevant to each of their functions. A public authority may decide that little or no action is required to discharge the gender equality duty in some of its services, for example those which are purely technical, such as traffic control or weather forecasting. Gender equality will always be relevant, however, to the employment side of any of a public authority's functions.

2.25. The requirement for proportionality and relevance should not be interpreted, however, as a simple question of the numbers of people affected. Public authorities should also take into account the seriousness or extent of the discrimination, harassment or gender inequality, even if the number of people affected is small. This would often be the case where, for example, transsexual people were affected, as their numbers would be likely to be small but the seriousness or extent of discrimination and harassment might be significant.

2.26. Where changing a function or proposed policy would lead to significant benefits to the gender equality of men and women, (or, in employment and vocational training – including further and higher education – for transsexual men and women), public authorities should give greater weight to the case for change and take steps accordingly.

2.27. For example, a Regional Development Agency has a target of increasing employment rates in a particular district. When developing this policy, it discovers that women are less economically active than men in that district but the employment services and training opportunities which they are providing are not being accessed by women, because of lack of childcare support. They decide to adjust their policy and resource allocations to provide childcare advice and support.

of opportunity between women and men. Ultimately, the key to the success of the duty is achieving culture change in public authorities, a process which will take time and commitment. An authority which makes the effort to meet the needs of women and of men will see the benefits, however, through delivering better quality services and having a more productive workforce.

MEETING THE GENDER EQUALITY DUTY IN POLICY DEVELOPMENT

2.49. To meet the duty effectively, public authorities must ensure that they have due regard to the need to eliminate unlawful discrimination and harassment against either women or men, (and, in employment and vocational training – including further and higher education – against transsexual men and women) and that their policies are not maintaining or leading to gender inequality. To assist public authorities to do this, it is recommended that they should:

- collect evidence on the impact of core policies on women and men
- when new policies are being developed, assess their likely consequences for women and men
- alter or amend proposed policies so that they have due regard to the need to promote gender equality and eliminate unlawful discrimination and harassment
- resource the above changes appropriately.

2.50. Conducting impact assessments on policies is a useful way of demonstrating that public authorities have had due regard to the need to eliminate unlawful discrimination and harassment and to promote equality of opportunity when developing policy. It is also a legal requirement if a public authority is subject to the specific duties. Even for those public authorities which are not, however, it can be a useful tool for meeting the duty. For more detail on conducting gender impact assessments, see Chapter 3.

2.51. The best way to find out if a policy is likely to have a negative or a positive impact on gender equality is to:

- find out if research or data already exist, and if so, analyse and apply it
- take action to develop relevant information if it does not exist
- ask and involve external and internal stakeholders, such as women's and men's voluntary sector groups, service user and consumer groups, trade unions and employee or staff networks.

2.52. Going through this process brings significant benefits to the effectiveness of policymaking. Developing a good base of evidence about differences in the impact of policies on women and men will avoid resources being misdirected and potentially wasted.

Women's current and future entitlement to pensions is significantly lower than men's. The DWP produced a report 'Women and Pensions – The Evidence' that specifically investigated the gender differences in pension provision between men and women. It showed that only 24% of recently retired women were entitled to a full Basic State Pension in their own right. Even when looking at working-age women, 2.2 million women are not building up rights to even the Basic State Pension.

Women's greater likelihood of undertaking unpaid parenting and caring commitments, and the subsequent impact on their ability to engage in paid employment, were identified as the key causes of the gender differences.

The subsequent DWP White Paper 'Security in retirement: towards a new pensions system' put forward several changes to the recognition of unpaid caring work within the state pension system that will mean for the first time paid work and unpaid care will be equally recognised within the state pension system.

This will benefit not just women, but also the increasing number of men undertaking unpaid care and help produce a pensions system that fully reflects working lives both now and in the future.

2.53–2.61. (*Outside the scope of this work.*)

MEETING THE GENDER EQUALITY DUTY IN EMPLOYMENT

2.62. To meet the gender equality duty as an employer, a public authority will need to ensure that it has due regard to the need to eliminate unlawful discrimination and harassment in its employment practices and actively promotes gender equality within its workforce. This includes discrimination and harassment of transsexual people on grounds of their gender reassignment.

2.63. In practice this will involve a cyclical process of: data collection, analysis of data, developing an action plan, implementing the plan and monitoring the outcomes to inform further action. It is recommended that the public authority involves the workforce in the process and agrees a timescale over which it will take action. Doing this will not only enable that authority to meet its obligations under the duty, but will also improve its ability to recruit and retain staff and improve service delivery. For more detail on data collection, see Chapter 3.

2.64. The following issues are usually the most common ones to be considered when a public authority is deciding employment priorities for action:

- ensuring fair recruitment processes
- avoiding concentration of women and men into particular areas of work and addressing it where it already exists ('occupational segregation')
- promoting and managing flexible working
- ensuring high-level part-time work and supporting part-time workers
- managing leave for parents and carers
- managing pregnancy and return from maternity leave
- eliminating harassment including sexual harassment
- eliminating discrimination against, and harassment of, transsexual staff and potential staff
- grievance and disciplinary procedures
- redundancy
- retirement
- equal pay
- work-based training opportunities.

> London Underground has targeted women in its recruitment of train drivers as part of a strategy that identified the lack of gender balance in the workforce as a central factor affecting its ability to move from being an asset-based organisation to a customer-focused organisation. In an 18-month campaign, it increased the number of female tube drivers from 75 to 167. It broadened its recruitment advertising by placing an advertisement in Cosmopolitan magazine, which produced 6,000 applications. The strategy also tackled ongoing workplace issues that were discouraging women:
>
> — sexual harassment and a culture that was unwelcoming to women
> — the lack of adequate physical facilities such as women's toilets and showers and difficulties accessing the facilities that did exist
> — inflexibility in working time and rostering
>
> A central feature of the work was the implementation of a Managing Equality and Diversity competence programme, which was rolled out to all managers, the introduction of a managing diversity competence statement and the development of personal diversity goals and measures for managers.
>
> *IDS Diversity at Work No 4, October 2004*

TRANSSEXUAL EMPLOYEES AND POTENTIAL EMPLOYEES

2.65. Discrimination on the grounds of sex includes discrimination on the grounds of gender reassignment in employment and vocational training (including further and higher education). Public authorities should review all employment policies and procedures to ensure that they adequately cover transsexual employees – especially those dealing with recruitment, confidentiality, harassment, access to training and development, occupational pensions and insurance.

2.66. It is important to remember that the legal obligation to prevent discrimination against transsexual people in employment and vocational training (including further and higher education) covers not only those who have undergone gender reassignment in the past but also those who intend to undergo gender reassignment and those who are undergoing it.

MEETING THE GENDER EQUALITY DUTY FOR EQUAL PAY

2.67. Public authorities are required to comply with the EqPA. The requirement to have due regard to the need to eliminate unlawful discrimination includes discrimination that is unlawful under the EqPA.

2.68. The right of an individual under the EqPA is set out in paragraph 2.9 above. 'Like work' means work which is the same or broadly similar. Work rated as equivalent means work that has been rated using a non-discriminatory job evaluation scheme as equivalent. Work of equal value is where the work done is different but considered to be of equal value or worth in terms of demands such as effort, skill and decision-making. More detail on this can be found in the Code of Practice on Equal Pay and the EOC website, at www.eoc.org.uk

> A public sector organisation based in Wales, with over five hundred staff undertook an equal pay review (EPR). Just under half the workforce was female. Part-time work was fairly common and this group was slightly more likely to be female than male. Prior to the review, the organisation had a fairly complicated pay structure which was felt to have too many grades for the number of staff. There were also several people outside of the pay structure. The organisation began a pay

and grading exercise in 1999 and this eventually evolved into a full EPR. There was significant union involvement throughout the process and members of each staff grade were also involved in the working group. The working group used consultants to help them draft the job evaluation system and set up the EPR. The review was thorough and included data on every aspect of recruitment, pay and progression. The review found that women were earning 81% of men's basic hourly wages, but only 71% once additional allowances were taken into account. Since action was taken, the pay gap has reduced to 13% for total pay – ie women are now earning 87% of men's total hourly pay.

Equal Pay Reviews in Practice, IES for EOC 2005

MEETING THE DUTY TO ELIMINATE HARASSMENT

2.69. Having due regard to the need to eliminate harassment, including sexual harassment, is a legal requirement under the general duty. The duty to have due regard to the need to promote equality of opportunity between men and women is also relevant here as this may help eliminate harassment. A public authority should consider the steps it needs to take to ensure that harassment is prevented across all its activities before it occurs.

2.70. In order to discharge this duty, it is recommended that public authorities develop and regularly review a clear policy for preventing and tackling harassment across all of its functions where relevant. This would include, for example:

- in employment, education and service delivery
- in relation to those not traditionally thought of as receiving a service, such as those who are subject to state powers, for example prisoners or asylum seekers
- in regulatory and enforcement functions
- in management of premises.

2.71. It is recommended that public authorities actively promote the policy to ensure that everyone is aware of and understands it. It is also recommended that public authorities provide training so that their managers and staff are equipped to deal with instances of harassment should they occur.

2.72. Public authorities should also adopt and communicate complaints and investigations procedures for dealing both formally and informally (as appropriate) with harassment, in a supportive manner. In the employment context, it is recommended that procedures for investigating harassment complaints should be linked to grievance and disciplinary procedures and should conform to the accepted standards for disciplinary action in the Acas Code of Practice on Disciplinary and Grievance Procedures.

2.73. Public authorities will need to determine the effectiveness of their policy and procedures. They can do this by monitoring the number of complaints of harassment and their outcome, and by reviewing policies and procedures periodically to ensure they are working effectively and that those who have made complaints are not victimised.

2.74. Where complaints of harassment are upheld, there should be a consistent and proportionate relationship between the severity of the harassment and the penalty imposed on the harasser. In the case of harassment by an employee, this may include disciplinary action and, in severe cases, dismissal. In the case of harassment by service users, tenants, pupils etc, public authorities should ensure that they deal with complaints of harassment by male and female employees consistently to avoid any direct discrimination. Appropriate action may involve warnings as to the consequences of repeated acts of harassment and, in serious cases, the withdrawal of services or the withdrawal of normal services.

2.75. 'Sexual Harassment: Guidance for Managers and Supervisors' explains how to prevent harassment taking place and how to handle complaints. It is available, along with other information and guidance on harassment, on the EOC website www.eoc.org.uk

2.76. A public authority is liable for any acts of harassment carried out by its employees in the course of their employment, or by any other person over whom the public authority has direct control and therefore for whose conduct it could reasonably be held responsible. This is the case, in most circumstances, even where those acts are carried out without either the knowledge or approval of the public authority. Public authorities will have a defence to claims of harassment which has been committed by their employees or agents if they have taken such prior measures as are reasonably practicable to prevent harassment taking place.

2.77. The harassment provisions in the employment and vocational training sections of the SDA do not expressly extend to harassment of employees by someone who is not under the direct control of the employer. An employee who has been subjected to serious harassment, however, which the employer could have prevented but did not, may be entitled to resign and claim constructive unfair dismissal.

CHAPTER 3: HOW TO MEET THE SPECIFIC DUTIES

INTRODUCTION

[4.264]

3.1. All the public authorities listed in Appendix D are subject to the specific duties described in this chapter. Further orders may be made by government from time to time to update the list of authorities.

3.2. The duties set out a framework to assist listed public authorities in planning, delivering and evaluating action to meet the general duty and to report on those activities. At the heart of this framework is the Gender Equality Scheme (the scheme), which is explained below. When developing and implementing the scheme, however, public authorities should bear in mind the scheme is a means of meeting the three elements of the general duty, not an end in itself. When public authorities are being assessed on whether or not they have met the duty, the existence of the scheme will not in itself be enough. They will have to demonstrate what action they have taken and the outcomes they have achieved.

3.3. The duties apply to all listed authorities whatever their size, but the way in which they are implemented should be appropriate to the size of the authority and its functions. A large NHS trust, for example, may have the capacity to undertake a significant change project to implement the duty. A small school, while still obliged to implement the specific duties, will do so on a scale appropriate to its size and resources.

WHAT DO THE SPECIFIC DUTIES REQUIRE PUBLIC AUTHORITIES TO DO?

3.4. The full text of the specific duties Order is set out at Appendix C, but in summary it provides that the public authority should:

- **prepare and publish a Gender Equality Scheme** showing how it intends to fulfil the general and specific duties and setting out its gender equality objectives
- **in preparing a scheme:**
  - **consult employees, service users and others** (including trade unions)
  - **take into account any information it has gathered or considers relevant** as to how its policies and practices affect gender equality in the workplace and in the delivery of its services
  - in formulating its overall gender equality objectives, **consider the need to have objectives to address the causes of any gender pay gap**
- **ensure that the scheme sets out the actions** the authority has taken or intends to take to—
  - gather information on the effect of its policies and practices on men and women, in employment, services and performance of its functions
  - use the information to review the implementation of the scheme objectives
  - assess the impact of its current and future policies and practices on gender equality
  - consult relevant employees, service users and others (including trade unions)
  - ensure implementation of the scheme objectives
- **implement the scheme and their actions for gathering and using information** within three years of publication of the scheme, unless it is unreasonable or impracticable to do so
- **review and revise the scheme** at least every three years
- **report on progress annually**.

3.5. All listed public authorities must publish their schemes no later than 30 April 2007.

3.6. All listed public authorities are required to comply with the same specific duties. This contrasts with the specific duties under the Race Relations Act 1976 (as amended), which have different requirements for different sectors, and the specific duties under the Disability Discrimination Act 1995 (as amended) which have different requirements in relation to information gathering.

PREPARING AND PUBLISHING A GENDER EQUALITY SCHEME

3.7. In order to prepare a scheme identifying gender equality objectives, and setting out the actions it intends to carry out to achieve them, each public authority will have to develop an understanding of the major gender equality issues in its functions. This should be based on a good evidence base and developed through consultation with stakeholders, and the specific duties set out these elements of the process as a legal requirement. Public authorities are then required to commit to a set of priority objectives, selected according to the principles of proportionality and relevance. Public authorities have discretion to decide those priorities themselves, but the priorities which they select should reflect the evidence. The general duty requires public authorities to focus on the issues within their remit which have the greatest importance and impact on gender equality.

3.8. The scheme should be published in a readily accessible format, for example, in a clearly signposted part of the public authority's website. It can be published as part of another published document or within a number of other published documents, for example within the business plan of a public authority or within a general equality scheme. Public authorities will have to ensure, however, that the individual elements of the scheme are easily identifiable, in order to show evidence of meeting the gender duty. This is also recommended in order to assure accountability to stakeholders.

WHAT SHOULD BE IN A GENDER EQUALITY SCHEME AND ACTION PLAN?

3.9. The gender equality scheme is legally required to contain the public authority's overall objectives for meeting the duty (see paragraphs 3.34–3.39) including any pay objectives (paragraphs 3.40–3.52). To demonstrate that the public authority is meeting the duty in full, it is recommended that the scheme should also contain a rationale for the choice of those objectives, based on:

- an overview of the remit and functions of the authority, including functions carried out through partnership and procurement
- the major findings of the information-gathering exercise
- the major findings of the consultation exercise.

3.10. Schemes are legally required to contain information on how the public authority will take action to:

- collect information (paras 3.12–3.23)
- use this information, and any other relevant information, to meet the general and specific duties
- use the information to review the effectiveness of its implementation of the duty and to prepare subsequent schemes (paras 3.22–3.23)
- assess the impact on gender equality of its existing and new policies and practices (paras 3.57–3.74)
- consult relevant employees, service users and others (including trade unions) (paras 3.24–3.33)
- achieve fulfilment of the objectives (paras 3.75–3.78)

3.11. Although not a formal legal requirement, evidence of effective practice which could usefully be included in the scheme might be:

- evidence of commitment from senior leaders
- evidence of the link to the authority's priorities and business plans
- the identification of individuals with clear responsibilities for taking action on the scheme or elements of the scheme
- the allocation of specific budgets, for example, for consultation or information gathering
- measurable and time bound indicators of progress towards the objectives
- measures to strengthen the capacity of the authority to meet the duty
- separate action plans for individual identifiable departments
- details of how impact assessment will be incorporated into the authority's decision-making process
- details of how the public authority will ensure the duty is met in procurement and partnerships.

GATHERING AND USING INFORMATION

3.12. In order to understand which of its functions have the greatest relevance to gender equality, a public authority will need to gather and use information on how women and men are affected by its activities. A public authority may already have this information, disaggregated by gender. This information will have a crucial role in helping the public authority to determine its gender equality priorities, conduct effective gender impact assessments of policies and practices, and monitor progress towards its gender equality objectives. Information can be both quantitative and qualitative, and from a variety of sources.

3.13. The specific duties require each listed public authority to gather information on the effect of its policies and practices on men and women, and in particular:

- the extent to which they promote equality between male and female staff
- the extent to which the services it provides and the functions it performs take account of the needs of women and men.

3.14. Policies and practices are very broad terms, and cover every aspect of a public authority's activities and functions.

3.15. The specific duties also require the public authority to take into account any other information which it considers relevant. This might include, for example, the national level gender equality policies and documents which relate to their business – for example, Public Service Agreements, national policy frameworks in their sector, or existing research which indicates the major gender issues in their area of work.

3.16. In order to meet the gender equality duty, public authorities will have to set up systems, or adapt existing systems, to ensure they obtain and monitor the relevant information. In many cases this should involve disaggregating existing information; in some cases this may require the collection of new information. Information should be collected on the gender profile of service users, on staff, and on any other people, such as tenants, who may be affected by decision-making and policy functions.

3.17. Information may also need to be collected to compare the profile of potential staff or service users with actual staff or service users. For example, to analyse the gender aspects of an employment scheme, a public authority would have to compare the percentage of women in the scheme with the pool of economically inactive or unemployed women relative to men.

3.18. Setting up these systems or adapting existing systems may be a significant task initially, in order to develop the evidence base for the initial scheme. It will, however, have major benefits in improving the performance management of the organisation overall. It is recommended that public authorities ensure their systems allow them to cross-reference information by ethnicity, disability, age and other categories, so that there is evidence of any issues for different groups of women and men.

3.19. Public authorities which do not already have data might look at collecting information in the following areas:

- gender differences in service use – needs, expectations, barriers, satisfaction rates, outcomes
- balance of women and men in key decision-making bodies, including public appointments
- the gender profile of their staff, including analysis of patterns for part-time staff and those with caring responsibilities
- the extent and causes of the gender pay gap in the authority for full-time and part-time staff – including data on pay systems, the impact of caring responsibilities and occupational segregation (see paras 3.40–3.56)
- the prevalence of harassment and sexual harassment of staff and service users, the number of formal complaints and the outcome of complaints
- return rates of women on maternity leave and whether they are returning to jobs at the same level of responsibility and pay
- issues and barriers affecting transsexual staff and potential staff.

3.20. Quantitative monitoring is likely to be difficult in relation to transsexual staff or job applicants because of very low numbers and privacy concerns. Staff and job applicants should be told why the information is being collected and what it will be used for and be assured of confidentiality and genuine anonymity. They should also be told that they are under no obligation to give such information. Further advice can be sought from Acas and transsexual groups.

3.21. Quantitative data can be supplemented by qualitative information from consultation with stakeholders, including voluntary sector groups and trade unions, and from focus groups or other sources.

3.22. The duty is not just about collecting information, however, but analysing and using it, so that public authorities know where they are being successful and where they need to take action. For example, information may indicate that very few men are accessing flexible working policies, relative to the proportion of women staff who do so, so a public authority may want to take steps to support more men to work on a flexible basis.

3.23. Once enough information has been collected to give a picture of gender equality priorities across the public authority, priority indicators in key areas should be identified for annual monitoring to allow the public authority to meet the specific duty to review progress.

Using data to develop the Women's Offending Reduction Programme – Home Office

Women make up 6% of the prison population and just one in five of known offenders[1] and are therefore often forgotten in debates around criminal justice policy. However, between 1992 and 2002 the male prison population increased by 50%, while the female prison population increased by 173%.[2] 71% of women sentenced to prison in 2002 received a sentence of less than 12 months.[3] 55% of women in prison have at least one child under 16.[4] In 1993 there was one female suicide in custody, in 2003 there were 14.[5] Half of women in prison have experienced domestic violence compared with 25% of the female population.[6] Women are twice as likely as men to have received help for mental or emotional problems in the twelve months prior to custody and more likely to have a serious mental illness.[7]

The Women's Offending Reduction Programme seeks to co-ordinate work across government departments and agencies to ensure that policies, services, programmes and other interventions respond more appropriately to the particular needs and characteristics of women offenders. A number of government departments, agencies and organisations are 'stakeholders' in the Programme. By ensuring the delivery of a co-ordinated multi-agency response to women's offending, the Programme seeks to tackle the variety of factors which can affect why women offend, including poor housing, mental health problems, substance misuse, abuse, child care, education and employment.

By gathering data on the patterns and trends in women's offending, sentencing and the characteristics of women offenders, they are better able to identify issues and to track the progress of their work. The ultimate measure of success of the Programme will be a reduction in offending by women and fewer women held in custody.

NOTES

1 www.homeoffice.gov.uk/rds/pdfs2/s95women03

2 www.homeoffice.gov.uk/rds/pdfs2/s95women03

3 www.homeoffice.gov.uk/rds/pdfs2/s95women03

4 Social Exclusion Unit Report (July 2002): Reducing Re-offending by Ex-prisoners.

5 www.homeoffice.gov.uk/rds/pdfs2/s95women03

6 Home Office & Prison Service, *Abuse, Interventions and Women in Prison: A Literature Review* (London, Home Office, 2003).

7 Department of Health, *Mainstreaming Gender and Women's Mental Health* (London, Department of Health, 2003).

CONSULTATION

3.24. The specific duties require listed public authorities to consult stakeholders when preparing a scheme. The requirement is to consult employees, service users and others (including trade unions) who appear to the authority to have an interest in the way the authority carries out its functions.

3.25. In addition, the scheme itself must include an outline of the actions which the authority intends to take or has taken in order to consult.

3.26. By consulting stakeholders, public authorities will be able to:

- build up a better picture of the most important gender issues in their work
- gather evidence to use in determining priorities and in the gender impact assessment process
- get feedback on their initial draft objectives
- develop greater ownership and understanding of their gender equality objectives
- improve accountability to their staff, service users and the general public.

3.27. Consultation will be especially important where one sex is under-represented in the formal decision-making processes of the public authority.

3.28. Using the information gathered during consultation will also be beneficial in conducting impact assessments, gathering evidence and monitoring progress. Public authorities may choose to consult stakeholders again at any relevant stages of the implementation or review process, although there is no legal requirement to do so.

3.29. The extent of consultation should be appropriate to the size, remit and resources of the authority and there is no prescribed means of carrying it out. Public authorities are free to adapt their existing processes of public consultation. It is important to remember, however, that the duty is to consult on gender equality. Women and men (and, where appropriate, girls and boys) should both be consulted, but public authorities will have to ensure that the consultation process gives adequate attention to issues of gender equality, and any questions are structured in such a way as to bring out any potential differences in views between women and men, or between groups of women and men.

3.30. It is also important that women and men are enabled to participate fully in a consultation process, in order to get a full picture of their concerns. Some women may be less likely to attend, or to speak out at a traditional public meeting if they do not feel sufficiently confident, if their community discourages women taking up public roles, or if there are language barriers.

3.31. Where one sex has been under-represented or disadvantaged in a policy area, service or employment issue, public authorities may need to make special efforts to encourage participation. For example, women have rarely been involved in decision-making on regeneration. Similarly, men may not have been previously included in discussions on childcare services. There may also be particular barriers to participation where a minority group has experienced multiple disadvantages, for example, on the grounds of ethnicity and sexual orientation. Public authorities may wish to consult such groups in a single-sex or group-specific environment.

3.32. It is recommended that consultation on employment issues with the transsexual community is conducted separately, although they should also be actively encouraged to participate in mainstream consultation processes.

3.33. Voluntary sector organisations, such as women's groups and men's groups, are likely to be useful sources of information through consultation. Public authorities should bear in mind, however, that such organisations may have limited capacity and resources and may need support to develop their capacity to engage with the process.

Overcoming consultation fatigue

One problem that has been faced in the implementation of positive equality duties in Northern Ireland is 'consultation fatigue', with community and voluntary groups being overloaded with lengthy consultation documents. In its review of the implementation of the duties, the Equality Commission for Northern Ireland (ECNI) stated that there was "consensus that blanket mail shots to everyone on a public authority's consultation list are rarely appropriate and should not be routinely advocated".

One means of tackling 'consultation fatigue' is to ensure that consultation is 'joined-up' within organisations, so that there can be one consultation exercise on related policies with affected groups. The ECNI has also recommended that "a number of public authorities should consolidate consultation exercises where possible on the same, or similar, policies". Health authorities in Northern Ireland undertake a region-wide equality impact assessment (EQIA) timetable so that each policy area is subject to equality impact assessment by all health authorities at the same time. This joined-up approach enables one consultation exercise for each EQIA.

PRIORITISING AND SETTING GENDER EQUALITY OBJECTIVES

3.34. The purpose of producing the scheme is to bring about change. It is therefore important that public authorities focus on achieving outcomes – specific identifiable improvements in policies, in the way services and functions are delivered and in the gender equality outcomes for employees. Focussing on outcomes rather than processes will be of benefit to smaller public authorities, which may not necessarily have the resources to undertake large-scale processes.

3.35. The specific duties require listed public authorities to ensure that their schemes set out overall objectives that the authority has identified for meeting the duty.

3.36. The duty does not prescribe which objectives should be chosen and it is up to the authority to select the priorities for action, in consultation with service users and employees, and taking into account all relevant information.

3.37. In deciding priorities for action, public authorities will also need to consider the resource implications – a major deep-seated inequality may take significant staff and cash resource to correct. It may be, however, that it is so clearly a significant gender inequality issue that not to address it could lay the public authority open to enforcement action by the EOC or CEHR.

3.38. The priorities are intended to cover a three-year period. It will clearly not be possible to address and resolve all issues of gender inequality in that 3 year period, but the requirement to have due regard means that public authorities are expected to begin to address the most significant problems.

3.39. Appropriate weight must be given to the three elements of the duty, as set out in Chapter 2, across all of the authority's functions. In determining priorities, therefore, public authorities must review questions of harassment, discrimination and the promotion of gender equality across employment, service provision, public functions and any other functions. In addition, they must take into account services and functions that are contracted out.

OBJECTIVES TO ADDRESS THE GENDER PAY GAP

3.40. The general duty includes a requirement to have due regard to the need to eliminate discrimination that is unlawful under the EqPA. The specific duties require listed public authorities, when setting their overall objectives, to 'consider the need to have objectives that address the causes of any differences between the pay of men and women that are related to their sex'.

3.41. These requirements, taken together with the specific duty to collect and make use of information on gender equality in the workforce and the duty to assess the impact of policies and practices, mean that listed public authorities have to undertake a process of determining whether their policies and practices are contributing to the causes of the gender pay gap. This should be done in consultation with employees and others, including trade unions.

3.42. The gender pay gap is determined by calculating women's overall average pay as a percentage of men's. The main factors which contribute to this gap are:

- discrimination, including pay discrimination (which is often inadvertent, but nonetheless unlawful)
- the impact of women's disproportionate share of caring responsibilities (which often results in women undertaking part-time work which is often poorly paid and often restricts career continuity and progression)
- the concentration of women in particular occupations ('occupational segregation'), usually characterised by lower levels of pay than in those numerically dominated by men.

3.43. The first step for a public authority considering the need for pay objectives should be to gather information to ascertain if there is a gender pay gap in its workforce. If there is, the authority should gather the information needed to identify the main cause or causes of that gap. These steps will enable it to give proper consideration to whether pay objectives are needed, and help it identify the causes those objectives may need to address. The size of the pay gap and the relative significance of each of the three causes will vary between different public authorities.

3.44. If a public authority fails to demonstrate that it has adequately collected and analysed information to establish whether or not there is a gender pay gap in its workforce, or fails to take action if there is a problem, it risks non-compliance with the duty, and subsequent enforcement action. Public authorities that do not set their own pay systems will still be expected to gather information and take appropriate action on any causes of the gender pay gap within their organisation which remain within their control.

3.45. Public authorities must be able to demonstrate that they have considered the need to have objectives that address the gender pay gap. For this reason, if a public authority does not include such objectives it should give reasons for that decision in its scheme. This might include providing evidence that there is no gender pay gap within its workforce, or within any wider group of women and men who are affected by its functions as an organisation, or that the alternative objectives which it has chosen have greater significance for gender equality. Public authorities should bear in mind, however, that pay discrimination is unlawful, and the general duty requires them to have due regard to the need to eliminate unlawful discrimination.

PAY DISCRIMINATION

3.46. In order to fulfil the general duty to have due regard to the need to eliminate discrimination that is unlawful under the EqPA, a public authority must be able to demonstrate that it has considered the need to take action on pay discrimination.

3.47. The gender equality duty does not require public authorities to undertake equal pay reviews. No specific course of action is prescribed to tackle pay discrimination. The statutory Code of Practice on Equal Pay recommends, however, that the most effective way of establishing whether a public authority's pay policies and pay systems are discriminatory is to undertake an equal pay review.

The fundamental components of an equal pay review are:

- comparing the pay of women and men doing equal work. Here employers need to check for one or more of the following: like work; work rated as equivalent; work of equal value – these checks are the foundation of an equal pay review
- identifying any equal pay gaps, including by differences between part-time and full-time workers' pay
- eliminating those pay gaps that cannot satisfactorily be explained on grounds other than sex.

The Code of Practice on Equal Pay and supporting toolkits are the recommended tools for undertaking this process. These can be found at www.eoc.org.uk

3.48. A public authority that has undertaken a pay review, containing the elements described above, in the preceding four years may not need to repeat it, unless it has undergone significant changes to its workforce, as it should already have evidence of the situation in its organisation and should be taking action.

3.49. Public authorities may also choose to collect pay information across a selected sample of their staff, for example administrators, manual workers, or departments or units such as IT or physiotherapy, to see if women and men carrying out the same jobs or jobs of equal value are receiving equal pay. Given the requirement to consult, any such approach should be discussed with the relevant trade union. Sampling may indicate a problem which suggests the need to proceed to a full pay review.

3.50. If a public authority decides not to undertake a full pay review, it may be appropriate for it to carry out a screening process, for example, to address areas known to pose a high risk of pay discrimination. These will include:

- starting salaries: checking whether women and men who have been recruited to the same jobs or jobs of equal value are being appointed on the same starting salary and whether any patterns are related to sex-based factors
- progression: whether unjustifiably long pay scales are inadvertently discriminating against women (who may be less likely to have continuous service)
- bonus payments: whether bonuses are paid, or higher bonuses are paid, in jobs where men predominate.

3.51. Many public authorities, such as schools, do not set their own pay systems. They are legally liable, however, under the EqPA, for the implementation of those pay systems. Some are likely to find the screening of high-risk factors, as set out above, which they, as employers, have control over, particularly useful in complying with the duty. Schools should ensure that decisions made within the school, which have an impact on an individual's pay (such as the allocation of Teaching and Learning Responsibility payments) are free of discrimination. Where a public authority does not set its own pay system, any pay review of that system would often be more appropriately carried out at a higher level (for example Local Education Authorities for schools).

3.52. Where public authorities do not set their own pay systems, but an authority becomes aware that there are elements in that system which are causing, or risk causing, pay discrimination, it is recommended that the public authority should alert the relevant pay body. The remit of pay review bodies in Great Britain includes a requirement to seek to ensure non-discriminatory pay systems, and to develop systems that support diversity.

CARING RESPONSIBILITIES AND OCCUPATIONAL SEGREGATION

3.53. Public authorities should also gather evidence on the impact of caring responsibilities on their workforces. Based on that evidence and on consultation with employees and trade unions, they should consider whether it is appropriate to set objectives to address any relevant issues. Women are significantly more likely than men to work part-time, often because of childcare and other caring responsibilities. Part-time work in Britain is characterised by particularly low rates of hourly pay and reduced access to promotion and development opportunities. In addition, lack of availability of suitable childcare restricts women's employment choices. Support to female and male employees with childcare responsibilities, through providing more flexible working and training opportunities or childcare provision or subsidy, will also contribute to the promotion of equality of opportunity between women and men.

3.54. Public authorities should also collect evidence on the extent of occupational segregation in their workforces. Based on that evidence and on consultation with employees and trade unions, they should consider whether it is appropriate to set objectives to address it. Employers who have strongly segregated workforces may be at higher risk of having equal pay claims taken against them. In a highly segregated workforce it can be easy for pay arrangements to evolve in which women are paid less than men when they are doing work of equal value, giving rise to equal pay tribunal claims.

3.55. Public authorities can check which issues are relevant to any gender pay gap in their organisation by:

- monitoring where women and men work in their organisation, what hours they work and at what grade. This will map any segregation by seniority and by types of work and will alert public authorities to the possible impact of caring responsibilities.
- using any annual staff monitoring exercise to ask staff if they have caring responsibilities, and whether this is for children or for older people.

CLOSING THE GENDER PAY GAP WITHIN THE WIDER REMIT OF A PUBLIC AUTHORITY

3.56. In addition to its functions as an employer, a public authority may have functions which have the potential to address the gender pay gap in a wider policy sense. This would be the case, for example, for a Regional Development Agency, a Learning and Skills Council or a local authority in its education functions. If this is the case, the public authority should also be considering whether it can address the causes of the gender pay gap within that wider remit where appropriate. This might include reviewing the high-level policy priorities of the authority overall, for example setting regional economic objectives that address the under-utilisation of the skills of part-time women workers. It might also include specific measures such as improving school careers advice so that boys and girls consider a wider range of career options, training women to fill areas of skills shortage in traditionally male-dominated areas and vice versa, or providing childcare support for male and female students in vocational training.

3.57–3.74. (*Outside the scope of this work.*)

IMPLEMENTING THE SCHEME

3.75. Listed public authorities are expected, within the three year period, to implement:

- their actions for gathering and using information
- the objectives in their scheme.

3.76. If a public authority does not comply with any specific duty imposed by the Order, including implementing the elements indicated above, the EOC or CEHR may issue a compliance notice (see Chapter 4 for further information about enforcement).

3.77. The public authority will not be under an obligation to implement their actions for gathering or using information or to implement the scheme objectives if, in all the circumstances of the case, it would be unreasonable or impracticable for it to do so. The words 'unreasonable' and 'impracticable' are intended to relate to particular and unforeseen circumstances. For example:

- where there are particular difficulties with implementing objectives in the scheme but these difficulties could not have been foreseen, then it is likely to be unreasonable to have to implement them
- where costs associated with an action unexpectedly escalate so as to be out of proportion to the duty, then it is unlikely to be practicable to implement the duty.

3.78. It is important, however, that public authorities consider other solutions where it is not reasonable or practicable for them to carry out a particular part of the scheme. Once barriers to equality have been identified, an authority will need to address them, considering alternative methods of overcoming them if those proposed originally are not practicable or reasonable.

ANNUAL REPORTS

3.79. Listed public authorities must take such steps as are reasonably practicable to publish annually a report, summarising the actions they have taken to implement their scheme objectives.

This report can be published as a separate document or within another published document, for example, the public authority's main annual report.

REVIEWING AND REVISING THE SCHEME

3.80. Listed public authorities have an obligation to review and revise the scheme every three years. It is recommended that this should involve a review of progress to date and of the appropriateness of the previous scheme objectives, with a view to continuous improvement in the implementation of the duty. Evidence for this process would include the information gathered to date, the results of impact assessments, and any feedback from stakeholders on the effectiveness of the preceding scheme.

3.81. In preparing the new scheme, public authorities are required to collect and make use of information, and to consult stakeholders as before. Stakeholders can also usefully be involved in the review of the previous scheme, although this is not a legal requirement.

(*Chapters 4, 5, 6 omitted: outside the scope of this work.*)

APPENDIX A: WHAT IS THE DEFINITION OF A PUBLIC AUTHORITY FOR THE PURPOSES OF THE GENERAL DUTY?

[4.265]

For the purposes of the gender duty, public authorities are bodies whose functions are those of a public nature. The most obvious examples of this are government departments, local authorities, the police and the armed forces. They will generally possess special powers, be democratically accountable, be publicly funded in whole or in part, be under an obligation to act only in the public interest and have a statutory constitution. These bodies are sometimes referred to as 'pure public authorities'. The gender duty will therefore apply for example to:

- Ministers, government departments and executive agencies (such as the Home Office and its executive agencies, including the Prison Service, and the Immigration and Nationality Directorate).
- The National Assembly for Wales.
- Army, Navy and Air Forces of the Crown (subject to a limited exception relating to work with the Government Communications Headquarters).
- Local government including local authorities, fire authorities, local probation boards, regional development agencies, magistrates courts committees, passenger transport executives and licensing boards.
- Governing bodies of further and higher education institutions, colleges and universities.
- Governing bodies of educational establishments maintained by local education authorities (including schools).
- The National Health Service including NHS Trusts, Health Authorities and primary care trusts, Local Health Boards (Wales).
- Police, including Chief Officers of Police, police authorities and the Independent Police Complaints Commission.
- Inspection and audit agencies such as the National Audit Office, Wales Audit Office, Audit Commissions, Her Majesty's Inspectorate of Constabulary (HMIC), the Healthcare Commission, the Health and Safety Executive.
- Some publicly-funded cultural bodies or institutions such as Sports Councils and Big Lottery Fund.
- Other bodies such as the Criminal Injuries Compensation Authority, the Crown Prosecution Service, Courts and tribunals (though not for judicial acts), Prison Boards of Visitors, the Children and Family Court Advisory and Support Service, the Community Development Foundation, Visiting Committees for Immigration Detention Centres, the Youth Justice Board for England and Wales, the Sentencing Advisory Panel.

This is not an exhaustive list.

Equivalent public authorities in Scotland are also covered by the general duty. Further detail is provided in the Scottish Code of Practice.

PRIVATE BODIES CARRYING OUT PUBLIC FUNCTIONS

The Equality Act 2006 is designed to ensure that a wide number of authorities are subject to the gender duty in relation to the performance of public functions. 'Public authority' therefore includes any person who has functions of a public nature. This will include private bodies or voluntary organisations who are carrying out public functions on behalf of a public authority. An organisation will be exercising a public function where it is in effect exercising a function which would otherwise be exercised by the state – and where individuals have to rely upon that person for the exercise of that function. These bodies are sometimes referred to as 'functional public bodies'. Whether or not an organisation is exercising a function of a public nature will ultimately be a matter for the courts. As the law presently stands, a private body may be held to be performing public functions and thus subject to the gender equality duty in relation to those functions if:

- it is publicly funded
- it is exercising powers of a public nature directly assigned to it by statute; or
- it is taking the place of central or local government
- it is providing a public service
- its structures and work are closely linked with the delegating or contracting-out state body
- there is a close relationship between the private body and any public authority.

Additional factors which may be relevant in determining whether or not a body is carrying out a function of a public nature include:

- the extent to which the private body is supervised by a state regulatory body
- the fact of supervision by a state regulatory body.

For example, the following bodies are likely to be deemed to be performing 'functions of a public nature' in relation to their public functions, and therefore subject to the gender equality duty in relation to those functions:

- the privatised utilities
- private security firms managing contracted-out prisons
- GPs when providing services under contract to a Primary Care Trust.

In relation to a particular act, a person is not a public authority if the nature of the act is private (for example, a private company running a prison will not be covered by the duty in relation to its private activities such as providing security guards for supermarkets).

A pure public authority contracting out services will always remain subject to the duty. It is possible that a 'pure' public authority which is subject to the duty could also be contracting out services to a 'functional' public authority (ie a private organisation providing a service of a public nature). In this case, both bodies will be subject to the duty in their own right. If there is a breach of the general duty, the legal responsibility for this could rest, depending on the circumstances, with either body. Actual responsibility would depend on the act which is the subject of the complaint, who was responsible for it and who was in breach of the general duty in respect of it. For example, a private prison might close down its childcare facilities for use by visitors, contrary to the terms of its contract with the Home Office. Whilst both the prison and the Home Office could be challenged in judicial review proceedings, the likelihood is that the Home Office would establish they had discharged their duty if they had included a requirement for childcare facilities in the contractual specifications. The private prison would be more likely to have difficulty in establishing that it had discharged the duty.

It is recommended that those authorities who may be carrying out functions of a public nature, but who are unsure whether they fall within the definition of a 'public authority' should safeguard their position by ensuring that they comply with the general duty in relation to those functions. It may also be advisable to seek legal advice on whether or not the gender equality duty applies in such a situation.

APPENDIX B: PUBLIC BODIES AND FUNCTIONS WHICH ARE EXEMPT FROM THE GENDER DUTY

[4.266]

S76A(3) SDA 1975

The Act currently exempts the following public authorities from the gender duty:

- both Houses of Parliament
- the Scottish Parliament
- the General Synod of the Church of England
- the Security Service
- the Secret Intelligence Service
- the Government Communications Headquarters
- a part of the armed forces of the Crown which is, in accordance with a requirement of the Secretary of State, assisting the Government Communications Headquarters, or
- a person specified by order of the Secretary of State.

S76A(4) SDA 1975

In addition there are certain functions of public authorities which the Act excludes from being subject to the duty. The general duty does not apply to the exercise of:

- a function in connection with proceedings in the House of Commons or the House of Lords
- a function in connection with proceedings in the Scottish Parliament (other than a function of the Scottish Parliamentary Corporate Body)
- a judicial function (whether in connection with a court or tribunal)
- a function exercised on behalf of or on the instructions of a person exercising a judicial function (whether in connection with a court or a tribunal)
- a function specified by order of the Secretary of State.

(*Appendices C–G omitted: outside the scope of this work.*)

PART 5
MISCELLANEOUS MATERIALS

A. INTERNATIONAL LAW MATERIALS

INTERNATIONAL LABOUR ORGANISATION CONVENTION (NO 87) ON FREEDOM OF ASSOCIATION AND PROTECTION OF THE RIGHT TO ORGANISE (1948)

NOTES

This Convention was adopted on 9 July 1948 and came into force on 4 July 1950. It was ratified by the UK on 27 June 1949.

PART I
FREEDOM OF ASSOCIATION

[5.1]
Article 1
Each Member of the International Labour Organisation for which this Convention is in force undertakes to give effect to the following provisions.

Article 2
Workers and employers, without distinction whatsoever, shall have the right to establish and, subject only to the rules of the organisation concerned, to join organisations of their own choosing without previous authorisation.

Article 3
1. Workers' and employers' organisations shall have the right to draw up their constitutions and rules, to elect their representatives in full freedom, to organise their administration and activities and to formulate their programmes.
2. The public authorities shall refrain from any interference which would restrict this right or impede the lawful exercise thereof.

Article 4
Workers' and employers' organisations shall not be liable to be dissolved or suspended by administrative authority.

Article 5
Workers' and employers' organisations shall have the right to establish and join federations and confederations and any such organisation, federation or confederation shall have the right to affiliate with international organisations of workers and employers.

Article 6
The provisions of Articles 2, 3 and 4 hereof apply to federations and confederations of workers' and employers' organisations.

Article 7
The acquisition of legal personality by workers' and employers' organisations, federations and confederations shall not be made subject to conditions of such a character as to restrict the application of the provisions of Articles 2, 3 and 4 hereof.

Article 8
1. In exercising the rights provided for in this Convention workers and employers and their respective organisations, like other persons or organised collectivities, shall respect the law of the land.
2. The law of the land shall not be such as to impair, nor shall it be so applied as to impair, the guarantees provided for in this Convention.

Article 9
1. The extent to which the guarantees provided for in this Convention shall apply to the armed forces and the police shall be determined by national laws or regulations.

2. In accordance with the principle set forth in paragraph 8 of Article 19 of the Constitution of the International Labour Organisation the ratification of this Convention by any Member shall not be deemed to affect any existing law, award, custom or agreement in virtue of which members of the armed forces or the police enjoy any right guaranteed by this Convention.

Article 10
In this Convention the term 'organisation' means any organisation of workers or of employers for furthering and defending the interests of workers or of employers.

PART II
PROTECTION OF THE RIGHT TO ORGANISE

[5.2]
Article 11
Each Member of the International Labour Organisation for which this Convention is in force undertakes to take all necessary and appropriate measures to ensure that workers and employers may exercise freely the right to organise.

PART III
MISCELLANEOUS PROVISIONS

[5.3]
Article 12
1. In respect of the territories referred to in Article 35 of the Constitution of the International Labour Organisation as amended by the Constitution of the International Labour Organisation Instrument of Amendment 1946, other than the territories referred to in paragraphs 4 and 5 of the said article as so amended, each Member of the Organisation which ratifies this Convention shall communicate to the Director-General of the International Labour Office with or as soon as possible after its ratification a declaration stating:
- (a) the territories in respect of which it undertakes that the provisions of the Convention shall be applied without modification;
- (b) the territories in respect of which it undertakes that the provisions of the Convention shall be applied subject to modifications, together with details of the said modifications;
- (c) the territories in respect of which the Convention is inapplicable and in such cases the grounds on which it is inapplicable;
- (d) the territories in respect of which it reserves its decision.

2. The undertakings referred to in subparagraphs (a) and (b) of paragraph 1 of this Article shall be deemed to be an integral part of the ratification and shall have the force of ratification.
3. Any Member may at any time by a subsequent declaration cancel in whole or in part any reservations made in its original declaration in virtue of subparagraphs (b), (c) or (d) of paragraph 1 of this Article.
4. Any Member may, at any time at which the Convention is subject to denunciation in accordance with the provisions of Article 16, communicate to the Director-General a declaration modifying in any other respect the terms of any former declaration and stating the present position in respect of such territories as it may specify.

Article 13
1. Where the subject-matter of this Convention is within the self-governing powers of any non-metropolitan territory, the Member responsible for the international relations of that territory may, in agreement with the government of the territory, communicate to the Director-General of the International Labour Office a declaration accepting on behalf of the territory the obligations of this Convention.
2. A declaration accepting the obligations of this Convention may be communicated to the Director-General of the International Labour Office:
- (a) by two or more Members of the Organisation in respect of any territory which is under their joint authority; or
- (b) by any international authority responsible for the administration of any territory, in virtue of the Charter of the United Nations or otherwise, in respect of any such territory.

3. Declarations communicated to the Director-General of the International Labour Office in accordance with the preceding paragraphs of this Article shall indicate whether the provisions of the Convention will be applied in the territory concerned without modification or subject to modifications; when the declaration indicates that the provisions of the Convention will be applied subject to modifications it shall give details of the said modifications.
4. The Member, Members or international authority concerned may at any time by a subsequent declaration renounce in whole or in part the right to have recourse to any modification indicated in any former declaration.

5. The Member, Members or international authority concerned may, at any time at which this Convention is subject to denunciation in accordance with the provisions of Article 16, communicate to the Director-General a declaration modifying in any other respect the terms of any former declaration and stating the present position in respect of the application of the Convention.

PART IV
FINAL PROVISIONS

[5.4]
Article 14
The formal ratifications of this Convention shall be communicated to the Director-General of the International Labour Office for registration.

Article 15
1. This Convention shall be binding only upon those Members of the International Labour Organisation whose ratifications have been registered with the Director-General.
2. It shall come into force twelve months after the date on which the ratifications of two Members have been registered with the Director-General.
3. Thereafter, this Convention shall come into force for any Member twelve months after the date on which its ratification has been registered.

Article 16
1. A Member which has ratified this Convention may denounce it after the expiration of ten years from the date on which the Convention first comes into force, by an act communicated to the Director-General of the International Labour Office for registration. Such denunciation shall not take effect until one year after the date on which it is registered.
2. Each Member which has ratified this Convention and which does not, within the year following the expiration of the period of ten years mentioned in the preceding paragraph, exercise the right of denunciation provided for in this article, will be bound for another period of ten years and, thereafter, may denounce this Convention at the expiration of each period of ten years under the terms provided for in this article.

Article 17
1. The Director-General of the International Labour Office shall notify all Members of the International Labour Organisation of the registration of all ratifications, declarations and denunciations communicated to him by the Members of the Organisation.
2. When notifying the Members of the Organisation of the registration of the second ratification communicated to him, the Director-General shall draw the attention of the Members of the Organisation to the date upon which the Convention will come into force.

Article 18
The Director-General of the International Labour Office shall communicate to the Secretary-General of the United Nations for registration in accordance with Article 102 of the Charter of the United Nations full particulars of all ratifications, declarations and acts of denunciation registered by him in accordance with the provisions of the preceding articles.

Article 19
At such times as it may consider necessary the Governing Body of the International Labour Office shall present to the General Conference a report on the working of this Convention and shall examine the desirability of placing on the agenda of the Conference the question of its revision in whole or in part.

Article 20
1. Should the Conference adopt a new Convention revising this Convention in whole or in part, then, unless the new Convention otherwise provides:
   (a) the ratification by a Member of the new revising Convention shall ipso jure involve the immediate denunciation of this Convention, notwithstanding the provisions of Article 16 above, if and when the new revising Convention shall have come into force;
   (b) as from the date when the new revising Convention comes into force this Convention shall cease to be open to ratification by the Members.
2. This Convention shall in any case remain in force in its actual form and content for those Members which have ratified it but have not ratified the revising Convention.

Article 21
The English and French versions of the text of this Convention are equally authoritative.

INTERNATIONAL LABOUR ORGANISATION CONVENTION (NO 98) ON THE RIGHT TO ORGANISE AND COLLECTIVE BARGAINING (1949)

NOTES

This Convention was adopted on 1 July 1949 and came into force on 18 July 1951. It was ratified by the UK on 30 June 1950.

[5.5]

Article 1

1. Workers shall enjoy adequate protection against acts of anti-union discrimination in respect of their employment.

2. Such protection shall apply more particularly in respect of acts calculated to:
   (a) Make the employment of a worker subject to the condition that he shall not join a union or shall relinquish trade union membership
   (b) Cause the dismissal of or otherwise prejudice a worker by reason of union membership or because of participation in union activities outside working hours or, with the consent of the employer, within working hours.

Article 2

1. Workers' and employers' organisations shall enjoy adequate protection against any acts of interference by each other or each others' agents or members in their establishment functioning or administration.

2. In particular, acts which are designed to promote the establishment of workers' organisations under the domination of employers or employers' organisations, or to support workers' organisations by financial or other means, with the object of placing such organisations under the control of employers or employers' organisations, shall be deemed to constitute acts of interference within the meaning of this article.

Article 3

Machinery appropriate to national conditions shall be established, where necessary, for the purpose of ensuring respect for the right to organise as defined in the preceding articles.

Article 4

Measures appropriate to national conditions shall be taken where necessary, to encourage and promote the full development and utilisation of machinery for voluntary negotiation between employers or employers' organisations and workers' organisations, with a view to the regulation of terms and conditions of employment by means of collective agreements.

Article 5

1. The extent to which the guarantees provided for in this Convention shall apply to the armed forces and the police shall be determined by national laws or regulations.

2. In accordance with the principle set forth in paragraph 8 of Article 19 of the Constitution of the International Labour Organisation the ratification of this Convention by any Member shall not be deemed to affect any existing law, award, custom or agreement in virtue of which members of the armed forces or the police enjoy any right guaranteed by this Convention.

Article 6

This Convention does not deal with the position of public servants engaged in the administration of the State, nor shall it be construed as prejudicing their rights or status in any way.

Article 7

The formal ratifications of this Convention shall be communicated to the Director-General of the International Labour Office for registration.

Article 8

1. This Convention shall be binding only upon those Members of the International Labour Organisation whose ratifications have been registered with the Director-General.

2. It shall come into force twelve months after the date on which the ratifications of two Members have been registered with the Director-General.

3. Thereafter, this Convention shall come into force for any Member twelve months after the date on which its ratification has been registered.

Article 9

1. Declarations communicated to the Director-General of the International Labour Office in accordance with paragraph 2 of Article 35 of the Constitution of the International Labour Organisation shall indicate—
   (a) the territories in respect of which the Member concerned undertakes that the provisions of the Convention shall be applied without modification;
   (b) the territories in respect of which it undertakes that the provisions of the Convention shall be applied subject to modifications, together with details of the said modifications;
   (c) the territories in respect of which the Convention is inapplicable and in such cases the grounds on which it is inapplicable;
   (d) the territories in respect of which it reserves its decision pending further consideration of the position.
2. The undertakings referred to in subparagraphs (a) and (b) of paragraph 1 of this Article shall be deemed to be an integral part of the ratification and shall have the force of ratification.
3. Any Member may at any time by a subsequent declaration cancel in whole or in part any reservation made in its original declaration in virtue of subparagraph (b), (c) or (d) of paragraph 1 of this Article.
4. Any Member may, at any time at which the Convention is subject to denunciation in accordance with the provisions of Article 11, communicate to the Director-General a declaration modifying in any other respect the terms of any former declaration and stating the present position in respect of such territories as it may specify.

Article 10

1. Declarations communicated to the Director-General of the International Labour Office in accordance with paragraph 4 or 5 of Article 35 of the Constitution of the International Labour Organisation shall indicate whether the provisions of the Convention will be applied in the territory concerned without modification or subject to modifications; when the declaration indicates that the provisions of the Convention will be applied subject to modifications, it shall give details of the said modifications.
2. The Member, Members or international authority concerned may at any time by a subsequent declaration renounce in whole or in part the right to have recourse to any modification indicated in any former declaration.
3. The Member, Members or international authority concerned may, at any time at which this Convention is subject to denunciation in accordance with the provisions of Article 11, communicate to the Director-General a declaration modifying in any other respect the terms of any former declaration and stating the present position in respect of the application of the Convention.

Article 11

1. A Member which has ratified this Convention may denounce it after the expiration of ten years from the date on which the Convention first comes into force, by an act communicated to the Director-General of the International Labour Office for registration. Such denunciation shall not take effect until one year after the date on which it is registered.
2. Each Member which has ratified this Convention and which does not, within the year following the expiration of the period of ten years mentioned in the preceding paragraph, exercise the right of denunciation provided for in this article, will be bound for another period of ten years and, thereafter, may denounce this Convention at the expiration of each period of ten years under the terms provided for in this Article.

Article 12

1. The Director-General of the International Labour Office shall notify all Members of the International Labour Organisation of the registration of all ratifications, declarations and denunciations communicated to him by the Members of the Organisation.
2. When notifying the Members of the Organisation of the registration of the second ratification communicated to him, the Director-General shall draw the attention of the Members of the Organisation to the date upon which the Convention will come into force.

Article 13

The Director-General of the International Labour Office shall communicate to the Secretary-General of the United Nations for registration in accordance with Article 102 of the Charter of the United Nations full particulars of all ratifications, declarations and acts of denunciation registered by him in accordance with the provisions of the preceding articles.

Article 14
At such times as it may consider necessary the Governing Body of the International Labour Office shall present to the General Conference a report on the working of this Convention and shall examine the desirability of placing on the agenda of the Conference the question of its revision in whole or in part.

Article 15
1. Should the Conference adopt a new Convention revising this Convention in whole or in part, then, unless the new Convention otherwise provides,
   (a) the ratification by a Member of the new revising Convention shall ipso jure involve the immediate denunciation of this Convention, notwithstanding the provisions of Article 11 above, if and when the new revising Convention shall have come into force;
   (b) as from the date when the new revising Convention comes into force, this Convention shall cease to be open to ratification by the Members.
2. This Convention shall in any case remain in force in its actual form and content for those Members which have ratified it but have not ratified the revising Convention.

Article 16
The English and French versions of the text of this Convention are equally authoritative.

EUROPEAN CONVENTION FOR THE PROTECTION OF HUMAN RIGHTS AND FUNDAMENTAL FREEDOMS (1950) (NOTE)

[5.6]

NOTES
Signed 4 November 1950; in force September 1953.
The European Convention is given domestic legal status by the Human Rights Act 1998. Sch 1 to that Act at **[1.1187]** et seq sets out the operative provisions of the Convention relevant to this work, except for Article 13, which provides that everyone whose Convention rights and freedoms are violated shall have an effective remedy before a national authority notwithstanding that the violation has been committed by persons acting in an official capacity.

INTERNATIONAL LABOUR ORGANISATION CONVENTION (NO 132) CONCERNING ANNUAL HOLIDAYS WITH PAY (REVISED), (1970)

NOTES
This Convention was adopted on 24 June 1970 and came into force on 30 June 1973. As of 6 April 2013, this Convention has not been ratified by the UK.

[5.7]
Article 1
The provisions of this Convention, in so far as they are not otherwise made effective by means of collective agreements, arbitration awards, court decisions, statutory wage fixing machinery, or in such other manner consistent with national practice as may be appropriate under national conditions, shall be given effect by national laws or regulations.

Article 2
1. This Convention applies to all employed persons, with the exception of seafarers.
2. In so far as necessary, measures may be taken by the competent authority or through the appropriate machinery in a country, after consultation with the organisations of employers and workers concerned, where such exist, to exclude from the application of this Convention limited categories of employed persons in respect of whose employment special problems of a substantial nature, relating to enforcement or to legislative or constitutional matters, arise.
3. Each Member which ratifies this Convention shall list in the first report on the application of the Convention submitted under Article 22 of the Constitution of the International Labour Organisation any categories which may have been excluded in pursuance of paragraph 2 of this Article, giving the reasons for such exclusion, and shall state in subsequent reports the position of its law and practice in respect of the categories excluded, and the extent to which effect has been given or is proposed to be given to the Convention in respect of such categories.

Article 3

1. Every person to whom this Convention applies shall be entitled to an annual paid holiday of a specified minimum length.
2. Each Member which ratifies this Convention shall specify the length of the holiday in a declaration appended to its ratification.
3. The holiday shall in no case be less than three working weeks for one year of service.
4. Each Member which has ratified this Convention may subsequently notify the Director-General of the International Labour Office, by a further declaration, that it specifies a holiday longer than that specified at the time of ratification.

Article 4

1. A person whose length of service in any year is less than that required for the full entitlement prescribed in the preceding Article shall be entitled in respect of that year to a holiday with pay proportionate to his length of service during that year.
2. The expression ***year*** in paragraph 1 of this Article shall mean the calendar year or any other period of the same length determined by the competent authority or through the appropriate machinery in the country concerned.

Article 5

1. A minimum period of service may be required for entitlement to any annual holiday with pay.
2. The length of any such qualifying period shall be determined by the competent authority or through the appropriate machinery in the country concerned but shall not exceed six months.
3. The manner in which length of service is calculated for the purpose of holiday entitlement shall be determined by the competent authority or through the appropriate machinery in each country.
4. Under conditions to be determined by the competent authority or through the appropriate machinery in each country, absence from work for such reasons beyond the control of the employed person concerned as illness, injury or maternity shall be counted as part of the period of service.

Article 6

1. Public and customary holidays, whether or not they fall during the annual holiday, shall not be counted as part of the minimum annual holiday with pay prescribed in Article 3, paragraph 3, of this Convention.
2. Under conditions to be determined by the competent authority or through the appropriate machinery in each country, periods of incapacity for work resulting from sickness or injury may not be counted as part of the minimum annual holiday with pay prescribed in Article 3, paragraph 3, of this Convention.

Article 7

1. Every person taking the holiday envisaged in this Convention shall receive in respect of the full period of that holiday at least his normal or average remuneration (including the cash equivalent of any part of that remuneration which is paid in kind and which is not a permanent benefit continuing whether or not the person concerned is on holiday), calculated in a manner to be determined by the competent authority or through the appropriate machinery in each country.
2. The amounts due in pursuance of paragraph 1 of this Article shall be paid to the person concerned in advance of the holiday, unless otherwise provided in an agreement applicable to him and the employer.

Article 8

1. The division of the annual holiday with pay into parts may be authorised by the competent authority or through the appropriate machinery in each country.
2. Unless otherwise provided in an agreement applicable to the employer and the employed person concerned, and on condition that the length of service of the person concerned entitles him to such a period, one of the parts shall consist of at least two uninterrupted working weeks.

Article 9

1. The uninterrupted part of the annual holiday with pay referred to in Article 8, paragraph 2, of this Convention shall be granted and taken no later than one year, and the remainder of the annual holiday with pay no later than eighteen months, from the end of the year in respect of which the holiday entitlement has arisen.
2. Any part of the annual holiday which exceeds a stated minimum may be postponed, with the consent of the employed person concerned, beyond the period specified in paragraph 1 of this Article and up to a further specified time limit.

3. The minimum and the time limit referred to in paragraph 2 of this Article shall be determined by the competent authority after consultation with the organisations of employers and workers concerned, or through collective bargaining, or in such other manner consistent with national practice as may be appropriate under national conditions.

Article 10
1. The time at which the holiday is to be taken shall, unless it is fixed by regulation, collective agreement, arbitration award or other means consistent with national practice, be determined by the employer after consultation with the employed person concerned or his representatives.
2. In fixing the time at which the holiday is to be taken, work requirements and the opportunities for rest and relaxation available to the employed person shall be taken into account.

Article 11
An employed person who has completed a minimum period of service corresponding to that which may be required under Article 5, paragraph 1, of this Convention shall receive, upon termination of employment, a holiday with pay proportionate to the length of service for which he has not received such a holiday, or compensation in lieu thereof, or the equivalent holiday credit.

Article 12
Agreements to relinquish the right to the minimum annual holiday with pay prescribed in Article 3, paragraph 3, of this Convention or to forgo such a holiday, for compensation or otherwise, shall, as appropriate to national conditions, be null and void or be prohibited.

Article 13
Special rules may be laid down by the competent authority or through the appropriate machinery in each country in respect of cases in which the employed person engages, during the holiday, in a gainful activity conflicting with the purpose of the holiday.

Article 14
Effective measures appropriate to the manner in which effect is given to the provisions of this Convention shall be taken to ensure the proper application and enforcement of regulations or provisions concerning holidays with pay, by means of adequate inspection or otherwise.

Article 15
1. Each Member may accept the obligations of this Convention separately—
   (a) in respect of employed persons in economic sectors other than agriculture;
   (b) in respect of employed persons in agriculture.
2. Each Member shall specify in its ratification whether it accepts the obligations of the Convention in respect of the persons covered by subparagraph (a) of paragraph 1 of this Article, in respect of the persons covered by subparagraph (b) of paragraph 1 of this Article, or in respect of both.
3. Each Member which has on ratification accepted the obligations of this Convention only in respect either of the persons covered by subparagraph (a) of paragraph 1 of this Article or of the persons covered by subparagraph (b) of paragraph 1 of this Article may subsequently notify the Director-General of the International Labour Office that it accepts the obligations of the Convention in respect of all persons to whom this Convention applies.

Article 16
This Convention revises the Holidays with Pay Convention, 1936, and the Holidays with Pay (Agriculture) Convention, 1952, on the following terms:
   (a) acceptance of the obligations of this Convention in respect of employed persons in economic sectors other than agriculture by a Member which is a party to the Holidays with Pay Convention, 1936, shall ipso jure involve the immediate denunciation of that Convention;
   (b) acceptance of the obligations of this Convention in respect of employed persons in agriculture by a Member which is a party to the Holidays with Pay (Agriculture) Convention, 1952, shall ipso jure involve the immediate denunciation of that Convention;
   (c) the coming into force of this Convention shall not close the Holidays with Pay (Agriculture) Convention, 1952, to further ratification.

Article 17
The formal ratifications of this Convention shall be communicated to the Director-General of the International Labour Office for registration.

Article 18

1. This Convention shall be binding only upon those Members of the International Labour Organisation whose ratifications have been registered with the Director-General.
2. It shall come into force twelve months after the date on which the ratifications of two Members have been registered with the Director-General.
3. Thereafter, this Convention shall come into force for any Member twelve months after the date on which its ratifications has been registered.

Article 19

1. A Member which has ratified this Convention may denounce it after the expiration of ten years from the date on which the Convention first comes into force, by an act communicated to the Director-General of the International Labour Office for registration. Such denunciation shall not take effect until one year after the date on which it is registered.
2. Each Member which has ratified this Convention and which does not, within the year following the expiration of the period of ten years mentioned in the preceding paragraph, exercise the right of denunciation provided for in this Article, will be bound for another period of ten years and, thereafter, may denounce this Convention at the expiration of each period of ten years under the terms provided for in this Article.

Article 20

1. The Director-General of the International Labour Office shall notify all Members of the International Labour Organisation of the registration of all ratifications and denunciations communicated to him by the Members of the Organisation.
2. When notifying the Members of the Organisation of the registration of the second ratification communicated to him, the Director-General shall draw the attention of the Members of the Organisation to the date upon which the Convention will come into force.

Article 21

The Director-General of the International Labour Office shall communicate to the Secretary-General of the United Nations for registration in accordance with Article 102 of the Charter of the United Nations full particulars of all ratifications and acts of denunciation registered by him in accordance with the provisions of the preceding Articles.

Article 22

At such times as it may consider necessary the Governing Body of the International Labour Office shall present to the General Conference a report on the working of this Convention and shall examine the desirability of placing on the agenda of the Conference the question of its revision in whole or in part.

Article 23

1. Should the Conference adopt a new Convention revising this Convention in whole or in part, then, unless the new Convention otherwise provides:
   (a) the ratification by a Member of the new revising Convention shall ipso jure involve the immediate denunciation of this Convention, notwithstanding the provisions of Article 19 above, if and when the new revising Convention shall have come into force;
   (b) as from the date when the new revising Convention comes into force this Convention shall cease to be open to ratification by the Members.
2. This Convention shall in any case remain in force in its actual form and content for those Members which have ratified it but have not ratified the revising Convention.

Article 24

The English and French versions of the text of this Convention are equally authoritative.

INTERNATIONAL LABOUR ORGANISATION CONVENTION (NO 135) CONCERNING PROTECTION AND FACILITIES TO BE AFFORDED TO WORKERS' REPRESENTATIVES IN THE UNDERTAKING (1971)

NOTES

This Convention was adopted on 23 June 1971 and came into force on 30 June 1973. It was ratified by the UK on 15 March 1973.

[5.8]

Article 1

Workers' representatives in the undertaking shall enjoy effective protection against any act prejudicial to them, including dismissal, based on their status or activities as a workers' representative or on union membership or participation in union activities, in so far as they act in conformity with existing laws or collective agreements or other jointly agreed arrangements.

Article 2

1. Such facilities in the undertaking shall be afforded to workers' representatives as may be appropriate in order to enable them to carry out their functions promptly and efficiently.
2. In this connection account shall be taken of the characteristics of the industrial relations system of the country and the needs, size and capabilities of the undertaking concerned.
3. The granting of such facilities shall not impair the efficient operation of the undertaking concerned.

Article 3

For the purpose of this Convention the term ***workers' representatives*** means persons who are recognised as such under national law or practice, whether they are—

(a) trade union representatives, namely, representatives designated or elected by trade unions or by members of such unions; or

(b) elected representatives, namely, representatives who are freely elected by the workers of the undertaking in accordance with provisions of national laws or regulations or of collective agreements and whose functions do not include activities which are recognised as the exclusive prerogative of trade unions in the country concerned.

Article 4

National laws or regulations, collective agreements, arbitration awards or court decisions may determine the type or types of workers' representatives which shall be entitled to the protection and facilities provided for in this Convention.

Article 5

Where there exist in the same undertaking both trade union representatives and elected representatives, appropriate measures shall be taken, wherever necessary, to ensure that the existence of elected representatives is not used to undermine the position of the trade unions concerned or their representatives and to encourage co-operation on all relevant matters between the elected representatives and the trade unions concerned and their representatives.

Article 6

Effect may be given to this Convention through national laws or regulations or collective agreements, or in any other manner consistent with national practice.

Article 7

The formal ratifications of this Convention shall be communicated to the Director-General of the International Labour Office for registration.

Article 8

1. This Convention shall be binding only upon those Members of the International Labour Organisation whose ratifications have been registered with the Director-General.
2. It shall come into force twelve months after the date on which the ratifications of two Members have been registered with the Director-General.
3. Thereafter, this Convention shall come into force for any Member twelve months after the date on which its ratification has been registered.

Article 9

1. A Member which has ratified this Convention may denounce it after the expiration of ten years from the date on which the Convention first comes into force, by an act communicated to the Director-General of the International Labour Office for registration. Such denunciation shall not take effect until one year after the date on which it is registered.

2. Each Member which has ratified this Convention and which does not, within the year following the expiration of the period of ten years mentioned in the preceding paragraph, exercise the right of denunciation provided for in this Article, will be bound for another period of ten years and, thereafter, may denounce this Convention at the expiration of each period of ten years under the terms provided for in this Article.

Article 10

1. The Director-General of the International Labour Office shall notify all Members of the International Labour Organisation of the registration of all ratifications and denunciations communicated to him by the Members of the Organisation.

2. When notifying the Members of the Organisation of the registration of the second ratification communicated to him, the Director-General shall draw the attention of the Members of the Organisation to the date upon which the Convention will come into force.

Article 11

The Director-General of the International Labour Office shall communicate to the Secretary-General of the United Nations for registration in accordance with Article 102 of the Charter of the United Nations full particulars of all ratifications and acts of denunciation registered by him in accordance with the provisions of the preceding Articles.

Article 12

At such times as it may consider necessary the Governing Body of the International Labour Office shall present to the General Conference a report on the working of this Convention and shall examine the desirability of placing on the agenda of the Conference the question of its revision in whole or in part.

Article 13

1. Should the Conference adopt a new Convention revising this Convention in whole or in part, then, unless the new Convention otherwise provides:

   (a) the ratification by a Member of the new revising Convention shall ipso jure involve the immediate denunciation of this Convention, notwithstanding the provisions of Article 9 above, if and when the new revising Convention shall have come into force;

   (b) as from the date when the new revising Convention comes into force this Convention shall cease to be open to ratification by the Members.

2. This Convention shall in any case remain in force in its actual form and content for those Members which have ratified it but have not ratified the revising Convention.

Article 14

The English and French versions of the text of this Convention are equally authoritative.

INTERNATIONAL LABOUR ORGANISATION CONVENTION (NO 154) CONCERNING THE PROMOTION OF COLLECTIVE BARGAINING (1981)

NOTES

This Convention was adopted on 19 June 1981 and came into force on 11 August 1983. As of 6 April 2013, this Convention has not been ratified by the UK.

PART I.
SCOPE AND DEFINITIONS

[5.9]

Article 1

1. This Convention applies to all branches of economic activity.

2. The extent to which the guarantees provided for in this Convention apply to the armed forces and the police may be determined by national laws or regulations or national practice.

3. As regards the public service, special modalities of application of this Convention may be fixed by national laws or regulations or national practice.

Article 2
For the purpose of this Convention the term ***collective bargaining*** extends to all negotiations which take place between an employer, a group of employers or one or more employers' organisations, on the one hand, and one or more workers' organisations, on the other, for—
(a) determining working conditions and terms of employment; and/or
(b) regulating relations between employers and workers; and/or
(c) regulating relations between employers or their organisations and a workers' organisation or workers' organisations.

Article 3
1. Where national law or practice recognises the existence of workers' representatives as defined in Article 3, subparagraph (b), of the Workers' Representatives Convention, 1971, national law or practice may determine the extent to which the term ***collective bargaining*** shall also extend, for the purpose of this Convention, to negotiations with these representatives.
2. Where, in pursuance of paragraph 1 of this Article, the term ***collective bargaining*** also includes negotiations with the workers' representatives referred to in that paragraph, appropriate measures shall be taken, wherever necessary, to ensure that the existence of these representatives is not used to undermine the position of the workers' organisations concerned.

PART II.
METHODS OF APPLICATION

[5.10]
Article 4
The provisions of this Convention shall, in so far as they are not otherwise made effective by means of collective agreements, arbitration awards or in such other manner as may be consistent with national practice, be given effect by national laws or regulations.

PART III.
PROMOTION OF COLLECTIVE BARGAINING

[5.11]
Article 5
1. Measures adapted to national conditions shall be taken to promote collective bargaining.
2. The aims of the measures referred to in paragraph 1 of this Article shall be the following:
(a) collective bargaining should be made possible for all employers and all groups of workers in the branches of activity covered by this Convention;
(b) collective bargaining should be progressively extended to all matters covered by subparagraphs (a), (b) and (c) of Article 2 of this Convention;
(c) the establishment of rules of procedure agreed between employers' and workers' organisations should be encouraged;
(d) collective bargaining should not be hampered by the absence of rules governing the procedure to be used or by the inadequacy or inappropriateness of such rules;
(e) bodies and procedures for the settlement of labour disputes should be so conceived as to contribute to the promotion of collective bargaining.

Article 6
The provisions of this Convention do not preclude the operation of industrial relations systems in which collective bargaining takes place within the framework of conciliation and/or arbitration machinery or institutions, in which machinery or institutions the parties to the collective bargaining process voluntarily participate.

Article 7
Measures taken by public authorities to encourage and promote the development of collective bargaining shall be the subject of prior consultation and, whenever possible, agreement between public authorities and employers' and workers' organisations.

Article 8
The measures taken with a view to promoting collective bargaining shall not be so conceived or applied as to hamper the freedom of collective bargaining.

PART IV.
FINAL PROVISIONS

[5.12]
Article 9
This Convention does not revise any existing Convention or Recommendation.

Article 10
The formal ratifications of this Convention shall be communicated to the Director-General of the International Labour Office for registration.

Article 11
1. This Convention shall be binding only upon those Members of the International Labour Organisation whose ratifications have been registered with the Director-General.
2. It shall come into force twelve months after the date on which the ratifications of two Members have been registered with the Director-General.
3. Thereafter, this Convention shall come into force for any Member twelve months after the date on which its ratification has been registered.

Article 12
1. A Member which has ratified this Convention may denounce it after the expiration of ten years from the date on which the Convention first comes into force, by an act communicated to the Director-General of the International Labour Office for registration. Such denunciation shall not take effect until one year after the date on which it is registered.
2. Each Member which has ratified this Convention and which does not, within the year following the expiration of the period of ten years mentioned in the preceding paragraph, exercise the right of denunciation provided for in this Article, will be bound for another period of ten years and, thereafter, may denounce this Convention at the expiration of each period of ten years under the terms provided for in this Article.

Article 13
1. The Director-General of the International Labour Office shall notify all Members of the International Labour Organisation of the registration of all ratifications and denunciations communicated to him by the Members of the Organisation.
2. When notifying the Members of the Organisation of the registration of the second ratification communicated to him, the Director-General shall draw the attention of the Members of the Organisation to the date upon which the Convention will come into force.

Article 14
The Director-General of the International Labour Office shall communicate to the Secretary-General of the United Nations for registration in accordance with Article 102 of the Charter of the United Nations full particulars of all ratifications and acts of denunciation registered by him in accordance with the provisions of the preceding Articles.

Article 15
At such times as it may consider necessary the Governing Body of the International Labour Office shall present to the General Conference a report on the working of this Convention and shall examine the desirability of placing on the agenda of the Conference the question of its revision in whole or in part.

Article 16
1. Should the Conference adopt a new Convention revising this Convention in whole or in part, then, unless the new Convention otherwise provides:
   (a) the ratification by a Member of the new revising Convention shall ipso jure involve the immediate denunciation of this Convention, notwithstanding the provisions of Article 12 above, if and when the new revising Convention shall have come into force;
   (b) as from the date when the new revising Convention comes into force this Convention shall cease to be open to ratification by the Members.
2. This Convention shall in any case remain in force in its actual form and content for those Members which have ratified it but have not ratified the revising Convention.

Article 17
The English and French versions of the text of this Convention are equally authoritative.

INTERNATIONAL LABOUR ORGANISATION CONVENTION (NO 158) CONCERNING TERMINATION OF EMPLOYMENT AT THE INITIATIVE OF THE EMPLOYER (1982)

NOTES

This Convention was adopted on 22 June 1982 and came into force on 23 November 1985. As of 6 April 2013, this Convention has not been ratified by the UK.

PART I. METHODS OF IMPLEMENTATION, SCOPE AND DEFINITIONS

[5.13]

Article 1

The provisions of this Convention shall, in so far as they are not otherwise made effective by means of collective agreements, arbitration awards or court decisions or in such other manner as may be consistent with national practice, be given effect by laws or regulations.

Article 2

1. This Convention applies to all branches of economic activity and to all employed persons.
2. A Member may exclude the following categories of employed persons from all or some of the provisions of this Convention:
   (a) workers engaged under a contract of employment for a specified period of time or a specified task;
   (b) workers serving a period of probation or a qualifying period of employment, determined in advance and of reasonable duration;
   (c) workers engaged on a casual basis for a short period.
3. Adequate safeguards shall be provided against recourse to contracts of employment for a specified period of time the aim of which is to avoid the protection resulting from this Convention.
4. In so far as necessary, measures may be taken by the competent authority or through the appropriate machinery in a country, after consultation with the organisations of employers and workers concerned, where such exist, to exclude from the application of this Convention or certain provisions thereof categories of employed persons whose terms and conditions of employment are governed by special arrangements which as a whole provide protection that is at least equivalent to the protection afforded under the Convention.
5. In so far as necessary, measures may be taken by the competent authority or through the appropriate machinery in a country, after consultation with the organisations of employers and workers concerned, where such exist, to exclude from the application of this Convention or certain provisions thereof other limited categories of employed persons in respect of which special problems of a substantial nature arise in the light of the particular conditions of employment of the workers concerned or the size or nature of the undertaking that employs them.
6. Each Member which ratifies this Convention shall list in the first report on the application of the Convention submitted under Article 22 of the Constitution of the International Labour Organisation any categories which may have been excluded in pursuance of paragraphs 4 and 5 of this Article, giving the reasons for such exclusion, and shall state in subsequent reports the position of its law and practice regarding the categories excluded, and the extent to which effect has been given or is proposed to be given to the Convention in respect of such categories.

Article 3

For the purpose of this Convention the terms ***termination*** and ***termination of employment*** mean termination of employment at the initiative of the employer.

PART II. STANDARD S OF GENERAL APPLICATION

DIVISION A. JUSTIFICATION FOR TERMINATION

[5.14]

Article 4

The employment of a worker shall not be terminated unless there is a valid reason for such termination connected with the capacity or conduct of the worker or based on the operational requirements of the undertaking, establishment or service.

Article 5

The following, inter alia, shall not constitute valid reasons for termination:

(a) union membership or participation in union activities outside working hours or, with the consent of the employer, within working hours;
(b) seeking office as, or acting or having acted in the capacity of, a workers' representative;
(c) the filing of a complaint or the participation in proceedings against an employer involving alleged violation of laws or regulations or recourse to competent administrative authorities;
(d) race, colour, sex, marital status, family responsibilities, pregnancy, religion, political opinion, national extraction or social origin;
(e) absence from work during maternity leave.

Article 6

1. Temporary absence from work because of illness or injury shall not constitute a valid reason for termination.
2. The definition of what constitutes temporary absence from work, the extent to which medical certification shall be required and possible limitations to the application of paragraph 1 of this Article shall be determined in accordance with the methods of implementation referred to in Article 1 of this Convention.

DIVISION B. PROCEDURE PRIOR TO OR AT THE TIME OF TERMINATION

Article 7

The employment of a worker shall not be terminated for reasons related to the worker's conduct or performance before he is provided an opportunity to defend himself against the allegations made, unless the employer cannot reasonably be expected to provide this opportunity.

DIVISION C. PROCEDURE OF APPEAL AGAINST TERMINATION

Article 8

1. A worker who considers that his employment has been unjustifiably terminated shall be entitled to appeal against that termination to an impartial body, such as a court, labour tribunal, arbitration committee or arbitrator.
2. Where termination has been authorised by a competent authority the application of paragraph 1 of this Article may be varied according to national law and practice.
3. A worker may be deemed to have waived his right to appeal against the termination of his employment if he has not exercised that right within a reasonable period of time after termination.

Article 9

1. The bodies referred to in Article 8 of this Convention shall be empowered to examine the reasons given for the termination and the other circumstances relating to the case and to render a decision on whether the termination was justified.
2. In order for the worker not to have to bear alone the burden of proving that the termination was not justified, the methods of implementation referred to in Article 1 of this Convention shall provide for one or the other or both of the following possibilities:
   (a) the burden of proving the existence of a valid reason for the termination as defined in Article 4 of this Convention shall rest on the employer;
   (b) the bodies referred to in Article 8 of this Convention shall be empowered to reach a conclusion on the reason for the termination having regard to the evidence provided by the parties and according to procedures provided for by national law and practice.
3. In cases of termination stated to be for reasons based on the operational requirements of the undertaking, establishment or service, the bodies referred to in Article 8 of this Convention shall be empowered to determine whether the termination was indeed for these reasons, but the extent to which they shall also be empowered to decide whether these reasons are sufficient to justify that termination shall be determined by the methods of implementation referred to in Article 1 of this Convention.

Article 10

If the bodies referred to in Article 8 of this Convention find that termination is unjustified and if they are not empowered or do not find it practicable, in accordance with national law and practice, to declare the termination invalid and/or order or propose reinstatement of the worker, they shall be empowered to order payment of adequate compensation or such other relief as may be deemed appropriate.

DIVISION D. PERIOD OF NOTICE

Article 11
A worker whose employment is to be terminated shall be entitled to a reasonable period of notice or compensation in lieu thereof, unless he is guilty of serious misconduct, that is, misconduct of such a nature that it would be unreasonable to require the employer to continue his employment during the notice period.

DIVISION E. SEVERANCE ALLOWANCE AND OTHER INCOME PROTECTION

Article 12
1. A worker whose employment has been terminated shall be entitled, in accordance with national law and practice, to-
   (a) a severance allowance or other separation benefits, the amount of which shall be based inter alia on length of service and the level of wages, and paid directly by the employer or by a fund constituted by employers' contributions; or
   (b) benefits from unemployment insurance or assistance or other forms of social security, such as old-age or invalidity benefits, under the normal conditions to which such benefits are subject; or
   (c) a combination of such allowance and benefits.
2. A worker who does not fulfil the qualifying conditions for unemployment insurance or assistance under a scheme of general scope need not be paid any allowance or benefit referred to in paragraph 1, subparagraph (a), of this Article solely because he is not receiving an unemployment benefit under paragraph 1, subparagraph (b).
3. Provision may be made by the methods of implementation referred to in Article 1 of this Convention for loss of entitlement to the allowance or benefits referred to in paragraph 1, subparagraph (a), of this Article in the event of termination for serious misconduct.

PART III.
SUPPLEMENTARY PROVISIONS CONCERNING TERMINATIONS OF EMPLOYMENT FOR ECONOMIC, TECHNOLOGICAL, STRUCTURAL OR SIMILAR REASONS

DIVISION A. CONSULTATION OF WORKERS' REPRESENTATIVES

[5.15]
Article 13
1. When the employer contemplates terminations for reasons of an economic, technological, structural or similar nature, the employer shall:
   (a) provide the workers' representatives concerned in good time with relevant information including the reasons for the terminations contemplated, the number and categories of workers likely to be affected and the period over which the terminations are intended to be carried out;
   (b) give, in accordance with national law and practice, the workers' representatives concerned, as early as possible, an opportunity for consultation on measures to be taken to avert or to minimise the terminations and measures to mitigate the adverse effects of any terminations on the workers concerned such as finding alternative employment.
2. The applicability of paragraph 1 of this Article may be limited by the methods of implementation referred to in Article 1 of this Convention to cases in which the number of workers whose termination of employment is contemplated is at least a specified number or percentage of the workforce.
3. For the purposes of this Article the term ***the workers' representatives concerned*** means the workers' representatives recognised as such by national law or practice, in conformity with the Workers' Representatives Convention, 1971.

DIVISION B. NOTIFICATION TO THE COMPETENT AUTHORITY

Article 14
1. When the employer contemplates terminations for reasons of an economic, technological, structural or similar nature, he shall notify, in accordance with national law and practice, the competent authority thereof as early as possible, giving relevant information, including a written statement of the reasons for the terminations, the number and categories of workers likely to be affected and the period over which the terminations are intended to be carried out.
2. National laws or regulations may limit the applicability of paragraph 1 of this Article to cases in which the number of workers whose termination of employment is contemplated is at least a specified number or percentage of the workforce.

3. The employer shall notify the competent authority of the terminations referred to in paragraph 1 of this Article a minimum period of time before carrying out the terminations, such period to be specified by national laws or regulations.

PART IV. FINAL PROVISIONS

[5.16]

Article 15

The formal ratifications of this Convention shall be communicated to the Director-General of the International Labour Office for registration.

Article 16

1. This Convention shall be binding only upon those Members of the International Labour Organisation whose ratifications have been registered with the Director-General.
2. It shall come into force twelve months after the date on which the ratifications of two Members have been registered with the Director-General.
3. Thereafter, this Convention shall come into force for any Member twelve months after the date on which its ratification has been registered.

Article 17

1. A Member which has ratified this Convention may denounce it after the expiration of ten years from the date on which the Convention first comes into force, by an act communicated to the Director-General of the International Labour Office for registration. Such denunciation shall not take effect until one year after the date on which it is registered.
2. Each Member which has ratified this Convention and which does not, within the year following the expiration of the period of ten years mentioned in the preceding paragraph, exercise the right of denunciation provided for in this Article, will be bound for another period of ten years and, thereafter, may denounce this Convention at the expiration of each period of ten years under the terms provided for in this Article.

Article 18

1. The Director-General of the International Labour Office shall notify all Members of the International Labour Organisation of the registration of all ratifications and denunciations communicated to him by the Members of the Organisation.
2. When notifying the Members of the Organisation of the registration of the second ratification communicated to him, the Director-General shall draw the attention of the Members of the Organisation to the date upon which the Convention will come into force.

Article 19

The Director-General of the International Labour Office shall communicate to the Secretary-General of the United Nations for registration in accordance with article 102 of the Charter of the United Nations full particulars of all ratifications and acts of denunciation registered by him in accordance with the provisions of the preceding Articles.

Article 20

At such times as it may consider necessary the Governing Body of the International Labour Office shall present to the General Conference a report on the working of this Convention and shall examine the desirability of placing on the agenda of the Conference the question of its revision in whole or in part.

Article 21

1. Should the Conference adopt a new Convention revising this Convention in whole or in part, then, unless the new Convention otherwise provides-
    - (a) the ratification by a Member of the new revising Convention shall ipso jure involve the immediate denunciation of this Convention, notwithstanding the provisions of Article 17 above, if and when the new revising Convention shall have come into force;
    - (b) as from the date when the new revising Convention comes into force this Convention shall cease to be open to ratification by the Members.
2. This Convention shall in any case remain in force in its actual form and content for those Members which have ratified it but have not ratified the revising Convention.

Article 22

The English and French versions of the text of this Convention are equally authoritative.

INTERNATIONAL LABOUR ORGANISATION CONVENTION (NO 175) CONCERNING PART-TIME WORK (1994)

NOTES

This Convention was adopted on 24 June 1994 and came into force on 28 February 1998. As of 6 April 2013, this Convention has not been ratified by the UK.

[5.17]

Article 1

For the purposes of this Convention:

(a) the term ***part-time worker*** means an employed person whose normal hours of work are less than those of comparable full-time workers;

(b) the normal hours of work referred to in subparagraph (a) may be calculated weekly or on average over a given period of employment;

(c) the term ***comparable full-time worker*** refers to a full-time worker who:

  (i) has the same type of employment relationship;

  (ii) is engaged in the same or a similar type of work or occupation; and

  (iii) is employed in the same establishment or, when there is no comparable full-time worker in that establishment, in the same enterprise or, when there is no comparable full-time worker in that enterprise, in the same branch of activity, as the part-time worker concerned;

(d) full-time workers affected by partial unemployment, that is by a collective and temporary reduction in their normal hours of work for economic, technical or structural reasons, are not considered to be part-time workers.

Article 2

This Convention does not affect more favourable provisions applicable to part-time workers under other international labour Conventions.

Article 3

1. This Convention applies to all part-time workers, it being understood that a Member may, after consulting the representative organisations of employers and workers concerned, exclude wholly or partly from its scope particular categories of workers or of establishments when its application to them would raise particular problems of a substantial nature.

2. Each Member having ratified this Convention which avails itself of the possibility afforded in the preceding paragraph shall, in its reports on the application of the Convention under article 22 of the Constitution of the International Labour Organisation, indicate any particular category of workers or of establishments thus excluded and the reasons why this exclusion was or is still judged necessary.

Article 4

Measures shall be taken to ensure that part-time workers receive the same protection as that accorded to comparable full-time workers in respect of:

(a) the right to organize, the right to bargain collectively and the right to act as workers' representatives;

(b) occupational safety and health;

(c) discrimination in employment and occupation.

Article 5

Measures appropriate to national law and practice shall be taken to ensure that part-time workers do not, solely because they work part time, receive a basic wage which, calculated proportionately on an hourly, performance-related, or piece-rate basis, is lower than the basic wage of comparable full-time workers, calculated according to the same method.

Article 6

Statutory social security schemes which are based on occupational activity shall be adapted so that part-time workers enjoy conditions equivalent to those of comparable full-time workers; these conditions may be determined in proportion to hours of work, contributions or earnings, or through other methods consistent with national law and practice.

Article 7
Measures shall be taken to ensure that part-time workers receive conditions equivalent to those of comparable full-time workers in the fields of:
(a) maternity protection;
(b) termination of employment;
(c) paid annual leave and paid public holidays; and
(d) sick leave,
it being understood that pecuniary entitlements may be determined in proportion to hours of work or earnings.

Article 8
1. Part-time workers whose hours of work or earnings are below specified thresholds may be excluded by a Member:
(a) from the scope of any of the statutory social security schemes referred to in Article 6, except in regard to employment injury benefits;
(b) from the scope of any of the measures taken in the fields covered by Article 7, except in regard to maternity protection measures other than those provided under statutory social security schemes.
2. The thresholds referred to in paragraph 1 shall be sufficiently low as not to exclude an unduly large percentage of part-time workers.
3. A Member which avails itself of the possibility provided for in paragraph 1 above shall:
(a) periodically review the thresholds in force;
(b) in its reports on the application of the Convention under article 22 of the Constitution of the International Labour Organisation, indicate the thresholds in force, the reasons therefor and whether consideration is being given to the progressive extension of protection to the workers excluded.
4. The most representative organisations of employers and workers shall be consulted on the establishment, review and revision of the thresholds referred to in this Article.

Article 9
1. Measures shall be taken to facilitate access to productive and freely chosen part-time work which meets the needs of both employers and workers, provided that the protection referred to in Articles 4 to 7 is ensured.
2. These measures shall include:
(a) the review of laws and regulations that may prevent or discourage recourse to or acceptance of part-time work;
(b) the use of employment services, where they exist, to identify and publicize possibilities for part-time work in their information and placement activities;
(c) special attention, in employment policies, to the needs and preferences of specific groups such as the unemployed, workers with family responsibilities, older workers, workers with disabilities and workers undergoing education or training.
3. These measures may also include research and dissemination of information on the degree to which part-time work responds to the economic and social aims of employers and workers.

Article 10
Where appropriate, measures shall be taken to ensure that transfer from full-time to part-time work or vice versa is voluntary, in accordance with national law and practice.

Article 11
The provisions of this Convention shall be implemented by laws or regulations, except in so far as effect is given to them by means of collective agreements or in any other manner consistent with national practice. The most representative organisations of employers and workers shall be consulted before any such laws or regulations are adopted.

Article 12
The formal ratifications of this Convention shall be communicated to the Director-General of the International Labour Office for registration.

Article 13
1. This Convention shall be binding only upon those Members of the International Labour Organisation whose ratifications have been registered with the Director-General.
2. It shall come into force 12 months after the date on which the ratifications of two Members have been registered with the Director-General.
3. Thereafter, this Convention shall come into force for any Member 12 months after the date on which its ratification has been registered.

Article 14

1. A Member which has ratified this Convention may denounce it after the expiration of ten years from the date on which the Convention first comes into force, by an act communicated to the Director-General of the International Labour Office for registration. Such denunciation shall not take effect until one year after the date on which it is registered.

2. Each Member which has ratified this Convention and which does not, within the year following the expiration of the period of ten years mentioned in the preceding paragraph, exercise the right of denunciation provided for in this Article, will be bound for another period of ten years and, thereafter, may denounce this Convention at the expiration of each period of ten years under the terms provided for in this Article.

Article 15

1. The Director-General of the International Labour Office shall notify all Members of the International Labour Organisation of the registration of all ratifications and denunciations communicated to him by the Members of the Organisation.

2. When notifying the Members of the Organisation of the registration of the second ratification communicated to him, the Director-General shall draw the attention of the Members of the Organisation to the date upon which the Convention will come into force.

Article 16

The Director-General of the International Labour Office shall communicate to the Secretary-General of the United Nations for registration in accordance with Article 102 of the Charter of the United Nations full particulars of all ratifications and acts of denunciations registered by him in accordance with the provisions of the preceding Articles.

Article 17

At such times as it may consider necessary, the Governing Body of the International Labour Office shall present to the General Conference a report on the working of this Convention and shall examine the desirability of placing on the agenda of the Conference the question of its revision in whole or in part.

Article 18

1. Should the Conference adopt a new Convention revising this Convention in whole or in part, then, unless the new Convention otherwise provides–

   (a) the ratification by a Member of the new revising Convention shall ipso jure involve the immediate denunciation of this Convention, notwithstanding the provisions of Article 14 above, if and when the new revising Convention shall have come into force;

   (b) as from the date when the new revising Convention comes into force this Convention shall cease to be open to ratification by the Members.

2. This Convention shall in any case remain in force in its actual form and content for those Members which have ratified it but have not ratified the revising Convention.

Article 19

The English and French versions of the text of this Convention are equally authoritative.

EUROPEAN SOCIAL CHARTER (1996)

(Revised)

Strasbourg, 3.V.1996

NOTES

The revised European Social Charter was adopted by the Council of Ministers of the Council of Europe on 3 May 1996 and came into force on 1 July 2009. It was signed by the United Kingdom on 7 November 1997 but has not yet been ratified (as at 6 April 2013). For provisions as to commencement see Art K at **[5.24]**.

[5.18]

PREAMBLE

The governments signatory hereto, being members of the Council of Europe,

Considering that the aim of the Council of Europe is the achievement of greater unity between its members for the purpose of safeguarding and realising the ideals and principles which are their common heritage and of facilitating their economic and social progress, in particular by the maintenance and further realisation of human rights and fundamental freedoms;

Considering that in the European Convention for the Protection of Human Rights and Fundamental Freedoms signed at Rome on 4 November 1950, and the Protocols thereto, the member States of the Council of Europe agreed to secure to their populations the civil and political rights and freedoms therein specified;

Considering that in the European Social Charter opened for signature in Turin on 18 October 1961 and the Protocols thereto, the member States of the Council of Europe agreed to secure to their populations the social rights specified therein in order to improve their standard of living and their social well-being;

Recalling that the Ministerial Conference on Human Rights held in Rome on 5 November 1990 stressed the need, on the one hand, to preserve the indivisible nature of all human rights, be they civil, political, economic, social or cultural and, on the other hand, to give the European Social Charter fresh impetus;

Resolved, as was decided during the Ministerial Conference held in Turin on 21 and 22 October 1991, to update and adapt the substantive contents of the Charter in order to take account in particular of the fundamental social changes which have occurred since the text was adopted;

Recognising the advantage of embodying in a Revised Charter, designed progressively to take the place of the European Social Charter, the rights guaranteed by the Charter as amended, the rights guaranteed by the Additional Protocol of 1988 and to add new rights,

Have agreed as follows—

PART I

[5.19]

The Parties accept as the aim of their policy, to be pursued by all appropriate means both national and international in character, the attainment of conditions in which the following rights and principles may be effectively realised—

1. Everyone shall have the opportunity to earn his living in an occupation freely entered upon.
2. All workers have the right to just conditions of work.
3. All workers have the right to safe and healthy working conditions.
4. All workers have the right to a fair remuneration sufficient for a decent standard of living for themselves and their families.
5. All workers and employers have the right to freedom of association in national or international organisations for the protection of their economic and social interests.
6. All workers and employers have the right to bargain collectively.
7. Children and young persons have the right to a special protection against the physical and moral hazards to which they are exposed.
8. Employed women, in case of maternity, have the right to a special protection.
9. Everyone has the right to appropriate facilities for vocational guidance with a view to helping him choose an occupation suited to his personal aptitude and interests.
10. Everyone has the right to appropriate facilities for vocational training.
11. Everyone has the right to benefit from any measures enabling him to enjoy the highest possible standard of health attainable.
12. All workers and their dependents have the right to social security.
13. Anyone without adequate resources has the right to social and medical assistance.
14. Everyone has the right to benefit from social welfare services.
15. Disabled persons have the right to independence, social integration and participation in the life of the community.
16. The family as a fundamental unit of society has the right to appropriate social, legal and economic protection to ensure its full development.
17. Children and young persons have the right to appropriate social, legal and economic protection.
18. The nationals of any one of the Parties have the right to engage in any gainful occupation in the territory of any one of the others on a footing of equality with the nationals of the latter, subject to restrictions based on cogent economic or social reasons.
19. Migrant workers who are nationals of a Party and their families have the right to protection and assistance in the territory of any other Party.
20. All workers have the right to equal opportunities and equal treatment in matters of employment and occupation without discrimination on the grounds of sex.
21. Workers have the right to be informed and to be consulted within the undertaking.
22. Workers have the right to take part in the determination and improvement of the working conditions and working environment in the undertaking.
23. Every elderly person has the right to social protection.
24. All workers have the right to protection in cases of termination of employment.
25. All workers have the right to protection of their claims in the event of the insolvency of their employer.
26. All workers have the right to dignity at work.

27. All persons with family responsibilities and who are engaged or wish to engage in employment have a right to do so without being subject to discrimination and as far as possible without conflict between their employment and family responsibilities.
28. Workers' representatives in undertakings have the right to protection against acts prejudicial to them and should be afforded appropriate facilities to carry out their functions.
29. All workers have the right to be informed and consulted in collective redundancy procedures.
30. Everyone has the right to protection against poverty and social exclusion.
31. Everyone has the right to housing.

PART II

[5.20]
The Parties undertake, as provided for in Part III, to consider themselves bound by the obligations laid down in the following articles and paragraphs.

Article 1
The right to work

With a view to ensuring the effective exercise of the right to work, the Parties undertake—

1. to accept as one of their primary aims and responsibilities the achievement and maintenance of as high and stable a level of employment as possible, with a view to the attainment of full employment;
2. to protect effectively the right of the worker to earn his living in an occupation freely entered upon;
3. to establish or maintain free employment services for all workers;
4. to provide or promote appropriate vocational guidance, training and rehabilitation.

Article 2
The right to just conditions of work

With a view to ensuring the effective exercise of the right to just conditions of work, the Parties undertake—

1. to provide for reasonable daily and weekly working hours, the working week to be progressively reduced to the extent that the increase of productivity and other relevant factors permit;
2. to provide for public holidays with pay;
3. to provide for a minimum of four weeks' annual holiday with pay;
4. to eliminate risks in inherently dangerous or unhealthy occupations, and where it has not yet been possible to eliminate or reduce sufficiently these risks, to provide for either a reduction of working hours or additional paid holidays for workers engaged in such occupations;
5. to ensure a weekly rest period which shall, as far as possible, coincide with the day recognised by tradition or custom in the country or region concerned as a day of rest;
6. to ensure that workers are informed in written form, as soon as possible, and in any event not later than two months after the date of commencing their employment, of the essential aspects of the contract or employment relationship;
7. to ensure that workers performing night work benefit from measures which take account of the special nature of the work.

Article 3
The right to safe and healthy working conditions

With a view to ensuring the effective exercise of the right to safe and healthy working conditions, the Parties undertake, in consultation with employers' and workers' organisations—

1. to formulate, implement and periodically review a coherent national policy on occupational safety, occupational health and the working environment. The primary aim of this policy shall be to improve occupational safety and health and to prevent accidents and injury to health arising out of, linked with or occurring in the course of work, particularly by minimising the causes of hazards inherent in the working environment;
2. to issue safety and health regulations;
3. to provide for the enforcement of such regulations by measures of supervision;
4. to promote the progressive development of occupational health services for all workers with essentially preventive and advisory functions.

Article 4
The right to a fair remuneration

With a view to ensuring the effective exercise of the right to a fair remuneration, the Parties undertake—

1. to recognise the right of workers to a remuneration such as will give them and their families a decent standard of living;
2. to recognise the right of workers to an increased rate of remuneration for overtime work, subject to exceptions in particular cases;
3. to recognise the right of men and women workers to equal pay for work of equal value;
4. to recognise the right of all workers to a reasonable period of notice for termination of employment;
5. to permit deductions from wages only under conditions and to the extent prescribed by national laws or regulations or fixed by collective agreements or arbitration awards.

The exercise of these rights shall be achieved by freely concluded collective agreements, by statutory wage-fixing machinery, or by other means appropriate to national conditions.

Article 5
The right to organise

With a view to ensuring or promoting the freedom of workers and employers to form local, national or international organisations for the protection of their economic and social interests and to join those organisations, the Parties undertake that national law shall not be such as to impair, nor shall it be so applied as to impair, this freedom. The extent to which the guarantees provided for in this article shall apply to the police shall be determined by national laws or regulations. The principle governing the application to the members of the armed forces of these guarantees and the extent to which they shall apply to persons in this category shall equally be determined by national laws or regulations.

Article 6
The right to bargain collectively

With a view to ensuring the effective exercise of the right to bargain collectively, the Parties undertake—

1. to promote joint consultation between workers and employers;
2. to promote, where necessary and appropriate, machinery for voluntary negotiations between employers or employers' organisations and workers' organisations, with a view to the regulation of terms and conditions of employment by means of collective agreements;
3. to promote the establishment and use of appropriate machinery for conciliation and voluntary arbitration for the settlement of labour disputes;

and recognise—

4. the right of workers and employers to collective action in cases of conflicts of interest, including the right to strike, subject to obligations that might arise out of collective agreements previously entered into.

Article 7
The right of children and young persons to protection

With a view to ensuring the effective exercise of the right of children and young persons to protection, the Parties undertake—

1. to provide that the minimum age of admission to employment shall be 15 years, subject to exceptions for children employed in prescribed light work without harm to their health, morals or education;
2. to provide that the minimum age of admission to employment shall be 18 years with respect to prescribed occupations regarded as dangerous or unhealthy;
3. to provide that persons who are still subject to compulsory education shall not be employed in such work as would deprive them of the full benefit of their education;
4. to provide that the working hours of persons under 18 years of age shall be limited in accordance with the needs of their development, and particularly with their need for vocational training;
5. to recognise the right of young workers and apprentices to a fair wage or other appropriate allowances;
6. to provide that the time spent by young persons in vocational training during the normal working hours with the consent of the employer shall be treated as forming part of the working day;
7. to provide that employed persons of under 18 years of age shall be entitled to a minimum of four weeks' annual holiday with pay;
8. to provide that persons under 18 years of age shall not be employed in night work with the exception of certain occupations provided for by national laws or regulations;
9. to provide that persons under 18 years of age employed in occupations prescribed by national laws or regulations shall be subject to regular medical control;
10. to ensure special protection against physical and moral dangers to which children and young persons are exposed, and particularly against those resulting directly or indirectly from their work.

Article 8
The right of employed women to protection of maternity
With a view to ensuring the effective exercise of the right of employed women to the protection of maternity, the Parties undertake—

1. to provide either by paid leave, by adequate social security benefits or by benefits from public funds for employed women to take leave before and after childbirth up to a total of at least fourteen weeks;
2. to consider it as unlawful for an employer to give a woman notice of dismissal during the period from the time she notifies her employer that she is pregnant until the end of her maternity leave, or to give her notice of dismissal at such a time that the notice would expire during such a period;
3. to provide that mothers who are nursing their infants shall be entitled to sufficient time off for this purpose;
4. to regulate the employment in night work of pregnant women, women who have recently given birth and women nursing their infants;
5. to prohibit the employment of pregnant women, women who have recently given birth or who are nursing their infants in underground mining and all other work which is unsuitable by reason of its dangerous, unhealthy or arduous nature and to take appropriate measures to protect the employment rights of these women.

Article 9
The right to vocational guidance
With a view to ensuring the effective exercise of the right to vocational guidance, the Parties undertake to provide or promote, as necessary, a service which will assist all persons, including the handicapped, to solve problems related to occupational choice and progress, with due regard to the individual's characteristics and their relation to occupational opportunity: this assistance should be available free of charge, both to young persons, including schoolchildren, and to adults.

Article 10
The right to vocational training
With a view to ensuring the effective exercise of the right to vocational training, the Parties undertake—

1. to provide or promote, as necessary, the technical and vocational training of all persons, including the handicapped, in consultation with employers' and workers' organisations, and to grant facilities for access to higher technical and university education, based solely on individual aptitude;
2. to provide or promote a system of apprenticeship and other systematic arrangements for training young boys and girls in their various employments;
3. to provide or promote, as necessary—
   (a) adequate and readily available training facilities for adult workers;
   (b) special facilities for the retraining of adult workers needed as a result of technological development or new trends in employment;
4. to provide or promote, as necessary, special measures for the retraining and reintegration of the long-term unemployed;
5. to encourage the full utilisation of the facilities provided by appropriate measures such as—
   (a) reducing or abolishing any fees or charges;
   (b) granting financial assistance in appropriate cases;
   (c) including in the normal working hours time spent on supplementary training taken by the worker, at the request of his employer, during employment;
   (d) ensuring, through adequate supervision, in consultation with the employers' and workers' organisations, the efficiency of apprenticeship and other training arrangements for young workers, and the adequate protection of young workers generally.

Article 11
The right to protection of health
With a view to ensuring the effective exercise of the right to protection of health, the Parties undertake, either directly or in co-operation with public or private organisations, to take appropriate measures designed *inter alia*—

1. to remove as far as possible the causes of ill-health;
2. to provide advisory and educational facilities for the promotion of health and the encouragement of individual responsibility in matters of health;
3. to prevent as far as possible epidemic, endemic and other diseases, as well as accidents.

Article 12
The right to social security

With a view to ensuring the effective exercise of the right to social security, the Parties undertake—

1. to establish or maintain a system of social security;
2. to maintain the social security system at a satisfactory level at least equal to that necessary for the ratification of the European Code of Social Security;
3. to endeavour to raise progressively the system of social security to a higher level;
4. to take steps, by the conclusion of appropriate bilateral and multilateral agreements or by other means, and subject to the conditions laid down in such agreements, in order to ensure—
   (a) equal treatment with their own nationals of the nationals of other Parties in respect of social security rights, including the retention of benefits arising out of social security legislation, whatever movements the persons protected may undertake between the territories of the Parties;
   (b) the granting, maintenance and resumption of social security rights by such means as the accumulation of insurance or employment periods completed under the legislation of each of the Parties.

Article 13
The right to social and medical assistance

With a view to ensuring the effective exercise of the right to social and medical assistance, the Parties undertake—

1. to ensure that any person who is without adequate resources and who is unable to secure such resources either by his own efforts or from other sources, in particular by benefits under a social security scheme, be granted adequate assistance, and, in case of sickness, the care necessitated by his condition;
2. to ensure that persons receiving such assistance shall not, for that reason, suffer from a diminution of their political or social rights;
3. to provide that everyone may receive by appropriate public or private services such advice and personal help as may be required to prevent, to remove, or to alleviate personal or family want;
4. to apply the provisions referred to in paragraphs 1, 2 and 3 of this article on an equal footing with their nationals to nationals of other Parties lawfully within their territories, in accordance with their obligations under the European Convention on Social and Medical Assistance, signed at Paris on 11 December 1953.

Article 14
The right to benefit from social welfare services

With a view to ensuring the effective exercise of the right to benefit from social welfare services, the Parties undertake—

1. to promote or provide services which, by using methods of social work, would contribute to the welfare and development of both individuals and groups in the community, and to their adjustment to the social environment;
2. to encourage the participation of individuals and voluntary or other organisations in the establishment and maintenance of such services.

Article 15
The right of persons with disabilities to independence, social integration and participation in the life of the community

With a view to ensuring to persons with disabilities, irrespective of age and the nature and origin of their disabilities, the effective exercise of the right to independence, social integration and participation in the life of the community, the Parties undertake, in particular—

1. to take the necessary measures to provide persons with disabilities with guidance, education and vocational training in the framework of general schemes wherever possible or, where this is not possible, through specialised bodies, public or private;
2. to promote their access to employment through all measures tending to encourage employers to hire and keep in employment persons with disabilities in the ordinary working environment and to adjust the working conditions to the needs of the disabled or, where this is not possible by reason of the disability, by arranging for or creating sheltered employment according to the level of disability. In certain cases, such measures may require recourse to specialised placement and support services;
3. to promote their full social integration and participation in the life of the community in particular through measures, including technical aids, aiming to overcome barriers to communication and mobility and enabling access to transport, housing, cultural activities and leisure.

Article 16
The right of the family to social, legal and economic protection
With a view to ensuring the necessary conditions for the full development of the family, which is a fundamental unit of society, the Parties undertake to promote the economic, legal and social protection of family life by such means as social and family benefits, fiscal arrangements, provision of family housing, benefits for the newly married and other appropriate means.

Article 17
The right of children and young persons to social, legal and economic protection
With a view to ensuring the effective exercise of the right of children and young persons to grow up in an environment which encourages the full development of their personality and of their physical and mental capacities, the Parties undertake, either directly or in co-operation with public and private organisations, to take all appropriate and necessary measures designed—

(a) to ensure that children and young persons, taking account of the rights and duties of their parents, have the care, the assistance, the education and the training they need, in particular by providing for the establishment or maintenance of institutions and services sufficient and adequate for this purpose;
(b) to protect children and young persons against negligence, violence or exploitation;
(c) to provide protection and special aid from the state for children and young persons temporarily or definitively deprived of their family's support;

to provide to children and young persons a free primary and secondary education as well as to encourage regular attendance at schools.

Article 18
The right to engage in a gainful occupation in the territory of other Parties
With a view to ensuring the effective exercise of the right to engage in a gainful occupation in the territory of any other Party, the Parties undertake—

1. to apply existing regulations in a spirit of liberality;
2. to simplify existing formalities and to reduce or abolish chancery dues and other charges payable by foreign workers or their employers;
3. to liberalise, individually or collectively, regulations governing the employment of foreign workers;

and recognise—

4. the right of their nationals to leave the country to engage in a gainful occupation in the territories of the other Parties.

Article 19
The right of migrant workers and their families to protection and assistance
With a view to ensuring the effective exercise of the right of migrant workers and their families to protection and assistance in the territory of any other Party, the Parties undertake—

1. to maintain or to satisfy themselves that there are maintained adequate and free services to assist such workers, particularly in obtaining accurate information, and to take all appropriate steps, so far as national laws and regulations permit, against misleading propaganda relating to emigration and immigration;
2. to adopt appropriate measures within their own jurisdiction to facilitate the departure, journey and reception of such workers and their families, and to provide, within their own jurisdiction, appropriate services for health, medical attention and good hygienic conditions during the journey;
3. to promote co-operation, as appropriate, between social services, public and private, in emigration and immigration countries;
4. to secure for such workers lawfully within their territories, insofar as such matters are regulated by law or regulations or are subject to the control of administrative authorities, treatment not less favourable than that of their own nationals in respect of the following matters—
    (a) remuneration and other employment and working conditions;
    (b) membership of trade unions and enjoyment of the benefits of collective bargaining;
    (c) accommodation;
5. to secure for such workers lawfully within their territories treatment not less favourable than that of their own nationals with regard to employment taxes, dues or contributions payable in respect of employed persons;
6. to facilitate as far as possible the reunion of the family of a foreign worker permitted to establish himself in the territory;
7. to secure for such workers lawfully within their territories treatment not less favourable than that of their own nationals in respect of legal proceedings relating to matters referred to in this article;

8. to secure that such workers lawfully residing within their territories are not expelled unless they endanger national security or offend against public interest or morality;
9. to permit, within legal limits, the transfer of such parts of the earnings and savings of such workers as they may desire;
10. to extend the protection and assistance provided for in this article to self-employed migrants insofar as such measures apply;
11. to promote and facilitate the teaching of the national language of the receiving state or, if there are several, one of these languages, to migrant workers and members of their families;
12. to promote and facilitate, as far as practicable, the teaching of the migrant worker's mother tongue to the children of the migrant worker.

Article 20
The right to equal opportunities and equal treatment in matters of employment and occupation without discrimination on the grounds of sex

With a view to ensuring the effective exercise of the right to equal opportunities and equal treatment in matters of employment and occupation without discrimination on the grounds of sex, the Parties undertake to recognise that right and to take appropriate measures to ensure or promote its application in the following fields—

(a) access to employment, protection against dismissal and occupational reintegration;
(b) vocational guidance, training, retraining and rehabilitation;
(c) terms of employment and working conditions, including remuneration;
(d) career development, including promotion.

Article 21
The right to information and consultation

With a view to ensuring the effective exercise of the right of workers to be informed and consulted within the undertaking, the Parties undertake to adopt or encourage measures enabling workers or their representatives, in accordance with national legislation and practice—

(a) to be informed regularly or at the appropriate time and in a comprehensible way about the economic and financial situation of the undertaking employing them, on the understanding that the disclosure of certain information which could be prejudicial to the undertaking may be refused or subject to confidentiality; and
(b) to be consulted in good time on proposed decisions which could substantially affect the interests of workers, particularly on those decisions which could have an important impact on the employment situation in the undertaking.

Article 22
The right to take part in the determination and improvement of the working conditions and working environment

With a view to ensuring the effective exercise of the right of workers to take part in the determination and improvement of the working conditions and working environment in the undertaking, the Parties undertake to adopt or encourage measures enabling workers or their representatives, in accordance with national legislation and practice, to contribute—

(a) to the determination and the improvement of the working conditions, work organisation and working environment;
(b) to the protection of health and safety within the undertaking;
(c) to the organisation of social and socio-cultural services and facilities within the undertaking;
(d) to the supervision of the observance of regulations on these matters.

Article 23
The right of elderly persons to social protection

With a view to ensuring the effective exercise of the right of elderly persons to social protection, the Parties undertake to adopt or encourage, either directly or in co-operation with public or private organisations, appropriate measures designed in particular—

to enable elderly persons to remain full members of society for as long as possible, by means of—

(a) adequate resources enabling them to lead a decent life and play an active part in public, social and cultural life;
(b) provision of information about services and facilities available for elderly persons and their opportunities to make use of them;

to enable elderly persons to choose their life-style freely and to lead independent lives in their familiar surroundings for as long as they wish and are able, by means of—

(a) provision of housing suited to their needs and their state of health or of adequate support for adapting their housing;

(b) the health care and the services necessitated by their state;

to guarantee elderly persons living in institutions appropriate support, while respecting their privacy, and participation in decisions concerning living conditions in the institution.

Article 24
The right to protection in cases of termination of employment

With a view to ensuring the effective exercise of the right of workers to protection in cases of termination of employment, the Parties undertake to recognise—

(a) the right of all workers not to have their employment terminated without valid reasons for such termination connected with their capacity or conduct or based on the operational requirements of the undertaking, establishment or service;

(b) the right of workers whose employment is terminated without a valid reason to adequate compensation or other appropriate relief.

To this end the Parties undertake to ensure that a worker who considers that his employment has been terminated without a valid reason shall have the right to appeal to an impartial body.

Article 25
The right of workers to the protection of their claims in the event of the insolvency of their employer

With a view to ensuring the effective exercise of the right of workers to the protection of their claims in the event of the insolvency of their employer, the Parties undertake to provide that workers' claims arising from contracts of employment or employment relationships be guaranteed by a guarantee institution or by any other effective form of protection.

Article 26
The right to dignity at work

With a view to ensuring the effective exercise of the right of all workers to protection of their dignity at work, the Parties undertake, in consultation with employers' and workers' organisations—

1. to promote awareness, information and prevention of sexual harassment in the workplace or in relation to work and to take all appropriate measures to protect workers from such conduct;
2. to promote awareness, information and prevention of recurrent reprehensible or distinctly negative and offensive actions directed against individual workers in the workplace or in relation to work and to take all appropriate measures to protect workers from such conduct.

Article 27
The right of workers with family responsibilities to equal opportunities and equal treatment

With a view to ensuring the exercise of the right to equality of opportunity and treatment for men and women workers with family responsibilities and between such workers and other workers, the Parties undertake—

1. to take appropriate measures—
   (a) to enable workers with family responsibilities to enter and remain in employment, as well as to re-enter employment after an absence due to those responsibilities, including measures in the field of vocational guidance and training;
   (b) to take account of their needs in terms of conditions of employment and social security;
   (c) to develop or promote services, public or private, in particular child daycare services and other childcare arrangements;
2. to provide a possibility for either parent to obtain, during a period after maternity leave, parental leave to take care of a child, the duration and conditions of which should be determined by national legislation, collective agreements or practice;
3. to ensure that family responsibilities shall not, as such, constitute a valid reason for termination of employment.

Article 28
The right of workers' representatives to protection in the undertaking and facilities to be accorded to them

With a view to ensuring the effective exercise of the right of workers' representatives to carry out their functions, the Parties undertake to ensure that in the undertaking—

(a) they enjoy effective protection against acts prejudicial to them, including dismissal, based on their status or activities as workers' representatives within the undertaking;

(b) they are afforded such facilities as may be appropriate in order to enable them to carry out their functions promptly and efficiently, account being taken of the industrial relations system of the country and the needs, size and capabilities of the undertaking concerned.

Article 29
The right to information and consultation in collective redundancy procedures
With a view to ensuring the effective exercise of the right of workers to be informed and consulted in situations of collective redundancies, the Parties undertake to ensure that employers shall inform and consult workers' representatives, in good time prior to such collective redundancies, on ways and means of avoiding collective redundancies or limiting their occurrence and mitigating their consequences, for example by recourse to accompanying social measures aimed, in particular, at aid for the redeployment or retraining of the workers concerned.

Article 30
The right to protection against poverty and social exclusion
With a view to ensuring the effective exercise of the right to protection against poverty and social exclusion, the Parties undertake—

(a) to take measures within the framework of an overall and co-ordinated approach to promote the effective access of persons who live or risk living in a situation of social exclusion or poverty, as well as their families, to, in particular, employment, housing, training, education, culture and social and medical assistance;

(b) to review these measures with a view to their adaptation if necessary.

Article 31
The right to housing
With a view to ensuring the effective exercise of the right to housing, the Parties undertake to take measures designed—

1. to promote access to housing of an adequate standard;
2. to prevent and reduce homelessness with a view to its gradual elimination;
3. to make the price of housing accessible to those without adequate resources.

PART III

[5.21]
Article A
Undertakings

1. Subject to the provisions of Article B below, each of the Parties undertakes—

(a) to consider Part I of this Charter as a declaration of the aims which it will pursue by all appropriate means, as stated in the introductory paragraph of that part;

(b) to consider itself bound by at least six of the following nine articles of Part II of this Charter: Articles 1, 5, 6, 7, 12, 13, 16, 19 and 20;

(c) to consider itself bound by an additional number of articles or numbered paragraphs of Part II of the Charter which it may select, provided that the total number of articles or numbered paragraphs by which it is bound is not less than sixteen articles or sixty-three numbered paragraphs.

2. The articles or paragraphs selected in accordance with sub-paragraphs b and c of paragraph 1 of this article shall be notified to the Secretary General of the Council of Europe at the time when the instrument of ratification, acceptance or approval is deposited.

3. Any Party may, at a later date, declare by notification addressed to the Secretary General that it considers itself bound by any articles or any numbered paragraphs of Part II of the Charter which it has not already accepted under the terms of paragraph 1 of this article. Such undertakings subsequently given shall be deemed to be an integral part of the ratification, acceptance or approval and shall have the same effect as from the first day of the month following the expiration of a period of one month after the date of the notification.

4. Each Party shall maintain a system of labour inspection appropriate to national conditions.

Article B
Links with the European Social Charter and the 1988 Additional Protocol
No Contracting Party to the European Social Charter or Party to the Additional Protocol of 5 May 1988 may ratify, accept or approve this Charter without considering itself bound by at least the provisions corresponding to the provisions of the European Social Charter and, where appropriate, of the Additional Protocol, to which it was bound.

Acceptance of the obligations of any provision of this Charter shall, from the date of entry into force of those obligations for the Party concerned, result in the corresponding provision of the European Social Charter and, where appropriate, of its Additional Protocol of 1988 ceasing to apply to the Party concerned in the event of that Party being bound by the first of those instruments or by both instruments.

PART IV

[5.22]
Article C
Supervision of the implementation of the undertakings contained in this Charter
The implementation of the legal obligations contained in this Charter shall be submitted to the same supervision as the European Social Charter.

Article D
Collective complaints
1. The provisions of the Additional Protocol to the European Social Charter providing for a system of collective complaints shall apply to the undertakings given in this Charter for the States which have ratified the said Protocol.
2. Any State which is not bound by the Additional Protocol to the European Social Charter providing for a system of collective complaints may when depositing its instrument of ratification, acceptance or approval of this Charter or at any time thereafter, declare by notification addressed to the Secretary General of the Council of Europe, that it accepts the supervision of its obligations under this Charter following the procedure provided for in the said Protocol.

PART V

[5.23]
Article E
Non-discrimination
The enjoyment of the rights set forth in this Charter shall be secured without discrimination on any ground such as race, colour, sex, language, religion, political or other opinion, national extraction or social origin, health, association with a national minority, birth or other status.

Article F
Derogations in time of war or public emergency
1. In time of war or other public emergency threatening the life of the nation any Party may take measures derogating from its obligations under this Charter to the extent strictly required by the exigencies of the situation, provided that such measures are not inconsistent with its other obligations under international law.
2. Any Party which has availed itself of this right of derogation shall, within a reasonable lapse of time, keep the Secretary General of the Council of Europe fully informed of the measures taken and of the reasons therefor. It shall likewise inform the Secretary General when such measures have ceased to operate and the provisions of the Charter which it has accepted are again being fully executed.

Article G
Restrictions
1. The rights and principles set forth in Part I when effectively realised, and their effective exercise as provided for in Part II, shall not be subject to any restrictions or limitations not specified in those parts, except such as are prescribed by law and are necessary in a democratic society for the protection of the rights and freedoms of others or for the protection of public interest, national security, public health, or morals.
2. The restrictions permitted under this Charter to the rights and obligations set forth herein shall not be applied for any purpose other than that for which they have been prescribed.

Article H
Relations between the Charter and domestic law or international agreements
The provisions of this Charter shall not prejudice the provisions of domestic law or of any bilateral or multilateral treaties, conventions or agreements which are already in force, or may come into force, under which more favourable treatment would be accorded to the persons protected.

Article I
Implementation of the undertakings given
1. Without prejudice to the methods of implementation foreseen in these articles the relevant provisions of Articles 1 to 31 of Part II of this Charter shall be implemented by—

(a) laws or regulations;
(b) agreements between employers or employers' organisations and workers' organisations;
(c) a combination of those two methods;
(d) other appropriate means.

2. Compliance with the undertakings deriving from the provisions of paragraphs 1, 2, 3, 4, 5 and 7 of Article 2, paragraphs 4, 6 and 7 of Article 7, paragraphs 1, 2, 3 and 5 of Article 10 and Articles 21 and 22 of Part II of this Charter shall be regarded as effective if the provisions are applied, in accordance with paragraph 1 of this article, to the great majority of the workers concerned.

Article J
Amendments

1. Any amendment to Parts I and II of this Charter with the purpose of extending the rights guaranteed in this Charter as well as any amendment to Parts III to VI, proposed by a Party or by the Governmental Committee, shall be communicated to the Secretary General of the Council of Europe and forwarded by the Secretary General to the Parties to this Charter.
2. Any amendment proposed in accordance with the provisions of the preceding paragraph shall be examined by the Governmental Committee which shall submit the text adopted to the Committee of Ministers for approval after consultation with the Parliamentary Assembly. After its approval by the Committee of Ministers this text shall be forwarded to the Parties for acceptance.
3. Any amendment to Part I and to Part II of this Charter shall enter into force, in respect of those Parties which have accepted it, on the first day of the month following the expiration of a period of one month after the date on which three Parties have informed the Secretary General that they have accepted it.

In respect of any Party which subsequently accepts it, the amendment shall enter into force on the first day of the month following the expiration of a period of one month after the date on which that Party has informed the Secretary General of its acceptance.

4. Any amendment to Parts III to VI of this Charter shall enter into force on the first day of the month following the expiration of a period of one month after the date on which all Parties have informed the Secretary General that they have accepted it.

PART VI

[5.24]
Article K
Signature, ratification and entry into force

1. This Charter shall be open for signature by the member States of the Council of Europe. It shall be subject to ratification, acceptance or approval. Instruments of ratification, acceptance or approval shall be deposited with the Secretary General of the Council of Europe.
2. This Charter shall enter into force on the first day of the month following the expiration of a period of one month after the date on which three member States of the Council of Europe have expressed their consent to be bound by this Charter in accordance with the preceding paragraph.
3. In respect of any member State which subsequently expresses its consent to be bound by this Charter, it shall enter into force on the first day of the month following the expiration of a period of one month after the date of the deposit of the instrument of ratification, acceptance or approval.

Article L
Territorial application

1. This Charter shall apply to the metropolitan territory of each Party. Each signatory may, at the time of signature or of the deposit of its instrument of ratification, acceptance or approval, specify, by declaration addressed to the Secretary General of the Council of Europe, the territory which shall be considered to be its metropolitan territory for this purpose.
2. Any signatory may, at the time of signature or of the deposit of its instrument of ratification, acceptance or approval, or at any time thereafter, declare by notification addressed to the Secretary General of the Council of Europe, that the Charter shall extend in whole or in part to a non-metropolitan territory or territories specified in the said declaration for whose international relations it is responsible or for which it assumes international responsibility. It shall specify in the declaration the articles or paragraphs of Part II of the Charter which it accepts as binding in respect of the territories named in the declaration.
3. The Charter shall extend its application to the territory or territories named in the aforesaid declaration as from the first day of the month following the expiration of a period of one month after the date of receipt of the notification of such declaration by the Secretary General.
4. Any Party may declare at a later date by notification addressed to the Secretary General of the Council of Europe that, in respect of one or more of the territories to which the Charter has been applied in accordance with paragraph 2 of this article, it accepts as binding any articles or any numbered paragraphs which it has not already accepted in respect of that territory or territories.

Such undertakings subsequently given shall be deemed to be an integral part of the original declaration in respect of the territory concerned, and shall have the same effect as from the first day of the month following the expiration of a period of one month after the date of receipt of such notification by the Secretary General.

Article M
Denunciation
1. Any Party may denounce this Charter only at the end of a period of five years from the date on which the Charter entered into force for it, or at the end of any subsequent period of two years, and in either case after giving six months' notice to the Secretary General of the Council of Europe who shall inform the other Parties accordingly.
2. Any Party may, in accordance with the provisions set out in the preceding paragraph, denounce any article or paragraph of Part II of the Charter accepted by it provided that the number of articles or paragraphs by which this Party is bound shall never be less than sixteen in the former case and sixty-three in the latter and that this number of articles or paragraphs shall continue to include the articles selected by the Party among those to which special reference is made in Article A, paragraph 1, sub-paragraph b.
3. Any Party may denounce the present Charter or any of the articles or paragraphs of Part II of the Charter under the conditions specified in paragraph 1 of this article in respect of any territory to which the said Charter is applicable, by virtue of a declaration made in accordance with paragraph 2 of Article L.

Article N
Appendix
The appendix to this Charter shall form an integral part of it.

Article O
Notifications
The Secretary General of the Council of Europe shall notify the member States of the Council and the Director General of the International Labour Office of—
- (a) any signature;
- (b) the deposit of any instrument of ratification, acceptance or approval;
- (c) any date of entry into force of this Charter in accordance with Article K;
- (d) any declaration made in application of Articles A, paragraphs 2 and 3, D, paragraphs 1 and 2, F, paragraph 2, L, paragraphs 1, 2, 3 and 4;
- (e) any amendment in accordance with Article J;
- (f) any denunciation in accordance with Article M;
- (g) any other act, notification or communication relating to this Charter.

In witness whereof, the undersigned, being duly authorised thereto, have signed this revised Charter.

Done at Strasbourg, this 3rd day of May 1996, in English and French, both texts being equally authentic, in a single copy which shall be deposited in the archives of the Council of Europe. The Secretary General of the Council of Europe shall transmit certified copies to each member State of the Council of Europe and to the Director General of the International Labour Office.

APPENDIX TO THE REVISED EUROPEAN SOCIAL CHARTER

SCOPE OF THE REVISED EUROPEAN SOCIAL CHARTER IN TERMS OF PERSONS PROTECTED

[5.25]
1. Without prejudice to Article 12, paragraph 4, and Article 13, paragraph 4, the persons covered by Articles 1 to 17 and 20 to 31 include foreigners only in so far as they are nationals of other Parties lawfully resident or working regularly within the territory of the Party concerned, subject to the understanding that these articles are to be interpreted in the light of the provisions of Articles 18 and 19.

This interpretation would not prejudice the extension of similar facilities to other persons by any of the Parties.

2. Each Party will grant to refugees as defined in the Convention relating to the Status of Refugees, signed in Geneva on 28 July 1951 and in the Protocol of 31 January 1967, and lawfully staying in its territory, treatment as favourable as possible, and in any case not less favourable than under the obligations accepted by the Party under the said convention and under any other existing international instruments applicable to those refugees.

3. Each Party will grant to stateless persons as defined in the Convention on the Status of Stateless Persons done in New York on 28 September 1954 and lawfully staying in its territory, treatment as favourable as possible and in any case not less favourable than under the obligations accepted by the Party under the said instrument and under any other existing international instruments applicable to those stateless persons.

PART I, PARAGRAPH 18, AND PART II, ARTICLE 18, PARAGRAPH 1

It is understood that these provisions are not concerned with the question of entry into the territories of the Parties and do not prejudice the provisions of the European Convention on Establishment, signed in Paris on 13 December 1955.

PART II

Article 1, paragraph 2
This provision shall not be interpreted as prohibiting or authorising any union security clause or practice.

Article 2, paragraph 6
Parties may provide that this provision shall not apply—
- (a) to workers having a contract or employment relationship with a total duration not exceeding one month and/or with a working week not exceeding eight hours;
- (b) where the contract or employment relationship is of a casual and/or specific nature, provided, in these cases, that its non-application is justified by objective considerations.

Article 3, paragraph 4
It is understood that for the purposes of this provision the functions, organisation and conditions of operation of these services shall be determined by national laws or regulations, collective agreements or other means appropriate to national conditions.

Article 4, paragraph 4
This provision shall be so understood as not to prohibit immediate dismissal for any serious offence.

Article 4, paragraph 5
It is understood that a Party may give the undertaking required in this paragraph if the great majority of workers are not permitted to suffer deductions from wages either by law or through collective agreements or arbitration awards, the exceptions being those persons not so covered.

Article 6, paragraph 4
It is understood that each Party may, insofar as it is concerned, regulate the exercise of the right to strike by law, provided that any further restriction that this might place on the right can be justified under the terms of Article G.

Article 7, paragraph 2
This provision does not prevent Parties from providing in their legislation that young persons not having reached the minimum age laid down may perform work in so far as it is absolutely necessary for their vocational training where such work is carried out in accordance with conditions prescribed by the competent authority and measures are taken to protect the health and safety of these young persons.

Article 7, paragraph 8
It is understood that a Party may give the undertaking required in this paragraph if it fulfils the spirit of the undertaking by providing by law that the great majority of persons under eighteen years of age shall not be employed in night work.

Article 8, paragraph 2
This provision shall not be interpreted as laying down an absolute prohibition. Exceptions could be made, for instance, in the following cases—
- (a) if an employed woman has been guilty of misconduct which justifies breaking off the employment relationship;
- (b) if the undertaking concerned ceases to operate;
- (c) if the period prescribed in the employment contract has expired.

Article 12, paragraph 4
The words "and subject to the conditions laid down in such agreements" in the introduction to this paragraph are taken to imply *inter alia* that with regard to benefits which are available independently of any insurance contribution, a Party may require the completion of a prescribed period of residence before granting such benefits to nationals of other Parties.

Article 13, paragraph 4
Governments not Parties to the European Convention on Social and Medical Assistance may ratify the Charter in respect of this paragraph provided that they grant to nationals of other Parties a treatment which is in conformity with the provisions of the said convention.

Article 16
It is understood that the protection afforded in this provision covers single-parent families.

Article 17
It is understood that this provision covers all persons below the age of 18 years, unless under the law applicable to the child majority is attained earlier, without prejudice to the other specific provisions provided by the Charter, particularly Article 7.

This does not imply an obligation to provide compulsory education up to the above-mentioned age.

Article 19, paragraph 6
For the purpose of applying this provision, the term "family of a foreign worker" is understood to mean at least the worker's spouse and unmarried children, as long as the latter are considered to be minors by the receiving State and are dependent on the migrant worker.

Article 20
1. It is understood that social security matters, as well as other provisions relating to unemployment benefit, old age benefit and survivor's benefit, may be excluded from the scope of this article.
2. Provisions concerning the protection of women, particularly as regards pregnancy, confinement and the post-natal period, shall not be deemed to be discrimination as referred to in this article.
3. This article shall not prevent the adoption of specific measures aimed at removing *de facto* inequalities.
4. Occupational activities which, by reason of their nature or the context in which they are carried out, can be entrusted only to persons of a particular sex may be excluded from the scope of this article or some of its provisions. This provision is not to be interpreted as requiring the Parties to embody in laws or regulations a list of occupations which, by reason of their nature or the context in which they are carried out, may be reserved to persons of a particular sex.

Articles 21 and 22
1. For the purpose of the application of these articles, the term "workers' representatives" means persons who are recognised as such under national legislation or practice.
2. The terms "national legislation and practice" embrace as the case may be, in addition to laws and regulations, collective agreements, other agreements between employers and workers' representatives, customs as well as relevant case law.
3. For the purpose of the application of these articles, the term "undertaking" is understood as referring to a set of tangible and intangible components, with or without legal personality, formed to produce goods or provide services for financial gain and with power to determine its own market policy.
4. It is understood that religious communities and their institutions may be excluded from the application of these articles, even if these institutions are "undertakings" within the meaning of paragraph 3. Establishments pursuing activities which are inspired by certain ideals or guided by certain moral concepts, ideals and concepts which are protected by national legislation, may be excluded from the application of these articles to such an extent as is necessary to protect the orientation of the undertaking.
5. It is understood that where in a state the rights set out in these articles are exercised in the various establishments of the undertaking, the Party concerned is to be considered as fulfilling the obligations deriving from these provisions.
6. The Parties may exclude from the field of application of these articles, those undertakings employing less than a certain number of workers, to be determined by national legislation or practice.

Article 22

1. This provision affects neither the powers and obligations of states as regards the adoption of health and safety regulations for workplaces, nor the powers and responsibilities of the bodies in charge of monitoring their application.
2. The terms "social and socio-cultural services and facilities" are understood as referring to the social and/or cultural facilities for workers provided by some undertakings such as welfare assistance, sports fields, rooms for nursing mothers, libraries, children's holiday camps, etc.

Article 23, paragraph 1

For the purpose of the application of this paragraph, the term "for as long as possible" refers to the elderly person's physical, psychological and intellectual capacities.

Article 24

1. It is understood that for the purposes of this article the terms "termination of employment" and "terminated" mean termination of employment at the initiative of the employer.
2. It is understood that this article covers all workers but that a Party may exclude from some or all of its protection the following categories of employed persons—
   (a) workers engaged under a contract of employment for a specified period of time or a specified task;
   (b) workers undergoing a period of probation or a qualifying period of employment, provided that this is determined in advance and is of a reasonable duration;
   (c) workers engaged on a casual basis for a short period.
3. For the purpose of this article the following, in particular, shall not constitute valid reasons for termination of employment—
   (a) trade union membership or participation in union activities outside working hours, or, with the consent of the employer, within working hours;
   (b) seeking office as, acting or having acted in the capacity of a workers' representative;
   (c) the filing of a complaint or the participation in proceedings against an employer involving alleged violation of laws or regulations or recourse to competent administrative authorities;
   (d) race, colour, sex, marital status, family responsibilities, pregnancy, religion, political opinion, national extraction or social origin;
   (e) maternity or parental leave;
   (f) temporary absence from work due to illness or injury.
4. It is understood that compensation or other appropriate relief in case of termination of employment without valid reasons shall be determined by national laws or regulations, collective agreements or other means appropriate to national conditions.

Article 25

1. It is understood that the competent national authority may, by way of exemption and after consulting organisations of employers and workers, exclude certain categories of workers from the protection provided in this provision by reason of the special nature of their employment relationship.
2. It is understood that the definition of the term "insolvency" must be determined by national law and practice.
3. The workers' claims covered by this provision shall include at least—
   (a) the workers' claims for wages relating to a prescribed period, which shall not be less than three months under a privilege system and eight weeks under a guarantee system, prior to the insolvency or to the termination of employment;
   (b) the workers' claims for holiday pay due as a result of work performed during the year in which the insolvency or the termination of employment occurred;
   (c) the workers' claims for amounts due in respect of other types of paid absence relating to a prescribed period, which shall not be less than three months under a privilege system and eight weeks under a guarantee system, prior to the insolvency or the termination of the employment.
4. National laws or regulations may limit the protection of workers' claims to a prescribed amount, which shall be of a socially acceptable level.

Article 26

It is understood that this article does not require that legislation be enacted by the Parties.

It is understood that paragraph 2 does not cover sexual harassment.

Article 27

It is understood that this article applies to men and women workers with family responsibilities in relation to their dependent children as well as in relation to other members of their immediate family who clearly need their care or support where such responsibilities restrict their possibilities of preparing for, entering, participating in or advancing in economic activity. The terms "dependent children" and "other members of their immediate family who clearly need their care and support" mean persons defined as such by the national legislation of the Party concerned.

Articles 28 and 29
For the purpose of the application of this article, the term "workers' representatives" means persons who are recognised as such under national legislation or practice.

PART III

It is understood that the Charter contains legal obligations of an international character, the application of which is submitted solely to the supervision provided for in Part IV thereof.

Article A, paragraph 1
It is understood that the numbered paragraphs may include articles consisting of only one paragraph.

Article B, paragraph 2
For the purpose of paragraph 2 of Article B, the provisions of the revised Charter correspond to the provisions of the Charter with the same article or paragraph number with the exception of—

(a) Article 3, paragraph 2, of the revised Charter which corresponds to Article 3, paragraphs 1 and 3, of the Charter;
(b) Article 3, paragraph 3, of the revised Charter which corresponds to Article 3, paragraphs 2 and 3, of the Charter;
(c) Article 10, paragraph 5, of the revised Charter which corresponds to Article 10, paragraph 4, of the Charter;
(d) Article 17, paragraph 1, of the revised Charter which corresponds to Article 17 of the Charter.

PART V

Article E
A differential treatment based on an objective and reasonable justification shall not be deemed discriminatory.

Article F
The terms "in time of war or other public emergency" shall be so understood as to cover also the *threat* of war.

Article I
It is understood that workers excluded in accordance with the appendix to Articles 21 and 22 are not taken into account in establishing the number of workers concerned.

Article J
The term "amendment" shall be extended so as to cover also the addition of new articles to the Charter.

INTERNATIONAL LABOUR ORGANISATION CONVENTION (NO 183) CONCERNING THE REVISION OF THE MATERNITY PROTECTION CONVENTION (REVISED), (2000)

NOTES

This Convention was adopted on 15 June 2000 and came into force on 7 February 2002. As of 6 April 2013, this Convention has not been ratified by the UK.

SCOPE

[5.26]
Article 1
For the purposes of this Convention, the term ***woman*** applies to any female person without discrimination whatsoever and the term ***child*** applies to any child without discrimination whatsoever.

Article 2

1. This Convention applies to all employed women, including those in atypical forms of dependent work.
2. However, each Member which ratifies this Convention may, after consulting the representative organisations of employers and workers concerned, exclude wholly or partly from the scope of the Convention limited categories of workers when its application to them would raise special problems of a substantial nature.
3. Each Member which avails itself of the possibility afforded in the preceding paragraph shall, in its first report on the application of the Convention under article 22 of the Constitution of the International Labour Organisation, list the categories of workers thus excluded and the reasons for their exclusion. In its subsequent reports, the Member shall describe the measures taken with a view to progressively extending the provisions of the Convention to these categories.

HEALTH PROTECTION

Article 3

Each Member shall, after consulting the representative organisations of employers and workers, adopt appropriate measures to ensure that pregnant or breastfeeding women are not obliged to perform work which has been determined by the competent authority to be prejudicial to the health of the mother or the child, or where an assessment has established a significant risk to the mother's health or that of her child.

MATERNITY LEAVE

Article 4

1. On production of a medical certificate or other appropriate certification, as determined by national law and practice, stating the presumed date of childbirth, a woman to whom this Convention applies shall be entitled to a period of maternity leave of not less than 14 weeks.
2. The length of the period of leave referred to above shall be specified by each Member in a declaration accompanying its ratification of this Convention.
3. Each Member may subsequently deposit with the Director-General of the International Labour Office a further declaration extending the period of maternity leave.
4. With due regard to the protection of the health of the mother and that of the child, maternity leave shall include a period of six weeks' compulsory leave after childbirth, unless otherwise agreed at the national level by the government and the representative organisations of employers and workers.
5. The prenatal portion of maternity leave shall be extended by any period elapsing between the presumed date of childbirth and the actual date of childbirth, without reduction in any compulsory portion of postnatal leave.

LEAVE IN CASE OF ILLNESS OR COMPLICATIONS

Article 5

On production of a medical certificate, leave shall be provided before or after the maternity leave period in the case of illness, complications or risk of complications arising out of pregnancy or childbirth. The nature and the maximum duration of such leave may be specified in accordance with national law and practice.

BENEFITS

Article 6

1. Cash benefits shall be provided, in accordance with national laws and regulations, or in any other manner consistent with national practice, to women who are absent from work on leave referred to in Articles 4 or 5.
2. Cash benefits shall be at a level which ensures that the woman can maintain herself and her child in proper conditions of health and with a suitable standard of living.
3. Where, under national law or practice, cash benefits paid with respect to leave referred to in Article 4 are based on previous earnings, the amount of such benefits shall not be less than two-thirds of the woman's previous earnings or of such of those earnings as are taken into account for the purpose of computing benefits.
4. Where, under national law or practice, other methods are used to determine the cash benefits paid with respect to leave referred to in Article 4, the amount of such benefits shall be comparable to the amount resulting on average from the application of the preceding paragraph.
5. Each Member shall ensure that the conditions to qualify for cash benefits can be satisfied by a large majority of the women to whom this Convention applies.

6. Where a woman does not meet the conditions to qualify for cash benefits under national laws and regulations or in any other manner consistent with national practice, she shall be entitled to adequate benefits out of social assistance funds, subject to the means test required for such assistance.
7. Medical benefits shall be provided for the woman and her child in accordance with national laws and regulations or in any other manner consistent with national practice. Medical benefits shall include prenatal, childbirth and postnatal care, as well as hospitalization care when necessary.
8. In order to protect the situation of women in the labour market, benefits in respect of the leave referred to in Articles 4 and 5 shall be provided through compulsory social insurance or public funds, or in a manner determined by national law and practice. An employer shall not be individually liable for the direct cost of any such monetary benefit to a woman employed by him or her without that employer's specific agreement except where:
   (a) such is provided for in national law or practice in a member State prior to the date of adoption of this Convention by the International Labour Conference; or
   (b) it is subsequently agreed at the national level by the government and the representative organisations of employers and workers.

Article 7
1. A Member whose economy and social security system are insufficiently developed shall be deemed to be in compliance with Article 6, paragraphs 3 and 4, if cash benefits are provided at a rate no lower than a rate payable for sickness or temporary disability in accordance with national laws and regulations.
2. A Member which avails itself of the possibility afforded in the preceding paragraph shall, in its first report on the application of this Convention under article 22 of the Constitution of the International Labour Organisation, explain the reasons therefor and indicate the rate at which cash benefits are provided. In its subsequent reports, the Member shall describe the measures taken with a view to progressively raising the rate of benefits.

EMPLOYMENT PROTECTION AND NON-DISCRIMINATION

Article 8
1. It shall be unlawful for an employer to terminate the employment of a woman during her pregnancy or absence on leave referred to in Articles 4 or 5 or during a period following her return to work to be prescribed by national laws or regulations, except on grounds unrelated to the pregnancy or birth of the child and its consequences or nursing. The burden of proving that the reasons for dismissal are unrelated to pregnancy or childbirth and its consequences or nursing shall rest on the employer.
2. A woman is guaranteed the right to return to the same position or an equivalent position paid at the same rate at the end of her maternity leave.

Article 9
1. Each Member shall adopt appropriate measures to ensure that maternity does not constitute a source of discrimination in employment, including - notwithstanding Article 2, paragraph 1 - access to employment.
2. Measures referred to in the preceding paragraph shall include a prohibition from requiring a test for pregnancy or a certificate of such a test when a woman is applying for employment, except where required by national laws or regulations in respect of work that is:
   (a) prohibited or restricted for pregnant or nursing women under national laws or regulations; or
   (b) where there is a recognized or significant risk to the health of the woman and child.

BREASTFEEDING MOTHERS

Article 10
1. A woman shall be provided with the right to one or more daily breaks or a daily reduction of hours of work to breastfeed her child.
2. The period during which nursing breaks or the reduction of daily hours of work are allowed, their number, the duration of nursing breaks and the procedures for the reduction of daily hours of work shall be determined by national law and practice. These breaks or the reduction of daily hours of work shall be counted as working time and remunerated accordingly.

PERIODIC REVIEW

Article 11
Each Member shall examine periodically, in consultation with the representative organisations of employers and workers, the appropriateness of extending the period of leave referred to in Article 4 or of increasing the amount or the rate of the cash benefits referred to in Article 6.

IMPLEMENTATION

Article 12
This Convention shall be implemented by means of laws or regulations, except in so far as effect is given to it by other means such as collective agreements, arbitration awards, court decisions, or in any other manner consistent with national practice.

FINAL PROVISIONS

Article 13
This Convention revises the Maternity Protection Convention (Revised), 1952.

Article 14
The formal ratifications of this Convention shall be communicated to the Director-General of the International Labour Office for registration.

Article 15
1. This Convention shall be binding only upon those Members of the International Labour Organisation whose ratifications have been registered with the Director-General of the International Labour Office.
2. It shall come into force 12 months after the date on which the ratifications of two Members have been registered with the Director-General.
3. Thereafter, this Convention shall come into force for any Member 12 months after the date on which its ratification has been registered.

Article 16
1. A Member which has ratified this Convention may denounce it after the expiration of ten years from the date on which the Convention first comes into force, by an act communicated to the Director-General of the International Labour Office for registration. Such denunciation shall not take effect until one year after the date on which it is registered.
2. Each Member which has ratified this Convention and which does not, within the year following the expiration of the period of ten years mentioned in the preceding paragraph, exercise the right of denunciation provided for in this Article, will be bound for another period of ten years and, thereafter, may denounce this Convention at the expiration of each period of ten years under the terms provided for in this Article.

Article 17
1. The Director-General of the International Labour Office shall notify all Members of the International Labour Organisation of the registration of all ratifications and acts of denunciation communicated by the Members of the Organisation.
2. When notifying the Members of the Organisation of the registration of the second ratification, the Director-General shall draw the attention of the Members of the Organisation to the date upon which the Convention shall come into force.

Article 18
The Director-General of the International Labour Office shall communicate to the Secretary-General of the United Nations, for registration in accordance with article 102 of the Charter of the United Nations, full particulars of all ratifications and acts of denunciation registered by the Director-General in accordance with the provisions of the preceding Articles.

Article 19
At such times as it may consider necessary, the Governing Body of the International Labour Office shall present to the General Conference a report on the working of this Convention and shall examine the desirability of placing on the agenda of the Conference the question of its revision in whole or in part.

Article 20

1. Should the Conference adopt a new Convention revising this Convention in whole or in part, then, unless the new Convention otherwise provides:

(a) the ratification by a Member of the new revising Convention shall ipso jure involve the immediate denunciation of this Convention, notwithstanding the provisions of Article 16 above, if and when the new revising Convention shall have come into force;

(b) as from the date when the new revising Convention comes into force, this Convention shall cease to be open to ratification by the Members.

2. This Convention shall in any case remain in force in its actual form and content for those Members which have ratified it but have not ratified the revising Convention.

Article 21

The English and French versions of the text of this Convention are equally authoritative.

UNITED NATIONS CONVENTION ON THE RIGHTS OF PERSONS WITH DISABILITIES

[13 December 2006]

NOTES

In accordance with Article 45(1) *post*, this Treaty entered into force on 3 May 2008 following ratification by the twentieth party. The UK ratified the Convention on 8 June 2009 and, in accordance with Article 45(2), the Treaty entered into force for the UK on 8 July 2009. The UK has entered a reservation in relation to Article 27 stating that "The United Kingdom accepts the provisions of the Convention, subject to the understanding that none of its obligations relating to equal treatment in employment and occupation, shall apply to the admission into or service in any of the naval, military or air forces of the Crown.". (Other reservations made by the UK relate to aspects of the Convention outside the scope of this work.)

The European Communities (Definition of Treaties) (United Nations Convention on the Rights of Persons with Disabilities) Order 2009, SI 2009/1181 **[2.1155]**, declares that the Convention is to be one of the European Union Treaties.

Arts 7–11, 13–25, 29–43, 47–49, which are outside the scope of this work, are omitted.

The Optional Protocol (which relates to the competence of the UN Committee on the Rights of Persons with Disabilities to receive communications from persons alleging violations of the Convention) is omitted for reasons of space; it was also ratified by the UK, on 7 August 2009, but is not within the scope of the designation in SI 2009/1181.

[5.27]

PREAMBLE

THE STATES PARTIES TO THE PRESENT CONVENTION,

(a) Recalling the principles proclaimed in the Charter of the United Nations[1] which recognize the inherent dignity and worth and the equal and inalienable rights of all members of the human family as the foundation of freedom, justice and peace in the world,

(b) Recognizing that the United Nations, in the Universal Declaration of Human Rights and in the International Covenants on Human Rights, has proclaimed and agreed that everyone is entitled to all the rights and freedoms set forth therein, without distinction of any kind,

(c) Reaffirming the universality, indivisibility, interdependence and interrelatedness of all human rights and fundamental freedoms and the need for persons with disabilities to be guaranteed their full enjoyment without discrimination,

(d) Recalling the International Covenant on Economic, Social and Cultural Rights,[2] the International Covenant on Civil and Political Rights,[3] the International Convention on the Elimination of All Forms of Racial Discrimination,[4] the Convention on the Elimination of All Forms of Discrimination against Women,[5] the Convention against Torture and Other Cruel, Inhuman or Degrading Treatment or Punishment,[6] the Convention on the Rights of the Child,[7] and the International Convention on the Protection of the Rights of All Migrant Workers and Members of Their Families,

(e) Recognizing that disability is an evolving concept and that disability results from the interaction between persons with impairments and attitudinal and environmental barriers that hinders their full and effective participation in society on an equal basis with others,

(f) Recognizing the importance of the principles and policy guidelines contained in the World Programme of Action concerning Disabled Persons and in the Standard Rules on the Equalization of Opportunities for Persons with Disabilities in influencing the promotion, formulation and evaluation of the policies, plans, programmes and actions at the national, regional and international levels to further equalize opportunities for persons with disabilities,

(g) Emphasizing the importance of mainstreaming disability issues as an integral part of relevant strategies of sustainable development,

(h) Recognizing also that discrimination against any person on the basis of disability is a violation of the inherent dignity and worth of the human person,

(i) Recognizing further the diversity of persons with disabilities,

(j) Recognizing the need to promote and protect the human rights of all persons with disabilities, including those who require more intensive support,

(k) Concerned that, despite these various instruments and undertakings, persons with disabilities continue to face barriers in their participation as equal members of society and violations of their human rights in all parts of the world,

(l) Recognizing the importance of international cooperation for improving the living conditions of persons with disabilities in every country, particularly in developing countries,

(m) Recognizing the valued existing and potential contributions made by persons with disabilities to the overall well-being and diversity of their communities, and that the promotion of the full enjoyment by persons with disabilities of their human rights and fundamental freedoms and of full participation by persons with disabilities will result in their enhanced sense of belonging and in significant advances in the human, social and economic development of society and the eradication of poverty,

(n) Recognizing the importance for persons with disabilities of their individual autonomy and independence, including the freedom to make their own choices,

(o) Considering that persons with disabilities should have the opportunity to be actively involved in decision-making processes about policies and programmes, including those directly concerning them,

(p) Concerned about the difficult conditions faced by persons with disabilities who are subject to multiple or aggravated forms of discrimination on the basis of race, colour, sex, language, religion, political or other opinion, national, ethnic, indigenous or social origin, property, birth, age or other status,

(q) Recognizing that women and girls with disabilities are often at greater risk, both within and outside the home, of violence, injury or abuse, neglect or negligent treatment, maltreatment or exploitation,

(r) Recognizing that children with disabilities should have full enjoyment of all human rights and fundamental freedoms on an equal basis with other children, and recalling obligations to that end undertaken by States Parties to the Convention on the Rights of the Child,

(s) Emphasizing the need to incorporate a gender perspective in all efforts to promote the full enjoyment of human rights and fundamental freedoms by persons with disabilities,

(t) Highlighting the fact that the majority of persons with disabilities live in conditions of poverty, and in this regard recognizing the critical need to address the negative impact of poverty on persons with disabilities,

(u) Bearing in mind that conditions of peace and security based on full respect for the purposes and principles contained in the Charter of the United Nations and observance of applicable human rights instruments are indispensable for the full protection of persons with disabilities, in particular during armed conflicts and foreign occupation,

(v) Recognizing the importance of accessibility to the physical, social, economic and cultural environment, to health and education and to information and communication, in enabling persons with disabilities to fully enjoy all human rights and fundamental freedoms,

(w) Realizing that the individual, having duties to other individuals and to the community to which he or she belongs, is under a responsibility to strive for the promotion and observance of the rights recognized in the International Bill of Human Rights,

(x) Convinced that the family is the natural and fundamental group unit of society and is entitled to protection by society and the State, and that persons with disabilities and their family members should receive the necessary protection and assistance to enable families to contribute towards the full and equal enjoyment of the rights of persons with disabilities,

(y) Convinced that a comprehensive and integral international convention to promote and protect the rights and dignity of persons with disabilities will make a significant contribution to redressing the profound social disadvantage of persons with disabilities and promote their participation in the civil, political, economic, social and cultural spheres with equal opportunities, in both developing and developed countries,

NOTES

1 Treaty Series No 67 (1946) Cmd 7015

2 Treaty Series No 6 (1977) Cmnd 6702

3 Treaty Series No 6 (1977) Cm 6702

4 Treaty Series No 77 (1969) Cmnd 4108

5 Treaty Series No 2 (1989) Cm 643

[6] Treaty Series No 107 (1991) Cm 1775

[7] Treaty Series No 44 (1992) Cm 1976

HAVE AGREED AS FOLLOWS:

Article 1
Purpose
The purpose of the present Convention is to promote, protect and ensure the full and equal enjoyment of all human rights and fundamental freedoms by all persons with disabilities, and to promote respect for their inherent dignity. Persons with disabilities include those who have long-term physical, mental, intellectual or sensory impairments which in interaction with various barriers may hinder their full and effective participation in society on an equal basis with others.

Article 2
Definitions
For the purposes of the present Convention:

"Communication" includes languages, display of text, Braille, tactile communication, large print, accessible multimedia as well as written, audio, plain language, human-reader and augmentative and alternative modes, means and formats of communication, including accessible information and communication technology;

"Language" includes spoken and signed languages and other forms of non spoken languages;

"Discrimination on the basis of disability" means any distinction, exclusion or restriction on the basis of disability which has the purpose or effect of impairing or nullifying the recognition, enjoyment or exercise, on an equal basis with others, of all human rights and fundamental freedoms in the political, economic, social, cultural, civil or any other field. It includes all forms of discrimination, including denial of reasonable accommodation;

"Reasonable accommodation" means necessary and appropriate modification and adjustments not imposing a disproportionate or undue burden, where needed in a particular case, to ensure to persons with disabilities the enjoyment or exercise on an equal basis with others of all human rights and fundamental freedoms;

"Universal design" means the design of products, environments, programmes and services to be usable by all people, to the greatest extent possible, without the need for adaptation or specialized design. "Universal design" shall not exclude assistive devices for particular groups of persons with disabilities where this is needed.

Article 3
General Principles
The principles of the present Convention shall be:

(a) Respect for inherent dignity, individual autonomy including the freedom to make one's own choices, and independence of persons;
(b) Non-discrimination;
(c) Full and effective participation and inclusion in society;
(d) Respect for difference and acceptance of persons with disabilities as part of human diversity and humanity;
(e) Equality of opportunity;
(f) Accessibility;
(g) Equality between men and women;
(h) Respect for the evolving capacities of children with disabilities and respect for the right of children with disabilities to preserve their identities.

Article 4
General Obligations
1. States Parties undertake to ensure and promote the full realization of all human rights and fundamental freedoms for all persons with disabilities without discrimination of any kind on the basis of disability. To this end, States Parties undertake:

(a) To adopt all appropriate legislative, administrative and other measures for the implementation of the rights recognized in the present Convention;
(b) To take all appropriate measures, including legislation, to modify or abolish existing laws, regulations, customs and practices that constitute discrimination against persons with disabilities;
(c) To take into account the protection and promotion of the human rights of persons with disabilities in all policies and programmes;
(d) To refrain from engaging in any act or practice that is inconsistent with the present Convention and to ensure that public authorities and institutions act in conformity with the present Convention;

(e) To take all appropriate measures to eliminate discrimination on the basis of disability by any person, organisation or private enterprise;

(f) To undertake or promote research and development of universally designed goods, services, equipment and facilities, as defined in article 2 of the present Convention, which should require the minimum possible adaptation and the least cost to meet the specific needs of a person with disabilities, to promote their availability and use, and to promote universal design in the development of standards and guidelines;

(g) To undertake or promote research and development of, and to promote the availability and use of new technologies, including information and communications technologies, mobility aids, devices and assistive technologies, suitable for persons with disabilities, giving priority to technologies at an affordable cost;

(h) To provide accessible information to persons with disabilities about mobility aids, devices and assistive technologies, including new technologies, as well as other forms of assistance, support services and facilities;

(i) To promote the training of professionals and staff working with persons with disabilities in the rights recognized in the present Convention so as to better provide the assistance and services guaranteed by those rights.

2. With regard to economic, social and cultural rights, each State Party undertakes to take measures to the maximum of its available resources and, where needed, within the framework of international cooperation, with a view to achieving progressively the full realization of these rights, without prejudice to those obligations contained in the present Convention that are immediately applicable according to international law.

3. In the development and implementation of legislation and policies to implement the present Convention, and in other decision-making processes concerning issues relating to persons with disabilities, States Parties shall closely consult with and actively involve persons with disabilities, including children with disabilities, through their representative organisations.

4. Nothing in the present Convention shall affect any provisions which are more conducive to the realization of the rights of persons with disabilities and which may be contained in the law of a State Party or international law in force for that State. There shall be no restriction upon or derogation from any of the human rights and fundamental freedoms recognized or existing in any State Party to the present Convention pursuant to law, conventions, regulation or custom on the pretext that the present Convention does not recognize such rights or freedoms or that it recognizes them to a lesser extent.

5. The provisions of the present Convention shall extend to all parts of federal States without any limitations or exceptions.

Article 5
Equality and Non-discrimination

1. States Parties recognize that all persons are equal before and under the law and are entitled without any discrimination to the equal protection and equal benefit of the law.

2. States Parties shall prohibit all discrimination on the basis of disability and guarantee to persons with disabilities equal and effective legal protection against discrimination on all grounds.

3. In order to promote equality and eliminate discrimination, States Parties shall take all appropriate steps to ensure that reasonable accommodation is provided.

4. Specific measures which are necessary to accelerate or achieve de facto equality of persons with disabilities shall not be considered discrimination under the terms of the present Convention.

Article 6
Women with Disabilities

1. States Parties recognize that women and girls with disabilities are subject to multiple discrimination, and in this regard shall take measures to ensure the full and equal enjoyment by them of all human rights and fundamental freedoms.

2. States Parties shall take all appropriate measures to ensure the full development, advancement and empowerment of women, for the purpose of guaranteeing them the exercise and enjoyment of the human rights and fundamental freedoms set out in the present Convention.

Article 12
Equal Recognition before the Law

1. States Parties reaffirm that persons with disabilities have the right to recognition everywhere as persons before the law.

2. States Parties shall recognize that persons with disabilities enjoy legal capacity on an equal basis with others in all aspects of life.

3. States Parties shall take appropriate measures to provide access by persons with disabilities to the support they may require in exercising their legal capacity.

4. States Parties shall ensure that all measures that relate to the exercise of legal capacity provide for appropriate and effective safeguards to prevent abuse in accordance with international human rights law. Such safeguards shall ensure that measures relating to the exercise of legal capacity respect the rights, will and preferences of the person, are free of conflict of interest and undue influence, are proportional and tailored to the person's circumstances, apply for the shortest time possible and are subject to regular review by a competent, independent and impartial authority or judicial body. The safeguards shall be proportional to the degree to which such measures affect the person's rights and interests.
5. Subject to the provisions of this article, States Parties shall take all appropriate and effective measures to ensure the equal right of persons with disabilities to own or inherit property, to control their own financial affairs and to have equal access to bank loans, mortgages and other forms of financial credit, and shall ensure that persons with disabilities are not arbitrarily deprived of their property.

Article 26
Habilitation and Rehabilitation
1. States Parties shall take effective and appropriate measures, including through peer support, to enable persons with disabilities to attain and maintain maximum independence, full physical, mental, social and vocational ability, and full inclusion and participation in all aspects of life. To that end, States Parties shall organize, strengthen and extend comprehensive habilitation and rehabilitation services and programmes, particularly in the areas of health, employment, education and social services, in such a way that these services and programmes:
   (a) Begin at the earliest possible stage, and are based on the multi-disciplinary assessment of individual needs and strengths;
   (b) Support participation and inclusion in the community and all aspects of society, are voluntary, and are available to persons with disabilities as close as possible to their own communities, including in rural areas.
2. States Parties shall promote the development of initial and continuing training for professionals and staff working in habilitation and rehabilitation services.
3. States Parties shall promote the availability, knowledge and use of assistive devices and technologies, designed for persons with disabilities, as they relate to habilitation and rehabilitation.

Article 27
Work and Employment
1. States Parties recognize the right of persons with disabilities to work, on an equal basis with others; this includes the right to the opportunity to gain a living by work freely chosen or accepted in a labour market and work environment that is open, inclusive and accessible to persons with disabilities. States Parties shall safeguard and promote the realization of the right to work, including for those who acquire a disability during the course of employment, by taking appropriate steps, including through legislation, to, inter alia:
   (a) Prohibit discrimination on the basis of disability with regard to all matters concerning all forms of employment, including conditions of recruitment, hiring and employment, continuance of employment, career advancement and safe and healthy working conditions;
   (b) Protect the rights of persons with disabilities, on an equal basis with others, to just and favourable conditions of work, including equal opportunities and equal remuneration for work of equal value, safe and healthy working conditions, including protection from harassment, and the redress of grievances;
   (c) Ensure that persons with disabilities are able to exercise their labour and trade union rights on an equal basis with others;
   (d) Enable persons with disabilities to have effective access to general technical and vocational guidance programmes, placement services and vocational and continuing training;
   (e) Promote employment opportunities and career advancement for persons with disabilities in the labour market, as well as assistance in finding, obtaining, maintaining and returning to employment;
   (f) Promote opportunities for self-employment, entrepreneurship, the development of cooperatives and starting one's own business;
   (g) Employ persons with disabilities in the public sector;
   (h) Promote the employment of persons with disabilities in the private sector through appropriate policies and measures, which may include affirmative action programmes, incentives and other measures;
   (i) Ensure that reasonable accommodation is provided to persons with disabilities in the workplace;
   (j) Promote the acquisition by persons with disabilities of work experience in the open labour market;
   (k) Promote vocational and professional rehabilitation, job retention and return-to-work programmes for persons with disabilities.

2. States Parties shall ensure that persons with disabilities are not held in slavery or in servitude, and are protected, on an equal basis with others, from forced or compulsory labour.

Article 28
Adequate Standard of Living and Social Protection

1. States Parties recognize the right of persons with disabilities to an adequate standard of living for themselves and their families, including adequate food, clothing and housing, and to the continuous improvement of living conditions, and shall take appropriate steps to safeguard and promote the realization of this right without discrimination on the basis of disability.
2. States Parties recognize the right of persons with disabilities to social protection and to the enjoyment of that right without discrimination on the basis of disability, and shall take appropriate steps to safeguard and promote the realization of this right, including measures:
   (a) To ensure equal access by persons with disabilities to clean water services, and to ensure access to appropriate and affordable services, devices and other assistance for disability-related needs;
   (b) To ensure access by persons with disabilities, in particular women and girls with disabilities and older persons with disabilities, to social protection programmes and poverty reduction programmes;
   (c) To ensure access by persons with disabilities and their families living in situations of poverty to assistance from the State with disability related expenses, including adequate training, counselling, financial assistance and respite care;
   (d) To ensure access by persons with disabilities to public housing programmes;
   (e) To ensure equal access by persons with disabilities to retirement benefits and programmes.

Article 44
Regional Integration Organisations

1. "Regional integration organisation" shall mean an organisation constituted by sovereign States of a given region, to which its member States have transferred competence in respect of matters governed by the present Convention. Such organisations shall declare, in their instruments of formal confirmation or accession, the extent of their competence with respect to matters governed by the present Convention. Subsequently, they shall inform the depositary of any substantial modification in the extent of their competence.
2. References to "States Parties" in the present Convention shall apply to such organisations within the limits of their competence.
3. For the purposes of article 45, paragraph 1, and article 47, paragraphs 2 and 3, of the present Convention, any instrument deposited by a regional integration organisation shall not be counted.
4. Regional integration organisations, in matters within their competence, may exercise their right to vote in the Conference of States Parties, with a number of votes equal to the number of their member States that are Parties to the present Convention. Such an organisation shall not exercise its right to vote if any of its member States exercises its right, and vice versa.

Article 45
Entry into Force

1. The present Convention shall enter into force on the thirtieth day after the deposit of the twentieth instrument of ratification or accession.
2. For each State or regional integration organisation ratifying, formally confirming or acceding to the present Convention after the deposit of the twentieth such instrument, the Convention shall enter into force on the thirtieth day after the deposit of its own such instrument.

Article 46
Reservations

1. Reservations incompatible with the object and purpose of the present Convention shall not be permitted.
2. Reservations may be withdrawn at any time

Article 50
Authentic Texts

The Arabic, Chinese, English, French, Russian and Spanish texts of the present Convention shall be equally authentic.

IN WITNESS THEREOF the undersigned plenipotentiaries, being duly authorized thereto by their respective Governments, have signed the present Convention.

B. EMPLOYMENT APPEAL TRIBUNAL PRACTICE DIRECTION AND PRACTICE STATEMENT

PRACTICE DIRECTION (EMPLOYMENT APPEAL TRIBUNAL – PROCEDURE) 2008

NOTES

Commencement: 22 May 2008 (see para 1.1).

CONTENTS

1. INTRODUCTION AND OBJECTIVE

[5.28]

1.1 This Practice Direction ("PD") supersedes all previous Practice Directions. It comes into force on 22 May 2008.

1.2 The Employment Appeal Tribunal Rules 1993 (SI 1993/2854) as amended by the Employment Appeal Tribunal (Amendment) Rules 2001 (SI 2001/1128 and 2001/1476) and the Employment Appeal Tribunal (Amendment) Rules 2004 (SI 2004/2526) ("the Rules") apply to all proceedings irrespective of when those proceedings were commenced.

1.3 By s 30(3) of the Employment Tribunals Act 1996 ("ETA 1996") the Employment Appeal Tribunal ("the EAT") has power, subject to the Rules, to regulate its own procedure. In so doing, the EAT regards itself as subject in all its actions to the duties imposed by Rule 2A. It will seek to apply the overriding objective when it exercises any power given to it by the Rules or interprets any Rule.

1.4 The overriding objective of this PD is to enable the EAT to deal with cases justly. Dealing with a case justly includes, so far as is practicable:

- 1.4.1 ensuring that the parties are on an equal footing;
- 1.4.2 dealing with the case in ways which are proportionate to the importance and complexity of the issues;
- 1.4.3 ensuring that it is dealt with expeditiously and fairly;
- 1.4.4 saving expense.

1.5 The parties are required to help the EAT to further the overriding objective.

1.6 Where the Rules do not otherwise provide, the following procedure will apply to all appeals to the EAT.

1.7 The provisions of this PD are subject to any specific directions which the EAT may make in any particular case. Otherwise, the directions set out below must be complied with in all appeals from Employment Tribunals. In national security appeals, and appeals from the Certification Officer and the Central Arbitration Committee, the Rules set out the separate procedures to be followed and the EAT will normally give specific directions.

1.8 Where it is appropriate to the EAT's jurisdiction, procedure, unrestricted rights of representation and restricted costs regime, the EAT is guided by the Civil Procedure Rules. So, for example:

1.8.1 For the purpose of serving a valid Notice of Appeal under Rule 3 and para 3 below, when an Employment Tribunal decision is sent to parties on a Wednesday, that day does not count and the Notice of Appeal must arrive at the EAT by 4.00 pm on or before the Wednesday 6 weeks (ie 42 days) later.

1.8.2 When a date is given for serving of a document or for doing some other act, the complete document must be received by the EAT or the relevant party by 4.00pm on that date. Any document received after 4.00 pm will be deemed to be lodged on the next working day.

1.8.3 Except as provided in 1.8.4 below, all days count, but if a time limit expires on a day when the central office of the EAT, or the EAT office in Edinburgh (as appropriate), is closed, it is extended to the next working day.

1.8.4 Where the time limit is 5 days (eg an appeal against a Registrar's order or direction), Saturdays, Sundays, Christmas Day, Good Friday and Bank Holidays do not count. For example an appeal against an order made on a Wednesday must arrive at the EAT on or before the following Wednesday.

1.9 In this PD any reference to the date of an order shall mean the date stamped upon the relevant order by the EAT ("the seal date").

1.10 The parties can expect the EAT normally to have read the documents (or the documents indicated in any essential reading list if permission is granted under para 6.3 below for an enlarged appeal bundle) in advance of any hearing.

2. INSTITUTION OF APPEAL

[5.29]

2.1 The Notice of Appeal must be, or be substantially, in accordance with Form 1 (in the amended form annexed to this Practice Direction) or Forms 1A or 2 of the Schedule to the Rules and must identify the date of the judgment, decision or order being appealed. Copies of the judgment, decision or order appealed against and of the Employment Tribunal's written reasons, together with a copy of the Claim (ET1) and the Response (ET3) must be attached, or if not, a written explanation must be given. A Notice of Appeal without such documentation will not be validly lodged.

2.2 If the appellant has made an application to the Employment Tribunal for a review of its judgment or decision, a copy of such application should accompany the Notice of Appeal together with the judgment and written reasons of the Employment Tribunal in respect of that review application, or a statement, if such be the case, that a judgment is awaited. If any of these documents cannot be included, a written explanation must be given. The appellant should also attach (where they are relevant to the appeal) copies of any orders including case management orders made by the Employment Tribunal.

2.3 Where written reasons of the Employment Tribunal are not attached to the Notice of Appeal, either (as set out in the written explanation) because a request for written reasons has been refused by the Employment Tribunal or for some other reason, an appellant must, when lodging the Notice of Appeal, apply in writing to the EAT to exercise its discretion to hear the appeal without written reasons or to exercise its power to request written reasons from the Employment Tribunal, setting out the full grounds of that application.

2.4 The Notice of Appeal must clearly identify the point(s) of law which form(s) the ground(s) of appeal from the judgment, decision or order of the Employment Tribunal to the EAT. It should also state the order which the appellant will ask the EAT to make at the hearing.

2.5 Rules 3(7)–(10) give a judge or the Registrar power to decide that no further action shall be taken in certain cases where it appears that the Notice of Appeal or any part of it (a) discloses no reasonable grounds for bringing the appeal, or (b) is an abuse of the Employment Appeal Tribunal's process or is otherwise likely to obstruct the just disposal of proceedings. The Rules specify the rights of the appellant and the procedure to be followed. The appellant can request an oral hearing before a judge to challenge the decision. If it appears to the judge or Registrar that a Notice of Appeal or an application gives insufficient grounds of, or lacks clarity in identifying, a point of law, the judge or Registrar may postpone any decision under Rule 3(7) pending the appellant's amplification or clarification of the Notice of Appeal or further information from the Employment Tribunal.

2.6 **Perversity Appeals**: an appellant may not state as a ground of appeal simply words to the effect that "the judgment or order was contrary to the evidence," or that "there was no evidence to support the judgment or order", or that "the judgment or order was one which no reasonable Tribunal could have reached and was perverse" unless the Notice of Appeal also sets out full particulars of the matters relied on in support of those general grounds.

2.7 A party cannot reserve a right to amend, alter or add, to a Notice of Appeal or a respondent's Answer. Any application for permission to amend must be made as soon as practicable and must be accompanied by a draft of the amended Notice of Appeal or amended Answer which makes clear the precise amendments for which permission is sought.

2.8 A respondent to the appeal who wishes to resist the appeal and/or to cross-appeal, but who has not delivered a respondent's Answer as directed by the Registrar, or otherwise ordered, may be precluded from taking part in the appeal unless permission is granted to serve an Answer out of time.

2.9 Where an application is made for permission to institute or continue relevant proceedings by a person who has been made the subject of a Restriction of Proceedings Order pursuant to s 33 of ETA 1996, that application will be considered on paper by a judge, who may make an order granting, refusing or otherwise dealing with such application on paper.

3. TIME FOR INSTITUTING APPEALS

[5.30]

3.1 The time within which an appeal must be instituted depends on whether the appeal is against a judgment or against an order or decision of the Employment Tribunal.

3.2 If the appeal is against an order or decision, the appeal must be instituted within 42 days of the date of the order or decision. The EAT will treat a Tribunal's refusal to make an order or decision as itself constituting an order or decision. The date of an order or decision is the date when the order or decision was sent to the parties, which is normally recorded on or in the order or decision.

3.3 If the appeal is against a judgment, the appeal must be instituted within 42 days from the date on which the written record of the judgment was sent to the parties. However in three situations the time for appealing against a judgment will be 42 days from the date when written reasons were sent to the parties. This will be the case only if (1) written reasons were requested orally at the hearing before the Tribunal or (2) written reasons were requested in writing within 14 days of the date on which the written record of the judgment was sent to the parties or (3) the Tribunal itself reserved its reasons and gave them subsequently in writing: such exception will not apply if the request to the Tribunal for written reasons is made out of time (whether or not such request is granted). The date of the written record and of the written reasons is the date when they are sent to the parties, which is normally recorded on or in the written record and the written reasons.

3.4 The time limit referred to in paras 3.1 to 3.3 above apply even though the question of remedy and assessment of compensation by the Employment Tribunal has been adjourned or has not been dealt with and even though an application has been made to the Employment Tribunal for a review.

3.5 An application for an extension of time for appealing cannot be considered until a Notice of Appeal in accordance with para 2(1) above has been lodged with the EAT.

3.6 Any application for an extension of time for appealing must be made as an interim application to the Registrar, who will normally determine the application after inviting and considering written representations from each side. An interim appeal lies from the Registrar's decision to a judge. Such an appeal must be notified to the EAT within 5 days of the date when the Registrar's decision was sent to the parties. [See para 4.3 below.]

3.7 In determining whether to extend the time for appealing, particular attention will be paid to whether any good excuse for the delay has been shown and to the guidance contained in the decisions of the EAT and the Court of Appeal, as summarised in ***United Arab Emirates v Abdelghafar*** [1995] ICR 65, ***Aziz v Bethnal Green City Challenge Co Ltd*** [2000] IRLR 111 and ***Jurkowska v HI Mad*** [2008] EWCA Civ 231.

3.8 It is not usually a good reason for late lodgment of a Notice of Appeal that an application for litigation support from public funds has been made, but not yet determined; or that support is being sought from, but has not yet been provided by, some other body, such as a trade union, employers' association or the Equality and Human Rights Commission.

3.9 In any case of doubt or difficulty, a Notice of Appeal should be lodged in time and an application made to the Registrar for directions.

4. INTERIM APPLICATIONS

[5.31]

4.1 Interim applications should be made in writing (no particular form is required) and will be initially referred to the Registrar who after considering the papers may deal with the case or refer it to a judge. The judge may dispose of it himself or refer it to a full EAT hearing. Parties are encouraged to make any such applications at a Preliminary Hearing ("PH") or an Appointment for Directions if one is ordered (see paras 9.7–9.18 and 11.2 below).

4.2 Unless otherwise ordered, any application for extension of time will be considered and determined as though it were an interim application to the Registrar, who will normally determine the application after inviting and considering written representations from each side.

4.3 An interim appeal lies from the Registrar's decision to a judge. Such an appeal must be notified to the EAT within 5 days of the date when the Registrar's decision was sent to the parties.

5. THE RIGHT TO INSPECT THE REGISTER AND CERTAIN DOCUMENTS AND TO TAKE COPIES

[5.32]

5.1 Any document lodged in the Central Office of the EAT in London or in the EAT office in Edinburgh in any proceedings before the EAT shall be sealed with the seal of the EAT showing the date (and time, if received after 4.00 pm) on which the document was lodged.

5.2 Particulars of the date of delivery at the Central Office of the EAT or in the EAT office in Edinburgh of any document for filing or lodgment together with the time, if received after 4.00 pm, the date of the document and the title of the appeal of which the document forms part of the record shall be entered in the Register of Cases kept in the Central Office and in Edinburgh or in the file which forms part of the Register of Cases.

5.3 Any person shall be entitled during office hours by appointment to inspect and request a copy of any of the following documents filed or lodged in the Central Office or the EAT office in Edinburgh, namely:

5.3.1 any Notice of Appeal or respondent's Answer or any copy thereof;
5.3.2 any judgment or order given or made in court or any copy of such judgment or order; and
5.3.3 with the permission of the EAT, which may be granted on an application, any other document.

5.4 A copying charge per page will be payable for those documents mentioned in para 5.3 above.

5.5 Nothing in this Direction shall be taken as preventing any party to an appeal from inspecting and requesting a copy of any document filed or lodged in the Central Office or the EAT office in Edinburgh before the commencement of the appeal, but made with a view to its commencement.

6. PAPERS FOR USE AT THE HEARING

[5.33]

6.1 It is the responsibility of the parties or their advisers (see paras 6.5 and 6.6 below) to prepare a core bundle of papers for use at any hearing. Ultimate responsibility lies with the appellant, following consultation with other parties. The bundle must include only those exhibits (productions in Scotland) and documents used before the Employment Tribunal which are considered to be necessary for the appeal. It is the duty of the parties or their advisers to ensure that only those documents are included which are (a) relevant to the point(s) of law raised in the appeal and (b) likely to be referred to at the hearing. It is also the responsibility of parties to retain copies of all documents and correspondence, including hearing bundles, sent to EAT. Bundles (see para 6.2 below) used at one EAT hearing will not be retained by the EAT for a subsequent hearing.

6.2 The documents in the core bundle should be numbered by item, then paginated continuously and indexed, in the following order:

6.2.1 Judgment, decision or order appealed from and written reasons
6.2.2 Sealed Notice of Appeal
6.2.3 Respondent's Answer if a Full Hearing ("FH"), respondent's Submissions if a PH
6.2.4 ET1 claim (and any Additional Information or Written Answers)
6.2.5 ET3 response (and any Additional Information or Written Answers)
6.2.6 Questionnaire and Replies (discrimination and equal pay cases)
6.2.7 Relevant orders, judgments and written reasons of the Employment Tribunal
6.2.8 Relevant orders and judgments of the EAT
6.2.9 Affidavits and Employment Tribunal comments (where ordered)
6.2.10 Any documents agreed or ordered pursuant to para 7 below.

6.3 Other documents relevant to the particular hearing (for example the particulars or contract of employment and any procedures) referred to at the Employment Tribunal may follow in the core bundle, if the total pages do not exceed 100. No bundle containing more than 100 pages should be agreed or lodged without the permission of the Registrar or order of a judge which will not be granted without the provision of an essential reading list as soon as practicable thereafter. If permitted or ordered, further pages should follow, with consecutive pagination, in an additional bundle or bundles if appropriate.

6.4 All documents must be legible and unmarked.

6.5 **PH cases** (see para 9.5.2 below)**, Appeals from Registrar's Order, Rule 3(10) hearings, Appointments for Directions**: the appellant must prepare and lodge 4 copies (2 copies if judge sitting alone) of the bundle as soon as possible after service of the Notice of Appeal and no later than 28 days from the seal date of the relevant order unless otherwise directed.

6.6 **FH cases** (see para 9.5.3 below): the parties must co-operate in agreeing a bundle of papers for the hearing. By no later than 28 days from the seal date of the relevant order, unless otherwise directed, the appellant is responsible for ensuring that 4 copies (2 copies if judge sitting alone) of a bundle agreed by the parties is lodged at the EAT.

6.7 Warned List and Fast Track FH cases: the bundles should be lodged as soon as possible and (unless the hearing date is within seven days) in any event within seven days after the parties have been notified that the case is expedited or in the Warned List.

6.8 In the event of disagreement between the parties or difficulty in preparing the bundles, the Registrar may give appropriate directions, whether on application in writing (on notice) by one or more of the parties or of his/her own initiative.

7. EVIDENCE BEFORE THE EMPLOYMENT TRIBUNAL

[5.34]
7.1 An appellant who considers that a point of law raised in the Notice of Appeal cannot be argued without reference to evidence given (or not given) at the Employment Tribunal, the nature or substance of which does not, or does not sufficiently, appear from the written reasons, must ordinarily submit an application with the Notice of Appeal. The application is for the nature of such evidence (or lack of it) to be admitted, or if necessary for the relevant parts of the employment judge's notes of evidence to be produced. If such application is not so made, then it should be made:

7.1.1 if a PH is ordered, in the skeleton or written submissions lodged prior to such PH; or
7.1.2 if the case is listed for FH without a PH, then within 14 days of the seal date of the order so providing.

Any such application by a respondent to an appeal, must, if not made earlier, accompany the respondent's Answer.

7.2 The application must explain why such a matter is considered necessary in order to argue the point of law raised in the Notice of Appeal or respondent's Answer. The application must identify:

7.2.1 the issue(s) in the Notice of Appeal or respondent's Answer to which the matter is relevant;
7.2.2 the names of the witnesses whose evidence is considered relevant, alternatively the nature of the evidence the absence of which is considered relevant;
7.2.3 (if applicable) the part of the hearing when the evidence was given;
7.2.4 the gist of the evidence (or absence of evidence) alleged to be relevant; and
7.2.5 (if the party has a record), saying so and by whom and when it was made, or producing an extract from a witness statement given in writing at the hearing.

7.3 The application will be considered on the papers, or if appropriate at a PH, by the Registrar or a judge. The Registrar or a judge may give directions for written representations (if they have not already been lodged), or may determine the application, but will ordinarily make an order requiring the party who seeks to raise such a matter to give notice to the other party(ies) to the appeal/cross-appeal. The notice will require the other party(ies) to co-operate in agreeing, within 21 days (unless a shorter period is ordered), a statement or note of the relevant evidence, alternatively a statement that there was no such evidence. All parties are required to use their best endeavours to agree such a statement or note.

7.4 In the absence of such agreement within 21 days (or such shorter period as may be ordered) of the requirement, any party may make an application within seven days thereafter to the EAT, for directions. The party must enclose all relevant correspondence and give notice to the other parties. The directions may include: the resolution of the disagreement on the papers or at a hearing; the administration by one party to the others of, or a request to the employment judge to respond to, a questionnaire; or, if the EAT is satisfied that such notes are necessary, a request that the employment judge produce his/her notes of evidence either in whole or in part.

7.5 If the EAT requests any documents from the employment judge, it will supply copies to the parties upon receipt.

7.6 In an appeal from an Employment Tribunal which ordered its proceedings to be tape recorded, the EAT will apply the principles above to any application for a transcript.

7.7 A note of evidence is not to be produced and supplied to the parties to enable the parties to embark on a "fishing expedition" to establish grounds or additional grounds of appeal or because they have not kept their own notes of the evidence. If an application for such a note is found by the EAT to have been unreasonably made or if there is unreasonable lack of co-operation in agreeing a relevant note or statement, the party behaving unreasonably is at risk of being ordered to pay costs.

8. FRESH EVIDENCE AND NEW POINTS OF LAW

[5.35]
8.1 Where an application is made by a party to an appeal to put in, at the hearing of the appeal, any document which was not before the Employment Tribunal, and which has not been agreed in writing by the other parties, the application and a copy of the documents sought to be admitted should be lodged at the EAT with the Notice of Appeal or the respondent's Answer, as appropriate.

The application and copy should be served on the other parties. The same principle applies to any oral evidence not given at the Employment Tribunal which is sought to be adduced on the appeal. The nature and substance of such evidence together with the date when the party first became aware of its existence must be disclosed in a document, where appropriate a witness statement from the relevant witness with signed statement of truth, which must be similarly lodged and served.

8.2 In exercising its discretion to admit any fresh evidence or new document, the EAT will apply the principles set out in ***Ladd v Marshall*** [1954] 1WLR 1489, having regard to the overriding objective, ie:

8.2.1 the evidence could not have been obtained with reasonable diligence for use at the Employment Tribunal hearing;
8.2.2 it is relevant and would probably have had an important influence on the hearing;
8.2.3 it is apparently credible.

Accordingly the evidence and representations in support of the application must address these principles.

8.3 A party wishing to resist the application must, within 14 days of its being sent, submit any representations in response to the EAT and other parties.

8.4 The application will be considered by the Registrar or a judge on the papers (or, if appropriate, at a PH) who may determine the issue or give directions for a hearing or may seek comments from the employment judge. A copy of any comments received from the employment judge will be sent to all parties.

8.5 If a respondent intends to contend at the FH that the appellant has raised a point which was not argued below, the respondent shall so state:

8.5.1 if a PH has been ordered, in writing to the EAT and all parties, within 14 days of receiving the Notice of Appeal;
8.5.2 if the case is listed for a FH without a PH, in a respondent's Answer.

In the event of dispute the employment judge should be asked for his/her comments as to whether a particular legal argument was deployed.

9. CASE TRACKS AND DIRECTIONS: THE SIFT OF APPEALS

[5.36]
9.1 Consistent with the overriding objective, the EAT will seek to give directions for case management so that the case can be dealt with quickly, or better considered, and in the most effective and just way.

9.2 Applications and directions for case management will usually be dealt with on the papers ("the sift") by a judge, or by the Registrar with an appeal to a judge. Any party seeking directions must serve a copy on all parties. Directions may be given at any stage, before or after the registration of a Notice of Appeal. An order made will contain a time for compliance, which must be observed or be the subject of an application by any party to vary or discharge it, or to seek an extension of time. Otherwise, failure to comply with an order in time or at all may result in the EAT exercising its power under Rule 26 to strike out the appeal, cross-appeal or respondent's Answer or debar the party from taking any further part in the proceedings or to make any other order it thinks fit, including an award of costs.

9.3 Any application to vary or discharge an order, or to seek an extension of time, must be lodged at the EAT and served on the other parties within the time fixed for compliance. Such other parties must, if opposing the application and within 14 days (or such shorter period as may be ordered) of receiving it, submit their representations to the EAT and the other parties.

9.4 An application to amend a Notice of Appeal or respondent's Answer must include the text of the original document with any changes clearly marked and identifiable, for example with deletions struck through in red and the text of the amendment either written or underlined in red. Any subsequent amendments will have to be in a different identifiable colour.

9.5 Notices of Appeal are sifted by a judge or the Registrar so as to determine the most effective case management of the appeal. The sift will result in a decision as to which track the appeal will occupy, and directions will be given. There are 4 tracks:

9.5.1 Rule 3(7) cases [see para 9.6 below].
9.5.2 Preliminary Hearing (PH) cases [see paras 9.7 – 9.18 below].
9.5.3 Full Hearing (FH) cases [see para 9.19 below].
9.5.4 Fast Track Full Hearing ("FTFH") cases [see paras 9.20 – 9.21 below].

The judge or Registrar may also stay (or sist in Scotland) the appeal for a period, normally 21 days pending the making or the conclusion of an application by the appellant to the Employment Tribunal (if necessary out of time) for a review or pending the response by the Employment Tribunal to an invitation from the judge or Registrar to clarify, supplement or give its written reasons.

RULE 3(7) CASES (9.5.1)

9.6 The judge or Registrar, having considered the Notice of Appeal and, if appropriate, having obtained any additional information, may decide that it or any of the grounds contained in it discloses no reasonable grounds for bringing the appeal or is an abuse of the process or otherwise likely to obstruct the just disposal of the proceedings. Reasons will be sent and within 28 days the appellant may submit a fresh Notice of Appeal for further consideration or request an oral hearing before a judge. At that hearing the judge may confirm the earlier decision or order that the appeal proceeds to a Preliminary or Full Hearing. A hearing under Rule 3(10), including judgment and any directions, will normally last not more than one and a half hours. A judge or Registrar may also follow the Rule 3(7) procedure, of his or her own initiative, or on application, at any later stage of the proceedings, if appropriate.

PRELIMINARY HEARING CASES (9.5.2)

9.7 The purpose of a PH is to determine whether:

9.7.1 the grounds in the Notice of Appeal raise a point of law which gives the appeal a reasonable prospect of success at a FH; or

9.7.2 for some other compelling reason the appeal should be heard eg that the appellant seeks a declaration of incompatibility under the Human Rights Act 1998; or to argue that a decision binding on the EAT should be considered by a higher court.

9.8 Prior to the PH there will be automatic directions. These include sending the Notice of Appeal to the respondent(s) to the appeal. The direction may order or in any event will enable the respondent(s) to lodge and serve, within 14 days of the seal date of the order (unless otherwise directed), concise written submissions in response to the Notice of Appeal, dedicated to showing that there is no reasonable prospect of success for all or any grounds of any appeal. Such submissions will be considered at the PH.

9.9 If the respondent to the appeal intends to serve a cross-appeal this must be accompanied by written submissions and must be lodged and served within 14 days of service of the Notice of Appeal. The respondent to the appeal must make clear whether it is intended to advance the cross-appeal:

9.9.1 in any event (an unconditional cross-appeal); or

9.9.2 only if the Appellant succeeds (a conditional cross-appeal).

In either case the respondent is entitled to attend the PH, which will also amount to a PH of the cross-appeal, and make submissions.

9.10 All parties will be notified of the date fixed for the PH. In the normal case, unless ordered otherwise, only the appellant and/or a representative should attend to make submissions to the EAT on the issue whether the Notice of Appeal raises a point of law with a reasonable prospect of success:

9.10.1 Except where the respondent to the appeal makes a cross-appeal, or the EAT orders a hearing with all parties present, the respondent to the appeal is not required to attend the hearing and is not usually permitted to take part in it. But any written submissions as referred to in (8) above will be considered at the PH.

9.10.2 If the appellant does not attend, the appeal may nevertheless be dealt with as above on written submissions, and be wholly or in part dismissed or allowed to proceed.

9.11 The PH, including judgment and directions, will normally last no more than one hour.

9.12 The sift procedure will be applied to cross-appeals as well as appeals. If an appeal has been assigned to the FH track, without a PH, and the respondent includes a cross-appeal in the respondent's Answer, the respondent must immediately apply to the EAT in writing on notice to the appellant for directions on the papers as to whether the EAT considers that there should be a PH of the cross-appeal.

9.13 If satisfied that the appeal (and/or the cross-appeal) should be heard at a FH on all or some of the grounds of appeal, the EAT will give directions relating to, for example, a time estimate, any application for fresh evidence, a procedure in respect of matters of evidence before the Employment Tribunal not sufficiently appearing from the written reasons, the exchange and lodging of skeleton arguments and an appellant's Chronology, and bundles of documents and authorities.

9.14 Permission to amend a Notice of Appeal (or cross-appeal) may be granted:

9.14.1 **If the proposed amendment is produced at the hearing**, then, if such amendment has not previously been notified to the other parties, and the appeal (or cross-appeal) might not have been permitted to proceed but for the amendment, the opposing party(ies) will have the opportunity to apply on notice to vary or discharge the permission to proceed, and for consequential directions as to the hearing or disposal of the appeal or cross-appeal.

9.14.2 **If a draft amendment is not available at the PH**, an application for permission to amend, in writing on notice to the other party(ies) in accordance with para 9.4 above, will be permitted to be made within 14 days. Where, but for such proposed amendment, the appeal (or cross-appeal) may not have been permitted to proceed to a FH, provision may be made in the order on the PH for the appeal (or cross-appeal) to be dismissed if the application for permission to amend is not made. Where such an application is made and refused, provision will be made for any party to have liberty to apply, in writing on notice to the other party(ies), as to the hearing or disposal of the appeal.

9.15 If not satisfied that the appeal, or any particular ground of it, should go forward to a FH, the EAT at the PH will dismiss the appeal, wholly or in part, and give a judgment setting out the reasons for doing so.

9.16 If an appeal is permitted to go forward to an FH on all grounds, a reasoned judgment will not normally be given.

9.17 Parties who become aware that a similar point is raised in other proceedings at an Employment Tribunal or the EAT are encouraged to co-operate in bringing this to the attention of the Registrar so that consideration can be given to the most expedient way of dealing with the cases, in particular to the possibility of having two or more appeals heard together.

9.18 If an appeal is permitted to go forward to an FH, a listing category will be assigned ie:

P (recommended to be heard in the President's list);

A (complex, and raising point(s) of law of public importance);

B (any other case);

The President reserves the discretion to alter any relevant category as circumstances require.

FULL HEARING CASES (9.5.3)

9.19 If a judge or the Registrar decides to list the case for an FH without a PH s/he will consider appropriate directions, relating for example to amendment, further information, any application for fresh evidence, a procedure in respect of matters of evidence at the Employment Tribunal not sufficiently appearing from the written reasons, allegations of bias, apparent bias or improper conduct, provisions for skeleton arguments, appellant's Chronology and bundles of documents and of authorities, time estimates and listing category (as set out in para 9.18 above).

FAST TRACK FULL HEARING CASES (9.5.4)

9.20 FH cases are normally heard in the order in which they are received. However, there are times when it is expedient to hear an appeal as soon as it can be fitted into the list. Appeals placed in this Fast Track, at the discretion of a judge or the Registrar, will normally fall into the following cases:

- 9.20.1 appeals where the parties have made a reasoned case on the merits for an expedited hearing;
- 9.20.2 appeals against interim orders or decisions of an Employment Tribunal, particularly those which involve the taking of a step in the proceedings within a specified period, for example adjournments, further information, amendments, disclosure, witness orders;
- 9.20.3 appeals on the outcome of which other applications to the Employment Tribunal or the EAT or the civil courts depend;
- 9.20.4 appeals in which a reference to the European Court of Justice (ECJ), or a declaration of incompatibility under the Human Rights Act 1998, is sought;
- 9.20.5 appeals involving reinstatement, re-engagement, interim relief or a recommendation for action (discrimination cases).

9.21 Category B cases estimated to take two hours or less may also be allocated to the Fast Track.

10. RESPONDENT'S ANSWER AND DIRECTIONS

[5.37]
10.1 After the sift stage or a PH, at which a decision is made to permit the appeal to go forward to an FH, the EAT will send the Notice of Appeal, with any amendments which have been permitted, and any submissions or skeleton argument lodged by the appellant, to all parties who are respondents to the appeal. Within 14 days of the seal date of the order (unless otherwise directed), respondents must lodge at the EAT and serve on the other parties a respondent's Answer. If it contains a cross-appeal, the appellant must within 14 days of service (unless otherwise directed), lodge and serve a Reply.

10.2 After lodgment and service of the respondent's Answer and of any Reply to a cross-appeal, the Registrar may, where necessary, invite applications from the parties in writing, on notice to all other parties, for directions, and may give any appropriate directions on the papers or may fix a day when the parties should attend on an Appointment for Directions.

10.3 A judge may at any time, upon consideration of the papers or at a hearing, make an order requiring or recommending consideration by the parties or any of them of compromise, conciliation, mediation or, in particular, reference to ACAS.

11. COMPLAINTS ABOUT THE CONDUCT OF THE EMPLOYMENT TRIBUNAL HEARING

[5.38]
11.1 An appellant who intends to complain about the conduct of the Employment Tribunal (for example bias, apparent bias or improper conduct by the employment judge or lay members or any procedural irregularity at the hearing) must include in the Notice of Appeal full particulars of each complaint made.

11.2 An appeal which is wholly or in part based on such a complaint will be sifted by a judge or the Registrar as set out in para 9.5 above and this may result in a decision as to the appropriate track which the appeal will occupy. At the sift stage or before, the judge or Registrar may postpone a decision as to track, and direct that the appellant or a representative provide an affidavit setting out full particulars of all allegations of bias or misconduct relied upon. At the sift stage the Registrar may enquire of the party making the complaint whether it is intended to proceed with it and may draw attention to para 11.6 below.

11.3 If the appeal is allocated to the PH or FH track, the EAT may take the following steps prior to such hearing within a time-limit set out in the relevant order:

11.3.1 require the appellant or a representative to provide, if not already provided, an affidavit as set out in para 11.2 above;

11.3.2 require any party to give an affidavit or to obtain a witness statement from any person who has represented any of the parties at the Tribunal hearing, and any other person present at the Tribunal hearing or a relevant part of it, giving their account of the events set out in the affidavit of the appellant or the appellant's representative. For the above purpose, the EAT will provide copies of any affidavits received from or on behalf of the appellant to any other person from whom an account is sought;

11.3.3 seek comments, upon all affidavits or witness statements received, from the employment judge of the Employment Tribunal from which the appeal is brought and may seek such comments from the lay members of the Tribunal. For the above purpose, copies of all relevant documents will be provided by the EAT to the employment judge and, if appropriate, the lay members; such documents will include any affidavits and witness statements received, the Notice of Appeal and other relevant documents.

11.3.4 the EAT will on receipt supply to the parties copies of all affidavits, statements and comments received.

11.4 A respondent who intends to make such a complaint must include such particulars as set out in paras 11.1 and 11.2 above:

11.4.1 (in the event of a PH being ordered in respect of the appellant's appeal, in accordance with para 9.5.2 above) in the cross-appeal referred to in para 9.9 above, or, in the absence of a cross-appeal, in written submissions, as referred to in para 9.8 above;

11.4.2 (in the event of no PH being ordered, in accordance with para 9.5.3 above) in his respondent's Answer.

A similar procedure will then be followed as in para 11.3 above.

11.5 In every case which is permitted to go forward to an FH the EAT will give appropriate directions, ordinarily on the papers after notice to the appellant and respondent, as to the procedure to be adopted at, and material to be provided to, the FH; but such directions may be given at the sift stage or at a PH.

11.6 Parties should note the following:

11.6.1 The EAT will not permit complaints of the kind mentioned above to be raised or developed at the hearing of the appeal unless this procedure has been followed.

11.6.2 The EAT recognises that employment judges and Employment Tribunals are themselves obliged to observe the overriding objective and are given wide powers and duties of case management (see Employment Tribunal (Constitution and Rules of Procedure) Regulations 2004 (SI No 1861)), so appeals in respect of the conduct of Employment Tribunals, which is in exercise of those powers and duties, are the less likely to succeed.

11.6.3 Unsuccessful pursuit of an allegation of bias or improper conduct, particularly in respect of case management decisions, may put the party raising it at risk of an order for costs.

12. LISTING OF APPEALS

[5.39]
12.1 **Estimate of Length of Hearing**: the lay members of the EAT are part-time members. They attend when available on pre-arranged dates. They do not sit for continuous periods. Consequently appeals which run beyond their estimated length have to be adjourned part-heard (often with substantial delay) until a day on which the judge and members are all available. To avoid inconvenience to the parties and to the EAT, and to avoid additional delay and costs suffered as a result of adjournment of part-heard appeals, all parties are required to ensure that the estimates of

length of hearing (allowing for the fact that the parties can expect the EAT to have pre-read the papers and for deliberation and the giving of a judgment) are accurate when first given. Any change in such estimate, or disagreement with an estimate made by the EAT on a sift or at a PH, is to be notified immediately to the Listing Officer.

12.2 If the EAT concludes that the hearing is likely to exceed the estimate, or if for other reasons the hearing may not be concluded within the time available, it may seek to avoid such adjournment by placing the parties under appropriate time limits in order to complete the presentation of the submissions within the estimated or available time.

12.3 Subject to para 12.6 below a date will be fixed for a PH as soon as practicable after the sift (referred to in para 9.5 above) and for an FH as soon as practicable after the sift if no PH is ordered, or otherwise after the PH.

12.4 The Listing Officer will normally consult the parties on dates, and will accommodate reasonable requests if practicable, but is not bound to do so. Once the date is fixed, the appeal will be set down in the list. A party finding that the date which has been fixed causes serious difficulties may apply to the Listing Officer for it to be changed, having first notified all other parties entitled to appear on the date, of their application and the reasons for it.

12.5 Parties receiving such an application must, as soon as possible and within seven days, notify the Listing Officer of their views.

12.6 In addition to this fixed date procedure, a list ("the warned list") may be drawn up. Cases will be placed in such warned list at the discretion of the Listing Officer or may be so placed by the direction of a judge or the Registrar. These will ordinarily be short cases, or cases where expedition has been ordered. Parties or their representatives will be notified that their case has been included in this list, and as much notice as possible will be given of the intention to list a case for hearing, when representations by way of objection from the parties will be considered by the Listing Officer and if necessary on appeal to the Registrar or a judge. The parties may apply on notice to all other parties for a fixed date for hearing.

12.7 Other cases may be put in the list by the Listing Officer with the consent of the parties at shorter notice: for example, where other cases have been settled or withdrawn or where it appears that they will take less time than originally estimated. Parties who wish their cases to be taken as soon as possible and at short notice should notify the Listing Officer. Representations by way of objection may be made by the parties to the Listing Officer and if necessary by appeal to a judge or the Registrar.

12.8 Each week an up-to-date list for the following week will be prepared, including any changes which have been made, in particular specifying cases which by then have been given fixed dates. The list appears on the EAT website.

13. SKELETON ARGUMENTS

[5.40]
(This part of the Practice Direction does not apply to an appeal heard in Scotland, unless otherwise directed in relation to that appeal by the EAT)

13.1 Skeleton arguments must be provided by all parties in all hearings, unless the EAT is notified by a party or representative in writing that the Notice of Appeal or respondent's Answer or relevant application contains the full argument, or the EAT otherwise directs in a particular case. It is the practice of the EAT for all the members to read the papers in advance. A well-structured skeleton argument helps the members and the parties to focus on the point(s) of law required to be decided and so make the oral hearing more effective.

13.2 The skeleton argument should be concise and should identify and summarise the point(s) of law, the steps in the legal argument and the statutory provisions and authorities to be relied upon, identifying them by name, page and paragraph and stating the legal proposition sought to be derived from them. It is not, however, the purpose of the skeleton argument to argue the case on paper in detail. The parties can be referred to by name or as they appeared at the Employment Tribunal ie claimant (C) and respondent (R).

13.3 The skeleton argument should state the form of order which the party will ask the EAT to make at the hearing: for example, in the case of an appellant, whether the EAT will be asked to remit the whole or part of the case to the same or to a different Employment Tribunal, or whether the EAT will be asked to substitute a different decision for that of the Employment Tribunal.

13.4 The appellant's skeleton argument must be accompanied by a Chronology of events relevant to the appeal which, if possible, should be agreed by the parties. That will normally be taken as an uncontroversial document, unless corrected by another party or the EAT.

13.5 Unless impracticable, the skeleton argument should be prepared using the pagination in the index to the appeal bundle. In a case where a note of the evidence at the Employment Tribunal has been produced, the skeleton argument should identify the parts of the record to which that party wishes to refer.

13.6 Represented parties should give the instructions necessary for their representative to comply with this procedure within the time limits.

13.7 The fact that conciliation or settlement negotiations are in progress in relation to the appeal does not excuse delay in lodging and exchanging skeleton arguments.

13.8 A skeleton argument may be lodged by the appellant with the Notice of Appeal or by the respondent with the respondent's Answer.

13.9 Skeleton arguments must (if not already so lodged):

13.9.1 be lodged at the EAT not less than 10 days (unless otherwise ordered) before the date fixed for the PH, appeal against Registrar's Order, Rule 3 (10) hearing or Appointment for Directions; or, if the hearing is fixed at less than seven days' notice, as soon as possible after the hearing date has been notified. In the event that the hearing has been ordered to be heard with all parties present, the skeleton arguments must also then be exchanged between the parties;

13.9.2 be lodged at the EAT, *and* exchanged between the parties, not less than 14 days before the FH;

13.9.3 in the case of warned list and fast track FH cases be lodged at the EAT and exchanged between the parties as soon as possible and (unless the hearing date is less than seven days later) in any event within seven days after the parties have been notified that the case is expedited or in the warned list.

13.10 Failure to follow this procedure may lead to an adjournment of an appeal or to dismissal for non-compliance with the PD pursuant to Rule 26, and to an award of costs. The party in default may also be required to attend before the EAT to explain their failure. It will always mean that the defaulting party must immediately despatch any delayed skeleton argument to the EAT by hand or by fax or by email to londoneat@tribunals.gsi.gov.uk or, as appropriate, edinburgheat@tribunals.gsi.gov.uk and (unless notified by the EAT to the contrary) bring to the hearing sufficient copies (a minimum of 6) of the skeleton argument and any authorities referred to. The EAT staff will not be responsible for supplying or copying these on the morning of the hearing.

14. CITATION OF AUTHORITIES

GENERAL

[5.41]

14.1 It is undesirable for parties to cite the same case from different sets of reports. The parties should, if practicable, agree which report will be used at the hearing. Where the Employment Tribunal has cited from a report it may be convenient to cite from the same report.

14.2 It is the responsibility of a party wishing to cite any authority to provide photocopies for the use of each member of the Tribunal and photocopies or at least a list for the other parties. All authorities should be indexed and incorporated in an agreed bundle.

14.3 Parties are advised not to cite an unnecessary number of authorities either in skeleton arguments or in oral argument at the hearing. It is of assistance to the EAT if parties could highlight or sideline passages relied on within the bundle of authorities.

14.4 It is unnecessary for a party citing a case in oral argument to read it in full to the EAT. Whenever a case is cited in a skeleton argument or in an oral argument it is helpful if the legal proposition for which it is cited is stated. References need only be made to the relevant passages in the report. If the formulation of the legal proposition based on the authority cited is not in dispute, further examination of the authority will often be unnecessary.

14.5 For decisions of the ECJ, the official report should be used where possible.

PH CASES

14.6 If it is thought necessary to cite any authority at a PH, appeal against Registrar's Order, Rule 3(10) hearing or Appointment for Directions, three copies should be provided for the EAT (one copy if a judge is sitting alone) no less than 10 days before the hearing, unless otherwise ordered: and additional copies for any other parties notified. All authorities should be bundled, indexed and incorporated in one agreed bundle.

FH CASES

14.7 The parties must co-operate in agreeing a list of authorities and must jointly or severally lodge a list and three bundles of copies (one copy if judge sitting alone) of such authorities at the EAT not less than seven days before the FH, unless otherwise ordered.

15. DISPOSAL OF APPEALS BY CONSENT

[5.42]

15.1 An appellant who wishes to abandon or withdraw an appeal should notify the other parties and the EAT immediately. If a settlement is reached, the parties should inform the EAT as soon as possible. The appellant should submit to the EAT a letter signed by or on behalf of the appellant and signed also by or on behalf of the respondent, asking the EAT for permission to withdraw the appeal and to make a consent order in the form of an attached draft signed by or for both parties dismissing the appeal, together with any other agreed order.

15.2 If the other parties do not agree to the proposed order the EAT should be informed. Written submissions should be lodged at the EAT and served on the parties. Any outstanding issue may be determined on the papers by the EAT, particularly if it relates to costs, but the EAT may fix an oral hearing to determine the outstanding matters in dispute between the parties.

15.3 If the parties reach an agreement that the appeal should be allowed by consent, and that an order made by the Employment Tribunal should be reversed or varied or the matter remitted to the Employment Tribunal on the ground that the decision contains an error of law, it is usually necessary for the matter to be heard by the EAT to determine whether there is a good reason for making the proposed order. On notification by the parties, the EAT will decide whether the appeal can be dealt with on the papers or by a hearing at which one or more parties or their representatives should attend to argue the case for allowing the appeal and making the order that the parties wish the EAT to make.

15.4 If the application for permission to withdraw an appeal is made close to the hearing date the EAT may require the attendance of the Appellant and/or a representative to explain the reasons for delay in making a decision not to pursue the appeal.

16. APPELLANT'S FAILURE TO PRESENT A RESPONSE

[5.43]
16.1 If the appellant in a case did not present a Response (ET3) to the Employment Tribunal and did not apply to the Employment Tribunal for an extension of time for doing so, or applied for such an extension and was refused, the Notice of Appeal must include particulars directed to the following issues, namely whether:

- 16.1.1 there is a good excuse for failing to present a Response (ET3) and (if that be the case) for failing to apply for such an extension of time; and
- 16.1.2 there is a reasonably arguable defence to the Claim (ET1).

16.2 In order to satisfy the EAT on these issues, the appellant must lodge at the EAT, together with the Notice of Appeal, a witness statement explaining in detail the circumstances in which there has been a failure to serve a Response (ET3) in time or apply for such an extension of time, the reason for that failure and the facts and matters relied upon for contesting the Claim (ET1) on the merits. There should be exhibited to the witness statement all relevant documents and a completed draft Response (ET3).

17. HEARINGS

[5.44]
17.1 Where consent is to be obtained from the parties pursuant to s 28(3) of the ETA 1996 to an appeal commencing or continuing to be heard by a judge together with only one lay member, the parties must, prior to the commencement or continuation of such hearing in front of a two-member court, themselves or by their representatives each sign a form containing the name of the one member remaining, and stating whether the member is a person falling within s 28(1)(a) or (b) of the ETA 1996.

17.2 **Video and Telephone Hearings**. Facilities can be arranged for the purpose of holding short PHs or short Appointments for Directions by video or telephone link, upon the application (in writing) of an appellant or respondent who, or whose representative, has a relevant disability (supported by appropriate medical evidence). Such facilities will only be made available for a hearing at which the party or, if more than one party will take part, both or all parties is or are legally represented. An application that a hearing should be so held will be determined by a judge or the Registrar, and must be made well in advance of the date intended for the hearing, so that arrangements may be made. So far as concerns video conferencing facilities, they may not always be available, dependent on the location of the parties: as for telephone hearings or, especially, telephone conferencing facilities, consideration may need to be given as to payment by a party or parties of any additional expenditure resulting.

18. HANDING DOWN OF JUDGMENTS

(ENGLAND AND WALES)

[5.45]
18.1 When the EAT reserves judgment to a later date, the parties will be notified of the date when it is ready to be handed down. It is not necessary for a party or representative to attend.

18.2 Copies of the judgment will be available to the parties or their representatives on the morning on which it is handed down or, if so directed by a judge, earlier to the parties' representatives in draft subject to terms as to confidentiality.

18.3 The judgment will be pronounced without being read aloud, by the judge who presided or by another judge, on behalf of the EAT. The judge may deal with any application or may refer it to the judge and/or the Tribunal who heard the appeal, whether to deal with on the papers or at a further oral hearing on notice. Applications for permission to appeal should be made pursuant to para 21 below. Applications for costs should be made pursuant to para 19 below.

18.4 Transcripts of unreserved judgments at a PH, appeal against Registrar's Order, Appointment for Directions and Rule 3(10) hearing will not (save as below) be produced and provided to the parties:

18.4.1 Where an appeal, or any ground of appeal, is dismissed in the presence of the appellant, no transcript of the judgment is produced unless, within 14 days of the seal date of the order, either party applies to the EAT for a transcript, or the EAT of its own initiative directs that a judgment be transcribed (in circumstances such as those set out in para 18.5.2 below).

18.4.2 Where an appeal or any ground of appeal is dismissed in the absence of the appellant, a transcript will be supplied to the appellant.

18.4.3 Where an appeal is allowed to go forward to a PH or an FH, a judgment will not normally be delivered, but, if it is, the judge may order it to be transcribed, in which case a transcript is provided to the parties.

18.5 Transcripts of unreserved judgments at an FH. Where judgment is delivered at the hearing, no transcript will be produced and provided to the parties unless:

18.5.1 either party applies for it to the EAT within 14 days of that hearing; or

18.5.2 the EAT of its own initiative directs that the judgment be transcribed, eg where it is considered that a point of general importance arises or that the matter is to be remitted to, or otherwise continued before, the Employment Tribunal.

18.6 Where judgment at either a PH or an FH is reserved, and later handed down in writing, a copy is provided to all parties, and to recognised law reporters.

(SCOTLAND)

18.7 Judgments are normally reserved in Scotland and will be handed down as soon as practicable thereafter on a provisional basis to both parties who will thereafter have a period of 14 days to make any representations with regard to expenses, leave to appeal or any other relevant matter. At the expiry of that period or after such representations have been dealt with, whichever shall be the later, an order will be issued to conform to the original judgment.

EAT WEBSITE

18.8 All FH judgments which are transcribed or handed down will be posted on the EAT website. Any other judgment may be posted on the EAT website if so directed by the Registrar or a Judge.

19. COSTS (REFERRED TO AS EXPENSES IN SCOTLAND)

[5.46]

19.1 In this PD "costs" includes legal costs, expenses, allowances paid by the Secretary of State and payment in respect of time spent in preparing a case. Such costs may relate to interim applications or hearings or to a PH or FH.

19.2 An application for costs must be made either during or at the end of a relevant hearing, or in writing to the Registrar within 14 days of the seal date of the relevant order of the EAT or, in the case of a reserved judgment, as provided for in paragraph 18.3 above, copied to all parties.

19.3 The party seeking the order must state the legal ground on which the application is based and the facts on which it is based and, by a schedule or otherwise, show how the costs have been incurred. If the application is made in respect of only part of the proceedings, particulars must be given showing how the costs have been incurred on that specific part. If the party against whom the order is sought wishes the EAT to have regard to means and/or an alleged inability to pay, a witness statement giving particulars and exhibiting any documents must be served on the other party(ies) and lodged with the EAT. Further directions may be required to be given by the EAT in such cases.

19.4 Such application may be resolved by the EAT on the papers, provided that the opportunity has been given for representations in writing by all relevant parties, or the EAT may refer the matter for an oral hearing, and may assess the costs either on the papers or at an oral hearing, or refer the matter for detailed assessment.

19.5 **Wasted Costs**: An application for a wasted costs order must be made in writing, setting out the nature of the case upon which the application is based and the best particulars of the costs sought to be recovered. Such application must be lodged with the EAT and served upon the party(ies) sought to be charged. Further directions may be required to be given by the EAT in such cases.

19.6 Where the EAT makes any costs order it shall provide written reasons for so doing if such order is made by decision on the papers. If such order is made at a hearing, then written reasons will be provided if a request is made at the hearing or within 21 days of the seal date of the costs order. The Registrar shall send a copy of the written reasons to all the parties to the proceedings.

20. REVIEW

[5.47]
Where an application is made for a review of a judgment or order of the EAT, it can be considered on paper by a judge who may, if he or she heard the original appeal or made the original order alone, without lay members, make such order, granting, refusing, adjourning or otherwise dealing with such application, as he or she may think fit. If the original judgment or order was made by the judge together with lay members, then the judge may, pursuant to Rule 33, consider and refuse such application for review on the papers. If the judge does not refuse such application, he or she may make any relevant further order, but would not grant such application without notice to the opposing party and reference to the lay members, for consideration with them, either on paper or in open court. A request to review a judgment or order of the EAT must be made within 14 days of the seal date of the order, or must include an application, with reasons for an extension of time copied to all parties.

21. APPEALS FROM THE EAT

APPEALS HEARD IN ENGLAND AND WALES

[5.48]
21.1 An application to the EAT for permission to appeal to the Court of Appeal must be made (unless the EAT otherwise orders) at the hearing or when a reserved judgment is handed down or in writing within 7 days thereafter as provided in para 18.3 above. If not made then, or if refused, or unless the EAT otherwise orders, any such applications must be made to the Court of Appeal within 21 days of the sealed order. An application for an extension of time for permission to appeal may be entertained by the EAT where a case is made out to the satisfaction of a judge or Registrar that there is a need to delay until after a transcript is received (expedited if appropriate). Applications for an extension of time for permission to appeal should however normally be made to the Court of Appeal.

21.2 The party seeking permission must state the point of law to be advanced and the grounds.

APPEALS HEARD IN SCOTLAND

21.3 An application to the EAT for permission to appeal to the Court of Session must be made within 42 days of the date of the hearing where judgment is delivered at that hearing: if judgment is reserved, within 42 days of the date the transcript was sent to parties.

21.4 The party seeking permission must state the point of law to be advanced and the grounds.

22. CONCILIATION

[5.49]
22.1 Pursuant to Rule 36 and the overriding objective, the EAT encourages alternative dispute resolution. To this end it has agreed a pilot scheme with ACAS for ACAS to provide conciliation in certain cases. See 2007 Protocol.

22.2 In all cases the parties should, and when so directed must, consider conciliation of their appeals. The Registrar or a Judge may at any stage make such a direction and require the parties to report on steps taken, but not the substance, to effect a conciliated settlement with the assistance of an ACAS officer notified by ACAS to the EAT.

EAT FORM 1
NOTICE OF APPEAL FROM DECISION OF EMPLOYMENT TRIBUNAL

[5.50]
1. The Appellant is (*name and address of the Appellant*):—

. . . .

. . . .

2. Any communication relating to this appeal may be sent to the Appellant at (*Appellant's address for service, including telephone number if any*):—

. . . .

. . . .

3. The Appellant appeals from (*here give particulars of the judgment, decision or order of the Employment Tribunal from which the appeal is brought including the location of the Employment Tribunal and the date*):—

. . . .

. . . .

4. The parties to the proceedings before the Employment Tribunal, other than the Appellant, were (*names and addresses of other parties to the proceedings resulting in judgment, decision or order appealed from*):—

. . . .

. . . .

5. Copies of—

(a) the written record of the employment tribunal's judgment, decision or order and the written reasons of the employment tribunal;

(b) the claim (ET1);

(c) the response (ET3);

(d) an explanation as to why any of these documents are not included;

are attached to this Notice.

6. If the appellant has made an application to the employment tribunal for a review of its judgment or decision, copies of—

(a) the review application;

(b) the judgment;

(c) the written reasons of the employment tribunal in respect of that review application; and/or

(d) a statement by or on behalf of the applicant, if such be the case, that a judgment is awaited;

are attached to this Notice. If any of these documents exist but cannot be included, then a written explanation must be given.

7. The grounds upon which this appeal is brought are that the employment tribunal erred in law in that (here set out in paragraphs the various grounds of appeal):—

. . . .

. . . .

. . . .

. . . .

. . . .

. . . .

Signed . . . . Date: . . . .

N.B. The details entered on your Notice of Appeal must be legible and suitable for photocopying or electronic scanning. The use of black ink or typescript is recommended

EMPLOYMENT APPEAL TRIBUNAL PRACTICE STATEMENT (2005)

[5.51]

This is a Practice Statement handed down by the President of the Employment Appeal Tribunal on 3 February 2005.

1. The attention of litigants and practitioners in the Employment Appeal Tribunal is expressly drawn to the wording and effect of Rules 3(1)(b) and 3(3) of the Employment Appeal Tribunal Rules (1993) (as amended). As is quite clear from the terms of paragraph 2.1 of the Employment Appeal Tribunal Practice Direction 2004 handed down on 9 December 2004, a Notice of Appeal without the specified documentation will not be validly lodged. The documentation required to accompany the Notice of Appeal in order for it to be valid now includes a copy of the Claim (ET1) and the Response (ET3) in the Employment Tribunal proceedings appealed from, if such be available to the appellant, and in any event if such not be available for whatever reason then a written explanation as to why they are not provided. Paragraph 2.1 of the Practice Direction makes this entirely clear:

> "2.1 . . . Copies of the judgment, decision or order appealed against and of the Employment Tribunal's written reasons, together with a copy of the Claim (ET1) and the Response (ET3) must be attached, or if not, a written explanation must be given. A Notice of Appeal without such documentation will not be validly lodged."

2. The reported decision of the Employment Appeal Tribunal in ***Kanapathiar v London Borough of Harrow*** [2003] IRLR 571 made quite clear that the effect of failure to lodge documents required by the Rules with the Notice of Appeal within the time limit specified for lodging of a Notice of

Appeal would mean that the Notice of Appeal had not been validly lodged in time. The same now applies to the additional documents required by the amended Rule, namely the Claim and the Response.

3. It is apparent that both practitioners and litigants in person are not complying with the new Rules and Practice Direction, and not appreciating the consequences of their non-compliance. Between 2 and 26 January 2005, 20 Notices of Appeal were received by the Employment Appeal Tribunal and returned as invalid (compared with 4 during the similar period in 2004). Of those 20 Notices of Appeal, 7 would have been invalid in any event under the old Rules. 13 however were only invalid because they were neither accompanied by the Claim nor the Response nor by any explanation as to their absence or unavailability. If the Notices of Appeal are relodged well within the very generous 42-day time limit, there may still be time for the missing documents to be supplied and the time limit to be complied with. If however, as is very often the case, such Notices of Appeal are delivered either at, or only immediately before, the expiry of the time limit, the absence of the relevant documents is, even if speedily pointed out by the Employment Appeal Tribunal, likely to lead to the Notice of Appeal being out of time.

4. Of the 20 Notices of Appeal which were invalidly lodged during the period above referred to, only 10 were lodged by litigants in person and 10 by solicitors or other representatives: and it is plain that the latter ought certainly to have known of the requirements, although, given the wide publication both of the Rules and the Practice Direction, together with the guidance given by the Employment Tribunals, both at the Tribunal and sent with their judgments, there can be no excuse for litigants in person either.

5. The reason for this Statement in open court is to re-emphasise these requirements and the consequence of failure to comply with them, namely that an appeal not lodged within the 42 days validly constituted, ie accompanied by the required documents, will be out of time, and extensions of time are only exceptionally granted (see paragraph 3.7 of the Practice Direction).

6. From the date of this Practice Statement, ignorance or misunderstanding of the requirements as to service of the documents required to make a Notice of Appeal within the 42 days valid will not be accepted by the Registrar as an excuse.

The Hon Mr Justice Burton

President of the Employment Appeal Tribunal

3 February 2005

EMPLOYMENT APPEAL TRIBUNAL PRACTICE STATEMENT (2012)

[5.52]

The President has issued the following Practice Statement (on 17 April 2012) for the assistance of parties and their representatives.

1. Fresh Evidence Appeals

Pending possible revision of the Practice Direction, parties should be aware that insofar as any appellant wishes to argue that the Employment Appeal Tribunal should consider evidence which was not placed before the Employment Tribunal, (a) it is likely that an order will be made by a judge of the Appeal Tribunal staying any further action on the appeal (or dismissing it as having no reasonable prospect of success, if appropriate) unless and until an application has first been made to the Employment Tribunal against whose judgment the appeal is brought for that tribunal to review its judgment; (b) it will remain open to him to contend that there has been an error of law if the Employment Tribunal thereafter is in error of law in refusing to review its decision.

There are three principal reasons for this. First the Employment Appeal Tribunal has a jurisdiction which is limited to appeals on a question of law. It will be rarely (if at all) that an Employment Tribunal will be in error of law by failing to have regard to evidence which was not placed before it by one or other party, where no attempt was made to invite the Employment Tribunal to pay regard to evidence which it then declined to hear. It has no jurisdiction on fact, save where the ET makes a decision which is perverse, or which materially misapprehends a relevant fact before it. Thus "fresh evidence" has no part to play similar to that which it plays in criminal appeals (where the test is the safety of a conviction) or civil appeals generally (the test being whether the court below was wrong). Secondly, it is logical that the Employment Tribunal should deal with these matters, since it will have heard the witnesses, evaluated the facts and reached judgments upon them, and will know how relevant and important the evidence is, is best placed to assess its credibility, and may be better informed than the Appeal Tribunal whether it could (and should) have been obtained with reasonable diligence for use at the hearing, Thirdly, of course, it relieves a certain amount of the burden on the Employment Appeal Tribunal.

In so advising, regard has been had in particular to the decision on this point by HHJ McMullen QC on 12 September 2011 in *Dr Korashi v Abertawe Bro Morgannwg University Local Health* [2012] IRLR 4 and similar expressions of view by both the present and immediate past Presidents, and by Elias LJ in particular at para 35 of his judgment in *The Governing Body Of St Andrew's Catholic Primary School v Blundell* [2011] EWCA Civ 427.

2. Authorities

For those parties who are represented, best practice is to use photo or online copies of formal reports, such as the ICR's or IRLR's rather than those available from other on-line sources. These reports have head notes and are more useful to the Court than other electronic copies of the same case. The reports should be presented in chronological order, because that assists the Court in seeing how the law has developed. Relevant passages on which a party intends to rely should be sidelined and/or highlighted clearly. If ring binders are used, they should be properly tabulated.

A number of familiar authorities are so frequently cited to the Appeal Tribunal that sufficient copies of those authorities for any hearing will be maintained at the Tribunal in every court. This will avoid unnecessary work for the parties, and avoid overuse of paper and copying resources. A list of such cases will be maintained on the website of the Appeal Tribunal, and any case on the list should not be photocopied. It may be relied on if necessary in argument before the Appeal Tribunal (which may refer to the maintained copy), and if so it will be sufficient for the party relying upon it to identify the principle contended for, or said to be inapplicable, by reference to the paragraph number(s) of the report.

Parties should note that in the Practice Direction in respect of civil appeals in England and Wales issued by the Lord Chief Justice and Heads of Division on 23 March 2012 (which parties should consider applicable to appeals to the EAT in England, subject only to necessary adaptations) it is directed that in the cases to which it relates reference should be made to no more than 10 authorities unless the scale of the appeal warrants more extensive citation. The same general principle applies to the Employment Appeal Tribunal in both Scotland and England (see the present Practice Direction). Cases should set out legal principle, rather than be merely illustrative of an application of it. Parties must be prepared to justify more extensive citation of authority.

The Hon Mr Justice Langstaff
President of the Employment Appeal Tribunal
17 April 2012

EMPLOYMENT APPEAL TRIBUNAL PRACTICE IN RELATION TO FAMILIAR AUTHORITIES

[5.53]

Certain key authorities (important court cases) have in the past been frequently included in the Bundles of Authorities prepared by parties for hearings at the EAT and regularly cited to the Appeal Tribunal.

As explained in the EAT President's **Practice Statement** of 17 April 2012 the Appeal Tribunal has adopted a new arrangement in relation to those frequently cited cases:

"A number of familiar authorities are so frequently cited to the Appeal Tribunal that sufficient copies of those authorities for any hearing will be maintained at the Tribunal in every court. This will avoid unnecessary work for the parties, and avoid overuse of paper and copying resources.
A list of such cases will be maintained on the website of the Appeal Tribunal, and any case on the list should not be photocopied. It may be relied on if necessary in argument before the Appeal Tribunal (which may refer to the maintained copy), and if so it will be sufficient for the party relying upon it to identify the principle contended for, or said to be inapplicable, by reference to the paragraph number(s) of the report."

Pursuant to that Statement, each EAT courtroom (in London and Edinburgh) is now supplied with sufficient copies of a *Bundle of Familiar Authorities* for use by each member of any Appeal Tribunal which is sitting.

The **Contents List** of those Bundles is attached.

Parties and their advisers should check the Contents List before assembling their own Bundles of Authorities and the cases shown in the Contents List should not be included in parties' bundles for hearings taking place from 25 June 2012 onwards.

Two particular points should be noted:

(1) the cases included in the Contents List are kept under review and the Appeal Tribunal expects to revise the Contents List from time to time. Parties and their advisers should always check this webpage for the current version before assembling their own bundles: and

(2) the cases included appear in the form of report available at the time of assembly of the bundles. Where cases have been reported in more than one source, a report has been selected which reflects paragraph 6 of the Practice Direction issued by the Lord Chief Justice on 23 March 2012 addressing Citation of Authorities.

Familiar Authorities Bundle—Contents

Amendment *(notice of appeal – whether to grant)*

1. Khudados v Leggate [2005] ICR 1013, EAT

2. Readman v Devon Primary Care Trust [2011] UKEAT 0116/11, EAT

Bias *(allegations – EAT procedure)*

3. Facey v Midas Retail Security [2001] ICR 287, EAT

Bias *(test for)*

4. Porter v Magill [2002] 2 AC 357, HL

Deciding a case on ground not argued

5. Chapman v Simon [1994] IRLR 124, CA

Error of law *(jurisdiction of EAT)*

6. British Telecommunications plc v Sheridan [1990] IRLR 27, CA

7. Brent London Borough Council v Fuller [2011] ICR 806, CA

New points of law *(taken for first time at the EAT)*

8. Kumchyk v Derby City Council [1978] ICR 1116, EAT

9. Jones v Governing Body of Burdett Coutts School [1999] ICR 38, CA

10. Glennie v Independent Magazines (UK) Ltd [1999] IRLR 719, CA

11. Secretary of State for Health v Rance [2007] IRLR 665, EAT

New points *(taken for first time during an employment tribunal hearing)*

12. Ladbrokes Racing Ltd v Traynor UKEATS 0067/06, EAT

Perversity

Yeboah v Crofton [2002] IRLR 634, CA

Polkey

14. Polkey v AE Dayton Services Ltd [1988] 1 AC 344, HL

Reasons *(duty to give)*

15. Meek v City of Birmingham District Council [1987] IRLR 250, CA

16. English v Emery Reimbold & Strick Ltd [2002] 1 WLR 2409, CA

17. Greenwood v NWF Retail [2011] ICR 896, EAT

Reasons *(EAT power to ask for further reasons)*

18. Barke v SEETEC Business Technology Centre Ltd [2005] IRLR 633, CA

Remission *(whether to the same or differently-constituted Tribunal)*

19. Sinclair Roche & Temperley v Heard [2004] IRLR 763, EAT

Time Limits *(whether to grant an extension of time for appealing)*

20. United Arab Emirates v Abdelghafar [1995] ICR 65, EAT

21. Aziz v Bethnal Green City Challenge Co Ltd [2000] IRLR 111, CA

22. Jurkowska v HLMAD Ltd [2008] ICR 841, CA

23. Muschett v London Borough of Hounslow [2009] ICR 424, EAT

Striking-out *(exercise of employment tribunal's powers)*

24. Tayside Public Transport Co Ltd v Reilly [2012] CSIH 46, CS

EMPLOYMENT TRIBUNALS (SCOTLAND) PRACTICE DIRECTION NO 1 (2006)

[5.54]

In consequence of the power given to me under Regulation 13 of the Employment Tribunals (Constitution and Rules of Procedure) Regulations 2004 I make the following Practice Direction:—

INTIMATION OF LIST OF DOCUMENTS 14 DAYS BEFORE A HEARING

When a party is legally represented their representative will intimate a list of the documents to be relied upon at any Hearing on the merits of the claim to the other party (or parties) or their representative (if represented) not later than 14 days before any such Hearing.

COLIN M MILNE

President of Employment Tribunals, Scotland

14 December 2006

NOTES

Many cases before the Employment Tribunal are subject to extensive case management by the judiciary, an element of which may involve orders being made regarding the identification and disclosure of documents. There is currently less opportunity to undertake in-depth case management of cases that might be regarded as more straightforward. Nevertheless, in keeping with one of the principal objectives identified in the Report of the Employment Tribunal System Taskforce, it is generally agreed that there is merit in each side having as much notice of the other side's case as possible in advance of the Hearing. The Rules of Procedure generally assist this objective but users have expressed concern about the lack of direction regarding the lodging of documents. There is no provision in the rules requiring the lodging of documents within a certain time span. It is not uncommon for a party to wait until the day of the Hearing to reveal the documents upon which they intend to rely to the other party (or parties, as the case may be). That on occasion leads to delay as the implications of that documentation are considered by the other side.

Following extensive consultation with Scottish users, I have agreed to make a Practice Direction requiring parties who are legally represented to provide a list of the documents they are going to rely upon to the other party/parties no later than 14 days before a Hearing on the merits of the case. It is expected that this list will be sufficiently detailed to enable the other party/parties to understand the nature of each of the documents which is to be produced. However, this direction is without prejudice to the right of any Employment Tribunal Chairman to impose a more onerous direction in respect of the provision of information about documents to be relied upon at any Hearing.

Consideration was given to the idea of actually requiring copies of the documents themselves to be provided to the other party/parties at least 14 days before the Hearing but that was considered to place too heavy a cost burden on parties, given the number of cases which settle in the 14 day period before the Hearing. Requiring a simple list however should at least put the other side on notice as to the documents which are going to be relied upon, thereby minimising the risk of delay arising from last minute surprises.

With regard to the general need for Employment Tribunals to be accessible to all users, it was felt unduly onerous to apply this Practice Direction to parties who are not legally represented. The imposition of a requirement, as here, which applies only to those who are legally represented finds a parallel in the provisions of the Rules themselves (see, for example, the obligations imposed when a party is legally represented under Rule 11).

NOTES

This Practice Direction applies to Scotland only.

EMPLOYMENT TRIBUNALS (SCOTLAND) PRACTICE DIRECTION NO 2 (2006)

[5.55]

In consequence of the power given to me under Regulation 13 of the Employment Tribunals (Constitution and Rules of Procedure) Regulations 2004 I make the following Practice Direction:—

SIST FOR MEDIATION

Where both (or, as the case may be, all) parties to a claim agree that it should be sisted for mediation a Chairman of Employment Tribunals shall sist it for that purpose. The Chairman shall nevertheless review the need for that sist within such timescale as he or she thinks necessary having regard to the interests of justice.

COLIN M MILNE

President of Employment Tribunals, Scotland

14 December 2006

NOTES

The sole purpose of this Practice Direction is to focus parties' minds on mediation as an option for the resolution of employment disputes. The role of Acas in providing a conciliation service is well known and highly valued but in certain circumstances Acas may also provide mediation. In recent times an employment dispute meditation service has also become more widely available from other providers. However, while mediation is on the increase in employment cases there is some evidence to suggest that not all parties are aware of this as an option which might be utilised.

While the direction directs that, where parties agree, a Chairman will sist the case, it must be borne in mind that Chairmen still have to consider the overriding objective, which involves taking account of what is in the interests of justice overall. It is therefore appropriate that any sist granted to allow for mediation to take place should be kept under regular review. The timing and circumstances of the review process are a matter for judicial discretion in each individual case in light of the interests of justice in that case.

This Practice Direction in relation to mediation clearly envisages what might be described as external mediation. It is without prejudice to the pilot being carried out in England and Wales (which pilot has not been extended to Scotland) in relation to judicial mediation.

NOTES

This Practice Direction applies to Scotland only.

EMPLOYMENT TRIBUNALS (SCOTLAND) PRACTICE DIRECTION NO 3 (2006)

[5.56]

In consequence of the power given to me under Regulation 13 of the Employment Tribunals (Constitution and Rules of Procedure) Regulations 2004 I make the following Practice Direction:—

COUNTER CLAIMS

(a) When a respondent wishes to present a claim against the claimant ("a counter claim") in accordance with Article 4 of the Employment Tribunals (Extension of Jurisdiction) (Scotland) Order 1994 they should, (if reasonably practicable) specify the amount claimed as part of the detail of the counter claim along with the other information provided for in Regulation 7 of the Employment Tribunals (Rules of Procedure) Regulations 2004.

(b) When a claimant receives notice of a counter claim the claimant will indicate to the Tribunal Office if it is intended to resist the counter claim and the reasons for so resisting within a period of 28 days from the date on which he or she was sent a copy of the counter claim, unless an order of the Tribunal is granted extending that period.

COLIN M MILNE

President of Employment Tribunals, Scotland

14 December 2006

NOTES

Consultation with Scottish users has established a desire to revert to the earlier Scottish practice in relation to counter claims. Rule 7 of Schedule 1 of the Employment Tribunals (Constitution and Rules of Procedure) Regulations 2004 does envisage the possibility of a Practice Direction being made in relation to counter claims.

The issues addressed in my Practice Direction concern the two items that users feel should be included so that parties have basic information available about the counterclaim and any response to it. The 28 day period referred to in paragraph (b) of the direction is without prejudice to the right of a party to seek an order from the Tribunal, in terms of rule 10(2)(e), extending the time limit for the lodging of a response to a counterclaim.

I also gave consideration to formally prescribing forms for use in making a counterclaim and responding to such a claim. In Scotland forms were in use under the Employment Tribunals (Constitution and Rules of Procedure) (Scotland) Regulations 1993, being issued by the employment tribunal office to respondents in every case in which a breach of contract claim was made and, in turn, issued to the claimant in every case in which a counterclaim was made. However, these forms are no longer issued. They were very basic in format and it seems to me that it is unnecessary to stipulate the use of a specific form, although parties may note that the old forms are still produced, by way of guidance, in Appendix 4 and Appendix 5 of Leslie's Employment Tribunal Practice in Scotland. Parties' representatives may find it convenient to use something similar to these forms although what matters, irrespective of the exact format used, is clear presentation of the information required to set out the basis of the counterclaim and any response to it.

NOTES

This Practice Direction applies to Scotland only.

C. CLAIM AND RESPONSE FORMS FOR TRIBUNAL CLAIMS

CLAIM TO AN EMPLOYMENT TRIBUNAL (ET1)

[5.57]

NOTES

The Forms reproduced in this Section are the current versions prescribed by HM Courts and Tribunals Service. The forms may be completed and submitted electronically or downloaded as PDFs for completion in hard copy, at www.justice.gov.uk.

Employment Tribunals Claim Form

Special Notice

This interactive form enables you to make a claim to an Employment Tribunal by completing and editing the form offline. You can save a part of fully completed form, email a saved form to another person to amend or for approval, and submit it securely online to the Employment Tribunals. Please make sure you have read the guidance notes on our website on how to make a claim before you fill in the form. We are unable to accept any attachments included or sent with this form.

Multiple Claims – If this claim is one of a number of claims arising out of the same or similar circumstances please fill in a claim form for the first claimant and then give the other claimants on the multiple form (maximum 28 claims). If more than 28 claims need to be submitted please create a multiple claims .csv file.
For guidelines please click here http://www.employmenttribunals.gov.uk/multiple/index.htm, enter the details in the correct column and attach the .csv file to this form below before submitting this claim form.

For Claimants in England and Wales - If someone is advising or representing you in relation to your claim, they must, unless they are a practising solicitor or barrister, be authorised to do so, wherever they are based (including Scotland, the Channel Islands and all of Europe). Trade Union officials, Citizens' Advice Bureau advisors or a personal friend helping you present your claim may be exempted from these requirements. However, to check your representatives status, and for more information, telephone 0845 450 6858 or go to www.claimsregulation.gov.uk

Select the type of claim you wish to make:

- [x] I want to make a claim.
- [ ] I want to make a claim on behalf of more than one person.

Select the reason(s) for the claim:

- [ ] Unfair dismissal or constructive dismissal
- [ ] Discrimination
- [ ] Redundancy payments
- [ ] Other payments you are owed
- [ ] Other complaints

Need Help?

If you require any help completing your form or have a general question about the tribunals process please contact the Employment Tribunals Enquiry Line on **08457 959 775** or minicom **08457 573 722** between 9am and 5pm Monday to Friday (closed on Bank Holidays).

If you require technical support please click below to email us.

Support Request

We regret we cannot provide any legal advice.

Please Note:
By law, your claim must be submitted using an approved form supplied by the Employment Tribunals (We are unable to accept any attachments included or sent with the form except for .csv file templates issued with multiple claims from our website), and you must provide the information marked with * and, if it is relevant, the information marked with (see' Information needed before a claim can be accepted')

General Information:

Once you have completed your form you can submit it securely on-line to the TS. On-line forms are processed faster than those sent by post.

POWERED by legatio | Email to client | Save | Print | Clear | New | Start Claim →

Version 7.9

1 Your details

1.1 Title: Mr Mrs Miss Ms Other

1.2* First name (or names):

1.3* Surname or family name:

1.4 Date of birth (date/month/year): Are you: male? female?

1.5* Address: Number or Name

Street

+ Town/City

County

Postcode

1.6 Phone number including area code **(where we can contact you in the day time):**

Mobile number **(if different):**

1.7 How would you prefer us to communicate with you? (Please tick only one box) E-mail Post

E-mail address:

2 Respondent's details

2.1* Give the name of your employer or the organisation you are claiming against.

2.2* Address: Number or Name

Street

+ Town/City

County

Postcode

Phone number:

2.3• If you worked at a different address from the one you have given at 2.2, please give the full address and postcode.

Postcode

Phone number:

If there are other respondents please complete **Section 11.**

3 Employment details

3.1 Please give the following information if possible.

When did your employment start?

Is your employment continuing? Yes No

If your employment has ceased, or you are in a period of notice, when did it, or will it, end?

3.2 Please say what job you do or did.

4 Earnings and benefits

4.1 How many hours on average do, or did, you work each week? hours each week

4.2 How much are, or were, you paid?

Pay before tax £ .00

Normal take-home pay (including overtime, commission, bonuses and so on) £ .00

Hourly
Weekly
Monthly
Yearly

4.3 If your employment has ended, did you work (or were you paid for) a period of notice? Yes No

If 'Yes', how many weeks' or months' notice did you work, or were you paid for? weeks months

4.4 Were you in your employer's pension scheme? Yes No

Please answer 4.5 to 4.9 if your claim, or part of it, is about unfair or constructive dismissal.

4.5 If you received any other benefits, e.g. company car, medical insurance, etc, from your employer, please give details.

4.6 Since leaving your employment have you got another job? Yes No
If 'No', please now go straight to section 4.9.

4.7 Please say when you started (or will start) work.

4.8 Please say how much you are now earning (or will earn). £ ______ .00 each ______

4.9 Please tick the box to say what you want if your case is successful:

a To get your old job back and compensation (reinstatement)

b To get another job with the same employer and compensation (re-engagement)

c Compensation only

5 Your claim

5.1* Please tick one or more of the boxes below. In the space provided, describe the event, or series of events, that have caused you to make this claim:

a I was unfairly dismissed (including constructive dismissal)

b I was discriminated against on the grounds of

Sex (including equal pay) | Race
Disability | Religion or belief
Sexual orientation | Age

c I am claiming a redundancy payment

d I am owed

notice pay
holiday pay
arrears of pay
other payments

e Other complaints

5.2* Please set out the background and details of your claim in the space below. The details of your claim should include **the date when the event(s) you are complaining about happened**; for example, if your claim relates to discrimination give the dates of all the incidents you are complaining about, or at least the date of the last incident. If your complaint is about payments you are owed please give the dates of the period covered. Please use the blank sheet at the end of the form if needed.

5.3 If your claim consists of, or includes, a claim that you are making a protected disclosure under the Employment Rights Act 1996 (otherwise known as a 'whistleblowing' claim), please tick the box below if you wish a copy of this form, or information from it, to be forwarded on your behalf to a relevant regulator (known as a 'prescribed person' under the relevant legislation) by the Tribunals Service.

☐

6 What compensation or remedy are you seeking?

6.1 Completion of this section is optional, but may help if you state what compensation or remedy you are seeking from your employer as a result of this complaint. If you specify an amount, please explain how you have calculated that figure.

7 Other information

7.1 Please do not send a covering letter with this form. You should add any extra information you want us to know here. Please use the blank sheet at the end of the form if needed.

8 Your representative

Please fill in this section only if you have appointed a representative. If you do fill in this section, we will in future only send correspondence to your representative and not to you.

8.1 Representative's name:

8.2 Name of the representative's organisation:

8.3 Address: Number or Name

Street

+ Town/City

County

Postcode

8.4 Phone number **(including area code):**

Mobile number **(if different):**

8.5 Reference:

8.6 How would they prefer us to communicate with them? (Please tick only one box) E-mail Post

E-mail address:

9 Disability

9.1 Please tick this box if you consider you have a disability Yes
Please say what this disability is and tell us what assistance, if any, you will need as your claim progresses through the system, including for any hearings that may need to be held at Tribunal Service premises.

10 Multiple cases

10.1 To your knowledge, is your claim one of a number of claims against the same employer arising from the same, or similar, circumstances? Yes No

11 Details of Additional Respondents

- Name of your employer or the organisation you are claiming against.
- Address: Number or Name
  Street
  + Town/City
  County
  Postcode

  Phone number:

- Name of your employer or the organisation you are claiming against.
- Address: Number or Name
  Street
  + Town/City
  County
  Postcode

  Phone number:

- Name of your employer or the organisation you are claiming against.
- Address: Number or Name
  Street
  + Town/City
  County
  Postcode

  Phone number:

Please read the form and check you have entered all the relevant information. Once you are satisfied, please tick this box.

Data Protection Act 1998. We will send a copy of this form to the respondent(s) and Acas. We will, if your claim consists of, or includes, a claim that you have made a protected disclosure under the Employment Rights Act 1996 (and you have given your consent that we should do so) send a copy of the form, or extracts from it, to the relevant regulator. We will put the information you give us on this form onto a computer. This helps us to monitor progress and produce statistics. Information provided on this form is passed to the Department for Business, Innovation and Skills to assist research into the use and effectiveness of employment tribunals.

Additional information for sections 5.2 and 7.

Additional information for sections 5.2 and 7.

Additional information for sections 5.2 and 7.

Equal Opportunities Monitoring Form

You are not obliged to fill in this section but, if you do so, it will enable us to monitor our processes and ensure that we provide equality of opportunity to all. The information you give here will be treated in strict confidence and this page will not form part of your case. It will be used only for monitoring and research purposes without identifying you.

1. What is your country of birth?

- England
- Wales
- Scotland
- Northern Ireland
- Republic of Ireland
- Elsewhere, *please write in the present name of the country*

2. What is your ethnic group?
Choose ONE section from A to E, then ✓ the appropriate box to indicate your cultural background.

A White

- British
- Irish
- Any other White background *please write in*

B Mixed

- White and Black Caribbean
- White and Black African
- White and Asian
- Any other Mixed background *please write in*

C Asian or Asian British

- Indian
- Pakistani
- Bangladeshi
- Any other Asian background *please write in*

D: Black or Black British

- Caribbean
- African
- Any other Black background *please write in*

E Chinese or other ethnic group

- Chinese
- Any other, *please write in*

3. What is your religion?
✓ box only

- None
- Christian (including Church of England, Catholic, Protestant and all other Christian denominations)
- Buddhist
- Hindu
- Jewish
- Muslim
- Sikh
- Any other religion, *please write in*

4. Sexual orientation

Which of these best describes you?
✓ box only

- Heterosexual
- Gay or lesbian or homosexual
- Bisexual
- Other

5. Disability

Do you have any health problems or disabilities that you expect will last for more than a year?
✓ box only

- Yes
- No

Click Here to return to the Home page when you have finished completing the form

Copy 1

Employment Tribunals - Multiple Claim Form

Please use this form if you wish to present two or more claims which arise from the same set of facts. Use additional sheets if necessary.

The following claimants are represented by ______ (if applicable) and the relevant required information for all the additional claimants is the same as stated in the main claim of

______ V

______

______

Title
First name (or names)
Surname or family name
Date of birth
Number or Name
Street
Town/City
County
Postcode

Title
First name (or names)
Surname or family name
Date of birth
Number or Name
Street
Town/City
County
Postcode

Title
First name (or names)
Surname or family name
Date of birth
Number or Name
Street
Town/City
County
Postcode

RESPONSE TO AN EMPLOYMENT TRIBUNAL CLAIM (ET3)

[5.58]

NOTES

See the notes to Form ET1 at **[5.57]**.

Employment Tribunals Response Form

Special Notice

You can make a response to an Employment Tribunal by completing and editing the form offline. You can save a part or fully completed form, email a saved form to another person to amend or for approval, and submit it securely online to the Employment Tribunal Service.

Please make sure you have read the guidance notes on our website or in our booklet on how to make a response before you fill in the form.

In order to proceed you must enter the case number and names of the parties printed on the form and letter we sent you.

Case number

Names of parties

V

Tribunal office dealing with claim --please select--

Print New Continue →

Need Help?

If you require any help completing your form or have a general question about the tribunals process please contact the Employment Tribunals Enquiry Line on

0845 795 9775

minicom 08457 573 722

between 9 am and 5 pm Monday to Friday, our lines are closed on Bank Holidays.

If you require technical support please click below to email us.

Support Request

We regret we cannot provide any legal advice.

Please Note:

By law, your claim must be submitted using an approved form supplied by the Employment Tribunals Service, and you must provide the information marked with ★ and, if it is relevant, the information marked with ● (see 'Information needed before a claim can be accepted')

General Information:

Once you have completed your form you can submit it securely on-line to the ETS. On-line forms are processed faster than those sent by post.

Version 7.4 POWERED by legatio

Case number:

1 Claimant's name

1.1 Claimant's name:

2 Respondent's details

2.1* Name of Individual, Company or Organisation

Contact name:

2.2* Address: Number or Name

Street

+ Town/City

County

Postcode

2.3 Phone number including area code **(where we can contact you in the day time)**:

Mobile number **(if different)**:

2.4 How would you prefer us to communicate with you? (Please tick only one box) E-mail Post

E-mail address:

2.5 What does this organisation mainly make or do?

2.6 How many people does this organisation employ in Great Britain?

2.7 Does this organisation have more than one site in Great Britain? Yes No

2.8 If 'Yes', how many people are employed at the place where the claimant worked?

3 Employment details

3.1 Are the dates of employment given by the claimant correct? Yes No
If 'Yes', please now go straight to section 3.3.

3.2 If 'No', please give dates and say why you disagree with the dates given by the claimant.

When their employment started

When their employment ended or will end

3 Employment details (continued)

Is their employment continuing? Yes ☐ No ☐

I disagree with the dates for the following reasons.

3.3 Is the claimant's description of their job or job title correct? Yes ☐ No ☐

If 'Yes', please now go straight to section 4

3.4 If 'No', please give the details you believe to be correct below.

4 Earnings and benefits

4.1 Are the claimant's hours of work correct? Yes ☐ No ☐

If 'No', please enter the details you believe to be correct. ☐ hours each week

4.2 Are the earnings details given by the claimant correct? Yes ☐ No ☐

If 'Yes', please now go straight to section 4.3

If 'No', please give the details you believe to be correct below.

Pay before tax £ ☐ .00

Normal take-home pay (including overtime, commission, bonuses and so on) £ ☐ .00

Hourly ☐
Weekly ☐
Monthly ☐
Yearly ☐

4.3 Is the information given by the claimant correct about being paid for, or working, a period of notice? Yes ☐ No ☐

If 'Yes', please now go straight to section 4.4

If 'No', please give the details you believe to be correct below. If you gave them no notice or didn't pay them instead of letting them work their notice, please explain what happened and why.

4.4 Are the details about pension and other benefits, e.g. company car, medical insurance, etc, given by the claimant correct? Yes ☐ No ☐

If 'Yes', please now go straight to section 5.

If 'No', please give the details you believe to be correct below.

ET3 v03 002

5 Response

5.1* Do you resist the claim? Yes No
If 'No', please now go straight to section 6.

5.2● If 'Yes', please set out in full the grounds on which you resist the claim.

6 Other information

6.1 Please do not send a covering letter with this form. You should add any extra information you want us to know here.

7 Your representative

If you have a representative, please fill in the following.

7.1 Representative's name:

7.2 Name of the representative's organisation:

7.3 Address: Number or Name

Street

+ Town/City

County

Postcode

7.4 Phone number:

7.5 Reference:

7.6 How would you prefer us to communicate with them? E-mail Post
(Please tick only one box)

E-mail address:

Please read the form and check you have entered all the relevant information.
Once you are satisfied, please tick this box.

Data Protection Act 1998. We will send a copy of this form to the claimant and Acas. We will put the information you give us on this form onto a computer. This helps us to monitor progress and produce statistics. Information provided on this form is passed to the Department for Business, Enterprise and Regulatory Reform to assist research into the use and effectiveness of employment tribunals. (URN 05/874)

ET3 v03 004

D. CABINET OFFICE MATERIALS

STAFF TRANSFERS IN THE PUBLIC SECTOR
Statement of Practice
January 2000 (Revised November 2007)

[5.59]

NOTES

This Statement of Practice was issued in January 2000 by the Cabinet Office. It has no statutory basis or force, but represents the policy which Government departments are required to follow and provides guidance for the rest of the public service, as to the application of the principles of TUPE in the contracting out or market testing of public service activities. The Statement was reissued in November 2007 with detailed revisions to reflect legislative changes (principally but not only the revision of the TUPE Regulations in 2006) and is reproduced here in its revised form. Both Annex A and Annex B are omitted for reasons of space. The full document can be accessed at www.gad.gov.uk/. Annex A is also reproduced in *Harvey* at **S[2925]** et seq.

GUIDING PRINCIPLES

- The Government is committed to ensuring that the public sector is a good employer and model contractor and client. The people employed in the public sector, directly and indirectly, are its biggest asset and critical in developing modern, high quality, efficient, responsive, customer focused and environmentally friendly public services.
- The Government's approach to modernising public services is a pragmatic one, based on finding the best supplier who can deliver quality services and value for money for the taxpayer. This involves some services or functions being provided by, or in partnership with, the private or voluntary sector, or restructured and organised in a new way within the public sector. The involvement, commitment and motivation of staff are vital for achieving smooth and seamless transition during such organisational change.
- Public Private Partnerships and the process of modernisation through organisational change in the public sector will be best achieved by clarity and certainty about the treatment of staff involved. The Government is committed to ensuring that staff involved in all such transfers are treated fairly and consistently and their rights respected. This will encourage a co-operative, partnership approach to the modernisation of the public sector with consequential benefits for all citizens.

INTRODUCTION

1. In order to meet these guiding principles the Government believes that there must be a clear and consistent policy for the treatment of staff, founded upon the provisions of the Transfer of Undertaking (Protection of Employment) Regulations 2006 (TUPE), which replaces the Transfer of Undertaking (Protection of Employment) Regulations 1981. This Statement of Practice[1] sets out the framework that the Government expects all public sector organisations to work within to achieve this aim (see paragraph 6 for the coverage of this Statement).

2. TUPE implements the 2001 European Council Acquired Rights Directive. In broad terms, TUPE protects employees' terms and conditions (except certain occupational pension arrangements) when the business or service in which they work is transferred from one employer to another. Employment with the new employer is treated as continuous from the date of the employee's start with the first employer. Terms and conditions cannot be changed where the operative reason for the change is the transfer although changes for other reasons may be negotiated, subject to certain conditions.

3. The Government takes a positive attitude towards TUPE, regarding it as an important aspect of employment rights legislation with the potential to promote a co-operative, partnership approach towards business restructuring and change in the public sector.

4. The Government's strategy in revising this legislation is based on the principle that it must be made to work effectively for all those whose interests depend upon it. This mirrors the Government's approach to employment relations issues generally.

5. In the area of Public Private Partnerships and change in the public sector, the consultations that the Government has undertaken and the representations which have been made, have showed a strong consensus between private sector employers, the voluntary sector, employee representatives and public sector organisations for the application of TUPE to situations where a service or function is contracted out, then retendered, brought back into the public sector, transferred within the public sector, or restructured and organised in a new way in a different part of the public sector. In any event, the TUPE Regulations 2006 have expanded the previous definition of what constitutes a transfer. It is accepted that there will still be some genuinely exceptional circumstances where TUPE will not apply but it is anticipated that there will be fewer than under the 1981 Regulations. Attempts to orchestrate a non-TUPE situation in other circumstances should not be tolerated. The policy in this Statement of Practice is therefore based on the following principles:

- contracting-out exercises with the private sector and voluntary organisations and transfers between different parts of the public sector, will be conducted on the basis that staff will transfer and TUPE should apply, unless there are genuinely exceptional reasons not to do so. Further guidance in relation to transferring staff from the public sector to a service provider and any subsequent re-tendering is provided at Annex B, 'Code of Practice on Workforce Matters in Public Sector Service Contracts' (issued in March 2003 and revised in March 2005);
- this includes second and subsequent round contracts that result in a new contractor and where a function is brought back into a public sector organisation where, in both cases, when the contract was first awarded staff transferred from the public sector;
- in circumstances where TUPE does not apply in strict legal terms to certain types of transfer between different parts of the public sector, the principles of TUPE should be followed (where possible using legislation to effect the transfer) and the staff involved should be treated no less favourably than had the Regulations applied; and
- there should be appropriate arrangements to protect occupational pensions, redundancy and severance terms of staff in all these types of transfer. Attached at Annex A is HM Treasury's Statement of Practice on Staff Transfers from Central Government "A fair deal for Staff Pensions" which sets out the policy on staff pensions announced by the Chief Secretary on 14 June 1999 that must be followed by Central Government Departments and Agencies, and which Ministers expect to be adopted by other public sector employers. This has been supplemented by further guidance issued in June 2004 'Fair deal for Staff Pensions: Procurement of Bulk Transfer Agreements and related issues', also attached at Annex A.

NOTES

[1] Further copies of this Statement can be obtained from Phillip Jones tel. 020 7276 1519 or by email to Phillip.Jones@cabinet-office.x.gsi.gov.uk

COVERAGE

6. This Statement of Practice sets out a framework to be followed by public sector organisations to implement the Government's policy on the treatment of staff transfers where the public sector is the employer when contracting out or the client in a subsequent retendering situation. It applies directly to Central Government Departments and Agencies and to the NHS. The Government expects other public sector organisations to follow this Statement of Practice. Local government is subject to some different considerations particularly the current restrictions in legislation contained in Parts I and II of the Local Government Act 1988. However abolition of CCT from January 2000 and proposals to modify Section 17 of the 1988 Act, as part of the introduction of Best Value, will remove in part obstacles to local authorities following this Statement of Practice. However, in doing so, they must have regard to the need to comply with their best value duties. The Personnel and Human Resources panel of the Local Government Association support the principles set out in this Statement of Practice and have encouraged their adoption by individual local authorities.

7. The Statement of Practice covers the following types of situation that may involve transfers of staff:

- Public Private Partnerships (eg following Better Quality Service reviews). This includes contracting-out; market testing; PFI; privatisation and other outsourcing and contracting exercises, (paragraphs 10–16);
- Second and subsequent generation contracting where, when the contract was first awarded, staff transferred from the public sector, (paragraph 12);
- Reorganisations and transfers from one part of the public sector to another, (paragraphs 17–20); and
- Reorganisations and transfers within the Civil Service (where TUPE cannot apply because there is no change in employer but TUPE principles should be followed), (paragraphs 21 and 22).

8. This Statement deals only with the policy framework for the treatment of staff involved in such transfers. It does not offer policy advice or guidance on:

- assessing the options for a particular service or function;
- project appraisal or procurement (except on the application of TUPE);
- managing a contracting exercise;
- how to discharge the obligations when TUPE applies or not;
- or how to secure appropriate pension provision, redundancy or severance terms.

Nor does it remove the need to seek legal advice in each individual case.

9. Detailed guidance on these aspects is provided separately, often tailored for different parts of the public sector to reflect their different needs, and for different types of Public Private Partnership. A list of relevant guidance for these aspects is at Annex B.

TRANSFERS AS A RESULT OF PUBLIC PRIVATE PARTNERSHIPS

10. This section of the Statement deals with the policy that should be adopted for the transfer of staff from the public sector to a private sector employer or a voluntary sector body. This will be as a result of a Public Private Partnership where a service or function currently performed by the public sector will in future be carried out by a private sector organisation. This may, for example, be a result of a PFI initiative, strategic contracting out or market testing exercises. All will involve some sort of contracting exercise where the public sector organisation (not necessarily the one in which the staff are employed) is the contracting authority.

11. In such transfers the application of TUPE will always be a matter of law based on the individual circumstances of the particular transfer. However, the policy adopted in defining the terms of the contracting exercise can help ensure that staff should be protected by TUPE and that all parties have a clear understanding that TUPE should apply and will be followed. In such transfers, therefore, the public sector contracting authority should, except in genuinely exceptional circumstances (see paragraph 14), ensure that:

- at the earliest appropriate stage in the contracting exercise, it states that staff are to transfer and this should normally have the effect of causing TUPE to apply, although legal advice should always be taken to confirm the applicability of TUPE in individual cases;
- at the earliest appropriate stage staff and recognised unions (or, if none, other independent staff representatives) are informed in writing of the intention that staff will transfer (and where possible when the transfer will take place) and that TUPE should apply;
- potential bidders are then invited to tender, drawing their attention in the Invitation to Tender letter to the intention that staff will transfer and TUPE should apply. The public sector contracting authority should also be aware of the new requirement in the 2006 TUPE Regulations in relation to notification of employee liability information, and legal advice should be taken as necessary. Potential bidders should be also advised that they can, if they wish, submit bids on the basis that staff do not transfer and TUPE does not apply, but that these will only be accepted if they fall within the genuinely exceptional circumstances ie unless the bid falls within one of the exceptions at paragraph 14 it must comply with the condition that staff transfer and TUPE should apply;
- the contracting exercise is then operated on the basis that the intention is that staff will transfer and TUPE should apply. Public sector contracting authorities should however consider all bids received. If a tenderer considers that staff should not transfer, they should be asked to give their reasons for this. Tenderers should be reminded if they do not consider that staff should transfer and the contract does not fall within the exceptions in paragraph 14, the contracting authority reserves the right not to accept the tender;
- in a very few cases bids made on the basis staff will not transfer and TUPE not apply will fall within the genuinely exceptional circumstances set out in paragraph 14 and cause the authority to accept the bid. The costs of redeploying staff and redundancies costs to the public sector employer must be taken into account when assessing such a bid. In all other cases the bid should not be accepted as it will not conform to the contracting authority's view that staff should transfer and TUPE apply; and
- where there is then a contractual requirement that staff should transfer, the requirements of TUPE should be scrupulously followed by the public sector contracting authority who should also ensure that it is satisfied that bidders' proposals fully meet the requirements of TUPE.

SECOND AND SUBSEQUENT TRANSFERS

12. This part of the Statement also extends to the retendering of contracts where, when the contract was first awarded staff transferred from the public sector (irrespective of whether TUPE applied at the time). Where a public contracting authority retenders such a contract then, except in exceptional circumstances (and where the incumbent contractor is successful), TUPE should apply and staff working on the contract should usually transfer. Views should be sought from the current contractor as to whether, from their point of view, there are any exceptional circumstances why staff should not transfer (by reference to paragraph 14). The retendering exercise should then be conducted as described above in paragraph 11.

TRANSFER OF SERVICES OR FUNCTIONS BACK INTO THE PUBLIC SECTOR

13. There may also be circumstances that require a function contracted-out to a private sector contractor or voluntary sector body to be brought back into the public sector on the termination of the contract. If, when the contract was first awarded staff transferred from the public sector (irrespective of whether TUPE applied at the time), then the public sector organisation should ensure that staff working on the contract transfer (and TUPE should therefore apply) into its organisation unless there are genuinely exceptional reasons not to do so. Views should be sought from the current contractor as to whether, from their point of view, there are any exceptional circumstances why staff should not transfer (by reference to paragraph 14). For transfers into the Civil Service, where TUPE applies, then the recruitment provisions of the Civil Service Order in Council and Civil Service Commissioners Recruitment Code are not relevant.[2] The Civil Service Nationality rules, which are statutorily based, will continue to apply.

NOTES

[2] Civil Service Management Code.

EXCEPTIONS

14. There may be a small number of cases where the policy set out in paragraphs 11–13 may not be followed and TUPE may not apply. There must be genuinely exceptional reasons why this should be the case. Circumstances that may qualify for such exceptions are, broadly:

- where a contract is for the provision of both goods and services, but the provision of services is ancillary in purpose to the provision of the goods; or
- where the activity for which the public sector organisation is contracting is essentially new or a one off project; or
- where services or goods are essentially a commodity bought 'off the shelf' and no grouping of staff are specifically and permanently assigned to a common task.

15. Where a public sector organisation believes such genuinely exceptional circumstances exist then it should be prepared to justify this, and the departure from the Government's policy (paras 11–13), publicly, if challenged. In central government, the agreement of the relevant departmental Ministers may need to be obtained before such an exception is made.

16. In such exceptional cases where staff do not transfer and TUPE does not apply, the public sector organisation should, in the case of first generation contracts, seek to identify as soon as possible with the contractor any staff that will be taken on voluntarily by the contractor,[3] and then, where possible, to redeploy those members of staff remaining within the public sector organisation (the costs of such redeployments and possible resulting redundancy payments must be taken into account when evaluating the bid).

NOTES

[3] Public Sector organisations should be aware that the transfer of a major part of the workforce, in terms of numbers or skills, may cause TUPE to apply.

TRANSFERS AND REORGANISATIONS WITHIN THE PUBLIC SECTOR

17. TUPE can apply to the transfers of a function from one part of the public sector to another where there is a change of employer. This, for example, can include:[4]

- Transfers between local government and civil service Departments and agencies
- Transfers between local government and NDPBs
- Transfers between local government and the NHS
- Transfers between the NHS and Civil Service Departments and Agencies
- Transfers between the NHS and NDPBs
- Transfers between NDPBs and civil service departments and agencies

18. The application of TUPE will, again, always be a matter of law based on the individual circumstances of the particular transfer. The amended Acquired Rights Directive directly legislates the *Henke* judgement of the European Court of Justice that: an administrative reorganisation of public administrative authorities or the transfer of administrative function is not a transfer and, therefore, as a matter of law, does not fall within the Directive. This provision in the Directive has been incorporated into the 2006 TUPE Regulations at 3(5). Case law[5] suggests that it excludes from the legislation's application only a relatively limited range of situations involving the transfer of entities pursuing non-economic objectives within the public sector. Nevertheless the issue has still to be tested fully in the tribunals and courts. The *Henke* exception has been thought to apply where: the reason for a transfer is only because there is a change of geographical boundaries and the type of public sector body carrying out the function does not change (eg the transfer of administrative staff as a result of changes to police authority boundaries); or where the main function is a judicial, quasi-judicial or quasi-judicial regulatory function (eg the creation of the Financial Services Authority) and incapable of being performed other than by a public sector authority. Officeholders who are not workers are also excluded from the scope of the Directive.

19. However, transfers at the instigation and under the control of Central Government will usually be effected through legislation, in particular those involving Officeholders. Provision can then be made for staff to transfer on TUPE terms, irrespective of whether the transfer is excluded from the scope of the Directive implemented by TUPE. Departments must therefore ensure that legislation effecting transfers of functions between public sector bodies makes provision for staff to transfer and on a basis that follows the principles of TUPE along with appropriate arrangements to protect occupational pension, redundancy and severance terms.

20. Section 38 of the Employment Relations Act also includes a power that can be used to apply the requirements of TUPE specifically to transfers outside the scope of the Directive eg Transfer of Undertakings (Protection of Employment) (Rent Officer Service) Regulations 1999 (SI 1999/2511). The DTI should be consulted about any proposal to exercise this power. Where, for whatever reason, this power or other legislation is not used there will be no legal requirement or obligation in such cases for staff to transfer to another part of the public sector where the function is to be performed (as to attempt to compel them would, in effect, constitute a unilateral change in their employment contract by imposing a change of employer). In such cases, as a matter of policy, public sector bodies should ensure that the principles underpinning TUPE are followed, so staff are offered the opportunity to transfer on terms that are, overall, no less favourable than had TUPE applied. They should also ensure appropriate pension provision and redundancy and severance terms. Staff who choose not to transfer should, where possible, be redeployed within the transferring public sector organisation.

NOTES

4 This list is not exhaustive.

5 *Mayeur v Association Promotion de l'Information Messine*: C-175/99 2000 IRLR 783, ECJ and *Collino v Telecom Italia SpA*: C-343/98 2000 IRLR 788, ECJ. These cases limit the application of the Henke exception to cases involving simply a re-organisation of public administrative structures or the transfer of administrative functions between public administrative authorities.

TRANSFERS AND REORGANISATIONS WITHIN THE CIVIL SERVICE

21. Reorganisation and transfers between Central Government Departments and agencies (ie within the Civil Service) do not involve a change in employer and TUPE therefore cannot apply. However, terms and conditions of employment do vary between different departments and many of the considerations addressed in the Statement for other types of transfer may also apply.

22. As a matter of policy, therefore, such reorganisations and transfers between Central Government Departments will be conducted on the basis that:

- as a general rule, when functions are transferred from one department to another staff will be transferred with the work;
- departments should, however, make every effort to provide an opportunity for those who wish to stay with or return to their original department to do so, having regard to ensuring consistent treatment of staff affected and the needs of the work;
- departments should ensure that wherever possible the principles of TUPE are followed. The existing terms and conditions of staff cannot be changed unilaterally, over time; the receiving department may aim to move, through negotiation with staff, towards fuller alignment of the terms of transferred staff to those of the main body of staff.
- staff and their recognised unions are informed at the earliest appropriate stage of the reorganisation and transfer.

(Annexes A and B omitted for reasons of space; see the note at the beginning of this Statement of Practice.)

PRINCIPLES OF GOOD EMPLOYMENT PRACTICE

A statement of principles that reflect good employment practice for Government, Contracting Authorities and Suppliers (2010)

[5.60]

NOTES

This Statement of Principles of Good Employment Practice is the replacement for the Code of practice on Workforce matters in Public Sector Employment Contracts, colloquially referred to as the 'Two-tier Code', which had been issued by the Cabinet Office in 2005, and was withdrawn with immediate effect on 13 December 2010. The Code had no statutory basis, and its revocation therefore required no legislation. However notes issued by the Cabinet Office in the statement announcing the withdrawal of the Code make it clear that provisions in contracts which have applied the Code continue to apply, unless the terms applying the Code are removed by renegotiation; in such an event the changes in the contractor's obligations will only apply to future new entrants to its workforce. However when contracts are re-competed, resulting in a new contract, the Code will not apply to the new contract. Revocation is also stated not to affect obligations under TUPE or the application of statutory equality duties.

The Code is available on the Cabinet Office website at:
www.gov.uk/government/publications/principles-of-good-employment-practice.

The Coalition Government has committed to opening up government procurement and reducing costs. It has also set itself the aspiration that 25% of government contracts should be awarded to small and medium-sized businesses.

Government understands that value for money means securing the best mix of quality and effectiveness for the least outlay. This applies to the whole lifetime of goods or services from purchase through to disposal.

In support of its aspirations, Government has developed a statement of principles of good employment practice that will form part of good practice literature and be shared with contracting authorities and suppliers.[1]

NOTES

1 This set of principles is voluntary and sits outside of the formal procurement decision making process, but will be disseminated to suppliers and commissioners

Government wants:

- employers of all sizes and from all sectors to have the freedom and flexibility to motivate and reward their workforce, to meet business needs.
- public, private, voluntary and community organisations to learn from each other and share best practice in the spirit of continuous improvement.
- employers to be aware of the best practice that fosters employee engagement, access to skills and development whilst securing quality outcomes in the provision of public services.

Six principles

This document is a statement of principles that reflect good employment practice. These principles are supported by Government and are voluntary.

1. Government as a good client

i. Through its commissioning, procurement standards and processes, central Government should encourage contracting authorities and suppliers to promote good workforce practices in the delivery of public services. Government will ensure that the workforce practices of the supplier are considered throughout the procurement process, where appropriate.

ii. Government will use outcome-based commissioning wherever possible; this is instead of prescribing how services are to be delivered. Using outcome-based commissioning will encourage more innovative approaches to the delivery of public services.

2. Training and skills

i. In letting and managing public contracts, the procurement process of contracting organisations will recognise the importance of basic skills such as literacy, numeracy and spoken English where these skills are relevant. These skills are often required in the delivery of public services, and enable the workforce to provide better quality services, particularly those in customer facing roles.

ii. Suppliers will be able to demonstrate that staff have appropriate training, qualifications and access to continuing professional development as befits their role; and that staff are supported to develop their skills and grow their experience in line with any future roles that maybe expected of them.

iii. Where there is a recognised trade union, suppliers will consult on workforce training and development issues.

3. A commitment to fair and reasonable terms and conditions

i. Where a supplier employs new entrants that sit alongside former public sector workers, new entrants should have fair and reasonable pay, terms and conditions. Suppliers should consult with their recognised trade unions on the terms and conditions to be offered to new entrants.

4. Equality

i. Contracting organisations will ensure that supplier policies and processes are entirely consistent with the responsibilities they have as employers under the Equality Act 2010. Government will ensure it delegates relevant legal obligations when suppliers are carrying out public functions.

ii. Government expects that suppliers will be able to demonstrate how working practices support their responsibilities as good employers.

5. Dispute resolution

i. All suppliers delivering public services should have regard to good industrial relations practice on dispute resolution. This includes treating employees fairly and ensuring compliance with the law on trade union membership.

ii. Suppliers will ensure that where there is a dispute, employees are aware of and have access to clear processes for dispute resolution. Government expects suppliers to consider the services of ACAS[2] as an option that is explored when disputes have not been resolved by internal support systems and processes.

iii. Where an employee has a right to be represented by a trade union, the employer will work with the employee and recognised trade union representative in resolving any dispute.

NOTES

[2] ACAS is the Advisory, Conciliation and Arbitration Service. ACAS provides free, confidential and impartial advice on a wide range of employment and industrial relations issues

6. Employee engagement

i. The themes identified in ***Drive for Change***[3] *place leadership, the design and delivery of service improvements, communications and a framework for staff engagement as vital components in ensuring and enhancing employee engagement.*

ii. The ***MacLeod Review***[4] *on employee engagement cited evidence of a positive correlation between an engaged workforce and improving performance. Building on the findings of the review, Government will encourage contractors to develop effective staff engagement strategies that enable people to be the best they can be at work.*

iii. Government recognises the premise that engagement between employee, employer and a recognised trade union where appropriate can be a key to unlocking productivity and creating a motivated workforce that feels respected, involved, heard, is well led and valued by those they work for and with.

NOTES

[3] Drive for Change is a practical tool for staff engagement in service improvement. The Drive for Change initiative was developed and supported by Cabinet Office and the Trades Union Congress and is currently in the process of being refreshed.

[4] The MacLeod Review was commissioned by the Department for Business, Innovation and Skills to take an in-depth look at employee engagement and to report on the potential benefits for organisations and employees.

Review

The impact of these principles on employment practice will be reviewed by the Public Services Forum in January 2012. The Forum will assess how the principles contribute to good employment practices in the delivery of contracted out services.

E. USEFUL ADDRESSES

USEFUL ADDRESSES

[5.61]

1. ADVISORY, CONCILIATION AND ARBITRATION SERVICE

NOTES

Further information is available on the ACAS website at www.acas.org.uk.

ACAS Helpline	Tel: 08457 47 47 47
	Text Relay service: 18001 08457 47 47 47
	Note that the telephone number for the Head Office and the regional offices is now 08457 38 37 36
Head Office	Euston Tower, 286 Euston Road, London, NW1 3JJ
Regional offices	
London	Euston Tower, 286 Euston Road, London, NW1 3JJ
East of England	Acas House, Kempson Way, Suffolk Business Park, Bury St Edmunds, Suffolk, IP32 7AR
East Midlands	Apex Court, City Link, Nottingham, NG2 4LA
West Midlands	Victoria Square House, Victoria Square, Birmingham, B2 4AJ
North West	7th Floor, Arndale House, Arndale Centre, Manchester M4 3AQ
	Redgrave Court, Merton Road, Bootle, Merseyside, Liverpool, L20 7HS
North East	Cross House, Westgate Road, Newcastle upon Tyne, NE1 4XX
Scotland	151 West George Street, Glasgow G2 7JJ
South West	Temple Quay House, 2 The Square, Bristol, BS1 6DG
South East	Cygnus House, Ground Floor, Waterfront Business Park, Fleet, Hampshire, GU51 3QT
Wales	Third Floor, Fusion Point 2, Dumballs Road, Cardiff, CF10 5BF
Yorkshire & Humber	The Cube, 123 Albion Street, Leeds, LS2 8ER

2. BAR COUNCIL

289–293 High Holborn, London, WC1V 7HZ
Tel: 020 7242 0082 Fax: 020 7831 9217
DX 240 LDE
Website: www.barcouncil.org.uk
Email: ContactUs@BarCouncil.org.uk

3. BAR PRO BONO UNIT

Bar Pro Bono Unit, The National Pro Bono Centre, 48 Chancery Lane, London, WC2A 1JF
Tel: 020 7092 3960 (Mon, Wed, Fri,10.00–14.00)
DX 188 London Chancery Lane
Website: www.barprobono.org.uk
Email: enquiries@barprobono.org.uk

4. BRITISH PSYCHOLOGICAL SOCIETY

St Andrews House, 48 Princess Road East, Leicester, LE1 7DR
Tel: 0116 254 9568 Fax: 0116 227 1314
Website: www.bps.org.uk
Email: enquiries@bps.org.uk

5. CENTRAL ARBITRATION COMMITTEE

22nd Floor, Euston Tower, 286 Euston Road, London, NW1 3JJ
Tel: 020 7904 2300 Fax: 020 7904 2301
Website: www.cac.gov.uk
Email: enquiries@cac.gov.uk

6. CHARTERED INSTITUTE OF PERSONNEL AND DEVELOPMENT

151 The Broadway, London, SW19 1JQ
Tel: 020 8612 6200 Fax: 020 8612 6201
Website: www.cipd.co.uk

7. CERTIFICATION OFFICER
22nd Floor, Euston Tower, 286 Euston Road, London, NW1 3JJ
Tel: 020 7210 3734 Fax: 020 7210 3612
Website: www.certoffice.org
Email: info@certoffice.org

8. DEPARTMENT FOR BUSINESS, INNOVATION & SKILLS (BIS) EMPLOYMENT MATTERS
Ministerial Correspondence Unit
Department for Business, Innovation & Skills
1 Victoria Street, London, SW1H 0ET
Tel: 020 7215 5000 Minicom: 020 7215 6740
Website: www.bis.gov.uk

9. DISCLOSURE AND BARRING SERVICE
(formerly the CRIMINAL RECORDS BUREAU)
The Criminal Records Bureau has been replaced by the Disclosure and Barring Service.
Telephone: 0870 909 0811 Minicom: 0870 909 0344
Website: www.gov.uk/disclosure-barring-service
Email: customerservices@dbs.gsi.gov.uk

10. DISCLOSURE SCOTLAND
PO Box 250, Glasgow, G51 1YU
Tel: 0870 609 6006 Fax: 0870 609 6996
Website: www.disclosurescotland.co.uk
Email: info@disclosurescotland.co.uk

11. EMPLOYMENT APPEAL TRIBUNAL
England & Wales
Fleetbank House, 2–6 Salisbury Square, London, EC4Y 8JX
Tel: 020 7273 1041 Fax: 020 7273 1045
Website: www.justice.gov.uk/tribunals/employment-appeals
Email: londoneat@hmcts.gsi.gov.uk

Scotland
52 Melville Street, Edinburgh, EH3 7HF
Tel: 0131 225 3963 Fax: 0131 220 6694
Email: edinburgheat@hmcts.gsi.gov.uk

12. EMPLOYMENT TRIBUNALS
NOTE: the Employment Tribunals Service has, since 1 April 2011, been part of the HM Courts and Tribunals Service, an executive agency of the Ministry of Justice. This section contains the contact details for employment tribunals. Location and contact details for hearing centres not listed below (and not permanently staffed) may be obtained at www.justice.gov.uk/tribunals/employment/venues.

Employment Tribunals Service
Public Enquiry Line
Tel: 0845 795 9775 Minicom: 0845 757 3722
Website: www.justice.gov.uk/tribunals/employment

Employment Tribunals Offices in England, Wales and Scotland

Aberdeen
Mezzanine Floor, Atholl House, 84–88 Guild Street, Aberdeen, AB11 6LT
Tel: 01224 593137 Fax: 01224 593138 DX AB77 Aberdeen
Email: aberdeenet@hmcts.gsi.gov.uk

Ashford
1st Floor, Ashford House, County Square Shopping Centre, Ashford, Kent, TN23 1YB
Tel: 01233 621346 Fax: 01233 624423 DX 157160 Ashford (Kent) 8
Email: ashfordet@hmcts.gsi.gov.uk

Bedford
All Bedford claims are administered by Huntingdon Employment Tribunal *(for details see below)*

Birmingham
Centre City Tower, 7 Hill Street, Birmingham, B5 4UU
Tel: 0121 600 7780 Fax: 0121 600 7882
Email: birminghamet@hmcts.gsi.gov.uk

Brighton
City Gate House, 185 Dyke Road, Brighton, East Sussex BN3 1TL
All correspondence and telephone enquiries should be addressed to the London South Office *(for details see below)*

Bristol
Ground Floor, The Crescent Centre, Temple Back, Bristol, BS1 6EZ
Tel: 0117 929 8261 Fax: 0117 925 3452
Email: bristolet@hmcts.gsi.gov.uk

Bury St Edmunds
100 Southgate Street, Bury St Edmunds, IP33 2AQ
Tel: 01284 762171 Fax: 01284 706064
Email: buryet@hmcts.gsi.gov.uk

Cardiff
Caradog House, 1–6 St Andrews Place, Cardiff, CF10 3BE
Tel: 02920 678100 Fax: 02920 225906 DX 33027 Cardiff
Email: cardiffet@hmcts.gsi.gov.uk

Dundee
Ground Floor, Block C, Caledonian House, Greenmarket, Dundee, DD1 4QX
Tel: 01382 221578 Fax: 01382 227136 DX DD51 Dundee
Email: dundeeet@hmcts.gsi.gov.uk

East London
2nd Floor, Anchorage House, 2 Clove Crescent, London, E14 2BE
Tel: 020 7538 6161 Fax: 020 7538 6210
Email: eastlondon@hmcts.gsi.gov.uk

Edinburgh
54–56 Melville Street, Edinburgh, EH3 7HF
Tel: 0131 226 5584 Fax: 0131 220 6847 DX ED147 Edinburgh
Email: edinburghet@hmcts.gsi.gov.uk

Exeter
2nd Floor, Keble House, Southernhay Gardens, Exeter, EX1 1NT
Tel: 01392 279665 Fax: 01392 430063
Email: exeteret@hmcts.gsi.gov.uk

Glasgow
3rd Floor Eagle Building, 215 Bothwell Street, Glasgow, G2 7TS
Tel: 0141 204 0730 Fax: 0141 204 0732 DX 580003 Glasgow 17
Email: glasgowet@hmcts.gsi.gov.uk

Huntingdon
Huntingdon Law Courts, Walden Road, Huntingdon, PE29 3DW
Tel: 01480 415600
Email: huntingdonet@hmcts.gsi.gov.uk

Leeds
4th Floor, City Exchange, 11 Albion Street, Leeds, LS1 5ES
Tel: 0113 245 9741 Fax: 0113 242 8843 DX 742940 Leeds 75
Email: leedset@hmcts.gsi.gov.uk

Leicester
5a New Walk, Leicester, LE1 6TE
Tel: 0116 255 0099 Fax: 0116 255 6099
Email: leicesteret@hmcts.gsi.gov.uk

Liverpool
All correspondence and telephone queries should be addressed to the Manchester office *(for details see below)*

London Central
Victory House, 30–34 Kingsway, London, WC2B 6EX
Tel: 020 7273 8603 Fax: 020 7273 8686 DX 141420 Bloomsbury
Email: londoncentralet@hmcts.gsi.gov.uk

London South
Montague Court, 101 London Road, West Croydon, CR0 2RF
Tel: 020 8667 9131 Fax: 020 8649 9470 DX 155062 Croydon 39
Email: londonsouthet@hmcts.gsi.gov.uk

Manchester
Alexandra House, 14–22 The Parsonage, Manchester M3, 2JA
Tel: 0161 833 6100 Fax: 0161 832 0249 DX 743570 Manchester 66
Email: manchesteret@hmcts.gsi.gov.uk

Newcastle
Quayside House, 110 Quayside, Newcastle upon Tyne, NE1 3DX
Tel: 0191 260 6900 Fax: 0870 739 4206 DX 742283 Newcastle U Tyne 35
Email: newcastleet@hmcts.gsi.gov.uk

Nottingham
3rd Floor, Byron House, 2a Maid Marian Way, Nottingham, NG1 6HS
Tel: 0115 947 5701 Fax: 0115 950 7612
Email: nottinghamet@hmcts.gsi.gov.uk

Reading
5th Floor, 30–31 Friar Street, Reading, RG1 1DY
Tel: 0118 959 4917 Fax: 0118 956 8066 DX 155830 Reading 31
Email: readinget@hmcts.gsi.gov.uk

Sheffield
All Sheffield claims are administered by Leeds Employment Tribunals (*see above for details*).

Shrewsbury
c/o Magistrates Court House, Preston Street, Shrewsbury, Shropshire SY2 5NX
All administration of Employment Tribunal claims for this region are undertaken at the Birmingham office (*see above for details*).

Southampton
Southampton Magistrates Court, 100 The Avenue, Southampton, Hampshire, SO17 1EY
Tel: 023 80 384200 Fax: 0870 739 4190
DX 135986 Southampton 32
Email: southamptonet@hmcts.gsi.gov.uk

Watford
3rd Floor, Radius House, 51 Clarendon Road, Watford, WD17 1HU
Tel: 01923 281750 Fax: 01923 281781 DX 155650 Watford 3
Email: watfordet@hmcts.gsi.gov.uk

Public Register of ET judgments

England & Wales
HM Courts and Tribunals Service, Field Support Unit, 1st Floor, 100 Southgate Street, Bury St Edmunds, IP33 2AQ
Tel: 0845 7959775 Fax: 01284 766334
Email: buryet@hmcts.gsi.gov.uk

Scotland
HM Courts and Tribunals Service, Eagle Building, 215 Bothwell Street, Glasgow, G2 7TS
Tel: 0141 204 0730 Fax: 0141 204 0732
Email: glasgowet@hmcts.gsi.gov.uk

President of Employment Tribunals

England & Wales
Victory House, 30–34 Kingsway, London, WC2B 6EX

Scotland
Eagle Building, 215 Bothwell Street, Glasgow, G2 7TS

13. EQUALITY AND HUMAN RIGHTS COMMISSION

NOTE: successor to the Equal Opportunities Commission, the Commission for Racial Equality, and the Disability Rights Commission.

Website: www.equalityhumanrights.com

Equality Advisory Support Service (EASS) *(formerly the Equality and Human Rights Commission Helpline)*

The EHRC Helpline has been replaced (as from 1 October 2012) by the Equality Advisory Support Service (EASS)
Tel: 0808 800 0082
Textphone: 0808 800 0084
Website: www.equalityadvisoryservice.com
Post: FREEPOST Equality Advisory Support Service FPN4431

Equality and Human Rights Commission Offices in England, Wales and Scotland

London
Fleetbank House, 2-6 Salisbury Square, London EC4Y 8JX
Tel: 0207 832 7800 Fax: 020 7832 7801

Manchester
Arndale House, The Arndale Centre, Manchester, M4 3AQ
Tel: 0161 829 8100 Fax: 0161 829 8110

Cardiff
3rd floor, 3 Callaghan Square, Cardiff, CF10 5BT
Tel: 02920 447710 Fax: 02920 447712
Email: wales@equalityhumanrights.com

Glasgow
151 West George Street, Glasgow G2 2JJ
Tel: 0141 228 5910 Fax: 0141 228 5912
Email: scotland@equalityhumanrights.com

14. FREE REPRESENTATION UNIT
Website: www.thefru.org.uk
London Office
Ground Floor, 60 Gray's Inn Road, London, WC1X 8LU
Tel: 020 7611 9555
Nottingham Office
Nottingham Law School Legal Advice Clinic, Belgrave Centre, Chaucer Street, Nottingham, NG1 5LP
Tel: 01158 484 262

15. HEALTH AND SAFETY EXECUTIVE
NOTE: successor since 1 April 2008 to the Health and Safety Commission and the Health and Safety Executive
HSE Head Office
Redgrave Court, Merton Road, Bootle, Merseyside, L20 7HS
Tel: 0151 951 4000
Website: www.hse.gov.uk
For details of London & regional offices see www.hse.gov.uk/contact

16. INFORMATION COMMISSIONER
(*Formerly* **Data Protection Commissioner**)
Information Commissioner's Office
Wycliffe House, Water Lane, Wilmslow, Cheshire, SK9 5AF
Helpline: 0303 123 1113 (or 01625 545745)
Textphone: 01625 545860
Fax: 01625 524510
Email (First contact team): casework@ico.org.uk
Website: www.ico.org.uk

Scotland
Information Commissioner's Office
45 Melville Street, Edinburgh, EH3 7HL
Tel: 0131 244 9001
Email: scotland@ico.org.uk

Wales
Information Commissioner's Office
2nd Floor, Churchill House, Churchill Way, Cardiff, CF10 2HH
Tel: 029 2067 8400
Fax: 029 2067 8399
Email: wales@ico.org.uk

17. THE LAW SOCIETY
Website: www.lawsociety.org.uk
England
The Law Society's Hall, 113 Chancery Lane, London, WC2A 1PL
Tel: 020 7242 1222
Fax: 020 7831 0344
DX 56 London Chancery Lane

Wales
The Law Society, Wales Office, Capital Tower, Greyfriars Road, Cardiff, CF10 3AG
Tel: 029 2064 5254
Fax: 29 2022 5944
Email: wales@lawsociety.org.uk

18. LAW SOCIETY OF SCOTLAND
26 Drumsheugh Gardens, Edinburgh, EH3 7YR
Tel: 0131 226 7411 Fax: 0131 225 2934
Textphone: 0131 476 8359
Email: lawscot@lawscot.org.uk
Website: www.lawscot.org.uk

19. PENSIONS OMBUDSMAN
11 Belgrave Road, London, SW1V 1RB
Tel: 020 7630 2200 Fax: 020 7821 0065
Website: www.pensions-ombudsman.org.uk
Email: enquiries@pensions-ombudsman.org.uk

20. PENSIONS REGULATOR
Website: www.thepensionsregulator.gov.uk
Pension scheme regulation enquiries
Napier House, Trafalgar Square, Brighton, BN1 4DW
Tel: 0845 600 0707 Fax: 0870 2411144
Email: customersupport@tpr.gov.uk

Automatic enrolment enquiries
PO Box 16314, Birmingham, B23 3JP
Tel: 0845 600 1011 Fax: 0845 606 9970
Email: customersupport@autoenrol.tpr.gov.uk

Levy, scheme return or exchange enquiries
Napier House, Trafalgar Square, Brighton, BN1 4DW
Tel: 0845 600 5666 Fax: 0870 2411144
Email: exchange@tpr.gov.uk

21. TPAS (THE PENSIONS ADVISORY SERVICE)
11 Belgrave Road, London, SW1V 1RB
Tel: 0845 601 2923 Fax: 020 7592 7000
Website: www.pensionsadvisoryservice.org.uk

22. TSO (THE STATIONERY OFFICE)
For general order and customer service enquiries:
Tel: 0870 600 5522
Email: customer.services@tso.co.uk
Website: www.tso.co.uk

23. TRADES UNION CONGRESS
Congress House, Great Russell Street, London, WC1B 3LS
Tel: 020 7636 4030
Email: info@tuc.org.uk
Website: www.tuc.org.uk

24. UK BORDER AGENCY
Immigration Inquiry Bureau
Lunar House, 40 Wellesley Road, Croydon, CR9 2BY
Tel: 0870 606 7766
Website: www.bia.homeoffice.gov.uk

Index

B

C

D

F

I

J

L

M

N

O

P

Q

R

T